THE LIVING BIBLE CONCORDANCE

COMPLETE

THE LIVING BIBLE CONCORDANCE

COMPLETE

Based on a paraphrased text by
Dr. Kenneth N. Taylor

Edited and Compiled under the supervision of
JACK ATKESON SPEER

PUBLISHED BY THE POOLESVILLE PRESBYTERIAN CHURCH
Poolesville, Maryland 20837

First Printing
Limited Edition — 2000
Printed by Hagerstown Bookbinding and Printing Co., Inc.

Speer, Jack Atkeson.
The Living Bible Concordance Complete.

"Based on Paraphrased text by Dr. Kenneth N. Taylor."
1. Bible — Concordances, English — Living Bible.
I. Taylor, Kenneth Nathaniel. The Living Bible,
paraphrased. II. Title.
BS425.S67 220.2 73-10013
ISBN 0-9600694-1-0

Dedicated to God
Through the Miracle of
Martin Fuller Speer

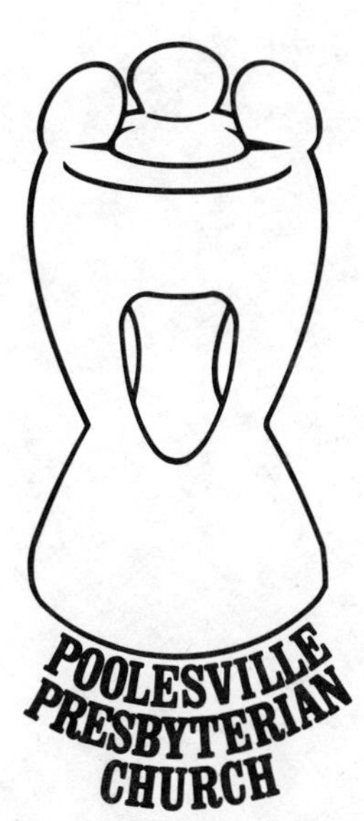

PREFACE
TO THE COMPLETE CONCORDANCE FOR THE LIVING BIBLE

THE LIVING BIBLE CONCORDANCE is the first complete word by word index ever offered for a truly popular English language Bible. The text is based upon THE LIVING BIBLE, a paraphrase by Dr. Kenneth N. Taylor. With record sales of over 7 million, the Bible soared to the number one non-fiction best seller for 1972 in America. It is apparent that many people are coming to grips with the Biblical message in a new and vital way.

How THE LIVING BIBLE CONCORDANCE came to be is as unique as the book itself. This concordance was created because a congregation came together in prayer for the life of a premature two pound baby boy, Martin Fuller Speer, born November 25, 1972. As God brought the tiny 58 member Poolesville Presbyterian Church together over the life of this child, so He brought these people together with their various gifts in the preparation of this concordance.

It began in the midst of personal suffering when the baby's father was led to THE LIVING BIBLE as the only complete Bible he could easily read and understand. Jack Speer, with his computer-library background, presented the idea for THE LIVING BIBLE CONCORDANCE to the Poolesville Presbyterian Church.

This church which had supported him in prayer now heard and endorsed his idea with the provision that Dr. Taylor would give his approval. This he graciously did with his personal endorsement, blessing, and the necessary computer tape from which THE LIVING BIBLE was generated. The Poolesville Presbyterian Church members then, in a leap of faith, pledged over and above their regular church offerings and the work of the concordance began.

A gift from God and a labor of love characterize the entire effort. Following the initial commitment, many members and friends of the church caught the vision and offered their gifts and talents. One man offered his copying machines for initial labels and drawings; another his computer at special rates to generate the concordance. A photo-composition man offered his services at cost, as did a newspaperman for the initial printed publicity. A printer offered to print the first edition as a gift, and a major paper company gave all the paper necessary to do this limited edition. Finally, as this concordance attests, a small but efficient binder offered to do the book with the care worthy of such a limited collector's edition.

It is important to remember that this was a cooperative effort, mostly volunteer. It is impossible to record the countless hours of labor given by so many members and friends of The Poolesville Presbyterian Church. In the end, it is they who have made this concordance possible. For this congregation the concordance project has been a labor of love to a God who has blessed us all. Our hope in preparing THE LIVING BIBLE CONCORDANCE is that you might be enriched in knowledge and understanding of God's will for your life.

Poolesville, Maryland
June 1973

Filbert L. Moore, Jr.
Pastor/Project Coordinator

ACKNOWLEDGEMENTS

The Members and Friends of The Poolesville Presbyterian Church gratefully wish to acknowledge those individuals and companies outside our Poolesville community whose contributions have made this LIVING BIBLE CONCORDANCE possible.

Artcraft Library Binders
Nancy Christ
COMNET-PUBLICATE, INC.
Composition Services, Inc.
COMRESS, INC.
Greg Cox
George Cozzens
Frederick News-Post
Gibson & Gray, Inc.
P. H. Glatfelter Company
Philip Glatfelter, III
Dale Graffus
Hagerstown Bookbinding & Printing Co., Inc.
Ronald Lee Henderson
Susan Ketron
Donald B. Lester
Michael Malloy
Vinita Mathur
William McKay
Bruce Metzger
Brower Murphy
Kenneth Taylor
Tyndale House Publishers
William Valiente
Gerald Wedinger
Glenn Wittig

DIRECTIONS AND EXPLANATIONS

THE LIVING BIBLE CONCORDANCE with over 734,000 entries, is designed as a complete study tool for THE LIVING BIBLE. Every word in this Bible has been concorded into at least one of three separate sections — a main body plus two appendices. This complete index will enable any reader of the Bible to locate quickly any text on any subject in the Bible.

To use THE LIVING BIBLE CONCORDANCE begin by looking for the Bible passage under any one of its words as spelled in the Bible. Do this alphabetically as searching in any dictionary or phone book. If you are searching for the passage "Christ makes us acceptable to God . . ." Hebrews 7:19, this passage will be found quickly if one searches for it under the least common word, "acceptable," which has but 17 Biblical occurrences, rather than under the more common word "God" which occurs 5004 times.

By way of further explanation note that when searching for hyphenated words, "be-", "el-" or "co-", such words will come before "bea" or "ela", or "coa." For example, the word "co-regent" is listed in the concordance before the word "coat."

Arriving at the page listing the word in the passage one hopes to find, the word will be seen in bold faced type with all its Biblical occurrences listed in a column in the order they appear in the Bible.

In each Biblical contextual phrase listed, readers will note an asterisk (*) denoting the Biblical word in its proper context. At the end of the Biblical contextual phrase there are the corresponding Biblical book, chapter and verse references which in some instances carry a small "f." This sign denotes a footnote as found in THE LIVING BIBLE.

Because THE LIVING BIBLE CONCORDANCE is a first for a paraphrased Bible, we felt it was important to include, for maximum clarity and understanding, the "literal" and "implied" meanings as indicated by Dr. Taylor in his footnotes.

After the main body of the concordance, readers will find two useful appendices. The first contains those many connecting words — articles, conjunctions, prepositions, some nouns and verbs which were not considered essential in the discovery of a Biblical text. But, since we dare not predict how students of the Bible might utilize THE LIVING BIBLE CONCORDANCE, we have included all such entries in an appendix with their corresponding Biblical book, chapter and verse references.

These references have been compacted by eliminating duplicate book names, chapter, and verse numbers. The number of occurrences within a verse is indicated by a superscript number (Gen. 2:14^{2}).

In a second appendix, readers will find concorded, an up-to-date listing of numerical quantities. For apparent clarity, Dr. Taylor has translated all ancient Biblical weights and measures into modern terminology. Students will find such quantities listed in ascending numerical sequence at the back of THE LIVING BIBLE CONCORDANCE complete with their appropriate contextual phrase.

ABBREVIATIONS

Below are listed the abbreviations for the Biblical books as they are used in THE LIVING BIBLE CONCORDANCE:

Gen	Genesis	Nah	Nahum
Ex	Exodus	Hab	Habakkuk
Lev	Leviticus	Zep	Zephaniah
Num	Numbers	Hag	Haggai
Deu	Deuteronomy	Zec	Zechariah
Jos	Joshua	Mal	Malachi
Ju	Judges	Mt	Matthew
Ru	Ruth	Mk	Mark
1Sa	1 Samuel	Lk	Luke
2Sa	2 Samuel	Jn	John
1Ki	1 Kings	Act	Acts
2Ki	2 Kings	Rom	Romans
1Ch	1 Chronicles	1Co	1 Corinthians
2Ch	2 Chronicles	2Co	2 Corinthians
Ez	Ezra	Gal	Galatians
Neh	Nehemiah	Eph	Ephesians
Est	Ester	Php	Philippians
Job	Job	Col	Colossians
Ps	Psalms	1Th	1 Thessalonians
Pro	Proverbs	2Th	2 Thessalonians
Ecc	Ecclesiastes	1Ti	1 Timothy
Sol	Song of Solomon	2Ti	2 Timothy
Is	Isaiah	Tit	Titus
Jer	Jeremiah	Phm	Philemon
Lam	Lamentations	Heb	Hebrews
Eze	Ezekiel	Jas	James
Dan	Daniel	1Pe	1 Peter
Hos	Hosea	2Pe	2 Peter
Joe	Joel	1Jn	1 John
Amo	Amos	2Jn	2 John
Ob	Obadiah	3Jn	3 John
Jon	Jonah	Jud	Jude
Mic	Micah	Rev	The Revelation

THE LIVING BIBLE CONCORDANCE

COMPLETE

D.
the destruction of Jerusalem in *. Dan 9:25f
M.
People don't get drunk by 9 *. Act 2:15
ARON
right," he said, "your brother * Ex 4:14
Now Jehovah said to *, "Go into Ex 4:27
meet Moses." So * traveled to Ex 4:27
Moses told * what God had said Ex 4:28
So Moses and * returned to Egypt Ex 4:29
council meeting. * told them what Ex 4:30
Moses and * went to see Pharaoh. Ex 5:1
But * and Moses persisted. Ex 5:3
When they met Moses and * Ex 5:20
Then the Lord ordered Moses and * Ex 6:13
and * and Moses were their sons. Ex 6:20
* married Elisheba, the daughter Ex 6:23
* and Moses, included in that Ex 6:26
list, are the same * and Moses to Ex 6:26
brother * shall be your spokesman. Ex 7:1
Tell * everything I say to you, Ex 7:2
So Moses and * did as the Lord Ex 7:6
Moses was eighty years old and * Ex 7:7
Then the Lord said to Moses and * Ex 7:8
when he does, * is to throw down Ex 7:9
So Moses and * went in to see Ex 7:10
instructed them—* threw down his Ex 7:10
Moses: "Tell * to point his rod Ex 7:19
So Moses and * did as the Lord Ex 7:20
officials watched, * hit the Ex 7:20
to Moses and *, just as the Lord Ex 7:22
Moses, "Instruct * to point the Ex 8:5
of the land." * did, and frogs Ex 8:6
Then Pharaoh summoned Moses and * Ex 8:8
So Moses and * went out from the Ex 8:12
to Moses, "Tell * to strike the Ex 8:16
So Moses and * did as God Ex 8:17
summoned Moses and * and said, Ex 8:25
Then Jehovah said to Moses and *, Ex 9:8
Then Pharaoh sent for Moses and * Ex 9:27
So Moses and * requested another Ex 10:3
So Moses and * were brought back Ex 10:8
call for Moses and * and said to Ex 10:16
So, although Moses and * did Ex 11:10
THEN THE LORD said to Moses and *, Ex 12:1
did as Moses and * had commanded. Ex 12:28
And Pharaoh summoned Moses and * Ex 12:31
Then Jehovah said to Moses and *, Ex 12:43
instructions to Moses and *. Ex 12:50
the sister of *, took a timbrel and Ex 15:20
bitterly against Moses and *. Ex 16:2
Then Moses and * called a meeting Ex 16:6
So * called them together and Ex 16:10
Moses told * to get a container Ex 16:33
to generation. * did this, just as Ex 16:34
Meanwhile Moses, *, and Hur Ex 17:10
rod any longer; so * and Hur rolled Ex 17:12
to God, and afterwards * and the Ex 18:12
on down, and bring * back with you, Ex 19:24
up here with *, Nadab, Abihu, and Ex 24:1
Then Moses, *, Nadab, Abihu, and Ex 24:9
am gone, consult with * and Hur." Ex 24:14
continually. * and his sons shall Ex 27:21
"CONSECRATE * YOUR brother, and Ex 28:1
Make special clothes for *, to Ex 28:2
people of Israel: * will carry Ex 28:12
In this way * shall carry the Ex 28:29
Jehovah. Thus * shall always be Ex 28:30,31
with gold bells. * shall wear the Ex 28:35
In this way * will be wearing it Ex 28:37,38
Clothe * and his sons with these Ex 28:41
These are to be worn whenever * Ex 28:43
ordinance for * and his sons. Ex 28:43
the dedication of * and his sons as Ex 29:1
"Bathe * and his sons there at Ex 29:3,4
thus you shall consecrate * and Ex 29:9
Tabernacle, and * and his sons Ex 29:10
"Next, * and his sons shall lay Ex 29:15,16
"Now take the other ram, and * Ex 29:19,20
the right ear of * and his sons, Ex 29:19,20
sprinkle it upon * and his sons and Ex 29:21
for ordination of * and his sons— Ex 29:22
in the hands of * and his sons, to Ex 29:24
ram to * and his sons. Ex 29:28
"These sacred garments of * Ex 29:29
High Priest after * shall wear Ex 29:30
in a sacred area. * and his sons Ex 29:32
* and his sons to their offices. Ex 29:35
and the altar and * and his sons Ex 29:44
"Every morning when * trims the Ex 30:7
"Once a year * must sanctify Ex 30:10
it with water. * and his sons Ex 30:19
These are instructions to * and Ex 30:21
Use it to anoint * and his sons, Ex 30:30
holy garments for * the priest, and Ex 31:10
right away, the people went to *. Ex 32:1
your golden earrings," * replied. Ex 32:2,3
boys and girls. * melted the gold, Ex 32:4
When * saw how happy the people Ex 32:5
Then he turned to *. Ex 32:21
"Don't get so upset," * Ex 32:22
upon his face, * and the people of Ex 34:30
over to him, and * and the leaders Ex 34:31
The holy garments for * the Ex 35:10-19
by Ithamar, son of * the priest. Ex 38:21
This robe was worn when * Ex 39:25,26
Robes were now made for * and his Ex 39:27
holy garments for * the priest and Ex 39:41
"Now bring * and his sons to the Ex 40:12
and clothe * with the holy Ex 40:13
Moses and * and Aaron's sons Ex 40:31
to * and his sons as their food; Lev 2:3
to Moses, "Give * and his sons Lev 6:9
to * and his sons for their food; Lev 6:16
male descendant of *, any priest, Lev 6:18
"On the day * and his sons are Lev 6:19,20
to Moses, "Tell * and his sons Lev 6:25
common property of all sons of *. Lev 7:10
shall belong to * and his sons, Lev 7:31
people of Israel to the sons of *. Lev 7:34
the sons of Aaron. * and his sons Lev 7:34
as priests—to * and to his sons. Lev 7:35
Moses, "Now bring * and his sons Lev 8:1
Then he took * and his sons and Lev 8:6
and he clothed * with the special Lev 8:7
sin offering, and * and his sons Lev 8:14
burnt offering. * and his sons laid Lev 8:18
of consecration; * and his sons Lev 8:22
in the hands of * and his sons to Lev 8:27
sprinkled it upon * and upon his Lev 8:30
* and his sons and their clothes. Lev 8:30
Then Moses said to * and his Lev 8:31
And again he warned * and his Lev 8:35
So * and his sons did all that Lev 8:36
Moses summoned * and Aaron's sons Lev 9:1
Israel, and told * to take a bull Lev 9:2
Moses then told * to proceed to Lev 9:7
had commanded. So * went up to the Lev 9:8
and * burned it upon the altar; Lev 9:20
the people, * blessed them and came Lev 9:22
Moses and * went into the Lev 9:23
BUT NADAB AND Abihu, the sons of * Lev 10:1
Then Moses said to *, "This is Lev 10:3
And * was speechless. Lev 10:3
Then Moses said to * and his sons Lev 10:6
Now the Lord instructed *, Lev 10:8,9
Then Moses said to * and to his Lev 10:12
Ithamar, the remaining sons of *. Lev 10:16
But * interceded with Moses. Lev 10:19
THEN THE LORD said to Moses and *, Lev 11:1
THE LORD SAID to Moses and *, "If Lev 13:1
He must be brought to * the Lev 13:1
Then the Lord said to Moses and * Lev 14:33,34
THE LORD TOLD Moses and * to give Lev 15:1
your brother * not to enter into Lev 16:1
sacrificed by * as a sin offering. Lev 16:9
"After * has sacrificed the Lev 16:11
Tabernacle when * enters to make Lev 16:17
"Then * shall go into the Lev 16:23
the Holy Place by *, to make Lev 16:27
in place of his ancestor *; Lev 16:32
And * followed all these Lev 16:35
instructions for * and the priests Lev 17:1
to Moses, "Tell * that any of his Lev 21:16,17
is a descendant of *—he is not Lev 21:21
instructions to * and his sons and Lev 21:24
THE LORD TOLD Moses, "Instruct * Lev 22:1
to Moses, "Tell * and his sons and Lev 22:17,18
Each morning and evening * shall Lev 24:3,4
The bread shall be eaten by * Lev 24:9
You and * are to direct the Num 1:2-15
Moses and * and the above- Num 1:17,18,19
to Moses and *: "Each tribe will Num 2:1
the generations of * and Moses." Num 3:2f
Ithamar to assist their father *. Num 3:4
them to * as his assistants. Num 3:6
However, only * and his sons may Num 3:10
of Moses and of * and his sons, who Num 3:38
by Moses and * at the command of Num 3:39
for each one to * and his sons." Num 3:47,48
And Moses gave it to * and his Num 3:51
THEN THE LORD said to Moses and *, Num 4:1
"When the camp moves, * and his Num 4:5
When * and his sons have Num 4:15
the Lord said to Moses and * Num 4:17,18,19
most holy things: * and his sons Num 4:17,18,19
of these items. * or any of his Num 4:27
So Moses and * and the other Num 4:34
Thus Moses and * and the leaders Num 4:46,47,48
to Moses, "Tell * and his sons Num 6:22,23
This is how * and his sons Num 6:27
THE LORD SAID to Moses, "Tell * Num 8:2
So * did this. Num 8:3
upon them, and *, with a gesture Num 8:11
to be presented to * and his sons, Num 8:13
as a gift to * and his sons. Num 8:19
So Moses and * and all the people Num 8:20
their clothes, and * presented them Num 8:21
as assistants to * and his sons; Num 8:22
They came to Moses and * and Num 9:6,7
ONE DAY MIRIAM and * were Num 12:1
Immediately he summoned Moses, * Num 12:3,4
the Tabernacle. "* and Miriam, Num 12:5
with leprosy. When * saw what had Num 12:10
report to Moses, *, and all the Num 13:26
of complaint against Moses and *. Num 14:2
Then Moses and * fell face Num 14:5
to Moses and to *, "How long will Num 14:26,27
Moses and * and the other judges. Num 15:33
They went to Moses and * and Num 16:3
And what has * done, that you are Num 16:11,12
your friends; * will be here too. Num 16:16
* will also be here with his." Num 16:17
the Tabernacle with Moses and *. Num 16:18
against Moses and *, and they all Num 16:19
said to Moses and *, "Get away Num 16:20
But Moses and * fell face Num 16:22
Eleazar the son of * the priest to Num 16:36,37
a descendant of *—may come before Num 16:40
against Moses and *, saying, "You Num 16:41
Moses and * came and stood at Num 16:43,44
But Moses and * fell face Num 16:45
And Moses said to *, "Quick, Num 16:46
* did as Moses had told him to, Num 16:47
Then * returned to Moses at the Num 16:50
(including *) brought him a rod. Num 17:6
Then each man except * claimed Num 17:9
THE LORD NOW spoke to *: "You Num 18:1
instructions to *: "I have given Num 18:8
shall be given to * the priest. Num 18:28,29
and wine press. * and his sons and Num 18:31
THE LORD SAID to Moses and *, Num 19:1
rebelled against Moses and *. Num 20:2
Moses and * turned away and went Num 20:6
then you and * must summon the Num 20:8
then Moses and * summoned the Num 20:10
But the Lord said to Moses and *, Num 20:12
Then the Lord said to Moses and * Num 20:23
time has come for * to die—for he Num 20:24
Now take * and his son Eleazar Num 20:25
his son; and * shall die there." Num 20:26
* and put them on his son Eleazar; Num 20:28
* died on the top of the mountain. Num 20:28
and grandson of * the priest) saw Num 25:7
and grandson of * the priest) has Num 25:10,11
to Eleazar (son of * the priest), Num 26:1
against Moses and *, and in fact Num 26:5-11
They were the parents of *, Num 26:58,59
and Miriam. To * were born Nadab, Num 26:60
you shall die as * your brother Num 27:13
Moses and * led them out of Egypt. Num 33:1
foot of Mount Hor, * the priest was Num 33:38,39
listened to me. * was in great Deu 9:20
where * died and was buried. Deu 10:6
ancestors, just as * your brother Deu 32:50
tribe of Levi, descendants of *). Jos 21:4
descendants of *, who was a member Jos 21:9-16
the priests—the descendants of *. Jos 21:19
"Then I sent Moses and * to Jos 24:5
Eleazar, the son of *, also died; Jos 24:33
and grandson of *, was the priest. Ju 20:27,28
Moses and *," Samuel continued. 1Sa 12:6
* to bring them into this land. 1Sa 12:8
*, Moses, Miriam. 1Ch 6:3
generations of * were as follows: 1Ch 6:4-15
But only * and his descendants 1Ch 6:49
The descendants of * were: 1Ch 6:50-53
the descendants of *, all of whom 1Ch 6:54
From the priests—descendants of * 1Ch 12:24-37
Amram was the ancestor of * and 1Ch 23:13
Literally, "the sons of Amram: * 1Ch 23:13f
* and his sons were set apart for 1Ch 23:13
*—in the sacrifices at the Temple; 1Ch 23:28
THE PRIESTS (THE descendants of *) 1Ch 24:1
were also sons of *, but they died 1Ch 24:1
by God through their ancestor *. 1Ch 24:19
Like the descendants of *, they 1Ch 24:31
Over the descendants of *, Zadok; 1Ch 27:16-22
Only the descendants of * are our 2Ch 13:10
alone, the sons of * who are 2Ch 26:17,18
the sons of *, to sacrifice them on 2Ch 29:21
Eleazar was the son of *, the Ez 7:1
A priest—a descendant of *—would Neh 10:38
the descendants of * the priest." Neh 12:47f
Moses and * as their shepherds. Ps 77:20
When Moses and * and Samuel, his Ps 99:6
and * with him, to call down Ps 105:26
yes, and *, too, the man anointed Ps 106:16
O priests of *, trust the Lord! Ps 115:10
and the priests of *, and all, Ps 115:12
And let the priests of * Ps 118:3
High priests of *, bless his Ps 135:19
I gave you Moses, *, and Miriam Mic 6:4
of the Jews, a descendant of *. Lk 1:5
They told *, 'Make idols for us, Act 7:40
work in the same way God chose *. Heb 5:4
with the rank of *—the same rank Heb 7:11
AARON'S
to listen to Moses' and * lies!" Ex 5:9
* son Eleazar married one of the Ex 6:25
serpents, too! But * serpent Ex 7:12
make special garments for * sons. Ex 28:4
to be carried over * heart when Ex 28:30,31

(AARON'S Con't)
with an opening for * head. Ex 28:32
ribbon to the front of * turban. Ex 28:37,38
"Weave * tunic from fine-twined Ex 28:39
"Then, for * sons, make robes, Ex 28:40
Then put * robe on him, and the Ex 29:5
Then take the breast of * Ex 29:26
adultery—at * encouragement, and Ex 32:25
because they had worshiped * calf. Ex 32:35
This same cloth was used for * Ex 39:1
Moses and Aaron and * sons Ex 40:31
the Lord, and * sons, the priests, Lev 1:5
of the altar, and * sons, the Lev 1:11
Tabernacle. Then * sons shall throw Lev 3:2
"* sons shall stand in front of Lev 6:14
and placed on * head the turban Lev 8:9
anointing oil upon * head, thus Lev 8:12
Next Moses placed the robes on * Lev 8:13
upon the lobe of * right ear and Lev 8:23
of the blood upon * sons—upon the Lev 8:24
summoned Aaron and * sons and the Lev 9:1
sacrifice; and * sons brought the Lev 9:18
and Elzaphon, * cousins, the sons Lev 10:4
AFTER * TWO sons died before the Lev 16:1
spoke to Moses on Mount Sinai, * Num 3:2
(Note: Eleazar, * son, shall be Num 3:31-35
"* son Eleazar shall be Num 4:16
responsible to * son Ithamar. Num 4:28
also report to * son Ithamar." Num 4:33
the leadership of Ithamar, * son. Num 7:8
inscribed upon it. * name is to be Num 17:1
day, he found that * rod, Num 17:8
The Lord told Moses to place * Num 17:10
complaints about * authority; Num 17:10
And he said to Moses, "Get * Num 20:8
There you shall remove * Num 20:26
were informed of * death, they Num 20:29
* sons were: 1Ch 6:3
two divisions named after * sons, 1Ch 24:1
then he divided * descendants 1Ch 24:3
was poured over * head, and ran Ps 133:2
it, and * wooden cane that budded. Heb 9:4

ABADDON
name in Hebrew is *, and in Greek, Rev 9:11

ABAGTHA
Harbona, Bigtha, *, Zethar, and Est 1:10

ABANA
Aren't the * River and Pharpar 2Ki 5:12

ABANDON
will not * you nor destroy you nor Deu 4:31
them and I will * them, hiding my Deu 31:17
He said, 'I will * them; Deu 32:20
I will not * you or fail to help Jos 1:5
Yet you continue to * me and to Ju 10:13
The Lord will not * his chosen 1Sa 12:22
He will * Israel because 1Ki 14:16
and induced him to * the Temple of 2Ch 24:17,18
mercy you did not * us to slavery; Ez 9:9
you didn't * them, even though Neh 9:17
* them to die in the wilderness! Neh 9:19
them completely or * them forever. Neh 9:31
Don't * me. Job 13:21
and mother should * me, you would Ps 27:10
he will never * his people. Ps 37:28
Don't * me—for you made me. Ps 138:8
Never * a friend—either yours or Pro 27:10
Then at last they will * their Is 2:20
he will * his siege. Is 37:30
I will never * the Jews, or David Jer 33:25,26
Let her go. * her and return to Jer 51:9
the Lord will not * him forever. Lam 3:31
I will * them and return to my Hos 5:15
God will * his people to their Mic 5:3
No, I will not * you or leave Jn 14:18
to * their children in the fields. Act 7:19
hidden, and had to * him, Pharaoh's Act 7:21
Some of the sailors planned to * Act 27:30

ABANDONED
live, and the land won't be *." Gen 47:19
and have quickly * all my laws. Ex 32:8
Unless their Rock had * them, Deu 32:30
They * Jehovah, the God loved Ju 2:12-14
But he was furious about it and * Ju 14:19
the Lord had seemingly * them. 1Sa 7:2
were dead, they * their cities; 1Sa 31:7
had been * by the Philistines. 2Sa 5:21
people of Israel * the Lord their 1Ki 9:9
they * their cities and fled. 1Ch 10:7
his people * the Lord God of their 2Ch 7:22
other tribes now * their homes and 2Ch 11:13,14
and power he * the Lord, and the 2Ch 12:1
you and * you to Shishak.' 2Ch 12:5
Lord our God; they * the Lord and 2Ch 29:6
of heaven, and he * them and let Ez 5:12
For once again we have * you and Ez 9:10
He who * us to our foes! Ps 60:9,10
Let their homes be desolate and *. Ps 69:25
Then he * his Tabernacle at Ps 78:60
these girls have * their husbands Pro 2:16,17
You stand there helpless and * Is 1:8
and for the * farms of Heshbon and Is 16:8
Israel will be as * as the Is 17:5
become like the * cities of the Is 17:9
everything is lost, * and Is 24:19
and empty, houses *, streets grown Is 27:10
parts of your * land shall soon be Is 49:19
for she who was * has more Is 54:1
young wife * by her husband. Is 54:6
For a brief moment I * you. Is 54:7
All the cities are *—all have Jer 4:29
Then the Lord said: I have * my Jer 12:7
is that they are permanently *. Jer 13:19f
I have * them because of all Jer 33:5
Judah and Israel and then * them! Jer 33:24
remain, and it will be * forever.' Jer 51:61,62
and burned, and the idol altars *. Eze 6:4-7
the Lord God, you * my flock, Eze 34:8
You will be * forever; Eze 35:9
tribe of Levi who * me when Israel Eze 44:10
Temple when Israel * me for idols. Eze 44:15
who have * their fathers' faith. Dan 11:30,31
evil ways, he * his plan to destroy Jon 3:10
rest in the * houses in Ashkelon. Zep 2:7
"Why has God * us?" Mal 2:14
it is a sign that you have * it Mk 6:11
to you that we have * our sins?" Lk 3:12
Or, "who * their original rank Jud 1:6f

ABANDONING
* that one, he dug again, and Gen 26:22
into the night, * their tents, 2Ki 7:7

ABANDONS
hunted down, but God never * us. 2Co 4:9

ABARIM
"Go up into Mount * and look Num 27:12
the mountains of *, near Mount Num 33:47
Mount Nebo in the * mountains, in Deu 32:49

ABATE
"And God does not * his anger. Job 9:13
the Lord will not * until it has Jer 23:20

ABBREVIATION
Coniah is an *—perhaps a Jer 22:24,25f

ABDA
Adoniram (son of *) was 1Ki 4:1
Bakbukiah and * (son of Neh 11:15,16,17

ABDEEL
Kedar, *,Mibsam, Mishma, Gen 25:12-15
*) to arrest Baruch and Jeremiah. Jer 36:26

ABDI
Kishi, *, Malluch, Hashabiah, 1Ch 6:44-47
clan, Kish (son of *) and Azariah 2Ch 29:12,13,14
*, Jeremoth, Elijah. Ez 10:26

ABDI-EL
Ahi, the son of * and grandson of 1Ch 5:15

ABDON
Mishal, *, Helkath, and Rehob. Jos 21:30,31
Next was * (son of Hillel) from Ju 12:13
The tribe of Asher gave them *, 1Ch 6:74
Ishpan, Eber, Eliel, *, Zichri, 1Ch 8:22-25
His oldest son was named *, 1Ch 8:30,31,32
Gibeon, * (the oldest), Zur, Kish, 1Ch 9:35,36,37
(son of Shaphan), * (son of Micah), 2Ch 34:20

ABEDNEGO
Azariah was called *. Dan 1:7
Meshach, and * as Daniel's Dan 2:49
Meshach, and *, whom you have put Dan 3:12
and * to be brought in before him. Dan 3:13
Meshach, and *," he asked, "that Dan 3:14
Shadrach, Meshach, and * replied, Dan 3:16
anger at Shadrach, Meshach, and *. Dan 3:19
*, and throw them into the fire. Dan 3:20
So Shadrach, Meshach, and * fell Dan 3:23
*, servants of the Most High God! Dan 3:26
Meshach, and *, for he sent his Dan 3:28
Meshach, and * shall be torn limb Dan 3:29
Meshach, and *, so that they Dan 3:30

ABEL
Her next child was his brother, *. Gen 4:2
* became a shepherd, while Cain Gen 4:2
farm produce, and * brought the Gen 4:4
Where is *?" Gen 4:9
at the city of * in Beth-maacah. 2Sa 20:14
they besieged * and built a mound 2Sa 20:15
an argument, ask advice at *.' 2Sa 20:18
men from righteous * to Zechariah Mt 23:35
from the murder of * to the murder Lk 11:51
It was by faith that * obeyed God Heb 11:4
God accepted * and proved it by Heb 11:4
and though * is long dead, we can Heb 11:4
vengeance as the blood of * did. Heb 12:24

ABEL-BETH-MAACAH
and he destroyed Ijon, Dan, *, 1Ki 15:20
He captured the cities of Ijon, * 2Ki 15:29

ABEL-MAIM
of Ijon, Dan, * and all of the 2Ch 16:4

ABEL-MEHOLAH
to the border of * near Tabbath. Ju 7:22
to * and over to Jokmeam; 1Ki 4:8-19
*) to replace you as my prophet. 1Ki 19:16

ABEL-MIZRAIM
renamed the place * (meaning Gen 50:11

ABEL-SHITTIM
far as *, on the plains of Moab. Num 33:49

ABEL'S
And the Lord accepted * offering, Gen 4:4

ABHOR
that is the reason I * them. Lev 20:23
and I will * you. Lev 26:30
"My best friends * me. Job 19:19
how you * all murder and Ps 5:6
help me to * all crooked deals of Ps 101:3
Do you * Jerusalem? Jer 14:19

ABHORRED
against his people, and he * them. Ps 106:40

ABHORRENT
This is * to the Lord your God. Deu 22:5

ABHORS
those the Lord *, whose only goal Ps 10:3
promises, and * those who don't. Pro 12:22

ABI
His mother's name: * (daughter of 2Ki 18:1

ABI-ALBON
* from Arbath; 2Sa 23:24-39

ABI-EZER
* from Anathoth; 2Sa 23:24-39
* from Anathoth; 1Ch 11:26-47
Ninth Division was * (from Anathoth 1Ch 27:12

ABIASAPH
sons of Korah:Assir, Elkanah, *. Ex 6:24

ABIATHAR
Only *, one of the sons of 1Sa 22:20
were saved. (* the priest went to 1Sa 23:6
plan and told * the priest to bring 1Sa 23:9
Then he said to * the priest, 1Sa 30:7
me the ephod!" So * brought it. 1Sa 30:7
Ahimelech (son of *) were the High 2Sa 8:17
into the country. * and Zadok and 2Sa 15:24
So Zadok and * carried the Ark of 2Sa 15:29
Zadok and *, the priests, are 2Sa 15:35,36
to Zadok and *, the priests, what 2Sa 17:15
Then David sent Zadok and * the 2Sa 19:11,12
and * were the chief priests. 2Sa 20:25
He took General Joab and * the 1Ki 1:7
and * the priest and General Joab. 1Ki 1:19
General Joab and * the priest; 1Ki 1:25
son of * the priest, rushed in. 1Ki 1:42
He and * the priest and General 1Ki 2:22
Then the king said to * the 1Ki 2:26
So Solomon forced * to give up 1Ki 2:27
and Zadok as priest instead of *. 1Ki 2:35
Zadok and * were priests; 1Ki 4:1
Then David called for Zadok and * 1Ch 15:11
(son of *) were the head priests; 1Ch 18:16
the son of *, and the heads of the 1Ch 24:6
(the son of Benaiah) and by *. 1Ch 27:34
the house of God—* was High Priest Mk 2:25,26

ABIATHAR'S
son Ahima-az and * son Jonathan. 2Sa 15:27

ABIB
Literally, "the tenth day of *." Ex 13:4,5f
Literally, "*"—the first month Deu 16:1f
me away to Tel *, another colony of Eze 3:14,15

ABIDA
Epher, Hanoch, *, and Eldaah. Gen 25:4
Ephah, Epher, Hanoch, *, and 1Ch 1:33

ABIDAN
Benjamin - * (son of Num 1:2-15
Leader: Gamaliel * Num 2:3-31
On the ninth day it was * the son Num 7:60-65
led by * the son of Gideoni. Num 10:24

ABIDING
to the wicked, but * love surrounds Ps 32:10

ABIEL
He was the son of *, grandson of 1Sa 9:1
both were the sons of *. 1Sa 14:50,51
* from Arbath; 1Ch 11:26-47

ABIEZER
was given to the clans of *, Jos 17:2
and the men of * came to him. Ju 6:34
than the entire crop of *?" Ju 8:2,3f
bore Ishhod, *, and Mahlah. 1Ch 7:18

ABIEZRITE
on the farm of Joash the *. Ju 6:11

ABIEZRITES
in Ophrah in the land of the *. Ju 6:24
in Ophrah, in the land of the *. Ju 8:32

ABIGAIL
intelligent woman, was named *. 1Sa 25:3
men went and told *, "David sent 1Sa 25:14
Then * hurriedly took two hundred 1Sa 25:18
When * saw David, she quickly 1Sa 25:23
David replied to *, "Bless the 1Sa 25:32
* to ask her to become his wife. 1Sa 25:39
and * of Carmel, Nabal's widow. 1Sa 27:2,3
Ahino-am and *, were among those 1Sa 30:5
from Jezreel and * the widow of 2Sa 2:2
*, the widow of Nabal of Carmel. 2Sa 3:3
Zeruiah and * 1Ch 2:16
*, whose husband was Jether from 1Ch 2:17
whose mother was * from Carmel. 1Ch 3:1

ABIGAL
and his mother was *, the daughter 2Sa 17:25

ABIHAIL
Zuriel (son of *) Num 3:31-35

ABIHAIL Con't)
his wife * were Ahban and Molid. 1Ch 2:29
Michael, Gilead, Jaroah, Huri, *. 1Ch 5:14
Jerimoth and of *, the daughter of 2Ch 11:18
the daughter of * who was Est 2:15f
(daughter of * and later adopted by Est 9:29-31
ABIHU
Their children were: Nadab, * Ex 6:23
with Aaron, Nadab, *, and seventy Ex 24:1
Then Moses, Aaron, Nadab, *, and Ex 24:9
his sons Nadab, *, Eleazer, and Ex 28:1
BUT NADAB AND *, the sons of Lev 10:1
death of Nadab and *, and mourn Lev 10:6
Nadab (his oldest), *, Eleazar, Num 3:2
But Nadab and * died before the Num 3:4
To Aaron were born Nadab, *, Num 26:60
But Nadab and * died when they Num 26:61
Nadab, *, Eleazar, Ithamar. 1Ch 6:3
Nadab and * were also sons of 1Ch 24:1
ABIHUD
Addar, Gera, *, Abishua, Naaman, 1Ch 8:3,4,5
ABIJAH
Joel and *, his oldest sons, 1Sa 8:2
JEROBOAM'S SON * now became very 1Ki 14:1
Rehoboam, *, Asa, Jehoshaphat, 1Ch 3:10-14
the oldest;*, the second. 1Ch 6:28
Eli-o-enai, Omri, Jeremoth, *, 1Ch 7:8
The children she bore him were *, 2Ch 11:20
Maacah's son * was his favorite, 2Ch 11:22
and his son * became the new king. 2Ch 12:16
* BECAME THE new king of Judah, in 2Ch 13:1
Judah, led by King *, fielded 2Ch 13:3
of Ephraim, King * shouted to King 2Ch 13:4
God used King * and the men of 2Ch 13:15,16
Meanwhile, King * of Judah became 2Ch 13:21
KING * WAS buried in Jerusalem. 2Ch 14:1
His mother's name was *, the 2Ch 29:1
Baruch, Meshullam, *, Neh 10:1
Ginnethoi, *, Mijamin, Neh 12:1
Zichri, leader of the * clan; Neh 12:12-21
Rehoboam was the father of *; Mt 1:7
Abijah; * was the father of Asa; Mt 1:7
Zacharias was a member of the * Lk 1:5
ABIJAH'S
his power during * lifetime, and 2Ch 13:20
ABIJAM
and his son * took the throne. 1Ki 14:31
* BEGAN HIS three-year reign as 1Ki 15:1
ABIJAM'S
reign in Israel. (* mother was 1Ki 15:1
But despite * sin, the Lord 1Ki 15:4
During * reign there was 1Ki 15:6
The rest of * history is 1Ki 15:7
ABILENE
Lysanias, over *; Lk 3:1
ABILITIES
with God-given * are to assist Ex 36:1
given me, and my * were constantly Job 29:20
their *—and then left on his trip. Mt 25:15
*, and with our help you believed. 1Co 3:5
about the special * the Holy Spirit 1Co 12:1
kinds of special *, but it is the 1Co 12:4
for the special * the Holy Spirit 1Co 14:1
of showing off my own power and *. 2Co 12:9
each of us special *—whatever he Eph 4:7
* to do certain things best? Eph 4:12
Be sure to use the * God has 1Ti 4:14
Put these * to work; 1Ti 4:15
certain special * from the Holy Heb 2:4
given each of you some special *; 1Pe 4:10
ABILITY
him great wisdom, *, and skill in Ex 31:3
more leadership * among the 1Ch 24:4
their ancestry and * at Jazer in 1Ch 26:31,32
* to give wise advice satisfies Pro 18:20
four youths great * to learn and Dan 1:17
to Daniel special * in Dan 1:17
for he had great *, and the king Dan 6:3
Some are born without the * to Mt 19:12
the Holy Spirit gave them this *. Act 2:4
God's * to know what is going on? Act 5:9
extent of my *, I am ready to come Rom 1:15
God has given each of us the * to Rom 12:6
So if God has given you the * to Rom 12:6
you administrative * and put you in Rom 12:8
gives the * to give wise advice; 1Co 12:8
Does God give all of us the * to 1Co 12:30
any other special * from the Holy 1Co 14:37
power and special * to do it well. Eph 3:7
been given special * as apostles; Eph 4:11
some have special * in winning Eph 4:11
character and *, and if they do 1Ti 3:10
God-given * you received as a gift 2Ti 1:14
ABIMA-EL
*, Sheba, Ophir, Havi-lah, Jobab. Gen 10:26-30
Diklah, Ebal, *, Sheba, Ophir, 1Ch 1:20-23
ABIMELECH
Then King * sent for her, and had Gen 20:2
But * hadn't slept with her yet, Gen 20:4
Then King * took sheep and oxen Gen 20:14
* for taking Abraham's wife. Gen 20:18
About this time King *, and Gen 21:22
Then King *, and Phicol, Gen 21:32
*, king of the Philistines, lived. Gen 26:1
But sometime later, King *, king Gen 26:8
* called for Isaac and exclaimed, Gen 26:9
treat us this way?" * exclaimed. Gen 26:10
Then * made a public Gen 26:11
And King * asked Isaac to leave Gen 26:16
from Gerar. King * arrived with his Gen 26:26
presented him with a son named *. Ju 8:31
ONE DAY GIDEON'S son * visited his Ju 9:1
so * felt close kinship there. Ju 9:2f
* was acclaimed king of Israel. Ju 9:6
thing in making * your king, that Ju 9:16
slave girl's son, *, to be your Ju 9:18
then may you and * have a long and Ju 9:19
Gideon, then may * destroy the Ju 9:20
and may they destroy *!" Ju 9:20
in Beer for fear of his brother *. Ju 9:21
between King * and the citizens of Ju 9:22,23
followed, both * and the citizens Ju 9:24
set an ambush for * along the trail Ju 9:25
But someone warned * about their Ju 9:25
and everyone began cursing *. Ju 9:27
"Who is *," Gaal shouted, "and Ju 9:28
Down with *! Ju 9:28
soon see what happens to *! Ju 9:29
I'll tell *, 'Get up an army and Ju 9:29
He sent messengers to * in Ju 9:31
So * and his men marched through Ju 9:34
the local leaders, * and his men Ju 9:35
"Who was it who said, 'Who is *, Ju 9:38
and fought with *, but was Ju 9:39
to the city gate. * was living at Ju 9:41
However, someone had told * about Ju 9:42
killing them. * stormed the city Ju 9:44
on all day before * finally Ju 9:45
When * learned of this, he led Ju 9:47,48
* next attacked the city of Ju 9:50
But as * was preparing to burn Ju 9:52
be said that a woman killed *!" Ju 9:54
Thus God punished both * and the Ju 9:56,57
Wasn't * killed at Thebez by a 2Sa 11:19,20,21
ABIMELECH'S
Of all of Gideon's wives, only * Ju 9:2f
of the city and proposed * scheme; Ju 9:3
where, following * example, the Ju 9:49
It landed on * head, crushing his Ju 9:53
AFTER * DEATH, the next judge of Ju 10:1
ABINADAB
the Ark to the hillside home of *; 1Sa 7:1
Then Jesse told his son * to step 1Sa 16:8
The three oldest—Eliab, *, and 1Sa 17:13
taken from the hillside home of *. 2Sa 6:3
his second was *, his third was 1Ch 2:13
Jonathan, Malchishua, *, Eshbaal. 1Ch 8:33
Malchishua, *, and Eshbaal. 1Ch 9:39
sons, Jonathan, *, and Malchishua, 1Ch 10:2
It was taken from the house of * 1Ch 13:7
ABINADAB'S
It was driven by * sons, Uzzah 2Sa 6:3
ABINIDAB
sons Jonathan, *, and Malchishua. 1Sa 31:2
ABINO-AM
O son of *, lead away your Ju 5:12
ABINOAM
Barak (son of *), who lived in Ju 4:6
ABIRAM
with Dathan and * (the sons of Num 16:1
Dathan and * (the sons of Eliab), Num 16:11,12
tents of Korah, Dathan, and *." Num 16:23,24
of Dathan and *, followed closely Num 16:25
the tents of Korah, Dathan, and *. Num 16:27
And Dathan and * came out and Num 16:27
of Nemu-el, *, and Dathan. Num 26:5-11
This Dathan and * were the two Num 26:5-11
* (the sons of Eliab, descendants Deu 11:6
his oldest son, *, died; 1Ki 16:34
Dathan, * and his friends; Ps 106:17
ABISHAG
in all the land. *, from Shunam, 1Ki 1:3,4
He was an old, old man now, and * 1Ki 1:15
*, the Shunammite, as my wife." 1Ki 2:17
Adonijah marry *," she replied. 1Ki 2:21
"If I were to give him *, I 1Ki 2:22
ABISHAI
(the Hittite) and * (Joab's brother 1Sa 26:5,6,7
"I'll go with you," * replied. 1Sa 26:5,6,7
So David and * went to Saul's 1Sa 26:5,6,7
for sure," * whispered to David. 1Sa 26:8
Joab's brothers, * and Asahel, 2Sa 2:18
Now Joab and * set out after 2Sa 2:24
So Joab and his brother * killed 2Sa 3:30
*, who was to attack the city. 2Sa 10:10
my lord the king?" * demanded. 2Sa 16:9
brother, * (the son of Zeruiah); 2Sa 18:2
And the king commanded Joab, *, 2Sa 18:5
say to you and * and Ittai, 'For my 2Sa 18:12
* asked, "Shall not Shime-i die, 2Sa 19:21
Then David said to *, "That 2Sa 20:6
So * and Joab set out after Sheba 2Sa 20:7
Joab and his brother * left him 2Sa 20:8,9,10
to kill him. But * the son of 2Sa 21:17
Of those three men, *, the 2Sa 23:18,19
Joab, *, Asahel, and Benaiah. 2Sa 23:24-39f
Zeruiah's sons were *, Joab, and 1Ch 2:16
*, Joab's brother, was commander 1Ch 11:20
* (son of Zeruiah) then destroyed 1Ch 18:12
*, moved against the Ammonites. 1Ch 19:11
ABISHAI'S
under attack by * troops, saw that 1Ch 19:15
ABISHALOM
was Maacah, the daughter of *. 1Ki 15:1
was Maacah, the daughter of *. 1Ki 15:10
ABISHU-A
Bukki was the son of *; Ez 7:1
* was the son of Phinehas; Ez 7:1
ABISHUA
*, the father of 1Ch 6:4-15
Eleazar, Phinehas, *, 1Ch 6:50-53
Addar, Gera, Abihud, *, Naaman, 1Ch 8:3,4,5
ABISHUR
Nadab and *. 1Ch 2:28
The sons of * and his wife 1Ch 2:29
ABITAL
Then Shephatiah was born to *, 2Sa 3:4
was Shephatiah, the son of *. 1Ch 3:3
ABITUB
His wife Hushim had borne him * 1Ch 8:11
ABIUD
Zerubbabel was the father of *; Mt 1:13
* was the father of Eliakim; Mt 1:13
ABJECT
So Israel was reduced to * Ju 6:6,7
ABLE
* to distinguish good from evil!" Gen 3:5
If they are * to accomplish all Gen 11:6
Isaac: "How were you * to find Gen 27:20
they were * to do the same thing Ex 7:11
you won't even be * to see the Ex 10:4,5
you will be * to endure the Ex 18:23
He chose * men from all over Ex 18:25
* to walk again, even with a limp, Ex 21:19
I will be * to obtain his Ex 32:30
He will be * to create beautiful Ex 35:32
Moses was not * to enter because Ex 40:35
he is * to afford—and use one of Lev 14:22
pair he is * to afford). Lev 14:30
but are not * to bring the Lev 14:32
the priest will be * to sprinkle Lev 17:6
owner is not * to redeem it, then Lev 25:28
and older who are * to go to war, Num 1:2-15
are * to work in the Tabernacle. Num 4:3
we are well * to conquer it!" Num 13:30
because he wasn't * to take care of Num 14:16
and clan are * to go to war." Num 26:2
and you will be * to go in and Deu 6:18
You will also be * to throw out Deu 6:19
No one will be * to stand against Deu 7:24
the Lord wasn't * to bring them to Deu 9:28
No one will be * to stand Deu 11:25
often as you are * to obtain it, Deu 12:15
Give as you are *, according as Deu 16:17
avenge the death will not be * to. Deu 19:6,7
In this way you will be * to Deu 19:10
you will not be * to help them. Deu 28:32
You will then be * to live safely Deu 30:20
I am no longer * to lead you, Deu 31:2
Literally, "I am no longer * to Deu 31:2f
No one will be * to oppose you Jos 1:5
will be * to stand up to you." Jos 10:8
"and if you are * to do it, you Jos 17:15
* to clear it all and live there. Jos 17:16,17,18
will not be * to say to ours, 'You Jos 22:26,27
no one has been * to defeat you. Jos 23:9
"Who is * to stand before 1Sa 6:20
If your man is * to kill me, 1Sa 17:9
For who by himself is * to carry 1Ki 3:9
had not been * to build it because 1Ki 5:2,3
had not been * to wipe them out 1Ki 9:20,21
Jeroboam was very *, and when 1Ki 11:27,28
so that he was * to run ahead of 1Ki 18:46
you won't be * to buy any of it!" 2Ki 7:2
you won't be * to buy any of it!" 2Ki 7:19
He was * to go on as far as 2Ki 9:27
He will never be * to save you 2Ki 18:29
What god has ever been * to save 2Ki 18:35
and that I will be * to go to the 2Ki 20:8
They were brave and * warriors, 1Ch 12:21
Semachiah, were also very * men. 1Ch 26:6,7
for who is * to govern by himself 2Ch 1:10
"The Lord is * to give you much 2Ch 25:9
will be * to return to this land. 2Ch 30:9
nations weren't * to do a thing to 2Ch 32:13
was * to resist us successfully. 2Ch 32:14
has ever yet been * to rescue his 2Ch 32:15
Some of the leaders were * to Ez 2:68
Then they will be * to offer Ez 6:10
and then they would be * to Neh 6:12,13
only then will I be * to face Job 13:20
again be * to enjoy his family. Job 21:21
Who is * to number his hosts of Job 25:3

(ABLE Con't)
Have you made him * to leap Job 39:20
Instead, the godly are * to be Ps 37:26
has been * to obey his laws and to Ps 78:7
with longing to be * to enter your Ps 84:2
My enemies have never been * to Ps 129:2
You won't be * to buy him off no Pro 6:35
it is to be * to say the right Pro 15:23
things, to be * to analyze them and Ecc 8:1
no one will be * to put it out. Is 1:31
none will be * to stop him. Is 22:22
not be * to prevail against you. Jer 1:18
And no one will be * to put the Jer 4:4
be * to put out the raging flames. Jer 17:27
face, for he won't be * to see. Eze 12:12
certainly be * to get it back!' Eze 33:24
nations be * to scoff at your land Eze 36:30
he is cleansed and * to perform his Eze 44:26
deep I wouldn't be * to get across Eze 47:5
our God is * to deliver us; Dan 3:17
for he is * to take those who Dan 4:37
* to deliver you from the lions?" Dan 6:20
me, so that I was * to break Dan 10:13
none will be * to stop him. Dan 11:16
be * to rescue her from my hand. Hos 1:10
Literally, "God is * of these Mt 3:9f
Those who hadn't been * to say a Mt 15:31
them, "Are you * to drink from the Mt 20:22
"Yes," they replied, "we are * Mt 20:22
man said, 'I am * to destroy the Mt 26:60,61
Literally, "as they were * to Mk 4:33f
Literally, "will be * to speak Mk 9:39f
Are you * to drink from the Mk 10:38
They will be * even to handle Mk 16:18
and they will be * to place their Mk 16:18
And so they are never * to help Lk 8:14
You won't be * to say, 'It has Lk 17:21
your opponents will be * to reply! Lk 21:15
And you won't be * to come where Jn 7:34
him and not being * to find him, Jn 7:36
won't be * to come where I am'?" Jn 7:36
When you were young, you were * Jn 21:18
you will not be * to stop them, Act 5:39
But none of them were * to stand Act 6:10
Alternatively, "Who will be * Act 8:33f
we nor our fathers were * to bear? Act 15:10
At last the mayor was * to quiet Act 19:35
words which are * to build your Act 20:32
he began, "to be * to present my Act 26:2
well * to do anything he promised. Rom 4:21
happens, we are * to hold our heads Rom 5:5
will ever be * to separate us from Rom 8:39
And God is * to make them do as Rom 14:4
* to teach others all about them. Rom 15:14
Then I will be * to come to you Rom 15:32
I commit you to God, who is * to Rom 16:25,26,27
So you should be * to decide your 1Co 6:3
church should be * to decide these 1Co 6:4f
Satan won't be * to tempt them 1Co 7:5
being * to stay happily unmarried. 1Co 7:7
Still another person is * to 1Co 12:10
IF I HAD the gift of being * to 1Co 13:1
* to preach the messages of God. 1Co 14:1
is that of being * to "speak in 1Co 14:2
they won't be * to understand you. 1Co 14:2
wish you were all * to prophesy, 1Co 14:5
So you see that being * to 1Co 14:22
I want to be * to do something 2Co 1:24
that he won't be * to recover. 2Co 2:7
God is * to make it up to you by 2Co 9:8
After that, we will be * to 2Co 10:16
and may you be * to feel and Eph 3:18,19
work within us is * to do far more Eph 3:20
gift of being * to preach well; Eph 4:11
Let no one be * to accuse you of Eph 5:3
that you will be * to stand safe Eph 6:11
Wear shoes that are * to speed Eph 6:15
no one being * to criticize you Php 1:10
We want to be * to present each Col 1:28
And these people will not be * to 1Th 5:3
then no one will be * to say 1Ti 5:14
am sure that he is * to safely 2Ti 1:12
that they will be * to teach it to Tit 1:9
he is wonderfully * to help us. Heb 2:18
You will never be * to eat solid Heb 5:14
laws had been * to save us, why Heb 7:11
He is * to save completely all Heb 7:25
of this she was * to become a Heb 11:11
for it is * to save our souls as it Jas 1:21
And he is * to keep you from Jud 1:24,25
won't be * to—death will not come. Rev 9:6
"Who is * to fight against Rev 13:4
Let those who are *, interpret Rev 13:18

ABLE-BODIED
his army—all the * men of Judah and 1Ki 12:21
asking every * man to help demolish 1Ki 15:22

ABNER
his cousin *, his uncle Ner's son. 1Sa 14:50,51
Goliath, he asked *, the general of 1Sa 17:55
of his army, "*, what sort of 1Sa 17:55
"I really don't know," * said. 1Sa 17:55
After David had killed Goliath, * 1Sa 17:57
Jonathan sat opposite him and * 1Sa 20:24,25
King Saul and General * were 1Sa 26:5,6,7
Then David shouted down to * and 1Sa 26:14
to Abner and Saul, "Wake up, *!" 1Sa 26:14
"Who is it?" * demanded. 1Sa 26:14
"Well, *, you're a great fellow, 1Sa 26:15
But *, Saul's commander-in-chief, 2Sa 2:8
One day General * led some of 2Sa 2:12
Then * suggested to Joab, 2Sa 2:14
the end of the day * and the men of 2Sa 2:17
a deer, and he began chasing *. 2Sa 2:19
on, singleminded, after * alone. 2Sa 2:19
When * looked behind and saw him 2Sa 2:20
"Go after someone else!" * 2Sa 2:21
Again * shouted to him, "Get 2Sa 2:22
But he refused to turn away, so * 2Sa 2:23
Joab and Abishai set out after *. 2Sa 2:24
of the hill, and * shouted down to 2Sa 2:26
That night * and his men 2Sa 2:29
As the war went on, * became a 2Sa 3:6
But when Ish-bosheth accused * of 2Sa 3:7
Abner of this, * was furious. 2Sa 3:8
no reply, for he was afraid of *. 2Sa 3:11
Then * sent messengers to David 2Sa 3:12
* told him, "Go on home now." 2Sa 3:16
Meanwhile, * consulted with the 2Sa 3:17
* also talked to the leaders of 2Sa 3:19
As * left, he promised David, 2Sa 3:21
So David let * return in 2Sa 3:21
But just after * left, Joab and 2Sa 3:22
When Joab was told that * had 2Sa 3:23
with * and tell him to come back. 2Sa 3:26
When * arrived at Hebron, Joab 2Sa 3:27
innocent of this crime against *. 2Sa 3:28
Abishai killed * because of the 2Sa 3:30
"Go into deep mourning for *." 2Sa 3:31
They buried * in Hebron. 2Sa 3:32
"Should * have died like a 2Sa 3:33,34
my two generals, * and Amasa. 1Ki 2:5
deaths of General *, 1Ki 2:32
the son of Kish, * the son of Ner, 1Ch 26:28
Over Benjamin, Ja-asiel (son of * 1Ch 27:16-22

ABNER'S
uncle Ner's son. (* father, Ner, 1Sa 14:50,51
Gibeon desert. * troops from the 2Sa 2:25
But three hundred and sixty of * 2Sa 2:31
in no way responsible for * death. 2Sa 3:37
heard about * death at Hebron, he 2Sa 4:1
and buried it in * tomb in Hebron. 2Sa 4:12

ABOARD
We went * a boat at Troas, and Act 16:11
he left us * ship while he went Act 18:19
Then we went * and they returned Act 21:6
bound for Italy, and put us *. Act 27:6
we hoisted * the lifeboat that was Act 27:16
all die unless everyone stays *." Act 27:31
that is the number we had *. Act 27:37

ABOLISH
I will * crop failures and Eze 36:29
made, and I will * the heathen Mic 5:14

ABOLISHED
And all idols will be utterly * Is 2:18

ABOMINABLE
must not do any of these * things; Lev 18:26
to me, and your * idol worship in Jer 13:27
by worshiping their * idols there. Jer 32:34

ABOMINATION
For such men are an * to the Pro 3:32
set up the * that astonished." Dan 11:30,31f
Literally, "the * of Mt 24:15f
it is an * in the sight of God. Lk 16:15

ABOMINATIONS
"Yes, all these * have been done Lev 18:27

ABOUND
Fish will * in the Dead Sea, for Eze 47:9

ABOUNDING
we see God's * grace forgiving us. Rom 5:20
and steady, always * in the Lord's 1Co 15:58

ABOVE-MENTIONED
made all of the * items for King 2Ch 4:12-16

ABOVE-NAMED
Moses and Aaron and the * Num 1:17,18,19

ABRAHAM
Father'), but '*' ('Father of Gen 17:5
Then * threw himself down in Gen 17:17
And * said to God, "Yes, do Gen 17:18
Then, that very day, * took Gen 17:23
had told him to. * was ninety-nine Gen 17:24-27
THE LORD APPEARED again to * Gen 18:1
Then * ran back to the tent and Gen 18:6
"In the tent," * replied. Gen 18:9
Now * and Sarah were both very Gen 18:11
Then God said to *, "Why did Gen 18:13
* went with them part of the way. Gen 18:16
"Should I hide my plan from *?" Gen 18:17
"For * shall become a mighty Gen 18:18
So the Lord told *, "I have Gen 18:20
the Lord remained with * a while. Gen 18:22,23
a while. Then * approached him and Gen 18:22,23
Then * spoke again. Gen 18:27
Then * went further with his Gen 18:29
"Please don't be angry," * Gen 18:30
Then * said, "Since I have dared Gen 18:31
Finally, * said, "Oh, let not Gen 18:32
finished his conversation with *. Gen 18:33
And * returned to his tent. Gen 18:33
That morning * was up early and Gen 19:27
NOW * MOVED south to the Negeb, Gen 20:1
Then the king called for *. Gen 20:9,10
"Well," * said, "I figured Gen 20:11,12
gave them to *, and returned Sarah Gen 20:14
Then * prayed, asking God to cure Gen 20:17
pregnant and gave * a baby son in Gen 21:2
God had said; and * named him Gen 21:3
Eight days after he was born, * Gen 21:4,5
(* was 100 years old at that time. Gen 21:4,5
Yet I have given * a child in his Gen 21:7
was weaned; and * gave a party to Gen 21:8
Ishmael—the son of * and the Gen 21:9
Isaac, she turned upon * and Gen 21:10
This upset * very much, for after Gen 21:11
But God told *, "Don't be upset Gen 21:12
So * got up early the next Gen 21:14
troops, came to * and said to him, Gen 21:22
* replied, "All right, I swear Gen 21:24
Then * complained to the king Gen 21:25
Then * gave sheep and oxen to the Gen 21:27
And * replied, "They are my gift Gen 21:30
home again. And * planted a Gen 21:33
And * lived in the Philistine Gen 21:34
"*!" Gen 22:1
The next morning * got up early, Gen 22:3
* saw the place in the distance. Gen 22:4
"Stay here with the donkey," * Gen 22:5
* placed the wood for the burnt Gen 22:6
"God will see to it, my son," * Gen 22:8
where God had told * to go, he Gen 22:9
the wood. And * took the knife and Gen 22:10
shouted to him from heaven, "*! Gen 22:11
him from heaven, "Abraham! *!" Gen 22:11
Then * noticed a ram caught by Gen 22:13
on the altar. * named the place Gen 22:14
God called again to * from heaven. Gen 22:15
there * mourned and wept for her. Gen 23:1
Then * bowed low before them and Gen 23:7
up, answering * as the others Gen 23:10
said to *, "please listen to me. Gen 23:11
* bowed again to the men of Heth, Gen 23:12
So * paid Ephron the price he had Gen 23:16
the city gate. So * buried Sarah Gen 23:19,20
* WAS NOW a very old man, and God Gen 24:1
One day * said to his household Gen 24:2
"No!" * warned. Gen 24:6
under the thigh of * his master and Gen 24:9f
to my master * and help me to Gen 24:12
God of my master *," he prayed; Gen 24:27
God of my master *, if you are Gen 24:42
God of my master *, because he had Gen 24:48
NOW * MARRIED again. Gen 25:1
* deeded everything he owned to Gen 25:5
Then * died, at the ripe old age Gen 25:7,8
in the field * had purchased from Gen 25:9,10
who was the son of * and Hagar the Gen 25:12-15
just as I promised * your father. Gen 26:3
I will do this because * obeyed Gen 26:5
by the servants of his father *. Gen 26:15
of his father *, the ones the Gen 26:18
"I am the God of * your Gen 26:24
my promise to *, who obeyed me." Gen 26:24
mighty blessings promised to *. Gen 28:4
for God has given it to *." Gen 28:4
of *, and of your father Isaac. Gen 28:13
of my grandfather *, even the Gen 31:42
I call upon the God of * and Gen 31:53
Then Jacob prayed, "O God of * Gen 32:9
the land I gave to * and Isaac. Gen 35:12
Hebron), where * too had lived. Gen 35:27
God of my fathers *, Isaac, the Gen 48:15
names of my fathers * and Isaac; Gen 48:16
Mamre—the field * bought from Gen 49:29,30
There they buried * and Sarah Gen 49:31
my grandfather * purchased from the Gen 49:32
cave * had bought in the field of Gen 50:12,13
of *, Isaac and Jacob." Gen 50:24
his promise to *, Isaac, and Jacob Ex 2:24
God of *, Isaac, and Jacob." Ex 3:6
the God of your ancestors *, Ex 3:15
of their ancestors *, Isaac, and Ex 4:5
who appeared to *, Isaac, and Ex 6:2,3
to give to *, Isaac, and Jacob. Ex 6:8,9
servants—to *, Isaac, and Israel. Ex 32:13
I promised *, Isaac, and Jacob; Ex 33:1
my promises to *, Isaac, and Jacob, Lev 26:42
land he promised *, Isaac, and Num 32:10,11
to your ancestors *, Isaac, and Deu 1:8
your ancestors, *, Isaac, and Deu 6:10,11,12
to your ancestors, *, Isaac, and Deu 9:5
your servants *, Isaac, and Jacob. Deu 9:27
ancestors, *, Isaac, and Jacob. Deu 29:13
ancestors, *, Isaac, and Jacob." Deu 30:20
"I promised *, Isaac, and Jacob Deu 34:4

ABRAHAM Con't)
the father of * and Nahor, lived Jos 24:2
But I took your father * from Jos 24:3
"O Lord God of *, Isaac, and 1Ki 18:36
contract with *, Isaac, and Jacob. 2Ki 13:23
was Abram (later known as *). 1Ch 1:24-27
* also had sons by his concubine 1Ch 1:32
These were the descendants of * 1Ch 1:33
O descendants of his servant *, 1Ch 16:12,13
His agreement with *, 1Ch 16:16
"O Lord God of our fathers: *, 1Ch 29:18
the descendants of your friend *? 2Ch 20:7
"Come back to the Lord God of *, 2Ch 30:6
the Chaldeans and renamed him *. Neh 9:7
the God of *—for the battle Ps 47:9
of God's servant *, and of Jacob. Ps 105:5,6
his covenant with * and Isaac, and Ps 105:8,9
sacred promises to * his servant. Ps 105:42
Lord who redeemed * says: My people Is 29:22
Yes, think about your ancestors * Is 51:1
* was only one when I called him. Is 51:1
Even if * and Jacob would disown Is 63:16
descendants of *, Isaac and Jacob. Jer 33:25,26
keep saying, "* was only one man Eze 33:24
us, as you promised our father *! Mic 7:20
*, all created by the same God. Mal 2:10
descendant of King David and of *: Mt 1:1
* was the father of Isaac; Mt 1:2
from * unto David are fourteen." Mt 1:17f
generations from * to King David; Mt 1:17
for we are Jews—descendants of *.' Mt 3:9
to raise up children unto *." Mt 3:9f
Heaven with *, Isaac, and Jacob. Mt 8:11
the God of *, Isaac, and Jacob'? Mt 22:32
e., if *, Isaac, and Jacob, long Mt 22:32f
said, "I was the God of *, etc." Mt 22:32f
'I am the God of *, and I am the Mk 12:26
For he promised our fathers—* Lk 1:55
ancestors, yes, to * himself, by Lk 1:72,73
because you are descendants of *. Lk 3:8
God can produce children of * Lk 3:8
Isaac's father was *; Lk 3:23-38
outside and see *, Isaac, Jacob, Lk 13:28
angels to be with * in the place of Lk 16:22
in the far distance with *. Lk 16:23
" 'Father *,' he shouted, 'have Lk 16:24
"But * said to him, 'Son, Lk 16:25
said, 'O Father *, then please send Lk 16:27
"But * said, 'The Scriptures Lk 16:29
*, they won't bother to read them. Lk 16:30
"But * said, 'If they won't Lk 16:31
sons of *, and I, the Messiah, Lk 19:9,10
God as 'the God of *, the God of Lk 20:37,38
"But we are descendants of *," Jn 8:33
that you are descendants of *! Jn 8:37
"Our father is *," they Jn 8:39
* wouldn't do a thing like that! Jn 8:40
by a demon. Even * and the Jn 8:52
than our father *, who died? Jn 8:53
Your father * rejoiced to see my Jn 8:56
years old—sure, you've seen *!" Jn 8:57
before * was ever born!" Jn 8:58
For it is the God of *, Isaac, Act 3:13
is the promise God gave to *. Act 3:25
appeared to our ancestor * in Iraq Act 7:2
"God also gave * the ceremony of Act 7:8
between God and the people of *. Act 7:8
buried in the tomb * bought from Act 7:16
his promise to * to free his Act 7:17,18
ancestors—of *, Isaac and Jacob.' Act 7:32
"Brothers—you sons of *, and Act 13:26
* WAS, HUMANLY speaking, the Rom 4:1
But from God's point of view * Rom 4:1
For the Scriptures tell us * Rom 4:3
Well, what about *? Rom 4:9
did God give this blessing to *? Rom 4:10
was a sign that * already had faith Rom 4:11
took place. So * is the spiritual Rom 4:11
faith. And * is also the spiritual Rom 4:12
saves them, for * found favor with Rom 4:12
the whole earth to * and his Rom 4:13
was not because * obeyed God's laws Rom 4:13
Abraham's, for * is the father of Rom 4:16
made * the father of many nations. Rom 4:17
nation who trust God as * did. Rom 4:17
So, when God told * that he would Rom 4:18
a great nation, * believed God even Rom 4:18
But * never doubted. Rom 4:20
way he accepted *—when we believe Rom 4:24
they come from * doesn't make them Rom 9:7
though * had other children too. Rom 9:7
of salvation which he made to *. Rom 9:8
a descendant of * and a member of Rom 11:1
And since * and the prophets are Rom 11:16
God has promised * and his Rom 11:17
promises to *, Isaac, and Jacob. Rom 11:28
And they are descendants of *? 2Co 11:22
* had the same experience—God Gal 3:6
real children of * are all the men Gal 3:7
God told * about this long ago Gal 3:8,9
the same blessing * received. Gal 3:8,9
same blessing he promised to *; Gal 3:14
Now, God gave some promises to * Gal 3:16
his promise to *, he did it by Gal 3:20
descendants of *, and all of God's Gal 3:29
For it is written that * had two Gal 4:22
say that God told * to send away Gal 4:30
God's promise to *: God took an Heb 6:13
he would bless * again and again, Heb 6:14
Then * waited patiently until Heb 6:15
High God. When * was returning home Heb 7:1
then * took a tenth of all he Heb 7:2
appearing to * in human form, or Heb 7:3f
(a) Even *, the first and most Heb 7:4
One could understand why * would Heb 7:5
a relative, and yet * paid him. Heb 7:6
upon mighty *, and as everyone Heb 7:6
tithes to Melchizedek through *. Heb 7:9
he came was in * when Abraham paid Heb 7:10
* paid the tithes to Melchizedek. Heb 7:10
* trusted God, and when God told Heb 11:8
he promised to give him, * obeyed. Heb 11:8
the same promise. * did this Heb 11:10
nation came from *, who was too old Heb 11:12
While God was testing him, * Heb 11:17
* a whole nation of descendants! Heb 11:18
for as far as * was concerned, Heb 11:19
even our father * was declared good Jas 2:21
say, that * trusted God, and the Jas 2:23
obeyed her husband *, honoring him 1Pe 3:6

ABRAHAM'S
year of * departure from Haran. Gen 11:32f
So God heeded * plea and kept Gen 19:29
Abimelech for taking * wife. Gen 20:18
violently away from * servants. Gen 21:25
LATER ON, GOD tested * [faith and Gen 22:1
the wife of * brother Nahor, had Gen 22:20-23
to follow * instructions. Gen 24:9
He took with him ten of * camels Gen 24:10
* brother. Gen 24:15,16f
"I am * servant," he explained. Gen 24:34
At this reply, * servant fell to Gen 24:52
where Sarah, * wife was buried. Gen 25:9,10
After * death, God poured out Gen 25:11
before, in * time, and so Isaac Gen 26:1
and daughter of Ishmael, * son. Gen 28:9
* sons were 1Ch 1:28-31
* son Isaac had two sons, 1Ch 1:34
for you are * family, and he was Is 41:8
Isaac's father was Abraham;* Lk 3:23-38
Literally, "into * bosom." Lk 16:22f
And so Isaac, * son, was Act 7:8
we have faith like *, for Abraham Rom 4:16
And because of * faith God Rom 4:23
faith—wasn't just for * benefit. Rom 4:23
make them truly * children. Rom 9:7
apply only to * son Isaac and Rom 9:7
This means that not all of * Rom 9:8
But some of these branches from * Rom 11:17
God's favor than * way, for he Gal 3:18
in my illustration * slave-wife Gal 4:24,25
could not inherit * home and lands Gal 4:30

ABRAM
three sons, *, Nahor, and Haran. Gen 11:26
Meanwhile, * married his Gen 11:29
Then Terah took his son *, his Gen 11:31
So * departed as the Lord had Gen 12:4
and Lot went too; * was Gen 12:4
Then Jehovah appeared to * and Gen 12:7
And * built an altar there to Gen 12:7
Afterwards * left that place and Gen 12:8
* went on down to Egypt to live. Gen 12:10
Then Pharaoh gave * many gifts Gen 12:16
Then Pharaoh called * before him Gen 12:18
under armed escort—*, his wife, and Gen 12:20
into the Negeb—* with his wife, and Gen 13:1
they owned, for * was very rich in Gen 13:1
not support both * and Lot with all Gen 13:6
the herdsmen of * and Lot, despite Gen 13:7
Then * talked it over with Lot. Gen 13:8
and thus he and * parted company. Gen 13:11
company. For * stayed in the land Gen 13:12
the Lord said to *, "Look as far Gen 13:14
Then * moved his tent to the Gen 13:18
came and told * the Hebrew, who was Gen 14:13
When * learned that Lot had been Gen 14:14
As * returned from his strike Gen 14:17
Then Melchizedek blessed * with Gen 14:19,20
heaven and earth, be upon you, *; Gen 14:19,20
Then * gave Melchizedek a tenth of Gen 14:19,20
But * replied, "I have solemnly Gen 14:22
lest you say, '* is rich because of Gen 14:23
JEHOVAH SPOKE to * in a Gen 15:1
fearful, *, for I will defend you. Gen 15:1
But * replied, "O Lord Jehovah, Gen 15:2,3
Then God brought * outside Gen 15:5
And * believed God; Gen 15:6
But * replied, "O Lord Jehovah, Gen 15:8
the carcasses, * shooed them away. Gen 15:11
sleep fell upon *, and a vision of Gen 15:12
Then Jehovah told *, "Your Gen 15:13
and it was dark, * saw a smoking Gen 15:17
this covenant with *: "I have Gen 15:18
BUT SARAI AND * had no children. Gen 16:1
her to * to be his second wife. Gen 16:2,3
And * agreed. (This took place ten Gen 16:2,3
ten years after * had first arrived Gen 16:2,3
Then Sarai said to *, "It's all Gen 16:5
girl as you see fit," * replied. Gen 16:6
So Hagar gave * a son, and Abram Gen 16:15
So Hagar gave Abram a son, and * Gen 16:15
him Ishmael. (* was eighty-six Gen 16:16
WHEN * WAS ninety-nine years old, Gen 17:1
of nations!" * fell face downward Gen 17:2,3,4
It is no longer '*' ('Exalted Gen 17:5
The son of Terah was * (later 1Ch 1:24-27
Lord God who chose * and brought Neh 9:7

ABRAM'S
AFTER THE DEATH of * father, God Gen 12:1
taking with them Lot—* nephew Gen 14:12
Literally, "* brother's son." Gen 14:12f
of Eshcol and Aner, * allies). Gen 14:13

ABREAST
by keeping * of the facts. Pro 24:3,4
chariots could go * on them, and Zep 2:15f

ABROAD
of Ham, spread * in many lands and Gen 10:20
Literally, "if he walks * with Ex 21:19f
and publish it *: The Lord who Jer 31:10
shout * when daybreak comes. Mt 10:27
be published * in all the earth." Rom 9:17f
Christ is already * in the world. 1Jn 4:3

ABRONAH
From Jotbathah to *; Num 33:15-37
From * to Ezion-geber; Num 33:15-37

ABRUPTLY
weather changed * and a heavy wind Act 27:14,15

ABSALOM
The third was *, born to Maacah, 2Sa 3:3
PRINCE *, DAVID'S son, had a 2Sa 13:1
Her brother * asked her, "Is it 2Sa 13:20
very angry, but * said nothing one 2Sa 13:21-24
in Ephraim, * invited his father 2Sa 13:21-24
* pressed him, but he wouldn't 2Sa 13:25
"Well, then," * said, "if you 2Sa 13:26
* kept on urging the matter until 2Sa 13:27
* told his men, "Wait until 2Sa 13:28
reached David: "* has killed all 2Sa 13:29,30
It was only Amnon! * has been 2Sa 13:32,33
(* got away. 2Sa 13:34
* fled to King Talmai of Geshur 2Sa 13:37,38,39
day for fellowship with his son *. 2Sa 13:37,38,39
was longing to see *, he sent for 2Sa 14:1
right, go and bring back *." 2Sa 14:21
and brought * back to Jerusalem. 2Sa 14:23
of manhood as *, and no one else 2Sa 14:25
After * had been in Jerusalem for 2Sa 14:28
but Joab wouldn't come. * sent 2Sa 14:29
So * said to his servants, "Go 2Sa 14:30
Then Joab came to * and demanded, 2Sa 14:31
And * replied, "Because I wanted 2Sa 14:32
So Joab told the king what * had 2Sa 14:33
Then at last David summoned *, 2Sa 14:33
* THEN BOUGHT a magnificent 2Sa 15:1
king for trial, * called him over 2Sa 15:2
to bow to him, * wouldn't let him, 2Sa 15:5
So in this way * stole the 2Sa 15:6
After four years, * said to the 2Sa 15:7,8
So * went to Hebron. 2Sa 15:9
* has been crowned in Hebron." 2Sa 15:10
Ahithophel declared for *, as did 2Sa 15:12
* in a conspiracy against you!" 2Sa 15:13
was backing *, David prayed, "O 2Sa 15:31
give * foolish advice!" 2Sa 15:31
return to Jerusalem and tell *, 2Sa 15:33,34
getting there just as * arrived. 2Sa 15:37
Lord has given it to your son *! 2Sa 16:7,8
Meanwhile, * and his men arrived 2Sa 16:15
he went immediately to see *. 2Sa 16:16
your friend David?" * asked him. 2Sa 16:17
Then * turned to Ahithophel and 2Sa 16:20
could see it, and * went into the 2Sa 16:22
father's wives. (* did whatever 2Sa 16:23
* and all the elders of Israel 2Sa 17:4
of the plan, but * said, "Ask 2Sa 17:5
When Hushai arrived, * told him 2Sa 17:6
"What is your opinion?" * asked 2Sa 17:6
Then * and all the men of Israel 2Sa 17:14
he could bring disaster upon *! 2Sa 17:14
to David, and he told * about it. 2Sa 17:18
disgraced when * refused his 2Sa 17:23
Meanwhile, * had mobilized the 2Sa 17:24
the Jordan River. * had appointed 2Sa 17:25
mother Zeruiah.) * and the Israeli 2Sa 17:26
sake, deal gently with young *." 2Sa 18:5
During the battle * came upon 2Sa 18:9
sake, please don't harm young *.' 2Sa 18:12
into the heart of * as he dangled 2Sa 18:14
surrounded * and finished him off. 2Sa 18:15
(* had built a monument to 2Sa 18:18
has saved him from his enemy *." 2Sa 18:19
"What of young *?" 2Sa 18:29
"What about young *? 2Sa 18:32

(ABSALOM Con't)
"O my son *, my son, my son 2Sa 18:33
my son Absalom, my son, my son *. 2Sa 18:33
for you! O *, my son, my son." 2Sa 18:33
was weeping and mourning for *. 2Sa 19:1
and kept on weeping, "O my son *! 2Sa 19:4
son Absalom! O * my son, my son!" 2Sa 19:4
to you; if * had lived and all of 2Sa 19:6
Philistines; and *, whom we made 2Sa 19:8,9,10
of the country, but now * is dead. 2Sa 19:8,9,10
going to hurt us more than * did. 2Sa 20:6
when I fled from your brother *. 1Ki 2:7
The third was *, the son of his 1Ch 3:2
married Maacah, the daughter of *. 2Ch 11:20
David when he fled from his son * Ps 3:1

ABSALOM'S
woman in her brother * quarters. 2Sa 13:20
Then, two years later, when * 2Sa 13:21-24
and it was also * home town, its 2Sa 15:9f
When * men arrived and asked her 2Sa 17:20
They threw * body into a deep 2Sa 18:17
He called it "* Monument," as 2Sa 18:18
man, and was * younger brother. 1Ki 1:6
revolt, though not *) he ran to the 1Ki 2:28

ABSENCE
had been harvested during her *. 2Ki 8:6

ABSENT
sings who, long * from her lovers, Is 23:15,16

ABSOLUTE
* loyalty and exclusive devotion. Ex 34:14
of Israel, and give you * power. 1Ki 11:37
His power is *! Ps 147:5
in God—this is the * truth—you can Mk 11:22,23
Jesus: "The * truth is that I Jn 8:58
am not telling the * truth: the 2Co 1:23
chosen—this is the * truth—as God's 1Ti 2:7

ABSOLUTELY
"Homosexuality is * forbidden, Lev 18:22
to take them, but he * refused. 2Ki 5:16
Even the heavens can't be * pure Job 15:15
return to me and * discard your Jer 4:1
for it is * true that the Lord Jer 26:15
And my judgment is * fair and Jn 5:30
but if I were, it would be an * Jn 8:16

ABSTAIN
on you than to * from eating food Act 15:27,28,29

ABSURD
that what he does is * or evil? Job 36:23
This is *, a hollow mockery, and Ecc 6:2

ABSURDITY
what an *! Ecc 3:19

ABUNDANCE
I have guaranteed him * of grain Gen 27:37
They shall be blessed with an * of Num 24:3-9
"The Lord will give you an * of Deu 28:11
There was an * of burnt 2Ch 29:35
Slaves among all this *! Neh 9:36
and there was an * of royal wine, Est 1:7
the people, giving them food in *. Job 36:31
us into wealth and great *. Ps 66:12
* of peace to the end of time. Ps 72:7
righteousness. An * of salvation Is 33:6
Yes, there will be an * of Is 35:2
priests with the * of offerings Jer 31:14
there will be such * of crops, that Amo 9:13
all shall be! The * of grain and Zec 9:16,17
given more, and he shall have *. Mt 25:29

ABUNDANT
and copper is * in the hills. Deu 8:9
many cattle, and * crops. Deu 28:11
He waters the furrows with * Ps 65:10
For the earth has yielded * Ps 67:6,7
You sent * rain upon your land, Ps 68:9,10
Bless us with * crops throughout Ps 72:16
But the * pastureland will yield Is 7:21,22
For I will give you * water for Is 44:3

ABUNDANTLY
they will breed * and reproduce in Gen 8:17
to our God, for he will * pardon! Is 55:7
the prophets will be * fulfilled. Lk 21:22

ABUSE
passing by hurled *, shaking their Mt 27:39
hurling * at Jesus, Paul shook off Act 18:6

ABUSED
to them, and they * her all night, Ju 19:25
possessions of those who * them. Eze 39:10

ABUSIVE
idols, or is a drunkard, or *. 1Co 5:11

ACACIA
skins, goat-skins, * wood, olive Ex 25:1
"Using * wood, make an Ark 3¾ Ex 25:10
Make poles from * wood overlaid Ex 25:13,14
"Then make a table of * wood Ex 25:23
Make the poles from * wood Ex 25:28
shall be made from * wood, each Ex 26:15,16
"Make bars of * wood to run Ex 26:26,27
Hang this upon four * pillars Ex 26:32
Hang up this curtain on five * Ex 26:37
"USING * WOOD, make a square Ex 27:1
from * wood overlaid with bronze. Ex 27:6
It shall be made from * wood. Ex 30:1
The poles are to be made of * Ex 30:5
* wood; Ex 35:5-9
and some brought the * wood Ex 35:24
frames of * wood standing on end. Ex 36:20
sets of bars from * wood to tie the Ex 36:31,32
into four posts of * wood, overlaid Ex 36:36
This was constructed of * wood Ex 37:1
Then he made poles from * wood, Ex 37:4
Then he made a table, using * Ex 37:10
The incense altar was made of * Ex 37:25
poles were gold-plated * wood. Ex 37:28
was also constructed of * wood; Ex 38:1
of * wood, overlaid with bronze. Ex 38:6
WHILE ISRAEL WAS camped at *, Num 25:1
So I made an Ark of * wood and Deu 10:3
Israeli camp at * to cross the Jos 2:1
of Israel left *, and arrived that Jos 3:1
dug a deep pit to trap them at *. Hos 5:2
of the Lord to water * Valley. Joe 3:18
what happened at * and Gilgal, and Mic 6:5

ACADEMIES
all the military * and training Mic 4:3

ACCAD
Babel, Erech, *, and Calneh in the Gen 10:10

ACCENT
Noticing the young Levite's *, Ju 18:3
by your Galilean * Mt 26:73

ACCEPT
All I'll * is what these young Gen 14:24
that you and they * this covenant. Gen 17:11
angel said, "I * your proposition Gen 19:21
"No, but please * them," Jacob Gen 33:10
Moses eventually decided to * Ex 2:21
of Israel will * your message. Ex 3:18
if they don't * you after these two Ex 4:9
And I will * them as my people Ex 6:7
* a fine instead, if they wish. Ex 21:30
and the owner must * his word, and Ex 22:11
and * her as his wife. Ex 22:16
our sins, and * us as your own." Ex 34:9
And you would * their daughters, Ex 34:16
will * your gift for the Lord. Lev 1:2,3
third day, the Lord will not * it; Lev 7:17,18
and the owner must * the money and Lev 25:27
humbled and they * the punishment I Lev 26:40,41
But then at last they shall * Lev 26:43
"* their gifts," the Lord told Num 7:4,5
Lord, "Do not * their sacrifices! Num 16:15
However, you may never * the Num 18:16
But if her husband refuses to * Num 30:8
then they must * land among the Num 32:30
a rich man, and never * bribes. Deu 16:19
If the defendant refuses to * Deu 17:12
and you must never * a widow's Deu 24:17
And * the work they do for you. Deu 33:11
"I * your terms," she replied. Jos 2:21
of the loaves, which you are to *. 1Sa 10:4
thought he should * the king's 1Sa 18:22
David was delighted to * the 1Sa 18:26
"I * all blame in this matter, 1Sa 25:24
then let him * my peace offering. 1Sa 26:19
the Lord God * your sacrifice." 2Sa 24:23
now please * my gifts." 2Ki 5:15
my God that I will not * them." 2Ki 5:16
refused to * him as their king; 2Ki 15:16
"And now I * your promise, Lord, 1Ch 17:23
other lands, you * as priests 2Ch 13:9
oath and vowed to * the curse of Neh 10:29
If they * bribes to denounce Job 17:5
you, and I will * his prayer on Job 42:8
* our praise, O Lord, for all Ps 21:13
They refused to * my laws. Ps 95:10
you promised me. * my grateful Ps 119:108
if you * criticism you are on the Pro 13:18
It is wrong to * a bribe to twist Pro 17:23
Don't refuse to * criticism; Pro 23:12
It is a badge of honor to * valid Pro 25:12
but refuses to * criticism will Pro 29:1
glass of wine, * his position in Ecc 5:18
To enjoy your work and to * your Ecc 5:19,20
too, when they * the Lord; Is 56:3
I will * their sacrifices and Is 56:7
God will not * their offerings. Is 66:3
I cannot * your offerings; Jer 6:20
They don't * the laws of God. Jer 8:7
Now I will no longer * you as my Jer 14:10
to me, I will not * them. Jer 14:12
And if they refuse to * the Jer 25:28
But now, because you * the false Jer 29:15
strike him, and * their awful Lam 3:30
There I will * you, and require Eze 20:40
feet, and don't * the food brought Eze 24:17
I will * you, says the Lord God." Eze 43:27
hard hearts would not * the truth. Hos 7:13
I will not * your burnt Amo 5:22
they will stay. * their gifts and Zec 6:10,11
"and I will not * your offerings. Mal 1:10
Should I * such offerings as Mal 1:13
you, but he won't * it, then the Mt 18:17
"Not everyone can * this Mt 19:11
Let anyone who can, * my Mt 19:12
laws to * money paid for murder." Mt 27:
of those who truly * God's message Mk 4:2
And he could hardly * the fact Mk 6:
"And whenever a village won't * Mk 6:11
'All right, why didn't you * him?' Mk 11:31
And don't hesitate to * Lk 10:7
You won't * it for yourselves, Lk 11:52
Who will * God's mighty miracles Jn 12:38
to * the mercies God was offering. Act 13:43
too, and they will * it." Act 28:28,29
Now God says he will * and acquit Rom 3:21,22
God will * all people in every Rom 4:17
us that God will * us in the same Rom 4:24
sacrifice, holy—the kind he can *. Rom 12:1
to * the money I am bringing them. Rom 15:31
and can't * these thoughts from 1Co 2:14
Why not just * mistreatment and 1Co 6:7
be supported by those who * it. 1Co 9:14
* the invitation if you want to. 1Co 10:27
want you to try to * me and be 2Co 1:13,14
both when they * the Good News Eph 3:6
is true, and if it is, then * it. 1Th 5:21
and who refuse to * his plan to 2Th 1:8
people * God's plan of faith. 1Ti 1:3,4
truth and everyone should * it. 1Ti 4:9,10
make you wise to * God's salvation 2Ti 3:15
and refusing to * the truth. 1Jn 1:8

ACCEPTABLE
they will be an * burnt offering Lev 1:9
it will only be * to the Lord if Lev 22:19
animal is * for this sacrifice." Lev 22:25
day onward it is * as a sacrifice Lev 22:26,27
All are fire offerings, very * to Lev 23:18
the list of those * to the Lord, Lev 27:27
be able to offer * sacrifices to Ez 6:10
* to him than human sacrifice. Is 66:3
making us holy and *, ready to Lk 1:75
Literally, "to proclaim the * Lk 4:18,19f
do good deeds and are * to him. Act 10:35
made * to God because he obeyed. Rom 5:19
by God to be his people and made * 1Co 1:2
he was the one who made us * to 1Co 1:30
* to God because of our faith. Gal 4:31
Christ makes us * to God, and now Heb 7:19
so come to him—[you who are * to 1Pe 2:5

ACCEPTABLY
you and walk * before you. Ex 33:13

ACCEPTANCE
enough to pray this prayer of *. 2Sa 7:27
I came to realize that * with God Gal 2:19

ACCEPTED
And the Lord * Abel's offering, Gen 4:4
insisted, and finally Esau * them. Gen 33:11
the people will be * and forgiven. Ex 28:37,38
the animal will be * by God instead Lev 1:4
so that it will be *: Eat it the Lev 19:5
to me, and will not be *. Lev 19:7
be offered, for it will not be *. Lev 22:20
or it will not be *: An animal Lev 22:21
be * by the Lord as your gift. Lev 23:9,10,11
to Moses, "I have * the Levites in Num 3:11,12
Israel, and I have * them in place Num 8:16
Yes, I have * the Levites in Num 8:18
die—no ransom may be * for him. Num 35:31
Nor may a payment be * from a Num 35:32
So Jephthah * the commission and Ju 11:11
he wouldn't have * our burnt Ju 13:23
for money. They * bribes and were 1Sa 8:3
Then David * her gifts and told 1Sa 25:35
and * Rehoboam as their king. 1Ki 12:16,17
The surrender was *, and 2Ki 24:12
and have not * my counsel." 2Ch 25:16
So the priests and the Levites * Ez 8:30
aides and I * no salaries or other Neh 5:14
turn to go to the king, she * the Est 2:15
* Job's prayer on their behalf. Job 42:9
But you have * the offer of my Ps 40:6
Sabbath, and have * his covenant Is 56:6
for they * Jesus as a prophet. Mt 21:46
So the police * the bribe and Mt 28:15
prophet is * in his own home town! Lk 4:24
lunch and Jesus * the invitation. Lk 7:36
people, the Jews, he was not *. Jn 1:11,12
their witness is * as fact. Jn 8:17
and they * them and know of a Jn 17:8
The Council * his advice, called Act 5:40
of Samaria had * God's message, Act 8:14
Then they * him, and after that Act 9:28
died—because he * the people's Act 12:23
she * all that Paul was saying. Act 16:14
of his good deeds that God * him? Rom 4:1
God had already * him and declared Rom 4:11
he was * and approved through his Rom 4:23
in the same way he * Abraham—when Rom 4:24
For God has * them to be his Rom 14:3
God, and he has * you because of 1Co 6:11
that we might be * by God because Gal 2:16
for he simply * God's promise. Gal 3:18
our own, but you * what we said as 1Th 2:13
we never * food from anyone 2Th 3:8
the nations, was * by men 1Ti 3:16

ACCEPTED Con't)
those who have * his salvation. 1Ti 4:9,10
offering did. God * Abel and proved Heb 11:4
one of those whom God has *. Heb 11:7
all who had * the Evil Creature's Rev 19:20
or his statue, nor * his mark on Rev 20:4

ACCEPTING
be held guilty for * the Lord's Num 18:32
Those * it become aware of the Pro 13:14
justice by * bribes, and sold into Amo 2:6
no doubts about." * them might Rom 14:1f
and help, and * whatever situation 1Co 7:17
Abel and proved it by * his gift; Heb 11:4
and his statue and * his mark on Rev 14:9

ACCEPTS
If it * the truce and opens its Deu 20:11
" 'Cursed is he who * a bribe to Deu 27:25
A WISE YOUTH * his father's Pro 13:1
the fact that he * Gentiles by Act 15:8

ACCESS
You had * to the holy mountain of Eze 28:14
their angels have constant * Mt 18:10
had opened up * to the holy God. Mk 15:38f

ACCESSORIES
gold for the lampstand and its *. Ex 25:39
the ropes, and all of the *. Num 4:26
and of its *, also the table of the 2Ch 29:18

ACCIDENT
from some ordinary * or disease, Num 16:29
"But if it is an *—a case in Num 35:22,23
or not it was an *, and whether or Num 35:24
in office at the time of the *. Jos 20:6

ACCIDENTAL
But if it is *—an act of God—and Ex 21:13
If it is decided that it was *, Num 35:25
to them, for the death was *. Jos 20:5
The man who caused the * death Jos 20:6

ACCIDENTALLY
a person who has * killed someone Num 35:6
into if he has killed someone *. Num 35:11
where anyone who * killed someone Deu 4:42
so that anyone who * kills someone Deu 19:2,3
so that anyone who * killed another Jos 20:9

ACCIDENTS
God even protects him from *. Ps 34:20

ACCLAIMED
Abimelech was * king of Israel. Ju 9:6

ACCO
the residents of *, Sidon, Ahlab, Ju 1:31,32

ACCOMMODATE
for the bronze altar to *. 2Ch 7:7

ACCOMMODATING
in circumference, * a population of Jon 3:3f

ACCOMPANIED
cavalry, and people * Joseph. Gen 50:9
and all who had * him to the Gen 50:14
sons of Jacob who * him to Egypt, Ex 1:1
* with loaves of leavened bread. Lev 7:13
the grain offerings that * them). Num 7:87
be * by a grain offering. Num 15:3,4
pints of oil, * by three pints of Num 15:5
Balaam * the king to Num 22:39
They are to be * by a grain Num 28:9,10
These shall be * by your grain Num 28:28,29
without defect— * by the usual Num 29:14
without defect— * by the usual Num 29:18
without defect—* by the usual grain Num 29:26,27
them into battle, * by the Ark, Num 31:6
started toward Ai, * by the elders Jos 8:10
of the Kenite tribe—* them. Ju 1:16
sons of Eli, * it into the battle. 1Sa 4:4
So Saul got up and Samuel * him to 1Sa 9:26,27
at night, * by two of his men. 1Sa 28:7,8
Twenty men * him, and David 2Sa 3:20
And King David * the bier to 2Sa 3:31
at Jerusalem, * by Ahithophel. 2Sa 16:15
joined them and * them to Egypt, 1Ki 11:16,17,18
great enthusiasm, * by singing and 1Ch 13:8
comprised an octet * by harps. 1Ch 15:20
the Lord (while * by the zither), 1Ch 25:3
The choir was * by 120 priests 2Ch 5:11,12
aides and servants * her, including 2Ch 9:1
They marched into Jerusalem * by 2Ch 20:28
singers singing, * by an orchestra 2Ch 23:12
of the Lord, * by the trumpets. 2Ch 29:27
of the leaders who * me from Ez 8:1
of the priests who * Zerubbabel Neh 12:1
to him, * skillfully on the harp; Ps 33:3
I will tell in song * by harps Ps 49:4
Sing, * by drums; Ps 81:2
Sing his praises, * by music Ps 92:3
Sing your praise * by music from Ps 98:5
sing praises to our God, * by Ps 147:7
Praise his name with dancing, * Ps 149:3
the Temple, * by the orchestra." Is 38:20
arrived in Mizpah, * by ten men. Jer 41:1
It is * by many kings called by Jer 50:41
to move away, * by the sound of a Eze 3:12
to be * by stringed instruments. Hab 3:19
years old he * his parents to Lk 2:41,42
Then, * by the disciples, he left Lk 22:39
The next day he went with them, * Act 10:23
These six brothers here * me, and Act 11:12
by the men who had * him to Act 13:31
them to Jerusalem, * by some local Act 15:2
Paul and * him on his journey. Act 16:10f
Then they * him down to the ship. Act 20:38
Some disciples from Caesarea * Act 21:16
with great pomp, * by military Act 25:23
It was the singing of a choir * Rev 14:2

ACCOMPANIMENT
* of zithers, harps, and cymbals. 1Ch 25:1

ACCOMPANY
A grain offering shall * it, Lev 23:13
for what is to * each sacrificial Num 15:11,12
without defect. * them with nine Num 28:12
Invite them to * you to the Deu 16:11
sailors to * Solomon's crews. 1Ki 9:27,28
and cymbals to * the singers with 1Ch 16:42
and small, to * him to the Temple. 2Ch 34:30
and cavalry to * us and protect us Ez 8:22
(The ambassadors, who * the gift Is 16:3
of soldiers and police to * him. Jn 18:3

ACCOMPANYING
Also * him were: Gen 46:16,17
and the * grain offering and Num 6:15
the grain offering * it must Num 15:8,9
and their * grain offerings. Num 29:9,10
sacrifice with its * grain Num 29:16
male goat with its * grain offering Num 29:19
offering, with its * grain offering Num 29:22
each with its * grain offering and Num 29:24
with their king, * him from the 2Sa 20:2
Those * Paul went on with him to Act 17:15

ACCOMPLISH
If they are able to * all this Gen 11:6
me to * the purpose of my journey. Gen 24:12
of war to * all of this. Jos 11:18
It took six months to * this, 1Ki 11:16,17,18
Two can * more than twice as much Ecc 4:9
king of Assyria to * his purpose, Is 10:12
It shall * all I want it to, and Is 55:11
* everything he sets out to do. Dan 11:3
himself, how can he * anything? Mk 3:26
he could live to * God's perfect Heb 5:7f

ACCOMPLISHED
This was all * in one campaign, Jos 10:42
of what God had * so quickly. 2Ch 29:36
you have * them, just as you said! Is 25:1
And when he sees all that is * Is 53:11
was * by later Persian kings. Jer 51:26f
So it was that Judah's exile was * Jer 52:27
has * all its terrors upon you! Eze 24:13
Literally, "until all things be * Mt 5:18f
of the things * among us." Lk 1:3f
how I am pent up until it is *! Lk 12:50
things God had * among the Gentiles Act 21:19
This is * from start to finish by Rom 1:17
Or, "I have fully * my Gospel Rom 15:19f
its value, and what was really *. 1Co 3:13
you have * something on your own? 1Co 4:7

ACCORD
of the world. In * with my words Jer 1:10
this opened to them of its own *! Act 12:10

ACCORDANCE
food to them in * with the number Gen 47:12
garments, in * with the Lord's Ex 39:1
all this was done in * with the Ex 39:6,7
to the Lord, in * with the Lev 9:16
In * with the Lord's directions, Num 31:47
(This was all done in * with the Jos 8:33
land was in strict * with the Jos 14:5
Israel in * with our daily needs. 1Ki 8:59
from day to day in * with the 2Ch 8:13
This was in * with the directions 2Ch 29:25,26
Have compassion upon me in * with Neh 13:22
in * with his mercy and love. Is 63:7
But I will judge each of you in * Eze 33:20
carried out in * with God's plan. Lk 9:31
in exact * with the plan shown to Act 7:44
or not marrying in * with God's 1Co 7:17

ACCORDING
his affairs * to God's will. Gen 6:9,10
Shem, classified * to their Gen 10:31
Literally, "* to their Ex 6:16f
Levites, listed * to their ages. Ex 6:19
Literally, "* to their Ex 6:19f
morning, each home * to its need; Ex 16:21
shall be * to the shekel of the Lev 27:25f
It was constructed * to the exact Num 8:4
Give as you are able, * as the Deu 16:17
Literally, "* to its families." Jos 13:15f
Literally, "* to its families." Jos 13:24f
Literally, "* to its families." Jos 13:29f
"Make me your wife * to God's Ru 3:9
* to Josephus, Chimham was 2Sa 19:37f
to Rehoboam is * to my wish." 1Ki 12:23,24
THE SONS OF Benjamin, * to age, 1Ch 8:1
and lamps, each * to its use. 1Ch 28:15
dressing * to his instructions. Est 2:15
Literally, "Judge me * to your Ps 35:24f
of us * to the work we do for him. Ps 62:12
living * to their own desires. Ps 81:12
For I have tried to live * to Ps 119:94
And he will reward everyone * to Pro 24:11,12
three years, * to the year of a Is 21:16f
* to his deeds—how he has lived. Jer 17:10
everyone * to his life and deeds. Jer 32:19
compassion too, * to the greatness Lam 3:32
because, * to Mesopotamian myths, Eze 8:14f
reward each * to your own actions. Eze 18:30
to be given land * to the tribe Eze 47:23
Literally, "* to Hab 3:1f
judge each person * to his deeds. Mt 16:27
just, for it is * to the will of Jn 5:30
his generation * to the will of Act 13:36
his head shaved * to Jewish custom, Act 18:18
and no other. * to some people, 1Co 8:5
So if you are suffering * to 1Pe 4:19
And the dead were judged * to the Rev 20:12
each * to the deeds he had done. Rev 20:12
Each was judged * to his deeds. Rev 20:13
* to the deeds he has done. Rev 22:12

ACCORDINGLY
later at Jerusalem, and I lived *. Act 26:4

ACCOUNT
household on * of her being there. Gen 12:17
him righteous on * of his faith. Gen 15:6
That is the true * of how Midian Ju 8:28
credit for your *," she declared. Ju 17:3
1 Samuel 31:3, 4 for the true *. 2Sa 1:10f
required to keep * of their 2Ki 22:7
This * includes a report of 2Ch 25:27
Judah very low on * of the evil 2Ch 28:19
and a frank * of his sins and 2Ch 33:19
and also the full * of the Est 10:2
not give * to you of what he does? Job 33:13
God will never call them to *. Ps 10:13
of man that you take * of him?" Ps 144:3f
* to God for everything you do. Ecc 11:9
Matthew * loses its significance. Is 7:14f
like me and who can call me to *? Jer 49:19
Who can call me to *? Jer 50:44
that you must give * on Judgment Mt 12:36
Literally, "on * of." Mt 14:3f
them to him to * for his money. Mt 25:19
Literally, "an * of the things Lk 1:3f
Literally, "on * of the Son of Lk 6:22f
And we all know that my * of Jn 21:24
of being called to * by the Roman Act 19:40
Yes, each of us will give an * Rom 14:12

ACCOUNTABLE
The governors were * to three Dan 6:2

ACCOUNTANT
rich man hired an * to handle his Lk 16:1
the * was thoroughly dishonest. Lk 16:1
"The * thought to himself, 'Now Lk 16:3
you signed,' the * told him. Lk 16:5,6
'Here,' the * said, 'take your Lk 16:7

ACCOUNTANTS
Still others assisted as *, 2Ch 34:13

ACCOUNTED
said, "We have * for all the men Num 31:48,49
all of them shall be * for Jer 23:4

ACCOUNTING
the building. No * was required 2Ki 12:15
to the king's * office where the 2Ch 24:11
High Priest for *, and then used 2Ch 34:9
men, and demand an * from them? Job 14:3
I will call for an * of their Hos 8:13

ACCOUNTS
decided to settle * with the nation 1Sa 15:2
These * tell of his reign and of 1Ch 29:30
decided to bring his * up to date. Mt 18:23
recheck all these * from first to Lk 1:3

ACCUMULATE
"The evil man may * money like Job 27:16

ACCUMULATED
their belongings * in the land of Gen 46:6
Yes, all the * judgment of the Mt 23:36

ACCURATE
in judgment. Use * Lev 19:35,36
you must use * scales and honest Deu 25:13,14,15
and have given an * report so that Jn 19:35
my account of these things is *. Jn 21:24
Literally, "having more * Act 24:22f

ACCURATELY
to him the way of God more *." Act 18:25,26f

ACCURSED
Literally, "This multitude is * Jn 7:49f

ACCUSATION
him a letter of * against the Ez 4:6
Let them answer your *! Mt 12:27
This * roused the crowds to fury Act 6:12
*, and ground their teeth in rage. Act 7:54

ACCUSATIONS
But if the man's * are true, and Deu 22:20
* and spreading vicious rumors! Is 58:9
* to the officials and the people. Jer 26:11
Temple has made * against you! Mic 1:2
said to Satan, "I reject your *, Zec 3:2
made their many * against him, Mt 27:12
stood there shouting their *. Lk 23:10

(ACCUSATIONS Con't)
asked him, "Are these * true?" Act 7:1
these * and a great riot followed. Act 21:30
Tertullus, to make their * Act 24:1
our * by examining him yourself." Act 24:8
* which they couldn't prove. Act 25:7
But the * made against him Act 25:18
behind their * is something else—it Act 26:6
trap him with many *, and leave him 1Ti 3:7
*, and evil suspicions. 1Ti 6:4

ACCUSE
we are, that you * us of such a Gen 44:7
Don't falsely * your neighbor of Lev 19:16
can never * me of robbing you." 1Sa 12:5
It's unfair for you to * me and 1Sa 22:15
would be the first to * me." 2Sa 18:13
* him of cursing God and the king. 1Ki 21:10
and then they would be able to * Neh 6:12,13
For they * me of things I never Ps 27:12
to a lie. They * me of things I Ps 35:11
for an excuse to * them and then Ps 37:32
The wicked *; Pro 12:6
he himself will * you. Pro 23:10,11
Don't tell anyone else, lest he * Pro 25:8,9,10
Never falsely * a man to his Pro 30:10
"Son of dust, you must * Eze 23:36
stand up and * these evil nations. Zep 3:8
he will love you and not * you." Zep 3:17,18
Literally, "*." Mt 12:10f
don't * anyone of what you know Lk 3:14
"Yet it is not I who will * you Jn 5:45
but it does hate me, because I * Jn 7:7
"Which of you can truthfully * Jn 8:46
the things they * me of doing. Act 24:13
Who dares * us whom God has Rom 8:33
Let no one be able to * you of Eph 5:3
Satan's power to * you of sin, and Col 2:15
two or three witnesses to * him. 1Ti 5:19
did not dare to * even Satan, or Jud 1:9

ACCUSED
before him and * him sharply. Gen 12:18
her, and has * her of shameful Deu 22:17,18
has falsely * a virgin of Israel. Deu 22:19
But when Ish-bosheth * Abner of 2Sa 3:7
"If a man is * of doing 1Ki 8:31
* him of cursing God and the king; 1Ki 21:13
but you have * me without the Job 6:14
Prisoners are falsely * and sent Eze 22:9
to the king and * some of the Jews Dan 3:8
the men who had * Daniel, and throw Dan 6:24
synagogues, and * before governors Mk 13:9
Then the chief priests * him of Mk 15:3,4
and even ate with them," they *. Act 11:3
They * Paul of "persuading men Act 18:13
onto earth—he * them day and night Rev 12:10

ACCUSER
Satan, the *, came with them. Job 1:6
"If you meet your * on the way Lk 12:58
for the * of our brothers has Rev 12:10

ACCUSERS
said to her, "Where are your *? Jn 8:10
governor. His * wouldn't go in Jn 18:28
turned to his * and said, "Listen, Act 18:14
and will tell his * to bring their Act 23:30
fully when your * arrive," the Act 23:35
to God. My * saw me in the Temple Act 24:18
himself face to face with his *. Act 25:16

ACCUSES
sleeping with her * her of having Deu 22:13,14
"Or if my land * me because I Job 31:38,39
their own conscience * them, or Rom 2:12-15
sues another and * his Christian 1Co 6:6

ACCUSING
are * honest men of evil deeds." Ps 31:18
hand, * Joshua of many things. Zec 3:1
"In saying that, you are * Mt 23:31
They began at once * him: "This Lk 23:2
"You brought this man to me, * Lk 23:14
What are you * him of doing?" Jn 18:29
for falsely * you when you have 1Pe 3:16

ACCUSTOMED
Ephraim is * to treading out the Hos 10:11

ACHAIA
became governor of *, the Jews rose Act 18:12
in Macedonia and * have taken up an Rom 15:26
Or, "throughout *." 2Co 1:1f

ACHAICUS
* have arrived here for a visit. 1Co 16:17

ACHAN
was disobeyed. For * (the son of Jos 7:1
* was found to be the guilty one. Jos 7:18
Joshua said to *, "My son, give Jos 7:19
* replied, "I have sinned Jos 7:20
there just as * had said, with the Jos 7:22
Israelites took *, the silver, the Jos 7:24
Then Joshua said to *, "Why have Jos 7:25
Don't you remember that when *, Jos 22:20
(*, the son of Carmi, was the man 1Ch 2:7

ACHBOR
by: King Baal-hanan (son of *). Gen 36:31-39
son), and * (Michaiah's son) to ask 2Ki 22:12,13
and Ahikam, and *, and Shaphan, and 2Ki 22:14
the son of * became king. 1Ch 1:49
Elnathan (son of *) to Egypt along Jer 26:22
Elnathan (son of *), Gemariah (son Jer 36:12

ACHE
Our hearts *, but at the same 2Co 6:10
a stomach * when I swallowed it. Rev 10:10

ACHIEVED
continue until its purpose is *. Mt 5:18

ACHIEVEMENTS
and his heroic * and his wars are 1Ki 22:45

ACHIM
Zadok was the father of *; Mt 1:14
Zadok was the father of Achim; * Mt 1:14

ACHISH
Saul, and went to King * of Gath. 1Sa 21:10
of what King * might do to him, so 1Sa 21:12
finally King * said to his men, 1Sa 21:14,15
under the protection of King *. 1Sa 27:2,3
One day David said to *, "My 1Sa 27:5
So * gave him Ziklag (which still 1Sa 27:6
your raid today?" * would ask. 1Sa 27:10
the Philistines. * believed David 1Sa 27:12
"Come and help us fight," King * 1Sa 28:1
bodyguard for life," * told him. 1Sa 28:2
marched at the rear with King *. 1Sa 29:2
And King * told them, "This is 1Sa 29:3
So * finally summoned David and 1Sa 29:6
But * insisted, "As far as I'm 1Sa 29:9
slaves escaped to King * of Gath. 1Ki 2:39

ACHISH'S
of Gath. But * officers weren't 1Sa 21:11

ACHOR
brought them to the valley of *. Jos 7:24
the Valley of * to Debir, where it Jos 15:7
and the valley of * shall be a Is 65:10

ACHSAH
give his daughter * to be the wife Jos 15:16
it, so * became Othni-el's wife. Jos 15:17
have my daughter * as his wife!" Ju 1:12
the city and won * as his bride. Ju 1:13
had a daughter, whose name was *. 1Ch 2:48,49

ACHSHAPH
The king of *; Jos 11:1
The king of *; Jos 12:8-24
Helkath, Hali, Beten, *, Jos 19:24,25,26

ACHZIB
Nezib, Keilah, *, and Mareshah. Jos 15:37-44
included Mahalab, *, Ummah, Aphek, Jos 19:29
Ahlab, *, Helbah, Aphik, or Rehob; Ju 1:31,32
The town of * has deceived the Mic 1:14

ACKNOWLEDGE
of Israel to * him as their king. 1Ki 12:21
And since you have refused to * 1Ki 14:9
said to me, "We * our sin against Ez 10:2
that I refused to * my sin and do Job 31:34
had sinned and to * that God had Job 32:2
And you that are near, * my Is 33:13
Only * your guilt; Jer 3:13
I will openly * him as my friend Mt 10:32
* me here on earth as your Friend. Lk 12:8
and would not * him as their king. Lk 19:14
"Then what beliefs did you * at Act 19:3
and would not even * him, God gave Rom 1:28
* that you are the ones I love. Rev 3:9

ACKNOWLEDGED
their wives and * their guilt by Ez 10:16-19

ACKNOWLEDGES
"If anyone publicly * me as his Mt 10:32

ACKNOWLEDGING
And the king is lying in bed, * 1Ki 1:46,47
power [instead of * it was by the Mk 3:30

ACKNOWLEDGMENT
'This gift is my * that the Lord my Deu 26:2,3

ACQUAINTANCE
Lover, friend, * —all are gone. Ps 88:18

ACQUAINTED
not * with the right and the good. Job 24:13
are not * with the light. Job 24:16
sorrows, * with bitterest grief. Is 53:3
who was * with the High Priest. Jn 18:15
There he became * with a Jew Act 18:2,3
so we could get * and I could tell Act 28:20
and become better * with our Lord 2Pe 3:18

ACQUIRED
and he * many towns, for God had 2Ch 32:28,29

ACQUIT
Literally, "I will not * the Ex 23:7f
Publicly * me, Lord, for you are Ps 17:2
Now God says he will accept and * Rom 3:21,22

ACQUITTAL
Because our * is not based on our Rom 3:27
and * are kings of life Rom 5:17
death) or else obedience (with *). Rom 6:16

ACQUITTED
with him, and be * by my Judge. Job 23:7
are * if they have faith. Rom 3:30
opportunity to be * by faith, even Rom 9:30

ACRE
over about half an * of land. 1Sa 14:14
An * of vineyard will not Is 5:10

ACREAGE
and Judah are his pleasant *! Is 5:7
the ruins. * will be cultivated Eze 36:34

ACRES
as well as to all your fertile *. Is 7:19

ACT
your mistress and * as you should, Gen 16:9-12
This is a strange way to *. Gen 31:28
But if it is accidental—an * of Ex 21:13
"If a thief is caught in the * Ex 22:2
"If he is caught in the * of Ex 22:4
God, so don't * like heathen—like Lev 18:3
in the *, he must pay a fine Deu 22:28,29
They * like men of Sodom and Deu 32:32
such a dastardly *," he begged, Ju 19:23
and * like a different person. 1Sa 10:6
So I am willing to * like a fool 2Sa 6:21
We must really * like men today 2Sa 10:12
and yet you * like this, making 2Sa 19:5
If you don't *, my son Solomon 1Ki 1:21
He pretended that it was an * of 1Ki 2:5
Be courageous and let us * like 1Ch 19:13
them: "You are to * always in the 2Ch 19:9
but I obeyed God and did not * Neh 5:15
You have noted each evil *. Ps 10:14
with people who * like that; Ps 12:3,4
doing nothing? * now and rescue me, Ps 35:17
wait patiently for him to *. Ps 37:7
be impatient for the Lord to *! Ps 37:34
They * so friendly when they Ps 41:6
Expect God to *! Ps 42:11
weeping, waiting for my God to *. Ps 69:3
I cannot sleep until you *. Ps 77:4
where I long to * as I should. Ps 101:2
They wouldn't wait for him to *, Ps 106:13
Lord, it is time for you to *. Ps 119:126
how to live—how to * in every Pro 1:2
he will not * sparingly. Is 30:14
Yet they * so pious! Is 58:2
Should I sit back and * as Jer 5:29
Don't * like the people who make Jer 10:2,3
they shall * like my people. Jer 31:1
For who can * against you Lam 3:37
this gracious *, for you did not Eze 16:61
whose every * is right and good; Dan 4:37
O Lord, listen to me and *! Dan 9:19
this time I was to * the part of Zec 11:15
by the way they *, just as you can Mt 7:16
do is done for show. They * holy Mt 23:5
Turn from your sins and * on this Mk 1:15
But shall I tell you to * that Lk 16:9
caught in the very * of adultery. Jn 8:4
real father when you * that way." Jn 8:41
Lord enough to induce him to *? Rom 11:35
Don't try to * big. Rom 12:16
is from God, why * as though you 1Co 4:7
easily, I don't * as though I know 1Co 9:22
sacrifices, are united by that *. 1Co 10:18
stand true to the Lord; * like 1Co 16:13
Lord by the way we *, so that no 2Co 6:3
You have made me * like a 2Co 12:11
like the way I will have to *. 2Co 12:20
Lord—to live and * in a way worthy Eph 4:1
So be careful how you *; Eph 5:15,16
Don't * thoughtlessly, but try Eph 5:17
way they *, one knows they don't. Tit 1:16
with this loving * and my weary Phm 1:20
I have faith by the way I *." Jas 2:18
you do; so * in reverent fear of 1Pe 1:17
In this * we see what real love 1Jn 4:10
into being by your * of will." Rev 4:11

ACTED
son of Nethanel, * as recording 1Ch 24:6
"But I didn't do it, for I * to Eze 20:9,10
Philistines have * against Judah Eze 25:15
* in treachery against their God. Eze 39:23
"Consider how you have *, and Hag 1:7
never have * as our fathers did.' Mt 23:29,30
The believers * at once, sending Act 17:14
the way we have * toward you. 2Co 1:12

ACTING
Shechem and Hamor, * dishonorably Gen 34:13
lost no time in * upon this Gen 34:18,19
them why they are * like this when Gen 44:4
must obey you, and * as though you Num 16:3
Quit * so proud and arrogant! 1Sa 2:3
never be guilty of * like that." 2Sa 11:11
And his son Jotham was the * 2Ki 15:5
was, and why he was * like that. Est 4:5
In that way you will be * as Mt 5:45
you will truly be * as sons of God: Lk 6:35
* under his own authority?" Lk 20:4
eat, you are not * in love if you Rom 14:15
In fact, you are * like people 1Co 3:3
them you will start * like them. 1Co 15:33
for I am * like a brainless fool. 2Co 11:17
each other, and * big, and saying 2Co 12:20

ACTION
behind the city, alert for *. Jos 8:3,4
to Barak, "Now is the time for *! Ju 4:14
was roused to * against the men of Ju 19:30

(ACTION Con't)
the men killed in * and to gather 1Ch 10:8
Then the Levites went into *: 2Ch 29:12,13,14
feeling that this * would clear the 2Ch 34:5
Levite opposed this course of *. Ez 10:15
* was determined by throwing dice. Est 3:7
observe the power of God in *. Ps 107:24
are like goads that spur to *. Ecc 12:11
but the * was only temporary. Jer 34:10
from now you will be called to *. Eze 38:8
This brutal * of Herod's Mt 2:17
rose in concerted * against Paul Act 18:12
for their first * was to dedicate 2Co 8:5
equalled by your realistic * now. 2Co 8:11

ACTIONS
with that? Your * at the end of the Ju 8:2,3
from David's * that he was in no 2Sa 3:37
Pride, lust, and evil * Pro 21:4
A man is known by his *. Pro 21:8
plans which end up in deadly *. Is 59:5
and you have proved it by your *. Jer 44:25
each according to your own *. Eze 18:30
brought forth fire from your own * Eze 28:18
and * of the other Jewish leaders. Lk 23:50,51,52
evil thoughts and *, yet now he has Col 1:21
lead to evil * and afterwards to Jas 1:15
he did, by his *, his good deeds. Jas 2:22
love them, and show it by our *. 1Jn 3:18
for sure, by our *, that we are on 1Jn 3:19

ACTIVE
the discharge is *, but also for a Lev 15:3
hill of Gibeon continued to be *. 1Ch 16:39
These units were called up for * 1Ch 27:1
not taking a more * part, so they 2Ch 30:15
These were the men who were * in Neh 12:26
The prophet Jeremiah was * during Zep 1:1f
When your old nature was still * Rom 7:5
and * church, but you are dead. Rev 3:1

ACTIVELY
You must * obey him in Deu 6:17
you have been * helping me Ps 74:12
leaders were * plotting Jesus' Lk 22:2

ACTIVITIES
The rest of Jeroboam's *—his wars 1Ki 14:19
The rest of Jehu's * are recorded 2Ki 10:34
his wars and other *, is written in 2Ch 27:7
of his life and * are recorded in 2Ch 28:26
The other * of Josiah, and his 2Ch 35:26
in Hezekiah's * in the west. Is 39:1f
and leave behind all their busy *. Jas 1:10,11
some of the future * soon to occur Rev 1:1

ACTIVITY
is defiled with this kind of *; Lev 18:25
earth—ceaseless *, day and night. Ecc 8:16,17
encouraging the * of demons), Gal 5:20

ACTS
See also * 7:4. Gen 11:32f
The penalty for homosexual * is Lev 20:13
in the book The * of Solomon. 1Ki 11:41
songs to celebrate your mighty *! Ps 21:13
* of God shall startle everyone. Ps 65:8
can be no joy for me until he *. Ps 77:2
Publish his glorious * throughout Ps 96:3
your many * of kindness to them. Ps 106:7
God we shall do mighty * of valor. Ps 108:13
by the way he *—whether what he Pro 20:11
"Christians"? See * 11:26. Is 65:15f
I have seen their despicable * Jer 23:11
to sinning and * like any other Eze 18:24
all your * of envy and of hate. Eze 35:11
* will boomerang upon your heads. Ob 1:15
attention to their * of charity! Mt 6:2
porches at that time. See * 10:9. Mt 24:17f
See * 6:5; 8:1-13. Act 21:8f
See * 19:29, 20:4, Philemon 24. Act 27:2f
in her immoral * and enjoyed her Rev 18:9

ACTUAL
The meaning is not of the * Hebrew Gen 30:6f
Note: The * value by today's Lev 27:3f
the * construction of the Temple. 1Ki 6:1
FINALLY THE * construction of the 2Ch 3:1
the Temple. The * construction 2Ch 3:2
The * construction of the Temple Ez 3:8
and 14 exceed the * damage done to Eze 26:14f
their bodies in * body Rom 2:29
is really being offered to * gods. 1Co 8:7

ACTUALLY
baby was * the first to be born. Gen 38:29
so that they were * a part of the Ex 37:8
whether or not it is * leprosy. Lev 14:57
(*, the half-tribe of Manasseh); Num 13:3-15
But * she had taken them up to Jos 2:6
were * living right here among us? Jos 9:22
And will Saul * come, as I have 1Sa 23:11
tell the king what * had happened. 2Sa 18:29f
though he was not * one of them. 2Sa 23:18,19
was not * one of the Top Three. 2Sa 23:23
of yours, when * he has determined 2Ch 18:22
God whether they * were descendants Ez 2:62,63
* were descendants of priests. Neh 7:64,65
the first, without * canceling it. Est 8:8f

to an enemy— (but * I have never Job 31:30
gone hungry— (* I have never Job 31:32
You have * fought against us and Ps 44:10
* came into my Temple to worship! Eze 23:39
* arrived and took them all away. Mt 24:39
No one has ever * seen God, but, Jn 1:18
(Not that anyone * sees the Jn 6:46
of circumcision (*, however, this Jn 7:21,22,23
gave them to me. *, they were Jn 17:6
from time to time, * alive, and Act 1:3
But it was Solomon who * built Act 7:47
look forward to * becoming all that Rom 5:2
And God has * given us his 1Co 2:12
we Christians * do have within us a 1Co 2:16
are * parts and members of Christ? 1Co 6:15
I am one who has * seen Jesus our 1Co 9:1
apostles, yet * I wasn't doing it, 1Co 15:10
But the fact is that Christ did * 1Co 15:20
* see in my life and my message. 2Co 12:6
when * you aren't at all? 2Co 13:5
* owns everything his father had. Gal 4:1
going so far as * to die a Php 2:8
jail, and you were * joyful when Heb 10:34
we ourselves have * seen and heard, 1Jn 1:3
* became man with a human body? 1Jn 4:2
this, he is * calling God a liar, 1Jn 5:10

ADADAH
Kinah, Dimonah, *, Kedesh, Hazor, Jos 15:21-32

ADAH
Lamech married two wives—* and Gen 4:19
To * was born a baby named Jabal. Gen 4:20
One day Lamech said to * and Gen 4:23
* (daughter of Elon the Hethite), Gen 36:2,3
Esau and * had a son named Gen 36:4
Descended from his wife *, born Gen 36:10,11,12
the oldest son of Esau and *. Gen 36:15,16

ADAIAH
Jedidah (daughter of * of Bozkath) 2Ki 22:1
Ethni, Zerah, *, Ethan, Zimmah, 1Ch 6:39-43
Eliel, *, Beraiah, Shimrath. 1Ch 8:19,20,21
priests was * (son of Jeroham, son 1Ch 9:12
Maaseiah (son of *), and Elishaphat 2Ch 23:1
Meshullam, Malluch, *, Jashub, Ez 10:29
Shelemiah, Nathan, *, Machnadebai, Ez 10:34-42
of Hazaiah, son of *, son of Neh 11:4,5,6
the leadership of * (son of Neh 11:10-14

ADALIA
Aspatha, Poratha, *, Aridatha, Est 9:7-10

ADAM
"This is it!" * exclaimed. Gen 2:23
The Lord God called to *, "Why Gen 3:9
And * replied, "I heard you Gen 3:10
"Yes," * admitted, "but it was Gen 3:12
And to *, God said, "Because you Gen 3:17
and the Lord God clothed * and Gen 3:21
THEN * HAD sexual intercourse with Gen 4:1
of the descendants of *—the man Gen 5:1
*: Adam was 130 years old when Gen 5:3,4,5
Adam: * was 130 years old when Gen 5:3,4,5
* lived another 800 years, Gen 5:3,4,5
at the city of *, near Zarethan, Jos 3:15,16
*, Seth, Enosh, Kenan, Mahalalel, 1Ch 1:1
all)— or if, like *, I have tried Job 31:33
But like *, you broke my Hos 6:7
Seth's father was *; Lk 3:23-38
of the world from one man, *, Act 17:26
When * sinned, sin entered the Rom 5:12
from the time of * until Moses, God Rom 5:13
the forbidden fruit, as * had. Rom 5:14
What a contrast between * and Rom 5:14
For this one man, *, brought death Rom 5:15
The sin of this one man, *, Rom 5:17
they can live. * caused many to be Rom 5:19
And *, the first man, was not 1Co 11:9
benefit, but Eve was made for *. 1Co 11:9
of what one man (*) did, and it is 1Co 15:21
us are related to *, being members 1Co 15:22
*, was given a natural, human body 1Co 15:45
Literally, "the last *." 1Co 15:45f
heavenly bodies. * was made from 1Co 15:47
Because God made * first, and 1Ti 2:13
And it was not * who was fooled 1Ti 2:14
generations after *, knew about Jud 1:14

ADAM'S
Literally, "This is the roll of * Gen 5:1f
Seth's father was Adam;* father Lk 3:23-38
[We know that it was * sin that Rom 5:13
God's mercy. * one sin brought the Rom 5:16
Yes, * sin brought punishment to Rom 5:18
a body just like *, made of dust, 1Co 15:48
has a body like *, so we shall some 1Co 15:49

ADAMAH
Chinnereth, *, Ramah, Hazor, Jos 19:35-39

ADAMANT
But the king of Edom was *. Num 20:20
But this time the man was *, so Ju 19:10

ADAMI-NEKEB
extended across to *, Jabneel, and Jos 19:33

ADAR
third day of the month of *." Ez 6:15f

ADBEEL
Nabaioth (the oldest), Kedar, *, 1Ch 1:28-31

ADD
he must * a fifth to its value. Lev 27:31
the Lord will * anything to what he Num 22:19
Do not * other laws or subtract Deu 4:2
Do not * to or subtract from Deu 12:32
I will * fifteen years to his 2Ki 20:6
into the walls to * to the beauty; 2Ch 3:6
(The king, I should *, had sent Neh 2:9
Do not * to his words, lest he Pro 30:6
incense to * to the praise of God. Is 60:6
Some manuscripts *: "And the Eze 40:28f
and he will *, "Shhh Amo 6:10
Some manuscripts * here, "For Mt 6:13f
Will all your worries * a single Mt 6:27
Many ancient authorities * verse Mk 11:26,f
Some ancient versions *, "Blessed Lk 1:28f
Later manuscripts * to verses 55 Lk 9:55f
Some ancient manuscripts * at this Lk 11:5,6f
Will it * a single day to your Lk 12:25
Some ancient authorities * verse Lk 23:17,f
I should * that Aristarchus, Act 27:2
Some of the ancient manuscripts *, Act 28:28,29f
Here I want to * some suggestions 1Co 7:12
Well, my brothers, let's * up 1Co 14:26
to * to what I was preaching. Gal 2:6
will * to my sorrows here in jail! Php 1:16,17
LET ME * this, dear brothers: You 1Th 4:1
the letters in his name * to 666! Rev 13:18
Some manuscripts *, "and be their Rev 21:3f
here, God shall * to him the Rev 22:18

ADDAN
Tel-harsha, Cherub, *, and Immer. Ez 2:59

ADDAR
*, Gera, Abihud, Abishua, Naaman, 1Ch 8:3,4,5

ADDED
Then God *, "Regarding Sarai Gen 17:15
and Jacob * them to his flock. Gen 30:39,40
has used, with twenty per cent *; Lev 22:14
* in the Hebrew text is this Num 1:17,18,19f
of Egypt. This * to the discontent Num 11:4,5
Then the Lord * to Moses and to Num 14:26,27
are to be * to spring water in a Num 19:17
Literally, "and he * no more." Deu 5:22f
And one of the neighbors *, 1Sa 10:12
"For now we have * to all our 1Sa 12:19
"What's more," he *, "the Lord 1Sa 16:18
The men who were with him * their 1Sa 28:23
replied Benaiah, and *, "May 1Ki 1:36
But," he *, "we should ask the 1Ki 22:5
Then he *, "He was Elijah's 2Ki 3:11
Ephraim also * their opposition. 2Ch 28:12
sin will be * to our many others. 2Ch 28:13
Then I * this to my request: "If Neh 2:7
But yet," he *, "all this is Est 5:13
For now you have * rebellion, Job 34:37
* years of life, as rich and full Ps 61:6
can be * or taken from it; Ecc 3:14
this time the Lord * a lot more! Jer 36:32
"And," the women *, "do you Jer 44:19
And now the Lord has * more! Jer 45:3
Then he *: "Son of dust, let all Eze 3:10
Then he *, "Come, and I Eze 8:13
And you * lustful Egypt to your Eze 16:26
But I have * to that rule, Mt 5:22
Then he *, "Now go away and Mt 9:13
Then he *, "Anyone who obeys Mt 12:50
Then he *, "Those experts in Mt 13:52
This sentence is * in some Mt 19:9f
And then he *, "It is the Mk 7:20
"And fasting" is * in some Mk 9:29f
Then he *, "These Scriptures Lk 4:21
And Jesus *, "I Lk 6:5
And he *, "Whoever stumbles Lk 20:18
and each day God * to them all who Act 2:47
believers were * to the Lord, Act 5:14
of people were * to the Lord. Act 11:24
They were * after the promise was Gal 3:19
system, he then *, "Here I am. Heb 10:9
And he *, "God himself has Rev 19:9

ADDER
it stings like an *. Pro 23:32
From the snake will be born an *, Is 14:29

ADDERS
* will pull it out unharmed. Is 11:8

ADDI
Melchi's father was *; Lk 3:23-38

ADDI'S
Melchi's father was Addi;* father Lk 3:23-38

ADDING
what he took, * a twenty percent Lev 6:4,5
* twenty percent and returning it Num 5:7
broken down and by * to the 2Ch 32:5
* this sin to all his many others. Lk 3:19,20

ADDITION
in * to grain and vegetables. Gen 9:2,3
offering. In *, the people are to Lev 9:4
* to the regular morning offering. Lev 9:17
(These are in * to your Sabbaths Lev 23:3
These annual festivals are in * Lev 23:38
are to be in * to your regular Lev 23:38
twenty percent in * to the priest's Lev 27:19

(ADDITION Con't)
dedication. In * to these Num 6:21
had died (in * to those who had Num 16:49
—in * to the regular offerings. Num 28:9,10
This is in * to the regular daily Num 28:15
These offerings shall be in * to Num 28:23
These special offerings are in * Num 28:31
seven lambs. In *, there shall be Num 29:5
sacrifices are in * to the regular Num 29:6
and also in * to the regular Num 29:6
This is in * to the sin offering Num 29:11
and in * to the regular daily Num 29:11
a sin offering, in * to the regular Num 29:16
Also, in * to the regular daily Num 29:19
And in * to the regular daily Num 29:22
* to the regular daily sacrifices. Num 29:25
* to the usual daily sacrifices. Num 29:28
offerings. In * to the usual daily Num 29:31
* to the regular daily sacrifices. Num 29:34
* to the regular daily sacrifices. Num 29:38
feasts, and are in * to sacrifices Num 29:39
the priests. In *, the priests Deu 18:4
of land (in * to the land of Gilead Jos 17:5,6
another altar in * to the only true Jos 22:19
* to the one man who had sinned?" Jos 22:20
* to thirty thousand from Judah. 1Sa 11:8
* to ten thousand men from Judah. 1Sa 15:4
men were missing, in * to Asahel. 2Sa 2:30
And now, in * to everything 2Sa 7:19
In * to the idolatry which God 2Ki 21:16
This is in * to the building 1Ch 29:3
tribute to him. In *, there was a 2Ch 9:13,14
In *, Solomon had 4,000 stalls of 2Ch 9:25
in Jerusalem in * to those placed 2Ch 17:19
and 200 lambs. In *, 600 oxen and 2Ch 29:32,33
In *, he required the people in 2Ch 31:4
to Judah; in * to 7,337 slaves and Ez 2:64,65
in * to a section of the wall. Neh 3:11
Feast of Purim. In *, letters were Est 9:29-31
"And then, in * to all your Eze 16:23
For you are thankless in * to all Eze 16:43
in * to all your other sins. Eze 44:7
him because in * to disobeying Jn 5:18
In * to the encouragement you 2Co 7:13

ADDITIONAL
and married two * wives from there, Gen 28:9
and worked the * seven years. Gen 29:30
with * money to buy more grain. Gen 43:22
by the people and * gifts were Ex 36:3
THE LORD GAVE to Moses these * Lev 17:1
three * Cities of Refuge. Deu 19:9
These were evidently * to the Jos 8:11,12,13f
Perhaps the * five thousand were Jos 8:11,12,13f
an * field as a wedding present. Jos 15:18,19
him to ask her father for an * Ju 1:14
David married * wives and 2Sa 5:13
were joined by * Syrian troops 2Sa 10:15,16
seventy thousand * laborers, eighty 1Ki 5:15
took the throne. * details about 2Ki 15:15
he married * wives and became the 1Ch 14:3
Syrians summoned * troops from east 1Ch 19:16
As a result, * vast quantities of 2Ch 14:14
Here are some * proverbs: Pro 24:21,22
for the Temple. An * 87½-foot strip Eze 45:2
an appendix giving * facts. Mk 16:9f
add at this point * portions of the Lk 11:5,6f

ADDITIONS
build on *; Is 54:2
to go after these * to faith is 2Pe 1:9

ADDON
Tel-harsha, Cherub, *, and Immer. Neh 7:61

ADDRESS
THIS BOOK RECORDS Moses' * to the Deu 1:1
At the time of this *, King Sihon Deu 1:1
Here, then, is Moses' * to Deu 1:1
of the army shall * the men in this Deu 20:5
into the temple to * the people: 2Ki 10:23
and encouraged them with this *: 2Ch 32:6
ANOTHER * FROM Eliphaz: Job 22:1
AFTER JESUS HAD finished this *, Mt 19:1
And don't * anyone here on earth Mt 23:9
the following * to the governor: Act 24:2

ADDRESSED
Then Shechem * Dinah's father and Gen 34:11
the Levite-priests * all Israel as Deu 27:9
Manasseh, and * them as follows: Jos 22:2,3
Then Joshua * them as follows: Jos 24:2
THEN SAMUEL * the people again: 1Sa 12:1
with his seal, and * them to the 1Ki 21:8
army officers, he * the assembled 1Ch 13:2
before them and * them as follows: 1Ch 28:2
of the Temple, and * them thus: 2Ch 29:4,5
Ezra the priest, arose and * them: Ez 10:10
from Massa, * to Ithiel and Ucal: Pro 30:1
from Gibeon, * me publicly in the Jer 28:1
* to everyone in his empire: Dan 6:25,26
The messages were * to both Mic 1:1
High Priest—for it was * to them. Hag 1:1
in heaven should be * like that. Mt 23:9
He turned around and * them as Lk 14:25
Then Jesus * the chief priests Lk 22:52
stood up and * them as follows: Act 1:15
Peter saw his opportunity and * Act 3:12
Then he * his colleagues as Act 5:35
He requested a letter * to Act 9:2
Peter stood and * them as follows: Act 15:7
Hill forum, * them as follows: Act 17:22
trades, and * them as follows: Act 19:25
he * them in Hebrew as follows: Act 21:40
Then Festus * the audience: Act 25:24

ADDRESSING
from Jerusalem, * it to the Jewish Jer 29:1

ADDS
The text *, "all these were the Gen 25:4f
The Hebrew text * here: Ps 9:16f
All our work * nothing to it! Pro 10:22
Or, "and he * no sorrow Pro 10:22f
Reverence for God * hours to each Pro 10:27
And now the Lord * this Jer 36:30
And then he *, "I will never Heb 10:17
book: If anyone * anything to what Rev 22:18

ADEQUATE
But who is * for such a task as 2Co 2:16

ADHERED
that unless they * to the ancient Act 15:1

ADI-EL
Asaiah, *, Jesimi-el, Benaiah, Ziza 1Ch 4:34-39
was Maasai (son of *, son of 1Ch 9:12
Azmaveth (son of *) was the chief 1Ch 27:25

ADIN
From the subclan of *, 454; Ez 2:3-35
From the clan of *—Ebed (son of Ez 8:2-14
From the subclan of *, 655; Neh 7:8-38
Adonijah, Bigvai, *, Neh 10:14-27

ADINA
* (son of Shiza) from the tribe of 1Ch 11:26-47

ADINO
known also as *, the Eznite. 2Sa 23:8

ADITHAIM
*, Gederah, and Gederothaim. Jos 15:33-36

ADJACENT
at the Temple. * to the holy lands Eze 45:6

ADJURE
O girls of Jerusalem, I * you by Sol 2:7
old bedroom. I * you, O women of Sol 3:5
off my veil. I * you, O women of Sol 5:8
embrace me. I * you, O women of Sol 8:4
on was this: "I * you by Jesus, Act 19:13

ADLAI
Shaphat (son of *) had charge of 1Ch 27:29

ADMAH
and to Sodom, Gomorrah, *, and Gen 10:15-19
Shinab, king of *, Gen 14:2
Sodom, Gomorrah, *, Zeboiim, and Gen 14:3
Sodom, Gomorrah, *, Zeboiim, and Gen 14:8,9
and Gomorrah and * and Zeboiim, Deu 29:23
How can I forsake you like * and Hos 11:8

ADMATHA
Carshena, Shethar, *, Tarshish, Est 1:13-15

ADMIN
Amminadab's father was *; Lk 3:23-38

ADMIN'S
Amminadab's father was Admin;* Lk 3:23-38

ADMINISTER
constantly available to * justice. Ex 18:26
They will * justice in every part Deu 16:18
could * the kingdom efficiently. Dan 6:2

ADMINISTERED
who * all public affairs. 2Ch 8:10

ADMINISTERING
of * a nation-wide farm program. Gen 41:33
preaching, not * a feeding Act 6:2

ADMINISTRATION
in charge of the * of Potiphar's Gen 39:4
the entire prison * to Joseph, so Gen 39:22
very corrupt in the * of justice. 1Sa 8:3
affairs and public * of that area. 1Ch 26:30
in all matters of public *. Neh 11:24
of the * of the storehouses; Neh 13:13
will come here to oversee my *. Jer 40:10

ADMINISTRATIVE
the complete * responsibility over Gen 39:6
Egypt into five * districts, Gen 41:34,35
appointed them as * assistants in Deu 1:15
"Appoint judges and * officials Deu 16:18
judges, and your * officers—are Deu 29:10
including officers and * staff. 1Ch 27:1
officers, and the * officers of the 1Ch 29:6,7
the * officials were meeting. Jer 36:12
entire empire as his * officer. Dan 6:3
persons—and the * district of Jon 3:3f
the chief * officer of the king, Zec 7:2
If God has given you * ability Rom 12:8

ADMINISTRATOR
*, who was his oldest servant, Gen 24:2
shall be the chief * over the Num 3:31-35
and the king's * Azrikam, and the 2Ch 28:7
Shebna, the palace *: "And who do Is 22:15,16

ADMINISTRATORS
appointed public * and judges. 1Ch 26:29

ADMIRATION
THE KING OF Syria had high * for 2Ki 5:1
receive praise and * because of all 2Th 1:10

ADMIRE
"The rich man had to * the Lk 16:8

ADMIRED
saw David, Saul * and loved him; 1Sa 16:21
Men with common sense are * Pro 10:13
and * throughout the earth. Is 62:6,7
publicly, to be *, for then you Mt 6:1

ADMIRER
been a great * of David, so when he 1Ki 5:1

ADMIRES
Everyone * a man with good sense, Pro 12:8

ADMIRING
things you are * will be knocked Lk 21:6

ADMIT
Would I not * it if I had sinned? Job 6:30
will only * that you were wrong. Job 22:21
Job refused to * he had sinned and Job 32:2
I wouldn't * what a sinner I was. Ps 32:3
For I * my shameful deed—it Ps 51:3
(let all Israel * it), if the Lord Ps 124:1
A man who refuses to * his Pro 28:13
making you * that he was right? Is 41:26
Only acknowledge your guilt; * Jer 3:13
my home until they * their guilt Hos 5:15
When will you * this calf you Hos 8:6
in shame, and * that your messages Mic 3:7
but wouldn't * it to anyone because Jn 12:42
If they would * it, they know Act 26:5
but they wouldn't * it or worship Rom 1:21
* your faults to one another and Jas 5:16
there, does not * my authority over 3Jn 1:9

ADMITTED
"Yes," Adam *, "but it was the Gen 3:12
Judah * that they were his and Gen 38:26
"No," he *. Num 22:30
a little honey," Jonathan *. 1Sa 14:43
and oxen," Saul *, "but they are 1Sa 15:15
"I have sinned," Saul finally * 1Sa 15:24
until I finally * all my sins to Ps 32:5
you have * me forever to your Ps 41:12
Note carefully who may be * to Eze 44:5
would get if they * that the cross Gal 6:12

ADMONISH
to * one another to know the Lord. Jer 31:34

ADNA
*, Chelal, Benaiah, Ma-aseiah, Ez 10:30
*, leader of the Harim clan; Neh 12:12-21

ADNAH
*, Jozabad, Jedia-el, Michael, 1Ch 12:20
troops were there under General *. 2Ch 17:14,15

ADONI-BEZEK
at Bezek. King * escaped, but the Ju 1:4,5,6
King * said. Ju 1:7

ADONI-ZEDEK
WHEN *, THE king of Jerusalem, Jos 10:1
So King * of Jerusalem sent Jos 10:3

ADONIJAH
The fourth was *, who was born 2Sa 3:4
* (his mother was Haggith) 1Ki 1:5
refused to endorse * were the 1Ki 1:8
* went to En-rogel where he 1Ki 1:9
Haggith's son, *, is now the king 1Ki 1:11
Then why is * reigning? 1Ki 1:13
But instead, * is the new king, 1Ki 1:18
as to whether * is the one you have 1Ki 1:20
appointed * to be the next king? 1Ki 1:24
and shouting, 'Long live King *!' 1Ki 1:25
along the way. * and his guests 1Ki 1:41
"Come in," * said to him, "for 1Ki 1:42
Then * and his guests jumped up 1Ki 1:49,50
for their lives. * rushed into the 1Ki 1:49,50
When word reached Solomon that * 1Ki 1:51
One day * the son of Haggith came 1Ki 2:13
"Then let your brother * marry 1Ki 2:21
strike me dead if * does not die 1Ki 2:23,24
The fourth was *, the son of 1Ch 3:2
*, Tobijah, and Tobadonijah; 2Ch 17:7,8,9
*, Bigvai, Adin, Neh 10:14-27

ADONIJAH'S
When Joab heard about * death 1Ki 2:28
(Joab had joined * revolt, though 1Ki 2:28

ADONIKAM
From the subclan of *, 666; Ez 2:3-35
From the clan of *—Eliphelet, Ez 8:2-14
From the subclan of *, 667; Neh 7:8-38

ADONIRAM
* (son of Abda) was superintendent 1Ki 4:1
months at home. * was the general 1Ki 5:14

ADOPT
I let them * Eze 20:25
could * us as his very own sons. Gal 4:5
has always been to * us into his Eph 1:5

ADOPTED
He also gave them the five * sons 2Sa 21:8
and whom he had * into his family Est 2:7
Mordecai's uncle, who had * her." Est 2:15f
So the Jews * Mordecai's Est 9:23
Abihail and later * by Mordecai the Est 9:29-31
worship God and be * into Israel as Zec 9:7
found him and * him as her own son, Act 7:21

ADOPTED Con't)
very own children, * into the bosom Rom 8:15

ADOPTING
I arrived, I am * them as my own, Gen 48:5

ADORAIM
*, Lachish, Azekah, 2Ch 11:5-10

ADORAM
* was in charge of the forced 2Sa 20:24
When King Rehoboam sent * (who 1Ki 12:18

ADORATION
stretch out her hands to God in *. Ps 68:31
other object of * and worship. 2Th 2:4

ADORE
your kingdom. We * you as being in 1Ch 29:11
* him, O his people! Ps 149:6,7

ADORNMENT
Literally, "a fair garland and * Pro 1:7,8,9f

ADRAMMELECH
of their gods * and Anammelech. 2Ki 17:31
sons * and Sharezer killed him. 2Ki 19:37
his god, his sons * and Sharezer Is 37:38

ADRAMYTTIUM
Literally, "a ship of *." Act 27:2f

ADRI-EL
daughter Merab, the wife of *. 2Sa 21:8

ADRIATIC
to and fro on the * Sea, the Act 27:27

ADRIEL
*, a man from Meholath, instead. 1Sa 18:19

ADULLAM
home and moved to * and lived there Gen 38:1
The king of *; Jos 12:8-24
Enam, Jarmuth, *, Socoh, Azekah, Jos 15:33-36
to the cave of *, where his 1Sa 22:1
in the cave of * and the invading 2Sa 23:13
he was hiding in the cave of *. 1Ch 11:15
Beth-zur, Soco, *, 2Ch 11:5-10
Zanoah, * (and their Neh 11:25-30

ADULLAMITE
friend Hirah, the *, went to Timnah Gen 38:12
friend Hirah the * to take the Gen 38:20

ADULLUM
They will penetrate to *, the Mic 1:15

ADULT
He will soften * hearts to become Lk 1:17

ADULTERERS
at night they are thieves and *, Job 24:14,15
you offspring of * and harlots! Is 57:3
Idolators! *! Eze 33:26
They are all *; Hos 7:4
innocent, against *, and liars, Mal 3:5
idol worshipers, * or 1Co 6:9,10

ADULTERESS
an * may cost him his very life. Pro 6:26

ADULTERESSES
they really are—* and murderers. Eze 23:45

ADULTERIES
defiled by your *—your worshiping Jer 3:2
that you stop your * with other Eze 16:40,41

ADULTEROUS
they are all *, treacherous men. Jer 9:2
take away their * hearts—their love Eze 6:9
Yes, you are an * wife who lives Eze 16:32
longer through the * worship of Eze 43:7

ADULTERY
"You must not commit *. Ex 20:14
been committing *—at Aaron's Ex 32:25
committing * against me Ex 34:15
sons would commit * against me by Ex 34:16
"If a man commits * with another Lev 20:10
man's wife commits *, but there is Num 5:11,12
But if you have committed *, Num 5:20
having committed * against her Num 5:27
has not committed *, she shall be Num 5:28
" 'You must not commit *. Deu 5:18
committing *, both he and the other Deu 22:22
The general law against * Deu 22:30f
" 'Cursed is he who commits * Deu 27:20
law would be needed to prohibit *. Deu 27:23f
him because of his * with Ps 51:1
idols was * in the sight of God. Ps 106:39
who commits * with another's wife. Pro 6:29
But the man who commits * is an Pro 6:32
You have committed * on the tops Is 57:7,8
This is *, for you are giving Is 57:7,8
God and committed * against him by Jer 3:13
was to commit * wholesale and to Jer 5:7
murder, commit *, lie, and worship Jer 7:9
For the land is full of * and Jer 23:10
they commit * and love Jer 23:14
They have committed * with their Jer 29:23
them, which is * against me. Eze 16:17
"And in all these years of * and Eze 16:22
"You have committed * with the Eze 16:28
After your * there, you still Eze 16:28
filthy sins, your * with your Eze 16:36
does not commit *, nor lie with any Eze 18:6
and commits *, and oppresses the Eze 18:11
does not commit *, and is fair to Eze 18:15
There are men who commit * Eze 22:10
menstruous women. * with a Eze 22:11
And they came and committed * Eze 23:17
For they have committed both * Eze 23:37
Will they commit * with these Eze 23:43
committing open * against me by Hos 1:2
For their mother has committed *. Hos 1:5
love her, even though she loves *. Hos 3:1
and kill and steal and commit *. Hos 4:2
and your brides commit *. Hos 4:13
for the spirit of * is deep within Hos 5:4
said, 'You shall not commit *.' Mt 5:27
committed * with her in his heart. Mt 5:28
to commit * if she marries again. Mt 5:32
And he who marries her commits *. Mt 5:32
thoughts, murder, *, fornication, Mt 15:19
and marries another, commits *." Mt 19:9
a divorced woman commits *." Mt 19:9f
kill, don't commit *, don't steal, Mt 19:18
theft, murder, *, wanting what Mk 7:21
else, he commits * against her. Mk 10:11
remarries, she, too, commits *." Mk 10:12
kill, don't commit *, don't steal, Mk 10:19
else commits *, and anyone who Lk 16:18
a divorced woman commits *." Lk 16:18
I don't commit *, I go without Lk 18:11
say—don't commit *, don't murder, Lk 18:20
a woman caught in * and placed her Jn 8:3
was caught in the very act of *. Jn 8:4
You say it is wrong to commit * Rom 2:22
drunk or in * and lust, or Rom 13:12,13
those who are immoral or commit *. Heb 13:4
laws by committing *, but have Jas 2:11
and of * they never have enough. 2Pe 2:14
all those who commit * with her." Rev 2:22f

ADUMMIM
* on the south side of the valley. Jos 15:7
is opposite the slope of *). Jos 18:17

ADVANCE
had agreed in * to run away so that Ju 20:32
The good man's earnings * the Pro 10:16
now * against the land of Israel. Is 18:4
you Egyptians and * to battle! Jer 46:3
their own lands as the enemies *. Jer 50:16
the enemies' * will all be dashed. Zec 9:5

ADVANCED
they were, and * against the rear Ju 20:34
they mobilized their army and *. 1Sa 7:7
As the Syrian army * upon them, 2Ki 6:18
Zerah. They * to the city of 2Ch 14:9,10
a man with an * case of leprosy. Lk 5:12

ADVANCING
the noise of the * army reaches the Zep 1:10

ADVANTAGE
"Do not take * of foreigners in Lev 19:33
" 'Cursed is he who takes * of a Deu 27:18
He took * of his position by 2Sa 3:7
to see you taken * of and Ez 4:14
For they have taken * of the Job 24:21
or if I have taken * of an orphan Job 31:21
So mankind has no real * over the Ecc 3:19
so what is the * of wealth—except Ecc 5:11
there is no * in a charmer." Ecc 10:11f
All take * of one another and Jer 9:4
Using his wealth for political *, Dan 11:2
hand, only to take * of them. Dan 11:34
And this has a real *: I am not 1Co 9:19
no one nor taken * of anyone. 2Co 7:2
you have, and take * of you, and 2Co 11:19,20
men I sent to you take * of you? 2Co 12:17

ADVANTAGES
money, but being wise has many *. Ecc 7:12
Yes, being a Jew has many *. Rom 3:2

ADVERSARIES
I will beat down his * before Ps 89:23

ADVERSITY
you can't stand the pressure of *. Pro 24:10
you the bread of * and water of Is 30:20

ADVICE
give you a word of *, and God will Ex 18:19,20
If you follow this *, and if the Ex 18:23
*, and followed this suggestion. Ex 18:24
gave insidious * that brought about Num 24:25f
followed Balaam's * and caused the Num 31:16
listened carefully to his *. 1Sa 3:19
upset and went to the Lord for *. 1Sa 8:6
give Absalom foolish *!" 2Sa 15:31
and counter Ahithophel's *. 2Sa 15:33,34
"Should we follow Ahithophel's * 2Sa 17:6
* is better than Ahithophel's." 2Sa 17:14
refused his *—saddled his donkey, 2Sa 17:23
an argument, ask * at Abel.' 2Sa 20:18
with her wise *, and they cut off 2Sa 20:22
ambassadors to him for his *. 1Ki 4:34
He ignored the old men's * and 1Ki 12:13,14
So on the * of his counselors, 1Ki 12:28
but my * to you is, be content 2Ki 14:10
But he rejected their * and asked 2Ch 10:8,9
for he refused the * of the old 2Ch 10:13
Following their evil *, Ahaziah 2Ch 22:5
"Since when have I asked your * 2Ch 25:16
Judah now took the * of his 2Ch 25:17
of Edom, but my * is to stay home 2Ch 25:19
he did nothing without their *. Est 1:13-15
she accepted the * of Hegai, the Est 2:15
"My * to you is this: Go to God Job 5:8
*, and were silent until I spoke. Job 29:21
follow evil men's *, who do not Ps 1:1
your back on me, spurning my *. Pro 1:30
Oh, why wouldn't I take *? Pro 5:13
Take to heart all of their *. Pro 6:21
For their * is a beam of light Pro 6:23
FOLLOW MY *, my son; Pro 7:1
My * is wholesome and good. Pro 8:8
"I, Wisdom, give good * and Pro 8:14,15
A godly man gives good *, but a Pro 10:21
The good man gives wise *, but Pro 10:31
A fool thinks he needs no *, but Pro 12:15
The good man asks * from friends; Pro 12:26
be humble, take * and become Pro 13:10
The * of a wise man refreshes Pro 13:14
If you are looking for *, stay Pro 14:7
a fool despises his father's *; Pro 15:5
Only the good can give good *. Pro 15:7
Everyone enjoys giving good *, Pro 15:23
Ability to give wise * satisfies Pro 18:20
Get all the * you can and be wise Pro 19:20
Though good * lies deep within a Pro 20:5
plans without the * of others; Pro 20:18
Listen to this wise *; Pro 22:17,18,19
He will despise the wisest *. Pro 23:9
Listen to your father's * and Pro 23:22
O my son, trust my *—stay away Pro 23:26,27,28
Timely * is as lovely as golden Pro 25:11
foolish king who refuses all *. Ecc 4:13
plead for * and help. Is 16:3
you ask * from everyone but me, Is 30:1
Has he ever needed anyone's *? Is 40:14
I make wise men give opposite * Is 44:25
and prophets—we don't need his *. Jer 18:18
you follow their * and refuse to Jer 27:10
prophet to ask for my help and *. Eze 14:6,7
these young men's * ten times Dan 1:20
he gave them this *: "If you are Lk 14:7
But you are following the * of Jn 8:38
"And so my * is, leave these men Act 5:38
The Council accepted his *, Act 5:40
gives the ability to give wise *; 1Co 12:8
with suggestions and godly *. Eph 6:4
"My * to you is to buy pure gold Rev 3:18

ADVISE
I will * you and watch your Ps 32:8
from Ophir. "I * you, O daughter, Ps 45:10,11
Who can * the Spirit of the Lord Is 40:13
Or, "who can * him?" 1Co 2:16f
I * you to obey only the Holy Gal 5:16

ADVISED
* that he be captured and killed. 2Sa 17:21
him anything more," the elders *. 1Ki 20:8
of the crew * trying to go further Act 27:12
The soldiers * their commanding Act 27:42

ADVISOR
King Abimelech arrived with his * Gen 26:26
Ahithophel, his *, was backing 2Sa 15:31
the Archite was his personal *. 1Ch 27:33
the king's *, and all the officials Jer 39:13

ADVISORS
Then Ahab summoned his *. 1Ki 20:7
family became his * after his 2Ch 22:4
The king and his * were in 2Ch 30:4
aides and teach the king's *. Ps 105:22
You have * by the ton—your Is 47:13
put on his regular staff of *. Dan 1:18,19
exclaimed to his *, "Didn't we Dan 3:24
Festus conferred with his * and Act 25:12

ADVOCATE
in heaven; my * is there on high. Job 16:19
And because I * your cause, your Ps 69:9

ADVOCATING
a political party * violent Mk 3:16-19

AENEAS
There he met a man named *, Act 9:33
Peter said to him, "*! Act 9:34
when they saw * walking around. Act 9:35

AENON
He was baptizing at *, near Jn 3:23,24

AFAR
See, the Lord comes from *, Is 30:27

AFFAIR
concerning this *, but his father Gen 37:11
* concerning Uriah the Hittite. 1Ki 15:5
of us involved in this sinful *. Ez 10:13
you may have no part in this *." Neh 2:20
authority in this * should return Act 25:5

AFFAIRS
He tried always to conduct his * Gen 6:9,10
and all of his business *. Gen 39:4
All his household * began to run Gen 39:5
for the * of fifty people; Ex 18:21
legal * were usually transacted. Ru 4:1f
* in order, and hanged himself; 2Sa 17:23
Ahishar was manager of palace *; 1Ki 4:1
Ahab's household * was Obadiah, who 1Ki 18:3,4
So the manager of palace * and 2Ki 10:5

(AFFAIRS Con't)
"Set your * in order and prepare 2Ki 20:1
for the religious * and public 1Ch 26:30
and public * of the tribes of 1Ch 26:31,32
who administered all public *. 2Ch 8:10
involving violation of sacred *; 2Ch 19:11
of the king's * and of the judging 2Ch 26:21
have watched human *: There was a Ecc 9:13
"Set your * in order, for you are Is 38:1
directing the * of generations of Is 41:4
these holy *, for you have hired Eze 44:8
the * of the province of Babylon; Dan 2:49
of Babylonian *—who have defied Dan 3:12
was handling his * so that they Dan 6:4
and domestic *), Susanna, and many Lk 8:3
to handle his *, but soon a rumor Lk 16:1
charge of all the * of the palace. Act 7:10
a judge of Jewish * for many years, Act 24:10
even children the * of God, for you Rom 2:20
Lord in these *, God will be glad; Rom 14:18
workers in the * of Christ Jesus. Rom 16:3
debaters of this world's great *? 1Co 1:20
about your own *, but be interested Php 2:4
tied up in worldly *, for then you 2Ti 2:4
truly my son in the * of the Lord. Tit 1:4
and prying into other people's *. 1Pe 4:15
about worldly * and the world pays 1Jn 4:5

AFFECT
But the plague will * only the Ex 9:4

AFFECTED
go on sinning, soon all will be *? 1Co 5:6
extent that this * me too) has been 2Co 2:10

AFFECTION
husband will feel * for me, since I Gen 29:34
with her, and tried to win her *. Gen 34:3
I will not share your * with any Ex 20:5
Love each other with brotherly * Rom 12:10

AFFECTIONATELY
and embraced him * and kissed him; Gen 33:4

AFFECTIONS
*, and he shall be your master." Gen 3:16
By giving my * Deu 32:21
test my motives and * too. Ps 26:2
Above all else, guard your *. Pro 4:23

AFFECTS
No other sin * the body as this 1Co 6:18

AFFIRMING
an evil man by * on the witness Ex 23:1

AFFLICTED
are enslaved and *, then he takes Job 36:8
Literally, "the *." Ps 22:26f
*, the fatherless, the destitute. Ps 82:3
But listen now to this, * Is 51:21
He was oppressed and he was *, Is 53:7
O my * people, tempest-tossed and Is 54:11
good news to the suffering and *. Is 61:1
In all their affliction he was * Is 63:9
* them far beyond my intentions. Zec 1:15

AFFLICTING
people, O Lord, * those you love. Ps 94:5
For he does not enjoy * men and Lam 3:33

AFFLICTION
Waves of * have come upon me. Job 30:27
and water of *, yet he will be with Is 30:20
of *, but found no silver there. Is 48:10
In all their * he was afflicted, Is 63:9
saved them out of their *." Is 63:9f
will melt them in a crucible of *. Jer 9:7
sickbed of intense *, along with Rev 2:22

AFFLICTIONS
I AM THE man who has seen the * Lam 3:1

AFFORD
"We can't * to let a rift Gen 13:8
that he cannot * two lambs, then he Lev 14:21
he is able to *—and use one of the Lev 14:22
(whichever pair he is able to *). Lev 14:30
what they could *, but far more; 2Co 8:3
have, and can't * it, so you start Jas 4:2

AFIRE
city shall be set * by the Jer 38:18
My anger is * against these Eze 36:5

AFLAME
See, the Lord comes from afar, * Is 30:27
as a baker's oven is constantly * Hos 7:4
people constantly * with lust. Hos 7:4
sets the dry fields of Edom *. Ob 1:18
sets the forest *—like a burning Zec 12:6

AFRAID
will be * of you," God told him; Gen 9:2,3
laugh," she lied, for she was *. Gen 18:15
Don't be *! Gen 21:17
he was * they would kill him to Gen 26:7
"Because I was * I would be Gen 26:9
"I sneaked away because I was * Gen 31:31
* that he is coming to kill me and Gen 32:11
Don't be * to go down to Egypt, Gen 46:3,4
told them, "Don't be * of me. Gen 50:19
No, don't be *. Gen 50:21
for he was * to look at God. Ex 3:6
to him, "Don't be * to return to Ex 4:19
told the people, "Don't be *. Ex 14:13
they were * and revered the Lord, Ex 14:31
"Don't be *," Moses told them, Ex 20:20
will be * to sin against him!" Ex 20:20
of Israel were * to come near him. Ex 34:30
Why then were you not * to Num 12:7,8
Don't be *, and bring back some Num 13:20
Don't be * of them!" Num 14:9
of Israel are so * of the Num 14:25
Don't be *! Deu 1:19,20,21
"But I said to them, 'Don't be * Deu 1:29
But the Lord told me not to be * Deu 3:1
Don't be * of the nations there, Deu 3:22
for you were * of the fire and did Deu 5:5
But don't be * of them! Deu 7:18
"No, do not be * of those Deu 7:21
and they will be * to defy the Deu 17:13
about it will be * to tell lies on Deu 19:20
Don't be * as you go out to fight Deu 20:3
And now, is anyone *? Deu 20:8
about what happened and will be *. Deu 21:21
Do not be * of them! Deu 31:6
Don't be *, for the Lord will go Deu 31:8
"We are all * of you; Jos 2:9
No wonder we are * of you! Jos 2:11
the people were * of the Israelis; Jos 6:1
"Don't be * or discouraged; Jos 8:1
"Don't be * of them," the Lord Jos 10:8
"Don't ever be * or Jos 10:25
Joshua, "Don't be * of them, for Jos 11:6
Don't be *." Ju 4:18
"Don't be *! Ju 6:23
But if you are *, first go down Ju 7:10
boy was only a lad and was * to. Ju 8:20
usual, for he was * to tell Eli 1Sa 3:15
And God caused the people to be * 1Sa 11:7
"But when you were * of Nahash, 1Sa 12:12
much * of the Lord and of Samuel. 1Sa 12:18
Lord, for I was * of the people and 1Sa 15:24
too, for Saul was * of him and 1Sa 18:11,12
he became even more * of him; 1Sa 18:15,16
became even more * of him, and grew 1Sa 18:29
comments and was * of what King 1Sa 21:12
But David's men said, "We're * 1Sa 23:3
"Don't be *," Jonathan 1Sa 23:17
But my commanders are * to have 1Sa 29:9
But his armor bearer was * to, 1Sa 31:3,4
no reply, for he was * of Abner. 2Sa 3:11
David was now * of the Lord and 2Sa 6:9
But David said, "Don't be *! 2Sa 9:7
And the Syrians were * to help 2Sa 10:19
David's aides were * to tell him. 2Sa 12:18
Don't be *. 2Sa 13:28
Ahima-az apparently was * to tell 2Sa 18:29f
Elijah said to her, "Don't be *! 1Ki 17:13
Lord said to Elijah, "Don't be *. 2Ki 1:15
"Don't be *!" 2Ki 6:16
daughter of Zion isn't * of you! 2Ki 19:21
for they were * of what the 2Ki 25:26
But the man was * to do it, so 1Ch 10:4
for they were * that David and his 1Ch 12:19
Now David was * of God and asked, 1Ch 13:12
Be very much * to give any other 2Ch 19:7
"The Lord says, 'Don't be *! 2Ch 20:15
Don't be * or discouraged! 2Ch 20:17
and do not be * of the king of 2Ch 32:7
and said to them, "Don't be *! Neh 4:14
Or, "the bars of heaven are * of Job 26:13f
renown to make you nervous and *. Job 33:7
he stands up, the strongest are *. Job 41:25
me on every side, I am not *. Ps 3:6
I will not be *, for you are close Ps 23:4
Everywhere I looked I was *, for Ps 31:13
again, * of what they have seen; Ps 48:6
But when I am *, I will put my Ps 56:3,4
I am not * of anything mere man Ps 56:10,11
deed is done, yet they are not *. Ps 64:4
them safe, so they were not *. Ps 78:53
Now you don't need to be * of Ps 91:5
That is why he is not *, but can Ps 112:8
How can I be *? Ps 118:6
you need not be * of disaster or Pro 3:24,25,26
You will be * of heights and of Ecc 12:5
don't be * of the Assyrians when Is 10:24
I will trust and not be *, for Is 12:2
strongest hearts melt, and are *. Is 13:8
Encourage those who are *. Is 35:4
Shout louder—don't be *—tell the Is 40:9
God—and I say to you, Don't be *; Is 41:13
be *, for I have ransomed you; Is 43:1
Don't be *, for I am with you. Is 43:5
O servant of mine, don't be *. Is 44:2
my chosen ones, don't be *. Is 44:2
Don't, don't be *. Is 44:8
hearts: don't be * of people's Is 51:7
Why were you more * of them than Is 57:11
And don't be * of the people, Jer 1:8
Don't be * of them, or else I Jer 1:17
Don't be * of such a god for it Jer 10:5
the farmers are *. Jer 14:4
their whispered threats, and am *. Jer 20:10
are so desperately *—to Jer 22:24,25
they shall not need to be * again; Jer 23:4
So don't be *, O Jacob my Jer 30:10
and no one shall make them *. Jer 30:10
country, we were * and decided to Jer 35:11
"But I am * to surrender," the Jer 38:19
For they were * of what the Jer 41:18
But don't you be *, O my people Jer 46:27
rest and nothing shall make her *. Jer 46:27
"Son of dust, don't be * of Eze 2:6
So don't be * of them, or fear Eze 3:9
Their kings are horribly * and Eze 27:35
* because of all I do to you. Eze 32:10
and no one shall make them *. Eze 34:28
bothering them or making them *. Eze 39:26
"I'm * you will become pale and Dan 1:10
be * to tell me what it means." Dan 4:19
"don't be *! Dan 10:19
But Jonah was * to go and ran Jon 1:3
But the Lord is not * of him! Nah 1:12
and no one will make them *." Zep 3:13
will be, "Cheer up, don't be *. Zep 3:16
so don't be *.' Hag 2:5
hearts like flint, * to hear the Zec 7:12
So don't be * or discouraged! Zec 8:13
But don't be * of those who Mt 10:26
"Don't be * of those who can Mt 10:28
John but was * of a riot, for all Mt 14:5
"Don't be *!" Mt 14:27
"Get up," he said, "don't be * Mt 17:7
of him, but were * to try because Mt 21:46
man, and I was * you would rob me Mt 25:24,25
scatter, and I was * ." Mt 25:24,25f
and said to Jairus, "Don't be *. Mk 5:36
Don't be *." Mk 6:50
were * to ask him what he meant. Mk 9:32
But they were * to touch him for Mk 12:12
Then Pilate, * of a riot and Mk 15:15
But the angel said, "Don't be *, Lk 1:13
"Don't be *!" Lk 2:10
Jesus replied, "Don't be *! Lk 5:10
said to the father, "Don't be *! Lk 8:50
sealed and they were * to ask him. Lk 9:45
"Dear friends, don't be * of Lk 12:4
"So don't be *, little flock. Lk 12:32
was * [you would demand my profits Lk 19:21
But they were * that if they Lk 20:19
to them and told them not to be *. Jn 6:20
said: "Don't be * of your King, Jn 12:15
So don't be troubled or *. Jn 14:27
for they were * the people would Act 5:26,27
but they were all * of him. Act 9:26
vision and told him, "Don't be *! Act 18:9
The sailors were * of being Act 27:17
said, 'Don't be *, Paul—for you Act 27:24
So if you don't want to be *, Rom 13:3
*, for he will have you punished. Rom 13:4
I am * to come to deal with you. 1Co 4:18
And we are not *, but are quite 2Co 5:8
he will be * to raise his voice!" 2Co 10:1
* I might be puffed up by them; 2Co 12:7
For I am * that when I come to 2Co 12:20
have to act. I am * that I will 2Co 12:20
Yes, I am * that when I come God 2Co 12:21
because he was * of what these Gal 2:12
I fear for you. I am * that all Gal 4:11
I am saying this because I am * Col 2:4
I was * that perhaps Satan had 1Th 3:5
For I am * that some of them 1Ti 5:15
not want you to be * of people, but 2Ti 1:7
you will never be * to tell others 2Ti 1:8
Stand steady, and don't be * of 2Ti 4:5
for three months, and were not *. Heb 11:23
and wasn't * of the king's anger. Heb 11:27
and I am not * of anything that Heb 13:6
If we are *, it is for fear of 1Jn 4:18
hand on me and said, "Don't be *! Rev 1:17,18
keys of hell and death—don't be *! Rev 1:17,18
Stop being * of what you are Rev 2:10

AFRESH
his lovingkindness begins * each Lam 3:23

AFRICA
Put and Lud were in North *; Is 66:19f
three cities of ancient North *. Eze 27:10f
from Cyrene, in *—Simon was his Mt 27:32

AFRICAN
to the quicksands of the * coast, Act 27:17

AFTERBIRTH
She will hide from them the * and Deu 28:56,57

AFTERNOON
One hot summer * as he was sitting Gen 18:1
"Well, this * when I came to the Gen 24:42
That * as he and his wife and Ju 19:9
They raved all * until the time 1Ki 18:29
At noon it has begun. All * it Jer 6:4
in the * he did the same thing. Mt 20:5
That *, the whole earth Mt 27:45
Late in the * his disciples came Mk 6:35,36
it was late in the *—and went out Mk 11:11
until three o'clock that *. Mk 15:33
Late that * Joseph from Mk 15:42,43
Late in the * all twelve of the Lk 9:12

AFTERNOON Con't)
This was done late on Friday *, Lk 23:54
o'clock that * until the evening. Jn 1:39
"Yesterday * at about one o'clock Jn 4:52
to the Temple one * to take part in Act 3:1
While wide awake one * he had a Act 10:3
this time of the *, when suddenly a Act 10:30

AFTERWARD
city on fire.) * the army of Judah Ju 1:9
and as long * as the old men of his Ju 2:7-9
Soon * the armies of Midian, Ju 6:33
* Delilah said to him, "You are Ju 16:10
and * they had supper together. Ju 19:21
and Jonathan and * commanded that 2Sa 1:17,18
are a prophet," she told him *, 1Ki 17:24
as they flee. But * I will restore Jer 49:6
Then, *, go to your people in Eze 3:11
bed of love, but * she hated them Eze 23:17
* HE BROUGHT me into the nave, the Eze 41:1
* HE BROUGHT me out again to the Eze 43:1
and on each day *, the priests will Eze 43:27
is all right. But * he must wait Eze 44:26
* King Darius wrote this message Dan 6:25,26
horn that came up * and destroyed Dan 7:20
for several days. * I was up and Dan 8:27
and for many years * he will leave Dan 11:8
* they will return to the Lord Hos 3:5
He cannot decide * to do Gal 3:15
deeds aren't known until long *. 1Ti 5:25

AFTERWARDS
to water it; * the river divided Gen 2:10
But * the Lord asked Cain, Gen 4:9
Enosh was born. * he lived another Gen 5:6,7,8
Kenan was born. * he lived another Gen 5:9,10,11
was born. * he lived another 840 Gen 5:12,13,14
Jared was born. * he lived 830 Gen 5:15,16,17
Enoch was born. * he lived another Gen 5:18,19,20
was born. * he lived another 300 Gen 5:21-24
Lamech was born; * he lived Gen 5:25,26,27
God has cursed." * Lamech lived Gen 5:28-31
In those days, and even *, when Gen 6:4
He lived another 430 years *, and Gen 11:16,17
He lived another 209 years *, and Gen 11:18,19
He lived 200 years *, with many Gen 11:22,23
He lived 119 years *, and had Gen 11:24,25
Jehovah's visit. * Abram left that Gen 12:8
* JEHOVAH SPOKE to Abram in a Gen 15:1
* Lot left Zoar, fearful of the Gen 19:30
at a big party. *, that night, Gen 29:23
him six sons." * she gave birth Gen 30:21
to a feast, and * spent the night Gen 31:54
* Jacob built a stone pillar at Gen 35:13,14
Isaac died soon *, at the ripe Gen 35:28,29
as a result. * she resumed wearing Gen 38:19
Then, soon *, the baby with the Gen 38:30
out first, and * they were still Gen 41:21
of Egypt; but * there will be Gen 41:30
And Joseph did. Soon * Jacob took Gen 47:31
and kissed him. * he commanded his Gen 50:2
I promise not to refuse * to let Ex 10:17
to God, and * Aaron and the Ex 18:12
Soon * Moses let his Ex 18:27
married *, only he shall be freed; Ex 21:3
to the Lord. *, take them from Ex 29:25
offering; *, keep it for yourself. Ex 29:26
a sin offering for atonement; *, Ex 29:36
to the calf-idol; * they sat down Ex 32:6
to his friend. * Moses would return Ex 33:11
talked with him. *, all the people Ex 34:32
his face aglow. * he would put the Ex 34:35
waving them. And * they shall Lev 10:15
his leprosy; and * the priest shall Lev 14:19
for seven days *, and during that Lev 15:19
is in her period of defilement *. Lev 15:33
shall * wash his clothes and Lev 16:26
internal organs. *, the person Lev 16:28
traveled again. * they left Num 12:16
and bathe, and * return to the camp Num 19:7
the water must * wash his clothes; Num 19:21
of the cattle. * you must pile all Deu 13:16
And ever * his house shall be Deu 25:10
and worship him. *, go and feast Deu 26:11
for Israel. (* Joshua and the Jos 10:15
upon Egypt; and * I brought my Jos 24:5
after that. * the army of Judah Ju 1:17
* Saul said, "Let's chase the 1Sa 14:36
* Jonathan called David and told 1Sa 19:7
SHORTLY *, SAMUEL died and all 1Sa 25:1
* Joab returned to Jerusalem. 2Sa 10:14
Soon * two young prostitutes came 1Ki 3:16
to the other. * Solomon sent the 1Ki 8:66
* he said to his sons, "When I 1Ki 13:31
Solomon had made. * Rehoboam made 1Ki 14:27
bread first; and * there will still 1Ki 17:13
him in to eat, and *, whenever he 2Ki 4:8
he asked Gehazi *. 2Ki 4:14
* Elisha went to Damascus (the 2Ki 8:7
palace for lunch. * he said, 2Ki 9:34
* the Lord said to Jehu, "You 2Ki 10:30
Soon * news reached the king 2Ki 19:9
to comfort him. *, his wife 1Ch 7:23
to Rehoboam. *, when King Rehoboam 2Ch 10:18
and * return them to the armory. 2Ch 12:11
trumpets blew. * the king and his 2Ch 29:29
* A MASSIVE campaign against idol 2Ch 31:1
people to eat. * the Levites 2Ch 35:14
reign of Josiah. * King Neco of 2Ch 35:20
And *, when King Ahasu-erus began Ez 4:6
of Israel. But * our ancestors Ez 5:12
SOON * KING Ahasuerus appointed Est 3:1
* Mordecai returned to his job, Est 6:12
not long * when Job's sons and Job 1:12,13
let me speak, and *, mock on. Job 21:2,3
every direction. * comes the Job 37:4
of my life, and * I will live with Ps 23:6
and counsel; and * receive me into Ps 73:24
But * only a bitter conscience Pro 5:4
Lest * you groan in anguish and Pro 5:11
But * he brags about his bargain! Pro 20:14
swaying mast. And * you will say, Pro 23:35
was rescued. But * no one thought Ecc 9:15
It was only a little while * Sol 3:4
And * I will give you good judges Is 1:26
SOON *, THE king of Babylon Is 39:1
Then, *, this faithless one Jer 3:10
from hers; but * I will return and Jer 12:15
Then, a long time *, the Lord Jer 13:6
Soon *, the Lord gave this Jer 28:12
away from God but I was sorry *. Jer 31:19
But soon * Johanan (son of Jer 40:13,14
and his army. But * the land shall Jer 46:26
ahead for Israel. *, turn over and Eze 4:6
* the Spirit of God carried me Eze 11:24
burned and certainly useless *! Eze 15:5,6
were picked up *, there were twelve Mt 14:20
Then * he went up into the hills Mt 14:23,24
and children! And *, when the Mt 15:37,38
* the disciples asked Jesus Mt 17:19
on the third day * I will be Mt 17:22,23
Satan's temptations to sin. And * Mk 1:12,13
* he went up into the hills and Mk 3:13
*, when he was alone with the Mk 4:10
teaching, but *, when he was alone Mk 4:34
SOON * HE left that section of the Mk 6:1
for that meal, and * twelve Mk 6:43,44
* he went up into the hills to Mk 6:46
full, and * he sent them home. Mk 8:8,9
of scraps did you pick up *?" Mk 8:19
he would rise again three days *. Mk 8:31
was all right! *, when Jesus was Mk 9:28
Soon * Elizabeth his wife became Lk 1:24
One day soon * he went out into Lk 6:12
Not long * Jesus went with his Lk 7:11
NOT LONG * he began a tour of the Lk 8:1
but whose faith * is choked out by Lk 8:14
of scraps were picked up *! Lk 9:17
what they had seen until long *. Lk 9:36
wine first, and *, when everyone is Jn 2:10
* Jesus and his disciples left Jn 3:22
* JESUS RETURNED to Jerusalem for Jn 5:1
step down into it * was healed). Jn 5:4
the crowd. But * Jesus found him Jn 5:14
* he did the same with the fish. Jn 6:11
* Joseph of Arimathea, who had Jn 19:38
It was not long * that he rose Act 1:9
God told him, 'and * my people will Act 7:7
the Messiah. * Cornelius begged him Act 10:48
to death. * he left to live in Act 12:19
* they preached from town to town Act 13:6,7
'*' [says the Lord Act 15:16
* they were thrown into prison. Act 16:23
a powerful sermon. * they met with Act 18:25,26
*, Paul felt impelled by the Holy Act 19:21
So shortly *, we packed our Act 21:15
As they talked it over * they Act 26:31
But shortly *, the weather Act 27:14,15
to prayer. *, they should come 1Co 7:5
can tell everyone * what you were 1Co 14:5
he can tell people *, plainly. 1Co 14:13
that three days * he arose from the 1Co 15:4
as well as * when I returned, so 2Co 1:15,16
But * when some Jewish friends Gal 2:12
Adam first, and * he made Eve. 1Ti 2:13
have spoken long * about "today" Heb 4:8
would rise to a better life *. Heb 11:35
of the joy he knew would be his *; Heb 12:2
hurts! But * we can see the result, Heb 12:11
single meal. And *, when he wanted Heb 12:17
he is tempted, for * he will get as Jas 1:12
* to the death penalty from God. Jas 1:15
suffering, and his great glory *. 1Pe 1:11
his suffering, and * you will have 1Pe 4:13
of him and then * turn his back on 2Pe 2:21
and a new earth *, where there will 2Pe 3:13
were finished. * he would be Rev 20:3

AGABUS
one of them, named *, stood up in Act 11:28
days, a man named *, who also had Act 21:10

AGAG
Their king will be greater than *; Num 24:3-9
He captured *, the king of the 1Sa 15:8
and I brought King * but killed 1Sa 15:20
Then Samuel said, "Bring King * 1Sa 15:32
King Agag to me." * arrived all 1Sa 15:32

AGAGITE
the *), as prime minister. Est 3:1
son of Hammedatha the *." Est 3:10f
of Hammedatha the *), the enemy of Est 9:24,25

AGAINST-CHRIST
These "*" people used to be 1Jn 2:19

AGATE
an amber, an *, and an amethyst. Ex 28:19
a jacinth, an *, and an amethyst. Ex 39:12
of sparkling *, and your gates and Is 54:12
linen, and jewelry of coral and *. Eze 27:16

AGE
and died at the * of 930. Gen 5:3,4,5
and died at the * of 912. Gen 5:6,7,8
and died at the * of 905. Gen 5:9,10,11
and died at the * of 910. Gen 5:12,13,14
and died at the * of 895. Gen 5:15,16,17
and died at the * of 962. Gen 5:18,19,20
and died at the * of 969. Gen 5:25,26,27
and died at the * of 777. Gen 5:28-31
And there Terah died at the * of Gen 11:32
die in peace, at a ripe old *. Gen 15:15
"A woman my * have a baby?" Gen 18:12
old *, at the time God had said; Gen 21:1
Abraham a child in his old *!" Gen 21:7
at the ripe old * of 175, and his Gen 25:7,8
Ishmael finally died at the * of Gen 25:17
Esau, at the * of forty, married Gen 26:34
ONE DAY, IN Isaac's old * when he Gen 27:1
at the ripe old * of 180. Gen 35:28,29
was born to him in his old *. Gen 37:3
child of his old *, a little one. Gen 44:20
Israel was half blind with *, so Gen 48:10
So Joseph died at the * of 110, Gen 50:26
Amram lived to the * of 137. Ex 6:20
A man from the * of twenty to Lev 27:3
a woman from the * of twenty to Lev 27:4
to fifty years of * who were Num 4:35
Tabernacle at the * of twenty-five, Num 8:23,24
are to retire at the * of fifty. Num 8:23,24
of *, and so were not counted. Num 26:64,65f
twenty years of * were now dead. Num 26:64,65f
twenty years of * would ever see Num 32:10,11
Soon after this he died at the * Jos 24:29
God, died at the * of 110, and was Ju 2:7-9
of marriageable * were saved. Ju 21:10,11,12
take care of you in your old *; Ru 4:15
almost blind with * by now), and 1Sa 3:2,3
IN HIS OLD *, Samuel retired and 1Sa 8:1
he will die in battle or of old *. 1Sa 26:10
years, since the * of thirty. 2Sa 5:4,5
* in Israel, and 500,000 in Judah. 2Sa 24:9
IN HIS OLD * King David was 1Ki 1:1
Lord, especially in his old *. 1Ki 11:4
In his old * his feet became 1Ki 15:23
became the new king at the * of 2Ki 14:21
His * at the beginning of his 2Ki 15:1
His * when he became king: 25 2Ki 15:32,33
*: 20 years old 2Ki 16:1
His * at the beginning of his 2Ki 18:1
His * at beginning of his reign:12 2Ki 21:1
His * at the beginning of his 2Ki 21:19,20
His * at the beginning of his 2Ki 22:1
His * when he became king: 23 2Ki 23:31,32
His * when he became king: 25 2Ki 23:36,37
His * at the beginning of his 2Ki 24:8,9
His * when he became king: 21 2Ki 24:18,19
daughter at the * of sixty, and she 1Ch 2:21
OF Benjamin, according to *, were: 1Ch 8:1
* in Israel and 470,000 in Judah. 1Ch 21:5
distinction as to * or rank. 1Ch 24:31
without regard to * or reputation. 1Ch 25:8
He died at an old *, wealthy and 1Ch 29:28
He had become king at the * of 2Ch 12:13
He lived to a very old *, 2Ch 24:15
*, and become great and powerful. Job 21:7
but it is not mere * that makes Job 32:8,9
And now, in my old *, don't set Ps 71:9
Even in old * they will still Ps 92:14
dignity, and has no fear of old *. Pro 31:25
will tremble with *, and your Ecc 12:3
when your hair is white with *, Is 46:4
And when you reached the * of Eze 16:6,7
other youths your *," he said, Dan 1:10
reigning at the * of sixty-two. Dan 5:31
Or, "*." Mt 13:39f
Or, "*." Mt 13:40f
Or, "*." Mt 13:49f
Literally "*." Mt 24:3f
Then at last this * will come to Mt 24:34
Or, "*." Mt 28:20f
that will signal the end of the *. Mk 13:30
her—became pregnant in her old *! Lk 1:36
things happen, the end of this * Lk 21:32
a father, at the * of one hundred, Rom 4:19
Jews of my own * in the whole Gal 1:14
reaches whatever * his father set. Gal 4:2
at the end of the *, to put away Heb 9:26
spite of her old *, for she Heb 11:11

AGE-OLD
disciples follow our * customs? Mk 7:5
AGED
(Ask your father and the * men; Deu 32:7
And * men. Deu 32:25
king in place of his * father. 1Ki 1:5
Like *, helpless lions they Job 4:11
On our side are * men much older Job 15:10
and even the * rose and stood up in Job 29:8
make me even wiser than the *. Ps 119:100
* men are treated with contempt. Lam 5:12
Listen, you * men of Israel! Joe 1:2
will once again be * men and women Zec 8:4
AGEE
Shammah, the son of * from Harar. 2Sa 23:11,12
AGENCY
be a missionary by any group or *. Gal 1:1
AGENT
I am the * of my Father in Lk 10:22
AGENTS
Turkey, where his * purchased them 1Ki 10:28
them by sending * to tell lies Ez 4:4,5
We will appoint * in each Est 2:3
he sent his * to the farmers to Mt 21:34
* pretending to be honest men. Lk 20:20
AGES
the order of their *, from the Gen 43:33
of Levi, in the order of their *: Ex 6:16
listed according to their *. Ex 6:19
of all males from * thirty to fifty Num 4:3
men between the * of thirty and Num 4:21,22,23
from everlasting * past—and on into Ps 41:13
* past—will answer them! Ps 55:19
God is my King from * past; Ps 74:12
my years! In * past you laid the Ps 102:25
From * past, I am. Pro 8:23
know it didn't exist long * ago? Ecc 1:8-11
Haven't I proclaimed from * past Is 44:8
Father, our Redeemer from * past. Is 63:16
shall be infamous through the *. Jer 23:40
is alive from everlasting * past! Mic 5:2
God through all the * of eternity. Gal 1:5
and long * ago he planned that we Eph 2:10
through endless * because of his Eph 3:21
He is the King of the *, the 1Ti 1:17
through the * ever since it was Rev 10:7
O King of *. Rev 15:3,4
AGGREGATE
In any event, he represents the * Eze 38:2,3f
AGGRESSIVE
and who delight in * wars." Ps 68:30f
AGHAST
* at the meaning of the dream. Dan 4:19
her people stand *, pale-faced Nah 2:10
AGING
David (the son of * Jesse, a 1Sa 17:12
AGLOW
the people would see his face *. Ex 34:35
Look down on us, your face * with Ps 80:19
AGO
"Some time * when you were Gen 41:10
remembered the dreams of long *! Gen 42:8,9
of what we did to Joseph long *. Gen 42:21
ancestors long *, where the Ex 13:11
"It was forty years *, at Mount Deu 1:6
Remember the days of long *! Deu 32:7
thing the Lord did forty years * Jos 4:23
LONG * WHEN judges ruled in Ru 1:1
days *, for they have been found. 1Sa 9:20
three days * because I was sick. 1Sa 30:13
in this land long *, and because he 2Ki 21:11
* by a great king of Israel. Ez 5:11
you did in the days of long *. Ps 44:1
miracles he did for me so long *. Ps 77:11
LONG * WHEN the Israelis escaped Ps 114:1
you did in days of long *. Ps 143:5
know it didn't exist long ages *? Ecc 1:8-11
Whatever is, has been long *; Ecc 3:15
it was known long * what each man Ecc 6:10
just as the Egyptians did long *. Is 10:24
* when they returned from Egypt. Is 11:16
Israelites approached (so long * Is 17:9
is the one who planned it long *. Is 22:9,10,11
You planned them long *, and now Is 25:1
was I who decided all this long *? Is 37:26
cities long * destroyed, reviving Is 61:4
a young bride long * and how you Jer 2:2
Long * you shook off my yoke and Jer 2:20
old days of long *" when you Jer 3:16
to walk in, in the days of long *. Jer 6:16
For long * the Lord had said to Jer 31:3
their fathers long *—a wonderful Jer 32:22
your fathers long * when I brought Jer 34:13
of doom he made so long *. Lam 2:17
of those days long * when you were Eze 16:22
to lie there with those of long *. Eze 26:20
* the nether world of the dead. Eze 26:20
which I gave your fathers long *. Eze 36:28
I spoke of long * through the Eze 38:17
who long * preceded you, a kingdom Dan 5:18
as in days long * in her youth, Hos 1:15
long *. The Lord does not forget. Hos 9:9
like those of Egypt long *. Amo 4:10
and Gilead as they did long *. Mic 7:14
us as you promised Jacob long *. Mic 7:20
Long years *, when Jerusalem was Zec 7:7
as the Jebusites did so long *. Zec 9:7
did long centuries * from the Zec 14:5
long * in shame and humility. Mt 11:21
as the prophets declared long *; Mk 14:21
Furthermore, six months * your Lk 1:36
holy prophets long *— someone to Lk 1:70
repentance long *, clothed in Lk 10:13
who killed the prophets long *. Lk 11:47
three days *— some women from our Lk 24:21
was written long * that the Messiah Lk 24:46
"only a few days * the Jewish Jn 11:8
was predicted long * by the Holy Act 1:16
centuries * by the prophet Joel— Act 2:16
Moses, for instance, said long *, Act 3:21,22
you spoke long * by the Holy Act 4:25,26
Some time * there was that Act 5:36
Cornelius replied, "Four days * Act 10:30
among you long * to preach the Good Act 15:7
who led a rebellion a few years * Act 21:37,38
than twelve days * that I arrived Act 24:11
was promised long * by God's Rom 1:2
Scriptures told about it long *). Rom 3:21,22
Scriptures so long * are to teach Rom 15:4
people in the wilderness long *. 1Co 10:1
to do a year *, for you were not 2Co 8:10
to send an offering a year *. 2Co 9:2
Fourteen years * I 2Co 12:2,3
about this long * when he said, "I Gal 3:8,9
was killed long *, and the world's Gal 6:14
Long *, even before he made the Eph 1:4
he decided on in mercy long *; Eph 1:9
him just as he decided long *. Eph 1:11
Spirit, who long * had been Eph 1:13
and long ages * he planned that Eph 2:10
LONG * GOD spoke in many different Heb 1:1
chose you long * and knew you would 1Pe 1:2
But God condemned them long * and 2Pe 2:3
was written long *, for they have Jud 1:4
AGONY
We too have writhed in *, but Is 26:18
for he was in such * of spirit that Lk 22:44
with tears and * of soul to the Heb 5:7
five months with * like the pain of Rev 9:5
AGREE
Come on, let's * to this so that Gen 34:23
people have said to you, and I *. Deu 5:28
us, we will * to your terms." 1Sa 11:3
pleasant reply and * to be good to 1Ki 12:7
"I hope you will * with them and 2Ch 18:12
For we * before our God to Ez 10:3
"Quit quarreling with God! * Job 22:21
I will never, never * that you Job 27:5
Anyone even half bright will * Job 34:34,35
If you can do that, then I'll * Job 40:14
Will he * to let you make him Job 41:4
don't go to war until they *. Pro 20:18
but you refuse to * it is so. Is 48:6
You will *, when you meet them, Eze 14:23
this—if two of you * down here on Mt 18:19
Didn't you * to work all day for Mt 20:13
Murderers! You * with your Lk 11:48
Your laws say that if two men * Jn 8:17
"If you * that I am faithful to Act 16:15
you to * to their request." Act 23:21
I * with these laws I am breaking. Rom 7:16
*, because I want to help them. 1Co 9:20
When with the heathen I * with 1Co 9:21
is something else I cannot * with. 1Co 11:17
truth, as all who know us will *. 2Co 4:2
I hope you can * that I have 2Co 13:6
and, I hoped, * that it was right. Gal 2:2
And they did *; Gal 2:3
Does it really * that Jesus Christ, 1Jn 4:2
They will mutually * to give their Rev 17:17
AGREED
And Abram *. Gen 16:2,3
is publicly * upon, and it will Gen 23:9
pieces of silver, as publicly *. Gen 23:16
* and had left for Paddan-aram. Gen 28:6,7,8
* - Laben replied Gen 29:19
So Jacob * to work seven more Gen 29:28
Hamor and Shechem gladly *, and Gen 34:18,19
So all the men *, and all were Gen 34:24
And his brothers *. Gen 37:26,27
To this they *. Gen 42:20
Pharaoh *. Gen 50:6
penalties she has * to are too Num 30:5
day, then he has already * to it. Num 30:14
to which she * shall come upon Num 30:15
"They * to this; Deu 1:14
"And the Lord * to your request, Deu 5:28
as the Lord * to help you do. Deu 6:19
To this they fully *, and pledged Jos 1:16
The men *. Jos 2:14
"All right," the Angel *. Ju 6:18
* to do whatever he told them to. Ju 9:4
"All right," they *, "let's Ju 14:1
The young man * to this, and Ju 17:10,1
But the armies of Israel had * Ju 20:3
For at that time it was * by Ju 21:5
you think best," Elkanah *. 1Sa 1:2
So Samuel * and sent the men home 1Sa 8:22
"All right," Saul *, "let's 1Sa 9:9,10,11
And the people *. 1Sa 14:40
So Samuel finally * and went with 1Sa 15:31
Finally Saul *, and vowed, "As 1Sa 19:6
The next morning, as *, Jonathan 1Sa 20:35
she readily * to his request. 1Sa 25:41
"Good," David *. 1Sa 28:2
Joab *, so twelve men were chosen 2Sa 2:14
David *, and sent word to Tamar 2Sa 13:7
finally the king *, and let all of 2Sa 13:27
"Good," the king *. 2Sa 19:38
they * to help him become king. 1Ki 1:7
Ben-hadad * and sent his armies 1Ki 15:20
And all the people * to this 1Ki 18:24
And all the others *. 1Ki 22:12
So the priests * to set up a 2Ki 12:8
consent, for everyone * with him. 1Ch 13:4
fathers, and * that anyone who 2Ch 15:13
Ben-hadad * to King Asa's request 2Ch 16:4
And all the others *. 2Ch 18:11
and it was * to use it for making 2Ch 24:14
and they all *. Ez 10:5
So it was *! Neh 2:5,6
and the plan to which he had *. Neh 2:18
So they * to do it and said that Neh 5:12
For we all heartily * to this Neh 10:29
We also * not to let our Neh 10:30
We further * that if the heathen Neh 10:31
And we * not to do any work every Neh 10:31
We also * to charge ourselves Neh 10:32
We also * always to bring the Neh 10:35
We * to give to God our oldest Neh 10:36
So we * together not to neglect Neh 10:39,40
The king *, confirming his Est 3:10
So the king *, and the decree was Est 9:14
the realm * to inaugurate this Est 9:27
So King Zedekiah *. Jer 38:5
The steward finally * to the Dan 1:14
field. He * to pay them $20 a day Mt 20:2
*, "for there would be a riot." Mt 26:5
found many who * to be false Mt 26:60,61
Jesus * that Elijah must come Mk 9:12,13
told them to, and then the men *. Mk 11:6
—* that God's requirements were Lk 7:29
"Correct," Jesus *. Lk 7:43
disciple, the man *—but wanted to Lk 9:59
his father * to divide his Lk 15:12
coming and had not * with the Lk 23:50,51,52
(His wife had * to this Act 5:2
about them. Some * with the Jewish Act 14:4
having unanimously * on our Act 15:25
Barnabas *, and wanted to take Act 15:37
So Paul * to their request and Act 21:26,27
The commander *, so Paul stood on Act 21:40
afterwards they *, "This man Act 26:31
glad, for they * that this earth Heb 11:13
AGREEING
was standing there *—keeping the Act 22:20
And so, by *, I can win their 1Co 9:21
each other and * wholeheartedly Php 2:2
AGREEMENT
And I will continue this * Gen 17:7,8
possession, by * in the presence of Gen 23:17,18
Your part of the * is to obey Ex 34:11
them of their * with Moses: "The Jos 1:12,13
the * with a binding oath. Jos 9:14,15
mutual-assistance * between King Ju 4:17
His * is eternal, final, sealed. 2Sa 23:5
your * and obeyed my commandment? 1Ki 2:43
have not kept our * and have not 1Ki 11:11
His * with Abraham, 1Ch 16:16
were in complete * in this matter, 2Ch 30:4
subject to your *, you issue a Est 1:19
"I have made a solemn * with my Ps 89:3,4
have trapped yourself by your *. Pro 6:2
I will cancel your * of Is 28:18
say, Remember this * that your Jer 11:6
idols. The * I made with their Jer 11:10
and violated his * with them, for Jer 22:9
That was the end of the *. Zec 11:11
the new * between God and man. Mk 14:24
token of God's new * to save you—an Lk 22:20
to save you—an * sealed with the Lk 22:20
PAUL WAS IN complete * with the Act 8:1
rule would be the * of both husband 1Co 7:5
cup is the new * between God and 1Co 11:25
about his new * to save them. 2Co 3:6
overwhelming glory of the new *. 2Co 3:10
because the new * which he passes Heb 8:6
The old * didn't even work. Heb 8:7
I will make a new * with the people Heb 8:8
This new * will not be like the Heb 8:9
in that *, so I had to cancel it. Heb 8:9
But this is the new * I will Heb 8:10
of this new *, as taking the place Heb 8:13

AGREEMENT Con't)
NOW IN THAT first * between God Heb 9:1
Christ came with this new * so Heb 9:15
before even the first * could go Heb 9:18
beginning of the * between you and Heb 9:20
you and God, the * God commanded me Heb 9:20
that under the old * almost Heb 9:22
Under the old * the priests Heb 10:11
"This is the * I will make with Heb 10:16
broke their first *: I will write Heb 10:16
brought us his wonderful new *; Heb 12:24
by an everlasting * between God and Heb 13:20,21

AGREES
and if the Lord *, you will be able Ex 18:23
who * to pay a stranger's debts. Pro 27:13
Gentile conversion * with what the Act 15:15
believe only what * with their 1Co 1:22

AGRIPPA
A few days later King * arrived Act 25:13
to hear the man myself," * said. Act 25:22
audience: "King * and all Act 25:24
you, King *, to examine him and Act 25:26
THEN * SAID to Paul, "Go ahead. Act 26:1
"I am fortunate, King *," he Act 26:2
"And so, O King *, I was not Act 26:19
And King * knows about these Act 26:26
King *, do you believe the Act 26:27
* interrupted him. Act 26:28
And * said to Festus, "He could Act 26:32

AGROUND
and ran *. Act 27:41

AGUR
These are the messages of *, son Pro 30:1

AH
*, let me express my anguish. Job 7:11
The Girl: "*, I hear him—my Sol 2:8
*, LAND BEYOND the upper reaches Is 18:1

AHA
sound of the bugle he shouts, '*!' Job 39:25
have seen me doing wrong! "*!" Ps 35:21
Don't let them say, "*! Ps 35:25

AHAB
son * became king in his place. 1Ki 16:28
when * became the king of Israel; 1Ki 16:29
* reigned for twenty-two years. 1Ki 16:29
Gilead, told King *, "As surely as 1Ki 17:1
"Go and tell King * that I will 1Ki 18:1
was on the way to see King *, 1Ki 18:5
isn't here,' King * forced the king 1Ki 18:10
where, and when * comes and can't 1Ki 18:12
will present myself to * today." 1Ki 18:15
So Obadiah went to tell * that 1Ki 18:16
come; and * went out to meet him. 1Ki 18:16
* exclaimed when he saw him. 1Ki 18:17
So * summoned all the people and 1Ki 18:20
Then Elijah said to *, "Go and 1Ki 18:41
So * prepared a feast. 1Ki 18:42
Then Elijah shouted, "Hurry to * 1Ki 18:44
rainstorm. * left hastily for 1Ki 18:45
WHEN * TOLD Queen Jezebel what 1Ki 19:1
the city to King * of Israel: 1Ki 20:2,3
"All right, my lord," * 1Ki 20:4
Then * summoned his advisors. 1Ki 20:7
this message to *: "May the gods 1Ki 20:10
Then a prophet came to see King * 1Ki 20:13
* asked, "How will he do it?" 1Ki 20:14
"Shall we attack first?" * 1Ki 20:14
approached King * and said, "Get 1Ki 20:22
and go out to King * to see if he 1Ki 20:31
So * went back to the palace 1Ki 21:4
it, and he refused!" * told her. 1Ki 21:6
news, she said to *, "You know the 1Ki 21:15
So * went down to the vineyard to 1Ki 21:16
"Go to Samaria to meet King *. 1Ki 21:18
"So my enemy has found me!" * 1Ki 21:20
to the devil as *, for his wife 1Ki 21:25
When * heard these prophecies, 1Ki 21:27
* has humbled himself before me? 1Ki 21:29
was visiting King * of Israel, 1Ki 22:2
Ahab of Israel, * said to his 1Ki 22:3
So King * summoned his four 1Ki 22:6
"Well, there's one," King * 1Ki 22:8
So King * called to one of his 1Ki 22:9
Turning to Jehoshaphat, * 1Ki 22:18
* to go and die at Ramoth-gilead?' 1Ki 22:20
Then King * ordered Micaiah's 1Ki 22:26
So King * of Israel and King 1Ki 22:29
* said to Jehoshaphat, "You wear 1Ki 22:30
So * went into the battle 1Ki 22:30
no one except King * himself. 1Ki 22:31
* between the joints of his armor. 1Ki 22:34
wore on, and King * went back in, 1Ki 22:35
of Israel. So * was buried among 1Ki 22:40
of the reign of King * of Israel. 1Ki 22:41
He also made peace with *, the 1Ki 22:44
Joram of Israel, the son of *. 2Ki 8:16
But he was as wicked as * and 2Ki 8:18
Joram of Israel, the son of *. 2Ki 8:24,25
he was related to * by marriage. 2Ki 8:27
of Israel (son of *) in his war 2Ki 8:28
are to destroy the family of *; 2Ki 9:7
The entire family of * must be 2Ki 9:8
I will destroy the family of * 2Ki 9:9
behind his father *, the Lord 2Ki 9:25
(These seventy sons of King * were 2Ki 10:6
of the family of * who were in 2Ki 10:11
the sons of King * and of the Queen 2Ki 10:13
said to them, "* hardly worshiped 2Ki 10:17
to destroy the dynasty of *. 2Ki 10:30
as * the king of Israel had done. 2Ki 21:3,4,5
King * of Israel. 2Ch 18:1
to visit King *, and King Ahab gave 2Ch 18:2
Ahab, and King * gave a great party 2Ch 18:2
So King * summoned 400 of his 2Ch 18:3,4,5
"Well," * told him, "there is 2Ch 18:6,7
'Who can get King * to go to battle 2Ch 18:19,20
that day, and King * went back in, 2Ch 18:34
Yes, as wicked as *, for Jehoram 2Ch 21:6
the daughters of *, and his whole 2Ch 21:6
the times of King *, and because 2Ch 21:13
the evil ways of *, for his mother 2Ch 22:3
Yes, he was as evil as *, for 2Ch 22:4
Israel (the son of *), who was at 2Ch 22:5
appointed to end the dynasty of *. 2Ch 22:7
and friends of *, he met King 2Ch 22:8
false prophets, * (son of Kolaiah) Jer 29:21
like Zedekiah and * whom the king Jer 29:22
to execute the family of *. Hos 1:4,5f
example you follow is that of *! Mic 6:16

AHAB'S
The man in charge of * household 1Ki 18:3,4
to run ahead of * chariot to the 1Ki 18:46
This reply of * reached Ben-hadad 1Ki 20:12
* troops marched out of the city. 1Ki 20:16
By now * entire army had joined 1Ki 20:19
of the city near King * palace. 1Ki 21:1
So she wrote letters in * name, 1Ki 21:8
The rest of * history—including 1Ki 22:39
Ahaziah, King * son and 1Ki 22:49
that Ahaziah, * son, began to reign 1Ki 22:51
AFTER KING * death the nation of 2Ki 1:1
* SON JEHORAM began his reign over 2Ki 3:1
but after * death, the king of 2Ki 3:5
he even married one of * 2Ki 8:18
as all of King * descendants 2Ki 8:27
Dogs shall eat * wife Jezebel at 2Ki 9:10
the guardians of * seventy sons—all 2Ki 10:1
the best one of * sons to be your 2Ki 10:2,3
of * sons, sent him this message: 2Ki 10:5
king instead of one of * sons." 2Ki 10:5
would happen to * descendants." 2Ki 10:9,10
butchered all of * friends and 2Ki 10:17
evil as Ahab, for * family became 2Ch 22:4

AHARAH
the second,*, the third,Nohah, the 1Ch 8:1

AHARHEL
named after *, the son of Harum. 1Ch 4:8

AHASBAI
Eliphelet (son of *) from Maacah; 2Sa 23:24-39

AHASU-ERUS
And afterwards, when King * began Ez 4:6

AHASUERUS
the reign of King *, emperor of Est 1:1
BUT AFTER KING *' anger had Est 2:1
night with King *, she was given Est 2:12,13,14
of the history of King *' reign. Est 2:23
SOON AFTERWARDS KING * Est 3:1
throughout the whole kingdom of *. Est 3:5,6
of the reign of *, and February of Est 3:7
King * and sealed with his ring. Est 3:12
King * demanded. Est 7:5
ON THAT SAME day King * gave the Est 8:1
Then King * said to Queen Esther Est 8:7
the name of King * and sealed the Est 8:9,10
* was the 28th day of February! Est 8:12
of the kingdom of * with messages Est 9:29-31
KING * NOT only laid tribute upon Est 10:1
next to that of King * himself. Est 10:3
of King Darius, the son of *. Dan 9:1

AHAVA
We assembled at the * River and Ez 8:15
we were at the * River so that we Ez 8:21
We broke camp at the * River at Ez 8:31

AHAZ
Then his son * became the new 2Ki 15:38
NEW KING OF Judah: * 2Ki 16:1
war on * and besieged Jerusalem; 2Ki 16:5
King * sent a messenger to King 2Ki 16:7
* took the silver and gold from 2Ki 16:8
King * now went to Damascus to 2Ki 16:10
Uriah the priest did as King * 2Ki 16:16
the reign of King * is recorded in 2Ki 16:19
When * died he was buried in the 2Ki 16:20
at this time: King *, who had been 2Ki 17:1
Father's name: * 2Ki 18:1
backward on the sundial of *! 2Ki 20:11
Or, "on the steps of *." 2Ki 20:11f
the palace roof above the * Room. 2Ki 23:12
Jotham, *, Hezekiah, 1Ch 3:10-14
Pithon, Melech, Tarea, *. 1Ch 8:35
* was the father of Jehoaddah, 1Ch 8:36
of Pithon, Melech, Tahre-a, and *; 1Ch 9:41
* was the father of Jarah; 1Ch 9:42
and his son * became the new king. 2Ch 27:9
* WAS TWENTY years old when he 2Ch 28:1
About that time King * of Judah 2Ch 28:16
evil deeds of King * of Israel, 2Ch 28:19
King * ruled two tribes of 2Ch 28:19f
for King * instead of helping him. 2Ch 28:20
So even though * had given him 2Ch 28:21
King * collapsed spiritually. 2Ch 28:22
When King * died, he was buried 2Ch 28:27
King * when he closed the Temple. 2Ch 29:19
King Jotham, King * and King Is 1:1
DURING THE REIGN of * (the son of Is 7:1
*, you and Shear-jashub, your son. Is 7:3
this further message to King *: Is 7:10
"Ask me for a sign, *, to prove Is 7:11
came to me the year King * died: Is 14:28
as measured on *' sun dial!" Is 38:8
when * paid "protection money" Eze 23:12f
Uzziah, Jotham, *, and Hos 1:1
King Jotham, King *, and King Mic 1:1
Jotham was the father of *; Mt 1:9
Jotham was the father of Ahaz; * Mt 1:9

AHAZIAH
his ancestors, and * his son became 1Ki 22:40
at Ezion-geber. *, King Ahab's son 1Ki 22:49
of Judah that *, Ahab's son, began 1Ki 22:51
idols. So * made the Lord God of 1Ki 22:52,53
Israel's new king, *, had fallen 2Ki 1:2
Because King * has done this, 2Ki 1:4,5
So * died as the Lord had 2Ki 1:17
the new king—for * did not have a 2Ki 1:17
Then his son * 2Ki 8:24,25
* is an alternate form of the name 2Ki 8:24,25f
the son of Ahab. * was twenty-two 2Ki 8:26
While he was there, King * of 2Ki 8:29
(King * of Judah was there too, 2Ki 9:16
Then he and King * of Judah rode 2Ki 9:21
*, "There is treachery, Ahaziah! 2Ki 9:23
Ahaziah, "There is treachery, *! 2Ki 9:23
Meanwhile, King * of Judah had 2Ki 9:27
the brothers of King * of Judah. 2Ki 10:13
of King *. 2Ki 10:13
THE mother of King * of Judah, 2Ki 11:1
a sister of King * (for she was a 2Ki 11:2,3
Jehoram, and *, the kings of 2Ki 12:18
*, Joash, Amaziah, Azariah, 1Ch 3:10-14
partnership with *, king of Israel, 2Ch 20:35
yourself with King *, the Lord has 2Ch 20:37
THE PEOPLE of Jerusalem chose *, 2Ch 22:1
sons). * was twenty-two years old 2Ch 22:2
Following their evil advice, * 2Ch 22:5
at Ramoth-gilead. * led his army 2Ch 22:5
to recover. * went to visit him, 2Ch 22:6
for God had decided to punish * 2Ch 22:7
It was during this visit that * 2Ch 22:7
were searching for *, they found 2Ch 22:9
Even so, * was given a royal 2Ch 22:9

AHAZIAH'S
The rest of the history of * 2Ki 1:18
royal cemetery. (* reign over 2Ki 9:29
of King Jehoram, * father). 2Ki 11:2,3
Ahab, he met King * nephews, the 2Ch 22:8
heard the news of her son * death. 2Ch 22:10
who was King * sister 2Ch 22:11

AHBAN
his wife Abihail were * and Molid. 1Ch 2:29

AHER
Hushim was one of the sons of *. 1Ch 7:12

AHI
*, the son of Abdi-el and 1Ch 5:15

AHI-EZER
Their chief was *, son of Shemaah 1Ch 12:3-7

AHIAH
Hashabnah, Ma-aseiah, *, Neh 10:14-27

AHIAM
* (the son of Sharar) from Harar; 2Sa 23:24-39
* (son of Sacher) from Harar; 1Ch 11:26-47

AHIAN
The sons of Shemida were *, 1Ch 7:19

AHIEZER
Dan - * (son of Num 1:2-15
Leader: * (son of Num 2:3-31
*, the son of Ammishaddai, Num 7:66-71
of *, the son of Ammishaddai; Num 10:25

AHIHUD
Asher * (son of Shelomi) Num 34:16-28
Heglam), the father of Uzza and *. 1Ch 8:6,7

AHIJAH
Among his men was * the priest 1Sa 14:3
Ark of God," Saul shouted to *. 1Sa 14:18
Elihoreph and * (sons of Shisha) 1Ki 4:1
the prophet * from Shiloh (who had 1Ki 11:29
in the field, * tore his new robe 1Ki 11:30
*, the prophet from Shiloh. 1Ki 12:15
queen, and go to * the prophet at 1Ki 14:2
So when * heard her at the door, 1Ki 14:6
Then * said to Jeroboam's wife, 1Ki 14:12
the Lord had predicted through *. 1Ki 14:18
Then Baasha (the son of *, from 1Ki 15:27
*, the prophet from Shiloh. 1Ki 15:29

(AHIJAH Con't)
Nebat) and of Baasha (son of *). 2Ki 9:9
oldest), Bunah, Oren, Ozem, and *. 1Ch 2:25
Naaman, *, 1Ch 8:6,7
* from Pelon; 1Ch 11:26-47
Eighth, the group led by *; 1Ch 24:7-18
Other Levites, led by *, were 1Ch 26:20,21,22
in the prophecy of * the Shilonite, 2Ch 9:29
spoken to Jeroboam by *, the 2Ch 10:15

AHIJAH'S
So his wife went to * home at 1Ki 14:4

AHIKAM
assistant, and * (Shaphan's son), 2Ki 22:12,13
So Hilkiah the priest, and *, and 2Ki 22:14
(the son of * and grandson of 2Ki 25:22
summoned Hilkiah, * (son of 2Ch 34:20
But * (son of Shaphan), the royal Jer 26:24
Gedaliah (son of *, son of Jer 39:14

AHILUD
state was Jehoshaphat (son of *). 2Sa 8:16
Jehoshaphat (son of *) was the 1Ki 4:1
Baana (son of *), whose area was 1Ki 4:8-19
Jehoshaphat (son of *) was the 1Ch 18:15

AHIMA-AZ
was Ahino-am, the daughter of *. 1Sa 14:50,51
son * and Abiathar's son Jonathan. 2Sa 15:27
send their sons * and Jonathan to 2Sa 15:35,36
Jonathan and * had been staying 2Sa 17:17
if she had seen * and Jonathan, she 2Sa 17:20
Then Zadok's son * said, "Let me 2Sa 18:19
But * pleaded with Joab, "Please 2Sa 18:22
Then * took a short cut across 2Sa 18:23
"The first man looks like *, the 2Sa 18:27
Then * cried out to the king, 2Sa 18:28
* apparently was afraid to tell 2Sa 18:29f
* answered. 2Sa 18:29
king told him. So * stepped aside. 2Sa 18:30
* (who married Princess Basemath, 1Ki 4:8-19
*, the father of 1Ch 6:4-15
Zadok, *. 1Ch 6:50-53

AHIMAN
of Anak: Talmai, Sheshai, and *. Jos 15:14
cities of Sheshai, *, and Talmai. Ju 1:10
Akkub, Talmon, and *—all Levites. 1Ch 9:17,18

AHIMANITES
There they saw the *, Sheshites, Num 13:22

AHIMELECH
city of Nob to see *, the priest. 1Sa 21:1
* trembled when he saw him. 1Sa 21:1
David asked * if he had a spear 1Sa 21:8
saw David talking to * the priest. 1Sa 22:9,10
the priest. * consulted the Lord to 1Sa 22:9,10
King Saul immediately summoned * 1Sa 22:11,12
quavered *. 1Sa 22:11,12
"But sir," * replied, "is 1Sa 22:14
"You shall die, *, along with 1Sa 22:16
of *, escaped and fled to David. 1Sa 22:20
David asked * (the Hittite) and 1Sa 26:5,6,7
Zadok (son of Ahitub) and * (son 2Sa 8:17
Zadok (son of Ahitub) and * (son 1Ch 18:16
clan, and with *, who represented 1Ch 24:3
Zadok the priest, * the son of 1Ch 24:6
King David, Zadok, *, and the 1Ch 24:31

AHIMOTH
Amasai, *, Elkanah, Zophai, 1Ch 6:25,26,27

AHINADAB
* (the son of Iddo), whose area 1Ki 4:8-19

AHINO-AM
Saul's wife was *, the daughter 1Sa 14:50,51
David also married * from 1Sa 25:43
He had his two wives with him—* 1Sa 27:2,3
(David's two wives, * and 1Sa 30:5
So David and his wives—* from 2Sa 2:2
was Amnon, born to his wife *. 2Sa 3:2
born to his wife, * of Jezreel. 1Ch 3:1

AHIO
by Abinadab's sons, Uzzah and *. 2Sa 6:3
Uzzah and Ahio. * was walking in 2Sa 6:4
*, Shashak, Jeremoth. 1Ch 8:14
Zur, Kish, Baal, Nadab, Gedor, *, 1Ch 8:30,31,32
Ner, Nadab, Gedor, *, Zechariah, 1Ch 9:35,36,37
Uzza and * drove the oxen. 1Ch 13:7

AHIRA
Naphtali - * (son of Enan Num 1:2-15
Leader: Ochran) * (son of Num 2:3-31
On the twelfth day came *, son of Num 7:78-83
led by *, the son of Enan. Num 10:27

AHIRAM
named after their ancestor *. Num 26:38-41

AHIRAMITES
The *, named after their ancestor Num 26:38-41

AHISAMACH
Oholiab (son of * of the tribe of Ex 31:6
(Oholiab is the son of *, of the Ex 35:34
(son of * of the tribe of Dan); Ex 38:23

AHISHAHAR
Chenaanah, Zethan, Tarshish, *. 1Ch 7:10

AHISHAR
* was manager of palace affairs; 1Ki 4:1

AHITHOPHEL
he sent for *, one of David's 2Sa 15:12
lived in Giloh. * declared for 2Sa 15:12
When someone told David that *, 2Sa 15:31
* give Absalom foolish advice!" 2Sa 15:31
at Jerusalem, accompanied by *. 2Sa 16:15
Then Absalom turned to * and 2Sa 16:20
* told him, "Go and sleep with 2Sa 16:21
(Absalom did whatever * told him 2Sa 16:23
for every word * spoke was as 2Sa 16:23
"NOW," * SAID, "give me twelve 2Sa 17:1
Absalom told him what * had said. 2Sa 17:6
time I think * has made a mistake. 2Sa 17:7
the counsel of *, which really was 2Sa 17:14
the priests, what * had said and 2Sa 17:15
And they told him how * had 2Sa 17:21
Meanwhile, *—publicly disgraced 2Sa 17:23
Eliam (the son of *) from Gilo; 2Sa 23:24-39
* was the king's official 1Ch 27:33
personal advisor. * was assisted 1Ch 27:34

AHITHOPHEL'S
frustrate and counter * advice. 2Sa 15:33,34
"Should we follow * advice? 2Sa 17:6
advice is better than *." 2Sa 17:14

AHITUB
(the son of *, Ichabod's brother; 1Sa 14:3
Ichabod's brother; * was the 1Sa 14:3
"Listen to me, you son of *!" 1Sa 22:11,12
Zadok (son of *) and Ahimelech 2Sa 8:17
*, the father of 1Ch 6:4-15
*, the father of 1Ch 6:4-15
Meraioth, Amariah, *, 1Ch 6:50-53
Zadok, son of Meraioth, son of *). 1Ch 9:10,11
Zadok (son of *) and Ahimelech 1Ch 18:16
Zadok was the son of *; Ez 7:1
* was the son of Amariah; Ez 7:1
son of * the chief priest). Neh 11:10-14

AHLAB
of Acco, Sidon, *, Achzib, Helbah, Ju 1:31,32

AHLAI
and Sheshan's son was *. 1Ch 2:31
Zabad (son of *); 1Ch 11:26-47

AHOAH
*, Gera, Shephuphan, Huram. 1Ch 8:3,4,5

AHOH
Zalmon from *; 2Sa 23:24-39
a member of the subclan of *. 1Ch 11:12
Ilai from *; 1Ch 11:26-47

AHOHI
the son of Dodo and grandson of *. 2Sa 23:9
was Dodai (a descendant of *). 1Ch 27:4

AHUMAI
the ancestor of * and Lahad. 1Ch 4:2

AHUZZAM
Naarah bore him *, Hepher, 1Ch 4:6

AHUZZATH
with his advisor, *, and also Gen 26:26

AHZAI
of Azarel, son of *, son of Neh 11:10-14

AI
on the west and * on the east. Gen 12:8
between Bethel and *—to the place Gen 13:3,4
on the city of *, east of Bethel. Jos 7:2
men of * as far as the quarries. Jos 7:5
take the entire army and go to *, Jos 8:1
I have given the king of * and Jos 8:1
Before the main army left for *, Jos 8:3,4
the men of * will come out to fight Jos 8:5
Bethel and the west side of *; Jos 8:9
and started toward *, accompanied Jos 8:10
The King of *, seeing the Jos 8:14
a soldier left in * or Bethel and Jos 8:17
*, for I will give you the city." Jos 8:18
When the men of * looked behind Jos 8:20,21
So the men of * were caught in a Jos 8:22
for the king of *, who was captured Jos 8:23
So the entire population of *, Jos 8:25
* until the last person was dead. Jos 8:26
they could.) So * became a Jos 8:28
Joshua hanged the king of * on a Jos 8:29
to Jericho and *, they resorted to Jos 9:3,4,5
and destroyed * and had killed its Jos 10:1
much larger than *—and its men were Jos 10:2
The king of *, near Bethel; Jos 12:8-24
From the subclans of Bethel and *, Ez 2:3-35
From the subclans of Bethel and *, Neh 7:8-38
Cry out, O Heshbon, for * is Jer 49:3

AIAH
*, Gen 36:24
grandsons of Saul by his wife *. 2Sa 21:8
Zibeon's sons were * and 1Ch 1:40

AIATH
Now they are at *, now at Migron; Is 10:28,29

AID
would * them in becoming pregnant. Gen 30:14f
Moses then came to their * and Ex 2:17
evil spirits for *, or be a fortune Deu 18:10
And peace to all who * you; 1Ch 12:18
And never again did the Syrians * 1Ch 19:19
to * in the construction. 1Ch 29:3
their gods, but none gives them *. Job 5:1
he sped swiftly to my * with Ps 18:10
May he send you * from his Ps 20:2
when they sought your *. Ps 22:5
O God my Strength, hurry to my *. Ps 22:19
replying when I call to you for *. Ps 31:17
Lord, hurry to my *! Ps 70:1
Rush to my *, for only you can Ps 70:5
of mercy for all who ask your *. Ps 86:5
Pekah to come and * them, Is 8:6
to Egypt to find * and have put Is 30:2
treasure to pay for Egypt's *. Is 30:6
and kings will send you *. Is 60:10
will not succeed despite their *. Jer 2:37
there was no one to give her *. Lam 1:7
you for * [instead of trusting me Eze 29:6
can * them whenever you want to; Mk 14:7
with money to * the Jews, and to Act 24:17
return is to give some material *. Rom 15:27

AIDE
and Asaiah, the king's personal *. 2Ch 34:20

AIDED
of Shechem who * him in butchering Ju 9:24

AIDES
When the palace * saw her, they Gen 12:15
Some of Saul's * suggested a 1Sa 16:15,16
SAUL NOW URGED his * and his son 1Sa 19:1
Saul then instructed his * to 1Sa 28:7,8
David's * were afraid to tell 2Sa 12:18
and ate. His * were amazed. 2Sa 12:21
to the ground. His * also tore 2Sa 13:31
"We are with you," his * 2Sa 15:15
"The cure for this," his * told 1Ki 1:2
the king's * told him, "Nathan the 1Ki 1:22,23
of servants and * who stood around 1Ki 10:5
and your palace * are content—but 1Ki 10:8
to one of his *, "Go get Micaiah. 1Ki 22:9
the son of Shomer—both trusted *. 2Ki 12:21
But his * conspired against him 2Ki 21:23
David's sons were his chief *. 1Ch 18:17
A very great retinue of * and 2Ch 9:1
many servants and * he had, and 2Ch 9:4
for him and his *, butchering great 2Ch 18:2
of Israel called one of his *. 2Ch 18:8
Afterwards the king and his * 2Ch 29:29
The king, his *, and all the 2Ch 30:2,3
Shime-i and the following *: 2Ch 31:12,13
battle," he exclaimed to his *. 2Ch 35:23
Ar-ta-xerxes—my * and I accepted no Neh 5:14
of their *, who tyrannized them; Neh 5:15
all his governors, *, and army Est 1:1
were his personal *—Mehuman, Est 1:10
properly sent through his *?" Est 1:13-15
The king and all his * thought Est 1:21
So his * suggested, "Let us go Est 2:2
The king turned to his *. Est 5:5
Then Harbona, one of the king's * Est 7:9
officials, and *—helped the Jews Est 9:3
* and teach the king's advisors. Ps 105:22
copied by the * of King Hezekiah Pro 25:1
A wicked ruler will have wicked * Pro 29:12
"Then the king said to his *, Mt 22:13
for his palace *, army officers, Mk 6:21

AIJA
Geba, Michmash, *, Bethel (and its Neh 11:31-35

AIJALON
its place over the valley of *!" Jos 10:12
Sha-alabbin, *, Ithlah, Elon, Jos 19:41-46
Elteke, Gibbethon, *, and Jos 21:23,24
into Mount Heres, *, and Sha-albim, Ju 1:35
and was buried at * in Zebulun. Ju 12:11,12
to *, growing more and more faint. 1Sa 14:31
Beth-horon; *; 1Ch 6:66-69
chiefs of subclans living in *; 1Ch 8:13
Zorah, *, and Hebron. 2Ch 11:5-10
Beth-shemesh, *, Gederoth, Soco, 2Ch 28:17,18

AIM
Evil men take * to slay the Ps 37:14
tongues; they * their bitter words Ps 64:3
For their tongues * lies like Jer 9:8
The archer's * will fail, the Amo 2:15
In this way * for harmony in the Rom 14:19
with the same *, though each of us 1Co 3:8
LET LOVE BE your greatest *; 1Co 14:1
So our * is to please him always 2Co 5:9
because your whole * is wrong—you Jas 4:3
I say it again, that if your * is Jas 4:4

AIMED
bowstrings, and * from ambush at Ps 11:2
your arrows * straight at them. Ps 21:12
He has bent his bow and * it Lam 3:12
fiery arrows * at you by Satan. Eph 6:16

AIMLESSLY
of Beer-sheba, wandering *. Gen 21:14

AIN
to Riblah at the east side of *. Num 34:10,11
Lebaoth, Shilhim, *, and Rimmon. Jos 15:21-32
*, Juttah, and Beth-shemesh. Jos 21:9-16
*, Rimmon, Tochen, and Ashan; 1Ch 4:32,33

AIR
David and tossing dust into the *. 2Sa 16:13
on, leaving him dangling in the *. 2Sa 18:9
dust into the * and put earth on Job 2:12
his nose in the *, yet he shall Job 20:6

AIR Con't)
tight seal, so no * can get between Job 41:15-17
They weigh less than * on scales. Ps 62:9
up and leave me dangling in the *; Ps 140:5
breathe the same *, and both die. Ecc 3:19
noses in the *, tinkling bracelets Is 3:16
You shall toss them in the *; Is 41:16
they rose into the * the wheels Eze 10:15,16
and rose into the * with their Eze 11:22
Even the birds of the * and the Zep 1:3
saw a scroll flying through the *. Zec 5:1
* and tossed up handfuls of dust. Act 22:23
the power of the *, who is at work Eph 2:2
the * and remain with him forever. 1Th 4:17
a breath of fresh *, and he was 2Ti 1:16
and * were darkened by the smoke. Rev 9:2
poured out his flask into the *; Rev 16:17

IRS
on *, and slap you in the face. 2Co 11:19,20

KAN
of Ezer:Bilhan, Zaavan, *. Gen 36:27

KKUB
Hodaviah, Eliashib, Pelaiah, *, 1Ch 3:24
*, Talmon, and Ahiman—all Levites. 1Ch 9:17,18
*, Hatita, and Shobai), 139. Ez 2:40,41,42
Lebanah, Hagabah, *, Hagab, Ez 2:43-54
Sherebiah, Jamin, *, Shabbethai, Neh 8:7,8
led by *, Talmon, and others of Neh 11:19
Meshullam, Talmon, *. Neh 12:25

AKRABBIM
Literally, "ascent of *." Num 34:4f
south of Mount *, on into the Jos 15:2,3,4

ALAMOTH
Literally, "set to *." 1Ch 15:20f

ALARM
but you shall not sound the *." Num 10:5,6,7f
sound the * with these trumpets. Num 10:9
stayed with me to sound the *. Neh 4:18
Literally, "I said in my *, all Ps 116:10,11f
sound the * throughout the land. Jer 4:5
Sound the * in Tekoa; Jer 6:1
and blows the * to warn them, then Eze 33:3
who hears the * and refuses to heed Eze 33:4
doesn't sound the * and warn the Eze 33:6
and north will * him and he will Dan 11:44
Sound the *! Hos 5:8
SOUND THE *! Hos 8:1
SOUND THE * in Jerusalem! Joe 2:1
The * has sounded—listen and fear! Amo 3:6
Sound the *! Nah 2:1
A cry of * will begin at the Zep 1:10

ALARMED
The Egyptians became *, and made Ex 1:12
But he was * by Daniel's Dan 1:10

ALARMS
war and hunger and *, then this is Jer 42:13,14

ALAS
"*, who can live when God does Num 24:23,24
he cried out, "*, O Lord God, for Ju 6:22
"*, my daughter!" Ju 11:35
exclaiming, "*, my brother!" 1Ki 13:30
"*, my master, what shall we do 2Ki 6:15
*, in all history when has there Jer 30:7
and say, "*, our king is dead!" Jer 34:5
with deep remorse and say, * for Eze 6:11
*, this terrible day of Joe 1:15
"*, Babylon, that mighty city! Rev 18:10
and crying, "*, that great city, Rev 18:16
"*, alas, for that great city! Rev 18:19
"Alas, *, for that great city! Rev 18:19

ALCHEMY
a strong dose of * and magic! Dan 1:3,4f

ALEMETH
Geba, *, and Anathoth—were given to 1Ch 6:60
Anathoth, *. 1Ch 7:8
*, Azmaveth, Zimri. 1Ch 8:36
Jarah was the father of *, 1Ch 9:42

ALERT
behind the city, * for action. Jos 8:3,4
are well informed, * and sensible, Dan 1:3,4
Keep * and pray. Mt 26:41
know when it will happen, stay *. Mk 13:33
be alive to God, * to him, through Rom 6:11

ALERTED
so the police were * and many men Ju 16:2

ALEXANDER
of the conquest by * the Great. Eze 26:14f
The Greek Empire, founded by * the Dan 2:39f
The four principal successors of * Dan 8:8f
Doubtless * the Great. Dan 11:3f
(Simon is the father of * and Mk 15:21
Caiaphas, John, *, and others of Act 4:6
* was spotted among the crowd by Act 19:33
Hymenaeus and * are two examples 1Ti 1:20
* the coppersmith has done me 2Ti 4:14

ALEXANDRIA
Jews from Cyrene, * in Egypt, and Act 6:9
in Ephesus from * in Egypt. Act 18:24
Egyptian ship from *, bound for Act 27:6
Twin Brothers of *, a ship that had Act 28:11

ALGUM
great supply of * trees and gems. 1Ki 10:11
Solomon used the * wood to make 1Ki 10:12
fir trees, and * trees from the 2Ch 2:8

ALIAH
Chief Timna, Chief *, Chief 1Ch 1:51-54

ALIAN
The sons of Shobal: *, Manahath, 1Ch 1:40

ALIENS
all the resident * in Israel to 1Ch 22:2
Protect the rights of * and Jer 22:3
needy and cruelly extort from *. Eze 22:29

ALIGHT
would not * on such floating Gen 8:7f

ALIKE
animals *, and reptiles and birds. Gen 7:23
"Will you kill good and bad *? Gen 18:22,23
plants, and animals *. Gen 19:25
animals *, throughout the land." Ex 9:9
animals * throughout all Egypt. Ex 9:10
men and animals *, was killed, and Ex 9:25
and the Egyptian people *. Ex 11:3
Cattle and wild animals * shall Lev 25:6,7
This applies to men and women *. Num 5:3
families, sons and daughters *. Num 18:11
be fair to great and small *. Deu 1:17
women, and children *. Deu 3:6
terrorize young men and girls *; Deu 32:25
capital cities and villages *. 1Sa 6:4,5
by the army and general public *. 1Sa 18:5
We share and share *—those who go 1Sa 30:24
and women *—of a loaf of bread, 2Sa 6:19
size and were made *, for each was 1Ki 7:37
(men and women *) a loaf of 1Ch 16:3
dividing it to young and old *. 2Ch 31:14,15
cabinet officials *—for seven days Est 1:5
Both rich and poor * are there, Job 3:19
Old and young * will be Job 18:20
Both * are buried in the same Job 21:26
for men and animals *. Ps 36:6
* are nothing in his sight. Ps 62:9
Day and night * belong to you; Ps 74:16
Darkness and light are both * to Ps 139:12
or bad, we'll treat them all *. Pro 1:12
The rich and the poor are * Pro 22:2
day and a cranky woman are much *! Pro 27:15
and death are * in this: neither Pro 27:20
Rich and poor are * in this: each Pro 29:13
wise and foolish *— just as the Ecc 2:13,14
Wise men and fools * spend their Ecc 6:7,8
sound very much *, as do those for Is 5:7f
small *, both officers and men. Is 10:33
and prophets—all are * in this. Jer 2:26,27
in it—the cities and people *. Jer 8:16
and priests * have made it their Jer 14:18
and shepherds * shall live together Jer 31:24
and animals * have disappeared. Jer 32:43
*, who had given him that answer: Jer 44:20
both young and old * shall be Jer 51:3
both young and old *, by tying Eze 13:18
man and beast *, though Noah, Eze 14:19
and sons *—and my rule is this: It Eze 18:4
tree will die, green and dry *. Eze 20:47
good and bad *— I will not spare Eze 21:3
their leaders. All * shall die. Eze 21:12
men and women *, and put strange Joe 2:29
and fine young men * will grow Amo 8:13
The governor and judge * demand Mic 7:3
sweep away both men and animals *. Zep 1:3
they could find, good and bad *; Mt 22:10
and residents of Jerusalem *! Act 2:14
women *, and they shall prophesy. Act 2:18
men and women * and jailing them. Act 8:3
to convince the Jews and Greeks *. Act 18:4
Ephesus, to Jews and Greeks *; Act 19:17
Jews and Gentiles *—the necessity Act 20:21
light to Jews and Gentiles *." Act 26:23
people and uncivilized *; Rom 1:14
to the educated and uneducated *. Rom 1:14
Gentiles * who keep on sinning. Rom 2:9
shown that all men * are sinners, Rom 3:9
he could have mercy upon all *. Rom 11:32
for every day * belongs to God. Rom 14:5
be stared at by men and angels *. 1Co 4:9
and Gentiles *—are seen to be Eph 3:10
until finally we all believe * Eph 4:13
and people *, all who fear your Rev 11:18

ALIVE
to keep them * through the flood. Gen 6:19,20
*, and those with him in the boat. Gen 7:23
throw him * into this well here; Gen 37:21,22
Is he still *?" Gen 43:27
"He is * and well." Gen 43:28
"Is my father still *?" Gen 45:3
and your families *, so that you Gen 45:7
"Joseph is *," they shouted to Gen 45:26
Joseph my son is *! Gen 45:28
you again and know you are *." Gen 46:30
know whether they are still *." Ex 4:18
the sea, not one remained *. Ex 14:28
The other goat shall be kept * Lev 16:10
All three shall be burned * to Lev 20:14
as her own, shall be burned *. Lev 21:9
"And for those who are left *, I Lev 26:36
Joshua and Caleb remained *. Num 14:36,37,38
and they go down * into Sheol, then Num 16:30
So they went down * into Sheol Num 16:33
We left nothing * except the Deu 2:33,34
Lord your God are still * today. Deu 4:4
but with you who are here * today. Deu 5:2,3
preserve us * as he has until now. Deu 6:24
and his children who are still *. Deu 28:54
and Israel shall come * again! Deu 30:6
in the entire city was left *. Jos 10:28
Not one person was left *. Jos 10:37
Lord has kept me * and well for all Jos 14:10
not one man was left *. Ju 4:16
and her father and burned them *. Ju 15:6
Those who are left * will live 1Sa 2:33
As long as that fellow is *, 1Sa 20:31
remains * by tomorrow morning!" 1Sa 25:22
men would be * tomorrow morning." 1Sa 25:34
They didn't leave one person * 1Sa 27:9
No one was left * to come to Gath 1Sa 27:11
lame son is still *." 2Sa 9:3
the child was *, for I said, 2Sa 12:22
sons, and not one is left *!" 2Sa 13:29,30
so that not one of them is left *. 2Sa 17:12
as he dangled * from the oak. 2Sa 18:14
while I am still * to see it.' 1Ki 1:48
do this while you are still *. 1Ki 11:12,13
returned, and he became * again! 1Ki 17:22
"See! He's *!" 1Ki 17:23
"Take them *," Ben-hadad 1Ki 20:18
"Oh, is he still *?" 1Ki 20:32
priests left * by Elijah at Carmel, 1Ki 22:6f
only enough to keep him * 1Ki 22:27
Another 10,000 were taken * to 2Ch 25:12
While Zechariah was * Uzziah was 2Ch 26:5
men found guilty, and impaled *. Est 2:23
They are * in the morning, but Job 4:20
grass without water to keep it *. Job 8:11-13
"Are you the wisest man *? Job 15:7,8
does a man wish to be swallowed *? Job 37:19,20
God is *! Ps 18:46
death itself, and here I am *! Ps 30:3
He protects them and keeps them *; Ps 41:2
been swallowed * by our enemies, Ps 124:2,3
Let everything * give praises to Ps 150:6
It is a wonderful thing to be *! Ecc 11:7
men will be left * that seven women Is 4:1
of all its people will be left *. Is 16:13,14
Few will be left *. Is 24:6
Not one of her sons is left * to Is 51:18
who are still left * shall long to Jer 8:3
the king of Babylon burned *!" Jer 29:22
and left without a soul *. Jer 46:19
and save your own souls *?" Eze 13:18f
isn't a man * who can tell others Dan 2:10
only ten will come back *." Amo 5:3
* inside, "Are any others left?" Amo 6:10
I'd rather be dead than * [when Jon 4:3
is * from everlasting ages past! Mic 5:2
dead, were not * in the presence of Mt 22:32f
were still very much *, for he Mk 12:27
she had seen Jesus, and he was *! Mk 16:10,11
who had seen him * from the dead. Mk 16:14
means that person is *, not dead! Lk 20:37,38
in a tomb for someone who is *? Lk 24:5
there who told them Jesus is *! Lk 24:22,23
been * and is himself God. Jn 1:1
my brother would still be *." Jn 11:32
to time, actually *, and proved to Act 1:3
after you killed him we saw him *! Act 3:15
who died, but Paul insists is *! Act 25:19
so that I am still * today to tell Act 26:22
and instead be * to God, alert to Rom 6:11
to her husband as long as he is *. Rom 7:2
wrong while he was *, but it is Rom 7:3
of idols as *, and have believed 1Co 8:7
are really * and are real gods, and 1Co 10:19
if I were burned * for preaching 1Co 13:3
*, though some have died by now. 1Co 15:6
his people will become * again. 1Co 15:23
suddenly become *, with new bodies 1Co 15:52
and then we who are still * shall 1Co 15:52
here we are, still very much *. 2Co 6:9
Literally, "he made us *." Eph 2:5f
of those who are * from the dead. Php 3:11
SINCE YOU BECAME * again, so to Col 3:1
Then we who are still * and 1Th 4:17
or * at the time of his return. 1Th 5:10
While he is still * no one can Heb 9:17
death, but he came back again *! Heb 11:19
CHRIST WAS * when the world began, 1Jn 1:1
who has been * from the beginning. 1Jn 2:13
died, who is now * forevermore, who Rev 1:17,18
upon the world to test everyone *. Rev 3:10
But the men left * after these Rev 9:20
He was * but isn't now. Rev 17:8
thrown * into the Lake of Fire that Rev 19:20

ALKALI
the whole land is * and salt, a Deu 29:23

ALL-CONSUMING
of this *, Everlasting Fire?" Is 33:14

ALL-OUT
an * effort against Greece. Dan 11:2f
ALL-POWERFUL
"Look, God is *. Job 36:22
is that man should fear the * God. Ecc 3:14
ALL-SEEING
to the * eyes of our living God; Heb 4:13
ALLAMMELECH
Helkath, Hali, Beten, Achshaph, *, Jos 19:24,25,26
ALLEGIANCE
had declared their * to the king of 2Ki 25:11
that tribe retained its * to Saul. 1Ch 12:24-37
pledged their * to King Solomon. 1Ch 29:24
On arrival they swore * to the 2Ch 23:2,3
For many in Judah had sworn * to Neh 6:18
tongue shall swear * to my name. Is 45:23
HEAR ME, MY people: you swear * to Is 48:1
ALLEYS
They lurk in dark * of the city Ps 10:8
the streets and * of the city and Lk 14:21
ALLIANCE
in one vast * against Israel. Ju 6:33
SOLOMON MADE AN * with Pharaoh, 1Ki 3:1
Solomon made a formal * of peace. 1Ki 5:12
Now break your * with King Baasha 1Ki 15:19
silver, and bronze, seeking an *. 1Ch 18:10
you to break your * with King 2Ch 16:3
made a marriage * [for his son 2Ch 18:1
Ahaziah made an * with King Jehoram 2Ch 22:5
Ahaziah for his * with Jehoram. 2Ch 22:7
token of * with the king of Judah. Is 16:1
Hezekiah was seeking a defensive * Is 30:2f
prostitutions by your * with her. Eze 16:26
"Several years later an * will Dan 11:6
too will form an * with the Dan 11:17
ALLIANCES
What have you gained by your * Jer 2:18
by forming * with each other Dan 2:43
ALLIED
at that time. * with him were the Ju 3:13
all the * forces of Midian!" Ju 7:14
left of the * armies of the east; Ju 8:10
with thirty-two * nations and their 1Ki 20:1
and the thirty-two * kings were 1Ki 20:16
"Because you have * yourself with 2Ch 20:37
is * with the descendants of Lot. Ps 83:8
is * with Israel against us!" Is 7:2
Judah and her * tribes.' Eze 37:16
ALLIES
* arrived and the slaughter began. Gen 14:5,6
attacked Ched-or-laomer and his * Gen 14:8,9
of Eshcol and Aner, Abram's *). Gen 14:13
Aner, Eshcol, and Mamre, my *." Gen 14:24
their *, he was very frightened. Jos 10:1
they had no local *, for they had Ju 18:28
are * and conspirators with David; 1Sa 22:17
When Hadadezer's * saw that the 2Sa 10:19
"Let us be * just as our fathers 1Ki 15:19
But which of your * will give you 2Ki 18:20,21
So the Hagrites and all their * 1Ch 5:20
against their * from Mount Seir and 2Ch 20:23
enemies, for men are useless *. Ps 108:12
their oppressors were powerful *. Ecc 4:1
them there and be their loyal *. Is 14:1
have done, and crush their * too. Is 31:2
the nations refusing to be your * Is 60:12
It will do you no good! Your * Jer 4:30
your * over you as your rulers? Jer 13:21
Weep, for your * are gone. Jer 22:20
And now all your * have Jer 22:22
and their * from Tyre and Sidon Jer 47:4
chariots, and her * from other Jer 50:37
Egypt and Israel's other former *. Lam 1:2f
I begged my * Lam 1:19
We look for our * Lam 4:17
your * and worshiping their gods Eze 16:28
together all your *—these lovers of Eze 16:37
payments to your * for their love. Eze 16:40,41
says: All Egypt's * shall fall, and Eze 30:6
Egypt on fire and destroyed her *. Eze 30:8
them in hell. Her * too are all Eze 31:17
of hell, surrounded by their *. Eze 32:23
You and all your *—a vast and Eze 38:9
and on all your * who live safely Eze 39:6
Then the Syrian king and his * Dan 11:15
All your * will turn against you Ob 1:7
were her mighty *, and she could Nah 3:9
ALLON
of Shiphi, son of *, son of 1Ch 4:34-39
ALLOTED
* to Judah and Benjamin, is 8 Eze 48:21,22
ALLOTMENT
A regular food * was given to all 2Ch 31:17,18
This then is your *, that which Jer 13:24,25
This shall be his *. Eze 45:8
ALLOTMENTS
These are the * to be made to Eze 48:29
ALLOTTED
The goat * to the Lord shall Lev 16:9
will be * to the smaller tribes. Num 33:54
permanently as it was first *. Num 36:7
territory * to one of the tribes. Deu 12:14
of Mount Seir, was * by Joshua to Jos 12:7
of Canaan were * to the remaining Jos 14:1
in the territory * to us," they Ju 1:3
And so to me also have been * Job 7:3
ALLOW
Because Edom refused to * Israel Num 20:21,22
but if he refuses to * it on the Num 30:12
So Joshua would not * the people Jos 9:26
things to me if I * anything but Ru 1:17
wouldn't * them for fear of their 1Sa 13:19
for refusing to * my people to 1Sa 15:2
to * them to continue as priests; Ez 2:62,63
they would not even * them to eat Ez 2:62,63
you will not * your beloved one Ps 16:10
How long, O God, will you * our Ps 74:9,10
But I will not * those who Ps 101:7
to * him not to defile Dan 1:8f
Will you, who cannot * sin in any Hab 1:13
(But he refused to * the demons Mk 1:34
And don't * us to be tempted." Lk 11:4
them, so God will * them to 2Th 2:11
own glory, should * Jesus to Heb 2:10
ALLOWANCE
cash * for the rest of his life. 2Ki 25:30
And he was given a regular * to Jer 52:34
each other, making * for each Eph 4:2
ALLOWANCES
gave them large * and arranged for 2Ch 11:23
ALLOWED
of Israel be * to leave Egypt. Ex 7:2
alike shall be * to graze there. Lev 25:6,7
since we are not * to plant or Lev 25:20
The Edomites at Seir * us to go Deu 2:29
no one was * to go in or out. Jos 6:1
If the people had been * to eat 1Sa 14:30
anyway, that he is * to defy the 1Sa 17:26
for I am not * to eat anything or 1Ki 13:16,17
and he continually * King Hazael of 2Ki 13:3
they would be * to live in the land 2Ki 25:24
And who am I to be * to build a 2Ch 2:6
That is why the Lord God * the 2Ch 28:5
He asked to be * to return to Ez 7:6
So they were not * to continue as Neh 7:64,65
So once again you * the heathen Neh 9:30
whom you have * to conquer us Neh 9:37
Why is a man * to be born if God Job 3:23
day of calamity, and * to escape. Job 21:30-32
These are the ones who are * to Ps 24:6
and * his Ark to be captured; Ps 78:61
heathen nations be * to scoff, Ps 79:10
wicked be * to triumph and exult? Ps 94:3
For the Lord who * you to be Is 22:17
sinner, should he be * to live? Eze 18:24
haircuts are all they are *. Eze 44:20
* to live a short time longer. Dan 7:12
ground when thrown or * to fall. Hos 4:12f
home, you are not * to pour out Hos 9:4
only priests were * to eat? Mk 2:25,26
never be * into his Kingdom." Mk 10:15
be * to eat the Passover lamb. Jn 18:28
even one person is * to go on 1Co 5:6
Even if I am * to do them, I'll 1Co 6:12
isn't * to drink some of the milk? 1Co 9:7
am not * to tell them to others). 2Co 12:4
No one will be * to bury them, Rev 11:8,9
ALLOWING
any other nation, * you to receive Deu 26:19
and on me too, not * me to have Php 2:27
ALLOWS
and courteous. It * discussion and Jas 3:17
loves us, for he * us to be called 1Jn 3:1
ALLOY
now mixed with worthless *! Is 1:22
ALLURE
all its * and its power over you. Rom 6:7
ALLUSION
Probably an * to the kings of Hos 13:11f
ALLY
Assyria to be his * in his war 2Ch 28:16
morning; they * themselves with the Job 24:16
signed a treaty to * themselves Ps 83:5
And Israel will be their *; Is 19:24
and their "glorious *," Egypt! Is 20:5,6
Egypt is a dangerous *. Is 36:6
one * to another for their help; Jer 2:36
For Babylon is Judah's * and has Eze 21:23
ALMIGHTY
to him and told him, "I am the *; Gen 17:1
Laban's daughters. God * bless Gen 28:2
I am God *," the Lord said to Gen 35:11
May God * give you mercy before Gen 43:14
"God * appeared to me at Luz in Gen 48:3
your fathers, the *, bless you with Gen 49:25
I am Jehovah, the * God who Ex 6:2,3
I have seen what God * showed me; Num 24:3-9
He sees what * God has shown Num 24:15-19
and strength of * God which he used Deu 7:19
Mara means "bitter") "for * Ru 1:20
and you begged * God for them— if Job 8:5
* God, or even reason with him? Job 9:14
Are you qualified to judge the *? Job 11:7
I long to speak directly to the *. Job 13:3
the *, stubbornly assaulting him. Job 15:25,26
" 'Who is * God?' Job 21:15
deeply of the anger of the *. Job 21:20
Is it any pleasure to the * if Job 22:3
* himself shall be your treasure; Job 22:25
he, the *, has terrified me with Job 23:16,17
rights, even the * God who has Job 27:2
himself in the * or pay any Job 27:10
the hand of the *: If he has a Job 27:13
when the * was still with me and Job 29:5
I know full well that * God Job 31:2,3
now let the * show me that I am Job 31:35
the * which makes him intelligent. Job 32:8,9
the breath of the * gives me life. Job 33:4
Are you going to condemn the * Job 34:17
"God is * and yet does not Job 36:5
the power of the *, and yet he is Job 37:23
still want to argue with the *? Job 40:2
themselves against * God— these Ps 83:5
WE LIVE WITHIN the shadow of the * Ps 91:1
the time for the * to crush you. Is 13:6
So King Zedekiah swore before * Jer 38:16
as the voice of * God when he Eze 10:5
Days—the * God—sat down to judge. Dan 7:9
arrogance against * God, and the Dan 7:11
Destruction from the * is almost Joe 1:15
shall be enthroned beside * Lk 22:69
their little plots against * God? Act 4:25,26
hushed and guilty before * God. Rom 3:19
blessed and only * God, the King of 1Ti 6:15
holy, Lord God *—the one who was, Rev 4:8
thanks, Lord God *, who is and was, Rev 11:17
Lord God *. Rev 15:3,4
say, "Yes, Lord God *, your Rev 16:7
coming Judgment Day of God *. Rev 16:14
For the Lord our God, the *, Rev 19:6
fierceness of the wrath of * God. Rev 19:15
for the Lord God * and the Lamb Rev 21:22
ALMODAD
*, Sheleph, Hazarmaveth, Jerah, Gen 10:26-30
*, Sheleph, Hazarmaveth, Jerah, 1Ch 1:20-23
ALMON
Gibeon, Gaba, Anathoth, and *. Jos 21:17,18
ALMON-DIBLATHAIM
and then to *, and on into the Num 33:46
ALMOND
from poplar, *, and plane trees, Gen 30:37
decorated with three * flowers. Ex 25:32,33
with four * flowers—one placed Ex 25:34,35
* flowers were all of one piece. Ex 37:17
decorated with * blossoms, a flower Ex 37:20,21
from the branch of an * tree." Jer 1:11
between shaqedh (*) in verse 11 and Jer 1:12f
ALMONDS
myrrh, pistachio nuts, and *. Gen 43:11
and had ripe * hanging from it! Num 17:8
ALOES
As * planted by the Lord himself; Num 24:3-9
perfumed with myrrh, * and cassia. Ps 45:8
with myrrh, * and cinnamon. Pro 7:16,17
*, and every other lovely spice. Sol 4:13,14
ointment made from myrrh and *. Jn 19:39
ALOFT
He will hold you * in his hands Is 62:3
ALONE
"It isn't good for man to be *; Gen 2:18
I consider you * to be righteous. Gen 7:1
But leave these men *, for they Gen 19:8
residents finally left him *. Gen 26:22
to the camp and was there *; Gen 32:22,23,24
of Egypt. I * will outrank you." Gen 41:40
is dead and he * is left of his Gen 42:38
And his brother is dead, and he * Gen 44:20
he was left * with his brothers. Gen 45:1
Then God let him *. Ex 4:25,26
we were slaves, to leave us *? Ex 14:12
to do all this *, with people Ex 18:14
Moses * shall come near to the Ex 24:2
They * shall eat those items Ex 29:33
Now let me * and my anger shall Ex 32:10
that you will not have the task *. Num 11:17
are 600,000 men * [besides all the Num 11:21
They live *, Num 23:7-10
shall be purified by the water *.' Num 31:23
Jehovah is our God, Jehovah *. Deu 6:4
name * to endorse your promises. Deu 6:13
" 'Let me * that I may destroy Deu 9:13,14
him and take oaths by his name *. Deu 10:20
This contract is not with you * Deu 29:14,15
When the Lord * was leading them, Deu 32:12
Don't you see that I * am God? Deu 32:39
Worship the Lord *. Jos 24:14
Yes, we choose the Lord, for he * Jos 24:18
worship and obey the Lord *." Jos 24:24
on and returned * to the king. Ju 3:17,18,19
down to the camp *—take along your Ju 7:10
But again she was *—Manoah was Ju 13:9
*, without her husband or sons. Ru 1:4,5
No one shall succeed by strength * 1Sa 2:9

(ALONE Con't)
"Leave us * and we will be your 1Sa 11:1
you and you * if you will only 1Sa 12:10
"Why are you *?" 1Sa 21:1
on, singleminded, after Abner *. 2Sa 2:19
Let him *, for no doubt the Lord 2Sa 16:11
"If he is *, he has news." 2Sa 18:25
Our Lord * is God; 2Sa 22:32
and fled, he stood * at the center 2Sa 23:11,12
And as the two of them were * in 1Ki 11:29
so that he will leave me *." 1Ki 15:19
So they did, each going *. 1Ki 18:6
Then he went on * into the 1Ki 19:4
but the prophet said, "Let her *; 2Ki 4:27
you * are the God of all the 2Ki 19:15
will know that you * are God." 2Ki 19:19
King Josiah replied, "Leave it *. 2Ki 23:18
Riches and honor come from you * 1Ch 29:12
* may help them in their work. 2Ch 13:10
For we trust in you * to rescue 2Ch 14:11
so that he will leave me *." 2Ch 16:3
of the priests *, the sons of Aaron 2Ch 26:17,18
and to burn incense upon it *? 2Ch 32:12
Leave me *! 2Ch 35:21
Then Ezra prayed, "You * are Neh 9:6
hands on Mordecai *, but to move Est 3:5,6
500 men in Shushan *," he Est 9:12
I * have escaped to tell you." Job 1:16
I * have escaped to tell you." Job 1:17
and I * escaped to tell you." Job 1:19
wild animals will leave you *. Job 5:22
monster, that you never let me *? Job 7:12
Oh, let me * for these few Job 7:16
Why won't you let me *—even long Job 7:19
sorrows. He * is strong and just. Job 9:19
Oh, let me * that I may have a Job 10:20,21
He * knows what we should do; Job 12:13
"Be silent now and let me *, Job 13:13
ancestors to whom * the land was Job 15:17-19
or unjust. He * has authority over Job 34:13
him up, let * try to conquer him. Job 41:10
my only hope. You * can lift my Ps 3:3
*, O Lord, you will keep me safe. Ps 4:8
With them * he shares the secrets Ps 25:14
for help, for he * can rescue me. Ps 25:15
LORD, I TRUST in you *. Ps 31:1
For you * are strong enough. Ps 31:4
I said, "You * are my God; Ps 31:14,15
We depend upon the Lord * to Ps 33:20
us, for our hopes are in you *. Ps 33:22
It is against you and you * I Ps 51:4
O my God, you * can rescue me. Ps 51:14,15
For salvation comes from him *. Ps 62:1
Yes, he * is my Rock, my Ps 62:2
For salvation comes from him *. Ps 62:5
Yes, he * is my Rock, my Ps 62:6
come from God *. Ps 62:7
O Lord, you * are my hope; Ps 71:5
I tell everyone that you * are Ps 71:16
learn that you *, Jehovah, are the Ps 83:18
do great miracles. You * are God. Ps 86:10
This I declare, that he * is my Ps 91:2
that God * is glorious and strong. Ps 96:7
or like an owl * in the desert. Ps 102:6
Praise him who * does mighty Ps 136:4
desperate, and you * know which way Ps 142:3
For he * is worthy. Ps 148:13
Let her love * fill you with Pro 5:19
the upright man *, and quit trying Pro 24:15,16
let * God. Who else but God goes Pro 30:3
a man who is quite *, without a son Ecc 4:8
but if a man falls when he is *, Ecc 4:10
other, but how can one be warm *? Ecc 4:11
And one standing * can be Ecc 4:12
the Lord * will be exalted. Is 2:11
and the Lord * will be exalted. Is 2:17
be * in the midst of the earth! Is 5:8
for he * is holy, just and good. Is 5:16
capital of Syria *, and King Is 7:8
capital of Ephraim * and King Is 7:9
Let me * to weep. Is 22:4
but now we worship you *. Is 26:13
the cherubim, you * are God of all Is 37:16,17
You * made heaven and earth. Is 37:16,17
that you are God, and you *." Is 37:20
the First and Last; I * am he. Is 41:4
must serve but me *, for I have Is 41:9
and to understand that I * am God. Is 43:10
I, yes, I * am he who blots away Is 43:25
me; I * stretched out the heavens. Is 44:24
there is no one else. I * am God. Is 45:6
You say, "I * am God! Is 47:8
my chosen ones! I * am God. Is 48:12
into exile, leaving me here *. Is 49:21
"I have trodden the winepress *. Is 63:3
So I executed vengeance *; Is 63:5
You sit * like a Bedouin in the Jer 3:2
will swear by me *, the living God, Jer 4:2
and weep * upon the mountains; Jer 7:29
it, let * commanded it to be done. Jer 7:31
Let them boast in this *: That Jer 9:24
(And that title belongs to you *! Jer 10:7
Who but you *, O Lord our God, Jer 14:22
I sit * beneath the hand of God. Jer 15:17,18
at last that I * am God. Jer 16:21
Lord, you * can heal me, you Jer 17:14
can heal me, you * can save, and my Jer 17:14
and my praises are for you *. Jer 17:14
Lord, don't desert me now! You * Jer 17:17
for you * are the Lord, my God. Jer 31:18
tribes living * in the desert Jer 49:31
grief, she sits * in her mourning. Lam 1:1
My Comforter is far away—he who * Lam 1:16
They will realize that I * am Eze 6:10
will realize that I * am God. Eze 6:13
fulfilling their orders, I was *. Eze 9:8
here today, they * would be saved Eze 14:14
that they * would be saved. Eze 14:18
and know that I * am God, I let Eze 20:26
you will know that I * am God." Eze 23:49
Then Israel will know that I * am Eze 29:16
that he is not * in having all his Eze 32:31
I replied, "Lord, you * know the Eze 37:3
of Zadok—for they * of all the Eze 40:46
he * has all wisdom and all power. Dan 2:20
I, Daniel, * saw this great Dan 10:7
ran to hide, and I was left *. Dan 10:8
he will leave the Syrian king *. Dan 11:8
"You must live * for many days; Hos 3:3
from them and they are left *. Hos 5:6
when I turn away and leave you *. Hos 9:12
I * am God, your Lord, and have Hos 13:4
for in you *, O Lord, the Hos 14:3
decide to let you * and give you a Joe 2:14
that I * am the Lord, your God. Joe 2:27
of the earth, I have chosen you *. Amo 3:2
She is left * to die." Amo 5:2
comes from the Lord *." Jon 2:9
* [as these Chaldeans do Hab 2:4
God, thinking he will let them *. Zep 1:12
that all was done by grace *." Zec 4:7
apart, to face their sorrow *. Zec 12:12,13,14
Lord—his name * will be worshiped. Zec 14:9
by yourself, all *, and shut the Mt 6:6
him to go away and leave them *. Mt 8:34
bread permitted to the priests *. Mt 12:4
a boat to a remote area to be *. Mt 14:13
"for God * is truly good. Mt 19:17
message: "Leave that good man *; Mt 27:19
But the rest said, "Leave him * Mt 27:49
There, for forty days, * except Mk 1:12,13
out * into the wilderness to pray. Mk 1:35
Afterwards, when he was * with Mk 4:10
when he was * with his disciples, Mk 4:34
Jesus to go away and leave them *! Mk 5:17
lake, and he was * on land, he saw Mk 6:47
Afterwards, when Jesus was * in Mk 9:28
Later, when he was * with his Mk 10:10
and Andrew got * with him and asked Mk 13:3,4
But Jesus said, "Let her *; Mk 14:6
"Man shall not live by bread *." Lk 4:4f
"We must worship God, and him *. Lk 4:8
and leave them * (for a deep wave Lk 8:37
One day as he was *, praying, Lk 9:18
was there * with his disciples. Lk 9:36
him and hardly ever leaves him *. Lk 9:39
He was * at the time as his Jn 4:8
went higher into the mountains *. Jn 6:15
shall we go? You * have the words Jn 6:68
If we let him * the whole nation Jn 11:48
Jesus replied, "Let her *. Jn 12:7
Unless I die I will be *—a single Jn 12:23,24
to his own home, leaving me *. Jn 16:32
Yet I will not be *, for the Jn 16:32
"I am not praying for these * Jn 17:20
my advice is, leave these men *. Act 5:38
first to the Jews *, but now Rom 1:16
Was it by faith *? Rom 4:9
*, before he was circumcised. Rom 4:12
For everything comes from God *. Rom 11:36
will pin their hopes on him *." Rom 15:12
To God, who * is wise, be the Rom 16:25,26,27
and some that they * are the true 1Co 1:12
For it is from God * that you 1Co 1:30
these ways. God * is the Judge of 1Co 5:13
And must Barnabas and I * keep 1Co 9:6
with the spirit *, speaking in 1Co 14:16
hands of God, who * could save us, 2Co 1:9
of God, giving ourselves to him *. 2Co 7:1
be for Christ *, just as a pure 2Co 11:2
did it by himself *, without angels Gal 3:20
faith in the cross of Christ *. Gal 5:11
off from you and leave you *! Gal 5:12
the cross of Christ * can save. Gal 6:12
put my trust and hope in Christ *. Php 3:7
on faith—counting on Christ *. Php 3:9
for we serve God *, who examines 1Th 2:4
I decided to stay * in Athens and 1Th 3:1
he * is God, and full of wisdom. 1Ti 1:17
who are poor and * in the world, if 1Ti 5:5
* and have nowhere else to turn. 1Ti 5:16
of lords, who * can never die, who 1Ti 6:16
once a year, all *, and always with Heb 9:7
God is by faith *, plus nothing; Jas 2:18
be filled with God * to make them Jas 4:8
* decides to save us or destroy. Jas 4:12
faith and hope can rest in him *. 1Pe 1:21
And now—all glory to him who * is Jud 1:24,25
In China *, in 1961, there were Rev 9:16f
For you * are holy. Rev 15:3,4
and authority belong to him *; Rev 19:1
Worship God *." Rev 22:9

ALONGSIDE
crews working * Solomon's men, went 2Ch 8:17,18
for three miles * the holy grounds, Eze 48:18

ALOOF
LORD, WHY ARE you standing * and Ps 10:1
stand silent and * while the Ps 109:1
You stood *, refusing to lift a Ob 1:11

ALOUD
Then he wept *. Gen 45:2
*, and they carried on all night. Num 14:1
foe, Joshua prayed *, "Let the sun Jos 10:12
Temple—wept *, while others were Ez 3:12
The laws of God were read * to Neh 9:3
and night, pleading * with God; Ps 55:17
chariot, reading * from the book of Act 8:28
and they wept * as they embraced Act 20:37
If you read this prophecy * to Rev 1:3

ALPHA
Literally, "I am * and Omega"; Rev 1:8f

ALPHABET
and last letters of the Greek *. Rev 1:8f

ALPHAEUS
James (*' son), Mt 10:2,3,4
Levi, the son of *, sitting at his Mk 2:14
James (the son of *), Mk 3:16-19
James (the son of *), Lk 6:14,15,16
James (son of *), Act 1:14

ALTAR
Then Noah built an * and Gen 8:20
And Abram built an * there to Gen 12:7
There he made camp, and made an * Gen 12:8
place where he had built the *. Gen 13:3,4
and built an * to Jehovah there. Gen 13:18
a fire upon the *, saddled his Gen 22:3
to go, he built an * and placed the Gen 22:9
laid him on the * over the wood. Gen 22:9
son, as a burnt offering on the *. Gen 22:13
Then Isaac built an * and Gen 26:25
And there he erected an * and Gen 33:20
"The * to the God of Israel." Gen 33:20
"and build an * to worship the God Gen 35:1
I will build an * there to the God Gen 35:3
And Jacob erected an * there and Gen 35:7
and named it "The * to the God who Gen 35:7
Moses built an * there and Ex 17:15,16
would make them unfit for my *. Ex 20:25
And don't make steps for the *, Ex 20:26
him even from my *, and kill him. Ex 21:14
he built an * at the foot of the Ex 24:4
pillars around the * because there Ex 24:4
half he splashed against the *. Ex 24:6
make a square * 7½ feet wide, and Ex 27:1
corners of the *, attach them Ex 27:2
For moving the *, make poles Ex 27:6
the rings at each side of the *. Ex 27:7
of the altar. The * is to be Ex 27:8
or to the * in the Holy Place, lest Ex 28:43
the horns of the *, smearing it on Ex 29:12
the rest at the base of the *. Ex 29:12
on them, and burn them upon the *. Ex 29:13
and sprinkled upon the *. Ex 29:15,16
body, and burn it all upon the *; Ex 29:18
the rest of the blood over the *. Ex 29:19,20
the blood from the * and mix it Ex 29:21
burn them on the * as a fragrant Ex 29:25
purge the * by making atonement Ex 29:36
Make atonement for the * and Ex 29:37
After this the * shall be Ex 29:37
lambs upon the *, one in the Ex 29:38
Tabernacle and the * and Aaron and Ex 29:44
"THEN MAKE A small * for burning Ex 30:1
the wood of the *—they are not to Ex 30:2
and horns of the * with pure gold, Ex 30:3
gold molding around the entire *. Ex 30:3
Place the * just outside the Ex 30:6
spices on the *, and each evening Ex 30:7
make an atonement for the *." Ex 30:10f
the *, smearing Ex 30:10
is the Lord's supremely holy *." Ex 30:10
and the *, and fill it with water. Ex 30:17,18
* to burn offerings to the Lord. Ex 30:20
the incense *, the burnt offering Ex 30:26,27
the burnt offering * with all its Ex 30:28
its instruments; the * of incense; Ex 31:8
the burnt offering * with its Ex 31:9
it, he built an * before the calf Ex 32:5
The incense * and its carrying Ex 35:10-19
The * for the burnt offerings; Ex 35:10-19
The bronze grating of the *, and Ex 35:10-19
The incense * was made of acacia Ex 37:25
* so that it was all one piece. Ex 37:25

(ALTAR Con't)
THE BURNT-OFFERING * was also Ex 38:1
This * was overlaid with bronze. Ex 38:2
be used with the *—the pots, Ex 38:3
the rings at the side of the *. Ex 38:7
* was hollow, with plank siding. Ex 38:7
and for the bronze *, the bronze Ex 38:29
grating, the * utensils, the bases Ex 38:29
The golden *; Ex 39:33-40
The bronze *; Ex 39:33-40
"Place the golden * for the Ex 40:5
and place the * for burnt Ex 40:6
and the *, and fill it with water. Ex 40:7
oil upon the * of burnt offering Ex 40:10
for the * shall then become most Ex 40:10
placed the golden * in the Ex 40:26
placed the outside * for the burnt Ex 40:29
the tent and the *, and filled it Ex 40:30
Whenever they walked past the * Ex 40:32
the tent and the *, and set up the Ex 40:33
all sides of the * at the entrance Lev 1:5
wood fire upon the *, and put the Lev 1:6,7
burn them upon the *, and they will Lev 1:9
north side of the *, and Aaron's Lev 1:11
blood back and forth upon the *. Lev 1:11
fat, on top of the wood on the *. Lev 1:12
the * as an offering to the Lord; Lev 1:13
the bird to the * and wring off its Lev 1:15,16,17
drained out at the side of the *. Lev 1:15,16,17
east side of the * with the ashes. Lev 1:15,16,17
burn it upon the *, and the Lord Lev 1:15,16,17
the *, an offering made by fire." Lev 2:2f
the * to present it to the Lord. Lev 2:8
not for a sweet savor on the *." Lev 2:12f
the sides of the *, and shall burn Lev 3:2
the sides of the *, and shall Lev 3:7,8
offer upon the * the fat, the tail Lev 3:9,10,11
the sides of the *, and shall Lev 3:13
offer upon the *, as a burnt Lev 3:14
of the incense * before the Lord in Lev 4:7
at the base of the * for burnt Lev 4:7
burn them on the * of burnt Lev 4:10
*—and burned there on a wood fire. Lev 4:11,12
the horns of the * there in the Lev 4:18
the burnt offering *, at the Lev 4:18
be removed and burned upon the *. Lev 4:19
the horns of the * of burnt Lev 4:25
poured out at the base of the *. Lev 4:25
be burned upon the *, just as if it Lev 4:26
the horns of the burnt offering *. Lev 4:30
of the blood at the base of the *. Lev 4:30
priest shall burn it upon the *; Lev 4:31
the burnt offering *, and all the Lev 4:34
poured out at the base of the *. Lev 4:34
the fat on the * as in any other Lev 4:35
at the side of the * and the rest Lev 5:9
drained out at the base of the *; Lev 5:9
and burn it on the * just as any Lev 5:12
the hearth of the * all night, with Lev 6:9
with the * fire kept burning. Lev 6:9
and put them beside the *. Lev 6:10
Meanwhile, the fire on the * Lev 6:12
burning upon the * continually. Lev 6:13
the * to offer it before the Lord. Lev 6:14
burn it upon the * as a Lev 6:15
back and forth upon the *. Lev 7:2
The priest will offer upon the * Lev 7:3
* as a guilt offering to the Lord. Lev 7:5
it before the *, then it shall be Lev 7:14
Lord by waving it before the *. Lev 7:30
the fat upon the *, but the breast Lev 7:31
When he came to the * he Lev 8:11
utensils of the * and the washbasin Lev 8:11
four horns of the *, and upon the Lev 8:15,16
and upon the * itself, to sanctify Lev 8:15,16
of the blood at the base of the *; Lev 8:15,16
thus he sanctified the *, making Lev 8:15,16
fat, and burned them all on the *. Lev 8:15,16
blood back and forth upon the *. Lev 8:19
them upon the *, so that the entire Lev 8:21
back and forth upon the *. Lev 8:24
blood upon the * round about." Lev 8:24f
of waving them before the *. Lev 8:27
*, along with the burnt offering Lev 8:28
Lord by waving it before the *; Lev 8:29
sprinkled upon the *, and sprinkled Lev 8:30
to proceed to the * and to offer Lev 9:7
So Aaron went up to the * and Lev 9:8
the horns of the *, and poured out Lev 9:9
out the rest at the base of the *. Lev 9:9
Then he burned upon the * the Lev 9:10
it back and forth upon the *; Lev 9:12
he burned each part upon the *. Lev 9:13
upon the * as a burnt offering. Lev 9:14
it upon the * in addition to the Lev 9:17
it back and forth upon the *. Lev 9:18
and Aaron burned it upon the *; Lev 9:20
them and came down from the *. Lev 9:22
burnt offering and fat on the *; Lev 9:24
burning it on the *—make sure there Lev 10:12
in it, and eat it beside the *. Lev 10:12

of waving them before the *. Lev 14:12
offering upon the *, making Lev 14:20
by waving it before the *; Lev 14:21
them before the * as a gesture of Lev 14:24
coals from the * of the Lord, and Lev 16:12
Then he shall go out to the * Lev 16:18
the horns of the *, and sprinkle Lev 16:18
blood upon the * seven times with Lev 16:19
and the *, he shall bring the live Lev 16:20
He shall also burn upon the * Lev 16:25
*, the priests, and the people. Lev 16:33
the blood upon the * of the Lord at Lev 17:6
* as an atonement for your souls; Lev 17:11
Molech, burning them upon his *; Lev 18:21
*, because of the physical defect; Lev 21:23
offering for the * of the Lord. Lev 22:22
Tabernacle, the *, and all the Num 3:25-30
over the gold *, cover it with a Num 4:11
the carrying poles into the *. Num 4:11
removed from the *, and the altar Num 4:13
the altar, and the * shall be Num 4:13
All of the * utensils are to be Num 4:14
the * and the Tabernacle. Num 4:26
They will also carry the *, the Num 4:26
Jehovah, and carry it to the *. Num 5:25
handful upon the *, and then Num 5:26
including the * and its utensils, Num 7:1
on the day the * was anointed, Num 7:10
placing them before the *. Num 7:10
day for the dedication of the *." Num 7:11
So, beginning the day the * was Num 7:84,85,86
forth before the * in a gesture of Num 15:19,20,21
a covering for the *, for these Num 16:38
and the * sheet shall be a Num 16:38
metal to cover the *, to be a Num 16:39
and place fire in it from the *; Num 16:46
articles or the *, lest I destroy Num 18:2,3
within the sanctuary and at the *. Num 18:5
including the * and all that is Num 18:7
them before the * belong to you and Num 18:8
to the Lord by burning upon the *. Num 18:9
them before the * are for you and Num 18:11
sprinkled upon the *, and their fat Num 18:17
gesture of waving before the *. Num 18:18
*, shall belong to the Levites; Num 18:24
gesture of waving before the *. Num 18:25,26
a ram were sacrificed on each *. Num 23:2
a young bull and a ram on each *. Num 23:14
a young bull and ram on every *. Num 23:30
you burn on the * for me are my Num 28:1
gesture of waving before the *. Num 31:29
waving before the *, your offerings Deu 12:6
Lord by waving them before his *. Deu 12:17
to the central * where you, your Deu 12:18
He will tell you where this * Deu 12:18
the central * is too far away from Deu 12:20-23
need be taken to the central *. Deu 12:26,27
upon the * of the Lord your God. Deu 12:26,27
the *, and you will eat the meat. Deu 12:26,27
beside the * of the Lord your God. Deu 16:21
brought to the * of the Lord and by Deu 18:1
your hand and set it before the *. Deu 26:4
And build an * there to the Lord Deu 27:5,6
Use uncut boulders, and on the * Deu 27:5,6
work before you at the incense * Deu 33:10
And the * of burnt offering. Deu 33:10
Then Joshua built an * to the Jos 8:30
laws: "Make me an * of boulders Jos 8:31
offerings to the Lord on the *. Jos 8:31
* each of the Ten Commandments. Jos 8:32
Israel and for the * of the Jos 9:27
to see, in the shape of an *. Jos 22:10
* of rebellion against the Lord. Jos 22:16
If you need the * because your Jos 22:19
building another * in addition to Jos 22:19
to the only true * of our God. Jos 22:19
* in rebellion against the Lord. Jos 22:22,23
have not built the * to sacrifice Jos 22:22,23
So we decided to build the * as Jos 22:26,27
'Look at the * of the Lord which Jos 22:28
patterned after the * of Jehovah. Jos 22:28
building our own * for burnt Jos 22:29
Only the * in front of the Jos 22:29
and Gad named the * "The Altar of Jos 22:34
the altar "The * of Witness," for Jos 22:34
And Gideon built an * there and Ju 6:24
"The * of Peace with Jehovah." Ju 6:24
(The * is still there in Ophrah Ju 6:24
ox to the family * of Baal, and Ju 6:25
"Replace it with an * for the Ju 6:26
as wood for the fire on the *." Ju 6:26
that the * of Baal was knocked Ju 6:28
gone, and a new * had been built Ju 6:28
"He must die for insulting the * Ju 6:30
the one who broke apart his *!" Ju 6:31
flames from the * were leaping up Ju 13:20
early and built an *, and offered Ju 21:4
the fat on the * had been 1Sa 2:15
sacrifice upon my *, and to burn 1Sa 2:28
And he built an * to the Lord at 1Sa 7:17
to worship God at the * at Bethel; 1Sa 10:3

he climbed the hill to the *. 1Sa 10:13
And Saul built an * to the 1Sa 14:35
"Go and build an * to the Lord on 2Sa 24:18
I can build an * to the Lord, and 2Sa 24:21
for wood to build a fire on the *. 2Sa 24:22
And David built an * there to 2Sa 24:25
hold of the horns of the sacred *. 1Ki 1:49,50
they brought him down from the *. 1Ki 1:53
caught hold of the horns of the *. 1Ki 2:28
"Kill him there beside the * and 1Ki 2:31
made a cedar-wood * for this room. 1Ki 6:20
the cedar *—with pure gold; 1Ki 6:21,22
This included the *, the table 1Ki 7:48
stood before the * of the Lord with 1Ki 8:22,23
here before your *, swears that he 1Ki 8:31
from before the * of Jehovah and 1Ki 8:54,55
* was too small to handle so much. 1Ki 8:64
a year on the * he had built. 1Ki 9:25
upon the * to the calves at Bethel, 1Ki 12:32,33
AS JEROBOAM APPROACHED the * 1Ki 13:1
shouted, "O *, the Lord says that 1Ki 13:2
the Lord: "This * will split 1Ki 13:3
appeared in the * and the ashes 1Ki 13:5
shout against the * in Bethel, and 1Ki 13:32
First he built a temple and an * 1Ki 16:32
the wood of their *, but without 1Ki 18:23
Lord's *, with no fire under it. 1Ki 18:23
bulls and placed it on the *; 1Ki 18:26
they began to dance around the *. 1Ki 18:26
as he repaired the * of the Lord 1Ki 18:30
stones to rebuild the Lord's *. 1Ki 18:32
around the *. 1Ki 18:32
He piled wood upon the * and cut 1Ki 18:33
and the water ran off the * and 1Ki 18:35
walked up to the * and prayed, "O 1Ki 18:36
and surrounded the *, which was 2Ki 11:11
priest of Baal, in front of the *. 2Ki 11:18
of the * at the Temple entrance. 2Ki 12:9
an unusual * in a heathen temple. 2Ki 16:10
Literally, "he saw the * that was 2Ki 16:10f
Then he removed the old bronze * 2Ki 16:14
and the new *), and placed it on 2Ki 16:14
it on the north side of the new *. 2Ki 16:14
to use the new * for the sacrifices 2Ki 16:15
to be sprinkled over the new *. 2Ki 16:15
So the old * was used only for 2Ki 16:15
"The old bronze *," he said, 2Ki 16:15
to worship at the * in Jerusalem!' 2Ki 18:22
a burnt offering on a heathen *. 2Ki 21:6
did not serve at the * of the 2Ki 23:9
Then the king destroyed the * of 2Ki 23:10
He also tore down the * and 2Ki 23:15
there upon the * at Bethel to 2Ki 23:16
would happen to Jeroboam's *. 2Ki 23:16
happen here at the * at Bethel!" 2Ki 23:17
evening upon the * set aside for 1Ch 16:40
in offering sacrifices on the *. 1Ch 18:8
David to build an * to the Lord at 1Ch 21:18
then I will build an * to the 1Ch 21:22
and built an * to the Lord 1Ch 21:26
to burn up the offering on the *. 1Ch 21:26
The Tabernacle and * made by 1Ch 21:29
* for Israel's burnt offering!" 1Ch 22:1
gold for the * of incense and for 1Ch 28:18
The bronze * made by Bezalel 2Ch 1:5,6
HE ALSO MADE a bronze * thirty 2Ch 4:1
the utensils, the *, and the table 2Ch 4:19
at the east side of the *. 2Ch 5:11,12
in front of the * of the Lord. 2Ch 6:12,13
before this *, then hear from 2Ch 6:22
for the bronze * to accommodate. 2Ch 7:7
to the Lord on the * he had built 2Ch 8:12
and he rebuilt the * of the Lord in 2Ch 15:8
around the * in the outer court. 2Ch 23:10
the priest of Baal before his *. 2Ch 23:15,16,17
burning incense upon the *. 2Ch 26:16
Temple and of the * of burnt 2Ch 29:18
They are beside the * of the 2Ch 29:19
them on the * of the Lord. 2Ch 29:21
it on the *, and they killed the 2Ch 29:22
blood upon the *, and did the same 2Ch 29:22
blood upon the *, to make atonement 2Ch 29:24
be placed upon the *, and as the 2Ch 29:27
use only the one * at the Temple, 2Ch 32:12
Then he rebuilt the * of the 2Ch 33:16
it upon the * as the Levites 2Ch 35:11
upon the * of the Lord, as Josiah 2Ch 35:16
the * of the God of Israel; Ez 3:1
man of God. The * was rebuilt on Ez 3:3
offered upon the * of your Temple Ez 7:17
They supplied wood for the * at Neh 13:31
come before your *, singing a song Ps 26:6
There I will go to the * of God Ps 43:4
upon my * have promised to obey Ps 50:5
*, for you bring them regularly. Ps 50:8
burned before you on the *. Ps 51:16
I bring to sacrifice upon your *. Ps 51:19
dressed in holy * robes. Ps 110:3
sacrifice upon the *, for you are Ps 118:27,28
flew over to the * and with a pair Is 6:6
And there will be an * to the Is 19:19

(ALTAR Con't)
means—an * covered with blood. Is 29:2
an ox on the * of God, it is no Is 66:3
or the blood of a swine on his *! Is 66:3
They have built the * called Jer 7:31
used at the *, and the snuffers, Jer 52:18
The Lord has rejected his own *, Lam 2:7
north of the * gate, in the Eze 8:5
and the bronze *, were about Eze 8:16
and stood beside the bronze *. Eze 9:2
before being taken to the *; Eze 40:38
in charge of the *—the descendants Eze 40:46
and there was an * in the court, Eze 40:47
be an *, but it was made of wood. Eze 41:21
This * was 3½ feet square, and Eze 41:22
are the measurements of the *: Eze 43:13
inches beyond the * on all sides. Eze 43:13
The first stage of the * is a Eze 43:14
is the top of the *, with four Eze 43:15
This top platform of the * is Eze 43:16
side are steps to climb the *." Eze 43:17
of the * to be made in the future, Eze 43:18
four horns of the * and on the four Eze 43:20
and make atonement for the *. Eze 43:20
Thus the * shall be cleansed, as Eze 43:22
for the *, thus consecrating it. Eze 43:26
sacrifice on the * the burnt Eze 43:27
of the base of the * and upon the Eze 45:19
the *, that is, on its south side. Eze 47:1
By offering swine on the *. Dan 11:30,31f
*, temple, priests, or even idols! Hos 3:4
all night before the *, weeping. Joe 1:13
the people and the *, weeping; Joe 2:17
The horns of the * will be cut Amo 3:14
beside the *, saying, "Smash the Amo 9:1
sacred as the bowls beside the *. Zec 14:20
polluted sacrifices on my *." Mal 1:7
to offer on the * of the Lord—yes, Mal 1:8
it, saying that my * is not Mal 1:12
Yet you cover the * with your Mal 2:13
before the * in the Temple, Mt 5:23
there beside the * and go and Mt 5:24
an oath 'By the * can be broken, Mt 23:18
the gifts on the *' is binding! Mt 23:18
the gift on the *, or the altar Mt 23:19
* itself that sanctifies the gift? Mt 23:19
When you swear 'By the *' you Mt 23:20
between the * and the sanctuary. Mt 23:35
on the * of the Temple." Mk 12:33
to the right of the * of incense! Lk 1:11,12
between the * and the sanctuary. Lk 11:51
And those who work at the * of 1Co 9:13
to lay as a sacrifice upon your *. Heb 10:5
stood before the * day after day Heb 10:11
to slay him on the * of sacrifice; Heb 11:17
We have an *—the cross where Heb 13:10
his son Isaac to die on the *? Jas 2:21
seal, I saw an *, and underneath it Rev 6:9
censer came and stood at the *; Rev 8:3
the golden * before the throne. Rev 8:3
up to God from the * where the Rev 8:4
with fire from the * and threw it Rev 8:5
of the golden * that stands before Rev 9:13
court where the * stands, and to Rev 11:1
of God, and the *, and them that Rev 11:1f
And I heard the angel of the * Rev 16:7
Literally, "I heard the * cry. Rev 16:7f

ALTARS
"The * you make for me must be Ex 20:24
for me must be simple * of earth. Ex 20:24
Build * only where I tell you to, Ex 20:24
You may also build * from stone, Ex 20:25
down their heathen *, smash the Ex 34:13
I will destroy the * on the hills Lev 26:30
down your incense *, leaving your Lev 26:30
the lampstand, the *, the various Num 3:31-35
"Build seven * here, and prepare Num 23:1
prepared seven *, and have Num 23:3,4
Pisgah, and built seven * there; Num 23:14
to build seven *, and to prepare Num 23:29
down the heathen * and shatter the Deu 7:5
all the heathen * wherever you find Deu 12:2
Break the *, smash the obelisks, Deu 12:3
you to destroy their heathen *. Ju 2:2
their offerings on * in the hills, 1Ki 3:2
of the hilltop * was at Gibeon and 1Ki 3:4
and torn down your * and killed 1Ki 19:10
and have torn down your *; 1Ki 19:14
down, breaking the * and images and 2Ki 11:18
numerous * in the groves of trees. 2Ki 16:4
and they had built * to other gods 2Ki 17:9
to death on the * of Molech; 2Ki 17:17
children on the * of their gods 2Ki 17:31
to the Lord on the hilltop *. 2Ki 17:32
whose hilltop * you've destroyed. 2Ki 18:22
He built * for Baal and made a 2Ki 21:3,4,5
Heathen * to the sun god, moon 2Ki 21:3,4,5
Then he tore down the * which 2Ki 23:12
He also destroyed the * which 2Ki 23:12
upon their own *, and he burned 2Ki 23:20
bones upon the * to defile them. 2Ki 23:20
He demolished the heathen * on 2Ch 14:3
and the incense * from every one of 2Ch 14:5
down the heathen * on the hills, 2Ch 17:6
and broke up the * and knocked 2Ch 23:15,16,17
there, and made * to the heathen 2Ch 28:24
the heathen * in Jerusalem, and 2Ch 30:14
all the incense *, and threw them 2Ch 30:14
tore down the idol *, the obelisks, 2Ch 31:1
He rebuilt the heathen * his 2Ch 33:3
had destroyed—the * of Baal, and of 2Ch 33:3
He even constructed heathen * in 2Ch 33:4,5
and tore down the * he had built on 2Ch 33:15
stood, and the * that were in 2Ch 33:15
upon the * on the hills, but only 2Ch 33:17
the heathen * and the shame-idols 2Ch 34:3
to watch as the * of Baal were 2Ch 34:4
obelisks above the * chopped down, 2Ch 34:4
upon their own *, feeling that this 2Ch 34:5
He broke down the heathen *, 2Ch 34:7
idols and * to other gods. Ps 78:58
nest among your * and there have Ps 84:3
of all her idol * and her idols. Is 27:9
his temples and * in the hills and Is 36:7
only at the * here in Jerusalem? Is 36:7
of Nabaioth for my *, and I will Is 60:7
cities, and your * of shame (your Jer 11:13
of shame (your * to burn incense to Jer 11:13
or on the corners of their *. Jer 17:1
They have built high * to Baal Jer 19:5
be a priest at my *, and he shall Jer 30:21
And they have built high * to Jer 32:35
burned, and the idol * abandoned. Eze 6:4-7
will lie scattered among the *. Eze 6:4-7
your idols and * on every hill and Eze 6:13
in the fires of strange *? Eze 16:21
lovers, and idol * on every street, Eze 16:24
*, your brothels, on every street. Eze 16:31
brothels and idol *, and strip you Eze 16:39
them as sacrifices on their *. Eze 23:37
burning their children on idol *. Eze 36:12
Ephraim has built many *, but Hos 8:11
They are * of sin! Hos 8:11
it on the * of her heathen gods; Hos 10:1
heathen * and smash their idols. Hos 10:2
And the idol * of Aven at Bethel Hos 10:8
Row on row of *—like furrows in a Hos 12:11
also destroy the idol * at Bethel. Amo 3:14
The idol * and temples of Israel Amo 7:9
I saw your many *, and one of them Act 17:23
prophets and torn down God's *; Rom 11:2,3

ALTERED
that cannot be * or revoked." Dan 6:12

ALTERNATE
Ahaziah is an * form of the name 2Ki 8:24,25f
of silver." An * rendering of Ps 68:30f
riddles"; an * rendering might Dan 8:23f
This * paraphrase interprets Jn 3:5f
to one side. An * rendering might Rev 7:17f

ALTERNATED
pomegranates, * with gold bells. Ex 28:33,34

ALTERNATING
* all around the edge. Ex 39:25,26
of palm trees * with the cherubim. Eze 41:17,18

ALTERNATIVE
and I have no * but to send him. Act 25:25
An * paraphrase of these verses 1Pe 2:2,3f

ALTERNATIVELY
his generation." *, "Who will be Act 8:33f

ALTERNATIVES
by simple "Yes" or "No" *. Lev 8:8f

ALTERS
any nation that * this commandment Ez 6:12

ALTHOUGH
Now * the man and his wife were Gen 2:25
on them! So * Laban searched the Gen 31:34
his own, and so, * he married her, Gen 38:9
So, * Moses and Aaron did Ex 11:10
the Philistines, * that was the Ex 13:17,18
badger (because * it chews the cud, Lev 11:4-7
The hare (because * it chews the Lev 11:4-7
The swine (because * it has cloven Lev 11:4-7
testicles— * he is a descendant of Lev 21:21
of Manasseh, that * the Lord had Deu 3:18
Pigs may not be eaten because, * Deu 14:8
ceremony was that * when Israel Jos 5:4,5
AFTER THE CONQUEST—* seven of Jos 18:1
father of Anak)—* the fields beyond Jos 21:9-16
of Manasseh, * the other half of Jos 22:7,8
her children; but * he loved 1Sa 1:5
declare that * I promised that your 1Sa 2:30
torturing you. But * I have done so 1Sa 10:18,19
for this work, * they became 1Ki 9:22
had no sons, * he had several 1Ch 2:34,35
* Joseph received the birthright, 1Ch 5:2
in Judah (* the fields and suburbs 1Ch 6:55,56,57
to curse them—* God turned the Neh 13:2
And now, * ten thousand enemies Ps 3:6
of evil men, * they prowl on every Ps 12:8
this: that * the wicked flourish Ps 92:7
he will abandon his siege. * it Is 37:30
when I call (* they see and hear! Is 43:8
him forever. * God gives him Lam 3:32
the Lord God says: * I have Eze 11:16
But * he made the world, the Jn 1:10
* Jesus was very fond of Martha, Jn 11:5
because *, of course, people Rom 5:13
And even we Christians, * we Rom 8:23
children. For * you may have ten 1Co 4:15
* I am not there with you, I have 1Co 5:3,4
the right one! But * being a 1Co 8:1
to do it too, * all the time he 1Co 8:10
each other. For * the first woman 1Co 11:12
When I come, * I can't do much 2Co 1:24
or anyone else, * as apostles of 1Th 2:6
* GOD'S PROMISE still stands—his Heb 4:1
Abraham. For * Levi wasn't born Heb 7:10
be a Priest, * he never said that Heb 7:21
us guilty sinners, * he himself was 1Pe 3:18
—so that * their bodies were 1Pe 4:6
without so much as trembling, * 2Pe 2:11

ALTOGETHER
villages. * there were twelve of Jos 19:15,16
So * the territory included Jos 19:35-39
so he reigned for forty years *. 2Sa 5:4,5
His mouth is * sweet, lovable in Sol 5:16
idols are * stupid and foolish. Jer 10:8
Literally, "You were * born in Jn 9:34f

ALUSH
Next was Dophkah, and then *; Num 33:13

ALVAH
Timna,The clan of *,The clan of Gen 36:40-43

ALVAN
The children of Shobal:*, Gen 36:23

AM
Cain retorted. "* I supposed Gen 4:9
For I * sorry I made them." Gen 6:7
"Look! I * going to cover the Gen 6:17
and said, "I * going to give this Gen 12:7
direction, for I * going to give Gen 13:15
And I * going to give you so Gen 13:16
new possessions I * giving you." Gen 13:17
And he told him, "I * Jehovah Gen 15:7
Hagar: "I * running away from my Gen 16:8
and told him, "I * the Almighty; Gen 17:1
him, "I * changing your name. Gen 17:5
do is wicked. I * going down to Gen 18:21
though I * but dust and ashes. Gen 18:27
"Look," he said, "I * giving Gen 20:16
"Here I *, a visitor in a Gen 23:4
See, here I *, standing beside Gen 24:13
I have told you why I * here." Gen 24:33
"I * Abraham's servant," he Gen 24:34
I *, standing beside this spring. Gen 24:43
Esau: "Boy, * I starved! Gen 25:30
his arrival. "I * the God of Gen 26:24
"Fear not, for I * with you and Gen 26:24
Isaac: "I * an old man now, and Gen 27:2,3,4
Esau: "Here I *, father, with the Gen 27:31
the Lord. "I * Jehovah," he said, Gen 28:13
What's more, I * with you, and Gen 28:15
giving you all I * promising." Gen 28:15
Jacob flew into a rage. "* I Gen 30:2
for she said, "I * in a fierce Gen 30:8
with my sister and I * winning!" Gen 30:8
"for I * hiring you with some Gen 30:16
Angel said. 'I * the God you met Gen 31:13
do me good— I * not worthy of the Gen 32:10
And now I * two armies! Gen 32:10
Esau, for I * frightened—terribly Gen 32:11
with God'). I * God Almighty," Gen 35:11
the right than I *, because I Gen 38:26
now this—here I * in jail when I Gen 40:15
in the country! I * hereby Gen 41:40
said to them, "I * a God-fearing Gen 42:18
"I * Joseph!" Gen 45:3
And he said again, "I * Joseph, Gen 45:4
"I * God," the voice replied, Gen 46:3,4
hard years, and I * not nearly as Gen 47:9
But when I * dead, take me out Gen 47:30
I arrived, I * adopting them as my Gen 48:5
Then Israel said to Joseph, "I * Gen 48:21
first no longer. I * demoting you, Gen 49:4
* I God, to judge and punish you? Gen 50:19
As far as I * concerned, God Gen 50:20
* a stranger in a foreign land." Ex 2:22
on holy ground. I * the God of Ex 3:6
Now I * going to send you to Ex 3:10
the proof that I * the one who is Ex 3:12
Literally, "I * what I am," Ex 3:14f
Literally, "I am what I *," Ex 3:14f
"Just say, 'I * has sent me!' Ex 3:14
of his land! I * Jehovah, the Ex 6:2,3
And they shall know that I * Ex 6:7
whom the Lord said, "I * Jehovah. Ex 6:28,29
find out that I * indeed God when I Ex 7:5
going to find out that I * God. Ex 7:17
thus you will know that I * the Ex 8:22
But I * warning you that you must Ex 8:29
This time I * going to send a Ex 9:14
things I * doing in Egypt! Ex 10:2
proved to you that I * Jehovah." Ex 10:2
the gods of Egypt—for I * Jehovah. Ex 12:12

(AM Con't)

shall know that I * the Lord."	Ex 14:4
shall know that I * Jehovah."	Ex 14:18
for I * the Lord who heals you."	Ex 15:26
know that I * Jehovah your God.'	Ex 16:11,12
"Don't they realize that I *	Ex 16:28,29
told him. "I * their judge,	Ex 18:15,16
Then he said to Moses, "I *	Ex 19:9
"I * Jehovah your God who	Ex 20:2
for I, the Lord your God, * very	Ex 20:5
for I * very compassionate.	Ex 22:27
"See, I * sending an Angel	Ex 23:20
problems while I * gone, consult	Ex 24:14
the pattern I * showing you here on	Ex 25:40
know that I * the Lord their God.	Ex 29:46
among them. I * Jehovah their God.	Ex 29:46
it helps you to remember that I *	Ex 31:12,13
"I * Jehovah, the merciful and	Ex 34:5,6
I * going to make with you.	Ex 34:10
to them, "What I * now going to do	Lev 8:5
for so I * commanded.	Lev 10:13
"I * the Lord your God.	Lev 11:44
things, and be holy, for I * holy;	Lev 11:44
For I * the Lord who brought you	Lev 11:45
therefore be holy, for I * holy."	Lev 11:45
"I * a leper, I am a leper."	Lev 13:45
"I am a leper, I * a leper."	Lev 13:45
For I myself * present in the	Lev 16:1
"I * Jehovah your God, so don't	Lev 18:1
where I * going to take you.	Lev 18:3
detail, for I * the Lord your God.	Lev 18:4,5
I * the Lord.	Lev 18:4,5
a near relative, for I * the	Lev 18:6
name of your God, for I * Jehovah.	Lev 18:21
and because they do them I *	Lev 18:24
that is why I * punishing the	Lev 18:25
the land where I * taking you, and	Lev 18:27
For I * Jehovah your God."	Lev 18:29,30
I, the Lord your God, * holy.	Lev 19:1
law, for I * the Lord your God.	Lev 19:1
idols, for I * Jehovah your God.	Lev 19:3,4
through, for I * Jehovah your God.	Lev 19:10
name of your God, for I * Jehovah.	Lev 19:12
Fear your God; I * Jehovah!	Lev 19:14
for I * Jehovah.	Lev 19:16
as yourself, for I * Jehovah.	Lev 19:18
"I * Jehovah your God!	Lev 19:26
with funeral rites; I * the Lord.	Lev 19:28
my Tabernacle, for I * the Lord.	Lev 19:30
wizards, for I * Jehovah your God.	Lev 19:31
in the fear of God. I * Jehovah.	Lev 19:32
of Egypt. I * Jehovah your God.	Lev 19:34
measure, for I * Jehovah your God	Lev 19:35,36
obeying them, for I * Jehovah."	Lev 19:37
holy, for I * the Lord your God.	Lev 20:7
I * the Lord who sanctifies you.	Lev 20:8
milk and honey.' I * the Lord your	Lev 20:24
me, for I the Lord * holy, and I	Lev 20:26
Lord who sanctifies you, * holy.	Lev 21:8
his God is upon him; I * Jehovah.	Lev 21:12
for I * Jehovah.	Lev 22:1
For I * Jehovah!	Lev 22:3
this will defile him. I * Jehovah.	Lev 22:8
I * the Lord who sanctifies them.	Lev 22:9
for I * Jehovah who sanctifies	Lev 22:16
the following day. I * the Lord.	Lev 22:29,30
my commandments, for I * the Lord.	Lev 22:31
be my own people! I * Jehovah!"	Lev 22:32,33
their own; I * Jehovah your God!	Lev 23:22
shelters. I * Jehovah your God."	Lev 23:43
for I * Jehovah your God."	Lev 24:22
"When you come into the land I *	Lev 25:1
For I * Jehovah.	Lev 25:17,18
of Egypt; I * the Lord your God.	Lev 25:55
stones, for I * the Lord your God.	Lev 26:1
my Tabernacle, for I * the Lord.	Lev 26:2
For I * the Lord your God who	Lev 26:13
them, for I * Jehovah their God.	Lev 26:44
watched in wonder. I * Jehovah."	Lev 26:45
They are mine; I * Jehovah."	Num 3:13
The Levites shall be mine (I *	Num 3:41
shall be mine; I * Jehovah.	Num 3:45
For I * Jehovah, your God."	Num 10:10
Are they my children? * I their	Num 11:12
Where * I supposed to get meat	Num 11:13
land I * giving to Israel;	Num 13:2
live in the land I * going to give	Num 15:1
in the land that I * going to give	Num 15:17,18
For I * Jehovah your God who	Num 15:41
yes, I * the Lord, your God."	Num 15:41
income, for I * all that you need.	Num 18:20
mankind, [before I * taken away	Num 27:16
land of Canaan (I * giving you the	Num 34:1
I * giving all of it to you!	Deu 1:8
as these I * giving you today?	Deu 4:8
" 'I * Jehovah your God who	Deu 5:6
way, for I * the Lord your God.	Deu 5:9,10
Lord your God. I * a jealous God,	Deu 5:9,10
in the land I * giving to them.'	Deu 5:31
commandments I * giving you today.	Deu 6:6
commandments I * giving you today.	Deu 7:11

the commandments I * giving you	Deu 10:12,13
Listen! I * not talking now to	Deu 11:2
commandments I * going to give you	Deu 11:8
that I * going to give you today,	Deu 11:13
"I * giving you the choice today	Deu 11:26
your God which I * giving you	Deu 11:27
all the laws I * giving you today.	Deu 11:32
which I * giving you today, and if	Deu 13:18
God that I * giving you today.	Deu 15:4,5
That is why I * giving you this	Deu 15:15
commandments I * giving you	Deu 19:9
why I * giving you this command.	Deu 24:22
God, the laws I * declaring to you	Deu 28:1
your God that I * giving you today,	Deu 28:13
obey these laws I * giving you	Deu 28:15-19
them, "I * now 120 years old!	Deu 31:2
I * no longer able to lead you,	Deu 31:2
Literally, "I * no longer able to	Deu 31:2f
"If even today, while I * still	Deu 31:27
Don't you see that I alone * God?	Deu 32:39
* giving to the people of Israel.	Deu 32:49
you the land I * giving the people	Deu 32:52
will know that I * with you just as	Jos 3:7
"I * the Commander-in-Chief of	Jos 5:14
O Lord, what * I to do now that	Jos 7:8
I * ready to drive these people	Jos 13:2-7
today I * eighty-five years old.	Jos 14:10
years old. I * as strong now as I	Jos 14:11
said to them, "I * an old man now,	Jos 23:2
of all the earth—I * going to die.	Jos 23:14
he said, "for I * very thirsty."	Ju 4:19
the Midianites! I * sending you!"	Ju 6:14
of Manasseh, and I * the least	Ju 6:15
Literally, "I * will be with	Ju 6:16f
"Yes," he replied, "I *."	Ju 13:11
"Well," he said, "if I * tied	Ju 16:11
"I * going to give it to the Lord	Ju 17:3
And he replied, "I * a priest	Ju 17:9
from Bethlehem, in Judah, and I *	Ju 17:9
for I * too old to have a husband.	Ru 1:12
"You must know I * only a	Ru 2:10,11
It's true that I * a close	Ru 3:12
closely related to you than I *.	Ru 3:12
to purchase it and I * next."	Ru 4:4
But I * very sad and I was	1Sa 1:15,16
Please don't think that I * just	1Sa 1:15,16
Hannah asked him. "I * the	1Sa 1:26
and now I * giving him to the	1Sa 1:28
"Here I *.	1Sa 3:4,5
to Samuel, "I * going to do a	1Sa 3:11
in Israel. I * going to do all of	1Sa 3:12
replied, "for I * the one they are	1Sa 8:7
"I * the seer!"	1Sa 9:19
"I * doing this because the Lord	1Sa 10:1
asking, 'How * I to find my son?'	1Sa 10:2
"I * sorry that I ever made Saul	1Sa 15:11
staff, for I * very fond of him."	1Sa 16:22
"When I * taking care of my	1Sa 17:34
"* I a dog," he roared at	1Sa 17:43
One day Saul said to David, "I *	1Sa 18:17
"Who * I that I should be the	1Sa 18:18
But the truth is that I * only a	1Sa 20:3
If your father asks where I *,	1Sa 20:6
not to tell anybody why I * here.	1Sa 21:2
destroy Keilah because I * here.	1Sa 23:10
say that I * trying to harm you?	1Sa 24:9,10
you that I * not trying to harm you	1Sa 24:11
better man than I *, for you have	1Sa 24:17
you own. I * told that you are	1Sa 25:7
"Because I * in deep trouble,"	1Sa 28:15
"I * an Egyptian—the servant of	1Sa 30:13
he begged, 'for I * in terrible	2Sa 1:9
And he replied, "I * an	2Sa 1:13
"* I a Judean dog to be kicked	2Sa 3:8
and even though I * God's chosen	2Sa 3:39
of the Lord! So I * willing to act	2Sa 6:21
Yes, and I * willing to look	2Sa 6:22
Here I * living in this beautiful	2Sa 7:2
an insignificant person as I *?	2Sa 7:18
For you know what I * like!	2Sa 7:20
of Israel, that I * the first of a	2Sa 7:27
"Yes, sir, I *," he replied.	2Sa 9:2
"I * going to show special	2Sa 10:2
So Amnon told him, "I * in love	2Sa 13:4
"I * a widow," she replied,	2Sa 14:5,6
then if he finds that I * guilty	2Sa 14:32
to curse me, who * I to say no?	2Sa 16:10
will see that I * being wronged and	2Sa 16:12
I * once more king of Israel!"	2Sa 19:22
For as you know I * lame.	2Sa 19:26
said. "I * content just to have	2Sa 19:30
"No," he replied, "I * far too	2Sa 19:34
old for that. I * eighty years old	2Sa 19:35
And he replied, "I *."	2Sa 20:17
For he sees that I * clean.	2Sa 22:25
David remarked, "How thirsty I *	2Sa 23:15
I * the one who has sinned!	2Sa 24:17
while I * still alive to see it.'	1Ki 1:48
"I * going where every man on	1Ki 2:2
some day go. I * counting on you to	1Ki 2:2
David, but I * as a little child	1Ki 3:7

And here I * among your own	1Ki 3:8
So I * planning to build a	1Ki 5:5
him not to. 'I * glad you want to	1Ki 8:18
"Yes," he replied, "I *."	1Ki 13:14
for I * not allowed to eat	1Ki 13:16,17
But the old man said, "I * a	1Ki 13:18
from the Lord. I * to take you home	1Ki 13:18
fathers were. I * sending you a	1Ki 15:19
made my people sin, and I * angry!	1Ki 16:2
widow with whom I * staying?"	1Ki 17:20
"Now go and tell the king I *	1Ki 18:8
Then Elijah spoke again. "I *	1Ki 18:22
Israel and that I * your servant;	1Ki 18:36
by the gods that I * going to kill	1Ki 19:2
Literally, "I * no better than my	1Ki 19:4f
your prophets, and only I * left;	1Ki 19:10
more to me than I * going to do to	1Ki 20:10
you will know that I * the Lord."	1Ki 20:13
know that I * indeed the Lord."	1Ki 20:28
the battle, for I * badly	1Ki 22:34
But Elijah replied, "If I * a	2Ki 1:10
Elijah replied, "If I * a man of	2Ki 1:12
grant you before I * taken away?"	2Ki 2:9
"If you see me when I * taken	2Ki 2:10
"No," she replied, "I *	2Ki 4:13
a leper to heal! * I God, that I	2Ki 5:7
"* I a dog?"	2Ki 8:13
as loyal to me as I * to you?"	2Ki 10:15
to the way I * going to!	2Ki 10:17
Literally, "saying, 'I * your	2Ki 16:7f
against me I * going to put a hook	2Ki 19:28
you to me, that I * going to	2Ki 22:15,16
my enemies when I * innocent, then	1Ch 12:17
and said, "Who * I, O Lord God,	1Ch 17:16
You know that I * but a dog, yet	1Ch 17:18
Then David declared, "I * going	1Ch 19:2,3
But David said to God, "I * the	1Ch 21:8
And David said to God, "I * the	1Ch 21:17
of our God, I * instructing you to	1Ch 28:8
Temple of God, I * giving all of my	1Ch 29:3
name, but who * I and who are my	1Ch 29:14
my people— yes, I * giving you the	2Ch 1:12
And I * also giving you such	2Ch 1:12
"I * about to build a temple for	2Ch 2:4
And who * I to be allowed to	2Ch 2:6
for the temple I * going to build	2Ch 2:9
"I * sending you a master	2Ch 2:13
Listen to my prayer that I *	2Ch 6:19
father's loins! I * going to be	2Ch 10:11
Go home, for I * behind their	2Ch 11:4
"for I * badly wounded."	2Ch 18:33
gods, and I * very angry with them	2Ch 34:25
power with which I * at war."	2Ch 35:21f
out, "O my God, I * ashamed;	Ez 9:6
blow you must rush to where I *;	Neh 4:19
"I * doing a great work!	Neh 6:3
"You can be very sure that I *	Neh 6:7
me. I * the only one left."	Job 1:14,15
I die? * I unfeeling, like stone?	Job 6:12
For I * utterly helpless,	Job 6:13
Stop assuming my guilt, for I *	Job 6:29
"O God, * I some monster, that	Job 7:12
And who * I that I should try to	Job 9:14
"But I? * I righteous?	Job 9:20
And even if I * utterly	Job 9:21
I despise what I *.	Job 9:21
for you are no mere man as I *.	Job 9:32,33
him boldly that I * not guilty.	Job 9:35
"I * WEARY of living.	Job 10:1
wickedness, and I * done for.	Job 10:15
I * filled with frustration.	Job 10:15
myself—you are no better than I *.	Job 12:3
Yes, I, a righteous man, * now	Job 12:4
I may speak—and I * willing to face	Job 13:13
Nevertheless I * going to argue	Job 13:15
my favor, that I * not godless, to	Job 13:16
Listen closely to what I * about	Job 13:17
case: I know that I * righteous.	Job 13:18
on every side. I * like a fallen,	Job 13:27,28
"Yet I * innocent, and my prayer	Job 16:17
"I * SICK and near to death;	Job 17:1
me. I * surrounded by mockers.	Job 17:2
* but a shadow of my former self.	Job 17:7
you have declared I * a sinner.	Job 19:3
on every side, and I * done for.	Job 19:10
I * like a foreigner to them.	Job 19:15
against me. I * skin and bones and	Job 19:20
"I * complaining about God,	Job 21:4
Even I * frightened when I see	Job 21:6
why he can't see what I * doing!	Job 22:13
"No wonder I * so terrified in	Job 23:15
a liar and claim that I * wrong?"	Job 24:25
my innocence. I * not a sinner—I	Job 27:6
song! I * a joke among them!	Job 30:9
They rush upon me when I * down.	Job 30:14
I * black, but not from sunburn.	Job 30:28,29
for I * considered a brother to	Job 30:28,29
God knows that I * innocent— or if	Job 31:6
have seen, or if I * guilty of any	Job 31:7,8
Almighty show me that I * wrong;	Job 31:35
and said, "I * young and you are	Job 32:6

(AM Con't)

For I * pent up and full of	Job 32:18
* like a wine cask without a vent!	Job 32:19
"Look, I * the one you were	Job 33:6
of me. I * not some person of	Job 33:7
I, too, * made of common clay.	Job 33:7
again— 'I * pure, I am innocent;	Job 33:9
again— 'I am pure, I * innocent;	Job 33:9
I want to hear it, for I *	Job 33:32
For Job has said, 'I * innocent,	Job 34:5
says I'm not. I * called a liar,	Job 34:6
a liar, even though I * innocent.	Job 34:6
I am innocent. I * horribly	Job 34:6
you the truth of what I * saying.	Job 36:2
of my Maker. I * telling you the	Job 36:4
* a man of well-rounded knowledge.	Job 36:4
Now get ready to fight, for I *	Job 38:3
"I * nothing—how could I ever	Job 40:4
"I * angry with you and with your	Job 42:7
Today I * giving you your glory.'	Ps 2:7
and you perish. I * warning you—his	Ps 2:12
me on every side, I * not afraid.	Ps 3:6
for though I * alone, O Lord, you	Ps 4:8
Pity me, O Lord, for I * weak.	Ps 6:2
and I * upset and disturbed.	Ps 6:3
I * worn out with pain;	Ps 6:6
I * DEPENDING on you, O Lord my	Ps 7:1
Oh, how grateful and thankful I *	Ps 7:17
when I * trusting in the Lord?	Ps 11:1
the other way when I * in need?	Ps 13:1
Don't let them gloat that I *	Ps 13:4
He sees that I * given pleasant	Ps 16:6
I * always thinking of the Lord;	Ps 16:8
I * PLEADING for your help, O	Ps 17:1
tested me and seen that I * good.	Ps 17:3
Why * I praying like this?	Ps 17:6
I * saved from all my enemies!	Ps 18:3
is right, and I * pure of heart.	Ps 18:24
But I * a worm, not a man,	Ps 22:6
I * surrounded by fearsome	Ps 22:12
Don't fail me, Lord, for I *	Ps 25:2
your mercy, for I * helpless,	Ps 25:16
No, I * not like that, O Lord;	Ps 26:11
* confident that God will save me.	Ps 27:3
responds, "Lord, I * coming."	Ps 27:8
Oh, do not hide yourself when I *	Ps 27:9
I * surrounded by waiting enemies.	Ps 27:11
cruelty. I * expecting the Lord to	Ps 27:13
death itself, and here I * alive!	Ps 30:3
imitation gods. I * radiant with	Ps 31:7
I * pining away with grief;	Ps 31:9,10
I * scorned by all my enemies	Ps 31:11
when I go by. I * forgotten like a	Ps 31:12
harm. I * sinking down to death.	Ps 35:12
But now that I * in trouble they	Ps 35:15
I have been young and now I *	Ps 37:25
Because of my sins I * bent and	Ps 38:5,6
I * exhausted and crushed;	Ps 38:8
fails, and I * going blind.	Ps 38:10
But I * deaf to all their	Ps 38:13,14
their threats; I * silent before	Ps 38:13,14
For I * waiting for you, O Lord	Ps 38:15
who gloat when I * cast down!	Ps 38:16
Literally, "I * ready to fall."	Ps 38:17f
I confess my sins; I * sorry for	Ps 38:18
Help me to know that I * here for	Ps 39:4
Lord, I * speechless before you.	Ps 39:9
Lord, don't hit me anymore—I *	Ps 39:10
For I * your guest.	Ps 39:12
For I am your guest. I * a	Ps 39:12
me and I * ashamed to look up.	Ps 40:12
I * poor and needy, yet the Lord	Ps 40:17
come to visit me while I * sick;	Ps 41:6
* lying there upon my bed of pain.	Ps 41:6
what they will do when I * dead.	Ps 41:7
Yet I * standing here depressed	Ps 42:6
by all. I * constantly despised,	Ps 44:15,16
to the King, for I * as full of	Ps 45:1
Know that I * God!	Ps 46:10
For I * your God.	Ps 50:7
But I * like a sheltered olive	Ps 52:8
But I * trusting you to save me.	Ps 55:23
But when I * afraid, I will put	Ps 56:3,4
And since I * trusting him, what	Ps 56:3,4
God is for me! I * trusting	Ps 56:10,11
his promises! I * not afraid of	Ps 56:10,11
O GOD, HAVE pity, for I * trusting	Ps 57:1
destroying me. I * surrounded by	Ps 57:4
For wherever I *, though far	Ps 61:2
That is why I * bringing you	Ps 66:15
I have wept until I * exhausted;	Ps 69:3
to kill me though I * innocent.	Ps 69:4
I *, and you know all my sins.	Ps 69:5
though I * mocked and cursed and	Ps 69:7
for my sins! I * the talk of the	Ps 69:12
and from these deep waters I * in.	Ps 69:14
for I * in deep trouble.	Ps 69:17
But I * in deep trouble.	Ps 70:5
Rock, where I * always welcome,	Ps 71:3
wonder I * always praising you!	Ps 71:6
And now that I * old and gray,	Ps 71:18
* ready, I will punish the wicked!	Ps 75:2
Oh, that he would listen. I * in	Ps 77:2
I * too distressed even to pray!	Ps 77:4
Open your ears to what I *	Ps 78:1
So I * letting them go their	Ps 81:12
I * listening carefully to all	Ps 85:8
me, for I * deep in trouble.	Ps 86:1
Save me, for I * serving you and	Ps 86:2
Be merciful, O Lord, for I *	Ps 86:3
I * in a trap with no way out.	Ps 88:8
miracles when I * in the grave?	Ps 88:10
he is my God, and I * trusting	Ps 91:2
No wonder I * glad!	Ps 92:4
How refreshed I * by your	Ps 92:10
my appetite. I * reduced to skin	Ps 102:5
and despair. I * like a vulture in	Ps 102:6
evening shadows. I * withering like	Ps 102:11
their requests. I * recording this	Ps 102:18
you are wise, to what I * saying.	Ps 107:43
I love them, but even while I *	Ps 109:4
I * slipping down the hill to	Ps 109:22,23
hill to death; I * shaken off from	Ps 109:22,23
fasting and I * skin and bones.	Ps 109:24
skin and bones. I * a symbol of	Ps 109:25
in your Word. I * but a pilgrim	Ps 119:19
I * completely discouraged—I lie	Ps 119:25
help me, undeserving as I *, to	Ps 119:29,30
I * very angry with those who	Ps 119:53
I * firmly anchored to your laws.	Ps 119:61
Lord, I * overflowing with your	Ps 119:65
I too * trusting in your Word.	Ps 119:74
with your help? I * shriveled like	Ps 119:83
my joy and health. I * yours!	Ps 119:94
I * ever thinking of your rules.	Ps 119:99
I * close to death at the hands	Ps 119:107
forever. I * determined to obey	Ps 119:112
for I * your servant;	Ps 119:125
just and right. I * indignant and	Ps 119:139
them so much. I * worthless and	Ps 119:141
I * praying with great	Ps 119:145
"Save me," I cry, "for I *	Ps 119:146
me, for I * obeying your commands.	Ps 119:153
and Kedar. I * tired of being here	Ps 120:5,6
who hate peace. I * for peace, but	Ps 120:7
LORD, I * not proud and haughty.	Ps 131:1
it all." I * quiet now before the	Ps 131:2
Though I * surrounded by	Ps 138:7
Every moment, you know where I *.	Ps 139:3
You know what I * going to say	Ps 139:4
But I * in constant prayer	Ps 141:5
know that I * trying to help them.	Ps 141:6,7
For I * overwhelmed and	Ps 142:3
"Hear my cry, for I * very low.	Ps 142:6
the grave. I * losing all hope;	Ps 143:4
I am losing all hope; I *	Ps 143:4
the morning, for I * trusting you.	Ps 143:8
for I * your servant.	Ps 143:12
I know what I * saying;	Pro 5:1
From ages past, I *.	Pro 8:23
cleansed my heart; I * sinless"?	Pro 20:9
Then believe what I * telling you	Pro 22:20,21
I * tired out, O God, and ready	Pro 30:2
ready to die. I * too stupid even	Pro 30:2
And if I * too poor, I may steal,	Pro 30:9
I said to myself, "Look, I *	Ecc 1:16-18
And I * disgusted about this,	Ecc 2:18
The Girl: "I * dark but	Sol 1:5
THE GIRL: "I * the rose of	Sol 2:1
other youths. I * seated in his	Sol 2:3
'apples'—for I * utterly lovesick.	Sol 2:5
"My beloved is mine and I * his.	Sol 2:16
one, my bride; I * overcome by one	Sol 4:9
KING SOLOMON: "I * here in my	Sol 5:1
the night and * covered with dew.'	Sol 5:2
him that I * sick with love."	Sol 5:8
the lilies. I * my beloved's and	Sol 6:3
The Girl: "I * my beloved's and	Sol 7:10
and I * the one he desires.	Sol 7:10
The Girl: "I * slim, tall,	Sol 8:10
Literally, "I * as a wall."	Sol 8:10f
Hear what he is telling you! I *	Is 1:11
is sealed, for I * a foul-mouthed	Is 6:5
of the son I * going to give you.	Is 8:1
Write down all these things I *	Is 8:16
I * not through with Dibon yet!	Is 15:9
* terrified, blinded with dismay.	Is 21:3
my heart races; I * gripped by	Is 21:4
But the Lord God says, See, I *	Is 28:16
the proof that I * the one who is	Is 37:30
leave it all. I * robbed of my	Is 38:10
'O God,' I cried, 'I * in	Is 38:14
I alone * he.	Is 41:4
Fear not, for I * with you.	Is 41:10
Do not be dismayed. I * your God.	Is 41:10
all be gone. I * holding you by	Is 41:13
be afraid; I * here to help you.	Is 41:13
for I will help you. I * the	Is 41:14
I am the Lord, your Redeemer; I *	Is 41:14
and despair. I * the Lord!	Is 42:8
For I * the Lord your God, your	Is 43:3
Don't be afraid, for I * with	Is 43:5
to understand that I alone * God.	Is 43:10
never will be. I * the Lord, and	Is 43:11
From eternity to eternity I *	Is 43:13
cries of fear. I * the Lord, your	Is 43:15
and King. I * the Lord, who opens	Is 43:16
I, yes, I alone * he who blots	Is 43:25
* the Lord's," they'll proudly	Is 44:5
say, or, "I * a Jew," and	Is 44:5
says it—I * the First and Last;	Is 44:6
I * the one who shows what liars	Is 44:25
and you will know that I * doing	Is 45:3
you didn't know me. I * Jehovah;	Is 45:5
is no other God. I * Jehovah and	Is 45:6
I alone * God.	Is 45:6
I, Jehovah, * he who does these	Is 45:7
an empty chaos. I * Jehovah, he	Is 45:18
For I * God;	Is 45:22
For I * God—I only—and there is	Is 46:9
For I * offering you my	Is 46:13
but right now! I * ready to save	Is 46:13
You say, "I alone * God!	Is 47:8
I alone * God.	Is 48:12
I alone am God. I * the First;	Is 48:12
I am the First; I * the Last.	Is 48:12
But I * saying it.	Is 48:15
of Israel, says, I * the Lord your	Is 48:17
of his hand; I * like a sharp arrow	Is 49:2
Through you I * saying to the	Is 49:8,9
out! I * giving you your freedom!'	Is 49:8,9
then you shall know I * the Lord.	Is 49:23
that I, the Lord, * your Savior and	Is 49:26
dying fish. I * the one who sends	Is 50:3
I, even I, * he who comforts you	Is 51:12
For I * the Lord your God, the	Is 51:15
all the earth. I * the one who says	Is 51:16
be routed, for I * on your side.	Is 54:15
is at stake. I * ready to make an	Is 55:3
Do what's right and good, for I *	Is 56:1
"Yes, I * here," he will	Is 58:9
that I, the Lord, * your Savior and	Is 60:16
righteousness. I * like a	Is 61:10
the Lord your God, * coming to save	Is 62:11
For I * holier than you!"	Is 65:5
For see, I * creating new	Is 65:17
verse 12: "For I * watching over	Jer 1:12f
of this land. I * calling the	Jer 1:15
For I * with you," says the	Jer 1:19
to me again, for I * merciful;	Jer 3:12
come home, for I * your Master and	Jer 3:14
For I the Lord * bringing vast	Jer 4:6
Though I * the one who gives them	Jer 5:23,24
For all this I * full of the	Jer 6:11
them. I * weary of holding it in.	Jer 6:11
and to their other idol-gods! *	Jer 7:19
understand that I * the Lord of	Jer 9:24
Therefore, the Lord says, I *	Jer 11:11
(And I * poor,	Jer 12:3
to utter shame. I * keenly aware	Jer 13:27
to destroy you. I * tired of always	Jer 15:6
For I * hated everywhere I go.	Jer 15:10
everywhere I go. I * neither a	Jer 15:10
for your sake that I * suffering.	Jer 15:15
How proud I * to bear your name,	Jer 15:16
conquer you for I * with you to	Jer 15:20
Now I * sending for many	Jer 16:16
from my wrath. I * sending for	Jer 16:16
For I * closely watching you and	Jer 16:17
at last that I alone * God.	Jer 16:21
of the Lord. I * planning evil	Jer 18:11
stronger than I *, but now I am the	Jer 20:7
I am, but now I * the laughingstock	Jer 20:7
whispered threats, and * afraid.	Jer 20:10
against you, for I * very angry.	Jer 21:5
the Lord says: I * ready to judge	Jer 21:12
their evil ways. * I a God who is	Jer 23:23
Can anyone hide from me? * I not	Jer 23:24
no more, for I * sending terrible	Jer 25:27
the punishment I * ready to pour	Jer 26:3
As for me, I * helpless and in	Jer 26:14
my name: Look, I * turning them	Jer 29:21
For I * with you and I will save	Jer 30:11
you will understand what I *	Jer 30:24
For I * a Father to Israel, and	Jer 31:9
I * as likely to reject my people	Jer 31:36
people Israel as I * to do away	Jer 31:36
I * the Lord, the God of all	Jer 32:27
so I * determined to be rid of it.	Jer 32:31
Baruch, "Since I * a prisoner	Jer 36:5
"But I * afraid to surrender,"	Jer 38:19
Now I * going to take off your	Jer 40:4
For I * sorry for all the	Jer 42:10
any more, for I * with you to save	Jer 42:11
has added more! I * weary of my own	Jer 45:3
says the Lord, for I * with you.	Jer 46:28
again, for see, I * raising up an	Jer 50:9
For see, I * against you, O	Jer 50:31
For see, I * against you, O	Jer 51:25
the evil I * bringing upon her.'	Jer 51:64
I * helpless in their hands.	Lam 1:14
I * THE man who has seen the	Lam 3:1
"Son of dust," he said, "I *	Eze 2:3

(AM Con't)
But I * sending you to give them Eze 2:4
I * giving you—eat this scroll! Eze 3:1
Then he said: "Son of dust, I * Eze 3:4
my messages. I * not sending you Eze 3:5
would listen!) I * sending you to Eze 3:7
says, I, even I, * against you and Eze 5:8
Then at last you will know I * Eze 6:4-7
They will realize that I alone * Eze 6:10
will realize that I alone * God. Eze 6:13
Then you will know I * the Eze 6:14
and you shall know I * the Lord." Eze 7:4
know that I, the Lord, * doing it. Eze 7:8,9
They shall learn that I * the Eze 7:26,27
and you will know I * the Lord. Eze 11:10
you will know I * the Lord—you who Eze 11:12
then they shall know I * the Lord. Eze 12:15
they shall know I * the Lord." Eze 12:16
and you shall know I * the Lord." Eze 12:20
For I * the Lord! Eze 12:25
And you shall know I * the Lord. Eze 13:9
and you shall know I * the Lord. Eze 13:14
and you shall know I * the Lord. Eze 13:21
and you shall know I * the Lord." Eze 13:23
and you shall know I * the Lord. Eze 14:8
and then you shall know I * the Eze 15:7
this is what I * going to do: I Eze 16:37
and you will know I * the Lord. Eze 16:62
people of Israel. * I the one who Eze 18:25
gods, for I * the Lord your God. Eze 20:7
idols, for I * the Lord your God. Eze 20:19
that I * the Lord your God. Eze 20:20
know that I alone * God, I let them Eze 20:26
you will know I * the Lord. Eze 20:38
you will know I * the Lord. Eze 20:42
you will know I * the Lord." Eze 20:44
For the Lord says: I * against Eze 21:3
and you shall know I * the Lord." Eze 22:16
her sister was Oholibah. (I * Eze 23:4,5
will know that I alone * God." Eze 23:49
"Son of dust, I * going to take Eze 24:16
then you will know I * the Lord." Eze 24:24
they shall know I * the Lord." Eze 24:27
Then you will know I * the Lord. Eze 25:5
then you shall know I * the Lord. Eze 25:7
and they shall know I * the Lord. Eze 25:11
they shall know I * the Lord." Eze 25:17
Then they shall know I * the Eze 26:6
You say, 'I * the most beautiful Eze 27:3
"The Lord God says: I * your Eze 28:22
who see shall know I * the Lord. Eze 28:22
Then you will know I * the Lord. Eze 28:23
know I * the Lord their God." Eze 28:26
Lord God says: I * your enemy, Eze 29:3
all of you shall know I * the Eze 29:6
therefore I * against you and Eze 29:10
will know that I alone * God." Eze 29:16
Egypt shall know I * the Lord." Eze 29:21
And they will know I * the Lord Eze 30:8
they shall know I * the Lord." Eze 30:19
For, the Lord God says, I * Eze 30:22
Egypt shall know I * the Lord. Eze 30:25
then they shall know I * the Eze 30:26
then they shall know I * the Lord. Eze 33:29
therefore I * against the Eze 34:9,10
they shall know I * the Lord. Eze 34:27
Lord their God, * with them, and Eze 34:30
You are my men and I * your God, Eze 34:31
"The Lord God says: I * against Eze 35:3
then you shall know I * the Lord. Eze 35:4,5
Then you shall know I * the Lord. Eze 35:9
And then you will know I * the Eze 35:15
Lord God says, I * full of fury Eze 36:6
See, I * for you, and I will Eze 36:9
Then you shall know I * the Lord. Eze 36:11
from harm!' I * concerned about my Eze 36:21
Lord God says, I * bringing you Eze 36:22
you deserve it; I * doing it to Eze 36:22
the world shall know I * the Lord. Eze 36:23
"The Lord God says: I * ready to Eze 36:37,38
everyone will know I * the Lord." Eze 36:37,38
God says, See! I * going to make Eze 37:5
live and know I * the Lord." Eze 37:6
you will know I * the Lord. Eze 37:13
"For the Lord God says: I * Eze 37:21
God says: I * against you, Gog. Eze 38:2,3
nations will know that I * God. Eze 38:15,16
have done, and know that I * God! Eze 38:23
and they shall know I * the Lord. Eze 39:6
too shall know I * the Lord, the Eze 39:7
will know I * the Lord their God. Eze 39:22
I * concerned about my reputation! Eze 39:25
Then my people will know I * the Eze 39:28
own any, for I * their heritage! Eze 44:28
it's not because I * wiser than any Dan 2:30
but they can't. I * told that you Dan 5:16
for I * innocent before God, nor, Dan 6:22
to my feet. "I * here," he said, Dan 8:19
to me, "Daniel, I * here to help Dan 9:22
was given. I * here to tell you Dan 9:23
Now I * here to tell you what Dan 10:14
heaven, "Sir, I * terrified by Dan 10:16
why I have come? I * here to tell Dan 10:20,21
of Jezreel I * about to punish King Hos 1:4,5
is not mine and I * not her God. Hos 1:9
wife—I * no longer her husband. Hos 1:2
off with him than I * now." Hos 1:7
Look, priest, I * pointing my Hos 4:4
recognize that I * watching them. Hos 7:2
For I * God and not man; Hos 11:9
For I am God and not man; I * the Hos 11:9
Ephraim boasts, "I * so rich! Hos 12:8
I * the same Lord, the same God, Hos 12:9
in Egypt, and I * the one who will Hos 12:9
I alone * God, your Lord, and Hos 13:4
Stay away from idols! I * living Hos 14:8
care for you. I * like an evergreen Hos 14:8
a thing as I * going to tell you? Joe 1:2
He will reply, "See, I * Joe 2:19
And you will know that I * here Joe 2:27
that I alone * the Lord, your God. Joe 2:27
at last that I * the Lord your God Joe 3:17
The fact is, I * getting ready to Amo 3:4
For I, the Lord, * sending Amo 3:6
But Amos replied, "I * not Amo 7:14
of prophets. I * just a herdsman Amo 7:14
from the Lord: 'I * going to Jon 1:2
And he said, "I * a Jew; Jon 1:9,10
after I * through with you. Mic 2:3
But as for me, I * filled with Mic 3:8
You will be astounded at what I * Hab 1:5
For I * going to do something in Hab 1:5
see to believe. I * raising a new Hab 1:6
That is why I * holding back the Hag 1:10
his messenger), "I * with you; Hag 1:13
take courage and work, for 'I * Hag 2:4
Notice, I * giving you this Hag 2:18,19
of Judah, "I * about to shake the Hag 2:21
and Jerusalem? I * as jealous as a Zec 1:14
captive wife. I * very angry with Zec 1:15
sins, and now I * giving you these Zec 3:4
"I * sending this curse into the Zec 5:4
"The Lord of Hosts says, I * Zec 8:2
Now I * going to return to my Zec 8:3
"For I * sowing peace and Zec 8:12
entering Israel. I * closely Zec 9:8
'Thank God, now I * rich!' Zec 11:5
me my pay, whatever I * worth; Zec 11:12
" 'No,' he will say. 'I * not a Zec 13:5
'I am not a prophet; I * a Zec 13:5
his master. I * your Father and Mal 1:6
For I * a Great King," says the Mal 1:14
"For I * the Lord—I do not Mal 3:6
far greater than I *, so great that Mt 3:11
I * not worthy to carry his shoes! Mt 3:11
he said. "I * the one who needs to Mt 3:14
* wonderfully pleased with him." Mt 3:17
Then the officer said, "Sir, I * Mt 8:8,9
I know, because I * under the Mt 8:8,9
"I * sending you out as sheep Mt 10:16
complain that I * 'a glutton and a Mt 11:19
for I * gentle and humble, and Mt 11:29,30
* master even of the Sabbath." Mt 12:8
And if, as you claim, I * Mt 12:27
But if I * casting out demons by Mt 12:28
* the farmer who sows the choice Mt 13:37
people saying I *? Mt 16:13
them, "Who do you think I *?" Mt 16:15
I * wonderfully pleased with him. Mt 17:5
told them, "I * going to be Mt 17:22,23
Should you be angry because I * Mt 20:15
cup I * about to drink from?" Mt 20:22
when he said, 'I * the God of Mt 22:32
each one asked, "* I the one?" Mt 26:22
to the man by whom I * betrayed. Mt 26:24
asked him, "Rabbi, * I the one?" Mt 26:25
* betrayed into the hands of evil Mt 26:45
to the crowd. "* I some dangerous Mt 26:55
man said, 'I * able to destroy the Mt 26:60,61
"Yes," Jesus said, "I *. Mt 26:64
crowd, saying, "I * innocent of Mt 27:24
Didn't he say, 'I * God's Son'?" Mt 27:41,42,43
and be sure of this—that I * with Mt 28:20
far greater than I *, so much Mk 1:7
* not even worthy to be his slave. Mk 1:7
Literally, "Whose shoes I * not Mk 1:7f
all the others I * going to tell? Mk 4:13
"Who do the people think I *? Mk 8:27
asked, "Who do you think I *?" Mk 8:29
* going to be betrayed and killed Mk 9:30,31
* not here to be served, but to Mk 10:45
God said to Moses, 'I * the God Mk 12:26
of Abraham, and I * the God of Mk 12:26
Isaac, and I * the God of Jacob.' Mk 12:26
not have said, 'I * the God' of Mk 12:27
near, that I * right at the door. Mk 13:29
they asked him, "* I the one?" Mk 14:19
* betrayed. Mk 14:21
But after I * raised to life Mk 14:28
* betrayed into the hands of Mk 14:41
Jesus asked them, "* I some Mk 14:48
Jesus said, "I *, and you will Mk 14:62
Then the angel said, "I * Lk 1:19
can I have a baby? I * a virgin." Lk 1:34
Mary said, "I * the Lord's Lk 1:38
* willing to do whatever he wants. Lk 1:38
in fact, I * not even worthy of Lk 3:16
* master even of the Sabbath." Lk 6:5
to my home, for I * not worthy of Lk 7:6,7,8
I know, because I * under the Lk 7:6,7,8
they say, 'Look! I * sending my Lk 7:27
But I * sure you can always Lk 7:35
"Who are the people saying I *?" Lk 9:18
them, "Who do you think I *?" Lk 9:20
* going to be betrayed." Lk 9:44
Go now, and remember that I * Lk 10:3
you wanted it. I * the Agent of my Lk 10:22
the next time I * here.' Lk 10:35
And if I * empowered by Satan, Lk 11:19
But if I * casting out demons Lk 11:20
skies [to prove I * the Messiah Lk 11:29,30
of me, and how I * pent up until it Lk 12:50
and here I *, dying of hunger! Lk 15:17
and you, and * no longer worthy of Lk 15:19
and you, and * not worthy of being Lk 15:21
I * in anguish in these flames.' Lk 16:24
children's souls. I * warning you! Lk 17:2,3
that I * in this place or that; Lk 17:23
Or, "the hour I * revealed." Lk 17:30f
'Thank God, I * not a sinner like Lk 18:11
For I * going to be a guest in Lk 19:5
'Hard, * I? Lk 19:22
me and how tough I *, then why Lk 19:22
For I * your servant. Lk 22:27
Simon said, "Lord, I * ready to Lk 22:33
headed the mob. "* I a robber," Lk 22:52
"No sir, I * not!" Lk 22:58
And he replied, "Yes, I *." Lk 22:70
Touch me and make sure that I * Lk 24:39
by far than I *—for he existed long Jn 1:15
He denied it flatly. "I * not Jn 1:20
He replied, "I * a voice from Jn 1:23
* not even fit to be his slave." Jn 1:27
far greater than I * is coming, who Jn 1:30
one, but I * here baptizing with Jn 1:31
"How do you know what I * Jn 1:48
Jesus replied, "What I * telling Jn 3:5
these things? I * telling you what Jn 3:10,11
told you that I * not the Messiah. Jn 3:28
not the Messiah. I * here to Jn 3:28
with him. I * the Bridegroom's Jn 3:29
* filled with joy at his success. Jn 3:29
anyone else. I * of the earth, and Jn 3:31
for you, and who I *, you would ask Jn 4:10
Then Jesus told her, "I * the Jn 4:26
While I * trying to get there, Jn 5:7
I judge as I * told. Jn 5:30
Jesus replied, "I * the Bread of Jn 6:35
Yes, I * the Bread of Life! Jn 6:48-51
who eats it. I * that Living Bread Jn 6:48-51
I * the true Bread from heaven; Jn 6:58
and you will see that I * right." Jn 7:24
and raised, but I * the Jn 7:28
I * to be here a little longer. Jn 7:33
won't be able to come where I *!" Jn 7:34
be able to come where I *'?" Jn 7:36
"I * the Light of the world. Jn 8:12
from and where I * going, but you Jn 8:14
facts. I * not judging you now; Jn 8:15
Well, I * one witness, and my Jn 8:18
don't know who I *, so you don't Jn 8:19
to them again, "I * going away; Jn 8:21
And you cannot come where I * Jn 8:21
cannot come where I * going'?" Jn 8:22
are from below; I * from above. Jn 8:23
You are of this world; I * not. Jn 8:23
for unless you believe that I * Jn 8:24
He replied, "I * the one I have Jn 8:25
* told to by the one who sent me; Jn 8:26
then you will realize that I * he Jn 8:28
your hearts. I * telling you what Jn 8:38
to you from God. I * not here on my Jn 8:42
you understand what I * saying? Jn 8:43
And since I * telling you the Jn 8:46
them this: "If I * merely boasting Jn 8:54
But while I * still here in the Jn 9:5
And the beggar said, "I * the Jn 9:9
"I * the Gate for the sheep," he Jn 10:7
Yes, I * the Gate. Jn 10:9
"I * the Good Shepherd. Jn 10:11
"I * the Good Shepherd and know Jn 10:14
Father says, 'I * the Son of God'? Jn 10:34,35,36
And for your sake, I * glad I Jn 11:15
Jesus told her, "I * the one who Jn 11:25
for my servants must be where I *. Jn 12:26
And when I * lifted up [on the Jn 12:32
doesn't obey me, I * not his Jn 12:47
understand now why I * doing it; Jn 13:7
"I * not saying these things to Jn 13:18
"And so I * giving a new Jn 13:34
he asked, "for I * ready to Jn 13:37
lives, and I * going to prepare Jn 14:2,3
can always be with me where I *. Jn 14:2,3

AM Con't)
And you know where I * going and Jn 14:4
Jesus told him, "I * the Jn 14:6
If you had known who I *, then Jn 14:7
yet know who I *, Philip, even Jn 14:9
Don't you believe that I * in Jn 14:10
Just believe it—that I * in the Jn 14:11
I * going to be with the Father. Jn 14:12,13
will know that I * in my Father, Jn 14:20
And remember, I * not making up Jn 14:24
who sent me. I * telling you these Jn 14:25
now while I * still with you. Jn 14:25
"I * leaving you with a Jn 14:27
Remember what I told you—I * Jn 14:28
Father, who is greater than I *. Jn 14:28
"I * THE true Vine, and my Father Jn 15:1
"Yes, I * the Vine; Jn 15:5
"But now I * going away to the Jn 16:5
is asking me whither I * going." Jn 16:5f
Now I * leaving the world, and Jn 17:11
"And now I * coming to you. Jn 17:13
of this world any more than I *. Jn 17:16
into the world, I * sending them Jn 17:18
"I * not praying for these alone Jn 17:20
are in me and I * in you, so they Jn 17:21
"I * he," Jesus said. Jn 18:4,5
"I told you I * he," Jesus Jn 18:8
"and since I * the one you are Jn 18:8
"No," he said, "I * not!" Jn 18:17
"* I a Jew?" Jn 18:35
Then Jesus answered, "I * not an Jn 18:36
to the Jews, "I * going to bring Jn 19:4
'He said, I * King of the Jews.' Jn 19:21
me, even so I * sending you." Jn 20:21
"You know I * your friend." Jn 21:15
"you know I * your friend." Jn 21:16
you know I *," he said. Jn 21:17
I * that disciple! Jn 21:24
out to him, 'I * the God of your Act 7:32
And the voice replied, "I * Act 9:5
'Do you think I * the Messiah? Act 13:25
with him, I * utterly worthless.' Act 13:25
for I * doing something in your Act 13:41
"If you agree that I * faithful Act 16:15
your own heads—I * innocent—from Act 18:6
For I * with you and no one can Act 18:10
Of course, I * not only talking Act 19:27
"And now I * going to Jerusalem, Act 20:22
For I * ready not only to be Act 21:13
"No," Paul replied, "I * a Jew Act 21:39
"I * a Jew," he said, "born Act 22:3
And he replied, 'I * Jesus of Act 22:8
"Yes, I certainly *." Act 22:27
"I * too," the commander Act 22:28
"But I * a citizen by birth!" Act 22:28
So he shouted, "Brothers, I * a Act 23:6
And I * being tried here today Act 23:6
when I shouted out, 'I * here Act 24:21
Paul denied the charges: "I * Act 25:8
You know very well I * not Act 25:10,11
But if I * innocent, neither you Act 25:10,11
"I * fortunate, King Agrippa," Act 26:2
is because I * looking forward to Act 26:6
"And the Lord replied, 'I * Act 26:15
Yes, I * going to send you to the Act 26:17
me so that I * still alive today to Act 26:22
But Paul replied, "I * not Act 26:25
I speak frankly for I * sure Act 26:26
as I *, except for these chains." Act 26:29
has come that I * bound with this Act 28:20
of my ability, I * ready to come Rom 1:15
For I * not ashamed of this Good Rom 1:16
Well then, * I suggesting that Rom 7:7
with me, because I * sold into Rom 7:14
well that what I * doing is wrong, Rom 7:16
with these laws I * breaking. Rom 7:16
is stronger than I * that makes me Rom 7:17
I know I * rotten through and Rom 7:18
Now if I * doing what I don't Rom 7:20
For I * convinced that nothing Rom 8:38
Remember that I myself * a Jew, a Rom 11:1
As for myself, I * perfectly sure Rom 14:14
for I *, by God's grace, a Rom 15:15,16
But now at last I * through with Rom 15:23
work here, and I * ready to come Rom 15:23
For I * planning to take a trip Rom 15:24
And I * sure that when I come Rom 15:29
the money I * bringing them. Rom 15:31
and I * not the only one who is Rom 16:4
to you for him. I * his guest, and Rom 16:23
Some of you are saying, "I * a 1Co 1:12
in my name? I * so thankful now 1Co 1:14
Yet when I * among mature 1Co 2:6
about whether I * greater than 1Co 3:4
Who * I, and who is Apollos, that 1Co 3:5
I * not writing about these 1Co 4:14
That is the very reason why I * 1Co 4:17
* afraid to come to deal with you. 1Co 4:18
Although I * not there with you, 1Co 5:3,4
I * trying to make you ashamed. 1Co 6:5
Even if I * allowed to do them, 1Co 6:12
unmarried if you can, just as I *. 1Co 7:8
I * saying this to help you, not 1Co 7:35
and I think I * giving you 1Co 7:40
I * AN apostle, God's messenger, 1Co 9:1
to no mere man. I * one who has 1Co 9:1
If in the opinion of others, I * 1Co 9:2
I certainly * to you, for you have 1Co 9:2
And I * not writing this to hint 1Co 9:15
real advantage: I * not bound to 1Co 9:19
When I * with the Jews I seem as 1Co 9:20
When I * with Gentiles who follow 1Co 9:20
When I * with those whose 1Co 9:22
what I * about to say is true. 1Co 10:15
What * I trying to say? 1Co 10:19
What am I trying to say? * I 1Co 10:19
What I * saying is that those 1Co 10:20
just because he thinks I * wrong? 1Co 10:30
Christ's. I * so glad, dear 1Co 11:2
For I * told that everyone 1Co 11:21
no food? What * I supposed to say 1Co 11:22
If the foot says, "I * not a 1Co 12:15
the body because I * not a hand," 1Co 12:15
an ear say, "I * not part of the 1Co 12:16
I * only an ear, and not an eye"? 1Co 12:16
Now here is what I * trying to 1Co 12:27
but I don't know what I * saying. 1Co 14:14
understand the praise I * giving; 1Co 14:15
let's add up what I * saying. 1Co 14:26
that what I * saying is a 1Co 14:37
For I * the least worthy of all 1Co 15:9
But whatever I * now it is all 1Co 15:10
But I * telling you this strange 1Co 15:51
I * coming to visit you after I 1Co 16:5
doing the Lord's work just as I *. 1Co 16:10
time among you; I * looking forward 1Co 16:11
real devotion. I * so glad that 1Co 16:17
as I * sure they were to you, too. 1Co 16:18
up my mind yet? Or * I like a man 2Co 1:17
As surely as God is true, I * not 2Co 1:18
against me if I * not telling the 2Co 1:23
No, I * giving you some good 2Co 5:12
and draw me in. I * talking to you 2Co 6:13
I * no longer sorry that I sent 2Co 7:8
Now I * glad I sent it, not 2Co 7:9
me, now that I * sure all is well 2Co 7:16
I * not giving you an order; 2Co 8:8
you an order; I * not saying you 2Co 8:8
I * thankful to God that he has 2Co 8:16
to see you! I * sending another 2Co 8:18
And I * sending you still another 2Co 8:22
But I * sending these men just 2Co 9:3
It is true that I * an ordinary, 2Co 10:3
will not think I * just blustering 2Co 10:9
dare say that I * as wonderful as 2Co 10:12
is on my heart. I * anxious for 2Co 11:2
But I * frightened, fearing that 2Co 11:3
are any better than I *. 2Co 11:5
If I * a poor speaker, at least 2Co 11:6
I know what I * talking about, as I 2Co 11:6
Yet I * not surprised! 2Co 11:14
I * acting like a brainless fool. 2Co 11:17
Well, so * I. 2Co 11:22
God's chosen people? So * I. 2Co 11:22
Well, I * too. 2Co 11:22
the things that show how weak I *. 2Co 11:30
(and anyway I * not allowed to tell 2Co 12:4
about, but I * not going to do it. 2Co 12:5
going to do it. I * going to boast 2Co 12:5
about how weak I * and how great 2Co 12:5
But I * with you; 2Co 12:9
Now I * glad to boast about how 2Co 12:9
glad to boast about how weak I *; 2Co 12:9
how weak I am; I * glad to be a 2Co 12:9
Christ's good, I * quite happy 2Co 12:10
for when I * weak, then I am 2Co 12:10
for when I am weak, then I * 2Co 12:10
I * really worth nothing at all. 2Co 12:11
Now I * coming to you again, the 2Co 12:14
their children. I * glad to give 2Co 12:15
I suppose you think I * saying 2Co 12:19
For I * afraid that when I come 2Co 12:20
have to act. I * afraid that I will 2Co 12:20
Yes, I * afraid that when I come 2Co 12:21
THIS IS THE third time I * coming 2Co 13:1
I * writing this to you now in 2Co 13:10
I * amazed that you are turning Gal 1:6
You can see that I * not trying Gal 1:10
no, I * trying to please God. Gal 1:10
(Listen to what I * saying, for Gal 1:20
I am saying, for I * telling you Gal 1:20
This is exactly what happened—I * Gal 1:20
himself for me. I * not one of Gal 2:21
Here's what I * trying to say: Gal 3:17
I fear for you. I * afraid that Gal 4:11
things, for I * as free from these Gal 4:12
doing it just when I * with you! Gal 4:18
are hurting me! I * once again Gal 4:19
For I * going to give you many Gal 4:27
I * trusting the Lord to bring Gal 5:10
say that I myself * preaching that Gal 5:11
The fact that I * still being Gal 5:11
proves that I * still preaching Gal 5:11
I PAUL, THE servant of Christ, * Eph 3:1
it, and though I * the most useless Eph 3:8
It is for you I * suffering and Eph 3:13
Gentiles too. I * in chains now Eph 6:20
all about how I * getting along. Eph 6:21
getting along. I * sending him to Eph 6:22
And I * sure that God who began Php 1:6
knows that I * in chains simply Php 1:13
simply because I * a Christian. Php 1:13
is being preached and I * glad. Php 1:18
I * going to keep on being glad, Php 1:19
for Christ while I * going through Php 1:20
Yes, I * still needed down here Php 1:25
and I * still in the midst of a Php 1:30
And now that I * away you must be Php 2:12
your faith which I * offering up to Php 2:17
is, if I * to die for you—even then Php 2:17
And I * trusting the Lord that Php 2:24
Now I * sending him home again, Php 2:26
So I * all the more anxious to Php 2:28
I don't mean to say I * perfect. Php 3:12
No, dear brothers, I * still not Php 3:13
I should be but I * bringing all my Php 3:13
How grateful I * and how I praise Php 4:10
than I need! I * generously Php 4:18
and I * glad, for I am helping to Col 1:24
and I am glad, for I * helping to Col 1:24
I * saying this because I am Col 2:4
I am saying this because I * Col 2:4
For though I * far away from you Col 2:5
Christ for which I * here in jail. Col 4:3
tell you how I * getting along. Col 4:7
encourage you. I * also sending Col 4:9
Now here is my greeting which I * 2Th 3:17
What I * eager for is that all 1Ti 1:5
blessed God, whose messenger I *. 1Ti 1:10,11
How thankful I * to Christ Jesus 1Ti 1:12
I * writing these things to you 1Ti 3:14
For I * afraid that some of them 1Ti 5:15
them know that I * your friend even 2Ti 1:8
* here in jail for Christ's sake. 2Ti 1:8
That is why I * suffering here in 2Ti 1:12
here in jail and I * certainly not 2Ti 1:12
I trust, and I * sure that he is 2Ti 1:12
truths that I * in trouble here and 2Ti 2:9
is not chained, even though I *. 2Ti 2:9
though I am. I * more than willing 2Ti 2:10
I * comforted by this truth, that 2Ti 2:11
that I * not that kind of person. 2Ti 3:10
I * planning to send either Tit 3:12
I always thank God when I * Phm 1:4
to both of us. I * sending him Phm 1:12
with me while I * in these chains Phm 1:13
If I * really your friend, give Phm 1:17
letter because I * positive that Phm 1:21
for me, for I * hoping that God Phm 1:22
Another time he said, "I * his Heb 1:5,6
time, "See, here * I and the Heb 2:13
Dear friends, even though I * Heb 6:9
what I * saying applies to you. Heb 6:9
applies to you. I * confident you Heb 6:9
he then added, "Here I *. Heb 10:9
is my Helper and I * not afraid of Heb 13:6
must be holy, for I * holy." 1Pe 1:16
it, "See, I * sending Christ to be 1Pe 2:6
I, too, * an elder; 1Pe 5:1
I * sending this note to you 1Pe 5:12
are numbered, and I * soon to die. 2Pe 1:13,14
As long as I * still here I 2Pe 1:13,14
Son; I * well pleased with him." 2Pe 1:17,18
I * warning you ahead of time, 2Pe 3:17
have seen him; I * speaking of 1Jn 1:2
MY LITTLE CHILDREN, I * telling 1Jn 2:1
Someone may say, "I * a 1Jn 2:4
I * on my way to heaven; 1Jn 2:4
Dear brothers, I * not writing 1Jn 2:7
I * writing these things to all 1Jn 2:12
our Savior. I * saying these 1Jn 2:13
And you young men, I * talking to 1Jn 2:13
And I * writing to you younger 1Jn 2:13
So I * not writing to you as to 1Jn 2:21
ordinary sins; I * speaking of that 1Jn 5:17
How happy I * to find some of 2Jn 1:4
Dear friend, I * praying that all 3Jn 1:2
loving deeds. I * glad when you 3Jn 1:6
"I * the A and the Z, Rev 1:8
Literally, "I * Alpha and Rev 1:8f
* A and Z, the First and Last!" Rev 1:11
Though I * the First and Last, Rev 1:17,18
sword. I * fully aware that you Rev 2:13
"I * aware of all your good Rev 2:19
Pay attention now to what I * Rev 2:22
shall know that I * he who searches Rev 2:23
Look, I * coming soon! Rev 3:11
"You say, 'I * rich, with Rev 3:17
door and I * constantly knocking. Rev 3:20
She boasts, 'I * queen upon my Rev 18:7
my throne. I * no helpless widow. Rev 18:7
For I * a servant of God just as Rev 19:10
I * making all things new!" Rev 21:5

(AM Con't)
It is finished! I * the A and the Rev 21:6
and true: 'I * coming soon!' Rev 22:6,7
I, too, * a servant of Jesus as Rev 22:9
"See, I * coming soon, Rev 22:12
he has done. I * the A and the Z, Rev 22:13
these things. I * both David's Root Rev 22:16
I * the bright Morning Star. Rev 22:16

AMAD
Allammelech, *, and Mishal. Jos 19:24,25,26

AMAL
Zophah, Imna, Shelesh, *. 1Ch 7:35

AMALEK
Gatam, Kenaz, * (born to Timna, Gen 36:10,11,12
clan of Gatam,The clan of *. Gen 36:15,16
But now the warriors of * came to Ex 17:8
to fight the army of *. Ex 17:9
went out to fight the army of *. Ex 17:10
the soldiers of * were winning. Ex 17:11
of *, putting them to the sword. Ex 17:13
blot out every trace of *." Ex 17:14
* generation after generation." Ex 17:15,16
of the people of * and prophesied: Num 24:20
"* was the first of the nations, Num 24:20
what the people of * did to you as Deu 25:17
the name of * from under heaven. Deu 25:19
from Midian, *, and other Ju 6:3,4
armies of Midian, *, and other Ju 6:33
The vast armies of Midian, *, Ju 7:12,13
with the nation of * for refusing 1Sa 15:2
destroy the entire * nation—men, 1Sa 15:3
when he was so angry with *. 1Sa 28:18
*, and King Hadadezer. 2Sa 8:11,12
Zephi, Gatam, Kenaz, Timna, and *. 1Ch 1:36
members of the tribe of *. 1Ch 4:43
against the * raiders at Ziklag. 1Ch 12:21
Ammon, *, and the Philistines. 1Ch 18:11
Ammon, *, Philistia and Tyre; Ps 83:7

AMALEKITE
servant of an *," he replied. 1Sa 30:13
So he led them to the * 1Sa 30:16
" 'An *,' I replied. 2Sa 1:8
And he replied, "I am an *." 2Sa 1:13

AMALEKITES
and destroyed the *, and also the Gen 14:7
giants there! The * live in the Num 13:29
so afraid of the * and the Num 14:25
Don't you remember? The * and Num 14:43
Then the * and the Canaanites Num 14:45
armies of the Ammonites and the *. Ju 3:13
the *, and the Maonites? Ju 10:12
in the hill country of the *. Ju 12:15
and conquered the * and saved 1Sa 14:48
from Judah. The * were camped in 1Sa 15:5
among the * or else die with them. 1Sa 15:6
Then Saul butchered the * from 1Sa 15:7
the *, but killed everyone else. 1Sa 15:8
the *, until they are all dead.' 1Sa 15:18
Girzites, and the *—people who had 1Sa 27:8
found that the * had raided the 1Sa 30:1
hundred men set out after the *. 1Sa 30:9,10
Ziklag after slaughtering the *. 2Sa 1:1

AMAM
(or, Hazor), *, Shema, Moladah, Jos 15:21-32

AMANA
from the peak of *, from the peak Sol 4:8f

AMARIAH
*, the father of 1Ch 6:4-15
*, the father of 1Ch 6:4-15
Meraioth, *, Ahitub, 1Ch 6:50-53
led by Jeriah. * was second in 1Ch 23:19
oldest son;*, his second son; 1Ch 24:23
Then he appointed *, the High 2Ch 19:11
Shemaiah, *, and Shecaniah. 2Ch 31:14,15
Ahitub was the son of *; Ez 7:1
* was the son of Meraioth; Ez 7:1
*, Joseph. Ez 10:34-42
Jeremiah, Pashhur, *, Neh 10:1
Zechariah, son of *, son of Neh 11:4,5,6
Seraiah, Jeremiah, Ezra, *, Neh 12:1
Jehohanan, leader of the * clan; Neh 12:12-21
great-grandson of *, and Zep 1:1

AMASA
Absalom had appointed * as 2Sa 17:25
Joab. (* was Joab's second cousin; 2Sa 17:25
And he told them to tell *, 2Sa 19:13
Then * convinced all the 2Sa 19:14
Then the king instructed * to 2Sa 20:4
at that time. So * went out to 2Sa 20:5
they came face to face with *. 2Sa 20:8,9,10
As he stepped forward to greet *, 2Sa 20:8,9,10
to kiss him. * didn't notice the 2Sa 20:8,9,10
But * lay in his blood in the 2Sa 20:12
my two generals, Abner and *. 1Ki 2:5
and General *, commander-in-chief 1Ki 2:32
of Ishmael, had a son named *. 1Ch 2:17
Shallum, and * the son of Hadlai. 2Ch 28:12

AMASA'S
shouted to * troops, "If you are 2Sa 20:11

AMASAI
*, Ahimoth, Elkanah, Zophai, 1Ch 6:25,26,27
II, Mahath, *, Elkanah I, Joel, 1Ch 6:33-38
upon them, and *, a leader of The 1Ch 12:18
Nethanel, *, Zechariah, Benaiah, 1Ch 15:24
of *) and Joel (son of Azariah); 2Ch 29:12,13,14

AMASHSAI
the leadership of * (son of Azarel, Neh 11:10-14

AMASIAH
Next was * (son of Zichri), a 2Ch 17:16

AMASIS
Pharaoh Hophra was killed by *, Jer 44:30f

AMASSED
of Israel, and he * even greater 1Ch 29:25

AMAZED
* at what I have done to you. Lev 26:32
His aides were *. 2Sa 12:21
passing by will be * and will 1Ki 9:8
so many stand *—is because you are Ps 71:7
You are *, incredulous? Is 29:9
miracle that makes us stare, *. Is 41:23
Yet many shall be * when they Is 52:14,15
I was * and appalled. Is 63:5
I stand *, silent, dumb with Jer 8:21
All the world will stand * at Mic 7:16
Lord replied: "Look, and be *! Hab 1:5
The crowds were * at Jesus' Mt 7:28
Jesus stood there *! Mt 8:10
The crowd was *. Mt 12:23
The disciples were utterly * and Mt 21:20
This * them. So Jesus said it Mk 10:24
of him and were * by the beautiful Lk 4:22
Here, too, the people were * at Lk 4:32
*, the people asked, "What is in Lk 4:36
Jesus was *. Lk 7:9
They stood there * and perplexed. Act 2:12
they were * and realized what being Act 4:13
and was * by the miracles he did. Act 8:13
All who heard him were *. Act 9:21
with Peter were * that the gift of Act 10:45
I am * that you are turning away Gal 1:6

AMAZEMENT
to the youngest, much to their *! Gen 43:33
"you will be speechless with *!" Ex 14:14f
objects of horror, *, and contempt, 2Ch 29:8
in * at its utter desolation. Jer 18:16
jumped up in * and exclaimed to his Dan 3:24
and left him. * gripped the Mk 1:27
they were overcome with utter *. Mk 7:37
said no more, much to Pilate's *. Mk 15:5

AMAZIAH
and his son * became the new king. 2Ki 12:21
wars against King * of Judah, are 2Ki 13:12
King * began his reign over Judah. 2Ki 14:1
reign over Judah. * was 2Ki 14:2
Once * killed ten thousand 2Ki 14:7
But * refused to listen, so King 2Ki 14:11
King * was captured, and the 2Ki 14:13
his war with King * of Judah are 2Ki 14:15
* lived fifteen years longer than 2Ki 14:17
of the reign of King * of Judah. 2Ki 14:23
Name of his father: *, the 2Ki 15:1
the Lord just as his father * had. 2Ki 15:3
Ahaziah, Joash, *, Azariah, 1Ch 3:10-14
Kishi, Abdi, Malluch, Hashabiah, * 1Ch 6:44-47
When Joash died, his son * became 2Ch 24:27
* WAS TWENTY-FIVE years old when 2Ch 25:1
Another thing * did was to 2Ch 25:5
"But the money!" * whined. 2Ch 25:9
So * sent them home again to 2Ch 25:10
Then * took courage and led his 2Ch 25:11
When King * returned from this 2Ch 25:14
King * of Judah now took the 2Ch 25:17
But * wouldn't listen, for God 2Ch 25:20
the defeated King * of Judah and 2Ch 25:23
However, King * of Judah lived on 2Ch 25:25
The complete biography of King * 2Ch 25:26
of his father *, and was, in 2Ch 26:4
But when *, the priest of Bethel, Amo 7:10
Then * sent orders to Amos, "Get Amo 7:12

AMAZIAH'S
a report of * turning away from 2Ch 25:27

AMAZING
such * power and mighty miracles. Deu 7:8
he performed * miracles which have Deu 34:11,12
of Israel of this * miracle." Jos 4:7
a reminder of this * miracle—that Jos 4:22
witnessed the * deeds which the Jos 24:31
at last they will realize what * Ps 64:9
LORD, YOU HAVE poured out * Ps 85:1
Tell everyone about the * things Ps 96:3
said, "What * things the Lord has Ps 126:2
It is * to think about. Ps 139:14
for he has done * things for you. Joe 2:21
what an * thing the Lord has Mt 21:42
and it is an * thing to see.' Mk 12:11
with them and * everyone with his Lk 2:46,47
came back with an * report that his Lk 24:22,23
man because of the * things he Act 8:9,10,11
to understand the * message we 2Co 4:4

AMBASSADOR
you as my * to Pharaoh, and your Ex 7:1
Then the Assyrian * shouted in 2Ki 18:28
Solomon sent an * to King Hiram 2Ch 2:3
Thus the * mocked the Lord 2Ch 32:16
The Assyrian * told them to go Is 36:4
of Egypt, and of her * and child. Dan 11:6
God has sent an * to the nations Ob 1:1
Hail to God's *!" Jn 12:13

AMBASSADORS
the Israeli *, "we will stay on Num 20:19
Israel now sent * to King Sihon Num 21:21
So King Balak's * returned Num 22:14
* than the former group. Num 22:15
and the * for their sacrifices. Num 22:40
of Kedemoth I sent * to King Sihon Deu 2:26
They sent * to Joshua wearing Jos 9:3,4,5
Then Phinehas and the ten * went Jos 22:32
So David sent * to express 2Sa 10:2
their * to him for his advice. 1Ki 4:34
of Israel, he sent * to extend 1Ki 5:1
of Babylon) sent * with greetings 2Ki 20:12
But when David's * arrived, King 1Ch 19:2,3
King David's * by shaving their 1Ch 19:4
of Lachish, sent * with this 2Ch 32:9
However, when * arrived from 2Ch 32:31
But King Neco sent * to Josiah 2Ch 35:21
(The *, who accompany the gift Is 16:3
Land that sends * in fast boats Is 18:2
But now your * weep in bitter Is 33:7
through their * in Jerusalem, Jer 27:3
Zedekiah's * to Nebuchadnezzar. Jer 29:3
Babylon, sending * to Egypt to seek Eze 17:15
We are Christ's *. 2Co 5:20

AMBER
The third row will be an *, an Ex 28:19
made of polished * and each wheel Eze 1:16

AMBER-COLORED
from his waist up, he was all * Eze 8:2

AMBITION
* and death are alike in Pro 27:20
But all the while my * has been Rom 15:20
This should be your *: to live a 1Th 4:11
he has a good *. 1Ti 3:1
or selfish *, there will be Jas 3:16
craze for sex, the * to buy 1Jn 2:16

AMBUSH
Set an * behind the city." Jos 8:2
troops to hide in * close behind Jos 8:3,4
jump up from your * and enter the Jos 8:7
night and lay in * between Bethel Jos 8:9
in * on the west side of the city. Jos 8:11,12,13
there was an * behind the city. Jos 8:14
And when the men in * saw his Jos 8:19
who had been in * were inside the Jos 8:20,21
For the men of Shechem set an * Ju 9:25
So the Israeli army set an * all Ju 20:29
thousand men in * west of Geba Ju 20:33
the * more room for maneuvering. Ju 20:35-39
But then the men in * rushed into Ju 20:35-39
who had set the * came out and Ju 20:42
behind the men of Judah to * them; 2Ch 13:13,14
traps, and robbers will * him. Job 18:8,9
aimed from * at the people of God. Ps 11:2
They lurk in * for my life. Ps 59:3
They shoot from * at the Ps 64:4
they wait in * with a net to Ps 140:5
send out an *, for the Lord will Jer 51:12
lying in * for their victims; Hos 6:9

AMBUSHING
at him, or * him, or angrily Num 35:20

AMEN
all the people shall reply, '*.' Deu 27:15
all the people shall reply, '*.' Deu 27:16
all the people shall reply, '*.' Deu 27:17
all the people shall reply, '*.' Deu 27:18
all the people shall reply, '*.' Deu 27:19
all the people shall reply, '*.' Deu 27:20
all the people shall reply, '*.' Deu 27:21
all the people shall reply, '*.' Deu 27:22
all the people shall reply, '*.' Deu 27:23
all the people shall reply, '*.' Deu 27:24
all the people shall reply, '*.' Deu 27:25
all the people shall reply, '*.' Deu 27:26
* - praise God replied 1Ki 1:36
And all the people shouted "*!" 1Ch 16:36
And all the people shouted, "*," Neh 5:13
the people said, "*," and lifted Neh 8:6
eternity ahead. * and amen! Ps 41:13
Amen and *! Ps 41:13
with his glory. *, and amen! Ps 72:19
Amen, and *! Ps 72:19
be the Lord forever! * and amen! Ps 89:52
Amen and *! Ps 89:52
Let all the people say, "*!" Ps 106:48
all the priests and people, "*! Jer 28:6
power and the glory forever. *." Mt 6:13f
*.' Your heavenly Father will Mt 6:13
gives peace, be with you all. *. Rom 15:33
through Jesus Christ our Lord. *. Rom 16:25,26,27
all the ages of eternity. *. Gal 1:5
be glory forever and ever. *. Php 4:20
"with all his saints. *." 1Th 3:13f
is God, and full of wisdom. *. 1Ti 1:17

(AMEN Con't)
and dominion forever and ever. *. 1Ti 6:16
be the glory forever and ever. *. 2Ti 4:18
him be glory forever and ever. *. Heb 13:20,21
and power forever and ever. *. 1Pe 4:11
all things, forever and ever. *. 1Pe 5:11
God's place in your hearts. *. 1Jn 5:21
shouts of everlasting joy. *. Jud 1:24,25
He rules forever! *! Rev 1:6
in terror when he comes. Yes! *! Rev 1:7
Literally, "from the *." Rev 3:14f
Living Beings kept saying, "*!" Rev 5:14
throne and worshiping God. "*!" Rev 7:12
our God forever and forever. *!" Rev 7:12
upon the throne, and said, "*! Rev 19:4

AMETHYST
be an amber, an agate, and an *. Ex 28:19
a jacinth, an agate, and an *. Ex 39:12
The twelfth with *. Rev 21:18,19,20

AMI
Hattil, Pochereth-hazzebaim, *. Ez 2:55,56,57

AMISS
and found nothing * and know that I Ps 17:3

AMITTAI
*) the prophet from Gath-hepher. 2Ki 14:25
message to Jonah, the son of *: Jon 1:1

AMMAH
as they arrived at * Hill near 2Sa 2:24

AMMI
Call your brother * (which means Hos 1:11

AMMI-EL
(the daughter of *) became the 1Ch 3:5
* (the sixth), 1Ch 26:4,5

AMMIEL
*, son of Gemalli, from the tribe Num 13:3-15
and Machir (son of * of Lodebar) 2Sa 17:27

AMMIHUD
Elishama (son of *) Num 1:2-15
Elishama (son of *) Num 2:3-31
the son of *, chief of the tribe of Num 7:48-53
led by Elishama, the son of *; Num 10:22
Shemuel (son of *) Num 34:16-28
Pedahel (son of *) Num 34:16-28
(the son of *) and stayed there 2Sa 13:37,38,39
*, the father of 1Ch 7:25,26,27
Uthai (the son of *, son of Omri, 1Ch 9:4

AMMINADAB
of * and sister of Nahshon. Ex 6:23
Judah - Nahshon (son of * Num 1:2-15
Nahshon (son of *) Num 2:3-31
So Nahshon, the son of * of the Num 7:12
and led by Nahshon, the son of *. Num 10:14
Perez, Hezron, Ram, *, Nashon, Ru 4:18-22
Ram was the father of *, and 1Ch 2:10
of Amminadab, and * was the father 1Ch 2:10
*, Korah, Assir, 1Ch 6:22,23,24
of Uzziel; with * as their leader. 1Ch 15:4-10
Joel, Shemaiah, Eliel, and *. 1Ch 15:11
Aram was the father of *; Mt 1:4
* was the father of Nahshon; Mt 1:4
Nahshon's father was *; Lk 3:23-38

AMMINADAB'S
Nahshon's father was Amminadab;* Lk 3:23-38

AMMISHADDAI
Ahiezer (son of *) Num 1:2-15
Ahiezer (son of *) Num 2:3-31
Ahiezer, the son of *, brought Num 7:66-71
of Ahiezer, the son of *; Num 10:25

AMMIZABAD
His son * succeeded him as 1Ch 27:5,6

AMMON
of the children of * was strong." Num 21:24f
from the people of * and from the Deu 2:37
as far as the borders of *. Jos 13:10
of * as far as Aroer near Rabbah. Jos 13:25
Sidon, Moab, * and Philistia. Ju 10:6
The armies of * were mobilized Ju 10:17
to the king of *, demanding to know Ju 11:12
The king of * replied that the Ju 11:13
land belonged to the people of *; Ju 11:13
of us is right—Israel or *." Ju 11:27
But the king of * paid no Ju 11:28
and attacked the army of *. Ju 11:29
us to help you fight against *? Ju 12:1
the king of *, you came to me and 1Sa 12:12
against Moab, *, Edom, the kings of 1Sa 14:47
from Syria, Moab, *, the 2Sa 8:11,12
Now the people of * realized how 2Sa 10:6
siege of Rabbah the capital of *. 2Sa 12:26,27
Zelek from *; 2Sa 23:24-39
—Moab, *, Edom, Sidon, and from 1Ki 11:1
Zelek from *; 1Ch 11:26-47
*, Amalek, and the Philistines. 1Ch 18:11
WHEN KING NAHASH of * died, his 1Ch 19:1
The army of * went out to meet 1Ch 19:9
and villages of the people of *. 1Ch 20:1
the kings of Moab, *, and of the 2Ch 20:1
*, Moab, and Mount Seir are doing. 2Ch 20:10
the armies of *, Moab, and Mount 2Ch 20:22
was Shime-ath, a woman from *; 2Ch 24:26
women from Ashdod, *, and Moab, Neh 13:23
*, Amalek, Philistia and Tyre; Ps 83:7
nations of Edom and Moab and *. Is 11:14
the nations of Edom, Moab and *; Jer 25:21
of Edom, Moab, *, Tyre and Sidon, Jer 27:3
* and prophesy against its people. Eze 25:2
her, just as they will upon *. Eze 25:9,10
Moab, Edom, and most of * will Dan 11:41
The Lord says, "The people of * Amo 1:13
people of Moab and *, mocking my Zep 2:8
Israel, "Moab and * will be Zep 2:9

AMMONITE
(which was the * frontier) to the Deu 3:16
"No * or Moabite may ever enter Deu 23:3
SOME TIME AFTER this the * king 2Sa 10:1
of Rabbah, an *) and Machir (son of 2Sa 17:27
mother was Naamah, an * woman. 1Ki 14:21
with all the conquered * peoples. 1Ch 20:3
and Tobiah (an * who was a Neh 2:10

AMMONITES
ancestor of the nation of the *. Gen 19:38
as far as the borders of the *; Num 21:24
the * to the descendants of Lot. Num 21:24f
at Ar, into the land of the *. Deu 2:19
called 'Zamzummim' by the *. Deu 2:20
them as the * came in, and the Deu 2:21
the * lived there in their place. Deu 2:21
the cities of the *, and measures Deu 3:11
the * or the Moabites in any way. Deu 23:6
which is the boundary of the *. Jos 12:2
of the * and the Amalekites. Ju 3:13
the * to begin tormenting them. Ju 10:7,8
For the * crossed the Jordan to Ju 10:9
the Amorites, the *, the Ju 10:11
lead our forces against the *?" Ju 10:18
* began their war against Israel. Ju 11:4
and lead their army against the *. Ju 11:6
against the *, we will make you the Ju 11:8
Israel conquer the *, then when he Ju 11:30,31
army against the *, and the Lord Ju 11:32
He destroyed the * with a Ju 11:33
Thus the * were subdued by the Ju 11:33
victory over your enemies, the *. Ju 11:36
the army of the * against the 1Sa 11:1
attack against the * and 1Sa 11:11
attack them. The * defended the 2Sa 10:7,8
"And if the * are too strong for 2Sa 10:11
Then, when the * saw the Syrians 2Sa 10:14
to help the * anymore after that. 2Sa 10:19
the Israeli army to destroy the *. 2Sa 11:1
all of the cities of the *. 2Sa 12:31
Milcom, the horrible god of the *. 1Ki 11:5
the unutterably vile god of the *. 1Ki 11:7
and Milcom, the god of the *. 1Ki 11:33
for Milcom, the evil god of the *. 2Ki 23:13
Moabites, and * against Judah in 2Ki 24:2
Abishai, moved against the *. 1Ch 19:11
"and if the * are too strong for 1Ch 19:12
When the *, under attack by 1Ch 19:15
aid the * in their battles. 1Ch 19:19
For the * and Moabites turned 2Ch 20:23
the Meunites. The * paid annual 2Ch 26:8
His war against the * was 2Ch 27:5
Jebusites, *, Moabites, Egyptians, Ez 9:1
and the Arabians, *, and Ashdodites Neh 4:7
said that the * and Moabites should Neh 13:1
The Moabites and * were among Ps 83:8f
Edomites, *, Moabites, Arabs, and Jer 9:25,26
Moab and among the * and in Edom Jer 40:11
king of the *, had sent Ishmael Jer 40:13,14
toward the country of the *. Jer 41:10
of his men into the land of the *. Jer 41:15
The * Jer 49:1
fortunes of the *, says the Lord. Jer 49:6
Literally, "Rabbah of the *." Eze 21:19,20f
"Son of dust, prophesy to the * Eze 21:28
the country of the * into a waste Eze 25:5

AMMONITESS
was Naamah the *—he was buried 1Ki 14:31
mother's name was Naamah the *. 2Ch 12:13

AMMUNITION
No, I am giving you some good *! 2Co 5:12

AMNON
The oldest was *, born to his 2Sa 3:2
And Prince * (her half brother) 2Sa 13:1
in love with her. * became so 2Sa 13:2
to * to do anything to her." 2Sa 13:2f
But * had a very crafty 2Sa 13:3
One day Jonadab said to *, 2Sa 13:4
So * told him, "I am in love with 2Sa 13:4
So * did. And when the king came 2Sa 13:6
came to see him, * asked him for 2Sa 13:6
"Oh, *," she cried. 2Sa 13:12
"Is it true that * raped you? 2Sa 13:20
way or the other about this to *. 2Sa 13:21-24
sending my brother * instead?" 2Sa 13:26
"Why *?" 2Sa 13:26
of his sons attend, including *. 2Sa 13:27
men, "Wait until * gets drunk, 2Sa 13:28
So they murdered *. 2Sa 13:29,30
It was only *! 2Sa 13:32,33
this ever since * raped Tamar. 2Sa 13:32,33
It was only *." 2Sa 13:32,33
KING DAVID'S OLDEST son was *, 1Ch 3:1
*, Rinnah, Ben-hanan, Tilon. 1Ch 4:20

AMNON'S
to Tamar to go to * quarters and 2Sa 13:7
now reconciled to * death, longed 2Sa 13:37,38,39

AMOK
Joiarib, Jedaiah, Sallu, *, Neh 12:1
Eber, leader of the * clan; Neh 12:12-21

AMON
"Take him to *, the mayor of the 1Ki 22:26
and his son * became the new king. 2Ki 21:18
Name of the new king of Judah: * 2Ki 21:19,20
Manasseh, *, 1Ch 3:10-14
back to Governor * and to my son 2Ch 18:25
and his son * became the new king. 2Ch 33:20,21
the new king. * was twenty-two 2Ch 33:20,21
Manasseh; for * sacrificed to all 2Ch 33:22
Pochereth-hazzebaim, *. Neh 7:57,58,59
of Josiah (son of *) king of Judah, Jer 25:2,3
I will punish *, god of Thebes, and Jer 46:25
Josiah (son of *) king of Judah. Zep 1:1

AMON'S
* son Josiah upon the throne. 2Ki 21:24
The rest of * biography is 2Ki 21:25
of * son Josiah, king of Judah. Jer 1:1

AMORITE
to Mamre the * (brother of Eshcol Gen 14:13
for the wickedness of the * Gen 15:16
While Israel was there in the * Num 21:31,32
arriving among the * hills to which Deu 1:19,20,21
King Sihon the *, king of Heshbon. Deu 2:24
two * kings east of the Jordan. Deu 4:47
and Og, the two * kings east of the Jos 2:10
So these five * kings combined Jos 10:5
an * and your mother a Hittite! Eze 16:3
a Hittite and your father an *. Eze 16:45

AMORITES
nations:Jebusites, *, Gen 10:15-19
the * living in Hazazan-tamar. Gen 14:7
Rephaim, *, Canaanites, Gen 15:19,20,21
* with my sword and with my bow." Gen 48:22
Hittites, *, Perizzites, Hivites, Ex 3:8
Hittites, *, Perizzites, Hivites, Ex 3:17
Hittites, *, Hivites, and Ex 13:4,5
the land of the *, Hittites, Ex 23:23
the Canaanites, *, Hittites, Ex 33:2
before you the *, Canaanites, Ex 34:11
the Hittites, Jebusites, and *; Num 13:29
River, near the borders of the *. Num 21:13
between the Moabites and the *. Num 21:13
the * and the people of Moab. Num 21:15
to King Sihon of the *. Num 21:21
the cities of the * and lived in Num 21:25,26
By King Sihon of the *. Num 21:27-30
the towns and driving out the *. Num 21:31,32
had done to the *, he and his Num 22:2,3
King Sihon of the *, and of King Og Num 32:33
out the * who were living there. Num 32:39
King Sihon of the * had already Deu 1:1
country of the *, the valley of the Deu 1:7
to be slaughtered by these *. Deu 1:27
But the * who lived there came Deu 1:44
King Sihon of the *, at Heshbon.' Deu 3:1
two kings of the * east of the Deu 3:8
while the * called it 'Senir.' Deu 3:9
occupied by the * under King Deu 4:44,45,46
The *, the Canaanites, Deu 7:1
the Hittites, the *, the Deu 20:17
Sihon and Og, the kings of the *. Deu 31:4
Girgashites, *, and Jebusites—all Jos 3:10
Jordan River—the * and Canaanites Jos 5:1
are going to let the * kill us? Jos 7:7
Hittites, *, Canaanites, Jos 9:1
two kings of the *—Sihon, king of Jos 9:10
For all the kings of the * who Jos 10:6
The kings of the *; Jos 11:1
King Sihon of the *, who lived in Jos 12:2
the Hittites, the *, the Jos 12:8-24
to Aphek at the boundary of the * Jos 13:2-7
King Sihon of the *, who reigned in Jos 13:10
* on the other side of the Jordan; Jos 24:8
kings of the * and their people. Jos 24:12
gods of the * here in this land? Jos 24:15
who drove out the * and the other Jos 24:18
As for the tribe of Dan, the * Ju 1:34
but when the * later spread into Ju 1:35
The boundary of the * begins at Ju 1:36
Perizzites, *, and Jebusites. Ju 3:5
the gods of the * who live around Ju 6:10
in the land of the * (that is, in Ju 10:7,8
the Egyptians, the *, the Ju 10:11
King Sihon of the *, who lived in Ju 11:19
from the * and gave it to Israel. Ju 11:23
Israel and the * in those days. 1Sa 7:14
was left of the nation of the *. 2Sa 21:2
of the * and King Og of Bashan. 1Ki 4:8-19
he conquered—the *, Hittites, 1Ki 9:20,21
idols just as the * did—the people 1Ki 21:26
wicked than the * who were in this 2Ki 21:11
of the Jebusites, *, Girgashites, 1Ch 1:13-16

(AMORITES Con't)
the Hittites, *, Perizzites, 2Ch 8:7,8
Moabites, Egyptians, and *. Ez 9:1
Hittites, *, Perizzites, Jebusites, Neh 9:8
mighty kings— Sihon, king of *; Ps 135:11
Sihon, king of *—for God's Ps 136:19
cities of the *, deserted when the Is 17:9
The * and Hittites were nations Eze 16:3f
I cleared the land of the * Amo 2:9
before them—the *, as tall as cedar Amo 2:9
to possess the land of the *. Amo 2:10

AMOS
* WAS A herdsman living in the Amo 1:1
And the Lord said to me, "*, Amo 7:8
Bethel, heard what * was saying, he Amo 7:10
the king: "* is a traitor to our Amo 7:10
Then Amaziah sent orders to *, Amo 7:12
But * replied, "I am not really Amo 7:14
"What do you see, *?" Amo 8:2
Manasseh was the father of *; Mt 1:10
Amos; * was the father of Josiah; Mt 1:10
Mattathias' father was *; Lk 3:23-38
Mattathias' father was Amos;*' Lk 3:23-38
In the book of *' prophecies the Act 7:42
to this passage from the prophet * Act 15:15
Implied. See * 9:11-15f. Act 15:15f
Implied. See * 9:11-12. Act 15:16f

AMOUNT
that no one kept track of the *. Gen 41:49
be fined whatever * the woman's Ex 21:22
The judges will determine the *. Ex 21:30
* of the best of his own crop. Ex 22:5
the same * of cassia as of Ex 30:24
The * of silver used was 9,575 Ex 38:25,26
representing the entire *, Lev 2:2
to the priest the * he has used, Lev 22:14
pay almost the * he received when Lev 25:51
small part of the * he received Lev 25:52
poor to pay this *, he shall be Lev 27:8
man shall pay that * plus twenty Lev 27:14,15
the * of seed required to sow it. Lev 27:16
judged by the * of your harvest. Deu 16:10
of the vast * of loot they had 1Sa 30:16
a very large * of bronze from 2Sa 8:8
To gather this *, King Hezekiah 2Ki 18:15
as well as a great * of bronze from 1Ch 18:8
as the specific * of gold needed 1Ch 28:15
An immense * of lumber will be 2Ch 2:9
990 gallons of wine; any * of Ez 7:22
* of money could begin to cover." Est 7:4
Babylon, and no * of silver or gold Is 13:17
of evil men? No * of soap or lye Jer 2:22
His life will * to nothing. Jer 22:30
ram, and whatever * he is willing Eze 46:5
greater than the * planted—thirty, Mt 13:23f
this small *,' he told him, 'so now Mt 25:21
over this small *, so now I will Mt 25:23
times as much as the original *! Lk 19:16
gain—five times the original *. Lk 19:18
this offering. The * depends on how 1Co 16:2
A Christian who doesn't * to much Jas 1:9

AMOUNTED
to the warriors—* to:337,500 Num 31:42-46
The total value of their gifts * Ez 2:69

AMOUNTS
out the same * of each, using the Ex 30:34
Tremendous * of loot were carried 2Sa 12:29,30
him large * of money every year. 1Ch 18:6
David also took great * of 1Ch 20:2
They also contributed great * of 1Ch 29:8
and tremendous * of booty which 2Ch 28:8
their worship * to mere words Is 29:13
Some who were rich put in large * Mk 12:41

AMOZ
to Isaiah (son of *), the prophet, 2Ki 19:2
by the prophet Isaiah (son of *). 2Ch 26:22
prophet (son of *) cried out in 2Ch 32:20
the son of *), and in The Annals of 2Ch 32:32
to Isaiah, son of *, in the visions Is 1:1
of *) concerning Babylon's doom. Is 13:1
Isaiah, the son of *, to take off Is 20:2
Isaiah the prophet, son of *. Is 37:2
Then Isaiah, the son of *, sent Is 37:21
the prophet (*' son) went to visit Is 38:1

AMPHIPOLIS
the cities of * and Apollonia and Act 17:1

AMPHITHEATER
Everyone rushed to the *, Act 19:29

AMPLE
* crops, Deu 28:2-6
and with * pastures for your cows. Is 30:23

AMPLIATUS
Say "hello" to *, whom I love Rom 16:8

AMPLIFIED
* New Testament. Eph 4:15,16f

AMRAM
The sons of Kohath:*, Ex 6:18
And * Ex 6:20
* lived to the age of 137. Ex 6:20
grandsons (clan names) * Num 3:25-30
the wife of *, son of Kohath. Num 26:58,59
*, Izhar, Hebron, Uzziel. 1Ch 6:2
The sons of Kohath were:*, Izhar, 1Ch 6:18
*, Izhar, Hebron, and 1Ch 23:12
* was the ancestor of Aaron and 1Ch 23:13
Literally, "the sons of *: Aaron 1Ch 23:13f
the other descendants of Levi: *; 1Ch 24:20
*, Izhar, Hebron, and Uzziel. 1Ch 26:23,24
Ma-adai, *, Uel, Banaiah, Bedeiah, Ez 10:34-42

AMRAM'S
* descendants included: 1Ch 6:3

AMRAPHEL
*, king of Shinar, Gen 14:1

AMUSED
He is * by all their puny plans. Ps 2:4

AMUSEMENT
he said in *. Gen 17:17
and much to the * of their enemies— Ex 32:25

AMZI
Amaziah, Hilkiah, *, Bani, Shemer, 1Ch 6:44-47
Pelaliah, son of *, son of Neh 11:10-14

ANAB
Debir, *, Judah, and Israel; Jos 11:21
(or, Debir), *, Eshtemoh, Anim, Jos 15:48-62

ANACHRONISTIC
paraphrase is of course highly *! Mt 13:52f

ANAH
Oholibamah (daughter of * and Gen 36:2,3
(daughter of *):The clan of Gen 36:18,19
tribe of *,The tribe of Dishon,The Gen 36:20,21
*. (This is the boy who discovered Gen 36:24
The children of *:Dishon, Gen 36:25
Lotan, Shobal, Zibeon, *, Dishon, 1Ch 1:38,39
were Aiah and * . 1Ch 1:40

ANAH'S
* son was 1Ch 1:41

ANAHARATH
Hapharaim, Shion, *, Rabbith, Jos 19:17-23

ANAIAH
*, Uriah, Hilkiah, and Ma-aseiah. Neh 8:1
Hanan, *, Hoshea, Neh 10:14-27

ANAK
all families descended from *. Num 13:22
Among them are the famed * Deu 9:1
descendants of * who lived in the Jos 11:21
of *: Talmai, Sheshai, and Ahiman. Jos 15:14
was the father of *)—although the Jos 21:9-16
of the three sons of *. Ju 1:20

ANAK'S
had been named after * father. Jos 15:13

ANAKIM
and what's more, we saw * giants Num 13:28
we saw some of the * there, Num 13:33
there—the descendants of the *!' Deu 1:28
tribe, tall as the giants of *; Deu 2:10
both the Emim and the * are Deu 2:11
powerful tribe, as tall as the *; Deu 2:21
spies we found the * living there Jos 14:12
after a great hero of the *. Jos 14:15
O descendants of the *, how you Jer 47:5

ANALYZE
able to * them and interpret them. Ecc 8:1

ANAMIM
Ludim, *, Lehabim, Naphtuhim, Gen 10:13,14
the Ludim, the *, the Lehabim, the 1Ch 1:11,12

ANAMMELECH
of their gods Adrammelech and *. 2Ki 17:31

ANAN
Hanan, *, Malluch, Neh 10:14-27

ANANI
Akkub, Johanan, Delaiah, *. 1Ch 3:24

ANANIAH
Ma-aseiah, son of *) repaired the Neh 3:23
Anathoth, Nob, *, Neh 11:31-35

ANANIAS
BUT THERE WAS a man named * (with Act 5:1
But Peter said, "*, Satan has Act 5:3
As soon as * heard these words, Act 5:5
in Damascus a believer named *. Act 9:10
him in a vision, calling, "*!" Act 9:10
of a man named * coming in and Act 9:12
"But Lord," exclaimed *, "I Act 9:13
So * went over and found Paul and Act 9:17
There a man named *, as godly a Act 22:12
Instantly * the High Priest Act 23:2
FIVE DAYS LATER * the High Priest Act 24:1

ANARCHY
And the worst sort of * will Is 3:5
no king in Egypt; * shall reign! Eze 30:13
peace and bring * to the earth; Rev 6:4

ANATH
after Ehud was Shamgar (son of *). Ju 3:31

ANATHOTH
Gibeon, Gaba, *, and Almon. Jos 21:17,18
Abi-ezer from *; 2Sa 23:24-39
"Go back to your home in *. 1Ki 2:26
Geba, Alemeth, and *—were given to 1Ch 6:60
*, Alemeth. 1Ch 7:8
Abi-ezer from *; 1Ch 11:26-47
Jehu from *; 1Ch 12:3-7
was Abi-ezer (from * in the tribe 1Ch 27:12
From the subclan of *, 128; Ez 2:3-35
From the subclan of *, 128; Neh 7:8-38
*, Nebai, Magpiash, Neh 10:14-27
*, Nob, Ananiah, Neh 11:31-35
O poor *, what a fate is yours! Is 10:30
town of * in the land of Benjamin. Jer 1:1
men of the city of * shall be Jer 11:21,22
Not one of these plotters of * Jer 11:23
with mere men—these men of * Jer 12:5
this false prophet Jeremiah of *? Jer 29:27
farm he owns in *, for by law you Jer 32:6,7
"Buy my field in *, in the land Jer 32:8

ANCESTOR
Or, "the * of." Gen 4:18f
Or, "the * of." Gen 4:18f
Or, "the * of." Gen 4:18f
Or, "the * of." Gen 4:18f
son, the * (of Seth) was born." Gen 5:3,4,5f
"After this * of Seth was born." Gen 5:3,4,5f
(Ham is the * of the Canaanites. Gen 9:18
Ham was not the * of the Negro, as Gen 9:18f
Mizraim was the * Gen 10:13,14
Or, "*." Gen 10:26-30f
born to him the * of Shelah, and Gen 11:12,13f
he became the * of the nation of Gen 19:37
he became the * of the nation of Gen 19:38
in place of his * Aaron; Lev 16:32
named after their * Hanoch. Num 26:5-11
The Palluites, named after their * Num 26:5-11
named after their * Hezron. Num 26:5-11
The Carmites, named after their * Num 26:5-11
named after their * Nemu-el. Num 26:12-14
The Jaminites, named after their * Num 26:12-14
named after their * Jachin. Num 26:12-14
The Zerahites, named after their * Num 26:12-14
The Shaulites, named after their * Num 26:12-14
named after their * Zephon. Num 26:15-18
The Haggites, named after their * Num 26:15-18
The Shunites, named after their * Num 26:15-18
The Oznites, named after their * Num 26:15-18
The Erites, named after their * Num 26:15-18
The Arodites, named after their * Num 26:15-18
The Arelites, named after their * Num 26:15-18
named after their * Shelah. Num 26:19-22
The Perezites, named after their * Num 26:19-22
The Zerahites, named after their * Num 26:19-22
named after their * Hezron. Num 26:19-22
The Hamulites, named after their * Num 26:19-22
The Tolaites, named after their * Num 26:23-25
The Punites, named after their * Num 26:23-25
named after their * Jashub. Num 26:23-25
named after their * Shimron. Num 26:23-25
The Seredites, named after their * Num 26:26,27
The Elonites, named after their * Num 26:26,27
named after their * Jahleel. Num 26:26,27
named after their * Machir. Num 26:28-37
named after their * Gilead. Num 26:28-37
The Jezerites, named after their * Num 26:28-37
The Helekites, named after their * Num 26:28-37
named after their * Asriel. Num 26:28-37
named after their * Shechem. Num 26:28-37
named after their * Shemida. Num 26:28-37
named after their * Hepher. Num 26:28-37
named after their * Shuthelah. Num 26:28-37
their * Eran, a son of Shuthelah. Num 26:28-37
named after their * Becher. Num 26:28-37
The Tahanites, named after their * Num 26:28-37
The Bela-ites, named after their * Num 26:38-41
The Ardites, named after their * Num 26:38-41
The Naamites, named after their * Num 26:38-41
named after their * Ashbel. Num 26:38-41
named after their * Ahiram. Num 26:38-41
named after their * Shephupham. Num 26:38-41
named after their * Hupham. Num 26:38-41
The Imnites, named after their * Num 26:44-47
The Ishvites, named after their * Num 26:44-47
The Beriites, named after their * Num 26:44-47
The Heberites, named after their * Num 26:44-47
named after their * Malchi-el. Num 26:44-47
named after their * Jahzeel. Num 26:48-50
The Gunites, named after their * Num 26:48-50
The Jezerites, named after their * Num 26:48-50
named after their * Shillem. Num 26:48-50
named after their * Gershon. Num 26:57
named after their * Kohath. Num 26:57
The Merarites, named after their * Num 26:57
Their * was Machir, son of Num 27:1
"Dan," naming it after their *. Jos 19:47,48
after their *, Israel's son, but it Ju 18:29
as those of our * Perez, the son of Ru 4:12
Boaz, beginning with his * Perez: Ru 4:18-22
Didn't I choose your * Levi from 1Sa 2:28
He pleased the Lord like his * 1Ki 15:11
though not quite like his * David; 2Ki 14:3
the Lord as his * David had; 2Ki 16:2
(similar to that of his * David). 2Ki 18:1
Lord God of his * David has heard 2Ki 20:5
the steps of his * King David, 2Ki 22:1
Canaan was also the * of the 1Ch 1:13-16
Kiriath-jearim and Haroeh, the * 1Ch 2:52
Jahath, the * of Ahumai and Lahad. 1Ch 4:2
(the * of Gedor),Ezer (the ancestor 1Ch 4:3-4

(ANCESTOR Con't)
of Gedor),Ezer (the * of Hushah), 1Ch 4:3-4
he was also the * of the clan 1Ch 4:8
of Joab, the * of the inhabitants 1Ch 4:14
Shammai, and Ishbah—an * of 1Ch 4:17
Amram was the * of Aaron and 1Ch 23:13
by God through their * Aaron. 1Ch 24:19
Lord God of your * David says that 2Ch 21:12
king, unlike his * King David. 2Ch 28:1
just as his * David's had been. 2Ch 29:2
good example of his * King David. 2Ch 34:2
search for the God of his * David; 2Ch 34:3
him the throne of his * David. Lk 1:32
are you greater than our * Jacob? Jn 4:12
Spirit through our * King David, Act 4:25,26
appeared to our * Abraham in Iraq Act 7:2
Levi himself (the * of all Jewish Heb 7:9

ANCESTORS
the age of 137, and joined his *. Gen 25:17
"We are shepherds like our *. Gen 47:3
nearly as old as many of my *." Gen 47:9
Egypt and bury me beside my *." Gen 47:30
the God of your * Abraham, Isaac, Ex 3:15
the God of their * Abraham, Isaac, Ex 4:5
promised to your * long ago, where Ex 13:11
to their *, to be their God. Lev 26:45
to the land you promised their *? Num 11:12
I promised to this people's *. Num 14:23
history, how our * went down to Num 20:15
promised to your * Abraham, Isaac, Deu 1:8
you by the Lord God of your *. Deu 4:1
promises he has made to your *. Deu 4:31
"It was because he loved your * Deu 4:37
with your *, but with you who are Deu 5:2,3
he promised your *, Abraham, Deu 6:10,11,12
which the Lord promised your *. Deu 6:18
land he had promised to our *. Deu 6:23
he kept his promise to your *. Deu 7:8
unknown to both you and your *. Deu 8:3
to fulfill his promise to your *. Deu 8:18
promises to your *, Abraham, Isaac, Deu 9:5
When your * went down into Egypt Deu 10:22
promised to your * and to you, Deu 11:9
nation just as he promised your *. Deu 13:17
he promised your *, and gives you Deu 19:8
me to the land he promised our *.' Deu 26:2,3
Lord your God, 'My * were migrant Deu 26:5
given us, as you promised our *; Deu 26:15
nor your * gave a second thought; Deu 28:36
you nor your * have known, gods Deu 28:64
your *, Abraham, Isaac, and Jacob. Deu 29:13
the God of their *, when he brought Deu 29:25
back again to the land of your *. Deu 30:5
you even more than he did your *! Deu 30:5
*, Abraham, Isaac, and Jacob." Deu 30:20
promised by the Lord to their *; Deu 31:7
"You shall die and join your *. Deu 31:16
I promised their *—a land 'flowing Deu 31:20
die and join your *, just as Aaron Deu 32:50
the land I promised to their *. Jos 1:6
promised to their *, and they went Jos 21:43
Israel says, 'Your *, including Jos 24:2
idols which your * worshiped when Jos 24:14
Will it be the gods of your * Jos 24:15
I promised to your *, and I said Ju 2:1
worshiped by their *—the God who Ju 2:12-14
faith of their *, for they refused Ju 2:17
even worse than their * had. Ju 2:19
I made with their *, I will no Ju 2:20
obey the Lord as their * did." Ju 2:22
the miracles our * have told us Ju 6:13
"He brought your * out of the 1Sa 12:6
has done for you and for your *: 1Sa 12:7
upon you as it was upon your *. 1Sa 12:15
instructions he has given our *. 1Ki 8:58
even worse than that of their *. 1Ki 14:22
buried among his * in Jerusalem, 1Ki 14:31
So Ahab was buried among his *, 1Ki 22:40
buried with his * in Jerusalem, the 1Ki 22:50
objects that his *—Jehoshaphat, 2Ki 12:18
buried with his * in the City of 2Ki 15:7
Lord's opinion, just like his *. 2Ki 15:9
had given to their * through these 2Ki 17:13
stubborn as their * and refused to 2Ki 17:14
*, and despised all his warnings. 2Ki 17:15
All the treasures of your * will 2Ki 20:17
I brought their * from Egypt." 2Ki 21:15
his back on the Lord God of his *. 2Ki 21:22
* have followed your commands." 2Ki 22:12,13
of * and descendants. 1Ch 1:1f
(the * of the Philistines). 1Ch 1:11,12
respectively, the * of the 1Ch 4:18
just as their * had supervised and 1Ch 9:19
of the Lord God of their *. 2Ch 14:4
to worship the God of their *. 2Ch 19:4
You wouldn't let our * invade 2Ch 20:10
to follow the God of their *. 2Ch 20:33
the God of their *, and to worship 2Ch 24:17,18
forsaken the Lord God of their *. 2Ch 24:24
Lord God of your *—clean all the 2Ch 29:4,5
rescue his people from me or my *; 2Ch 32:15
this land which I gave your *." 2Ch 33:8
us is that our * have not obeyed 2Ch 34:21
Jehovah, the God of their *. 2Ch 34:33
corps of your *, as first organized 2Ch 35:4,5
But afterwards our * angered the Ez 5:12
Lord God of our *, who made the Ez 7:27
For the city where my * are Neh 2:3
own sins and those of their *. Neh 9:3
and sorrows of our * in Egypt, and Neh 9:9
You led our * by a pillar of Neh 9:12
but our * were a proud and Neh 9:16
land you had promised to their *. Neh 9:23
and prophets and * from the days Neh 9:32
priests, and * didn't obey your Neh 9:34
of plenty which you gave to our *! Neh 9:36
their fathers—our * to whom alone Job 15:17-19
From the very first your * Is 43:27
Yes, think about your * Abraham Is 51:1
gave to you and to your * forever. Jer 25:5
THESE ARE THE * of Jesus Christ, a Mt 1:1
"He has been merciful to our *, Lk 1:72,73
For you are exactly like your * Lk 11:47
where our * worshiped?" Jn 4:20
and of all our * who has brought Act 3:13
promise to your * to bless the Act 3:25
The God of our * brought Jesus Act 5:30
there was great misery for our *. Act 7:11
*—of Abraham, Isaac and Jacob.' Act 7:32
"Our * carried along with them a Act 7:44
Name one prophet your * didn't Act 7:52
Israel chose our * and honored them Act 13:17
promise to our * has come true in Act 13:32,33
I am a Pharisee, as were all my *! Act 23:6
of serving the God of our *; Act 24:14
of God's promise made to our *. Act 26:6
nor violated the customs of our *. Act 28:17
is no record of any of his *. Heb 7:3

ANCESTRAL
Heshbon—Sihon's * home—and devours Jer 48:45
his * home for this registration. Lk 2:3

ANCESTRIES
These are the names and * 1Ch 6:33-38

ANCESTRY
Merari's * was traced back 1Ch 6:44-47
Shallum's * went back through 1Ch 9:19
the basis of their * and ability at 1Ch 26:31,32
could not prove their Jewish *; Neh 7:61

ANCHOR
But the good man has a strong *. Pro 10:25
so they pulled up * and sailed Act 27:13
and trustworthy * for our souls, Heb 6:19

ANCHORED
but I am firmly * to your laws. Ps 119:61

ANCHORS
threw out four * from the stern and Act 27:29
going to put out * from the prow. Act 27:30
Cutting off the * and leaving Act 27:40

ANCIENT
In many of the languages of the * Lev 2:13f
(By the way, Hebron was very *, Num 13:22
was pronounced in * times) was Num 13:22f
of the * race of giants. Num 13:33
capital. The * poets had referred Num 21:27-30
road to Egypt ever since * times. 1Sa 27:8
You are destroying an *, 2Sa 20:19
These names all come from very * 1Ch 4:21-22
of this division in * times. 1Ch 9:20
We suggest that you search the * Ez 4:15
those treading the * paths of sin Job 22:15,16
Open up, O * gates, and let the Ps 24:7
who rides upon the * heavens, whose Ps 68:33
ones you chose in * times from Ps 74:2
Do not move the * boundary marks. Pro 22:28
by moving their * boundary marks, Pro 23:10,11
Or, "Rezin's enemies," in some * Is 9:11,12f
you all this power from * times? Is 37:26
do as I have done since * times. Is 44:7
In * Babylonia (and in many Is 47:2f
And they shall rebuild the * Is 61:4
the Lord—a mighty nation, an * Jer 5:15
They have turned away from the * Jer 18:15
these people. The * prophets who Jer 28:8
at the site of * Mizpah. Jer 41:9f
These were three cities of * North Eze 27:10f
A region in * Cilicia known from Eze 27:11f
I will cause the * glory of Israel Eze 29:21
and claimed your * heights as Eze 36:2
other of the * manuscripts, reads, Eze 40:29,30f
in place and the * of Days—the Dan 7:9
he approached the * of Days and Dan 7:13
until the * of Days came and Dan 7:22
"But then the * of Days will Dan 7:26
parallel to this * practice used by Hos 4:12f
And remember, the * prophets were Mt 5:12
disobey the * Jewish traditions?" Mt 15:2
in many of the * manuscripts. Mt 17:21f
in many manuscripts, some *. Mt 18:11f
is added in some * manuscripts. Mt 19:9f
This was done to fulfill the * Mt 21:4
Many * manuscripts omit this Mt 24:36f
Some * manuscripts read, "the Mk 1:3f
was Elijah the * prophet, now Mk 6:15
as required by their * Mk 7:3
in many of the * manuscripts. Mk 7:15,16f
or some other * prophet come back Mk 8:28
manuscripts, but not the most *. Mk 9:29f
in some of the * manuscripts. Mk 9:43,44f
in some of the * manuscripts. Mk 9:45,46f
Some of the * manuscripts do not Mk 10:24f
Many * authorities add verse 26, Mk 11:26,f
Some * manuscripts read, "new Mk 14:24f
in some of the * manuscripts. Mk 15:28f
found in the most * manuscripts, Mk 16:9f
Some * manuscripts omit Mk 16:17f
Some * versions add, "Blessed are Lk 1:28f
King David's * home—journeying Lk 2:4
good company—the * prophets were Lk 6:23
just as the * prophets predicted. Lk 8:10
in some of the * manuscripts. Lk 8:43,44f
* prophet risen from the dead." Lk 9:8
* prophets risen from the dead." Lk 9:19
Some * manuscripts add at this Lk 11:5,6f
Implied by * custom. Lk 12:53f
predictions of the * prophets Lk 18:31
and the words of the * Scriptures Lk 21:22
Some * authorities add verse 17, Lk 23:17,f
Many of the * manuscripts omit the Jn 5:4f
in the text of many * manuscripts. Jn 7:8f
Most * manuscripts omit John Jn 7:53f
sin, as prophesied from * times. Act 3:21,22
Many * manuscripts omit verse 37 Act 8:37f
adhered to the * Jewish custom of Act 15:1
in many of the * manuscripts. Act 18:21f
Some of the * manuscripts add, Act 28:28,29f
Some * manuscripts read, 1Co 11:24f
We are told in the * Scriptures 1Co 14:21
who lived in * times before the 2Pe 2:5
This great Dragon—the * serpent Rev 12:9

ANCIENTS
by which * thought they could Eze 21:21f

ANDREW
called Peter, and *—out in a boat Mt 4:18
* (Peter's brother), Mt 10:2,3,4
and his brother * fishing with Mk 1:16
*, Philip Mk 3:16-19
James, John, and * got alone with Mk 13:3,4
* (Simon's brother), Lk 6:14,15,16
(One of these men was *, Simon Jn 1:40
* then went to find his brother Jn 1:41
(Philip was from Bethsaida, * Jn 1:44
Then *, Simon Peter's brother, Jn 6:8,9
Philip told * about it, and Jn 12:22
*, Philip Act 1:14

ANDREW'S
over to Simon and * home, where Mk 1:29,30

ANDRONICUS
Then there are * and Junias, my Rom 16:7

ANEM
Ramoth, and *, and the surrounding 1Ch 6:73

ANER
of Eshcol and *, Abram's allies). Gen 14:13
*, Eshcol, and Mamre, my allies." Gen 14:24
*, Bile-am. 1Ch 6:70

ANEW
to set its hope * on God and not Ps 78:7

ANGEL
she ran away. The * of the Lord Gen 16:7
The *: "Hagar, Sarai's maid, Gen 16:8
The *: "Return to your mistress Gen 16:9-12
"All right," the * said, "I Gen 19:21
cries, and the * of God called to Gen 21:17
At that moment the * of God Gen 22:11
in any way," the * said, "for I Gen 22:12
Then the * of God called again to Gen 22:15
He will send his * on ahead of Gen 24:7
will send his * with you and make Gen 24:40
Then, in my dream, the * of God Gen 31:11
has done to you,' the * said. Gen 31:12
He is the * who has kept me from Gen 48:16
God, suddenly the * of Jehovah Ex 3:2
Then the * of God, who was Ex 14:19
"See, I am sending an * before Ex 23:20
For my * shall go before you and Ex 23:23
my * shall travel on ahead of you; Ex 32:34
I will send an * before you to Ex 33:2
us and sent an * who brought us out Num 20:16
so he sent an * to stand in the Num 22:22,23
suddenly saw the * of the Lord Num 22:22,23
Now the * of the Lord stood at a Num 22:24
Then the * of the Lord moved Num 22:26
and he saw the * standing in the Num 22:31
the * demanded. Num 22:32
But the * told him, "Go with the Num 22:35
the death * passed over the oldest Num 28:16
gave each of them a supervising *! Deu 32:8
ONE DAY THE * of the Lord arrived Ju 2:1
tears as the * finished speaking; Ju 2:4
But the * of Jehovah Ju 5:23
But one day the * of the Lord Ju 6:11
The * of the Lord appeared to him Ju 6:12
"All right," the * agreed. Ju 6:18
took it out to the *, who was Ju 6:19

(ANGEL Con't)
The * said to him, "Place the Ju 6:20
instructions, the * touched the Ju 6:21
And suddenly the * was gone! Ju 6:21
indeed been the * of the Lord, he Ju 6:22
the * of the Lord face to face!" Ju 6:22
Then one day the * of the Lord Ju 13:2,3
She had no children, but the * Ju 13:2,3
he must be the * of the Lord, for Ju 13:6
prayer, and the * of God appeared Ju 13:9
And the * replied, "Be sure that Ju 13:13,14
Then Manoah said to the *, Ju 13:15
"I'll stay," the * replied, Ju 13:16
that he was the * of the Lord. Ju 13:16
he said to the *, "we will Ju 13:17
"Don't even ask my name," the * Ju 13:18
and the * did a strange and Ju 13:19
the * ascended in the fire! Ju 13:20
it had been the * of the Lord. Ju 13:21
you're as perfect as an * of God. 1Sa 29:9
I know that you are like the * 2Sa 14:17
But you are as wise as an * of 2Sa 14:20
But I know that you are as an * 2Sa 19:27
But as the death * was preparing 2Sa 24:16
When David saw the *, he said to 2Sa 24:17
feet long, so each * measured 1Ki 6:23-28
and an * gave me a message from 1Ki 13:18
But as he was sleeping, an * 1Ki 19:5
Then the * of the Lord came again 1Ki 19:7
made, until one * approached the 1Ki 22:21
But an * of the Lord told Elijah 2Ki 1:3
Then the * of the Lord said to 2Ki 1:15
That very night the * of the Lord 2Ki 19:35
plague as the * of the Lord brings 1Ch 21:12
During the plague God sent an * 1Ch 21:15
the destroying *, "Stop! 1Ch 21:15
(The * of the Lord was standing 1Ch 21:15
When David saw the * of the 1Ch 21:16
Then the * of the Lord told Gad 1Ch 21:18
Ornan saw the * as he turned, and 1Ch 21:19,20
Then the Lord commanded the * to 1Ch 21:27
drawn sword of the * of Jehovah. 1Ch 21:30
the Lord sent an * who destroyed 2Ch 32:21
Or, "and if the * says." Job 33:23,24f
For the * of the Lord guards and Ps 34:7
sent by the * of the Lord. Ps 35:5
the * of the Lord pursuing them. Ps 35:6
What mightiest * Ps 89:6
The Lord of Hosts will send his * Is 10:26
That night the * of the Lord went Is 37:36
Or, "The * of his Presence saved Is 63:9f
for he sent his * to deliver his Dan 3:28
"Then you saw God's * Dan 4:23
"My God has sent his *," he Dan 6:22
Only Michael, the * who guards Dan 10:20,21
of God's * (Isaiah 36-37). Hos 1:7f
Yes, he wrestled with the * and Hos 12:4
An * stood beside me, and I asked Zec 1:9
horse—he was the * of the Zec 1:10
reported to the * of the Lord, "We Zec 1:11
Upon hearing this, the * of the Zec 1:12
And the Lord answered the * who Zec 1:13
Then the * said, "Shout out this Zec 1:14
I asked the *. Zec 1:19
The * replied, "They have come to Zec 1:21
Then the * who was talking to me Zec 2:3
meet another * coming toward him. Zec 2:3
said the other *, "that Jerusalem Zec 2:4
THEN THE * showed me (in my Zec 3:1
standing before the * of the Lord; Zec 3:1
he stood before the * of the Lord. Zec 3:3
Then the * said to the others Zec 3:4
Then the * of the Lord spoke very Zec 3:5,6
THEN THE * who had been talking Zec 4:1
the * asked. Zec 4:5
Then the * left me for awhile, Zec 5:5
I asked the *. Zec 5:10
I asked the *. Zec 6:4
as God, like the * of the Lord who Zec 12:8
and saw an * standing beside him. Mt 1:20
"Joseph, son of David," the * Mt 1:20
he did as the * commanded, and Mt 1:24
After they were gone, an * of the Mt 2:13
his mother," the * said, "and Mt 2:13
When Herod died, an * of the Lord Mt 2:19
for an * of the Lord came down Mt 28:2
Then the * spoke to the women. Mt 28:5
* said, "Don't be so surprised. Mk 16:6
when suddenly an * appeared, Lk 1:11,12
But the * said, "Don't be Lk 1:13
Zacharias said to the *, "But Lk 1:18
Then the * said, "I am Gabriel! Lk 1:19
month God sent the * Gabriel to Lk 1:26
to think what the * could mean. Lk 1:29
Mary," the * told her, "for God Lk 1:30
Mary asked the *, "But how can I Lk 1:34
The * replied, "The Holy Spirit Lk 1:35
And then the * disappeared. Lk 1:38
Suddenly an * appeared among Lk 2:9
but the * reassured them. Lk 2:10
Suddenly, the * was joined by a Lk 2:13
and what the * had said to them Lk 2:17
just as the * had told them. Lk 2:20
* before he was even conceived. Lk 2:21
Then an * from heaven appeared Lk 22:43
the water, for an * of the Lord Jn 5:4
declared an * had spoken to him. Jn 12:29
But an * of the Lord came at Act 5:19
Mount Sinai, an * appeared to him Act 7:30
of Israel and the * who gave them Act 7:38
the plan shown to Moses by the *. Act 7:44
But as for Philip, an * of the Act 8:26
saw an * of God coming toward him. Act 10:3
the * said. Act 10:3
he asked the *. Act 10:4
And the * replied, "Your prayers Act 10:4
As soon as the * was gone, Act 10:7
Jews, and how an * had instructed Act 10:22
He told us how an * had appeared Act 11:13
can be saved!' the * had told him. Act 11:14
* of the Lord stood beside Peter! Act 12:7
beside Peter! The * slapped him on Act 12:7
Then the * told him, "Get Act 12:8
the * ordered. Act 12:8
left the cell, following the *. Act 12:9
a block, and then the * left him. Act 12:10
"The Lord has sent his * and Act 12:11
they decided, "It must be his *. Act 12:15
Instantly, an * of the Lord Act 12:23
"Perhaps a spirit or * spoke to Act 23:9
"For last night an * of the God Act 27:23
God sent his * to destroy them. 1Co 10:10
himself into an * of light, so is 2Co 11:14
yes, if an * comes from heaven Gal 1:8
though I were an * from God, or Gal 4:14
For God never said to any *, Heb 1:5,6
And did God ever say to an *, as Heb 1:13
* but as a human being—yes, a Jew. Heb 2:16
death: for an * was sent to Heb 5:7f
God's terrible * of Death could not Heb 11:28
and then an * was sent from Rev 1:1
Literally, "*," as in 1:20. Rev 2:1f
Literally, "*." Rev 2:8f
Literally, "*." Rev 2:12f
Literally, "*." Rev 2:18f
Literally, "*." Rev 3:1f
Literally, "*." Rev 3:7f
Literally, "*." Rev 3:14f
A mighty * with a loud voice was Rev 5:2
And I saw another * coming from Rev 7:2
Then another * with a golden Rev 8:3
where the * had poured them out. Rev 8:4
Then the * filled the censer with Rev 8:5
The first * blew his trumpet, and Rev 8:7
Then the second * blew his Rev 8:8,9
The third * blew, and a great Rev 8:10
The fourth * blew his trumpet and Rev 8:12
THEN THE FIFTH * blew his trumpet Rev 9:1
The sixth * blew his trumpet and Rev 9:13
to the sixth *, "Release the four Rev 9:14
THEN I SAW another mighty * coming Rev 10:1
Then the mighty * standing on the Rev 10:5
when the seventh * blew his Rev 10:7
from the mighty * standing there Rev 10:8
For just then the seventh * blew Rev 11:15
And I saw another * flying Rev 14:6
Then another * followed him Rev 14:8
Then a third * followed them Rev 14:9
Then an * came from the temple Rev 14:15
After that another * came from Rev 14:17
Just then the * who has power to Rev 14:18
shouted to the * with the sickle, Rev 14:18
So the * swung his sickle on Rev 14:19
So the first * left the temple Rev 16:2
The second * poured out his flask Rev 16:3
The third * poured out his flask Rev 16:4
And I heard this * of the waters Rev 16:5
And I heard the * of the altar Rev 16:7
Then the fourth * poured out his Rev 16:8
Then the fifth * poured out his Rev 16:10
The sixth * poured out his flask Rev 16:12
Then the seventh * poured out his Rev 16:17
So the * took me in spirit into Rev 17:3
the * asked. Rev 17:7
AFTER ALL THIS I saw another * Rev 18:1
Then a mighty * picked up a Rev 18:21
And the * Rev 19:9
Then I saw an * standing in the Rev 19:17
THEN I SAW an * come down from Rev 20:1
The * held in his hand a golden Rev 21:15
feet across (the * called out these Rev 21:17
an angel's! The * used normal units Rev 21:17f
Then the * said to me, "These Rev 22:6,7
has sent his * to tell you this Rev 22:6,7
the * who showed them to me; Rev 22:8
I, Jesus, have sent my * to you Rev 22:16

ANGEL'S
They ate * food! Ps 78:25
and Satan was there too, at the * Zec 3:1
to give them the * message. Mt 28:8
face become as radiant as an *! Act 6:15
length of a man's arm—not an *! Rev 21:17f

ANGELIC
The highest of * powers Ps 89:7
the mighty * prince who stands Dan 12:1
believe from this that an * Rev 1:20f

ANGELS
and placed mighty * at the east of Gen 3:24
THAT EVENING THE two * came to Gen 19:1
At dawn the next morning the * Gen 19:15
When Lot still hesitated, the * Gen 19:16
"Flee for your lives," the * Gen 19:17
and he saw the * of God going up Gen 28:12
And the * of God came to meet Gen 32:1
Then make images of *, Ex 25:18
The cherubim—the *—shall be Ex 25:20
by ten thousands of holy *, Deu 33:2
who is enthroned above the *. 1Sa 4:4
Solomon placed two statues of * 1Ki 6:23-28
The two * were identical in all 1Ki 6:23-28
Figures of *, palm trees, and 1Ki 6:29
back upon itself. *, palm trees, 1Ki 6:35
with carved lions, oxen, and *. 1Ki 7:27-30
it under the wings of the *. 1Ki 8:6
the angels. The * had been 1Ki 8:7
stuck out past the * and could be 1Ki 8:8
on your throne high above the *, 2Ki 19:15
Lord God enthroned above the *. 1Ch 13:6
and for the gold * whose wings were 1Ch 28:18
with * engraved on the walls. 2Ch 3:7
of *, and plated them with gold. 2Ch 3:10
fine-spun linen, decorated with *. 2Ch 3:14
placed it beneath the *' wings; 2Ch 5:7,8
surrounded by vast throngs of *. 2Ch 18:18
and all the * of heaven worship Neh 9:6
One day as the * Job 1:6
NOW THE * Job 2:1
(for even * make mistakes), how Job 4:18,19
Why, God doesn't even trust the *! Job 15:15
is able to number his hosts of *? Job 25:3
and all the * shouted for joy? Job 38:6,7
only a little lower than the *, Ps 8:5
PRAISE THE LORD, you * of his; Ps 29:1
them a band of destroying *. Ps 78:49
myriads of * Ps 89:5
For he orders his * to protect Ps 91:11
Bless the Lord, you mighty * of Ps 103:20
of his * who serve him constantly. Ps 103:21
upon the wings of the wind. The * Ps 104:4
praises before the armies of * Ps 138:1
Praise him, all his *, all the Ps 148:2
ascend to heaven and rule the *. Is 14:13
punish the fallen * in the heavens, Is 24:21
Probably a symbol of the *. Eze 28:14f
dreaming, I saw one of God's * Dan 4:13
Millions of * ministered to him Dan 7:10
Then I heard two of the holy * Dan 8:13
Hebrew: "two others," probably * Dan 12:5f
out of my presence with these *. Zec 3:7
come, and all his saints and * Zec 14:5
* to keep you from harm,' Mt 4:6
Then Satan went away, and * came Mt 4:11
and the reapers are the *. Mt 13:39
will send my * and they will Mt 13:41
—the * will come and separate the Mt 13:49
shall come with my * in the glory Mt 16:27
their * have constant access Mt 18:10
everyone is as the * in heaven. Mt 22:30
And I shall send forth my * with Mt 24:31
the end will be—not even the *. Mt 24:36
glory, and all the * with me, then Mt 25:31
for thousands of * to protect us, Mt 26:53
the * came and cared for him. Mk 1:12,13
of my Father, with the holy *." Mk 8:38
married—they will be like the *. Mk 12:25
And I will send out the * to Mk 13:27
"However, no one, not even the * Mk 13:32
When this great army of * had Lk 2:15
the visit of the *, and because Lk 2:20
God will send his * to guard you Lk 4:9,10,11
and the holy *, I will be ashamed Lk 9:26
presence of God's * if you publicly Lk 12:8
But I will deny before the * Lk 12:9
presence of the * of God when one Lk 15:10
was carried by the * to be with Lk 16:22
in these respects they are like * Lk 20:36
they had seen some * there who told Lk 24:22,23
open and the * of God coming back Jn 1:51
two white-robed * sitting at the Jn 20:12
the * asked her. Jn 20:13
them from the hands of *." Act 7:53
Law as it was ordained by *." Act 7:53f
no resurrection or * or even Act 23:8
life can't. The * won't, and all Rom 8:38
be stared at by men and * alike. 1Co 4:9
and reward the very * in heaven? 1Co 6:3
a fact for all the * to notice 1Co 11:10
Literally, "because of the *." 1Co 11:10f
The * 1Co 15:40
God gave his laws to * to give to Gal 3:19
without * or Moses as go-betweens. Gal 3:20
worship *, as they say you must. Col 2:18
with his mighty *, bringing 2Th 1:7

ANGELS Con't)

endless chain of * leading up to 1Ti 1:3,4
was served by *, was preached among 1Ti 3:16
and of the holy * to do this 1Ti 5:21
greater than the *, as proved by Heb 1:4
the names and titles of the *. Heb 1:4
all the * of God worship him." Heb 1:5,6
God speaks of his * as messengers Heb 1:7
No, for the * are only Heb 1:14
For since the messages from * Heb 2:2
about will not be controlled by *. Heb 2:5
him lower than the * for a little Heb 2:7
lower than the *—crowned now by God Heb 2:9
were statues of * called the Heb 9:5
gathering of countless happy *; Heb 12:22
* without realizing it! Heb 13:2
that even the * in heaven would 1Pe 1:12
with all the * and powers of heaven 1Pe 3:22
For God did not spare even the * 2Pe 2:4
although the * in heaven who stand 2Pe 2:11
And I remind you of those * who Jud 1:6
mightiest of the *, when he was Jud 1:9
Literally, "*." Rev 1:20f
Father and his * that he is mine. Rev 3:5
of millions of * surrounding the Rev 5:11
THEN I SAW four * standing at the Rev 7:1
out to those four * who had been Rev 7:2
And now all the * were crowding Rev 7:11
And I saw the seven * that stand Rev 8:2
Then the seven * with the seven Rev 8:6
remaining * blow their trumpets." Rev 8:13
Literally, "(fallen) *." Rev 9:14f
Michael and the * under his Rev 12:7
Dragon and his hosts of fallen *. Rev 12:7
of the holy * and the Lamb. Rev 14:10
to come: Seven * were assigned to Rev 15:1
The seven * who were assigned to Rev 15:6
until the seven * had completed Rev 15:8
to the seven *, "Now go your ways Rev 16:1
ONE OF THE seven * who had poured Rev 17:1
Then one of the seven *, who had Rev 21:9
twelve gates guarded by twelve *. Rev 21:12

ANGER

So he called it, "The Well of * Gen 26:21
For in their * they murdered a Gen 49:6
Cursed be their *, for it is Gen 49:7
Then, red-faced with *, Moses Ex 11:8
You sent forth your *, and it Ex 15:7
And my * shall flame out against Ex 22:24
Now let me alone and my * shall Ex 32:10
"why is your * so hot against your Ex 32:11
and in terrible * he threw the Ex 32:19
he said, "slow to * and rich in Ex 34:5,6
let loose my great * and send you Lev 26:28
his fierce * against their sins." Num 1:53
heard them. His * flared out Num 11:1
and the * of the Lord grew hot; Num 11:10
the meat, the * of the Lord rose Num 11:33
Then the * of the Lord grew hot Num 12:9
for God's * has gone out among Num 16:46
Let your * rise on Israel.' Num 23:7-10
Striking his hands together in * Num 24:10
and the * of the Lord was hot Num 25:3
so that his fierce * will turn away Num 25:4
has turned away my *, for he was Num 25:10,11
And the Lord's * was hot against Num 32:10,11
you, so Jehovah's * against Israel Num 32:14
is thrown without *, without Num 35:22,23
God, and his * may rise quickly Deu 6:15
Then the * of the Lord would be Deu 7:4
thus provoking him to great *. Deu 9:18
For if you do, the * of the Lord Deu 11:17
from his fierce * and be merciful Deu 13:17
not pardon! His * and jealousy will Deu 29:20
destroyed by the Lord in his *. Deu 29:23
That is why the * of the Lord Deu 29:27
In great * the Lord rooted them Deu 29:28
Then my * will flame out against Deu 31:17
For my * has kindled a fire Deu 32:22
And so the fierce * of the Lord Jos 7:26
has given you. His * will rise hot Jos 23:15,16
So the * of the Lord flamed out Ju 2:12-14
Then the * of the Lord would Ju 2:20
Then the * of the Lord flamed out Ju 3:8
afraid of Saul's *, and they came 1Sa 11:7
table in fierce * and refused to 1Sa 20:34
Then the * of the Lord flared 2Sa 6:7
ONCE AGAIN THE * of the Lord 2Sa 24:1
Let your * be only against me and 2Sa 24:17
and did more to * the Lord God of 1Ki 16:33
and my * can't be stopped. 2Ki 22:17
back his great * against Judah, 2Ki 23:26
So the Lord finally, in his *, 2Ki 24:20
Then the * of the Lord blazed 1Ch 13:10
* of God broke out upon Israel; 1Ch 27:24
to pour out my * upon Jerusalem. 2Ch 12:7
the Lord's * was turned aside and 2Ch 12:12
* of the Lord is upon you." 2Ch 28:11
fierce * will turn away from us. 2Ch 29:10
fierce * will turn away from you. 2Ch 30:8
proud, and so the * of God was upon 2Ch 32:25
the Lord's great * has been poured 2Ch 34:21
prophets until the * of the Lord 2Ch 36:16
Surely your * will destroy us now Ez 9:14
and * throughout your realm. Est 1:18
BUT AFTER KING Ahasuerus' * had Est 2:1
overcome by their own *. Job 5:2
overturning them in his *. Job 9:5
"And God does not abate his *. Job 9:13
forget me there until your * ends; Job 14:13
by your *, with flashing eyes? Job 15:12
your clothes in *, is this going to Job 18:4
he distributes his sorrows and *. Job 21:17
Let him drink deeply of the * of Job 21:20
does not instantly respond in *? Job 35:14,15
But the godless reap his *. Job 36:13
Don't let your * at others lead Job 36:18
Give vent to your *. Job 40:11
before his * is roused and you Ps 2:12
punish me in the heat of your *. Ps 6:1
Arise in * against the anger of Ps 7:6
Arise in anger against the * of Ps 7:6
holy name. His * lasts a moment; Ps 30:5
Stop your *! Ps 37:8
Because of your * my body is Ps 38:3,4
The nations rant and rave in * Ps 46:6
Don't let them, Lord. In * cast Ps 56:7
with the fierceness of your *. Ps 69:24
Why is your * hot against us—the Ps 74:1
Has he slammed the door in * on Ps 77:9
mouths, when the * of the Lord Ps 78:31
many a time he held back his *. Ps 78:38
his *, sending sorrow and trouble. Ps 78:49
He gave free course to his * and Ps 78:50
because his * was intense. Ps 78:62
your blazing *, is now ended. Ps 85:3
O Lord, so that your * will never Ps 85:4
We die beneath your *; Ps 90:7
can realize the terrors of your *? Ps 90:11
Turn away your * from us. Ps 90:13
because of your * against me, Ps 102:9,10
That is why Jehovah's * burned Ps 106:40
many kings in the day of his *. Ps 110:5
they will gnash their teeth in * Ps 112:10
our enemies, destroyed by their *. Ps 124:2,3
his family to * and resentment will Pro 11:29
He knows that * causes mistakes. Pro 14:29
The * of the king is a messenger Pro 16:14
His * shuts you out like iron Pro 18:19
A wise man restrains his * and Pro 19:11
The king's * is as dangerous as a Pro 19:12
to rouse his * is to risk your Pro 20:2
just as surely a retort causes *! Pro 25:23
more dangerous and cruel than *. Pro 27:4
A rebel shouts in *; Pro 29:11
bleeding, so * causes quarrels. Pro 30:33
pour out my * on you, my enemies! Is 1:24
That is why the * of the Lord is Is 5:25
But even so, his * is not ended; Is 5:25
by the fierce * of those two Is 7:4
And even then the Lord's * Is 9:11,12
That is why his * is not yet Is 9:17
God's * is not yet satisfied. Is 9:21
And even then my * will not be Is 10:4
Assyria is the whip of my *; Is 10:5,6
in a little while my * against Is 10:25
to do this work, to satisfy my *. Is 13:3
They carry his * with them and Is 13:5
day of his wrath and fierce *. Is 13:9
wrath and fierce *, and the earth Is 13:13
enemies away. My * against Israel Is 27:4,5
suddenly and in *, as at Mount Is 28:21
Because of your * against the Is 37:29
back my * and not wipe you out. Is 48:9
save you from my * and not destroy Is 48:11
and fear their * all day long? Is 51:13
In a moment of * I turned my Is 54:8
again pour out my * on you as I Is 54:9
you in my *, I will have mercy on Is 60:10
nations in my * and made them Is 63:6
for I will put aside my * and Is 65:16
the fury of his * and his hot Is 66:15
"I haven't done a thing to * God. Jer 2:35
bodies, or else my * will burn you Jer 4:4
* of the Lord has not stopped yet. Jer 4:8
Lord, and crushed by his fierce *. Jer 4:26
They shall die beneath my *. Jer 6:15
No wonder my * is great! Jer 7:18
I will pour out my *, yes, my fury Jer 7:20
by the unquenchable fire of my *. Jer 7:20
earth shall tremble at his *; Jer 10:10
Don't do it in your *, for I Jer 10:24
fierce * of the Lord is upon them. Jer 12:13
before, for my * burns like fire, Jer 15:14
of my * that shall burn forever. Jer 17:4
tried to defend them from your *. Jer 18:20
deal with them in your *. Jer 18:23
The terrible * of the Lord will Jer 23:20
Don't * me by worshiping idols; Jer 25:6
fierceness of the * of the Lord. Jer 25:37
of the fierce * of the Lord. Jer 25:38
now it has done nothing but * me; Jer 32:31
to destroy them in my furious *. Jer 33:5
of fear or * at what he had done. Jer 36:24,25
says: Just as my * and fury were Jer 42:18
For my * rose high against them Jer 44:2,3
And so my fury and * boiled Jer 44:6
For you are rousing my * with Jer 44:8
My fierce * will bring great Jer 49:37
Because of the * of the Lord, Jer 50:13
save yourselves from the fierce * Jer 51:45
the Lord, in his *, saw to it that Jer 52:3
A CLOUD OF * from the Lord has Lam 2:1
have killed them, Lord, in your *; Lam 2:21
in the day of your * none escaped Lam 2:22
You have engulfed us by your *, Lam 3:43
But now at last the * of the Lord Lam 4:11
his fiercest * has been poured Lam 4:11
But you too will feel the awful * Lam 4:21
I went in bitterness and *, Eze 3:14,15
necessarily *, but indicated here Eze 3:14,15f
Then at last my * will be Eze 5:13
I will loose my * on you for your Eze 7:3
of * and with hailstones of wrath. Eze 13:13
alliance with her. My * is great. Eze 16:26
and fulfill my * against them while Eze 20:8
and in great * and with power. Eze 20:33
I will pour out my * upon you; Eze 22:31
all around: My * is afire against Eze 36:5
I consumed them in my *. Eze 43:8
became dark with * at Shadrach, Dan 3:19
And because the king, in his *, Dan 3:22
away your furious * from Jerusalem, Dan 9:16
in great *, will rally against Dan 11:10,11
in great * to destroy as he goes. Dan 11:44
Therefore, I will pour my * down Hos 5:10
much as my fierce * tells me to. Hos 11:9
I gave you kings in my *, and I Hos 13:11
for my * will be forever gone! Hos 14:4
he was pitiless in unrelenting *. Amo 1:11
his fierce * from destroying us." Jon 3:9
tumble down before his *. Nah 1:6
will rise up in * and turn on you Hab 2:7
Was it in *, Lord, you smote the Hab 3:8,9
land in awesome *, and trampled Hab 3:12
before the fierce * of the Lord Zep 2:2
my fiercest * and wrath upon them. Zep 3:8
seventy years your * has raged Zec 1:12
judgment and quieted my * there." Zec 6:8
"My * burns against your Zec 10:3
demonstrating God's * against it Lk 9:5
again Jesus was moved with deep *. Jn 11:37,38
At this their * boiled and they Act 19:28
But God shows his * from heaven Rom 1:18
* will be poured out upon them. Rom 2:8
and to end all God's * against us. Rom 3:25
end up under his *, for we always Rom 4:15
jealousy and *, constant effort to Gal 5:20
God's * just like everyone else. Eph 2:3
As parts of the same body, our * Eph 2:16
God's terrible * is upon those Col 3:6
rotten garments of *, hatred, Col 3:8
from God's terrible * against sin. 1Th 1:10
But the * of God has caught up 1Th 2:16
to pour out his * upon us, but to 1Th 5:9
from sin and * and resentment. 1Ti 2:8
in jealousy and *, which only lead 1Ti 6:4
into the sin of * with each other. 2Ti 2:16
Then God, full of this * against Heb 3:11
have sworn in my * that those who Heb 4:3
of God's awful * which will consume Heb 10:27
and wasn't afraid of the king's *. Heb 11:27
become angry; for * doesn't make Jas 1:20
satisfy God's * against our sins. 1Jn 4:10
and from the * of the Lamb. Rev 6:16
great day of their * has come, and Rev 6:17
to you in great *, knowing that he Rev 12:12
drink the wine of the * of God; Rev 14:10
at last God's * will be finished. Rev 15:1
the last drop of * in the cup of Rev 16:19

ANGERED

at Massah you * the Lord, and yet Deu 9:22
seriously they had * David, so they 2Sa 10:6
for they have * the Lord by 1Ki 14:15
did wrong and * the Lord with their 1Ki 14:22
Jeroboam had * the Lord God of 1Ki 15:30
* the Lord by all his evil deeds. 1Ki 16:4-7
evil and have * me ever since I 2Ki 21:15
But afterwards our ancestors * Ez 5:12
With all these things they * Ps 106:29
At Meribah, too, Israel * God, Ps 106:32
The word of God has * them; Jer 6:10
"Oh, why have they * me with Jer 8:19
youth, but have * me by all these Eze 16:43
and return home. * by having to Dan 11:30,31
He is not easily *; Joe 2:13
when your fathers * me and I Zec 8:14,15

ANGERING

* the Lord God of his fathers. 2Ch 28:25

ANGRIER

And the closer he came, the * he Dan 8:7

ANGRILY

But Leah * replied, "Wasn't it Gen 30:15

(ANGRILY Con't)
ambushing him, or * striking him Num 35:21
they shouted *. 2Ch 10:16
God hates me and * tears at my Job 16:9
he spoke out *, and said, "I am Job 32:5
Do not * reject your servant. Ps 27:9
They are proud, cursing liars. * Ps 59:12,13
talking about," he * declared. Mt 26:70
Looking around at them *, for he Mk 3:5
Spirit, glared * at the sorcerer Act 13:9

ANGRY
dejected and very *, and his face Gen 4:5
"Why are you *?" Gen 4:6
"Please don't be *," Abraham Gen 18:30
said, "Oh, let not the Lord be *; Gen 18:32
too shocked and * to overlook the Gen 34:6,7
of Egypt became * with his chief Gen 40:1
"Some time ago when you were * Gen 41:10
But don't be * with yourselves Gen 45:5
Then the Lord became *. Ex 4:14
and Moses was very * with them. Ex 16:20
He was very * about this with Lev 10:16
Then Moses was very * and said to Num 16:15
"must you be * with all the people Num 16:22
But God was * about Balaam's Num 22:22,23
Literally, "God was * because he Num 22:22,23f
as * as I, concerning my honor; Num 25:10,11
but Moses was very * with the army Num 31:14
their complaining and was very *. Deu 1:34,35
"And the Lord was even * with me Deu 1:37
"But the Lord was * with me Deu 3:26
But he was * with me because of Deu 4:21,22
your God is very * because of your Deu 4:25
how continually * you made the Deu 9:7
"Don't you remember how * you Deu 9:8
the Lord was so * with him; Deu 9:20
otherwise the * avenger might Deu 19:6,7
of fierce and * men who will have Deu 28:50
'Why was he so *?' Deu 29:24
says is evil, making him very *." Deu 31:29
And Jehovah was very *; Deu 32:16
the Lord was very * with the entire Jos 7:1
The people of Israel were * with Jos 9:18
will be * with all of us tomorrow. Jos 22:17,18
"Please don't be * with me, but Ju 6:39
were violently * with Gideon. Ju 8:1
This made Jehovah very * with Ju 10:7,8
"Somebody's apt to get * and Ju 18:25
But she became * with him and Ju 19:2
upon Saul and he became very *. 1Sa 11:6
David talking like that, he was *. 1Sa 17:28
Of course Saul was very *. 1Sa 18:8
But if he is *, then I'll know 1Sa 20:7
whether or not your father is *?" 1Sa 20:10
If he is * and wants you killed, 1Sa 20:13
when he was so * with Amalek. 1Sa 28:18
But the Philistine leaders were * 1Sa 29:4
David was * at what the Lord had 2Sa 6:8
"If the king is * and asks, 'Why 2Sa 11:19,20,21
he was very *, but Absalom said 2Sa 13:21-24
Why should this make you *? 2Sa 19:42
and you become * with them and 1Ki 8:46
Jehovah was very * with Solomon 1Ki 11:9,10
The king was very * with the 1Ki 13:4
made my people sin, and I am *! 1Ki 16:2
and the Lord was very * about it. 1Ki 16:13
So God was very *. 1Ki 16:26
went home to Samaria * and sullen. 1Ki 20:43
So Ahab went back to the palace * 1Ki 21:4
What has made you so upset and * 1Ki 21:5
have made him very * and have led 1Ki 21:22
the Lord God of Israel very *. 1Ki 22:52,53
But Naaman was * and stalked 2Ki 5:11
So the Lord was very * with 2Ki 13:3
But the prophet was * with him. 2Ki 13:19
things, and the Lord was very *. 2Ki 17:11
So the Lord was very *. 2Ki 17:17
So the Lord was very *, for 2Ki 21:6
you must be very * with us, for 2Ki 22:12,13
gods and have made me very *; 2Ki 22:17
and had made the Lord very *. 2Ki 23:19
David was * at the Lord for what 1Ch 13:11
and you become * with them, and 2Ch 6:36
Asa was so * with the prophet for 2Ch 16:10
made them very * and insulted. 2Ch 25:10
This made the Lord very * and he 2Ch 25:15
your fathers was * with Judah and 2Ch 28:9
"If you do, the Lord will be *, 2Ch 28:13
of evil, making the Lord very *. 2Ch 33:6
very * with them for their deeds. 2Ch 34:25
they were very * that anyone was Neh 2:10
SANBALLAT WAS VERY * when he Neh 4:1
I was very * when I heard this; Neh 5:6
*, and full of love and mercy; Neh 9:17
palace gate—became * at the king Est 2:21
Turn away your * gaze and let him Job 14:6
the * hand of God has touched me. Job 19:21
of Ram) became * because Job Job 32:2
But he was also * with Job's Job 32:3
"I am * with you and with your Job 42:7
Or, "Be ye *." Ps 4:4f
he is * with the wicked every day. Ps 7:11
For he was *. Ps 18:7
DON'T punish me while you are *! Ps 38:1
you have become * and deserted Ps 60:1
Who can stand before an * God? Ps 76:7
Jehovah heard them and was *; Ps 78:21
They made him * by erecting Ps 78:58
O Jehovah, how long will you be * Ps 79:5
you be * and reject our prayers? Ps 80:4
(Or will you be always *—on and Ps 85:5
slow in getting *, full of constant Ps 86:15
Why be so * with the one you Ps 89:38
he is slow to get * and full of Ps 103:8
a grudge, nor remains * forever. Ps 103:9
he became * and spoke foolishly. Ps 106:33
I am very * with those who spurn Ps 119:53
I am indignant and * because of Ps 119:139
your fist against my * enemies! Ps 138:7
slow to get *, full of love. Ps 145:8
he is * with those who cause Pro 14:35
An * man is silenced by giving Pro 21:14
Keep away from *, short-tempered Pro 22:24,25
That would make God very *; Ecc 5:6,7
discouraged, frustrated, and *. Ecc 5:17
If the boss is * with you, don't Ecc 10:4
My brothers were * with me and Sol 1:6
He was * with me, but now he Is 12:1
held the nations in your * grip. Is 14:6
his enemies with * indignation and Is 30:30
See, all your * enemies lie Is 41:11
And all who were * with him shall Is 45:24
For I was * with my people Is 47:6
I was * and smote these greedy Is 57:17
Oh, be not so * with us, Lord, Is 64:9
I'm sure he isn't *!" Jer 2:35
surely you won't be * about such Jer 3:4,5
I will not be forever * with you. Jer 3:12
against you, for I am very *. Jer 21:5
Are you * with us still? Lam 5:22
fear their sullen, * looks, even Eze 3:9
was that had made the Lord so *. Eze 8:3
and not be * with you anymore. Eze 16:42
will pay back your * deeds with Eze 35:11
asking, "Why is the king so *? Dan 2:15
Hearing this, the king was very * Dan 6:14
morally rotten, an * king shall Dan 8:23
CHANGE OF plans made Jonah very *. Jon 4:1
to get *, and full of kindness; Jon 4:2
it right to be * about this?" Jon 4:4
to be * because the plant died?" Jon 4:9
it is right for me to be * enough Jon 4:9
You cannot stay * with your Mic 7:18
He is slow in getting *, but Nah 1:3
Who can stand before an * God? Nah 1:6
Were you * with them? Hab 3:8,9f
The Lord of Hosts was very * with Zec 1:2
I am very * with the heathen Zec 1:15
furiously *—because of all that Zec 8:2
are only *, even in your own home, Mt 5:22
And they became * with him! Mt 13:57
"Then the * king sent the man to Mt 18:34
Should you be * because I am Mt 20:15
"Then the * king sent out his Mt 22:7
synagogue was very * about it Lk 13:14
His master was * and told him to Lk 14:21
"The older brother was * and Lk 15:28
Are you tempting the Lord to be * 1Co 10:22
put in jail, faced * mobs, worked 2Co 6:5
other, and being * with each other, 2Co 12:20
By his death he ended the * Eph 2:15
If you are *, don't sin by Eph 4:26
you still *—get over it quickly; Eph 4:26
for when you are * you give a Eph 4:27
being mean, bad-tempered and *. Eph 4:31
making them * and resentful. Eph 6:4
only upset people and make them *. 2Ti 2:23
says, "I was very * with them, for Heb 3:10
And who was it who made God * Heb 3:17
He said, "My son, don't be * Heb 12:5
speak little, and not become *; Jas 1:19
The nations were * with you, but Rev 11:18
it is your turn to be * with them. Rev 11:18

ANGUISH
his clothes in * and frustration. Gen 37:29
to him for all the * of his youth, Gen 41:51
We saw his terror and * and heard Gen 42:21
And if I must bear the * of their Gen 43:14
*, and it will never be again. Ex 11:6
saw her he tore his clothes in *. Ju 11:35
She was in deep * and was crying 1Sa 1:10
Ah, let me express my *. Job 7:11
my * I eagerly await sweet death! Job 14:14
He lives in fear, distress, and * Job 15:23,24
aren't you satisfied with my *? Job 19:22
I be hiding daily * in my heart? Ps 13:2
O Lord, have mercy on me in my *. Ps 31:9,10
My days are filled with *. Ps 38:5,6
My heart is in * within me. Ps 55:4
In my distress and *, your Ps 119:143
are engulfed by * and distress, Pro 1:27
Lest afterwards you groan in * Pro 5:11
Whose heart is filled with * and Pro 23:29,30
be trouble and * and dark despair. Is 8:22
Moab will pray in * to their idols Is 16:12
by the * of his soul, he shall be Is 53:11
In a moment, just as Israel's * Is 66:7,8
from their time of * and despair. Jer 11:12
I will cause * and terror to fall Jer 15:8
*—anguish as of a woman in labor. Jer 22:23
anguish—* as of a woman in labor. Jer 22:23
and beards in *, and slash their Jer 48:37
Fear, * and sorrow have gripped Jer 49:24
behold and see my * and despair, Lam 1:18
See, O Lord, my *; Lam 1:20
what can I compare your * to? Lam 2:13
surrounded me with * and distress. Lam 3:5
It is a day of shouts of *, not Eze 7:7
son of dust, in your bitter *; Eze 21:6
In deep * you will drain that Eze 23:34
Israel in her *, and laughed at Eze 25:3
and called out in *, "O Daniel, Dan 6:20
and there will be a time of * Dan 12:1
in the dust in your * and shame. Mic 1:10
distress and *, a day of ruin and Zep 1:15
"Screams of * come from Ramah, Mt 2:18
to be filled with * and despair. Mt 26:37
the early stages of the * ahead. Mk 13:8
for I am in * in these flames.' Lk 16:24
being comforted and you are in *. Lk 16:25
Now Jesus was in great * of Jn 13:21
child is born—her * gives place to Jn 16:21
out of all of his *, and gave him Act 7:10
I have seen the * of my people Act 7:34
their tongues in *, and cursed the Rev 16:10

ANGUISHED
and answered his * cry in Heb 5:7f
cry and groan with * grief because Jas 5:1

ANIAM
were Ahian, Shechem, Likhi, and *. 1Ch 7:19

ANIM
Anab, Eshtemoh, *, Goshen, Holon, Jos 15:48-62

ANIMAL
every kind of *—cattle and reptiles Gen 1:24
soil every kind of * and bird, and Gen 2:19,20
Bring a pair of every *—a male Gen 6:19,20
kind of bird and * and reptile. Gen 6:19,20
of every kind of *—domestic and Gen 7:14,15
You made me pay for every * Gen 31:39
that a wild * has eaten him. Gen 37:19,20
A wild * has eaten him. Gen 37:33
torn to pieces by some wild *; Gen 44:28
for every man and * left out in the Ex 9:19
This * shall be a year-old male, Ex 12:5
and every firstborn male *; Ex 13:1
with arrows, whether man or *.' Ex 19:13
the owner of the *, and the dead Ex 21:34
the dead * shall belong to him. Ex 21:34
lets his * loose and it gets into Ex 22:5
or any other * for him, and it Ex 22:10
But if the * or property has Ex 22:12
by some wild *, he shall bring the Ex 22:13
"If a man borrows an * (or Ex 22:14
an * shall certainly be executed. Ex 22:19
not eat any * that has been Ex 22:31
attacked and killed by a wild *. Ex 22:31
Bring the * to the entrance of Lev 1:2,3
the death of the * will be accepted Lev 1:4
The man shall then kill the * Lev 1:5
Then the priests will skin the * Lev 1:6,7
sections of the * and its head and Lev 1:8
"If the * used as a burnt Lev 1:10
or a cow, but the * must be Lev 3:1
The man who brings the * shall Lev 3:2
dead body of an * forbidden for Lev 5:2
"The sacrificial * shall be Lev 7:2
the * presented for the sacrifice. Lev 7:14
After the * has been sacrificed Lev 7:15
The fat of an * that dies of Lev 7:24
the burnt offering *, and his sons Lev 9:12
they brought the * to him piece Lev 9:13
food include any * with cloven Lev 11:2,3
by touching any * with only Lev 11:26
any * that does not chew the cud. Lev 11:26
chew the cud. Any * that walks on Lev 11:27
* shall be defiled until evening. Lev 11:27
"If the dead body of such an * Lev 11:35
"If an * which you are permitted Lev 11:39
among all * life upon the earth. Lev 11:47
and kills an * or bird of a kind Lev 17:13
for the life of every bird and * Lev 17:14
dead body of an * that dies of Lev 17:15
female *, thus defiling himself; Lev 18:23
to a male *, to mate with it; Lev 18:23
with an *, he shall be executed and Lev 20:15
be executed and the * killed. Lev 20:15
with an *, kill the woman and the Lev 20:16
the woman and the *, for they Lev 20:16
me by eating any * or bird which I Lev 20:25
He may not eat any * that dies Lev 22:8
if it is a male * without defect; Lev 22:19
must sacrifice an * that has no Lev 22:21
be accepted: An * that is blind or Lev 22:22

ANIMAL Con't)

not for a vow. An * that has	Lev 22:24
for no defective * is acceptable	Lev 22:25
slaughter a mother * and her	Lev 22:28
* the same day it is slain.	Lev 22:29,30
Anyone who kills an * [that	Lev 24:18
"To repeat, whoever kills an *	Lev 24:21
"But if it is an * that is vowed	Lev 27:9
But if the * given to the Lord	Lev 27:11,12
If the * is a kind that may be	Lev 27:13
firstborn of an * that cannot be	Lev 27:27
And the Lord owns every tenth *	Lev 27:32
must be an * from their flocks of	Num 15:3,4
And the one who burns the * must	Num 19:8
of a man, woman, *, bird, a small	Deu 4:16,17
bird, a small * that runs along	Deu 4:18
"You are not to eat any * I have	Deu 14:3,4,5
"Any * that has cloven hooves	Deu 14:6
eaten, but if the * doesn't have	Deu 14:7
However, if this firstborn * has	Deu 15:21
has sexual intercourse with an *.'	Deu 27:21
of the sacrificed * was boiling,	1Sa 2:13,14
But just then a wild * passed by	2Ki 14:9
Just then a wild * came by and	2Ch 25:18
No wild * has ever walked upon	Job 28:8
all his pomp must die like any *.	Ps 49:12
must die like any *.	Ps 49:20
I must seem like an * to you, O	Ps 73:22
moving in on some wild *!	Jer 4:17
earth and all mankind and every *;	Jer 27:5
This land—though every man and *	Jer 33:12
never eaten any * that died of	Eze 4:14
neither man nor * will disturb	Eze 32:13
prey to every * that comes along.	Eze 34:5
from any bird or * that dies a	Eze 44:31
the mind of an * instead of a man.	Dan 4:16
the fields like an *, eating grass	Dan 4:25
became those of an *, and he lived	Dan 5:21
The second * looked like a bear	Dan 7:5
my dream, a fourth * rose up out of	Dan 7:7
As I watched, the brutal fourth *	Dan 7:11
Then I asked about the fourth *,	Dan 7:19
"This fourth *," he told me,	Dan 7:23
Then I looked and saw four *	Zec 1:18
the daily blood of * sacrifices, as	Heb 7:27
on earth offers * blood in the Holy	Heb 9:25
satisfied with the * sacrifices,	Heb 10:6
that if even an * touched the	Heb 12:20
every kind of * or bird that lives	Jas 3:7
Then I saw another strange *,	Rev 13:11
on a scarlet * that had seven heads	Rev 17:3
the * she is riding represents.	Rev 17:7
The scarlet * that died is the	Rev 17:11
"The scarlet * and his ten	Rev 17:16
to the scarlet *, so that the words	Rev 17:17

ANIMAL'S

Then the priest shall take the *	Lev 4:5
hands upon the * head and kill it	Lev 4:15
shall also be given the * hide.	Lev 7:8

ANIMALS

God made all sorts of wild * and	Gen 1:25
the fish and birds and all the *.	Gen 1:28
the * and birds for their food."	Gen 1:30
* of the whole earth—to be cursed.	Gen 3:14
garments made from skins of *.	Gen 3:21
Yes, and the * too, and the	Gen 6:7
Bring in the *, too—a pair of	Gen 7:2
and all the * and birds and	Gen 7:4
various kinds of *—those for eating	Gen 7:8,9
domestic and wild *, and reptiles	Gen 7:21
* alike, and reptiles and birds.	Gen 7:23
Noah and all the * in the boat!	Gen 8:1
of dead * floating on the water.	Gen 8:7f
Release all the *, birds, and	Gen 8:17
along with all the *, reptiles, and	Gen 8:18,19
the * and birds God had designated	Gen 8:20
"All wild * and birds and fish	Gen 9:2,3
But never eat * unless their	Gen 9:4
Man-killing * must die, and any	Gen 9:5,6
and the * you brought with	Gen 9:9,10,11
cattle and wild *—that I will never	Gen 9:9,10,11
There were too many * for the	Gen 13:6
life—people, plants, and * alike.	Gen 19:25
for the stronger * to mate, and	Gen 30:41
For if he said the speckled *	Gen 31:8
and killed by wild *, did I show	Gen 31:39
each group of * by itself,	Gen 32:16
Whose * are these?"	Gen 32:17
to load their pack * and return	Gen 45:17
the Egyptians and their *.	Ex 8:17
* alike, throughout the land."	Ex 9:9
and * alike throughout all Egypt.	Ex 9:10
upon the people, *, and trees."	Ex 9:22
fields, men and * alike, was	Ex 9:25
and even the firstborn of the *.	Ex 11:5
nor shall any of their * die.	Ex 11:7
and firstborn male * in all the	Ex 12:12
and firstborn male * belong to the	Ex 13:12
land of Egypt, both of men and *;	Ex 13:15
resembling *, birds, or fish.	Ex 20:4
leave the rest for the * to	Ex 23:11
and the wild * would become too	Ex 23:29
*, and drew it off into basins.	Ex 24:6
use * from your herds and flocks.	Lev 1:2,3
place where the * for burnt	Lev 4:29
and killed by wild *, may be used	Lev 7:24
eat blood, whether of birds or *.	Lev 7:26,27
breasts of these *, and Aaron	Lev 9:20
of Israel that the * which may be	Lev 11:2,3
"These are the forbidden small *	Lev 11:29,30
"* that crawl shall not be	Lev 11:41,42
laws concerning *, birds, and	Lev 11:46
or is torn by wild *, must wash his	Lev 17:15
the birds and * I have given you	Lev 20:25
sacrifices the * brought by the	Lev 22:3
wild *, for this will defile him.	Lev 22:8
Cattle and wild * alike shall be	Lev 25:6,7
I will chase away the dangerous *	Lev 26:6
I will send wild * to kill your	Lev 26:22
the Lord—people, *, or inherited	Lev 27:28
*, as they pass by for counting.	Lev 27:32
in Israel of both men and *!	Num 3:13
Israel are mine, both men and *;	Num 8:17
and the firstborn of their *.	Num 18:14,15
* that I do not permit for food.	Num 18:16
The meat of these * shall be	Num 18:18
sheep, and gave * to Balaam and the	Num 22:40
Make sure that the * you	Num 28:31
booty, including the people and *;	Num 31:26
whether of birds, *, or fish.	Deu 5:8
ground and to your *, so that you	Deu 7:13
he did, the wild * would multiply	Deu 7:22
* of your flocks and herds.	Deu 12:6
These are the * you may eat:	Deu 14:3,4,5
touch the dead bodies of such *.	Deu 14:8
"Only sea * with fins and scales	Deu 14:9
shall eat these * before the Lord	Deu 15:20
the birds and wild *, and no one	Deu 28:26
use your * for his personal gain.	1Sa 8:16
and wild *," Goliath yelled.	1Sa 17:44
the birds and wild *, and the whole	1Sa 17:46
wild * from eating them at night.	2Sa 21:10
with interest in *, birds, snakes,	1Ki 4:33
water for the men or their pack *.	2Ki 3:9
for yourselves and for your *!	2Ki 3:17
happens to the * it won't be any	2Ki 7:13
he pastured his * eastward to the	1Ch 5:9
Then the priests killed the *	2Ch 29:24
contribution of * for the daily	2Ch 31:3
stalls for his *, and folds for the	2Ch 32:28,29
us, drove away the * and killed all	Job 1:14,15
wild * will leave you alone.	Job 5:22
Dangerous * will be at peace	Job 5:23
Have we become like * to you,	Job 18:3
They sound like * among the	Job 30:7
wiser than the * and birds?'	Job 35:11
The wild * hide in the rocks or	Job 37:8
them, or the wild * destroy them.	Job 39:15
other wild * on which he preys.	Job 40:20
and oxen, and wild * too, the	Ps 8:7
for men and * alike.	Ps 36:6
Burnt * bring no special joy to	Ps 40:6
For all the * of field and	Ps 50:10,11
lie exposed—food for birds and *.	Ps 79:2
us, and the wild * feed on us.	Ps 80:13
They give water for all the * to	Ps 104:11
He feeds the wild * and the	Ps 147:9
cedars, the wild * and cattle, the	Ps 148:10
the welfare of his *, but even the	Pro 12:10
Cliff badgers: delicate little *	Pro 30:24-28
The lion, king of the *.	Pro 30:29,30,31
For men and * both breathe the	Ecc 3:19
of * goes downward into dust?	Ecc 3:21
Even the *—the donkey and the	Is 1:3
The wild * of the desert will	Is 13:21
mountain birds and wild * to eat;	Is 18:6
wild * will gnaw bones all winter.	Is 18:6
The wild * of the desert will	Is 34:14
its * enough to offer to our God.	Is 40:16
The wild * in the fields will	Is 43:20
Come, wild * of the field;	Is 56:9
come, wild * of the forest,	Is 56:9
this place—people, *, trees and	Jer 7:20
for the birds and *, and no one	Jer 7:33
cattle, gone the birds and wild *.	Jer 9:10
The wild * and birds have moved	Jer 12:4
vultures and wild * to pick the	Jer 12:9
wild * to finish up what's left.	Jer 15:3
apart by vultures and wild *.	Jer 16:4
vultures and wild * to feed upon.	Jer 19:7
and both men and * shall die.	Jer 21:6
men and * alike have disappeared.	Jer 32:43
bodies to the vultures and wild *.	Jer 34:20
Hazor shall be a home for wild *	Jer 49:33
all shall be gone—both men and *	Jer 50:3
it shall be a home for the wild *	Jer 50:39
but wild * lurking in the ruins.	Lam 5:18
the kinds of * our law forbids."	Eze 4:14
come, but wild * will attack you	Eze 5:17
of dangerous wild * into the land	Eze 14:15
and bearing fruit. * of every sort	Eze 17:22,23
as food to the wild * and birds.	Eze 29:5
pass that way, neither men nor *.	Eze 29:11
* will lie among her branches;	Eze 31:13
you and the wild * of the whole	Eze 32:4
be eaten by wild *, and those in	Eze 33:27
away the dangerous * from the land	Eze 34:25
conquer them nor wild * attack.	Eze 34:28
vultures and wild * to devour you.	Eze 39:4
all the birds and * and say to	Eze 39:17
tables where the * for sacrifice	Eze 40:39
they may slay the * brought for	Eze 44:11
after being attacked by other *.	Eze 44:31
and even * and birds are under your	Dan 2:38
to eat. Wild * rested beneath its	Dan 4:12
Get the * out from under it and	Dan 4:14
let him eat grass with the wild *!	Dan 4:15
to eat, the wild * living in its	Dan 4:21
grass with the * of the field.'	Dan 4:23
to live with the * in the fields,	Dan 4:32
Then four huge * came up out of	Dan 7:3
The third of these strange *	Dan 7:6
the other *, and it had ten horns.	Dan 7:7
As for the other three *, their	Dan 7:12
"These four huge *," he said,	Dan 7:17
wild * will eat their fruit.	Hos 1:12
you and the wild *, birds, and	Hos 1:18
sick and die; the *, the birds, and	Hos 4:3
Even the wild * cry to you for	Joe 1:20
one, not even the *, eat anything	Jon 3:7
You terrified the wild * you	Hab 2:17
I will sweep away both men and *	Zep 1:3
All sorts of wild * will have	Zep 2:14
ruins, a place for * to live!	Zep 2:15
all the other * in the enemy camp.	Zec 14:15
You tell the people, 'Lame *	Mal 1:8
sick * to offer to me on it.	Mal 1:12
Stolen *, lame and sick—as	Mal 1:13
manure of these * you offer me, and	Mal 2:3
and brought the * to him and threw	Mt 21:7
except for desert *, he was	Mk 1:12,13
In the sheet were all sorts of *	Act 10:12
were all sorts of *, reptiles and	Act 11:6
eating unbled meat of strangled *.	Act 15:20
from unbled meat of strangled *,	Act 15:27,28,29
from strangled *, and not to commit	Act 21:25
birds and * and snakes and puny	Rom 1:23
of nature, like * and plants,	Rom 8:22
Humans, *, fish, and birds are	1Co 15:39
they are like lazy *, living only	Tit 1:12
him the blood of * that are	Heb 5:1
sprinkled with the blood of *.	Heb 9:23
blood of the slain * into the	Heb 13:11
* were burned outside the city.	Heb 13:11
are fools—no better than *.	2Pe 2:12
and, like *, they do whatever they	Jud 1:10
and famine and disease and wild *.	Rev 6:8

ANKLE

their scarves and * chains,	Is 3:20

ANKLE-BONES

the man's feet and * were healed	Act 3:7,8

ANKLES

bracelets on their *, with wanton	Is 3:16
point the water was up to my *.	Eze 47:3

ANKLETS

*, rings, earrings, and necklaces.	Num 31:50

ANNA

*, a prophetess, was also there	Lk 2:36,37

ANNALS

in The * of the Kings of Israel.	1Ki 14:19
in The * of the Kings of Judah.	1Ki 14:29
in The * of the Kings of Judah.	1Ki 15:7
in The * of the Kings of Judah.	1Ki 15:23
in The * of the Kings of Israel.	1Ki 15:31
in The * of the Kings of Israel.	1Ki 16:4-7
in The * of the Kings of Israel.	1Ki 16:14
in The * of the Kings of Israel.	1Ki 16:20
in The * of the Kings of Israel.	1Ki 16:27
in The * of the Kings of Israel.	1Ki 22:39
in The * of the Kings of Judah.	1Ki 22:45
in The * of the Kings of Israel.	2Ki 1:18
in The * of the Kings of Judah.	2Ki 8:23
in The * of the Kings of Israel.	2Ki 10:34
in The * of the Kings of Judah.	2Ki 12:19
in The * of the Kings of Israel.	2Ki 13:8
in The * of the Kings of Israel.	2Ki 13:12
in The * of the Kings of Israel.	2Ki 14:15
in The * of the Kings of Judah.	2Ki 14:18
in The * of the Kings of Israel.	2Ki 14:28
in The * of the Kings of Judah.	2Ki 15:6
in The * of the Kings of Israel.	2Ki 15:11
are recorded in The * of the	2Ki 15:15
in The * of the Kings of Israel.	2Ki 15:21
in The * of the Kings of Israel.	2Ki 15:26
in The * of the Kings of Israel.	2Ki 15:31
in The * of the Kings of Judah.	2Ki 15:36
in The * of the Kings of Judah.	2Ki 16:19
in The * of the Kings of Judah.	2Ki 20:20
in The * of the Kings of Judah.	2Ki 21:17
in The * of the Kings of Judah.	2Ki 21:25
in The * of the Kings of Judah.	2Ki 23:28
in The * of the Kings of Judah.	2Ki 24:5
in The * of the Kings of Israel.	1Ch 9:1

(ANNALS Con't)
put into the * of King David. 1Ch 27:24
is written in The * of the Kings of 2Ch 16:11
in The * of the Kings of Israel. 2Ch 20:34
Temple, see The * of the Kings. 2Ch 24:27
is written in The * of the Kings of 2Ch 25:26
is written in The * of the Kings of 2Ch 27:7
recorded in The * of the Kings of 2Ch 28:26
Amoz), and in The * of the Kings of 2Ch 32:32
in The * of the Kings of Israel. 2Ch 33:18
recorded in The * of the Prophets. 2Ch 33:19
are written in The * of the Kings 2Ch 35:27
in The * of the Kings of Judah; 2Ch 36:8

ANNAS
Lysanias, over Abilene; and * and Lk 3:1
First they took him to *, the Jn 18:13
Then * sent Jesus, bound, to Jn 18:24
in Jerusalem— * the High Priest Act 4:6

ANNEX
An * of rooms was built along the 1Ki 6:5
there was an * on each side of the 1Ki 6:10
Each story of the * was 7½ feet 1Ki 6:10

ANNIHILATE
* all the cities of that area. Num 21:2
* them, as I have commanded you. Jer 50:21

ANNIVERSARY
Sacrifice it there on the * Deu 16:6

ANNOUNCE
you, and he will * it to Pharaoh, Ex 7:2
day of this month (* this to all Ex 12:3,4
forever, and * to Joshua that I Ex 17:14
* to you the meaning of my name Ex 33:19
THE LORD SAID to Moses, "* to the Lev 23:1
men, they will * the names of the Deu 20:9
broken-hearted, to * liberty to Is 61:1
Whenever I * that a certain Jer 18:7
And if I * that I will make a Jer 18:9
grain and wine for you. * a fast; Joe 1:14
* this far and wide: Get ready Joe 3:9
He will issue his laws and * his Mic 4:2
Go and * to them that the Mt 10:7
to precede me, to * my coming, and Mt 11:10
and to * that captives shall be Lk 4:18,19
to * the coming of the Kingdom of Lk 8:1
Life, but I will * before my Father Rev 3:5

ANNOUNCED
"Listen to this," he proudly *. Gen 37:6
The Lord * that the plague would Ex 9:5
Now Moses * to Pharaoh, Ex 11:4
Then Moses * to the people all Ex 24:3
the calf and *, "Tomorrow there Ex 32:5
him and * the meaning of his name. Ex 34:5,6
That day shall be * as a time of Lev 23:21
be * by loud blowing of trumpets. Lev 23:23,24
So Moses * these annual festivals Lev 23:44
So Moses * that the Passover Num 9:4,5
from Gilgal, and * to the people of Ju 2:1
Saul and Samuel to battle!" he *. 1Sa 11:7
Israel. He * that he had destroyed 1Sa 13:3,4
Jeroboam also * that the annual 1Ki 12:32,33
so he * that all the people of 2Ch 20:3
THEN JOSIAH * that the Passover 2Ch 35:1
and the decree was * at Shushan, Est 9:14
enemies * and seen them destroyed. Ps 92:11
He has * this victory and Ps 98:2,3
Ephraim your doom has been *. Jer 4:15
* by Jeremiah against the nations. Jer 25:13
punishment he has * against you. Jer 26:13
God * that he would send his Son Mk 1:2
last the time has come!" he *. Mk 1:15
closely and then *, "You were with Mk 14:66,67
ever *, and it is for everyone! Lk 2:10
he * the Good News to the people. Lk 3:18
the people, and * his verdict: Lk 23:14
leaders who had * that anyone Jn 9:22,23
had publicly * that anyone seeing Jn 11:57
won't believe when you hear it *.' Act 13:41
great salvation * by the Lord Jesus Heb 2:3
time is now. He * this through King Heb 4:7
has been plainly * to all of us. 1Pe 1:12
ever since it was * by his servants Rev 10:7

ANNOUNCEMENT
on it the birth * of the son I am Is 8:1
Make this * to Judah and to Jer 5:20
Lord and make an * to all the Jer 26:2
Hear this *, Israel: When your Hos 5:9
"Listen to this *, and publish Amo 3:13
and give them this * from the Lord: Jon 1:2
On that day the * to Jerusalem Zep 3:16
as a public * of their decision to Mk 1:4
feet as a public * of your doom. Lk 10:11
—I heard an * of how many there Rev 9:16

ANNOUNCES
"Cyrus, King of Persia, hereby * Ez 1:2

ANNOUNCING
the camp * that no more donations Ex 36:4-7
"It is I, the Lord, * your Is 63:1
Lord, fearlessly * God's punishment Mic 3:8
The mighty deep cried out, * its Hab 3:10
* the Good News about the Kingdom. Mt 9:35
cross above his head, * his crime. Mk 15:26
For many will come * themselves Lk 21:8

ANNOYS
wife * like constant dripping. Pro 19:13

ANNUAL
"This * 'Celebration with Ex 12:17
as the date of the * celebration of Ex 12:42
Now remember, during the * Ex 13:3
This * memorial week will brand Ex 13:9
"There are three * religious Ex 23:14
This celebration is to be an * Ex 23:15
This shall be a regular, * event Ex 30:10
these three * religious festivals: Ex 34:22
celebrate several * festivals of Lev 23:1
"(These, then, are the regular * Lev 23:37
These * festivals are in Lev 23:38
This seven-day * feast is a law Lev 23:41
So Moses announced these * Lev 23:44
them at your * festivals and at the Num 10:10
at any of the * festivals—must be Num 15:3,4
It is an * offering from your Num 15:19,20,21
the times of your * feasts, and are Num 29:39
the first sample from each * Deu 26:2,3
to carry Israel's * tax money to Ju 3:15
Suddenly someone thought of the * Ju 21:19
went on the * trip to the 1Sa 1:21,22
Bethlehem for an * family reunion. 1Sa 20:6
and brought him * tribute money. 2Sa 8:6
sent him an * payment of 125,000 1Ki 5:11
They brought him * tribute of 1Ki 10:25
announced that the * Tabernacle 1Ki 12:32,33
This was a month later than the * 1Ki 12:32,33f
to the * festival at Jerusalem; 1Ki 12:32,33
They paid Israel an * tribute of 2Ki 3:4
to pay heavy * taxes to Assyria. 2Ki 17:3
to pay the * tribute to Assyria. 2Ki 17:4
the * Day of Atonement for Israel. 1Ch 6:49
at the * Festival of Tabernacles. 2Ch 5:3
and at the three * festivals—the 2Ch 8:13
lands that paid * tribute to him. 2Ch 9:13,14
Each brought him * tribute of 2Ch 9:24
But you must pay * tribute to 2Ch 12:8
him presents and * tribute, and the 2Ch 17:11
The Ammonites paid * tribute to 2Ch 26:8
from them an * tribute of $200,000 2Ch 27:5
for the * Passover celebration. 2Ch 30:1
and for the other * feasts as 2Ch 31:3
* tribute from Judah of $250,000. 2Ch 36:3
regular * feasts of the Lord. Ez 3:5
new moon feasts, and the * feasts. Neh 10:33
this day have an * celebration on Est 9:19
them to declare an * holiday on the Est 9:21
and began this * custom, as a Est 9:23
It would be an * event from Est 9:28
inaugurating his * Feast of Purim. Est 9:29-31
seven days of the * feast, he shall Eze 45:25
two days later—an * Jewish holiday Mk 14:1
Jerusalem for the * Passover Lk 2:41,42
Then it was time for the * Jewish Jn 2:13
for the * Passover celebration Jn 6:2-5
one of the * Jewish holidays, and Jn 7:2
This * celebration came fifty days Act 2:1f

ANNUALLY
Jewish calendar. *, on the tenth Ex 12:3,4
*, generation after generation. Ex 12:17
"So celebrate the event * in Ex 13:10
the Passover * on the fourteenth Num 9:2,3
Atonement [offered * on that day Num 29:11
He rode circuit *, setting up 1Sa 7:16
large sums of money * to David. 1Ch 18:13
charge ourselves * with a Temple Neh 10:32
these two days * as the Feast of Est 9:29-31

ANNUL
for he died to * that whole system Eph 2:15

ANOINT
"Use this," he said, "to * the Ex 30:26,27
Use it to * Aaron and his sons, Ex 30:30
Then * the washbasin and its Ex 40:11
holy garments and * him, Ex 40:13
upon them, and * them as you did Ex 40:15
shall be used to * the man's head. Lev 14:18
enough olive oil to * yourselves! Deu 28:40
You are to * him as the leader of 1Sa 9:16
show you which of his sons to *." 1Sa 16:3
said, "This is the one; * him." 1Sa 16:12
to * him there as king of Israel. 1Ki 1:34
* Hazael to be king of Syria. 1Ki 19:15
Then * Jehu (son of Himshi) to 1Ki 19:16
of Israel, and * Elisha (the son of 1Ki 19:16
of Israel says, 'I * you king of 2Ki 9:6
who was sent to * David as king. Ps 89:19f
not get enough to * Mic 6:15
of olive oil to * my head, but she Lk 7:46

ANOINTED
place where you * the pillar and Gen 31:13
then * the pillar with olive oil. Gen 35:13,14
and his sons are * and inducted Lev 6:19,20
For on the day the Lord * them, Lev 7:36
performed by the * High Priest, Lev 16:32
"The High Priest—* with the Lev 21:10
All were * as priests and set Num 3:3
MOSES * AND sanctified each part Num 7:1
*, placing them before the altar. Num 7:10
day the altar was *, it was Num 7:84,85,86
And gives great glory to his * 1Sa 2:10
him that he had been * as king! 1Sa 10:16
and before his * king—whose ox or 1Sa 12:3
"The Lord and his * king are my 1Sa 12:5
And shows mercy to his *— 2Sa 22:51
David, the * of the God of Jacob; 2Sa 23:1
And Zadok and Nathan have * him 1Ki 1:44,45
Tell him that the Lord has * him 2Ki 9:3
that he had been * king of Israel! 2Ki 9:12
Commandments, and * him as king. 2Ki 11:12
the Lord, and they * him as king of 1Ch 11:3
their king. They * him before the 1Ch 29:22
and they * Zadok as their priest. 1Ch 29:22
face away from me, your * one. 2Ch 6:42
as Jehoiada and his sons * him. 2Ch 23:11
Literally, "his *." Ps 2:2f
Literally, "You have * my head Ps 23:5f
and gives victory to his * king. Ps 28:8
the one you have * as your king. Ps 84:9
Literally, "your *." Ps 84:9f
I have * him with my holy oil. Ps 89:20
me, the one you * as their king. Ps 89:51
Literally, "* with fresh oil." Ps 92:10f
yes, and Aaron, too, the man * Ps 106:16
to the Messiah, the * One. Is 10:27f
to Cyrus, God's *, whom he has Is 45:1
the Lord has * me to bring good Is 61:1
*—was captured in their snares. Lam 4:20
I appointed you to be the * Eze 28:14
Jerusalem, until the * One comes! Dan 9:25
of 434 years, the * One will be Dan 9:26
represent the two * ones who assist Zec 4:14
she could, and has * my body ahead Mk 14:8
he had seen him—God's * King. Lk 2:26
of nard, and * Jesus' feet with it Jn 12:3
and against the * Son of God!' Act 4:25,26
your * Son, your holy servant. Act 4:27
of Nazareth was * by God with the Act 10:38
Or, "The Lord and his * shall now Rev 11:15f

ANOINTING
spices for the * oil and for the Ex 25:1
their ministry by * their heads Ex 28:41
Then take the * oil and pour it Ex 29:7
with some of the * oil and sprinkle Ex 29:21
to generation, for his * ceremony. Ex 29:29
all this into a holy * oil. Ex 30:25
shall always be my holy * oil. Ex 30:31
minister as priests; the * oil; Ex 31:11
Spices for the * oil and for the Ex 35:5-9
The * oil and sweet incense; Ex 35:10-19
the * oil and the sweet incense. Ex 35:28
the sacred oil for * the priests, Ex 37:29
The * oil; Ex 39:33-40
"Take the * oil and sprinkle it Ex 40:9
Sprinkle the * oil upon the Ex 40:10
their * shall be permanent from Ex 40:15
sacrifice on the day of their *. Lev 6:22,23
garments, the * oil, the young bull Lev 8:1
Then Moses took the * oil and Lev 8:10
Then he poured the * oil upon Lev 8:12
Next he took some of the * oil Lev 8:30
* oil of Jehovah is upon you." Lev 10:7
with the special * oil and wearing Lev 21:10
the * oil of his God is upon him; Lev 21:12
offering, and the * oil—in fact, Num 4:16
as the fragrant * oil that was Ps 133:2
people, * them with olive oil. Mk 6:13

ANOTHER'S
who commits adultery with * wife. Pro 6:29
to countersign * note, to become Pro 17:18
rewarded who protects * interests. Pro 27:18
a man gouges out * eye, he must pay Mt 5:38

ANSWER
who eats it must * for his sin. Lev 7:17,18
The * is, 'I will bless you Lev 25:21,22
God's * came, "Judah. Ju 1:2
food there, but got the same *. Ju 8:8
wife, "Get the * from your Ju 14:15
and haven't told me the *!" Ju 14:16
he told her the * and she, of Ju 14:17
gave the * to the young men. Ju 14:17
have found the * to my riddle!" Ju 14:18
had told him the * to his riddle. Ju 14:19
But there was no *, for she was Ju 19:28
upon my sorrow and * my prayer and 1Sa 1:11
Now I have an * for my enemies, 1Sa 2:1
thing and received the same *. 1Sa 17:30
But the Lord refused to * him, 1Sa 28:5,6
But he refused to *. 2Sa 22:42
me know what * to give to God." 2Sa 24:13
listen to me and * my requests. 1Ki 8:29
and forgive and * all who have made 1Ki 8:39
from heaven and * their prayers. 1Ki 8:43
O Lord, hear and * them whenever 1Ki 8:52
And the * will be, 'The people 1Ki 9:9
"Come back then for my *." 1Ki 12:5
was no reply, no voice, no *. 1Ki 18:29
O Lord, * me! 1Ki 18:37
O Lord, answer me! * me so these 1Ki 18:37

ANSWER Con't)
will have the * to your question 1Ki 22:25
let me know what * to return to the 1Ch 21:12
May you always hear and * the 2Ch 6:20,21
"And the * will be, 'Because his 2Ch 7:22
Their * was, 'We are the Ez 5:11
All I want is a reasonable * Job 6:24
your prayer, and * you, and bless Job 8:6
him, can a man * even one question Job 9:3
me to come—how quickly I will *! Job 13:22
THE * OF Eliphaz the Temanite: Job 15:1
"Listen, and I will * you from Job 15:17-19
some sense if you want us to *! Job 18:2
reply, for I have the * for you. Job 20:2
to you, O God, but you don't * me. Job 30:20
had been unable to * Job's Job 32:3
not * with that kind of logic! Job 32:14
No, I will give my * too. Job 32:17
Don't hesitate to * me if you Job 33:5
God will hear and * and receive him Job 33:26
The * must be obvious even to you! Job 34:33
"I will * you, and all your Job 35:4
you a question, and give me the *. Job 40:7
See if you can * them!' Job 42:4
to me and * when I call to him. Ps 4:3
He will * all my prayers. Ps 6:9
upper hand? * me, O Lord my God; Ps 13:3
Because I know you will * me, O Ps 17:6
Lord, but he refused to * them. Ps 18:41
May he * all your prayers! Ps 20:5
Yes, God will * me and rescue me. Ps 22:21
If you refuse to * me, I might as Ps 28:1
* quickly when I cry to you; Ps 31:2
by harps the * to one of life's Ps 49:4
and he will hear and *. Ps 55:17
everlasting ages past—will * them! Ps 55:19
And because you * prayer, all Ps 65:1
Literally, "will * us in Ps 65:5f
and kindness. Now * my prayer and Ps 69:13
O Jehovah, * my prayers, for Ps 69:16
and inactive when we pray. * us! Ps 83:1
* me, for I am deep in trouble. Ps 86:1
When he calls on me I will *; Ps 91:15
Then I will have an * for those Ps 119:40,41,42
great earnestness; * me, O Lord, Ps 119:145
cry for your help: "Hear me! *! Ps 130:2
can ever get an * to his prayers? Ps 130:3,4
When I pray, you * me, and Ps 138:3
QUICK, LORD, * me—for I have Ps 141:1
HEAR MY PRAYER, O Lord; * my Ps 143:1
Literally, "* me in faithfulness Ps 143:1f
Come quickly, Lord, and * me, Ps 143:7
I will not * your cry for help. Pro 1:28
A SOFT * turns away wrath, but Pro 15:1
* to my search for satisfaction. Ecc 2:20-23
He will * you. Is 30:19
says, This is my * to your prayer Is 37:21
then I will * when they cry to me. Is 41:17
Not one gave any * when I asked. Is 41:28
to it there is no *, for it cannot Is 46:7
when you call, the Lord will *. Is 58:9
for when I called, you didn't *; Is 65:12
I will * them before they even Is 65:24
will go ahead and * their prayers! Is 65:24
they refused to *, and when I spoke Is 66:4
but you refused to hear or *. Jer 7:13,14
And the * will be, "Because Jer 22:9
to listen or * when I call, I will Jer 35:17
alike, who had given him that *: Jer 44:20
you alone know the * to that." Eze 37:3
the Lord, I will * the pleading of Hos 1:21,22
earth in * to its cry for rain. Hos 1:21,22
Then the earth can * the parched Hos 1:21,22
And the * will be, "No," and Amo 6:10
your patience is exhausted? * me! Mic 6:3
there is no *. Hab 1:2
* God will give to my complaint. Hab 2:1
me, "Write my * on a billboard, Hab 2:2
will * with lightning and showers. Zec 10:1
This was his *: "If you had Mt 12:11
Let them * your accusation! Mt 12:27
But to * your question, you can Mt 19:17
"I'll tell you if you * one Mt 21:24
And Jesus said, "Then I won't * Mt 21:27
They had no *. Mt 22:46
"And I will *, 'When you refused Mt 25:45
But they wouldn't * him. Mk 3:4
But they were ashamed to *, for Mk 9:34
tell you if you * one question! Mk 11:29
Was he sent by God, or not? * Mk 11:30
So they said, "We can't *. Mk 11:33
I won't * your question either!" Mk 11:33
"Do you refuse to * this charge? Mk 14:60
And when they refused to *, Jesus Lk 14:4
Again they had no *. Lk 14:6
keep praying until the * comes. Lk 18:1
He will * them quickly! Lk 18:8
question before I *," he replied. Lk 20:3
I won't * your question either." Lk 20:8
and marveling at his *, they were Lk 20:26
about how to * the charges against Lk 21:14
Tell us, so we can give an * to Jn 1:22
They kept demanding an *, so he Jn 8:7
making up this * to your question! Jn 14:24
It is the * given by the Father Jn 14:24
"Is that the way to * the High Jn 18:22
but Jesus gave no *. Jn 19:9
able to present my * before you, Act 26:2
For the * to that question, Rom 4:10
to that question, * this one: When Rom 4:10
last letter: my * is that if you do 1Co 7:1
Now I will try to * your other 1Co 7:25
to do so? In * to this question, I 1Co 7:25
that only his * is the right one! 1Co 8:1
This is my * to those who 1Co 9:3
lest the * hurt your conscience. 1Co 10:25
You will find the * in your own 1Co 15:36
only God can * that. 2Co 12:2,3
have the right * for everyone. Col 4:6
But the * lies in Christ, who 1Ti 3:16
that God will * your prayers and Phm 1:22
the Lord to give you any solid *. Jas 1:7,8
we can be sure that he will * us. 1Jn 5:15
My * to them is: Remember this Jud 1:5

ANSWERED
Then God * the lad's cries, and Gen 21:17
"Yes, Lord!" he *. Gen 22:11
And God * her prayers and she Gen 30:17
plight, and * her prayers by giving Gen 30:22
because I was afraid," Jacob *. Gen 31:31
to the God who * my prayers in the Gen 35:3
Jacob *. Gen 46:2
and the people * in unison, "We Ex 24:3
But the people *, "We choose the Jos 24:21
The Lord * his prayer, and the Ju 13:9
and the Lord has * your request. 1Sa 12:13
why haven't you * my question? 1Sa 14:41
Ahima-az *. 2Sa 18:29
Then at last God * prayer and 2Sa 21:12,13,14
And the Lord * his prayer, and 2Sa 24:25
you have heard and * my request: 1Ki 8:28
Solomon * all her questions; 1Ki 10:3
the new king * them roughly. 1Ki 12:13,14
about yourself," Elijah *. 1Ki 18:18
"Yes," the prophet *. 1Ki 20:14
"Yes," Elijah *, "I have come 1Ki 21:20
Jehu *, "What do you know about 2Ki 9:19
to the Lord, who * by sending down 1Ch 21:26
that the Lord had * his plea, he 1Ch 21:28
And Solomon * all her problems. 2Ch 9:2
And the Lord listened, and * his 2Ch 33:13
His prayer, and the way God *, 2Ch 33:19
Memucan * for the others, "Queen Est 1:16
And even if my prayers were * I Job 9:16
for help, and God * him, have Job 12:4
THEN THE LORD * Job from the Job 38:1
you listened to my plea and * me. Ps 31:22
For I cried to him and he * me! Ps 34:4
I saved you; I * from Mount Sinai Ps 81:7
cried to him for help, he * them. Ps 99:6
O Jehovah our God! You * them Ps 99:8
Lord and he * me and rescued me. Ps 118:5
But the people were silent and * Is 36:21
in southern Egypt) * Jeremiah: Jer 44:15
And I *, "The Lord told me to Eze 24:20,21
Daniel *, "Keep your gifts, or Dan 5:17
in heaven and was * the very first Dan 10:12
I *, "A plumbline." Amo 7:8
I cried to the Lord and he * me; Jon 2:2
And the priests *, "Yes." Hag 2:13
Angel of the Lord—* me, "The Lord Zec 1:10
And the Lord * the angel who Zec 1:13
I *, "I see a golden lampstand Zec 4:2
think prayers are * only by Mt 6:7,8
But Jesus *, "O you men of Mt 8:26
Simon Peter *, "The Christ, the Mt 16:16
" 'Friend,' he * one of them, 'I Mt 20:13
'I won't,' he *, but later he Mt 21:29
he said, "You have * well—so Mk 7:29
But Jesus *, "You don't know Mk 10:38
realized that Jesus had * well. Mk 12:28
John * the question by saying, Lk 3:16
Jesus * them, "It is the sick Lk 5:31
Then Jesus spoke up and * his Lk 7:40
had owed him the most," Simon *. Lk 7:43
one more chance,' the gardener *. Lk 13:8
seed," Jesus *, "it would be Lk 17:6
Jesus *, "You don't know who I Jn 8:19
"Neither," Jesus *. Jn 9:3
The man *, "Who is he, sir, for Jn 9:36
Jesus *, "Die for me? Jn 13:38
Then Jesus *, "I am not an Jn 18:36
"You can," Philip *, "if you Act 8:37
* and they began praising God! Act 11:18
in thanksgiving for * prayer. Act 18:18f
in thanksgiving for * prayer. Act 18:22f
"Cilicia," Paul *. Act 23:34
But God graciously heard and * Heb 5:7f
lie, never * back when insulted; 1Pe 2:23

ANSWERING
now he spoke up, * Abraham as the Gen 23:10
O Lord, thank you so much for * Ps 118:21

ANSWERS
to get * for David from the Lord. 1Sa 23:6
gave him the right * every time. 1Ki 10:3
and the god who * by sending fire 1Ki 18:24
find relief, so let me give my *. Job 32:20
* from you, and you must reply. Job 38:3
Do you—God's critic—have the *?" Job 40:2
could I ever find the *? Job 40:4
and give me speedy *, for my days Ps 102:2
he hears my prayers and * them. Ps 116:1
and the rich man * with insults. Pro 18:23
by his *— but not the Pharisees! Mt 22:33
with his understanding and *. Lk 2:46,47
he knows all the *, he is just 1Co 8:2
* to your prayers for our safety! 2Co 1:11
forget to thank him for his *. Php 4:6
wrong and shallow * built on men's Col 2:8
watch for God's * and remember to Col 4:2
your prayers will not get ready *. 1Pe 3:7

ANTECEDENT
the exact * is unclear. Rev 19:9f

ANTELOPE
The *, and the mountain sheep. Deu 14:3,4,5

ANTHEM
let this * be their song: Is 27:2

ANTHOTHIJAH
Elam, *, Iphdeiah, Penuel. 1Ch 8:22-25

ANTI-BABYLONIAN
The * party in Judah looked to Eze 23:17f

ANTI-SEMITES
The sons of * will come and bow Is 60:14

ANTICHRIST
Probably the future * of 2 Dan 7:24f
the * at the end of human history. Dan 8:23f
from view and the * of the last Dan 11:40f
You have heard about the * who is 1Jn 2:18
Such a person is *, for he does 1Jn 2:22
These remarks of mine about the * 1Jn 2:26
Christ, like the "*" you have 1Jn 4:3

ANTICIPATION
Hell is licking its chops in * of Is 5:14

ANTIGONUS
of Babylonia, * of Syria and Asia Dan 8:8f

ANTIOCH
Berenice, murdered in * by Dan 11:7f
Nicolaus of * (a Gentile convert Act 6:5
Cyprus, and *, scattering the Good Act 11:19
who went to * from Cyprus and Act 11:20
to * to help the new converts. Act 11:22
him, he brought him back to *; Act 11:26
(It was there at * that the Act 11:26
from Jerusalem to *, and one of Act 11:27
their business, returned to *, Act 12:25
of the church at * were Barnabas Act 13:1
Paul went on to *, a city in the Act 13:14
Jews arrived from * and Iconium and Act 14:19
Iconium and *, where they helped Act 14:21
by ship to *, where their journey Act 14:26
believers at * for a long while. Act 14:28
WHILE PAUL AND Barnabas were at *, Act 15:1
send delegates to * with Paul and Act 15:22
"To: The Gentile brothers in *, Act 15:23
went at once to *, where they Act 15:30
Paul and Barnabas stayed on at * Act 15:34,35
and then sailed on to *. Act 18:22
But when Peter came to * I had to Gal 2:11
I was visiting in *, Iconium and 2Ti 3:11

ANTIOCHUS
Israel was attacked by * IV Dan 8:9f
Probably a reference to * Dan 8:23f
in marriage to * II of Syria to Dan 11:6f
in Antioch by * II's former wife Dan 11:7f
Possibly * III the Great, who was Dan 11:13f
Seleucus IV, successor of * III, Dan 11:20f
This may refer to * IV Epiphanes Dan 11:21f
Probably * IV and Ptolemy IV. Dan 11:27f
who conspired with * against the Dan 11:32f
The prophecy takes a turn here. * Dan 11:40f

ANTIPAS
deny me, even when *, my faithful Rev 2:13

ANTIPATER
and * of Macedonia and Greece. Dan 8:8f

ANTIPATRIS
the soldiers took Paul to *. Act 23:31

ANTIPHONAL
In a great * chorus they sang, Is 6:3

ANTIQUITY
looked like has been lost in *. Ex 28:30,31f

ANTS
Take a lesson from the *, you Pro 6:6
*: they aren't strong, but store Pro 30:24-28

ANUB
Koz was the father of * and 1Ch 4:8

ANVIL
and the molder helps at the *. Is 41:7
on the * and throw them away." Zec 1:21

ANXIETY
They lie there sleepless with *, Hos 7:14
freedom from all * and fear. 1Pe 1:2

ANXIOUS
in fact, he will be so * to get Ex 11:1

(ANXIOUS Con't)
They were all * to see David 1Ch 12:23
and who are * to do your will. 2Ch 6:14
in fact, he himself was as * to 2Ch 26:20
I want to hear it, for I am * to Job 33:32
Happy is the man who is so * to Pro 8:34
* hearts are very heavy but a Pro 12:25
* they are to worship correctly; Is 58:2
he is full of kindness, and * not Joe 2:13
"So don't be * about tomorrow. Mt 6:34
of a riot and * to please the Mk 15:15
with deep longing, * to eat this Lk 22:15
before the Lord, * to hear what he Act 10:33
I became very * to honor God in Act 22:3
Then Festus, * to please the Act 25:9
meat, he, too, is * to please the Rom 14:6
A girl who is not married is * to 1Co 7:34
Since you are so * to have 1Co 14:12
sincere, and very * to get rid of 2Co 7:11
for we are * that no one should 2Co 8:20
I am * for you with the deep 2Co 11:2
of God himself—* that your love 2Co 11:2
Those false teachers who are so * Gal 4:17
So I am all the more * to get him Php 2:28
I know you have always been * to Php 4:10
And we are * that you keep right Heb 6:11
but you will be * to follow the Heb 6:12
will be * to do the will of God. 1Pe 4:2

ANXIOUSLY
you search for me ever so *. Pro 1:28
Those in Aroer stand * beside Jer 48:19
We, too, wait * for that day when Rom 8:23
so * and with such deep concern. 2Co 7:15

ANYBODY
"He told me not to tell * why I 1Sa 21:2
accept as priests * who comes along 2Ch 13:9
or *—no one can show her the way. Is 19:15
But talk is cheap—* could say Mt 9:5,6
But talk is cheap—* could say Mk 2:9,10,11
But talk is cheap—* could say Lk 5:23,24
your Lord and if * asks why you 1Pe 3:15

ANYMORE
getting pregnant *, she gave her Gen 30:9
"It isn't *!" Gen 32:28
help the Ammonites * after that. 2Sa 10:19
Lord, don't hit me *—I am Ps 39:10
no one will live there *. Is 34:10
from you and will not listen *. Is 59:2
even think about the old ones *. Is 65:17
No one will live there *. Jer 49:18
quiet and not be angry with you *. Eze 16:42
I will not let it be mocked at *. Eze 39:7
their names will not be spoken *. Hos 1:17
to your offerings *, and you Mal 2:13
it because he doesn't love us *? Rom 8:35
with the Gentiles * because he was Gal 2:12
They don't care * about right Eph 4:19
* or remember what he looks like. Jas 1:24

ANYONE'S
Has he ever needed * advice? Is 40:14
And the prince may never take * Eze 46:18
If you forgive * sins, they are Jn 20:23
And if * name was not found Rev 20:15

ANYTHING
a baby?' Is * too hard for God? Gen 18:14
intention of doing * wrong." Gen 20:5
children. If * should happen to Gen 42:38
anyone who eats * that has yeast in Ex 12:19
must not eat * made with yeast; Ex 12:20
at all times. * that is too Ex 18:22
Literally, "of * in heaven or Ex 20:4f
oxen, donkeys, or * else he has." Ex 20:17
of silver or gold or of * else! Ex 20:23
clothing, or * else is lost, and Ex 22:9
an animal (or * else) from a Ex 22:14
nor have * to do with their gods. Ex 23:32
"Anyone touching * ceremonially Lev 5:2
the next day. But * left over Lev 7:17,18
into contact with * that is Lev 7:19
Anyone who touches * that is Lev 7:21
you to do. * left of the meat and Lev 8:32
evening, and * upon which the Lev 11:32
a rug, or a sack; * it touches must Lev 11:32
a pottery bowl, * in the bowl is Lev 11:33
she must not touch * sacred, nor Lev 12:4
in a garment or * made of skin or Lev 13:59
Any bed he lies on and * he sits Lev 15:4
Anyone touching or carrying * Lev 15:10
until evening. * she lies on or Lev 15:20
Anyone touching her bed or * she Lev 15:21,22,23
above, so that * she lies upon Lev 15:26
Anyone touching her bed or * she Lev 15:27
sheep or a goat. * that has a Lev 22:20
to the Lord has * superfluous or Lev 22:23
However, * utterly devoted to Lev 27:28
and don't touch * that belongs to Num 16:26
evening. And * a defiled person Num 19:22
add * to what he said before." Num 22:19
"Have I ever done * like this Num 22:30
* except what God tells me to say; Num 22:38
But Balaam replied, "Can I say * Num 23:12
has given Moses: '* that will Num 31:22
water. But * that won't stand heat Num 31:23
if you can find * like this: An Deu 4:32
donkeys, nor * else he owns.' Deu 5:21
and herds, nor * you have vowed to Deu 12:17
"Don't eat * that has died a Deu 14:21
or blind, or if * else is wrong Deu 15:21
clothing, or * else you find. Deu 22:3
not want to see * indecent lest he Deu 23:14
form of money, food, or * else. Deu 23:19
"If you lend * to another man, Deu 24:10
leave * remaining for the Deu 24:20
You shall not prosper in * you Deu 28:29
Is that * for you to fight us Ju 12:3
or eat * that isn't kosher." Ju 13:13,14
replied, "but I'll not eat *. Ju 13:16
* but death to separate us." Ru 1:17
you if you hide * from me!" 1Sa 3:16,17
had to face * like this before! 1Sa 4:7
"But we don't have * to pay him 1Sa 9:7
anyone who eats * before 1Sa 14:24,25
So no one ate * all day, even 1Sa 14:24,25
"He's never done * to harm you," 1Sa 19:4
Saul didn't say * about it that 1Sa 20:26
of bread, or * else you can." 1Sa 21:3
them, nor stolen * from them the 1Sa 25:7
didn't tell him * about her meeting 1Sa 25:36
He had not had * to eat or drink 1Sa 30:11,12
He wouldn't stop for *, but kept 2Sa 2:19
David had refused to eat * the 2Sa 3:35,36
to Amnon to do * to her." 2Sa 13:2f
It's not * to worry about!" 2Sa 13:20
Apparently we don't mean * to 2Sa 19:6
"Use * you like," Araunah told 2Sa 24:22
I know he will do * you request) 1Ki 2:17
him to ask for * he wanted, and it 1Ki 3:5
than * I've ever heard of ! 1Ki 10:7
orders not to eat * or drink any 1Ki 13:9
for I am not allowed to eat * or 1Ki 13:16,17
and told him, "I didn't see *." 1Ki 18:43
"Don't give him * more," the 1Ki 20:8
for he never prophesies * good. 1Ki 22:8
He never tells me * good. 1Ki 22:18
and will do * you tell us to. 2Ki 10:5
you done * about the Temple? 2Ki 12:7
be permitted to give * to you? 1Ch 29:14
*, and I will give it to you!" 2Ch 1:7
he never prophesies * but evil! 2Ch 18:6,7
He never prophesies * but evil 2Ch 18:17
"You may do * you like with his Job 1:12,13
"A man will give * to save his Job 2:4,5
of God and never * unpleasant?" Job 2:10
You're not telling me * new. Job 9:2
who have never known * good. Job 21:25
men of importance * they wanted, Job 22:8
that I dread more than * else. Job 31:23
But if you have * to say at this Job 33:32
I owe no one *. Job 41:11
"I know that you can do * and Job 42:2
love to say * that will do harm, O Ps 52:4
Can't they understand *? Ps 53:4
I am not afraid of * mere man can Ps 56:10,11
is * like him? Ps 89:6
Point out * you find in me that Ps 139:24
before he created * else. Pro 8:22
but if he is hungry, he'll eat *! Pro 27:7
hold onto * with oil-slick hands. Pro 27:16
all these things. * I wanted, I Ecc 2:10
You can get * by either wisdom Ecc 7:12
part in * here on earth any more. Ecc 9:6
you will never get * done. Ecc 11:4
I have said. Ask * you like, in Is 7:11
the Lord with * like that." Is 7:12
Don't fear * except the Lord of Is 8:13
Egypt cannot be saved by * or Is 19:15
Where are the witnesses of * they Is 43:9
Can't you do * right at all?" Is 45:10
Who has heard or seen * as Is 66:7,8
we won't have * to do with him Jer 2:31
don't care * about you any more; Jer 30:14
is there * too hard for me? Jer 32:27
well and give him * he wants." Jer 39:11,12
in the streets for * at all. Lam 4:5
I have never told them * at all. Eze 13:2,3
hearts—should I let them ask me *? Eze 14:3
There has never been * like it Eze 16:16
they must not wear * that would Eze 44:18
see nor hear, nor know * at all. Dan 5:23
But they couldn't find * to Dan 6:4
the animals, eat * at all, nor even Jon 3:7
see if * would happen to the city. Jon 4:5
No one can tell her *; Zep 3:2
to ask the idols for * like that! Zec 10:2
* very valuable to offer to God!' Mal 1:7
* like this," they exclaimed. Mt 9:33
he vowed to give her * she wanted. Mt 14:7
"Don't you see that * you eat Mt 15:17
earth concerning * you ask for, my Mt 18:19
You can get *—anything you ask Mt 21:22
You can get anything—* you ask Mt 21:22
say, but above * else, don't follow Mt 23:3
Or thirsty and give you * to Mt 25:37
you wouldn't give me * to drink; Mt 25:42
"We've never seen * like this Mk 2:12
himself, how can he accomplish *? Mk 3:26
"Ask me for * you like," the Mk 6:22,23
Don't you remember * at all? Mk 8:18
"Can you see * now?" Mk 8:23
For is * worth more than his Mk 8:37
Jesus asked. "* is possible if Mk 9:23
it can't season *. Mk 9:50
has ever given up *—home, brothers, Mk 10:29
You can pray for *, and if you Mk 11:24
* poisonous, it won't hurt them; Mk 16:18
refused to have * to do with them Lk 9:53
them, "More than * else, beware of Lk 12:1
And no one gave him *. Lk 15:16
"Do you have * here to eat?" Lk 24:41
BEFORE * ELSE existed, Jn 1:1
"Can * good come from there?" Jn 1:46
Samaritan" for *—usually they Jn 4:9
"We've never heard * like it." Jn 7:46
we don't know * about him." Jn 9:29
yet you don't know * about him! Jn 9:30
You can ask him for *, using my Jn 14:12,13
Yes, ask *, using my name, and I Jn 14:14
need to ask me for *, for you can Jn 16:23
don't need anyone to tell you *. Jn 16:30
They won't stop at * that you in Act 4:28
'For I have never yet eaten * Act 11:8
When he couldn't find out * in Act 21:34
have * against me) — but look! Act 24:19
man hasn't done * worthy of death Act 26:31
out the tackle and * else they Act 27:19
was well able to do * he promised. Rom 4:21
had done * either good or bad. Rom 9:10-13
what is his, or do * else the Ten Rom 13:9
Don't do * that will cause Rom 14:16
wine or doing * else that offends Rom 14:21
him it is wrong. * that is done Rom 14:23
you couldn't digest * stronger. 1Co 3:2
I can do * I want to if Christ 1Co 6:12
life aren't * new and different. 1Co 10:13
But a man should not wear * on 1Co 11:7
we never teach * else than 1Co 11:16
big ear, how could you smell *? 1Co 12:17
* of lasting value by ourselves. 2Co 3:5
to you without charging you *? 2Co 11:7
didn't ask you for *, for the 2Co 11:8,9
*, for I don't want your money. 2Co 12:14
seem to cost us *, but he is a 2Co 12:16
As sure as * he must have made 2Co 12:16
should boast about * except the Gal 6:14
Ask God for * in line with the Eph 6:18
I will never do * that will cause Php 1:20
Does it mean * to you that we are Php 2:1
Don't worry about *; Php 4:6
He existed before God made * at Col 1:15
We can bear * as long as we know 1Th 3:8
I really don't need to say * about 1Th 5:1
then no one will be able to say * 1Ti 5:14
Anyone who says * different is 1Ti 6:4
Run from * that gives you the 2Ti 2:22
* that makes you want to do right. 2Ti 2:22
won't really believe * they hear. 2Ti 3:5
far as doing * good is concerned. Tit 1:16
there won't be * to criticize in Tit 2:8
to criticize in * you say! Tit 2:8
* from you, charge me for it. Phm 1:18
dies—no one gets * until it is Heb 9:16
let us strip off * that slows us Heb 12:1
of * that mere man can do to me." Heb 13:6
will be ready for *, strong in Jas 1:4
by heaven or earth or * else; Jas 5:12
you * to get hold of your money. 2Pe 2:3
him for * in line with his will. 1Jn 5:14
Dear children, keep away from * 1Jn 5:21
mock and curse at * they do not Jud 1:10
and, like Balaam, they will do * Jud 1:11
Don't do * yet—hurt neither earth Rev 7:3
said, "No, don't do * like that. Rev 22:9
If anyone adds * to what is written Rev 22:18

ANYTIME
But you can go * and it will make Jn 7:6

ANYWAY
father's wealth will come to us *! Gen 31:14
But some of the people went out * Ex 16:27
then he shall pay the money *. Ex 22:17
it is guilty *, and must bring his Lev 5:17,18
offering *, shall be cut off from Lev 7:20
been found. And *, you own all the 1Sa 9:20
Philistine, *, that he is allowed 1Sa 17:26
are you doing around here, *?" 1Sa 17:28
king of Israel trying to catch, *? 1Sa 24:14
since it's all in the family *. 2Sa 13:20
"And *, why shouldn't I? 2Sa 16:19
"Yes, but let me go *," he 2Sa 18:23
Yet Solomon did it *. 1Ki 11:2
kill us, we would have died *." 2Ki 7:4
eat the Passover *, even though 2Ch 30:17,18,19
He will supply your every need *! Job 12:6
the consequence but does it *. Pro 29:24

(ANYWAY Con't)
is nothing but death ahead *. Ecc 9:2,3
they do, but I will heal them *! Is 57:18
And you won't listen to me *." Jer 38:15
him a message *, it is a lie. Eze 14:9
We don't need one *!" Hos 10:3
A curse upon them *!" Jn 7:49
haven't seen me and believe *." Jn 20:29
asked Pilate to have him killed *. Act 13:28
ahead and did them *, and Rom 1:32
I try not to do wrong, I do it *. Rom 7:19
but Paul says to welcome them *. Rom 14:1f
to stay with him *, he must not 1Co 7:12
decide to go ahead * and get 1Co 7:28
he would have come *, for he is 2Co 8:17
do, listen to me *—a witless man, a 2Co 11:16
only God can answer that. But *, 2Co 12:2,3
put in words (and * I am not 2Co 12:4
I want you! And *, you are my 2Co 12:14
on following them *, still bound by Col 2:20
"the Lord will be merciful *." 1Jn 3:20f

APART
and to cut them * down the middle, Gen 15:10
as solid walls to hold the seas *. Ex 15:8
I will cut them * with my sword Ex 15:9
that will set him * from others, so Ex 28:3
these things are set * and holy. Ex 29:33
touches it shall be set * for God. Ex 29:37
Or, "shall be set * for God," Ex 30:29f
tear it *, but not completely. Lev 1:15,16,17
It is to be set * from the burnt Lev 7:35
thus setting him * for his work. Lev 8:12
and I have set you * from all other Lev 20:26
The priest is set * to offer the Lev 21:8
in a place set * for the purpose. Lev 24:9
* to minister at the Tabernacle. Num 3:3
Moses, "Now set * the Levites from Num 8:5,6
of Israel to set * three cities Deu 4:41
It was there that Jehovah set * Deu 10:8
you must set * three Cities of Deu 19:2,3
To rip them * with their teeth; Deu 32:24
Baal was knocked *, the idol beside Ju 6:28
the one who broke * his altar!" Ju 6:31
the lion's jaws *, and did it as Ju 14:6
young men were kept strictly *. 2Sa 13:2
then we will break the rafts * 1Ki 5:9
of ornaments an inch or two *, 1Ki 7:24
altar will split *, and the ashes 1Ki 13:3
* the body of your wife, Jezebel. 1Ki 21:23
and they cut * all the gold bowls 2Ki 24:13
Aaron and his sons were set * for 1Ch 23:13
Baal were knocked *, the obelisks 2Ch 34:4
quietly until he broke me *. Job 16:12
Men know how to tear * flinty Job 28:9
set * the redeemed for himself. Ps 4:3
eager to tear me *, like young Ps 17:12
*—and no one can help you then. Ps 50:22
you have torn it *. Ps 60:2
so that it would never fall *. Ps 104:5
done to them * from his decision. Ps 105:14
brass and cut * their iron bars. Ps 107:16
and quickly broke * before them. Ps 114:3
For who can eat or enjoy * from Ecc 2:24-26
I, the Lord, have set * these Is 13:3
it was like being torn * by Is 38:13
*, making chaff of mountains. Is 41:15
come, tear * the sheep; Is 56:9
all who go out shall be torn *. Jer 5:6
now it was mildewed and falling *. Jer 13:7
* by vultures and wild animals. Jer 16:4
I will cut you * just as you cut Jer 34:18,19
just as you cut * the calf when you Jer 34:18,19
causes him to sit * in silence Lam 3:28
wolves, who tear * their victims, Eze 22:27
will be torn *, Memphis will be in Eze 30:16
Israel * for special blessings." Eze 37:28
land shall be set * for the Eze 45:7
them and tore them * before they Dan 6:24
by tearing them * with its huge Dan 7:7
that tore men * and that stamped Dan 7:19
kingdom will break * and be divided Dan 11:4
For his empire will be torn * and Dan 11:4
Judah as a lion rips * its prey; Hos 5:14
*, to face their sorrow alone. Zec 12:12,13,14
Olives will split *, making a very Zec 14:4
are wolves and will tear you *. Mt 7:15
broke the loaves * and gave them to Mt 14:19
it and broke it * and gave it to Mt 26:26
in the Temple was split * from Mt 27:51
in the Temple was split * from Mk 15:38
will be split *, three in favor of Lk 12:52
it, he broke it * and gave it to Lk 22:19
hanging in the Temple split *. Lk 23:45
Nor can you be fruitful * from Jn 15:4
* from me you can't do a thing. Jn 15:5
those who are set * for himself. Act 20:32
would tear him *, ordered his Act 23:10
who are set * by faith in me.' Act 26:18
of the waves and began to break *. Act 27:41
Anything that is done * from what Rom 14:23
and you are set * for God, and he 1Co 6:11

were living utterly * from Christ; Eph 2:12
whom God has set * for himself—you Heb 3:1
looking for some victim to tear *. 1Pe 5:8

APARTMENT
so they all left the *. 2Sa 13:9
the most luxurious * in the harem. Est 2:9
She was taken to the king's * in Est 2:12,13,14
From your * came the sound of Eze 23:42

APELLES
Then there is *, a good man whom Rom 16:10

APES
silver, ivory, *, and peacocks 1Ki 10:22
silver, ivory, *, and peacocks. 2Ch 9:21

APHEK
The king of *; Jos 12:8-24
to * at the boundary of the Jos 13:2-7
Achzib, Ummah, *, and Rehob—an Jos 19:30,31
Ebenezer, the Philistines at *. 1Sa 4:1
now mobilized at *, and the 1Sa 29:1
Israel again, this time at *. 1Ki 20:26
the walls of *, but the wall fell 1Ki 20:30
conquer the Syrians at *. 2Ki 13:16,17

APHEKAH
Beth-tappu-ah, *, Humtah, Jos 15:48-62

APHIAH
and great-great-grandson of *. 1Sa 9:1

APHIK
Achzib, Helbah, *, or Rehob; Ju 1:31,32

APIECE
for everyone—three quarts *; Ex 16:18
Literally, "five shekels * by the Num 3:47,48f
weighing about four ounces *); Num 7:84,85,86
for them to have several wives *. 2Ch 11:23

APIS
Why has *, your bull god, fled Jer 46:15

APOLLONIA
of Amphipolis and * and came to Act 17:1

APOLLOS
As it happened, a Jew named *, a Act 18:24
* had been thinking about going Act 18:27
WHILE * WAS in Corinth, Paul Act 19:1
that they are for * or for Peter; 1Co 1:12
than *, and dividing the church. 1Co 3:4
Who am I, and who is *, that we 1Co 3:5
your hearts, and *' work was to 1Co 3:6
things grow. * and I are working 1Co 3:8
I have laid the foundation and * 1Co 3:10
He has given you Paul and * and 1Co 3:22
SO * AND I should be looked upon 1Co 4:1
I have used * and myself as 1Co 4:6
I begged * to visit you along 1Co 16:12
the lawyer and * with their trip; Tit 3:13

APOLLYON
* [and in English, the Destroyer Rev 9:11

APOLOGIZE
altar and go and * and be Mt 5:24

APOLOGY
very hour there has been no *; Jer 44:10

APOSTASY
I am keenly aware of your *, Jer 13:27

APOSTLE
chosen to be an * just as we were. Act 1:17
have chosen as an * to replace Act 1:24,25
became an * with the other eleven. Act 1:26
the believers, and killed the * Act 12:2
I AM AN *, God's messenger, 1Co 9:1
I am not an *, I certainly am to 1Co 9:2
Is everyone an *? 1Co 12:29
even be called an * at all after 1Co 15:9
I was truly an *, sent to you by 2Co 12:12
And the only other * I met at Gal 1:19

APOSTLES
one of the twelve *, went to the Mt 26:14
The * now returned to Jesus from Mk 6:30
(They were appointed as his * Lk 6:13
His * asked him what the story Lk 8:9
his twelve * and gave them Lk 9:1
After the * returned to Jesus and Lk 9:10
send prophets and * to you, and you Lk 11:49
One day the * said to the Lord, Lk 17:5
giving his chosen * further Act 1:1
he appeared to the * from time to Act 1:3
with the eleven *, and shouted to Act 2:14
and to the other *, "Brothers, Act 2:37
attendance at the *' teaching Act 2:42
all, and the * did many miracles. Act 2:43
And the * preached powerful Act 4:33
the * to give to others in need. Act 4:34,35
(the one the * nicknamed "Barny Act 4:36
the money to the * for distribution Act 4:37
Meanwhile, the * were meeting Act 5:12
and arrested the *, and put them Act 5:18
for the * to be brought for trial. Act 5:21
But Peter and the * replied, "We Act 5:29
requested that the * be sent Act 5:34
called in the *, had them beaten, Act 5:40
presented to the *, who prayed for Act 6:6
the * fled into Judea and Samaria. Act 8:1
When the * back in Jerusalem Act 8:14
was given when the * placed their Act 8:18
brought him to the * and told them Act 9:27

"And we * are witnesses of all Act 10:39
SOON THE NEWS reached the * and Act 11:1
leaders, and some backed the *. Act 14:4
to talk to the * and elders there Act 15:2
leaders—all the * and elders were Act 15:4
So the * and church elders set a Act 15:6
Then the * and elders and the Act 15:22
"From: The *, elders and brothers Act 15:23
by the * and elders in Jerusalem. Act 16:4
They are respected by the *, and Rom 16:7
God has put us * at the very end of 1Co 4:9
the other * have of being a guest 1Co 9:4
*, Prophets - those who 1Co 12:28
James saw him and later all the *. 1Co 15:7
worthy of all the *, and I 1Co 15:9
than all the other *, yet actually 1Co 15:10
and we * are all liars because 1Co 15:15
us * to preach the Good News. 2Co 1:21
into thinking they are Christ's *. 2Co 11:13
those who were * before I was. Gal 1:17
on now: the * and the prophets; Eph 2:20
Holy Spirit to his * and prophets. Eph 3:5
been given special ability as *; Eph 4:11
else, although as * of Christ we 1Th 2:6
and from us * who brought you the 2Pe 3:1
Dear friends, remember what the * Jud 1:17
who say they are * but aren't. Rev 2:2
of God and the prophets and the *! Rev 18:20
names of the twelve * of the Lamb. Rev 21:14

APPA-IM
*. Seled died without children, 1Ch 2:30
children, but * had a son named 1Ch 2:31

APPALLED
The leaders of Edom are *, Ex 15:15
I was amazed and *. Is 63:5
all who go by will be *, and gasp Jer 49:17
pass by shall be * and shall mock Jer 50:13
All who know you are * at your Eze 28:19

APPARENTLY
* lighting from time to time upon Gen 8:7f
* a sort of sleeveless tunic Ex 28:4f
* a kind of sacred lot used to Lev 8:8f
he had married." * they were Num 12:1f
Ahima-az * was afraid to tell the 2Sa 18:29f
* we don't mean anything to you; 2Sa 19:6
and Benaiah. * new names were 2Sa 23:24-39f
* Jehu in his zeal exceeded the 2Ki 10:11f
* a different Sheshan than in 1Ch 2:34,35f
Literally, "your saint"; * a Ps 89:19f
* God's patience with their Is 6:10f
This is * an early message to Jer 35:1f
with his eyes." * a reference to Eze 12:12f
with his eyes." * a reference to Eze 12:13f
* the Roman Empire. Dan 2:40f
shall touch Azel"—* a hamlet on Zec 14:5f
Zacharias was * stone deaf as well Lk 1:62f
but * not in this deeper sense. Jn 16:5f
him out of the city, * dead. Act 14:19
He is * quoting some in the 1Co 6:12f
11:5), * in public meetings, but 1Co 14:34f

APPEAL
His decision is without * and is Deu 17:10
the court of final * in cases 2Ch 19:11
of final * in all civil cases; 2Ch 19:11
him frequently to * for justice Lk 18:3
men to kill me. I * to Caesar." Act 25:10,11
against them, to * to Caesar. Act 28:19
Jesus Christ we * to such people—we 2Th 3:12

APPEALED
in fact, that * to them. 1Sa 15:9
You have * to Caesar, and to Act 25:12
But Paul * to Caesar! Act 25:21
However, he * his case to Caesar, Act 25:25
free if he hadn't * to Caesar!" Act 26:32

APPEALS
not the kind that * to the great 1Co 2:6
everything that * to you, and the 1Jn 2:16

APPEAR
shall * before the Lord God. Ex 23:17
the Tabernacle to * before the Ex 30:20
And no one shall * before me Ex 34:20
of Israel shall * before the Lord. Ex 34:23
when you go up to * before the Lord Ex 34:24
said, "Jehovah will * to them." Lev 9:4
his glory will * to you." Lev 9:6
the spot does not * to be deeper Lev 13:21
"But if the spots * again, the Lev 14:43
where leprosy may *: in a garment Lev 14:54
"Every man in Israel shall * Deu 16:16
who suddenly * from nowhere?" 1Sa 25:11
everyone should * at Jerusalem Ez 10:7,8
the morning to *, and caused the Job 38:12
Can you make lightning * and Job 38:35
When you *, they will be Ps 21:9,10
the oceans back to let dry land *. Ps 24:2
He will * in his glory! Ps 102:16
Let them *! Is 50:8
with it and * there in my glory," Hag 1:8
And many false prophets will * Mt 24:11
will * in the heavens and there Mt 24:30
for Zacharias to * and wondered why Lk 1:21

(APPEAR Con't)
when Christ comes, he will just * Jn 7:27
wolves, will * among you, not Act 20:29
occasions when I shall * to you. Act 26:16
Literally, "not that we may * 2Co 13:7f
Then this wicked one will *, 2Th 2:8
God our Savior to *, then he saved Tit 3:4
to * now before God as our Friend. Heb 9:24

APPEARANCE
ready for God's * two days from Ex 19:15
changed to the * of fire, and Num 9:15
to the * of fire at night. Num 9:16
Men judge by outward *, but I 1Sa 16:7
very embarrassed over their *. 2Sa 10:5
He will not judge by *, false Is 11:3
Tell them its * and its plan so Eze 43:10
by your * and have no strength. Dan 10:16
they watched, his * changed so that Mt 17:2
and motionless, to all * dead. Mk 9:26
because he had changed his *. Mk 16:12
Literally, "the * of his face Lk 9:29f
They were splendid in *, Lk 9:31

APPEARED
And light *. Gen 1:3
go down, other mountain peaks *. Gen 8:5
Then Jehovah * to Abram and said, Gen 12:7
it was he who * to her—as "the God Gen 16:13
years old, God * to him and told Gen 17:1
THE LORD * again to Abraham while Gen 18:1
Jehovah * to him there and told Gen 26:2
Jehovah * to him on the night of Gen 26:24
That night God * to Laban in a Gen 31:24
God of your father * to me last Gen 31:29
is why he * to you last night." Gen 31:42
So Hamor and Shechem * before Gen 34:20
the God who * to you when you fled Gen 35:1
at Bethel that God * to him when he Gen 35:7
Paddan-aram, God * to him once Gen 35:9
the place where God had * to him; Gen 35:13,14
of the child who * first, but he Gen 38:28
seven more heads * on the stalk, Gen 41:6
"God Almighty * to me at Luz in Gen 48:3
Angel of Jehovah * to him as a Ex 3:2
They'll say, 'Jehovah never * to Ex 4:1
and Jacob, has really * to you. Ex 4:5
the night, Jehovah * to Moses and Ex 4:24
Almighty God who * to Abraham, Ex 6:2,3
for the boils * upon them too. Ex 9:11
* the awesome glory of Jehovah. Ex 16:10
and the glory of the Lord * to Lev 9:23
no yellow hair has *, and if the Lev 13:32
Then the glory of the Lord *, and Num 14:10,11
Then the glory of Jehovah * to Num 16:19
the Cloud * and the awesome glory Num 16:42
and the glory of Jehovah * to Num 20:6
He * to them in a great cloud at Deu 31:15
And with the favor of God who * Deu 33:16
a man * nearby with a drawn sword. Jos 5:13
The Angel of the Lord * to him Ju 6:12
the same one who * to Moses and Ju 6:16f
Angel of the Lord * to the wife of Ju 13:2,3
"A man from God * to me and I Ju 13:6
the Angel of God * once again to Ju 13:9
and wouldn't have * to us and told Ju 13:23
The bottom of the sea *. 2Sa 22:16
The Lord * to him in a dream 1Ki 3:5
wanted, the Lord * to him the 1Ki 9:2,3
of Israel who had * to him twice to 1Ki 11:9,10
a wide crack * in the altar and the 1Ki 13:5
by horses of fire, * and drove 2Ki 2:11
previously * in bold face type. 1Ch 1:5-9f
That night God * to Solomon and 2Ch 1:7
where the Lord had * to Solomon's 2Ch 3:1
One night the Lord * to Solomon 2Ch 7:12
Suddenly—leprosy * in his 2Ch 26:19
world began! It * at his command! Ps 33:9
Hophra of Egypt * at the southern Jer 37:5
four strange forms * that looked Eze 1:5
it sat someone who * to be a Man. Eze 1:26
way the glory of the Lord * to me. Eze 1:27,28
I saw what * to be a Man; Eze 8:2
Six men * at his call, coming Eze 9:2
* in the sky above the heads of Eze 10:1
what * to be a city opposite me. Eze 40:2
of Holies was what * to be an Eze 41:21
the God of Israel * from the east. Eze 43:2
another small horn * among them, Dan 7:8
a buck goat * from the west, so Dan 8:5
The star * to them again, Mt 2:9
the Lord * to Joseph in a dream. Mt 2:13
first * to them two years before. Mt 2:16
angel of the Lord * in a dream to Mt 2:19
Then John *, and if you are Mt 11:13
Suddenly Moses and Elijah * and Mt 17:3
a place, or has * here or there,' Mt 24:23
and * to many people there. Mt 27:53
Then Elijah and Moses * and Mk 9:4
he * to two who were walking from Mk 16:12
Still later he * to the eleven Mk 16:14
suddenly an angel *, standing to Lk 1:11,12
Gabriel * to her and said, Lk 1:28
Suddenly an angel * among them, Lk 2:9
Then two men * and began talking Lk 9:30
For when he describes how God * Lk 20:37,38
Then an angel from heaven * Lk 22:43
Suddenly two men * before them, Lk 24:4
has really risen! He * to Peter!" Lk 24:33,34
of how Jesus had * to them as they Lk 24:35
LATER JESUS * again to the Jn 21:1
time Jesus had * to us since his Jn 21:14
his crucifixion he * to the Act 1:3
And another time when he * to Act 1:6
fire * and settled on their heads. Act 2:3
* to our ancestor Abraham in Iraq Act 7:2
Sinai, an Angel * to him in a flame Act 7:30
Lord Jesus, who * to you on the Act 9:17
He told us how an angel had * to Act 11:13
For I have * to you to appoint Act 26:16
already many such persons have *. 1Jn 2:18
Then the stars of heaven * to be Rev 6:13
trumpet, and what * to be a huge Rev 8:8,9
THEN A GREAT pageant * in heaven, Rev 12:1
Suddenly a red Dragon *, with Rev 12:3

APPEARING
them about Jehovah * to you here in Ex 3:16
me, though not * to you personally, Jn 5:37
was Christ * to Abraham in human Heb 7:3f

APPEARS
This clause * in some versions, Gen 27:38f
and the brightness * to be no Lev 13:26
not spread, and it * to be no Lev 13:34
But if it * that the spreading Lev 13:37
22, where the total * in the text. Jos 21:20,21,22f
and the new crop *, and the Pro 27:25,26,27
the Man * who has a right to it. Eze 21:27
I replied. "It * to be about Zec 5:2
"But who can live when he *? Mal 3:2
book of Isaiah, * in Malachi 3:1. Mk 1:3f
42 which * in all the manuscripts. Lk 1:28f
prediction of this * in the Book of Act 1:20
the Lord Jesus * suddenly from 2Th 1:7
the dead when he * to set up his 2Ti 4:1

APPEASE
Jacob's strategy was to * Esau Gen 32:20
of death and a wise man will * it. Pro 16:14

APPEASED
Then at last my anger will be *. Eze 5:13

APPENDIX
an * giving additional facts. Mk 16:9f

APPETITE
* is gone when I look at it; Job 6:5,6,7
all taste and * for food and Job 33:20
tasteless, and I have lost my *. Ps 102:3,4
My son, honey whets the *, and so Pro 24:13,14
God has given us an * for food 1Co 6:13
their god is their *: they are Php 3:19

APPETITES
the young lions' * as they lie in Job 38:39,40
Their * were gone and death was Ps 107:18

APPHIA
your home, and to * our sister, and Phm 1:1

APPIAN
on the * Way. Act 28:15

APPLAUDED
which was * by the army and general 1Sa 18:5

APPLAUDS
the world loudly * success— yet in Ps 49:18

APPLE
As though they were the * of his Deu 32:10
rotten * can spoil a barrelful. Ecc 9:18
The Girl: "My lover is an * Sol 2:3
King Solomon: "Under the * tree Sol 8:5

APPLES
stolen * Pro 9:17
as golden * in a silver basket. Pro 25:11
'*'—for I am utterly lovesick. Sol 2:5
your breath like *, and your Sol 7:8
the pomegranates wither; the * Joe 1:12

APPLICABLE
instructions are * whether her baby Lev 12:6

APPLIED
This prohibition * not only while Lev 18:14f
Note that this rule * to the High Lev 21:11f
in verse 1 * to ordinary priests. Lev 21:11f
And I * myself to search for Ecc 1:12-15
word because * to idols, so it will Hos 1:16f
they * to someone far away. Hos 8:12

APPLIES
after birth. This * to every Gen 17:12
and it * to all your posterity. Gen 17:12
The same law * to those born in Ex 12:49
The same rule * to your vineyards Ex 23:11
This rule * whether the sacrifice Lev 7:9
and this rule * to your sons and Lev 10:8,9
This * not only while the Lev 15:3
and humility. This * whether you Lev 16:29,30
This restriction * to the Lev 22:25
this law * to the foreigner as Lev 24:15,16
This * to men and women alike. Num 5:3
This same law * to individual Num 15:29
sanctuary; this * to your tithes of Deu 14:23
The same * to donkeys, clothing, Deu 22:3
In Matthew 22:41–45, Jesus * Ps 110:1f
well as the next * to Israelites Is 65:1f
well as the next * to Israelites Is 65:1f
that what I am saying * to you. Heb 6:9

APPLY
These same rules * to foreigners Ex 12:19
in God's ways. I * the laws of God Ex 18:15,16
"The same instructions * to both Lev 7:7
The same instructions * to Lev 15:7
the same rules * as indicated Lev 15:25
these laws * both to you who are Lev 18:26
These instructions * both to Num 15:13,14
(This release does not * to Deu 15:3
These instructions * only to Deu 20:15
but could * themselves fully to 2Ch 31:4
* your rules to everything I do. Ps 119:125
Won't even one of you * these Is 42:23
phrases * to a human king of Tyre, Eze 28:12f
Tyre, and some seem to * to Satan. Eze 28:12f
* these verses with discernment. Eze 28:12f
Don't let the prophets' words * Act 13:40
the laws of marriage no longer * Rom 7:2
that the promises * only to Rom 9:7
through Christ * to them both when Eph 3:6
to understand how they * to you. 2Ti 2:7

APPLYING
quoted by Christ as * to himself. Ps 40:7f

APPOINT
Or, "Let Pharaoh * officials to Gen 41:34,35f
hate bribes, and * them as judges, Ex 18:21
then I will * a place where he can Ex 21:13
please * a new leader for the Num 27:16
I will * them as your leaders.' Deu 1:13
"* judges and administrative Deu 16:18
dead if I do not * you as 2Sa 19:13
Egypt, I didn't * a place for my 1Ki 8:16
you to select and * judges and Ez 7:25
We will * agents in each Est 2:3
And I will * some of those Is 66:21
I will * over them four kinds of Jer 15:3
And I will * responsible Jer 23:4
Babylon, did not * Coniah (King Jer 37:1
and I will * over the Edomites the Jer 49:19
* over them whomsoever I please. Jer 50:44
Minni, and Ashkenaz. * a leader; Jer 51:27
months, they will * men to search Eze 39:14
our hills, he will * seven Mic 5:5
For I have appeared to you to * Act 26:16
and I asked you to * pastors Tit 1:5

APPOINTED
—let her be the one you have * as Gen 24:14
who should be * for the job, Gen 41:38
"See, I have * you as my Ex 7:1
the Lord has * tomorrow as a day of Ex 16:23
"See, I have * Bezalel (son of Ex 31:1
"And I have * Oholiab (son of Ex 31:6
at the dates * each year in March; Ex 34:18
has specifically * Bezalel (the son Ex 35:30,31
all who have been * to minister to Lev 7:35
led by a man * for the task. Lev 16:21
to the Lord at the time he had *. Num 9:6,7
of the men I have * to handle the Num 34:16-28
of the men I have * to oversee the Num 34:29
every tribe, and * them as Deu 1:15
priest or judge * by God for this Deu 17:12
But he * none for Israel; Deu 32:9
Then they set up the idols and * Ju 18:30
* his sons as judges in his place. 1Sa 8:1
the Lord has * you to be the king 1Sa 10:1
"It was the Lord who * Moses and 1Sa 12:6
* him as king over his people; 1Sa 13:14
that you killed God's * king." 2Sa 1:16
He is God's * king no more. 2Sa 1:21
who have * me as their new king." 2Sa 2:7
his family and who * me as leader 2Sa 6:21
Absalom had * Amasa as general 2Sa 17:25
DAVID NOW * regimental colonels 2Sa 18:1
* Adonijah to be the next king? 1Ki 1:24
for I have * him king of Israel 1Ki 1:35
Then the king * Benaiah as 1Ki 2:35
* a man to be my people's leader.' 1Ki 8:16
The king * his special assistant 2Ki 7:17
from Judah and * their own king. 2Ki 8:20
the Lord, and they * from among 2Ki 17:32
who had been * by the previous 2Ki 23:5
Then the king of Babylon * King 2Ki 24:17
Then King Nebuchadnezzar * 2Ki 25:22
of Babylon had * Gedaliah as 2Ki 25:23
King David * songleaders and 1Ch 6:31
other Levites—were * to various 1Ch 6:48
and they were * by David and Samuel 1Ch 9:22
He * certain of the Levites to 1Ch 16:4
David also * Heman, Jeduthun, 1Ch 16:41
And Jeduthun's sons were * as 1Ch 16:42
shepherds I * to care for my 1Ch 17:6
the throne and * his son Solomon as 1Ch 23:1
Tabernacle then * men to prophesy 1Ch 25:1
The singers were * to their 1Ch 25:8
The sons of Obed-edom were also * 1Ch 26:4,5
the Merari group, * Shimri as the 1Ch 26:10
his brothers were * to care for the 1Ch 26:26

(APPOINTED Con't)
of Izhar) were * public 1Ch 26:29
of Jerijah, were * to control the 1Ch 26:31,32
were * on the basis of their 1Ch 26:31,32
So God * Solomon to take the 1Ch 29:23
* by my lord David, your father. 2Ch 2:14
He had * other priests instead 2Ch 11:15
have * heathen priests instead. 2Ch 13:9
ancestors. He * judges throughout 2Ch 19:5
"Watch your step—I have not * 2Ch 19:6
Then he * Amariah, the High 2Ch 19:11
had * to end the dynasty of Ahab. 2Ch 22:7
Jehoiada now * the Levite 2Ch 23:18
One of the priests was * in each 2Ch 31:19
He recruited an army and * 2Ch 32:6
at the Temple, he * Shaphan (son of 2Ch 34:8
The king of Egypt now * Eliakim, 2Ch 36:4
Nebuchadnezzar * Jehoiachin's 2Ch 36:10
were * to supervise the workmen. Ez 3:8
King Cyrus * as governor of Judah. Ez 5:14
I * twelve leaders of the Ez 8:24
He also reports that you have * Neh 6:7
the gates and had * the Neh 7:1
instead, they rebelled and * a Neh 9:17
He was * by King David, Neh 11:22,23
On that day men were * to be in Neh 12:44
who had been * as custodian of the Neh 13:4
and I * Hanan (son of Zaccur, son Neh 13:13
AFTERWARDS KING Ahasuerus * Est 3:1
to do their duty on the * day." Est 3:14
who had been * as her attendant, Est 4:5
and Esther * Mordecai to be in Est 8:2
But the Jews went ahead on that * Est 9:5
two days at the * time each year. Est 9:27
rescued me, the king you *. Ps 18:50
sanctified you and * you as my Jer 1:5
They all return at God's * time Jer 8:7
of Babylon (I have * him as my Jer 25:8,9
"The Lord has * you to replace Jer 29:26
King Jehoiakim * his son Coniah as Jer 37:1f
who has been * as governor of Judah Jer 40:5
of Babylon had * Gedaliah as Jer 40:7
and * by the Babylonian emperor. Jer 41:18
"Son of dust, I have * you as a Eze 3:17
were created. I * you to be the Eze 28:14
I have * you as a watchman for Eze 33:7
* place outside the Temple area. Eze 43:21
steward who was * by the Dan 1:11
costly gifts, and * him to be ruler Dan 2:48
request, the king * Shadrach, Dan 2:49
until God's * time has come. Dan 11:27
all their trials, at God's * time. Dan 11:35
She has * kings and princes, but Hos 8:4
I * the prophets to guard my Hos 9:8
"The Lord * seventy others and Mt 11:1f
he has * me to preach Good News Lk 4:18,19
(They were * as his "apostles," Lk 6:13
I chose you! I * you to go and Jn 15:16
so that Pharaoh * him governor over Act 7:10
Paul and Barnabas also * elders Act 14:23
by the man he has *, and has Act 17:31
As you know, God has * me as a Rom 11:13
This letter is from me, Paul, * by 2Co 1:1
to God who * him High Priest, just Heb 3:2
but later God * by his oath his Son Heb 7:28
And since every high priest is * Heb 8:3
angelic being is * by God to Rev 1:20f
they will be * to their kingdoms Rev 17:12

APPOINTING
I am hereby * you to be in Gen 41:40
to Mordecai, [* him Prime Minister Est 8:2
who submit to him, * them to Dan 11:39

APPOINTMENT
of his troops, an * which was 1Sa 18:5
her to ask for an * with the king. 2Sa 14:2,3
Daniel held this * as the king's Dan 1:21
country. An * with Herod was Act 12:21

APPOINTMENTS
These * were made by King Hezekiah 2Ch 31:12,13
Those * have already been made." Mk 10:40

APPOINTS
men, and that he * anyone he Dan 5:21
John replied, "God in heaven * Jn 3:27

APPORTION
you are to * among yourselves by Num 34:13

APPORTIONED
of Israel its * place as its home. Ps 78:55

APPRECIATE
and the Lord will * it. Lev 4:31
the Lord will * and enjoy— for in Lev 17:5
the Lord will * and enjoy— instead Lev 17:6
which the Lord will * and enjoy. Num 29:2
her that we * her kindness to us. 2Ki 4:13
In the end, people * frankness Pro 28:23
their owner and * his care for Is 1:3
I hope you properly * the work of 1Co 16:18
But though I * your gifts, what Php 4:17

APPRECIATED
of it will be fully * by the Lord. Lev 2:9
people of Judah * the priests and Neh 12:44
They also * the work of the Neh 12:45
A man with good sense is *. Pro 13:15
and what he says will not be *. Ecc 9:16
Hezekiah * this and took the Is 39:2
should be highly *, especially 1Ti 5:17

APPRECIATION
to show special * and thanksgiving Lev 7:15
words of * for their "kindness." Pro 23:6,7,8
a special * for Daniel, and Dan 1:9
and * to those who had sent them. Act 15:33
joy, and show your *, for he Php 2:29

APPRECIATIVELY
(King Hezekiah spoke very * to 2Ch 30:22

APPREHENSION
My mind is filled with * and with Ps 6:3

APPREHENSIVE
And Solomon became *, for Hadad 1Ki 11:14

APPRENTICE
* than from a skilled rebel! Pro 26:10

APPROACH
Lord, or when they * the altar to Ex 30:20
among those who * me, and I will be Lev 10:3
"As you * a city to fight Deu 20:10
rest of us how we should * God. Job 37:19,20
would we then dare to * him? Job 37:19,20
veiling his * with dense clouds Ps 18:11
The whole land trembles at the * Jer 8:16
and he shall * me, for who would Jer 30:21
that no human being can * him. 1Ti 6:16

APPROACHED
Then Abraham * him and said, Gen 18:22,23
As he * his brother he bowed low Gen 33:3
was over, Joseph * Pharaoh's staff Gen 50:4
Then the baby's sister * the Ex 2:7
As the Egyptian army *, the Ex 14:10
Just then Saul * Samuel and 1Sa 9:18
As Goliath *, David ran out to 1Sa 17:48,49
When the woman * the king, she 2Sa 14:4
As he *, the woman asked, "Are 2Sa 20:17
King David's death *, he gave this 1Ki 2:1
AS JEROBOAM * the altar to burn 1Ki 13:1
As they *, Ben-hadad's scouts 1Ki 20:17
Then the prophet * King Ahab and 1Ki 20:22
* the Lord and said, 'I'll do it!' 1Ki 22:21
As she * Mount Carmel, Elisha saw 2Ki 4:25
has * his record of obedience. 2Ki 23:25
the Temple, they * Zerubbabel and Ez 4:2
Haman now * the king about the Est 3:8
So Esther * and touched its tip. Est 5:2
a prostitute. She * him, saucy and Pro 7:10
when the Israelites * (so long ago Is 17:9
eighty men * Mizpah from Shechem, Jer 41:5
from heaven; he * the Ancient of Dan 7:13
his report), so I * one of those Dan 7:16
But as he *, I was too frightened Dan 8:17
AS JESUS AND the disciples * Mt 21:1
out as he * the village gate. Lk 7:12
As they * Jericho, a blind man Lk 18:35
But even as he said this, a mob * Lk 22:47
Literally, "* Jesus to kiss Lk 22:47f
As they *, Jesus said, "Here Jn 1:47
around noon as he * the village of Jn 4:5,6
As they * the Temple, they saw a Act 3:2
So I * him and asked him to give Rev 10:9

APPROACHES
the day of the Lord's judgment *. Joe 2:1
surely, the time * when the vision Hab 2:3
the evil prince of this world *. Jn 14:30

APPROACHING
But as he was * the borders of Gen 12:11,12,13
frightened of you as though * God! Gen 33:10
the Israelis were * (for they were Num 21:1
people of Israel were * his land. Num 33:40
that the Philistines were *. 1Sa 7:7
and the sounds of a great army *. 2Ki 7:6
and his company * and shouted, 2Ki 9:17
Then Ornan saw the king *. 1Ch 21:21
hear the first rumor of * forces. Jer 51:46
A leper is *. Mt 8:2

APPROPRIATE
Everything is * in its own time. Ecc 3:11

APPROVAL
So Moses gave his * by saying to Num 32:28
God has given his *, let us send 1Ch 13:2
life and wins * from the Lord. Pro 8:35
But his * is as refreshing as the Pro 19:12
trusted God—let God show his * Mt 27:41,42,43
Herod's * she was powerless. Mk 6:19
"Your * or disapproval means Jn 5:41,42
"and your * is required." Jn 18:31
and the breastplate of God's *. Eph 6:14
God and won his *, none of them Heb 11:39

APPROVE
shall demand, and as the judges *. Ex 21:22
let him * the indictments made Job 31:35
Do you * of those who condemn Ps 94:21,22
will know that you * of this custom Act 21:24
so that all can * your behavior. Rom 13:12,13
it will look as if you * of them. 1Ti 5:22

APPROVED
ritually * by God. Gen 8:20f
This was an * custom for those who 1Sa 1:11f
elders of Israel * of the plan, 2Sa 17:4
was accepted and * through his Rom 4:23
"not that we may appear *." 2Co 13:7f

APPROVES
a good man whom the Lord *; Rom 16:10
the Lord himself *, with Eph 6:4

APPROXIMATE
The above figures are *. Lev 27:3f
And all of them—the * count of Jn 6:10

APPROXIMATELY
it is * a tenth of a bushel. Ex 16:36
* to our first day of April. Num 9:2,3f
Note: This was * May 5. Num 10:11f
So * three thousand soldiers were Jos 7:4
of silver," * 800,000 pounds 1Ch 19:6f
shall surround the city for * Eze 48:17
Literally, "10,000 talents." * Mt 18:24f
* L700. Mt 18:28f
* £3,500. Act 19:18,19f

APRIES
Hophra, or *, ruled Egypt from 588 Jer 44:30f

APRIL
IT WAS ON the fifteenth day of * Num 1:1
to our first day of *. Num 9:2,3f
in the wilderness of Zin in * Num 20:1
Egypt, on the first day of *, Num 33:3,4
Passover during the month of *, Deu 16:1
six months, from * until October. 2Sa 21:10f
seventeenth day of * in the fourth 2Ch 3:2
the first day of *, and by the 2Ch 29:17
the normal time in *, because not 2Ch 30:2,3
the first day of *, in Jerusalem. 2Ch 35:1
celebrated on the first day of *. Ez 6:19
ONE DAY IN * four months later, as Neh 2:1
This was done in * of the twelfth Est 3:7
EARLY IN * of the twenty-fifth Eze 40:1
* was the first month of the Eze 45:18f
Then one day early in *, as I was Dan 10:4
Press Release, * 24, 1964). Rev 9:16f

APT
his idol, you are * to do it. Ex 34:15
"Somebody's * to get angry and Ju 18:25
Gomorrah were. An * comparison! Is 1:10

AQABA
boundary was on the Gulf of *. Ob 1:1f

AQUEDUCT
down through an * to the west side 2Ch 32:30
at the end of the * which leads Is 7:3

AQUILA
with a Jew named *, born in Pontus, Act 18:2,3
taking Priscilla and * with him. Act 18:18
Priscilla and * were there and Act 18:25,26
Tell Priscilla and * "hello." Rom 16:3
loving greetings. * and Priscilla 1Co 16:19
to Priscilla and * and those living 2Ti 4:19

AR
The city of * in Moab, Num 21:27-30
borders of Moab at *, into the Deu 2:18
Moabites, whose capital is at *. Deu 2:29
In one night your cities of * and Is 15:1

AR-TA-XERXES
same thing during the reign of *. Ez 4:7
of the letter they sent to King *: Ez 4:11
When this letter from King * was Ez 4:23
and *, the kings of Persia. Ez 6:14
during the reign of King * of Ez 7:1
of the reign of * and arrived at Ez 7:7,8,9
King * presented this letter to Ez 7:11
"From: *, the king of kings. Ez 7:12
"I, * the king, send this decree Ez 7:21
during the reign of King *: Ez 8:1
of the reign of King * of Persia, Neh 1:1
the reign of King *—my aides and I Neh 5:14
interesting comments on to King *! Neh 6:7
the reign of King * (though I later Neh 13:6

ARA
Jephunneh, Pispa, *. 1Ch 7:38

ARAB
Holon, Giloh, *, Dumah, Eshan, Jos 15:48-62
and Geshem the * heard of our plan, Neh 2:19
TOBIAH, Geshem the *, and the rest Neh 6:1
An * tribe living in the desert Jer 49:28f
but rather, a group of * tribes. Jer 49:30f

ARABAH
the valley of the * in the Deu 1:1
the valley of the *, and the Negeb, Deu 1:7
crossing the * Road that goes south Deu 2:8
They also received the * (or, Deu 3:17
(also called the Sea of the *). Deu 3:17
and all the * east of the Jordan Deu 4:49
and attacked at the Plain of *. Jos 8:14
The kings in the *, south of Jos 11:1
the lowlands, the *, and the hills Jos 11:16
the lowlands, the *, the mountain Jos 12:8-24
along the north edge of the *. Jos 18:18
went down into the *, ran south Jos 18:18
out toward the * through a gate 2Ki 25:4,5
it across the fields, toward *. Jer 52:7
to the brook of *," says the Lord, Amo 6:14

ARABIA
with the kings of * and the other 1Ki 10:15

(ARABIA Con't)
from the kings of * and many other 2Ch 9:13,14
is God's message concerning *: Is 21:13
you will hide in the deserts of *. Is 21:13
and all the kings of * and of Jer 25:24
Dedan was in Northern * and was a Jer 49:8f
For Cush and Put and Lud, * and Eze 30:5
Great trading centers in *. Eze 38:13f
the deserts of *, and then came Gal 1:17

ARABIAN
Vedan and Javan bring * yarn, Eze 27:19

ARABIANS
and Tobiah and the *, Ammonites, Neh 4:7
"The *, and Kedar's wealthy Eze 27:21
Jewish converts— Cretans, and *. Act 2:11

ARABS
tribute, and the * donated 7,700 2Ch 17:11
and the * living next to the 2Ch 21:16
of * had killed his older sons). 2Ch 22:1
battles with the * of Gurbaal and 2Ch 26:7
Moabites, *, and yes, even you Jer 9:25,26
Hagar" by the *—and in my Gal 4:24,25

ARAD
WHEN THE KING of * heard that the Num 21:1
the king of * and his people, they Num 21:2
Canaanite king of *, who lived in Num 33:40
The king of *; Jos 12:8-24
south of *, the descendants of Ju 1:16
Zebadiah, *, Eder, Michael, 1Ch 8:15,16

ARAH
*, Hanniel, Rizia. 1Ch 7:39
From the subclan of *, 775; Ez 2:3-35
Shecaniah (son of *) and because Neh 6:18
From the subclan of *, 652; Neh 7:8-38

ARAM
Asshur,Arpachshad, Lud, *. Gen 10:22
(father of *),Chesed, Hazo, Gen 22:20-23
From the land of *, Num 23:7-10
Arpachshad, Lud, *, Uz, Hul, 1Ch 1:17
But Geshur and * wrested these 1Ch 2:23
Rohgah, Jehubbah, *. 1Ch 7:34
Hezron was the father of *; Mt 1:3
* was the father of Amminadab; Mt 1:4

ARAM-MAACAH
from Mesopotamia, *, and Zobah. 1Ch 19:6

ARAM'S
* sons Gen 10:23

ARAMAEAN
his * concubine, were Asri-el and 1Ch 7:14

ARAMAIC
speak in *, for we understand it. 2Ki 18:26
to him in the * language, and it Ez 4:7
to him, "Please talk to us in * Is 36:11
* was the language used in Is 36:11f
the corresponding * expression is Eze 2:1f
The language was *; Dan 1:3,4f
(speaking in *) said to the king, Dan 2:4
was in familiar *, they could read Dan 5:8f
your father"—the * word for Dan 5:11f
He spoke here in *. Mk 15:34f

ARAMEAN
of Bethuel the * from Paddam-aram, Gen 25:20
brother—the son of Bethuel the *. Gen 28:5

ARAMEANS
* who went to Egypt for refuge. Deu 26:5

ARAN
The children of Dishan:Uz, *. Gen 36:28,29,30
Dishan's sons were Uz and *. 1Ch 1:42

ARARAT
to rest upon the mountains of *. Gen 8:3,4
Turkey—the land of *—and his son 2Ki 19:37
into the land of *, and Esar-haddon Is 37:38
bring out the armies of *, Minni, Jer 51:27

ARAUNAH
of * the Jebusite at the time. 2Sa 24:16
floor of * the Jebusite." 2Sa 24:18
When * saw the king and his men 2Sa 24:20
"Why have you come?" * asked. 2Sa 24:21
"Use anything you like," * told 2Sa 24:22
But the king said to *, "No, I 2Sa 24:24

ARBA
given the city of * (also called Jos 15:13
Kiriath-arba (* was the father of Jos 21:9-16
Paarai from *; 2Sa 23:24-39

ARBATH
Abi-albon from *; 2Sa 23:24-39
Abiel from *; 1Ch 11:26-47

ARBITRATE
Your duties will be to * for the Lev 10:10
He will * among the nations, and Mic 4:3

ARCH
now become the capstone of the *! Ps 118:22
became the capstone of the *.' Act 4:11

ARCHANGEL
cry of the * and the great 1Th 4:16

ARCHELAUS
the new king was Herod's son, *. Mt 2:22

ARCHER
of Paran, and became an expert *. Gen 21:20,21

ARCHER'S
themselves. The * aim will fail, Amo 2:15

ARCHERS
Then the * overtook Saul and 1Sa 31:3,4
Philistine * shot and wounded him. 1Ch 10:3
All of them were expert * and 1Ch 12:2
The enemy * struck King Josiah 2Ch 35:23
his target. His * surround me, Job 16:13
Only a few of its stalwart * Is 21:17
Elamites are the *; Is 22:6,7
let the * shoot at her; Jer 50:14
Send out a call for * to come to Jer 50:29

ARCHES
Some manuscripts add: "And the * Eze 40:28f

ARCHIPPUS
And say to *, "Be sure that you Col 4:17
our sister, and to * who like Phm 1:1

ARCHITE
found Hushai the * waiting for him 2Sa 15:32
friend, Hushai the *, arrived, he 2Sa 16:16
the * what he thinks about this." 2Sa 17:5
the * was his personal advisor. 1Ch 27:33

ARCHITECTS
your * have made you glorious. Eze 27:4

ARCHITES
in the territory of the *; Jos 16:1

ARCHIVES
historian and in charge of the *; 1Ki 4:1
*, where documents were stored. Ez 6:1

ARD
Huppim, and *. Gen 46:19-22
named after their ancestor *. Num 26:38-41

ARDENT
until now, * multitudes have been Mt 11:12

ARDITES
The *, named after their ancestor Num 26:38-41

ARDON
Jesher, Shobab, and *. 1Ch 2:18

AREA
(This * was inhabited by Gen 12:6
The men of this * were unusually Gen 13:13
in this entire * that our father Gen 19:31
its name to the * it occupied. Gen 36:40-43
boil its meat in a sacred *. Ex 29:31
camping * with its own flag. Num 1:52
have its own tent *, with its Num 2:1
The * east of the Tabernacle was Num 3:38
Ever after, the * was known as Num 11:3
all the cities of that *. Num 21:2
spies to look over the Jazer *; Num 21:31,32
name of their * to Havroth-jair. Num 32:41
the * Nobah, after his own name. Num 32:42
While in that * they camped at Num 33:49
In this way the total * of our Num 36:3
(Cities in the * included Suph, Deu 1:1
Lebanon—the entire * from the Deu 1:7
be easy to conquer the whole *. Deu 1:41
around in the * of Mount Seir. Deu 2:1
to live in that *, a very large Deu 2:10
"(That *, too, used to be Deu 2:20
and Gad I gave the * beginning at Deu 3:12
Gad received the * extending from Deu 3:16
Israel also conquered all the * Deu 4:48
The toilet * shall be outside Deu 23:12
of the surrounding * heard what had Jos 9:1
the Israelis: (The * involved Jos 12:1
of the present * of Gilead, which Jos 12:2
of Israel. The * included the hill Jos 12:8-24
and all of the Lebanon mountain * Jos 13:2-7
the following * to the tribe of Jos 13:15
receive which * was decided by Jos 14:1
The cities within its * Jos 19:41-46
by sacred lot in the * of Bashan. Jos 21:6
To Esau I gave the * around Mount Jos 24:4
arrived in that * of Ephraim, Ju 17:7,8
in the * strong enough to try it. Ju 18:7
the Shaalim *, and the entire land 1Sa 9:4
And if he is in the * at all, 1Sa 23:23
Ben-hur, whose * for this taxation 1Ki 4:8-19
Ben-deker, whose * was Makaz, 1Ki 4:8-19
Ben-hesed, whose * was Arubboth, 1Ki 4:8-19
whose * was the highlands of Dor; 1Ki 4:8-19
Baana (son of Ahilud), whose * was 1Ki 4:8-19
Ben-geber, whose * was 1Ki 4:8-19
of Iddo), whose * was Mahanaim; 1Ki 4:8-19
daughters), whose * was Naphtali; 1Ki 4:8-19
of Paruah), whose * was Issachar; 1Ki 4:8-19
Shime-i (son of Ela), whose * was 1Ki 4:8-19
Geber (son of Uri), whose * was 1Ki 4:8-19
King Solomon ruled the whole * 1Ki 4:21
the entire * claimed by Egypt—all 2Ki 24:7
in the Bashan * from the tribes of 1Ch 6:62
They lived in an * bounded on one 1Ch 7:28
in the * of the Netophathites). 1Ch 9:15,16
that is why that * of Jerusalem is 1Ch 11:7
public administration of that *. 1Ch 26:30
Netophah in the * of Othni-el, who 1Ch 27:15
the cities in that *, and terror 2Ch 14:14
in the Ashdod * and in other parts 2Ch 26:6
*, and to all registered Levites. 2Ch 31:19
the * west of the Euphrates River: Ez 4:17
the mayor of the Beth-haccherem *; Neh 3:14
and the * of Geba and Azmaveth, for Neh 12:29
cattleman in that entire *. Job 1:2,3
Literally, "bamah"—a hilltop * Eze 20:29f
in the mountainous * southeast of Eze 38:2,3f
of the Temple * with his measuring Eze 40:5
yards. The * was 175 feet square. Eze 41:13
to measure the entire Temple *. Eze 42:15
* from the public places. Eze 42:16-20
place outside the Temple *. Eze 43:21
be built within the * which is 8 Eze 45:3
be the residence * for the Levites Eze 45:5
This Temple * will be 8 Eze 48:9
Next to it lies the * where the Eze 48:12
grounds, is garden * belonging to Eze 48:18
"The entire *—including sacred Eze 48:20
both sides of this *, extending Eze 48:21,22
South of Benjamin's * lies that Eze 48:24
site, covering the * all the way Zec 14:10
no one could go through that *. Mt 8:28
villages of that *, teaching in the Mt 9:35
"kings" over the *, his Mt 14:1f
a boat to a remote * to be alone. Mt 14:13
Then they went out to an * known Mt 27:33
through that entire * of Galilee. Mk 1:28
the whole * to spread the news of Mk 6:55
the * east of the Jordan River. Mk 10:1
through the Temple *, the chief Mk 11:27,28
*, he asked them this question: Mk 12:35
on a large, level *, surrounded by Lk 6:17,18
In the Temple * he saw merchants Jn 2:14
the Temple in the * known as Act 5:12
in the * we now know as Syria. Act 7:2f
the surrounding *, and preaching Act 14:5,6
In deference to the Jews of the * Act 16:3
* was stirred by God's message. Act 19:20

AREAS
of the people inhabiting these *: Gen 10:13,14
white, transparent * in the skin, Lev 13:38
called Cush. But * of Ethiopia and Num 12:1f
the plains, divided by tribal *. Num 24:2
The kings in the mountain * of Jos 11:1
Here is a list of the * still to Jos 13:2-7
situated in the * assigned to Jos 17:11
The cities in these *, besides Jos 19:15,16
Baana (son of Hushai), whose * 1Ki 4:8-19
their surrounding *: Beth-shean, 1Ch 7:29
road, and two to the nearby *. 1Ch 26:18
the Temple storage *, and the 1Ch 28:12
all idols from the * occupied by 2Ch 34:33
and placed in the storage *. Neh 10:38
He will enter the richest * of Dan 11:24
Cyrene language * of Libya, Act 2:10

ARELI
Ezbon, Eri, Arodi, and *. Gen 46:16,17
named after their ancestor *. Num 26:15-18

ARELITES
The *, named after their ancestor Num 26:15-18

ARETAS
under King * kept guards at the 2Co 11:32

ARGOB
the entire * region of Bashan. Deu 3:4
kingdom of King Og, the * region. Deu 3:13
over the whole * region (Bashan) to Deu 3:14
and the region of * in Bashan, 1Ki 4:8-19
palace at Samaria (* and Arieh were 2Ki 15:25

ARGUE
If God decides to * with him, Job 9:3
I should try to * with Almighty Job 9:14
Nevertheless I am going to * my Job 13:15
I will * my case before him." Job 13:15f
Who can * with me over this? Job 13:19
"Do you still want to * with the Job 40:2
Does the pot * with its maker? Is 45:9
Consult together, * your case Is 45:21
men who love to * and to fight. Hab 1:3
arrival they came to * with him. Mk 8:11
And they began to * among Lk 22:24
Jesus Christ, who was I to *?" Act 11:17
jumped up to * that Paul was all Act 23:9
For instance, don't * with him Rom 14:2
ceremonies I don't *, even though I 1Co 9:20
But if anyone wants to * about 1Co 11:16
From now on please don't * with Gal 6:17
not to * over unimportant things. 2Ti 2:14
who wants to * will be ashamed of Tit 2:8
But someone may well *, "You say Jas 2:18
Try to help those who * against Jud 1:22

ARGUED
* over it with Isaac's herdsmen. Gen 26:20
This is that Moses who * with the Ex 6:30
people of Israel * against God and Ex 17:7
And so they * back and forth 1Ki 3:22
So I * with these parents and Neh 13:25
some Jewish leaders * with them. Mk 9:14
Pilate * with them, for he Lk 23:20
he had * plotted to murder him. Act 9:29
the Jewish believers * with him. Act 11:2
and * against whatever Paul said. Act 13:45
Paul and Barnabas * and Act 15:2
" 'But Lord,' I *, 'they Act 22:19
But after they had * back and Act 28:25

ARGUERS
These *—their minds warped by 1Ti 6:5

ARGUING
If Job had been * with me, I Job 32:14
he needs when * with his enemies. Ps 127:5
When * with a rebel, don't use Pro 26:4,5
There's no use * with a fool. Pro 29:9
So there's no use * with God Ecc 6:10
for they had been * about which of Mk 9:34
Then the Jews began * with each Jn 6:52
hands to the Jews, but they keep * Rom 10:21
Christ to stop * among yourselves. 1Co 1:10
me about the * that goes on in 1Co 11:18
complaining and *, so that no one Php 2:14
time * and talking foolishness. 1Ti 1:6
Don't waste time * over foolish 1Ti 4:7
Don't get involved in * over Tit 3:9
when he was * with Satan about Jud 1:9
ARGUMENT
named the well, "The Well of *!" Gen 26:20
(meaning "*" and "strife!" Ex 17:7
discussion and * going on all 2Sa 19:8,9,10
The * continued back and forth, 2Sa 19:43
settle an *, ask advice at Abel.' 2Sa 20:18
to the king to have an * settled. 1Ki 3:16
But the king won the *, and Joab 1Ch 21:4
my side of this *, and listen to Job 23:4,5
and try to see my side of this *. Job 31:35
man wins his case by careful *; Pro 13:2
every day along with * and strife. Pro 17:1
* that isn't any of your business. Pro 26:17
"What's all the * about?" Mk 9:16
Now came an * among them as to Lk 9:46
so is a home filled with * and Lk 11:17
One day someone began an * with Jn 3:25
started an * with him, and they Act 6:9
down every proud * against God and 2Co 10:5
love of *, are men like that. 2Ti 2:17
the oath ends all * about it. Heb 6:16
This will be their line of *: 2Pe 3:4
ARGUMENTS
Job's * and yet had condemned him. Job 32:3
carefully to your *, but not one of Job 32:11,12
deciding all the people's *. Ps 122:5
Pride leads to *; Pro 13:10
ends * and settles disputes Pro 18:18
don't use foolish * as he does, or Pro 26:4,5
Bring your strongest *. Is 41:1
all the Jewish * in public debate, Act 18:28
that whether my * are trivial or Act 26:29
* and quarrels, dear brothers. 1Co 1:11
is wise enough to decide these *? 1Co 6:5
up questions and * instead of 1Ti 1:3,4
and stirring up * ending in 1Ti 6:4
Keep out of foolish * with those 1Ti 6:20
things. Such * are confusing and 2Ti 2:14
in foolish * which only upset 2Ti 2:23
keep out of * and quarrels about Tit 3:9
They stir up *; Jud 1:19
ARI-EL
So I sent for Eliezer, *, Ez 8:16
ARI-OCH
But when *, the chief Dan 2:14
Then * told him all that had Dan 2:15
Then Daniel went in to see *, who Dan 2:24
Then * hurried Daniel in to the Dan 2:25
ARIDAI
*, and Vaizatha. Est 9:7-10
ARIDATHA
Aspatha, Poratha, Adalia, *, Est 9:7-10
ARIEH
* were also slain in the revolt). 2Ki 15:25
ARIEL
sons of * of Moab. 2Sa 23:20
Literally, "to *." Is 29:1f
as her name "*" means—an altar Is 29:2
ARIELS
Literally, "*." 1Ch 11:22f
ARIMATHEA
a rich man from * named Joseph, one Mt 27:57
Late that afternoon Joseph from * Mk 15:42,43
from the city of * in Judea, went Lk 23:50,51,52
Afterwards Joseph of *, who had Jn 19:38
ARIOCH
*, king of Ellasar, Gen 14:1
ARISAI
Parmashta, *, Est 9:7-10
ARISE
Moses cried out, "*, O Lord, and Num 10:35
Jacob shall * in power Num 24:15-19
"But he said to me, '* and lead Deu 10:11
Let those gods *, Deu 32:38
*, O Barak! Ju 5:12
And now, O Lord God, * and enter 2Ch 6:41
I will cry to him, "*, O Lord! Ps 3:7
But Lord! * in anger against the Ps 7:6
O Lord, * and judge and punish Ps 9:19
O Lord, *! Ps 10:12
The Lord replies, "I will * Ps 12:5
Lord, * and stand against them. Ps 17:13,14
we will * to stand firm and sure! Ps 20:8
Rouse yourself, my soul! *, O Ps 57:8
God of Israel, * and punish the Ps 59:5
*, O GOD, and scatter all your Ps 68:1
praise your name! *, O God, and Ps 74:22
their waves * in fearful storms; Ps 89:9
shine out. * and judge the earth; Ps 94:1
*, O Lord, and enter your Temple Ps 132:8
How delicious they smell! *, my Sol 2:13
Ethiopian Dynasty would soon *. Is 7:18f
*, MY PEOPLE! Is 60:1
out and say, "*, and let us go up Jer 31:6
will * to take your place. Dan 2:39
will *, more brutal than the Dan 7:24
and a king will * whose armies Dan 9:26
wooden idols to * and save them, Hab 2:19
The men of Nineveh shall * Mt 12:41
For false Christs shall *, and Mt 24:24
shall * and point her finger at Lk 11:31
too, shall * and condemn this Lk 11:32
of all those who * from the dead, Col 1:18
ARISES
"If a case * that is too hard Deu 17:8
ARISING
'Who is this,' they ask, '* as Sol 6:10
ARISTARCHUS
along Gaius and *, Paul's traveling Act 19:29
* and Secundus, from Thessalonica; Act 20:4
I should add that *, Act 27:2
*, who is with me here as a Col 4:10
So do Mark, *, Demas and Luke, Phm 1:24
ARISTOBULUS
those working at the house of *. Rom 16:10
ARK
left the * in pairs and groups. Gen 8:18,19
kept in the * in the Tabernacle. Ex 16:34
"Using acacia wood, make an * 3¾ Ex 25:10
the sides of the *, to carry it. Ex 25:13,14
When the * is finished, place Ex 25:16
Literally, "Put into the * the Ex 25:16f
the two ends of the lid of the *. Ex 25:18
Install the lid upon the *, and Ex 25:21
place within the * the tablets of Ex 25:21
and the * will contain the laws Ex 25:22
Behind this curtain place the * Ex 26:33
of the *—in the Most Holy Place. Ex 26:34
* containing the Ten Commandments. Ex 30:6
Tabernacle, the *, the table and Ex 30:26,27
it in front of the * where I meet Ex 30:36
* with the place of mercy upon it; Ex 31:7
The * and its poles; Ex 35:10-19
NEXT BEZALEL MADE the *. Ex 37:1
the sides of the *, to carry it. Ex 37:5
to house the *, so that the Levites Ex 38:21
* with the Ten Commandments in it; Ex 39:33-40
In it, place the * containing Ex 40:3
the * within the Holy of Holies. Ex 40:3
for the incense in front of the *. Ex 40:5
Inside the * he placed the stones Ex 40:20
poles to the * and installed the Ex 40:20
Then he brought the * into the Ex 40:21
veil, where the * and the place of Lev 16:1
place above the * (containing the Lev 16:13
the care of the *, the table, the Num 3:31-35
the veil and cover the * with it. Num 4:5
poles of the * in their rings. Num 4:6
of mercy over the *, the spot Num 7:89
with the * at the front of the Num 10:33
As the * was carried forward, Num 10:35
And when the * was set down he Num 10:36
the * nor Moses left the camp. Num 14:44
meet with you, in front of the *. Num 17:4
* as a reminder of this rebellion. Num 17:10
into battle, accompanied by the *, Num 31:6
to make a wooden * to keep them in, Deu 10:1
that I should place them in the *. Deu 10:2
So I made an * of acacia wood Deu 10:3
the tablets in the * I had made, Deu 10:5
Levi to carry the * containing the Deu 10:8
who carried the * containing the Deu 31:9
who carried the * containing the Deu 31:25
the law beside the *, as a solemn Deu 31:26
the priests carrying the * of God, Jos 3:2,3,4
Literally, "the * of the covenant Jos 3:2,3,4f
clear space between you and the *; Jos 3:2,3,4
* and lead us across the river!" Jos 3:6
are carrying the * to stop at the Jos 3:8
Think of it! The * of God, who Jos 3:11
are carrying the * touch the water Jos 3:13,14
were carrying the * touched the Jos 3:13,14
were carrying the * stood on dry Jos 3:17
of the Jordan where the * is. Jos 4:5
when the * of God went across!' Jos 4:7
were carrying the * stood in the Jos 4:10
carry the * up out of the river. Jos 4:11
to the priests carrying the *. Jos 4:15,16
ahead of the *, each carrying a Jos 6:3,4
the *, followed by a rearguard. Jos 6:6-9
The * was carried around the city Jos 6:11
before the * of the Lord until Jos 7:6
priests with the *, ready to Jos 8:33
(The * of God was in Bethel in Ju 20:27,28
*, the Lord called out, "Samuel! 1Sa 3:2,3
"Let's bring the * here from 1Sa 4:3
So they sent for the * of the 1Sa 4:4
When the Israelis saw the * 1Sa 4:5
it was because the * of the Lord 1Sa 4:6
And the * of God was captured 1Sa 4:11
for the safety of the * of God. 1Sa 4:13
and the * has been captured." 1Sa 4:17
happened to the *, Eli fell 1Sa 4:18
heard that the * had been captured 1Sa 4:19
this because the * of God had been 1Sa 4:21,22
TOOK the captured * of God from the 1Sa 5:1
ground before the * of Jehovah! 1Sa 5:3
before the * of the Lord again. 1Sa 5:4
can't keep the * of the God of 1Sa 5:7
to decide how to dispose of the *. 1Sa 5:8
But when the * arrived at Gath, 1Sa 5:9
So they sent the * to Ekron, but 1Sa 5:10
are bringing the * of the God of 1Sa 5:10
them to send the * back to its own 1Sa 5:11
THE * REMAINED in the Philistine 1Sa 6:1
shall we do about the * of God? 1Sa 6:2
Place the * of God on the cart 1Sa 6:8
Then the * of the Lord and the 1Sa 6:11
saw the * they went wild with joy! 1Sa 6:13
of Levi lifted the * and the chest 1Sa 6:15
because they looked into the *. 1Sa 6:19
"Where can we send the * from 1Sa 6:20
brought back the * of the Lord. 1Sa 6:21
came and took the * to the hillside 1Sa 7:1
charge of it. The * remained there 1Sa 7:2
"Bring the * of God," Saul 1Sa 14:18
(For the * was among the people 1Sa 14:18
to bring home the * of the Lord of 2Sa 6:1
the cherubim. The * was placed 2Sa 6:3
put out his hand to steady the *. 2Sa 6:6
so he died there beside the *. 2Sa 6:7
can I ever bring the * home?" 2Sa 6:9
he brought the * to the City of 2Sa 6:12
So Israel brought home the * of 2Sa 6:15
The * was placed inside the tent 2Sa 6:17
the * of God is out in a tent!" 2Sa 7:2
Uriah replied, "The * and the 2Sa 11:11
Levites took the * of the Covenant 2Sa 15:24
took the * back into the city. 2Sa 15:25,26
the * and the Tabernacle again. 2Sa 15:25,26
carried the * of God back into the 2Sa 15:29
For you carried the * of the Lord 1Ki 2:26
And as he stood before the * of 1Ki 3:15
The inner room was where the * of 1Ki 6:19
of the * of the Covenant of the 1Ki 8:1
carried the * to the Temple, along 1Ki 8:3,4
before the *, sacrificing uncounted 1Ki 8:5
Then the priests took the * into 1Ki 8:6
spot where the * would be placed; 1Ki 8:7
the * and its carrying poles. 1Ki 8:7
There was nothing in the * at 1Ki 8:9
the Temple for the * which contains 1Ki 8:21
after he had placed the * in it. 1Ch 6:31
And let us bring back the * of 1Ch 13:3
present when the * of God was 1Ch 13:5
to bring back the * of the Lord God 1Ch 13:6
out his hand to steady the * 1Ch 13:9
him because he had touched the *. 1Ch 13:10
I ever get the * of God home?" 1Ch 13:12
of David. The * remained there 1Ch 13:14
to house the * of God, and issued 1Ch 15:1
we transfer the * to its new home 1Ch 15:2
of the * into the new Tabernacle. 1Ch 15:3
you may bring the * of Jehovah, the 1Ch 15:12
* of Jehovah, the God of Israel. 1Ch 15:14
Then the Levites carried the * 1Ch 15:15
and Elkanah were guards for the *. 1Ch 15:23
and Jehiah guarded the *. 1Ch 15:24
to take the * to Jerusalem. 1Ch 15:25
were carrying the *, they 1Ch 15:26
carrying the *, the singers, and 1Ch 15:27
of Israel took the * to Jerusalem 1Ch 15:28
(But as the * arrived in 1Ch 15:29
SO THE * of God was brought into 1Ch 16:1
before the * by giving constant 1Ch 16:4
trumpets regularly before the *. 1Ch 16:6
Literally, "before the * of the 1Ch 16:37f
home while the * of the Covenant of 1Ch 17:1
be bringing the * and the other 1Ch 22:19
in which the * of the Covenant of 1Ch 28:2
the * of the Covenant of the Lord. 1Ch 28:18
King David for the * of God when he 2Ch 1:4
the * from the [Tabernacle in the 2Ch 5:2
Levites lifted the * and carried it 2Ch 5:4,5
oxen before the * in such numbers 2Ch 5:6
Then the priests carried the * 2Ch 5:7,8
their wings spread over the * and 2Ch 5:7,8
The * is still there at the time 2Ch 5:9
Nothing was in the * except the 2Ch 5:10
Israel, and placed the * there. 2Ch 6:11
And in the * is the Covenant 2Ch 6:11
of yours where the * of your 2Ch 6:41
palace, for the * of the Lord was 2Ch 8:11
"Since the * is now in Solomon's 2Ch 35:3
and allowed his * to be captured; Ps 78:61
build a permanent home for the * Ps 132:2-5
First the * was in Ps 132:6

(ARK Con't)
the *, the symbol of your power. Ps 132:8
possessed the * of God's covenant. Jer 3:16
about, and the * will not be Jer 3:16
Noah went into the * and the flood Lk 17:27
chest, called the * of the Heb 9:4
Inside the * were the tablets of Heb 9:4
built the * and saved his family. Heb 11:7
while Noah was building the *. 1Pe 3:20
was opened and the * of his Rev 11:19

ARK'S
out over the * golden cover, called Heb 9:5

ARKITES
*, Sinites,Arvadites, Zemarites, Gen 10:15-19
Hivites, *, Sinites, Arvadites, 1Ch 1:13-16

ARM
you have said and * yourselves for Num 32:20
great power and your mighty *.' Deu 9:29
With savage * and face and head. Deu 33:20
and a rounded back, with * rests; 1Ki 10:19
Instantly the king's * became 1Ki 13:4
your God to restore my * again." 1Ki 13:6
the king's * became normal again. 1Ki 13:6
reward because you healed my *." 1Ki 13:7
and leans on my *, may the Lord 2Ki 5:18
let my * be torn from its socket! Job 31:22
stopped the * raised to strike? Job 38:15
* yourself, O Mighty One, Ps 45:3
Use your strong right * to rescue Ps 60:4,5
protected by your strong right *. Ps 63:8
Strong is your *! Ps 89:13
brushes a grasshopper from his *. Ps 109:22,23
The strong * of the Lord has done Ps 118:15,16
down his mighty * upon his enemies Is 30:30
The Lord has bared his holy * Is 52:10
lie there with your * bared [to Eze 4:7
"Son of dust, I have broken the * Eze 30:21
means by the first "broken *." Eze 30:21f
God's sword will cut his * and Zec 11:17
his right eye; his * will become Zec 11:17
the man, "Stretch out your *." Mt 12:13
"that you had to * yourselves with Mt 26:55
"How powerful is his mighty *! Lk 1:51
Literally, "To whom has the * of Jn 12:38f
of a man's *—not an angel's! Rev 21:17f

ARMAGEDDON
Hebrew, *—the Mountain of Megiddo. Rev 16:16

ARMED
the country under * escort—Abram, Gen 12:20
even though they had left Egypt *; Ex 13:17,18
he followed up with an * attack, Num 21:31,32
of Israel, 12,000 * men were sent Num 31:4,5
will go over *, ahead of the rest Num 32:17
the Lord fully * into Canaan, but Num 32:32
down until their * men led the Deu 3:18
your troops, fully *, must lead the Jos 1:14
of Manasseh—fully * as Moses had Jos 4:12,13
instructions: the * men would lead Jos 6:6-9
So six hundred * troops of the Ju 18:11
with all of the * men standing just Ju 18:15,16
bag and, * only with his shepherd's 1Sa 17:40
One must be * to chop them down; 2Sa 23:7
Another time, * only with a 2Sa 23:21
warrior who was * with a spear; 2Sa 23:21
on duty, and he * them from the 2Ki 11:10
There were 44,760 *, trained, and 1Ch 5:18
From Judah, 6,800 troops * with 1Ch 12:24-37
they were fully * and totally 1Ch 12:24-37
* with large shields and bows. 2Ch 14:8
These officers, fully *, formed 2Ch 23:10
So I placed * guards from each Neh 4:13
defeats his foes. * with his tin Job 15:25,26
For you have * me with strong Ps 18:39
though fully *, turned their backs Ps 78:9
people, fully *, mounted for war. Jer 6:23
They are fully * for slaughter; Jer 50:27
you a mighty host, all fully *. Eze 38:4
I will overthrow their * might, Hag 2:22
Though Tyre has * herself to the Zec 9:3
Then the Lord will go out fully * Zec 14:3
with a great crowd * with swords Mt 26:47
* to the teeth to capture me? Mk 14:48
send Jesus under * guard to Pilate, Mk 15:1
strong and fully *, guards his Lk 11:21
* with swords and clubs to get me? Lk 22:52
to Damascus, * with the authority Act 26:12
200,000,000 * and organized Rev 9:16f

ARMENIA
Tubal were in Asia Minor and *. Is 66:19f

ARMFUL
As Paul gathered an * of sticks Act 28:3

ARMIES
mobilized their * in Siddim Valley Gen 14:3
And now I am two *! Gen 32:10
and all his *, and the Egyptians Ex 14:4
all his *, chariots, and horsemen. Ex 14:17
Pharaoh's chariots and *, Ex 15:4
you with enemy *, so that your Ex 22:24
In summary, the * of Israel Num 2:32,33
God did to the * of Egypt and to Deu 11:4
destroyed, for the * of Israel kept Jos 8:27
combined their * to fight for their Jos 9:1
* for a united attack on Gibeon. Jos 10:5
the hills are here with their *." Jos 10:6
and took the enemy * by surprise. Jos 10:9
wiped out the five * except for a Jos 10:20
*, and uniting to crush Israel. Jos 11:4
by Joshua and the * of Israel on Jos 12:7
disbanded the * of Israel, the Ju 2:6
Allied with him were the * of Ju 3:13
Soon afterward the * of Midian, Ju 6:33
of Harod. The * of Midian were Ju 7:1
The vast * of Midian, Amalek, Ju 7:12,13
all the vast * of Midian!" Ju 7:15
left of the allied * of the east; Ju 8:10
their misery. The * of Ammon were Ju 10:17
But the * of Israel had agreed Ju 20:32
I defy the * of Israel! 1Sa 17:10
strutted before the * of Israel. 1Sa 17:16
to defy the * of the living God?" 1Sa 17:26
defied the * of the living God! 1Sa 17:36
of the Lord of the * of heaven and 1Sa 17:45
* for another war with Israel. 1Sa 28:1
the * of Israel were at Gilboa. 1Sa 28:4
The two * then began to fight 2Sa 2:17
combined * of Israel and Judah. 2Sa 3:12
"The Ark and the * and the general 2Sa 11:11
Ben-hadad agreed and sent his * 1Ki 15:20
Lord God of the * of heaven, in 1Ki 18:15
Lord God of the * of heaven, but 1Ki 19:14
The two * camped opposite each 1Ki 20:29
the * of heaven stood around him. 1Ki 22:19
led their * to Ramoth-gilead. 1Ki 22:29
So their two *, now joined also 2Ki 3:9
about the three * marching against 2Ki 3:21
"The three * have attacked and 2Ki 3:23
attacking * of Syria and Israel. 2Ki 16:7
During his reign the * of King 2Ki 24:10
one who led our * to battle and 1Ch 11:2
mobilized the * of Judah and 2Ch 11:1
and bows. Both * were composed of 2Ch 14:8
Listen, * of Judah and 2Ch 15:2
mobilized his * to attack Israel. 2Ch 16:4
led their * to Ramoth-gilead. 2Ch 18:28
LATER ON, THE * of the kings of 2Ch 20:1
"And now see what the * of 2Ch 20:10
Lord caused the * of Ammon, Moab, 2Ch 20:22
gods of Edom. The * met at 2Ch 25:21
to Damascus. The * from Israel also 2Ch 28:5
Elkanah. The * from Israel also 2Ch 28:8
in his war against the * of Edom. 2Ch 28:16
So God sent the Assyrian *, and 2Ch 33:11
me and bring fresh * against me. Job 10:17
Some nations boast of * and of Ps 20:7
Commander of all of heaven's *! Ps 24:10
The Commander of the * of heaven Ps 46:7
The Commander of the heavenly * Ps 46:11
* of the world are his trophies. Ps 47:9
the Commander of the * of heaven. Ps 48:8
God of heaven's *, God of Israel, Ps 59:5
cry out the happy news: "The * Ps 68:11,12,13
O Lord God of the * of heaven, Ps 69:6
O Jehovah, God of heaven's *, Ps 80:4
of the * of heaven, and bless us. Ps 80:14
O God of the * of heaven. Ps 80:19
Temple, O Lord of the * of heaven. Ps 84:1
of heaven's *, my King and my God! Ps 84:3
O Jehovah, God of the heavenly *, Ps 84:8
O Lord of the * of heaven, Ps 84:12
of the heavenly *, where is there Ps 89:8
Yes, bless the Lord, you * of Ps 103:21
* of Babylon captured Jerusalem. Ps 137:7
praises before the * of angels Ps 138:1
his angels, all the * of heaven. Ps 148:2
"as upon a dance before two *." Sol 6:13f
he will destroy her *, judges, Is 3:2
King, the Lord of heaven's *." Is 6:5
fell to the Assyrian * in 722 B.C. Is 7:8f
mighty * will rage against them. Is 8:7,8
the Lord of the * of heaven! Is 8:13
Lord of heaven's * for his people: Is 8:18
* has dedicated himself to do it! Is 9:7
to him, the Lord of heaven's *. Is 9:13
wrath of the Lord of heaven's *. Is 9:19,20
drowned the Egyptian * in the sea. Is 10:26
Look, the mighty * of Assyria are Is 10:28,29
The Lord, the Lord of the * of Is 10:33
set apart these * for this task; Is 13:3
Listen as the * march! Is 13:4
The * of Babylon will run until Is 13:14
The attacking * will have no Is 13:18
Lord of heaven's *, and will cut Is 14:22
says the Lord of the * of heaven. Is 14:23
their * spread out as far as Is 16:8
Look, see the * thundering toward Is 17:12
from the Lord God of heaven's *! Is 22:5
Lord God of the * of heaven has Is 22:15,16
The Commander of the * of heaven Is 23:9
Then the Lord of heaven's * will Is 24:23
Your * will be burned to lime, Is 33:12
his fury is against their *. Is 34:2
Lord will deliver you from my *. Is 36:18
over the * of the king of Assyria? Is 36:18
all its * is no obstacle to you! Is 37:25
of Assyria, his * shall not enter Is 37:33
and to put entire * to the sword. Is 41:2
He will utterly rout the * of the Is 48:14
And I have created the * that Is 54:16
by invading * as in the past. Is 65:21,22
survivors of the * of the nations, Is 66:19f
I am calling the * of the Jer 1:15
I see great * marching on Jer 2:15
I see the * of Egypt rising Jer 2:16
noise of marching * coming near. Jer 4:29
The Lord God says, See the * Jer 6:22
We have heard the fame of their * Jer 6:24
For suddenly the destroying * Jer 6:26
of great * coming from the north. Jer 10:22
Destroying * plunder the land; Jer 12:12
See the * marching from the Jer 13:20
will let invading * kill you here Jer 19:7
together all the * of the north Jer 25:8,9
waste by warring *—because of the Jer 25:38
and all his * from all the kingdoms Jer 34:1
I will summon the Babylonian * Jer 34:22
With you I will crush *, Jer 51:21
bring out the * of Ararat, Minni, Jer 51:27
Bring against her the * of the Jer 51:28
* of all the countries they rule. Jer 51:28
* against Babylon, says the Lord. Jer 51:48
Destroying * come and slay her Jer 51:56
land and tell the * of the enemy to Eze 14:17
Then the * of the nations Eze 19:8
He and his *—the terror of the Eze 30:11
of all their *—all of them Eze 32:26
his hordes and the * of Togarmah Eze 38:6
You and all your vast * will die Eze 39:4
for Gog and his * in the Valley of Eze 39:11
There Gog and all his * will be Eze 39:11
Jerusalem with his *, and the Lord Dan 1:1
him, though their * be mighty, and Dan 8:24
and a king will arise whose * Dan 9:26
* of Egypt will go down to defeat. Dan 11:15
again turn his * southward, as he Dan 11:29
help from her * or her weapons." Hos 1:7
I will gather the * of the Hos 10:10
great * can make a nation safe! Hos 10:13
I will remove these * from the Joe 2:20
will gather the * of the world into Joe 3:2
collect all your *. Joe 3:9
* will pass through her any more. Joe 3:17
You are to send your * against Ob 1:1
The * of destruction are coming; Mic 6:9
when the combined * of the Nah 2:1f
are already surrounded by enemy *! Nah 2:1
and disperse the * of your enemy. Zep 3:15
invading * from entering Israel. Zec 9:8
their * to surround Jerusalem. Zec 12:2
will bewilder the * drawn up Zec 12:4
* of heaven—praising God: Lk 2:13
surrounded by *, then you will know Lk 21:20
they made whole * turn and run Heb 11:34
* westward without hindrance. Rev 16:12
And they gathered all the * of Rev 16:16
The * of heaven, dressed in Rev 19:14
earth and their * to fight against Rev 19:19
the attacking * and consume them. Rev 20:9

ARMLOADS
comes to us with * of salvation. Ps 130:7

ARMONI
two sons of Rizpah—* and 2Sa 21:8

ARMOR
he groaned to his youthful * Ju 9:54
spearhead, and his * bearer walked 1Sa 17:4-7
Then Saul gave David his own *—a 1Sa 17:38,39
but stored his * in his tent. 1Sa 17:54
He groaned to his * bearer, 1Sa 31:3,4
But his * bearer was afraid to, 1Sa 31:3,4
When his * bearer saw that he 1Sa 31:5
So Saul, his * bearer, his three 1Sa 31:6
stripped off his * and sent the 1Sa 31:9
His * was placed in the temple of 1Sa 31:10
Ten of Joab's young * bearers 2Sa 18:15
a new suit of *, closed in on David 2Sa 21:16
Naharai from Be-eroth, the * 2Sa 23:24-39
hundred pieces of * (gold worth 1Ki 10:16,17
Ahab between the joints of his *. 1Ki 22:34
When his chariot and * were 1Ki 22:38
So they stripped off Saul's * 1Ch 10:9
They fastened his * to the walls 1Ch 10:10
was General Joab's * bearer; 1Ch 11:26-47
*, spices, horses, and mules. 2Ch 9:24
lower * and the breastplate meet. 2Ch 18:33
me with strong * for the battle. Ps 18:39
Put on your *, take your shield Ps 35:2
His faithful promises are your *. Ps 91:4
want attacks you in full *. Pro 6:11
He put on righteousness as *, Is 59:17
Buckle on your *, you Egyptians Jer 46:3
your spears, put on your *. Jer 46:4
and put on the * of right living, Rom 13:12,13
Put on all of God's * so that Eph 6:11
So use every piece of God's * to Eph 6:13

ARMOR Con't)	
protected by the * of faith and	1Th 5:8
ARMORED	
on every side with * men and I will	Eze 23:24
I will mobilize your troops and *	Eze 38:4
The locusts looked like horses *	Rev 9:7
ARMORIES	
were placed in * in every city as a	2Ch 11:12
ARMORY	
and a fortified city and an *."	2Ki 10:2,3
aromatic oils, the *—everything.	2Ki 20:13
afterwards return them to the *.	2Ch 12:11
from the *, where the wall turns.	Neh 3:19
You run to the * for your	Is 22:8
The Lord has opened his * and	Jer 50:25
took him into the * and called out	Mt 27:27
ordered Paul to be taken to the *.	Act 21:34
force and bring him back to the *.	Act 23:10
and came to the * and told Paul.	Act 23:16
They returned to the * the next	Act 23:32
ARMPITS	
* to protect you from the ropes."	Jer 38:12
ARMRESTS	
also gold *, each flanked by a	2Ch 9:18
ARMS	
other's * and wept a long while.	Gen 46:29
But Israel crossed his * as he	Gen 48:14
to issue a call to * to the	Ex 17:9
but whenever he rested his * at	Ex 17:11
Moses' * finally became too	Ex 17:12
of you must take * to wage	Num 31:3
old enough to bear *, had died.	Deu 2:14,15
underneath are the everlasting *.	Deu 33:27
old enough to bear * had been	Jos 5:4,5
* when they left Egypt were dead;	Jos 5:6
as a call to * and mustered an army	Ju 3:27
as a call to *, and the men of	Ju 6:34
But he broke the ropes from his *	Ju 16:12
the call to * throughout Israel.	1Sa 13:3,4
he cuddled it in his * like a	2Sa 12:3
She will lie in your * and keep	1Ki 1:2
and she lay in his * to warm him	1Ki 1:3,4
dead child in my * and took mine to	1Ki 3:20
reached out his * toward heaven,	2Ch 6:12,13
them, and broke the * of orphans.	Job 22:9
Break the * of these wicked men.	Ps 10:15
and carry them forever in your *.	Ps 28:9
She put her * around him and	Pro 7:13
like myrrh. His * are round bars	Sol 5:14
Your * lie paralyzed with fear;	Is 13:7
he will carry the lambs in his *	Is 40:11
Now we can solder on the *."	Is 41:7
to you in their *, and your	Is 49:22
spreading out my * to welcome them	Is 65:2
Judah, not even the babies in *.	Jer 44:7
are cut off; her * are broken.	Jer 48:25
break both his *—the strong one and	Eze 30:22
And I will strengthen the * of	Eze 30:24
But I will break the * of	Eze 30:24
Babylon, while the * of Pharaoh	Eze 30:25
its chest and * were of silver, its	Dan 2:32
pools of fire; his * and feet shone	Dan 10:5,6
him to walk, I held him in my *.	Hos 11:3
in the upraised * of the cavalry!	Nah 3:3
missing * and legs had new ones;	Mt 15:31
by wearing on their * little	Mt 23:5
sprinkled their * to the elbows,	Mk 7:3
and taking the child in his * he	Mk 9:36
children into his * and placed his	Mk 10:16
the child in his *, praising God.	Lk 2:28
him with open *, for they had been	Lk 8:40
him with open *, for they had been	Jn 4:45
down and took him into his *.	Act 20:10,11,12
ARMY	
But now the other *, that of the	Gen 14:8,9
And as the * of the kings of	Gen 14:10
the retiring * as far as Dan.	Gen 14:14
the fleeing * to Hobah, north of	Gen 14:15
of his *, returned home again.	Gen 21:32
and also Phicol, his * commander.	Gen 26:26
meet Jacob—with an * of 400 men!	Gen 32:6
* of Midian when it invaded Moab.	Gen 36:31-39
and the Egyptian * overtook the	Ex 14:9
As the Egyptian * approached, the	Ex 14:10
And of all the * of Pharaoh that	Ex 14:28
to fight the * of Amalek.	Ex 17:9
went out to fight the * of Amalek.	Ex 17:10
troops crushed the * of Amalek,	Ex 17:13
land I will meet you with an *!"	Num 20:18
mobilizing his *, he marched to the	Num 20:20
he mobilized his * and attacked	Num 21:1
Instead he mobilized his * and	Num 21:23
met them with his * at Edre-i.	Num 21:33
And the mighty * of the king of	Num 24:21,22
Then the Israeli * took as	Num 31:9,10,11
the victorious *, but Moses was	Num 31:13
* officers and battalion leaders.	Num 31:14
donkeys, and flocks kept by the *.	Num 31:28
So the half given to the *	Num 31:36-40
a man named Nobah led an *	Num 32:42
He immediately mobilized his *	Deu 3:1
and chariots, an * far greater than	Deu 20:1
before the Israeli * and say,	Deu 20:2
"Then the officers of the *	Deu 20:5
drafted into the * nor given any	Deu 24:5
* across to the plains of Jericho.	Jos 4:12,13
of the Lord's *," he replied.	Jos 5:14
Your entire * is to walk around	Jos 6:3,4
The Israeli * was paralyzed with	Jos 7:5
take the entire * and go to Ai,	Jos 8:1
Before the main * left for Ai,	Jos 8:3,4
"When our main * attacks, the	Jos 8:5
but Joshua and the rest of the *	Jos 8:9
Joshua and the Israeli * fled	Jos 8:15
When the * of Israel had finished	Jos 8:24
The Israeli * set out at once to	Jos 9:17
So Joshua and the Israeli * left	Jos 10:7
panic so that the * of Israel	Jos 10:10
until the Israeli * had finished	Jos 10:13
the Israeli * returned to Gilgal.	Jos 10:15
the rest of the *, "Go on chasing	Jos 10:19
So Joshua and the Israeli *	Jos 10:20
captains of his * to put their feet	Jos 10:24
arrived with his * to try to help	Jos 10:33
him and destroyed his entire *.	Jos 10:33
The Israeli * then captured Eglon	Jos 10:34,35
So Joshua and his * conquered the	Jos 10:40
Then Joshua and his * returned	Jos 10:43
gave all that vast * to the	Jos 11:8
Manasseh left the * of Israel at	Jos 22:9
they mustered an * at Shiloh and	Jos 22:12
So the * of Simeon went with	Ju 1:3
Simeon went with the * of Judah.	Ju 1:3
but the Israeli * soon captured him	Ju 1:4,5,6
Afterward the * of Judah fought	Ju 1:9
Afterwards the * of Judah joined	Ju 1:17
The * of Judah also conquered the	Ju 1:18
Israel against the * of King	Ju 3:10
an * under his own command.	Ju 3:27
The * then proceeded to seize the	Ju 3:28
The commander-in-chief of his *	Ju 4:2,3
Jabin's mighty * with all his	Ju 4:7
that Barak and his * were camped at	Ju 4:12
his entire *, including the nine	Ju 4:13
all of Sisera's * was destroyed;	Ju 4:16
With an * of peasants!	Ju 5:11
name) and his * got an early start	Ju 7:1
whole vast enemy * began rushing	Ju 7:21
destroy the fleeing * of Midian.	Ju 7:23
the generals of the * of Midian!	Ju 8:2,3
the Midianite * in surprise raids.	Ju 8:11
I'll tell Abimelech, 'Get up an *	Ju 9:29
Come by night with an * and hide	Ju 9:32
to attack Israel's * at Mizpah.	Ju 10:17
their * against the Ammonites.	Ju 11:6
an * at Jahaz and attacked them.	Ju 11:20
and he led his * across the land of	Ju 11:29
and attacked the * of Ammon.	Ju 11:29
So Jephthah led his * against the	Ju 11:32
mobilized its * at Zaphon and sent	Ju 12:1
mobilized his * and attacked the	Ju 12:4
and attacked the * of Ephraim.	Ju 12:4
Jordan behind the * of Ephraim, and	Ju 12:5
grounds of the * of the tribe of	Ju 13:25
So the men of Dan chose five *	Ju 18:2
A tenth of the * will be selected	Ju 20:8,9,10
The * of Israel, not counting	Ju 20:17
Before the battle the Israeli *	Ju 20:18
So the entire * left early the	Ju 20:19,20
Then the Israeli * wept before	Ju 20:22,23,24
Then the entire * went up to	Ju 20:26
So the Israeli * set an ambush	Ju 20:29
When the * of Benjamin came out	Ju 20:31
Then the * of Benjamin shouted,	Ju 20:32
away so that the * of Benjamin	Ju 20:32
But when the main * of Israel	Ju 20:33
the rear of the * of Benjamin, who	Ju 20:34
and the Israeli * killed 25,100 men	Ju 20:35-39
The * of Israel retreated from the	Ju 20:35-39
for the Israeli * to turn around	Ju 20:35-39
and attack the * of Benjamin, who	Ju 20:35-39
They encircled the * of Benjamin	Ju 20:43
The rest of the * fled into the	Ju 20:45
Then the Israeli * returned and	Ju 20:48
The Israeli * was camped near	1Sa 4:1
After the battle was over, the *	1Sa 4:3
mobilized their * and advanced.	1Sa 7:7
for the Israeli * rescued them from	1Sa 7:14
AT THIS TIME Nahash led the * of	1Sa 11:1
having divided his * into three	1Sa 11:11
The remnant of their * was so	1Sa 11:11
of King Hazor's *, and by the	1Sa 12:9
The rest of the * was sent home.	1Sa 13:2
So the entire Israeli * mobilized	1Sa 13:3,4
recruited a mighty * of three	1Sa 13:5
in the entire "*" of Israel that	1Sa 13:22
a contingent of the Philistine *.	1Sa 13:23
*, and even among the raiders.	1Sa 14:15
sight—the vast * of the Philistines	1Sa 14:16
the Philistine * revolted and	1Sa 14:21
Then Saul called back the *, and	1Sa 14:46
sent the Israeli * out in every	1Sa 14:47
And the general-in-chief of his *	1Sa 14:50,51
he conscripted him into his *.	1Sa 14:52
So Saul mobilized his * at	1Sa 15:4
"It's true that the * spared the	1Sa 15:15
NOW mustered their * for battle and	1Sa 17:1
you need a whole * to settle this?	1Sa 17:8
and the Israeli * heard this,	1Sa 17:11
Saul's * to fight the Philistines.	1Sa 17:13
(Saul and the Israeli * were	1Sa 17:19
as the Israeli * was leaving for	1Sa 17:20
facing each other, * against army.	1Sa 17:21
facing each other, army against *.	1Sa 17:21
his challenge to the * of Israel.	1Sa 17:23
* began to run away in fright.	1Sa 17:24
"He has insulted the entire * of	1Sa 17:25
in the * since he was a boy!"	1Sa 17:33
Then the Israeli * returned and	1Sa 17:53
the general of his *, "Abner, what	1Sa 17:55
by the * and general public alike.	1Sa 18:5
victorious Israeli * was returning	1Sa 18:6
Whenever the Philistine *	1Sa 18:30
and put to flight their entire *.	1Sa 19:8
and commissions in his *?	1Sa 22:7
to fight the whole Philistine *!"	1Sa 23:3
So Saul mobilized his entire * to	1Sa 23:8
When Saul saw the vast * of the	1Sa 28:5,6
the entire Israeli * will be routed	1Sa 28:19
THE PHILISTINE * now mobilized at	1Sa 29:1
Philistine * went on to Jezreel.	1Sa 29:11
from the Israeli * with his clothes	2Sa 1:1
"From the Israeli *," he	2Sa 1:3
man replied, "Our entire * fled.	2Sa 1:4
David placed several * garrisons	2Sa 8:6
victory over the * of Hadadezer,	2Sa 8:9
The general of his * was Joab	2Sa 8:16
entire Israeli * to attack them.	2Sa 10:7,8
fighters in his *, placed them	2Sa 10:9
He left the rest of the * to his	2Sa 10:10
led the Israeli * to Helam, where	2Sa 10:17
* to destroy the Ammonites.	2Sa 11:1
how Joab and the * were getting	2Sa 11:7
you may return to the *."	2Sa 11:12
Meanwhile Joab and the Israeli *	2Sa 12:26,27
Now bring the rest of the * and	2Sa 12:28
So David led his * to Rabbah and	2Sa 12:29,30
Then David and the * returned to	2Sa 12:31
the entire * of Israel, bringing	2Sa 17:11
destroy his entire * so that not	2Sa 17:12
have the entire * of Israel there	2Sa 17:13
die, and his entire * with him."	2Sa 17:16
the entire * of Israel and was	2Sa 17:24
general of the *, replacing Joab.	2Sa 17:25
Absalom and the Israeli * now	2Sa 17:26
The king planned to lead the *	2Sa 18:2
from chasing the * of Israel.	2Sa 18:16
And the * of Israel fled to their	2Sa 18:17
The entire * crept back into the	2Sa 19:3
of my * in place of Joab."	2Sa 19:13
the king and his * during their	2Sa 19:31,32
to mobilize the * of Judah within	2Sa 20:4
* and the king's own bodyguard.	2Sa 20:7
of the *, and Benaiah was in charge	2Sa 20:23
By your power I can crush an *;	2Sa 22:30
men in David's *: the first was	2Sa 23:8
the rest of the Israeli * fled.	2Sa 23:9
(The rest of the * did not return	2Sa 23:10
of the Israeli *—went down at	2Sa 23:13
of the *—and was their leader.	2Sa 23:18,19
of his *, "Take a census of all	2Sa 24:2
so Joab and the other * officers	2Sa 24:4
Rei, and David's * chiefs.	1Ki 1:8
Benaiah, the loyal * officers, or	1Ki 1:10
of the * of Israel, and General	1Ki 2:32
of the * of Judah.	1Ki 2:32
was commander-in-chief of the *;	1Ki 4:1
officials, * officers, chariot	1Ki 9:22
the Israeli * had killed nearly	1Ki 11:15
he summoned his *—all the	1Ki 12:21
So the * went home as the Lord	1Ki 12:23,24
with the Israeli * laying siege to	1Ki 15:27
for when the * of Israel, which	1Ki 16:15,16
of the *, as their new ruler.	1Ki 16:15,16
So Omri led the * of Gibbethon	1Ki 16:17
now mobilized his * and, with	1Ki 20:1
the rest of his * of 7,000 men.	1Ki 20:15
By now Ahab's entire * had joined	1Ki 20:19
entire Syrian * panicked and fled.	1Ki 20:20
* was killed in a great slaughter.	1Ki 20:21
Recruit another * like the one	1Ki 20:25
up the Syrian * and marched out	1Ki 20:26
Israel then mustered its *, set	1Ki 20:27
but the Israeli * looked like two	1Ki 20:27
defeat this vast *, and you shall	1Ki 20:28
you send your * with mine to	1Ki 22:4
Then he sent an * captain with	2Ki 1:9
the Israeli * and sent this message	2Ki 3:6,7,8
you victorious over the * of Moab!	2Ki 3:18
Israeli camp, the * of Israel	2Ki 3:24
and the * of Moab fled.	2Ki 3:24
of the Israeli *, killed him and	2Ki 3:27
So the * of Israel turned back in	2Ki 3:27

(ARMY Con't)
king or to the general of the *?" 2Ki 4:13
of his *, for he had led his troops 2Ki 5:1
Syria sent a great * with many 2Ki 6:14
"For our * is bigger than 2Ki 6:16
As the Syrian * advanced upon 2Ki 6:18
his entire * and besieged Samaria. 2Ki 6:24
out and surrender to the Syrian *. 2Ki 7:4
the whole Syrian * hear the clatter 2Ki 7:6
sounds of a great * approaching. 2Ki 7:6
surrounded by the * of Edom. 2Ki 8:21
but his * deserted him and fled. 2Ki 8:21
around with the other * officers. 2Ki 9:5
(King Joram had been with the * 2Ki 9:14
reduced Jehoahaz's * to fifty 2Ki 13:7
his * and come out and fight. 2Ki 14:8
Joash of Israel mustered his *. 2Ki 14:11
was defeated and the * fled home. 2Ki 14:12
captured, and the * of Israel 2Ki 14:13
general of his *, conspired against 2Ki 15:25
staff from Lachish with a great *; 2Ki 18:17
And with an * as small as yours, 2Ki 18:24
contingent in my master's *. 2Ki 18:24
his entire * and laid siege to 2Ki 25:1
the Babylonian * in tearing down 2Ki 25:10
A commander of the * of Judah, 2Ki 25:19
who destroyed the * of Midian in 1Ch 1:46
troops in the * of Reuben, Gad, and 1Ch 5:18
became the general of David's *. 1Ch 11:5,6
The Israeli * was in a barley 1Ch 11:13
highest-ranking officers in the *. 1Ch 11:15f
These men were * officers; 1Ch 12:14
he made them captains of his *. 1Ch 12:18
the Israeli * and joined David just 1Ch 12:19
a tremendous *—the army of God. 1Ch 12:22
a tremendous army—the * of God. 1Ch 12:22
with all of his * officers, he 1Ch 13:1
way, so he called together his *. 1Ch 14:8
and he cut down the * of the 1Ch 14:16
officers of the * went with great 1Ch 15:25
Hadadezer's *, he sent his son 1Ch 18:9
was commander-in-chief of the *; 1Ch 18:15
king of Maacah and his entire *. 1Ch 19:7
of Israel. The * of Ammon went out 1Ch 19:9
he divided his * and sent one group 1Ch 19:10
of the Syrian *. 1Ch 19:17,18
led the Israeli * in successful 1Ch 20:1
Then David and all his * returned 1Ch 20:3
officers and generals of the *. 1Ch 26:26
THE ISRAELI * was divided into 1Ch 27:1
officers in David's *. 1Ch 27:5,6
of the Israeli *. 1Ch 27:34
of the twelve * divisions, the 1Ch 28:1
the other * officers, those in 1Ch 28:1
volunteer, and the * and the entire 1Ch 28:21
of the tribes, the * officers, and 1Ch 29:6,7
The national leaders, the * 1Ch 29:24
He summoned all the * officers 2Ch 1:2,3
When the * of Judah arrived at 2Ch 13:4
King Jeroboam and the Israeli *: 2Ch 13:4
of David? Your * is twice as large 2Ch 13:8
sent part of his * around behind 2Ch 13:13,14
Jeroboam and the * of Israel, and 2Ch 13:15,16
King Asa's Judean * was 300,000 2Ch 14:8
and spears. His * of Benjaminites 2Ch 14:8
But now he was attacked by an * 2Ch 14:9,10
powerless against this mighty *. 2Ch 14:11
and Asa and the * of Judah 2Ch 14:12
entire Ethiopian * was wiped out so 2Ch 14:13
for the Lord and his * destroyed 2Ch 14:13
Then the * of Judah carried off 2Ch 14:13
Lord your God, the * of the king of 2Ch 16:7
and their vast *, with all of their 2Ch 16:8
and he had a huge * stationed at 2Ch 17:13
with an * of 280,000 men. 2Ch 17:14,15
that "a vast * is marching against 2Ch 20:2
ourselves against this mighty *. 2Ch 20:12
be paralyzed by this mighty *! 2Ch 20:15
Early the next morning the * of 2Ch 20:20
So, when the * of Judah arrived 2Ch 20:24
him with his full * and with all of 2Ch 21:9
Ahaziah led his * there to join 2Ch 22:5
took some of the * officers into 2Ch 23:1
and shields to all the * officers. 2Ch 23:9
entrance, with the * officers and 2Ch 23:12
priest shouted to the * officers. 2Ch 23:13,14
Then the * officers, nobles, 2Ch 23:20
A few months later the Syrian * 2Ch 24:23
the tiny Syrian *, but the Lord let 2Ch 24:24
Lord let the great * of Judah be 2Ch 24:24
to organize the *, assigning 2Ch 25:5,6
that he had an * of 300,000 men 2Ch 25:5,6
and led his * to the Valley of 2Ch 25:11
Meanwhile, the * of Israel that 2Ch 25:13
was defeated, and its * fled home. 2Ch 25:22
He organized his * into regiments 2Ch 26:11
*, and his assistant, Ma-aseiah. 2Ch 26:11
regiments. The * consisted of 2Ch 26:13
went out to meet the returning *. 2Ch 28:9
So the * officers turned over the 2Ch 28:14
He recruited an * and appointed 2Ch 32:6
or his mighty *, for there is 2Ch 32:7
He has a great *, but they are 2Ch 32:8
the Assyrian * with all its 2Ch 32:21
And he stationed his * generals 2Ch 33:14
led his * [against the Assyrians 2Ch 35:20
Instead he led his * into the 2Ch 35:22
Then his * burned the Temple and 2Ch 36:19
had sent along * officers and Neh 2:9
and the Samaritan * officers. Neh 4:1
They plotted to lead an * Neh 4:8
aides, and * officers, bringing Est 1:1
king instructs his *, and as one Job 29:25
Yes, though a mighty * marches Ps 27:3
The best-equipped * cannot save a Ps 33:16,17
Have you deserted our *? Ps 108:11
drowned Pharaoh's * in the sea, for Ps 136:15
self-control than to control an *. Pro 16:32
A king as he leads his *. Pro 30:29,30,31
came with his * and besieged it. Ecc 9:14
men of his * surrounding it. Sol 3:7
terrible as an * with banners." Sol 6:4f
Literally, "terrible as an * with Sol 6:10f
prophets, elders, * officers, Is 3:3
will come with his great *! Is 7:17
whistle for the * of Upper Egypt, Is 7:18
Assyria's vast * is like a Is 10:18
all that mighty * will be left; Is 10:19
to Laish, for the mighty * comes. Is 10:30
all of that vast *, great and small Is 10:33
break the Assyrian * when they are Is 14:25
For a perfectly trained * Is 14:31
Let your mighty * now advance Is 18:4
Your mighty * will be left dead Is 18:6
of his * against the Philistine Is 20:1
* (the Assyrians) against you; Is 28:2
strip the fallen * of Assyria! Is 33:4
with a great * from Lachish to Is 36:2
2,000 men left in your entire *! Is 36:8,9
With that tiny *, how can you Is 36:8,9
an * against him [from the south Is 37:8,9
* against the nations of the west. Is 37:24
send an invading * against Babylon, Is 43:14
I called forth the mighty * of Is 43:17
warn everyone that a powerful * Jer 6:1
The noise of their * is like a Jer 6:23
of the terrible *, for the enemy is Jer 8:16
and destroyed by the invading *. Jer 13:22
* against a high city wall. Jer 15:20
to the Chaldean * and live. Jer 21:9
king of Babylon, and his mighty *. Jer 22:24,25
Jehoiakim and the * officers and Jer 26:21
* was besieging Jerusalem. Jer 32:2
At this time the Babylonian * Jer 34:7
officials to the * of the king of Jer 34:21
over the Egyptian * at Carchemish. Jer 36:1f
When the * of Pharaoh Hophra of Jer 37:5
the Babylonian * withdrew from Jer 37:5
that Pharaoh's *, though it came Jer 37:7
entire Babylonian * until there was Jer 37:10
When the Babylonian * set out Jer 37:11
engage Pharaoh's * in battle, Jer 37:11
* and you will not escape." Jer 38:18
the officers of the Babylonian *; Jer 38:21,22
and all his * came against Jer 39:1
of the Babylonian * came in and sat Jer 39:3
Meanwhile the * burned Jerusalem, Jer 39:8
THEN JOHANAN AND the * captains Jer 42:1
of Egypt, and his * were defeated Jer 46:2
The Egyptian * flees in terror; Jer 46:5
What is this mighty *, rising Jer 46:7
It is the Egyptian *, boasting Jer 46:8
the invading * marches in. Jer 46:22,23
king of Babylon, and his *. Jer 46:26
by the Egyptian *. Jer 47:1
your entire * shall be destroyed Jer 49:26
I will destroy the * of Elam, and Jer 49:35
I am raising up an * of great Jer 50:9
A great * from the north! Jer 50:41
are burning and the * is in panic. Jer 51:32
was quartermaster of Zedekiah's *. Jer 51:59
came with all his * against Jer 52:4
all his * was scattered from him. Jer 52:8
set the Chaldean * to work tearing Jer 52:14
to the Babylonian *, and the Jer 52:15
officers of the *, seven of the Jer 52:24,25
of the Jewish * (who was in charge Jer 52:24,25
A great * has come at his command Lam 1:15
like the shouting of a mighty *. Eze 1:24
Demonstrate how an enemy * will Eze 4:3
shout to Israel's *, 'Mobilize!' Eze 7:14
seek for a great * and many horses Eze 17:15
Pharaoh and all his mighty * Eze 17:17
fine steeds, those * officers in Eze 23:12
great * fully prepared for attack. Eze 23:24
"The Lord God says: Bring an * Eze 23:46
great * and cavalry and chariots. Eze 26:7
"Your * includes men from Eze 27:10
as God, an enemy *, the terror of Eze 28:7
of disease and an * to destroy; Eze 28:23
I will bring an * against you, O Eze 29:8
"Son of dust, the * of King Eze 29:18
not pay the * for all this work. Eze 29:1
everything she has, for his *. Eze 29:1
When Pharaoh Hophra sent an * to Eze 30:21
A foreign * (from Babylon)—the Eze 31:1
great * to catch you with my net. Eze 32:
*—the terror of the nations. Eze 32:1
his * slain, says the Lord God. Eze 32:3
And Pharaoh and his * shall lie Eze 32:3
When I bring an * against a Eze 33:
when he sees the * coming, and Eze 33:
and stood up—a very great *. Eze 37:1
vast and awesome *—will roll down Eze 38:
of your * in the mountains. Eze 39:
to "The Valley of Gog's *." Eze 39:1
Valley of Gog's * to bury them. Eze 39:15,16
men of his * to bind Shadrach, Dan 3:20
of the * of heaven by canceling Dan 8:11
But the * of heaven was Dan 8:12
of the heavenly *, came to help me, Dan 10:13
he will raise an * against the king Dan 11:7
assemble a mighty * that will Dan 11:10,11
a fully-equipped * far greater than Dan 11:13
and raise a great * against Egypt; Dan 11:25
raise a mighty *, but to no avail, Dan 11:25
* will desert, and many be killed. Dan 11:26
his vast * and navy will rush out Dan 11:40
by the invading *, her babies Hos 13:16
A vast * of locusts Joe 1:6
It is a terrible * too numerous Joe 1:6
What a mighty *! Joe 2:2
a mighty * moving into battle. Joe 2:5
This is his mighty * and they Joe 2:11
—my great destroying * that I sent Joe 2:25
"Though he build his * millions Nah 1:12
of the advancing * reaches the very Zep 1:10
Capernaum, a Roman * captain came Mt 8:5,6
king sent out his * and destroyed Mt 22:7
his palace aides, * officers, and Mk 6:21
When this great * of angels had Lk 2:15
* captain was sick and near Lk 7:2
whether his * of 10,000 is strong Lk 14:31
then the Roman * will come and kill Jn 11:48
CAESAREA THERE lived a Roman * Act 10:1
What soldier in the * has to pay 1Co 9:7
And if the * bugler doesn't play 1Co 14:8
one who has enlisted you in his *. 2Ti 2:4
* of evil desires within you? Jas 4:1
* of chariots rushing into battle. Rev 9:9
They led an * of 200,000,000 Rev 9:16
onto the earth with all his *. Rev 12:9
sitting on the horse and his *. Rev 19:19
And their entire * was killed Rev 19:21

ARNAN
Rephaiah's son was *; 1Ch 3:21,22

ARNAN'S
* son was Obadiah; 1Ch 3:21,22

ARNI
Admin's father was *; Lk 3:23-38

ARNI'S
Admin's father was Arni;* father Lk 3:23-38

ARNON
far side of the * River, near the Num 21:13
the Amorites. (The * River is the Num 21:13
the valley of the * River, and the Num 21:14
land from the * River to the Jabbok Num 21:24
On the heights of the * River. Num 21:27-30
to meet him at the * River, at the Num 22:36
said, 'Cross the * River into the Deu 2:24
the edge of the * River valley, and Deu 2:35,36
valley of the * to Mount Hermon. Deu 3:8
at Aroer on the * River, plus half Deu 3:12
of the valley of the * River. Deu 3:16
at the edge of the * River valley Deu 4:48
the valley of the * River to Mount Jos 12:1
on the edge of the * Valley, and Jos 12:2
the valley of the * River to the Jos 12:2
the valley of the * River, included Jos 13:9
the valley of the * River, past the Jos 13:16
past the city of * in the middle of Jos 13:16
the whole territory from the * Ju 11:13
boundary of Moab at the * River; Ju 11:18
your land from the * River to the Ju 11:21,22
Aroer, and all along the * River. Ju 11:26
the * as far as Gilead and Bashan. 2Ki 10:32,33
the * River like homeless birds. Is 16:2
Tell it by the banks of the *, Jer 48:20

AROD
named after their ancestor *. Num 26:15-18

ARODI
Ezbon, Eri, *, and Areli. Gen 46:16,17

ARODITES
The *, named after their ancestor Num 26:15-18

AROER
Dibon, Ataroth, *, Num 32:34,35,36
We conquered everything from * to Deu 2:35,36
area beginning at * on the Arnon Deu 3:12
all the area from * at the edge of Deu 4:48
His kingdom extended from *, on Jos 12:2
Their territory ran from *, on Jos 13:9
land extended from * on the edge of Jos 13:16
of Ammon as far as * near Rabbah. Jos 13:25

AROER Con't)
*, and all along the Arnon River. Ju 11:26
all the way from * to Minnith, Ju 11:33
Bethel, South Ramoth, Jattir, *, 1Sa 30:27-31
and camped at *, south of the city 2Sa 24:5
Manasseh from the * River in the 2Ki 10:32,33
lived in * and as far distant as 1Ch 5:7,8
Je-iel (sons of Hotham) from *; 1Ch 11:26-47
The cities of * are deserted. Is 17:2
Those in * stand anxiously Jer 48:19

AROMA
*, and some fresh-baked bread. Gen 27:17
within us, an * to both the saved 2Co 2:15

AROMATIC
* oils, the armory—everything. 2Ki 20:13

AROSE
went the shout *, "Kneel down!" Gen 41:43
a great cry * throughout the city. 1Sa 4:13
Literally, "* from his bed." 2Sa 11:2f
Then I, Ezra the priest, * and Ez 10:10
So she * and stood before him, Est 8:4
to you there"— I * and went, and Eze 3:23
But soon a terrible storm *. Mk 4:37
So a great clamor *. Act 23:9
days afterwards he * from the grave 1Co 15:4
speak, when Christ * from the dead, Col 3:1

AROUSE
Who dares * him? Num 24:3-9
her and * my wrath and vengeance. Eze 24:8

AROUSED
like a mighty man * by wine, he Ps 78:65
angry, but when *, his power is Nah 1:3

AROUSING
and now they are * the city to Ju 9:31
at me and * my fury against them? Eze 8:17
are wrong and * all kinds of Rom 7:8

ARPACHSHAD
Asshur,*, Lud, Aram. Gen 10:22
included *, born two years after Gen 11:10,11
When * was thirty-five years old, Gen 11:12,13
*, Lud, Aram, Uz, Hul, Gether, 1Ch 1:17
of Shem was *, the son of 1Ch 1:24-27
the son of * was Shelah, 1Ch 1:24-27

ARPACHSHAD'S
* son was Shelah, and Shelah's Gen 10:24
* son was 1Ch 1:18

ARPAD
*, Sepharvaim, Hena, and Ivvah? 2Ki 18:34
king of Hamoth and the king of *? 2Ki 19:13
will go down before us as * did; Is 10:9
what I did to Hamath and *? Is 36:19
to the king of *, and to the kings Is 37:13
of Hamath and * are stricken with Jer 49:23

ARPHAXAD
Cainan's father was *; Lk 3:23-38

ARPHAXAD'S
Cainan's father was Arphaxad;* Lk 3:23-38

ARRANGE
how to * a bloody death for him." 1Ki 2:9
Edom with Joab to * for the burial 1Ki 11:15
Let our leaders * trials for us. Ez 10:14
until I can * to take you to a Is 36:17
to * to betray Jesus to them. Mk 14:10
* to get him to the Emperor." Act 25:21

ARRANGED
And his mother * a marriage for Gen 21:20,21
Jacob now * his family into a Gen 33:2
Er grew up, Judah * for him to Gen 38:6
For the Lord had * to defeat 2Sa 17:14
she had done, he * for the men's 2Sa 21:12,13,14
Each of them * provisions for one 1Ki 4:7
Five of these vats were * on the 1Ki 7:39
David * for Asaph and his fellow 1Ch 16:37
allowances and * for them to have 2Ch 11:23
Jehoiada * two marriages for 2Ch 24:3
court, * the same as the other. Eze 42:9,10
Now the Lord had * for a great Jon 1:17
the heat, the Lord * for a vine to Jon 4:6

ARRANGEMENT
to build it). This * is still in Jos 9:27
This * was practical because 2Ki 11:2,3f
That is why we have made this *. 2Co 8:21
success of this new and better *. Heb 7:22
Under the old * there had to be Heb 7:23
or beautiful clothes, or hair *. 1Pe 3:3

ARRANGEMENTS
who were with her. * were made for Jos 6:23
he wanted, so the * were made. Ju 14:7
As his father was making final * Ju 14:10,11
leaving the city. * had been made 2Sa 17:17
As to the financial *, I will 2Ch 2:10
So all the * were made. 2Ch 23:8
them into Jerusalem to make the *. Mk 14:13
* WERE FINALLY made to start us on Act 27:1

ARRANGES
And if he * an engagement Ex 21:9

ARRANGING
for God was * to destroy him for 2Ch 25:20

ARRAY
of fire upon the * of the Ex 14:24
along with a vast * of horses and Jos 11:4
All these men came in battle * to 1Ch 12:38
Literally, "in holy *." Ps 110:3f

ARRAYED
All God's terrors are * against Job 6:4

ARREST
They remained under * there for Gen 40:4
When the soldiers came to * 1Sa 19:14
He shouted to his guards, "* 1Ki 13:4
King Ahab ordered Micaiah's *. 1Ki 22:26
with fifty soldiers to * him. 2Ki 1:9
king had come to * him, and the 2Ki 7:17
years that he was under house *: 1Ch 3:17,18
"* this man and take him back to 2Ch 18:25
If you do this again, I will * Neh 13:21
If he rushes in and makes an *, Job 11:10
responsibility to * any madman who Jer 29:26
Abdeel) to * Baruch and Jeremiah. Jer 36:26
The guard making the * was Irijah Jer 37:13
order for Daniel's *, and he was Dan 6:16
would say "Yes," so they could * Mt 12:10
to plot Jesus' * and death. Mt 12:14
for which they could * him. Mt 22:15
Judas had told them to * the man Mt 26:48
and clubs before you could * me? Mt 26:55
If he did, they planned to * him! Mk 3:2
For Herod had sent soldiers to * Mk 6:17,18
The Jewish leaders wanted to * Mk 12:12
an opportunity to * Jesus secretly Mk 14:1
one to * when I go over and greet Mk 14:44
Why didn't you * me in the Mk 14:49
governor as reason for * by him. Lk 20:19
for them to * Jesus quietly when Lk 22:6
Why didn't you * me in the Lk 22:53
Jewish leaders sought to * him; Jn 7:30
priests sent officers to * Jesus. Jn 7:32
had been sent to * him returned to Jn 7:45
Once again they started to * him. Jn 10:39
so that they could * him. Jn 11:57
And we hear that he has * Act 9:14
to * every believer in Damascus!" Act 9:14
he came here to * them all and take Act 9:21

ARRESTED
he ordered Moses * and executed. Ex 2:15
He was * and taken before Moses Num 15:33
and I will be * and executed as 1Ki 1:21
was saying, he * Jeremiah and had Jer 20:2
Gate, a sentry * him as a traitor, Jer 37:13
*, he left Judea and returned home Mt 4:12,13
For you will be * and tried, and Mt 10:17
"When you are *, don't worry Mt 10:19
For Herod had * John and Mt 14:3
He had the man * and jailed until Mt 18:30
Jewish leaders had * Jesus out of Mt 27:18
Later on, after John was * by Mk 1:14
will be * and taken before the Mk 10:33
something he could be * for. Mk 12:13
But when you are * and stand Mk 13:11
Then the mob * Jesus and held Mk 14:46
for which they could have him *. Lk 11:53,54
they wanted him * immediately, for Lk 20:19
* him there would be a riot. Lk 20:19
will betray you and have you *; Lk 21:16
religious leaders * him and handed Lk 24:20
And some wanted him *, but no Jn 7:44
But he was not *, for his time Jn 8:20
lieutenant, * Jesus and tied him. Jn 18:12
"We wouldn't have * him if he Jn 18:30
I was * by the Jewish leaders. Jn 18:36
They * them and since it was Act 4:3
jealousy and * the apostles, and Act 5:18
his officers and * them (without Act 5:26,27
* him and brought him before the Act 6:12
Jewish leaders, he * Peter during Act 12:3
the sixteen guards *, Act 12:19
The commander * him and ordered Act 21:33
defile the Temple when we * him. Act 24:6
The Jews * me in the Temple for Act 26:21
"Brothers, I was * by the Jews in Act 28:17
prison will be * and taken away; Rev 13:10

ARRIVAL
to him on the night of his *. Gen 26:24
heard of Jacob's *, he rushed out Gen 29:12,13
Upon Jacob's * at Bethel, en Gen 35:9
During this time before the * of Gen 41:50
ready for Joseph's * at noon, for Gen 43:25
UPON THEIR *, Joseph went in to Gen 47:1
years after his *, so that he was Gen 47:28
But upon *, there was no water! Ex 17:1
because of you, and dread your *.' Deu 2:25
the wilderness, until your * here. Deu 11:5
village was stirred by their *. Ru 1:19
(Their return from Moab and * in Ru 1:22
seven days for his *, but when he 1Sa 13:8
The news of his * in Judah soon 1Sa 22:6
knew of Saul's * and sent out spies 1Sa 26:3,4
had been made for their *. 1Ch 12:39
UPON * AT Jerusalem, Rehoboam 2Ch 11:1
to Jerusalem. On * they swore 2Ch 23:2,3
year of their * at Jerusalem. Ez 3:8
On the fourth day after our * the Ez 8:33
heard of my *, they were very angry Neh 2:10
Three days after my * at Neh 2:11,12
And on the day of his *, your Eze 24:27
Next I saw the * of a Man—or so Dan 7:13
The news of their * spread Mt 14:35
On their * in Capernaum, the Mt 17:24
to be ready for the Lord's *." Mk 1:3
* spread quickly through the city. Mk 2:1
the news of his *, and began Mk 6:55
For as usual the news of his * Mk 7:24
his * they came to argue with him. Mk 8:11
expecting the * of God's Kingdom), Mk 15:42,43
preparing the people for his *. Lk 1:17
heard of his *, they flocked to see Jn 12:9
Upon * in Jerusalem he tried to Act 9:26
Upon * they called together the Act 14:27
And after the * of Silas and Act 18:5
And upon his * in Greece, he was Act 18:27
us, and on * we were guests at the Act 21:16
told the Jews to wait for the * Act 24:22
On Paul's * in court the Jews Act 25:7
Three days after his *, he Act 28:17
refreshed us by the * of Titus. 2Co 7:6

ARRIVE
soon * in Goshen—which they did. Gen 46:28
Jehovah told him, "When you * Ex 4:21
Aaron, "When you * in the land of Lev 14:33,34
Fruits: When you * in the land I Lev 23:9,10,11
"When you * in the Promised Land Num 10:9
that when they * in the land that I Num 15:17,18
that when they * in the land, Num 35:9,10
* in the land where you will live. Deu 4:5
when you * in the Promised Land. Deu 4:14
and goats when you * in the land he Deu 7:13
must obey when you * in the land Deu 12:1
effect until you * in the place of Deu 12:9
When you *, use the money to buy Deu 14:26
"But if, when you * in the land Deu 15:7
"When you * in the land the Lord Deu 17:14
"When you * in the Promised Land Deu 18:9
"When you * in the land the Lord Deu 19:14
"IF, WHEN YOU * in the Promised Deu 21:1
when you * in the Promised Land. Deu 23:20
"WHEN YOU * in the land and have Deu 26:1
you do when you * in the land the Deu 28:8
"When we * at the outer Ju 7:17
As you * there you will meet a 1Sa 10:5
further instructions when I *." 1Sa 10:8
without waiting for you to *." 1Sa 13:12
the Jordan to * ahead of the king. 2Sa 19:17
and when you *, anoint Hazael to be 1Ki 19:15
Temple when you * in Jerusalem. Ez 7:17
Shallum) will soon * to ask you to Jer 32:6,7
The same day they *, meet them at Zec 6:10,11
world will see me * in the clouds Mt 24:30
your Lord will * unannounced and Mt 24:50
messenger would * first to prepare Mk 1:2
Kingdom of God * in great power!" Mk 9:1
that it was time for them to *. Lk 14:17
possible you may * in my presence Lk 21:36
Possibly in order to * in Act 18:20f
when your accusers *," the Act 23:35
about the other matters after I *. 1Co 11:34
other brothers to * ahead of me to 2Co 9:5

ARRIVED
in Haran—and finally * in Canaan. Gen 12:5
And sure enough, when they * Gen 12:14
allies * and the slaughter began. Gen 14:5,6
had first * in the land of Canaan. Gen 16:2,3
Lot was sitting there as they *. Gen 19:1
When they * at the place where Gen 22:9
After this, a message * that Gen 22:20-23
named Rebekah * with a water jug Gen 24:15,16
had * from her great-uncle. Gen 24:28f
* home exhausted from the hunt. Gen 25:29
King Abimelech * with his Gen 26:26
going on, Rachel * with her Gen 29:9
Then they * safely at Gen 33:18
Finally they * at Luz (also Gen 35:6
delivery * and she had twin sons. Gen 38:27
WHEN JOSEPH * in Egypt as a Gen 39:1
So it was that Israel's sons * Gen 42:5
As they * at the entrance to the Gen 43:19
and his brothers *, and they fell Gen 44:14
that Joseph had *, he gathered his Gen 48:2
of Egypt before I *, I am adopting Gen 48:5
When they * at Atad Gen 50:10
numbers of quail * and covered the Ex 16:13
years until they * in the land of Ex 16:35
They * while Moses and the Ex 18:5,6
THE ISRAELIS * in the Sinai Ex 19:1
price shall be * at by counting the Lev 25:14,15,16
new location by the time they *. Num 10:21
through the Negeb and * at Hebron. Num 13:22
This was their report: "We * in Num 13:27
THE PEOPLE OF Israel * in the Num 20:1
"A vast horde of people has * Num 22:5,6
from Egypt has * at his border, and Num 22:11
WHEN ISRAEL * in the land of Jazar Num 32:1
at Jericho. They * at an inn Jos 2:1
had * in the city that evening. Jos 2:2
left Acacia, and * that evening at Jos 3:1

(ARRIVED Con't)
When they * at the camp of Jos 9:6
Horam of Gezer * with his army to Jos 10:33
Joshua and his troops * Jos 11:7
When they * in the land of Jos 22:15
But when they * at the Red Sea, Jos 24:6
ONE DAY THE Angel of the Lord * at Ju 2:1
When he * in the hill country of Ju 3:27
These enemy hordes * on droves Ju 6:5
people of Israel * at Kadesh, on Ju 11:16
until at last they * beyond the Ju 11:18
As Samson and his captors * at Ju 15:14
in Judah, * in that area of Ju 17:7,8
men of Dan * at the city of Laish. Ju 18:27
When he * at her home, she let Ju 19:3
"We * one evening at Gibe-ah, a Ju 20:4
thousand of them * in Gibe-ah to Ju 20:14,15
Boaz * from the city while she Ru 2:4,5
Naomi asked her when she * Ru 3:15-18
of the Lord had *, they panicked. 1Sa 4:6
the battle and * at Shiloh the same 1Sa 4:12
the battlefront * and told what had 1Sa 4:13
But when the Ark * at Gath, the 1Sa 5:9
the Philistines * for battle, but 1Sa 7:10
He has just * back from a trip to 1Sa 9:12,13
When Saul and the servant * at 1Sa 10:10
the city when that message *! 1Sa 11:9
But early the next morning Saul * 1Sa 11:11
as he was finishing, Samuel *. 1Sa 13:10
that you hadn't * by the time you 1Sa 13:11
Agag * all full of smiles, for 1Sa 15:32
When he * at Bethlehem, the 1Sa 16:4
When they *, Samuel took one 1Sa 16:6
with the gifts. He * at the 1Sa 17:20
But when the time * for the 1Sa 18:19
but when they * and saw Samuel 1Sa 19:20
and * at the great well in Secu. 1Sa 19:22
When they * Saul shouted at him, 1Sa 22:11,12
When she * home she found that 1Sa 25:36
When the messengers * at Carmel 1Sa 25:40
one fault in him since he *." 1Sa 29:3
David and his men * home at their 1Sa 30:1
When he * at Ziklag, he sent part 1Sa 30:26
Three days later a man * from the 2Sa 1:1
going down as they * at Ammah Hill 2Sa 2:24
morning until they * at Mahanaim. 2Sa 2:29
When Abner * at Hebron, Joab 2Sa 3:27
Rechab and Baanah * at King 2Sa 4:5
The Philistines * and spread out 2Sa 5:18
But when they * at the threshing 2Sa 6:6
Mephibosheth * in great fear and 2Sa 9:5,6
These troops * at Helam under the 2Sa 10:15,16
When he *, David asked him how 2Sa 11:7
So the messenger * at Jerusalem, 2Sa 11:22
Recently a guest * at the home 2Sa 12:4
brother Shime-ah) * and said, "No, 2Sa 13:32,33
They soon *, weeping and sobbing, 2Sa 13:36
A messenger soon * in Jerusalem 2Sa 15:13
It seems but yesterday that you * 2Sa 15:19,20
getting there just as Absalom *. 2Sa 15:37
Meanwhile, Absalom and his men * 2Sa 16:15
the Archite, *, he went immediately 2Sa 16:16
When Hushai *, Absalom told him 2Sa 17:6
When Absalom's men * and asked 2Sa 17:20
David soon * at Mahanaim. 2Sa 17:24
When David * at Mahanaim, he was 2Sa 17:27
Then the man from Cush * and 2Sa 18:31
And when he * at the Jordan 2Sa 19:15
* from Jerusalem to meet the king. 2Sa 19:24,25
exile in Mahanaim, * from Rogelim 2Sa 19:31,32
When he * at his palace in 2Sa 20:3
As they * at the great stone in 2Sa 20:8,9,10
When Joab's forces *, they 2Sa 20:15
When they *, he said to them, 1Ki 1:32
questions. She * in Jerusalem with 1Ki 10:2
peacocks * at the Israeli ports. 1Ki 10:22
When King Rehoboam * in 1Ki 12:21
As he * at the gates of the city 1Ki 17:10
And when Ben-hadad *, he invited 1Ki 20:33
When he *, the king asked him, 1Ki 22:15
but they never *, for they were 1Ki 22:48
When they * on the other side 2Ki 2:9
But when they * at the Israeli 2Ki 3:24
When Elisha *, the child was 2Ki 4:32
So Naaman * with his horses and 2Ki 5:9
Ephraim have just *, and he would 2Ki 5:22
But when they * at the hill 2Ki 5:24
When they * at the Jordan, they 2Ki 6:4
As soon as they * Elisha prayed, 2Ki 6:20
But before the messenger * Elisha 2Ki 6:32
messenger * [followed by the king 2Ki 6:33
When the lepers * at the edge of 2Ki 7:8
When he * in Ramoth-gilead, he 2Ki 9:4
When the letter *, all seventy 2Ki 10:7
king's sons had *, he said to pile 2Ki 10:8
When he * in Samaria he 2Ki 10:17
when they first *, the Lord sent 2Ki 17:25
Nebuchadnezzar himself * during 2Ki 24:11
royal bodyguard, * at Jerusalem 2Ki 25:8
and Manasseh * in Jerusalem: 1Ch 9:3
But as they * at the 1Ch 13:9
(But as the Ark * in Jerusalem, 1Ch 15:29
When the Syrians * from Damascus 1Ch 18:5
But when David's ambassadors *, 1Ch 19:2,3
When David * on the scene, he 1Ch 20:2
over Israel; they * from as far 2Ch 7:8
cities and soon * at Jerusalem. 2Ch 12:4
When the army of Judah * at 2Ch 13:4
When he * before the king, the 2Ch 18:14
in this land when your people *? 2Ch 20:7
So, when the army of Judah * at 2Ch 20:24
disaster and never * at Tarshish. 2Ch 20:37
the Syrian army * and conquered 2Ch 24:23
But a prophet * with this message 2Ch 25:7
king of Assyria, *, he caused 2Ch 28:20
The first of these tithes * in 2Ch 31:7,8
And when he * at the temple of 2Ch 32:21
gifts for the Lord * at Jerusalem, 2Ch 32:23
However, when ambassadors * from 2Ch 32:31
companions soon * in Jerusalem and Ez 5:3
Ar-ta-xerxes and * at Jerusalem in Ez 7:7,8,9
men (they * at a later time); Ez 8:2-14
people and the priests who had *; Ez 8:15
So at last we * safely at Ez 8:32
and Benjamin had * and were sitting Ez 10:9
some men who had * from Judah. Neh 1:2
When I * in the provinces west of Neh 2:9
When they * at the Fountain Gate Neh 12:37
When I * back in Jerusalem and Neh 13:7
Haman had just * in the outer court Est 6:4
king's messengers * to conduct Est 6:14
the king's decree *, the Jews were Est 8:17
speaking, another * with more bad Job 1:16
speaking, another * to say, "Your Job 1:18
and former friends * and feasted Job 42:11
The kings of the earth have * Ps 48:4
Then Jacob (Israel) * in Egypt Ps 105:23
king of Babylon, * in this country, Jer 35:11
*, while he was still in prison: Jer 39:15
top officials, * in Mizpah, Jer 41:1
And so they * in Egypt at the Jer 43:7
of the guard, * in Jerusalem, and Jer 52:12
from Jerusalem * to tell me, "The Eze 33:21
speak again by the time the man *. Eze 33:22
When they had all * and were Dan 3:3
and when they * he and his princes, Dan 5:2,3,4
For the Lord your God has * to Zep 3:17,18
For the Lord of Hosts has * to Zec 10:3
from eastern lands * in Jerusalem, Mt 2:1
Or, "has *." Mt 3:2f
Or, "is at hand," or, "has *." Mt 4:17f
When Jesus * in Capernaum, a Mt 8:5,6
When Jesus * at Peter's house, Mt 8:14
When they * on the other side of Mt 8:28
When Jesus * at the rabbi's home Mt 9:23
Or, "at hand," or, "has *." Mt 10:7f
Kingdom of God has * among you. Mt 12:28
Jewish leaders now * from Jerusalem Mt 15:1
When they * at the bottom of the Mt 17:14
would happen to him when they *. Mt 20:18
'The Messiah has * at such and such Mt 24:23
actually * and took them all away. Mt 24:39
one of the Twelve, * with a great Mt 26:47
Jesus and his companions now * at Mk 1:21
Four men * carrying a paralyzed Mk 2:3
religion who had * from Jerusalem Mk 3:22
Now his mother and brothers * at Mk 3:31,32
WHEN THEY * at the other side of Mk 5:1
to her, messengers * from Jairus' Mk 5:35
When they *, Jesus saw that all Mk 5:38
When they * at Gennesaret on the Mk 6:53
religious leaders * from Jerusalem Mk 7:1
And when she * home, her little Mk 7:30
When they * at Bethsaida, some Mk 8:22
And so they * at Capernaum. Mk 9:33
to him when they * at Jerusalem. Mk 10:32
When they * back to Jerusalem he Mk 11:15
By this time they had * in Mk 11:27,28
In the evening Jesus * with the Mk 14:17
of his disciples) * with a mob Mk 14:43
So as soon as they * he walked Mk 14:45
But when they * they looked up Mk 16:4
and so, when Mary and Joseph * to Lk 2:27
that the Messiah had finally *. Lk 2:38
So they * at the other side, in Lk 8:26
her, a messenger * from the Jairus' Lk 8:49
When they * at the house Jesus Lk 8:51
of mine has just * for a visit and Lk 11:5,6
that the Kingdom of God has *. Lk 11:20
When Jesus *, he sat down to eat Lk 11:37,38
When you * you would call Lk 15:6
When Jesus * at the spot, he Lk 18:40
the time of its destruction has *. Lk 21:20
celebration *, when the Passover Lk 22:7
Then Jesus and the others *, and Lk 22:14
is the true Light * to shine on Jn 1:9
Just then his disciples *. Jn 4:27
through Galilee he * at the town of Jn 4:46,47
When they * and found him, they Jn 6:25
When they * at Bethany, they were Jn 11:17
When Mary * where Jesus was, she Jn 11:32
country people * in Jerusalem Jn 11:55
began, Jesus * in Bethany where Jn 12:
weapons they * at the olive grove. Jn 18:
Then Simon Peter * and went on Jn 20:
the Day of Pentecost had now *. Act 2:
having * from many nations. Act 2:
They * at the Temple about Act 5:21
and his courtiers * at the Temple, Act 5:21
But when the police * at the Act 5:22
Then someone * with the news Act 5:25
As soon as they *, they began Act 8:15
as soon as he *, they took him Act 9:39
They * in Caesarea the following Act 10:24
But when Peter * back in Act 11:2
them to Caesarea * at the house Act 11:11
me, and we soon * at the home of Act 11:12
When he * and saw the wonderful Act 11:23
from Tyre and Sidon * to see him. Act 12:20
and when the day * he put on his Act 12:21
later, some Jews * from Antioch and Act 14:19
men from Judea * and began to teach Act 15:1
who had recently * from Italy with Act 18:2,3
preacher, had just * in Ephesus Act 18:24
through Turkey and * in Ephesus, Act 19:1
five days later * in Troas, Turkey, Act 20:6
and a day later we * at Miletus. Act 20:15
When they * he told them, "You Act 20:18
* from Judea and visited us. Act 21:10
When they * in Caesarea, they Act 23:33
* with some of the Jewish leaders Act 24:1
days ago that I * in Jerusalem to Act 24:11
THREE DAYS AFTER Festus * in Act 25:1
A few days later King Agrippa * Act 25:13
and Bernice had * at the courtroom Act 25:23
southern coast, we * at Fair Act 27:7,8
following day we * at Puteoli, Act 28:13
When we * in Rome, Paul was Act 28:16
Achaicus have * here for a visit. 1Co 16:17
When we * in Macedonia there was 2Co 7:5
For when he first * he ate with Gal 2:12

ARRIVES

*, coming in from his hunting. Gen 27:30
Year of Jubilee *, then he and his Lev 25:54
the guests can't eat until he * 1Sa 9:12,13
not sit down to eat until he *." 1Sa 16:10,11
the city before he *, both we and 2Sa 15:14
When he *, shut the door and keep 2Ki 6:32
he is killed when he * there." 2Ki 19:7
welcome her as she * with all her Eze 32:21
"When Pharaoh *, he will be Eze 32:31
him in the moment he * and knocks. Lk 12:36
that awesome Day of the Lord *. Act 2:20
As soon as one of them *, please Tit 3:12

ARRIVING

JACOB TRAVELED ON, finally * in Gen 29:1
talk with Jacob, * just as Jacob's Gen 34:6,7
without water. * at Marah, they Ex 15:23
Sinai, * there on the fifteenth Ex 16:1
desert, finally * among the Amorite Deu 1:19,20,21
Upon * at Timnah he talked with Ju 14:7
to settle in. * in the hill country Ju 18:2
to Jerusalem, * on March 25 of the 2Ki 25:1
of the priests * for duty that 2Ch 23:8
Since many of the people * from 2Ch 30:17,18,19
* across the lake, the disciples Mt 16:5
but just before * at the house, Lk 7:6,7,8
the Gaza Desert, * around noon." Act 8:26
* in Jerusalem, they met with the Act 15:4
* at the port of Ephesus, he Act 18:19
from those * from Jerusalem. Act 28:21
He is *, surrounded by clouds; Rev 1:7

ARROGANCE

And because of your * against 2Ki 19:28
added rebellion, * and blasphemy to Job 34:37
Put an end to their *, these who Ps 38:16
"Look at these men of *; Ps 73:12
warned the proud to cease their *! Ps 75:4
See their *! Ps 94:4
name and stand in * against you—how Ps 139:20
For wisdom hates pride, *, Pro 8:13
I will crush the * of the proud Is 13:11
* and insolence are all gone now! Is 16:6
We know your loftiness, your * Jer 48:29
because of its * against Almighty Dan 7:11
The very * of Israel testifies Hos 5:5

ARROGANT

and * toward her mistress Sarai. Gen 16:4
Quit acting so proud and *! 1Sa 2:3
"Who else is as * as Job? Job 34:7,8
They are pitiless and *. Ps 17:10
lips of these * men who are Ps 31:18
O Jehovah, an * nation has Ps 74:18
Mockers are proud, haughty and *. Pro 21:24
beyond description, *, disdainful. Pro 30:13,14
has become proud and *, the Lord Eze 31:10
What's more, these * Chaldeans Hab 2:5
proud and * men from among you; Zep 3:11
been proud and *," says the Lord. Mal 3:13
concerned, "Blessed are the *." Mal 3:14,15

ARROW

and Jonathan shot an * beyond him. 1Sa 20:36
almost reached the *, Jonathan 1Sa 20:37

ARROW Con't)
"The * is still ahead of you. 1Sa 20:37
However, someone shot an * at 1Ki 22:34
and the * pierced his heart, and 2Ki 9:24
*, full of victory over Syria; 2Ki 13:16,17
wall, nor even shoot an * into it. 2Ki 19:32
soldiers shot an * haphazardly at 2Ch 18:33
struck down. The * is pulled from Job 20:25
Suddenly his * will pierce them. Ps 64:7
Like a crooked *, they missed the Ps 78:57
with an * through its heart. Pro 7:23
or shooting him with a sharp *. Pro 25:18
I am like a sharp * in his Is 49:2
Ephraim, you are my *! Zec 9:13

ARROWS
Take your bow and * out into the Gen 27:2,3,4
with *, whether man or animal.' Ex 19:13
And shall shoot them with many *. Num 24:3-9
And shoot them down with my *. Deu 32:23
My * shall be drunk with blood! Deu 32:40,41
and shoot three * in front of the 1Sa 20:20
send a lad to bring the * back. 1Sa 20:21
'Go farther—the * are still ahead 1Sa 20:22
boy with him to gather his *. 1Sa 20:35
can find the * as I shoot them." 1Sa 20:36
the * and ran back to his master. 1Sa 20:38
Then Jonathan gave his bow and * 1Sa 20:40
He shot forth his * of lightning 2Sa 22:15
a bow and some *," and he did. 2Ki 13:15
Now pick up the other * and 2Ki 13:18
men to shoot * and huge stones from 2Ch 26:15
their * and fatally wounded him. 2Ch 35:23
has struck me down with his *; Job 6:4
he has sent his poisoned * deep Job 6:4
letting fly their *, so that the Job 16:13
away though the * rattle against Job 39:21-23
wood. * cannot make him flee. Job 41:27,28
deadly * made from shafts of fire. Ps 7:13
bows, drawn their * tight against Ps 11:2
He flashed his fearful * of Ps 18:14
see your * aimed straight at them. Ps 21:12
Your * have struck deep; Ps 38:2
Your * are sharp Ps 45:5
teeth are sharp as spears and *. Ps 57:4
words like * straight at my heart. Ps 64:3
* and burned with glowing coals. Ps 120:4
are like sharp * to defend him. Ps 127:4
bolts, your *, Lord, upon your Ps 144:6
around firebrands, * and death! Pro 26:18,19
Their * are sharp; Is 5:28
sharp * and the terrors of war! Is 21:15
nor shoot their * there, nor march Is 37:33
bows to shoot their * of untruth. Jer 9:3
The enemies' * go straight to the Jer 50:9
spare no *, for she has sinned Jer 50:14
of trouble. The * of the enemy Jer 51:3
Sharpen the *! Jer 51:11
sent his * deep within my heart. Lam 3:13
"I will shower you with deadly * Eze 5:16
they will cast lots by shaking * Eze 21:21
bucklers, bows and *, javelins and Eze 39:9
and you put * to the string. Hab 3:8,9f
from your * and the flashing of Hab 3:11
His * shall fly like lightning; Zec 9:14
the fiery * aimed at you by Satan. Eph 6:16

ARSENAL
All of the godly man's *—weapons 2Co 6:7

ARTEMAS
I am planning to send either * or Tit 3:12

ARTFUL
strip away their * beauty and their Is 3:18

ARTICLE
by finding a lost * and lying about Lev 6:3
be defiled—any * of wood, or of Lev 11:32
the defiled * touches any food, all Lev 11:34
or leather *, for it is contagious Lev 13:52
the suspected * to be washed, then Lev 13:54
* is infected through and through. Lev 13:55

ARTICLES
any of the sacred * or the altar, Num 18:2,3
or similar *, but only for repairs 2Ki 12:13,14
and the other holy * of worship 1Ch 22:19
This will be used for the * made 1Ch 29:4,5
and to foundrymen who made * of 2Ch 24:12
other ceremonial * left here by Jer 27:19,20,21

ARTISTIC
He is highly capable as an * Ex 31:4
silver and for the * decorations. 1Ch 29:4,5

ARTS
same thing with their magical *! Ex 7:11
used their secret * and they, too, Ex 7:22
with their secret *, and they, too, Ex 8:7
*, but this time they failed. Ex 8:18
In the cultural *, I organized Ecc 2:7,8

ARUBBOTH
Ben-hesed, whose area was *, 1Ki 4:8-19

ARUMAH
to Abimelech in * telling him, Ju 9:31
Abimelech was living at * at Ju 9:41

ARVAD
sailors come from Sidon and *; Eze 27:8
Men from * and from Helech Eze 27:11

ARVADITES
Sinites,*, Zemarites, Hamathites. Gen 10:15-19
*, Zemarites, and Hamathites. 1Ch 1:13-16

ARZA
at the home of *, the 1Ki 16:9

ASA
his son * reigned in his place. 1Ki 15:8
* became king of Judah, in 1Ki 15:9
not removed, for * did not realize 1Ki 15:14
the heart of * was perfect toward 1Ki 15:14f
war between King * of Judah and 1Ki 15:16
Then * took all the silver and 1Ki 15:18
Then King * made a proclamation 1Ki 15:22
And King * used these materials 1Ki 15:22
of the reign of King * of Judah. 1Ki 15:25
of the reign of King * of Judah. 1Ki 15:28
between King * of Judah and King 1Ki 15:32,33
the reign of King * of Judah, but 1Ki 16:8
of the reign of King * of Judah. 1Ki 16:10
King * of Judah had been on the 1Ki 16:23
King * of Judah had been on the 1Ki 16:29
the son of * had become king during 1Ki 22:41
He did as his father * had done, 1Ki 22:43
from the days of his father *. 1Ki 22:46
Rehoboam, Abijah, *, Jehoshaphat, 1Ch 3:10-14
Berechiah (the son of *, son of 1Ch 9:15,16
Then his son * became the new 2Ch 14:1
of his reign, for * was careful to 2Ch 14:2
and King * sent his troops to meet 2Ch 14:9,10
Ethiopians, and * and the army of 2Ch 14:12
out to meet King * as he was 2Ch 15:2
"Listen to me, *! 2Ch 15:2
When King * heard this message 2Ch 15:8
the Lord God was with King *). 2Ch 15:9
King * even removed his mother 2Ch 15:16
the heart of King * was perfect 2Ch 15:17
Then King * and the people of 2Ch 16:6
came to King * and told him, 2Ch 16:7
* was so angry with the prophet 2Ch 16:10
him into jail. And * oppressed all 2Ch 16:10
The rest of the biography of * is 2Ch 16:11
year of his reign, * became 2Ch 16:12
king, just as his father * was. 2Ch 20:32
good ways of King *, but you have 2Ch 21:12
by King * when he fortified Mizpah Jer 41:9
Abijah was the father of *; Mt 1:7
* was the father of Jehoshaphat; Mt 1:8

ASA'S
The rest of * biography—his 1Ki 15:23
King * Judean army was 300,000 2Ch 14:8
year of King * reign, and 2Ch 15:10
thirty-fifth year of King * reign. 2Ch 15:19
IN THE THIRTY-SIXTH year of King * 2Ch 16:1
road to Judah. * response was to 2Ch 16:2
Ben-hadad agreed to King * 2Ch 16:4

ASAHEL
Joab's brothers, Abishai and *, 2Sa 2:18
in the battle. * could run like a 2Sa 2:18
out to him, "Is that you, *?" 2Sa 2:20
Abner warned. But * refused and 2Sa 2:21
were missing, in addition to *. 2Sa 2:30
for the death of his brother *. 2Sa 3:27
brother * at the battle of Gibeon. 2Sa 3:30
*, the brother of Joab, was also 2Sa 23:24-39
Joab, Abishai, *, and Benaiah. 2Sa 23:24-39f
sons were Abishai, Joab, and *. 1Ch 2:16
* (Joab's brother); 1Ch 11:26-47
Division was * (the brother of 1Ch 27:7
Zebadiah, *, Shemiramoth, 2Ch 17:7,8,9
Jehiel, Azaziah, Nahath, *, 2Ch 31:12,13
Only Jonathan (son of *), Ez 10:15

ASAHEL'S
Joab and his men took * body to 2Sa 2:32

ASAIAH
and Shaphan, and *, the king's 2Ki 22:12,13
and Shaphan, and * went to the 2Ki 22:14
Jeshohaiah, *, Adi-el, Jesimi-el, 1Ch 4:34-39
Uzzah, Shime-a, Haggiah, *. 1Ch 6:29,30
return, including * (Shilon's 1Ch 9:5
of Merari; with * as their leader; 1Ch 15:4-10
leaders: Uriel, *, Joel, Shemaiah, 1Ch 15:11
and *, the king's personal aide. 2Ch 34:20

ASAPH
and Joah (son of *) the historian 2Ki 18:37
was his colleague *, whose 1Ch 6:39-43
of Zichri, who was the son of *). 1Ch 9:15,16
Heman (son of Joel), * (son of 1Ch 15:17
Heman, *, and Ethan were chosen 1Ch 15:19
this assignment: *, the leader of 1Ch 16:5
to the Lord. * was the director of 1Ch 16:7
David arranged for * and his 1Ch 16:37
groups of *, Heman, and Jeduthun. 1Ch 25:1
Under the leadership of *, the 1Ch 25:2
*, Jeduthun, and Heman reported 1Ch 25:6,7
indicated Joseph of the * clan; 1Ch 25:9-31
TEMPLE GUARDS were from the * 1Ch 26:1
The singers were *, Heman, 2Ch 5:11,12
who was one of the sons of *). 2Ch 20:14
From the * clan, Zechariah and 2Ch 29:12,13,14
and of the prophet *, which they 2Ch 29:30
The singers (the sons of *) were 2Ch 35:15
by King David, *, Heman, and 2Ch 35:15
members from the clan of *, 128; Ez 2:40,41,42
and the descendants of * crashed Ez 3:10
also a letter to *, the manager Neh 2:8
members from the clan of *, 148; Neh 7:43,44,45
of Zabdi, son of *) was the one Neh 11:15,16,17
a descendant of *, whose clan Neh 11:22,23
Micaiah, son of Zaccur, son of *), Neh 12:35,36
days of David and * that the custom Neh 12:46
and Joah (son of *), the royal Is 36:22

ASAPH'S
scribe, and Joah (* son), the royal Is 36:3

ASAREL
sons were:Ziph, Ziphah, Tiri-a, *. 1Ch 4:16

ASCEND
* to heaven and rule the angels. Is 14:13
tell them that I * to my Father and Jn 20:17
watch the smoke *, and saying, Rev 18:18

ASCENDED
the mountain, and Moses * to God. Ex 19:20
watched, the Angel * in the fire! Ju 13:20
years old when he * the throne, and 1Ki 22:42
years old when he * the throne. 2Ch 36:9
God has * with a mighty shout, Ps 47:5
III, who now * the Egyptian throne Dan 11:7f
I haven't yet * to the Father. Jn 20:17
for he never * into the skies. Act 2:34
mixed with prayers * up to God from Rev 8:4

ASCENDS
Mount Zion. He * the heights, Ps 68:18
The smoke from her burning * Rev 19:3

ASCENT
Literally, "* of Akrabbim." Num 34:4f
begins at the * of Scorpion Pass, Ju 1:36

ASCERTAINED
The exact weight cannot be *. Ex 30:22,23f
The exact weight cannot be *. Ex 38:27f

ASCRIBE
* great strength and glory to his 1Ch 16:28
Yes, * to the Lord 1Ch 16:29

ASENATH
wife, a girl named *, daughter of Gen 41:45
born to Joseph by *, the daughter Gen 41:50
(their mother was *, the daughter Gen 46:19-22

ASH
with bronze. The * buckets, Ex 27:3
oak, he plants the * in the forest Is 44:14
the graveyard and * dump in the Jer 31:40
and kettles, and * shovels used at Jer 52:18

ASHAMED
of them was embarrassed or *. Gen 2:25
* and had been beaten in battle. 2Sa 19:3
making us feel *, as though we had 2Sa 19:5
and Levites became * of themselves 2Ch 30:15
For I was * to ask the king for Ez 8:22
and cried out, "O my God, I am *; Ez 9:6
God, shouldn't someone make you *? Job 11:3
Why aren't you * to deal with me Job 19:3
You have tried to make me feel * Job 20:3
God, he will be * and repent? Job 36:19
up with me and I am * to look up. Ps 40:12
let them be * and terrified Ps 83:17
then I will never have to be * of Ps 119:80
This will make him feel * of Pro 25:21,22
they are not even *. Is 3:9
mart of the world. Be *, O Sidon, Is 23:4
Perhaps then they will be *! Is 26:11
no longer pale with fear, or be *. Is 29:22
those who worship them are so *. Is 44:9
idols shall be disappointed and *. Is 45:16
him shall come to him and be *. Is 45:24
wait for me shall never be *." Is 49:23
you shall be sad and *, but they Is 65:13
Were my people * when they Jer 6:15
Are they * because they worship Jer 8:12
will see your wickedness and be *. Jer 22:22
I was thoroughly * of all I did Jer 31:19
Then at last Moab shall be * of Jer 48:13
"We are * because the Temple of Jer 51:51
even they are * of you. Eze 16:27
jewels and leave you naked and *. Eze 16:39
O my people Israel, be utterly * Eze 36:32
they will be * of all their sins. Eze 43:10
And if they are truly * of what Eze 43:11
for all to see; * and defenseless, Ob 1:10
as slaves—stripped, naked and *. Mic 1:11
is for me, and be * for taunting Mic 7:10
longer need to be * of yourselves, Zep 3:11
And anyone who is * of me and my Mk 8:38
will be * of him when I return in Mk 8:38
But they were * to answer, for Mk 9:34
angels, I will be * then of all who Lk 9:26
are * of me and of my words now. Lk 9:26
For I am not * of this Good News Rom 1:16
since you are * now even to think Rom 6:21
In other words, he will feel * Rom 12:20
things to make you *, but to warn 1Co 4:14
I am trying to make you *. 1Co 6:5
man with long hair tends to be *. 1Co 11:14,15
I would be very much *—and so 2Co 9:4

(ASHAMED Con't)
in the face. I'm * to say that I'm 2Co 11:21
cause me to be * of myself but that Php 1:20
proud of what they should be * of; Php 3:19
him, that he may be * of himself. 2Th 3:14
I am certainly not * of it, for I 2Ti 1:12
was never * of my being in jail. 2Ti 1:16
be * when God examines your work. 2Ti 2:15
to argue will be * of himself Tit 2:8
That is why Jesus is not * to Heb 2:11
And now God is not * to be called Heb 11:16
they will become * of themselves 1Pe 3:16
not have to be * and shrink back 1Jn 2:28
so we will not be * and 1Jn 4:17
pure, so you won't be naked and *; Rev 3:18
not need to walk naked and *." Rev 16:15

ASHAN
Libnah, Ether, *, Iphtah, Ashnah, Jos 15:37-44
Sharuhen, En-rimmon, Ether, and *. Jos 19:2-7
Etam, Ain, Rimmon, Tochen, and *; 1Ch 4:32,33
Hilen, Debir, *, Beth-shemesh. 1Ch 6:58,59

ASHARELAH
Zaccur, Joseph, Nethaniah, and *. 1Ch 25:2

ASHBEL
*, Gera, Naaman, Gen 46:19-22
named after their ancestor *. Num 26:38-41
Bela, the first,*, the 1Ch 8:1

ASHBELITES
The *, named after their ancestor Num 26:38-41

ASHDOD
remained in Gaza, Gath, and *. Jos 11:22
Gaza, *, Ashkelon, Gath Jos 13:2-7
of * with their nearby villages; Jos 15:46
also the city of * with its Jos 15:47
their idol Dagon in the city of *. 1Sa 5:1
of the temple of Dagon in *. 1Sa 5:5
the people of * and the nearby 1Sa 5:6
capital cities, *, Gaza, Ashkelon, 1Sa 6:17
walls, also those of Jabneh and *. 2Ch 26:6
Then he built new cities in the * 2Ch 26:6
married women from *, Ammon, and Neh 13:23
in the language of * and couldn't Neh 13:24
Philistine city of * and captured Is 20:1
what remains of *, and I visited Jer 25:19,20
I will kill the people of *, and Amo 1:8
Gaza, Ashkelon, *, Ekron—these Zep 2:4
over the city of *, the rich city Zec 9:6

ASHDODITES
Ammonites, and * heard that the Neh 4:7

ASHEN-FACED
Then why do they stand there, *, Jer 30:6

ASHER
to the east of the city of *. Gen 2:14
and Leah named him * (meaning Gen 30:13
Leah's servant-girl:Gad, *. Gen 35:26
* and his sons: Imnah, Ishvah, Gen 46:16,17
"* shall produce rich foods, fit Gen 49:20
Dan, Naphtali,Gad, *. Ex 1:1
* - Pagiel (son of Ochran Num 1:2-15
* - 41,500 Num 1:20-46
Tribe: Dan * Naphtali Num 2:3-31
Next to * Num 2:3-31
of the tribe of *, brought his Num 7:72-77
the tribe of *, led by Pagiel, Num 10:26
of Michael, from the tribe of *; Num 13:3-15
The tribe of *: 53,400. Num 26:44-47
clans named after the sons of *: Num 26:44-47
* also had a daughter named Serah. Num 26:44-47
* Ahihud (son of Shelomi) Num 34:16-28
of Reuben, Gad, *, Zebulun, Dan, Deu 27:13
Of the tribe of *: Deu 33:24
"* is a favorite son, Deu 33:24
from the border of * to Jos 17:7
the territory of * and the eastern Jos 17:10
to Issachar and *: Beth-shean, Jos 17:11
The Land Given to the Tribe of *: Jos 19:24,25,26
to be assigned its land was *. Jos 19:24,25,26
the boundary of * on the west, and Jos 19:34
of Issachar, *, Naphtali, and the Jos 21:6
The tribe of * gave four cities Jos 21:30,31
nor did the tribe of * drive out Ju 1:31,32
And why did * sit unmoved Ju 5:17
Manasseh, *, Zebulun, and Naphtali, Ju 6:35
of Naphtali, *, and Manasseh and Ju 7:23
whose areas were * and Bealoth; 1Ki 4:8-19
Benjamin, Naphtali, Gad, *. 1Ch 2:1
*, Naphtali, and Manasseh. 1Ch 6:62
The tribe of * gave them Abdon, 1Ch 6:74
The children of *: 1Ch 7:30
These descendants of * were heads 1Ch 7:40
From the tribe of *, there were 1Ch 12:24-37
from the tribes of *, Manasseh, and 2Ch 30:11
be named for Gad, * and Naphtali. Eze 48:34
Jewish tribe of *, and was very Lk 2:36,37
* 12,000 Rev 7:4-8

ASHER'S
of the land. * territory lies Eze 48:2
Naphtali's land lies south of *, Eze 48:3

ASHERAH
the goddess * that stood nearby. Ju 6:25
and for cutting down the * idol." Ju 6:30
* who are supported by Jezebel." 1Ki 18:19
These were evidently the 400 * 1Ki 22:6f
worship the goddess * at Samaria. 2Ki 13:6
shameful idols of *, and broke up 2Ki 18:4
made a shameful * idol, just as 2Ki 21:3,4,5
*, and the sun, moon, and stars. 2Ki 23:4
shameful idol of * from the Temple 2Ki 23:6
cut down the shameful idols of *; 2Ki 23:14
and burned the shameful idol of *. 2Ki 23:15

ASHERAH-IDOL
set up a shameful * in the 2Ki 21:7
the women wove robes for the *. 2Ki 23:7
mother because she made an *; 2Ch 15:16

ASHERIM
Literally, "*." Ex 34:13f
hills, and destroying the * idols. 2Ch 17:6

ASHERIM-IDOLS
down the shameful *, and demanded 2Ch 14:3

ASHEROTH
worshiped Baal and the * idols. Ju 3:7

ASHES
Lord, though I am but dust and *. Gen 18:27
and Aaron, "Take * from the kiln. Ex 9:8
So they took * from the kiln and Ex 9:10
east side of the altar with the *. Lev 1:15,16,17
place where the * are brought from Lev 4:11,12
and clean out the * of the burnt Lev 6:10
and carry the * outside the camp to Lev 6:11
"The * are to be removed from Num 4:13
gather up the * of the heifer and Num 19:9
And the one who gathers up the * Num 19:10
through the * of the red heifer Num 19:12
To become purified again, * from Num 19:17
Literally, "* of the burnt sin Num 19:17f
Yes, from a pile of *— 1Sa 2:8
Now she tore the robe and put * 2Sa 13:19
apart, and the * on it will spill 1Ki 13:3
the altar and the * poured out, 1Ki 13:5
and he carried the * to Bethel. 2Ki 23:4
on sackcloth and *, and went out Est 4:1
and many lay in sackcloth and *. Est 4:3
himself, and sat among the *. Job 2:8
have about as much value as *. Job 13:12
I have become as dust and *. Job 30:19
myself and repent in dust and *.' Job 42:6
turn to * and their peace Ps 69:22
I eat * instead of bread. Ps 102:9,10
The poor, deluded fool feeds on *; Is 44:20
and covering yourselves with *? Is 58:5
Israel he will give:Beauty for *; Is 61:3
clothes and sit in * and weep Jer 6:26
and he shall reduce it to *. Jer 21:10
and *, without a living soul. Jer 44:2,3
he has rolled me in * and dirt. Lam 3:16
to be burned to * as you do even Eze 20:31
their heads and wallowing in *. Eze 27:30
and let it burn you to * upon the Eze 28:18
myself with *, and confessed my Dan 9:3
and put on sackcloth and sat in *. Jon 3:6
will turn to * in their hands? Hab 2:13
upon the wicked as * underfoot," Mal 4:3
and throwing * on their heads to Lk 10:13
and goats and the * of young cows Heb 9:13
into heaps of * and blotted them 2Pe 2:6

ASHHUR
birth to *, the father of Tekoa. 1Ch 2:24
*, the father of Tekoa, had two 1Ch 4:5

ASHIMA
and the men of Hamath worshiped * 2Ki 17:30

ASHKELON
Gaza, Ashdad, *, Gath Jos 13:2-7
cities of Gaza, *, and Ekron, with Ju 1:18
to the city of *, killed thirty Ju 14:19
Ashdod, Gaza, *, Gath, and Ekron. 1Sa 6:17
it from the cities of Gath and *, 2Sa 1:20
Philistine cities: *, Gaza, Ekron, Jer 25:19,20
The cities of Gaza and * will be Jer 47:5
For the city of * and those Jer 47:7
destroy Ekron and the king of *; Amo 1:8
Gaza, *, Ashdod, Ekron—these Zep 2:4
rest in the abandoned houses in *. Zep 2:7
"* will see it happen and be Zec 9:5
* will be completely destroyed. Zec 9:5

ASHKENAZ
The sons of Gomer:*, Riphath, Gen 10:3
*, Diphath, and Togarmah. 1Ch 1:5-9
armies of Ararat, Minni, and *. Jer 51:27

ASHNAH
Eshtaol, Zorah, *, Zanoah, Jos 15:33-36
Ashan, Iphtah, *, Nezib, Keilah, Jos 15:37-44

ASHORE
the boat *, but couldn't make it. Jon 1:13
jumped into the water [and swam * Jn 21:7
went out and dragged the net *. Jn 21:11
We went *, found the local Act 21:4
and let him go * to visit with Act 27:3
knew they would soon be driven *; Act 27:29
raised the foresail and headed *. Act 27:40
any of them swim * and escape. Act 27:42
So everyone escaped safely *! Act 27:44

ASHPENAZ
Then he ordered *, who was in Dan 1:3,4

ASHTAROTH
been defeated at *, near Edre-i. Deu 1:1
who lived at * and Edre-i: He Jos 12:4
who had reigned in * and Edre-i. Jos 13:12
royal cities of * and Edre-i were Jos 13:31
worshiping Baal and the * idols. Ju 2:12-14
gods Baal and *, and the gods of Ju 10:6
foreign gods and your * idols. 1Sa 7:3
and * and worshiped only the Lord. 1Sa 7:4
worshiping the Baal and * idols. 1Sa 12:10
in the temple of *, and his body 1Sa 31:10
Golan, in Bashan; *. 1Ch 6:71
the images of * and the sun-idols. Is 17:8

ASHTERATH
Uzzia from *; 1Ch 11:26-47

ASHTEROTH-KARNAIM
The Rephaim in *; Gen 14:5,6

ASHTORETH
Solomon worshiped *, the goddess 1Ki 11:5
*, the goddess of the Sidonians; 1Ki 11:33
these shrines for *, the evil 2Ki 23:13

ASHTRAYS
and the *, all of pure gold. Ex 37:23,24

ASHURI
His territory included Gilead, * 2Sa 2:9

ASHVATH
Pasach, Bimhal, *. 1Ch 7:33

ASIA
Meshech, Rosh and Tubal were in * Is 66:19f
Regions of * Minor, now in Turkey. Eze 27:13f
Regions of * Minor, now in Turkey. Eze 27:14f
of Syria and * Minor, and Antipater Dan 8:8f
Those exiled in * Minor shall Ob 1:20
Literally, "*," a province of Act 2:9f
Literally, "*." Act 20:4f
Literally, "the coast of *." Act 27:2f
person to become a Christian in *. Rom 16:5
The churches here in * send you 1Co 16:19
hard time we went through in *. 2Co 1:8
came here from * have deserted me; 2Ti 1:15
Literally, "in *." Rev 1:4f
"The seven churches in *." Rev 1:11f

ASIDE
grown, she laid * her widow's Gen 38:14
Sabbath day and set it * for rest. Ex 20:11
shall be set * for sacrificing. Lev 7:4
thigh that was set *, along with Lev 10:15
"You shall set * for God all the Deu 15:19
clothing, laying * that which she Deu 21:13
your not turning * in any way from Deu 28:14
told Joshua to set * a day to Jos 5:2,3
cities be set * for this purpose on Jos 20:8
they took him * and asked him, Ju 18:3
But you have put * your personal Ru 3:10
been set * for the guest of honor. 1Sa 9:23
But David jumped * and escaped. 1Sa 18:11,12
Joab took him * at the city gate as 2Sa 3:27
So Ahima-az stepped *. 2Sa 18:30
and called him * to talk to him. 1Ki 11:29
them * as they are filled!" 2Ki 4:4
have thrown me * and have worshiped 2Ki 22:17
upon the altar set * for that 1Ch 16:40
he will permanently throw you *. 1Ch 28:9
anger was turned * and he didn't 2Ch 12:12
(He laid * his royal robes so 2Ch 35:22
The caravans turn * to be Job 6:15-18
I have not turned *. Job 23:11
The needy are kicked *; Job 24:4
The young saw me and stepped *, Job 29:8
For they turned * from following Job 34:27
Why have you tossed me *? Ps 43:2
you have tossed us * in dishonor, Ps 44:9
Don't toss me *, banished Ps 51:11
in my old age, don't set me *. Ps 71:9
I will never lay * your laws, Ps 119:93
your path, but I will not turn *. Ps 119:110
He won't turn * for anyone. Pro 30:29,30,31
for I will put * my anger and Is 65:16
thrones and lay * their robes and Eze 26:16
is the land set * for the Temple. Eze 48:8
in the dust and kick * the meek. Amo 2:7
throne and laid * his royal robes Jon 3:6
But Peter took him * to Mt 16:22
twelve disciples *, and talked to Mt 20:17
rolled * the stone and sat on it. Mt 28:2
Peter took him * and chided him. Mk 8:32
"you must put * your own pleasures Mk 8:34
Taking them *, Jesus once more Mk 10:32
it *, jumped up and came to Jesus. Mk 10:50
could ever roll * the huge stone Mk 16:3
follow me must put * his own Lk 9:23
the entrance had been rolled *. Lk 24:2
and, calling her * from the Jn 11:28
"Roll the stone *," Jesus told Jn 11:39
So they rolled the stone *. Jn 11:41
was rolled * from the entrance. Jn 20:1
they laid * as they stoned him.' Act 22:20
and leading him * asked, "What is Act 23:19
put this all * and be a fool rather 1Co 3:18
unfit and ordered to stand *. 1Co 9:27
of you should put * something from 1Co 16:2

ASIDE Con't)
you not to toss * this marvelous 2Co 6:1
as God, but laid * his mighty Php 2:7
I have put * all else, counting Php 3:8
now and has been put * forever. Heb 8:13
Next, learn to put * your own 2Pe 1:6

SLEEP
Soon he fell * again and had a Gen 41:5
and so he died, for he was fast * Ju 4:21
camp and found him *, with his 1Sa 26:5,6,7
the Lord had put them sound *. 1Sa 26:12
me while I was *, and laid her dead 1Ki 3:20
or is * and needs to be wakened!" 1Ki 18:27
be quiet now, * and at rest, along Job 3:13
of those who are * to speak." Sol 7:9
was sound * down in the hold. Jon 1:5
woke me, as though I had been *. Zec 4:1
But Jesus was *. Mt 8:24
three disciples and found them *. Mt 26:40
they had all been * when Jesus' Mt 28:12,13
Jesus was * at the back of the Mk 4:38
she is only *!" Mk 5:39
three disciples and found them *. Mk 14:37
he said. "*? Mk 14:37
she is only *!" Lk 8:52
been very drowsy and had fallen *. Lk 9:32
That night two men will be * in Lk 17:34
find them *, exhausted from grief. Lk 22:45
*! he said Lk 22:46
executed, he was *, double-chained Act 12:6
sill, went fast * and fell three Act 20:9
first-fruits of them that are *." 1Co 15:20f
So be on your guard, not * like 1Th 5:6

SNAH
Paseah, Besai, *, Me-unim, Ez 2:43-54
*, Me-unim, Nephushesim, Neh 7:46-56

SPATHA
Parshandatha, Dalphon, *, Poratha, Est 9:7-10

SPECTS
Certain * of verses 12 and 14 Eze 26:14f
about the business * of this Act 19:27
where various * of the Holy Spirit Rev 1:4f

SPHALT
the valley was full of * pits. Gen 14:10

SRI-EL
*, Shechem, Shemida, and Hepher. Jos 17:2
Aramaean concubine, were * and 1Ch 7:14

SRIEL
named after their ancestor *. Num 26:28-37

SRIELITES
The *, named after their ancestor Num 26:28-37

SS
one—free and untamed as a wild *! Gen 16:9-12
She is a lonely, wandering wild *. Hos 8:9

ASSASSINATE
and his son Jonathan to * David. 1Sa 19:1
at the king and plotted to * him. Est 2:21
gates, who had plotted to * him. Est 6:1
(son of Nethaniah) to * him. Jer 40:13,14

ASSASSINATED
against him and * him while he was 1Ki 15:27
that Zimri had * the king, they 1Ki 16:15,16
against him and * him in his royal 2Ki 12:20
the men who had * his father; 2Ki 14:5
against him and * him at Ibleam and 2Ki 15:10
and * him and took the throne. 2Ki 15:14
from Gilead, and * him in the 2Ki 15:25
plotted against Pekah and * him; 2Ki 15:30
the priest. They * him as he lay in 2Ch 24:25
the men who had * his father. 2Ch 25:3
At last his own officers * him 2Ch 33:24
all of those who * him, and 2Ch 33:25
The people of Jerusalem who had * Jer 37:1f
Seleucus was *, ingratiated himself Dan 11:21f
Three Israelite kings were * Hos 7:7f
kings of Israel * during her last Hos 13:11f

ASSASSINATION
the man who saved the king from *! Est 7:9

ASSASSINS
to Silla. The * were Jozachar, the 2Ki 12:21
but his enemies sent * and killed 2Ki 14:19
killed all the * and placed Amon's 2Ki 21:24
and took 4,000 members of the * Act 21:37,38

ASSAULTING
the Almighty, stubbornly * him. Job 15:25,26

ASSAYER
Jeremiah, I have made you an * of Jer 6:27

ASSEMBLE
all Israel will * and worship me. Lev 23:1
the people to * and for signaling Num 10:1
the summons to * and the signal to Num 10:5,6,7
all Israel would * before the Lord Deu 31:10,11
450,000 troops to * with one mind Ju 20:1
Syrian king will * a mighty army Dan 11:10,11

ASSEMBLED
by the women who * at the entrance Ex 38:8
So all the people *, and Moses Lev 8:4
Aaron, and they all * to watch. Num 16:19
So Gideon * them at the water. Ju 7:5,6
the * men of Israel as follows: 1Ch 13:2
he had invited * themselves before 2Ch 1:5,6
a very large crowd * at Jerusalem 2Ch 30:13
We * at the Ahava River and Ez 8:15
all the people * at the plaza in Neh 8:1
Supreme Court * there and looked Mt 26:59
Supreme Court *, including the Lk 22:66
went in where the others were *. Act 10:27

ASSEMBLIES
religious feasts and solemn *. Amo 5:21
represent the * here and are 2Co 8:23

ASSEMBLING
home, times for * to worship, and Lev 23:3

ASSEMBLY
the Lord appeared to the whole *. Lev 9:23
be a sacred * of all the people; Lev 23:35
"But when the * is to be gathered Num 10:5,6,7f
members of the *, were involved. Num 16:2
festival a holy * of all the people Num 28:18
a holy and solemn * of all the Num 28:25
a special, solemn * of all the Num 28:26
there shall be a solemn * of all Num 29:1
there shall be yet another * of Num 29:12
the people to another solemn *; Num 29:35
song to the whole * of Israel: Deu 31:30
before the entire *, including the Jos 8:35
at a general * of all the people. Ju 11:11
to the entire * and said: "My son 1Ch 29:1
of the whole *, David expressed his 1Ch 29:10
aides, and all the * of Jerusalem 2Ch 30:2,3
immediately expelled from the *. Neh 13:3
I stand up and cry to the * for Job 30:28,29
* places where we worshiped you. Ps 74:8
Literally, "the * of the holy Ps 89:5f
Literally, "the * of the holy Ps 89:7f
I will preside on the Mount of * Is 14:13
just off the upper * hall of the Jer 36:10
The * nominated two men: Joseph Act 1:23
*, and they elected the following: Act 6:5

ASSERT
home, and should * his authority. Est 1:22
Gulf, who began to * themselves Hab 1:6f

ASSES
riders on *, riders on camels." Is 21:6,7f
is that the * and camels were Is 21:6,7f

ASSESSED
servant of God had * upon Israel. 2Ch 24:9

ASSESSING
from the rich, * each one $2,000 in 2Ki 15:19,20

ASSESSMENT
it is a regular * or some special 2Ki 12:4,5

ASSESSMENTS
Do kings levy * against their own Mt 17:25

ASSHUR
*,Arpachshad, Lud, Aram. Gen 10:22
Elam, *, 1Ch 1:17
Haran and Canneh, Eden, * and Eze 27:23

ASSHURIM
Dedan's sons were *, Letushim, Gen 25:3

ASSIGN
Tell them, 'Pharaoh will * to you Gen 45:18
Aaron or any of his sons may * Num 4:27
"* duties to each man by name. Num 4:32
The Lord instructed Joshua to * Jos 15:13
Then the Lord could * the Jos 18:8
And didn't I * the sacrificial 1Sa 2:28
Lots were then drawn to * land 1Ch 6:61
* me Godliness and Integrity as Ps 25:21
people, but shall * all the Eze 45:8
of trust and * him to the place of Lk 12:46

ASSIGNED
Potiphar * Joseph to wait on them. Gen 40:4
So Joseph * the best land of Gen 47:11
for they were * food from Pharaoh Gen 47:22
For the Levites are * for the Num 1:50
For they are * to him as Num 3:7,8,9
The half of the booty * to the Num 31:42-46
So Moses * the territory of King Num 32:33
have already been * land on the Num 34:14,15
had been * to Israel by the Lord. Deu 2:12
previously * this land to them. Jos 13:8
Moses hadn't * any land to the Jos 13:14
Moses had * the following area to Jos 13:15
Moses also * land to the tribe of Jos 13:24
Moses had * the following Jos 13:29
of Judah (as * by sacred lot): Jos 15:1
the number of cities * to Judah. Jos 15:48-62f
Sea was * to Ephraim, and the land Jos 17:10
in the areas * to Issachar and Jos 17:11
section will be * to each tribe. Jos 18:5,6
The section of land * to the Jos 18:11
previously * to the tribes of Judah Jos 18:11
This was the land * to the tribe Jos 18:20
of the land previously * to Judah. Jos 19:1
The fourth tribe to be * its land Jos 19:17-23
The fifth tribe to be * its land Jos 19:24,25,26
The last tribe to be * its land Jos 19:40
cities had been * originally to the Jos 21:4
* by the toss of the sacred dice. Jos 21:8
were * to the division of Gershon. Jos 21:33
(Moses had * the land of Bashan Jos 22:7,8
* to the tribes of Joseph. Jos 24:32
living in the land * to them. Ju 18:1
So Joab * Uriah to a spot close 2Sa 11:16
had been * to him by King Solomon. 1Ki 7:40
cities and land * by lot to the 1Ch 6:54
were also * by lot to the Levites 1Ch 6:64,65
They were * to each of the four 1Ch 9:24
the villages were * to them from 1Ch 9:25
Some of them were * to care for 1Ch 9:28
and they were all * to the 1Ch 23:24
All tasks were * to the various 1Ch 24:5
of Ithamar were * to each task. 1Ch 24:6
The work was * (by coin-toss) in 1Ch 24:7-18
as originally * by God through 1Ch 24:19
Aaron, they were * to their duties 1Ch 24:31
They were * guard duty at the 1Ch 26:13
Six guards were * daily to the 1Ch 26:17
Six guards were * each day to 1Ch 26:18
So at last he completed the work * 2Ch 4:11
he also * the Levites to their 2Ch 8:14
and he * the gatekeepers to their 2Ch 8:14
These offerings were * to the Neh 12:44
foreigners, and * tasks to the Neh 13:30
He * the moon to mark the months, Ps 104:19
into the room * for the use of the Jer 35:4
The king * them the best of food Dan 1:5
Begin the joyous tasks I have * Mt 25:21
these have been * me by the Jn 5:36
out the tasks * us by the one who Jn 9:4
for doing the work * me by the Lord Act 20:24
yes, God has * such gifts to each Heb 2:4
Seven angels were * to carry down Rev 15:1
The seven angels who were * to Rev 15:6

ASSIGNING
Tabernacles. In * the priests to 2Ch 8:14
organize the army, * leaders to 2Ch 25:5,6

ASSIGNMENT
So this was the * of land to the Jos 15:20
received the next * of Jos 19:1
The third tribe to receive its * Jos 19:10
The sixth tribe to receive its * Jos 19:32
First to receive their * were the Jos 21:9-16
those given this *: Asaph, the 1Ch 16:4

ASSIGNMENTS
The Territorial * Jos 13:14
carried out his * successfully. 1Sa 18:5
down the names and * in the 1Ch 24:6
He made the identical * of the 2Ch 23:18

ASSIR
The sons of Korah:*, Elkanah, Ex 6:24
Amminadab, Korah, *, 1Ch 6:22,23,24
Elkanah, Ebiasaph, *, Tahath, 1Ch 6:22,23,24
Zephaniah, Tahath, *, Ebiasaph, 1Ch 6:33-38

ASSIST
men to * you and be your guides." Gen 33:15
who wanted to * in the work given Ex 35:29
abilities are to * Bezalel and Ex 36:1
Ithamar to * their father Aaron. Num 3:4
After retirement they can * with Num 8:25,26
of Levi shall * you in any way. Num 18:4
quarrels and * them in every way. Deu 1:15
to * him in hearing these cases. 2Sa 15:3
Now please * me with this 1Ki 5:6
and King Josiah went to * him; 2Ki 23:29
to * his son in this project. 1Ch 22:17
the Levites was to * the 1Ch 23:28
Each corps will * particular 2Ch 35:4,5
prepare to * the people who come. 2Ch 35:6
to Israel and to * in the Ez 6:21,22
that they would * their brothers Neh 5:12
to Jerusalem to * in the ceremonies Neh 12:27
let your laws * me. Ps 119:175
to * the people in a general way. Eze 44:14
who * the Lord of all the earth." Zec 4:14
on at Antioch to * several others Act 15:34,35

ASSISTANCE
"If I need * against the 2Sa 10:11
you live, and come to their *. 1Ki 8:49
gave them whatever * they could, as Ez 1:6
They have even given us their * Ez 9:9
other * from the people of Israel. Neh 5:14
*, as well as Put and Libya. Nah 3:9
all who need their *, that their Tit 3:14

ASSISTANT
"The king's chief * spoke very Gen 42:30
So Moses and Joshua, his *, Ex 24:13
of the tribe of Dan) to be his *; Ex 31:6
Instead, your *, Joshua (the son Deu 1:38
spoke to Moses' *, whose name was Jos 1:1
He was Saul's special *, and he 1Sa 18:5
he went with Elijah, as his *. 1Ki 19:21
he added, "He was Elijah's *." 2Ki 3:11
The king appointed his special * 2Ki 7:17
Jehu said to Bidkar, his *, 2Ki 9:25
Asaiah, the king's *, and Ahikam 2Ki 22:12,13
chief priest, his * Zephaniah, and 2Ki 25:18
Heman's * 1Ch 6:39-43
Heman's second * was Ethan, a 1Ch 6:44-47
Shavsha was the king's special * 1Ch 18:16
*, while he was in the wilderness. 2Ch 1:2,3
of the army, and his *, Ma-aseiah. 2Ch 26:11
son of Mattaniah) as their *. Neh 13:13
king's chief *, and many others. Jer 39:3

(ASSISTANT Con't)
and Zephaniah his *, the three Jer 52:24,25
sent priests and * priests from Jn 1:19
Mark went with them as their *. Act 13:5

ASSISTANTS
received by Pharaoh and his *. Gen 41:37
counselors and *—all the senior Gen 50:7
present them to Aaron as his *. Num 3:6
as * to Aaron and his sons; Num 8:22
personally chosen *, protested, Num 11:28
the tribe of Levi, are your *; Num 18:2,3
* for the work of the Tabernacle. Num 18:6
as administrative * in charge of Deu 1:15
and David's sons were his *. 2Sa 8:18
the Levites, and the Temple *. 1Ch 9:2
men were chosen as their *: 1Ch 15:18
with the Levites as their *. 2Ch 19:11
His faithful * were Eden, 2Ch 31:14,15
of the Temple * were represented: Ez 2:43-54
The Temple * and the descendants Ez 2:58
(The Temple attendants were * to Ez 8:20
"Of the Temple *, the following Neh 7:46-56
"In all, the Temple * and the Neh 7:60
the Temple *, and the descendants Neh 11:3
son of Jeduthun) were his *. Neh 11:15,16,17
where the Temple *—the Levites—boil Eze 46:24
as Daniel's *, to be in charge of Dan 2:49
together ten * and gave them each Lk 19:13
He sent his two *, Timothy and Act 19:22

ASSISTED
the young man who * him, Joshua Ex 33:11
master craftsman, * by Oholiab Ex 38:23
* by leaders from each tribe:" Num 1:2-15
helper, for he * Eli the priest. 1Sa 2:11
young women who * at the entrance 1Sa 2:22
warriors, and they * David when he 1Ch 12:21
They * in the special sacrifices 1Ch 23:31
and the Temple and * the priests in 1Ch 23:32
Ahithophel was * by Jehoiada 1Ch 27:34
was put in charge, * by his brother 2Ch 31:12,13
Still others * as accountants, 2Ch 34:13
was * by Judah, son of Hassenu-ah. Neh 11:7,8,9
who was * by Zabdiel (son of Neh 11:10-14
a son of Judah) * in all matters of Neh 11:24
gatekeepers, who * them in Neh 12:45

ASSISTING
be given to the * priest, the one Lev 7:14
was helping the Lord by * Eli. 1Sa 3:1
The officer * the king said, 2Ki 7:2
Levites who were * me, said to Neh 8:9

ASSISTS
A man who * a thief must really Pro 29:24

ASSOCIATE
Don't * with evil men; Pro 23:6,7,8
king, and don't * with radicals. Pro 24:21,22
the man who is my * and equal," Zec 13:7
"Why does your teacher * with Mt 9:11
Don't even * with such people. Eph 5:7

ASSOCIATED
(* Press Release, April 24, 1964). Rev 9:16f

ASSOCIATES
as happened to Korah and his *. Num 16:40
the cymbals. His * were Zechariah, 1Ch 16:5
Tabe-el and their * wrote a letter Ez 4:7

ASSOCIATING
law because he was * with such Lk 15:2

ASSOCIATION
from our first * with the Lord—from Act 1:21,22

ASSOS
Paul was going by land to *, and Act 20:13

ASSUME
anyone else who presumes to * Num 3:10
we * no responsibility whatsoever; Jos 2:19
we may rightly * that all those who 1Jn 2:29

ASSUMED
for it must be * that she Deu 22:25,26,27
* they would receive much more. Mt 20:10
They all * the baby's name would Lk 1:59
day, for they * he was with Lk 2:44
so hastily, they * she was going to Jn 11:31
from Ephesus in Turkey, and * Act 21:29
for now you have * your great power Rev 11:17

ASSUMING
Stop * my guilt, for I am Job 6:29
wide open, and * the prisoners had Act 16:27

ASSURANCE
Yet we have this *: Those who Is 26:19
speaking words of comfort and *. Zec 1:13
city, there was no * you would ever Zec 8:10
For, after all, there is no * to 1Co 7:16
full * that what we said was true. 1Th 1:5
It is the confident * that Heb 11:1
Lord with perfect * and trust, and 1Jn 3:21

ASSURANCES
give * of peace when all is war. Jer 6:14
when they hear such * from God; Heb 6:18

ASSURE
bury my father; * him that I will Gen 50:5
you about, and I * you that my Ex 32:34
I can * you he will never 2Sa 14:10
wounds, for they * them all is well Jer 8:11
And Jesus replied, "Let me * you Mk 10:29
"And I * you of this: I, the Lk 12:8
and I can * you that all he says Jn 5:32,33
I can * you that he has worked Col 4:13

ASSURED
at Heshbon," the Lord * him. Num 21:34
Moses," they * him, "and may the Jos 1:17,18
"Rest *," David replied. 1Sa 21:5
And Gedaliah * them that it Jer 40:9
God's presence, * of his glad Eph 3:12

ASSURES
No, our faith in him * our souls' Heb 10:39

ASSURING
It was for us, too, * us that Rom 4:24

ASSYRIA
there he extended his reign to *. Gen 10:11,12
border in the direction of *). Gen 25:18
of the king of * shall deport you Num 24:21,22
And shall oppress both Eber and *. Num 24:23,24
Then King Pul of * invaded the 2Ki 15:19,20
and he took the people away to * 2Ki 15:29
Tiglath-pileser of *, begging him 2Ki 16:7
In deference to the king of * he 2Ki 16:18
King Shalmaneser of * attacked 2Ki 17:3
to pay heavy annual taxes to *. 2Ki 17:3
the king of * by asking King So of 2Ki 17:4
to pay the annual tribute to *. 2Ki 17:4
So the king of * put him in 2Ki 17:4
people of Israel were exiled to *. 2Ki 17:6
* where they remain to this day. 2Ki 17:23
And the king of * transported 2Ki 17:24
to the king of *: "We colonists 2Ki 17:26
The king of * then decreed that 2Ki 17:27,28
the king of * and refused to pay 2Ki 18:7
Shalmaneser of * attacked Israel 2Ki 18:9
that the king of * transported the 2Ki 18:11
the Israelis to * and put them in 2Ki 18:11
Sennacherib of * besieged and 2Ki 18:13
* at Lachish: "I have done wrong. 2Ki 18:14
The king of * then demanded a 2Ki 18:14
Nevertheless the king of * sent 2Ki 18:17
great King of * says, 'No one can 2Ki 18:19
bet with my master, the king of *! 2Ki 18:23
"Listen to the great king of *! 2Ki 18:28
their people from the king of *? 2Ki 18:33
For the king of * will receive 2Ki 19:7
what the kings of * have done 2Ki 19:11
The former kings of * destroyed 2Ki 19:12
that the kings of * have destroyed 2Ki 19:17
the king of * is that he shall not 2Ki 19:32
and this city from the king of *. 2Ki 20:6
the king of * at the Euphrates 2Ki 23:29
by King Tilgath-pilneser of *. 1Ch 5:6
So God caused King Pul of * 1Ch 5:26
asked the king of * to be his ally 2Ch 28:16
king of *, arrived, he caused 2Ch 28:20
from the power of the kings of *. 2Ch 30:6
Sennacherib of * invaded Judah and 2Ch 32:1
"Why should the king of * come 2Ch 32:4
of the king of * or his mighty 2Ch 32:7
Then King Sennacherib of *, while 2Ch 32:9
"King Sennacherib of * asks, 'Do 2Ch 32:10
deliver us from the king of *"! 2Ch 32:11
the other kings of * before me have 2Ch 32:13
come only to fight the king of *! 2Ch 35:21
of * brought us here." Ez 4:2
caused the king of * to be generous Ez 6:21,22
when the kings of * first triumphed Neh 9:32
and Tyre; * has joined them too, Ps 83:8
* will come with his great army! Is 7:17
and of * too, to swarm down upon Is 7:18
the king of * will invade both Is 8:4
the king of * and all his mighty Is 8:7,8
you. * is the whip of my anger; Is 10:5,6
But the king of * will not know Is 10:7
used the king of * to accomplish Is 10:12
O king of *, the Lord of Hosts will Is 10:16
Look, the mighty armies of * are Is 10:28,29
of Israel from *, Upper and Lower Is 11:11
He will make a highway from * Is 11:16
Shalmaneser V of *. Is 14:29f
Sargon of *. Is 14:31f
Literally, "*." Is 19:23f
IN THE YEAR when Sargon, king of * Is 20:1
For the king of * will take away Is 20:4
their enemies, * and Egypt, will be Is 27:13
dynasty against Sennacherib of *. Is 30:2f
will strip the fallen army of *! Is 33:4
* has refused their cry for peace. Is 33:7
king of *, came to fight against Is 36:1
mighty king of * says you are a Is 36:4
My master, the king of *, wants Is 36:8,9
of the great king, the king of *: Is 36:13
you be conquered by the king of *. Is 36:15
over the armies of the king of *? Is 36:18
the king of *, and his blasphemy. Is 37:6
For a report from * will reach Is 37:7
not be captured by the king of *! Is 37:10
the kings of * have gone, for they Is 37:11
that the kings of * have destroyed Is 37:18
city from the king of *: This year Is 37:30
"As for the king of *, his Is 37:3
Then Sennacherib, king of *, Is 37:3
and this city from the king of *. Is 38:
Egypt and *, and I delivered them. Is 52:
alliances with Egypt and with *? Jer 2:1
will forsake you as * did before. Jer 2:3
king of *, in the days of Hezekiah Jer 21:
First the king of * ate them up; Jer 50:1
land as I punished the king of *. Jer 50:1
for bread from Egypt, and * too. Lam 5:
choicest men of *—worshiping their Eze 23:
people: You are as * was—a great Eze 31:2,
"The princes of * lie there Eze 32:2
will turn to *, to the great king Hos 5:1
calling to Egypt, flying to *. Hos 7:1
those she hires; * is one of them. Hos 8:
off to Egypt and *, and live there Hos 9:
are carried off to * as slaves? Hos 9:
go as slaves to *, a present to the Hos 10:
* because they won't return to me. Hos 11:
Egypt—like doves flying from *. Hos 11:1
gifts to Egypt and * to get their Hos 12:
of praise. * cannot save us, nor Hos 14:
They will rule * with drawn Mic 5:
and honor you—from * to Egypt, and Mic 7:1
he will destroy * and make its Zep 2:1
from Egypt and *, and resettle them Zec 10:1
dry—the rule of * and Egypt over my Zec 10:1

ASSYRIA'S
him shake free of * power, but this 2Ki 17:4
* vast army is like a glorious Is 10:18
is the king of * offer to you: Give Is 36:16
of the king of * representative as Is 37:4
against Sennacherib, * king. Is 37:21

ASSYRIAN
it as a payment to the * king. 2Ki 16:8
was filled with * troops for three 2Ki 17:5
But since these * colonists did 2Ki 17:25
and gave it all to the * king. 2Ki 18:16
Then the * general sent this 2Ki 18:19
But the * general replied, "Has 2Ki 18:27
Then the * ambassador shouted in 2Ki 18:28
him what the * general had said. 2Ki 18:37
God has heard the * general defying 2Ki 19:4
Then the * general returned to 2Ki 19:8
killed 185,000 * troops, and dead 2Ki 19:35
who destroyed the * army with all 2Ch 32:21
So God sent the * armies, and 2Ch 33:11
fell to the * armies in 722 B.C. Is 7:8f
I have decided to break the * Is 14:25
prepared for Molech, the * god; Is 30:33
of terror when the * officers Is 33:18
with him. The * ambassador told Is 36:4
Now the * envoy left Jerusalem Is 37:8,9
But at this point the * king Is 37:8,9
No, the * kings completely Is 37:12
She fawned over her * neighbors, Eze 23:12
known from * records as Hilakku. Eze 27:11f
A prediction of the * conquest of Hos 1:4,5f
Soon after defeating Israel, the * Hos 1:7f
The * invasion came about twenty Hos 4:19f
Call together the * and Egyptian Amo 3:9
And when the * invades our land Mic 5:5
Nineveh was the * capital. Nah 1:1f
yoke of slavery to this * king." Nah 1:13
O * king, your princes lie dead Nah 3:18

ASSYRIANS
So the * attacked Damascus, the 2Ki 16:9
So the * took over Samaria and 2Ki 17:24
these * have made against me.' 2Ki 19:5,6
Egypt led his army [against the * 2Ch 35:20
* you have hired to save you Is 7:20
will turn upon the * and punish Is 10:12
and briars, the * who destroyed the Is 10:17
Israel, instead of fearing the *. Is 10:20
be afraid of the * when they Is 10:24
not the *, who consign Tyre to the Is 23:13
a mighty army (the *) against you; Is 28:2
for his protection against the *. Is 28:15
shall punish the *, who had been Is 30:31
And the * will be destroyed, but Is 31:8
* will be taken away as slaves. Is 31:8
quietly at home, but the * Is 32:19
WOE TO YOU, *, Is 33:1
The * have broken their peace pact Is 33:8
and might. You * will gain nothing Is 33:11
Of course the * could destroy Is 37:19
the * and killed 185,000 soldiers; Is 37:36
taken away by the * as slaves. Jer 31:15f
adultery with the * too [by making Eze 16:28
her love to the *, her neighbors, Eze 23:4,5
* whose gods she loved so much. Eze 23:9
and all the * with them—handsome Eze 23:23
He will deliver us from the * Mic 5:6
Thebes was conquered by the * Nah 3:8f
against the * around 630 B.C. Hab 1:6f

ASTONISHED
Fair-minded men are * when they Job 17:8
set up the abomination that *." Dan 11:30,31f
the synagogue and * everyone with Mt 13:53,54
the people were * at his wisdom and Mk 6:2,3

(ASTONISHED Con't)
* at the power of God's message. Act 13:12

ASTONISHMENT
will whistle with *, asking, 'Why 1Ki 9:8
* at all that I have done to her. Jer 19:8
story expressed *, but Mary Lk 2:18

ASTOUNDED
You will be * at what I am about Hab 1:5

ASTOUNDING
heard things so * that they are 2Co 12:4

ASTRAY
are leading you *, as you have just Num 25:18
tries to lead you * must be Deu 13:5
fellow citizens * with the Deu 13:12,13,14
the proper path to all who go *; Ps 25:8
A curse on those who lead * the Pro 28:10
God's paths and go *, you will hear Is 30:21
Their shepherds led them * and Jer 50:6
You who lead his people *! Mic 3:5
Judah and Israel have been led * Zec 10:2
the Messiah, and will lead many *. Mt 24:5
will appear and lead many *. Mt 24:11
Messiah, and will lead many *. Mk 13:6
"So you also have been led *?" Jn 7:47
Not one of you was led *. 2Co 7:2
church and been led * by Satan. 1Ti 5:15
to blindfold you and lead you *. 1Jn 2:26

ASTROLOGER
Daniel replied, "No wise man, *, Dan 2:27

ASTROLOGERS
by the ton—your * and stargazers, Is 47:13
magicians and wise * in his realm. Dan 1:20
sorcerers, and *, and demanded that Dan 2:1
Then the * (speaking in Aramaic) Dan 2:4
magicians, *, fortune-tellers, and Dan 4:7
"Bring the magicians and *!" Dan 5:7
all the magicians, *, Chaldeans and Dan 5:11
My wise men and * have tried to Dan 5:15
At about that time some * from Mt 2:1
*, asking them to come to see him; Mt 2:7
After this interview the * Mt 2:9
that the * had disobeyed him. Mt 2:16
farms, for the * had told him the Mt 2:16

ASTRONOMY
mathematics, * and history—plus a Dan 1:3,4f

ASTUTE
he was a very * man and a Ez 8:18

ASYNCRITUS
my greetings to *, Phlegon, Hermes, Rom 16:14

ATAD
When they arrived at * Gen 50:10

ATARAH
Jerahmeel's second wife * was the 1Ch 2:26

ATAROTH
whole countryside—*, Dibon, Jazer, Num 32:3,4
Dibon, *, Aroer, Num 32:34,35,36
to Luz, then on to *, in the Jos 16:1
southward to * and Naarah, and Jos 16:7

ATAROTH-ADDAR
The eastern boundary began at *. Jos 16:5,6
proceeded down to * in the hill Jos 18:13

ATE
So she * some of the fruit and Gen 3:6
to her husband, and he * it too. Gen 3:6
And as they * it, suddenly they Gen 3:7
who brought me some, and I * it." Gen 3:12
to your wife and * the fruit when I Gen 3:17
the trees beside them as they *. Gen 18:8
so he * and drank and went on Gen 25:34
for them, and they * and drank in Gen 26:30
Jacob and Laban * together beside Gen 31:46
but the birds came and * them." Gen 40:17
Then the skinny cows * the fat Gen 41:4
And these skinny cattle * up the Gen 41:20
Joseph * by himself, his brothers Gen 43:32
and they * every bit of Ex 10:15
So the people of Israel * the Ex 16:35
and they all * the sacrificial meal Ex 18:12
that time he neither * nor drank. Ex 34:28
and all that time I * nothing. Deu 9:9
you * as you escaped from Egypt. Deu 16:3
Literally, "* the parched grain Ru 2:14f
So Saul * with Samuel. 1Sa 9:24
So no one * anything all day, 1Sa 14:24,25
upon anyone who * food that day, 1Sa 14:28
and * the raw, bloody meat. 1Sa 14:32
king and his men, and they * it. 1Sa 28:25
on, Mephibosheth * regularly with 2Sa 9:10,11
he returned to the palace and *. 2Sa 12:20
and the prophet * some food and 1Ki 13:19
So he * and drank and lay down 1Ki 19:6
So he got up and * and drank, and 1Ki 19:8
So we boiled my son and * him, 2Ki 6:26-30
they * with the other priests. 2Ki 23:9
* regularly at the king's table. 2Ki 25:29
They, with the entire nation, * Ez 6:21,22
so they * and were full and Neh 9:25
how often we * together. Ps 41:9
They * angel's food! Ps 78:25
The people * their fill. Ps 78:29
locusts came, and * up everything Ps 105:35
crops; they * what others planted. Ps 105:44
First the king of Assyria * them Jer 50:17
And when I * it, it tasted sweet Eze 3:3
embroidered. You * the finest foods Eze 16:13
other fellows who * the king's rich Dan 1:13
his palace and * grass like the Dan 4:33
wild donkeys; he * grass like the Dan 5:21
you back the crops the locusts *! Joe 2:25
the locusts * your figs and olive Amo 4:9
They * everything in sight. Amo 7:2
The next morning the worm * Jon 4:7
* nothing and became very hungry. Mt 4:2
Temple and they * the special bread Mt 12:4
path, and the birds came and * it. Mt 13:4
And everyone * until full! Mt 14:20
And everyone * until full—4,000 Mt 15:37,38
then—and they * the special bread Mk 2:25,26
it off the hard ground and * it. Mk 4:4
And the crowd * until they could Mk 6:42
And the whole crowd * until they Mk 8:8,9
for forty days. He * nothing all Lk 4:1
the Lord, and * it—illegal as this Lk 6:4
and the birds came and * it as it Lk 8:5
And everyone * and ate; Lk 9:17
And everyone ate and *; Lk 9:17
" 'But we * with you, and you Lk 13:26
They * and drank and Lk 17:27
and he * it as they watched! Lk 24:43
And everyone * until full! Jn 6:11
in the wilderness * bread from the Jn 6:48-51
they * bread from heaven." Jn 6:58
Then he * and was strengthened. Act 9:19
but to us who * and drank with him Act 10:40,41
even * with them," they accused. Act 11:3
They all went back upstairs and * Act 20:10,11,12
and broke off a piece and * it. Act 27:35
Literally, "all * the same 1Co 10:3,4f
For when he first arrived he * Gal 2:12
I took it from his hand, and * it! Rev 10:10

ATER
From the subclan of * (the Ez 2:3-35
of Shallum, *, Talmon, Akkub, Ez 2:40,41,42
Hezekiah of the subclan of *, 98; Neh 7:8-38
*, Hezekiah, Azzur, Hodiah, Neh 10:14-27

ATHACH
Hormah, Borashan, *, Hebron. 1Sa 30:27-31

ATHAIAH
* (son of Uzziah, son of Neh 11:4,5,6

ATHALIAH
His mother was *, the 2Ki 8:26
WHEN *, THE mother of King Ahaziah 2Ki 11:1
years while * reigned as queen. 2Ki 11:2,3
When * heard all the noise, she 2Ki 11:13,14
Shamsherai, Shehariah, *, 1Ch 8:26,27
His mother's name was *, 2Ch 22:2
their grandmother * killed them 2Ch 22:10
years while * reigned as queen. 2Ch 22:12
the reign of Queen *, Jehoiada the 2Ch 23:1
When Queen * heard all the noise 2Ch 23:12
* ripped her clothes and screamed, 2Ch 23:12
peaceful because Queen * was dead. 2Ch 23:21
(The followers of wicked * had 2Ch 24:7,8
(son of *), and 70 other men; Ez 8:2-14

ATHALIAH'S
In the seventh year of Queen * 2Ki 11:4
back into quietness after * death. 2Ki 11:20

ATHEISTS
In those days the ungodly, the *, Is 32:5

ATHENIANS
that all the * as well as the Act 17:21

ATHENS
on with him to *, and then returned Act 17:15
for them in *, he was deeply Act 17:16
the foreigners in * seemed to spend Act 17:21
"Men of *, I notice that you are Act 17:22
THEN PAUL LEFT * and went to Act 18:1
to stay alone in * and send 1Th 3:1

ATHLAI
Zabbai, *. Ez 10:28

ATHLETE
or as joyous as an * looking Ps 19:5
your best. An * goes to all this 1Co 9:25
Like an * I punish my body, 1Co 9:27
work, just as an * either follows 2Ti 2:5

ATHLETES
fifty of our best * will search the 2Ki 2:16

ATOMS
Perhaps the reference is to *, Heb 11:3f

ATONE
without defect to * for his sin. Lev 4:28
Literally, "* for." Is 27:9f

ATONED
Iniquity is * for by mercy and Pro 16:6

ATONEMENT
used in their * (that is, in their Ex 29:33
bull as a sin offering for *; Ex 29:36
purge the altar by making * for Ex 29:36
Make * for the altar and Ex 29:37
Literally, "shall make an * for Ex 30:10f
blood of the sin offering for *. Ex 30:10
the Lord to make * for yourselves. Ex 30:15
and to make * for you." Ex 30:16
Literally, "to make * for him." Lev 1:4f
priest shall make * for the nation, Lev 4:20
thus the priest shall make * for Lev 4:26
Thus the priest shall make * for Lev 4:31
and the priest shall make * for Lev 4:35
priest shall make * for him, and he Lev 5:6
so the priest shall make * for Lev 5:10
priest shall make * for him for any Lev 5:13
priest shall make * for him with Lev 5:16
with it the priest shall make * Lev 5:17,18
priest shall make * for him before Lev 6:7
to make * in the Holy Place. Lev 6:30
of the * ceremony, for his food. Lev 7:7
the altar, making * for it. Lev 8:15,16
Lord in order to make * for them. Lev 8:34
offering, making * for himself Lev 9:7
make * for them before the Lord?" Lev 10:17
the Lord and make * for her; Lev 12:7
The priest will make * for her Lev 12:8
Thus the priest shall make * for Lev 14:18
perform the rite of * for the Lev 14:19
the altar, making * for the man, Lev 14:20
* by waving it before the altar; Lev 14:21
to make * for him before the Lord. Lev 14:29
and the priest shall make * for Lev 14:31
This is the method for making * Lev 14:53
thus the priest shall make * Lev 15:15
offering, and make * for her before Lev 15:30
* for himself and his family. Lev 16:6
The rite of * shall be performed Lev 16:10
Thus he shall make * for the Lev 16:16
enters to make * in the Holy Lev 16:17
again and has made * for himself Lev 16:17
before the Lord and make * for it. Lev 16:18
the rite of * for the Holy Place, Lev 16:20
making * for himself and for them. Lev 16:24
by Aaron, to make *) shall be Lev 16:27
commemorating the *, cleansing you Lev 16:29,30
and make * for the holy sanctuary, Lev 16:33
for you, to make * for the people Lev 16:34
the altar as an * for your souls; Lev 17:11
it is the blood that makes *, Lev 17:11
The priest shall make * with the Lev 19:22
"The Day of * follows nine days Lev 23:26,27
making * before the Lord your God. Lev 23:28
this time for * begins on the Lev 23:32
fiftieth year, on the Day of *, Lev 25:9
priest, along with a lamb for *. Num 5:8
and make * for his defilement. Num 6:11
to make * for the Levites. Num 8:12
sacrifices, making * for them. Num 8:19
He then performed the rite of * Num 8:21
And the priest shall make * for Num 15:25
priest shall make * for him before Num 15:28
the people and make * for them; Num 16:46
the incense and made * for them. Num 16:47
he has made * for the people of Num 25:12,13
to make * for yourselves. Num 28:22
goat to make * for yourselves. Num 28:30
a sin offering, to make * for you. Num 29:5
of * [offered annually on that day Num 29:11
This is to make * for our souls Num 31:50
the land, and no * can be made for Num 35:33
to the annual Day of * for Israel. 1Ch 6:49
the altar, to make * for all Israel 2Ch 29:24
Temple and for the * of Israel. Neh 10:33
And there will be no * then to Is 47:11
This will cleanse and make * for Eze 43:20
cleanse and make * for the altar, Eze 43:26
offerings to make * for those who Eze 45:15

ATONING
Or, "* sacrifice." 1Jn 2:2f

ATROTH-BETH-JOAB
the Netophathites, *, half the 1Ch 2:54

ATROTH-SHOPHAN
*, Jazer, Num 32:34,35,36

ATTACH
of gold for it and * them to the Ex 25:12
of the altar, * them firmly, and Ex 27:2
forming a pouch. * to it four rows Ex 28:17
"* the top of the chestpiece to Ex 28:22,23,24
at the sash. Now * the bottom of Ex 28:28
[To * the chestpiece to the ephod Ex 39:15-18
generation) and to * the tassels to Num 15:37,38
of one of these snakes and * it Num 21:8
One pair stretched out to * to Eze 1:11

ATTACHED
with silver hooks * to silver rods, Ex 27:9,10
to silver rods, * to the posts. Ex 27:9,10
linen, and * to four posts imbedded Ex 27:16
shall be made and * to golden Ex 28:13,14
One end of each cord is * to Ex 28:22,23,24
the two cords are * to the front Ex 28:25
This plate is to be * by means Ex 28:37,38
merely separate parts that are *. Ex 30:2
Five of these sheets were * end Ex 36:10
*, forming two long roof-sheets. Ex 36:10
were firmly * to each other. Ex 36:18
The veil was then * to four gold Ex 36:36
onyx stones, * to the [two Ex 39:6,7

(ATTACHED Con't)
of twined gold * to gold clasps on Ex 39:15-18
Pomegranates were * to the Ex 39:24
on them, and * the carrying poles Ex 40:20
He * the curtain at the entrance Ex 40:28
of the building, * to the Temple 1Ki 6:10
100 pomegranates * to the chains. 2Ch 3:16
came together and * to each other Eze 37:7
* to the Temple wall for support. Eze 41:6
He had * himself to the governor, Act 13:6,7

ATTACHES
muscle where it * to the hip. Gen 32:32

ATTACHING
into their bases and * the bars. Ex 40:18

ATTACHMENT
Levi (meaning "*") for she said, Gen 29:34

ATTACK
Sin is waiting to * you, longing Gen 4:7
cross this line to * you and you Gen 31:51,52
and you will not cross it to * me. Gen 31:51,52
your great power they won't * us! Ex 15:16
No one will * and conquer your Ex 34:24
he followed up with an armed *, Num 21:31,32
from * by the local inhabitants. Num 32:17
warned us, 'Don't * the Moabites Deu 2:9
But do not * them, for I will not Deu 2:19
discover the best way to * us." Jos 2:3
killed during the *, and many Jos 7:5
us and * us and wipe us out. Jos 7:9
armies for a united * on Gibeon. Jos 10:5
And after that no one dared to * Jos 10:21
During the * on Lachish, King Jos 10:33
"Who will lead the * against Ju 1:12
Kenaz, volunteered to lead the *; Ju 1:13
Take your troops and * the Ju 7:8,9
encouraged and be eager to *!" Ju 7:11
city went out to *, he and his men Ju 9:43
the Jordan to * the Israelis. Ju 10:9
to * Israel's army at Mizpah. Ju 10:17
unprepared for an *, for there were Ju 18:7
And the men replied, "Let's *! Ju 18:9,10
Gibe-ah, to * the men of Benjamin. Ju 20:19,20
out of the town to *, the Israeli Ju 20:31
to turn around and * the army of Ju 20:35-39
a surprise * against the Ammonites 1Sa 11:11
me and to come here and * me?" 1Sa 22:13
Lord, "Shall I go and * them?" 1Sa 23:2
"It is a serious sin to * God's 1Sa 24:6
he plans to return and * us!" 2Sa 3:24,25
replied, "Don't make a frontal *. 2Sa 5:23
the tops of the balsam trees, *! 2Sa 5:24
the entire Israeli army to * them. 2Sa 10:7,8
Abishai, who was to * the city. 2Sa 10:10
back from the *, and they returned 2Sa 20:22
Once during a Philistine *, when 2Sa 23:11,12
word of the *, he discontinued 1Ki 15:21
"Prepare to *!" 1Ki 20:12
"Shall we * first?" 1Ki 20:14
entire army had joined the *. 1Ki 20:19
another * by the king of Syria." 1Ki 20:22
I * Ramoth-gilead, or not?" 1Ki 22:6
"Go ahead and * Ramoth-gilead," 1Ki 22:12
we * Ramoth-gilead, or not?" 1Ki 22:15
So they wheeled around to * 1Ki 22:32,33
"We'll * from the wilderness of 2Ki 3:6,7,8
to * us," they cried out. 2Ki 7:6
Then they will * us and make 2Ki 7:12
moved on toward Jerusalem to * it. 2Ki 12:17
So Hazael called off the *. 2Ki 12:18
led an * against Israel. 2Ki 15:29
King Pekah of Israel to * Judah. 2Ki 15:37
of Ethiopia was coming to * him. 2Ki 19:9
Before leaving to meet the *, he 2Ki 19:9
mulberry trees and * from there. 1Ch 14:14
is your signal to *, for God will 1Ch 14:15
When the Ammonites, under * by 1Ch 19:15
in your name we * this vast horde. 2Ch 14:11
mobilized his armies to * Israel. 2Ch 16:4
and gave up his plan to * Judah. 2Ch 16:5
Tomorrow, go down and * them! 2Ch 20:16
to the Ethiopians to * Jehoram. 2Ch 21:16
was intending to * Jerusalem, 2Ch 32:2
for the people were fearful of *. Ez 3:3
mounted a massive * against me. Ps 18:4
I can scale any wall, * any troop. Ps 18:29
of the world * me, I will march out Ps 118:10
Yes, they surround and * me; Ps 118:11
Here come these lawless men to * Ps 119:150
But before you have begun the *, Is 18:5
and camels were paired for the *. Is 21:6,7f
"Let us * by night and destroy Jer 6:5
king of Babylon, to * Egypt: Jer 46:13
Nebuchadnezzar. "* those wealthy Jer 49:31
are permitted to * them freely, for Jer 50:7
* her, and she shall be destroyed. Jer 50:9
like a lion, waiting to * me. Lam 3:10
and power in the * against her Eze 4:7
wild animals will * you and kill Eze 5:17
whether to * Jerusalem or Rabbah. Eze 21:21
He will * and defeat them. Eze 21:23
a great army fully prepared for *. Eze 23:24
then he will * your mainland city Eze 26:8
the terrible waves of enemy *. Eze 26:19
conquer them nor wild animals *. Eze 34:28
the king of the south will * him Dan 11:40
watch for the enemy * to begin! Nah 2:1
red in the sunlight! The * begins! Nah 2:3
the pearls and turn and * you. Mt 7:6
Jewish leaders to * and stone them, Act 14:5,6
and weapons of *—have been ours. 2Co 6:7
curse and swear, * their fathers 1Ti 1:9
or trees, but to * those people who Rev 9:4
Dragon set out to * the rest of her Rev 12:17
woman, and will * her and leave her Rev 17:16

ATTACKED
Cain * and killed his brother. Gen 4:8
I have killed a youth who * and Gen 4:23
* Ched-or-laomer and his allies Gen 14:8,9
That night he successfully * Gen 14:15
If any were * and killed by wild Gen 31:39
through, so that they were not *. Gen 35:5
If it was * by some wild animal, Ex 22:13
* and killed by a wild animal. Ex 22:31
of disease, or is * and killed by Lev 7:24
* them and chased them to Hormah. Num 14:45
his army and * Israel, taking some Num 21:1
his army and * Israel in the Num 21:23
his army and * us at Edre-i. Deu 3:1
and * at the Plain of Arabah. Jos 8:14
they went to Lachish and * it. Jos 10:31
at the Springs of Merom and *. Jos 11:7
Then he * and destroyed all the Jos 11:12
had * them and driven them out. Jos 13:12
Later they * the city of Debir Ju 1:11
of Joseph, they * the city of Ju 1:22,23
Then they * the Moabites and Ju 3:29
Abimelech next * the city of Ju 9:50
to know why Israel was being *. Ju 11:12
an army at Jahaz and * them. Ju 11:20
Gilead, and * the army of Ammon. Ju 11:29
army and * the army of Ephraim. Ju 12:4
a young lion * Samson in the Ju 14:5
So he * them with great fury and Ju 15:8
it turned and *, and the ten Ju 20:33
Then Jonathan * and destroyed 1Sa 13:3,4
Whenever the Philistine army *, 1Sa 18:30
spirit from the Lord * him. 1Sa 19:9,10
And when Joab and his troops *, 2Sa 10:13
to Helam, where the Syrians * him. 2Sa 10:17
gates, the men on the wall * us; 2Sa 11:24
eaten the body nor * the donkey. 1Ki 13:28
Egypt * and conquered Jerusalem. 1Ki 14:25
to go a lion * and killed him. 1Ki 20:36
"The three armies have * and 2Ki 3:23
Jordan River and * the city of 2Ki 8:21
So the Assyrians * Damascus, the 2Ki 16:9
King Shalmaneser of Assyria * and 2Ki 17:3
of Assyria * Israel and began a 2Ki 18:9
King Neco of Egypt * the king of 2Ki 23:29
of Babylon * Jerusalem. 2Ki 24:1
THE PHILISTINES * and defeated the 1Ch 10:1
So he * them at Baal-perazim and 1Ch 14:11
So Joab and his troops * the 1Ch 19:14
Shishak of Egypt * Jerusalem in the 2Ch 12:2
But now he was * by an army of 2Ch 14:9,10
While they were at Gerar they * 2Ch 14:14
Jehoram * him with his full army 2Ch 21:9
failed to conquer a nation we *? 2Ch 32:13
If you are * and knocked down, Job 22:29
day when I was weakest, they *. Ps 18:18
And one standing alone can be * Ecc 4:12
Jerusalem was * by King Rezin of Is 7:1
You are being *! Is 21:5
who tries a better life is soon *. Is 59:15
and Nebuchadnezzar II soon *. Jer 4:6f
those attacking you shall be *. Jer 30:16
king of Babylon has * Jerusalem. Eze 24:2
leaving them to be * and destroyed, Eze 34:8
after being * by other animals. Eze 44:31
Nebuchadnezzar * Jerusalem with his Dan 1:1
very strong and * the south and Dan 8:9
Israel was * by Antiochus IV Dan 8:9f
Israel; they * and conquered him, Amo 1:9
But the farmers * his men, beat Mt 21:35
to Jericho was * by bandits. Lk 10:30
start a riot. They * the home of Act 17:5

ATTACKERS
and you will flee before your *; Lev 26:17
their * until they were destroyed. 2Ki 17:20

ATTACKING
after * the Lord's chosen king? 1Sa 26:9
to spy out the city before * it!" 2Sa 10:3
then engaged in * the Philistine 1Ki 16:15,16
the * armies of Syria and Israel. 2Ki 16:7
or unjustly * those I dislike. Ps 7:4
like roaring lions * their prey. Ps 22:13
No enemy * the walls, but peace Ps 144:12-15
the poor as a lion or bear * them. Pro 28:15
your plans of * us, and perish! Is 8:9,10
think of Syria and Israel * you. Is 8:12
He will merely think he is * my Is 10:7
their wives raped by the * hordes. Is 13:16
buy them off. The * armies will Is 13:18
and those * you shall be Jer 30:16
on the * armies and consume them. Rev 20:9

ATTACKS
for he said, "If Esau * one Gen 32:8
However, if a man deliberately * Ex 21:14
"When our main army *, the men Jos 8:5
These * took place east of the Ju 10:7,8
And when he comes out and * and a 2Sa 17:9
army in successful * against the 1Ch 20:1
crop disease, or * of locusts or 2Ch 6:28
Again and again he * me, running Job 16:14
declare war on them for their * Ps 35:1
Why must I suffer these * from my Ps 42:9
always welcome, safe from all *. Ps 71:3
you; want * you in full armor. Pro 6:11
the flags waving as their enemy *. Is 13:2
made you impervious to their *. Jer 1:18
his protection as the enemy *. Lam 2:3
my just *, but I found not one. Eze 22:30
broken after your * but the Lord Nah 2:2
everyone * them, for they have no Zec 10:2
and better-armed * and overcomes Lk 11:22
enemy whenever he *, and when it is Eph 6:13
you from satanic * of every kind. 2Th 3:3
who keeps you safe from all *. 1Pe 2:25
Be careful—watch out for * from 1Pe 5:8
Stand firm when he *. 1Pe 5:9

ATTAI
they named *. 1Ch 2:34,35
* was sixth in command; 1Ch 12:8-13
Abijah, *, Ziza, and Shelomith. 2Ch 11:20

ATTAI'S
* son was Nathan; 1Ch 2:36

ATTAIN
but to * this honor and renown Deu 26:19
of them they could not * life. Eze 20:25
Literally, "his hand shall * Eze 46:7f
day to * this same hope I have! Act 26:7

ATTALIA
again in Perga, and went on to *. Act 14:25

ATTEMPT
If you * to enter my land I will Num 20:18
failed in their * to conquer the Ju 1:19
it at David in an * to kill him. 1Sa 19:9,10
of Ramah in an * to cut off all 1Ki 15:17
a last desperate * to break through 2Ki 3:26
in an * to reunite the kingdom. 2Ch 11:1
earth unite in an * to move her, Zec 12:3
Thus their * to outwit him before Lk 20:26
the city must not * to return. Lk 21:21

ATTEMPTED
for he has * to foment rebellion Deu 13:5
had * to regain his power. 2Sa 8:3
Ele-ad and Ezer * to rustle cattle 1Ch 7:20,21
and countries who * to control it. Ez 4:15

ATTEMPTING
table, * to deceive each other. Dan 11:27
by evil means, * to live beyond the Hab 2:9

ATTEMPTS
Anyone else who * to perform Num 18:7
Anyone who * to change this Ez 6:11
The fool * to fool himself and Pro 14:8
* to lead her in green pastures. Hos 4:16

ATTEND
invited them to * the sacrifices to Num 25:2
of his sons *, including Amnon. 2Sa 13:27
your sons to * the festivities. 1Ki 1:25
They urged him to *, so he joined 1Ki 12:2,3,4
all over Judah to * the services at Jer 36:9
cities to * these celebrations. Zec 8:20,21
to Jerusalem to * the Passover Jn 12:20

ATTENDANCE
in regular * at the apostles' Act 2:42

ATTENDANT
The * to the king's sons was 1Ch 27:32
gatekeeper, Temple *, or other Ez 7:24
appointed as her *, and told him to Est 4:5
it back to the * and sat down, Lk 4:20

ATTENDANTS
cried out to his *, and he was left Gen 45:1
serving girls as *, mounted her 1Sa 25:42
and the Temple * to send us priests Ez 8:17
and 220 Temple *. Ez 8:20
(The Temple * were assistants to Ez 8:20
The Temple * living in Ophel Neh 3:26
far as the Temple *' and merchants' Neh 3:31
the Temple *, and the rest of the Neh 7:73
Truth walk before you as your *. Ps 89:14,15

ATTENDED
the men had just * a funeral, and Num 9:6.7
no one had * from Jabesh-gilead. Ju 21:8,9
Festival, which they * each year. Lk 2:41,42

ATTENDING
men were not only * the feasts, but Num 25:2
the women who were * her told her 1Sa 4:20

ATTENTION
to the Lord's *, and to make Ex 30:16
is called to his * he must bring as Lev 4:23
They next turned their * to the Num 21:33
But the king of Ammon paid no * Ju 11:28

(ATTENTION Con't)
don't pay any * to what he said. 1Sa 25:25
"to catch the * of your god! 1Ki 18:27
stopped and called them to *. 2Ch 20:20
enough to understand paid close *. Neh 8:1
and didn't pay any * to the Neh 9:17
or pay any * to God except in times Job 27:10
* to the rich than to the poor. Job 34:19
the poor to come to the * of God. Job 34:28
puny man, to pay any * to him! Ps 8:4
he gives * when they cry to him. Ps 34:15
He paid * to it! Ps 66:19
taught me to pay * to your laws. Ps 119:71,72
sheep, he pays no * to the Is 31:4,5
Pay *, Israel, for you are my Is 44:21
shall stand at * when you pass by; Is 49:7
Yet she paid no *, even though Jer 3:8
We won't pay any *!" Jer 6:17
they fast, I will not pay any *; Jer 14:12
They stubbornly refused to pay * Jer 17:23
But if you refuse to pay * to Jer 22:5
you say but don't pay any * to it! Eze 33:32
is paying no * to you or your law. Dan 6:13
"After this he will turn his * Dan 11:18
center of * from this point on. Dan 11:40f
the nations with this message: '*! Ob 1:1
*! Mic 1:2
they paid no * at all. Zec 1:4
Lord doesn't pay * to your Mal 2:13
call * to their acts of charity! Mt 6:2
—reader, pay *! Mk 13:14
'That one is,' don't pay any *. Mk 13:21
Solomon is here [and few pay any * Lk 11:31
* and plenty of fertilizer. Lk 13:8
governor to pay no * to what Paul Act 13:8
give me your * for only a moment as Act 24:4
to distract your * from him. 1Co 7:35
Pay * to what I have said. 2Co 13:11
that you will pay more * to them. Gal 4:17
You will do well to pay close * 2Pe 1:19
and the world pays * to them. 1Jn 4:5
she refused. Pay * now to what I Rev 2:22

ATTENTIVE
be wide awake and * to all the 2Ch 6:40

ATTIC
the corner of an * than with a Pro 21:9
in a corner of an * than in a Pro 25:24

ATTITUDE
cooling in Laban's * towards him. Gen 31:2
for the dream and for his cocky *. Gen 37:8
was angry about Balaam's eager *, Num 22:22,23
God gave him a new *, and all of 1Sa 10:9
change in his *) is recorded in The 2Ch 33:19
danger of punishment for your *." Job 19:29
A relaxed * lengthens a man's Pro 14:30
them that this * would surely lead Zec 7:7
"Your * toward me has been proud Mal 3:13
Your * Mt 20:28
Now change your mind and * to Act 3:19
the * of Christ toward the other. Rom 15:5
Your * should be the kind that Php 2:5
you must have the same * he did; 1Pe 4:1
to come, and his * of enmity 1Jn 4:3
"Change your mind and *, or else Rev 2:16
her mind and *, but she refused. Rev 2:21
their mind and * about all their Rev 9:21
mind and * to give him glory. Rev 16:9

ATTITUDES
with selfish * and evil hearts—and Hag 2:14
Now your * and thoughts must all Eph 4:23

ATTORNEY
He is the great Prosecuting * Is 3:13

ATTRACTED
truth from him, will be * to me. Jn 6:45
So do not be * by strange, new Heb 13:9

ATTRACTION
become the world's greatest *, Is 2:2
will naturally go to the main * Jn 3:29

ATTRACTIONS
too quickly the * of this world and Mk 4:19

ATTRACTIVE
to get her, for she was very *. Gen 26:7
Kindness makes a man *. Pro 19:22
for they were all * young men, Eze 23:6
in all the * things of the world Gal 6:14

ATTRACTIVENESS
But in our eyes there was no * at Is 53:2

ATTRACTS
unless the Father * him to me." Jn 6:65

AUDIENCE
requested another * with Pharaoh Ex 10:3
Don't demand an * with the king Pro 25:6,7
Amazement gripped the * and they Mk 1:27
Then Festus addressed the *: Act 25:24
here in this * might become the Act 26:29

AUGUST
at Jerusalem in the month of *; Ez 7:7,8,9
THEN, LATE IN * of the sixth year Eze 8:1
When: In late * of the second Hag 1:1
the month of * each year, as they Zec 7:3
and mourned in * and October, were Zec 7:5
in July, *, October, and January Zec 8:19

AUGUSTUS
ABOUT THIS TIME Caesar *, the Lk 2:1

AUNT
that he was her * Rebekah's son. Gen 29:12,13
nor your *—your father's Lev 18:12
nor your *—your mother's Lev 18:13
nor your *—the wife of your Lev 18:14
man and his maiden *—whether the Lev 20:19
Joash was rescued by his * 2Ki 11:2,3
Joash was rescued by his * 2Ch 22:11
his nurse and by his * and uncle. 2Ch 22:12
Furthermore, six months ago your * Lk 1:36
mother, Mary, his *, the wife of Jn 19:25

AUSIA
Judea, Cappadocia, Pontus, *, Act 2:9
provinces of Cilicia, and *. Act 6:9
province of * at that time. Act 16:6
province of *—both Jews and Act 19:10
Cappadocia, *, and Bithynia. 1Pe 1:1

AUTHOR
He was the * of 3,000 proverbs 1Ki 4:32
THE *: SOLOMON Ecc 1:1
And you killed the * of Life; Act 3:15
with himself, the * and Giver of Eph 1:23

AUTHORITIES
Many ancient * add verse 26, "but Mk 11:26,f
Jewish rulers and * in the Lk 12:11
the top religious * of the nation. Lk 22:66
Some ancient * add verse 17, "For Lk 23:17,f
and kingdoms, its rulers and *; Col 1:16

AUTHORITY
he himself has no more * here Gen 39:9
as a token of his *, and dressed Gen 41:41,42
complaints about Aaron's *; Num 17:10
fact challenged the very * of God! Num 26:5-11
Publicly give him your * so that Num 27:20
And his *: 1Ch 16:12,13
His * is seen throughout the 1Ch 16:14
of great * in their clan. 1Ch 26:6,7
the other men of * in his kingdom. 1Ch 28:1
his home, and should assert his *. Est 1:22
Minister, with * next to that of Est 10:3
He alone has * over the earth Job 34:13
everything is put under his *: Ps 8:6
With good men in *, the people Pro 29:2
men given great *, and rich men not Ecc 10:6
revolting against *, criminals Is 3:5
and title and *, and he will be a Is 22:21
full of words with no divine *. Jer 5:13
to positions of * and dividing the Dan 11:39
one who had great *, and not as Mt 7:29
I know, because I am under the * Mt 8:8,9
and I have * over my soldiers, and Mt 8:8,9
And I know you have * to tell his Mt 8:8,9
have the * on earth to forgive Mt 9:5,6
God for giving such * to a man! Mt 9:8
him, and gave them * to cast out Mt 10:1
to know by whose * he had thrown Mt 21:23
Literally, "By what * do you do Mt 21:23f
They did not have the * Mt 27:1f
given all * in heaven and earth. Mt 28:18
he spoke as an *, and didn't try to Mk 1:22
have the * on earth to forgive Mk 2:9,10,11
have * even to decide what men Mk 2:28
Who gave you the * to drive out Mk 11:27,28
shall use my * to cast out demons, Mk 16:17
who has far higher * than mine; Lk 3:16
the opinions of others as his *. Lk 4:32
have the * on earth to forgive Lk 5:23,24
I know, because I am under the * Lk 7:6,7,8
and I have * over my men. Lk 7:6,7,8
and gave them * over all Lk 9:1
And I have given you * over all Lk 10:19
They demanded to know by what * Lk 20:2
merely acting under his own *?" Lk 20:4
"If you have this * from God, Jn 2:18
For you have given him * over Jn 17:2
gave him the * to send the Holy Act 2:33
"By what power, or by whose * Act 4:7
It is by his * that this man Act 4:10
great * under Candace the queen. Act 8:27
soon, those with * in this affair Act 25:5
armed with the * and commission of Act 26:12
sure on the * of the Lord Jesus Rom 14:14
a sign that she is under man's *, 1Co 11:10
For the rule and * over all 1Co 15:27
by Christ's *, and for your good. 2Co 2:10
and * of Christ, I certainly can. 2Co 10:7
I should about my * over 2Co 10:8
authority over you—* to help you, 2Co 10:8
But we will not boast of * we do 2Co 10:13
far when we claim * over you, for 2Co 10:14
for I want to use the Lord's * 2Co 13:10
God has placed them in * over you. Eph 6:1
He is the highest Ruler, with * Col 2:10
Christ by his *: Stay away from any 2Th 3:6
others who are in * over us, or are 1Ti 2:2
does not admit my * over him and 3Jn 1:9
at those in * over them, even Jud 1:8
and * are his from the beginning; Jud 1:24,25
Father gave me the * to rule them; Rev 2:27
long sword and the * to banish Rev 6:4
* of his Christ are finally here; Rev 12:10
own power and throne and great *. Rev 13:2
and gave him * to control the Rev 13:5
He exercised all the * of the Rev 13:12
to give their * to the scarlet Rev 17:17
heaven with great *, and the earth Rev 18:1
Honor and * belong to him alone; Rev 19:1

AUTHORIZED
as * by the High Priests; Act 26:10
Literally, "They are not * to 1Co 14:34f

AUTHORIZING
the chief priests, * him to arrest Act 9:14

AUTOBIOGRAPHY
THE * OF Nehemiah, the son of Neh 1:1

AUTOMATICALLY
her promise will * become invalid. Num 30:5

AUTUMN
* morning during harvest time. Is 18:4
Like * leaves we fade, wither and Is 64:6
Once more the * rains will come, Joe 2:23
about the time of the * equinox. Act 27:9f
waits until the * for his precious Jas 5:7

AVAIL
plans will not *, for you never ask Is 22:9,10,11
writhed in agony, but all to no *. Is 26:18
conquest, but all to no *. Is 29:8
army, but to no *, for plots Dan 11:25

AVAILABILITY
sin, and of the * of God's Jn 16:8

AVAILABLE
many animals for the * pasture. Gen 13:6
there was grain * in Egypt he said Gen 42:1
that there is grain * in Egypt. Gen 42:2
They were constantly * to Ex 18:26
bread * for ten entire families; Lev 26:26
was no other food *, the priest 1Sa 21:6
The total number of men * for 1Ch 7:5
and unnumbered virgins * to me; Sol 6:8
there is righteousness * because Jn 16:10
from God is * to the Gentiles too, Act 28:28,29
make his salvation * to the Rom 11:11
treasures * to them in Christ; Eph 3:8
and he is equally * to all. Col 3:11

AVEN
And the idol altars of * at Hos 10:8
as the plain of *, and the people Amo 1:5

AVENGE
relatives who want to * his death; Num 35:12
Anyone seeking to * the death Deu 19:6,7
For he will * his people, Deu 32:40,41
you will * the murder of my 2Ki 9:7
Publicly * this slaughter of Ps 79:10
has come for me to * my people, to Is 63:4
I will * you. Jer 51:36
to * his sister's murder. Dan 11:7f
Jehu's dynasty to * the murders Hos 1:4,5
For I will * the blood of my Joe 3:21
Dear friends, never * yourselves. Rom 12:19
When will you * our blood against Rev 6:10

AVENGED
"Shall not my soul be * on such Jer 9:9
is * and God's people triumph?" Dan 8:13
and he has * the murder of his Rev 19:2

AVENGER
weapon. The * of his death shall Num 35:19
shall be executed by the *. Num 35:21
over to the * of the dead man. Num 35:24
shall save the killer from the *; Num 35:25
the City, and the * finds him Num 35:27
otherwise the angry * might catch Deu 19:6,7
to the dead man's *, to kill him. Deu 19:12

AVENGES
He who * murder has an open ear Ps 9:12

AVENGING
so greatly by * themselves upon the Eze 25:12

AVERAGE
If you count yourself above * in 1Co 3:18
A cubit was the * length of a Rev 21:17f

AVERT
Can promises and sacrifices now * Jer 11:15

AVITH
His city was *. Gen 36:31-39
king and ruled from the city of *. 1Ch 1:46

AVOID
will be able to * the death of Deu 19:10
they checked them in and out to * 1Ch 9:28
Don't do as the wicked do. * Pro 4:15
for how can he * what he doesn't Ecc 8:6,7
They do it here to * the Eze 46:19,20
them, so you can * trouble by Mt 24:44
where he tried to * all publicity Mk 9:30,31
So, dear friends, carefully * 1Co 10:14
at home, to * disgracing the church 1Co 11:22
can be popular and * the Gal 6:12

AVOIDED
can't be *, then at least do this. Gen 43:11
evil is * by reverence for God. Pro 16:6
have * all this injury and loss! Act 27:21

AVOIDS
A wise man is cautious and * Pro 14:16

AVVA
Babylon, Cuthah, *, Hamath, and 2Ki 17:24
AVVIM
the tribe of * living in villages Deu 2:23
The land of the * in the south; Jos 13:2-7
Zimaraim, Bethel, *, Parah, Jos 18:21-28
AVVITES
worshiped by the *, and the people 2Ki 17:31
AWAIT
anguish I eagerly * sweet death! Job 14:14
What joys * us among all the good Ps 65:4
great punishments * Jerusalem to Eze 14:21
that * you when it's finished. Zec 8:9
"But, oh, the sorrows that * the Lk 6:24
What horrors * you, you cities Lk 10:13
Jesus, "the same horrors * you! Lk 11:46
What joys * the sower and the Jn 4:36
and * my further instructions." Act 9:6
death as they * this great event. Rom 8:22
AWAITED
trembled with fear at what * them. 1Sa 13:7
God, the one we have so long *." Jn 11:27
AWAITING
Oh, the joys * Israel, Num 24:3-9
the good life * you in the land the Deu 11:21
"This is the fate * the wicked Job 27:13
They do not see your punishment * Ps 10:5
We are like sheep * slaughter. Ps 44:22
not knowing the fate * it there. Pro 7:23
because of the awful fate * them, Jer 23:9
That is the fate * every one of Jer 42:17
and sat before me * his reply. Eze 20:1
of punishment * you, but by your Amo 6:3
awful hour * him might never come. Mk 14:35
been * the coming of the Savior Lk 2:38
a great reward * you in heaven. Lk 6:23
Yes, awesome judgment is * you. Lk 11:44
But, oh, the horror * that man Lk 22:22
"There is no eternal doom * Jn 3:18
SO THERE IS now no condemnation * Rom 8:1
day—we are like sheep * slaughter; Rom 8:36
better things were * you in heaven, Heb 10:34
but they saw it all * them on Heb 11:13
pain of her labor, * her delivery. Rev 12:2
Blessed are all who are * me, who Rev 16:15
AWAITS
This is what * the wicked man, Job 20:29
see the ruin that * you up ahead? Is 42:23
In the streets the sword * me; Lam 1:20
for I fear some tragedy * me." Dan 2:1
The land will tremble as it * Amo 8:8
only bitterness * them as the Lord Mic 1:12
for a tremendous reward * you up Mt 5:12
heaviest sentence * these men." Lk 20:47
not knowing what * me, except Act 20:22
what * you in the years ahead.' Act 22:10
what terrible fate * those who have 1Pe 4:17
AWAKE
*, O Deborah, and sing! Ju 5:12
"Yes, O my God, be wide * and 2Ch 6:40
I will listen, wide *, to every 2Ch 7:15
the anger of my enemies. *! Ps 7:6
And when I * in heaven, I will be Ps 17:15
They lie * at night to hatch Ps 36:4
I lie * at night thinking of you— Ps 63:6
I lie *, lonely as a solitary Ps 102:7
I stay * through the night to Ps 119:148
in poverty. Stay *, work hard, and Pro 20:13
of the park, not to * my lover. Sol 3:5
I lie *, trembling. Is 21:4
the dust shall * and sing for joy! Is 26:19
*, O Lord! Is 51:9
full of deceit. I * with fear and Jer 23:9
WOE TO YOU who lie * at night, Mic 2:1
"*, O sword, against my Zec 13:7
As he lay * Mt 1:20
"So stay * and be prepared, for Mt 25:13
stay * with me." Mt 26:38
you even stay * with me one hour? Mt 26:40
While wide * one afternoon he Act 10:3
exhaustion, stayed * through 2Co 6:5
the Scriptures, "*, O sleeper, and Eph 5:14
AWAKEN
he shall not *, nor be roused Job 14:11,12
They will * to the truth as one Ps 73:20
park, that you do not * my lover. Sol 2:7
up nor * love until it please." Sol 2:7f
The Girl: "Come, north wind, *; Sol 4:16
not to * him until he please." Sol 8:4
side to * him and said, "Quick! Act 12:7
AWAKENED
sleeping, my heart * in a dream. Sol 5:2
travail, there I * your love." Sol 8:5
AWAKENING
rose up as though * from sleep, and Ps 78:65
AWAKENS
the truth as one * from a dream of Ps 73:20
AWARE
eyes to make you * of right and Gen 2:16,17
they became * of their nakedness, Gen 3:7
though he wasn't * of touching it. Lev 5:2
land, who are well * that you are Num 14:14
* of what was going on around him. 1Sa 2:22
to you, as my father is well *." 1Sa 23:17
to God when he is * of them, while Ps 32:6
The Lord is fully * of how Ps 94:11
Those accepting it become * of Pro 13:14
I am keenly * of your apostasy, Jer 13:27
"But anyone who is not * that he Lk 12:48
"As the Jews are well *, I was Act 26:4
They were fully * of God's death Rom 1:32
I am fully * that you live in Rev 2:13
"I am * of all your good Rev 2:19
AWARENESS
an * of the glory of the Lord. Hab 2:14
AWAY
Store * in the boat all the food Gen 6:21
carcasses, Abram shooed them *. Gen 15:11
will come * with great wealth. Gen 15:14
So Sarai beat her and she ran *. Gen 16:6
Hagar: "I am running * from my Gen 16:8
and sent her * with their son. Gen 21:14
sat down a hundred yards or so *. Gen 21:16
* from Abraham's servants. Gen 21:25
off into the east, * from Isaac. Gen 25:6
of the rights he had thrown *. Gen 25:34
you and have sent you * in peace; Gen 26:29
and has carried * your blessing." Gen 27:35
So Isaac sent Jacob *, and he Gen 28:5
"We don't roll * the stone and Gen 29:8
well and rolled * the stone and Gen 29:10
you have rushed them * like this? Gen 31:26
"I sneaked * because I was Gen 31:31
they were still a long way *. Gen 35:16
Canaan—and moved * from his Gen 36:6,7,8
was * when the traders came by) Gen 37:29
He tore himself *, but as he Gen 39:12
one of them went * and never Gen 44:28
And if you take * his brother Gen 44:29
Come down to me right *! Gen 45:9
O my soul, stay * from them. Gen 49:6
But Moses ran * into the land of Ex 2:15
the shepherds chased the girls *. Ex 2:17
you to let him go * and worship me, Ex 4:23
to take the frogs *, and I will let Ex 8:8
replied, "but don't go too far *. Ex 8:28
your God to take * this death. Ex 10:17
please go *, all of you; Ex 12:31
letting all these slaves get *?" Ex 14:5
Stay * from the mountain Ex 19:13
is hurt, or gets *, and there is no Ex 22:10
that has strayed *, you must take Ex 23:4
"Keep far * from falsely Ex 23:7
take * sickness from among you. Ex 23:25
right *, the people went to Aaron. Ex 32:1
fierce wrath. Turn * from this Ex 32:12
it to you to take * the iniquity Lev 10:17
Anyone carrying * the carcass Lev 11:28
meat or carrying * its carcass Lev 11:40
The priest will put it * for Lev 13:50
the live bird fly * into an open Lev 14:53
Lord's and which is to be sent *. Lev 16:8
don't let him get * with it, or Lev 19:17
If the Jubilee is many years *, Lev 25:14,15,16
I will chase * the dangerous Lev 26:6
and your life shall ebb *; Lev 26:16
them to be dragged * to distant Lev 26:36
Those left shall pine * in enemy Lev 26:39
thigh rot * and your body swell.' Num 5:21,22
anyone who is not * on a trip, and Num 9:13
body is half rotted * at birth." Num 12:12
and Aaron, "Get * from these Num 16:21
the people to get * from the tents Num 16:23,24
he told the people, "get * Num 16:26
"Get * from these people so that Num 16:45
Moses and Aaron turned * and went Num 20:6
Pray to him to take * the Num 21:7
donkey saw me and shied * from me; Num 22:33
which stretched * across the Num 24:2
will turn * from the people." Num 25:4
priest) has turned * my anger, for Num 25:10,11
all mankind, [before I am taken * Num 27:16
If you turn * from God like Num 32:15
the countryside as far * as Gaza. Deu 2:23
However, we stayed * from the Deu 2:37
to get * with this, but not you. Deu 4:19
There, far *, you will worship Deu 4:28
He drove * other nations greater Deu 4:38
And the Lord will take * all Deu 7:15
quickly turning * from the laws of Deu 9:12
How quickly you turned * from Deu 9:16
altar is too far * from you, then Deu 12:20-23
tried to draw you * from the Lord Deu 13:10
is so far * that it isn't Deu 14:24
and don't send him * empty-handed! Deu 15:13
heart be turned * from the Lord, Deu 17:17
him from turning * from God's laws Deu 17:20
In this way you will put * the Deu 21:9
In this way you shall put * this Deu 21:21
or sheep wandering *, don't pretend Deu 22:1
camps must stay * from all evil. Deu 23:9,10
indecent lest he turn * from you. Deu 23:14
do not take any * in a container. Deu 23:24
her the letter, and send her *. Deu 24:1
he is poor he needs it right *; Deu 24:14,15
one will be there to chase them *. Deu 28:26
Your donkeys will be driven * as Deu 28:31
daughters are taken * as slaves. Deu 28:32
for the Lord will thrust you *. Deu 28:37
be snatched * from you as slaves. Deu 28:41
to turn * from the Lord our God and Deu 29:18
and threw them * into another land, Deu 29:28
But if your hearts turn * and Deu 30:17
you are drawn * to worship other Deu 30:17
I will turn * from them because Deu 31:18
turn * from God and his commands; Deu 31:29
They shrugged * the Rock of their Deu 32:15
He will watch their power ebb *, Deu 32:36
courage melted * completely and Jos 5:1
Literally, "to roll" (*). Jos 5:8,9f
did before, and we will run *. Jos 8:5
* again just as they did before!' Jos 8:6
As Joshua sent * these troops, Jos 22:7,8
Israel by turning * from him and Jos 22:16
Far be it from us to turn * Jos 22:29
and truth. Put * forever the idols Jos 24:14
Then Joshua sent the people * to Jos 24:28
How quickly they turned * from Ju 2:17
Hobab—had moved * from the rest of Ju 4:11
places as far * as the Oak of Ju 4:11
O son of Abino-am, lead * your Ju 5:12
Swept them *. Ju 5:21
countryside as far * as Gaza, Ju 6:3,4
to eat, and taking * all their Ju 6:3,4
Now the Lord has thrown us * and Ju 6:13
a panic, shouting and running *. Ju 7:21
to places as far * as Beth-shittah Ju 7:22
of Israel turned * from the Lord Ju 10:6
So go *; Ju 10:13
of Israel who took * the land from Ju 11:23
and as far * as Vineyard Meadow. Ju 11:33
young girls went * for four days Ju 11:40
he was dragged * and killed. Ju 12:6
with two new ropes and led him *. Ju 15:12,13
Tossing * the jawbone, he Ju 15:16,17
his hair *, breaking the loom. Ju 16:14
"You've taken * all my gods and Ju 18:24
they were too far * from Sidon, and Ju 18:28
with him and ran *, and returned to Ju 19:2
They came from as far * as Dan Ju 20:1
Benjamin was drawn * from the town Ju 20:31
in advance to run * so that the Ju 20:32
them and be drawn * from the town. Ju 20:32
let me know right *, for if you Ru 4:4
"Throw * your bottle." 1Sa 1:14
calves * from them in the barn. 1Sa 6:7
He will take * the best of your 1Sa 8:14
One day Kish's donkeys strayed *, 1Sa 9:3
sinned by turning * from him and 1Sa 12:10
rapidly slipping *, he decided to 1Sa 13:8
began to melt * in all directions. 1Sa 14:16
the Philistines were running *. 1Sa 14:22
and the evil spirit would go *. 1Sa 16:23
army began to run * in fright. 1Sa 17:24
"If you don't get * tonight," 1Sa 19:11
In that way David got * and went 1Sa 19:18
I am only a step * from death! 1Sa 20:3
So they parted, David going * 1Sa 20:42
that I came * without a weapon!" 1Sa 21:8
they knew he was running * from 1Sa 22:17
* when he had him in his power? 1Sa 24:19
days who run * from their masters. 1Sa 25:10
and they got * without anyone 1Sa 26:12
sent me * to worship heathen gods. 1Sa 26:19
Then David went * and Saul 1Sa 26:25
shouted to him, "Get * from here. 2Sa 2:22
But he refused to turn *, so 2Sa 2:23
I can to take * the entire kingdom 2Sa 3:9,10
So Ish-bosheth took her * from 2Sa 3:15
and had been sent * in peace, he 2Sa 3:23
do you mean by letting him get *? 2Sa 3:24,25
the Syrians began to run *. 2Sa 10:13
night after being * for so long?" 2Sa 11:10
head in her hands went * crying. 2Sa 13:19
(Absalom got *. 2Sa 13:34
Or, "God does not sweep life *, 2Sa 14:14f
a panic and everyone will run *; 2Sa 17:2,3
them from as far * as Dan and 2Sa 17:11
Turn and run *; 2Sa 22:41
are as thorns to be thrown *, 2Sa 23:6
enemies lead them * as captives to 1Ki 8:46
your children turn * from me and 1Ki 9:6
then I will take * the people of 1Ki 9:7
turned his heart * from the Lord, 1Ki 11:3
tear the kingdom * from you and 1Ki 11:11
I will take the kingdom * from 1Ki 11:12,13
" 'But I will take * the kingdom 1Ki 11:35
did not turn * from his evil ways; 1Ki 13:33
I ripped the kingdom * from the 1Ki 14:8
I will sweep * your family as a 1Ki 14:10
and haul * its stones and timbers. 1Ki 15:22
will carry you *, who knows where, 1Ki 18:12
or maybe he is * on a trip, or is 1Ki 18:27

AWAY Con't)
"Take * my life. 1Ki 19:4
his shoulders and walked * again. 1Ki 19:19
will take * whatever they like!" 1Ki 20:5,6
if he gets *, you must die, or 1Ki 20:39
great harm to you and sweep you *; 1Ki 21:21
that you must come down right *." 2Ki 1:11
to take Elijah * from you today?" 2Ki 2:3
to take * your master today?" 2Ki 2:5
I grant you before I am taken *?" 2Ki 2:9
Gehazi began to push her *, but 2Ki 4:27
Naaman was angry and stalked *. 2Ki 5:11
So he went * in a rage. 2Ki 5:12
get * without taking his gifts. 2Ki 5:20
stayed * from the land of Israel. 2Ki 6:23
* by the Syrians in their haste. 2Ki 7:15
Call him into a private room * 2Ki 9:2
She stole him * from among the 2Ki 11:2,3
and he took the people * to 2Ki 15:29
They took * the population of the 2Ki 16:9
Then Jeroboam drew Israel * from 2Ki 17:21
finally swept them *, just as all 2Ki 17:23
demand if you will only go *." 2Ki 18:14
"From far * in Babylon," 2Ki 20:14
sons will be taken * and made into 2Ki 20:18
as far * as Geba and Beersheba. 2Ki 23:8
chains and taken * to Babylon. 2Ki 25:7
some were as far * as Baal. 1Ch 4:32,33
had begun to run *, but he held 1Ch 11:13
pulled the spear * from him and 1Ch 11:23
and from as far * as Issachar, 1Ch 12:40
used me to sweep * my enemies like 1Ch 14:11
them and take them * as captives to 2Ch 6:36
face * from me, your anointed one. 2Ch 6:42
they arrived from as far * as 2Ch 7:8
as far * as the border of Egypt. 2Ch 9:26
Jerusalem and took * all the 2Ch 12:9
And you have driven * the 2Ch 13:9
Ramah and carried * the building 2Ch 16:6
bodies and came * loaded with 2Ch 20:25
them three days to cart it all *! 2Ch 20:25
Jehoram had turned * from the Lord 2Ch 21:10
and your bowels will rot *." 2Ch 21:15
and carried * everything of value 2Ch 21:17
and was hidden * in a storage 2Ch 22:11
Get at it right *. 2Ch 24:5
Amaziah's turning * from God, and 2Ch 25:27
they had turned * from the Lord God 2Ch 28:6
fierce anger will turn * from us. 2Ch 29:10
utensils thrown * by King Ahaz when 2Ch 29:19
fierce anger will turn * from you. 2Ch 30:8
continue to turn * his face from 2Ch 30:9
and carted him * to Babylon. 2Ch 33:11
* the king in chains to Babylon. 2Ch 36:6
Temple were taken * to Babylon at 2Ch 36:10
Those who survived were taken * 2Ch 36:20
that could be heard from far *! Ez 3:13
to send them * with our children; Ez 10:3
God will be turned * from us." Ez 10:14
the governor, run * from danger? Neh 6:11
So the people went * to eat a Neh 8:12
They threw * your law, killed the Neh 9:26
of Jerusalem was heard far *! Neh 12:43
you get * with this sinful deed?" Neh 13:27
Mordecai could get * with it Est 3:3,4
man who feared God and stayed * Job 1:1
have sinned and turned * from God Job 1:5
But just take * his wealth, and Job 1:11
So Satan went *; Job 1:12,13
raided us, drove * the animals and Job 1:14,15
had, and they were his to take *. Job 1:21
God and turns * from all evil. Job 2:3
dashed—you turn * from me in terror Job 6:19-21
who die shall go * forever— gone Job 7:9
pardon my sin and take it all *? Job 7:21
God will not cast * a good man, Job 8:20
he sends death to snatch a man *, Job 9:12
"My life passes swiftly *, Job 9:25
Priests are led * as slaves. Job 12:19
He takes * the voice of orators, Job 12:20
He takes * the understanding of Job 12:24,25
Why do you turn * from me? Job 13:24
won't you? Turn * your angry gaze Job 14:6
"Mountains wear * and disappear. Job 14:18,19
Torrents tear * the soil. Job 14:18,19
So every hope of man is worn *. Job 14:18,19
old and wrinkled, then send him *. Job 14:20,21
getting carried * by your anger, Job 15:12
I would try to take * your grief. Job 16:5
me down, and taken * my family. Job 16:7
for you—all of you please go *; Job 17:10
"He has sent * my brothers, and Job 19:13
forever, cast * like his own dung. Job 20:7
they ordered God * and wanted no Job 21:14
Yet the wicked get * with it Job 21:17
Are they carried * by the storm? Job 21:18
You sent widows * without Job 22:9
sin are snatched * in youth, and Job 22:15,16
For they said to God, 'Go *, Job 22:17
throw your gold *, then the Job 22:24
God, who has taken * my rights, Job 27:2
cuts him off and takes * his life? Job 27:8
* in the storms of the night. Job 27:20
The east wind carries him *, and Job 27:21
I could get * with it— if I have Job 31:21
have never turned * even a stranger Job 31:32
pass *, removed by no human hand. Job 34:20
to turn * from their sin. Job 36:10
"How he wanted to lure you * Job 36:16
winds have cleared * the clouds, Job 37:21
and does not run * though the Job 39:21-23
He smells the battle when far *. Job 39:25
a ring in his nose and lead him *. Job 40:24
They blow * like chaff before the Ps 1:4
me * with no one to rescue me. Ps 7:2
The wicked shall be sent * to Ps 9:17
ARE you standing aloof and far *? Ps 10:1
Why do you let the wicked get * Ps 10:13
But no, all have strayed *; Ps 14:3
I threw them * like sweepings Ps 18:42
For they warn us * from harm and Ps 19:11
My strength has drained * like Ps 22:14
O Lord, don't stay *. Ps 22:19
he has not turned and walked *. Ps 22:24
turned your face * from me and cut Ps 30:6,7
He took * my clothes of mourning Ps 30:11
I am pining * with grief; Ps 31:9,10
my years are shortened, drained * Ps 31:9,10
"Even my bones are rotting *." Ps 31:9,10f
Blow them * like chaff in the Ps 35:5
planning how to keep * from wrong. Ps 36:4
Soon they fade * like grass and Ps 37:2
My loved ones and friends stay * Ps 38:11
don't go *! Ps 38:21
If we had turned * from Ps 44:20
parents in your homeland far *. Ps 45:10,11
Have pity upon me and take * the Ps 51:1
you * from the land of the living. Ps 52:5
like a dove, to fly * and rest! Ps 55:6
They expect to get * with it. Ps 56:7
God will sweep * both old and Ps 58:9
For wherever I am, though far * Ps 61:2
the world and far * upon the sea. Ps 65:5
Blessed be God who didn't turn * Ps 66:20
Chase them *! Ps 68:1
O God, don't stay *! Ps 71:12
O GOD, WHY have you cast us * Ps 74:1
Will you let them get * with this Ps 74:9,10
their hearts were far *. Ps 78:37
Again and again they turned * Ps 78:41
vine and drove * the heathen from Ps 80:8
O my God, blow them * like dust; Ps 83:13
loathe me, and they have gone *. Ps 88:8
why have you thrown my life *? Ps 88:14
completely take * my lovingkindness Ps 89:33
How long will you delay? Turn * Ps 90:13
and heart were far * from me. Ps 95:10
and stay * from every evil. Ps 101:4
Don't turn * from me in this time Ps 102:2
shirt and throwing * the old one! Ps 102:26
He has removed our sins as far * Ps 103:12
But if you turn * from them, then Ps 104:29
* to distant lands as exiles. Ps 106:27
idols, and were led * from God. Ps 106:36
Lord, have you thrown us *? Ps 108:11
and slink *, their hopes thwarted. Ps 112:10
Turn me * from wanting any other Ps 119:37
No, I haven't turned * from what Ps 119:102,103
the scum you skim off and throw *; Ps 119:119
I have wandered * like a lost Ps 119:176
turned * from your commandments. Ps 119:176
We have put * our lyres, hanging Ps 137:2
When far * you know my every Ps 139:2
I can never get * from my God! Ps 139:7
wicked, Lord! *, bloodthirsty men! Ps 139:19
Take * my lust for evil things; Ps 141:4
don't turn * from me or I shall Ps 143:7
it stays *, but not these men; Pro 1:17
For you turned * from me—to Pro 1:32
the sense to stay * from evil men Pro 2:11,12,13
Don't let them slip *, for they Pro 3:21
I speak the truth—don't turn *. Pro 4:1
Avoid their haunts—turn *, go Pro 4:15
literally, "Put * from you a Pro 4:24f
he has let himself be led * into Pro 5:23
will keep you far * from Pro 6:24
my husband is * on a long trip. Pro 7:19
Don't go near her; stay * from Pro 7:25
sleeps * his hour of opportunity. Pro 10:5
and the wicked are whirled *. Pro 10:25
It is possible to give * and Pro 11:24,25
only a fool idles * his time. Pro 12:11
for advice, stay * from fools. Pro 14:7
evil shall wander * and be lost, Pro 14:22
jealousy rots it *. Pro 14:30
A SOFT ANSWER turns * wrath, but Pro 15:1
A mocker stays * from wise men Pro 15:12
The path of the godly leads * Pro 16:17
A poor man's own brothers turn * Pro 19:7
The man who strays * from common Pro 21:16
who values his soul will stay *. Pro 22:5
Keep * from angry, short-tempered Pro 22:24,25
my son, trust my advice—stay * Pro 23:26,27,28
Good news from far * is like cold Pro 25:25
flood sweeping * their last hope. Pro 28:3
the wicked prosper, good men go *; Pro 28:28
good men stay * and sing for joy. Pro 29:5,6
takes the wealth * from him and Ecc 2:24-26
A time for throwing *; Ecc 3:6
seeks what has been driven *." Ecc 3:15f
It is all swept *. Ecc 5:16
Wisdom is far *, and very Ecc 7:24
* to follow his own downward road. Ecc 7:29
days shall pass * as quickly as Ecc 8:13
my love, my fair one, and come *. Sol 2:10
my love, my fair one, and come *.' Sol 2:13
the shadows flee *, come to me, my Sol 2:17
the shadows flee *, I will go to Sol 4:6
to try to get * from the terror of Is 2:21
them * and shows their guilt. Is 3:9
For the Lord will strip * their Is 3:18
you into exile far * because you Is 5:13
they have thrown * the laws of God Is 5:24
to the nations far *, whistling to Is 5:26
they are all taken * as slaves to Is 6:12
countries far *, and all the land Is 6:12
and carry * their riches." Is 8:4
My people will be led * captive, Is 8:21
body, as when a sick man wastes *. Is 10:18
them here, from countries far *. Is 13:5
of Assembly far * in the north. Is 14:13
are heard far *, even in Jahaz. Is 15:4
with no one to chase them *. Is 17:2
river bank will wither and blow *. Is 19:7
Assyria will take * the Egyptians Is 20:4
The people slip * but they are Is 22:3
will hurl you *, sending you into Is 22:17
you * into a distant, barren land; Is 22:18
sun and moon will seem to fade *. Is 24:23
The Lord God will wipe * all Is 25:8
all tears and take * forever all Is 25:8
will people turn * from wickedness Is 26:9
I'll watch to keep all enemies *. Is 27:3
blown * in a storm from the east. Is 27:7,8
It was to purge * Is 27:9
people, for they turn * from God. Is 27:11
greedily snatched * as an early fig Is 28:4
He who believes need never run * Is 28:16
it *, and you will be drowned. Is 28:17
* like chaff before the wind. Is 29:5
its chaff blown * by the wind. Is 30:24
them all, to sweep them all *. Is 30:28
He will not be frightened *! Is 31:4,5
of you will throw * his golden Is 31:7
will be taken * as slaves. Is 31:8
what I have done, O nations far *! Is 33:13
and the highlands of heaven far *. Is 33:17
above will melt * and disappear Is 34:4
Surely God won't let him get * Is 37:4
My life is blown * like a Is 38:12
"From far * in Babylon," Is 39:3
grass that dies *, and all his Is 40:6
He chases them * and goes on Is 41:3
you and will not throw you *. Is 41:9
the wind shall blow them all *; Is 41:16
they will be turned *. Is 42:17
Whenever you have thrown * your Is 43:12
I, yes, I alone am he who blots * Is 43:25
are being hauled * on ox carts! Is 46:1
east—that man Cyrus from far *. Is 46:11
caused you to turn * from me and Is 47:10
then to cleanse * your sins. Is 47:11
* and disappear, unable to help. Is 47:15
return from far *, from north and Is 49:12
chase * all those destroying you. Is 49:17
who enslaved you shall be far *. Is 49:19
rest were carried * into exile, Is 49:21
I divorced her and sent her *? Is 50:1
I do not rebel nor turn *. Is 50:5
We are the ones who strayed * Is 53:6
trial they led him * to his death. Is 53:8
Your enemies will stay far *; Is 54:14
them * from evil days ahead. Is 57:1
A breath can puff them *. Is 57:13
Clear * the rocks and stones. Is 57:14
turned his face * from you and will Is 59:2
He has turned *. Is 59:11
Zion who have turned * from sin. Is 59:20
again from far *, bringing their Is 60:9
and take * your grain and wine. Is 62:8
sins, like the wind, sweep us *. Is 64:6
Therefore you have turned * from Is 64:7
throw them all *—there are some Is 65:8
the people were taken * as slaves. Jer 1:3
that turned them * and changed them Jer 2:4,5
Why is she captured and led far * Jer 2:14
my yoke and broke * from my ties. Jer 2:20
that cannot ever be washed *. Jer 2:22
would never turn * from me again. Jer 3:19
backs on God and wandered far *. Jer 3:21
have turned *, and worship gods Jer 5:7
And so I have taken * these Jer 5:25
of Israel says, * with your Jer 7:21

(AWAY Con't)
one shall be left to scare them *. Jer 7:33
Oh, that I could go * and forget Jer 9:2
my children have been taken * and Jer 10:20
*, leaving the land deserted. Jer 12:4
But then they turned *. Jer 13:11
shall be carried * as slaves. Jer 13:17
and all Judah shall be taken * as Jer 13:19
or a leopard take * his spots? Jer 13:23
I wouldn't help them—* with them! Jer 15:1
from them—taken * my lovingkindness Jer 16:5
I will send you * as slaves to your Jer 17:4
and turns his heart * from God. Jer 17:5
desert her and fly *, so is the man Jer 17:11
all who turn * from you shall be Jer 17:13
They have turned * from the Jer 18:15
and he shall take * these people as Jer 20:4
weep for the captives led *! Jer 22:10
and was taken * as a captive: He Jer 22:11
to sweep * these wicked men. Jer 23:19
who turned * to the idols of Baal. Jer 23:27
for the Lord has cast you *!" Jer 23:33
I will take * your joy, your Jer 25:10
land and send you far * to perish. Jer 27:10
be carried * with you to Babylon! Jer 27:18
all yet be carried * to Babylon and Jer 27:22
Don't dwindle *! Jer 29:6
* by the Assyrians as slaves. Jer 31:15f
I turned * from God but I was Jer 31:19
to do * with these laws of nature! Jer 31:36
them * forever for their sins! Jer 31:37
And I will cleanse * all their Jer 33:8
send him * to Babylon as a slave. Jer 39:7
and olives and store them *." Jer 40:10
not taken them all *, and that Jer 40:11
oil and honey they had hidden *. Jer 41:8
* from all this slaughter here!" Jer 46:16
Silent as a serpent gliding *, Jer 46:22,23
for I will save you from far * Jer 46:27
Her crying will be heard as far * Jer 48:2,3,4
shall be taken * to distant lands! Jer 48:7
that she could fly *, for her Jer 48:9
you do not get *, for the time of Jer 48:44
daughters are taken * as slaves. Jer 48:46
will be dragged * as slaves! Jer 49:20
is heard as far * as the Red Sea. Jer 49:21
Their camels will be taken *, and Jer 49:29
shall be dragged * as slaves; Jer 50:45
and winnow her and blow her *; Jer 51:2
and return to Jerusalem far *! Jer 51:50
taken * as captives to Babylon. Jer 52:3
Why is Judah led *, a slave? Lam 1:3
Now she sits in exile far *. Lam 1:3
her virgins have been dragged *. Lam 1:4
and taken far * as slaves. Lam 1:5
therefore she is tossed * like Lam 1:8
My Comforter is far *—he who Lam 1:16
far * as slaves to distant lands. Lam 1:18
Their lives ebb * like those Lam 2:12
gone, for you have taken them *. Lam 3:17
"Get *!" Lam 4:15
They take * the young men to Lam 5:13
Lord began to move *, accompanied Eze 3:12
me up and took me * to Tel Abib, Eze 3:14,15
waste * beneath their punishment. Eze 4:17
for she has turned * from my laws Eze 5:5,6,7
for I will take * their adulterous Eze 6:9
I will turn my eyes * and show Eze 7:4
All your boasting will die *, and Eze 7:10,11
"Throw * your money! Eze 7:19
Therefore I will take it all * Eze 7:20
he has gone *!' Eze 8:12
He has gone *!' Eze 9:9
and walk * into the night; Eze 12:6
their homes and sent * into exile. Eze 12:11
I will sweep it * with a storm of Eze 13:13
will you turn * my people from me? Eze 13:19
my fury against you will die *; Eze 16:42
No, it will wither * completely Eze 17:10
came to Jerusalem and took * Eze 17:12,13
and stays * from sin, and is Eze 18:8
But if a wicked person turns * Eze 18:21
When a good man turns * from Eze 18:26
And if a wicked person turns * Eze 18:27
the others and noticed from far *. Eze 19:11
* her children as their slaves. Eze 23:10
which you turned *, disgusted. Eze 23:22
your children will be taken * as Eze 23:25
"You even sent * to distant Eze 23:40
scorch * the rust and corruption. Eze 24:11
going to take * your lovely wife. Eze 24:16
she was marched * captive, Eze 25:3
was taken * to captivity). Eze 26:1
I will scrape * her soil and make Eze 26:4
Her wealth is taken *, her Eze 30:4
women will be taken * as slaves. Eze 30:17
will be taken * as captives. Eze 30:18
go * and leave her lying there. Eze 31:12
we pine * with guilt. Eze 33:10
who have wandered * and are lost. Eze 34:4
I will take * their right to feed Eze 34:9,10
take * their right to eat. Eze 34:9,10
those who strayed *, and bring them Eze 34:15,16
until they're scattered far *. Eze 34:21
them, and drive * the dangerous Eze 34:25
you * as slaves to many lands. Eze 36:3
washed *, your idol worship gone. Eze 36:25
I will cleanse * your sins. Eze 36:29
and I was carried * by the Spirit Eze 37:1
and gold and drive * their cattle Eze 38:13
Israel was sent * to exile—it was Eze 39:23
Therefore I turned my face * from Eze 39:23
I turned my face * and punished Eze 39:24
for sending them * to exile, and Eze 39:28
Thirty-five feet * from the Eze 41:10
Now let them put * their idols Eze 43:9
Israel strayed * from God to idols Eze 44:10
property and having to move *." Eze 46:18
and the wind blew them all *. Dan 2:35
throne and took * his glory, and Dan 5:20
we have turned * from you and Dan 9:11
Lord, please turn * your furious Dan 9:16
will learn to stay * from sin, and Dan 9:24
this prophecy is many years *." Dan 10:14
him and take * his kingdom and make Dan 11:5
will be swept * before him, Dan 11:22
sacrifice is taken * and the Dan 12:11
cause her to waste * and die of Hos 1:3
Stay * from her, for she is Hos 4:17
shall sweep them *; Hos 4:19
I will sap * the strength of Hos 5:12
them off and chase all rescuers *. Hos 5:14
Their sinful deeds give them * on Hos 7:2
Israel has thrown * her chance Hos 8:3
they applied to someone far *. Hos 8:12
The glory of Israel flies * like Hos 9:11
when I turn * and leave you alone. Hos 9:12
the Lord and he took * our king. Hos 10:3
that quickly dries *, like chaff Hos 13:3
have been taken *, and like a lion Hos 13:8
in my anger, and I took them * Hos 13:11
and stored * for punishment. Hos 13:12
dry *, and he will die of thirst. Hos 13:15
say, "O Lord, take * our sins; Hos 14:2
far * and rest beneath my shadow. Hos 14:7
O Ephraim! Stay * from idols! Hos 14:8
the north and send them far *; Joe 2:20
sell them to the Sabeans far *. Joe 3:8
her people as far * as the plain of Amo 1:5
you * like the cattle you are; Amo 4:2
they will drag the last of you * Amo 4:2
in war and drove * your horses. Amo 4:10
firebrands snatched * from fire. Amo 4:11
of peace. * with your hymns of Amo 5:23
You push * all thought of Amo 6:3
I will no longer turn * from Amo 7:8
far * into exile and slavery." Amo 7:11
took him far * to foreign lands; Ob 1:12
to go and ran * from the Lord. Jon 1:3
he was running * from the Lord. Jon 1:9,10
have rejected me and cast me *. Jon 2:4
That's why I ran * to Tarshish. Jon 4:2
so that it withered * and died. Jon 4:7
which had been taken * from them. Mic 1:11f
led * as slaves—stripped, naked Mic 1:11
which had been taken * from them. Mic 1:11f
which had been taken * from them. Mic 1:11f
are swept *—the very ground on Mic 1:11
For they are snatched * and you Mic 1:16
and sent us far *, and given what Mic 2:4
dictate to strong nations far *. Mic 4:3
you will be sent far * into exile Mic 4:10
that makes you turn * from me? Mic 6:3
of Bashan and Carmel fade *; Nah 1:4
But he sweeps * his enemies with Nah 1:8
streets, and led *, a slave, with Nah 2:7
Her soldiers slip *, deserting Nah 2:8
uncounted wealth is stripped *. Nah 2:9
swarm like locusts and carry it *. Nah 3:16
of them will flee * and disappear, Nah 3:17
All opposition melts * before Hab 1:9
Will you let them get * with this Hab 1:17
I plan won't happen right *. Hab 2:3
"I will sweep * everything in Zep 1:2
I will sweep * both men and Zep 1:3
opportunity is blown * like chaff; Zep 2:2
wounded and taken * your reproach. Zep 3:17,18
together those who were chased *. Zep 3:19
blow it *—it doesn't last at all." Hag 1:9
on the anvil and throw them *." Zec 1:21
I have taken * your sins, and now I Zec 3:4
come from so far * represent many Zec 6:15
They turned stubbornly * and put Zec 7:11
when they cried to me, I turned *. Zec 7:13
movements and I will keep them *; Zec 9:8
cast them all *, for I, the Lord Zec 10:6
will be taken * as slaves, and half Zec 14:1
corpses, their flesh rotting *; Zec 14:12
watch as the dross is burned *. Mal 3:3
say, 'We have never even gone *!' Mal 3:7
Your grapes won't shrivel * Mal 3:11
fire, and storing * the grain." Mt 3:12
Then Satan went *, and angels Mt 4:1
be healed from as far * as Syria. Mt 4:2
lust, gouge it out and throw it *. Mt 5:2
to sin, cut it off and throw it *. Mt 5:3
* from those who want to borrow. Mt 5:4
But when you pray, go * by Mt 6:
they can erode * or may be stolen. Mt 6:1
Go *, for your deeds are evil.' Mt 7:2
him to go * and leave them alone. Mt 8:3
Then he added, "Now go * and Mt 9:1
For the patch would tear * and Mt 9:1
the little he has will be taken *. Mt 13:12,1
comes and snatches * the seeds Mt 13:1
crates and throws the others *. Mt 13:47,4
send the crowds * so they can go Mt 14:1
me, but their hearts are far *. Mt 15:
disciples urged him to send her *. Mt 15:2
I don't want to send them * Mt 15:3
said, "Get * from me, you Satan! Mt 16:2
and it would go far *. Mt 17:2
to sin, cut it off and throw it *. Mt 18:
sin, gouge it out and throw it *. Mt 18:
* and is lost, what will he do? Mt 18:1
* sadly, for he was very rich. Mt 19:2
is it against the law to give * Mt 20:1
went * to live in another country. Mt 21:3
God shall be taken * from you, and Mt 21:4
and baffled them and they went *. Mt 22:2
this generation shall pass *." Mt 24:34
arrived and took them all *. Mt 24:39
"But he called back, 'Go *! Mt 25:12
my left and say, '* with you, you Mt 25:41
"And they shall go * into Mt 25:46
let this cup be taken * from me. Mt 26:39
If this cup cannot go * until I Mt 26:42
"Put * your sword," Jesus told Mt 26:52
And he went *, crying bitterly. Mt 26:75
soldiers to take * and crucify. Mt 27:26
They told Jesus about her right * Mk 1:29,30
But some day he will be taken * Mk 2:20
The patch pulls * and leaves the Mk 2:21
went * and met with the Herodians Mk 3:6
from as far * as Tyre and Sidon. Mk 3:7,8
shall be taken * even what he has. Mk 4:25
field, and went *, and as the days Mk 4:27
smashed the shackles and walked *. Mk 5:3,4
to go * and leave them alone! Mk 5:17
"Let's get * from the crowds for a Mk 6:31
the people to go * to the nearby Mk 6:35,36
a house to get * from the crowds, Mk 7:17
About fifty miles *. Mk 7:24f
Right * a woman came to him whose Mk 7:25
Jesus led him * from the crowd Mk 7:33
Only those who throw * their Mk 8:35
*, telling them not to bother him. Mk 10:13
Don't send them *! Mk 10:14
sadly *, for he was very rich. Mk 10:22
'The Rock the builders threw * Mk 12:10
So they left him and went *. Mk 12:12
the hour might pass * from him." Mk 14:35f
for you. Take * this cup from me. Mk 14:36
And he went * again and prayed, Mk 14:39
so that he ran * completely naked. Mk 14:51,52
fists on him as they led him *. Mk 14:65
and led him * to be crucified. Mk 15:20
were watching as Jesus was laid *. Mk 15:47
moved * and the entrance was open! Mk 16:4
"to take * my disgrace of having Lk 1:25
sent the rich * with empty hands. Lk 1:53
and his mother stored * all these Lk 2:51
turned to God and * from their Lk 3:3
If you have extra food, give it * Lk 3:11
fire and store * the grain." Lk 3:17
left Jesus for a while and went *. Lk 4:13
But he walked * through the Lk 4:30
began shouting at Jesus, "Go *! Lk 4:34
Literally, "taken * from them." Lk 5:35f
and when things are taken * from Lk 6:30
steals the words * and prevents Lk 8:12
has shall be taken * from him." Lk 8:18
The herdsmen rushed * to the Lk 8:34
begged Jesus to go * and leave them Lk 8:37
Then he sent them * to tell Lk 9:2
he slipped quietly * with them Lk 9:10
to send the people * to the nearby Lk 9:12
Then, as the voice died *, Jesus Lk 9:36
But they were turned *! Lk 9:53
I won't take it * from her!" Lk 10:42
of them and chase * the others.' Lk 11:49
enough stored * for years to come. Lk 12:19
barns to store * their food, and Lk 12:24
in here, guilty as you are. Go *.' Lk 13:27
and healed him and sent him *. Lk 14:4
are still far *, he will send a Lk 14:32
of them strayed * and was lost in Lk 15:3,4
others who haven't strayed *! Lk 15:7
a long distance *, his father saw Lk 15:20
"Those * from home that day must Lk 17:31
will be taken *, the other left. Lk 17:34
the disciples told them to go *. Lk 18:15
Never send them *! Lk 18:16,17

(AWAY Con't)
sadly *, for he was very rich. Lk 18:23
of God would begin right *. Lk 19:11
was called * to the distant capital Lk 19:12
'Take the money * from him and give Lk 19:24
farmers, and went * to a distant Lk 20:9
and sent * without collecting. Lk 20:11
He, too, was wounded and chased * Lk 20:12
weapons, or sent * as exiles and Lk 21:24
earth shall pass *, yet my words Lk 21:33
He walked *, perhaps a stone's Lk 22:41,42
take * this cup of horror from me. Lk 22:41,42
As the crowd led Jesus * to his Lk 23:26
As the body was taken *, the Lk 23:55
Bethany was a mile or so *, Lk 24:50f
God who takes * the world's sin! Jn 1:29
They stayed * from that Light for Jn 3:20
turned * and deserted him. Jn 6:66
And the Jewish leaders slipped * Jn 8:9
to them again, "I am going *; Jn 8:21
it was washed *, he could see! Jn 9:15
No one shall snatch them * from Jn 10:28
But he walked * and left them, Jn 10:39
But some went * to the Pharisees Jn 11:46
went * and was hidden from them. Jn 12:36
before I must go * and leave you! Jn 13:33
you—I am going *, but I will come Jn 14:28
me, he is thrown * like a useless Jn 15:6
"But now I am going * to the one Jn 16:5
for you that I go *, for if I Jn 16:7
said to Peter, "Put your sword *. Jn 18:11
"Then take him * and judge him Jn 18:31
"* with him," they yelled. Jn 19:15
"* with him—crucify him!" Jn 19:15
So he came and took it *. Jn 19:38
"Because they have taken * my Jn 20:13
you have taken him *, tell me where Jn 20:15
to the beach, about 300 feet *. Jn 21:8
Jesus has gone * to heaven, and Act 1:11
so he can cleanse * your sins and Act 3:19
He drew * some people as Act 5:37
"Then God turned * from them and Act 7:42
captivity far * beyond Babylon.' Act 7:43
of the Lord caught * Philip, and Act 8:39
put * idols and worship only him. Act 17:30
"* with him, away with him!" Act 21:36
"Away with him, * with him!" Act 21:36
send you far * to the Gentiles!' Act 22:21
shouted, "* with such a fellow! Act 22:22
to take him * from them by force Act 23:10
took him violently * from us, Act 24:7
"After several years *, I Act 24:17
"Go * for now," he replied, Act 24:25
sins are cleansed *, who are set Act 26:18
who push * the truth from them. Rom 1:18
Every one has turned *; Rom 3:12
Jesus Christ to take * our sins. Rom 3:21,22
kindness freely takes * our sins. Rom 3:24
would come and take * those sins. Rom 3:25
because Jesus took * their sins. Rom 3:26
in Jesus who took * their sins. Rom 3:26
freely takes * many sins and gives Rom 5:16
itself cannot keep God's love *. Rom 8:38
Not all the Jews have turned * Rom 11:5
When God turned * from them it Rom 11:15
who were so far * from him—being Rom 11:24
At that time I will take * their Rom 11:27
this letter. Stay * from those who Rom 16:17
sins are washed *, and you are set 1Co 6:11
do * with both stomachs and food. 1Co 6:13
I have put * the childish things. 1Co 13:11
brightness was already fading *. 2Co 3:7
will never go *, we can preach with 2Co 3:12
could not see the glory fade *. 2Co 3:13
sins, then the veil is taken *. 2Co 3:16
is time spent * from our eternal 2Co 5:6
in this body or * from this body 2Co 5:9
let us turn * from everything 2Co 7:1
* from sin and seek eternal life. 2Co 7:10
that you can give * more and more 2Co 9:10
that you can give * much, and when 2Co 9:11
when he is far *; but when he gets 2Co 10:1
you will be led * from your pure 2Co 11:3
in the city wall, and so I got *! 2Co 11:33
you are turning * so soon from God Gal 1:6
No, I went * into the deserts of Gal 1:17
Jesus Christ to take * our sins. Gal 2:16
didn't reject me and turn me *. Gal 4:14
Abraham to send * the slave-wife Gal 4:30
death to clear * our sins and make Gal 5:5
ignore God and get * with it: a man Gal 6:7
us that he took * all our sins Eph 1:7
you once were far * from God, now Eph 2:13
who were very far * from him, and Eph 2:17
they are far * from the life of Eph 4:17,18
a sacrifice to take * your sins. Eph 5:2
And now that I am * you must be Php 2:12
In everything you do, stay * from Php 2:14
do because you were far *. Php 2:30
thrown them all * so that I can put Php 3:7
who were once so far * from God. Col 1:21
For though I am far * from you Col 2:5
sinful desires were not yet cut *. Col 2:13
In this way God took * Satan's Col 2:15
where your sins were all taken *. Col 2:15
* then with sinful, earthly Col 3:5
cast off and throw * all these Col 3:8
who can get * with shirking. Col 3:25
and how you turned * from your 1Th 1:9
you and had been * from you but a 1Th 2:17
not be able to get * anywhere—there 1Th 5:3
Keep * from every kind of evil. 1Th 5:22
Don't be carried * and deceived 2Th 2:3
authority: Stay * from any 2Th 3:6
who he is and stay * from him, that 2Th 3:14
church will turn * from Christ and 1Ti 4:1
already turned * from the church 1Ti 5:15
Be sure that you yourself stay * 1Ti 5:22
of making money. Keep * from them. 1Ti 6:5
* a single penny when we die. 1Ti 6:7
Some people have even turned * 1Ti 6:10
If you stay * from sin you will 2Ti 2:21
help, to turn * from their wrong 2Ti 2:25
But they won't get * with all 2Ti 3:9
Everyone had run *. 2Ti 4:16
turned * from the grace of God. Tit 1:11
pity—by washing * our sins and Tit 3:5
way: that he ran * from you for a Phm 1:15
or we may drift * from them. Heb 2:1
leading you * from the living God. Heb 3:12
things to be given * to certain Heb 9:16
of the age, to put * the power of Heb 9:26
and goats really to take * sins. Heb 10:4
which forever took those sins *. Heb 10:4f
that could never take * our sins. Heb 10:11
die *, no matter what happens. Heb 10:35
him * to heaven without dying; Heb 11:5
home and go far * to another land Heb 11:8
Abraham obeyed. * he went, not even Heb 11:8
made whole armies turn and run *. Heb 11:34
Stay * from the love of money; Heb 13:5
where his blood washed our sins *. Heb 13:12
beauty and fades *, withered—killed Jas 1:10,11
as soon as he walks *, he can't Jas 1:24
them safely * by a different road. Jas 2:25
a fight to take it * from them. Jas 4:2
even now rotting *, and your fine Jas 5:2
anyone has slipped * from God and Jas 5:19
life they gave you will fade *. 1Pe 1:23
been to you, put * all evil, 1Pe 2:2,3
I beg you to keep * from the evil 1Pe 2:11
Like sheep you wandered * from 1Pe 2:25
Turn * from evil and do good. 1Pe 3:11
you will never stumble or fall *. 2Pe 1:10
heavens be stored * for a great 2Pe 3:7
heavens will pass * with a terrible 2Pe 3:10
is going to melt *, what holy, 2Pe 3:11
and not be carried * by the 2Pe 3:17
Christ died to wash * our sins. 1Jn 1:9
so that you will stay * from sin. 1Jn 2:1
And this world is fading *, and 1Jn 2:17
that he could take * our sins, and 1Jn 3:5
terrible end of those who fall *. 1Jn 5:17f
Dear children, keep * from 1Jn 5:21
and falling *, and to bring you, Jud 1:24,25
no one will take * your crown Rev 3:11
up like a scroll and taken *; Rev 6:14
And God will wipe their tears* Rev 7:17
long to die—but death will flee *! Rev 9:6
will be arrested and taken *; Rev 13:10
"Come * from her, my people; Rev 18:4
shall be thrown * as I have thrown Rev 18:21
as I have thrown * this stone, and Rev 18:21
earth and sky fled *, but they Rev 20:11
He will wipe * all tears from Rev 21:4
who have strayed * from God, and Rev 22:15
God shall take * his share in the Rev 22:19

AWE

Lord, and they will stand in *. Deu 28:10
He is to be held in * above all 1Ch 16:25
Stand before the Lord in *, Ps 4:4
I will worship you with deepest * Ps 5:7
the Lord and stand in * of him. Ps 33:8
me, and stand in * before the Lord, Ps 40:3
They will watch in *. Ps 52:6
Then everyone shall stand in * Ps 64:9
What * we feel, kneeling here Ps 68:35
stand in dread and * of him. Ps 89:7
I stand in * of only your words. Ps 119:161
of Israel, and stand in * of him. Is 29:23
my people and will tremble with *! Jer 33:9
The men stood there in * before Jon 1:16
They will stand in silent *, deaf Mic 7:16
they will stand in *. Mic 7:17
I worship you in * for the fearful Hab 3:2
and * for me, by keeping them. Mal 2:5
And they were filled with * and Mk 4:41
The crowd watched Jesus in * as Mk 9:15
was gripped with * and fear. Lk 5:26
And they were filled with * and Lk 8:25
* gripped the people as they saw Lk 9:43
was stricken with * before God and Lk 23:47
A deep sense of * was on them Act 2:43
hearts, and with holy fear and *. Heb 12:28
and followed the Creature in *. Rev 13:3

AWE-INSPIRING

Go forth to * deeds! Ps 45:4
How * are your deeds, O God! Ps 66:3
(what a holy, * name that is). Ps 111:9
Your * deeds shall be on every Ps 145:6

AWED

the people were * as they realized 1Ki 3:28
The disciples just sat there, *! Mt 8:27
Everyone stood there * by the Act 3:11

AWESOME

This is the * entrance to Gen 28:16,17
Who is so * in splendor, Ex 15:11
appeared the * glory of Jehovah. Ex 16:10
to show you his * power, so that Ex 20:20
mountain saw the * sight: the glory Ex 24:17
the * glory of the Lord was seen. Num 16:42
This * fire will consume us. Deu 5:25
you, and he is a great and * God. Deu 7:21
his greatness and his * power. Deu 11:2
again, or see the * fire on the Deu 18:16
He did great and * miracles Deu 26:8
of the * horrors surrounding you. Deu 28:67
"O great and * God who keeps his Neh 1:5
"And now, O great and * God, you Neh 9:32
And don't terrify me with your * Job 13:21
above all gods, is * beyond words; Ps 47:2
With dread deeds and * power you Ps 65:5
princes and does * things to the Ps 76:12
You still demonstrate your * Ps 77:14
are scattered by your * power. Ps 89:10
What an * thing this is! Ps 130:3,4
I see an * vision: oh, the Is 21:2
I will take * vengeance on these Is 29:14
he will rule with * strength. Is 40:10
down, for you did * things beyond Is 64:3
In his day of * fury he has shown Lam 2:1
the world and an * example to Eze 5:15
allies—a vast and * army—will roll Eze 38:9
"you are a great and * God; Dan 9:4
And so the * curse of God has Dan 9:11
the Lord is an *, terrible thing. Joe 2:11
Therefore I will make an * Mic 6:16
in his * power. Hab 3:4
You marched across the land in * Hab 3:12
For the * Day of his Judgment has Zep 1:7
And so the * curse of God is Mal 3:9
Yes, * judgment is awaiting you. Lk 11:44
and the Son will do far more * Jn 5:20
that * Day of the Lord arrives. Act 2:20
What a wave of * joy swept Act 20:10,11,12
of displaying the * power of God Rom 9:17
For there was an * trumpet Heb 12:19

AWESTRUCK

The others sat there, *. Mt 14:33
and they were * by his story. Mk 5:20
For he was * by the size of Lk 5:9

AWFUL

Oh, please overlook the * Deu 9:27
the siege and the * distress caused Deu 28:56,57
Benjamin because of this * deed. Ju 19:30
"It is an * thing to make the 1Sa 2:23,24,25
with people who do these * things. Ez 9:14
the * stain of my transgressions. Ps 51:1
for my * thirst they offered me Ps 69:21
Walk through the * ruins of the Ps 74:3
has sworn your * fate—with my own Is 5:9
I am gripped by * fear. Is 21:4
Face the * sins that you have Jer 2:23
of the * fate awaiting them, Jer 23:9
Instead the * cries of terror Jer 48:34
For I can never forget these * Lam 3:20
and accept their * insults, for Lam 3:30
But you too will feel the * anger Lam 4:21
For your sins are so * that in Eze 16:52
beneath the * blows of sorrow and Eze 23:33
and Samaria of all their * deeds. Eze 23:36
O Israel, ever since that * night Hos 10:9
pass the * story down from Joe 1:3
"to bring this * storm upon us? Jon 1:8
and correct us for our * sins. Hab 1:12
were possible the * hour awaiting Mk 14:35
a time of * hunger is before them. Lk 6:25
you free from the * power of sin; 1Co 7:22
of God's * anger which will consume Heb 10:27

AWHILE

So he let it shine for *, and Gen 1:4,5
any further. Stop * and rest here Gen 18:3,4
Do stay * before continuing your Gen 18:5
Stay there with him * until your Gen 27:44
to Hazeroth, where they stayed *. Num 11:35
Her father urged him to stay *, Ju 19:4
had watched for *, they returned to 1Sa 6:16
not slept with any women for *." 1Sa 21:4
so they stayed there * and rested. 2Sa 16:14
me and rest * and have some food; 1Ki 13:7
But after * the brook dried up, 1Ki 17:7
sleeping and decided to read *. Est 6:1
So listen to me * and let me Job 32:10

(AWHILE Con't)
them, they walked * behind him; Ps 78:34
Then the angel left me for *, but Zec 5:5
true, and sort of believe for *; Lk 8:13
be stricken * with blindness." Act 13:11
he stayed * longer in Turkey. Act 19:22
And after * they began to think Rom 1:21
I want to come and stay *, if the 1Co 16:7
I don't come for * you will know 1Ti 3:15
because after * they are likely to 1Ti 5:11
see Jesus—who for * was a little Heb 2:9

AWL
his ear with an *, and after that Ex 21:6
you— then take an * and pierce his Deu 15:17

AWNINGS
you stand beneath * bright with Eze 27:7

AWOKE
When Noah * from his drunken Gen 9:24,25
and * trembling with fear. Dan 2:1
When I *, I was greatly Dan 7:28
When Joseph *, he did as the Mt 1:24

AXE
chop wood, and the * head flies off Deu 19:5
For sharpening an *, 30Ç 1Sa 13:21
sound of hammer, *, or any other 1Ki 6:7
him with an *, or wounding him with Pro 25:18
is risk in each stroke of your *! Ecc 10:8,9
A dull * requires great strength; Ecc 10:10
But the Lord says, "Shall the * Is 10:15
as a woodsman's * cuts down the Is 10:34
forge to make an *, pounding on it Is 44:12
Then the woodcarver takes the * Is 44:13
"And even now the * of God's Mt 3:10
stones! The * of his judgment is Lk 3:9

AXES
plowshares, discs, *, or sickles, 1Sa 13:20
and * and work in the brick kilns; 2Sa 12:31
work with saws, iron picks, and *, 1Ch 20:3
They came with their * and Ps 74:5,6

AXHEAD
his * fell into the river. 2Ki 6:5
and the * rose to the surface and 2Ki 6:6

AXLES
wheels and bronze *, and at each 1Ki 7:27-30
were connected to * that had been 1Ki 7:32
the *, spokes, rims, and hubs. 1Ki 7:33

AYYAH
as far as * and its towns. 1Ch 7:28

AZALIAH
Shaphan (son of *, son of 2Ki 22:3,4
Shaphan (son of *) and Ma-aseiah, 2Ch 34:8

AZANIAH
Jeshua (son of *), Binnui Neh 10:9-13

AZAREL
Elkanah, Isshiah, *, Jo-ezer, 1Ch 12:3-7
Eleventh, * and twelve of his sons 1Ch 25:9-31
Over Dan, * (son of Jeroham). 1Ch 27:16-22
*, Shelemiah, Shemariah, Shallum, Ez 10:34-42
Amashsai (son of *, son of Ahzai, Neh 11:10-14
Shemaiah, *, Milalai, Neh 12:35,36

AZARIAH
* (son of Zadok) was the High 1Ki 4:1
* (son of Nathan) was secretary of 1Ki 4:1
Then his son * 2Ki 14:21
NEW KING OF Judah: * 2Ki 15:1
* was a good king, and he pleased 2Ki 15:3
The rest of the history of * is 2Ki 15:6
When * died, he was buried with 2Ki 15:7
at that time: King *, who had been 2Ki 15:8
Concurrent with: King * of Judah 2Ki 15:17
Concurrent with: King * of Judah, 2Ki 15:23
Concurrent with: King * of Judah, 2Ki 15:27
Also called *. 2Ki 15:34,35f
Ethan's son was *. 1Ch 2:8
Jehu's son was *; 1Ch 2:38
Ahaziah, Joash, Amaziah, *, 1Ch 3:10-14
*, the father of 1Ch 6:4-15
* (the High Priest in Solomon's 1Ch 6:4-15
*, the father of 1Ch 6:4-15
Elkanah I, Joel, *, Zephaniah, 1Ch 6:33-38
* (the son of Hilkiah, son of 1Ch 9:10,11
THEN THE SPIRIT of God came upon * 2Ch 15:1
Jehoshaphat—were *, Jehiel, 2Ch 21:2
*, Michael, and Sheph-atiah. 2Ch 21:2
his confidence: * (son of Jeroham), 2Ch 23:1
of Jehohanan), * (son of Obed), 2Ch 23:1
upon the altar. * the High Priest 2Ch 26:17,18
When * and the others saw it, 2Ch 26:20
These men were * the son of 2Ch 28:12
of Amasai) and Joel (son of *); 2Ch 29:12,13,14
Abdi) and * (son of Jehallelel); 2Ch 29:12,13,14
And * the High Priest from the 2Ch 31:10
Hezekiah and * the High Priest. 2Ch 31:12,13
Seriah was the son of *; Ez 7:1
* was the son of Hilkiah; Ez 7:1
Benjamin, Hasshub, and * (son of Neh 3:23
Nehemiah; *, Ra-amiah, Nahamani; Neh 7:7
Ma-aseiah, Kelita, *, Jozabad, Neh 8:7,8
Zedekiah, Seraiah, *, Neh 10:1
Hoshaiah, *, Ezra, Meshullam, Neh 12:33
all the people, * (son of Jer 43:2,3
Daniel, Hananiah, Misha-el, and * Dan 1:6
Misha-el was called Meshach;* was Dan 1:7
Misha-el, and *, and suggested a Dan 1:11
Daniel, Hananiah, Misha-el, and *. Dan 1:18,19
Misha-el, and *, his companions. Dan 2:17

AZARIAH'S
Jehu's son was Azariah; * son 1Ch 2:39
wall from * house to the corner. Neh 3:24

AZAZ
Bela (the son of *, grandson of 1Ch 5:7,8

AZAZEL
Literally, "for *" or "for Lev 16:8f
Literally, "for *" or "for Lev 16:10f
Literally, "for *" or "for Lev 16:26f

AZAZIAH
Je-iel, and * were the harpists. 1Ch 15:21
Over Ephraim, Hoshea (son of *); 1Ch 27:16-22
Jehiel, *, Nahath, Asahel, 2Ch 31:12,13

AZBUK
Nehemiah (son of *), the mayor of Neh 3:16

AZEKAH
to Beth-horon and * and Makkedah, Jos 10:10
that continued all the way to *; Jos 10:11
Adullam, Socoh, *, Sha-araim, Jos 15:33-36
in Judah and * in Ephes-dammim. 1Sa 17:1
Adoraim, Lachish, *, 2Ch 11:5-10
and its nearby fields, * Neh 11:25-30
Lachish and *—the only walled Jer 34:7

AZEL
Raphah, Eleasah, *. 1Ch 8:37
* had six sons: 1Ch 8:38
Bine-a, Rephaiah, Eleasah, and *. 1Ch 9:43
* had six sons: 1Ch 9:44
shall touch *"—apparently a hamlet Zec 14:5f

AZEL'S
* brother Eshek had three sons: 1Ch 8:39

AZGAD
From the subclan of *, 1,222; Ez 2:3-35
From the clan of *—Johanan (son of Ez 8:2-14
From the subclan of *, 2,322; Neh 7:8-38
Bani, Bunni, *, Bebai, Neh 10:14-27

AZI-EL
and Zechariah, *, Shemiramoth, 1Ch 15:20

AZIZA
Mattaniah, Jeremoth, Zabad, *. Ez 10:27

AZMAVETH
* from Bahurim; 2Sa 23:24-39
Alemeth, *, Zimri. 1Ch 8:36
Jarah was the father of Alemeth, * 1Ch 9:42
* from Baharum; 1Ch 11:26-47
Jezi-el and Pelet, sons of *; 1Ch 12:3-7
* (son of Adi-el) was the chief 1Ch 27:25
From the subclan of *, 42; Ez 2:3-35
area of Geba and *, for the singers Neh 12:29

AZMON
go to Hazaraddar, and on to *. Num 34:4
From * the boundary will follow Num 34:5
through Karka and *, until it Jos 15:2,3,4

AZNOTH-TABOR
and ran past *, then to Hukkok, and Jos 19:34

AZOR
Eliakim was the father of *; Mt 1:13
* was the father of Zadok; Mt 1:14

AZOTUS
Philip found himself at *! Act 8:40

AZRI-EL
Epher, Ishi, Eliel, *, Jeremiah, 1Ch 5:24
and Seraiah (son of *) and Jer 36:26

AZRIEL
Over Naphtali, Jeremoth (son of * 1Ch 27:16-22

AZRIKAM
Eli-o-enai, Hizkiah, *. 1Ch 3:23
*, Bocheru, Ishmael, She-ariah, 1Ch 8:38
of Hasshub, son of *, son of 1Ch 9:14
*, Bocheru, Ishmael, 1Ch 9:44
administrator *, and the king's 2Ch 28:7
(son of Hasshub, son of * Neh 11:15,16,17

AZUBAH
His mother was *, the daughter of 1Ki 22:42
* and Jerioth. 1Ch 2:18
These are the children of *: 1Ch 2:18
His mother's name was *, the 2Ch 20:31

AZUBAH'S
After * death, Caleb married 1Ch 2:19

AZZAN
Paltiel (son of *) Num 34:16-28

AZZUR
Ater, Hezekiah, *, Hodiah, Neh 10:14-27
(son of *), a false prophet from Jer 28:1
*) and Pelatiah (son of Benaiah). Eze 11:1

B
(*) Melchizedek placed a blessing Heb 7:6

B.C.
times) was founded about 1720 *. Num 13:22f
to the Assyrian armies in 722 *. Is 7:8f
Egyptian Dynasty (730–660 *). Is 18:1f
in Jeremiah's time (around 626 *. Jer 5:15f
Empire lasted from about 1900 *. Jer 5:15f
to 1550 *. Jer 5:15f
soil as early as 3000 *. Jer 5:15f
dating from the 5th century *. Jer 7:18f
ruler before the exile of 597 *. Jer 21:1f
brief months in the year 609 *. Jer 22:11f
He ruled from 609–598 *. Jer 22:13f
Great entered Babylon in 539 *. Jer 25:12f
Probably in the summer of 605 *. Jer 36:1f
ruled Egypt from 588 to 568 *. Jer 44:30f
In 609 *. Jer 47:1f
Late in July, 587 *. Jer 52:12f
of a 13-year siege (587–574 *). Eze 29:18f
of a 13-year siege (587–574 *). Eze 29:20f
587 *., the year Jerusalem fell to Eze 30:20f
It was the year 587 *. Eze 31:1f
In 252 *. Dan 11:6f
event was fulfilled in 168–167 *. Dan 11:30,31f
who invaded Gilead around 740 *. Hos 10:14f
the events of the year 612 *. Nah 2:1f
the Assyrians around 630 *. Hab 1:6f
coast of Palestine around 1200 *. Zep 2:5f

BA-ASEIAH
Berechiah, Shime-a, Michael, *, 1Ch 6:39-43

BAAL
the worship of *, the god of Moab; Num 25:3
execute all who had worshiped *. Num 25:5
They are causing you to worship * Num 25:18
* and the Ashtaroth idols. Ju 2:12-14
* and the Asheroth idols. Ju 3:7
family altar of *, and pull it Ju 6:25
that the altar of * was knocked Ju 6:28
the altar of *, and for cutting Ju 6:30
mob, "Does * need your help? Ju 6:31
who should die for insulting *! Ju 6:31
insulting Baal! If * is really a Ju 6:31
* take care of himself0,6▮!" Ju 6:32
Literally, "Let * bring Ju 6:32f
mockingly, "Let * be honored!" Ju 6:32f
the idols * and Baal-berith. Ju 8:33
the heathen gods * and Ashtaroth, Ju 10:6
their idols of * and Ashtaroth and 1Sa 7:4
the * and Ashtaroth idols. 1Sa 12:10
and then began worshiping *. 1Ki 16:31
and an altar for * in Samaria. 1Ki 16:32
and have worshiped * instead. 1Ki 18:18
450 prophets of * and the 400 1Ki 18:19
But if * is God, then follow 1Ki 18:21
them, "but * has 450 prophets. 1Ki 18:22
The prophets of * may choose 1Ki 18:23
turned to the prophets of *. 1Ki 18:25
and they called to * all morning, 1Ki 18:26
shouting, "O *, hear us!" 1Ki 18:26
them to grab the prophets of *. 1Ki 18:40
the prophets of *, she sent this 1Ki 19:1
never bowed to * nor kissed him!" 1Ki 19:18
the 450 prophets of * were slain. 1Ki 22:6f
to * that his father had made. 2Ki 3:2
hardly worshiped * at all in 2Ki 10:17
and priests of *, and call together 2Ki 10:18,19
we worshipers of * are going to 2Ki 10:18,19
summoning those who worshiped *; 2Ki 10:20,21
of * from one end to the other. 2Ki 10:20,21
only those who worship * are here; 2Ki 10:23
As the priests of * began 2Ki 10:24
the worship of *, and burned it. 2Ki 10:26
every trace of * from Israel. 2Ki 10:28
to the temple of * and tore it 2Ki 11:18
of *, in front of the altar. 2Ki 11:18
* and the sun, moon, and stars. 2Ki 17:16
He built altars for * and made a 2Ki 21:3,4,5
in the worship of *, Asherah, and 2Ki 23:4
offered incense to * and to the 2Ki 23:5
some were as far away as *. 1Ch 4:32,33
his great-grandson was *. 1Ch 5:5
Zur, Kish, *, Nadab, Gedor, Ahio, 1Ch 8:30,31,32
Abdon (the oldest), Zur, Kish, *, 1Ch 9:35,36,37
to the temple of * and knocked it 2Ch 23:15,16,17
the priest of * before his altar. 2Ch 23:15,16,17
and worshiped the idols of *. 2Ch 28:2
altars of *, and of the 2Ch 33:3
as the altars of * were knocked 2Ch 34:4
the worshipers of * at Peor and Ps 106:28
prophets worshiped * and wasted Jer 2:8
lie, and worship * and all of those Jer 7:9
*, as their fathers told them to. Jer 9:14
to burn incense to *) are along Jer 11:13
incense to * that the Lord of Hosts Jer 11:17
God instead of * (whom they taught Jer 12:16
They have built high altars to * Jer 19:5
they prophesied by * and led my Jer 23:13
who turned away to the idols of *. Jer 23:27
offer incense to *, and to pour out Jer 32:29
to * in the Valley of Hinnom. Jer 32:35
she used in worshiping *, her god! Hos 1:8
that she burned to * her idol and Hos 1:13
Literally, "my *," meaning "my Hos 1:16f
to * and burning incense to idols. Hos 11:2
but he worshiped * and sealed his Hos 13:1
remnant of those who worship *; Zep 1:4

BAAL-BERITH
to worship the idols Baal and *. Ju 8:33

BAAL-BERITH Con't)
of the idol *, which he used to Ju 9:4
the fort next to the temple of *. Ju 9:46

AAL-GAD
near Seir, to * in the valley of Jos 11:17
(This land which lay between * in Jos 12:7
mountain area from * beneath Mount Jos 13:2-7

AAL-HAMON
Solomon had a vineyard at * Sol 8:11

AAL-HANAN
Succeeded by: King * (son of Gen 36:31-39
When Shaul died, * the son of 1Ch 1:49
When * died, Hadad became king 1Ch 1:50
and storage. * from Gedera was 1Ch 27:28

AAL-HAZOR
being sheared at * in Ephraim, 2Sa 13:21-24

AAL-HERMON
from * to the entrance of Hamath. Ju 3:1
to *, Senir, and Mount Hermon. 1Ch 5:23

AAL-JUDAH
and led them to * to bring home the 2Sa 6:1

AAL-MEON
*, Sibmah. Num 32:37,38
far distant as Mount Nebo and *. 1Ch 5:7,8
* and Kiriathaim. Eze 25:9,10

AAL-PEOR
Lord did to you at *, where he Deu 4:3
But then you deserted me for *, Hos 9:10
*, the god of Peor, a city of Hos 9:10f

AAL-PERAZIM
with them at *, and defeated them. 2Sa 5:20
So he attacked them at * and 1Ch 14:11
has been known as * ever since 1Ch 14:11

BAAL-SHALISHAH
One day a man from * brought 2Ki 4:42

BAAL-TAMAR
of Israel reached *, it turned and Ju 20:33

BAAL-WORSHIP
Gilgal, the town where * Hos 9:15f

BAAL-ZEBUB
temple of the god * at Ekron to ask 2Ki 1:2
Is that why you are going to *, 2Ki 1:3
questions of *, the god of Ekron. 2Ki 1:6
send messengers to *, the god of 2Ki 1:16

BAAL-ZEPHON
the sea, opposite *, and to camp Ex 14:2
near Piha-hiroth, across from *. Ex 14:9
Pihahiroth (near *, where they Num 33:7

BAAL'S
Any of * worshipers who don't 2Ki 10:18,19
* son was Beerah. 1Ch 5:6

BAALAH
to circle around * (which is Jos 15:9
circled west of * to Mount Seir, Jos 15:10,11
south of Shikkeron and Mount *. Jos 15:10,11
Biziothiah, *, Iim, Ezem, Eltolad, Jos 15:21-32
and all Israel went to * (i.e. 1Ch 13:6

BAALAM
been removed to the temple of *. 2Ch 24:7,8

BAALATH
Gibbethon, *, Jehud, Bene-berak, Jos 19:41-46
*, and Tamar, a desert city. 1Ki 9:17,18
He also built * and other supply 2Ch 8:6

BAALATH-BEER
The cities as far south as * Jos 19:8

BAALIS
warn Gedaliah that *, king of the Jer 40:13,14

BAANA
* (son of Ahilud), whose area was 1Ki 4:8-19
* (son of Hushai), whose areas 1Ki 4:8-19
Meshezabel) and Zadok (son of *). Neh 3:4
Har *. Neh 10:14-27

BAANAH
to two brothers, * and Rechab, who 2Sa 4:2,3
Rechab and * arrived at King 2Sa 4:5
Heleb (son of *) from Netophah; 2Sa 23:24-39
Heled (son of *) from Netophah; 1Ch 11:26-47
Rehum, *. Ez 2:2
Bigvai, Nehum, *. Neh 7:7

BAARA
Hushim and *, but he had children 1Ch 8:8,9,10

BAASHA
Asa of Judah and King * of Israel. 1Ki 15:16
King * built the fortress city 1Ki 15:17
alliance with King * of Israel so 1Ki 15:19
When * received word of the 1Ki 15:21
Then * (the son of Ahijah, from 1Ki 15:27
of Gibbethon. So * replaced Nadab 1Ki 15:28
Asa of Judah and King * of Israel. 1Ki 15:32,33
Baasha of Israel. * reigned for 1Ki 15:32,33
delivered to King * at this time by 1Ki 16:1
The message was sent to * and his 1Ki 16:4-7
the descendants of * was in line 1Ki 16:12
the family of King *, for you have 1Ki 21:22
Nebat) and of * (son of Ahijah). 2Ki 9:9
Asa's reign, King * of Israel 2Ch 16:1
alliance with King * of Israel, so 2Ch 16:3
As soon as King * of Israel 2Ch 16:5
himself against *, king of Israel. Jer 41:9

BAASHA'S
Further details of * reign are 1Ki 15:31

The rest of * biography—his deeds 1Ki 16:4-7
Elah, * son, began reigning 1Ki 16:8

BABEL
empire included *, Erech, Accad, Gen 10:10
city was called * (meaning Gen 11:9

BABIES
women have their * so quickly that Ex 1:19
them along like * until we get to Num 11:12
including the women and *. Deu 2:33,34
nation—men, women, *, little 1Sa 15:3
children, and *, and also all the 1Sa 22:19
men, dash their * against the 2Ki 8:12
man who takes your * and smashes Ps 137:9
Israel's kings will be like *, Is 3:4
like the cows. * will crawl safely Is 11:8
Babylon or the * or the children. Is 13:18
No longer will * die when only a Is 65:20
Judah, not even the * in arms. Jer 44:7
little children and tiny * are Lam 2:11
heedless of their *' cries. Lam 4:3,4
of water left. * cry for bread but Lam 4:3,4
invading army, her * dashed to Hos 13:16
the children, and even the *. Joe 2:16
off as slaves; her * were dashed to Nah 3:10
For they say, 'Even little * Mt 21:16
and to those with * in those days. Mt 24:19
Literally, "*." Lk 10:21f
their * to him to touch and bless. Lk 18:15
those days, and those with tiny *. Lk 21:23
were still just * in the Christian 1Co 3:1
are still *, wanting your own way? 1Co 3:3
Be innocent * when it comes to 1Co 14:20
You are like * who can drink only Heb 5:12,13

BABY
him with a * son named Enoch; Gen 4:17
To Adah was born a * named Gen 4:20
Yes, you are pregnant and your * Gen 16:9-12
And Sarah, to have a * at 90?" Gen 17:17
the time when she could have a *. Gen 18:11
"A woman my age have a *?" Gen 18:12
an old woman like me have a *?' Gen 18:13
The older girl's * was named Gen 19:37
The name of the younger girl's * Gen 19:38
and gave Abraham a * son in his old Gen 21:1
that I would ever have a *? Gen 21:7
to prevent her from having a * Gen 38:9
hand and the other * was actually Gen 38:29
Then, soon afterwards, the * Gen 38:30
command and let the * boys live?" Ex 1:18
and a * son was born to them. Ex 2:1
beautiful *, she hid him at home Ex 2:1
with tar, put the * in it, and laid Ex 2:3
When she opened it, there was a *! Ex 2:6
women to nurse the * for you?" Ex 2:7
They had a * named Gershom Ex 2:22
can also mean "kid"—a * goat. Ex 12:3,4f
in exchange for a lamb or * goat; Ex 13:13
"When a * boy is born, the Lev 12:2
"When a * girl is born, the Lev 12:5
whether her * is a boy or girl), Lev 12:6
and the new * she has borne, so Deu 28:56,57
The * nursing at the breast, Deu 32:25
'You are going to have a * boy!' Ju 13:7
kosher, for the * is going to be a Ju 13:7
raise the * after he is born?" Ju 13:12
comes true and the * is born," he Ju 13:17
Naomi took care of the *, and the Ru 4:16,17
in the process of time, a * boy 1Sa 1:19,20
"Wait until the * is weaned, and 1Sa 1:21,22
So she stayed home until the * was 1Sa 1:23
right and that the * was a boy. 1Sa 4:20
it in his arms like a * daughter. 2Sa 12:3
And the Lord made Bath-sheba's * 2Sa 12:15
Then, on the seventh day, the * 2Sa 12:18
"He was so broken up about the * 2Sa 12:18
"Is the * dead?" 2Sa 12:19
"While the * was still living, 2Sa 12:21
but now that the * is dead, you 2Sa 12:21
And the Lord loved the *, and 2Sa 12:24
David nicknamed the * Jedidiah 2Sa 12:25
two of us, and recently I had a *. 1Ki 3:17,18
old, this woman's * was born too. 1Ki 3:17,18
But her * died during the night 1Ki 3:19
I tried to feed my * it was dead! 1Ki 3:21
Then the king said, "Give the * 1Ki 3:27
little flocks of * goats in 1Ki 20:27
and had a * boy the following year, 2Ki 4:17
take a poor man's * as a pledge Job 24:9
little body of a * while it is yet Ecc 11:5
Woe to the * just being born who Is 45:10
anguish starts, the * is born; Is 66:7,8
and stood over where the * was." Mt 2:9f
Entering the house where the * Mt 2:11
to Egypt with the * and his Mt 2:13
with Mary and the *, and stayed Mt 2:14
them to kill every * boy two years Mt 2:16
up and take the * and his mother Mt 2:20
and have a * boy, and you are to Lk 1:31
angel, "But how can I have a *? Lk 1:34
so the * born to you will be Lk 1:35
voice, my * moved in me for joy! Lk 1:44
the * to be born—and it was a boy. Lk 1:57
When the * was eight days old, Lk 1:59
time came for her * to be born; Lk 2:6
You will find a * wrapped in a Lk 2:12
And there was the *, lying in the Lk 2:16
to present the * Jesus to the Lord Lk 2:27
came as a human *, born into King Rom 1:3
was also much too old to have a * Rom 4:19
For you are still only * 1Co 3:3
the birth of the slave-wife's *. Gal 4:23
But the * of the freeborn wife Gal 4:23
for more, as a * cries for milk. 1Pe 2:2,3f
cry for this as a * cries for his 1Pe 2:2,3
eat the * as soon as it was born. Rev 12:4

BABY-CHRISTIAN
He is still a *! Heb 5:12,13

BABY'S
When the * mother saw that he was Ex 2:1
river's edge. The * sister watched Ex 2:4
Then the * sister approached the Ex 2:7
instructed the * mother, "and I Ex 2:9
They all assumed the * name would Lk 1:59
So they asked the * father, Lk 1:62
Eight days later, at the * Lk 2:21

BABYLON
was discovered in the land of *, Gen 11:2
But areas of Ethiopia and * were Num 12:1f
robe imported from *, and some Jos 7:21
of people from *, Cuthah, Avva, 2Ki 17:24
from * how to worship the Lord. 2Ki 17:27,28
Those from * worshiped idols of 2Ki 17:30
These colonists from * worshiped 2Ki 17:41
of King Baladan of *) sent 2Ki 20:12
"From far away in *," Hezekiah 2Ki 20:14
this palace shall be carried to *. 2Ki 20:17
in the palace of the king of *." 2Ki 20:18
of * attacked Jerusalem. 2Ki 24:1
for the king of * occupied the 2Ki 24:7
* besieged the city of Jerusalem. 2Ki 24:10
was imprisoned in * during the 2Ki 24:12
and the queen mother, to *. 2Ki 24:15
Then the king of * appointed 2Ki 24:17
rebelled against the king of *. 2Ki 24:20
KING NEBUCHADNEZZAR of * 2Ki 25:1
sentenced before the king of *. 2Ki 25:6
with chains and taken away to *. 2Ki 25:7
at Jerusalem from * on July 22 of 2Ki 25:8
to the king of * were all taken as 2Ki 25:11
were all taken as exiles to *. 2Ki 25:11
and carried all the bronze to *. 2Ki 25:13
Temple guards to * as captives. 2Ki 25:18
to the king of * at Riblah, where 2Ki 25:20
that the king of * had appointed 2Ki 25:23
reign of King Evil-merodach of *. 2Ki 25:27
were being held as prisoners in *. 2Ki 25:28
Judah was exiled to * because the 1Ch 9:1
arrived from * to find out about 2Ch 32:31
chains and carted him away to *. 2Ch 33:11
Finally Nebuchadnezzar king of * 2Ch 36:6
took away the king in chains to *. 2Ch 36:6
them in his own temple in *. 2Ch 36:7
to * by King Nebuchadnezzar. 2Ch 36:10
were taken away to * at that time, 2Ch 36:10
the king of * against them and 2Ch 36:17
The Lord used the king of * to 2Ch 36:17
were taken away to * as slaves to 2Ch 36:20
the kingdom of Persia conquered *. 2Ch 36:20
had been deported to * by King Ez 2:1
to Jerusalem from * are rebuilding Ez 4:12
that King Cyrus of *, during the Ez 5:13
and had placed in the temple of *. Ez 5:14
royal library of * to discover Ez 5:17
who traveled from * to Jerusalem Ez 7:1
They left * in the middle of Ez 7:7,8,9
in all of the provinces of *. Ez 7:16
me from * during the reign of King Ez 8:1
by King Nebuchadnezzar of *. Neh 7:6
I had returned to * in the Neh 13:6
had been exiled to * along with Est 2:6
rivers of * thinking of Jerusalem. Ps 137:1
armies of * captured Jerusalem. Ps 137:7
they yelled. O *, evil beast, Ps 137:8
they march against * to destroy the Is 13:2
are his weapons against you, O *. Is 13:5
The armies of * will run until Is 13:14
the Medes against *, and no amount Is 13:17
* or the babies or the children. Is 13:18
And so *, the most glorious of Is 13:19
heaven; * will never rise again. Is 13:20
*, in Iraq, still lies in utter Is 13:20f
of * and say, "You bully, you! Is 14:4
I will make * into a desolate Is 14:23
THIS IS GOD'S message concerning * Is 21:1
part in the siege. * will fall, and Is 21:2
out, "* is fallen, is fallen; Is 21:8,9
and all the idols of * lie broken Is 21:8,9
SOON AFTERWARDS, THE king of * Is 39:1
the envoys from * on a tour of the Is 39:2
"From far away in *," Hezekiah Is 39:3
fathers—will be carried off to *. Is 39:6
in the palace of the king of *." Is 39:7

(BABYLON Con't)
army against *, that will walk in Is 43:14
God shall open the gates of * to Is 45:1
THE IDOLS OF *, Bel and Nebo, Is 46:1
O *, THE unconquered, come sit in Is 47:1
Sit in darkness and silence, O *; Is 47:5
them fall into your hands, O *. Is 47:6
Leave *, singing as you go; Is 48:20
and slavery. Put * and all it Is 52:11
from *. Jer 4:6f
to the king of *, says the Lord, Jer 20:4
as slaves to * and kill them. Jer 20:4
kings, shall be carried off to *. Jer 20:5
become slaves in * and die Jer 20:6
king of *, has declared war on us! Jer 21:1
* and the Chaldeans besieging you. Jer 21:3,4
Nebuchadnezzar of *, to slaughter Jer 21:7
* and he shall reduce it to ashes. Jer 21:10
king of *, and his mighty army. Jer 22:24,25
NEBUCHADNEZZAR, KING of *, Jer 24:1
and exiled him to * along with the Jer 24:1
represent the exiles sent to *. Jer 24:4,5
king of *, began his reign. Jer 25:1
king of * (I have appointed him as Jer 25:8,9
the king of * for seventy years. Jer 25:11
ended, I will punish the king of * Jer 25:12
the Great entered * in 539 B.C. Jer 25:12f
And finally, the king of * Jer 25:26
of *, who is my deputy. Jer 27:6
* and make him their slave. Jer 27:7
king of * will not enslave you. Jer 27:9
to the king of *, I will drive you Jer 27:10
to the king of * will be permitted Jer 27:11
to the king of *," he said. Jer 27:12
you the king of * will not conquer Jer 27:14
Temple will be returned from *. Jer 27:16
Surrender to the king of * and Jer 27:17
not be carried away with you to *! Jer 27:18
king of *, when he exiled all the Jer 27:19,20,21
and Jerusalem to *, along with Jer 27:19,20,21
be carried away to * and will stay Jer 27:22
of the king of * from your necks. Jer 28:2
carried off to *, and I will bring Jer 28:3
exiled to *, says the Lord. Jer 28:4
on your necks by the king of *." Jer 28:4
bring back from * the treasures of Jer 28:6
to King Nebuchadnezzar of *." Jer 28:11
to Nebuchadnezzar, king of *. Jer 28:14
been deported to * by Jer 29:1
when they went to * as King Jer 29:3
he has exiled to * from Jerusalem: Jer 29:4
for the peace and prosperity of *. Jer 29:7
Pray for her, for if * has peace, Jer 29:7
You will be in * for a lifetime. Jer 29:10
were not exiled to *, and on the Jer 29:16,17
Jewish captives over there in *. Jer 29:20
whom the king of * burned alive!" Jer 29:22
to us here in * saying that our Jer 29:28
all the exiles in * and tell them Jer 29:31
by the king of *, and that King Jer 32:3
of * for trial and sentencing. Jer 32:4
"He shall take you to * and Jer 32:5
and to Nebuchadnezzar, king of *; Jer 32:28
to the king of * through warfare, Jer 32:36
king of *, and all his armies from Jer 34:1
king of * and he shall burn it. Jer 34:2
before the king of * and he shall Jer 34:3
you and you shall be exiled to *. Jer 34:3
of the king of *, though he has Jer 34:21
king of *, arrived in this country, Jer 35:11
said the king of * would destroy Jer 36:29
NEBUCHADNEZZAR, KING OF *, did Jer 37:1
The Babylonians took Coniah to * Jer 37:1f
be defeated by the king of *!" Jer 37:17
that the king of * would not come? Jer 37:19
by the king of *— they went to the Jer 38:3
will surrender to *, you and your Jer 38:17
*, and this city will be burned." Jer 38:23
king of * who was at Riblah, in the Jer 39:5
The king of * made Zedekiah Jer 39:6
to send him away to * as a slave. Jer 39:7
who had defected to him to *. Jer 39:9
sent to *, but then released him. Jer 40:1
If you want to come with me to *, Jer 40:4
by the king of *, and stay with the Jer 40:5
that the king of * had appointed Jer 40:7
exiled everyone to *, they came to Jer 40:7
serve the king of *," he said, Jer 40:9
that the king of * had not taken Jer 40:11
Don't fear the king of * any Jer 42:11
or carried off to * as slaves." Jer 43:2,3
king of *, here to Egypt, for he is Jer 43:10
to Nebuchadnezzar, king of *." Jer 44:30
king of *, in the fourth year of Jer 46:2
king of *, to attack Egypt: Jer 46:13
king of *, and his army. Jer 46:26
king of *, for the Lord will send Jer 49:28
for Nebuchadnezzar, king of *, Jer 49:30
* This is the message Jer 50:1
the Lord against * and the Jer 50:1
Tell all the world that * will be Jer 50:2
But now, flee from *, the land of Jer 50:8
bring them against * to attack her, Jer 50:9
they do not miss! And * shall be Jer 50:10
anger of the Lord, * shall become Jer 50:13
Yes, prepare to fight with *, all Jer 50:14
king of *, crunched their bones. Jer 50:17
punish the king of * and his land Jer 50:18
Yes, march against *, the land of Jer 50:21
destruction. *, the mightiest Jer 50:23
* is desolate among the nations! Jer 50:23
the nations! O *, I have set a Jer 50:24
The terror that befalls * will be Jer 50:25
For the time has come for * to be Jer 50:27
a call for archers to come to *; Jer 50:29
in the cities of * that will burn Jer 50:32
As for the people of *—there is no Jer 50:34
It shall smite the people of * Jer 50:35
Therefore this city of * shall Jer 50:39
he will destroy * just as he Jer 50:40
and no one will live again in *. Jer 50:40
the shoreline. O *, they ride Jer 50:42
When the king of * received the Jer 50:43
*, the land of the Chaldeans. Jer 50:45
destroyer against *, against that Jer 51:1
down the bowmen of * and pierce her Jer 51:3
Flee from *! Jer 51:6
Babylon's sins. * has been as a Jer 51:7
But now, suddenly * too has Jer 51:8
to march on * and destroy her. Jer 51:11
Prepare your defenses, *! Jer 51:12
he has said he would concerning *. Jer 51:12
was used of God to conquer *. Jer 51:20f
before your eyes I will repay * Jer 51:24
*, destroyer of the earth! Jer 51:25
of the city of * was accomplished Jer 51:26f
nations to mobilize for war on *. Jer 51:27
* trembles and writhes in pain, Jer 51:29
stands unchanged. * will be left Jer 51:29
of Israel, says: * is like the Jer 51:33
The Jews in * say, Jer 51:34,35
king of *, has eaten and crushed us Jer 51:34,35
* be repaid for all she did to us! Jer 51:34,35
water supply, and * shall become a Jer 51:37
the men of * roar like lions. Jer 51:38
How * is fallen—great Babylon, Jer 51:41
How Babylon is fallen—great *, Jer 51:41
The sea has risen upon *; Jer 51:42
Bel, the god of *, and pull from Jer 51:44
the wall of * has fallen. Jer 51:44
O my people, flee from *; Jer 51:45
of * fight against each other. Jer 51:46
armies against *, says the Lord. Jer 51:48
Just as * killed the people of Jer 51:49
defiled by foreigners from *." Jer 51:51
the destruction of the idols of *. Jer 51:52
Though * be as powerful as Jer 51:53
of *, the land the Chaldeans rule! Jer 51:54
For the Lord is destroying *; Jer 51:55
and is giving * all her due. Jer 51:56
For the wide walls of * shall be Jer 51:58
and exile to * along with Jer 51:59
scheduled against *—all the words Jer 51:60
"When you get to *, read what I Jer 51:61,62
you will destroy * so that not a Jer 51:61,62
and say, 'So shall * sink, never Jer 51:64
the king of * until he and the Jer 52:3
were taken away as captives to *. Jer 52:3
king of *, came with all his army Jer 52:4
him to the king of * who was Jer 52:9
taken in chains to * and put in Jer 52:11
king of *, Nebuzaradan, captain of Jer 52:12
Then he took to *, as captives, Jer 52:15
stood, and carted them off to *. Jer 52:17
He took them to the king of * at Jer 52:26
captives taken to * in the seventh Jer 52:28
imprisonment in * of Jehoiachin, Jer 52:31
who became king of * that year, was Jer 52:31
the other kings in *, and gave him Jer 52:32
beside the Chebar Canal in *. Eze 1:1
to *, to the Jews in exile there. Eze 11:24
he was taken to *, Jeremiah 52:11. Eze 12:12f
to *, the land of the Chaldeans; Eze 12:13
he was taken to *, Jeremiah 52:11. Eze 12:13f
you as exiles in *, you will see Eze 14:22
*—and you still weren't satisfied. Eze 16:29
Nebuchadnezzar, king of * [the Eze 17:12,13
and brought them to *. Eze 17:12,13
rebelled against *, sending Eze 17:15
shall die in *, where the king Eze 17:16
when the king of * lays siege to Eze 17:17
will bring him to * and deal with Eze 17:20
brought him before the king of *. Eze 19:9
in returning to Israel from *. Eze 20:35,36f
for the king of * to follow—one to Eze 21:19,20
at the fork in the road from *. Eze 21:19,20
For the king of * stands at a Eze 21:21
mistake? For * is Judah's ally and Eze 21:23
But (the king of *) will think Eze 21:23
will save you from the king of *. Eze 21:29
the embassy from * (Isaiah 38–39), Eze 23:16f
king of * has attacked Jerusalem. Eze 24:2
* to tell you what has happened. Eze 24:
king of *—the king of kings from Eze 26
of * fought hard against Tyre. Eze 29:
king of *, and he will carrry off Eze 29:
king of *, will destroy the Eze 30:
* and place my sword in his hand. Eze 30:
before the king of * as one who has Eze 30:
of the king of *, while the arms of Eze 30:
of the king of *, and he swings it Eze 30:
A foreign army (from *)—the Eze 31:
the king of * shall come upon you. Eze 32:
When he returned to *, he took Dan 1:
to execute all the wise men of *. Dan 2:
of *, and said, "Don't kill them. Dan 2:
whole province of *, as well as Dan 2:4
the affairs of the province of *; Dan 2:4
of Dura, in the province of *; Dan 3:
there in the province of *. Dan 3:3
the wise men of * to tell me the Dan 4:
royal palace in *, and saying, Dan 4:2
reign, and brought to *. Dan 5:2,3,
Chaldeans and soothsayers of *. Dan 5:1
be sent far away into exile in *. Mic 4:1
living between * and the Persian Hab 1:
from * to rebuild Jerusalem. Hag 1:
of the north, from *,' says the Zec 2:6,
He replied, "To * Zec 5:1
* had, by the time of Zechariah, Zec 5:1
gold from the Jews exiled in *. Zec 6:10,1
at the time of the exile to *). Mt 1:1
into captivity far away beyond *.' Act 7:4
Literally, "She who is at * is 1Pe 5:1
chosen"; but * was the Christian 1Pe 5:1
church here in * salutes you, and 1Pe 5:1
skies, saying, "* is fal en, is Rev 14:
The great city of "*" split Rev 16:1
on her forehead: "* the Great, Rev 17:
He gave a mighty shout, "* the Rev 18:
out, "Alas, *, that mighty city! Rev 18:1
and shouted, "*, that great city, Rev 18:2

BABYLON'S
(son of Amoz) concerning * doom. Is 13:
the palaces. * days are numbered; Is 13:2
save Israel from * mighty power; Is 47:
him—put your neck under * yoke! Jer 27:
that will not submit to * king? Jer 27:1
The whole earth shall shake at * Jer 50:4
his vengeance on all of * sins. Jer 51:
believe its eyes at * fall! Jer 51:4
I will destroy you with * mighty Eze 32:1
to rule in Judah, * King Dan 1:
and so all of "*" sins were Rev 16:1

BABYLONIA
Located along the border of *. Gen 2:11,12
Temple and exile the people to *.' Ez 5:1
names of Egypt and *, Philistia and Ps 87:
Ethiopia, Elam, *, Hamath and all Is 11:1
In ancient * (and in many eastern Is 47:2
to put an end to the empire of *. Is 48:1
The kingdom of *, being revived in Jer 5:15
In southern *. Jer 50:21
In eastern *. Jer 50:21
Nebuchadnezzar of *. Eze 27:26
Egypt, Seleucus of *, Antigonus of Dan 8:8

BABYLONIAN
king's garden. The * troops 2Ki 25:4,
He then supervised the * army in 2Ki 25:1
be made in the * archives, where Ez 6:1
principal gods in the * pantheon. Is 46:1
The old * Empire lasted from Jer 5:15
on * soil as early as 3000 B.C. Jer 5:15
and killed Belshazzar, the last * Jer 25:12
after the * captivity (the rulers Jer 30:21
the palace, while the * army was Jer 32:2
At this time the * army was Jer 34:7
I will summon the * armies back Jer 34:22
of Jerusalem, the * army withdrew Jer 37:5
the entire * army until there was Jer 37:1
When the * army set out from Jer 37:11
* army and you will not escape." Jer 38:18
to the officers of the * army; Jer 38:21,22
officers of the * army came in and Jer 39:3
officials and * soldiers who were Jer 41:3
and appointed by the * emperor. Jer 41:18
come over to the * army, and the Jer 52:15
They were pictures of * military Eze 23:14,15
gave them * names, as Dan 1:7
put in charge of * affairs—who have Dan 3:12
reign over the * empire, Daniel had Dan 7:1
Tammuz-Adonis, a * god. Dan 11:37f

BABYLONIANS
The * carried home all the 2Ki 24:13
The * broke up the bronze pillars 2Ki 25:13
and submit to the *, they would be 2Ki 25:24
his court—both the Jews and the *. 2Ki 25:25
of what the * would do to them. 2Ki 25:26
to the * for seventy years. Ez 1:1f
the Persians, the *, the men of Ez 4:8,9
It will be the *, not the Is 23:13
The boasts of the * will turn to Is 43:14
walls, and the * shall conquer the Jer 32:24

BABYLONIANS Con't)
this city to the * and to Jer 32:28
And the * outside the walls Jer 32:29
now ravaged by the *, where men and Jer 32:43
enemy, yet the * will enter, and Jer 33:5
the city. The * took Coniah to Jer 37:1f
to Egypt! The * shall defeat them Jer 37:7
These * shall capture this city Jer 37:8
Don't fool yourselves that the * Jer 37:9
he was defecting to the *. Jer 37:13
to the * would live, and that the Jer 38:2
said, "for the * will hand me over Jer 38:19
to the *, and you will not escape. Jer 38:23
Jerusalem was retaken by the *. Jer 38:28
But the * chased the king and Jer 39:5
before the * arrived, while he was Jer 39:15
be safe to surrender to the *. Jer 40:9
for you with the * who will come Jer 40:10
afraid of what the * would do when Jer 41:18
be killed by the * or carried off Jer 43:2,3
The * dismantled the two large Jer 52:17
For the * will come, and all the Eze 23:23
when the combined armies of the * Nah 2:1f

BACK
a raven that flew * and forth Gen 8:7
and drew the dove * into the boat. Gen 8:9
and this time she didn't come *. Gen 8:12
me * my people who were captured; Gen 14:21
Then Abraham ran * to the tent Gen 18:6
"Stand *," they yelled. Gen 19:9
"And don't look *. Gen 19:17
But Lot's wife looked * as she Gen 19:26
"That is why I held you * from Gen 20:6
worship, and then come right *." Gen 22:5
family, and to bring * a girl Gen 24:38
said, "Send me * to my master!" Gen 24:54
I want to report * to my master." Gen 24:56
bring you * safely to this land; Gen 28:15
and will bring me * safely to my Gen 28:21
and I will give you * a tenth of Gen 28:22
stone was rolled * over the mouth Gen 29:3
so they can get * to grazing?" Gen 29:7
to Laban, "I want to go * home. Gen 30:25
thing, I'll go * to work for you. Gen 30:31,32
I'll give it * without question." Gen 31:32
So Esau started * to Seir that Gen 33:16
the young goat * to her, and to Gen 38:20
of the town to go * again." Gen 38:23
but he drew * his hand and the Gen 38:29
He has held * nothing from me Gen 39:9
you * your job as his wine taster. Gen 40:13
on me when you are * in his favor, Gen 40:14
your youngest brother * to me. Gen 42:20
your youngest brother * to me. Gen 42:34
I will give you * your brother and Gen 42:34
didn't come *, Simeon is gone, and Gen 42:36
I don't bring Benjamin * to you. Gen 42:37
'Don't ever come * again unless Gen 43:3,4,5
If I don't bring him * to you, Gen 43:9
that you can pay * what was in the Gen 43:12
we have brought it * again, Gen 43:21
time bantering * and forth, and the Gen 43:34
Didn't we bring * the money we Gen 44:8
But you told us, 'Don't come * Gen 44:23
And when he said, 'Go * again Gen 44:25
And now, sir, if I go * to my Gen 44:30
I don't bring him * to you, I shall Gen 44:32
bring your descendants * again; Gen 46:3,4
his sons, he lay * in the bed, Gen 49:33
to take his body * to the land of Gen 50:5
"Now Joseph will pay us * for all Gen 50:15
Egypt and take you * to the land he Gen 50:24
take his body * with them when they Gen 50:25
she brought him * to the princess Ex 2:10
* into the land of Canaan Ex 2:24
* to Egypt and visit my relatives. Ex 4:18
"When you arrive * in Egypt you Ex 4:21
their work? Get * to your jobs!" Ex 5:4,5
Get * to work. Ex 5:18
Then Moses went * to the Lord. Ex 5:22
told him, "Go * again to Pharaoh Ex 6:11
Lord said, "go * to Pharaoh in the Ex 7:15
has sent me * to demand that you Ex 7:16
"GO * TO Pharaoh," the Lord Ex 9:1
to Moses, "Go * again and make Ex 10:1
So Moses and Aaron were brought * Ex 10:8
may be purchased * from the Lord in Ex 13:13
However, you must buy * your Ex 13:13
eldest sons are always bought *.' Ex 13:15
waters will come * over the Ex 14:26
"Oh, that we were * in Egypt," Ex 16:3
But the Lord told Moses, "Go * Ex 19:21
and bring Aaron * with you, and Ex 19:24
shall let her be bought * again; Ex 21:8
must let him have it * at night. Ex 22:26
you must take it * to its owner. Ex 23:4
and wait for us until we come *; Ex 24:14
down from the * of the tent, and a Ex 26:12
and *, joined at the shoulders. Ex 28:7
WHEN MOSES DIDN'T come * down Ex 32:1
Turn * from your fierce wrath. Ex 32:12
your swords and go * and forth from Ex 32:27
shall see my *, but not my face." Ex 33:23
realize as he came * down the Ex 34:29
blood * and forth upon the altar. Lev 1:11
* and forth upon the altar. Lev 7:2
blood * and forth upon the altar. Lev 8:19
* and forth upon the altar. Lev 8:24
Moses then took it all * from Lev 8:28
it * and forth upon the altar; Lev 9:12
it * and forth upon the altar. Lev 9:18
he must come * to the priest again, Lev 13:7
it can be put * into service after Lev 13:58
and then come * into the camp. Lev 16:26
or has a humped *, or is a dwarf, Lev 21:20
may always buy it * at a price Lev 25:27
If anyone wants to buy * this Lev 27:31
Lord, and may not be bought *!" Lev 27:33
then wave it all * and forth before Num 6:20
after that she can come * again." Num 12:14
* in before they traveled again. Num 12:15
Don't be afraid, and bring * some Num 13:20
a leader to take us * to Egypt!" Num 14:4
you must turn * into the wilderness Num 14:25
This loaf must be waved * and Num 15:19,20,21
So all the people stood * from Num 16:27
or goats may not be bought *; Num 18:17
Israel turned * and journeyed from Num 20:21,22
Balaam beat her * onto the road. Num 22:22,23
I will go * home if you don't Num 22:34
Get out of here! Go * home! Num 24:11
you may come * into the camp." Num 31:24
"The Lord made us wander * and Num 32:13
now and go on * across the desert Deu 1:40
"THEN WE TURNED * across the Deu 2:1
"In all history, going * to the Deu 4:32
Then you come * and stand here Deu 5:31
* to your homes the next morning. Deu 16:7
take it * to its owner. Deu 22:1
Take it * to him at sundown so Deu 24:12,13
the field, don't go * after it. Deu 24:19
Then the Lord will send you * to Deu 28:68
you and bring you * again to the Deu 30:4
as though held * by a dam, and will Jos 3:13,14
had traveled * and forth across the Jos 5:6
city, they went * and finished off Jos 8:24
Don't let them get * to their Jos 10:19
Then they turned * to Debir, Jos 10:38
On the way *, Joshua captured Jos 11:10
and bring * a report of its size Jos 18:4
to bring * their report to Joshua. Jos 18:8
their relatives * home—their booty Jos 22:7,8
ambassadors went * to the people of Jos 22:32
you if you go * on your word." Jos 24:27
"Now God has paid me *." Ju 1:7
the people * to God, was Deborah, a Ju 4:4
from getting * in, while his other Ju 9:44
and carried it * to the town where, Ju 9:49
"Give us * our land peaceably," Ju 11:13
the Lord and I cannot take it *." Ju 11:35
man from God come * to us again and Ju 13:8
Manoah ran * with his wife and Ju 13:11
his wife and went * home to live Ju 14:19
them * for what they did to me." Ju 15:11
so that I may pay * the Philistines Ju 16:28
they brought him * home and buried Ju 16:31
him to handle, he turned * home. Ju 18:26
see her to try to win her * again. Ju 19:3
the donkey's * and took her home. Ju 19:28
* to her people and to her gods; Ru 1:15
* on me and sent such calamity!" Ru 1:21
of Moab who came * with Naomi. Ru 2:6
And when she went * to work Ru 2:15
She carried it * into the city Ru 2:18
"he said to come * and stay close Ru 2:21
and laid it on her *. Ru 3:15-18
Naomi, who came * to us from Moab. Ru 4:3
I will give him * to you, and he'll 1Sa 1:11
and went happily *, and began to 1Sa 1:18
"Go on * to bed." 1Sa 3:4,5
"Go on * to bed." 1Sa 3:6
So Samuel went * to bed. 1Sa 3:9
to send the Ark * to its own 1Sa 5:11
"Yes, send it * with a gift," 1Sa 6:3
had brought * the Ark of the Lord. 1Sa 6:21
Then he would come * to Ramah, 1Sa 7:17
He has just arrived * from a trip 1Sa 9:12,13
So he sent the messengers * to 1Sa 11:9
turn your * on him in any way. 1Sa 12:20
Philistines fell * as Jonathan and 1Sa 14:13
Then Saul called * the army, and 1Sa 14:46
to hold him *, and tore his robe. 1Sa 15:27
He went * and forth to Bethlehem 1Sa 17:14,15
and bring us * a letter 1Sa 17:18
When Saul's men reported this * 1Sa 18:24
send a lad to bring the arrows *. 1Sa 20:21
arrows and ran * to his master. 1Sa 20:38
him to take them * to the city. 1Sa 20:40
and then come * and give me a more 1Sa 23:23
The Lord placed you at my mercy * 1Sa 24:9,10
Saul called *, "Is it really you, 1Sa 24:15
and his men went * to their cave. 1Sa 24:22
God has paid * Nabal and kept me 1Sa 25:39
and followed the men * to David. 1Sa 25:42
NOW THE MEN from Ziph came * to 1Sa 26:1
done wrong. Come * home, my son, 1Sa 26:21
disturbed me by bringing me *?" 1Sa 28:15
your strength for the trip *." 1Sa 28:22
"Send them *!" 1Sa 29:4
upset them, but go * quietly." 1Sa 29:7
So David headed * into the land 1Sa 29:11
We were on our way * from 1Sa 30:14
kill me or give me * to my master, 1Sa 30:15
David got * everything they had 1Sa 30:18,19
Lord, "Shall I move * to Judah?" 2Sa 2:1
"Yes," he called *, "it is." 2Sa 2:20
his body and came out his *. 2Sa 2:23
Joab shouted *, "I swear by God 2Sa 2:27
"Give me * my wife Michal, for I 2Sa 3:14
"When I get * I will call a 2Sa 3:21
with Abner and tell him to come *. 2Sa 3:26
So Nathan went * to David and 2Sa 7:17
He also carried * to Jerusalem a 2Sa 8:8
pull * and leave him there to die! 2Sa 11:15
as we chased them * to the city 2Sa 11:23
Can I bring him * again? 2Sa 12:23
loot were carried * to Jerusalem, 2Sa 12:29,30
* to bed and pretend you are sick; 2Sa 13:5
As they were on the way * to 2Sa 13:29,30
bring your son * from his exile. 2Sa 14:14
provision to bring * those he 2Sa 14:14f
right, go and bring * Absalom." 2Sa 14:21
brought Absalom * to Jerusalem. 2Sa 14:23
why he brought me * from Geshur if 2Sa 14:32
he would bring me * to Jerusalem, I 2Sa 15:7,8
Go on * with your men to 2Sa 15:19,20
Go on * and take your troops with 2Sa 15:19,20
took the Ark * into the city. 2Sa 15:25,26
"he will bring me * to see the Ark 2Sa 15:25,26
* into the city and stayed there. 2Sa 15:29
Today I will get * the kingdom of 2Sa 16:3
"The Lord is paying you * for 2Sa 16:7,8
were beaten * by David's men. 2Sa 18:7
The entire army crept * into the 2Sa 19:3
about bringing the king *?" 2Sa 19:8,9,10
* all those who are with you." 2Sa 19:14
So the king started * to 2Sa 19:15
"I am content just to have you * 2Sa 19:30
him * to be our king again." 2Sa 19:43
The argument continued * and 2Sa 19:43
days and to report * at that time. 2Sa 20:4
called his troops * from the 2Sa 20:22
with David, held * the Philistines 2Sa 23:9
and beat * the Philistines; 2Sa 23:11,12
So she came * in and stood before 1Ki 1:28
When you bring him * here, 1Ki 1:35
"Go * to your home in Anathoth. 1Ki 2:26
he took them * to Jerusalem. 1Ki 2:40
And so they argued * and forth 1Ki 3:22
was hinged to fold * upon itself. 1Ki 6:34
Bring them * again to this land 1Ki 8:33,34
They used to run * and forth from 1Ki 9:27,28
It had six steps and a rounded * 1Ki 10:19
even so, I'd like to go * home." 1Ki 11:22
Here is the story * of his 1Ki 11:27,28
"Come * then for my answer." 1Ki 12:5
he couldn't pull it * again! 1Ki 13:4
So he went * another way. 1Ki 13:10
So they went * together, and the 1Ki 13:19
donkey and took it * to the city to 1Ki 13:29
shields * to the guard chamber. 1Ki 14:28
have brought them * to yourself." 1Ki 18:37
Then the Lord told him, "Go * by 1Ki 19:15
Elijah replied, "Go on *! 1Ki 19:20
So Ahab went * to the palace 1Ki 21:4
they turned *! 1Ki 22:32,33
and King Ahab went * in, propped up 1Ki 22:35
told us to go * to the king and 2Ki 1:6
So the army of Israel turned * in 2Ki 3:27
the creditor was demanding it *. 2Ki 4:1
"Call her * again," Elisha told 2Ki 4:15,16
to the prophet and come right *." 2Ki 4:22
down and walked * and forth in the 2Ki 4:35
and came * with some wild gourds. 2Ki 4:39
party went * to find the prophet; 2Ki 5:15
of earth to take * with me, for 2Ki 5:17
servants to carry * with Gehazi. 2Ki 5:23
the servants and sent the men *. 2Ki 5:24
And the report came *, "Elisha is 2Ki 6:13
starve if we go * into the city; 2Ki 7:4
come on, let's go * and tell the 2Ki 7:9
So they went * to the city and 2Ki 7:10
son he had brought * to life, 2Ki 8:1
getting * her house and land. 2Ki 8:3
brought a little boy * to life. 2Ki 8:5
one Elisha brought * to life!" 2Ki 8:5
When Hazael went *, the king 2Ki 8:14
Jehu went * to his friends and 2Ki 9:11
or foe," King Joram shouted *. 2Ki 9:17
the city settled * into quietness 2Ki 11:20
sketch and sent it * to Uriah the 2Ki 16:10
* this message to King Hezekiah: 2Ki 19:9
* on the road by which you came. 2Ki 19:28

(BACK Con't)
"Go * to Hezekiah, the leader of 2Ki 20:5
and turned his * on the Lord God 2Ki 21:22
He brought * to Jerusalem the 2Ki 23:8
But the Lord still did not hold * 2Ki 23:26
His officers took his body * in 2Ki 23:30
his genealogy was traced * 1Ch 6:33-38
genealogy was traced * through: 1Ch 6:39-43
Merari's ancestry was traced * 1Ch 6:44-47
Shallum's ancestry went * 1Ch 9:19
When the Philistines went * the 1Ch 10:8
and brought * his body and the 1Ch 10:12
and brought them safely * again. 1Ch 11:2
well, and brought it * to David. 1Ch 11:18,19
they sent them *, for they were 1Ch 12:19
And let us bring * the Ark of 1Ch 13:3
in Judah to bring * the Ark of the 1Ch 13:6
Bring us safely * from among the 1Ch 16:35
then he sent them * to David in 1Ch 19:4
put * his sword into its sheath; 1Ch 21:27
* to Jerusalem to rule Israel. 2Ch 1:13
sins and give them * this land you 2Ch 6:25
Ophir and brought * $13,000,000 2Ch 8:17,18
Hiram, to bring * gold, silver, 2Ch 9:21
He brought * into the Temple the 2Ch 15:18
of the Lord search * and forth 2Ch 16:9
"Arrest this man and take him * 2Ch 18:25
and King Ahab went * in, propped up 2Ch 18:34
the chest * to the Temple again. 2Ch 24:11
to bring them * to the Lord, but 2Ch 24:19
they are doing and pay them *." 2Ch 24:22
nation and sending * great 2Ch 24:23
And they brought him * on horses 2Ch 25:28
and took them * to their families 2Ch 28:15
Then they went * to the palace 2Ch 29:18
"Come * to the Lord God of 2Ch 30:6
So they brought * to the king 2Ch 34:28
need to carry it * and forth upon 2Ch 35:3
But Josiah refused to turn *. 2Ch 35:22
him * to Jerusalem where he died. 2Ch 35:24,25
to take * to Jerusalem. Ez 1:11
shall be taken * to Jerusalem and Ez 6:5
and to send * a report of the Ez 7:14
I will bring you * to Jerusalem. Neh 1:9
May their scoffing fall * upon Neh 4:4
them right * into slavery again. Neh 5:8
by sending * this message to them: Neh 6:3
many letters went * and forth Neh 6:17
they came * to Jerusalem. Neh 7:73
take them * into slavery in Egypt! Neh 9:17
to go * again to Jerusalem). Neh 13:6
When I arrived * in Jerusalem Neh 13:7
and I brought * the Temple bowls, Neh 13:9
Then I called all the Levites * Neh 13:11
Esther told Hathach to go * and Est 4:10
he had taken * from Haman—and gave Est 8:2
change me * again to dust so soon? Job 10:9
But you, O God, have kept them * Job 17:3,4
on ropes, swinging * and forth. Job 28:3,4
are old, so I held * and did not Job 32:6
for man— brings * his soul from Job 33:30
Turn * from evil, for it was to Job 36:21
"Can you hold * the stars? Job 38:31
God will turn them * in shame. Ps 6:10
if I were paying * evil for good Ps 7:4
My enemies will fall * and perish Ps 9:3
Lord, snatch me * from the jaws Ps 9:13
Push them *! Ps 17:13,14
by turning * from following him. Ps 18:21
holding myself * from doing wrong. Ps 18:23
turn * until all were conquered. Ps 18:37
He is the God who pays * those Ps 18:47
oceans * to let dry land appear. Ps 24:2
pay them * for all their evil Ps 28:4
You brought me * from the brink Ps 30:3
Turn them * and confuse them. Ps 35:4
no fear of God to hold them *. Ps 36:1
borrow and "cannot pay it *"! Ps 37:21
Don't sit *, unmindful of my Ps 39:12
O Lord, don't hold * your tender Ps 40:11
me well again so I can pay them *! Ps 41:10
me, give me * my joy again. Ps 51:8
Let these evil men slink * at Ps 59:14,15
Literally, "I will bring * from Ps 68:22f
But you will bring me * to life Ps 71:20
Why hold * your power? Ps 74:11
Many and many a time he held * Ps 78:38
They turned * from entering the Ps 78:57
* and sent them to eternal shame. Ps 78:66
Come *, we beg of you, O God of Ps 80:14
Literally, "brought * the Ps 85:1f
Now bring us * to loving you, Ps 85:4
I will not take * one word of Ps 89:34
You speak, and man turns * to Ps 90:3
At dawn they slink * into their Ps 104:22
He brought the exiles * from the Ps 107:3
Why were they held *? Ps 114:5
and let me slip * into sin again. Ps 119:8
they would hold me * from sin. Ps 119:11
around and came running * to you. Ps 119:59,60
oh, give me * my life again, just Ps 119:107

Yes, rescue me and give me * my Ps 119:154
oh, give me * my life again. Ps 119:156
Now give me * my life and health Ps 119:159
WHEN JEHOVAH BROUGHT * his Ps 126:1
Though my * is cut to ribbons Ps 129:3,4
And surely you will never go * on Ps 132:11
and bringing * the exiles. Ps 147:2
and join us"—turn your * on them! Pro 1:10
your * on me, spurning my advice. Pro 1:30
the Lord, and turn your * on evil; Pro 3:7,8
Don't sidetrack; pull * your Pro 4:27
in his house to pay it *. Pro 6:31
Let her hold you * from visiting Pro 7:5
lashes on the * of a rebel. Pro 17:10
It is harder to win * the Pro 18:19
and have to take * your words of Pro 23:6,7,8
don't stand * and let them die. Pro 24:11,12
Don't say, "Now I can pay him * Pro 24:28,29
than to be sent * to the end of the Pro 25:6,7
and a rebel with a rod to his *! Pro 26:3
and it will roll * and crush you. Pro 26:27
Who else but God goes * and Pro 30:4
* and forth, getting nowhere. Ecc 1:3-7
remember what we have done * here. Ecc 1:8-11
one can bring them * to life to Ecc 3:22
The man who speculates is soon * Ecc 5:15
not need to look * with sorrow on Ecc 5:19,20
No one can hold * his spirit from Ecc 8:8
and the * is inlaid with these Sol 3:10
myrrh as I pulled * the bolt. Sol 5:5
to be * among my own people." Sol 6:12
of Shulam. Come *, come back, that Sol 6:13
Come back, come *, that we may Sol 6:13
Lord will bring * a remnant of his Is 11:11
exhausted, fleeing * to their own Is 13:14
He will bring them * to settle Is 14:1
will move freely * and forth Is 19:23
city will come * to life again; Is 23:15,16
and brought * to Jerusalem to Is 27:13
travelers detour on * roads. Is 33:8
by fraud, who hold * their hands Is 33:15
Your mind will think * to this Is 33:18
secretary, went * to Hezekiah with Is 36:22
he sent messengers * to Jerusalem Is 37:8,9
mouth and led you * to your own Is 37:29
I have called you * from the Is 41:9
sons and daughters * to Israel from Is 43:6
Bring them * to me—blind as they Is 43:8
I will never go * on my word, for Is 45:23
* my anger and not wipe you out. Is 48:9
your little sons * to you in their Is 49:22
I give my * to the whip, and my Is 50:6
now I can take you * again and Is 52:3
For the Lord has called you * Is 54:6
For the Lord God who brings * Is 56:8
I will pay them * in full. Is 65:7
And they shall bring * all your Is 66:20
and shrink * in horror and dismay. Jer 2:12
is not to take her * again, for she Jer 3:1
but she didn't come *. Jer 3:7
O my rebellious children, come * Jer 3:22
Should I sit * and act as though Jer 5:29
—only to go right * to all these Jer 7:10
mistake, he goes * to the fork Jer 8:4,5
why he was holding * the rain: Jer 14:1
* to me from all their evil ways. Jer 15:7
You will look * no longer to the Jer 16:14,15
Yes, I will bring you * again, Jer 16:14,15
of good; turn * from your evil Jer 18:11
I will turn my * on them and refuse Jer 18:17
Jeremiah replied, "Go * to King Jer 21:3,4
they took * to Egypt with them. Jer 22:13f
and bring them * into their own Jer 23:3
brought the Jews * to their own Jer 23:8
of turning them * from their sins. Jer 23:14
I will bring them * here again. Jer 24:6
"The decision is right; for * in Jer 26:18
and the Lord held * the terrible Jer 26:19
and brought him * to King Jer 26:23
Then I will bring them all * to Jer 27:22
Within two years I will bring * Jer 28:3
and I will bring * King Jeconiah, Jer 28:4
you say and bring * from Babylon Jer 28:6
you * home again to your own land. Jer 29:14
I will give you * your health Jer 30:17
will gather them * together again Jer 31:10
they will come * to you from the Jer 31:16
road signs pointing * to Israel. Jer 31:21
When I bring them * again they Jer 31:23
bring my people * again from all Jer 32:37
I will bring them * to this very Jer 32:37
Babylonian armies * again and they Jer 34:22
tell you to turn * from your wicked Jer 35:15
Begin with the first message * in Jer 36:2
you, don't send me * to that Jer 37:20
me not to send you * to the dungeon Jer 38:26
the two walls * of the palace Jer 39:4
to take him * to his home. Jer 39:14
turn * from their wicked ways; Jer 44:5
who refuse to go *—who insist on Jer 44:28
again? Go * into your scabbard; Jer 47:6

Then Israel shall come and take * Jer 49:2
bring the people *, says the Lord. Jer 49:39
to Zion and start * home again. Jer 50:5
remember how to get * to the fold. Jer 50:6
Let them rush * to their own Jer 50:16
they will escape * to their own Jer 50:28
in my path and turned me *. Lam 1:13
They have not tried to hold you * Lam 2:14
Turn us around and bring us * to Lam 5:21
Give us * the joys we used to Lam 5:21
of an eagle at the * of his head! Eze 1:10
out from the middle of his *. Eze 1:11
case, reported * and said, "I have Eze 9:11
I will gather you * from the Eze 11:17
of God carried me * again to Eze 11:24
can carry on your * and leave your Eze 12:3
couldn't keep them * from harm. Eze 20:9,10
they would draw * in horror, and Eze 20:26
when I bring you * from exile, and Eze 20:41
Then you will look * at all your Eze 20:43
For I will gather them * again Eze 28:25
bring her people * to the land of Eze 29:14
"the great waters were held *." Eze 31:15f
if he gives * the borrower's Eze 33:15
certainly be able to get it *!' Eze 33:24
are whispering behind your *. Eze 33:30
And I will bring them * from Eze 34:13
where they were, * home to their Eze 34:13
says, I will pay * your angry deeds Eze 35:11
I am bringing you * again, but not Eze 36:22
For I will bring you * home Eze 36:24
But when I bring you * they will Eze 36:35
out of the Temple, * into the inner Eze 42:1
were set * from the ground floor. Eze 42:6
THEN THE LORD brought me * to the Eze 44:1
and then return * to the entrance, Eze 46:2
THEN HE BROUGHT me * to the door Eze 47:1
then led me * along the bank. Eze 47:6
youths brought * as captives—young Dan 1:3,4
your * wet with dew from heaven. Dan 4:25
get your kingdom * again, when you Dan 4:26
My counselors and officers came * Dan 4:36
They rushed * to the king and Dan 6:12
but on its * it had wings like Dan 7:6
and send us * to our own land Dan 9:3
way *, past the prince of Persia; Dan 10:20,21
he will carry * their idols with Dan 11:8
But now I will take * the wine Hos 1:9
There I will give * her Hos 1:15
and bring her * to you and love Hos 3:1
So I bought her [* from her Hos 3:2
Oh, come * to God. Hos 12:6
I will turn them * into the Joe 2:20
And I will give you * the crops Joe 2:25
Beware, for I will strike * Joe 3:4
But I will bring them * again Joe 3:7
you * for all that you have done. Joe 3:7
Syrians should go * to Kir as Amo 1:5f
that they must go * to Egypt as Amo 1:5f
I ruined your crops by holding * Amo 4:7
only ten will come * alive." Amo 5:3
yes, drink and stagger * and Ob 1:16
and will hold * his fierce anger Jon 3:9
of captivity, * to your own land. Mic 2:13
that he will bring * his punished Mic 4:6
* to you again, just as before. Mic 4:8
she cannot hold them *. Nah 2:8
Never again will you bring * Nah 2:13
All who see you will shrink * Nah 3:7
That is why I am holding * the Hag 1:10
but I will bring you * again. Zec 2:6,7
and he pushed her * into the basket Zec 5:8
be off, to patrol * and forth Zec 6:7
sins behind, and coming * to me? Zec 7:5
for I have bought them * again. Zec 10:8
I will bring them * from Egypt Zec 10:10
for the waves will be held *. Zec 10:11
scars on your chest and your *?' Zec 13:6
but I will come * and comfort and Zec 13:7
And when you find him, come * and Mt 2:8
and his mother * to Israel, for Mt 2:20
the self-righteous, * to God." Mt 9:13
you can bring her * to life again Mt 9:18
Jesus told them, "Go * to John Mt 11:4
Literally, "brings * out of his Mt 13:52f
the Baptist, come * to life again. Mt 14:2
he didn't want to * down in front Mt 14:9
And when they had climbed * Mt 14:32
will be brought * to life again." Mt 17:22,23
it, you have won * a brother. Mt 18:15
with you and go * to him again, Mt 18:16
and circled * to Judea from across Mt 19:1
of you shall fall * into sin and Mt 24:10
"But he called *, 'Go away! Mt 25:12
But after I have been brought * Mt 26:32
heavy, so he went * to prayer the Mt 26:44
and brought * the money to the Mt 27:3
the crowd shouted * their Mt 27:21
And the mob yelled *, "His blood Mt 27:25
who had died came * to life again. Mt 27:52
days I will come * to life again.' Mt 27:63

(BACK Con't)
everyone he came * to life! Mt 27:64
For he has come * to life again, Mt 28:6
Jesus was asleep at the * of the Mk 4:38
So he got * into the boat. Mk 5:18
the Baptist come * to life again. Mk 6:14
He has come * from the dead." Mk 6:16
So she hurried * to the king and Mk 6:25
and brought * his head on a tray, Mk 6:28
They came * to report that there Mk 6:38
disciples to get * into the boat Mk 6:45
to Sidon, then * to the Sea of Mk 7:31
So he got * into the boat and Mk 8:13
"Don't even go * to the village Mk 8:26
prophet come * to life again." Mk 8:28
who won't be given *, a hundred Mk 10:30
I will come * to life again." Mk 10:34
across its * for him to ride on. Mk 11:7
When they arrived * to Jerusalem Mk 11:15
man and sent him * empty-handed. Mk 12:3
don't even go * into the house. Mk 13:15,16
They shouted *, "Crucify him!" Mk 15:13
He has come * to life! Mk 16:6
when Jesus came * to life, and the Mk 16:9
was, they rushed * to Jerusalem to Mk 16:13
and then went * to her own home. Lk 1:56
Then the shepherds went * again Lk 2:20
him, they went * to Jerusalem to Lk 2:45
book and handed it * to the Lk 4:20
don't worry about getting them *. Lk 6:30
it will all come * on you. Lk 6:37
measure what is given * to you." Lk 6:38
went * into the city of Capernaum. Lk 7:1
"Laddie," he said, "come * to Lk 7:14
And Jesus gave him * to his Lk 7:15
his reply: "Go * to John and tell Lk 7:20,21,22
The dead come * to life. Lk 7:20,21,22
them could pay him *, so he kindly Lk 7:42
* to the other side of the lake. Lk 8:37
"Go * to your family," he told Lk 8:39
Baptist come * to life again"; Lk 9:7
I will come * to life again!" Lk 9:22
When word came * of what had Lk 9:54
And I'll sit * and say to Lk 12:19
'My Lord won't be * for a long Lk 12:45
" 'Your brother is *,' he was Lk 15:27
son of yours comes * after spending Lk 15:30
and he was dead and has come * to Lk 15:32
One of them came * to Jesus, Lk 17:15
giving him * four times as much!" Lk 19:8
"But the third man brought * Lk 19:20
across its * for Jesus to sit on. Lk 19:35
up and sent him * empty-handed. Lk 20:10
pour out to purchase * your souls. Lk 22:20
on him, they sent him * to Pilate. Lk 23:11
and sent him * to us—nothing this Lk 23:15
He has come * to life again! Lk 24:6,7
you * in Galilee—that the Messiah Lk 24:6,7
and rushed * to Jerusalem Lk 24:9
and then he went * home again, Lk 24:12
morning and came * with an amazing Lk 24:22,23
were on their way * to Jerusalem, Lk 24:33,34
* and forth to me, the Messiah." Jn 1:51
After he came * to life again, Jn 2:22
How can an old man go * into his Jn 3:4
the well and went * to the village Jn 4:28,29
Then Jesus told him, "Go * home. Jn 4:50
still hadn't come *, they got into Jn 6:17
The next morning, * across the Jn 6:22,23
he was * again at the Temple. Jn 8:2
sent and washed and came * seeing! Jn 9:7
life that I may have it * again. Jn 10:17
bring my brother * to life again, Jn 11:22
will come * to life again." Jn 11:23
man he had brought * to life. Jn 12:1
man who had come * to life again. Jn 12:9
Jesus call Lazarus * to life were Jn 12:17
Literally, "leaning * against Jn 13:25f
When I come * to life again, you Jn 14:20
but I will come * to you again. Jn 14:28
you by pruning you * for greater Jn 15:3
he can give the glory * to you. Jn 17:1
and you have given them * to me Jn 17:10
Then Pilate went * into the Jn 18:33
But they screamed *, "No! Jn 18:40
THEN PILATE LAID open Jesus' * Jn 19:1
He took Jesus * into the palace Jn 19:9
the chief priests shouted *. Jn 19:15
the half mile * to Jerusalem and Act 1:12
and brought him * to life again, Act 2:24
'You will give me * my life, and Act 2:28
but God brought him * to life Act 3:15
Jesus your Messiah * to you again. Act 3:20
by turning you * from your sins." Act 3:26
God raised * to life again. Act 4:10
So they called them * in, and Act 4:18
brought Jesus * to life again after Act 5:30
And so God sent * the same man Act 7:35
the Red Sea, and * and forth Act 7:36
we will have gods to lead us *; Act 7:40
When the apostles * in Jerusalem Act 8:14
Spirit and get your sight *." Act 9:17
But God brought him * to life Act 10:40,41
But when Peter arrived * in Act 11:2
him, he brought him * to Antioch; Act 11:26
that she ran * inside to tell Act 12:14
"But God brought him * to life Act 13:30
God brought Jesus * to life again. Act 13:32,33
* to life again, no more to die. Act 13:34
—someone God brought * to life, Act 13:37
got up and went * into the city! Act 14:20
Then they traveled * through Act 14:24
and his coming * to life, and Act 17:3
by bringing him * to life again." Act 17:31
They all went * upstairs and ate Act 20:10,11,12
and bring him * to the armory. Act 23:10
to bring Paul * to the Council Act 23:15
So I ordered him * to jail until Act 25:21
God can bring men * to life again? Act 26:8
They tried at first to face * to Act 27:14,15
But after they had argued * and Act 28:25
* Jesus our Lord from the dead. Rom 4:24
we were brought * to God by the Rom 5:10
power, brought him * to life again, Rom 6:4
of you—for you are * from death and Rom 6:13
Then you came * to life again Rom 7:4
for us and came * to life again for Rom 8:34
to bring Christ * to life again." Rom 10:7
Yes, for even * in the time of Rom 10:19
on them and fall * upon their heads Rom 11:9
like dead people coming * to life. Rom 11:15
them and come * to God, God will Rom 11:23
graft them * into the tree again. Rom 11:23
to put the Jews * again, who were Rom 11:24
he will never go * on his Rom 11:29
Never pay * evil for evil. Rom 12:17
* from the true wisdom from above. 1Co 3:18
* to God, because he owns it. 1Co 6:20
you might fall * into sin. 1Co 7:2
remain single or else go * to him. 1Co 7:11
will never come * to life again? 1Co 15:12
dead do not come * to life again. 1Co 15:15
who will come * to life again 1Co 15:20
then when Christ comes *, all his 1Co 15:23
If the dead will not come * to 1Co 15:29
dead be brought * to life again? 1Co 15:35
have when we come * to life again, 1Co 15:42
when we come * to life again. 1Co 15:43
but when they come * to life they 1Co 15:44
but send him * to me happy with 1Co 16:11
when our Lord Jesus comes * again. 2Co 1:13,14
the Lord Jesus * from death will 2Co 4:14
will also bring us * to life again 2Co 4:14
to pat ourselves on the * again? 2Co 5:12
God who brought us * to himself 2Co 5:18
offended or kept * from finding the 2Co 6:3
and bring them * to God, and change 2Co 10:5
to get * into your good graces. 2Co 12:19
came * to the city of Damascus. Gal 1:17
FOURTEEN YEARS later I went * Gal 2:1
you want to go * again and become Gal 4:9
you * from following the truth? Gal 5:7
Lord to bring you * to believing as Gal 5:10
humbly help him * onto the right Gal 6:1
sins, he gave us * our lives again Eph 2:5
the one who went * up, that he Eph 4:10
shrinking * from all that might Php 2:12
Then when he comes * he can cheer Php 2:19
to send Epaphroditus * to you. Php 2:25
anxious to get him * to you again, Php 2:28
that brought him * to life again, Php 3:10
When he comes * he will take Php 3:21
has brought you * as his friends. Col 1:21
real life comes * again, you will Col 3:4
whom God brought * to life—and he 1Th 1:10
to come * to see you once more. 1Th 2:17
Christ when he comes * again. 1Th 2:19
Lord Jesus send us * to you again. 1Th 3:11
died and then came * to life again, 1Th 4:14
God will bring * with him all the 1Th 4:14
See that no one pays * evil for 1Th 5:15
Lord Jesus Christ comes * again. 1Th 5:23
him * steps out of the way. 2Th 2:7
forward to his coming * again. 2Ti 4:8
They must not talk *, nor steal, Tit 2:9
I am sending him * to you, and Phm 1:12
I will pay it * (I, Paul, Phm 1:19
you have dropped * to the place Heb 5:12,13
to bring you * to the Lord again if Heb 6:4
coming * again is drawing near. Heb 10:25
Otherwise, if they shrink *, God Heb 10:38
could have gone * to the good Heb 11:15
would bring him * to life again; Heb 11:19
death, but he came * again alive! Heb 11:19
loved ones * again from death. Heb 11:35
down or holds us *, and especially Heb 12:1
those rights * again, it was too Heb 12:17
They staggered * under God's Heb 12:20
that I can come * to you sooner. Heb 13:19
who brings him * to God will have Jas 5:20
don't slip * into your old 1Pe 1:14
never answered * when insulted; 1Pe 2:23
Don't snap * at those who say 1Pe 3:9
future to look * upon and fear. 2Pe 2:6
bait, they lure * into sin those 2Pe 2:18
turn his * on the holy commandments 2Pe 2:21
that "A dog comes * to what he has 2Pe 2:22
* and wallow in the mud again." 2Pe 2:22
Jesus promised to come *, did he? 2Pe 3:4
Why, as far * as anyone can 2Pe 3:4
and shrink * from meeting him. 1Jn 2:28
and turn * to me again and work Rev 2:5
was dead and then came * to life. Rev 2:8
sight of God. Go * to what you Rev 3:3
eyes and give you * your sight. Rev 3:18
dotted front and * with eyes, stood Rev 4:6
*, and sealed with seven seals. Rev 5:1
the earth, holding * the four winds Rev 7:1
wounded and then came * to life. Rev 13:14
dead did not come * to life until Rev 20:5
But cowards who turn * from Rev 21:8

BACK-TO-BACK
but two can stand * and conquer; Ecc 4:12

BACKBITERS
They were *, haters of God, Rom 1:30

BACKBONE
close to the *, the fat covering Lev 3:9,10,11

BACKED
* by all the honor of your name. Ps 138:2
The king's command is * by great Ecc 8:4
was a frameup, * by the chief Mk 15:10
leaders, and some * the apostles. Act 14:4

BACKFIRE
Honoring a rebel will * like a Pro 26:8

BACKGROUND
* music while the work progressed. 2Ch 34:12

BACKGROUNDS
scarlet on linen *, and as Ex 35:35

BACKING
his advisor, was * Absalom, David 2Sa 15:31

BACKS
sacks from the * of their donkeys Gen 44:11
And you shall trample on their * Deu 33:29
tank from the * of the bronze oxen 2Ki 16:17
This tank was set on the * of 2Ch 4:3
Temple and turned their * on it. 2Ch 29:6
Oh, they have strong * all Job 30:2
But all have turned their * on Ps 53:3
and laid great burdens on our *. Ps 66:11
turned their * and fled when the Ps 78:9
have turned their * upon the Lord, Is 1:4
on turning your * and refusing to Is 1:20
the dust and walked upon your *." Is 51:23
We turned our * on him and looked Is 53:3
* on God and wandered far away. Jer 3:21
me and turned your * upon me. Jer 15:6
They have turned their * upon me Jer 32:33
with their * to the Temple of the Eze 8:16
their * to all knowledge of God. Eze 16:3f
me and turned your * upon me, Eze 23:35
have turned their * on all the Jon 2:8
right off the * of those who Mic 2:8
and rip open the * of others with Mt 23:34
to turn their * on sin, so that God Mk 1:4
slashed down across their bared *; Act 16:23
each other's *, filled with conceit 2Co 12:20
have turned their * on the truth. Tit 1:14
But we have never turned our * on Heb 10:39
Some were laughed at and their * Heb 11:36
about others behind their *. 1Pe 2:1

BACKSLIDER
The * gets bored with himself; Pro 14:14

BACKWARD
the Ark, Eli fell * from his seat 1Sa 4:18
ten points or * ten points?" 2Ki 20:9
"make it go *." 2Ki 20:10
points * on the sundial of Ahaz! 2Ki 20:11
They will stagger *, destroyed Ps 64:8
They went * instead of forward. Jer 7:24
soldiers run without a * glance. Jer 46:5
fathers flee without a * glance Jer 47:3

BACKWARDS
and, walking * into the tent, let Gen 9:23
will send the sun * ten degrees as Is 38:8
it, they all fell * to the ground! Jn 18:6

BACKYARD
hid them inside a well in his *. 2Sa 17:18

BAD
giving knowledge of Good and *. Gen 2:9
of right and wrong, good and *. Gen 2:16,17
knowing good from *, what if he Gen 3:22
As God observed how * it was, and Gen 6:12,13
"Will you kill good and * alike? Gen 18:22,23
of the * things they were doing. Gen 37:2
they were indeed in a * situation. Ex 5:19
the vow is good or *, when he Lev 5:4
good for * or bad for good; Lev 27:10
good for bad or * for good; Lev 27:10
it is good or *, and there shall be Lev 27:33
you must not feel *, for remember Deu 15:18
For rebellion is as * as the sin 1Sa 15:23
is as * as worshiping idols. 1Sa 15:23
but he has repaid me * for good. 1Sa 25:21

(BAD Con't)
I discern between good and *?" 2Sa 19:35f
'Isn't killing Naboth * enough? 1Ki 21:19
It's always *." 1Ki 22:18
but the water is *, and causes 2Ki 2:19
evil—but not as * as some of the 2Ki 17:1
will receive * news from home and 2Ki 19:7
arrived with more * news: "The Job 1:16
my problems go from * to worse. Ps 25:17
He does not fear * news, nor Ps 112:7
"Good or *, we'll treat them Pro 1:12
A fool's fun is being *; Pro 10:23
that * is good, and good is bad. Pro 17:15
that bad is good, and good is *. Pro 17:15
is heavy is as * as stealing his Pro 25:20
so also it is * for men to think Pro 25:27
man does, both good and *." Ecc 3:17
whether good or *, religious or Ecc 9:2,3
he is going to run into * luck. Ecc 9:12
A quiet spirit will quiet his * Ecc 10:4
every hidden thing, good or *. Ecc 12:14
Born to be *, they have turned Is 1:4
I send good times and *. Is 45:7
among a cluster of * ones (and Is 65:8
for right and go from * to worse; Jer 9:3
No one can really know how * it Jer 17:9
some very good and some very *." Jer 24:3
like spoiled figs, too * to use. Jer 24:8
like rotting figs, too * to eat. Jer 29:16,17
Things became so * at last that Jer 52:3
And if a good man becomes *, and Eze 3:20
people, good and * alike— I will Eze 21:3
of good men and *, between those Mal 3:18
they could find, good and * alike; Mt 22:10
to repent, but the * ones." Mk 2:17
he is good or *," the man replied, Jn 9:25
You are just as *. Rom 2:1
God is when they see how * we are. Rom 3:5
is wrong, and my * conscience Rom 7:16
done anything either good or *. Rom 9:10-13
a * conscience over eating it. 1Co 10:27
for the good or * things he has 2Co 5:10
We started out *, being born with Eph 2:3
Don't use * language. Eph 4:29
to them, and thoroughly *. 2Ti 3:2
say, "so you might as well be *. 2Pe 2:19
But if we have * consciences and 1Jn 3:20
Dear friend, don't let this * 3Jn 1:11

BAD-TEMPERED
Nabal is a * boor, but please 1Sa 25:25
Stop being mean, * and angry. Eph 4:31

BADGE
It is a * of honor to accept Pro 25:12

BADGER
The coney, or rock * (because Lev 11:4-7

BADGERS
Cliff *: delicate little animals Pro 30:24-28

BADLANDS
On through the * they go, where Is 30:6

BADLY
They were * frightened when they Gen 43:18
as though * beaten, and all the Jos 8:15
The Israelis were * frightened 1Sa 7:7
their army was so * scattered that 1Sa 11:11
overtook Saul and wounded him *. 1Sa 31:3,4
his people too were * frightened. 2Sa 4:1
battle, for I am * wounded," he 1Ki 22:34
chariot, "for I am * wounded." 2Ch 18:33
Jehoshaphat was * shaken by this 2Ch 20:3
you and all Judah get * hurt." 2Ch 25:19
I was * frightened, but I Neh 2:1
trouble and I need his help so *. Ps 77:2
finished they were * frightened. Jer 36:16
and was * mistreated by many. Mt 17:12
The women ran from the tomb, * Mt 28:8
you, and they * need your help, and Mk 14:7
They were * frightened, but the Lk 2:9
And the whole crowd was * Lk 8:35
of his house naked and * injured. Act 19:16
You know how * we had been 1Th 2:2

BADNESS
The good hate the * of the Pro 29:27

BAFFLED
and beard and sat down utterly *. Ez 9:3
"You sit there *, with no Job 32:15
The servants return, * and Jer 14:3
Are you also *? Jer 14:9
His reply surprised and * them Mt 22:22

BAFFLEMENT
their heads in * at his reply. Mk 12:17

BAFFLES
that bothers and * the man of the 1Co 2:15

BAG
in his shepherd's * and, armed only 1Sa 17:40
his shepherd's *, took out a stone, 1Sa 17:48,49
all the weights in the * are his Pro 16:11f
don't even carry a duffle * with Mt 10:10
a beggar's *, nor food, nor money. Lk 9:3
*, or even an extra pair of shoes. Lk 10:4
money, duffle *, or extra clothing, Lk 22:35
* if you have one, and your money. Lk 22:36

BAGGAGE
"He is hiding in the *." 1Sa 10:22
David left his luggage with a * 1Sa 17:22
Bring your * outside your house Eze 12:4

BAGS
burden resting among the saddle *. Gen 49:14
the money in two *, and gave them 2Ki 5:23
Gehazi took the * from the 2Ki 5:24
it, put it into *, and gave it to 2Ki 12:10
Pack your *, he says. Jer 10:17
* of false, deceitful weights? Mic 6:11
These were leather * for storing Mt 9:17f

BAHARUM
Azmaveth from *; 1Ch 11:26-47

BAHURIM
As David and his party passed *, 2Sa 16:5
time they reached *, so they stayed 2Sa 16:14
Meanwhile, they escaped to * 2Sa 17:18
the man from *, hurried across with 2Sa 19:16
Azmaveth from *; 2Sa 23:24-39
of Gera the Benjaminite from *? 1Ki 2:8

BAIL
go only after they had posted *. Act 17:8,9

BAILIFFS
thousand are to be * and judges, 1Ch 23:4,5
And even the * were using their Mk 14:65

BAIT
lust as their *, they lure back 2Pe 2:18

BAKAH
Weep, men of *. Mic 1:10

BAKBAKKAR
*, Heresh, Galal, 1Ch 9:15,16

BAKBUK
Me-unim, Nephisim, *, Hakupha, Ez 2:43-54
*, Hakupha, Harhur, Neh 7:46-56

BAKBUKIAH
* and Abda (son of Shammua, son Neh 11:15,16,17
* and Unno, their fellow Neh 12:9
Mattaniah, *, Obadiah, Neh 12:25

BAKE
of offering. * this bread from a Lev 23:17
be large enough to * all the bread Lev 26:26
and * and make perfumes for him. 1Sa 8:13
* me a little loaf of bread first; 1Ki 17:13
warm himself and * his bread, and Is 44:15
to * my bread and roast my meat. Is 44:19
are watching, * it over a fire, Eze 4:12
sin offering and * the flour of the Eze 46:19,20

BAKED
with freshly * unleavened bread. Gen 19:3
When they stopped to eat, they * Ex 12:39
"If bread * in the oven is Lev 2:4
ground flour, * with olive oil but Lev 2:4
prepared—whether *, fried, or Lev 2:8
it is * it must be without yeast. Lev 6:17
sacrifice is *, fried, or grilled. Lev 7:9
These loaves shall be * from Lev 24:5-8
a young goat, and * some unleavened Ju 6:19
dough and * unleavened bread. 1Sa 28:24
then she * some special bread for 2Sa 13:8

BAKER
with his chief * and his wine Gen 40:1
When the chief * saw that the Gen 40:16
taster and chief *, and they were Gen 40:20
but he sentenced the chief * to Gen 40:22
me and the chief * in jail in the Gen 41:10
guard, the chief * and I each had Gen 41:11
and the chief * was executed, and Gen 41:13

BAKER'S
They are all adulterers; as a * Hos 7:4

BAKERY
were all kinds of * goods for Gen 40:17

BAKING
and saw some bread * on hot stones, 1Ki 19:6

BALAAM
sent messengers to * (son of Beor) Num 22:5,6
He begged * to come and help him. Num 22:5,6
They went to * with money in Num 22:7
"Stay here overnight," * said, Num 22:8
That night God came to * and Num 22:9
The next morning * told the men, Num 22:13
They came to * with this Num 22:16,17
But * replied, "If he were to Num 22:18
That night God told *, "Get up Num 22:20
to kill him. As * and two servants Num 22:22,23
but * beat her back onto the road. Num 22:22,23
In a great fit of temper * beat Num 22:27
me look like a fool!" * shouted. Num 22:29
Then * confessed, "I have Num 22:34
to say." So * went on with them. Num 22:35
When King Balak heard that * was Num 22:36
he asked *. Num 22:37
* replied, "I have come, but I Num 22:38
I shall speak." * accompanied the Num 22:39
gave animals to * and the Num 22:40
The next morning Balak took * to Num 22:41
* SAID TO the king, "Build seven Num 23:1
Then * said to the king, "Stand Num 23:3,4
God met him there. * told the Lord, Num 23:3,4
Then the Lord gave * a message Num 23:5
When * returned, the king was Num 23:6
But * replied, "Can I say Num 23:12
So King Balak took * into the Num 23:14
Then * said to the king, "Stand Num 23:15
And the Lord met * and told Num 23:16
the king exclaimed to *. Num 23:25
But * replied, "Didn't I tell Num 23:26
Then the king said to *, "I will Num 23:27
So King Balak took * to the top Num 23:28
the desert. * again told the king Num 23:29
The king did as * said, and Num 23:30
* REALIZED BY now that Jehovah Num 24:1
"* the son of Beor says that Num 24:3-9
* replied, "Didn't I tell your Num 24:12
"* the son of Beor is the man Num 24:15-19
Then * looked over at the homes Num 24:20
So * and Balak returned to their Num 24:25
But not before * gave insidious Num 24:25f
Hur, and Reba. *, the son of Beor, Num 31:8
they even tried to hire *, the Deu 23:4
But the Lord wouldn't listen to *; Deu 23:5
* the magician, the son of Beor. Jos 13:22
*, the son of Beor, to curse you. Jos 24:9
Instead, they had hired * to Neh 13:2
the curse of *, son of Beor, but I Mic 6:5
become lost like *, the son of 2Pe 2:15
doing wrong; but * was stopped 2Pe 2:16
and, like *, they will do Jud 1:11
you who do as * did when he taught Rev 2:14
of these very same followers of * Rev 2:15

BALAAM'S
But God was angry about * eager Num 22:22,23
were riding along, * donkey Num 22:22,23
crushing * foot in the process. Num 22:25
Then the Lord opened * eyes and Num 22:31
This was * message: Num 23:7-10
ones who followed * advice and Num 31:16

BALAAMITES
from Greek to Hebrew, becomes *; Rev 2:6f
Greek form of "*." Rev 2:15f

BALADAN
(the son of King * of Babylon) sent 2Ki 20:12
the son of *) sent Hezekiah a Is 39:1

BALAH
Hazar-shual, *, Ezem, Eltolad, Jos 19:2-7

BALAK
When King * of Moab (the son of Num 22:2,3
So King * sent messengers to Num 22:4
explained to him what * wanted. Num 22:7
"They have come from King * of Num 22:10
his refusal. * tried again. Num 22:15
"King * pleads with you to come. Num 22:16,17
When King * heard that Balaam Num 22:36
where King * sacrificed oxen and Num 22:40
The next morning * took Balaam Num 22:41
* followed his instructions, and Num 23:2
gave Balaam a message for King *. Num 23:5
"King *, king of Moab, has Num 23:7-10
demanded King *. Num 23:11
Then * told him, "Come with me Num 23:13
So King * took Balaam into the Num 23:14
"Rise up, *, and hear: Num 23:18-24
So King * took Balaam to the top Num 23:28
King * was livid with rage by Num 24:10
So Balaam and * returned to their Num 24:25
Then King * of Moab started a Jos 24:9
Are you better than King *, the Ju 11:25
O my people, how *, king of Moab, Mic 6:5
did when he taught * how to ruin Rev 2:14

BALAK'S
So King * ambassadors returned Num 22:14

BALANCE
In addition, there was a trade * 2Ch 9:13,14
My life hangs in the *, but I Ps 119:109
Literally, "a just * and scales Pro 16:11f

BALANCED
information and * judgment, the Dan 1:20

BALANCES
and beard; use * to weigh the hair Eze 5:1
God's * and have failed the test. Dan 5:27
holding a pair of * in his hand. Rev 6:5

BALANCING
Do you understand the * of the Job 37:16,17

BALCONIES
as three thousand people in the * Ju 16:27

BALD
locusts, * locusts, crickets, and Lev 11:21,22
him a leper even though he is *! Lev 13:40
he simply has a * forehead, but Lev 13:41
"whether it be * in the head Lev 13:55f
"The priests shall not clip * Lev 21:5
fun of him because of his * head. 2Ki 2:23
The soldiers' heads were * (from Eze 29:18

BALDNESS
However, if in the * there is a Lev 13:42

BALL
his hands like a * and toss you Is 22:18
Having started the * rolling so 2Co 8:11

BALLAD
Again and again they sing the * Ju 5:11

BALLADS
here from the book, Heroic *. 2Sa 1:17,18

BALM	
Take them to the man as gifts—*,	Gen 43:11
and with honey, oil and *.	Eze 27:17
BALSAM	
them and come out by the * trees.	2Sa 5:23
the tops of the * trees, attack!	2Sa 5:24
BAMAH	
Literally, "*"—a hilltop area	Eze 20:29f
BAMOTH	
Mattanah, Nahaliel, and *;	Num 21:19
BAMOTH-BAAL	
the top of Mount *, from which he	Num 22:41
the plain—Dibon, *, Beth-baal-meon,	Jos 13:17
BAN	
who is under the * of God to be put	Lev 27:29f
BANAIAH	
Ma-adai, Amram, Uel, *, Bedeiah,	Ez 10:34-42
BAND	
"A marauding * shall stamp upon	Gen 49:19
It shall have a woven * around	Ex 28:32
Soon he had quite a * of	Ju 11:3
you will meet a * of prophets	1Sa 10:5
home at Gibe-ah, a * of men whose	1Sa 10:26
of the * wherever there was room.	1Ki 7:36
and harps. The * and chorus united	2Ch 5:13,14
accompanied by a * of harps, lyres,	2Ch 20:28
He dispatched against them a * of	Ps 78:49
Midianites by Gideon's little *.	Is 9:4
leads a pilgrim * to Jerusalem to	Is 30:29
"When the *	Dan 3:5
So when the *	Dan 3:7
the golden statue when the *	Dan 3:10
with a golden * across his chest.	Rev 1:13
BANDAGE	
having placed a * over his eyes to	1Ki 20:38
Then the prophet yanked off the *	1Ki 20:41
BANDAGED	
wounds with medicine and * them.	Lk 10:34
BANDAGES	
I will put splints and * upon	Eze 34:15,16
BANDED	
tip of each stand, * with lugs.	1Ki 7:35
in the ground, * with a chain of	Dan 4:15
* with a chain of iron and brass.	Dan 4:23
us, and then * the ship with ropes	Act 27:17
BANDIT	
In those days * gangs of Moabites	2Ki 13:20,21
a robber, and violently like a *.	Pro 24:34
being a liar, thief, and *!	Hos 7:1
BANDITRY	
the loot from their thefts and *.	Amo 3:10
BANDITS	
living off the land as *.	Ju 11:3
of a gang of *—men who fled with	1Ki 11:24
from enemies and * along the way.	Ez 8:31
to Jericho was attacked by *.	Lk 10:30
was a neighbor to the *' victim?"	Lk 10:36
BANDS	
of King Ish-bosheth's raiding *.	2Sa 4:2,3
he was a leper. * of Syrians had	2Ki 5:2
And the Lord sent * of	2Ki 24:2
(for the marauding * of Arabs had	2Ch 22:1
rushed in: "Three * of Chaldeans	Job 1:17
take off the slave * from your	Is 52:2
Jewish guerrilla * in the	Jer 40:7
Literally, "lay * upon you."	Eze 3:25f
Literally, "I will lay * upon	Eze 4:8f
BANI	
* from Gad;	2Sa 23:24-39
Hilkiah, Amzi, *, Shemer, Mahli,	1Ch 6:44-47
of Imri, son of *) of the clan of	1Ch 9:4
From the subclan of *, 642;	Ez 2:3-35
From the clan of *—Shelomith (son	Ez 8:2-14
From the clan of *:	Ez 10:29
From the clan of *:	Ez 10:34-42
Mattenai, Jaasu, *, Binnui,	Ez 10:34-42
supervision of Rehum (son of *).	Neh 3:17
scroll, Jeshua, *, Sherebiah,	Neh 8:7,8
Jeshua, Kadmi-el, *, Shebaniah,	Neh 9:4
Bunni, Sherebiah, *, and Chenani.	Neh 9:4
Jeshua, Kadmi-el, *, Hashabneiah,	Neh 9:5
*, Beninu.	Neh 10:9-13
*, Bunni, Azgad, Bebai,	Neh 10:14-27
was Uzzi (son of *, son of	Neh 11:22,23
BANISH	
Yes, be bold and strong! * fear	Jos 1:9
you do. So * grief and pain, but	Ecc 11:10
let them * from their minds the	Is 55:7
And I will * the Egyptians to	Eze 30:23
the authority to * peace and bring	Rev 6:4
BANISHED	
So the Lord God * him forever	Gen 3:23
You are hereby * from this	Gen 4:11
For you have * me from my farm	Gen 4:14
to bring home your own * son.	2Sa 14:13
Vashti be forever * from your	Est 1:19
Don't toss me aside, * forever	Ps 51:11
gladness has been * from the	Is 24:11
nations to which they will be *.	Eze 29:13
BANISHES	
back those he *, so that they will	2Sa 14:14f
BANISHMENT	
by death, *, confiscation of goods,	Ez 7:26
BANK	
standing on the * of the Nile	Gen 41:1
"I was standing upon the * of	Gen 41:17
began grazing along the river *.	Gen 41:18
along the river *, she spied the	Ex 2:5
Stand beside the river * and meet	Ex 7:15
along the river * to get drinking	Ex 7:24
followed the north * of the Brook	Jos 17:9
all on the other * before dawn.	2Sa 17:22
returned to the * of the Jordan	2Ki 2:13,14
along a river * bearing luscious	Ps 1:3
river * will wither and blow away.	Is 19:7
up an earthen * against its walls.	Is 37:33
grass, like willows on a river *.	Is 44:4
then led me back along the *.	Eze 47:6
horns standing on the river *;	Dan 8:3
on each * of a river.	Dan 12:5
* so I could have some interest.	Mt 25:27
the money in the * so that I could	Lk 19:23
city to a river * where we	Act 16:13
BANKED	
The water stood * up along both	Ps 78:13
BANKERS	
* and debtors—none will be spared.	Is 24:2
BANKS	
evening at the * of the Jordan	Jos 3:1
Jordan was overflowing all its *;	Jos 3:13,14
the * of the river as before!	Jos 4:18
and along the * of the Habor River	2Ki 17:6
and along the * of the Habor River	2Ki 18:11
on both the east and west *.	1Ch 12:15
The grassy * are dried up and the	Is 15:6
Tell it by the * of the Arnon,	Jer 48:20
along the * of the Nile, making	Eze 32:2
trees will grow along the river *.	Eze 47:12
BANNED	
Finally Saul * him from his	1Sa 18:13
King Saul had * all mediums and	1Sa 28:3
BANNER	
"Raise the * of the Lord!"	Ex 17:15,16
with its flagpole and tribal *;	Num 2:1
under its own *, in the locations	Num 2:34
But you have given us a * to	Ps 60:4,5
out behind his * and destroy them.	Ps 118:10
will be a * of salvation to all	Is 11:10
BANNERS	
terrible as an army with *."	Sol 6:4f
"terrible as an army with *."	Sol 6:10f
BANQUET	
as they were finishing their *.	1Ki 1:41
the * table and fled in panic;	1Ki 1:49,50
all of his officials to a great *.	1Ki 3:15
* I have prepared for you today."	Est 5:4
king and Haman came to Esther's *.	Est 5:5
to the * I shall prepare for you.	Est 5:7,8
man was Haman as he left the *!	Est 5:9
to the * she prepared for us;	Est 5:12
way with the king to the *."	Est 5:14
to the * Esther had prepared.	Est 6:14
KING and Haman came to Esther's *.	Est 7:1
prepared a great *, and mixed the	Pro 9:2
come to wisdom's * and drink the	Pro 9:5
He brings me to the * hall and	Sol 2:4
They are preparing a great *!	Is 21:5
Feast at my * table—feast on	Eze 39:20
she rushed to the * hall and said	Dan 5:10
and when the * was ready he sent	Mt 22:3
and the * hall was filled with	Mt 22:10
A * was prepared in Jesus' honor.	Jn 12:2
for the wedding * of the Lamb, and	Rev 19:7
BANQUETS	
the head table at *, and in the	Mt 23:6
—* and parties and weddings—just	Mt 24:37,38
places of honor at *— but they	Mk 12:39
BANTERING	
They had a wonderful time * back	Gen 43:34
BAPTISM	
After his *, as soon as Jesus	Mt 3:16
Literally, "preaching a * of	Mk 1:4f
Or to be baptized with the * of	Mk 10:38
baptized with my *, but I do not	Mk 10:39
Or, "preaching the * of	Lk 3:3f
came for *: "You brood of snakes!	Lk 3:7
for them and refused John's *.	Lk 7:30
There is a terrible * ahead of	Lk 12:50
Some think this means water *.	Jn 3:5f
them that Jesus' * was best.	Jn 3:25
did you acknowledge at your *?"	Act 19:3
them that John's * was to	Act 19:4
receiving his * must then go on to	Act 19:4
buried with him by * when he died,	Rom 6:4
This might be called their *	1Co 10:2
one faith, one *, and we all have	Eph 4:5
her holy and clean, washed by *	Eph 5:26
operation, the * of your souls.	Col 2:11
For in * you see how your old,	Col 2:12
about * and spiritual gifts	Heb 6:2
(That, by the way, is what *	1Pe 3:21
for us: In * we show that we have	1Pe 3:21
Or, "*, which corresponds to	1Pe 3:21f
—yes, not only at his * but also	1Jn 5:6,7,8
*, and the voice before he died.	1Jn 5:6,7,8
BAPTIST	
John the * began preaching out in	Mt 3:1
of John the * came to Jesus and	Mt 9:14
John the *, who was now in	Mt 11:2
more brightly than John the *.	Mt 11:11
And from the time John the *	Mt 11:12
For John the * doesn't even	Mt 11:18
the *, come back to life again.	Mt 14:2
replied, "some say John the *;	Mt 16:14
he was speaking of John the *.	Mt 17:13
"Was John the * sent from God,	Mt 21:25
For John the * told you to	Mt 21:32
This messenger was John the *.	Mk 1:4
the * come back to life again.	Mk 6:14
John the *—right now—on a tray!"	Mk 6:25
you are John the *," the disciples	Mk 8:28
What about John the *?	Mk 11:30
The disciples of John the * soon	Lk 7:18
For John the * used to go	Lk 7:33
the * come back to life again";	Lk 9:7
"John the *," they told him,	Lk 9:19
Until John the * began to	Lk 16:16
God sent John the * as a witness	Jn 1:6,7
At this time John the * was not	Jn 3:23,24
but someone else, yes, John the *,	Jn 5:32,33
with John the * in Galilee.	Act 10:36,37
"But before he came, John the *	Act 13:24
him about John the * and what John	Act 18:25,26
"What John the * taught."	Act 19:3
BAPTIST'S	
for John the * head on a tray.	Mt 14:8
her, "Ask for John the * head!"	Mk 6:24
"John the * disciples are	Lk.5:33
BAPTIZE	
water I * those who repent of	Mt 3:11
He shall * you with	Mt 3:11
I * you with	Mk 1:8
water but he will * you with	Mk 1:8
by saying, "I * only with water;	Lk 3:16
He will * you with fire—with the	Lk 3:16
what right do you have to *?"	Jn 1:24,25
John told them, "I merely * with	Jn 1:26
God sent me to * he told me, 'When	Jn 1:33
himself didn't * them, but his	Jn 4:1
now that I didn't * any of you	1Co 1:14
For Christ didn't send me to *,	1Co 1:17
BAPTIZED	
he * them in the Jordan River.	Mt 3:6
coming to be *, he denounced	Mt 3:7
Before being *, prove that you	Mt 3:8
River to be * there by John.	Mt 3:13
"I am the one who needs to be *	Mt 3:14
So then John * him.	Mt 3:15
that all should be * as a public	Mk 1:4
he * them in the Jordan River.	Mk 1:5
Galilee, and was * by John there in	Mk 1:9
Or to be * with the baptism of	Mk 10:38
of suffering I must be * with?"	Mk 10:38
from my cup and be * with my	Mk 10:39
Those who believe and are * will	Mk 16:16
people should be * to show that	Lk 3:3
That is why you want to be *!	Lk 3:7
to be * and asked, "How shall we	Lk 3:12
*, Jesus himself was baptized;	Lk 3:21
baptized, Jesus himself was *;	Lk 3:21
right, and they were * by him.	Lk 7:29
for a while in Judea and * there.	Jn 3:22
than to John to be * and to become	Jn 4:1
"John * you with	Act 1:5
them, "but you shall be * with	Act 1:5
the time he was * by John until the	Act 1:21,22
to God, and be * in the name of	Act 2:38
Peter were *—about 3,000 in all!	Act 2:41
and many men and women were *.	Act 8:12
believed and was * and began	Act 8:13
For they had only been * in the	Act 8:16
Why can't I be *?"	Act 8:36
into the water and Philip * him.	Act 8:38
could see, and was immediately *.	Act 9:18
when he said, 'Yes, John * with	Act 11:16
water, but you shall be * with	Act 11:16
She was * along with all her	Act 16:15
and he and all his family were *.	Act 16:33
*—as were many others in Corinth.	Act 18:8
as they heard this, they were * in	Act 19:5
Go and be *, and be cleansed from	Act 22:16
and were * to become a part of	Rom 6:2,3
Were any of you * in my name?	1Co 1:13
Oh, yes, and I * the family of	1Co 1:16
* both in sea and cloud!	1Co 10:2
We have been * into Christ's body	1Co 12:13
being * for those who are gone?	1Co 15:29
we who have been * into union with	Gal 3:27
because in being * we are turning	1Pe 3:21
when Jesus was *, and again as he	1Jn 5:6,7,8
BAPTIZES	
He is the one who * with	Jn 1:33
BAPTIZING	
preaching and * until now, ardent	Mt 11:12

(BAPTIZING Con't)
all the nations, * them into the Mt 28:19
the Jordan River where John was *. Jn 1:28
was the one, but I am here * with Jn 1:31
He was * at Aenon, near Salim, Jn 3:23,24
the Messiah—he is * too, and Jn 3:26
the place where John was first *. Jn 10:40
object to my * them, now that they Act 10:46,47
So he did, * them in the name Act 10:48
I don't remember ever * anyone 1Co 1:16

BAR
The middle *, halfway up the Ex 26:28
The middle * of the five was Ex 36:33
$200, and a * of gold worth $500. Jos 7:21

BAR-JESUS
sorcerer, a fake prophet named *. Act 13:6,7

BARABBAS
in jail named *, and as the crowds Mt 27:16
to you—*, or Jesus your Messiah?" Mt 27:17
*' release, and for Jesus' death. Mt 27:20
shouted back their reply: "*!" Mt 27:21
Then Pilate released * to them. Mt 27:26
at that time was *, convicted along Mk 15:7
the release of * instead of Jesus. Mk 15:11
"But if I release *," Pilate Mk 15:12
the people, released * to them. Mk 15:15
"Kill him, and release * to us!" Lk 23:18
to us!" (* was in prison for Lk 23:19
And he released *, the man in Lk 23:25
Not this man, but *!" Jn 18:40
Not this man, but Barabbas!" * Jn 18:40

BARACHEL
Then Elihu (son of *, the Buzite, Job 32:2

BARACHIAH
Zechariah (son of *), slain by you Mt 23:35

BARAK
One day she summoned * (son of Ju 4:6
if you go with me!" * told her. Ju 4:8
When * summoned the men of Ju 4:10
was told that * and his army were Ju 4:12
Then Deborah said to *, "Now is Ju 4:14
So * led his ten thousand men down Ju 4:14
escaped on foot. * and his men Ju 4:16
When * came by looking for Ju 4:22
THEN DEBORAH AND * sang this Ju 5:1
Arise, O *! Ju 5:12
With Deborah and *. Ju 5:15
Then the Lord sent Gideon, *, 1Sa 12:11
of Gideon and * and Samson and Heb 11:32

BARBED
and * and sting like scorpions. Eze 2:6

BARBER
in a * and cut off his hair. Ju 16:19

BARBER'S
and use it as a * razor to shave Eze 5:1

BARE
before the Lord on the * earth. 2Sa 12:16
feet were * as a sign of mourning. 2Sa 15:30
They quickly carpeted the * steps 2Ki 9:13
rocks and lay * precious stones. Job 28:10
breath the depths were laid *. Ps 18:15
It strips the forests *. Ps 29:9
them * of everything they own. Ps 35:26
they own. * them to dishonor. Ps 35:26
Israel—stripped * of people except Is 17:6
stand upon the * hills panting like Jer 14:6
He has plucked you *! Jer 48:32
but I will strip * the land of Jer 49:9,10
you own, leaving you naked and *. Eze 23:29
don't * your head nor feet, and Eze 24:17
her soil and make her a * rock! Eze 26:4
I will make your island a * Eze 26:14
trunks and branches white and *. Joe 1:7
The fields are * of crops. Joe 1:10
laid * his bones from head to toe. Hab 3:13
the Pleasant Land lay * and Zec 7:14
will be laid * and he will fall 1Co 14:25
have our lives laid *—before him. 2Co 5:10
Everything about us is * and wide Heb 4:13

BARED
* fangs they will devour Israel. Is 9:11,12
The Lord has * his holy arm Is 52:10
lie there with your arm * [to Eze 4:7
Your head and feet shall not be *; Eze 24:23
slashed down across their * backs; Act 16:23

BAREFOOT
and to walk around naked and *. Is 20:2
walking naked and * for the last Is 20:3
walk naked and *, both young and Is 20:4
I will walk naked and * in sorrow Mic 1:8

BARELY
But when they were * out of the Gen 44:4
time just getting * enough to keep Job 24:5
to be lazy and * get by, than to Ecc 4:5,6
Are we little children, * old Is 28:9
They hardly get started, * take Is 40:24
course, that might be * possible. Rom 5:7
If the righteous are * saved, 1Pe 4:18

BARENESS
▮ Literally, "whether the * be Lev 13:55f

BARGAIN
that we keep this * when we are out Gen 31:49
afterwards he brags about his *! Pro 20:14
You have struck a * with Death, Is 28:15
He discovered a real *—a pearl Mt 13:46

BARGAINS
a hard worker, and watches for *. Pro 31:18

BARIAH
sons, including Hattush, Igal, *, 1Ch 3:21,22

BARK
of gum from the * of a tree. Num 11:7
and stripped the * from the fig Joe 1:7

BARKOS
*, Sisera, Temah, Neziah, Hatipha. Ez 2:43-54
*, Sisera, Temah, Neh 7:46-56

BARLEY
All the flax and * were Ex 9:31
destroyed (for the * was ripe, and Ex 9:31
ten bushels of * seed for sowing is Lev 27:16
of a bushel of * meal without oil Num 5:15
it is a land of wheat and *, of Deu 8:8
this huge loaf of * bread that came Ju 7:12,13
at the beginning of the * harvest. Ru 1:22
off some heads of * and drop them Ru 2:16
had beaten out the * she had Ru 2:17
the end of the * harvest, and then Ru 2:23
will be winnowing * tonight out on Ru 3:2
and a half of * in it as a present Ru 3:15-18
and gave her the * from Boaz, and Ru 3:15-18
set fire to that * field of Joab's 2Sa 14:30
bowls, wheat and * flour, parched 2Sa 17:28,29
at the beginning of the * harvest. 2Sa 21:9
also the * and straw for the 1Ki 4:28
and twenty individual loaves of * 2Ki 4:42
or four gallons of * grain will be 2Ki 7:1
four gallons of * were sold that 2Ki 7:16
that flour and * would sell for so 2Ki 7:18
The Israeli army was in a * field 1Ch 11:13
20,000 barrels of *, 20,000 barrels 2Ch 2:10
So send along the wheat, *, 2Ch 2:15
of wheat, and 10,000 sacks of *. 2Ch 27:5
wheat, and weeds instead of *." Job 31:40
with wheat and * and overflow your Pro 3:9,10
of wheat, *, oil and honey they had Jer 41:8
*, beans, lentils, and spelt. Eze 4:9
prepare it as you would * cakes. Eze 4:12
paltry handfuls of * or a piece of Eze 13:19
or * for every sixty you reap; Eze 45:13
eight bushels of *, and I said to Hos 3:2
Weep for the wheat and the * too, Joe 1:11
* loaves and a couple of fish! Jn 6:8,9
$20, or three pounds of * flour, Rev 6:6
of * for a denarius. " Rev 6:6f

BARN
calves away from them in the *. 1Sa 6:7
calves were shut up in the *. 1Sa 6:10
it is too late to lock the *. Ecc 10:11
them, and put the wheat in the *.' Mt 13:30

BARNABAS
Then * brought him to the Act 9:27
they sent * to Antioch to help the Act 11:22
the cost. * was a kindly person, Act 11:24
Then * went on to Tarsus to hunt Act 11:25
their gifts to * and Paul to take Act 11:30
* and Paul now visited Jerusalem Act 12:25
at Antioch were * and Symeon (also Act 13:1
said, "Dedicate * and Paul for a Act 13:2
The governor invited * and Paul Act 13:6,7
to what Paul and * said, trying to Act 13:8
to Jerusalem. But * and Paul went Act 13:14
"And now * and I are here to Act 13:32,33
followed Paul and * down the street Act 13:43
Then Paul and * spoke out boldly Act 13:46
and *, and ran them out of town. Act 13:50
AT ICONIUM, PAUL and * went Act 14:1
against Paul and *, saying all Act 14:2
When Paul and * learned of a plot Act 14:5,6
They decided that * was the Act 14:12
But when * and Paul saw what was Act 14:14
But even so, Paul and * could Act 14:18
The next day he left with * for Act 14:20
Paul and * also appointed elders Act 14:23
WHILE PAUL AND * were at Antioch, Act 15:1
Paul and * argued and discussed Act 15:2
Paul and * reported on what God had Act 15:4
now listened as * and Paul told Act 15:12
and *, to report on this decision. Act 15:22
along with our beloved * and Paul. Act 15:25
Paul and * stayed on at Antioch Act 15:34,35
Paul suggested to * that they Act 15:36
getting along. * agreed, and Act 15:37
they separated. * took Mark with Act 15:39
And must * and I alone keep 1Co 9:6
Jerusalem again, this time with *; Gal 2:1
shook hands with * and me and Gal 2:7,8,9
and even * became hypocrites too, Gal 2:13
and so does Mark, a relative of *. Col 4:10

BARNS
shall be stolen from your *. Job 5:24
* full to the brim with crops of Ps 144:12-15
* with plenty of the finest wheat. Ps 147:14
he will fill your * with wheat and Pro 3:9,10
They have filled their * with Is 3:14
the * and granaries are empty; Joe 1:17
and the cattle * are empty, yet I Hab 3:17
In fact, his * were full to Lk 12:17
down my * and build bigger ones! Lk 12:18
or harvest or have * to store away Lk 12:24

BARNY
nicknamed "* the Preacher"! Act 4:36

BARRACKS
they stay in their *. Jer 51:30
took him into the * of the palace, Mk 15:16,17
over at the *, knows that I am in Php 1:13

BARRAGE
beneath a fiery * of brimstone. Job 18:15

BARRED
with high walls and * gates. Deu 3:5
walls and installing * gates. 2Ch 8:5
darkness, and * them by limiting Job 38:10

BARREL
of grapes, and a small * of wine. 2Sa 16:1
Each day take flour from the * Eze 4:12

BARRELFUL
one rotten apple can spoil a *. Ecc 9:18

BARRELS
of bread, two * of wine, five 1Sa 25:18
"Fill four * with water," he 1Ki 18:33
wheat, 20,000 * of barley, 20,000 2Ch 2:10
of barley, 20,000 * of wine, and 2Ch 2:10
wine, and 20,000 * of olive oil." 2Ch 2:10
It held 3,000 * of water. 2Ch 4:5

BARREN
But Sarai was *; Gen 11:30
have a child, while Rachel was *. Gen 29:31
RACHEL, REALIZING SHE was *, Gen 30:1
So he went up to a * height, Num 23:3,4
shall be *, not even your cattle. Deu 7:14
The curse of * wombs; Deu 28:15-19
you have been * so long, you will Ju 13:2,3
The * woman now has seven 1Sa 2:5
For the godless are *: they can Job 15:34
to fall upon the * deserts, so that Job 38:25-27
the parched and * ground is Job 38:25-27
us in the * wilderness and sending Ps 44:19
river through the dry and * land; Ps 105:41
HellThe * wombA barren desertFire Pro 30:15,16
HellThe barren wombA * desertFire Pro 30:15,16
you away into a distant, * land; Is 22:18
cypress, fir and pine—on * land. Is 41:19
blossom; her * wilderness will Is 51:3
me even through the * deserts. Jer 2:2
them through the * wilderness, a Jer 2:6
all its beauty into * wilderness. Jer 12:10
plains in the * wilderness; Jer 17:6
exile lay empty as a * wilderness; Eze 36:34
Their cornstalks stand there *, Hos 8:7
all fail, and the fields lie *; Hab 3:17
"When you went out into the * Mt 11:7
out in the * wilderness," Isaiah Mk 1:3
to stay out in the * wastelands. Mk 1:45
no children, for Elizabeth was *; Lk 1:7
Elizabeth—'the * one,' they Lk 1:36
shouting from the * wilderness, Lk 3:4
out into the * wastelands of Judea, Lk 4:1
a voice from the * wilderness, Jn 1:23

BARRENNESS
all the women with * to punish Gen 20:18
who is responsible for your *." Gen 30:2
miscarriages nor * throughout your Ex 23:26
taunting Hannah because of her *. 1Sa 1:6

BARRICADED
fled into it, * the gates, and Ju 9:51

BARRIER
Jordan River as a * between our Jos 22:24,25
rooms was a low * eighteen inches Eze 40:7-12

BARS
"Make * of acacia wood to run Ex 26:26,27
* on each side of the Tabernacle. Ex 26:26,27
Also five * for the rear of the Ex 26:26,27
and make gold rings to hold the *; Ex 26:29
and also overlay the * with gold. Ex 26:29
frames, *, pillars, and bases; Ex 35:10-19
Then he made five sets of * from Ex 36:31,32
The frames and * were all Ex 36:34
frames; *; Ex 39:33-40
their bases and attaching the *. Ex 40:18
* the way to the Holy of Holies. Lev 4:6
Tabernacle, the *, the bases, the Num 4:30,31
of bread, some fig *, and a jar of 1Ki 14:3
walls, towers, gates, and *." 2Ch 14:7
doors, and made the bolts and *. Neh 3:3
and installed the bolts and *. Neh 3:6
and installed the bolts and *; Neh 3:13
and installed the bolts and *. Neh 3:14
and installed its locks and *. Neh 3:15
Or, "the * of heaven are afraid Job 26:13f
His ribs are like iron *. Job 40:18
brass and cut apart their iron *. Ps 107:16
anger shuts you out like iron *. Pro 18:19
His arms are round * of gold set Sol 5:14
city gates of brass and iron *. Is 45:2
Can a man break * of northern Jer 15:12,13
All their locks and * are broken, Lam 2:9

(BARS Con't)
I will snap the * that locked Amo 1:5

BARSABBAS
(also called *) and Matthias. Act 1:23
(also called *) and Silas. Act 15:22

BARTER
their goods to * for your trade. Eze 27:9

BARTHOLOMEW
*, Thomas Mt 10:2,3,4
*, Matthew Mk 3:16-19
*, Matthew Lk 6:14,15,16
*, Matthew Act 1:14

BARTIMAEUS
blind beggar named * (the son of Mk 10:46
When * heard that Jesus from Mk 10:47
calling you!" * yanked off his Mk 10:50

BARUCH
Next to him was * (son of Neh 3:20
*, Meshullam, Abijah, Neh 10:1
Ma-aseiah (son of *, son of Neh 11:4,5,6
the papers to * (son of Neriah, who Jer 32:12
given the papers to * I prayed: Jer 32:16
So Jeremiah sent for * (son of Jer 36:4
* wrote down all the prophecies. Jer 36:4
Jeremiah said to *, "Since I am a Jer 36:5
* did as Jeremiah told him to, Jer 36:8
Temple that day. * went to the Jer 36:10
about the messages * was reading to Jer 36:13
of Cushi) to ask * to come and read Jer 36:14,15
messages to them too, and * did. Jer 36:14,15
So * explained that Jeremiah Jer 36:18
hide," the officials said to *. Jer 36:19
Abdeel) to arrest * and Jeremiah. Jer 36:26
dictated again to * all he had Jer 36:32
to go to Egypt! * (son of Neriah) Jer 43:2,3
They even forced Jeremiah and * Jer 43:6
Jeremiah gave to * in the fourth Jer 45:1
of Josiah), after * had written Jer 45:1
O *, the Lord God of Israel says Jer 45:2
But tell * this, The Lord says: Jer 45:4

BARZILLAI
and * (a Gileadite of Rogelim). 2Sa 17:27
*, who had fed the king and his 2Sa 19:31,32
Jerusalem," the king said to *. 2Sa 19:33
and blessed *, he returned home. 2Sa 19:39
But be kind to the sons of * the 1Ki 2:7
Hakkoz, and * (he married one of Ez 2:61
the daughters of * the Gileadite Ez 2:61
Hakkoz, and * (he married one of Neh 7:63
the daughters of * the Gileadite Neh 7:63

BARZILLAI'S
to Josephus, Chimham was * son. 2Sa 19:37f

BASE
they came to the * of Mt. Ex 19:2,3
*, shaft, lamps, and blossoms. Ex 25:31
the rest at the * of the altar. Ex 29:12
Each frame was connected to its * Ex 36:24
beaten gold. Its *, shaft, Ex 37:17
Each post had a bronze *, and Ex 38:17
The washbasin and its *; Ex 39:33-40
poured out at the * of the altar Lev 4:7
poured out at the * of the burnt Lev 4:18
poured out at the * of the altar. Lev 4:25
the blood at the * of the altar. Lev 4:30
poured out at the * of the altar. Lev 4:34
drained out at the * of the altar; Lev 5:9
the blood at the * of the altar; Lev 8:15,16
the rest at the * of the altar. Lev 9:9
decorations on the * and branches, Num 8:4
and down to the * of the mountain Jos 18:16
Or, "because of man's * pride." Job 35:12f
its corners, * and sides were all Eze 41:22
The * is twenty-one inches high, Eze 43:13
than the * block on all sides. Eze 43:14
corners of the * of the altar and Eze 45:19

BASED
Many Hebrew names are * on puns. Gen 3:20f
should be * on whatever seems best 1Sa 10:7
your criticisms are not * on fact. Job 6:25,26
Your words are * on clever Job 15:4,5
Our power is * on your favor! Ps 89:17
all your commandments are * on Ps 119:151
they are * upon this earthly life. Pro 11:7
Your lawsuits are * on lies; Is 59:4
Their decisions must be * upon my Eze 44:24
predictions were * on how their Hos 4:12f
Their sentence is * on this Jn 3:19
Because our acquittal is not * on Rom 3:27
it is * on what Christ has done Rom 3:27
I preach is not * on some mere Gal 1:11
of priesthood * on family lines was Heb 7:18

BASEMATH
and he also married *, daughter Gen 26:34
* (his cousin Gen 36:2,3
Esau and * had a son named Reuel. Gen 36:4
had grandchildren from his wife *. Gen 36:13,14
Esau and his wife * while they Gen 36:17
Ahima-az (who married Princess *, 1Ki 4:8-19

BASES
with forty silver * for the frames Ex 26:18,19
* under each piece of the frame. Ex 26:18,19
their forty silver *, two bases for Ex 26:21
silver bases, two * for each frame, Ex 26:21
sixteen silver * for the frames—two Ex 26:25
the frames—two * under each frame. Ex 26:25
are to rest in four silver *. Ex 26:32
being imbedded in solid bronze *. Ex 27:17
frames, bars, pillars, and *; Ex 35:10-19
The pillars and their *; Ex 35:10-19
fitting into forty silver *. Ex 36:24
silver *, two for each frame. Ex 36:25,26
sixteen silver * beneath them, two Ex 36:30
gold and set into four silver *. Ex 36:36
their five * were molded from Ex 36:38
hold drapes, with * of bronze and Ex 38:10
* and with silver hooks and rods. Ex 38:11
*, and with silver hooks and rods. Ex 38:12
each with three posts and three *. Ex 38:14,15
*, and with silver hooks and rods; Ex 38:19
603,550 men. The * for the frames Ex 38:27
for casting the * for the posts at Ex 38:29
utensils, the * for the posts Ex 38:29
Posts; *; Ex 39:33-40
The * and the drapes at the gate Ex 39:33-40
their * and attaching the bars. Ex 40:18
the posts; the * for the posts, Num 3:36,37
and their *, pegs, and ropes. Num 3:36,37
the bars, the *, the frames for Num 4:30,31
fence with their *, pegs, cords, Num 4:32
Latticework covering the * of the 1Ki 7:41-46
cover the * of the two capitals; 1Ki 7:41-46
tank and its * and carried all the 2Ki 25:13
great tank and its *—all made for 2Ki 25:16
The * for the vats, and the vats 2Ch 4:12-16

BASHAN
to the city of *, but King Og of Num 21:33
but King Og of * met them with his Num 21:33
and of King Og of *—all the land Num 32:33
and King Og of * had been defeated Deu 1:1
TURNED toward King Og's land of *. Deu 3:1
the entire Argob region of *. Deu 3:4
the kingdom of * just as we had Deu 3:6
all of Gilead and * as far as the Deu 3:10
"Incidentally, King Og of * was Deu 3:11
the Argob region. (* is sometimes Deu 3:13
Argob region (*) to the borders of Deu 3:14
and Golan, in *, for the tribe of Deu 4:43
that of King Og of *—they were two Deu 4:47
and King Og of * came out against Deu 29:7
Choice * rams, and goats— Deu 32:14
Leaping out from *." Deu 33:22
of Heshbon, and Og, king of *. Jos 9:10
King Og of *, the last of the Jos 12:4
Salecah on Mount * in the east, and Jos 12:5
Mount * with its city of Salecah; Jos 13:11
of King Og of *, who had reigned in Jos 13:12
included all of *, the former Jos 13:30
and the sixty cities of Jair in *. Jos 13:30
land of Gilead and * [on the east Jos 17:1
and * across the Jordan River). Jos 17:5,6
and Golan of *, in the land of Jos 20:8
by sacred lot in the area of *. Jos 21:6
Golan, in * (a City of Refuge), Jos 21:27
the land of * to the half-tribe of Jos 22:7,8
and the region of Argob in *, 1Ki 4:8-19
of the Amorites and King Og of *. 1Ki 4:8-19
the Arnon as far as Gilead and *. 2Ki 10:32,33
in the land of *, lived the 1Ch 5:11
(in the land of *) and throughout 1Ch 5:16
the land from * to Baal-hermon, 1Ch 5:23
cities in the * area from the 1Ch 6:62
Golan, in *; 1Ch 6:71
Sihon of Heshbon and King Og of *. Neh 9:22
strong as the giant bulls from *. Ps 22:12
O mighty mountains in *! Ps 68:15,16
"I will bring back from *." Ps 68:22f
and Og, the king of *; Ps 135:11
*—for his lovingkindness to Israel Ps 136:20
the mighty oaks of * shall bend Is 2:13
Sharon has become a wilderness; * Is 33:9
shout for them at *; Jer 22:20
of Carmel and * and to be happy Jer 50:19
made your oars from oaks of *. Eze 27:6
fat young bulls of * for my feast! Eze 39:18
"fat cows" of * living in Amo 4:1
* and Gilead as they did long ago. Mic 7:14
the lush pastures of * and Carmel Nah 1:4
Cry in fear, you oaks of *, as Zec 11:2

BASIC
fear of God are * to all wisdom. Pro 9:10
Then I observed that the * motive Ecc 4:4
And this is the * law of the Eze 43:12

BASIN
Drain the lamb's blood into a *, Ex 12:22
a bronze * with a bronze pedestal. Ex 30:17,18
The * with its pedestal; Ex 35:10-19
the great bronze * in the Temple Jer 27:19,20,21
poured water into a *, and began Jn 13:5

BASINS
animals, and drew it off into *. Ex 24:6
the blood from the * towards the Ex 24:8
The ash buckets, shovels, *, Ex 27:3
*, meat hooks, and fire pans. Ex 38:3
hooks, shovels, *, and other Num 4:14
pots, shovels, and * and at last 1Ki 7:40
pots, shovels, * 1Ki 7:41-46
cups, snuffers, *, spoons, 1Ki 7:50
meat and for the *, cups, and bowls 1Ch 28:17
pots, shovels, and * for use in 2Ch 4:11
lamp snuffers, *, spoons, and 2Ch 4:22

BASIS
Language is the * on which science Gen 11:6f
be selected on the * of whether it Lev 27:33
on Saul's staff on a part-time *. 1Sa 17:14,15
villages on the * of their 1Ch 9:22
appointed on the * of their 1Ch 26:31,32
Verse 14 is the * for the Dan 8:26f
on a sharecrop *, and went away to Mt 21:33
No, for he does it on the * of Rom 3:26
Abraham had no * at all for pride. Rom 4:1
Levi, but on the * of power flowing Heb 7:16

BASK
not the wise man * in his wisdom, Jer 9:23
guard as they * in false security. Dan 8:25

BASKET
In the top * were all kinds of Gen 40:17
Place the bread in a * and Ex 29:3,4
one wafer from the * of unleavened Ex 29:23
*, at the door of the Tabernacle. Ex 29:32
the * of bread made without yeast; Lev 8:1
all taken from the * which had been Lev 8:26
that is in the * of consecration, Lev 8:31
a * of bread made without yeast; Num 6:15
the * of bread made without yeast; Num 6:17
Bring it in a * and hand it to Deu 26:2,3
The priest will then take the * Deu 26:4
Then, carrying the meat in a * Ju 6:19
as golden apples in a silver *. Pro 25:11
In one * there were fresh, Jer 24:2
a vision, a * full of ripe fruit. Amo 8:1
I replied, "A * full of ripe Amo 8:2
He replied, "It is a bushel * Zec 5:6
lead cover on the * was lifted off, Zec 5:7
see a woman sitting inside the *! Zec 5:7
her back into the * and clamped Zec 5:8
And they took the bushel * Zec 5:9
let him down in a * through an Act 9:25
but I was let down by rope and * 2Co 11:33

BASKETFULS
(from carrying heavy * of earth); Eze 29:18
there were twelve * left over! Mt 14:20
up, there were seven * left over! Mt 15:37,38
five loaves, and the * left over? Mt 16:9
afterwards twelve * of scraps were Mk 6:43,44
were seven very large * left over! Mk 8:8,9
How many * of scraps did you pick Mk 8:19
"Seven *," they said. Mk 8:20
still, twelve * of scraps were Lk 9:17

BASKETS
three * of pastries on my head. Gen 40:16
"The three * mean three days," Gen 40:18,19
were packed into * and presented to 2Ki 10:7
I saw two * of figs placed in Jer 24:2
And twelve * were filled with Jn 6:13

BASTARD
the sanctuary. A * may not enter Deu 23:2
"You illegitimate *, Jn 9:34

BAT
The hoopoe, the *. Lev 11:13-19
The hoopoe, the *. Deu 14:11-18

BATH
take a complete * and be unclean Lev 15:16
beauty taking her evening *. 2Sa 11:2
you a blood *—your turn has come! Eze 35:6
measure, and the * (one-tenth of a Eze 45:11

BATH-RABBIM
pools in Heshbon by the gate of *. Sol 7:4

BATH-SHEBA
told that she was *, the daughter 2Sa 11:3
When * heard that her husband was 2Sa 11:26
Then David comforted *; 2Sa 12:24
Then Nathan the prophet went to * 1Ki 1:11
So * went into the king's 1Ki 1:15
for him. * bowed low before him. 1Ki 1:16
"Call *," David said. 1Ki 1:28
Then * bowed low before him again 1Ki 1:31
came to see Solomon's mother, *. 1Ki 2:13
"All right," * replied, "I'll 1Ki 2:18

BATH-SHEBA'S
And the Lord made * baby deathly 2Sa 12:15

BATH-SHUA
Judah had three sons by *, a girl 1Ch 2:3
Literally, "*." 1Ch 3:5f

BATHE
came down to * in the river, and as Ex 2:5
to the river to *, and say to him, Ex 8:20
"* Aaron and his sons there at Ex 29:3,4
all his hair, and * himself, and Lev 14:8
his clothes and *, and shall then Lev 14:9
wash his clothes and * himself. Lev 15:5
wash his clothes and * himself. Lev 15:6
wash his clothes and * himself. Lev 15:8
wash his clothes and * himself. Lev 15:10

(BATHE Con't)
his clothes and * himself and be Lev 15:11
as the man must *, and they are Lev 15:18
his clothes and * himself and be Lev 15:21,22,23
* and be defiled until evening. Lev 15:27
He must * himself and put on the Lev 16:4
Then he shall * in a sacred Lev 16:24
his clothes and * himself and then Lev 16:26
* himself and then return to camp. Lev 16:28
his clothes and * himself and be Lev 17:15
his clothes and *, he shall suffer Lev 17:16
his clothes, and *, and afterwards Num 19:7
his clothes, and *, and he too Num 19:8
his clothes and * himself, and that Num 19:19
then he shall * himself and Deu 23:11
Now do what I tell you—* and put Ru 3:3

BATHED
until after he has * that evening. Lev 22:6
the prostitutes *, dogs came and 1Ki 22:38
been welcomed! You * yourself, Eze 23:40
Jesus replied, "One who has * Jn 13:10

BATHES
He * his feet in soothing olive Deu 33:24

BATHING
clothes and * in running water. Lev 15:13

BATHROOM
that perhaps he was using the *. Ju 3:24
cave to go to the *, but as it 1Sa 24:3

BATHSHEBA
he was in Jerusalem, his wife * 1Ch 3:5
his adultery with *, and his murder Ps 51:1

BATS
to the moles and *, and crawl into Is 2:20

BATTALION
the army officers and * leaders. Num 31:14
Then the officers and * leaders Num 31:48,49
the captains and * leaders and Num 31:51,52
the names of the * leaders. Deu 20:9

BATTALIONS
their troops by * and companies, 1Sa 29:2
the forced labor *, and Jehoshaphat 2Sa 20:24
labor * from the tribe of Joseph. 1Ki 11:27,28

BATTER
a * of flour mixed with olive oil. Lev 7:12

BATTERED
its gates are * down. Is 24:12

BATTERING
portable towers, and * rams Deu 20:20
the city wall and began * it down. 2Sa 20:15
Cut down her trees for * rams; Jer 6:6
and * rams surrounding the walls. Eze 4:1
Jerusalem! With * rams they will go Eze 21:22
He will set up * rams against Eze 26:9

BATTLE
captured in a *, that you have Gen 31:26
though fleeing in *, with no power Lev 26:37
has been killed in *, or who has Num 19:16
that he can * them successfully." Num 22:11
lead them into * and care for them, Num 27:17
armed men were sent to * by Moses. Num 31:4,5
into *, accompanied by the Ark, Num 31:6
man of Midian was killed in *! Num 31:7
who were in the *, "This is the Num 31:21
who were in the *, and the other Num 31:27
*, and not one of us is missing! Num 31:48,49
will go over to * for the Lord, Num 32:27
Before you begin the *, a priest Deu 20:2
For you might be killed in the *, Deu 20:5
You might die in * and someone Deu 20:6
For you might die in the *, and Deu 20:7
You will march out to * Deu 28:25
out against us in *, but we Deu 29:7
During the * the five kings Jos 10:16
one enemy troop survived the *. Jos 11:8
Israel went out to * against its Ju 2:15
the slopes of Mount Tabor into *. Ju 4:14
Dared to die upon the fields of *. Ju 5:18
Your actions at the end of the * Ju 8:2,3
Shechem into the * and fought with Ju 9:39
of Shechem went out to * again. Ju 9:42
the fields. The * went on all day Ju 9:45
life and went to * without you, and Ju 12:3
Before the * the Israeli army Ju 20:18
in their usual * formation. Ju 20:30
Summary of the *: Ju 20:35-39
troops died in that day's *. Ju 20:44
After the * was over, the army 1Sa 4:3
"If we carry it into * with us, 1Sa 4:3
of Eli, accompanied it into the *. 1Sa 4:4
ran from the * and arrived at 1Sa 4:12
the news of the *, for his heart 1Sa 4:13
"I have just come from the *—I 1Sa 4:16
arrived for *, but the Lord spoke 1Sa 7:10
his troops into *, while others 1Sa 8:12
will govern us and lead us to *." 1Sa 8:20
to follow Saul and Samuel to *!" 1Sa 11:7
ready for *, I said, 'The 1Sa 13:11
rushed out to the * and found the 1Sa 14:20
* continued out beyond Beth-aven. 1Sa 14:23
they flew upon the spoils of * 1Sa 14:32
their army for * and camped between 1Sa 17:1
with shouts and * cries. 1Sa 17:20
you just want to see the *!" 1Sa 17:28
AFTER SAUL'S RETURN from his * 1Sa 24:1
or he will die in * or of old age. 1Sa 26:10
"They aren't going into the * 1Sa 29:4
by turning against us in the *? 1Sa 29:4
to have you with them in the *. 1Sa 29:9
who go to * and those who guard the 1Sa 30:24
had begun the * against Israel, and 1Sa 31:1
"Tell me how the * went." 2Sa 1:4
And did not return from * 2Sa 1:22
have fallen in the midst of the *. 2Sa 1:25
and Asahel, were also in the *. 2Sa 2:18
brother Asahel at the * of Gibeon. 2Sa 3:30
were killed at the * of Jezreel. 2Sa 4:4
the outcome of the * reached the 2Sa 4:4
of Zobah in a * at the Euphrates 2Sa 8:3
part of the *—and then pull back 2Sa 11:15
David of how the * was going, he 2Sa 11:18
So the * began in the forest of 2Sa 18:6
that day. The * raged all across 2Sa 18:8
During the * Absalom came upon 2Sa 18:9
ashamed and had been beaten in *. 2Sa 19:3
had died in * on Mount Gilboa. 2Sa 21:12,13,14
the thick of the *, David became 2Sa 21:15
are not going out to * again! 2Sa 21:17
have given me strength for the * 2Sa 22:40
killed eight hundred men in one *. 2Sa 23:8
your people out to * against their 1Ki 8:44
who had died in *, the Israeli army 1Ki 11:15
lines, and moved into the *; 1Ki 20:27
on the seventh day the * began. 1Ki 20:29
I was in the *, and a man brought 1Ki 20:39
So Ahab went into the * disguised 1Ki 22:30
"Take me out of the *, for I am 1Ki 22:34
The * became more and more 1Ki 22:35
What are your * plans?" 2Ki 3:6,7,8
Moab saw that the * had been lost, 2Ki 3:26
King Joram was wounded in the *, 2Ki 8:28
his army. The * began at 2Ki 14:11
also died in the *, for God was 1Ch 5:22
led our armies to * and brought 1Ch 11:2
He was with David in the * 1Ch 11:13
he was going into * with the 1Ch 12:19
All these men came in * array to 1Ch 12:38
After the * the Israelis picked 1Ch 14:12
them and began the * at the gates 1Ch 19:9
and engaged the enemy troops in *. 1Ch 19:17,18
During another *, at Gath, a 1Ch 20:6,7
will lead us into * against you. 2Ch 13:12
turn the tide of * against King 2Ch 13:15,16
as he was returning from the *. 2Ch 15:2
they had captured in the *. 2Ch 15:11
King Ahab to go to * against 2Ch 18:19,20
until I return safely from the *!' 2Ch 18:26
The * grew hotter and hotter 2Ch 18:34
For the * is not yours, but 2Ch 20:15
led his army there to join the *. 2Ch 22:5
your troops to *, you will be 2Ch 25:8
the * at the Valley of Megiddo. 2Ch 35:22
"Take me out of the *," he 2Ch 35:23
shall perish in * and die because Job 36:12
into * when the trumpet blows. Job 39:24
He smells the * when far away. Job 39:25
He rejoices at the shouts of * Job 39:25
a man and brace yourself for *. Job 40:7
long remember the * that ensues, Job 41:8
He prepares me for * and gives Ps 18:34
me with strong armor for the *. Ps 18:39
You gave me victory in every *. Ps 18:43,44,45
and mighty, invincible in *. Ps 24:8
the God of Abraham—for the * Ps 47:9
Though the tide of * runs Ps 55:18
for help, the tide of * turns. Ps 56:9
There they shouted their * cry Ps 74:4
when the day of * came, because Ps 78:9
and refused to help him in *. Ps 89:43
in the heat of *, and now he has Ps 118:14
gives me strength and skill in *. Ps 144:1
prepared against the day of *." Pro 21:31f
that obligation and that dark * Ecc 8:8
strongest man the *, and that wise Ecc 9:11
Their husbands shall die in *; Is 3:25,26
longer be the issuing of * gear; Is 9:5
dead bodies of those slain in *. Is 14:19
The Lord, the God of *, has Is 14:27
When I raise my * flag upon the Is 18:3
your shields and prepare for *! Is 21:5
us swift horses for riding to *." Is 30:16
* flags of Israel, says the Lord. Is 31:9
people and destroyed them in *. Is 42:25
trumpets and the enemies' * cries. Jer 4:19
See them prepare for *. Jer 6:4
as a horse rushing to the *! Jer 8:6
so their young men shall die in *; Jer 11:21,22
and their youths die in *! Jer 18:21
For I will upset the * plans Jer 19:7
Terrify him all day long with * Jer 20:16
Pharaoh's army in *, Jeremiah Jer 37:11
occasion of the * of Carchemish Jer 46:2
you Egyptians and advance to *! Jer 46:3
Mobilize for *, for the sword of Jer 46:14
And then the roar of * will surge Jer 48:2,3,4
Let there be the shout of * in Jer 50:22
their * cry roars like the surf Jer 50:42
against you fully ready for the *. Jer 50:42
Sound the * cry; Jer 51:27
ebb away like those wounded in *. Lam 2:12
in a mighty * of the end times. Eze 38:2,3f
on the Prince of Princes in *; Dan 8:25
neither in * nor in riot. Dan 11:20
us, nor can our strength in *; Hos 14:3
like a mighty army moving into *. Joe 2:5
there will be wild shouts of * Amo 1:14
men to *, a hundred will return. Amo 5:3
Trumpet calls and * cries; Zep 1:16
glorious like a proud steed in *. Zec 10:3
*, the Ruler over all the earth. Zec 10:4
that they are being called to *? 1Co 14:8
finally won the * against all his 1Co 15:28
In every * you will need faith Eph 6:16
winning a great * against many Heb 7:1
the * and gave it to Melchizedek. Heb 7:2
were given great power in *; Heb 11:34
you have won your * with Satan. 1Jn 2:13
fight and win this * except by 1Jn 5:5
looked like horses armored for *. Rev 9:7
army of chariots rushing into *. Rev 9:9
And the Dragon lost the * and Rev 12:8
to gather them for * against the Rev 16:14
Gog and Magog, for *—a mighty host, Rev 20:8

BATTLEAXE
is God's * and sword. Jer 51:20

BATTLEFIELD
Israeli troops are dead on the *. 1Sa 4:17
* with shouts and battle cries. 1Sa 17:20
the booty from the *, they found 1Ch 10:8
heroic warriors went out to the * 1Ch 10:12

BATTLEFIELDS
those slain on *, from whom your Ps 88:5

BATTLEFRONT
As the messenger from the * 1Sa 4:13

BATTLEGROUND
of God from the * at Ebenezer to 1Sa 5:1

BATTLEMENT
we will build upon her a * of Sol 8:9

BATTLEMENTS
huge stones from the towers and *. 2Ch 26:15
the walled cities and strongest *! Zep 1:16

BATTLES
for the Lord's * go with you over Num 32:29
by fighting the Lord's *." 1Sa 18:17
for you are fighting his *; 1Sa 25:28
aid the Ammonites in their *. 1Ch 19:19
but also in his * with the Arabs of 2Ch 26:7
our God to fight our * for us!" 2Ch 32:8
and have not helped us in our *. Ps 44:9
Joshua led the * against the Act 7:45
plans and methods to win my *. 2Co 10:3
well in the Lord's *, just as the 1Ti 1:18
as a result won *, overthrew Heb 11:33
he rode out to conquer in many * Rev 6:2

BATTLING
the wilderness, * them at Jahaz. Num 21:23
* to the last before your gates. Is 28:6
working and * side by side. Php 2:25

BAVVAI
brothers led by * (son of Henadad), Neh 3:18

BAY
began at the south * of the Salt Jos 15:2,3,4
began at the * where the Jordan Jos 15:5
ended at the north * of the Salt Jos 18:19
* and white, each with its rider. Zec 1:8
but noticed a * with a beach and Act 27:39

BAZLITH
*, Mehida, Harsha, Neh 7:46-56

BAZLUTH
Hakupha, Harhur, *, Mehida, Harsha, Ez 2:43-54

BDELLIUM
beautiful * and even lapis lazuli. Gen 2:11,12

BE-ALOTH
Ziph, Telem, *, Hazor-hadattah, Jos 15:21-32

BE-ERA
Ithran, *. 1Ch 7:36,37

BE-ERI
Judith, daughter of * the Hethite; Gen 26:34

BE-EROTH
journeyed from * of Bene-jaakan to Deu 10:6
Chephirah, *, and Kiriath-jearim. Jos 9:17
Gibeon, Ramah, *, Mizpeh, Jos 18:21-28
who was from * in Benjamin. 2Sa 4:2,3
(People from * are counted as 2Sa 4:2,3
Naharai from *, the armor bearer 2Sa 23:24-39
Naharai from *—he was General 1Ch 11:26-47
Chephirah, and *, 743; Ez 2:3-35
Chephirah, and *, 743; Neh 7:8-38

BE-ESHTERAH
Bashan (a City of Refuge), and *. Jos 21:27

BEACH
upon a *, God will silence them. Is 17:13
up Jonah on the *, and it did. Jon 2:10
walking along the * beside the Lake Mt 4:18

(BEACH Con't)
A little farther up the * he saw Mt 4:21
the people listened on the *. Mt 13:2,3
it up onto the * and sits down and Mt 13:47,48
A little farther up the *, he saw Mk 1:19
As he was walking up the * he Mk 2:14
withdrew to the *, followed by a Mk 3:7,8
in case he was crowded off the *. Mk 3:9
around him on the * as he was Mk 4:1
the * but couldn't see who he was. Jn 21:4
net to the *, about 300 feet away. Jn 21:8
walked down to the * with us where Act 21:5
a bay with a * and wondered whether Act 27:39
rocks and be driven up onto the *. Act 27:39
a bonfire on the * to welcome and Act 28:1
along the * by the wild waves. Jud 1:13
He stood waiting on an ocean *. Rev 12:17

BEACON
You think of yourselves as * Rom 2:19
Shine out among them like * Php 2:15

BEAD
by a single * of your necklace. Sol 4:9

BEADS
golden earrings and silver *." Sol 1:11

BEAK
him with an olive leaf in her *. Gen 8:11

BEALIAH
Jerimoth; *; 1Ch 12:3-7

BEALOTH
whose areas were Asher and *; 1Ki 4:8-19

BEAM
was as huge as a weaver's *! 2Sa 21:19
was as thick as a weaver's *. 1Ch 11:23
his spear was like a weaver's *! 1Ch 20:5
let your face * with joy as you Ps 67:1
For their advice is a * of light Pro 6:23

BEAMED
He's alive!" he *. 1Ki 17:23
a floodlight is * upon you." Lk 11:36

BEAMS
of the Temple by * resting on 1Ki 6:6
the wall—so the * were not inserted 1Ki 6:6
the * and pillars, with cedar. 1Ki 6:9
stone and one layer of cedar *. 1Ki 6:36
The great cedar ceiling * rested 1Ki 7:2
and were topped with cedar *. 1Ki 7:11
topped with cedar *, just like the 1Ki 7:12
All the walls, *, doors, and 2Ch 3:7
blocks, timber, lumber, and *. 2Ch 34:10,11
way shall have the * pulled from Ez 6:11
me timber for the * and for the Neh 2:8
thing—cut the *, hung the doors, Neh 3:3
They laid the *, set up the Neh 3:6
* and throw them on the fire. Jer 22:7
you, and the * in the ceilings echo Hab 2:11

BEANS
parched grain, *, lentils, honey, 2Sa 17:28,29
barley, *, lentils, and spelt. Eze 4:9

BEAR
woman, "You shall * children in Gen 3:16
is greater than I can *. Gen 4:13
Sarah shall * you a son; Gen 17:19
then let me * the blame forever. Gen 43:9
And if I must * the anguish of Gen 43:14
you, I shall * the blame forever.' Gen 44:32
I cannot * to see what this would Gen 44:34
forehead, and thus * the guilt Ex 28:37,38
Don't * a grudge; Lev 19:18
He shall * his guilt. Lev 20:17
they shall * their guilt. Lev 20:19
* their sin and die childless. Lev 20:20
he must * his guilt. Num 9:13
they shall * the burden of the Num 11:17
old enough to * arms, had died. Deu 2:14,15
been old enough to * arms had been Jos 5:4,5
been old enough to * arms when they Jos 5:6
"and a lion or a * comes and grabs 1Sa 17:34
the lion and the * will save me 1Sa 17:37
* who has been robbed of her cubs. 2Sa 17:8
in the soil and * fruit for God. 2Ki 19:30
He made the *, Orion and the Job 9:9
of the * with her satellites across Job 38:32
they are a burden too heavy to *. Ps 38:3,4
It is safer to meet a * robbed of Pro 17:12
A short-tempered man must * his Pro 19:19
as a lion or * attacking them. Pro 28:15
for he shall * all their sins. Is 53:11
is incurable, but I must * it. Jer 10:19
How proud I am to * your name, O Jer 15:16
he could no longer * all the evil Jer 44:22
He lurks like a *, like a lion, Lam 3:10
see what sorrows we must *! Lam 5:1
* the consequence of all your sin. Eze 23:35
for they must * their shame for all Eze 44:13
looked like a * with its paw Dan 7:5
and your city * your name." Dan 9:19
she shall * no more fruit. Hos 9:16
to pieces like a * whose cubs have Hos 13:8
Samaria must * her guilt, for Hos 13:16
The trees will * their fruit; Joe 2:22
lion—and met by a *, or a man in a Amo 5:19
How long shall I * with you? Mt 17:17
Then he said to it, "Never * Mt 21:19
"You shall never * fruit again!" Mk 11:14
wife Elizabeth will * you a son! Lk 1:13
* fruit for even larger crops. Jn 15:2
we nor our fathers were able to *? Act 15:10
wife was about to * him twin Rom 9:10-13
for we must * the "burden" of Rom 15:1
you can * up patiently against it. 1Co 10:13
not * to look at Moses' face. 2Co 3:7
like a fool. Do * with me and let 2Co 11:1
Each of us must * some faults Gal 6:5
all my energies to * on this one Php 3:13
As I was saying, when I could * 1Th 3:5
We can * anything as long as we 1Th 3:8
Christ, whose noble name you *. Jas 2:7

BEAR'S
but had * feet and a lion's mouth! Rev 13:2

BEARD
from his head, *, and eyebrows, and Lev 14:9
of your *, as the heathen do. Lev 19:27
flow down his *, until finally 1Sa 21:13
nor trimmed his * since the day the 2Sa 19:24,25
took him by the * with his right 2Sa 20:8,9,10
* and sat down utterly baffled. Ez 9:3
ran down onto his *, and onto the Ps 133:2
Literally, "head-hair, *, Is 7:20f
to those who pull out the *. Is 50:6
razor to shave your head and *; Eze 5:1

BEARDS
hair or *, nor cut their flesh. Lev 21:5
off half their * and cut their 2Sa 10:4
at Jericho until their * grew out; 2Sa 10:5
by shaving their * and cutting 1Ch 19:4
until their * had grown out again. 1Ch 19:5
in sorrow and cut off their *. Is 15:2
They had shaved off their *, torn Jer 41:5
They shave their heads and * in Jer 48:37

BEARER
groaned to his youthful armor *. Ju 9:54
and his armor * walked ahead of him 1Sa 17:4-7
with his shield * ahead of him, 1Sa 17:41,42
He groaned to his armor *, "Kill 1Sa 31:3,4
But his armor * was afraid to, 1Sa 31:3,4
When his armor * saw that he was 1Sa 31:5
So Saul, his armor *, his three 1Sa 31:6
Naharai from Be-eroth, the armor * 2Sa 23:24-39
was General Joab's armor *; 1Ch 11:26-47

BEARERS
Ten of Joab's young armor * then 2Sa 18:15
and touched it, and the * stopped. Lk 7:14
then you will become light *." Jn 12:36

BEARING
day, * the burden of your sins. Num 14:34,35
along a river bank * luscious fruit Ps 1:3
You are like a lovely orchard * Sol 4:13,14
forth branches and * fruit. Eze 17:22,23
Lord, * children that aren't his. Hos 5:7
to suffer with him there, * his Heb 13:13
of Life, * twelve crops of fruit, Rev 22:2

BEARS
—he * my name. Ex 23:21
The first son she * to him shall Deu 25:6
to both lions and *, and I'll do it 1Sa 17:36
and two female * came out of the 2Ki 2:24
stole the fruit it *, or if I have Job 31:38,39
He who daily * our burdens also Ps 68:19
He never * a grudge, nor remains Ps 103:9
child, as one who * your name! Ps 109:21
a tree that * life-giving fruit, Pro 11:30
The cows will graze among *; Is 11:7
You roar like hungry *; Is 59:11

BEAST
"Issachar is a strong * of Gen 49:14
from man or *, and then eats the Lev 7:21
Ask the dumbest *—he knows that Job 12:7,8,9
O Babylon, evil *, you shall be Ps 137:8
famine to destroy both man and *. Eze 14:13
kills man and * alike, though Eze 14:19

BEASTS
I will set wild * upon them, Deu 32:24
Of all the *, he is the Job 41:34
Literally, "the wild *." Ps 74:19f
your beloved people from these *. Ps 74:19
that they are no better than *. Ecc 3:18
has no real advantage over the *; Ecc 3:19
who consign Tyre to the wild *. Is 23:13
But look! The * are stumbling! Is 46:1
to him, all men are stupid *. Jer 51:17
war, famine, ferocious *, plague. Eze 14:21
taught him to be 'king of the *.' Eze 19:5
in fighting wild *—those men of 1Co 15:32

BEAT
So Sarai * her and she ran away. Gen 16:6
and holy incense. * some of it Ex 30:36
Bezalel * gold into thin plates Ex 39:3
He shall then * the metal into a Num 16:38
bronze censers and * them out into Num 16:39
Balaam * her back onto the road. Num 22:22,23
So he * her again. Num 22:25
In a great fit of temper Balaam * Num 22:27
"Why did you * your donkey those Num 22:32
When you * the olives from your Deu 24:20
I * them into dust; 2Sa 22:43
and * back the Philistines; 2Sa 23:11,12
But we can * them easily on the 1Ki 20:23
of a doubt that we will * them." 1Ki 20:25
there he burned it and * it to 2Ki 23:6
I will * down his adversaries Ps 89:23
know it when they * me up . Pro 23:35
Literally, "* their swords into Is 2:4f
waits in hiding to * up the judge Is 29:21
for your grief. * your breasts in Is 32:12
let the leaders of mankind * Jer 25:34
Son of dust, with sobbing, * Eze 21:12
* your pruning hooks into spears. Joe 3:10
Jonah, and the sun * down upon his Jon 4:8
They will * their swords into Mic 4:3
like doves, and * their breasts! Nah 2:7
the storm winds * against his Mt 7:25
and storm winds * against his Mt 7:27
attacked his men, * one, killed one Mt 21:35
others * up his messengers and Mt 22:6
and * him on the head with it. Mt 27:30
But the farmers * up the man and Mk 12:3
And they * him on the head Mk 15:19
and money and * him up and left him Lk 10:30
as he prayed, but * upon his chest Lk 18:13
But the tenants * him up and sent Lk 20:10
and * him outside the courtroom. Act 18:17
on two of them and * them up, so Act 19:16
I imprisoned and * those in every Act 22:19

BEATEN
before, and we are * for something Ex 5:16
using * gold, and place them at Ex 25:18
"Make a lampstand of pure, * Ex 25:31
to be one piece of pure, * gold. Ex 25:36
He made two cherubim of * gold Ex 37:7
again using pure, * gold. Ex 37:17
all one piece of pure, * gold. Ex 37:22
with sweet incense * into fine Lev 16:12
was made entirely of * gold. Num 8:4
two trumpets of * silver to be used Num 10:1
to lie down and be * in his Deu 25:1
as though badly *, and all the Jos 8:15
when she had * out the barley she Ru 2:17
troops were * back by David's men. 2Sa 18:7
ashamed and had been * in battle. 2Sa 19:3
Solomon had some of the gold * 1Ki 10:16,17
you would have * Syria until they 2Ki 13:19
those without it are * as Pro 10:13
on dill, but it is * with a stick. Is 28:27
but it is * softly with a flail. Is 28:27
They shall see my Servant * and Is 52:14,15
They bring * sheets of silver Jer 10:9
and later, others were either * Mk 12:5
the courts, and * in the Mk 13:9
he was * up and insulted and sent Lk 20:11
apostles, had them *, and then told Act 5:40
stripped and * with wooden whips. Act 16:22
They have publicly * us without Act 16:37
We have been *, put in jail, 2Co 6:5
Three times I was * with rods. 2Co 11:25
laughed at and *, and sometimes you Heb 10:33
But others trusted God and were * Heb 11:35
if you are * for doing wrong; 1Pe 2:20

BEATING
your * me these three times?" Num 22:28
the penalty is a *, the judge shall Deu 25:1
house and began * at the door and Ju 19:22
Oh, let him stop * me, so that I Job 9:34
troops coming, they quit * Paul. Act 21:32
port of Salmone. * into the wind Act 27:7,8

BEATS
"If a man * his slave to Ex 21:20
My heart * wildly, my strength Ps 38:10

BEAUTIFUL
all sorts of * trees there in the Gen 2:9
* bdellium and even lapis lazuli. Gen 2:11,12
looked upon the * earth women and Gen 6:1
"You are very *," he told her, Gen 12:11,12,13
or like the * countryside around Gen 13:10
Lord about this, a * young girl Gen 24:15,16
and dressed him in * clothing and Gen 41:41,42
was an unusually * baby, she hid Ex 2:1
separation to God—* garments that Ex 28:2
The * clothing for the priests, to Ex 35:10-19
He will be able to create * Ex 35:32
a jeweler, and can do * carving; Ex 35:33
the people made * garments of blue, Ex 39:1
it was a skillful and * piece of Ex 39:3
The chestpiece was a * piece of Ex 39:8
The chestpiece, the * turbans, Ex 39:28,29
the captives a * girl you want as Deu 21:11
For I saw a * robe imported from Jos 7:21
And she gave him milk in a * cup! Ju 5:25
and his wife, a * and very 1Sa 25:3
Here I am living in this * cedar 2Sa 7:2
you built me a * cedar temple?' 2Sa 7:7
and its * harbor are ours! 2Sa 12:26,27
son, had a * sister named Tamar. 2Sa 13:1
Tamar, who was a very * girl. 2Sa 14:27

(BEAUTIFUL Con't)
the most * girl in all the land. 1Ki 1:3,4
She also saw the * palace he had 1Ki 10:4
been such a supply of * wood. 1Ki 10:12
and gold dishes, * cloth, myrrh, 1Ki 10:25
"This city is located in * 2Ki 2:19
highest heaven would be * enough! 2Ch 2:6
will be huge and incredibly *. 2Ch 2:9
trees and chains. * jewels were 2Ch 3:6
there been such * instruments in 2Ch 9:11
Solomon's * Temple—wept aloud, Ez 3:12
There were also two * pieces of Ez 8:26,27
into a * guest room for Tobiah. Neh 13:5
beauty—for she was a very * woman. Est 1:11
and find the most * girls in the Est 2:2
This man had a * and lovely Est 2:7
demanded a second bevy of * girls. Est 2:19
The heavens are made * by his Job 26:13
MY HEART IS overflowing with a * Ps 45:1
in * clothing woven with gold. Ps 45:13
shines from the * Temple Ps 50:2
she will place a * crown upon Pro 4:8,9
A * woman lacking discretion and Pro 11:22
an attic than in a * home with a Pro 25:24
And then there were my many * Ecc 2:7,8
The Girl: "I am dark but *, O Sol 1:5
don't know, O most * woman in all Sol 1:8
* you are, my love, how beautiful! Sol 1:15
beautiful you are, my love, how *! Sol 1:15
KING SOLOMON: "How * you are, my Sol 4:1
beautiful you are, my love, how *! Sol 4:1
of scarlet—and how * your mouth. Sol 4:3
You are so *, my love, in every Sol 4:7
"O rarest of * women, where has Sol 6:1
you are as * as the lovely land of Sol 6:4
of Tirzah, yes, * as Jerusalem, and Sol 6:4
KING SOLOMON: "How * your Sol 7:1
lingerie, * dresses and veils. Is 3:23
him say, "Many a * home will lie Is 5:9
are, building this * sepulchre in Is 22:15,16
turned to rubble. * palaces in Is 25:2
become as * as the Garden of Eden. Is 51:3
Put on your * clothes, O Zion, Is 52:1
How * upon the mountains are the Is 52:7
all, you will be * forever, a joy Is 60:15
Our holy, * Temple where our Is 64:11
* land, the finest in the world. Jer 3:19
Why do you put on your most * Jer 4:30
Helpless as a girl, you are * Jer 6:2
* to see and full of good fruit; Jer 11:16
your * flock I gave you to take Jer 13:20
But a * palace does not make a Jer 22:15
graciously in a * palace among the Jer 22:23
See how the strong, the * is Jer 48:17
city called 'Most * in All the Lam 2:15
it was inexpressibly *. Eze 1:22
a throne made of * blue sapphire Eze 1:26
SUDDENLY A THRONE of * blue Eze 10:1
place, I gave you * clothes of Eze 16:9,10
bracelets and * necklaces, a ring Eze 16:11
And so you were made * with gold Eze 16:13
foods and became more * than ever. Eze 16:13
you and take your * jewels and Eze 16:39
They will strip you of your * Eze 23:26
and * crowns upon your head. Eze 23:42
destroy my lovely, * Temple, the Eze 24:20,21
their robes and * garments and sit Eze 26:16
You say, 'I am the most * city in Eze 27:3
in * settings of finest gold. Eze 28:13
It was strong and *, for its Eze 31:7
What nation is as * as you, O Eze 32:19
songs with a * voice or plays well Eze 33:32
have built this * city as my royal Dan 4:30
give her, the more * the statues Hos 10:1
spread out, as * as olive trees, Hos 14:6
"Their * homes are full of the Amo 3:10
forts and plunder those * homes." Amo 3:11
"And I will destroy the * homes Amo 3:15
You will be hauled from your * Amo 4:3
"* Israel lies broken and Amo 5:2
never live in the * stone houses Amo 5:11
of Israel, and hate their * homes. Amo 6:8
"* girls and fine young men Amo 8:13
of God. The * and faithless city, Nah 3:4
Or, "with mighty shouts, 'How * Zec 4:7f
How wonderful and * all shall be! Zec 9:16,17
the tallest and most * of them Zec 11:2
You are like * mausoleums—full of Mt 23:27
what * buildings these are! Mk 13:1
a * flask of expensive perfume. Mk 14:3
* words that fell from his lips. Lk 4:22
talking about the * stonework of Lk 21:5
one called The * Gate—was his Act 3:2
so often at The * Gate, they were Act 3:10
to make one jar *, to be used for Rom 9:21
they say, "How * are the feet of Rom 10:15
God gives it a * new body—just the 1Co 15:38
as parts of a *, constantly growing Eph 2:21
or * clothes, or hair arrangement. 1Pe 3:3
arrangement. Be * inside, in your 1Pe 3:4
clothing and * jewelry made of gold Rev 17:4
great city, so *—like a woman Rev 18:16
It was a glorious sight, * as a Rev 21:2

BEAUTIFULLY
curtain, made of * embroidered Ex 27:16
its pedestal; the * made, holy Ex 31:10
fine-twined linen, * embroidered Ex 38:18
the ephod joined its * woven sash. Ex 39:20
securely above the * woven sash of Ex 39:21
the linen belt was * embroidered Ex 39:28,29
his inspection the * tailored Ex 39:41
with its * woven belt. Lev 8:7
her own clothing is * made—a Pro 31:22
"Because you dance so *." Sol 6:13
silk and linen and * embroidered. Eze 16:13
You used the * embroidered Eze 16:18
You sat together on a * Eze 23:41
was not clothed as * as they. Mt 6:29

BEAUTIFY
the king want to * the Temple of Ez 7:27
and box trees—to * my sanctuary. Is 60:13

BEAUTY
in Egypt everyone spoke of her *. Gen 12:14
was shapely, and in every way a *. Gen 29:17
unusual * taking her evening bath. 2Sa 11:2
into the walls to add to the *; 2Ch 3:6
breathtaking the * of his palace, 2Ch 9:3
gaze upon her *—for she was a very Est 1:11
they are given * treatments, and Est 2:3
her for the * treatments, gave her Est 2:9
six months of * treatments with oil Est 2:12,13,14
she wished, to enhance her *. Est 2:12,13,14
royal husband delights in your *. Ps 45:10,11
Literally, "their * shall be for Ps 49:14f
of Zion, the perfection of *." Ps 50:2f
strength and * are in his Temple. Ps 96:6
Worship the Lord with the * of Ps 96:9
Daughters of graceful * like the Ps 144:12-15
Don't lust for their *. Pro 6:25
Charm can be deceptive and * Pro 31:30
"O woman of rare *, what is it Sol 5:9
away their artful * and their Is 3:18
All their * will be gone; Is 3:24
Woe to her fading *, the crowning Is 28:1
Once glorious, her fading * Is 28:4
of * to his people who are left. Is 28:5
the King in his *, and the Is 33:17
his * fades like dying flowers. Is 40:6
Israel he will give:* for ashes; Is 61:3
all the things of * are destroyed. Is 64:11
all its * into barren wilderness. Jer 12:10
All her * and her majesty are Lam 1:6
among the nations for your *; Eze 16:14
me—you trusted in your * instead; Eze 16:15
Your * was his for the asking. Eze 16:15
you offered your * to every man who Eze 16:25
or be given * here in the land of Eze 26:20
the perfection of wisdom and *. Eze 28:12
with pride because of all your *; Eze 28:17
none equaled it in *. Eze 31:8
Garden in all its *, but they Joe 2:3
Hebrew word for "*," here Mic 1:11f
Hebrew word for "*," here Mic 1:11f
Hebrew word for "*," here Mic 1:11f
nations with her *, then taught Nah 3:4
was born—a child of divine *. Act 7:20
from ours, and the * and the glory 1Co 15:40
from the * and the glory of ours. 1Co 15:40
other in their * and brightness. 1Co 15:41
that has lost its * and fades away, Jas 1:10,11
about the outward * that depends on 1Pe 3:3
That kind of deep * was seen in 1Pe 3:5

BEBAI
From the subclan of *, 623; Ez 2:3-35
From the clan of *—Zechariah (son Ez 8:2-14
(son of *), and 28 other men; Ez 8:2-14
From the clan of *: Ez 10:28
From the subclan of *, 628; Neh 7:8-38
Bani, Bunni, Azgad, *, Neh 10:14-27

BECAME
And man * a living person. Gen 2:7
it, suddenly they * aware of their Gen 3:7
Abel * a shepherd, while Cain was Gen 4:2
named Jabal. He * the first of the Gen 4:20
their children * giants, of whom so Gen 6:4
Noah * a farmer and planted a Gen 9:20,21
Their descendants * the maritime Gen 10:5
of Cush was Nimrod, who * the Gen 10:8
and his name * proverbial. Gen 10:9
was pregnant, she * very proud and Gen 16:4
next morning the angels * urgent. Gen 19:15
him, and * a pillar of salt. Gen 19:26
And so it was that both girls * Gen 19:36
was named Moab; he * the ancestor Gen 19:37
was Benammi; he * the ancestor of Gen 19:38
and Sarah * pregnant and gave Gen 21:1
of Paran, and * an expert archer. Gen 21:20,21
in the field. They * his permanent Gen 23:17,18
mother's tent, and she * his wife. Gen 24:67
These twelve sons of his * the Gen 25:16
Then at last she * pregnant. Gen 25:21
As the boys grew, Esau * a Gen 25:27
wealth, and * richer and richer. Gen 26:13
And the Philistines * jealous of Gen 26:14
So Leah * pregnant and had a Gen 29:32
She soon * pregnant again and Gen 29:33
Again she * pregnant and had a Gen 29:34
barren, * envious of her sister. Gen 30:1
with her, and she * pregnant and Gen 30:5
servant-girl, * pregnant again and Gen 30:7
prayers and she * pregnant again, Gen 30:17
Then once again she * Gen 30:19
For she * pregnant and gave Gen 30:23,24
rapidly and he * very wealthy, with Gen 30:43
* the heads of clans, as listed Gen 36:15,16
and she * pregnant as a result. Gen 38:18
So Joseph naturally * quite a Gen 39:4
the king of Egypt * angry with his Gen 40:1
about it, he * very concerned as to Gen 41:8
So Joseph * famous throughout the Gen 41:45
The famine * worse and worse, so Gen 47:13
And the land * Pharaoh's. Gen 47:20
Thus all the people of Egypt * Gen 47:21
so that they soon * a large nation, Ex 1:7
The Egyptians * alarmed, and Ex 1:12
to the princess and he * her son. Ex 2:10
So he threw it down—and it * a Ex 4:3
He did, and it * a rod in his Ex 4:4
Then the Lord * angry. Ex 4:14
and his court, and it * a serpent. Ex 7:10
Their rods * serpents, too! Ex 7:12
The fish died and the water * so Ex 7:21
the sky, and it * boils that broke Ex 9:10
and his staff * bold again. Ex 14:5
the water, and the water * sweet. Ex 15:25
and when the sun * hot upon the Ex 16:21
And the food * known as "manna" Ex 16:31
Moses' arms finally * too tired Ex 17:12
but if he was married before he * Ex 21:3
suddenly * white with leprosy. Num 12:10
and * slaves of the Egyptians. Num 20:15
to him and she * the wife of Num 26:58,59
His son Eleazar * the next Deu 10:6
in Egypt they * a mighty nation. Deu 26:5
The Lord * king in Jerusalem, Deu 33:5
and his name * famous everywhere. Jos 6:27
So Ai * a desolate mound of Jos 8:28
So they * servants of the Jos 9:21
them, but they * wood-choppers and Jos 9:27
it, so Achsah * Othni-el's wife. Jos 15:17
when the Israelis * strong enough, Jos 17:13
they * concerned and got a key. Ju 3:25
And from that time on Israel * Ju 4:24
Until Deborah * a mother to Ju 5:7
it, so it * an evil deed that Ju 8:27
he * one of the leading citizens. Ju 9:26
And after that it * a custom in Ju 11:39
and * as one of Micah's sons. Ju 17:10,11
But she * angry with him and ran Ju 19:2
possible, and I * pregnant tonight, Ru 1:12
and the child * the Lord's 1Sa 2:11
So it was at Mizpah that Samuel * 1Sa 7:6
touched * his constant companions. 1Sa 10:26
upon Saul and he * very angry. 1Sa 11:6
and David * his bodyguard. 1Sa 16:21
When King Saul saw this, he * 1Sa 18:15,16
the people, he * even more afraid 1Sa 18:29
So David's name * very famous 1Sa 18:30
within him and he * as stone." 1Sa 25:37,38f
So she * his wife. 1Sa 25:42
David's position now * stronger 2Sa 3:1
dynasty * weaker and weaker. 2Sa 3:1
As the war went on, Abner * a 2Sa 3:6
as she was running, and he * lame. 2Sa 4:4
So David * greater and greater, 2Sa 5:10
people forever, and you * our God. 2Sa 7:24
and the Syrians * David's subjects 2Sa 8:6
So David * very famous. 2Sa 8:13
All the household of Ziba * 2Sa 9:12
to David and * his servants. 2Sa 10:19
palace and she * one of his wives; 2Sa 11:27
Amnon * so tormented by his love 2Sa 13:2
by his love for her that he * ill. 2Sa 13:2
So the conspiracy * very strong. 2Sa 15:12
David * weak and exhausted. 2Sa 21:15
And Solomon * the new king, 1Ki 2:12
grip upon the kingdom * secure. 1Ki 2:46
But when it * light outside, I 1Ki 3:21
although they * soldiers, 1Ki 9:22
And Solomon * apprehensive, for 1Ki 11:14
Hadad * one of Pharaoh's closest 1Ki 11:19
(where he later * king) when David 1Ki 11:24
of Ephraim, and it * his capital. 1Ki 12:25
Instantly the king's arm * 1Ki 13:4
and the king's arm * normal again. 1Ki 13:6
JEROBOAM'S SON ABIJAH now * 1Ki 14:1
people of Judah * as depraved as 1Ki 14:24
Asa * king of Judah, in 1Ki 15:9
In his old age his feet * 1Ki 15:23
Then his son Jehoshaphat * the 1Ki 15:24
his son Ahab * king in his place. 1Ki 16:28
when Ahab * the king of Israel; 1Ki 16:29
But one day the woman's son * 1Ki 17:17

(BECAME Con't)
returned, and he * alive again! 1Ki 17:22
The battle * more and more 1Ki 22:35
his son * the new king of Israel. 1Ki 22:40
brother Jehoram * the new king—for 2Ki 1:17
And his flesh * as healthy as a 2Ki 5:14
at Hazael until he * embarrassed, 2Ki 8:11
And Hazael * king instead. 2Ki 8:15
years old when he * king, and he 2Ki 8:17
* the new king during the twelfth 2Ki 8:24,25
and his son Jehoahaz * the new 2Ki 10:35
seven years old when he * king. 2Ki 11:21
Israel that Joash * king of Judah. 2Ki 12:1
Whenever the chest * full, the 2Ki 12:10
his son Amaziah * the new king. 2Ki 12:21
and Jeroboam II * the new king. 2Ki 13:13
And his son Jeroboam * the new 2Ki 14:16
* the new king at the age of 2Ki 14:21
* the new king of Israel. 2Ki 14:29
David, and his son Jotham * king. 2Ki 15:7
One month after Shallum * king, 2Ki 15:14
When he died, his son Pekahiah * 2Ki 15:22
So Pekah * the new king. 2Ki 15:25
His age when he * king: 25 years 2Ki 15:32,33
Then his son Ahaz * the new king. 2Ki 15:38
his son Hezekiah * the new king. 2Ki 16:20
and his son Esarhaddon * the new king. 2Ki 19:37
HEZEKIAH NOW * deathly sick, and 2Ki 20:1
When he died, his son Manasseh * 2Ki 20:21
and his son Amon * the new king. 2Ki 21:18
and his son Josiah * the new king. 2Ki 21:26
His age when he * king: 23 years 2Ki 23:31,32
His age when he * king: 25 years 2Ki 23:36,37
his son Jehoiachin * the new king. 2Ki 24:6
His age when he * king: 21 years 2Ki 24:18,19
was Nimrod, who * a great hero. 1Ch 1:10
Zerah from Bozrah * the new king. 1Ch 1:44
of the Temanites * the king. 1Ch 1:45
the fields of Moab—* king and ruled 1Ch 1:46
town of Rehoboth * the new king. 1Ch 1:48
the son of Achbor * king. 1Ch 1:49
When Baal-hanan died, Hadad * 1Ch 1:50
* the parents of twin sons, 1Ch 2:4
(the daughter of Ammi-el) * the 1Ch 3:5
His relatives * heads of clans 1Ch 5:7,8
Machir (who * the father of 1Ch 7:14
These sons all * chiefs of 1Ch 8:8,9,10
he * the general of David's army. 1Ch 11:5,6
And David * more and more famous 1Ch 11:9
it ever since Saul * king." 1Ch 13:3
wives and * the father of many sons 1Ch 14:3
his son Hanun * the new king. 1Ch 19:1
to King David and * his subjects. 1Ch 19:19
his son Rehoboam * the new king. 2Ch 9:31
and his son Abijah * the new king. 2Ch 12:16
ABIJAH * THE new king of Judah, in 2Ch 13:1
Meanwhile, King Abijah of Judah * 2Ch 13:21
Then his son Asa * the new king 2Ch 14:1
of his reign, Asa * seriously 2Ch 16:12
THEN HIS SON Jehoshaphat * the 2Ch 17:1
their taxes, so he * very wealthy 2Ch 17:5
So Jehoshaphat * very strong, 2Ch 17:12
Jehoshaphat: He * king of Judah 2Ch 20:31
Jehoram * the new ruler of Judah. 2Ch 21:1
for Ahab's family * his advisors 2Ch 22:4
years old when he * king, and he 2Ch 24:1
When Joash died, his son Amaziah * 2Ch 24:27
years old when he * king, and he 2Ch 25:1
So he * very famous, for the Lord 2Ch 26:15
But at that point he * proud—and 2Ch 26:16
His son Jotham * vice-regent, in 2Ch 26:21
and his son Jotham * the new king. 2Ch 26:23
old at the time he * king, and he 2Ch 27:1
even so his people * very corrupt. 2Ch 27:2
King Jotham * powerful because 2Ch 27:6
and his son Ahaz * the new king. 2Ch 27:9
years old when he * king and he 2Ch 28:1
his son Hezekiah * the new king. 2Ch 28:27
years old when he * the king of 2Ch 29:1
Then the priests and Levites * 2Ch 30:15
From then on King Hezekiah * 2Ch 32:23
But about that time Hezekiah * 2Ch 32:24
So Hezekiah * very wealthy and 2Ch 32:27
Then his son Manasseh * the new 2Ch 32:33
years old when he * king, and he 2Ch 33:1
and his son Amon * the new king. 2Ch 33:20,21
eight years old when he * king. 2Ch 34:1
years old when he * king, and he 2Ch 36:5
and his son Jehoiachin * the new 2Ch 36:8
years old when he * king and he 2Ch 36:11
being repaired, they * furious. Neh 4:7
clan * the Tabernacle singers. Neh 11:22,23
at the palace gate—* angry at the Est 2:21
descendants and to all who * Jews; Est 9:27
the Clan of Ram) * angry because Job 32:2
he * angry and spoke foolishly. Ps 106:33
* God's new home and kingdom. Ps 114:2
So I * greater than any of the Ecc 2:9
and Esar-haddon his son * king. Is 37:38
this that Hezekiah * deathly sick Is 38:1
But when I blessed him, he * a Is 51:1
And he * their Savior. Is 63:8
That is why he * their enemy and Is 63:10
* bold and returned to their sins. Jer 34:11f
years old when he * king, and he Jer 52:1
Things * so bad at last that the Jer 52:3
Evil-merodach, who * king of Jer 52:31
You grew up and * tall, slender Eze 16:6,7
covenant with you, and you * mine. Eze 16:8
You ate the finest foods and * Eze 16:13
It took root and grew and * a Eze 17:6
to catch prey and * a man-eater. Eze 19:3
the beasts.' He * a leader among Eze 19:6
prey, and he too * a man-eater. Eze 19:6
Its strongest branch * a ruler's Eze 19:11
girls * prostitutes in Egypt. Eze 23:2,3
the statue down * a great mountain Dan 2:35
fury and his face * dark with anger Dan 3:19
His thoughts and feelings * those Dan 5:21
It did as it pleased and * very Dan 8:4
The victor * both proud and Dan 8:8
at first, soon * very strong and Dan 8:9
(Darius was a Mede but * king of Dan 9:1
when he * a man, he even fought Hos 12:3
then you * proud and forgot me. Hos 13:6
Their land * desolate; Zec 7:14
But I * impatient with these Zec 11:8
of you * one person in his sight. Mal 2:15
she * pregnant by the Holy Spirit. Mt 1:18
he ate nothing and * very hungry. Mt 4:2
And as he did, his hand * Mt 12:13
And they * angry with him! Mt 13:57
and his clothing * dazzling white. Mt 17:2
widow * the second brother's wife. Mt 22:25
and his clothing * dazzling white, Mk 9:3
threw away * the cornerstone, the Mk 12:10
Elizabeth his wife * pregnant and Lk 1:24
her—* pregnant in her old age! Lk 1:36
Literally, "* strong in spirit." Lk 1:80f
There the child * a strong, Lk 2:40
Soon he * well known throughout Lk 4:14
And as he did, it * completely Lk 6:10
and his clothes * dazzling white Lk 9:29
The boy * so hungry that even Lk 15:16
Then they * desperate. Lk 23:5
before—* fast friends. Lk 23:12
* a human being and lived here on Jn 1:14
Jesus replied that people soon * Jn 4:13
was chosen and * an apostle with Act 1:26
which * the capstone of the arch.' Act 4:11
Literally, "* the head of the Act 4:11f
Isaac * the father of Jacob, and Act 7:8
he * a mighty prince and orator. Act 7:22
Paul * more and more fervent in Act 9:22
About this time she * ill and Act 9:37
of these Gentiles * believers. Act 11:21
were persuaded and * Act 17:4
a few joined him and * believers. Act 17:34
There he * acquainted with a Jew Act 18:2,3
But when Gallio * governor of Act 18:12
very carefully. I * very anxious to Act 22:3
foolish minds * dark and confused. Rom 1:21
God, they * utter fools instead. Rom 1:22
Their lives * full of every kind Rom 1:29
It was before he * a Jew—before Rom 4:10
was broken when we * Christians and Rom 6:2,3
Now if the whole world * rich as Rom 11:12
and * Christians before I did. Rom 16:7
before he * a Christian shouldn't 1Co 7:18
that before you * Christians you 1Co 12:2
But when I * a man my thoughts 1Co 13:11
shoulders, but * earnest and 2Co 7:11
you about. You * frightened about 2Co 7:11
yet to help you he * so very poor, 2Co 8:9
who have sinned * sinners and don't 2Co 12:21
and even Barnabas * hypocrites too, Gal 2:13
Literally, "* obedient unto Php 2:8f
you Philippians * my partners in Php 4:15
SINCE YOU * alive again, so to Col 3:1
So you * our followers and the 1Th 1:6
Then you yourselves * an example 1Th 1:7
we were misled by others and * Tit 3:3
Thus he * far greater than the Heb 1:4
flesh and blood—he * flesh and Heb 2:14
did when we first * Christians, we Heb 3:14
that Jesus * the Giver of eternal Heb 5:9
of his faith he * one of those whom Heb 11:7
May he who * the great Shepherd Heb 13:20,21
his Word, and we *, as it were, the Jas 1:18
And you know that he * a man so 1Jn 3:5
actually * man with a human body? 1Jn 4:2
and the sun * dark like black Rev 6:12
the ocean * as smooth as glass. Rev 7:1
Literally, "* blood." Rev 8:8,9f
oceans, and they * like the watery Rev 16:3
and springs and they * blood. Rev 16:4

BECHER

Benjamin's sons: Bela, *, Gen 46:19-22
named after their ancestor *. Num 26:28-37
Bela, *, Jedia-el. 1Ch 7:6
The sons of * were: 1Ch 7:8

BECHERITES

The *, named after their ancestor Num 26:28-37

BECKONING

Literally, "* with the hand." Act 13:16f

BECOME

a way that the two * one person. Gen 2:24
eat it you will * like him, for Gen 3:5
* the mother of all mankind"; Gen 3:20
that the man has * as we are, Gen 3:22
If you do, I will cause you to * Gen 12:2
to multiply and * a great nation. Gen 17:20
"For Abraham shall * a mighty Gen 18:18
upon, and it will * a permanent Gen 23:9
you *The mother of many millions! Gen 24:60
womb shall * two rival nations. Gen 25:23
to * as numerous as the stars! Gen 26:4
* too rich and powerful for us." Gen 26:16
that they will * a great Gen 26:24
may you * a great nation of many Gen 28:2
And this memorial pillar shall * Gen 28:22
until they * as the sands along the Gen 32:12
business among us and * rich!" Gen 34:9,10
unite with you to * one people. Gen 34:16
all they have will * ours and the Gen 34:23
to multiply and to * a great Gen 35:11
Then we'll see what will * of all Gen 37:19,20
so that you will * a great nation. Gen 45:7
that you will * a great nation there. Gen 46:3,4
and may they * a mighty nation." Gen 48:16
"Manasseh too shall * a great Gen 48:19
brother shall * even greater." Gen 48:19
multiply and to * a mighty nation. Ex 1:20
when Moses had grown up and * a Ex 2:11
rod, and it will * a serpent." Ex 7:9
rod, and it will * lice, throughout Ex 8:16
the people might * discouraged by Ex 13:17,18
for the land would * a wilderness, Ex 23:29
would * too many to control. Ex 23:29
Thus the two widths * one. Ex 26:10,11
Or, "shall * holy," or, "only Ex 29:37f
whatever touches them shall * Ex 30:29
If you * friendly with them and Ex 34:15
and it shall * holy. Ex 40:9
for the altar shall then * most Ex 40:10
touches them shall * holy." Lev 6:18f
the disease have * fainter and have Lev 13:6
* full of enormous wickedness. Lev 19:29
the water will * bitter within her, Num 5:27
unharmed and will soon * pregnant. Num 5:28
he took his vow to * a Nazirite." Num 6:21
to Moses, "When did I * weak? Num 11:23
and little ones will * slaves. Num 14:3
children would * slaves of the Num 14:31
seven days. To * purified again, Num 19:17
will automatically * invalid. Num 30:5
commands you will * a great nation Deu 6:3
too quickly and * dangerous. Deu 7:22
For when you have * full and Deu 8:12,13
and herds have * very large, and Deu 8:12,13
out that you don't * proud, and Deu 8:14
so that you would * humble and so Deu 8:16
gives you power to * rich, and he Deu 8:18
No one will * poor because of Deu 15:4,5
Has anyone just * engaged? Deu 20:7
its people shall * your servants. Deu 20:11
Today you have * the people of Deu 27:9
The land will * as dry as dust Deu 28:24
You will * an object of horror, Deu 28:37
among you shall * richer and richer Deu 28:43
while you * poorer and poorer. Deu 28:43
warning: You will * slaves to your Deu 28:47,48
clothes haven't * old, and your Deu 29:5
you will live and * a great nation, Deu 30:16
when they have * fat and Deu 31:20
But Israel has * corrupt, Deu 32:5
Literally, they have * "something Jos 7:12f
or else * totally God's. Jos 7:12f
our clothing and shoes have * Jos 9:13
The tribe of Joseph had * two Jos 14:3,4
would * as weak as anyone else." Ju 16:7
would * as weak as anyone else." Ju 16:16,17
"For her son would * an heir to Ru 4:6
you and they have * fat from the 1Sa 2:29
or we will * their slaves just as 1Sa 4:9
proposition and * his son-in-law. 1Sa 18:22
Abigail to ask her to * his wife. 1Sa 25:39
has left you and has * your enemy? 1Sa 28:16
were spared to * David's 2Sa 8:2
wilderness for any who * faint." 2Sa 16:2
they agreed to help him * king. 1Ki 1:7
and you * angry with them and 1Ki 8:46
and Israel will * a joke to the 1Ki 9:7
This Temple will * a heap of 1Ki 9:8
He had * the leader of a gang of 1Ki 11:24
* friendly with King Rehoboam; 1Ki 12:27
who told me that I would * king. 1Ki 14:2
the son of Jeroboam had * king. 1Ki 15:25
Meanwhile the famine had * very 1Ki 18:2
the son of Asa had * king during 1Ki 22:41
after Jehu had * the king of Israel 2Ki 12:1
Jeroboam II had * king during the 2Ki 14:23
shall * a great nation again; 2Ki 19:30
A remnant of my people shall * 2Ki 19:31

(BECOME Con't)
be cursed and * desolate, and 2Ki 22:18,19
to see David * king instead of 1Ch 12:23
purpose of helping David * king. 1Ch 12:24-37
forever, and you have * their God. 1Ch 17:22
for I have * king in my father's 2Ch 6:10
and you * angry with them, and 2Ch 6:36
since Solomon had * king, and the 2Ch 8:1
He made silver * as plentiful in 2Ch 9:27
He had * king at the age of 2Ch 12:13
But when Jehoram had * solidly 2Ch 21:3,4
praise, for he had * proud, and so 2Ch 32:25
of the Lord and to * a Bible Ez 7:10
this rule could we * a prosperous Ez 9:12
* captives in a foreign land! Neh 4:4
merciful, slow to * angry, and full Neh 9:17
gone through * as nothing to you. Neh 9:32
By that time Mordecai had * a Est 2:19
and how he had * the greatest man Est 5:11
he had * more and more powerful. Est 9:4
"Your sons shall * important Job 5:25
* a laughingstock to my neighbors. Job 12:4
futility will * evident to him. Job 15:32
those with pure hearts shall * Job 17:9
Have we * like animals to you, Job 18:3
old age, and * great and powerful. Job 21:7
"And now I have * the subject of Job 30:9
I have * as dust and ashes. Job 30:19
You have * cruel toward me, and Job 30:21
and someone else * her husband. Job 31:10
Then his body will * as healthy Job 33:25
Do you know why you * warm when Job 37:16,17
their wealth, and * ever more bold Ps 52:7
you have * angry and deserted us. Ps 60:1
Moab shall * my lowly servant, Ps 60:8
Don't * rich by extortion and Ps 62:10,11
sword, to * the food of jackals. Ps 63:10
of Weeping it will * a place of Ps 84:6
But others * poor through Ps 107:39
May his children * fatherless Ps 109:9,10
now * the capstone of the arch! Ps 118:22
Those who make them * like them! Ps 135:18
I want those already wise to * Pro 1:5,6
the wiser and * leaders by Pro 1:5,6
How does a man * wise? Pro 1:7,8,9
and you * a slave of foreigners. Pro 5:10
end in shame, but the meek * wise. Pro 11:2
It is possible to give away and * Pro 11:24,25
Work hard and * a leader; Pro 12:24
be humble, take advice and * Pro 13:10
Those accepting it * aware of the Pro 13:14
Be with wise men and * wise. Pro 13:20
Be with evil men and * evil. Pro 13:20
to * responsible for his debts. Pro 17:18
if you * a man of common sense. Pro 23:15,16
* unfaithful to their wives. Pro 23:26,27,28
or you will * as foolish as he is! Pro 26:4,5
For if I grow rich, I may * Pro 30:9
He might even * king, though born Ecc 4:14
He can * the leader of millions Ecc 4:16
strong legs will * weak, and your Ecc 12:3
on forever, and * very exhausting! Ecc 12:12
* the world's greatest attraction, Is 2:2
will * patches of briars. Is 7:23
It is no longer a city—it has * a Is 17:1
mountain tops and * like the Is 17:9
For Jerusalem shall * as her name Is 29:2
Sharon has * a wilderness; Is 33:9
forts, and it will * the haunt of Is 34:13
The deserts will * as green as Is 35:2
The parched ground will * a Is 35:7
And some of your own sons will * Is 39:7
Then you would have * as Is 48:19
her barren wilderness will * as Is 51:3
Why has Israel * a nation of Jer 2:14
Why have you * this degenerate Jer 2:21
again, for she has * corrupted. Jer 3:1
The cities of Judah shall * dens Jer 10:22
therefore it shall * as this Jer 13:10
end of his life * a poor old fool. Jer 17:11
Therefore their land shall * Jer 18:16
household shall * slaves in Babylon Jer 20:6
this palace shall * a shambles. Jer 22:5
This entire land shall * a Jer 25:11
Their fate shall * proverbial of Jer 29:22
Even her famed mercenaries have * Jer 46:20,21
It shall * a desolate heap, and Jer 49:2
that Bozrah shall * heaps of ruins, Jer 49:13
Your cities will * as silent as Jer 49:18
Damascus has * feeble and all Jer 49:24
for you shall * the least of the Jer 50:12
Babylon shall * deserted wasteland, Jer 50:13
All her wise counselors shall * Jer 50:36
lands shall * as weak as women. Jer 50:37
of Babylon shall * inhabited by Jer 50:39
they have * as women. Jer 51:30
and Babylon shall * a heap of Jer 51:37
Our former servants have * our Lam 5:8
You will * a laughingstock to Eze 5:15
The famine will * more and more Eze 5:16
plenty of water to * a splendid Eze 17:8
It shall * a noble cedar, Eze 17:22,23
strong knees will tremble and * Eze 21:7
these who have * old harlot hags? Eze 23:43
laid waste, I shall * wealthy!' Eze 26:2
Her island shall * uninhabited, Eze 26:5
Tyre shall * the prey of many Eze 26:5
The land of Egypt shall * a Eze 29:9
has * proud and arrogant, the Eze 31:10
They have * a prey to every Eze 34:5
land has * like Eden's garden! Eze 36:35
"Son of dust, can these bones * Eze 37:3
They say: 'We have * a heap of Eze 37:11
Another 1,500 feet and it had * a Eze 47:5
"I'm afraid you will * pale and Dan 1:10
his neck, and * the third ruler Dan 5:7
when they have * morally rotten, an Dan 8:23
of followers, he will * strong. Dan 11:23
prosper and * a great nation; Hos 1:10
for she has * another man's wife—I Hos 1:2
you will * a heap of rubble. Hos 5:9
The leaders of Judah have * the Hos 5:10
thus they * as good-for-nothing Hos 7:8
your wife will * a prostitute in Amo 7:17
will certainly * slaves in exile, Amo 7:17
But Jerusalem will * a refuge, a Ob 1:17
said, "and it will * calm again. Jon 1:12
of rubble, and * an open field, her Mic 1:6
a field, and * a heap of rubble; Mic 3:12
the oceans and rivers * dry sand; Nah 1:4
The coastland will * a pasture, Zep 2:6
and Gomorrah, and * a place of Zep 2:9
That once proud city will * a Zep 2:14
But now—see how she has * a Zep 2:15
or meat, will it too * holy?" Hag 2:12
does it * contaminated?" Hag 2:13
time of Zechariah, * a symbol, the Zec 5:11f
to the hilt, and * so rich that Zec 9:3
Every field will * a lush Zec 10:1
The Nile will * dry—the rule of Zec 10:11
his arm will * useless and his Zec 11:17
border) will * one vast plain, but Zec 14:10
They will * like walking corpses, Zec 14:12
plots will * public information. Mt 10:26
from your sins and * as little Mt 18:3
The two shall * one—no longer Mt 19:5,6
so that you will * guilty of all Mt 23:35
yet it grows to * one of the Mk 4:31,32
the years and had * poor from Mk 5:26
and grind his teeth and * rigid. Mk 9:18
When its buds * tender and its Mk 13:28
He will soften adult hearts to * Lk 1:17
Very soon now, you will * Lk 1:31
this stone to * a loaf of bread." Lk 4:3
It will * as evident as yeast in Lk 12:2
So no one can * my disciple Lk 14:33
the poor—it will * treasure for you Lk 18:22
all will * one vast heap of Lk 21:6
the right to * children of God. Jn 1:11,12
He must * greater and greater, Jn 3:30
and I must * less and less. Jn 3:30
be baptized and to * his Jn 4:1
Do you want to * his disciples Jn 9:27
Then you will * convinced that Jn 10:38
then you will * light bearers." Jn 12:36
'Let his home * desolate with no Act 1:20
faith, who had * a Christian). Act 6:5
face * as radiant as an angel's! Act 6:15
and there * slaves for 400 years. Act 7:6
for we don't know what has * of Act 7:40
why the crowd had * so furious! Act 22:24
you expect me to * a Christian?" Act 26:28
audience might * the same as I am, Act 26:29
but the winds had * too strong, Act 27:7,8
descendants and * a great nation, Rom 4:18
to * a part of Jesus Christ; Rom 6:2,3
For you have * a part of him, and Rom 6:5
of your bodies * tools of Rom 6:13
and you have * slaves to your new Rom 6:18
who would—should * like his Son, so Rom 8:29
it will be when they * Christians! Rom 11:15
He was the very first person to * Rom 16:5
of you will have * proud, thinking 1Co 4:18
in his sight the two * one person. 1Co 6:16
a Christian may * a Christian with 1Co 7:14
a Christian may * a Christian with 1Co 7:14
Literally, "* not bondservants of 1Co 7:23f
Then he will * bold enough to do 1Co 8:10
yet I have freely and happily * a 1Co 9:19
right will * known and recognized! 1Co 11:19
and has * the first of millions 1Co 15:20
all his people will * alive again. 1Co 15:23
us for they * sick and die; 1Co 15:43
dust, but all who * Christ's will 1Co 15:48
died will suddenly * alive, with 1Co 15:52
They were the first to * 1Co 16:15
Otherwise he may * so bitter and 2Co 2:7
us, we * more and more like him. 2Co 3:18
that we might * the righteousness 2Co 5:21f
churches, was to * a burden to 2Co 12:13
that you will * mature Christians. 2Co 13:9
that we cannot * right with God by Gal 2:16
go back again and * slaves once Gal 4:9
And now have I * your enemy Gal 4:16
has done we have * gifts to God Eph 1:11
thus he fused us together to * Eph 2:15
God's Son, and all * full-grown in Eph 4:13
—and so * more and more in every Eph 4:15,16
them may even * children of light! Eph 5:13
them and they have * more and more Php 1:14
grow and * happy in your faith; Php 1:25
have Christ, and * one with him, Php 3:9
in the Lord, and * strong and Col 2:7
* discouraged and quit trying. Col 3:21
God, who called you to * his 1Th 5:24
They want to * famous as 1Ti 1:7
to trust him and * full of the love 1Ti 1:14
from Christ and * eager followers 1Ti 4:1
A widow who wants to * one of the 1Ti 5:9
The younger widows should not * 1Ti 5:11
not let yourself * tied up in 2Ti 2:4
teachers will * worse and worse, 2Ti 3:13
They will * worn out like old Heb 1:11
not let our hearts * set against Heb 3:7,8
none of you will * hardened against Heb 3:13
Word until you * better Christians Heb 5:14
other things and * mature in our Heb 6:1
for you, you won't * bored with Heb 6:12
a Christian, nor * spiritually dull Heb 6:12
Literally, "having * our High Heb 6:20f
did not * a priest by meeting the Heb 7:16
she was able to * a mother in spite Heb 11:11
and hurt themselves, but * strong. Heb 12:13
speak little, and not * angry; Jas 1:19
should * masters (teachers)." Jas 3:1f
and knew you would * his children. 1Pe 1:2
And now you have * living 1Pe 2:5
the builders has * the Cornerstone, 1Pe 2:7
names, they will * ashamed of 1Pe 3:16
so that you will * patient and 2Pe 1:6
spiritually and * fruitful and 2Pe 1:8
off the road and * lost like 2Pe 2:15
you yourselves * mixed up too. 2Pe 3:17
strength and * better acquainted 2Pe 3:18
never really known him or * his. 1Jn 3:6
No one who has * part of God's 1Jn 5:18
order that we may * partners with 3Jn 1:8
that after we * Christians we can Jud 1:4
indifference and * enthusiastic Rev 3:19
she has * a den of demons, a Rev 18:2
And so the merchants who have * Rev 18:15
the vile will * more vile; Rev 22:11

BECOMES

payment, and thus * your slave." Ex 21:2f
place of God, * a single unit. Ex 26:6
head, and it then * his substitute: Lev 1:4
of any kind, he * guilty as soon as Lev 5:3
the burned place * bright Lev 13:24
The daughter of any priest who * Lev 21:9
If anyone * poor and sells some Lev 25:25
"If your brother * poor, you are Lev 25:35
"If a fellow Israelite * poor Lev 25:39
living among you * rich, and an Lev 25:47
and an Israelite * poor and sells Lev 25:47
the water, it * bitter within her Num 5:24
Any man who * ceremonially Deu 23:9,10
rain, and the earth * a desert; Job 12:15
dessert. He * thin, mere skin and Job 33:21
so that she * a happy mother. Ps 113:9
the night * light around me. Ps 139:11
A man who loves pleasure * poor; Pro 21:17
by wise planning, * strong through Pro 24:3,4
* as useless as a paralyzed leg. Pro 26:7
A slave who * a king. Pro 30:21,22,23
but if a sinner * wealthy, God Ecc 2:24-26
And if a good man * bad, and you Eze 3:20
"Then you will see what * of all Eze 12:24
my wrath until it * a roaring Eze 21:31
of the last days * the center of Dan 11:40f
person, and so * ceremonially Hag 2:13
of all seeds, but * the largest of Mt 13:31,32
them," he said, "* a perpetual Jn 4:14
it * that we aren't obeying them; Rom 3:20
heart that a man * right with God; Rom 10:10
a prostitute she * a part of him 1Co 6:16
of him and he * a part of her? 1Co 6:16
is in when he * a Christian, let 1Co 7:24
When someone * a Christian he 2Co 5:17
he * a brand new person inside. 2Co 5:17
Watch out that no one * involved Heb 12:16
in sexual sin or * careless about Heb 12:16
does when it * all brown and dry. 1Pe 1:24
up with sin and * its slave again, 2Pe 2:20
Greek to Hebrew, * Balaamites; Rev 2:6f

BECOMING

this would aid them in * pregnant. Gen 30:14f
Israelis are * dangerous to us Ex 1:9
taller, and he was * everyone's 1Sa 2:26
worldly Saul * religious, 1Sa 10:12f
in exchange for * 2Sa 3:12
that the workmen were * tired; Neh 4:10
is the first step toward * wise! Pro 4:7
When you enjoy * wise, there is Pro 24:13,14

BECOMING Con't)
The weather was * dangerous for Act 27:9
For your faith in God is * known Rom 1:8
to actually * all that God has had Rom 5:2
temptation from * so strong that 1Co 10:13
of a slave and * like men. Php 2:7
to keep you from * fainthearted in 1Th 3:2,3
If you want to keep from * Heb 12:3
are * mere moth-eaten rags. Jas 5:2

BECORATH
great-grandson of *, and 1Sa 9:1

BED
gave him straw to * down the Gen 24:32
her, he spilled the sperm on the * Gen 38:9
afterwards Jacob took to his *. Gen 47:31
* to greet him, and said to him, Gen 48:2
*, breathed his last, and died. Gen 49:33
be confined to *, but doesn't die, Ex 21:18
it heals. Any * he lies on and Lev 15:4
so anyone touching the man's * Lev 15:5
Anyone touching her * or Lev 15:21,22,23
* he lies upon shall be defiled. Lev 15:24
Anyone touching her * or Lev 15:27
Samson stayed in * with the girl Ju 16:3
Eli had gone to * (he was almost 1Sa 3:2,3
"Go on back to *." 1Sa 3:4,5
"Go on back to *." 1Sa 3:6
So Samuel went back to *. 1Sa 3:9
Samuel stayed in * until morning, 1Sa 3:15
and put it in his *, and covered 1Sa 19:13
sick and couldn't get out of *. 1Sa 19:14
Saul said to bring him in his *, 1Sa 19:15
and got up and sat on the *. 1Sa 28:23
man in his own house and on his *! 2Sa 4:11
Literally, "arose from his *." 2Sa 11:2f
go to * with them in public view. 2Sa 12:11
Go back to * and pretend you are 2Sa 13:5
"Come to * with me, my darling." 2Sa 13:11
King David was confined to his *; 1Ki 1:1
And the king is lying in *, 1Ki 1:46,47
the body on his *, and then cried 1Ki 17:19
He refused to eat and went to * 1Ki 21:4
never leave the * he is lying on; 2Ki 1:4,5
not leave the * you are lying on; 2Ki 1:6
this, you shall not leave this *; 2Ki 1:16
we can put in a *, a table, a 2Ki 4:10
She carried him up to the * of 2Ki 4:21
lying there upon the prophet's *. 2Ki 4:32
The king got out of * and told 2Ki 7:12
be out of * and at the Temple! 2Ki 20:5
He was laid on a * perfumed with 2Ch 16:13,14
him as he lay in *, and buried him 2Ch 24:25
to the king's *, each would be Est 2:12,13,14
When I go to * I think, 'Oh, Job 7:4
"He goes to * rich, but wakes up Job 27:19
Lie quietly upon your * in silent Ps 4:4
Literally, "You make all his * in Ps 41:3f
am lying there upon my * of pain. Ps 41:6
"He'll never get out of that * Ps 41:8
here you are! My * is spread with Pro 7:16,17
They'll even take your *! Pro 22:26,27
He sticks to his * like a door Pro 26:14
king lies on his *, enchanted by Sol 1:12
my lover was missing from my *. Sol 3:1
The * you have made is far too Is 28:20
decorate your * of prostitution. Eze 16:16
her in the * of love, but afterward Eze 23:17
embroidered * and put my incense Eze 23:41
and went to * without dinner. Dan 6:18
* paralyzed and racked with pain. Mt 8:5,6
was in * with a high fever. Mt 8:14
sick in * with a high fever. Mk 1:29,30
in *, and the demon was gone. Mk 7:30
for the night and we are all in *. Lk 11:7
Get up and make your *." Act 9:34

BEDAD
by: King Hadad (son of * Gen 36:31-39
Hadad the son of *—the one who 1Ch 1:46

BEDAN
Ulam's son was *. 1Ch 7:17

BEDDING
Any clothing or * the semen Lev 15:17

BEDEIAH
Ma-adai, Amram, Uel, Banaiah, *, Ez 10:34-42

BEDOUIN
You sit alone like a * in the Jer 3:2
"Attack those wealthy * tribes Jer 49:31
Kiriathaim. And * tribes from the Eze 25:9,10

BEDOUINS
I will let the * from the desert to Eze 25:4

BEDRIDDEN
paralyzed and * for eight years. Act 9:33

BEDROOM
Going into his *, he wept there. Gen 43:30
sneaked into his * and murdered him 2Sa 4:6,7
So she did, and went into his * 2Sa 13:8
here in my * and feed it to me." 2Sa 13:10
Bath-sheba went into the king's *. 1Ki 1:15
speak in the privacy of your *!" 2Ki 6:12
home, into my mother's old *. Sol 3:4
he was knocking at my * door. Sol 5:2
in his upstairs *, with its windows Dan 6:10
He would call down from his *, Lk 11:7

BEDROOMS
your * and right into your beds! Ex 8:3,4

BEDS
bedrooms and right into your *! Ex 8:3,4
on men as they lie on their *. Job 33:15
its vast ocean *, and mountains Ps 104:7,8
for joy as they lie upon their *. Ps 149:4,5
like sweetly scented * of spices. Sol 5:13
to his spice *, to pasture his Sol 6:2
Water will fill the dry stream * Joe 3:18
You lie on ivory * surrounded Amo 6:4
the streets on * and mats so that Act 5:15

BEDSIDE
He went to her *, and as he took Mk 1:31
Standing at her * he spoke to the Lk 4:39

BEDSTEAD
His iron * is kept in a museum at Deu 3:11

BEDTIME
out for a walk; at * and the first Deu 6:7
at *, and before breakfast! Deu 11:19

BEEF
well-aged wine and choice *. Is 25:6

BEELIADA
Japhia, Elishama, *, Eliphelet. 1Ch 14:4-7

BEELZEBUB
Literally, "*." Mt 12:24f
Literally, "from *." Lk 11:15f

BEER
Then Israel traveled to * Num 21:16
and lived in * for fear of his Ju 9:21
Don't drink any wine or *, and Ju 13:4
drink any wine or *, and not to eat Ju 13:7
drink any wine or *, or eat Ju 13:13,14

BEER-LAHAI-ROI
in the Negeb, had returned to *. Gen 24:62
(Isaac had now moved south to * Gen 25:11

BEER-SHEBA
of *, wandering aimlessly. Gen 21:14
well was called * ("Well of the Gen 21:31
men, and traveled home again to *. Gen 22:19
When he went to *, Jehovah Gen 26:23
*. Gen 26:33f
So Jacob left * and journeyed Gen 28:10
and came to *, and offered Gen 46:1
So Jacob left *, and his sons Gen 46:5
Hazar-shual, *, Biziothiah, Baalah, Jos 15:21-32
*, Sheba, Moladah, Hazar-shual, Jos 19:2-7
And all Israel from Dan to * 1Sa 3:20
his oldest sons, held court in *; 1Sa 8:2
way from Dan to *, and give it to 2Sa 3:9,10
away as Dan and *, so that you will 2Sa 17:11
and south to Judah as far as *. 2Sa 24:7
he went to *, a city of Judah, 1Ki 19:3
(His mother was Zibiah, from *. 2Ki 12:1
They lived at *, Moladah, 1Ch 4:28
Literally, "from * to Dan." 1Ch 21:2f
traveling from * to the hill 2Ch 19:4
mother's name was Zibiah, from *. 2Ch 24:1
from Dan to *, inviting everyone. 2Ch 30:5
Hazar-shual, * (and its Neh 11:25-30
So the people spread from * to the Neh 11:25-30
the idols of Bethel, Gilgal, or *; Amo 5:5

BEERAH
Baal's son was *. 1Ch 5:6

BEERI
to Hosea, son of *, during the Hos 1:1

BEERSHEBA
away as Dan and *, and everywhere Ju 20:1
those as far away as Geba and *. 2Ki 23:8
Samaria, Dan, and * shall fall and Amo 8:14

BEES
chased them like * and killed them Deu 1:44
And he found a swarm of * in it, Ju 14:8
They swarm around me like *; Ps 118:12
you, like * to sting and to kill. Is 7:18

BEFALL
These horrors shall * you and Deu 28:46
* those who break this contract. Deu 29:21
Disaster on disaster shall * Jer 6:9
Calamity upon calamity will * Eze 7:26,27
great terror shall * them at that Eze 30:9

BEFALLEN
tragedy that had * him, they got in Job 2:11
Disaster has * us! Jer 9:19
things have * you is because you Jer 44:23
O LORD, REMEMBER all that has * Lam 5:1

BEFALLS
* him, I shall die with sorrow.' Gen 44:29
harm * the good, but there is Pro 12:21
at the disaster that * you. Jer 25:11
I will see to it that evil * you, Jer 44:27
The terror that * Babylon will be Jer 50:25
* me that the dream foretells. Dan 2:8,9

BEFELL
these disasters * Judah at the 2Ki 24:3,4

BEFOREHAND
God had selected *—not to the Act 10:40,41
He decided * which should rise Act 17:26

BEFRIEND
to * you when you get to heaven." Lk 16:9f

BEG
your father * you to forgive us." Gen 50:16,17
wrong all along. * God to end this Ex 9:28
this once, and * Jehovah your God Ex 10:17
"Heal her, O God, I * you!" Num 12:13
Now I * for this one thing: Jos 2:12,13
to the prophet, "* the Lord your 1Ki 13:6
to * for help from the Lord; 2Ch 20:3
any interest. I * you, gentlemen, Neh 5:10
"O God, there are two things I * Job 13:20
I even * him! Job 19:16
"His children shall * from the Job 20:10
Will he * you to desist or try Job 41:3
Come back, we * of you, O God of Ps 80:14
Each day I * your help; Ps 88:9
Go and * to have your name Pro 6:3
Many * favors from a man who is Pro 19:6
O God, I * two favors from you Pro 30:7
and * for peace and my protection. Is 27:4,5
them nor pray nor * that I should Jer 7:16
desperate enough to * me for help. Jer 11:14
Listen, O my lord the king: I * Jer 37:20
we were before. * the Lord your Jer 42:3
now our lot. We * for bread from Lam 5:6
her husband. * her to stop her Hos 1:2
his wrath begins. * him to save Zep 2:3
Please, I * you, oh, don't Lk 8:28
ditches, and I'm too proud to *. Lk 16:3
Mankind will * the mountains to Lk 23:30
sent two men to * him to return Act 9:38
But, dear brothers, I * you in 1Co 1:10
So I * you to follow my example, 1Co 4:16
speak to you: we * you, as though 2Co 5:20
AS GOD'S PARTNERS we * you not to 2Co 6:1
I * YOU—I, a prisoner here in jail Eph 4:1
Now we * you—yes, we demand of 1Th 4:1
Even so, dear friends, we * you 1Th 4:10
I * my God to bless you richly. 2Ti 1:3
is in heaven I * you to keep away 1Pe 2:11

BEGAN
WHEN GOD * creating Gen 1:1
that men first * to call themselves Gen 4:26
and the floods * to disappear, for Gen 8:1
150 days after it *, the boat came Gen 8:3,4
The people who lived there * to Gen 11:3,4
arrived and the slaughter *. Gen 14:5,6
And they lunged at Lot and * Gen 19:9
of childbirth * while they were Gen 35:16
At once the Lord * blessing Gen 39:5
All his household affairs * to Gen 39:5
Potiphar's wife * making eyes at Gen 39:7
he had fled, she * screaming; Gen 39:14,15
branches that * to bud and blossom, Gen 40:9,10
river and * grazing in the grass. Gen 41:2
* grazing along the river bank. Gen 41:18
* traveling all across the land. Gen 41:46
Then the seven years of famine * Gen 41:54
The people * to starve. Gen 41:55
opened them. He * searching the Gen 44:12
and Benjamin * weeping too. Gen 45:14
people of Israel * to prosper, and Gen 47:27
of the Egyptians * dying, but not Ex 9:6
Egyptians, and * to harass them. Ex 14:24
Their chariot wheels * coming Ex 14:25
next morning and * offering burnt Ex 32:6
of them as they * their march. Num 10:34
fire of the Lord * destroying those Num 11:1
had come with them * to long for Num 11:4,5
But as everyone * eating the Num 11:33
THEN ALL THE people * weeping Num 14:1
all the people * muttering again Num 16:41
they * to murmur against God and Num 21:5
of the young men * going to wild Num 25:1
Israel * to follow foreign gods, Deu 32:16
the water * piling up as though Jos 3:15,16
The next day they * to eat from Jos 5:11,12
their pursuers and * killing them. Jos 8:20,21
city came out and * destroying the Jos 8:22
Judah's southern boundary * at the Jos 15:1
this boundary * at the south bay of Jos 15:2,3,4
The northern boundary * at the bay Jos 15:5
boundary * at Ataroth-addar. Jos 16:5,6
The northern boundary * at the Jos 16:5,6
The northern boundary * at the Jos 18:12
Its boundary * at Judah, at the Jos 19:33
The western boundary * near Jos 19:34
THEN THE PEOPLE of Israel * once Ju 6:1
* to cry out to the Lord for help. Ju 6:6,7
as the city * to stir, someone Ju 6:28
vast enemy army * rushing around in Ju 7:21
But all Israel soon * worshiping Ju 8:27
dead, the Israelis * to worship the Ju 8:33
and everyone * cursing Abimelech. Ju 9:27
men * their march upon the city. Ju 9:35
hiding places and * killing them. Ju 9:43
Zalmon where he * chopping a bundle Ju 9:47,48
* their war against Israel. Ju 11:4
And the Spirit of the Lord * to Ju 13:25
Delilah * to hit him, but she Ju 16:19
But before long his hair * to Ju 16:22
the house and * beating at the door Ju 19:22

(BEGAN Con't)
a village in Benjamin," he *. Ju 20:4
Benjamin * to kill the men of Ju 20:31
and * to take her meals again. 1Sa 1:18
Then the Lord * to give messages 1Sa 3:21,4:1
dead, her labor pains suddenly *. 1Sa 4:19
Then the Lord * to destroy the 1Sa 5:6
at Gath, the Lord * destroying its 1Sa 5:9
him, and he too * to prophesy. 1Sa 10:10
years old when he * to reign, and 1Sa 13:1f
* to melt away in all directions. 1Sa 14:16
army * to run away in fright. 1Sa 17:24
and he * to rave like a madman. 1Sa 18:10
David * to soothe him by playing 1Sa 18:10
them and they also * to prophesy. 1Sa 19:20
Saul, and he too * to prophesy! 1Sa 19:23
When the new moon celebration *, 1Sa 20:24,25
Then others * coming—those who 1Sa 22:2
and * roaming the countryside. 1Sa 23:13
As Saul and his men * to close 1Sa 23:26
But then his conscience * 1Sa 24:5
Then he * to cry. 1Sa 24:15
his men * talking of killing him. 1Sa 30:6
The two armies then * to fight 2Sa 2:17
a deer, and he * chasing Abner. 2Sa 2:19
ONE DAY DAVID * wondering if any 2Sa 9:1
the Syrians * to run away. 2Sa 10:13
Ammonites. They * by laying siege 2Sa 11:1
So the battle * in the forest of 2Sa 18:6
city wall and * battering it down. 2Sa 20:15
David's conscience * to bother him, 2Sa 24:10
"Sir," one of them *, "we live 1Ki 3:17,18
reign that he * the actual 1Ki 6:1
to them, they * shouting, "Down 1Ki 12:16,17
years old when he * to reign, and 1Ki 14:21
ABIJAM * HIS three-year reign as 1Ki 15:1
Elah, Baasha's son, * reigning 1Ki 16:8
years when Omri * his reign over 1Ki 16:23
and then * worshiping Baal. 1Ki 16:31
Then they * to dance around the 1Ki 18:26
About noontime, Elijah * mocking 1Ki 18:27
on the seventh day the battle *. 1Ki 20:29
* to reign over Israel in Samaria; 1Ki 22:51
boys from the city * mocking and 2Ki 2:23
AHAB'S SON JEHORAM * his reign 2Ki 3:1
rushed out and * killing them; 2Ki 3:24
Gehazi * to push her away, but 2Ki 4:27
And the child's body * to grow 2Ki 4:34
Jordan, they * cutting down trees; 2Ki 6:4
of Judah, * his reign during the 2Ki 8:16
years old when he * to reign but he 2Ki 8:26
As the priests of Baal * offering 2Ki 10:24
At about that time the Lord * to 2Ki 10:32,33
she screamed, and * to tear her 2Ki 11:13,14
JEHOAHAZ (THE SON of Jehu) * a 2Ki 13:1
Amaziah * his reign over Judah. 2Ki 14:1
The battle * at Beth-shemesh, one 2Ki 14:11
* a siege on the city of Samaria. 2Ki 18:9
before the kingdom of Israel *: 1Ch 1:43
At that time David * the custom 1Ch 16:7
to meet them and * the battle at 1Ch 19:9
when wars usually *) Joab led the 1Ch 20:1
Joab * the census, but he never 1Ch 27:24
construction of the Temple *. 2Ch 3:1
The actual construction * on the 2Ch 3:2
He * the practice that still 2Ch 8:7,8
all over Israel * moving to 2Ch 11:16
The men of Judah * to shout. 2Ch 13:15,16
of his reign he * a nationwide 2Ch 17:7,8,9
And at the moment they * to sing 2Ch 20:22
years old when he * to reign, and 2Ch 21:5
years old when he * to reign and he 2Ch 21:20
when he * to reign, and he 2Ch 22:2
years old when he * to reign and he 2Ch 27:8
themselves, and * to clean up and 2Ch 29:15
This all * on the first day of 2Ch 29:17
as the sacrifice *, the instruments 2Ch 29:27
of music * to play the songs of the 2Ch 29:27
years old when he * to reign in 2Ch 33:20,21
of his reign, he * to search for 2Ch 34:3
and four years later he * to 2Ch 34:3
years old when he * to reign, but 2Ch 36:2
that the priests * sacrificing Ez 3:6
(This was before they * building Ez 3:6
of the Temple * in June of the Ez 3:8
King Ahasu-erus * to reign, they Ez 4:6
as judges; we * our work on Ez 10:16-19
And so the work *. Neh 2:18
Then some of the leaders * Neh 4:10
All the people * sobbing when Neh 8:9
was the one who * the Neh 11:15,16,17
that the custom * of having choir Neh 12:46
people of Judah * bringing their Neh 13:12
had cooled, he * brooding over the Est 2:1
your kingdom," he *, "and their Est 3:8
suggestion and * this annual Est 9:23
when he but spoke, the world *! Ps 33:9
of my life before I * to breathe. Ps 139:16
I existed before the earth *. Pro 8:23
Now I * a study of the Ecc 2:12
back to where he *—with nothing. Ecc 5:15
words he gave before the worlds *? Is 40:21
* his meteoric rise to power. Is 44:28f
people Israel and * to punish them Is 47:6
For since the world * no one has Is 64:4
king of Babylon, * his reign. Jer 25:1
Recently you * doing what was Jer 34:15
they all * to return to Judah from Jer 40:12
glory of the Lord * to move away, Eze 3:12
And so they * by killing the Eze 9:6
Though the vine * so well, will Eze 17:10
me and the bodies * breathing; Eze 37:10
The man * to measure the wall Eze 40:5
YEARS AFTER King Jehoiakim * Dan 1:1
* to play, everyone—whatever his Dan 3:7
entered the city and * reigning Dan 5:31
and the king * to think of placing Dan 6:3
jealous, and they * searching for Dan 6:4
Then the court * its session and Dan 7:10
one of these horns * to grow, so Dan 8:3
The moment you * praying, a Dan 9:23
very first day you * to fast before Dan 10:12
All their wickedness * at Gilgal; Hos 9:15
there I * to hate them. Hos 9:15
* to preach, the people repented. Jon 3:4,5
south * to follow your example. Mic 1:13
Persian Gulf, who * to assert Hab 1:6f
The lofty sun and moon * to Hab 3:11
they * to worship him in earnest. Hag 1:12
For since you * laying the Zec 8:9
Before the work * there were no Zec 8:10
John the Baptist * preaching out Mt 3:1
From then on, Jesus * to preach, Mt 4:17
They * screaming at him, "What Mt 8:29
* talking about him to the crowds. Mt 11:7
John the Baptist * preaching and Mt 11:12
Then he * to pour out his Mt 11:20
so they * breaking off heads of Mt 12:1
When the crop * to grow, the Mt 13:26
he was terrified and * to sink. Mt 14:30
From then on Jesus * to speak Mt 16:21
that way, they * shouting, "Sir, Mt 20:30
the $5,000 * immediately to buy and Mt 25:16
and John, and * to be filled with Mt 26:37
Peter * to curse and swear. Mt 26:74
was present and * shouting, "Why Mk 1:23
* discussing what had happened. Mk 1:27
went on his way he * to shout the Mk 1:45
the crowds * to gather again, and Mk 3:20
High waves * to break into the Mk 4:37
it, and the crowd * pleading with Mk 5:17
of that region and * to tell Mk 5:20
his arrival, and * carrying sick Mk 6:55
Then he * to tell them about the Mk 8:31
Literally, "Peter * to rebuke Mk 8:32f
Suddenly his face * to shine with Mk 9:2
appeared and * talking with Jesus! Mk 9:4
Now they * asking him about Mk 9:11
Then Peter * to mention all that Mk 10:28
Jesus once more * describing all Mk 10:32
was near, he * to shout out, Mk 10:47
to the Temple and * to drive out Mk 11:15
he had done they * planning how Mk 11:18
THE PASSOVER OBSERVANCE * two Mk 14:1
So he * looking for the right Mk 14:11
John with him and * to be filled Mk 14:33
Then some of them * to spit at Mk 14:65
him and * to hammer his face with Mk 14:65
standing there and * telling the Mk 14:69
around the fire * saying to Peter, Mk 14:70
He * to curse and swear. Mk 14:71
And he * to cry. Mk 14:72
Now a mob * to crowd in toward Mk 15:8
again, and he * praising God. Lk 1:64
* his public ministry to Israel. Lk 1:80
and she also * thanking God and Lk 2:38
old when he * his public ministry. Lk 3:23-38
* shouting at Jesus, "Go away! Lk 4:33
were so full that they * to tear! Lk 5:6
rage, and * to plot his murder. Lk 6:11
So they * pleading earnestly Lk 7:4
Then the boy sat up and * to talk Lk 7:15
NOT LONG AFTERWARDS he * a Lk 8:1
This seed * to grow, but soon Lk 8:6
was sleeping the wind * to rise. Lk 8:23
Jesus knew, she * to tremble and Lk 8:47
So they * their circuit of the Lk 9:6
was praying, his face * to shine, Lk 9:29
Then two men appeared and * Lk 9:30
Now he * teaching them again Lk 13:18
But they all * making excuses. Lk 14:18
over the land, and he * to starve. Lk 15:14
So the party *. Lk 15:24
Until John the Baptist * to Lk 16:16
going by, so he * shouting, Lk 18:38
whole procession * to shout and Lk 19:36,37
saw the city ahead, he * to cry. Lk 19:41
Then he entered the Temple and * Lk 19:45
Some of his disciples * talking Lk 21:5
and the crowds * gathering early in Lk 21:37,38
So he * to look for an Lk 22:6
And they * to argue among Lk 22:24
firelight and * staring at him. Lk 22:56
in charge of Jesus * mocking him. Lk 22:63,64
They * at once accusing him: Lk 23:2
Now Herod and his soldiers * Lk 23:11
them and * walking beside them. Lk 24:15
They * telling each other how Lk 24:32
them, and then * rising into the Lk 24:51
One day someone * an argument Jn 3:25
He rolled up the mat and * Jn 5:9
So they * harassing Jesus as a Jn 5:16
the lake, crowds * gathering on the Jn 6:22,23
Then the Jews * to murmur against Jn 6:41
Then the Jews * arguing with each Jn 6:52
* believing him to be the Messiah. Jn 8:30,31
Since the world * there has Jn 9:32
leaders * plotting Jesus' death. Jn 11:53
ceremony before the Passover *. Jn 11:55
ceremonies *, Jesus arrived in Jn 12:1
poured water into a basin, and * Jn 13:5
we shared before the world *. Jn 17:5
you loved me before the world *! Jn 17:24
Inside, the High Priest * asking Jn 18:19
officials * yelling, "Crucify! Jn 19:6
Holy Spirit and * speaking in Act 2:4
there a moment and * walking! Act 3:7,8
and immediately * preaching! Act 5:21
of the believers * that day, Act 8:1
was baptized and * following Philip Act 8:13
As soon as they arrived, they * Act 8:15
So Philip * with this same Act 8:35
"Well, I * telling them the Good Act 11:15
answered and they * praising God! Act 11:18
upon him, and he * wandering around Act 13:11
and *. "Men of Israel," he Act 13:16
Judea arrived and * to teach the Act 15:1
Pulling out the believers, he * a Act 19:9
Christians. It * with Demetrius, a Act 19:24
boiled and they * shouting, "Great Act 19:28
A crowd * to gather and soon the Act 19:29
INTENTLY AT the Council, Paul *: Act 23:1
Paul *: "I know, sir, that you Act 24:10
King Agrippa," he *, "to be able Act 26:2
Just then a light wind * blowing Act 27:13
* throwing the cargo overboard. Act 27:18
felt better and * eating, all two Act 27:36
of the waves and * to break apart. Act 27:41
a day later a south wind * Act 28:13
of prophecy. He * lecturing in the Act 28:23
And after awhile they * to think Rom 1:21
everything * to grow old and die, Rom 5:12
our benefit before the world *. 1Co 2:7
that led to death * with such glory 2Co 3:7
And I am sure that God who * the Php 1:6
He was before all else * and it Col 1:17
is, his church—which he *; Col 1:18
before the world *—to show his love 2Ti 1:9
the world *—and he cannot lie. Tit 1:1
for them since the world *. Heb 4:3
and again, ever since the world *. Heb 9:26
and the gardens * to grow again. Jas 5:18
before the world *, but only 1Pe 1:20
CHRIST WAS ALIVE when the world *, 1Jn 1:1
* to sin has kept steadily at it. 1Jn 3:8
seal and * to unroll the scroll. Rev 6:1
before the world *, will be Rev 17:8

BEGET
to a brother to * children from her Lev 18:16f
Why should you * children with Pro 5:16

BEGGAR
When you give a gift to a *, Mt 6:2
Now it happened that a blind * Mk 10:46
One day Lazarus, a diseased *, Lk 16:20
Finally the * died and was Lk 16:22
him as a blind * asked each other, Jn 9:8
this the same fellow—that *?" Jn 9:8
And the * said, "I am the same Jn 9:9
he was the lame * they had seen so Act 3:10

BEGGAR'S
a * bag, nor food, nor money. Lk 9:3
with you, or a * bag, or even an Lk 10:4

BEGGARS
the *, crippled, lame, and blind. Lk 14:21

BEGGED
"Please, fellows," he *, Gen 19:7
"Oh no, sirs, please," Lot *, Gen 19:18,19,20
Rachel * Leah to give some of Gen 30:14
me have her as my wife," he *. Gen 34:11
treat us like this," they *. Ex 5:15
and Aaron and *, "Plead with God Ex 8:8
But Moses * God not to do it. Ex 32:11
He * Balaam to come and help him. Num 22:5,6
* of God at Mount Horeb. Deu 18:16
the mountain you * that you might Deu 18:16
But finally they * the Lord for Ju 4:2,3
again and * him to save them. Ju 10:10
So Delilah * Samson to tell her Ju 16:6
act," he *, "for he is my guest. Ju 19:23
mayors again and * them to send the 1Sa 5:11
they *. 1Sa 6:21
they * Samuel. 1Sa 7:8
and * him not to be against David. 1Sa 19:4

BEGGED Con't)
me what I can do," Jonathan *. 1Sa 20:4
of my misery,' he *, 'for I am in 2Sa 1:9
* him to take a bite of supper. 2Sa 3:35,36
David * him to spare the child, 2Sa 12:16
but let me go anyway," he *. 2Sa 18:23
king of Israel and *, "Your 1Ki 20:32
And I * you not to lie to me!" 2Ki 4:28
So we fasted and * God to take Ez 8:23
Have I * you for a present? Job 6:22
them, and you * Almighty God for Job 8:5
I, the man who * God for help, Job 12:4
and their God and * him to turn Ps 106:23
behalf—how I have * you to spare Jer 15:11
to Jeremiah, and *, "Ask the Lord Jer 21:1
the Lord and * the Lord to have Jer 26:19
just say that you * me not to send Jer 38:26
I * my allies Lam 1:19
so the demons *, "If you cast us Mt 8:31
to see Jesus, and * him to go away Mt 8:34
The sick * him to let them touch Mt 14:36
* him to give him a little time. Mt 18:29
who hadn't any oil * the others to Mt 25:7,8
front of him and * to be healed. Mk 1:40
Then the demons * him again and Mk 5:10
into those hogs," the demons *. Mk 5:12
* Jesus to let him go along. Mk 5:18
and streets, and * him to let them Mk 6:56
him, and everyone * Jesus to lay Mk 7:32
and * him to touch and heal him. Mk 8:22
So I * your disciples to cast out Mk 9:18
"Please heal her," everyone *. Lk 4:38
found him they * him not to leave Lk 4:42
And everyone * Jesus to go away Lk 8:37
* to go too, but Jesus said no. Lk 8:38
at Jesus' feet and * him to come Lk 8:41
him alone. I * your disciples to Lk 9:40
His father came out and * him, Lk 15:28
gone on, but they * him to stay Lk 24:29
* him to stay at their village; Jn 4:40,41
found Jesus, and * him to come to Jn 4:46,47
And he * Philip to come up into Act 8:31
Afterwards Cornelius * him to Act 10:48
"Then the people * for a king, Act 13:21
He brought them out and * them, Act 16:30
So they came to the jail and * Act 16:39
* Paul not to go on to Jerusalem. Act 21:12
They * him to bring Paul to Act 25:3
light, Paul * everyone to eat. Act 27:33
* us to stay with them seven days. Act 28:14
are returning. I * Apollos to 1Co 16:12
They * us to take the money so 2Co 8:4
Three different times I * God to 2Co 12:8
the people * God to stop speaking. Heb 12:19

BEGGING
me, bowing low and *, 'Please leave Ex 11:8
for Jephthah, * him to come and Ju 11:6
before him, * for money and food. 1Sa 2:36
of Assyria, * him to help him fight 2Ki 16:7
at his feet and * him with tears to Est 8:3
He wanders around * for food. Job 15:23,24
Yes, my * has been stilled. Ps 131:2
fastidiously are * in the streets Lam 4:5
is bothering us with all her *." Mt 15:23
in the dust, * to be healed. Lk 5:12
They kept * him not to order Lk 8:31
beside the road, * from travelers. Lk 18:35
wandering around * for someone to Act 13:11
a message to him, * him not to risk Act 19:31

BEGIN
One week from today I will * Gen 7:4
away the stone and * the watering Gen 29:8
ours and our children's to * with! Gen 31:16
* the very next day, and it did. Ex 9:5
who felt called to the work to *. Ex 36:1
stops, he shall * a seven-day Lev 15:13
and let his hair * to grow again. Num 6:11
He must * all over again with a Num 6:12
Levites are to * serving in the Num 8:23,24
celebration would * on the evening Num 9:4,5
festival will *, but no leavened Num 28:17
The southern boundary will * at Num 34:3
"Your northern border will * at Num 34:7,8,9
War against him and * to take Deu 2:24
they could not * settling down Deu 3:18
"But you will also * to search Deu 4:29
your God and * to disobey him. Deu 8:11
Jordan River and * to dispossess Deu 9:1
conquered it, and * to think, 'We Deu 17:14
Before you * the battle, a Deu 20:2
so today you must * to obey all of Deu 27:10
these people will * worshiping Deu 31:16
"If you don't, and if you * to Jos 23:12
enemy troops to * fighting and Ju 7:22
Ammonites to * tormenting them. Ju 10:7,8
and he will * to rescue Israel Ju 13:5
the time when wars *, David sent 2Sa 11:1
so I will * the preparations for 1Ch 22:5
father's family to * a dynasty that 1Ch 28:4
and we will * cutting wood from 2Ch 2:16
and Mount Seir to * fighting among 2Ch 20:22
* their work at the Temple again. 2Ch 35:2
them to * building again! Ez 5:1
For women everywhere will * to Est 1:17
of money could * to cover." Est 7:4
that we cannot * to know him. Job 36:26
No one can * to understand Job 36:26
warning you—his wrath will soon *. Ps 2:12
O Lord, make these enemies * to Ps 55:9
they could even * their lament. Ps 78:64
The only way to * is by reverence Ps 111:10
your foolishness and * to live; Pro 9:6
so don't let it *. Pro 17:14
and soon the rafters * to rot. Ecc 10:18
* to speak the Hebrew language. Is 19:18
living God, and * to live good, Jer 4:2
Quick! * your crying! Jer 9:17,18
the siege will soon *. Jer 10:17
trapped inside * to eat their own Jer 19:9
these you judge! * doing what is Jer 21:12
your sinning and * obeying the Lord Jer 26:13
the other nations. * with the first Jer 36:2
little while the flailing will *. Jer 51:33
And * right here at the Temple." Eze 9:6
do when they * their long march to Eze 12:4
was and what it means. So, *!" Dan 2:6
righteousness will *, and the Most Dan 9:24
and even the fish * to disappear. Hos 4:3
and the earth and sky * to shake. Joe 3:16
watch for the enemy attack to *! Nah 2:1
In this time of our deep need, * Hab 3:2
A cry of alarm will * at the Zep 1:10
while I will * to shake the heavens Hag 2:6
to see the work *, to see the Zec 4:10
Lord said, "Go. * your patrol." Zec 6:7
and the leaves * to sprout, you Mt 24:32
for a while,' and * oppressing Mt 24:49
responsibilities. * the joyous Mt 25:21
But when these things * to Mk 13:9
and its leaves * to sprout, you Mk 13:28
"But don't * until you count the Lk 14:28
For who would * construction of a Lk 14:28
will the Kingdom of God *?" Lk 17:20
And Jesus said, "All right, * Lk 18:42
Kingdom of God would * right away. Lk 19:11
So when all these things * to Lk 21:28
Don't * telling others Lk 24:49
who will soon * his ministry among Jn 1:27
will not * until the summer ends Jn 4:35
to * to do it!" Jn 6:7
tried this before, [but * now Jn 16:24
* my remarks with a bit of history Act 13:16
The people waited for him to * Act 28:6
be jealous and * to want God's Rom 11:11
to * doing something about it. 2Co 8:10
up many of them to * helping. 2Co 9:2
I pray that you will * to Eph 1:19
must stop it and * using those Eph 4:28
for you we always * by giving Col 1:3
pains * when her child is born. 1Th 5:3
kindness should * at home, 1Ti 5:4
to be rich soon * to do all kinds 1Ti 6:9
will * living with him in heaven. 2Ti 2:11
they can * doing the will of God. 2Ti 2:26
so that we can * really to live? Heb 12:9
* first among God's own children. 1Pe 4:17
out to him, "* to use the sickle, Rev 14:15

BEGINNING
Or, "In the * God created . . ." Gen 1:1f
This was the * of an explosion of Gen 11:6f
seven days before * to minister in Ex 29:30
* the day following the Passover. Lev 23:6
So, * the day the altar was Num 7:84,85,86
* in the evening. Num 9:2,3
second month, * in the evening. Num 9:11
and at the * of each month to Num 10:10
it is the * of a seven-day Num 29:12
of his land. * today I will make Deu 2:25
I gave the area * at Aroer on the Deu 3:12
people's * to worship their gods. Deu 7:4
son, who is the * of his strength Deu 21:17
important than ours at the *!" Ju 8:2,3
Just as they were * to warm to Ju 19:22
at the * of the barley harvest. Ru 1:22
Boaz, * with his ancestor Perez: Ru 4:18-22
"Tomorrow is the * of the 1Sa 20:5
THAT WAS THE * of a long war 2Sa 3:1
Then, * at the old Millo section 2Sa 5:9
at the * of the barley harvest. 2Sa 21:9
He reigned two years, * in the 1Ki 15:25
But this is only the *, for the 2Ki 3:18
His age at the * of his reign: 16 2Ki 15:1
His age at the * of his reign: 25 2Ki 18:1
His age at * of his reign:12 years 2Ki 21:1
His age at the * of his reign: 22 2Ki 21:19,20
His age at the * of his reign: 8 2Ki 22:1
His age at the * of his reign: 18 2Ki 24:8,9
This is at least a *, something 1Ch 22:14
of his life more than at the *. Job 42:12
was the * of its strength and joy. Ps 78:51
you are God without * or end. Ps 90:2
The Lord formed me in the *, Pro 8:22
scope of God's work from * to end. Ecc 3:11
at the * of the reign of Jehoiakim Jer 27:1
to Jeremiah in the * of the reign Jer 49:34
Do not despise this small *, Zec 4:10
hidden since the * of time." Mt 13:34,35
that at the * God created man and Mt 19:4
them, * with the last men first. Mt 20:8
When you hear of wars *, this Mt 24:6
But all this will be only the * Mt 24:8
* to happen, you can know that my Mt 24:33
been since the * of God's creation, Mk 13:19
you see clouds * to form in the Lk 12:54
and insurrections *, don't panic. Lk 21:9
of the prophets, * with the book of Lk 24:27
Literally, "In the *." Jn 1:1f
Literally, "In the *." Jn 1:1f
(For Jesus knew from the * who Jn 6:64
away one by one, * with the eldest, Jn 8:9
He was a murderer from the * and Jn 8:44
you have been with me from the *. Jn 15:27
all through Judea, * with John the Act 10:36,37
just as he fell on us at the *! Act 11:15
reveals his plans made from the *. Act 15:18
For from the very * God decided Rom 8:29
what he had decided from the *; Rom 9:10-13
whom he chose from the very *. Rom 11:2,3
kept secret from the * of time. Rom 16:25,26,27
new, * a "Church of Paul." 1Co 1:15
ARE WE * to be like those false 2Co 3:1
chosen from the * to be his, and Eph 1:11
secretly planned from the very *. Eph 3:9
Literally, "he is the *, the Col 1:18f
"Lord, in the * you made the Heb 1:10
that marks the * of the agreement Heb 9:20
one who has been alive from the *. 1Jn 2:13
you have been taught from the *. 1Jn 2:24
for the message to us from the * 1Jn 3:11
us right from the *, that 2Jn 1:5
and authority are his from the *; Jud 1:24,25
the * and the Ending of all Rev 1:8
I am the A and the Z—the * and Rev 21:6
I am the A and the Z, the * and Rev 22:13

BEGINS
(Isaac * to tremble noticeably. Gen 27:33
(Esau * to sob with deep and Gen 27:34
But if, later on, this spot * to Lev 13:35
this time for atonement * on the Lev 23:32
"Seven weeks after the harvest * Deu 16:9
or tribe of Israel—* to turn away Deu 29:18
The boundary of the Amorites * Ju 1:36
Suddenly it * to wither, even Job 8:11-13
Since he * with a foolish Ecc 10:12,13
All the world * to sing! Is 14:7
So it will be when the Lord * to Is 30:26
the nation *. Is 66:7,8
Today your work *, to warn the Jer 1:10
his lovingkindness * afresh each Lam 3:23
all his sins and * to obey my laws Eze 18:21
being good and * sinning and dies Eze 18:26
where the northern boundary *. Eze 47:20
* to play, and that anyone who Dan 3:10
The attack *! Nah 2:3
judgment *, and your opportunity is Zep 2:2
the terrible day of his wrath *. Zep 2:2
and if anyone * false prophecy Zec 13:3
come [at the time the Kingdom * Mt 11:14
or persecution * because of his Mt 13:21
celebration * in two days, and I Mt 26:2
HERE * THE wonderful story of Mk 1:1
soon as persecution *, they wilt. Mk 4:17
My story * with a Jewish priest, Lk 1:5
"But if the man * to think, 'My Lk 12:45
a long time,' and * to whip the men Lk 12:45
with you before my suffering *. Lk 22:15
* and ends with you Corinthians? 1Co 14:36

BEGONE
of hope. *, you evil-minded men. Ps 119:115
Away, bloodthirsty men! *! Ps 139:19
of every God-given right. Up! *! Mic 2:10
right," Jesus told them. "*." Mt 8:32

BEGOTTEN
Literally, "This day have I * Ps 2:7f
Literally, "This day have I * Act 13:32,33f
Literally, "this day I have * Heb 1:5,6f
Literally, "* you." Heb 5:5f

BEGS
nature to do what it * you to do. Rom 8:12

BEGUN
they have just * to exploit their Gen 11:6
"Since I have *, let me go on Gen 18:27
them—the plague has already *." Num 16:46
the plague had indeed already *; Num 16:47
to me, 'I have * to give you the Deu 2:31
your children have * wholeheartedly Deu 30:2
But after they had * their Ru 1:8
For the plague had already * and 1Sa 5:11
THE PHILISTINES had * 1Sa 31:1
over Judah had * in the twelfth 2Ki 9:29
the idol-worship * by Jeroboam I 2Ki 15:24
of Israel had * to worship it by 2Ki 18:4
field and had * to run away, but 1Ch 11:13

(BEGUN Con't)
against idol worship was *. 2Ch 31:1
fifty-two days after we had *! Neh 6:15
I have * to speak; Job 33:2
But before you have * the Is 18:5
See, I have already *! Is 43:19
At noon it has *. Jer 6:4
I have * to punish my own Jer 25:29
*, and there is more ahead." Eze 19:14
you have * to build the Temple. Hag 2:15
you have even * to rebuild the Hag 2:18,19
to say, 'It has * here in this Lk 17:21
He asked them when the lad had * Jn 4:52
their journey had *, and where they Act 14:26
A new life has *! 2Co 5:17
day of the Lord has already *. 2Th 2:1
great power and have * to reign. Rev 11:17

BEHALF
them to speak to Pharaoh on his *. Gen 50:4
man on whose * the ceremony is Lev 14:25
on * of all the people of Israel. Num 3:7,8,9
on * of the people of Israel. Num 3:38
King Solomon on my * (for I know he 1Ki 2:17
sacrifices on * of all Israel. 1Ch 29:21
These men signed on * of the Neh 10:28
Job 16:18
Let it protest on my *.
his prayer on your *, and won't Job 42:8
accepted Job's prayer on their *. Job 42:9
out to God on her * until she Is 62:1
with you on their *—how I have Jer 15:11
he made sin on our *, that we might 2Co 5:21f

BEHAVE
but we should * like God's very own Rom 8:15
I would never * like that"—let 1Co 10:12
own little family *, how can he 1Ti 3:5
the young men to * carefully, Tit 2:6
Be careful how you * among your 1Pe 2:12

BEHAVED
doing right and * even worse than Ju 2:19
wrong, or how they have * proudly. Job 36:9

BEHAVES
* himself, he will not be harmed; 1Ki 1:52

BEHAVIOR
father's shameful * toward David. 1Sa 20:34
Don't copy the * and customs of Rom 12:2
do so that all can approve your *. Rom 13:12,13
Lord, and your * should show it! Eph 5:8
be won by your respectful, pure *. 1Pe 3:1

BEHEAD
then the king will * me for Dan 1:10

BEHEADED
So John was * in the prison, and Mt 14:10
said, "it is John, the man I *. Mk 6:16
"I * John," Herod said, "so Lk 9:9
those who had been * for their Rev 20:4

BEHEMOTH
"Take a look at the *! Job 40:15

BEHIND
your own country * you, and your Gen 12:1
from the tent door * him. Gen 18:10
to them, shutting the door * him. Gen 19:6
following along * him, and became a Gen 19:26
He is coming right * us!" Gen 32:18
He fled, leaving his jacket *!" Gen 39:18
Not a hoof shall be left *; Ex 10:26
the cloud around * them, and it Ex 14:19
from the hooks. * this curtain Ex 26:33
Nun), stayed * in the Tabernacle. Ex 33:11
the Holy Place * the veil, where Lev 16:1
wore when he went * the veil, and Lev 16:23
That is the reasoning * my Lev 17:12
But he shall not go in * the Lev 21:23
of Judah grouped * its flag, and Num 10:14
tribe of Ephraim * its flag, led by Num 10:22
about all you left * in Egypt, and Num 11:18
*, with no respect or fear of God. Deu 25:18
However, stay about a half mile * Jos 3:2,3,4
on their trumpets. * them would Jos 6:6-9
Set an ambush * the city." Jos 8:2
* the city, alert for action. Jos 8:3,4
there was an ambush * the city. Jos 8:14
When the men of Ai looked * Jos 8:20,21
locked the doors * him and escaped Ju 3:22,23
of the Jordan * the army of Ju 12:5
that the Lord was * the request, Ju 14:4
who now looked * them and were Ju 20:40,41
* his reapers." Ru 2:2
Stay right * my women workers; Ru 2:8,9
and stay close * his reapers until Ru 2:21
"Come on, climb right * me," 1Sa 14:12
Literally, "* the ephod." 1Sa 21:9f
remained * to guard their gear. 1Sa 25:13
"My master left me * three days 1Sa 30:13
When Abner looked * and saw him 2Sa 2:20
He followed along * her as far 2Sa 3:16
frontal attack. Go * them and come 2Sa 5:23
out and lock the door * her." 2Sa 13:17,18
He left no one * except ten of 2Sa 15:16
they will all close ranks * you." 2Sa 16:21
He shields all who hide * him. 2Sa 22:31
a courtyard * this hall. 1Ki 7:8
The rest fled * the walls of 1Ki 20:30
your sons and shut the door * you. 2Ki 4:4
He went in and shut the door * 2Ki 4:33
you know about peace? Get * me!" 2Ki 9:18
about friendliness? Get * me!" 2Ki 9:19
were riding along * his father 2Ki 9:25
both in front and * him, he divided 1Ch 19:10
Go home, for I am * their 2Ch 11:4
* the men of Judah to ambush them; 2Ch 13:13,14
with the enemy before and * them. 2Ch 13:13,14
in the cleared spaces * the walls. Neh 4:13
the other half stood guard * them. Neh 4:16
her full support * Mordecai's Est 9:29-31
sins and leave all iniquity * you. Job 11:13,14
for fear—his enemy is close * him! Job 18:11
a shining wake of froth * him. Job 41:31,32
for everyone who hides * him. Ps 18:30
I follow close * you, protected Ps 63:8
front, musicians *, girls playing Ps 68:25
Zebulun and Naphtali are right *. Ps 68:27
them, they walked awhile * him; Ps 78:34
out * his banner and destroy them. Ps 118:10
Leave * your foolishness and Pro 9:6
leads upward, leaving hell *. Pro 15:24
Look, there he is * the wall, now Sol 2:9
"My dove is hiding * some rocks, Sol 2:14
rocks, * an outcrop of the cliff. Sol 2:14
* your locks. Sol 4:3
Literally, "* your veil." Sol 4:3f
* your hair. Sol 6:7
their sins * them like a bullock Is 5:18
* you say, "No, this is the way; Is 30:21
far * you—it is unclean to you. Is 52:11
Israel, will protect you from *. Is 52:12
the cities left * during the exile, Is 54:3
deserting me. * closed doors you Is 57:7,8
the Lord will protect you from *. Is 58:8
* a trail of misery and death. Is 59:7
that are hidden * a tree in the Is 66:17
all its sorrows will be * them. Jer 31:13
land who were left *, and had not Jer 40:7
* you and you will perish there. Jer 42:16
Literally, "I heard * me the Eze 3:12f
Put them * you and receive a new Eze 18:31
of prostitution *, but was still as Eze 23:8
right along * her older sister. Eze 23:13
gates, pulling chariots * them. Eze 26:10
people are whispering * your back. Eze 33:30
with a hallway 12¼ feet deep * it. Eze 41:3
The rows of rooms * this Eze 42:3
the passage shall be shut * him. Eze 46:12
inherit your possessions left *? Hos 9:6
plague follows close *. Hab 3:5
beside a river. * him were other Zec 1:8
sins *, and coming back to me? Zec 7:5
their father *, went with him. Mt 4:22
and shut the door * you and pray to Mt 6:6
bleeding came up * him and touched Mt 9:20
men followed along *, shouting, "O Mt 9:27
a vast crowd surged along *. Mt 20:29
and pressed along *, shouting, Mt 21:9
* (though other boats followed). Mk 4:36
him, and the crowd thronged *. Mk 5:24
is why she came up * him through Mk 5:27
very sternly, "Satan, get * me! Mk 8:33
the other disciples had left *. Mk 10:28
crowds ahead and *, and all of them Mk 11:9
following along *, clothed only in Mk 14:51,52
Peter followed far * and then Mk 14:54
but Jesus stayed * in Jerusalem. Lk 2:43
Going in, she knelt * him at his Lk 7:38
be healed came up * and touched Lk 8:43,44
lanes and out * the hedges and urge Lk 14:23
Great crowds trailed along *, Lk 23:27
money changers * their counters. Jn 2:14
off in their boat, leaving him *. Jn 6:22,23
leaving them *, and coming to you. Jn 17:11
Simon Peter followed along *, Jn 18:15
and saw someone standing * her. Jn 20:14
were meeting * locked doors, in Jn 20:19
She followed along * us Act 16:17
Silas and Timothy remained *. Act 17:14
the gates were closed * him. Act 21:30
the crowd surged * shouting, "Away Act 21:36
But the real reason * their Act 26:6
We finally sailed * a small Act 27:16
was being towed * us, and then Act 27:16
misery and trouble * them, and Rom 3:16
their unbelief * them and come back Rom 11:23
on your thrones, leaving us far *! 1Co 4:8
leaving entirely * us the cancerous 1Co 5:8
and whispering * each other's 2Co 12:20
with God himself * the sacred Heb 6:19
Then there was a curtain and * Heb 9:3
They will soon die and leave * Jas 1:10,11
about others * their backs. 1Pe 2:1
of Christ, you will leave God *; 2Jn 1:9
All they leave * them is shame Jud 1:13
heard a loud voice * me, a voice Rev 1:10
speaking, there * me were seven Rev 1:12
His tail drew along * him a Rev 12:4

BEHOLD
Literally, "Therefore, *, I will Jer 16:21
And yet, O people everywhere, * Lam 1:1
"Do always * . " Mt 18:10
And Pilate said, "* the man!" Jn 19:

BEHOLDING
Literally, "from * vanity." Ps 119:37

BEHURIM
as far as *, weeping as he went. 2Sa 3:16

BEING
every living *—everything in which Gen 6:1
you and to every *, that never Gen 9:1
to every living * on the earth." Gen 9:16,1
of someone as * "like Nimrod—a Gen 10:
on account of her * there. Gen 12:1
her the privilege of * your wife. Gen 16:
"thank you for * so kind and Gen 24:2
his life was * threatened by Esau. Gen 27:42
He explained about * her cousin Gen 29:12,1
are all because of your * here. Gen 30:2
As they were * born, the midwife Gen 38:28
his father-in-law * a major Gen 41:45
they saw where they were * taken. Gen 43:18
"If the field is * burned off Ex 22:6
each frame-piece * fifteen feet Ex 26:15,16
* imbedded in solid bronze bases. Ex 27:17
from * in the presence of God. Ex 34:29
sheets, each loop * opposite its Ex 36:11,12
as * ceremonially defiled. Lev 11:25
ear of the man * cleansed, and upon Lev 14:14
* cleansed from his leprosy; Lev 14:19
the ceremony is * performed—and Lev 14:25
head of the man * cleansed, to make Lev 14:29
not be defiled by * eaten by Lev 22:15
is no proof, there * no witness, Num 5:13
of * in the presence of death. Num 6:9
and protested at * forbidden from Num 9:6,7
(The first of the grapes were * Num 13:20
If a lamb is * sacrificed, use Num 15:3,4
been defiled by * in the tent, or Num 19:18
any defect such as * lame or blind, Deu 15:21
by flagrant crime, * a prostitute Deu 22:21
were suspected of * spies had Jos 2:2
your shame of not * circumcised." Jos 5:8,9
others died while * chased by the Jos 7:5
people of Israel are * defeated. Jos 7:12
troops of Midian, * Ishmaelites, Ju 8:23,24
to know why Israel was * attacked. Ju 11:12
to them without * guilty.' Ju 21:22
"For you are * even kinder to Ru 3:10
he has rejected you from * king." 1Sa 15:23
you from * the king of Israel." 1Sa 15:26
weren't happy about his * there. 1Sa 21:11
trouble, such as * in debt, or 1Sa 22:2
doing good and for * loyal, and I 1Sa 26:23
Lord bless you for * so loyal to 2Sa 2:5
a sacred vow by * kind to him." 2Sa 9:3
night after * away for so long?" 2Sa 11:10
up about the baby * sick," they 2Sa 12:18
sheep were * sheared at Baal-hazor 2Sa 13:21-24
Tell them the plans that are * 2Sa 15:35,36
will see that I am * wronged and 2Sa 16:12
that your men are * slaughtered. 2Sa 17:9
the lower floor * 7½ feet wide, the 1Ki 6:6
He was half Jewish, * the son of 1Ki 7:14
* held as prisoners in Babylon. 2Ki 25:28
I took you from * a shepherd and 1Ch 17:7
of my children * kings too! 1Ch 17:17
fiber of your * to obey the Lord 1Ch 22:19
We adore you as * in control of 1Ch 29:11
Instead of its * famous, all who 2Ch 7:21
Beth-horon, both * supply centers, 2Ch 8:5
to stop * priests of the Lord. 2Ch 11:13,14
mother Maacah from * the queen 2Ch 15:16
wealthy as well as * very popular. 2Ch 17:5
the miracle of his * healed, God 2Ch 32:31
was good progress * made in the 2Ch 34:15,16
It is * built with huge stones, Ez 5:8
is * laid in the city walls. Ez 5:8
religious progress * made there. Ez 7:14
So the holy people of God were * Ez 9:2
for God was * gracious to me. Neh 2:8
O Lord God, for we are * mocked. Neh 4:4
* repaired, they became furious. Neh 4:7
their king—that is what is * said. Neh 6:5,6
the Temple, not * a priest, I would Neh 6:11
to Judah after * exiled by King Neh 7:6
of the passage that was * read. Neh 8:7,8
us you were * perfectly fair; Neh 9:33
laws of Moses were * read, the Neh 13:1
friends as well as * the chief Est 1:13-15
were that before * taken to the Est 2:12,13,14
it because of his * a Jew, which Est 3:3,4
couriers, after * first proclaimed Est 3:15
the cries of those * oppressed. Job 34:28
me for doing right and * pure. Ps 18:20
Save me from * overpowered by my Ps 39:8
is * played for your enjoyment. Ps 45:8
and to stop * stubborn and Ps 75:5
May every fiber of my * unite in Ps 86:11
to the Lord for * so good, for Ps 107:1

3EING Con't)
'or always * so loving and kind. Ps 107:1
How I dread * mocked for obeying, Ps 119:39
' am tired of * here among these Ps 120:5,6
You were there while I was * Ps 139:15
nis command, and they came into *; Ps 148:5
When a bird sees a trap * set, Pro 1:17
'How long will you go on * Pro 1:22
*, filling your life with joy. Pro 2:10
A fool's fun is * bad; Pro 10:23
a wise man's fun is * wise! Pro 10:23
* destroyed by their wickedness. Pro 13:6
* kidnapped and held for ransom Pro 13:8
good men from * sentenced to death, Pro 14:25
There is treasure in * good, but Pro 15:6
to fine the godly for * good! Pro 17:26
And to punish nobles for * Pro 17:26
to harm others; * a good neighbor Pro 21:10
* happy-go-lucky around a person Pro 25:20
even to call myself a human *! Pro 30:2
If you have been a fool by * Pro 30:32
Just as * too busy gives you Ecc 5:1
* a fool makes you a blabbermouth. Ecc 5:1
If you see some poor man * Ecc 5:8
quick-tempered—that is * a fool. Ecc 7:9
To be wise is as good as * rich; Ecc 7:11
but * wise has many advantages. Ecc 7:12
DON'T LET THE excitement of * Ecc 12:1
there, the rent * one thousand Sol 8:11
You are * attacked! Is 21:5
as I watch them * destroyed. Is 22:4
it was like * torn apart by Is 38:13
your troubles and isn't * fair? Is 40:27
Woe to the baby just * born who Is 45:10
are * hauled away on ox carts! Is 46:1
I spoke and they came into *. Is 48:13
You worry at * so small and few, Is 51:1
(but not from * drunk)— this is Is 51:21
No one cares about * fair and Is 59:4
you out for * loyal to my name. Is 66:5
The kingdom of Babylonia, * Jer 5:15f
to doing evil now start * good. Jer 13:23
and Judah who were * sent to Jer 40:1
cut her off from * a nation." Jer 48:2,3,4
for all Moab is * destroyed. Jer 48:2,3,4
Draw a picture of siege mounds * Eze 4:1
counsel * given out in this city. Eze 11:1
them what * exiled will be like. Eze 12:3
things are * done to Israel." Eze 14:23
and after * put in the fire! Eze 15:5,6
before * burned and certainly Eze 15:5,6
"Yet you say: 'The Lord isn't * Eze 18:25
turns away from * good and begins Eze 18:26
this: A sword is * sharpened and Eze 21:9,10,11
I will cut you off from * a Eze 25:7
I will save my flock from * taken Eze 34:9,10
have their turn of * covered with Eze 36:7
before * taken to the altar; Eze 40:38
defile himself by * in the presence Eze 44:25
after * attacked by other animals. Eze 44:31
and sword, or * jailed and robbed. Dan 11:33
* a liar, thief, and bandit! Hos 7:1
flock * fattened for the butcher. Zec 11:4
* a man of stern principle, Mt 1:19
Before * baptized, prove that Mt 3:8
of * brought before the court. Mt 5:22
me, you are not worthy of * mine; Mt 10:37
me, you are not worthy of * mine. Mt 10:37
me, you are not worthy of * mine. Mt 10:38
Highly honored by Christ's * Mt 11:23f
sovereignty * Galilee and Peraea. Mt 14:1f
came to test Jesus' claim of * Mt 16:1
of * the sons of wicked men. Mt 23:31
Literally, "roof tops" which, * Mt 24:17f
* ready for my unannounced return. Mt 24:44
* sealed at each end with clay. Mt 27:66f
and kings of * my followers. Mk 13:9
when the incense was * burned. Lk 1:10
at what was * said about Jesus. Lk 2:33
and was * discussed everywhere. Lk 3:15
am not even worthy of * his slave. Lk 3:16
* urged by the Spirit out into the Lk 4:1
people from believing and * saved. Lk 8:12
one thing worth * concerned about. Lk 10:42
prove his claim of * the Messiah. Lk 11:16
Your eyes light up your inward * Lk 11:34
worthy of * called your son. Lk 15:19
not worthy of * called your son— Lk 15:21
admire the rascal for * so shrewd. Lk 16:8
the scoundrel for * so shrewd?" Lk 16:8f
So now he is here * comforted and Lk 16:25
as * only "half-breed" Hebrews. Lk 17:16f
counted worthy of * raised from the Lk 20:34,35
* told that summer is near. Lk 21:30
became a human * and lived here Jn 1:14
a denarius * a full day's wage. Jn 6:7f
for him and not * able to find him, Jn 7:36
of anyone who believes in me." Jn 7:38
to Jesus at the table, * his Jn 13:23
glorious unity of * one, as we are— Jn 17:22
and you in me, all * perfected into Jn 17:23

* spoken by the disciples. Act 2:6
to them all who were * saved. Act 2:47
* with Jesus had done for them! Act 4:13
their widows were * discriminated Act 6:1
that they were not * given as much Act 6:1
* prepared, he fell into a trance. Act 10:9,10
Gentiles also were * converted! Act 11:1
to worry about their * Gentiles! Act 11:12
Gentiles, too, were * converted. Act 15:3
Then Judas and Silas, both * Act 15:32
for we are in danger of * called Act 19:40
And I am * tried here today Act 23:6
lifeboat that was * towed behind Act 27:16
The sailors were afraid of * Act 27:17
storm, as we were * driven to and Act 27:27
and by * raised from the dead he Rom 1:4
I go I hear you * talked about! Rom 1:8
* disobedient to their parents. Rom 1:30
how patient he is * with you? Rom 2:4
* a Jew is worth something if you Rom 2:25
THEN WHAT'S THE use of * a Jew? Rom 3:1
Yes, * a Jew has many Rom 3:2
—not by "* good enough" and Rom 3:21,22
In this way he was * entirely Rom 3:25
this question of * saved by faith? Rom 4:1
No, for * saved is a gift; Rom 4:4,5
if a person could earn it by * Rom 4:4,5
in my * given the death penalty. Rom 7:10
Was God * unfair? Rom 9:14
the law and * good instead of by Rom 9:32
there are a few * saved as a Rom 11:5
it is not by their * good enough. Rom 11:6
not to brag about * put in to Rom 11:18
far away from him—* part of a wild Rom 11:24
to keep from * punished, and Rom 13:5
the "burden" of * considerate of Rom 15:1
this message is * preached Rom 16:25,26,27
Or, "are *." 1Co 1:18f
without * with people like that. 1Co 5:10
* able to stay happily unmarried. 1Co 7:7
But although * a "know-it-all" 1Co 8:1
really * offered to actual gods. 1Co 8:7
have of * a guest in your homes? 1Co 9:4
IF I HAD the gift of * able to 1Co 13:1
gift of prophecy, * able to preach 1Co 14:1
But if your gift is that of * 1Co 14:2
that they are * called to battle? 1Co 14:8
So you see that * able to 1Co 14:22
And if * a Christian is of value 1Co 15:19
related to Adam, * members of his 1Co 15:22
* baptized for those who are gone? 1Co 15:29
Every human * has a body just 1Co 15:48
keep from * outsmarted by Satan; 2Co 2:11
To those who are not * saved, we 2Co 2:16
merely as a human * like myself. 2Co 5:16
when salvation was * offered." 2Co 6:2
by * poor he could make you rich. 2Co 8:9
if it were * given under pressure. 2Co 9:5
weak human *, but I don't use human 2Co 10:3
about * in someone else's field. 2Co 10:16
each other, and * angry with each 2Co 12:20
you are * fooled by those who Gal 1:7
can be earned by * circumcised and Gal 2:5
(By the way, their * great Gal 2:6
that they weren't * honest about Gal 2:14
be saved without * circumcised and Gal 2:17
the Jews—were * spoken of, but to Gal 3:16
favor with God by * circumcised Gal 5:3
The fact that I am still * Gal 5:11
cut yourselves by * circumcised Gal 5:12
We started out bad, * born with Eph 2:3
the gift of * able to preach well; Eph 4:11
of * filled full with Christ. Eph 4:13
They stop at nothing, * driven by Eph 4:19
Stop * mean, bad-tempered and Eph 4:31
* holy and without a single fault. Eph 5:27
clean, no one * able to criticize Php 1:10
is * preached and I am glad. Php 1:18
I am going to keep on * glad, for Php 1:19
How much happier for me than * Php 1:23
that result from * saved, obeying Php 2:12
longer counting on * saved by being Php 3:9
on being saved by * good enough or Php 3:9
words we spoke as * just our own, 1Th 2:13
in your hearts * made strong, 1Th 3:13
* gathered together to meet him? 2Th 2:1
keeping him from * here already; 2Th 2:6
and their idea of * saved by 1Ti 1:3,4
be noticed for * kind and good, not 1Ti 2:9,10
might be proud of * chosen so soon, 1Ti 3:6
and practice * a better Christian, 1Ti 4:8
is * helped by their efforts. 1Ti 6:2
that no human * can approach him. 1Ti 6:16
in need, always * ready to share 1Ti 6:18
This * so, I want to remind you 2Ti 1:6
love them and enjoy * with them. 2Ti 1:7
was never ashamed of my * in jail. 2Ti 1:16
And he saved me from * thrown to 2Ti 4:17
a reputation for * wild or Tit 1:6
their own homes, * kind and Tit 2:5
is now * offered to everyone; Tit 2:11

blood too by * born in human form; Heb 2:14
for only as a human * could he Heb 2:14
angel but as a human *—yes, a Jew. Heb 2:16
God, * blinded by the glamor Heb 3:13
"today" * the time to get in. Heb 4:8
of rest, too, * careful not to Heb 4:11
to the honor of * High Priest; Heb 5:5
Christ's body, * human, was frail Heb 5:7f
to be saved by * good, or about the Heb 6:1
become bored with * a Christian, Heb 6:12
This certain hope of * saved is a Heb 6:19
for our sins—he * perfect, without Heb 9:14
in this way, by * sprinkled with Heb 9:23
this, about not * satisfied with Heb 10:8
each other in * helpful and kind to Heb 10:24
and some by * sawed in two; Heb 11:37,38
his holiness. * punished isn't Heb 12:11
Share the sorrow of those * Heb 13:3
world, * willing to be despised Heb 13:13
no human * can tame the tongue. Jas 3:8
don't brag about * wise and good if Jas 3:14
the privilege of * born again, so 1Pe 1:3
It is * tested as fire tests gold 1Pe 1:7
strong after * tried in the test 1Pe 1:7
get no credit for * patient if you 1Pe 2:20
of your wives, * thoughtful of 1Pe 3:7
but because in * baptized we are 1Pe 3:21
and insulted for * a Christian, for 1Pe 4:14
Spirit of God is * seen in you." 1Pe 4:14f
making trouble or * a busybody and 1Pe 4:15
shame to suffer for * a Christian. 1Pe 4:16
Praise God for the privilege of * 1Pe 4:16
* called by his wonderful name! 1Pe 4:16
"You aren't saved by * good," 2Pe 2:19
He isn't really * slow about his 2Pe 3:9
a human * with a body like ours. 2Jn 1:7
Beware of * like them, and 2Jn 1:8
find the Lord by * kind to them, Jud 1:23
* merciful to them as sinners. Jud 1:23
Those who listen to it * read and Rev 1:3
that an angelic * is appointed by Rev 1:20f
Stop * afraid of what you are Rev 2:10
into * by your act of will." Rev 4:11
And I heard the second Living * Rev 6:3
the third Living * say, "Come!" Rev 6:5
the fourth Living * say, "Come!" Rev 6:7
* faithful in their witnessing. Rev 6:9
at his reappearance after * dead. Rev 17:8

BEING'S
Each * wings stretched straight Eze 1:23

BEINGS
It was at this time that * from Gen 6:1
supernatural *, but no longer godly Gen 6:1f
when the evil * from the spirit Gen 6:4
shall it be lived in by human *; Jer 50:39
The four living * were joined Eze 1:9
of the living * on each side, and Eze 1:11
The living * darted to and fro, Eze 1:14
When the four living * flew Eze 1:19,20,21
When the living * stopped, the Eze 1:19,20,21
four living * was in the wheels; Eze 1:19,20,21
and the living * went there too. Eze 1:19,20,21
of the living * as they touched Eze 3:13
These were the same * I had seen Eze 10:15,16
These were the living * I had Eze 10:20
We are merely human * like Act 14:15
mighty satanic * and great evil Eph 6:12
are human *—made of flesh and Heb 2:14
Four Living *, dotted front and Rev 4:6
The first of these Living * was Rev 4:7
Each of these Living * had six Rev 4:8
And when the Living * gave glory Rev 4:9
and the Living *, and on the Lamb Rev 5:6
and the Living * and the Elders: Rev 5:11
And the four Living * kept Rev 5:14
Then one of the four Living *, Rev 6:1
the four Living * said, "A loaf of Rev 6:6
the four Living *, and falling face Rev 7:11
* and the twenty-four Elders; Rev 14:3
And one of the four Living * Rev 15:7
and four Living * fell down and Rev 19:4

BEJEWELED
your clothing was * with every Eze 28:13

BEL
THE IDOLS OF Babylon, * and Nebo, Is 46:1
And I will punish *, the god of Jer 51:44

BELA
The king of * (later called Zoar). Gen 14:2
Zeboiim, and *) mobilized their Gen 14:3
and * (Zoar), unsuccessfully Gen 14:8,9
King * (son of Beor), from Gen 36:31-39
Benjamin's sons: *, Becher, Gen 46:19-22
named after their ancestor *. Num 26:38-41
Sub-clans named after sons of * Num 26:38-41
* (the son of Beor), who lived in 1Ch 1:43
When * died, Jobab the son of 1Ch 1:44
* (the son of Azaz, grandson of 1Ch 5:7,8
*, Becher, Jedia-el. 1Ch 7:6
The sons of *: 1Ch 7:7

(BELA Con't)
*, the first,Ashbel, the 1Ch 8:1
The sons of * were: 1Ch 8:3,4,5

BELA-ITES
The *, named after their ancestor Num 26:38-41

BELIEF
women in the * that this would aid Gen 30:14f
* in the resurrection of the dead. Act 28:20f
Their * in the truth which they Tit 1:9
Noah's * in God was in direct Heb 11:7

BELIEFS
because of his *, his enthusiasm Mt 13:21
"Then what * did you acknowledge Act 19:3
about their Jewish *, certainly Act 23:29

BELIEVE
Some commentators * that the Gen 6:1f
BUT MOSES SAID, "They won't * me! Ex 4:1
"Do that and they will * you!" Ex 4:5
"If they don't * the first Ex 4:8
and then they will always * you. Ex 19:9
Will they never * me, even after Num 14:10,11
Aaron, "Because you did not * me Num 20:12
"Didn't you * me when I said I Num 22:37
"They refused to * the Lord our Deu 1:32
wouldn't * that he would help you; Deu 9:23
have no reason to * that you will Deu 28:66
"Do you expect me to * that?" Ju 11:9
I didn't * it until I came, but 1Ki 10:7
to * in the Lord their God. 2Ki 17:14
Don't * it when he says that I 2Ki 19:10
she could scarcely * it! 2Ch 9:4
I didn't * it until I got here 2Ch 9:6
he said. "* in the Lord your God, 2Ch 20:20
have success! * his prophets, and 2Ch 20:20
Don't * him. 2Ch 32:15
Josiah refused to * that Neco's 2Ch 35:22
Shouldn't you * that God will Job 4:6
scarce * that he had heard my cry. Job 9:16
We'll * it when we see God rescue Ps 22:8
they didn't * in God or trust in Ps 78:22
and refused to * in miracles. Ps 78:32
for they wouldn't * his solemn oath Ps 106:24
too glorious, too wonderful to *! Ps 139:6
I been right? Then * what I am Pro 22:20,21
pleasant enough, but don't * him; Pro 26:24,25,26
Some linguists * the meaning Pro 30:18,19f
You don't * me? Is 7:9
you must learn to * what I say." Is 7:9
You don't * it? Is 29:9
Those in error will * the truth, Is 29:24
to know and to * me and to Is 43:10
BUT, OH, HOW few * it! Is 53:1
Some * this verse as well as Is 65:1f
Some * this verse as well as Is 65:1f
Don't * them. Jer 12:6
But Gedaliah wouldn't * them. Jer 40:13,14
The world can scarcely * its eyes Jer 51:41
me to * your interpretation!" Dan 2:8,9
that you will have to see to *. Hab 1:5
"Do you * I can make you see?" Mt 9:28
is here—and you refuse to * him. Mt 12:41
is here—and you refuse to * him. Mt 12:42
you ask for in prayer—if you *." Mt 21:22
why we didn't * what John said. Mt 21:25
to repent, and so you couldn't *. Mt 21:32
here or there,' don't * it. Mt 24:23
at a certain place, don't * it! Mt 24:26
people wouldn't * Mt 24:39
from the cross and we'll * you! Mt 27:41,42,43
fact that they wouldn't * in him. Mk 6:6
For they didn't want to *! Mk 6:52
Then we will * in you." Mk 8:11
must I be with you until you *? Mk 9:19
little ones who * in me to lose Mk 9:42
you really * and have no doubt! Mk 11:22,23
and if you *, you have it; Mk 11:24
from the cross and we'll * you!" Mk 15:32
Pilate couldn't * that Jesus was Mk 15:44
But they didn't * her! Mk 16:10,11
refusal to * those who had seen him Mk 16:14
Those who * and are baptized Mk 16:16
But those who refuse to * will be Mk 16:16
"And those who * shall use my Mk 16:17
is true, and sort of * for awhile; Lk 8:13
who listen and * God's words but Lk 8:14
anyone else to * the Good News. Lk 8:14
them to others who also soon *." Lk 8:15
from having a chance to * it." Lk 11:52
don't * it or go out to look for Lk 17:23
ask, 'Then why didn't you * him?' Lk 20:5
But don't * them! Lk 21:8
* me or let me present my case. Lk 22:67,68
tale to the men—they didn't * it. Lk 24:11
You find it so hard to * all that Lk 24:25
Literally, "to * on his name." Jn 1:11,12f
All those who * this are reborn! Jn 1:13
Jesus asked him, "Do you * all Jn 1:50
have seen—and yet you won't * me. Jn 3:10,11
But if you don't even * me when Jn 3:12
can you possibly * if I tell you Jn 3:12
but how few * what he tells them! Jn 3:32
Those who * him discover that Jn 3:33,34
those who don't * and obey him Jn 3:36
to * in him after hearing him. Jn 4:40,41
woman, "Now we * because we have Jn 4:42
"Won't any of you * in me unless I Jn 4:48
However, most commentators * the Jn 5:32,33f
you will * in me and be saved. Jn 5:34
for you refuse to * me—the one sent Jn 5:38
you * they give you eternal life. Jn 5:39
No wonder you can't *! Jn 5:44
For you have refused to * Moses. Jn 5:46
but you refuse to * him, so you Jn 5:46
him, so you refuse to * in me. Jn 5:46
And since you don't * what he Jn 5:47
no wonder you don't * me either." Jn 5:47
fed you, not because you * in me. Jn 6:26
you * in the one he has sent." Jn 6:29
want us to * you are the Messiah. Jn 6:30,31
But some of you don't * me." Jn 6:64
who didn't * and knew the one who Jn 6:64
life, and we * them and know you Jn 6:69
For even his brothers didn't * Jn 7:5
for unless you * that I am the Jn 8:24
you just naturally don't * it! Jn 8:45
you the truth, why don't you * me? Jn 8:46
The Jewish leaders wouldn't * he Jn 9:18
said, "Do you * in the Messiah?" Jn 9:35
Lord," the man said, "I *!" Jn 9:38
and you don't * me," Jesus Jn 10:25
But you don't * me because you Jn 10:26
Don't * me unless I do miracles Jn 10:37
But if I do, * them even if you Jn 10:38
them even if you don't * me. Jn 10:38
another opportunity to * in me. Jn 11:15
Do you * this, Martha?" Jn 11:26
she told him. "I * you are the Jn 11:27
miracle from God if you *?" Jn 11:40
so that they will * you sent me. Jn 11:42
would not * he was the Messiah. Jn 12:37
predicted: "Lord, who will * us? Jn 12:38
But they couldn't *, for as Jn 12:39
when it happens, you will * on me. Jn 13:19
All commentators * him to be Jn 13:23f
Don't you * that I am in the Jn 14:10
Just * it—that I am in the Jn 14:11
Or else * it because of the Jn 14:11
when they do, you will * [in me Jn 14:29
and * that I came from the Father. Jn 16:27
From this we * that you came from Jn 16:30
"Do you finally * this?" Jn 16:31
from you, and they * you sent me. Jn 17:8
and the world will * you sent me. Jn 17:21
report so that you also can *. Jn 19:35
is true, that you also may *." Jn 19:35f
replied, "I won't * it unless I Jn 20:25
Don't be faithless any longer.* Jn 20:27
Then Jesus told him, "You * Jn 20:29
haven't seen me and * anyway." Jn 20:29
so that you will * that he is the Jn 20:30,31
"if you * with all your heart." Act 8:37
And the eunuch replied, "I * that Act 8:37
didn't * it was really happening. Act 12:9
They didn't * her. Act 12:15
* when you hear it announced.' Act 13:41
so that they also could *. Act 15:7
Don't you * that all are saved Act 15:11
They replied, "* on the Lord Act 16:31
must then go on to * in Jesus, the Act 19:4
and persuading many to * in Jesus. Act 19:8
people here won't * you when you Act 22:17,18
today because I * in the Act 23:6
but the Pharisees * in all of Act 23:8
do confess, that I * in the way of Act 24:14
I firmly * in the Jewish law and Act 24:14
and I *, just as these men do, Act 24:15
But is it a crime to * in the Act 26:8
"I used to * that I ought to do Act 26:9
King Agrippa, do you * the Act 26:27
"Sirs," he said, "I * there is Act 27:10
For I * God! Act 27:25
that it is because I * the Messiah Act 28:20
But we want to hear what you *, Act 28:22
they, too, will * and obey him. Rom 1:5
bringing all who * it to heaven. Rom 1:16
they deliberately chose to * lies. Rom 1:25
of those who * and are saved Rom 4:11
Abraham—when we * the promises of Rom 4:24
but only those who * the promise of Rom 9:8
Those who * in him will never be Rom 9:33
is your Lord, and * in your own Rom 10:9
to save them unless they * in him? Rom 10:14
And how can they * in him if they Rom 10:14
they didn't * God, and you are Rom 11:20
You may * there is no harm in Rom 14:2
EVEN IF WE * that it makes no Rom 15:1
and full of peace as you * in him. Rom 15:13
because they * only what agrees 1Co 1:22
you, and I can just about * it. 1Co 11:18
You will always * in him, always 1Co 13:7
you still firmly * it, unless of 1Co 15:2
Since you * what we preach, that 1Co 15:12
Why do it unless you * that the 1Co 15:2
We never try to get anyone to * 2Co 4:
We boldly say what we * [trusting 2Co 4:1
"I * and therefore I speak." 2Co 4:1
Since we * that Christ died for 2Co 5:13,1
us, we should also * that we have 2Co 5:13,1
a partner with one who doesn't *? 2Co 6:1
You seem so gullible: you * 2Co 11:
I can hardly * it! Gal 3:
It is when you * in Christ and Gal 3:
escape is open to all who * him. Gal 3:21,2
we could * in the coming Savior. Gal 3:2
power is to help those who * him. Eph 1:1
We who * are carefully joined Eph 2:21
until finally we all * alike Eph 4:1
about what we * because someone has Eph 4:14
on some point, I * that God will Php 3:15
is that you fully * the Truth, Col 1:23
For since we * that Jesus died 1Th 4:14
again, we can also * that when 1Th 4:14
have come from me, don't * them. 2Th 2:
they have refused to * it and 2Th 2:10
will allow them to * lies with all 2Th 2:11
you to be among the first to *." 2Th 2:13
that people will * it, for our hope 1Ti 4:9,1
the faith of some who * them. 2Ti 2:18
wrong ideas and * what is true. 2Ti 2:25
yes, but they won't really * 2Ti 3:5
You know what I * and the way I 2Ti 3:10
want to * in our Savior and God. Tit 2:10
the Holy Spirit to those who *; Heb 2:4
any good because they didn't * it. Heb 4:2
For only we who * God can enter Heb 4:3
those who don't * me will never get Heb 4:3
I really don't * that what I am Heb 6:9
come to God must * that there is a Heb 11:6
Well, remember that the demons * Jas 2:19
he is very precious to you who *; 1Pe 2:7
asks why you * as you do, be ready 1Pe 3:15
Others * this should read: "Your 1Pe 5:13f
for he does not * in God the Father 1Jn 2:22
For a person who doesn't * in 1Jn 2:23
says we must do: * on the name of 1Jn 3:23
don't always * everything you hear 1Jn 4:1
and because we * him when he tells 1Jn 4:16
IF YOU * that Jesus is the 1Jn 5:1
We * men who witness in our 1Jn 5:9
we can * whatever God declares. 1Jn 5:9
All who * this know in their 1Jn 5:10
If anyone doesn't * this, he is 1Jn 5:10
* what God has said about his Son. 1Jn 5:10
I have written this to you who * 1Jn 5:13
around—who don't * that Jesus 2Jn 1:7
and he doesn't * what Christ 2Jn 1:10
Jerome, etc.) * from this that an Rev 1:20f
most commentators *, or whether the Rev 9:1f
Blessed are those who * it and Rev 22:6,7

BELIEVED
And Abram * God; Gen 15:6
Then the elders * that God had Ex 4:31
* in him and in his servant Moses. Ex 14:31
the other leaders finally * them. Jos 9:14,15
Achish * David and thought that 1Sa 27:12
Testament saints * in a conscious Ps 6:5f
Then at last his people * him. Ps 106:12
world—would have * an enemy could Lam 4:12
on him, because he * in his God. Dan 6:23
Usually * to be a revived Roman Dan 7:23f
And they * him and declared a Jon 3:4,5
What you have * has happened!" Mt 8:13
the people * John was a prophet. Mt 14:5
still * by them to this very day. Mt 28:15
how strongly they * that he would Mk 2:5
(For the people all * strongly Mk 11:32
the others, but no one * them. Mk 16:13
And now, because you haven't * Lk 1:20
* that God would do what he said; Lk 1:45
Then some Sadducees—men who * Lk 20:27
And his disciples * that he Jn 2:11
Literally, "His disciples * on Jn 2:11f
Many from the Samaritan village * Jn 4:39
And the man * Jesus and started Jn 4:50
* that Jesus was the Messiah. Jn 4:53
myself they aren't *, but someone Jn 5:31
* even though you have seen me. Jn 6:36
the crowds at the Temple * on him. Jn 7:31
Literally, "Many * on him Jn 10:42f
saw it happen, finally * on him. Jn 11:45
and * in Jesus as their Messiah. Jn 12:11
the Jewish leaders * him to be the Jn 12:42
and saw, and * [that he had risen Jn 20:8
And those who * Peter were Act 2:41
their message * it, so that the Act 4:4
But now they * Philip's message Act 8:12
Then Simon himself * and was Act 8:13
the town, and many * in the Lord. Act 9:42
he gave us when we * on the Lord Act 11:17
what happened he * and was Act 13:12
eternal life, *. Act 13:48
many—both Jews and Gentiles—*. Act 14:1
As a result, many of them *, Act 17:12

BELIEVED Con't)
all his household * in the Lord and Act 18:8
the Holy Spirit when you *?" Act 19:2
he * and why, and persuading many Act 19:8
of Jews have also *, and they are Act 21:20
in every synagogue who * on you. Act 22:19
Some *, and some didn't. Act 28:24
tell us Abraham * God, and that is Rom 4:3
nation, Abraham * God even though Rom 4:18
But Abraham never doubted. He * Rom 4:20
who has * me when I told them?" Rom 10:16
nearer now than when we first *. Rom 13:11
all those who * his message, which 1Co 1:21
and with our help you *. 1Co 3:5
as alive, and have * that food 1Co 8:7
really * it in the first place. 1Co 15:2
the Gospel to you, and you * it. 1Co 15:11
what they really *, and weren't Gal 2:14
only because he * God's promises. Gal 3:6
changed your lives when you * it. 1Th 2:13
have * what we told you about him. 2Th 1:10
the future, Noah * him even though Heb 11:7
descendants! He * that if Isaac Heb 11:19
And it was because he * God Heb 11:28
By faith—because she * in God Heb 11:31
who have never * in the Lord? 1Pe 4:17
Go back to what you heard and * Rev 3:3

BELIEVER
Now I say that each * should Ps 32:6
Now there was in Damascus a * Act 9:10
to arrest every * in Damascus!" Act 9:14
("Gazelle"), a * who was always Act 9:36
met Timothy, a * whose mother was a Act 16:1
lead about a wife that is a *?" 1Co 9:5f
lead about a wife that is a *?" 1Co 9:5f
she were a *, couldn't I bring 1Co 9:5

BELIEVERS
for the future * who will come to Jn 17:20
As the * met together that day, Act 2:1
They joined with the other * in Act 2:42
And all the * met together Act 2:44
that the number of * now reached a Act 4:4
Then all the * united in this Act 4:24
All the * were of one heart and Act 4:32
among all the *, and no Act 4:33
The other * didn't dare join Act 5:13
And more and more * were added Act 5:14
BUT WITH THE * multiplying Act 6:1
called a meeting of all the *. Act 6:2
persecution of the * began that Act 8:1
to devastate the *, even entering Act 8:3
But the * Act 8:4
hands upon these *, and they Act 8:17
persecution of any * he found Act 9:2
has done to the * in Jerusalem! Act 9:13
He stayed with the * in Damascus Act 9:19
to meet with the *, but they were Act 9:26
with the * and preached boldly in Act 9:28
However, when the other * heard Act 9:30
and numbers. The * learned how to Act 9:31
and in his travels came to the * Act 9:32
and called in the * and widows, Act 9:41
by some other * from Joppa. Act 10:23
the Jewish * argued with him. Act 11:2
Meanwhile, the * who fled from Act 11:19
However, some of the * who went Act 11:20
of these Gentiles became *. Act 11:21
and encouraged the * to stay close Act 11:23
Antioch that the * were first Act 11:26
So the * decided to send relief Act 11:29
of the *, and killed the apostle Act 12:1
rapidly and there were many new *. Act 12:24
But as the * stood around him, Act 14:20
they helped the * to grow in love Act 14:22
together the * and reported on Act 14:27
And they stayed there with the * Act 14:28
began to teach the * that unless Act 15:1
and finally the * sent them to Act 15:2
to visit the *, telling them—much Act 15:3
"We understand that some * from Act 15:24
preached long sermons to the *, Act 15:32
blessing of the *, left for Syria Act 15:40,41
rejoiced because all were now *! Act 16:34
they met with the * and preached to Act 16:40
some of the other *, and took them Act 17:6
up trouble. The * acted at once, Act 17:14
but a few joined him and became *. Act 17:34
visiting all the *, encouraging Act 18:23
and the * encouraged him in this. Act 18:27
Pulling out the *, he began a Act 19:9
Many of the * who had been Act 19:18,19
preaching to the * along the way, Act 20:2
* and stayed with them a week. Act 21:4
the *, but stayed only one day. Act 21:7
of us—the local * and his traveling Act 21:12
from Cyprus, one of the early *; Act 21:16
and all the * at Jerusalem Act 21:17
that Jewish * must continue to Act 21:20
Puteoli, where we found some *! Act 28:14
such preaching is mostly for * 1Co 14:24
So, my fellow *, long to be 1Co 14:39
And the * who are dead will be 1Th 4:16
leaders and to the other * there. Heb 13:24,25

BELIEVES
and the owner * he has found it in Ex 22:9
Only a simpleton * what he is Pro 14:15
He who * need never run away Is 28:16
* in me will have eternal life. Jn 3:15
Son so that anyone who * in him Jn 3:16
to my message and * in God who sent Jn 5:24
sees his Son and * on him should Jn 6:40
* in me already has eternal life! Jn 6:47
being of anyone who * in me." Jn 7:38
Pharisees who * he is the Messiah? Jn 7:48
Anyone who * in me, even though Jn 11:25
that everyone who * in him will Act 10:43
us that no one who * in Christ will Rom 10:11
But if someone * it is wrong, Rom 14:14
But anyone who * that something Rom 14:23
he does, as well as by what he *. Jas 2:24
And everyone who really * this 1Jn 3:3
Anyone who * and says that Jesus 1Jn 4:15

BELIEVING
for you, truly * that in a time 2Ch 20:9
and the people are * your lies. Jer 28:15
fooled you into * his lies, I will Jer 29:31
trusting in a lie—* that military Hos 10:13
people from * and being saved. Lk 8:12
condemned for not * in the only Jn 3:18
Those * in me will never thirst. Jn 6:35
be given to everyone * in him; Jn 7:39
began * him to be the Messiah. Jn 8:30,31
He is given eternal life for * Jn 11:26
I tell you, anyone * in me shall do Jn 14:12,13
that * in him you will have life. Jn 20:30,31
* that the dead will rise again!' Act 24:21
Instead of * what they knew was Rom 1:25
For it is by * in his heart that Rom 10:10
be removed only by * in Christ. 2Co 3:14
trick people into *—we are not 2Co 4:2
are true by *, not by seeing. 2Co 5:7
with God comes by * in Christ. Gal 2:19
to * as I do about these things. Gal 5:10
justly judged for * falsehood, 2Th 2:12
But you must keep on * the things 2Ti 3:14
knowing and * the truth and doing Tit 2:2
By faith—by * God—we know that Heb 11:3
hold that "only *" is enough? Jas 2:19
is enough? * in one God? Jas 2:19
When will you ever learn that "* Jas 2:20
So keep on * what you have been 1Jn 2:24
battle except by * that Jesus is 1Jn 5:5

BELLIES
* as well as those that have legs. Lev 11:41,42
the * of the pregnant women!" 2Ki 8:12

BELLOWS
as iron. The * blow fiercely; Jer 6:29

BELLS
alternated with gold *. Ex 28:33,34
to the Lord; the * will tinkle as Ex 28:35
and scarlet. * of pure gold were Ex 39:25,26
of the skirt, with * and Ex 39:25,26
In that day the * on the horses Zec 14:20
No more joyous wedding * and Rev 18:23

BELLY
live, crawling along on your *. Gen 3:14
plunged it deep into the king's *. Ju 3:21
* with the butt end of his spear. 2Sa 2:23
about to fill his *, God will rain Job 20:23
loins and the muscles of his *. Job 40:16
at him. His * is covered with Job 41:30
Literally, "*." Sol 7:2f
and filled his * with our riches Jer 51:34,35
of silver, its * and thighs of Dan 2:32
—represented by the bronze * of Dan 2:39

BELONG
will give you the blessings that * Gen 27:2,3,4
— they should reply: "These * Gen 32:18
It shall * to my people." Ex 6:8,9
male animals * to the Lord, and you Ex 13:12
shall still * to the master, and he Ex 21:4
the dead animal shall * to him. Ex 21:34
The rest of the flour shall * to Lev 5:13
of the flour will * to Aaron and Lev 6:16
the breast shall * to Aaron and his Lev 7:31
And afterwards they shall * to Lev 10:15
it, then it shall * to the new Lev 25:28
year, then it will * permanently to Lev 25:30
and they must * to no one else. Lev 25:34
the second shall * to the Lord! Lev 27:10
Jubilee, it shall * to the Lord as Lev 27:21
substitution shall * to the Lord, Lev 27:33
before the altar * to you and your Num 18:8
the altar, shall * to the Levites; Num 18:24
it shall * to his brothers. Num 27:9
when you possess it, it shall * Deu 2:31
Earth and highest heaven * to Deu 10:14
for funerals. You * exclusively to Deu 14:2
shall see that you * to the Lord, Deu 28:10
were just in shall * to you and Jos 14:9
your people Israel * to you 1Ch 17:22
If you * to the Lord, reverence Ps 34:9
Day and night alike * to you; Ps 74:16
The heavens * to the Lord, but Ps 115:16
who * to God shall live again. Is 26:19
Return and help us, for we who * Is 63:17
the city will * to our enemies." Jer 32:25
and you will * to them again; Eze 36:12
sons, it will * to him forever. Eze 46:16
of Israel, shall * to the prince. Eze 48:21,22
my children; they * to other men. Hos 1:4
rule them, for they * to you. Joe 2:17
of all the nations that * to me." Amo 9:12
Or, "for the cities of Syria * to Zec 9:1f
hate you because you * to me. Mt 10:22
will legally * to the dead man, to Lk 20:28
you because you * to me, for they Jn 15:21
given me because they * to you. Jn 17:9
since they are mine, * to you; Jn 17:10
country would * to him and his Act 7:5
Many people here in this city * Act 18:10
the God to whom I * and whom I Act 27:23
those who * to Christ Jesus. Rom 8:1
So we * to each other, and each Rom 12:4,5
who don't * to the Lord at all. 1Co 3:3
All are yours, and you * to 1Co 3:23
Your own body does not * to you. 1Co 6:19
by Christ, so you * to him—be free 1Co 7:23
you, for we all * to Christ Jesus. 1Co 16:24
guarantee that we * to him, and as 2Co 1:22
of those who * to the Lord. 2Co 8:23
that test and truly * to the Lord. 2Co 13:6
of God's promises to him * to us. Gal 3:29
Those who * to Christ have nailed Gal 5:24
in heaven because we * to Christ. Eph 1:3
we * to his dearly loved Son. Eph 1:6
But now you * to Christ Jesus, Eph 2:13
country, and you * in God's Eph 2:19
both are invited to * to his Eph 3:6
you because you * to Christ. Eph 4:32
of God will never * to anyone who Eph 5:5
things that * to those who live in Col 1:12
you who * to God the Father and the 1Th 1:1
with all those who * to him. 1Th 3:13
do not * to darkness and night. 1Th 5:5
for you who * to Christ Jesus. 1Th 5:18
glory will be that you * to him. 2Th 1:12
As we all know, Christ did not * Heb 7:12,13,14
you don't really * in his family. Heb 12:8
you claim that you * to the Lord Jas 2:1
And how can we be sure that we * 1Jn 2:3
I am on my way to heaven; I * to 1Jn 2:4
it shows that you * to Satan, who 1Jn 3:8
Dear young friends, you * to God 1Jn 4:4
These men * to this world, so, 1Jn 4:5
and the power * to the one sitting Rev 5:13
confessing that they * to Jesus. Rev 12:17
Honor and authority * to him Rev 19:1

BELONGED
since she * to his father. Deu 22:30
(The land of Tappu-ah * to Jos 17:8
land, * to the tribe of Ephraim. Jos 17:8
south of the brook * to the tribe Jos 17:9
the land * to the people of Ammon; Ju 11:13
she found herself * to Boaz, this Ru 2:3
everything that * to Saul and his 2Sa 9:9
Temple that had * to King David. 2Ki 11:10
but the land * to the descendants 1Ch 4:40,41
These had once * to King David 2Ch 23:9
these offerings * to the Levites, Neh 13:5
prison yard. (It * to Malchiah, a Jer 38:6
would love you if you * to it; Jn 15:19
they never really * with us or else 1Jn 2:19
We are not to be like Cain, who * 1Jn 3:12

BELONGING
among the oaks * to Mamre the Gen 14:13
buy was that * to the priests, for Gen 47:22
it from the half * to the Num 31:42-46
the country * to their brothers the Deu 2:4
The territory now * to the Jos 13:2-7
beneath them, one wheel * to each. Eze 1:15
* to the city, for public use. Eze 48:18
the thistles are the people * to Mt 13:38
was an estate * to Publius, the Act 28:7
were marked as * to Christ by the Eph 1:13
old requirement of * to the tribe Heb 7:16

BELONGINGS
too, and all their * accumulated in Gen 46:6
their *, as all Israel watched! Deu 11:6
have hidden it among their *. Jos 7:10,11
and all of their *, and David 1Sa 30:18,19
out all of his * from the room. Neh 13:8
his weapons and carries off his *. Lk 11:22
son packed all his * and took a Lk 15:13

BELONGS
everything you get * to Pharaoh. Gen 47:24
Which means, "he to whom it *." Gen 49:10f
The remainder * to the priests Lev 2:10
a holy place. It * to you and to Lev 10:13
any holy place. It * to you and to Lev 10:14
he has taken what * to his uncle; Lev 20:20
for he has taken what * to his Lev 20:21
anything that * to them, lest you Num 16:26

(BELONGS Con't)
everything that * to them, and they Num 16:30
wives, for she * to his father.' Deu 27:20
tribe to which the guilty man *. Jos 7:14
stolen that which * to the Lord Jos 7:15
Me-arah (which * to the Sidonians), Jos 13:2-7
(which still * to the kings of 1Sa 27:6
the dead child * to the other. 1Ki 3:23
It all * to you! 1Ch 29:16
THE EARTH * to God! Ps 24:1
Power * to God! Ps 68:34
For all of it * to you. Ps 82:8
LORD GOD, TO whom vengeance *, let Ps 94:1
(And that title * to you alone! Jer 10:7
by others, for it * to the Lord; Eze 48:14
where she * and where she will Zec 5:11
To him * the royal title. Zec 6:13
for the whole wide world * to Mt 5:5
God everything that * to God." Mt 22:21
wanting what * to others, Mk 7:22
Kingdom of God * to such as they. Mk 10:14
But everything that * to God must Mk 12:17
For the Kingdom of God * to men Lk 18:16,17
for every day alike * to God. Rom 14:5
body, for it * also to his wife. 1Co 7:4
good thing in it * to the Lord and 1Co 10:26
everything he has * to us, for that Gal 4:7
share in all that * to Christ. Heb 3:14
him who said, "Justice * to me; Heb 10:30
a child of God and who * to Satan. 1Jn 3:10
* to our Lord, and to his Christ; Rev 11:15

BELOVED
even your * son from me." Gen 22:12
withheld even your * son from me, Gen 22:16
son, daughter, or * wife whispers Deu 13:6,7
brother and his * wife and his Deu 28:54
her * husband, son, and daughter. Deu 28:56,57
"He is * of God Deu 33:12
(meaning, "* of Jehovah") because 2Sa 12:25
you will not allow your * one to Ps 16:10
then you can deliver your * Ps 60:4,5
Save your * people from these Ps 74:19
Hear the cry of your * Ps 108:6
make her a * member of your Pro 7:4
of my perfume. My * one is a Sol 1:13
King Solomon: "My * is a bouquet Sol 1:14
thorns, so is my * as compared with Sol 2:2
The Girl: "Ah, I hear him—my *! Sol 2:8
* is like a gazelle or young deer. Sol 2:9
"My * said to me, 'Rise up, my Sol 2:10
"My * is mine and I am his. Sol 2:16
come to me, my *, and be like a Sol 2:17
waft its lovely perfume to my *. Sol 4:16
"Oh, lover and *, eat and drink! Sol 5:1
I heard the voice of my *; Sol 5:2
"My * tried to unlatch the door Sol 5:4
I opened to my *, but he was Sol 5:6
if you find my * one, tell him that Sol 5:8
The Girl: "My * one is tanned Sol 5:10
Jerusalem, is my *, my friend." Sol 5:16
I am my beloved's and my * is Sol 6:3
King Solomon: "O my *, you are Sol 6:4
sit beside my * in his chariot." Sol 6:12f
Come, my *, let us go out into Sol 7:11
I have stored them up for my *." Sol 7:13
the desert, leaning on her *?" Sol 8:5
"O my *, living in the gardens, Sol 8:13
Come quickly, my *, and be like Sol 8:14
the one I love. My * has a vineyard Is 5:1
What right do my * people have Jer 11:15
palace: You are as * to me as Jer 22:6
The Lord has trampled his * city Lam 1:15
Daniel, greatly * of God," he Dan 10:11
nor for the god * of women, Dan 11:37
I will slay even her * child. Hos 9:16
God's holy and * Temple by marrying Mal 2:11
said, "This is my * Son, and I am Mt 3:17
He is my *, in whom my soul Mt 12:18
said, "This is my * Son, and I am Mt 17:5
heaven said, "You are my * Son; Mk 1:11
cloud said, "This is my * Son. Mk 9:7
with our * Barnabas and Paul. Act 15:25
Yet the Jews are still * of God Rom 11:28
our fellow worker, and * Stachys. Rom 16:9
and counsel you as * children. 1Co 4:14
I won to Christ, a * and 1Co 4:17
* friends, stay true to the Lord. Php 4:1
you, dear brothers, much * of God. 1Th 1:4
* brother, especially to me. Phm 1:16
Our wise and * brother Paul has 2Pe 3:15,16
To: Christians everywhere—* of God Jud 1:1
people and the * city of Jerusalem Rev 20:9

BELOVED'S
I am my * and my beloved is Sol 6:3
The Girl: "I am my * and I am Sol 7:10

BELOW
the sky above and the oceans *." Gen 1:6
the vapor above from the water *. Gen 1:7,8
ship, eighteen inches * the roof; Gen 6:16
Laban, meanwhile, camped * him in Gen 31:25
oak tree in the valley * Bethel. Gen 35:8
branches and one * the bottom set. Ex 25:34,35
from the shoulders to * the knees. Ex 28:4f
When Joshua heard the noise * Ex 32:17
also a flower * the bottom pair Ex 37:20,21
if the infection seems to be * Lev 13:29,30
from each tribe, as listed *: Num 34:16-28
Listed * are the laws Moses Deu 4:44,45,46
Sea, * the slopes of Mount Pisgah. Deu 4:49
while the people had watched *. Deu 9:10,11
There * me I could see the calf Deu 9:16
the mountain as you all watched *. Deu 10:4
And of the earth that lies *. Deu 33:13
And the water * that point flowed Jos 3:15,16
cities listed *, with their Jos 21:9-16
in the valley just *, the Lord said Ju 7:8,9
were camped in the valley * them. 1Sa 15:5
near Zarethan * Jezreel, and all 1Ki 4:8-19
Above and * the lions and oxen 1Ki 7:27-30
When the Israelis in the valley * 1Ch 10:7
were crushed upon the rocks *. 2Ch 25:12
on high? Far * him are the heavens Ps 113:6
(The people * must seem to him Is 40:22
or in the open country down *. Jer 17:2,3
of terror rise from the city *. Jer 48:5
wider than the one * it, Eze 41:7
with wood above and * the windows. Eze 41:15,16
crashes down upon the people *. Amo 9:1
their stones into the valleys *. Mic 1:6
from smashing on the rocks *." Mt 4:6
cliff and drowned in the water *. Mt 8:32
Meanwhile Peter was * in the Mk 14:66,67
from crashing to the pavement *!" Lk 4:9,10,11
the lake *, where they drowned. Lk 8:33
he said to them, "You are from *; Jn 8:23
fell three stories to his death *. Act 20:9
found 120 feet of water * them. Act 27:28
onto the people *, and they cursed Rev 16:21

BELSHAZZAR
and killed *, the last Babylonian Jer 25:12f
* THE KING invited a thousand of Dan 5:1
While * was drinking he was Dan 5:2,3,4
to Babylon. * ordered that these Dan 5:2,3,4
* was the second under Nabonidus Dan 5:7f
hall and said to *, "Calm Dan 5:10
"And you, his successor, O *—you Dan 5:22
That very night *, the Chaldean Dan 5:30
the reign of King *, I had another Dan 8:1

BELSHAZZAR'S
Then at * command, Daniel was Dan 5:29
the first year of * reign over the Dan 7:1

BELT
and the linen * was beautifully Ex 39:28,29
with its beautifully woven *. Lev 8:7
linen coat, shorts, *, and turban. Lev 16:4
him his robe, sword, bow, and *. 1Sa 18:4
ten pieces of silver and a *." 2Sa 18:11f
of the silver. The * was probably 2Sa 18:11f
"with a wide leather *." 2Ki 1:8
to him like his clothing or his *. Ps 109:19
garments, with a * of purest gold Dan 10:5,6
hair and he wore a leather *; Mt 3:4
hair and he wore a leather *; Mk 1:6
He took Paul's *, bound his own Act 21:11
the owner of this * be bound by the Act 21:11
need the strong * of truth and the Eph 6:14

BELTED
or with swords * to their sides. Neh 4:18
She makes * linen garments to Pro 31:24

BELTESHAZZAR
as follows:Daniel was called *; Dan 1:7
in—the man I named * after my Dan 4:8
"O *, master magician," I said, Dan 4:9
"O *, that was my dream; Dan 4:18
"Daniel, whose name was *." Dan 4:19f
Finally the king said to him: "* Dan 4:19
Call for this man, Daniel—or *, Dan 5:12
called *) had another vision. Dan 10:1

BELTS
sons, with the * and caps, as the Lev 8:13
their * are tight, their Is 5:27
with handsome *, and flowing Eze 23:14,15
with golden * across their chests. Rev 15:6

BEN-ABINADAB
* (who married Solomon's daughter, 1Ki 4:8-19

BEN-DEKER
*, whose area was Makaz, 1Ki 4:8-19

BEN-GEBER
*, whose area was Ramoth-gilead, 1Ki 4:8-19

BEN-HADAD
* of Syria, with this message: 1Ki 15:18
* agreed and sent his armies 1Ki 15:20
KING * OF Syria now mobilized his 1Ki 20:1
So he told the messengers from *, 1Ki 20:9
So the messengers returned to *. 1Ki 20:9
This reply of Ahab's reached * 1Ki 20:12
"Prepare to attack!" * commanded 1Ki 20:12
About noontime, as * and the 1Ki 20:16
"Take them alive," * commanded, 1Ki 20:18
them, but King * and a few others 1Ki 20:20
So King * did as they 1Ki 20:25
another 27,000. * fled into the 1Ki 20:30
servant * pleads, 'Let me live!' 1Ki 20:32
"Yes, your brother *!" 1Ki 20:33
And when * arrived, he invited 1Ki 20:33
* told him, "I will restore the 1Ki 20:34
Later on, however, King * of 2Ki 6:24
of Syria), where King * lay sick. 2Ki 8:7
to him, "Your son *, the king of 2Ki 8:8,9
and his son * to conquer them. 2Ki 13:3
his son * reigned in his place. 2Ki 13:24
that his father had lost to *. 2Ki 13:25
to send it to King * of Syria, at 2Ch 16:2
* agreed to King Asa's request 2Ch 16:4
the strong fortress of *. Amo 1:4

BEN-HADAD'S
Soon * messengers returned again 1Ki 20:5,6
As they approached, * scouts 1Ki 20:17
For after their defeat, * 1Ki 20:23

BEN-HAIL
These men included *, Obadiah, 2Ch 17:7,8,9

BEN-HANAN
Amnon, Rinnah, *, Tilon. 1Ch 4:20

BEN-HESED
*, whose area was Arubboth, 1Ki 4:8-19

BEN-HINNOM
in the Valley of *, and there they Jer 7:31
or the "Valley of *," to the Jer 7:32
of * by the east gate of the city. Jer 19:1
"Topheth" or "* Valley," but Jer 19:6

BEN-HUR
*, whose area for this taxation 1Ki 4:8-19

BEN-ONI
him "*" ("Son of my sorrow"); Gen 35:18

BEN-ZOHETH
The sons of Ishi:Zoheth, *. 1Ch 4:20

BENAIAH
secretary. * (son of Jehoiada) was 2Sa 8:18
of the army, and * was in charge of 2Sa 20:23
There was also * (son of 2Sa 23:20
from Kabzeel. * killed two giants, 2Sa 23:20
deeds that gave * almost as much 2Sa 23:22
* of Pirathon; 2Sa 23:24-39
Joab, Abishai, Asahel, and *. 2Sa 23:24-39f
priests Zadok and *, the prophet 1Ki 1:8
the prophet, *, the loyal army 1Ki 1:10
But Zadok the priest and * and 1Ki 1:26
"and Nathan the prophet, and *." 1Ki 1:32
replied *, and added, "May 1Ki 1:36
the prophet, *, and David's 1Ki 1:38
the prophet and *, protected by the 1Ki 1:44,45
So King Solomon sent * to execute 1Ki 2:25
Solomon, he sent * to execute him. 1Ki 2:29
* went into the Tabernacle and 1Ki 2:30
So * returned to the king for 1Ki 2:30
So * returned to the Tabernacle 1Ki 2:34
Then the king appointed * as 1Ki 2:35
Then, at the king's command, * 1Ki 2:46
* (son of Jehoiada) was 1Ki 4:1
Adi-el, Jesimi-el, *, Ziza (the son 1Ch 4:34-39
*, whose father was a mighty 1Ch 11:22
weaver's beam. But * went up to him 1Ch 11:23
* from Pirathon; 1Ch 11:26-47
Unni, Eliab, *, Ma-asseiah, 1Ch 15:18
Ma-aseiah, and * comprised an octet 1Ch 15:20
Amasai, Zechariah, *, and 1Ch 15:24
Eliab, *, Obed-edom, and Je-iel; 1Ch 16:5
The priests * and Jahaziel 1Ch 16:6
* (son of Jehoiada) was in 1Ch 18:17
of the Third Division was *. 1Ch 27:5,6
Division was * from Pirathon in 1Ch 27:14
(the son of *) and by Abiathar. 1Ch 27:34
Zechariah, son of *, son of Je-iel, 2Ch 20:14
Eliel, Ismachiah, Mahath, *. 2Ch 31:12,13
Hashabiah, *. Ez 10:25
Adna, Chelal, *, Ma-aseiah, Ez 10:30
Zabad, Zebina, Jaddai, Joel, *. Ez 10:43
of Azzur) and Pelatiah (son of *). Eze 11:1
Pelatiah (son of *) suddenly died. Eze 11:13

BENAMMI
of the younger girl's baby was *; Gen 19:38

BENCH
* on the stone-paved platform. Jn 19:13

BENCHES
Gold and silver * stood on Est 1:6

BEND
And strength to * a bow of bronze. 2Sa 22:35
earth. * low, O Lord, and listen. 2Ki 19:16
you; * low and hear my whispered Ps 31:2
Rescue me! * down your ear and Ps 71:2
the cherubim, * down your ear and Ps 80:1
* DOWN AND hear my prayer, O Lord, Ps 86:1
of my distress. * down your ear and Ps 102:2
* down the heavens, Lord, and Ps 144:5
of Bashan shall * low, and all the Is 2:13
"They * their tongues like bows Jer 9:3
handle the shield and * the bow! Jer 46:9
where it will * westward to the Eze 47:18
"O my God, * down your ear and Dan 9:18

BENDING
For now is the time—you are * Ps 69:13

BENDS
Because he * down and listens, I Ps 116:2

BENDS Con't)
He * his bow against his people Lam 2:4

BENE-BERAK
Baalath, Jehud, *, Gath-rimmon, Jos 19:41-46

BENE-JAAKAN
From Moseroth to *; Num 33:15-37
From * to Hor-haggidgad; Num 33:15-37
from Be-eroth of * to Moserah, Deu 10:6

BENEFACTOR
their * has been so kind to them? Gen 44:4

BENEFACTORS
and great men) are called '*.' Lk 22:25f

BENEFIT
this is a permanent law for the * Num 19:10
Never twist justice to * a rich Deu 16:19
God showed it to me for your *. Dan 2:30
But the Sabbath was made to * Mk 2:27
man, and not man to * the Sabbath. Mk 2:27
"And how does a man * if he Mk 8:36
voice was for your *, not mine. Jn 12:30
faith—wasn't just for Abraham's *. Rom 4:23
But this has been a * to you, for Rom 11:28
for our * before the world began. 1Co 2:7
*, but Eve was made for Adam. 1Co 11:9
sufferings of ours are for your *. 2Co 4:15
our right minds, it is for your *. 2Co 5:13,14

BENEFITED
We have all * from the rich Jn 1:16
a while, and you * and rejoiced, Jn 5:35

BENEFITS
Are there any special * for them Rom 3:1
of God, and his * to you include Rom 6:22
together in the * of his body. 1Co 10:16

BENHADAD
shall burn up the palaces of *. Jer 49:27

BENINU
Bani, *. Neh 10:9-13

BENJAMIN
She was pregnant with *, but Gen 31:35f
but his father called him "*" Gen 35:18
The sons of Rachel:Joseph, *. Gen 35:24
younger brother * go with them, for Gen 42:4
and now you want to take * too! Gen 42:36
if I don't bring * back to you. Gen 42:37
We cannot go unless you let * go Gen 43:3,4,5
will release Simeon and return *. Gen 43:14
When Joseph saw that * was with Gen 43:16
Literally, "his brother *, his Gen 43:29f
*, he asked, "Is this your Gen 43:29
He gave the largest serving to * Gen 43:34
and my brother * has heard me say Gen 45:11,12
* and Benjamin began weeping too. Gen 45:14
Benjamin and * began weeping too. Gen 45:14
new clothes—but to * he gave five Gen 45:22
Joseph and *; Gen 46:19-22
"* is a wolf that prowls. Gen 49:27
* Dan, Naphtali,Gad, Asher. Ex 1:1
* - Abidan (son of Num 1:2-15
* - 35,400 Num 1:20-46
Tribe: Ephraim Manasseh * Num 2:3-31
of the tribe of *, with his gifts, Num 7:60-65
and the tribe of *, led by Num 10:24
son of Raphu, from the tribe of *; Num 13:3-15
The tribe of *: 45,600. Num 26:38-41
clans named after the sons of *: Num 26:38-41
* Elidad (son of Chislon) Num 34:16-28
Joseph, and * shall stand upon Deu 27:12
Concerning the tribe of *, Moses Deu 33:12
The Land Given to the Tribe of *: Jos 18:11
of the tribe of * lay between the Jos 18:11
land assigned to the tribe of *. Jos 18:20
the land given to the tribe of *: Jos 18:21-28
were given to the tribe of *. Jos 18:21-28
tribes of Judah, Simeon, and *. Jos 21:4
The tribe of * gave them these Jos 21:17,18
The tribe of * failed to Ju 1:21
They came from Ephraim and *, Ju 5:13,14
and also in Judah, *, and Ephraim. Ju 10:9
of the tribe of *, so they went Ju 19:14
it was in the territory of *. Ju 19:16
of * because of this awful deed. Ju 19:30
Mizpah soon reached the land of *. Ju 20:3
a village in *," he began. Ju 20:4
to the tribe of *, asking, "Did Ju 20:12
But the people of * wouldn't Ju 20:13
men of *, numbered 400,000 men. Ju 20:17
lead us against the people of *?" Ju 20:18
Gibe-ah, to attack the men of *. Ju 20:19,20
further against our brother *?" Ju 20:22,23,24
our brother *, or shall we stop?" Ju 20:27,28
it that you defeat the men of *." Ju 20:27,28
When the army of * came out of Ju 20:31
retreated and * was drawn away from Ju 20:31
done previously, * began to kill Ju 20:31
Then the army of * shouted, Ju 20:32
that the army of * would chase them Ju 20:32
of the army of *, who still didn't Ju 20:34
Israel defeat *, and the Israeli Ju 20:35-39
25,100 men of * that day, leaving Ju 20:35-39
from the men of * in order to give Ju 20:35-39
When the men of * had killed Ju 20:35-39
attack the army of *, who now Ju 20:35-39
They encircled the army of * Ju 20:43
Eighteen thousand of the * Ju 20:44
So the tribe of * lost Ju 20:46,47
of the tribe of *—men, women, Ju 20:48
marry a man from the tribe of *. Ju 21:1
loss of their brother tribe, *. Ju 21:6
of the men of * at Rimmon Rock. Ju 21:13
of the tribe of * are dead?" Ju 21:16
They told the men of * who still Ju 21:20
So the men of * did as they were Ju 21:23
A man from the tribe of * ran 1Sa 4:12
man from the tribe of *. 1Sa 9:1
the entire land of *, but couldn't 1Sa 9:4
send you a man from the land of *. 1Sa 9:16
"I'm from the tribe of *, the 1Sa 9:21
tomb at Zelzah, in the land of *; 1Sa 10:2
of * was chosen by sacred lot. 1Sa 10:20
of the tribe of * before the Lord, 1Sa 10:21
son, in Gibe-ah in the land of *. 1Sa 13:2
went to Gibe-ah in the land of *. 1Sa 13:15
camp in Geba in the land of *; 1Sa 13:16
"Listen here, you men of *!" 1Sa 22:7
of *, and all the rest of Israel. 2Sa 2:9
from the tribe of * regrouped there 2Sa 2:25
from the tribe of *) were dead. 2Sa 2:31
to the leaders of the tribe of *; 2Sa 3:19
with the people of Israel and *. 2Sa 3:19
who was from Be-eroth in *. 2Sa 4:2,3
Gittaim is not in *. 2Sa 4:2,3f
from the tribe of * were with him, 2Sa 19:17
So all except Judah and * turned 2Sa 20:2
from Gibe-ah, of the tribe of *; 2Sa 23:24-39
(son of Ela), whose area was *; 1Ki 4:8-19
Of the twelve tribes, Judah and * 1Ki 11:32f
Judah and * were sometimes (as in 1Ki 12:20f
men of Judah and *: 180,000 special 1Ki 12:21
of Judah and * that they must not 1Ki 12:23,24
Geba in * and the city of Mizpah. 1Ki 15:22
Joseph, *, Naphtali, Gad, Asher. 1Ch 2:1
to the priests by the tribe of *. 1Ch 6:60
tribes of Judah, Simeon, and *. 1Ch 6:64,65
The sons of * were: 1Ch 7:6
Jeush, *, Ehud, Chenaanah, Zethan, 1Ch 7:10
THE SONS OF *, according to age, 1Ch 8:1
they were all from the tribe of *. 1Ch 8:40
tribes of Judah, *, Ephraim, and 1Ch 9:3
of * who returned were these: 1Ch 9:7,8
they were all of the tribe of *. 1Ch 12:2
Others came to David from * and 1Ch 12:16
From the tribe of *, the same 1Ch 12:24-37
tribes of Levi and * in his figures 1Ch 21:6
in the tribe of *), who commanded 1Ch 27:12
Over *, Ja-asiel (son of Abner); 1Ch 27:16-22
of Judah and *, 180,000 strong, and 2Ch 11:1
to the people of Judah and of *: 2Ch 11:3
For only Judah and * remained 2Ch 11:12
land of Judah and *, and gave them 2Ch 11:23
Listen, armies of Judah and *!" 2Ch 15:2
land of Judah and *, and in the 2Ch 15:8
of Judah and *, and the immigrants 2Ch 15:9
But here in Judah and * the heart 2Ch 15:17
200,000 troops. * supplied 200,000 2Ch 17:17
to each clan from Judah and *. 2Ch 25:5,6
Israel—Judah and *—and so is 2Ch 28:19f
cities of Judah, *, Ephraim, and 2Ch 31:1
in Jerusalem and * to subscribe to 2Ch 34:32
of Judah and *, and to the priests Ez 1:5
WHEN THE ENEMIES of Judah and * Ez 4:1
all the men of Judah and * had Ez 10:9
Shime-on, *, Malluch, Shemariah. Ez 10:31,32
*, Hasshub, and Azariah (son of Neh 3:23
towns of Judah and * were selected Neh 11:1
Leaders from the tribe of *: Neh 11:7,8,9
The people of the tribe of * Neh 11:31-35
sent to live with the tribe of *. Neh 11:36
Judah, *, Shemaiah, and Jeremiah. Neh 12:34
The little tribe of * leads the Ps 68:27
Let Ephraim, * and Manasseh see Ps 80:2
town of Anathoth in the land of *. Jer 1:1
RUN, PEOPLE OF *, run for your Jer 6:1
of Judah and *, and from the Negeb Jer 17:26
stocks at * Gate near the Temple. Jer 20:2
in the land of *," he said, "for Jer 32:8
the country of * and here in Jer 32:44
in the land of *, in the vicinity Jer 33:13
go to the land of *, to see the Jer 37:12
through the * Gate, a sentry Jer 37:13
out to the Gate of * where the king Jer 38:8
alloted to Judah and *, is 8 Eze 48:21,22
be named for Joseph, * and Dan. Eze 48:32
tremble, land of *! Hos 5:8
And the people of * shall possess Ob 1:19
from the Gate of * over to the site Zec 14:10
of *, who reigned for forty years. Act 13:21
of the old original * family. Php 3:5
* 12,000 Rev 7:4-8

BENJAMIN'S
cup at the top of * sack, along Gen 44:2
And the cup was found in *! Gen 44:12
* sons: Bela, Becher, Gen 46:19-22
are as follows: * section extends Eze 48:23
South of * area lies that of Eze 48:24
Abraham and a member of * family. Rom 11:1

BENJAMINITE
Gera, a *), who was left-handed. Ju 3:15
and this * is merely cursing me. 2Sa 16:11
son of Gera the *), the man from 2Sa 19:16
(son of Bichri, a *) blew a trumpet 2Sa 20:1
son of Gera the * from Bahurim? 1Ki 2:8
Ithai (son of Ribai) a * from 1Ch 11:26-47
son of Shime-i, son of Kish, a *). Est 2:5

BENJAMINITES
are counted as * even though they 2Sa 4:2,3
A total of 956 * returned. 1Ch 9:9
His army of * numbered 280,000, 2Ch 14:8

BENO
led by his son *, included his 1Ch 24:26,27

BENT
even though man's * is always Gen 8:21
land, he willingly * his shoulder Gen 49:15
of Ekron, where it * to the left, Jos 15:10,11
He * the heavens down and came to 2Sa 22:10
He has * and strung his bow and Ps 7:12
his nostrils. He * the heavens Ps 18:9
Because of my sins I am * and Ps 38:5,6
and those * beneath their loads. Ps 145:14
he lifts the burdens from those * Ps 146:8
their bows are *; Is 5:28
He has * his bow and aimed it Lam 3:12
within your walls is * on murder. Eze 22:6
woman who had been * double for Lk 13:11
old sinful selves, * on following Rom 8:8

BENT-BACKED
They walk * beneath their load of Is 1:4
* forever with a heavy load." Rom 11:10

BEON
Elealeh, Sebam, Nebo, and *. Num 32:3,4

BEOR
King Bela (son of *), from Gen 36:31-39
to Balaam (son of *) who was living Num 22:5,6
"Balaam the son of * says that Num 24:3-9
"Balaam the son of * is the man Num 24:15-19
Balaam, the son of *, was also Num 31:8
Balaam, the son of * from Pethor, Deu 23:4
Balaam the magician, the son of *. Jos 13:22
the son of *, to curse you. Jos 24:9
Bela (the son of *), who lived in 1Ch 1:43
of Balaam, son of *, but I made him Mic 6:5
Balaam, the son of *, who fell in 2Pe 2:15

BERA
*, king of Sodom, Gen 14:2

BERACAH
and Pelet, sons of Azmaveth; *; 1Ch 12:3-7

BERAIAH
Eliel, Adaiah, *, Shimrath. 1Ch 8:19,20,21

BERATE
why * her for doing a good thing? Mk 14:6

BEREAVED
For why should I be * of both of Gen 27:45
"You have * me of my Gen 42:36

BERECHIAH
Hananiah, Hashubah, Ohel, *, 1Ch 3:19,20
*, Shime-a, Michael, Ba-aseiah, 1Ch 6:39-43
* (the son of Asa, son of 1Ch 9:15,16
Asaph (son of *), and Ethan (son of 1Ch 15:17
for his skill. * and Elkanah were 1Ch 15:23
son of Johanan, * the son of 2Ch 28:12
Meshullam (son of *, son of Neh 3:4
and Meshullam (son of *), who Neh 3:30
daughter of Meshullam (son of *). Neh 6:18
Zechariah (son of *, and grandson Zec 1:1
Zechariah (son of * and grandson of Zec 1:7

BERED
It lies between Kadesh and *. Gen 16:14
Shuthelah, *, Tahath, Eleadah, 1Ch 7:20,21

BEREFT
and be * of all their children! Jer 18:21

BERENICE
gave his daughter * in marriage to Dan 11:6f
Literally, "from a branch." *, Dan 11:7f

BERI
Suah, Harnepher, Shual, *, Imrah, 1Ch 7:36,37

BERIAH
*, and a sister, Serah. Gen 46:16,17
named after their ancestor *. Num 26:44-47
named after the sons of * were: Num 26:44-47
son whom he called * (meaning "a 1Ch 7:23
Ishvi, *, Serah 1Ch 7:30
The sons of * were: 1Ch 7:31
* and Shema, chiefs of subclans 1Ch 8:13
The sons of * were: 1Ch 8:15,16
was next, and Jeush and * were 1Ch 23:10,11

BERIAH'S
* sons were Heber and Malchiel. Gen 46:16,17

BERIITES
The *, named after their ancestor Num 26:44-47

BERNICE
later King Agrippa arrived with * Act 25:13
after the king and * had arrived at Act 25:23
Then the king, the governor, *, Act 26:30

BEROEA
and Silas to *, and, as usual, Act 17:10

(BEROEA Con't)
But the people of * were more Act 17:11
was preaching in *, they went over Act 17:13
then returned to * with a message Act 17:15
they were Sopater of *, the son Act 20:4

BEROTHAH
then to * and Sibraim, which are Eze 47:16

BEROTHAI
Hadadezer's cities of Betah and *. 2Sa 8:8

BERYL
will be an onyx, a *, and a Ex 28:20
In the fourth row, a *, an onyx, Ex 39:13
The eighth with *; Rev 21:18,19,20

BESAI
Uzza, Paseah, *, Asnah, Me-unim, Ez 2:43-54
Gazzam, Uzza, Paseah, *, Neh 7:46-56

BESIDE
set up camp * the oak at Moreh. Gen 12:6
the Lord found her * a desert Gen 16:7
the trees * them as they ate. Gen 18:8
a tamarisk tree * the well, and Gen 21:33
Then, standing * her body, he Gen 23:3
down outside the town, * a spring. Gen 24:11
See, here I am, standing * this Gen 24:13
was still standing * his camels, Gen 24:29,30
Here I am, standing * this spring. Gen 24:43
of sheep lying * a well in an open Gen 29:2
placed these rods * the watering Gen 30:38
ate together * the pile of rocks. Gen 31:46
herself, and sat * the road at the Gen 38:14
was soliciting out * the road at Gen 38:21
They went over and stood * the Gen 41:3
and bury me * my ancestors." Gen 47:30
her * the road to Bethlehem." Gen 48:7
"Joseph is a fruitful tree * a Gen 49:22
As he was sitting there * a well, Ex 2:15
Stand * the river bank and meet Ex 7:15
they were camped * the shore near Ex 14:9
and they camped there * the Ex 15:27
stand here on this rock * me. Ex 33:21
offering and put them * the altar. Lev 6:10
in it, and eat it * the altar. Lev 10:12
someone fall dead * him, then seven Num 6:9
rod permanently * the Ark as a Num 17:10
king was standing * the burnt Num 23:6
standing * their burnt offerings. Num 23:17
As cedar trees * the waters. Num 24:3-9
the plains of Moab * the Jordan Num 26:3,4
the plains of Moab * the Jordan Num 26:63
the plains of Moab * the Jordan Num 31:12
Leaving Elim, they camped * the Num 33:10
the plains of Moab * the river Num 33:48
WHILE ISRAEL WAS camped * the Num 35:1
the plains of Moab * the Jordan Num 36:13
and stand here * me, and I will Deu 5:31
* the altar of the Lord your God. Deu 16:21
book of the law * the Ark, as a Deu 31:26
And lives in safety * him. Deu 33:12
of the mountain * the valley of Jos 18:16
tree that was * the Tabernacle. Jos 24:26
At ease * his harbors? Ju 5:17
apart, the idol * it was gone, and Ju 6:28
in the valley * the hill of Moreh. Ju 7:1
under the oak * the garrison at Ju 9:6
very contentedly * a heap of grain Ru 3:6,7
customary place * the entrance. 1Sa 1:9
Eli was waiting * the road to 1Sa 4:13
from his seat * the gate and his 1Sa 4:18
of God on the cart * a chest 1Sa 6:8
Joshua and stopped * a large rock. 1Sa 6:14
will see two men * Rachel's tomb at 1Sa 10:2
Abner was sitting * Saul, but 1Sa 20:24,25
spear in the ground * his head. 1Sa 26:5,6,7
jug of water that was * his head? 1Sa 26:16
and buried him * his father; 2Sa 2:32
their bodies * the pool in Hebron. 2Sa 4:12
this, so he died there * the Ark. 2Sa 6:7
and set it down * the road until 2Sa 15:24
so he died and was buried * his 2Sa 17:23
for his mother be placed * his; 1Ki 2:19
"Kill him there * the altar and 1Ki 2:31
and he was buried * his house in 1Ki 2:34
took my son from * me while I was 1Ki 3:20
arms and took mine to sleep * her. 1Ki 3:20
my men to work * them, and I will 1Ki 5:6
donkey and the lion standing * it. 1Ki 13:24,25
standing quietly * it, reported it 1Ki 13:24,25
standing there * it, for the lion 1Ki 13:28
Lay my bones * his bones. 1Ki 13:31
him to, and camped * the brook. 1Ki 17:5
The prophet waited for the king * 1Ki 20:38
armor were washed * the pool of 1Ki 22:38
together and stood * the Jordan 2Ki 2:6,7
a new one down * the Jordan River, 2Ki 6:1
new king standing * the pillar, as 2Ki 11:13,14
along the highway * the field where 2Ki 18:17
He stood * the pillar in front 2Ki 23:3
the Bethlehem well * the gate, and 1Ch 11:17
Strength and gladness walk * him. 1Ch 16:27
and skilled engravers to work * 2Ch 2:7
and he will stand * you and help 2Ch 19:6
Stay right * the king." 2Ch 23:7
They are * the altar of the 2Ch 29:19
the queen sitting * him, "How long Neh 2:5,6
repaired the wall * his own house, Neh 3:10
king's castle * the prison yard. Neh 3:25
Tobiah, who was standing * him, Neh 4:3
within easy reach * them, or with Neh 4:17
or on the plaza * the Water Gate, Neh 8:16
their cries from * the Red Sea. Neh 9:9
stairs which go up * the castle to Neh 12:37
donkeys feeding * them, when the Job 1:14,15
Will he stay * your feeding crib? Job 39:9
the willows there * the stream. Job 40:22
and leads me * the quiet streams. Ps 23:2,3
for you are close * me, guarding, Ps 23:4
Standing * you is the queen, Ps 45:9
she is, led * her maids of honor Ps 45:14
they hide * the trail, listening Ps 56:6
place a checkmark * the names of Ps 87:6
and the birds nest * the streams Ps 104:12
For he stands * the poor and Ps 109:31
God stands * you to protect you. Ps 110:5
holding court * the city gates, Ps 122:5
WEEPING, WE SAT * the rivers of Ps 137:1
His eyes are like doves * the Sol 5:12
sit * my beloved in his chariot." Sol 6:12f
Theirs is no fire to sit * to Is 47:14
will lead them * the cool waters. Is 49:10
You sit like a prostitute * the Jer 3:2
But the Lord stands * me like a Jer 20:11
They shall walk * the quiet Jer 31:9
army were defeated * the Euphrates Jer 46:2
country * the river Euphrates! Jer 46:10
Those in Aroer stand anxiously * Jer 48:19
* the Chebar Canal in Babylon. Eze 1:1
the sound of their wheels * them. Eze 3:13
Jewish exiles * the Chebar River. Eze 3:14,15
and stood * the bronze altar. Eze 9:2
went in and stood * one of the Eze 10:6
had a wheel * him—"The Eze 10:9-13
beings I had seen * the Chebar Eze 10:15,16
and stayed * them as they flew. Eze 10:15,16
with their wheels * them to the Eze 10:19
God of Israel * the Chebar Canal. Eze 10:20
with their wheels * them, and the Eze 11:22
in fertile ground * a broad Eze 17:5
in fertile ground * a broad river Eze 17:12,13
"Your mother was like a vine * Eze 19:10
herds that graze * the streams, and Eze 32:13
you will be laid * the people you Eze 32:19
to lie there * the nations she Eze 32:21
with their weapons * them, with Eze 32:27
put up a marker * them so that the Eze 39:15,16
standing * the Temple gate, Eze 40:3
buildings, one * the northern Eze 40:44
south, and one * the southern Eze 40:44
me: "The building * the inner Eze 40:45
The building * the inner Eze 40:46
hall, the hallways * the Temple, Eze 41:26
tiers had wider walkways * them. Eze 42:5
was still standing * me). Eze 43:6
They built their idol temples * Eze 43:8
The king was * himself with joy Dan 6:23
of those standing * the throne and Dan 7:16
Elam, standing * the Ulai River. Dan 8:2
as I was standing * the great Dan 10:4
Lord was standing * a wall built Amo 7:7
I SAW THE Lord standing * the Amo 9:1
among the myrtle trees * a river. Zec 1:8
An angel stood * me, and I asked Zec 1:9
angel who stood * me, speaking Zec 1:13
Joshua is standing *, and I will Zec 3:9
sacred as the bowls * the altar. Zec 14:20
and saw an angel standing * him. Mt 1:20
but soon he moved to Capernaum, * Mt 4:12,13
land of Naphtali, * the Lake, and Mt 4:15,16
along the beach * the Lake of Mt 4:18
sacrifice there * the altar and go Mt 5:24
ground, some fell * a path, and the Mt 13:4
Two blind men were sitting * the Mt 20:30
tied there, with its colt * it. Mt 21:2
and noticed a fig tree * the road. Mt 21:19
walking along * them they screamed Mk 6:49
* the road as Jesus was going by. Mk 10:46
* a fire among the servants. Mk 14:54
When the Roman officer standing * Mk 15:39
a little child * him and said to Lk 9:47
him lying half dead * the road. Lk 10:30
Kneeling * him the Samaritan Lk 10:34
and walked along * him till they Lk 10:34
man was sitting * the road, begging Lk 18:35
* the road, to watch from there. Lk 19:4
look for a donkey tied * the road. Lk 19:30
shall be enthroned * Almighty Lk 22:69
One of the criminals hanging * Lk 23:39
them and began walking * them. Lk 24:15
sun and sat wearily * the well. Jn 4:5,6
left her waterpot * the well and Jn 4:28,29
there * me, his close friend, Jn 19:26
disciples * the Lake of Galilee. Jn 21:1
Sit here in honor * me until I Act 2:34
street and laid * the Temple Act 3:2
was standing right there * them! Act 4:14
out and buried her * her husband. Act 5:10
standing * God, at his right Act 7:56
and walk along * the chariot." Act 8:29
angel of the Lord stood * Peter! Act 12:7
place of prayer * the river, we met Act 16:16
me, and standing * me said, Act 22:13
That night the Lord stood * Paul Act 23:11
whom I serve stood * me, and said, Act 27:23
where he sits * God in the place of Col 3:1
honor * the great God of heaven. Heb 1:3
Son, "Sit here * me in honor until Heb 1:13
who conquers sit * me on my throne, Rev 3:21

BESIDES
I thought. And *, she is my Gen 20:11,12
there, * the wives he already had. Gen 28:9
thousand of them, * all the women Ex 12:37
[* all the women and children Num 11:21
The total booty (* the jewelry, Num 31:32-35
and forty-two other cities *. Num 35:6
The cities in these areas, * Jos 19:15,16
*, just who do you think you are? Ju 11:25
she asked him for, * the presents 1Ki 10:13
$20,000,000, * sales taxes and 1Ki 10:15
girls * the Egyptian princess. 1Ki 11:1
He is an engraver *, and an 2Ch 2:14
* visitors from other countries! Neh 5:17
what he owes with some extra *. Ps 37:21
looking," they say, "and *, he Ps 94:6,7
others too * my people Israel. Is 56:8
hideous creatures, * all the Eze 8:10
day, * all the women and children. Mt 14:21
men * the women and children! Mt 15:37,38
they will mourn. [*, going without Mk 2:21
your coat, give him your shirt *. Lk 6:29
"And *, what's the use of Lk 12:25
in anguish. And *, there is a Lk 16:26
"And now, * all this—which Lk 24:21
living water? And *, are you Jn 4:12
other miracles * the ones told Jn 20:30,31
I have seven thousand others * Rom 11:4
Then, * all this, I have the 2Co 11:28
first promise. *, they are likely 1Ti 5:13

BESIEGE
peace with you, you must * it. Deu 20:12
"When you * a city, don't Deu 20:19
to Keilah and * David and his men. 1Sa 23:8
Israel's enemies * one of her 1Ki 8:37
to * Tirzah, Israel's capital. 1Ki 16:17
With great success he will * and Dan 11:24

BESIEGED
spot close to the * city where he 2Sa 11:16
arrived, they * Abel and built a 2Sa 20:15
* Samaria, the Israeli capital. 1Ki 20:1
his entire army and * Samaria. 2Ki 6:24
war on Ahaz and * Jerusalem; 2Ki 16:5
of Assyria * and captured all the 2Ki 18:13
Babylon * the city of Jerusalem. 2Ki 24:10
king came with his army and * it. Ecc 9:14
to relieve the * city of Jerusalem, Jer 37:5
against Jerusalem again and * it. Jer 39:1
invaded Judah and * Jerusalem. Hos 1:7f

BESIEGING
for three years * Samaria, the 2Ki 17:5
are in the land * our 2Ch 6:28
while still * the city of Lachish, 2Ch 32:9
had left Lachish and was * Libnah. Is 37:8,9
a * army against a high city wall. Jer 15:20
Babylon and the Chaldeans * you. Jer 21:3,4
Babylonian army was * Jerusalem. Jer 32:2
army was * Jerusalem, Lachish and Jer 34:7

BESMIRCHED
yours are hearts * with every sort Mt 23:28

BESODEIAH
Paseah) and Meshullam (son of *). Neh 3:6

BESOR
When they reached * Brook, two 1Sa 30:9,10
When they reached * Brook and the 1Sa 30:21

BEST
of meat from his * lambs, and Gen 4:4
Use your * flour, and make enough Gen 18:6
samples of the * of everything his Gen 24:10
Then she took Esau's * Gen 27:15
"We tried our *. Gen 38:23
Load your donkeys with the * Gen 43:11
* territory in the land of Egypt. Gen 45:18
property, for the * of all the land Gen 45:20
Give them the * land of Egypt. Gen 47:5,6
So Joseph assigned the * land of Gen 47:11
daughters with the * of Egypt!" Ex 3:22
amount of the * of his own crop. Ex 22:5
And you must bring the * of the Ex 34:26
to the Lord—the * of the olive oil, Num 18:12
give the * tenth to the priests. Num 18:32
to discover the * route of entry, Deu 1:22
had selected the * places for them Deu 1:33
With the * of what the sun makes Deu 33:14
May he be blessed with the * Deu 33:16
He chose the * of the land for Deu 33:21
discover the * way to attack us." Jos 2:3

BEST Con't)
hitch his father's * ox to the Ju 6:25
Punish us in any way you think *, Ju 10:15
been * man at Samson's wedding. Ju 14:20
"so I married her to your * man. Ju 15:2
thousand of their * soldiers to Ju 21:10,11,12
"Well, whatever you think *," 1Sa 1:23
* of the offerings of my people! 1Sa 2:29
"let him do what he thinks *." 1Sa 3:18
He will take away the * of your 1Sa 8:14
on whatever seems * under the 1Sa 10:7
"Do as you think *; 1Sa 14:7
"Do as you think *." 1Sa 14:36
his men kept the * of the sheep and 1Sa 15:9
army spared the * of the sheep and 1Sa 15:15
let them keep the * of the sheep 1Sa 15:21
and was obviously the * match! 1Sa 17:11f
* to escape, but it was no use. 1Sa 23:26
he selected the * fighters in his 2Sa 10:9
the enemies' * men were fighting; 2Sa 11:16
"Do as you think *." 2Sa 15:15
let him do what seems * to him." 2Sa 15:25,26
"Well, whatever you think *," 2Sa 18:4
of God, so do what you think *. 2Sa 19:27
man who did his * to destroy us. 2Sa 21:5,6
they do their * to do your will. 1Ki 8:22,23
and the * of your children!" 1Ki 20:2,3
and fifty of our * athletes will 2Ki 2:16
You will conquer the * of their 2Ki 3:19
camel-loads of the * produce of the 2Ki 8:8,9
letter, select the * one of Ahab's 2Ki 10:2,3
princes and the * of the soldiers, 2Ki 24:14
thousand of the * troops and one 2Ki 24:16
the * course for Israel to take. 1Ch 12:24-37
And may the Lord do what is *." 1Ch 19:13
way, was of the *, from Parvaim. 2Ch 3:6
of our God—the * of our grain Neh 10:37
and did his * to make her happy; Est 2:9
people—whatever you think *." Est 3:11
because he did his * for his Est 10:3
"My * friends abhor me. Job 19:19
The mountains offer their * food Job 40:20
I did my * to keep them all, Ps 18:23
* to those who humbly turn to him. Ps 25:9
teach him how to choose the *. Ps 25:12
along the * pathway for your life; Ps 32:8
Even my * friend has turned Ps 41:9
—the very * for those he loves. Ps 47:4
But even the * of these years are Ps 90:10
You did your * to kill me, O my Ps 118:13
I have tried my * to find Ps 119:10
gave me was the * thing that could Ps 119:71,72
taste the *!" Pro 9:17
yourself and your own * interests. Pro 15:31,32
and a pleasant teacher is the *. Pro 16:21
gossip separates the * of Pro 16:28
nagging about them parts the * of Pro 17:9
* interest and will be a success. Pro 19:8
but you are the * of them all!" Pro 31:29
say how one's days can * be spent? Ecc 6:12
Who can know what will prove * Ecc 6:12
I have tried my * to be wise. Ecc 7:23
gives you is your * reward down Ecc 9:9
as exciting as the * of wine, Sol 7:9
cut down the * of the grape vines; Is 16:8
Their * counsel to the king of Is 19:11
They are the * you can find, but Is 19:13
a present and his * wishes, Is 39:1
as to what is right and *? Is 40:14
Is that the * that they can do? Is 46:1
ships of many lands, the very *, Is 60:9
my seed so carefully—the very *. Jer 2:21
power—do with me as you think *. Jer 26:14
And all the * soldiers of Israel Eze 17:21
the * of all lands anywhere. Eze 20:5,6
Use only the * sheep from the Eze 24:5
choicest and the * of Lebanon, the Eze 31:16
You eat the * food and wear the Eze 34:3
not only keep the * of the pastures Eze 34:18
That you take the * water for Eze 34:18
The king assigned them the * of Dan 1:5
he does whatever he thinks * Dan 4:35
Conscript your * soldiers; Joe 3:9
flee, and even the * of horsemen Amo 2:15
and it is, at *, short-lived. Jon 4:10
Even the * of them are prickly Mic 7:4
Don't trust anyone, not your * Mic 7:5
if your eye—even if it is your * Mt 5:29
planning how * to get rid of him. Mk 11:18
They love to sit in the * seats Mk 12:39
'The old ways are *,' they say." Lk 5:39
Purity is * demonstrated by Lk 11:41
don't always head for the * seat. Lk 14:8
the * way to betray Jesus to them. Lk 22:4
serves you * will be your leader. Lk 22:26
Usually a host uses the * wine Jn 2:10
But you have kept the * for the Jn 2:10
them that Jesus' baptism was *. Jn 3:25
is that it is * for you that I go Jn 16:7
And give my * regards to those Rom 16:10
be, and ignore the * ideas of men, 1Co 1:19
But usually it is * to be 1Co 7:2
I think it is * for a person to 1Co 7:26
you serve the Lord *, with as few 1Co 7:35
would keep you from doing your *. 1Co 9:25
but it may not be * and helpful. 1Co 10:23
too, and what is * for him. 1Co 10:24
I like or what is * for me, but 1Co 10:33
me, but what is * for them, so that 1Co 10:33
No, but try your * to have the 1Co 12:31
always expect the * of him, and 1Co 13:7
him for the very *, for those that 1Co 14:12
in Jerusalem. * of all, they went 2Co 8:5
My power shows up * in weak 2Co 12:9
here send you their * regards. 2Co 13:13
doing my * to get rid of them all. Gal 1:13
effort to get the * for yourself, Gal 5:20
is doing his very *, for then he Gal 6:4
what is * for us at all times. Eph 1:8
abilities to do certain things *? Eph 4:12
be eager to give them your very * Eph 6:5
And if you don't do your * for Col 3:25
had gotten the * of you and that 1Th 3:5
gold—the very * in the house—so 2Ti 2:21
to try their * to satisfy them. Tit 2:9
Let us do our * to go into that Heb 4:11
years, doing the * for us that they Heb 12:10
right and for our * good, that we Heb 12:10
fail to find God's * blessings. Heb 12:15
forget that it is * to listen much, Jas 1:19
and give him the * seat in the Jas 2:3

BEST-EQUIPPED
The * army cannot save a king—for Ps 33:16,17

BESTOW
next * this life from heaven." Jn 3:8

BET
I'll tell you what: Make a * 2Ki 18:23
wants to make a little * with you! Is 36:8,9

BETAH
cities of * and Berothai. 2Sa 8:8

BETEN
Helkath, Hali, *, Achshaph, Jos 19:24,25,26

BETH-ANATH
Horem, *, and Beth-shemesh. Jos 19:35-39
Beth-shemesh or of *, so these Ju 1:33

BETH-ANOTH
Gedor, Maarath, *, Eltekon, Jos 15:48-62

BETH-ARABAH
proceeded north of * to the stone Jos 15:6
Rabbah, *, Middin, Secacah, Jos 15:48-62
Emek-keziz, *, Zimaraim, Bethel, Jos 18:21-28

BETH-ARBEL
fall, just as at *, which Shalman Hos 10:14

BETH-ASHBEA
the linen workers who worked at *, 1Ch 4:21-22

BETH-AVEN
country and the Wilderness of *. Jos 18:12
they camped at Michmash east of *. 1Sa 13:5
the battle continued out beyond *. 1Sa 14:23
and Ramah, and on over to *; Hos 5:8
idols at * should be hurt; Hos 10:5

BETH-AZMAVETH
From the subclan of *, 42; Neh 7:8-38

BETH-BAAL-MEON
Bamoth-baal, *, Jahaz, Kedemoth, Jos 13:17

BETH-BARAH
Jordan River at *, thus preventing Ju 7:24

BETH-BIRI
Hazar-susim, *, and Sha-araim. 1Ch 4:31

BETH-CAR
*, killing them all along the way. 1Sa 7:11

BETH-DAGON
Gederoth, *, Naamah, Makkedah, Jos 15:37-44
turned east toward *, and ran as Jos 19:27

BETH-DIBLATHAIM
Dibon and Nebo and *, and Jer 48:22

BETH-EMEK
running north of * and Neiel. Jos 19:27

BETH-EZEL
venture outside; * sounds like a Mic 1:11f
venture outside; * sounds like a Mic 1:11f
The foundations of * Mic 1:11
venture outside; * sounds like a Mic 1:11f

BETH-GADER
and Hareph (the father of *). 1Ch 2:51

BETH-GAMUL
and Kiriathaim and * and Beth-meon, Jer 48:23

BETH-GILGAL
they also came from * and the Neh 12:29

BETH-HACCHEREM
Rechab), the mayor of the * area; Neh 3:14
send up a smoke signal at *; Jer 6:1

BETH-HAGGAN
had fled along the road to *. 2Ki 9:27

BETH-HARAM
In the valley were *, and Jos 13:27,28

BETH-HARAN
Beth-nimrah, * Num 32:34,35,36

BETH-HOGLAH
Sea, crossed to *, then proceeded Jos 15:6
ran south past *, and ended at the Jos 18:19
Jericho, *, Emek-keziz, Jos 18:21-28

BETH-HORON
all the way to * and Azekah and Jos 10:10
down the hill to *, the Lord Jos 10:11
as far as Lower *, then to Gezer Jos 16:1
From there it ran to Upper *, Jos 16:5,6
the hill country south of Lower *. Jos 18:13
the mountain near * and ending at Jos 18:14
Refuge), Gezer, Kibza-im, and *. Jos 21:20,21,22
another went to *, and the third 1Sa 13:18
along with Lower *, Baalath, and 1Ki 9:17,18
Jokme-am; *; 1Ch 6:66-69
She built Lower and Upper * and 1Ch 7:24
cities of upper * and lower 2Ch 8:5
and lower *, both being supply 2Ch 8:5
in the vicinity of *, toward 2Ch 25:13

BETH-JESHIMOTH
Jordan River, from * as far as Num 33:49
*, and the slopes of Mount Pisgah. Jos 13:20
*Baal-meon and Kiriathaim. Eze 25:9,10

BETH-LE-APHRAH
Weep, men of Bakah. In * roll in Mic 1:10

BETH-LEBAOTH
Hazar-susah, *, Sharuhen, Jos 19:2-7

BETH-MAACAH
Bichri at the city of Abel in *. 2Sa 20:14

BETH-MARCABOTH
Hormah, Ziklag, *, Hazar-susah, Jos 19:2-7
Hormah, Ziklag, *, Hazar-susim, 1Ch 4:31

BETH-MEON
and Beth-gamul and *, and Keri-oth Jer 48:23

BETH-MILLO
of Shechem and * called a meeting Ju 9:6
the citizens of Shechem and *; Ju 9:20

BETH-NIMRAH
Jogbehah, *, Num 32:34,35,36
Beth-haram, and *, Succoth, Zaphon, Jos 13:27,28

BETH-PAZZEZ
En-haddah, *, Tabor, Shahazumah, Jos 19:17-23

BETH-PELET
Heshmon, *, Hazar-shual, Jos 15:21-32
Jeshua, Moladah, *, Neh 11:25-30

BETH-PEOR
we remained in the valley near *. Deu 3:29
Jordan River near the city of *. Deu 4:44,45,46
in a valley near * in Moab, but no Deu 34:6
above the valley, *, Jos 13:20

BETH-REHOB
happened in the valley next to *. Ju 18:28

BETH-SHAN
was fastened to the wall of *. 1Sa 31:10
all night to * and took down the 1Sa 31:12
public square at * where the 2Sa 21:12,13,14

BETH-SHEAN
and Asher: *, Ible-am, Dor, En-dor, Jos 17:11
lowlands around * and the Valley ofJos 17:16,17,18
people living in *, Taanach, Dor, Ju 1:27
Megiddo, all of * near Zarethan 1Ki 4:8-19
the territory from * to 1Ki 4:8-19
*, Taanach, Megiddo, and Dor. 1Ch 7:29

BETH-SHEMESH
Mount Jearim, and went down to *. Jos 15:10,11
Tabor, Shahazumah, and *— Jos 19:17-23
Horem, Beth-anath, and *. Jos 19:35-39
Holon, Debir, Ain, Juttah, and *. Jos 21:9-16
out the people of * or of Ju 1:33
land and go into *, then you will 1Sa 6:9
toward *, lowing as they went; 1Sa 6:12
them as far as the border of *. 1Sa 6:12
The people of * were reaping 1Sa 6:13
the Lord that day by the men of *. 1Sa 6:15
(By the way, that large rock at * 1Sa 6:18
of the men of * because they looked 1Sa 6:19
Sha-albim, *, and Elon-beth-hanan; 1Ki 4:8-19
The battle began at *, one of the 2Ki 14:11
Eshtemoa, Hilen, Debir, Ashan, *. 1Ch 6:58,59
The armies met at *, in Judah, 2Ch 25:21
already captured *, Aijalon, 2Ch 28:17,18

BETH-SHITTAH
as far away as * near Zererah, and Ju 7:22

BETH-TAPPU-AH
Eshan, Janim, *, Aphekah, Humtah, Jos 15:48-62

BETH-TOGARMAH
Tubal, Gomer, *) can be identified Eze 38:2,3f

BETH-ZUR
Timnah, Halhul, *, Gedor, Maarath, Jos 15:48-62
*, Soco, Adullam, 2Ch 11:5-10
the mayor of half the * district; Neh 3:16

BETHANY
Then he returned to *, where he Mt 21:17
Jesus now proceeded to *, to the Mt 26:6
AS THEY NEARED Bethphage and * Mk 11:1
to * with the twelve disciples. Mk 11:11
The next morning as they left *, Mk 11:12
Meanwhile Jesus was in *, at the Mk 14:3
of Bethphage and *, on the Mount of Lk 19:29
Implied. * was a mile or so away, Lk 24:50f
to *, and lifting his hands to Lk 24:50
This incident took place at *, a Jn 1:28
who lived in * with Mary and her Jn 11:1
When they arrived at *, they were Jn 11:17
for four days. * was only a couple Jn 11:18

(BETHANY Con't)
Jesus arrived in * where Lazarus — Jn 12:1

BETHEL
to the hilly country between * on — Gen 12:8
northward toward * where he had — Gen 13:3,4
before, between * and Ai—to the — Gen 13:3,4
He named the place * ("House of — Gen 28:19
'I am the God you met at *,' he — Gen 31:13
"MOVE ON TO * now, and settle — Gen 35:1
"For we are going to *," he — Gen 35:3
at Luz (also called *), in Canaan. — Gen 35:6
to the God who met me here at *" — Gen 35:7
Literally, "The God of *." — Gen 35:7f
because it was there at * that — Gen 35:7
oak tree in the valley below *. — Gen 35:8
Upon Jacob's arrival at *, en — Gen 35:9
Jacob named the spot * ("House — Gen 35:15
Leaving *, he and his household — Gen 35:16
spy on the city of Ai, east of *. — Jos 7:2
between * and the west side of Ai; — Jos 8:9
forces expected from * (verse 17). — Jos 8:11,12,13f
left in Ai or * and the city gates — Jos 8:17
The king of Ai, near *; — Jos 12:8-24
The king of *; — Jos 12:8-24
and the hill country to *. — Jos 16:1
It then went from * to Luz, then — Jos 16:1
Luz (also called *) and proceeded — Jos 18:13
Zimaraim, *, Avvim, Parah, Ophrah, — Jos 18:21-28
the city of *, formerly known as — Ju 1:22,23
*, in the hill country of Ephraim; — Ju 4:5
* first to ask counsel from God. — Ju 20:18
Then the entire army went up to * — Ju 20:26
(The Ark of God was in * in — Ju 20:27,28
running between * and Gibe-ah, so — Ju 20:31
leaders met at * and sat before God — Ju 21:2
Lebonah and *, along the east side — Ju 21:19
road that goes from * to Shechem. — Ju 21:19
his court first at *, then Gilgal, — 1Sa 7:16
to worship God at the altar at *; — 1Sa 10:3
Michmash and Mount * while the — 1Sa 13:2
*, South Ramoth, Jattir, Aroer, — 1Sa 30:27-31
placed in * and the other in Dan. — 1Ki 12:29
held at * on the first of November — 1Ki 12:32,33
at *, and burned incense to them. — 1Ki 12:32,33
And it was there at * that he — 1Ki 12:32,33
prophet living in *, and his sons — 1Ki 13:11
or to drink any water at *. — 1Ki 13:16,17
in * where the old prophet lived. — 1Ki 13:24,25
the altar in *, and his curse — 1Ki 13:32
a man from *, rebuilt Jericho. — 1Ki 16:34
the Lord has told me to go to *." — 2Ki 2:1
So they went on together to *. — 2Ki 2:1
There the young prophets of * — 2Ki 2:3
stay here in *, for the Lord has — 2Ki 2:4
From Jericho he went to *. — 2Ki 2:23
golden calves at * and Dan—this was — 2Ki 10:29
So one of them returned to * and — 2Ki 17:27,28
and he carried the ashes to *. — 2Ki 23:4
and shrine at * which Jeroboam I — 2Ki 23:15
upon the altar at * to defile it, — 2Ki 23:16
happen here at the altar at *!" — 2Ki 23:17
dust, just as he had done at *. — 2Ki 23:19
on one side by * and its — 1Ch 7:28
some of his cities—*, Jeshanah, — 2Ch 13:18,19
From the subclans of * and Ai, — Ez 2:3-35
From the subclans of * and Ai, — Neh 7:8-38
Geba, Michmash, Aija, * (and its — Neh 11:31-35
Israel was of her calf-idol at *. — Jer 48:13
worship me at Gilgal and at *. — Hos 4:15
And the idol altars of Aven at * — Hos 10:8
He met God there at * face to — Hos 12:4
also destroy the idol altars at *. — Amo 3:14
to idols at * and Gilgal. — Amo 4:4
Don't seek the idols of *, — Amo 5:5
of * shall surely come to grief." — Amo 5:5
of the idols in * can put it out. — Amo 5:6
But when Amaziah, the priest of * — Amo 7:10
The Jews of the city of * had — Zec 7:2
"When you return to *, say to — Zec 7:5

BETHESDA
Sheep Gate, was * Pool, with five — Jn 5:2

BETHLEHEM
traveled on toward Ephrath (*). — Gen 35:16
road to Ephrath (also called *). — Gen 35:19
buried her beside the road to *." — Gen 48:7
Shimron, Idalah, *, and each of — Jos 19:15,16
judge was Ibzan, who lived in *. — Ju 12:8
he died, and was buried at *. — Ju 12:9,10
from the town of *, in Judah, — Ju 17:7,8
from *, in Judah, and I am — Ju 17:9
* in Judah to be his concubine. — Ju 19:1
father's home in *, and was there — Ju 19:2
"We're on the way home from *, — Ju 19:18
a man named Elimelech, from *, — Ru 1:1
Ephrathites from * in Judah." — Ru 1:1f
So they both came to * and the — Ru 1:19
and arrival in * was at the — Ru 1:22
NOW NAOMI HAD an in-law there in * — Ru 2:1
successful man in *, and may the — Ru 4:11
oil and go to * and find a man — 1Sa 16:1
When he arrived at *, the elders — 1Sa 16:4
a young fellow in *, the son of a — 1Sa 16:18
He went back and forth to * to — 1Sa 17:14,15
name is Jesse and we live in *." — 1Sa 17:58
to * for an annual family reunion. — 1Sa 20:6
"He asked me if he could go to * — 1Sa 20:28,29
Asahel's body to * and buried him — 2Sa 2:32
had occupied the nearby city of *. — 2Sa 23:14
Elhanan (son of Dodo) from *; — 2Sa 23:24-39
Salma (the father of *), and — 1Ch 2:51
Salma were his son *, the — 1Ch 2:54
who was the father of *. — 1Ch 4:3-4
of the Philistines had occupied *. — 1Ch 11:16
David wanted a drink from the * — 1Ch 11:17
Elhanan, the son of Dodo from *; — 1Ch 11:26-47
*, Etam, Tekoa, — 2Ch 11:5-10
From the subclan of *, 123; — Ez 2:3-35
From the subclans of * and — Neh 7:8-38
Chimham, near *, taking with them — Jer 41:16,17
O * Ephrathah, you are but a — Mic 5:2
JESUS WAS BORN in the town of *, — Mt 2:1
"Yes, in *," they said, "for — Mt 2:5
'O little town of *, you are not — Mt 2:6
Then he told them, "Go to * and — Mt 2:8
to them again, standing over *. — Mt 2:9
Sending soldiers to *, he ordered — Mt 2:16
he had to go to * in Judea, King — Lk 2:4
Lord—has been born tonight in *! — Lk 2:11
Let's go to *! — Lk 2:15
line of David, in *, the village — Jn 7:41,42

BETHLEHEM-JUDAH
in *) had seven older brothers. — 1Sa 17:12

BETHPHAGE
near the town of * on the Mount of — Mt 21:1
AS THEY NEARED * and Bethany on — Mk 11:1
As they came to the towns of * — Lk 19:29

BETHRAPHA
Eshton was the father of *, — 1Ch 4:11,12

BETHSAIDA
you, Chorazin, and woe to you, *! — Mt 11:21
*, where he would join them later. — Mk 6:45
When they arrived at *, some — Mk 8:22
with them toward the city of *. — Lk 9:10
you, you cities of Chorazin and *! — Lk 10:13
(Philip was from *, Andrew and — Jn 1:44
who was from *, and said, "Sir, — Jn 12:21

BETHUEL
Jidlaph,* (father of Rebekah). — Gen 22:20-23
(Her father was * the son of — Gen 24:15,16
"My father is *, the son of — Gen 24:24
My father is *, the son of Nahor — Gen 24:47
Then Laban and * replied, "The — Gen 24:50
the daughter of * the Aramean from — Gen 25:20
*, and marry one of your — Gen 28:2
brother—the son of * the Aramean. — Gen 28:5
Ezem, Tolad, *, Hormah, Ziklag, — 1Ch 4:30

BETHUL
Ezem, Eltolad, *, Hormah, Ziklag, — Jos 19:2-7

BETHZUR
son was Maon, the father of *. — 1Ch 2:45

BETONIM
*, and from Mahanaim to Lo-debar. — Jos 13:26

BETRAY
"If you won't * us, we'll see to — Jos 2:14
However, if you * us, then this — Jos 2:20
father, but don't * me to him!" — 1Sa 20:8
"And will these men of Keilah * — 1Sa 23:12
replied, "Yes, they will * you." — 1Sa 23:12
oath that he wouldn't * her. — 1Sa 28:10
but if you have come to * me to — 1Ch 12:17
of Ziph tried to * him to Saul. — Ps 54:1
and * some vital information. — Pro 5:2
promises to you, while you * them! — Is 33:1
to blaspheme and * me when I — Eze 20:27,28
"Brother shall * brother to — Mt 10:21
shall * their own children. — Mt 10:21
sin and * and hate each other. — Mt 24:10
an opportunity to * Jesus to them. — Mt 26:16
he said, "One of you will * me." — Mt 26:20,21
"Brothers will * each other to — Mk 13:12
fathers will * their own children, — Mk 13:12
will * their parents to be killed. — Mk 13:12
to arrange to * Jesus to them. — Mk 14:10
right time and place to * Jesus. — Mk 14:11
one of you will * me, one of you — Mk 14:18
will * you and have you arrested; — Lk 21:16
the best way to * Jesus to them. — Lk 22:4
friend, is the man who will * me. — Lk 22:21
this—* the Messiah with a kiss?" — Lk 22:48
and knew the one who would * him. — Jn 6:64
of the Twelve, who would * him. — Jn 6:71
one who would * him—said, "That — Jn 12:4
to carry out his plan to * Jesus. — Jn 13:1
For Jesus knew who would * — Jn 13:11
with me will * me,' and this will — Jn 13:18
it is true—one of you will * me." — Jn 13:21
which of us will * you?" — Jn 21:20
They will * their friends; — 2Ti 3:4

BETRAYED
in Gibe-ah and * David to him. — 1Sa 23:19
And if I had * the king by — 2Sa 18:13
This friend of mine * me—I who — Ps 55:20
Now you, too, will be * and — Is 33:1
But you have * me; — Jer 3:20
They have * you and left you to — Jer 38:21,22
For they have * the honor of the — Hos 5:7
Chaldeans are * by all their wine, — Hab 2:5
say those who have * them—their — Zec 11:5
Judas Iscariot (the one who * — Mt 10:2,3,4
"I am going to be * into the power — Mt 17:22,23
will be * to the chief priests — Mt 20:18
shall be * and crucified." — Mt 26:2
but woe to the man by whom I am *. — Mt 26:24
am * into the hands of evil men! — Mt 26:45
About that time Judas, who * him, — Mt 27:3
"for I have * an innocent man." — Mt 27:4
Judas Iscariot (who later * him). — Mk 3:16-19
am going to be * and killed and — Mk 9:30,31
am *. Oh, that he had never been — Mk 14:21
am * into the hands of wicked — Mk 14:41
Judas Iscariot (who later * him). — Lk 6:14,15,16
am going to be *." — Lk 9:44
must be * into the power of evil — Lk 24:6,7
Judas, who * Jesus by guiding the — Act 1:16
Messiah whom you * and murdered. — Act 7:52
night when Judas * him, the Lord — 1Co 11:23
Then the devil who had * them — Rev 20:10

BETRAYER
Look! My * is here!" — Mk 14:42
Judas, the *, knew this place, — Jn 18:2

BETRAYING
the Lord by * a trust, it is sin. — Num 5:5,6
your father by not * you to David, — 2Sa 3:8
Here comes the man who is * me!" — Mt 26:46

BETRAYS
man or woman, * the Lord by — Num 5:5,6
Literally, "who * nations with — Nah 3:4f
awaiting that man who * me." — Lk 22:22

BETROTH
I will * you to me in — Hos 1:20

BETROTHAL
with permanent *, for love is — Sol 8:6

BETTER
"Who could do it * than Joseph? — Gen 41:38
We said it would be * to be — Ex 14:12
you are no * than anyone else; — Num 16:3
he is * than his fellow citizens. — Deu 17:20
at least two, and three is even *. — Deu 19:15
grapes of Ephraim * than the entire — Ju 8:2,3f
Are you * than King Balak, the — Ju 11:25
Isn't it * for you to be a priest — Ju 18:19
But Naomi replied, "It is * for — Ru 1:11
Isn't having me * than having ten — 1Sa 1:8
eaten the honey he felt much *. — 1Sa 14:27
See how much * I feel now that I — 1Sa 14:29
Obedience is far * than — 1Sa 15:22
of yours who is * than you are. — 1Sa 15:28
Saul would feel *, and the evil — 1Sa 16:23
David, "You are a * man than I am, — 1Sa 24:17
You'd * think fast, for there is — 1Sa 25:17
Is there any * way for him to — 1Sa 29:4
Tell him you'll feel * if she — 2Sa 13:5
advice is * than Ahithophel's." — 2Sa 17:14
really was the * plan, so that he — 2Sa 17:14
of us, and it is * that you stay — 2Sa 18:3
"but it is * to fall into the hand — 2Sa 24:14
of two men who were * than he. — 1Ki 2:32
to treat us * than he did." — 1Ki 12:2,3,4
Literally, "I am no * than my — 1Ki 19:4f
a piece of * land in trade. — 1Ki 21:2
River of Damascus * than all the — 2Ki 5:12
they let us live, so much the *; — 2Ki 7:4
"We'd * send out scouts to see. — 2Ki 7:13
Then you will realize how much * — 2Ch 12:8
brothers who were * than you, now — 2Ch 21:13
in much * condition than before. — 2Ch 24:13
you think your God can do any *? — 2Ch 32:14
they see no * in the daytime than — Job 5:14
myself—you are no * than I am. — Job 12:3
* off before God than if I had'? — Job 35:2,3
Don't they really know any *? — Ps 14:4
It is * to have little and be — Ps 37:16
are * to me than life itself. — Ps 63:3
* than a thousand anywhere else! — Ps 84:10
him to act, but demanded * food, — Ps 106:14
It is * to trust the Lord than to — Ps 118:8
It is * to take refuge in him — Ps 118:9
I don't think myself * than — Ps 131:1
Yes, if you want * insight and — Pro 2:3,4,5
him *, so the Lord corrects you. — Pro 3:11,12
My gifts are * than the purest — Pro 8:19
* refuse than suffer later. — Pro 11:15
It is * to get your hands — Pro 12:9
* a little with reverence for — Pro 15:16
It is * to eat soup with someone — Pro 15:17
A little, gained honestly, is * — Pro 16:8
How much * is wisdom than gold, — Pro 16:16
* poor and humble than proud and — Pro 16:19
It is * to be slow-tempered than — Pro 16:32
it is * to have self-control than — Pro 16:32
A DRY CRUST eaten in peace is * — Pro 17:1
* BE POOR and honest than rich — Pro 19:1
And it is * to be poor than — Pro 19:22

(BETTER Con't)
It is * to live in the corner of Pro 21:9
* to live in the desert than with Pro 21:19
esteem is * than silver and gold. Pro 22:1
It is * to wait for an invitation Pro 25:6,7
It is * to live in a corner of an Pro 25:24
The master may get * work from an Pro 26:10
Open rebuke is * than hidden Pro 27:5
Wounds from a friend are * than Pro 27:6
* to be poor and honest than rich Pro 28:6
is no * than a murderer. Pro 28:24
I said to myself, "Look, I am * Ecc 1:16-18
just as light is * than darkness; Ecc 2:13,14
there was nothing * for a man to do Ecc 2:24-26
there is nothing * for a man than Ecc 3:12
that they are no * than beasts. Ecc 3:18
So I saw that there is nothing * Ecc 3:22
So I felt that the dead were * Ecc 4:2
feels that it is * to be lazy and Ecc 4:5,6
for the results can be much *. Ecc 4:9
three is even *, for a Ecc 4:12
It is * to be a poor but wise Ecc 4:13
It is far * not to say you'll do Ecc 5:5
that he would be * off born dead. Ecc 6:3
* than to be an old, unhappy man. Ecc 6:5
who is wise lives a far * life. Ecc 6:7,8
The day one dies is * than the day Ecc 7:1
It is * to spend your time at Ecc 7:2
Sorrow is * than laughter, for Ecc 7:3
It is * to be criticized by a Ecc 7:5
Finishing is * than starting! Ecc 7:8
Patience is * than pride! Ecc 7:8
they were any * than these! Ecc 7:10
in fact, it is *. Ecc 7:11
fear God will be * off, unlike the Ecc 8:12
there was nothing * in all the Ecc 8:15
"It is * to be a live dog than a Ecc 9:4
though wisdom is * than strength, Ecc 9:16
of a wise man are * than the shout Ecc 9:17
Wisdom is * than weapons of war, Ecc 9:18
Your love is * than wine. Sol 1:4
How much * it is than mere wine. Sol 4:10
loved one that is * than any other, Sol 5:9
* than ten thousand others! Sol 5:10
we will rebuild it * than before. Is 9:8,9,10
so that I can give you * news. Is 21:12
on, and tomorrow will be * yet!" Is 56:12
tries a * life is soon attacked. Is 59:15
the sword are far * off than those Lam 4:9
says: You are no * than the people Eze 16:3
none is * than any other. Eze 24:6
that Judah is no * off than any Eze 25:8
Or, probably *, "They exchanged Eze 27:19f
healthier and * nourished than the Dan 1:15
advice ten times * than that of all Dan 1:20
* off with him than I am now." Hos 1:7
Once they were * and greater than Amo 6:2
Far * it would be for you if Ob 1:5
For he said, "Death is * than Jon 4:8
vainly hope for * days, but only Mic 1:12
Are you any * than Thebes, Nah 3:8
destroy those who are * than they? Hab 1:13
and throw it away. * for part of Mt 5:29
* that than find yourself in hell. Mt 5:30
* off at Judgment Day than they. Mt 10:15
Truly, Tyre and Sidon will be * Mt 11:22
Truly, Sodom will be * off at Mt 11:24
it would be * for you to have a Mt 18:6
and throw it away. * to enter Mt 18:8
and throw it away. * to enter Mt 18:9
how it is, it is * not to marry!" Mt 19:10
I am betrayed. Far * for that one Mt 26:24
You know * than to put new wine Mk 2:22
was no * but, in fact, was worse. Mk 5:26
"He's no * than we are," they Mk 6:2,3
faith—it would be * for that man if Mk 9:42
wrong, cut it off. * live forever Mk 9:43,44
evil, cut it off! * be lame and Mk 9:45,46
gouge it out. * enter the Kingdom Mk 9:47
Even wicked Sodom will be * off Lk 10:12
have a * place than this for you!' Lk 14:10
he would be far * off than facing Lk 17:2,3
And if you don't have a sword, * Lk 22:36
How can you offer * water than Jn 4:12
had begun to feel *, and they Jn 4:52
"That means he is getting *!" Jn 11:12,13
"* that one should die for all." Jn 18:14
Suddenly everyone felt * and Act 27:36
you are no * off than the heathen. Rom 2:25
heathen will be much * off Rom 2:27
worse we are, the * God likes it! Rom 3:8
Well, then, are we Jews * than Rom 3:9
standards, you had * put this all 1Co 3:18
and to widows—* to stay unmarried 1Co 7:8
It is * to marry than to burn 1Co 7:9
who doesn't marry does even *. 1Co 7:38
eat it, and no * off if we do. 1Co 8:8
else that is * than any of them! 1Co 12:31
themselves, are any * than I am. 2Co 11:5
though they certainly knew *. Gal 2:13
child is not much * off than a Gal 4:1
be equipped to do * work for him, Eph 4:12
be constantly changing for the *. Eph 4:23
and dying—well, that's * yet! Php 1:21
know which is *, to live or die! Php 1:22
of others as * than yourself. Php 2:3
learning to know God * and better. Col 1:10
learning to know God better and *. Col 1:10
practice being a * Christian, 1Ti 4:8
So I think it is * for these 1Ti 5:14
And you know * than I can tell 2Ti 1:18
but something much *—a beloved Phm 1:16
until you become * Christians and Heb 5:14
But now we have a far * hope, for Heb 7:19
of this new and * arrangement. Heb 7:22
The sacrifice he offers is far * Heb 8:4
came with God's new and * way. Heb 9:10
He came as High Priest of this * Heb 9:11
system in favor of a far * one. Heb 10:9
you, knowing that * things were Heb 10:34
He thought that it was * to Heb 11:26
would rise to a * life afterwards. Heb 11:35
and share the even * rewards that Heb 11:40
who should know *, do wrong, our Jas 3:1
evil because you knew no *. 1Pe 1:14
speak to them * than any words. 1Pe 3:1
to suffer, it is * to suffer for 1Pe 3:17
Then learn to know him * and 2Pe 1:2
learn to know him better and *. 2Pe 1:2
For as you know him *, he will 2Pe 1:3
learn to know God * and discover 2Pe 1:5
But false teachers are fools—no * 2Pe 2:12
It would be * if he had never 2Pe 2:21
and become * acquainted with our 2Pe 3:18
his brother's life was * than his. 1Jn 3:12
they are getting to know him *. 1Jn 4:7
good men will be *; Rev 22:11

BETTER-ARMED
stronger and * attacks and Lk 11:22

BETWEEN
and * your offspring and hers. Gen 3:15
(which is located * Nineveh and Gen 10:11,12
to the hilly country * Bethel on Gen 12:8
had camped before, * Bethel and Gen 13:3,4
So fights broke out * the Gen 13:7
"This fighting * our men has got Gen 13:8
to let a rift develop * our clans. Gen 13:8
* the halves of the carcasses. Gen 15:17
Literally, "Let the Lord judge * Gen 16:5f
It lies * Kadesh and Bered. Gen 16:14
I will prepare a contract * us, Gen 17:2,3,4
this agreement * us generation Gen 17:7,8
be * me and your children as well. Gen 17:7,8
and settled * Kadesh and Shur. Gen 20:1
"but what is that * friends? Gen 23:14,15
decided to ask for a treaty * us. Gen 26:28
"stands * us as a witness of our Gen 31:51,52
itself, separated by a distance *. Gen 32:16
* your people and my people. Ex 8:23
* Egyptians and Israelis.' Ex 11:7
toward Piha-hiroth * Migdol and the Ex 14:2
now, * the desert and the sea!' Ex 14:3
and it stood * the people of Ex 14:20
followed them * the walls of water Ex 14:23
Sihn Wilderness, * Elim and Mt. Ex 16:1
an engagement * a Hebrew slave-girl Ex 21:9
divide the price * them—and each Ex 21:35
the place of mercy * the cherubim; Ex 25:22
placed * each set of branches; Ex 25:34,35
Put it * the Tabernacle and the Ex 30:17,18
the covenant * me and you forever; Ex 31:12,13
* me and the people of Israel. Ex 31:17
Bells of pure gold were placed * Ex 39:25,26
Set the washbasin * the Ex 40:7
Next he placed the washbasin * Ex 40:30
the difference * what is holy and Lev 10:10
These are the distinctions * Lev 11:47
is outlawed * a man and his maiden Lev 20:19
made a distinction * you and the Lev 20:24
make a distinction * the birds and Lev 20:25
as a wall * the people of Israel Num 1:53
all of the men * the ages of thirty Num 4:21,22,23
Ark, the spot * the two cherubim. Num 7:89
to distinguish * the summons to Num 10:5,6,7
them to carry it on a pole * them! Num 13:23
And he stood * the living and Num 16:48
* the Lord and you and your Num 18:19
* the Moabites and the Amorites. Num 21:13
of Waheb, lie * the Amorites and Num 21:15
road went * two vineyard walls. Num 22:24
relationships * a man and his wife Num 30:16
and his wife and * a father and his Num 30:16
Thus there will be 3000 feet * Num 35:5
I stood as an intermediary * you Deu 5:5
them to your forehead * your eyes! Deu 11:18
* God's blessing or God's curse! Deu 11:26
Then the Levites standing * Deu 27:14
* his land and his neighbor's.' Deu 27:17
a clear space * you and the Ark; Jos 3:2,3,4
* Bethel and the west side of Ai; Jos 8:9
of Mount Ebal. * them stood the Jos 8:33
(This land which lay * Baal-gad Jos 12:7
of Benjamin lay * the territory Jos 18:11
* our people and your people! Jos 22:24,25
"It is a witness * us and them Jos 22:34
darkness * them and the Egyptians; Jos 24:7
contract * themselves and God. Jos 24:25
Palm Tree," * Ramah and Bethel, in Ju 4:5
agreement * King Jabin of Hazor and Ju 4:17
stirred up trouble * King Abimelech Ju 9:22,23
of Dan, located * the cities of Ju 13:25
pairs, with a torch * each pair. Ju 15:4
of the temple, * the two pillars Ju 16:25,26
and buried him * Zorah and Ju 16:31
and everywhere *, and from across Ju 20:1
roadway running * Bethel and Ju 20:31
fields of Shiloh, * Lebonah and Ju 21:19
and placed it * Mizpah and Jeshanah 1Sa 7:12
The Israeli cities * Ekron and 1Sa 7:14
And there was peace * Israel and 1Sa 7:14
over a narrow pass * two rocky 1Sa 14:4
Then Saul said, "Now draw lots * 1Sa 14:42
battle and camped * Socoh in Judah 1Sa 17:1
hills, with the valley * them. 1Sa 17:3
an immediate bond of love * them. 1Sa 18:1
"The Lord will decide * us. 1Sa 24:12
some sword play * our young men!" 2Sa 2:14
of a long war * the followers of 2Sa 3:1
divide the land equally * you." 2Sa 19:29
Literally, "can I discern * good 2Sa 19:35f
the oath * himself and Jonathan. 2Sa 21:7
* what is right and what is wrong. 1Ki 3:9
divide it * us!" 1Ki 3:26
River * Succoth and Zarethan. 1Ki 7:41-46
There was constant war * 1Ki 14:30
constant war * Israel and Judah. 1Ki 15:6
Literally, "* Rehoboam and 1Ki 15:6f
There was lifelong war * King Asa 1Ki 15:16
There was continuous warfare * 1Ki 15:32,33
going to waver * two opinions?" 1Ki 18:21
with his face * his knees, and 1Ki 18:42
THREE YEARS there was no war * 1Ki 22:1
Ahab * the joints of his armor. 1Ki 22:34
appeared and drove * them, 2Ki 2:11
and shot Joram * the shoulders; 2Ki 9:24
Jehoiada made a treaty * the 2Ki 11:17
He also made a contract * the 2Ki 11:17
of Israel * Hamath and the Dead 2Ki 14:25
(it had stood * the Temple entrance 2Ki 16:14
* the palace and the Temple. 2Ki 16:18
a gate that lay * the double walls 2Ki 25:4,5
there had been many wars * them. 1Ch 18:10
the Lord standing * heaven and 1Ch 21:16
valley * Succoth and Zeredah. 2Ch 4:17,18
And in the Ark is the Covenant * 2Ch 6:11
There were continual wars * 2Ch 12:15
Early in his reign war broke out * 2Ch 13:1
was * your father and my father. 2Ch 16:3
back and forth * Tobiah and the Neh 6:17
Don't I know the difference * Job 6:30
there is no umpire * us, no middle Job 9:32,33
someone to stand * you and God and Job 33:6
* them, and nothing can penetrate. Job 41:15-17
you and knowing all is well * us. Ps 17:15
girls playing the timbrels in *. Ps 68:25
into the breach * the people and Ps 106:23
disputes * powerful opponents. Pro 18:18
The growth of love * a man and a Pro 30:18,19
of myrrh lying * my breasts." Sol 1:13
Then, at last, the jealousy * Is 11:13
back and forth * their lands, and Is 19:23
for fixing walls. * the city walls, Is 22:9,10,11
the sea, * the roaring waves. Is 51:15
There is word play here * shaqedh Jer 1:12f
There is a difference * chaff and Jer 23:28
when you walked * its halves to Jer 34:18,19
through the gate * the two walls Jer 39:4
bury large rocks * the pavement Jer 43:9
out by the gate * the two walls Jer 52:7
And put an iron plate * you and Eze 4:3
there at the door, * the porch and Eze 8:16
and said: "Go in * the whirling Eze 10:2
clothing to go * the cherubim and Eze 10:6
burning coals from * the wheels, Eze 10:6
from the flames * the cherubim and Eze 10:7,8
day—as a symbol * them and me, to Eze 20:12
of the contract * us to help you Eze 20:20
the difference * right and wrong, Eze 22:26
will surely judge * these fat Eze 34:20
of 8¾ feet along the wall * them. Eze 40:7-12
in front of (or *) the guardrooms, Eze 40:7-12f
The distance * the two Eze 40:23
And the distance * the Eze 40:27
A 17½-foot walk ran * the Eze 42:4
the inner court, * the Temple and Eze 42:9,10
There was a walk * the two wings Eze 42:11
Literally, "* the holy and the Eze 42:16-20f
wall *, and worshiped their idols. Eze 43:8
the difference * what is holy and Eze 44:23
Literally, "* what is ritually Eze 44:23f
are on the border * Damascus and Eze 47:16
on the border * Damascus to the Eze 48:1
This land, lying * the sections Eze 48:21,22

(BETWEEN Con't)
It held three ribs * its teeth, Dan 7:5
very large horn * its eyes, rushed Dan 8:5
will be formed * the king of Syria Dan 11:6
Seleucid wars * Egypt and Syria. Dan 11:6f
treaty of peace * their two lands. Dan 11:6f
He will halt * Jerusalem and the Dan 11:45
will make a treaty * you and the Hos 1:18
of God, will stand * the people and Joe 2:17
walk together with your sins * us? Amo 3:3
no distinction * the city Jon 3:3f
Justice is twisted * them. Mic 7:3
of Semites living * Babylon and the Hab 1:6f
coming from * what looked like two Zec 6:1
with perfect harmony * the two!' Zec 6:13
* Judah and Israel was broken. Zec 11:14
see the difference * God's Mal 3:18
good men and bad, * those who serve Mal 3:18
* the altar and the sanctuary. Mt 23:35
the new agreement * God and man. Mk 14:24
* the altar and the sanctuary. Lk 11:51
to divide his wealth * his sons. Lk 15:12
reached the border * Galilee and Lk 17:11
you something. * now and tomorrow Lk 22:34
on either side, with Jesus * them. Jn 19:18
* God and the people of Abraham. Act 7:8
mediator * the people of Israel and Act 7:38
double-chained * two soldiers with Act 12:6
He made no distinction * them Act 15:9
* the island and the mainland, Act 27:4
they could get * the rocks and be Act 27:39
You Jews think all is well * Rom 2:17
What a contrast * Adam and Christ Rom 5:14
And what a difference * man's Rom 5:15
all is well * themselves and God. Rom 11:9
the new agreement * God and you 1Co 11:25
nothing is written * the lines! 2Co 1:13,14
Any coldness still * us is not 2Co 6:12
And what harmony can there be * 2Co 6:15
And what union can there be * 2Co 6:16
I am sure all is well * us again. 2Co 7:16
He has made peace * us Jews and Eph 2:14
angry resentment * us, caused by Eph 2:15
the difference * right and wrong, Php 1:10
himself man, is * them to bring 1Ti 2:5
the difference * right and wrong. Heb 5:12,13
NOW IN THAT first agreement * God Heb 9:1
of the agreement * you and God, the Heb 9:20
agreement * God and you, signed Heb 13:20,21
the difference * true and false. 1Jn 2:21

BEVY
a second * of beautiful girls. Est 2:19

BEWAIL
one will be left to * your fate. Eze 7:10,11

BEWAILING
And so she did, * her fate with Ju 11:38

BEWARE
may not pass, and tell them, '*! Ex 19:12
the priests. But * that you do not Num 18:32
"But *! Deu 4:15
of the river. * lest you break the Deu 4:23
hold no more, then * lest you Deu 6:10,11,12
be careful! * that in your plenty Deu 8:11
land of Egypt. * that you don't Deu 8:15
"But * that your hearts do not Deu 11:16
them as much as they need. *! Deu 15:9
Let those who hate me *. Ps 118:7
* of your neighbor! Jer 9:4
Beware of your neighbor! * of Jer 9:4
of Philistia? *, for I will strike Joe 3:4
"* of false teachers who come Mt 7:15
and harmless as doves. But *! Mt 10:17
Jesus warned them; "* of the Mt 16:6
But again I say, '* of the yeast Mt 16:11
"* that you don't look down upon Mt 18:10
very solemnly, "* of the yeast of Mk 8:15
"* of the teachers of religion! Mk 12:38
anything else, * of these Pharisees Lk 12:1
to decide such things as that? *! Lk 12:15
and said, "* of these experts in Lk 20:46
"And now *! Act 20:28
out! * of ruining each other. Gal 5:15
* then of your own hearts, dear Heb 3:12
against Christ. * of being like 2Jn 1:8

BEWILDER
the Lord, "I will * the armies Zec 12:4

BEWILDERED
and *, too frightened to talk. Mk 16:8
Dear friends, don't be * or 1Pe 4:12

BEWILDERMENT
land with helpless *—from the king Jer 13:13

BEWITCHING
* people everywhere. Nah 3:4

BEYOND
on and camped * the Tower of Eder. Gen 35:21
of Brambles"), * the Jordan River, Gen 50:10
It was terrible * description. Ex 9:24
we have passed * your borders. Num 21:22
They are * numbering. Num 23:7-10
I could not go * the words of Num 24:13
Land—the good land * the Jordan Deu 3:23,24,25
* your strength and reach; Deu 30:11
nor are they * the ocean, so far Deu 30:13
to * the tableland near Medeba. Jos 13:16
the fields * the city and the Jos 21:9-16
when they lived * the Euphrates Jos 24:14
of your ancestors * the Euphrates Jos 24:15
last they arrived * the boundary of Ju 11:18
battle continued out * Beth-aven. 1Sa 14:23
and Jonathan shot an arrow * him. 1Sa 20:36
of the valley and * the Jordan 1Sa 31:7
Such generosity is far * any 2Sa 7:19
have insulted him * the possibility 2Sa 16:21
at once into the wilderness *; 2Sa 17:16
The moment you go * Kidron Brook, 1Ki 2:36,37
and scatter them * the Euphrates 1Ki 14:15
from * the Salt Sea, from Syria. 2Ch 20:2
of your empire * the Euphrates, for Ez 4:16
the entire land * the Euphrates Ez 4:20
next to them, and * them was the Neh 3:2
of wall, and * him were Meshullam Neh 3:4
on the wall. * him was Hananiah, a Neh 3:8
The priests repaired the wall * Neh 3:28
his own house, and * him was Neh 3:29
inner court just * the royal hall Est 5:1
Your faithfulness reaches * the Ps 36:5
all gods, is awesome * words; Ps 47:2
The reference seems to look * Ps 72:6f
For the Lord is great * Ps 96:4
* measure, high as the heavens. Ps 108:4
in him are blessed * expression. Ps 112:1
His greatness is * discovery! Ps 145:3
broken * hope of healing. Pro 6:15
not to spread * their boundaries. Pro 8:27,28,29
They are proud * description, Pro 30:13,14
AH, LAND * the upper reaches of Is 18:1
Literally, "land * the rivers of Is 18:1f
before me, O lands * the sea. Is 41:1
The lands * the sea watch in fear Is 41:5
even distant lands * the seas have Is 42:4
live in distant lands * the sea! Is 42:10
did awesome things * our highest Is 64:3
and to the lands * the sea that Is 66:19
My grief is * healing; Jer 8:18
on the garbage dump * the gate! Jer 22:19
* the guardrooms was a 10½-foot Eze 40:7-12
3½-foot columns. * this hall, at Eze 40:7-12
inches * the altar on all sides. Eze 43:13
He reveals profound mysteries * Dan 2:22
He went far * God's command to Hos 1:4,5f
to live * the reach of danger. Hab 2:9
Those who live far * the rivers Zep 3:10
them far * my intentions. Zec 1:15
power goes far * our borders!" Mal 1:5
the countryside * the Jordan River, Mt 4:15,16
spread far * the borders of Galilee Mt 4:24
Idumea, from * the Jordan River, Mk 3:7,8
was known for wisdom * his years; Lk 2:40
you will know it * all doubt. Lk 17:24
them, and went * the Jordan River Jn 10:40
verse—that goes * the limits of Jn 18:34f
captivity far away * Babylon.' Act 7:43
thoughts grew far * those of my 1Co 13:11
Best of all, they went * our 2Co 8:5
real, that it goes * mere words. 2Co 8:8
that are far * you, where no one 2Co 10:16
that they are * a man's power to 2Co 12:4
of—infinitely * our highest Eph 3:20
everywhere, far * your boundaries, 1Th 1:8
So let us go out to him * the Heb 13:13
* the reach of change and decay. 1Pe 1:4
For if you wander * the teaching 2Jn 1:9
seemed wounded * recovery—but the Rev 13:3

BEZAI
From the subclan of *, 323; Ez 2:3-35
From the subclan of *, 324; Neh 7:8-38
Hashum, *, Hariph, Neh 10:14-27

BEZALEL
He was the grandfather of * Ex 17:10f
I have appointed * (son of Uri, and Ex 31:1
appointed * (the son of Uri and Ex 35:30,31
are to assist * and Oholiab in Ex 36:1
So Moses told * and Oholiab and Ex 36:1
six feet wide). * coupled five of Ex 36:16
NEXT * MADE the Ark. Ex 37:1
Aaron the priest. * (son of Uri Ex 38:22
linen thread. * beat gold into Ex 39:3
Uri, and Uri's son was *. 1Ch 2:20
The bronze altar made by * (son 2Ch 1:5,6
Mattaniah, *, Binnui, Manasseh. Ez 10:30

BEZEK
of the enemy were slain at *. Ju 1:4,5,6
He counted them in * and found 1Sa 11:8

BEZER
These cities were *, on the Deu 4:43
They were *, in the wilderness of Jos 20:8
*, Jahaz, Kedemoth, and Mepha-ath. Jos 21:36,37
Reuben gave them * (a desert town), 1Ch 6:78,79
Imrah, *, Hod, Shamma, Shilshah, 1Ch 7:36,37

BIBLE
and to become a * teacher, teaching Ez 7:10
and in their home * classes, they Act 5:42
a wonderful * teacher and preacher, Act 18:24
the * teaches what it doesn't. 2Co 4:2
and must be a good * teacher. 1Ti 3:2
The whole * 2Ti 3:16
They won't listen to what the * 2Ti 4:4

BICHRI
was Sheba (son of *, a Benjaminite) 2Sa 20:1
his own clan of * at the city of 2Sa 20:14

BID
Literally, "* them farewell at Lk 9:61f

BIDDING
And he will come and do my *. Is 46:11

BIDKAR
Jehu said to *, his assistant, 2Ki 9:25

BIER
accompanied the * to the cemetery. 2Sa 3:31

BIG
celebrate with Jacob at a * party. Gen 29:22
Take them home and prepare a * Gen 43:16
the * toes of their right feet; Ex 29:19,20
upon the * toe of his right foot. Lev 8:23
the * toes of their right feet. Lev 8:24
upon the * toe of his right foot. Lev 14:14
right hand and the * toe of his Lev 14:17
on the * toe of his right foot. Lev 14:25
hand, and upon the * toe of his Lev 14:28
and cut off his thumbs and * toes. Ju 1:4,5,6
"Now where is that * mouth of Ju 9:38
that Nabal had thrown a * party. 1Sa 25:36
he threw another * party for all Est 2:18
problems far too * for me to solve Ps 40:12
They raise * families there, and Ps 107:38
than the mayors of ten * cities! Ecc 7:19
won't take a * crew or a lot of Eze 17:9
Though they do a * business as Hos 4:10
"I want to see whether it is * Zec 2:2
the * dinner she was preparing. Lk 10:40
But about that time, a * blowup Act 19:23
Don't try to act *. Rom 12:16
have * names or power or wealth. 1Co 1:26
proud men are just * talkers or 1Co 4:19
body were just one * ear, how could 1Co 12:17
"He sounds *, but it's all 2Co 10:10
other, and acting *, and saying 2Co 12:20
should be like one * happy family, 1Pe 3:8

BIGGER
"For our army is * than 2Ki 6:16
down my barns and build * ones! Lk 12:18
the use of worrying over * things? Lk 12:26

BIGGEST
She was their * customer for Rev 18:12

BIGTHA
Biztha, Harbona, *, Abagtha, Est 1:10

BIGTHAN
king's eunuchs, * and Teresh—who Est 2:21

BIGTHANA
the plot of * and Teresh, two of Est 6:1

BIGVAI
Mordecai, Bilshan, Mispar, *, Ez 2:2
From the subclan of *, 2,056; Ez 2:3-35
From the clan of *—Uthai, Zaccur, Ez 8:2-14
Mordecai, Bilshan, Mispereth; *, Neh 7:7
From the subclan of *, 2,067; Neh 7:8-38
Adonijah, *, Adin, Neh 10:14-27

BILDAD
the Temanite, * the Shuhite, and Job 2:11
* THE SHUHITE replies to Job: Job 8:1
THE FURTHER REPLY of * the Job 18:1
THE FURTHER REPLY of * the Job 25:1
So Eliphaz the Temanite, and * Job 42:9

BILE-AM
Aner, *. 1Ch 6:70

BILGAH
Fifteenth, the group led by *; 1Ch 24:7-18
Ma-adiah, *, Shemaiah, Neh 12:1
Shammu-a, leader of the * clan; Neh 12:12-21

BILGAI
Mija-min, Ma-aziah, *, Neh 10:1

BILHAH
a servant girl, *, to be her maid. Gen 29:29
my servant-girl *, and her children Gen 30:3
So she gave him * to be his Gen 30:4
Then *, Rachel's servant-girl, Gen 30:7
Reuben slept with *, his father's Gen 35:22
The sons of *, Rachel's Gen 35:25
his father's wives * and Zilpah, Gen 37:2
of Jacob and *, the slave-girl Gen 46:23,24,25
Hazar-shual, *, Ezem, Tolad, 1Ch 4:29
*) were: 1Ch 7:13

BILHAN
The children of Ezer:*, Zaavan, Gen 36:27
The sons of Ezer: *, Zaavan, and 1Ch 1:42
son of Jedia-el was * 1Ch 7:10
The sons of * were: 1Ch 7:10

BILL
* the child was named 'Bill'!" Gen 30:6f
bill the child was named '*!" Gen 30:6f
'If his * runs higher than that,' Lk 10:35

BILLBOARD
to me, "Write my answer on a *, Hab 2:2

BILLION
Solomon received a * dollars 2Ch 9:13,14

BILLOWED
the smoke * into the sky as from Ex 19:18
flaming sulphur * from their Rev 9:17,18

BILLOWING
and the smoke * from the mountain, Ex 20:18
of smoke * up from their burning. Is 9:18
clouds are * dust beneath his Nah 1:3

BILLOWS
All your waves and * have gone Ps 42:7

BILLS
the innkeeper two twenty-dollar * Lk 10:35
he has enough money to pay the *? Lk 14:28
for enough money to pay your *. 1Th 4:12

BILLY
nanny goats,20 * goats,200 Gen 32:13,14,15
or ewe, * goat or nanny goat. Lev 3:6
as his sacrifice a * goat without Lev 4:23
from kids and rams from * goats! Eze 34:17

BILSHAN
Mordecai, *, Mispar, Bigvai, Ez 2:2
Mordecai, *, Mispereth; Neh 7:7

BIMHAL
Pasach, *, Ashvath. 1Ch 7:33

BIND
will no longer * us in any way." Jos 2:20
But that promise doesn't * you! 1Ki 2:9
turn, and my garments * about me. Job 30:18
upon the nations. * their kings Ps 149:8
Literally, "* them upon your Pro 7:3f
the chains that * his people and Is 9:4
he will heal us and * our wounds. Jer 14:19
to help you or to * up your wound Jer 30:13
men of his army to * Shadrach, Dan 3:20
and I will * you to me forever Hos 1:19
He has wounded—he will * us up. Hos 6:1
this—whatever you * on earth is Mt 18:18
to his aides, '* him hand and foot Mt 22:13

BINDER
by the reaper, despised by the *. Ps 129:6,7

BINDING
"We were out in the field * Gen 37:7
the agreement with a * oath. Jos 9:14,15
to a permanent and * contract Jos 24:25
He heals the brokenhearted, * up Ps 147:3
kingdom without first * Satan. Mt 12:29
'By the gold in the Temple' is *! Mt 23:16
'By the gifts on the altar' is *! Mt 23:18
them to death, * and delivering Act 22:4

BINDS
For though he wounds, he * and Job 5:18
marries, the law * her to her Rom 7:2

BINE-A
Moza was the father of *, whose 1Ch 8:37
Moza was the father of *, 1Ch 9:43

BINGE
was one constant * of doing evil. 2Ch 21:6

BINNUI
of *)—all of whom were Levites. Ez 8:33
Mattaniah, Bezalel, *, Manasseh. Ez 10:30
Jaasu, Bani, *, Shime-i, Shelemiah, Ez 10:34-42
Next was * (son of Henadad), who Neh 3:24
From the subclan of *, 648; Neh 7:8-38
Jeshua (son of Azaniah), * Neh 10:9-13
Jeshua, *, Kadmi-el, Sherebiah, Neh 12:8

BIOGRAPHIES
Detailed * of King David have 1Ch 29:29
Several * of Christ have already Lk 1:1,2

BIOGRAPHY
The rest of Asa's *—his conquests 1Ki 15:23
The rest of Baasha's *—his deeds 1Ki 16:4-7
the rest of his * is recorded in 2Ki 14:18
The rest of Jeroboam's *—all that 2Ki 14:28
The rest of Amon's * is recorded 2Ki 21:25
The rest of the * of Josiah is 2Ki 23:28
The rest of Solomon's * is 2Ch 9:29
The complete * of Rehoboam is 2Ch 12:15
His complete * and speeches are 2Ch 13:22
The rest of the * of Asa is 2Ch 16:11
The complete * of King Amaziah 2Ch 25:26

BIRD
sort of fish and every kind of *. Gen 1:21,22
kind of animal and *, and brought Gen 2:19,20
Bring in a pair of each kind of * Gen 6:19,20
of every kind of *. Gen 7:3
evening, the * returned to him with Gen 8:11
"If anyone wishes to use a * as Lev 1:14
A priest will take the * to the Lev 1:15,16,17
whichever * is handed to him first, Lev 5:8
He shall offer the second * as a Lev 5:10
The other *, still living, shall Lev 14:6
living * fly into the open field. Lev 14:7
well as the living *, into the Lev 14:51,52
the blood of the * that was killed Lev 14:51,52
Then he shall let the live * fly Lev 14:53
kills an animal or * of a kind Lev 17:13
for the life of every * and animal Lev 17:14
any animal or * which I have Lev 20:25
woman, animal, *, a small animal Deu 4:16,17
"You may eat any * except the Deu 14:11-18
treasures that no * of prey can Job 28:7
pet of him like a *, or give him to Job 41:5
Literally, "Flee as a *." Ps 11:1f
as a * from a hunter's snare. Ps 124:7
When a * sees a trap being set, Pro 1:17
a hunter, or a * from the net. Pro 6:5
He was as a * flying into a Pro 7:23
though they had the wings of a *! Pro 23:4,5
a * that wanders from its nest. Pro 27:8
better life. A * in the hand is Ecc 6:9
a net, or a * caught in a snare. Ecc 9:12
for a little * will tell them Ecc 10:20
I will call that swift * of prey Is 46:11
Like a * that fills her nest with Jer 17:11
chased me as though I were a *. Lam 3:52
will shelter every kind of *. Eze 17:22,23
eat meat from any * or animal that Eze 44:31
her down like a * from the sky; Hos 7:12
flies away like a *, for your Hos 9:11
kind of animal or * that lives and Jas 3:7
"of every foul and hateful *." Rev 18:2f

BIRD'S
"If a * nest is lying on the Deu 22:6

BIRDS
be filled with * of every kind." Gen 1:20
them, and to the * he said, "Let Gen 1:21,22
you are masters of the fish and * Gen 1:28
animals and * for their food." Gen 1:30
too, and the reptiles and the *. Gen 6:7
and all the animals and * and Gen 7:4
were not, and the * and reptiles. Gen 7:8,9
reptiles and * of every sort. Gen 7:14,15
the earth perished—*, domestic and Gen 7:21
animals alike, and reptiles and *. Gen 7:23
Release all the animals, *, and Gen 8:17
reptiles, and *—all left the ark in Gen 8:18,19
animals and * God had designated Gen 8:20
"All wild animals and * and fish Gen 9:2,3
with you—all these * and cattle and Gen 9:9,10,11
halves, but not to divide the *. Gen 15:10
but the * came and ate them." Gen 40:17
on a pole, and the * will come and Gen 40:18,19
resembling animals, *, or fish. Ex 20:4
one of the * shall be his sin Lev 5:7
"Never eat blood, whether of * Lev 7:26,27
"Among the *, these are the ones Lev 11:13-19
animals, *, and whatever swims in Lev 11:46
require two living * of a kind Lev 14:4
order one of the * killed in an Lev 14:5
using two *, cedar wood, scarlet Lev 14:49
He shall kill one of the * over Lev 14:50
between the * and animals I have Lev 20:25
offer one of the * for a sin Num 6:11
whether of *, animals, or fish. Deu 5:8
be food to the * and wild animals, Deu 28:26
your flesh to the * and wild 1Sa 17:44
of your men to the * and wild 1Sa 17:46
in animals, *, snakes, fish, and 1Ki 4:33
in the field shall be eaten by *.' 1Ki 14:11
fields will be eaten by the *." 1Ki 16:4-7
ask the *—they will tell you; Job 12:7,8,9
even the sharp-eyed * in the sky Job 28:21
wiser than the animals and *?' Job 35:11
animals too, the * and fish, and Ps 8:8
And all the * upon the mountains! Ps 50:10,11
He rained down * as thick as Ps 78:27
He caused the * to fall to the Ps 78:28
exposed—food for * and animals. Ps 79:2
thirst, and the * nest beside the Ps 104:12
There the * make their nests, Ps 104:17
the snakes and *, the kings and Ps 148:10
dawn with the first note of the *; Ecc 12:4
time of the singing of * has come. Sol 2:12
the Arnon River like homeless *. Is 16:2
* and wild animals to eat; Is 18:6
over Jerusalem as * hover round Is 31:4,5
and the * of the heavens had fled. Jer 4:25
be food for the * and animals, and Jer 7:33
gone the * and wild animals. Jer 9:10
The wild animals and * have moved Jer 12:4
my people free like * from cages. Eze 13:20
as food to the wild animals and *. Eze 29:5
at its roots. The * nested in its Eze 31:6
lying there. The * will pluck off Eze 31:13
And all the * of the heavens will Eze 32:4
dust, call all the * and animals Eze 39:17
even animals and * are under your Dan 2:38
its shade and * sheltered in its Dan 4:12
under it and the * from its Dan 4:14
branches full of *— that tree, Dan 4:21
and his nails were like *' claws. Dan 4:33
those of *, and it had four heads! Dan 7:6
the wild animals, *, and snakes, Hos 1:18
the animals, the *, and even the Hos 4:3
Like a flock of *, they will Hos 11:11
Even the * of the air and the Zep 1:3
Look at the *! Mt 6:26
* have nests, but I, the Messiah, Mt 8:20
a path, and the * came and ate it. Mt 13:4
* can come and find shelter." Mt 13:31,32
on a path, and the * came and Mk 4:4
branches where * can build their Mk 4:31,32
and the * came and ate it as it Lk 8:5
Foxes have dens to live in, and * Lk 9:58
more valuable to him than any *! Lk 12:24
and the * live among its branches. Lk 13:19
* [forbidden to the Jews for food Act 10:12
and * [which we are not to eat Act 11:6
* and animals and snakes and puny Rom 1:23
Humans, animals, fish, and * are 1Co 15:39
shouting loudly to the *, "Come! Rev 19:17
horse, and all the * of heaven were Rev 19:21

BIRSHA
*, king of Gomorrah, Gen 14:2

BIRTH
conceived and gave * to a son, Cain Gen 4:1
Later on Eve gave * to another Gen 4:25
old at the * of his son Terah. Gen 11:24,25
on the eighth day after *. Gen 17:12
very old, she gave * to my master's Gen 24:36
and gave * to her fifth son. Gen 30:17
Afterwards she gave * to a Gen 30:21
pregnant and gave * to a son. Gen 30:23,24
Soon after the * of Joseph to Gen 30:25
and return to the land of your *.' Gen 31:13
He lived to see the * of his son Gen 50:23
Moses said at his *, "The God of Ex 18:4
body is half rotted away at *." Num 12:12
it was God who had given them *. Deu 32:18
of God from the time of his *; Ju 13:5
* until the day of his death!" Ju 13:7
Nazirite to God since before my *. Ju 16:16,17
and she gave * to his son. 2Sa 11:27
* to a son and named him Solomon. 2Sa 12:24
* to Ashhur, the father of Tekoa. 1Ch 2:24
a hard time at his * (Jabez means 1Ch 4:9
and cursed the day of his *. Job 3:1
"Let the day of my * be Job 3:2,3
"Why didn't I die at *? Job 3:11
For if only I had died at *, Job 3:13
Why didn't you let me die at *? Job 10:18
give * only to wickedness." Job 15:35
KNOW how mountain goats give *? Job 39:1
Have you ever seen them giving * Job 39:1
themselves to give * to their Job 39:2,3
to * his treachery and lies; Ps 7:14
I have depended upon you since *; Ps 22:9,10,11
and as those who die at *, who Ps 58:8
been with me from * and have helped Ps 71:6
For though his * would then be Ecc 6:4
your mother gave * to you in her Sol 8:5
of course, was not a virgin *. Is 7:14f
write on it the * announcement of Is 8:1
of a woman giving * to a child. Is 21:3
We suffered as a woman giving *, Is 26:17
For when they see the surging * Is 29:23
*, and the child does not come. Is 37:3
The Lord called me before my *. Is 49:1
even before the * pains come. Is 66:7,8
Shall I bring to the point of * Is 66:9
woman giving * to her first child; Jer 4:31
oh, that I had died at *. Jer 15:10
he did not kill me at my *! Jer 20:17
Do men give *? Jer 30:6
ones, those ready to give *. Jer 31:8
if not the same as, the new *. Jer 31:33f
women in the pains of giving *. Jer 48:41
flocks and herds gave * to young. Eze 31:6
any more. Your * rate will rise and Eze 36:14
and this time gave * to a son. Hos 1:8
will die at *, or perish in the Hos 9:11
that don't give *, for breasts that Hos 9:14
And if she gives *, I will slay Hos 9:16
New * is offered him, but he is Hos 13:13
concerning the * of Jesus Christ: Mt 1:18
She shall give * to a Son, and he Mt 1:23
*, and many will rejoice with you. Lk 1:14
Spirit, even from before his *! Lk 1:15
and she gave * to her first Lk 2:7
of Moses after the * of a child, Lk 2:22
Or, "Physical * is not enough. Jn 3:5f
observed during every human *. Jn 3:5f
born only once, with physical * Jn 6:63
along, he saw a man blind from *. Jn 9:1
a man lame from * carried along the Act 3:2
from *, so he had never walked. Act 14:8
"But I am a citizen by *!" Act 22:28
you are a Jew by *, you have long Gal 2:14
You and I are Jews by *, not Gal 2:15
the * of the slave-wife's baby. Gal 4:23
as a woman's * pains begin when her 1Th 5:3
were, no record of his * or death. Heb 7:3f
was about to give * to her child, Rev 12:4
She gave * to a boy who was to Rev 12:5
who had given * to the child. Rev 12:13

BIRTHDAY
Pharaoh's * came three days Gen 40:20
* shall give this offering. Ex 30:14
Job's sons had a *, he invited his Job 1:4
When these * parties ended—and Job 1:5
On the king's *, the princes get Hos 7:5
But at a * party for Herod, Mt 14:6
It was Herod's * and he gave a Mk 6:21
his fortieth *, it came into his Act 7:23

BIRTHPLACE
you will be the * of my King who is Mic 5:2
BIRTHRIGHT
right, trade me your * for it!" Gen 25:31
starvation, what good is his *?" Gen 25:32
his * to be of no value." Gen 25:34f
For he took my *, and now he has Gen 27:36
wives, his * was given to his half 1Ch 5:1
Although Joseph received the *, 1Ch 5:2
BIRTHS
the order of their *, of the Gen 25:12-15
are named in the order of their *. Ex 28:10
BIRZAITH
Heber, Malchi-el (the father of * 1Ch 7:31
BISHLAM
of Ar-ta-xerxes. *, Mithredath, and Ez 4:7
BIT
gave it quite a * of thought and Gen 37:11
wasn't fooling one * when he said, Gen 43:3,4,5
and they ate every * of Ex 10:15
from them the least little *. Jos 23:6
have eaten this little * of honey. 1Sa 14:29
"It was only a little * on the 1Sa 14:43
There isn't one * of truth to the Neh 6:8
Not one * longer may he live. Job 14:5
* in its mouth to keep it in line! Ps 32:9
no one cares a * what happens to Ps 142:4
shame—he won't help one little *! Is 30:5
in your nose and a * in your mouth Is 37:29
Keep just a * of the hair and Eze 5:3
until every * of bread is gone. Eze 5:16
my remarks with a * of history Act 13:16
In the end they will get every * 2Co 11:15
we change his message not one * 1Th 2:4
means of a small * in his mouth. Jas 3:3
struck and * with fatal wounds. Rev 9:19
BITCH
"You son of a *!" 1Sa 20:30
BITE
and a * to eat to strengthen you. Gen 18:5
Give me a * of that red stuff Gen 25:30
* we eat and everything we drink; Deu 2:28
won't get a single * of the meat. Deu 28:31
begged him to take a * of supper. 2Sa 3:35,36
"Bring me a * of bread, too." 1Ki 17:11
But after the men had eaten a * 2Ki 4:40
they shall * you and you will die. Jer 8:17
after them to * and destroy them. Amo 9:3
BITES
in the path that * the horses' Gen 49:17
wept, "Oh, for a few * of meat! Num 11:4,5
For in the end it * like a Pro 23:32
Literally, "If the serpent * Ecc 10:11f
did, and died from snake *. 1Co 10:9
BITHI-AH
Mered married *, an Egyptian 1Ch 4:17
BITHYNIA
the province of *, but again the Act 16:7
Galatia, Cappadocia, Ausia, and *. 1Pe 1:1
BITS
he smashed them to * and 2Ki 23:12
iron and clay, smashing them to *. Dan 2:34
it must be smashed to *. Hos 8:6
BITTEN
and many of them were * and died. Num 21:6
anyone who is * shall live if he Num 21:8
who had been * looked at the bronze Num 21:9
Demolish an old wall—and be * by Ecc 10:8,9
BITTER
But Isaac and Rebekah were * Gen 26:35
to sob with deep and * sobs. Gen 27:34
Canaan—the famine is very * there. Gen 47:4
slavery more * still, forcing them Ex 1:13,14
with unleavened bread and * herbs. Ex 12:8
and there was * crying throughout Ex 12:30
because it was * (that is why the Ex 15:23
was called Marah, meaning "*"). Ex 15:23
of * water that brings a curse. Num 5:18
* water that causes the curse. Num 5:19
wash them off into the * water. Num 5:23
* within her [if she is guilty Num 5:24
water will become * within her, and Num 5:27
with unleavened bread and * herbs. Num 9:11
When those * days have come upon Deu 4:30
will grow * and poisonous fruit. Deu 29:18
are * with poison; Deu 32:32
Mara means "*") "for Almighty Ru 1:20
Almighty God has dealt me * blows. Ru 1:20
You will shed * tears because of 1Sa 8:18
for in their * grief for their 1Sa 30:6
For the Lord saw the * plight of 2Ki 14:26
crying with a loud and * wail. Est 4:1
but fills me with * sorrows. Job 9:18
"You write * things against me Job 13:26
"My complaint today is still a * Job 23:2
they aim their * words like Ps 64:3
That is why you must eat the * Pro 1:31
But afterwards only a * Pro 5:4
in the end she is * as wormwood." Pro 5:4f
father and a * blow to his mother. Pro 17:25
A * woman when she finally Pro 30:21,22,23
and grief, and restless, * nights. Ecc 2:20-23
A prostitute is more * than Ecc 7:26
* is sweet and sweet is bitter. Is 5:20
bitter is sweet and sweet is *. Is 5:20
strong drink turns * in the Is 24:9
weep in * disappointment, for Is 33:7
You will see what an evil, * Jer 2:19
it is a * dose of your own Jer 4:18
Ramah there is * weeping, Rachel Jer 31:15
son of dust, in your * anguish; Eze 21:6
* pill for the poor and oppressed. Amo 5:7
died; *, bitter will be that day. Amo 8:10
bitter, * will be that day. Amo 8:10
They laughed at him in * Mk 5:40
Are you able to drink from the * Mk 10:38
Wine drugged with * herbs was Mk 15:23
Otherwise he may become so * and 2Co 2:7
and not * against them, nor harsh. Col 3:19
he wept * tears of repentance. Heb 12:17
fresh water and then with * water? Jas 3:11
you are * and jealous and selfish; Jas 3:14
BITTEREST
sorrows, acquainted with * grief. Is 53:3
BITTERLY
Esau: (*) "No wonder they call Gen 27:36
and weeping * before the Lord. Ex 2:23
There too, the people spoke * Ex 16:2
'Curse them *,' he said, Ju 5:23
God until evening, weeping *. Ju 21:2
* as she prayed to the Lord. 1Sa 1:10
of Israel must hate him * by now. 1Sa 27:12
and weep * as for an only son. Jer 6:26
of Luhith, weeping *, while cries Jer 48:5
been dragged away. * she weeps. Lam 1:4
shore, weeping * and casting dust Eze 27:30
But Ephraim has * provoked the Hos 12:14
a nation that will * oppress you Amo 6:14
Micah * declaims each town, Mic 1:11f
Micah * declaims each town, Mic 1:11f
Micah * declaims each town, Mic 1:11f
day when strong men will weep *. Zep 1:14
son, and grieve * for him as for an Zec 12:10
And he went away, crying *. Mt 26:75
the Law complained * to Jesus' Lk 5:30
out of the courtyard, crying *. Lk 22:62
followers so * in Jerusalem?" Act 9:21
* day and night because of you. Rom 9:1
BITTERNESS
in misery and *, who long for Job 3:20,21
to speak out of the * of my soul. Job 7:11
I will speak in my sorrow and *. Job 10:1
can know his own * or joy—no one Pro 14:10
has fled because of my soul's *. Is 38:15
me to undergo this *, for you have Is 38:17
* and give them poison to drink. Jer 9:15
* and give them poison to drink. Jer 23:15
these women will taunt you with *. Jer 38:21,22
He has filled me with *, and Lam 3:15
Oh, remember the * and suffering Lam 3:19
I went in * and anger, Eze 3:14,15
with * of heart and deep mourning. Eze 27:31
days, but only * awaits them as the Mic 1:12
Literally, "the gall of *." Act 8:23f
fighting, lying, *, and gossip. Rom 1:29
mouths are full of cursing and *. Rom 3:14
Watch out that no * takes root Heb 12:15
The star was called "*" Rev 8:11
BITUMEN
and collected * to use as mortar. Gen 11:3,4
BIZIOTHIAH
Beer-sheba, *, Baalah, Iim, Ezem, Jos 15:21-32
BIZTHA
aides—Mehuman, *, Harbona, Bigtha, Est 1:10
BLABBERMOUTH
so being a fool makes you a *. Ecc 5:1
BLACK
or spotted, and all the * sheep. Gen 30:31,32
patches, and all of the * sheep. Gen 30:35,36
mate only with Jacob's * rams. Gen 30:39,40
and that there is * hair in it, Lev 13:31
has stopped and * hairs are found Lev 13:37
by * clouds and deep darkness. Deu 4:11
No Israeli may practice * magic, Deu 18:10
the sky was soon * with clouds, and 1Ki 18:45
He practiced * magic and used 2Ki 21:6
*, red, white, and yellow marble. Est 1:6
and may a * cloud overshadow it. Job 3:5
The * night is their morning; Job 24:17
Into the * rock, shadowed by Job 28:3,4
I am *, but not from sunburn. Job 30:28,29
My skin is * and peeling. Job 30:30
* is white and white is black; Is 5:20
black is white and white is *; Is 5:20
and sorrow and the heavens are *. Is 5:30
The heavens will be * above Is 13:10
Darkness as * as night shall Is 60:2
be draped with *, because of my Jer 4:28
but now their faces are as * as Lam 4:8
Our skin was * from famine. Lam 5:10
I clothed Lebanon in * and caused Eze 31:15
southeast of the * Sea and Eze 38:2,3f
of * clouds and thick darkness. Joe 2:2
the second by * ones, the third by Zec 6:2
The chariot pulled by the * Zec 6:6
can't turn one hair white or *. Mt 5:36
the sun shall turn * and the Act 2:20
(also called "The * Man"), Lucius Act 13:1
been practicing * magic confessed Act 19:18,19
And I saw a * horse, with its Rev 6:5
and the sun became dark like * Rev 6:12
BLACKENED
The land is * by that fire, by Is 9:19,20
BLACKMAIL
Perhaps the reference is to *, or Pro 5:9f
BLACKNESS
skin is filled with worms and *. Job 7:5
gloom, clouds, *, Trumpet calls Zep 1:15
BLACKSMITH
to take them to a Philistine *. 1Sa 13:20
BLACKSMITHS
There were no * at all in the 1Sa 13:19
*—the Lord gave me this vision. Jer 24:1
Then the Lord showed me four *. Zec 1:20
BLADDER
also the gall * and two kidneys, Ex 29:13
also the gall * and the two kidneys Ex 29:22
loin-fat on them, and the gall *. Lev 3:3,4,5
them, and the gall *, as a burnt Lev 3:9,10,11
loin-fat on them, and the gall *. Lev 3:15,16
them, and the gall *, and shall Lev 4:9
and the gall *—all shall be set Lev 7:4
organs, the gall *, the two kidneys Lev 8:25
kidneys, and gall * from this sin Lev 9:10
BLADDERS
organs—and the kidneys and gall *. Lev 9:19
BLADE
the *, and it pierced him through. 1Sa 31:3,4
there they search for every * of Job 39:8
be wise and sharpen the *. Ecc 10:10
BLADES
thorns choked out the tender *. Mt 13:7
BLAME
then let me bear the * forever. Gen 43:9
you, I shall bear the * forever.' Gen 44:32
"You can't * me for whatever Ju 15:3
"I accept all * in this matter, 1Sa 25:24
"You aren't to *," he told 2Ki 10:9,10
Would you * a leaf that is blown Job 13:25
and then * it on the Lord! Pro 19:3
and try to pass the * to him! Hos 4:4
* for this man's death on us!" Act 5:28
Well then, why does God * them Rom 9:19
with us and * it on the Lord. 2Co 6:3
this to scold or * you, for, as I 2Co 7:3
can speak a word of * against you. Php 2:15
BLAMED
for he was * for it by the prophet 2Ki 10:11f
I hope that they will not be * 2Ti 4:16
BLAMELESS
To the *. 2Sa 22:26
Anyone who leads a * life and is Ps 15:2
For the good man—the *, the Ps 37:37
I will try to walk a * path, but Ps 101:2
are *—you have done all you could. Eze 3:19
be kept strong and * until that day 1Th 5:23
must be men of * lives because Tit 1:7
for he is holy and *, unstained Heb 7:26
they are *. Rev 14:5
BLAMELESSLY
You must walk * before the Lord Deu 18:13
BLANCHED
His face * with fear, and such Dan 5:6
BLANKET
tent and she covered him with a *. Ju 4:18
But the next day Hazael took a * 2Ki 8:15
two under the same * gain warmth Ecc 4:11
are your sheet, worms your *! Is 14:11
She wrapped him in a * Lk 2:7
will find a baby wrapped in a *, Lk 2:12
BLANKETS
On top of these * is placed a Ex 26:14
covered it with *, with its head on 1Sa 19:13
but no matter how many * were 1Ki 1:1
and * the tops of the mountains. Job 36:30
the * are too narrow to cover you. Is 28:20
BLARE
the warriors shout and trumpets *. Amo 2:2
BLARING
with trumpets *. Num 31:6
trumpets * and horns sounding. 2Ch 15:14
a mighty shout, with trumpets *. Ps 47:5
BLASPHEME
"You shall not * God, nor curse Ex 22:28
* him, so your child shall die." 2Sa 12:14
They * your name and stand in Ps 139:20
continued to * and betray me when I Eze 20:27,28
BLASPHEMED
Literally, "* the Name." Lev 24:11f
Whom have you defied and *? 2Ki 19:22
arrogant nation has * your name. Ps 74:18
name is constantly *, day by day. Is 52:5
Or, "*." Act 13:45f

(BLASPHEMED Con't)
opposed him and *, hurling abuse at Act 18:6
All that time he * God's Name Rev 13:6

BLASPHEMES
who * the name of Jehovah. Lev 24:15,16

BLASPHEMIES
to speak great * against the Lord; Rev 13:5
written all over with * against Rev 17:3

BLASPHEMING
or a foreigner, is * Jehovah, and Num 15:30
* God, and he doesn't stop them. 1Sa 3:13
god there is, even * the God of Dan 11:36

BLASPHEMOUS
And written on each head were * Rev 13:1

BLASPHEMY
and * to your other sins." Job 34:37
of trouble and frustration and *; Is 37:3
your God heard the * of the king of Is 37:4
of the king of Assyria, and his *. Is 37:6
*! This man is saying Mt 9:3
"Even * against me Mt 12:31,32
his own clothing, shouting, "*! Mt 26:65,66
This is *! Mk 2:7
be forgiven, even * against me; Mk 3:28
against me; but * against the Holy Mk 3:29
You have heard his *. Mk 14:63,64
"This is *! Lk 5:21
and he replied, "Why is it *? Lk 5:22
for any good work, but for * Jn 10:33
do you call it * when the one Jn 10:34,35,36
spiritual death. * against the Holy 1Jn 5:17f

BLAST
At the * of your breath Ex 15:8
a ram's horn sounding one long *; Ex 19:13
long, loud * as from a ram's horn; Ex 19:16
As the trumpet * grew louder and Ex 19:19
the long, frightening trumpet *; Ex 20:18
one long, loud *, all the people Jos 6:5
long, loud trumpet *, Joshua yelled Jos 6:16
heard the trumpet *, they shouted Jos 6:20
By the * of his breath 2Sa 22:16
it was such a terrible * that the 1Ki 19:11
At the * of your breath the Ps 18:15
They whirl and sway beneath the * Ps 29:9
hear the joyful * of the trumpet, Ps 89:14,15
WITH THE voice of a trumpet *; Is 58:1
but in a roaring *—and he will Jer 4:11,12
O my soul, the * of the enemies' Jer 4:19
Let the * of the warning trumpet Joe 2:1
a mighty trumpet *, and they shall Mt 24:31
For there will be a trumpet * 1Co 15:52
an awesome trumpet *, and a voice Heb 12:19
like a trumpet *, saying, "I am A Rev 1:10
a mighty trumpet *, spoke to me and Rev 4:1
Everyone was burned by this * of Rev 16:9

BLASTS
"Different trumpet * will be Num 10:5,6,7
Warn with trumpet * in Gibeah and Hos 5:8
prepared to blow their mighty *. Rev 8:6

BLASTUS
made friends with *, the royal Act 12:20

BLAZE
and my anger shall * out against Ex 32:10
* against me like a roaring flame. Ps 118:12
Their hearts * like a furnace Hos 7:6

BLAZED
So fire * forth from the Lev 10:2
their torches * into the night. Ju 7:19,20
Then the anger of the Lord * out 1Ch 13:10
dazzling white and * with light. Lk 9:29

BLAZING
He will vindicate you with the * Ps 37:6
the * fire of thorns beneath it. Ps 58:9
wrath, your * anger, is now ended. Ps 85:3
For in my jealousy and * wrath, Eze 38:19
For he is like a * fire refining Mal 3:2
Now with * torches, lanterns, and Jn 18:3
whole lives into a * flame of Jas 3:6

BLEACH
he can * the dirtiest garments! Mal 3:2

BLEACHED
where cloth was *, near the conduit 2Ki 18:17
past the field where cloth is *. Is 36:2

BLEACHING
that leads down to the * field. Is 7:3

BLEAK
Let that night be * and joyless. Job 3:7

BLEAT
the sheep * in misery. Joe 1:18

BLEATING
"Then what was all the * of 1Sa 15:14

BLEEDING
again after her * at childbirth. Lev 12:7
*, so anger causes quarrels. Pro 30:33
claws, and left me * and desolate. Lam 3:11
with internal * came up behind him Mt 9:20
touched him, the * stopped and she Mk 5:29
had been slowly * for twelve years, Lk 8:43,44
edge of his robe, the * stopped. Lk 8:43,44

BLEMISH
be a ram without * taken to the Lev 5:17,18
bulls and seven rams without *. Eze 45:23
and one ram, all without any *. Eze 46:6
or any other *, being holy and Eph 5:27

BLEMISHES
must be a male, and without any *. Lev 1:10
sacrifice a young bull with no *, Eze 45:18

BLESS
"God * Shem, Gen 9:26,27
God * Japheth, Gen 9:26,27
I will * you and make your name Gen 12:2
I will * those who bless you and Gen 12:3
I will bless those who * you and Gen 12:3
Or, "The nations will * Gen 12:3f
And I will * her and give you a Gen 17:16
Yes, I will * her richly, and Gen 17:16
to God, "Yes, do * Ishmael!" Gen 17:18
all right, I will * him also, just Gen 17:20
from me, I will * you with Gen 22:17
be with you and * you, and I will Gen 26:3
with you and will * you, and will Gen 26:24
* you in the name of the Lord." Gen 26:29
enjoyed it he will * you before his Gen 27:8,9,10
will * me with all your heart!" Gen 27:19
it and * you with all my heart." Gen 27:25
and blessed are all who * you." Gen 27:27,28,29
Esau: "O my father, * me, bless Gen 27:34
Esau: "O my father, bless me, * Gen 27:34
O my father, * me too." Gen 27:38
God Almighty * you and give you Gen 28:2
not let you go until you * me." Gen 32:26
over to me and I will * them." Gen 48:9
my life, wonderfully * these boys. Gen 48:15
people of Israel * each other by Gen 48:20
the Almighty, * you with blessings Gen 49:25
"* the Lord," Jethro said, Ex 18:10
and God will * you: Be these Ex 18:19,20
and I will come and * you there. Ex 20:24
then I will * you with food and Ex 23:25
The answer is, 'I will * you Lev 25:21,22
'May the Lord * and protect you; Num 6:24,25,26
and I myself will personally * Num 6:27
on those whom you *, and I also Num 22:5,6
I have received a command to * Num 23:18-24
them, at least don't * them!" Num 23:25
Jehovah planned to * Israel, so he Num 24:1
times more, and * you as he Deu 1:11
and chose to * their descendants Deu 4:37
And he will love you and * you Deu 7:13
When you have eaten your fill, * Deu 8:10
* his name, just as is done today. Deu 10:8
and then Jehovah your God will * Deu 14:29
Lord will greatly * you in the land Deu 15:4,5
He will * you as he has Deu 15:6
The Lord will * you for it. Deu 22:7
your God won't * you when you Deu 23:20
it through the night and * you; Deu 24:12,13
then the Lord your God will * and Deu 24:19
home in heaven and * your people Deu 26:15
The Lord will * you with good Deu 28:8
He will * everything you do; Deu 28:12
do you good and * you even more Deu 30:5
Lord your God will * you and the Deu 30:16
Instead I made him * you; Jos 24:10
Yes, * the Lord! Ju 5:2
"God * you for confessing it," Ju 17:2
"I know the Lord will really * Ju 17:13
And may he * you with another Ru 1:9
to take refuge, * you for it." Ru 2:12
said to Naomi, "* the Lord who has Ru 4:14
home Eli would * Elkanah and Hannah 1Sa 2:20
I will * his descendants, and his 1Sa 2:35
David replied to Abigail, "* the 1Sa 25:32
Thank God for your good sense! * 1Sa 25:33
"May the Lord * you for being so 2Sa 2:5
David returned to * his family. 2Sa 6:20
* me and my family forever! 2Sa 7:29
But God will * you with a longer 2Sa 14:14
* me because of these curses." 2Sa 16:12
induce you to ask God to * us?" 2Sa 21:3
saying, 'May God * you even more 1Ki 1:46,47
David did, then I will * you; 1Ki 11:38
* me and help me in my work; 1Ch 4:10
returned to * his own household. 1Ch 16:43
for these people and * me for it. Neh 5:19
you, and * you with a happy home. Job 8:6
For you * the godly man, O Lord; Ps 5:12
and * all who truly worship God; Ps 7:9
I will * the Lord who counsels Ps 16:7
defend and * your chosen ones. Ps 28:9
He will * them with peace. Ps 29:11
* the Lord, the God of Israel, Ps 41:13
I will * you as long as I live, Ps 63:4
Let everyone * God and sing his Ps 66:8
O GOD, IN mercy * us; Ps 67:1
God, even our own God, will * us. Ps 67:6,7
will * him all day long. Ps 72:15
will bless him all day long. * Ps 72:16
of the armies of heaven, and * us. Ps 80:14
gods will personally * this city. Ps 87:5
I will protect and * him Ps 89:24
O Jehovah, come and * us! Ps 90:13
Sing out his praises! * his Ps 96:2
Give thanks to him and * his Ps 100:4
I * THE holy name of God with all Ps 103:1
Yes, I will * the Lord and not Ps 103:2
there is. * the Lord, you mighty Ps 103:20
Yes, * the Lord, you armies of Ps 103:21
Let everything everywhere * the Ps 103:22
And how I * him too! Ps 103:22
I * THE Lord: O Lord my God, how Ps 104:1
now don't you * him. Ps 109:17
about us and he will surely * us. Ps 115:12
He will * the people of Israel Ps 115:12
May the Lord richly * both you Ps 115:14
and earth will personally * you! Ps 115:15
by the Lord. We * you from the Ps 118:26
* me with life Ps 119:17
Commit yourself to * me! Ps 119:122
May the Lord continually * you Ps 128:5
And may God * Israel! Ps 128:6
by refuse to * them by saying, Ps 129:8
you; we * you in Jehovah's name." Ps 129:8
OH, * THE Lord, you who serve him Ps 134:1
hands in holiness and * the Lord. Ps 134:2
The Lord * you from Zion—the Lord Ps 134:3
O Israel, * Jehovah! Ps 135:19
High priests of Aaron, * his Ps 135:19
O Levite priests, * the Lord Ps 135:20
Lord Jehovah! Oh, * his name, all Ps 135:20
* THE LORD who is my immovable Ps 144:1
* your name each day and forever. Ps 145:1
Lord, and your people will * you. Ps 145:10
men everywhere to * his holy name Ps 145:21
prices, but they * the man who Pro 11:26
Her children stand and * her; Pro 31:28
For the Lord will * Egypt and Is 19:25
he will conquer you to * you, Is 30:18
Then God will * you with rain at Is 30:23
And God will greatly * his Is 32:20
them their sins and * them. Is 33:24
And the Lord will * Israel Is 51:3
ask me any more to * this people. Jer 14:11
them peace, that you will * them. Jer 14:13
by forsaking your promise to * us! Jer 14:21
my mind and not * that nation as I Jer 18:10
cities, "The Lord * you, O center Jer 31:23
If you do, I will * you and no Jer 42:10
I will * them and multiply them Eze 37:26
that the Lord will * your homes. Eze 44:30
"forget" to * your children. Hos 4:6
I wanted so much to * you! Hos 6:11
but I made him * you instead? Mic 6:5
You will * us as you promised Mic 7:20
I will * you." Hag 1:13
this day onward, I will * you. Hag 2:18,19
From this day I will * you." Hag 2:18,19
and * her and live in her." Zec 1:17
once more choose to * Jerusalem.' Zec 2:11,12
or, "The Lord * it!" Zec 4:7f
If you do, I will certainly * Zec 8:14,15
this decision of mine to * you. Zec 8:14,15
to * us, and be merciful to us. Zec 8:20,21
"God * King David's Son!" Mt 21:9
* him, Lord!" Mt 21:9
shouting, "God * the Son of Mt 21:15
to Jesus to * them, the disciples Mk 10:13
has decided to wonderfully * you! Lk 1:30
called out, "God * your mother—the Lk 11:27
babies to him to touch and *. Lk 18:15
Savior! God * the King of Israel! Jn 12:13
your ancestors to * the entire Act 3:25
men of Israel, to * you by turning Act 3:26
had promised to * him because of Rom 4:11
how very much he wanted to * you. Rom 9:4
chose to * Jacob, but not Esau." Rom 9:10-13
pray that God will * him. Rom 12:14
but God working in me, to * me. 1Co 15:10
Christ mightily * each one of you, 2Co 1:2
he said, "I will * those in every Gal 3:8,9
Now God can * the Gentiles, too, Gal 3:14
May God * you all. Php 1:2
if we ask God to * it, for it is 1Ti 4:5
* you and use you to help others. 1Ti 4:16
I beg my God to * you richly. 2Ti 1:3
May the Lord * Onesiphorus and 2Ti 1:16
by, that he would * Abraham again Heb 6:14
has the power to * is always Heb 7:7
* him in everything he does. Jas 1:25
"Well, good-bye and God * you; Jas 2:16
May God * you richly and grant 1Pe 1:2
others, and God will * us for it. 1Pe 3:9
his Son will * us with great mercy 2Jn 1:3
God's love can reach and * you. Jud 1:21

BLESSED
with pleasure, and * them all. Gen 1:21,22
And God * them and told them, Gen 1:28
doing, and God * the seventh day Gen 2:3
God created man and woman and * Gen 5:2
GOD * NOAH and his sons and told Gen 9:1
Or, "* be Jehovah, the God of Gen 9:26,27f
He was a mighty hunter, * of Gen 10:9
mighty hunter, * of God." Gen 10:9

(BLESSED Con't)
and the entire world will be * Gen 12:3
Then Melchizedek * Abram with Gen 14:19,20
you, Abram; and * be God, who has Gen 14:19,20
And God * the boy and he grew up Gen 21:20,21
man, and God * him in every way. Gen 24:1
Literally, "* of Jehovah." Gen 24:31f
and worshiped and * Jehovah, the Gen 24:48
nurse, and * her with this Gen 24:60
For Jehovah * him. Gen 26:12
and fields that Jehovah has *. Gen 27:27,28,29
and * are all who bless you." Gen 27:27,28,29
(As soon as Isaac has * Jacob, Gen 27:30
* him with irrevocable blessing?" Gen 27:33
SO ISAAC CALLED for Jacob and * Gen 28:1
the earth will be * through you and Gen 28:14
The other women will think me * Gen 30:13
Jehovah has * you from everything Gen 30:30
and * them, and returned home. Gen 31:55
And he * him there. Gen 32:29
to him once again and * him. Gen 35:9
The Lord greatly * Joseph there Gen 39:2
And Jacob * Pharaoh. Gen 47:7
Then Jacob * Pharaoh again Gen 47:10
land of Canaan and * me, and said Gen 48:3
Then he * Joseph with this Gen 48:15
So Jacob * the boys that day with Gen 48:20
father * his twelve sons with. Gen 49:28
And God * the midwives. Ex 1:20
so he * the Sabbath day and set Ex 20:11
all their work and * them because Ex 39:43
the people, Aaron * them and came Lev 9:22
came out again they * the people; Lev 9:23
curse them, for I have * them!" Num 22:12
and now you have * them!" Num 23:11
For God has * them, Num 23:18-24
They shall be * with an abundance Num 24:3-9
* is everyone who blesses you, O Num 24:3-9
you have * them three times. Num 24:10
over you and * you every step of Deu 2:7
You will be * above all the Deu 7:14
as the Lord your God has * you. Deu 15:14
according as the Lord has * you. Deu 16:17
"May his land be * by God Deu 33:13
May he be * Deu 33:14
May he be * with the best gifts Deu 33:16
So Joshua * him and gave him Jos 14:13,14
So Joshua * them and sent them Jos 22:6
these troops, he * them and told Jos 22:7,8
* be Jael, Ju 5:24
Yes, may she be * Ju 5:24
and the Lord * him as he grew up. Ju 13:24
that the Lord had * his people by Ru 1:6,7
How he has * me! 1Sa 2:1
him the king and * his kingdom so 2Sa 5:12
* Obed-edom and all his household. 2Sa 6:11
Then he * the people in the name 2Sa 6:18
the king and * him and said, "At 2Sa 14:22
and after David had kissed and * 2Sa 19:39
* be my Rock. 2Sa 22:47
* be God 2Sa 22:48
than he has * you personally! 1Ki 1:46,47
He is saying, '* be the Lord God 1Ki 1:48
they stood before him, and * them. 1Ki 8:14
"* be the Lord God of Israel," 1Ki 8:15
"* be the Lord who has fulfilled 1Ki 8:56
And they * the king. 1Ki 8:66
Lord had * Solomon with wisdom, 1Ki 10:1
to your wisdom! * be the Lord your 1Ki 10:9
and the Lord * him and his family. 1Ch 13:14
offerings David * the people in the 1Ch 16:2
* be Jehovah, God of Israel, 1Ch 16:36
you their king! * be the Lord God 2Ch 2:12
"* be the Lord God of Israel," 2Ch 6:4
you talk! * be the Lord your God! 2Ch 9:8
God, he prospered, for God * him. 2Ch 26:5
Levites stood and * the people, and 2Ch 30:27
* the Lord and praised his people! 2Ch 31:7,8
for the Lord has * his people." 2Ch 31:10
Then Ezra * the Lord, the great Neh 8:6
away. * be the name of the Lord." Job 1:21
What * relief when at last they Job 3:22
ready to perish and they * me. Job 29:13
then they will be * with prosperity Job 36:11
So the Lord * Job at the end of Job 42:12
because he has * me so richly. Ps 13:6
conspiring men. * is the Lord, for Ps 31:21
* is the nation whose God is the Ps 33:12
Those * by the Lord shall Ps 37:22
* be God who didn't turn away Ps 66:20
power to his people. * be God! Ps 68:35
and all will be * in him; Ps 72:17
* be Jehovah God, the God of Ps 72:18
* be his glorious name forever! Ps 72:19
O Lord of the armies of heaven, * Ps 84:12
your attendants. * are those who Ps 89:14,15
And yet—* be the Lord forever! Ps 89:52
* be the Lord, the God of Israel, Ps 106:48
He never * others; Ps 109:17
in him are * beyond expression. Ps 112:1
* is his name forever and forever. Ps 113:2
Give us success. * is the one Ps 118:26
* Lord, teach me your rules. Ps 119:12
* be Jehovah who has not let them Ps 124:6
Literally, "the Lord be * from Ps 135:21f
be destroyed. * is the man who Ps 137:8
destroyed us. * is the man who Ps 137:9
be paraphrased, "* is he who Ps 137:9f
all enemies, and * your children. Ps 147:13
To despise the poor is to sin. * Pro 14:21
* is the man who reveres God, but Pro 28:14
He will say, "* be Egypt, my Is 19:25
* be Iraq, the land I have made; Is 19:25
* be Israel, my inheritance!" Is 19:25
to his promises. * are all those Is 30:18
will be * of God for all they do. Is 32:8
But when I * him, he became a Is 51:1
to rescue you. * is the man who Is 56:2
honors them; and * is the man who Is 56:2
that they are a people God has *. Is 61:9
and "The City God Has *." Is 62:12
children of those the Lord has *; Is 65:23
their children, too, shall be *. Is 65:23
the same as though they * an idol. Is 66:3
But * is the man who trusts in Jer 17:7
That is why God * him. Jer 22:15
heaven, saying, "* be the name of Dan 2:20
Then Nebuchadnezzar said, "* be Dan 3:28
And * are those who wait and Dan 12:12
and Gilgal, and how I * you there? Mic 6:5
will call you *, for you will be a Mal 3:12
concerned, "* are the arrogant." Mal 3:14,15
Then give him this message, '* Mt 11:6
But * are your eyes, for they see; Mt 13:16
"God has * you, Simon, son of Mt 16:17
heads and * them before he left. Mt 19:15
Literally, "* is he who comes in Mt 21:9f
my right, 'Come, * of my Father, Mt 25:34
loaf of bread and * it and broke it Mt 26:26
too, so Jesus also * these and told Mk 8:7
on their heads and he * them. Mk 10:16
Some ancient versions add, "* are Lk 1:28f
Simeon * them but then said to Lk 2:34,35
And tell him, '* is the one who Lk 7:23
Literally, "* is he who keeps Lk 7:23f
but even more * are all who hear Lk 11:28
to heaven, he * them, and then Lk 24:50
have seen me. But * are those who Jn 20:29
"God * David greatly, and David Act 7:46
more * to give than to receive.' Act 20:35
the * God who made these things. Rom 1:25
by God. "*, and to be envied," Rom 4:7
We have * those who cursed us. 1Co 4:12
as Peter had been * so greatly in Gal 2:7,8,9
Christ, who has * us with every Eph 1:3
our * God, whose messenger I am. 1Ti 1:10,11
from heaven by the * and only 1Ti 6:15
my hands upon your head and * you. 2Ti 1:6
Melchizedek met him and * him; Heb 7:1
was old and dying, * each of Heb 11:21
do what it says will also be *. Rev 1:3
as a thief ! * are all who are Rev 16:15
dictated this sentence to me: "* Rev 19:9
years had ended.) * and holy are Rev 20:6
will happen soon. * are those who Rev 22:6,7
First and Last. * forever are all Rev 22:14

BLESSEDNESS
was unaware of the * of the future Is 38:18f

BLESSES
Blessed is everyone who * you, O Num 24:3-9
the olive oil that * God and man, Ju 9:9
until he arrives and * the food." 1Sa 9:12,13
he punishes or * the people, giving Job 36:31
GOD * THOSE who are kind to the Ps 41:1
How he * them! Ps 107:38
The Lord * good men and condemns Pro 12:2
God * those who obey him; Pro 16:20
greater than the person he *. Heb 7:7
a true statement of the way God *. 1Pe 5:12

BLESSING
you will be a * to many others. Gen 12:2
blessed Abram with this *: Gen 14:19,20
"The * of the supreme God, Gen 14:19,20
be a source of * for all the Gen 18:18
enemies, and be a * to all the Gen 22:18
her with this * as they Gen 24:60
and they shall be a * to all the Gen 26:4
plainly see that Jehovah is * you. Gen 26:28
and curse me instead of * me!" Gen 27:11,12
blessed him with irrevocable *?" Gen 27:33
me and has carried away your *." Gen 27:35
and now he has stolen my *. Gen 27:36
Oh, haven't you saved even one * Gen 27:36
Esau: "Not one * left for me? Gen 27:38
with his father's *, to get a wife Gen 28:6,7,8
"Don't give him your * and don't Gen 31:24
At once the Lord began * Gen 39:5
Joseph with this *: "May God, the Gen 48:15
that day with this *: "May the Gen 48:20
"Go with my *," Jethro replied. Ex 4:18
and oh, give me a * Ex 12:32
now he will give you a great *." Ex 32:29
give this special * to the people Num 6:22,23
between God's * or God's curse! Deu 11:26
There will be * if you obey the Deu 11:27
to possess it, a * shall be Deu 11:29
The only prerequisite for his * Deu 15:4,5
in size to his * upon you as judged Deu 16:10
to the Lord for * you with a good Deu 16:15
curse into a * for you, because the Deu 23:5
to proclaim a *, and the tribes of Deu 27:12
you life or death, * or curse. Deu 30:19
THIS IS THE * that Moses, the man Deu 33:1
This is my * on the multitudes of Deu 33:17
"A * upon those who help Gad. Deu 33:20
Ark, ready to pronounce their *. Jos 8:33
the statements of * and curses that Jos 8:34
you want God's *, listen to me! Ju 9:7
and to receive his *, but Samuel 1Sa 13:10
* upon all the people of Israel: 1Ki 8:54,55
May this * rest upon my children 1Ch 17:27
when you grant a *, Lord, it is an 1Ch 17:27
Lord, it is an eternal *!" 1Ch 17:27
What a * God gave him with all 1Ch 26:4,5
and they stood to receive his *: 2Ch 6:3
while the Lord is * us with peace 2Ch 14:7
in the Valley of *, as it is called 2Ch 20:26
for the Lord his God was * him. Ez 7:6
God turned the curse into a *. Neh 13:2
as their * from him, planted in Ps 24:5
God's circle of *, and his children Ps 25:13
the Lord shall be given every *. Ps 37:9
*, and shall have wonderful peace. Ps 37:11
and their children are a *. Ps 37:26
he will honor you with every *, Ps 37:34
God himself is * you forever. Ps 45:2
of his land of *, to this land of Ps 78:54
You will receive every * you can Ps 81:10
where pools of * and refreshment Ps 84:6
you are * and saving your people. Ps 106:4
What a * is that stillness, as Ps 107:30
won't mind that if you are * me! Ps 109:28
What a * this has been to me—to Ps 119:56
this eternal * on Jerusalem, Ps 133:3
place your hand of * on my head. Ps 139:5
but his * is on the upright. Pro 3:33
Let your manhood be a *; Pro 5:18
The Lord's * is our greatest Pro 10:22
she is a * to him from the Lord. Pro 18:22
you fear God you can expect his *. Ecc 7:18
and Israel will be a * to them. Is 19:24
This is the * I have given you, Is 54:17
when all who invoke a * or take Is 65:16
seek my help and * any more, Jer 44:26
honored my name by * you despite Eze 20:44
their homes around my hill a *. Eze 34:26
showers of *, for I will not shut Eze 34:26
He wept and pleaded for a * from Hos 12:4
a * instead of his terrible curse. Joe 2:14
to seek his *, and to speak with Zec 7:2
For now 'Judah' is a word of *, Zec 8:13
to ask for his * and help. Zec 8:22
and you receive no * from him. Mal 2:13
you and pour out a * so great you Mal 3:10
be a godly home, give it your *; Mt 10:13
if not, keep the *. Mt 10:13
and asked God's * on the meal, then Mt 14:19
and asked God's * on it and broke Mk 14:22
has given you this wonderful *." Lk 1:45
implore God's * on those who hurt Lk 6:28
you enter a home, give it your *. Lk 10:5
If it is worthy of the *, the Lk 10:6
of the blessing, the * will stand; Lk 10:6
if not, the * will return to you. Lk 10:6
he asked God's * on the food and Lk 24:30
us—* upon blessing heaped upon us! Jn 1:16
us—blessing upon * heaped upon us! Jn 1:16
That is the path of *. Jn 13:17
and laid their hands on them in *. Act 6:6
and, with the * of the believers, Act 15:40,41
of us will be a * to the other. Rom 1:11,12
to feel secure or enjoy God's *. Rom 3:17
Now then, the question: Is this * Rom 4:9
laws, or is the * also given to Rom 4:9
did God give this * to Abraham? Rom 4:10
try to gain God's * and salvation Rom 4:15
this * even before it happened. Rom 4:20
how much greater a * the world will Rom 11:12
So now you, too, receive the * Rom 11:17
will give me a great * for you. Rom 15:29
Now you have every grace and *; 1Co 1:7
grace and * that God has given us. 1Co 2:12
and also for the * I myself receive 1Co 9:23
When we ask the Lord's * upon 1Co 10:16
together the * of Christ's blood? 1Co 10:16
could be a double * to you and so 2Co 1:15,16
* upon us forever and ever! 2Co 4:17
May peace and * be yours from Gal 1:3
share the same * Abraham received. Gal 3:8,9
same * he promised to Abraham; Gal 3:14
reap a harvest of * if we don't get Gal 6:9
us with every * in heaven because Eph 1:3
to, and what will give them a *. Eph 4:29

(BLESSING Con't)
will be a long life, full of *. Eph 6:3
May God's grace and * be upon Eph 6:24
Jesus Christ: May * and peace of 1Th 1:1
May the * of our Lord Jesus 2Th 3:18
* at the day of Christ's return. 2Ti 1:18
has experienced God's * upon it. Heb 6:7
(b) Melchizedek placed a * upon Heb 7:6
And so * and cursing come Jas 3:10
in these last days, as a * to you. 1Pe 1:20
receive a special * from the Lord. Rev 1:3
honor, and the glory, and the *." Rev 5:12
exclaiming, "The * and the honor Rev 5:13
they said. "*, and glory, and Rev 7:12

BLESSINGS
used to pronounce * on others." Gen 12:2f
And I will give you great *." Gen 15:1
are all your * when I have no son? Gen 15:2,3
with incredible * and multiply your Gen 22:17
my master with * so that he is a Gen 24:35
God poured out rich * upon Isaac. Gen 25:11
I will give you the * that belong Gen 27:2,3,4
Isaac and he gives Jacob his *): Gen 27:23
you can give me your finest *!" Gen 27:31
the mighty * promised to Abraham. Gen 28:4
told me that the many * I've been Gen 30:27
bless you with * of heaven above Gen 49:25
the earth beneath—* of the breasts Gen 49:25
and of the womb, * of the grain Gen 49:26
grain and flowers, * reaching to Gen 49:26
These shall be the * upon the Gen 49:26
So these are the * that Israel Gen 49:28
and his sons shall call down my * Num 6:27
for I know what fantastic * fall Num 22:5,6
to pronounce his * and decide Deu 21:5
These are the * that will come Deu 28:2-6
* in the city, Deu 28:2-6
* in the field; Deu 28:2-6
* of fruit and bread; Deu 28:2-6
* when you come in, Deu 28:2-6
* when you go out. Deu 28:2-6
But each of these * depends on Deu 28:14
to you—the * and the curses I have Deu 30:1
Let all these * come upon Joseph, Deu 33:16
With all the * of the Lord; Deu 33:23
What * are yours, O Israel! Deu 33:29
And Saul said to David, "* on 1Sa 26:25
you showered your * on such an 2Sa 7:18
such * as Israel, your people? 2Sa 7:23
and * through Nathan the prophet. 2Sa 12:25
in bed, acknowledging their *. 1Ki 1:46,47
receive God's rich *, and may one 1Ki 2:45
asking for his * upon his people. 1Ch 16:4
* in his name at all times. 1Ch 23:13
May his * rest upon you. Ez 1:3
enjoyed themselves in all your *. Neh 9:25
wicked with his *, but gives them Job 36:6
paid me with his *, for I have done Ps 18:24
You give * to the pure but pain Ps 18:26
* overflow! Ps 23:5
me and cut off your river of *. Ps 30:6,7
For you have stored up great * Ps 31:19
You feed them with * from your Ps 36:8
Many * are given to those who Ps 40:4
choicest * for his Jewish people Ps 47:4
have given me the * you reserve for Ps 61:5
the * of God have changed to hate. Ps 77:10
of Israel from giving them his *. Ps 78:41
poured out amazing * on this land! Ps 85:1
Yes, the Lord pours down his * on Ps 85:12
and old shall hear about your *. Ps 89:1
How refreshed I am by your *! Ps 92:10
With all my heart I want your *. Ps 119:58
with your *, just as you promised. Ps 119:65
* ON ALL who reverence and trust Ps 128:1
bless you with heaven's * Ps 128:5
saying, "Jehovah's * be upon you; Ps 129:8
The good man is covered with * Pro 10:6
The good shall never lose God's * Pro 10:30
hard work returns many * to him. Pro 12:14
Curses chase sinners, while * Pro 13:21
many nations; but * shall be Pro 24:25
her twice as many * as he gave her Is 40:2
Spirit and my * on your children. Is 44:3
she who was abandoned has more * Is 54:1
And my * are for Gentiles, too, Is 56:3
full share of the * I promised to Is 58:14
that you aren't finding God's *; Is 59:9
you promised great * on Jerusalem. Jer 4:10
away these wondrous * from them. Jer 5:25
prayers for these *, and to grant Eze 36:37,38
set Israel apart for special *." Eze 37:28
and to his *, in the end times. Hos 3:5
you about the * that await you when Zec 8:9
all these * will be given to the Zec 8:12
of giving you * as I would like to, Mal 2:1
day by day? * on you if I return Mt 24:46
and God poured out his * on him. Lk 2:40
give * to all who come to him." Lk 4:18,19
and counts his *—and then renounces Lk 14:33
from the rich * he brought to Jn 1:16
We say that he received these * Rom 4:9
claim that God's * go to those who Rom 4:14
So God's * are given to us by Rom 4:16
of his Son, what * he must have for Rom 5:10
And so God's * are not given Rom 9:16
food and other * trap them into Rom 11:9
in their spiritual *, they ought Rom 15:27f
service to them in material *." Rom 15:27f
your feet. The * from our Lord Rom 16:20
you all of his *, and great peace 1Co 1:3
* by explaining God's secrets. 1Co 4:1
May his * and peace be yours, Eph 1:2
promises of mighty * through Christ Eph 3:6
for such wonderful * as these. Eph 4:1
of you his fullest *, and his peace Php 1:2
We have shared together the * of Php 1:7
palace. The * of our Lord Jesus Php 4:23
shower you with * and fill you with Col 1:2
May God's * surround you. Col 4:18
And may rich * from our Lord 1Th 5:28
give you rich * and peace-filled 2Th 1:2
give you his * and his peace. Tit 1:4
May God's * be with you all. Tit 3:15
give you his * and his peace. Phm 1:3
The * of our Lord Jesus Christ be Phm 1:25
* to his two sons, Jacob and Esau. Heb 11:20
will fail to find God's best *. Heb 12:15
in receiving God's *, and if you 1Pe 3:7
to others God's many kinds of *. 1Pe 4:10
God gives special * to those who 1Pe 5:5
rich and wonderful * he promised; 2Pe 1:4
inherit all these *, and I will be Rev 21:7

BLESSSED
ground and said, "* be the Lord 2Sa 18:28

BLEST
forever shall call me * of God. Lk 1:48
Yes, says the Spirit, they are * Rev 14:13

BLEW
west wind that * the locusts out Ex 10:19
and a strong east wind * all that Ex 14:21
But God * with his wind, and the Ex 15:10
as the priests * a long, loud Jos 6:16
of Ephraim, he * a trumpet as a Ju 3:27
Gideon, and he * a trumpet as a Ju 6:34
Suddenly they * their trumpets and Ju 7:19,20
Then he * his trumpet and his 2Sa 2:28
Then Joab * the trumpet, and his 2Sa 18:16
a Benjaminite) * a trumpet and 2Sa 20:1
And he * the trumpet and called 2Sa 20:22
their coats and * a trumpet, 2Ki 9:13
Then, when the priests * the 2Ch 7:6
and the priests * the trumpets. 2Ch 13:13,14
singers sang and the trumpets *. 2Ch 29:28
robes and * their trumpets; Ez 3:10
smoke * from his nostrils. Ps 18:8
and the wind * them all away. Dan 2:35
the ship and * it out to sea. Act 27:14,15
The first angel * his trumpet, Rev 8:7
Then the second angel * his Rev 8:8,9
The third angel *, and a great Rev 8:10
The fourth angel * his trumpet Rev 8:12
THEN THE FIFTH angel * his trumpet Rev 9:1
The sixth angel * his trumpet and Rev 9:13
the seventh angel * his trumpet, Rev 10:7
For just then the seventh angel * Rev 11:15

BLIGHT
He will * your crops, covering Deu 28:22
and hills and * their greenery. Is 42:15
then they were a * upon my holy Eze 36:20
your grapes will * upon the vine. Hos 9:2
"I sent * and mildew on your Amo 4:9

BLIGHTED
grain * before it is half grown. 2Ki 19:26
will her hopes be *, but those of Dan 11:6
the Pleasant Land lay bare and* Zec 7:14
of the sun was * and darkened, and Rev 8:12

BLIND
Israel was half * with age, so Gen 48:10
nor trip up a * man as he walks. Lev 19:14
For instance, if a man is * or Lev 21:18
An animal that is * or disabled or Lev 22:22
as being lame or *, or if anything Deu 15:21
For bribes * the eyes of the Deu 16:19
who takes advantage of a * man.' Deu 27:18
as the * man gropes in darkness. Deu 28:29
bed (he was almost * with age by 1Sa 3:2,3
ninety-eight years old and was * 1Sa 4:15
"Even the * and lame could keep 2Sa 5:6
those 'lame' and '*' Jebusites. 2Sa 5:8
saying, "Even the * and the lame 2Sa 5:8
"Lord, please make them *." 2Ki 6:18
They grope like * men in the Job 5:14
their children shall go *. Job 17:5
I served as eyes for the * and Job 29:15
strength fails, and I am going *. Ps 38:10
So I am letting them go their * Ps 81:12
Is God deaf and *—he who makes Ps 94:9
and opens the eyes of the *; Ps 146:8
man sees, while the fool is *. Ecc 2:13,14
Then go ahead and be * if you Is 29:9
darkness the * will see my plans. Is 29:18
the eyes of the *, and unstop the Is 35:5
You will open the eyes of the *, Is 42:7
He will bring * Israel along a Is 42:16
Oh, how * and deaf you are Is 42:18
Who in all the world is as * as Is 42:19
Who is so * as my "dedicated Is 42:19
Bring them back to me—* as they Is 43:8
all * to every danger. Is 56:10
No wonder you grope like * men Is 59:10
and to open the eyes of the *. Is 61:1
like a hunter hiding in a *. Jer 5:26
forgetting their * and lame, young Jer 31:8
idols—and I will * their lecherous Eze 6:9
as helpless as a * man searching Zep 1:17
of Judah, but * all her enemies. Zec 12:4
even the sick and the * ones.' Mal 1:8
her home, two * men followed along Mt 9:27
seen me do— the * people I've Mt 11:5
man—he was both * and unable to Mt 12:22
They are * guides leading the Mt 15:13,14
guides leading the *, and both will Mt 15:13,14
him their lame, *, maimed, and Mt 15:30
had been * were gazing about them! Mt 15:31
Two * men were sitting beside the Mt 20:30
And now the * and crippled came Mt 21:14
you are yourselves. * guides! Mt 23:16
the Temple' is binding! * fools! Mt 23:17
on the altar' is binding! *! Mt 23:19
things undone. * guides! Mt 23:24
extortion and greed. * Pharisees! Mt 23:26
people brought a * man to him and Mk 8:22
Jesus took the * man by the hand Mk 8:23
of God half * than have two eyes Mk 9:47
Now it happened that a * beggar Mk 10:46
So they called the * man. Mk 10:49
"O Teacher," the * man said, "I Mk 10:51
And instantly the * man could see, Mk 10:52
released and the * shall see, that Lk 4:18,19
it for one * man to lead another? Lk 6:39
* and casting out evil spirits. Lk 7:20,21,22
how those who were * can see. Lk 7:20,21,22
the crippled, the lame, and the *. Lk 14:13
beggars, crippled, lame, and *. Lk 14:21
As they approached Jericho, a * Lk 18:35
"Bring the * man over here," he Lk 18:40
Crowds of sick folks—lame, *, or Jn 5:3
along, he saw a man * from birth. Jn 9:1
him, "why was this man born *? Jn 9:2
the mud over the * man's eyes, and Jn 9:6
who knew him as a * beggar asked Jn 9:8
man who had been * and demanded, Jn 9:17
he had been *, until they called in Jn 9:18
Was he born *? Jn 9:19
that he was born *, but we don't Jn 9:20
man who had been * and told him, Jn 9:24
this: I was *, and now I see!" Jn 9:25
"He can heal * men, and yet you Jn 9:30
open the eyes of someone born *. Jn 9:32
are spiritually * and to show those Jn 9:39
think they see that they are *." Jn 9:39
"Are you saying we are *?" Jn 9:40
"If you were *, you wouldn't be Jn 9:41
Can a demon open the eyes of * Jn 10:21
fellow healed a * man—why couldn't Jn 11:37,38
ground, he found that he was *. Act 9:8,9
there three days, *, going without Act 9:8,9
you could point it out to a * man. Rom 2:19
their hearts are * and they think 2Co 3:15
has made him *, unable to see the 2Co 4:4
to faith is * indeed, or at least 2Pe 1:9
* so that he cannot see the way. 1Jn 2:11
and poor and * and naked. Rev 3:17

BLINDED
and temporarily * the men of Sodom Gen 19:11
and the eye is *, then the slave Ex 21:26
I am terrified, * with dismay. Is 21:3
Kings shall be * by your glory; Is 62:2
useless and his right eye *." Zec 11:17
has * their eyes and hardened Jn 12:40
"I was * by the intense light, Act 22:11
eyes of the others have been *. Rom 11:7
were veiled and * too. 2Co 3:14
do, for they are * and confused. Eph 4:17,18
against God, being * by the glamor Heb 3:13

BLINDFOLD
love to * you and lead you astray. 1Jn 2:26

BLINDFOLDED
at him, and they * him and began to Mk 14:65
mocking him. They * him and hit him Lk 22:63,64

BLINDING
From his face came * flashes like Dan 10:5,6
With * speed and violence he Amo 5:9

BLINDLY
the simpleton goes * on and Pro 22:3
Now these same men are * Lam 4:14
him, worshiping *, while we Jews Jn 4:21-24

BLINDNESS
He will send madness, *, fear, Deu 28:28
let darkness, * and great Ps 69:23
work, and there will be *, too. Ecc 12:3
will be stricken awhile with *." Act 13:11

BLINDS
of the wicked. God * the eyes of Job 9:24
But this is foolish talk; it * Tit 1:10

BLISTER
on hot coals and not * his feet? Pro 6:28

BLISTERED
feet haven't been * or swollen. Deu 8:4
their shoulders were raw and * Eze 29:18

BLITHELY
"Let no one * think, when he Deu 29:19
says but will * follow their own 2Ti 4:4

BLOATED
Yes, fat and *; Deu 32:15

BLOCK
huge work crew to * them, and to 2Ch 32:4
They * my road and do everything Job 30:13
* to those who trust in you. Ps 69:6
He measures and marks out a * of Is 44:13
out, "Why, it's just a * of wood! Is 44:19
It will * the path of the Eze 39:11
than the base * on all sides. Eze 43:14
entrance to the * of sacred Eze 46:19,20
thornbushes; I'll * the road before Hos 1:6
a *, and then the angel left him. Act 12:10
So don't be a stumbling * to 1Co 10:32

BLOCKED
enemies, the Lord * their path. Ju 2:15
God has * my path and turned my Job 19:8
All the escape routes are *; Jer 51:32
* my way. Then Michael, one of Dan 10:13
the people have * them at every Hos 9:8

BLOCKS
and shaped huge * of stone—a very 1Ki 5:17
beams resting on * built out from 1Ki 6:6
* of squared stone for the Temple. 1Ch 22:2
*, timber, lumber, and beams. 2Ch 34:10,11
and second cell * and came to the Act 12:10

BLOOD
* calls to me from the ground. Gen 4:10
defiled with your brother's *. Gen 4:11
flesh and *," Laban exclaimed. Gen 29:14
"we'll shed no *—let's throw him Gen 37:21,22
and spattered its * on Joseph's Gen 37:31
dry land, and it will turn to *." Ex 4:9
rod, and the river will turn to *! Ex 7:17
in the homes will turn to *." Ex 7:19
rod, and the river turned to *. Ex 7:20
and there was * throughout the Ex 7:21
they, too, turned water into *; Ex 7:22
killed, and their * shall be Ex 12:7
Use the * of the lamb eaten in Ex 12:7
I am Jehovah. The * you have Ex 12:13
and when I see the * I will pass Ex 12:13
Drain the lamb's * into a basin, Ex 12:22
into the lamb's *, and strike the Ex 12:22
that there will be * upon them, and Ex 12:22
but when he sees the * upon the Ex 12:23
"No sacrificial * shall be Ex 23:18
Moses took half of the * of Ex 24:6
Then Moses threw the * from the Ex 24:8
and said, "This * confirms and Ex 24:8
Place its * upon the horns of Ex 29:12
it is killed. Its * shall also be Ex 29:15,16
Collect the * and place some of Ex 29:19,20
sprinkle the rest of the * over Ex 29:19,20
Then scrape off some of the * Ex 29:21
upon its horns the * of the sin Ex 30:10
will present the * before the Lord, Lev 1:5
* back and forth upon the altar. Lev 1:11
its head, and the * shall be Lev 1:15,16,17
shall throw the * against the sides Lev 3:2
the priests shall throw the * Lev 3:7,8
The priest shall throw its * Lev 3:13
you shall eat neither fat nor *." Lev 3:17
take the animal's * into the Lev 4:5
his finger in the * and sprinkle it Lev 4:6
put some of the * upon the horns of Lev 4:7
the remainder of the * shall be Lev 4:7
shall bring its * into the Lev 4:16
his finger in the * and sprinkle it Lev 4:17
Then he shall put * upon the Lev 4:18
remainder of the * shall be poured Lev 4:18
take some of the * of this sin Lev 4:25
the rest of the * shall be poured Lev 4:25
take some of the * with his finger Lev 4:30
of the * at the base of the altar. Lev 4:30
take some of the * with his finger Lev 4:34
the rest of the * shall be poured Lev 4:34
some of the * at the side of the Lev 5:9
if any * sprinkles onto their Lev 6:27
if any of its * is taken into the Lev 6:30
are slain, and its * shall be Lev 7:2
who sprinkles the * of the animal Lev 7:14
"Never eat *, whether of birds Lev 7:26,27
He smeared some of the * with his Lev 8:15,16
of the * at the base of the altar; Lev 8:15,16
* back and forth upon the altar. Lev 8:19
took some of its * and smeared it Lev 8:23
Next he smeared some of the * Lev 8:24
The rest of the * he sprinkled Lev 8:24
Literally, "Moses threw the * Lev 8:24f
and some of the * that had been Lev 8:30
his sons caught the * for him, Lev 9:9
sons caught the * and he sprinkled Lev 9:12
and Aaron's sons brought the * to Lev 9:18
"Since its * was not taken Lev 10:18
in her * of purification." Lev 12:5f
be dipped in the *, along with the Lev 14:6
shall sprinkle the * seven times Lev 14:7
The priest shall take the * from Lev 14:14
with the * of the guilt offering. Lev 14:17
smear some of its * upon the tip of Lev 14:25
with the * of the guilt offering. Lev 14:28
bird, into the * of the bird that Lev 14:51,52
And he shall bring some of the * Lev 16:14
and bring its * within the veil, Lev 16:15
did with the * of the young bull. Lev 16:15
He must smear the * of the young Lev 16:18
and sprinkle * upon the altar Lev 16:19
offering (their * was taken into Lev 16:27
to sprinkle the * upon the altar of Lev 17:6
among you, who eats * in any form. Lev 17:10
flesh is in the *, and I have given Lev 17:11
have given you the * to sprinkle Lev 17:11
it is the * that makes atonement, Lev 17:11
living among them, may eat *. Lev 17:12
must pour out the * and cover it Lev 17:13
with dust, for the * is the life. Lev 17:14
is its *. Lev 17:14
Therefore, anyone who eats * must Lev 17:14
against the * of your neighbor." Lev 19:16f
not eat meat with undrained *; Lev 19:26
he has cursed his own flesh and *. Lev 20:9
Literally, "their * shall be upon Lev 20:16f
children of mixed *—half priestly Lev 21:14,15
Their * is to be sprinkled upon Num 18:17
Eleazar shall take some of her * Num 19:4
hide, meat, *, and dung. Num 19:5
And have drunk the * of the Num 23:18-24
are not to eat the *—pour it out on Deu 12:16
never to eat the *, for the blood Deu 12:20-23
the blood, for the * is the life, Deu 12:20-23
Instead, pour the * out upon the Deu 12:24,25
Lord your God. The * will be poured Deu 12:26,27
But don't eat the *; Deu 15:23
*, neither have our eyes seen it. Deu 21:7
us the guilt of this man's *.' Deu 21:8
My arrows shall be drunk with *! Deu 32:40,41
My sword devours the flesh and * Deu 32:40,41
Are gory with *.' Deu 32:40,41
me, your own flesh and *!" Ju 9:2
against the Lord by eating *. 1Sa 14:33
the Lord by eating the *." 1Sa 14:34
Jonathan swore to be his * 1Sa 18:1
"We are your * brothers," they 2Sa 5:1
own tribe, my own flesh and *!" 2Sa 19:11,12
But Amasa lay in his * in the 2Sa 20:12
This is the * of these men who 2Sa 23:17
and swords until the * gushed out. 1Ki 18:28
shall lick your * outside the city 1Ki 21:19
as they licked the * of Naboth!' 1Ki 21:19
chariot with the * from his wound 1Ki 22:35
licked the king's * just as the 1Ki 22:38
"*!" 2Ki 3:23
window, and her * spattered against 2Ki 9:33
the * of peace offerings upon it. 2Ki 16:13
offerings. The * from the burnt 2Ki 16:15
Jerusalem with *, and the Lord 2Ki 24:3,4
It is the very * of these men who 1Ch 11:18,19
before me with *: so you are not to 1Ch 22:8
a warrior and have shed much *.' 1Ch 28:3
priests took the * and sprinkled it 2Ch 29:22
sprinkled their * upon the altar, 2Ch 29:22
with their * upon the altar, to 2Ch 29:24
and the priests sprinkled the * 2Ch 30:16
and presented the * to the priests, 2Ch 35:11
O earth, do not conceal my *. Job 16:18
Her nestlings gulp down *, for Job 39:30
your sacrifices of flesh and *. Ps 50:13
Sprinkle me with the cleansing * Ps 51:7
Cover your feet with their *; Ps 68:23
their rivers into *, so that no one Ps 78:44
* has flowed like water. Ps 79:3
water into *, poisoning the fish. Ps 105:29
innocent * and polluting the land Ps 106:37,38
I don't want to see the * from Is 1:11
they are covered with the * of Is 1:15
will run red with *, but I am not Is 15:9
means—an altar covered with *. Is 29:2
mountains will flow with their *. Is 34:3
sword of the Lord is sated with *; Is 34:6
The land will be soaked with *, Is 34:7
drunk with rivers of their own *. Is 49:26
It is their * you see upon my Is 63:3
or the * of a swine on his altar! Is 66:3
* of the innocent and the poor. Jer 2:34
let the sword pour out their *! Jer 18:21
with the * of innocent children. Jer 19:4
drunk with your *, for the Lord God Jer 46:10
swords from your *, refusing to do Jer 48:10
full for all our * she spilled!" Jer 51:34,35
the city by shedding innocent *. Lam 4:13
*, defiling everything they touch. Lam 4:1
I will demand your * for theirs. Eze 3:1
your own *, and I said, 'Live! Eze 16:6,
you were naked and covered with *. Eze 16:2
for the fire; your * will be Eze 21:3
murders, leaving * upon the rocks Eze 24:
with your gushing *, filling the Eze 32:
You eat meat with the *; Eze 33:2
since you enjoy * so much, I will Eze 35:
you a * bath—your turn has come! Eze 35:
eat the flesh and drink the *! Eze 39:17
men and drink the * of princes—they Eze 39:18
drink * until you are drunk; Eze 39:19
and the sprinkling of * upon it. Eze 43:18
You shall take some of its * and Eze 43:20
me my food, the fat and the *. Eze 44:7
offer the fat and * of the Eze 44:15
take some of the * of this sin Eze 45:19
tracked with footprints of *. Hos 6:8
* and fire and pillars of smoke. Joe 2:30
and the moon to * before the great Joe 2:31
For I will avenge the * of my Joe 3:21
for your *, eager to destroy you. Mic 4:11
WOE TO NINEVEH, City of *, full of Nah 3:1
therefore your * will be poured Zep 1:17
sacrifices that she eats with *. Zec 9:7
I made with you, sealed with *. Zec 9:11
guilty of all the * of murdered Mt 23:35
is my *, sealing the New Covenant. Mt 26:28
still called "The Field of *." Mt 27:8
of the * of this good man. Mt 27:24
And the mob yelled back, "His * Mt 27:25
my *, poured out for many, sealing Mk 14:24
Literally, "This is my * of the Mk 14:24f
sealed with the * I shall pour out Lk 22:20
in my *, poured out for you." Lk 22:20f
into a sweat of *, with great drops Lk 22:44
Literally, "not of *." Jn 1:13f
and drink his *, you cannot have Jn 6:53
flesh and drink my * has eternal Jn 6:54
food, and my * is the true drink. Jn 6:55
my * is in me, and I in him. Jn 6:56
spear, and * and water flowed out. Jn 19:34
named the place 'The Field of *.' Act 1:19
* and fire and clouds of smoke; Act 2:19
Literally, "and from *." Act 15:27,28,29f
and said, "Your * be upon your own Act 18:6
that no man's * can be laid at my Act 20:26
purchased with his *—for the Holy Act 20:28
He used Christ's * and our faith Rom 3:25
And since by his * he did all Rom 5:9
the blessing of Christ's *? 1Co 10:16
and set in motion by my *. 1Co 11:25
the body and the * of the Lord. 1Co 11:27
* cannot get into God's kingdom. 1Co 15:50
sins through the * of his Son, by Eph 1:7
has done for you with his *. Eph 2:13
made of flesh and *, but against Eph 6:12
his * and forgave us all our sins. Col 1:14
peace with God for all by his *. Col 1:20
of flesh and *—he became flesh and Heb 2:14
* too by being born in human form; Heb 2:14
offers to him the * of animals that Heb 5:1
sweating of great drops of *? Heb 5:7f
paid for their sins with his *. Heb 7:25
He never needs the daily * of Heb 7:27
and always with * which he Heb 9:7
once for all took * into that inner Heb 9:12
but it was not the * of goats and Heb 9:12
No, he took his own *, and with Heb 9:12
And if under the old system the * Heb 9:13
more surely the * of Christ will Heb 9:14
That is why * was sprinkled [as Heb 9:18
laws, he took the * of calves and Heb 9:19
and sprinkled the * over the book Heb 9:19
Then he said, "This is the * Heb 9:20
way he sprinkled * on the sacred Heb 9:21
sprinkling it with *, and without Heb 9:22
* there is no forgiveness of sins. Heb 9:22
sprinkled with the * of animals. Heb 9:23
* in the Holy of Holies each year. Heb 9:25
For it is not possible for the * Heb 10:4
The * of bulls and goats merely Heb 10:4f
There he gave his own * which Heb 10:4f
"O God, the * of bulls and goats Heb 10:5
God is, because of the * of Jesus. Heb 10:19
with Christ's * to make us clean, Heb 10:22
his cleansing * as though it were Heb 10:29
and sprinkle the * on the doorposts Heb 11:28
until you sweat great drops of *. Heb 12:4
and to the sprinkled * which Heb 12:24
vengeance as the * of Abel did. Heb 12:24
priest brought the * of the slain Heb 13:11
where his * washed our sins away. Heb 13:12
signed with his *, produce in you Heb 13:20,21
you with the * of Jesus Christ and 1Pe 1:2
other, and the * of Jesus his Son 1Jn 1:7
is he who came by water and *." 1Jn 5:6,7,8f
water only, but by water and *." 1Jn 5:6,7,8f
and the water, and the *." 1Jn 5:6,7,8f
for you were slain, and your * Rev 5:9

BLOOD Con't)
When will you avenge our * Rev 6:10
them by the * of the Lamb. Rev 7:14
* were thrown down upon the earth. Rev 8:7
Literally, "became *." Rev 8:8,9f
*; and a third of the fish were Rev 8:8,9
and oceans to *, and to send every Rev 11:6
They defeated him by the * of Rev 12:11
the city, and * flowed out in a Rev 14:20
like the watery * of a dead man; Rev 16:3
and springs and they became *. Rev 16:4
their * poured out upon the earth; Rev 16:6
the * of those who murdered them; Rev 16:6
with the * of the martyrs of Jesus Rev 17:6
for the * of all the martyred Rev 18:24
garments dipped in *, and his title Rev 19:13

BLOOD-RED
black and the moon * before that Act 2:20
black cloth, and the moon was *. Rev 6:12

BLOOD-SMEARED
"What a * husband you've turned Ex 4:25,26

BLOOD-STAINED
they shall walk the * fields of Ps 58:10
no more the * uniforms of war; Is 9:5

BLOODBATH
command in this *, for he was 2Ki 10:11f

BLOODIED
Servant beaten and *, so disfigured Is 52:14,15

BLOODSHED
responsible for unjustified *. Deu 19:10
I want no more *." 2Sa 14:11
of justice, but found * instead. Is 5:7
"justice" and "*" sound very Is 5:7f
halt to your dishonest gain and *. Eze 22:13

BLOODSHOT
Who is the man with * eyes and Pro 23:29,30

BLOODTHIRSTY
Away, * men! Ps 139:19

BLOODY
calves, and ate the raw, * meat. 1Sa 14:32
to arrange a * death for him." 1Ki 2:9
for the land is full of * crimes. Eze 7:23

BLOOM
the flax was in *), but the wheat Ex 9:31
is finally in full *, then you will Jas 1:4

BLOSSOM
began to bud and *, and soon there Gen 40:9,10
hillsides * with joy. Ps 65:11,12
and the grape vines are in *. Sol 2:13
them, for the grapes are all in *. Sol 2:15
well that it will * on the very Is 17:11
root and bud and * and fill the Is 27:6
the desert will * with flowers. Is 35:1
again, and make her deserts *; Is 51:3
she will * as the lily and root Hos 14:5
watered garden and * like grapes Hos 14:7
there is neither * left nor fruit, Hab 3:17

BLOSSOMING
had budded and was *, and had ripe Num 17:8
or the pomegranates were * yet. Sol 6:11

BLOSSOMS
base, shaft, lamps, and *. Ex 25:31
with identical carvings of *. Ex 37:19
with almond *, a flower on the stem Ex 37:20,21
of trouble! He * for a moment like Job 14:2
and whether the * have opened and Sol 7:12

BLOT
And he said, "I will * out from Gen 6:7
* out every trace of Amalek." Ex 17:14
if not, then * me out of the book Ex 32:32
the Lord told me, 'and I will * Deu 9:13,14
* out his name from under heaven. Deu 29:20
said that he would * out the name 2Ki 14:27
Do not * it out, for they have Neh 4:5
But I will not completely * you Jer 5:18
Don't forgive them, don't * out Jer 18:23
I will * out your names and you Eze 13:9
I will * you out, and I will Eze 32:7

BLOTS
I, yes, I alone am he who * away Is 43:25

BLOTTED
All existence on the earth was * Gen 7:23
of the earth and * out the sun so Ex 10:15
me will be * out of my book. Ex 32:33
May it be * off the calendar, Job 3:6
Let these men be * from the list Ps 69:28
Or, "Let them be * out of the Ps 69:28f
May his family name be * out in a Ps 109:12,13
I've * out your sins; Is 44:22
out that the sunshine isn't * out. Lk 11:35
your sins, and * out the charges Col 2:14
heaps of ashes and * them off the 2Pe 2:6

BLOTTING
the wicked, * out their names Ps 9:5
covered them, * out the sun, and a Mk 9:7
sins against them but * them out. 2Co 5:19

BLOW
He sent a wind to * across the Gen 8:1
wind to * all that day and night; Ex 10:13
let the trumpets * loud and long Lev 25:9
you shall * but you shall not sound Num 10:5,6,7f
are permitted to * the trumpets. Num 10:8
men in my group * our trumpets, you Ju 7:18
our trumpets, you * yours on all Ju 7:18
of Israel. Then * the trumpets and 1Ki 1:34
* you must rush to where I am; Neh 4:19
He makes the winds * and sets Job 28:25
* away like chaff before the wind. Ps 1:4
and confuse them. * them away like Ps 35:5
your fist and give them a final *. Ps 74:11
O my God, * them away like dust; Ps 83:13
* and all the river ice is broken. Ps 147:18
and a bitter * to his mother. Pro 17:25
butter, and a * to the nose causes Pro 30:33
come, south wind, * upon my Sol 4:16
When I * the trumpet, listen! Is 18:3
river bank will wither and * away. Is 19:7
the wind shall * them all away; Is 41:16
The bellows * fiercely; Jer 6:29
and winnow her and * her away; Jer 51:2
We have borne the * that they Lam 5:7
The Lord God says: "With one * Eze 7:5,6
fury upon you and * upon the fire Eze 21:31
I will * the fire of my wrath Eze 22:21
the desert—will * hard upon him and Hos 13:15
again be dealt a * like this. Joe 2:27
east wind to * on Jonah, and the Jon 4:8
He will stop you with one *; Nah 1:9
And when you bring it home, I * Hag 1:9
persecution *, they lose interest. Lk 8:13
prepared to * their mighty blasts. Rev 8:6
angels * their trumpets." Rev 8:13

BLOWING
announced by loud * of trumpets. Lev 23:23,24
of gladness, too, * them at your Num 10:10
with the priests * their trumpets. Jos 6:3,4
* continually on their trumpets. Jos 6:6-9
men did the same, * the trumpets in Ju 7:19,20
much shouting and * of trumpets. 2Sa 6:15
and everyone was rejoicing and * 2Ki 11:13,14
shouts of joy, the * of horns and 1Ch 15:28
land rejoicing and * trumpets, and 2Ch 23:12
Job, * words around like wind? Job 8:2
wind is * and everything is still? Job 37:16,17
is like a cloud * over a desert Pro 25:14
winds * from every direction. Dan 7:2
the hypocrites do—* trumpets in the Mt 6:2
Grass * in the wind? Mt 11:7
Just then a light wind began * Act 27:13
a day later a south wind began *, Act 28:13
They are like clouds * over dry Jud 1:12
four winds from *, so that not a Rev 7:1

BLOWN
When both trumpets are *, the Num 10:3
But if only one is *, then only Num 10:4
When the travel signal is *, the Num 10:5,6,7
and the trumpets were * and all 1Ki 1:39
Would you blame a leaf that is * Job 13:25
* away in the storms of the night. Job 27:20
* by the wind and gone forever. Ps 103:16
* away in a storm from the east. Is 27:7,8
trumpet will be *, and many about Is 27:13
its chaff * away by the wind. Is 30:24
My life is * away like a Is 38:12
away, like chaff * by the wind, Hos 13:3
opportunity is * away like chaff; Zep 2:2
eye, when the last trumpet is *. 1Co 15:52

BLOWS
terrible * against Egypt and Deu 6:22
God has dealt me bitter *. Ru 1:20
from the north, the cold. God * Job 37:10
into battle when the trumpet *. Job 39:24
strength and fall beneath their *. Ps 10:10
deep; your * are crushing me. Ps 38:2
even if the world * up, and the Ps 46:2
and made us reel beneath your *. Ps 60:3
The wind * south and north, here Ecc 1:3-7
with unceasing * of rage and held Is 14:6
take root, when he * on them and Is 40:24
I have created the smith who * Is 54:16
by the death * I rain upon them." Jer 25:16
beneath the awful * of sorrow and Eze 23:33
army coming, and * the alarm to Eze 33:3
beneath your *, and then gloating Hab 2:15
"When the south wind * you say, Lk 12:55
the *, God is well pleased. 1Pe 2:20

BLOWUP
But about that time, a big * Act 19:23

BLUE
Gold, silver, bronze, * cloth, Ex 25:1
feet wide, dyed *, purple, and Ex 26:1
make a veil from *, purple, and Ex 26:31
embroidered *, purple, and scarlet Ex 26:36
embroidered *, purple, and scarlet Ex 27:16
the workmen, using *, purple, and Ex 28:5,6
of gold, *, purple, and scarlet Ex 28:8
use the same gold, *, purple, and Ex 28:15
the ephod by means of * ribbons; Ex 28:28
"The ephod shall be made of * Ex 28:30,31
embroidered with *, purple, and Ex 28:33,34
by means of a * ribbon to the front Ex 28:37,38
*, purple, and scarlet cloth, made Ex 35:5-9
Others brought *, purple, and Ex 35:23
spinning prepared *, purple, and Ex 35:25
designers in *, purple, and scarlet Ex 35:35
from finely-twined *, purple, and Ex 36:8,9
Fifty * ribbons were looped Ex 36:11,12
The *, purple, and scarlet inner Ex 36:35
with *, purple, and scarlet. Ex 36:37
*, purple, and scarlet thread. Ex 38:18
at embroidering *, purple, and Ex 38:23
garments of *, purple, and scarlet Ex 39:1
the *, purple, and scarlet linen; Ex 39:3
of the same gold, *, purple, and Ex 39:4,5
*, purple, and scarlet linen. Ex 39:8
of the ephod, with a * ribbon. Ex 39:21
was woven, all of *, and there was Ex 39:22
with *, purple, and scarlet. Ex 39:24
embroidered with *, purple, and Ex 39:28,29
the turban with a * cord, just as Ex 39:31
goatskins with a * cloth, and place Num 4:6
"Next they must spread a * cloth Num 4:7
"Next they must cover with a * Num 4:9
"They must then spread a * cloth Num 4:11
to be wrapped in a * cloth, covered Num 4:12
to their clothes with a * cord. Num 15:37,38
purple, crimson, and * cloth; 2Ch 2:7
and * linen and crimson cloth. 2Ch 2:14
placed a veil of * and crimson 2Ch 3:14
*, fastened with purple ribbons Est 1:6
the royal robes of * and white and Est 8:15
made of beautiful * sapphire Eze 1:26
SUDDENLY A THRONE of beautiful * Eze 10:1
*, dashing about on their horses. Eze 23:6
fabrics to trade—* cloth, Eze 27:24
to win a * ribbon or a silver cup, 1Co 9:25

BLUEPRINT
Then David gave Solomon the * of 1Ch 28:11
"Every part of this *," David 1Ch 28:19
I was there when he made the * Pro 8:27,28,29

BLURRED
Now all that I know is hazy and * 1Co 13:12

BLURTED
Peter * out, "Sir, it's Mt 17:4
he was saying, * out, "Master, Lk 9:33

BLURTS
Only a fool * out everything he Pro 10:14

BLUSH
I am ashamed; I * to lift up my Ez 9:6
you, and you will * to think of all Is 1:29
No, not at all—they didn't even * Jer 6:15
they don't even know how to *! Jer 8:12

BLUSTERING
* when I scold you in my letters. 2Co 10:9

BOAR
protection. The * from the forest Ps 80:13

BOARD
a new suit and your * and room." Ju 17:10,11
He bought a ticket, went on *, Jon 1:3
when you have a * in your own? Mt 7:3
see because of the * in your own? Mt 7:4
First get rid of the *. Mt 7:5
—when a * is in your own? Lk 6:41
you can't see past the * in yours? Lk 6:42
First get rid of the *, and then Lk 6:42
people put on * all sorts of things Act 28:10

BOARDED
flood came. He * the boat with his Gen 7:7
ended, we * ship at Philippi in Act 20:6
There we * a ship sailing for Act 21:2

BOARDS
and making the *, and in preparing 1Ki 5:18
the floors were made of cypress *. 1Ki 6:15
floor to the ceiling with cedar *. 1Ki 6:16
will enclose her with cedar *." Sol 8:9

BOAST
'My enemies will *, Deu 32:27
of Israel will * to me that they Ju 7:2
I remain silent while you *? Job 11:3
Who in all the earth can * that Job 25:4
They * that neither God nor man Ps 10:6
Some nations * of armies and of Ps 20:7
but our * is in the Lord our God. Ps 20:7
I will * of all his kindness to Ps 34:2
let these who * against me and Ps 35:26
My constant * is God. Ps 44:8
They trust in their wealth and * Ps 49:6
hero, do you? You * about this evil Ps 52:1
They * against the very heavens, Ps 73:9
How these men of evil *! Ps 94:4
And they * that their sin is Is 3:9
* about the liquor they can hold. Is 5:22
They *, "We in our own power and Is 10:13
"Shall the axe * greater power Is 10:15
Will they still * of their Is 19:11
mock the Lord. You *, 'I came with Is 37:24
"You * of wells you've dug in Is 37:25
of it, when you * of living in the Is 48:1
Let them * in this alone: That Jer 9:24
Do you remember that * of yours: Jer 48:14
over her and * of their power. Lam 2:17
you * yourself to be like God. Eze 28:2,3
Then will you * as a god? Eze 28:9

(BOAST Con't)
nor any other god, for he will * Dan 11:37
you *. Ob 1:3
Then what can we * about doing, Rom 3:27
would have something to * about. Rom 4:1
anyone is going to *, let him boast 1Co 1:31
to boast, let him * only of what 1Co 1:31
You can * about us that we, at 2Co 5:12
But we will not * of authority we 2Co 10:13
anyone is going to *, let him boast 2Co 10:17
to boast, let him * about what the 2Co 10:17
feet of those who * that they are 2Co 11:12
I also * a little as they do. 2Co 11:16
But whatever they can * about—I'm 2Co 11:21
fool again—I can * about it, too. 2Co 11:21
(Have I gone mad to * like this? 2Co 11:23
I am going to * only about how 2Co 12:5
I have plenty to * about and 2Co 12:6
Now I am glad to * about how 2Co 12:9
* that you are their disciples. Gal 6:13
that I should * about anything Gal 6:14
with those who * of their 1Ti 6:20
They proudly * about their sins 2Pe 2:18

BOASTED
to my latest dream," he *. Gen 37:9
" 'You have *, "My chariots 2Ki 19:23
his wife, and * to them about his Est 5:11
for she has * against the Lord. Jer 48:42
about whom we had * that under his Lam 4:20
Saying that, you * great words Eze 35:13
story to some who * of their virtue Lk 18:9
that I have publicly * you would. 2Co 8:24
do it, and I have * to the friends 2Co 9:2

BOASTFUL
or envious, never * or proud, 1Co 13:4
they will be proud and *, 2Ti 3:2

BOASTING
They are always * of their evil Ps 10:7
Listen to their *. Ps 17:10
Sinners love to fight; * is Pro 17:19
Because of all your evil *, O Is 10:16
It is the Egyptian army, * that Jer 46:8
care in the world, * that they are Jer 49:31
All your * will die away, and no Eze 7:10,11
God, and the * of its little horn. Dan 7:11
"No one will be * then of his Zec 13:4
replied, "You are *—and lying!" Jn 8:13
* about myself, it doesn't count. Jn 8:54
it is that you are * about your 1Co 5:6
* to Titus has also proved true! 2Co 7:14
I was wrong in my * about you. 2Co 9:3
I may seem to be * more than I 2Co 10:8
THIS * IS all so foolish, but let 2Co 12:1
me act like a fool—* like this—for 2Co 12:11

BOASTS
Ethiopia, someone * that he was Ps 87:4
unscathed. The * of the Babylonians Is 43:14
Jerusalem, which *, 'We are safe; Jer 21:13
has said, but her * are false—her Jer 48:30
Ephraim *, "I am so rich! Hos 12:8
When someone * about himself 2Co 10:18
She *, 'I am queen upon my throne. Rev 18:7

BOAT
Make a * from resinous wood, Gen 6:14
and make three decks inside the * Gen 6:16
a female—into the * with you, to Gen 6:19,20
Store away in the * all the food Gen 6:21
"Go into the * with all your Gen 7:1
He boarded the * with his wife Gen 7:7
They came into the * in pairs, Gen 7:8,9
But Noah had gone into the * Gen 7:13
With them in the * were pairs of Gen 7:14,15
the * high above the earth. Gen 7:17
the * floated safely upon it; Gen 7:18
and those with him in the *. Gen 7:23
Noah and all the animals in the *! Gen 8:1
it began, the * came to rest upon Gen 8:3,4
and drew the dove back into the *. Gen 8:9
So the * was soon empty. Gen 8:18,19
she made a little * from papyrus Ex 2:3
spied the little * among the reeds Ex 2:5
They tried harder to row the * Jon 1:13
Peter, and Andrew—out in a * Mt 4:18
John, sitting in a * with their Mt 4:21
Then he got into a * and started Mt 8:23
up, with waves higher than the *. Mt 8:24
SO JESUS CLIMBED into a * and went Mt 9:1
He got into a * and taught from Mt 13:2,3
a * to a remote area to be alone. Mt 14:13
to get into their * and cross to Mt 14:22
the side of the * and walked on the Mt 14:29
back into the *, the wind stopped. Mt 14:32
into the * and crossed to Magadan. Mt 15:39
John, in a * mending their nets. Mk 1:19
Zebedee in the * with the hired men Mk 1:20
to bring around a * and to have it Mk 3:9
so he got into a * and sat down and Mk 4:1
to break into the * until it was Mk 4:37
the * with his head on a cushion. Mk 4:38
as Jesus was climbing from the *. Mk 5:1
So he got back into the *. Mk 5:18
When Jesus had gone across by * Mk 5:21
So they left by * for a quieter Mk 6:32
there as he stepped from the *; Mk 6:34
get back into the * and strike out Mk 6:45
disciples in their * were out in Mk 6:47
Then he climbed into the * and Mk 6:51
moored the *, and climbed out. Mk 6:53
this he got into a * with his Mk 8:10
So he got back into the * and Mk 8:13
only one loaf of bread in the *. Mk 8:14
could sit in the * and speak to the Lk 5:3
in the other * and soon both boats Lk 5:7
were out in a *, he suggested that Lk 8:22
As he was climbing out of the * Lk 8:27
So he returned to the * and left, Lk 8:37
they got into the * and headed out Jn 6:17
saw Jesus walking toward the *! Jn 6:18,19
the * was where they were going! Jn 6:21
Literally, "and straightway the * Jn 6:21f
in their *, leaving him behind. Jn 6:22,23
side of the *, and you'll get Jn 21:6
The rest of us stayed in the * Jn 21:8
We went aboard a * at Troas, and Act 16:11
to come down to the * to meet him. Act 20:17
We left on a * Act 27:2
the emergency * as though they were Act 27:30
the ropes and let the * fall off. Act 27:32

BOATS
in fast * down the Nile! Is 18:2
behind (though other * followed). Mk 4:36
He noticed two empty * standing Lk 5:2
Stepping into one of the *, Lk 5:3
boat and soon both * were filled Lk 5:7
Several small * from Tiberias Jn 6:22,23
they got into the * and went across Jn 6:24

BOAZ
His name was *. Ru 2:1
belonged to *, this relative of Ru 2:3
* arrived from the city while she Ru 2:4,5
* went over and talked to her. Ru 2:8,9
"Yes, I know," * replied, "and Ru 2:10,11
At lunch time * called to her, Ru 2:14
to work again, * told his young men Ru 2:15
that the owner of the field was *. Ru 2:19
The man I'm thinking of is *! Ru 3:2
After * had finished a good meal, Ru 3:6,7
the barley from *, and mentioned Ru 3:15-18
what happens, for * won't rest Ru 3:15-18
SO * WENT down to the market place Ru 4:1
Then * called for ten of the Ru 4:2
* said to his relative, "You Ru 4:3
Then * told him, "Your purchase Ru 4:5
So, as the man said to *, "You Ru 4:8
Then * said to the witnesses and Ru 4:9
So * married Ruth, and when he Ru 4:13
This is the family tree of *, Ru 4:18-22
Salmon, *, Obed, Jesse, David. Ru 4:18-22
one on the north, the * Pillar. 1Ki 7:16-22
and * means "strength." 1Ki 7:16-22f
and Salma was the father of *. 1Ch 2:11
* was the father of Obed, and 1Ch 2:12
and * (the one on the left). 2Ch 3:17
Salmon was the father of * (Rahab Mt 1:5
was his mother); * was the father Mt 1:5
Obed's father was *; Lk 3:23-38
Obed's father was Boaz;*' father Lk 3:23-38

BOCHERU
Azrikam, *, Ishmael, She-ariah, 1Ch 8:38
Azrikam, *, Ishmael, 1Ch 9:44

BOCHIM
Lord arrived at *, coming from Ju 2:1
place was called "*" (meaning, Ju 2:5

BODIES
All must be circumcised. Your * Gen 17:13
nothing left but our * and land. Gen 47:18
*, reaching from hips to knees. Ex 28:42
get the charred * from before the Lev 10:4
meat or even touch their dead *; Lev 11:8
meat or even touch their dead *. Lev 11:11
"Anyone touching their dead * Lev 11:24
Anyone touching their dead * Lev 11:31
dead * to rot among your idols; Lev 26:30
shave their entire * and wash their Num 8:7
But as for you, your dead * Num 14:32
You may not even touch the dead * Deu 14:8
Your dead * will be food to the Deu 28:26
and * wasted from sorrow and fear. Deu 28:65
and burned their *, and piled a Jos 7:25
that their * be taken down and Jos 10:27
in all, and their * were scattered 1Sa 14:14
and then I will give the dead * 1Sa 17:46
of Ekron. The * of the dead and 1Sa 17:52
they found the * of Saul and his 1Sa 31:8
and took down the * of Saul and his 1Sa 31:12
their * beside the pool in Hebron. 2Sa 4:12
tearing at their * during the day 2Sa 21:10
They had stolen their * from the 2Sa 21:12,13,14
all and dragged their * outside. 2Ki 10:25
troops, and dead * were seen all 2Ki 19:35
other with the * of his victims. 2Ki 21:16
day to strip the * of the men 1Ch 10:8
found the * of Saul and his sons. 1Ch 10:8
body and the * of his three sons. 1Ch 10:12
there were dead * lying on the 2Ch 20:24
out to plunder the * and came away 2Ch 20:25
They have power over our * and Neh 9:37
hung up the * of Haman's ten sons. Est 9:14
to ride across our broken *. Ps 66:12
of ruins. The * of your people lie Ps 79:2
and the rotting * of his people Is 5:25
dead * of those slain in battle. Is 14:19
the vultures will tear * all Is 18:6
*! Is 22:2
Their * shall rise again! Is 26:19
stench of rotting * will fill the Is 34:3
is, "Dead * cannot praise you." Is 38:18f
look at the dead * of those who Is 66:24
not just your *, or else my anger Jer 4:4
will dump the * in that valley. Jer 7:32
that valley. The * of my people Jer 7:33
Tell them this, says the Lord: * Jer 9:22
prophesy—their * shall be thrown Jer 14:16
* of those the sword has killed; Jer 14:18
them, but their * shall lie on the Jer 16:4
famine, and their * shall be picked Jer 16:4
leave your dead * for vultures and Jer 19:7
* shall be heaped in this valley. Jer 19:11
fill Jerusalem with dead * too. Jer 19:12
nor gather up the * to bury them; Jer 25:33
I will feed your dead * to the Jer 34:20
and threw their * into a cistern. Jer 41:7
Ishmael dumped the * of the men he Jer 41:9
Fill its courts with the * of Eze 9:7
part of the * of the cherubim. Eze 10:17f
dead, like the * of those in the Eze 26:20
them, but the * had no breath. Eze 37:8
*, that they may live again." Eze 37:9
me and the * began breathing; Eze 37:10
people of Israel to bury the *. Eze 39:12
"And many of those whose * lie Dan 12:2
* will be scattered everywhere. Amo 8:3
heaps of * everywhere. Nah 3:3
heaps of *, everywhere. Nah 3:3
the dust and your * will lie there Zep 1:17
your *—but can't touch your souls! Mt 10:28
and their * left to the vultures. Lk 17:37f
For ghosts don't have *, as you Lk 24:39
then their * could be taken down. Jn 19:31
"These men are gods in human *!" Act 14:11
sinful things with each other's *. Rom 1:24
who cut their * in actual body Rom 2:29
So when their * died it was not Rom 5:14
Do not let any part of your * Rom 6:13
make your dying * live again after Rom 8:11
including the new * he has promised Rom 8:23
he has promised us—* that will Rom 8:23
with you to give your * to God. Rom 12:1
*, so it is with Christ's body. Rom 12:4,5
never right: our * were not made 1Co 6:13
wants to fill our * with himself. 1Co 6:13
And God is going to raise our * 1Co 6:14
Don't you realize that your * 1Co 6:15
Our * have many parts, but the 1Co 12:12
He has made many parts for our * 1Co 12:18
What kind of * will they have?" 1Co 15:35
Literally, "There are celestial * 1Co 15:40f
in heaven have * far different 1Co 15:40
the glory of their * is different 1Co 15:40
In the same way, our earthly * 1Co 15:42
different from the * we shall have 1Co 15:42
never die. The * we have now 1Co 15:43
Yes, they are weak, dying * now, 1Co 15:43
They are just human * at death, 1Co 15:44
to life they will be superhuman *. 1Co 15:44
are natural, human *, there are 1Co 15:44
also supernatural, spiritual *. 1Co 15:44
have these human * and later on God 1Co 15:46
gives us spiritual, heavenly *. 1Co 15:46
These perishable * of ours are 1Co 15:50
but we shall all be given new *! 1Co 15:51
new * that will never, never die; 1Co 15:52
shall suddenly have new * too. 1Co 15:52
For our earthly *, the ones we 1Co 15:53
into heavenly * that cannot perish 1Co 15:53
container, that is, in our weak *. 2Co 4:7
These * of ours are constantly 2Co 4:10
Jesus Christ within our dying *. 2Co 4:11
Though our * are dying, our inner 2Co 4:16
and leave these *—we will have 2Co 5:1
have wonderful new * in heaven, 2Co 5:1
weary we grow of our present *. 2Co 5:2
have heavenly * which we shall put 2Co 5:2
not be merely spirits without *. 2Co 5:3
These earthly * make us groan 2Co 5:4
of dying and having no * at all. 2Co 5:4
We want to slip into our new * so 2Co 5:4
that these dying * will, as it 2Co 5:4
to our heavenly *, realizing that 2Co 5:6
in these earthly * is time spent 2Co 5:6
We, too, are weak in our *, as he 2Co 13:4
persons without *—the evil rulers Eph 6:12
* that makes us children of God; Php 3:3

BODIES Con't)
take these dying * of ours and Php 3:21
them into glorious * like his own, Php 3:21
cleanse men's * from sin, just Heb 9:13
and because our * have been washed Heb 10:22
sin, and then the * of the animals Heb 13:11
not because our * are washed 1Pe 3:21
—so that although their * were 1Pe 4:6
and the heavenly * will disappear 2Pe 3:10
and the heavenly * will melt and 2Pe 3:12
degrading their * and laughing at Jud 1:8
a half days their * will be exposed Rev 11:8,9
The oceans surrendered the * Rev 20:13

BODILY
and a ram without * defect for a Lev 9:2
lamb, all without * defect, for Lev 9:3
who have any * defect may not offer Lev 21:16,17
desires, not by a * operation of Col 2:11
spiritually fit. * exercise is all 1Ti 4:8

BODY
* from the dust of the ground Gen 2:7
Then, standing beside her *, he Gen 23:3
and impale your * on a pole, and Gen 40:18,19
upon his father's * and wept over Gen 50:1
his morticians to embalm the *. Gen 50:2
swear to take his * back to the Gen 50:5
and carried his * into the land of Gen 50:12,13
would take his * back with them Gen 50:25
* was placed in a coffin in Egypt. Gen 50:26
and hid his * in the sand. Ex 2:12
Then take the *, including the Ex 29:14
pieces of the *, and burn it all Ex 29:17
as the dead * of an animal Lev 5:2
or the dead * of some forbidden Lev 5:2
not severing its head from its *. Lev 5:8
Anyone touching the dead * of Lev 11:27
"If the dead * of such an animal Lev 11:35
If the * falls into a spring or Lev 11:36
all over his * from head to foot Lev 13:12
eats the dead * of an animal that Lev 17:15
or lacking in its * parts, it may Lev 22:23
thigh rot away and your * swell.' Num 5:21,22
her, and her * will swell and her Num 5:27
go near any dead * during the Num 6:6,7
even if it is the * of his father, Num 6:6,7
of touching a dead *, or if they Num 9:10
* is half rotted away at birth." Num 12:12
a dead human * shall be defiled for Num 19:11
the man's * and into her stomach. Num 25:8
killed anyone or touched a dead *. Num 31:19
from the * to the nearest city. Deu 21:2
on a tree, his * shall not remain Deu 21:23
he took down the * and threw it in Jos 8:29
down to get his *, and they brought Ju 16:31
knife and cut her * into twelve Ju 19:29
So I cut her * into twelve Ju 20:6
only the trunk of his * was left 1Sa 5:4
to you will be over my dead *." 1Sa 22:23
Ashtaroth, and his * was fastened 1Sa 31:10
It went right through his * and 2Sa 2:23
Joab and his men took Asahel's * 2Sa 2:32
They threw Absalom's * into a 2Sa 18:17
With the * out of the way, 2Sa 20:13
to, therefore your * shall not be 1Ki 13:21,22
killed him. His * lay there on the 1Ki 13:24,25
Those who came by and saw the * 1Ki 13:24,25
He found the prophet's * lying in 1Ki 13:28
the * nor attacked the donkey. 1Ki 13:28
So the prophet laid the * upon 1Ki 13:29
He laid the * in his own grave, 1Ki 13:30
And he took the boy's * from her 1Ki 17:19
and laid the * on his bed, and 1Ki 17:19
apart the * of your wife, Jezebel. 1Ki 21:23
And his * was taken to Samaria and 1Ki 22:36,37
Then he lay upon the child's *, 2Ki 4:34
And the child's * began to grow 2Ki 4:34
flesh and that her * would be 2Ki 9:36
his * into the tomb of Elisha. 2Ki 13:20,21
And as soon as the * touched 2Ki 13:20,21
him there. His * was returned on 2Ki 14:20
His officers took his * back in 2Ki 23:30
and it pierced his *. 1Ch 10:4
and brought back his * and the 1Ch 10:12
Touch his * with sickness and he Job 2:4,5
And I know that after this * has Job 19:26
has decayed, this * shall see God! Job 19:26
The arrow is pulled from his * Job 20:25
to keep soul and * together. Job 24:5
Then his * will become as Job 33:25
Heal me, for my * is sick, and I Ps 6:2
Heart, *, and soul are filled Ps 16:9
I can count every bone in my *. Ps 22:17
Because of your anger my * is Ps 38:3,4
and my whole * is diseased. Ps 38:7
You made my *, Lord; Ps 119:73
inner parts of my *, and knit them Ps 139:13
consumes your *, and you say, Pro 5:11
can sustain his broken *, but Pro 18:14
into the little * of a baby while Ecc 11:5
with topaz; his * is bright ivory Sol 5:14
*, as when a sick man wastes away. Is 10:18
graves, but your * is thrown out Is 14:19
are circumcised in * but not in Jer 9:25,26
His dead * shall be thrown out to Jer 36:30
and the other pair covered his *. Eze 1:11
each had two wings covering his *. Eze 1:23
the bones of each * came together Eze 37:7
cows, and his * was wet with dew; Dan 4:33
the cows and his * was wet with the Dan 5:21
was killed and its * handed over to Dan 7:11
in to carry his * from the house, Amo 6:10
For you already have life and a * Mt 6:25
destroy both soul and * in hell. Mt 10:28
came for his * and buried it, and Mt 14:12
on me to prepare my * for burial. Mt 26:12
it and eat it, for this is my *." Mt 26:26
willing, but how weak the * is!" Mt 26:41
to Pilate and asked for Jesus' *. Mt 27:58
Joseph took the * and wrapped it Mt 27:59
and stealing his * and then telling Mt 27:64
Come in and see where his * was Mt 28:6
during the night and stole his *. Mt 28:12,13
for his * and buried it in a tomb. Mk 6:29
threw his * out of the vineyard. Mk 12:8
my * ahead of time for burial. Mk 14:8
and said, "Eat it—this is my *." Mk 14:22
willing enough, the * is weak." Mk 14:38
to Pilate and asked for Jesus' *. Mk 15:42,43
told Joseph he could have the *. Mk 15:45
and, taking Jesus' * down from the Mk 15:46
Look, that's where his * was Mk 16:6
They can only kill the *; Lk 12:4
Jesus replied, "Where the * is, Lk 17:37
"This is my *, given for you. Lk 22:19
and asked for the * of Jesus. Lk 23:50,51,52
So he took down Jesus' * and Lk 23:53
As the * was taken away, the Lk 23:55
in—but the Lord Jesus' * was gone. Lk 24:3
report that his * was missing, and Lk 24:22,23
enough, Jesus' * was gone, just as Lk 24:24
"this sanctuary" he meant his *. Jn 2:21
permission to take Jesus' * down; Jn 19:38
Together they wrapped Jesus' * Jn 19:40
taken the Lord's * out of the tomb, Jn 20:2
the * of Jesus had been lying. Jn 20:12
let the * of your Holy Son decay. Act 2:27
in hell and his * would not decay. Act 2:31
came to a small * of water, and the Act 8:36
Turning to the * he said, "Get Act 9:40
and was buried, and his * decayed. Act 13:36
to life, whose * was not touched at Act 13:37
bodies in actual * circumcision, Rom 2:29
your sin-loving * is no longer Rom 6:6
control your puny * any longer; Rom 6:12
He sent his own Son in a human * Rom 8:3
your * will die because of sin; Rom 8:10
bodies, so it is with Christ's *. Rom 12:4,5
No other sin affects the * as 1Co 6:18
this sin it is against your own *. 1Co 6:18
learned that your * is the home of 1Co 6:19
Your own * does not belong to 1Co 6:19
So use every part of your * to 1Co 6:20
right to her own *, for her husband 1Co 7:4
right to his own *, for it belongs 1Co 7:4
Literally, "pure in * and in 1Co 7:34f
Like an athlete I punish my *, 1Co 9:27
together in the benefits of his *. 1Co 10:16
all parts of the one * of Christ. 1Co 10:17
This is my *, which is given 1Co 11:24
the * and the blood of the Lord. 1Co 11:27
thinking about the * of Christ and 1Co 11:29
* when they are all put together. 1Co 12:12
So it is with the "*" of 1Co 12:12
is a part of the one * of Christ. 1Co 12:13
fitted us all together into one *. 1Co 12:13
into Christ's * by the one Spirit, 1Co 12:13
Yes, the * has many parts, not 1Co 12:14
not a part of the * because I am 1Co 12:15
make it any less a part of the *. 1Co 12:15
am not part of the * because I am 1Co 12:16
make it any less a part of the *? 1Co 12:16
Suppose the whole * were an 1Co 12:17
Or if your whole * were just one 1Co 12:17
What a strange thing a * would 1Co 12:19
but still there is only one *. 1Co 12:20
So God has put the * together in 1Co 12:24
are the one * of Christ and each 1Co 12:27
in his church, which is his *: 1Co 12:28
it a beautiful new *—just the kind 1Co 15:38
Adam, was given a natural, human * 1Co 15:45
Every human being has a * just 1Co 15:48
of * as his—a body from heaven. 1Co 15:48
of body as his—a * from heaven. 1Co 15:48
Just as each of us now has a * 1Co 15:49
some day have a * like Christ's. 1Co 15:49
an earthly * made of flesh and 1Co 15:50
are here in this * or away from 2Co 5:9
this * and with him in heaven. 2Co 5:9
he has done in his earthly *. 2Co 5:10
wrong, whether of * or spirit, and 2Co 7:1
Don't ask me whether my * was 2Co 12:2,3
His weak, human * died on the 2Co 13:4
have within this * is a result of Gal 2:20
for I carry on my * the scars of Gal 6:17
which is his *, filled with Eph 1:23
As parts of the same *, our Eph 2:16
We are all parts of one *, we Eph 4:4
up the church, the * of Christ, to Eph 4:12
is the Head of his *, the church. Eph 4:15,16
Under his direction the whole * Eph 4:15,16
so that the whole * is healthy and Eph 4:15,16
is in charge of his * the church. Eph 5:23
No one hates his own * but Eph 5:29,30
cares for his * the church, of Eph 5:29,30
and wife are one * is proved by the Eph 5:31
we are parts of the * of Christ. Eph 5:32
He is the Head of the * made up Col 1:18
of his own human *, and now as a Col 1:22
sufferings for his *, the church. Col 1:24
there is all of God in a human *; Col 2:9
of us who are his * are joined; Col 2:19
and hard on the *, but they have no Col 2:23
and privilege as members of his *. Col 3:15
and soul and * be kept strong and 1Th 5:23
Christ's *, being human, was Heb 5:7f
And can a human * live long Heb 5:7f
made ready this * of mine for me to Heb 10:5
curtain—his human *—to let us into Heb 10:20
Just as the * is dead when there Jas 2:26
and poisons every part of the *. Jas 3:6
sins in his own * when he died on 1Pe 2:24
But though his * died, his spirit 1Pe 3:18
For remember, when your * 1Pe 4:1
became man with a human *? 1Jn 4:2
a human being with a * like ours. 2Jn 1:7
you and that your * is as healthy 3Jn 1:2
Satan about Moses' *, did not dare Jud 1:9

BODY-HAIR
Literally, "head-hair, beard,* Is 7:20f

BODYGUARD
* and his chief executioner. Gen 39:1
said to his young *, "Come on, 1Sa 14:1
Jonathan had said to his *. 1Sa 14:6
exclaimed to his *, "for the Lord 1Sa 14:12
that Jonathan and his * were gone. 1Sa 14:17
and David became his *. 1Sa 16:21
Why, he is the captain of your * 1Sa 22:14
* for life," Achish told him. 1Sa 28:2
of Jehoiada) was captain of his *, 2Sa 8:18
Quick, take my * and chase after 2Sa 20:6
Joab's army and the king's own *. 2Sa 20:7
was in charge of the king's *. 2Sa 20:23
And David made him chief of his * 2Sa 23:23
and David's * took Solomon to 1Ki 1:38
protected by the king's own *; 1Ki 1:44,45
palace guard and the queen's *. 2Ki 11:4
by her * and many trumpeters; 2Ki 11:13,14
of the royal *, arrived at 2Ki 25:8
He cried out to his *, "Quick, 1Ch 10:4
Then his *, seeing that Saul was 1Ch 10:5
David made him captain of his *. 1Ch 11:24,25
of the king's *—the Cherethites and 1Ch 18:17
*, she could scarcely believe it! 2Ch 9:4
the care of the captain of his *. 2Ch 12:10
You Levites, form a * for the 2Ch 23:7
of his personal *, and told them Act 10:7

BODYGUARDS
He ordered his *, "Kill these 1Sa 22:17
Integrity as my *, for I expect you Ps 25:21
swordsmen and experienced *. Sol 3:8
So he sent one of his * to the Mk 6:27

BOG
out from the * and the mire, and Ps 40:2

BOHAN
to the stone of * (son of Reuben). Jos 15:6
to the Stone of * (who was a son of Jos 18:17

BOIL
"Do not * a young goat in its Ex 23:19
* its meat in a sacred area. Ex 29:31
and his sons, "* the meat at the Lev 8:31
skin, or a scab or * or pimple with Lev 13:1
of a man who has a * in his skin Lev 13:18
leprosy has broken out from the *. Lev 13:20
the scar from the *, and the priest Lev 13:23
"You must not * a young goat in Deu 14:21
Hezekiah to * some dried figs and 2Ki 20:7
of them and spread it on the *. 2Ki 20:7
"He makes the water * with his Job 41:31,32
*, and he will get well again." Is 38:21
the forests and * the oceans dry. Is 64:2
the north will * out upon all the Jer 1:14
a pot of water on the fire to *. Eze 24:3
beneath the pot. * the meat well, Eze 24:5
let the fire roar and the pot *. Eze 24:10
me, the priests * the meat of the Eze 46:19,20
—* the sacrifices the people offer. Eze 46:24
charge to * their sacrifices in; Zec 14:21

BOILED
be eaten raw or *, but roasted, Ex 12:9
the clothing is * shall be broken; Lev 6:28
it in mortars, * it, and then made Num 11:8
meat before it was *, so that it 1Sa 2:15
Saul * with rage. 1Sa 20:30

(BOILED Con't)
So we * my son and ate him, but — 2Ki 6:26-30
Passover lambs and * the holy — 2Ch 35:13
And so my fury and anger * — Jer 44:6
At this their anger * and they — Act 19:28

BOILING
animal was *, the servant would put — 1Sa 2:13,14
* pot that is fired by dry rushes. — Job 41:20
And I replied, "I see a pot of * — Jer 1:13
* vats, with ovens underneath. — Eze 46:23

BOILS
of Egypt and cause * to break out — Ex 9:9
sky, and it became * that broke out — Ex 9:10
because of the *, for the boils — Ex 9:11
for the * appeared upon them too. — Ex 9:11
upon you Egyptian *, tumors, — Deu 28:27
The Lord will cover you with * — Deu 28:35
villages with a plague of *. — 1Sa 5:6
case of * from head to foot. — Job 2:7

BOLD
and his staff became * again. — Ex 14:5
Yes, be * and strong! — Jos 1:9
that is why I have been * enough — 2Sa 7:27
The names in * face type are — 1Ch 1:1f
The use of * type or italic type — 1Ch 1:1f
appeared in * face type. — 1Ch 1:5-9f
ever more * in their wickedness." — Ps 52:7
Winking at sin leads to sorrow; * — Pro 10:10
But the godly are * as lions! — Pro 28:1
I publicly proclaim * promises; — Is 45:19
* and returned to their sins. — Jer 34:11f
But even so I have been * enough — Rom 15:15,16
Then he will become * enough to — 1Co 8:10
letters are * enough when he is far — 2Co 10:1
* in telling others about Christ. — Php 1:14
Pray that I will be * enough to — Col 4:4
and * trust in the Lord. — 1Ti 3:13

BOLDEST
When it comes true, the * heart — Eze 21:7

BOLDLY
very popular. He * followed the — 2Ch 17:6
tell him * that I am not guilty. — Job 9:35
evident to all—she * murders, — Eze 24:7
Jewish leaders, * asked Pilate for — Jn 19:38
and * preached God's message. — Act 4:31
* in the name of the Lord. — Act 9:29
Barnabas spoke out * and declared, — Act 13:46
time, preaching *, and the Lord — Act 14:3
So he was preaching * and — Act 18:25,26
and preached * each Sabbath day — Act 19:8
And later on Isaiah said * that — Rom 10:20
We * say what we believe — 2Co 4:13
right words as I * tell others — Eph 6:19
on speaking out * for him even here — Eph 6:20
ready to speak out * for Christ — Php 1:20
Yet God gave us the courage to * — 1Th 2:2
the opportunity to * preach a whole — 2Ti 4:17
So let us come * to the very — Heb 4:16

BOLDNESS
Forgive me for my * in coming — 1Sa 25:28
full of fight and *, where even the — Nah 2:11
When the Council saw the * of — Act 4:13
servants great * in their — Act 4:29
them with all * about the Kingdom — Act 28:31
preach with great *, and not as — 2Co 3:12
stir into flame the strength and * — 2Ti 1:6

BOLT
"Let us hide in the Temple and * — Neh 6:10
myrrh as I pulled back the *. — Sol 5:5

BOLTED
pulled Lot in and * the door, and — Gen 19:10
a drawn sword. She * off the road — Num 22:22,23

BOLTS
May you be protected with strong * — Deu 33:25
doors, and made the * and bars. — Neh 3:3
and installed the * and bars. — Neh 3:6
and installed the * and bars; — Neh 3:13
and installed the * and bars. — Neh 3:14
fills his hands with lightning *. — Job 36:32
The lightning * are directed by — Job 37:12
Let loose your lightning *, your — Ps 144:6

BOND
immediate * of love between them. — 1Sa 18:1
Literally, "every male, both * — 1Ki 14:10f
The common * of rebels is their — Pro 14:9
The common * of godly people is — Pro 14:9
to show that the * of unity between — Zec 11:14

BONDAGE
broken spirit and the cruel *." — Ex 6:8,9f
On that day God will end the * — Is 10:27
woman from the * in which Satan has — Lk 13:16

BONDS
my * and I will serve you forever. — Ps 116:16
Go now, leave your * and slavery. — Is 52:11

BONDSERVANTS
Literally, "Become not * of — 1Co 7:23f

BONE
"She is part of my own * and — Gen 2:23
must not break a * of it, and must — Num 9:12
he even touches a * or a grave, he — Num 19:16
or by touching a *, or touching — Num 19:18
Literally, "your * and flesh." — 1Ch 11:1f
must have stripped them to the *. — Job 22:6
even though no * is broken, so — Job 33:19
I can count every * in my body. — Ps 22:17
flood, sometimes as dry as a *." — Jer 15:17,18
my people and strip them to the *. — Mic 3:2

BONES
you shall not break any of its *. — Ex 12:46
Moses took the * of Joseph with — Ex 13:19
would take his * with them when God — Ex 13:19
He shall break their * in pieces, — Num 24:3-9
The * of Joseph, which the people — Jos 24:32
for the men's * to be buried in the — 2Sa 21:12,13,14
him the * of Saul and Jonathan. — 2Sa 21:12,13,14
So their * were brought to him. — 2Sa 21:12,13,14
and men's * shall be burned upon — 1Ki 13:2
Lay my * beside his bones. — 1Ki 13:31
Lay my bones beside his *. — 1Ki 13:31
touched Elisha's *, the dead man — 2Ki 13:20,21
by scattering human * over them. — 2Ki 23:14
to bring out the * in them and to — 2Ki 23:16
Don't disturb his *." — 2Ki 23:18
So they didn't burn his * or those — 2Ki 23:18
* upon the altars to defile them. — 2Ki 23:20
Then he burned the * of the — 2Ch 34:5
and knit together * and sinews. — Job 10:11
me to skin and *—as a proof, they — Job 16:8
I am skin and * and have escaped — Job 19:20
Though still a young man, his * — Job 20:11
* of the dying cry from the city; — Job 24:12
were relentlessly gnawing at my *. — Job 30:17
and peeling. My * burn with fever. — Job 30:30
He becomes thin, mere skin and * — Job 33:21
and all my * are out of joint. — Ps 22:14
Literally, "Even my * are rotting — Ps 31:9,10f
God will scatter the * of these, — Ps 53:5
I am reduced to skin and * — Ps 102:5
from fasting and I am skin and *. — Ps 109:24
* are strewn across the ground, — Ps 141:6,7
the earth, our * are scattered at — Ps 141:6,7f
a soft tongue can break hard *. — Pro 25:15
animals will gnaw * all winter. — Is 18:6
and dig out their * and spread — Jer 8:2
Their * shall not be gathered up — Jer 8:2
that burns in my *, and I can't — Jer 20:9
king of Babylon, crunched their *. — Jer 50:17
heaven that burns within my *; — Lam 1:13
made me old and has broken my *. — Lam 3:4
Their skin sticks to their *; — Lam 4:8
be shattered; the * of their — Eze 6:4-7
until the flesh falls off the *. — Eze 24:5
then empty the pot and burn the *. — Eze 24:10
and fill the valleys with your *. — Eze 32:5
(iniquities) upon their *." — Eze 32:27f
up the broken * nor gone looking — Eze 34:4
full of old, dry * that were — Eze 37:1
"Son of dust, can these * become — Eze 37:3
Then he told me to speak to the * — Eze 37:4
and say: "O dry *, listen to the — Eze 37:4
valley, and the * of each body came — Eze 37:7
formed over the *, and skin covered — Eze 37:8
meant: "These *," he said, — Eze 37:11
of dried-out *—all hope is gone.' — Eze 37:11
Whenever anyone sees some *, he — Eze 39:15,16
them, break their *, and chop them — Mic 3:3
laid bare his * from head to toe. — Hab 3:13
heal the broken *, nor feed the — Zec 11:16
*, and of foulness and corruption. — Mt 23:27
"Not one of his * shall be — Jn 19:36,37
his * with them when they left! — Heb 11:22

BONFIRE
and burned them at a public *. — Act 19:18,19
to us, building a * on the beach to — Act 28:1
away for a great * at the judgment — 2Pe 3:7

BONY
very skinny and *—in fact, I've — Gen 41:19

BOO
death, and * him into eternity. — Job 27:23

BOOBY
They lay a * trap for their own — Pro 1:18

BOOBY-TRAP
There is a * in every path he — Job 18:10

BOOK
And he read to the people the * — Ex 24:7
he had written—the * of the — Ex 24:7
out of the * you have written." — Ex 32:32
me will be blotted out of my *. — Ex 32:33
these curses in a * and wash them — Num 5:23
This fact is mentioned in The * — Num 21:14
THIS * RECORDS Moses' address to — Deu 1:1
the * kept by the Levite-priests. — Deu 17:18
written in this *, thus refusing — Deu 28:58,59
this *, until you are destroyed. — Deu 28:61
written in this * shall lie heavily — Deu 29:20
recorded in this *) that befall — Deu 29:21
in this *) broke forth upon them. — Deu 29:27
written in this * of the law, and — Deu 30:10
recorded in this *, he instructed — Deu 31:24
to put this * of the law beside — Deu 31:26
in the * of his laws: "Make me — Jos 8:31
written in the * of God's laws. — Jos 8:34
greater detail in The * of Jashar. — Jos 10:1
in the * of the laws of Moses; — Jos 23:
reply in the * of the laws of God, — Jos 24:2
he wrote them in a * and put it — 1Sa 10:2
It is quoted here from the *, — 2Sa 1:17,1
in the * The Acts of Solomon. — 1Ki 11:4
of this *: you must be very angry — 2Ki 22:12,1
as I stated in that * you read. — 2Ki 22:15,1
when you read the * and its — 2Ki 22:18,1
to them the entire * of God's laws — 2Ki 23:
to do everything the * commanded. — 2Ki 23:
God in The * of the Covenant. — 2Ki 23:2
written in the * that Hilkiah the — 2Ki 23:2
They took copies of The * of the — 2Ch 17:7,8,
are written in The * of Isaiah (the — 2Ch 32:3
the remainder of the *, is Ezra. — Ez 7:28
In The * of the Chronicles the — Neh 12:2
recorded in the * of the history of — Est 2:2
are written in The * of the — Est 10:
have recorded every one in your *. — Ps 56:
be blotted out of the * of life." — Ps 69:28
Every day was recorded in your *! — Ps 139:1
events are a sealed * to them. — Is 29:1
the words of a *, and out of their — Is 29:1
Search the * of the Lord and see — Is 34:1
promised in this *—all the — Jer 25:1
times throughout the * of Ezekiel. — Eze 2:1
learned from the * of Jeremiah the — Dan 9:
written in the '* of the Future.' — Dan 10:20,2
written in the * will endure it. — Dan 12:
And he had a * of Remembrance — Mal 3:1
Every law in the * will continue — Mt 5:1
The Matthew who wrote this *. — Mt 9:9
In the * written by the prophet — Mk 1:2
unrecorded in the * of Isaiah, — Mk 1:3
never read in the * of Exodus about — Mk 12:2
Scriptures. The * of Isaiah the — Lk 4:17
He closed the * and handed it — Lk 4:20
For David himself wrote in the * — Lk 20:42,4
beginning with the * of Genesis and — Lk 24:2
to be John, the writer of this *. — Jn 13:23
told about in this *, but these are — Jn 20:30,31
e., the * of Luke; — Act 1:1
appears in the * of Psalms, where — Act 1:20
really throw the * at them." — Act 4:17
In the * of Amos' prophecies the — Act 7:42
from the * of the prophet Isaiah. — Act 8:28
Luke, the writer of this *, now — Act 16:10f
Do you remember what the * of — Rom 3:4
As it says in the * of Job, God — 1Co 3:19
And again, in the * of Psalms, — 1Co 3:20
written in God's * of the Law." — Gal 3:10
are written in the * of Life. — Php 4:3
No, for in the * of Psalms David — Heb 2:6
For he says in the * of Psalms, — Heb 2:12
the blood over the * of God's laws — Heb 9:19
THIS * UNVEILS some of the future — Rev 1:1
his name from the * of Life, but I — Rev 3:5
not written in the * of Life of the — Rev 13:8f
Lamb's * of Life—worshiped the — Rev 13:8
written in the * of Life before the — Rev 17:8
opened, including the * of Life. — Rev 20:12
recorded in the * of Life, he was — Rev 20:15
written in the Lamb's * of Life. — Rev 21:27
heed the truth stated in this *. — Rev 22:9
who reads this *: If anyone adds — Rev 22:18
the plagues described in this *. — Rev 22:18

BOOK'S
the limits of this * — Jn 18:34f

BOOKS
"Read the history * and see— — Job 8:8
frequent puns in the prophetic *. — Jer 29:24f
its session and The * were opened. — Dan 7:10
world could hardly contain the *! — Jn 21:25
readings from the * of Moses and — Act 13:15
their incantation * and charms and — Act 19:18,19
the value of the * at $10,000. — Act 19:18,19
written in the * of prophecy; — Act 24:14
the five * of Moses and the books — Act 28:23
of Moses and the * of prophecy. — Act 28:23
*, but especially the parchments. — 2Ti 4:13
and The * were opened, including — Rev 20:12
written in The *, each according to — Rev 20:12

BOOMERANG
Haman's plot to *, and he and his — Est 9:24,25
plans for others * upon himself; — Ps 7:16
of my enemies to * upon them. — Ps 54:5
sins of evil men to * upon them! — Ps 94:23
Let their plots *! — Ps 140:9
Your acts will * upon your heads. — Ob 1:15
Let these good things * on them — Rom 11:9

BOOMERANGS
violence * and destroys them. — Pro 21:7

BOOR
Nabal is a bad-tempered *, but — 1Sa 25:25

BOOST
has been a great * in getting out — Php 1:12

BOOTH
as full of cracks as a leafy *! — Job 27:18
though it were a * of leaves and — Lam 2:6
sitting at a tax collection *. — Mt 9:9

BOOTH Con't)
sitting at his tax collection *. Mk 2:14
at a tax collection *. Lk 5:27

BOOTHS
Feast of Tabernacles" or "*." Zec 14:16f

BOOTSTRAPS
their belts are tight, their * Is 5:27

BOOTY
keep for yourself the * stolen Gen 14:21
but give a share of the * to Gen 14:24
And divide the captured *." Ex 15:9
and a lot of miscellaneous *. Num 31:9,10,11
a list of all the *, including the Num 31:26
The total * (besides the Num 31:32-35
The half of the * assigned to the Num 31:42-46
the Lord from our *—gold jewelry, Num 31:50
kept personal * for themselves. Num 31:53
along with the * gained from Deu 2:35,36
must pile all the * into the middle Deu 13:16
Keep none of the *! Deu 13:17
women, children, cattle, and *. Deu 20:14
back home—their * of cattle, Jos 22:7,8
defeated. The * included 50,000 1Ch 5:21
and to gather the * from the 1Ch 10:8
of * to the king of Damascus. 2Ch 24:23
off great quantities of *. 2Ch 25:13
of * which they took to Samaria. 2Ch 28:8
the captives and * to the political 2Ch 28:14
of Israel are dividing the *. Ps 68:11,12,13
foreigners and to wicked men as *. Eze 7:21
capture vast * and many slaves. Eze 38:12

BORASHAN
Hormah, *, Athach, Hebron. 1Sa 30:27-31

BORDER
Located along the * of Babylonia. Gen 2:11,12f
at the southern * of Judah. Gen 15:18f
* in the direction of Assyria). Gen 25:18
your land from one * to the other. Ex 8:2
land of Egypt from * to border; Ex 10:14
land of Egypt from border to *; Ex 10:14
after wave of them crossing the *. Ex 12:51
your * on the other side." Num 20:17
and Aaron at the * of the land of Num 20:23
Literally, "For the * of the Num 21:24f
has arrived at his *, and he wants Num 22:11
Arnon River, at the * of his land. Num 22:36
then Iyeabarim (at the * of Moab). Num 33:44
"Your northern * will begin at Num 34:7,8,9
"The eastern * will be from Num 34:10,11
[on the * of the Promised Land Deu 1:19,20,21
touched the * of the kingdom of Jos 12:5
was the western *, extending as far Jos 13:27,28
then the * turned east from the Jos 13:27,28
at the northern * of Edom, crossed Jos 15:1
From there the * extended to the Jos 15:7
From there the * extended from Jos 15:9
Then the * circled west of Jos 15:10,11
The western * was the shoreline Jos 15:12
and west to the * of the Jos 16:1
southward from the * of Asher to Jos 17:7
Tappu-ah, on the * of Manasseh's Jos 17:8
of Tappu-ah the * of Manasseh Jos 17:9
There the * turned south, Jos 18:14
The southern * ran from the edge Jos 18:15
of the Arabah. The * then went down Jos 18:18
The eastern * was the Jordan Jos 18:20
went east to the * of Jos 19:12
* of Abel-meholah near Tabbath. Ju 7:22
along the eastern * until at last Ju 11:18
If they cross the * of our land 1Sa 6:9
as far as the * of Beth-shemesh. 1Sa 6:12
moved toward the * above the valley 1Sa 13:18
and as far away as the * of Egypt. 2Ch 9:26
the * in the land of Israel. 2Ch 17:4
broke across the *, and carried 2Ch 21:17
He brought them to the * of his Ps 78:54
beard, and onto the * of his robe. Ps 133:2
a monument to the Lord at its *. Is 19:19
war resounds from the northern *. Jer 8:16
at the southern * of Judah to Jer 37:5
as far south as the * of Ethiopia. Eze 29:10
which are on the * between Damascus Eze 47:16
on the * of Hauran. Eze 47:16
So the northern * will be from Eze 47:17
Hazar-enon, on the * with Hamath to Eze 47:17
"The eastern * will run south Eze 47:18
"The southern * will go west Eze 47:19
Hazar-enon on the * between Eze 48:1
from its eastern * clear across to Eze 48:23
clear across to the western *. Eze 48:23
while its south * runs from Tamar Eze 48:27,28
Geba (the northern * of Judah) to Zec 14:10
(the southern *) will become one Zec 14:10
they reached the * between Galilee Lk 17:11
*, and stayed there several days. Act 16:12

BORDERING
in the lowlands * Philistine 1Ch 27:28
When I punish all the * nations Eze 28:26

BORDERS
But as he was approaching the * Gen 12:11,12,13
with his * extending to Sidon. Gen 49:13
within the * of your land! Ex 13:6,7
encamped on the * of your land. Num 20:16
River, near the * of the Amorites. Num 21:13
we have passed beyond your *. Num 21:22
as far as the * of the Ammonites; Num 21:24
shall cross the * of Moab at Ar, Deu 2:18
(Bashan) to the * of the Geshurites Deu 3:14
Lord enlarges your *, the central Deu 12:20-23
extended as far as the * of Ammon. Jos 13:10
* of Edom in the Negeb, namely: Jos 15:21-32
cities along the * of Ashdod with Jos 15:46
and down to the * of Egypt. 1Ki 4:21
engraved on the * of the band 1Ki 7:36
and have conquered the farthest *. 2Ki 19:23
all the way to the * of Israel, and Eze 11:10
I will chase you even to the * of Eze 11:11
from the Negeb to your northern *. Eze 21:4
these same eastern and western *. Eze 48:24
Then Gad, with the same * on Eze 48:27,28
to enlarge their *, they committed Amo 1:13
them waste to their farthest *; Zep 3:6
power goes far beyond our *!" Mal 1:5
far beyond the * of Galilee so that Mt 4:24
to the Judean * and into the area Mk 10:1
Judea and even out across the *. Lk 7:17
Then going along the * of Mysia Act 16:7

BORE
new wife, and she * him several Gen 25:1
twelve tribes that * their names. Gen 25:16
and shall publicly * his ear with Ex 21:6
tonight, and * sons, would you Ru 1:12
Caleb's concubine Ephah * him 1Ch 2:46
Maacah, * him Sheber, Tirhanah, 1Ch 2:48,49
Naarah * him Ahuzzam, Hepher, 1Ch 4:6
and Helah * him Zereth, Izhar, 1Ch 4:7
* him a son whom she named Peresh; 1Ch 7:16
Hammolecheth, Machir's sister, * 1Ch 7:18
wife conceived and * a son whom he 1Ch 7:23
The children she * him were 2Ch 11:20
and * a son, Immanuel, the Christ. Is 7:14f
she conceived, and * me a son, and Is 8:3
me here alone. Who * these? Is 49:21
Yet it was our grief he *, our Is 53:4
a sinner, and he * the sins of Is 53:12
I married them, and they * me Eze 23:4,5
children whom they * to me, burning Eze 23:37
and she conceived and * him a son. Hos 1:3
sicknesses and * our diseases." Mt 8:17
But lest I * you, kindly give me Act 24:4

BORED
Jehoiada the priest * a hole in 2Ki 12:9
The backslider gets * with Pro 14:14
you won't become * with being a Heb 6:12

BORN
To Adah was * a baby named Gen 4:20
wife, Zillah, was * Tubal-cain. Gen 4:22
the ancestor (of Seth) was *." Gen 5:3,4,5f
Seth was *, the very image of his Gen 5:3,4,5
After Seth was *, Gen 5:3,4,5
this ancestor of Seth was *." Gen 5:3,4,5f
old when his son Enosh was *. Gen 5:6,7,8
old when his son Kenan was *. Gen 5:9,10,11
old when his son Mahalalel was *. Gen 5:12,13,14
old when his son Jared was *. Gen 5:15,16,17
old when his son Enoch was *. Gen 5:18,19,20
old when his son Methuselah was *. Gen 5:21-24
old when his son Lamech was *; Gen 5:25,26,27
years old when his son Noah was *. Gen 5:28-31
for sons were * to them after the Gen 10:1
Two sons were * to Eber: Gen 10:25
Arpachshad, * two years after the Gen 11:10,11
Or, by Hebrew usage, "there was * Gen 11:12,13f
Shelah was *, and after that he Gen 11:12,13
his son Eber was *, living 403 Gen 11:14,15
old when his son Peleg was * Gen 11:16,17
years old when his son Reu was *. Gen 11:18,19
years old when Serug was *. Gen 11:20,21
old when his son Nahor was *. Gen 11:22,23
land where he was * (in Ur of the Gen 11:28
together the men * into his Gen 14:14
to everyone * in your household. Gen 17:12
Isaac, who will be * to you and Gen 17:21
every other male—* in his household Gen 17:23
* there or bought as slaves. Gen 17:24-27
Eight days after he was *, Gen 21:4,5
The first was * so covered with Gen 25:25
Then the other twin was * with Gen 25:26
years old when the twins were *. Gen 25:26
All these were * to him at Gen 35:26
All these sons were * to Esau in Gen 36:5
Edomites, * to him in Mount Seir: Gen 36:9
Descended from his wife Adah, * Gen 36:10,11,12
(* to Timna, Eliphaz' concubine). Gen 36:10,11,12
his wife Basemath. * to her son Gen 36:13,14
of Reuel, * to Esau and his wife Gen 36:17
was * to him in his old age. Gen 37:3
As they were being *, the Gen 38:28
was actually the first to be *. Gen 38:29
was *, and he was named Zerah. Gen 38:30
two sons were * to Joseph by Gen 41:50
daughter Dinah, * to Jacob in Gen 46:15
Joseph's sons, * in the land of Gen 46:19-22
and Manasseh, * here in the land of Gen 48:5
But any other children * to you Gen 48:6
were *, but to let the girls live. Ex 1:15,16
and a baby son was * to them. Ex 2:1
as much as to those * in the land. Ex 12:19
though they had been * among you; Ex 12:48
The same law applies to those * Ex 12:49
said when he was *, "I have been Ex 18:3
"When a baby boy is *, the Lev 12:2
"When a baby girl is *, the Lev 12:5
This applies whether you are * in Lev 16:29,30
"And anyone—native * or Lev 17:15
* in the same house or elsewhere. Lev 18:9
to you who are * in the nation of Lev 18:26
* in his household may eat it. Lev 22:11
sheep, or goat is *, it shall be Lev 22:26,27
they have been * in your land. Lev 25:45
Jochebed, was * to him and she Num 26:58,59
To Aaron were * Nadab, Abihu, Num 26:60
grandchildren are * and you have Deu 4:25
none of the boys * since that time Jos 5:4,5
raise the baby after he is *?" Ju 13:12
and the baby is *," he said to the Ju 13:17
When her son was * they named him Ju 13:24
of time, a baby boy was * to her. 1Sa 1:19,20
Several sons were * to David 2Sa 3:2
The oldest was Amnon, * to his 2Sa 3:2
His second son, Chileab, was * 2Sa 3:3
The third was Absalom, * to 2Sa 3:3
Adonijah, who was * to Haggith. 2Sa 3:4
Then Shephatiah was * to Abital, 2Sa 3:4
and Ithream was * to Eglah. 2Sa 3:5
children who were * at Jerusalem: 2Sa 5:14,15,16
old, this woman's baby was * too. 1Ki 3:17,18
Josiah shall be * into the family 1Ki 13:2
is ready to be *, but the mother 2Ki 19:3
was Amnon, who was * to his wife, 1Ch 3:1
These six were * to him in 1Ch 3:4
These are the sons who were * to 1Ch 3:17,18
The sons of Manasseh, * to his 1Ch 7:14
These are the names of the sons * 1Ch 14:4-7
Three sons were * from this 2Ch 11:19
be * to come to all this trouble. Job 3:10
Why is a man allowed to be * if Job 3:23
see— for we were * but yesterday Job 8:9
then did you even let me be *? Job 10:18
colt is likely to be * a man! Job 11:12
you demand purity in one * impure? Job 14:4
Were you * before the hills were Job 15:7,8
For you were * before it was all Job 38:21
mortal—* to die—shall worship him. Ps 22:29
But I was * a sinner, yes, from Ps 51:5
These men are * sinners, lying Ps 58:3
boasts that he was * in one or Ps 87:4
names of those who were * here. Ps 87:6
your Spirit, and new life is * Ps 104:30
Children * to a young man are Ps 127:4
You saw me before I was * and Ps 139:16
Yes, I was * before God made the Pro 8:26
is * to help in time of need. Pro 17:17
others were * within my household. Ecc 2:7,8
A time to be *, a time to die; Ecc 3:2
have never been *, and have never Ecc 4:3
become king, though * in poverty. Ecc 4:14
he would be better off * dead. Ecc 6:3
is better than the day he is *! Ecc 7:1
were evil too. * to be bad, they Is 1:4
child shall be * to a virgin! Is 7:14
For unto us a Child is *; Is 9:6
From the snake will be * an Is 14:29
Woe to the baby just being * who Is 45:10
cared for you since you were *. Is 46:3
The generations * in exile shall Is 49:20
their children will not be * to Is 65:23
Israel, shall be *, even before the Is 66:7,8
anguish starts, the baby is *; Is 66:7,8
before you were * I sanctified Jer 1:5
For the children * in this city, Jer 16:3
cursed be the day that I was *! Jer 20:14
father the news that a son was *. Jer 20:15
Why was I ever *? Jer 20:18
where we were * and get away from Jer 46:16
When you were *, no one cared Eze 16:4
On that day when you were *, you Eze 16:5
your own country where you were *. Eze 21:30
where they were *, but she will be Eze 29:14
All children * in the Eze 47:22
will be * to you from other men. Hos 1:2
as the day she was *, and cause her Hos 1:3
When he was *, he struggled with Hos 12:3
and his brothers (* at the time of Mt 1:11
a virgin until her Son was *; Mt 1:25
JESUS WAS * in the town of Mt 2:1
us where the Messiah would be *?" Mt 2:4
"Truly, of all men ever *, none Mt 11:11
Some are * without the ability Mt 19:12
Literally, "* eunuchs," or, Mt 19:12f
eunuchs," or, "* emasculated." Mt 19:12f
that one if he had never been *." Mt 26:24
Oh, that he had never been *!" Mk 14:21

(BORN Con't)
to speak until the child is *. Lk 1:20
so the baby * to you will be Lk 1:35
the baby to be *—and it was a boy. Lk 1:57
time came for her baby to be *; Lk 2:6
been * tonight in Bethlehem! Lk 2:11
Unless you are * again, you can Jn 3:3
"* again!" Jn 3:4
mother's womb and be * again?" Jn 3:4
is this: Unless one is * of water Jn 3:5
You must also be * Jn 3:5f
interprets "* of water" as Jn 3:5f
that you must be * again! Jn 3:7
Those * only once, with physical Jn 6:63
For we know where this man was *; Jn 7:27
me and where I was * and raised, Jn 7:28
Messiah will be * of the royal line Jn 7:41,42
the village where David was *." Jn 7:41,42
They replied, "We were not * out Jn 8:41
before Abraham was ever *!" Jn 8:58
him, "why was this man * blind? Jn 9:2
Was he * blind? Jn 9:19
and that he was * blind, but we Jn 9:20
open the eyes of someone * blind. Jn 9:32
Literally, "You were altogether * Jn 9:34f
when her child is *—her anguish Jn 16:21
"I was * for that purpose. Jn 18:37
of the lands where we were *! Act 2:8
"About that time Moses was *—a Act 7:20
Midian, where his two sons were *. Act 7:29
Jew named Aquila, * in Pontus, who Act 18:2,3
"I am a Jew," he said, "* in Act 22:3
as a human baby, * into King Rom 1:3
because you were * of Jewish Rom 2:28
And not everyone * into a Jewish Rom 9:6
Esau, the child * first, would be a Rom 9:10-13
children were even *, before they Rom 9:10-13
all men have been * from women ever 1Co 11:12
been * almost too late for this. 1Co 15:8
For even before I was * God had Gal 1:15
he sent his Son, * of a woman, born Gal 4:4
born of a woman, * as a Jew, to Gal 4:4
her child to be *—longing for the Gal 4:19
freeborn wife was * only after God Gal 4:23
And so we who are * of the Holy Gal 4:29
We started out bad, being * with Eph 2:3
old, having been * into a Php 3:5
pains begin when her child is *. 1Th 5:3
their children are *, but he will 1Ti 2:15
a Man, * into King David's family; 2Ti 2:8
too by being * in human form; Heb 2:14
He was never * and he never died Heb 7:3
For although Levi wasn't * yet, Heb 7:10
privilege of being * again, so that 1Pe 1:3
they feel like; * only to be caught 2Pe 2:12
The person who has been * into 1Jn 3:9
new life has been * into him and 1Jn 3:9
controls him—he has been * again. 1Jn 3:9
eat the baby as soon as it was *. Rev 12:4

BORNE
Nahor, had * him eight sons. Gen 22:20-23
and both have * him children, and Deu 21:15
new baby she has *, so that she Deu 28:56,57
His wife Hushim had * him Abitub 1Ch 8:11
taunted me—then I could have * it; Ps 55:12
We have * the blow that they Lam 5:7
daughters you had * to me, and Eze 16:20
who has seen has * witness, and his Jn 19:35f

BORROW
nations but will never need to *! Deu 15:6
but shall not * from them. Deu 28:12
"Then * many pots and pans from 2Ki 4:3
Evil men * and "cannot pay it Ps 37:21
fair to those who * from him and Eze 18:16
away from those who want to *. Mt 5:42
to * three loaves of bread. Lk 11:5,6

BORROWED
the man who * it must pay for it. Ex 22:14
on something * or rented, or by Lev 6:2
"Oh, sir," he cried, "it was* 2Ki 6:5
* to the limit to pay their taxes. Neh 5:2,3,4

BORROWER
so the * is servant to the lender. Pro 22:7

BORROWER'S
he gives back the * pledge and Eze 33:15

BORROWERS
lenders and *, bankers and Is 24:2

BORROWS
"If a man * an animal (or Ex 22:14

BOSOM
Literally, "into Abraham's *." Lk 16:22f
Literally, "reclining on Jesus' * Jn 13:23f
adopted into the * of his family, Rom 8:15

BOSS
If the * is angry with you, don't Ecc 10:4

BOSSES
whipped the Israeli work-crew *. Ex 5:14
We are not our own * to live or Rom 14:7

BOTH
and his wife were * naked, neither Gen 2:25
This made Cain * dejected and Gen 4:5
But the land could not support * Gen 13:6
was thirteen. * were circumcised Gen 17:24-27
Now Abraham and Sarah were * Gen 18:11
And so it was that * girls Gen 19:36
a half-sister (we * have the same Gen 20:11,12
oxen and servants—* men and Gen 20:14
For why should I be bereaved of * Gen 27:45
many servants, * men and women. Gen 32:5
him; and * of them were in tears! Gen 33:4
their hands on, * inside the city Gen 34:28
* because of all their cattle. Gen 36:6,7,8
And they hated him * for the Gen 37:8
so he jailed them * in the prison Gen 40:1
And they replied, "We * had Gen 40:8
"* dreams mean the same thing," Gen 41:25
to be your slaves, * we and he in Gen 44:16
and I will help * of you to speak Ex 4:15
of Egypt, * of men and animals; Ex 13:15
He has thrown * horse and rider Ex 15:1
who denies it, * parties to the Ex 22:9
on * sides of two stone tablets. Ex 32:15
holy garments. * men and women Ex 35:22
God has filled them * with Ex 35:35
at * top and bottom by rings. Ex 36:29
apply to * the sin offering and the Lev 7:7
goat and, laying * hands upon its Lev 16:21
You may not marry * a woman and Lev 18:17
these laws apply * to you who are Lev 18:26
man's wife, * the man and woman Lev 20:10
is his father's; * the man and the Lev 20:11
daughter-in-law, * shall be Lev 20:12
acts is death to * parties. Lev 20:13
of menstruation, * shall be Lev 20:18
sacrificed to God, * from the holy Lev 21:22
if he does, * the first and the Lev 27:10
change made, then * the original Lev 27:33
in Israel of * men and animals! Num 3:13
about one pound, * filled with Num 7:13
are mine, * men and animals; Num 8:17
When * trumpets are blown, the Num 10:3
the miracles I did * in Egypt and Num 14:22
These instructions apply * to Num 15:13,14
lest I destroy * them and you. Num 18:2,3
And shall oppress * Eber and Num 24:23,24
male lambs—* without defect —in Num 28:9,10
giants of Anakim; * the Emim and Deu 2:11
Jehovah is God * in heaven and down Deu 4:39
to * you and your ancestors. Deu 8:3
continue to send * the early and Deu 11:14
have *, it may not be eaten. Deu 14:7
when he hasn't, * men shall be Deu 19:17
not the other, and * have borne him Deu 21:15
to * the house and its owner. Deu 22:8
If you do, * the crops and the Deu 22:9
adultery, * he and the other man's Deu 22:22
walls of a city, * she and the man Deu 22:23,24
a homosexual, for * are detestable Deu 23:17,18
* slave and free. Deu 32:36
The kings of Canaan, * east and Jos 11:1
with God that * of us have.' Jos 22:28
into a panic, * the soldiers and Ju 4:15
wine that cheers * God and man, Ju 9:13
In the events that followed, * Ju 9:24
Thus God punished * Abimelech Ju 9:56,57
But later, * men died, so that Ru 1:4,5
So they * came to Bethlehem and Ru 1:19
Philistine cities, * the fortified 1Sa 6:18
the Lord, and if * you and your 1Sa 12:14
* were the sons of Abiel. 1Sa 14:50,51
I have done this to * lions and 1Sa 17:36
* Saul and Jonathan slew their 2Sa 1:22
* Saul and Jonathan! 2Sa 1:23
Thus the whole nation, * Judah 2Sa 3:37
as king of * Israel and Judah; 2Sa 5:4,5
(who was lame in * feet) moved to 2Sa 9:13
before he arrives, * we and the 2Sa 15:14
facts straight: * of you claim the 1Ki 3:23
I can supply * cedar and cypress. 1Ki 5:8
the full length of * sides of the 1Ki 6:5
all the walls of * rooms of the 1Ki 6:29
of * rooms was overlaid with gold. 1Ki 6:30
and Joab were * dead, he asked 1Ki 11:21
Literally, "every male, * bond 1Ki 14:10f
the son of Shomer—* trusted aides. 2Ki 12:21
Why provoke disaster for * 2Ki 14:10
prophets to warn * Israel and Judah 2Ki 17:13
cities * large and small. 2Ki 18:8
of idol worship, * in Jerusalem and 2Ki 23:24
* the Jews and the Babylonians. 2Ki 25:25
They were experts with * shield 1Ch 12:8-13
on * the east and west banks. 1Ch 12:15
enemy forces were * in front and 1Ch 19:10
lower Beth-horon, * being supply 2Ch 8:5
shields and bows. * armies were 2Ch 14:8
and vineyards, * on the hillsides 2Ch 26:10
heathen altars in * courts of the 2Ch 33:4,5
by * Manasseh and his people. 2Ch 33:10
and treasures from * the Temple and 2Ch 36:18
choir members, * men and women. Ez 2:64,65
choir members, * men and women. Neh 7:67
* choirs then proceeded to the Neh 12:40,41
Purim, decreed by * Mordecai the Est 9:29-3
to curse them. * rich and poor Job 3:1
to him, for he destroys * kinds. Job 9:2
Deceivers and deceived are * his Job 12:1
anything good. * alike are buried Job 21:2
dust, * eaten by the same worms. Job 21:2
He created us *. Job 31:1
be * his representative and yours. Job 33:
the nations. * proud and humble Ps 22:2
God will sweep away * old and Ps 58:
* alike are nothing in his sight. Ps 62:
The water stood banked up along * Ps 78:1
of every kind, * great and small. Ps 104:2
* we and our fathers have sinned Ps 106:
Aaron, and all, * great and small, Ps 115:1
May the Lord richly bless * you Ps 115:14
Your laws are * my light and my Ps 119:24
even say it. You * precede and Ps 139:
Darkness and light are * alike to Ps 139:12
the God who made * earth and Ps 146:6
If you want favor with * God and Pro 3:4,5
eye on * the evil and the good. Pro 15:3
will make you * wise and honored. Pro 15:33
lies from a king are * unexpected. Pro 17:7
Next I bought slaves, * men and Ecc 2:7,8
For the wise and fool * die, and Ecc 2:16
to come * will be long forgotten. Ecc 2:16
man does, * good and bad." Ecc 3:17
For men and animals * breathe Ecc 3:19
breathe the same air, and * die. Ecc 3:19
to get enough. * have the same Ecc 6:7,8
—will * be dead. Is 7:15,16
of Jeberechiah, * known as honest Is 8:2
will invade * Damascus and Samaria Is 8:4
Manasseh—and * against Judah. Is 9:21
small alike, * officers and men. Is 10:33
the survivors, * those who escape Is 15:9
a terror to all * far and near, Is 18:7
and barefoot, * young and old, Is 20:4
Peace, peace to them, * near and Is 57:19
My hand has made * earth and Is 66:2
and my mercies. * great and small Jer 16:6
and * men and animals shall die. Jer 21:6
For everyone, * great and small, Jer 31:34
Israel, says: Take * this sealed Jer 32:14
I will rebuild the cities of * Jer 33:7
Hebrew slaves, * men and women. Jer 34:9
"You and Jeremiah * hide," the Jer 36:19
of Israel, says: * you and your Jer 44:25
all shall be gone—* men and Jer 50:3
No one shall be spared; * young Jer 51:3
the civilians too, * old and young, Jer 51:22
It is good * to hope and wait Lam 3:26
a scroll, with writing on * sides. Eze 2:9,10
the people to lack * bread and Eze 4:17
wall and its builders * are gone. Eze 13:15
of my people, of * young and old Eze 13:18
famine to destroy * man and beast. Eze 14:13
So they are useless * before and Eze 15:5,6
have sinned with, * those you loved Eze 16:37
guilty * of murder and idolatry. Eze 22:4
For they have committed * Eze 23:37
and destroy * men and herds. Eze 29:8
and I will break * his arms—the Eze 30:22
"For you said, '* Israel and Eze 35:10
the walls along * sides of the Eze 40:16
the terrace, the same on * sides. Eze 41:9
the terrace, on * sides of the Eze 41:10
* the nave and the Holy of Holies Eze 41:23
palm trees on * sides of the entry Eze 41:26
for * liquid and dry measure. Eze 45:11
many trees were growing on * Eze 47:7
"The land on * sides of this Eze 48:21,22
the ram and broke off * his horns. Dan 8:7
The victor became * proud and Dan 8:8
"* these kings Dan 11:27
He replied, with * hands lifted Dan 12:7
Therefore, I will punish * Hos 4:9
the Lord against * Israel and Amo 3:1
this: That homes * great and small Amo 6:11
The messages were addressed to * Mic 1:1
evil deeds with * hands, and how Mic 7:3
I will sweep away * men and Zep 1:3
drought to starve * you and all Hag 1:11
He will rule * as King and as Zec 6:13
Ephraim, you are my arrow! * of Zec 9:13
* in winter and in summer. Zec 14:8
old and under, * in the town and on Mt 2:16
For he gives his sunlight to * Mt 5:45
That way * are preserved." Mt 9:17
Fear only God who can destroy * Mt 10:28
man—he was * blind and unable to Mt 12:22
so that he could * speak and see. Mt 12:22
if you do. Let * grow together Mt 13:30
treasure things * new and old." Mt 13:52f
and * will fall into a ditch." Mt 15:13,14
to cover the taxes for * of us; Mt 17:26,27
with * of your hands and feet. Mt 18:8
for * of you are from Galilee." Mt 26:69
as he left. * Mary Magdalene and Mt 27:61
and now they were * very old. Lk 1:7

(BOTH Con't)
You will * have great joy and Lk 1:14
So Jesus grew * tall and wise, Lk 2:52
place to place on * sides of the Lk 3:3
boat and soon * boats were filled Lk 5:7
*, letting them keep the money! Lk 7:42
sinned against * heaven and you, Lk 15:18
You cannot serve * God and Lk 16:13
How can the Messiah be * Lk 20:44
for * are from Galilee." Lk 22:59
highly regarded by * God and man. Lk 24:19
sower and the reaper, * together! Jn 4:36
hated * of us—me and my Father. Jn 15:24
visitors from Rome—* Jews and Act 2:10
Lord, crowds * of men and women. Act 5:14
Didn't I make * heaven and Act 7:50
he found there, * men and women, so Act 9:2
to Antioch; and * of them stayed Act 11:26
leaders stirred up * the godly Act 13:50
many—* Jews and Gentiles—believed. Act 14:1
Then Judas and Silas, * being Act 15:32
province of Ausia—* Jews and Act 19:10
* men and women to prison. Act 22:4
at Paul from * sides, pulling him Act 23:10
of * the righteous and ungodly. Act 24:15
death is demanded * by the local Act 25:24
And I will protect you from * Act 26:17
to everyone, * great and small. Act 26:22
trivial or strong, * you and Act 26:29
to everyone else, * to civilized Rom 1:14
Notice how God is * kind and Rom 11:22
* while we live and when we die. Rom 14:9
to salvation, * Jews and Gentiles, 1Co 1:24
* interpretations are possible. 1Co 6:4f
do away with * stomachs and food. 1Co 6:13
the agreement of * husband and wife 1Co 7:5
gods, * in heaven and on earth. 1Co 8:5
* in sea and cloud! 1Co 10:2
You cannot eat bread * at the 1Co 10:21
ever since, and * men and women 1Co 11:12
I will do *. 1Co 14:15
us, an aroma to * the saved and the 2Co 2:15
disappeared, for * of us have been Eph 2:16
by God's sons; * are invited to Eph 3:6
apply to them * when they accept Eph 3:6
blessings of God, * when I was in Php 1:7
They are against * God and man, 1Th 2:15
be well rewarded * by respect from 1Ti 3:13
hard at * preaching and teaching. 1Ti 5:17
different is * proud and stupid. 1Ti 6:4
to be of real use to * of us. Phm 1:11
who would be * merciful to us and Heb 2:17
He has given us * his promise and Heb 6:18
in your life, * inside and outside, Jas 1:21
brothers, and in * of them I have 2Pe 3:1
honor, * now and forevermore. 2Pe 3:18
with * God the Father and his Son. 1Jn 2:24
Then you will have * the Father 2Jn 1:9
fear your Name, * great and Rev 11:18
and of all humanity, * great and Rev 19:18
his statue. * of them—the Evil Rev 19:20
* David's Root and his Descendant. Rev 22:16

BOTHER
They did not * to ask the Lord, Jos 9:14,15
warned the young men not to * you; Ru 2:8,9
nations won't * them as they did 2Sa 7:10,11
began to * him, and he said to the 2Sa 24:10
"No," Elisha said, "don't *." 2Ki 2:16
that I wouldn't * with you except 2Ki 3:14
you and you don't * to look. Job 30:20
how you can * with mere puny man, Ps 8:4
Why * at all with the human race? Ps 144:3
So don't * with him; Pro 9:7,8
mean, so why * to speak at all? Ecc 6:11
"No," he said, "I'll not * the Is 7:12
no one will * us now; Is 14:8
lied and said, "He won't * us! Jer 5:12
Who will even * to ask how you Jer 15:5
more against us, nor * us again." Jer 18:18
but you replied, "Don't * me." Jer 22:21
But that didn't * her. Eze 23:19,20
Don't * us here with your Amo 7:13
"Every time you say, 'Don't * Mal 1:7
"Don't * him," they said. Mt 19:13
desert, don't * to go and look. Mt 24:26
at once, "Why does this * you? Mk 2:8
away, telling them not to * him. Mk 10:13
home, you didn't * to offer me Lk 7:44
he said. 'Why * with it any Lk 13:7
they won't * to read them. Lk 16:30
you didn't * much with goodness. Rom 6:20
whose consciences * them easily, I 1Co 9:22
"Don't * about his letters," 2Co 10:10
hurt and * me, and prick my pride. 2Co 12:7
[who don't * with circumcision and Gal 2:12
consciences won't even * them. 1Ti 4:2

BOTHERED
water—a tree not * by the heat nor Jer 17:8
And if your brother is * by what Rom 14:15

BOTHERING
spirit is * you," they said. 1Sa 16:15,16

But then his conscience began * 1Sa 24:5
If I find thorns and briars * Is 27:4,5
one * them or making them afraid. Eze 39:26
is * us with all her begging." Mt 15:23
"Why are you * us, Jesus of Mk 1:24

BOTHERS
to himself, 'but this woman * me. Lk 18:4,5
and that * and baffles the man of 1Co 2:15
So when they eat such food it * 1Co 8:7

BOTTLE
"Throw away your *." 1Sa 1:14
the third will have a * of wine. 1Sa 10:3
poured me from * to bottle like Job 10:10
me from bottle to * like milk, and Job 10:10
and preserved them in your *! Ps 56:8
DEAD FLIES WILL cause even a * of Ecc 10:1
Literally, "that every * shall be Jer 13:12f
Moab like an old, unwanted *. Jer 48:38
came in with a * of very expensive Mt 26:7

BOTTOM
inside the boat—a *, middle, and Gen 6:16
all that night, drying the sea *. Ex 14:21
of water along the * of the sea—all Ex 14:23
Those at the * of the mountain Ex 24:17
branches and one below the * set. Ex 25:34,35
at the * and top with clasps. Ex 26:24
rings for the * front edge of the Ex 28:27
Now attach the * of the Ex 28:28
chestpiece to the * rings of the Ex 28:28
not fray. The * edge of the ephod Ex 28:33,34
other at both top and * by rings. Ex 36:29
also a flower below the * pair Ex 37:20,21
to the * edge of the robe; Ex 39:24
along the * edge of the skirt, with Ex 39:25,26
from the river * and immediately Deu 27:2,3,4
by hand in the * of a grape press—a Ju 6:11
slit off the * of Saul's robe! 1Sa 24:4
The * of the sea appeared. 2Sa 22:16
The * floor of the side rooms was 1Ki 6:8
cooking oil in the * of the jar. 1Ki 17:12
From the * of my heart praise Ps 35:10
forming a dry road across its *. Ps 106:9
Who led them through the * of Is 63:13
*, and Jeremiah sank down into it. Jer 38:6
terror to the very * and will lick Eze 23:34
and that the * row of rooms Eze 41:8
they even hit the * of the den. Dan 6:24
Though they hide at the * of the Amo 9:3
threatened to send them to the *. Jon 1:4
When they arrived at the * of the Mt 17:14
was split apart from top to *; Mt 27:51
At the * of the mountain they Mk 9:14
was split apart from top to *. Mk 15:38

BOTTOMLESS
not to order them into the * Pit. Lk 8:31
was given the key to the * pit. Rev 9:1
the Prince of the * pit whose name Rev 9:11
tyrant who comes out of the * pit Rev 11:7
come up out of the * pit and go to Rev 17:8
the key to the * pit and a heavy Rev 20:1
threw him into the * pit, which he Rev 20:3

BOTTOMS
* fitting into forty silver bases. Ex 36:24
I went down to the * of the Jon 2:6

BOUGHS
On the first day, take * of Lev 23:40
fronds, and the * of leafy Lev 23:40
trees, don't go over the * twice; Deu 24:20
beneath the thick * of a great oak 2Sa 18:9
none had * to compare; Eze 31:8

BOUGHT
his household or * from outside—and Gen 17:23
whether born there or * as slaves. Gen 17:24-27
This is the land he *: Ephron's Gen 23:17,18
the city. (He * the land he camped Gen 33:19
So Joseph * all the land of Egypt Gen 47:20
* you and your land for Pharaoh. Gen 47:23
field Abraham * from Ephron the Gen 49:29,30
cave Abraham had * in the field of Gen 50:12,13
eldest sons are always * back.' Ex 13:15
please the man who * her, then he Ex 21:8
he shall let her be * back again; Ex 21:8
land is sold or * during the Lev 25:14,15,16
a field he has *, but which is not Lev 27:22
original owner from whom it was *. Lev 27:24
the Lord, and may not be * back!" Lev 27:33
sheep, or goats may not be * back; Num 18:17
* for $200 from the sons of Hamor. Jos 24:32
that today I have * all the Ru 4:9
wife Michal, for I * her with the 2Sa 3:14
ABSALOM THEN * a magnificent 2Sa 15:1
Then Omri * the hill now known 1Ki 16:24
but King Menahem * him off with a 2Ki 15:19,20
carpenters, and * cedar logs from Ez 3:7
"It cannot be * for gold or Job 28:15
It cannot be * for jewels mounted Job 28:17
Next I * slaves, both men and Ecc 2:7,8
every other spice that can be *? Sol 3:6
So I * the loincloth and put it Jer 13:2
So I * the field, paying Hanamel Jer 32:9
Fields will again be * and sold Jer 32:43

once again be * and sold—deeds Jer 32:44
to see the property he had *. Jer 37:12
So I * her [back from her slavery Hos 3:2
for Tarshish. He * a ticket, went Jon 1:3
for I have * them back again. Zec 10:8
people have been * and slain by Zec 11:5
Then those who * and sold sheep, Zec 11:11
Joseph * a long sheet of linen Mk 15:46
One said he had just * a field Lk 14:18
Another said he had just * five Lk 14:19
as we were. He * a field with the Act 1:18
the tomb Abraham * from the sons of Act 7:16
for thinking God's gift can be *! Act 8:20
For God has * you with a great 1Co 6:20
You have been * and paid for by 1Co 7:23
But Christ has * us out from Gal 3:13
his dear Son, who * our freedom Col 1:14
even their Master who * them; 2Pe 2:1
and your blood has * people from Rev 5:9

BOULDER
Roll a * down on someone, and it Pro 26:27
Then a mighty angel picked up a * Rev 18:21

BOULDERS
then use only uncut stones and *. Ex 20:25
honey'—take out * from the river Deu 27:2,3,4
Use uncut *, and on the altar Deu 27:5,6
me an altar of * that have neither Jos 8:31
Build the roads, pull out the *, Is 62:10

BOUNCED
those they * upon their knees? Lam 2:20

BOUND
I'll keep the rest of you here, * Gen 42:16
and had him * before their eyes. Gen 42:24
father's life is * up in the lad's Gen 44:30
without yeast, and * their kneading Ex 12:34
Gaza, where he was * with bronze Ju 16:21
"Your hands were not *, 2Sa 3:33,34
I was trapped, and * 2Sa 22:6
put out and he was * with chains 2Ki 25:7
him with hooks and * him with 2Ch 33:11
Death * me with chains, and the Ps 18:4
You * the world together so that Ps 104:5
that evil men had * me with. Ps 129:3,4
eyes and * him in chains to send Jer 39:7
* with cords and made secure. Eze 27:24
the sick nor * up the broken bones Eze 34:4
So they * them tight with ropes Dan 3:21
down * into the roaring flames. Dan 3:23
All her leaders were * in chains. Nah 3:10
bind on earth is * in heaven, and Mt 18:18
[Satan must be * before his Mk 3:27
And Lazarus came—* up in the Jn 11:44
Then Annas sent Jesus, *, to Jn 18:24
He took Paul's belt, * his own Act 21:11
of this belt be * by the Jews in Act 21:11
ordered him * with double chains. Act 21:33
he had ordered him * and whipped. Act 22:29
got together and * themselves by a Act 23:12,13
They have * themselves under a Act 23:21
* for Italy, and put us aboard. Act 27:6
has come that I am * with this Act 28:20
dies, she is no longer * to him; Rom 7:2
I am not * to obey anyone just 1Co 9:19
happiness was so * up in mine that 2Co 2:3
them anyway, still * by such rules Col 2:20
against them, * himself with an Heb 3:11
God also * himself with an oath, Heb 6:17
held * at the great River Rev 9:14
devil, Satan—and * him in chains Rev 20:2

BOUNDARIES
the mountain, or even touch its *; Ex 19:12
the people not to cross the *. Ex 19:21
You told me to set * around the Ex 19:23
break across the * to try to come Ex 19:24
And I will set your enlarged * Ex 23:31
before you and enlarge your *. Ex 34:24
*, with the city in the center. Num 35:5
"If the Lord enlarges your * as Deu 19:8
"For in the cities within the * Deu 20:16
* included the following cities: Jos 19:17-23
The * included these cities: Jos 19:24,25,26
the tribes, with the * indicated; Jos 19:49
blow and sets the * of the oceans. Job 28:25
"Who decreed the * of the seas Job 38:8,9
Can you find its *, or go to its Job 38:20
not to spread beyond their *. Pro 8:27,28,29
kingdom will not increase its *. Is 7:8
He has widened the * of our land! Is 26:15
I have reduced your * and Eze 16:27
You have extended your * out Eze 27:4
and western * are the same as those Eze 45:7
"Divide the land within these * Eze 47:21
and has the same east and west *. Eze 48:2
same * on the east and the west. Eze 48:5,6,7
and western * as the tribal units, Eze 48:8
and western * of Israel, shall Eze 48:21,22
Next is Issachar, with the same *. Eze 48:25
Others will set your * then. Mic 2:5
He determined their *. Act 17:26
far beyond your *, for wherever we 1Th 1:8
Stay always within the * where Jud 1:21

BOUNDARY
Isaac, to respect the * line. Gen 31:53
people watch. Set * lines the Ex 19:12
(The Arnon River is the * line Num 21:13
The southern * will begin at the Num 34:3
From Azmon the * will follow the Num 34:5
"Your western * will be the Num 34:6
man's land by moving the * marker. Deu 19:14
" 'Cursed is he who moves the * Deu 27:17
which is the * of the Ammonites. Jos 12:2
extending to the * of the kingdoms Jos 12:5
Gilead where the * touched the Jos 12:5
Egypt to the southern * of Ekron; Jos 13:2-7
to Aphek at the * of the Jos 13:2-7
western * of the tribe of Reuben. Jos 13:23
Judah's southern * began at the Jos 15:1
More specifically, this * began Jos 15:2,3,4
The eastern * extended along the Jos 15:5
The northern * began at the bay Jos 15:5
to En-rogel. The * then passed Jos 15:8
Turning northwest again, the * Jos 15:10,11
From Ekron the * extended to the Jos 15:46
THE SOUTHERN * of the Tribes of Jos 16:1
This * extended from the Jordan Jos 16:1
eastern * began at Ataroth-addar. Jos 16:5,6
The northern * began at the Sea, Jos 16:5,6
western half of the northern * Jos 16:8
The northern * of the tribe of Jos 17:7
On the south the * went from Jos 17:7
Manasseh's northern * was the Jos 17:10
* was the territory of Issachar. Jos 17:10
The northern * began at the Jos 18:12
From there the * went south to Jos 18:13
This was the western *. Jos 18:14
From En-rogel the * proceeded Jos 18:17
was Zebulun. Its * started on the Jos 19:10
In the other direction, the * Jos 19:12
The northern * of Zebulun passed Jos 19:14
villages. The * of Issachar ended Jos 19:17-23
The * on the west side went from Jos 19:24,25,26
Then the * turned toward Ramah Jos 19:29
of Naphtali. Its * began at Judah, Jos 19:33
The western * began near Heleph Jos 19:34
with the Zebulun * in the south, Jos 19:34
and with the * of Asher on the Jos 19:34
their slaves. The * of the Ju 1:36
the * of Moab at the Arnon River; Ju 11:18
He sets a * for the ocean, yes, Job 26:10
a * for the day and for the night. Job 26:10
Literally, "The * lines are Ps 16:6f
And then you set a * for the Ps 104:9
Do not move the ancient * marks. Pro 22:28
their ancient * marks, for their Pro 23:10,11
Euphrates River to the Egyptian *. Is 27:12
"The northern * will run from Eze 47:15
will be your *, from the southern Eze 47:20
from the southern * to the point Eze 47:20
point where the northern * begins. Eze 47:20
For Dan: From the northwest * at Eze 48:1
* lines on the east and the west. Eze 48:3
same eastern and western * lines. Eze 48:4
Literally, "as those who move a * Hos 5:10f
from your northern * to your Amo 6:14
her southern * was on the Gulf of Ob 1:1f

BOUNDED
(or, wasteland), * by the Jordan Deu 3:17
They lived in an area * on one 1Ch 7:28

BOUNDING
mountains and * over the hills. Sol 2:8

BOUNDLESS
our guilt is as * as the heavens. Ez 9:6
for it is his * mercy that has 1Pe 1:3

BOUNDS
utmost * of the everlasting hills. Gen 49:26
and roar, can never pass those *. Jer 5:22
love will know no *, for my anger Hos 14:4
Their joy knew no *! Mt 2:10
farthest * of earth and heaven. Mk 13:27
door, their surprise knew no *. Act 12:16

BOUNTIFUL
year they will have a * harvest. 2Ki 19:29
as they gaze at their * crops. Ps 4:7
land and it yields its * crops. Ps 85:12
with all your * provision. Ps 104:28
sorrow for those * farms of yours Is 32:12
Wherever they plant, * crops will Is 32:20
where there are * harvests of grain Is 36:17
My true disciples produce * Jn 15:8
ready to give a * supply of wisdom Jas 1:5

BOUNTIFULLY
Literally, "deal * that I may Ps 119:17f

BOUNTY
lushest * and its richest fruit. Is 4:2,3,4
to eat of its * and goodness, but Jer 2:7
people with my *, says the Lord. Jer 31:14

BOUQUET
King Solomon: "My beloved is a * Sol 1:14

BOUTS
on long drinking * that last till Is 5:11
up their drinking *, and off they Hos 4:18
parties, drinking *, and the 1Pe 4:3

BOW
Take your * and arrows out into Gen 27:2,3,4
May all your relatives * low Gen 27:27,28,29
brothers come and * before you?" Gen 37:10
with my sword and with my *." Gen 48:22
Your father's sons shall * before Gen 49:8
You must never * to an image or Ex 20:5
You shall not * down to any Deu 5:9,10
Your enemies shall * low before Deu 33:29
descendants shall * before him, 1Sa 2:36
him his robe, sword, *, and belt. 1Sa 18:4
Then Jonathan gave his * and 1Sa 20:40
And when anyone came to * to him, 2Sa 15:5
And strength to bend a * of 2Sa 22:35
He came to * low before the king; 1Ki 1:53
the Lord pardon me when I * too." 2Ki 5:18
Then Jehu drew his * with his 2Ki 9:24
Elisha told him, "Get a * and 2Ki 13:15
his hand upon the *, and Elisha 2Ki 13:16,17
But Mordecai refused to *. Est 3:2
gate, refusing to * to me." Est 5:13
have before they * themselves to Job 39:2,3
He has bent and strung his * and Ps 7:12
Literally, "a * of bronze." Ps 18:34f
draw an iron *! Ps 18:34
before come now and * before me. Ps 18:43,44,45
The desert nomads shall * before Ps 72:9
All will * before him! Ps 72:11
one—will come and * before you, Ps 86:9
gods—for every god must * to him! Ps 97:7
Exalt the Lord our holy God! * Ps 99:5
and make them * low before you." Ps 110:1
Evil men shall * before the Pro 14:19
Small and great, all * before Is 2:9
All the glory of mankind will * Is 2:17
the world shall * to me, and every Is 45:23
princes shall * low because the Is 49:7
They shall * to the earth before Is 49:23
will come and * before you! Is 60:14
of God * before their idols. Jer 10:14
handle the shield and bend the *! Jer 46:9
He bends his * against his people Lam 2:4
He has bent his * and aimed it Lam 3:12
of prices. We * our necks beneath Lam 5:5
They are like a crooked * that Hos 7:16
"Shall we * before the Lord with Mic 6:6
salvation. Your * was pulled from Hab 3:8,9f
They go up on their roofs and * Zep 1:5
Judah, you are my *! Zec 9:13
hope hangs, the * that wins the Zec 10:4
to have everyone * to them as they Mk 12:38
and ran aground. The * of the Act 27:41
"every knee shall * to me and Rom 14:11
every knee shall * in heaven and on Php 2:10
Its rider carried a *, and a Rev 6:2

BOWED
Then Abraham * low before them Gen 23:7
Abraham * again to the men of Gen 23:12
with head *, worshiping Jehovah. Gen 24:26
Then I * my head and worshiped Gen 24:48
As he approached his brother he * Gen 33:3
children, and * low before him. Gen 33:6
her children, and *, and finally Gen 33:7
around it and * low before it!" Gen 37:7
eleven stars * low before me!" Gen 37:9
brothers came, and * low before Gen 42:6
Then again they * before him. Gen 43:28
boys by the hand, * deeply to him, Gen 48:12,13
and * their heads and worshiped. Ex 4:31
And all the people * their Ex 12:27
Literally, "David * himself 1Sa 20:41f
around, David * low before him. 1Sa 24:7,8
dismounted and * low before him. 1Sa 25:23
was Samuel and * low before him. 1Sa 28:14
and he came and * low before the 2Sa 14:33
The man * and ran off. 2Sa 18:21
is well!" He * low with his face 2Sa 18:28
Bath-sheba * low before him. 1Ki 1:16
Nathan came in and * low before 1Ki 1:22,23
Then Bath-sheba * low before him 1Ki 1:31
as she entered and * low to her. 1Ki 2:19
never * to Baal nor kissed him!" 1Ki 19:18
* to the ground before King David. 1Ch 21:21
up as gods, and * before them, and 2Ch 25:14
* low before the Lord in worship. 2Ch 29:29
and * their heads and worshiped. 2Ch 29:30
then they * and worshiped the Neh 8:6
Now all the king's officials * Est 3:2
You alone can lift my head, now * Ps 3:3
tree you've * low before idols. Jer 2:20
The whole nation will be * down Zec 12:12,13,14
robes and to be * to by the people Lk 20:46
The women were terrified and * Lk 24:5
is finished," and * his head and Jn 19:30
me and have not * down to idols!" Rom 11:4

BOWEL
after every * movement he must Deu 23:13
down with the incurable * disease. 2Ch 21:18

BOWELS
his * gushed out onto the ground. 2Sa 20:8,9,10
and your * will rot away." 2Ch 21:15

he burst open, spilling out his *. Act 1:18

BOWING
their presents, * low before him. Gen 43:26
running to me, * low and begging, Ex 11:8
* low to the pillar of cloud. Ex 33:10
* down and worshiping the idols. Num 25:2
worshiping and * low before the Ju 2:12-14
deep humility, * low before him. 2Sa 9:5,6
And they did, * low before the 1Ch 29:20
of penance and * like reeds in the Is 58:5
* before him and obeying him. 1Pe 3:22

BOWL
If it falls into a pottery *, Lev 11:33
anything in the * is defiled, and Lev 11:33
and you shall smash the *. Lev 11:33
defiled * is also contaminated. Lev 11:34
in an earthenware *, and dip the Lev 14:50
and a silver * of about one pound, Num 7:13
me a new * filled with salt." 2Ki 2:20
and the golden * is broken, and the Ecc 12:6
he sent for a * of water and washed Mt 27:24

BOWLFUL
and wrung out a whole * of water! Ju 6:38

BOWLS
water stored in * and pots in the Ex 7:19
your ovens and your kneading *; Ex 8:3,4
gold, he made the *, flagons, Ex 37:15,16
dishes, spoons, *, cups, and the Num 4:7
12 silver * (each weighing about Num 7:84,85,86
pots, serving *, wheat and barley 2Sa 17:28,29
gold snuffers, *, trumpets, or 2Ki 12:13,14
and they cut apart all the gold * 2Ki 24:13
The gold and silver *, with all 2Ki 25:14,15
cups, and * of gold and silver. 1Ch 28:17
And he molded 100 solid gold *. 2Ch 4:8
of silver and gold *, clothing, 2Ch 9:24
silver and gold * which he and his 2Ch 15:18
silver spoons and * used for 2Ch 24:14
and golden * from the Temple, as 2Ch 25:24
The king took the gold * from 2Ch 28:24
and for his shields and gold *. 2Ch 32:27
some of the golden * and other 2Ch 36:7
donated the gold * and other Ez 1:7
30 * of solid gold, Ez 1:9,10
2,410 silver * (of various Ez 1:9,10
gold and silver * which Ez 5:14
him to return the * to Jerusalem Ez 5:15
And the gold and silver * which Ez 6:5
And take with you the gold * and Ez 7:19
gold, the golden *, and the other Ez 8:25
and twenty gold * worth a total Ez 8:26,27
and money and * which had been Ez 8:28
in gold, 50 golden *, and 530 sets Neh 7:70
frankincense, *, and tithes of Neh 13:5
back the Temple *, the grain Neh 13:9
snuffers, spoons, *, and all the Jer 52:18
candlesticks and cups and *. Jer 52:19
golden * through two golden tubes. Zec 4:12
sacred as the * beside the altar. Zec 14:20

BOWMEN
strike down the * of Babylon and Jer 51:3

BOWS
and Joseph came and made their *. Gen 33:7
It was not your swords or * that Jos 24:12
were expert marksmen with their *. 1Ch 8:40
armed with large shields and *. 2Ch 14:8
men equipped with * and shields 2Ch 17:17
coats of mail, *, and slingstones. 2Ch 26:14
have strung their *, drawn their Ps 11:2
their * are bent; Is 5:28
"They bend their tongues like * Jer 9:3
and bucklers, * and arrows, Eze 39:9

BOWSTRINGS
seven raw-leather *, I would become Ju 16:7
So they brought her the seven *, Ju 16:8
Then he snapped the * like cotton Ju 16:9
tight against the *, and aimed from Ps 11:2

BOX
down into the fire *, resting it Ex 27:5
about halfway up [in the fire * Ex 38:4
gold * of incense which weighed Num 7:14
* trees—to beautify my sanctuary. Is 60:13
a * over it to shut out the light? Mk 4:21
their gifts into the collection *. Lk 21:1

BOXES
* with Scripture verses inside, Mt 23:5
to the collection * in the Temple Mk 12:41

BOY
the * or your slave-girl wife; Gen 21:12
Go and get the * and comfort Gen 21:18
And God blessed the * and he Gen 21:20,21
Esau: "*, am I starved! Gen 25:30
"Wonderful—another *!" Gen 35:17
(This is the * who discovered a Gen 36:24
The second * was named Ephraim Gen 41:52
he sees that the * is not with us, Gen 44:31
the younger *, and his left hand Gen 48:14
if the ox gores a * or a girl. Ex 21:31
"When a baby * is born, the Lev 12:2
her baby is a * or girl), she must Lev 12:6
dollars; a * from five to twenty Lev 27:5

(BOY Con't)
a girl, five dollars. A * one Lev 27:6
But the * was only a lad and was Ju 8:20
'You are going to have a baby *!' Ju 13:7
Samson said to the * who was Ju 16:25,26
in the process of time, a baby * 1Sa 1:19,20
right and that the baby was a *. 1Sa 4:20
He was a fine looking *, 1Sa 16:12
You are only a * and he has been 1Sa 17:33
in the army since he was a *!" 1Sa 17:33
at this nice little red-cheeked *! 1Sa 17:41,42
"Tell me about your father, my * 1Sa 17:58
* with him to gather his arrows. 1Sa 20:35
"Start running," he told the *, 1Sa 20:36
So the * ran and Jonathan shot 1Sa 20:36
When the * had almost reached 1Sa 20:37
So the * quickly gathered up 1Sa 20:38
and arrows to the * and told him to 1Sa 20:40
The king replied, "No, my *; 2Sa 13:25
But a * saw them leaving 2Sa 17:18
"No, we don't need you now, my * 2Sa 18:22
him whether the * will recover." 1Ki 14:3
of your sons—this * who is sick and 1Ki 14:10
and had a baby * the following 2Ki 4:17
This time the little * sneezed 2Ki 4:35
brought a little * back to life. 2Ki 8:5
the mother of the * walked in! 2Ki 8:5
to kill every baby * two years old Mt 2:16
heal his servant * who was in bed Mt 8:5,6
and to my slave *, 'Do this or Mt 8:8,9
And the * was healed that same Mt 8:13
him a paralyzed * on a mat. Mt 9:2
to the sick *, "Cheer up, son! Mt 9:2
And the * jumped up and left! Mt 9:7
the demon in the * and it left him, Mt 17:18
from that moment the * was well. Mt 17:18
told the older *, 'Son, go out and Mt 21:28
"He's just a carpenter, Mary's * Mk 6:2,3
Bring the * to me." Mk 9:19
So they brought the *, but when Mk 9:20
the * again and left him; Mk 9:26
and the * lay there limp and Mk 9:26
and have a baby *, and you are to Lk 1:31
baby to be born—and it was a *. Lk 1:57
The little * greatly loved God Lk 1:80
first child is a *, he shall be Lk 2:23
and my servant * will be healed! Lk 7:6,7,8
village gate. The * who had died Lk 7:12
Then the * sat up and began to Lk 7:15
"Teacher, this * here is my only Lk 9:38
As the * was coming the demon Lk 9:42
and healed the * and handed him Lk 9:42
fathers—if your * asks for bread, Lk 11:11
his pigs. The * became so hungry Lk 15:16
"Take this * to the commander. Act 23:17
The commander took the * by the Act 23:19
commander warned the * as he left. Act 23:22
She gave birth to a * who was to Rev 12:5

BOY'S
And he took the * body from her 1Ki 17:19
But the * mother said, "I swear 2Ki 4:30

BOYHOOD
of Nazareth, his * home, he went as Lk 4:16

BOYS
the other men and * of the Gen 17:24-27
As the * grew, Esau became a Gen 25:27
Israel looked over at the two *. Gen 48:8
So Joseph brought the * close to Gen 48:10
Joseph took the * by the hand, Gen 48:12,13
him, and led the * to their Gen 48:12,13
his hands upon the *' heads, so Gen 48:14
life, wonderfully bless these *. Gen 48:15
May these * be an honor to my Gen 48:16
So Jacob blessed the * that day Gen 48:20
to kill all Hebrew * as soon as Ex 1:15,16
the king—they let the * live too. Ex 1:17
command and let the baby * live?" Ex 1:18
Hebrew * into the Nile River. Ex 1:22
So they all did—men and women, * Ex 32:2,3
all the men and * of Israel shall Ex 34:23
Now kill all the * and all the Num 31:17
and none of the * born since that Jos 5:4,5
see how the * are getting along; 1Sa 17:18
road, some young * from the city 2Ki 2:23
perish, young * and veterans too. Is 34:7
their * and girls shall starve. Jer 11:21,22
and young, * and girls, killed by Lam 2:21
filled with * and girls at play. Zec 8:5
He called, "Any fish, *?" Jn 21:5
And I am writing to you younger * 1Jn 2:13

BOZEZ
which had been named * and Seneh. 1Sa 14:4

BOZKATH
Lachish, *, Eglon, Cabbon, Lahmam, Jos 15:37-44
Jedidah (daughter of Adaiah of *) 2Ki 22:1

BOZRAH
of *. Gen 36:31-39
Zerah from * became the new king. 1Ch 1:44
from the city of *, with his Is 63:1
and Keri-oth and *—and all the Jer 48:24
the Lord, that * shall become heaps Jer 49:13
will spread his wings against *. Jer 49:22
burn down all the forts of *." Amo 1:12
north of Edom, and * in the south. Amo 1:12f

BRACE
"Stand up like a man and * Job 40:7

BRACED
with undercarriages * with square 1Ki 7:27-30

BRACELETS
and two five-ounce golden * for Gen 24:22
the ring, and the * on his sister's Gen 24:29,30
So I gave her the ring and the * Gen 24:47
jewelry, *, anklets, rings, Num 31:50
his * to bring to you, my lord." 2Sa 1:10
the air, tinkling * on their Is 3:16
* and veils of shimmering gauze. Is 3:19
I gave you lovely ornaments, * Eze 16:11
who put * on your wrists and Eze 23:42

BRAG
For these men * of all their Ps 10:3
disgraced—all who * about their Ps 97:7
DON'T * ABOUT your plans for Pro 27:1
evil, don't * about it—cover your Pro 30:32
the Holy City and * about depending Is 48:1
No one will ever * of Moab any Jer 48:2,3,4
you * that you are his special Rom 2:17
But you must be careful not to * Rom 11:18
can ever * in the presence of God. 1Co 1:29
of yours who * about how well they 2Co 5:12
They * that they are Hebrews, do 2Co 11:22
But if I must *, I would rather 2Co 11:30
I would rather * about the things 2Co 11:30
And if you don't * about them, Jas 3:13
And by all means don't * about Jas 3:14

BRAGGART
out against that * Israel who says Is 9:8,9,10

BRAGGARTS
insolent, proud *, always thinking Rom 1:30

BRAGGING
The Lord's reply to your * is to Is 9:11,12
living at ease, * as the greatest Is 47:8
had a man's eyes and a * mouth. Dan 7:8
and the loud, * mouth, the one Dan 7:20
will not feel proud and start * Rom 11:25
Such * isn't something the Lord 2Co 11:17
is something worth * about, but I 2Co 12:5
Otherwise you will be * about Jas 4:16

BRAGS
a fool doesn't, and even * about Pro 13:16
But afterwards he * about his Pro 20:14

BRAINLESS
do, for I am acting like a * fool. 2Co 11:17

BRAINS
have robbed my people of their *. Hos 4:11

BRAMBLE
on thorns, or grapes on * bushes. Lk 6:44

BRAMBLES
(meaning "Threshing Place of * Gen 50:10

BRANCH
The second * is called the Gen 2:13
The third * is the Tigris, which Gen 2:14
center shaft, each * decorated with Ex 25:32,33
scarlet thread, and the hyssop *. Lev 14:6
cedar wood, hyssop *, and scarlet Lev 14:51,52
promised that your * of the tribe 1Sa 2:30
The term used here, "* of the Is 4:2,3,4f
—yes, a new * Is 11:1
is thrown out like a broken *; Is 14:19
from the * of an almond tree." Jer 1:11
* upon King David's throne. Jer 23:5,6
even as valuable as a single *? Eze 15:2
Its strongest * became a ruler's Eze 19:11
no strong * remains. Eze 19:14
Literally, "from a *." Dan 11:7f
represents my servant The * Zec 3:8
name is "The *"—he will grow up Zec 6:12
When her * is tender and the Mt 24:32
He lops off every * that doesn't Jn 15:2
For a * can't produce fruit when Jn 15:4
like a useless *, withers, and is Jn 15:6
hyssop * and held up to his lips. Jn 19:29
you are just a *, not a root. Rom 11:18
home that was a * of the old Php 3:5

BRANCHES
the river divided into four *. Gen 2:10
placed the peeled * before them, Gen 30:41
a vine with three * that began to Gen 40:9,10
"The three * mean three days! Gen 40:12
a fountain. His * shade the wall. Gen 49:22
cluster of hyssop * and dip them Ex 12:22
It will have three * going out Ex 25:32,33
placed between each set of *; Ex 25:34,35
of * and one below the bottom set. Ex 25:34,35
These decorations and * and the Ex 25:36
The lampstand had six *, three Ex 37:18
Each of the * was decorated with Ex 37:19
the stem beneath each pair of *; Ex 37:20,21
The decorations and * were all Ex 37:22
at the ends of the *, the snuffers, Ex 37:23,24
and some hyssop *, to be used for Lev 14:4
scarlet thread, and hyssop *. Lev 14:49
on the base and *, was made Num 8:4
wood and hyssop * and scarlet Num 19:6
shall take hyssop * and dip them Num 19:18
joyously waving * of juniper trees 2Sa 6:5
and his hair caught in the *. 2Sa 18:9
the hills to get * from olive, Neh 8:15
So the people went out and cut * Neh 8:16
his * spread across the garden. Job 8:16
again, and grows tender, new *. Job 14:7
and all his * will be lopped off. Job 18:16
and sing among the * of the trees. Ps 104:12
them upon the * of the willow Ps 137:2
tree and take hold of its *. Sol 7:8
in the highest *, four or five out Is 17:6
the city munching on twigs and *. Is 27:10
My people are like the dead * of Is 27:11
Strip the * from each vine, for Jer 5:10
booth of leaves and * in a garden! Lam 2:6
strong * and luxuriant leaves. Eze 17:6
sent its roots and * out toward him Eze 17:7
I will cut off its * and let its Eze 17:9
forth * and bearing fruit. Eze 17:22,23
* will shelter every kind of bird. Eze 17:22,23
to the ground. Its * were broken Eze 19:12
of its * and devoured its fruit." Eze 19:14f
full of thick * and forest shade, Eze 31:2,3
grew long thick * because of all Eze 31:5
The birds nested in its *, and Eze 31:6
no cypress had * equal to it; Eze 31:8
on the ground. Her * will be Eze 31:12
wild animals will lie among her *; Eze 31:13
and green, and its * were weighted Dan 4:12
sheltered in its *, and all the Dan 4:12
lop off its *; Dan 4:14
the birds from its *, but leave Dan 4:14
shade, with its * full of birds— Dan 4:21
in Lebanon. Her * will spread out, Hos 14:6
trunks and * white and bare. Joe 1:7
the two olive * that emptied oil Zec 4:12
and others cut * from the trees and Mt 21:8
plants, with long * where birds can Mk 4:31,32
down leafy * from the fields. Mk 11:8
and the birds live among its *. Lk 13:19
took palm * and went down the road Jn 12:13
And he prunes those * that bear Jn 15:2
you are the *. Jn 15:5
tree are holy, the * will be too. Rom 11:16
But some of these * from Rom 11:17
And you Gentiles who were * from, Rom 11:17
the * that were broken off. Rom 11:18
be saying, "those * were broken Rom 11:19
Remember that those *, the Jews, Rom 11:20
For if God did not spare the * Rom 11:21
the people, using * of hyssop Heb 9:19
white, with palm * in their hands. Rev 7:9

BRAND
This annual memorial week will * Ex 13:9
as much as if his * of ownership Ex 13:16
I am tied with * new ropes which Ju 16:11
For I'm going to do a * new Is 43:19
Is not this a * plucked out of Zec 3:2f
He has put his * upon us—his 2Co 1:22
he becomes a * new person inside. 2Co 5:17
You are living a * new kind of Col 3:10

BRANDED
as though he had * his mark of Ex 13:9

BRANDISH
take a sword and * it twice, Eze 21:14
when I * my sword before them. Eze 32:10

BRANDISHED
* against the sons of Greece." Zec 9:13

BRANDS
brings out the less expensive *. Jn 2:10

BRASH
She was the *, coarse type, seen Pro 7:11,12
A prostitute is loud and *, and Pro 9:13

BRASS
Then he made ten * vats, and 1Ki 7:38
silversmiths, * and iron workers; 2Ch 2:7
work with * and iron, and knows all 2Ch 2:14
who made articles of iron and *. 2Ch 24:12
* which were as precious as gold. Ez 8:26,27
Is my flesh made of *? Job 6:12
lie straight as a tube of *. Job 40:18
to him, and * is rotten wood. Job 41:27,28
* and cut apart their iron bars. Ps 107:16
the city gates of * and iron bars. Is 45:2
you are as hardheaded as *. Is 48:4
I will exchange your * for gold, Is 60:17
wood for *, your stones for iron. Is 60:17
iron pillar and heavy gates of *. Jer 1:18
They are insolent as *, hard and Jer 6:28
that shone like polished *. Eze 1:4
feet, and shone like burnished *. Eze 1:7
*, the tin, the iron and the lead. Eze 22:18,19,20
and thighs of *, its legs of iron, Dan 2:32
iron, clay, *, silver, and gold; Dan 2:35
all the iron and *, the clay, the Dan 2:45
*, surrounded by the tender grass. Dan 4:15
banded with a chain of iron and *. Dan 4:23
* and iron, wood and stone. Dan 5:2,3,4
of silver, gold, *, iron, wood, and Dan 5:23

(BRASS Con't)
its iron teeth and * claws that Dan 7:19
like polished *, and his voice was Dan 10:5,6
iron and hoofs of * and you will Mic 4:13
like two mountains made of *. Zec 6:1
whose feet are like glowing *. Rev 2:18
gold and silver, *, stone, and Rev 9:20
and * and iron and marble; Rev 18:12

BRAT
I know what a cocky * you are; 1Sa 17:28

BRAVE
"Be strong and *, for you will Jos 1:6
thousand * warriors that day, Ju 20:46,47
And whenever Saul saw any *, 1Sa 14:52
but was handsome, *, and strong, 1Sa 16:18
trained, and * troops in the army 1Ch 5:18
Ishmaiah from Gibeon (a * warrior 1Ch 12:3-7
Great and * warriors from the 1Ch 12:8-13
They were * and able warriors, 1Ch 12:21
Their * brothers, Elihu and 1Ch 26:6,7
composed of well-trained, * men. 2Ch 14:8
Twenty-six hundred * clan 2Ch 26:12
other priests, all * men, and 2Ch 26:17,18
"Be strong, be *, and do not be 2Ch 32:7
Be *, stouthearted and courageous. Ps 27:14

BRAVED
Christians who * the persecution, Act 8:2f

BRAVELY
Israel's leaders * led; Ju 5:2

BRAVEST
thousand of his * troops to hide in Jos 8:3,4
Then even the * of them, though 2Sa 17:10
of some of the * of David's 1Ch 11:10
120,000 of his * soldiers because 2Ch 28:6
even in Jahaz. The * warriors of Is 15:4

BRAWL
he will say, 'I got into a * at Zec 13:6

BRAWLS
hard liquor leads to *; Pro 20:1

BRAY
When wild donkeys *, it is Job 6:5,6,7

BRAZEN
Or, "The wicked man is *; Pro 21:29f
you are a * prostitute, building Eze 16:30

BRAZENLY
* you murder without a cause. Jer 2:34

BRAZIER
More literally, "a large * in Jer 36:22f

BREACH
made a * in the tribes of Israel. Ju 21:15
stepped into the * between the Ps 106:23
through the nearest * in the wall. Amo 4:3
"He who opens the *." Mic 2:13f

BREACHED
The walls of Jerusalem are * and Is 22:5
of July, they * the wall, and the Jer 39:2

BREAD
Heaven, brought him * and wine. Gen 14:18
with freshly baked unleavened *. Gen 19:3
Then Jacob gave Esau *, peas, Gen 25:34
aroma, and some fresh-baked *. Gen 27:17
they said, "but give us *; Gen 47:15
unleavened * and bitter herbs. Ex 12:8
to eat only * made without yeast. Ex 12:15
with Unleavened *' will cause you Ex 12:17
Only * without yeast may be Ex 12:18
serve only yeastless *." Ex 12:20
with them their * dough without Ex 12:34
to eat, they baked * from the Ex 12:39
time to wait for * to rise to take Ex 12:39
you shall eat only * without yeast, Ex 13:6,7
the evening, and * in the morning. Ex 16:7,8,9
be stuffed with *, and you shall Ex 16:11,12
and flat, and tasted like honey *. Ex 16:31
could see the * the Lord had fed Ex 16:32
of Unleavened *, when for seven Ex 23:15
you are not to eat * with yeast, Ex 23:15
shall be offered with leavened *; Ex 23:18
and always keep the special * of Ex 25:30
no defects, and * made without Ex 29:2
of sweetened * mingled with oil, Ex 29:2
(The various kinds of * shall be Ex 29:2
Place the * in a basket and Ex 29:3,4
and one loaf of *, one cake of Ex 29:23
cake of shortening *, and one wafer Ex 29:23
of unleavened * that was placed Ex 29:23
the meat, also the * in the basket, Ex 29:32
If any of the meat or * remains Ex 29:34
of Unleavened * for seven days, Ex 34:18
"You must not use leavened * Ex 34:25
The * of the Presence; Ex 35:10-19
The * of the Presence; Ex 39:33-40
veil, and set the * of the Ex 40:23
"If * baked in the oven is Lev 2:4
You may offer yeast * and honey Lev 2:12
thanksgiving, unleavened short * Lev 7:12
with loaves of leavened *. Lev 7:13
basket of * made without yeast; Lev 8:1
and a slice of *, all taken from Lev 8:26
it along with the * that is in the Lev 8:31
Anything left of the meat and * Lev 8:32
"The Festival of Unleavened *: Lev 23:6
kernels nor * nor parched grain. Lev 23:14
of two loaves of * from your homes Lev 23:17
Bake this * from a fifth of a Lev 23:17
Along with the * and the wine, Lev 23:18
twelve loaves of * in two rows upon Lev 24:5-8
of Israel. The * shall be eaten by Lev 24:9
to bake all the * available for ten Lev 26:26
table where the * of the Presence Num 4:7
cups, and the * upon the cloth. Num 4:7
a basket of * made without Num 6:15
basket of * made without yeast; Num 6:17
unleavened * and bitter herbs. Num 9:11
For they are but * for us to eat! Num 14:9
but no leavened * shall be served. Num 28:17
(it was a kind of * unknown before) Deu 8:16
neither eating * nor drinking Deu 9:18
the sacrifice with unleavened *. Deu 16:3
Eat unleavened * for seven days Deu 16:3
a reminder of the * you ate as you Deu 16:3
was no time for the * to rise. Deu 16:3
shall eat no * made with yeast. Deu 16:8
The Festival of Unleavened *, Deu 16:16
Blessings of fruit and *; Deu 28:2-6
Curses on your fruit and *; Deu 28:15-19
to grow grain for * or grapes for Deu 29:6
and they made unleavened *. Jos 5:11,12
wineskins and dry, moldy *. Jos 9:3,4,5
This * was hot from the ovens Jos 9:12
* from a bushel of flour. Ju 6:19
the meat and the * upon that rock Ju 6:20
the meat and * with his staff, and Ju 6:21
loaf of barley * that came tumbling Ju 7:12,13
three loaves of *, and the third 1Sa 10:3
ten loaves of * to your brothers. 1Sa 17:17
Give me five loaves of *, or 1Sa 21:3
"We don't have any regular *," 1Sa 21:4
there is the holy *, which I guess 1Sa 21:4
gave him the holy *—the Bread of 1Sa 21:6
the holy bread—the * of the 1Sa 21:6
replaced that day with fresh *. 1Sa 21:6
Should I take my * and my water 1Sa 25:11
hundred loaves of *, two barrels of 1Sa 25:18
dough and baked unleavened *. 1Sa 28:24
alike—of a loaf of *, some wine, 2Sa 6:19
then she baked some special * for 2Sa 13:8
hundred loaves of *, one hundred 2Sa 16:1
ride on, and the * and summer fruit 2Sa 16:2
table where the * of the Presence 1Ki 7:48
of ten loaves of *, some fig bars, 1Ki 14:3
The ravens brought him * and 1Ki 17:6
"Bring me a bite of *, too." 1Ki 17:11
a single piece of * in the house. 1Ki 17:12
bake me a little loaf of * first; 1Ki 17:13
had fed them with * and water. 1Ki 18:3,4
and fed them with * and water? 1Ki 18:13
He looked around and saw some * 1Ki 19:6
and feed him with * and water—and 1Ki 22:27
loaves of barley * made from the 2Ki 4:42
the preparation of the special * 1Ch 9:32
(men and women alike) a loaf of * 1Ch 16:3
They provided the * of the 1Ch 23:29
table on which the * of the 1Ch 28:16
display the special sacrificial *, 2Ch 2:4
Literally, "The * of the 2Ch 2:4f
the table for the * of the Presence 2Ch 4:19
and they place the * of the 2Ch 13:11
and feed him with * and water until 2Ch 18:26
the table of the * of the Presence 2Ch 29:18
* for the next seven days. 2Ch 35:17
of Unleavened * for seven days. Ez 6:21,22
"You gave them * from heaven Neh 9:15
stop giving them * from heaven or Neh 9:20
of the special * of the Presence, Neh 10:33
thirsty, and * to the starving. Job 22:7
They eat my people like * and Ps 14:4
For they devour my people like * Ps 53:4
He gave them * from heaven! Ps 78:24
I eat ashes instead of *. Ps 102:9,10
skin, and * to give him strength. Ps 104:15
and gave them manna—* from heaven. Ps 105:40
ground shall have his fill of *." Pro 12:11f
one's soul for a piece of *. Pro 28:21
with a flail. * grain is easily Is 28:28
Though he give you the * of Is 30:20
and bake his *, and then—he really Is 44:15
it to bake my * and roast my meat. Is 44:19
for the farmer and * for the Is 55:10
your children's *, and your flocks Jer 5:17
loaf of fresh * every day as long Jer 37:21
all the * in the city is gone." Jer 38:9
Her people groan and cry for *; Lam 1:11
through the garbage dumps for *. Lam 1:19
Babies cry for * but no one can Lam 4:3,4
We beg for * from Egypt, and Lam 5:6
"During the first 390 days eat * Eze 4:9
shall eat defiled * in the Gentile Eze 4:13
Then he told me, "Son of dust, * Eze 4:16
to lack both * and water, and to Eze 4:17
until every bit of * is gone. Eze 5:16
or a piece of * will you turn away Eze 13:19
feast. Only * without yeast shall Eze 45:21
of the flour offerings into *. Eze 46:19,20
a famine of * or water, but of Amo 8:11
brush against some * or wine or Hag 2:12
changing stones into loaves of *. Mt 4:3
For the Scriptures tell us that * Mt 4:4
for a loaf of *, will he be given a Mt 7:9
* permitted to the priests alone. Mt 12:4
be compared to a woman making *. Mt 13:33
small loaves of * and two fish!" Mt 14:17
"It doesn't seem right to take * Mt 15:26
of * and a few small fish!" Mt 15:34
they had forgotten to bring *. Mt 16:7
ceremonies, when * made with yeast Mt 26:17
a small loaf of * and blessed it Mt 26:26
then—and they ate the special * Mk 2:25,26
five loaves of * and two fish. Mk 6:38
gave some of the * and fish to each Mk 6:41
"How many loaves of * do you Mk 8:5
only one loaf of * in the boat. Mk 8:14
about their forgetting to bring *. Mk 8:16
men I fed with five loaves of *? Mk 8:19
I'm worried that we have no *?" Mk 8:21
no * made with yeast was eaten. Mk 14:1
As they were eating, Jesus took * Mk 14:22
stone to become a loaf of *." Lk 4:3
are much more important than *!' Lk 4:4
"Man shall not live by * alone." Lk 4:4f
the special * that was placed Lk 6:4
five loaves of * and two fish among Lk 9:13
to borrow three loaves of *. Lk 11:5,6
for *, do you give him a stone? Lk 11:11
for its daily *, but your heavenly Lk 12:30
* made without yeast was used. Lk 22:1
and eaten with the unleavened *. Lk 22:7
Then he took a loaf of *; Lk 22:19
a small loaf of * and broke it and Lk 24:30
him as he was breaking the *. Lk 24:35
buy * to feed all these people?" Jn 6:2-5
Give us free * every day, like Jn 6:30,31
'Moses gave them * from heaven.' Jn 6:30,31
And now he offers you true * from Jn 6:32
The true * is a Person—the one Jn 6:33
that * every day of our lives!" Jn 6:34
Jesus replied, "I am the * of Jn 6:35
claimed to be the * from heaven. Jn 6:41
Yes, I am the * of Life! Jn 6:48-51
* from the skies, they all died. Jn 6:48-51
But the * from heaven gives Jn 6:48-51
I am that Living * that came down Jn 6:48-51
Anyone eating this * shall live Jn 6:48-51
live forever; this * is my flesh Jn 6:48-51
I am the true * from heaven; Jn 6:58
and anyone who eats this * shall Jn 6:58
they ate * from heaven." Jn 6:58
the * dipped in the sauce." Jn 13:26
frying over it, and there was *. Jn 21:9
around serving us the * and fish. Jn 21:13
Literally, "the breaking of *," Act 2:42f
upon the pure * of honor and 1Co 5:8
off pieces of the * from the loaf 1Co 10:16
You cannot eat * both at the 1Co 10:21
Lord Jesus took *, and when he had 1Co 11:23
For every time you eat this * 1Co 11:26
So if anyone eats this * and 1Co 11:27
the * and drinking from the cup. 1Co 11:28
For if he eats the * and drinks 1Co 11:29
special loaves of holy * upon it; Heb 9:1
said, "A loaf of * for $20, or Rev 6:6

BREADTH
within a hair's *, never missing! Ju 20:16

BREAK
say, and then * down and cry. Gen 37:35
and cause boils to * out upon Ex 9:9
and you shall not * any of its Ex 12:46
and the people * across the Ex 19:24
and * down their shameful idols. Ex 23:24
Instead, you must * down their Ex 34:13
with olive oil. * it into pieces Lev 2:6
I will * your proud power and Lev 26:19
and must not * a bone of it, and Num 9:12
signal to * camp and move onward. Num 10:5,6,7
He shall * their bones in pieces, Num 24:3-9
Beware lest you * the contract Deu 4:23
You will * it if you make any Deu 4:23
"You must * down the heathen Deu 7:5
under the trees. * the altars, Deu 12:3
nor sowed—and there * its neck. Deu 21:4
Your heart will * with longing Deu 28:32
befall those who * this contract. Deu 29:21
They will forget about me and * Deu 31:16
and despise me and * my contract, Deu 31:20
live, for if we * our oath the Jos 9:20
that I would never * my covenant Ju 2:1
return and * down this tower." Ju 8:9
then we will * the rafts apart 1Ki 5:9
and silver. Now * your alliance 1Ki 15:19
to * through to the king of Edom; 2Ki 3:26
anyone who tries to * through. 2Ki 11:6,7,8
to induce you to * your alliance 2Ch 16:3
and try to * me with your words? Job 19:2

(BREAK Con't)
They * into houses at night and Job 24:16
"Come, let us * his chains," Ps 2:3
* the arms of these wicked men. Ps 10:15
O God, * off their fangs. Ps 58:6
No, I will not * my covenant; Ps 89:34
means that poverty will * in upon Pro 24:34
a soft tongue can * hard bones. Pro 25:15
For God will * the chains that Is 9:4
He will * the slave-yoke off Is 10:27
I have decided to * the Assyrian Is 14:25
He will not * the bruised reed, Is 42:3
Shout, O earth; * forth into Is 44:23
shout, O earth. * forth with Is 49:13
Let the ruins of Jerusalem * Is 52:9
SING, O CHILDLESS woman! * out Is 54:1
the enemy shall * open the graves Jer 8:1
Can a man * bars of northern iron Jer 15:12,13
of Hosts, I will * the yoke from Jer 30:8
If you can * my covenant with the Jer 33:20,21
And he shall * down the obelisks Jer 43:13
lands; * open her granaries; Jer 50:26
says the Lord, to * nations in Jer 51:20
all her weapons * in her hands, Jer 51:56
occupy your homes, * down your Eze 7:24
I will * down your whitewashed Eze 13:14
with my fist and * off their food Eze 14:13
merchandise and * down your walls. Eze 26:12
When I come to * the power of Eze 30:18
Egypt, and I will * both his Eze 30:22
But I will * the arms of Pharaoh, Eze 30:24
When you saw the horn * off, and Dan 8:22
Empire will * into four sections Dan 8:22
that time, he will * his pledge and Dan 9:27
that I was able to * through these Dan 10:13
his kingdom will * apart and be Dan 11:4
God will * down their heathen Hos 10:2
You devour them, flog them, * Mic 3:3
Now I will * your chains and Nah 1:13
* the law without rebuke." Mal 2:9
decided to * the engagement but Mt 1:19
'You shall not * your vows to God, Mt 5:33
nothing—you can * that oath, but to Mt 23:16
centuries shall * upon the heads of Mt 23:36
High waves began to * into the Mk 4:37
* his oath in front of his guests. Mk 6:26
And so you * the law of God in Mk 7:12,13
And wars will * out near and Mk 13:7
dawn is about to * upon us, to Lk 1:78
When the floodwaters rise and * Lk 6:47,48
already, so they didn't * his. Jn 19:33
What kind of judge are you to * Act 23:3
of the waves and began to * apart. Act 27:41
that mean God will * his promises? Rom 3:3
laws is not to have any to *! Rom 4:15
Only if there were no laws to * Rom 7:8
And when we * off pieces of the 1Co 10:16
them they will * out into 2Co 9:11
These weapons can * down every 2Co 10:5
die and in dying * the power of the Heb 2:14
"Who is worthy to * the seals on Rev 5:2
scroll and to * its seven seals." Rev 5:5
and * its seals and open it; Rev 5:9

BREAKER
harassing Jesus as a Sabbath *. Jn 5:16

BREAKERS
You are mightier than all the * Ps 93:4
But though they roar like * Is 17:13

BREAKFAST
walking, at bedtime, and before *! Deu 11:19
insisted on their having * first. Ju 19:5
dawn to prepare * for her Pro 31:15
"Now come and have some *!" Jn 21:12
After * Jesus said to Simon Jn 21:15

BREAKING
at Lot and began * down the door. Gen 19:9
After * camp at Rephidim, they Ex 19:2,3
in the act of * into a house and is Ex 22:2
spot, it may be leprosy * out. Lev 13:42
I will revenge the * of my Lev 26:25
and for signaling the * of camp. Num 10:1
yanked his hair away, * the loom. Ju 16:14
and tore it down, * the altars and 2Ki 11:18
"The Place of * Through"). 1Ch 14:11
majesty of God * forth upon us from Job 37:22
them and * off their teeth. Ps 3:7
close to those whose hearts are *; Ps 34:18
earth, * and burning every weapon. Ps 46:9
testing God's patience to the * Ps 106:14
a sad face means a * heart. Pro 15:13
Then in loneliness my * heart Jer 13:17
My heart is * over what is Lam 3:51
* wedlock living with other men. Eze 16:38
But will Israel prosper after * Eze 17:15
kingdom, * the power of the nation Hos 1:4,5
forward they march, never * ranks. Joe 2:7
on the strong, * all defenses. Amo 5:9
so they began * off heads of Mt 12:1
"Your disciples are * the law. Mt 12:2
That was * the law too. Mt 12:4
the disciples were * off heads of Mk 2:23
for the food. * the loaves into Mk 6:41
Then, * the seal, she poured it Mk 14:3
they were * off the heads of wheat, Lk 6:1
him as he was * the bread. Lk 24:35
So why pick on me for * them? Jn 7:19
Literally, "the * of bread," Act 2:42f
You are * my heart! Act 21:13
but you dishonor him by * them. Rom 2:23
"But," some say, "our * faith Rom 3:5
The only way we can keep from * Rom 4:15
of death for * his laws—because he Rom 5:13
I agree with these laws I am *. Rom 7:16
guilty they are of * God's laws. Gal 3:19
* down the wall of contempt Eph 2:14
But you are * this law of our Jas 2:9

BREAKS
If we don't, and war * out, they Ex 1:10
* any of my commandments. Lev 4:2
to be a stick that * beneath your 2Ki 18:20,21
ahead and that the * in the wall Neh 4:7
My flesh * open, full of pus. Job 7:5
so full of majesty. It * down Ps 29:5,6
There he * the weapons of our Ps 76:3
That is why the earth * out in Ps 98:4
And so if anyone * the least Mt 5:19
who at any time * a single one of Gal 3:10
and sometimes it * out into curses Jas 3:9

BREAST
Then take the * of Aaron's Ex 29:26
"Give the * and thigh of the Ex 29:27
of the fat and *, which is to be Lev 7:30
the altar, but the * shall belong Lev 7:31
For I have designated the * and Lev 7:34
Now Moses took the * and Lev 8:29
But the * and the thigh, which Lev 10:14
along with the * that was offered Lev 10:15
including the * and right thigh Num 18:18
The baby nursing at the *, Deu 32:25
a child who is weaned from the *. Ps 131:2

BREASTPLATE
be set in the ephod and in the *. Ex 25:1
the lower armor and the * meet. 2Ch 18:33
truth and the * of God's approval. Eph 6:14

BREASTPLATES
They wore * that seemed to be of Rev 9:9
their riders wore fiery-red *, Rev 9:17,18

BREASTS
of the * and of the womb, Gen 49:25
The fat was placed upon the * of Lev 9:20
but he waved the * and right Lev 9:21
Why did she nurse me at her *? Job 3:12
their mother's *, and take a poor Job 24:9
Literally, "*." Pro 5:19f
of myrrh lying between my *." Sol 1:13
Your * are like twin fawns of a Sol 4:5
Your two * are like two fawns, Sol 7:3
* are like its clusters of dates. Sol 7:7
Now may your * be like grape Sol 7:8
a little sister too young for * Sol 8:8
King Solomon: "If she has no * Sol 8:9
Literally, "My * are its Sol 8:10f
Beat your * in sorrow for those Is 32:12
infant at a mother's generous *. Is 66:11
be nursed at her *, carried on her Is 66:12
upon their mothers' shrunken *. Lam 2:12
of maidenhood your * were Eze 16:6,7
birth, for * that cannot nourish. Hos 9:14
like doves, and beat their *! Nah 2:7
and the * that gave you suck!" Lk 11:27

BREATH
and breathed into it the * of Gen 2:7
in which there is the * of life. Gen 6:17
And with Rachel's last * (for Gen 35:18
At the blast of your * Ex 15:8
By the blast of his * 2Sa 22:16
My life is but a *, and nothing Job 7:7
of God, and the * of all mankind. Job 12:10
the * of God shall destroy him; Job 15:30
live, while I have * from God, my Job 27:3
[But I might as well save my *, Job 30:28,29
in a man, the * of the Almighty Job 32:8,9
* of the Almighty gives me life. Job 33:4
Yes, his * would kindle Job 41:21
At the blast of your * the depths Ps 18:15
And with a * he can scatter the Ps 33:10
Frail as *! Ps 39:5,6
yes, man is frail as *. Ps 39:11
warships with a * of wind. Ps 48:7
gone in a moment like a * of wind. Ps 78:39
And when you gather up their *, Ps 104:29
I will praise God to my last *! Ps 104:33
For man is but a *; Ps 144:4
I live, yes, even with my dying *. Ps 146:2
Don't waste your * on a rebel. Pro 23:9
perfumed lilies, his * like myrrh. Sol 5:13
the scent of your * like apples, Sol 7:8
Frail as his *! Is 2:22
it is piled high with wood. The * Is 30:33
Your own * will turn to fire and Is 33:11
flower fades beneath the * of God. Is 40:7
and gives life and * and spirit to Is 42:5
off! A * can puff them away. Is 57:13
flood-tide driven by Jehovah's *. Is 59:19
But you say, "Don't waste your * Jer 2:25
people gasping for *, pleading for Jer 4:31
replied, "Don't waste your *. Jer 18:12
is not a * of life in them at all! Jer 51:17
I will put * into you, and you Eze 37:6
them, but the bodies had no *. Eze 37:8
who gives you the * of life and Dan 5:23
but there is no * at all inside! Hab 2:19
grass, moved by every * of wind? Lk 7:24
PAUL, THREATENING with every * Act 9:1
He himself gives life and * to Act 17:25
burn up with the * of his mouth and 2Th 2:8
His visits revived me like a * of 2Ti 1:16
He was permitted to give * to Rev 13:15

BREATHE
He will not let me *, but fills Job 9:18
I will pray as long as I *! Ps 116:2
they cannot even *. Ps 135:17
of my life before I began to *. Ps 139:16
For men and animals both * the Ecc 3:19
I am going to make you live and * Eze 37:5
O Spirit, and * upon these slain Eze 37:9
is gone and I can hardly *." Dan 10:17

BREATHED
and * into it the breath of life. Gen 2:7
that * and lived upon dry land. Gen 7:22
in the bed, * his last, and died. Gen 49:33
—to have never * or seen the Job 3:16
Then he * on them and told Jn 20:22

BREATHING
for every man must die. His * Ps 146:4
me and the bodies began *; Eze 37:10

BREATHTAKING
was, and how * the beauty of his 2Ch 9:3

BRED
I also * great herds and flocks, Ecc 2:7,8

BREED
so that they will * abundantly and Gen 8:17

BRETHREN
at his words: Your * hate you and Is 66:5
back all your * from every nation Is 66:20
rejoin their * in their own land. Mic 5:3
*, please listen patiently to Heb 13:22

BREWED
evil deeds. She * many a cup of woe Rev 18:6

BRIARS
thorns and * of the wilderness." Ju 8:7
with wild thorns and *. Ju 8:16
it be overgrown with * and thorns. Is 5:6
will become patches of *. Is 7:23
wickedness, these thorns and *; Is 9:18
those thorns and *, the Assyrians Is 10:17
If I find thorns and * bothering Is 27:4,5
will thrive with thorns and *; Is 32:13
where * grew, the myrtle trees Is 55:13
like thorns and *, though they Eze 28:24
But I will fence her in with * Hos 1:6
the best of them are prickly as *; Mic 7:4

BRIBE
"Take no bribes, for a * makes Ex 23:8
you clearly see! A * hurts the Ex 23:8
" 'Cursed is he who accepts a * Deu 27:25
Have I ever taken a *? 1Sa 12:3
never taken even one single *." 1Sa 12:4
A * works like magic. Pro 17:8
It is wrong to accept a * to Pro 17:23
A * does wonders; Pro 18:16
if they are trying to * him! Pro 21:27
for he is trying to * you, and no Pro 23:1
man is turned into a fool by a *; Ecc 7:7
it was decided to * the police to Mt 28:12,13
So the police accepted the * and Mt 28:15
He also hoped that Paul would * Act 24:26

BRIBERY
is oppression and * and men who Hab 1:3

BRIBES
men who hate *, and appoint them as Ex 18:21
"Take no *, for a bribe makes Ex 23:8
no partiality and takes no *. Deu 10:17
a rich man, and never accept *. Deu 16:19
accept bribes. For * blind the eyes Deu 16:19
They accepted * and were very 1Sa 8:3
no partiality, no taking of *." 2Ch 19:7
If they accept * to denounce Job 17:5
despite the * offered him—such a Ps 15:5
the innocent and demands *. Ps 26:9,10
"justice" in exchange for *. Ps 58:1
but hating * brings happiness. Pro 15:27
if he hates dishonesty and *. Pro 28:16
but one who demands * destroys it. Pro 29:4
all of them take * and won't Is 1:23
They take * to pervert justice, Is 5:23
hands from taking *, who refuse to Is 33:15
by accepting *, and sold into Amo 2:6
you take *; Amo 5:12
kind— you leaders who take *; Mic 3:11
governor and judge alike demand *. Mic 7:3
and * and trickery prevail. Hab 1:4
not to take *—and to be merciful Zec 7:8,9

BRIBING
* the rich shall end in poverty. Pro 22:16
them gifts, * them to come to you! Eze 16:33,34

BRICK
of hard-burned *, and collected Gen 11:3,4
carry heavy loads of mortar and *. Ex 1:13,14
quotas by a single *, for they Ex 5:7,8
and axes and work in the * kilns; 2Sa 12:31
iron harrows, and in * kilns." 2Sa 12:31f
dust, take a large * and lay it Eze 4:1
ran a line of * boiling vats, with Eze 46:23

BRICKS
any more straw for making *! Ex 5:7,8
just as many * as before!" Ex 5:10,11
to make as many * as before, and we Ex 5:16
deliver the regular quota of *." Ex 5:18
Prepare many * for repairing your Nah 3:14

BRIDAL
"Wait until the * week is over Gen 29:27
jewels to display, as * ornaments. Is 49:18

BRIDE
the city and won Achsah as his *. Ju 1:13
The *, Ps 45:13
"Come with me from Lebanon, my * Sol 4:8
my heart, my lovely one, my *; Sol 4:9
is your love, my darling, my *. Sol 4:10
"My darling * is like a private Sol 4:12
in my garden, my darling, my *! Sol 5:1
suit or a * with her jewels. Is 61:10
and "The *," for the Lord Is 62:4
you as a bridegroom with his *. Is 62:5
me as a young * long ago and how Jer 2:2
her jewels? What * will seek to Jer 2:32
and the * from her privacy. Joe 2:16
the * curses her mother-in-law. Mic 7:6
—the * will go where the Jn 3:29
and his * has prepared herself. Rev 19:7
beautiful as a * at her wedding. Rev 21:2
show you the *, the Lamb's wife." Rev 21:9
The Spirit and the * say, Rev 22:17

BRIDE'S
a bridegroom to the * parents." Ex 22:16f

BRIDEGROOM
from a * to the bride's parents." Ex 22:16f
Literally, "is like a *." Ps 19:5f
as a * going to his wedding, Ps 19:5
I am like a * in his wedding suit Is 61:10
over you as a * with his bride. Is 62:5
Call the * from his quarters and Joe 2:16
Literally, "the *." Mt 9:15f
lamps and went to meet the *. Mt 25:1
"So, when the * was delayed, Mt 25:5,6
by the shout, 'The * is coming! Mt 25:5,6
"But while they were gone, the * Mt 25:10
friends of the * refuse to eat at Mk 2:19
come when the * will be killed; Lk 5:35
did), he called the * over. Jn 2:9
—the bride will go where the * is! Jn 3:29

BRIDEGROOM'S
"Should the * friends mourn and Mt 9:15
is! A * friends rejoice with him. Jn 3:29
I am the * friend, and I am Jn 3:29

BRIDEGROOMS
joyous voices of the * and brides. Jer 7:34
the songs of * and of brides. Jer 16:9
happy voices of * and of brides, Jer 33:10,11
voices of the * and the brides. Rev 18:23

BRIDES
voices of the bridegrooms and *. Jer 7:34
the songs of bridegrooms and of *. Jer 16:9
bridegrooms and of *, and the Jer 33:10,11
and your * commit adultery. Hos 4:13
of the bridegrooms and the *. Rev 18:23

BRIDESMAIDS
illustrated by the story of ten * Mt 25:1

BRIDLE
in your nose and a * in your mouth 2Ki 19:28
a donkey with a *, and a rebel with Pro 26:3
proud nations and * them and lead Is 30:28
long and as high as a horse's *. Rev 14:20

BRIEF
But your days there will be *; Deu 4:26
You have set mankind so * a span Job 14:5
how * my time on earth will be. Ps 39:4
days are few and *, like grass, Ps 103:15
Let his years be few and *; Ps 109:8
For a * moment I abandoned you. Is 54:7
* months in the year 609 B.C. Jer 22:11f
but after a very * reign, he will Dan 11:20
Dear, dear children, how * are Jn 13:33
us for a few * years, doing the Heb 12:10
I sent a * letter to the church 3Jn 1:9
to come, but his reign will be *. Rev 17:10
one * moment, to reign with him. Rev 17:12

BRIEFLY
How * we possessed Jerusalem! Is 63:18
was * governor, but not king. Jer 22:30f
will invade Egypt *, but will Dan 11:9
only a moment as I * outline our Act 24:4
you Gentiles, as I * mentioned Eph 3:2,3

BRIGHT
Then God said, "Let there be * Gen 1:14,15
It can be * with joy if you will Gen 4:7
swelling or a * spot, sort of Lev 13:19
But if the * spot grows no Lev 13:23
place becomes * reddish-white or Lev 13:24
If the hair in the * spot turns Lev 13:25
white hairs in the * spot, and the Lev 13:26
But if the * spot does not move Lev 13:28
a scab from a burn, or a * spot. Lev 14:56
You shall grope in the * Deu 28:29
You make my darkness *. 2Sa 22:29
a * cloud fills the Temple! 1Ki 8:10
Lord, coming as a * cloud, filled 2Ch 5:13,14
any darkness will be as * as Job 11:17
And your * flame shall be put Job 18:5
Anyone even half * will agree Job 34:34,35
to you the night shines as * as Ps 139:12
for you! A * future lies ahead! Pro 24:13,14
his body is * ivory encrusted Sol 5:14
The moon will be as * as the Is 30:26
He will make the darkness * Is 42:16
around you shall be as * as day. Is 58:10
that glowed like * coals of fire or Eze 1:13
you stand beneath awnings * with Eze 27:7
* stars will be dark above you. Eze 32:8
But even as he said it, a * cloud Mt 17:5
* with the glory of the Lord. Lk 2:9
even as he was saying this, a * Lk 9:34
so * their eyes were dazzled. Lk 24:4
about noon a very * light from Act 22:6
you along with a * cloud of glory Rom 9:4
They wander around looking as * Jud 1:13
earth grew * with his splendor. Rev 18:1
I am the * Morning Star. Rev 22:16

BRIGHTEN
and * your eyes with mascara? Jer 4:30

BRIGHTER
the sunlight * than seven days! Is 30:26
light from heaven * than the sun Act 26:13

BRIGHTEST
the * light is dark as midnight.' Job 10:22
yes, even at * noontime, as though Is 59:10

BRIGHTLY
For the flame of God burns * in Is 31:9
God—shall shine as * as the sun's Dan 12:3
more * than John the Baptist. Mt 11:11
John shone * for a while, and Jn 5:35
we can be mirrors that * reflect 2Co 3:18

BRIGHTLY-COLORED
gave him a special gift—a * coat. Gen 37:3
pulled off his * robe, and threw Gen 37:23

BRIGHTNESS
spot, and the * appears to be no Lev 13:26
The earth was radiant with his *. 2Sa 22:13
at the sun for its * when the winds Job 37:21
be that all the * of the sun and Is 24:23
up, he was all amber-colored *. Eze 8:2
the * of the glory of the Lord. Eze 10:4
Jesus covered with * and glory, and Lk 9:32
each other in their beauty and *. 1Co 15:41
the * was already fading away. 2Co 3:7
that it is the * of his glory that 2Co 4:6

BRILLIANCE
Suddenly the * of his presence Ps 18:12
as the sun's *, and those who turn Dan 12:3
fade, obscured by * from your Hab 3:11
God through human *, and then he 1Co 1:21
God uses man's own * to trap him; 1Co 3:19
power of the sun in unclouded *. Rev 1:16

BRILLIANT
be a pavement of * sapphire stones, Ex 24:10
He is a * man, the son of a 2Ch 2:13
invented by * men to shoot arrows 2Ch 26:15
think of all these * comments? Job 26:4
shrine where the *, dazzling Ps 26:8
coals of fire or * torches, and it Eze 1:13
His * splendor fills the earth Hab 3:3
From his hands flash rays of * Hab 3:4
of sinners!' But * men like you can Mt 11:19
and his clothing was a * white. Mt 28:3
suddenly a * light from heaven Act 9:3
of men, even the most * of them." 1Co 1:19
scholars, these * debaters of this 1Co 1:20
* ideas to tell you God's message. 1Co 2:1

BRILLIANTLY
*, frightening and terrible. Dan 2:31

BRIM
high and 15 feet from * to brim; 1Ki 7:23
high and 15 feet from brim to *; 1Ki 7:23
inches thick; its * was shaped like 1Ki 7:26
every container was full to the *! 2Ki 4:6
Their hearts are filled to the * Ps 5:9
Barns full to the * with crops of Ps 144:12-15
cup filled to the * with my fury, Jer 25:15
warehouse is filled to the *! Eze 27:25
to fill them to the * with water. Jn 2:7,8

BRIMSTONE
beneath a fiery barrage of *. Job 18:15
He will rain down fire and * on Ps 11:6
great hailstones, fire and *! Eze 38:22
Then fire and * rained down from Lk 17:29

BRING
they shall * about the seasons on Gen 1:14,15
And God said, "Let the earth * Gen 1:24
he said, "He will * us relief from Gen 5:28-31
and their wives. * a pair of every Gen 6:19,20
through the flood. * in a pair of Gen 6:19,20
to be righteous. * in the animals, Gen 7:2
shouted to Lot, "* out those men Gen 19:5
family, and to * back a girl from Gen 24:38
and good—and * it here for me to Gen 27:2,3,4
Go out to the flocks and * me two Gen 27:8,9,10
Isaac: "Then * me the venison, Gen 27:25
* you back safely to this land; Gen 28:15
clothes, and will * me back safely Gen 28:21
with the flocks, and * me word." Gen 37:13,14
"* her out and burn her," Judah Gen 38:24
"My husband had to * in this Gen 39:14,15
families; but * your youngest Gen 42:20
go on home, but * your youngest Gen 42:34
if I don't * Benjamin back to you. Gen 42:37
to say, '* me your brother'?" Gen 43:7
If I don't * him back to you, Gen 43:9
Didn't we * back the money we Gen 44:8
And you said to us, '* him here Gen 44:21
I told him, 'If I don't * him Gen 44:32
me. And * him to me quickly." Gen 45:13
in Canaan, and to * your father Gen 45:18
ones, and to * your father here. Gen 45:19
* your descendants back again; Gen 46:3,4
And Israel said, "* them over to Gen 48:9
with you and will * you again to Gen 48:21
and get you, and * you out of this Gen 50:24
one of the maids to * it to her. Ex 2:5
and Jacob [to * their descendants Ex 2:24
They told him, "We * you a Ex 5:1
I will * them into the land I Ex 6:8,9
Quick! * in your cattle from the Ex 9:19
land of Egypt to * locusts—they Ex 10:12
by the Lord to * his people out Ex 12:42
You will * them in and plant them Ex 15:17
Why did you * us here to die, Ex 17:3
"Go on down, and * Aaron back with Ex 19:24
his master shall * him before the Ex 21:6
animal, he shall * the torn carcass Ex 22:13
everyone must * me a sacrifice at Ex 23:15
* to me the first of your crops. Ex 23:16
of your crops, * me the choicest Ex 23:19
Literally, "you shall * [it] into Ex 23:19f
go before you and * you into the Ex 23:23
* me an offering from this list: Ex 25:1
of Israel to * you pure olive oil Ex 27:20
in a basket and * it to the Ex 29:3,4
"Then * the young bull to the Ex 29:10
it is to * you, the people of Ex 30:16
* such a terrible sin upon them?" Ex 32:21
Well, I told them, '* me your Ex 32:24
And you must * the best of the Ex 34:26
may * these offerings to Jehovah: Ex 35:5-9
Then * in the table and place Ex 40:4
on it, and * in the lampstand and Ex 40:4
"Now * Aaron and his sons to the Ex 40:12
Then * his sons and put their Ex 40:14
physical defects. * the animal to Lev 1:2,3
to the Lord is to * fine flour and Lev 2:1
grilled—you are to * this grain Lev 2:8
He shall * it to the door of the Lev 4:4
Then the priest shall * its Lev 4:16
attention he must * as his Lev 4:23
it, he is to * as his sacrifice a Lev 4:28
He shall * it to the place where Lev 4:29
"However, if he chooses to * a Lev 4:32
He shall * it to the place where Lev 4:33
his sin and * his guilt offering Lev 5:6
"If he is too poor to * a lamb Lev 5:7
then he shall * two turtledoves or Lev 5:7
"If he is too poor to * Lev 5:11
then he shall * a tenth of a bushel Lev 5:11
He shall * it to the priest and Lev 5:12
then he shall * a ram without Lev 5:15
he shall * it to the priest, and Lev 5:16
anyway, and must * his sacrifice of Lev 5:17,18
and on the same day he shall * Lev 6:4,5
He shall * it to the priest, and Lev 6:6
they shall * to the Lord a regular Lev 6:19,20
to the Lord must * it personally Lev 7:29
He shall * the offering of the Lev 7:30
THE LORD SAID to Moses, "Now * Lev 8:1
In addition, the people are to * Lev 9:4
The people are to * the thigh Lev 10:15
or girl), she must * a yearling Lev 12:6
But if she is too poor to * a Lev 12:8
then she must * two turtledoves or Lev 12:8
then he shall * only one, a male Lev 14:21
"He shall also * two turtledoves Lev 14:22
He shall * them to the priest at Lev 14:23
are not able to * the sacrifices Lev 14:32
young pigeons and * them to the Lev 15:29
there: He must * a young bull for a Lev 16:3
Israel shall then * him two male Lev 16:5
Then he shall * the two goats Lev 16:7
powder, and * it inside the veil. Lev 16:12
And he shall * some of the blood Lev 16:14
offering goat, and * its blood Lev 16:15

(BRING Con't)
altar, he shall * the live goat Lev 16:20
to cause them to * their sacrifices Lev 17:5
The man involved shall * his Lev 19:21
first harvest, * the first sheaf of Lev 23:9,10,11
later you shall * to the Lord an Lev 23:15,16
of Israel to * you pure olive oil Lev 24:1
the owner shall * it to the priest Lev 27:11,12
When the people of Israel * a Num 5:9,10
the man shall * his wife to the Num 5:15
offering—to * out the truth Num 5:15
"The priest shall * her before Num 5:16
He shall * her before the Lord Num 5:30
day, he must * two turtledoves or Num 6:10
new vow, and must * a male lamb a Num 6:12
sacrifices he must * any further Num 6:21
"Let each of them * his gift on a Num 7:11
Have them * a young bull and a Num 8:8
Then * the Levites to the door Num 8:9
leaders of Israel; * them to the Num 11:16
Don't be afraid, and * back some Num 13:20
He will * us safely into the land Num 14:8
He wasn't strong enough to * them Num 14:16
I will * him into the land he Num 14:24
Well, instead I will * them Num 14:31
Be sure to * your censers with Num 16:17
chiefs is to * you a wooden rod Num 17:1
He was to [* it out and show it Num 17:10
gifts the people * as offerings to Num 18:12
"Tell the people of Israel to * Num 19:1
and * us here to this evil place? Num 20:5
Must we * you water from this Num 20:10
you shall not * them into the land Num 20:12
the place of God. * me any cases Deu 1:17
I am a jealous God, and I will * Deu 5:9,10
he used to * you out of Egypt? Deu 7:19
Do not * an idol into your home Deu 7:26
wasn't able to * them to the land Deu 9:28
There you shall * to the Lord Deu 12:6
then you must * all your burnt Deu 12:11
sacrifices and * your offerings. Deu 12:14
crops every year. * this tithe to Deu 14:23
At that time * to him a free-will Deu 16:10
"On each of these occasions * a Deu 16:16
offerings the people * to him. Deu 18:1
for him and shall * him home and Deu 19:12
and mother shall * the proof of her Deu 22:15
you must not * to the Lord any Deu 23:17,18
this would * guilt upon the land Deu 24:4
The owner will * it out to you. Deu 24:11
you forget to * in a sheaf from the Deu 24:19
harvest. * it in a basket and Deu 26:2,3
"The Lord will * a distant Deu 28:49
He will * upon you all the Deu 28:60
The Lord will * upon you every Deu 28:61
and find you and * you back again Deu 30:4
with no one to * them down to you; Deu 30:12
no one can * you their message; Deu 30:13
to him, "You must * the people of Deu 31:23
The Lord will now * calamity upon Jos 7:25
of the cave and to * out the five Jos 10:22,23
territory and * back a report of Jos 18:4
to * back their report to Joshua. Jos 18:8
certainly he will * evil upon you Jos 23:15,16
to * terrible plagues upon Egypt; Jos 24:5
And he will * home Ju 5:30
"* out your son," they shouted Ju 6:30
Literally, "Let Baal * charges," Ju 6:32f
still too many! * them down to the Ju 7:4
However, if you wish to * Ju 13:16
bring something, * an offering to Ju 13:16
people demanded, "* out Samson so Ju 16:25,26
at the old man to * out the man who Ju 19:22
man's wife. I'll * them out and you Ju 19:24
a supply line to * us food, and the Ju 20:8,9,10
"* your shawl," he told her. Ru 3:15-18
"Let's * the Ark here from 1Sa 4:3
the chef to * Saul the choicest cut 1Sa 9:23
him and refused to * him presents, 1Sa 10:27
be our king? * them here and we 1Sa 11:12
Aaron to * them into this land. 1Sa 12:8
were gone. "* the Ark of God," 1Sa 14:18
and tell them to * the oxen and 1Sa 14:34
Then Samuel said, "* King Agag 1Sa 15:32
along; and * us back a letter 1Sa 17:18
Saul said to * him in his bed, 1Sa 19:15
Then I'll send a lad to * the 1Sa 20:21
"Must you * me a madman? 1Sa 21:14,15
the priest to * the ephod and to 1Sa 23:9
"Will you * his spirit up?" 1Sa 28:7,8
whom do you want me to * up?" 1Sa 28:11
"* me Samuel," Saul replied. 1Sa 28:11
the priest, "* me the ephod!" 1Sa 30:7
bracelets to * to you, my lord." 2Sa 1:10
you unless you * me my wife Michal, 2Sa 3:13
to Baal-judah to * home the Ark of 2Sa 6:1
"How can I ever * the Ark home?" 2Sa 6:9
in order to * glory to your name. 2Sa 7:23
Can I * him back again? 2Sa 12:23
Now * the rest of the army and 2Sa 12:28
Then he said to Tamar, "Now * me 2Sa 13:10
"If anyone objects, * him to me; 2Sa 14:10
to * home your own banished son. 2Sa 14:13
to * your son back from his exile. 2Sa 14:14
made provision to * back those he 2Sa 14:14f
right, go and * back Absalom." 2Sa 14:21
and when anyone came to * a case 2Sa 15:2
if he would * me back to Jerusalem, 2Sa 15:7,8
said, "he will * me back to see 2Sa 15:25,26
he could * disaster upon Absalom! 2Sa 17:14
"Return to us and * back all those 2Sa 19:14
asking them to * him the bones of 2Sa 21:12,13,14
But you * down the haughty; 2Sa 22:28
When you * him back here, place 1Ki 1:35
All right, * me a sword." 1Ki 3:24
My men will * the logs from the 1Ki 5:9
you are their God. * them back 1Ki 8:33,34
me, I will * disaster upon your 1Ki 14:10
what the ravens * you, for I have 1Ki 17:4
"* me a bite of bread, too." 1Ki 17:11
Baal instead. Now * all the people 1Ki 18:19
prophets. Now * two young bulls. 1Ki 18:23
The Lord is going to * great 1Ki 21:21
"Well," he said, "* me a new 2Ki 2:20
"Now * me someone to play the 2Ki 3:15
"* me another jar," she said to 2Ki 4:6
"* me some meal," Elisha said. 2Ki 4:41
going to obey me, * the heads of 2Ki 10:6
idolatry: I will * such evil upon 2Ki 21:12
which I will * upon this place." 2Ki 22:20
He ordered his men to * out the 2Ki 23:16
And let us * back the Ark of our 1Ch 13:3
Kiriath-jearim) in Judah to * 1Ch 13:6
so that you may * the Ark of 1Ch 15:12
* an offering and come before him; 1Ch 16:29
* us safely back from among the 1Ch 16:35
And may this * eternal honor to 1Ch 17:24
and * me the totals," he told 1Ch 21:2
as you need, and * it to you in log 2Ch 2:16
by King Hiram, to * back gold, 2Ch 9:21
the people to * to the Lord the tax 2Ch 24:9
God sent prophets to * them back 2Ch 24:19
"You must not * the captives 2Ch 28:13
"Now * your sacrifices and thank 2Ch 29:31
in Jerusalem to * their tithes to 2Ch 31:4
of the people who * in their 2Ch 35:4,5
I will * you back to Jerusalem. Neh 1:9
to * about riots and confusion. Neh 4:8
in the land should * any grain or Neh 10:31
We also agreed always to * the Neh 10:35
And we promised to * to the Neh 10:37
required by law to * these Neh 10:39,40
and Carkas— to * Queen Vashti to Est 1:11
in the empire and * them to the Est 2:2
"* him in," the king ordered. Est 6:5
So he replied, "* out some of Est 6:7,8
man, no mediator to * us together. Job 9:32,33
me and * fresh armies against me. Job 10:17
* up all the follies of my youth. Job 13:26
He does * about justice at last, Job 35:14,15
Can you send him out to * in the Job 39:12
to master him * a sharp sword! Job 40:19
Then I will * him sacrifices and Ps 27:6
Burnt animals * no special joy to Ps 40:6
the sacrifices you * to my altar, Ps 50:8
altar, for you * them regularly. Ps 50:8
and in the bullocks I * to Ps 51:19
Gladly I * my sacrifices to you; Ps 54:6
power and * them to their knees. Ps 59:11
to their knees. * them to the dust, Ps 59:11
Who will * me in triumph into Ps 60:9,10
Literally, "I will * back from Ps 68:22f
Rebuke our enemies, O Lord. * Ps 68:30
But you will * me back to life Ps 71:20
from Seba—all will * their gifts. Ps 72:10
Or, "you will * me unto honor." Ps 73:24f
Man's futile wrath will * you Ps 76:10
Let everyone * him presents. Ps 76:11
Now * us back to loving you, Ps 85:4
glory he deserves! * your offering Ps 96:8
Let lies be told about him, and * Ps 109:6
I will * him an offering of wine Ps 116:13
I will publicly * him the Ps 116:14
the lightning to * down the rain; Ps 135:7
you will * me safely through them. Ps 138:7
strong for me. * me out of prison, Ps 142:7
Don't * me to trial! Ps 143:2
Lord, saving me will * glory to Ps 143:11
to your name. * me out of all this Ps 143:11
For a prostitute will * a man to Pro 6:26
many counselors * success. Pro 15:22
it will * you before men of Pro 18:16
These good deeds of hers shall * Pro 31:31
and no one can * them back to life Ecc 3:22
Only he can * order from this Ecc 5:9
I would * you to my childhood Sol 8:2
Don't * me any more of them. Is 1:11
The incense you * me is a stench Is 1:12,13
haughty and * them to the dust. Is 2:12
the Lord will * a terrible curse Is 7:17
He will * true justice and peace Is 9:7
to your bragging is to * your Is 9:11,12
At that time the Lord will * Is 11:11
He will * them back to settle Is 14:1
divide, will * gifts to the Lord of Is 18:7
I will * upon Egypt and Ethiopia. Is 20:3
O people of Tema, * food and Is 21:14
With this news * cheer to all Is 35:3
sea. * your strongest arguments. Is 41:1
He will * blind Israel along a Is 42:16
I will * my sons and daughters Is 43:6
I created them. * them back to Is 43:8
Yet he cannot * himself to ask, Is 44:20
with God, and you shall * me Is 49:3
to * my salvation to them too." Is 49:6
feet of those who * the happy news Is 52:7
Lord God * his people home again. Is 52:8
promises, I will * them also to my Is 56:7
says, I will * others too besides Is 56:8
the hungry and * right into your Is 58:7
to * the sons of Israel home Is 60:9
this will * me glory. Is 60:21
I, the Lord, will * it all to Is 60:22
has anointed me to * good news to Is 61:1
you and will * you many gifts." Is 62:11
If they sacrifice a lamb, or * an Is 66:3
Shall I * to the point of birth Is 66:9
And they shall * back all your Is 66:20
Master and I will * you again to Jer 3:14
See, I will * a distant nation Jer 5:15
I will * evil upon this people; Jer 6:18,19
is no pureness in them to * out. Jer 6:29
They * beaten sheets of silver Jer 10:9
I am going to * calamity down upon Jer 11:11
will * a great disaster upon them. Jer 11:23
I * a case before you to decide. Jer 12:1
Now let me * you this complaint: Jer 12:1
Yet the people say, "God won't * Jer 12:4
I will * upon them swarms of Jer 12:9
of you, and will * you home to your Jer 12:15
at noon time I will * death to Jer 15:8
hungry soul. They * joy to my Jer 15:16
Yes, I will * you back again, Jer 16:14,15
You alone are my hope. * Jer 17:18
* double destruction upon them! Jer 17:18
on the Sabbath you * in loads of Jer 17:27
says, I will * terrible evil upon Jer 19:3
says: I will * upon this city and Jer 19:15
In fact, I will * your enemies Jer 21:3,4
* out its tools to dismantle you. Jer 22:7
sent them, and * them back into Jer 23:3
For I will * evil upon them and Jer 23:12
And I will * reproach upon you Jer 23:40
and I will * them back here again. Jer 24:6
and I will * them all against this Jer 25:8,9
I will * upon them all the Jer 25:13
Then I will * them all back to Jer 27:22
Within two years I will * back Jer 28:3
and I will * back King Jeconiah, Jer 28:4
you say and * back from Babylon the Jer 28:6
promised, and * you home again. Jer 29:10
I sent you and * you back home Jer 29:14
Judah, and I will * them home to Jer 30:3
for I will * you home again from Jer 30:10
But, says the Lord, when I * you Jer 30:18
For I will * them from the Jer 31:8
says: When I * them back again they Jer 31:23
by the hand to * them out of the Jer 31:32
but I will * my people back again Jer 32:37
I will * them back to this very Jer 32:37
At that time I will * to the Jer 33:15
They sent soldiers to * Jeremiah Jer 39:14
go by promising to * him their Jer 41:8
the evil I will * upon you there. Jer 42:17
I will surely * Nebuchadnezzar, Jer 43:10
For though I will * great evil Jer 45:5
from far away and * your children Jer 46:27
But see, I will * terror upon Jer 49:5
I will * you down, says the Lord. Jer 49:16
From all directions I will * Jer 49:32
My fierce anger will * great Jer 49:37
But in the latter days I will * Jer 49:39
north and I will * them against Jer 50:9
And I will * Israel home again Jer 50:19
Sound the battle cry; * out the Jer 51:27
Appoint a leader; * a multitude Jer 51:27
bring a multitude of horses! * Jer 51:28
I will * them like lambs to the Jer 51:40
Turn us around and * us back to Lam 5:21
I, even I the Lord, will * war Eze 6:3
Tell them to * their weapons with Eze 9:1
are such rebels. * your baggage Eze 12:4
him in my net and * him to Babylon, Eze 12:13
"Or when I * war against that Eze 14:17
snare, and I will * him to Babylon Eze 17:20
that I would * them out of Egypt to Eze 20:5,6
nations who saw me * them out of Eze 20:14
that I would not * them into the Eze 20:15
With might and fury I will * you Eze 20:34
and will * you into my desert Eze 20:35,36
Israel, but I will * them out of Eze 20:38
don't * your gifts to me as well! Eze 20:39
and require you to * me your Eze 20:40

(BRING Con't)

incense when I * you back from	Eze 20:41
dross, I will * you to my crucible	Eze 22:18,19,20
"The Lord God says: * an army	Eze 23:46
Thus I will * down my judgment	Eze 25:11
Tyre, and I will * nations against	Eze 26:3
"For the Lord God says: I will *	Eze 26:7
I will * you to a dreadful end;	Eze 26:21
* slaves and bronze dishes,	Eze 27:13
many wares. They * emeralds, purple	Eze 27:16
Vedan and Javan * Arabian yarn,	Eze 27:19
* you lambs and rams and goats.	Eze 27:21
They * choice fabrics to	Eze 27:24
"But now your statesmen * your	Eze 27:26
They will * you to the pit of	Eze 28:8
God says: I will * an army against	Eze 29:8
years he will * the Egyptians home	Eze 29:13
of Egypt and * her people back to	Eze 29:14
to * panic to the Ethiopians;	Eze 30:9
people: When I * an army against a	Eze 33:2
And I will * them back from	Eze 34:13
and * them safely home again.	Eze 34:15,16
For I will * you back home again	Eze 36:24
your sins, I will * you home again	Eze 36:33
But when I * you back they will	Eze 36:35
I will * you against my land, and	Eze 38:15,16
I would * you against my people.	Eze 38:17
my greatness and * honor upon my	Eze 38:23
I will * them home from the	Eze 39:27
who * them, says the Lord God.	Eze 45:15
All the people of Israel shall *	Eze 45:16
And he shall * 1½ gallons of	Eze 46:5
he shall * one young bull, in	Eze 46:6
With the young bull, he must * a	Eze 46:7
With the ram, he is to * one	Eze 46:7
With the lamb, he is to *	Eze 46:7
With each bushel he is to * 1½	Eze 46:7
"* the magicians and	Dan 5:7
he screamed. "* the Chaldeans!	Dan 5:7
a command to * the men who had	Dan 6:24
own household will * his downfall;	Dan 11:26
But I will court her again, and *	Hos 1:14
wife again and * her back to you	Hos 3:1
net over her and * her down like a	Hos 7:12
And I will * them home again;	Hos 11:11
O Death, * forth your terrors for	Hos 13:14
by your sins. * your petition.	Hos 14:2
to * to the Temple of the Lord;	Joe 1:9
a solemn meeting. * everyone—the	Joe 2:16
But I will * them back again	Joe 3:7
And now, O Lord, * down your	Joe 3:11
Collect the nations; * them to	Joe 3:12
Sacrifice each morning and * your	Amo 4:4
"Therefore I will * upon you all	Amo 4:12
you * the Day of Judgment near.	Amo 6:3
"O Israel, I will * against you	Amo 6:14
the heavens, I will * them down.	Amo 9:2
the stars, I will * you plummeting	Ob 1:4
"to * this awful storm upon us?	Jon 1:8
that are left—and * you together	Mic 2:12
will lead you out of exile and *	Mic 2:13
says that he will * back his	Mic 4:6
God will * me out of my darkness	Mic 7:9
Never again will you * back	Nah 2:13
* me safely over the mountains.	Hab 3:19
helpless ones, and * together those	Zep 3:19
you together and * you home again,	Zep 3:20
the mountains and * down timber,	Hag 1:8
And when you * it home, I blow it	Hag 1:9
winds but I will * you back again.	Zec 2:6,7
Literally, "He will * forth the	Zec 4:7f
and Jedaiah will * gifts of silver	Zec 6:10,11
I will * them home again to live	Zec 8:8
shall * peace among the nations.	Zec 9:10
I will * them back from Egypt	Zec 10:10
I will * the third that remain	Zec 13:9
But when you * that kind of	Mal 1:9
people to * cheap, sick animals to	Mal 1:12
promises, to * you great joy.	Mal 3:1
been robbing me. * all the tithes	Mal 3:10
Don't * us into temptation, but	Mt 6:13
"but you can * her back to life	Mt 9:18
"Don't imagine that I came to *	Mt 10:34
"* them here," he said.	Mt 14:18
to * in their sick to be healed.	Mt 14:35
they had forgotten to * any food.	Mt 16:5
they had forgotten to * bread.	Mt 16:7
How long shall I bear with you? *	Mt 17:17
to * his accounts up to date.	Mt 18:23
Untie them and * them here.	Mt 21:2
He instructed his disciples to *	Mk 3:9
off John's head and * it to him.	Mk 6:27
about their forgetting to * bread.	Mk 8:16
with you? * the boy to me."	Mk 9:19
Untie him and * him here.	Mk 11:2
he said. "I * you the most	Lk 2:10
find some charge to * against him.	Lk 6:7
I put up with you? * him here."	Lk 9:41
"I have come to * fire to the	Lk 12:49
up, the host will * him over to	Lk 14:9
slaves, 'Quick! * the finest robe	Lk 15:22
Your command would * immediate	Lk 17:6
he stopped. "* the blind man over	Lk 18:40
mine who revolted—* them in and	Lk 19:27
"Untie him," Jesus said, "and *	Lk 19:30
"Why didn't you * him in?"	Jn 7:45
I must * them also, and they will	Jn 10:16
know that God will * my brother	Jn 11:22
Father, * glory and honor to	Jn 12:28
it, for this will * praise to the	Jn 14:12,13
He shall praise me and * me	Jn 16:14
And I came to * truth to the	Jn 18:37
"I am going to * him out to you	Jn 19:4
"* some of the fish you've just	Jn 21:10
beside me until I * your enemies	Act 2:35
and intend to * the blame for this	Act 5:28
* them in chains to Jerusalem.	Act 9:2
and I are here to * you this Good	Act 13:32,33
"For God had promised to * him	Act 13:34
We have come to * you the Good	Act 14:15
a people to * honor to his name.	Act 15:14
to let me * any Christians I found	Act 22:5
and * him back to the armory.	Act 23:10
"Ask the commander to * Paul	Act 23:15
and asked me to * this young man to	Act 23:18
to ask you to * Paul before the	Act 23:20
to * their charges before you."	Act 23:30
They begged him to * Paul to	Act 25:3
God can * men back to life again?	Act 26:8
from the dead, to * light to Jews	Act 26:23
Day and night I * you and your	Rom 1:9
good to * about my condemnation.	Rom 7:13
to find Christ and * him down to	Rom 10:6
to * Christ back to life again."	Rom 10:7
* glad tidings of good things."	Rom 10:15
and used it to * down to nothing	1Co 1:28
* us into the glories of heaven.	1Co 2:7
However, marriage will * extra	1Co 7:28
she were a believer, couldn't I *	1Co 9:5
whom the heathen * sacrifices are	1Co 10:19
who are poor and can * no food?	1Co 11:22
so that he won't * punishment upon	1Co 11:34
themselves and * long letters of	2Co 3:1
death will also * us back to life	2Co 4:14
If so, it is to * glory to God.	2Co 5:13,14
capture rebels and * them back to	2Co 10:5
I am trusting the Lord to * you	Gal 5:10
he guarantees to * us to himself.	Eph 1:14
Rather, * them up with the loving	Eph 6:4
God, for this will * much praise	Php 1:11
embarrass God, but * joy to him who	1Th 2:12
Yes, you will * us much joy as we	1Th 2:19
returns, God will * back with him	1Th 4:14
May the Lord * you into an ever	2Th 3:5
to * shame to the name of Christ.	1Ti 1:20
is between them to * them together,	1Ti 2:5
After all, we didn't * any money	1Ti 6:7
if that will * salvation and	2Ti 2:10
for the Lord. * others to Christ.	2Ti 4:5
Only Luke is with me. * Mark	2Ti 4:11
When you come, be sure to * the	2Ti 4:13
* me into his heavenly kingdom.	2Ti 4:18
I have been sent to * faith to	Tit 1:1
to * them into their salvation.	Heb 2:10
There is no use trying to * you	Heb 6:4
You cannot * yourself to repent	Heb 6:6
waiting for God to * him to that	Heb 11:10
would * him back to life again;	Heb 11:19
trials, it will * you much praise	1Pe 1:7
he might * us safely home to God.	1Pe 3:18
wicked world to * to us eternal	1Jn 4:9
He will * the people of the	Jud 1:15
away, and to * you, sinless and	Jud 1:24,25
peace and * anarchy to the earth;	Rev 6:4
will come and * their glory to it.	Rev 21:24

BRINGING

instructions, * the dressed kids,	Gen 27:14
and we will be responsible for *	Gen 44:31
and about his * them out of Egypt.	Ex 18:9
* him their questions to decide;	Ex 18:19,20
were restrained from * more!	Ex 36:4-7
The person * it is to lay his	Lev 1:4
a sin offering, * it to the	Lev 4:14
Israel that anyone * a thanksgiving	Lev 7:29
a falsehood, thus * reproach upon	Lev 19:12
my covenant by * war against you.	Lev 26:25
his people and * disaster to this	Num 32:15
Lord must hate us, * us here from	Deu 1:27
For the Lord your God is * you	Deu 8:7
falling off and * guilt to both the	Deu 22:8
responsible for * the people back	Ju 4:4
out, "They are * the Ark of the	1Sa 5:10
"Why have you disturbed me by *	1Sa 28:15
a raid, * much loot with them.	2Sa 3:22
was * me good news, I killed him;	2Sa 4:10
army of Israel, * them from as far	2Sa 17:11
talking about * the king back?"	2Sa 19:8,9,10
* him back to be our king again."	2Sa 19:43
forth from Ophir, * gold to King	1Ki 9:27,28
said: "The man * this letter is my	2Ki 5:6
of * it to the City of David.	1Ch 13:13
to celebrate the * of the Ark into	1Ch 15:3
in preparation for * home the Ark	1Ch 15:14
you will soon be * the Ark and the	1Ch 22:19
before, since * my people from the	2Ch 6:5,6
of Judah began * their tithes of	Neh 13:12
some men from Tyre * in fish and	Neh 13:16
And now you are * more wrath upon	Neh 13:18
and army officers, * them in from	Est 1:1
That is why I am * you these fat	Ps 66:15
The kings of the earth are *	Ps 68:29
He is rebuilding Jerusalem and *	Ps 147:2
ships from Sidon, * merchandise	Is 23:2,3
* you the wealth of many lands.	Is 60:5
and Ephah, too, * gold and incense	Is 60:6
away, * their wealth with them.	Is 60:9
For I the Lord am * vast	Jer 4:6
be that God is * his people home	Jer 16:14,15
and incense, * their sacrifices to	Jer 17:26
song of those * thanksgiving	Jer 33:10,11
and were * offerings and incense.	Jer 41:5
of the evil I am * upon her.'	Jer 51:64
I will crush your pride by * to	Eze 7:24
It shall become a noble cedar, *	Eze 17:22,23
my power in * them out of Egypt.	Eze 20:22
God says, I am * you back again,	Eze 36:22
the nations, and * them home from	Eze 37:21
* you from the distant north.	Eze 39:2
and responsible for * them home.	Eze 39:28
But the Lord is * a lawsuit	Hos 12:2
say, 'Don't bother * anything very	Mal 1:7
Literally, "* forth the fruits."	Mt 21:43f
were * their children to Jesus to	Mk 10:13
from * in loads of merchandise.	Mk 11:16
came too, * a hundred pounds of	Jn 19:39
Jerusalem suburbs, * their sick	Act 5:16
out by * him back to life again."	Act 17:31
and defiles it by * Gentiles in!"	Act 21:28
visiting him or * him gifts to make	Act 24:23
It is God's powerful method of *	Rom 1:16
to you Gentiles, * you the Gospel	Rom 15:15,16
to accept the money I am * them.	Rom 15:31
We are in deep trouble for * you	2Co 1:6,7
should be but I am * all my	Php 3:13
mighty angels, * judgment on those	2Th 1:8
doing this he was * vast multitudes	Heb 2:10
This time he will come * salvation	Heb 9:28
spoke of God * the people of Israel	Heb 11:22
soul from death, * about the	Jas 5:20

BRINGS

he also drinks the wine Jacob *	Gen 27:25
favorite dish and * it to him.	Gen 27:31
each year, when Jehovah * you	Ex 13:4,5
And remember, when the Lord *	Ex 13:11
* it, as the penalty for his sins.	Lev 1:4
The man who * it will kill it	Lev 1:11
The man who * the animal shall	Lev 3:2
"If it is a lamb, the man who *	Lev 3:7,8
"If anyone * a goat as his	Lev 3:12
and so * guilt upon the people, he	Lev 4:3
"However, if someone * a	Lev 7:16
of bitter water that * a curse.	Num 5:18
"WHEN THE LORD * you into the	Deu 7:1
When the Lord your God * you	Deu 11:29
Whenever anyone * a contribution	2Ki 12:4,5
Lord * destruction to the land.	1Ch 21:12
Literally, "He * forth to the	Job 28:11f
things for man— * back his soul	Job 33:30
* to birth his treachery and lies;	Ps 7:14
God does, how he * ruin upon the	Ps 46:8
as he * them safely into harbor!	Ps 107:30
valleys. He * the hungry to settle	Ps 107:36
but * the wicked into the dust.	Ps 147:6
Ill-gotten gain * no lasting	Pro 10:2
Wickedness never * real success;	Pro 12:3
Work * profit; talk brings	Pro 14:23
Work brings profit; talk *	Pro 14:23
griping * discouragement.	Pro 15:4
Dishonest money * grief to all	Pro 15:27
but hating bribes * happiness.	Pro 15:27
Sin * disgrace.	Pro 18:3
Steady plodding * prosperity;	Pro 21:5
hasty speculation * poverty.	Pro 21:5
as a wind from the north * cold,	Pro 25:23
Hard work * prosperity;	Pro 28:19
playing around * poverty.	Pro 28:19
Left to himself, he * shame to	Pro 29:15
in a fall, while humility * honor.	Pro 29:23
been before; God * to pass again	Ecc 3:15
thinking that wealth * happiness!	Ecc 5:10
but a fool's speech * him to ruin.	Ecc 10:12,13
lovely to eat. He * me to the	Sol 2:4
He humbles the proud and * the	Is 26:5
world and * them all to naught.	Is 40:23
For the Lord God who * back the	Is 56:8
he sends the lightning and * the	Jer 10:13
from his treasuries he * the wind.	Jer 10:13
the world; he * the lightning with	Jer 51:16
Damascus comes. She * wines from	Eze 27:18
while Dedan * expensive	Eze 27:20
and violence he * destruction on	Amo 5:9
and goes out and * thirty, sixty,	Mt 13:23
Literally, "* back out of his	Mt 13:52f

BRINGS Con't)
is anyone who * God's message to Mk 4:14
Your pretense * you honor from Lk 16:15
* out the less expensive brands. Jn 2:10
This * great glory to my Father. Jn 15:8
just returned and * the welcome 1Th 3:6
not only right, but it * results. Tit 3:8
who * God's mercy to his people. Heb 10:29
that person who * him back to God Jas 5:20

BRINK
You brought me back from the * Ps 30:3
sick men at the * of death, and Pro 31:6,7

BROACHED
Then Jeremiah * the subject of Jer 37:18

BROAD
Hang them up before the Lord in * Num 25:4
for the taking—a *, fertile, Ju 18:9,10
and a mind with * interests. 1Ki 4:29
needed from there to the * Wall. Neh 3:8
of Furnaces to the * Wall, then Neh 12:38
stumble along in * daylight, yes, Is 59:10
"A great eagle with * wings full Eze 17:3,4
in fertile ground beside a * Eze 17:5
ground beside a * river and he Eze 17:12,13
it were 37½ feet by 8¾ feet *." Eze 40:28f
37½ feet long and 8¾ feet *." Eze 40:29,30f
will stumble in * daylight as well Hos 4:5
and spread its * leaves over Jon 4:6
is *, and its gate is wide enough Mt 7:13
They will go up across the * Rev 20:9
Its walls were * and high, with Rev 21:12

BROAD-WINGED
But when another great, *, Eze 17:7

BROADCAST
as law, must be * to all the people Est 8:13
you want them * to the world. Pro 20:19
Then the Lord said: * this Jer 11:6
rooms shall be * from the housetops Lk 12:3

BROADER
His Spirit is * than the earth Job 11:9

BROILED
They gave him a piece of * fish, Lk 24:42

BROKE
he had made them. It * his heart. Gen 6:6
So fights * out between the Gen 13:7
the message, he * down and cried. Gen 50:16,17
became boils that * out on men and Ex 9:10
that were on the tablets you *. Ex 34:1
the people * camp and followed. Num 9:20,21
people of the land * the contract Deu 29:25
in this book) * forth upon them. Deu 29:27
The people * into tears as the Ju 2:4
to the judges, but * faith with Ju 2:17
the one who * apart his altar!" Ju 6:31
their trumpets and * their clay Ju 7:19,20
So Samson's wife * down in tears Ju 14:16
But he * the ropes from his arms Ju 16:12
and they all * down and cried. Ru 1:9
So the people * up the wood of 1Sa 6:14
plight, everyone * into tears. 1Sa 11:4
Suddenly panic * out throughout 1Sa 14:15
been before. War * out shortly 1Sa 19:8
Then the king * into tears, and 2Sa 18:33
So the three men * through the 2Sa 23:16
Under cover of night he * through 2Ki 8:21
on Jerusalem and * down its wall 2Ki 14:13
on the hills, * down the obelisks, 2Ki 18:4
of Asherah, and * up the bronze 2Ki 18:4
Then he * down and cried. 2Ki 20:3
The Babylonians * up the bronze 2Ki 25:13
men, these three * through to the 1Ch 11:18,19
anger of God * out upon Israel; 1Ch 27:24
Early in his reign war * out 2Ch 13:1
on the hills, and * down the 2Ch 14:3
They marched against Judah, * 2Ch 21:17
it down, and * up the altars and 2Ch 23:15,16,17
city of Gath and * down its walls, 2Ch 26:6
thing there. He * down the heathen 2Ch 34:7
the Temple and * down the walls of 2Ch 36:19
in Jerusalem. We * camp at the Ez 8:31
"I was living quietly until he * Job 16:12
them, and * the arms of orphans. Job 22:9
of his presence * through the Ps 18:12
peace with him. He * his promises. Ps 55:20
so a plague * out upon them and Ps 106:29
That is why he * them with hard Ps 107:12
For he * down their prison gates Ps 107:16
and quickly * apart before them. Ps 114:3
By our own strength we * down the Is 10:13
Then he * down with great sobs. Is 38:3
my yoke and * away from my ties. Jer 2:20
yoke off Jeremiah's neck and * it. Jer 28:10
they *, forcing me to reject them, Jer 31:32
"a covenant they *, even though I Jer 31:32f
You lightly * your solemn vows to Eze 16:59,60
whose covenant he despised and *. Eze 17:16
For the king of Israel * his Eze 17:18
and * off all relations with them. Eze 23:17
He charged into the ram and * off Dan 8:7
But like Adam, you * my covenant; Hos 6:7
For they * their treaty with Amo 1:9
Then I * my other staff, Zec 11:14
the Light * through upon them." Mt 4:15,16
on the meal, then * the loaves Mt 14:19
and blessed it and * it apart and Mt 26:26
and the earth shook, and rocks *, Mt 27:51
God for them, * them into pieces Mk 8:6
blessing on it and * it in pieces Mk 14:22
chains he simply * them and rushed Lk 8:29
then he * off pieces for his Lk 9:16
God for it, he * it apart and gave Lk 22:19
of spirit that he * into a sweat of Lk 22:44
loaf of bread and * it and was Lk 24:30
Then the meeting * up and Jn 7:53
So the soldiers came and * the Jn 19:32
all, and * off a piece and ate it. Act 27:35
* their promises, and were Rom 1:31
just because they * their promises Rom 3:3
to God for it, he * it and gave it 1Co 11:24
It almost * my heart and I tell 2Co 2:4
they * their first promise. 1Ti 5:12
Jesus Christ, who * the power of 2Ti 1:10
though they * their first Heb 10:16
AS I WATCHED, the Lamb * the first Rev 6:1
second seal, and * it open too. Rev 6:3
war and killing * out everywhere. Rev 6:4
And when he * open the fifth Rev 6:9
I watched as he * the sixth seal, Rev 6:12
malignant sores * out on everyone Rev 16:2

BROKEN
and has * his wage contract with me Gen 31:7
Literally, "because of their * Ex 6:8,9f
lay * at the foot of the mountain. Ex 32:19
it, then its neck must be *. Ex 34:20
the clothing is boiled shall be *; Lev 6:28
leprosy has * out from the boil. Lev 13:20
leprosy that has * out from the Lev 13:25
that has * out in the skin. Lev 13:39
man must be *, and every wooden Lev 15:12
or lame, or has a * nose or any Lev 21:18
or toes, or has a * foot or hand, Lev 21:19
I have * your chains and will Lev 26:13
vow must not be *: the person Num 30:1
have neither been * nor carved," Jos 8:31
And now since you have * the Ju 2:3
fight against the Lord shall be *; 1Sa 2:10
and his neck was * by the fall and 1Sa 4:18
"He was so * up about the baby 2Sa 12:18
but the people of Israel have * 1Ki 19:10
the people have * their covenant 1Ki 19:14
wherever it was * down and by 2Ch 32:5
abandoned you and * your laws! Ez 9:10
return, we have * your Ez 9:14
see the * walls and burned gates. Neh 2:13
Then Job took a * piece of Job 2:8
strikes, you faint and are *. Job 4:5
they shall all be * and destroyed. Job 4:10
and the fangs of the wicked are *. Job 5:16
My heart's desires are *. Job 17:11
He has * me down on every side, Job 19:10
For wicked men are * like a tree Job 24:20
My heart is *. Job 30:16
I expected my fall to be *, just Job 30:24
though no bone is *, so that a man Job 33:19
my health is * from sorrow. Ps 31:9,10
man, like a * and discarded pot. Ps 31:12
and all their weapons will be *. Ps 37:15
evil men shall be *, but the Lord Ps 37:17
my health is * beneath my sins. Ps 38:3,4
It is a * spirit you Ps 51:17
and penitence. A * and a contrite Ps 51:17
O GOD, YOU have rejected us and * Ps 60:1
to ride across our * bodies. Ps 66:12
Their contempt has * my heart; Ps 69:20
But now you have * down our Ps 80:12
You have * down the walls Ps 89:40
My health is * and my heart is Ps 102:3,4
all the trees lay * on the Ps 105:33
The snare is * and we are free! Ps 124:7
blow and all the river ice is *. Ps 147:18
of the earth were * open by his Pro 3:20
* beyond hope of healing. Pro 6:15
but a * spirit makes one sick. Pro 17:22
can sustain his * body, but when Pro 18:14
and its walls were * down. Pro 24:30,31
or trying to run on a * foot. Pro 25:19
* and never have another chance. Pro 29:1
cord is not easily *. Ecc 4:12
the golden bowl is *, and the Ecc 12:6
and the pitcher is * at the Ecc 12:6
and the wheel is * at the cistern; Ecc 12:6
too, will be crushed and *. Is 7:8
power, and * your evil rule." Is 14:5
joyous song: "Your power is *; Is 14:8
is thrown out like a * branch; Is 14:19
That rod is *, yes; Is 14:29
small—all will be crushed and *. Is 19:10
of Babylon lie * on the ground." Is 21:8,9
and * his everlasting commands. Is 24:4,5
The earth has * down in utter Is 24:19
of a tree, * off and used to burn Is 27:11
and be *, trapped and captured. Is 28:13
God will smash you like a * Is 30:14
The Assyrians have * their peace Is 33:8
on * masts with useless tackle. Is 33:23
you will never be *, says the Lord Is 54:10
* cisterns that can't hold water! Jer 2:13
and weep with * hearts, for the Jer 4:8
the cities were * down before the Jer 4:26
my heart is *. Jer 8:18
their fathers is * and canceled. Jer 11:10
up and leave you * and charred. Jer 11:16
stubborn will can't be * either. Jer 15:12,13
is like a discarded, * dish. Jer 22:28
My heart is * for the false Jer 23:9
says, You have * a wooden yoke but Jer 28:13
my servant, be * so that he shall Jer 33:20,21
people—for you have * your oath. Jer 34:18,19
her arms are *. Jer 48:25
is * for the men of Kir-heres. Jer 48:31
How it is *! Jer 48:39
that will never be * again." Jer 50:5
the earth, lies * and shattered. Jer 50:23
Lord their God has * forth in fury Jer 50:28
houses and * down the city gates. Jer 51:30
Like a widow * with grief, she Lam 1:1
my heart is * and my soul Lam 1:20
In his wrath he has * every Lam 2:2
He has violently * down his Lam 2:6
All their locks and bars are *, Lam 2:9
my heart is *, my spirit poured Lam 2:11
He has made me old and has * my Lam 3:4
He has made me eat gravel and * Lam 3:16
repay you for your * promises. Eze 16:59,60
Its branches were * and withered Eze 19:12
sigh with grief and * heart. Eze 21:6
has been *, and I have fallen Eze 26:2
through your * gates, pulling Eze 26:10
Now you lie * beneath the sea; Eze 27:34
"Son of dust, I have * the arm Eze 30:21
means by the first "* arm." Eze 30:21f
the one that was * before, and I Eze 30:22
Now you will lie crushed and * Eze 32:28
nor bound up the * bones nor gone Eze 34:4
their * limbs and heal the sick. Eze 34:15,16
When I have * off their chains of Eze 34:27
Thus you have * my covenant in Eze 44:7
his horn was *, and in its place Dan 8:8
for he shall be * by the hand of Dan 8:25
be crushed and * by my sentence Hos 5:11
because they have * my treaty and Hos 8:1
she lies among the nations as a * Hos 8:8
"Beautiful Israel lies * and Amo 5:2
God lies empty and * after your Nah 2:2
showing that I had * my contract to Zec 11:10
between Judah and Israel was *. Zec 11:14
nor heal the * bones, nor feed the Zec 11:16
shall be *, but those it falls on Mt 21:44
the altar' can be *, but to swear Mt 23:18
* a single one of those laws." Mk 10:20
It would be a colt, not yet * for Lk 19:30
over that Stone shall be *; Lk 20:18
of the very heavens will be * up. Lk 21:26
legs of the men * to hasten death; Jn 19:31
his bones shall be *," and, "They Jn 19:36,37
'I will return and renew the * Act 15:16
Your long studying has * your Act 26:24
planks and debris from the * ship. Act 27:44
For sin's power over us was * Rom 6:2,3
that I had * the law and was a Rom 7:9
some of the Jews, have been * off. Rom 11:17
the branches that were * off. Rom 11:18
branches were * off to make room Rom 11:19
the Jews, were * off because they Rom 11:20
And so, in effect, you have * 1Co 1:13
Some ancient manuscripts read, "* 1Co 11:24f
troubles, but not crushed and *. 2Co 4:8
who has * every law there is. Jas 2:10
you have not * the marriage laws by Jas 2:11
you have entirely * God's laws and Jas 2:11
clay that is * into tiny pieces. Rev 2:27
When he had * the third seal, I Rev 6:5
And when the fourth seal was *, I Rev 6:7
WHEN THE LAMB had * the seventh Rev 8:1

BROKEN-DOWN
as a city with * walls. Pro 25:28

BROKEN-HEARTED
He has sent me to comfort the *, Is 61:1

BROKENHEARTED
need, and hounded * ones to death. Ps 109:16
He heals the *, binding up their Ps 147:3
he has sent me to heal the * and Lk 4:18,19

BRONZE
all metal workers in * and iron." Gen 4:22f
forging instruments of * and Gen 4:22
Gold, silver, *, blue cloth, Ex 25:1
them together with fifty * clasps. Ex 26:10,11
and a * socket for each pillar. Ex 26:37
and overlay everything with *. Ex 27:2
fire pans are all to be made of *. Ex 27:3
Make a * grating, with a metal Ex 27:4
from acacia wood overlaid with *. Ex 27:6
into twenty * post holders. Ex 27:9,10

(BRONZE Con't)
posts fitted into * sockets, with Ex 27:11
being imbedded in solid * bases. Ex 27:17
on the walls, will be made of *. Ex 27:19
a * basin with a bronze pedestal. Ex 30:17,18
a bronze basin with a * pedestal. Ex 30:17,18
made of gold, silver, and *. Ex 31:4
Gold, silver, and *; Ex 35:5-9
The * grating of the altar, and Ex 35:10-19
Others brought silver and * as Ex 35:24
from gold, silver, and *; Ex 35:32
and fifty small * clasps to couple Ex 36:18
five bases were molded from *. Ex 36:38
This altar was overlaid with *. Ex 38:2
Then he made * utensils to be Ex 38:3
Next he made a * grating that Ex 38:4
of acacia wood, overlaid with *. Ex 38:6
The * washbasin and its bronze Ex 38:8
The bronze washbasin and its * Ex 38:8
from the solid * mirrors donated by Ex 38:8
* and with silver hooks and rods. Ex 38:10
long, with twenty * posts and bases Ex 38:11
Each post had a * base, and all Ex 38:17
posts, with four * bases, and with Ex 38:19
the Tabernacle and court were *. Ex 38:20
7,540 pounds of *, which was used Ex 38:29
and for the * altar, the bronze Ex 38:29
bronze altar, the * grating, the Ex 38:29
The * altar; Ex 39:33-40
The * grating; Ex 39:33-40
or if a * kettle is used, it must Lev 6:28
as iron, and your earth as *. Lev 26:19
took the 250 * censers and beat Num 16:39
Lord told him, "Make a * replica Num 21:8
at the * snake, he recovered! Num 21:9
as gold, silver, *, iron, tin, or Num 31:22
as unyielding as *, and the earth Deu 28:23
Of iron and *, Deu 33:25
the utensils of * and iron will be Jos 6:19
and gold and the * and iron Jos 6:24
gold, *, iron, and clothing. Jos 22:7,8
he was bound with * chains and made Ju 16:21
He wore a * helmet, a 1Sa 17:4-7
coat of mail, * leggings, and 1Sa 17:4-7
and carried a * javelin several 1Sa 17:4-7
* helmet and a coat of mail. 1Sa 17:38,39
large amount of * from Hadadezer's 2Sa 8:8
made from silver, gold, and *. 2Sa 8:10
And strength to bend a bow of *. 2Sa 22:35
sixty walled cities with * gates; 1Ki 4:8-19
was a skilled craftsman in * work. 1Ki 7:13
He cast two hollow * pillars, 1Ki 7:15
capitals of molten *, each 7½ feet 1Ki 7:16-22
with seven sets of *, 1Ki 7:16-22
Then Hiram cast a round * tank, 1Ki 7:23
It rested on twelve * 1Ki 7:25
stands had four * wheels and bronze 1Ki 7:27-30
bronze wheels and * axles, and at 1Ki 7:27-30
posts made of * and decorated with 1Ki 7:27-30
cast from molten *, including the 1Ki 7:33
made of burnished *, and were cast 1Ki 7:41-46
offerings: for the * altar was too 1Ki 8:64
Afterwards Rehoboam made * 1Ki 14:27
the Temple of the * shields his 1Ki 15:15
Then he removed the old * altar 2Ki 16:14
"The old * altar," he said, 2Ki 16:15
the backs of the * oxen and placed 2Ki 16:17
and broke up the * serpent that 2Ki 18:4
them, it was merely a piece of *. 2Ki 18:4
The Babylonians broke up the * 2Ki 25:13
the Temple and the * tank and its 2Ki 25:13
and carried all the * to Babylon. 2Ki 25:13
spoons, and other * instruments 2Ki 25:14,15
with an intricate * network of 2Ki 25:17
chosen to sound the * cymbals; 1Ch 15:19
a great amount of * from 1Ch 18:8
(King Solomon later melted the * 1Ch 18:8
He molded it into the * tank, the 1Ch 18:8
and *, seeking an alliance. 1Ch 18:10
and they smelted so much * that 1Ch 22:3
and so much iron and * that I 1Ch 22:14
smiths and * and iron workers. 1Ch 22:16
gold, silver, *, iron, wood, and 1Ch 29:2
800 tons of *; 1Ch 29:6,7
The * altar made by Bezalel 2Ch 1:5,6
HE ALSO MADE a * altar thirty feet 2Ch 4:1
the doors of these courts with *. 2Ch 4:9
King Solomon, using polished *. 2Ch 4:12-16
Great quantities of * were used, 2Ch 4:17,18
The platform was made of *, 7½ 2Ch 6:12,13
for the * altar to accommodate. 2Ch 7:7
replaced them with * shields and 2Ch 12:10
and bound him with * chains and 2Ch 33:11
Literally, "a bow of *." Ps 18:34f
break bars of northern iron or *? Jer 15:12,13
The pillars of * standing before Jer 27:19,20,21
and the great * basin in the Temple Jer 27:19,20,21
the two large * pillars that stood Jer 52:17
Temple, and the * laver and bronze Jer 52:17
bronze laver and * bulls on which Jer 52:17
And he took along all the * pots Jer 52:18
of each column had * carvings, a Jer 52:22
a network of * pomegranates. Jer 52:22
all glowing *, dazzling like fire; Eze 1:27,28
the porch and the * altar, were Eze 8:16
and stood beside the * altar. Eze 9:2
bring slaves and * dishes, while Eze 27:13
face shone like *, standing beside Eze 40:3
—represented by the * belly of the Dan 2:39
lifted up the * image of a serpent Jn 3:14
like burnished *, and his voice Rev 1:15

BROOD
But here you are, a * of sinners Num 32:14
poor varieties don't. You * of Mt 12:34
for baptism: "You * of snakes! Lk 3:7
a hen protects her * under her Lk 13:34

BROODING
with the Spirit of God * over the Gen 1:2
cooled, he began * over the loss of Est 2:1

BROOK
of the * Zared and set up camp. Num 21:12
Literally, "the * of Egypt." Num 34:5f
" 'Now cross Zered *,' the Lord Deu 2:13
get across Zered * from Kadesh! Deu 2:14,15
from the * of Egypt to the southern Jos 13:2-7
reached the * of Egypt, and along Jos 15:2,3,4
villages as far as the * of Egypt; Jos 15:47
the mouth of the * of Egypt on the Jos 15:47
Kanah * to the Mediterranean Sea. Jos 16:8
north bank of the * of Kanah to the Jos 17:9
(Several cities south of the * Jos 17:9
The land south of the * and as Jos 17:10
land north of the * and east of the Jos 17:10
reached the * east of Jeokne-am. Jos 19:11
When they reached Besor *, two 1Sa 30:9,10
When they reached Besor * and the 1Sa 30:21
*, and went out into the country. 2Sa 15:23
had crossed the * and were gone. 2Sa 17:20
The moment you go beyond Kidron * 1Ki 2:36,37
cut down and burned at Kidron *. 1Ki 15:13
hide by Cherith * at a place east 1Ki 17:3
Drink from the * and eat what 1Ki 17:4
him to, and camped beside the *. 1Ki 17:5
evening, and he drank from the *. 1Ki 17:6
But after awhile the * dried up, 1Ki 17:7
every stream and * to see if we can 1Ki 18:5
to Kishon * and killed them there. 1Ki 18:40
it outside Jerusalem to Kidron *; 2Ki 23:6
* of Egypt to the Euphrates River. 2Ki 24:7
Literally, "from Shihor—the * of 1Ch 13:5f
to the * of Egypt at the other. 2Ch 7:8
crushed and burned it at Kidron *. 2Ch 15:16
carted it out to the * Kidron. 2Ch 29:16
and threw them into Kidron *. 2Ch 30:14
the * running through the fields. 2Ch 32:4
and I followed the *, inspecting Neh 2:14,15
have proved as unreliable as a *; Job 6:15-18
and flee across the * of Willows. Is 15:7
seasonal mountain *—sometimes a Jer 15:17,18
fields out to the * of Kidron, and Jer 31:40
the course of the * of Egypt (Wadi Eze 47:19
then follows the * of Egypt (Wadi Eze 48:27,28
from Hamath to the * of Arabah," Amo 6:14

BROOKS
*—and [build shelters with them Lev 23:40
a good land of *, pools, gushing Deu 8:7
Jotbathah, a land of * and water. Deu 10:7
Hiddai from the * of Gaash; 2Sa 23:24-39
Hurai from near the * of Gaash; 1Ch 11:26-47
* and meadows as my share! Ps 16:6
the water *, deep and quiet. Sol 5:12

BROOM
sat down under a * bush and prayed 1Ki 19:4
down and slept beneath the * bush. 1Ki 19:5
Literally, "with coals of the * Ps 120:4f
I will sweep the land with the * Is 14:23

BROTH
in a basket and * in a pot, he took Ju 6:19
there, and pour the * over it." Ju 6:20

BROTHEL
built a spacious * for your lovers, Eze 16:24

BROTHELS
and to gang up at the city's *. Jer 5:7
altars, your *, on every street. Eze 16:31
knock down your * and idol altars, Eze 16:39

BROTHER
Her next child was his *, Gen 4:2
One day Cain suggested to his *, Gen 4:8
Cain attacked and killed his *. Gen 4:8
asked Cain, "Where is your *? Gen 4:9
Shem, the oldest * of Japheth. Gen 10:21
and Joktan (Peleg's *). Gen 10:25
Sarai, while his * Nahor married Gen 11:29
who was the daughter of their * Gen 11:29
and she had a * named Iscah. Gen 11:29
Mamre the Amorite (* of Eshcol and Gen 14:13
herself said, 'Yes, he is my *.' Gen 20:5
am giving your '*' a thousand Gen 20:16
* Nahor, had borne him eight sons. Gen 22:20-23
Abraham's *. Gen 24:15,16f
and when her * Laban saw the Gen 24:29,30
of my master's *. Gen 24:48
presents to her mother and *. Gen 24:53
her mother and * exclaimed. Gen 24:55
rights to his younger *. Gen 25:33
what his father had said to his *. Gen 27:6,7
Isaac: "Your * was here and Gen 27:35
For a time you will serve your *, Gen 27:39,40
Literally, "your mother's *." Gen 28:2f
*—the son of Bethuel the Aramean. Gen 28:5
of his mother's *—and because the Gen 29:10
messengers to his * Esau in Edom, Gen 32:3
at the hand of my * Esau, for I am Gen 32:11
a present for his * Esau:200 Gen 32:13,14,15
As he approached his * he bowed Gen 33:3
"*, I have plenty," Esau Gen 33:9
when you fled from your * Esau." Gen 35:1
from his * Jacob to Mount Seir. Gen 36:6,7,8
for, after all, he is our *!" Gen 37:26,27
Then Judah said to Er's *, Onan, Gen 38:8
law requires of a dead man's *; Gen 38:8
[to deny a child to his deceased * Gen 38:10
Joseph's younger * Benjamin go with Gen 42:4
to him [as it had to his * Joseph Gen 42:4
Our youngest * is there with our Gen 42:13
until this youngest * comes here. Gen 42:15
One of you go and get your *! Gen 42:16
*, then I'll know you are spies." Gen 42:16
but bring your youngest * back Gen 42:20
bring your youngest * back to me. Gen 42:34
give you back your * and you can Gen 42:34
with you, for his * Joseph is dead Gen 42:38
again unless your * is with you.' Gen 43:3,4,5
ever tell him you had another *?" Gen 43:6
we had another *, so we told him. Gen 43:7
going to say, 'Bring me your *'?" Gen 43:7
mistake, and take your * and go. Gen 43:13
Looking at his * Gen 43:29
Literally, "his * Benjamin, his Gen 43:29f
*, the one you told me about? Gen 43:29
his * and had to go out and cry. Gen 43:30
had a father or a *, and we said, Gen 44:19
And his * is dead, and he alone Gen 44:20
your youngest * is with you.' Gen 44:23
you let our youngest * go with us. Gen 44:26
And if you take away his * from Gen 44:29
your * whom you sold into Egypt! Gen 45:4
my promise, and my * Benjamin has Gen 45:11,12
* shall become even greater." Gen 48:19
your own Hebrew * like that?" Ex 2:13
"All right," he said, "your * Ex 4:14
Literally, "your * the Levite." Ex 4:14f
* Aaron shall be your spokesman. Ex 7:1
"CONSECRATE AARON YOUR *, and Ex 28:1
Moses, "Warn your * Aaron not to Lev 16:1
aunt—the wife of your father's *. Lev 18:14
Except when the * died and left no Lev 18:16f
wife was left to a * to beget Lev 18:16f
"Don't hate your *. Lev 19:17
*, and they shall be childless. Lev 20:21
son, daughter, *, or unmarried Lev 21:2,3
"If your * becomes poor, you are Lev 25:35
Fear your God and let your * Lev 25:36
his father, mother, *, or sister; Num 6:6,7
"We are the descendants of your * Num 20:14
descended from his * Jacob, whose Num 20:14f
And if he has no *, then it Num 27:10
die as Aaron your * did, for you Num 27:13
our * Zelophehad to his daughters. Num 36:1
Land, as their * tribes do; Deu 10:9
friend, even a *, son, daughter, or Deu 13:6,7
just like his * Levites who work Deu 18:6,7
you make to a * Israelite, whether Deu 23:19
For if you take interest from a * Deu 23:20
If anyone kidnaps a * Israelite, Deu 24:7
your * be degraded in your eyes. Deu 25:1
"If a man's * dies without a Deu 25:5
instead, her husband's * must Deu 25:5
son of the dead *, so that his name Deu 25:6
But if the dead man's * refuses Deu 25:7
'My husband's * refuses to let his Deu 25:7
toward his own * and his beloved Deu 28:54
just as Aaron your * died in Mount Deu 32:50
You have not deserted your * Jos 22:2,3
go to war against their * tribes. Jos 22:12
son of his younger * Kenaz, Ju 1:13
Caleb's younger *) to save them. Ju 3:9
Beer for fear of his * Abimelech. Ju 9:21
further against our * Benjamin?" Ju 20:22,23,24
* Benjamin, or shall we stop?" Ju 20:27,28
loss of their * tribe, Benjamin. Ju 21:6
a younger * of her former husband. Ru 1:11f
She is selling our * Elimelech's Ru 4:3
(the son of Ahitub, Ichabod's *; 1Sa 14:3
But when David's oldest *, Eliab, 1Sa 17:28
Jonathan swore to be his blood *, 1Sa 18:1
Do this for me as my sworn *. 1Sa 20:8
"His * demanded that he be 1Sa 20:28,29
(Joab's * and the son of Zeruiah). 1Sa 26:5,6,7
How I weep for you, my * 2Sa 1:26
I could never face your * Joab if 2Sa 2:22
for the death of his * Asahel. 2Sa 3:27
So Joab and his * Abishai killed 2Sa 3:30

(BROTHER Con't)
* Asahel at the battle of Gibeon. 2Sa 3:30
of the army to his * Abishai, who 2Sa 10:10
And Prince Amnon (her half *) 2Sa 13:1
(the son of David's * Shime-ah). 2Sa 13:3
Her * Absalom asked her, "Is it 2Sa 13:20
woman in her * Absalom's quarters. 2Sa 13:20
sending my * Amnon instead?" 2Sa 13:26
son of David's * Shime-ah) arrived 2Sa 13:32,33
be executed for murdering his *. 2Sa 14:7
*, Abishai (the son of Zeruiah); 2Sa 18:2
"I'm glad to see you, my *," 2Sa 20:8,9,10
Joab and his * Abishai left him 2Sa 20:8,9,10
the * of Goliath the Gittite, 2Sa 21:19
of David's * Shime-i—killed him. 2Sa 21:20,21
men, Abishai, the * of Joab (son of 2Sa 23:18,19
Asahel, the * of Joab, was also 2Sa 23:24-39
man, and was Absalom's younger *. 1Ki 1:6
army officers, or his * Solomon. 1Ki 1:10
when I fled from your * Absalom. 1Ki 2:7
everything went to my * instead; 1Ki 2:15
"Then let your * Adonijah marry 1Ki 2:21
For he is my older *! 1Ki 2:22
"What sort of deal is this, my * 1Ki 9:13
grave, exclaiming, "Alas, my *!" 1Ki 13:30
"He is my *!" 1Ki 20:32
"Yes, your * Ben-hadad!" 1Ki 20:33
Elijah, and his * Jehoram became 2Ki 1:17
Shammai's * Jada had two sons, 1Ch 2:32
Caleb (Jerahmeel's *) was Mesha; 1Ch 2:42
Chelub (the * of Shuhah), whose 1Ch 4:11,12
was given to his half *, Joseph. 1Ch 5:1
Literally, "*," or "kinsman." 1Ch 6:39-43f
His * Shomer's 1Ch 7:34
The sons of his * Hotham 1Ch 7:35
Azel's * Eshek had three sons: 1Ch 8:39
Abishai, Joab's *, was commander 1Ch 11:20
Asahel (Joab's *); 1Ch 11:26-47
Joel (* of Nathan); 1Ch 11:26-47
Joha (his *) from Tiza; 1Ch 11:26-47
His * Joash; Jezi-el and Pelet, 1Ch 12:3-7
the command of his * Abishai, moved 1Ch 19:11
and help me," Joab told his *; 1Ch 19:12
Lahmi, the * of Goliath the giant; 1Ch 20:5
the son of David's * Shimea. 1Ch 20:6,7
was Asahel (the * of Joab), who was 1Ch 27:7
Over Judah, Elihu (a * of King 1Ch 27:16-22
the daughter of David's * Eliab. 2Ch 11:18
* Shime-i and the following aides: 2Ch 31:12,13
Eliakim, the * of Jehoahaz, as the 2Ch 36:4
Jehoiachin's * Zedekiah as the new 2Ch 36:10
Jerusalem to my * Hanani and to Neh 7:2
cancel the debts of our * Jews. Neh 10:31
fear of God. My *, you have proved Job 6:15-18
for I am considered a * to Job 30:28,29
* who was sick and nearing death. Ps 35:14
his own * from the penalty of sin! Ps 49:7
You slander your own *. Ps 50:20
Anyone is my * who fears and Ps 119:63
* is born to help in time of need. Pro 17:17
A lazy man is * to the saboteur. Pro 18:9
of an offended * than to capture a Pro 18:19
friend who sticks closer than a *. Pro 18:24
without a son or *, yet he works Ecc 4:8
GIRL: "Oh, if only you were my *; Sol 8:1
will say to his *, "You have some Is 3:6
Each fights against his * to Is 9:19,20
against each other—* against Is 19:2
against *, neighbor against Is 19:2
Beware of your *! Jer 9:4
saying about your * exiles: 'It is Eze 11:15
child, * or unmarried sister. Eze 44:25
But when her * Dan 11:7
who, when his * Seleucus was Dan 11:21f
RENAME your * and sister. Hos 1:11
Call your * Ammi (which means Hos 1:11
was born, he struggled with his *; Hos 12:3
their treaty with their *, Israel; Amo 1:9
For he chased his *, Israel, with Amo 1:11
Because of what you did to your * Ob 1:10
I even rejected his very own *, Mal 1:2,3
Literally, "with your *." Mt 5:22f
in the eye of a * when you have a Mt 7:3
Then you can see to help your *. Mt 7:5
Andrew (Peter's *), Mt 10:2,3,4
John (James' *), Mt 10:2,3,4
"* shall betray brother to Mt 10:21
"Brother shall betray * to Mt 10:21
is my *, sister and mother!" Mt 12:50
his wife Herodias, his * Philip's Mt 14:3
James, and his * John to the top of Mt 17:1
"If a * sins against you, go to Mt 18:15
it, you have won back a *. Mt 18:15
I forgive a * who sins against me? Mt 18:21
children, his * should marry the Mt 22:24
This * also died without Mt 22:26
passed to the next *, and so on Mt 22:26
saw Simon and his * Andrew fishing Mk 1:16
*, and my sister, and my mother." Mk 3:35
Mary's boy, and a * of James and Mk 6:2,3
Herodias, his * Philip's wife. Mk 6:17,18
the man's * should marry his widow Mk 12:19
So the second * married the Mk 12:20,21,22
Then the next * married her, and Mk 12:20,21,22
Herod, over Galilee; his * Lk 3:1
Andrew (Simon's *), Lk 6:14,15,16
of saying to him, "*, let me help Lk 6:42
please tell my * to divide my Lk 12:13
" 'Your * is back,' he was told, Lk 15:27
"The older * was angry and Lk 15:28
For he is your *; Lk 15:32
"Rebuke your * if he sins, and Lk 17:2,3
the man's * shall marry the widow Lk 20:28
any children. His * married the Lk 20:30
men was Andrew, Simon Peter's *. Jn 1:40
Andrew then went to find his * Jn 1:41
Then Andrew, Simon Peter's *, Jn 6:8,9
Well, her * Lazarus, who lived in Jn 11:1
here, my * wouldn't have died. Jn 11:21
God will bring my * back to life Jn 11:22
Jesus told her, "Your * will Jn 11:23
here, my * would still be alive." Jn 11:32
Cana in Galilee, my * James and I Jn 21:2
on him and said, "* Paul, the Lord Act 9:17
James (John's *). Act 12:2
"You know, dear *, how many Act 21:20
'* Saul, receive your sight!' Act 22:13
be a servant to Jacob, his twin *. Rom 9:10-13
GIVE A WARM welcome to any * Rom 14:1
your * or look down on him. Rom 14:10
never make your * stumble by Rom 14:13
And if your * is bothered by Rom 14:15
offends your * or makes him sin. Rom 14:21
greetings too, as a Christian *. Rom 16:22
so does Quartus, a Christian *. Rom 16:23
missionary, and from * Sosthenes. 1Co 1:1
who claims to be a * Christian but 1Co 5:11
* in front of unbelievers. 1Co 6:6
* to sin whose conscience 1Co 8:9
damage to a * with a tender 1Co 8:11
sin against your * by encouraging 1Co 8:12
going to make my * sin, I'll not 1Co 8:13
and from our dear * Timothy. 2Co 1:1
But Titus, my dear *, wasn't 2Co 2:13
another well-known * with him, who 2Co 8:18
you still another *, whom we know 2Co 8:22
and sent our other * with him, did 2Co 12:18
that time was James, our Lord's *. Gal 1:19
Tychicus, who is a much loved * Eph 6:21
DEAR * CHRISTIANS, I love you and Php 4:1
messenger, and from * Timothy. Col 1:1
Tychicus, our much loved *, will Col 4:7
loved *, one of your own people. Col 4:9
send Timothy, our * and fellow 1Th 3:2,3
to a * who needs to be warned. 2Th 3:15
harder because a * in the faith is 1Ti 6:2
left at Troas with * Carpus, and 2Ti 4:13
Jesus Christ, and from * Timothy. Phm 1:1
from your love, my *, because your Phm 1:7
beloved *, especially to me. Phm 1:16
servant but also your * in Christ. Phm 1:16
Yes, dear *, give me joy with Phm 1:20
or neighbor or *, saying, 'You, Heb 8:11
I want you to know that * Heb 13:23
in my opinion, a very faithful *. 1Pe 5:12
Our wise and beloved * Paul has 2Pe 3:15,16
For he who dislikes his * is 1Jn 2:11
doesn't love his * shows that he is 1Jn 3:10
to Satan and killed his *. 1Jn 3:12
Anyone who hates his Christian * 1Jn 3:15
well, and sees a * in need, and 1Jn 3:17
on hating his *, he is a liar; 1Jn 4:20
for if he doesn't love his * who 1Jn 4:20
love not only God, but his * too. 1Jn 4:21
of Jesus Christ, and a * of James. Jud 1:1
example of Cain who killed his *; Jud 1:11
It is I, your * John, a fellow Rev 1:9
are, and as your * Christians are, Rev 19:10

BROTHER-IN-LAW
One day Moses said to his * Hobab Num 10:29
But his * replied, "No, I must Num 10:30

BROTHER-TRIBES
land holdings, as were their *. Gen 49:7f

BROTHER'S
But the Lord said, "Your * blood Gen 4:10
have defiled with your * blood. Gen 4:11
in tents. His * name was Jubal, Gen 4:21
Literally, "Abram's * son." Gen 14:12f
in this far-off land, to his * Gen 24:38
my relatives, from my * family. Gen 24:40
Literally, "my master's * Gen 24:48f
awhile until your * fury is spent, Gen 27:44
from you will be your * heirs." Gen 38:8
a baby which would be his *. Gen 38:9
* payment at the top of his sack! Gen 42:25
He began searching the oldest * Gen 44:12
nor your * wife, for she is your Lev 18:16
brother's wife, for she is your *. Lev 18:16
If a man marries his * widow, Lev 20:21
Literally, "his * wife." Lev 20:21f
refuses to let his * name Deu 25:7
who refuses to build his * house.' Deu 25:9
named Peresh; his * name was 1Ch 7:16
oldest * house, tragedy struck. Job 1:12,13
in their oldest * home, when Job 1:18
widow became the second * wife. Mt 22:25
and have children in his * name. Mk 12:19
Herodias, his * wife, and for many Lk 3:19,20
his * life was better than his. 1Jn 3:12

BROTHERHOOD
So the rumor spread among the * Jn 21:23

BROTHERLY
Love each other with * affection Rom 12:10
But concerning the pure * love 1Th 4:9
LOVE each other with true * love. Heb 13:1

BROTHERS
went outside and told his two *. Gen 9:22
Be the master of your *. Gen 27:27,28,29
addressed Dinah's father and *. Gen 34:11
Her * then lied to Shechem and Gen 34:13
two of Dinah's *, Simeon and Levi, Gen 34:25
His * of course noticed their Gen 37:4
his *, causing even deeper hatred. Gen 37:5
his * derided. Gen 37:8
dream and told it to his *. Gen 37:9
told his father as well as his *; Gen 37:10
and * come and bow before you?" Gen 37:10
His * were fit to be tied Gen 37:11
One day Joseph's * took their Gen 37:12
told him, "Your * are over in Gen 37:13,14
"For my * and their flocks," Gen 37:16
I heard your * say they were Gen 37:17
And his * agreed. Gen 37:26,27
came by, his * pulled Joseph out Gen 37:28
he wept to his *. Gen 37:30
Then the * killed a goat and Gen 37:31
too, just as he had his two *. Gen 38:11
* went down to Egypt to buy Gen 42:3
to him that his * came, and bowed Gen 42:6
We are all * and honest men, Gen 42:11
are twelve of us *, and our father Gen 42:13
and one of our * is dead." Gen 42:13
"Look," he exclaimed to his *, Gen 42:28
We are twelve *, sons of one Gen 42:32
Leave one of your * here with me Gen 42:33
Joseph ate by himself, his * were Gen 43:32
WHEN HIS * were ready to leave, Gen 44:1
he was told. The * were up at dawn Gen 44:3
when Judah and his * arrived, and Gen 44:14
and let the lad return with his *. Gen 44:33
and he was left alone with his *. Gen 45:1
he said to his *. Gen 45:3
But his * couldn't say a word, Gen 45:3
with each of his *, who finally Gen 45:15
Pharaoh—"Joseph's * have come"; Gen 45:16
"Tell your * to load their pack Gen 45:17
And tell your * to take wagons Gen 45:19
So he sent his * off. Gen 45:24
And Joseph said to his * and to Gen 46:31
"My father and my * are here from Gen 47:1
He took five of his * with him, Gen 47:2
*, just as Pharaoh had commanded. Gen 47:11
instead of to your *, as your Gen 48:22
"Judah, your * shall praise you. Gen 49:8
Joseph who was exiled from his *. Gen 49:26
people—his * and their families. Gen 50:8
to Egypt with his * and all who had Gen 50:14
dead, Joseph's * were frightened. Gen 50:15
Then his * came and fell down Gen 50:18
So Joseph and his * and their Gen 50:22
Joseph told his *, "but God will Gen 50:24
Then Joseph made his * promise Gen 50:25
* died, ending that generation. Ex 1:6
ground—one of his own Hebrew *! Ex 2:11
your *, friends, and neighbors.' Ex 32:27
meant killing your own sons and *; Ex 32:29
but your *, the people of Israel, Lev 25:46
by one of his *, his uncle, Lev 25:48
with our dear * the Lord killed!" Num 20:3
along with our father's *." Num 27:3,4
it shall belong to his *. Num 27:9
here while your * go across and do Num 32:6
What are we getting into? Our * Deu 1:28
belonging to their * the Edomites, Deu 2:4
Edom where our * lived, crossing Deu 2:8
the Edomites are your * and you Deu 23:7
Even his own children, *, fathers, Deu 33:9
The prince among his *. Deu 33:16
Esteemed above his *; Deu 33:24
and mother, my * and sisters, and Jos 2:12,13
father, mother, my * and anyone Jos 2:17,18
father, mother, *, and other Jos 6:23
truth, but our * who went with us Jos 14:8
"They must have been my *!" Ju 8:19
uncles—his mother's *—in Shechem. Ju 9:1
Shechem with his *, and he became Ju 9:26
when these half * grew up, they Ju 11:1
Later, his * and other relatives Ju 16:31
"No, my *, don't do such a Ju 19:23
And when their fathers and * Ju 21:22
from among all his * to be my 1Sa 2:28
"If none of our * will come and 1Sa 11:3
and Saul's father, Kish, were *; 1Sa 14:50,51

(BROTHERS Con't)
there among his *, Samuel took the 1Sa 16:13
had seven older *. 1Sa 17:12
ten loaves of bread to your *. 1Sa 17:17
out to the ranks to find his *. 1Sa 17:22
Adullam, where his * and other 1Sa 22:1
But David said, "No, my *! 1Sa 30:23
Joab's *, Abishai and Asahel, 2Sa 2:18
people from chasing their *?" 2Sa 2:26
then fell to two *, Baanah and 2Sa 4:2,3
"We are your blood *," they 2Sa 5:1
father and all his * to come to a 2Sa 13:21-24
Yet you are my own *, my own 2Sa 19:11,12
Then he summoned all of his *—the 1Ki 1:9
their *, the people of Israel. 1Ki 12:23,24
You and I are *; 1Ki 22:4
While he was there he met the * 2Ki 10:13
And they replied, "We are * 2Ki 10:13
distinguished than any of his *. 1Ch 4:9
but none of his * had large 1Ch 4:27
and his * tried to comfort him. 1Ch 7:22
messages to our * throughout the 1Ch 13:2
with all your * so that you may 1Ch 15:12
his * Shoham, Zaccur, and Ibri. 1Ch 24:26,27
with twelve of his sons and *; 1Ch 25:9-31
and twelve of his sons and *; 1Ch 25:9-31
Izri and twelve of his sons and *; 1Ch 25:9-31
and twelve of his sons and *; 1Ch 25:9-31
and twelve of his sons and *; 1Ch 25:9-31
and twelve of his sons and *; 1Ch 25:9-31
and twelve of his sons and *; 1Ch 25:9-31
and twelve of his sons and *; 1Ch 25:9-31
and twelve of his sons and *; 1Ch 25:9-31
and twelve of his sons and *; 1Ch 25:9-31
and twelve of his sons and *; 1Ch 25:9-31
and twelve of his sons and *; 1Ch 25:9-31
and twelve of his sons and *; 1Ch 25:9-31
and twelve of his sons and *; 1Ch 25:9-31
and twelve of his sons and *; 1Ch 25:9-31
and twelve of his sons and *; 1Ch 25:9-31
and twelve of his sons and *; 1Ch 25:9-31
and twelve of his sons and *; 1Ch 25:9-31
and twelve of his sons and *; 1Ch 25:9-31
and twelve of his sons and *; 1Ch 25:9-31
and twelve of his sons and *; 1Ch 25:9-31
and twelve of his sons and *; 1Ch 25:9-31
and twelve of his sons and *; 1Ch 25:9-31
and twelve of his sons and *. 1Ch 25:9-31
Their brave *, Elihu and 1Ch 26:6,7
and *, too, were real leaders. 1Ch 26:9
Hosah's sons and * numbered 1Ch 26:11
Shelomoth and his * were 1Ch 26:26
Shelomoth and his * were also 1Ch 26:28
"My * and my people! 1Ch 28:2
officers, and his * all pledged 1Ch 29:24
all their sons and *, dressed in 2Ch 5:11,12
says, Do not fight against your *. 2Ch 11:4
of Judah. His *—other sons of 2Ch 21:2
killed all of his * and many other 2Ch 21:3,4
have killed your * who were better 2Ch 21:13
so their * the Levites helped them 2Ch 29:34
your fathers and * who sinned 2Ch 30:7
Lord again, your * and your 2Ch 30:9
Nethanel, and his * Hashabiah, 2Ch 35:9
brought to them by their Levite *. 2Ch 35:15
* feel is the will of your God. Ez 7:18
to ask him and his * and the Temple Ez 8:17
with eighteen of his sons and *; Ez 8:18
with twenty of his sons and *; Ez 8:19
line were his clan * led by Bavvai Neh 3:18
of us—I, nor my *, nor the Neh 4:23
"We are their *, and our Neh 5:5
to help our Jewish * who have Neh 5:8
would assist their * without Neh 5:12
he invited his * and sisters to his Job 1:4
"He has sent away my *, and my Job 19:13
My own wife and * refuse to Job 19:17
Then all of his *, sisters, and Job 42:11
into his will along with their *. Job 42:15
I will praise you to all my *; Ps 22:22
Even my own * pretend they don't Ps 69:8
my * and my friends who live here; Ps 122:8
pleasant, when * live in harmony! Ps 133:1
witnessSowing discord among * Pro 6:16-19
A poor man's own * turn away from Pro 19:7
has tanned me. My * were angry with Sol 1:6
did your *, the people of Ephraim. Jer 7:15
Even your own *, your own Jer 12:6
of another Jew for all were *. Jer 34:9
him and all his * and Jer 35:3
Her children, her *, her Jer 49:9,10
of all his *, but the east wind—a Hos 13:15
at all that your * need your help. Amo 6:6
turning against even their own *. Mic 7:1
armed might, and * and companions Hag 2:22
was the father of Judah and his *. Mt 1:2
Jechoniah and his * (born at the Mt 1:11
he saw two *—Simon, also called Mt 4:18
he saw two other *, James and John, Mt 4:21
his mother and * were outside, Mt 12:46,47
Who are my *?" Mt 12:48
"these are my mother and *." Mt 12:49
*—James, Joseph, Simon, and Judas. Mt 13:55
refuse to truly forgive your *." Mt 18:35
*, sisters, father, mother, wife, Mt 19:29
had among us a family of seven *. Mt 22:25
you are on the same level, as *. Mt 23:8
my * you were doing it to me!' Mt 25:40
*, you were refusing help to me.' Mt 25:45
Go tell my * to leave at once for Mt 28:10
Now his mother and * arrived at Mk 3:31,32
"Your mother and * are outside Mk 3:31,32
Who are my *?" Mk 3:33
said, "These are my mother and *! Mk 3:34
up anything—home, *, sisters, Mk 10:29
times over, homes, *, sisters, Mk 10:30
Well, there were seven * and the Mk 12:20,21,22
For when these seven * and the Mk 12:25
"* will betray each other to Mk 13:12
Once when his mother and * came Lk 8:19
"My mother and my * are all those Lk 8:21
*, relatives, and rich neighbors! Lk 14:12
wife, children, *, or sisters—yes, Lk 14:26
for I have five *—to warn them Lk 16:28
and again. Your * can read them any Lk 16:29
home, wife, *, parents, or children Lk 18:29
We know of a family of seven *. Lk 20:29
you—your parents, *, relatives, and Lk 21:16
build up the faith of your *." Lk 22:32
with his mother, *, and disciples. Jn 2:12
and Jesus' * urged him to go to Jn 7:3
For even his * didn't believe Jn 7:5
But after his * had left for the Jn 7:10
But go find my * and tell them Jn 20:17
And the * of Jesus. Act 1:14
"*, it was necessary for the Act 1:16
"Dear *, think! Act 2:29
"*, what should we do?" Act 2:37
"Dear *, I realize that what you Act 3:17
yourselves, dear *, and select Act 6:3
identity to his *, and they were Act 7:13
Jacob and all his *' families to Act 7:14
visit his *, the people of Israel. Act 7:23
Moses supposed his * would Act 7:25
'Gentlemen,' he said, 'you are * Act 7:26
from among your *.' Act 7:37
apostles and other * in Judea that Act 11:1
These six * here accompanied me, Act 11:12
this message: "*, if you have any Act 13:15
"*—you sons of Abraham, and also Act 13:26
* -Listen Act 13:38
them as follows: "*, you all know Act 15:7
"*," he said, "listen to me. Act 15:13
"From: The apostles, elders and * Act 15:23
"To: The Gentile * in Antioch, Act 15:23
thought of by the * in Lystra and Act 16:2
"* AND FATHERS, listen to me as I Act 22:1
"*, I have always lived before Act 23:1
the High Priest, *," Paul replied, Act 23:5
So he shouted, "*, I am a Act 23:6
it was in The Twin * of Alexandria, Act 28:11
The * in Rome had heard we were Act 28:15
"*, I was arrested by the Jews in Act 28:17
I want you to know, dear *, that Rom 1:13
* in Christ, that when a person Rom 7:1
So, dear *, you have no Rom 8:12
would be the First, with many *. Rom 8:29
Oh, my Jewish *! Rom 9:1
DEAR *, THE longing of my heart Rom 10:1
from God, dear *, so that you will Rom 11:25
AND SO, DEAR *, I plead with you Rom 12:1
wise and good, my *, and that you Rom 15:14
and the other * who are with them. Rom 16:14
But, dear *, I beg you in the 1Co 1:10
arguments and quarrels, dear *. 1Co 1:11
Notice among yourselves, dear *, 1Co 1:26
DEAR *, EVEN when I first came to 1Co 2:1
DEAR *, I have been talking to you 1Co 3:1
cheating others, even your own *. 1Co 6:8
So, dear *, whatever situation a 1Co 7:24
Lord's * do, and as Peter does? 1Co 9:5
FOR WE MUST never forget, dear *, 1Co 10:1
I am so glad, dear *, that you 1Co 11:2
So, dear *, when you gather for 1Co 11:33
AND NOW, *, I want to write about 1Co 12:1
Dear *, don't be childish in your 1Co 14:20
Well, my *, let's add up what I 1Co 14:26
NOW LET ME remind you, *, of what 1Co 15:1
hundred Christian * at one time, 1Co 15:6
I tell you this, my *: an earthly 1Co 15:50
So, my dear *, since future 1Co 15:58
I think you ought to know, dear * 2Co 1:8
that the other two * represent the 2Co 8:23
So I have asked these other * to 2Co 9:5
to be * in Christ but are not. 2Co 11:26
to confer with the * there about Gal 2:2
Dear *, even in everyday life a Gal 3:15
Dear *, please feel as I do about Gal 4:12
You and I, dear *, are the Gal 4:28
Dear *, we are not slave Gal 4:31
For, dear *, you have been given Gal 5:13
DEAR *, IF a Christian is overcome Gal 6:1
and especially to our Christian *. Gal 6:10
Dear *, may the grace of our Lord Gal 6:18
you, my Christian *, and love, with Eph 6:23
to know this, dear *: Everything Php 1:12
to you that we are * in the Lord, Php 2:1
well, he and I have been real *, Php 2:25
No, dear *, I am still not all I Php 3:13
Dear *, pattern your lives after Php 3:17
And now, *, as I close this Php 4:8
there; the * with me send their Php 4:21
To: The faithful Christian * Col 1:2
you, dear *, much beloved of God. 1Th 1:4
YOU YOURSELVES KNOW, dear *, 1Th 2:1
Don't you remember, dear *, how 1Th 2:9
And then, dear *, you suffered 1Th 2:14
Dear *, after we left you and had 1Th 2:17
comforted, dear *, in all of our 1Th 3:7
LET ME ADD this, dear *: You 1Th 4:1
* throughout your whole nation. 1Th 4:10
And now, dear *, I want you to 1Th 4:13
about that, dear *, for you know 1Th 5:1
But, dear *, you are not in the 1Th 5:4
Dear *, honor the officers of 1Th 5:12
Dear *, warn those who are lazy; 1Th 5:14
Dear *, pray for us. 1Th 5:25
hands for me with all the * there. 1Th 5:26
Dear *, giving thanks to God for 2Th 1:3
and excited, dear *, by the rumor 2Th 2:1
God for you, our * loved by the 2Th 2:13
in mind, dear *, stand firm and 2Th 2:15
FINALLY, DEAR *, as I come to the 2Th 3:1
Now here is a command, dear *, 2Th 3:6
*, never be tired of doing right. 2Th 3:13
men as you would to much loved *. 1Ti 5:1
is not ashamed to call us his *. Heb 2:11
will talk to my * about God my Heb 2:12
my trust in God along with my *." Heb 2:13
to be like us, his *, so that he Heb 2:17
THEREFORE, DEAR * whom God has Heb 3:1
own hearts, dear *, lest you find Heb 3:12
And so, dear *, now we may walk Heb 10:19
Dear *, is your life full of Jas 1:2
So don't be misled, dear *. Jas 1:16
Dear *, don't ever forget that it Jas 1:19
DEAR *, HOW can you claim that you Jas 2:1
Listen to me, dear *: God has Jas 2:5
Dear *, what's the use of saying Jas 2:14
DEAR *, DON'T be too eager to tell Jas 3:1
Dear *, surely this is not right! Jas 3:10
evil about each other, dear *. Jas 4:11
Now as for you, dear * who are Jas 5:7
Don't grumble about each other, * Jas 5:9
But most of all, dear *, do not Jas 5:12
Dear *, if anyone has slipped Jas 5:19
Dear *, you are only visitors 1Pe 2:11
So, dear *, work hard to prove 2Pe 1:10
to you, dear *, and in both of them 2Pe 3:1
of time, dear *, so that you can 2Pe 3:17
Dear *, I am not writing out a 1Jn 2:7
our lives for our Christian *. 1Jn 3:16
children—your * and sisters in the 1Jn 5:2
Some of the * traveling by have 3Jn 1:3
until their other *, fellow Rev 6:11
for the Accuser of our * has been Rev 12:10
are, and as your * the prophets Rev 22:9

BROUGHT

and bird, and * them to the man to Gen 2:19,20
a woman, and * her to the man. Gen 2:22
me who * me some, and I ate it." Gen 3:12
At harvest time Cain * the Lord Gen 4:3
produce, and Abel * the fatty cuts Gen 4:4
and the animals you * with Gen 9:9,10,11
Heaven, * him bread and wine. Gen 14:18
Then God * Abram outside beneath Gen 15:5
"I am Jehovah who * you out of the Gen 15:7
had her * to him at his palace. Gen 20:2
And Sarah declared, "God has * Gen 21:6
* you here, so what can we say? Gen 24:50
Then he * out jewels set in Gen 24:53
And Isaac * Rebekah into his Gen 24:67
of the venison he * home, and Gen 25:28
greeted him warmly and * him home. Gen 29:12,13
growing in a field and * them to Gen 30:14
the idols they had * with them, and Gen 35:2
were * to him from the prison. Gen 40:20
He was * hastily from the Gen 41:14
When the grain they had * from Gen 43:2
we have * it back again, along Gen 43:21
Then he released Simeon and * him Gen 43:23
and his sons * him to Egypt, along Gen 46:5
They * their livestock too, and Gen 46:6
They have * with them their Gen 46:32
Then Joseph * his father Jacob to Gen 47:7
for grain, and he * the money to Gen 47:14
So they * their cattle to Joseph Gen 47:17
So Joseph * the boys close to him Gen 48:10
for evil, for he * me to this high Gen 50:20
Later, when he was older, she * Ex 2:10
by this threat, * their cattle and Ex 9:20
So Moses and Aaron were * back to Ex 10:8
the east wind had * the locusts. Ex 10:13
I * you out of the land of Egypt; Ex 12:17

BROUGHT Con't)

yeastless dough they had * along.	Ex 12:39
That very day the Lord * out the	Ex 12:51
for the Lord has * you out with	Ex 13:3
miracles Jehovah * us out of Egypt	Ex 13:14
It is a reminder that the Lord *	Ex 13:16
"Have you * us out here to die in	Ex 14:11
But now you have * us into this	Ex 16:3
* you out of the land of Egypt.	Ex 16:6
when he * them from Egypt.	Ex 16:32
the Lord had * them out of Egypt.	Ex 18:1
* your wife and your two sons."	Ex 18:5,6
or complicated can be * to you.	Ex 18:22
justice. They * the hard cases to	Ex 18:26
and how I * you to myself as though	Ex 19:4
entrusted shall be * before God to	Ex 22:8
Lord their God. I * them out of	Ex 29:46
fellow Moses who * us here from	Ex 32:1
the god that * you out of Egypt!"	Ex 32:4
people that you * from Egypt have	Ex 32:7
Israel, that * you out of Egypt.'	Ex 32:8
people whom you * from the land of	Ex 32:11
So they * them to me and I threw	Ex 32:24
these people you * from Egypt to	Ex 33:1
They * to the Lord their offerings	Ex 35:22
Others * blue, purple, and	Ex 35:23
Others * silver and bronze as	Ex 35:24
and some * the acacia wood needed	Ex 35:24
fine-twined linen, and * them in.	Ex 35:25
The leaders * onyx stones to be	Ex 35:27
—* their freewill offerings to him.	Ex 35:29
The people * gifts of 3,140	Ex 38:24
The people * 7,540 pounds of	Ex 38:29
Then they * the entire Tabernacle	Ex 39:33-40
They also * for his inspection	Ex 39:41
Then he * the Ark into the	Ex 40:21
"If bread baked in the oven is *	Lev 2:4
the ashes are * from the altar—and	Lev 4:11,12
well cooked, then * to the Lord as	Lev 6:21
to the one who * it to be offered;	Lev 7:17,18
So they * all these things to the	Lev 9:5
they * the animal to him piece	Lev 9:13
and Aaron's sons * the blood to	Lev 9:18
For I am the Lord who * you out	Lev 11:45
He must be * to Aaron the priest	Lev 13:1
having leprosy is * to the priest,	Lev 13:9,10
Other stones shall be * to	Lev 14:42
who * you from the land of Egypt.	Lev 19:35,36
they have * it upon themselves by	Lev 20:12
They have * it upon themselves.	Lev 20:13
the animals * by the people or	Lev 22:3
for the holy sacrifices * by the	Lev 22:15
and was * to Moses for judgment.	Lev 24:11
For I, the Lord your God, * you	Lev 25:38
For I * you from the land of	Lev 25:42
I * them from the land of Egypt;	Lev 25:55
For I am the Lord your God who *	Lev 26:13
against them, and * them into the	Lev 26:40,41
For I * their forefathers out of	Lev 26:45
he shall be * to the priest and the	Lev 27:8
was 157,600. They * up the rear	Num 2:3-31
Her husband shall not be * to	Num 5:31
the census—* their offerings.	Num 7:2
They * six covered wagons, each	Num 7:3
Judah, * his gift the first day.	Num 7:12
He also * a tiny	Num 7:14
six ounces. He * a young bull, a	Num 7:15
* his gifts and offerings.	Num 7:18-23
tribe of Ephraim, * his gifts, the	Num 7:48-53
* his gifts on the tenth day.	Num 7:66-71
tribe of Asher, * his gifts on the	Num 7:72-77
they were identical to those * by	Num 7:78-83
For the burnt offerings they *:	Num 7:87
For sin offerings they *:	Num 7:87
For the peace offerings they *:	Num 7:88
The Lord sent a wind that * quail	Num 11:31
until she was * back in before they	Num 12:15
the fruit they had * with them.	Num 13:26
Here is some fruit we have * as	Num 13:27
For I am Jehovah your God who *	Num 15:41
"that you * us out of lovely	Num 16:13
What's more, you haven't * us	Num 16:14
(including Aaron) * him a rod.	Num 17:6
When Moses * them out to show the	Num 17:9
are * to the Lord by the people;	Num 18:8
It is to be * when he is one	Num 18:16
'wave offerings' * by the people of	Num 18:19
"You have deliberately * us	Num 20:4
sent an Angel who * us out of	Num 20:16
"Why have you * us out of Egypt	Num 21:5
"King Balak, king of Moab, has *	Num 23:7-10
God has * them out of Egypt.	Num 23:18-24
God has * them from Egypt.	Num 24:3-9
advice that * about the situation	Num 24:25f
men insolently * a Midianite girl	Num 25:6
So Moses * their case before the	Num 27:5
so see to it that they are *	Num 28:1
spoils of war were * to Moses and	Num 31:12
So we have * a special	Num 31:50
until we have * them safely to	Num 32:17
that he personally * you out from	Deu 4:37
the Lord your God * you out with a	Deu 5:15
"When the Lord your God has *	Deu 6:10,11,12
the Lord who * you out of the land	Deu 6:10,11,12
and the Lord * us out of Egypt with	Deu 6:21
our own eyes. He * us out of Egypt	Deu 6:23
That is why he * you out of	Deu 7:8
Lord your God who * you out of your	Deu 8:14
he hated them: he * them into the	Deu 9:28
which you * from Egypt by your	Deu 9:29
All these must be * to the	Deu 12:18
Lord your God who * you out of	Deu 13:5
Lord your God who * you from the	Deu 13:10
God * you out of Egypt by night.	Deu 16:1
by the sacrifices * to the altar of	Deu 18:1
every ox or sheep * for sacrifice	Deu 18:3
harvest samples * in thanksgiving	Deu 18:4
both men shall be * before the	Deu 19:17
God who * you safely out of Egypt!	Deu 20:1
Lord my God has * me to the land he	Deu 26:2,3
oppression, and * us out of Egypt	Deu 26:8
and has * us to this place and	Deu 26:9
And now, O Lord, see, I have *	Deu 26:10
that the Lord * upon Pharaoh and	Deu 29:2,3
* them out of the land of Egypt.	Deu 29:25
When I have * them into the land	Deu 31:20
and must be * into his treasury."	Jos 6:19
why have you * us over the Jordan	Jos 7:7
* calamity upon all of Israel.'	Jos 7:15
morning, Joshua * the tribes of	Jos 7:16
Then he * the clans of Judah,	Jos 7:17
of that clan were * before the Lord	Jos 7:17
Zabdi's family was * man by man,	Jos 7:18
They * it all to Joshua and laid	Jos 7:23
and * them to the valley of Achor.	Jos 7:24
"Why have you * calamity upon us?	Jos 7:25
who was captured and * to Joshua.	Jos 8:23
When the news was * to Joshua	Jos 10:17
given the offerings * to the Lord.	Jos 13:14
and afterwards I * my people out	Jos 24:5
and I * the sea crashing in upon	Jos 24:7
"Finally I * you into the land	Jos 24:8
swords or bows that * you victory!	Jos 24:12
of Israel had * with them when they	Jos 24:32
of Israel, "I * you out of Egypt	Ju 2:1
God who had * them out of Egypt.	Ju 2:12-14
Lord God of Israel * you out of	Ju 6:8
as when God * them out of Egypt?	Ju 6:13
"You have * me to the dust.	Ju 11:35
his clan, and * in thirty girls to	Ju 12:9,10
So they * her the seven	Ju 16:8
So they * the money with them.	Ju 16:18
her lap, and they * in a barber and	Ju 16:19
So he was * from the prison and	Ju 16:25,26
his body, and they * him back home	Ju 16:31
of Ephraim, who * home a girl from	Ju 19:1
they were * to the camp at Shiloh.	Ju 21:10,11,12
and the Lord has * me home empty;	Ru 1:21
it * up be given to Eli's sons.	1Sa 2:13,14
coat for him and * it to him when	1Sa 2:19
other offerings which are * to me?	1Sa 2:29
God who * this great evil upon us;	1Sa 6:9
had * back the Ark of the Lord.	1Sa 6:21
of dispute were * to him in each of	1Sa 7:16
Ever since I * them from Egypt.	1Sa 8:8
So the chef * it in and placed	1Sa 9:24
the Lord God: "I * you from Egypt	1Sa 10:18,19
Then he * each family of the	1Sa 10:21
So they found him and * him out,	1Sa 10:23
continued. "He * your ancestors	1Sa 12:6
and I * King Agag but killed	1Sa 15:20
* and poured it upon David's head;	1Sa 16:13
Goliath, Abner * him to Saul with	1Sa 17:57
and how the Lord * a great victory	1Sa 19:5
have * to you and your young men.	1Sa 25:27
bread. She * the meal to the king	1Sa 28:25
So Abiathar * it.	1Sa 30:7
in a field and * him to David.	1Sa 30:11,12
from the wall and * them to Jabesh,	1Sa 31:12
young man who had * the news,	2Sa 1:13
When David heard this, he * the	2Sa 6:12
So Israel * home the Ark of the	2Sa 6:15
the time I * Israel out of Egypt.	2Sa 7:6
and * him annual tribute money.	2Sa 8:6
David * the gold shields to	2Sa 8:7
sent for her and * her to the	2Sa 11:27
Then Joab went to Geshur and *	2Sa 14:23
the king why he * me back from	2Sa 14:32
They * him and those who were	2Sa 17:28,29
of Michal that she * up for Saul's	2Sa 21:8
So their bones were * to him.	2Sa 21:12,13,14
from the well and * it to David.	2Sa 23:16
selected. They * her to the king	1Ki 1:3,4
they * him down from the altar.	1Ki 1:53
his daughters. He * her to	1Ki 3:1
So a sword was * to the king.	1Ki 3:24
to him, 'When I * my people from	1Ki 8:16
* them out of the land of Egypt."	1Ki 8:21
* out from the Egyptian furnace.	1Ki 8:51
you, for when you * our fathers	1Ki 8:53
* them out of the land of Egypt;	1Ki 9:9
That is why the Lord has * this	1Ki 9:9
(And when King Hiram's ships *	1Ki 10:11
Ophir, they also * along a great	1Ki 10:11
They * him annual tribute of	1Ki 10:25
Solomon's horses were * to him	1Ki 10:28
Genubath, who was * up in Pharaoh's	1Ki 11:20
The ravens * him bread and meat	1Ki 17:6
—the man who * this disaster upon	1Ki 18:17
have * them back to yourself."	1Ki 18:37
heavy wind * a terrific rainstorm.	1Ki 18:45
battle, and a man * me a prisoner	1Ki 20:39
So they * it to him.	2Ki 2:20
"The Lord has * us here to let	2Ki 3:10
Her sons * the pots and pans to	2Ki 4:5
* Elisha a sack of fresh corn	2Ki 4:42
of dove's dung * three dollars!	2Ki 6:25
whose son he had * back to life,	2Ki 8:1
* a little boy back to life.	2Ki 8:5
very one Elisha * back to life!"	2Ki 8:5
instructions. They * to Jehoiada	2Ki 11:9
Then Jehoiada * out the young	2Ki 11:12
their God who had * them safely out	2Ki 17:7
the Lord who had * them out of the	2Ki 17:35,36
he made and how he * water into the	2Ki 20:20
I * their ancestors from Egypt."	2Ki 21:15
He * back to Jerusalem the	2Ki 23:8
and * back his body and the	1Ch 10:12
and * them safely back again.	1Ch 11:2
the well, and * it back to David.	1Ch 11:18,19
and Naphtali * food on donkeys,	1Ch 12:40
and sheep were * to the	1Ch 12:40
of God was * from Kiriath-jearim.	1Ch 13:5
SO THE ARK of God was * into the	1Ch 16:1
the time I * Israel out of Egypt.	1Ch 17:5
he went. He * the gold shields of	1Ch 18:7
THEN SATAN * disaster upon Israel,	1Ch 21:1
The men of Tyre and Sidon *	1Ch 22:4
care of the gifts * to the Lord and	1Ch 26:20,21,22
who * gifts to the Lord.	1Ch 26:28
The next day they * a thousand	1Ch 29:21
Then Solomon * in the gifts	2Ch 5:1
the God who * them out of the land	2Ch 7:22
went to Ophir and * back	2Ch 8:17,18
Solomon's crews * gold from Ophir,	2Ch 9:10
value as she had * to him, plus	2Ch 9:12
Each * him annual tribute of	2Ch 9:24
Horses were * to him from Egypt	2Ch 9:28
his lifetime. He * back into the	2Ch 15:18
Even some of the Philistines *	2Ch 17:11
and * him to Jehu, who killed him.	2Ch 22:9
Then they * out the little	2Ch 23:11
were glad, and * the money and	2Ch 24:10
money was * to the king and	2Ch 24:14
the Edomites, he * with him idols	2Ch 25:14
And they * him back on horses to	2Ch 25:28
For the Lord * Judah very low on	2Ch 28:19
of the Temple, and * out into the	2Ch 29:16
offering were then * before the	2Ch 29:23
part of the nation * their	2Ch 29:31
wished to, * burnt offerings too.	2Ch 29:31
3,000 sheep were * as holy gifts.	2Ch 29:32,33
* burnt offerings into the Temple.	2Ch 30:15
the provinces also * in the tithes	2Ch 31:5,6
and sheep, and * a tithe of the	2Ch 31:5,6
were * into the Lord's house.	2Ch 31:12,13
The messengers who * the letters	2Ch 32:18
of Gihon and * the water down	2Ch 32:30
Gifts were * by the people coming	2Ch 34:9
So they * back to the king	2Ch 34:28
their meals were * to them by their	2Ch 35:15
second chariot and * him back to	2Ch 35:24,25
Then the Lord * the king of	2Ch 36:17
The logs were * down from the	Ez 3:7
of Assyria * us here."	Ez 4:2
son of Iddo)—who * messages from	Ez 5:1
So Ezra the priest * out to them	Neh 8:1
chose Abram and * him from Ur of	Neh 9:7
is our God! He * us out of Egypt!'	Neh 9:18
the Israelis and * them into the	Neh 9:23
the people * a daily supply of food	Neh 12:47
cleaned, and I * back the Temple	Neh 13:9
sort of thing and * the present	Neh 13:18
could be * in on the Sabbath day.	Neh 13:19
decree, Esther was * to the king's	Est 2:8
but that God has * you into the	Est 4:14
Then Mordecai was * before the	Est 8:1
be * down to the King of Terrors.	Job 18:14
Those who survive shall be *	Job 27:15
trials the Lord had * upon him.	Job 42:11
And each of them * him a gift of	Job 42:11
* me through the years of infancy.	Ps 22:9,10,11
health again. You * me back from	Ps 30:3
when they are * before the judge.	Ps 37:33
But in the end, you * us into	Ps 66:12
them. He * them to the border of	Ps 78:54
for we are * low to the dust.	Ps 79:8
we be saved. You * us from Egypt	Ps 80:8
* you out of the land of Egypt.	Ps 81:10
Literally, "* back the	Ps 85:1f
and joy— and * his people safely	Ps 105:37
So he * his chosen ones singing	Ps 105:43
He * the exiles back from the	Ps 107:3

(BROUGHT Con't)
Their lies have * me into deep Ps 119:85,86
WHEN JEHOVAH * back his exiles to Ps 126:1
May all who hate the Jews be * to Ps 129:5
continues forever. He * them out Ps 136:11,12
She buys imported foods, * by Pro 31:14
The Girl: "The king has * me into Sol 1:4
him go until I had * him into my Sol 3:4
your proud looks will be * low; Is 2:11
shall be * down to the dust; Is 5:15
The Lord of Hosts has * them Is 13:4
But instead, you will be * Is 14:15
Who has * this disaster on Tyre, Is 23:8
will be demolished and * to dust. Is 25:12
be rescued and * back to Jerusalem Is 27:13
They * him this message from Is 37:3
You have not * me the lambs for Is 43:23
You have * me no sweet-smelling Is 43:24
He was * as a lamb to the Is 53:7
is the one who * Israel through the Is 63:11
I, the Lord, who * them safely out Jer 2:6
And I * them into a fruitful Jer 2:7
And you have * this on Jer 2:17
Your ways have * this down upon Jer 4:18
For I told them at the time I * Jer 11:4
fathers when I * them out of Jer 11:7
I * you out from slavery in Egypt. Jer 16:14,15
smash the jar you * with you, and Jer 19:10
Cursed be the man who * my Jer 20:15
the Lord lives who * the Jews back Jer 23:8
So you have * upon yourselves all Jer 25:7
They took him prisoner and * him Jer 26:23
offerings * to them at the Temple; Jer 31:14
"You * Israel out of Egypt with Jer 32:21
long ago when I * them from their Jer 34:13
Habazziniah), and * him and all his Jer 35:3
Jehudi * it from Elishama the Jer 36:21
palace will be * out and given to Jer 38:21,22
of Jericho and * him to Jer 39:5
Lord your God has * this disaster Jer 40:2,3
his armory and * out weapons to Jer 50:25
They * him to the king of Jer 52:9
Jehoiachin and * him out of prison, Jer 52:31
He has * the kingdom to dust, Lam 2:2
He has * me into deepest Lam 3:2
Those * up in palaces now scratch Lam 4:5
Then he * me to the door of the Eze 8:7
He * me to the north gate of the Eze 8:14
Then he * me into the inner court Eze 8:16
THEN THE SPIRIT lifted me and * me Eze 11:1
but you will be * out from it." Eze 11:7f
So I did as I was told. I * my Eze 12:7
and * them to Babylon. Eze 17:12,13
pit and * him in chains to Egypt. Eze 19:4
* him before the king of Babylon. Eze 19:9
from harm. So I * my people out of Eze 20:9,10
betray me when I * them into the Eze 20:27,28
They * their perfumes and Eze 20:27,28
after I * you out of Egypt. Eze 20:35,36
Then, when I have * you home to Eze 20:42
exalted, and the rich * very low. Eze 21:26
* from the land of Egypt; Eze 23:27
"You * all this upon yourself by Eze 23:30
* to you by consoling friends." Eze 24:17
* to you by sympathetic friends. Eze 24:22
therefore I * forth fire from Eze 28:18
Literally, "I * fire from the Eze 28:18f
And you will be * down to the pit Eze 31:18
None of his past sins shall be * Eze 33:16
for you have been * here so I can Eze 40:4
Then he * me to the entrance Eze 40:48,49
AFTERWARD HE * me into the nave, Eze 41:1
AFTERWARD HE * me out again to the Eze 43:1
Then the Spirit took me up and * Eze 43:5
THEN THE LORD * me back to the Eze 44:1
Then he * me through the north Eze 44:4
they may slay the animals * for Eze 44:11
and sacrifices * to the Temple by Eze 44:29
Then he * me out to the outer Eze 46:21,22
THEN HE * me back to the door of Eze 47:1
Then he * me outside the wall Eze 47:2
the Jewish youths * back as Dan 1:3,4
the superintendent * all the young Dan 1:18,19
Abednego to be * in before him. Dan 3:13
reign, and * to Babylon. Dan 5:2,3,4
sacred cups be * in to the feast, Dan 5:2,3,4
* from Israel as a Jewish captive? Dan 5:13
* here these cups from his Temple; Dan 5:23
A stone was * and placed over Dan 6:17
He sat upon a fiery throne * in Dan 7:9
be—* there on clouds from heaven; Dan 7:13
O Lord our God, you * lasting Dan 9:15
as a son and * him out of Egypt. Hos 11:1
ever since I * you out from Egypt. Hos 13:4
And I * you out from Egypt and Amo 2:10
the entire family I * from Egypt: Amo 3:1
Have not I, who * you out of Amo 9:7
people, too? I * the Philistines Amo 9:7
who is in travail has * forth." Mic 5:3f
For I * you out of Egypt, and Mic 6:4
I * you out of slavery in Egypt. Mic 7:15
The queen of Nineveh is * out Nah 2:7
were miraculously * through when Zec 10:11f
through when God * them out of Zec 10:11f
the offerings * to him by the Mal 3:4
commanded, and * Mary home to be Mt 1:24
of being * before the court. Mt 5:22
people were * to Jesus; Mt 8:16
Soon some men * him a paralyzed Mt 9:2
unable to talk—was * to Jesus, and Mt 12:22
and his head was * on a tray and Mt 14:11
And a vast crowd * him their Mt 15:30
so I * him to your disciples, Mt 17:16
I will be * back to life again." Mt 17:22,23
was * in who owed him $10,000,000! Mt 18:24
Little children were * for Jesus Mt 19:13
scolded those who * them. Mt 19:13
sons of Zebedee, * them to Jesus Mt 20:20
Jesus said, and * the animals to Mt 21:7
"So the servants did, and * in Mt 22:10
the $5,000 * him $10,000. Mt 25:20
But after I have been * back to Mt 26:32
Then Jesus * them to a garden Mt 26:36
and * back the money to the chief Mt 27:3
* to him for healing; Mk 1:32,33
the prison, and * back his head on Mk 6:28
impediment was * to him, and Mk 7:32
some people * a blind man to him Mk 8:22
said, "Teacher, I * my son for you Mk 9:17
So they * the boy, but when he Mk 9:20
they * up the subject again. Mk 10:10
So the colt was * to Jesus and Mk 11:7
And they * Jesus to a place Mk 15:22
diseases were, * them to Jesus; Lk 4:40
A shout for help * their Lk 5:7
he was there and * an exquisite Lk 7:37
shall be * to light and made Lk 8:17
This * scoffing and laughter, Lk 8:53
No, you shall be * down to Lk 10:15
"And when you are * to trial Lk 12:11
One day some mothers * their Lk 18:15
"But the third man * back only Lk 19:20
So they * the colt to Jesus Lk 19:35
we fight? We * along the swords!" Lk 22:49
"You * this man to me, accusing Lk 23:14
rich blessings he * to us—blessing Jn 1:16
* us loving forgiveness as well. Jn 1:17
And he * Peter to meet Jesus. Jn 1:42
"Who * it to him?" Jn 4:33
and Pharisees * a woman caught in Jn 8:3
was—the man he had * back to life. Jn 12:1
sent to earth! I * glory to you Jn 17:4
called for Jesus to be * to him. Jn 18:33
their chief priests * you here. Jn 18:35
who * me to you have the greater Jn 19:11
At these words Pilate * Jesus out Jn 19:13
of death and * him back to life Act 2:24
ancestors who has * glory to his Act 3:13
but God * him back to life again. Act 3:15
And as soon as God had * his Act 3:26
So the two disciples were * in Act 4:7
sold them and * the money to the Act 4:34,35
field he owned and * the money to Act 4:37
property, and * only part of the Act 5:2
Sick people were * out into the Act 5:15
gates of the jail and * them out. Act 5:19
the apostles to be * for trial. Act 5:21
and * them in before the Council. Act 5:26,27
The God of our ancestors * Jesus Act 5:30
So they * in some men to lie Act 6:11
arrested him and * him before the Act 6:12
Then God * him here to the land Act 7:4
Moses, who * us out of Egypt.' Act 7:40
Then Barnabas * him to the Act 9:27
But God * him back to life again Act 10:40,41
When he found him, he * him back Act 11:26
the Lord had * him out of jail. Act 12:17
"But God * him back to life Act 13:30
God * Jesus back to life again. Act 13:32,33
—someone God * back to life, Act 13:37
of the city, * them cartloads of Act 14:13
and Silas. He * them out and Act 16:30
Then he * them up into his house Act 16:34
them to go, and * them out and pled Act 16:39
against Paul and * him before the Act 18:12
their deeds and * their incantation Act 19:18,19
Yet you have * these men here Act 19:37
So the commander * him inside and Act 22:24
He had Paul * in before them to Act 22:30
next day and ordered Paul * in. Act 25:17
city, Festus ordered Paul * in. Act 25:23
So I have * him before you all, Act 25:26
if my dishonesty * him glory by Rom 3:7
of God who * back Jesus our Lord Rom 4:24
our faith, he has * us into this Rom 5:2
enemies, we were * back to God by Rom 5:10
For this one man, Adam, * death to Rom 5:15
But this one man, Jesus Christ, * Rom 5:15
Adam's one sin * the penalty of Rom 5:16
Yes, Adam's sin * punishment to Rom 5:18
over all men and * them to death, Rom 5:21
glorious power, * him back to life Rom 6:4
Or, "he * us near to God." 1Co 1:30
For I was the one who * you to 1Co 4:15
the food * there as gifts to him? 1Co 9:13
the food that is * by those 1Co 9:13
and he * them all safely through 1Co 10:1
the dead be * back to life again? 1Co 15:35
the same God who * the Lord Jesus 2Co 4:14
are from God who * us back to 2Co 5:18
the news that he * of the wonderful 2Co 7:7
from Macedonia * me another gift. 2Co 11:8,9
* you the Good News of Christ. Gal 4:13
now you have been * very near to Eph 2:13
And he has * this Good News of Eph 2:17
that the Lord has * me here to use Php 1:16,17
mighty power that * him back to Php 3:10
As you well know, when I first * Php 4:15
the one who * you this Good News. Col 1:7
kingdom and * us into the kingdom Col 1:13
he has * you back as his friends. Col 1:21
result Christ has * you into the Col 1:22
For when we * you the Good News, 1Th 1:5
the trials and sorrows it * you. 1Th 1:6
whom God * back to life—and he is 1Th 1:10
Has she * up her children well? 1Ti 5:10
The first time I was * before the 2Ti 4:16
hearts of the people who * them. Heb 9:9
obeyed God and * an offering that Heb 11:4
It was faith that * the walls of Heb 11:30
and to Jesus himself, who has * Heb 12:24
the high priest * the blood of the Heb 13:11
God of peace, who * again from the Heb 13:20,21
recently was he * into public view, 1Pe 1:20
us apostles who * you the words of 2Pe 3:1
and * us into fellowship with God; 1Jn 2:2
the nations shall be * into it. Rev 21:26

BROWN
The leaves will never turn * and Eze 47:12
—Jamieson, Fausset and * Zep 2:15f
when it becomes all * and dry. 1Pe 1:24

BRUISE
to * him and fill him with grief. Is 53:10
For your sin is an incurable *, a Jer 30:12

BRUISED
burn part of the * grain mixed with Lev 2:16
He will not break the * reed, Is 42:3
burn dimly or be * until . . ." Is 42:4f
But he was wounded and * for our Is 53:5

BRUISES
covered with * and welts and Is 1:5,6

BRUISING
iron—smashing, *, and conquering. Dan 2:40

BRUSH
stands will be overgrown with *. Mic 3:12
and happens to * against some bread Hag 2:12

BRUSHED
washed himself, * his hair, changed 2Sa 12:20

BRUSHES
man * a grasshopper from his arm. Ps 109:22,23
impure, and then * against Hag 2:13

BRUTAL
of them and put * taskmasters over Ex 1:11
The taskmasters were *. Ex 5:13
been more and more * to them, and Ex 5:23
with no * jailer to curse them. Job 3:18
It was far more * and vicious Dan 7:7
As I watched, the * fourth animal Dan 7:11
animal, the one so * and shocking, Dan 7:19
It will be more * than any of the Dan 7:23
will arise, more * than the other Dan 7:24
This * action of Herod's Mt 2:17

BRUTALLY
for you knew how * the Egyptians Neh 9:10
They will be * killed by enemy Lk 21:24
and now they have * persecuted us 1Th 2:15

BUBASTIS
of Heliopolis and * shall die by Eze 30:17

BUBBLE
Does a spring of water * out Jas 3:11

BUBBLED
before the springs * forth their Pro 8:24

BUBBLES
making * and muddying the stream. Eze 32:2

BUCK
mean, suddenly a * goat appeared Dan 8:5
helpless and the * goat knocked him Dan 8:7

BUCKET
drop in the *, dust on the scales. Is 40:15
have a rope or a *," she said, Jn 4:11

BUCKETFUL
You drink wine by the * and Amo 6:6

BUCKETS
The ash *, shovels, basins, Ex 27:3

BUCKLE
* on your armor, you Egyptians Jer 46:3

BUCKLERS
your shields and *, bows and Eze 39:9

BUD
nipped in the * because of wrong Gen 11:6f
that began to * and blossom, and Gen 40:9,10
it may sprout and * again at the Job 14:8,9
will take root and * and blossom Is 27:6

BUDDED
tribe of Levi, had * and was Num 17:8
the vines have * and whether the Sol 7:12
and Aaron's wooden cane that *. Heb 9:4

BUDDING
grape vines were * or the Sol 6:11
shall be like a * tree, or like a Is 61:11

BUDGE
truth and don't * an inch in the Lk 20:21

BUDS
for * will grow on his rod! Num 17:5
princes [her topmost * and shoots Eze 17:12,13
When its * become tender and its Mk 13:28

BUFFETED
—like green fruit from fig trees * Rev 6:13

BUGLE
priests—formed a * corps to march 1Ch 15:24
At the sound of the * he shouts, Job 39:25

BUGLER
And if the army * doesn't play 1Co 14:8

BUILD
to Jacob, "and * an altar to Gen 35:1
them, "and I will * an altar there Gen 35:3
of sheep and oxen. * altars only Ex 20:24
You may also * altars from Ex 20:25
and quarter it, and * a wood fire Lev 1:6,7
brooks—and [* shelters with them Lev 23:40
BALAAM SAID TO the king, "* seven Num 23:1
Balaam again told the king to * Num 23:29
"We will * sheepfolds for our Num 32:16
But first we will need to * Num 32:17
Go ahead and * cities for your Num 32:24
you didn't *, wells you didn't dig, Deu 6:10,11,12
Rather, you must * a sanctuary Deu 12:4,5
Be sure that he doesn't * up a Deu 17:16
refuses to * his brother's house.' Deu 25:9
in the lime. And * an altar there Deu 27:5,6
else will live in the house you *; Deu 28:30
We will use them to * a monument Jos 4:6
yet told them where to * it). Jos 9:27
So we decided to * the altar as Jos 22:26,27
cities you did not *—these cities Jos 24:13
plagues. Now * a new cart and 1Sa 6:7
masons to * a palace for David. 2Sa 5:11
Literally, "Shall you * me a 2Sa 7:5f
He is the one who shall * me a 2Sa 7:13
to him, "Go and * an altar to the 2Sa 24:18
so that I can * an altar to the 2Sa 24:21
for wood to * a fire on the altar. 2Sa 24:22
and told him, "* a house here in 1Ki 2:36,37
Temple of the Lord he wanted to *. 1Ki 5:2,3
not been able to * it because of 1Ki 5:2,3
So I am planning to * a Temple 1Ki 5:5
your throne, shall * me a Temple.' 1Ki 5:5
Sea and * them into rafts. 1Ki 5:9
So it took seven years to *. 1Ki 6:38
He wanted to * a Temple for the 1Ki 8:17
is the one who shall * my Temple.' 1Ki 8:19
forced labor to * the Temple, his 1Ki 9:15
these materials to * the city of 1Ki 15:22
to * a fire to roast their flesh. 1Ki 19:21
whether we can * a new one down 2Ki 6:1
with a shield, nor * a ramp against 2Ki 19:32
carpenters to help * David's palace 1Ch 14:1
'You are not to * my temple! 1Ch 17:4
should * me a cedar-lined temple.' 1Ch 17:6
He is the one who shall * me a 1Ch 17:12
instruct David to * an altar to the 1Ch 21:18
then I will * an altar to the 1Ch 21:22
place where I'll * the Temple of 1Ch 22:1
his son Solomon to * a temple for 1Ch 22:6
"I wanted to * it myself," 1Ch 22:7
so you are not to * my Temple. 1Ch 22:8
He shall * my temple, and he 1Ch 22:10
do and * the Temple of the Lord. 1Ch 22:11
It was my desire to * a temple in 1Ch 28:2
'You are not to * my temple, for 1Ch 28:3
son Solomon shall * my temple; 1Ch 28:6
chosen you to * his holy temple. 1Ch 28:10
for the temple he will * is not 1Ch 29:1
have gathered to * a temple for 1Ch 29:16
time had come to * a temple for the 2Ch 2:1
"I am about to * a temple for 2Ch 2:4
But who can ever * him a worthy 2Ch 2:6
And who am I to be allowed to * a 2Ch 2:6
I am going to * will be huge and 2Ch 2:9
son to * God's Temple, and a royal 2Ch 2:12
"My father David wanted to * 2Ch 6:7
was not the one to * it: his son 2Ch 6:9
* walled cities throughout Judah. 2Ch 14:6
"Let us * and fortify cities 2Ch 14:7
them to * Geba and Mizpah instead. 2Ch 16:6
instructed me to * him a Temple in 2Ch 36:22,23
"Do they think they can * the Neh 4:1
and used them to * huts on the Neh 8:16
rich and * their lovely homes. Ps 49:16
Zion; * the walls of Jerusalem." Ps 51:18f
settle there and * their cities, Ps 107:36
to * a permanent home for the Ark Ps 132:2-5
we will * upon her a battlement Sol 8:9
Between the city walls, you * a Is 22:9,10,11
Cornerstone that is safe to * on. Is 28:16
* forts around it to destroy it. Is 29:3
its gates, nor * up an earthen bank Is 37:33
Enlarge your house; * on Is 54:2
Foreigners will come and * your Is 60:10
people to return! * the roads, pull Is 62:10
can you * for me as good as that? Is 66:1
and the fathers * fires, and the Jer 7:18
You say, "I will * a Jer 22:14
* homes and plan to stay; Jer 29:5
and that we should * permanent Jer 29:28
but now I will carefully * it up. Jer 31:28
He also told us not to * houses Jer 35:7
My people * a flimsy wall and Eze 13:10
they will * siege towers and make Eze 21:22
anyone who would * again the wall Eze 22:30
in Israel, and * their homes and Eze 28:26
as eagles, and * your nest among Ob 1:4
"Though he * his army millions Nah 1:12
"Woe to you who * cities with Hab 2:12
you have begun to * the Temple. Hag 2:15
—and will * the Temple of the Zec 6:12
and upon this rock I will * my Mt 16:18
For you * monuments to the Mt 23:29,30
Jesus, in order to * a case against Mt 26:59
You can destroy the Temple and * Mt 27:40
* their nests and be sheltered." Mk 4:31,32
three days I will * another, made Mk 14:58
personally to * us a synagogue!" Lk 7:5
down my barns and * bigger ones! Lk 12:18
* up the faith of your brothers." Lk 22:32
"It took forty-six years to * Jn 2:20
What kind of home could you *?' Act 7:48,49
which are able to * your faith and Act 20:32
church and try to * each other up. Rom 14:19
and thus * him up in the Lord. Rom 15:1
be used to * on that foundation. 1Co 3:12
and some * with sticks, and hay, 1Co 3:12
needed to * the church is love. 1Co 8:1
to all, and * them up in the Lord. 1Co 14:26
dear friends—to * you up 2Co 12:19
So encourage each other to * 1Th 5:11
And many people can * houses, Heb 3:4
getting ready to * the tabernacle, Heb 8:5
But you, dear friends, must * up Jud 1:20

BUILDER
* and top trader of the world? Is 23:8
taught me how to be an expert *. 1Co 3:10
kind of material each * has used. 1Co 3:13
city whose designer and * is God. Heb 11:10

BUILDER'S
was laid, the * oldest son would Jos 6:26

BUILDERS
and Hiram's * in cutting the timber 1Ki 5:18
When the * completed the Ez 3:10
The stone rejected by the * has Ps 118:22
a house, the *' work is useless. Ps 127:1
be burned; the * from many lands Jer 51:58
"Tell these evil * that their Eze 13:11
The wall and its * both are gone. Eze 13:15
rejected by the * has been made the Mt 21:42
'The Rock the * threw away became Mk 12:10
the * was made the cornerstone'?" Lk 20:17
discarded by the * which became the Act 4:11
rejected by the * has become the 1Pe 2:7

BUILDING
to talk about * a great city, with Gen 11:3,4
and that ended the * of the city. Gen 11:8
burdens while * the store-cities Ex 1:11
on that end of the * with sixteen Ex 26:25
rear of the *, facing westward. Ex 26:26,27
various steps in * the Tabernacle Ex 38:21
of the frames of the Tabernacle *; Num 3:36,37
away from him and * an altar of Jos 22:16
the Lord by * another altar in Jos 22:19
against him by * our own altar for Jos 22:29
he could finish * his palace and 1Ki 3:1
or any other tool at the * site. 1Ki 6:7
each side of the *, attached to the 1Ki 6:10
the Temple he was *: "If you do as 1Ki 6:11,12
and the entire * was completed in 1Ki 6:38
the Lord is filling the entire *! 1Ki 8:11
WHEN SOLOMON HAD finished * the 1Ki 9:1
he discontinued * the city of Ramah 1Ki 15:21
surrounded the * with eighty of his 2Ki 10:24
"The Temple * needs repairing. 2Ki 12:4,5
but only for repairs to the *. 2Ki 12:13,14
the very city and * which the Lord 2Ki 21:3,4,5
Give this money to the * 2Ki 22:5,6
(The * superintendents were not 2Ki 22:7
necessary for the *, but God has 1Ch 28:2
not just another *—it is for the 1Ch 29:1
as I could for * it—enough gold, 1Ch 29:2
This is in addition to the * 1Ch 29:3
to finishing the * of your temple, 1Ch 29:19
to David when he was * his palace. 2Ch 2:3
So Solomon finished * the Temple 2Ch 7:11
and the great * projects of the 2Ch 8:1
supply centers, * their walls and 2Ch 8:5
he discontinued * Ramah and gave up 2Ch 16:5
carried away the * stones and 2Ch 16:6
offerings for the * fund, so that 2Ch 24:5
the money to the * superintendents, 2Ch 24:12
and to purchase * materials—stone 2Ch 34:10,11
materials—stone * blocks, timber, 2Ch 34:10,11
were the * superintendents. 2Ch 34:12
responsibility of * him a Temple in Ez 1:2
(This was before they began * the Ez 3:6
men must stop * the Temple until I Ez 4:21
and forced the Jews to stop *. Ez 4:23
encouraging them to begin * again! Ez 5:1
force us to stop *, but let us Ez 5:5
and after * it, he hung the doors Neh 3:14
and the old Officers' Club *. Neh 3:16
* of the wall in his own district. Neh 3:17
us who are * your wall." Neh 4:5
that is why you are * the wall. Neh 6:5,6
from the gallows he was *. Est 6:4
first before * your house. Pro 24:27
you think you are, * this beautiful Is 22:15,16
for you are * your great palace Jer 22:13
By not paying wages you are * Jer 22:13
shall never be used for * again. Jer 51:26
you are a brazen prostitute, * Eze 16:31
mainland city by * a siege wall and Eze 26:8
And he said to me: "The * beside Eze 40:45
maintenance. The * beside the Eze 40:46
A large * stood on the west, Eze 41:12
and so was the * west of the Eze 41:15,16
the Temple yard, and to another *. Eze 42:1
The rows of rooms behind this * Eze 42:3
ran between the * and the tiers of Eze 42:4
the doors of the * facing north. Eze 42:4
And since the * was not built Eze 42:6
Temple a similar * composed of two Eze 42:9,10
two wings of the *, the same as in Eze 42:11
as in the other * across the Eze 42:11
of the * open to the public." Eze 42:14
houses you are *, nor drink the Amo 5:11
And Zerubbabel will finish * this Zec 4:7
the most honored stone in the *! Mk 12:10
construction of a * without first Lk 14:28
'He started that * and ran out of Lk 14:30
farming and *— until the morning Lk 17:28
After this prayer, the * where Act 4:31
on them. This * was constructed in Act 7:44
the privilege of * a permanent Act 7:46
very kind to us, * a bonfire on the Act 28:1
you are God's *, not ours. 1Co 3:9
and the cornerstone of the * is Eph 2:20
work for him, * up the church, the Eph 4:12
for God's use in * his house. 1Pe 2:5
and important part of the *." 1Pe 2:7
for them while Noah was * the ark. 1Pe 3:20

BUILDING-STONES
And now you have become living * 1Pe 2:5

BUILDINGS
These * were constructed 1Ki 7:9
and all the other * he had always 1Ki 9:1
for overlaying the walls of the *. 1Ch 29:4,5
special treasury * for his silver, 2Ch 32:27
old *, never to be rebuilt again. Ps 28:5
were two one-room *, one beside the Eze 40:44
on a tour of the various Temple *. Mt 24:1
But he told them, "All these * Mt 24:2
what beautiful * these are! Mk 13:1

BUILDS
UNLESS THE LORD * a house, the Ps 127:1
A WISE WOMAN * her house, while a Pro 14:1
In those days, when a man * a Is 65:21,22
man who * his house on solid rock. Mt 7:24
a man who * his house on sand. Mt 7:26
are like a man who * a house on a Lk 6:47,48
* a house without a foundation. Lk 6:49
But he who * on the foundation 1Co 3:10
just as a man who * a fine house Heb 3:3
of Rock upon which God *; 1Pe 2:4

BUILDUP
Saul countered with a * of 1Sa 17:2

BUILT
Then Noah * an altar and Gen 8:20
to Assyria. He * Nineveh, Gen 10:11,12
And Abram * an altar there to Gen 12:7
place where he had * the altar. Gen 13:3,4
and * an altar to Jehovah there. Gen 13:18
Abraham to go, he * an altar and Gen 22:9
Then Isaac * an altar and Gen 26:25
Thus he * his flocks from Gen 30:39,40
There he * himself a camp, with Gen 33:17
Afterwards Jacob * a stone pillar Gen 35:13,14
Moses * an altar there and Ex 17:15,16
and early the next morning he * Ex 24:4
resting it upon the ledge * there. Ex 27:5
were about it, he * an altar before Ex 32:5
are powerfully *, and we saw some Num 13:32
Pisgah, and * seven altars there; Num 23:14
The people of Gad * these cities: Num 32:34,35,36
The children of Reuben * the Num 32:37,38
and have * fine homes to live in, Deu 8:12,13
'Has anyone just * a new house, but Deu 20:5
Joshua also * another monument Jos 4:9
Then Joshua * an altar to the Jos 8:30

(BUILT Con't)
it would be * (for the Lord hadn't Jos 9:27
* on mounds except for Hazor. Jos 11:13
in Canaan, they * a large monument Jos 22:10
that we have not * the altar in Jos 22:22,23
that we have not * the altar to Jos 22:22,23
And Gideon * an altar there and Ju 6:24
the Lord your God, * here on this Ju 6:26
new altar had been * instead, with Ju 6:28
were up early and * an altar, and Ju 21:4
And he * an altar to the Lord at 1Sa 7:17
And Saul * an altar to the 1Sa 14:35
of the city, he * northward toward 2Sa 5:9
* me a beautiful cedar temple?' 2Sa 7:7
(Absalom had * a monument to 2Sa 18:18
besieged Abel and * a mound to the 2Sa 20:15
And David * an altar there to 2Sa 24:25
of the Lord hadn't yet been *. 1Ki 3:2
An annex of rooms was * along the 1Ki 6:5
resting on blocks * out from the 1Ki 6:6
structure was * without the sound 1Ki 6:7
THEN SOLOMON * his own palace, 1Ki 7:1
palace which he * for Pharaoh's 1Ki 7:8
But, O Lord, I have * you a lovely 1Ki 8:12,13
been * for the Lord God of Israel. 1Ki 8:20
much less this Temple I have *! 1Ki 8:27
which I have * for your name, hear 1Ki 8:44
which I have * for your name, hear 1Ki 8:48
which you have * and have put my 1Ki 9:2,3
which Solomon * the Temple and the 1Ki 9:10
He also * cities for grain 1Ki 9:19
he had * for her in the palace. 1Ki 9:24
Then he * Fort Millo. 1Ki 9:24
a year on the altar he had *. 1Ki 9:25
Edom, where he * a fleet of ships. 1Ki 9:26
palace he had *, and when she saw 1Ki 10:4
Solomon * up a great stable of 1Ki 10:26
He even * a temple on the Mount 1Ki 11:7
Solomon * temples for these 1Ki 11:8
of this city his father had *. 1Ki 11:27,28
Jeroboam now * the city of 1Ki 12:25
Later he * Penuel. 1Ki 12:25
They * shrines and obelisks and 1Ki 14:23
King Baasha * the fortress city 1Ki 15:17
of the cities he *—is found in The 1Ki 15:23
for $4,000 and * a city on it, 1Ki 16:24
First he * a temple and an altar 1Ki 16:32
and the cities he *—is written in 1Ki 22:39
King Jehoshaphat * great 1Ki 22:48
After his father's death he * 2Ki 14:22
of the Temple of the Lord was *. 2Ki 15:34,35
Uriah * one just like it by 2Ki 16:11,12
and they had * altars to other gods 2Ki 17:9
Literally, "* them high places in 2Ki 17:9f
had destroyed. He * altars for Baal 2Ki 21:3,4,5
kings of Judah had * on the palace 2Ki 23:12
* in the two courts of the Temple; 2Ki 23:12
(Solomon had * these shrines for 2Ki 23:13
They had been * by the various 2Ki 23:19
Then, when Solomon * the Temple 1Ch 6:32
was Sheerah. She * Lower and Upper 1Ch 7:24
Shemed (who * Ono and Lod and 1Ch 8:12
DAVID NOW * several palaces for 1Ch 15:1
and he also * a new Tabernacle to 1Ch 15:1
and * an altar to the Lord 1Ch 21:26
Moses had * the Tabernacle 500 2Ch 1:2,3f
in Jerusalem, * by King David for 2Ch 1:4
rule Israel. He * up a huge force 2Ch 1:14
he also * ten tables and placed 2Ch 4:8
place, and I have * the Temple for 2Ch 6:10
less this Temple which I have *! 2Ch 6:18
Temple I have * is truly yours. 2Ch 6:33
which I have * for your name, then 2Ch 6:34
your Temple I have *, and plead 2Ch 6:37,38
conquered it. He * Tadmor in the 2Ch 8:4
in the desert, and * cities in 2Ch 8:4
He also * Baalath and other 2Ch 8:6
were kept. He * to his heart's 2Ch 8:6
the new palace he had * for her. 2Ch 8:11
the altar he had * in front of the 2Ch 8:12
war on him and * the fortress 2Ch 16:1
very strong, and * fortresses and 2Ch 17:12
Your people settled here and * 2Ch 20:8
Then he * new cities in the 2Ch 26:6
He * fortified towers in 2Ch 26:9
He * the Upper Gate of the 2Ch 27:3
And he * cities in the hill 2Ch 27:4
He also * many storehouses for 2Ch 32:28,29
Hill, where it was * very high. 2Ch 33:14
the altars he had * on the mountain 2Ch 33:15
locations where he * idols on the 2Ch 33:19
of Israel must be * by the Ez 4:3
It is being * with huge stones, Ez 5:8
of God be * there as before. Ez 5:15
from his house and * into a gallows Ez 6:11
The Fish Gate was * by the sons Neh 3:3
led by Hanun, * the Valley Gate, Neh 3:13
district; he * as far as the royal Neh 3:16
of Zabbai), who * from the turn in Neh 3:20
son of Hakkoz) * a section of the Neh 3:21
of Henadad), who * the portion of Neh 3:24
who * next to his own house. Neh 3:30
the singers had * their own Neh 12:29
and he ordered the gallows *. Est 5:14
Every house * by the wicked is Job 27:18
There he * his towering temple, Ps 78:69
WISDOM HAS * a palace supported on Pro 9:1
Any enterprise is * by wise Pro 24:3,4
choicest vines. He * a watchtower Is 5:2
Your homes are * on great estates Is 5:8
check the foundation wall you *; Is 28:17
and they have * for themselves Jer 2:13
They have * the altar called Jer 7:31
They have * high altars to Baal Jer 19:5
mounds have been * against the city Jer 32:24
From the time this city was * Jer 32:31
And they have * high altars to Jer 32:35
We haven't * houses or owned Jer 35:9
will destroy this nation that I *; Jer 45:4
Jerusalem and * forts around it, Jer 52:4
He has * forts against me and Lam 3:5
siege mounds being * against the Eze 4:1
the Lord God— you * a spacious Eze 16:24
You are like a ship * of finest Eze 27:5
thirty rooms were * against the Eze 40:17
I noticed that the Temple was * Eze 41:8
And since the building was not * Eze 42:6
They * their idol temples beside Eze 43:8
where the Temple is * is holy. Eze 43:12
The Temple shall be * within the Eze 45:3
mighty power, have * this beautiful Dan 4:30
Ephraim has * many altars, but Hos 8:11
Israel has * great palaces; Hos 8:14
beside a wall * with a plumbline, Amo 7:7
her ornate idol temples, * with Mic 1:7
of the hill where the city is *. Zep 1:10
live in the new homes they have *. Zep 1:13
collapse, for it is * on rock. Mt 7:25
around it, and * a platform for the Mt 21:33
"A man planted a vineyard and * a Mk 12:1
juice, and * a watchman's tower. Mk 12:1
was *, to push him over the cliff. Lk 4:29
stands firm, for it is strongly *. Lk 6:47,48
it was Solomon who actually * it. Act 7:47
and Apollos has * on it. 1Co 3:10
Then every workman who has * on 1Co 3:14
But if the house he has * burns 1Co 3:15
* upon this wonderful message; 1Co 15:1
be * to keep men from finding him. 2Co 10:5
shallow answers * on men's thoughts Col 2:8
place of worship * by the Lord and Heb 8:2
he * the ark and saved his family. Heb 11:7
* on seven hills where this woman Rev 17:9
of jasper, and was * on twelve Rev 21:18,19,20

BUKKI
Dan * (son of Jogli) Num 34:16-28
*, the father of 1Ch 6:4-15
*, Uzzi, Zerahiah, 1Ch 6:50-53
Uzzi was the son of *; Ez 7:1
* was the son of Abishu-a; Ez 7:1

BUKKIAH
were his sons: *, Mattaniah, 1Ch 25:4,5
Sixth, * and twelve of his sons 1Ch 25:9-31

BULGING
a * wall that bursts and falls; Is 30:13

BULK
However, the great * of the 1Ki 20:21

BULL
get a young * and two rams with no Ex 29:1
with the young * and the two rams. Ex 29:3,4
"Then bring the young * to the Ex 29:10
* as a sin offering for atonement; Ex 29:36
only a * with no physical defects. Lev 1:2,3
may use either a * or a cow, but Lev 3:1
must offer a young * without defect Lev 4:3
in the case of a * or cow Lev 4:10
But the remainder of the young * Lev 4:11,12
offer a young * for a sin offering, Lev 4:14
cart the young * outside the camp Lev 4:21
oil, the young * for the sin Lev 8:1
Then he took the young * for the Lev 8:14
The carcass of the young *, with Lev 8:17
Aaron to take a * calf from the Lev 9:2
must bring a young * for a sin Lev 16:3
the Lord the young * as a sin Lev 16:6
the young * as a sin offering for Lev 16:11
blood of the young * and sprinkle Lev 16:14
did with the blood of the young *. Lev 16:15
blood of the young * and the goat Lev 16:18
And the young * and the goat Lev 16:27
it must be a young * or a sheep Lev 22:19
If the young * or lamb presented Lev 22:23
one young *, and two rams. Lev 23:18
He brought a young *, a ram, and Num 7:15
Have them bring a young * and a Num 8:8
young * for a sin offering. Num 8:8
"If the sacrifice is a young *, Num 15:8,9
*, ram, lamb, or young goat. Num 15:11,12
one young * for a burnt offering. Num 15:23,24
and a young * and a ram were Num 23:2
a young * and a ram on each." Num 23:3,4
and he offered up a young * and a Num 23:14
a young * and ram on every altar. Num 23:30
as a grain offering with each *; Num 28:12
of wine with each *, four pints for Num 28:14
With each * there shall be a Num 28:20,21
with oil with each *, six quarts Num 28:28,29
of one young *, one ram, and seven Num 29:2
offered with the *, six quarts with Num 29:3,4
him—of one young *, one ram, seven Num 29:8
oil are to be offered with the *; Num 29:9,10
Lord—of one young *, one ram, seven Num 29:36
He is a young * in strength and Deu 33:17
a three-year-old * for the 1Sa 1:24
the other young * and lay it on the 1Ki 18:23
and cut the young * into pieces and 1Ki 18:33
up the young *, the wood, the 1Ki 18:38
horn of a mighty fighting *. Ps 18:2
made me as strong as a wild *. Ps 92:10
Why has Apis, your * god, fled Jer 46:15
sacrifice a young * with no Eze 45:18
provide a young * for a sin Eze 45:22
one young *, in perfect condition; Eze 46:6
With the young *, he must bring Eze 46:7
be one bushel with the young *; Eze 46:11

BULLIES
One of Israel. * will vanish and Is 29:20

BULLION
and silver, were melted down to *. 2Ki 25:14,15
*, $2,000,000 worth of silver, 1Ch 22:14

BULLOCK
to Moses, "When a *, sheep, or Lev 22:26,27
* and seven rams for consecration. 2Ch 13:9
than sacrificing a * or an ox. Ps 69:31
their sins behind them like a * Is 5:18
be given a * for a sin offering. Eze 43:19
Then take the * for the sin Eze 43:21
be cleansed, as it was by the *. Eze 43:22
another perfect * and a perfect ram Eze 43:23
a male goat, a * and a ram from the Eze 43:25
bushel for each * and ram; Eze 45:24

BULLOCKS
But it isn't sacrificial * and Ps 50:9
and in the * I bring to sacrifice Ps 51:19

BULLS
colts,40 cows,10 *,20 female Gen 32:13,14,15
12 *, 12 rams, Num 7:87
24 young *, Num 7:88
* and offer them before the Lord; Num 8:12
* and seven rams for sacrifice." Num 23:1
seven young * and seven rams for Num 23:29
Lord of two young *, one ram, and Num 28:11
the Lord two young *, one ram, and Num 28:19
It shall consist of two young *, Num 28:27
be thirteen young *, two rams, and Num 29:13
for each of the thirteen young *; Num 29:14
twelve young *, two rams, and Num 29:17
offer eleven young *, two rams, Num 29:20
ten young *, two rams, and fourteen Num 29:23
nine young *, two rams, and Num 29:26,27
eight young *, two rams, and Num 29:29
seven young *, two rams, and Num 29:32
Now bring two young *. 1Ki 18:23
choose one of the * and prepare 1Ki 18:25
* and placed it on the altar; 1Ki 18:26
seven * and seven lambs. 1Ch 15:26
a thousand young *, a thousand 1Ch 29:21
taking seven young *, seven rams, 2Ch 29:21
So they killed the young *, and 2Ch 29:22
In all, there were 70 young * 2Ch 29:32,33
* for offerings, and 7,000 sheep; 2Ch 30:24
1,000 young * and 10,000 sheep. 2Ch 30:24
offerings, and 3,000 young *. 2Ch 35:7
in Jerusalem young *, rams, and Ez 6:9
100 young *, 200 rams, and 400 Ez 6:17
Now take seven young * and seven Job 42:8
strong as the giant * from Bashan. Ps 22:12
laver and bronze * on which it Jer 52:17
laver and twelve * was tremendous. Jer 52:20
young * of Bashan for my feast! Eze 39:18
* and seven rams without blemish. Eze 45:23
the blood of * and goats and the Heb 9:13
for the blood of * and goats really Heb 10:4
The blood of * and goats merely Heb 10:4f
God, the blood of * and goats Heb 10:5

BULLY
of Babylon and say, "You *, you! Is 14:4

BUM
that I am just some drunken *!" 1Sa 1:15,16

BUMP
they * wildly through the streets! Nah 3:2

BUMPER
there were * crops everywhere. Gen 41:47
land will yield * crops and you can Lev 25:19
bless you with * crops the sixth Lev 25:21,22
land will yield * crops, and the Lev 26:4,5
vineyards, and reap their * crops! Ps 107:37
from then would yield a * crop. Is 37:30f
fields will yield * crops, and Eze 34:27
is, "I will give them * crops." Eze 34:29f

BUMS
There were, however, some * and 1Sa 10:27
at night—woe to you drunken *. Is 5:11

BUNAH
Ram (the oldest), *, Oren, Ozem, 1Ch 2:25
BUNCH
and what a wicked * they are. Ex 32:22
in and kill the whole * of them. 2Ki 10:25
"What does this * of poor, Neh 4:1
are all a * of silly lies; Zec 10:2
Jesus replied, "You * of Mk 7:6,7
it is merely a * of questions of Act 18:15
BUNCHES
one hundred * of grapes, and a 2Sa 16:1
BUNDLE
leather, and the * shall be placed Num 4:10
began chopping a * of firewood, and Ju 9:47,48
So each of them quickly cut a * Ju 9:49
I make. You * them all together as Job 14:17
in a * and was lying at the side. Jn 20:7
BUNDLES
example, the * were piled against Ju 9:49
BUNNI
*, Sherebiah, Bani, and Chenani. Neh 9:4
Bani, *, Azgad, Bebai, Neh 10:14-27
son of Hashabiah, son of *); Neh 11:15,16,17
BURDEN
"Issachar is a strong beast of * Gen 49:14
Moses, this job is too heavy a * Ex 18:18
you will share the * with them. Ex 18:22
me the * of a people like this? Num 11:11
they shall bear the * of the Num 11:17
day, bearing the * of your sins. Num 14:34,35
You are a great * for me to carry Deu 1:9
would be too much of a * on you." 2Sa 13:25
go with me, you will only be a *; 2Sa 15:33,34
I would only be a * to my lord 2Sa 19:35
made my life so heavy a * to me? Job 7:20
and carry their * no longer? Job 39:2,3
who rolled his * on the Lord?" Ps 22:8
they are a * too heavy to bear. Ps 38:3,4
For I groan and weep beneath my * Ps 55:2
relieve your shoulder of its *; Ps 81:6
it, but a fool's * is his folly. Pro 16:22
God, will unburden myself of the * Jer 23:38,39
Literally, either, "the * of the Jer 23:38,39f
peace has the * of proof on him to Jer 28:9
of the * of her wonderful king! Hos 8:10
to lay no greater * of Jewish laws Act 15:27,28,29
for we must bear the "*" of Rom 15:1
was to become a * to you—I didn't 2Co 12:13
would not be a * to anyone there, 1Th 2:9
we would not be a * to any of you. 2Th 3:8
BURDENING
will be a heavy stone * the world. Zec 12:3
to correct God by * the Gentiles Act 15:10
BURDENS
down under heavy * while building Ex 1:11
beneath their *, in deep trouble Ex 2:23
"My father gave you heavy * but I 2Ch 10:14
Give your * to the Lord. Ps 55:22
net and laid great * on our backs. Ps 66:11
He who daily bears our * also Ps 68:19
he lifts the * from those bent Ps 146:8
even the old folks carry heavy *. Is 47:6
(from * of stones for the siege). Eze 29:18
for I give you only light *." Mt 11:29,30
bear some faults and * of his own. Gal 6:5
BUREAUCRACY
matter is lost in red tape and *. Ecc 5:8
BURIAL
by the men of Heth as a * plot. Gen 23:19,20
Ephron the Hethite for a * ground. Gen 49:29,30
king and giving him a decent *. 2Sa 2:5
to arrange for the * of some 1Ki 11:15
was given a royal * because he was 2Ch 22:9
give him a decent *—I say that he Ecc 6:3
enough for decent * anywhere, and Jer 19:11
on me to prepare my body for *. Mt 26:12
my body ahead of time for *. Mk 14:8
did it in preparation for my *. Jn 12:7
as is the Jewish custom of *. Jn 19:40
Her friends prepared her for * Act 9:37
BURIED
So Abraham * Sarah there, in the Gen 23:19,20
Isaac and Ishmael * him in the cave Gen 25:9,10
where Sarah, Abraham's wife was *. Gen 25:9,10
earrings, and he * them beneath the Gen 35:4
died and was * beneath the oak tree Gen 35:8
So Rachel died, and was * near Gen 35:19
And his sons Esau and Jacob * Gen 35:28,29
Ephrath, and I * her beside the Gen 48:7
There they * Abraham and Sarah Gen 49:31
there they * Isaac and Rebekah Gen 49:31
and there I * Leah. Gen 49:31
land of Canaan and * it there in Gen 50:12,13
because they * the people there Num 11:34
where Miriam died and was *. Num 20:1
where Aaron died and was *. Deu 10:6
The Lord * him in a valley near Deu 34:6
silver * deeper than the rest." Jos 7:21
the silver * beneath the rest. Jos 7:22
He was * on his own estate at Jos 24:30
left Egypt, were * in Shechem, in Jos 24:32
he was * in the hill country of Jos 24:33
of 110, and was * at the edge of Ju 2:7-9
old man, and was * in the sepulcher Ju 8:32
When he died, he was * in Shamir, Ju 10:2
When Jair died he was * in Ju 10:5
At his death he was * in one of Ju 12:7
he died, and was * at Bethlehem. Ju 12:9,10
and was * at Aijalon in Zebulun. Ju 12:11,12
Then he died and was * in Ju 12:15
him back home and * him between Ju 16:31
where his father, Manoah, was *. Ju 16:31
die where you die, and be * there. Ru 1:17
* him in his family plot at Ramah. 1Sa 25:1
He was * in Ramah, his home town. 1Sa 28:3
Then they * their remains 1Sa 31:13
Jabesh-gilead had * Saul, he sent 2Sa 2:4
and * him beside his father; 2Sa 2:32
They * Abner in Hebron. 2Sa 3:32
* it in Abner's tomb in Hebron. 2Sa 4:12
so he died and was * beside his 2Sa 17:23
where my father and mother are *. 2Sa 19:37
men's bones to be * in the grave 2Sa 21:12,13,14
Then David died and was * in 1Ki 2:10
and he was * beside his house in 1Ki 2:34
* in the city of his father David; 1Ki 11:43
* in the grave of your fathers." 1Ki 13:21,22
the grave where the prophet is *. 1Ki 13:31
Ammonitess—he was * among his 1Ki 14:31
When he died he was * in 1Ki 15:8
he died he was * in the royal 1Ki 15:24
When Omri died he was * in 1Ki 16:28
was taken to Samaria and * there. 1Ki 22:36,37
So Ahab was * among his 1Ki 22:40
died he was * with his ancestors in 1Ki 22:50
He died and was * in the royal 2Ki 8:24,25
they * him in the royal cemetery. 2Ki 9:28
When Jehu died, he was * in 2Ki 10:35
He was * in the royal cemetery in 2Ki 12:21
Jehoahaz died and was * in 2Ki 13:9,10
Joash died and was * in Samaria 2Ki 13:13
So Elisha died and was *. 2Ki 13:20,21
When Joash died, he was * in 2Ki 14:16
horses, and he was * in the royal 2Ki 14:20
When Jeroboam II died he was * 2Ki 14:29
When Azariah died, he was * with 2Ki 15:7
When Jotham died he was * with 2Ki 15:38
When Ahaz died he was * in the 2Ki 16:20
When he died he was * in the 2Ki 21:18
He was * in a crypt in the 2Ki 21:26
to Jerusalem and * him in the grave 2Ki 23:30
Then they * them beneath the oak 1Ch 10:12
Then he died and was * in 2Ch 9:31
When Rehoboam died he was * in 2Ch 12:16
KING ABIJAH WAS * in Jerusalem. 2Ch 14:1
his reign, and was * in his own 2Ch 16:13,14
JEHOSHAPHAT DIED, he was * in 2Ch 21:1
He was * in Jerusalem, but not in 2Ch 21:20
He was * in the City of David 2Ch 24:16
he lay in bed, and * him in the 2Ch 24:25
and * him in the royal cemetery. 2Ch 25:28
When Uzziah died, he was * in 2Ch 26:23
When he died, he was * in 2Ch 27:9
When King Ahaz died, he was * in 2Ch 28:27
When Hezekiah died he was * in 2Ch 32:33
When Manasseh died he was * 2Ch 33:20,21
He was * there, in the royal 2Ch 35:24,25
my ancestors are * is in ruins, and Neh 2:3
But when a man dies and is *, Job 14:10
Both alike are * in the same Job 21:26
I have seen wicked men * and as Ecc 8:9,10
they are * with you. Is 14:11
from the earth where you lie *. Is 29:4
He was * like a criminal in a Is 53:9
up again nor * but shall be Jer 8:2
He shall be * like a dead Jer 22:19
had him * in an unmarked grave. Jer 26:23
and distress. He * me in dark Lam 3:6
and you won't be *, for I have Eze 29:5
They are * in a common grave, Eze 32:27
lords who are * in great honor with Eze 32:27
Gog and all his armies will be *. Eze 39:11
lie dead and * will rise up, some Dan 12:2
for his body and * it, and came to Mt 14:12
for his body and * it in a tomb. Mk 6:29
The rich man also died and was *, Lk 16:22
"Where is he *?" Jn 11:34
for he died and was *, and his Act 2:29
sheet and took him out and * him. Act 5:6
the young men who * your husband, Act 5:9
out and * her beside her husband. Act 5:10
to Shechem and * in the tomb Act 7:16
came and with great sorrow * Act 8:2
and was *, and his body decayed. Act 13:36
Your old sin-loving nature was * Rom 6:4
and that he was *, and that three 1Co 15:4
died with him and was * with him; Col 2:12
surrendered the bodies * in them; Rev 20:13
BURIERS
them so that the * will see them Eze 39:15,16
BURN
"Bring her out and * her," Judah Gen 38:24
and that it didn't * up, he went Ex 3:2
if all is not eaten that night, * Ex 12:10
foot for foot, * for burn, wound Ex 21:25
*, wound for wound, lash for lash. Ex 21:25
to * there continually. Ex 27:20
them, and * them upon the altar. Ex 29:13
camp and * it as a sin offering. Ex 29:14
and * it all upon the altar; Ex 29:18
their hands and * them on the altar Ex 29:25
remains until the morning, * it; Ex 29:34
lamps, he shall * sweet spices on Ex 30:7
the lamps he shall * the incense Ex 30:8
altar to * offerings to the Lord. Ex 30:20
the priests will * them upon the Lev 1:9
Then the priests shall * it all Lev 1:13
And the priest shall * it upon Lev 1:15,16,17
Literally, "shall * the memorial Lev 2:2f
to one of the priests to *, and Lev 2:2
"The priests are to * only a Lev 2:9
Then the priests shall * part of Lev 2:16
altar, and shall * before the Lord Lev 3:3,4,5
and shall * them on the altar of Lev 4:10
the camp and * it there, just as Lev 4:21
sacrifice, and the priest shall * Lev 4:31
lamb—the priest shall * the fat Lev 4:35
portion, and * it on the altar just Lev 5:12
on it, and * the fat of the daily Lev 6:12
mixed into it, and * it upon the Lev 6:15
The priests will * them upon the Lev 7:5
Then the priest shall * the fat Lev 7:31
out from the *, and the priest must Lev 13:25
a scar from the *, and the priest Lev 13:28
and he must * the clothing, Lev 13:52
it is leprosy and he must * it. Lev 13:57
a scab from a *, or a bright spot. Lev 14:56
He shall also * upon the altar Lev 16:25
Tabernacle, and to * the fat as a Lev 17:5
Tabernacle, and to * the fat as a Lev 17:6
all of it, and * the handful upon Num 5:26
before the Lord to * incense, lest Num 16:40
Then someone shall * the heifer Num 19:5
which you * on the altar for me are Num 28:1
" 'You must not * with desire Deu 5:21
shameful images and * the idols. Deu 7:5
"* their idols and do not touch Deu 7:25
the obelisks, * the shameful Deu 12:3
of the street and * it, then put Deu 13:16
Hamstring their horses and * Jos 11:6
(However, Joshua did not * any Jos 11:13
forth from me and * down the great Ju 9:15
was preparing to * it, a woman on Ju 9:52
We are going to * down your Ju 12:1
husband, or we'll * down your Ju 14:15
my altar, and to * incense, and to 1Sa 2:28
the altar to * incense to the 1Ki 13:1
hills who come here to * incense; 1Ki 13:2
Israel: you will * their forts, 2Ki 8:12
again use it to * his son or 2Ki 23:10
in them and to * them there upon 2Ki 23:16
So they didn't * his bones or 2Ki 23:18
to * up the offering on the altar. 1Ch 21:26
place where I can * incense and 2Ch 2:4
Literally, "a place to * incense 2Ch 2:6f
They * sacrifices to the Lord 2Ch 13:11
"It is not for you, Uzziah, to * 2Ch 26:17,18
it was not just to * incense to the 2Ch 28:3
to him and to * incense." 2Ch 29:11
and to * incense upon it alone? 2Ch 32:12
the flames shall * up all he has. Job 15:30
My bones * with fever. Job 30:30
My loins * with inflammation Ps 38:7
Will your jealousy * till every Ps 79:5
How long will your wrath * like Ps 89:46
will deal with them and * them. Is 5:24
He will * up all this Is 9:18
In a single night he will * those Is 10:17
her, I will * them up, unless these Is 27:4,5
and used to * beneath the pots. Is 27:11
Literally, "He will not * dimly Is 42:4f
your glory would * down the forests Is 64:2
When they * incense to him, he Is 66:3
else my anger will * you to a crisp Jer 4:4
raging fire and * up these people Jer 5:14
and there they * to death their Jer 7:31
to their idols and * incense before Jer 11:12
(your altars to * incense to Baal) Jer 11:13
of your enemies to * you up and Jer 11:16
of my anger that shall * forever. Jer 17:4
The people * incense to Jer 19:4
and there they * their sons in Jer 19:5
* up everything in its path." Jer 21:14
Does not my word * like fire? Jer 23:29
to the city and * down all these Jer 32:29
king of Babylon and he shall * it. Jer 34:2
and they will * incense in your Jer 34:5
it and capture this city and * it. Jer 34:22
They pled with the king not to * Jer 36:24,25
this city and * it to the ground. Jer 37:8
gods of Egypt and * the idols and Jer 43:12
of Heliopolis, and * down the Jer 43:13
We will * incense to the 'Queen Jer 44:17

(BURN Con't)
* up the palaces of Benhadad. Jer 49:27
will * everything around them. Jer 50:32
After your siege, * it there. Eze 5:2
even so, they * but poorly! Eze 15:4
They will * your homes, Eze 16:40,41
* out the wickedness within you. Eze 22:15
and daughters and * their homes. Eze 23:47
empty the pot and * the bones. Eze 24:10
and let it * you to ashes upon Eze 28:18
sin offering and * it at the Eze 43:21
and * sweet incense before him. Dan 2:46
they go up into the hills to * Hos 4:13
palaces and * those fortresses. Hos 8:14
Tyre, and it will * down all his Amo 1:10
* down all the forts of Bozrah." Amo 1:12
* down their forts and palaces; Amo 1:14
with fire, and * down all Amo 2:5
nets and * incense before them! Hab 1:16
they will * up all the Zec 12:6
the thistles and * them, and put Mt 13:30
them into the furnace and * them. Mt 13:42
and * incense before the Lord. Lk 1:8,9
from grain, and * up the chaff with Lk 3:17
down from heaven to * them up?" Lk 9:54
It is better to marry than to * 1Co 7:9
Lord Jesus will * up with the 2Th 2:8
Things will be said that will * 2Ti 2:17

BURNED
"If the field is being * off and Ex 22:6
to the veil, and * upon it the Ex 40:27
altar—and * there on a wood fire. Lev 4:11,12
be removed and * upon the altar. Lev 4:19
All the fat shall be * upon the Lev 4:26
be entirely * up before the Lord; Lev 6:22,23
That carcass must be entirely * Lev 6:30
until the third day shall be *. Lev 7:17,18
unclean shall not be eaten, but *; Lev 7:19
fat, and * them all on the altar. Lev 8:15,16
hide and dung, was * outside the Lev 8:17
Next he quartered the ram and * Lev 8:20
with water, and * them upon the Lev 8:21
back from them and * it upon the Lev 8:28
of the meat and bread must be *." Lev 8:32
Then he * upon the altar the Lev 9:10
Moses, but he * the meat and hide Lev 9:11
and he * each part upon the altar. Lev 9:13
and Aaron * it upon the altar; Lev 9:20
when the fat was *, and they shall Lev 10:15
and discovered that it had been *! Lev 10:16
"If a man is * in some way, and Lev 13:24
some way, and the * place becomes Lev 13:24
and shall be *, for the article is Lev 13:55
the camp and *, including the hides Lev 16:27
until the third day must be *. Lev 19:6
All three shall be * alive to Lev 20:14
well as her own, shall be * alive. Lev 21:9
because the fire from the Lord * Num 11:3
from Jehovah and * up the 250 men Num 16:35
fat shall be * as a fire offering; Num 18:17
villages of Midian were then *. Num 31:9,10,11
and the mountain * with fire; Deu 4:11
you had made—and * it and ground it Deu 9:21
his child to be * to death as a Deu 18:10
alkali and salt, a * over Deu 29:23
Then the Israelis * the city and Jos 6:24
the Lord shall be * with fire, Jos 7:15
them to death and * their bodies, Jos 7:25
the horses and * all the chariots. Jos 11:9
was killed and the city was *. Jos 11:11
and her father and * them alive. Ju 15:6
and * the city to the ground. Ju 18:27
and cattle—and * down every city Ju 20:48
first be *," [as the law requires 1Sa 2:16
the city and * it to the ground, 1Sa 30:1
land of Caleb, and had * Ziklag." 1Sa 30:14
And * up all before him, 2Sa 22:9
They shall be *." 2Sa 23:7
*, killing the Israeli population; 1Ki 9:16
And he also * incense upon it. 1Ki 9:25
at Bethel, and * incense to them. 1Ki 12:32,33
and men's bones shall be * upon 1Ki 13:2
he cut down and * at Kidron Brook. 1Ki 15:13
the palace and * it over him and 1Ki 16:18
from heaven and * up the young 1Ki 18:38
sacrificed and * incense there. 1Ki 22:43
And again the fire from God * 2Ki 1:12
for the worship of Baal, and * it. 2Ki 10:26
sacrificed and * incense there. 2Ki 12:3
sacrificed and * incense there. 2Ki 14:4
people sacrificed and * incense. 2Ki 15:4
people sacrificed and * incense. 2Ki 15:34,35
He also sacrificed and * incense 2Ki 16:4
and they had * incense to the 2Ki 17:11
They even * their own sons and 2Ki 17:17
from Sephar even * their own 2Ki 17:31
and have * their idol-gods. 2Ki 19:18
The king had it all * in the 2Ki 23:4
for they had * incense in the 2Ki 23:5
there he * it and beat it to dust 2Ki 23:6
where they had * incense, even 2Ki 23:8
* the shameful idol of Asherah. 2Ki 23:15
own altars, and he * human bones 2Ki 23:20
He * down the Temple, the palace, 2Ki 25:9
but David ordered them *. 1Ch 14:12
heaven and * up the sacrifices! 2Ch 7:1
crushed and * it at Kidron Brook. 2Ch 15:16
them, and * incense to them! 2Ch 25:14
Yes, he sacrificed and * incense 2Ch 28:4
Then he * the bones of the 2Ch 34:5
Then his army * the Temple and 2Ch 36:19
of Jerusalem and * all the palaces 2Ch 36:19
torn down, and the gates are *." Neh 1:3
and the gates have been * down." Neh 2:3
see the broken walls and * gates. Neh 2:13
lies in ruins and its gates are *. Neh 2:17
from heaven and * up your sheep and Job 1:16
* before you on the altar. Ps 51:16
the fire of his wrath * against Ps 78:21
For we are chopped and * by our Ps 80:16
That is why Jehovah's anger * Ps 106:40
arrows and * with glowing coals. Ps 120:4
against his chest and not be *? Pro 6:27
your cities are *; Is 1:7
all such will be *. Is 9:5
Yes, let them be * up by the fire Is 26:11
Your armies will be * to lime, Is 33:12
Yet, though set on fire and *, Is 42:25
you will not be * up—the flames Is 43:2
of wood! I've * it for heat and Is 44:19
praised you is * down, and all the Is 64:11
for they also * incense on the Is 65:7
cities in ruins, * and desolate. Jer 2:15
incense has been * upon the roofs Jer 19:13
the king of Babylon * alive!" Jer 29:22
After the king had * the scroll, Jer 36:27
Lord says, You * the scroll because Jer 36:29
live and the city will not be *. Jer 38:17
and this city will be *." Jer 38:23
Meanwhile the army * Jerusalem, Jer 39:8
their wives had * incense to idols Jer 44:15
because you have * incense and Jer 44:23
the neighboring towns shall be *. Jer 49:2
The invaders have * the houses Jer 51:30
and her high gates shall be *; Jer 51:58
in Jerusalem; and * the Temple and Jer 52:13
that * it down to its foundations. Lam 4:11
*, and the idol altars abandoned. Eze 6:4-7
before being * and certainly Eze 15:5,6
little sons to be * to ashes as you Eze 20:31
and everything left will be *. Eze 23:25
handed over to be * because of its Dan 7:11
For all the incense that she * to Hos 1:13
pastures and * up all the trees. Joe 1:19
it had * up the waters and was Amo 7:4
of worshipers, will all be *. Mic 1:7
the enemy and set on fire and *. Nah 3:13
set on fire and * to the ground. Zec 9:4
watch as the dross is * away. Mal 3:3
The proud and wicked will be * up Mal 4:1
They will be chopped and *. Mt 3:10
are separated and *, so shall it be Mt 13:40
the murderers and * their city. Mt 22:7
when the incense was being *. Lk 1:10
a pile with all the others and *. Jn 15:6
and * them at a public bonfire. Act 19:18,19
with women, * with lust for each Rom 1:27
and if I were * alive for preaching 1Co 13:3
animals were * outside the city. Heb 13:11
and everything on it will be * up. 2Pe 3:10
out, roots and all, to be *. Jud 1:12
were *, and all the green grass. Rev 8:7
Everyone was * by this blast of Rev 16:9

BURNER
down the incense * he was holding. 2Ch 26:19

BURNING
you here in this * bush and that he Ex 3:16
"THEN MAKE A small altar for * Ex 30:1
night, with the altar fire kept *. Lev 6:9
must be kept *—it must not go out. Lev 6:12
The fire must be kept * upon the Lev 6:13
a handful and * it upon the altar Lev 9:17
to the Lord by * it on the Lev 10:12
person doing the * shall wash his Lev 16:28
to Molech, * them upon his altar; Lev 18:21
and with tuberculosis and * fever; Lev 26:16
was known as "The Place of *," Num 11:3
He must also scatter the * Num 16:36,37
to the Lord by * upon the altar. Num 18:9
and throw them into the * pile. Num 19:6
"I came down from the * Deu 9:15
* fever, and fatal disease. Deu 32:24
In the * bush. Deu 33:16
the Philistines, * the grain to the Ju 15:5
before the rite of * the fat on the 1Sa 2:15
wives to use for * incense and 1Ki 11:8
to worship it by * incense to it; 2Ki 18:4
made a very great * of incense for 2Ch 16:13,14
* incense upon the altar. 2Ch 26:16
and scorch them with his * wind. Ps 11:6
breaking and * every weapon. Ps 46:9
the entire country * down the Ps 74:8
them from the * sun, and gave them Ps 105:39
for me. Let * coals fall down upon Ps 140:10
you will disappear like * straw; Is 1:31
pair of tongs picked out a * coal. Is 6:6
smoke billowing up from their *. Is 9:18
the flames of the * city reflect Is 13:8
be filled with * pitch, and the Is 34:9
nor quench the dimly * flame. Is 42:3
as dried grass * in the fire. Is 47:14
many gardens and * incense on the Is 65:3
At that time he will send a * Jer 4:11,12
There is no use now in * sweet Jer 6:20
is right before my * fury flashes Jer 21:12
brazier in which a fire was *." Jer 36:22f
here in Egypt, * incense to them, Jer 44:8
But ever since we quit * incense Jer 44:18
the people were * incense to idols Jer 44:21
false gods and * incense to idols. Jer 48:35
the fortifications are * and the Jer 51:32
Each of them held a censer of * Eze 8:11
and take some * coals from between Eze 10:6
they bore to me, * them as Eze 23:37
* their children on idol altars. Eze 36:12
is erected for the * of offerings Eze 43:18
to Baal and * incense to idols. Hos 11:2
they are like a * stick pulled Zec 3:2
a * match among the sheaves; Zec 12:6
is coming, * like a furnace. Mal 4:1
from the grain, * the chaff with Mt 3:12
Exodus about Moses and the * bush? Mk 12:26
to him in the * bush, he speaks of Lk 20:37,38
ready for condemnation and * off. Heb 6:8
to be a huge * mountain was thrown Rev 8:8,9
with fire and * sulphur in the Rev 14:10
The smoke from her * ascends Rev 19:3
be thrown into the Lake of Fire * Rev 20:10

BURNISHED
All these items were made of * 1Ki 7:41-46
feet, and shone like * brass. Eze 1:7
His feet gleamed like * bronze, Rev 1:15

BURNS
And the one who * the animal Num 19:8
That * to the depths of the Deu 32:22
His fury * against me; Job 19:11
* hot within me. Ps 69:9
Fire goes forth before him and * Ps 97:3
My stomach constricts and * with Is 21:3
For the flame of God * brightly Is 31:9
Part of the tree he * to roast Is 44:16
for my anger * like fire, and it Jer 15:14
is like fire that * in my bones, Jer 20:9
heaven that * within my bones; Lam 1:13
enemy attacks. God * across the Lam 2:3
My fury * against you. Hos 8:5
"My anger * against your Zec 10:3
But if the house he has built * 1Co 3:15
Lake of Fire that * with sulphur. Rev 19:20
Lake that * with fire and sulphur. Rev 21:8

BURNT
him there as a * offering upon one Gen 22:2
Abraham placed the wood for the * Gen 22:6
son, as a * offering on the altar. Gen 22:13
* offerings to Jehovah our God. Ex 10:25
Literally, "a * offering and Ex 18:12f
to me—your * offerings and peace Ex 20:24
to sacrifice the * offerings and Ex 24:5
it is a * offering to the Lord, Ex 29:18
as a fragrant * offering to him. Ex 29:25
a fragrant * offering to the Lord. Ex 29:41
Offer no unauthorized incense, * Ex 30:9
altar, the * offering altar with Ex 30:28
the altar of incense; the * Ex 31:9
and began offering * offerings and Ex 32:6
The altar for the * offerings; Ex 35:10-19
the altar for * offerings in front Ex 40:6
upon the altar of * offering and Ex 40:10
altar for the * offerings near the Ex 40:29
offered upon it a * offering and a Ex 40:29
an ox given as a * offering, use Lev 1:2,3
be an acceptable * offering with Lev 1:9
"If the animal used as a * Lev 1:10
to the Lord; for * offerings give Lev 1:13
use a bird as his * offering, he Lev 1:14
as a holy * offering to the Lord. Lev 2:3
as a holy * offering to the Lord. Lev 2:10
in * offerings to the Lord. Lev 2:11
time, but not as * offerings. Lev 2:12
as a * offering to the Lord. Lev 3:9,10,11
the altar, as a * offering to the Lev 3:14
gall bladder. This * offering is Lev 3:15,16
of the altar for * offerings, at Lev 4:7
on the altar of * offering, just as Lev 4:10
at the base of the * offering Lev 4:18
place where the * offerings are Lev 4:24
of the altar of * offerings, and Lev 4:25
the animals for * offerings are Lev 4:29
the horns of the * offering altar. Lev 4:30
place where the * offerings are Lev 4:33
the horns of the * offering altar, Lev 4:34
and the other his * offering. Lev 5:7
second bird as a * offering, Lev 5:10

BURNT Con't)	
concerning the * offering:	Lev 6:9
"The * offering shall be left	Lev 6:9
the ashes of the * offering and put	Lev 6:10
and lay the daily * offering on it,	Lev 6:12
of the * offerings made to me.	Lev 6:17
where the * offerings are killed.	Lev 6:25
place where the * offering	Lev 7:2
(When the offering is a *	Lev 7:8
It is to be set apart from the *	Lev 7:35
concerning the * offering, grain	Lev 7:37
Lord the ram for the * offering.	Lev 8:18
it was a * offering that pleased	Lev 8:21
altar, along with the * offering	Lev 8:28
Literally, "upon the *	Lev 8:28f
defect for a * offering, and to	Lev 9:2
defect, for their * offering.	Lev 9:3
offering and the * offering, making	Lev 9:7
Next he killed the * offering	Lev 9:12
upon the altar as a * offering.	Lev 9:14
Thus he sacrificed their *	Lev 9:16
* offering and fat on the altar;	Lev 9:24
sin offering and * offering before	Lev 10:19
yearling lamb as a * offering, and	Lev 12:6
One will be for a * offering and	Lev 12:8
sin offerings and * offerings are	Lev 14:13
shall kill the * offering, and	Lev 14:19
and the other for a * offering.	Lev 14:22
the other for a * offering, to be	Lev 14:31
and the other for a * offering;	Lev 15:15
the other for a * offering, and	Lev 15:30
and a ram for a * offering.	Lev 16:3
and a ram for their * offering.	Lev 16:5
sacrifice his own * offering and	Lev 16:24
offering and the * offering for the	Lev 16:24
you who offers a * offering or a	Lev 17:8,9
his child as a * offering to Molech	Lev 20:1
among you offers a * offering	Lev 22:17,18
it is not a fit * offering for	Lev 22:22
without defect as a * offering.	Lev 23:12
shall sacrifice as * offerings to	Lev 23:18
the other for a * offering, and	Num 6:11
and offer a * sacrifice to the	Num 6:14
sin offering and the * offering;	Num 6:16
male yearling lamb as * offerings;	Num 7:15
For the * offerings they brought:	Num 7:87
the other for a * offering, to make	Num 8:12
* offerings and peace offerings.	Num 10:10
the Lord with a * offering or any	Num 15:3,4
one young bull for a * offering.	Num 15:23,24
Literally, "ashes of the * sin	Num 19:17f
here by your * offerings and I will	Num 23:3,4
beside the * offerings with all the	Num 23:6
here by your * offering while I go	Num 23:15
standing beside their * offerings.	Num 23:17
each day as a regular * offering.	Num 28:3
This is the * offering ordained	Num 28:6
shall be an extra * offering to the	Num 28:11
offering. This * offering shall be	Num 28:13
This, then, will be the *	Num 28:14
* offering and its drink offering.	Num 28:15
You shall offer as * sacrifices	Num 28:19
A special * offering, very	Num 28:27
the regular daily * offerings and	Num 28:31
On that day you shall offer a *	Num 29:2
monthly * offering for that day,	Num 29:6
Literally, "* offerings of the	Num 29:6f
the regular daily * sacrifices,	Num 29:6
On that day you shall offer a *	Num 29:8
the regular daily * sacrifices,	Num 29:11
Your special * sacrifice that	Num 29:13
the regular daily * sacrifice with	Num 29:16
the regular daily * sacrifice, you	Num 29:19
the regular daily * sacrifices,	Num 29:22
Sacrifice a * offering—they are	Num 29:36
offerings, * sacrifices, grain	Num 29:39
to the Lord your * offerings and	Deu 12:6
bring all your * sacrifices and	Deu 12:11
"You are not to sacrifice your *	Deu 12:13
vows, and your * offerings need be	Deu 12:26,27
a * offering to Jehovah your God.	Deu 13:16
* offerings to the Lord your God.	Deu 27:5,6
And the altar of * offering.	Deu 33:10
Then the priests offered *	Jos 8:31
altar to sacrifice * offerings or	Jos 22:22,23
the Lord with our * offerings and	Jos 22:26,27
It is not for * offerings or	Jos 22:28
our own altar for * offerings,	Jos 22:29
Then sacrifice the ox as a *	Ju 6:26
as a * offering to the Lord!	Ju 11:30,31
have accepted our * offerings and	Ju 13:23
* sacrifices and peace offerings.	Ju 20:26
them to the Lord as a * offering.	1Sa 6:14
And many * offerings and	1Sa 6:15
Lord as a whole * offering and	1Sa 7:9
sacrificing the * offering, the	1Sa 7:10
* offerings and peace offerings.	1Sa 10:8
to sacrifice the * offering and the	1Sa 13:9
So I reluctantly offered the *	1Sa 13:12
pleasure in your * offerings and	1Sa 15:22
and he sacrificed * offerings and	2Sa 6:17
"Here are oxen for the *	2Sa 24:22
to the Lord my God * offerings that	2Sa 24:24
* offerings and peace offerings.	2Sa 24:25
one thousand * offerings!	1Ki 3:4
* offerings and peace offerings.	1Ki 3:15
the Temple for the * offerings,	1Ki 8:64
Solomon offered * offerings and	1Ki 9:25
him as a * offering upon the wall.	2Ki 3:27
again offer any * offerings or	2Ki 5:17
sacrifices and * offerings, Jehu	2Ki 10:24
sacrificing the * offering, Jehu	2Ki 10:25
offering him as a * sacrifice to	2Ki 16:3
The king presented a * offering	2Ki 16:13
the sacrifices of * offering, the	2Ki 16:15
the king's * offering and grain	2Ki 16:15
The blood from the * offerings	2Ki 16:15
a * offering on a heathen altar.	2Ki 21:6
sacrificing * offerings and	1Ch 6:49
Israel sacrificed * offerings and	1Ch 16:1
They sacrificed * offerings to	1Ch 16:40
"Take the oxen, too, for *	1Ch 21:23
I will not offer a * offering	1Ch 21:24
and sacrificed * offerings and	1Ch 21:26
altar for Israel's * offering!"	1Ch 22:1
sacrifices of * offerings, the	1Ch 23:31
lambs as * offerings to the Lord;	1Ch 29:21
it 1,000 * offerings to the Lord.	2Ch 1:5,6
and sacrifice * offerings each	2Ch 2:4
* offerings to the Lord.	2Ch 7:4,5
Then Solomon sacrificed *	2Ch 8:12
* offerings and sweet incense;	2Ch 13:11
to sacrifice the * offering to the	2Ch 23:18
* offerings were sacrificed	2Ch 24:14
* offerings have not been offered.	2Ch 29:7
of the altar of * offerings and of	2Ch 29:18
specified that the * offering and	2Ch 29:24
Then Hezekiah ordered the *	2Ch 29:27
to, brought * offerings too.	2Ch 29:31
70 young bulls for * offerings, 100	2Ch 29:32,33
to prepare the * offerings, so	2Ch 29:34
There was an abundance of *	2Ch 29:35
* offerings into the Temple.	2Ch 30:15
corps to offer the * offerings and	2Ch 31:2
and evening * offerings, as well as	2Ch 31:3
own children as * offerings in the	2Ch 33:6
to present its own * sacrifices to	2Ch 35:12
the fat of the * offerings.	2Ch 35:14
All the * offerings were	2Ch 35:16
and sacrificed * offerings upon	Ez 3:1
evening * offerings to the Lord;	Ez 3:3
sacrificing the * offerings	Ez 3:4
the * offerings to the Lord.	Ez 3:6
* offerings to the God of heaven;	Ez 6:9
party sacrificed * offerings to the	Ez 8:35
time of the evening * offering.	Ez 9:4
offerings and * offerings for the	Neh 10:33
the wood for the * offerings at the	Neh 10:34
a * offering for each of them.	Job 1:5
offer a * offering for yourselves;	Job 42:8
your sacrifices and * offerings.	Ps 20:3
from your people. * animals bring	Ps 40:6
housetops, * yellow by the sun.	Is 37:27
me the lambs for * offerings;	Is 43:23
come with their * offerings and	Jer 17:26
There they have * their children	Jer 32:35
Levites to offer * offerings and	Jer 33:18
I gave them. They * their firstborn	Eze 20:26
for the * offerings, sin offerings	Eze 40:39
salt upon them as a * offering.	Eze 43:24
on the altar the * offerings and	Eze 43:27
brought for * offerings and be	Eze 44:11
These are the meal offerings, *	Eze 45:15
offerings, * offerings, meal	Eze 45:17
prepare a * offering to the Lord.	Eze 45:23
the sin offering, * offering, meal	Eze 45:25
his * offering and peace offering.	Eze 46:2
"The * offering which the prince	Eze 46:4
offers an extra * offering or peace	Eze 46:12
as a * offering to the Lord.	Eze 46:13
I will not accept your *	Amo 5:22
* before you as offerings for sin.	Heb 10:6
BURNT-OFFERING	
THE * ALTAR was also constructed	Ex 38:1
BURNT-OFFERINGS	
your Temple with * to pay my vows.	Ps 66:13
BURNT-OUT	
and leave you, a * mountain.	Jer 51:25
BURROW	
and rock-badgers * in among the	Ps 104:18
Hedgehogs will * there;	Zep 2:14
BURST	
And he said, "Let the earth *	Gen 1:11,12
waters * forth upon the earth for	Gen 7:10,11,12
and * into tears, sobbing wildly.	Gen 21:16
he exclaimed. "He * through my	2Sa 5:20
Floods of evil * upon me;	2Sa 22:5
My words are ready to * out!	Job 32:19
Joy rises in my heart until I *	Ps 28:7
At your command the springs *	Ps 74:15
the mountains * into flame at his	Ps 104:32
streams to * from flinty rock.	Ps 114:8
like a mighty hailstorm he will *	Is 28:2
Springs will * forth in the	Is 35:6
OH, THAT YOU would * forth from	Is 64:1
* with indignation at their sins.	Jer 15:17,18
it shall * upon the heads of the	Jer 30:23
a fountain will * forth from the	Joe 3:18
They * into flames like straw.	Nah 1:10
Then springs * forth upon the	Hab 3:8,9
For the old skins would * with	Mt 9:17
They would *.	Mk 2:22
the road will * into cheers!"	Lk 19:40
* open, spilling out his bowels.	Act 1:18
BURSTING	
called Perez (meaning "* Out").	Gen 38:29
So he named the place "*."	2Sa 5:20
like water * through a dam!"	1Ch 14:11
within me grew to the * point.	Ps 39:2,3
him, light will come * in.	Ps 112:4
For you will soon be * at the	Is 54:3
BURSTS	
a bulging wall that * and falls;	Is 30:13
for the new wine * the old skins,	Lk 5:37
Great * of light flashed forth	Rev 4:3
will be killed by * of fire	Rev 11:5
BURY	
land, with no place to * my wife.	Gen 23:4
so that you can * her there."	Gen 23:5,6
Go and * your dead."	Gen 23:11
and then I will * my dead."	Gen 23:13
Go ahead and * your dead."	Gen 23:14,15
request: do not * me in Egypt.	Gen 47:29
and * me beside my ancestors."	Gen 47:30
You must * me with my fathers in	Gen 49:29,30
land of Canaan, to * him there.	Gen 50:5
permit me to go and * my father;	Gen 50:5
"Go and * your father, as you	Gen 50:6
You must * him the same day, for	Deu 21:23
there beside the altar and * him.	1Ki 2:31
city to mourn over it and * it.	1Ki 13:29
"When I die, * me in the grave	1Ki 13:31
mourn for him and * him, but he is	1Ki 14:13
Jezreel, and no one will * her.'	2Ki 9:10
"Someone go and * this cursed	2Ki 9:34
But when they went out to * her,	2Ki 9:35
No one is left even to * them.	Ps 79:3
so many slain to * that there won't	Jer 7:32
the mower, and no one will * them.	Jer 9:22
there shall be no one to * them.	Jer 14:16
No one shall mourn for them or *	Jer 16:4
gather up the bodies to * them;	Jer 25:33
as they watch you, * large rocks	Jer 43:9
people of Israel to * the bodies.	Eze 39:12
skeletons left and * them, so that	Eze 39:14
Valley of Gog's Army to * them.	Eze 39:15,16
out to * him with their might.	Dan 11:40
Memphis will * them.	Hos 9:6
only one left to * him, and when he	Amo 6:10
and temples, and I will * you!	Nah 1:14
Or, "Let me first go and * my	Mt 8:21f
me first to go and * my father,'	Lk 9:59f
them, and the hills to * them.	Lk 23:30
No one will be allowed to * them,	Rev 11:8,9
BURYING	
Egyptians who were * all their	Num 33:3,4
Once some men who were * a friend	2Ki 13:20,21
BUSH	
child beneath a * and went off and	Gen 21:15
a ram caught by its horns in a *.	Gen 22:13
to him as a flame of fire in a *.	Ex 3:2
When Moses saw that the * was on	Ex 3:2
in this burning * and that he said	Ex 3:16
In the burning *.	Deu 33:16
finally turned to the thorn *.	Ju 9:14
"And the thorn * replied, 'If	Ju 9:15
* and prayed that he might die.	1Ki 19:4
and slept beneath the broom *.	1Ki 19:5
in the hand is worth two in the *;	Ecc 6:9
about Moses and the burning *?	Mk 12:26
soon it grows into a tall *, and	Lk 13:19
him in the burning *, he speaks of	Lk 20:37,38
to him in a flame of fire in a *.	Act 7:30
BUSHEL	
is approximately a tenth of a *.	Ex 16:36
a tenth of a * of fine flour.	Lev 5:11
tenth of a * of fine flour, half to	Lev 6:19,20
of a fifth of a * of finely ground	Lev 23:13
* of fine flour containing yeast.	Lev 23:17
using a fifth of a * for each.	Lev 24:5-8
of a tenth of a * of barley meal	Num 5:15
bread from a * of flour.	Ju 6:19
had gleaned, it came to a whole *!	Ru 2:17
Then he tied up a * and a half of	Ru 3:15-18
and a * of flour and some wine.	1Sa 1:24
David, "Take this * of roasted	1Sa 17:17
to the prince: a * of wheat or	Eze 45:13
* for each bullock and ram;	Eze 45:24
oil—1½ gallons to go with each *.	Eze 45:24
offering of one * of flour to go	Eze 46:5
of olive oil for each * of flour.	Eze 46:5
the young bull, he must bring a *	Eze 46:7
With the ram, he is to bring one *	Eze 46:7

(BUSHEL Con't)
With each * he is to bring 1½ Eze 46:7
be one * with the young bull; Eze 46:11
young bull; one * with the ram; Eze 46:11
and 1½ gallons of oil with each * Eze 46:11
* of flour with half a gallon of Eze 46:14,15
He replied, "It is a * basket Zec 5:6
And they took the * basket and Zec 5:9

BUSHELS
that requires ten * of barley seed Lev 27:16
least anyone gathered was 100 *! Num 11:32
dressed sheep, two * of roasted 1Sa 25:18
palace were 195 * of fine flour, 1Ki 4:22
of fine flour, 390 * of meal, 10 1Ki 4:22
payment of 125,000 * of wheat for 1Ki 5:11
1,225 * of wheat; Ez 7:22
of juice! Ten * of seed will yield Is 5:10
scales, honest *, honest gallons. Eze 45:10
was about 220 litres, or 6½ *. Eze 45:11f
provide fourteen * of grain for the Eze 45:24
dollars and eight * of barley, and Hos 3:2
'A thousand * of wheat,' was the Lk 16:7
it with one for only 800 *!' Lk 16:7

BUSHES
animals among the *, huddling Job 30:7
The people hide in the * and flee Jer 4:29
thorn * or figs with thistles. Mt 7:16
on thorns, or grapes on bramble *. Lk 6:44
branches of hyssop * and scarlet Heb 9:19

BUSIEST
She calls from the * Pro 9:3

BUSILY
She finds wool and flax and * Pro 31:13

BUSINESS
went on about his *, indifferent to Gen 25:34
your * among us and become rich!" Gen 34:9,10
and all of his * affairs. Gen 39:4
"Interpreting dreams is God's * Gen 40:8
from the normal * of the week. Lev 23:3
"The king's * required such 1Sa 21:8
men: Eliakam, his * manager; 2Ki 18:18
of Hilkiah) the * manager, and 2Ki 18:37
I beg you, gentlemen, stop this * Neh 5:10
men who are minding their own *. Ps 35:20
man who conducts his * fairly. Ps 112:5
and to those minding their own *. Pro 9:15
demands fairness in every * deal. Pro 16:11
Develop your * first before Pro 24:27
argument that isn't any of your *. Pro 26:17
his family forever—so watch your * Pro 27:23,24
your own fun and * on that day, but Is 58:13
It is a shameful * that these men Jer 10:14
They take root and their * grows. Jer 12:2
Judah mourns; * has ground to a Jer 14:2
have made it their * to travel Jer 14:18
lives, his * will be gone, for God Eze 7:13
Though they do a big * as Hos 4:10
on about their *, one to his farm, Mt 22:5
was King Herod's * manager and was Lk 8:3
about their daily *—eating and Lk 17:28
Yes, it will be '* as usual' Lk 17:30
tax-collecting * (and, of course, a Lk 19:1
leaders and the * community Lk 19:47
will put them in charge of this *. Act 6:3
told Moses to mind his own *. Act 7:27
their *, returned to Antioch, Act 12:25
"Gentlemen, this * is our income. Act 19:25
talking about the * aspects of this Act 19:27
minding your own * and doing your 1Th 4:11
getting into other people's *. 1Ti 5:13
and open up a profitable *." Jas 4:13

BUSINESSES
her * will give their profits to Is 23:18
feasts; your * shall fail and all Jer 25:10

BUSINESSMEN
army officers, *, lawyers, Is 3:3
All your greedy *, all your loan Zep 1:11
with her, and * throughout the Rev 18:3
the brides. Her * were known around Rev 18:23

BUSY
But while I was * doing 1Ki 20:40
for they had been * from morning 2Ch 35:14
And all his * rushing ends in Ps 39:5,6
too * to heed their requests. Ps 102:17
Just as being too * gives you Ecc 5:1
What's the trouble in this *, Is 22:2
behind all their * activities. Jas 1:10,11

BUSYBODY
trouble or being a * and prying 1Pe 4:15

BUTCHER
told a servant to hurry and * it. Gen 18:7
If we * all our flocks and herds Num 11:22
they are ready to * those who do Ps 37:14
an ox going to the *, or as a stag Pro 7:22
Yes, I will * you, whether you Jer 34:18,19
they will * their sons and Eze 23:47
they will * your people, and your Eze 26:11
a flock being fattened for the *. Zec 11:4

BUTCHERED
you eat may be * anywhere, just as Deu 12:15
and herds may be * on your own Deu 12:20-23
Your oxen shall be * before your Deu 28:31
of battle and * the sheep, oxen, 1Sa 14:32
Then Saul * the Amalekites from 1Sa 15:7
with a tape, were *, and one-third 2Sa 8:2
When he arrived in Samaria he * 2Ki 10:17
them, but you have * them without 2Ch 28:9
see my people * and destroyed?" Est 8:6
He caused his people to be * Ps 78:62
The enemy has * the entire Ps 79:3
Those who don't run will be *. Is 13:15
Jehoiakim, who * him with a sword Jer 26:23
I am the Lord. You * my people when Eze 35:4,5
that Pilate had * some Jews from Lk 13:1

BUTCHERING
who aided him in * Gideon's seventy Ju 9:24
him and his aides, * great numbers 2Ch 18:2
tables where the * knives and other Eze 40:42

BUTT
belly with the * end of his spear. 2Sa 2:23
For these shepherds push and * Eze 34:21

BUTTED
The ram * everything out of its Dan 8:4

BUTTER
lentils, honey, *, and cheese. 2Sa 17:28,29
they will not be * and honey to Job 20:17
As the churning of cream yields * Pro 30:33

BUTTOCKS
* and sent them home half naked. 2Sa 10:4
at the middle to expose their *; 1Ch 19:4
and old, their * uncovered, to the Is 20:4

BUY
"No, let me * it from you. Gen 23:13
to Egypt to * grain from Joseph. Gen 41:56,57
Go down and * some for us before Gen 42:2
brothers went down to Egypt to * Gen 42:3
from many lands to * food, for the Gen 42:5
"We have come to * grain." Gen 42:7
"We have come to * food. Gen 42:10
again and * us a little food." Gen 43:2
trip to Egypt to * food, as we Gen 43:20
additional money to * more grain. Gen 43:22
'Go back again and * us a little Gen 44:25
Why should we die? * us and our Gen 47:19
The only land he didn't * was Gen 47:22
However, you must * back your Ex 13:13
"If you * Ex 21:2
then he may always * it back at a Lev 25:27
If anyone wants to * back this Lev 27:31
use the money to * an ox, a sheep, Deu 14:26
"If you * a Hebrew slave, Deu 15:12
no one will even want to * you." Deu 28:68
it so that you can * it if you Ru 4:4
replied, "All right, I'll * it." Ru 4:4
you * it." Ru 4:6
to Boaz, "You * it for yourself," Ru 4:8
a little lamb he had managed to *. 2Sa 12:3
And David replied, "To * your 2Sa 24:21
I will * it, for I don't want to 2Sa 24:24
won't be able to * any of it!" 2Ki 7:2
won't be able to * any of it!" 2Ki 7:19
merchants, and to * the other 2Ki 12:11,12
It was not used to * silver 2Ki 12:13,14
and to * lumber and stone." 2Ki 22:5,6
David said to Ornan, "Let me * 1Ch 21:22
"I will * it for the full price; 1Ch 21:24
holy day, we would refuse to * it. Neh 10:31
all the earth to * eternal life for Ps 49:8,9
You won't be able to * him off Pro 6:35
but the cake they * with such Pro 20:17
If a man tried to * it with Sol 8:7
You * up property so others have Is 5:8
of silver or gold will * them off. Is 13:17
The man too poor to * expensive Is 40:20
THE LORD SAID to me, Go and * a Jer 13:1
THE LORD SAID, * a clay jar and Jer 19:1
to ask you to * the farm he owns in Jer 32:6,7
have a chance to * before it is Jer 32:6,7
in the prison. "* my field in Jer 32:8
And yet you say to * the Jer 32:25
There will be nothing to * or Eze 7:12
Edom sends her traders to * your Eze 27:16
enough money to * the field—and get Mt 13:44
to the villages and * some food." Mt 14:15
Go instead to the shops and * Mt 25:9
immediately to * and sell with it Mt 25:16
finally decided to * a certain Mt 27:7
and farms and * themselves some Mk 6:35,36
to * food for all this crowd!" Mk 6:37
and * enough for this whole mob?" Lk 9:13
to * friendship through cheating? Lk 16:9
sell your clothes and * one! Lk 22:36
into the village to * some food. Jn 4:8
where can we * bread to feed all Jn 6:2-5
to * some. The second time they Act 7:12
offered money to * this power. Act 8:18
born as a Jew, to * freedom for us Gal 4:5
the ambition to * everything that 1Jn 2:16
"My advice to you is to * pure Rev 3:18
get a job or even * in any store Rev 13:17
is no one left to * their goods. Rev 18:11

BUYER
says the * as he haggles over Pro 20:14

BUYERS
and mistresses, * and sellers, Is 24:2

BUYING
and will be * and selling houses Jer 32:15
of the poor, * them for their debt Amo 8:6
and drinking, * and selling, Lk 17:28
food from anyone without * it; 2Th 3:8

BUYS
the priest * a slave with his own Lev 22:11
spins it. She * imported foods, Pro 31:14
out to inspect a field, and * it; Pro 31:16

BUZ
Their names were:Uz, the oldest,* Gen 22:20-23
The descendants of *, in the 1Ch 5:14
Dedan and Tema and *, and the Jer 25:23

BUZI
Ezekiel was a priest (the son of * Eze 1:1

BUZITE
of Barachel, the *, of the Clan of Job 32:2

BUZZARD
The osprey, the *, Deu 14:11-18

BYGONE
she remembers happy * days. Lam 1:7
in them. In * days he permitted Act 14:16

BYSTANDERS
Some of the * misunderstood and Mt 27:47

BYWORD
a proverb and a * among all the Deu 28:37
the word "Jew" a * of contempt Ps 44:14
make you a * of contempt forever. Jer 25:8,9

C
(*) The Jewish priests, though Heb 7:8

CABBON
Bozkath, Eglon, *, Lahmam, Jos 15:37-44

CABIN
The walls of your * are of Eze 27:6

CABINET
HERE IS A list of King Solomon's * 1Ki 4:1
and * officials alike—for seven Est 1:5

CAE
was at the port of * sarea from Act 18:22

CAESAR
said, "give it to * if it is his, Mt 22:21
ABOUT THIS TIME * Augustus, the Lk 2:1
Emperor Tiberius *, a message came Lk 3:1
a king is a rebel against *." Jn 19:12
"We have no king but *," the Jn 19:15
king, Jesus, instead of *." Act 17:7
I appeal to *." Act 25:10,11
You have appealed to *, and to Act 25:12
Caesar, and to * you shall go!" Act 25:12
But Paul appealed to *! Act 25:21
his case to *, and I have no Act 25:25
free if he hadn't appealed to *!" Act 26:32
will surely stand trial before *! Act 27:24
against them, to appeal to *. Act 28:19

CAESAR'S
"*," they replied. Mt 22:21
They replied, "*—the Roman Lk 20:24
this man, you are no friend of *. Jn 19:12
result of Claudius * order to Act 18:2,3
those who work in * palace. Php 4:22

CAESAREA
When Jesus came to * Philippi, he Mt 16:13
out to the villages of * Philippi. Mk 8:27
the way, as he traveled to *. Act 8:40
to * and then sent him to his home Act 9:30
IN * THERE lived a Roman army Act 10:1
They arrived in * the following Act 10:24
me with them to * arrived at the Act 11:11
Afterwards he left to live in * Act 12:19
While he was in *, a delegation Act 12:20
Then we went on to * and stayed Act 21:8
Some disciples from * Act 21:16
for * at nine o'clock tonight! Act 23:23,24
the cavalry to take him on to *. Act 23:32
When they arrived in *, they Act 23:33
Festus arrived in * to take over Act 25:1
since Paul was at * and he himself Act 25:4
he returned to * and the following Act 25:6

CAGE
They prodded him into a * and Eze 19:9

CAGES
my people free like birds from *. Eze 13:20

CAIAPHAS
the residence of * the High Priest, Mt 26:3
him to the home of * the High Mt 26:57
and Annas and * were High Lk 3:1
And one of them, *, who was High Jn 11:49
nation came from * in his position Jn 11:51
of *, the High Priest that year. Jn 18:13
Priest that year. * was the one Jn 18:14
bound, to * the High Priest. Jn 18:24
Jesus' trial before * ended in Jn 18:28
was there, and *, John, Alexander, Act 4:6

CAIN
* (meaning "I have created"). Gen 4:1
Abel became a shepherd, while * Gen 4:2
At harvest time * brought the Gen 4:3
This made * both dejected and Gen 4:5
One day * suggested to his Gen 4:8

CAIN Con't)
* attacked and killed his brother. Gen 4:8
But afterwards the Lord asked *, Gen 4:9
"How should I know?" * retorted. Gen 4:9
* replied to the Lord, "My Gen 4:13
on * as a warning not to kill him. Gen 4:15
to kill him. So * went out from Gen 4:16
so when * founded a city, he Gen 4:17
If anyone who kills * will be Gen 4:24
son for the one * killed." Gen 4:25
men" to the men of the line of *. Gen 6:1f
We are not to be like *, who 1Jn 3:12
Because * had been doing wrong 1Jn 3:12
For they follow the example of * Jud 1:11

CAIN'S
Abel's offering, but not *. Gen 4:5
Then * wife conceived and Gen 4:17
God more than * offering did. Heb 11:4

CAINAN
Shelah's father was *; Lk 3:23-38
Mahalaleel's father was *; Lk 3:23-38

CAINAN'S
Shelah's father was Cainan;* Lk 3:23-38
Mahalaleel's father was Cainan;* Lk 3:23-38

CAKE
loaf of bread, one * of shortening Ex 29:23
him part of a fig *, two clusters 1Sa 30:11,12
some wine, and a * of raisins. 2Sa 6:19
some wine, and a * of raisins. 1Ch 16:3
cheating, but the * they buy with Pro 20:17
as a half-baked *! Hos 7:8

CAKES
one hundred raisin *, and two 1Sa 25:18
*, and packed them onto donkeys. 1Sa 25:18
the flat * for grain offerings. 1Ch 9:31
Vast supplies of flour, fig *, 1Ch 12:40
dough and make * to offer to "The Jer 7:18
to her and making * for her with Jer 44:19
prepare it as you would barley *. Eze 4:12

CALAH
He built Nineveh, Rehoboth-Ir, *, Gen 10:11,12
*), the main city of the empire. Gen 10:11,12

CALAMITY
has brought * upon all of Israel.' Jos 7:15
"Why have you brought * upon us? Jos 7:25
The Lord will now bring * upon Jos 7:25
is called "The Valley of *." Jos 7:26
his back on me and sent such *!" Ru 1:21
In the day of my *, 2Sa 22:19
* will certainly fall upon us; 2Ki 7:9
are faced with any * such as war, 2Ch 20:9
He will laugh when * crushes the Job 9:23
* stands ready to pounce upon him. Job 18:12
day of *, and allowed to escape. Job 21:30-32
can to hasten my *, knowing full Job 30:13
hand or cries for help in his *. Job 30:24
God above sends * on those who do. Job 31:2,3
* will surely overtake the Ps 34:21
A rebellious son is a * to his Pro 19:13
but it is a * to evil-doers. Pro 21:15
But one * is enough to lay you Pro 24:15,16
repent, therefore * will come upon Is 30:13
am going to bring * down upon them Jer 11:11
the people crushed by terrible *. Jer 17:16
the day of great * for Egypt, a Jer 46:20,21
Hosts. * is coming fast to Moab. Jer 48:16
I will bring * upon them." Jer 49:32
* upon calamity will befall you; Eze 7:26,27
Calamity upon * will befall you; Eze 7:26,27
for time until the * befalls me Dan 2:8,9
crushed us with the * he prepared; Dan 9:14
the day of his * and looted him. Ob 1:13
that time of *, not a soul in all Mk 13:20
When we have trouble or *, when Rom 8:35

CALAMUS
nard and saffron, * and cinnamon, Sol 4:13,14
wrought iron, cassia and *, Eze 27:19

CALCOL
*, and Darda, the sons of Mahol; 1Ki 4:31
*, and Dara. 1Ch 2:6

CALDRON
Literally, "this city the * and Eze 11:3f
are the flesh and this is the *; Eze 11:7f

CALEB
house of * (1 Chronicles 2:18,19). Ex 17:10f
*, son of Jephunneh, from the Num 13:3-15
But * reassured the people as Num 13:30
son of Nun), and * (the son of Num 14:6
But my servant * is a different Num 14:24
Land. Only * (son of Jephunneh) and Num 14:30
only Joshua and * remained alive. Num 14:36,37,38
The only exceptions were * (son Num 26:64,65
The only exceptions were * (son Num 32:12
Judah * (son of Jephunneh Num 34:16-28
fathers, except * (the son of Deu 1:36
The Land Given to *: Jos 14:6
by *, came to Joshua in Gilgal. Jos 14:6
Kadesh-barnea?" * asked Joshua. Jos 14:6
The Land Given to *: Jos 15:13
territory to * (son of Jephunneh), Jos 15:13
Anak's father. * drove out the Jos 15:14
* said that he would give his Jos 15:16
donkey to speak to * about this. Jos 15:18,19
given to *, the son of Jephunneh; Jos 21:9-16
Debir?" * challenged them. Ju 1:12
her donkey to speak to * about it. Ju 1:14
So * gave her the upper and lower Ju 1:15
The city of Hebron was given to * Ju 1:20
had promised; so * drove out the Ju 1:20
a descendant of *, was uncouth, 1Sa 25:3
of *, and had burned Ziklag." 1Sa 30:14
* (the son of 1Ch 2:18
After Azubah's death, * married 1Ch 2:19
Hezron's death, * married 1Ch 2:24
* (Jerahmeel's brother) was Mesha; 1Ch 2:42
and of Gibe-a). * also had a 1Ch 2:48,49
Hur (who was the oldest son of * 1Ch 2:50
The sons of * (the son of 1Ch 4:15
were given to * the son of 1Ch 6:55,56,57

CALEB'S
Othni-el (son of Kenaz), * Jos 15:17
* nephew, Othni-el, son of his Ju 1:13
Lord, he gave them * nephew, Ju 3:9
* younger brother) to save them. Ju 3:9
* concubine Ephah bore him 1Ch 2:46
Another of * concubines, Maacah, 1Ch 2:48,49

CALENDAR
important month of the Jewish *. Ex 12:2
seventh month" of the Hebrew *. Lev 16:29,30f
first month" (of the Hebrew *). Lev 23:5f
seventh month" (of the Hebrew *). Lev 23:23,24f
seventh month" (of the Hebrew *). Lev 23:26,27f
seventh month" (of the Hebrew *). Lev 23:33,34f
seventh month" (of the Hebrew *). Lev 25:9f
second month" (of the Jewish *). Num 1:1f
second month" (of the Jewish *). Num 1:17,18,19f
of the Hebrew * corresponds Num 9:2,3f
seventh month" (of the Hebrew *). Num 29:1f
seventh month" (of the Hebrew *). Num 29:7f
seventh month" (of the Hebrew *). Num 29:12f
first month" (of the Hebrew *). Num 33:3,4f
fifth month" (of the Hebrew *). Num 33:38,39f
month" (of the Hebrew *). Deu 1:1f
first month of the Hebrew *. Deu 16:1f
first month" (of the Jewish *). Jos 4:19f
eighth month" of the Hebrew *. 1Ki 12:32,33f
seventh month" of the Hebrew *. Ez 3:6f
the first month" of the Hebrew *. Ez 6:19f
the first month" of the Hebrew *. Ez 8:31f
the ninth month" of the Hebrew *. Ez 10:9f
May it be blotted off the *, Job 3:6
but mark your * to think of me Job 14:13

CALF
and selected a fat * and told a Gen 18:7
tooled it into the form of a *. Ex 32:4
altar before the * and announced, Ex 32:5
They have molded themselves a *, Ex 32:8
Moses saw the * and the dancing, Ex 32:19
He took the * and melted it in Ex 32:20
this * came out Ex 32:24
they had worshiped Aaron's *. Ex 32:35
to take a bull * from the herd for Lev 9:2
also a yearling * and a yearling Lev 9:3
* as a sacrifice for his own sin; Lev 9:8
There below me I could see the * Deu 9:16
I took your sin—the * you had Deu 9:21
The woman had been fattening a * 1Sa 28:24
but I needed it all, as a * must Jer 31:18
you cut apart the * when you walked Jer 34:18,19
O Samaria, I reject this *—this Hos 8:5
When will you admit this * you Hos 8:6
And kill the * we have in the Lk 15:23
has killed the * we were fattening Lk 15:27
finest * we have on the place.' Lk 15:30
in worship of the golden *. 1Co 10:7

CALF-GOD
tremble lest their * idols at Hos 10:5
This idol—this * thing—will be Hos 10:6

CALF-IDOL
and peace offerings to the *; Ex 32:6
to the golden *, a prophet of the 1Ki 13:1
though they made a * and Neh 9:18
as Israel was of her * at Bethel. Jer 48:13
So they made a * and sacrificed Act 7:41

CALF-IDOLS
king had two gold * made and told 1Ki 12:28
One of these * was placed in 1Ki 12:29

CALKING
old craftsmen from Gebal do the *. Eze 27:9

CALL
man to see what he would * them; Gen 2:19,20
men first began to * themselves Gen 4:26
"Well," they said, "we'll * Gen 24:57
wonder they * him 'The Cheater.' Gen 27:36
to attack me. I * upon the God of Gen 31:53
"* together all the elders of Ex 3:16
Then Pharaoh sent an urgent * for Ex 10:16
Joshua to issue a * to arms to the Ex 17:9
his upper lip and * out as he goes, Lev 13:45
his sons shall * down my blessings Num 6:27
but the Moabites * them Emim. Deu 2:11
among us whenever we * upon him? Deu 4:7
black magic, or * on the evil Deu 18:10
* forth the spirits of the dead. Deu 18:11
"I * heaven and earth to witness Deu 30:19
"* them all together," the Lord Deu 31:12
speak to them, and * heaven and Deu 31:28
a trumpet as a * to arms and Ju 3:27
a trumpet as a * to arms, and the Ju 6:34
"Why didn't you * for us to help Ju 12:1
But she told them, "Don't * me Ru 1:20
call me Naomi. * me Mara," (Naomi Ru 1:20
why should you * me Naomi when Ru 1:21
"I didn't * you," Eli said. 1Sa 3:4,5
"No, I didn't * you, my son," 1Sa 3:6
the * to arms throughout Israel. 1Sa 13:3,4
Then * Jesse to the sacrifice 1Sa 16:3
How long will it be before you * 2Sa 2:26
I get back I will * a convention of 2Sa 3:21
I will * upon the Lord, 2Sa 22:4
"* Bath-sheba," David said. 1Ki 1:28
"* Zadok the priest," the king 1Ki 1:32
and prepare it and * to your god; 1Ki 18:25
In her letter she commanded: "* 1Ki 21:9
"* her back again," Elisha told 2Ki 4:15,16
summoned Gehazi. "* her!" 2Ki 4:36
the leprosy and * upon the name of 2Ki 5:11
son of Nimshi). * him into a 2Ki 9:2
and * together all his worshipers. 2Ki 10:18,19
turn to you and * themselves your 2Ch 6:24
Then the Lord told me to * Neh 7:5
awesome presence. * to me to Job 13:22
You would * and I would come, Job 14:15
into darkness, and * the grave my Job 17:13,14
* my servant, but he doesn't come; Job 19:16
now hear me as I * again. Ps 4:1
to me and answer when I * to him. Ps 4:3
when they * to him for help. Ps 9:12
God will never * them to account. Ps 10:13
replying when I * to you for aid. Ps 31:17
YOU * YOURSELF a hero, do you? Ps 52:1
But I will * upon the Lord to Ps 55:16
The very day I * for help, the Ps 56:9
I CRY TO the Lord; I * and call to Ps 77:1
I call and * to him. Ps 77:1
that will not * upon your name! Ps 79:6
I will * to you whenever trouble Ps 86:7
with him, to * down miracles of Ps 105:27
"Come, come to me," I * to Ps 119:48
He is close to all who * on him Ps 145:18
I will praise the Lord and * on Ps 145:21
I am too stupid even to * myself Pro 30:2
of the cliff. * to me and let me Sol 2:14
and Gomorrah, as I * you now. Is 1:10
And she shall * him Immanuel Is 7:14
"* him Maher-shalal-hash-baz. Is 8:3
Perish! * your councils of war, Is 8:9,10
Don't let people * you a traitor Is 8:12
for wisdom, and * upon mediums, Is 19:3
And then I will * my servant Is 22:20
Does a machine * its inventor Is 29:16
I * her! Is 30:7
the nations and * on my name, and I Is 41:25
trust in idols and * them gods will Is 42:17
I * (although they see and hear! Is 43:8
I will * that swift bird of prey Is 46:11
* out the demon hordes you've Is 47:12
all these years. * on them to help Is 47:12
* upon him now while he is near. Is 55:6
Is this what you * fasting? Is 58:5
Then, when you *, the Lord will Is 58:9
He can hear you when you *! Is 59:1
They will * Jerusalem "The City Is 60:14
will slay you and * his true Is 65:15
them before they even * to me. Is 65:24
in this. They * a carved-up wooden Jer 2:26,27
Why don't you * on these gods Jer 2:28
The Lord used to * you his green Jer 11:16
They have plotted to * for a mob Jer 12:6
He says from now on to * you 'The Jer 20:3
I will * for a wrecking crew to Jer 22:7
I will * for war against all the Jer 25:29
The Lord will not * off the Jer 30:24
of Ephraim will * out and say, Jer 31:6
or answer when I *, I will send Jer 35:17
"* together the men of Judah Jer 43:9
Rename Pharaoh Hophra and * him Jer 46:17
He has sent a messenger to * the Jer 49:14
For who is like me and who can * Jer 49:19
Send out a * for archers to come Jer 50:29
Who can * me to account? Jer 50:44
THEN HE THUNDERED, "* those to Eze 9:1
Six men appeared at his *, coming Eze 9:2
He will * his magicians to use Eze 21:21
"But now I snap my fingers and * Eze 22:13
Then he told me to * to the wind Eze 37:9
"And now, son of dust, * all the Eze 39:17
of Babylon. * for this man, Dan 5:12
And God said, "* him Lo-ammi Hos 1:9
RENAME your brother and sister. * Hos 1:11
the Lord, she will * me "My Hos 1:16
I will * for an accounting of Hos 8:13
Why don't you * on him for help? Hos 13:10

(CALL Con't)
never again will we * the idols Hos 14:3
Announce a fast; * a solemn Joe 1:14
Sound the trumpet in Zion! * a Joe 2:15
even the babies. * the bridegroom Joe 2:16
* together the Assyrian and Amo 3:9
and every road. * for the farmers Amo 5:16
with you, too; * for professional Amo 5:16
and she could * on them for Nah 3:9
O Lord, how long must I * for Hab 1:2
and save them, who * out to the Hab 2:19
sound the trumpet * and go out Zec 9:14
They will * upon my name and I Zec 13:9
"And all nations will * you Mal 3:12
If you * your friend an idiot, Mt 5:22
and streets to * attention to their Mt 6:2
"When you * me good you are Mt 19:17
the paymaster to * the men in and Mt 20:8
the Holy Spirit, * him 'Lord'?" Mt 22:43
Don't ever let anyone * you Mt 23:8
"Why do you * me good?" Mk 10:18
with this man you * your king?" Mk 15:12
forever shall * me blest of God. Lk 1:48
"So why do you * me 'Lord' when Lk 6:46
He would * down from his Lk 11:7
When you arrived you would * Lk 15:6
And then won't she * in her Lk 15:9
are saying when you * me 'good'?" Lk 18:19
come—the one they * Christ—and when Jn 4:25
And he told them, "A man they * Jn 9:11
God came, do you * it blasphemy Jn 10:34,35,36
who had seen Jesus * Lazarus back Jn 12:17
I was doing? You * me 'Master' and Jn 13:13
I no longer * you slaves, for a Jn 15:15
for men to * upon to save them." Act 4:12
time, I'll * for you again." Act 24:25
For God's gifts and his * can Rom 11:29
You are to * a meeting of the 1Co 5:3,4
I * upon this God to witness 2Co 1:23
We are honest, but they * us 2Co 6:8
God," as they * themselves, are 2Co 11:5
or agency. My * is from Jesus Gal 1:1
dogs, I * them—who say you must be Php 3:2
not ashamed to * us his brothers. Heb 2:11
He should * for the elders of the Jas 5:14
truths,' as they * them—depths of Rev 2:24,25

CALLED
darkness again. He * the light Gen 1:4,5
The second branch is * the Gen 2:13
and whatever he * them, that was Gen 2:19,20
The Lord God * to Adam, "Why Gen 3:9
and * them Man from the start. Gen 5:2
That is why the city was * Babel Gen 11:9
Then Pharaoh * Abram before him Gen 12:18
The king of Bela (later * Zoar). Gen 14:2
Enmishpat (later * Kadesh) and Gen 14:7
been captured, he * together the Gen 14:14
of Shaveh (later * King's Valley), Gen 14:17
and hastily * a meeting of all the Gen 20:8
Then the king * for Abraham. Gen 20:9,10
the Angel of God * to Hagar from Gen 21:17
on the well was * Beer-sheba Gen 21:31
God *. Gen 22:1
Then the Angel of God * again to Gen 22:15
So they * Rebekah. Gen 24:58
So they * him "Esau." Gen 25:25
So they * him Jacob (meaning Gen 25:26
Abimelech * for Isaac and Gen 26:9
So he * it, "The Well of Gen 26:21
So he * it, "The Well of Room Gen 26:22
and is * that to this day. Gen 26:33
he * for Esau his oldest son. Gen 27:1
the venison, she * her son Jacob Gen 27:6,7
SO ISAAC * for Jacob and blessed Gen 28:1
the Angel of God * to me and told Gen 31:11
So it was also * "The Gen 31:49
(That is why the place is * Gen 33:17
an altar and * it Gen 33:20
at Luz (also * Bethel), in Canaan. Gen 35:6
And ever after it was * "The Oak Gen 35:8
shall no longer be * Jacob Gen 35:10
but his father * him "Benjamin" Gen 35:18
to Ephrath (also * Bethlehem). Gen 35:19
Kiriath-arba (now * Hebron), where Gen 35:27
descendants of Esau (also * Edom): Gen 36:1
A few days later Israel * for Gen 37:13,14
And ever after he was * Perez Gen 38:29
might mean; he * for all the Gen 41:8
that is why I have * for you." Gen 41:15
Jacob!" he *. Gen 46:2
for him to die, he * for his son Gen 47:29
THEN JACOB * together all his sons Gen 49:1
girl rushed home and * her mother! Ex 2:8
Then God * out to him, Ex 3:3,4
Then Pharaoh * in his Ex 7:11
Then Pharaoh * for Moses and Ex 10:24
This observance shall be * the Ex 12:11
Then Moses * for all the elders Ex 12:21
was * Marah, meaning "bitter"). Ex 15:23
Then Moses and Aaron * a meeting Ex 16:6
So Aaron * them together and Ex 16:10
an altar there and * it Ex 17:15,16
mountain God * to him and said, Ex 19:2,3
the mountain and * together the Ex 19:7
Sinai and * Moses up to the top Ex 19:20
the seventh day he * to Moses Ex 24:16
with God," he * it) far outside Ex 33:7
But Moses * them over to him, and Ex 34:31
NOW MOSES * a meeting of all the Ex 35:1
who felt * to the work to begin. Ex 36:1
a lid * "the place of mercy"; Ex 37:6
as soon as it is * to his Lev 4:23
Then Moses * for Misha-el and Lev 10:4
So the name of that place was *, Num 11:34
she came was sometimes * Cush. Num 12:1f
was thereafter * Hormah (meaning Num 21:3
he shouted, "I * you to curse my Num 24:10
people shall be *, and no hard work Num 28:18
First-fruits (also * the Festival Num 28:26
them, and he * the area Nobah, Num 32:42
* 'Zamzummim' by the Ammonites. Deu 2:20
(The Sidonians * Mount Hermon Deu 3:9
while the Amorites * it 'Senir.' Deu 3:9
(Bashan is sometimes * 'The Land Deu 3:13
(also * the Sea of the Arabah). Deu 3:17
Hermon, as it is sometimes *; Deu 4:48
your God * the Festival of Weeks. Deu 16:10
Then Moses * for Joshua and said Deu 31:7
was * Gilgal (meaning, "to end" Jos 5:8,9
and is still * that today. Jos 5:8,9
is * "The Valley of Calamity." Jos 7:26
were * out to chase after them; Jos 8:16
Sidon and a place * the Salt Pits, Jos 11:8
Hebron had been * Kiriath-arba, Jos 14:15
city of Arba (also * Hebron), which Jos 15:13
Debir (formerly * Kiriath-sepher). Jos 15:15
south to Luz (also * Bethel) and Jos 18:13
(sometimes * Kiriath-jearim), one Jos 18:14
and they * the city "Dan," Jos 19:47,48
Refuge—it was also * Kiriath-arba Jos 21:9-16
JOSHUA NOW * together the troops Jos 22:1
was very old, he * for the leaders Jos 23:2
Hebron (formerly * Kiriath-arba), Ju 1:10
Debir (formerly * Kiriath-sepher). Ju 1:11
runs to a spot * The Rock, and Ju 1:36
so the name of that place was * Ju 2:5
* "The City of Palm Trees." Ju 3:13
She held court at a place now * Ju 4:5
From then on Gideon was * Ju 6:32
winepress of Zeeb, as it is now *; Ju 7:25
and Beth-millo * a meeting under Ju 9:6
still * "The Cities of Jair." Ju 10:4
(The place has been * "Jawbone Ju 15:16,17
(which is still * "The Camp of Ju 18:12
it had originally been * Laish. Ju 18:29
(also * Jebus) before dark. Ju 19:10
The chiefs of Israel now * for Ju 20:3
At lunch time Boaz * to her, Ru 2:14
"Say, come over here," he * to Ru 4:1
Then Boaz * for ten of the chief Ru 4:2
Ark, the Lord * out, "Samuel! 1Sa 3:4,5
Then the Lord * again, 1Sa 3:6
So now the Lord * the third 1Sa 3:8
And the Lord came and * as 1Sa 3:10
But Eli * him. 1Sa 3:16,17
So they * a conference of the 1Sa 5:8
Then the Philistines * for their 1Sa 6:2
(In those days prophets were * 1Sa 9:9,10,11
Samuel * up to him, "Get up; 1Sa 9:26,27
Samuel now * a convocation of all 1Sa 10:17
So Samuel * the tribal leaders 1Sa 10:20
So Samuel * to the Lord, and the 1Sa 12:18
Then Saul * back the army, and 1Sa 14:46
Afterwards Jonathan * David and 1Sa 19:7
been *, "The Rock of Escape!" 1Sa 23:28
Saul * back, "Is it really you, 1Sa 24:15
so I have * for you to ask you 1Sa 28:15
saw him coming, he * out to him, 2Sa 2:20
"Yes," he * back, "it is." 2Sa 2:20
of Zion, now * the City of David. 2Sa 5:7
of Zion (also * the City of David) 2Sa 5:9
(which it is still * to this day). 2Sa 6:8
And you would be * one of the 2Sa 13:13
for trial, Absalom * him over and 2Sa 15:2
on my name." He * it "Absalom's 2Sa 18:18
But a wise woman in the city * 2Sa 20:16
And he blew the trumpet and * his 2Sa 20:22
But I * upon the Lord in my 2Sa 22:7
in the palace was * the Hall of the 1Ki 7:2
Another room was * the Hall of 1Ki 7:6
THEN SOLOMON * a convocation at 1Ki 8:1
and * him aside to talk to him. 1Ki 11:29
men's counsel and * in the young 1Ki 12:8
at the door, he * out, "Come in, 1Ki 14:6
As she was going to get it, he * 1Ki 17:11
and they * to Baal all morning, 1Ki 18:26
Then Elijah * to the people, 1Ki 18:30
The following year he * up the 1Ki 20:26
by, the prophet * out to him, 1Ki 20:39
They * the meeting and put 1Ki 21:12
So King Ahab * to one of his 1Ki 22:9
For it is the Lord who has * us 2Ki 3:13
was puzzled. He * together his 2Ki 6:11
the city, a woman * to him, "Help, 2Ki 6:26-30
for the Lord has * down a famine on 2Ki 8:1
The watchman * out to the king 2Ki 9:18
Then Jehu * a meeting of all the 2Ki 10:17
So Joash * for Jehoiada and the 2Ki 12:7
So Hazael * off the attack. 2Ki 12:18
Jokthe-el, as it is * to this day. 2Ki 14:7
Also * Uzziah. 2Ki 15:1f
Also * Pul, in verse 19 above. 2Ki 15:29f
Also * Azariah. 2Ki 15:34,35f
Craftsman Valley (* that because 1Ch 4:14
bore a son whom he * Beriah 1Ch 7:23
Gera (also * Heglam), the father 1Ch 8:6,7
as it used to be *) where the 1Ch 11:4
of Zion, later * the City of David, 1Ch 11:5,6
Jerusalem is * the City of David. 1Ch 11:7
And it is still * that today. 1Ch 13:11
way, so he * together his army. 1Ch 14:8
Then David * for Zadok and 1Ch 15:11
and he * out to the Lord, who 1Ch 21:26
These units were * up for active 1Ch 27:1
So the king of Israel * one of 2Ch 18:8
Hazazon-tamar" (also * Engedi). 2Ch 20:2
stopped and * them to attention. 2Ch 20:20
Blessing, as it is * today, and how 2Ch 20:26
Also * "Jehoahaz." 2Ch 22:1f
So the king * for Jehoiada, the 2Ch 24:6
He * a meeting of all the people. 2Ch 24:20
Kelaiah (also * Kelita), Ez 10:23
the situation, I * together the Neh 4:14
Then I * a public trial to deal Neh 5:7
Then the Levite leaders * out to Neh 9:5
Then I * all the Levites back Neh 13:11
Hadassah (also * Esther), whose Est 2:7
her, and * for her by name. Est 2:12,13,14
Haman * in the king's secretaries Est 3:12
and the king has not * for me to Est 4:11
secretaries were * in—it was now Est 8:9,10
Shushan, he * for Queen Esther. Est 9:12
celebration is * "Purim," because Est 9:26
Are you * into his counsel room? Job 15:7,8
I am * a liar, even though I am Job 34:6
a man is * before God in judgment. Job 34:23
nations has been * to plot against Ps 2:2
I have * you all "gods" and Ps 82:6
He * for a famine on the land of Ps 105:16
When his case is * for judgment, Ps 109:7
I have * you so often but still Pro 1:24
* to him, but there was no reply. Sol 5:6
Then your city shall again be * Is 1:26
only let us be * by your name so Is 4:1
I have * those rejoicing in their Is 13:3
The Lord God of Hosts * you to Is 22:12
It will be * "The Land of Is 34:12
I have * you back from the ends Is 41:9
"I the Lord have * you to Is 42:6
I have * you by name; Is 43:1
the sea. I * forth the mighty army Is 43:17
my chosen. I * you by name when you Is 45:4
never again will you be * "The Is 47:5
I have * Cyrus; Is 48:15
The Lord * me before my birth. Is 49:1
From within the womb he * me by Is 49:1
Abraham was only one when I * him. Is 51:1
For the Lord has * you back from Is 54:6
my Temple shall be * "A House of Is 56:7
You shall be * priests of the Is 61:6
Never again shall you be * "The Is 62:4
And they shall be * "The Holy Is 62:12
Jerusalem shall be * "The Land of Is 62:12
nation that never * you "Lord"? Is 63:19
for when I *, you didn't answer; Is 65:12
feared, for when I * them, they Is 66:4
Shiloh—this Temple * by my name, Jer 7:13,14
goddess of love and war, was *. Jer 7:18f
They have built the altar * Jer 7:31
shall no longer be * "Topheth" or Jer 19:6
"Jehoiachin," as he is also *. Jer 28:4f
Now you are * "The Outcast" and Jer 30:17
Jehoiachin (also * Coniah and Jer 36:30f
Ebed-melech * down to Jeremiah, Jer 38:12
him why the king had * for him. Jer 38:27
The captain * for Jeremiah and Jer 40:2,3
So he * for Johanan and the Jer 42:8
It is accompanied by many kings * Jer 50:41
"Is this the city * 'Most Lam 2:15
You have deliberately * for this Lam 2:22
But I * upon your name, O Lord, Lam 3:55
names they have * me, and all they Lam 3:61
And the Lord * to the man with the Eze 9:3
as I heard them *, for each one had Eze 10:9-13
Then the nations * out their Eze 19:4
And so it is still * 'The Place Eze 20:29
when Israel * on you for aid Eze 29:6
from now you will be * to action. Eze 38:8
This was * "the lower Eze 40:18
court (which was * "the outer Eze 40:19
It was originally * Lebo-Hamath. Eze 47:15f
follows:Daniel was * Belteshazzar; Dan 1:7
Hananiah was * Shadrach; Dan 1:7

CALLED Con't)
Misha-el was * Meshach; Dan 1:7
Azariah was * Abednego. Dan 1:7
He immediately * in all his Dan 2:1
than usual, and * for some of the Dan 3:20
frightened me. I * in all the wise Dan 4:6
words, a voice * down from heaven, Dan 4:31
as the king * him—for his mind is Dan 5:12
lions' den, and * out in anguish, Dan 6:20
Daniel (also * Belteshazzar) had Dan 10:1
But the more I * to him, the Hos 11:2
He was * the most fruitful of all Hos 13:15
from the depths of death I *, and Jon 2:2
Let the mountains and hills be * Mic 6:1
In fact, I have * for a drought Hag 1:11
them from God. I * but they Zec 7:13
Jerusalem shall be * 'The Faithful Zec 8:3
And I took my staff * "Grace" Zec 11:10
their people are * 'Those Whom God Mal 1:4
and he shall be * "Emmanuel" Mt 1:23
He * a meeting of the Jewish Mt 2:4
"I have * my Son from Egypt." Mt 2:15
"He shall be * a Nazarene." Mt 2:23
* Peter, and Andrew—out in a boat Mt 4:18
Jesus * out, "Come along with me Mt 4:19
and he * to them to come too. Mt 4:21
shall be * the sons of God. Mt 5:9
JESUS * HIS twelve disciples to Mt 10:1
Simon (also * Peter), Mt 10:2,3,4
household, have been * 'Satan,' Mt 10:25
See Matthew 9:34, where they * him Mt 10:25f
Then the Pharisees * a meeting to Mt 12:14
Then Peter * to him: "Sir, if it Mt 14:28
Then Jesus * to the crowds and Mt 15:10
Then Jesus * his disciples to him Mt 15:32
Jesus * a small child over to him Mt 18:2
And the king * before him the Mt 18:32
But Jesus * them together and Mt 20:25
in the road and *, "What do you Mt 20:32,33
For many are *, but few are Mt 22:14
Since David * him 'Lord,' how Mt 22:45
and to be * 'Rabbi' and 'Master'! Mt 23:7
And don't be * 'Master,' for Mt 23:10
"But he * back, 'Go away! Mt 25:12
country, who * together his Mt 25:14
from his trip and * them to him to Mt 25:19
"Peter," he *, "couldn't you Mt 26:40
is still * "The Field of Blood." Mt 27:8
Literally, "Jesus who is * Mt 27:17f
and * out the entire contingent. Mt 27:27
Jewish leaders was *, and it was Mt 28:12,13
Jesus * out to them, "Come, Mk 1:17
their nets. He * them too, and Mk 1:20
Jesus * them "Sons of Thunder"), Mk 3:16-19
And he * his twelve disciples Mk 6:7
Then Jesus * to the crowd to come Mk 7:14
Jesus * his disciples to discuss Mk 8:1
Then he * his disciples and the Mk 8:34
He sat down and * them around him Mk 9:35
So Jesus * them to him and said, Mk 10:42
So they * the blind man. Mk 10:49
Since David * him his Lord, how Mk 12:37
He * his disciples to him and Mk 12:43,44
this "waste," as they * it. Mk 14:4,5
to an olive grove * the Garden of Mk 14:32
of the palace, * out the entire Mk 15:16,17
Jesus to a place * Golgotha. Mk 15:22
Then Jesus * out with a loud Mk 15:34
room in the Temple * "The Holy of Mk 15:38f
already dead so he * for the Roman Mk 15:44
and shall be * the Son of God. Lk 1:32
barren one,' they * her—became Lk 1:36
son, shall be * the prophet of the Lk 1:76
At daybreak he * together his Lk 6:13
Simon (he also * him Peter), Lk 6:14,15,16
and *, "Get up, little girl!" Lk 8:54
ONE DAY JESUS * together his Lk 9:1
a man in the crowd * out to him, Lk 9:38
The Jews * the Samaritans Lk 9:53f
woman in the crowd * out, "God Lk 11:27
Then someone * from the crowd, Lk 12:13
longer worthy of being * your son. Lk 15:19
not worthy of being * your son—' Lk 15:21
"So his employer * him in and Lk 16:2
Then Jesus * the children over to Lk 18:16,17
up at Zacchaeus and * him by name! Lk 19:5
province was * away to the distant Lk 19:12
Before he left he * together ten Lk 19:13
"Upon his return he * in the men Lk 19:15
you are mine and are * by my Name. Lk 21:17
great men) are * 'benefactors.' Lk 22:25f
Then Pilate * together the chief Lk 23:13
him at a place * "The Skull." Lk 23:32,33
And they * to him, "If you are Lk 23:37
you shall be * Peter, the rock!" Jn 1:42
did), he * the bridegroom over. Jn 2:9
They were terrified, but he * Jn 6:20
in the Temple, * out, "Yes, you Jn 7:28
blind, until they * in his parents Jn 9:18
So for the second time they * in Jn 9:24
* for Jesus to be brought to him. Jn 18:33
he * himself the Son of God." Jn 19:7
in a place that is * The Pavement, Jn 19:13f
He *, "Any fish, boys?" Jn 21:5
Simon (also * "The Zealot"), Act 1:14
(also * Barsabbas) and Matthias. Act 1:23
you who has been * by the Lord our Act 2:39
gate—the one * The Beautiful Act 3:2
So they * them back in, and Act 4:18
his advice, * in the apostles, had Act 5:40
So the Twelve * a meeting of all Act 6:2
voice of the Lord * out to him, 'I Act 7:31
Power of God which is * great." Act 8:9,10,11f
helped her up and * in the Act 9:41
gone, Cornelius * two of his Act 10:7
for him, and had * together his Act 10:24
were first * "Christians." Act 11:26
and Symeon (also * "The Black Act 13:1
So Paul * to him, "Stand up!" Act 14:10
Upon arrival they * together the Act 14:27
(also * Barsabbas) and Silas. Act 15:22
where they * a general meeting of Act 15:30
Trembling with fear, the jailer * Act 16:29
goddess Diana. He * a meeting of Act 19:25
for we are in danger of being * Act 19:40
Paul * one of the officers and Act 23:17
the prisoner, * me over and asked Act 23:18
Then the commander * two of his Act 23:23,24
When Tertullus was * forward, he Act 24:2
for the trial, I * the case the Act 25:17
and about someone * Jesus who died, Act 25:19
they * it) caught the ship and blew Act 27:14,15
but finally Paul * the crew Act 27:21
his arrival, he * together the Act 28:17
And having chosen us, he * us to Rom 8:30
be * "sons of the Living God." Rom 9:26
the eyes of those * to salvation, 1Co 1:24
work he was doing when God * him. 1Co 7:20
and if he has * you and you are 1Co 7:22
This might be * their 1Co 10:2
that they are being * to battle? 1Co 14:8
shouldn't even be * an apostle at 1Co 15:9
province in what is now * Turkey. Gal 1:1f
I was not * to be a missionary by Gal 1:1
me to be his, and * me—what Gal 1:15
Mount Sinai, by the way, is * Gal 4:24,25
has * you to freedom in Christ. Gal 5:8
the future he has * you to share. Eph 1:18
and that you were * godless and Eph 2:11
* to the same glorious future. Eph 4:4
For God has not * us to be 1Th 4:7
God, who * you to become his 1Th 5:24
Through us he * you to share in 2Th 2:14
God also * him "Lord" when he Heb 1:10
He has to be * by God for this Heb 5:4
this part was * the Holy Place. Heb 9:1
was a room * the Holy of Holies. Heb 9:3
the golden chest, * the ark of the Heb 9:4
statues of angels * the Heb 9:5
golden cover, * the mercy seat. Heb 9:5
not ashamed to be * their God, for Heb 11:16
was even * "the friend of God." Jas 2:23
to others how God * you out of the 1Pe 2:9
Are you * to preach? 1Pe 4:11
Are you * to help others? 1Pe 4:11
and being * by his wonderful name! 1Pe 4:16
those God has * and chosen, and 2Pe 1:10
he allows us to be * his 1Jn 3:1
who * himself the Son of Man, Rev 1:13
They were created and * into Rev 4:11
They * loudly to the Lord and Rev 6:10
The star was * "Bitterness" Rev 8:11
heaven * to me, "Don't do it. Rev 10:4
ancient serpent * the devil, or Rev 12:9
who was * "The Son of Man," Rev 14:14
the temple and * out to him, Rev 14:15
world near a place *, in Hebrew, Rev 16:16
* and chosen and faithful ones. Rev 17:14
across (the angel * out these Rev 21:17

CALLING
there to the Lord, * upon the Gen 21:33
after themselves, * it Havvoth-jair Deu 3:14
* it Samaria in honor of Shemer. 1Ki 16:24
of myself for * you a sinner, but Job 20:3
Oh, that you would hear him * you Ps 95:7
Someone from among you keeps *, Is 21:11
you keeps calling, * to me: Is 21:11
leads his sheep, * each by its Is 40:26
I am * the armies of the Jer 1:15
I looked forward to your * me Jer 3:19
up early and *, but you refused to Jer 7:13,14
a man's voice * from across the Dan 8:16
* to Egypt, flying to Assyria. Hos 7:11
against you, * for your blood, Mic 4:11
"When you call me good you are * Mt 19:17
*, 'Sir, open the door for us!' Mt 25:11
and thought he was * for Elijah. Mt 27:47
they said, "come on, he's * Mk 10:49
he was * for the prophet Elijah. Mk 15:34f
he was * for the prophet Elijah. Mk 15:35
* her over to him Jesus said, Lk 13:12
to Mary and, * her aside from the Jn 11:28
him in a vision, *, "Ananias!" Act 9:10
sins, * on the name of the Lord.' Act 22:16
and * to him, "Father, Father." Rom 8:15
for which God is * us up to heaven Php 3:14
when you hear him *, do not harden Heb 4:7
When a man takes an oath, he is * Heb 6:16
him, * on the Lord to heal him. Jas 5:14
then if men speak against you, * 1Pe 3:16
majestic voice * down from heaven, 2Pe 1:17,18
we are lying and * God a liar, for 1Jn 1:10
he is actually * God a liar, 1Jn 5:10
If anyone hears me * him and Rev 3:20
Then I heard another voice * from Rev 18:4

CALLOUS
will be utterly * toward his own Deu 28:54

CALLS
blood * to me from the ground. Gen 4:10
So when Pharaoh * for you and Gen 46:33
again, and if he * again, say, 1Sa 3:9
made for you—he * them your gods! 2Ch 13:8
an arrest, and * the court to Job 11:10
good man when he * to him for help, Ps 34:17
Literally, "deep * to deep at the Ps 42:7f
Though a man * himself happy all Ps 49:18
When he * on me I will answer; Ps 91:15
action. He * to the storm winds; Ps 107:25
He counts the stars and * them Ps 147:4
But then he * for warmer Ps 147:18
a hearing. She * out to the crowds Pro 1:21
she *. Pro 8:4,5
all to come. She * from the busiest Pro 9:3
how much more his friends! He * Pro 19:7
the one who * you by your name. Is 45:3
Yet no one * upon your name or Is 64:7
for he * them gods, when there is Jer 51:17
"Everyone who * upon the name of Joe 2:32
into night, who * forth the water Amo 5:8
on the earth. He * for the vapor to Amo 9:6
The Lord's voice * out to all Mic 6:9
Trumpet * and battle cries; Zep 1:16
has done * for the death penalty. Lk 23:15
and he * his own sheep by name Jn 10:3
Anyone who * upon the name of Rom 10:13
everywhere—whoever * upon the name 1Co 1:2
the world * foolish and silly. 1Co 1:21
If the Lord * you, and you are a 1Co 7:22
and "A person who * himself a 2Ti 2:19
woman Jezebel, who * herself a Rev 2:20
Here is a puzzle that * for Rev 13:18

CALM
And by his power the sea grows * Job 26:12
to Belshazzar, "* yourself, Your Dan 5:10
"don't be afraid! * yourself; Dan 10:19
"and it will become * again. Jon 1:12
the storm subsided and all was *. Mt 8:26
fell, and there was a great *! Mk 4:39
and waves subsided and all was *! Lk 8:24

CALMED
So they * down. Ju 8:2,3

CALMLY
afraid, but can * face his foes. Ps 112:8

CALMS
* the storm and stills the waves. Ps 107:29

CALNEH
and * in the land of Shinar. Gen 10:10
Go over to * and see what Amo 6:2

CALNO
"We will destroy * just as we Is 10:9

CALVE
Or, "makes the hinds to *." Ps 29:9f

CALVES
*, and lambs will all disappear. Deu 28:51
that have just had *—cows that 1Sa 6:7
* away from them in the barn. 1Sa 6:7
don't, [but return to their *, 1Sa 6:9
their * were shut up in the barn. 1Sa 6:10
*, and ate the raw, bloody meat. 1Sa 14:32
the altar to the * at Bethel, and 1Ki 12:32,33
made me furious with your gold *. 1Ki 14:9
destroy the golden * at Bethel and 2Ki 10:29
Jeroboam's gold * that had been the 2Ki 10:31
and made two * from molten gold. 2Ki 17:16
* which he placed on the hills. 2Ch 11:15
with those gold * you have with 2Ch 13:8
and skip before him like young *! Ps 29:5,6
these fat he-goats, rams and *. Ps 66:15
Lambs and * and kids will pasture Is 5:17
will be at peace. * and fat cattle Is 11:6
cubs and * will lie down Is 11:7
have become like frightened *. Jer 46:20,21
were cloven like *' feet, and shone Eze 1:7
they say—men kissing *! Hos 13:2
lambs and the choicest *. Amo 6:4
with offerings of yearling *?" Mic 6:6
joy like * let out to pasture. Mal 4:2
was not the blood of goats and *. Heb 9:12
took the blood of * and goats, Heb 9:19

CAME
plants and fruits they * from." Gen 1:11,12
The time * when the Lord God Gen 2:7
So the serpent * to the woman. Gen 3:1

(CAME Con't)

to the ground from which you *.	Gen 3:19
FINALLY THE DAY * when the Lord	Gen 7:1
600 years old when the flood *.	Gen 7:6
and reptiles. They * into the boat	Gen 7:8,9
days old, the rain * down in mighty	Gen 7:10,11,12
Two by two they *, male and	Gen 7:16
it began, the boat * to rest upon	Gen 8:3,4
From these three sons of Noah *	Gen 9:19
* the Philistines), and Caphtorim.	Gen 10:13,14
But when God * down to see the	Gen 11:5
Traveling through Canaan, they *	Gen 12:6
One of the men who escaped * and	Gen 14:13
the king of Sodom * out to meet	Gen 14:17
And when the vultures * down	Gen 15:11
THAT EVENING THE two angels * to	Gen 19:1
But that night God * to him in a	Gen 20:3
of his troops, * to Abraham and	Gen 21:22
"Well, this afternoon when I *	Gen 24:42
(From this * his nickname	Gen 25:30
Then the local shepherds * and	Gen 26:20
Isaac's servants * to tell him,	Gen 26:32
Finally the time * for him to	Gen 29:21
you had before I *, and your wealth	Gen 30:30
see them when they * to drink;	Gen 30:38
And the angels of God * to meet	Gen 32:1
Then the concubines * forward	Gen 33:6
Next * Leah with her children,	Gen 33:7
and Joseph * and made their bows.	Gen 33:7
flocks and herds I met as I *?"	Gen 33:8
as Jacob's sons * in from the	Gen 34:6,7
Literally, "* into the gate of	Gen 34:20f
So Jacob * at last to Isaac his	Gen 35:27
* by, his brothers pulled Joseph	Gen 37:28
was away when the traders * by)	Gen 37:29
at the time— she * and grabbed him	Gen 39:12
around the place * running in to	Gen 39:14,15
when her husband * home that night,	Gen 39:16
but the birds * and ate them."	Gen 40:17
Pharaoh's birthday * three days	Gen 40:20
sleek, fat cows * up out of the	Gen 41:2
Then seven other cows * up from	Gen 41:3
of clothes, * in before Pharaoh.	Gen 41:14
cows * up out of the river and	Gen 41:18
But then seven other cows * up	Gen 41:19
Then, out of the same stalk, *	Gen 41:23
seven years of plenty * to an end.	Gen 41:53
other lands who * to Egypt to buy	Gen 41:56,57
that his brothers *, and bowed low	Gen 42:6
So they * to their father	Gen 42:29
When Joseph * home they gave him	Gen 43:26
Then he washed his face and *	Gen 43:31
So they * closer.	Gen 45:4
possessions, and * to Beer-sheba,	Gen 46:1
of Canaan, and * to Egypt—Jacob and	Gen 46:6
* to Joseph crying again for food.	Gen 47:15
The next year they * again and	Gen 47:18
after this, word * to Joseph that	Gen 48:1
when I * from Paddan-aram, as we	Gen 48:7
Then his brothers * and fell down	Gen 50:18
a new king * to the throne of	Ex 1:8
daughters, * down to bathe in the	Ex 2:5
priest of Midian * to draw water	Ex 2:16
Moses then * to their aid and	Ex 2:17
palace, as they * out from their	Ex 5:20
The court officials now * to	Ex 10:7
And they * to Elim where there	Ex 15:27
then the leaders of the people *	Ex 16:22
But now the warriors of Amalek *	Ex 17:8
leaders of Israel * to meet Jethro,	Ex 18:12
they * to the base of Mt.	Ex 19:2,3
and a huge cloud * down upon the	Ex 19:16
So the Lord * down upon the top	Ex 19:20
When they * near the camp, Moses	Ex 32:19
this calf * out!"	Ex 32:24
And all the Levites *.	Ex 32:26
Moses didn't realize as he *	Ex 34:29
* and talked with him.	Ex 34:31
Afterwards, all the people * to	Ex 34:32
the veil until he * out again;	Ex 34:34
Both men and women *, all who	Ex 35:22
pounds, which * from the fifty-cent	Ex 38:25,26
When he * to the altar he	Lev 8:11
* and stood there before the Lord.	Lev 9:5
them and * down from the altar.	Lev 9:22
and when they * out again they	Lev 9:23
Then fire * from the Lord and	Lev 9:24
or Levite, but * into the	Num 3:38
The money collected * to a	Num 3:50
tribe of Zebulun, * with his	Num 7:24-29
On the fifth day * Shelumi-el,	Num 7:36-41
tribe of Manasseh, * the eighth day	Num 7:54-59
On the twelfth day * Ahira, son	Num 7:78-83
that night. They * to Moses and	Num 9:6,7
Next * the tribe of Issachar,	Num 10:15
Then * the flag of the camp of	Num 10:18
Next * the Kohathites carrying	Num 10:21
And the Lord * down in the Cloud	Num 11:25
she * was sometimes called Cush.	Num 12:1f
Then they * to what is now known	Num 13:23
lived in the hills * down and	Num 14:45
So they did. They * with their	Num 16:18
And Dathan and Abiram * out and	Num 16:27
Then fire * forth from Jehovah	Num 16:35
Moses and Aaron * and stood at	Num 16:43,44
Then the people * to Moses and	Num 21:7
That night God * to Balaam and	Num 22:9
They * to Balaam with this	Num 22:16,17
Then the Spirit of God * upon him,	Num 24:2
of Zelophehad * to the entrance of	Num 27:1
battalion leaders * to Moses and	Num 31:48,49
So they * to Moses and Eleazar	Num 32:2
Leaving Marah, they * to Elim,	Num 33:9
sons of Joseph) * to Moses and the	Num 36:1
into the hills and * to the Valley	Deu 1:24,25
who lived there * out against them,	Deu 1:44
as the Ammonites * in, and the	Deu 2:21
tribal leaders * to me and	Deu 5:23
"I * down from the burning	Deu 9:15
Then I * down and placed the	Deu 10:5
and water when you * out of Egypt;	Deu 23:4
the Egyptians who * with you from	Deu 23:8
did to you as you * from Egypt.	Deu 25:17
"When we * here, King Sihon of	Deu 29:7
King Og of Bashan * out against us	Deu 29:7
how as we left, we * safely through	Deu 29:16
So Moses and Joshua * and stood	Deu 31:14
"The Lord * to us at Mount	Deu 33:2
Then the two spies * down from	Jos 2:23
And as soon as the priests *	Jos 4:18
inside the city * out and began	Jos 8:22
Three days later the facts *	Jos 9:16
by Caleb, * to Joshua in Gilgal.	Jos 14:6
These women * to Eleazar the	Jos 17:4
total inheritance * to ten sections	Jos 17:5,6
Then the two tribes of Joseph *	Jos 17:14
inheritance * from what had earlier	Jos 19:9
city of Tyre and * to the	Jos 19:29
the tribe of Levi * to Shiloh to	Jos 21:1
to the Levites * to forty-eight.	Jos 21:41,42
the Lord had promised them * true.	Jos 21:45
So they * and presented	Jos 24:1
the Jordan River and * to Jericho.	Jos 24:11
God's answer *, "Judah.	Ju 1:2
Literally, "when she * to him."	Ju 1:14f
and the Israelites * to her to	Ju 4:5
When Barak * by looking for	Ju 4:22
They * from Ephraim and Benjamin,	Ju 5:13,14
nations * and destroyed their crops	Ju 6:3,4
Angel of the Lord * and sat beneath	Ju 6:11
Then the Spirit of the Lord *	Ju 6:34
and the men of Abiezer * to him.	Ju 6:34
* tumbling down into our camp.	Ju 7:12,13
of Jotham, Gideon's son, * true.	Ju 9:56,57
when the Israelis * from Egypt;	Ju 11:13
Spirit of the Lord * upon Jephthah	Ju 11:29
Spirit of the Lord * mightily upon	Ju 14:6
This was his riddle: "Food * out	Ju 14:14
Then the Spirit of the Lord *	Ju 14:19
So the Philistines * and got	Ju 15:6
of the Lord * upon Samson, and the	Ju 15:14
other relatives * down to get his	Ju 16:31
of his neighbors * chasing after	Ju 18:22
just as they * to Gibe-ah, a	Ju 19:14
Just then an old man * by on his	Ju 19:16
at Mizpah. They * from as far away	Ju 20:1
When the army of Benjamin * out	Ju 20:31
had set the ambush * out and joined	Ju 20:42
So they both * to Bethlehem and	Ru 1:19
of Moab who * back with Naomi.	Ru 2:6
gleaned, it * to a whole bushel!	Ru 2:17
Then Ruth * quietly and lifted	Ru 3:6,7
Naomi, who * back to us from Moab.	Ru 4:3
when they * to Shiloh to worship.	1Sa 2:13,14
it to him when she * with her	1Sa 2:19
* to Eli and gave him this	1Sa 2:27
And the Lord * and called as	1Sa 3:10
The cart * into the field of a	1Sa 6:14
SO THE MEN of Kiriath-jearim * and	1Sa 7:1
prophecies * true that day.	1Sa 10:9
the Spirit of God * upon him, and	1Sa 10:10
When a messenger * to Gibe-ah,	1Sa 11:4
Then the Spirit of God *	1Sa 11:6
and they * to him as one man.	1Sa 11:7
king of Ammon, you * to me and said	1Sa 12:12
when Israel * from Egypt.	1Sa 15:2
Israel when they * out of the land	1Sa 15:6
the city * trembling to meet him.	1Sa 16:4
and the Spirit of Jehovah * upon	1Sa 16:13
from Gath, * out of the Philistine	1Sa 17:4-7
Women * out from all the towns	1Sa 18:6
him when he * out in the morning.	1Sa 19:11
When the soldiers * to arrest	1Sa 19:14
But when they * to carry him	1Sa 19:16
the Spirit of God * upon them and	1Sa 19:20
the Spirit of God * upon Saul, and	1Sa 19:23
As soon as he was gone, David *	1Sa 20:41
that I * away without a weapon!"	1Sa 21:8
ONE DAY NEWS * to David that the	1Sa 23:1
on his way, David * out and shouted	1Sa 24:7,8
NOW THE MEN from Ziph * back to	1Sa 26:1
king when someone * to kill him?	1Sa 26:15
Then the leaders of Judah * to	2Sa 2:4
his body and * out his back.	2Sa 2:23
they * to the place where he lay.	2Sa 2:23
You know perfectly well that he *	2Sa 3:24,25
tribes of Israel * to David at	2Sa 5:1
(But as the procession * into the	2Sa 6:16
But Michal * out to meet him and	2Sa 6:20
when they * to help Hadadezer.	2Sa 8:5
and when she * he slept with her.	2Sa 11:4
"The enemy * out against us,"	2Sa 11:23
And when the king * to see him,	2Sa 13:6
if we all *, we would be too much	2Sa 13:25
Then Joab * to Absalom and	2Sa 14:31
Absalom, and he * and bowed low	2Sa 14:33
and when anyone * to bring a case	2Sa 15:2
And when anyone * to bow to him,	2Sa 15:5
* out of the village cursing them.	2Sa 16:5
During the battle Absalom * upon	2Sa 18:9
As the messenger * closer, the	2Sa 18:25
they * face to face with Amasa.	2Sa 20:8,9,10
But Abishai the son of Zeruiah *	2Sa 21:17
He bent the heavens down and * to	2Sa 22:10
They * upon me	2Sa 22:19
word of the Lord * to the prophet	2Sa 24:11
So Gad * to David and asked him,	2Sa 24:13
That day Gad * to David and said	2Sa 24:18
towards him, he * forward and fell	2Sa 24:20
Nathan * in and bowed low before	1Ki 1:22,23
So she * back in and stood before	1Ki 1:28
He * to bow low before the king;	1Ki 1:53
but when he * down to meet me at	1Ki 2:8
the son of Haggith * to see	1Ki 2:13
young prostitutes * to the king to	1Ki 3:16
So he * to work for King Solomon.	1Ki 7:14
and a great crowd * from one end of	1Ki 8:65
Hiram * from Tyre to see the	1Ki 9:11,12
I didn't believe it until I *,	1Ki 10:7
Great men from many lands * to	1Ki 10:24
Many of them * from nations where	1Ki 11:1
son of Nebat), who * from the city	1Ki 11:26
* for the coronation ceremony.	1Ki 12:1
to Judah by the road I * on."	1Ki 13:9
"Are you the prophet who * from	1Ki 13:14
home by the same road I * on."	1Ki 13:16,17
from the Lord * to the old man,	1Ki 13:20
a lion * out and killed him.	1Ki 13:24,25
Those who * by and saw the body	1Ki 13:24,25
Then the angel of the Lord *	1Ki 19:7
Then a prophet * to see King Ahab	1Ki 20:13
Then another message * to Elijah:	1Ki 21:28
bathed, dogs * and licked the	1Ki 22:38
"A man * up to us," they said,	2Ki 1:6
NOW THE TIME * for the Lord to	2Ki 2:1
of Bethel Seminary * out to meet	2Ki 2:3
Jericho Seminary * to Elisha and	2Ki 2:5
and two female bears * out of the	2Ki 2:24
message of the Lord * to Elisha:	2Ki 3:15
seminary students * to Elisha to	2Ki 4:1
When she *, he said to Gehazi,	2Ki 4:11,12
But when she * to Elisha at the	2Ki 4:27
And when she * in, he said,	2Ki 4:36
and * back with some wild gourds.	2Ki 4:39
ONE DAY THE seminary students * to	2Ki 6:1
And the report * back, "Elisha is	2Ki 6:13
Just as she * in, the king was	2Ki 8:4
(son of Jehoram) * to visit him.	2Ki 8:29
and they all * and filled the	2Ki 10:20,21
sixteen years. He * to the throne	2Ki 13:9,10
statement to Jehu * true, that	2Ki 15:12
(the son of Gadi) * to Samaria from	2Ki 15:14
This disaster * upon the nation	2Ki 17:7
out of the land when Israel * in.	2Ki 17:11
of the nations from which they *.	2Ki 17:33
back on the road by which you *.	2Ki 19:28
He shall return by the road he *	2Ki 19:33
of the prophet who * from Judah and	2Ki 23:17
city of Masrekah * to the throne.	1Ch 1:47
Israel, and from Judah * a Prince.	1Ch 5:2
And the Philistines * and lived	1Ch 10:7
Others * to David from Benjamin	1Ch 12:16
Then the Holy Spirit * upon them,	1Ch 12:18
All these men * in battle array	1Ch 12:38
which he gave * to 1,100,000 men of	1Ch 21:5
The total * to 38,000.	1Ch 23:3
* out of the Holy of Holies!	2Ch 5:11,12
fabled wisdom, she * to Jerusalem	2Ch 9:1
Kings from every nation * to	2Ch 9:23
ALL THE LEADERS of Israel * to	2Ch 10:1
the Lord * upon the residents.	2Ch 14:14
THEN THE SPIRIT of God * upon	2Ch 15:1
They all * to Jerusalem in June	2Ch 15:10
the prophet Hanani * to King Asa	2Ch 16:7
across the nation * to Jerusalem to	2Ch 20:4
Spirit of the Lord * upon one of	2Ch 20:14
the bodies and * away loaded with	2Ch 20:25
his intestines * out and he died in	2Ch 21:19
leaders of Judah * to King Joash	2Ch 24:17,18
So the wrath of God * down upon	2Ch 24:17,18
Then the Spirit of God * upon	2Ch 24:20
Just then a wild animal * by and	2Ch 25:18
turned to God and * to Jerusalem.	2Ch 30:11

CAME Con't)

When Hezekiah and his officials *	2Ch 31:7,8
Then at last he * to his senses	2Ch 33:12
through Jeremiah * true, that the	2Ch 36:21
returned to Judah * to Jerusalem	Ez 3:1
So Shesh-bazzar * and laid the	Ez 5:16
BUT THEN THE Jewish leaders * to	Ez 9:1
sin of his people * and sat with me	Ez 9:4
Jews named Hanani * to visit me	Neh 1:2
Then * Malchijah (son of Harim)	Neh 3:11
of Bani). Then * Hashabiah, the	Neh 3:17
Then * the priests from the	Neh 3:22
Then * the Tekoites, who	Neh 3:27
servant * with an open letter in	Neh 6:5,6
they * back to Jerusalem.	Neh 7:73
"You * down upon Mount Sinai and	Neh 9:13
officials who * to Jerusalem	Neh 11:3
the land * to Jerusalem to assist	Neh 12:27
The choir members also * to	Neh 12:28
they also * from Beth-gilgal and	Neh 12:29
last time they * on the Sabbath.	Neh 13:21
said not to. He * daily to the	Est 2:11
Then, as each girl's turn * for	Est 2:12,13,14
When Esther's maids and eunuchs *	Est 4:4
So the king and Haman * to	Est 5:5
and in them he * across the item	Est 6:1
So Haman * in and the king said	Est 6:6
SO THE KING and Haman * to	Est 7:1
And now once more Esther * before	Est 8:3
when the matter * before the king,	Est 9:24,25
* to present themselves before	Job 1:6
Satan, the Accuser, * with them.	Job 1:6
before God. "I * naked from my	Job 1:21
* again to present themselves	Job 2:1
in my ear. It * in a nighttime	Job 4:13
the dreadful silence * this voice:	Job 4:16
and wicked men who * to disaster	Job 21:28
for good to come. Evil * instead.	Job 30:26
Darkness *.	Job 30:26
He bent the heavens down and *	Ps 18:9
The nations * and served me.	Ps 18:43,44,45
I cried to him, he heard and *."	Ps 22:24
that * to destroy us have fled!"	Ps 68:11,12,13
But as for me, I * so close to	Ps 73:2
the ground. They * with their axes	Ps 74:5,6
the day of battle *, because they	Ps 78:9
the earth * to worship him.	Ps 102:21,22
*—how God tested his patience!	Ps 105:19
hordes of locusts *, and ate up	Ps 105:34
around and * running back to you.	Ps 119:59,60
command, and they * into being;	Ps 148:5
* and to which they must return.	Ecc 3:20
Step by step I * to this result	Ecc 7:27,28
* with his army and besieged it.	Ecc 9:14
These are the messages that * to	Is 1:1
However, when the news * to the	Is 7:2
This is the message that * to me	Is 14:28
they return. You * against them and	Is 26:14
king of Assyria, * to fight against	Is 36:1
You boast, 'I * with my mighty	Is 37:24
own land by the same road you *."	Is 37:29
by the road he * on, and will not	Is 37:34
Then Isaiah the prophet * to the	Is 39:3
Everything I prophesied * true,	Is 42:9
I spoke and they * into being.	Is 48:13
and Sarah, from whom you *.	Is 51:1
I looked but no one * to help	Is 63:5
So it was before when you *	Is 64:3
The first of these messages * to	Jer 1:1
Others * during the reign of	Jer 1:3
This message from the Lord * to	Jer 3:6
We expected peace, but no peace *;	Jer 8:15
Then the Lord's message * to me	Jer 13:3
THIS MESSAGE * to Jeremiah from	Jer 14:1
people of Judah * from the Lord to	Jer 25:1
THIS MESSAGE * to Jeremiah from	Jer 26:1
THIS MESSAGE * to Jeremiah from	Jer 27:1
THE FOLLOWING MESSAGE * to	Jer 32:1
Then this message from the Lord *	Jer 32:6,7
So Hanamel *, as the Lord had	Jer 32:8
Our fathers * and conquered it	Jer 32:23
Then this message * to Jeremiah:	Jer 32:26
Then this message * to Jeremiah	Jer 33:19
THIS IS THE message that * to	Jer 34:1
kingdoms he ruled, * and fought	Jer 34:1
This is the message that * to	Jer 34:8
People * from all over Judah to	Jer 36:9
army, though it * here to help you,	Jer 37:7
the city officials * to Jeremiah	Jer 38:27
and all his army * against	Jer 39:1
Babylonian army * in and sat in	Jer 39:3
to Babylon, they * to see Gedaliah	Jer 40:8
of the leaders who *: Ishmael (son	Jer 40:8
guerrilla leaders * to Mizpah to	Jer 40:13,14
great and small, * to Jeremiah and	Jer 42:1
against Elam * to Jeremiah in the	Jer 49:34
this message * to Jeremiah to give	Jer 51:59
king of Babylon, * with all his	Jer 52:4
Yes, you * at my despairing cry	Lam 3:57
* a voice from the crystal sky	Eze 1:25
AGAIN A MESSAGE * from the Lord:	Eze 6:1
THIS FURTHER MESSAGE * to me	Eze 7:1
Then the Spirit of the Lord *	Eze 11:5
Again a message * from the Lord:	Eze 11:14
AGAIN A MESSAGE * to me from the	Eze 12:1
The next morning this message *	Eze 12:8
Then this message * to me from	Eze 12:17
Again a message * to me from the	Eze 12:21
Then this message *:	Eze 12:26
THEN THIS MESSAGE * to me:	Eze 13:1
that * to me to give to them:	Eze 14:2
Then this message of the Lord *	Eze 14:12
THEN THIS MESSAGE * to me from	Eze 15:1
THEN AGAIN A message * to me from	Eze 16:1
"But I * by and saw you there,	Eze 16:6,7
to every man who * along.	Eze 16:15
to every man who * by, in an	Eze 16:25
THEN THIS MESSAGE * to me from	Eze 17:1
feathers * to Lebanon and plucked	Eze 17:3,4
eagle * along, this tree sent its	Eze 17:7
Then this message * to me from	Eze 17:11
* to Jerusalem and took away	Eze 17:12,13
THEN THE LORD'S message * to me	Eze 18:1
elders of Israel * to ask	Eze 20:1
Then this message * to me from	Eze 20:45
THEN THIS MESSAGE * to me from	Eze 21:1
Then again this message * to me	Eze 21:8
Then this message * to me.	Eze 21:18
NOW ANOTHER MESSAGE * from	Eze 22:1
Again the message of the Lord *	Eze 22:23
THE LORD'S MESSAGE * to me again,	Eze 23:1
And they * and committed	Eze 23:17
* into my Temple to worship!	Eze 23:39
From your apartment * the sound	Eze 23:42
message * to me from the Lord.	Eze 24:1
Again a message * to me from the	Eze 24:15
THEN THE LORD'S message * to me	Eze 25:1
ANOTHER MESSAGE * to me from	Eze 26:1
THEN THIS MESSAGE * to me from	Eze 27:1
Then this further message * to me	Eze 28:11
Then another message * to me from	Eze 28:20
message * to me from the Lord:	Eze 29:1
message * to me from the Lord:	Eze 29:17
captivity, this message * to me:	Eze 30:20
this message * to me from the	Eze 31:1
message * to me from the Lord:	Eze 32:1
another message * to me from the	Eze 32:17
ONCE AGAIN A message * to me from	Eze 33:1
Then this message * to me:	Eze 33:23
THEN THIS MESSAGE * to me from	Eze 34:1
AGAIN A MESSAGE * from the Lord.	Eze 35:1
Then this further word * to me	Eze 36:16
bones of each body * together and	Eze 37:7
Again a message from the Lord *	Eze 37:15
across it, he * to an inner wall	Eze 40:23
across it, he * to the inner wall	Eze 40:27
when he * to destroy the city.	Eze 43:3
And the glory of the Lord * into	Eze 43:4
chief executioner, * to kill them,	Dan 2:14
by supernatural means. It *	Dan 2:34
Then Nebuchadnezzar * as close as	Dan 3:26
but when they *—the magicians,	Dan 4:7
At last Daniel * in—the man I	Dan 4:8
My counselors and officers * back	Dan 4:36
But when they *, none of them	Dan 5:8
In the evening the men * again to	Dan 6:15
Then four huge animals * up out	Dan 7:3
little horn that * up afterward and	Dan 7:20
Ancient of Days * and opened his	Dan 7:22
And the closer he *, the angrier	Dan 8:7
When this vision * to me (Daniel	Dan 10:2
From his face * blinding flashes	Dan 10:5,6
the heavenly army, * to help me, so	Dan 10:13
The Assyrian invasion * about	Hos 4:19f
THIS MESSAGE * from the Lord to	Joe 1:1
This vision * to him at the time	Amo 1:2
* to Micah in the form of visions.	Mic 1:1
THIS IS THE message that * to the	Hab 1:1
weapons those who * out like a	Hab 3:14
later, * often to this Temple.	Hag 2:8,9f
this message * from the Lord	Hag 2:10
When you * to draw fifty gallons	Hag 2:16,17
Another message * to Haggai from	Hag 2:20
from the Lord * to Zechariah (son	Zec 1:7
ANOTHER MESSAGE * to me from	Zec 7:1
Then this message from the Lord *	Zec 7:8,9
That is why such great wrath *	Zec 7:12
AGAIN THE LORD'S message * to me:	Zec 8:1
Here is another message that * to	Zec 8:18
them until it * and stood over	Mt 2:9f
as soon as Jesus * up out of the	Mt 3:16
and angels * and cared for Jesus.	Mt 4:11
No, I * to fulfill them, and to	Mt 5:17
Jesus as he * down the hillside.	Mt 8:1
Roman army captain * and pled with	Mt 8:5,6
Suddenly a terrible storm * up,	Mt 8:24
And they * out of the men and	Mt 8:32
entire population * rushing out to	Mt 8:34
John the Baptist * to Jesus and	Mt 9:14
synagogue * and worshiped him.	Mt 9:18
internal bleeding * up behind him	Mt 9:20
the crowds that *, because their	Mt 9:36
"Don't imagine that I * to bring	Mt 10:34
some Pharisees, * to Jesus asking	Mt 12:38
for she * from a distant land to	Mt 12:42
will return to the man I * from.'	Mt 12:43,44,45
path, and the birds * and ate it.	Mt 13:4
His disciples * and asked him,	Mt 13:10
slept, his enemy * and sowed	Mt 13:25
"The farmer's men * and told	Mt 13:27
Then John's disciples * for his	Mt 14:12
* to tell Jesus what had happened.	Mt 14:12
So when Jesus * out of the	Mt 14:14
That evening the disciples * to	Mt 14:15
* to them, walking on the water!	Mt 14:25
Then the disciples * and told	Mt 15:12
was living there * to him,	Mt 15:22
But she * and worshiped him and	Mt 15:25
* to test Jesus' claim of being	Mt 16:1
When Jesus * to Caesarea	Mt 16:13
it, a bright cloud * over them, and	Mt 17:5
Jesus * over and touched them.	Mt 17:7
A man * and knelt before Jesus	Mt 17:14
tax collectors * to Peter and asked	Mt 17:24
ABOUT THAT TIME the disciples * to	Mt 18:1
* to save the lost.	Mt 18:11
Then Peter * to him and asked,	Mt 18:21
Some Pharisees * to interview	Mt 19:3
Someone * to Jesus with this	Mt 19:16
So when the men hired earlier *	Mt 20:10
When Jesus * to the place where	Mt 20:32,33
And now the blind and crippled *	Mt 21:14
Jewish leaders * up to him and	Mt 21:23
But when the king * in to meet	Mt 22:11
after death, * to him and asked,	Mt 22:23
his disciples * along and wanted to	Mt 24:1
the bridegroom *, and those who	Mt 25:10
"Next * the man who had received	Mt 25:22
"Then the man with the $1,000 *	Mt 25:24,25
While he was eating, a woman *	Mt 26:7
the disciples * to Jesus and asked,	Mt 26:17
Then he * to the disciples and	Mt 26:45
So now Judas * straight to Jesus	Mt 26:49
to the rear, and * to the courtyard	Mt 26:58
courtyard a girl * over and said to	Mt 26:69
standing there * over to him and	Mt 26:73
grounds they * across a man from	Mt 27:32
who had died * back to life again.	Mt 27:52
When evening *, a rich man from	Mt 27:57
everyone he * back to life!	Mt 27:64
for an angel of the Lord * down	Mt 28:2
Jesus' disciples * during the night	Mt 28:12,13
Then one day Jesus * from	Mk 1:9
The moment Jesus * up out of the	Mk 1:10
the angels * and cared for him.	Mk 1:12,13
them too, for that is why I *."	Mk 1:38
Once a leper * and knelt in	Mk 1:40
And people from everywhere * to	Mk 1:45
One day some people * to Jesus	Mk 2:18
* to see him for themselves.	Mk 3:7,8
was happening they * to try to take	Mk 3:21
and the birds * and picked it off	Mk 4:4
then the farmer * at once with his	Mk 4:29
Then the evil spirits * out of	Mk 5:13
name was Jairus, * and fell down	Mk 5:22
that is why she * up behind him	Mk 5:27
happened to her, * and fell at his	Mk 5:33
Herodias' chance finally *.	Mk 6:21
Then Herodias' daughter * in and	Mk 6:22,23
had happened, they * for his body	Mk 6:29
his disciples * to him and said,	Mk 6:35,36
They * back to report that there	Mk 6:38
Right away a woman * to him whose	Mk 7:25
Jesus and now she * and fell at his	Mk 7:25
and * to the region of Dalmanutha.	Mk 8:10
arrival they * to argue with him.	Mk 8:11
Jesus in awe as he * toward them,	Mk 9:15
Some Pharisees * and asked him,	Mk 10:2
on a trip, a man * running to him	Mk 10:17
sons of Zebedee, * over and spoke	Mk 10:35
Literally, "* up to him."	Mk 10:35f
aside, jumped up and * to Jesus.	Mk 10:50
of Jerusalem and * to the Mount of	Mk 11:1
* up to him demanding, "What's	Mk 11:27,28
Then a poor widow * and dropped	Mk 12:42
during supper a woman * in with a	Mk 14:3
And now they * to an olive grove	Mk 14:32
morning when Jesus * back to life,	Mk 16:9
When he finally * out, he	Lk 1:22
When you * in and greeted me,	Lk 1:44
* for the circumcision ceremony.	Lk 1:59
time * for her baby to be born;	Lk 2:6
When the time * for Mary's	Lk 2:22
She * along just as Simeon was	Lk 2:38
Caesar, a message * from God to	Lk 3:1
to the crowds that * for baptism:	Lk 3:7
their corruption—* to be baptized	Lk 3:12
When he * to the village of	Lk 4:16
"These Scriptures * true today!"	Lk 4:21
and the demons * out at his	Lk 4:41
and vast crowds * to hear him	Lk 5:15
Some men * carrying a paralyzed	Lk 5:18,19
When they * down the slopes of	Lk 6:17,18

(CAME Con't)
again from the time I first * in. Lk 7:45
and the birds * and ate it as it Lk 8:5
and brothers * to see him, they Lk 8:19
the city of Gadara * to meet him, a Lk 8:27
Soon a crowd * out to see for Lk 8:35
Jewish synagogue, * and fell down Lk 8:41
to be healed * up behind and Lk 8:43,44
of the disciples * and urged him to Lk 9:12
nearby, he * over and asked them, Lk 9:18
Now * an argument among them as Lk 9:46
His disciple John * to him and Lk 9:49
When word * back of what had Lk 9:54
on Moses' laws * to test Jesus' Lk 10:25
"By chance a Jewish priest * Lk 10:31
* along, and when he saw him, he Lk 10:33
him till they * to an inn, where he Lk 10:34
they * to a village where a woman Lk 10:38
She * to Jesus and said, "Sir, Lk 10:40
of his disciples * to him as he Lk 11:1
from which you *, and the breasts Lk 11:27
in his garden and * again and again Lk 13:6
When he noticed that all who * to Lk 14:7
* to listen to Jesus' sermons; Lk 15:1
"When he finally * to his Lk 15:17
His father * out and begged him, Lk 15:28
One of them * back to Jesus, Lk 17:15
flood * and destroyed them all. Lk 17:27
A widow of that city * to him Lk 18:3
When Jesus * by he looked up at Lk 19:5
As they * to the towns of Lk 19:29
But as they * closer to Jerusalem Lk 19:41
When harvest time *, he sent one Lk 20:10
* to Jesus with this: Lk 20:28
Then a poor widow * by and Lk 21:2
Herod * to the same conclusion Lk 23:15
And when the crowd that * to see Lk 23:48
Jesus himself * along and joined Lk 24:15
this morning and * back with an Lk 24:22,23
didn't recognize him when he *. Jn 1:10
mother * to him with the problem. Jn 2:3
After he * back to life again, Jn 2:22
* for an interview with Jesus. Jn 3:1
Light from heaven * into the world, Jn 3:19
So they * to John and said, Jn 3:26
of Sychar, he * to Jacob's Well, Jn 4:5,6
Soon a Samaritan woman * to draw Jn 4:7
So the people * streaming from Jn 4:30
When they * out to see him at Jn 4:40,41
angel of the Lord * from time to Jn 5:4
that he * down from heaven?" Jn 6:42
I am that Living Bread that * Jn 6:48-51
He was the Jewish leader who * Jn 7:50
For I know where I * from and Jn 8:14
sent and washed and * back seeing! Jn 9:7
"All others who * before me Jn 10:8
the message of God *, do you call Jn 10:34,35,36
And many * to the decision Jn 10:42
Tears * to Jesus' eyes. Jn 11:35
Then they * to the tomb. Jn 11:37,38
And Lazarus *—bound up in the Jn 11:44
the entire nation * from Caiaphas Jn 11:51
that is the very reason why I *! Jn 12:27
When he * to Simon Peter, Peter Jn 13:6
believe that I * from the Father. Jn 16:27
Yes, I * from the Father into Jn 16:28
From this we believe that you * Jn 16:30
a certainty that I * down to earth Jn 17:8
And I * to bring truth to the Jn 18:37
Then Jesus * out wearing the Jn 19:5
So the soldiers * and broke the Jn 19:32
but when they * to him, they saw Jn 19:33
So he * and took it away. Jn 19:38
* too, bringing a hundred pounds Jn 19:39
Mary Magdalene * to the tomb and Jn 20:1
disciple also, who * first." Jn 20:3,4f
the Holy Spirit * upon them in Act 1:4
This annual celebration * fifty Act 2:1f
the house, crowds * running to see Act 2:6
so that he * up with a leap, stood Act 3:7,8
* over to them, very disturbed Act 4:1
later his wife * in, not knowing Act 5:7
and the young men * in and, seeing Act 5:10
And crowds * in from the Act 5:16
But an angel of the Lord * at Act 5:19
So Jacob * to Egypt, where he Act 7:15
birthday, it * into his mind to Act 7:23
And as the murderous stones * Act 7:59
* and with great sorrow buried Act 8:2
As they rode along, they * to a Act 8:36
And when they * up out of the Act 8:39
"And we understand that he * Act 9:21
and in his travels * to the Act 9:32
So I * as soon as I was sent Act 10:29
The Jews who * with Peter were Act 10:45
"But the voice * again, 'Don't Act 11:9
During this time some prophets * Act 11:27
cell blocks and * to the iron gate Act 12:10
a girl named Rhoda * to open it. Act 12:13
"But before he *, John the Act 13:24
While they were at Lystra, they * Act 14:8
Scriptures to some women who *. Act 16:13
So they * to the jail and begged Act 16:39
and Apollonia and * to Act 17:1
the Holy Spirit * on them, and they Act 19:6
and any demons within them * out. Act 19:12
Jews of Damascus, * to me, and Act 22:13
The crowd listened until Paul * Act 22:22
and * to the armory and told Paul. Act 23:16
of the garrison, * and took him Act 24:7
A few days later Felix * with Act 24:24
"When they * here for the trial, Act 25:17
gone by." It * at about the time Act 27:9f
time and no harm * to him, they Act 28:6
in the island * and were cured. Act 28:9
and when the time * to sail, Act 28:10
and * to meet us at the Forum Act 28:15
day large numbers * to his house. Act 28:23
our Lord, who * as a human baby, Rom 1:3
of escape, Christ * at just the Rom 5:6
Then you * back to life again Rom 7:9
that those who * to him—and all Rom 8:29
and when we *, he declared us Rom 8:30
died for us and * back to life Rom 8:34
As the Psalmist said, "He * for Rom 15:3
Remember that Jesus Christ * to Rom 15:8
And remember that he * also that Rom 15:9
Because the news about Christ * Rom 15:27
BROTHERS, EVEN when I first * 1Co 2:1
on the cross. I * to you in 1Co 2:3
but the first woman * out of man. 1Co 11:8
For although the first woman * 1Co 11:12
Death * into the world because of 1Co 15:21
but Christ * from heaven above. 1Co 15:47
happy either, unless I * with joy. 2Co 2:3
For God says, "Your cry * to me 2Co 6:2
* back to the city of Damascus. Gal 1:17
and Titus * along too. Gal 2:1
ones, really—who * to spy on us and Gal 2:4
But when Peter * to Antioch I had Gal 2:11
friends of James *, he wouldn't eat Gal 2:12
Scripture that I * to realize that Gal 2:19
obey the laws. I * to realize that Gal 2:19
the Holy Spirit * upon you only Gal 3:2
Until Christ * we were guarded by Gal 3:23
guide until Christ * to give us Gal 3:24
it was with us before Christ *. Gal 4:3
But when the right time *, the Gal 4:4
The same one who * down is the Eph 4:10
you sent me when Epaphroditus *. Php 4:18
The same Good News that * to you Col 1:6
This is the wonderful news that * Col 1:23
When you * to Christ he set you Col 2:11
and then you * up out of death Col 2:12
rules that ended when Christ *. Col 2:17
just before we * to you, and how 1Th 2:2
died and then * back to life again, 1Th 4:14
as it did when it * to you. 2Th 3:1
that Christ Jesus * into the world 1Ti 1:15
in Christ, who * to earth as a man, 1Ti 3:16
with us when we * into the world, 1Ti 6:7
* here from Asia have deserted me; 2Ti 1:15
In fact, when he * to Rome he 2Ti 1:17
But when the time * for the Tit 3:4
his firstborn Son * to earth—God Heb 1:5,6
They were the ones who * out of Heb 3:16
seed from which he * was in Abraham Heb 7:10
of Levi, but * from the tribe of Heb 7:12,13,14
High Priest who * with the rank of Heb 7:15
* with God's new and better way. Heb 9:10
He * as High Priest of this Heb 9:11
Christ * with this new agreement Heb 9:15
But no! He * once for all, at the Heb 9:26
Christ * to die on the cross. Heb 10:4f
That is why Christ said, as he * Heb 10:5
And so a whole nation * from Heb 11:12
death, but he * back again alive! Heb 11:19
what the prophets said * true. 2Pe 1:19
But the Son of God * to destroy 1Jn 3:8
Literally, "This is he who * by 1Jn 5:6,7,8f
that Jesus Christ * to earth as a 2Jn 1:7
was dead and then * back to life. Rev 2:8
censer * and stood at the altar; Rev 8:3
Then locusts * from the smoke and Rev 9:3
wounded and then * back to life. Rev 13:14
Then an angel * from the temple Rev 14:15
After that another angel * from Rev 14:17
seven plagues then * from the Rev 15:6
and a mighty shout * from the Rev 16:17
plagues * over and talked with me. Rev 17:1
And out of the throne * a voice Rev 19:5
last plagues, * and said to me, Rev 21:9

CAMEL
the * drivers to wash their feet. Gen 24:32
she had stuffed them into her * Gen 31:34
The * (it chews the cud but does Lev 11:4-7
So you may not eat the *, the Deu 14:7
female *, seeking for a male! Jer 2:23
is easier for a * to go through the Mt 19:24
strain out a gnat and swallow a *. Mt 23:24
It is easier for a * to go Mk 10:25
It is easier for a * to go Lk 18:25

CAMEL-LOADS
So Hazael took forty * of the best 2Ki 8:8,9
* of spices, gold, and jewels. 2Ch 9:1

CAMEL'S
John's clothing was woven from * Mt 3:4
His clothes were woven from * Mk 1:6

CAMELS
men and women slaves, and *. Gen 12:16
ten of Abraham's * loaded with Gen 24:10
There he made the * kneel down Gen 24:11
and I will water your * too!' Gen 24:14
*, too, until they have enough!" Gen 24:19
to the * until they had enough. Gen 24:20
Then at last, when the * had Gen 24:22
for the *, and a guest room." Gen 24:25
beside his *, and said to him, Gen 24:29,30
and a place prepared for the *!" Gen 24:31
to bed down the *, and feed for Gen 24:32
and many slaves and * and donkeys. Gen 24:35
And I'll water your * too!" Gen 24:44
sir, and I will water your * too!' Gen 24:46
mounted the * and went with him. Gen 24:61
he looked up and saw the * coming. Gen 24:63
many servants, *, and donkeys. Gen 30:43
wives and sons on *, and fled Gen 31:17-20
and herds and *, into two groups; Gen 32:7
rams,30 milk *, with their colts,40 Gen 32:13,14,15
a string of * coming towards them Gen 37:25
donkeys, *, flocks, and herds. Ex 9:3
on droves of * too numerous to Ju 6:5
were too many * even to count! Ju 7:12,13
the ornaments from their *' necks. Ju 8:21
or the chains around the *' necks. Ju 8:26
oxen, sheep, *, and donkeys.' 1Sa 15:3
oxen, donkeys, *, and clothing 1Sa 27:9
hundred young men who fled on *. 1Sa 30:17
a long train of * carrying spices, 1Ki 10:2
The booty included 50,000 *, 1Ch 5:21
on donkeys, *, mules, and oxen. 1Ch 12:40
had charge of the *, and Jehdeiah 1Ch 27:30
herds of sheep and * before finally 2Ch 14:15
mules, 435 *, and 6,720 donkeys. Ez 2:66,67
mules, 435 *, and 6,720 donkeys. Neh 7:68,69
carriers—riders on *, mules, and Est 8:9,10
for he owned 7,000 sheep, 3,000 * Job 1:2,3
driven off your * and killed your Job 1:17
sheep, 6,000 *, 1,000 teams of Job 42:12
riders in pairs on donkeys and *, Is 21:6,7
riders on asses, riders on *." Is 21:6,7f
and * were paired for the attack. Is 21:6,7f
Egypt—donkeys and * laden down with Is 30:6
Vast droves of * will converge Is 60:6
and on mules and *, to my holy Is 66:20
Their * will be taken away, and Jer 49:29
Their * and cattle shall all be Jer 49:32
into a pasture for * and all the Eze 25:5
the horses, mules, *, donkeys, and Zec 14:15

CAMP
set up * beside the oak at Moreh. Gen 12:6
There he made *, and made an Gen 12:8
That night, when he stopped to * Gen 28:11
Jacob spent that night in the *. Gen 32:21
to the * and was there alone; Gen 32:22,23,24
There he built himself a *, with Gen 33:17
and returned to their * again. Gen 34:26
and to * there along the shore. Ex 14:2
and covered the *, and in the Ex 16:13
all around the * was wet with dew; Ex 16:13
be peace and harmony in the *." Ex 18:23
After breaking * at Rephidim, Ex 19:2,3
Sinai and set up * there. Ex 19:2,3
Moses led them out from the * to Ex 19:17
* and burn it as a sin offering. Ex 29:14
When they came near the *, Moses Ex 32:19
he stood at the * entrance and Ex 32:26
one end of the * to the other and Ex 32:27
far outside the *, and everyone who Ex 33:7
return to the *, but the young man Ex 33:11
throughout the * announcing that no Ex 36:4-7
place outside the *—a place where Lev 4:11,12
bull outside the * and burn it Lev 4:21
ashes outside the * to a place that Lev 6:11
burned outside the *, as the Lord Lev 8:17
the meat and hide outside the *. Lev 9:11
and carry them outside the *." Lev 10:4
and must live outside the *. Lev 13:46
go out of the * to examine him. Lev 14:3
and return to live inside the *; Lev 14:8
and then come back into the *. Lev 16:26
outside the * and burned, including Lev 16:27
himself and then return to *. Lev 16:28
Out in the * one day, a young man Lev 24:10
him outside the * and tell all who Lev 24:13,14
youth out of the * and stoned him Lev 24:23
Tabernacle at the * of Israel on Num 1:1
Judah's side of the * was 186,400. Num 2:3-31
Reuben side of the * was 151,450. Num 2:3-31
was separate from the others in *. Num 2:3-31
side of the * was 108,100, and they Num 2:3-31
Dan's side of the * was 157,600. Num 2:3-31
* Location Num 3:16-24

CAMP Con't)
* Location Num 3:25-30
* Location Num 3:31-35
"When the * moves, Aaron and his Num 4:5
to wherever the * is traveling; Num 4:15
lepers from the *, and all who have Num 5:1
the * where I live among you." Num 5:3
the people broke * and followed. Num 9:20,21
for signaling the breaking of *. Num 10:1
signal to break * and move onward. Num 10:5,6,7
Then came the flag of the * of Num 10:18
those at the far end of the *. Num 11:1
still in the *, and when the Spirit Num 11:26
Then Moses returned to the * Num 11:30
fall into the * and all around it! Num 11:31
the *. But as everyone began Num 11:32
Let her be confined outside the * Num 12:14
So Miriam was excluded from the * Num 12:15
The idea swept the *. Num 14:4
was throughout the * when Moses Num 14:39
the Ark nor Moses left the *. Num 14:44
him to death outside the *." Num 15:35
So they took him outside the * Num 15:36
her outside the * and someone shall Num 19:1
return to the * and be ceremonially Num 19:7
place outside the *, where they Num 19:9
of the brook Zared and set up *. Num 21:12
out toward the * of Israel which Num 24:1
girl into the *, right before the Num 25:6
Now stay outside of the * for Num 31:19
you may come back into the *." Num 31:24
places for them to *, and had Deu 1:33
must leave the *, and stay outside Deu 23:9,10
area shall be outside the *. Deu 23:12
excrement. The * must be holy, for Deu 23:14
from the Israeli * at Acacia to Jos 2:1
went through the * giving these Jos 3:2,3,4
the place where you * tonight." Jos 4:2,3
nation rested in * until the raw Jos 5:8,9
* again and spent the night there. Jos 6:11
and returned again to the *. Jos 6:12,13,14
to live outside the * of Israel. Jos 6:23
army remained in the * at Jericho. Jos 8:9
When they arrived at the * of Jos 9:6
returned to their * at Makkedah Jos 10:21
returned to their * at Gilgal. Jos 10:43
for they established their * at Jos 11:5
to Joshua and the * at Shiloh. Jos 18:9
go down to the * alone—take along Ju 7:10
to the outposts of the enemy *. Ju 7:11
came tumbling down into our *. Ju 7:12,13
guardposts of the *," he told Ju 7:17
all sides of the * and shout, 'We Ju 7:18
the outer edge of the * of Midian. Ju 7:19,20
one end of the * to the other, and Ju 7:22
still called "The * of Dan"), Ju 18:12
were brought to the * at Shiloh. Ju 21:10,11,12
returned to their * and their 1Sa 4:3
over in the * of the Hebrews?" 1Sa 4:6
"God has come into their *!" 1Sa 4:7
* in Geba in the land of Benjamin; 1Sa 13:16
left the * of the Philistines; 1Sa 13:17
the tumult in the * of the 1Sa 14:19
outskirts of the * just as the 1Sa 17:20
the deserted Philistine *. 1Sa 17:53
David slipped over to Saul's * 1Sa 26:5,6,7
went to Saul's * and found him 1Sa 26:5,6,7
slope opposite the * until they 1Sa 26:13
The Philistines set up their * at 1Sa 28:4
superintendent of this labor *. 1Ki 5:14
at the Israeli *, the army of 2Ki 3:24
went out to the * of the Syrians, 2Ki 7:5
at the edge of the * they went into 2Ki 7:8
the Syrian * and no one was there! 2Ki 7:10
have left their * and have hidden 2Ki 7:12
plundered the * of the Syrians. 2Ki 7:16
to the Philistine *, drew some 1Ch 11:18,19
We broke * at the Ahava River at Ez 8:31
The nomads will not even * there. Is 13:20
went out to the * of the Assyrians Is 37:36
They shall set up * around the Jer 6:3
people can safely * in the wildest Eze 34:25
the other animals in the enemy *. Zec 14:15

CAMPAIGN
in one *, for the Lord God of Jos 10:42
* has lasted for such a long time. Jos 22:2,3
AFTERWARDS A MASSIVE * against 2Ch 31:1
prophets to * for you at Jerusalem Neh 6:7

CAMPAIGNS
and wait for word of Cyrus' new *. Is 41:5

CAMPED
where he had * before, between Gen 13:3,4
as he was * at the top of a ridge; Gen 31:25
Laban, meanwhile, * below him in Gen 31:25
in Canaan, and * outside the city. Gen 33:18
(He bought the land he * on from Gen 33:19
Then Israel journeyed on and * Gen 35:21
Leaving Succoth, they * in Etham Ex 13:20
So they * where they were told. Ex 14:4
as they were * beside the shore Ex 14:9
and they * there beside the Ex 15:27
Moses and the people were * at Mt. Ex 18:5,6
wherever it stopped, and * there. Num 9:17
So it was that they * or Num 9:23
blown, the tribes * on the east Num 10:5,6,7
and * in the wilderness of Paran. Num 12:16
(The Israelis were * in the Num 13:3-15
and * at Kadesh, where Miriam Num 20:1
next to Oboth and * there. Num 21:10
plains of Moab and * east of the Num 22:1
WHILE ISRAEL WAS * at Acacia, Num 25:1
(The entire nation was * in the Num 26:3,4
of Israel who were * on the plains Num 31:12
* at the foot of Mount Migdol). Num 33:7
Leaving Elim, they * beside the Num 33:10
from Mount Hor and * in Zalmonah, Num 33:41
While in that area they * at Num 33:49
It was while they were * there Num 33:50,51
WHILE ISRAEL WAS * beside the Num 35:1
while they were * on the plains of Num 36:13
when they were * in the valley of Deu 1:1
and as they were * east of the Deu 4:44,45,46
* for a few days before crossing. Jos 3:1
where they were * for the night and Jos 4:8
Jordan River and * in Gilgal at the Jos 4:19
While they were * at Gilgal on Jos 5:10
the people were * at that time Jos 13:32
and his army were * at Mount Tabor, Ju 4:12
They crossed the Jordan and * in Ju 6:33
The armies of Midian were * north Ju 7:1
the Midianites * in the valley just Ju 7:8,9
They * first at a place west of Ju 18:12
in, they * in the village square. Ju 19:15
When he saw the travelers * in Ju 19:17
The Israeli army was * near 1Sa 4:1
and they * at Michmash east of 1Sa 13:5
hundred men were * at the edge of 1Sa 14:2
The Amalekites were * in the 1Sa 15:5
for battle and * between Socoh in 1Sa 17:1
(Saul and the Israeli army were * 1Sa 17:19
where David was * has been called, 1Sa 23:28
Saul * along the road at the 1Sa 26:3,4
* at the springs in Jezreel. 1Sa 29:1
army now * in the land of Gilead. 2Sa 17:26
the Jordan and * at Aroer, south of 2Sa 24:5
him to, and * beside the brook. 1Ki 17:5
The two armies * opposite each 1Ki 20:29
and they * along the highway 2Ki 18:17
The Philistines were * in the 1Ch 11:15
These forces * at Medeba where 1Ch 19:7
Ahava River and * there for three Ez 8:15
The merchants and tradesmen * Neh 13:20
in Jerusalem. He * near the outlet Is 36:2

CAMPING
Hebrew, who was * among the oaks Gen 14:13
separate * area with its own flag. Num 1:52
the Etham wilderness, * at Marah. Num 33:8
his officers are * out in open 2Sa 11:11
doing out here, * around the wall? Neh 13:21

CAMPS
set up their *, each tribe under Num 2:34
* must stay away from all evil. Deu 23:9,10
city, and enemy * around it, and Eze 4:1
training * will be closed down. Mic 4:3
of shepherd * and folds for sheep. Zep 2:6

CAMPSITE
Israelites traveled to a new *. Num 2:3-31

CANA
in the village of * in Galilee, Jn 2:1
This miracle at * in Galilee was Jn 2:11
at the town of *, where he had Jn 4:46,47
This man went over to *, found Jn 4:46,47
Nathanael from * in Galilee, my Jn 21:2

CANAAN
Ham, the father of *, saw his Gen 9:22
Literally, "cursed be *." Gen 9:24,25f
And may * be his slave. Gen 9:26,27
And let * be his slave." Gen 9:26,27
of Ham were:Cush, Mizraim,Put, *. Gen 10:6
of Heth; from * descended these Gen 10:15-19
Eventually the descendants of * Gen 10:15-19
Chaldeans to go to the land of *; Gen 11:31
in Haran—and finally arrived in *. Gen 12:5
Traveling through *, they came Gen 12:6
in the land of *, while Lot lived Gen 13:12
first arrived in the land of *. Gen 16:2,3
of * to you and them, forever. Gen 17:7,8
died in Hebron in the land of *; Gen 23:1
his father Isaac in the land of *. Gen 31:17-20
in *, and camped outside the city. Gen 33:18
at Luz (also called Bethel), in *. Gen 35:6
married three local girls from *: Gen 36:2,3
born to Esau in the land of *. Gen 36:5
in the land of *—and moved away Gen 36:6,7,8
they lived in *:The clan of Gen 36:17
of *, where his father had lived. Gen 37:1
in * as it was everywhere else. Gen 42:5
"From the land of *," they Gen 42:7
our father is in the land of *. Gen 42:13
in the land of * and told him all Gen 42:29
with our father in the land of *.' Gen 42:32
to their homes in *, and to bring Gen 45:17
land of *, to Jacob their father. Gen 45:25
in the land of *, and came to Gen 46:6
mother was a girl from *). Gen 46:8-14
*, before Israel went to Egypt). Gen 46:8-14
from the land of * to join me. Gen 46:31
are here from *," he reported, Gen 47:1
*—the famine is very bitter there. Gen 47:4
land of Egypt and * were starving. Gen 47:13
money in Egypt and * in exchange Gen 47:14
Luz in the land of * and blessed Gen 48:3
give this land of * to you and to Gen 48:4
to *, the land of your fathers. Gen 48:21
in the land of *, in the cave in Gen 49:29,30
the land of *, to bury him there. Gen 50:5
into the land of * and buried it Gen 50:12,13
with them when they returned to *. Gen 50:25
back into the land of * Ex 2:24
land of * where they were living. Ex 6:4
All the people of * melt with Ex 15:15
*, where there were crops to eat. Ex 16:35
in the land of * which I have given Lev 14:33,34
of * where I am going to take you. Lev 18:3
the land of *, and to be your God. Lev 25:38
*—the land I am giving to Israel; Num 13:2
Onan who died in the land of *: Num 26:19-22
rest of you in the land of *." Num 32:30
fully armed into *, but our own Num 32:32
in the land of *, heard that the Num 33:40
into the land of *, you must drive Num 33:50,51
into the land of * (I am giving you Num 34:1
in the land of *, and three on the Num 35:13,14
all the land of * and Lebanon—the Deu 1:7
the peoples of *, whose land had Deu 2:12
across the land of *, the land I am Deu 32:49
on they lived on the crops of *. Jos 5:11,12
The kings of *, both east and Jos 11:1
THE CONQUERED LANDS of * were Jos 14:1
to spy out the land of *. Jos 14:7
'The section of * you were just in Jos 14:9
at Shiloh in * and crossed the Jos 22:9
they were still in *, they built a Jos 22:10
into the land of * and gave him Jos 24:3
had not experienced the wars of *. Ju 3:1
by King Jabin of Hazor, in *. Ju 4:2,3
Israel to subdue King Jabin of *. Ju 4:23
The kings of * fought in Taanach Ju 5:19
Cush, Misream, *, and 1Ch 1:5-9
* was also the ancestor of the 1Ch 1:13-16
sons by Bath-shua, a girl from *: 1Ch 2:3
'I will give you the land of * 1Ch 16:18
land of * as your inheritance." Ps 105:10,11
few, and were only visitors in *. Ps 105:12
of *, cutting off its food supply. Ps 105:16
idols of *—shedding innocent blood Ps 106:37,38
and the kings of *— and gave Ps 135:11
Literally, "the language of *." Is 19:18f
than the people of *—your father Eze 16:3
and in the land of *, for the Zep 2:5
A woman from * who was living Mt 15:22
in Egypt and * and there was great Act 7:11
seven nations in *, and gave Israel Act 13:19,20

CANAAN'S
* oldest son was Sidon, and he Gen 10:15-19
Among * sons were: 1Ch 1:13-16

CANAANITE
marry one of these * girls. Gen 28:1
against marrying a * girl, and that Gen 28:6,7,8
There he met and married a * Gen 38:2
Shaul (whose mother was a *). Ex 6:15
It was then that the * king of Num 33:40

CANAANITES
(Ham is the ancestor of the *. Gen 9:18
The * were Ham's descendants. Gen 9:24,25f
"A curse upon the *," he swore. Gen 9:24,25
and may the * be Shem's slaves." Gen 9:26,27f
(This area was inhabited by * at Gen 12:6
from the tribes of * and Gen 13:7
*, Girgashites, Jebusites." Gen 15:19,20,21
one of these local girls, these *. Gen 24:3
Literally, "daughters of the *." Gen 24:37f
land—all the * and Perizzites. Gen 34:30
The local residents, the *, Gen 50:11
land where the *, Hittites, Ex 3:8
occupied by the *, Hittites, Ex 3:17
the land of the *, Hittites, Ex 13:4,5
ago, where the * are now living, Ex 13:11
Perizzites, *, Hivites, and Ex 23:23
*, and Hittites from before you. Ex 23:28
to drive out the *, Amorites, Ex 33:2
you the Amorites, *, Hittites, Ex 34:11
Jordan River valley are the *." Num 13:29
Amalekites and the * living in the Num 14:25
The Amalekites and the * are Num 14:43
Then the Amalekites and the * Num 14:45
their request and defeated the *; Num 21:3
The Amorites, the *, Deu 7:1
River, where the * live, in the Deu 11:30
the Amorites, the *, the Deu 20:17
drive out the *, Hittites, Hivites, Jos 3:10
Amorites and * who lived along the Jos 5:1
For when the * and the other Jos 7:9

(CANAANITES Con't)
Amorites, *, Perizzites, Hivites, Jos 9:1
the Amorites, the *, the Jos 12:8-24
belonging to the * from the brook Jos 13:2-7
all the land of the *, including Jos 13:2-7
of Manasseh. The * living in Gezer Jos 16:10
in those cities, the * remained. Jos 17:12
forced the * to work as slaves. Jos 17:13
Joseph, "for the * in the lowlands Jos 17:16,17,18
can drive out the * from the Jos 17:16,17,18
Perizzites, the *, the Hittites, Jos 24:11
to go to war against the *?" Ju 1:1
them defeat the * and Perizzites, Ju 1:4,5,6
Judah fought the * in the hill Ju 1:9
Then Judah marched against the * Ju 1:10
they fought the * at the city of Ju 1:17
so the * stayed there. Ju 1:27
they put the * to work as slaves, Ju 1:28
This was also true of the * Ju 1:29
live among the *, who were the Ju 1:31,32
The *, Ju 3:1
So Israel lived among the *, Ju 3:5
of the Hivites and *, and south to 2Sa 24:7
in the land—the *, Hittites, Ez 9:1
the land of the *, Hittites, Neh 9:8
people of the * were powerless! Neh 9:24

CANAL
beside the Chebar * in Babylon. Eze 1:1
beside the Chebar *, and when they Eze 10:15,16
God of Israel beside the Chebar *. Eze 10:20
I had seen at the *, and they Eze 10:22
*, and then later at Jerusalem Eze 43:3

CANALS
all its rivers, *, marshes, and Ex 7:19

CANCEL
* the debts of our brother Jews. Neh 10:31
I will * your agreement of Is 28:18
your God, he will * all the Jer 26:13
I knew how easily you could * Jon 4:2
come—it isn't to * the laws of Mt 5:17
that agreement, so I had to * it. Heb 8:9

CANCELED
their fathers is broken and *. Jer 11:10
sign it so that it cannot be * or Dan 6:8
that is why God * his sins and Rom 4:3
it—could not be * or changed four Gal 3:17
was * because it didn't work. Heb 7:18

CANCELING
* of all public and private debts. Lev 25:10
there is to be a * of all debts! Deu 15:1
the first, without actually * it. Est 8:8f
of the army of heaven by * the Dan 8:11

CANCELLATION
year of debt * is close at hand! Deu 15:9

CANCELS
He * the first system in favor of Heb 10:9

CANCER
be victims of *, or be lepers, or 2Sa 3:29
Remove this evil *—this wicked 1Co 5:7

CANCEROUS
behind us the * old life with all 1Co 5:8

CANDACE
great authority under * the queen. Act 8:27

CANDLE
Their * of life is snuffed out. Job 4:21

CANDLESTICK
the golden * and a table with Heb 9:1
and remove your * from its place Rev 2:5

CANDLESTICKS
for the silver * and lamps, each 1Ch 28:15
and silver * and cups and bowls. Jer 52:19
behind me were seven * of gold. Rev 1:12
*: The seven stars are the leaders Rev 1:20
* are the churches themselves. Rev 1:20
and walks among the golden *." Rev 2:1f
and two * standing before the God Rev 11:4

CANDLEWICKS
their lives snuffed out like *. Is 43:17

CANE
much of cinnamon and of sweet *; Ex 30:22,23
Can a * walk by itself?" Is 10:15
on the head with a *, and spit on Mk 15:19
and Aaron's wooden * that budded. Heb 9:4
leaning on the top of his *. Heb 11:21

CANES
her streets on *, and the streets Zec 8:4

CANNEH
Haran and *, Eden, Asshur and Eze 27:23

CANNON
will not be born to be * fodder. Is 65:23

CANOPY
* which was supported by pillars. 1Ki 7:6
Its posts are silver, its * Sol 3:10
public grounds—a * of smoke and Is 4:5
He shall spread his royal * over Jer 43:10
And there was a wooden * over the Eze 41:25
and on the * over the entrance. Eze 41:26

CANS
and the trash * in the Temple of Zec 14:20

CANTEEN
and strapped a * of water to Gen 21:14
so she refilled the * and gave Gen 21:19

CANTOR
of choir leaders: Heman the * was 1Ch 6:33-38

CANTORS
The * were all prominent Levites. 1Ch 9:33,34

CANVAS
He saw the sky open, and a great * Act 10:11

CAP
and are a feather in your *. Pro 3:22
a feather in your * to have their Eze 27:10

CAPABLE
And if any of them are *, put Gen 47:5,6
"Find some *, godly, honest men Ex 18:21
He is highly * as an artistic Ex 31:4
Daniel soon proved himself more * Dan 6:3
Or, "Even the least * people in 1Co 6:4f

CAPACITY
it had a twelve thousand gallon *. 1Ki 7:26

CAPERNAUM
but soon he moved to *, beside Mt 4:12,13
When Jesus arrived in *, a Roman Mt 8:5,6
the lake to *, his home town. Mt 9:1
And *, though highly honored, Mt 11:23
On their arrival in *, the Temple Mt 17:24
at the town of * and on Saturday Mk 1:21
over the city of * gathered outside Mk 1:32,33
he returned to *, and the news of Mk 2:1
WHILE IN * Jesus went over to the Mk 3:1
And so they arrived at *. Mk 9:33
THEN HE LEFT * Mk 10:1
town like those you did in *?' Lk 4:23
Then he returned to *, a city in Lk 4:31
to leave them, but to stay at *. Lk 4:42
he went back into the city of *. Lk 7:1
And you people of *, what shall Lk 10:15
After the wedding he left for * Jn 2:12
man in the city of *, a government Jn 4:46,47
him to come to * with him and heal Jn 4:46,47
out across the lake toward *. Jn 6:17
went across to * to look for him. Jn 6:24
this sermon in the synagogue in *. Jn 6:59

CAPES
and * and ornate combs and purses; Is 3:22

CAPHTOR
when the people of * invaded and Deu 2:23
those colonists from *. Jer 47:4
I brought the Philistines from * Amo 9:7

CAPHTORIM
whom came the Philistines), and *. Gen 10:13,14
the Pathrusim, the *, and the 1Ch 1:11,12

CAPITAL
which had been King Sihon's *. Num 21:25,26
King Sihon's *, Num 21:27-30
way, he left the * and went out to Num 22:36
the Moabites, whose * is at Ar. Deu 2:29
King Sihon, whose * was Heshbon; Deu 4:44,45,46
(Hazor had at one time been the * Jos 11:10
annual tax money to the Moabite *. Ju 3:15
* cities and villages alike. 1Sa 6:4,5
the mayors of the * cities, Ashdod, 1Sa 6:17
battle reached the *, the child's 2Sa 4:4
siege of Rabbah the * of Ammon. 2Sa 12:26,27
Hebron was King David's first *, 2Sa 15:9f
6 feet wide. Each * was decorated 1Ki 7:16-22
A * at the top of each pillar; 1Ki 7:41-46
of Ephraim, and it became his *. 1Ki 12:25
palace, in the * city of Tirzah. 1Ki 16:9
to besiege Tirzah, Israel's *. 1Ki 16:17
besieged Samaria, the Israeli *. 1Ki 20:1
twelve years. His * was Samaria. 2Ki 3:1
in Samaria, the * city of Israel! 2Ki 6:20
to Damascus (the * of Syria), where 2Ki 8:7
attacked Damascus, the * of Syria. 2Ki 16:9
Samaria, the * city of Israel. 2Ki 17:5
Then he moved the * to Jerusalem, 1Ch 3:4
troops in Damascus, the Syrian *. 1Ch 18:6
7½-foot * flaring out to the roof. 2Ch 3:15
stationed at Jerusalem, his *. 2Ch 17:13
will remain the * of Syria alone, Is 7:8
Samaria, the * of "Ephraim," Is 7:8f
Samaria is the * of Ephraim Is 7:9
going to give you. Use * letters! Is 8:1
message to Damascus, * of Syria: Is 17:1
and as the * of my empire." Dan 4:30
This time I was at Susa, the * Dan 8:2
*, where the king's chapel is!" Amo 7:13
* cities, Samaria and Jerusalem! Mic 1:5
Nineveh was the Assyrian *. Nah 1:1f
and make its great * Nineveh a Zep 2:13
than that the * of so vast an Zep 2:15f
for Jerusalem is the * of the Mt 5:35
to the distant * of the empire to Lk 19:12

CAPITALS
The posts and their * and rods Ex 36:38
villages controlled by the five *. 1Sa 6:18
two lily-shaped * of molten bronze, 1Ki 7:16-22
the bases of the * of each pillar; 1Ki 7:41-46
to cover the bases of the two *; 1Ki 7:41-46
* at the tops of the pillars. 2Ki 25:17
The two flared * on the tops of 2Ch 4:12-16
The two sets of chains on the *, 2Ch 4:12-16
the two sets of chains on the *, 2Ch 4:12-16
Susa was one of several * of the Dan 8:2f

CAPITULATED
Tyre * to Nebuchadnezzar at the Eze 29:18f
Tyre * to Nebuchadnezzar at the Eze 29:20f

CAPPADOCIA
Judea, *, Pontus, Ausia, Act 2:9
Galatia, *, Ausia, and Bithynia. 1Pe 1:1

CAPPED
They threw me in a well and * it Lam 3:53

CAPS
and place * on their heads. Ex 29:9
turbans, and the * and the Ex 39:28,29
*, as the Lord had commanded him. Lev 8:13
that will be a feather in our * 2Co 13:7

CAPSTONE
has now become the * of the arch! Ps 118:22
"He will bring forth the *." Zec 4:7f
which became the * of the arch.' Act 4:11

CAPTAIN
Potiphar was * of the palace Gen 37:36
Now this man Potiphar was the * Gen 39:1
of Potiphar, the * of the guard, Gen 40:1
the castle of the * of the guard, Gen 41:10
was a slave of the * of the guard, Gen 41:12
Give this cheese to their * and 1Sa 17:18
and demoted him to the rank of *. 1Sa 18:13
Why, he is the * of your 1Sa 22:14
Benaiah (son of Jehoiada) was * 2Sa 8:18
to Ittai, the * of the six hundred 2Sa 15:19,20
Then he sent an army * with 2Ki 1:9
top of a hill. The * said to him, 2Ki 1:9
So the king sent another * with 2Ki 1:11
but this time the * fell to his 2Ki 1:13
General Nebuzaradan, the * of the 2Ki 25:8
David made him * of his 1Ch 11:24,25
Korah clan. The * of the guard was 1Ch 26:1
care of the * of his bodyguard. 2Ch 12:10
this was when Joab, * of his Ps 60:1
Then Nebuzaradan, the * of the Jer 39:9
So Nebuzaradan, the * of the Jer 39:13
NEBUZARADAN, * OF the guard, took Jer 40:1
The * called for Jeremiah and Jer 40:2,3
by Nebuzaradan, * of the guard. Jer 41:10
Nebuzaradan, the * of the guard, Jer 43:6
Nebuzaradan, * of the guard, Jer 52:12
The * of the guard took along Jer 52:24,25
Nebuzaradan, his * of the guard, Jer 52:30
So the * went down after him. Jon 1:6
a Roman army * came and pled with Mt 8:5,6
army * was sick and near death. Lk 7:2
When the * heard about Jesus, he Lk 7:3
what a wonderful person the * was. Lk 7:4
at the house, the * sent some Lk 7:6,7,8
When the * of the Roman military Lk 23:47
chief priests, the * of the Temple Act 4:1
When the police * Act 5:24
Literally, "the * of the Act 5:24f
The police * went with his Act 5:26,27
a * of an Italian regiment. Act 10:1
* and the owner than to Paul. Act 27:11

CAPTAIN'S
and the roar of the * commands. Job 39:25
And when the * friends returned Lk 7:10

CAPTAINS
The famous Egyptian * are dead Ex 15:4
offering from the * and battalion Num 31:51,52
Joshua told the * of his army to Jos 10:24
As the Philistine * were leading 1Sa 29:2
Rechab, who were * of King 2Sa 4:2,3
thirty-two chariot * to fight no 1Ki 22:31
and he made them * of his army. 1Ch 12:18
THEN JOHANAN AND the army * and Jer 42:1
Johanan and the * of his forces, Jer 42:8
and the other * in command. Jer 43:5
farmers and oxen, * and rulers; Jer 51:23
wise men, rulers, *, warriors. Jer 51:57
young men, * and commanders, in Eze 23:6
governors, *, judges, treasurers, Dan 3:2
Then the princes, governors, *, Dan 3:27
chief priests and * of the Temple Lk 22:4
chief priests and * of the Temple Lk 22:52
And all the shipowners and * of Rev 18:17
kings, and *, and great generals; Rev 19:18

CAPTION
A mysterious * was written on her Rev 17:5

CAPTIVATING
pure as the sun, so utterly *?' Sol 6:10

CAPTIVE
in Egypt as a * of the Ishmaelite Gen 39:1
son of the * in the dungeon; Ex 12:29
The king is held * in your Sol 7:5
My people will be led away *, Is 8:21
my * people—and not for a reward! Is 45:13
your neck, O * daughter of Zion. Is 52:2
*: He shall die in a distant land Jer 22:11
was marched away *, therefore I Eze 25:3
are your * markets, giving payment Eze 27:15
Or, "when I carry you * among the Eze 32:9f
brought from Israel as a Jewish *? Dan 5:13
as a husband for his * wife. Zec 1:14

CAPTIVES
including the women and other *. Gen 14:16
that you are * in enemy lands. Lev 26:34,35
Then the Israeli army took as * Num 31:9,10,11
then burned. The * and other Num 31:12
Then purify yourselves and your * Num 31:19
a share of all the *, oxen, Num 31:28
tribute of all the *, flocks, and Num 31:30
you see among the * a beautiful Deu 21:11
Of all the slain and *. Deu 32:40,41
son of Abino-am, lead away your *! Ju 5:12
lead them away as * to some foreign 1Ki 8:46
and among their * was a little girl 2Ki 5:2
the people away to Assyria as *. 2Ki 15:29
of the city as *, resettling them 2Ki 16:9
took ten thousand * from Jerusalem, 2Ki 24:14
Temple guards to Babylon as *. 2Ki 25:18
2,000 donkeys, and 100,000 *. 1Ch 5:21
take them away as * to some foreign 2Ch 6:36
"You must not bring the * 2Ch 28:13
turned over the * and booty to the 2Ch 28:14
become * in a foreign land! Neh 4:4
leading many * in his train. Ps 68:18
demand that a tyrant let his * go? Is 49:24
But the Lord says, "Even the * Is 49:25
liberty to * and to open the eyes Is 61:1
Instead weep for the * led away! Jer 22:10
and all the other * exiled to Jer 28:4
message to all the * he has exiled Jer 29:4
Jewish * over there in Babylon. Jer 29:20
Ishmael made * of the king's Jer 41:10
and carry off the people as his *. Jer 43:12
were taken away as * to Babylon. Jer 52:3
Then he took to Babylon, as *, Jer 52:15
The number of * taken to Babylon Jer 52:28
745—a total of 4,600 * in all. Jer 52:30
at night, just as * do when they Eze 12:4
daughters will be taken away as *. Eze 30:18
brought back as *—young men of the Dan 1:3,4
* who will tell you your dream!" Dan 2:25
one of the Jewish *, is paying no Dan 6:13
They collect * like sand. Hab 1:9
when all their * will taunt them, Hab 2:6
to announce that * shall be Lk 4:18,19
* to all the nations of the world; Lk 21:24

CAPTIVITY
God will rescue you from your *! Deu 30:3
you from your * in Egypt!" 1Ki 12:28
the thirty-seventh year of his *. 2Ki 25:27
and was taken into * by King 1Ch 5:6
into * under Nebuchadnezzar). 1Ch 6:4-15
wives are in * because of this. 2Ch 29:9
would remain in * to the Ez 1:1f
Literally, "brought back the *." Ps 85:1f
into * with none to rescue them. Is 5:29
sending you into *, O strong man! Is 22:17
Terror and the * of hell are Is 24:17
Yet even now, be free from your * Is 48:20
for my people's return from *. Is 57:14
and those for *, to captivity. Jer 15:2
and those for captivity, to *. Jer 15:2
saying that our * will be long, and Jer 29:28
again from your * and restore your Jer 30:18
the Babylonian * (the rulers of the Jer 30:21f
rejoice, for their * with all its Jer 31:13
for 390 years by * and doom. Eze 4:4,5
sixth year of King Jehoiachin's *, Eze 8:1
He was held in * so that his Eze 19:9
seventh year of Jeconiah's *." Eze 20:1f
King Jehoiachin's *), another Eze 24:1
Jehoiachin was taken away to *). Eze 26:1
year of King Jehoiachin's *, Eze 29:17
*, this message came to me: Eze 30:20
year of King Jehoiachin's *, Eze 31:1
King Jehoiachin's *, this message Eze 32:1
I will end the * of my people and Eze 39:25
* and send us back to our own land Dan 9:3
I had freed her from * in Egypt. Hos 1:15
So I will send them into * with Amo 5:25,26,27
of *, back to your own land. Mic 2:13
So I will send you into * far Act 7:43
while in their *, and now you can Rom 7:6

CAPTORS
As Samson and his * arrived at Ju 15:14
them from their Philistine *. 1Sa 7:14
and make their * merciful to them; 1Ki 8:50
by their *, and they will be able 2Ch 30:9
Yet our *, our tormentors, demand Ps 137:3,4
Their * hold them and refuse to Jer 50:33

CAPTURE
Until they have eaten what they * Num 23:18-24
which cities we should * first.' Deu 1:22
who would go and * Kiriath-sepher. Jos 15:16
"God let you * Oreb and Zeeb, the Ju 8:2,3
replied, "To * Samson and do to Ju 15:10
"We have come to * you and take Ju 15:12,13
to * him if he tried to leave. Ju 16:2
think anyone could ever * you!" Ju 16:6
The Philistines have come to * Ju 16:12
are here to * you, Samson!" Ju 16:20
to celebrate the * of Samson. Ju 16:23,24
Ramah, he sent soldiers to * him; 1Sa 19:20
Philistines * me and torture me." 1Sa 31:3,4
of Israel, they tried to * him; 2Sa 5:17
are being made to * me, and they 2Sa 15:35,36
went on with Joab to * Sheba. 2Sa 20:13
heathen * and torture me." 1Ch 10:4
mobilized their forces to * him. 1Ch 14:8
Judah and let you * them, but you 2Ch 28:9
No, it's useless to try to * Job 41:9
at his home to * and kill him. Ps 59:1
than to * a fortified city. Pro 18:19
Jerusalem, and how you * my heart. Sol 6:4
with several other men to * Uriah. Jer 26:22
it and * this city and burn it. Jer 34:22
These Babylonians shall * this Jer 37:8
Mahseiah), concerning Seraiah's * Jer 51:59
an enemy army will * Jerusalem! Eze 4:3
I will * him in my net and bring Eze 12:13
will * vast booty and many slaves. Eze 38:12
city of Egypt and * it, and the Dan 11:15
will besiege and * powerful Dan 11:24
He will * all the treasures of Dan 11:43
I will search them out and * them. Amo 9:3
against their walls and * them! Hab 1:10
this, armed to the teeth to * me? Mk 14:48
With these weapons I can * rebels 2Co 10:5

CAPTURED
that Lot had been *, he called Gen 14:14
give me back my people who were *; Gen 14:21
"Are my daughters prisoners, * Gen 31:26
And divide the * booty." Ex 15:9
"If a thief is *, he must make Ex 22:3
So Israel * all the cities of the Num 21:25,26
And his daughters are * Num 21:27-30
when she was *, then remain in your Deu 21:13
the city from every side and * it! Jos 6:20
who was * and brought to Joshua. Jos 8:23
how Joshua had * and destroyed Ai Jos 10:1
The Israeli army then * Eglon on Jos 10:34,35
to Hebron, and * it and all of its Jos 10:37
which they quickly * with all of Jos 10:39
On the way back, Joshua * Hazor Jos 11:10
the tribe of Dan * the city of Jos 19:47,48
Israeli army soon * him and cut off Ju 1:4,5,6
First they sent scouts, who * a Ju 1:24
two generals of Midian, were *. Ju 7:25
Gideon chased and * them, routing Ju 8:12
There he * a young fellow from Ju 8:14
Abimelech finally * the city, Ju 9:45
the city of Thebez, and * it. Ju 9:50
of Ephraim. He * the fords of the Ju 12:5
Please tell me how you can be * Ju 16:10
tell me how you can really be *." Ju 16:13
So the Philistines * him and Ju 16:21
And the Ark of God was * and 1Sa 4:11
too, and the Ark has been *." 1Sa 4:17
the Ark had been * and that her 1Sa 4:19
of God had been * and because her 1Sa 4:21,22
THE PHILISTINES TOOK the * Ark of 1Sa 5:1
east of Egypt. He * Agag, the king 1Sa 15:8
were among those who had been *. 1Sa 30:5
defeated them and * the stronghold 2Sa 5:7
David * seventeen hundred 2Sa 8:4
led his army to Rabbah and * it. 2Sa 12:29,30
advised that he be * and killed. 2Sa 17:21
and chariots were *, and most of 1Ki 20:21
went to war against Gath and * it; 2Ki 12:17
King Amaziah was *, and the army 2Ki 14:13
(which had been * by Judah)—is 2Ki 14:28
against Israel. He * the cities of 2Ki 15:29
besieged and * all the fortified 2Ki 18:13
out after him and * him in the 2Ki 25:4,5
* in war and exiled to Manahath. 1Ch 8:6,7
So David * the fortress of Zion, 1Ch 11:5,6
David * a thousand of his 1Ch 18:4
troops, and * some of his 2Ch 13:18,19
cattle tents and * great herds of 2Ch 14:15
the cities he had * in the hill 2Ch 15:8
plunder they had * in the battle. 2Ch 15:11
King Joash of Israel * the 2Ch 25:23
Philistines and * the city of Gath 2Ch 26:6
The armies from Israel also * 2Ch 28:8
distributed * stores of clothing to 2Ch 28:15
and had already * Beth-shemesh, 2Ch 28:17,18
kings—we were *, robbed, and Ez 9:7
Your people * fortified cities Neh 9:25
He had been * when Jerusalem was Est 2:6
a crucible. You * us in your net Ps 66:11
and allowed his Ark to be *; Ps 78:61
enemies who * them to pity them. Ps 106:46
the armies of Babylon * Jerusalem. Ps 137:7
city of Ashdod and * it, the Lord Is 20:1
fulfilled when Cyrus * the city. Is 21:5f
slip away but they are *, too. Is 22:3
fall and be broken, trapped and *. Is 28:13
not be * by the king of Assyria! Is 37:10
when Jerusalem was * and the people Jer 1:3
that cannot be *, like an iron Jer 1:18
Why is she * and led far away? Jer 2:14
It shall be * by the king of Jer 21:10
of Babylon, had * and enslaved Jer 24:1
it shall never again be * or Jer 31:40
you shall be * and taken before Jer 34:3
before Nebuchadnezzar * the city. Jer 37:1f
would surely be * by the king of Jer 38:3
*, and many shall die of plague. Jer 43:11
of Gaza, before the city was * Jer 47:1
its forts are overwhelmed and *. Jer 48:1
tents will be *, says the Lord, Jer 49:29
her young children are * and Lam 1:5
anointed—was * in their snares. Lam 4:20
and he shall be * in my snare, and Eze 17:20
trapped him in a pit and * him. Eze 19:8
years after King Jeconiah was *, Eze 20:1
Jerusalem was *—the hand of the Eze 40:1
to escape; you * the survivors and Ob 1:14
homes with * goods and slaves. Nah 2:12
And the Evil Creature was *, and Rev 19:20

CAPTURING
an armed attack, * all of the towns Num 21:31,32
For Edom was invading Judah and * 2Ch 28:16
I want killed, and * those I want Jer 43:11
* Jesus quietly, and killing him. Mt 26:4

CARAVAN
around by the * route east of Nobah Ju 8:11
was a flourishing * city at the Jer 49:8f

CARAVANS
disappears. The * turn aside to be Job 6:15-18
When * from Tema and from Sheba Job 6:19-21
O * from Dedam, you will hide in Is 21:13
of Tarshish are your ocean *; Eze 27:25

CARBUNCLE
were a sardius, a topaz, and a *; Ex 39:10
jasper, sapphire, *, and Eze 28:13

CARCASS
bring the torn * to confirm the Ex 22:13
Leave its * for the dogs to eat. Ex 22:31
Holy Place. That * must be entirely Lev 6:30
may then eat the *, and it must be Lev 7:6
guilt offering—the * shall be given Lev 7:7
on the altar. The * of the young Lev 8:17
Anyone carrying away the * shall Lev 11:28
upon which the * falls shall be Lev 11:32
yet anyone who pulls out the * is Lev 11:36
And if the * touches grain to be Lev 11:37
are wet and the * falls upon it, Lev 11:38
* shall be defiled until evening. Lev 11:39
carrying away its * shall wash his Lev 11:40
path to look at the * of the lion. Ju 14:8
water over the * and the wood." 1Ki 18:33
It lies as a * in the road, Is 14:19
And wherever the * is, there the Mt 24:28

CARCASS-HOOKS
shovels, basins, *, and fire pans Ex 27:3

CARCASSES
time to time upon * of dead animals Gen 8:7f
the *, Abram shooed them away. Gen 15:11
between the halves of the *. Gen 15:17
They piled up the * for each 2Ch 35:12

CARCHEMISH
at * on the Euphrates River, and 2Ch 35:20
just as we did *," he will say, Is 10:9
over the Egyptian army at *. Jer 36:1f
of the battle of * when Pharaoh Jer 46:2

CARE
gardener, to tend and * for it. Gen 2:15
for Joseph took * of everything, Gen 39:23
that I would take * of the lad. Gen 44:32
I will take * of you there" ' Gen 45:11,12
Indeed, I myself will take * of Gen 50:21
going to take * of us or not?" Ex 17:7
they can take * of themselves. Ex 18:22
Use this money for the * of the Ex 30:16
of Levites was the * of the Num 3:25-30
of Levites was the * of the Ark, Num 3:31-35
two clans was the * of the frames Num 3:36,37
take * of them in the wilderness. Num 14:16
into battle and * for them, so that Num 27:17
You will plant vineyards and * Deu 28:39
surrounds him with his loving *, Deu 33:12
He would take * of them in other Jos 13:33
* of you for such a long time." Jos 24:20
God, and did not * about the mighty Ju 2:10
god, let him take * of himself and Ju 6:31
Baal take * of himself !" Ju 6:32
The Lord is taking * of you." Ju 18:6
and take * of you in your old age; Ru 4:15
Naomi took * of the baby, and the Ru 4:16,17
you're supposed to be taking * of? 1Sa 17:28
"I'll take * of this 1Sa 17:32
"When I am taking * of my 1Sa 17:34
are safe in the * of the Lord your 1Sa 25:29
"I will take * of you there." 2Sa 19:33
for they took * of me when I fled 1Ki 2:7
to * for their personal needs. 2Ki 12:8
Some of them were assigned to * 1Ch 9:28
I appointed to * for my people—that 1Ch 17:6
And they took * of the 1Ch 23:32
were given the * of the gifts 1Ch 26:20,21,22
were appointed to * for the gifts 1Ch 26:26
for the * of the items dedicated to 1Ch 26:28
The sheep were under the * of 1Ch 27:31

(CARE Con't)
* of the captain of his bodyguard. 2Ch 12:10
and begged God to take * of us. Ez 8:23
to * for the Temple of our God; Neh 10:32
There she was under the * of Est 2:12,13,14
God will * for those who are good? Job 4:6
me, and I was preserved by your *. Job 10:12
by when God took * of me, when he Job 29:2
* for even the daintiest dessert. Job 33:20
For he doesn't * how great a man Job 34:19
They * nothing for God or what Ps 28:5
takes * of those he has forgiven. Ps 37:17
thought I didn't *—but now your Ps 50:21
men who * nothing for God are Ps 54:3
and of your constant, daily *. Ps 71:15
He will take * of the helpless Ps 72:12
miracles give proof that you *. Ps 75:1
or trust in him to * for them, Ps 78:22
plight and * for this your vine! Ps 80:14
and are under his personal *. Ps 92:13
Lord, and exhibits his faithful *. Ps 92:15
doesn't *." Ps 94:6,7
his solemn oath to * for them. Ps 106:24
God's constant * of him will make Ps 112:6
that Jehovah will take * of him. Ps 112:7
for they do not * for your laws. Ps 119:155
they * nothing for your laws. Ps 119:158
A rebel doesn't * about the Pro 18:2
* is headed for serious trouble. Pro 28:14
the godless don't *. Pro 29:7
pieces to those who * for it. Sol 8:12
and appreciate his * for them, but Is 1:3
I do for them, they still don't *. Is 1:3
king and take * of this mess." Is 3:6
the Lord you have no thought or *. Is 5:12
neither know nor * that I have done Is 5:13
are planning to refuse my gentle * Is 8:6
have refused his * and thereby Is 8:14,15
God has removed his protecting *. Is 22:8
we are under the * of one who will Is 28:15
you'll *, O careless ones. Is 32:10
and * nothing for the promises Is 33:8
he will * for us and save us. Is 33:22
And after his *, he uses part of Is 44:15
I made you and I will * for you. Is 46:4
You didn't * a whit about my Is 47:7
they shall * for all your needs. Is 49:23
He was despised and we didn't *. Is 53:3
no one seems to * or wonder why. Is 57:1
Your children will * for you, O Is 62:5
of untruth. They * nothing for Jer 9:3
* nothing for me," says the Lord. Jer 9:3
flock I gave you to take * of? Jer 13:20
His subjects will not even * that Jer 22:18
the very ones they were to * for. Jer 23:1
shepherds to * for them, and they Jer 23:4
* anything about you any more; Jer 30:14
I will * for them as I did those Jer 31:2
will lead them home with great *. Jer 31:9
put him into the * of Gedaliah (son Jer 39:14
under Gedaliah's * in Mizpah by Jer 41:10
desert without a * in the world, Jer 49:31
poorest people to * for the crops Jer 52:16
with great * and eaten fearfully. Eze 4:16
food with utmost * and sip their Eze 12:19
* for them that I destroyed them. Eze 20:14
Great * must therefore be taken Eze 28:12f
You haven't taken * of the weak Eze 34:4
search for them or * about them. Eze 34:6
What do we * that God is there!' Eze 35:10
But he doesn't know or even * Hos 11:3
I took * of you in the Hos 13:5
I look after you and * for you. Hos 14:8
lies in ruins and you don't *. Hag 1:9
Don't you think I * about what has Zec 1:14
will be under my personal *." Zec 10:12
if you are killed, I don't *. Zec 11:9
who will not * for the dying ones, Zec 11:16
who doesn't * for the flock. Zec 11:17
and comfort and * for the lambs. Zec 13:7
you promised to * for and keep. Mal 2:14
God won't punish us—he doesn't *. Mal 2:17
"TAKE *! Mt 6:1
* for you, O men of little faith? Mt 6:30
God will take * of your tomorrow Mt 6:34
dead * for their own dead." Mt 8:22
help should feed and * for you. Mt 10:10
to honor and * for your parents. Mt 15:5,6
with Jesus to * for him were Mt 27:55
don't you even * that we are all Mk 4:38
Take *! Mk 13:23
"Anyone who takes * of a little Lk 9:48
who sent me. Your * for others is Lk 9:48
dead * for their own dead." Lk 9:60f
Literally, "took * of him." Lk 10:34f
and told him to take * of the Lk 10:35
to take * of me when I leave!' Lk 16:4
plowing or taking * of sheep, he Lk 17:7,8,9
full and doesn't *, then he brings Jn 2:10
but you don't * about the honor Jn 5:44
Take * to live in me, and let me Jn 15:4
them in your own *—all those you Jn 17:11
"Then take * of my sheep," Jesus Jn 21:16
"Men of Israel, take * what you Act 5:35
them over to the * of the Lord in Act 14:23
Jewish laws, you take * of it. Act 18:15
you to God and his * and to his Act 20:32
thank him for all his daily *. Rom 1:21
Or don't you *? Rom 2:4
They * nothing about God nor what Rom 3:18
Just remember that God doesn't * 1Co 8:8
What shepherd takes * of a flock 1Co 9:7
do not require this special *. 1Co 12:24
extra honor and * are given to 1Co 12:24
have the same * for each other that 1Co 12:25
believe [trusting God to * for us 2Co 4:13
how much you really do * for us. 2Co 7:12
and don't even * about the wicked, 2Co 12:21
They don't * anymore about right Eph 4:19
(He gave his very life to take * Eph 5:23
take tender * of those who are 1Th 5:14
The church should take loving * 1Ti 5:3
The church should * for widows 1Ti 5:5
But anyone who won't * for his 1Ti 5:8
and take * of their own homes; 1Ti 5:14
must take * of her, and not leave 1Ti 5:16
its money for the * of widows who 1Ti 5:16
out to help and * for those who are Heb 1:14
the one who takes * of orphans and Jas 1:27
you love and take * of yourself." Jas 2:8
the flock of God; * for it 1Pe 5:2
for God in taking * of the 3Jn 1:5
So we ourselves should take * of 3Jn 1:8
to take * of her for 1,260 days. Rev 12:6

CARED
stayed and * for Laban's flock. Gen 30:35,36
all that time I * for your ewes and Gen 31:38
And you know how he has * for Deu 1:31
They didn't see how the Lord * Deu 11:5
Their needs were to be * for, he 2Sa 20:3
He was * for by his nurse and by 2Ch 22:12
proper times and * for the Neh 13:31
we have always * for orphans in our Job 31:18
you have always * for me in my Ps 4:1
shepherd and he * for them with a Ps 78:71,72
The children I raised and * for so Is 1:2
I have created you and * for you Is 46:3
Even their priests * nothing for Jer 2:8
Has even one of them * enough to Jer 23:18
even though I * for them as a Jer 31:32f
I will see that you are well * Jer 40:4
When you were born, no one * for Eze 16:4
no one pitied you or * for you. Eze 16:5
and angels came and * for Jesus. Mt 4:11
the angels came and * for him. Mk 1:12,13
Not that he * for the poor, Jn 12:6
But Gallio couldn't have * less. Act 18:17
* about what was happening to you. 2Co 2:4
No, you took me in and * for me Gal 4:14
her, where she was * for and Rev 12:14

CAREFUL
Abraham warned. "Be * that you Gen 24:6
* not to be too hard on Jacob!' Gen 31:29
But if you are * to obey him, Ex 23:22
"Then, using the most * Ex 28:15
"Be very, very * never to Ex 34:12
sons to be very * not to defile my Lev 22:1
The Levites must be * not to Num 18:2,3
We will be * not to go through Num 20:17
Edomites will be nervous, so be *. Deu 2:4
Be very * never to forget what Deu 4:9
command and be * to obey it, so Deu 6:3
"But that is the time to be *! Deu 8:11
(By the way, be very * not to Deu 12:19
"Be * to obey all of these Deu 12:28
you must be very * lest you be Deu 18:9
vow, you must be * to do as you Deu 23:23
"Be very * to follow the Deu 24:8
for if you are * to obey every one Jos 1:7
So be very * to keep on loving Jos 23:11
"Be * how you talk, mister," Ju 18:25
Jeroboam thought, "Unless I'm * 1Ki 12:26
So be very *, for the Lord has 1Ch 28:10
night, for we are * to follow the 2Ch 13:11
was * to obey the Lord his God. 2Ch 14:2
because he was * to follow the path 2Ch 27:6
truth for him? Be * that he Job 13:9
The good man wins his case by * Pro 13:2
From a wise mind comes * and Pro 16:23
That is why men are not more * to Ecc 9:2,3
You are so * to polish the Mt 23:25
were godly folk, * to obey all of Lk 1:6
So be * how you listen; Lk 8:18
For though you are * to tithe Lk 11:42
Oh, be *! Act 13:40
But you must be * not to brag Rom 11:18
be humble and grateful—and *. Rom 11:20
on the foundation must be very *. 1Co 3:10
So be * not to jump to 1Co 4:5
But be * not to use your freedom 1Co 8:9
So be *. 1Co 10:12
So be * how you act; Eph 5:15,16
so * to follow my instructions. Php 2:12
must be even more * to do the good Php 2:12
him, but be * of him, for he 2Ti 4:1
Christians will be * to do good Tit 3:8
to him, to be * to hear his voice Heb 3:7,8
rest, too, being * not to disobey Heb 4:1
So remember, and be *. Heb 12:1
Be * how you behave among your 1Pe 2:1
You husbands must be * of your 1Pe 3:7
Be *—watch out for attacks from 1Pe 5:8
to them, but be * that you Jud 1:23
calls for * thought to solve it. Rev 13:18

CAREFULLY
but watched her * to see if she Gen 24:21
and ordinances, * obeying them, for Lev 19:37
these instructions *, lest they be Lev 22:9
the Levites, * following Jehovah's Num 8:20
"AND NOW, O Israel, listen * to Deu 4:1
and said, "Listen * now to all Deu 5:1
except to listen * to all he says Deu 10:12,13
miracles! How *, then, you should Deu 11:8
"And if you will * obey all of Deu 11:13
So keep these commandments * in Deu 11:18
"If you * obey all the Deu 11:22
is that you * heed all the commands Deu 15:4,5
first check the rumor very *; Deu 17:4
had been told: he * obeyed all of Jos 11:15
on this hill, laying the stones *. Ju 6:26
people listened * to his advice. 1Sa 3:19
doors and * overlaid with gold. 1Ki 6:35
in everything, and * obeyed all of 2Ki 18:6
in Israel was * recorded in The 1Ch 9:1
For if you * obey the rules and 1Ch 22:13
* following God's instructions, 2Ch 4:7
His was a good reign, as he * 2Ch 34:2
Listen * to what I say! Neh 1:6,7
listening very * to your arguments, Job 32:11,12
"For God * watches the goings on Job 34:21
I am listening * to all the Lord Ps 85:8
Listen *. Pro 4:20
and he weighs * everything you do. Pro 5:21
all the evidence *, distinguishing Pro 20:8
She watches * all that goes on Pro 31:27
THIS, TOO, I * explored—that godly Ecc 9:1
on the arms." * they join the Is 41:7
we are, for we * plan our lies. Is 59:13
chose my seed so *—the very best. Jer 2:21
but now I will * build it up. Jer 31:28
listen to them * for yourself. Eze 3:10
I will count you * and let only Eze 20:37
"Son of dust, notice *; Eze 44:5
of the Lord. Note * who may be Eze 44:5
up and listen * to what I have to Dan 10:11
happen unless you * obey the Zec 6:15
He looked around * at everything Mk 11:11
Listen * to everything he tells Act 3:21,22
Jewish laws and customs very *. Act 22:3
So, dear friends, * avoid 1Co 10:14
examine himself * before eating the 1Co 11:28
But if you * examine yourselves 1Co 11:31
And we * protect from the eyes of 1Co 12:23
We who believe are * joined Eph 2:21
behave *, taking life seriously. Tit 2:6
SO WE MUST listen very * to the Heb 2:1
Christ to be the * chosen, precious 1Pe 2:6
and you have * examined the claims Rev 2:2
Anyone who can hear, listen *: Rev 13:9

CARELESS
He speaks no * word; Ps 12:6
Spurn the * kiss of a Pro 4:24
you'll care, O * ones. Is 32:10
Their * laughter now means sorrow Lk 6:25
don't let me find you living in * Lk 21:34,35
sin or becomes * about God as Esau Heb 12:16

CARELESSLY
"Someone might * have raped her, Gen 26:10
Yet these false teachers * go Jud 1:8

CARELESSNESS
that you ought to die for your *. 1Sa 26:16

CARES
just as a father * for his child!' Deu 1:31
Lord your God personally * for! Deu 11:12
They die and no one *. Job 4:21
He * for them when times are hard; Ps 37:19
no one * a bit what happens to Ps 142:4
and * for the orphans and widows. Ps 146:9
of the proud but * for widows. Pro 15:25
A worthless witness * nothing for Pro 19:28
Lord your God who * for his people: Is 51:22
No one * about being fair and Is 59:4
land is desolate and no one *. Jer 12:11
And if God * so wonderfully for Mt 6:30
message, but the * of this life and Mt 13:22
And whoever * for me is caring Lk 9:48
body but lovingly * for it, just as Eph 5:29,30
it, just as Christ * for his body Eph 5:29,30
me happy and lighten all my *. Php 2:28
your worries and *, for he is 1Pe 5:7

CARETAKERS
They are the Temple *, to do Eze 44:14

CARGO
* overboard to lighten the ship. Jon 1:5

'ARGO Con't)
loss of *, injuries, and death." Act 27:10
began throwing the * overboard. Act 27:18
'ARING
* for it must repay the owner. Ex 22:12
has given you, * for your many Deu 3:19
your God who has been * for you. Deu 29:6
now, and Abishag was * for him. 1Ki 1:15
Jehovah himself is * for you! Ps 121:5
sweet ointments, * nothing at all Amo 6:6
But the Lord took me from * for Amo 7:15
as a Shepherd * for his sheep. Zec 9:16,17
is welcoming me and * for me. Mt 18:5
child like this is * for me! Lk 9:48
And whoever cares for me is * for Lk 9:48
still others have a gift for * Eph 4:11
and * for her own children. 1Th 2:7
'ARKAS
Zethar, and *— to bring Queen Est 1:10
'ARMEL
The king of Jokne-am, in *; Jos 12:8-24
Zior, Maon, *, Ziph, Juttah, Jos 15:48-62
side went from * to Shihor-libnath, Jos 19:24,25,26
had gone to Mount * to erect a 1Sa 15:12
there, near the village of *. 1Sa 25:2
his young men to * to give him this 1Sa 25:5
whole time they have been in *. 1Sa 25:7
When the messengers arrived at * 1Sa 25:40
and Abigail of *, Nabal's widow. 1Sa 27:2,3
of Nabal from *— and his men and 2Sa 2:2
Abigail, the widow of Nabal of *. 2Sa 3:3
Hezro from *; 2Sa 23:24-39
of Israel to Mount *, with all 450 1Ki 18:19
and the prophets to Mount *. 1Ki 18:20
the top of Mount * and got down on 1Ki 18:42
alive by Elijah at *, though the 1Ki 22:6f
Then he went to Mount * and 2Ki 2:25
As she approached Mount *, Elisha 2Ki 4:25
whose mother was Abigail from *. 1Ch 3:1
Hezro from *; 1Ch 11:26-47
"As Mount * crowns the Sol 7:5
Bashan and * are plundered. Is 33:9
Mount Tabor or Mount * by the sea! Jer 46:18
in the fields of * and Bashan and Jer 50:19
pastures of Mount * withered and Amo 1:2
at the top of *, I will search them Amo 9:3
the lush pastures of Bashan and * Nah 1:4
CARMEL'S
* pastures and Sharon's meadows; Is 35:2
CARMI
Hanoch, Pallu, Hezron, and *. Gen 46:8-14
son:Hanoch, Pallu,Hezron, *. Ex 6:14
named after their ancestor *. Num 26:5-11
For Achan (the son of *, grandson Jos 7:1
(Achan, the son of *, was the man 1Ch 2:7
Perez, Hezron, *, Hur, 1Ch 4:1
Hanoch, Pallu, Hezron, *. 1Ch 5:3
CARMITES
The *, named after their ancestor Num 26:5-11
CARNAGE
killed in war and *, but that you Jer 34:4
leaving horrible * everywhere. Zec 9:15
CAROUSE
don't * with drunkards and Pro 23:19,20,21
their enemies, who * in the Temple Lam 2:7
CAROUSING
sound of many men *—lewd men and Eze 23:42
in careless ease, * and drinking, Lk 21:34,35
CARPENTER
"He's just a *, Mary's boy, and Mk 6:2,3
CARPENTER'S
"He's just a * son, and we know Mt 13:55
CARPENTERS
as jewelers, *, embroidery Ex 35:35
sent cedar lumber, *, and masons to 2Sa 5:11
to pay the *, stonemasons, 2Ki 12:11,12
that they can hire * and masons to 2Ki 22:5,6
sent masons and * to help build 1Ch 14:1
and * and craftsmen of every kind. 1Ch 22:15
and * to restore the Temple; 2Ch 24:12
Levites to pay the * and 2Ch 34:10,11
Then they hired masons and *, and Ez 3:7
with all these *—mere men—who claim Is 44:11
tradesmen—the * and blacksmiths—the Jer 24:1
CARPENTRY
about stonework, *, and weaving; 2Ch 2:14
CARPETED
They quickly * the bare steps 2Ki 9:13
and the valleys are * with grain. Ps 65:13
CARPETS
And sit on rich *, Ju 5:10
and many-colored * bound with cords Eze 27:24
CARPUS
Troas with Brother *, and also the 2Ti 4:13
CARRIED
Sodom and Gomorrah and * off all Gen 14:11
while he himself * the knife and Gen 22:6
Jacob * the platter of food into Gen 27:18
me and has * away your blessing." Gen 27:35
was quickly * to Pharaoh's palace. Gen 45:2
them, and * his body into the land Gen 50:12,13
and * them on their shoulders. Ex 12:34
to be * over Aaron's heart when Ex 28:30,31
be * to a ceremonially clean place Lev 4:11,12
and got them, and * them out in Lev 10:5
mortar shall be * out of the city Lev 14:45
shall be * outside the camp and Lev 16:27
As the Ark was * forward, Moses Num 10:35
aloud, and they * on all night. Num 14:1
directions to Moses were * out. Num 16:40
sons of Levi, who * the Ark Deu 31:9
the Levites who * the Ark Deu 31:25
Because he * out God's penalties Deu 33:21
Joshua. They * them to the place Jos 4:8
Joshua by Moses, had been * out. Jos 4:10
The Ark was * around the city Jos 6:11
cut a bundle and * it back to the Ju 9:49
his shoulders and * them to the top Ju 16:3
and * them off to their own land. Ju 21:23
whole bushel! She * it back into Ru 2:18
So these instructions were * out. 1Sa 6:10
"Well, I have * out the Lord's 1Sa 15:13
leggings, and * a bronze javelin 1Sa 17:4-7
and he always * out his assignments 1Sa 18:5
City of David, but * it instead to 2Sa 6:10
He also * back to Jerusalem a 2Sa 8:8
Tremendous amounts of loot were * 2Sa 12:29,30
So Zadok and Abiathar * the Ark 2Sa 15:29
For you * the Ark of the Lord 1Ki 2:26
the priests * the Ark to the 1Ki 8:3,4
body from her and * it upstairs to 1Ki 17:19
was * by a whirlwind into heaven. 2Ki 2:11
he died. She * him up to the bed 2Ki 4:21
So Israel was * off to the land 2Ki 17:23
this palace shall be * to Babylon. 2Ki 20:17
and he * the ashes to Bethel. 2Ki 23:4
The Babylonians * home all the 2Ki 24:13
and * all the bronze to Babylon. 2Ki 25:13
the choirs * on their work there. 1Ch 6:32
Then the Levites * the Ark on 1Ch 15:15
Each group * out the Temple 1Ch 24:19
lifted the Ark and * it out of the 2Ch 5:4,5
Then the priests * the Ark into 2Ch 5:7,8
Then the army of Judah * off vast 2Ch 14:13
out to Ramah and * away the 2Ch 16:6
the border, and * away everything 2Ch 21:17
Then the Levites * the chest to 2Ch 24:11
Corner Gate. He * off all the 2Ch 25:24
* in the materials to the workmen. 2Ch 34:13
Palal (son of Uzai) * on the Neh 3:25
And we * our weapons with us at Neh 4:23
(This procedure had not been * Neh 8:17
So the mail went out swiftly, * Est 8:14
are doing, getting * away by your Job 15:12
Are they * away by the storm? Job 21:18
people and * off their treasures. Is 10:13
fathers—will be * off to Babylon. Is 39:6
and the rest were * away into Is 49:21
and * them through all the years. Is 63:9
at her breasts, * on her hips and Is 66:12
at harvest time, * in vessels Is 66:20
It cannot speak, and it must be * Jer 10:5
flock shall be * away as slaves. Jer 13:17
kings, shall be * off to Babylon. Jer 20:5
abate until it has * out the full Jer 23:20
not be * away with you to Babylon! Jer 27:18
will all yet be * away to Babylon Jer 27:22
Nebuchadnezzar * off to Babylon, Jer 28:3
or * off to Babylon as slaves." Jer 43:2,3
linen clothing and * a writer's Eze 9:2
Afterwards the Spirit of God * me Eze 11:24
cedar tree and * it into a city Eze 17:3,4
upon me and I was * away by the Eze 37:1
you will be * off to Egypt and Hos 9:3
are * off to Assyria as slaves? Hos 9:6
treasures and * them off to your Joe 3:5
of Gilgal will be * off to exile, Amo 5:5
They will be * out of the city in Amo 8:3
him when invaders * off his wealth Ob 1:11
they * them out to the tomb. Mk 16:1
Jerusalem, to be * out in Lk 9:31
died and was * by the angels to be Lk 16:22
and saw it * into the tomb. Lk 23:55
lame from birth * along the street Act 3:2
that she was dead, * her out and Act 5:10
"Our ancestors * along with them Act 7:44
Don't be * away and deceived 2Th 2:3
could still be * on by others who Heb 7:23
He personally * the load of our 1Pe 2:24
out and not be * away by the 2Pe 3:17
Its rider * a bow, and a crown Rev 6:2
CARRIERS
accountants, supervisors, and *. 2Ch 34:13
letters by swift *—riders on Est 8:9,10
CARRIES
She * them upon her wings— Deu 32:11
The east wind * him away, and he Job 27:21
the wind * them off like straw. Is 40:24
If your foot * you toward evil, Mk 9:45,46
weapons and * off his belongings. Lk 11:22
what he says. He * out and 2Co 1:20
CARRION
on such floating *, and was thus a Gen 8:7f
CARRRY
and he will * off her wealth, Eze 29:19
CARRY
you wish and * on your business Gen 34:9,10
as they could *—and to put into the Gen 44:1
from Egypt to * their wives and Gen 45:19
* heavy loads of mortar and brick. Ex 1:13,14
one house, and not * it outside; Ex 12:46
at the sides of the Ark, to * it. Ex 25:13,14
that will be used to * the table. Ex 25:26,27
with bronze. To * it, put the Ex 27:7
Israel: Aaron will * their names Ex 28:12
In this way Aaron shall * the Ex 28:29
at the sides of the Ark, to * it. Ex 37:5
Levites could * on their ministry. Ex 38:21
his clothes and * the ashes outside Lev 6:11
and * them outside the camp." Lev 10:4
So the goat shall * all the sins Lev 16:22
laws, and you must * them out in Lev 18:4,5
from her to * on the name and Lev 18:16f
and his sons may * out the duties Num 3:10
shall come and * the units to Num 4:15
not die when they * the most Num 4:17,18,19
and point out what each is to *. Num 4:17,18,19
"They will * the curtains of the Num 4:25
They are also to * the drapes Num 4:26
They will also * the altar, the Num 4:26
moved, they are to * the frames of Num 4:30,31
All this was done to * out the Num 4:37
Jehovah, and * it to the altar. Num 5:25
were required to * their portion of Num 7:9
The Levites will * out the sacred Num 8:19
I can't * this nation by Num 11:14
to * it on a pole between them! Num 13:23
fail to * out all of these Num 15:22
lay incense on it, and * it Num 16:46
burden for me to * all by myself, Deu 1:9
tribe of Levi to * the Ark Deu 10:8
convenient to * your tithes to that Deu 14:24
so be sure to * out this command. Deu 16:12
chop your wood and * your water. Deu 29:11
the Jordan, and to * them out and Jos 4:2,3
Each of you is to * out a stone Jos 4:5
* the Ark up out of the river. Jos 4:11
to chop wood and * water for the Jos 9:23
Ehud was the man chosen to * Ju 3:15
have children to * on her husband's Ru 4:5
can have a son to * on the family Ru 4:10
"If we * it into battle with us, 1Sa 4:3
to * them throughout all Israel. 1Sa 11:7
But when they came to * him out, 1Sa 19:16
too much of a load to * around! 2Sa 14:26
a servant girl to * to them the 2Sa 17:17
have no sons to * on my name." 2Sa 18:18
For who by himself is able to * 1Ki 3:9
of the Lord will * you away, who 1Ki 18:12
"* him home to his mother." 2Ki 4:19
you to * to the king of Israel." 2Ki 5:5
servants to * back with Gehazi. 2Ki 5:23
no one except the Levites may * 1Ch 15:2
And Nathan replied, "* out your 1Ch 17:2
no longer need to * the Tabernacle 1Ch 23:26
and Ithamar were left to * on. 1Ch 24:1
And now, O God of Israel, * out 2Ch 6:16
the guards would * them, and 2Ch 12:11
you don't need to * it back and 2Ch 35:3
vow to * out their promises. Neh 5:12
to * food while they are starving. Job 24:10
and * their burden no longer? Job 39:2,3
Lead them like a shepherd and * Ps 28:9
For when they die they * nothing Ps 49:17
He will * them. Ps 55:22
angels of his who * out his orders, Ps 103:20
you run. * out my instructions; Pro 4:13
They seize my people and * them Is 5:29
Samaria and * away their riches." Is 8:4
O Babylon. They * his anger with Is 13:5
they can *, and flee across the Is 15:7
will come and * you off, until at Is 28:19
he will * the lambs in his arms Is 40:11
What fools they are who * around Is 45:20
I will * you along and be your Is 46:4
They * it around on their Is 46:7
the old folks * heavy burdens. Is 47:6
and they shall * your little sons Is 49:22
purify yourselves, all you who * Is 52:11
that the wind can * them off! Is 57:13
* out my threats of punishment." Jer 1:12
here among us, and we * your name; Jer 14:9
* off the people as his captives. Jer 43:12
Then go ahead and * out your Jer 44:25
* out my judgments against you. Eze 11:9
Pack whatever you can * on your Eze 12:3
are observing and * your Eze 12:5
only what he can * with him, with Eze 12:12
They will * out my furious Eze 25:14
Or, "when I * you captive among Eze 32:9f
to Egypt he will * back their idols Dan 11:8
I will * them off and chase all Hos 5:14
when he goes in to * his body from Amo 6:10
them, and didn't * it through. Jon 3:10

(CARRY Con't)
you rise at dawn to * out your Mic 2:1
swarm like locusts and * it away. Nah 3:16
nor * the lame that cannot walk; Zec 11:16
I am not worthy to * his shoes! Mt 3:11
demand that you * their gear for a Mt 5:41
their gear for a mile, * it two. Mt 5:41
don't even * a duffle bag with Mt 10:10
forced him to * Jesus' cross. Mt 27:32
have two feet that * you to hell. Mk 9:45,46
into service to * Jesus' cross. Mk 15:21
conveniences and * his cross with Lk 9:23
not * his own cross and follow me. Lk 14:27
And then you would joyfully * it Lk 15:5
to the dead man, to * on his name. Lk 20:28
It's illegal to * that sleeping Jn 5:10
All of us must quickly * out the Jn 9:4
to * out his plan to betray Jesus. Jn 13:1
He did this to * out the Jn 18:9
and they will * you out too." Act 5:9
you should * this project through 2Co 8:11
I don't want to * out my present 2Co 10:2
things, for I * on my body the Gal 6:17
* away a single penny when we die. 1Ti 6:7
always * out his promises to us. 2Ti 2:13
them promise to * his bones with Heb 11:22
were assigned to * down to earth Rev 15:1
a plan that will * out his Rev 17:17

CARRYING
again and kept * water to the Gen 24:20
walking shoes and * your walking Ex 12:11
These * poles shall never be Ex 25:15
Thus Aaron shall always be * the Ex 28:30,31
gold rings to hold the * poles. Ex 30:4
The table, its * poles, and all of Ex 35:10-19
The incense altar and its * poles; Ex 35:10-19
and its * poles and utensils; Ex 35:10-19
to hold the * poles in place. Ex 37:14
this molding, to hold the * poles. Ex 37:27
poles. The * poles were Ex 37:28
grating, to insert the * poles. Ex 38:5
poles. The * poles themselves were Ex 38:6
with bronze. The * poles were Ex 38:7
The * poles; Ex 39:33-40
and attached the * poles to the Ark Ex 40:20
Anyone * away the carcass shall Lev 11:28
eating its meat or * away its Lev 11:40
Anyone touching or * anything Lev 15:10
* poles of the Ark in their rings. Num 4:6
Then they shall insert the * Num 4:8
shall be placed upon a * frame. Num 4:10
insert the * poles into the altar. Num 4:11
and placed on the * frame. Num 4:12
Finally, the * poles are to be Num 4:14
the line of march, * the Tabernacle Num 10:17
Next came the Kohathites * the Num 10:21
see the priests * the Ark of God, Jos 3:2,3,4
Instruct the priests who are * Jos 3:8
When the priests who are * the Jos 3:13,14
priests who were * the Ark touched Jos 3:13,14
priests who were * the Ark stood on Jos 3:17
The priests who were * the Ark Jos 4:10
orders to the priests * the Ark. Jos 4:15,16
of the Ark, each * a trumpet made Jos 6:3,4
come the priests * the Ark, Jos 6:6-9
their wood and * their water. Jos 9:21
Then, * the meat in a basket and Ju 6:19
when he saw them * them out. Ju 18:18
one will be * three young goats, 1Sa 10:3
donkey * a load of food and wine. 1Sa 16:20
* out vengeance with my own hands. 1Sa 25:33
* off all the women and children. 1Sa 30:2
After the men who were * it had 2Sa 6:13
the Ark and its * poles. 1Ki 8:7
camels * spices, gold, and jewels; 1Ki 10:2
drinking wine, and * out silver and 2Ki 7:8
improperly—you were not * it." 1Ch 15:13
shoulders with its * poles, just as 1Ch 15:15
Levites who were * the Ark, they 1Ch 15:26
David, the Levites * the Ark, 1Ch 15:27
over the Ark and its * poles. 2Ch 5:7,8
These * poles were so long that 2Ch 5:9
* off great quantities of booty. 2Ch 25:13
Yes, they go out weeping, * seed Ps 126:6
return singing, * their sheaves. Ps 126:6
enough to use for * coals from the Is 30:14
in linen clothing, * the writer's Eze 9:11
* heavy basketfuls of earth); Eze 29:18
the necessity of * the sacrifices Eze 46:19,20
"If one of you is * a holy Hag 2:12
a man * a yardstick in his hand. Zec 2:1
Four men arrived * a paralyzed Mk 2:3
arrival, and began * sick folks to Mk 6:55
towards you * a pot of water. Mk 14:13
Some men came * a paralyzed man Lk 5:18,19
along * a pitcher of water. Lk 22:10
forced to follow, * Jesus' cross. Lk 23:26
out of the city, * his cross to the Jn 19:17
you, laughing and * on, gorging and Jud 1:12
from the east, * the Great Seal of Rev 7:2
the heavens, * the everlasting Good Rev 14:6

CARSHENA
These men were *, Shethar, Est 1:13-15

CART
The priest shall then * the Lev 4:21
Now build a new * and hitch to 1Sa 6:7
Place the Ark of God on the * 1Sa 6:8
hitched to the * and their calves 1Sa 6:10
and tumors were placed upon the *. 1Sa 6:11
The * came into the field of a 1Sa 6:14
up the wood of the * for a fire and 1Sa 6:14
the * and laid them on the rock. 1Sa 6:15
The Ark was placed upon a new * 2Sa 6:3
the house of Abinadab on a new *. 1Ch 13:7
them three days to * it all away! 2Ch 20:25
The beasts are stumbling! The * Is 46:1

CARTED
The Levites then * it out to the 2Ch 29:16
chains and * him away to Babylon. 2Ch 33:11
stood, and * them off to Babylon. Jer 52:17
thing—will be * with them when they Hos 10:6

CARTLOADS
city, brought them * of flowers and Act 14:13

CARTS
are being hauled away on ox *! Is 46:1

CARVE
and hire a man to * a face on it, Is 40:20
They cut down a tree and * an Jer 10:2,3
"Take a stick and * on it these Eze 37:16
Then take another stick and * Eze 37:16

CARVED
high, with horns * from the wood of Ex 30:2
These were * statues of male Ex 34:13f
you must never worship * images, Lev 26:1
their idols—their * stones, molten Num 33:52
in secret, whether * of wood or Deu 27:15
been broken nor *," the Lord had Jos 8:31
watched, Joshua * upon the stones Jos 8:32
"I'll have an idol * for you and Ju 17:3
stone walls was * with designs of 1Ki 6:18
open flowers were * on all the 1Ki 6:29
doors were * with cherubim, palm 1Ki 6:32
open flowers were * on these doors 1Ki 6:35
with * lions, oxen, and angels. 1Ki 7:27-30
to sacrifice to * statues of goats 2Ch 11:15
and chopped the * paneling, and Ps 74:5,6
* by men from wood and stone. Is 37:19
I will not share my praise with * Is 42:8
left he makes his god: a * idol! Is 44:17
* image commanded it to happen!" Is 48:5
* idols and strange evil rites?" Jer 8:19
windows and * palm trees on both Eze 41:26
All her * images will be smashed Mic 1:7
And I see two olive trees * upon Zec 4:3
not one * on stone, but in human 2Co 3:3

CARVED-UP
They call a * wooden post their Jer 2:26,27

CARVER
a new idol; the * hurries the Is 41:7

CARVES
of wood and * the figure of a man. Is 44:13

CARVING
too, as a jeweler and in * wood. Ex 31:5
a jeweler, and can do beautiful *; Ex 35:33
for themselves, * them to look like Rom 1:23

CARVINGS
with identical * of blossoms. Ex 37:19
column had bronze *, a network of Jer 52:22
The walls were decorated with * Eze 41:17,18
*, and brass and iron and marble; Rev 18:12

CASCADED
stream that * out of the mountain. Deu 9:21

CASE
In this * for instance, the Gen 3:20f
in that *, if it kills someone, Ex 21:29
"In every * in which an ox, Ex 22:9
just as in the * of a bull or cow Lev 4:10
as in the * of a thank-offering Lev 4:35
the * with the grain offering." Lev 5:13
is an established * of leprosy, and Lev 13:11
"In the * of a man who has a Lev 13:18
In that * the priest shall Lev 13:43
as in the * of a sin offering. Lev 14:13
no heir, in which * his wife was Lev 18:16f
So Moses brought their * before Num 27:5
"But if it is an accident—a * in Num 35:22,23
"If a * arises that is too hard Deu 17:8
shall take the * to the sanctuary Deu 17:8
In this * the ephod evidently was Ju 8:27f
"In that *," Eli said, "cheer 1Sa 1:17
and when anyone came to bring a * 2Sa 15:2
"In that *," the king told 2Sa 16:4
in each * that comes before you. 2Ch 19:6
Whenever a * is referred to you 2Ch 19:10
then each * will be decided and Ez 10:14
* of boils from head to foot. Job 2:7
I am going to argue my * with him. Job 13:15
I will argue my * before him." Job 13:15f
"This is my *: I know that I am Job 13:18
open the court and listen to my *? Job 24:1
Without making a federal * of Job 34:24
But that is not our *. Ps 44:22
Arise, O God, and state your * Ps 74:2
life is ebbing out—a hopeless *. Ps 88:
When his * is called for Ps 109:
The good man wins his * by Pro 13:
people is a clear * of selling Pro 28:2
This is the * of a man who is Ecc 4:
In that *, your mouth is making Ecc 5:6,
his * against his people! Is 3:1
and Judah, you have heard the *! Is 5:
The court is ready for your *. Is 41:
Plead your * for my forgiving Is 43:2
Consult together, argue your * Is 45:2
I bring a * before you to decide. Jer 12:
for the Lord has a * against all Jer 25:3
I will plead your *; Jer 51:3
Plead my *! Lam 3:5
a writer's * strapped to his side. Eze 9:
with the writer's *, and said to Eze 9:
the writer's *, reported back and Eze 9:1
in * they sanctify the people. Eze 46:19,20
Stand up and state your * against Mic 6:
For he has a * against his people Mic 6:2
then take your * to the church, and Mt 18:17
order to build a * against him that Mt 26:5
in * he was crowded off the beach. Mk 3:9
man with an advanced * of leprosy. Lk 5:12
A typical * of discrimination (cf. Lk 9:53
believe me or let me present my *. Lk 22:67,68
if this were a * involving some Act 18:14
craftsmen have a * against them, Act 19:38
the judges can take the * at once. Act 19:38
"I will hear your * fully when Act 23:35
outline our * against this man. Act 24:4
and then he would decide the *. Act 24:22
discussed Paul's * with the king. Act 25:14
* was left for me by Felix. Act 25:14
I called the * the very next day Act 25:17
to how to decide a * of this kind Act 25:20
However, he appealed his * to Act 25:25
For in that * the free gift would Rom 11:6
In this * his feeling about it 1Co 10:29
in that * all Christians who 1Co 15:18
There is a strong * to be made Heb 5:7f
he left his * in the hands of God 1Pe 2:23

CASES
They brought the hard * to Moses Ex 18:26
"In any of these *, he shall Lev 5:5
Bring me any * too difficult for Deu 1:17
this is your rule in such *. Deu 19:21
of the priest in * of leprosy, for Deu 24:8
then Mizpah, and * of dispute were 1Sa 7:16
and he would hear * there, too. 1Sa 7:17
to assist him in hearing these *. 2Sa 15:3
whether murder * or other 2Ch 19:10
of final appeal in * involving 2Ch 19:11
of final appeal in all civil *; 2Ch 19:11
In such * it is all right. Eze 44:25
Jesus replied, "* like this Mk 9:29
In such * the Christian husband 1Co 7:15
But in other * only the judgment 1Ti 5:24
himself will handle these *." Heb 10:30

CASH
He offered * or, if Naboth 1Ki 21:2
The king also gave him a daily * 2Ki 25:30
and $100 a day in *, and had put Neh 5:15
Unless you have the extra * on Pro 22:26,27

CASIPHIA
of the Jews at *, to ask him and Ez 8:17

CASK
I am like a wine * without a Job 32:19

CASLUHIM
Pathrusim, * (from whom came the Gen 10:13,14
Caphtorim, and the * (the ancestors 1Ch 1:11,12

CASPIAN
*, currently in central Turkey. Eze 38:2,3f

CASSIA
the same amount of * as of Ex 30:24
perfumed with myrrh, aloes and *. Ps 45:8
wrought iron, * and calamus, Eze 27:19

CAST
all around it. * four rings of Ex 25:12
Then he * four rings of gold and Ex 37:13
Four rings were * for each side Ex 38:5
pedestal were * from the solid Ex 38:8
Tabernacle, and * lots to Lev 16:8
them I am going to * them out from Lev 18:24
of the nations I * out before you, Lev 20:23
He will * them out a little at a Deu 7:22
He * two hollow bronze pillars, 1Ki 7:15
Then Hiram * a round bronze tank, 1Ki 7:23
which were * along with the tank. 1Ki 7:24
had been * as part of the stands. 1Ki 7:32
of the stands were * from molten 1Ki 7:33
too, were * with the stands. 1Ki 7:34
All was * as one unit with the 1Ki 7:35
for each was * from the same mold. 1Ki 7:37
bronze, and were * at the plains of 1Ki 7:41-46
and I will * them out of my sight; 1Ki 9:7
Lord had * out from before them. 2Ki 17:8
The tank and oxen were * as one 2Ch 4:3
he then * ten gold lampstands and 2Ch 4:7

(CAST Con't)
Literally, "* lots," a form of Neh 10:34f
God will not * away a good man, Job 8:20
Literally, "shall * off his Job 15:33f
forever, * away like his own dung. Job 20:7
and have been * out into deserts Job 30:3
now * off all restraint before me. Job 30:11
as dust and * them to the wind. Ps 18:42
these who gloat when I am * down! Ps 38:16
Are we * off forever? Ps 44:23
In anger * them to the ground. Ps 56:7
He who * us off! Ps 60:9,10
O GOD, WHY have you * us away Ps 74:1
Then why * me off, rejected? Ps 89:38
upon Edom I * my shoe." Ps 108:9f
Literally, "* dice into the Pro 16:33f
the die is *, for there it lies. Ecc 11:3
golden images and * them out like Is 30:22
Let men * off their wicked Is 55:7
hate you and * you out for being Is 66:5
for the Lord has * you away!" Jer 23:33
I will * you out of my presence, Jer 23:38,39
and * us out of our own country. Jer 51:34,35
dust of the earth, * from the Lam 2:1
they will * lots by shaking Eze 21:21
Therefore, I * you out of the Eze 28:16
Therefore I have * you down to Eze 28:17
set nor put into a * to make it Eze 30:21
have rejected me and * me away. Jon 2:4
though I had never * them all away, Zec 10:6
Syriac version. "* it to the Zec 11:13f
for all of you to be * into hell. Mt 5:29
used your name to * out demons and Mt 7:22
prepared—shall be * into outer Mt 8:12
begged, "If you * us out, send us Mt 8:31
So Jesus * out the demon, and Mt 9:33
reason he can * out demons is that Mt 9:34
them authority to * out evil Mt 10:1
cure the lepers, and * out demons. Mt 10:8
* out demons because he is Satan, Mt 12:24
people use when they * them out? Mt 12:27
Only then can his demons be * Mt 12:29
couldn't we * that demon out?" Mt 17:19
out to preach and to * out demons. Mk 3:14,15
"How can Satan * out Satan? Mk 3:23
bound before his demons are * out Mk 3:27
two, with power to * out demons. Mk 6:7
And they * out many demons, and Mk 6:13
So I begged your disciples to * Mk 9:18
couldn't we * that demon out?" Mk 9:28
using your name to * out demons; Mk 9:38
whom he had * out seven demons. Mk 16:9
my authority to * out demons, and Mk 16:17
And he * out many demons. Lk 6:17,18
from whom he had * out demons or Lk 8:2
(Jesus had * out seven demons from Lk 8:2
demons—power to * them out—and to Lk 9:1
I begged your disciples to * the Lk 9:40
using your name to * out demons. Lk 9:49
Once, when Jesus * out a demon Lk 11:14
"No wonder he can * them out. Lk 11:15
empowering me to * out his demons, Lk 11:18
For they * out demons! Lk 11:19
"When a demon is * out of a man, Lk 11:24
to kill and then * into hell. Lk 12:5
of this world, shall be * out. Jn 12:31
them, and * lots for my robe." Jn 19:23,24
Literally, "* lots," or, "threw Act 1:26f
Many evil spirits were * out, Act 8:7
death, I * my vote against them. Act 26:10
should be * upon the Syrtis." Act 27:17f
in spirit— and * out this man from 1Co 5:5
you and * an evil spell upon you? Gal 3:1
but now is the time to * off and Col 3:8
Living One, and * their crowns Rev 4:10
found himself * down to earth, he Rev 12:13

CASTANETS
tambourines, *, and cymbals. 2Sa 6:5

CASTING
which was used for * the bases for Ex 38:29
The king did the * at the 2Ch 4:17,18
You can yet be saved by * out Jer 4:14
will I consider * them away forever Jer 31:37
bitterly and * dust upon their Eze 27:30
And if Satan is * out Satan, he Mt 12:26
And if, as you claim, I am * out Mt 12:27
But if I am * out demons by the Mt 12:28
* the wicked into the fire; Mt 13:50
the blind and * out evil spirits. Lk 7:20,21,22
But if I am * out demons because Lk 11:20
I will keep on * out demons and Lk 13:32
from town to town * out demons Act 19:13

CASTLE
Joseph was, in the * of Potiphar, Gen 40:1
in jail in the * of the captain of Gen 41:10
king's * beside the prison yard. Neh 3:25
opposite the * Tower and over to Neh 3:27
the * to the old City of David; Neh 12:37
Literally, "*," or "fort." Act 21:34f

CASTLES
* are full of rich treasures. Job 3:14,15

CASTRATE
you would go and * themselves." Gal 5:12f

CASTRATED
or *—shall not be offered to the Lev 22:24

CASTS
by a fisherman—he * a net into the Mt 13:47,48

CASUALTIES
he counted his *, he learned that 2Sa 2:30

CATARACT
pour upon me like a thundering *. Ps 42:7

CATASTROPHE
this would ward off further * to Num 17:10
What a *! Is 3:9

CATCH
* up with them, destroy them. Ex 15:9
We would have to * every fish in Num 11:22
that your sin will * up with you. Num 32:23
avenger might * and kill the Deu 19:6,7
If you hurry you can probably * Jos 2:5
that I would never * King Zebah and Ju 8:15
rush out and * them and take them Ju 21:21
If it turns on me I * it by the 1Sa 17:35
Come on down, sir, and we will * 1Sa 23:20
of Israel trying to *, anyway? 1Sa 24:14
Will I * them?" 1Sa 30:8
Then Joab sent messengers to * up 2Sa 3:26
"to * the attention of your god! 1Ki 18:27
No one can * him off guard or Job 40:24
"CAN YOU * leviathan with a hook Job 41:1
O God, hold them responsible. * Ps 5:10
Like hunters they * their victims Ps 10:9
have set a trap to * me, a noose to Ps 140:5
they are ropes that * and hold Pro 5:22
The lizards: they are easy to * Pro 30:24-28
the vineyards. * them, for the Sol 2:15
to * the glances of the men. Is 3:16
to * prey and became a man-eater. Eze 19:3
and learned to * prey, and he too Eze 19:6
a great army to * you with my net. Eze 32:3
she will not * up with them. Hos 1:7
the mouth of the first fish you *. Mt 17:26,27
and you will * a lot of fish!" Lk 5:4
last night and didn't * a thing. Lk 5:5
the size of their *, as were the Lk 5:9
Don't let my sudden coming * you Lk 21:34,35
guards at the city gates to * me; 2Co 11:32
which he uses to * them whenever he 2Ti 2:26
run after it to * and hold it! 1Pe 3:11

CATCHING
defeating many by * them off guard Dan 8:25

CATER
The kings of the world will * to Is 60:11

CATERPILLARS
of locusts or *, or if your 2Ch 6:28
He gave their crops to *. Ps 78:46

CATERPILLERS
or locusts or *, or if Israel's 1Ki 8:37

CATS
These fat * have everything Ps 73:7

CATTLE
kind of animal—* and reptiles and Gen 1:24
wild animals and * and reptiles. Gen 1:25
these birds and * and wild Gen 9:9,10,11
all his wealth—the * and slaves he Gen 12:5
sheep and * and many servants. Gen 13:5
sheep and herds of *, and a fortune Gen 24:35
herds of *, and many servants. Gen 26:14
the fields herding *, so he did Gen 34:5
servants, * and flocks—all the Gen 36:6,7,8
them both because of all their *. Gen 36:6,7,8
And these skinny * ate up the Gen 41:20
So they brought their * to Joseph Gen 47:17
is gone, and our * are yours, and Gen 47:18
to destroy your *, horses, donkeys, Ex 9:3
will affect only the * of Egypt; Ex 9:4
The next morning all the * of the Ex 9:6
of the Israeli * were dead, yet Ex 9:7
Bring in your * from the fields, Ex 9:19
* and slaves in from the fields; Ex 9:20
also all the firstborn of the *. Ex 12:29
and herds—a vast exodus of *. Ex 12:38
with our children and * too?" Ex 17:3
your * or your house guests. Ex 20:10
is mine—*, sheep, and goats. Ex 34:19
mate your * with a different kind; Lev 19:19
living among you. * and wild Lev 25:6,7
and destroy your * and reduce your Lev 26:22
and the Levites' * are mine as Num 3:41
firstborn * of the whole nation." Num 3:41
and give me the * of the Levites Num 3:45
* of the people of Israel; Num 3:45
goats, or from their herds of *. Num 15:3,4
all the people and all their *!" Num 20:8
and the people and their * drank. Num 20:11
and seized the * and flocks and a Num 31:9,10,11
flocks, and * that are given to the Num 31:30
wives, flocks, and * shall stay Num 32:26
*, flocks, and other livestock. Num 35:3
alive except the *, which we took Deu 2:35,36
But we kept the * and loot for Deu 3:7
for your many * until you return Deu 3:19
servants, oxen, donkeys, or *; Deu 5:14
great flocks of *, sheep, and goats Deu 7:13
shall be barren, not even your *. Deu 7:14
for your * to graze in, and you Deu 11:15
and even all of the *. Deu 13:15
the women, children, *, and booty. Deu 20:14
crops and healthy *, and prosper Deu 28:8
many *, and abundant crops. Deu 28:11
fertility of your * and flocks; Deu 28:15-19
until your * and crops are gone. Deu 28:51
and much * and wonderful crops; Deu 30:9
and children and * may remain here, Jos 1:14
the loot and the * for yourselves. Jos 8:2
Only the * and the loot were not Jos 8:27
All the loot and * of the Jos 11:14
pasturelands for their *. Jos 14:3,4
for our *," they said. Jos 21:2
booty of *, silver, gold, bronze, Jos 22:7,8
their children, *, and household Ju 18:21
children, and *—and burned down Ju 20:48
confiscated their *, and so the 1Sa 23:5
20 pasture-fed *, 100 sheep, and, 1Ki 4:23
Joel was a * man, and he pastured 1Ch 5:9
were many * in the land of Gilead. 1Ch 5:9
to rustle * at Gath, but they were 1Ch 7:20,21
wine, oil, *, and sheep were 1Ch 12:40
in charge of the * on the Plains of 1Ch 27:29
but destroyed the * tents and 2Ch 14:15
had great herds of * out in the 2Ch 26:10
tithes of their * and sheep, and 2Ch 31:5,6
our bodies and our *, and we serve Neh 9:37
of all our *, herds, and flocks, Neh 10:36
Their * are productive, they Job 21:10
Literally, "(even) the * (warn Job 36:33f
mine! The * on a thousand hills! Ps 50:10,11
Their * died in the fields, Ps 78:48
to feed the *, and there are fruit Ps 104:14
big families there, and many *. Ps 107:38
wild animals and *, the snakes and Ps 148:10
to be trampled by * and sheep. Is 5:5
will cover them; *, sheep and goats Is 7:25
Calves and fat * will be safe Is 11:6
Like * grazing in the valleys, Is 63:14
*, yes, and your grapes and figs; Jer 5:17
Gone is the lowing of *, gone the Jer 9:10
to him all your * for his use. Jer 27:6
the number of * here in Israel. Jer 31:27
Their camels and * shall all be Jer 49:32
Not even her *—woe to them, too! Jer 50:27
your fruit and steal your dairy *. Eze 25:4
her people, her * and her flocks. Eze 25:13
For the people are rich with * Eze 38:12
drive away their * and seize their Eze 38:13
fields. The * groan with hunger; Joe 1:18
lead you away like the * you are; Amo 4:2
and all its *?" Jon 4:11
the fields and the * barns are Hab 3:17
you and all your *, and ruin Hag 1:11
many *—and yet they will be safe. Zec 2:4
Don't you untie your * from their Lk 13:15
merchants selling *, sheep, and Jn 2:14
he and his sons and * enjoyed?" Jn 4:12
wheat, *, sheep, horses, Rev 18:13

CATTLEMAN
He was, in fact, the richest * in Job 1:2,3

CATTLEMEN
He became the first of the * and Gen 4:20

CATTY
always critical and *, watch out! Gal 5:15

CAUGHT
or you will be * in the destruction Gen 19:15
Then Abraham noticed a ram * by Gen 22:13
in hot pursuit and * up with them Gen 31:23
Laban finally * up with Jacob Gen 31:25
So he * up with them and Gen 44:6
whether he is * in possession of Ex 21:16
"If a thief is * in the act of Ex 22:2
"If he is * in the act of Ex 22:4
his sons * the blood for him, Lev 9:9
and his sons * the blood and he Lev 9:12
So the people * and killed quail Num 11:32
one of them was * gathering wood on Num 15:32
* in the act, he must pay a fine Deu 22:28,29
So the men of Ai were * in a trap Jos 8:22
replied, "You haven't * them yet! Ju 8:6
So he went out and * three Ju 15:4
household, * up with him. 2Sa 16:1
and his hair * in the branches. 2Sa 18:9
that was * there and killed it. 2Sa 23:20
the Tabernacle and * hold of the 1Ki 1:49,50
* hold of the horns of the altar. 1Ki 2:28
before him and * hold of his feet. 2Ki 4:27
So Gehazi * up with him. 2Ki 5:21
They * up with Saul and his 1Ch 10:2
They are * in their own traps; Job 5:13
overthrown me and * me in his net. Job 19:6
I chased my enemies; I * up with Ps 18:37
* in their own net, and destroyed. Ps 35:8
their evil deeds and not get *. Ps 36:2
to count, have all * up with me and Ps 40:12
My enemies chased and * me. Ps 143:3

(CAUGHT Con't)
cubs than a fool * in his folly. Pro 17:12
be punished and a liar shall be *. Pro 19:9
those cursed of God are * in it. Pro 22:14
A man who is * lying to his Pro 26:18,19
others will get * in it himself. Pro 26:27
evil men are * in it, but good Pro 29:5,6
He is like a fish * in a net, or Ecc 9:12
in a net, or a bird * in a snare. Ecc 9:12
helpless as wild goats * in a net. Is 51:20
that Israel knows is getting *. Jer 2:26,27
Zedekiah would be * and taken as a Jer 32:4
the king and * him on the plains of Jer 39:5
to stop him. They * up with him at Jer 41:12
you and you are *, for you have Jer 50:24
chased them and * King Zedekiah in Jer 52:8
Are we but fish, to be * and Hab 1:14
At last justice has * up with Hab 2:6
wild animals you * in your Hab 2:17
* up with them and punished them. Zec 1:5,6
by demons * sight of him they would Mk 3:11
So they * him and murdered him Mk 12:8
brought a woman * in adultery and Jn 8:3
was * in the very act of adultery. Jn 8:4
We did, but * nothing all night. Jn 21:3
fish you've just *," Jesus said. Jn 21:10
Spirit of the Lord * away Philip, Act 8:39
* the ship and blew it out to sea. Act 27:14,15
But the anger of God has * up 1Th 2:16
the earth will be * up with them in 1Th 4:17
born only to be * and killed, 2Pe 2:12
was * up to God and to his throne. Rev 12:5

CAUSE
If you do, I will * you to Gen 12:2
I will * him to multiply and Gen 17:20
And I will * your descendants to Gen 26:4
him, "and I will * you to be Gen 35:11
But I will * Pharaoh to Ex 7:3
will ask him to * the swarms of Ex 8:29
land of Egypt and * boils to break Ex 9:9
toward heaven and * the hail to Ex 9:22
Bread' will * you always to Ex 12:17
A bribe hurts the * of the person Ex 23:8
and I will * you to defeat the Ex 23:31
fields, and to * them to bring Lev 17:5
left alive, I will * them to be Lev 26:36
* of the plague that destroyed us. Num 31:16
these laws is to * you, your sons, Deu 6:2
* your enemies to fall before you; Deu 23:14
"The Lord will * you to be Deu 28:25
for I will * you to defeat them! Ju 7:8,9
come true, I will * your two sons, 1Sa 2:34
have done I will * your own 2Sa 12:11
Literally, "He will * my help and 2Sa 23:5f
me, then I will * your descendants 1Ki 9:5
the Lord will * you to triumph!" 1Ki 22:12
the Lord will * you to conquer!" 1Ki 22:15
They shall no longer * death or 2Ki 2:21
Because of this I will * your 2Ki 10:30
the * of such great sin in Israel. 2Ki 10:31
The Lord is eager to * this to 2Ki 19:31
I will * the kings of Israel to 2Ki 21:13
And I now declare that I will * 1Ch 17:10
Why must you * Israel to sin?" 1Ch 21:3
and I will * his sons and his 1Ch 22:10
the Lord will * you to conquer." 2Ch 18:11
God had given us * for great joy. Neh 12:43
let you harm him without any *." Job 2:3
and to God would I commit my *." Job 5:8f
multiplies my wounds without a *. Job 9:17
He has good * for fear—his enemy Job 18:11
God had just * for punishing him. Job 32:2
* it to strike as you direct it? Job 38:35
"I will * your name to be Ps 45:17
He will * the evil deeds of my Ps 54:5
all those who hate me without *. Ps 69:4
O God of Israel, don't let me * Ps 69:6
And because I advocate your *, Ps 69:9
insulted. Give * for these poor and Ps 74:21
Literally, "* your face to shine Ps 80:3f
Literally, "* your face to shine Ps 80:7f
not ours, O Lord! * everyone to Ps 115:1
They can't rest unless they * Pro 4:16
advance the * of righteousness. Pro 10:16
An unreliable messenger can * a Pro 13:17
he is angry with those who * Pro 14:35
wrath, but harsh words * quarrels. Pro 15:1
Gentle words * life and health; Pro 15:4
The father of a godly man has * Pro 23:24,25
DEAD FLIES WILL * even a bottle of Ecc 10:1
of being young * you to forget Ecc 12:1
And the Lord shall * his Is 30:30
will * all this to come to pass. Is 37:32
tyrannized without * by Egypt and Is 52:4
the earth, and * the grain to grow Is 55:10
Brazenly you murder without a *. Jer 2:34
I will * anguish and terror to Jer 15:8
I will * them to know . . ." Jer 16:21f
For I have committed my * to you. Jer 20:12
and justice and * righteousness to Jer 23:5,6
For the Lord will * something new Jer 31:22
* her enemies to wipe her out. Jer 49:37
I will * the people to lack both Eze 4:17
it is not without * that all these Eze 14:23
come when I will * the ancient Eze 29:21
of my sheep, and * them to lie down Eze 34:15,16
of exile and * you to rise again Eze 37:12
that would * them to perspire. Eze 44:18
But a general will stop him and * Dan 11:18
she was born, and * her to waste Hos 1:3
O Israel, I will * you to forget Hos 1:17
their parents and * their deaths. Mt 10:21
Literally, "* to stumble." Mt 18:6f
helping me, he is hurting my *. Lk 11:23
God and the first * of all things; Jn 1:1f
God and the first * of all things; Jn 1:14f
Last Day I will * all such to rise Jn 6:44
And I will * strange Act 2:19
They found no just * to execute Act 13:28
riot, since there is no * for it. Act 19:40
for they found no * for the death Act 28:18
Didn't the law * my doom? Rom 7:13
Accepting them might * discord Rom 14:1f
Don't do anything that will * Rom 14:16
Stay away from those who * Rom 16:17
we should be the * of a quarrel? 1Co 3:5
eat it, lest you * some Christian 1Co 8:9
Literally, "For this * ought the 1Co 11:10f
and how can you if I * you pain? 2Co 2:2
Don't * the Holy Spirit sorrow by Eph 4:30
anything that will * me to be Php 1:20
for they support the * of Satan. Rev 2:9

CAUSED
Then the Lord God * the man to Gen 2:21
later Mosaic law, * ceremonial Gen 31:35f
* frogs to come up upon the land. Ex 8:7
as Moses asked and * the swarms to Ex 8:31,32
rod and Jehovah * an east wind to Ex 10:13
(For God * the Egyptians to be Ex 11:3
They have * their own doom." Lev 20:27
and * you to live in shelters. Lev 23:43
Place of the Graves * by Lust," Num 11:34
Then the Lord * the donkey to Num 22:28
advice and * the people of Israel Num 31:16
as the Lord has * other nations in Deu 8:20
* by your enemies at your gates. Deu 28:56,57
the Lord, and he * them to turn up Jos 14:1
The man who * the accidental Jos 20:6
For in the confusion the Lord * Ju 7:22
So the Lord * water to gush Ju 15:19
of the tumor * by the plague, and 1Sa 6:4,5
And God * the people to be afraid 1Sa 11:7
mental condition * forgetfulness, 1Sa 17:55f
Now I have * the death of all of 1Sa 22:22
And have * me to subdue 2Sa 22:40
famine in the land * by plant 1Ki 8:37
So the Lord * Hadad the Edomite 1Ki 11:14
hand was in it—he * the new king to 1Ki 12:15
whose sins had * the famine. 1Ki 21:9f
"The Lord has * this mess," the 2Ki 6:33
Jeroboam, who had * Israel to sin. 2Ki 13:2
In those days the Lord * King 2Ki 15:37
to do this, and he * the shadow to 2Ki 20:11
* by the evils of King Manasseh. 2Ki 23:26
So God * King Pul of Assyria 1Ch 5:26
* all the nations to fear him. 1Ch 14:17
demands. (God * him to do it in 2Ch 10:15
praise, the Lord * the armies of 2Ch 20:22
arrived, he * trouble for King Ahaz 2Ch 28:20
He has * us to be objects of 2Ch 29:8
the Lord had * the king of Assyria Ez 6:21,22
instead you * the kings of Persia Ez 9:9
Og of Bashan. You * a population Neh 9:23
And I * the widows' hearts to Job 29:13
"If I have hurt the poor or * Job 31:16
* the dawn to rise in the east? Job 38:12
trouble and grief they have *. Ps 10:14
You have * this nation to Ps 60:2
Literally, "You * men to ride Ps 66:12f
the shore! He * the birds to fall Ps 78:28
enemy hands. He * his people to be Ps 78:62
sins had * the plague to start. Ps 106:30
great love, and * even their Ps 106:46
For he * gushing streams to Ps 114:8
I have * all this to happen as I Is 37:26
"knowledge" have * you to turn Is 47:10
without mercy and * her enemies to Lam 2:17
Thus they have * your death along Eze 21:29
I clothed Lebanon in black and * Eze 31:15
For I have * my terror to fall Eze 32:32
"But you * the Nazirites to sin Amo 2:12
gods and * this terrible storm; Jon 1:7
Your 'guidance' has * many to Mal 2:8
But Jesus said, "Your error is * Mt 22:29
but this * complaints from the Lk 15:2
God—has * this perfect healing. Act 3:16
that it was Adam's sin that * this Rom 5:13
The sin of this one man, Adam, * Rom 5:17
Adam * many to be sinners Rom 5:19
God, and Christ * many to be made Rom 5:19
I wrote about, who * all the 2Co 2:5,6
trouble, has not * sorrow to me as 2Co 2:5,6
between us, * by the Jewish laws Eph 2:15
the Garden, that * sweating of Heb 5:7f
and if his sickness was * by some Jas 5:15
wounds that once had * his death. Rev 5:6
* destruction upon the earth." Rev 11:18

CAUSES
bitter water that * the curse. Num 5:19
Some he * to be poor 1Sa 2:7
He * the good to walk a steady 2Sa 22:34
but the water is bad, and * our 2Ki 2:19
all nature, and * the lightning to Job 37:15
the world, and * wars to end Ps 46:9
* princes to wander among ruins; Ps 107:40
of godly citizens * a city to Pro 11:11
He knows that anger * mistakes. Pro 14:29
just as surely a retort * anger! Pro 25:23
Greed * fighting; Pro 28:25
a blow to the nose * bleeding, so Pro 30:33
bleeding, so anger * quarrels. Pro 30:33
He * mist to rise upon the earth; Jer 10:13
late, before he * deep, Jer 13:16
the heavens and he * the vapors to Jer 51:16
for it * him to sit apart in Lam 3:28
eye!—* you to lust, gouge it out Mt 5:29
your right hand—* you to sin, cut Mt 5:30
for fornication, * her to commit Mt 5:32
But if any of you * one of these Mt 18:6
So if your hand or foot * you to Mt 18:8
And if your eye * you to sin, Mt 18:9
But if someone * one of these Mk 9:42
For sin—the sting that * 1Co 15:55,56
it springs up it * deep trouble, Heb 12:15
is, and whether it * physical death 1Jn 5:17f
supporting the * of Satan while Rev 3:9

CAUSING
brothers, * even deeper hatred. Gen 37:5
to trial for * her horrible Num 5:31
They are * you to worship Baal, Num 25:18
by * the lion to kill him." 1Ki 13:26
he issued a decree * Haman's plot Est 9:24,25
and instruction, * them to change Job 33:17,18
following him, * the cry of the Job 34:28
for the lightning, * the rain to Job 38:25-27
* seeds to sprout across the land. Ps 65:10
angered God, * Moses serious Ps 106:32
smooth and sweet, * the lips of Sol 7:9
prophets are, by * something else Is 44:25
to other gods, * my fury to rise! Jer 32:29
What an incredible evil, * Judah Jer 32:35
to them, and * me to destroy you Jer 44:8
enjoy afflicting men and * sorrow. Lam 3:33
other gods, * Israel to fall into Eze 44:12
wind over the sea, * a great storm Jon 1:4
"But he is * riots against the Lk 23:5
be responsible for * great 1Co 8:11
If anyone is * divisions among Tit 3:10
WHAT IS * the quarrels and fights Jas 4:1
upon the sun, * it to scorch all Rev 16:8

CAUTIONED
them, but he * them against Mt 12:16
"Don't touch me," he *, "for I Jn 20:17

CAUTIOUS
Don't insist that I be * lest I Job 32:21,22
A wise man is * and avoids Pro 14:16

CAVALRY
*, and people accompanied Joseph. Gen 50:9
Pharaoh's entire *—horses, Ex 14:9
after them with chariots and *. Jos 24:6
* and twenty thousand infantry; 2Sa 8:4
for homes for his * and chariot 1Ki 9:19
of chariots and *—1,400 chariots in 1Ki 10:26
*, and twenty thousand troops. 1Ch 18:4
chariots, and * from Mesopotamia, 1Ch 19:6
recruited 12,000 * to guard the 2Ch 1:14
for soldiers and * to accompany us Ez 8:22
their mighty * and chariots instead Is 31:1
a great army and * and chariots. Eze 26:7
The hoofs of his * will choke Eze 26:10
troops and armored *, and make you Eze 38:4
* and cover the land like a cloud. Eze 38:15,16
in the upraised arms of the *! Nah 3:3
Their * move proudly forward from Hab 1:8
200 spearmen and 70 mounted *. Act 23:23,24
the * to take him on to Caesarea. Act 23:32

CAVALRYMEN
*, including General Shobach. 2Sa 10:18
chariot commanders, and *. 1Ki 9:22
in all, and 12,000 * who lived in 1Ki 10:26
officers, charioteers, and *; 2Ch 8:9
and 12,000 * stationed in the 2Ch 9:25
sixty thousand * and an unnumbered 2Ch 12:3
with all of their chariots and *? 2Ch 16:8

CAVE
went to live in a * in the Gen 19:30
to sell me the * of Mach-pelah, Gen 23:9
I will give you the * and the Gen 23:11
Mamre, and the * at the end of the Gen 23:17,18
in the field and * deeded to him by Gen 23:19,20
buried him in the * of Mach-pelah Gen 25:9,10
of Canaan, in the * in the field of Gen 49:29,30
It is the * which my grandfather Gen 49:32

(CAVE Con't)
it there in the * of Mach-pelah—the Gen 50:12,13
of Mach-pelah—the * Abraham had Gen 50:12,13
and hid in a * at Makkedah. Jos 10:16
the mouth of the * and that guards Jos 10:18
the mouth of the * and to bring out Jos 10:22,23
the * where they had been hiding; Jos 10:27
was placed at the mouth of the *. Jos 10:27
Then he went to live in a * in Ju 15:8
at the * in the rock of Etam. Ju 15:11
and escaped to the * of Adullam, 1Sa 22:1
when David was living in the *. 1Sa 22:4
* and return to the land of Judah. 1Sa 22:5
Saul went into a * to go to the 1Sa 24:3
and his men were hiding in the *! 1Sa 24:3
After Saul had left the * and gone 1Sa 24:7,8
back there in the * and some of my 1Sa 24:9,10
and his men went back to their *. 1Sa 24:22
already hidden in some pit or *. 2Sa 17:9
was living in the * of Adullam and 2Sa 23:13
of God, where he lived in a *. 1Ki 19:9
stood at the entrance of the *. 1Ki 19:13
he was hiding in the * of Adullam. 1Ch 11:15
It was a * with a heavy stone Jn 11:37,38

CAVERNS
and crawl into the * to hide among Is 2:21

CAVES
mountains, living in * and dens. Ju 6:2
tried to hide in *, thickets, 1Sa 13:6
* in the hill country of Ziph. 1Sa 23:14,15
"He is in the * of Horesh on 1Sa 23:19
went to live in the * of Engedi. 1Sa 23:29
of them in two *—fifty in each—and 1Ki 18:3,4
of them in two * and fed them with 1Ki 18:13
and live in * for want of a home. Job 24:8
and in *, and among the rocks. Job 30:6
Crawl into the * in the rocks and Is 2:10
rocks and into the * because of the Is 2:19
valleys and * and thorny parts, as Is 7:19
the graves and * to worship evil Is 65:4
and live in the * like doves that Jer 48:28
forts and * shall die of disease. Eze 33:27
mountains, hiding in dens and *. Heb 11:37,38
chained in gloomy * and darkness 2Pe 2:4
themselves in the * and rocks of Rev 6:15

CEASE
and all ordinary work shall *. Lev 23:7
For there in death the wicked * Job 3:17
only tell us, and we will * at Job 34:32
I warned the proud to * their Ps 75:4
and scoffers will *, and all those Is 29:20
I will not * to pray for her or to Is 62:1
and idolatry to * from the land. Eze 23:48

CEASED
his task, God * from this work he Gen 2:2
when he * this work of creation. Gen 2:3
water sources * their gushing, and Gen 8:2
and the rain * pouring down. Ex 9:33
music in your palace has *; Is 14:11
in the wine presses has * forever. Is 16:10

CEASELESS
earth—* activity, day and night. Ecc 8:16,17

CEDAR
shall take some * wood, a scarlet Lev 14:4
along with the * wood, the scarlet Lev 14:6
using two birds, * wood, scarlet Lev 14:49
bowl, and dip the * wood, hyssop Lev 14:51,52
Eleazar shall take * wood and Num 19:6
As * trees beside the waters. Num 24:3-9
Then King Hiram of Tyre sent * 2Sa 5:11
in this beautiful * palace while 2Sa 7:2
built me a beautiful * temple?' 2Sa 7:7
of Lebanon to cut * timber for me, 1Ki 5:6
I can supply both * and cypress. 1Ki 5:8
Solomon as much * and cypress 1Ki 5:10
the beams and pillars, with *. 1Ki 6:9
to the Temple walls by * timbers. 1Ki 6:10
was paneled with *, and the floors 1Ki 6:15
to the ceiling with * boards. 1Ki 6:16
Throughout the Temple the * 1Ki 6:18
the * altar—with pure gold; 1Ki 6:21,22
stone and one layer of * beams. 1Ki 6:36
The great * ceiling beams rested 1Ki 7:2
upon four rows of * pillars. 1Ki 7:2
it was paneled with * from the 1Ki 7:7
and were topped with * beams. 1Ki 7:11
walls, topped with * beams, just 1Ki 7:12
for all the * and cypress lumber 1Ki 9:11,12
in those days, and * was of no 1Ki 10:27
of the mighty * tree, 'Give your 2Ki 14:9
supplied him with much * lumber. 1Ch 14:1
great rafts of * logs to David. 1Ch 22:4
And expensive * lumber was used 2Ch 1:15
shipments of * lumber such as Hiram 2Ch 2:3
Also send me * trees, fir trees, 2Ch 2:8
in the road! And * was used as 2Ch 9:27
demanded of a * tree, 'Give your 2Ch 25:18
and bought * logs from the people Ez 3:7
His tail is as straight as a * Job 40:17
towering like a * of Lebanon, but Ps 37:35,36
we were like the mighty * trees, Ps 80:10
shaded by the * trees and firs." Sol 1:17
will enclose her with * boards." Sol 8:9
all of your fine * beams and throw Jer 22:7
* and painted a lovely red." Jer 22:14
top of the tallest * tree and Eze 17:3,4
top of the highest *, and I, Eze 17:22,23
It shall become a noble *, Eze 17:22,23
They took a * from Lebanon to Eze 27:5
nation—like a * of Lebanon, full of Eze 31:2,3
as * trees, and strong as oaks! Amo 2:9
All her * paneling will lie open Zep 2:14

CEDAR-LINED
they should build me a * temple.' 1Ch 17:6

CEDAR-PANELED
His * living quarters surrounded 1Ki 7:8
I'm living here in a * home while 1Ch 17:1

CEDAR-WOOD
made a * altar for this room. 1Ki 6:20

CEDARS
burn down the great * of Lebanon!' Ju 9:15
the great * of Lebanon down to the 1Ki 4:33
I have cut down the tallest * and 2Ki 19:23
It breaks down the *. Ps 29:5,6
Literally, "the * of God." Ps 80:10f
and grow tall as the * of Lebanon. Ps 92:12
The Lord planted the * of Ps 104:16
fruit trees and *, the wild Ps 148:9
of the mountains and * of Lebanon. Sol 4:11
of finest gold, like * of Lebanon; Sol 5:15
All the tall * of Lebanon and Is 2:13
but we will replace them with *! Is 9:8,9,10
fir trees and * of Lebanon—sing out Is 14:8
I cut down the tallest * and Is 37:24
I will plant trees—*, myrtle, Is 41:19
He cuts down *, he selects the Is 44:14
palace among the * of Lebanon, but Jer 22:23
in the soil like * in Lebanon. Hos 14:5
trees, for all the ruined *; Zec 11:2

CEILING
to form the * of the Tabernacle. Ex 36:13
Above the * was a second layer Ex 36:14,15
from floor to *, was paneled with 1Ki 6:15
floor to the * with cedar boards. 1Ki 6:16
Its walls and * were overlaid 1Ki 6:20
The great cedar * beams rested 1Ki 7:2
and * overlaid with pure gold! 2Ch 3:4

CEILINGS
into its doorframes and *. Jer 22:13
beams in the * echo what they say. Hab 2:11

CELEBRATE
and Abraham gave a party to * the Gen 21:8
to * with Jacob at a big party. Gen 29:22
"You shall * this event each Ex 12:14
so it is a law that you must * Ex 12:17
they may come and * with you—then Ex 12:48
"So * the event annually in late Ex 13:10
Or, "feasts you must *." Ex 23:14f
"Be sure to * the Feast of Ex 34:18
"And you must remember to * Ex 34:22
that they are to * several annual Lev 23:1
is the time to * this seven-day Lev 23:39
"The people of Israel must * the Num 9:2,3
they may still * the Passover, but Num 9:10
and yet refuses to * the Passover Num 9:13
you and wants to * the Passover to Num 9:14
year, you shall * the Num 28:16
the people to * the new harvest. Num 28:26
"ALWAYS REMEMBER TO * the Deu 16:1
he has given you. * with your Deu 26:11
To * their sacrifices with them. Deu 33:19
to * the capture of Samson. Ju 16:23,24
Elkanah would * the happy occasion 1Sa 1:4
along the way to * and to cheer for 1Sa 18:6
come to a feast to * the occasion. 2Sa 13:21-24
to Jerusalem to * the bringing of 1Ch 15:3
For God wants Israel always to * 2Ch 2:4
had voted to * the Passover in May 2Ch 30:2,3
it is a time to * with a hearty Neh 8:10
of Vashti. To * the occasion, he Est 2:18
of the month, to * with feasting, Est 9:22
never fail to * these two days at Est 9:27
We will write songs to * your Ps 21:13
who come to * the Temple feasts; Lam 1:4
No longer can the people * their Lam 2:6
month, you shall * the Passover. Eze 45:21
the Lord of Hosts, to * a time Zec 14:16
We must * with a feast, for this Lk 15:23
* his coming home again unharmed.' Lk 15:27
prostitutes, you * by killing the Lk 15:30
But it is right to *. Lk 15:32
throw parties to * the death of the Rev 11:10

CELEBRATED
is to be * at the end of March. Lev 23:5
This is to be * beginning the day Lev 23:6
to be * before the Lord for seven Lev 23:33,34
Trumpets shall be * on the Num 29:1
of Jericho, they * the Passover Jos 5:10
He has * his coronation by 1Ki 1:19
Today he * his coronation by 1Ki 1:25
Josiah, and it was * in Jerusalem. 2Ki 23:23
the nation and * the wonderful news 1Ch 10:9
For the next seven days, they * 2Ch 7:8
Or, "The Passover had not been * 2Ch 30:5f
So the people of Israel * the 2Ch 30:21
Passover would be * on the first 2Ch 35:1
And they * the Feast of Ez 3:4
The Passover was * on the first Ez 6:19
Passover feast and * the Feast of Ez 6:21,22
to generation, * by every family Est 9:28
And thus you * those former days Eze 23:21

CELEBRATES
The whole city * a good man's Pro 11:10

CELEBRATING
and when you are * the Passover, Ex 12:25
why you are *—it is a celebration Ex 13:8
the whole city is * and rejoicing. 1Ki 1:44,45
day they rested, * their victory Est 9:17
go hungry while * with the groom? Lk 5:34
drink, or for not * Jewish holidays Col 2:16

CELEBRATION
The * shall last seven days. Ex 12:15
seven days of the * shall be Ex 12:15
On the first day of the *, and Ex 12:16
"This annual '* with Unleavened Ex 12:17
you will reply, 'It is the * of Ex 12:27
the annual * of God's deliverance. Ex 12:42
Now remember, during the annual * Ex 13:3
"During those * days each year Ex 13:8
is a * of what the Lord did for you Ex 13:8
Again I say, this * shall Ex 13:16
you before. This * is to be an Ex 23:15
on the day of the *, but offer a Lev 23:25
It is a joyous *, and no heavy Lev 23:36
instructions concerning this *." Num 9:2,3
that the Passover * would begin on Num 9:4,5
you to the * at the sanctuary. Deu 16:11
"Another *, the Festival of Deu 16:13
seven days of the *," he said, Ju 14:12
it up for the remainder of the *. Ju 14:17
took part in the *, and carried Ju 21:23
of the * of the new moon. 1Sa 20:5
When the new moon * began, the 1Sa 20:24,25
in a family *," Jonathan replied. 1Sa 20:28,29
the City of David with a great *. 2Sa 6:12
not a day for execution but for *! 2Sa 19:22
and noisy * all along the way. 1Ki 1:40
This * occurred at the time of 1Ki 8:2
so much. The * lasted for fourteen 1Ki 8:65
than the annual * in Jerusalem, 1Ki 12:32,33f
to have a great * to praise him. 2Ki 10:18,19
There had not been a Passover * 2Ki 23:22
brought to the *, for joy had 1Ch 12:40
At last the * ended and the 1Ch 16:43
at the new moon * and other regular 2Ch 2:4
This * took place in October at 2Ch 5:3
Passover *, the Festival of Weeks, 2Ch 8:13
for the annual Passover *. 2Ch 30:1
month of May for the Passover *. 2Ch 30:13
For Jerusalem hadn't seen a * 2Ch 30:26
During the dedication * 100 Ez 6:17
great and joyful * because they Neh 8:12
This was the year of the great * Est 1:1
the occasion. The * lasted six Est 1:4
a great * and declared a holiday. Est 8:17
day have an annual * on the second Est 9:19
That is why this * is called Est 9:26
and sisters to his home for a *. Job 1:4
At the new moon *, he shall Eze 46:6
"As you know, the Passover * Mt 26:2
"But not during the Passover * Mt 26:5
the Passover *—anyone they wanted. Mt 27:15
After the * was over they Lk 2:43
AND NOW THE Passover * was Lk 22:1
Now the day of the Passover * Lk 22:7
*, and Jesus went to Jerusalem. Jn 2:13
at the Passover *, many people were Jn 2:23
at the Passover * and had seen some Jn 4:45
for the annual Passover * Jn 6:2-5
him to go to Judea for the *. Jn 7:3
had left for the *, then he went Jn 7:10
to find him at the * and kept Jn 7:11
* of the cleansing of the Temple. Jn 10:22,23f
at the time of the Dedication *. Jn 10:22,23
This annual * came fifty days Act 2:1f
the Passover * and imprisoned him, Act 12:3
possible, for the * of Pentecost. Act 20:16

CELEBRATIONS
moon *, and at all the festivals. 1Ch 23:31
the new moon *, and the other Ez 3:5
Come to the joyous * at full Ps 81:3
Your holy * of the new moon and Is 1:12,13
and on the days of the new moon *. Eze 46:1
and on the days of the new moon *. Eze 46:3
foreign cities to attend these *. Zec 8:20,21
for the religious *, having arrived Act 2:5

CELESTIAL
Literally, "There are * bodies." 1Co 15:40f

CELL
They took Jeremiah from his * and Jer 38:6
into a debtor's *, for you will Mt 5:25
was a light in the * and an angel Act 12:7
So Peter left the *, following Act 12:9

(CELL Con't)
first and second * blocks and came Act 12:10

CEMETERY
a permanent * for my family." Gen 23:9
accompanied the bier to the *. 2Sa 3:31
in the royal * in Jerusalem. 1Ki 15:24
in the royal * in the City of 2Ki 8:24,25
they buried him in the royal *. 2Ki 9:28
He was buried in the royal * in 2Ki 12:21
in the royal *, in the City of 2Ki 14:20
Judah in the royal *, in the City 2Ki 15:38
in the royal *, in the City of 2Ki 16:20
was buried in the * of the kings in 2Ch 21:1
Jerusalem, but not in the royal *. 2Ch 21:20
but not in the * of the kings. 2Ch 24:25
and buried him in the royal *. 2Ch 25:28
in the royal * even though he was a 2Ch 26:23
the royal hillside * among the 2Ch 32:33
was buried there, in the royal *. 2Ch 35:24,25
he built as far as the royal *, Neh 3:16
returned from the *, having Ecc 8:9,10
They lived in a * and were so Mt 8:28
to make it into a * for foreigners Mt 27:7
That is why the * is still Mt 27:8
they left the * and went into Mt 27:53
he lived in a * among the tombs. Lk 8:27

CEN-SERS
incense from the * of these men Num 16:38

CENCHREAE
with him. At *, Paul had his head Act 18:18
*, will be coming to see you soon. Rom 16:1

CENSER
he shall take a * full of live Lev 16:12
a * for each man, 250 in all; Num 16:17
"Quick, take a * and place fire in Num 16:46
Each of them held a * of burning Eze 8:11
* came and stood at the altar; Rev 8:3
Then the angel filled the * with Rev 8:5

CENSERS
fire in their *, laid incense on Lev 10:1
Or, "placed fire in their * Lev 10:1f
with you, take * tomorrow and light Num 16:6,7
Be sure to bring your * with Num 16:17
They came with their * and lit Num 16:18
to pull those * from the fire; Num 16:36,37
altar, for these * are holy because Num 16:38
the 250 bronze * and beat them out Num 16:39
29 *, Ez 1:9,10

CENSUS
you take a * of the people of Ex 30:11,12
registered in the * who were twenty Ex 38:25,26
"Take a * of all the men twenty Num 1:2-15
not include their number in the *. Num 1:47,48,49
*: 74,600 54,400 57,400 Num 2:3-31
him, "Take a * of the tribe of Num 3:14,15
* Num 3:16-24
* Num 3:25-30
* Num 3:31-35
"Now take a * of all the eldest Num 3:40
So Moses took a * of the eldest Num 3:42
Aaron, "Take a * of the Kohath Num 4:1
This * will be of all males from Num 4:3
to Moses, "Take a * of the Num 4:21,22,23
"Now take a * of the Merari Num 4:29
leaders took a * of the Kohath Num 4:34
A similar * of the Gershon Num 4:38-41
This * was taken in response to Num 4:49
the *—brought their offerings. Num 7:2
priest), "Take a * of all the men Num 26:2
So Moses and Eleazar issued * Num 26:3,4
Here are the results of the *: Num 26:3,4
This * also included the sub-clans Num 26:19-22
indicated by the *— the larger Num 26:52,53
of the Levites numbered in the *: Num 26:57
of Levites in the * was 23,000, Num 26:62
in the total * figure of the people Num 26:62
So these are the * figures as Num 26:63
Not one person in this entire * Num 26:64,65
time of the first *, they had been Num 26:64,65f
in the previous * taken in the Num 26:64,65
harm them by taking a national *. 2Sa 24:1
his army, "Take a * of all the 2Sa 24:2
But after he had taken the *, 2Sa 24:10
he made David decide to take a *. 1Ch 21:1
"Take a complete * throughout 1Ch 21:2
the * and punished Israel for it. 1Ch 21:7
one who sinned by ordering the *. 1Ch 21:17
At this time a * was taken of 1Ch 23:3
In the *, all the men of Levi who 1Ch 23:24
(This * of the tribe of Levi was 1Ch 23:27
When David took his * he didn't 1Ch 27:23
Joab began the *, but he never 1Ch 27:24
Solomon now took a * of all 2Ch 2:17
Then he took a * and found that 2Ch 25:5,6
Here is a * of those who returned Ez 2:2
decreed that a * should be taken Lk 2:1
(This * was taken when Quirinius Lk 2:2

CENT
has used, with twenty per * added; Lev 22:14
tenth of one per * of the men I Ecc 7:27,28
back again and owe them not a *! Is 52:3
and one per * of your olive oil; Eze 45:14
you for one *, and I never will. 2Co 11:8,9

CENTER
At the * of the garden he placed Gen 2:9
the tree at the * of the garden Gen 3:2,3
each side of the * shaft, each Ex 25:32,33
was a hole at the * just as in a Ex 39:23
and at the * of these tribal Num 2:1
with the city in the *. Num 35:5
his words from the * of the fire. Deu 4:36
to face from the * of the fire, Deu 5:4
to stand at the * of the temple, Ju 16:25,26
toward the present city *. 2Sa 5:9
stood alone at the * of a field of 2Sa 23:11,12
each other at the * of the room; 1Ki 6:23-28
1½ feet high. Its * was concave, 2¼ 1Ki 7:31
a platform in the * of the outer 2Ch 6:12,13
enter the very * of your being, Pro 2:10
* of righteousness, O holy hill!" Jer 31:23
O wealthy port, great * of Jer 51:13
Then from the * of the cloud, Eze 1:5
Place a third of it at the * of Eze 5:2
city, merchant * of the world, the Eze 27:3
units, with the Temple in the *. Eze 48:8
and parks, with a city in the *. Eze 48:15
* of attention from this point on. Dan 11:40f
a symbol, the * of world idolatry Zec 5:11f
He was in the * of the procession Mk 11:9
on the * cross, and the two Lk 23:32,33
knows that Ephesus is the * Act 19:35
Christ himself is the * of God's 1Co 1:24
of the Jews, the * of that system Gal 4:24,25
is, at the * of satanic worship; Rev 2:13
Literally, "in the * of the Rev 7:17f
down the * of the main street. Rev 22:2

CENTERING
The idolatry and oppression * in Mic 1:5

CENTERS
cities in Hamath as supply *. 2Ch 8:4
both being supply *, building their 2Ch 8:5
and other supply * at this time, 2Ch 8:6
all of the supply * in Naphtali. 2Ch 16:4
and other heathen * of worship. 2Ch 31:1
collection * at the gates were: Neh 12:25
Great trading * in Arabia. Eze 38:13f

CENTRAL
flowers. The * shaft itself will Ex 25:34,35
be brought to the * altar where Deu 12:18
your borders, the * altar is too Deu 12:20-23
need be taken to the * altar. Deu 12:26,27
Caspian, currently in * Turkey. Eze 38:2,3f
six wings, and the * sections of Rev 4:8

CENTURIES
directions issued * earlier by King 2Ch 35:15
* ago by a great king of Israel. Ez 5:11
people did long * ago from the Zec 14:5
about John's ministry * before! Mt 3:3
judgment of the * shall break upon Mt 23:36
have clung to for *, and still Mk 7:4
was predicted * ago by the prophet Act 2:16
He has kept this secret for * Col 1:26,27

CENTURY
A papyrus dating from the 5th * Jer 7:18f

CEREAL
and store them—the * offerings, sin Eze 42:13
by the people—the * offerings, the Eze 44:29

CEREMONIAL
Mosaic law, caused * defilement of Gen 31:35f
from her * impurity, she must not Lev 12:4
born, the mother's * impurity shall Lev 12:5
be in a state of * defilement for Lev 15:19
at that time for * purification. 1Sa 21:7
and all the other * articles left Jer 27:19,20,21
"For they ignore our ritual of * Mt 15:2
the ritual of * handwashing!" Mt 15:20
performing the * washing required Lk 11:37,38
they were used for Jewish * Jn 2:6
from God, not from * rules about Heb 13:9

CEREMONIALLY
be carried to a * clean place Lev 4:11,12
"Anyone touching anything * Lev 5:2
camp to a place that is * clean. Lev 6:11
anything that is * unclean shall Lev 7:19
only by a person who is * clean. Lev 7:19
Any priest who is * unclean but Lev 7:20
anything that is * unclean, whether Lev 7:21
nightfall, as being * defiled. Lev 11:25
and be * defiled until evening; Lev 11:28
between what is * clean and may be Lev 11:47
eaten, and what is * defiled and Lev 11:47
mother shall be * defiled for seven Lev 12:2
then she will be * clean again Lev 12:7
that she will be * pure again." Lev 12:8
is * defiled. Lev 15:1
the man's bed is * defiled until Lev 15:5
defiled is himself * unclean until Lev 15:6
Anyone he spits on is * unclean Lev 15:8
remain * defiled until evening. Lev 15:17
* defiled until the next evening. Lev 15:18
and be * defiled until evening. Lev 15:21,22,23
this time is * defiled for seven Lev 15:24
stops, she is no longer * defiled. Lev 15:2
for they are considered * defiled. Lev 19:2
and he may not * defile himself as Lev 21:4
if a priest who is * defiled Lev 22:3
anyone who is * defiled for any Lev 22:5
funeral, and were * defiled by Num 9:6,7
anyone is * impure at the time. Num 18:1
they are * defiled at the time. Num 18:13
be * defiled until the evening. Num 19:7
Then someone who is not * Num 19:9
fire in order to be made * pure; Num 31:23
Those who are * defiled may eat Deu 12:15
And even persons who are * Deu 12:20-23
I have declared to be * defiled. Deu 14:3,4,5
all other kinds are * defiled. Deu 14:10
Anyone, even if * defiled at the Deu 15:22
Any man who becomes * defiled Deu 23:9,10
tithe while I was * defiled (for Deu 26:14
so that David was * impure. 1Sa 20:26
and Zebulun were * impure 2Ch 30:17,18,19
and so becomes * impure, and then Hag 2:13

CEREMONIES
in preparation for the treaty *. Gen 26:30
the consecration *), Moses summoned Lev 9:1
*, for removal of sin. Num 19:9
the Passover * as recorded by the 2Ki 23:21
underwent the * of sanctification 1Ch 15:14
perform the * of purification. 1Ch 23:28
took part in the * without regard 2Ch 5:11,12
them during the * of praise and Neh 12:24
to assist in the * and to take part Neh 12:27
the purification * as required by Neh 12:45
He has made known his laws and * Ps 147:19
the new moon *, the Sabbaths and Eze 45:17
against the Temple *, so truth and Dan 8:12f
of the Passover *, when bread made Mt 26:17
of the first day of the Passover * Mt 27:62
and take it to the master of *." Jn 2:7,8
When the master of * tasted the Jn 2:9
for the Tabernacle *, one of the Jn 7:2
SIX DAYS BEFORE the Passover * Jn 12:1
*, when Christ was crucified. Act 2:1f
all the Jewish customs and *. Act 15:5
As soon as the Passover * ended, Act 20:6
Jewish customs and * I don't argue, 1Co 9:20
of slavery to Jewish laws and *. Gal 5:1
are obeying the Jewish * or not; Gal 5:6
going through the * and rituals of Eph 2:11
feasts or new moon * or Sabbaths. Col 2:16

CEREMONY
What is this * about?' Ex 12:26
"THIS IS THE * for the dedication Ex 29:1
generation, for his anointing *. Ex 29:29
in the ordination *—and boil its Ex 29:31
is, in their consecration *). Ex 29:33
The priest who performs the * Lev 6:26
of the atonement *, for his food. Lev 7:7
after the * is completed. Lev 7:9
* of the one who is healed. Lev 14:4
* of cleansing before the Lord. Lev 14:23
whose behalf the * is being Lev 14:25
required for the * of cleansing. Lev 14:32
He shall also perform the * of Lev 14:49
cleansing * by washing his clothes Lev 15:13
This *, in later generations, Lev 16:32
the purification * for themselves. Jos 3:5
circumcision * was that although Jos 5:4,5
After the * the entire nation Jos 5:8,9
and, in a great *, drew water from 1Sa 7:6
and in a solemn * before the Lord 1Sa 11:15
Israel came for the coronation *. 1Ki 12:1
of Israel for the coronation *. 1Ch 23:2
and clans—for the * of transferring 2Ch 5:2
(The customary pomp and * was 2Ch 21:19
Throughout the entire * everyone 2Ch 29:28
"The consecration * is now 2Ch 29:31
properly sanctified for the *." 2Ch 30:17,18,19
The entire Passover * was 2Ch 35:16
this cleansing *, offer another Eze 43:23
such as their * of cleansing for Mk 7:4
first performing the washing *." Mk 7:5
came for the circumcision *. Lk 1:59
circumcision *, he was named Jesus, Lk 2:21
* before the Passover began. Jn 11:55
"God also gave Abraham the * of Act 7:8
the Temple for the *, thus Act 21:26,27
initiation * of circumcision. Rom 2:28
in the Jewish circumcision *? Rom 3:1
initiation * of circumcision. Rom 4:10
The circumcision * was a sign Rom 4:11
his sight—before the * took place. Rom 4:11
it is not this * that saves them, Rom 4:12
through the Jewish * of 1Co 7:18
has gone through this * or not. 1Co 7:19
Jewish initiation * when I was Php 3:5

CERTAIN
from the ground at * places and Gen 2:6
their inheritance * cities and Num 35:2
it is, that it is * that such a Deu 13:12,13,14
"With * exceptions, Deu 14:19,20
he noticed a * Philistine girl, Ju 14:1

CERTAIN Con't)
"There were two men in a * city, 2Sa 12:1
to make * demands upon Rehoboam. 1Ki 12:2,3,4
He appointed * of the Levites to 1Ch 16:4
making * that each knew his work. Neh 13:30
Now there was a * Jew at the Est 2:5
"There is a * race of people Est 3:8
I walked by the field of a * lazy Pro 24:30,31
that nothing is * in this life. Ecc 7:14
But your doom is *. Jer 5:31
Whenever I announce that a * Jer 18:7
that I will make a * nation strong Jer 18:9
* aspects of verses 12 and 14 Eze 26:14f
and * as my description of it." Dan 2:45
It concerned events * to happen Dan 10:1
You want a * piece of land, or Mic 2:2
punishments will be quick and *; Mal 3:5
"Now listen to this story: A * Mt 21:33
Or, that he is hiding at a * Mt 24:26
decided to buy a * field where the Mt 27:7
hills and summoned * ones he chose, Mk 3:13
One day in a * village he was Lk 5:12
"There was a * rich man," Jesus Lk 16:19
"A nobleman living in a * Lk 19:12
(waiting for a * movement of the Jn 5:3
and showed him to * witnesses God Act 10:40,41
we are * to get them whether or Rom 4:16
the ability to do * things well. Rom 12:6
each of us with * special 1Co 3:5
do or don't do on * days or months Gal 4:10
abilities to do * things best? Eph 4:12
here and so I feel * I will be Php 1:25
tasting, or even touching * foods? Col 2:21
and by giving * special abilities Heb 2:4
This * hope of being saved is a Heb 6:19
dealt only with * rituals—what Heb 9:10
be given away to * people when he Heb 9:16
rules about eating * foods—a method Heb 13:9
This makes us all the more * that 1Jn 2:18
be tattooed with a * mark on the Rev 13:16
his seven heads represent a * city Rev 17:9

CERTAINLY
I told you, I will * see to it that Gen 18:14
"*," the men replied, "for you Gen 23:5,6
she says, 'Yes, *, and I will water Gen 24:14
"*, sir," she said, and quickly Gen 24:18
And she will reply, "*! Gen 24:44
and told me, '*, sir, and I will Gen 24:46
I have told you is * going to Gen 41:32
Then God told him, "I will * be Ex 3:12
* do everything he asks of us." Ex 19:8
an animal shall * be executed. Ex 22:19
for you have * found favor with me, Ex 33:17
he is * guilty before the Lord." Lev 5:19
you should * have eaten it there, Lev 10:18
otherwise I would * have killed Num 22:33
The Lord had * defeated all the Num 33:3,4
ways, you shall * perish, just as Deu 8:19
"The Lord will * give us the Jos 2:24
But as * as the Lord has given Jos 23:15,16
promised, just as * he will bring Jos 23:15,16
Angel, "we will * want to tell Ju 13:17
"The Lord has * helped us!" 1Sa 7:12
"You have * done wrong, but make 1Sa 12:20
You were * happy about it then. 1Sa 19:5
This was * not the first time I 1Sa 22:15
here in Judah; we * don't want to 1Sa 23:3
he said, 'I will * put Saul into 1Sa 24:4
the king would * find out who did 2Sa 18:13
interrupted, "It * was her son, 1Ki 3:22
So you should * obey him when he 2Ki 5:13
calamity will * fall upon us; 2Ki 7:9
that dark battle. * a man's Ecc 8:8
"He is my shepherd," he will * Is 44:28
Yes, I will * deliver you from Jer 15:21
Take note: The Lord will * do Jer 49:20
burned and * useless afterwards! Eze 15:5,6
We are many, so we should * be Eze 33:24
me the dream, you * can't expect me Dan 2:8,9
of Israel will * become slaves in Amo 7:17
If you do, I will * bless you. Zec 8:14,15
heaven even more * give good gifts Mt 7:11
here now will * live to see me Mt 16:28
you my disciples shall * sit on Mt 19:28
and say, 'We * would never have Mt 23:29,30
heard this and he said, "* not. Mk 8:12
But it * isn't God's way. Mk 10:6,7
For my words will * come true at Lk 1:20
you are * not honoring the Father. Jn 5:23
then you will * know whether my Jn 7:17
"For this man * does miracles. Jn 11:47
For they will * hear that you Act 21:22
" 'But Lord,' I argued, 'they * Act 22:19
"Yes, I * am." Act 22:27
Jewish beliefs, * nothing worthy of Act 23:29
and these men * cannot prove the Act 24:13
How could he? For * he has never 1Co 2:16
But it * is our job to judge and 1Co 5:12
but you * may if you wish. 1Co 7:6
not an apostle, I * am to you, for 1Co 9:2
to demons, * not to God. 1Co 10:20
You are * free to eat food 1Co 10:23
Well, I * do not! 1Co 11:22
I * have my share in it too. 2Co 2:5,6
is * far greater, for it is 2Co 3:11
Whatever we do, it is * not for 2Co 5:13,14
and authority of Christ, I * can. 2Co 10:7
When I was there I * gave you 2Co 12:12
though they * knew better. Gal 2:13
the truth? It * isn't God who has Gal 5:8
saved by what they are, * I could! Php 3:4
of Christ we * had a right to some 1Th 2:6
in jail and I am * not ashamed of 2Ti 1:12
promise, would * do what he said. Heb 11:11

CERTAINTY
then know for a * that the Lord Jos 23:13
Therefore know for a * that you Jer 42:22
them and know of a * that I came Jn 17:8
with as much * as though they were Rom 4:17
real * and clear understanding. Col 2:2
It is the * that what we hope for Heb 11:1

CHAFF
They blow away like * before the Ps 1:4
Blow them away like * in the Ps 35:5
like dust; like * before the wind— Ps 83:13
They will flee, scattered like * Is 17:13
away like * before the wind. Is 29:5
its * blown away by the wind. Is 30:24
apart, making * of mountains. Is 41:15
scatter you as * is scattered by Jer 13:24,25
There is a difference between * Jer 23:28
as small as *, and the wind blew Dan 2:35
dries away, like * blown by the Hos 13:3
opportunity is blown away like *; Zep 2:2
He will separate the * from the Mt 3:12
grain, burning the * with Mt 3:12
He will separate * from grain, Lk 3:17
and burn up the * with eternal fire Lk 3:17

CHAIN
the royal golden * about his neck Gen 41:41,42
banded with a * of iron and brass, Dan 4:15
banded with a * of iron and brass. Dan 4:23
honor with a gold * around his Dan 5:7
with a golden * around your neck, Dan 5:16
and a golden * was hung around his Dan 5:29
that I am bound with this *." Act 28:20
with an endless * of angels leading 1Ti 1:3,4
pit and a heavy * in his hand. Rev 20:1

CHAIN-DESIGNED
sets of bronze, * lattices and four 1Ki 7:16-22

CHAINED
He has * his steed to the Gen 49:11
* him in prison at the demand of Mt 14:3
But the Word of God is not *, 2Ti 2:9
and others were * in dungeons. Heb 11:36
them into hell, * in gloomy caves 2Pe 2:4
Now God has them * up in prisons Jud 1:6

CHAINS
king's prisoners were kept in *. Gen 39:20
only one of you shall remain in * Gen 42:19
reminder. Two * of pure, twisted Ex 28:13,14
I have broken your * and will Lev 26:13
or the * around the camels' necks. Ju 8:26
and subdue him and put him in *. Ju 16:5
bound with bronze * and made to Ju 16:21
as they saw him there in *. Ju 16:23,24
and he made gold * to protect the 1Ki 6:21,22
prison and in * for his rebellion. 2Ki 17:4
with * and taken away to Babylon. 2Ki 25:7
engraved with palm trees and *. 2Ch 3:5
He made * 2Ch 3:16
Literally, "* in the Holy of 2Ch 3:16f
pomegranates attached to the *. 2Ch 3:16
The two sets of * on the capitals, 2Ch 4:12-16
the two sets of * on the capitals, 2Ch 4:12-16
* and carted him away to Babylon. 2Ch 33:11
away the king in * to Babylon. 2Ch 36:6
"Come, let us break his *," Ps 2:3
Death bound me with *, and the Ps 18:4
of death and snapped their *. Ps 107:14
For he has snapped the * that Ps 129:3,4
*, and execute their sentences. Ps 149:8
scarves and ankle *, headbands, Is 3:20
For God will break the * that Is 9:4
from slavery and *, you will jeer Is 14:3
and with silver * around its neck? Is 40:19
as prisoners in *, and fall down on Is 45:14
and snap their *, and foreigners Jer 30:8
and bound him in * to send him away Jer 39:7
to take off your * and let you go. Jer 40:4
he was taken in * to Babylon and Jer 52:11
he has fastened me with heavy *. Lam 3:7
"Prepare * for my people, for Eze 7:23
pit and brought him in * to Egypt. Eze 19:4
When I have broken off their * of Eze 34:27
to me forever with * of Hos 1:19
Egypt, and cut your * of slavery. Mic 6:4
Now I will break your * and Nah 1:13
All her leaders were bound in *. Nah 3:10
Then they sent him in * to Mt 27:2
when shackled with * he simply Lk 8:29
bring them in * to Jerusalem. Act 9:2
them in * to the chief priests." Act 9:21
And the * fell off his wrists! Act 12:7
* of every prisoner fell off! Act 16:26
ordered him bound with double *. Act 21:33
to Jerusalem in * to be punished. Act 22:5
freed him from his * and ordered Act 22:30
with the Jews, he left Paul in *. Act 24:27
as I am, except for these *." Act 26:29
in their rules, like slaves in *. Gal 2:4
from these * as you used to be. Gal 4:12
up again in the * of slavery to Gal 5:1
I am in * now for preaching this Eph 6:20
* simply because I am a Christian. Php 1:13
seem to have lost their fear of *! Php 1:14
to the Lord while here in my *. Phm 1:10
I am in these * for preaching the Phm 1:13
bound him in * for 1,000 years, Rev 20:2

CHAIR
we can put in a bed, a table, a * 2Ki 4:10
is half a * and a tattered pillow. Amo 3:12

CHAIRS
they pull up their * Is 21:5

CHALCEDONY
The third with *; Rev 21:18,19,20

CHALDEA
O daughter of *, never again will Is 47:1
I will make the land of * an Jer 25:12
to * to invite them to come to Eze 23:16

CHALDEAN
the flower of * culture, will be as Is 13:19
surrender to the * army and live. Jer 21:9
But the * soldiers chased them Jer 52:8
and set the * army to work tearing Jer 52:14
the * language and literature. Dan 1:3,4
That very night Belshazzar, the * Dan 5:30

CHALDEANS
born (in Ur of the *), and was Gen 11:28
the * to go to the land of Canaan; Gen 11:31
city of Ur of the *, to give you Gen 15:7
And the Lord sent bands of *, 2Ki 24:2
of the * and renamed him Abraham. Neh 9:7
"Three bands of * have driven off Job 1:17
rout the armies of the *"? Is 48:14
Babylon and the * besieging you. Jer 21:3,4
shall enslave the *, just as they Jer 25:14
*, spoken by Jeremiah the prophet: Jer 50:1
from Babylon, the land of the *; Jer 50:8
Though you were glad, O *, Jer 50:11
shall smite the *, says the Lord. Jer 50:35
Babylon, the land of the *. Jer 50:45
land of the *, and destroy it. Jer 51:1
in the land of the *, slashed to Jer 51:4
their God, but the land of the * Jer 51:5
and all the * for all the evil they Jer 51:24
of Babylon, the land the * rule! Jer 51:54
surrounded by the *), and made a Jer 52:7
him to Babylon, the land of the *; Eze 12:13
the * from Pekod and Shoa and Koa; Eze 23:23
The * replied to the king, Dan 2:10
"Bring the *! Dan 5:7
* and soothsayers of Babylon. Dan 5:11
a Mede but became king of the *. Dan 9:1
force on the world scene, the *, Hab 1:6
*: a tribe of Semites living Hab 1:6f
the rise of these * to chasten and Hab 1:12
themselves alone [as these * do Hab 2:4
What's more, these arrogant * Hab 2:5
So he left the land of the * and Act 7:4

CHALLENGE
shout his * to the army of Israel. 1Sa 17:23
with Jehoram to * Jehu (son of 2Ch 22:7
No one can stop him or * him, Dan 4:35

CHALLENGED
fact * the very authority of God! Num 26:5-11
Caleb * them. Ju 1:12
river, the Gilead guards * him. Ju 12:5
He even * the Commander Dan 8:11

CHAMBER
the shields back to the guard *. 1Ki 14:28
"going forth from his *." Ps 19:5f
a princess, waits within her *, Ps 45:13
* with the other civic leaders. Pro 31:23
man to the torture * until he had Mt 18:34
* and conferred among themselves. Act 4:15
the Council * while he talked. Act 5:34
They left the Council * Act 5:41
in the Council * saw Stephen's face Act 6:15

CHAMBERS
them in the sacred *, and put on Eze 44:19
of sacred * that faced north. Eze 46:19,20

CHAMELEON
The snail, the *. Lev 11:29,30

CHAMPION
Then Goliath, a Philistine * from 1Sa 17:4-7
* was dead, they turned and ran. 1Sa 17:50,51

CHANCE
Why didn't you give me a * to Gen 31:27
I'm going to take a * that you Gen 42:19
lions hiding and waiting their *. Ps 17:12
This is the last * for all of Ps 50:22
Anyone refusing has lost his *. Pro 10:17

(CHANCE Con't)
forsakes them, he gets another *. Pro 28:13
broken and never have another *. Pro 29:1
All is *! Ecc 9:1
but it is all by *, by happening Ecc 9:11
happen to Egypt, what * have we?" Is 20:5,6
other men at every *, so Israel has Jer 3:6
of always giving you another *. Jer 15:6
by law you have a * to buy before Jer 32:6,7
the test—and what * do they have? Eze 21:13
I'll give you one more *. Dan 3:15
So they concluded, "Our only * Dan 6:5
Israel has thrown away her * with Hos 8:3
they will never have a * to live Zep 1:13
before he had a * to speak, Jesus Mt 17:25
Herodias' * finally came. Mk 6:21
"By * a Jewish priest came Lk 10:31
from having a * to believe it." Lk 11:52
" 'Give it one more *,' the Lk 13:8
son, they said, 'This is our *! Lk 20:14
you get a * to be free, take it. 1Co 7:21
for a while you didn't have the *. Php 4:10
you get the *, in season and out, 2Ti 4:2
who had the first *, for they Heb 4:6
your patience has a * to grow. Jas 1:3
what * will the godless have? 1Pe 4:18

CHANCELLERY
the Jew, who works at the *. Est 6:10

CHANCES
A man may ruin his * by his own Pro 19:3
so he took no *, but put them Act 16:24
will give us many * to preach the Col 4:3
Make the most of your * to tell Col 4:5

CHANGE
a quick shave and * of clothes, Gen 41:14
Then he shall * his clothes and Lev 6:11
the donor may neither * his mind Lev 27:10
for if there is any * made, then Lev 27:33
He doesn't * his mind like humans Num 23:18-24
her nails and * her clothing, Deu 21:13
He will * you into a holy people Deu 28:9
midnight and the * of guards when Ju 7:19,20
* his mind, for he is not a man!" 1Sa 15:29
of Israel was ready for this *. 1Ch 12:38
before the great * in his attitude) 2Ch 33:19
But he didn't * as his father 2Ch 33:23
Anyone who attempts to * this Ez 6:11
* me back again to dust so soon? Job 10:9
causing them to * their minds, and Job 33:17,18
Must he * the order of the Job 34:33
and you will * them like a man Ps 102:26
has spoken—who can * his plans? Is 14:27
people and will not * his mind. Is 31:2
up my mind and I will not * it." Jer 4:28
punished them, but they won't *! Jer 5:3
Can the Ethiopian * the color of Jer 13:23
then I too will * my mind and not Jer 18:10
And nothing will * this decree, Jer 28:14
to disobey. This * seems to Jer 31:33f
than I would * my laws of night and Jer 33:25,26
my servant, or * the plan that his Jer 33:25,26
see the great * in your hearts. Eze 20:41
And they will * the name of the Eze 39:11
Temple—they must * their clothes Eze 42:14
* all laws, morals, and customs. Dan 7:25
Literally, "* the times and the Dan 7:25f
Perhaps the meaning is, "* Dan 7:25f
THIS * OF plans made Jonah very Jon 4:1
"At that time I will * the Zep 3:9
I will * the speech of the Zep 3:9f
And don't think that I might * my Zec 8:14,15
them, and I won't * this decision Zec 8:14,15
"If you don't * your ways and Mal 2:1
"For I am the Lord—I do not *. Mal 3:6
God can * these stones here into Mt 3:9
pair of shoes or a * of clothes. Mk 6:8,9
and will * disobedient minds to the Lk 1:17
said to Pilate, "* it from 'The Jn 19:21
these things. Now * your mind and Act 3:19
Whoever has that kind of * in his Rom 2:29
may be asking, did I * my plan? 2Co 1:17
By looking at the good * in your 2Co 3:2
back to God, and * them into men 2Co 10:5
Satan can * himself into an angel 2Co 11:14
and * the truth concerning Christ. Gal 1:7
bodies of ours and * them into Php 3:21
tell the truth; we * his message 1Th 2:4
But you yourself will never *, Heb 1:12
whether he might * his plans. Heb 6:17
and will never * his mind: You are Heb 7:21
forever without * or shadow. Jas 1:17
beyond the reach of * and decay. 1Pe 1:4
keep without * through the years. Jud 1:3
"* your mind and attitude, or Rev 2:16
I gave her time to * her mind Rev 2:21
Neither did they * their mind Rev 9:21
did not * their mind and attitude Rev 16:9

CHANGEABLE
No one needed to tell him how * Jn 2:24,25

CHANGED
and when he * and said I could Gen 31:8
And that night, as it * to a Ex 14:20
So the Lord * his mind and spared Ex 32:14
the spot has not * and has not Lev 13:5
the spot has not * its color, even Lev 13:55
The vow may not be *; Lev 27:10
and that evening the Cloud * to Num 9:15
It was at this time that Moses * Num 13:16
whose name was later * to Israel. Num 20:14f
(The Israelites later * the names Num 32:37,38
in Gilead, and * the name of their Num 32:41
journey, she * her mind and said to Ru 1:8
brushed his hair, * his clothes, 2Sa 12:20
he also conquered Sela and * its 2Ki 14:7
name was later * to Israel). 2Ki 17:34
and he * his name to Jehoiakim. 2Ki 23:34
and he * his name to Zedekiah. 2Ki 24:17
compassion that he * his mind and 1Ch 21:15
(Eliakim's name was * to 2Ch 36:4
that can never be *, that Queen Est 1:19
Job was so * that they could Job 2:12
are pure and need never be *." Ps 19:9f
blessings of God have * to hate. Ps 77:10
hand of the Most High has *." Ps 77:10f
Your royal decrees cannot be *. Ps 93:5
Next I * my course again and Ecc 2:3
them away and * them into fools who Jer 2:4,5
name will be * from "Topheth," or Jer 7:32
the Lord has * your name. Jer 20:3
They * their minds and made Jer 34:11
they did not turn when they * Eze 10:9-13
that it cannot be canceled or *; Dan 6:8
the law and it cannot be *." Dan 6:15
They will be * to joyous Zec 8:19
his appearance * so that his face Mt 17:2
but later he * his mind and went. Mt 21:29
condemned to die, * his mind and Mt 27:3
because he had * his appearance. Mk 16:12
"the appearance of his face *." Lk 9:29f
the weather * abruptly and a heavy Act 27:14,15
came to him, they * their minds and Act 28:6
for those with * hearts and minds. Rom 2:29
And your * lives are the result 1Co 9:1
is, for it has not *—it is the same 1Co 15:1
down and signed, cannot be *. Gal 3:15
not be canceled or * four hundred Gal 3:17
* into new and different people. Gal 6:15
just as it * yours that very first Col 1:6
* your lives when you believed it. 1Th 2:13
his law must be * to permit it. Heb 7:12,13,14
that God's method *, for Christ, Heb 7:15
now your very lives have been * 1Pe 2:10
Then the scene * and I saw a Rev 14:14

CHANGELESS
My God is * in his love for me Ps 59:10

CHANGERS
and money * behind their counters. Jn 2:14
the money *' coins over the floor Jn 2:15

CHANGES
he gave five * of clothes and three Gen 45:22
But if the raw flesh later * to Lev 13:16,17
that their love for you never *. 1Ch 29:18
For the water * and turns to Job 38:30
days that your will never *. Ps 119:152
then that nation * its mind and Jer 18:10
The old order *. Eze 21:26
kind of truth that * lives—so that Tit 1:1

CHANGING
God told him, "I am * your name. Gen 17:5
people go and then * your mind." Ex 8:29
daytime Cloud * to the appearance Num 9:16
by * stones into loaves of bread. Mt 4:3
children, forever * our minds about Eph 4:14
be constantly * for the better. Eph 4:23
over the world and * lives Col 1:6

CHANNELS
overflow all its * and sweep into Is 8:7,8
their * fouled with rotting reeds. Is 19:6
Let them go through legal *. Act 19:38

CHANT
And let the priests of Aaron * Ps 118:3
Let the Gentile converts *, Ps 118:4

CHANT,"WE
Temple and chant,"* are saved!" Jer 7:10

CHAOS
he can bring order from this *. Ecc 5:9
The city lies in *; Is 24:10
be lived in, not to be an empty *. Is 45:18

CHAOTIC
a shapeless, * mass, Gen 1:2

CHAPEL
capital, where the king's * is!" Amo 7:13

CHAPLAIN
Jairite was David's personal *. 2Sa 20:26
the king's private *, were his 1Ch 25:4,5

CHAPLAINS
personal friends, and private *. 2Ki 10:11

CHAPTER
throughout the remainder of the *. Gen 11:12,13f
week(continued in next *) Ex 7:25
Deuel in * 1. Num 2:3-31f
Their duties are explained in * 4, Jos 3:12f
Implied in * 2, verse 22; Ju 3:1
2, verse 22; and * 3, verse 4. Ju 3:1
Implied in * 2, verse 22; Ju 3:1
2, verse 22; and * 3, verse 4. Ju 3:1
* 1, verse 17, says King Jehoram 2Ki 3:1
deals with events preceding * 9. 1Ch 10:1
seen in Daniel, * 5, as this Is 21:5
Not Cyrus, as in * 41, but Christ. Is 42:1
continued to worship her (* 44). Jer 7:18
See * 32:6–15. Jer 37:12
see note on * 7, verse 18. Jer 44:17
in point of time, follows * 36. Jer 45:1f
(Events told about in * 39. Jer 52:1
in the preceding * and verse. Hos 1:11
See * 1, verses 6, 9, and 10. Hos 1:23f
See Numbers, * 23. Hos 9:10f
See Numbers, * 6. Amo 2:11f
See verse 1 of * 1. Mic 1:14f
This * predicts the events of the Nah 2:1f
See 1 Kings, * 10. Lk 11:31f
* 5:19; 8:36, 56, 58, etc. Jn 10:25f
See * 3. Jn 19:39f
see footnote * 1, verse 1. Act 1:1f
See * 15, verse 38. Act 13:13f
See * 13, verses 11–16. Rev 19:20f

CHAPTERS
in these *, Jethro and Reuel. Ex 3:1f
Judges, * 19 and 20. Hos 10:9f
this event, see Ezekiel, * 26-28. Lk 10:13f

CHARACTER
no longer godly in * (verse 3). Gen 6:1f
* of his reign: evil 2Ki 16:1
* of his reign: evil—but not as 2Ki 17:1
* of his reign: good (similar to 2Ki 18:1
* of his reign: evil 2Ki 21:1
* of his reign: evil 2Ki 21:19,20
* of his reign: good; 2Ki 22:1
* of his reign: evil, like the 2Ki 23:31,32
* of his reign: evil, like the 2Ki 23:36,37
* of his reign: evil, like that of 2Ki 24:18,19
Faithfulness is your very *. Ps 89:8
The * of even a child can be Pro 20:11
strength of * in us and helps us Rom 5:4
as a test of their * and ability, 1Ti 3:10
a quiet growth in grace and *. Heb 12:11
strong in *, full and complete. Jas 1:4
us, and to give us his own *. 2Pe 1:4

CHARGE
cave and the field without any *. Gen 23:11
Soon he was put in * of the Gen 39:4
and put him in * of administering a Gen 41:33
to be in * of this entire project. Gen 41:40
in * of all the land of Egypt." Gen 41:41,42
* over all the land of Egypt." Gen 41:44
all Egypt, and in * of the sale of Gen 42:6
put them in * of my flocks, too." Gen 47:5,6
under him, each in * of a hundred; Ex 18:21
you * against him, as his guilt Lev 5:15
priest who is in * of the atonement Lev 7:7
priest who is in * shall also be Lev 7:8
and don't * him interest on the Lev 25:36
They are in * of all the Num 3:7,8,9
the people watch, * him with the Num 27:19
Present this to the Levites in * Num 31:30
assistants in * of thousands, Deu 1:15
and do not * them with murdering an Deu 21:8
That same day Moses gave this * Deu 27:11
the officer in *, "The men were Jos 2:4
his son Eleazar to be in * of it. 1Sa 7:1
heard the king give them this *. 2Sa 18:5
was in * of the king's bodyguard. 2Sa 20:23
Adoram was in * of the forced 2Sa 20:24
he gave this * to his son Solomon: 1Ki 2:1
and in * of the archives; 1Ki 4:1
was, he put him in * of his labor 1Ki 11:27,28
Adoram (who was in * of the draft) 1Ki 12:18
Then General Zimri, who had * of 1Ki 16:9
The man in * of Ahab's household 1Ki 18:3,4
lieutenant in * of the smallest 2Ki 18:24
in * of the palace tailor shop. 2Ki 22:14
Korahites were in * of the 1Ch 9:19
in * of the Lord's Tabernacle. 1Ch 9:23
clan were in * of the preparation 1Ch 9:32
Jehoiada) was in * of the king's 1Ch 18:17
were given * of the storehouses); 1Ch 26:14,15
He was in * of the divisions 1Ch 26:23,24
were placed in * of the territory 1Ch 26:30
He had * of 24,000 troops who 1Ch 27:2,3
He had * of 24,000 troops who 1Ch 27:4
officer in * of the palace 1Ch 27:25
* of the supplies of olive oil. 1Ch 27:28
Shitrai from Sharon was in * of 1Ch 27:29
had * of those in the valleys. 1Ch 27:29
of Ishmael, had * of the camels, 1Ch 27:30
Meronoth had * of the donkeys. 1Ch 27:30
officers, those in * of his 1Ch 28:1
vice-regent, in * of the king's 2Ch 26:21
Levite, was put in *, assisted by 2Ch 31:12,13
Gate, was put in * of distributing 2Ch 31:14,15
priests— to be in * of Ez 8:25
We also agreed to * ourselves Neh 10:32

(CHARGE Con't)
* of the work outside the Temple; Neh 11:15,16,17
in * of the thanksgiving service. Neh 12:8
The gatekeepers who had * of the Neh 12:25
appointed to be in * of the Neh 12:44
the Levite in * of the Neh 13:13
Hegai, the eunuch in *, will see Est 2:3
the eunuch in * of the harem, Est 2:15
to be in * of Haman's estate. Est 8:2
You have put him in * of Ps 8:6
in supreme * of all the earth. Ps 83:18
He was put in * of all the Ps 105:21
all my efforts, free of *. Ecc 2:20-23
the priest in * of the Temple of Jer 20:1
army (who was in * of recruitment) Jer 52:24,25
Prostitutes * for their Eze 16:33,34
* the watchman with their deaths. Eze 33:6
for the priests in * of the Eze 40:46
to take * of my sanctuary. Eze 44:8
was in * of his palace personnel, Dan 1:3,4
to be in * of all the affairs of Dan 2:49
you have put in * of Babylonian Dan 3:12
These "soldiers" * like Joe 2:7
* of my Temple, to keep it holy; Zec 3:7
of * to boil their sacrifices in; Zec 14:21
"So pray to the one in * of the Mt 9:38
ones in * of everything I own! Mt 24:47
tell the man in *, 'Our Master sent Mk 14:14
"Do you refuse to answer this *? Mk 14:60
Roman officer in * and asked him. Mk 15:44
find some * to bring against him. Lk 6:7
manager and was in * of his palace Lk 8:3
will put him in * of all he owns. Lk 12:42,43,44
But the local Jewish leader in * Lk 13:14
Now the guards in * of Jesus Lk 22:63,64
but he was in * of the disciples' Jn 12:6
"What is your * against this man? Jn 18:29
and we will put them in * of this Act 6:3
as putting him in * of all the Act 7:10
don't * them with this sin!" Act 7:60
Prophets, those in * of the service Act 13:15
For there is no real * against Act 25:26
But the officers in * of the Act 27:11
and put you in * of the work of Rom 12:8
from preaching to you without *. 1Co 9:15
For a husband is in * of his Eph 5:23
is in * of his body the church. Eph 5:23
anything from you, * me for it. Phm 1:18
complete * of everything there is. Heb 2:8
is in complete * of God's house. Heb 3:6
drink the Water of Life without *. Rev 22:17

CHARGED
Then he * Joshua (son of Nun) to Deu 31:23
We have * him nothing—he hasn't 2Sa 19:42
you have not even * for your love! Eze 16:31
angrier he was. He * into the ram Dan 8:7
Yes, it will surely be * against Lk 11:51
No falsehood can be * against Rev 14:5

CHARGES
Literally, "Let Baal bring *," Ju 6:32f
(The schedule of * was as 1Sa 13:21
DISMISS ALL THE * against me, Ps 26:1
O GOD, DEFEND me from the * of Ps 43:1
Here are my * against you: I Ps 50:7
list all the above * against you. Ps 50:21
his neighbor, the * won't stick Pro 11:9f
the following *: There is no Hos 4:1
What about all these * against Mk 15:3,4
how to answer the * against you, Lk 21:14
to bring their * before you." Act 23:30
forward, he laid * against Paul in Act 24:2
Paul denied the *: "I am not Act 25:8
trial on these * in Jerusalem. Act 25:20
without any * against him!" Act 25:27
blotted out the * proved against Col 2:14

CHARGING
"Keep far away from falsely * Ex 23:7
to you without * you anything? 2Co 11:7

CHARIOT
Pharaoh also gave Joseph the * of Gen 41:43
Joseph jumped into his * and Gen 46:29
the chase in his *, followed by Ex 14:6
pick of Egypt's * corps—600 Ex 14:7
Their * wheels began coming off, Ex 14:25
from his * and escaped on foot. Ju 4:15
'Why is his * so long in coming? Ju 5:28
and make his weapons and * 1Sa 8:12
then he lamed all of the * horses 2Sa 8:4
a magnificent * and chariot horses, 2Sa 15:1
chariot and * horses, and hired 2Sa 15:1
Solomon owned forty thousand * 1Ki 4:26
and were similar to * wheels. 1Ki 7:33
his cavalry and * drivers, and 1Ki 9:19
* commanders, and cavalrymen. 1Ki 9:22
who lived in the * cities and with 1Ki 10:26
An Egyptian * delivered to 1Ki 10:29
But King Rehoboam escaped by * 1Ki 12:18
* troops, plotted against him. 1Ki 16:9
to get into his * and get down the 1Ki 18:44
* to the entrance of the city! 1Ki 18:46
he invited him up into his *! 1Ki 20:33
his thirty-two * captains to fight 1Ki 22:31
he groaned to his * driver. 1Ki 22:34
propped up in his * with the blood 1Ki 22:35
When his * and armor were washed 1Ki 22:38
suddenly a * of fire, drawn by 2Ki 2:11
My father! The * of Israel and 2Ki 2:12
from his * and ran to meet him. 2Ki 5:21
down from his * to meet you? 2Ki 5:26
Then Jehu jumped into a * and 2Ki 9:16
Get my * ready!" 2Ki 9:21
and he sank down dead in his *. 2Ki 9:24
So they shot him in his * at the 2Ki 9:27
His officials took him by * to 2Ki 9:28
he helped him into the royal *. 2Ki 10:15
his body back in a * from Megiddo 2Ki 23:30
He crippled all the * teams 1Ch 18:4
stationed in the * cities, as well 2Ch 9:25
into his * and fled to Jerusalem. 2Ch 10:18
his *, "for I am badly wounded." 2Ch 18:33
propped up in his *, to fight the 2Ch 18:34
So they lifted him out of his * 2Ch 35:24,25
him in his second * and brought him 2Ch 35:24,25
mare harnessed to Pharaoh's *." Sol 1:9f
Look, it is the * Sol 3:7
a * from the wood of Lebanon. Sol 3:9
sit beside my beloved in his *." Sol 6:12f
and his rider, the * and the Jer 51:21
come * horses, steeds and mules. Eze 27:14
The first * was pulled by red Zec 6:2
do his work. The * pulled by the Zec 6:6
returning in his *, reading aloud Act 8:28
and walk along beside the *." Act 8:29
up into the * and sit with him. Act 8:31
He stopped the *, and they went Act 8:38

CHARIOT-HORSES
Four * were found and the king 2Ki 7:14
Then King Joram reined the * 2Ki 9:23

CHARIOTEER
chariot and the *— yes, and the Jer 51:21

CHARIOTEERS
and *—was used in the chase; Ex 14:9
soldiers and the *, and Sisera Ju 4:15
seven hundred * dead on the field, 2Sa 10:18
and employed twelve thousand *. 1Ki 4:26
The Chariot of Israel and the * 2Ki 2:12
king sent out two * to see where 2Ki 7:14
seven thousand * and forty thousand 1Ch 19:17,18
officers, *, and cavalrymen; 2Ch 8:9
to his *: "Ignore everyone but the 2Ch 18:30
So when the Syrian * saw King 2Ch 18:31
* see their mistake and leave him. 2Ch 18:31

CHARIOTS
So a very great number of *, Gen 50:9
chariot corps—600 * in all—and Ex 14:7
* driven by Egyptian officers. Ex 14:7
cavalry—horses, *, and Ex 14:9
all his armies, *, and horsemen. Ex 14:17
Pharaoh's horses, *, and horsemen. Ex 14:23
* scraped along the dry ground. Ex 14:25
and their * and horsemen." Ex 14:26
the path and the * and horsemen. Ex 14:28
He has overthrown Pharaoh's * and Ex 15:4
Pharaoh, his horsemen, and his * Ex 15:19
their horses and *—how he drowned Deu 11:4
of horses and *, an army far Deu 20:1
of horses and *, covered the Jos 11:4
their horses and burn their *." Jos 11:6
the horses and burned all the *. Jos 11:9
* and are too strong for us." Jos 17:16,17,18
they are strong and have iron *." Jos 17:16,17,18
after them with * and cavalry. Jos 24:6
of the valley, who had iron *. Ju 1:19
He had nine hundred iron *, and Ju 4:2,3
*, under General Sisera's command. Ju 4:7
nine hundred iron *, and marched Ju 4:13
the enemy and the * as far as Ju 4:16
and make them run before his *; 1Sa 8:11
of three thousand *, six thousand 1Sa 13:5
the enemy * closing in upon him. 2Sa 1:6
So he hired * and drivers and 1Ki 1:5
which to keep his *, cities for 1Ki 9:19
a vast number of * and 1Ki 10:26
and cavalry—1,400 * in all, and 1Ki 10:26
their hordes of * and horses, 1Ki 20:1
of the horses and * were captured, 1Ki 20:21
number of horses, *, and men, and 1Ki 20:25
his horses and * and stood at the 2Ki 5:9
* and horses to surround the city. 2Ki 6:14
troops, horses, and * everywhere. 2Ki 6:15
horses of fire and * of fire 2Ki 6:17
of speeding * and a loud galloping 2Ki 7:6
For you have * and horses and a 2Ki 10:2,3
ten *, and ten thousand infantry; 2Ki 13:7
Literally, "The * of Israel and 2Ki 13:14f
horses and *, it will do no good. 2Ki 18:24
" 'You have boasted, "My * have 2Ki 19:23
of horses and * located near the 2Ki 23:11
a thousand of his *, seven thousand 1Ch 18:4
to enlist mercenary troops, *, 1Ch 19:6
He hired thirty-two thousand *, 1Ch 19:7
force of 1,400 * and recruited 2Ch 1:14
cities where the * were garaged, 2Ch 1:14
At that time Egyptian * sold for 2Ch 1:17
where his * and horses were kept. 2Ch 8:6
of horses and *, and 12,000 2Ch 9:25
twelve hundred *, sixty thousand 2Ch 12:3
Ethiopia with 300 *, under the 2Ch 14:9,10
all of their * and cavalrymen? 2Ch 16:8
*, marching by night, and almost 2Ch 21:9
Surrounded by unnumbered *, the Ps 68:17
The clouds are his *. Ps 104:3
Literally, "the * of my princely Sol 6:12f
of horses and * and idols—the land Is 2:7
of their * spin like the wind. Is 5:28
Syrians drive the *; Is 22:6,7
mighty cavalry and * instead of Is 31:1
Egypt with all its * and horses, to Is 43:17
and with swift * of doom to pour Is 66:15
on horses and in *, and in Is 66:20
wind; his * are like a whirlwind; Jer 4:13
Then come, O horses and * and Jer 46:9
wheels as the * go rushing by; Jer 47:3
her horses and *, and her allies Jer 50:37
the north with * and wagons and a Eze 23:24
a great army and cavalry and *. Eze 26:7
gates, pulling * behind them. Eze 26:10
the rumbling of *, or the roar of Joe 2:5
Use your swiftest * and flee, O Mic 1:13
See their glittering * moving Nah 2:3
Your own * race recklessly along Nah 2:4
He destroys your weapons. Your * Nah 2:13
the whips as the * rush forward Nah 3:2
pounding, and * clattering as they Nah 3:2
horses? Your * were salvation. Hab 3:8,9f
No, you were sending your * of Hab 3:8,9
thick that three * could go abreast Zep 2:15f
again and saw four * coming from Zec 6:1
an army of * rushing into battle. Rev 9:9
wheat, cattle, sheep, horses, *, Rev 18:13

CHARITIES
* have not gone unnoticed by God! Act 10:4
your * have been noticed by God! Act 10:31

CHARITY
call attention to their acts of *! Mt 6:2
He gave generously to * and was a Act 10:2

CHARM
* can be deceptive and beauty Pro 31:30
snakes which you cannot *. Jer 8:17
with the lasting * of a gentle and 1Pe 3:4

CHARMED
bites before it is *, there is no Ecc 10:11f

CHARMER
or be a serpent *, medium, or Deu 18:11
there is no advantage in a *." Ecc 10:11f

CHARMERS
ears to the most expert of *. Ps 58:4,5

CHARMS
Let her * Pro 5:19
by tying magic * on their wrists Eze 13:18
souls with all your magic *. Eze 13:20
I will tear off the * and set my Eze 13:20
mistress of deadly *, enticed the Nah 3:4
books and * and burned them at a Act 19:18,19

CHARRED
"Go and get the * bodies from Lev 10:4
And look at those * stones they Neh 4:1
you up and leave you broken and *. Jer 11:16
smoke rising from her * remains. Rev 18:9

CHART
* prepared by his father David; 2Ch 8:14
your commands are my * and guide. Ps 119:19
thought. You * the path ahead of Ps 139:3

CHASE
manager, "* after them and stop Gen 44:4
heart and he will * after you. Ex 14:4
So Pharaoh led the * in his Ex 14:6
and charioteers—was used in the *; Ex 14:9
The enemy said, "I will * after Ex 15:9
I will * away the dangerous Lev 26:6
You will * your enemies; Lev 26:7
Five of you will * a hundred, Lev 26:8
one will be there to * them away. Deu 28:26
How could one single enemy * a Deu 32:30
We will let them * us until they Jos 8:6
were called out to * after them; Jos 8:16
* those nations from your land. Jos 23:13
them to come and * and destroy the Ju 7:23
of Benjamin would * them and be Ju 20:32
hills joined the * when they saw 1Sa 14:22
Afterwards Saul said, "Let's * 1Sa 14:36
so Saul quit the * and returned to 1Sa 23:28
David asked the Lord, "Shall I * 1Sa 30:8
Quick, take my bodyguard and * 2Sa 20:6
I will * after him and get 2Ki 5:20
Will you * dry, useless straws? Job 13:25
all your enemies! * them away! Ps 68:1
a mountain. * them with your fiery Ps 83:15
Curses * sinners, while blessings Pro 13:21
while blessings * the righteous! Pro 13:21
with no one to * them away. Is 17:2
One of them will * a thousand of Is 30:17
* away all those destroying you. Is 49:17

(CHASE Con't)
destruction shall * them until I Jer 9:16
of this land and * you into a Jer 16:13
I am sending for hunters to * you Jer 16:16
are like sheep the lions *. Jer 50:17
I will * my people with the sword. Eze 5:2
I will * you even to the borders Eze 11:11
your people will * you from your Dan 4:25
I will carry them off and * all Hos 5:14
and now her enemies will * her. Hos 8:3
of them and * away the others.' Lk 11:49

CHASED
them in all, and * after the Gen 14:14
But the shepherds * the girls Ex 2:17
of Pharaoh that * after Israel Ex 14:28
as though * by a man with a sword; Lev 26:36
them and * them to Hormah. Num 14:45
against them, and * them like bees Deu 1:44
died while being * by the men of Ai Jos 7:5
them at Gibeon and * the others all Jos 10:10
the Israelis, who * them as far as Jos 11:8
Sea, the Egyptians * after them Jos 24:6
Barak and his men * the enemy Ju 4:16
The two kings fled, but Gideon * Ju 8:12
* Jephthah out of the country. Ju 11:1
the town as they * after Israel. Ju 20:31
but the Israelis * after them, and Ju 20:42
routed them, and * them from 1Sa 7:11
But hungry as they were, they * 1Sa 14:31
Even when you are * by those who 1Sa 25:29
said, "and as we * them back to 2Sa 11:23
our king instead, * him out of the 2Sa 19:8,9,10
I have * my enemies 2Sa 22:38
The Israelis * them, but King 1Ki 20:20
whom the Lord had * out of the land 1Ki 21:26
* out the inhabitants of Gath. 1Ch 8:13
Israel, and * King Jeroboam's 2Ch 13:18,19
They * them as far as Gerar, and 2Ch 14:13
so I * him out of the Temple. Neh 13:28
darkness, and * out of the world. Job 18:18
He will be * and struck down. Job 20:24
need never slip. I * my enemies; Ps 18:37
My enemies * and caught me. Ps 143:3
own land like deer * by dogs, Is 13:14
they will be * down dark and Jer 23:12
But the Babylonians * the king Jer 39:5
But the Chaldean soldiers * them Jer 52:8
* me as though I were a bird. Lam 3:52
Nebuchadnezzar was * from his Dan 4:33
glory, and he was * out of his Dan 5:21
For he * his brother, Israel, Amo 1:11
be as a man who is * by a lion—and Amo 5:19
together those who were * away. Zep 3:19
He, too, was wounded and * away. Lk 20:12
some ropes and * them all out, and Jn 2:15

CHASES
Punishment that hurts * evil from Pro 20:30
to the sword. He * them away and Is 41:3

CHASING
as though you were * a criminal and Gen 31:36,37
even run when no one is * you! Lev 26:17
Sea as they were * you, and how the Deu 11:4
the men who were * them had Jos 2:22
the army, "Go on * the enemy and Jos 10:19
They were very tired, but still * Ju 8:4
"We are weary from * after Zebah Ju 8:5
his neighbors came * after them, Ju 18:22
"What do you want, * after us Ju 18:23
the Philistines, * them as far as 1Sa 17:52
Should he spend his time * one 1Sa 24:14
Why are you * me? 1Sa 26:17,18
a deer, and he began * Abner. 2Sa 2:19
people from * their brothers?" 2Sa 2:26
stopped * the troops of Israel. 2Sa 2:28
from * the army of Israel. 2Sa 18:16
of Israel, they stopped * him. 2Ch 18:32
THE WICKED FLEE when no one is * Pro 28:1
It is all foolishness, * the Ecc 1:12-15
even this was like * the wind. Ecc 1:16-18
all so useless, a * of the wind, Ecc 2:11
all is foolishness, * the wind. Ecc 2:17
example of foolishly * the wind. Ecc 2:24-26
But this, too, is foolishness, * Ecc 4:4
it is all foolishness, * the wind. Ecc 4:16
is foolish; it's * the wind. Ecc 6:9
swiftness of your enemies * you! Is 30:16
sword of the enemy * after you. Eze 5:12
in Israel—Ephraim * other gods, Hos 6:10
ISRAEL IS * the wind, yes, Hos 12:1
But when the Egyptians * them Heb 11:29
rest of your life * after evil 1Pe 4:2

CHASM
And besides, there is a great * Lk 16:26

CHASTEN
these Chaldeans to * and correct us Hab 1:12

CHASTENING
Oh, do not despise the * of the Job 5:17

CHASTENS
resent it when God * and corrects Pro 3:11,12

CHASTISED
He was * that we might have Is 53:5

CHASTISEMENT
Will this put an end to your *? Job 36:19

CHATTER
was not just meaningless * to you; 1Th 1:5

CHATTERED
Delirious, I * like a swallow Is 38:14

CHEAP
Silver was too * to count for 2Ch 9:20
people to bring *, sick animals to Mal 1:12
But talk is *—anybody could say Mt 9:5,6
But talk is *—anybody could say Mk 2:9,10,11
But talk is *—anybody could say Lk 5:23,24
guests, and the * ones are used in 2Ti 2:20

CHEAPEN
Did I do wrong and * myself and 2Co 11:7

CHEAT
All who * with unjust weights Deu 25:16
trying to * him out of his rights. Pro 24:15,16
You * and shortchange everyone. Is 59:6
dishonest scales—they love to *. Hos 12:7
He did not lie or *; Mal 2:6
all those who * their hired hands, Mal 3:5
don't lie, don't *, respect your Mk 10:19
they shamelessly * widows out of Mk 12:40
If you * even a little, you won't Lk 16:10
For I never *, I don't commit Lk 18:11
to * widows out of their property. Lk 20:47
want to harm or * him, or kill him Rom 13:9
that you never * in this matter by 1Th 4:6

CHEATED
Their children are *, with no Job 5:4
the Lord to let yourselves be *. 1Co 6:7
We have * no one nor taken 2Co 7:2
whom you have * of their pay. Jas 5:4

CHEATER
"No wonder they call him 'The *.' Gen 27:36
"Jacob" means "*." Gen 27:36f
poor and honest than rich and a *. Pro 28:6

CHEATERS
harm, but * will be destroyed. Pro 28:18
Wealthy * will not be spoken of Is 32:5

CHEATING
robbery there, and * in the markets Ps 55:11
THE LORD HATES * and delights in Pro 11:1
The Lord despises every kind of * Pro 20:10
Some men enjoy *, but the cake Pro 20:17
A fortune can be made from *, Pro 20:21
The Lord loathes all * and Pro 20:23
days plotting violence and *. Pro 24:2
Their lies about God and their * Is 32:6
Quit robbing and * my people out of Eze 45:9
get out and start * again—using Amo 8:5
to be no end of getting rich by *? Mic 6:10
reputation for *—sitting at a tax Lk 5:27
way, to buy friendship through *? Lk 16:9
and the other a * tax collector. Lk 18:10
* others, even your own brothers. 1Co 6:8

CHEATS
* and thieves and idol worshipers. 1Co 5:10

CHEBAR
beside the * Canal in Babylon. Eze 1:1
Jewish exiles beside the * River. Eze 3:14,15
seen beside the * Canal, and when Eze 10:15,16
God of Israel beside the * Canal. Eze 10:20
first by the * Canal, and then Eze 43:3

CHECK
gods, first * the facts to see if Deu 13:12,13,14
first * the rumor very carefully; Deu 17:4
the river and * out the situation Jos 2:1
Go and * again to be sure of 1Sa 23:22
Obadiah, "We must * every stream 1Ki 18:5
the people: "* to be sure that 2Ki 10:23
However, let's * with the Lord 2Ch 18:3,4,5
"* these witches' words against Is 8:20
needs repair! You * over the houses Is 22:9,10,11
* the foundation wall you built; Is 28:17
day by day to * up on Paul and Act 17:11
* up on yourselves. 2Co 13:5

CHECKED
And when they had *, they found 1Sa 14:17
* them in and out to avoid loss. 1Ch 9:28
they also * all the weights and 1Ch 23:29

CHECKERBOARD
linen, using a * pattern; Ex 28:39

CHECKERED
a robe, a * tunic, a turban, and Ex 28:4

CHECKING
with a plumbline, * it with a Amo 7:7
estimates and then * to see if he Lk 14:28

CHECKMARK
he will place a * beside the names Ps 87:6

CHECKS
A prudent man * to see where he Pro 14:15
and blessed is the man who * Is 56:2
for as a grape-gatherer * each Jer 6:9

CHED-OR-LAOMER
*, king of Elam, and Gen 14:1
subject to King *, but now in the Gen 14:4
One year later, * and his allies Gen 14:5,6
attacked * and his allies as they Gen 14:8,9
his strike against * and the other Gen 14:17

CHEEK
goes over and kisses him on the *. Gen 27:26
and kissed him on the * and said, 1Sa 10:1
they slap my *. Job 16:10
Let him turn the other * to Lam 3:30
If you are slapped on one *, turn Mt 5:39
"If someone slaps you on one *, Lk 6:29
him on the * in friendly greeting. Lk 22:47

CHEEKS
The shoulder, the *, and the Deu 18:3
* until David could weep no more. 1Sa 20:41
How lovely your * are, with your Sol 1:10
Your * are matched loveliness Sol 4:3
and quiet. His * are like sweetly Sol 5:13
Your * are matched loveliness Sol 6:7
* to those who pull out the beard. Is 50:6
tears run down her *. Lam 1:2
tears flow down my *. Lam 1:16

CHEER
"In that case," Eli said, "* 1Sa 1:17
celebrate and to * for King Saul, 1Sa 18:6
said to David, "* up, for we have 1Sa 20:42
Everyone will * at his death, Job 27:23
haughtily reject him. So * up! Ps 31:24
me and give me renewed hope and *. Ps 94:19
encourage and * me with your Ps 119:28
With this news bring * to all Is 35:3
will be, "* up, don't be afraid. Zep 3:16
said to the sick boy, "* up, son! Mt 9:2
Literally, "Be of good *." Mk 10:49f
and sorrows; but * up, for I have Jn 16:33
this injury and loss! But * up! Act 27:22
should do so with Christian *. Rom 12:8
Then when he comes back he can * Php 2:19

CHEERED
and stamped and * with glee at the Eze 25:6
They have * me greatly and have 1Co 16:18

CHEERFUL
always been * when I was with him. Neh 2:1
my sadness and be *, then he would Job 9:27
when he is *, everything seems Pro 15:15
A * heart does good like Pro 17:22
also in the spirit of * giving. 2Co 8:7
* givers are the ones God prizes. 2Co 9:7

CHEERFULLY
found him, Saul greeted him *. 1Sa 15:13
You welcome those who * do good, Is 64:5
Work hard and * at all you do, Col 3:23
not all the more * submit to God's Heb 12:9
* share your home with those who 1Pe 4:9

CHEERING
as Christians * each other up? Php 2:1

CHEERS
the wine that * both God and man, Ju 9:13
the road will burst into *!" Lk 19:40
Then God who * those who are 2Co 7:6

CHEESE
Soon, taking them * and milk and Gen 18:8
Give this * to their captain and 1Sa 17:18
lentils, honey, butter, and *. 2Sa 17:28,29
like milk, and curdled me like *. Job 10:10

CHEF
Samuel then instructed the * to 1Sa 9:23
So the * brought it in and 1Sa 9:24

CHELAL
Adna, *, Benaiah, Ma-aseiah, Ez 10:30

CHELUB
* (the brother of Shuhah), whose 1Ch 4:11,12
Ezri (son of *) was manager of 1Ch 27:26

CHELUBAI
Hezron were Jerahmeel, Ram, and *. 1Ch 2:9

CHELUHI
Banaiah, Bedeiah, *, Vaniah, Ez 10:34-42

CHEMOSH
O people of *; Num 21:27-30
You keep whatever your god * Ju 11:24
Jerusalem, for *, the depraved god 1Ki 11:7
Sidonians; and *, the god of Moab; 1Ki 11:33
and for *, the evil god of Moab; 2Ki 23:13
Your god *, with his priests and Jer 48:7
of her idol *, as Israel was of her Jer 48:13
the people of the god * are Jer 48:46

CHENAANAH
Zedekiah (son of *), made some iron 1Ki 22:11
Then Zedekiah (son of *) walked 1Ki 22:24
Jeush, Benjamin, Ehud, *, Zethan, 1Ch 7:10
One of them, Zedekiah (son of * 2Ch 18:10
Then Zedekiah (son of *) walked 2Ch 18:23

CHENANI
Bunni, Sherebiah, Bani, and *. Neh 9:4

CHENANIAH
The song leader was *, the chief 1Ch 15:22
the singers, and * the song leader 1Ch 15:27
* and his sons (from the subclan 1Ch 26:29

CHEPHAR-AMMONI
Parah, Ophrah, *, Ophni, Geba, Jos 18:21-28

CHEPHIRAH
*, Be-eroth, and Kiriath-jearim. Jos 9:17
Be-eroth, Mizpeh, *, Mozah, Rekem, Jos 18:21-28
Kiriatharim, *, and Be-eroth, 743; Ez 2:3-35
*, and Be-eroth, 743; Neh 7:8-38

CHERAN
Dishon:Hemdan, Eshban,Ithran, *. Gen 36:26
Hamran, Eshban, Ithran, and *. 1Ch 1:41
CHERETHITES
from raiding the * in the Negeb, 1Sa 30:14
Literally, "the * and 2Sa 8:18f
Gath, and the * and Pelethites. 2Sa 15:17,18
Literally, "the * and 2Sa 20:23f
bodyguard—the * and Pelethites—and 1Ch 18:17
Literally, "* (or Cretans)." Zep 2:5f
CHERISH
from wrong and * my laws in your Is 51:7
CHERISHED
I'll send my * son. Lk 20:13
CHERITH
east and hide by * Brook at a place 1Ki 17:3
CHERITHITES
will wipe out the * and utterly Eze 25:16
CHERUB
Literally, "one wing of a *, five 2Ch 3:11,12,13f
Tel-harsha, *, Addan, and Immer. Ez 2:59
Tel-harsha, *, Addon, and Immer. Neh 7:61
Literally, "a *." Ps 18:10f
his hand (for each * had, beneath Eze 10:7,8
you to be the anointed guardian *. Eze 28:14
O overshadowing *, from the midst Eze 28:16
Or, "and the guardian * drove you Eze 28:16f
CHERUB'S
Literally, "* face." Eze 10:14f
CHERUBIM
Literally, "*." Ex 25:18f
at each end. The *—the Ex 25:20
the place of mercy between the *; Ex 25:22
with * embroidered on them. Ex 26:1
with * embroidered into the cloth. Ex 26:31
linen, with * skillfully Ex 36:8,9
* skillfully embroidered into it. Ex 36:35
He made two * of beaten gold and Ex 37:7
one piece. The * faced each other, Ex 37:9
Ark, the spot between the two *. Num 7:89
of heaven enthroned above the *. 2Sa 6:1
Literally, "he made two *." 1Ki 6:23-28f
were carved with *, palm trees, and 1Ki 6:32
with the stand. *, lions, and palm 1Ki 7:36
Literally, "*." 2Ki 19:15f
Literally, "above the *." 1Ch 13:6f
Mounted on the *, Ps 18:10
O God enthroned above the *, bend Ps 80:1
He is enthroned upon the *. Ps 99:1
above the *, you alone are God of Is 37:16,17
rose from the * where it had rested Eze 9:3
the sky above the heads of the *. Eze 10:1
wheels beneath the * and take a Eze 10:2
He did so while I watched. The * Eze 10:3
from above the * and went over to Eze 10:4
the wings of the * was as the voice Eze 10:5
to go between the * and take some Eze 10:6
and one of the * reached out his Eze 10:7,8
flames between the * and put them Eze 10:7,8
Each of the four * had a wheel Eze 10:9-13
the * could go straight forward Eze 10:9-13
Each of the four * had four Eze 10:14
When the * stood still, so did Eze 10:17
part of the bodies of the *. Eze 10:17f
could not be separated from the *. Eze 10:17f
of the * was in the wheels. Eze 10:17
the Temple and stood above the *. Eze 10:18
And as I watched, the * flew Eze 10:19
Then the * lifted their wings and Eze 11:22
with carvings of *, each with two Eze 41:17,18
palm trees alternating with the *. Eze 41:17,18
decorated with * and palm trees, Eze 41:25
angels called the *—the guardians Heb 9:5
CHESALON
to the town of * on the northern Jos 15:10,11
CHESED
(father of Aram),*, Hazo, Pildash, Gen 22:20-23
CHESIL
Ezem, Eltolad, *, Hormah, Ziklag, Jos 15:21-32
CHEST
your robe, next to your *." Ex 4:6
the cart beside a * containing the 1Sa 6:8
the Lord and the * containing the 1Sa 6:11
the Ark and the * containing the 1Sa 6:15
the lid of a large * and set it on 2Ki 12:9
Whenever the * became full, the 2Ki 12:10
It was not put into the *. 2Ki 12:16
instructed that a * be made and set 2Ch 24:7,8
it in the * until it was full. 2Ch 24:10
Then the Levites carried the * to 2Ch 24:11
the * back to the Temple again. 2Ch 24:11
against his * and not be burned? Pro 6:27
purest gold, its * and arms were of Dan 2:32
scars on your * and your back?' Zec 13:6
but beat upon his * in sorrow, Lk 18:13
*," to whisper his inquiry. Jn 13:25f
and the golden *, called the ark of Heb 9:4
Above the golden * were statues Heb 9:5
with a golden band across his *. Rev 1:13
CHESTPIECE
they shall make: a *, an ephod, Ex 28:4
a * to be used as God's oracle; Ex 28:15
This * is to be of two folds of Ex 28:16
"Attach the top of the * to the Ex 28:22,23,24
at the outer top edge of the *. Ex 28:22,23,24
two lower, inside edges of the *; Ex 28:26
Now attach the bottom of the * Ex 28:28
this will prevent the * from Ex 28:28
of Israel on the * over his heart Ex 28:29
Insert into the pocket of the * Ex 28:30,31
the tunic, ephod, *, and sash, and Ex 29:5
to be used for the ephod and *. Ex 35:5-9
be used for the ephod and the *; Ex 35:27
The * was a beautiful piece of Ex 39:8
[To attach the * to the ephod Ex 39:15-18
on the top corners of the *. Ex 39:15-18
lower edge of the *, on the under Ex 39:19
woven sash. The * was held Ex 39:21
the rings of the * to the rings of Ex 39:21
linen thread. The *, the beautiful Ex 39:28,29
Then he put on him the * and Lev 8:8
CHESTS
pouch worn by priests on their *. Ju 8:27f
"The money * have been opened 2Ch 34:17
with golden belts across their *. Rev 15:6
CHESULLOTH
Jezreel, *, Shunem, Hapharaim, Jos 19:17-23
CHEW
hooves, it does not * the cud). Lev 11:4-7
animal that does not * the cud. Lev 11:26
"They * the cud but do not have Deu 14:7
hooves, they don't * the cud. Deu 14:8
CHEWING
man is like * with a sore tooth, or Pro 25:19
CHEWS
cloven hooves which * its cud. Lev 11:2,3
The camel (it * the cud but does Lev 11:4-7
although it * the cud, it does not Lev 11:4-7
The hare (because although it * Lev 11:4-7
cloven hooves and * the cud may be Deu 14:6
CHEZIB
They lived at * and had three Gen 38:3,4,5
CHICKENS
count your * before they hatch!" 1Ki 20:11
Like a coop full of * their Jer 5:27
CHICKS
a hen gathers her * beneath her Mt 23:37
CHIDE
left that he could even * you for; Col 1:22
CHIDED
so Peter took him aside and * him. Mk 8:32
CHIDON
threshing-floor of *, the oxen 1Ch 13:9
CHIEF
palace guard, the * executioner. Gen 37:36
bodyguard and his * executioner. Gen 39:1
him favor with the * jailer. Gen 39:21
to him. The * jailer had no more Gen 39:23
angry with his * baker and his wine Gen 40:1
guard, who was the * executioner. Gen 40:1
When the * baker saw that the Gen 40:16
He sent for his wine taster and * Gen 40:20
but he sentenced the * baker to Gen 40:22
and put me and the * baker in jail Gen 41:10
of the guard, the * baker and I Gen 41:11
taster, and the * baker was Gen 41:13
"The king's * assistant spoke Gen 42:30
me * of all the land of Egypt. Gen 45:9
son, shall be the * administrator Num 3:31-35
the son of Zuar, * of the tribe of Num 7:18-23
the son of Helon, * of the tribe of Num 7:24-29
Shedeur, * of the tribe of Reuben; Num 7:30-35
of Zuri-shaddai, * of the tribe of Num 7:36-41
of Deuel, * of the tribe of Gad. Num 7:42-47
son of Ammihud, * of the tribe of Num 7:48-53
son of Gideoni, * of the tribe of Num 7:60-65
He was the * of the tribe of Dan Num 7:66-71
Pagiel, son of Ochran, * of the Num 7:72-77
son of Enan, * of the tribe of Num 7:78-83
Levites, and the * judge on duty at Deu 17:9
for ten of the * men of the Ru 4:2
Edomite, Saul's * herdsman, was 1Sa 21:7
and Abiathar were the * priests. 2Sa 20:25
And David made him * of his 2Sa 23:23
the homes of the * men of the city, 2Ki 10:6
field marshal, his * treasurer, and 2Ki 18:17
treasurer, and his * of staff from 2Ki 18:17
The general took Seraiah, the * 2Ki 25:18
army of Judah, the * recruiting 2Ki 25:19
* Timna, Chief Aliah, Chief 1Ch 1:51-54
Chief Timna, * Aliah, Chief 1Ch 1:51-54
Chief Timna, Chief Aliah, * 1Ch 1:51-54
Chief Jetheth, * Oholibamah, Chief 1Ch 1:51-54
Chief Oholibamah, * Elah, Chief 1Ch 1:51-54
Chief Elah, * Pinon, Chief Kenaz, 1Ch 1:51-54
Elah, Chief Pinon, * Kenaz, Chief 1Ch 1:51-54
Chief Kenaz, * Teman, Chief Mibzar, 1Ch 1:51-54
Chief Teman, * Mibzar, Chief 1Ch 1:51-54
Mibzar, * Magdi-el, Chief Iram. 1Ch 1:51-54
Mibzar, Chief Magdi-el, * Iram. 1Ch 1:51-54
He was the * custodian of the 1Ch 9:10,11
were Shallum (the * gatekeeper), 1Ch 9:17,18
He was the * and the most famous 1Ch 11:21
Their * was Ahi-ezer, son of 1Ch 12:3-7
Ezer was the *; 1Ch 12:8-13
was Chenaniah, the * of the 1Ch 15:22
David's sons were his * aides. 1Ch 18:17
was the * officer of the treasury. 1Ch 26:23,24
and was the * of the thirty 1Ch 27:5,6
of Adi-el) was the * financial 1Ch 27:25
of Uzziah) was * of the regional 1Ch 27:25
Jehoiada the * priest didn't 2Ch 23:8
the son of Aaron, the * priest. Ez 7:1
Their * was Joel, son of Zichri, Neh 11:7,8,9
son of Ahitub the * priest). Neh 11:10-14
the * officers of the government. Est 1:13-15
them as their *, or as a king Job 29:25
* assistant, and many others. Jer 39:3
Nebushazban, the * of the eunuchs, Jer 39:13
Seraiah the * priest, and Zephaniah Jer 52:24,25
the three * Temple guards, one of Jer 52:24,25
Literally, "his * eunuch." Dan 1:3,4f
But when Ari-och, the * Dan 2:14
well as * over all his wise men. Dan 2:48
Daniel served as * magistrate in Dan 2:49
he was made * of all the Dan 5:11
by Sharezer, the * administrative Zec 7:2
Literally, "of the elders, and * Mt 16:21f
will be betrayed to the * priests Mt 20:18
But when the * priests and other Mt 21:15
was teaching, the * priests and Mt 21:23
When the * priests and other Mt 21:45
At that very moment the * priests Mt 26:3
went to the * priests, and asked, Mt 26:14
The * priests and, in fact, the Mt 26:59
WHEN IT WAS morning, the * priests Mt 27:1
the money to the * priests and Mt 27:3
The * priests picked the money up. Mt 27:6
But when the * priests and other Mt 27:12
Meanwhile the * priests and Mt 27:20
And the * priests and Jewish Mt 27:41,42,43
—the * priests and Pharisees went Mt 27:62
tomb went to the * priests and told Mt 28:11
the elders and the * Priests and Mk 8:31
taken before the * priests and the Mk 10:33
When the * priests and other Mk 11:18
* priests and other Jewish leaders Mk 11:27,28
was eaten. The * priests and other Mk 14:1
went to the * priests to arrange to Mk 14:10
When the * priests heard why he Mk 14:11
sent out by the * priests and other Mk 14:43
where all of the * priests and Mk 14:53
Inside, the * priests and the Mk 14:55
EARLY IN THE morning the * Mk 15:1
Then the * priests accused him of Mk 15:3,4
backed by the * priests because Mk 15:10
But at this point the * priests Mk 15:11
The * priests and religious Mk 15:31
elders, * priests, and teachers of Lk 9:22
Temple, but the * priests and other Lk 19:47
confronted by the * priests and Lk 20:1
When the * priests and religious Lk 20:19
was used. The * priests and other Lk 22:2
went over to the * priests and Lk 22:4
Then Jesus addressed the * Lk 22:52
including the * priests and all the Lk 22:66
Then Pilate turned to the * Lk 23:4
Meanwhile, the * priests and the Lk 23:10
Then Pilate called together the * Lk 23:13
But the * priests and our Lk 24:20
mood, they and the * priests sent Jn 7:32
to the * priests and Pharisees. Jn 7:45
Then the * priests and Pharisees Jn 11:47
Meanwhile the * priests and Jn 11:57
Then the * priests decided to Jn 12:10
The * priests and Pharisees had Jn 18:3
"Your own people and their * Jn 18:35
At sight of him the * priests and Jn 19:6
the * priests shouted back. Jn 19:15
Then the * priests said to Jn 19:21
to the people, the * priests, the Act 4:1
and the * priests heard this, Act 5:24
with him from the * priests, Act 9:14
them in chains to the * priests." Act 9:21
he was the * speaker, was Mercury! Act 14:12
and ordered the * priests into Act 22:30
Then they went to the * priests Act 23:14
where the * priests and other Act 25:2
When I was in Jerusalem, the * Act 25:15
commission of the * priests, when Act 26:12
CHIEFS
Then the leaders of Israel—the * Num 7:2
the * of the tribes of Israel. Num 7:84,85,86
then only the * of the tribes of Num 10:4
of their tribal * is to bring you a Num 17:1
each of the twelve * (including Num 17:6
with the other * of Midian—Evi, Jos 13:21
of Benjamin.) The * of Israel now Ju 20:3
Shime-i, Rei, and David's army *. 1Ki 1:8
The * of their clans were these 1Ch 5:24
and Isshiah, all * of subclans. 1Ch 7:3
These five mighty warriors were * 1Ch 7:7
and they were led by their clan * 1Ch 7:9

(CHIEFS Con't)
They were the * of the subclans 1Ch 7:11
were all skilled warriors and *. 1Ch 7:40
The sons of Ehud, * of the 1Ch 8:6,7
These sons all became * of 1Ch 8:8,9,10
Beriah and Shema, * of subclans 1Ch 8:13
These were the * of the subclans 1Ch 8:28
These men were all * of subclans. 1Ch 9:9
These were the * of the Levites Neh 12:24

CHILD
Her next * was his brother, Gen 4:2
(his son Haran's *), and his Gen 11:31
Yet I have given Abraham a * in Gen 21:7
Time went by and the * grew and Gen 21:8
gone she left the * beneath a bush Gen 21:15
to give Rebekah a *, for even after Gen 25:21
have a *, while Rachel was barren. Gen 29:31
bill the * was named 'Bill'!" Gen 30:6f
her prayers by giving her a *. Gen 30:22
Reuben, Jacob's oldest *, Simeon, Gen 35:23
"The * is gone; Gen 37:30
willing to have a * who would not Gen 38:9
deny a * to his deceased brother Gen 38:10
stick is the father of my *. Gen 38:25
the wrist of the * who appeared Gen 38:28
a * of his old age, a little one. Gen 44:20
son, the * of my vigorous youth. Gen 49:3
"Take this * home and nurse him Ex 2:9
from the oldest * of Pharaoh, heir Ex 11:5
oldest * of his lowliest slave; Ex 11:5
sacrifices his * as a burnt Lev 20:1
he has given his * to Molech, thus Lev 20:3
dollars made for each firstborn *. Num 18:16
just as a father cares for his *!' Deu 1:31
who presents his * to be burned to Deu 18:10
daughter—his only *—ran out to meet Ju 11:34
the * you are going to give us." Ju 13:8
"Listen, my *," he said to her. Ru 2:8,9
don't worry about a thing, my *; Ru 3:11
sacrifice they took the * to Eli. 1Sa 1:25
I asked him to give me this *, 1Sa 1:27
and the * became the Lord's 1Sa 2:11
Samuel, though only a *, was the 1Sa 2:18
the Lord who had spoken to the *. 1Sa 3:8
Then she murmured, "Name the * 1Sa 4:21,22
him, so your * shall die." 2Sa 12:14
David begged him to spare the *, 2Sa 12:16
when we tell him the * is dead?" 2Sa 12:18
and wept while the * was alive, for 2Sa 12:22
to me and let the * live.' 2Sa 12:22
* who doesn't know his way around. 1Ki 3:7
and laid her dead * in my arms and 1Ki 3:20
son, and the living * is mine." 1Ki 3:22
claim the living *, and each says 1Ki 3:23
the dead * belongs to the other. 1Ki 3:23
the living * in two and give half 1Ki 3:25
the mother of the *, and who loved 1Ki 3:26
Give her the *—don't kill him!" 1Ki 3:26
was a very small * at the time). 1Ki 11:16,17,18
Lord says that a * named Josiah 1Ki 13:2
into the city, the * will die. 1Ki 14:12
For this * is the only good 1Ki 14:13
and the * died just as she walked 1Ki 14:17
not a single male *. 1Ki 16:11
himself upon the * three times, and 1Ki 17:21
and the spirit of the * returned, 1Ki 17:22
One day when her * was older, he 2Ki 4:18
all right and if the * is well." 2Ki 4:26
told him, "The * is still dead." 2Ki 4:31
When Elisha arrived, the * was 2Ki 4:32
himself again upon the *. 2Ki 4:35
It is as when a * is ready to be 2Ki 19:3
Lord who enjoys helping his *!" Ps 35:27
Then he killed the oldest * in Ps 105:36
Hear the cry of your beloved * Ps 108:6
*, as one who bears your name! Ps 109:21
a * who is weaned from the breast. Ps 131:2
He destroyed the eldest * in Ps 135:8
*, and the companion of my father. Pro 4:3
at his side like a little *. Pro 8:30
The character of even a * can be Pro 20:11
Teach a * to choose the right Pro 22:6
Scolding and spanking a * helps Pro 29:15
Woe to the land whose king is a * Ecc 10:16,17
* shall be born to a virgin! Is 7:14
God's sign was that before this * Is 7:14f
By the time this * is weaned Is 7:15,16
Literally, "For before this * Is 7:15,16f
the * was even on the way). Is 8:2
years, before this * is even old Is 8:4
For unto us a * is born; Is 9:6
so few a * could count them! Is 10:19
a little * shall lead them all. Is 11:6
and a little * who puts his hand in Is 11:8
of a woman giving birth to a *. Is 21:3
birth, and the * does not come. Is 37:3
cry like a woman delivering her *. Is 42:14
Can a mother forget her little * Is 49:15
woman giving birth to her first *; Jer 4:31
in pain like a woman having a *. Jer 13:21
and Ephraim is my oldest *. Jer 31:9
is still my son, my darling *. Jer 31:20
the plan that his * will someday Jer 33:25,26
a man, woman or * among you who has Jer 44:7
From the time I was a * until now Eze 4:14
*, brother or unmarried sister. Eze 44:25
and of her ambassador and *. Dan 11:6
And the Lord said, "Name the * Hos 1:4,5
Soon Gomer had another *—this one Hos 1:6
I will slay even her beloved *. Hos 9:16
WHEN ISRAEL WAS a * I loved him as Hos 11:1
but he is like a * resisting in the Hos 13:13
If you sacrificed your oldest *, Mic 6:7
him as for an oldest * who died. Zec 12:10
For the * within her has been Mt 1:20
The virgin shall conceive a *! Mt 1:23
to Bethlehem and search for the *. Mt 2:8
is going to try to kill the *." Mt 2:13
trying to kill the * are dead." Mt 2:20
If a * asks his father for a Mt 7:9
*, you will surely be rewarded." Mt 10:42
Jesus called a small * over to Mt 18:2
as this little *, is the greatest Mt 18:4
welcomes a little * like this Mt 18:5
"The * isn't dead; Mk 5:39
her * from the demon's control. Mk 7:26
convulsed the * horribly, and he Mk 9:20
of this * and enter him no more!" Mk 9:25
Then he placed a little * among Mk 9:36
and taking the * in his arms he Mk 9:36
welcomes a little * like this in my Mk 9:37
to God as a little * will never be Mk 10:15
to speak until the * is born. Lk 1:20
Elizabeth's * leaped within her and Lk 1:41
women, and your * is destined for Lk 1:42
what this * will turn out to be? Lk 1:66
gave birth to her first *, a son. Lk 2:7
had said to them about this *. Lk 2:17
they had seen the *, just as the Lk 2:20
the birth of a *, his parents took Lk 2:22
a woman's first * is a boy, he Lk 2:23
the * in his arms, praising God. Lk 2:28
soul, for this * shall be rejected Lk 2:34,35
There the * became a strong, Lk 2:40
him, for his only * was dying, a Lk 8:42
he stood a little * beside him and Lk 9:47
* like this is caring for me! Lk 9:48
laws since I was a small *." Lk 18:21
come now before my * dies." Jn 4:49
in labor when her * is born—her Jn 16:21
was born—a * of divine beauty. Act 7:20
her that Esau, the * born first, Rom 9:10-13
and trustworthy * in the Lord. 1Co 4:17
It's like this: when I was a * I 1Co 13:11
thought and reasoned as a * does. 1Co 13:11
promises to Abraham and his *. Gal 3:16
of, but to his *—and that, of Gal 3:16
* to whom God's promise was made. Gal 3:19
little son, that * is not much Gal 4:1
waiting for her * to be Gal 4:19
though you never before had a *. Gal 4:27
just as Isaac the * of promise was Gal 4:29
much loved * imitates his father. Eph 5:1
that you are a * of God, for this Php 1:11
pains begin when her * is born. 1Th 5:3
you to become his *, will do all 1Th 5:24
you were a small *, you were taught 2Ti 3:15
kindness to my * Onesimus, whom I Phm 1:10
to have even one *—a nation with so Heb 11:12
them an unusual *, they trusted Heb 11:23
touch the oldest * in those homes, Heb 11:28
words God spoke to you, his *? Heb 12:5
it proves you are really his *." Heb 12:6
holy, who invited you to be his *. 1Pe 1:15
So now we can tell who is a * of 1Jn 3:10
Savior—then you are a * of God. 1Jn 5:1
for every * of God can obey him, 1Jn 5:4
sister—another choice * of God. 2Jn 1:13
give birth to her *, ready to eat Rev 12:4
who had given birth to the *. Rev 12:13

CHILD'S
the capital, the * nurse grabbed 2Sa 4:4
let this * spirit return to him." 1Ki 17:21
Lay the staff upon the * face." 2Ki 4:29
the * face, but nothing happened. 2Ki 4:31
Then he lay upon the * body, 2Ki 4:34
his mouth upon the * mouth, and his 2Ki 4:34
his eyes upon the * eyes, and his 2Ki 4:34
and his hands upon the * hands. 2Ki 4:34
And the * body began to grow warm 2Ki 4:34
as a little *, and he was healed! 2Ki 5:14
as a *, firm and youthful again. Job 33:25
glory. A * glory is his father. Pro 17:6

CHILDBIRTH
But Rachel's pains of * began Gen 35:16
again after her bleeding at *. Lev 12:7
then, are the procedures after *. Lev 12:7

CHILDHOOD
far from my * home, I told her, Gen 20:13
who had been her * nurse, and Gen 24:59
intensely for your * home—why have Gen 31:30
to return to her * home and to her Gen 38:11
and returned to her * home; Ru 1:14
they had been raised since *. 2Ki 10:6
I've trusted you from *. Ps 71:5
from my earliest *—and I have Ps 71:17
Pamper a servant from *, and he Pro 29:21
him into my * home, into my Sol 3:4
I would bring you to my * home, Sol 8:2
And all your friends of * days Is 47:15
*, rotten through and through. Is 48:8
From our * we have seen Jer 3:24
from * against the Lord our God; Jer 3:25
Since * you have been that Jer 22:21
from my earliest * in Tarsus Act 26:4
beyond those of my *, and now I 1Co 13:11

CHILDISH
now I have put away the * things. 1Co 13:11
Dear brothers, don't be * in your 1Co 14:20

CHILDISHLY
will be like babies, ruling *. Is 3:4

CHILDLESS
shall bear their sin and die *. Lev 20:20
his brother, and they shall be *. Lev 20:21
now your mother shall be *." 1Sa 15:33
So Michal was * throughout her 2Sa 6:23
the * who have no protecting sons. Job 24:21
He gives children to the * wife, Ps 113:9
For you are * now! Is 23:4
SING, O * woman! Is 54:1
She sits * now, disgraced, for Jer 15:9
Record this man Coniah as *, for Jer 22:30
"Now you can rejoice, O * woman; Gal 4:27

CHILDLIKE
protects the simple and the *; Ps 116:6

CHILDREN
* in intense pain and suffering; Gen 3:16
human women, their * became giants, Gen 6:4
* and to repopulate the earth. Gen 9:1
Yes, have many * and repopulate Gen 9:7
solemnly promise you and your * Gen 9:9,10,11
she had no *. Gen 11:30
BUT SARAI AND Abram had no *. Gen 16:1
"Since the Lord has given me no * Gen 16:2,3
girl, and her * shall be mine." Gen 16:2,3
be between me and your * as well. Gen 17:7,8
will soon be too old for having *. Gen 19:31
so that they could have *; Gen 20:17
He also had four other * from his Gen 22:24
to give me and my * this land. Gen 24:7
bore him several *:Zimran, Jokshan, Gen 25:1
these were the * of Keturah." Gen 25:4f
This is the story of Isaac's *: Gen 25:19
she had no *. Gen 25:21
And it seemed as though * were Gen 25:22
bless you and give you many *; Gen 28:2
And then she stopped having *. Gen 29:35
"Give me * or I'll die," she Gen 30:1
Bilhah, and her * will be mine." Gen 30:3
Let me take my wives and *—for I Gen 30:26
and these * are mine, and these Gen 31:43
me and these mothers and my *. Gen 32:11
and eleven *, and took them Gen 32:22,23,24
and their * at the head, Leah and Gen 33:2
head, Leah and her * next, and Gen 33:2
at the women and * and asked, "Who Gen 33:5
"My *," Jacob replied. Gen 33:5
their *, and bowed low before him. Gen 33:6
Next came Leah with her *, and Gen 33:7
some of the * are small, and the Gen 33:13
and *, and wealth of every kind. Gen 34:29
Then Esau took his wives, *, Gen 36:6,7,8
The * of Lotan (the son of Seir) Gen 36:22
The * of Shobal:Alvan, Manahath, Gen 36:23
The * of Zibeon: Gen 36:24
The * of Anah:Dishon, Oholibamah. Gen 36:25
The * of Dishon:Hemdan, Gen 36:26
The * of Ezer:Bilhan, Zaavan, Gen 36:27
The * of Dishan:Uz, Aran. Gen 36:28,29,30
any of his other *, because Joseph Gen 37:3
bereaved me of my *—Joseph didn't Gen 42:36
alone is left of his mother's *. Gen 42:38
of his mother's *, and his father Gen 44:20
me with all your *, your Gen 45:10
and all his *, sons and daughters, Gen 46:6
*, for an everlasting possession.' Gen 48:4
But any other * born to you Gen 48:6
Rachel died after only two * Gen 48:7
God has let me see your * too." Gen 48:11
But they left their little * and Gen 50:8
his son Ephraim's *, and the Gen 50:23
children, and the * of Machir, Gen 50:23
God, he gave them * of their own. Ex 1:21
"He must be one of the Hebrew * Ex 2:6
Their * were:Nadab, Ex 6:23
and Phinehas was one of his *. Ex 6:25
What stories you can tell your * Ex 10:2
you can even take your * with Ex 10:24
* when I smite the land of Egypt. Ex 12:13
* ask, 'What does all this mean? Ex 12:26
the women and *, going on foot. Ex 12:37
explain to your * why you are Ex 13:8
"And in the future, when your * Ex 13:14

HILDREN Con't)
die, with our * and cattle too?" Ex 17:3
continues upon the *, Ex 20:5
the wife and * shall still belong Ex 21:4
my wife, and my *, and I would Ex 21:5
be widows and your * fatherless. Ex 22:24
of memorial for the * of Israel." Ex 39:6,7f
all their * and children's children Ex 40:15
* shall forever be my priests." Ex 40:15
a brother to beget * from her to Lev 18:16f
give any of your * to Molech, Lev 18:21
was required if she had no *. Lev 20:21f
be the father of * of mixed Lev 21:14,15
it, and any slave * born in his Lev 22:11
can leave with his *, and return to Lev 25:41
may purchase the * of the Lev 25:45
to pass on to your * after you; Lev 25:46
his * shall be freed at that time. Lev 25:54
to kill your * and destroy your Lev 26:22
And since they had no *, this Num 3:4
all the firstborn * of the Num 8:16
Are they my *? Num 11:12
alone [besides all the women and * Num 11:21
fault in the * to the third and Num 14:17,18
" 'You said your * would become Num 14:31
"When your * finally live in the Num 15:1
of the * of Ammon was strong." Num 21:24f
The little * Num 21:27-30
all the women and *, and seized Num 31:9,10,11
"Our *, wives, flocks, and Num 32:26
The * of Reuben built the Num 32:37,38
I will give the land to the * Deu 1:39
women, and * alike. Deu 3:6
" 'But your wives and *,' I told Deu 3:19
Tell your * and your Deu 4:9
can teach my laws to their *.' Deu 4:10
"In the future, when your * and Deu 4:25
with you and your *, and so that Deu 4:40
of the * of those who hate me; Deu 5:9,10
* throughout all generations! Deu 5:29
and so that you will have many *. Deu 6:3
You must teach them to your * Deu 6:7
chose you, their *, to be above Deu 10:15
I am not talking now to your * Deu 11:2
Teach them to your *. Deu 11:19
you and your * will enjoy the good Deu 11:21
where you, your *, and the Levites Deu 12:18
will be well with you and your *. Deu 12:24,25
well with you and your * forever. Deu 12:28
the women, *, cattle, and booty. Deu 20:14
have borne him *, and the mother of Deu 21:15
Many *, Deu 28:2-6
he promised: many *, many cattle, Deu 28:11
and his * who are still alive. Deu 28:54
flesh of his own *—because he is Deu 28:55
plagues upon you and upon your *. Deu 28:58,59
Then your * and the generations Deu 29:22
for us and our * to obey forever. Deu 29:29
and you and your * have begun Deu 30:2
the hearts of your * and of your Deu 30:6
of your children's * so that you Deu 30:6
and give you many * and much cattle Deu 30:9
that you and your * might live! Deu 30:19
"—men, women, *, and foreigners Deu 31:12
Do this so that your little * Deu 31:13
today, and pass them on to your *. Deu 32:46
Even his own *, brothers, fathers, Deu 33:9
your wives and * and cattle may Jos 1:14
future, when your * ask, 'What is Jos 4:6
said, "when your * ask you why Jos 4:21
circumcised their *—the men who had Jos 5:7
the women and * and the foreigners Jos 8:35
in the future your * will say to Jos 22:24,25
And your * may make our children Jos 22:24,25
And your children may make our * Jos 22:24,25
symbol to show our * and your Jos 22:26,27
children and your * that we, too, Jos 22:26,27
and your * will not be able to say Jos 22:26,27
If they say this, our * can Jos 22:28
Isaac's *, whom I gave him, were Jos 24:4
Jacob and his * went into Egypt. Jos 24:4
She had no *, but the Angel said Ju 13:2,3
placing their *, cattle, and Ju 18:21
women, *, and cattle—and burned Ju 20:48
All the men, married women, and * Ju 21:10,11,12
that she can have * to carry on her Ru 4:5
complicate his estate for the * Ru 4:6f
Peninnah had some *, but Hannah 1Sa 1:2
presents to Peninnah and her *; 1Sa 1:4
so she had no * to give presents 1Sa 1:5
make such a fuss over having no *? 1Sa 1:8
Peninnah and her * went on the 1Sa 1:21,22
The barren woman now has seven *; 1Sa 2:5
She with many * has no more! 1Sa 2:5
to give them other * to take the 1Sa 2:20
and their * shall die by the 1Sa 2:33
babies, little *, oxen, sheep, 1Sa 15:3
but also to my * after the Lord 1Sa 20:15
* into God's hands forever." 1Sa 20:42
women, *, and babies, and also all 1Sa 22:19
carrying off all the women and *. 1Sa 30:2
grief for their *, his men began 1Sa 30:6
Give them their wives and their * 1Sa 30:22
May each of his * be victims of 2Sa 3:29
These are his * who were born at 2Sa 5:14,15,16
me, that if my * and their 1Ki 2:4
"However, if you or your * turn 1Ki 9:6
wives and the best of your *!" 1Ki 20:2,3
gold, wives, and *, but about this 1Ki 20:5,6
have my wives and * and silver and 1Ki 20:7
you and upon your * and your 2Ki 5:27
and your children's * forever." 2Ki 5:27
of his *, except for his year-old 2Ki 11:1
rest of the king's * who were 2Ki 11:2,3
but he didn't kill their *, for 2Ki 14:6
killed for their *, nor children 2Ki 14:6
children, nor * for the sins of 2Ki 14:6
burned their own * on the altars of 2Ki 17:31
These are the * of Azubah: 1Ch 2:18
Seled died without *, but 1Ch 2:30
Jether died without *, but 1Ch 2:32
Zerubbabel's * were: 1Ch 3:19,20
fewer * than was normal in Judah. 1Ch 4:27
The * of Asher: 1Ch 7:30
Heber's * were: 1Ch 7:32
Hushim and Baara, but he had * in 1Ch 8:8,9,10
of my * being kings too! 1Ch 17:17
my * will always rule this nation. 1Ch 17:23
ruled by my * and their posterity! 1Ch 17:24
May this blessing rest upon my * 1Ch 17:27
of his clan, for he had many *. 1Ch 23:17
their father did and had no *; 1Ch 24:1
has given me many *—he has chosen 1Ch 28:5
it to your * to rule forever. 1Ch 28:8
of Absalom. The * she bore him were 2Ch 11:20
ones, wives, and *, the Spirit of 2Ch 20:13
You, your *, your wives, and all 2Ch 21:14
However, he didn't kill their * 2Ch 25:4
nor the * for the father's sins. 2Ch 25:4
sacrificed his own * in the fire, 2Ch 28:3
Judean women and *, and tremendous 2Ch 28:8
to the women and * who needed it, 2Ch 28:15
away from us. My *, don't neglect 2Ch 29:11
brothers and your * will be treated 2Ch 30:9
sacrificed his own * as burnt 2Ch 33:6
*, and our goods as we traveled. Ez 8:21
to our * as an inheritance. Ez 9:12
of men, women, and * gathered Ez 10:1
and to send them away with our *; Ez 10:3
and many had * by these wives. Ez 10:44
had to sell their * or mortgage Neh 5:2,3,4
brothers, and our * are just like Neh 5:5
"Yet we must sell our * into Neh 5:5
their lands and sell them their *. Neh 5:12
The women and * rejoiced too, and Neh 12:43
that many of their * spoke in the Neh 13:24
their * intermarry with non-Jews. Neh 13:25
and old, women and *—must all be Est 3:13
and his many *, and promotions the Est 5:11
would summon his * to him and Job 1:5
all their * shall be scattered. Job 4:11
Their * are cheated, with no one Job 5:4
If your * sinned against him, Job 8:4
friends, their * shall go blind. Job 17:5
Even young * despise me. Job 19:18
"His * shall beg from the poor, Job 20:10
They live to see their * grow to Job 21:8
have many happy *, they spend Job 21:11
least God will punish their *!' Job 21:19
the man who sins, not his *! Job 21:19
to search for food for their *. Job 24:5
"The wicked snatch fatherless * Job 24:9
leave no property for their *. Job 24:18
has a multitude of *, it is so that Job 27:14
with me and my * were around me; Job 29:5
to be fools, yes, * of no name, Job 30:8
them as our own *)— or if I have Job 31:18
Making a total of twenty *, twice Job 42:13,14f
You have taught the little * to Ps 8:2
so that their * and grandchildren Ps 17:13,14
will destroy them and their *. Ps 21:9,10
worship him. Our * too shall serve Ps 22:30
and his * shall inherit the earth. Ps 25:13
women and *—fear the Lord and stand Ps 33:8
nor have I seen the * of the Ps 37:25
and their * are a blessing. Ps 37:26
so that you can tell your *. Ps 48:13
Their * shall inherit the land; Ps 69:36
(and their * too) about all your Ps 71:18
of Jehovah to your *, and tell them Ps 78:4
them to their *, so that they in Ps 78:5
in turn could teach their * too. Ps 78:6
If his * forsake my laws and Ps 89:30,31,32
let our * see glorious things, Ps 90:16
slavery—they were * of death—and Ps 102:20
his salvation is to children's * Ps 103:17,18
* away to distant lands as exiles. Ps 106:27
their little * to the demons—the Ps 106:37,38
them many * and much prosperity. Ps 107:41
May his * become fatherless and Ps 109:9,10
let no one pity his fatherless *. Ps 109:12,13
His * shall be honored Ps 112:2
He gives * to the childless Ps 113:9
richly bless both you and your *. Ps 115:14
* are a gift from God; Ps 127:3
they are his reward. * born to a Ps 127:4
And look at all those *! Ps 128:3
Let each generation tell its * Ps 145:4
all enemies, and blessed your *. Ps 147:13
*— all praise the Lord together. Ps 148:12
Why should you beget * with Pro 5:16
Why share your * with those Pro 5:17
will rescue the * of the godly. Pro 11:21
deep strength; his * have a place Pro 14:26
Don't fail to correct your *; Pro 23:13,14
lazy. Her * stand and bless her; Pro 31:28
his death that his * can't even Ecc 6:3
The * I raised and cared for so Is 1:2
Foolish as little * playing king. Is 3:12
I and the * God has given me Is 8:18
they will even eat their own *! Is 9:19,20
rob the widows and fatherless *. Is 10:2
Their little * will be dashed to Is 13:16
of Babylon or the babies or the *. Is 13:18
Slay the * of this sinner. Is 14:21
will cut off his * and his Is 14:22
* from ever sitting on his throne. Is 14:22
Are we little *, barely old Is 28:9
Literally, "when he sees his *, Is 29:23f
WOE TO MY rebellious *, says the Is 30:1
Spirit and my blessings on your *. Is 44:3
I'll never lose my *." Is 47:8
the loss of your *, despite all Is 47:9
For most of my * were killed and Is 49:21
fight you, and I will save your *. Is 49:25
have a multitude of *, many heirs. Is 53:10
Literally, "*." Is 54:1f
You * of sinners and liars! Is 57:4
and slay your * as human sacrifices Is 57:5
and their * and their children's Is 59:21
and their children's * forever." Is 59:21
Your * will care for you, O Is 62:5
their * will not be born to be Is 65:23
For they are the * of those the Is 65:23
and their *, too, shall be Is 65:23
flow to her. Her * shall be nursed Is 66:12
a holy people, the first of my *. Jer 2:3
yes, even with your children's * Jer 2:9
I have punished your * but it Jer 2:30
O sinful *, come home, for I am Jer 3:14
be for you to be here among my *. Jer 3:19
O my rebellious *, come back to Jer 3:22
they are dull, retarded * who Jer 4:22
For even your * have turned away, Jer 5:7
even upon the * playing in the Jer 6:11
Watch how the * gather wood and Jer 7:18
* no longer play in the streets; Jer 9:21
My home is gone; my * have been Jer 10:20
they and all their * would be mine Jer 11:4
for all her * have been killed. Jer 15:9
You must not marry and have * Jer 16:2
For the * born in this city, and Jer 16:3
Now, Lord, let their * starve to Jer 18:21
and be bereft of all their *! Jer 18:21
with the blood of innocent *. Jer 19:4
to eat their own * and friends. Jer 19:9
He and his * will be exiled to Jer 22:28
for none of his * shall ever sit Jer 22:30
Marry and have *, and then find Jer 29:6
and your * from their exile. Jer 30:10
Their * shall prosper as in Jer 30:20
is weeping for her * and she Jer 31:15
the Lord, and your * will come Jer 31:17
* pay for their fathers' sins." Jer 31:29
* suffer for their fathers' sins; Jer 32:18
There they have burnt their * as Jer 32:35
neither we nor our * forever. Jer 35:6
All your wives and * will be Jer 38:23
his * and all the nobles of Judah. Jer 39:6
women, * and eunuchs, to prepare to Jer 41:16,17
men, women and *, the king's Jer 43:6
bring your * from a distant land. Jer 46:27
at their helpless *, for the time Jer 47:3
place to hide. Her *, her brothers, Jer 49:9,10
your fatherless * who remain, and Jer 49:11
* will be dragged away as slaves! Jer 49:20
For even little * shall be Jer 50:45
her young * are captured and Lam 1:5
help me. My * have no future; Lam 1:16
little * and tiny babies are Lam 2:11
plead for your * as they faint Lam 2:19
Shall mothers eat their little *, Lam 2:20
All my little * lie dead upon the Lam 2:22
have cooked and eaten their own *; Lam 4:10
and the little * stagger beneath Lam 5:13
young, girls, women and little *; Eze 9:6
Must you also slay my * in the Eze 16:21
slaying of your * as sacrifices to Eze 16:36
husband and her *, and you do too. Eze 16:45
their husbands and their *. Eze 16:45
of Israel: The * are punished for Eze 18:2
Her * were like lion's cubs! Eze 19:2
"Then I spoke to their * and Eze 20:18

(CHILDREN Con't)
"But their * too rebelled Eze 20:21
They burnt their firstborn * as Eze 20:26
took away her * as their slaves. Eze 23:10
be killed; your * will be taken Eze 23:25
and murdered my * whom they bore to Eze 23:37
had murdered their * in front of Eze 23:39
burning their * on idol altars. Eze 36:12
They and their * after them shall Eze 37:25
families. All * born in the Eze 47:22
the same rights your own * have. Eze 47:22
along with their * and wives, and Dan 6:24
that some of her * will be born to Hos 1:2
are my sons, * of the Living God.' Hos 1:10
favors to her * as I would to my Hos 1:4
to my own, for they are not my *; Hos 1:4
I will "forget" to bless your *. Hos 4:6
they shall have no *, for they have Hos 4:10
Lord, bearing * that aren't his. Hos 5:7
a bird, for your * will die at Hos 9:11
And if your * grow, I will take Hos 9:12
even mothers and * were dashed to Hos 10:14
In years to come, tell your * Joe 1:3
Bring everyone—the elders, the * Joe 2:16
Or, "with its 120,000 * who don't Jon 4:11f
their * of every God-given right. Mic 2:9
to feed your * and your wives, and Nah 2:12
Their *, too, shall see the Zec 10:7
with all their *, they will come Zec 10:9
I will rebuke your * and I will Mal 2:3
We are * of the same father, Mal 2:10
Godly * from your union. Mal 2:15
Rachel weeping for her *, Mt 2:18
to raise up * unto Abraham." Mt 3:9f
good gifts to your *, won't your Mt 7:11
fathers shall betray their own *. Mt 10:21
own children. And * shall rise Mt 10:21
These people are like * playing, Mt 11:16
"wisdom is justified by her *." Mt 11:19f
and for revealing it to little *. Mt 11:25
day, besides all the women and *. Mt 14:21
bread from the * and throw it to Mt 15:26
men besides the women and *! Mt 15:37,38
become as little *, you will never Mt 18:3
a single one of these little *. Mt 18:10
wife and * and everything he had. Mt 18:25
Little * were brought for Jesus Mt 19:13
"Let the little * come to me, and Mt 19:14
*, or property, to follow me, Mt 19:29
even the little * in the Temple Mt 21:15
hear what these * are saying?" Mt 21:15
a man died without *, his brother Mt 22:24
widow and their * would get all the Mt 22:24
then died, without *, so his widow Mt 22:25
This brother also died without * Mt 22:26
to gather your * together as a hen Mt 23:37
to feed my * day by day? Mt 24:45
blood be on us and on our *!" Mt 27:25
Literally, "Let the * eat Mk 7:27f
were bringing their * to Jesus to Mk 10:13
to them, "Let the * come to me, Mk 10:14
Then he took the * into his arms Mk 10:16
So Jesus said it again: "Dear * Mk 10:24
mother, father, *, or property—for Mk 10:29
*, and land—with persecutions! Mk 10:30
a man dies without *, the man's Mk 12:19
and have * in his brother's name. Mk 12:19
married and died, and left no *. Mk 12:20,21,22
soon he died too, and left no *. Mk 12:20,21,22
and died without *, and so on Mk 12:20,21,22
dead, and still there were no *; Mk 12:20,21,22
betray their own *, and children Mk 13:12
own children, and * will betray Mk 13:12
and to mothers nursing their *. Mk 13:17
if possible, even God's own *. Mk 13:22
But they had no *, for Elizabeth Lk 1:7
the fathers to the *, and the Lk 1:17f
away my disgrace of having no *!" Lk 1:25
and his *—to be merciful to them Lk 1:55
God can produce * of Abraham from Lk 3:8
They are like a group of * who Lk 7:32
is justified of all her *." Lk 7:35f
who are as trusting as little *. Lk 10:21
yourselves give * what they need, Lk 11:13
to gather your * together even as a Lk 13:34
mother, wife, *, brothers, or Lk 14:26
Then Jesus called the * over to Lk 18:16,17
"Let the little * come to me! Lk 18:16,17
parents, or * for the sake of the Lk 18:29
the ground, and your * within you; Lk 19:44
a man dies without *, the man's Lk 20:28
widow and their * will legally Lk 20:28
and then died without any *. Lk 20:29
Still no *. Lk 20:30
her and died, leaving no *. Lk 20:31
but for yourselves and for your *. Lk 23:28
women who have no * will be counted Lk 23:29
gave the right to become * of God. Jn 1:11,12
circumcising your * falls on the Jn 7:21,22,23
For you are the * of your father Jn 8:44
it proves you aren't his *." Jn 8:47
but for all the * of God scattered Jn 11:52
Dear, dear *, how brief are Jn 13:33
Literally, "*." Jn 21:5f
God, and to your * and even to Act 2:39
You are the * of those prophets; Act 3:25
as yet he had no *! Act 7:5
to abandon their * in the fields. Act 7:19
wives and * walked down to the Act 21:5
the circumcision of their *. Act 21:21
and teach even * the affairs of Rom 2:20
God's very own *, adopted into the Rom 8:15
us that we really are God's *. Rom 8:16
And since we are his *, we will Rom 8:17
day when God will resurrect his *. Rom 8:19
from sin which God's * enjoy. Rom 8:20,21
full rights as his *, including the Rom 8:23
make them truly Abraham's *. Rom 9:7
though Abraham had other * too. Rom 9:7
all of Abraham's * are children of Rom 9:8
children are * of God, but only Rom 9:8
to bear him twin *, God told her Rom 9:10-13
And God said this before the * Rom 9:10-13
it was not because of what the * Rom 9:10-13
he will find other * for himself Rom 9:25
God's people, their * will be too. Rom 11:16
Abraham and his *, sharing in God's Rom 11:17
When God's * are in need, you be Rom 12:13
God has accepted them to be his *. Rom 14:3
one of God's own *, and Urbanus, Rom 16:8
warn and counsel you as beloved *. 1Co 4:14
separates, the * might never come 1Co 7:14
* to live in peace and harmony. 1Co 7:15
a sign to God's * concerning his 1Co 14:22
if you truly were my very own *. 2Co 6:13
And anyway, you are my *, and 2Co 12:14
and little * don't pay for their 2Co 12:14
parents supply food for their *. 2Co 12:14
this that the real * of Abraham are Gal 3:7
were to his *, as it would if all Gal 3:16
For now we are all * of God Gal 3:26
Oh, my *, how you are hurting Gal 4:19
that system, are her slave *. Gal 4:24,25
For I am going to give you many * Gal 4:27
* than the slave-wife has." Gal 4:27
brothers, are the * that God Gal 4:28
we are not slave *, obligated to Gal 4:31
Jewish laws, but * of the free Gal 4:31
you were enemies of God's * and Eph 2:12
as all God's * should, how long, Eph 3:18,19
Then we will no longer be like *, Eph 4:14
them may even become * of light! Eph 5:13
*, OBEY YOUR parents; Eph 6:1
and nagging your *, making them Eph 6:4
innocent lives as * of God in a Php 2:15
our bodies that makes us * of God; Php 3:3
You * must always obey your Col 3:20
Fathers, don't scold your * so Col 3:21
feeding and caring for her own *. 1Th 2:7
to his own *—don't you remember? 1Th 2:11
For you are all * of the light 1Th 5:5
you the kind of * he wants to 2Th 1:11
women when their * are born, but he 1Ti 2:15
* who obey quickly and quietly. 1Ti 3:4
But if they have * or 1Ti 5:4
Has she brought up her * well? 1Ti 5:10
again and have *, and take care of 1Ti 5:14
one wife and their * must love the Tit 1:6
husbands and their *, and to be Tit 2:4
here am I and the * God gave me." Heb 2:13
Since we, God's *, are human Heb 2:14
disobey God as the * of Israel did, Heb 4:11
him—and still do—by helping his *? Heb 6:10
any loving father does for his *. Heb 12:7
the first * in his new family. Jas 1:18
and knew you would become his *. 1Pe 1:2
And God has reserved for his * 1Pe 1:4
Obey God because you are his *; 1Pe 1:14
For the Lord is watching his *, 1Pe 3:12
begin first among God's own *. 1Pe 4:17
MY LITTLE *, I am telling you this 1Jn 2:1
of you, my little *, because your 1Jn 2:12
Dear *, this world's last hour 1Jn 2:18
And now, my little *, stay in 1Jn 2:28
all those who do right are his *. 1Jn 2:29
*—think of it—and we really are! 1Jn 3:1
understand that we are his *. 1Jn 3:1
are already God's *, right now, and 1Jn 3:2
Oh, dear *, don't let anyone 1Jn 3:7
Little *, let us stop just 1Jn 3:18
But we are * of God; 1Jn 4:6
that they are the * of God, and 1Jn 4:7
love the Father love his * too. 1Jn 5:1
you love God's *—your brothers and 1Jn 5:2
We know that we are * of God and 1Jn 5:19
Dear *, keep away from anything 1Jn 5:21
own, and to her * whom I love so 2Jn 1:1
find some of your * here, and to 2Jn 1:4
Greetings from the * of your 2Jn 1:13
to hear such things about my *. 3Jn 1:4
right prove that they are God's *; 3Jn 1:11
they are Jews—the * of God—but they Rev 2:9
and I will strike her * dead. Rev 2:23
the rest of her *—all who were Rev 12:17
and you, O * of God and the Rev 18:20

CHILDREN'S
ours and our * to begin with! Gen 31:16
to you and to your * children, for Gen 48:4
their children and * children shall Ex 40:15
and of your * children so that you Deu 30:6
It was his * pet and he fed it 2Sa 12:3
and your * children forever." 2Ki 5:27
not die for the * sins, nor the 2Ch 25:4
his salvation is to * children of Ps 103:17,18
children and his * children from Is 14:22
and their * children forever." Is 59:21
yes, even with your * children in Jer 2:9
harvest and your * bread, and your Jer 5:17
and the * teeth are set on edge." Jer 31:29f
babies' cries. The * tongues stick Lam 4:3,4
and the * teeth are set on edge." Eze 18:2f
It isn't right to take the * food Mk 7:27
some scraps from the * plates." Mk 7:28
become like little *, and will Lk 1:17
who harm these little * souls. Lk 17:2,3
as trusting as these little *. Lk 18:16,17
plan, result in the * salvation. 1Co 7:14

CHILEAB
His second son, *, was born to 2Sa 3:3

CHILION
and his two sons, Mahlon and *. Ru 1:1
These young men, Mahlon and *, Ru 1:4,5
of Elimelech, *, and Mahlon, from Ru 4:9

CHILL
A * of fear swept through the Mt 9:8

CHILLED
Sorrow * their hearts, and each Mt 26:22

CHILMAD
Asshur and * all send their wares. Eze 27:23

CHIMED
Then all the other Jews * in, Act 24:9

CHIMHAM
But here is *. 2Sa 19:37
According to Josephus, * was 2Sa 19:37f
"Good," the king agreed. "* 2Sa 19:38
on to Gilgal, taking * with him. 2Sa 19:40
village of Geruth *, near Jer 41:16,17

CHIN
or *, the priest must examine him; Lev 13:29,30

CHINA
near future. In * alone, in 1961, Rev 9:16f

CHINNERETH
on the west, from * to Mount Pisgah Deu 3:17
Ziddim, Zer, Hammath, Rakkath, *, Jos 19:35-39

CHINNEROTH
kings in the Arabah, south of *; Jos 11:1
all of *, and all the cities in the 1Ki 15:20

CHIOS
the next day we passed *; Act 20:15

CHIP
Don't * or shape the stones with Ex 20:25
a * of wood upon an ocean wave. Hos 10:7

CHIPPED
gold or silver or * from stone. Act 17:29

CHISELED
have an idol * out from stone. Jer 2:26,27
evil were laws * with an iron pen Jer 17:1

CHISLON
Elidad (son of *) Num 34:16-28

CHISLOTH-TABOR
to the border of *, and from there Jos 19:12

CHITLISH
Cabbon, Lahmam, *, Gederoth, Jos 15:37-44

CHLOE'S
For some of those who live at * 1Co 1:11

CHOENIX
Literally, "A * of wheat for a Rev 6:6f
and three * of barley for a Rev 6:6f

CHOICE
Take your * of any section of the Gen 13:9
And I have given the * land of Gen 48:22
"I am giving you the * today Deu 11:26
it was your own *, and you have Deu 23:23
* Bashan rams, and goats— Deu 32:14
she was given her * of clothing or Est 2:12,13,14
"This is the King of my *, and I Ps 2:6
the son of your *, Ps 80:17
but my * is clear—I love your Ps 119:113
clear, well-aged wine and * beef. Is 25:6
Come, take your * of wine and Is 55:1
Take your * of life or death! Jer 21:8
the Edomites the person of my *. Jer 49:19
dying in the same * soil where it Eze 17:10
They bring * fabrics to Eze 27:24
gods and offered them * gifts." Hos 3:1
or "that which is *." Hag 2:7f
that * seed is full of thistles!' Mt 13:27
am the farmer who sows the * Mt 13:37
on the lookout for * pearls. Mt 13:45
from poor stock produce * fruit. Lk 6:43
slaves have no * but to like it! Lk 22:25
this sacred trust and I have no *. 1Co 9:17
sister—another * child of God. 2Jn 1:13

CHOICES
that I will give him three *." 2Sa 24:12
'The Lord has offered you three *. 1Ch 21:10,11

CHOICEST
trees producing the * of fruit. Gen 2:9
his steed to the * vine, and washed Gen 49:11
bring me the * sample of the first Ex 23:19
the * of spices—eighteen pounds Ex 30:22,23
selected from the * part of the Num 18:28,29
With the * gifts of heaven Deu 33:13
to bring Saul the * cut of meat, 1Sa 9:23
tallest cedars and * cypress tree 2Ki 19:23
* blessings for his Jewish people Ps 47:4
made the * of your possessions. Ps 74:2
But he would feed you with the * Ps 81:16
his garden and eat its * fruits." Sol 4:16
his vineyard with the * vines. Is 5:2
They fill your * valleys and Is 22:6,7
cedars and * cypress trees. Is 37:24
you with the * of their goods to Is 60:16
is on the way; her * youth are Jer 48:15
and honey, the * spot on earth, Eze 20:15
with them—the * men of Eze 23:7
Fill it with * mutton, the rump Eze 24:4
trees of Eden, the * and the best Eze 31:16
tenderest lambs and the * calves. Amo 6:4

CHOIR
of * leaders: Heman the Cantor 1Ch 6:33-38
of the altar. The * was accompanied 2Ch 5:11,12
harps and lyres for the *. 2Ch 9:11
there should be a * leading the 2Ch 20:21
The * members from the clan of Ez 2:40,41,42
200 * members, both men and women. Ez 2:64,65
no priest, Levite, * member, Ez 7:24
The * members from the clan of Neh 7:43,44,45
also, 7,337 slaves and 245 * Neh 7:67
gatekeepers, the * members, the Neh 7:73
the gatekeepers; the * members; Neh 10:28
gatekeepers, and the * singers. Neh 10:39,40
and harps. The * members also came Neh 12:28
began of having * directors to lead Neh 12:46
the members of the *, the Neh 12:47
of the *, and the gatekeepers. Neh 13:5
so they and the * singers who were Neh 13:10
(A note to the * director: When Hab 3:19
this ode, the * is to be Hab 3:19
Is that a joyous * I hear? Zep 3:17,18
It was the singing of a * Rev 14:2
This tremendous *—144,000 Rev 14:3

CHOIRMASTER
the direction of Jezrahiah the *. Neh 12:42

CHOIRS
harps and harpsichords for his *. 1Ki 10:12
songleaders and * to praise God in 1Ch 6:31
the * carried on their work there. 1Ch 6:32
custom of using * in the Tabernacle 1Ch 16:7
for him, as did the Temple *. 2Ch 35:24,25
Both * then proceeded to the Neh 12:40,41
to lead the * in hymns of praise Neh 12:46
and women's * and orchestras. Ecc 2:7,8

CHOKE
The hoofs of his cavalry will * Eze 26:10
longing for money * out God's Word, Mt 13:22

CHOKED
thorns * out the tender blades. Mt 13:7
grain stalks were soon * out. Lk 8:7
afterwards is * out by worry and Lk 8:14

CHOOSE
"Look my kingdom over, and * the Gen 20:15
to have you * the finest of our Gen 23:5,6
then I will * Jehovah as my God! Gen 28:21
And Pharaoh said to Joseph, "* Gen 47:5,6
he will * until we get there." Ex 10:26
offering, he may * either Lev 1:14
to * a place for them to stop. Num 10:33
and problems? So * some men from Deu 1:13
He didn't * you and pour out his Deu 7:7
the place he will * as his home. Deu 12:11
so in the place the Lord will *. Deu 12:14
place he shall * as his sanctuary; Deu 14:23
the Lord shall * as his sanctuary. Deu 16:6
the man the Lord your God shall *. Deu 17:15
shall *, and do not oppress him. Deu 23:15,16
the king you will *, to a nation to Deu 28:36
Oh, that you would * life; Deu 30:19
might live! * to love the Lord Deu 30:20
Yes, we * the Lord, for he alone Jos 24:18
But the people answered, "We * Jos 24:21
Didn't I * your ancestor Levi 1Sa 2:28
and you * someone to represent you, 1Sa 17:8
him, "Will you * seven years of 2Sa 24:13
The prophets of Baal may * 1Ki 18:23
are many of you; * one of the bulls 1Ki 18:25
Which will you *? 1Ch 21:10,11
and that you * another queen more Est 1:19
We can * the sounds we want to Job 34:3
we can * the taste we want in Job 34:3
should * to follow what is right. Job 34:4
God will teach him how to * the Ps 25:12
For Jehovah is my refuge! I * Ps 91:9
facts and did not * to reverence Pro 1:29
IF YOU MUST *, take a good name Pro 22:1
Teach a child to * the right Pro 22:6
good, but instead * their own mad Ecc 9:2,3
Lord himself will * the sign—a Is 7:14
the evil and to * the good . . . Is 7:15,16f
Sabbaths holy and * the things that Is 56:4
But those who * their own ways, Is 66:3
Why should you * war and famine Jer 27:13
of that land * a watchman, and Eze 33:2
once more * to bless Jerusalem.' Zec 2:11,12
the multitudes who * its easy way. Mt 7:13
"You didn't * me! Jn 15:16
"So now we must * someone else Act 1:21,22
Don't you realize that you can * Rom 6:16
You can * sin (with death) or Rom 6:16
or die as we ourselves might *. Rom 14:7
not words that we as men might *. 1Co 2:13
Which do you *? 1Co 4:21
messengers you yourselves will *. 1Co 16:3
of men you should * as officers for 1Ti 3:15
The men you * must be well Tit 1:6

CHOOSES
"However, if he * to bring a Lev 4:32
of mercy are, just whenever he *. Lev 16:1
Literally, "whom Jehovah * to be Num 16:6,7f
If the place the Lord * for his Deu 14:24
Yet when he * not to speak, who Job 34:29,30
shown by the kind of friends he *. Pro 27:19
Anyone who * you needs to have Is 41:24
the Holy One of Israel, * you." Is 49:7
and gives power to anyone he *. Dan 4:25
and gives them to anyone he *." Dan 4:32
to whom the Son * to reveal him." Lk 10:22

CHOOSING
Those * other gods shall all be Ps 16:4
* to do what you know I despise. Is 65:12
of God's kindness in * them. Rom 11:5
Jesus our Lord for * me as one of 1Ti 1:12
Never be in a hurry about * a 1Ti 5:22

CHOP
his neighbor to * wood, and the axe Deu 19:5
* your wood and carry your water. Deu 29:11
with servants to * wood and carry Jos 9:23
One must be armed to * them down; 2Sa 23:7
their bones, and * them up like Mic 3:3
to * down every unproductive tree. Mt 3:10

CHOPPED
got up early, * wood for a fire Gen 22:3
And Samuel * him in pieces 1Sa 15:33
the obelisks, and * down the 2Ch 14:3
above the altars * down, and the 2Ch 34:4
and * down the obelisks. 2Ch 34:7
like a forest * to the ground. Ps 74:5,6
and smashed and * the carved Ps 74:5,6
For we are * and burned by our Ps 80:16
will be cut off, * down like a Is 11:1
They will be * and burned. Mt 3:10
are * down and thrown on the fire. Mt 7:19
* down and thrown into the fire." Lk 3:9

CHOPPING
of the Israelis, * their wood and Jos 9:21
where he began * a bundle of Ju 9:47,48
but as one of them was *, his 2Ki 6:5
heaven, is * down the mighty tree! Is 10:33

CHOPS
Hell is licking its * in Is 5:14

CHORAL
Asaph was the director of this * 1Ch 16:7

CHORAZIN
"Woe to you, *, and woe to you, Mt 11:21
you cities of * and Bethsaida! Lk 10:13

CHORDS
The melodious * of the harp and Is 24:8

CHORUS
Their voices rose in a great * Num 14:2
The band and * united as one to 2Ch 5:13,14
In a great antiphonal * they Is 6:3
Join in the *, you desert Is 42:11
the whole grand * shall sing Hos 1:21,22

CHORUSED
"Yes," they *, "go up to 2Ch 18:11

CHOSE
So that is what Lot *—the Jordan Gen 13:11
suggestion. He * able men from all Ex 18:25
a good idea, so I * twelve spies, Deu 1:23
your ancestors and * to bless their Deu 4:37
so much that he * you, their Deu 10:15
He * the best of the land for Deu 33:21
city he wanted. He * Timnath-serah Jos 19:50
When Israel * new gods, Ju 5:8
So the men of Dan * five army Ju 18:2
the Lord who * me above your father 2Sa 6:21
Lord of heaven: 'I * you to be the 2Sa 7:8
and its gods. You * Israel to be 2Sa 7:24
Lord your God who * you and set you 1Ki 10:9
of David and * Jeroboam I (the son 2Ki 17:21
The Egyptian king then * 2Ki 23:34
THEN THE PEOPLE of Jerusalem * 2Ch 22:1
who * to remain in Persia gave Ez 1:6
"You are the Lord God who * Neh 9:7
the wealthy live wherever they *. Job 22:8
ones you * in ancient times from Ps 74:2
your possessions. You * Jerusalem Ps 74:2
of Ephraim, and * the tribe of Ps 78:68
and the earth. He * his servant Ps 78:70
angry with the one you * as king? Ps 89:38
king you * for your people. Ps 132:10
and * what they knew I despised. Is 66:4
For when I planted you, I * my Jer 2:21
—that the Lord * Judah and Israel Jer 33:24
Instead he * Zedekiah (son of Jer 37:1
God says: When I * Israel and Eze 20:5,6
And I * your sons to be Amo 2:11
certain ones he *, inviting them to Mk 3:13
are the names of the twelve he *: Mk 3:16-19
his followers and * twelve of them Lk 6:13
THE LORD NOW * seventy other Lk 10:1
Then Jesus said, "I * the twelve Jn 6:70
know so well each one of you I *. Jn 13:18
"You didn't choose me! I * you! Jn 15:16
but you don't—for I * you to come Jn 15:19
"The God of this nation Israel * Act 13:17
all know that God * me from among Act 15:7
while Paul * Silas and, with the Act 15:40,41
deliberately * to believe lies. Rom 1:25
Thank God that though you once * Rom 6:17
* to bless Jacob, but not Esau." Rom 9:10-13
because of what God wanted and *. Rom 9:10-13
whom he * from the very beginning. Rom 11:2,3
the world, God * us to be his very Eph 1:4
Lord, because God * from the very 2Th 2:13
Or, "because God * you to be 2Th 2:13f
It is he who saved us and * us 2Ti 1:9
work in the same way God * Aaron. Heb 5:4
of the king, but * to share Heb 11:24,25
Dear friends, God the Father * 1Pe 1:2
Lamb of God. God * him for this 1Pe 1:20

CHOSEN
those kinds I have * for eating and Gen 7:2
Moses' personally * assistants, Num 11:28
everyone in Israel has been * of Num 16:3
and whom he has * as his priest. Num 16:5
will find out whom the Lord has *. Num 16:6,7
God of Israel has * you from among Num 16:8,9
*: for buds will grow on his rod! Num 17:5
He has * you from all the people Deu 7:6
whole earth to be his own * ones. Deu 7:6
God, and he has * you to be his own Deu 14:2
For the Lord your God has * the Deu 18:5
Lord your God has * them to Deu 21:5
"Tell the twelve men * for a Jos 4:2,3
The cities * as Cities of Refuge Jos 20:7
have * to obey the Lord." Jos 24:22
Ehud was the man * to carry Ju 3:15
And now you have * his slave Ju 9:18
cry to the new gods you have *! Ju 10:14
of Benjamin was * by sacred lot. 1Sa 10:20
the family of the Matrites was *. 1Sa 10:21
man the Lord has * as your king. 1Sa 10:24
here is the king you have *. 1Sa 12:13
The Lord will not abandon his * 1Sa 12:22
And Jonathan and Saul were * by 1Sa 14:41
And Jonathan was * as the 1Sa 14:42
this is the man the Lord has *!" 1Sa 16:6
"The Lord has not * any of 1Sa 16:10,11
attack God's * king in any way." 1Sa 24:6
harm him—he is the Lord's * king.' 1Sa 24:9,10
after attacking the Lord's * king? 1Sa 26:9
kill the man he has * to be king! 1Sa 26:11
"Why did you kill God's * 2Sa 1:14
Joab agreed, so twelve men were * 2Sa 2:15
and even though I am God's * 2Sa 3:39
kindness on Israel, his * people. 2Sa 5:12
For you have rescued your * 2Sa 7:23
for the man who is * by the Lord 2Sa 16:18
for he cursed the Lord's * king!" 2Sa 19:21
He has *! 2Sa 23:5
the one you have * to succeed you. 1Ki 1:20
you have * to be the next king." 1Ki 1:27
And here I am among your own * 1Ki 3:8
toward your * city of Jerusalem and 1Ki 8:44
which you have *, and toward this 1Ki 8:48
Moses that you had * Israel from 1Ki 8:53
sake of Jerusalem, my * city." 1Ki 11:12,13
which I have * above all the other 1Ki 11:32
servant David, my * one who obeyed 1Ki 11:34
the city I have * to be the place 1Ki 11:36
Israel, the Lord had * to live in. 1Ki 14:21
city I have * from among all the 2Ki 21:7
and I will discard my * city of 2Ki 23:27
And his son Jehoahaz was * by the 2Ki 23:30
They were * from their villages 1Ch 9:22
God has * them for this purpose; 1Ch 15:2
The following men were * as their 1Ch 15:18
Heman, Asaph, and Ethan were * to 1Ch 15:19
O * sons of Jacob, 1Ch 16:12,13
'Don't harm my * people,' he 1Ch 16:22
others who were * by name to give 1Ch 16:41
The Temple guards were * from 1Ch 26:19
God of Israel has * me from among 1Ch 28:4
he has * the tribe of Judah, and 1Ch 28:4
children—he has * Solomon to 1Ch 28:5

(CHOSEN Con't)
for I have * him as my son and I 1Ch 28:6
* you to build his holy temple. 1Ch 28:10
whom God has * to be the next king 1Ch 29:1
the land of Egypt, * a city 2Ch 6:5,6
and never before have I * a king 2Ch 6:5,6
But now I have * Jerusalem as 2Ch 6:5,6
it: his son was * for that task. 2Ch 6:9
which you have *, and this Temple 2Ch 6:34
prayer and have * this Temple as 2Ch 7:12
For I have * this Temple and 2Ch 7:16
the city God had * as his residence 2Ch 12:13
for the Lord has * you to minister 2Ch 29:11
city I have * to be honored forever 2Ch 33:7
The God who has * the city of Ez 6:12
place in which I have * to live.' Neh 1:9
The day * for this throughout Est 8:12
His * one replies, Ps 2:7
defend and bless your * ones. Ps 28:9
whose people he has * as his own. Ps 33:12
are those you have * to come and Ps 65:4
where God has * to live forever. Ps 68:15,16
I have * him and I will tell Ps 73:28
agreement with my * servant David. Ps 89:3,4
and said, "I have * a splendid Ps 89:19
he did for us, his * Ps 105:5,6
"Touch not these * ones of Ps 105:15
So he brought his * ones singing Ps 105:43
Let me share in your * ones' Ps 106:5
But Moses, his * one, stepped Ps 106:23
laws, for I have * to do right. Ps 119:29,30
I have * to follow your will. Ps 119:173
O Lord, you have * Jerusalem Ps 132:13
For the Lord has * Israel as his Ps 135:4
terrors of the pathway you have *. Pro 1:31
He'll not be * as a counselor! Pro 24:7
O Israel, you are mine, my * ones; Is 41:8
* you and will not throw you away. Is 41:9
whom I uphold; my * One, in whom Is 42:1
and my servants, * to know and to Is 43:10
my * ones, can be refreshed. Is 43:20
O my servant Israel, O my * ones: Is 44:1
O Jerusalem, my * ones, don't be Is 44:2
he has * to conquer many lands. Is 45:1
of Jacob, my servant—Israel, my *. Is 45:4
Listen to me, my people, my * Is 48:12
low because the Lord has * you; Is 49:7
all, and Israel is his * nation. Jer 10:16
He was * by the Egyptians to Jer 22:13f
for he had been * and appointed by Jer 41:18
*, all from the tribe of Judah. Dan 1:6
for he has * some to survive. Joe 2:32
of the earth, I have * you alone. Amo 3:2
You went out to save your * Hab 3:13
and has * their executioners. Zep 1:7
for I have specially * you," Hag 2:23
even the Lord, who has * Zec 3:2f
See my * One. Mt 12:18
many are called, but few are *." Mt 22:14
shortened for the sake of God's * Mt 24:22
if it were possible, even God's * Mt 24:24
shall gather my * ones from the Mt 24:31
But for the sake of his * ones he Mk 13:20
gather together my * ones from all Mk 13:27
said, "This is my Son, my * One; Lk 9:35
really God's * One, the Messiah." Lk 23:35
after giving his * apostles further Act 1:1
Judas was one of us, * to be an Act 1:17
prayed for the right man to be *. Act 1:24,25
these men you have * as an apostle Act 1:24,25
and in this manner Matthias was * Act 1:26
For Paul is my * instrument to Act 9:15
The men * were two of the church Act 15:22
of our fathers has * you to know Act 22:14
Christ's slave, * to be a Rom 1:1
And having * us, he called us to Rom 8:30
us whom God has * for his own? Rom 8:33
He took you as his own special, * Rom 9:4
FROM: PAUL, * by God to be Jesus 1Co 1:1
Or, "* by Christ Jesus." 1Co 1:2f
Instead, God has deliberately * 1Co 1:27
He has * a plan despised by the 1Co 1:28
are Israelites, God's * people? 2Co 11:22
I was born God had * me to be his, Gal 1:15
writing to you, * by God to be Eph 1:1
plan we were * from the beginning Eph 1:11
yet I was the one * for this Eph 3:8
who have been * for such wonderful Eph 4:1
FROM: PAUL, * by God to be Jesus Col 1:1
Since you have been * by God who Col 3:12
We know that God has * you, dear 1Th 1:4
For God has not * to pour out his 1Th 5:9
And I have been *—this is the 1Ti 2:7
be proud of being * so soon, and 1Ti 3:6
then they may be * as deacons. 1Ti 3:10
And God has * me to be his 2Ti 1:11
Christ Jesus to those God has *. 2Ti 2:10
to those God has * and to teach Tit 1:1
who are * for heaven—I want you to Heb 3:1
else, but he is * to speak for all Heb 5:1
no, he was * by God. Heb 5:5
"You have been * to be a priest Heb 5:6
For remember that God has * him Heb 5:10
of all God's * people, gave Heb 7:4
had not been * for priesthood; Heb 7:12,13,14
brothers: God has * poor people to Jas 2:5
who has * him above all others. 1Pe 2:4
be the carefully *, precious 1Pe 2:6
for you have been * by God 1Pe 2:9
who is at Babylon is likewise *"; 1Pe 5:13f
God has called and *, and then you 2Pe 1:10
of God and * by him. Jud 1:1
called and * and faithful ones. Rev 17:14

CHRIST
Lord and his Messiah, * the King. Ps 2:2
This verse was quoted by * as Ps 40:7f
and bore a son, Immanuel, the *. Is 7:14f
*, the Messiah. Is 11:1f
*, the Messiah. Is 11:1f
Not Cyrus, as in chapter 41, but * Is 42:1f
is also to * in the more distant Is 45:13f
of this passage by * himself, and Is 52:13f
to the final restoration under *. Jer 30:21f
roots of David." * was the true Jer 33:15f
* was "the greater David." Hos 3:5f
i.e., *, the Messiah. Hag 2:7f
Peace with God through * who, 500 Hag 2:8,9f
the Messiah, *. Zec 3:8f
to *, is clear from the context. Zec 13:6f
THESE ARE THE ancestors of Jesus * Mt 1:1
mother of Jesus * the Messiah). Mt 1:16
and fourteen from the exile to *. Mt 1:17
the birth of Jesus *: His mother, Mt 1:18
Simon Peter answered, "The *, Mt 16:16
Literally, "Jesus who is called * Mt 27:17f
Several biographies of * have Lk 1:1,2
knew he was the *, he stopped them Lk 4:41
Peter replied, "The Messiah—the * Lk 9:20
the person is neutral about *. Lk 11:25f
"Why is it," he asked, "that * Lk 20:41
there was *, Jn 1:1
Literally, "the Word," meaning * Jn 1:1f
that Jesus * is the true Light. Jn 1:6,7
And * Jn 1:14
Literally, "the Word," meaning * Jn 1:14f
while Jesus * brought us loving Jn 1:17
"I am not the *," he said. Jn 1:20
one they call *—and when he does, Jn 4:25
man was born; when * comes, he will Jn 7:27
*, the one you sent to earth! Jn 17:3
ceremonies, when * was crucified. Act 2:1f
the name of Jesus * for the Act 2:38
Holy Spirit. For * promised him to Act 2:39
of Jesus * of Nazareth, walk!" Act 3:6
and told the people there about *. Act 8:5
that Jesus * is the Son of God." Act 8:37
that Jesus was indeed the *. Act 9:22
Jesus * has healed you! Act 9:34
Jesus *, who was I to argue?" Act 11:17
of our Lord Jesus *—will confirm Act 15:26
* to come out of her," he said. Act 16:18
spoke against *, so he left, Act 19:9
through faith in our Lord Jesus *. Act 20:21
told them about faith in * Jesus. Act 24:24
Christians everywhere curse *. Act 26:11
of God and about the Lord Jesus *; Act 28:31
his Son, Jesus * our Lord, who came Rom 1:3
And now, through *, all the Rom 1:5
you, too, are invited by Jesus * Rom 1:6,7
Father and from Jesus * our Lord. Rom 1:6,7
How I thank God through Jesus * Rom 1:8
ashamed of this Good News about *. Rom 1:16
faith and trust in * to save us. Rom 1:17
command Jesus * will judge the Rom 2:16
Jesus * to take away our sins. Rom 3:21,22
way, by coming to *, no matter who Rom 3:21,22
we trust in Jesus *, who in his Rom 3:24
For God sent * Jesus to take the Rom 3:25
to the time when * would come and Rom 3:25
it is based on what * has done Rom 3:27
by faith in * and not by the good Rom 3:28
* to save them from God's wrath. Rom 4:4,5
who have faith in * but also keep Rom 4:9
Jewish rules, but only trust in *? Rom 4:9
Jesus * our Lord has done for us. Rom 5:1
no way of escape, * came at just Rom 5:6
for us by sending * to die for us Rom 5:8
our Lord Jesus * has done in dying Rom 5:11
What a contrast between Adam and * Rom 5:14
But this one man, Jesus *, Rom 5:15
to many, while * freely takes away Rom 5:16
because of this one man, Jesus *. Rom 5:17
disobeyed God, and * caused many to Rom 5:19
life through Jesus * our Lord. Rom 5:21
to become a part of Jesus *; Rom 6:2,3
"died" with *, we know that you Rom 6:8
his new life. * rose from the dead Rom 6:9
to him, through Jesus * our Lord. Rom 6:11
life through Jesus * our Lord. Rom 6:23
brothers in *, that when a person Rom 7:1
as it were, with * on the cross; Rom 7:4
when * did, and are a new person. Rom 7:4
God through Jesus * our Lord." Rom 7:23,24,25f
by Jesus * our Lord. Rom 7:23,24,25
those who belong to * Jesus. Rom 8:1
is mine through * Jesus—has freed Rom 8:2
have the Spirit of * living in him, Rom 8:9
Yet, even though * lives within Rom 8:10
but your spirit will live, for * Rom 8:10
Who then will condemn us? Will *? Rom 8:34
is ours through * who loved us Rom 8:37
Lord Jesus * when he died for us. Rom 8:39
How I long for you to come to *. Rom 9:1
because of you. * knows and the Rom 9:1
your fathers, and * himself was one Rom 9:5
For they don't understand that * Rom 10:3
They don't understand that * Rom 10:4
heavens to find * and bring him Rom 10:6
to bring * back to life again." Rom 10:7
from trusting *—which is what we Rom 10:8
mouth that Jesus * is your Lord, Rom 10:9
in * will ever be disappointed. Rom 10:11
Good News—the Good News about *. Rom 10:17
about when we tell them of *. Rom 11:8
on when the Jews, too, come to *. Rom 11:12
wonderful when the Jews come to *. Rom 11:15
come to *—those of you who will. Rom 11:25
But ask the Lord Jesus * to help Rom 13:14
Either way we are his. * died Rom 14:9
ruin someone for whom * died. Rom 14:15
If you let * be Lord in these Rom 14:18
Lord. * didn't please himself. Rom 15:3
attitude of * toward the other. Rom 15:5
the Father of our Lord Jesus *. Rom 15:6
just as * has warmly welcomed you; Rom 15:7
Remember that Jesus * came to Rom 15:8
from Jesus * to you Gentiles, Rom 15:15,16
all * Jesus has done through me. Rom 15:17
Gospel of * all the way from Rom 15:19
where the name of * has never yet Rom 15:20
* before will see and understand. Rom 15:21
Because the news about * came to Rom 15:27
workers in the affairs of * Jesus. Rom 16:3
things about * that are contrary to Rom 16:17
from our Lord Jesus * be upon you. Rom 16:20
May the grace of our Lord Jesus * Rom 16:24
will have faith in * and obey him. Rom 16:25,26,27
forever through Jesus * our Lord. Rom 16:25,26,27
Or, "chosen by * Jesus." 1Co 1:2f
Literally, "sanctified in * 1Co 1:2f
to him by * Jesus. 1Co 1:2
of Jesus *, our Lord and theirs. 1Co 1:2
and the Lord Jesus * give you all 1Co 1:3
what I told you * could do for 1Co 1:6
the return of our Lord Jesus *. 1Co 1:7
with his Son, even * our Lord. 1Co 1:9
of the Lord Jesus * to stop arguing 1Co 1:10
alone are the true followers of *. 1Co 1:12
have broken * into many pieces. 1Co 1:13
anyone else. For * didn't send me 1Co 1:17
simple message of the cross of *. 1Co 1:17
So when we preach about * dying 1Co 1:23
to see that * is the mighty power 1Co 1:24
God to save them; * himself is the 1Co 1:24
in his weakness—* dying on the 1Co 1:25
of you who follow * have big names 1Co 1:26
have your life through * Jesus. 1Co 1:30
* and his death on the cross. 1Co 2:2
the very thoughts and mind of *. 1Co 2:16
that one we already have—Jesus *. 1Co 3:11
belong to *, and Christ is God's. 1Co 3:23
belong to Christ, and * is God's. 1Co 3:23
to teach you about *, remember that 1Co 4:15
who brought you to * when I 1Co 4:15
For he is one of those I won to * 1Co 4:17
of the Lord Jesus * I have already 1Co 5:3,4
when our Lord Jesus * returns. 1Co 5:5
you can stay pure. *, God's Lamb, 1Co 5:7
the Lord Jesus * and the Spirit of 1Co 6:11
I can do anything I want to if * 1Co 6:12
as he raised up the Lord Jesus *. 1Co 6:14
actually parts and members of *? 1Co 6:15
So should I take part of * and 1Co 6:15
the Lord, you and * are joined 1Co 6:17
remember that * has set you free 1Co 7:22
that you are now a slave of *. 1Co 7:22
and paid for by *, so you belong to 1Co 7:23
and one Lord Jesus *, who made 1Co 8:6
tender conscience for whom * died. 1Co 8:11
And it is a sin against * to sin 1Co 8:12
you have been won to * through me. 1Co 9:2
in our message to you from *. 1Co 9:12
all so that I can win them to *. 1Co 9:19
Gospel and I can win them to *. 1Co 9:20
about * and let Christ save him. 1Co 9:22
about Christ and let * save him. 1Co 9:22
receive when I see them come to *. 1Co 9:23
they drank the water that * gave 1Co 10:3,4
them, and the Rock was *." 1Co 10:3,4f
all parts of the one body of *. 1Co 10:17
is responsible to *, and Christ is 1Co 11:3
and * is responsible to God. 1Co 11:3
or preaching, he dishonors *. 1Co 11:4

HRIST Con't)
about the body of * and what it 1Co 11:29
is trifling with the death of *. 1Co 11:29
So it is with the "body" of *. 1Co 12:12
us is a part of the one body of *. 1Co 12:13
the one body of * and each one of 1Co 12:27
told to me, that * died for our 1Co 15:3
we preach, that * rose from the 1Co 15:12
dead, then * must still be dead. 1Co 15:13
that God raised * from the grave, 1Co 15:15
If they don't, then * is still 1Co 15:16
But the fact is that * did 1Co 15:20
this other man (*) has done that 1Co 15:21
But all who are related to * will 1Co 15:22
in his own turn: * rose first; 1Co 15:23
then when * comes back, all his 1Co 15:23
every kind. For * will be King 1Co 15:25
has been given to * by his Father; 1Co 15:27
except, of course, * does not 1Co 15:27
When * has finally won the 1Co 15:28
but * 1Co 15:45
but * came from heaven above. 1Co 15:47
through Jesus * our Lord! 1Co 15:57
of the Lord Jesus * rest upon you. 1Co 16:23
you, for we all belong to * Jesus. 1Co 16:24
and the Lord Jesus * mightily bless 2Co 1:2
of our Lord Jesus *, the source of 2Co 1:3,4
sufferings for *, the more he will 2Co 1:5
you about Jesus * the Son of God. 2Co 1:19
For through what * has done, he 2Co 2:14
It is the fragrance of * within 2Co 2:15
* we are a life-giving perfume. 2Co 2:16
a letter from *, written by us. 2Co 3:3
in God through *, that he will help 2Co 3:4
be removed only by believing in *. 2Co 3:14
about the glory of *, who is God. 2Co 4:4
but about * Jesus as Lord. 2Co 4:5
is seen in the face of Jesus *. 2Co 4:6
living * within [who keeps us safe 2Co 4:10
Jesus * within our dying bodies. 2Co 4:11
you who are won to *, the more 2Co 4:15
For we must all stand before * 2Co 5:10
Since we believe that * died for 2Co 5:13,14
lives pleasing * who died and rose 2Co 5:15
Once I mistakenly thought of * 2Co 5:16
himself through what * Jesus did. 2Co 5:18
For God was in *, restoring the 2Co 5:19
beg you, as though * himself were 2Co 5:20
For God took the sinless * and 2Co 5:21
there be between * and the devil? 2Co 6:15
gently, as * himself would do. 2Co 10:1
hearts' desire is obedience to *. 2Co 10:5
and you surrender to *. 2Co 10:6
authority of *, I certainly can. 2Co 10:7
with the Good News concerning *. 2Co 10:14
love should be for * alone, just as 2Co 11:2
They say they serve *? 2Co 11:23
to be brothers in * but are not. 2Co 11:26
of our Lord Jesus *, who is to be 2Co 11:31
Literally, "A man in *." 2Co 12:2,3f
you want that * speaks through me. 2Co 13:3
speaks through me. * is not weak in 2Co 13:3
Grow in *. 2Co 13:11
our Lord Jesus * be with you all. 2Co 13:14
My call is from Jesus * himself, Gal 1:1
Father and from the Lord Jesus *. Gal 1:3
eternal life he gives through *; Gal 1:6
and change the truth concerning *. Gal 1:7
person than Jesus * himself, who Gal 1:12
we enjoyed in * Jesus, as to Gal 2:4
in Jesus * to take away our sins. Gal 2:16
have trusted Jesus *, that we might Gal 2:16
But what if we trust * to save us Gal 2:17
say that faith in * had ruined us? Gal 2:17
with God comes by believing in *. Gal 2:19
I have been crucified with *: and Gal 2:20
no longer live, but * lives in me. Gal 2:20
there was no need for * to die. Gal 2:21
on it of * dying on the cross. Gal 3:1
* and trusted him to save you. Gal 3:2
It is when you believe in * and Gal 3:5
all who trust in * share the same Gal 3:8,9
one slip. But * has bought us out Gal 3:13
that, of course, means *. Gal 3:16
the coming of *, the Child to whom Gal 3:19
out is through faith in Jesus *; Gal 3:21,22
Until * came we were guarded by Gal 3:23
and guide until * came to give us Gal 3:24
But now that * has come, we Gal 3:25
faith in Jesus *, and we who have Gal 3:26
union with * are enveloped by him. Gal 3:27
we are one in * Jesus. Gal 3:28
way it was with us before * came. Gal 4:3
brought you the Good News of *. Gal 4:13
from God, or even Jesus * himself. Gal 4:14
you will finally be filled with *. Gal 4:19
SO * HAS made us free. Gal 5:1
with God, then * cannot save you. Gal 5:2
law or perish. * is useless to you Gal 5:4
And we to whom * has given Gal 5:6
has called you to freedom in *. Gal 5:8
faith in the cross of * alone. Gal 5:11
Those who belong to * have nailed Gal 5:24
the cross of * alone can save. Gal 6:12
the cross of our Lord Jesus *. Gal 6:14
our Lord Jesus * be with you all. Gal 6:18
our Father and Jesus * our Lord. Eph 1:2
of our Lord Jesus *, who has Eph 1:3
in heaven because we belong to *. Eph 1:3
through what * would do for us; Eph 1:4
by sending Jesus * to die for us. Eph 1:5
reason for sending *, a plan he Eph 1:9
be with him in *, forever. Eph 1:10
Moreover, because of what * has Eph 1:11
who were the first to trust in *. Eph 1:12
And because of what * did, all Eph 1:13
saved, and trusted *, were marked Eph 1:13
as belonging to * by the Holy Eph 1:13
of our Lord Jesus *, to give you Eph 1:16,17
understand who * is and all that he Eph 1:16,17
power that raised * from the dead Eph 1:20
when he raised * from the Eph 2:5
glory along with *, where we sit Eph 2:6
because of what * Jesus did. Eph 2:6
has done for us through Jesus *. Eph 2:7
been saved through trusting *. Eph 2:8
given us new lives from * Jesus; Eph 2:10
were living utterly apart from *; Eph 2:12
But now you belong to * Jesus, Eph 2:13
* has done for you with his blood. Eph 2:13
For * himself is our way of Eph 2:14
because of what * has done for us. Eph 2:18
the building is Jesus * himself! Eph 2:20
together with * as parts of a Eph 2:21
I PAUL, THE servant of *, am here Eph 3:1
blessings through * apply to them Eph 3:6
* and what he has done for them. Eph 3:6
treasures available to them in *; Eph 3:8
it through Jesus * our Lord. Eph 3:11
we come with * and trust in him. Eph 3:12
And I pray that * will be more Eph 3:17
for the church through Jesus *. Eph 3:21
However, * has given each of us Eph 4:7
he says that when * returned Eph 4:8
winning people to *, helping them Eph 4:11
the body of *, to a position of Eph 4:12
point of being filled full with *. Eph 4:13
in every way like * who is the Head Eph 4:15,16
But that isn't the way * taught Eph 4:20
you because you belong to *. Eph 4:32
the example of * who loved you and Eph 5:2
The kingdom of * and of God will Eph 5:5
and * shall give you light." Eph 5:14
in the name of our Lord Jesus *. Eph 5:20
Honor * by submitting to each Eph 5:21
in the same way * is in charge of Eph 5:23
just as the church obeys *. Eph 5:24
to your wives as * showed to the Eph 5:25
for it, just as * cares for his Eph 5:29,30
way we are parts of the body of *. Eph 5:32
Serve them as you would *. Eph 6:5
though working for *, doing the Eph 6:6,7
you yourselves are slaves to *; Eph 6:9
the Father and the Lord Jesus *. Eph 6:23
sincerely love our Lord Jesus *. Eph 6:24
AND Timothy, slaves of Jesus *. Php 1:1
and the Lord Jesus * will give each Php 1:2
Good News about * from the time you Php 1:5
on that day when Jesus * returns. Php 1:6
truth and telling others about *. Php 1:7
the tenderness of Jesus *. Php 1:8
out the Good News concerning *. Php 1:12
bold in telling others about *. Php 1:14
* is being preached and I am glad. Php 1:18
out boldly for * while I am going Php 1:20
be an honor to *, whether I live or Php 1:20
opportunities for *, and Php 1:21
to win people to *, then I really Php 1:22
for I long to go and be with *. Php 1:23
reason to glorify * Jesus for Php 1:26
shown us by Jesus *, who, though Php 2:5
confess that Jesus * is Lord, to Php 2:11
Then when * returns how glad I Php 2:16
plans and not those of Jesus *. Php 2:21
for the work of * and was at the Php 2:30
We Christians glory in what * Php 3:3
put my trust and hope in * alone. Php 3:7
gain of knowing * Jesus my Lord. Php 3:8
that I can have *, and become one Php 3:8
but by trusting * to save me; Php 3:9
on faith—counting on * alone. Php 3:9
way to really know * and to Php 3:10
* saved me for and wants me to be. Php 3:12
of what * Jesus did for us. Php 3:14
really enemies of the cross of *. Php 3:18
our Savior the Lord Jesus * is; Php 3:20
at rest as you trust in * Jesus. Php 4:7
with the help of * who gives me the Php 4:13
of what * Jesus has done for us. Php 4:19
Lord Jesus * be upon your spirits. Php 4:23
of our Lord Jesus *, for we have Col 1:3
* is the exact likeness of the Col 1:15
and, in fact, * himself is the Col 1:16
all were made by * for his own Col 1:16
now as a result * has brought you Col 1:22
And this is the secret: that * in Col 1:26,27
go we talk about * to all who will Col 1:28
what * has done for each of them. Col 1:28
of knowing * with real certainty Col 2:2
at last made known, is * himself. Col 2:2
because of your strong faith in *. Col 2:5
And now just as you trusted * to Col 2:6
instead of on what * has said. Col 2:8
For in * there is all of God in Col 2:9
when you have *, and you are filled Col 2:10
God through your union with *. Col 2:10
When you came to * he set you Col 2:11
God who raised * from the dead. Col 2:12
the very life of *, for he forgave Col 2:13
rules that ended when * came. Col 2:17
of the real thing—of * himself. Col 2:17
But they are not connected to *, Col 2:19
as it were, with * and this has set Col 2:20
so to speak, when * arose from the Col 3:1
life is in heaven with * and God. Col 3:3
And when * who is our real life Col 3:4
more and more like * who created Col 3:10
Whether a person has * is what Col 3:11
which comes from * be always Col 3:15
Remember what * taught and let Col 3:16
it is the Lord * who is going to Col 3:24
of * for which I am here in jail. Col 4:3
of * Jesus, sends you his love. Col 4:12
and the Lord Jesus *: May blessing 1Th 1:1
Father, and from Jesus * our Lord. 1Th 1:1
to the return of our Lord Jesus *. 1Th 1:3
as apostles of * we certainly had a 1Th 2:6
Jesus * when he comes back again. 1Th 2:19
our Lord Jesus * returns with all 1Th 3:13
save us through our Lord Jesus *; 1Th 5:9
for you who belong to * Jesus. 1Th 5:18
our Lord Jesus * comes back again. 1Th 5:23
Jesus * be with you, every one. 1Th 5:28
Father and in the Lord Jesus *. 2Th 1:1
and the Lord Jesus * give you rich 2Th 1:2
them through our Lord Jesus *. 2Th 1:8
of the Lord Jesus * because of the 2Th 1:12
of the Lord Jesus * has made all 2Th 1:12
of our Lord Jesus *, and our being 2Th 2:1
in the glory of our Lord Jesus *. 2Th 2:14
May our Lord Jesus * himself and 2Th 2:16
of the patience that comes from *. 2Th 3:5
of our Lord Jesus * by his 2Th 3:6
In the name of the Lord Jesus * 2Th 3:12
our Lord Jesus * be upon you all. 2Th 3:18
of Jesus *, sent out by the direct 1Ti 1:1
by Jesus * our Lord—our only hope. 1Ti 1:1
May God our Father and Jesus * 1Ti 1:2
How thankful I am to * Jesus our 1Ti 1:12
I used to scoff at the name of *. 1Ti 1:13
for I didn't know * at that time. 1Ti 1:13
full of the love of * Jesus. 1Ti 1:14
know it, that * Jesus came into the 1Ti 1:15
on me so that * Jesus could use me 1Ti 1:16
Cling tightly to your faith in * 1Ti 1:19
in * after defying God like that. 1Ti 1:19
to bring shame to the name of *. 1Ti 1:20
other side, and * Jesus, himself 1Ti 2:5
followers of * who is the hidden 1Ti 3:9
But the answer lies in *, who 1Ti 3:16
turn away from * and become eager 1Ti 4:1
their vow to * and marry again. 1Ti 5:11
and the Lord Jesus * and of the 1Ti 5:21
of the Lord Jesus * and are the 1Ti 6:3
to all, and before * Jesus who gave 1Ti 6:13
until our Lord Jesus * returns. 1Ti 6:14
For in due season * will be 1Ti 6:15
them through faith in Jesus *. 2Ti 1:1
May God the Father and * Jesus 2Ti 1:2
love and kindness to us through *. 2Ti 1:9
our Savior Jesus *, who broke the 2Ti 1:10
faith and love * Jesus offers you. 2Ti 1:13
Literally, "and love that is in * 2Ti 1:13f
the strength * Jesus gives you. 2Ti 2:1
soldier of Jesus *, just as I do, 2Ti 2:3
fact that Jesus * was a Man, born 2Ti 2:8
* Jesus to those God has chosen. 2Ti 2:10
suffer and die for * it only means 2Ti 2:11
*, then he must turn against us. 2Ti 2:12
the house—so that * himself can use 2Ti 2:21
You know my faith in * and how I 2Ti 3:10
decide to please * Jesus by living 2Ti 3:12
salvation by trusting in * Jesus. 2Ti 3:15
God and before * Jesus—who will 2Ti 4:1
Bring others to *. 2Ti 4:5
May the Lord Jesus * be with 2Ti 4:22
God and the messenger of Jesus *. Tit 1:1
May God the Father and * Jesus our Tit 1:4
our great God and Savior Jesus *. Tit 2:13
of what Jesus * our Savior did so Tit 3:6
Jesus *, and from Brother Timothy. Phm 1:1
and the Lord Jesus * give you his Phm 1:3
in you that come from * Jesus. Phm 1:6

(CHRIST Con't)
you in the name of * because it is Phm 1:8,9
in jail for the sake of Jesus *. Phm 1:8,9
but also your brother in *. Phm 1:16
* Jesus, sends you his greetings. Phm 1:23
The blessings of our Lord Jesus * Phm 1:25
later on. But *, God's faithful Heb 3:6
And since * is so much superior, Heb 3:7,8
share in all that belongs to *. Heb 3:14
God. * has already entered there. Heb 4:10
That is why * did not elect Heb 5:5
Yet while * was here on earth he Heb 5:7
desire was that * should die Heb 5:7f
those first lessons about *. Heb 6:1
of heaven, where * has gone ahead Heb 6:20
Melchizedek was * appearing to Heb 7:3f
God need to send * as a priest with Heb 7:11
As we all know, * did not belong Heb 7:12,13,14
changed, for *, the new High Priest Heb 7:15
when he says of *, "You are a Heb 7:17
better hope, for * makes us Heb 7:19
God took an oath that * would Heb 7:20
Only to * he said, "The Lord has Heb 7:21
Because of God's oath, * can Heb 7:22
WHAT WE ARE saying is this: *, Heb 8:1
* must make an offering too. Heb 8:3
Mount Sinai. But *, as a Minister Heb 8:6
them over until * came with God's Heb 9:10
the blood of * will transform our Heb 9:14
Holy Spirit, * willingly gave Heb 9:14
sin or fault. * came with this new Heb 9:15
promised them. For * died to rescue Heb 9:15
For * has entered into heaven Heb 9:24
judgment, so also * died only once Heb 9:28
the good things * would do for us. Heb 10:1
Jesus * came to die on the cross. Heb 10:4f
That is why * said, as he came Heb 10:5
After * said this, about not Heb 10:8
our sins. But * gave himself to Heb 10:12
way which * has opened up for us by Heb 10:20
when you first learned about *. Heb 10:32
for the promised * than to own all Heb 11:26
Jesus * is the same yesterday, Heb 13:8
cross where * was sacrificed—where Heb 13:10
of * all that is pleasing to him. Heb 13:20,21
of God and of the Lord Jesus *. Jas 1:1
to the Lord Jesus *, the Lord of Jas 2:1
*, whose noble name you bear. Jas 2:7
you are doing what * wants you to. Jas 2:12
* and making you to please him. 1Pe 1:2
and Father of our Lord Jesus *; 1Pe 1:3
* rose again from the dead. 1Pe 1:3
what the Spirit of * within them 1Pe 1:11
have happened to *: his suffering, 1Pe 1:11
to you when Jesus * returns. 1Pe 1:13
lifeblood of *, the sinless, 1Pe 1:19
in God who raised * from the dead 1Pe 1:21
when you trusted * to save you; 1Pe 1:22
for it comes from *, God's 1Pe 1:23
Come to *, who is the living 1Pe 2:4
to him because of Jesus * 1Pe 2:5
I am sending * to be the carefully 1Pe 2:6
your good works when * returns. 1Pe 2:12
God has given you. *, who suffered 1Pe 2:21
Quietly trust yourself to * your 1Pe 3:15
* also suffered. 1Pe 3:18
and doom by the resurrection of *; 1Pe 3:21
And now * is in heaven, sitting 1Pe 3:22
SINCE * SUFFERED and underwent 1Pe 4:1
through Jesus *—to him be glory and 1Pe 4:11
you partners with * in his 1Pe 4:13
with my own eyes I saw * dying on 1Pe 5:1
kindness through *, will give you 1Pe 5:10
be to all of you who are in *. 1Pe 5:14
servant and missionary of Jesus *. 2Pe 1:1
* our God and Savior gives to us. 2Pe 1:1
and useful to our Lord Jesus *. 2Pe 1:8
of our Lord and Savior Jesus *. 2Pe 1:11
But the Lord Jesus * has showed 2Pe 1:13,14
Lord Jesus * and his coming again. 2Pe 1:16
in your souls and * the Morning 2Pe 1:19
And because of them * and his way 2Pe 2:2
and Savior Jesus *, and then gets 2Pe 2:20
never known about * at all than to 2Pe 2:21
with our Lord and Savior Jesus *. 2Pe 3:18
* WAS ALIVE when the world began, 1Jn 1:1
I am speaking of *, who is 1Jn 1:2
Father and with Jesus * his Son. 1Jn 1:3
presence, just as * does, then we 1Jn 1:7
* died to wash away our sins. 1Jn 1:9
His name is Jesus *, the one who 1Jn 2:1
I belong to *." 1Jn 2:4
But if he doesn't do what * 1Jn 2:4
But those who do what * tells 1Jn 2:5
a Christian should live as * did. 1Jn 2:6
for you just as it did for *; 1Jn 2:8
new light of life in * shines in. 1Jn 2:8
in the light of * but dislikes his 1Jn 2:9
you really know *, the one who has 1Jn 2:13
one who is against *—and already 1Jn 2:18
one who says that Jesus is not *. 1Jn 2:22
doesn't believe in *, God's Son, 1Jn 2:23
But he who has *, God's Son, has 1Jn 2:23
in *, never to depart from him. 1Jn 2:27
to stay pure because * is pure. 1Jn 3:3
Son Jesus *, and love one another. 1Jn 3:23
agree that Jesus *, God's Son, 1Jn 4:2
one who is against *, like the 1Jn 4:3
* is already abroad in the world. 1Jn 4:3
who are against *, because there is 1Jn 4:4
And as we live with *, our love 1Jn 4:17
IF YOU BELIEVE that Jesus is the * 1Jn 5:1
by trusting * to help him. 1Jn 5:4
that Jesus * is the Son of God. 1Jn 5:6,7,8
of sinning, for *, God's Son, holds 1Jn 5:18
And we know that *, God's Son, 1Jn 5:20
we are in Jesus * his Son, who is 1Jn 5:20
Father and Jesus * his Son will 2Jn 1:3
believe that Jesus * came to earth 2Jn 1:7
against the truth and against *. 2Jn 1:7
of *, you will leave God behind; 2Jn 1:9
believe what * taught, don't even 2Jn 1:10
FROM: JUDE, A servant of Jesus *, Jud 1:1
our only Master and Lord, Jesus *. Jud 1:4
of our Lord Jesus * told you, that Jud 1:17
our Lord Jesus * in his mercy is Jud 1:21
saves us through Jesus * our Lord; Jud 1:24,25
to occur in the life of Jesus *. Rev 1:1
(concerning, or, from) Jesus *." Rev 1:1f
* and everything he heard and saw. Rev 1:2
and from Jesus * who faithfully Rev 1:5
telling what I knew about Jesus *. Rev 1:9
or whether the reference is to *. Rev 9:1f
belongs to our Lord, and to his *; Rev 11:15
of his * are finally here; Rev 12:10
with * for a thousand years. Rev 20:4
of God and of *, and shall reign Rev 20:6

CHRIST'S
indicate * universal rule. Zec 9:10f
Highly honored by * being there. Mt 11:23f
because you are *—I say this Mk 9:41
showing that * death, for man's Mk 15:38f
Even * resurrection failed to Lk 16:31f
from Paul, Jesus * slave, chosen to Rom 1:1
He used * blood and our faith as Rom 3:25
to all, but * righteousness makes Rom 5:18
filled us with * goodness, gave us Rom 8:30
Who then can ever keep * love Rom 8:35
our bodies, so it is with * body. Rom 12:4,5
For the Lord Jesus * sake, and Rom 15:30
by God to be Jesus * missionary, 1Co 1:1
now that you are *: he has 1Co 1:4
time of testing at * Judgment Day 1Co 3:13
be looked upon as * servants who 1Co 4:1
together the blessing of * blood? 1Co 10:16
my example, just as I follow *. 1Co 11:1
We have been baptized into * body 1Co 12:13
but all who become * will have the 1Co 15:48
shall some day have a body like *. 1Co 15:49
by God to be Jesus * messenger; 2Co 1:1
by * authority, and for your good. 2Co 2:10
* power, with God's eye upon us. 2Co 2:17
because * love controls us now. 2Co 5:13,14
We are * ambassadors. 2Co 5:20
into thinking they are * apostles. 2Co 11:13
demonstration of * power, instead 2Co 12:9
Since I know it is all for * 2Co 12:10
Do you feel * presence and power 2Co 13:5
men I could not be * servant. Gal 1:10
who treats * death as meaningless. Gal 2:21
meaning of Jesus * death as clearly Gal 3:1
And now that we are * we are the Gal 3:29
are counting on * death to clear Gal 5:5
by God to be Jesus * messenger. Eph 1:1
who are * have been given to him! Eph 1:18
And God was pleased, for * love Eph 5:2
by God to be Jesus * messenger, and Col 1:1
He is Jesus * faithful slave, Col 1:7
and on earth—for * death on the Col 1:20
the remainder of * sufferings for Col 1:24
do it only because * mighty energy Col 1:29
it by nailing it to * cross. Col 2:14
to the whole world * triumph at the Col 2:15
never let it be said that * 1Ti 6:1
the meaning of * words and stirring 1Ti 6:4
FROM: PAUL, JESUS * missionary, 2Ti 1:1
I am here in jail for * sake. 2Ti 1:8
blessing at the day of * return. 2Ti 1:18
as I do, and as * soldier do not 2Ti 2:4
is to the day of * resurrection. Heb 5:5f
Implied. * longing was to live Heb 5:7f
be performed. * body, being human, Heb 5:7f
explanation that * plea was that he Heb 5:7f
was sprinkled [as proof of * death Heb 9:18
* dying for us once and for all. Heb 10:10
sprinkled with * blood to make us Heb 10:22
sin is not covered by * death; Heb 10:26
FROM: PETER, JESUS * missionary. 1Pe 1:1
of being in * family and being 1Pe 4:16
We know what real love is from * 1Jn 3:16
from heaven at * baptism, and the 1Jn 5:6,7,8
while if you are loyal to * 2Jn 1:9
death from persecution for * sake. Rev 14:13

CHRISTIAN
Jewish faith, who had become a *). Act 6:5
to destroy every *, went to the Act 9:1
a * Jewess but his father a Greek. Act 16:1
you expect me to become a *?" Act 26:28
in him, he is not a * at all. Rom 8:9
should do so with * cheer. Rom 12:8
you are a *, don't curse him; Rom 12:14
PHOEBE, A DEAR * woman from the Rom 16:1
Lord, giving her a warm * welcome. Rom 16:1
person to become a * in Asia. Rom 16:5
Remember me to the * slaves over Rom 16:11
my greetings too, as a * brother. Rom 16:22
and so does Quartus, a * brother. Rom 16:23
But the man who isn't a * can't 1Co 2:14
just babies in the * life, who are 1Co 3:1
grow strong in the * life, leaving 1Co 5:8
to be a brother * but indulges in 1Co 5:11
against another *, you "go to 1Co 6:1
But, instead, one * sues another 1Co 6:6
* brother in front of unbelievers. 1Co 6:6
right to me: If a * has a wife who 1Co 7:12
wife who is not a *, but she wants 1Co 7:12
And if a * woman has a husband 1Co 7:13
who isn't a *, and he wants her to 1Co 7:13
who isn't a * may become a 1Co 7:14
may become a * with the help of his 1Co 7:14
with the help of his * wife. 1Co 7:14
And the wife who isn't a * may 1Co 7:14
may become a * with the help of her 1Co 7:14
with the help of her * husband. 1Co 7:14
wife who isn't a * is eager to 1Co 7:15
In such cases the * husband or 1Co 7:15
a * shouldn't worry about it; 1Co 7:18
at all whether a * has gone through 1Co 7:19
when he becomes a *, let him stay 1Co 7:24
but only if she marries a *. 1Co 7:39
* brother to sin whose conscience 1Co 8:9
He said this to show us that * 1Co 9:10
always do what is right as a *. 1Co 9:21
If someone who isn't a * asks you 1Co 10:27
and an unsaved person or a new * 1Co 14:24
than five hundred * brothers at one 1Co 15:6
And if being a * is of value to 1Co 15:19
When someone becomes a * he 2Co 5:17
How can a * be a partner with one 2Co 6:15
man who is not a * is not the 2Co 7:10
experience to be an earnest *. 2Co 8:22
DEAR BROTHERS, IF a * is overcome Gal 6:1
and especially to our * brothers. Gal 6:10
DEAR * FRIENDS at Ephesus, ever Eph 1:1
household with every other *. Eph 2:19
the most useless * there is, yet I Eph 3:8
May God give peace to you, my * Eph 6:23
in chains simply because I am a *. Php 1:13
who walk along the * road who are Php 3:18
To: The faithful * brothers—God's Col 1:2
Please give my greeting to the * Col 4:15
toward all the * brothers 1Th 4:10
what happens to a * when he dies so 1Th 4:13
Stay away from any * who spends his 2Th 3:6
and clothing. * women should be 1Ti 2:9,10
The pastor must not be a new *, 1Ti 3:6
being a better *, because that will 1Ti 4:8
has no right to say he is a *. 1Ti 5:8
* SLAVES SHOULD work hard for 1Ti 6:1
If their owner is a *, that is 1Ti 6:2
fruitful * life down here as well. 1Ti 6:19
calls himself a * should not be 2Ti 2:19
to be very difficult to be a *. 2Ti 3:1
have turned against the * faith. 2Ti 3:8
so that the * faith can't be spoken Tit 2:5
to all of the * friends there. Tit 3:15
far along in the * life, and Heb 5:12,13
bored with being a *, nor become Heb 6:12
A * who doesn't amount to much in Jas 1:9
Anyone who says he is a * but Jas 1:26
worth much. The * who is pure and Jas 1:27
for being a *, for when that 1Pe 4:14
no shame to suffer for being a *. 1Pe 4:16
but Babylon was the * nickname 1Pe 5:13f
other the handshake of * love. 1Pe 5:14
Someone may say, "I am a *; 1Jn 2:4
know whether or not you are a *. 1Jn 2:5
Anyone who says he is a * should 1Jn 2:6
Anyone who hates his * brother 1Jn 3:15
down our lives for our * brothers. 1Jn 3:16
supposed to be a * has money enough 1Jn 3:17
If you see a * sinning in a way 1Jn 5:16
can a * ever sin in such a way? 1Jn 5:17f

CHRISTIANITY
and orthodox * ever since. Is 52:13f
that goes along with true *. Tit 2:1

CHRISTIANS
i.e., "*"? Is 65:15f
whether these were * who braved the Act 8:2f
for these new * to receive the Holy Act 8:15
believers were first called "*." Act 11:26
send relief to the * in Judea, each Act 11:29
of the * and gave them the letter. Act 15:30

CHRISTIANS Con't)

That night the * hurried Paul and Act 17:10
good-bye to the * and sailed for Act 18:18
in Ephesus concerning the *. Act 19:23
Our Jewish * here at Jerusalem Act 21:21
for the Hebrew * and that you Act 21:24
"As for the Gentile *, we aren't Act 21:25
And I persecuted the *, hounding Act 22:4
let me bring any * I found to Act 22:5
Felix, who knew * didn't go Act 24:22
I used torture to try to make * Act 26:11
know about these * is that they are Act 28:22
when we became * and were baptized Rom 6:2,3
And even we *, although we have Rom 8:23
it will be when they become *! Rom 11:15
Some think that * should observe Rom 14:5
thing for us as * is not what we Rom 14:17
take a gift to the Jewish * there. Rom 15:25
For you see, the * in Macedonia Rom 15:26
a real debt to the Jerusalem *. Rom 15:27
from those who are not *. Rom 15:31
Pray also that the * there will Rom 15:31
and became * before I did. Rom 16:7
and all the * who are with them. Rom 16:15
To: The * in Corinth, invited by 1Co 1:2
And to: All * everywhere—whoever 1Co 1:2
Yet when I am among mature * I do 1Co 2:6
But, strange as it seems, we * 1Co 2:16
*, who are filled with the Spirit. 1Co 3:1
For you are still only baby *, 1Co 3:3
are all such wise and sensible *! 1Co 4:10
* to decide which of you is right? 1Co 6:1
that some day we * are going to 1Co 6:2
Don't you realize that we * will 1Co 6:3
outside judges who are not even *? 1Co 6:4
all is a real defeat for you as *. 1Co 6:7
Here is the problem: We * are 1Co 7:26
However, some * don't realize 1Co 8:7
they are Jews or Gentiles or *. 1Co 10:32
before you became * you went around 1Co 12:2
God) is what the * need, and 1Co 14:22
in that case all * who have died 1Co 15:18
you are not even * at all and have 1Co 15:34
and all the * who have died will 1Co 15:52
to send to the * in Jerusalem; 1Co 16:1
They were the first to become * 1Co 16:15
helping and serving * everywhere. 1Co 16:15
We are writing to all of you * 2Co 1:1
me into faithful * and commissioned 2Co 1:21
But we * have no veil over our 2Co 3:18
So stop evaluating * by what the 2Co 5:16
joy of helping the * in Jerusalem. 2Co 8:4
anything, for the * from Macedonia 2Co 11:8,9
Are you really *? 2Co 13:5
* when actually you aren't at all? 2Co 13:5
is that you will become mature *. 2Co 13:9
All the * here send you their 2Co 13:13
and all the other * here. Gal 1:1
I went after the * mercilessly, Gal 1:13
And still the * in Judea didn't Gal 1:22
some so-called "*" there—false Gal 2:4
with the Gentile * [who don't Gal 2:12
and then all the other Jewish * Gal 2:13
and yet we Jewish * know very well Gal 2:16
them now will make you stronger *? Gal 3:3
and all of us as * can have the Gal 3:14
but we are all the same—we are *; Gal 3:28
had been promised to all of us *. Eph 1:13
love you have for * everywhere, I Eph 1:15
earnestly for all * everywhere. Eph 6:18
all the * in the city of Philippi. Php 1:1
many of the * here seem to have Php 1:14
always to live as * should, so Php 1:27
IS THERE ANY such thing as * Php 2:1
We * glory in what Christ Jesus has Php 3:3
you who are mature * will see Php 3:15
DEAR BROTHER *, I love you and Php 4:1
Say "hello" for me to all the * Php 4:21
And all the other * here want to Php 4:22
These are the only Jewish * Col 4:11
the * in Laodicea and Hierapolis. Col 4:13
to all the other * in Greece. 1Th 1:7
are a part of God's plan for us *. 1Th 3:2,3
people who are not * will trust and 1Th 4:12
with him all the * who have died. 1Th 4:14
to read this letter to all the *. 1Th 5:27
is that all the * there will be 1Ti 1:5
who aren't *—so that Satan can't 1Ti 3:7
* to enjoy and be thankful for. 1Ti 4:3
* will know and do what is right. 1Ti 5:7
strangers as well as to other *? 1Ti 5:10
As you know, all the * who came 2Ti 1:15
all * must obey the Jewish laws. Tit 1:10
So speak to the * there as Tit 1:13
Insist on them so that * will be Tit 3:8
And we * are God's house—he lives Heb 3:6
we first became *, we will share in Heb 3:14
You have been * a long time now, Heb 5:12,13
you become better * and learn right Heb 5:14
as strong * ought to be. Heb 6:1
there. The * from Italy who are Heb 13:24,25
To: Jewish * scattered everywhere. Jas 1:1
have faith and are * if you aren't Jas 2:14
To: The Jewish * driven out of 1Pe 1:1
Show respect for everyone. Love * 1Pe 2:17
And if even we who are * must be 1Pe 4:17
and remember that other * all 1Pe 5:9
If we love other * it proves that 1Jn 3:14
that * should love one another. 2Jn 1:5
those who are not *, even though 3Jn 1:7
the leader of the * there, does not 3Jn 1:9
To: * everywhere—beloved of God Jud 1:1
after we become * we can do just as Jud 1:4
as your brother * are, who testify Rev 19:10

CHRISTS

For false * shall arise, and Mt 24:24

CHRONIC

* rebellion was finally exhausted. Is 6:10f

CHRONICLES

house of Caleb (1 * 2:18,19). Ex 17:10f
See Numbers 35 and 1 * 6. Jos 20:2f
See 1 * 18:17. 2Sa 8:18f
(See 1 * 20:5. 2Sa 21:19f
The remainder of 1 * deals with 1Ch 10:1
In The Book of the * the Levite Neh 12:23
in The Book of the * of the Kings Est 10:2
Implied in 2 * 35:24, 25. Zec 12:11f

CHRONOLOGICAL

* order with the other messages. Jer 35:1f

CHRYSOLITE

sparkled like *, giving off a Eze 10:9-13
topaz, diamond, *, onyx, jasper, Eze 28:13
The seventh with *; Rev 21:18,19,20

CHRYSOPRASE

The tenth with *; Rev 21:18,19,20

CHUNK

Should I fall down before a * of Is 44:19
So take out the meat * by chunk Eze 24:6
So take out the meat chunk by * Eze 24:6
the work of God for a * of meat. Rom 14:20

CHURCH

give their support money to the * Mt 15:5,6
upon this rock I will build my *; Mt 16:18
your case to the *, and if the Mt 18:17
the * should excommunicate him. Mt 18:17
Terror gripped the entire * and Act 5:11
sweeping over the * in Jerusalem, Act 8:1
Literally, "the *." Act 8:4f
Meanwhile, the * had peace Act 9:31
When the * at Jerusalem heard Act 11:22
the elders of the * in Jerusalem. Act 11:30
up to God from the * for his safety Act 12:5
teachers of the * at Antioch were Act 13:1
elders in every * and prayed for Act 14:23
they met with the * leaders—all the Act 15:4
So the apostles and * elders set Act 15:6
The men chosen were two of the * Act 15:22
the * that day as they read it. Act 15:31
So the * grew daily in faith and Act 16:5
he visited the * [at Jerusalem Act 18:22
to strengthen the *, for he Act 18:27
the elders of the * at Ephesus Act 20:17
God's flock—his *, purchased with Act 20:28
and the elders of the Jerusalem *. Act 21:18
that will help your * grow strong Rom 1:11,12
discord in the *, but Paul says to Rom 14:1f
* and try to build each other up. Rom 14:19
other into the *, just as Christ Rom 15:7
than where a * has already been Rom 15:20
Gentiles from the * in Jerusalem. Rom 15:27
She has worked hard in the * Rom 16:1
I am his guest, and the * meets Rom 16:23
there won't be splits in the *. 1Co 1:10
new, beginning a "* of Paul." 1Co 1:15
than Apollos, and dividing the *. 1Co 3:4
have a man in your * who is living 1Co 5:1
a meeting of the *—and the power of 1Co 5:3,4
fellowship of the * and into 1Co 5:5
are members of the *, and who are 1Co 5:12
man and put him out of your *. 1Co 5:13
people in the * should be able to 1Co 6:4f
Isn't there anyone in all the * 1Co 6:5
some in the * of lustful Corinth 1Co 6:12f
needed to build the * is love. 1Co 8:1
publicly in the *, and all the 1Co 11:16
disgracing the * and shaming those 1Co 11:22
a means of helping the entire *. 1Co 12:7
in his *, which is his body: 1Co 12:28
* grow in holiness and happiness. 1Co 14:4
be of real help to the whole *. 1Co 14:12
gifts, comes to * and hears you all 1Co 14:23
be silent during the * meetings. 1Co 14:34
their opinions in * meetings. 1Co 14:35
the way I treated the * of God. 1Co 15:9
in their home for their * service. 1Co 16:19
the leaders of the * so that they Gal 2:2
And the great leaders of the * Gal 2:6
the pillars of the *, saw how Gal 2:7,8,9
Head of the *— which is his body, Eph 1:22
to belong to his *, and all of Eph 3:6
together in his *, in just the way Eph 3:10
for the * through Jesus Christ. Eph 3:21
building up the *, the body of Eph 4:12
is the Head of his body, the *. Eph 4:15,16
is in charge of his body the *. Eph 5:23
just as the * obeys Christ. Eph 5:24
showed to the * when he died for Eph 5:25
as a glorious * without a single Eph 5:27
body the *, of which we are parts. Eph 5:29,30
that I greatly persecuted the *; Php 3:6
No other * did this. Php 4:15
is, his *—which he began; Col 1:18
sufferings for his body, the *. Col 1:24
God has sent me to help his * and Col 1:25
you and for the * at Laodicea, and Col 2:1
for then the whole * will stay Col 3:14
pass it on to the * at Laodicea? Col 4:16
To: The * at Thessalonica—to you 1Th 1:1
officers of your * who work hard 1Th 5:12
To: The * of Thessalonica—kept 2Th 1:1
Let them be silent in your * 1Ti 2:12
More literally, "* leader" or 1Ti 3:1f
how can he help the whole *? 1Ti 3:5
people outside the *—those who 1Ti 3:7
other jobs in the * as a test of 1Ti 3:10
officers for the * of the living 1Ti 3:15
times some in the * will turn away 1Ti 4:1
explain the Scriptures to the *; 1Ti 4:13
* laid their hands upon your head. 1Ti 4:14
The * should take loving care of 1Ti 5:3
The * should care for widows who 1Ti 5:5
This should be your * rule so 1Ti 5:7
one of the special * workers 1Ti 5:9
* and been led astray by Satan. 1Ti 5:15
and not leave this to the * to do. 1Ti 5:16
Then the * can spend its money 1Ti 5:16
front of the whole * so that no one 1Ti 5:20
They will go to *, 2Ti 3:5
worker, and to the * that meets in Phm 1:1
Let us not neglect our * Heb 10:25
and to the *, composed of all Heb 12:23
If a man comes into your * Jas 2:2
the elders of the * and they should Jas 5:14
Cornerstone of my *, and I will 1Pe 2:6
A word to you elders of the *. 1Pe 5:1
The * here in Rome 1Pe 5:13
"Your sister * here in Babylon 1Pe 5:13f
FROM: JOHN, THE old Elder of the * 2Jn 1:1
as does everyone else in the *. 2Jn 1:1
They have told the * here of 3Jn 1:6
I sent a brief letter to the * 3Jn 1:9
he tries to put them out of the *. 3Jn 1:10
love feasts of the *, they are evil Jud 1:12
aloud to the *, you will receive a Rev 1:3
to the * in Ephesus, the one in Rev 1:11
by God to oversee each local *. Rev 1:20f
of the * at Ephesus and tell him Rev 2:1
of the * in Smyrna write this Rev 2:8
of the * in Pergamos: Rev 2:12
of the * in Thyatira: Rev 2:18
of the * in Sardis write this Rev 3:1
and active *, but you are dead. Rev 3:1
of the * in Philadelphia. Rev 3:7
of the * in Laodicea: Rev 3:14

CHURCH'S

church, and if the * verdict favors Mt 18:17

CHURCHES

Cilicia, to encourage the * there. Act 15:40,41
I have among the other Gentile *. Rom 1:13
to them: so are all the Gentile *. Rom 16:4
All the * here send you their Rom 16:16
teach in all the * wherever I go. 1Co 4:17
This is my rule for all the *. 1Co 7:17
the * feel the same way about it. 1Co 11:16
he finds it in all the other *. 1Co 14:33
I gave to the * in Galatia). 1Co 16:1
The * here in Asia send you their 1Co 16:19
has done for the * in Macedonia. 2Co 8:1
of the Good News in all the *. 2Co 8:18
was elected by the * to travel with 2Co 8:19
Instead I "robbed" other * by 2Co 11:8,9
worry of how the * are getting 2Co 11:28
else in all other *, was to become 2Co 12:13
To: The * of Galatia. Gal 1:1
suffered what the * in Judea did, 1Th 2:14
We are happy to tell other * 2Th 1:4
each of its *, and I asked you to Tit 1:5
be members of our *, but they never 1Jn 2:19
To: The seven * in Turkey. Rev 1:4
letter to the seven * in Turkey: Rev 1:11
"The seven * in Asia." Rev 1:11f
of the seven *, and the seven Rev 1:20
candlesticks are the * themselves. Rev 1:20
from him who walks among the * Rev 2:1
from its place among the *. Rev 2:5
is saying to the *: To everyone who Rev 2:7
is saying to the *: He who is Rev 2:11
is saying to the *: Every one who Rev 2:17
And all the * shall know that I Rev 2:23
to what the Spirit says to the *. Rev 2:29
the Spirit is saying to the *. Rev 3:6
the Spirit is saying to the *. Rev 3:13
the Spirit is saying to the *." Rev 3:22

(CHURCHES Con't)
to tell the * all these things. Rev 22:16
CHURLISH
*, stubborn, and ill-mannered. 1Sa 25:3
CHURNING
As the * of cream yields butter, Pro 30:33
CHURNS
his commotion. He * the depths. Job 41:31,32
but always * up mire and dirt. Is 57:20
CHUZA
Chuza's wife (* was King Herod's Lk 8:3
CHUZA'S
her), Joanna, * wife (Chuza was Lk 8:3
CILICIA
A region in ancient * known from Eze 27:11f
Turkish provinces of *, and Ausia. Act 6:9
brothers in Antioch, Syria and *. Act 15:23
left for Syria and *, to encourage Act 15:40,41
in * which is no small town. Act 21:39
Tarsus, a city in *, but educated Act 22:3
"*," Paul answered. Act 23:34
the provinces of * and Pamphylia, Act 27:5
this visit I went to Syria and *. Gal 1:21
CINDERS
remain will be as * in your eyes Num 33:55
CINNAMON
half as much of * and of sweet Ex 30:22,23
perfumed with myrrh, aloes and *. Pro 7:16,17
nard and saffron, calamus and *, Sol 4:13,14
CIRCLE
northward to * around Baalah (which Jos 15:9
He shall live within God's * of Ps 25:13
It is God who sits above the * Is 40:22
be the inner * of his disciples. Lk 6:13
the vicious * of sin and death. Rom 8:2
CIRCLED
Then the border * west of Baalah Jos 15:10,11
From there it * to the west, Jos 19:11
Then Gideon * around by the Ju 8:11
So we * the city, and I followed Neh 2:14,15
left Galilee and * back to Judea Mt 19:1
From there we * around to Act 28:13
wearing a long robe * with a Rev 1:13
CIRCLES
men, * me like a pack of dogs; Ps 22:16
A vulture * ominously above the Jer 48:40
in ever-widening *, and the number Act 6:7
CIRCUIT
He rode * annually, setting up 1Sa 7:16
So they began their * of the Lk 9:6
CIRCULATING
the reports * among us from the Lk 1:1,2
These rumors were * all over Lk 9:8
CIRCUMCISE
set aside a day to * the entire Jos 5:2,3
Literally, "* yourselves . . . Jer 4:4f
pagan nations also * themselves. Jer 9:25,26
Unless you * your hearts by Jer 9:25,26
CIRCUMCISED
every male among you shall be *; Gen 17:9,10
Every male shall be * on the Gen 17:12
All must be *. Gen 17:13
Both were * the same day, along Gen 17:24-27
Abraham * him, as God required. Gen 21:4,5
For you are not *. Gen 34:14
man of you will be *, then we will Gen 34:15
us men be *, the same as they are. Gen 34:22
the men agreed, and all were *. Gen 34:24
may eat it if he has been *. Ex 12:44
all the males be *, and then they Ex 12:48
the eighth day, her son must be *. Lev 12:3
bear arms had been *, that entire Jos 5:4,5
born since that time had been *. Jos 5:4,5
So now Joshua * their Jos 5:7
ended your shame of not being *." Jos 5:8,9
all those who are * in body but not Jer 9:25,26
been * and does not love the Lord. Eze 44:9
was * when he was eight days old. Act 7:8
converts must be * and required to Act 15:5
of the area, he * Timothy before Act 16:3
of his faith, that he was *. Rom 4:11
of those Jews who have been *. Rom 4:12
by faith alone, before he was *. Rom 4:12
and if he hasn't been *, he 1Co 7:18
be *, though he was a Gentile. Gal 2:3
* and by obeying Jewish laws. Gal 2:5
without being * and obeying all the Gal 2:17
with God by being * must always Gal 5:3
we have been * or not, or whether Gal 5:6
by being * would cut themselves off Gal 5:12
convince you to be * are doing it Gal 6:12
but they want you to be * in Gal 6:13
now whether we have been * or not; Gal 6:15
godly, for they * themselves as a Eph 2:11
say you must be * to be saved. Php 3:2
CIRCUMCISING
for if the correct time for * Jn 7:21,22,23
CIRCUMCISION
The place where the * rite took Jos 5:2,3
The reason for this second * Jos 5:4,5
by loving me, your * is only a Jer 9:25,26
friends came for the * ceremony. Lk 1:59
Eight days later, at the baby's * Lk 2:21
obey Moses' law of * (actually, Jn 7:21,22,23
* is older than the Mosaic law); Jn 7:21,22,23
the ceremony of * at that time, as Act 7:8
of *, they could not be saved. Act 15:1
forbid the * of their children. Act 21:21
Jewish initiation ceremony of *. Rom 2:28
in actual body *, but he is looking Rom 2:29
value in the Jewish * ceremony? Rom 3:1
Jewish initiation ceremony of *. Rom 4:10
circumcised. The * ceremony was a Rom 4:11
Jewish ceremony of * before he 1Co 7:18
* and the many other Jewish laws Gal 2:12
who insisted that * was necessary Gal 2:12
are counting on * and keeping the Gal 5:2
am preaching that * and Jewish laws Gal 5:11
who submit to * don't try to keep Gal 6:13
That is the only true "*." Php 3:3
operation of * but by a spiritual Col 2:11
CIRCUMFERENCE
45 feet in *. 1Ki 7:23
*, hollow, with three-inch walls. Jer 52:21
"The entire * of the city is six Eze 48:35
eight miles in *, accommodating a Jon 3:3f
CIRCUMSTANCE
you don't do that under any *. Gen 24:6
as Mount Zion, unmoved by any *. Ps 125:1
to act in every *, for he wanted Pro 1:2
never under any * serve your gods Dan 3:18
under any *, that for the next Dan 6:7
Under this *, what is my pay? 1Co 9:18
CIRCUMSTANCES
but under no * are you to take my Gen 24:8
"Never, under any *, are you to Deu 16:21
*, for the Lord will guide you. 1Sa 10:7
will not be overthrown by evil *. Ps 112:6
Do not under any *, go along with Is 8:11
CISTERN
into a spring or * where there is Lev 11:36
And he took them out to the * and 2Ki 10:14
and the wheel is broken at the *; Ecc 12:6
an empty * in the prison yard. Jer 38:6
was in the *, he rushed out to the Jer 38:7
in putting Jeremiah into the *. Jer 38:9
he took to the * and lowered to Jer 38:11
and threw their bodies into a *. Jer 41:7
hidden away. The * where Ishmael Jer 41:9
CISTERNS
rocks, and even in tombs and *. 1Sa 13:6
good things, with * and vineyards Neh 9:25
broken * that can't hold water! Jer 2:13
Fifty-three * have been uncovered Jer 41:9f
CITADEL
Gate, and around * Hill, where it 2Ch 33:14
CITIES
lived among the * of the plain, Gen 13:12
with the other * and villages of Gen 19:25
furnace, rising from the * there. Gen 19:28
of death that engulfed the *. Gen 19:29
was upon all the * they journeyed Gen 35:5
Egypt, storing them in nearby *. Gen 41:48
though in walled *, may be redeemed Lev 25:32
*, and the surrounding fields. Lev 25:33
surrounding their *, for these are Lev 25:34
You will flee to your *, and I Lev 26:25
I will make your * desolate, Lev 26:31
be desolate and your * destroyed. Lev 26:33
and what * there are, and whether Num 13:19
* are fortified and very large; Num 13:28
annihilate all the * of that area. Num 21:2
destroyed them and their *. Num 21:3
So Israel captured all the * of Num 21:25,26
And shall destroy many *." Num 24:15-19
All of the *, towns, and villages Num 31:9,10,11
for our flocks and * for our little Num 32:16
to build walled * here for our Num 32:17
Go ahead and build * for your Num 32:24
stay here in the * of Gilead. Num 32:26
the land and *—to the tribes of Num 32:33
The people of Gad built these *: Num 32:34,35,36
They were all fortified * with Num 32:34,35,36
of Reuben built the following *: Num 32:37,38
* they had conquered and rebuilt. Num 32:37,38
* and surrounding pasture lands. Num 35:2
These * are for their homes, and Num 35:3
Levites the six * of Refuge where a Num 35:6
and forty-two other * besides. Num 35:6
be forty-eight * with the Num 35:7
These * shall be in various Num 35:8
the larger tribes with many * Num 35:8
in the land, * of Refuge shall be Num 35:11
These * will be places of Num 35:12
Three of these six * of Refuge Num 35:13,14
the Jordan River. (* in the area Deu 1:1
which * we should capture first.' Deu 1:22
of their * rise high into the sky! Deu 1:28
conquered all his *, and utterly Deu 2:33,34
ransacking the * we had taken. Deu 2:35,36
including all the * in the valley. Deu 2:35,36
the hill country *, the places Deu 2:37
We conquered all sixty of his *, Deu 3:4
These were well-fortified * with Deu 3:5
We had now conquered all the * Deu 3:10
as the * of Salecah and Edre-i. Deu 3:10
Rabbah, one of the * of the Deu 3:11
of Mount Gilead, including its *. Deu 3:12
live here in the * the Lord has Deu 3:19
to set apart three * east of the Deu 4:41
These * were Bezer, on the Deu 4:43
given you great * full of good Deu 6:10,11,12
of good things—* you didn't build, Deu 6:10,11,12
They live in high walled *. Deu 9:1
about one of the * of Israel that Deu 13:12,13,14
you in one of the * the Lord has Deu 13:12,13,14
* the Lord your God is giving you. Deu 16:18
living in their * and homes, you Deu 19:1
set apart three * of Refuge so that Deu 19:2,3
one of these * in each district; Deu 19:2,3
and keep the roads to these * in Deu 19:2,3
purpose of these *: If a man goes Deu 19:4
to one of those * and be safe. Deu 19:5
These * must be scattered so that Deu 19:6,7
three additional * of Refuge. Deu 19:9
into one of the * of Refuge, the Deu 19:11
only to distant *, not to those in Deu 20:15
not of the * of these nations." Deu 20:15f
"For in the * within the Deu 20:16
lay siege to your * and knock down Deu 28:52
the midst of the siege of your *. Deu 28:55
and reached their * in three days. Jos 9:17
(The names of the * were Gibeon, Jos 9:17
But the * were not harmed Jos 9:18
great as the royal * and much Jos 10:2
get back to their *, for the Lord Jos 10:19
to reach their fortified *. Jos 10:20
The Hivite kings in the * on the Jos 11:1
all the other * of those kings. Jos 11:12
burn any of the * built on mounds Jos 11:13
of the ravaged * were taken by the Jos 11:14
None of the * was given a peace Jos 11:19
and completely destroyed their *. Jos 11:21
Jordan River whose * were destroyed Jos 12:1
the * of the eastern desert. Jos 12:1
kings and their * were destroyed. Jos 12:8-24
Five * of the Philistines: Jos 13:2-7
it also included all the * of Jos 13:10
and the other * on the plain—Dibon, Jos 13:17
also included the * of the Jos 13:21
Jazer, all the * of Gilead and half Jos 13:25
and the sixty * of Jair in Bashan. Jos 13:30
King Og's royal * of Ashtaroth and Jos 13:31
at all, except * in which to live Jos 14:3,4
in great, walled *, but if the Lord Jos 14:12
from there to the * of Mount Ephron Jos 15:9
The * of Judah which were Jos 15:21-32
* with their surrounding villages. Jos 15:21-32
The following * situated in the Jos 15:33-36
* with their surrounding villages. Jos 15:33-36
other * with their villages: Jos 15:37-44
and included the * along the Jos 15:46
the number of * assigned to Judah. Jos 15:48-62f
* in the hill country with their Jos 15:48-62
given some of the * in the Jos 16:9
(Several * south of the brook Jos 17:9
the following * which were situated Jos 17:11
those *, the Canaanites remained. Jos 17:12
listing the * in each section. Jos 18:9
of the * of the tribe of Judah. Jos 18:14
* were included in the land given Jos 18:21-28
All of these * and their Jos 18:21-28
* with their respective villages: Jos 19:2-7
The * as far south as Jos 19:8
of Iphtahel. The * in these areas, Jos 19:15,16
there were twelve of these *. Jos 19:15,16
included the following *: Jos 19:17-23
sixteen * in all, each with its Jos 19:17-23
The boundaries included these *: Jos 19:24,25,26
* and their surrounding villages. Jos 19:30,31
The fortified * included in this Jos 19:35-39
* with their surrounding villages. Jos 19:35-39
The * within its area included: Jos 19:41-46
designate now the * of Refuge, as I Jos 20:2
to one of these * and be protected Jos 20:3
any of these *, he will meet with Jos 20:4
The * chosen as Cities of Refuge Jos 20:7
The cities chosen as * of Refuge Jos 20:7
that three * be set aside for this Jos 20:8
These * of Refuge were for Jos 20:9
Moses to give * to us Levites for Jos 21:2
* with their pasturelands. Jos 21:3
Thirteen of these * had been Jos 21:4
were given ten * from the Jos 21:5
received thirteen *, selected by Jos 21:6
These * were given by the tribes Jos 21:6
received twelve * from the tribes Jos 21:7
obeyed, and the * and pasturelands Jos 21:8
* listed below, with their Jos 21:9-16
four * and their pasturelands: Jos 21:17,18
So in all, thirteen * were given Jos 21:19
* and pasturelands from the tribe Jos 21:20,21,22
The following four * and Jos 21:23,24

(CITIES Con't)

Manasseh gave the * of Taanach and	Jos 21:25
So the total number of * and	Jos 21:26
received two * and pasturelands	Jos 21:27
The tribe of Issachar gave four *	Jos 21:28,29
The tribe of Asher gave four *	Jos 21:30,31
So thirteen * with their	Jos 21:33
four * by the tribe of Zebulun:	Jos 21:34,35
Gad gave them four * with	Jos 21:38,39
Levites was given twelve * in all.	Jos 21:40
The total number of * and	Jos 21:41,42
not worked for and * you did not	Jos 24:13
* where you are now living.	Jos 24:13
* of Sheshai, Ahiman, and Talmai.	Ju 1:10
also conquered the * of Gaza,	Ju 1:18
The Philistines (five *),	Ju 3:1
they owned thirty * in the land of	Ju 10:4
still called "The * of Jair."	Ju 10:4
including twenty *, and as far away	Ju 11:33
buried in one of the * of Gilead.	Ju 12:7
the * of Zorah and Eshta-ol.	Ju 13:25
heroes from the * of Zorah and	Ju 18:2
Then they rebuilt their * and	Ju 21:23
mayors of the five * of the	1Sa 5:8
capital * and villages alike.	1Sa 6:4,5
of the capital *, Ashdod, Gaza,	1Sa 6:17
other Philistine *, both the	1Sa 6:18
both the fortified * and the	1Sa 6:18
The Israeli * between Ekron and	1Sa 7:14
of those three * from all the	1Sa 7:16
in the following * where David and	1Sa 30:27-31
Racal, the * of the Jerahmeelites,	1Sa 30:27-31
Jerahmeelites, the * of the	1Sa 30:27-31
were dead, they abandoned their *;	1Sa 31:7
Hide it from the * of Gath and	2Sa 1:20
* of Betah and Berothai.	2Sa 8:8
our people and the * of our God.	2Sa 10:12
all of the * of the Ammonites.	2Sa 12:31
Tyre, and all the * of the Hivites	2Sa 24:7
sixty walled * with bronze gates;	1Ki 4:8-19
besiege one of her *, or if the	1Ki 8:37
he gave twenty * in the land of	1Ki 9:11,12
Hiram came from Tyre to see the *	1Ki 9:11,12
"These * are a wasteland!"	1Ki 9:13
* of Hazor, Megiddo, and Gezer.	1Ki 9:15
He also built * for grain	1Ki 9:19
for grain storage, * in which to	1Ki 9:19
keep his chariots, * for homes for	1Ki 9:19
and resort * near Jerusalem and in	1Ki 9:19
* and with the king at Jerusalem.	1Ki 10:26
above all the other * of Israel.	1Ki 11:32
the shrines in the * of Samaria	1Ki 13:32
among all the * of Israel, the Lord	1Ki 14:21
against some of the * of Israel;	1Ki 15:20
all the * in the land of Naphtali.	1Ki 15:20
the names of the * he built—is	1Ki 15:23
will restore the * my father took	1Ki 20:34
palace and the * he built—is	1Ki 22:39
the best of their *—even those that	2Ki 3:19
They destroyed the *, threw	2Ki 3:25
reconquering the * that his father	2Ki 13:25
one of the * of Judah, and Judah	2Ki 14:11
He captured the * of Ijon,	2Ki 15:29
and among the * of the Medes.	2Ki 17:6
them high places in all their *."	2Ki 17:9f
them in the * of Samaria, replacing	2Ki 17:24
Samaria and the other * of Israel.	2Ki 17:24
shrines on the hills near their *.	2Ki 17:29
destroying * both large and small.	2Ki 18:8
the watchman to the fortified *."	2Ki 18:8f
Gozan, and in the * of the Medes.	2Ki 18:11
all the fortified * of Judah.	2Ki 18:13
conquest of all those fortified *!	2Ki 19:25
all the * of the tribes of Israel.	2Ki 21:7
living in other * of Judah, and	2Ki 23:8
twenty-three * in the land of	1Ch 2:22
Aram wrested these * from him and	1Ch 2:23
These * were under their control	1Ch 4:31
This is a record of the * and	1Ch 6:54
and the following * of Refuge with	1Ch 6:58,59
Thirteen other * with surrounding	1Ch 6:60
they received ten * in the	1Ch 6:61
by lot thirteen * in the Bashan	1Ch 6:62
by lot twelve * from the tribes of	1Ch 6:63
* and pasturelands were also	1Ch 6:64,65
The tribe of Ephraim gave these *	1Ch 6:66-69
The following * of Refuge and	1Ch 6:70
* of Refuge and pastureland given	1Ch 6:71
to the Merari clan as * of Refuge.	1Ch 6:77
the following * and their	1Ch 7:29
in their former * were families	1Ch 9:2
they abandoned their * and fled.	1Ch 10:7
Hadadezer's * of Tibhath and Cun.	1Ch 18:8
Hanun had recruited from his *.	1Ch 19:7
our people and the * of our God.	1Ch 19:13
against the * and villages of the	1Ch 20:1
throughout the *, villages, and	1Ch 27:25
to guard the * where the chariots	2Ch 1:14
land besieging our *—whatever the	2Ch 6:28
to rebuilding the * which King	2Ch 8:2
* in Hamath as supply centers.	2Ch 8:4
He fortified the * of upper	2Ch 8:5
and constructed * where his	2Ch 8:6
in the chariot *, as well as in	2Ch 9:25
fortified these * of Judah with	2Ch 11:5-10
in the fortified * throughout the	2Ch 11:23
* and soon arrived at Jerusalem.	2Ch 12:4
all the other * of Israel.	2Ch 12:13
some of his *—Bethel, Jeshanah,	2Ch 13:18,19
from every one of Judah's *.	2Ch 14:5
build walled * throughout Judah.	2Ch 14:6
"Let us build and fortify * now,	2Ch 14:7
attacked all the * in that area,	2Ch 14:14
were collected from these * too.	2Ch 14:14
They not only plundered the *,	2Ch 14:15
and in the * he had captured in the	2Ch 15:8
They destroyed the * of Ijon,	2Ch 16:4
of the fortified * of Judah, in	2Ch 17:2
and in the * of Ephraim that his	2Ch 17:2
as teachers in all the * of Judah.	2Ch 17:7,8,9
Lord to all the * of Judah, to	2Ch 17:7,8,9
and supply * throughout Judah.	2Ch 17:12
fortified * throughout the nation.	2Ch 17:19
larger *, and instructed them:	2Ch 19:5
some of the fortified * of Judah.	2Ch 21:3,4
"Go to all the * of Judah and	2Ch 24:5
* of Judah, and from Jerusalem?	2Ch 24:6
sent to all the * of Judah and	2Ch 24:9
several of the * of Judah in the	2Ch 25:13
Then he built new * in the Ashdod	2Ch 26:6
And he built * in the hill	2Ch 27:4
the lowland * and the Negeb and had	2Ch 28:17,18
went out to the * of Judah,	2Ch 31:1
priests in their *, dividing it to	2Ch 31:14,15
in each of the * of the priests to	2Ch 31:19
to the fortified *, planning to	2Ch 32:1
above all the other * of Israel.	2Ch 33:7
all of the fortified * of Judah.	2Ch 33:14
Then he went to the * of	2Ch 34:6
and to the other * of Judah, from	Ez 2:1
from the Persian * of Tel-melah,	Ez 2:59
to the other * of Judah from which	Ez 2:70
in the nearby * went home for a	Neh 4:12
from the Persian * of Tel-melah,	Neh 7:61
throughout the * of the land,	Neh 8:15
Your people captured fortified *	Neh 9:25
from the other * and towns of Judah	Neh 11:1
homes in the various * of Judah).	Neh 11:3
gathered in their * throughout all	Est 9:1
countryside and * of the empire, so	Est 9:28
* after killing off its citizens.	Job 15:27,28
The Lord will destroy your *;	Ps 9:6
in triumph into Edom's strong *?	Ps 60:9,10
he rebuilds the * of Judah.	Ps 69:35
may the * be as full of people as	Ps 72:16
Jerusalem and all the * of Judah	Ps 97:8,9
and build their *, to sow their	Ps 107:36
to conquer these fortified *?	Ps 108:10
than the mayors of ten big *!	Ecc 7:19
lies in ruins; your * are burned;	Is 1:7
"Not until their * are	Is 6:11
its greatest * and had no mercy on	Is 14:17
nor rebuild the * of the world.	Is 14:21
Weep, Philistine *—you are	Is 14:31
In one night your * of Ar and Kir	Is 15:1
The cries from the * of Heshbon	Is 15:4
The * of Aroer are deserted.	Is 17:2
Their largest * will be as	Is 17:9
like the abandoned * of the	Is 17:9
At that time five of the * of	Is 19:18
You turn mighty * into heaps of	Is 25:2
Her walled * will be silent and	Is 27:10
your joyous homes and happy *	Is 32:13
be deserted, the crowded * empty.	Is 32:14
will be destroyed and their *	Is 32:19
* of Judah and conquered them.	Is 36:1
Did their gods save the * of	Is 37:12
the kings of the * of Sepharvaim,	Is 37:13
crush walled * into ruined heaps.	Is 37:26
be afraid—tell the * of Judah,	Is 40:9
Join in the chorus, you desert *	Is 42:11
delivered and the * of Judah lived	Is 44:26
will possess the * left behind	Is 54:3
ruins of your *, and you will be	Is 58:12
Who Rebuild Their Walls and *."	Is 58:12
will come and build your *.	Is 60:10
ruins, repairing * long ago	Is 61:4
Your holy * are destroyed;	Is 64:10
and in all the other * of Judah.	Jer 1:15
to destroy her and leave her * in	Jer 2:15
from their * of Memphis and	Jer 2:16
many gods as there are * in Judah.	Jer 2:28
Flee to the fortified *!"	Jer 4:5
your land. Your * will lie in ruin	Jer 4:7
Jerusalem and the * of Judah.	Jer 4:16
and all the * were broken down	Jer 4:26
All the * flee in terror at the	Jer 4:29
All the * are abandoned—all have	Jer 4:29
lurk around their * so that all who	Jer 5:6
and they shall sack your walled *	Jer 5:17
throughout the * of Judah and in	Jer 7:17
and in the * of Judah, and the	Jer 7:34
Come, let us go to the walled *	Jer 8:14
in it—the * and people alike.	Jer 8:16
their dens. The * of Judah shall be	Jer 9:11
the north. The * of Judah shall	Jer 10:22
gods as there are *, and your	Jer 11:13
They are no longer yours. The *	Jer 13:19
Literally, "the * are closed and	Jer 13:19f
the gates of your * and take from	Jer 15:7
and from the * of Judah and	Jer 17:26
destroyed like the * of old which	Jer 20:16
I went to Jerusalem and to the *	Jer 25:18
of the Philistine *: Ashkelon,	Jer 25:19,20
was before. The * will be filled	Jer 30:19
O virgin Israel, to your * here.	Jer 31:21
in Judah and her *, "The Lord	Jer 31:23
Jerusalem, in the * of Judah and in	Jer 32:44
I will rebuild the * of both	Jer 33:7
and in the * east of the Philistine	Jer 33:13
plain, in all the * of the Negeb,	Jer 33:13
and in all the * of Judah.	Jer 33:13
Jerusalem and the * of Judah:	Jer 34:1
walled * of Judah still standing.	Jer 34:7
And I will see to it that the *	Jer 34:22
of Egypt in the * of Migdol,	Jer 44:1
and to all the * of Judah.	Jer 44:2,3
as fire upon the * of Judah and	Jer 44:6
always done in the * of Judah and	Jer 44:17
to idols in the * of Judah and in	Jer 44:21
publish it in the * of Migdol,	Jer 46:14
it will destroy their * and	Jer 47:2
from Caphtor. The * of Gaza and	Jer 47:5
All the villages and *, whether	Jer 48:8
fly away, for her * shall be left	Jer 48:9
All the * of the tableland lie in	Jer 48:21
Bozrah—and all the * of the land of	Jer 48:24
flee from your * and live in the	Jer 48:28
says the Lord. Her * are fallen;	Jer 48:41
Why are you living in the * of	Jer 49:1
taken over Gad and all its *?	Jer 49:1
and her * shall be eternal	Jer 49:13
Your * will become as silent as	Jer 49:18
Damascus The * of Hamath and	Jer 49:23
a fire in the * of Babylon that	Jer 50:32
his own name: Your * shall be	Jer 51:14
by its waves. Her * lie in	Jer 51:43
and the girls in Judah's *.	Lam 5:11
All your * will be smashed and	Eze 6:4-7
I will crush you and make your *	Eze 6:14
Your * shall be destroyed and	Eze 12:20
nations and ruined their *;	Eze 19:7
out her frontier *, the glory of	Eze 25:9,10
These were three * of ancient	Eze 27:10f
Judah and the * in what was once	Eze 27:17
"The surrounding * quake at the	Eze 27:28
nations, and her * will lie as	Eze 29:12
nations, and her * shall be in	Eze 30:7
surrounded by other ruined *.	Eze 30:7
"The * of Pathros [along the	Eze 30:14
among the ruined * keep saying,	Eze 33:24
will demolish your * and make you	Eze 35:4,5
your * will never be rebuilt.	Eze 35:9
the long-deserted *, destroyed and	Eze 36:4
and the ruined * will be rebuilt	Eze 36:10
The ruined * are rebuilt and	Eze 36:35
The ruined * will be crowded once	Eze 36:37,38
once-desolate * that are now filled	Eze 38:12
You will never reach the *—you	Eze 39:5
"The people of the * of Israel	Eze 39:9
to the coastal * and conquer many.	Dan 11:18
defenses for her *, but they have	Hos 8:14
War will swirl through their *;	Hos 11:6
* of the plain that perished with	Hos 11:8f
revenge on me, you * of Philistia?	Joe 3:4
People from two or three * would	Amo 4:8
I destroyed some of your *, as I	Amo 4:11
their ruined *, and live in them	Amo 9:14
capital *, Samaria and Jerusalem!	Mic 1:5
the first of the * of Judah to	Mic 1:13
Then all the * of the south began	Mic 1:13
the gates of your * of captivity,	Mic 2:13
demolish the defenses of your *.	Mic 5:11
* where your idol temples stand.	Mic 5:14
Your *, people of God, will be	Mic 7:11
lawlessness and all the * too.	Hab 2:8
"Woe to you who build * with	Hab 2:12
and violence in * everywhere.	Hab 2:17
down go the walled * and	Zep 1:16
Philistine *, too, will be rooted	Zep 2:4
ruin and their * deserted without a	Zep 3:6
Jerusalem and the * of Judah.	Zec 1:12
declares that the * of Israel will	Zec 1:17
* to attend these celebrations.	Zec 8:20,21
friends in other * and say, 'Let's	Zec 8:20,21
Or, "for the * of Syria belong to	Zec 9:1f
and the Ten *, and Jerusalem, and	Mt 4:25
through all the * and villages of	Mt 9:35
Truly, the wicked * of Sodom and	Mt 10:15
* where they were scheduled to go.	Mt 11:1
teach and preach in their *."	Mt 11:1f
against the * where he had done	Mt 11:20
* destroyed by God for their	Mt 11:21f

(CITIES Con't)
* destroyed by God for their villages and *, and out on the — Mt 11:23f
villages and *, and out on the — Mk 6:56
of the * and villages of Galilee — Lk 8:1
What horrors await you, you * of — Lk 10:13
done in the * of Tyre and Sidon, — Lk 10:13
* destroyed by God in judgment for — Lk 10:13f
you shall be governor of ten *.' — Lk 19:17
'You can be governor over five * — Lk 19:19
of those two *, but the delegates — Act 12:20
peace, for their * were — Act 12:20
going to the * of Lycaonia, Lystra, — Act 14:5,6
the way in the * of Phoenicia and — Act 15:3
NOW THEY TRAVELED through the * — Act 17:1
in all the * he passed through. — Act 20:2
in distant * in foreign lands. — Act 26:11
* of Sodom and Gomorrah perished. — Rom 9:29
Good News to other * that are far — 2Co 10:16
from mobs in the * and from death — 2Co 11:26
Later, he turned the * of Sodom — 2Pe 2:6
And don't forget the * of Sodom — Jud 1:7
Those * were destroyed by fire — Jud 1:7
sections, and * around the world — Rev 16:19

CITIZEN

must be treated like any other *; — Lev 19:34
*, for I am Jehovah your God." — Lev 24:22
of Elnathan, a * of Jerusalem) — 2Ki 24:8,9
official and * of your empire. — Est 1:16
And yet the least * of the — Lk 7:28
* who hasn't even been tried?" — Act 22:25
This man is a Roman *!" — Act 22:26
"Tell me, are you a Roman *?" — Act 22:27
"But I am a * by birth!" — Act 22:28
Paul was a Roman *, and the — Act 22:29
I learned that he was a Roman *. — Act 23:27
and he will be a * in the city of — Rev 3:12

CITIZENS

before all the * of the town: — Gen 23:10
led their fellow * astray with the — Deu 13:12,13,14
he is better than his fellow *. — Deu 17:20
Then the * of Shechem and — Ju 9:6
the * of Shechem and Beth-millo; — Ju 9:20
* of Shechem, and they revolted. — Ju 9:22,23
Abimelech and the * of Shechem who — Ju 9:24
he became one of the leading *. — Ju 9:26
But when the local * went to see — 1Sa 5:3
But the * of Jabesh asked for — 1Sa 11:1
* together for fasting and prayer. — 1Ki 21:9
for its * refused to accept him as — 2Ki 15:16
any of the Israeli *, but used them — 2Ch 8:9
Hezekiah and the * of Jerusalem: — 2Ch 32:9
But some public-spirited * — 2Ch 33:25
Here is the list of ordinary * — Ez 10:25
who were * of the province. — Neh 3:7
the ordinary *, for registration. — Neh 7:5
There was a total of 42,360 * who — Neh 7:66
cities after killing off its *. — Job 15:27,28
When he registers her * he will — Ps 87:6
former guests are now * of hell. — Pro 9:18
The good influence of godly * — Pro 11:11
* of Gebim are preparing to run. — Is 10:31
And all your * shall be taught — Is 54:13
I will make them second-class *. — Is 56:3
and all you * of Jerusalem. — Jer 17:20
kings of Judah and * of Jerusalem! — Jer 19:3
* of Judah who are here in Egypt! — Jer 44:24
for exile, you * of Egypt, for the — Jer 46:19
to be considered * and have the — Eze 47:22
of blood. Her * are gangs of — Hos 6:9
and violence; your * are so used to — Mic 6:12
than before. * of many lands will — Mic 7:12
Jesus said, "the * are free! — Mt 17:26,27
and the leading * of Galilee. — Mk 6:21
are registered as * of heaven." — Lk 10:20
And it is true that the * of this — Lk 16:8
and jailed us—and we are Roman *! — Act 16:37
heard Paul and Silas were Roman *. — Act 16:38
very own family, * of God's — Eph 2:19
Rejoice, O heavens! You * of — Rev 12:12

CITY

to the east of the * of Asher. — Gen 2:14
so when Cain founded a *, he — Gen 4:17
Calah), the main * of the empire. — Gen 10:11,12
building a great *, with a — Gen 11:3,4
down to see the * and the tower — Gen 11:5
that ended the building of the *. — Gen 11:8
That is why the * was called — Gen 11:9
but they stopped instead at the * — Gen 11:31
at a place near the * of Sodom. — Gen 13:12
the booty stolen from my *." — Gen 14:21
you out of the * of Ur of the — Gen 15:7
there within the *—will you destroy — Gen 18:24
the entire * for their sake." — Gen 18:26
Will you destroy the * for lack — Gen 18:28
entrance of the * of Sodom, and Lot — Gen 19:1
the men of the *—yes, Sodomites, — Gen 19:4
from all over the *—surrounded the — Gen 19:4
do you have here in the *?" — Gen 19:12
For we will destroy the * — Gen 19:13
get out of the *, for the Lord is — Gen 19:14
in the destruction of the *." — Gen 19:15
the *, for the Lord was merciful. — Gen 19:16
and won't destroy that little *. — Gen 19:21
named Zoar, meaning "Little *." — Gen 19:22
One day, when visiting the * of — Gen 20:1
of the men of Heth at the * gate. — Gen 23:17,18
why stand here outside the * when — Gen 24:31
Isaac moved to the * of Gerar where — Gen 26:1
and the * that grew up there was — Gen 26:33
Literally, "of the *." — Gen 28:19f
Canaan, and camped outside the *. — Gen 33:18
other men of the *—for he was — Gen 34:18,19
appeared before the * council — Gen 34:20
"came into the gate of their *." — Gen 34:20f
entered the * without opposition, — Gen 34:25
and plundered the * because their — Gen 34:27
both inside the * and outside in — Gen 34:28
Jobab (son of Zerah), from the * — Gen 36:31-39
it invaded Moab. His * was Avith. — Gen 36:31-39
by: King Hadad, from the * of Pau. — Gen 36:31-39
of the men of the *, "Where does — Gen 38:21
barely out of the *, Joseph said to — Gen 44:4
again, and returned to the *. — Gen 44:13
as I have left the * I will spread — Ex 9:29
went out of the * and lifted his — Ex 9:33
a defiled place outside the *. — Lev 14:40
in a defiled place outside the *. — Lev 14:41
out of the * to a defiled place. — Lev 14:45
into an open field outside the *. — Lev 14:53
"If a man sells a house in the * — Lev 25:29
Literally, "in a walled *." — Lev 25:29f
River, and the * of Waheb, lie — Num 21:14
including the * of Heshbon, which — Num 21:25,26
The * of Ar in Moab, — Num 21:27-30
attention to the * of Bashan, but — Num 21:33
They left the * of Rameses, — Num 33:3,4
outward from the * walls for 1500 — Num 35:4
with the * in the center. — Num 35:5
to stay in the * of Refuge; — Num 35:25
"If the slayer leaves the *, — Num 35:26
stayed inside the * until the death — Num 35:28
a refugee in a * of Refuge, — Num 35:32
Not one * was too strong for us, — Deu 2:35,36
River near the * of Beth-peor. — Deu 4:44,45,46
war against that * and utterly — Deu 13:15
put the entire * to the torch, as a — Deu 13:16
your God. That * shall forever — Deu 13:16
within your *, so that they can eat — Deu 14:29
each * before the Lord your God. — Deu 16:8
* and shall be stoned to death. — Deu 17:5
"As you approach a * to fight — Deu 20:10
to you, kill every male in the *; — Deu 20:13
"When you besiege a *, don't — Deu 20:19
from the body to the nearest *. — Deu 21:2
Then the elders of that * shall — Deu 21:3
the elders of the * and declare, — Deu 21:19
Then the men of the * shall — Deu 21:21
of her virginity to the * judges. — Deu 22:15
of the * shall stone her to death. — Deu 22:21
the walls of a *, both she and the — Deu 22:23,24
shall go to the * elders and say to — Deu 25:7
The elders of the * will then — Deu 25:8
Blessings in the *, — Deu 28:2-6
Curses in the *; — Deu 28:15-19
and Jericho, the * of palm trees; — Deu 34:3
had arrived in the * that evening. — Jos 2:2
They left the * at dusk as the — Jos 2:5
at dusk as the * gates were about — Jos 2:5
meanwhile, the * gates were kept — Jos 2:7
was on top of the * wall, she let — Jos 2:15
returned to the * after searching — Jos 2:22
the river at the * of Adam, near — Jos 3:15,16
was close to the * of Jericho, and — Jos 3:15,16
eastern edge of the * of Jericho; — Jos 4:19
As Joshua was sizing up the * of — Jos 5:13
to walk around the * once a day for — Jos 6:3,4
to walk around the * seven times, — Jos 6:3,4
the walls of the * will fall down; — Jos 6:5
then move in upon the * from — Jos 6:5
The Ark was carried around the * — Jos 6:11
the * not once, but seven times. — Jos 6:15
The Lord has given us the *!" — Jos 6:16
* from every side and captured it! — Jos 6:20
Then the Israelis burned the * — Jos 6:24
on the * of Ai, east of Bethel. — Jos 7:2
"It's a small * and it won't take — Jos 7:3
Set an ambush behind the *." — Jos 8:2
behind the *, alert for action. — Jos 8:3,4
us until they have all left the *; — Jos 8:6
and enter the *, for the Lord will — Jos 8:7
Set the * on fire, as the Lord — Jos 8:8
edge of a valley north of the *. — Jos 8:11,12,13
ambush on the west side of the *. — Jos 8:11,12,13
there was an ambush behind the *. — Jos 8:14
soldiers in the * were called out — Jos 8:16
so the * was left defenseless; — Jos 8:16
the * gates were left wide open. — Jos 8:17
Ai, for I will give you the *." — Jos 8:18
into the * and set it on fire. — Jos 8:19
smoke from the * was filling the — Jos 8:20,21
were inside the *, so they turned — Jos 8:20,21
were inside the * came out and — Jos 8:22
men outside the *, they went back — Jos 8:2
threw it in front of the * gate. — Jos 8:2
For Gibeon was a great *—as great — Jos 10:
destroyed the * of Makkedah and — Jos 10:2
Not one person in the entire * — Jos 10:2
Lord gave them the * and its king. — Jos 10:3
to help defend the *, but Joshua's — Jos 10:3
they killed everyone in the *. — Jos 10:34,3
was killed and the * was burned. — Jos 11:1
The king of Dor in the * of — Jos 12:8-24
included the * in the valley, and — Jos 13:9
Mount Bashan with its * of — Jos 13:1
River, past the * of Arnon in the — Jos 13:16
Jebus (where the * of Jerusalem is — Jos 15:8
he was given the * of Arba (also — Jos 15:13
living in the * of Debir (formerly — Jos 15:15
also the * of Ashdod with its — Jos 15:47
The * of Salt, and En-gedi. — Jos 15:48-62
who lived in the * of Jerusalem, so — Jos 15:63
Manasseh, but the * of Tappu-ah, on — Jos 17:8
south of the old * of Jerusalem — Jos 18:16
and the fortified * of Tyre and — Jos 19:29
Dan captured the * of Leshem, — Jos 19:47,48
and they called the * "Dan," — Jos 19:47,48
he could have any * he wanted. — Jos 19:50
will meet with the * council and — Jos 20:4
must stay in that * until he has — Jos 20:6
to return to his own * and home." — Jos 20:6
Judean hills, as a * of Refuge—it — Jos 21:9-16
fields beyond the * and the — Jos 21:9-16
Shechem (a * of Refuge), Gezer, — Jos 21:20,21,22
Golan, in Bashan (a * of Refuge), — Jos 21:27
Kedesh, in Galilee (a * of — Jos 21:32
Ramoth (a * of Refuge), Mahanaim, — Jos 21:38,39
at Gibe-ah, the * which had been — Jos 24:33
its people, setting the * on fire. — Ju 1:8
Later they attacked the * of — Ju 1:11
and he conquered the * and won — Ju 1:13
in Jericho, "The * of Palm — Ju 1:16
Canaanites at the * of Zephath and — Ju 1:17
So now the * is named Hormah — Ju 1:17
The * of Hebron was given to — Ju 1:20
out the inhabitants of the *; — Ju 1:20
they attacked the * of Bethel, — Ju 1:22,23
a man coming out of the *. — Ju 1:24
Literally, "the way into the *." — Ju 1:24f
does not mean via the * gates. — Ju 1:24f
and founded a * there, naming it — Ju 1:26
called "The * of Palm Trees." — Ju 3:13
But outside the *, at the — Ju 3:17,18,19
and for fear of the men of the *; — Ju 6:27
Early the next morning, as the * — Ju 6:28
and religious leaders of the *. — Ju 8:14
Then he took the leaders of the * — Ju 8:16
knocked down the * tower and killed — Ju 8:17
* and proposed Abimelech's scheme; — Ju 9:3
the mayor of the *, heard what Gaal — Ju 9:30
the * to rebellion against you. — Ju 9:31
as it is daylight, storm the *. — Ju 9:33
themselves around the *. — Ju 9:34
as Gaal sat at the * gates, — Ju 9:35
men began their march upon the *. — Ju 9:35
cursed are right outside the *! — Ju 9:38
wounded all the way to the * gate. — Ju 9:40
And when the men of the * went — Ju 9:43
Abimelech stormed the * gate to — Ju 9:44
captured the *, killed its people, — Ju 9:45
Abimelech next attacked the * of — Ju 9:50
a fort inside the * and the entire — Ju 9:51
but lived in the * of Shamir in the — Ju 10:1
Dan, who lived in the * of Zorah. — Ju 13:2,3
and he went to the * of Ashkelon, — Ju 14:19
to the Philistine * of Gaza and — Ju 16:1
been seen in the *, so the police — Ju 16:2
many men of the * lay in wait all — Ju 16:2
all night at the * gate to capture — Ju 16:2
went out to the * gates and lifted — Ju 16:3
of Dan arrived at the * of Laish. — Ju 18:27
and burned the * to the ground. — Ju 18:27
Dan rebuilt the * and lived there. — Ju 18:28
lived there. The * was named — Ju 18:29
priests until the * was finally — Ju 18:30
in this heathen * where there are — Ju 19:12,13
evil men from the * of Gibe-ah so — Ju 20:13
that their * was on fire, and that — Ju 20:40,41
* and village in the entire land. — Ju 20:48
Boaz arrived from the * while she — Ru 2:4,5
She carried it back into the * — Ru 2:18
Then she returned to the *. — Ru 3:15-18
Literally, "the gate" of the *, — Ru 4:1f
And the women of the * said to — Ru 4:14
great cry arose throughout the *. — 1Sa 4:13
idol Dagon in the * of Ashdod. — 1Sa 5:1
country, lest the entire * die. — 1Sa 5:11
fear was sweeping across the *. — 1Sa 5:11
prophet who lives here in this *; — 1Sa 9:6
So they started into the * where — 1Sa 9:9,10,11
a hill toward the *, they saw some — 1Sa 9:9,10,11
He lives just inside the * gates. — 1Sa 9:12,13
So they went into the *, and as — 1Sa 9:14
returned to the *, Samuel took Saul — 1Sa 9:25

(CITY Con't)
him to the edge of the *. 1Sa 9:26,27
When they reached the * walls 1Sa 9:26,27
the Israeli * of Jabesh-gilead. 1Sa 11:1
the * when that message arrived! 1Sa 11:9
the * came trembling to meet him. 1Sa 16:4
him to take them back to the *. 1Sa 20:40
and Jonathan returning to the *. 1Sa 20:42
DAVID WENT TO the * of Nob to see 1Sa 21:1
Then he went to Nob, the * of 1Sa 22:19
trapped himself in a walled *!" 1Sa 23:7
instead of here in the royal *." 1Sa 27:5
home at their * of Ziklag, they 1Sa 30:1
had raided the * and burned it to 1Sa 30:1
"Which * shall I go to?" 2Sa 2:1
him aside at the * gate as if to 2Sa 3:27
Zion, now called the * of David. 2Sa 5:7
defenders of the * reached David, 2Sa 5:8
tunnel into the * and destroy those 2Sa 5:8
the * of David) his headquarters. 2Sa 5:9
section of the *, he built 2Sa 5:9
toward the present * center. 2Sa 5:9
taking it into the * of David, but 2Sa 6:10
the Ark to the * of David with a 2Sa 6:12
came into the *, Michal, Saul's 2Sa 6:16
conquering Gath, their largest *. 2Sa 8:1
out the * before attacking it!" 2Sa 10:3
the gates of their * while the 2Sa 10:7,8
Abishai, who was to attack the *. 2Sa 10:10
ran too, and retreated into the *. 2Sa 10:14
laying siege to the * of Rabbah. 2Sa 11:1
As he looked out over the *, he 2Sa 11:2
to the besieged * where he knew 2Sa 11:16
the troops go so close to the *? 2Sa 11:19,20,21
them back to the * gates, the men 2Sa 11:23
next time, and conquer the *; 2Sa 11:25
men in a certain *, one very rich, 2Sa 12:1
"I have taken the * of Waters." 2Sa 12:26,27f
the people of the * and made them 2Sa 12:31
coming toward the * along the road 2Sa 13:34
and went out to the gate of the *; 2Sa 15:2
"If we get out of the * before 2Sa 15:14
* of Jerusalem will be saved." 2Sa 15:14
at the edge of the * to let his 2Sa 15:17,18
throughout the * as the king and 2Sa 15:23
took the Ark back into the *. 2Sa 15:25,26
Return quietly to the * with your 2Sa 15:27
back into the * and stayed there. 2Sa 15:29
returned to the *, getting there 2Sa 15:37
escaped into some *, you will have 2Sa 17:13
the walls of the * into the nearest 2Sa 17:13
seen entering and leaving the *. 2Sa 17:17
stay here in the * and send us help 2Sa 18:3
So he stood at the gate of the * 2Sa 18:4
was sitting at the gate of the *. 2Sa 18:24
back into the * as though they were 2Sa 19:3
out and sat at the * gates, and as 2Sa 19:8,9,10
throughout the * that he was there, 2Sa 19:8,9,10
to die in my own *, where my father 2Sa 19:37
* where we can't reach him." 2Sa 20:6
at the * of Abel in Beth-maacah. 2Sa 20:14
to the top of the * wall and began 2Sa 20:15
But a wise woman in the * called 2Sa 20:16
peace-loving *, loyal to Israel. 2Sa 20:19
we will leave the * in peace." 2Sa 20:21
in Gibeon, the * of King Saul." 2Sa 21:5,6
the nearby * of Bethlehem. 2Sa 23:14
that good water in the * well!" 2Sa 23:15
(The well was near the * gate. 2Sa 23:15
south of the * that lies in the 2Sa 24:5
"Why is the * in such an 1Ki 1:41
* is celebrating and rejoicing. 1Ki 1:44,45
outside the * on pain of death. 1Ki 2:36,37
to live in the * of David until he 1Ki 3:1
Temple and the wall around the *. 1Ki 3:1
the * of David, to the Temple. 1Ki 8:1
toward your chosen * of Jerusalem 1Ki 8:44
and toward this * of Jerusalem 1Ki 8:48
Gezer was the * the king of 1Ki 9:16
later he had given the * to his 1Ki 9:16
Baalath, and Tamar, a desert *. 1Ki 9:17,18
daughter from the * of David—the 1Ki 9:24
sake of Jerusalem, my chosen *." 1Ki 11:12,13
from the * of Zeredah in Ephraim; 1Ki 11:26
of this * his father had built. 1Ki 11:27,28
in Jerusalem, the * I have chosen 1Ki 11:36
in the * of his father David; 1Ki 11:43
Jeroboam now built the * of 1Ki 12:25
* to mourn over it and bury it. 1Ki 13:29
who die in the * shall be eaten by 1Ki 14:11
into the *, the child will die. 1Ki 14:12
in Jerusalem, the * which, among 1Ki 14:21
King Baasha built the fortress * 1Ki 15:17
* of Ramah and returned to Tirzah. 1Ki 15:21
to build the * of Geba in Benjamin 1Ki 15:22
in Benjamin and the * of Mizpah. 1Ki 15:22
to the Philistine * of Gibbethon. 1Ki 15:27
who die in the * will be eaten by 1Ki 16:4-7
in the capital * of Tirzah. 1Ki 16:9
the Philistine * of Gibbethon, 1Ki 16:15,16
When Zimri saw that the * had 1Ki 16:18
$4,000 and built a * on it, calling 1Ki 16:24
of Zarephath, near the * of Sidon. 1Ki 17:8,9
* he saw a widow gathering sticks; 1Ki 17:10
chariot to the entrance of the *! 1Ki 18:46
he went to Beer-sheba, a * of 1Ki 19:3
He sent this message into the * 1Ki 20:2,3
troops marched out of the *. 1Ki 20:16
Ben-hadad fled into the * and hid 1Ki 20:30
of the * near King Ahab's palace. 1Ki 21:1
The * fathers followed the 1Ki 21:11
and he was dragged outside the * 1Ki 21:13
to death. The * officials then 1Ki 21:14
blood outside the * just as they 1Ki 21:19
who die in the * shall be eaten by 1Ki 21:24
occupying our * of Ramoth-gilead? 1Ki 22:3
threshing floor near the * gate. 1Ki 22:10
of the *, and to my son Joash. 1Ki 22:26
Literally, "as though the * were 1Ki 22:27f
the * of his forefather David; 1Ki 22:50
Now a delegation of the * 2Ki 2:19
"This * is located in beautiful 2Ki 2:19
Then he went out to the * well 2Ki 2:21
boys from the * began mocking and 2Ki 2:23
A prominent woman of the * 2Ki 4:8
and horses to surround the *. 2Ki 6:14
This isn't the right *! 2Ki 6:19
Samaria, the capital * of Israel! 2Ki 6:20
famine in the *, and after a long 2Ki 6:25
the wall of the *, a woman called 2Ki 6:26-30
sitting outside the * gates. 2Ki 7:3
starve if we go back into the *; 2Ki 7:4
So they went back to the * and 2Ki 7:10
we will be lured out of the *. 2Ki 7:12
and attacked the * of Zair, but was 2Ki 8:21
cemetery in the * of David—the old 2Ki 8:24,25
THEN JEHU WROTE a letter to the * 2Ki 10:1
and a fortified * and an armory." 2Ki 10:2,3
affairs and the * manager, together 2Ki 10:5
together with the * council and the 2Ki 10:5
chief men of the *, where they had 2Ki 10:6
entrance of the * gate, and to 2Ki 10:8
the people of the * and said to 2Ki 10:17
So everyone was happy, and the * 2Ki 11:20
* of David section of Jerusalem. 2Ki 14:20
ancestors in the * of David, and 2Ki 15:7
Menahem destroyed the * of 2Ki 15:16
* of David section of Jerusalem. 2Ki 15:38
the * of Elath for Syria; 2Ki 16:6
population of the * as captives, 2Ki 16:9
cemetery, in the * of David sector 2Ki 16:20
Samaria, the capital * of Israel. 2Ki 17:5
in colonies in the * of Halah and 2Ki 17:6
began a siege on the * of Samaria. 2Ki 18:9
in colonies in the * of Halath and 2Ki 18:11
is that he shall not enter this *. 2Ki 19:32
and save this * for the sake of my 2Ki 19:34
this * from the king of Assyria. 2Ki 20:6
water into the *—are recorded in 2Ki 20:20
Lord—in the very * and building 2Ki 21:3,4,5
in Jerusalem—the * I have chosen 2Ki 21:7
to destroy this * and its people, 2Ki 22:15,16
side as one enters the * gate. 2Ki 23:8
And the men of the * told him, 2Ki 23:17
and I will discard my chosen * of 2Ki 23:27
besieged the * of Jerusalem. 2Ki 24:10
The last food in the * was eaten 2Ki 25:3
surrounding the * took out after 2Ki 25:4,5
the people in the * and the Jewish 2Ki 25:11
hiding in the *, were taken by 2Ki 25:19
who lived in the * of Dinhabah. 1Ch 1:43
and ruled from the * of Avith. 1Ch 1:46
* of Masrekah came to the throne. 1Ch 1:47
and ruled from the * of Pai (his 1Ch 1:50
refused to let them enter the *. 1Ch 11:5,6
later called the * of David, and 1Ch 11:5,6
is called the * of David. 1Ch 11:7
He extended the * out around the 1Ch 11:8
of bringing it to the * of David. 1Ch 13:13
at the gates of the * of Medeba. 1Ch 19:9
retreating, they fled into the *. 1Ch 19:15
amounts of plunder from the *. 1Ch 20:2
He drove the people from the * 1Ch 20:3
* of David, also known as Zion, 2Ch 5:2
of Egypt, chosen a * anywhere in 2Ch 6:5,6
that *, and David as that king.' 2Ch 6:5,6
pray toward this * of Jerusalem 2Ch 6:34
fathers, and this * and your Temple 2Ch 6:37,38
fought against the * of 2Ch 8:3
daughter) from the * of David 2Ch 8:11
* as a further safety measure. 2Ch 11:12
in Jerusalem, the * God had chosen 2Ch 12:13
They advanced to the * of 2Ch 14:9,10
fighting of * against city, for God 2Ch 15:6
of city against *, for God was 2Ch 15:6
him hiding in the * of Samaria, and 2Ch 22:9
rejoiced, and the * was quiet and 2Ch 23:21
He was buried in the * of David 2Ch 24:16
buried him in the * of David, but 2Ch 24:25
he rebuilt the * of Eloth and 2Ch 26:2
and captured the * of Gath and 2Ch 26:6
in Jericho, the * of Palm Trees. 2Ch 28:15
And he did the same in every * 2Ch 28:25
Temple with the * officials, 2Ch 29:20
So the messengers went from * to 2Ch 30:10
went from city to * throughout 2Ch 30:10
to plug the springs outside the *. 2Ch 32:3
Fort Millo in the * of David, and 2Ch 32:5
plains before the *, and encouraged 2Ch 32:6
besieging the * of Lachish, sent 2Ch 32:9
the walls of the *, trying to 2Ch 32:18
* of David sector in Jerusalem. 2Ch 32:30
in Jerusalem—the * I have chosen to 2Ch 33:7
outer wall of the * of David and 2Ch 33:14
and dumped them outside the *. 2Ch 33:15
* treasurer, to repair the Temple. 2Ch 34:8
destroy this * and its people. 2Ch 34:24
words against this * and its 2Ch 34:27
evil upon this * and its people 2Ch 34:28
rebellious and evil *; Ez 4:12
know that if this * is rebuilt, it Ez 4:13
* this has been in the past; Ez 4:15
that if this * is rebuilt and the Ez 4:16
is being laid in the * walls. Ez 5:8
The God who has chosen the * of Ez 6:12
Jerusalem as a walled * in Judah. Ez 9:9
the elders and judges of his *; Ez 10:14
For the * where my ancestors are Neh 2:3
to rebuild the * of my fathers!" Neh 2:4
and for the * walls, and for a Neh 2:8
So we circled the *, and I Neh 2:14,15
The * officials did not know I Neh 2:16
full well the tragedy of our *; Neh 2:17
Men from the * of Jericho worked Neh 3:2
* of David section of Jerusalem. Neh 3:15
from the plains outside the *. Neh 3:22
*—for the workers worked hard. Neh 4:6
and guarded the * day and night to Neh 4:9
For the * was large, but the Neh 7:4
were scattered throughout the *. Neh 7:4
the leaders of the *, along with Neh 7:5
the Holy *, at this time; Neh 11:1
the castle to the old * of David; Neh 12:37
evil days upon us and upon our *? Neh 13:18
the gates of the * be shut as Neh 13:19
proclaimed in the * of Shushan. Est 3:15
* fell into confusion and panic. Est 3:15
went out into the *, crying with a Est 4:1
So Hathach went out to the * Est 4:6
the streets of the *, shouting, Est 6:11
king through the * streets filled Est 8:15
And in every * and province, as Est 8:17
bones of the dying cry from the *; Job 24:12
I went out to the * gate and took Job 29:7
The highest officials of the * Job 29:10
For they hate the noise of the * Job 39:7
him in Jerusalem, my holy *." Ps 2:6
of the * and murder passersby. Ps 10:8
through the * of our God—the sacred Ps 46:4
God himself is living in that *; Ps 46:5
Mount Zion rising north of the * Ps 48:2
arrived together to inspect the *. Ps 48:4
city's glory—the * of our God, the Ps 48:8
Go, inspect the *! Ps 48:12
violence and strife in the *." Ps 55:9f
entrenched in the heart of the *. Ps 55:10
around like dogs that prowl the *. Ps 59:6
and prowl the * all night before Ps 59:14,15
awful ruins of the *, and see what Ps 74:3
the * of God, the city he loves Ps 87:1
the city of God, the * he loves Ps 87:1
O * of God, what wondrous tales Ps 87:3
gods will personally bless this *. Ps 87:5
free the * of God from their grip. Ps 101:8
were sung throughout the *; Ps 102:21,22
here inside the crowded *. Ps 122:2,3
court beside the * gates, deciding Ps 122:5
May all who love this * prosper. Ps 122:6
Unless the Lord protects a *, Ps 127:1
I will make this * prosperous Ps 132:15
he who invades and sacks your *." Ps 137:9f
She is standing at the * gates Pro 8:1
in the *, "Come, you simple ones Pro 9:3
corners of the *, whispering to Pro 9:14
The whole * celebrates a good Pro 11:10
citizens causes a * to prosper, but Pro 11:11
than to capture a fortified *. Pro 18:19
as a * with broken-down walls. Pro 25:28
in the very * where they had Ecc 8:9,10
There was a small * with only a Ecc 9:14
There was in the * a wise man, Ecc 9:15
save the *, and so it was rescued. Ecc 9:15
Literally, "for a trip to the * Ecc 10:15f
look down on me, you * girls, Sol 1:6
the streets of the * and the roads Sol 3:2
Once "The * of Fair Play," but Is 1:21
Then your * shall again be called Is 1:26
be called "The * of Justice," and Is 1:26
But it was not taken; the * Is 7:1
Fear strikes the * of Ramah; Is 10:28,29
all the people of Gibeah—the * of Is 10:28,29
* reflect upon your pallid faces. Is 13:8
It is no longer a *—it has become Is 17:1

(CITY Con't)
against neighbor, * against city, Is 19:2
*, province against province. Is 19:2
Heliopolis, "The * of the Sun." Is 19:18
the Philistine * of Ashdod and Is 20:1
when Cyrus captured the *. Is 21:5f
* wall to shout out what he sees. Is 21:6,7
the attack. The * fell to the Medes Is 21:6,7f
The whole * is in terrible Is 22:2
the trouble in this busy, happy *? Is 22:2
Between the * walls, you build a Is 22:9,10,11
*, to destroy its strength. Is 23:11
* will come back to life again; Is 23:15,16
The * lies in chaos; Is 24:10
the land. The * is left in ruins; Is 24:12
"Our * is strong! Is 26:1
brings the haughty * to the dust; Is 26:5
* munching on twigs and branches. Is 27:10
WOE TO THE * of Samaria, Is 28:1
The proud * of Samaria—yes, the Is 28:3
the * of David. Is 29:1
will defend the * and deliver it. Is 31:4,5
they will get from your fallen *. Is 33:18
worshiped, a * quiet and unmoved. Is 33:20
out of the * to meet with him. Is 36:3
surrender, this * will be put under Is 36:12
is delivering this * from the king Is 37:30
not enter this *, says the Lord. Is 37:34
He will deliver you and this * Is 38:6
* gates of brass and iron bars. Is 45:2
He shall restore my * and free my Is 45:13
living in the Holy * and brag about Is 48:1
beautiful clothes, O Zion, Holy *; Is 52:1
They will call Jerusalem "The * Is 60:14
and "The * God Has Blessed." Is 62:12
Edom, from the * of Bozrah, with Is 63:1
is all the commotion in the *? Is 66:6
the gates of the * and all along Jer 1:15
You are strong like a fortified * Jer 1:18
you, and the whole * of Jerusalem Jer 3:17
just one, I'll not destroy the *! Jer 5:1
up camp around the *, and divide Jer 6:3
This is the * to be punished, for Jer 6:6
Go to Shiloh, the * I first Jer 7:12
streets—go from * to city Jer 11:6
from city to * throughout the land Jer 11:6
The men of the * of Anathoth shall Jer 11:21,22
army against a high * wall. Jer 15:20
For the children born in this *, Jer 16:3
and this * shall remain forever. Jer 17:25
by the east gate of the *. Jer 19:1
lay siege to the * until all food Jer 19:9
bring upon this * and her Jer 19:15
All the famed treasures of the *, Jer 20:5
of the *, mocked by all. Jer 20:7
the heart of this *, and I myself Jer 21:3,4
plague on this *, and both men and Jer 21:6
left in the * into the hands of Jer 21:7
I have set my face against this *; Jer 21:10
I will fight against this * of Jer 21:13
the ruins of this * and say to one Jer 22:8
Why did he destroy such a great * Jer 22:8
* I gave to you and your fathers. Jer 23:38,39
has prophesied against this *." Jer 26:11
against this Temple and this *. Jer 26:12
you and upon this * and upon every Jer 26:15
field and this * of Jerusalem razed Jer 26:18
denouncing the * and the nation at Jer 26:20
this whole * will be destroyed. Jer 27:17
And * dwellers and farmers and Jer 31:24
And the entire * including the Jer 31:40
Gate on the east side of the *; Jer 31:40
prophesy that the * would be Jer 32:3
built against the * walls, and the Jer 32:24
* by sword, famine and disease. Jer 32:24
* will belong to our enemies." Jer 32:25
Yes, I will give this * to the Jer 32:28
set fire to the * and burn down all Jer 32:29
From the time this * was built Jer 32:31
concerning this * that it will fall Jer 32:36
back to this very *, and make them Jer 32:37
the houses of this *, and the Jer 33:4
the men of this * are already as Jer 33:5
Then this * will be an honor to Jer 33:9
man and animal and * is doomed—will Jer 33:12
I will give this * to the king of Jer 34:2
from the * for a little while. Jer 34:21
it and capture this * and burn it. Jer 34:22
Nebuchadnezzar captured the *. Jer 37:1f
the besieged * of Jerusalem, the Jer 37:5
this * and burn it to the ground. Jer 37:8
you and put this * to the torch!" Jer 37:10
to leave the * to go to the land of Jer 37:12
he took Jeremiah before the * Jer 37:14
as there was any left in the *. Jer 37:21
and that the * of Jerusalem would Jer 38:3
all the bread in the * is gone." Jer 38:9
live and the * will not be burned. Jer 38:17
to surrender, this * shall be set Jer 38:18
and this * will be burned." Jer 38:23
before all the * officials came to Jer 38:27
the wall, and the * fell, and all Jer 39:2
realized that the * was lost, they Jer 39:4
and tore down the walls of the *. Jer 39:8
to this * everything I threatened; Jer 39:16
Settle in any * you wish and live Jer 40:10
Ishmael went out from the * to Jer 41:6
all inside the *, Ishmael and his Jer 41:7
in Egypt at the * of Tahpanhes, for Jer 43:7
standing in the * of Heliopolis, Jer 43:13
of Egypt, for the * of Memphis Jer 46:19
of Gaza, before the * was captured Jer 47:1
For the * of Ashkelon and those Jer 47:7
Woe to the * of Nebo, for it shall Jer 48:1
lie in ruins. The * of Kiriathaim Jer 48:1
of terror rise from the * below. Jer 48:5
by destroying your * of Rabbah. Jer 49:2
caravan * at the time of Jeremiah Jer 49:8f
O famous *, city of joy, how you Jer 49:25
O famous city, * of joy, how you Jer 49:25
* north of the Sea of Galilee; Jer 49:30f
surround the * so that none can Jer 50:29
Therefore this * of Babylon shall Jer 50:39
This complete destruction of the * Jer 51:26f
and broken down the * gates. Jer 51:30
this great * and all her idols; Jer 51:47
laid siege to the * for two years. Jer 52:5
the famine in the * was very Jer 52:6
the people in the * tore a hole in Jer 52:7
tore a hole in the * wall and all Jer 52:7
fled from the * during the night, Jer 52:7
gardens (for the * was surrounded Jer 52:7
was staying in the * of Riblah in Jer 52:9
tearing down the walls of the *. Jer 52:14
discovered in the *, and the Jer 52:24,25
Temple feasts; the * gates are Lam 1:4
* as grapes in a winepress. Lam 1:15
the fairest * of Israel lies in Lam 2:1
say, "Is this the * called 'Most Lam 2:15
the * by shedding innocent blood. Lam 4:13
men sit no longer in the * gates; Lam 5:14
a map of the * of Jerusalem on it. Eze 4:1
built against the *, and enemy Eze 4:1
and the * like a wall of iron. Eze 4:3
those to whom I have given the *! Eze 9:1
him through the * and kill everyone Eze 9:5
And they went out through the * Eze 9:7
and scatter them over the *." Eze 10:2
men of the *, including two Eze 11:1
counsel being given out in this *. Eze 11:1
Jerusalem, for our * is an iron Eze 11:3
Literally, "this * the caldron Eze 11:3f
think this * is an iron shield? Eze 11:7
No, this * will not be an iron Eze 11:11
rose from over the * and stood Eze 11:23
Dig a tunnel through the * wall Eze 12:5
it into a * filled with merchants. Eze 17:3,4
remaining in the * will be Eze 17:21
Jerusalem as the * of Murder. Eze 22:2
terrible deeds. * of Murder, Eze 22:3
doomed and damned—* of Idols, Eze 22:3
mock you, a * of infamous rebels. Eze 22:5
Woe to Jerusalem, * of Murderers; Eze 24:6
"Woe to Jerusalem, * of Eze 24:9
And I will turn the * of Rabbah Eze 25:5
* shall perish by the sword. Eze 26:6
your mainland * by building a siege Eze 26:8
will choke the * with dust, and Eze 26:10
will occupy every street in the *; Eze 26:11
'O mighty island *, with your naval Eze 26:17
of long ago. Your * will lie in Eze 26:20
"O mighty seaport *, merchant Eze 27:3
beautiful * in all the world.' Eze 27:3
such a wondrous * as Tyre, Eze 27:32
"Son of dust, look toward the * Eze 28:21
to tell me, "The * has fallen!" Eze 33:21
A * named 'Multitude' is there! Eze 39:15,16
appeared to be a * opposite me. Eze 40:2
when he came to destroy the *. Eze 43:3
miles for a * open to everyone in Eze 45:6
each side of the holy lands and *; Eze 45:7
and parks, with a * in the center. Eze 48:15
* itself is to be 1½ miles square. Eze 48:16
surround the * for approximately Eze 48:17
Outside the *, stretching east Eze 48:18
to the *, for public use. Eze 48:18
working in the *, no matter where Eze 48:19
sacred lands and * lands—is 8 Eze 48:20
side of the sacred and * lands. Eze 48:21,22
"Each * gate will be named in Eze 48:30,31
of the * is six miles. Eze 48:35
And the name of the * will be Eze 48:35
the city will be 'The * of God.' Eze 48:35
this beautiful * as my royal Dan 4:30
entered the * and began reigning Dan 5:31
your own *, your holy mountain. Dan 9:16
your * lies in ruins for our sins. Dan 9:16
how your * lies in ruins—for Dan 9:18
and your * bear your name." Dan 9:19
will destroy the * and the Temple. Dan 9:26
to a fortified * of Egypt and Dan 11:15
Gilead is a * of sinners, Hos 6:8
Baal-peor, the god of Peor, a * of Hos 9:10
They swarm upon the *; Joe 2:9
I sent rain on one *, but not Amo 4:7
of water to a * that had rain, but Amo 4:8
For the Lord God says, "The * Amo 5:3
will return. The * that sends a Amo 5:3
I will turn over this * and Amo 6:8
prostitute in this *, and your sons Amo 7:17
They will be carried out of the * Amo 8:3
I will rebuild the * of David, Amo 9:11
Petra, the * hewn from rocks; Ob 1:1f
"Go to the great * of Nineveh, Jon 1:2
"Go to that great *, Nineveh," he Jon 3:1
Now Nineveh was a very large *, Jon 3:3
between the * proper—the walls of Jon 3:3f
Jonah entered the * and began to Jon 3:4,5
throughout the *: "Let no one, not Jon 3:7
on the east side of the *, and he Jon 4:5
if anything would happen to the *. Jon 4:5
sorry for a great * like Nineveh Jon 4:11
Therefore the entire * of Samaria Mic 1:6
Woe to the * of Gath. Mic 1:10
this * and live in the fields; Mic 4:10
Soon the * is an empty shambles; Nah 2:10
and filled your * and your homes Nah 2:12
WOE TO NINEVEH, * of Blood, full Nah 3:1
The beautiful and faithless *, Nah 3:4
stars, filled your * with vast Nah 3:16
of the hill where the * is built. Zep 1:10
That once proud * will become a Zep 2:14
vast, prosperous * that lived in Zep 2:15
there is no * as great as I." Zep 2:15
vast an empire, a * of sixty miles Zep 2:15f
WOE TO FILTHY, sinful Jerusalem, * Zep 3:1
the *, and he does no wrong. Zep 3:5
Many will live outside the * Zec 2:4
he will be the glory of the *. Zec 2:5
The Jews of the * of Bethel had Zec 7:2
'The Faithful *,' and 'The Holy Zec 8:3
if you left the *, there was no Zec 8:10
"Foreigners will take over the * Zec 9:6
the rich * of the Philistines. Zec 9:6
Jerusalem; the * will be taken, the Zec 14:1
be left in what remains of the *. Zec 14:1
will reach across to the * gate. Zec 14:5
You are the world's light—a * on Mt 5:14
to the nearest * with the story of Mt 8:33
Literally, "his own *." Mt 9:1f
Whenever you enter a * or Mt 10:11
if not, keep the blessing. Any * Mt 10:14
in one *, flee to the next! Mt 10:23
face, into every * and place where Mt 11:1f
ends in ruin. A * or home divided Mt 12:25
throughout the *, and soon people Mt 14:35
disciples left the * of Jericho, a Mt 20:29
The entire * of Jerusalem was Mt 21:10
the murderers and burned their *. Mt 22:7
hound them from * to city, so that Mt 23:34
them from city to *, so that you Mt 23:34
"O Jerusalem, Jerusalem, the * Mt 23:37
The * gates were closed on the Mt 24:20f
He replied, "Go into the * and Mt 26:18
the way into the *, some of the Mt 28:11
from all over the * of Capernaum Mk 1:32,33
publicly enter a * anywhere, but Mk 1:45
spread quickly through the *. Mk 2:1
evening as usual they left the *. Mk 11:19
on ahead into the * and found Mk 14:16
Literally, "in the * of David." Lk 2:11f
hill on which the * was built, to Lk 4:29
to Capernaum, a * in Galilee, and Lk 4:31
went back into the * of Capernaum. Lk 7:1
a man from the * of Gadara came to Lk 8:27
*, spreading the news as they ran. Lk 8:34
So he went all through the * Lk 8:39
them toward the * of Bethsaida. Lk 9:10
than such a * on the Judgment Day. Lk 10:12
He went from * to city and Lk 13:22
He went from city to * and Lk 13:22
"O Jerusalem, Jerusalem! The * Lk 13:34
the prophets. The * that stones Lk 13:34
and alleys of the * and to invite Lk 14:21
"There was a * judge," he said, Lk 18:2
A widow of that * came to him Lk 18:3
saw the * ahead, he began to cry. Lk 19:41
the * must not attempt to return. Lk 21:21
Literally, "the *." Lk 22:10f
They went off to the * and found Lk 22:13
Court, from the * of Arimathea in Lk 23:50,51,52
wait here in the * until. . . ." Lk 24:49f
yet—stay here in the * until the Lk 24:49
a man in the * of Capernaum, a Jn 4:46,47
Inside the *, near the Sheep Jn 5:2
swept through the *, and a huge Jn 12:12
taken out of the *, carrying his Jn 19:17
was crucified was near the *; Jn 19:20
The whole * was favorable to Act 2:47
is happening here in this * today! Act 4:27
Literally, "Haran," a * in the Act 7:2f
him out of the * to stone him. Act 7:58
went to the * of Samaria and told Act 8:5

(CITY Con't)
so there was much joy in that *! Act 8:8
there and in every * along the way, Act 8:40
Now get up and go into the * and Act 9:6
the gates of the * day and night Act 9:24
through an opening in the * wall! Act 9:25
In the * of Joppa there was a Act 9:36
were nearing the *, Peter went up Act 10:9,10
a * in the province of Pisidia. Act 13:14
almost the entire * turned out to Act 13:44
leaders of the * and incited a mob Act 13:50
and went on to the * of Iconium. Act 13:51
But the people of the * were Act 14:4
outskirts of the *, brought them Act 14:13
at the * gates before the crowds. Act 14:13
him out of the *, apparently dead. Act 14:19
got up and went back into the *! Act 14:20
them out of the * the delegates Act 15:3
in every * on every Sabbath for Act 15:21
* where they had preached before, Act 15:36
and visit every * wherein we Act 15:36f
Then they went from * to city, Act 16:4
Then they went from city to *, Act 16:4
Mysia province to the * of Troas. Act 16:8
way outside the * to a river bank Act 16:13
"These Jews are corrupting our * Act 16:20,21
and pled with them to leave the *. Act 16:39
many important women of the *. Act 17:4
to the * Council for punishment. Act 17:5
disturbing our *," they shouted, Act 17:6
The people of the *, as well as Act 17:8,9
saw everywhere throughout the *. Act 17:16
a member of the * Council, and a Act 17:34
Many people here in this * belong Act 18:10
Paul stayed in the * several days Act 18:18
descended on the *, and the name of Act 19:17
the * was filled with confusion. Act 19:29
at the regular * Council meetings; Act 19:39
has told me in * after city that Act 20:23
me in city after * that jail and Act 20:23
(For down in the * earlier Act 21:29
The whole population of the * was Act 21:30
in Tarsus, a * in Cilicia, but Act 22:3
or on the streets of any *; Act 24:12
*, Festus ordered Paul brought in. Act 25:23
Fair Havens, near the * of Lasea. Act 27:7,8
Erastus, the * treasurer, sends Rom 16:23
Well, when I got as far as the * 2Co 2:12
guards at the * gates to catch me; 2Co 11:32
in the * wall, and so I got away! 2Co 11:33
came back to the * of Damascus. Gal 1:17
Christians in the * of Philippi. Php 1:1
people—in the * of Colosse. Col 1:2
Epaphras, from your *, a servant Col 4:12
in every * who would follow the Tit 1:5
MELCHIZEDEK WAS king of the * Heb 7:1
*, Salem, which means "Peace." Heb 7:2
strong heavenly * whose designer Heb 11:10
he has made a heavenly * for them. Heb 11:16
the others in her * when they Heb 11:31
Mount Zion, to the * of the living Heb 12:22
animals were burned outside the *. Heb 13:11
died outside the *, where his blood Heb 13:12
to him beyond the * walls [that is, Heb 13:13
you live in the * where Satan's Rev 2:13
a citizen in the * of my God—the Rev 3:12
They will trample the Holy * for Rev 11:2
of Jerusalem (the * fittingly Rev 11:8,9
of the *, leaving 7,000 dead. Rev 11:13
fallen—that great *—because she Rev 14:8
outside the *, and blood flowed out Rev 14:20
The great * of "Babylon" split Rev 16:19
seven heads represent a certain * Rev 17:9
the great * that rules over the Rev 17:18
"Alas, Babylon, that mighty *! Rev 18:10
"Alas, that great *, so Rev 18:16
all the wealth of the * is gone!" Rev 18:17
is there another * such as this?" Rev 18:18
"Alas, alas, for that great *! Rev 18:19
that great *, shall be thrown away Rev 18:21
and the beloved * of Jerusalem Rev 20:9
And I, John, saw the Holy *, the Rev 21:2
that wondrous *, the holy Rev 21:10
the * and its gates and walls. Rev 21:15
The * itself was pure, Rev 21:18,19,20
No temple could be seen in the *, Rev 21:22
And the * has no need of sun or Rev 21:23
There shall be nothing in the * Rev 22:3
the gates of the *, and to eat the Rev 22:14
"Outside the * are those who Rev 22:15

CITY'S
We have heard of the * glory—the Ps 48:8
and to gang up at the * brothels. Jer 5:7
picture of the * history, and does Jer 51:26f
who survived the * destruction, and Jer 52:15

CIVIC
them to the * leaders of Jezreel, 1Ki 21:8
chamber with the other * leaders. Pro 31:23
women and the * leaders of the city Act 13:50

CIVIL
of final appeal in all * cases; 2Ch 19:11
Israel's * government will be in Is 3:8
Then there will be a time of * Jer 51:46
filled with * war is doomed; Lk 11:17

CIVILIAN
Jehoiachin was given * clothing 2Ki 25:29

CIVILIANS
Then a posse of * killed all the 2Ki 21:24
yes, and the * too, both old and Jer 51:22

CIVILIZATION
having been driven from *. Job 30:5
of no name, outcasts of *. Job 30:8

CIVILIZED
to * people and uncivilized alike; Rom 1:14

CLAIM
and to settle any * against me Gen 20:16
out if you are what you * to be. Gen 42:33
both of you * the living child, and 1Ki 3:23
to swear to the truth of his *. 1Ki 18:10
went down to the vineyard to * it. 1Ki 21:16
this Temple and * you as our God, 2Ch 6:26
Yes, let the darkness * it for Job 3:5
* you are pure in the eyes of God! Job 11:4
pure and righteous as you * to be? Job 15:14
Can anyone * otherwise? Job 24:25
Who can prove me a liar and * Job 24:25
before God and * to be righteous? Job 25:4
right for you to *, 'I haven't Job 35:2,3
* that's made for them is false?" Ps 4:2
they will * I never warned them. Is 30:9
All who * me as their God will Is 43:7
* that they have made a god. Is 44:11
* that you yourself are Jehovah. Is 47:10
in you and will * you as his own. Is 62:4
people's ways and * me as their God Jer 12:16
yet they * to speak for me; Jer 23:21
messages they * are from God, when Eze 22:28
says: Because you * that you are as Eze 28:6
is deep, for they * their power is Hab 1:11
And you * this isn't evil? Mal 1:8
And if, as you *, I am casting Mt 12:27
came to test Jesus' * of being Mt 16:1
us whether you * to be the Messiah, Mt 26:63
a farce, for they * that God Mk 7:6,7
"Why do your religious teachers * Mk 12:35
prove his * of being the Messiah. Lk 11:16
They all shouted, "Then you * Lk 22:70
* it is here [at Mount Gerazim Jn 4:20
But it is my Father—and you * him Jn 8:54
you * to know what you are doing. Jn 9:41
treason, for they * another king, Act 17:7
Yet some * that this is what I Rom 3:8
So if you still * that God's Rom 4:14
Can't I * the same privilege the 1Co 9:4
meeting people who * to speak 1Co 12:3
through those who * to be giving 1Co 12:10
You who * to have the gift of 1Co 14:37
to be what we * by our wholesome 2Co 6:6
Yet if anyone can * the power and 2Co 10:7
you—but I shall make good every *. 2Co 10:8
too far when we * authority over 2Co 10:14
we were trying to * credit for the 2Co 10:15
and from men who * to be brothers 2Co 11:26
These proud men (though they * to Col 2:18
Such persons * they know God, Tit 1:16
DEAR BROTHERS, HOW can you * Jas 2:1
If we * we have not sinned, we 1Jn 1:10

CLAIMED
the local shepherds came and * it. Gen 26:20
men and animals; I * them for Num 8:17
Then each man except Aaron * his Num 17:9
The rocks they * to be their Deu 32:37
and the Jordan was his, he *. Ju 11:13
the entire area * by Egypt—all of 2Ki 24:7
Can you deny that you have * to Eze 13:7
sneered at you and * your ancient Eze 36:2
your Helper, as you have * he is. Amo 5:14
still others * he was a new Mk 6:15
or not he * to be the Messiah. Lk 22:67,68
whether he * to be the Messiah. Jn 1:19
he * to be the Bread from heaven. Jn 6:41
am the one I have always * to be. Jn 8:25
When you * this was the full Act 5:3
Elijah * that he was the only one Rom 11:2,3

CLAIMING
have been falsely * her menstrual Gen 31:35f
forward, * that we must obey you, Num 16:3
If anyone gives false witness, * Deu 19:16
shameful things, * that she was not Deu 22:17,18
that Adonijah was * sanctuary in 1Ki 1:51
longer, and stop * my promises, Ps 50:16
him as a traitor, * he was Jer 37:13
own visions and * to have messages Eze 13:2,3
For they were lying prophets, * Eze 13:16
as he pleases, * to be greater than Dan 11:36
him costly gifts! * his help he Dan 11:39
For many will come * to be the Mt 24:5
by * he is our Messiah—a King." Lk 23:2
and John were * that Jesus had Act 4:2
money, * it was the full price. Act 5:2
to lie about him, * they had heard Act 6:11
and confused. * themselves to be Rom 1:22
of God, * that he himself is God. 2Th 2:4
causes of Satan while * to be mine Rev 3:9

CLAIMS
he is a God who * absolute loyalty Ex 34:14
you, or one who * to foretell the Deu 13:1
But any prophet who falsely * Deu 18:20
And any prophet who * to give a Deu 18:20
and drop your * against them." Neh 5:11
the wall. He * you plan to be their Neh 6:5,6
"Is this the one who * the Lord Ps 22:8
the wisdom he * he is looking for, Pro 14:6
Can your idols make such * as Is 41:21
Their * of doom will fall upon Jer 5:13
any madman who * to be a prophet, Jer 29:26
My soul * the Lord as my Lam 3:24
orchards—gifts she * her lovers Hos 1:12
"When I make * about myself they Jn 5:31
is making these * for me too. Jn 5:32,33
Jesus told them, "These * are Jn 8:14
with anyone who * to be a brother 1Co 5:11
examined the * of those who say Rev 2:2

CLAMBERED
So they * up on their hands and 1Sa 14:13

CLAMOR
oceans and all the world's *. Ps 65:7
So a great * arose. Act 23:9

CLAMPED
and * down the heavy lid again. Zec 5:8
and * their feet into the stocks. Act 16:24

CLAMPS
doors in the gates and for the *; 1Ch 22:3

CLAN
our * will not come to an end." Gen 19:32
as listed here:The * of Teman,The Gen 36:15,16
clan of Teman,The * of Omar,The Gen 36:15,16
clan of Omar,The * of Zepho,The Gen 36:15,16
clan of Zepho,The * of Kenaz,The Gen 36:15,16
clan of Kenaz,The * of Korah,The Gen 36:15,16
* of Gatam,The clan of Amalek. Gen 36:15,16
clan of Gatam,The * of Amalek. Gen 36:15,16
in Canaan:The * of Nahath,The clan Gen 36:17
clan of Nahath,The * of Zerah,The Gen 36:17
* of Shammah,The clan of Mizzah. Gen 36:17
clan of Shammah,The * of Mizzah. Gen 36:17
of Anah):The * of Jeush,The clan of Gen 36:18,19
* of Jalam,The clan of Korah. Gen 36:18,19
clan of Jalam,The * of Korah. Gen 36:18,19
themselves:The * of Timna,The clan Gen 36:40-43
clan of Timna,The * of Alvah,The Gen 36:40-43
clan of Alvah,The * of Jetheth,The Gen 36:40-43
of Jetheth,The * of Oholibamah,The Gen 36:40-43
of Oholibamah,The * of Elah,The Gen 36:40-43
clan of Elah,The * of Pinon,The Gen 36:40-43
clan of Pinon,The * of Kenaz,The Gen 36:40-43
clan of Kenaz,The * of Teman,The Gen 36:40-43
clan of Teman,The * of Mibzar,The Gen 36:40-43
* of Magdiel,The clan of Iram. Gen 36:40-43
clan of Magdiel,The * of Iram. Gen 36:40-43
families within the * of Korah. Ex 6:24
Levi, indicating each person's *; Num 3:14,15
Levi's grandsons (* names Num 3:16-24
Levi's grandsons (* names Num 3:25-30
Levi's grandsons (* names Num 3:31-35
the utensils, the * of Kohath shall Num 4:15
and * are able to go to war." Num 26:2
was the following * of Machirites, Num 26:28-37
In this tribe was the * of the Num 26:42,43
Then the * of Machir of the tribe Num 32:39
The men of Jair, another * of Num 32:41
of Gilead (of the * of Machir, of Num 36:1
The * of Jair, of the tribe of Deu 3:14
Then I gave Gilead to the * of Deu 3:15
Lord will point out the guilty *; Jos 7:14
and the * must come by its Jos 7:14
the * of Zerah was singled out. Jos 7:17
Then the families of that * were Jos 7:17
* Machir, who was Manasseh's son. Jos 13:31
The * of Machir (Manasseh's oldest Jos 17:1
ten tribes, and each a * leader. Jos 22:14
the rest of his *, and had been Ju 4:11
Jabin of Hazor and the * of Heber. Ju 4:17
to men outside his *, and brought Ju 12:9,10
mobilize his own * of Bichri at the 2Sa 20:14
he was also the ancestor of the * 1Ch 4:8
of Guni, was the leader of the *. 1Ch 5:15
of the clan. The * lived in and 1Ch 5:16
In the Gershom *: 1Ch 6:19,20,21
In the Kohath *: 1Ch 6:22,23,24
The subclans of the * of Merari 1Ch 6:29,30
Cantor was from the * of Kohath; 1Ch 6:33-38
from the * of Merari, who stood on 1Ch 6:44-47
whom were members of the Kohath *: 1Ch 6:54
The subclans of the Gershom * 1Ch 6:62
given to the * of Gershom by the 1Ch 6:71
the Merari * as Cities of Refuge. 1Ch 6:77
and they were led by their * 1Ch 7:9
of the * of Perez (son of Judah). 1Ch 9:4
Some members of the Kohath * were 1Ch 9:32
each famous in his respective *. 1Ch 12:24-37
120 from the * of Kohath; 1Ch 15:4-10
220 from the * of Merari; 1Ch 15:4-10

(CLAN Con't)
130 from the * of Gershom; 1Ch 15:4-10
Kushaiah) from the * of Merari were 1Ch 15:17
his *, for he had many children. 1Ch 23:17
the Eleazar *, and with Ahimelech, 1Ch 24:3
who represented the Ithamar *; 1Ch 24:3
indicated Joseph of the Asaph *; 1Ch 25:9-31
the Asaph division of the Korah *. 1Ch 26:1
of great authority in their *. 1Ch 26:6,7
subclan from the * of Gershom 1Ch 26:20,21,22
men of the * of the Hebronites, 1Ch 26:31,32
Then the * leaders, the heads of 1Ch 29:6,7
priests and * leaders and judges. 2Ch 19:8
Then the Levites of the Kohath * 2Ch 20:19
clan and the Korah * stood to 2Ch 20:19
the Levites and * leaders about his 2Ch 23:2,3
to each * from Judah and Benjamin. 2Ch 25:5,6
Twenty-six hundred brave * 2Ch 26:12
From the Kohath *, Mahath (son 2Ch 29:12,13,14
From the Merari *, Kish (son of 2Ch 29:12,13,14
From the Gershon *, Joah (son of 2Ch 29:12,13,14
From the Elizaphan *, Shimri and 2Ch 29:12,13,14
From the Asaph *, Zechariah and 2Ch 29:12,13,14
From the Hemanite *, Jehuel and 2Ch 29:12,13,14
From the Jeduthun *, Shemaiah 2Ch 29:12,13,14
Priest from the * of Zadok replied, 2Ch 31:10
The choir members from the * of Ez 2:40,41,42
and his *, rebuilt the altar of the Ez 3:1
From the * of Phinehas—Gershom; Ez 8:2-14
From the * of Ithamar—Daniel; Ez 8:2-14
From the subclan of David of the * Ez 8:2-14
From the * of Parosh—Zechariah, Ez 8:2-14
From the * of Ez 8:2-14
From the * of Shecaniah—the son of Ez 8:2-14
From the * of Adin—Ebed (son of Ez 8:2-14
From the * of Elam—Jeshaiah (son Ez 8:2-14
From the * of Shephatiah—Zebadiah Ez 8:2-14
From the * of Joab—Obadiah (son of Ez 8:2-14
From the * of Bani—Shelomith (son Ez 8:2-14
From the * of Bebai—Zechariah (son Ez 8:2-14
From the * of Azgad—Johanan (son Ez 8:2-14
From the * of Adonikam—Eliphelet, Ez 8:2-14
From the * of Bigvai—Uthai, Ez 8:2-14
of Jehiel of the * of Elam) said to Ez 10:2
Some of the * leaders and I were Ez 10:16-19
From the * of Parosh: Ez 10:25
From the * of Elam: Ez 10:26
From the * of Zattu: Ez 10:27
From the * of Bebai: Ez 10:28
From the * of Bani: Ez 10:29
From the * of Pahath-moab: Ez 10:30
From the * of Harim: Ez 10:31,32
From the * of Hashum: Ez 10:33
From the * of Bani: Ez 10:34-42
From the * of Nebo: Ez 10:43
Next down the line were his * Neh 3:18
of Hodevah of the * of Jeshua, 74; Neh 7:43,44,45
The choir members from the * of Neh 7:43,44,45
The next day the * leaders and Neh 8:13
Talmon, and others of their *. Neh 11:19
* became the Tabernacle singers. Neh 11:22,23
The following were the * leaders Neh 12:12-21
Meraiah, leader of the Seraiah *; Neh 12:12-21
Hananiah, leader of the Jeremiah * Neh 12:12-21
Meshullam, leader of the Ezra *; Neh 12:12-21
Jehohanan, leader of the Amariah * Neh 12:12-21
Jonathan, leader of the Malluchi * Neh 12:12-21
Joseph, leader of the Shebaniah *; Neh 12:12-21
Adna, leader of the Harim *; Neh 12:12-21
Helkai, leader of the Meraioth *; Neh 12:12-21
Zechariah, leader of the Iddo *; Neh 12:12-21
leader of the Ginnethon *; Neh 12:12-21
Zichri, leader of the Abijah *; Neh 12:12-21
Shammu-a, leader of the Bilgah *; Neh 12:12-21
leader of the Shemaiah *; Neh 12:12-21
Mattenai, leader of the Joiarib *; Neh 12:12-21
Uzzi, leader of the Jedaiah *; Neh 12:12-21
Kallai, leader of the Sallai *; Neh 12:12-21
Eber, leader of the Amok *; Neh 12:12-21
Hashabiah, leader of the Hilkiah * Neh 12:12-21
Nethanel, leader of the Jedaiah *. Neh 12:12-21
the Buzite, of the * of Ram) became Job 32:2
family shall multiply into a *; Is 60:22
Israel as a new *: the Philistines Zec 9:7

CLANGING
the cymbals, yes, loud * cymbals. Ps 150:5

CLANS
let a rift develop between our *. Gen 13:8
became the heads of *, as listed Gen 36:15,16
The above * were the descendants Gen 36:15,16
The following * were the Gen 36:17
And these are the * named after Gen 36:18,19
* of the various tribes of Israel: Ex 6:14
The heads of the * of the tribe Ex 6:15
the heads of the * of the tribe of Ex 6:16
were:Libni, Shime-i,(and their *). Ex 6:17
the heads of the * of the Levites, Ex 6:25
and the families within the *. Ex 6:25
The responsibility of these two * Num 3:25-30
The responsibility of these four * Num 3:31-35
The responsibility of these two * Num 3:36,37
*, named after Reuben's sons: Num 26:5-11
In this tribe were the following * Num 26:12-14
In this tribe were the following * Num 26:15-18
In this tribe were the following * Num 26:19-22
In this tribe were the following * Num 26:23-25
In this tribe were the following * Num 26:26,27
the following *, named after the Num 26:28-37
In this tribe were the following * Num 26:38-41
In this tribe were the following * Num 26:44-47
In this tribe were the following * Num 26:48-50
These are the * of the Levites Num 26:57
And that tribe must come by its * Jos 7:14
Then he brought the * of Judah, Jos 7:17
was given to the * of Abiezer, Jos 17:2
before the Lord by tribes and *." 1Sa 10:18,19
of the tribes and *—to observe the 1Ki 8:1
The * named after the sons of 1Ch 1:11,12
were known as the Zorathite *. 1Ch 4:2
The * of Cozeba, 1Ch 4:21-22
These * were noted for their 1Ch 4:23
princes of wealthy * who traveled 1Ch 4:34-39
His relatives became heads of * 1Ch 5:7,8
heads of the seven *, were Michael, 1Ch 5:13
The chiefs of their * were the 1Ch 5:24
from all the * of the tribe of 1Ch 7:5
"You are the leaders of the * of 1Ch 15:12
the names of these * and subclans; 1Ch 23:24
of Levi in their various *. 1Ch 24:30
from the * of Korah and Merari. 1Ch 26:19
of the tribes and *—for the 2Ch 5:2
the Levite * that King David had. 2Ch 23:18
the gifts to the * of priests in 2Ch 31:14,15
register by *, and the Levites 2Ch 31:17,18
assist particular * of the people 2Ch 35:4,5
From the * of Shallum, (all of Neh 7:43,44,45
the Modiah and Miniamin * Neh 12:12-21
the heads of the * of the priests Neh 12:22
"And the * of Judah shall say to Zec 12:5
"In that day I will make the * Zec 12:6

CLANSMEN
Hashabiah and 1,700 of his * 1Ch 26:30
*, helped them during the service. Neh 12:9

CLAP
COME, EVERYONE, AND * for joy! Ps 47:1
Let the waves * their hands in Ps 98:8,9
Literally, "* your hands and Eze 6:11f
"Prophesy to them in this way: * Eze 21:14
All who hear your fate will * Nah 3:19

CLAPPED
Then everyone * and shouted, 2Ki 11:12
says: Because you * and stamped and Eze 25:6

CLAPPING
And you have prophesied with * Eze 21:17

CLARIFY
of God, you are to * the evidence 2Ch 19:10

CLASHING
obbligatos, the * of cymbals, and 2Ch 5:13,14

CLASPS
Then make fifty golden * to Ex 26:6
them together with fifty bronze *. Ex 26:10,11
at the bottom and top with *. Ex 26:24
* on the shoulder of the ephod. Ex 28:13,14
and its coverings, *, frames, bars, Ex 35:10-19
Then fifty * of gold were made Ex 36:13
fifty small bronze * to couple the Ex 36:18
Each frame had two * joining it Ex 36:22
connected to its base by two *. Ex 36:24
attached to gold * on the top Ex 39:15-18
Furniture; *; Ex 39:33-40

CLASSES
their home Bible *, they continued Act 5:42

CLASSIFICATION
the Levites—a job * of Temple Ez 8:20

CLASSIFIED
of Shem, * according to their Gen 10:31
old or older were * under the names 1Ch 23:24
and he collected proverbs and * Ecc 12:9

CLATTER
army hear the * of speeding 2Ki 7:6
make his sword * to the ground. Eze 30:22

CLATTERING
Hear the * hoofs and rumbling Jer 47:3
and chariots * as they bump wildly Nah 3:2

CLAUDA
small island named *, where with Act 27:16

CLAUDIA
Linus, *, and all the others. 2Ti 4:21

CLAUDIUS
fulfilled during the reign of *. Act 11:28
as a result of * Caesar's order to Act 18:2,3
"From: * Lysias Act 23:26

CLAUSE
This * appears in some versions, Gen 27:38f
This * is not included in some of Lk 8:43,44f

CLAWS
The Lord who saved me from the * 1Sa 17:37
torn me with his *, and left me Lam 3:11
and his nails were like birds' *. Dan 4:33
teeth and brass * that tore men Dan 7:19

CLAY
soil," or, "from a clod of *." Gen 2:7f
Then the * pot in which the Lev 6:2
animal touches any * oven, it is Lev 11:3
holy water in a * jar and mix into Num 5:1
collected all the * jars and Ju 7:8,
and a * jar with a torch in it. Ju 7:1
and broke their * jars so that Ju 7:19,2
of God is as fragile as a * vase! Job 13:1
I, too, am made of common *. Job 33:
smash them like * pots!" Ps 2:
has dried up like sun-baked *; Ps 22:1
glaze covers a common * pot. Pro 26:2
tread them as a potter tramples *. Is 41:2
Does the * dispute with him who Is 45:
We are the * and you are the Is 64:8
Go down to the shop where * pots Jer 18:2
as this potter has done to his *? Jer 18:6
As the * is in the potter's hand, Jer 18:6
THE LORD SAID, Buy a * jar and Jer 19:1
its feet part iron and part *. Dan 2:33
iron and *, smashing them to bits. Dan 2:34
iron, *, brass, silver, and gold; Dan 2:35
iron and part *—show that later on, Dan 2:41,42
as iron, and some as weak as *. Dan 2:41,42
This mixture of iron with * also Dan 2:43
succeed, for iron and * don't mix. Dan 2:43
the *, the silver, and the gold. Dan 2:45
Go into the pits to trample the * Nah 3:14
field where the * was used by Mt 27:7
being sealed at each end with *. Mt 27:66f
dug through the * roof above his Mk 2:4
makes a jar out of *, doesn't he Rom 9:21
the same lump of * to make one jar Rom 9:21
well as some made from wood and *. 2Ti 2:20
* that is broken into tiny pieces. Rev 2:27

CLAYBANKS
the casting at the * of the Jordan 2Ch 4:17,18

CLEAN
Literally, "*," i.e. Gen 8:20f
to a ceremonially * place outside Lev 4:11,12
outer garments and * out the ashes Lev 6:10
to a place that is ceremonially *. Lev 6:11
by a person who is ceremonially *. Lev 7:19
is ceremonially * and may be eaten, Lev 11:47
then she will be ceremonially * Lev 12:7
Literally, "he is *." Lev 13:34f
since they stay * even on ordinary 1Sa 21:5
For my hands were *; 2Sa 22:21
For he sees that I am *. 2Sa 22:25
Worship and serve him with a * 1Ch 28:9
of your ancestors—* all the debris 2Ch 29:4,5
and began to * up and sanctify the 2Ch 29:15
took eight days to * up, so the 2Ch 29:17
later he began to * up Judah and 2Ch 34:3
make them utterly *, even so you Job 9:30
the earth can boast that he is *? Job 25:4
and I shall be * again. Ps 51:7
Create in me a new, * heart, O Ps 51:10
with * thoughts and right desires. Ps 51:10
for I will have a * record. Ps 119:6
An empty stable stays *—but there Pro 14:4
Oh, wash yourselves! Be *! Is 1:16
you as * as freshly fallen snow. Is 1:18
of soap or lye can make you *. Jer 2:22
live good, honest, * lives, then Jer 4:2
I will make a * sweep throughout Eze 21:4
I had sprinkled * water on you, for Eze 36:25
for you will be *—your filthiness Eze 36:25
ritually * and ritually unclean." Eze 44:23f
have a * turban on his head?" Zec 3:5,6
finds the man's heart * but empty! Mt 12:43,44,45
and then the whole cup will be *. Mt 23:26
wrapped it in a * linen cloth, and Mt 27:59
former home is all swept and *. Lk 11:25
his feet washed to be entirely *. Jn 13:10
Now you are *—but that isn't true Jn 13:10
he said, "Not all of you are *." Jn 13:11
For God's home is holy and *, and 1Co 3:17
her holy and *, washed by baptism Eph 5:26
and to be inwardly *, no one being Php 1:10
You are to live *, innocent lives Php 2:15
of lust, but to be holy and *. 1Th 4:7
will be * and their faith strong. 1Ti 1:5
your faith, and your * thoughts. 1Ti 4:12
They must be * minded and level Tit 1:8
to be sensible and * minded, Tit 2:5
forgiven and made * by Christ's Heb 10:10
blood to make us *, and because our Heb 10:22
and seek to live a * and holy life, Heb 12:14
bodies are washed * by the water, 1Pe 3:21
your life stays * and true, and 3Jn 1:3
me white garments, * and pure, so Rev 3:18
*, followed him on white horses. Rev 19:14

CLEANED
The priests * up the inner room 2Ch 29:16
the land and * up the situation at 2Ch 34:8
room be thoroughly *, and I brought Neh 13:9

CLEANEST
She is permitted to wear the * Rev 19:8

CLEANSE
If the water used to * the Lev 11:34
In this way you shall * the Lev 15:31

(CLEANSE Con't)
and the water to * him has not been Num 19:20
Therefore, * your sinful hearts Deu 10:16
He will * your hearts and the Deu 30:6
purest water and * my hands with Job 9:30
* me from these hidden faults. Ps 19:12
Oh, wash me, * me from this Ps 51:2
then to * away your sins. Is 47:11
So shall he * Is 52:14,15
be wasted among the thorns. * Jer 4:4
O Jerusalem, * your hearts while Jer 4:14
but it can never * them, for there Jer 6:29
And I will * away all their sins Jer 33:8
And now, because I wanted to * Eze 24:13
I will * away your sins. Eze 36:29
"The Lord God says: When I * you Eze 36:33
This will * and make atonement Eze 43:20
for seven days to * and make Eze 43:26
only refine and * them and make Dan 11:35
a Fountain to * them from all their Zec 13:1
First * the inside of the cup, Mt 23:26
to him so he can * away your sins Act 3:19
He is the one who died to * us Heb 1:3
these failed to * the hearts of the Heb 9:9
young cows could * men's bodies Heb 9:13
him to * our hearts from sin. 1Pe 3:21
us and to * us from every wrong. 1Jn 1:9

CLEANSED
of the man being *, and upon the Lev 14:14
person being * from his leprosy; Lev 14:19
then be pronounced finally *. Lev 14:20
of the man being *, to make Lev 14:29
those who are * of leprosy but are Lev 14:32
*, and declare the leprosy gone. Lev 14:48
In this way the house shall be *. Lev 14:51,52
after that he shall be declared * Lev 17:15
he will then be * from the Num 6:9
and such evil must be * from Deu 22:21
in this way evil will be * from Deu 22:22
not even yet been * despite the Jos 22:17,18
Who can ever say, "I have * my Pro 20:9
them, so that the land will be *. Eze 39:14
And so the land will finally be * Eze 39:15,16
Thus the altar shall be *, as it Eze 43:22
days before he is * and able to Eze 44:26
and so the Temple will be *. Eze 45:20
sin, and their guilt will be *; Dan 9:24
and us, for he * their lives Act 15:9
Go and be baptized, and be * from Act 22:16
whose sins are * away, who are set Act 26:18
Literally, "having * it by Eph 5:26f
own people, with * hearts and real Tit 2:14
everything was * by sprinkling it Heb 9:22
the worshipers would have been * Heb 10:2
souls have been * from selfishness 1Pe 1:22

CLEANSES
Jesus his Son * us from every sin. 1Jn 1:7

CLEANSING
his ceremony of * before the Lord. Lev 14:23
required for the ceremony of *. Lev 14:32
the ceremony of *, using two birds, Lev 14:49
for the house and * it." Lev 14:53
begin a seven-day * ceremony by Lev 15:13
his finger, thus * it from the Lev 16:19
the atonement, * you in the Lord's Lev 16:29,30
from Israel. The * water was not Num 19:13
have completed the * of the Temple 2Ch 29:18
Sprinkle me with the * blood Ps 51:7
When you have finished this * Eze 43:23
of * for pots, pans and dishes. Mk 7:4
of the * of the Temple. Jn 10:22,23f
go through the * ceremony before Jn 11:55
* you by the work of the Holy 2Th 2:13
and treated his * blood as though Heb 10:29
in your hearts, * you with the 1Pe 1:2

CLEAR
or otherwise is not * in the text. Gen 21:9f
The meaning is not *. Ex 12:38f
stones, as * as the heavens. Ex 24:10
I refuse to * the guilty, and Ex 34:7
By executing him you will * out Deu 13:5
a * space between you and the Ark; Jos 3:2,3,4
to do it, you may * out the forest Jos 17:15
able to * it all and live there. Jos 17:16,17,18
It is not * whether he killed her Ju 11:39f
disobedient to his * command, and 1Ki 13:21,22
It is * that these disasters 2Ki 24:3,4
praise that rang out strong and *. 2Ch 20:19
When it was * that Sennacherib 2Ch 32:2
this action would * the people of 2Ch 34:5
My conscience is * for as long as Job 27:6
Your innocence will be * to Ps 37:6
but my choice is *—I love your Ps 119:113
My words are plain and * to Pro 8:9
The Hebrew of this verse is not *. Pro 18:19f
rich people is a * case of selling Pro 28:21
*, well-aged wine and choice beef. Is 25:6
I will say, Rebuild the road! * Is 57:14
It is not * from the Hebrew Is 66:19f
who * a forest of its trees. Jer 46:22,23
* across to Elealeh and to Jahaz; Jer 48:34
be heard * out in the outer court. Eze 10:5
Egypt will be as * and flow as Eze 32:14
area, extending * out to the Eze 48:21,22
* across to the western border. Eze 48:23
I will not * their oppressors of Joe 3:21
large and *, so that anyone can Hab 2:2
Haggai then made his meaning *. Hag 2:14
to Christ, is * from the context. Zec 13:6f
The Greek word is not * on this Mk 1:8f
The Greek word is not * on this Mk 1:8f
only will, you can * me of every Lk 5:12
It is not * whether these were Act 8:2f
When it was * that he wouldn't Act 21:14
a * conscience before God and man. Act 24:16
It is *, then, that God's promise Rom 4:13
can see you are honest * through. Rom 12:17
Jerusalem * over into Illyricum. Rom 15:19
to remain very * about what is Rom 16:19
My conscience is *, but even 1Co 4:4
so it is * to all that it is only 2Co 4:10
Consequently, it is * that no Gal 3:11
Christ's death to * away our sins Gal 5:5
you it will be a * sign from God Php 1:28
certainty and * understanding. Col 2:2
pure, and to keep * of all sexual 1Th 4:3,4
*, doing what you know is right. 1Ti 1:19
Steer * of foolish discussions 2Ti 2:16
to cleanse us and * our record of Heb 1:3
* and we want to keep it that way. Heb 13:18
will be *, even when we stand 1Jn 3:19
consciences are *, we can come to 1Jn 3:21
The inference is not * in the Rev 3:10f
gem, crystal * like jasper. Rev 21:11
Water of Life, * as crystal, Rev 22:1

CLEAR-EYED
it all I remained *, so that I Ecc 2:9

CLEARED
which the Lord had * out of the 2Ki 17:11
situation will be * up and the Ez 10:14
in the * spaces behind the walls. Neh 4:13
the winds have * away the clouds, Job 37:21
sins and God has * their record. Ps 32:1
planted us. You * the ground and Ps 80:9
I did for them! I * the land of the Amo 2:9
on the problem and * it up 2Co 7:11
Son did that God * a path for Col 1:20

CLEARER
of God's laws, the * it becomes Rom 3:20

CLEARING
to wait before * out the people Jos 18:3
"Join us in * out the people Ju 1:3
are counting on * your debt to God Gal 5:4

CLEARLY
you unaware of what you * see! Ex 23:8
so, guide me * along the way you Ex 33:13
Their fatal error is not * Lev 10:1f
the Lord had * instructed his 1Ki 11:2
Thus Solomon did what was * 1Ki 11:6
They sang loudly and * under the Neh 12:42
Tell me * what to do, which way Ps 5:8
the many times I * told you what Is 46:9
so that you could * understand. Is 48:16
against them loudly and *." Eze 11:4
But I can't see them very *; Mk 8:24
he saw everything *, drinking in Mk 8:25
Wasn't it * predicted by the Lk 24:26
For the Scriptures * state that Jn 7:41,42
* that I find him not guilty." Jn 19:4
"Therefore I * state to everyone Act 2:36
healed, let me * state to you and Act 4:10
"I see very * that the Jews are Act 10:34
see everything *, just as clearly 1Co 13:12
clearly, just as * as God sees into 1Co 13:12
unless each note is sounded *. 1Co 14:7
Christ's death as * as though I had Gal 3:1
point out very *, "Cursed is Gal 3:10
you wisdom to see * and really Eph 1:16,17
you always to see * the difference Php 1:10
BUT THE HOLY Spirit tells us * 1Ti 4:1
to impress them so * upon you that 2Pe 1:15

CLEAVES
when one plows and * the earth, our Ps 141:6,7f

CLEFT
put you in the * of the rock and Ex 33:22

CLEFTS
that nest in the * of the rocks. Jer 48:28
of Petra, in the * of the rocks. Jer 49:16

CLEMENCY
and pleading for *, Solomon 1Ki 1:51

CLEMENT
and they worked with *, too, and Php 4:3

CLENCH
You will * your fist against my Ps 138:7
Therefore I will * my fists Jer 15:6

CLENCHES
Armed with his tin shield, he * Job 15:25,26
When the Lord * his fist against Is 31:3

CLEOPAS
And one of them, *, replied, Lk 24:18
the wife of *, and Mary Magdalene. Jn 19:25

CLERGY
soldiers refused to harm the *. 1Sa 22:17

CLEVER
Your words are based on * Job 15:4,5
"He's quite * at 'saving' Mk 15:31
world are more * [in dishonesty! Lk 16:8
humble) have a very * imagination. Col 2:18

CLEVERLY
They speak * to their neighbors Jer 9:8
different, or has * lied to us and Eph 4:14
They will * tell their lies about 2Pe 2:1

CLIENT
beside the road waiting for a *! Jer 3:2

CLIFF
I see them from the * tops, Num 23:7-10
to the top of a * and thrown over, 2Ch 25:12
so close to the edge of the *! Ps 73:2
the edge of the * and down to their Ps 73:18
* badgers: delicate little animals Pro 30:24-28
rocks, behind an outcrop of the *. Sol 2:14
* and drowned in the water below. Mt 8:32
was built, to push him over the *. Lk 4:29
and fell over a * into the lake Lk 8:33

CLIFFS
are the three *), with their Jos 17:11
high upon the * to make her nest? Job 39:27
She lives upon the *, making her Job 39:28
me safely along the top of the *. Ps 18:33
at the tops of the * to try to get Is 2:21
mountains shall be thrown down; * Eze 38:20
in those high, inaccessible *. Ob 1:3

CLIMAX
and reached their *—none of these Eze 7:10,11
then, as a * to all his terrible Dan 9:27
On the last day, the * of the Jn 7:37

CLIMB
from Jericho. * to its heights, and Deu 32:49
"Come on, * right behind me," 1Sa 14:12
Who may * the mountain of the Ps 24:3
I said, I will * up into the Sol 7:8
I will * to the highest heavens Is 14:14
Weeping, they * the upward road Is 15:5
Her refugees will * the hills of Jer 48:5
On the east side are steps to * Eze 43:17
they run upon the walls; they * Joe 2:9
though they * into the heavens, I Amo 9:2
I WILL * my watchtower now, and Hab 2:1

CLIMBED
Moses * the rugged mountain to Ex 19:2,3
was up early and * Mount Sinai, as Ex 34:4
THEN MOSES * from the plains of Deu 34:1
* to the top of the roof to watch. Ju 9:51
he * the hill to the altar. 1Sa 10:13
They * the mountain slope 1Sa 26:13
and wept as they * the mountain. 2Sa 15:30
When the watchman * the stairs to 2Sa 18:24
But Elijah * to the top of Mount 1Ki 18:42
straight ahead and * the stairs Neh 12:37
We * the seven steps into the Eze 40:6
went on board, and * down into the Jon 1:3
SO JESUS * into a boat and went Mt 9:1
And when they had * back into Mt 14:32
and * a hill and sat there. Mt 15:29
Then he * into the boat and Mk 6:51
they moored the boat, and * out. Mk 6:54
So he ran ahead and * into a Lk 19:4
Zacchaeus hurriedly * down and Lk 19:6

CLIMBING
As they were * a hill toward the 1Sa 9:9,10,11
just as Jesus was * from the boat. Mk 5:1
As he was * out of the boat a Lk 8:27
* the hill, looking for him. Jn 6:2-5

CLIMBS
the road * to Gur, near Ibleam. 2Ki 9:27

CLINCH
and hurried to * the matter by 1Ki 20:33

CLING
worship him and * to him and take Deu 10:20
obey only his commands and * to Deu 13:4
to obey him and to * to him, for he Deu 30:20
for your lives. * to him and serve Jos 22:5
Now may those curses return and * Ps 109:19
to do right. I * to your commands Ps 119:31
But still I * to your laws and Ps 119:83
* to wisdom—she will protect Pro 4:6
Israel to * to me, says the Lord. Jer 13:11
"If you * to your life, you will Mt 10:39
They listen to God's words and * Lk 8:15
did not demand and * to his rights Php 2:6
that you would. * tightly to your 1Ti 1:19

CLINGING
all his ways, and * to him, then Deu 11:22
at sea, * to a swaying mast. Pro 23:34

CLINGS
Even as a loincloth * to a man's Jer 13:11
Whoever * to his life shall lose Lk 17:33

CLIP
on your temples or * the edges of Lev 19:27
"The priests shall not * bald Lev 21:5

CLOAK
and gives you his * as security, Deu 24:12,13
Then Elijah folded his * 2Ki 2:8
Then he picked up Elijah's * and 2Ki 2:13,14

(CLOAK Con't)
with an outer * of fine linen and Est 8:15
and wraps up the oceans in his *? Pro 30:4
a shepherd picks fleas from his *! Jer 43:12
and I wrapped my * around you to Eze 16:8

CLOAKS
on the four corners of your *. Deu 22:12
threw their * across its back for Mk 11:7

CLOCK
open around the * to receive the Is 60:11

CLOD
soil," or, "from a * of clay." Gen 2:7f

CLODS
soil," or, "from * in the soil," Gen 2:7f
when everything is dust and *? Job 38:37,38
earth, melting the * and causing Ps 65:10

CLOSE
between our clans. * relatives such Gen 13:8
See, the village is * by and it Gen 19:18,19,20
So Joseph brought the boys * to Gen 48:10
of Ephron the Hethite, * to Mamre. Gen 50:12,13
of the four legs, * to the top; Ex 25:26,27
or herds feed * to the mountain." Ex 34:3
four table legs, * to the molding, Ex 37:14
of the ephod, * to where the ephod Ex 39:20
the tail removed * to the backbone, Lev 3:9,10,11
wall, he shall * up the house for Lev 14:38
daughter—for she is a * relative. Lev 18:10
is a * relative of your mother; Lev 18:13
"Everyone who even comes * to Num 17:12,13
of debt cancellation is * at hand! Deu 15:9
will be reasonably * to everyone; Deu 19:6,7
but they are very * at hand —in Deu 30:14
were about to *, and I don't know Jos 2:5
the river was * to the city of Jos 3:15,16
to hide in ambush * behind the Jos 8:3,4
out—these men were * neighbors. Jos 9:16
so Abimelech felt * kinship there. Ju 9:2f
come back and stay * behind his Ru 2:21
kind to us, and is a * relative. Ru 3:2
law, for you are my * relative." Ru 3:9
It's true that I am a * relative, Ru 3:12
But Jonathan, because of his * 1Sa 19:1
As Saul and his men began to * 1Sa 23:26
Uriah to a spot * to the besieged 2Sa 11:16
the troops go so * to the city? 2Sa 11:19,20,21
will all * ranks behind you." 2Sa 16:21
who had been * to him in any way. 2Ki 10:11
him were as * to God as he was. 2Ki 18:5
He and his * relatives the 1Ch 9:19
But at the * of his life, 2Ch 20:35
sunrise, and to * and lock them Neh 7:3
to understand paid * attention. Neh 8:1
fear—his enemy is * behind him! Job 18:11
They * in upon me and are ready Ps 17:11
I kept * watch on all his laws; Ps 18:22
for you are * beside me, guarding, Ps 23:4
The Lord is * to those whose Ps 34:18
my pursuers are getting very *. Ps 35:3
cobras that * their ears to the Ps 58:4,5
I follow * behind you, protected Ps 63:8
But as for me, I came so * to Ps 73:2
But as for me, I get as * to him Ps 73:28
I am * to death at the hands of Ps 119:107
He is * to all who call on him Ps 145:18
But a curse upon those who * Pro 28:27
Dull their understanding, * Is 6:10
come too *, you'll defile me! Is 65:5
This is how a man lives * to God. Jer 22:16
prophets who lives * enough to God Jer 23:18
fear will follow * behind you and Jer 42:16
Then Nebuchadnezzar came as * as Dan 3:26
The night will * about you and cut Mic 3:6
plague follows * behind. Hab 3:5
* to Zebulun and Naphtali. Mt 4:12,13
last this age will come to its *. Mt 24:34
The next day—at the * of the Mt 27:62
him every day and keep * to me! Lk 9:23
Never forget how * you were to Lk 10:11
*, and everything I have is yours. Lk 15:31
encircle you and * in on you, and Lk 19:43
"They were * friends," the Jn 11:36
there beside me, his * friend, Jn 19:26
* at hand, they laid him there. Jn 19:42
and * friends to meet Peter. Act 10:24
* to the Lord, whatever the cost. Act 11:23
commanded those * to Paul to slap Act 23:2
and sailed along * to shore. Act 27:13
we live * to death, but here we 2Co 6:9
I * my letter with these last 2Co 13:11
And now, brothers, as I * this Php 4:8
Keep a * watch on all you do and 1Ti 4:16
have, but stay * to anything that 2Ti 2:22
And when you draw * to God, God Jas 4:8
to God, God will draw * to you. Jas 4:8
You will do well to pay * 2Pe 1:19
will always be in * fellowship with 1Jn 2:24
So if we stay * to him, obedient 1Jn 3:6
Its gates never *; Rev 21:25

CLOSED
of his ribs and * up the place from Gen 2:21
* the door and shut them in. Gen 7:16
* shall be defiled until evening. Lev 14:46
* upon them, and they perished. Num 16:33
flesh, and the fat * over it as the Ju 3:22,23
The Philistines * in on Saul, 1Sa 31:2
new suit of armor, * in on David 2Sa 21:16
He also * all the houses of male 1Ki 22:46
by King Ahaz when he * the Temple. 2Ch 29:19
But the Sea * in upon their Ps 78:53
"For you * your eyes to the Pro 1:29
Keep your mouth * and you'll stay Pro 21:23
Then let your lips be tightly * Ecc 12:4
He has * the eyes of your Is 29:10
* their minds from understanding. Is 44:18
Behind * doors you set your idols Is 57:7,8
Their ears are * and they refuse Jer 6:10
* their gates against the enemy. Jer 13:19
Literally, "the cities are * and Jer 13:19f
eastern passageway, but it was *. Eze 44:1
"This gate shall remain *; Eze 44:2
entrance shall be * during the six Eze 46:1
shall not be * until evening. Eze 46:2
The eastern passageway was *. Eze 47:2f
The waters * above me; Jon 2:5
and training camps will be * down. Mic 4:3
* their eyes in sleep, Mt 13:15
The city gates were * on the Mt 24:20f
He * the book and handed it back Lk 4:20
the gates were * behind him. Act 21:30
and you have * your eyes against Act 28:27
Their * hearts are full of Eph 4:17,18

CLOSELY
is so * related to your father; Lev 18:12
* by the 250 Israeli leaders. Num 16:25
Therefore, O Israel, listen * to Deu 6:3
They must be * questioned, and Deu 19:18
more * related to you than I am. Ru 3:12
Listen * to what I am about to Job 13:17
about ways to follow him more *. Ps 1:2
he still rules from heaven. He * Ps 11:4
He has made their hearts and * Ps 33:13,14,15
Listen * to my prayer, O God. Ps 86:6
and follow them as * as I can. Ps 119:31
will follow your laws even more *. Ps 119:32
now I * follow all you say. Ps 119:67
life, * follow my instructions. Pro 3:1
For God is * watching you, and Pro 5:21
follow it *, for it will do you Pro 22:17,18,19
interests *. Pro 27:23,24
For I am * watching you and I Jer 16:17
Lord is * watching all mankind, Zec 9:1
Israel. I am * watching their Zec 9:8
he will sit and * watch as the Mal 3:3
Jesus' enemies watched him *. Mk 3:2
your cross, and follow me *. Mk 8:34
She looked at him * and then Mk 14:66,67
Pharisees watched * to see whether Lk 6:7
in heaven who is * watching you. Col 4:1
more and more * to that ideal. 1Th 4:1

CLOSER
So they came *. Gen 45:4
"Don't come any *," God told Ex 3:5
be sure that you don't get any * Jos 3:2,3,4
As the messenger came *, the 2Sa 18:25
who sticks * than a brother. Pro 18:24
Come * and listen. Is 48:16
And the * he came, the angrier Dan 8:7
Jerusalem, coming * and closer Zep 1:10
coming closer and * until the noise Zep 1:10
But as they came * to Jerusalem Lk 19:41

CLOSES
When he * in on a man, there is Job 12:14

CLOSEST
If your nearest relative or * Deu 13:6,7
"Why, that man is one of our * Ru 2:20
Hadad became one of Pharaoh's * 1Ki 11:19
of Israel, the people * to him. Ps 148:14
Even those * to you—your Lk 21:16
table, being his * friend, Simon Jn 13:23

CLOSET
in a cloth in the clothes *. 1Sa 21:9

CLOSETS
like dust, with * jammed full of Job 27:16

CLOSING
the enemy chariots * in upon him. 2Sa 1:6
there was a solemn * service as Neh 8:18
I will write these * words in my Gal 6:11

CLOTH
Gold, silver, bronze, blue *, Ex 25:1
blue cloth, purple *, scarlet Ex 25:1
cloth, scarlet *, fine-twined Ex 25:1
and scarlet *, the fine-twined Ex 26:31
cherubim embroidered into the *. Ex 26:31
two folds of *, forming a pouch. Ex 28:16
be made of blue *, with an opening Ex 28:30,31
Blue, purple, and scarlet *, made Ex 35:5-9
and scarlet * made from the Ex 35:23
scarlet thread and *, and Ex 35:25
to spin the goats' hair into *. Ex 35:26
scarlet threads into fine linen *. Ex 38:23
and scarlet *—garments to be used Ex 39:1
This same * was used for Aaron's Ex 39:1
The ephod was made from this * Ex 39:2
and scarlet * cut from fine-twined Ex 39:4,5
these were made of linen *, Ex 39:24
with a blue *, and place the Num 4:6
"Next they must spread a blue * Num 4:7
cups, and the Bread upon the *. Num 4:7
They will spread a scarlet * Num 4:8
leather on top of the scarlet *. Num 4:8
cover with a blue * the lampstand, Num 4:9
"They must then spread a blue * Num 4:11
wrapped in a blue *, covered with Num 4:12
shall be covered with a purple *. Num 4:13
be placed upon the *—the firepans, Num 4:14
It is wrapped in a * in the 1Sa 21:9
The man's wife put a * over the 2Sa 17:19
dishes, beautiful *, myrrh, spices, 1Ki 10:25
the field where * was bleached, 2Ki 18:17
make purple, crimson, and blue *; 2Ch 2:7
and blue linen and crimson *. 2Ch 2:14
as fragile as a moth-infested *; Ps 39:11
the field where * is bleached. Is 36:2
himself in coarse * used for making Is 37:1
to trade—blue *, embroidery and Eze 27:24
Literally, "as a menstruous *." Eze 36:17f
an old garment with unshrunk *? Mt 9:16
in a clean linen *, and placed it Mt 27:59
an old garment with unshrunk *! Mk 2:21
"wearing only a linen *." Mk 14:51,52f
sheet of linen * and, taking Jesus' Mk 15:46
wound it in the * and laid it in a Mk 15:46
it in a long linen * and laid it in Lk 23:53
in a long linen * saturated with Jn 19:40
* lying there, but I didn't go in. Jn 20:5
He also noticed the * lying Jn 20:6
Thyatira, a merchant of purple *. Act 16:14
*, and the moon was blood-red. Rev 6:12

CLOTHE
You will * your sons and Ex 3:22
and respect. * Aaron and his sons Ex 28:41
with water; and * Aaron with the Ex 40:13
older priests to * themselves in 2Ki 19:2
they do. * them with disgrace. Ps 109:29
We will * the priests in white, Ps 132:9
I will * her priests with Ps 132:16
I'll * his enemies with shame, Ps 132:18
WAKE UP, WAKE up, Jerusalem, and * Is 52:1
and destitute. * those who are cold Is 58:7
then they * these gods in kingly Jer 10:9
You shall * yourselves with Eze 7:18
words, I will * you in purple Dan 5:16
Or naked, and * you? Mt 25:38
naked, and you wouldn't * me; Mt 25:43
* yourself with this new nature. Eph 4:24

CLOTHED
and the Lord God * Adam and his Gen 3:21
water, and he * Aaron with the Lev 8:7
Worship the Lord when * with 1Ch 16:29
elders of Israel * themselves in 1Ch 21:16
O Lord God, be * with salvation, 2Ch 6:41
leading the march, * in sanctified 2Ch 20:21
this time they fasted and * Neh 9:1
Those who hate you shall be * Job 8:22
heaven, * in dazzling splendor. Job 37:22
the depths? Who * them with clouds Job 38:8,9
* his neck with a quivering mane? Job 39:19
You have * him with splendor and Ps 21:5
Come before him * in sacred Ps 29:2
fall apart. You * the earth with Ps 104:6
For he will be * with fairness Is 11:5
allowed you to be * so gorgeously Is 22:17
on his head. He * himself with Is 59:17
For he has * me with garments of Is 61:10
ground in silence, * in sackcloth; Lam 2:10
washed nor rubbed with salt nor *. Eze 16:4
I * Lebanon in black and caused Eze 31:15
them into the furnace, fully *. Dan 3:21
was not * as beautifully as they. Mt 6:29
naked and you * me; Mt 25:36
there, fully * and perfectly sane, Mk 5:15
* only in a linen nightshirt. Mk 14:51,52
right sat a young man * in white. Mk 16:5
at Jesus' feet, * and sane! Lk 8:35
long ago, * in sackcloth and Lk 10:13
was splendidly * and lived each day Lk 16:19
before them, * in shining robes so Lk 24:4
before me * in a radiant robe! Act 10:30
Everyone who conquers will be * Rev 3:5
all were * in white, with golden Rev 4:4
before the Lamb, * in white, with Rev 7:9
these are, who are * in white, and Rev 7:13
* in sackcloth." Rev 11:3
I saw a woman * with the sun, Rev 12:1
from the temple, * in spotless Rev 15:6
a woman * in finest purple and Rev 18:16
He was * with garments dipped in Rev 19:13

CLOTHES
Then she took Esau's best *—they Gen 27:15
Isaac sniffs his *, and finally Gen 27:26
give me food and *, and will bring Gen 28:20
his * in anguish and frustration. Gen 37:29

CLOTHES Con't)
of *, came in before Pharaoh. Gen 41:14
each of them new *—but to Benjamin Gen 45:22
five changes of * and three hundred Gen 45:22
vine, and washed his * in wine. Gen 49:11
and the finest of * from her Ex 3:22
"Eat it with your traveling * Ex 12:11
into their spare *, and carried Ex 12:34
and have them wash their *. Ex 19:10
Make special * for Aaron, to Ex 28:2
and his sons and upon their *; Ex 29:21
shall wear these * for seven days Ex 29:30
Then he shall change his * and Lev 6:11
Aaron and upon his * and upon his Lev 8:30
and upon their *, thus consecrating Lev 8:30
Aaron and his sons and their *. Lev 8:30
mourning, and do not tear your *. Lev 10:6
and must wash his * immediately. Lev 11:25
shall wash his * and be Lev 11:28
* and be defiled until evening. Lev 11:40
need only wash his * and everything Lev 13:6
after washing his *, he is free. Lev 13:34
must tear his * and let his hair Lev 13:45
shall wash his *, shave off all his Lev 14:8
and wash his * and bathe, and shall Lev 14:9
must wash his * and bathe himself. Lev 15:5
must wash his * and bathe himself. Lev 15:6
must wash his * and bathe himself. Lev 15:8
must wash his * and bathe himself. Lev 15:10
must wash his * and bathe himself Lev 15:11
* and bathing in running water. Lev 15:13
shall wash his * and bathe himself Lev 15:21,22,23
and shall wash his * and bathe and Lev 15:27
place, put on his * again, and go Lev 16:24
shall afterwards wash his * and Lev 16:26
shall wash his * and bathe himself Lev 16:28
must wash his * and bathe himself Lev 17:15
But if he does not wash his * Lev 17:16
don't wear * made of half wool Lev 19:19
and washed their *, and Aaron Num 8:21
the hems of their * (this is a Num 15:37,38
to their * with a blue cord. Num 15:37,38
"Then he must wash his *, and Num 19:7
must wash his *, and bathe, and he Num 19:8
* and be defiled until evening; Num 19:10
must wash his * and bathe himself, Num 19:19
water must afterwards wash his *; Num 19:21
you must wash your * and be Num 31:24
For all these forty years your * Deu 8:4
yet your * haven't become old, and Deu 29:5
When he saw her he tore his * in Ju 11:35
and some nice * and go on down to Ru 3:3
his * torn and dirt on his head. 1Sa 4:12
He tore off his * and lay naked 1Sa 19:24
It is wrapped in a cloth in the * 1Sa 21:9
army with his * torn and with dirt 2Sa 1:1
David and his men tore their * in 2Sa 1:11
hair, changed his *, and went into 2Sa 12:20
His aides also tore their * in 2Sa 13:31
"Wear mourning *, and dishevel 2Sa 14:2,3
He had not washed his feet or * 2Sa 19:24,25
it, he tore his * and said, "This 2Ki 5:7
the king heard this he tore his *. 2Ki 6:26-30
screamed, and began to tear her *. 2Ki 11:13,14
with their * torn and told him what 2Ki 18:37
report he tore his * and put on 2Ki 19:1
in it, he tore his * in terror. 2Ki 22:11
Athaliah ripped her * and 2Ch 23:12
were with me—ever took off our *. Neh 4:23
Their * didn't wear out and their Neh 9:21
done, he tore his * and put on Est 4:1
permitted to enter in mourning *. Est 4:2
Just because you tear your * in Job 18:4
they divide my * among Ps 22:18
He took away my * of mourning and Ps 30:11
too much sleep * a man with rags. Pro 23:19,20,21
has made warm * for all of them. Pro 31:21
Wear fine *—with a dash of Ecc 9:8
I have no extra food or *. Is 3:7
jewels, and party * and negligees Is 3:22
sins, and to wear * made of Is 22:12
* for the priests of the Lord! Is 23:18
Strip off your pretty *—wear Is 32:11
to Hezekiah with * ripped to shreds Is 36:22
like old * eaten up by moths! Is 50:9
Put on your beautiful *, O Zion, Is 52:1
"Why are your * so red, as from Is 63:2
is their blood you see upon my *. Is 63:3
Put on * of mourning and weep Jer 4:8
put on mourning * and sit in ashes Jer 6:26
beards, torn their * and cut Jer 41:5
hands and put on * of sackcloth. Jer 48:37
and gave him new * and fed him Jer 52:33
*, who took them and went out. Eze 10:7,8
gave you beautiful * of linens and Eze 16:9,10
silver, and your * were silk and Eze 16:13
* I gave you—to cover your idols! Eze 16:18
to the hungry and * to those in Eze 18:7
the hungry and * the needy, and Eze 18:16
of your beautiful * and jewels. Eze 23:26
*, but you let your flocks starve. Eze 34:3
must change their * before going Eze 42:14
They must put on other * before Eze 42:14
must take off the * they wear while Eze 44:19
and put on other * lest they Eze 44:19
them for food and drinks and *." Hos 1:5
supplied, and the * I gave her to Hos 1:9
You will wear funeral * and shave Amo 8:10
and not enough * to keep you warm. Hag 1:6
am giving you these fine new *." Zec 3:4
No one will wear prophet's * to Zec 13:4
about things—food, drink, and *. Mt 6:25
"And why worry about your *? Mt 6:28
bag with extra * and shoes, or even Mt 10:10
return to their homes for their *. Mt 24:18
divide up his * among themselves. Mt 27:35
Jordan River. His * were woven Mk 1:6
the crowd and touched his *. Mk 5:27
and asked, "Who touched my *?" Mk 5:30
pair of shoes or a change of *. Mk 6:8,9
least touch the fringes of his *; Mk 6:56
even return for your money or *. Mk 13:15,16
though his * were torn off in the Mk 14:51,52
Priest tore at his * and said, Mk 14:63,64
and put his own * on him again, and Mk 15:20
him—and threw dice for his *. Mk 15:24
Literally, "swaddling *." Lk 2:7f
Literally, "swaddling *." Lk 2:12f
find him dressed in expensive *? Lk 7:25
and his * became dazzling white Lk 9:29
They stripped him of his * and Lk 10:30
enough food to eat or * to wear. Lk 12:22
of far more than food and *. Lk 12:23
better sell your * and buy one! Lk 22:36
divided my * among them, and cast Jn 19:23,24
even enough * to keep us warm. 1Co 4:11
which we shall put on like new *. 2Co 5:2
of their jewels or fancy *. 1Ti 2:9,10
worn out like old *, and some day Heb 1:11
in expensive * and with valuable Jas 2:2
in threadbare *, and you make a Jas 2:2
* or food, what good does that do? Jas 2:16
and your fine * are becoming mere Jas 5:2
beautiful *, or hair arrangement. 1Pe 3:3

CLOTHING
silver for Rebekah, and lovely *; Gen 24:53
themselves and to put on fresh *. Gen 35:2
aside her widow's * and covered Gen 38:14
wearing her widow's * as usual. Gen 38:19
him in beautiful * and placed the Gen 41:41,42
They ripped their * in despair, Gen 44:13
and gold jewelry, and for *. Ex 12:35
them and they washed their *. Ex 19:14
of your * and see your nakedness. Ex 20:26
reduce her food or *, or fail to Ex 21:10
ox, donkey, sheep, *, or anything Ex 22:9
If you take his * as a pledge of Ex 22:26
and they and their * shall be Ex 29:21
The beautiful * for the priests, Ex 35:10-19
onto their *, it must be washed in Lev 6:27
Then the clay pot in which the * Lev 6:28
wood, or of *, a rug, or a sack; Lev 11:32
he must burn the *, fabric, linen Lev 13:52
in the house shall wash his *. Lev 14:47
the evening. Any * or bedding the Lev 15:17
nor tear his *, nor be in the Lev 21:10
and wash their * and themselves. Num 8:7
ripped their * and said to all the Num 14:6
(besides the jewelry, *, etc. Num 31:32-35
and gives them food and *. Deu 10:18
and change her *, laying aside Deu 21:13
The same applies to donkeys, *, Deu 22:3
"A woman must not wear men's *, Deu 22:5
and a man must not wear women's *. Deu 22:5
"Don't wear * woven from two Deu 22:11
Israel tore their * and lay Jos 7:6
wearing worn-out *, as though from Jos 9:3,4,5
and cracked; our * and shoes have Jos 9:13
silver, gold, bronze, iron, and *. Jos 22:7,8
and hid it in his *, strapped Ju 3:16
or the royal * of the kings, or the Ju 8:26
men, took their *, and gave it to Ju 14:19
* before returning to their homes. 1Sa 27:9
* instead of his royal robes. 1Sa 28:7,8
With fine * and golden ornaments. 2Sa 1:24
might, and was wearing priests' *. 2Sa 6:14
torn * and earth upon his head. 2Sa 15:32
he tore his *, put on rags, fasted, 1Ki 21:27
in gold, and ten suits of *. 2Ki 5:5
receive money and * and olive farms 2Ki 5:26
and gold and * and hiding it. 2Ki 7:8
They followed a trail of * and 2Ki 7:15
you have torn your * and wept 2Ki 22:18,19
Jehoiachin was given civilian * 2Ki 25:29
and gold bowls, *, armor, spices, 2Ch 9:24
captured stores of * to the women 2Ch 28:15
he ripped his * in despair, and 2Ch 34:19
have ripped your * in despair and 2Ch 34:27
supply them with *, transportation, Ez 1:4
When I heard this, I tore my * Ez 9:3
and 530 sets of * for the priests. Neh 7:70
sets of * for the priests. Neh 7:72
her choice of * or jewelry she Est 2:12,13,14
and sent * to him to replace the Est 4:4
and even my * would be less Job 9:31
gave you all their * as a Job 22:6
the cold, without * or covering. Job 24:7
naked, without *, and are forced to Job 24:10
jammed full of *— yes, he may Job 27:16
shall wear that *, and shall divide Job 27:17
for righteousness was my *! Job 29:14
and not given him *, or fleece from Job 31:19,20
in beautiful * woven with gold. Ps 45:13
and their * is woven of cruelty! Ps 73:6
old, like worn-out *, and you will Ps 102:26
part of him as his *, or as the Ps 109:18
to him like his * or his belt. Ps 109:19
wool enough for *, and goat's Pro 27:25,26,27
her own * is beautifully made—a Pro 31:22
have some extra *, so you be our Is 3:6
will furnish our own food and *; Is 4:1
to take off his *, including his Is 20:2
Your * is stained with the blood Jer 2:34
most beautiful * and jewelry and Jer 4:30
supplies where used * was kept. Jer 38:11
One of them wore linen * and Eze 9:2
Just then the man in linen *, Eze 9:11
the man in linen * and said: "Go Eze 10:2
the man in linen * to go between Eze 10:6
of God; your * was bejeweled with Eze 28:13
"They must wear only linen * Eze 44:17
by touching them with this *. Eze 44:19
down to judge. His * was as white Dan 7:9
in * stolen from their debtors, Amo 2:8
pledged * of debtors overnight. Amo 2:8f
and all others wearing heathen *. Zep 1:8
Joshua's * was filthy as he stood Zec 3:3
there, "Remove his filthy *." Zec 3:4
of gold and silver and fine *. Zec 14:14
John's * was woven from camel's Mt 3:4
put on festive *, so that no one Mt 6:17
about having enough food and *. Mt 6:31,32
and his * became dazzling white. Mt 17:2
his own *, shouting, "Blasphemy! Mt 26:65,66
and his * was a brilliant white. Mt 28:3
touch his *, I will be healed." Mk 5:28
glory, and his * became dazzling Mk 9:3
And if God provides * for the Lk 12:28
provide * for you, you doubters? Lk 12:28
some of their * across its back for Lk 19:35
extra *, how did you get along?" Lk 22:35
And the soldiers gambled for his * Lk 23:34
ripped at their * in dismay and ran Act 14:14
or parts of his * were placed upon Act 19:12
for money or fine *— you know that Act 20:33
in return, for mere food and *? 1Co 9:11
without enough * to keep me warm. 2Co 11:27
and sensible in manner and *. 1Ti 2:9,10
if we have enough food and *. 1Ti 6:8
need of food and *, and you say to Jas 2:15
take neither food, *, shelter, nor 3Jn 1:7
purple and scarlet * and beautiful Rev 17:4

CLOUD
Or, "over the * of darkness," Gen 1:2f
the rainbow in the * and remember Gen 9:16,17
by a pillar of * during the Ex 13:21
day or night. The * and fire were Ex 13:22
Israel, moved the * around behind Ex 14:19
down from the * of fire upon the Ex 14:24
within the guiding *, there Ex 16:10
the form of a dark *, so that the Ex 19:9
storm, and a huge * came down upon Ex 19:16
disappeared into the * at the top. Ex 24:15
Sinai and the * covered it six Ex 24:16
day he called to Moses from the *. Ex 24:16
As he entered, the pillar of * Ex 33:9
bowing low to the pillar of *. Ex 33:10
of a pillar of * and stood there Ex 34:5,6
Then the * covered the Tabernacle Ex 40:34
enter because the * was standing Ex 40:35
Whenever the * lifted and moved, Ex 40:36
But if the * stayed, they stayed Ex 40:37
it moved. The * rested upon the Ex 40:38
was fire in the * so that all the Ex 40:38
For I myself am present in the * Lev 16:1
coals, so that a * of incense will Lev 16:13
was raised, the * covered it; Num 9:15
and that evening the * changed to Num 9:15
It was always so—the daytime * Num 9:16
When the * lifted, the people of Num 9:17
there as long as the * stayed. Num 9:18
If the * stayed above the Num 9:22
The * lifted from the Tabernacle Num 10:11
and followed the * until it stopped Num 10:12
left, with the * moving along ahead Num 10:34
And the Lord came down in the * Num 11:25
Then the Lord descended in the * Num 12:5
As the * moved from above the Num 12:10
They see the pillar of * and fire Num 14:14
Tabernacle, the * appeared and the Num 16:42
and a pillar of * during the day. Deu 1:33
He appeared to them in a great * Deu 31:15
The great * of smoke pouring into Ju 20:35-39

(CLOUD Con't)
a bright * fills the Temple! 1Ki 8:10
"I saw a little * about the size 1Ki 18:44
coming as a bright *, filled the 2Ch 5:13,14
by a pillar of * during the day and Neh 9:12
The pillar of * led them forward Neh 9:19
and may a black * overshadow it. Job 3:5
As a * disperses and vanishes, Job 7:9
as the shadow of a passing *, he Job 14:2
as a * before a strong wind. Job 30:15
he led them by a *, and at night by Ps 78:14
from the pillar of * and they Ps 99:7
He spread out a * above them to Ps 105:39
promised is like a * blowing over a Pro 25:14
life he is under a *—gloomy, Ecc 5:17
the deserts like a * of smoke along Sol 3:6
of smoke and * throughout the day, Is 4:5
and send a vast * of smoke Is 9:18
Egypt, riding on a swift *; Is 19:1
he will remove the * of gloom, the Is 25:7
who fly like a * to Israel, like Is 60:8
A * OF anger from the Lord has Lam 2:1
yourself as with a * so that our Lam 3:44
before it a huge * glowing with Eze 1:4
Then from the center of the *, Eze 1:5
* of smoke above their heads. Eze 8:11
And the * of glory filled the Eze 10:3
The Temple was filled with the * Eze 10:4
a dark * will cover her, and her Eze 30:18
I will cover the sun with a *, Eze 32:7
storm and cover the land like a *. Eze 38:9
and cover the land like a *. Eze 38:15,16
by the wind, like a * of smoke. Hos 13:3
said it, a bright * came over them, Mt 17:5
a voice from the * said, "This is Mt 17:5
these words, a * covered them, Mk 9:7
* said, "This is my beloved Son. Mk 9:7
* formed above them; Lk 9:34
And a voice from the * said, Lk 9:35
the Messiah, coming in a * with Lk 21:27
*, leaving them staring after him. Act 1:9
with a bright * of glory and told Rom 9:4
God guided them by sending a * 1Co 10:1
both in sea and *! 1Co 10:2
a *, with a rainbow over his head; Rev 10:1
in a * as their enemies watch. Rev 11:12
and I saw a white *, and someone Rev 14:14
So the one sitting on the * Rev 14:16

CLOUD-COVERED
And Moses disappeared into the * Ex 24:18

CLOUDED
But if your eye is * with evil Mt 6:23

CLOUDLESS
A * sunrise 2Sa 23:4
And your life will be *; Job 11:17

CLOUDS
my rainbow in the * as a sign of my Gen 9:13
When I send * over the earth, Gen 9:14
be seen in the *, and I will Gen 9:14
by black * and deep darkness. Deu 4:11
surrounded by the * and thick Deu 5:22
He walked upon dark *. 2Sa 22:10
And * were thick around him; 2Sa 22:12
soon black with *, and a heavy wind 1Ki 18:45
For thick * swirl about him so Job 22:14
He wraps the rain in his thick * Job 26:8
the * are not split by the weight. Job 26:8
He shrouds his throne with his * Job 26:9
of the *, and the thunders within? Job 36:29
He loads the * with moisture and Job 37:11
to flash forth from the *? Job 37:15
balancing of the * with wonderful Job 37:16,17
cleared away the *, neither can we Job 37:21
Who clothed them with * and thick Job 38:8,9
Can you shout to the * and make Job 38:34
wise enough to number all the *? Job 38:37,38
with dense * dark as murky waters. Ps 18:11
broke through the * with lightning Ps 18:12
of the Lord echoes from the *. Ps 29:3
faithfulness reaches beyond the *. Ps 36:5
song to him who rides upon the *! Ps 68:4
It trembled to its depths! The * Ps 77:17
as thick as dust, * of them like Ps 78:27
* and darkness surround him. Ps 97:2
the seas. The * are his chariots. Ps 104:3
swarmed in vast * from one end of Ps 105:31
He covers the heavens with *, Ps 147:8
him, vapors high above the *. Ps 148:4
When the * are heavy, the rains Ecc 11:3
regardeth the * shall not reap." Ecc 11:4f
silver lining left among your *, Ecc 12:2
the day, and * of fire at night, Is 4:5
I will command the * not to rain Is 5:6
land is cooled by *, you will cool Is 25:5
in the thunder of the storm *. Jer 10:13
a day of * and gloom; Eze 30:2,3
with its head high up among the *. Eze 31:2,3
reaching to the *, I will deliver Eze 31:10
be higher than the *, for all are Eze 31:14
be—brought there on * from heaven; Dan 7:13
of the sky for *, to pour down Hos 1:21,22
*, and disappears like dew. Hos 6:4
of black * and thick darkness. Joe 2:2
the raging storms; * are billowing Nah 1:3
darkness, gloom, *, blackness, Zep 1:15
me arrive in the * of heaven, with Mt 24:30
returning on the * of heaven." Mt 26:64
coming in the * with great power Mk 13:26
to earth in the * of heaven." Mk 14:62
"When you see * beginning to form Lk 12:54
and fire and * of smoke; Act 2:19
with them in the * to meet the Lord 1Th 4:17
they are as unstable as * driven 2Pe 2:17
They are like * blowing over dry Jud 1:12
He is arriving, surrounded by *; Rev 1:7

CLOUDY
scattered in that dark and * day. Eze 34:12

CLOVEN
with * hooves which chews its cud. Lev 11:2,3
cud but does not have * hooves); Lev 11:4-7
cud, it does not have * hooves); Lev 11:4-7
cud, it does not have * hooves); Lev 11:4-7
although it has * hooves, it does Lev 11:4-7
"Any animal that has * hooves Deu 14:6
the cud but do not have * hooves. Deu 14:7
* hooves, they don't chew the cud. Deu 14:8
their feet were * like calves' Eze 1:7

CLUB
go after it with a * and take the 1Sa 17:35
it by the jaw and * it to death. 1Sa 17:35
to him with only a * in his hand 1Ch 11:23
and the old Officers' * building. Neh 3:16

CLUBS
as straw. * do no good, and he Job 41:29
and *, sent by the Jewish leaders. Mt 26:47
and * before you could arrest me? Mt 26:55
with swords and *, sent out by the Mk 14:43
armed with swords and * to get me? Lk 22:52

CLUMSY
or the pot exclaim, "How * can Is 45:9

CLUNG
Nevertheless he still * to the 2Ki 3:3
they have * to for centuries, and Mk 7:4

CLUSTER
and then take a * of hyssop Ex 12:22
cut down a single * of grapes so Num 13:23
time (meaning "*") because of the Num 13:24
of the * of grapes they found! Num 13:24
are found among a * of bad ones Is 65:8
Not a * to eat, not a single Mic 7:1

CLUSTERED
The Levites' tents shall be * Num 1:53

CLUSTERS
soon there were * of ripe grapes. Gen 40:9,10
of a fig cake, two * of raisins, 1Sa 30:11,12
bread, one hundred * of raisins, 2Sa 16:1
breasts are like its * of dates. Sol 7:7
be like grape *, and the scent of Sol 7:8
now to cut off the * of grapes from Rev 14:18

CLUTCH
nations will * at the coat sleeves Zec 8:23

CLUTCHES
Rescue me from their *, and give Jer 15:15
her into the evil * of the Eze 23:9
them fall into the * of their own Zec 11:6
saved out of the * of evil men, for 2Th 3:2

CNIDUS
sailing, and finally neared *; Act 27:7,8
* was a port on the southeast Act 27:7,8f

CO-REGENCY
Possibly there was a *. 2Ki 3:1f

CO-REGENT
Or, "and they installed him as* 1Ch 29:22f

CO-WORKERS
We are only God's *. 1Co 3:9

COAL
of tongs picked out a burning *. Is 6:6
this * has touched your lips. Is 6:7

COALITION
a * against Edom and destroy her. Jer 49:14

COALS
full of live * from the altar of Lev 16:12
incense upon the *, so that a cloud Lev 16:13
Literally, "* were kindled by 2Sa 22:9f
Yes, his breath would kindle * Job 41:21
Literally, "* were kindled by Ps 18:8f
Literally, "* of fire." Ps 18:12f
arrows and burned with glowing *. Ps 120:4
Literally, "with * of the broom Ps 120:4f
Let burning * fall down upon Ps 140:10
Can he walk on hot * and not Pro 6:28
Literally, "like hot embers to * Pro 26:21f
use for carrying * from the hearth, Is 30:14
who blows the * beneath the forge Is 54:16
glowed like bright * of fire or Eze 1:13
handful of glowing * and scatter Eze 10:2
take some burning * from between Eze 10:6
and took some live * from the Eze 10:7,8
Now set it empty on the * to Eze 24:11
"heaping * of fire on his head." Rom 12:20

COARSE
a loaf, using * flour from the Num 15:19,20,21
She was the brash, * type, seen Pro 7:11,12
wound himself in * cloth used for Is 37:1
rough, * garments worn at times of Jon 3:4,5
Dirty stories, foul talk and * Eph 5:4

COAST
to the Philistine *, and from the Ex 23:31
down along the * of the Num 13:29
The Mediterranean * and the Negeb Deu 33:23
the Mediterranean *—heard that the Jos 5:1
The land of the Gebalites on the * Jos 13:2-7
also the entire Mediterranean * Jos 15:47
We will float them along the * to 1Ki 5:9
floated along the * of the Ez 3:7
Kings along the Mediterranean* Ps 72:10
destroy those along the sea *. Eze 25:16
routes along the * and along the Eze 26:2
from the southern * of Cyprus. Eze 27:6
* of Palestine around 1200 B.C. Zep 2:5f
living on the * and in the land Zep 2:5
Paul on to the *, while Silas and Act 17:14
and sailed for the * of Syria, Act 18:18
several stops along the Turkish *. Act 27:2
Literally, "the * of Asia." Act 27:2f
and passed along the * of the Act 27:5
port on the southeast * of Turkey. Act 27:7,8f
along the southern *, we arrived at Act 27:7,8
go further up the * to Phoenix, in Act 27:12
the quicksands of the African *, Act 27:17
and fearing rocks along the *, Act 27:29

COASTAL
Negeb, as well as on the * plains. Ju 1:9
and all the distant * lands. Is 11:11
to the * cities and conquer many. Dan 11:18
* strip as far north as Zarephath. Ob 1:20

COASTLAND
Literally, "inhabitants of the* Is 20:5,6f
you is left. The * will become a Zep 2:6

COASTLANDS
Let the western * glorify the Is 42:12
Rhodes, and many * are your captive Eze 27:15
All who live along the * watch, Eze 27:35

COASTLINE
be the * of the Mediterranean Sea. Num 34:6
recognize the *, but noticed a bay Act 27:39

COASTS
Ships shall come from the * of Num 24:23,24
live safely on the *, and they Eze 39:6

COAT
think he was wearing a fur *! Gen 25:25
special gift—a brightly-colored *. Gen 37:3
blood on Joseph's *, and took the Gen 37:31
and took the * to their father and Gen 37:32
"Is it Joseph's * or not?" Gen 37:32
he sobbed, "it is my son's *. Gen 37:33
on the neck of a * of mail, so that Ex 28:32
just as in a * of mail, for the Ex 39:23
with the special *, sash, robe, and Lev 8:7
linen *, shorts, belt, and turban. Lev 16:4
made a little * for him and brought 1Sa 2:19
two-hundred-pound * of mail, bronze 1Sa 17:4-7
bronze helmet and a * of mail. 1Sa 17:38,39
him and threw his * across his 1Ki 19:19
rotten tree, like a moth-eaten *. Job 13:27,28
will clutch at the * sleeves of one Zec 8:23
taken from you, give your * too. Mt 5:40
yanked off his old * and flung it Mk 10:50
If someone demands your *, give Lk 6:29
Not even an extra *. Lk 9:3
"Now put on your * and follow Act 12:8
sure to bring the * I left at Troas 2Ti 4:13

COATING
Face the stones with a * of lime Deu 27:2,3,4

COATS
their * as Moses had told them to. Lev 10:5
steps with their * and blew a 2Ki 9:13
* of mail, bows, and slingstones. 2Ch 26:14
her warriors in their * of mail. Jer 51:3
their * were unscorched, and they Dan 3:27
threw down their * along the road Mt 21:8
spread out their * along the road Mk 11:8
"If you have two *," he Lk 3:11
off their * and laid them at the Act 7:58
one another the * and other Act 9:39
the * they laid aside as they Act 22:20
They yelled and threw their * Act 22:23

COAXING
pretty speech, her * and her Pro 7:21

COBRAS
as deadly snakes, * that close Ps 58:4,5

COCK
night, before the * crows at dawn, Mt 26:34
And immediately the * crowed. Mt 26:74
said, "Before the * crows, you Mt 26:75
said, "before the * crows a second Mk 14:30
mind: "Before the * crows twice, Mk 14:72
No—three times before the * crows Jn 13:38

COCKY
the dream and for his * attitude. Gen 37:8
I know what a * brat you are; 1Sa 17:28
toward whom have you felt so *? 2Ki 19:22

CODE
or the * number of his name. Rev 13:17

(CODE Con't)
interpret this *: the numerical Rev 13:18
tattooed with the * of his name. Rev 14:11

COFFIN
body was placed in a * in Egypt. Gen 50:26
Then he walked over to the * and Lk 7:14

COILING
serpent, the *, writhing serpent, Is 27:1

COIN
Then we tossed a * Neh 10:34
We toss the *, Pro 16:33
A * toss Pro 18:18
You will find a * to cover the Mt 17:26,27
Here, show me a *." Mt 22:19
"Show me a * and I'll tell you." Mk 12:15
and title is this on the *?" Mk 12:16
trickery and said, "Show me a *. Lk 20:24

COIN-TOSS
to the various groups by * 1Ch 24:5
The work was assigned (by *) in 1Ch 24:7-18
to their duties by * without 1Ch 24:31
term of service by *, without 1Ch 25:8
for it was all done by *. 1Ch 26:13

COINCIDED
to Hukkok, and * with the Zebulun Jos 19:34

COINCIDENCE
was simply a * and was not sent by 1Sa 6:9

COINS
counted out thirty little silver * Zec 11:12
So I took the thirty * and threw Zec 11:13
And they gave him thirty silver *. Mt 26:15
valuable silver * and loses one. Lk 15:8
and dropped in two small copper *. Lk 21:2
money changers' * over the floor Jn 2:15

COL-HOZEH
Ma-aseiah (son of Baruch, son of * Neh 11:4,5,6

COLD
and harvest, * and heat, winter and Gen 8:22
the * and sleepless nights. Gen 31:40
heaped upon him, he was always *. 1Ki 1:1
*, without clothing or covering. Job 24:7
from the north, the *. Job 37:9
can stand before his freezing *? Ps 147:17
If you won't plow in the *, you Pro 20:4
his jacket in * weather, or rubbing Pro 25:20
as a wind from the north brings *, Pro 25:23
Good news from far away is like * Pro 25:25
Also, on a * night, two under the Ecc 4:11
Clothe those who are * and don't Is 58:7
mountains. The *, flowing streams Jer 18:14
for it was December, and *. Jer 36:22
the hedges in the *, but all of Nah 3:17
give even a cup of * water to a Mt 10:42
fire they had made, for it was *. Jn 18:18
and warm us in the rain and *. Act 28:1
often I have shivered with *, 2Co 11:27
well—you are neither hot nor *; Rev 3:15

COLDNESS
all my heart. Any * still between 2Co 6:12

COLHOZEH
Shallum (son of *), the mayor of Neh 3:15

COLLAPSE
top of their wall, it would *!" Neh 4:3
Everything he counts on will *. Job 8:14
Those nations will * and perish; Ps 20:8
earth has broken down in utter *; Is 24:19
neighbors and friends shall * Jer 6:21
they cry, and then * upon their Lam 2:12
won't *, for it is built on rock. Mt 7:25
divided against itself will *. Mk 3:24

COLLAPSED
Everything *. Ju 5:8
trial, King Ahaz * spiritually. 2Ch 28:22
"Law and order have *," Ps 11:3
"Because of the way your might * Eze 29:6
Then the whole statue * into a Dan 2:35

COLLAPSES
* before him. Job 9:13

COLLAR
neck in an iron *, until God's Ps 105:18
to put him in the stocks and *. Jer 29:26

COLLEAGUE
was his * Asaph, whose genealogy 1Ch 6:39-43

COLLEAGUES
sixty-eight of their * as guards. 1Ch 16:38
Then he addressed his * as Act 5:35

COLLECT
* a fifth of all the crops . . ." Gen 41:34,35f
as it is killed. * the blood and Ex 29:19,20
Then the Lord told Moses to * the Ex 30:22,23
until it was time to * the loot! 2Sa 23:10
Let's go and * the loot!" 2Ki 3:23
"* the money given to the priests 2Ki 22:3,4
of Judah and * offerings for the 2Ch 24:5
Levites go out and * the Temple 2Ch 24:6
Moreover, you are to * voluntary Ez 7:16
responsible to * the tithes in all Neh 10:37
offerings, and to * these from the Neh 12:44
and refreshment * after rains! Ps 84:6
Conscript your best soldiers; * Joe 3:9
your warriors! * the nations; Joe 3:12
They * captives like sand. Hab 1:9
to the farmers to * his share. Mt 21:34
of his men to * for him, but the Mt 21:36
men to * his share of the crop. Mk 12:2
"Make sure you * no more taxes Lk 3:13
his father died, * the inheritance Lk 9:59f
farm to * his share of the crops. Lk 20:10
and then try to * it all at once. 1Co 16:2

COLLECTED
and * bitumen to use as mortar. Gen 11:3,4
for we * your money all right." Gen 43:23
Joseph * all the money in Egypt Gen 47:14
Its blood shall also be * and Ex 29:15,16
head tax * from all those Ex 38:25,26
Then he * the fat of the ox and Lev 9:19
The money * came to a total of Num 3:50
So after Gideon had * all the Ju 7:8,9
Give me all the earrings * from Ju 8:23,24
So David * the construction 1Ch 22:5
"By hard work I have * 1Ch 22:14
I have now * everything that is 1Ch 28:2
materials I have already *. 1Ch 29:3
were * from these cities too. 2Ch 14:14
The money was * at the Temple 2Ch 34:9
the money * at the gates, he found 2Ch 34:14
from my taxes * in your territory. Ez 6:8
of all that was * as tithes was Neh 10:38
You have * all my tears and Ps 56:8
shout the water * into its vast Ps 104:7,8
kings before me. I * silver and Ecc 2:7,8
and he * proverbs and classified Ecc 12:9
In their greed they have * many Hab 2:5
would be, with your money all *; 2Co 9:3

COLLECTING
insulted and sent away without *. Lk 20:11
the money you are * to send to the 1Co 16:1

COLLECTION
Micah had many idols in his *, Ju 17:4,5
They set up a * system for gifts 2Ch 34:9
the * centers at the gates were: Neh 12:25
Let's see if the whole * of your Is 57:13
sitting at a tax * booth. Mt 9:9
"We can't put it in the *," Mt 27:6
sitting at his tax * booth. Mk 2:14
Then he went over to the * boxes Mk 12:41
cheating—sitting at a tax * booth. Lk 5:27
their gifts into the * box. Lk 21:1

COLLECTIVE
as a * noun, implying plurality. Rev 22:2f

COLLECTOR
who sent a tax * into Israel, but Dan 11:20
the road, he saw a tax *, Matthew, Mt 9:9
Matthew (the tax *), Mt 10:2,3,4
town he saw a tax *—with the usual Lk 5:27
and the other a cheating tax *. Lk 18:10
like that tax * over there! Lk 18:11
"But the corrupt tax * stood at Lk 18:13

COLLECTORS
the Temple tax * came to Peter and Mt 17:24
his fellow tax * and many other Mk 2:15
Even tax *—notorious for their Lk 3:12
Many of Levi's fellow tax * and Lk 5:29
Literally, "even the tax *"; Lk 7:29f
DISHONEST TAX * and other Lk 15:1

COLOGNE
fine clothes—with a dash of *! Ecc 9:8
How fragrant your *, and how Sol 1:3

COLONELS
NOW APPOINTED regimental * 2Sa 18:1

COLONIES
They were placed in * in the city 2Ki 17:6
transported * of people from 2Ki 17:24
and put them in * in the city of 2Ki 18:11

COLONISTS
But since these Assyrian * did 2Ki 17:25
of Assyria: "We * here in Israel 2Ki 17:26
and taught the * from Babylon how 2Ki 17:27,28
These * from Babylon worshiped 2Ki 17:41
Think of all the * you sent to Is 23:7
Philistines, those * from Caphtor. Jer 47:4

COLONY
Tyre was originally a * of the Is 23:1f
Tyre was originally a * of the Is 23:4f
Tel Abib, another * of Jewish Eze 3:14,15
* just inside the Macedonian Act 16:12

COLOR
skin, and if the * is gray, then Lev 13:21
not changed its *, even though it Lev 13:55
from Ethiopia) because of her *. Num 12:1f
Can the Ethiopian change the * of Jer 13:23
heart * all he sees and hears. Tit 1:15

COLORED
from ten * sheets of fine-twined Ex 26:1
My bed is spread with lovely, * Pro 7:16,17

COLORFUL
sit down, and soon * groups of Mk 6:39,40

COLOSSE
people—in the city of *. Col 1:2

COLT
The firstborn * of a donkey may Ex 34:20
* is likely to be born a man! Job 11:12
is lowly, riding on a donkey's *! Zec 9:9
tied there, with its * beside it. Mt 21:2
riding humbly on a donkey's *!" Mt 21:5
threw their garments over the * Mt 21:7
you will see a * tied up that has Mk 11:2
men and found the * standing in the Mk 11:4,5
are you doing, untying that *?" Mk 11:4,5
So the * was brought to Jesus and Mk 11:7
It would be a *, not yet broken Lk 19:30
They found the * as Jesus said, Lk 19:32
"Why are you untying our *?" Lk 19:33
So they brought the * to Jesus Lk 19:35
meekly, sitting on a donkey's *!" Jn 12:15

COLTS
camels, with their *,40 cows,10 Gen 32:13,14,15

COLUMN
his family into a *, with his two Gen 33:2
the front of the * to choose a Num 10:33
goods at the front of the *. Ju 18:21
The top 7½ feet of each * had Jer 52:22

COLUMNS
Gomorrah and saw * of smoke and Gen 19:28
three or four *, the king would Jer 36:23
a 14-foot hall with 3½-foot *. Eze 40:7-12
decorations on its *, but there Eze 40:34
and measured the * at the entrance Eze 41:3

COMB
a fine-toothed * to try to find a Job 33:10

COMBAT
we will settle this in single *! 1Sa 17:8
each side to fight in mortal *. 2Sa 2:15
against yourselves in mortal *! Eze 38:21
each other in hand-to-hand *. Zec 14:13

COMBED
I neither washed nor shaved nor * Dan 10:3

COMBINED
Their * offerings were as Num 7:84,85,86
they quickly * their armies to Jos 9:1
So these five Amorite kings * Jos 10:5
Their * troops, along with a vast Jos 11:4
the * armies of Israel and Judah. 2Sa 3:12
and Beriah were * into a single 1Ch 23:10,11
when the * armies of the Nah 2:1f
more than all the rest of them *. Lk 21:3

COMBS
and capes and ornate * and purses; Is 3:22

COME
and this time she didn't * back. Gen 8:12
the floods * and destroy all life. Gen 9:15
*, let us go down and give them Gen 11:7
will * away with great wealth. Gen 15:14
* from, and where are you going?" Gen 16:8
"Sirs," he said, "* to my home Gen 19:2
having children. *, let's fill him Gen 19:32
our clan will not * to an end." Gen 19:32
we *, that you are my sister.' Gen 20:13
worship, and then * right back." Gen 22:5
who will * so far from home?" Gen 24:5
"* and stay with us, friend; Gen 24:31
but to * to his relatives here Gen 24:38
I can't find a girl who will *?' Gen 24:39
"Why have you *?" Gen 26:27
Isaac: "* over here. Gen 27:21
Isaac: "* here and kiss me, my Gen 27:26
Rachel and Leah to * out to the Gen 31:4
my fathers has * and spoken to me. Gen 31:5
wealth will * to us anyway! Gen 31:14
You have * rushing after me as Gen 31:36,37
grandchildren? * now and we will Gen 31:44
will be enriched. * on, let's agree Gen 34:23
We are so few that they will * Gen 34:30
brothers * and bow before you?" Gen 37:10
they exclaimed. "* on, let's kill Gen 37:19,20
"Here * some Ishmaelites. Gen 37:26,27
she let him * and sleep with her; Gen 38:18
"Where did you * from!" Gen 38:29
that he * and sleep with her. Gen 39:7
will * and pick off your flesh!" Gen 40:18,19
fat ones that had * out first, and Gen 41:20
when the seven years of famine *. Gen 41:36
"We have * to buy grain." Gen 42:7
You have * to see how destitute Gen 42:8,9
"We have * to buy food. Gen 42:10
"You have * to see how weak we Gen 42:12
and you can * as often as you like Gen 42:34
didn't * back, Simeon is gone, and Gen 42:36
said, 'Don't ever * back again Gen 43:3,4,5
this time if you had let him *." Gen 43:10
But you told us, 'Don't * back Gen 44:23
Only then may we *.' Gen 44:26
"* over here," he said. Gen 45:4
of Egypt. * down to me right away! Gen 45:9
Otherwise you will * to utter Gen 45:11,12
brothers have *"; Gen 45:16
and * here to Egypt to live. Gen 45:18
and that you have * from the land Gen 46:31
We have * to live here in Egypt, Gen 47:4
to happen to you in the days to *. Gen 49:1
God will surely * and get you, and Gen 50:24
the time had * for their rescue. Ex 2:25
"Don't * any closer," God told Ex 3:5

(COME Con't)

I have * to deliver them from	Ex 3:8
and they will * out into your	Ex 8:3,4
frogs to * up upon the land.	Ex 8:7
of yours will * running to me,	Ex 11:8
And when you * into the land	Ex 12:25
and did not * in to destroy us.'	Ex 12:27
and then they may * and celebrate	Ex 12:48
the waters will * back over the	Ex 14:26
in the morning. * now before	Ex 16:7,8,9
water will * pouring out, enough	Ex 17:5,6
father-in-law, has * to visit	Ex 18:5,6
"Well, because the people * to	Ex 18:15,16
"I am going to * to you in the	Ex 19:9
tomorrow, I will * down upon Mt.	Ex 19:11
They must not * up here to try to	Ex 19:21
Literally, "The priests who *	Ex 19:22f
"But the people won't * up into	Ex 19:23
to try to * up here, or I will	Ex 19:24
"for God has * in this way to show	Ex 20:20
and I will * and bless you there.	Ex 20:24
the dispute shall * before God for	Ex 22:9
"If you * upon an enemy's ox or	Ex 23:4
any volunteer crop that may * up;	Ex 23:11
THE LORD NOW instructed Moses, "*	Ex 24:1
Moses alone shall * near to the	Ex 24:2
* up into the mountain at all."	Ex 24:2
And the Lord said to Moses, "*	Ex 24:12
and wait for us until we * back;	Ex 24:14
WHEN MOSES DIDN'T * back down	Ex 32:1
side, * over here and join me."	Ex 32:26
however, when I * to visit these	Ex 32:34
of cloud would * down and stand at	Ex 33:9
Be ready in the morning to * up	Ex 34:2
No one shall * with you and no	Ex 34:3
Israel were afraid to * near him.	Ex 34:30
"*, all of you who are skilled	Ex 35:10-19
* upon all the people of Israel.	Lev 10:6
skin after he has * to the priest	Lev 13:7
examined, he must * back to the	Lev 13:7
of the house shall * and report to	Lev 14:35
the priest shall * again and look,	Lev 14:44
young pigeons and * before the Lord	Lev 15:14
and then * back into the camp.	Lev 16:26
the veil, nor * near the altar,	Lev 21:23
All the people are to * together	Lev 23:26,27
"When you * into the land I am	Lev 25:1
crops that * up, and don't gather	Lev 25:5
old or older to * and register,	Num 1:17,18,19
of Kohath shall * and carry the	Num 4:15
the generations to *, are defiled	Num 9:10
tribes of Israel shall * to you.	Num 10:4
* with us and we will do you good;	Num 10:29
If you *, you will share in all	Num 10:32
Then the Egyptians who had * with	Num 11:4,5
I will * down and talk with you	Num 11:17
"* here, you three," he commanded.	Num 12:3,4
after that she can * back again."	Num 12:14
of Eliab), but they refused to *.	Num 16:11,12
We refuse to *."	Num 16:14
And Moses said to Korah, "* here	Num 16:16
of Aaron—may * before the Lord to	Num 16:40
to * and gather at the rock;	Num 20:10
"The time has * for Aaron to	Num 20:24
* to Heshbon,	Num 21:27-30
He begged Balaam to * and help	Num 22:5,6
"Please * and curse them for me,	Num 22:5,6
"They have * from King Balak of	Num 22:10
"King Balak pleads with you to *.	Num 22:16,17
Name your own figure! Only * and	Num 22:16,17
"I have * to stop you because	Num 22:32
Balaam replied, "I have *, but I	Num 22:38
'*,' he told me, 'curse Jacob for	Num 23:7-10
Then Balak told him, "* with me	Num 23:13
That there shall * a star from	Num 24:15-19
Ships shall * from the coasts of	Num 24:23,24
water to * out of the rock."	Num 27:14
she agreed shall * upon him—he	Num 30:15
you may * back into the camp."	Num 31:24
"When they * into the land of	Num 34:1
When those bitter days have *	Deu 4:30
God says, then * and tell us, and	Deu 5:26,27
Then you * back and stand here	Deu 5:31
"In the years to * when your son	Deu 6:20
where you have * from, where	Deu 11:10
if his predictions * true but he	Deu 13:2
true but he says, '*, let us	Deu 13:2
whispers to you to * and worship	Deu 13:6,7
has the right to * to the sanctuary	Deu 18:6,7
"Then the priests shall * (for	Deu 21:5
blessings that will * upon you:	Deu 28:2-6
Blessings when you * in,	Deu 28:2-6
of these curses shall * upon you:	Deu 28:15-19
Curses when you * in;	Deu 28:15-19
the generations to * and the	Deu 29:22
He will have mercy upon you and *	Deu 30:3
and Israel shall * alive again!	Deu 30:6
longer able to go out and * in."	Deu 31:2f
time has * when you must die.	Deu 31:14
Summon Joshua and * into the	Deu 31:14
Terrible trouble will * upon	Deu 31:17
great disasters * upon them, then	Deu 31:21
and in the days to * evil will	Deu 31:29
Let all these blessings * upon	Deu 33:16
and told them, "* and listen to	Jos 3:9
"* up from the riverbed," the	Jos 4:15,16
Behind them would * the priests	Jos 6:6-9
In the morning you must * by	Jos 7:14
And that tribe must * by its	Jos 7:14
and the clan must * by its	Jos 7:14
guilty family must * one by one.	Jos 7:14
the men of Ai will * out to fight	Jos 8:5
Israel, "We have * from a distant	Jos 9:6
"Where do you * from?"	Jos 9:8
"* and help me destroy Gibeon,"	Jos 10:4
"* and help your servants!"	Jos 10:6
they demanded. "* quickly and	Jos 10:6
they must let him * in and must	Jos 20:4
promises to you have all * true.	Jos 23:14
let them * down into the valley;	Ju 1:34
he still didn't * out, they became	Ju 3:25
to him, "* into my tent, sir.	Ju 4:18
him and said, "*, and I will show	Ju 4:22
'Because they did not * to help	Ju 5:23
is going to * and massacre all the	Ju 7:14
and told them to * and chase and	Ju 7:23
really want me, * and humble	Ju 9:15
waiting for him to * along, they	Ju 9:25
an army and * on out and fight!'	Ju 9:29
his relatives have * to live in	Ju 9:31
against you. * by night with an	Ju 9:32
who are with him * out against you,	Ju 9:33
begging him to * and lead their	Ju 11:6
them, "Why do you * to me when you	Ju 11:7
* now when you're in trouble?"	Ju 11:7
you, but you refused to *!"	Ju 12:2
the man from God * back to us again	Ju 13:8
"Why have you * here?"	Ju 15:10
"We have * to capture you and	Ju 15:12,13
The Philistines have * to capture	Ju 16:12
Philistines have *, Samson!"	Ju 16:14
"* just this once more," she	Ju 16:18
Why did you *?"	Ju 18:3
defend themselves! * on, let's go!	Ju 18:9,10
"Be quiet and * with us," they	Ju 18:19
"Well, * on," he said.	Ju 19:28
anyone who refused to * must die.	Ju 21:5
who refused to * to Mizpah, and	Ju 21:8,9
girls of Shiloh * out for their	Ju 21:21
and brothers * to us in protest, we	Ju 21:22
* here to live among strangers.	Ru 2:10,11
wings you have * to take refuge,	Ru 2:12
to her, "* and eat with us."	Ru 2:14
her, "he said to * back and stay	Ru 2:21
"Say, * over here," he called to	Ru 4:1
woman, who has now * into your	Ru 4:11
"Must you * here drunk?"	1Sa 1:14
Sometimes the servant would *	1Sa 2:15
I have said will * true, I will	1Sa 2:34
"God has * into their camp!"	1Sa 4:7
"I have just * from the battle—I	1Sa 4:16
"* and get it!"	1Sa 6:21
Then Samuel told them, "* to	1Sa 7:5
Then he would * back to Ramah,	1Sa 7:17
After that you will * to	1Sa 10:5
a harp, and prophesying as they *.	1Sa 10:5
of the Lord will * mightily upon	1Sa 10:6
"If none of our brothers will *	1Sa 11:3
Tomorrow we will * out to you and	1Sa 11:10
to the people, "*, let us all go	1Sa 11:14
he still didn't *, and Saul's	1Sa 13:8
young bodyguard, "* on, let's	1Sa 14:1
But if they say, '* on up and	1Sa 14:10
to Jonathan, "* on up here and	1Sa 14:12
"* on, climb right behind me,"	1Sa 14:12
* to make a sacrifice to the Lord.	1Sa 16:2
"Why have you *?"	1Sa 16:4
I have * to sacrifice to the	1Sa 16:5
Purify yourselves and * with me	1Sa 16:5
"that you * at me with a stick?"	1Sa 17:43
of his gods. "* over here and	1Sa 17:44
David shouted in reply, "You *	1Sa 17:45
and a spear, but I * to you in the	1Sa 17:45
does this young fellow * from?"	1Sa 17:55
"* out to the field with me,"	1Sa 20:11
I will * out and shoot three	1Sa 20:20
My own son—encouraging David to *	1Sa 22:8
me and to * here and attack me?"	1Sa 22:13
is planning to * and destroy Keilah	1Sa 23:10
And will Saul actually *, as I	1Sa 23:11
And the Lord said, "He will *."	1Sa 23:11
the wilderness. * on down, sir,	1Sa 23:20
places and then * back and give me	1Sa 23:23
have * at a happy time of holiday.	1Sa 25:8
Literally, "to men who * from God	1Sa 25:11f
if you had not * out to meet me,	1Sa 25:34
her why they had *, she readily	1Sa 25:40
Why should the king of Israel *	1Sa 26:20
have done wrong. * back home, my	1Sa 26:21
"Let one of your young men *	1Sa 26:22
No one was left alive to * to	1Sa 27:11
"* and help us fight," King	1Sa 28:1
All this has * upon you because	1Sa 28:18
"Who are you and where do you *	1Sa 30:13
"Where do you * from?"	2Sa 1:3
he cried out for me to * to him.	2Sa 1:7
" '* and put me out of my	2Sa 1:9
with Abner and tell him to * back.	2Sa 3:26
"You'll never * in here," they	2Sa 5:6
Go behind them and * out by the	2Sa 5:23
of Obed-edom, who had * from Gath.	2Sa 6:10
this land for generations to *!	2Sa 7:10,11
I've asked you to * so that I can	2Sa 9:7
the Syrians, * out and help me,"	2Sa 10:11
for you, I will * and help you.	2Sa 10:11
* and prepare some food for you.	2Sa 13:5
be permitted to * and cook a little	2Sa 13:6
"* to bed with me, my darling."	2Sa 13:11
his brothers to * to a feast to	2Sa 13:21-24
*, though he sent his thanks.	2Sa 13:25
"if you can't *, how about sending	2Sa 13:26
But I have * to plead with you	2Sa 14:15,16
"but he must never * here.	2Sa 14:24
but Joab wouldn't *.	2Sa 14:29
again, but again he refused to *.	2Sa 14:29
a lawsuit could * to me, and I	2Sa 15:4
Gittites who had * with him from	2Sa 15:17,18
So David replied, "All right, *	2Sa 15:22
* directly from the mouth of God.	2Sa 16:23
I will * upon him while he is	2Sa 17:2,3
"When Joab told me to *, there	2Sa 18:29
in Judah had * to Gilgal to meet	2Sa 19:15
That is why I have * here today,	2Sa 19:20
"Why didn't you * with me,	2Sa 19:24,25
me by saying that I refused to *.	2Sa 19:27
"* across with me and live in	2Sa 19:33
to do with David. * on, you men of	2Sa 20:1
for David, * and follow Joab."	2Sa 20:11
to me, Joab. * over here so I can	2Sa 20:16
And *, trembling,	2Sa 22:46
'One shall * who rules	2Sa 23:3
"Why have you *?"	2Sa 24:21
that they * to his coronation.	1Ki 1:9
with him, I'll * and confirm	1Ki 1:14
"* in," Adonijah said to him,	1Ki 1:42
"Have you * to make trouble?"	1Ki 2:13
"No," he replied, "I * in	1Ki 2:13
Joab, "The king says to * out!"	1Ki 2:30
man named Hiram to * from Tyre, for	1Ki 7:13
great name and * from distant lands	1Ki 8:41,42
or near, and they * to their	1Ki 8:47
live, and * to their assistance.	1Ki 8:49
"* back then for my answer."	1Ki 12:5
he was asked to * before an open	1Ki 12:20
hills who * here to burn incense;	1Ki 13:2
to the prophet, "* to the palace	1Ki 13:7
"* home with me and eat."	1Ki 13:15
command, and have * here, and have	1Ki 13:21,22
else, would * to ask about her son,	1Ki 14:5
out, "* in, wife of Jeroboam!	1Ki 14:6
family who will * to a quiet end.	1Ki 14:13
Have you * here to punish my sins	1Ki 17:18
to tell Ahab that Elijah had *;	1Ki 18:16
to the people, "* over here."	1Ki 18:30
have * for truce or for war."	1Ki 20:18
answered, "I have * to place God's	1Ki 21:20
"Oh, * now!"	1Ki 22:8
you to * along with us."	2Ki 1:9
of God, let fire * down from heaven	2Ki 1:10
that you must * down right away."	2Ki 1:11
of God, let fire * down from heaven	2Ki 1:12
to the prophet and * right back."	2Ki 4:22
he would * out and talk to me!	2Ki 5:11
"Please, sir, * with us,"	2Ki 6:3
them, "You've * the wrong way!	2Ki 6:19
fall upon us; * on, let's go back	2Ki 7:9
when the king had * to arrest him,	2Ki 7:17
the king that the prophet had *.	2Ki 8:7
"Do you * in peace?"	2Ki 9:18
"Do you * as a friend, Jehu?"	2Ki 9:22
that Jehu had * to Jezreel, she	2Ki 9:30
"Now * along with me," Jehu	2Ki 10:16
don't * will be put to death."	2Ki 10:18,19
But kill anyone who tries to * to	2Ki 11:15
his army and * out and fight.	2Ki 14:8
and your son. * and rescue me.'	2Ki 16:7f
that King Hezekiah * out to speak	2Ki 18:18
And do you think we have * here	2Ki 18:25
The time will * when everything in	2Ki 20:17
when the people * to worship.	2Ki 22:3,4
These names all * from very	1Ch 4:21-22
have * to help me, we are friends;	1Ch 12:17
but if you have * to betray me to	1Ch 12:17
inviting them to * and join us.	1Ch 13:2
Bring an offering and * before	1Ch 16:29
they can * in and conquer it!"	1Ch 19:2,3
too strong for me, * and help me,"	1Ch 19:12
for you, I'll * and help you.	1Ch 19:12
Riches and honor * from you	1Ch 29:12
Everything we have has * from	1Ch 29:14
that the time had * to build a	2Ch 2:1
of your power, and * from distant	2Ch 6:32
(for many had * from the	2Ch 15:9

(COME Con't)
"Oh, * now, don't talk like 2Ch 18:6,7
of God * down upon you and them; 2Ch 19:10
For they have * to throw us out 2Ch 20:11
"At last the time has * for the 2Ch 23:2,3
and Levites who * off duty on the 2Ch 23:4
everyone to * to the Temple at 2Ch 30:1
"* back to the Lord God of 2Ch 30:6
to the Lord and * to his Temple 2Ch 30:8
Then the people who had * to the 2Ch 31:1
"Where did all this * from?" 2Ch 31:9
"Why should the king of Assyria * 2Ch 32:4
written in the scroll will * true. 2Ch 34:24
to assist the people who *. 2Ch 35:6
I have * only to fight the king 2Ch 35:21
of Judah from which they had *. Ez 2:70
disaster could * only to those who Ez 8:22
who refused to * would be Ez 10:7,8
heathen wife will * at the Ez 10:14
Why should I stop to * and visit Neh 6:3
I suggest that you * and talk it Neh 6:7
Great trouble has * upon us and Neh 9:32
to Queen Vashti, she refused to *. Est 1:12
* to him in more than a month." Est 4:11
you and Haman to * to a banquet I Est 5:4
request, that you * again with Est 5:7,8
"Where have you * from?" Job 1:7
"Where have you * from?" Job 2:2
be born to * to all this trouble. Job 3:10
long for death, and it won't *; Job 3:20,21
Call to me to *—how quickly I Job 13:22
You would call and I would *, Job 14:15
How little will * of his hopes! Job 15:33
* out on top, above the godless; Job 17:8
call my servant, but he doesn't *; Job 19:16
They despise me and won't * near Job 30:10
They * at me from all Job 30:14
I therefore looked for good to * Job 30:26
Waves of affliction have * upon Job 30:27
poor to * to the attention of God. Job 34:28
If troubles * upon them, and Job 36:8
farther shall you *, and here shall Job 38:11
which the seas *, or walked in the Job 38:16
Where does the light * from, and Job 38:19
Where does it * from? Job 38:19
Where does dew * from? Job 38:28
dares * within reach of his jaws? Job 41:13
"*, let us break his chains," Ps 2:3
But as for me, I will * into your Ps 5:7
*, O Lord, and make me well. Ps 6:4
All who are oppressed may * to Ps 9:9
* and deal with all these proud Ps 10:2
that God would * from Zion now to Ps 14:7
SAVE ME, O God, because I have * Ps 16:1
You have * even in the night and Ps 17:3
Push them back! * and save me Ps 17:13,14
Even those I didn't know before * Ps 18:43,44,45
instantly. They * trembling from Ps 18:43,44,45
They * at me with open jaws, Ps 22:13
can rescue me. *, Lord, and show Ps 25:16
my innocence and * before your Ps 26:6
When evil men * to destroy me, Ps 27:2
There I'll be when troubles *. Ps 27:5
My heart has heard you say, "* Ps 27:8
Wait for the Lord, and he will * Ps 27:14
glory of his name. * before him Ps 29:2
Many sorrows * to the wicked, but Ps 32:10
Sons and daughters, * and listen Ps 34:11
are glad; they * together in Ps 35:15
O Lord my God. * and protect me. Ps 38:15
don't go away! * quickly! Ps 38:22
said, "See, I have *, just as Ps 40:7
Quick! * and help me! Ps 40:13
You are my Savior; * quickly, and Ps 40:17
* to visit me while I am sick; Ps 41:6
Where can I find him to * and Ps 42:2
Rise up, O Lord, and * and help Ps 44:26
He, the God of Jacob, has * to Ps 46:7
to rescue us. *, see the glorious Ps 46:8
He, the God of Jacob, has * to Ps 46:11
*, EVERYONE, AND clap for joy! Ps 47:1
times of trouble *, even though Ps 49:5
For God's forgiveness does not * Ps 49:7
He has * to judge his people. Ps 50:4
of punishment has *, and I list all Ps 50:21
the prophet had * to inform David Ps 51:1
like bread and refuse to * to God. Ps 53:4
Oh, that God would * from Zion Ps 53:6
* WITH GREAT power, Ps 54:1
Protect me from these who have *. Ps 59:1
At evening they * to spy, Ps 59:6
for me and he will * and help me. Ps 59:10
He will let me see my wish * true Ps 59:10
tense with fear when troubles *? Ps 62:2
tense with fear when troubles *? Ps 62:6
* from God alone. Ps 62:7
will * to you with their requests. Ps 65:1
you have chosen to * and live with Ps 65:4
of your glories. *, see the Ps 66:5
Now I have * to your Temple with Ps 66:13
* and hear, all of you who Ps 66:16

The Lord says, "*," to all his Ps 68:22
Quick! * and save me. Ps 69:17
Come and save me. *, Lord, and Ps 69:18
O God, don't stay away! * Ps 71:12
For promotion and power * from Ps 75:6,7
* back, we beg of you, O God of Ps 80:14
Sound the trumpet! * to the Ps 81:3
precious ones. *, they say, and Ps 83:4
and * near to the Living God. Ps 84:2
are welcome to * and nest among Ps 84:3
made each one—will * and bow before Ps 86:9
O Jehovah, * and bless us! Ps 90:13
overtake me or any plague * near? Ps 91:10
OH, *, LET us sing to the Lord! Ps 95:1
* before him with thankful Ps 95:2
they too are his. *, kneel Ps 95:6
calling you today and * to him! Ps 95:7
Bring your offering and * to Ps 96:8
Obey him gladly; * before him, Ps 100:2
I know that you will * and have Ps 102:13
when all the forest folk * out. Ps 104:20
—* with mighty power and rescue me. Ps 108:6
your people shall * to you Ps 110:3
now they are always free to * to Ps 111:9
him, light will * bursting in. Ps 112:4
How I enjoy your commands! "*, Ps 119:48
"Come, * to me," I call to Ps 119:48
to see your promises * true. Ps 119:82
* and have mercy on me as is your Ps 119:132
Here * these lawless men to Ps 119:150
like a lost sheep; * and find me Ps 119:176
* and go, and always guards you. Ps 121:8
people—have * to worship as the law Ps 122:4
thirsts for rain. * quickly, Lord, Ps 143:7
down the heavens, Lord, and *. Ps 144:5
If young toughs tell you, "* and Pro 1:10
All kinds of stuff ! * on, Pro 1:14
facts? * here and listen to me! Pro 1:23
so often but still you won't *. Pro 1:24
and cinnamon. * on, let's take our Pro 7:18
out her maidens inviting all to *. Pro 9:3
in the city, "*, you simple ones Pro 9:4
good judgment; * to wisdom's Pro 9:5
own business. "* home with me," Pro 9:16
The wicked man's fears will all * Pro 10:24
constantly and * to shame. Pro 13:5
but when dreams * true at last, Pro 13:12
is going to * of his invitation. Pro 23:1
finally * to light for all to see. Pro 26:24,25,26
He defends all who * to him for Pro 30:5
Generations * and go but it makes Ecc 1:3-7
I SAID TO myself, "* now, be Ecc 2:1
would * to the same conclusion Ecc 2:12
to * both will be long forgotten. Ecc 2:16
Such a lad could * from prison Ecc 4:14
are heavy, the rains * down; Ecc 11:3
the evil years *—when you'll no Ecc 12:1
For there will * a time when Ecc 12:3
Take me with you; *, let's Sol 1:4
For I will * and join you there Sol 1:7
my love, my fair one, and * away. Sol 2:10
of the singing of birds has *. Sol 2:12
my love, my fair one, and * away.' Sol 2:13
shadows flee away, * to me, my Sol 2:17
"* with me from Lebanon, my Sol 4:8
The Girl: "*, north wind, Sol 4:16
wind, awaken; *, south wind, blow Sol 4:16
Let him * into his garden and eat Sol 4:16
O maid of Shulam. * back, come Sol 6:13
Come back, * back, that we may Sol 6:13
one he desires. *, my beloved, let Sol 7:11
let me hear it too. * quickly, Sol 8:14
*, let's talk this over! Is 1:18
for they refuse to * to me. Is 1:28
"*," everyone will say, "let Is 2:3
O Israel, *, let us walk in the Is 2:5
will * racing toward Jerusalem. Is 5:26
will * with his great army! Is 7:17
They will * in vast hordes, Is 7:19
and despoiling (will) * quickly." Is 8:1f
and King Pekah to * and aid them, Is 8:6
harvest time has *, and like that Is 9:3
See, God has * to save me! Is 12:2
Lord's time has *, the time for the Is 13:6
generation will * and go, but the Is 13:20
the demons will * there to dance. Is 13:21
And many nationalities will * and Is 14:1
destruction has * upon their summer Is 16:9
but none will * to save them. Is 16:12
But the time will * when that Is 18:7
line of wise men they have * from? Is 19:11
Now at last—look! Here * riders Is 21:8,9
Seek for him, then * and ask Is 21:12
God, who lets this * upon you. Is 22:9,10,11
It will * out and fall to the Is 22:25
city will * back to life again; Is 23:15,16
Yet [the distant time will * Is 23:18
its walls * crashing down. Is 26:5
for only when you * in judgment Is 26:9
for all we have and are has * Is 26:12
No deliverance has * from all our Is 26:18

The time will * when Israel will Is 27:6
Yet the time will * when the Is 27:12
The enemy will * like a flood and Is 28:17
that flood will * and carry you Is 28:19
The Lord will * suddenly and in Is 28:21
of Hosts, will * upon them with Is 29:6
calamity will * upon you suddenly, Is 30:13
waits for you to * to him, so he Is 30:18
In such manner the Lord will * Is 31:4,5
wicked rebels, *, return to God. Is 31:6
I know the glorious day will * Is 31:7
once again enormous crops will *. Is 32:15
* HERE AND listen, O nations of Is 34:1
the demons will * there to rest. Is 34:14
will *, each one with its mate. Is 34:15
Spirit will make it all * true. Is 34:16
you think I have * here without the Is 36:10
open the gates and * out, and I Is 36:16
birth, and the child does not *. Is 37:3
will cause all this to * to pass. Is 37:32
Bring your strongest arguments. * Is 41:1
Let them * and show what they can Is 41:21
he will * against the nations and Is 41:25
as their God will *, for I have Is 43:7
They shall * to you with all Is 45:14
Gather together and *, you Is 45:20
concerning Cyrus would * true? Is 45:21
him shall * to him and be ashamed. Is 45:24
All I say will * to pass, for I Is 46:10
And he will * and do my bidding. Is 46:11
O BABYLON, THE unconquered, * sit Is 47:1
Well, those two things shall * Is 47:9
*, all of you, and listen. Is 48:14
* closer and listen. Is 48:16
request has * at a favorable time. Is 49:8,9
the prisoners of darkness, '* out! Is 49:8,9
Soon your rebuilders shall * and Is 49:17
shall * and be your slaves. Is 49:18
is silent and empty when I * home? Is 50:2
wait for me and long for me to *. Is 51:5
The time will * when God's Is 51:11
redeemed will all * home again. Is 51:11
They shall * with singing to Is 51:11
Terror shall not * near. Is 54:14
IS anyone thirsty? * and Is 55:1
you have no money! *, take your Is 55:1
* to me with your ears wide open. Is 55:3
and they will * running to obey, Is 55:5
As the rain and snow * down from Is 55:10
please him, and * to grips with his Is 56:4
*, wild animals of the field; Is 56:9
field; *, tear apart the sheep; Is 56:9
come, tear apart the sheep; *, Is 56:9
"*," they say. Is 56:12
But you—* here, you witches' Is 57:3
Yet they act so pious! They * to Is 58:2
For he will * like a flood-tide Is 59:19
He will * as a Redeemer to those Is 59:20
All nations will * to your Is 60:3
mighty kings will * to see the Is 60:3
Foreigners will * and build your Is 60:10
The sons of anti-Semites will * Is 60:14
favor to them has *, and the day of Is 61:2
foreign soldiers * and take away Is 62:8
For the time has * for me to Is 63:4
forth from the skies and * down! Is 64:1
* too close, you'll defile me! Is 65:5
And yet, the days will * Is 65:16
even before the birth pains *. Is 66:7,8
For see, the Lord will * with Is 66:15
* to an evil end, says Jehovah. Is 66:17
All mankind shall * to worship Is 66:23
of the north to * to Jerusalem and Jer 1:15
children in the years to *! Jer 2:9
search, for you * running to him! Jer 2:24
Don't * to me—you are all Jer 2:29
to * to me again, the Lord says. Jer 3:1
but she didn't * back. Jer 3:7
my sinful people, * home to me Jer 3:12
O sinful children, * home, for I Jer 3:14
all nations will * to him there and Jer 3:17
O my rebellious children, * back Jer 3:22
And they reply, Yes, we will *, Jer 3:22
will * to me and glorify my name. Jer 4:2
No evil will * upon us! Jer 5:12
shadows fall. "*," they say. Jer 6:5
yours, and then * here and stand Jer 7:10
wait here to die? *, let us go to Jer 8:14
to * to me," says the Lord. Jer 9:6
have to * any more to my Temple? Jer 11:15
Their time has *. Jer 11:23
* down from your thrones and sit Jer 13:18
well—that no war or famine will *. Jer 14:13
who say no war shall * nor famine. Jer 14:15
But no peace has * and there is Jer 14:19
But there will * a glorious day, Jer 16:14,15
the world will * to you saying, Jer 16:19
And when they * in that Jer 16:21
from God, why don't they * true?" Jer 17:15
the people shall * with their burnt Jer 17:26
Then the people said, "*, let's Jer 18:18

(COME Con't)

troops of soldiers * suddenly upon Jer 18:22
their time has *, that they pay Jer 23:12
all the evil that has * your way. Jer 25:7
* to be slaughtered and scattered; Jer 25:34
people who have * there to worship Jer 26:2
May your prophecies * true! Jer 28:6
But then I will * and do for you Jer 29:10
from them for a long time to *." Jer 29:28
would dare to * unless invited. Jer 30:21
The day shall * when watchmen on Jer 31:6
They shall * home and sing songs Jer 31:12
they will * back to you from the Jer 31:16
will * again to their own land. Jer 31:17
The Lord says: The time will * Jer 31:27
The day will *, says the Lord, Jer 31:31
the walls shall * in and set fire Jer 32:29
Nevertheless the time will * when Jer 33:6
Yes, the day will *, says the Jer 33:14
and night don't * on their usual Jer 33:20,21
to ask Baruch to * and read the Jer 36:14,15
he could go and * as he pleased. Jer 37:4
him to * to the palace secretly. Jer 37:17
the king of Babylon would not *? Jer 37:19
If you want to * with me to Jer 40:4
But if you don't want to *, Jer 40:4
who will * here to oversee my Jer 40:10
"Why should we let him * and Jer 40:15
he said, "Oh, * and see what has Jer 41:6
among you who has * here from Jer 44:7
Then *, O horses and chariots Jer 46:9
soldiers of Egypt! *, all of you Jer 46:9
Jews will say, "*, let us return Jer 46:16
for the time has * when all the Jer 47:4
to destroy her. "*," they say, Jer 48:2,3,4
is shattered! * down from your Jer 48:18
the time of your judgment has *. Jer 48:44
Then Israel shall * and take back Jer 49:2
them one who will * like a lion Jer 49:19
The one who will * will fly as Jer 49:22
For a nation shall * down upon Jer 50:3
back home again. "*," they will Jer 50:5
Yes, * against her from distant Jer 50:26
For the time has * for Babylon to Jer 50:27
Send out a call for archers to * Jer 50:29
now your day of reckoning has *. Jer 50:31
invader who will * upon them Jer 50:44
Winnowers shall * and winnow her Jer 51:2
they shall * from every side to Jer 51:2
The Lord has vindicated us. *, Jer 51:10
of commerce, your end has *; Jer 51:13
when God will * and see, and shall Jer 51:18
Messengers from every side * Jer 51:31
The nations shall no longer * and Jer 51:44
of the north shall * destroying Jer 51:48
Destroying armies * and slay her Jer 51:56
Zedekiah and had * over to the Jer 52:15
* to celebrate the Temple feasts; Lam 1:4
that punishment was sure to *. Lam 1:9
A great army has * at his command Lam 1:15
time will surely *—for you have Lam 1:21
cried until the tears no longer *; Lam 2:11
* from the rod of God's wrath. Lam 3:1
to * and save us, but we look in Lam 4:17
for a fire shall * from this Eze 5:4
And not only famine will *, but Eze 5:17
The end has *; Eze 7:5,6
the time has *; Eze 7:7
The day of judgment has *; Eze 7:10,11
"Yes, the time has *; Eze 7:12
For the time has * for the Eze 7:25
my Temple? But *, and I will show Eze 8:6
Then he added, "*, and I Eze 8:13
evil that will * upon Jerusalem." Eze 12:6
'The time has * for all these Eze 12:23
* true for a long, long time.' Eze 12:27
His prophecy will not * true, and Eze 14:9
of the enemy to * and destroy Eze 14:17
survivors and they * here to join Eze 14:22
gifts, bribing them to * to you! Eze 16:33,34
How dare you * to ask my help? Eze 20:3
though you have * to me to ask. Eze 20:31
now the time of punishment has *. Eze 21:24
* you will be wounded unto death. Eze 21:29
to Chaldea to invite them to * to Eze 23:16
For the Babylonians will *, and Eze 23:23
They will * against you from the Eze 23:24
for priests to * with other gods Eze 23:40
and they have * and been welcomed! Eze 23:40
it shall * to pass and I will do Eze 24:14
on a journey to * to you in Babylon Eze 24:26
rulers shall * down from their Eze 26:16
"Your sailors * from Sidon and Eze 27:8
Ships * from every land with all Eze 27:9
"From Tarshish * all kinds of Eze 27:12
* chariot horses, steeds and Eze 27:14
"Merchants * to you from Rhodes, Eze 27:15
Sheba and Raamah * with all kinds Eze 27:22
All your sailors out at sea * to Eze 27:29
And the day will * when I will Eze 29:21
This will all * true. Eze 30:9
When I * to break the power of Eze 30:18
king of Babylon shall * upon you. Eze 32:11
and her power shall * to an end. Eze 33:28
"* on, let's have some fun! Eze 33:30
Literally, "* and let us hear Eze 33:30f
So they * as though they are Eze 33:31
you a blood bath—your turn has *! Eze 35:6
See, I am for you, and I will * Eze 36:9
Lord God says: * from the four Eze 37:9
thought will have * to your mind. Eze 38:10
You will * from all over the Eze 38:15,16
But when you * to destroy the Eze 38:18
That day of judgment will *; Eze 39:8
sacrificial feast. * from far and Eze 39:17
of Israel. *, eat the flesh and Eze 39:17
the Levites may * near to the Lord Eze 40:46
But he shall go and * only Eze 44:3
They shall not * near me to Eze 44:13
* to my Table to minister to me; Eze 44:16
but when the people * in through Eze 46:9
the same way they * in, but must Eze 46:9
"But after your kingdom has * to Dan 2:39
* to the dedication of his statue. Dan 3:2
of the Most High God! * out! Dan 3:26
Come out! * here!" Dan 3:26
then the Ancient of Days will * Dan 7:26
place until the end times *." Dan 8:17
in the law of Moses has * true; Dan 9:13
the evils he predicted—all have *. Dan 9:13
"Do you know why I have *? Dan 10:20,21
his allies will * and lay siege to Dan 11:15
"Next to * to power will be an Dan 11:21
until God's appointed time has *. Dan 11:27
ungodly men will *, pretending to Dan 11:34
"Sir, how will this all * out?" Dan 12:8
"Yet the time will * when Israel Hos 1:10
that all she has, has * from me. Hos 1:8
and they shall * trembling, Hos 3:5
Your deeds won't let you * to Hos 5:4
Then at last, they will * with Hos 5:6
"*, LET US return to the Lord; Hos 6:1
time of Israel's punishment has *; Hos 9:7
I will * against you for your Hos 10:10
* and shower salvation upon you. Hos 10:12
you, and I did not * to destroy. Hos 11:9
birds, they will * from Egypt—like Hos 11:11
Oh, * back to God. Hos 12:6
So I will * upon you like a Hos 13:7
Bring your petition. * to the Hos 14:2
In years to *, tell your Joe 1:3
After them will * the Joe 1:4
Give me all your hearts. * with Joe 2:12
Once more the autumn rains will * Joe 2:23
terrible Day of the Lord shall *. Joe 2:31
Gather together and *, all Joe 3:11
the time will * when no foreign Joe 3:17
that the time will * when he will Amo 4:2
And yet you refused to *. Amo 4:10
only ten will * back alive." Amo 5:3
Bethel shall surely * to grief." Amo 5:5
I do not * from a family of Amo 7:14
"The time will * when there will Amo 9:13
"A report has * from the Lord," Ob 1:1
you if thieves had * at night to Ob 1:5
For deliverers will * to Ob 1:21
storm has * because of me." Jon 1:12
and you first told me to * here. Jon 4:2
Such evils surely will not * our Mic 2:6
The time will *, O Israel, when I Mic 2:12
No harm can * to us." Mic 3:11
"*," they will say to one Mic 4:2
and power will * back to you again, Mic 4:8
for the time will * when the Lord Mic 4:12
money, it will * to nothing at the Mic 6:14
Citizens of many lands will * Mic 7:12
O Lord, * and rule your people; Mic 7:14
They will * trembling out from Mic 7:17
See, the messengers * running Nah 1:15
from Nineveh will never * again. Nah 1:15
like eagles they * swooping down Hab 1:8
things will surely * to pass. Hab 2:3
("The time will * when all the Hab 2:14
* upon the people who invade us. Hab 3:16
awesome Day of his Judgment has *; Zep 1:7
of Ethiopia will * with their Zep 3:10
shall * to this Temple, and I Hag 2:7
"*, return to me," the Lord God Zec 1:4
"What have these men * to do?" Zec 1:21
The angel replied, "They have * Zec 1:21
" "*, flee from the land of the Zec 2:6,7
For I have * to live among you,' Zec 2:10
Lord, for he has * to earth from Zec 2:13
of the good things to *. Zec 3:8
the Man who will *, whose name is Zec 6:12
These three who have * from so Zec 6:15
who will some day * from distant Zec 6:15
the world will * on pilgrimages and Zec 8:20,21
Please * with me. Zec 8:20,21
nations, will * to the Lord of Zec 8:22
with blood. * to the place of Zec 9:12
in promises that don't * true? Zec 10:2
From them will * the Zec 10:4
to them, they'll * running, for I Zec 10:8
they will * home again to Israel. Zec 10:9
nations that * against Jerusalem. Zec 12:9
but I will * back and comfort and Zec 13:7
*, and all his saints and angels Zec 14:5
that refuses to * to Jerusalem to Zec 14:17
But if Egypt refuses to *, God Zec 14:18
be punished if they refuse to *. Zec 14:19
all who * to worship may use any Zec 14:21
men should * to them for guidance. Mal 2:7
you are looking for will * Mal 3:1
Hosts. "* and I will forgive you. Mal 3:7
and have * to worship him." Mt 2:2
asking them to * to see him; Mt 2:7
And when you find him, * back and Mt 2:8
"Screams of anguish * from Mt 2:18
Jesus called out, "* along with Mt 4:19
and he called to them to * too. Mt 4:21
why I have *—it isn't to cancel the Mt 5:17
them, and to make them all * true. Mt 5:17
* and offer your sacrifice to God. Mt 5:24
sacrifice to God. * to terms Mt 5:25
We ask that your kingdom will * Mt 6:10
"Beware of false teachers who * Mt 7:15
For when the rains and floods *, Mt 7:27
pled with him to * to his home and Mt 8:5,6
"Yes," Jesus said, "I will * Mt 8:7
it isn't necessary for you to * Mt 8:8,9
and to another, '*,' and he comes, Mt 8:8,9
shall * from all over the world Mt 8:11
Literally, "Have you * here to Mt 8:29f
booth. "* and be my disciple," Mt 9:9
For I have * to urge sinners, not Mt 9:13
you will only * and touch her." Mt 9:18
I have * to set a man against Mt 10:35
where he himself was about to *." Mt 11:1f
* [at the time the Kingdom begins Mt 11:14
Son reveals him. * to me and I Mt 11:28
this world or in the world to *. Mt 12:31,32
birds can * and find shelter." Mt 13:31,32
—the angels will * and separate Mt 13:49
the Baptist, * back to life again. Mt 14:2
you, tell me to * over to you, Mt 14:28
"All right," the Lord said, "* Mt 14:29
But evil words * from an evil Mt 15:18
For from the heart * evil Mt 15:19
of Mankind, shall * with my angels Mt 16:27
Literally, "that Elijah must * Mt 17:10f
Elijah must * and set everything Mt 17:11
And, in fact, he has already *, Mt 17:12
* to me, and don't prevent them. Mt 19:14
in heaven; and *, follow me." Mt 19:21
did not * to be served, but to Mt 20:28
to this estate; * on, let's kill Mt 21:38
everyone that it was time to *. Mt 22:3
For many will * claiming to be Mt 24:5
these must *, but the end is not Mt 24:6
the beginning of the horrors to *. Mt 24:8
and then, finally, the end will *. Mt 24:14
Then at last this age will * to Mt 24:34
is coming! * out and welcome him!' Mt 25:5,6
shall * in my glory, and all the Mt 25:31
at my right, '*, blessed of my Mt 25:34
says, my time has *, and I will eat Mt 26:18
The time has *! Mt 26:45
and do what you have * for." Mt 26:50
Well, then, * on down from the Mt 27:40
Israel, are you? * down from the Mt 27:41,42,43
Let's see whether Elijah will * Mt 27:49
And many women who had * down Mt 27:55
days I will * back to life again.' Mt 27:63
For he has * back to life again, Mt 28:6
he said he would. * in and see Mt 28:6
"At last the time has *!" Mk 1:15
Jesus called out to them, "*, Mk 1:17
you * to destroy us demons? Mk 1:24
no more and to * out of the man. Mk 1:25
demons to * out of their victims. Mk 1:34
"* with me," Jesus told him. Mk 2:14
told him. "* be my disciple." Mk 2:14
I haven't * to tell good people Mk 2:17
Jesus asked the man to * and Mk 3:3
them to * and join him there; Mk 3:13
him to * out and talk with them. Mk 3:31,32
of nice things * in and crowd out Mk 4:19
hidden will someday * to light. Mk 4:22
said, "* out, you evil spirit." Mk 5:7,8
"Please * and place your hands Mk 5:23
the Baptist * back to life again. Mk 6:14
He has * back from the dead." Mk 6:16
So when they * home from the Mk 7:4
called to the crowd to * and hear. Mk 7:14
For food doesn't * in contact Mk 7:19
of men's hearts, * evil thoughts of Mk 7:21
All these vile things * from Mk 7:23
For some of them have * a long Mk 8:3
prophet * back to life again." Mk 8:28
the crowds to * over and listen. Mk 8:34
return [before the Messiah could * Mk 9:11
Jesus agreed that Elijah must * Mk 9:12,13

COME Con't)

that he had, in fact, already *!	Mk 9:12,13
"I command you to * out of this	Mk 9:25
"Let the children * to me, for the	Mk 10:14
who refuses to * to God as a little	Mk 10:15
in heaven—and *, follow me."	Mk 10:21
to * he shall have eternal life.	Mk 10:30
but after three days I will *	Mk 10:34
and said, "Tell him to * here."	Mk 10:49
they said, "* on, he's calling	Mk 10:49
his father dies. * on, let's kill	Mk 12:7
He will * and kill them all, and	Mk 12:9
"for many will * declaring	Mk 13:6
you know that spring has *.	Mk 13:28
the master of the house will *."	Mk 13:34f
will *, at evening, at midnight,	Mk 13:35,36,37
heard why he had *, they were	Mk 14:11
hour awaiting him might never *.	Mk 14:35
into the hands of wicked men. *!	Mk 14:42
robber, that you * like this, armed	Mk 14:48
and * down from the cross."	Mk 15:29,30
"You 'King of Israel'! * on down	Mk 15:32
"Let's see if Elijah will * and	Mk 15:36
and had * with him to Jerusalem.	Mk 15:41
He has * back to life!	Mk 16:6
For I have * to tell you that God	Lk 1:13
For my words will certainly *	Lk 1:20
Holy Spirit shall * upon you, and	Lk 1:35
from God shall surely * true."	Lk 1:37
May everything you said * true."	Lk 1:38
for the time had * for the baby to	Lk 1:57
Israel, for he has * to visit his	Lk 1:68
said to each other, "* on!	Lk 2:15
to * soon. For the Holy Spirit	Lk 2:25
the Messiah to * soon, and eager to	Lk 3:15
blessings to all who * to him."	Lk 4:18,19
You have * to destroy us.	Lk 4:34
he told the demon. "* out!"	Lk 4:35
Jesus said to him, "* and be one	Lk 5:27
But the time will * when the	Lk 5:35
deformed hand, "* and stand here	Lk 6:8
had * to hear him or to be healed.	Lk 6:17,18
* when you shall laugh with joy!	Lk 6:21
it will all * back on you.	Lk 6:37
But all those who * and listen	Lk 6:47,48
ask him to * and heal his slave.	Lk 7:3
to * with them and help the man.	Lk 7:4
honor or even to * and meet you.	Lk 7:6,7,8
and they go; or '*!'	Lk 7:6,7,8
and they *;	Lk 7:6,7,8
"Laddie," he said, "* back to	Lk 7:14
The dead * back to life.	Lk 7:20,21,22
asked Jesus to * to his home for	Lk 7:36
and begged him to * home with him,	Lk 8:41
Baptist * back to life again";	Lk 9:7
and three days later I will *	Lk 9:22
* in my glory and in the glory of	Lk 9:26
But Jesus ordered the demon to *	Lk 9:42
For the Son of Man has not * to	Lk 9:55f
invited a man to * with him and to	Lk 9:59
Your duty is to * and preach the	Lk 9:60
Lord, I will *, but first let me	Lk 9:61
Tell her to * and help me."	Lk 10:40
enough stored away for years to *.	Lk 12:19
He may * at nine o'clock at	Lk 12:38
will * when least expected."	Lk 12:40
"I have * to bring fire to the	Lk 12:49
"Do you think I have * to give	Lk 12:51
"Those are the days to * for	Lk 13:14
You can't * in here, guilty as	Lk 13:27
for people will * from all over	Lk 13:29
sees you he will * and say,	Lk 14:10
and for that reason couldn't *.	Lk 14:20
*, so that the house will be full.	Lk 14:23
and he was dead and has * back to	Lk 15:32
to * and discuss the situation.	Lk 16:5,6
the Kingdom of God would * soon.	Lk 16:16
would * and lick his open sores.	Lk 16:21
anyone wanting to * to you from	Lk 16:26
lest they * here when they die.'	Lk 16:28
"Let the little children * to me!	Lk 18:16,17
you in heaven—and *, follow me."	Lk 18:22
eternal life in the world to *."	Lk 18:30
concerning me will * true.	Lk 18:31
"Quick! * down!	Lk 19:5
that salvation has * to this home	Lk 19:9,10
have * to search for and to save	Lk 19:9,10
land when his father dies. * on.	Lk 20:14
I'll tell you—he will * and kill	Lk 20:16
For many will * announcing	Lk 21:8
Literally, "will * in my Name."	Lk 21:8f
and saying, 'The time has *.'	Lk 21:8
True, wars must *, but the end	Lk 21:9
When the leaves * out, you know	Lk 21:30
has *. And though all heaven and	Lk 21:32
until the Kingdom of God has *."	Lk 22:18
For the time has * for this	Lk 22:37
about me to * true: 'He will be	Lk 22:37
me by the prophets will * true."	Lk 22:37
"that you have * armed with swords	Lk 22:52
me when you * into your Kingdom."	Lk 23:42
He has * back to life again!	Lk 24:6,7
that he had * to rescue Israel.	Lk 24:21
in the Psalms must all * true?"	Lk 24:44
You have seen these prophecies *	Lk 24:48
"* and see," he said.	Jn 1:39
He found Philip and told him, "*	Jn 1:43
"Can anything good * from	Jn 1:46
"Just * and see for yourself,"	Jn 1:46
where it had * from (though, of	Jn 2:9
refer to him, and had all * true!	Jn 2:22
have * to earth and will return	Jn 3:13
But those doing right * gladly	Jn 3:21
"He has * from heaven and is	Jn 3:31
the Messiah will *—the one they	Jn 4:25
told everyone, "* and meet a man	Jn 4:28,29
that Jesus had * from Judea and was	Jn 4:46,47
and begged him to * to Capernaum	Jn 4:46,47
* now before my child dies."	Jn 4:49
Yet you won't * to me so that I	Jn 5:40
I know, because I have * to you	Jn 5:43
Jesus still hadn't * back, they got	Jn 6:17
his disciples had * over together	Jn 6:22,23
But some will * to me—those the	Jn 6:37
For I have * here from heaven to	Jn 6:38
For no one can * to me unless	Jn 6:44
that no one can * to me unless the	Jn 6:65
You go on, and I'll * later	Jn 7:8
him, for God's time had not yet *.	Jn 7:30
And you won't be able to * where	Jn 7:34
won't be able to * where I am'?"	Jn 7:36
let him * to me and drink.	Jn 7:37
will * just before the Messiah."	Jn 7:40
Will the Messiah * from Galilee?	Jn 7:41,42
prophets will * from Galilee!"	Jn 7:52
And you cannot * where I am	Jn 8:21
What does he mean, 'You cannot *	Jn 8:22
me, for I have * to you from God.	Jn 8:42
Then Jesus told him, "I have *	Jn 9:39
sheep hear his voice and * to him;	Jn 10:3
Those who * in by way of the Gate	Jn 10:9
concerning this man have * true."	Jn 10:41
in me. *, let's go to him."	Jn 11:15
Jewish leaders had * to pay their	Jn 11:19
will * back to life again."	Jn 11:23
They told him, "* and see."	Jn 11:34
Then he shouted, "Lazarus, *	Jn 11:43
Roman army will * and kill us and	Jn 11:48
Will he * for the Passover?"	Jn 11:56
man who had * back to life again.	Jn 12:9
for he will * to you meekly,	Jn 12:15
had * true before their eyes.	Jn 12:16
Some Greeks who had * to	Jn 12:20
Jesus replied that the time had *	Jn 12:23,24
tell them to * and follow me, for	Jn 12:26
has *—and the time when Satan,	Jn 12:31
I have * as a Light to shine in	Jn 12:46
judge—for I have * to save the	Jn 12:47
and that he had * from God and	Jn 13:1
me,' and this will soon * true.	Jn 13:18
room, Jesus said, "My time has *;	Jn 13:31
for me, you cannot * to me—just as	Jn 13:33
"But why can't I * now?"	Jn 13:37
ready, then I will * and get you,	Jn 14:2,3
in the storm—I will * to you.	Jn 14:18
When I * back to life again, you	Jn 14:20
will * to them and live with them.	Jn 14:23
but I will * back to you again.	Jn 14:28
the Father. *, let's be going.	Jn 14:31
I chose you to * out of the world,	Jn 15:19
if I had not * and spoken to them.	Jn 15:22
He will * to you from the Father	Jn 15:26
if I don't, the Comforter won't *.	Jn 16:7
"And when he has * he will	Jn 16:8
but the time will * when this will	Jn 16:25
said, "Father, the time has *.	Jn 17:1
believers who will * to me because	Jn 17:20
Nicodemus, the man who had * to	Jn 19:39
said he would * to life again!	Jn 20:9
"We'll * too," we all said.	Jn 21:3
"Now * and have some	Jn 21:12
until I *, what is that to you?"	Jn 21:23
But when the Holy Spirit has *	Act 1:8
the Scriptures to * true concerning	Act 1:16
Yes, the Holy Spirit shall *	Act 2:18
families to * to Egypt,	Act 7:14
I have * down to deliver them.	Act 7:34
*, I will send you to Egypt.'	Act 7:34
yet he had not * upon any of them.	Act 8:16
And he begged Philip to * up	Act 8:31
and ask him to * and visit you."	Act 10:5,6
"Three men have * to see you.	Act 10:19
send for Peter to * and tell him	Act 10:22
* into a Gentile home like this.	Act 10:28
you have done well to * so soon.	Act 10:33
Just then three men who had * to	Act 11:11
for us * and give it!"	Act 13:15
our ancestors has * true in our own	Act 13:32,33
We have * to bring you the Good	Act 14:15
him, "* over here and help us."	Act 16:9
said, "* and stay at my home."	Act 16:15
God and they have * to tell you how	Act 16:17
Christ to * out of her," he said.	Act 16:18
Let them * themselves and release	Act 16:37
at Mars Hill. "* and tell us more	Act 17:19
the one John said would * later.	Act 19:4
whom Paul preaches, to * out!"	Act 19:13
to * down to the boat to meet him.	Act 20:17
certainly hear that you have *.	Act 21:22
to *, Felix was terrified.	Act 24:25
I asked you to * here today so	Act 28:20
has * that I am bound with this	Act 28:20
to * at last to see you and, if	Rom 1:10
that I planned to * many times	Rom 1:13
I am ready to * also to you in Rome	Rom 1:15
to * to God in this same way.	Rom 1:16
for there is going to * a day of	Rom 2:5
The day will surely * when at	Rom 2:16
with that idea you * to this: the	Rom 3:8
would * and take away those sins.	Rom 3:25
No, the Gentiles, too, may * to	Rom 3:29
a promise just couldn't * to pass!	Rom 4:18
us from all of God's wrath to *.	Rom 5:9
Adam and Christ who was yet to *!	Rom 5:14
us, he called us to * to him;	Rom 8:30
How I long for you to * to	Rom 9:1
Just the fact that they * from	Rom 9:7
who * preaching God's Good News!	Rom 10:15
and refusing to *.	Rom 10:21
when the Jews, too, * to Christ.	Rom 11:12
when the Jews * to Christ.	Rom 11:15
behind them and * back to God, God	Rom 11:23
* to Christ—those of you who will.	Rom 11:25
"There shall * out of Zion a	Rom 11:26
and I am ready to * after all these	Rom 15:23
But before I *, I must go down to	Rom 15:25
the Gentiles have * to share in	Rom 15:27f
* to see you on my way to Spain.	Rom 15:28
And I am sure that when I * the	Rom 15:29
Then I will be able to * to you	Rom 15:32
There is going to * a time of	1Co 3:13
I am afraid to * to deal with you.	1Co 4:18
But I will *, and soon, if the	1Co 4:19
Shall I * with punishment and	1Co 4:21
* with quiet love and gentleness?	1Co 4:21
Afterwards, they should *	1Co 7:5
might never * to know the Lord;	1Co 7:14
when I see them * to Christ.	1Co 9:23
wrong desires that * into your life	1Co 10:13
The first man didn't * from	1Co 11:8
women * from God their Creator.	1Co 11:12
When you * together to eat, it	1Co 11:20
God will someday * to an end, but	1Co 13:8
special gifts will * to an end, and	1Co 13:10
if I myself should * to you talking	1Co 14:6
will never * back to life again?	1Co 15:12
dead do not * back to life again.	1Co 15:15
who will * back to life again	1Co 15:20
After that the end will * when he	1Co 15:24
If the dead will not * back to	1Co 15:29
shall have when we * back to life	1Co 15:42
when we * back to life again.	1Co 15:43
but when they * back to life they	1Co 15:44
Scripture will * true—"Death is	1Co 15:54
When I * I will send your loving	1Co 16:3
I want to * and stay awhile, if	1Co 16:7
Lord Jesus, *!	1Co 16:22
reason I haven't * to visit you yet	2Co 1:23
When I *, although I can't do	2Co 1:24
straightened out before I *.	2Co 2:3
Then, when I do *, I will not be	2Co 2:3
the joys to * will last forever.	2Co 4:18
urging everyone to * into his favor	2Co 5:18
need not * to you with harshness.	2Co 7:9
and longed for me to * and help.	2Co 7:11
he would have * anyway, for he is	2Co 8:17
Macedonian people * with me, only	2Co 9:4
I * how harsh and rough I can be.	2Co 10:2
were the first to * to you with the	2Co 10:14
For I am afraid that when I * to	2Co 12:20
Yes, I am afraid that when I *	2Co 12:21
as I * now for this visit.	2Co 13:1
that this time I * ready to punish	2Co 13:2
need to scold and punish when I *;	2Co 13:10
wouldn't have * up except for some	Gal 2:4
But now that Christ has *, we	Gal 3:25
especially promised he would *.	Gal 4:23
this world or in the world to *.	Eph 1:21
or Gentiles, may * to God the	Eph 2:18
Now we can * fearlessly right	Eph 3:12
we * with Christ and trust in him.	Eph 3:12
This means that he had first *	Eph 4:9
your strength must * from the	Eph 6:10
soon I myself may * to see you.	Php 2:24
for everything to * to him—all	Col 1:20
Lord Jesus, and * with him into the	Col 3:17
to be thankful when they *.	Col 4:2
to * back to see you once more.	1Th 2:17
We wanted very much to * and I,	1Th 2:18
suffering would soon *—and it did.	1Th 3:4
For the Lord himself will * down	1Th 4:16
That day of the Lord will *	1Th 5:2
* from me, don't believe them.	2Th 2:1

(COME Con't)
For that day will not * until two 2Th 2:3
rebellion will *—the son of hell. 2Th 2:3
for he can * only when his time 2Th 2:6
but he himself will not * until 2Th 2:7
This man of sin will * as 2Th 2:9
FINALLY, DEAR BROTHERS, as I * 2Th 3:1
so that if I don't * for awhile you 1Ti 3:15
and hurt for a long time to *. 2Ti 2:17
Then they will * to their senses 2Ti 2:26
For there is going to * a time 2Ti 4:3
And now the time has * for me to 2Ti 4:7
Please * as soon as you can, for 2Ti 4:9
Bring Mark with you when you *, 2Ti 4:11
When you *, be sure to bring 2Ti 4:13
in you that * from Christ Jesus. Phm 1:6
prayers and let me * to you soon. Phm 1:22
We all know he did not * as an Heb 2:16
let them * to his place of rest. Heb 3:11
So let us * boldly to the very Heb 4:16
of the world to *, and then have Heb 6:5
it and good crops * up, that land Heb 6:7
all who * to God through him. Heb 7:25
"The day will * when I will make a Heb 8:8
are invited may * and have forever Heb 9:15
and he will * again, but not to Heb 9:28
This time he will * bringing Heb 9:28
Then I said, 'See, I have * to Heb 10:7
I have * to give my life." Heb 10:9
Anyone who wants to * to God must Heb 11:6
But you have * right up into Heb 12:22
Think of all the good that has * Heb 13:7
that I can * back to you sooner. Heb 13:19
if he comes here soon, I will * Heb 13:23
And so blessing and cursing * Jas 3:10
for his milk. * to Christ, who is 1Pe 2:4
holy priests; so * to him—[you who 1Pe 2:5
will * upon you with great glory. 1Pe 4:14
For the time has * for judgment, 1Pe 4:17
He personally will * and pick you 1Pe 5:10
is washed only to * back and wallow 2Pe 2:22
days there will * scoffers who will 2Pe 3:3
Jesus promised to * back, did he? 2Pe 3:4
He'll never *! 2Pe 3:4
and for him to *, try hard to live 2Pe 3:14
this world's last hour has *. 1Jn 2:18
Holy Spirit has * upon you, and you 1Jn 2:20
are clear, we can * to the Lord 1Jn 3:21
who is going to *, and his attitude 1Jn 4:3
God's Son, has * to help us 1Jn 5:20
for I hope to * to see you soon and 2Jn 1:12
When I * I will tell you some of 3Jn 1:10
times there would * these scoffers Jud 1:18
when these things will all * true. Rev 1:3
God who is, and was, and is to *! Rev 1:4
"who comes" or "who is to *." Rev 1:8f
or else I will * and remove your Rev 2:5
or else I will * to you suddenly Rev 2:16
to what you have until I *. Rev 2:24,25
Unless you do, I will * suddenly Rev 3:3
which will * upon the world to test Rev 3:10
the door, I will * in and Rev 3:20
to me and said, "* up here and I Rev 4:1
who was, and is, and is to *." Rev 4:8
sounded like thunder, said, "*!" Rev 6:1
second Living Being say, "*!" Rev 6:3
the third Living Being say, "*!" Rev 6:5
fourth Living Being say, "*!" Rev 6:7
has *, and who can survive it?" Rev 6:17
in white, and where they * from?" Rev 7:13
won't be able to—death will not *. Rev 9:6
will shout from heaven, "* up!" Rev 11:12
in heaven, portraying things to *. Rev 12:1
for the devil has * down to you in Rev 12:12
For the time has * when he will Rev 14:7
the time has * for his martyrs Rev 14:13
the time has * for you to reap; Rev 14:15
showing things to *: Seven angels Rev 15:1
All nations will * Rev 15:3,4
"Take note: I will * as Rev 16:15
An epoch of human history has * Rev 16:17f
talked with me. "* with me," he Rev 17:1
And yet, soon he will * up out of Rev 17:8
to *, but his reign will be brief. Rev 17:10
saw another angel * down from Rev 18:1
"* away from her, my people; Rev 18:4
for the time has * for the Rev 19:7
shouting loudly to the birds, "*! Rev 19:17
of the Great God! * and eat the Rev 19:18
THEN I SAW an angel * down from Rev 20:1
They had * to life again and now Rev 20:4
(The rest of the dead did not * Rev 20:5
and said to me, "* with me and I Rev 21:9
* and bring their glory to it. Rev 21:24
The Spirit and the bride say, "* Rev 22:17
who hears them say the same, '*.' Rev 22:17
Let the thirsty one *—anyone who Rev 22:17
let him * and drink the Water of Rev 22:17

COMES
I will say to some girl who * out Gen 24:43
Look, there * his daughter Rachel Gen 29:6
"Here * that master-dreamer," Gen 37:19,20
this youngest brother * here. Gen 42:15
*, whom all people shall obey. Gen 49:10
meet Pharaoh as he * out to the Ex 8:20
But if any harm * to the woman Ex 21:23
"Any meat that * into contact Lev 7:19
"But if, when the priest * again Lev 14:48
until after he * out again and has Lev 16:17
ripening when sowing time * again. Lev 26:4,5
He may eat nothing that * from Num 6:3,4
whether my word * true or not!" Num 11:23
"Everyone who even * close to Num 17:12,13
* by obeying every command of God. Deu 8:3
until the owner * looking for it, Deu 22:2
If a relative of the dead man * Jos 20:5
"and if anyone * by, looking for Ju 4:20
"When all this * true and the Ju 13:17
because everything he says * true; 1Sa 9:6
a lion or a bear * and grabs a lamb 1Sa 17:34
when your father * to see you, 2Sa 13:5
And when he * out and attacks and 2Sa 17:9
He shouted down, "Here * another 2Sa 18:26
"He is a good man and * with good 2Sa 18:27
and when Ahab * and can't find you, 1Ki 18:12
place to stay whenever he * by." 2Ki 4:10
for everything he says * true. 2Ki 10:9,10
every one of them *, for we 2Ki 10:18,19
For he * to judge the earth. 1Ch 16:33
for your holy name * from you! 1Ch 29:16
anybody who * along with a young 2Ch 13:9
in each case that * before you. 2Ch 19:6
but then * sudden disaster. Job 5:3
Misery * upon them to punish Job 5:6
point * out from his gall. Job 20:25
his cry when trouble * upon him? Job 27:9
Afterwards * the roaring of the Job 37:4
"From the south * the rain; Job 37:9
For salvation * from God. Ps 3:8
and their refuge when trouble *. Ps 37:39
on Mount Zion. He * with the Ps 50:3
Literally, "*, and does not keep Ps 50:3f
For salvation * from him alone. Ps 62:1
For salvation * from him alone. Ps 62:5
Mount Sinai and * to his holy Ps 68:17
Everyone who * along has robbed Ps 89:41
Happiness * to those who are fair Ps 106:3
For growth in wisdom * from Ps 111:10
for he is loving and kind, and * Ps 130:7
for, yet it * easily to the man Pro 14:6
From a wise mind * careful and Pro 16:23
but victory * from God. Pro 21:31
the man do who * after the king?" Ecc 2:12f
Tackle every task that * along, Ecc 7:18
so unfair, that one fate * to all. Ecc 9:2,3
Here he *, leaping upon the Sol 2:8
Before the dawn * and the Sol 2:17
"heroes" when it * to drinking, Is 5:22
to Laish, for the mighty army *. Is 10:30
every home * the sound of weeping. Is 15:3
in one moment it * crashing down. Is 30:13
See, the Lord * from afar, aflame Is 30:27
And when he *, he will open Is 35:5
you won't know where it * from. Is 47:11
If any nation * to fight you, it Is 54:15
and give no warning when danger *. Is 56:10
WHO IS THIS who * from Edom, from Is 63:1
When danger *, let them go out Jer 2:28
let you know when trouble *." Jer 6:17
Only when his message * true can Jer 28:9
It will be a great company who *. Jer 31:8
And when he * he shall destroy Jer 43:11
But a fire * from Heshbon—Sihon's Jer 48:45
thought that * into your minds. Eze 11:5
idols and then * to ask my help. Eze 14:4
idols, and then * to a prophet to Eze 14:6,7
When it * true, the boldest heart Eze 21:7
idolatry. Now * your day of doom. Eze 22:4
whatever order it *—for none is Eze 24:6
And when that time *, then you Eze 24:24
Damascus *. Eze 27:18
word is that * from the Lord!" Eze 33:30f
prey to every animal that * along. Eze 34:5
Then * Manasseh, south of Eze 48:4
matter where he * from in Israel. Eze 48:19
Then * Zebulun, also extending Eze 48:26
until the Anointed One *! Dan 9:25
of the holy people * to an end." Dan 12:7f
"Divine Truth" * to them Hos 4:12
day of punishment *, you will Hos 5:9
as soon as trouble *, they will Hos 5:15
For my deliverance * from the Jon 2:9
in heaven and * to earth, walking Mic 1:3
But first * terrible destruction Mic 7:13
When trouble *, he is the place Nah 1:7
the sun * up and warms the earth. Nah 3:17
I cry, but no one * to save. Hab 1:2
Swiftly it *—a day when strong Zep 1:14
Though the rain * in torrents, Mt 7:25
'Come,' and he *, and to my slave Mt 8:8,9
shout abroad when daybreak *. Mt 10:27
* and snatches away the seeds Mt 13:19
while when trouble *, or Mt 13:21
Literally, "what * out of a man Mt 15:11f
return before the Messiah *?" Mt 17:10
Literally, "Blessed is he who * Mt 21:9f
'Here * the heir to this estate; Mt 21:38
Look! Here * the man who is Mt 26:46
Satan * at once to try to make Mk 4:15
"Praise God for him who * in Mk 11:9
before the end-time finally *. Mk 13:10
but then the devil * and steals the Lk 8:12
But whenever he * there will be Lk 12:38
west, you say, 'Here * a shower.' Lk 12:54
who * in the name of the Lord.' Lk 13:35
Literally, "If anyone * to me and Lk 14:26f
Yet when this son of yours * Lk 15:30
When a servant * in from plowing Lk 17:7,8,9
keep praying until the answer *. Lk 18:1
the Holy Spirit * and fills you Lk 24:49
Jesus said, "Here * an honest Jn 1:47
tell where it * from or where it Jn 3:8
* to the world through the Jews." Jn 4:21-24
"My nourishment * from doing the Jn 4:34
honor that * from the only God! Jn 5:44
when Christ *, he will just Jn 7:27
one will know where he * from." Jn 7:27
falls and all work * to an end. Jn 9:4
For a shepherd * through the Jn 10:2
who is truth, *, he shall guide you Jn 16:13
Pharisees when it * to obedience to Act 26:5
it * to these matters of faith. Rom 4:16
But the salvation that * through Rom 10:6
For salvation that * from Rom 10:8
Yet faith * from listening to Rom 10:17
For everything * from God alone. Rom 11:36
not the kind that * from here on 1Co 2:6
When the Lord *, he will turn on 1Co 4:5
for when that time * you can be 1Co 4:8
Do this until he * again. 1Co 11:26
Be innocent babies when it * to 1Co 14:20
have these gifts, * to church and 1Co 14:23
or a new Christian * in who does 1Co 14:24
then when Christ * back, all his 1Co 15:23
And when the green shoot * up 1Co 15:37
If Timothy * make him feel at 1Co 16:10
when our Lord Jesus * back again. 2Co 1:13,14
Our only power and success * from 2Co 3:5
yes, if an angel * from heaven Gal 1:8
For my message * from no less a Gal 1:12
with God * by believing in Christ. Gal 2:19
Then when he * back he can cheer Php 2:19
When he * back he will take Php 3:21
no effect when it * to conquering a Col 2:23
is our real life * back again, you Col 3:4
Let the peace of heart which * Col 3:15
if he * your way. Col 4:10
Jesus Christ when he * back again. 1Th 2:19
thief when that day of the Lord *. 1Th 5:4
Lord Jesus Christ * back again. 1Th 5:23
power, when he * to receive praise 2Th 1:10
when he *, it is already going on, 2Th 2:7
the patience that * from Christ. 2Th 3:5
with love that * from pure hearts, 1Ti 1:5
soon, and pride * before a fall. 1Ti 3:6
and along with this gift * the Tit 2:12
you, and with him * my own heart. Phm 1:12
that * along with your salvation. Heb 6:9
and after that * judgment, so also Heb 9:27
Your spiritual strength * as a Heb 13:9
if he * here soon, I will come Heb 13:23
good and perfect * to us from God, Jas 1:17
If a man * into your church Jas 2:2
moment another man * in who is poor Jas 2:2
But the wisdom that * from heaven Jas 3:17
joy that * from heaven itself. 1Pe 1:8
forever, for it * from Christ, 1Pe 1:23
the Head Shepherd *, your reward 1Pe 5:4
until the day of final judgment *. 2Pe 2:9
that "A dog * back to what he has 2Pe 2:22
and the pride that * from wealth 1Jn 2:16
so that when he * you will be sure 1Jn 2:28
this, that when he * we will be 1Jn 3:2
other, for love * from God and 1Jn 4:7
So you see, our love for him * 1Jn 4:19
If anyone * to teach you, and he 2Jn 1:10
in sorrow and in terror when he *. Rev 1:7
Literally, "who *" or "who is Rev 1:8f
shout, "Salvation * from our God Rev 7:10
who * out of the bottomless pit Rev 11:7
And when that time *, all doing Rev 22:11

COMFORT
Go and get the boy and * him, Gen 21:18
she was a special * to him after Gen 24:67
His family all tried to * him, Gen 37:35
Don't slow down for my * unless I 2Ki 4:24
and his brothers tried to * him. 1Ch 7:22
their homes to * and console him. Job 2:11
This, at least, gives me * Job 6:10
a little moment of * before I leave Job 10:20,21
Is God's * too little for you? Job 15:11
How can you * me when your whole Job 21:34
* their hearts by helping them. Ps 10:17

(COMFORT Con't)
"Your rod and your staff * me." Ps 23:4f
me, you would welcome and * me. Ps 27:10
some pity, if even one would * me! Ps 69:20
before, and turn again and * me. Ps 71:21
face because you help and * me. Ps 86:17
your Word has been my *. Ps 119:52
Now let your lovingkindness * Ps 119:75,76,77
When will you * me with your Ps 119:82
anguish, your commandments * me. Ps 119:143
Don't try to * me—let me cry for Is 22:4
*, OH, COMFORT my people, says Is 40:1
COMFORT, OH, * my people, says Is 40:1
Who is left to * you? Is 51:19
I will lead them and * them, Is 57:18
He has sent me to * the Is 61:1
I will * you there as a little Is 66:13
No one shall * the mourners with Jer 16:7
joy and I will * them and make them Jer 31:13
How can I * you? Lam 2:13
speaking words of * and assurance. Zec 1:13
Lord will again * Jerusalem and Zec 1:17
silly lies; what * is there in Zec 10:2
back and * and care for the lambs. Zec 13:7
and in the * of the Holy Spirit. Act 9:31
Those who offer * to the Rom 12:8
same help and * God has given us. 2Co 1:3,4
us with his * and encouragement. 2Co 1:5
you God's * and salvation. 2Co 1:6,7
God will tenderly * you when you 2Co 1:6,7
is time to forgive him and * him. 2Co 2:7
are, and to * and encourage you. Col 4:8
here, and what a * they have been! Col 4:11
him forever. So * and encourage 1Th 4:18
lazy; * those who are frightened; 1Th 5:14
us everlasting * and hope which we 2Th 2:16
we don't deserve, * your hearts 2Th 2:17
hearts with all *, and help you in 2Th 2:17
much joy and * from your love, my Phm 1:7

COMFORTABLE
This made him * and very Jon 4:6
him gifts to make his stay more *. Act 24:23

COMFORTED
Then David * Bath-sheba; 2Sa 12:24
for the Lord has * his people, and Is 49:13
for the Lord has * his people; Is 52:9
a little one is * by its mother. Is 66:13
cannot be *, for they are gone. Jer 31:15
the water, are * to find her there Eze 31:16
he will be * to find that he is not Eze 32:31
for they shall be *. Mt 5:4
So now he is here being * and you Lk 16:25
But in our trouble God had * 2Co 1:6,7
So we are greatly *, dear 1Th 3:7
I am * by this truth, that when 2Ti 2:11

COMFORTER
tears flow down my cheeks. My * Lam 1:16
*, and he will never leave you. Jn 14:15,16
But when the Father sends the * Jn 14:26
— and by the * I mean the Holy Jn 14:26
"But I will send you the *—the Jn 15:26
for if I don't, the * won't come. Jn 16:7

COMFORTERS
What miserable * all of you are. Job 16:2
These '*' have gaping jaws to Job 16:10

COMFORTING
his sorrow, and * him because of Job 42:11
the Lord, encouraging and * them. 1Co 14:3

COMFORTS
and as one who * those who mourn. Job 29:25
angry with me, but now he * me. Is 12:1
I, even I, am he who * you and Is 51:12
pleads for help but no one * her. Lam 1:17
who so wonderfully * and 2Co 1:3,4

COMING
And Adam replied, "I heard you * Gen 3:10
noticed three men * toward him. Gen 18:2
the village were * to draw water. Gen 24:11
village are * out to draw water. Gen 24:13
words, Rebekah was * along with her Gen 24:45
he looked up and saw the camels *. Gen 24:63
arrives, * in from his hunting. Gen 27:30
That evening as Jacob was * home Gen 30:16
inform you of my *, hoping that you Gen 32:5
afraid that he is * to kill me and Gen 32:11
He is * right behind us!" Gen 32:18
Jacob saw Esau * with his 400 men. Gen 33:1
But when they saw him *, Gen 37:18
a string of camels * towards them Gen 37:25
And he is * here to look for you, Ex 4:14
Their chariot wheels began * Ex 14:25
from * loose from the ephod. Ex 28:28
tricked them into * to the Ex 32:12
Miriam as you were * from Egypt. Deu 24:9
captured a man * out of the city. Ju 1:24
arrived at Bochim, * from Gilgal, Ju 2:1
'Why is his chariot so long in *? Ju 5:28
Doesn't it look like people * Ju 9:36
"I'm sure I see people * towards Ju 9:37
There are others * along the road Ju 9:37
rather, you have wronged me by * Ju 11:27
the first person * out of his house Ju 11:30,31
homes instead of * with me? Ru 1:8
When the Israelis saw the Ark *, 1Sa 4:5
of Ekron saw it * they cried out, 1Sa 5:10
they saw Samuel * out toward them 1Sa 9:14
will see three men * toward you who 1Sa 10:3
a band of prophets * down the hill 1Sa 10:5
me, for I will be * to sacrifice 1Sa 10:8
saw the prophets * toward them, and 1Sa 10:10
When the Philistines saw them * 1Sa 14:11
Then others began *—those who 1Sa 22:2
she met David * towards her. 1Sa 25:20
Forgive me for my boldness in * 1Sa 25:28
"I see a specter * up out of the 1Sa 28:13
behind and saw him *, he called out 2Sa 2:20
But Asahel refused and kept on *. 2Sa 2:21
* and went into the stronghold. 2Sa 5:17
saw a great crowd * toward the city 2Sa 13:34
Your sons are *, just as I 2Sa 13:35
king and his men * towards him, he 2Sa 24:20
Suddenly Obadiah saw Elijah * 1Ki 18:7
For I hear a mighty rainstorm * 1Ki 18:41
to him, "Some troops are *!" 1Ki 20:17
that woman from Shunem is *. 2Ki 4:25
When Naaman saw him *, he jumped 2Ki 5:21
and shouted, "Someone is *." 2Ki 9:17
of Rechab, who was * to meet him. 2Ki 10:15
and those who were * on duty, and 2Ki 11:9
of Ethiopia was * to attack him. 2Ki 19:9
glory of the Lord, * as a bright 2Ch 5:13,14
crowds * in from all over Israel; 2Ch 7:8
You will find them * up the 2Ch 20:16
by the people * from Manasseh, 2Ch 34:9
they are * tonight to kill you." Neh 6:10
and stood up in respect at my *. Job 29:8
cattle (warn us) of the * storm." Job 36:33f
heart responds, "Lord, I am *." Ps 27:8
he knows their judgment day is *. Ps 37:12,13
For the Lord is * to judge the Ps 96:13
Lord, for he is * to judge the Ps 98:8,9
The Red Sea saw them * and Ps 114:3
Blessed is the one who is *, the Ps 118:26
I was just * to look for you and Pro 7:15
The leaves are * out Sol 2:13
"Who is this * up from the Sol 8:5
for the day is * when your proud Is 2:11
refers to the * Messiah (Jeremiah Is 4:2,3,4f
and Israel are * against you. Is 7:5
mighty armies of Assyria are *! Is 10:28,29
day of the Lord is *, the terrible Is 13:9
return, and those * to live in Is 14:2
At last you have what was * to Is 14:4
is * down from the north against Is 14:31
Look, the Lord is * against Egypt, Is 19:1
The Lord is * from the heavens to Is 26:21
LOOK, A RIGHTEOUS King is *, with Is 32:1
God is * to destroy your enemies. Is 35:4
He is * to save you." Is 35:4
"The time is * when everything Is 39:6
of Judah, "Your God is *!" Is 40:9
Yes, the Lord God is * with Is 40:10
"It's * along fine. Is 41:7
My mercy and justice are * soon; Is 51:5
But in that * day, no weapon Is 54:17
for I am * soon to rescue you. Is 56:1
For your sons and daughters are * Is 60:4
Lord your God, am * to save you and Is 62:11
that the enemy is * from a distant Jer 4:16
noise of marching armies * near. Jer 4:29
north, * to destroy this nation! Jer 6:1
The time is *, says the Lord, Jer 7:32
for the enemy is *, and is Jer 8:16
A time is *, says the Lord, when Jer 9:25,26
of great armies * from the north. Jer 10:22
The day is *, says the Lord, when Jer 19:6
For the time is *, says the Lord, Jer 23:5,6
For the time is * when I will Jer 30:3
of terror such as in that * day? Jer 30:7
But in that * day, all who are Jer 30:16
For the time is *, says the Lord, Jer 31:38,39
that insisted on * here to Egypt Jer 44:12
repent of their * and escape from Jer 44:14
concerning the * of Nebuchadnezzar, Jer 46:13
of Hosts, one is * against Egypt Jer 46:18
The Lord says: A flood is * from Jer 47:2
The time is * soon, the Lord has Jer 48:12
Calamity is * fast to Moab. Jer 48:16
See them *! Jer 50:41
And the time is * when God will Jer 51:18
For rumors will keep * year by Jer 51:46
For the time is surely * when I Jer 51:47
But the time is * for the Jer 51:52
a great storm * toward me from the Eze 1:4
Six men appeared at his call, * Eze 9:2
surrounded him, * from every side, Eze 19:8
he sees the army *, and blows the Eze 33:3
sees the enemy * and doesn't sound Eze 33:6
they will be * home again soon! Eze 36:8
The sound of his * was like the Eze 43:2
wine before * to the inner court. Eze 44:21
Those * in from the south must go Eze 46:9
"You dreamed of * events. Dan 2:29
* down from heaven. Dan 4:13
* down from heaven and saying, Dan 4:23
last days of the * time of Dan 8:19
In that * day, says the Lord, she Hos 1:16
as surely as the * of dawn or the Hos 6:3
They are *! Hos 8:1
they climb up into the houses, * Joe 2:9
Lord God says, "an enemy is *! Amo 3:11
The time is surely *," says the Amo 8:11
He is *! Mic 1:3
In that * day, the Lord says that Mic 4:6
The armies of destruction are *; Mic 6:9
But your judgment day is * Mic 7:4
The time is * when all their Hab 2:6
gate of Jerusalem, * closer and Zep 1:10
the time is * soon when I will Zep 3:8
meet another angel * toward him. Zec 2:3
saw four chariots * from between Zec 6:1
sins behind, and * back to me? Zec 7:5
For look—your King is *! Zec 9:9
FOR THE day of the Lord is * soon! Zec 14:1
Yes, he is surely *," says the Mal 3:1
Who can endure his *? Mal 3:2
is *, burning like a furnace. Mal 4:1
for the Kingdom of Heaven is * Mt 3:2
* to be baptized, he denounced Mt 3:7
could escape the * wrath of God? Mt 3:7
but someone else is *, far Mt 3:11
God * down in the form of a dove. Mt 3:16
folk were soon * to be healed from Mt 4:24
"But the time is * when I Mt 9:15
For the time is * when the truth Mt 10:26
me, to announce my *, and prepare Mt 11:10
live to see me * in my Kingdom." Mt 16:28
that Jesus was * that way, they Mt 20:30
her King is * to her, riding humbly Mt 21:5
saw the son * they said among Mt 21:38
my * be, when I, the Messiah, Mt 24:27
then at last the signal of my * Mt 24:30
Literally, "of the * of the Son Mt 24:30f
before the sudden * of the flood; Mt 24:37,38
So shall my * be. Mt 24:39
know what day your Lord is *. Mt 24:42
'My Lord won't be * for a while,' Mt 24:48
the shout, 'The bridegroom is *! Mt 25:5,6
his disciples from * and stealing Mt 27:64
to prepare the world for his *. Mk 1:2
"Someone is * soon who is far Mk 1:7
was no point in Jesus' * now. Mk 5:35
For so many people were * and Mk 6:31
"But when the farmers saw him * Mk 12:7
* in the clouds with great power Mk 13:26
"My * Mk 13:34
will see a man * towards you Mk 14:13
Simon of Cyrene, who was * in Mk 15:21
and he will precede the * of the Lk 1:17
been awaiting the * of the Savior Lk 2:38
but someone is * soon who has far Lk 3:16
yourself by * to my home, for I am Lk 7:6,7,8
A funeral procession was * out Lk 7:12
Literally, "the one who is *." Lk 7:19f
to announce the * of the Kingdom Lk 8:1
on the way, * from other towns. Lk 8:4
everyone about the * of the Kingdom Lk 9:2
As the boy was * the demon Lk 9:42
be greatest [in the * Kingdom Lk 9:46
and preach the * of the Kingdom of Lk 9:60
thief if they knew when he was *. Lk 12:39
his father saw him *, and was Lk 15:20
heard dance music * from the house, Lk 15:25
his * home again unharmed.' Lk 15:27
"The time is * when you will Lk 17:22
me out with her constant *!' Lk 18:4,5
But Jesus said, "The time is * Lk 21:6
fate they see * upon the earth, for Lk 21:26
the Messiah, * in a cloud with Lk 21:27
Don't let my sudden * catch you Lk 21:34,35
safely through these * horrors." Lk 21:36f
the highest rank [in the * Kingdom Lk 22:24
But the time is soon * when I, Lk 22:69
who was just * into Jerusalem from Lk 23:26
For the days are * when the Lk 23:29
the Messiah's * and had not agreed Lk 23:50,51,52
on everyone * into the world. Jn 1:9
said, 'Someone is * who is greater Jn 1:15
'Get ready for the * of the Lord!' Jn 1:23
The next day John saw Jesus * Jn 1:29
is *, who existed long before me!' Jn 1:30
the angels of God * back and forth Jn 1:51
there instead of * here to us." Jn 3:26
the greater crowds * to him than to Jn 4:1
Jesus replied, "The time is *, Jn 4:21-24
in Galilee after * from Judea. Jn 4:54
that the time is *, in fact, it is Jn 5:25
Indeed the time is * when all the Jn 5:28
No one * to me will ever be Jn 6:35
He knew I was * and was glad." Jn 8:56
he sees a wolf * and will leave the Jn 10:12
Jesus was *, she went to meet him. Jn 11:20
going to prepare them for your *. Jn 14:2,3

(COMING Con't)
indeed the time is * when those who Jn 16:2
"But the time is *—in fact, it Jn 16:32
leaving them behind, and * to you. Jn 17:11
"And now I am * to you. Jn 17:13
who predicted the * of the Act 7:52
So he did, and who should be * Act 8:27
man named Ananias * in and laying Act 9:12
saw an angel of God * toward him. Act 10:3
was * upon the land of Israel. Act 11:28
But he is * soon—and in Act 13:25
Messiah and his * back to life, and Act 17:3
the synagogue, "The Messiah is *! Act 18:25,26
When the mob saw the troops *, Act 21:32
* and came to meet us at the Forum Act 28:15
I will finally succeed in *." Rom 1:10f
this same way, by * to Christ, no Rom 3:21,22
It will be like dead people * Rom 11:15
Wake up, for the * of the Lord Rom 13:11
been so long in * to visit you. Rom 15:22
will be * to see you soon. Rom 16:1
one whatever praise is * to him. 1Co 4:5
I am * to visit you after I have 1Co 16:5
Now I am * to you again, the 2Co 12:14
THIS IS THE third time I am * to 2Co 13:1
only until the * of Christ, the Gal 3:19
we could believe in the * Savior. Gal 3:23
Remember that the Lord is * soon. Php 4:5
AND NOW, WHAT about the * again of 2Th 2:1
plain to us by the * of our Savior 2Ti 1:10
forward to his * back again. 2Ti 4:8
to me if I were the one who was *. Phm 1:17
But he has set another time for * Heb 4:7
his * back again is drawing near. Heb 10:25
* will not be delayed much longer. Heb 10:37
receive on that * day of judgment. Jas 5:3
And take courage, for the * of Jas 5:8
The great Judge is *. Jas 5:9
It will be yours in that * last 1Pe 1:5
The end of the world is * soon. 1Pe 4:7
* day when it will be displayed. 1Pe 4:13
Lord Jesus Christ and his * again. 2Pe 1:16
The day of the Lord is surely *, 2Pe 3:10
Antichrist who is *—the one who is 1Jn 2:18
* with millions of his holy ones. Jud 1:14
who is, and was, and is * again! Rev 1:8
Literally, "* out from his Rev 1:16f
or "kept through" the * horror. Rev 3:10f
Look, I am * soon! Rev 3:11
* down from heaven from my God; Rev 3:12
And I saw another angel * from Rev 7:2
"These are the ones * out of the Rev 7:14
ends, but there are two more *! Rev 9:12
THEN I SAW another mighty angel * Rev 10:1
animal, this one * up out of the Rev 13:11
* Judgment Day of God Almighty. Rev 16:14
* down from God out of heaven. Rev 21:2
and true: 'I am * soon!' Rev 22:6,7
"See, I am * soon, Rev 22:12

COMINGS
But I know you well—your * and Is 37:28

COMMAND
my * and let the baby boys live?" Ex 1:18
NOW, AT GOD'S *, the people of Ex 17:1
Anyone who does not obey this * Ex 31:14,15
them by the Lord's * to Ex 35:29
and Aaron at the * of the Lord, Num 3:39
journeyed at the * of the Lord and Num 9:18
to the * of the Lord my God. Num 22:18
I have received a * to bless Num 23:18-24
He issued the following * to Num 25:4
and rebelled against the Lord's *. Deu 1:26
This is my *. Deu 5:12
closely to each * and be careful to Deu 6:3
comes by obeying every * of God. Deu 8:3
is giving you if you obey this *. Deu 15:4,5
is why I am giving you this *. Deu 15:15
so be sure to carry out this *. Deu 16:12
The purpose of this * is to Deu 20:18
is why I have given you this *. Deu 24:18
is why I am giving you this *. Deu 24:22
the judge shall * him to lie down Deu 25:1
gods, violating his express *. Deu 29:26
that I * you today, the Lord your Deu 30:7,8
And at God's * he performed Deu 34:11,12
who, at the Lord's *, issued the Jos 4:15,16
the Lord now told him to * them. Jos 4:15,16
God's * to destroy everything Jos 7:1
he issued a * that a great stone Jos 10:18
So the Lord's * to Moses was Jos 21:8
mustered an army under his own *. Ju 3:27
under General Sisera's *. Ju 4:7
At God's * they rushed into the Ju 5:15
had not heard his father's *; 1Sa 14:27
Jonathan exclaimed. "A * like 1Sa 14:29
I have carried out the Lord's *!" 1Sa 15:13
and the * of the Lord, for I was 1Sa 15:24
your * at the risk of my life. 1Sa 28:21
frightened. The * of the Israeli 2Sa 4:2,3
under his personal *, and took them 2Sa 10:9
at Helam under the * of Shobach, 2Sa 10:15,16
around here, and this is a *. 2Sa 13:28
there at your *, and we can take 2Sa 17:13
But the king's * overcame Joab's 2Sa 24:4
"Didn't I * you in the name of God 1Ki 2:42
Then, at the king's *, Benaiah 1Ki 2:46
Then, at the Lord's *, the 1Ki 13:2
to his clear *, and have come here, 1Ki 13:21,22
who disobeyed the Lord's *; 1Ki 13:26
I have done all this at your *. 1Ki 18:36
my people are yours to *, and my 1Ki 22:4
people and horses are yours to *. 2Ki 3:6,7,8
the Lord's * in this bloodbath, for 2Ki 10:11f
" 'And my * concerning the king 2Ki 19:32
Judah at the direct * of the Lord. 2Ki 24:3,4
Obadiah was second in *; 1Ch 12:8-13
Eliab was third in *; 1Ch 12:8-13
Mishmannah was fourth in *; 1Ch 12:8-13
Jeremiah was fifth in *; 1Ch 12:8-13
Attai was sixth in *; 1Ch 12:8-13
Eliel was seventh in *; 1Ch 12:8-13
Johanan was eighth in *; 1Ch 12:8-13
Elzabad was ninth in *; 1Ch 12:8-13
Jeremiah was tenth in *; 1Ch 12:8-13
Machbannai was eleventh in *. 1Ch 12:8-13
troops under the * of Zadok, a 1Ch 12:24-37
The other group, under the * of 1Ch 19:11
Amariah was second in *, Jahaziel 1Ch 23:19
and Isshiah was the second in *. 1Ch 23:20
the entire nation are at your *." 1Ch 28:21
Using every resource at my *, I 1Ch 29:2
"If your people go out at your * 2Ch 6:34
no rain, or if I * the locust 2Ch 7:13
Next in * was Jeho-hanan with an 2Ch 17:14,15
the * of Eliada, a great general. 2Ch 17:17
His second in * was Jehozabad, 2Ch 17:18
My troops are at your *! 2Ch 18:3,4,5
but followed the * of the Lord 2Ch 25:4
Therefore, I * that these men Ez 4:21
at once with the * of King Darius. Ez 6:13
Is it at your * that the eagle Job 39:27
Then at your *, O Lord, the sea Ps 18:15
It appeared at his *! Ps 33:9
At your * the springs burst Ps 74:15
grows up at his * to feed the Ps 104:14
and mourned and despised his *. Ps 106:25
For he issued his *, and they Ps 148:5
The king's * is backed by great Ecc 8:4
any other, that you * us this?" Sol 5:9
I will * the clouds not to rain Is 5:6
Who are you to * me concerning Is 45:11
You also will * the nations and Is 55:5
That was not the point of my *. Jer 7:22
until this day: Obey my every *! Jer 11:7
obeyed the king's * and freed their Jer 34:10
and the other captains in *. Jer 43:5
A great army has come at his * to Lam 1:15
the heights of heaven at his *. Lam 2:1
obey my laws and do whatever I *. Eze 36:27
languages, this is the king's *: Dan 3:4
Then at Belshazzar's *, Daniel Dan 5:29
Then the king issued a * to bring Dan 6:24
you began praying, a * was given. Dan 9:23
from the time the * is given to Dan 9:25
He went far beyond God's * to Hos 1:4,5f
* the sword to kill them there. Amo 9:4
At his * the oceans and rivers Nah 1:4
Woe to those who * their Hab 2:19
forth upon the earth at your *! Hab 3:8,9
nullify the direct * of God to Mt 15:5,6
* in the laws of Moses?" Mt 22:36
he said, "I * you to come out of Mk 9:25
and your * will be obeyed. Mk 11:22,23
and the demons came out at his *, Lk 4:41
* would bring immediate results! Lk 17:6
something else! I * you in the name Act 3:6
within her. "I * you in the name Act 16:18
come when at God's * Jesus Christ Rom 2:16
its will at God's *—will all Rom 8:20,21
I have a *, not just a suggestion. 1Co 7:10
And it is not a * from me, for 1Co 7:10
special * for them from the Lord. 1Co 7:25
up in this one *: "Love others as Gal 5:14
and so obey our Lord's *. Gal 6:2
brothers there. I * you in the 1Th 5:27
Now here is a *, dear brothers, 2Th 3:6
to such people—we * them—to quiet 2Th 3:12
out by the direct * of God our 1Ti 1:1
my son, here is my * to you: Fight 1Ti 1:18
I solemnly * you in the presence 1Ti 5:21
I * you before God who gives life 1Ti 6:13
great facts, and * them in the name 2Ti 2:14
it to everyone. By * of God our Tit 1:3
by the mighty power of his *. Heb 1:3
all things—were made at God's *; Heb 11:3
back under God's * that if even an Heb 12:20
obey our Lord's *, "You must love Jas 2:8
by the word of his *, and had used 2Pe 3:5,6
the Truth, obeying God's *. 2Jn 1:4
angels under his * fought the Rev 12:7

COMMANDED
Noah did everything as God * him. Gen 6:22
So Noah did everything the Lord * Gen 7:5
and female, just as God * Noah. Gen 7:8,9
and female, just as God had *. Gen 7:16
as Pharaoh had *, and provisions Gen 45:21
brothers, just as Pharaoh had *. Gen 47:11
Afterwards he * his morticians Gen 50:2
So his sons did as Israel * Gen 50:12,13
Then Pharaoh * all of his people Ex 1:22
son, and I have * you to let him Ex 4:23
and Aaron did as the Lord * them. Ex 7:6
and Aaron did as the Lord * them. Ex 7:20
Aaron did as God *, and suddenly Ex 8:17
to Jehovah our God, as he * us." Ex 8:27
"GO BACK TO Pharaoh," the Lord * Ex 9:1
did as Moses and Aaron had *. Ex 12:28
Moses why this had been * them. Ex 16:22
Moses *. Ex 17:2
yeast, just as I * you before. Ex 23:15
what the Lord has *: All of you Ex 35:4
and construct what God has * us: Ex 35:10-19
All this was * to Moses by the Ex 39:21
just as the Lord had * Moses. Ex 39:25,26
just as Jehovah had * Moses. Ex 39:28,29
to do all as the Lord had * him. Ex 40:16
just as the Lord had * him. Ex 40:19
screen it, just as the Lord had *. Ex 40:21
the Lord, just as the Lord had *. Ex 40:23
spices, just as the Lord had *. Ex 40:27
just as the Lord had * him. Ex 40:29
just as the Lord had * Moses. Ex 40:32
Tabernacle, and * him to give the Lev 1:2,3
anointed them, he * that the people Lev 7:36
to do has been * by Jehovah." Lev 8:5
crown—as the Lord had * Moses. Lev 8:9
and caps, as the Lord had * him. Lev 8:13
the camp, as the Lord had * Moses. Lev 8:17
that day had been * by the Lord in Lev 8:34
did all that the Lord had * Moses. Lev 8:36
as Moses had *, and the people came Lev 9:5
for the people, as the Lord had *. Lev 9:7
as the Lord had * Moses, but he Lev 9:10
it to him, just as Moses had *. Lev 9:21
to what the Lord had just * them! Lev 10:1
And they did as Moses *. Lev 10:7
for so I am *. Lev 10:13
family, for the Lord has * this." Lev 10:15
he died, as Jehovah had * Moses. Lev 24:23
family, as the Lord had * Moses. Num 1:17,18,19
as the Lord had *, and found the Num 3:42
and his sons as the Lord had *. Num 3:51
done just as the Lord had * Moses. Num 8:22
peninsula, just as the Lord had *. Num 9:4,5
"Come here, you three," he *. Num 12:3,4
and Miriam, step forward," he *; Num 12:5
Moses did as the Lord had * and Num 13:3-15
and killed him as the Lord had *. Num 15:36
So Moses did as the Lord * him. Num 17:11
So Moses did as the Lord * him. Num 20:27
So Moses did as Jehovah *, and Num 27:22
as the Lord had *. Num 27:23
"The Lord has * that when anyone Num 30:1
the priest did as the Lord *. Num 31:31
"As the Lord has *, so we will do— Num 32:31
Lord has further * concerning the Num 36:6
did as the Lord * Moses. Num 36:10
God had * him to pass on to them: Deu 1:1
time that the Lord * me to issue Deu 4:14
And he has * us to obey all of Deu 6:24
this day, just as the Lord * me. Deu 10:5
and the widows, just as you * me; Deu 26:13
and have done everything you * me. Deu 26:14
I have * you today to love the Deu 30:16
destroy them as I have * you. Deu 31:5
The Lord * that these laws be Deu 31:10,11
just as the Lord had * Joshua. Jos 4:8
for the trumpets," Joshua *. Jos 6:10
city on fire, as the Lord has *. Jos 8:8
at Mount Ebal, as Moses had * Jos 8:31
Then Joshua * the rest of the Jos 10:19
God of Israel had *, slaughtering Jos 10:40
just as Moses had * long before. Jos 11:12
For so the Lord had * his Jos 11:15
killed, as the Lord had * Moses. Jos 11:20
of Manasseh as I have * you." Jos 13:2-7
So, as the Lord had * through Jos 17:5,6
disciple Moses * you, and have Jos 22:2,3
God of Israel has * you to mobilize Ju 4:6
and did as the Lord had *. Ju 6:27
and afterward * that it be sung 2Sa 1:17,18
I will do all that you have *." 2Sa 9:10,11
And the king * Joab, Abishai, and 2Sa 18:5
to do what the Lord had * him. 2Sa 24:19
army went home as the Lord had *. 1Ki 12:23,24
for I have * them to feed you." 1Ki 17:4
let a single one escape," he *. 1Ki 18:40
Ben-hadad * his officers. 1Ki 20:12
"Take them alive," Ben-hadad *, 1Ki 20:18
In her letter she *: "Call the 1Ki 21:9
For the king of Syria had * his 1Ki 22:31
has * you to come along with us." 2Ki 1:9
"Will you please be quiet?" he * 2Ki 2:5

(COMMANDED Con't)
King Joram *. 2Ki 9:21
Elisha *, and he did. 2Ki 13:16,17
for the Lord had * through the law 2Ki 14:6
in terror. He * Hilkiah the 2Ki 22:12,13
and to do everything the book *. 2Ki 23:3
all the details * by Moses the 1Ch 6:49
So David did as the Lord * him; 1Ch 14:16
The words he * 1Ch 16:15
just as the Lord had * Israel. 1Ch 16:40
* the destroying angel, "Stop! 1Ch 21:15
Then the Lord * the angel to put 1Ch 21:27
He now * his son Solomon to 1Ch 22:6
of Benjamin), who * 24,000 troops 1Ch 27:12
of Othni-el, who * 24,000 men on 1Ch 27:15
For Solomon * that all of the 2Ch 4:19
clan leaders * these regiments. 2Ch 26:12
speaking for the Lord) had * them. 2Ch 29:15
as the king had *—for the king had 2Ch 29:24
as * by the king and his officers. 2Ch 30:12
all the idols, and * Judah and 2Ch 32:12
just as King Cyrus has *." Ez 4:3
as had been * by God and decreed by Ez 6:14
and you * them, through Moses Neh 9:14
were thirsty. You * them to go in Neh 9:15
as * by David, the man of God. Neh 12:24
So from then on I * that the Neh 13:19
Then I * the Levites to purify Neh 13:22
passed by, for so the king had *. Est 3:2
"Have you ever once * the Job 38:12
did as the Lord * them, and the Job 42:9
to Israel, and * our fathers to Ps 78:5
even though he * the skies to Ps 78:23
the world. You * the Red Sea to Ps 106:9
* all the vast myriads of stars. Is 45:12
my carved image * it to happen!" Is 48:5
of it, let alone * it to be done. Jer 7:31
and do whatever I * them, then they Jer 11:4
MY PEOPLE SIN as though * to, as Jer 17:1
* them nor even thought of! Jer 19:5
*, and cannot imagine suggesting. Jer 32:35
as I * you, and freed your slaves. Jer 34:15
(son of Rechab) * that none of us Jer 35:6
that Jonadab our father * us. Jer 35:10
Then the king * Jerahmeel (a Jer 36:26
Then King Zedekiah * that Jer 37:21
Then the king * Ebedmelech to Jer 38:10
steps to do as the king had *. Jer 39:13
Annihilate them, as I have * you. Jer 50:21
to the winds as he * me and the Eze 37:10
worshiped him, and * his people to Dan 2:46
and Abednego. He * that the furnace Dan 3:19
"The Lord has * 490 years Dan 9:24
For the Lord * this: That homes Amo 6:11
For I have * that Israel be Amo 9:9
the Lord of Hosts, * them—the laws Zec 7:12
did as the angel *, and brought Mt 1:24
paralyzed man, he *, "Pick up your Mt 9:5,6
mountain, Jesus * them not to tell Mt 17:9
Jesus curtly * the demon to say Mk 1:25
paralyzed man, he *, "Pick up your Mk 2:9,10,11
heaven, he sighed and *, "Open!" Mk 7:34
paralyzed man, he *, "Pick up your Lk 5:23,24
For this is as the Lord * when Act 13:47
the High Priest * those close to Act 23:2
something the Lord * me to do, for 2Co 11:17
God * me to make with you." Heb 9:20
the death the king *, and they hid Heb 11:23
his people that he * them to kill a Heb 11:28
seven days, as God had * them. Heb 11:30
And God has * that the earth and 2Pe 3:7

COMMANDER
and Phicol, * of his troops, came Gen 21:22
and Phicol, * of his army, returned Gen 21:32
and also Phicol, his army *. Gen 26:26
Joshua is your new *, as the Lord Deu 31:3
"Take off your shoes," the * Jos 5:15
So Saul made him * of his troops, 1Sa 18:5
as captives. A * of the army of 2Ki 25:19
Abishai, Joab's brother, was * of 1Ch 11:20
The * of the First Division was 1Ch 27:2,3
The * of the Second Division was 1Ch 27:4
The * of the Third Division was 1Ch 27:5,6
succeeded him as division *. 1Ch 27:5,6
The * of the Fourth Division was 1Ch 27:7
The * of the Fifth Division was 1Ch 27:8
The * of the Sixth Division was 1Ch 27:9
The * of the Seventh Division was 1Ch 27:10
The * of the Eighth Division was 1Ch 27:11
The * of the Ninth Division was 1Ch 27:12
The * of the Tenth Division was 1Ch 27:13
The * of the Eleventh Division 1Ch 27:14
The * of the Twelfth Division was 1Ch 27:15
to Hananiah, the * of the Neh 7:2
Who is this King of Glory? The * Ps 24:10
The * of the armies of heaven is Ps 46:7
The * of the heavenly armies is Ps 46:11
the * of the armies of heaven. Ps 48:8
O Jehovah, * of the heavenly Ps 89:8
of the world? The * of the armies Is 23:9
He even challenged the * Dan 8:11
word reached the * of the Roman Act 21:31
beating Paul. The * arrested him Act 21:33
*, "May I have a word with you?" Act 21:37,38
the * asked, surprised. Act 21:37,38
The * agreed, so Paul stood on Act 21:40
So the * brought him inside and Act 22:24
The officer went to the * and Act 22:26
So the * went over and asked Act 22:27
"I am too," the * muttered, Act 22:28
citizen, and the * was frightened Act 22:29
The next day the * freed him from Act 22:30
Finally the *, fearing they would Act 23:10
"Ask the * to bring Paul back Act 23:15
said, "Take this boy to the *. Act 23:17
The * took the boy by the hand, Act 23:19
the * warned the boy as he left. Act 23:22
Then the * called two of his Act 23:23,24
but Lysias, the * of the garrison, Act 24:7
the garrison *, and then he would Act 24:22

COMMANDER-IN-CHIEF
to obey Joshua as their *. Jos 1:16
"I am the * of the Lord's Jos 5:14
in Canaan. The * of his army was Ju 4:2,3
"If you will be our * against Ju 11:8
and was made * and king. Ju 11:11
But Abner, Saul's *, had gone to 2Sa 2:8
for becoming * of the combined 2Sa 3:12
* of all of Hadadezer's forces. 2Sa 10:15,16
* of my army in place of Joab." 2Sa 19:13
Joab was * of the army, and 2Sa 20:23
The king said to Joab, * of his 2Sa 24:2
of General Abner, * of the army of 1Ki 2:32
Amasa, * of the army of Judah. 1Ki 2:32
Benaiah as *, and Zadok as priest 1Ki 2:35
Benaiah (son of Jehoiada) was * of 1Ki 4:1
* of the army, as their new ruler. 1Ki 16:15,16
for Naaman, the * of his army, for 2Ki 5:1
a Jebusite shall be made *!" 1Ch 11:5,6
Joab (son of Zeruiah) was * of 1Ch 18:15
by Shophach, King Hadadezer's *. 1Ch 19:16
He also killed Shophach, the * of 1Ch 19:17,18
Joab was * of the Israeli army. 1Ch 27:34
The * was General Hananiah. 2Ch 26:11
Assyria, sent the * of his army Is 20:1

COMMANDERS
and company *, and found its total Num 31:51,52
But the Philistine * demanded, 1Sa 29:3
go with us, but my * say no. 1Sa 29:6
But my * are afraid to have you 1Sa 29:9
and company * over his troops. 2Sa 18:1
chariot *, and cavalrymen. 1Ki 9:22
the units and their regimental *: 1Ch 27:1
leaders, the * of the twelve army 1Ch 28:1
men, captains and *, in handsome Eze 23:6

COMMANDING
of Remaliah), the * general of his 2Ki 15:25
guards, one of the * officers of Jer 52:24,25
For Jesus was already * the demon Lk 8:29
the soldiers and * officer, "You Act 27:31
The soldiers advised their * Act 27:42

COMMANDMENT
exempted by Jehovah's * to Moses). Num 2:32,33
or traveled at the * of the Lord; Num 9:23
For he has despised the * of the Num 15:31
"This is the * Jehovah has given Num 31:21
against the Lord's * and went on up Deu 1:43
this is a * of the Lord your God); Deu 5:16
that is why this * is necessary. Deu 15:11
This is the * of the Lord your Deu 20:17
and disobeyed my * and has taken Jos 7:10,11
Every * Moses had ever given was Jos 8:35
and Moses had passed the * on to Jos 11:15
"You have disobeyed the * of the 1Sa 13:13
have not obeyed the Lord's *." 1Sa 13:14
Here is his * to you: 'I have 1Sa 15:2
Since you have rejected the * of 1Sa 15:26
your agreement and obeyed my *? 1Ki 2:43
search out every * of the Lord so 1Ch 28:8
this * and destroys this Temple. Ez 6:12
Literally, "There was a * from Neh 11:22,23f
are you disobeying the king's *?" Est 3:3,4
and speeded by the king's *. Est 8:14
So the * of Esther confirmed Est 9:32
I gave this * to your fathers, Jer 17:21,22
defied the king's *, and were Dan 3:28
breaks the least *, and teaches Mt 5:19
This is the first and greatest *. Mt 22:38,39
"And so I am giving a new * to Jn 13:34
is a * from the Lord himself. 1Co 14:37
and as we obey this *, to love 1Jn 2:8

COMMANDMENTS
Abraham obeyed my * and laws." Gen 26:5
those who love me and obey my *. Ex 20:6
you the laws and * I have written Ex 24:12
with the Ten * engraved on them. Ex 25:16
There I will tell you my * for Ex 25:22
the Ark containing the Ten *. Ex 30:6
on which the Ten * were written Ex 31:18
his hands the Ten * written on both Ex 32:15
(God himself had written the * Ex 32:16
agreement is to obey all of my *; Ex 34:11
wrote out the Covenant—the Ten* Ex 34:28
he gave them the * the Lord had Ex 34:32
the Ark with the Ten * in it; Ex 39:33-40
the Ark containing the Ten *; Ex 40:3
with the Ten * engraved on them, Ex 40:20
breaks any of my *. Lev 4:2
the stone tablets of the Ten *); Lev 16:13
You must heed all of my * and Lev 19:37
You must obey all of my *, for I Lev 20:8
"You must keep all of my *, for Lev 22:31
"If you obey all of my *, I Lev 26:3
These are the * the Lord gave to Lev 27:34
tassels, of the * of the Lord, and Num 15:39
These, then, are the * the Lord Num 30:16
These are the * and ordinances Num 36:13
must obey—the Ten *—and wrote them Deu 4:13
those who love me and keep my *. Deu 5:9,10
Those were the only * he gave you Deu 5:22
for me, wanting to obey my *. Deu 5:29
give you all my *, and you shall Deu 5:31
must obey all the * of the Lord Deu 5:32
give you all these * which you are Deu 6:1
these * I am giving you today. Deu 6:6
Therefore, obey all these * I am Deu 7:11
"YOU MUST OBEY all the * I give Deu 8:1
he had written the * he had spoken Deu 9:10,11
tablets the same * that were on the Deu 10:2
He again wrote the Ten * on them Deu 10:4
(They were the same * he had Deu 10:4
containing the Ten * of Jehovah, Deu 10:8
your own good the * I am giving you Deu 10:12,13
should obey these * I am going to Deu 11:8
If you obey the *, you will have Deu 11:9
obey all of his * that I am going Deu 11:13
So keep these * carefully in Deu 11:18
"If you carefully obey all the * Deu 11:22
if you obey the * of the Lord your Deu 11:27
careful to obey all of these *. Deu 12:28
Obey all the * I give you. Deu 12:32
to him and to his * which I am Deu 13:18
to all these * I am giving you Deu 19:9
obey all of these * and ordinances Deu 26:16
Literally, "Keep all the * I Deu 27:1f
all of these * I have given you." Deu 27:10
"IF YOU FULLY obey all of these * Deu 28:1
and obey the * of the Lord your God Deu 28:13
to obey all of the * I have given Deu 30:2
and obey all the * that I command Deu 30:7,8
you but obey the * written in this Deu 30:10
Obeying these * is not something Deu 30:11
containing the Ten * of the Lord. Deu 31:9
containing the Ten * to put this Deu 31:25
and followed the * that the Lord Deu 34:9
of the altar each of the Ten *. Jos 8:32
obey all of the * Moses gave you. Jos 22:5
would obey the * the Lord had given Ju 3:4
and listen to his * and not rebel 1Sa 12:14
against the Lord's * and refuse to 1Sa 12:15
follow all of my * and 1Ki 6:11,12
to obey all the * and instructions 1Ki 8:58
*, just as you are doing today." 1Ki 8:61
one who obeyed my *, I will let 1Ki 11:34
right, obeying my * as my servant 1Ki 11:38
my * as my servant David did. 1Ki 14:8
Ten *, and anointed him as king. 2Ki 11:12
he had warned them to obey his * 2Ki 17:13
They defied all the * of the 2Ki 17:16
obey the * of the Lord their God; 2Ki 17:19
And if he continues to obey my * 1Ch 28:7
nation obey the * of the Lord God 2Ch 14:4
He obeyed the * of his father's 2Ch 17:4
know why you are disobeying his *. 2Ch 24:20
Lord to follow his * with all his 2Ch 34:31
have broken your * again and Ez 9:14
of not obeying the * you gave us Neh 1:6,7
good laws and true *, including Neh 9:13
they refused to listen to your *. Neh 9:16
I have not refused his * but Job 23:12
your * more than the finest gold. Ps 119:127
and anguish, your * comfort me. Ps 119:143
all your * are based on truth. Ps 119:151
I have looked for your * and I Ps 119:167
have not turned away from your *. Ps 119:176
Keep the * and keep your life; Pro 19:16
God and obey his *, for this is the Ecc 12:13
don't despise the * of their God! Is 58:2
my * and not obeyed my laws. Jer 9:13
of stone, as were the Ten *. Jer 31:33f
obey the * of the Lord your God." Zec 6:15
violate the direct * of God? Mt 15:3
get to heaven if you keep the *." Mt 19:17
All the other * and all the Mt 22:40
know the *: don't kill, don't Mk 10:19
So he asked, "Of all the *, Mk 12:28
No other * are greater than Mk 12:31
know what the ten * say—don't Lk 18:20
with the Ten * written on them. Act 7:44
The Ten * were given so that all Rom 5:20
by knowing the * of God, because we Rom 8:3
else the Ten * say is wrong. Rom 13:9
pleasing God and keeping God's *. 1Co 7:19

(COMMANDMENTS Con't)
keeping the Ten *, ends in death; 2Co 3:6
the Ten * is the way to be saved. 2Co 3:15
later when God gave the Ten *. Gal 3:17
when he gave the Ten * to Moses. Gal 4:24,25
God by trying to obey the *; Gal 4:24,25
This is the first of God's Ten * Eph 6:2
of his * which you had not obeyed. Col 2:14
stone with the Ten * written on Heb 9:4
the holy * that were given to him. 2Pe 2:21
were keeping God's * and confessing Rev 12:17

COMMANDOS
walls like picked and trained *. Joe 2:7

COMMANDS
upon them the same * that were on Ex 34:1
If you obey these * you will Deu 6:3
obey him in everything he *. Deu 6:17
who love him and who obey his *. Deu 7:9
God and obey every one of his *. Deu 11:1
obey only his * and cling to him. Deu 13:4
heed all the * of the Lord your God Deu 15:4,5
his God by obeying all of his *. Deu 17:19
and turn away from God and his *; Deu 31:29
against your *, he shall die. Jos 1:17,18
him and said, "Give me your *." Jos 5:14
for they refused to obey God's *. Ju 2:17
keep each of his * written in the 1Ki 2:3
to you, and obeyed your *. 1Ki 3:6
obeyed all of God's * to Moses. 2Ki 18:6
ancestors have followed your *." 2Ki 22:12,13
Be strong and do as he *." 1Ch 28:10
And if you will only obey my * 2Ch 33:8
priest, the student of God's *: Ez 7:11
we will follow your *, and the Ez 10:3
* of the others who fear our God. Ez 10:3
when they heard the * of the law. Neh 8:9
stars won't shine, if he * it so! Job 9:7
he * throughout the earth. Job 37:12
and the roar of the captain's *. Job 39:25
I have followed your * and have Ps 17:4
For I have followed his * and Ps 18:21
to fear him or even honor his *. Ps 55:19
gods, and refused to follow his *. Ps 78:56
listening for each of his *. Ps 103:20
man who delights in doing his *. Ps 112:1
your * are my chart and guide. Ps 119:19
who refuse your *— don't let them Ps 119:21
I cling to your * and follow Ps 119:31
How I enjoy your *! Ps 119:47
angry with those who spurn your *. Ps 119:53
to stop me from obeying God's *. Ps 119:115
expectantly for each of your *. Ps 119:131
me, for I am obeying your *. Ps 119:153
they have not known his *. Ps 147:20
God and broken his everlasting *. Is 24:4,5
of me and my *, the Lord God says. Eze 22:12
against you and scorned your *. Dan 9:5
The only * you keep are those of Mic 6:16
obey all the * I have given you; Mt 28:20
claim that God * the people to obey Mk 7:6,7
by means of the * I gave you. Jn 15:3
in me and obey my *, you may ask Jn 15:7
on to them the * you gave me; Jn 17:8
I have given them your *. Jn 17:14
things, but now he * everyone to Act 17:30
sight by doing what the law *. Rom 3:20
and as God *, this message is Rom 16:25,26,27
These are not direct * from the 1Co 7:12
for you know the * we gave you from 1Th 4:1
its * are always just and right. Heb 1:8
to his * and trust in Jesus." Rev 14:12

COMMEMORATE
altar there to * Jehovah's visit. Gen 12:7

COMMEMORATING
for this is the day * the Lev 16:29,30

COMMEND
whether they criticize us or * us. 2Co 6:8

COMMENDED
Or, "Do you think the rich man * Lk 16:8f

COMMENDS
committing it, * the faithful Ps 15:4
But when the Lord * him, that's 2Co 10:18

COMMENTARY
—Jamieson, Fausset and Brown * Zep 2:15f

COMMENTATORS
(verse 3). Some * believe that the Gen 6:1f
But many * prefer this Hag 2:7f
Some * would interpret this to Lk 16:9f
However, most * believe the Jn 5:32,33f
All * believe him to be John, Jn 13:23f
* differ widely in their thoughts 1Jn 5:17f
origin, as most * believe, or Rev 9:1f

COMMENTS
the people, Moses made these *: Deu 32:46
David heard these * and was 1Sa 21:12
* on to King Ar-ta-xerxes! Neh 6:7
think of all these brilliant *? Job 26:4
But Jesus ignored their * and Mk 5:36
Some of his * are not easy to 2Pe 3:15,16

COMMERCE
center of *, your end has come; Jer 51:13

COMMERCIAL
a net, for they were * fishermen. Mt 4:18
nets, for they were * fishermen. Mk 1:16

COMMISSION
the Jordan River. * Joshua to Deu 3:28
So Jephthah accepted the * and Ju 11:11
We also * you to take with you Ez 7:15
the authority and * of the chief Act 26:12

COMMISSIONED
and made you a * officer." 2Sa 18:11
probably that worn by a * officer. 2Sa 18:11f
to serve him who * me to restore to Is 49:5
Christians and * us apostles to 2Co 1:21

COMMISSIONS
and vineyards and * in his army? 1Sa 22:7

COMMIT
"You must not * adultery. Ex 20:14
your sons would * adultery against Ex 34:16
" 'You must not * adultery. Deu 5:18
to persuade you to * suicide by 2Ch 32:11
and to God would I * my cause." Job 5:8f
Into your hand I * my spirit. Ps 31:5,6
* everything you do to the Lord. Ps 37:5
I've been perfectly fair. * Ps 119:122
* your work to the Lord, then it Pro 16:3
thanks was to * adultery wholesale Jer 5:7
can steal, murder, * adultery, lie, Jer 7:9
* adultery and love dishonesty. Jer 23:14
of Judah that they * these terrible Eze 8:17
them, and does not * adultery, nor Eze 18:6
them, and does not * adultery, and Eze 18:15
There are men who * adultery Eze 22:10
Will they * adultery with these Eze 23:43
and kill and steal and * adultery. Hos 4:2
and your brides * adultery. Hos 4:13
By the murders you *, you have Hab 2:10
said, 'You shall not * adultery.' Mt 5:27
* adultery if she marries again. Mt 5:32
kill, don't * adultery, don't Mt 19:18
don't kill, don't * adultery, don't Mk 10:19
For I never cheat, I don't * Lk 18:11
say—don't * adultery, don't murder, Lk 18:20
Then Jesus shouted, "Father, I * Lk 23:46
and not to * fornication." Act 21:25
You say it is wrong to * Rom 2:22
I * you to God, who is able to Rom 16:25,26,27
who are immoral or * adultery. Heb 13:4
those who * adultery with her." Rev 2:22f

COMMITMENT
to test their * to him: "If you Ex 15:25
—as followers of Moses—their * to 1Co 10:2

COMMITS
"If a man * adultery with Lev 20:10
if a man's wife * adultery, but Num 5:11,12
" 'Cursed is he who * adultery Deu 27:20
"Whenever someone * a crime, and 2Ch 6:22
So it is with the man who * Pro 6:29
But the man who * adultery is an Pro 6:32
the mountains and * adultery, and Eze 18:11
And he who marries her * Mt 5:32
and marries another, * adultery." Mt 19:9
a divorced woman * adultery." Mt 19:9f
else, he * adultery against her. Mk 10:11
remarries, she, too, * adultery." Mk 10:12
someone else * adultery, and anyone Lk 16:18
a divorced woman * adultery." Lk 16:18

COMMITTED
*, and it shall be forgiven him. Lev 19:22
But if you have * adultery, Num 5:20
defiled, having * adultery against Num 5:27
But if she is pure and has not * Num 5:28
"If a man has * a crime worthy Deu 21:22
these men have * a terrible crime. Ju 20:6
has been * against the Lord?" 1Sa 2:23,24,25
We must find out what sin was * 1Sa 14:38
bronze shields and * them to the 2Ch 12:10
For our fathers have * a deep 2Ch 29:6
yes, I and my people have * the Neh 1:6,7
you know full well I've not *? Job 10:4-7
they had * their many crimes! Ecc 8:9,10
You have * adultery on the tops Is 57:7,8
Lord your God and * adultery Jer 3:13
For I have * my cause to you. Jer 20:12
They have * adultery with their Jer 29:23
"What crime have I *? Jer 37:18
sins you have *, I will punish you Eze 5:9
"You have * adultery with the Eze 16:28
"Even Samaria has not * half Eze 16:51
And they came and * adultery Eze 23:17
For they have * both adultery Eze 23:37
for all the sins they have *. Eze 44:13
he *; in fact, I will put an end Hos 1:4,5
For their mother has * adultery. Hos 1:5
borders, they * cruel crimes, Amo 1:13
* adultery with her in his heart. Mt 5:28
What crime has he *? Lk 23:22
they had been * to God for the work Act 14:26
teaching to which God has * you. Rom 6:17
the sins they had * while still Heb 9:15
Literally, "have * fornication Rev 18:3f

COMMITTING
people had been * adultery—at Ex 32:25
prostitutes, * adultery against me Ex 34:15
"If a man is discovered * Deu 22:22
day at Shechem, * them to a Jos 24:25
criticizes those * it, commends the Ps 15:4
been untrue to me, * open adultery Hos 1:2
marriage laws by * adultery, but Jas 2:11

COMMODITIES
If these were *, their Eze 27:17f

COMMON
"If any one of the * people sins Lev 4:27
* property of all sons of Aaron. Lev 7:10
You must not treat me as * and Lev 22:32,33
sell the fields of * land Lev 25:34
they were *, lest you die." Num 18:32
it is a land where iron is as * Deu 8:9
This was a * expression of grief 1Sa 4:12f
the street like a * pervert!" 2Sa 6:20
Silver was as * as stones in 1Ki 10:27
greater value than the * sycamore! 1Ki 10:27
than ever from the * people, to 1Ki 13:33
the ranks of the * people and made 1Ki 14:7
on the graves of the * people. 2Ki 23:6
lumber was used like * sycamore! 2Ch 1:15
He indentured 70,000 as * 2Ch 2:18
used as though it were * sycamore. 2Ch 9:27
and some of the * people settled in Ez 2:70
and the * people gave $100,000 Neh 7:72
entire nation—for the * people; Neh 10:28
I, too, am made of * clay. Job 33:7
Don't treat me as a * sinner or Ps 26:9,10
young man from the * people to be Ps 89:19
therefore give me * sense to Ps 119:125
give me the * sense you promised. Ps 119:169
good judgment and * sense, then Pro 3:4,5
and has good judgment and * sense Pro 3:13,14,15
and doing right—and * sense. Pro 3:21
develop good judgment and * sense! Pro 4:5
And with your wisdom, develop * Pro 4:7
young man lacking * sense, walking Pro 7:7
O foolish ones, let me show you * Pro 8:4,5
give good advice and * sense. Pro 8:14,15
Men with * sense are admired Pro 10:13
is destroyed by lack of * sense. Pro 10:21
easily to the man with * sense. Pro 14:6
The * bond of rebels is their Pro 14:9
The * bond of godly people is Pro 14:9
hearts of men of * sense, but it Pro 14:33
The wise man is known by his * Pro 16:21
A rebuke to a man of * sense is Pro 17:10
The man who strays away from * Pro 21:16
if you become a man of * sense. Pro 23:15,16
strong through * sense, and profits Pro 24:3,4
pretty glaze covers a * clay pot. Pro 26:23
the * people will die of thirst. Is 5:13
A very * type of divination by Eze 21:21f
a half sister—this is *. Eze 22:11
Even the * people oppress and Eze 22:29
mountain of God like a * sinner. Eze 28:16
They are buried in a * grave, Eze 32:27
"between the holy and the *." Eze 42:16-20f
the * people on these occasions. Eze 46:10
I try to find * ground with him so 1Co 9:22
have in * with the people of sin? 2Co 6:14
the old system the * people could Heb 9:8
as though it were * and unhallowed, Heb 10:29

COMMOTION
guests heard the * and shouting 1Ki 1:41
all the noise and *, and the shouts 2Ch 23:12
together in a loud * that could be Ez 3:13
makes the water boil with his *. Job 41:31,32
Don't you hear the tumult and * Ps 83:2
What is all the * in the city? Is 66:6
"Why all this weeping and *?" Mk 5:39
At dawn, the jail was in great *. Act 12:18

COMMUNICATE
I would * by visions and dreams; Num 12:6
but that is not how I * with my Num 12:7,8
practice magic and * with evil Is 2:6

COMMUNICATION
Reliable * permits progress. Pro 13:17

COMMUNION
sessions and at the * services Act 2:42
in homes for *, and shared their Act 2:46
we gathered for a * service, with Act 20:7
meet together for your * services. 1Co 11:17
* service—wait for each other; 1Co 11:33
Impenitence at the * Table 1Jn 5:17f

COMMUNITIES
of Egypt, all of the * of them." Ex 12:51f

COMMUNITY
Levites in your *, for they have no Deu 14:27
the gods honored by the Jewish *. Jer 7:18f
leaders and the business * Lk 19:47

COMPANIES
Three * of raiders soon left the 1Sa 13:17
by battalions and *, David and his 1Sa 29:2
manned them with * of soldiers 2Ch 11:11

COMPANION
I will make a * for him, a helper Gen 2:18
the laws shall be his constant *. Deu 17:19
to jackals and a * to ostriches. Job 30:28,29

COMPANION Con't)
like myself, my * and my friend. Ps 55:13
child, and the * of my father. Pro 4:3
has, for he is the * of the Father Jn 1:18
that Titus, my *, should be Gal 2:3

COMPANIONS
and invited his * to a feast, and Gen 31:54
he sent his * on and returned alone Ju 3:17,18,19
had touched became his constant *. 1Sa 10:26
and to their * living in Samaria Ez 4:17
and their * soon arrived in Ez 5:3
and their * complied at once with Ez 6:13
among the flocks of your *." Sol 1:7
your * may listen to your voice; Sol 8:13
Your leaders are rebels, * of Is 1:23
And Daniel and his * were Dan 2:13
Misha-el, and Azariah, his *. Dan 2:17
and * will kill each other. Hag 2:22
the years, the * you promised to Mal 2:14
Jesus and his * now arrived at Mk 1:21
King David and his * were hungry, Mk 2:25,26
to be his regular * and to go out Mk 3:14,15
Paul's traveling *, for trial. Act 19:29
and his traveling *—begged Paul not Act 21:12
to be led into Damascus by my *. Act 22:11
the sun shone down on me and my *. Act 26:13

COMPANIONSHIP
and enjoy the * of those who love 2Ti 2:22

COMPANY
and thus he and Abram parted *. Gen 13:11
leaders and * commanders, and Num 31:51,52
and * commanders over his troops. 2Sa 18:1
saw Jehu and his * approaching and 2Ki 9:17
I want the * of the godly men Ps 16:3
Wickedness loves *—and leads Pro 16:29
Literally, "* not with him." Pro 20:19f
don't even enjoy their *. Pro 24:1
It will be a great * who comes. Jer 31:8
And you will be in good *—the Lk 6:23
but enjoy the * of ordinary folks. Rom 12:16
are not to keep * with anyone who 1Co 5:11

COMPARATIVE
Now I began a study of the * Ecc 2:12

COMPARE
"There was no king who could * Neh 13:26
cannot * with you in glory! Ps 76:4
Literally, "I * you to my mare Sol 1:9f
With what can we * him? Is 40:18
"With whom will you * me? Is 40:25
in all of heaven and earth do I *? Is 46:5
Will you * me with an idol made Is 46:6
O Jerusalem, what can I * your Lam 2:13
none had boughs to *; Eze 31:8
* Joshua 5:13-15. Dan 8:11f
Romans at Magnesia. * verse 18. Dan 11:13f
"With what shall I * them? Lk 7:31
to * himself with someone else. Gal 6:4

COMPARED
all the world could be * with it! 2Ch 9:19
be absolutely pure * with him! Job 15:15
are less than nothing as * to him. Job 25:5
No one else can be * with you. Ps 40:5
all of heaven can be * with God? Ps 89:6
Who can be * with God enthroned Ps 113:5
For as * with you, no one is Ps 143:2
nothing can be * with it. Pro 8:11
as * with any other girls." Sol 2:2
as * with any of the other youths. Sol 2:3
nothing * to what I'm going to do! Is 43:18
when * with vigorous young men! Is 59:10
his treasuries. * to him, all men Jer 51:17
pale and thin * with the other Dan 1:10
earth are nothing when * to him; Dan 4:35
"The Kingdom of Heaven can be * Mt 13:33
What can be * with the value of Mt 16:26
"The Kingdom of Heaven can be * Mt 18:23
can be * with that of a man who Mk 13:34
now is nothing * to the glory he Rom 8:18
is worthless when * with the Php 3:8

COMPARES
Nothing else * with it. Pro 3:13,14,15

COMPARING
that they are only * themselves 2Co 10:12

COMPARISON
What have I done in * with that? Ju 8:2,3
of baby goats in * to the vast 1Ki 20:27
all in * to the way I am going to! 2Ki 10:17
me are nothing in * to what you 1Ch 17:17
fathomless—what can you know in *? Job 11:8
down here is futile in *. Ecc 11:8
An apt *! Is 1:10
are nothing in * with him—they are Is 40:15
they seem almost righteous in * Eze 16:51
so awful that in * with you, your Eze 16:52
how they looked in * with the other Dan 1:13
How glorious it was! In *, it is Hag 2:3
But he is coming soon—and in * Act 13:25
nothing at all in * with the 2Co 3:10

COMPASSION
to you, and have * upon you, and Deu 13:17
And will have * on them when they Deu 32:36
but then he felt such * that he 1Ch 21:15
* on his people and on his Temple. 2Ch 36:15
O my God! Have * upon me in Neh 13:22
and have * on his servants. Ps 135:14
everyone, and his * is intertwined Ps 145:9
have * upon them in their sorrow. Is 49:13
But with great * I will gather Is 54:7
power, your mercy and your *? Is 63:15
return and have * on all of you, Jer 12:15
ray of hope: his * never ends. Lam 3:22
yet he will show * too, according Lam 3:32
Once again you will have * on Mic 7:19
"Try to show as much * as your Lk 6:36

COMPASSIONATE
for I am very *. Ex 22:27

COMPEL
cursed wherever I * them to go. Jer 24:9

COMPELLED
in fact, he * his people to 2Ch 21:11
no one should be * to take more Est 1:8

COMPENSATE
for what I did, to * for any Gen 20:16

COMPENSATION
for it is their * for their service Num 18:31
And Nebuchadnezzar received no * Eze 29:18

COMPILED
and Levites was * during the reign Neh 12:22

COMPLACENCY
your own * will kill you. Pro 1:32

COMPLAIN
these wicked people * about me? Num 14:26,27
God and to * against Moses. Num 21:5
I can assure you he will never * 2Sa 14:10
So how can I *?" 2Sa 19:28
Let me * freely. Job 10:1
To * about the law is to praise Pro 28:4
and * when punished for our sins? Lam 3:39
could * to the king about him. Dan 6:4
feast and drink, and you * that I Mt 11:19
of children who * to their friends, Lk 7:32

COMPLAINED
Then Abraham * to the king Gen 21:25
the people growled and * to Moses. Ex 17:2
and older, who has * against me, Num 14:29
"They murmured and * in their Deu 1:27
when you * against him at Massah. Deu 6:16
Delilah *. Ju 16:13
And I have never once * to 2Sa 7:7
But the men of Israel * to the 2Sa 19:41
this man is doing," he * to them. 1Ki 20:7
Turning to Jehoshaphat, Ahab *, 1Ki 22:18
the reapers. He * about a 2Ki 4:19
They murmured and *, demanding Ps 78:18
when you * there was no water. Ps 81:7
very angry. He * to the Lord about Jon 4:2
of the Law * bitterly to Jesus' Lk 5:30
Those who spoke only Greek * that Act 6:1
his love and * against him in the Heb 3:7,8

COMPLAINERS
* will be willing to be taught! Is 29:24

COMPLAINING
really * against us—who are we? Ex 16:7,8,9
THE PEOPLE WERE soon * about all Num 11:1
Then at last this murmuring and * Num 17:5
"Well, the Lord heard their * Deu 1:34,35
Then some of the leaders began * Neh 4:10
"I am * about God, Job 21:4
TO myself, I'm going to quit *! Ps 39:1
than with a quarrelsome, * woman. Pro 21:19
his disciples were * and said to Jn 6:61
Elijah the prophet was * to God Rom 11:2,3
do, stay away from * and arguing, Php 2:14

COMPLAINS
a man * when there is no salt in Job 6:5,6,7

COMPLAINT
of * against Moses and Aaron. Num 14:2
tribe of Joseph have a proper *. Num 36:5
"My * today is still a bitter Job 23:2
*, for my punishment is from you. Ps 39:9
you: I have no * about the Ps 50:8
LORD, LISTEN TO my *: Oh, preserve Ps 64:1
Now let me bring you this *: Why Jer 12:1
hills be called to witness your *. Mic 6:1
mountains, listen to the Lord's *! Mic 6:2
what answer God will give to my *. Hab 2:1
Their next * was that Jesus' Lk 5:33

COMPLAINTS
for he has heard your * against Ex 16:7,8,9
and hear his reply to your *." Ex 16:7,8,9
to Moses, "I have heard their *. Ex 16:11,12
hear the people's * against each Ex 18:13
because of their *, so the fire of Num 11:1
heard your tearful * about all you Num 11:18
if there were any further * Num 17:10
"If I decided to forget my * Job 9:27
was severely tried by their *. Ps 95:9
You can no more stop her * than Pro 27:16
but this caused * from the Lk 15:2
And if there are * about other Act 19:39
best for yourself, * and Gal 5:20
Don't listen to * against the 1Ti 5:19

COMPLETE
feast before them, * with freshly Gen 19:3
So Potiphar gave Joseph the * Gen 39:6
you shall have * charge over all Gen 41:44
on hand now to * the job!" Ex 36:4-7
he shall take a * bath and be Lev 15:16
be destroyed, do a * job of Deu 7:2
stay with them until they * the Jos 1:15
"Let there be * silence except Jos 6:10
"Take a * census throughout the 1Ch 21:2
the Lord. The * biography of 2Ch 12:15
daughters. His * biography and 2Ch 13:22
of Israel. The * biography of King 2Ch 25:26
advisors were in * agreement in 2Ch 30:4
God will judge them with * Ps 50:6
* with their growing crops; Ps 105:44
This * destruction of the city of Jer 51:26f
have kept us from * destruction. Lam 3:22
of this Temple, and he will * it. Zec 4:9
Otherwise he might * only the Lk 14:29
your enemies into * subjection.' Act 2:35
PAUL WAS IN * agreement with the Act 8:1
of us to make it *, for we each Rom 12:4,5
you to live in * harmony with each Rom 15:5
made perfect and *, then the need 1Co 13:10
encourage you to * your share in 2Co 8:6
when salvation from sin will be *. Eph 4:30
your patience and * faith in God, 2Th 1:4
And you have put him in * charge Heb 2:8
is in * charge of God's house. Heb 3:6
So there is a full * rest still Heb 4:9
strong in character, full and *. Jas 1:4
his faith was made * by what he Jas 2:22
our love grows more perfect and *; 1Jn 4:17
When they * the three and a half Rev 11:7

COMPLETED
*, with all that they contained. Gen 2:1
sacrifice after the ceremony is *. Lev 7:9
be *—for it takes seven days. Lev 8:33
"When he has * the rite of Lev 16:20
(She had just * the purification 2Sa 11:4
entire land, they * their task in 2Sa 24:8
building was * in every detail in 1Ki 6:38
basins and at last * the work in 1Ki 7:40
After the Temple was *, Solomon 1Ki 9:25
and when he finally * it by 1Ki 16:34
So at last he * the work assigned 2Ch 4:11
He * what he had planned to do. 2Ch 7:11
and his own royal palace were *. 2Ch 8:1
Thus Solomon successfully * the 2Ch 8:16
entire job was * in sixteen days. 2Ch 29:17
"We have * the cleansing of the 2Ch 29:18
ceremony was * in that one day. 2Ch 35:16
When the builders * the Ez 3:10
since, though it is not yet *. Ez 5:16
and merchants * the wall from that Neh 3:32
At last the wall was * to half Neh 4:6
that we had almost * the rebuilding Neh 6:1
In Heshbon, plans have been * to Jer 48:2,3,4
have * all the days of your siege. Eze 4:8
wrath against the wall will be *; Eze 13:15
period was *, the superintendent Dan 1:18,19
and, oh, that my task were *! Lk 12:49
to God for the work now *. Act 14:26
this money and * this good deed of Rom 15:28
* pouring out the seven plagues. Rev 15:8

COMPLETELY
For we will destroy the city *. Gen 19:13
but he has been * unscrupulous and Gen 31:7
"Are you going to destroy us *? Ex 10:7
he shall tear it apart, but not *. Lev 1:15,16,17
If the spot has indeed turned * Lev 13:16,17
He is * at home in my house! Num 12:7,8
people, they would * annihilate all Num 21:2
and the Israelis * destroyed them Num 21:3
land and * destroyed their people. Jos 2:10
melted away * and they were Jos 5:1
you * rid yourselves of this sin. Jos 7:12
will help you to * destroy them." Jos 10:19
he killed them all and * Jos 11:21
other gods he will * wipe you out Jos 23:15,16
Lord helped Israel conquer him *. Ju 3:10
was * stripped and devastated. Ju 6:5
let the Midianites * ruin us." Ju 6:13
By then the temple was * filled Ju 16:27
Now go and * destroy the entire 1Sa 15:3
told you, 'Go and * destroy the 1Sa 15:18
to wipe them out * at the time of 1Ki 9:20,21
of trusting * in the Lord as his 1Ki 11:4
No one else was so * sold out to 1Ki 21:25
for you will * conquer the 2Ki 13:16,17
they have * destroyed everything. 2Ki 19:11
King David, obeying the Lord * 2Ki 22:1
There was no other king who so * 2Ki 23:25
the Israelis had not * wiped out. 2Ch 8:7,8
I will not * destroy you; 2Ch 12:7
king of Babylon to destroy them *. 2Ch 36:17
of the land; they * took over the Neh 9:22
them * or abandon them forever. Neh 9:31
* innocent—as pure as solid gold! Job 23:10
against me—a man I * trusted; Ps 41:9

(COMPLETELY Con't)
but I will never * take away my Ps 89:33
I am * discouraged—I lie in the Ps 119:25
sense, then trust the Lord *; Pro 3:4,5
The land will be * emptied and Is 24:3
No, the Assyrian kings * Is 37:12
For you are a prostitute, and * Jer 3:3
But I will not * blot you out. Jer 5:18
cry, "have you * rejected Judah? Jer 14:19
of Judah are * destroyed and left Jer 34:22
their father *, but you have Jer 35:16
me to destroy you * and to make you Jer 44:8
You shall be * wiped out. Jer 51:26
Her enemies have plundered her *, Lam 1:10
No, it will wither away * when Eze 17:10
It will be * uninhabited. Eze 29:11
upon his home and * destroy it." Zec 5:4
and Ashkelon will be * destroyed. Zec 9:5
for they shall be * satisfied. Mt 5:6
his sight was * restored, and he Mk 8:25
so that he ran away * naked. Mk 14:51,52
And as he did, it became * Lk 6:10
they found the slave * healed. Lk 7:10
The lepers are * healed. Lk 7:20,21,22
desert, * under the demon's power. Lk 8:29
your income, you * forget about Lk 11:42
that your faith should not * fail. Lk 22:32
a man * well on the Sabbath? Jn 7:21,22,23
He was * sure that God was well Rom 4:21
but give yourselves * to Rom 6:13
give themselves more * to prayer. 1Co 7:5
Then have you gone * crazy? Gal 3:3
He will * fool those who are on 2Th 2:10
should * give up drinking wine. 1Ti 5:23
two things we can * count on, for Heb 6:18
He is able to save * all who Heb 7:25
of the covenant, * covered on all Heb 9:4
Elijah was as * human as we are, Jas 5:17
At that time God * destroyed the 2Pe 2:5
is good and who pleases God *. 1Jn 2:1

COMPLETENESS
to see him in his *, face to face. 1Co 13:12

COMPLETES
This * the roof-covering. Ex 26:14

COMPLETING
After * the Temple, Solomon 1Ki 6:9

COMPLETION
The * date was February 18 Ez 6:15
project through to * just as 2Co 8:11

COMPLEX
for making me so wonderfully *! Ps 139:14

COMPLEXION
just because my * is so dark—the Sol 1:6

COMPLICATE
i.e., * his estate for the children Ru 4:6f

COMPLICATED
or * can be brought to you. Ex 18:22

COMPLIED
their companions * at once with the Ez 6:13

COMPLIMENT
For a fool's * is as quickly Ecc 7:6
They encourage and * those who Jer 23:14

COMPOSE
and on the harp. * new songs of Ps 33:3

COMPOSED
Then David * a dirge for Saul and 2Sa 1:17,18
Both armies were * of 2Ch 14:8
was * by King Solomon:The Girl: Sol 1:1
a similar building * of two units Eze 42:9,10
and to the church, * of all Heb 12:23

COMPOSING
drapes * the walls of the court. Ex 38:18

COMPOSURE
Or, "I sought to learn about * Ecc 1:16-18f

COMPOUND
perfume-makers to * all this into a Ex 30:25

COMPOUNDED
They are the dross, * from the Eze 22:18,19,20

COMPOUNDING
the light, and for * the anointing Ex 35:28

COMPOUNDS
Anyone who * any incense like it Ex 30:33
tribal * will be the Tabernacle." Num 2:1

COMPREHEND
We cannot * the greatness of his Job 37:5
No fool can * this: that Ps 92:6

COMPRISED
* an octet accompanied by harps. 1Ch 15:20

COMPROMISE
careful never to * with the people Ex 34:12
will, rejecting * with evil, and Ps 119:3
your agreement of * with Death and Is 28:18

COMPROMISES
If a godly man * with the wicked, Pro 25:26

COMPULSION
Or, "by an inner *." Act 20:22f

COMPULSORY
These offerings are * at the Num 29:39

COMRADES
heard that their * had fled and 1Sa 31:7

CONANIAH
the Lord's house. *, the Levite, 2Ch 31:12,13
The Levite leaders—*, Shemaiah, 2Ch 35:9

CONCAVE
Its center was *, 2¼ feet deep, 1Ki 7:31

CONCEAL
don't * his horrible suggestion. Deu 13:8
O earth, do not * my blood. Job 16:18
It is God's privilege to * Pro 25:2,3

CONCEALS
mouth of the wicked * violence." Pro 10:6f

CONCEIT
Instead, in their *, they think Ps 36:2
I will not permit * and pride. Ps 101:5
his * with silly replies! Pro 26:4,5
backs, filled with * and disunity. 2Co 12:20

CONCEITED
Don't be *, sure of your own Pro 3:7,8
fool, and that is a man who is *. Pro 26:12
Rich men are *, but their real Pro 28:11
And are you still so *, so 1Co 5:2

CONCEIVE
you will soon * and have a son! Ju 13:2,3
The only thing they can '*' is Job 15:35
The virgin shall * a child! Mt 1:23

CONCEIVED
his wife, and she * and gave birth Gen 4:1
Then Cain's wife * and presented Gen 4:17
So he slept with Hagar, and she *; Gen 16:4
and when he slept with her, she * 2Sa 12:24
the woman soon * and had a baby 2Ki 4:17
Afterwards, his wife * and bore 1Ch 7:23
"and the night when I was *. Job 3:2,3
from the moment my mother * me. Ps 51:5
a virgin (Mary) * and bore a son, Is 7:14f
my wife and she *, and bore me a Is 8:3
and she * and bore him a son. Hos 1:3
she again * and this time gave Hos 1:8
in the womb, or never even be *. Hos 9:11
her has been * by the Holy Spirit. Mt 1:20
by the angel before he was even *. Lk 2:21

CONCEIVES
The wicked man * an evil plot, Ps 7:14

CONCENTRATE
But I will * my thoughts upon Ps 119:78

CONCERN
world whose only * is earthly Ps 17:13,14
Your only * is your own fine Hag 1:9
eternal life * themselves with Lk 9:60
the Kingdom of God your primary *. Lk 12:31
the Scriptures: "* for God's House Jn 2:17
and has no real * for the sheep. Jn 10:13
so anxiously and with such deep *. 2Co 7:15
same real * for you that I have. 2Co 8:16
you with the deep * of God 2Co 11:2
his deep love and * for you, you Col 3:12

CONCERNED
So far as the Lord was *, it was Gen 38:10
it, he became very * as to what the Gen 41:8
As far as I am *, God turned Gen 50:20
out, they became * and got a key. Ju 3:25
as far as the Philistines were *. 1Sa 13:3,4
"As far as I'm *, you're as 1Sa 29:9
But because you were sorry and * 2Ki 22:18,19
the Lord's opinion of him was *. 2Ch 26:4
reign as far as the Lord was *. 2Ch 36:9
as the Lord was *, for he refused 2Ch 36:12
*, for he refused to follow him. 2Ch 36:13
You are * Ps 36:6
A good man is * for the welfare Pro 12:10
the Lord are much * about it. Pro 28:5
I am * about my reputation that Eze 36:21
for I am * about my reputation! Eze 39:25
another vision. It * events certain Dan 10:1
says, I am greatly *—yes, furiously Zec 8:2
From now on, as far as we're *, Mal 3:14,15
and are deeply * about them. Mt 6:31,32
And don't be * about the fact Lk 6:35
one thing worth being * about. Lk 10:42
don't be * about what to say in Lk 12:11
Therefore, don't be * about how Lk 21:14
"What are you so * about?" Lk 24:17
will no longer be * about whether Jn 4:21-24
But you shouldn't be so * about Jn 6:27
the judges, were * at these reports Act 17:8,9
So as far as I was *, the good Rom 7:10
far as my old sinful nature is *. Rom 7:18
will so far as my new nature is *; Rom 7:22
human nature is *, he who now rules Rom 9:5
As far as God is * there is a 2Co 2:15
far as doing anything good is *. Tit 1:16
man that you are so * about him? Heb 2:6
far as Abraham was *, Isaac was Heb 11:19
Don't be * about the outward 1Pe 3:3
they are * about worldly affairs 1Jn 4:5

CONCERNING
fit to be tied * this affair, but Gen 37:11
the Lord * the frogs he had sent. Ex 8:12
* the observance of the Passover. Ex 12:43
to Moses * the incense: "Use sweet Ex 30:34
to Jehovah * the people of Israel; Ex 39:6,7
these are the laws * anyone who Lev 4:2
for the leader * his sin, and he Lev 4:26
TO give testimony * what he knows Lev 5:
atonement for him * his sin and he Lev 5:1
regulations * the burnt offering: Lev 6
"These are the regulations * the Lev 6:1
instructions * the sin offering: Lev 6:2
"HERE ARE THE instructions * the Lev 7:
"Here are the instructions * the Lev 7:1
These were the instructions * the Lev 7:3
offering, and * the consecration Lev 7:3
Keep yourselves pure * these Lev 11:4
These are the laws * animals, Lev 11:4
These are the regulations * Lev 13:5
these regulations * a person whose Lev 14:
These, then, are the laws * those Lev 14:3
These, then, are the laws * the Lev 14:5
"This, then, is the law * a Num 5:2
"These are the regulations * a Num 6:2
instructions * this celebration." Num 9:2,
instructions * the Passover. Num 9:1
find out the Lord's mind * him. Num 15:3
* the water at Meribah. Num 20:2
and he spoke this prophecy * them: Num 24:3-
he was as angry as I, * my honor; Num 25:10,1
Lord gave Moses * relationships Num 30:1
further commanded * the daughters Num 36:
Then Moses said * the tribe of Deu 33:
* the tribe of Benjamin, Moses Deu 33:1
* the tribe of Joseph, he said: Deu 33:1
* the tribe of Gad, Moses said: Deu 33:2
the Lord had said * Mount Ebal. Jos 8:3
tell you what to do * marriage." Ru 3:4
of surprise * worldly Saul becoming 1Sa 10:12
have promised * me and my family. 2Sa 7:2
Shiloh * the descendants of Eli. 1Ki 2:2
guiltless * their deaths." 1Ki 2:3
do as you have asked * the timber. 1Ki 5:8
message to Solomon * the Temple he 1Ki 6:11,12
Solomon * the name of the Lord." 1Ki 10:1
the affair * Uriah the Hittite. 1Ki 15:5
" 'And my command * the king of 2Ki 19:32
the instructions * the work of the 1Ch 28:13
prayer * his private sorrow, as 2Ch 6:29
instructions * these matters and 2Ch 8:15
and * the treasury personnel. 2Ch 8:15
seer * Jeroboam the son of Nebat. 2Ch 9:29
Here are the statistics * the Ez 2:36-39
Here are the statistics * the Ez 2:40,41,42
has been sent out * the Temple of Ez 6:3
"Here are the statistics * the Neh 7:39-42
"Here are the statistics * the Neh 7:43,44,45
from the king * them." Neh 11:22,23f
The instructions * these girls Est 2:12,13,14
Nevertheless, his mind * me Job 23:13
speak rightly * my servant Job." Job 42:8
a sad situation * kings and rulers: Ecc 10:5
the Lord * Judah and Jerusalem: Is 2:1
(son of Amoz) * Babylon's doom. Is 13:1
Is this proud Moab, * which we Is 16:6
All this * Moab has been said Is 16:13,14
THIS IS GOD'S message * Egypt: Is 19:1
THIS IS GOD'S message * Babylon: Is 21:1
This is God's message * Arabia: Is 21:13
THIS IS GOD'S message * Jerusalem: Is 22:1
him in the dark * what they do! Is 29:15
this word of mine * Egypt, so that Is 30:8
Who are you to command me * the Is 45:11
things * Cyrus would come true? Is 45:21
For this is the Lord's message * Jer 22:6
And write this also * Israel and Jer 30:4
God of Israel says * this city that Jer 32:36
And now the Lord adds this * Jer 36:30
gave to Jeremiah * all the Jews who Jer 44:1
to Jeremiah * foreign nations. Jer 46:1
this message * the coming of Jer 46:13
to Jeremiah * the Philistines of Jer 47:1
(Here the prophecy * Moab ends. Jer 48:47
he has said he would * Babylon. Jer 51:12
of Mahseiah), * Seraiah's capture Jer 51:59
be completed; and * those who Eze 13:15
Yes, this is the primary law * Eze 43:12
laws I gave you * these holy Eze 44:8
* the impending doom of Nineveh: Nah 1:1
THIS IS THE message * God's curse Zec 9:1
These are the facts * the birth Mt 1:18
of the prophets * the Messiah, Mt 2:23
the prophecy of Isaiah * him: Mt 12:17
down here on earth * anything you Mt 18:19
for I had a terrible nightmare * Mt 27:19
prophets * me will come true. Lk 18:31
even though I make them * myself. Jn 8:14
* this man have come true." Jn 10:41
the prophets said * the Messiah, Jn 15:25
* the method of his execution. Jn 18:32
to come true * Judas, who betrayed Act 1:16
his words * the Kingdom of God; Act 8:12
all the prophecies * his death, he Act 13:29
about when it says * Jesus, 'Today Act 13:32,33
we have decided * your question. Act 15:26
known the decision * the Gentiles, Act 16:4
Literally, "* the Kingdom of Act 19:8f
in Ephesus * the Christians. Act 19:23

CONCERNING Con't)
- What were his experiences * this Rom 4:1
- Isaiah the prophet cried out * Rom 9:27
- said to you husbands * your wives. 1Co 7:16
- to God's children * his power, but 1Co 14:22
- you with the Good News * Christ. 2Co 10:14
- and change the truth * Christ. Gal 1:7
- him the truths * himself, then Eph 4:21
- out the Good News * Christ. Php 1:12
- But * the pure brotherly love 1Th 4:9
- you, especially * the faith and 2Ti 1:13
- who are mixed up * the truth. 2Ti 2:25
- Literally, "the revelation of (*, Rev 1:1f

CONCERNS
- of God is right, whatever it *. Ps 119:128
- watching everything that * you. 1Pe 5:7

CONCERTED
- the Jews rose in * action against Act 18:12

CONCESSION
- "I'll tell you why—it was a * to Mk 10:5

CONCLUDE
- So I * that, first, there is Ecc 3:12
- II of Syria to * a treaty of peace Dan 11:6f
- for we could only * that God was Act 16:10

CONCLUDED
- He * his prophecies by saying: Num 24:23,24
- Jeremiah *: "Never forget the Jer 42:19
- So they *, "Our only chance is Dan 6:5

CONCLUSION
- "At the * of the period of his Num 6:13
- sacrifices at the * of his period Num 6:21
- At the * of these offerings 1Ch 16:2
- else would come to the same * Ecc 2:12
- This is my *, says the Preacher. Ecc 7:27,28
- premise, his * is sheer madness. Ecc 10:12,13
- Here is my final *: fear God and Ecc 12:13
- Herod came to the same * and Lk 23:15
- At its * the people gave him a Act 12:22

CONCLUSIONS
- So be careful not to jump to * 1Co 4:5

CONCOCTED
- they speak foolishness * out of Jer 14:14

CONCUBINE
- children from his *, Reumah:Tebah, Gen 22:24
- his father's *, and someone told Gen 35:22
- (born to Timna, Eliphaz' *). Gen 36:10,11,12
- He also had a * in Shechem, who Ju 8:31
- Bethlehem in Judah to be his *. Ju 19:1
- virgin to be your * and nurse. 1Ki 1:2
- Abraham also had sons by his * 1Ch 1:32
- of Abraham by his * Keturah. 1Ch 1:33
- Caleb's * Ephah bore him 1Ch 2:46
- his Aramaean *, were Asri-el and 1Ch 7:14

CONCUBINES
- to the sons of his * and sent them Gen 25:6
- of the *, but didn't find them. Gen 31:33
- his two wives and his two * and Gen 32:22,23,24
- with his two * and their children Gen 33:2
- Then the * came forward with Gen 33:6
- of Saul's *, a girl named Rizpah. 2Sa 3:7
- wives and *, and had many sons and 2Sa 5:13
- your daughters, your wives and *; 2Sa 19:5
- hundred wives and three hundred *; 1Ki 11:3
- Another of Caleb's *, Maacah, 1Ch 2:48,49
- not include the sons of his *. 1Ch 3:9
- other wives and * (he had eighteen 2Ch 11:21
- wives and sixty *—with twenty-eight 2Ch 11:21
- Kings' daughters are among your *. Ps 45:9
- there were my many beautiful *. Ecc 2:7,8
- queens, and eighty *, and Sol 6:8
- even the queens and * praise you. Sol 6:9
- wives, and * drank toasts from them Dan 5:2,3,4
- and wives and * have been drinking Dan 5:23

CONCURRENT
- * with: King Azariah of Judah who 2Ki 15:17
- * with: King Azariah of Judah, who 2Ki 15:23
- * with: King Azariah of Judah, who 2Ki 15:27
- * with: Jotham (son of Uzziah) 2Ki 15:30

CONDEMN
- Are you going to * me just Job 6:25,26
- innocent, O God, but will * me. Job 9:29
- I will say to God, 'Don't just * Job 10:2
- but why should I * you? Job 15:6
- Are you going to * the Almighty Job 34:17
- Are you going to * this God who Job 34:18
- my justice and * me, so that you Job 40:8
- You deliver the humble but * the Ps 18:27
- Do you approve of those who * Ps 94:21,22
- the wicked and * the innocent. Pro 18:5
- Judge them, son of dust; * them; Eze 20:4
- nation at the judgment and * you. Mt 12:41
- nation in the judgment, and * it; Mt 12:42
- and they will * me to die. Mt 20:18
- be sufficient to * him to death. Mk 14:55
- Never criticize or *—or it will Lk 6:37
- shall arise and * this nation, for Lk 11:32
- the world to * it, but to save it. Jn 3:17
- Didn't even one of them * you?" Jn 8:10
- I could * you for much and teach Jn 8:26
- God will judge and * others for Rom 2:3
- Literally, "will *" you. Rom 2:27f
- How could he ever * anyone? Rom 3:6
- For he could not judge and * me Rom 3:7
- Who then will * us? Rom 8:34
- who foolishly * the Gospel without 1Pe 2:15

CONDEMNATION
- A MESSAGE OF * from the Lord was 1Ki 16:1
- under God's * than we were before. Ez 10:10
- what was good to bring about my *. Rom 7:13
- SO THERE IS now no * awaiting Rom 8:1
- are still under * for your sins; 1Co 15:17
- is ready for * and burning off. Heb 6:8

CONDEMNED
- Job's arguments and yet had * him. Job 32:3
- let the godly be * when they are Ps 37:33
- the prisoners and those * to die. Ps 79:11
- When their leaders are *, and Ps 141:6,7
- until they are tried and *. Is 24:22
- in other gods has openly * him; Hos 7:10
- have * those who aren't guilty! Mt 12:7
- by them or you will be *." Mt 12:37
- Jesus had been * to die, changed Mt 27:3
- who refuse to believe will be *. Mk 16:16
- 'He will be * as a criminal!' Lk 22:37
- government to be * to death, and Lk 24:20
- * for not believing in the only Jn 3:18
- So why should I be * for making a Jn 7:21,22,23
- and when they were * to death, I Act 26:10
- be * with the rest of the world. 1Co 11:32
- And so they will stand * because 1Ti 5:12
- You have * and killed good men Jas 5:6
- you will not sin and be * for it. Jas 5:12
- But God * them long ago and their 2Pe 2:3

CONDEMNING
- silent before the ones * him. Is 53:7
- this generation, * it, for she went Lk 11:31

CONDEMNS
- The Lord blesses good men and * Pro 12:2
- Literally, "If our heart * us, 1Jn 3:20f

CONDITION
- here on one *—that every one of us Gen 34:22
- Literally, "knew their *." Ex 2:25f
- "but only on one *: I will gouge 1Sa 11:2
- unstable mental * caused 1Sa 17:55f
- getting the Temple into good *." 2Ki 12:7
- was in much better * than before. 2Ch 24:13
- * for helping another Israelite?" Neh 5:7
- one young bull, in perfect *; Eze 46:6
- eyes to their true * so that they Act 26:18
- so I was given a physical * which 2Co 12:7
- the only * is that you fully Col 1:23

CONDITIONS
- the terrible * they were under. Ex 2:11
- them the following *, to test their Ex 15:25
- "Here are the * for his entering Lev 16:3
- If you wait for perfect *, you Ecc 11:4
- You may remain under these * Jer 7:5
- the terms and *, and also the Jer 32:11

CONDUCT
- He tried always to * his affairs Gen 6:9,10
- to * the king across the river. 2Sa 19:31,32
- were supposed to * the worship Neh 13:10
- arrived to * Haman quickly to the Est 6:14
- of * by demanding his own way. Pro 18:1

CONDUCTED
- They were then * into the palace Gen 43:24
- Literally, "he * them to the 1Ch 20:3f

CONDUCTS
- man who * his business fairly. Ps 112:5

CONDUIT
- near the * of the upper pool. 2Ki 18:17
- the pool and * he made and how he 2Ki 20:20

CONEY
- The *, or rock badger (because Lev 11:4-7
- eat the camel, the hare, or the *. Deu 14:7

CONFEDERACY
- crowned him king of the Judean *. 2Sa 2:4
- * for seven and one-half years. 2Sa 2:10,11

CONFEDERATES
- The names of Gog's * (Meshech, Eze 38:2,3f

CONFER
- * with King Hezekiah in Jerusalem. Is 36:2
- and God will * on you a new name. Is 62:2
- orders from God to * with the Gal 2:2

CONFERENCE
- So they called a * of the mayors 1Sa 5:8
- For a summit * of the nations Ps 2:2
- at their summit *—they signed a Ps 83:5
- the palace to the * room where the Jer 36:12
- Then Johanan had a private * Jer 40:15
- each other at the * table, Dan 11:27

CONFERRED
- chamber and * among themselves. Act 4:15
- Festus * with his advisors and Act 25:12
- These miracle-working demons * Rev 16:14

CONFESS
- said to them, "I * my sin against Ex 10:16
- cases, he shall * his sin and Lev 5:5
- upon its head, * over it all the Lev 16:21
- "But at last they shall * their Lev 26:40,41
- He must * his sin and make full Num 5:7
- and * that you are their God. 1Ki 8:33,34
- toward this place and * your name. 1Ki 8:35,36
- we were before. * your sin to the Ez 10:11
- * that we have sinned against you; Neh 1:6,7
- is this: Go to God and * your sins Job 5:8
- I said to myself, "I will * them Ps 32:5
- believer should * his sins to God Ps 32:6
- me in the face. I * my sins; Ps 38:18
- stand in awe and * the greatness of Ps 64:9
- O nations of the world, * that Ps 96:7
- must * that only God can prophesy. Is 43:9
- them to mourn and to * their sins. Is 57:18
- * that you refused to follow me. Jer 3:13
- O Lord, we * our wickedness, and Jer 14:20
- I will save them to * to the Eze 12:16
- whips to make him * his crime. Act 22:24
- "But one thing I do *, that I Act 24:14
- to me and every tongue * to God." Rom 14:11
- every tongue shall * that Jesus Php 2:11
- But if we * our sins to him, 1Jn 1:9
- Literally, "if we * our sins." 1Jn 1:9f

CONFESSED
- "I finally see my fault," he *. Ex 9:27
- Then Balaam *, "I have sinned. Num 22:34
- "Then they *, 'We have sinned! Deu 1:41
- have worshiped idols," they *. Ju 10:10
- been cut," he *, "for I've been a Ju 16:16,17
- the Lord again and * that they had 1Sa 12:10
- Then Saul *, "I have done wrong. 1Sa 26:21
- "for you yourself * that you 2Sa 1:16
- the Lord," David * to Nathan. 2Sa 12:13
- leaders of Israel * their sins and 2Ch 12:6
- and the people * their sins to the 2Ch 30:22
- What relief for those who have * Ps 32:1
- heal me, for I have * my sins." Ps 41:4
- listened if I had not * my sins. Ps 66:18
- * my sins and those of my people. Dan 9:4
- and when they * their sins, he Mt 3:6
- and when they * their sins he Mk 1:5
- black magic * their deeds and Act 19:18,19
- and which you have * with such a 1Ti 6:12

CONFESSES
- But if he * and forsakes them, he Pro 28:13
- If he listens and * it, you have Mt 18:15

CONFESSING
- "God bless you for * it," his Ju 17:2
- they took turns * their own sins Neh 9:3
- Even while I was praying and * my Dan 9:20
- and * that they belong to Jesus. Rev 12:17

CONFESSION
- the God of Israel and make your *. Jos 7:19
- all who have made an honest *; 1Ki 8:39
- and making this *, a large crowd of Ez 10:1
- Literally, "* is made unto Rom 10:10f
- a ringing * before many witnesses. 1Ti 6:12

CONFIDE
- love me when you don't * in me?" Ju 16:15
- a master doesn't * in his slaves; Jn 15:15

CONFIDENCE
- priest into his *, and they agreed 1Ki 1:7
- officers into his *: Azariah (son 2Ch 23:1
- not trust in God still be your *? Job 4:6
- God gives them * and strength, Job 24:22,23
- Lord, and have no * in those who Ps 40:4
- am afraid, I will put my * in you. Ps 56:3,4
- the Lord than to put * in men. Ps 118:8
- a fool plunges ahead with great * Pro 14:16
- Putting * in an unreliable man is Pro 25:19
- in quietness and * is your Is 30:15
- Quietness and * will reign Is 32:17
- has made the Lord his hope and *. Jer 17:7
- these people living in such *! Eze 38:11
- Don't you even yet have * in Mk 4:40
- gives me * as I make my defense. Act 24:10
- so, by agreeing, I can win their * 1Co 9:21
- Now we look forward with * to our 2Co 5:6
- I have the highest * in you, and 2Co 7:4
- Once again I can have perfect * 2Co 7:16
- own * and bold trust in the Lord. 1Ti 3:13
- can face him with * and joy, 1Jn 4:17
- opportunity for endurance and *. Rev 13:10

CONFIDENT
- they were * of a massive slaughter Ju 20:35-39
- "The * stride of the wicked man Job 18:7
- I am * that God will save me. Ps 27:3
- O God, my heart is quiet and *. Ps 57:7
- to you. I am * you are producing Heb 6:9
- It is the * assurance that Heb 11:1

CONFIDENTIALLY
- his men to say * to David that the 1Sa 18:22

CONFIDENTLY
- now stand, and we * and joyfully Rom 5:2
- us to wait patiently and *. Rom 8:25
- because he was * waiting for God to Heb 11:10
- end of his life, * spoke of God Heb 11:22

CONFINE
- and does not * himself to Cyrus. Jer 51:26f

CONFINED
- so that he must be * to bed, but Ex 21:18
- Let her be * outside the camp for Num 12:14
- IN HIS OLD age King David was * to 1Ki 1:1
- And Jeremiah remained * to the Jer 38:28

CONFIRM
torn carcass to * the fact, and Ex 22:13
So her husband may either * or Num 30:13
He wants to * you today as his Deu 29:13
his people, and to * that he is Deu 29:13
and * everything you've said." 1Ki 1:14
encouragement to * these two days Est 9:29-31
Will no one anywhere * my Job 17:3,4
Jesus Christ—will * orally what we Act 15:26
CONFIRMATION
public * that this well is mine." Gen 21:30
And his * to Jacob. 1Ch 16:17
* of my covenant with them. Is 42:6
CONFIRMED
So the commandment of Esther * Est 9:32
my own experience, * by the Job 15:17-19
and Isaac, and * with Jacob. Ps 105:10,11
The officer * the fact, and Mk 15:45
was with them and * what they said Mk 16:20
God, who knows men's hearts, * Act 15:8
CONFIRMING
The king agreed, * his decision Est 3:10
of his faith, * his salvation. Rom 10:10
CONFIRMS
said, "This blood * and seals the Ex 24:8
CONFISCATE
enemies will not * it. Is 65:21,22
CONFISCATED
They * all the flocks and herds Gen 34:28
grapes shall be * by the priests. Deu 22:9
Philistines and * their cattle, and 1Sa 23:5
and his troops * many idols which 2Sa 5:21
God has * our land and sent us Mic 2:4
nations will be *—great quantities Zec 14:14
CONFISCATING
* the crops that others plant.' Lk 19:21
CONFISCATION
* of goods, or imprisonment." Ez 7:26
CONFLAGRATION
becomes a roaring *, and I will Eze 21:31
CONFLICT
Go ahead and prepare for the *, Pro 21:31
He will end all * with his final Mt 12:20
and here there is no * with Gal 5:23
CONFOUNDED
This remark * the disciples. Mt 19:25
CONFRONT
and * him with his fault. Mt 18:15
CONFRONTATION
this time of their * with Pharaoh. Ex 7:7
CONFRONTED
I immediately * the leaders and Neh 13:11
the Temple, he was * by the chief Lk 20:1
CONFRONTS
The same providence * everyone, Ecc 9:2,3
CONFUSE
Turn them back and * them. Ps 35:4
Come and help me! * them! Ps 40:14,15
and delight in hurting me. * them! Ps 70:2,3
You need never * grapevines with Mt 7:16
we did not want to * you into Gal 2:5
CONFUSED
there that Jehovah * them by giving Gen 11:9
You will be * and a failure in Deu 28:20
cause them to be *, though I am Ps 69:6
and *, and drink it all in. Ps 73:10
is lost, abandoned and *. Is 24:19
See, all your angry enemies lie * Is 41:11
This Darius is not to be * with Dan 5:31f
I was * and disturbed by all I Dan 7:15
of Teman will be *, and helpless to Ob 1:9
* and disturbed, Mary tried to Lk 1:29
leave, Peter, all * and not even Lk 9:33
foolish minds became dark and *. Rom 1:21
Or, "were * fools." Rom 1:31f
do, for they are blinded and *. Eph 4:17,18
CONFUSING
The other explanation of this * 1Sa 17:55f
who has been troubling and * you. Gal 5:10
Such arguments are * and useless, 2Ti 2:14
CONFUSION
Babel (meaning "*"), because it Gen 11:9
before your enemies in utter *; Deu 28:25
For in the * the Lord caused the Ju 7:22
were thrown into *, and the 1Sa 7:10
there was terrible * everywhere. 1Sa 14:20
to bring about riots and *. Neh 4:8
as the city fell into * and panic. Est 3:15
death where only * reigns, and Job 10:22
What a day of * and terror from Is 22:5
Bring * and trouble on all who Jer 17:18
is almost here; *, destruction, and Mic 7:4
all was in great *, with Mk 5:38
soon the city was filled with *. Act 19:29
some another—everything was in *. Act 19:32
all the uproar and *, he ordered Act 21:34
CONGRATULATE
his son Joram to * him, for 2Sa 8:10
Now go out there and * the 2Sa 19:7
to greet and * King David on his 1Ch 18:10
they revile God and * those the Ps 10:3
CONGRATULATING
all the people are * King David, 1Ki 1:46,47
CONGRATULATIONS
Lord loved the baby, and sent * 2Sa 12:25
to extend * and good wishes. 1Ki 5:1
her and said, "*, favored lady! Lk 1:28
CONGREGATION
for the entire *, and no work of Ex 12:16
from the * of Israel. Ex 12:19
All the * of Israel shall Ex 12:47
of the * came and talked with him. Ex 34:31
All the * shall stone him; Lev 24:15,16
Literally, "to all the *." Num 15:33f
"The whole * of the Lord demands Jos 22:16
I will stand up before the * and Ps 22:22
before the entire *, before the Ps 35:18
and truth to all the *. Ps 40:10
before the *, and before the Ps 107:32
Let the * of Israel praise him Ps 118:2
the mount of the * in the sides of Is 14:13f
he preached. The * was surprised Mk 1:22
come and stand in front of the *. Mk 3:3
After the entire * had escorted Act 15:3
and the whole * voted to send Act 15:22
ship, the entire * including wives Act 21:5
CONIAH
Also known as Jehoiachin or *. 1Ch 3:16f
And as for you, *, Jer 22:24,25
* is an abbreviation—perhaps a Jer 22:24,25f
This man * is like a discarded, Jer 22:28
Record this man * as childless, Jer 22:30
(also called * and Jeconiah) Jer 36:30f
did not appoint * (King Jehoiakim's Jer 37:1
appointed his son * as ruler before Jer 37:1f
The Babylonians took * to Babylon Jer 37:1f
CONIAH'S
This man * grandson, Zerubbabel, Jer 22:30f
CONJECTURES
the speakers are * and are not in Sol 1:1f
CONNECT
six feet wide. * five of these Ex 26:9
gold were made to * the loops, thus Ex 36:13
CONNECTED
These corner frames will be * at Ex 26:24
court are to be * by silver rods, Ex 27:17
bear the guilt * with any errors Ex 28:37,38
Each frame was * to its base by Ex 36:24
This drapery was * by five hooks Ex 36:38
for the work * with the Tabernacle Num 1:50
else * with their use and repair. Num 4:32
The rooms were * to the walls of 1Ki 6:6
wheels which were * to axles that 1Ki 7:32
will be * by a highway, and the Is 19:23
But they are not * to Christ, Col 2:19
Their work is * with a mere Heb 8:5
CONNECTING
for our souls, * us with God Heb 6:19
CONNECTION
in * with funeral rites; Lev 19:28
you present in * with vows, or as Num 29:39
for use in * with the sacrifices. 2Ch 4:11
I have thought about this in * Ecc 3:10
CONNOTATION
Ezekiel. The * is "mortal man." Eze 2:1f
CONQUER
But you can * it!" Gen 4:7
These descendants of yours will * Gen 22:17
you must utterly * them and break Ex 23:24
No one will attack and * your Ex 34:24
"for we are well able to * it!" Num 13:30
he would help them * the king of Num 21:2
would be easy to * the whole area. Deu 1:41
When they * the land the Lord Deu 3:20
people across to * the land you Deu 3:28
the Jordan River and * that land. Deu 4:26
'How can we ever * these nations Deu 7:17
quickly * them and drive them out. Deu 9:3
see to it that they * it. Deu 31:7
and they shall * all the land I Jos 1:6
will go across and * and live in Jos 1:10,11
River to help them * their Jos 1:14
to Ai, for it is now yours to *. Jos 8:1
disciple Moses to * this entire Jos 9:24
impossible to *, so the tribe of Jos 19:47,48
then we will help you * yours." Ju 1:3
their attempt to * the people of Ju 1:19
of eastern Syria * them. Ju 3:8
helped Israel * him completely. Ju 3:10
to * part of Israel at that time. Ju 3:12
"I'll * the Midianites with Ju 7:7
* all the vast armies of Midian!" Ju 7:15
would help Israel * the Ammonites, Ju 11:30,31
the Lord helped me to * the enemy. Ju 12:3
Today the Lord will * you and I 1Sa 17:46
will help you * the Philistines." 1Sa 23:4
blind and the lame could * you!" 2Sa 5:8
Fight harder next time, and * 2Sa 11:25
for God will help you * it." 1Ki 22:6
the Lord will cause you to *!" 1Ki 22:15
You will * the best of their 2Ki 3:19
and his son Ben-hadad to * them. 2Ki 13:3
for you will completely * the 2Ki 13:16,1
but they did not * it. 2Ki 16:
he says that I won't * Jerusalem. 2Ki 19:1
kings of Israel to * Jerusalem, and 2Ki 21:1
the wicked nations won't * them 1Ch 17:
that they can come in and * it!" 1Ch 19:2,
the Lord will cause you to *." 2Ch 18:1
failed to * a nation we attacked? 2Ch 32:1
You commanded them to go in and * Neh 9:1
"Then you helped them * great Neh 9:2
more you let their enemies * them. Neh 9:2
the heathen nations to * them. Neh 9:3
to * us because of our sins. Neh 9:3
His enemies * him as a king Job 15:23,2
him up, let alone try to * him. Job 41:1
otherwise my enemies will * me. Ps 5:
don't let them * you! Ps 9:1
They did not * by their own Ps 44:
how they long to * me. Ps 56:
to * these fortified cities? Ps 108:1
two can stand back-to-back and *; Ecc 4:1
part of his plan to * the world. Is 10:
Do not let them rise and * the Is 14:2
he will * you to bless you, just Is 30:1
he has chosen to * many lands. Is 45:
But they will not * you for I am Jer 15:2
great kings shall * Babylon and Jer 27:
not * you, for they are liars. Jer 27:1
Babylonians shall * the city by Jer 32:2
he shall * it. Jer 32:2
Cyrus was used of God to * Jer 51:20
No more will other nations * Eze 34:2
no one will ever * it. Dan 2:44
to the coastal cities and * many. Dan 11:1
* the Negeb's outlying villages. Ob 1:2
up I'll give to those who * you! Mic 6:14
march across the world and * it. Hab 1:6
hand but * evil by doing good. Rom 12:21
when God will * sin and death. Rom 15:4
will use to * all else everywhere. Php 3:21
he rode out to * in many battles Rev 6:2
against them and * and kill them; Rev 11:7
Lamb, and the Lamb will * them; Rev 17:14
CONQUERED
and you will be * by your Lev 26:25
fear—that the enemy was already *! Num 21:34
when the land is *, you must give Num 32:29
cities they had * and rebuilt. Num 32:37,38
went to Gilead and * it, and drove Num 32:39
him, and we * all his cities, and Deu 2:33,34
we had taken. We * everything from Deu 2:35,36
them all. We * all sixty of his Deu 3:4
We had now * all the cities on Deu 3:10
"At that time I gave the * land Deu 3:12
Israel * his land and that of Deu 4:47
Israel also * all the area from Deu 4:48
give you, and have * it, and begin Deu 17:14
the land and have * it and are Deu 26:1
when Jericho is * you will let me Jos 2:12,13
So Joshua and his army * the Jos 10:40
So Joshua * the entire land—the Jos 11:16
are still many nations to be *. Jos 13:1
THE * LANDS of Canaan were Jos 14:1
was the one who * it, so Achsah Jos 15:17
yet entered and * the land God had Jos 18:1
* cities with their pasturelands. Jos 21:3
went in and * it and lived there. Jos 21:43
(Judah had * Jerusalem, and Ju 1:8
and he * the city and won Achsah Ju 1:13
The army of Judah also * the Ju 1:18
* them and made them their slaves. Ju 1:35
So Moab was * by Israel that Ju 3:30
Lord let them be * by King Jabin of Ju 4:2,3
Lord let them be * by the Ju 13:1
city was finally * by its enemies. Ju 18:30
which had been * by the 1Sa 7:14
so he let them be * by Sisera, the 1Sa 12:9
He did great deeds and * the 1Sa 14:48
So David * the Philistine giant 1Sa 17:50,51
of Egypt. The * peoples of those 1Ki 4:21
the king of Egypt * and burned, 1Ki 9:16
in the nations he *—the Amorites, 1Ki 9:20,21
of Egypt attacked and * Jerusalem. 1Ki 14:25
slingers surrounded and * it." 2Ki 3:25f
King Hazael * several sections of 2Ki 10:32,33
he also * parts of Manasseh from 2Ki 10:32,33
He also * Sela and changed its 2Ki 14:7
He also * the Philistines as far 2Ki 18:8
"My chariots have * the highest 2Ki 19:23
and have * the farthest borders. 2Ki 19:23
I have been refreshed at many * 2Ki 19:24
So of course the nations you * 2Ki 19:26
flooding and * the lowlands on both 1Ch 12:15
* Gath and its surrounding towns. 1Ch 18:1
He also * Moab and required its 1Ch 18:2
every year. He * the dominion of 1Ch 18:3
he laid siege to Rabbah and * it. 1Ch 20:1
as was his custom with all the * 1Ch 20:3
for I have * them in the name of 1Ch 22:18
the city of Hamath-zobah and * it. 2Ch 8:3
He quickly * Judah's fortified 2Ch 12:4

CONQUERED Con't)
So King Shishak of Egypt * 2Ch 12:9
of Ephraim that his father had *. 2Ch 17:2
army arrived and * Judah and 2Ch 24:23
army of Judah be * by them because 2Ch 24:24
king of Babylon * Jerusalem, and 2Ch 36:6
the kingdom of Persia * Babylon. 2Ch 36:20
and has lived in * cities after Job 15:27,28
my enemies say, "We have * him!" Ps 13:4
not turn back until all were *. Ps 18:37
mightiest of our enemies are *. Ps 76:5
O GOD, YOUR land has been * by the Ps 79:1
soon be a king, ruling a * land. Is 10:8
walled cities of Judah and * them. Is 36:1
you be * by the king of Assyria. Is 36:15
cypress trees. I * their highest Is 37:24
dug in many a * land, and Egypt Is 37:25
heathen say their gods have * me. Is 48:11
that nation until he has * it. Jer 27:8
the city would be * by the king of Jer 32:3
Our fathers came and * it and Jer 32:23
persecuted have turned and * her. Lam 1:3
we are a * land. Lam 1:16
they attacked and * him, and led Amo 1:9
bring back slaves from * nations; Nah 2:13
Thebes was * by the Assyrians Nah 3:8f
Gaza will be *, her king killed, Zec 9:5
people, or against * foreigners?" Mt 17:25
and Jerusalem shall be * and Lk 21:24
Father on his throne when I had *. Rev 3:21
Root of David, has *, and proved Rev 5:5

CONQUERING
in * their enemies: Ju 3:1
that the honor of * Sisera will go Ju 4:9
by * Gath, their largest city. 2Sa 8:1
far and wide, a *, destroying Is 18:2
far and near, that *, destroying Is 18:7
He proved my power by * foreign Is 55:4
as iron—smashing, bruising, and *. Dan 2:40
This will be his plot for * all Dan 11:17
when it comes to * a person's evil Col 2:23

CONQUEROR
heroic deeds and be a great *." 1Sa 26:25

CONQUERORS
all those who had been their *. 1Sa 14:48

CONQUERS
"Whoever * it shall have my Ju 1:12
The wise man * the strong man and Pro 21:22
Everyone who * will be clothed Rev 3:5
"As for the one who *, I will Rev 3:12
I will let every one who * sit Rev 3:21
Everyone who * will inherit all Rev 21:7

CONQUEST
them until they complete the *. Jos 1:15
AFTER THE *—although seven of the Jos 18:1
the invasion and * of Israel, and 1Ki 9:20,21
I decreed your * of all those 2Ki 19:25
You are very proud about your * 2Ch 25:19
victorious *, but all to no avail. Is 29:8
of the * by Alexander the Great. Eze 26:14f
hungry nor be shamed by heathen *. Eze 34:29
A prediction of the Assyrian * of Hos 1:4,5f

CONQUESTS
The rest of Asa's biography—his * 1Ki 15:23
deeds and *—are written in The 1Ki 16:4-7
their sins and *, and, using lust 2Pe 2:18

CONSCIENCE
also the Tree of *, giving Gen 2:9
from the Tree of *—for its fruit Gen 2:16,17
Why kill him and have a guilty *? Gen 37:26,27
tribe of Reuben has an uneasy *. Ju 5:16
But then his * began bothering 1Sa 24:5
you won't want the * of a murderer 1Sa 25:30,31
census, David's * began to bother 2Sa 24:10
Then two men who had no * 1Ki 21:13
* is clear for as long as I live. Job 27:6
But afterwards only a bitter * Pro 5:4
A man's * Pro 20:27
A murderer's * will drive him Pro 28:17
lived before God in all good *!" Act 23:1
a clear * before God and man. Act 24:16
their own * accuses them, or Rom 2:12-15
wrong, and my bad * proves that I Rom 7:16
on this point. My * is clear, but 1Co 4:4
Christian brother to sin whose * 1Co 8:9
a tender * for whom Christ died. 1Co 8:11
lest the answer hurt your * 1Co 10:25
having a bad * over eating it. 1Co 10:27
man who told you, and of his *. 1Co 10:28
a sinner, and his * will be pricked 1Co 14:24
always keep your * clear, doing 1Ti 1:19
Pray for us, for our * is clear Heb 13:18

CONSCIENCES
those whose * hurt them when they Rom 14:1f
them and hurts their tender *. 1Co 8:7
When I am with those whose * 1Co 9:22
disobeyed their * and have 1Ti 1:19
their * won't even bother them. 1Ti 4:2
side, and our * will be clear, even 1Jn 3:19
But if we have bad * and feel 1Jn 3:20
friends, if our * are clear, we can 1Jn 3:21

CONSCIOUS
believed in a * and pleasant Ps 6:5f

CONSCRIPT
* 1,000 men from each tribe." Num 31:4,5
a king, he will * your sons and 1Sa 8:11
Solomon didn't * any Israelis 1Ki 9:22
of the draft) to * men from the 1Ki 12:18
for war! * your best soldiers; Joe 3:9

CONSCRIPTED
But all of us who are * will go Num 32:27
and Reuben who are * for the Lord's Num 32:29
young man, he * him into his army. 1Sa 14:52
Solomon had * forced labor to 1Ki 9:15
Solomon * his labor forces from 1Ki 9:20,21

CONSCRIPTING
still continues of * as slave 2Ch 8:7,8

CONSCRIPTION
men of * age in Israel, and 500,000 2Sa 24:9

CONSECRATE
"* AARON YOUR brother, and his Ex 28:1
thus you shall * Aaron and his Ex 29:9
for the altar and * it to God every Ex 29:37
clothes lest they * the people by Eze 44:19
the world, and I * myself to meet Jn 17:19

CONSECRATED
would upon a seal, '* to Jehovah.' Ex 28:36
with the words, "* to Jehovah." Ex 39:30
* in place of his ancestor Aaron; Lev 16:32
for he is holy and * to the Lord; Num 6:5
effect, and he is * to the Lord Num 6:8
the fulness of the fruit be *." Deu 22:9f
So Micah * him as his personal Ju 17:12
Solomon * the inner court of the 2Ch 7:7
* and all unauthorized personnel. 2Ch 23:19
of Aaron who are * to this work. 2Ch 26:17,18
and Levites had * themselves. Ez 6:20
as gold. I * these men to the Ez 8:28
the Lord, and then * the treas Ez 8:28
carried in vessels * to the Lord. Is 66:20
a * offering to God and the Lamb. Rev 14:4

CONSECRATING
clothes, thus * to the Lord's use Lev 8:30
vow of a Nazirite, * himself to the Num 6:1
by * her to perpetual virginity. Ju 11:39f
for the altar, thus * it. Eze 43:26

CONSECRATION
the * ram to Aaron and his sons. Ex 29:27
preserved for the * of his son who Ex 29:29
"Take the ram of *—the ram used Ex 29:31
(that is, in their * ceremony). Ex 29:33
* offering and the peace offering; Lev 7:37
the other ram, the ram of *; Lev 8:22
of the ram of *, just as the Lord Lev 8:29
*, just as I instructed you to do. Lev 8:31
which time their * would be Lev 8:33
ON THE EIGHTH day (of the * Lev 9:1
house, for the * of the anointing Lev 21:12
of his special * to the Lord, taste Num 6:3,4
for his vow of * remains in Num 6:6,7
bullock and seven rams for *. 2Ch 13:9
"The * ceremony is now ended," 2Ch 29:31

CONSENT
gods, do not * nor listen, and Deu 13:8
There was unanimous *, for 1Ch 13:4
and princes, but not with my *. Hos 8:4
No one can kill me without my * Jn 10:18
want to do it without your *. Phm 1:14

CONSENTED
Saul finally *, "All right, go 1Sa 17:37

CONSEQUENCE
* of what he had said before. Ex 6:8,9
bathe, he shall suffer the *." Lev 17:16
For he knows the * but does it Pro 29:24
must bear the * of all your sin. Eze 23:35

CONSEQUENCES
I am willing to face the *. Job 13:13
love to talk will suffer the *. Pro 18:21
goes blindly on and suffers the *. Pro 22:3
never looks, and suffers the *. Pro 27:12
to warn him of the *, and the Lord Eze 3:20
of the *, without fear or favor. Mt 22:16

CONSEQUENTLY
partiality, and * hated Joseph; Gen 37:4
she wanted. *, at her mother's Mt 14:8
of the Law." *, it is clear that Gal 3:11

CONSIDER
I * you alone to be righteous. Gen 7:1
Literally, "thus did Esau * his Gen 25:34f
But they will only * staying Gen 34:22
The Lord will * this as your Num 18:27
and has not done what I * right; 1Ki 11:33
and do whatever I * right, obeying 1Ki 11:38
less filthy than you * me to be! Job 9:31
"Listen, O Job, stop and * the Job 37:14
who seek the Lord! * the quarry Is 51:1
explored, will I * casting them Jer 31:37
even yet they will * what this Eze 12:3
Revelation. Or, * the destruction Dan 9:25f
Lord of Hosts. "* how you have Hag 1:7
not * yourselves worthy of praise. Lk 17:10
But a married woman must * other 1Co 7:34

But when you * the wonderful 2Pe 1:19

CONSIDERABLE
Soon Jacob noticed a * cooling Gen 31:2
of * insight and understanding. Act 13:6,7

CONSIDERATE
of being * of the doubts and fears Rom 15:1
are unselfish and * in all you do. Php 4:5

CONSIDERED
then God * him righteous on Gen 15:6
they are * ceremonially defiled. Lev 19:23
They no longer * the Lord as Ju 8:34
it wasn't * to be of much value! 1Ki 10:21
for I am * a brother to jackals Job 30:28,29
no longer will men be * old at Is 65:20
to be * citizens and have the same Eze 47:22
and many who are * least here Mk 10:31
but may be * an appendix giving Mk 16:9f
* by the world as wise and great. 1Co 1:27
the land is * no good and is ready Heb 6:8

CONSIDERING
* all the other cities of Israel. 2Ch 12:13
* this, he fell into a dream, and Mt 1:20

CONSIDERS
a wise son * each suggestion. Pro 15:5
ideas the world * foolish and of 1Co 1:27
those the world * great, so that 1Co 1:28

CONSIGN
who * Tyre to the wild beasts. Is 23:13
the one who will * you to living in Hos 12:9

CONSIGNING
This they did, * their gifts to Act 11:30

CONSIST
It will * of two pieces, front Ex 28:7
This shall * of two loaves of Lev 23:17
it must * of nine quarts of fine Num 15:8,9
It shall * of two young bulls, Num 28:27
These personal contributions * 1Ch 29:4,5
This daily offering will * of Eze 45:23

CONSISTED
150 feet long; it * of drapes woven Ex 38:9
the first day. It * of a silver Num 7:13
The army * of 307,500 men, all 2Ch 26:13
the Dung Gate * of half of the Neh 12:31,32
a legion * of 6,000 troops. Lk 8:30f

CONSISTENT
This is more * with Genesis 11:26 Gen 11:32f

CONSISTENTLY
oh, how I want to follow them *. Ps 119:5

CONSISTING
accompany it, * of a fifth of a Lev 23:13
Also offer a drink offering * of Lev 23:13
drink offering, * of three pints of Num 28:7
a burnt sacrifice * of one young Num 29:2
the Izhar group, * of Shelamoth 1Ch 24:22

CONSISTS
For life * of far more than food Lk 12:23

CONSOLATION
will be a * to them, for it will be Eze 16:54
Literally, "the * of Israel." Lk 2:25f

CONSOLE
their homes to comfort and * him. Job 2:11
you may not mourn in public or * Eze 24:22
* Martha and Mary on their loss. Jn 11:19
house trying to * Mary saw her Jn 11:31

CONSOLING
him in his home, * him for all his Job 42:11
brought to you by * friends." Eze 24:17

CONSPIRACY
So the * became very strong. 2Sa 15:12
Absalom in a * against you!" 2Sa 15:13
about King Shallum and his * 2Ki 15:15
my life from the * of these wicked Ps 64:1
have discovered a * against me Jer 11:9

CONSPIRATORS
they are allies and * with David; 1Sa 22:17
of the kings. The * were Zabad, 2Ch 24:26

CONSPIRED
Every one of you who has * Num 14:34,35
of Levi) * with Dathan and Abiram Num 16:1
two leaders who * with Korah Num 26:5-11
"Why have you and David * 1Sa 22:13
he told them. "I * against my 2Ki 10:9,10
son of Jabesh) * against him and 2Ki 15:10
of his army, * against him with 2Ki 15:25
Then Hoshea * against the king 2Ki 17:4
But his aides * against him and 2Ki 21:23
and how his people * against him in 2Ch 25:27
Menelaus, the High Priest, who * Dan 11:32f

CONSPIRING
your hand, safe from all * men. Ps 31:20
a thing like this—* together to Act 5:9

CONSTABLE
So the * and his men went all Jos 2:7

CONSTANT
then, when he was 365, and in * Gen 5:21-24
before the Lord as a * reminder. Ex 28:12
There they shall live in * fear. Lev 26:36
the laws shall be his * companion. Deu 17:19
will be a * temptation to you." Ju 2:3
touched became his * companions. 1Sa 10:26
Therefore murder shall be a * 2Sa 12:10

(CONSTANT Con't)
There was * war between Rehoboam 1Ki 14:30
* war between Rehoboam and Judah. 1Ki 15:6
the Ark by giving * praise and 1Ch 16:4
the Lord for his * love and mercy. 1Ch 16:41
was one * binge of doing evil. 2Ch 21:6
Yes, Lord, let your * love Ps 33:22
How precious is your * love, O Ps 36:7
My * boast is God. Ps 44:8
Save us by your * love. Ps 44:26
are, and of your *, daily care. Ps 71:15
Sheba, and there will be * praise Ps 72:15
I am looking up to you in * hope. Ps 86:3
of * lovingkindness and of truth; Ps 86:15
us * joy to the end of our lives. Ps 90:14
God's * care of him will make a Ps 112:6
because they are my * guide. Ps 119:98
But I am in * prayer against the Ps 141:5
first, he is a * liar; Pro 6:12,13
Wounds and * disgrace are his Pro 6:33
I was his * delight, laughing and Pro 8:30
there is * trouble for the wicked. Pro 12:21
and tumbles into * trouble. Pro 17:20
A fool gets into * fights. Pro 18:6,7
wife annoys like * dripping. Pro 19:13
A * dripping on a rainy day and a Pro 27:15
Will you be in * dread of men's Is 51:13
we are * sinners and have been Is 64:5
But they will be in * danger, Dan 11:33
wilderness. His * theme was, Mt 3:1
heaven their angels have * access Mt 18:10
their need for * prayer and to show Lk 18:1
wearing me out with her * coming!' Lk 18:4,5
Keep a * watch. Lk 21:36
I was with you—my * watchcare over Act 20:31
And I was a * example to you in Act 20:35
Yes, we live under * danger to 2Co 4:11
but this gives us * opportunities 2Co 4:11
this, I have the * worry of how the 2Co 11:28
and anger, * effort to get the best Gal 5:20
they will be * liars and 2Ti 3:3
rescue us from * falling into sin Tit 2:14
their lives as slaves to * dread. Heb 2:15
These men are * gripers, never Jud 1:16
* improvement in all these things. Rev 2:19

CONSTANTLY
And they were * at war with one Gen 25:18
I will be with you * until I have Gen 28:15
They were * available to Ex 18:26
And you must think * about these Deu 6:6
his promises and * loves those who Deu 7:9
For all this time you have * Deu 9:7
you do. * remind the people about Jos 1:8
The Israelis fought * with the 1Sa 14:52
again, but he mourned * for him; 1Sa 15:35
He will * look after 2Sa 23:5
of my prayer be * before him day 1Ki 8:59
I will * watch over it and 1Ki 9:2,3
He served the Lord * and 1Ch 23:13
Fresh honors were * given me, Job 29:20
were * refreshed and renewed. Job 29:20
I will * speak of his glories and Ps 34:1
How * I find myself upon the Ps 38:17
May they * exclaim, "How great Ps 40:16
I am * despised, mocked, taunted Ps 44:15,16
For we are facing death threats * Ps 44:22
and have helped me *—no wonder I am Ps 71:6
I have * testified to others of the Ps 71:17
needy revere you *, as long as sun Ps 72:5
downtrodden people be * insulted. Ps 74:21
Those wonderful deeds are * in Ps 77:12
They will grow * in strength and Ps 84:7
You are * so kind! Ps 86:13
I will protect and bless him * Ps 89:24
of his angels who serve him *. Ps 103:21
Think * about the evil things he Ps 109:15
Jehovah is * thinking about us Ps 115:12
this has been to me—to * obey. Ps 119:56
that you are thinking about me *! Ps 139:17,18
they need it. You * satisfy the Ps 145:16
* and come to shame. Pro 13:5
name is * blasphemed, day by day. Is 52:5
and ripened corn I * supplied, and Hos 1:9
as a baker's oven is * Hos 7:4
these people * aflame with lust. Hos 7:4
Jesus * used these illustrations Mt 13:34,35
her, and it torments her *." Mt 15:22
Spirit and * expecting the Messiah Lk 2:25
disciples are * going without food, Lk 5:33
But Jesus replied, "My Father * Jn 5:17
has been with us * from our first Act 1:21,22
met together * and shared Act 2:44
that Stephen was * speaking against Act 6:13
after that he was * with the Act 9:28
men have * testified to this in Act 13:31
a man who is * inciting the Jews Act 24:5
These bodies of ours are * 2Co 4:10
These two forces within us are * Gal 5:17
I pray for you *, asking God, the Eph 1:16,17
* growing temple for God. Eph 2:21
all be * changing for the better. Eph 4:23
right, and trying * to be more and Col 3:10
God for you and pray for you *. 1Th 1:2
this: if you are * doing what is 1Jn 3:7
at the door and I am * knocking. Rev 3:20

CONSTELLATION
or guide the * of the Bear with her Job 38:32
Stars and the * Orion, who turns Amo 5:8

CONSTELLATIONS
and the * of the southern Zodiac. Job 9:9

CONSTRICTS
My stomach * and burns with Is 21:3

CONSTRUCT
it with tar; and * decks and stalls Gen 6:14
and 45 feet high. * a skylight all Gen 6:16
each of two sides, * two gold rings Ex 30:4
and * what God has commanded us: Ex 35:10-19
which took thirteen years to *. 1Ki 7:1
of the Lord and * the altar for 1Ch 22:1
* harps and lyres for the choir. 2Ch 9:11
He had to * special treasury 2Ch 32:27

CONSTRUCTED
This was * of acacia wood and was Ex 37:1
A rim four inches high was * Ex 37:12
ALTAR was also * of acacia wood; Ex 38:1
Then he * the courtyard. Ex 38:9
It was * according to the exact Num 8:4
the night and * a monument there. Jos 4:8
These buildings were * entirely 1Ki 7:9
They were * with undercarriages 1Ki 7:27-30
The angels had been * in such a 1Ki 8:7
passageway he had * between the 2Ki 16:18
Tabernacle * by Moses, the Lord's 2Ch 1:2,3
He also * ten vats for water to 2Ch 4:6
Then he * a court for the 2Ch 4:9
at this time, and * cities where 2Ch 8:6
What's more, Jehoram * idol 2Ch 21:11
He also * forts in the Negeb, 2Ch 26:10
He even * heathen altars in both 2Ch 33:4,5
Temple that was * here many Ez 5:11
a 75-foot gallows *, to hang Est 7:9
was the large one * by King Asa Jer 41:9
and each wheel was * with a second Eze 1:16
Judah has * great defenses for Hos 8:14
This building was * in exact Act 7:44

CONSTRUCTING
and skill in * the Tabernacle and Ex 31:3
* and furnishing the Tabernacle." Ex 36:1
All the nails used in * the Ex 38:20
and * a second wall outside it. 2Ch 32:5

CONSTRUCTION
a drawing of the * plan, and the Ex 25:9
the acacia wood needed in the *. Ex 35:24
* of the Tabernacle and the court. Ex 38:29
began the actual * of the Temple. 1Ki 6:1
The stones used in the * of the 1Ki 6:7
the * of the palace and Temple. 1Ki 9:11,12
and gave it to the * 2Ki 12:11,12
required from the * 2Ki 12:15
So David collected the * materials 1Ch 22:5
private treasures to aid in the *. 1Ch 29:3
FINALLY THE ACTUAL * of the 2Ch 3:1
The actual * began on the 2Ch 3:2
The * of the two pillars, 2Ch 4:12-16
completed the * of the Temple. 2Ch 8:16
The actual * of the Temple began Ez 3:8
we went to the * site of the Temple Ez 5:8
"Do not disturb the * of the Ez 6:6
to pay the full * costs without Ez 6:8
to assist in the * of the Temple. Ez 6:21,22
of money for the * of the Temple or Ez 7:20
Because of the * of these wheels, Eze 10:9-13
the details of its *—its doors and Eze 43:11
For who would begin * of a Lk 14:28

CONSTRUCTIVE
If you profit from * criticism Pro 15:31,32

CONSULT
I am gone, * with Aaron and Hur." Ex 24:14
to * with Jehovah went out there. Ex 33:7
He shall be the one to * with Num 27:21
came to Shiloh to * with Eleazar Jos 21:1
Judah, and Edom went to * Elisha. 2Ki 3:12
and went to * his king, who had Is 37:8,9
that cannot save! * together, Is 45:21
to *— and destroy all your idols. Mic 5:12
I didn't go up to Jerusalem to * Gal 1:17

CONSULTATION
After * with the leaders of the 2Ch 20:21

CONSULTED
"for a fortune-teller that I * Gen 30:27
They quickly * with the leaders Num 22:4
Ahimelech * the Lord to find out 1Sa 22:9,10
first time I had * God for him! 1Sa 22:15
Meanwhile, Abner * with the 2Sa 3:17
they * fortune-tellers and used 2Ki 17:17
and because he had * a medium, 1Ch 10:13
AFTER DAVID HAD * with all of his 1Ch 13:1
David * with Zadok, who 1Ch 24:3
of Hinnom. He * spirit-mediums, 2Ch 33:6
Thummim could be * to find out Ez 2:62,63
Thummim had been * to find out Neh 7:64,65
but first * his lawyers, for he Est 1:13-15
She went out and * her mother, Mk 6:24

CONSULTING
"Do not defile yourselves by * Lev 19:31
future by * witches and mediums? Is 8:19
For without * me you have gone Is 30:2
the Holy One of Israel and * him. Is 31:1
no judgment without * the Father. Jn 5:30

CONSULTS
against anyone who * mediums and Lev 20:6

CONSUME
famine will * the land. Gen 41:30
This awesome fire will * us. Deu 5:25
as drought and heat * snow. Job 24:19
beauty shall be for Sheol to *." Ps 49:14f
Pour out your fury upon them; * Ps 69:24
and fire fell from heaven to * Ps 106:18
and the flames will * the Is 9:18
the Lord God of Hosts to * them. Is 10:23
his words * like fire. Is 30:27
sufficient fuel to * a sacrifice Is 40:16
up—the flames will not * you. Is 43:2
like fire, and it shall * you. Jer 15:14
here to Egypt and I will * them. Jer 44:12
and utterly * them in the desert. Eze 20:13
I will * you with the fire of my Eze 22:31
to * and destroy it until the end. Dan 7:26
through Israel and * her, and none Amo 5:6
the enemy will * you like young Nah 3:15
which will * all his enemies. Heb 10:27
the attacking armies and * them. Rev 20:9

CONSUMED
it * them as fire consumes straw. Ex 15:7
entire ram was * before the Lord; Lev 8:21
from the Lord and * the burnt Lev 9:24
your eyes shall be * and your Lev 26:16
up from the rock and * them! Ju 6:21
Their harvest was * by locusts. Ps 78:46
and plants will be * by the Jer 7:20
wickedness, I * them in my anger. Eze 43:8
like a tree, they will be *—roots Mal 4:1
she shall be utterly * by fire; Rev 18:8

CONSUMES
it consumed them as fire * straw. Ex 15:7
God's fire * them with all their Job 15:34
Death * sinners as drought and Job 24:19
* your body, and you say, "Oh, Pro 5:11

CONSUMING
* the earth and all of its crops, Deu 32:22
his goods, * all he has left. Job 20:26
presence! The * fire of your glory Is 64:2
For our God is a * fire. Heb 12:29

CONTACT
"Any meat that comes into * with Lev 7:19
or no * with the nearby villages. Ju 18:7
Gad, who was David's * with God. 2Sa 24:11
For food doesn't come in * with Mk 7:19
Those in frequent * with the 1Co 7:31

CONTACTS
Be wise in all your * with them. Col 4:5
dirtied by his * with the world. Jas 1:27

CONTAGIOUS
If the spot has spread, it is a * Lev 13:51
* and must be destroyed by fire. Lev 13:52

CONTAIN
and the Ark will * the laws of my Ex 25:22
heavens cannot * you, much less 1Ki 8:27
Literally, "as great as would * 1Ki 18:32f
of heavens cannot * you—how much 2Ch 6:18
forests do not * sufficient fuel to Is 40:16
manuscripts do not * the words, Mk 10:24f
world could hardly * the books! Jn 21:25

CONTAINED
completed, with all that they *. Gen 2:1
square and * 240 gallons of water. 1Ki 7:38
all it * disappeared into heaven. Act 11:10
The first one * the golden Heb 9:1

CONTAINER
Moses told Aaron to get a * and Ex 16:33
The omer—the * used to measure Ex 16:36
seven days. Any * in the tent Num 19:15
but do not take any away in a *. Deu 23:24
Soon every * was full to the 2Ki 4:6
In fact, every * in Jerusalem Zec 14:21
—is held in a perishable *, that 2Co 4:7

CONTAINERS
basins, and other *—and a cover of Num 4:14
oil left in your * until the time 1Ki 17:14
plenty left in the *, just as the 1Ki 17:16
them in the sacred * for use by the Neh 10:39,40

CONTAINING
* God's directions and laws. Ex 24:7
place the Ark * the stone tablets Ex 26:33
the Ark * the Ten Commandments. Ex 30:6
In it, place the Ark * the Ten Ex 40:3
above the Ark (* the stone tablets Lev 16:13
of a bushel of fine flour * yeast. Lev 23:17
to carry the Ark * the Ten Deu 10:8
carried the Ark * the Ten Deu 31:9
carried the Ark * the Ten Deu 31:25
beside a chest * the gold models of 1Sa 6:8
Lord and the chest * the gold rats 1Sa 6:11

'ONTAINING Con't)
Ark and the chest * the golden rats 1Sa 6:15
Then I took the sealed deed * Jer 32:11
emptied the flasks * the seven last Rev 21:9
ONTAINS
Tabernacle and everything it *. Ex 31:3
for the Ark which * the covenant 1Ki 8:21
* and holds high the truth of God. 1Ti 3:15
God * far more wonderful promises. Heb 8:6
and all that it * and the sea and Rev 10:6
ONTAMINATE
You shall not * yourselves and Lev 20:25
ONTAMINATED
is in the defiled bowl is also *. Lev 11:34
be sown in the field, it is not *; Lev 11:37
not be declared * if he decides Lev 14:36
on and anything he sits on is *; Lev 15:4
something, does it become *?" Hag 2:13
ONTAMINATING
the Lord), "were * your sacrifices Hag 2:14
ONTAMINATION
cleansed from the * of being in the Num 6:9
ONTEMPT
offerings to the Lord with *. 1Sa 2:17
him, sneering in * at this nice 1Sa 17:41,42
and she was filled with * for 2Sa 6:16
and *, as you see us today. 2Ch 29:8
* and anger throughout your realm. Est 1:18
He pours * upon princes, and Job 12:21
They hold me in * and my Job 30:15
the crowd and its *, so that I Job 31:34
get away with this * for God? Ps 10:13
a byword of * and shame among the Ps 44:14
Their * has broken my heart; Ps 69:20
They heap * on us. Ps 79:4
For God pours * upon the haughty Ps 107:40
Proud men hold me in * for Ps 119:51
For we have had our fill of * and Ps 123:3,4
be under God's * and judgment, yet Is 9:1
pride and show his * for all the Is 23:9
make you a byword of * forever. Jer 25:8,9
Even aged men are treated with *. Lam 5:12
you held Sodom in unspeakable *. Eze 16:56
her and treated her with great *. Eze 28:24
them with such *, then they shall Eze 28:26
relish, in utter * for me, to take Eze 36:5
some to shame and everlasting *. Dan 12:2
her chance with *, and now her Hos 8:3
ways, and their * for the Lord. Zep 1:8f
and be treated with utter *. Mk 9:12,13
man who had great * for everyone. Lk 18:2
breaking down the wall of * Eph 2:14
will laugh at you in * and scorn. 1Pe 4:4
ONTEMPTIBLE
"Therefore I have made you * in Mal 2:9
ONTEMPTUOUSLY
Fathers and mothers are * Eze 22:7
ONTENT
have plenty to eat and be fully *. Deu 11:15
Why weren't we * with what we Jos 7:7
"I am * just to have you back 2Sa 19:30
palace aides are *—but how could it 1Ki 10:8
she replied, "I am perfectly *." 2Ki 4:13
but my advice to you is, be * 2Ki 14:10
"We will lie to our hearts' *. Ps 12:3,4
rich, I may become * without God. Pro 30:9
how much we hear, we are not *. Ecc 1:8-11
and fed and well *, and with Is 44:16
You follow evil to your hearts' * Jer 16:12
he said, "now I can die *! Lk 2:29,30,31
and be * with your pay!" Lk 3:14
but are quite * to die, for then we 2Co 5:8
ONTENTED
populous, * nation at this time. 1Ki 4:20
Your wife shall be * in your Ps 128:3
those who sit * in their sins, Zep 1:12
You are full and spiritually *, 1Co 4:8
CONTENTEDLY
he lay down very * beside a heap of Ru 3:6,7
CONTENTMENT
But as for me, my * is not in Ps 17:15
find *—well, what's the use? Ecc 6:6
I have learned the secret of * in Php 4:12
CONTEST
"I am in a fierce * with my sister Gen 30:8
To win the * you must deny 1Co 9:25
CONTEXT
Implied in *. Gen 14:11f
Implied from *. Gen 29:26f
See * for validity of the Ps 116:15f
The * seems to favor the former. Is 66:19f
But from the * Gog seems to be a Eze 38:2,3f
to Christ, is clear from the *. Zec 13:6f
CONTIGUOUS
it is * with them in length, and Eze 45:7
CONTINGENT
by a * of the Philistine army. 1Sa 13:23
smallest * in my master's army. 2Ki 18:24
and worst * of my master's troops? Is 36:8,9
and called out the entire *. Mt 27:27
CONTINUAL
have this * responsibility: that Gen 17:9,10
There were * wars between Rehoboam 2Ch 12:15
CONTINUALLY
the Tabernacle, to burn there *. Ex 27:20
will be reminded of them *. Ex 28:29
be kept burning upon the altar *. Lev 6:13
have been done * by the people of Lev 18:27
forget it!) how * angry you made Deu 9:7
*, and nothing will save you. Deu 28:29
blowing * on their trumpets. Jos 6:6-9
I have * threatened him and his 1Sa 3:13
Egypt they have * forsaken me and 1Sa 8:8
that time he * disobeyed the Lord. 1Ki 15:34
Israel, and he * allowed King 2Ki 13:3
* walk where you tell them to go. 2Ch 6:31
father Asa was. He * tried to 2Ch 20:32
Burnt offerings were sacrificed * 2Ch 24:14
Literally, "His praise shall * be Ps 34:1f
"the lovingkindness of God *." Ps 52:1f
praise your name *, fulfilling my Ps 61:8
"men shall pray for him *." Ps 72:15f
May the Lord * bless you with Ps 128:5
And the Lord will guide you *, Is 58:11
just and good; you * do wrong and Is 59:8
of them shall be accounted for *. Jer 23:4
of fire inside that flashed *; Eze 1:4
whom you worship *, deliver you." Dan 6:16
whom you worship *, able to deliver Dan 6:20
* in the Temple, praising God. Lk 24:53
of sinning and * being disobedient Rom 1:30
And why should we ourselves be * 1Co 15:30
of life that is * learning more and Col 3:10
With Jesus' help we will * offer Heb 13:15
* be singing praises to the Lord. Jas 5:13
your sight. I * discipline and Rev 3:19
CONTINUE
And I will * this agreement Gen 17:7,8
*—Suppose there are only twenty?" Gen 18:31
so that our family line will *." Gen 19:34
* to refuse to let the people go. Ex 7:14
days she shall * her recovery. Lev 12:5
Literally, "shall * in her blood Lev 12:5f
you, but you * to walk against my Lev 26:23
third day, he will * to be defiled Num 19:12
In this way the Lord will * to Num 27:21
will * south past Scorpion Pass Num 34:4
him, then he will * to send both Deu 11:14
name *—he refuses to marry me.' Deu 25:7
Be sure to * to obey all of the Jos 22:5
* to live among them as servants. Ju 1:33
Yet you * to abandon me and to Ju 10:13
that what you are doing can *. 1Sa 2:30
and I will * to teach you those 1Sa 12:23
But if you * to sin, you and 1Sa 12:25
* to kill each other forever? 2Sa 2:26
And I will * his kingdom into 2Sa 7:13
May our dynasty * on and on 2Sa 7:29
you as they * to live in this land 1Ki 8:40
and they * as slaves even today. 1Ki 9:20,21
of David will * to reign in 1Ki 11:36
so that you may * to rule this good 1Ch 28:8
priests could not * their work. 2Ch 5:13,14
mercy and will not * to turn away 2Ch 30:9
decided to * the observance for 2Ch 30:23
to allow them to * as priests; Ez 2:62,63
but let us * while King Darius Ez 5:5
So they were not allowed to * as Neh 7:64,65
* to oppose him will be fatal." Est 6:13
But he will not * to be rich, or Job 15:29
his prosperity shall not *. Job 20:21
Shall I then * to wait when you Job 32:16
now let me *. Job 33:2
with vigor, and * to hate me—though Ps 38:19
"Judah shall * to produce kings, Ps 60:6,7
as sun and moon * in the skies! Ps 72:5
it will * as the sun; Ps 72:17
throne will * to the end of time. Ps 89:35,36
But our families will *; Ps 102:28
so that I can * to obey you. Ps 119:17
me, but I will * in your plans. Ps 119:23
then I can * to obey you. Ps 119:88
then I can * to obey your laws. Ps 119:117
the wicked man's riches * forever. Pro 10:3
Don't envy evil men but * to Pro 23:17,18
out. Why * the process longer? Jer 6:29
fire, they * in their wicked ways. Jer 6:29
will I let you * as my spokesman. Jer 15:19
then this nation shall * forever. Jer 17:25
We will * to live as we want to, Jer 18:12
How long will this *? Jer 23:26
Only then can you * to live here Jer 25:5
"Meanwhile * your demonstration Eze 4:7
life, though they * in their sins. Eze 13:22
or not to let them * their diet. Dan 1:13
But the wicked shall * in their Dan 12:10
punish them, they * all their evil Zep 3:7
whether they must * their Zec 7:3
* until its purpose is achieved. Mt 5:18
They encouraged them to * in the Act 14:22
believers must * to follow the Act 21:20
if you * to love and trust him. Rom 11:22
and so their sins * to grow. 1Th 2:16
* TO LOVE each other with true Heb 13:1
those who * to seek salvation by Heb 13:10
Most important of all, * to show 1Pe 4:8
surround us, and * to punish the 2Pe 2:9
and those who * in evil prove 3Jn 1:11
by fire and * to be a warning to us Jud 1:7
those who are holy will * on in Rev 22:11
CONTINUED
as the waters * to go down, other Gen 8:5
Thus he * slowly southward to Gen 12:9
Then they * northward toward Gen 13:3,4
met at Bethel,' he *, 'the place Gen 31:13
This heap," Laban *, "stands Gen 31:51,52
their families * to live in Egypt. Gen 50:22
So the people of Israel * to Ex 1:20
The following week(* in next Ex 7:25
This * throughout all their Ex 40:38
and from there * southward along Num 21:4
MOSES * SPEAKING to the people of Deu 5:1
that * all the way to Azekah; Jos 10:11
So Joshua and the Israeli army * Jos 10:20
Michmethath, then * on past Jos 16:5,6
From there it * across the valley Jos 18:16
where the Jebusites lived, and * Jos 18:16
then it * east of Gath-hepher, Jos 19:13
This family * as priests until Ju 18:30
God has * his kindness to us as Ru 2:20
Samuel * as Israel's judge for 1Sa 7:15
Moses and Aaron," Samuel *. 1Sa 12:6
the battle * out beyond Beth-aven. 1Sa 14:23
David * to succeed in everything 1Sa 18:14
So David and his men * on, and 2Sa 16:13
The argument * back and forth, and 2Sa 19:43
him lying there and * after Sheba. 2Sa 20:8,9,10
except that he * to sacrifice in 1Ki 3:3
And you have * your kindness to 1Ki 3:6
to Solomon and * to serve him 1Ki 4:21
* under the kingship of the 1Ki 12:20
Elijah and her son * to eat from 1Ki 17:15
Meanwhile, all the prophets * 1Ki 22:10
* from the days of his father Asa. 1Ki 22:46
his heart, for he * to worship 2Ki 10:31
But they * to sin, following the 2Ki 13:6
and they * to worship the goddess 2Ki 13:6
evil king, and he * the 2Ki 15:24
evil king, and he * in the example 2Ki 15:28
But they * to follow the 2Ki 17:33
people * to worship other gods. 2Ki 17:40
The siege * into the eleventh 2Ki 25:2
the hill of Gibeon * to be active. 1Ch 16:39
Then he *, "Be strong and 1Ch 28:20
the Lord has told me," Micaiah *. 2Ch 18:18
after day, and money * to pour in. 2Ch 24:11
the observance *, and peace 2Ch 30:22
The enthusiasm *, so it was 2Ch 30:23
the piles * to grow until October. 2Ch 31:7,8
his lifetime they * serving 2Ch 34:33
So the Jewish leaders * in their Ez 6:14
and wouldn't listen, and * to sin. Neh 9:29
Solomon's servants * to live in Neh 11:3
then we * on to the Sheep Gate Neh 12:39
JOB *: Job 29:1
ELIHU *: Job 34:1
ELIHU *: Job 35:1
ELIHU *: Job 36:1
out upon them and * until Phineas Ps 106:30
slavery, but they * to rebel Ps 106:43
saw the * rebellion of Israel. Jer 3:7
* to worship her (chapter 44). Jer 7:18f
And you have * to do great Jer 32:20
says: Your fathers * to blaspheme Eze 20:27,28
the tribe of Levi, * as my priests Eze 44:15
So he * to travel around Lk 4:44
As Jesus and the disciples * on Lk 10:38
As they * onward toward Lk 17:11
Literally, "you have * with me in Lk 22:28f
and those who have * in evil, to Jn 5:29
classes, they * to teach and preach Act 5:42
Meanwhile Peter * knocking. Act 12:16
they * their work with the Jews. Gal 2:7,8,9
Job is an example of a man who * Jas 5:11
CONTINUES
the punishment * upon the children, Ex 20:5
"If the menstrual flow * after Lev 15:25
upon him, so the defilement *. Num 19:13
The Rock, and * upward from there. Ju 1:36
And if he * to obey my 1Ch 28:7
that still * of conscripting as 2Ch 8:7,8
Now he * to unveil his power. Ps 29:10
But the Lord * forever, exalted Ps 92:8
Your love for us * on forever. Ps 106:1
his lovingkindness * forever. Ps 136:1
for his lovingkindness * forever. Ps 136:2
for his lovingkindness * forever. Ps 136:3
for his lovingkindness * forever. Ps 136:4
for his lovingkindness * forever. Ps 136:5
for his lovingkindness * forever. Ps 136:6
his lovingkindness * forever: the Ps 136:7
for his lovingkindness * forever; Ps 136:8
for his lovingkindness * forever. Ps 136:9
* forever. Ps 136:10

(CONTINUES Con't)
* forever. Ps 136:11,12
his lovingkindness * forever, and Ps 136:13
his lovingkindness * forever— but Ps 136:14
* forever. Ps 136:15
for his lovingkindness * forever. Ps 136:16
his lovingkindness * forever, and Ps 136:17
* forever: Sihon, king of Ps 136:18
* forever— and Og, king of Ps 136:19
* forever. Ps 136:20
* forever; Ps 136:21
for his lovingkindness * forever. Ps 136:22
for his lovingkindness * forever. Ps 136:23
for his lovingkindness * forever. Ps 136:24
for his lovingkindness * forever. Ps 136:25
for his lovingkindness * forever. Ps 136:26
lovingkindness, Lord, * forever. Ps 138:8
to be taught. She * to live a lie. Jer 7:28
Your throne * from generation to Lam 5:19
But Jesus lives forever and * to Heb 7:24

CONTINUING
Do stay awhile before * your Gen 18:5
put him there for * to prophesy Jer 32:3

CONTINUOUS
There was * warfare between King 1Ki 15:32,33
yet there will be * day! Zec 14:7

CONTINUOUSLY
* both in winter and in summer. Zec 14:8

CONTRACT
I will prepare a * between us, Gen 17:2,3,4
It is a * that I shall be your Gen 17:7,8
"Your part of the *," God told Gen 17:9,10
part of this *, and it applies to Gen 17:12
for he has violated my *." Gen 17:14
But my * is with Isaac, who will Gen 17:21
"I have fulfilled my *," Jacob Gen 29:21
broken his wage * with me again and Gen 31:7
your part of my * with you, you Ex 19:5
the * I am going to make with you. Ex 34:10
"In every * of sale there must Lev 25:24
this is a permanent * Num 18:19
Beware lest you break the * the Deu 4:23
"The Lord our God made a * with Deu 5:2,3
his part of the * which, in his Deu 7:12
receiving the * which Jehovah had Deu 9:9
Lord gave me the *, the tablets on Deu 9:10,11
to enter into a * with Jehovah your Deu 29:12
a * he is making with you today. Deu 29:12
This * is not with you alone as Deu 29:14,15
befall those who break this *. Deu 29:21
the land broke the * made with them Deu 29:25
break the * I have made with them. Deu 31:16
me and break my *, and great Deu 31:20
* between themselves and God. Jos 24:25
have broken the *, it is no longer Ju 2:3
and king. The * was ratified before Ju 11:11
He told them about his * with Ju 18:4
So David made a * before the Lord 2Sa 5:3
He also made a * between the king 2Ki 11:17
* with Abraham, Isaac, and Jacob. 2Ki 13:23
For the Lord had made a * with 2Ki 17:35,36
So David made a * with them 1Ch 11:3
Then they entered into a * to 2Ch 15:12
Then Jehoiada made a solemn * 2Ch 23:15,16,17
to you, you made a * with him to Neh 9:8
the terms of your * with me, then Ps 132:12
that I made a * with their Jer 11:1
all the evils stated in the *. Jer 11:8
I will make a new * with the people Jer 31:31
land of Egypt—a * they broke, Jer 31:32
But this is the new * I will Jer 31:33
the terms of our * I will cut you Jer 34:18,19
for they are a symbol of the * Eze 20:20
my * to lead and protect them. Zec 11:10
'Yes, here is the * you signed,' Lk 16:5,6
and renew the broken * with David, Act 15:16

CONTRADICT
The voice spoke again, "Don't * Act 10:15
who do things that * the glorious 1Ti 1:10,11

CONTRADICTED
these always * each other. Mt 26:60,61
but they * each other. Mk 14:56

CONTRADICTS
Stop listening to teaching that * Pro 19:27

CONTRARY
—* to what the Lord had just Lev 10:1
Priest, while the * instructions in Lev 21:11f
I could do nothing * to the command Num 22:18
though this was * to God's rules. 2Ch 30:17,18,19
out quite to the *—the Jews Est 9:1
in ways that are * to Roman law." Act 18:13
* to what you have been taught. Rom 16:17

CONTRAST
This was quite a * to the former Neh 5:15
18 and 26. In *, see verse 11. Eze 20:25f
in * to "hearts of stone." Eze 36:26f
up his honesty in * to my lies. Rom 3:7
What a * between Adam and Christ Rom 5:14
God was in direct * to the sin and Heb 11:7

CONTRASTED
here * with their shame; Mic 1:11f
go forth," here * with the fear of Mic 1:11f
here * with their shame; Mic 1:11f
go forth," here * with the fear of Mic 1:11f
here * with their shame; Mic 1:11f
go forth," here * with the fear of Mic 1:11f

CONTRIBUTE
Israel must always * this portion Ex 29:28
who do not go should * toward the Ez 1:4

CONTRIBUTED
However, the money that was * 2Ki 12:16
They also * great amounts of 1Ch 29:8
Then the king * 30,000 lambs and 2Ch 35:7

CONTRIBUTING
others who were * from their Lk 8:3

CONTRIBUTION
offerings—as their * to the Lord. Ex 29:28
ask for a little * from you, for we 1Sa 25:8
Whenever anyone brings a * to the 2Ki 12:4,5
King Solomon's * for this purpose 2Ch 7:4,5
He also made a personal * of 2Ch 31:3

CONTRIBUTIONS
put all of the people's * into it. 2Ki 12:9
These personal * consist of 1Ch 29:4,5
* to the priests and Levites. 2Ch 35:8
crops, and other *, the first of Neh 10:37

CONTRITE
A broken and a * heart, O God, Ps 51:17
with *, humble spirits dwell; Is 57:15
* heart, who trembles at my word. Is 66:2

CONTRITION
in *, I will listen to your plea. 2Ki 22:18,19

CONTROL
came out, keeping himself under *. Gen 43:31
still the ox was not kept under *; Ex 21:29
not kept it under *, then there Ex 21:36
fire gets out of * and goes into Ex 22:6
would become too many to *. Ex 23:29
The Spirit of the Lord took * of Ju 3:10
assistant to * the traffic at the 2Ki 7:17
These cities were under their * 1Ch 4:31
were appointed to * the religious 1Ch 26:31,32
We adore you as being in * of 1Ch 29:11
of Ramah in order to * the road 2Ch 16:1
countries who attempted to * it. Ez 4:15
the situation to get out of *!" Ez 4:22
Lord showed his * of all creation. Ps 29:10
self-control than to * an army. Pro 16:32
World events are under his *. Dan 2:21
are under your *, as God decreed. Dan 2:38
Therefore * your passions—let Mal 2:16
No one was strong enough to * Mk 5:3,4
her child from the demon's *. Mk 7:26
And whenever the demon is in * Mk 9:18
This demon had often taken * of Lk 8:29
longer under sin's *, no longer Rom 6:6
Do not let sin * your puny body Rom 6:12
and it has no more * over you. Rom 7:4
destroyed sin's * over us by giving Rom 8:3
still under the * of their old Rom 8:8
But if you can't * yourselves, 1Co 7:9
each other to win * over us, and Gal 5:17
but doesn't * his sharp tongue is Jas 1:26
If anyone can * his tongue, it Jas 3:1
* over himself in every other way. Jas 3:1
good life, keep * of your tongue, 1Pe 3:10
us is under Satan's power and *. 1Jn 5:19
They were given * of one-fourth Rev 6:8
and gave him authority to * the Rev 13:5

CONTROLLED
that the earth is * by Jehovah. Ex 9:29
Sihon also * the Jordan River Jos 12:3
the Philistines still * the land. Ju 15:20
villages * by the five capitals. 1Sa 6:18
the son of Israel, * the following 1Ch 7:29
She who * the lucrative Eze 26:2
Those who let themselves be * by Rom 8:5
You are * by your new nature if Rom 8:9
* by your own desires, not God's. 1Co 3:3
the Holy Spirit, and * by him. Eph 5:18
about will not be * by angels. Heb 2:5

CONTROLLING
Self-control means * the tongue! Pro 13:3
he has trouble * his passions, it 1Co 7:36

CONTROLS
your hand * power and might, and 1Ch 29:12
Do you know how God * all Job 37:15
all gods. He * the formation of Ps 95:4
A wise man * his temper. Pro 14:29
but it is the Lord who * its Pro 16:33
breath of life and * your destiny! Dan 5:23
because Christ's love * us now. 2Co 5:13,14
But when the Holy Spirit * our Gal 5:22
man is a slave to whatever * him. 2Pe 2:19
and * him—he has been born again. 1Jn 3:9

CONTROVERSIAL
The * Hebrew word used here Is 7:14f
word is not clear on this * point. Mk 1:8f
word is not clear on this * point. Mk 1:8f
questions and * theological ideas; Tit 3:9

CONTROVERSY
But the * put David more than 1Sa 18:13

CONVENANT
Ark will contain the laws of my *. Ex 25:2

CONVENED
and Pharisees * a council to Jn 11:4

CONVENIENCES
own desires and * and carry his Lk 9:2

CONVENIENT
away that it isn't * to carry your Deu 14:2
it's so * to the palace." 1Ki 21:
* time, I'll call for you again." Act 24:2
when it is * and when it is not. 2Ti 4:

CONVENING
the Temple, and, * the Jewish Act 5:2

CONVENTION
back I will call a * of all the 2Sa 3:2

CONVERGE
Vast droves of camels will * Is 60:

CONVERSATION
That ended the * and God left. Gen 17:2
had finished his * with Abraham. Gen 18:3
But Rebekah overheard the *. Gen 27:
As this * was going on, Rachel Gen 29:
AFTER KING SAUL had finished his * 1Sa 18:
heart, and of my * with the king, Neh 2:1
I listen to their * and what do Jer 8:
the whole topic of * will be that Jer 16:14,1
the truth, for the * had not been Jer 38:2
Let your * be gracious as well Col 4:
Your * should be so sensible and Tit 2:

CONVERSING
immoral, and those * with demons, Rev 21:

CONVERSION
before their * stood to their feet Act 15:
And this fact of Gentile * Act 15:1

CONVERT
all the nations will * their Is 2:4
to make one *, and then turn him Mt 23:15
Nicolaus of Antioch (a Gentile * Act 6:5

CONVERTED
They wrecked the temple and * it 2Ki 10:27
of Tobiah, had * a storage room Neh 13:5
which had been * into a prison. Jer 37:15,16
nations will be * to the Lord, and Zec 2:11,12
of the Jewish priests were * too. Act 6:7
that Gentiles also were being *! Act 11:1
the Gentiles, too, were being *. Act 15:3
husbands will be * if they stay; 1Co 7:16

CONVERTS
Let the Gentile * chant, "His Ps 118:4
Jewish *— Cretans, and Arabians. Act 2:10
night some of his * let him down in Act 9:25
to Antioch to help the new *. Act 11:22
year, teaching the many new *. Act 11:26
And their * Act 13:52
that all Gentile * must be Act 15:5
to see how the new * were getting Act 15:36
and became *—including a large Act 17:4
it goes, winning * everywhere as it 2Th 3:1

CONVEY
To trust a rebel to * a message Pro 26:6

CONVEYED
But when they * the emperor's Est 1:12

CONVICT
"Never * anyone on the testimony Deu 19:15
"Is it legal to * a man before Jn 7:51
Literally, "he will * the world Jn 16:8f
not * a man before he is tried. Act 25:16

CONVICTED
"You have * yourself in making 2Sa 14:13
time was Barabbas, * along with Mk 15:7

CONVINCE
One look was enough to * us that Deu 1:24,25
Doesn't this * you that I am not 1Sa 24:11
God can * the sinner of his sin.' Job 32:13
failed to * the Pharisees, to whom Lk 16:31f
"And when he has come he will * Jn 16:8
to * the Jews and Greeks alike. Act 18:4
these sermons will * him of the 1Co 14:24
who are trying to * you to be Gal 6:12

CONVINCED
The woman was *. Gen 3:6
his clothes, and finally seems *. Gen 27:26
Then Amasa * all the leaders 2Sa 19:14
one of them has * Job that he is a Job 32:11,12
we are right, but is the Lord *? Pro 16:2
are * that he was a prophet." Lk 20:6
* that he was indeed the Messiah. Jn 2:23
Then you will become * that the Jn 10:38
For I am * that nothing can ever Rom 8:38
in the Lord, * of the Good News Col 1:23
fully * that he really loves us. 1Jn 4:18

CONVINCES
(The ruse * Isaac and he gives Gen 27:23

CONVOCATION
of sacred * of all the people; Lev 23:21
another sacred * of all the people, Lev 23:36
another * of all the people shall Num 29:7
Elected by a * of the leaders of Deu 33:5
Samuel now called a * of all 1Sa 10:17
THEN SOLOMON CALLED A * at 1Ki 8:1

CONVOCATIONS
festivals—sacred * of all Lev 23:37

CONVULSE
will fall—the heavens will *. Mk 13:25
CONVULSED
overshadowing the earth will be *. Mt 24:29
* the man violently and left him. Mk 1:26
Jesus the demon * the child Mk 9:20
and * the boy again and left him; Mk 9:26
CONVULSION
and threw him into a violent *. Lk 9:42
CONVULSIONS
and it throws him into * so that Lk 9:39
COOK
daily tasks. So * as much as you Ex 16:23
You must not * a young goat in Ex 34:26
and force them to * and bake and 1Sa 8:13
to come and * a little something 2Sa 13:6
a few sticks to * this last meal, 1Ki 17:12
Go ahead and * that 'last meal,' 1Ki 17:13
and the pot boil. * the meat well Eze 24:10
COOKED
If your offering is * in a pan, Lev 2:7
It shall be * on a griddle, Lev 6:21
and should be well *, then brought Lev 6:21
Tender-hearted women have * and Lam 4:10
COOKING
One day Jacob was * stew when Gen 25:29
mats to sleep on, * pots, serving 2Sa 17:28,29
* oil in the bottom of the jar. 1Ki 17:12
quickly than a * pot can feel the Ps 58:9
like meat for the * pot— and then Mic 3:3
COOL
was sitting in a * upstairs room Ju 3:20
a wise man stays * when insulted. Pro 12:16
is as refreshing as a * day Pro 25:13
* the pride of ruthless nations. Is 25:5
lead them beside the * waters. Is 49:10
and will * the love of many. Mt 24:12
in water and * my tongue, for I am Lk 16:24
COOL-TEMPERED
a * man tries to stop them. Pro 15:18
COOLED
and when the metal *, he ground it Ex 32:20
anger had *, he began brooding over Est 2:1
As a hot, dry land is * by Is 25:5
COOLING
* in Laban's attitude towards him. Gen 31:2
desert and as the * shadow of a Is 32:2
COOLS
man holds his temper in and * it. Pro 29:11
COOP
Like a * full of chickens their Jer 5:27
COOPERATE
Do not * with an evil man by Ex 23:1
straight, and we will fully *." Ez 10:4
COOPERATED
All the people of Judah * by 2Ch 17:5
course they then * in the Ez 8:36
COOPERATION
requiring their * in the Act 9:2
COPIED
were discovered and * by the Pro 25:1
* the nations all around you." Eze 11:12
in it—all * from things in Heb 9:23
COPIES
Moses also gave * of the laws to Deu 31:9
They took * of The Book of the 2Ch 17:7,8,9
priest, and sent * to all the other Jer 29:25
down here are *, were made pure Heb 9:23
COPPER
and * is abundant in the hills. Deu 8:9
the earth and melt * from stone. Job 28:2
and dropped in two small * coins. Lk 21:2
COPPERSMITH
Alexander the * has done me much 2Ti 4:14
COPY
king, then he must * these laws Deu 17:18
That * of the laws shall be his Deu 17:19
and gave him a * of the Ten 2Ki 11:12
and handed him a * of the law of 2Ch 23:11
you to take a * of God's laws to Ez 7:14
killed them. "A * of this Est 3:14
Mordecai also gave Hathach a * Est 4:8
It further stated that a * of Est 8:13
Don't * their ways. Pro 3:31
also the unsealed *, and publicly, Jer 32:11
deed and the * and put them into a Jer 32:14
Don't * the behavior and customs Rom 12:2
a * of the real temple in heaven. Heb 9:24
COPYING
out in *, reads: "Saul was . . . 1Sa 13:1f
COR
to pray and prophesy (1 *. 1Co 14:34f
ends in physical death (1 *. 1Jn 5:17f
CORAL
in fine gold. * or crystal is Job 28:18
linen, and jewelry of * and agate. Eze 27:16
CORD
One end of each * is attached to Ex 28:22,23,24
turban with a blue *, just as the Ex 39:31
to their clothes with a blue *. Num 15:37,38
* is not easily broken. Ecc 4:12
before the silver * of life snaps, Ecc 12:6
your umbilical * was uncut, and you Eze 16:4
This was done by stringing a * Mt 27:66f
the rock, the * being sealed at Mt 27:66f
CORDIALLY
at Jerusalem welcomed us *. Act 21:17
CORDS
of two twisted * of pure gold. Ex 28:22,23,24
The other ends of the two * are Ex 28:25
the Tabernacle court, and their *; Ex 35:10-19
The * and nails; Ex 39:33-40
their bases, pegs, *, and Num 4:32
Literally, "fastened with * of Est 1:6f
Or, "with * of falsehood." Is 5:18f
bound with * and made secure. Eze 27:24
CORE
the world was rotten to the *. Gen 6:11
are shaken to the *. Ps 82:5
foolish things, false to the *. Lam 2:14
for he knew mankind to the *. Jn 2:24,25
CORIANDER
it was white, like * seed, and Ex 16:31
The manna was about the size of * Num 11:7
CORINTH
PAUL LEFT Athens and went to *. Act 18:1
baptized—as were many others in *. Act 18:8
WHILE APOLLOS WAS in *, Paul Act 19:1
To: The Christians in *, invited 1Co 1:2
* who were excusing their sins. 1Co 6:12f
there in * and throughout Greece. 2Co 1:1
Erastus stayed at *, and I left 2Ti 4:20
CORINTHIAN
Oh, my dear * friends! 2Co 6:11
CORINTHIANS
See 2 * 3:13. Ex 34:33f
See 2 * 4:4, and Ephesians 2:2 Jn 12:31f
will begins and ends with you *? 1Co 14:36
2 * 2Co 1:24
in Matthew 8:14, 1 * 9:5, etc. 1Pe 5:13f
CORMORANT
The *, the ibis, Lev 11:13-19
The vulture, the *, Deu 14:11-18
CORN
Prospering in a land of * and Deu 33:28
brought Elisha a sack of fresh * 2Ki 4:42
heavy millstones and grind the *; Is 47:2
wine and ripened * I constantly Hos 1:9
sending you much * and wine and Joe 2:19
CORNELIUS
army officer, *, a captain of an Act 10:1
* -the angel said Act 10:3
* stared at him in terror. Act 10:4
As soon as the angel was gone, * Act 10:7
Just then the men sent by * had Act 10:17
Then they told him about * the Act 10:22
following day, and * was waiting Act 10:24
As Peter entered his home, * Act 10:25
* replied, "Four days ago I was Act 10:30
He told me, '*, your prayers are Act 10:31
Afterwards * begged him to stay Act 10:48
CORNER
be frogs in every * of the land." Ex 8:5
at the outside * of the four legs, Ex 25:26,27
frames, and two frames at each *. Ex 26:23
These * frames will be connected Ex 26:24
metal ring at each *, and fit the Ex 27:4
frames, plus another at each *. Ex 36:28
axles, and at each * of the stands 1Ki 7:27-30
The tank was in the southeast *, 1Ki 7:39
of Ephraim to the * Gate, a 2Ki 14:13
* of the outer room of the Temple. 2Ch 4:10
the gate of Ephraim to the * Gate. 2Ch 25:23
Jerusalem at the * Gate, and the 2Ch 26:9
gods in every * of Jerusalem. 2Ch 28:24
from Azariah's house to the *. Neh 3:24
the work from the * to the Neh 3:25
then to the upper room at the *. Neh 3:31
from that * to the Sheep Gate. Neh 3:32
people in every * of the land; Neh 9:22
Literally, "the head of the *." Ps 118:22f
every * for men to be her lovers. Pro 7:11,12
It is better to live in the * of Pro 21:9
It is better to live in a * of an Pro 25:24
in some dark * so that no one can Is 45:19
of Hananel at the northeast *, Jer 31:38,39
to the * Gate at the northwest; Jer 31:38,39
I saw that in each * there was a Eze 46:21,22
gate, then to the * Gate, and from Zec 14:10
Literally, "the head of the *." Mt 21:42f
and look in every * of the house Lk 15:8
"became the head of the *." Act 4:11f
for they were not done in a *! Act 26:26
CORNER-HORNS
high, with its * made as part of Ex 37:25
CORNERS
lower *, two rings on each side. Ex 25:12
Make horns for the four * of the Ex 27:2
those at the *, were linked to each Ex 36:29
*, all of one piece with the rest. Ex 38:2
on the top * of the chestpiece. Ex 39:15-18
don't reap the * of your fields, Lev 19:9
reap all the * of the fields, nor Lev 23:22
on the four * of your cloaks. Deu 22:12
each of the four * of the stands, 1Ki 7:34
to the farthest * of the universe, Neh 1:9
In the farthest * of the earth Ps 65:8
from the farthest * of the earth. Ps 107:3
into the dark * of your mind to Pro 6:23
at the street * of the city, Pro 9:14
who live in earth's remotest *! Is 42:10
from the farthest * of the earth. Is 43:6
or on the * of their altars. Jer 17:1
the farthest * of the earth. Jer 25:32
Literally, "those who cut the * Jer 49:32f
5¼ feet high; its *, base and sides Eze 41:22
twenty-one inches up from the *. Eze 43:15
and on the four * of the top Eze 43:20
and upon the four * of the base of Eze 45:19
each of the four * of the court. Eze 46:21,22
darkest * to find and punish those Zep 1:12
publicly on street * and in the Mt 6:5
Now go out to the street * and Mt 22:9
with no dark *, then your face will Lk 11:36
sheet, suspended by its four *, Act 10:11
down by its four * from the sky. Act 11:5
* of the earth to my salvation.' Act 13:47
shining into dark *, their words 2Pe 1:19
at the four * of the earth, holding Rev 7:1
CORNERSTONE
and who laid its *, as the morning Job 38:6,7
* that is safe to build on. Is 28:16
From them will come the *, the Zec 10:4
has been made the honored *; Mt 21:42
away became the *, the most honored Mk 12:10
by the builders was made the *'?" Lk 20:17
and the * of the building is Eph 2:20
chosen, precious * of my church, 1Pe 2:6
has become the *, the most honored 1Pe 2:7
CORNET
Literally, "the *, flute, harp, Dan 3:5f
Literally, "the *, flute, harp, Dan 3:7f
Literally, "the *, flute, harp, Dan 3:10f
CORNETS
Let the * and trumpets shout! Ps 98:6
CORNSTALKS
Their * stand there barren, Hos 8:7
CORONATION
that they come to his *. 1Ki 1:9
He has celebrated his * by 1Ki 1:19
Today he celebrated his * by 1Ki 1:25
Israel came for the * ceremony. 1Ki 12:1
custom at times of *, surrounded by 2Ki 11:13,14
of Israel for the * ceremony. 1Ch 23:2
came to Shechem for Rehoboam's *. 2Ch 10:1
was present at the *, and led the 2Ch 10:2,3
This is your * Day. Ps 2:7
CORPS
of Egypt's chariot *—600 chariots Ex 14:7
So Saul took his elite * of 1Sa 26:2
a bugle * to march at the head of 1Ch 15:24
Subdivisions of the Gershom * 1Ch 23:7
The priests formed a trumpet *. 2Ch 29:25,26
into service * to offer the burnt 2Ch 31:2
under the names of their work *. 2Ch 31:17,18
service * of your ancestors, as 2Ch 35:4,5
son Solomon. Each * will assist 2Ch 35:4,5
into service * as the king had 2Ch 35:10
various service *, to do the work Ez 6:18
division of the Temple service *. Lk 1:5
CORPSE
field touches the * of someone who Num 19:16
CORPSES
stripped from the *—so much that it 2Ch 20:25
decaying * fertilized the soil. Ps 83:10
No wonder you are like * when Is 59:10
to pick the flesh from their *. Jer 12:9
They will become like walking *, Zec 14:12
CORRECT
daughters of Zelophehad are *. Num 27:6,7
Don't fail to * your children; Pro 23:13,14
his course— so you * me, Lord; Jer 10:24
you, but only enough to * you. Jer 46:28
and * us for our awful sins. Hab 1:12
"*," Jesus agreed. Lk 7:43
he told a story to * the impression Lk 19:11
for if the * time for Jn 7:21,22,23
be an absolutely * judgment in Jn 8:16
And now are you going to * God Act 15:10
when it is not. * and rebuke your 2Ti 4:2
CORRECTED
and they have * it with their Num 15:25
should do, and * them as their Job 29:25
After you have * Ps 119:7
Anyone willing to be * is on the Pro 10:17
heard of a son who was never *? Heb 12:7
CORRECTING
people to do them, * them when Tit 2:15
CORRECTION
she refuses all *. Zep 3:2
how, but God's * is always right Heb 12:10
CORRECTLY
the Lord, offer it * so that it Lev 19:5

(CORRECTLY Con't)
it that everything is finished *. 1Ch 28:20
How anxious they are to worship * Is 58:2

CORRECTS
"How enviable the man whom God * Job 5:17
God chastens and * you, for his Pro 3:11,12
him better, so the Lord * you. Pro 3:11,12
he even * deafness and Mk 7:37

CORRESPONDING
In Daniel 7:13, the * Aramaic Eze 2:1f
the one below it, * to the Eze 41:7

CORRESPONDS
Hebrew calendar * approximately to Num 9:2,3f
This * to early in our Hag 2:18,19f
Or, "Baptism, which * to this, 1Pe 3:21f

CORRODED
His life is * with sin. Ps 53:1

CORRODES
the other kind * his strength and Pro 12:4

CORRUPT
the wisest and * their decisions. Deu 16:19
But Israel has become *, Deu 32:5
and were very * in the 1Sa 8:3
that point he became proud—and *. 2Ch 26:16
even so his people became very *. 2Ch 27:2
like you, who is * and sinful, Job 15:16
they are filthy with sin—* and Ps 53:3
Will you permit a * government Ps 94:20
When you remove * men from the Pro 25:4,5
and even the police courts are *. Ecc 3:16
of justice, and * and sour all that Amo 6:12
"But the * tax collector stood Lk 18:13
to me, and the *, and murderers, Rev 21:8

CORRUPTED
lest you be * by the horrible Deu 18:9
back again, for she has become *. Jer 3:1
your beauty; you * your wisdom for Eze 28:17
who * the earth with her sin; Rev 19:2

CORRUPTING
same temple-girl, * my holy name. Amo 2:7
"These Jews are * our city," Act 16:20,21

CORRUPTION
to the other it is filled with *. Ez 9:11
* and deceit of every kind. Pro 8:13
a land of sin and * and turned my Jer 2:7
to scorch away the rust and *. Eze 24:11
It is the rust and * of your Eze 24:13
bones, and of foulness and *. Mt 23:27
for their *—came to be baptized and Lk 3:12
of the * they are passing." Lk 11:44
Literally, "saw no *." Act 13:37f

COS
elders, we sailed straight to *. Act 21:1

COSAM
Addi's father was *; Lk 3:23-38

COSAM'S
Addi's father was Cosam;* father Lk 3:23-38

COST
*: don't try to make a profit! Lev 25:37
it would * to hire a servant for Lev 25:50
sinned at the * of their lives. Num 16:38
six years he has * you less than Deu 15:18
that have * me nothing. 2Sa 24:24
to Jerusalem * $400, and the horses 1Ki 10:29
offering that has * me nothing!" 1Ch 21:24
may * him his very life. Pro 6:26
to the Lord before counting the *. Pro 20:25
If you go, it will be at the * Jer 42:20
Not one sparrow (What do they *? Mt 10:29
don't begin until you count the *. Lk 14:28
close to the Lord, whatever the *. Act 11:23
muttered, "and it * me plenty!" Act 22:28
loyal to him no matter what the *. 1Co 13:7
that I could serve you without *. 2Co 11:8,9
and it is still not going to * 2Co 12:14
didn't seem to * us anything, but 2Co 12:16

COSTLY
for * gold and silver jewelry." Ex 11:2
stones, * jewels, and marble. 1Ch 29:2
he gave him many * gifts, and Dan 2:48
knew—and lavish on him * gifts! Dan 11:38
who poured the * perfume on Jesus' Jn 11:1
Then Mary took a jar of * Jn 12:3

COSTS
full construction * without delay Ez 6:8

COTTON
the bowstrings like * thread, Ju 16:9
or *, for the crops will fail. Is 19:9

COUCH
In despair he fell upon the * Est 7:8

COUNCIL
Shechem appeared before the city * Gen 34:20
people of Israel to a * meeting. Ex 4:29
meet with the city * and explain Jos 20:4
our * before the Lord at Mizpah?" Ju 21:5
letter to the city * of Samaria and 2Ki 10:1
with the city * and the guardians 2Ki 10:5
and officers for a * of war, and it 2Ch 32:3
I and my * of Seven hereby Ez 7:14
the king and his * of Seven and Ez 7:28
the king and his * and the leaders Ez 8:25
for he sits in the * chamber with Pro 31:23
about it," the * promised, "we'll Mt 28:14
of the Jewish *, the Pharisees were Lk 14:1
Jesus was led before this *, and Lk 22:66
THEN THE ENTIRE * took Jesus over Lk 23:1
a * to discuss the situation. Jn 11:47
happened that the * of all the Act 4:5
the * demanded. Act 4:7
When the * saw the boldness of Act 4:13
And the * could hardly discredit Act 4:14
So they sent them out of the * Act 4:15
The * then threatened them Act 4:21
and told them what the * had said. Act 4:23
the Jewish * and the entire Senate, Act 5:21
returned to the * and reported, Act 5:22
and brought them in before the *. Act 5:26,27
At this, the * was furious, and Act 5:33
the * chamber while he talked. Act 5:34
The * accepted his advice, called Act 5:40
They left the * chamber Act 5:41
him and brought him before the *. Act 6:12
everyone in the * chamber saw Act 6:15
to the City * for punishment. Act 17:5
took them before the * instead. Act 17:6
member of the City *, and a woman Act 17:34
at the regular City * meetings; Act 19:39
the * can testify that this is so. Act 22:5
into session with the Jewish *. Act 22:30
GAZING INTENTLY AT the *, Paul Act 23:1
Part of the * were Sadducees, and Act 23:6
This divided the * right down the Act 23:7
to the * again," they requested. Act 23:15
Paul before the * again, pretending Act 23:20
Then I took him to their * to Act 23:28
wrongdoing their * found in me, Act 24:20
am here before the * to defend Act 24:21

COUNCILMEN
and other religious leaders and *. Lk 20:1

COUNCILS
my voice goes unheeded in their *. Ps 120:7
Call your * of war, develop your Is 8:9,10

COUNSEL
your mind and give me your *!" Ju 20:7
to Bethel first to ask * from God. Ju 20:18
will * you as I did your father.' 2Sa 15:33,34
to defeat the * of Ahithophel, 2Sa 17:14
For we always give wise *. 2Sa 20:18
the old men's * and called in the 1Ki 12:8
the * of the younger ones. 2Ch 10:14
and have not accepted my *." 2Ch 25:16
to take the * of Jeremiah the 2Ch 36:12
followed Memucan's *, and sent Est 1:21
For your own good, listen to my * Job 5:27
Have you heard the secret * of Job 15:7,8
Are you called into his * room? Job 15:7,8
no more, for my * satisfied them. Job 29:22
my life with your wisdom and *; Ps 73:24
For you have spurned my * and Pro 1:25
night long their * will lead you Pro 6:22
Their * will keep you far away Pro 6:24
"Listen to my *—oh, don't refuse Pro 8:33
but the liar's * is shunned. Pro 10:31
understanding, * and might; Is 11:2
Their best * to the king of Egypt Is 19:11
ruined Egypt with their foolish *. Is 19:13
or be his teacher or give him *? Is 40:13
* being given out in this city. Eze 11:1
"So my * is: Don't worry about Mt 6:25
Literally, "took * against Jesus Mt 27:1f
and * you as beloved children. 1Co 4:14
and I think I am giving you * 1Co 7:40

COUNSELED
men who had * his father Solomon. 1Ki 12:6
men who had * his father Solomon. 2Ch 10:6

COUNSELING
beneath him, each * ten persons. Ex 18:21

COUNSELOR
And he has made me a * to Gen 45:8
a wise * and an educated man. 1Ch 27:32
king's official * and Hushai the 1Ch 27:33
The godly man is a good * Ps 37:30,31
He'll not be chosen as a *! Pro 24:7
"Wonderful," "*," "The Mighty Is 9:6
as the king's * until the first Dan 1:21
Who knows enough to be his * and Rom 11:34

COUNSELOR'S
lies deep within a * heart, the Pro 20:5

COUNSELORS
of Pharaoh's * and assistants—all Gen 50:7
of David's * who lived in Giloh. 2Sa 15:12
So on the advice of his *, the 1Ki 12:28
five of the king's *, and sixty 2Ki 25:19
King Hanun's * warned him, "Don't 1Ch 19:2,3
the advice of his * and declared 2Ch 25:17
"He makes fools of * and judges. Job 12:17
laws are both my light and my *. Ps 119:24
as *; those without it are beaten Pro 10:13
but with good * there is safety. Pro 11:14
Plans go wrong with too few *; Pro 15:22
counselors; many * bring success. Pro 15:22
there is safety in many *. Pro 24:6
* like those you used to have. Is 1:26
Her wise * are all at their Is 19:3
What fools the * of Zoan are! Is 19:11
to your "wise *," O Pharaoh? Is 19:12
make their wisest * as fools." Is 29:14
All her wise * shall become Jer 50:36
the king's special * discovered in Jer 52:24,25
them his * when they graduated. Dan 1:5
treasurers, *, sheriffs, and rulers Dan 3:2
captains, and * crowded around them Dan 3:27
and kingdom. My * and officers came Dan 4:36
We presidents, governors, * and Dan 6:7
down with his * and discussing Lk 14:31

COUNSELS
I will bless the Lord who * me; Ps 16:7

COUNT
and * the stars if you can. Gen 15:5
will be like that—too many to *!" Gen 15:5
you to reduce the * of your flock? Gen 31:39
along the shores—too many to *." Gen 32:12
Literally, "you shall * the fruit Lev 19:23f
person's clan; * every male down to Num 3:14,15
before his defilement no longer *. Num 6:12
and the Lord your God will * it Deu 24:12,13
too numerous to * and stayed until Ju 6:5
were too many camels even to *! Ju 7:12,13
out to * the people of Israel. 2Sa 24:4
are almost too many people to *! 1Ki 3:8
retorted, "Don't * your chickens 1Ki 20:11
that no one tried to keep *! 2Ch 5:6
Silver was too cheap to * for 2Ch 9:20
miracles, too many to *. Job 9:10
And if I'm good, that doesn't *. Job 10:15
and so to * you as his enemy. Job 33:10
Lord, will * on you for help. Ps 9:10
I can * every bone in my body. Ps 22:17
Meanwhile my sins, too many to *, Ps 40:12
Walk around and * her many Ps 48:12
I cannot even * all those who Ps 69:4
I cannot * the times when you Ps 71:15
guilty. * his prayers as sins. Ps 109:7
I can't even * how many times a Ps 139:17,18
morning, he will * it as a curse! Pro 27:14
so few a child could * them! Is 10:19
world, too many to *, and there Is 48:19
I will * you carefully and let Eze 20:37
to *—like sand along a seashore! Hos 1:10
too numerous to *, with teeth as Joe 1:6
"But don't begin until you * the Lk 14:28
And all of them—the approximate * Jn 6:10
about myself, it doesn't *. Jn 8:54
By his * there were 153 large Jn 21:11
If you * yourself above average 1Co 3:18
has done, it doesn't * for much. 2Co 10:18
we can completely * on, for it is Heb 6:18
shores, there is no way to * them. Heb 11:12
too great to *, from all nations Rev 7:9
and to * the number of worshipers. Rev 11:1

COUNTED
that, like dust, they can't be *! Gen 13:16
who would not be * as his own, and Gen 38:9
but all of it is * as a holy Lev 2:3
use, but it is all * as a holy Lev 2:10
in this entire census had been * Num 26:64,65
years of age, and so were not *. Num 26:64,65f
For all who had been * then had Num 26:64,65
it will be * against you as a sin. Deu 15:9
would be * as a sin against you. Deu 24:14,15
to him shall be * as the son of the Deu 25:6
as one man. He * them in Bezek and 1Sa 11:8
When Saul * the soldiers who were 1Sa 13:15
too, and when he * his casualties, 2Sa 2:30
(People from Be-eroth are * as 2Sa 4:2,3
instance) * together as one tribe. 1Ki 12:20f
the High Priest * it, put it into 2Ki 12:10
of the High Priest * the money, and 2Ch 24:11
been opened and *, and the money 2Ch 34:17
never again to be * among the days Job 3:6
For all he * on will disappear, Job 15:32
will be, who * on "Ethiopia's Is 20:5,6
make many to be * righteous before Is 53:11
He was * as a sinner, and he bore Is 53:12
All who harmed them were * deeply Jer 2:3
These can be * on. Jer 18:15
And as the stars cannot be * nor Jer 33:22
isn't worthy to be * as a nation. Jer 33:24
And Moab will no longer be * Eze 25:9,10
So they * out thirty little silver Zec 11:12
said, "He was * among evil men." Mk 15:28
when those who are * worthy of Lk 20:34,35
will be * fortunate indeed. Lk 23:29
them they would not be * guilty. Jn 15:24
that God had * them worthy to Act 5:41
* against him by the Lord." Rom 4:8
that you will be * free from all 1Co 1:8
by the world, * as nothing at all, 1Co 1:28

COUNTENANCE
Literally, "for the help of his * Ps 42:4,5f
"He is the help of my *." Ps 43:5f

COUNTER
Then you can frustrate and * 2Sa 15:33,34

COUNTERED
Saul * with a buildup of forces 1Sa 17:2
COUNTERS
and money changers behind their *. Jn 2:14
COUNTERSIGN
It is poor judgment to * Pro 17:18
cash on hand, don't * a note. Pro 22:26,27
COUNTERSTRATEGY
for you and all your * will fail. Ob 1:7
COUNTING
descendants, not * the wives of Gen 46:26
be arrived at by * the number of Lev 25:14,15,16
animals, as they pass by for *. Lev 27:32
census was 23,000, * all the males Num 26:62
The army of Israel, not * the Ju 20:17
some day go. I am * on you to be a 1Ki 2:2
We should make plans—* on God to Pro 16:9
to the Lord before * the cost. Pro 20:25
your walls are * your towers and Is 33:18
himself, no longer * men's sins 2Co 5:19
if you are * on circumcision and Gal 5:2
to you if you are * on clearing Gal 5:4
Holy Spirit are * on Christ's death Gal 5:5
I have put aside all else, * it Php 3:8
him, no longer * on being saved by Php 3:9
on faith—* on Christ alone. Php 3:9
COUNTLESS
descendants into * thousands and Gen 22:17
There shall be * widows; Jer 15:8
the gathering of * happy angels; Heb 12:22
COUNTRIES
the surrounding * too, but in Egypt Gen 41:54
to him from Egypt and other *. 2Ch 9:28
and * who attempted to control it. Ez 4:15
their * on my way to Judah; Neh 2:7
besides visitors from other *! Neh 5:17
born in one or another of those *. Ps 87:4
as slaves to other * far away, and Is 6:12
them here, from * far away. Is 13:5
home from the * of the north, where Jer 16:14,15
* to which he had exiled them." Jer 23:8
of the northern *, far and near, Jer 25:26
So now I have given all your * Jer 27:6
again from all the * where in my Jer 32:37
the other nearby * heard that a few Jer 40:11
from the nearby * where they had Jer 43:5
they shall be exiled to * Jer 49:36
the armies of all the * they rule. Jer 51:28
you in the * of the world, yet I Eze 11:16
of the * where they are in exile. Eze 20:38
Libya and all the * leagued with Eze 30:5
COUNTRY
"Leave your own * behind you, and Gen 12:1
to the hilly * between Bethel on Gen 12:8
them out of the * under armed Gen 12:20
my *, as I have been toward you." Gen 21:23
the Philistine * for a long time. Gen 21:34
across the * from Havilah to Shur Gen 25:18
asked Isaac to leave the *. Gen 26:16
Now leave this * and return to Gen 31:13
you are the wisest man in the *! Gen 41:39
us and escape out of the *." Ex 1:10
throw you out of the *. Ex 11:1
That entire * is defiled with Lev 18:25
into the hill * of the Negeb, and Num 13:17
a magnificent *—a land 'flowing Num 13:27
while in the hill * there are the Num 13:29
be taken into this * ahead of us. Num 14:3
* ahead, and the Lord loves us. Num 14:7
into the hill *, despite the fact Num 14:44
into the wonderful * you promised, Num 16:14
Please let us pass through your *. Num 20:17
pass through their *, Israel turned Num 20:21,22
in the Amorite *, Moses sent spies Num 21:31,32
what wonderful sheep * it was. Num 32:1
And it is all wonderful sheep *, Num 32:3,4
portion of the * will be the Num 34:3
Now go and occupy the hill * of Deu 1:7
on up into the hill * to fight. Deu 1:43
through the * belonging to their Deu 2:4
Mount Seir hill * as their Deu 2:5
go through their *, and so did the Deu 2:29
River and the hill * cities, the Deu 2:37
They renamed their * after Deu 3:14
Divide the * into three Deu 19:2,3
in the *, only the man shall die. Deu 22:25,26,27
give my * to you," she told them. Jos 2:9
"We are from a very distant *; Jos 9:9
the whole *—the nations and kings Jos 10:40
kings of the hill *, the Negeb, the Jos 10:40
the kings of the northern hill *; Jos 11:1
The kings in the Jebusite hill *; Jos 11:1
land—the hill *, the Negeb, the Jos 11:16
lived in the hill * in Hebron, Jos 11:21
The area included the hill *, Jos 12:8-24
All the hill * from Lebanon to Jos 13:2-7
hill * which the Lord promised me. Jos 14:12
cities in the hill * with their Jos 15:48-62
and the hill * to Bethel. Jos 16:1
"If the hill * of Ephraim is not Jos 17:15
out to map the * and to bring back Jos 18:8
* and the Wilderness of Beth-aven. Jos 18:12
hill * south of Lower Beth-horon. Jos 18:13
in the hill * of Ephraim; Jos 19:50
Galilee in the hill * of Naphtali; Jos 20:7
Shechem, in the hill * of Jos 20:7
as Hebron) in the hill * of Judah. Jos 20:7
to their own sections of the *. Jos 24:28
in the hill * of Ephraim, on the Jos 24:30
he was buried in the hill * of Jos 24:33
in the hill * and in the Negeb, as Ju 1:9
people of the hill *, though they Ju 1:19
did force them to leave the *. Ju 1:28
them into the hill * and wouldn't Ju 1:34
in the hill * of Ephraim, north of Ju 2:7-9
When he arrived in the hill * of Ju 3:27
Bethel, in the hill * of Ephraim; Ju 4:5
the hill * of Ephraim summoning Ju 7:24
Shamir in the hill * of Ephraim. Ju 10:1
they chased Jephthah out of the *. Ju 11:1
in the hill * of the Amalekites. Ju 12:15
IN THE HILL * of Ephraim lived a Ju 17:1
Arriving in the hill * of Ju 18:2
on up into the hill * of Ephraim. Ju 18:13
side of the hill * of Ephraim, who Ju 19:1
from the hill * of Ephraim, but was Ju 19:16
the Ephraim hill *, near Shiloh. Ju 19:18
left the * because of a famine Ru 1:1
own *, lest the entire city die. 1Sa 5:11
* for seven months in all. 1Sa 6:1
cities and the * villages 1Sa 6:18
through the hill * of Ephraim, the 1Sa 9:4
caves in the hill * of Ziph. 1Sa 23:14,15
live in one of the * towns instead 1Sa 27:5
Brook, and went out into the *. 2Sa 15:23
of the *, but now Absalom is dead. 2Sa 19:8,9,10
from the hill * of Ephraim, who has 2Sa 20:21
So they searched the * from one 1Ki 1:3,4
was the hill * of Ephraim; 1Ki 4:8-19
in the hill *, and thirty-three 1Ki 5:15
I heard in my own * about your 1Ki 10:6
nearly every male in the entire *. 1Ki 11:15
deserted his post and fled the *. 1Ki 11:23
in the hill * of Ephraim, and it 1Ki 12:25
* shall be eaten by vultures." 1Ki 21:24
move to some other *, for the Lord 2Ki 8:1
sections of the * east of the 2Ki 10:32,33
Husham from the * of the Temanites 1Ch 1:45
the entire pasture * of Sharon. 1Ch 5:16
When they wandered from * to 1Ch 16:20
they wandered from country to *, 1Ch 16:20
foreigners in the * (just as his 2Ch 2:17
at one end of the * to the brook of 2Ch 7:8
about you in my own * is true! 2Ch 9:5
in the hill * of Ephraim, King 2Ch 13:4
in the hill * of Ephraim, and he 2Ch 15:8
throughout the *, and in the cities 2Ch 17:2
to the hill * of Ephraim to 2Ch 19:4
other parts of the Philistine *. 2Ch 26:6
cities in the hill * of Judah, and 2Ch 27:4
one end of the * to the other. Ps 44:1
through the entire * burning down Ps 74:8
a king who is devoted to his *! Ecc 5:9
Your * lies in ruins; Is 1:7
left—and the whole * is an utter Is 6:11
to take you to a * very similar to Is 36:17
to this one—a * where there are Is 36:17
He will return to his own * by Is 37:34
returned to his own *, to Nineveh. Is 37:37
made a wasteland of this entire *. Jer 10:25
through the whole *, reassuring Jer 14:18
or in the open * down below. Jer 17:2,3
and never again see his own *. Jer 22:12
mother out of this *, and you shall Jer 22:26
* and farm the land as usual." Jer 27:11
here in this * and will be buying Jer 32:15
witnessed—in the * of Benjamin and Jer 32:44
and in the hill *, in the Jer 32:44
arrived in this *, we were afraid Jer 35:11
this * and everything in it. Jer 36:29
toward the * of the Ammonites. Jer 41:10
* beside the river Euphrates! Jer 46:10
back to their own * to tell how the Jer 50:28
and cast us out of our own *. Jer 51:34,35
will never see your own * again. Eze 13:9
in your own * where you were born. Eze 21:30
in your own * and you will be Eze 21:32
camels and all the * of the Eze 25:5
The whole * will shake with your Eze 26:15
an army against a *, and the people Eze 33:2
he got possession of the whole *! Eze 33:24
in their own *, they defiled it by Eze 36:17
across the entire * of Israel, from Eze 48:23
the first great king of that *. Dan 8:21
The entire * would be devastated. Amo 1:12f
shall occupy the hill * of Edom; Ob 1:19
What is your work? What * are you Jon 1:8
there in my own * and you first Jon 4:2
again,' for their * is named 'The Mal 1:4
the lake, in the * of the Mt 8:28
own *, and among his own people!" Mt 13:57
the * and walked the fifty miles Mt 15:21
went away to live in another *. Mt 21:33
going into another *, who called Mt 25:14
section of the * and returned with Mk 6:1
farmers and moved to another *. Mk 12:1
who went on a trip to another *. Mk 13:34
coming in from the * just then, was Mk 15:21
Jerusalem into the *, but they Mk 16:12
* across the lake from Galilee. Lk 8:26
'go out into the * lanes and out Lk 14:23
or there in that part of the *.' Lk 17:21
Jerusalem from the *, was forced to Lk 23:26
everywhere except in his own *!" Jn 4:43,44
of leaving the * and going as a Jn 7:35
was near, and many * people arrived Jn 11:55
a * that God would direct him to. Act 7:3
the whole * would belong to him and Act 7:5
live in a foreign * and there Act 7:6
"At this, Moses fled the *, and Act 7:29
upon trade with Herod's *. Act 12:20
age in the whole *, and tried as Gal 1:14
citizens of God's *, and you belong Eph 2:19
COUNTRYMAN
has given it to a * of yours who is 1Sa 15:28
COUNTRYMEN
by all his * because he did his Est 10:3
from your own *, just as they 1Th 2:14
COUNTRYSIDE
or like the beautiful * around Gen 13:10
When he saw how good the * was, Gen 49:15
* and filled the nation's homes. Ex 8:13
of this whole *—Ataroth, Dibon, Num 32:3,4
across the * as far away as Gaza. Deu 2:23
and plundered the * as far away as Ju 6:3,4
Keilah and began roaming the *. 1Sa 23:13
all across the *, and more men 2Sa 18:8
Syrian forces that filled the *! 1Ki 20:27
the surrounding *, for its citizens 2Ki 15:16
Let the * and everything in it 1Ch 16:32
throughout the * and cities of the Est 9:28
our land and pillaged the *. Ps 44:10
Ephrathah, then in the distant * Ps 132:6
bands in the * heard that the king Jer 40:7
You have filled the * with Hab 2:8
the Lake, and the * beyond the Mt 4:15,16
miracle swept the entire *. Mt 9:26
*, spreading the news as they ran. Mk 5:14
COUNTS
Everything he * on will collapse. Job 8:14
If he * on his home for Job 8:15
His fury burns against me; he * Job 19:11
their wounds. He * the stars and Ps 147:4
only righteousness * then. Pro 11:4
its pet name, and * them to see Is 40:26
incense to him, he * it the same as Is 66:3
sits down and * his blessings—and Lk 14:33
we worship that *, but how we Jn 4:21-24
or not; what * is whether we really Gal 6:15
COUPLE
were angry with a * of us and put Gen 41:10
does not die for a * of days, then Ex 21:21
bronze clasps to * the loops so Ex 36:18
that within a * of years, before Is 8:4
for a * of dollars and eight Hos 3:2
In just a * of days, Hos 6:2
"A * of hours later he was Mt 20:3
of five sparrows? A * of pennies? Lk 12:6
barley loaves and a * of fish! Jn 6:8,9
Bethany was only a * of miles Jn 11:18
COUPLED
Bezalel * five of these Ex 36:16
COURAGE
So lead on with * and strength!" Jos 1:17,18
could cross, their * melted away Jos 5:1
So the men of Israel took * and Ju 20:22,23,24
you, I will come and help you. *! 2Sa 10:12
is a command. Take * and do it!" 2Sa 13:28
man of unusual *, and Jehoiada. 1Ch 12:24-37
Now I have the * to pray to you, 1Ch 17:25
from God, he took * and destroyed 2Ch 15:8
priest got up his * and took some 2Ch 23:1
Then Amaziah took * and led his 2Ch 25:11
Take * and tell us how to Ez 10:4
"You will have * because you Job 11:18
Suddenly my * was gone; Ps 30:6,7
So cheer up! Take * if you are Ps 31:24
Take *, my soul! Ps 42:4,5
A man's * Pro 18:14
when * dies, what hope is left? Pro 18:14
WINE GIVES FALSE *; Pro 20:1
judges and great * to your soldiers Is 28:6
* to those with repentant hearts. Is 57:15
Then the * of the mightiest Jer 49:22
Their * is gone; Jer 51:30
Then he will stir up his * and Dan 11:25
But take *, O Zerubbabel and Hag 2:4
the people; take * and work, for 'I Hag 2:4
gathered his * and went to Pilate Mk 15:42,43
tides. The * of many people will Lk 21:26
But no one had the * to speak Jn 7:13
So take *! Act 27:25
them, he thanked God and took *. Act 28:15

(COURAGE Con't)
Yet God gave us the * to boldly 1Th 2:2
—if we keep up our * firm to the Heb 3:6
them can take new * when they hear Heb 6:18
And take *, for the coming of the Jas 5:8

COURAGEOUS
Be strong! Be *! Deu 31:6
Israel watched, "Be strong! Be *! Deu 31:7
to be strong and *, and said to Deu 31:23
You need only to be strong and * Jos 1:7
"Be strong and *, for the Lord Jos 10:25
is and how * his soldiers are. 2Sa 17:10
and help you. Be * and let us act 1Ch 19:13
Be strong and *, fearless and 1Ch 22:13
"Be strong and * and get to work. 1Ch 28:20
* men led by King Jeroboam. 2Ch 13:3
Be brave, stouthearted and *. Ps 27:14
How strong and * will you be Eze 22:14
The most * of your mighty men Amo 2:16

COURIERS
king's speediest *, after being Est 3:15
by the king's * and speeded by the Est 8:14

COURSE
"Of * we may eat it," the woman Gen 3:2,3
I will of * pay the full price Gen 23:9
Jacob: "Yes, of *." Gen 27:24
Esau: "Why, it's me, of *! Gen 27:32
His brothers of * noticed their Gen 37:4
not realizing of * that she was his Gen 38:16
Of * they didn't know that Joseph Gen 42:23
But of * some of them wouldn't Ex 16:20
barred gates. Of * we also took all Deu 3:5
ancestors. Of *, the Lord your God Deu 13:18
But of * he didn't realize that Jos 8:14
And of * the tribes of Gad and Jos 18:7
No, of * not. Ju 11:25
answer and she, of *, gave the Ju 14:17
No, of * not, my daughters; Ru 1:13
Of * Saul was very angry. 1Sa 18:8
"Of * you don't know about it!" 1Sa 20:3
"Of * not!" 1Sa 20:9
He, of *, didn't understand what 1Sa 20:39
This was of * a great sin, for 1Ki 12:30
of Judah replied, "Of *! 1Ki 22:4
"Why, of *! 1Ki 22:15
Elisha snapped. "Of * I know 2Ki 2:3
he commanded. "Of * I know 2Ki 2:5
"Of * I will," Jehoshaphat 2Ki 3:6,7,8
"Of * not!" 2Ki 6:22
So of * the nations you 2Ki 19:26
the best * for Israel to take. 1Ch 12:24-37
though some, of *, were stationed 2Ch 1:14
"Why, of *!" 2Ch 18:3,4,5
images (this of * was before the 2Ch 33:19
River, and of * they then Ez 8:36
Levite opposed this * of action. Ez 10:15
During the wine * the king said Est 5:6
Again, during the wine *, the Est 7:2
He was, of *, very great among Est 10:3
But of * you know all this! Job 38:21
He gave free * to his anger and Ps 78:50
to my * of seeking wisdom. Ecc 2:3
Next I changed my * again and Ecc 2:3
And, of *, it is very good if a Ecc 5:19,20
day and night. (Of *, only God can Ecc 8:16,17
their own mad *, for they have no Ecc 9:2,3
This, of *, was not a virgin Is 7:14f
No lion will lurk along its *, Is 35:9
wood and stone. Of * the Assyrians Is 37:19
I will make an obstacle * of the Jer 6:21
his *— so you correct me, Lord; Jer 10:23
And they will reply, Of *, you Jer 13:12
it and helping us? Of * not!" Jer 44:19
have run their * and reached their Eze 7:10,11
asks the Lord. Of * not! Eze 18:23
No, of * not. Eze 18:24
along the * of the Jordan River Eze 26:2
then follow the * of the Brook of Eze 47:19
and of * I went without desserts. Dan 10:3
he forgive your sins? Of * not! Mic 6:7
given a poisonous snake? Of * not! Mt 7:10
(They were, of *, hoping he Mt 12:10
it that day? Of * you would. Mt 12:11
The paraphrase is of * highly Mt 13:52f
"Of * he does," Peter replied. Mt 17:25
They replied, "The first, of *." Mt 21:31
And of * you should obey their Mt 23:3
to shut out the light? Of * not! Mk 4:21
Of * they were trying to trap him. Mk 10:2
the man and said, "Of * I will. Lk 5:13
literally is, of *, unknown. Lk 8:30f
give him a scorpion? [Of * not! Lk 11:12
single day to your life? Of * not! Lk 12:25
business (and, of *, a very rich Lk 19:1
They were, of *, delighted to Lk 22:5
seen God, but, of *, his only Son Jn 1:18
from (though, of *, the servants Jn 2:9
In the * of his journey through Jn 4:46,47
(You always hear me, of *, but I Jn 11:42
"Of * not," he replied. Jn 18:25
"Of * not!" Act 8:31
local dialect, of *), "These men Act 14:11
and, of *, from fornication. Act 15:27,28,29
province! Of *, I am not only Act 19:27
him killed. Of * I quickly pointed Act 25:16
keep the ship on *, so we sailed Act 27:4
break his promises? Of * not! Rom 3:4
*, that might be barely possible. Rom 5:7
because although, of *, people Rom 5:13
Of * not! Rom 6:2,3
receiving God's grace!) Of * not! Rom 6:15
laws of God are evil? Of * not! Rom 7:7
hearts knows, of *, what the Spirit Rom 8:27
Was God being unfair? Of * not. Rom 9:14
Jewish people forever? Of * not! Rom 11:11
wrong, of * you should be afraid, Rom 13:4
you say, but of * you are all such 1Co 4:10
Don't let that worry you—but of * 1Co 7:21
unmarried. Of *, if you already 1Co 7:27
thinking about us? Of * he was. 1Co 9:10
I can, except of * that I must 1Co 9:21
be seen, while of * the parts that 1Co 12:24
Is everyone an apostle? Of * 1Co 12:29
Can everyone heal the sick? Of * 1Co 12:30
of *, you can tell everyone 1Co 14:5
it, unless of * you never really 1Co 15:2
the grave, and of * that isn't true 1Co 15:15
except, of *, Christ does not 1Co 15:27
Of *, I don't mean that those who 2Co 8:13
No, of * not. 2Co 12:18
Jewish laws? Of * not, for the Holy Gal 3:2
No, of * not. Gal 3:5
that, of *, means Christ. Gal 3:16
against each other? Of * not! Gal 3:21,22
Some, of *, are preaching the Php 1:15
make it plain, as, of *, I should. Col 4:4
of God—which, of *, it was—and it 1Th 2:13
(But of * you know that such 1Th 3:2,3
doing right! Of *, you get no 1Pe 2:20
Of *, your former friends will be 1Pe 4:4
from his mad * when his donkey 2Pe 2:16
Every wrong is a sin, of *. 1Jn 5:17

COURSES
The Great Court had three * of 1Ki 7:12

COURSING
God and the Lamb, * down the Rev 22:2

COURT
his *, and it became a serpent. Ex 7:10
The * officials now came to Ex 10:7
not give false testimony in *." Ex 20:16f
north side of the *—150 feet of Ex 27:11
The west side of the * will be Ex 27:12
"The entrance to the * will be a Ex 27:16
All the posts around the * are Ex 27:17
So the entire * will be 150 feet Ex 27:18
The drapes for the walls of the *; Ex 35:10-19
Drapes for the entrance to the *; Ex 35:10-19
The posts of the Tabernacle *, and Ex 35:10-19
* were woven of fine-twined linen. Ex 38:16
entrance to the * was made of Ex 38:18
composing the walls of the *. Ex 38:18
the Tabernacle and * were bronze. Ex 38:20
enclosing the *, and for all the Ex 38:29
of the Tabernacle and the *. Ex 38:29
The drapes for the walls of the * Ex 39:33-40
the drapes at the gate of the *; Ex 39:33-40
be tried in a * but not put to Lev 19:20
and his entire * in Egypt, and Deu 34:11,12
She held * at a place now called Ju 4:5
setting up his * first at Bethel, 1Sa 7:16
oldest sons, held * in Beer-sheba; 1Sa 8:2
of Solomon's *—one man from each 1Ki 4:7
food for King Solomon and his *; 1Ki 4:27
The wall of the inner * had three 1Ki 6:36
The Great * had three courses of 1Ki 7:12
like the inner * of the Temple and 1Ki 7:12
room, but not from the outer *; 1Ki 8:8
sanctified the * in front of the 1Ki 8:64
Gedaliah and his *—both the Jews 2Ki 25:25
for the outer *, the outside rooms, 1Ch 28:12
Then he constructed a * for the 2Ch 4:9
also the public *, and overlaid the 2Ch 4:9
of the outer *, in front of the 2Ch 6:12,13
Solomon consecrated the inner * 2Ch 7:7
Priest, to be the * of final appeal 2Ch 19:11
in Judah, as the * of final appeal 2Ch 19:11
at the new * of the Temple, and 2Ch 20:5
around the altar in the outer *. 2Ch 23:10
executed in the * of the Temple. 2Ch 24:21
out into the * all the filth and 2Ch 29:16
reached the outer *, which took 2Ch 29:17
or in the * of the Temple, or on Neh 8:16
He came daily to the * of the Est 2:11
the king's inner * without his Est 4:11
entered the inner * just beyond the Est 5:1
there in the inner *, he welcomed Est 5:2
"Who is on duty in the outer * Est 6:4
in the outer * of the palace to ask Est 6:4
was a friend at * for all of them. Est 10:3
and calls the * to order, who is Job 11:10
"WHY DOESN'T GOD open the * and Job 24:1
GOD STANDS UP to open heaven's *. Ps 82:1
him to * before an unfair judge. Ps 109:6
There are the judges holding * Ps 122:5
from the king's *, his reign will Pro 25:4,5
Don't be hot-headed and rush to * Pro 25:8,9,10
came to the royal *, "Syria is Is 7:2
Come now and speak. The * is Is 41:1
sentence of my * upon your sins. Is 47:8
his * and all his evil priests? Jer 12:5
the door of the Temple to hold *. Jer 26:10
and persuaded the * not to turn him Jer 26:24
in the Temple *, and the metal Jer 27:19,20,21
and the * officials, and the tribal Jer 29:1
Literally, "a woman shall * a Jer 31:22f
Literally, "in the * of the Jer 32:2f
you are princes, * officials, Jer 34:18,19
Literally, "the * of the guard." Jer 37:21f
where the king was holding *. Jer 38:8
door of the Temple *, where I made Eze 8:7
me into the inner * of the Temple Eze 8:16
cloud of glory filled the inner *. Eze 10:3
of glory, and the * of the Temple Eze 10:4
be heard clear out in the outer *. Eze 10:5
the passageway to the * inside. Eze 40:17
the walls into the * the same Eze 40:18
other side of this * (which was Eze 40:19
"the outer *" of the Temple Eze 40:19
into the *, and straight across it, Eze 40:23
through it to an inner *. Eze 40:23
into the * and straight across it, Eze 40:27
through it to the inner *. Eze 40:27
Then he took me along the * to Eze 40:32
Its entry hall faced the outer * Eze 40:34
toward the outer *, and it had palm Eze 40:37
In the inner *, there were two Eze 40:44
Then he measured the inner * [in Eze 40:47
an altar in the *, standing in Eze 40:47
led up to it from the inner *. Eze 40:48,49
row of rooms down in the inner *. Eze 41:10
The inner * at the east of the Eze 41:14
into the inner * to the rooms north Eze 42:1
were the inner wall of the *. Eze 42:3
the outer * on one side, and having Eze 42:3
strip of inner * on the other. Eze 42:3
those in the outer * were, the Eze 42:6
next to the outer *, were 87½ feet Eze 42:7,8
Temple *, which was 175 feet long. Eze 42:7,8
* to these rooms from the east. Eze 42:9,10
side of the inner *, between the Eze 42:9,10
*, arranged the same as the other. Eze 42:9,10
across the *—the same length and Eze 42:11
there was a door from the outer * Eze 42:12
before going out to the outer *. Eze 42:14
and brought me into the inner *; Eze 43:5
to the inner *, for they must wear Eze 44:17
in the inner * or in the Temple. Eze 44:17
When they return to the outer *, Eze 44:19
wine before coming to the inner *. Eze 44:21
enters the inner * and the Eze 44:27
walls at the entry of the inner *. Eze 45:19
through the outer *, in case they Eze 46:19,20
out to the outer * again and led me Eze 46:21,22
each of the four corners of the *. Eze 46:21,22
chief magistrate in the king's *. Dan 2:49
Then the * began its session and Dan 7:10
and opened his * and vindicated his Dan 7:22
and open his * of justice and Dan 7:26
But I will * her again, and bring Hos 1:14
testifies against her in my *. Hos 5:5
of being brought before the *. Mt 5:22
he drags you into * and you are Mt 5:25
If you are ordered to *, and Mt 5:40
Jewish Supreme * assembled there Mt 26:59
presiding over the *, Pilate's wife Mt 27:19
Jewish Supreme * were trying to Mk 14:55
up before the * and asked Jesus, Mk 14:60
*—met to discuss their next steps. Mk 15:1
the Jewish Supreme * (who Mk 15:42,43
in the Temple *, praying as they Lk 1:10
on the way to *, try to settle the Lk 12:58
the Jewish Supreme * assembled, Lk 22:66
the Jewish Supreme *, from the city Lk 23:50,51,52
On Paul's arrival in * the Jews Act 25:7
and ask a heathen * to decide the 1Co 6:1
pick on you and drag you into *? Jas 2:6
the inner * where the altar stands, Rev 11:1
"But do not measure the outer * Rev 11:2

COURT-MARTIALED
* and sentenced to death. Act 12:19

COURT'S
defy the * judgment a second time. Deu 17:13

COURTEOUS
but be gentle and truly * to all. Tit 3:2
Then it is peace-loving and *. Jas 3:17

COURTEOUSLY
He welcomed us * and fed us for Act 28:7
For if you talk meekly and * to 2Ti 2:25

COURTESY
You neglected the usual * of Lk 7:46
to you through the * of Silvanus 1Pe 5:12

COURTIERS
His * replied, "Nothing!" Est 6:3

(COURTIERS Con't)
So the * replied to the king, Est 6:5
the High Priest and his * arrived Act 5:21

COURTROOM
have justice against every * lie. Is 54:17
And he drove them out of the * Act 18:16
and beat him outside the *. Act 18:17
had arrived at the * with great Act 25:23

COURTS
No one sentenced by the * to die Lev 27:29
built in the two * of the Temple; 2Ki 23:12
the doors of these * with bronze. 2Ch 4:9
Jehoshaphat set up * in 2Ch 19:8
stay in the outer * of the Temple, 2Ch 23:5,6
altars in both * of the Temple of 2Ch 33:4,5
you within the holy tabernacle *! Ps 65:4
Literally, "enter his *." Ps 96:8f
enter his * with praise. Ps 100:4
Here in the * of the Temple in Ps 116:18,19
him as they stand in his Temple *. Ps 135:1
judges in their *, and to everyone Pro 1:21
and even the police * are corrupt. Ecc 3:16
use to oppress the poor in the *. Is 32:7
Our * oppose the righteous man; Is 59:14
Within the Temple * you Is 62:9
Fill its * with the bodies of Eze 9:7
remodel your * into true halls of Amo 5:15
given in the *, for the wicked far Hab 1:4
You will be dragged before the *, Mk 13:9
against them, the * are currently Act 19:38
who witness in our *, and so surely 1Jn 5:9

COURTYARD
"Then make a * for the Ex 27:9,10
Then he constructed the *. Ex 38:9
Then make the * around the Ex 40:8
at the entrance to the *. Ex 40:8
yeast in the * of the Tabernacle. Lev 6:16
eat it in the * of the Tabernacle. Lev 6:26
surrounding the *, the screen at Num 3:25-30
entrance of the * surrounding the Num 3:25-30
the posts around the * and their Num 3:36,37
covering the * fence, and the Num 4:26
entrance to the * that surrounds Num 4:26
the frames for the * fence with Num 4:32
surrounded a * behind this hall. 1Ki 7:8
So before Isaiah had left the *, 2Ki 20:4
in the * of the palace garden. Est 1:5
It stands in Haman's *." Est 7:9
* and come near to the Living God. Ps 84:2
and came to the * of the High Mt 26:58
was sitting in the * a girl came Mt 26:69
By sunset the * was filled with Mk 1:32,33
Peter was below in the *. Mk 14:66,67
walked over to the edge of the *. Mk 14:68
The soldiers lit a fire in the * Lk 22:55
And Peter walked out of the *, Lk 22:62
permitted into the * along with Jn 18:15

COURTYARDS
or in their *, or in the court of Neh 8:16

COUSIN
And because she was his *—the Gen 29:10
He explained about being her * Gen 29:12,13
Basemath (his * Gen 36:2,3
his * Abner, his uncle Ner's son. 1Sa 14:50,51
crafty friend—his * Jonadab (the 2Sa 13:3
(Amasa was Joab's second *; 2Sa 17:25
Rehoboam married his * 2Ch 11:18
a beautiful and lovely young *, Est 2:7
he was her * and foster father. Est 8:1
to Jeremiah: Your * Hanamel (son of Jer 32:6,7
the presence of my * Hanamel and Jer 32:12

COUSINS
Bethuel, and marry one of your * Gen 28:2
Elzaphon, Aaron's *, the sons of Lev 10:4
to their *, the sons of Kish. 1Ch 23:22

COVENANT
So that day Jehovah made this * Gen 15:18
that you and they accept this *. Gen 17:11
participants in my everlasting *. Gen 17:13
and I will sign my * with him Gen 17:19
the place where they made their *. Gen 21:31
the Eternal God [to witness the * Gen 21:33
And I entered into a solemn * Ex 6:4
"You must make no * with them, Ex 23:32
Book of the *—containing God's Ex 24:7
and seals the * the Lord has made Ex 24:8
the * between me and you forever; Ex 31:12,13
This law is a perpetual * and Ex 31:16
It is an eternal symbol of the * Ex 31:17
my * with you and with Israel." Ex 34:27
wrote out the *—the Ten Ex 34:28
the salt is a reminder of God's *. Lev 2:13
* with the people of Israel. Lev 24:5-8
you, and fulfill my * with you. Lev 26:9
my * by bringing war against you. Lev 26:25
them and my * with them, for I am Lev 26:44
And God will be reminded of his * Num 10:10
Literally, "a * of salt." Num 18:19f
land violates your * with God by Deu 17:2,3
Moses restated the * which the Lord Deu 29:1
the terms of this * so that you Deu 29:9
Literally, "the Ark of the * of Jos 3:2,3,4f
has violated the * of the Lord and Jos 7:15
So Joshua made a * with them that Jos 24:25
never break my * with you, if you, Ju 2:1
So Jonathan made a * with the 1Sa 20:16
the Ark of the * of God and set it 2Sa 15:24
An everlasting * with me; 2Sa 23:5
the Ark of the * of the Lord, he 1Ki 3:15
of the * of the Lord was placed. 1Ki 6:19
of the Ark of the * of the Lord 1Ki 8:1
the Lord made his * with the people 1Ki 8:9
which contains the * made by the 1Ki 8:21
have broken their * with you and 1Ki 19:10
* and have torn down your altars; 1Ki 19:14
They rejected his laws and the * 2Ki 17:15
forget the * I made with you; 2Ki 17:38
transgressed his * and disobeyed 2Ki 18:12
their God in The Book of the *. 2Ki 23:21
Remember his * forever— 1Ch 16:15
the Ark of the * of the Lord." 1Ch 16:37f
* of God is out there in a tent!" 1Ch 17:1
the Ark of the * of the Lord could 1Ch 28:2
over the Ark of the * of the Lord. 1Ch 28:18
the Lord made a * with the people 2Ch 5:10
And in the Ark is the * between 2Ch 6:11
All were happy for this * with 2Ch 15:15
for he had made a * with David 2Ch 21:7
"But now I want to make a * with 2Ch 29:10
scroll to them—the * of God that 2Ch 34:30
priests put our names to this *." Neh 9:38
THE governor, signed the *. Neh 10:1
"I MADE A * with my eyes not to Job 31:1
We have not violated your *. Ps 44:17
Literally, "who made a * with me Ps 50:5f
my * with him will never end. Ps 89:28
No, I will not break my *; Ps 89:34
Have you renounced your * with Ps 89:39
to his * and remember to obey him! Ps 103:17,18
his promise, his * with Abraham and Ps 105:8,9
confirmation of my * with them. Is 42:6
Or, "You will be my * with all Is 42:6f
an everlasting * with you, to give Is 55:3
* with David, here remembered. Is 55:3f
have accepted his * and promises, Is 56:6
make an everlasting * with them. Is 61:8
you possessed the Ark of God's *. Jer 3:16
Some versions read, "a * they Jer 31:32f
And I will make an everlasting * Jer 32:40
If you can break my * with the Jer 33:20,21
only then will my * with David, my Jer 33:20,21
and my * with the Levite priests, Jer 33:20,21
I made a * with your fathers long Jer 34:13
I signed a * with you, and you Eze 16:8
I will establish an everlasting * Eze 16:59,60
act, for you did not keep my *. Eze 16:61
I will reaffirm my * with you, Eze 16:62
Nebuchadnezzar made a * with a Eze 17:12,13
and whose * he despised and broke. Eze 17:16
And I will make a * of peace Eze 37:26
Thus you have broken my * in Eze 44:7
But like Adam, you broke my *; Hos 6:7
pit because of the * I made with Zec 9:11
You have distorted the * of Levi, Mal 2:8
violating the * of our fathers! Mal 2:10
May the Lord cut off from his * Mal 2:12
is my blood, sealing the New *. Mt 26:28
"This is my blood of the *." Mk 14:24f
manuscripts read, "new *." Mk 14:24f
Literally, "This cup is the new * Lk 22:20f
as evidence of the * between God Act 7:8
the ark of the *, completely Heb 9:4
ark of his * could be seen inside. Rev 11:19

COVENANTS
for "goodness" in making *. Lev 2:13f

COVER
to * themselves around the hips. Gen 3:7
I am going to * the earth with a Gen 6:17
their father to * his nakedness as Gen 9:23
They will * the land from east to Gen 28:14
If you refuse, tomorrow I will * Ex 10:4,5
locusts—they will * the land and Ex 10:12
a well and doesn't * it, and an ox Ex 21:33
of the rock and * you with my hand Ex 33:22
wild disarray, and * his upper lip Lev 13:45
of incense will * the mercy place Lev 16:13
out the blood and * it with dust, Lev 17:13
the veil and * the Ark with it. Num 4:5
Then they will * the veil with Num 4:6
goatskin leather, * the goatskins Num 4:6
"Next they must * with a blue Num 4:9
the gold altar, * it with a Num 4:11
containers—and a * of goatskin Num 4:14
sheet of metal to * the altar, to Num 16:39
Egypt, and they * the face of the Num 22:5,6
the spade and * the excrement. Deu 23:13
The Lord will * you with boils Deu 28:35
then go and lift the * off his Ru 3:4
* the bases of the two capitals; 1Ki 7:41-46
Under * of night he broke through 2Ki 8:21
of money could begin to *." Est 7:4
covered all over as wings * doves! Ps 68:11,12,13
His people must destroy them. * Ps 68:23
Destroy them! * them with Ps 71:13
would never again * the earth. Ps 104:9
brag about it—* your mouth with Pro 30:32
Shame will * you, and you will Is 1:29
grew, for thorns will * them; Is 7:25
the blankets are too narrow to * Is 28:20
of a flood to * the earth and Is 54:9
as night shall * all the peoples of Is 60:2
in despair, and * your face with Jer 2:37
and * their heads in grief. Jer 14:3
that it will * the earth like a Jer 46:8
allowance to * his daily needs Jer 52:34
and horror and shame shall * you; Eze 7:18
for it—and * it with whitewash! Eze 13:10
Why did you whitewash it and * up Eze 13:12
I gave you—to * your idols! Eze 16:18
you will * your mouth in silence Eze 16:63
she does not even try to * it. Eze 24:7
the slain shall * the ground. Eze 30:4
and * the ground with the slain. Eze 30:11
a dark cloud will * her, and her Eze 30:18
And I will * the hills with your Eze 32:5
I will * the sun with a cloud, Eze 32:7
on you and * you with skin. Eze 37:6
storm and * the land like a cloud. Eze 38:9
and * the land like a cloud. Eze 38:15,16
I gave her to * her nakedness—I Hos 1:9
darkness will * you, with never a Mic 3:6
Then at last you will * your Mic 3:7
I will * you with filth and show Nah 3:6
Suddenly the heavy lead * on the Zec 5:7
Yet you * the altar with your Mal 2:13
You will find a coin to * the Mt 17:26,27
homes and then, to * up the kind of Mk 12:40
are sacrificed to * the sins of the Heb 5:1
priests did, to * over first their Heb 7:27
golden *, called the mercy seat. Heb 9:5
offering to God to * his own Heb 9:7

COVERED
until finally the water * all Gen 7:19
And the water * the earth 150 Gen 7:24
So she * her face with her veil. Gen 24:65
The first was born so * with Gen 25:25
But a heavy stone * the mouth of Gen 29:2
clothing and * herself with a veil Gen 38:14
(Moses * his face with his Ex 3:6
Aaron did, and frogs * the Ex 8:6
frogs * the countryside and filled Ex 8:13
the ground will be * with them. Ex 8:21
And the locusts * the land of Ex 10:14
For the locusts * the face of Ex 10:15
The water * the path and the Ex 14:28
with his wind, and the sea * them. Ex 15:10
quail arrived and * the camp, and Ex 16:13
Sinai was * with smoke because Ex 19:18
Sinai and the cloud * it six Ex 24:16
Then the cloud * the Tabernacle Ex 40:34
shall then be * with goatskin Num 4:10
in a blue cloth, * with goatskin Num 4:12
shall be * with a purple cloth. Num 4:13
They brought six * wagons, each Num 7:3
was raised, the Cloud * it; Num 9:15
Or, "The ground was * with them, Num 11:31f
and chariots, * the landscape Jos 11:4
tent and she * him with a blanket. Ju 4:18
So she gave him some milk and * Ju 4:19
but the ground was * with dew! Ju 6:40
and put it in his bed, and * it 1Sa 19:13
His head was * and his feet were 2Sa 15:30
who were with him * their heads and 2Sa 15:30
The king * his face with his 2Sa 19:4
a porch in front * by a canopy 1Ki 7:6
feet wide. A * porch ran along the 2Ch 3:4
by the reeds, * by their shade Job 40:22
His belly is * with scales as Job 41:30
What joys when sins are * over! Ps 32:1
* all over as wings cover doves! Ps 68:11,12,13
how the frogs had * all of Egypt! Ps 78:45
The mountains were * with our Ps 80:10
your people—yes, * over each one, Ps 85:2
Then the water returned and * Ps 106:11
The good man is * with blessings Pro 10:6
with thorns, and * with weeds; Pro 24:30,31
in the night and am * with dew.' Sol 5:2
weak and faint, * with bruises and Is 1:5,6
they are * with the blood of your Is 1:15
With two of their wings they * Is 6:2
with two others they * their Is 6:2
it lies in an open grave, * with Is 14:19
Their tables are * with vomit; Is 28:8
means—an altar * with blood. Is 29:2
the ground will be * with fire. Is 34:9
into deserts, * with dying fish. Is 50:2
she is * by its waves. Jer 51:42
the streets, * with blood, defiling Lam 4:14
and the other pair * his body. Eze 1:11
The walls were * with pictures of Eze 8:10
Each of the four wheels was * Eze 10:9-13
and saw you there, * with your own Eze 16:6,7
you were naked and * with blood. Eze 16:22

(COVERED Con't)
turn of being * with shame, but Eze 36:7
bones, and skin * them, but the Eze 37:8
mountain that * the whole earth. Dan 2:35
* by your wild and stormy waves. Jon 2:3
The ground * with thistles Mt 13:22
was * with darkness for three Mt 27:45
words, a cloud * them, blotting out Mk 9:7
has * my feet with rare perfume. Lk 7:46
Now they woke up and saw Jesus * Lk 9:32
and terror gripped them as it * Lk 9:34
Pool, with five * platforms or Jn 5:2
the swath that had * Jesus' head Jn 20:7
the younger men * him with a sheet Act 5:6
us that women's heads should be *? 1Co 11:14,15
and minds are * by a thick veil, 2Co 3:14
stand before him * with his love. Eph 1:4
* on all sides with pure gold. Heb 9:4
and goats merely * over the sins, Heb 10:4f
sin is not * by Christ's death; Heb 10:26
of their wings were * with eyes. Rev 4:8

COVERING
floods prevailed, * the ground and Gen 7:17
* the Egyptians and their animals. Ex 8:17
The drapery * the entrance to the Ex 38:18
layers of * for the roof and Ex 39:33-40
backbone, the fat * the internal Lev 3:9,10,11
He took all the fat * the Lev 8:15,16
tails and the fat * the inner Lev 9:19
linen or woolen *, or leather Lev 13:52
drapes, the drapes * the fence Num 3:25-30
and finally a * of goatskin leather Num 4:8
cover it with a * of goatskin Num 4:11
carry the drapes * the courtyard Num 4:26
into a sheet as a * for the altar, Num 16:38
He will blight your crops, * them Deu 28:22
the * off his feet and lay there. Ru 3:6,7
Latticework * the bases of the 1Ki 7:41-46
the cold, without clothing or *. Job 24:7
* the entire land from the Ps 80:11
of waters * up the mountains. Ps 104:6
of fire at night, * the Glorious Is 4:5
and * yourselves with ashes? Is 58:5
and each had two wings * his body. Eze 1:23
with their shields * them and Eze 32:27
an elevated site, * the area all Zec 14:10
* it up to keep it from shining? Lk 8:16
the huge stone * the entrance had Lk 24:2
without a * on her head dishonors 1Co 11:5
husband [for her * is a sign of her 1Co 11:5
to wear a head *, then she should 1Co 11:6
shaved, then she should wear a *. 1Co 11:6
So a woman should wear a * on 1Co 11:10
pray in public without * her head? 1Co 11:13
should wear a * when prophesying or 1Co 11:16

COVERINGS
The Tabernacle tent, and its *, Ex 35:10-19
Then he spread the * over the Ex 40:19
Tabernacle: its *, its entry Num 3:25-30
itself with its *, the goatskin Num 4:25

COVERS
The water * them. Ex 15:5
Then take all the fat that * the Ex 29:13
and the fat that * the insides, Ex 29:22
Lord the fat that * the inward Lev 3:3,4,5
the fat which * the insides, the Lev 3:14
tail, the fat that * the insides, Lev 7:3
him as the soft earth * him. Job 21:33
by harps. He * the heavens with Ps 147:8
pretty glaze * a common clay pot. Pro 26:23
of desolation * all the land. Jer 4:27
* the land. Joe 1:6
What a mighty army! It * the Joe 2:2

COVERTS
caves, thickets, *, among the 1Sa 13:6

COVET
Don't * his riches. Pro 24:19,20

COW
either a bull or a *, but the Lev 3:1
* sacrificed as a thank-offering. Lev 4:10
day, whether she is a * or ewe. Lev 22:28
to have a * and two sheep left. Is 7:21,22
* dung instead of human dung." Eze 4:15
grass like a *, your back wet with Dan 4:25
"If your * falls into a pit, Lk 14:5

COWARDS
be my son. But * who turn back Rev 21:8

COWERING
as weak as women, * in fear beneath Is 19:16

COWS
their colts,40 *,10 bulls,20 female Gen 32:13,14,15
seven sleek, fat * came up out of Gen 41:2
Then seven other * came up from Gen 41:3
over and stood beside the fat *. Gen 41:3
Then the skinny * ate the fat Gen 41:4
healthy-looking * came up out of Gen 41:18
But then seven other * came up Gen 41:19
The seven fat * (and also the Gen 41:26
The seven skinny * (and also the Gen 41:27
"However, the firstborn of *, Num 18:17
hitch to it two * that have just 1Sa 6:7
just had calves—* that never before 1Sa 6:7
the * go wherever they want to. 1Sa 6:8
Two fresh * were hitched to the 1Sa 6:10
And sure enough, the * went 1Sa 6:12
and killed the * and sacrificed 1Sa 6:14
The * will graze among bears; Is 11:7
lions will eat grass like the *. Is 11:7
up with grass, * grazing through Is 27:10
with ample pastures for your *. Is 30:23
and are fat as * that feed in lush Jer 50:11
eat grass like the * for seven Dan 4:32
*, and his body was wet with dew; Dan 4:33
he ate grass like the * and his Dan 5:21
LISTEN TO ME, you "fat *" of Amo 4:1
the ashes of young * could cleanse Heb 9:13

COYNESS
Don't let their * seduce you. Pro 6:25

COZBI
The girl's name was *, daughter Num 25:15
just seen by the death of *." Num 25:18

COZEBA
The clans of *, 1Ch 4:21-22

CRABBY
with a * woman in a lovely home. Pro 21:9

CRACK
At the same moment a wide * 1Ki 13:5
Hear the * of the whips as the Nah 3:2

CRACKED
new, but now they are old and *; Jos 9:13
The ground is parched and * for Jer 14:4
on you but, like a * staff, you Eze 29:7

CRACKLED
thunder rolled and * in the sky. Ps 77:17

CRACKS
which grows in * in the wall. 1Ki 4:33
as full of * as a leafy booth! Job 27:18
* there may yet be in your faith. 1Th 3:10

CRAFT
and trim harbor *—all shall be Is 2:16

CRAFTIEST
THE SERPENT WAS the * of all the Gen 3:1

CRAFTILY
They are the kind who * sneak 2Ti 3:6

CRAFTINESS
They are full of * and plot Ps 83:3

CRAFTS
* we will be needing in the work. Ex 35:35

CRAFTS-MAN
"I am sending you a master *—my 2Ch 2:13

CRAFTSMAN
was the master *, assisted by Ex 38:22
he too was a skilled * and also Ex 38:23
he was a skilled * in bronze work. 1Ki 7:13
the inhabitants of * Valley (called 1Ch 4:14
This skillful *, Huramabi, made 2Ch 4:12-16

CRAFTSMANSHIP
are a marvelous display of his *. Ps 19:1

CRAFTSMEN
who are skilled * having special Ex 35:10-19
"ALL THE OTHER * with God-given Ex 36:1
of the soldiers, *, and smiths. 2Ki 24:14
and one thousand * and smiths, all 2Ki 24:16
that because many * lived there). 1Ch 4:14
carpenters and * of every kind. 1Ch 22:15
"So send me skilled *—goldsmiths 2Ch 2:7
to work beside the * of Judah and 2Ch 2:7
He will work with your * and 2Ch 2:14
Lod, Ono (the Valley of the *). Neh 11:31-35
the work of the most skilled of *. Sol 7:1
officers and * had been deported to Jer 29:1
Wise old * from Gebal do the Eze 27:9
who employed many * to manufacture Act 19:24
If Demetrius and the * have a Act 19:38

CRAFTY
for I know that he is very *. 1Sa 23:22
But Amnon had a very * 2Sa 13:3
"He frustrates the plans of * Job 5:12
But no, my people are like * Hos 12:7

CRAG
and Seneh. The * on the north was 1Sa 14:5

CRAGS
between two rocky * which had been 1Sa 14:4
of a mountain goat upon the *. Ps 18:33
mountain goats on inaccessible *. Jer 16:16
* of Mount Hermon never run dry. Jer 18:14

CRAMMED
an evil man's mind is * with Pro 12:5
full of lies, * with plunder. Nah 3:1

CRANE
and the *, and the swallow. Jer 8:7

CRANKY
home with a *, quarrelsome woman. Pro 25:24
day and a * woman are much alike! Pro 27:15

CRANNY
Every nook and * will be Ob 1:6
nook and * until she finds it? Lk 15:8

CRASH
their enemies will * through Hos 11:6
it will fall with a mighty *." Mt 7:27

CRASHED
And the temple * down upon the Ju 16:30
and the descendants of Asaph * Ez 3:10
and thunder * and rumbled, Rev 8:5
the seven thunders * their reply. Rev 10:3
Lightning flashed and thunder * Rev 11:19
Then the thunder * and rolled, Rev 16:18

CRASHES
roof * down upon the people below. Amo 9:1

CRASHING
and I brought the sea * in upon Jos 24:7
and trumpets, the * of cymbals, and 1Ch 15:28
its walls come * down. Is 26:5
in one moment it comes * down. Is 30:13
from * to the pavement below!" Lk 4:9,10,11
a hundred oceans * on the shore, or Rev 19:6

CRATES
into * and throws the others away. Mt 13:47,48

CRAVING
forever * more: no, three things! Pro 30:15,16

CRAWL
your feet or * upon the ground: Lev 11:29,30
"Animals that * shall not be Lev 11:41,42
things that * upon the earth. Lev 11:44
* into the caves in the rocks and Is 2:10
his enemies will * with fear into Is 2:19
and bats, and * into the caverns Is 2:21
Babies will * safely among Is 11:8

CRAWLED
Then the two men * out of the 2Sa 17:21

CRAWLING
you live, * along on your belly. Gen 3:14
that have legs. No * thing with Lev 11:41,42
* in the dust. Deu 32:24
The Israelis are * out of their 1Sa 14:11
lowly as worms * from their holes. Mic 7:17

CRAWLS
in the water or * upon the ground. Lev 11:46
How a serpent * upon a rock. Pro 30:18,19

CRAZE
evil desires—the * for sex, the 1Jn 2:16

CRAZED
from it and reel, * by the death Jer 25:16

CRAZY
"Are you *?" 1Ki 2:22
"What did that * fellow want? 2Ki 9:11
"The prophets are *"; Hos 9:7
food, and you say, 'He's *.' Mt 11:18
and you said, 'He must be *!' Lk 7:33
"He has a demon or else is *. Jn 10:20
he is likely to think you are *. 1Co 14:23
Then have you gone completely *? Gal 3:3

CREAM
As the churning of * yields Pro 30:33
Yes, honey and * are under your Sol 4:11
the streets! The * of our Lam 4:2

CREATE
He will be able to * beautiful Ex 35:32
from your sight. * in me a new, Ps 51:10
* rivers for them in the desert! Is 43:19

CREATED
Or, "In the beginning God * Gen 1:1f
So God * great sea creatures, Gen 1:21,22
son, Cain (meaning "I have *"). Gen 4:1
God's help, I have * a man!" Gen 4:1
his creation. God * man and woman Gen 5:2
the sense of his *, supernatural Gen 6:1f
of the earth all mankind that I *. Gen 6:7
the time when God * man upon the Deu 4:32
Has he not * you? Deu 32:6
You * the heavens and the earth. 2Ki 19:15
made my servant too. He * us both. Job 31:15
before it was all *, and you are so Job 38:21
everything—for you * them all. Ps 89:11
them all. You * north and south! Ps 89:12
Before the mountains were *, Ps 90:2
And a people that shall be * Ps 102:18
Literally, "*." Ps 104:30f
generation, like the earth you *; Ps 119:90,91
before he * anything else. Pro 8:22
I lived before the oceans were * Pro 8:24
I was with what he *—his wide world Pro 8:31
Who but God has * the world? Pro 30:4
In that day he who * the royal Is 11:10
Look up into the heavens! Who * Is 40:26
The Lord God who * the heavens Is 42:5
them out and * the earth and Is 42:5
BUT NOW THE Lord who * you, O Is 43:1
made them for my glory; I * them. Is 43:7
I, Jehovah, * them. Is 45:8
I have made the earth and * man Is 45:12
For Jehovah * the heavens and Is 45:18
I have * you and cared for you Is 46:3
I have * the smith who blows the Is 54:16
And I have * the armies that Is 54:16
to you on the day you were *. Eze 28:13
the day you were * until that time Eze 28:15
Seek him who * the Seven Stars Amo 5:8
Abraham, all * by the same God. Mal 2:10
the beginning God * man and woman, Mt 19:4
himself God. He * everything Jn 1:3
need there is. He * all the people Act 17:26
God, the Father, who * all things 1Co 8:6

(CREATED Con't)
who * this new life within you. Col 3:10
power, for you have * all things. Rev 4:11
They were * and called into being Rev 4:11
and ever, who * heaven and Rev 10:6

CREATING
WHEN GOD BEGAN * Gen 1:1
For see, I am * new heavens and Is 65:17

CREATION
day when he ceased this work of *. Gen 2:3
the events in the * of the heavens Gen 2:4
God from the day of his *. Gen 5:1
among all of God's *, so let Job 40:19
Lord showed his control of all *. Ps 29:10
rejoice forever in my *. Is 65:18
God's *, nor will ever be again. Mk 13:19
the Messiah, who is Lord of all *. Act 10:36,37
For all * is waiting patiently Rom 8:19
Literally, "The whole * has been Rom 8:22f
"he is the firstborn of all *." Col 1:15f
the seventh day of *, having Heb 4:4
work, just as God did after the *. Heb 4:10
it was since the first day of *." 2Pe 3:4
the primeval source of God's *: Rev 3:14

CREATOR
the supreme God, * of heaven and Gen 14:19,20
the supreme God, * of heaven and Gen 14:22
More pure than his *?' Job 4:17
cause you to forget about your *. Ecc 12:1
Yes, remember your * now while Ecc 12:6
think of God their * and have Is 17:7
God, the * of the farthest parts of Is 40:28
Holy One, Israel's * and King. Is 43:15
to the man who fights with his *. Is 45:9
Israel, Israel's *, says: What Is 45:11
your * will be your "husband." Is 54:5
He is the * of all, and Israel is Jer 10:16
Almighty God his * that he would Jer 38:16
"O Lord, * of heaven and earth Act 4:24
and women come from God their *. 1Co 11:12
himself is the * who made Col 1:16
us from God, the * of all light, Jas 1:17

CREATURE
I'll repeat it again—any water * Lev 11:12
Literally, "every *." Lev 17:14f
that not a living * will remain, Jer 51:61,62
* rising up out of the sea. Rev 13:1
This * looked like a leopard but Rev 13:2
miracle and followed the * in awe. Rev 13:3
and they worshiped the strange *. Rev 13:4
Then the Dragon encouraged the * Rev 13:5
Book of Life—worshiped the evil *. Rev 13:8
authority of the * whose Rev 13:12
first * was there to watch him. Rev 13:14
of the first *, who was fatally Rev 13:14
* or the code number of his name. Rev 13:17
worshiping the * from the sea Rev 14:9
have worshiped the * and his Rev 14:11
over the Evil * and his statue and Rev 15:2
* and was worshiping his statue. Rev 16:2
the throne of the * from the sea, Rev 16:10
the *, and his False Prophet. Rev 16:13
The Dragon—Satan—and the * from Rev 17:3f
Then I saw the Evil * gathering Rev 19:19
And the Evil * was captured, and Rev 19:20
when the Evil * was Rev 19:20
Both of them—the Evil * and his Rev 19:20
not worshiped the * or his statue, Rev 20:4
sulphur where the * and False Rev 20:10

CREATURE'S
accepted the Evil * mark, and who Rev 19:20

CREATURES
So God created great sea *, Gen 1:21,22
all the * the Lord God had made. Gen 3:1
but all other water * are Lev 11:10
earth, you * of the ocean depths. Ps 148:7
will be haunted by howling *. Is 13:21
and deeded it to those doleful *; Is 34:17
and hideous *, besides all the Eze 8:10
my life eaten such *, for they are Act 10:14
we are the most miserable of *. 1Co 15:19

CREDIT
there will be no * to the one who Lev 7:17,18
to the Lord as a * for your Ju 17:3
"They * David with ten thousands 1Sa 18:8
* for the victory instead of me." 2Sa 12:28
well before you vouch for his *! Pro 11:15
This is to his *. Pro 19:11
The world's poorest * risk is the Pro 27:13
hearts they give no * to you. Jer 12:2
"Do you think you deserve * for Lk 6:32
isn't any special * to me—I 1Co 9:16
trying to claim * for the work 2Co 10:15
none of us can take any * for it. Eph 2:9
Of course, you get no * for 1Pe 2:20

CREDITED
It shall be * to you just as Num 18:30

CREDITING
* Mordecai with the information. Est 2:22

CREDITOR
Every * shall write "Paid in Deu 15:2
now the * was demanding it back. 2Ki 4:1
I am neither a * soon to Jer 15:10
and is a merciful *, not holding Eze 18:7
"But his * wouldn't wait. Mt 18:30

CREDITORS
their home. May * seize his entire Ps 109:11
LORD ASKS, Did I sell you to my *? Is 50:1

CREEKS
for them. The * are dry and the Joe 1:20

CREEPING
and, quietly * up to him as he Ju 4:21
Are we but * things that have no Hab 1:14

CREEPS
And as you sleep, poverty * upon Pro 6:11

CREMATED
them to Jabesh, where they * them. 1Sa 31:12

CREPT
So he took Purah and * down Ju 7:11
Gideon * up to one of the tents Ju 7:12,13
men with him * to the outer edge of Ju 7:19,20
Then David * forward and 1Sa 24:4
The entire army * back into the 2Sa 19:3
For death has * in through your Jer 9:21

CRESCENS
to Thessalonica. * has gone to 2Ti 4:10

CRESCENTS
not including the * and pendants or Ju 8:26

CRETANS
Literally, "Cherethites (or *)." Zep 2:5f
Jewish converts— *, and Arabians. Act 2:11

CRETE
to *, passing the port of Salmone. Act 27:7,8
on the island of * so that you Tit 1:5
a prophet from *, has said about Tit 1:12
"These men of * are all liars; Tit 1:12

CREW
They organized a huge work * to 2Ch 32:4
* led by Zaccur (son of Imri). Neh 3:2
I will call for a wrecking * to Jer 22:7
won't take a big * or a lot of Eze 17:9
all your * have perished with you. Eze 27:34
Then the * decided to draw straws Jon 1:7
winter—most of the * advised trying Act 27:12
grew higher, the * began throwing Act 27:18
Paul called the * together and Act 27:21
After eating, the * lightened Act 27:38

CREWS
sailors to accompany Solomon's *. 1Ki 9:27,28
experienced * working alongside 2Ch 8:17,18
King Hiram's and King Solomon's * 2Ch 9:10
merchant ships and * will stand a Rev 18:17

CRIB
he stay beside your feeding *? Job 39:9

CRICKETS
*, and grasshoppers—may be eaten. Lev 11:21,22

CRIED
"Out, all of you," he * out to Gen 45:1
the message, he broke down and *. Gen 50:16,17
* out to the Lord to help them. Ex 14:10
But, tormented by thirst, they * Ex 17:3
forward, Moses * out, "Arise, O Num 10:35
had happened, he * out to Moses, Num 12:11
And Moses * out to the Lord, Num 12:13
But when we * to the Lord he Num 20:16
came to Moses and * out, "We have Num 21:7
us and we * to the Lord God. Deu 26:6,7
Joshua * out to the Lord, "O Jos 7:7
Then Israel * out to me and I Jos 24:7
But when Israel * out to the Ju 3:9
But when they * to the Lord, he Ju 3:15
of the Lord, he * out, "Alas, O Ju 6:22
a time when you * out to me that I Ju 10:12
"Alas, my daughter!" he * out. Ju 11:35
"We will die," Manoah * out to Ju 13:22
So she * whenever she was with Ju 14:17
"O Lord God of Israel," they * Ju 21:3
and they all broke down and *. Ru 1:9
And again they * together, and Ru 1:14
Naomi * excitedly. Ru 2:20
they * out. 1Sa 4:7
saw it coming they * out, "They 1Sa 5:10
they * out. 1Sa 6:20
were in Egypt and * out to the 1Sa 12:8
"Then they * to the Lord again 1Sa 12:10
they * out to Samuel. 1Sa 12:19
that he * to the Lord all night. 1Sa 15:11
When he saw me he * out for me 2Sa 1:7
"Oh, Amnon," she *. 2Sa 13:12
she *. 2Sa 13:16
front of him, and * out, "O king! 2Sa 14:4
Then Ahima-az * out to the king, 2Sa 18:28
They * to God, 2Sa 22:42
very much, * out, "Oh, no, sir! 1Ki 3:26
of Jehovah and * out this blessing 1Ki 8:54,55
please," the king * out to the 1Ki 13:6
"O man of God," she *, "what 1Ki 17:18
his bed, and then * out to the 1Ki 17:20
three times, and * out to the Lord, 1Ki 17:21
Elisha saw it and * out, "My 2Ki 2:12
Lord God of Elijah?" he * out. 2Ki 2:13,14
the king of Israel * out. 2Ki 3:10
a bite or two they * out, "Oh, 2Ki 4:40
"Oh, sir," he *, "it was 2Ki 6:5
we do now?" he * out to Elisha. 2Ki 6:15
to attack us," they * out. 2Ki 7:6
he *. 2Ki 13:14
Then he broke down and *. 2Ki 20:3
They * out to God to help them, 1Ch 5:20
He * out to his bodyguard, 1Ch 10:4
Then they * out to the Lord for 2Ch 13:13,14
"O Lord," he * out to God, "no 2Ch 14:11
But Jehoshaphat * out to the Lord 2Ch 18:31
(son of Amoz) * out in prayer to 2Ch 32:20
and * out humbly to God for help. 2Ch 33:12
* out, "O my God, I am ashamed; Ez 9:6
gathered around and * with me. Ez 10:1
I heard this, I sat down and *. Neh 1:4
"O Lord God," I * out; Neh 1:5
of trouble they * to you and you Neh 9:27
to you and * to you for help, once Neh 9:28
impulsively * out in desperation? Job 6:25,26
I * out to the Lord, and he heard Ps 3:4
rescue them; they * to the Lord, Ps 18:41
When I * to him, he heard and Ps 22:24
I * to you, O Lord; Ps 30:8
For I * to him and he answered Ps 34:4
This poor man * to the Lord—and Ps 34:6
did for me: For I * to him for Ps 66:17
He said, "You * to me in Ps 81:7
his prophet, * to him for help, he Ps 99:6
But I * to him, "O God, you Ps 102:24
they *, and he did! Ps 107:6
Then they * to the Lord in their Ps 107:13
Then they * to the Lord in their Ps 107:19
Then I *, "Lord, save me!" Ps 116:4
'O God,' I *, 'I am in Is 38:14
of Egypt and they * out, "Where is Is 63:11
I have * until the tears no Lam 2:11
my face and * out: "O Lord God! Eze 9:8
on my face and * out: "O Lord God, Eze 11:13
"In my great trouble I * to the Jon 2:2
The mighty deep * out, announcing Hab 3:10
when they * to me, I turned away. Zec 7:13
Isaiah the prophet * out Rom 9:27
you honestly that I * over it. 2Co 2:4
* to the mountains to crush them. Rev 6:16

CRIER
O * of Good News, shout to Is 40:9

CRIES
Then God answered the lad's *, Gen 21:17
For God has heard the lad's * as Gen 21:17
He heard their * from heaven, Ex 2:23
If you don't return it, and he * Ex 22:27
and the needy man * out to the Deu 15:9
It is he who *, 'Destroy them!' Deu 33:27
with shouts and battle *. 1Sa 17:20
their * from beside the Red Sea. Neh 9:9
or * for help in his calamity. Job 30:24
Yes, he hears the * of those Job 34:28
to say he doesn't hear those *; Job 35:13
Surely you will hear their * and Ps 10:17
You heard their * for help and Ps 22:5
not despised my * of deep despair; Ps 22:24
For Jehovah hears the * of his Ps 69:33
their * and heeded their distress; Ps 106:44
he hears their * for help and Ps 145:19
she *. Pro 1:22
He who shuts his ears to the * of Pro 21:13
* of deep oppression met his ears. Is 5:7
of weeping. The * from the cities Is 15:4
birth, who * and writhes in pain. Is 26:17
will turn to * of fear. Is 43:14
you moan with mournful * like Is 59:11
and the enemies' battle *. Jer 4:19
Listen to the frantic * of the Jer 25:36
bitterly, while * of terror rise Jer 48:5
Instead the awful * of terror Jer 48:34
"O Lord," she *, "see my Lam 1:9
heedless of their babies' *. Lam 4:3,4
again your guilt * out against you, Eze 21:24
and none * out to me for help. Hos 7:7
My heart * out within me; Hos 11:8
will be turned to * of despair. Amo 8:10
Trumpet calls and battle *; Zep 1:16
Lord their God, will hear their *. Zec 10:6
in Egypt and have heard their *. Act 7:34
Hear the * of the field workers Jas 5:4
Their * have reached the ears of Jas 5:4
for more, as a baby * for milk. 1Pe 2:2,3f
cry for this as a baby * for his 1Pe 2:2,3

CRIME
Meanwhile, the * rate was rising Gen 6:11
for the earth is filled with * Gen 6:12,13
"What is my *? Gen 31:36,37
what he knows about a * is guilty. Lev 5:1
accuse your neighbor of some *, Lev 19:16
"If a man has committed a * Deu 21:22
Israel by flagrant *, being a Deu 22:21
In this way you will reduce * Deu 22:25,26,27
shall be executed for his own *. Deu 24:16
"IF A MAN is guilty of a *, and Deu 25:1
to the seriousness of the *; Deu 25:1

(CRIME Con't)
such a horrible * since Israel left Ju 19:30
men have committed a terrible *. Ju 20:6
What is my *? 1Sa 26:17,18
innocent of this * against Abner. 2Sa 3:28
You know what a serious * it is 2Sa 13:12
"To reject me now is a greater * 2Sa 13:16
"Whenever someone commits a *, 2Ch 6:22
* was on the increase everywhere. 2Ch 15:5
For a * wave has engulfed Job 24:2
For lust is a shameful sin, a * Job 31:11
for some great * before a man is Job 34:23
with its opportunities for *. Job 36:20
and innocent of some great *. Ps 19:13
lookout for opportunities of *. Ps 64:6
No * in our streets. Ps 144:12-15
like that, for * is their way of Pro 1:16
their partners in *—men who turn Pro 2:11,12,13
A wise king stamps out * by Pro 20:26
is giving way to * and even the Ecc 3:16
evil and * throughout the earth. Ecc 4:3
The land is defiled by *; Is 24:4,5
"What * have I committed? Jer 37:18
Jerusalem, city of violence and *. Zep 3:1
ever return, for * was rampant. Zec 8:10
above his head, announcing his *. Mk 15:26
That isn't a *!" Lk 23:4
"Why? What * has he committed? Lk 23:22
them, "He is not guilty of any *. Jn 18:38
involving some *, I would be Act 18:14
whips to make him confess his *. Act 22:24
Yet, O King, for me it is a *, Act 26:7
But is it a * to believe in the Act 26:8

CRIMES
they had committed their many *! Ecc 8:9,10
for the land is full of bloody *. Eze 7:23
As a sentence for your *, you Hos 4:5
committed cruel *, ripping open Amo 1:13
spectacle of all Israel's *. Amo 3:9
him of many *, and Pilate asked Mk 15:3,4
penalty for these *, yet they went Rom 1:32
is ready to judge her for her *. Rev 18:5

CRIMINAL
you were chasing a * and have Gen 31:36,37
He was buried like a * in a rich Is 53:9
"Am I some dangerous *," he Mt 26:55
notorious * in jail named Barabbas, Mt 27:16
'He will be condemned as a *!' Lk 22:37
But the other * protested. Lk 23:40,41
arrested him if he weren't a *!" Jn 18:30
have been put in jail like a *. 2Ti 2:9

CRIMINAL'S
to die a * death on a cross. Php 2:8

CRIMINALS
as * as soon as you are dead." 1Ki 1:21
Preserve me from these *, these Ps 59:2
wicked men, these gangs of *. Ps 64:1
be to ferret out * and free the Ps 101:8
* sneering at honorable men. Is 3:5
Two others, *, were led out to be Lk 23:32,33
and the two * on either side. Lk 23:32,33
One of the * hanging beside him Lk 23:39
for God to let * go free, and say Rom 3:26

CRIMSON
make purple, *, and blue cloth; 2Ch 2:7
purple and blue linen and * cloth. 2Ch 2:14
a veil of blue and * fine-spun 2Ch 3:14
*, I can make you white as wool! Is 1:18
his magnificent garments of *? Is 63:1

CRINGE
Those who hate the Lord would * Ps 81:15
the sailors * in terror. Ps 107:26

CRINGING
And so we should not be like *, Rom 8:15

CRIPPLE
deed done to the *, and how he was Act 4:9

CRIPPLED
troops. He * all the chariot teams 1Ch 18:4
had new ones; the * were walking Mt 15:31
Better to enter heaven * than to Mt 18:8
And now the blind and * came to Mt 21:14
Instead, invite the poor, the *, Lk 14:13
the beggars, *, lame, and blind. Lk 14:21
upon a man with * feet who had been Act 14:8

CRISIS
to God except in times of *. Job 27:10
and have seen the * in my soul. Ps 31:7
But during a * he will take over Dan 11:21
all around you about the * ahead. Lk 12:56

CRISP
to a * because of all your sins. Jer 4:4

CRISPUS
However, *, the leader of the Act 18:8
any of you except * and Gaius. 1Co 1:14

CRISSCROSSING
years since * the wilderness, and Jos 14:10

CRITIC
Do you—God's *—have the Job 40:2

CRITICAL
are always * and catty, watch out! Gal 5:15

CRITICISM
as to whether the * was because she Num 12:1f
If you refuse * you will end in Pro 13:18
if you accept * you are on the Pro 13:18
If you profit from constructive * Pro 15:31,32
But to reject * is to harm Pro 15:31,32
Don't refuse to accept *; Pro 23:12
badge of honor to accept valid *. Pro 25:12
refuses to accept * will suddenly Pro 29:1
that will cause * against yourself Rom 14:16
Are you yourselves above *? Jas 5:9

CRITICISMS
but your * are not based on fact. Job 6:25,26
I would spout off my * against Job 16:4
complaints and *, the feeling that Gal 5:20

CRITICIZE
Why then were you not afraid to * Num 12:7,8
chooses not to speak, who can *? Job 34:29,30
they couldn't find anything to *! Dan 6:4
"DON'T *, AND then you won't be Mt 7:1
Never * or condemn—or it will Lk 6:37
Who are you to * God? Rom 9:20
Don't * him for having different Rom 14:1
You have no right to * your Rom 14:10
So don't * each other any more. Rom 14:13
whether they * us or commend us. 2Co 6:8
one being able to * you from now Php 1:10
So don't let anyone * you for Col 2:16
anything to * in anything you say! Tit 2:8
Don't * and speak evil about each Jas 4:11
do you have to judge or * others? Jas 4:12

CRITICIZED
are * for helping me like this." 2Sa 14:9
It is better to be * by a wise Ecc 7:5
AND then you won't be *. Mt 7:1
(But after John had publicly * Lk 3:19,20

CRITICIZES
out against sin, * those committing Ps 15:4

CRITICIZING
DAY MIRIAM and Aaron were * Num 12:1
and said, "Why are you * her? Mt 26:10
[Let him do whatever * must be Jas 5:9

CROAK
the ravens will * from her doors. Zep 2:14

CROCODILE
nations, but you are merely a * Eze 32:2

CROOK
but a * will slip and fall. Pro 10:9

CROOKED
Travelers used the narrow, * side Ju 5:6
Everything they say is * and Ps 36:3
All your dealings are *: you give Ps 58:1
Like a * arrow, they missed the Ps 78:57
help me to abhor all * deals of Ps 101:3
Everything they do is * and Pro 2:15
She staggers down a * trail, and Pro 5:6
straighten out the * paths and Is 40:4
They are like a * bow that always Hos 7:16
the straightest is more * than a Mic 7:4
of people who are * and stubborn. Php 2:15

CROOKS
* are jealous of each other's Pro 12:12

CROP
There were * failures in all the Gen 41:54
amount of the best of his own *. Ex 22:5
any volunteer * that may come up; Ex 23:11
of each year's * to the Tabernacle Ex 34:26
Then the priest will remove the * Lev 1:15,16,17
It is the same with your grape * Lev 19:10
And the fourth year the entire * Lev 19:24
in the fifth year, the * is yours. Lev 19:25
wine, grain, and every other *. Num 18:13
first of the new * of grain as a Num 28:26
than the entire * of Abiezer?" Ju 8:2,3f
use it as seed for next year's *; 2Ki 19:29
or plagues, or * disease, or 2Ch 6:28
part of every * to the Neh 10:35
it be a ground * or from our fruit Neh 10:35
and the new * appears, and the Pro 27:25,26,27
when the * is stripped and robbed. Is 1:8
He expected them to yield a * of Is 5:7
will yield but a one-bushel *! Is 5:10
a wonderful, rare * of greatest Is 17:10
from then would yield a bumper *. Is 37:30f
They shall harvest a * of shame, Jer 12:13
I will abolish * failures and Eze 36:29
There will be a new * every Eze 47:12
At that time I will sow a * of Hos 1:23
and you will reap a * of my love; Hos 10:12
and raised a thriving * of sins. Hos 10:13
all the main * that sprang up after Amo 7:1
to sow another *, and the terraces Amo 9:13
*, there were only ten. Hag 2:16,17
and produced a * that was thirty, Mt 13:8
Literally, "produces a * many Mt 13:23f
When the * began to grow, the Mt 13:26
will give God his share of the *. Mt 21:43
hearts, so that no * is produced. Mk 4:19
men to collect his share of the *. Mk 12:2
this seed grew and produced a * Lk 8:8
shall produce a large * of fruit. Jn 15:5
who harvests his * and doesn't have 1Co 9:7
get only a small *, but if he 2Co 9:6
reap just the kind of * he sows! Gal 6:7
paid well if he raises a large *. 2Ti 2:6
fruit, with a fresh * each month; Rev 22:2

CROPS
No longer will it yield * for Gen 4:12
That year Isaac's * were Gen 26:12
of rain for your *, and good Gen 27:27,28,29
run smoothly, his * flourished and Gen 39:5
a fifth of all the * . . ." Gen 41:34,35f
all the excess * of the next seven Gen 41:34,35
there were bumper * everywhere. Gen 41:47
portion of all the * grown Gen 41:48
percent of all the * except those Gen 47:26
and the * were destroyed. Ex 9:25
Canaan, where there were * to eat. Ex 16:35
the tithe of your * and your wine, Ex 22:29
"Sow and reap your * for six Ex 23:10
bring to me the first of your *. Ex 23:16
"As you reap each of your *, Ex 23:19
"When you harvest your *, don't Lev 19:9
the first three *, for they are Lev 19:23
of the new grain of your later *. Lev 23:15,16
first sampling of your later *. Lev 23:17
first sampling of your later *. Lev 23:20
and harvest your *, but during the Lev 25:3
Don't sow your * and don't prune Lev 25:4
the volunteer * that come up, and Lev 25:5
for the land. Any * that do grow Lev 25:6,7
not sow, nor gather * nor grapes; Lev 25:11
* that grow wild in the fields. Lev 25:12
the number of * the new owner Lev 25:14,15,16
will yield bumper * and you can eat Lev 25:19
to plant or harvest * that year?' Lev 25:20
you with bumper * the sixth year Lev 25:21,22
last you until the * of the eighth Lev 25:21,22
will yield bumper *, and the trees Lev 26:4,5
such a surplus of * that you won't Lev 26:10
you will sow your * in vain, for Lev 26:16
its *, nor your trees their fruit. Lev 26:20
some samples of the * you see." Num 13:20
of each year's new * by making a Num 15:19,20,21
land of wonderful *—the figs, Num 20:5
will have large * of grain, grapes, Deu 7:13
produce wonderful * of grain, Deu 11:14
"You must tithe all of your * Deu 14:22
portion of your * and herds and Deu 14:25
have no property or * as you do. Deu 14:27
"Do not sow other * in the rows Deu 22:9
If you do, both the * and the Deu 22:9
the first of the * from the ground Deu 26:10
Ample *, Deu 28:2-6
you with good * and healthy cattle, Deu 28:8
many cattle, and abundant *. Deu 28:11
to give you fine * every season. Deu 28:12
Curses upon your *; Deu 28:15-19
He will blight your *, covering Deu 28:22
of will eat the * you will have Deu 28:33
for the locusts will eat your *. Deu 28:38
until your cattle and * are gone. Deu 28:51
unsown, without *, without a shred Deu 29:23
and much cattle and wonderful *; Deu 30:9
the earth and all of its *, Deu 32:22
With the finest of mountain * Deu 33:15
on they lived on the * of Canaan. Jos 5:11,12
destroyed their * and plundered the Ju 6:3,4
by giving them good * again. Ru 1:6,7
and harvest his * without pay; 1Sa 8:12
Let no * of grain grow on your 2Sa 1:21
rain, and the * grow again!" 1Ki 17:14
the value of any * that had been 2Ki 8:6
one—with plentiful *, grain, wine, 2Ki 18:31,32
eat up all of your *, or if I send 2Ch 7:13
the first of their * and grain, new 2Ch 31:5,6
best of our grain *, and other Neh 10:37
else reap the * I have sown and let Job 31:7,8
as they gaze at their bountiful *. Ps 4:7
Bless us with abundant * Ps 72:16
He gave their * to caterpillars. Ps 78:46
and it yields its bountiful *. Ps 85:12
green, destroying all the *. Ps 105:35
complete with their growing *; Ps 105:44
and reap their bumper *! Ps 107:37
Barns full to the brim with * of Ps 144:12-15
your land, your *, your people. Is 7:20
and blow away. All * will perish; Is 19:7
or cotton, for the * will fail. Is 19:9
The earth languishes, the * Is 24:4,5
For the * of fruit will fail; Is 32:10
Then once again enormous * will Is 32:15
Wherever they plant, bountiful * Is 32:20
now to plant your *, and you will Is 37:30
the Lord—the good *, the wheat and Jer 31:12
houses or plant * or vineyards and Jer 35:7
or owned farms or planted *. Jer 35:9
of wine grapes and other *. Jer 40:12
the * as vinedressers and plowmen. Jer 52:16
were desolated, their * destroyed; Eze 19:7
will yield bumper *, and everyone Eze 34:27
is, "I will give them bumper *." Eze 34:29f
There will be heavy * of fruit to Eze 36:8
prepare the ground and sow your *. Eze 36:9

CROPS Con't)
planted lush * in the wilderness. Eze 36:36
them for * and for prosperity. Hos 7:14
finish eating your *, the Joe 1:4
The fields are bare of *. Joe 1:10
And I will give you back the * Joe 2:25
I ruined your * by holding back Amo 4:7
such abundance of *, that the Amo 9:13
eat their * and drink their wine. Amo 9:14
You will plant * but not harvest Mic 6:15
though the olive * all fail, and Hab 3:17
and giving you such scant *. Hag 1:10
and all your other *, a drought to Hag 1:11
their next *: From this day I will Hag 2:18,19
among you. Your * will prosper; Zec 8:12
Your * will be large, for I will Mal 3:11
fertile farm that produced fine *. Lk 12:16
the * that others plant.' Lk 19:21
to collect his share of the *. Lk 20:10
that bear fruit for even larger *. Jn 15:2
you rain and good * and giving you Act 14:17
and later on, good * to harvest and 2Co 9:10
upon it and good * come up, that Heb 6:7
But if it keeps on having * of Heb 6:8
of Life, bearing twelve * of Rev 22:2

CROSS
that I will not * this line to Gen 31:51,52
you will not * it to attack me. Gen 31:51,52
people not to * the boundaries. Ex 19:21
" 'Now * Zered Brook,' the Lord Deu 2:13
" 'Today Israel shall * the Deu 2:18
"Then the Lord said, '* the Deu 2:24
God, please let me * over into the Deu 3:23,24,25
you, and would not let me * over. Deu 3:26
But you shall not * the Jordan Deu 3:27
Soon, now, you will * the Jordan Deu 4:26
Today you are to * the Jordan Deu 9:1
For you are to * the Jordan and Deu 11:31
But when you * the Jordan River Deu 12:10
"When you * the Jordan River and Deu 27:2,3,4
"When you * into the Promised Deu 27:12
I shall not * the Jordan River. Deu 31:2
get ready to * the Jordan River. Jos 1:10,11
camp at Acacia to * the river and Jos 2:1
but as the people set out to * Jos 3:13,14
of Israel could *, their courage Jos 5:1
permission to * through his land to Ju 11:19
Ephraim tried to * the river, the Ju 12:5
If they * the border of our land 1Sa 6:9
"Come on, let's * the valley to 1Sa 14:1
allow my people to * their 1Sa 15:2
too exhausted to *, but the other 1Sa 30:9,10
they told him, "* the Jordan 2Sa 17:21
opened up a path for them to *. Ps 114:3
of protection, and no enemy can *. Is 33:21
1,500 feet and told me to * again. Eze 47:4
It was too deep to * on foot. Eze 47:5
* to the other side of the lake. Mt 8:18
If you refuse to take up your * Mt 10:38
their boat and * to the other side Mt 14:22
and take up his * and follow me. Mt 16:24
forced him to carry Jesus' *. Mt 27:32
the * if you are the Son of God!" Mt 27:40
Come down from the * and we'll Mt 27:41,42,43
* to the other side of the lake." Mk 4:35
your *, and follow me closely. Mk 8:34
into service to carry Jesus' *. Mk 15:21
A signboard was fastened to the * Mk 15:26
and come down from the *." Mk 15:29,30
Come on down from the * and we'll Mk 15:32
beside his * saw how he dismissed Mk 15:39
body down from the *, wound it in Mk 15:46
* to the other side of the lake. Lk 8:22
and carry his * with him every day Lk 9:23
not carry his own * and follow me. Lk 14:27
and no one over there can * to Lk 16:26
to follow, carrying Jesus' *. Lk 23:26
on the center *, and the two Lk 23:32,33
A signboard was nailed to the * Lk 23:38
And when I am lifted up [on the * Jn 12:32
city, carrying his * to the place Jn 19:17
Standing near the * were Jesus' Jn 19:25
government to nail him to the * Act 2:23
killed him by hanging him on a *. Act 5:30
where he was murdered on a * Act 10:39
from the * and placed in a tomb. Act 13:29
were nailed to the * with him; Rom 6:6
as it were, with Christ on the *; Rom 7:4
simple message of the * of Christ. 1Co 1:17
*—is far stronger than any man. 1Co 1:25
Christ and his death on the *. 1Co 2:2
body died on the *, but now he 2Co 13:4
on it of Christ dying on the *. Gal 3:1
[as Jesus was hung upon a wooden * Gal 3:13
faith in the * of Christ alone. Gal 5:11
to his * and crucified them there. Gal 5:24
the * of Christ alone can save. Gal 6:12
the * of our Lord Jesus Christ. Gal 6:14
Because of that * my interest in Gal 6:14
the feud ended at last at the *. Eph 2:16
to die a criminal's death on a *. Php 2:8
death, even the death of the *." Php 2:8f
really enemies of the * of Christ. Php 3:18
death on the * has made peace with Col 1:20
the death on the * of his own human Col 1:22
it by nailing it to Christ's *. Col 2:14
triumph at the * where your sins Col 2:15
like myself is a soldier of the *. Phm 1:1
die on the * for all mankind. Heb 5:7f
work at the * could be performed. Heb 5:7f
God's perfect will at the *. . . Heb 5:7f
Son of God to the * again by Heb 6:6
he sacrificed himself on the *. Heb 7:27
Jesus Christ came to die on the *. Heb 10:4f
death on the * because of the joy Heb 12:2
We have an altar—the * where Heb 13:10
he died on the *, so that we can be 1Pe 2:24
eyes I saw Christ dying on the *; 1Pe 5:1

CROSS-EXAMINE
without wavering. * me, O Lord, Ps 26:2

CROSSED
them with her) and * the Euphrates Gen 31:21
But Israel * his arms as he Gen 48:14
* your border on the other side." Num 20:17
They * into the hills and came Deu 1:24,25
the mountain and * the river and Jos 2:23
Then all the people * at a spot Jos 3:15,16
That day the entire nation * the Jos 4:19
* the Jordan River on dry ground! Jos 4:22
in the valley, and * the tableland Jos 13:9
border of Edom, * the Wilderness of Jos 15:1
the Salt Sea, * to Beth-hoglah, Jos 15:6
valley of Hinnom, * south of the Jos 18:16
in Canaan and * the Jordan River to Jos 22:9
the priest. They * the river and Jos 22:13
"Then you * the Jordan River and Jos 24:11
Israel. They * the Jordan and Ju 6:33
Gideon now * the Jordan River Ju 8:4
For the Ammonites * the Jordan to Ju 10:9
but they never once * into Moab. Ju 11:18
Some of them * the Jordan River 1Sa 13:7
the Jordan Valley, * the river, and 2Sa 2:29
retinue passed by, * Kidron Brook, 2Sa 15:23
had * the brook and were gone. 2Sa 17:20
So all the people * the Jordan 2Sa 19:39
First they * the Jordan and 2Sa 24:5
the rebellion: he * the Jordan 2Ki 8:21
They * the Jordan River during 1Ch 12:15
all Israel, * the Jordan River, and 1Ch 19:17,18
streams that can easily be *. Is 11:15
into the boat and * to Magadan. Mt 15:39
* to the other side of the lake. Mk 8:13
lying there, he * to the other side Lk 10:31
AFTER THIS, JESUS * over the Sea Jn 6:1
AFTER SAYING THESE things Jesus * Jn 18:1

CROSSES
The sun * the heavens from end Ps 19:6
their * on either side of his. Mk 15:27

CROSSING
called the Gihon, * the entire Gen 2:13
after wave of them * the border. Ex 12:51
brothers lived, * the Arabah Road Deu 2:8
camped for a few days before *. Jos 3:1
Moab, preventing anyone from *. Ju 3:28
from Egypt after * the Red Sea, Ju 11:16
As the king was *, Shime-i fell 2Sa 19:18
at Michmash and * over the pass; Is 10:28,29
As they were *, Jesus said to Mk 8:15
the boat and left, * back to the Lk 8:37

CROSSPIECES
*. These crosspieces were 1Ki 7:27-30
These * were decorated with 1Ki 7:27-30
removed their * and the water vats 2Ki 16:17

CROSSROADS
You stood at the * and killed Ob 1:14

CROSSWISE
with a second wheel * inside. Eze 1:16
had a second wheel * within, Eze 10:9-13

CROUCH
Like lions they * silently, Ps 10:9

CROUCHED
residence and * beside a fire among Mk 14:54

CROUCHES
He * like a lion, Deu 33:20

CROW
How you pride yourselves and * Amo 4:5

CROWD
great fear swept through the *. Gen 20:8
and to the * standing around, "You Ru 4:9
wall saw a great * coming toward 2Sa 13:34
saw that a * was gathering around 2Sa 20:12
days, and a great * came from one 1Ki 8:65
* that had gathered around them. 2Ki 10:9,10
So the * opened up for them to 2Ch 23:15,16,17
that a very large * assembled at 2Ch 30:13
a large * of men, women, and Ez 10:1
sins, fearing the * and its Job 31:34
before the largest * I can find. Ps 35:18
The denizens of hell * to meet Is 14:9
valleys and * against your gates. Is 22:6,7
And Hananiah said again to the * Jer 28:11
In the * were men, women and Jer 43:6
(it was a great * of all the Jews Jer 44:15
push and butt and * my sick and Eze 34:21
They never * each other. Joe 2:8
in a pasture—a noisy, happy *. Mic 2:12
Your princes and officials * Nah 3:17
Turning to the * he said, "I Mt 8:10
how large the * was growing, he Mt 8:18
swept through the * as they saw Mt 9:8
When the * was finally outside, Mt 9:25
speak and see. The * was amazed. Mt 12:23
where an immense * soon gathered. Mt 13:2,3
wilderness, a vast * was waiting Mt 14:14
(About 5,000 men were in the * Mt 14:21
And a vast * brought him their Mt 15:30
who presented them to the *. Mt 15:36
a huge * was waiting for them. Mt 17:14
a vast * surged along behind. Mt 20:29
The * told them to be quiet, but Mt 20:31
And some in the * threw down Mt 21:8
* all think he was a prophet." Mt 21:26
with a great * armed with swords Mt 26:47
Then Jesus spoke to the *. Mt 26:55
the * shouted back their reply: Mt 27:21
hands before the *, saying, "I am Mt 27:24
and a huge * of people from all Mk 1:32,33
Jesus through the *, so they dug Mk 2:4
followed by a huge * from all over Mk 3:7,8
ONCE AGAIN AN immense * gathered Mk 4:1
things come in and * out God's Mk 4:19
And a large * soon gathered Mk 5:15
about it, and the * began pleading Mk 5:17
the lake, a vast * gathered around Mk 5:21
Jesus went with him, and the * Mk 5:24
In the * was a woman who had Mk 5:25
the * and touched his clothes. Mk 5:27
around in the * and asked, "Who Mk 5:30
to him, "All this * pressing Mk 5:31
Then Jesus halted the * and Mk 5:37
So the usual vast * was there as Mk 6:34
to buy food for all this *!" Mk 6:37
Then Jesus told the * to sit Mk 6:39,40
And the * ate until they could Mk 6:42
Then Jesus called to the * to Mk 7:14
Jesus led him away from the * and Mk 7:33
Jesus told the * not to spread Mk 7:36
as another great * gathered, the Mk 8:1
So he told the * to sit down on Mk 8:6
And the whole * ate until they Mk 8:8,9
people in the * that day and when Mk 8:8,9
they found a great * surrounding Mk 9:14
with them. The * watched Jesus in Mk 9:15
One of the men in the * spoke up Mk 9:17
When Jesus saw the * was growing Mk 9:25
A murmur ran through the *—"He Mk 9:26
town, a great * was following. Mk 10:46
Then many in the * spread out Mk 11:8
delighted the * and they listened Mk 12:37
Now a mob began to * in toward Mk 15:8
Meanwhile, a great * stood Lk 1:10
The * replied, "What do you want Lk 3:10
But he walked away through the * Lk 4:30
the floor as the * watched, and Lk 4:35
They tried to push through the * Lk 5:18,19
man down into the *, still on his Lk 5:18,19
Turning to the * he said, "Never Lk 7:9
the usual great * at his heels. Lk 7:11
A great fear swept the *, and Lk 7:16
Jesus talked to the * about John. Lk 7:24
to a large * that was gathering to Lk 8:4
Soon a * came out to see for Lk 8:35
And the whole * was badly Lk 8:35
his disciples to set before the *. Lk 9:16
the hill, a huge * met him, and a Lk 9:37
and a man in the * called out to Lk 9:38
to him. The * was excited and Lk 11:14
a woman in the * called out, "God Lk 11:27
As the * pressed in upon him, he Lk 11:29,30
Then someone called from the *, Lk 12:13
Then he turned to the * and said, Lk 12:54
to work," he shouted to the *. Lk 13:14
When he heard the noise of a * Lk 18:36
among the * said, "Sir, rebuke Lk 19:39
roar rose from the * as with one Lk 23:18
As the * led Jesus away to his Lk 23:26
for each piece. The * watched. Lk 23:35
And when the * that came to see Lk 23:48
water, but right here in the * is Jn 1:26
Jesus had disappeared into the *. Jn 5:13
And a huge *, many of them Jn 6:2-5
The * replied, "You're out of Jn 7:20
So the * was divided about Jn 7:43
at the Temple. A * soon gathered, Jn 8:2
her out in front of the staring *. Jn 8:3
in front of the * with the woman. Jn 8:9
city, and a huge * of Passover Jn 12:12
And those in the * who had seen Jn 12:17
When the * heard the voice, Jn 12:29
asked the *. Jn 12:34
But others in the * were mocking. Act 2:13
and shouted to the *, "Listen, all Act 2:14
opportunity and addressed the *. Act 3:12

(CROWD Con't)
When the listening * saw what Act 14:11
A * began to gather and soon the Act 19:29
Alexander was spotted among the * Act 19:33
But when the * realized he was a Act 19:34
awesome joy swept through the *! Act 20:10,11,12
officers and ran down among the *. Act 21:32
Then he asked the * who he was Act 21:33
him, and the * surged behind Act 21:36
enveloped the *, and he addressed Act 21:40
The * listened until Paul came to Act 22:22
He wanted to find out why the * Act 22:24
no * around me, and no rioting! Act 24:18
You went along with the * and Eph 2:2
SINCE WE HAVE such a huge * of men Heb 12:1
After this I saw a vast *, too Rev 7:9
will * around to gaze at them. Rev 11:8,9
a vast * in heaven, "Hallelujah! Rev 19:1
shouting of a huge *, or like the Rev 19:6

CROWDED
of the East were * across the Ju 7:12,13
And they all * around him as he 1Ki 18:30
standing here inside the * city. Ps 122:2,3
be deserted, the * cities empty. Is 32:14
land shall soon be * with your Is 49:19
'We need more room! It's * here!' Is 49:20
The ruined cities will be * once Eze 36:37,38
and counselors * around them and Dan 3:27
As Jesus was speaking in a * Mt 12:46,47
in case he was * off the beach. Mk 3:9
arrived at the * house where he was Mk 3:31,32
that shot up and * the young plants Mk 4:7

CROWDING
* toward the Kingdom of Heaven, Mt 11:12
* around him, trying to touch him. Mk 3:10
many are * against you . . . ." Lk 8:45
And now all the angels were * Rev 7:11

CROWDS
about the great * at Mizpah, they 1Sa 7:7
* coming in from all over Israel; 2Ch 7:8
She calls out to the * along Pro 1:21
* to catch the glances of the men. Is 3:16
Jonah shouted to the * that Jon 3:4,5
Enormous * followed him wherever Mt 4:25
ONE DAY AS the * were gathering, Mt 5:1
The * were amazed at Jesus' Mt 7:28
LARGE * FOLLOWED Jesus as he Mt 8:1
and saw the noisy * and heard the Mt 9:23
How the * marveled! Mt 9:33
And what pity he felt for the * Mt 9:36
began talking about him to the *. Mt 11:7
when speaking to the *. Mt 13:34,35
Then, leaving the * outside, he Mt 13:36
But the * saw where he was Mt 14:13
send the * away so they can go to Mt 14:15
Then Jesus called to the * and Mt 15:10
about them! The * just marveled, Mt 15:31
Vast * followed him, and he Mt 19:2
Then the * surged on ahead and Mt 21:9
And the * replied, "It's Jesus, Mt 21:11
try because of the *, for they Mt 21:46
The * were profoundly impressed Mt 22:33
THEN JESUS SAID to the *, and to Mt 23:1
and as the * gathered before Mt 27:17
persuaded the * to ask for Mt 27:20
to the * that gathered around him. Mk 2:13
among the * that followed him. Mk 2:15
was staying, the * began to gather Mk 3:20
out, leaving the * behind (though Mk 4:36
from the * for a while and rest." Mk 6:31
stay and tell the * good-bye and Mk 6:45
get away from the *, and his Mk 7:17
and the * to come over and listen. Mk 8:34
And as always there were the *; Mk 10:1
procession with * ahead and behind, Mk 11:9
as the * dropped in their money. Mk 12:41
Meanwhile the * outside were Lk 1:21
preaching to the * that came for Lk 3:7
Then one day, after the * had Lk 3:21
the desert. The * searched Lk 4:42
Gennesaret, great * pressed in on Lk 5:1
and speak to the * from there. Lk 5:3
faster and vast * came to hear him Lk 5:15
in turn, were surrounded by the *. Lk 6:17,18
praised by the *—for false prophets Lk 6:26
But these * hear the words and do Lk 8:10
he was teaching, because of the *. Lk 8:19
of the lake the * received him with Lk 8:40
with him, pushing through the *. Lk 8:42
But the * found out where he was Lk 9:11
MEANWHILE THE * grew until Lk 12:1
Great * were following him. Lk 14:25
The * ahead of Jesus tried to Lk 18:39
was too short to see over the *. Lk 19:3
But the * were displeased. Lk 19:7
Then the * spread out their robes Lk 19:36,37
Then, with the * listening, he Lk 20:45
to teach, and the * began gathering Lk 21:37,38
quietly when the * weren't around. Lk 22:6
Great * trailed along behind, Lk 23:27
telling the *, "This is the one I Jn 1:15
is all. The * will naturally go to Jn 3:29
about the greater * coming to him Jn 4:1
surrounding it. * of sick Jn 5:3
across the lake, * began gathering Jn 6:22,23
discussion about him among the *. Jn 7:12
Many among the * at the Temple Jn 7:31
heard that the * were in this mood, Jn 7:32
shouted to the *, "If anyone is Jn 7:37
When the * heard him say this, Jn 7:40
These stupid * do, yes; Jn 7:49
Jesus shouted to the *, "If you Jn 12:44
above the house, * came running to Act 2:6
the Lord, * both of men and women. Act 5:14
he went by! And * came in from the Act 5:16
This accusation roused the * to Act 6:12
about Christ. * listened intently Act 8:6
saw the *, they were jealous, and Act 13:45
at the city gates before the *. Act 14:13
and turned the * into a murderous Act 14:19

CROWED
And immediately the cock *. Mt 26:74
Just then, a rooster *. Mk 14:68
And immediately the rooster * the Mk 14:72
as he said the words, a rooster *. Lk 22:60
And immediately a rooster *. Jn 18:27

CROWN
*—as the Lord had commanded Moses. Lev 8:9
Then I took his * and one of his 2Sa 1:10
* Saul's son Ish-bosheth as king. 2Sa 2:8
king of Rabbah's *—a $50,000 2Sa 12:29,30
decided to * himself king in place 1Ki 1:5
prince and put the * upon his head 2Ki 11:12
at Ibleam and took the * himself. 2Ki 15:10
the * from the head of King Milcom 1Ch 20:2
and placed the * upon his head and 2Ch 23:11
him with the royal * upon her head Est 1:11
he set the royal * on her head and Est 2:17
and the royal *, and instruct one Est 6:7,8
and the great * of gold, with an Est 8:15
and removed the * from my head. Job 19:9
I would treasure it like a *. Job 31:36
and placed a * of glory and honor Ps 8:5
You set a kingly * of purest gold Ps 21:3
For you have thrown his * in the Ps 89:39
godly be happy in the Lord and * Ps 97:12
and * your efforts with success. Pro 3:6
she will place a beautiful * upon Pro 4:8,9
wife is her husband's joy and *; Pro 12:4
White hair is a * of glory and is Pro 16:31
And the king's * doesn't stay in Pro 27:23,24
see the * with which his mother Sol 3:11
mountains, so your hair is your *. Sol 7:5
that Tirhakah, * prince of Is 37:8,9
splendid * for the King of kings. Is 62:3
Our glory is gone. The * is Lam 5:16
Take off your jeweled *, the Eze 21:26
them a * from the silver and gold. Zec 6:10,11
Then put the * on the head of Zec 6:10,11
"Then put the * in the Temple of Zec 6:14
land as glittering jewels in a *. Zec 9:16,17
him, and made a * from long thorns Mt 27:29
robe, and made a * of long, sharp Mk 15:16,17
soldiers made a * of thorns and Jn 19:2
Then Jesus came out wearing the * Jn 19:5
joy and is our proud reward and *? 1Th 2:19
In heaven a * is waiting for me 2Ti 4:8
as his reward the * of life that Jas 1:12
will give you the * of life—an Rev 2:10
that no one will take away your *. Rev 3:11
Its rider carried a bow, and a * Rev 6:2
a * of twelve stars on her head. Rev 12:1
with a * of solid gold upon his Rev 14:14

CROWNED
"And when he has been * and sits Deu 17:18
before the Lord they * him king. 1Sa 11:15
ONE DAY SAMUEL said to Saul, "I * 1Sa 15:1
came to David and * him king of the 2Sa 2:4
and they * him king of Israel. 2Sa 5:3
David had been * king of Israel, 2Sa 5:17
Absalom has been * in Hebron." 2Sa 15:10
they * King David's son Solomon 1Ch 29:22
THE PEOPLE OF Judah now * 2Ch 26:1
The simpleton is * with folly; Pro 14:18
the wise man is * with knowledge. Pro 14:18
which his mother * him on his Sol 3:11
and who was then * in his place. Jer 44:30f
to be * king of his province. Lk 19:12
but then a king was * who had no Act 7:17,18
have * him with glory and honor. Heb 2:7
than the angels—* now by God with Heb 2:9

CROWNING
grandchildren are his * glory. Pro 17:6
Woe to her fading beauty, the * Is 28:1
will be their * glory, the diadem Is 28:5

CROWNS
Then he * it all with green, Ps 65:11,12
"As Mount Carmel * the Sol 7:5
* are removed from your heads. Jer 13:18
and beautiful * upon your head. Eze 23:42
with golden * upon their heads. Rev 4:4
and cast their * before the throne, Rev 4:10
looked like golden * on their Rev 9:
horns, and seven * on his heads. Rev 12:
horns, and ten * upon its horns. Rev 13:
and on his head were many *. Rev 19:1

CROWS
before the cock * at dawn, you will Mt 26:3
*, you will deny me three times." Mt 26:7
"before the cock * a second time Mk 14:3
"Before the cock * twice, you will Mk 14:7
when the rooster *, you will deny Lk 22:3
the rooster * tomorrow morning, you Lk 22:6
No—three times before the cock * Jn 13:3

CRUCIBLE
O Lord, like silver in a *. Ps 66:1
can be tested in a *, but a man is Pro 27:2
melt them in a * of affliction. Jer 9:
bring you to my * in Jerusalem, Eze 22:18,19,2

CRUCIFIED
the meaning is that they were *. Est 2:23
will be mocked and *, and the third Mt 20:1
shall be betrayed and *." Mt 26:
Two robbers were also * there Mt 27:3
who was *, but he isn't here! Mt 28:
whip, and handed him over to be *. Mk 15:1
again, and led him away to be *. Mk 15:2
And then they * him—and threw Mk 15:24
Two robbers were also * that Mk 15:27
for Jesus, the Nazarene who was *? Mk 16:6
There all three were *—Jesus on Lk 23:32,33
of evil men and be * and that he Lk 24:6,7
to death, and they * him. Lk 24:20
"But we want him *," they Jn 18:31
Pilate gave Jesus to them to be *. Jn 19:16
There they * him and two Jn 19:18
The place where Jesus was * Jn 19:20
When the soldiers had * Jesus, Jn 19:23,24
legs of the two men * with Jesus; Jn 19:32
ceremonies, when Christ was *. Act 2:1f
* to be the Lord, the Messiah!" Act 2:36
the man you *—but God raised back Act 4:10
would have * the Lord of Glory. 1Co 2:8
I have been * with Christ: and I Gal 2:20
to his cross and * them there. Gal 5:24
very place where their Lord was *. Rev 11:8,9

CRUCIFIXION
will kill some by *, and rip open Mt 23:34
After the *, the soldiers threw Mt 27:35
The soldiers at the * and their Mt 27:54
the morning when the * took place. Mk 15:25
came to see the * saw that Jesus Lk 23:48
by *, a practice under Roman law. Jn 18:32f
The place of * was near a grove Jn 19:41
days after his * he appeared to the Act 1:3

CRUCIFY
And they shouted, "* him!" Mt 27:22
But they kept shouting, "*! Mt 27:23
kept shouting, "Crucify! *!" Mt 27:23
Roman soldiers to take away and *. Mt 27:26
again, and took him out to * him. Mt 27:31
They shouted back, "* him!" Mk 15:13
only roared the louder, "* him!" Mk 15:14
But they shouted, "* him! Lk 23:21
shouted, "Crucify him! * him!" Lk 23:21
officials began yelling, "*! Jn 19:6
began yelling, "Crucify! *!" Jn 19:6
"You * him," Pilate said. Jn 19:6
to release you or to * you?" Jn 19:10
"Away with him—* him!" Jn 19:15
"What? * your king?" Jn 19:15

CRUEL
anger, for it is fierce and *. Gen 49:7
broken spirit and the * bondage." Ex 6:8,9f
from the proud and * Egyptians." Ex 18:11
The Midianites were so * that Ju 6:2
from all who were * to you, and Ju 6:9
You have become * toward me, and Job 30:21
gone along with * and evil men. Ps 17:4
God, from these unjust and * men. Ps 71:4
is full of darkness and * men. Ps 74:20
your life to the * and merciless; Pro 5:9
money to * men. Pro 11:16
it is destroyed when you are *. Pro 11:17
the kindness of godless men is *. Pro 12:10
Jealousy is more dangerous and * Pro 27:4
and jealousy is as * as Sheol. Sol 8:6
Egypt to a hard, * master, to a Is 19:4
They are a *, merciless people, Jer 6:23
as brass, hard and * as iron. Jer 6:28
they are * and show no mercy; Jer 50:42
They are like * desert ostriches, Lam 4:3,4
he is * and robs and does wrong. Eze 18:18
of * men skilled in destruction. Eze 21:31
they committed * crimes, ripping Amo 1:13
a * and violent nation who will Hab 1:6
says he hates divorce and * men. Mal 2:16
They will be rough and *, and 2Ti 3:3
but even if they are tough and *. 1Pe 2:18

CRUELLY
is a form of hatred and wounds *. Pro 26:28
for I have wounded you *, as Jer 30:14
needy and * extort from aliens. Eze 22:29

CRUELTY
But God has seen your * and my Gen 31:42
and all the while are plotting *. Ps 27:12
and their clothing is woven of *! Ps 73:6
have ruled them with force and *. Eze 34:4
who has not suffered from your *? Nah 3:19
They are notorious for their *. Hab 1:7

CRUMB
their smallest * by all your taxes, Amo 5:11

CRUMBLE
and the mountains * into the sea. Ps 46:2
walls shall * to the earth. Eze 38:20
Bethel where Israel sinned will *. Hos 10:8
until the pillars * and the roof Amo 9:1
of Samaria will * into a heap of Mic 1:6

CRUMBLED
walls of Jericho * and fell before Jos 6:20

CRUMBLES
the earth * and its people are Nah 1:5
it * into a heap of ruins." Lk 6:49

CRUMBS
to eat the * that fall." Mt 15:27

CRUNCHED
king of Babylon, * their bones. Jer 50:17

CRUSADE
join him in a * against Egypt. Dan 11:14

CRUSH
I could * you, but the God of Gen 31:29
* us, and we will all be killed." Gen 34:30
so I will * Egypt with a final Ex 7:4
from a fresh ear, * and roast them, Lev 2:14
"They would * us!" Num 13:31
to come evil will * you for you Deu 31:29
* those who are their enemies; Deu 33:11
armies, and uniting to * Israel. Jos 11:4
By your power I can * an army; 2Sa 22:30
tried unsuccessfully to * the 2Ki 8:21
step on them and * them, or the Job 39:15
destroy me, * me to the ground, and Ps 7:5
O God, * them! Ps 10:12
him, does not * his debtors with Ps 15:5
But he will * his enemies, for Ps 68:21
needy and to * their oppressors. Ps 72:4
he let the heathen nations * them. Ps 106:41,42
He will * many heads. Ps 110:6
and it will roll back and * you. Pro 26:27
though you * him to powder. Pro 27:22
stones will fall and * you! Ecc 10:8,9
* your enemies as I have said. Is 7:11
still heavy upon them, to * them. Is 9:21
time for the Almighty to * you. Is 13:6
I will * the arrogance of the Is 13:11
and to * them on my mountains; Is 14:25
me that he is determined to * you. Is 28:22
be heard and shall * down his Is 30:30
have done, and * their allies too. Is 31:2
* walled cities into ruined heaps. Is 37:26
* the strength of mighty kings. Is 45:1
With you I will * armies, Jer 51:21
command to * the noblest youth. Lam 1:15
I will * you and make your Eze 6:14
I will * your pride by bringing Eze 7:24
fall on you and * you, and you Eze 13:14
"And so the Lord says: I will * Eze 13:20
me, then I will * them with my fist Eze 14:13
to fall upon them and * them. Hos 10:8
rob the poor and * the needy—you Amo 4:1
I will * Judah and Jerusalem Zep 1:4
He does not * the weak, Mt 12:20
and scorpions and to * them. Lk 10:19
For you * men beneath impossible Lk 11:46
in on you, and * you to the Lk 19:44
fall on them and * them, and the Lk 23:30
Holy Spirit you * it and its evil Rom 8:13
upon their heads to justly * them. Rom 11:9
The God of peace will soon * Rom 16:20
in honor until I * all your enemies Heb 1:13
cried to the mountains to * them. Rev 6:16

CRUSHED
and his troops * the army of Ex 17:13
injured genitals—* or Lev 22:24
the ground and * it into flour or Num 11:8
or you will be * by your enemies, Num 14:42
But the Lord our God * him, and Deu 2:33,34
"IF A MAN'S testicles are * or Deu 23:1
will always be oppressed and *. Deu 28:33
I * and scattered them 2Sa 22:43
into sin. He * the stones to dust 2Ki 23:15
But now he * them into dust, just 2Ki 23:19
20,000 sacks of * wheat, 20,000 2Ch 2:10
he cut down the idol and * and 2Ch 15:16
they were * upon the rocks below. 2Ch 25:12
or falling, or lie * upon the Job 4:3,4
are * to death as easily as moths! Job 4:18,19
of the poor shall not always be *. Ps 9:18
So I * them fine as dust and Ps 18:42
I am exhausted and *; Ps 38:8
you * the sea-god's heads! Ps 74:13,14
of death, * by misery and slavery? Ps 107:10
the wicked are * by their sins. Pro 14:32
be * before the Lord that day. Is 2:16
too, will be * and broken. Is 7:8
and lie fallen and * beneath it: Is 8:14,15
For the Lord has * your wicked Is 14:5
small—all will be * and broken. Is 19:10
and Moab will be * as straw beneath Is 25:10
Bread grain is easily *, so he Is 28:28
* everyone who has opposed them. Is 37:11
out judgment. I * the heathen Is 63:6
in a moment, every house is *. Jer 4:20
Lord, and * by his fierce anger. Jer 4:26
they will be * when their makers Jer 10:15
Lord, I don't want the people * Jer 17:16
* us and emptied out our strength; Jer 51:34,35
are broken, for he has * them. Lam 2:9
But you have trampled and * Lam 3:34,35,36
"Therefore I have * you with my Eze 16:27
Therefore I * her. Eze 16:50
them out to be * and despised. Eze 23:46
Now you will lie * and broken Eze 32:28
the statue and * the feet of iron Dan 2:34
its pieces were * as small as Dan 2:35
Rock that * to powder all the iron Dan 2:45
and others it * beneath its feet. Dan 7:7
curse of God has * us—the curse Dan 9:11
"And so the Lord deliberately * Dan 9:14
power of God's people has been *. Dan 12:7
Ephraim will be * and broken by my Hos 5:11
for you have been * by your sins. Hos 14:1
* upon the ground and cannot rise. Amo 5:2
mighty lion! You * your enemies to Nah 2:12
chosen people. You * the head of Hab 3:13
to move her, they will all be *. Zec 12:3
Then he told them, "My soul is * Mt 26:38
* by sorrow to the point of death; Mk 14:34
whom it falls will be * to dust." Lk 20:18
loves to sin was * and fatally Rom 6:6
We were really * and overwhelmed, 2Co 1:8
by troubles, but not * and broken. 2Co 4:8

CRUSHES
He will laugh when calamity * Job 9:23
to darkness and * down the Amo 4:13

CRUSHING
* Balaam's foot in the process. Num 22:25
people under their * oppressions; Ju 2:18
to pay * taxes to King Eglon. Ju 3:14
* his head. Ju 5:26
It landed on Abimelech's head, * Ju 9:53
and stepped on the thistle, * it! 2Ch 25:18
he is skilled at * its pride! Job 26:12
your blows are * me. Ps 38:2
Oh, what a day of * trouble! Is 22:5
milling about and * each other. Lk 12:1
in all of our own * troubles and 1Th 3:7
spite of all the * troubles and 2Th 1:4

CRUST
A DRY * eaten in peace is better Pro 17:1

CRY
say, and then break down and *. Gen 37:35
brother and had to go out and *. Gen 43:30
any way, and they * to me for my Ex 22:23
"No, it's not a * of victory or Ex 32:18
otherwise he may * out to the Deu 24:14,15
"O Lord, hear the * of Judah Deu 33:7
to * out to the Lord for help. Ju 6:6,7
Go and * to the new gods you Ju 10:14
her * so much she couldn't eat. 1Sa 1:7
great * arose throughout the city. 1Sa 4:13
in mercy and have heard their *." 1Sa 9:16
Then he began to *. 1Sa 24:15
My * reached his ears. 2Sa 22:7
turn to you and * to you saying, 1Ki 8:47
them whenever they * out to you, 1Ki 8:52
down the * ran through his troops. 1Ki 22:36,37
* out to him, 'Oh, save us, God 1Ch 16:35
* out to you to save us; 2Ch 20:9
"Don't * on such a day as this! Neh 8:9
"THEY * FOR help but no one Job 5:1
believe that he had heard my *. Job 9:16
The bones of the dying * from Job 24:12
the wounded * for help; Job 24:12
Will God listen to his * when Job 27:9
"I * to you, O God, but you Job 30:20
I stand up and * to the assembly Job 30:28,29
him, causing the * of the poor to Job 34:28
yet none of them * to God, Job 35:9,10
"But when anyone does * out this Job 35:12
But do you * out against him Job 35:14,15
when their young * out to God as Job 38:41
I will * to him, "Arise, O Ps 3:7
to those who * to him for justice. Ps 9:12
you must listen to my earnest *! Ps 17:1
All I need to do is * to him—oh, Ps 18:3
my * reached his ears. Ps 18:6
Oh, listen to my *. Ps 28:2
Answer quickly when I * to you; Ps 31:2
attention when they * to him. Ps 34:15
listen to my *! Ps 39:12
then he listened and heard my *. Ps 40:1
"O God my Rock," I *, "why Ps 42:9
don't hide yourself when I * to Ps 55:1
I will * to the God of heaven Ps 57:2
earth, I will * to you for help. Ps 61:2
* out the happy news: "The Ps 68:11,12,13
and poor when they * to him; Ps 72:12
their battle * and erected their Ps 74:4
I * TO the Lord; Ps 77:1
Hear my urgent *. Ps 86:6
oh, listen to my *, for my life Ps 88:2
And he will * to me, 'You are my Ps 89:26
Then they * to the Lord in their Ps 107:28
Hear the * of your beloved Ps 108:6
"Save me," I *, "for I am Ps 119:146
I * for your help: "Hear me! Ps 130:1
Listen when I * to you for help! Ps 141:1
"Hear my *, for I am very low. Ps 142:6
young ravens * to him for food. Ps 147:9
I will not answer your * for help. Pro 1:28
A time to *; Ecc 3:4
for "righteousness" and "*." Is 5:7f
With one voice they all * out, Is 14:10
The bravest warriors of Moab * in Is 15:4
they will * to their gods in Is 16:12
then when they * to the Lord for Is 19:20
Don't try to comfort me—let me * Is 22:4
breached and the * of death echoes Is 22:5
to you at the sound of your *. Is 30:19
has refused their * for peace. Is 33:7
"Which one of us," they *, Is 33:14
I will answer when they * to me. Is 41:17
he will groan and * like a woman Is 42:14
when you * to them to save you! Is 57:13
pray for her or to * out to God on Is 62:1
on your walls who shall * to God Is 62:6,7
You shall * in sorrow and Is 65:14
Yet in time of trouble they * to Jer 2:26,27
it is the * of my people gasping Jer 4:31
them to listen. * out your Jer 7:27
Though they * for mercy, I will Jer 11:11
I hear its mournful *. Jer 12:11
a great * rises from Jerusalem. Jer 14:2
"O Lord," the people will *, Jer 14:19
but soon you will * and groan in Jer 22:23
That * of judgment will reach Jer 25:31
they *. Jer 30:5
But the Lord says: Don't * any Jer 31:16
pity them when they * for help. Jer 33:5
The earth is filled with your * Jer 46:12
of Moab, weep for her and *! Jer 48:17
* out, O Heshbon, for Ai is Jer 49:3
Edom's fall; the * of the people is Jer 49:21
their battle * roars like the Jer 50:42
fall, and her * of despair shall be Jer 50:46
Sound the battle *; Jer 51:27
Hear the * of great destruction Jer 51:54
Her people groan and * for bread; Lam 1:11
want food," they *, and then Lam 2:12
Rise in the night and * to your Lam 2:19
And though I * and shout, he Lam 3:8
from heaven and respond to my *! Lam 3:50
Yes, you came at my despairing * Lam 3:57
Babies * for bread but no one can Lam 4:3,4
the people will * out, 'Why didn't Eze 13:12
Yes, * for the sorrows of Egypt. Eze 32:16
earth in answer to its * for rain. Hos 1:21,22
answer the parched * of the grain, Hos 1:21,22
And the people will * to the Hos 10:8
Even the wild animals * to you Joe 1:20
Get up and * to your god, and see Jon 1:6
wear sackcloth and * mightily to Jon 3:8
You who * "Peace" to those who Mic 3:5
Murder!" I *, but no one comes Hab 1:2
of your homes * out against you, Hab 2:11
and fraud. A * of alarm will begin Zep 1:10
them are fallen. * in fear, you Zec 11:2
you *. Mal 2:14
And he began to *. Mk 14:72
Then Jesus uttered another loud * Mk 15:37
She gave a glad * and exclaimed Lk 1:42
"Don't *!" Lk 7:13
saw the city ahead, he began to *. Lk 19:41
For God says, "Your * came to 2Co 6:2
the soul-stirring * of the 1Th 4:16
his anguished * in Gethsemane Heb 5:7f
now is the time to * and groan with Jas 5:1
and kindness, * for more, as a baby 1Pe 2:2,3f
of your salvation; * for this as a 1Pe 2:2,3
Literally, "I heard the altar *. Rev 16:7f
loved so much are gone," they *. Rev 18:14

CRYING
Jacob kissed Rachel and started *! Gen 29:11
happened, she was * hysterically. Gen 39:14,15
came to Joseph * again for food. Gen 47:15
And he was *. Ex 2:6
and there was bitter * throughout Ex 12:30
anguish and was * bitterly as she 1Sa 1:10
Why is everyone *?" 1Sa 11:5
her head in her hands went away *. 2Sa 13:19
room over the gate, * as he went. 2Sa 18:33
and then Elisha started *. 2Ki 8:11
* with a loud and bitter wail. Est 4:1
I keep on weeping, * for your help, Ps 22:2
the women, ravaged, shall sit * Is 3:25,26

(CRYING Con't)
Luhith, and their * will be heard Is 15:5
Mobs form in the streets, * for Is 24:11
and the voice of weeping and * Is 65:19
windswept mountains, *, crying. Jer 3:21
windswept mountains, crying, *. Jer 3:21
I have heard great * like that of Jer 4:31
Begin your *! Jer 9:17,18
I cannot stop my *, for my people Jer 14:17
city to meet them, * as he went. Jer 41:6
destroyed. Her * will be heard as Jer 48:2,3,4
of sackcloth. * and sorrow will be Jer 48:38
Hear the * of these ministers of Joe 1:9
"There will be * in all the Amo 5:16
There will be sorrow and * in Amo 5:17
as an ostrich * across the desert Mic 1:8
And he went away, * bitterly. Mt 26:75
at a distance, * out, "Jesus, Lk 17:13
out of the courtyard, * bitterly. Lk 22:62
and was standing outside *. Jn 20:11
"Why are you *?" Jn 20:13
"Why are you *?" Jn 20:15
instead of * out for vengeance as Heb 12:24
said to me, "Stop *, for look! Rev 5:5
the heavens * loudly, "Woe, woe, Rev 8:13
with fear and * out, "Alas, Rev 18:10
weeping and *, "Alas, that great Rev 18:15
a long way off, * as they watch Rev 18:18
nor sorrow, nor *, nor pain. Rev 21:4

CRYPT
He was buried in a * in the 2Ki 21:26

CRYSTAL
Coral or * is worthless in Job 28:18
as though it were made of *; Eze 1:22
there came a voice from the * sky Eze 1:25
out before it was a shiny * sea. Rev 4:6
precious gem, * clear like jasper. Rev 21:11
of Life, clear as *, flowing from Rev 22:1

CUB
"Dan is like a lion's * Deu 33:22

CUBE
in fact it was in the form of a * Rev 21:16

CUBIT
Literally, "ten in a *." 1Ki 7:24f
measurements." A * was the average Rev 21:17f

CUBITS
wing of a cherub, five * long." 2Ch 3:11,12,13f
Literally, "144 * by human Rev 21:17f

CUBS
bear who has been robbed of her *. 2Sa 17:8
* than a fool caught in his folly. Pro 17:12
graze among bears; * and calves Is 11:7
Her children were like lion's *! Eze 19:2
One of her * [King Jehoahaz Eze 19:3
another of her * [King Jehoiachin Eze 19:5
like a bear whose * have been taken Hos 13:8

CUCUMBERS
and the wonderful * and melons, Num 11:4,5

CUD
cloven hooves which chews its *. Lev 11:2,3
The camel (it chews the * but does Lev 11:4-7
it chews the *, it does not have Lev 11:4-7
it chews the *, it does not have Lev 11:4-7
hooves, it does not chew the *). Lev 11:4-7
animal that does not chew the *. Lev 11:26
and chews the * may be eaten, but Deu 14:6
"They chew the * but do not have Deu 14:7
hooves, they don't chew the *. Deu 14:8

CUDDLED
his own cup; he * it in his arms 2Sa 12:3

CULT
from the Jewish * of "The Act 6:9

CULTIVATE
grain for man to *, and wine to Ps 104:14

CULTIVATED
Acreage will be * again that Eze 36:34
But you have * wickedness and Hos 10:13

CULTURAL
In the * arts, I organized men's Ecc 2:7,8

CULTURE
flower of Chaldean *, will be as Is 13:19

CUMMIN
is never rolled on *, but it is Is 28:27

CUN
cities of Tibhath and *. 1Ch 18:8

CUNNING
So you can see how * and deadly Rom 7:13

CUP
I was holding Pharaoh's wine * Gen 40:11
own silver * at the top of Gen 44:2
silver drinking *, which he uses Gen 44:5
If you find his * with any one Gen 44:9
And the * was found in Gen 44:12
in whose sack the * was found." Gen 44:16
"Only the man who stole the * Gen 44:17
gave him milk in a beautiful *! Ju 5:25
be all the men who * the water in Ju 7:5,6
and let it drink from his own *; 2Sa 12:3
and he asked her for a * of 1Ki 17:10
flaring out like the * of a lily. 2Ch 4:5
head with oil, my * runs over." Ps 23:5f
In Jehovah's hand there is a * Ps 75:8
They must drain that * to the Ps 75:8
Literally, "the * of salvation," Ps 116:13f
You have drunk enough from the * Is 51:17
You have drunk to the dregs the * Is 51:17
from your hands the terrible *; Is 51:22
But I will put that terrible * Is 51:23
and given us a * of poison to drink Jer 8:14
or send them a * of wine expressing Jer 16:7
my hand this wine * filled to the Jer 25:15
So I took the * of fury from the Jer 25:17
drank of the * so that from that Jer 25:18
from that terrible *, along with Jer 25:19,20
drank from this * of God's wrath. Jer 25:26
Drink from this * of my wrath until Jer 25:27
to accept the *, tell them, "The Jer 25:28
You must drink this * of Jer 49:12
Babylon has been as a golden * Jer 51:7
Lord's hands, a * from which he Jer 51:7
a * of deepest sorrows to drink. Lam 3:15
upon you—and the * from which she Eze 23:32
will drain that * of terror to the Eze 23:34
You drank my * of punishment Ob 1:16
and Judah like a * of poison to all Zec 12:2
you give even a * of cold water to Mt 10:42
* I am about to drink from?" Mt 20:22
the outside of the *, but the Mt 23:25
First cleanse the inside of the * Mt 23:26
then the whole * will be clean. Mt 23:26
And he took a * of wine and gave Mt 26:27
If it is possible, let this * be Mt 26:39
If this * cannot go away until I Mt 26:42
as gives you a * of water because Mk 9:41
* of sorrow I must drink from? Mk 10:38
drink from my * and be baptized Mk 10:39
Then he took a * of wine and gave Mk 14:23
Take away this * from me. Mk 14:36
Literally, "This * is the new Lk 22:20f
away this * of horror from me. Lk 22:41,42
Yes, your * of joy will overflow! Jn 15:11
and your * of joy will overflow. Jn 16:24
Shall I not drink from the * the Jn 18:11
win a blue ribbon or a silver *, 1Co 9:25
drinking from the * of wine at the 1Co 10:16
You cannot drink from the * at 1Co 10:21
In the same way, he took the * 1Co 11:25
saying, "This * is the new 1Co 11:25
and drink this * you are re-telling 1Co 11:26
drinks from this * of the Lord in 1Co 11:27
the bread and drinking from the *. 1Co 11:28
drinks from the * unworthily, not 1Co 11:29
("Let this * pass from me") and Heb 5:7f
undiluted into God's * of wrath. Rev 14:10
of anger in the * of the wine of Rev 16:19
She brewed many a * of woe for Rev 18:6

CUPBEARER
(I was the king's *. Neh 1:11

CUPBEARERS
uniforms, his *, and the many 1Ki 10:5

CUPS
*, and the Bread upon the cloth. Num 4:7
lamps, tongs, *, snuffers, basins, 1Ki 7:50
All of King Solomon's * were of 1Ki 10:21
It was not used to buy silver *, 2Ki 12:13,14
palace treasury, also the gold *. 2Ki 14:14
*, and bowls of gold and silver. 1Ch 28:17
All of King Solomon's * were 2Ch 9:20
I set * and jugs of wine before Jer 35:5
candlesticks and * and bowls. Jer 52:19
some of the sacred * from the Dan 1:1
gold and silver * taken long before Dan 5:2,3,4
that these sacred * be brought in Dan 5:2,3,4
from these *, they saw the fingers Dan 5:5
here these * from his Temple; Dan 5:23

CURB
a 10½-inch * around the edges. Eze 43:17
platform and in the * around it. Eze 43:20

CURDLED
like milk, and * me like cheese. Job 10:10

CURDS
and (is old enough to) eat * and Is 7:15,16f
will live on * and wild honey. Is 7:21,22

CURE
asking God to * the king and queen Gen 20:17
To * them by drying. Num 11:32f
of Saul's aides suggested a *. 1Sa 16:15,16
"The * for this," his aides 1Ki 1:2
and to * the wounds he gave them. Is 30:26
Yet there is no * for your Jer 46:11
but he can neither help nor *. Hos 5:13
Then I will * you of idolatry and Hos 14:4
wound—it is far too deep to *. Nah 3:19
public testimony of your *." Mt 8:4
Heal the sick, raise the dead, * Mt 10:8
but they couldn't * him." Mt 17:16
and could find no * (though she had Lk 8:43,44

CURED
the priest shall pronounce him *; Lev 13:6
pronounce him * of leprosy, for it Lev 13:13
he is *. Lev 13:13
the priest will pronounce him *. Lev 13:16,17
times upon the man * of his Lev 14:
pronounce him *, and shall let the Lev 14:
"Then the man who is * shall Lev 14:
declared fully * of his leprosy. Lev 14:
simply to go and wash and be *!" 2Ki 5:1
help, and the * lepers, and the Mt 11:
went out from him and they were *. Lk 6:1
They said to the man who was *, Jn 5:1
in the island came and were *. Act 28:

CURING
Jesus while he was * many sick Lk 7:20,21,2
of God and * those who were ill. Lk 9:1

CURIOUS
before the * gaze of kings. Eze 28:17

CURRENCY
$50,000 in foreign *; 1Ch 29:6,7

CURRENT
pounds sterling at * value. 1Ch 19:6

CURRENTLY
the Caspian, * in central Turkey. Eze 38:2,3
the courts are * in session and the Act 19:38

CURRY
are my gifts, to * your favor!" Gen 33:8

CURSE
I have placed a * upon the soil. Gen 3:17
will never again * the earth, Gen 8:21
"A * upon the Canaanites," he Gen 9:24,25
you and * those who curse you; Gen 12:3
you and curse those who * you; Gen 12:3
and * me instead of blessing me!" Gen 27:11,12
Cursed are all who * you, and Gen 27:27,28,29
your blessing and don't * him." Gen 31:24
a * upon anyone who took them. Gen 31:32
blaspheme God, nor * government Ex 22:28
"You must not * the deaf nor Lev 19:14
of bitter water that brings a *. Num 5:18
bitter water that causes the *. Num 5:19
shall make you a * among your Num 5:21,22
she shall be a * among her people. Num 5:27
"Please come and * them for me, Num 22:5,6
those whom you * are doomed." Num 22:5,6
to go at once and * them, in the Num 22:11
"You are not to * them, for I Num 22:12
Only come and * these people for Num 22:16,17
'Come,' he told me, '* Jacob for Num 23:7-10
But how can I * Num 23:7-10
"I told you to * my enemies, and Num 23:11
of Israel. * at least that many!" Num 23:13
No * can be placed on Jacob, Num 23:18-24
"If you aren't going to * them, Num 23:25
to let you * them from there." Num 23:27
"I called you to * my enemies and Num 24:10
I will bring the * of a father's Deu 5:9,10
between God's blessing or God's *! Deu 11:26
you today, and a * if you refuse Deu 11:28
Gerizim, and a * from Mount Ebal! Deu 11:29
Pethor, Mesopotamia, to * you. Deu 23:4
instead, he turned the intended * Deu 23:5
upon Mount Ebal to proclaim a *. Deu 27:13
" 'The * of God be upon anyone Deu 27:15
The * of barren wombs; Deu 28:15-19
will send his personal * upon you. Deu 28:20
warnings of this *, 'I shall Deu 29:19
you life or death, blessing or *. Deu 30:19
Then Joshua declared a terrible * Jos 6:26
for the fulfillment of this *. Jos 6:26f
Now a * shall be upon you! Jos 9:23
the * of God be on us if we did. Jos 22:22,23
Balaam, the son of Beor, to * you. Jos 24:9
Put a * on Meroz. Ju 5:23
'* them bitterly,' he said, Ju 5:23
So the * of Jotham, Gideon's son, Ju 9:56,57
Saul had declared, "A * upon 1Sa 14:24,25
for they all feared Saul's *. 1Sa 14:26
father had laid a * upon anyone who 1Sa 14:28
it with a terrible * against 1Sa 20:16
May God * me if even one of his 1Sa 25:22
May God * me if I don't do 2Sa 3:9,10
"Why should this dead dog * my 2Sa 16:9
"If the Lord has told him to * 2Sa 16:10
He cursed me with a terrible * as 1Ki 2:8
in Bethel, and his * against the 1Ki 13:32
For this was the Lord's * upon 1Ki 16:34
to place God's * upon you because 1Ki 21:20
asked me to * your enemies, and you 2Ch 1:11
And I invoked the * of God upon Neh 5:13
to accept the * of God unless we Neh 10:29
hired Balaam to * them—although God Neh 13:2
God turned the * into a blessing. Neh 13:2
see him * you to your face!" Job 1:11
and he will * you to your face!" Job 2:4,5
all this to you? * him and die." Job 2:9
who are experts at cursing * it. Job 3:8
Literally, "Let them who can * Job 3:8f
to rouse the sea monster, * it." Job 3:8f
morning light. * it for its Job 3:10
with no brutal jailer to * them. Job 3:18
immoral men. You * and lie, and Ps 50:19
me day after day and * at me. Ps 102:8
He loved to * others; Ps 109:17
now you * him. Ps 109:17

CURSE Con't)
Then let them * me if they Ps 109:28
The * of God is on the wicked, Pro 3:33
Poverty is his only *. Pro 10:15
People * the man who holds his Pro 11:26
for evil you will find his *. Pro 11:27
If you repay evil for good, a * Pro 17:13
but there is a * that goes with Pro 20:21
An undeserved * has no effect. Pro 26:2
morning, he will count it as a *! Pro 27:14
A * on those who lead astray the Pro 28:10
But a * upon those who close Pro 28:27
lest he * you for your sin. Pro 30:10
There are those who * their Pro 30:11,12
how often you yourself * others! Ecc 7:21,22
Never * the king, not even in Ecc 10:20
the Lord will bring a terrible * Is 7:17
and * their King and their God. Is 8:21
Therefore the * of God is upon Is 24:6
Your name shall be a * word Is 65:15
refusing to pay—yet they all * me. Jer 15:10
Well, let them *! Jer 15:11
and the * of God is on it. Jer 23:10
make Jerusalem a * word in every Jer 26:6
anyone wants to * someone he will Jer 29:22
"May the * of God be on us if we Jer 42:5
and to make you a * and a stench in Jer 44:8
Harden their hearts and * them, Lam 3:65
And so the awesome * of God has Dan 9:11
has crushed us—the * written in the Dan 9:11
Every * against us written in Dan 9:13
instead of his terrible *. Joe 2:14
you through the * of Balaam, son of Mic 6:5
* going out over the entire land. Zec 5:3
"I am sending this * into the Zec 5:4
"And my * shall remain upon his Zec 5:4
is a word of blessing, not a *. Zec 8:13
concerning God's * on the lands of Zec 9:1
And so the awesome * of God is Mal 3:9
And if you * him, you are in Mt 5:22
Peter began to * and swear. Mt 26:74
He began to * and swear. Mk 14:71
the happiness of those who * you; Lk 6:28
about it? A * upon them anyway!" Jn 7:49
Stephen * Moses, and even God. Act 6:11
themselves by a * neither to eat Act 23:12,13
themselves under a * to neither eat Act 23:21
Christians everywhere * Christ. Act 26:11
you are a Christian, don't * him; Rom 12:14
Spirit of God can * Jesus, and no 1Co 12:3
let God's * fall upon him. Gal 1:9
are under God's *, for the Gal 3:10
* for our wrongdoing upon himself. Gal 3:13
ONCE YOU WERE under God's *, Eph 2:1
rebellious hearts, * and swear, 1Ti 1:9
But these men mock and * at Jud 1:10
God and will die under his *. Jud 1:11

CURSED
of the whole earth—to be *. Gen 3:14
this ground which God has *." Gen 5:28-31
had done, he * Ham's descendants: Gen 9:24,25
Literally, "* be Canaan." Gen 9:24,25f
low before you. * are all who Gen 27:27,28,29
just for fun. * be their anger, Gen 49:7
he has * his own flesh and blood. Lev 20:9
* God, Lev 24:11
What God has not *? Num 23:7-10
Utterly detest it, for it is a * Deu 7:26
hanging on a tree is * of God. Deu 21:23
"'* is anyone who despises his Deu 27:16
"'* is he who moves the Deu 27:17
"'* is he who takes advantage Deu 27:18
"'* is he who is unjust to the Deu 27:19
"'* is he who commits adultery Deu 27:20
"'* is he who has sexual Deu 27:21
"'* is he who has sexual Deu 27:22
"'* is he who has sexual Deu 27:23
"'* is he who secretly slays Deu 27:24
"'* is he who accepts a bribe Deu 27:25
"'* is anyone who does not obey Deu 27:26
from their enemies—for they are *. Jos 7:12
The men you taunted and * are Ju 9:38
who does this shall be * of God." Ju 21:18
And he * David by the names of 1Sa 17:43
enemies shall be as * as Nabal is. 1Sa 25:26
of a man, then may he be * by God. 1Sa 26:19
for he * the Lord's chosen king!" 2Sa 19:21
from Bahurim? He * me with a 1Ki 2:8
He turned around and * them in 2Ki 2:24
go and bury this * woman, for she 2Ki 9:34
this land would be * and become 2Ki 22:18,19
mine, but you are * with those gold 2Ch 13:8
these parents and * them and Neh 13:25
Literally, "have * God." Job 1:5f
AT LAST JOB spoke, and * the day Job 3:1
"Let the day of my birth be *," Job 3:2,3
Everything they own is *. Job 24:18
I have never * anyone nor asked for Job 31:30
but those * by him shall die. Ps 37:22
and * by my vengeful enemies. Ps 44:15,16
and * and shamed for your sake. Ps 69:7
You rebuke those * proud ones who Ps 119:21
those * of God are caught in it. Pro 22:14
* by many people of many nations; Pro 24:24
delighting in their sins, are *. Is 66:3
* is the man who does not heed it! Jer 11:1
The Lord says: * is the man who Jer 17:5
Yet, * be the day that I was Jer 20:14
that I was born! * be the man who Jer 20:15
* wherever I compel them to go. Jer 24:9
and *, just as they are today. Jer 25:18
them they will be * and hissed and Jer 29:18
hatred—you will be * and reviled. Jer 42:18
despised and loathed, * and hated. Jer 44:12
incredible ruin, *, without an Jer 44:22
a living soul. * be those Jer 48:10
heaps of ruins, * and mocked; Jer 49:13
used to say to those they *! Zec 8:13
never again to be * and destroyed. Zec 14:11
asks the Lord. "* is that man Mal 1:14
Indeed, I have * you already Mal 2:1
with you, you * ones, into the Mt 25:41
fig tree he had *, they saw that it Mk 11:20
The fig tree you * has Mk 11:21
two robbers dying with him, * him. Mk 15:32
Then they * him and said, "You Jn 9:28
crowds, they were jealous, and * Act 13:45
We have blessed those who * us. 1Co 4:12
love the Lord, that person is *. 1Co 16:22
message, let him be forever *. Gal 1:8
very clearly, "* is everyone who Gal 3:10
on a tree is *" [as Jesus was hung Gal 3:13
Be happy if you are * and 1Pe 4:14
and are doomed and *. 2Pe 2:14
of heat, and they * the name of God Rev 16:9
in anguish, and * the God of Rev 16:11
below, and they * God because of Rev 16:21

CURSES
Rebekah: "Let his * be on me, Gen 27:13
"Anyone who reviles or * his Ex 21:17
"Anyone who * his father or Lev 20:9
that anyone who * his God must pay Lev 24:15,16
shall write these * in a book and Num 5:23
And * shall fall upon everyone who Num 24:3-9
fall upon everyone who * you.' Num 24:3-9
of these * shall come upon you: Deu 28:15-19
* in the city; Deu 28:15-19
* in the fields; Deu 28:15-19
* on your fruit and bread; Deu 28:15-19
* upon your crops; Deu 28:15-19
* upon the fertility of your Deu 28:15-19
* when you come in; Deu 28:15-19
* when you go out. Deu 28:15-19
"All these * shall pursue and Deu 28:45
And all the * written in this Deu 29:20
upon him all the * (which are Deu 29:21
so that all his * (which are Deu 29:27
blessings and the * I have Deu 30:1
God will take his * and turn them Deu 30:7,8
of blessing and * that Moses had Jos 8:34
bless me because of these *." 2Sa 16:12
of Joash, and the * laid upon 2Ch 24:27
All the * written in the scroll 2Ch 34:24
Now may those * return and cling Ps 109:19
an evil man inwardly * his luck. Pro 10:6
of the evil man is filled with *. Pro 10:11
* chase sinners, while blessings Pro 13:21
man who * his father or mother. Pro 20:20
even though these * of God have Jer 36:7
the bride * her mother-in-law. Mic 7:6
to, I will turn on you with *. Mal 2:1
Let God's * fall on anyone, Gal 1:8
it breaks out into * against men Jas 3:9

CURSING
and everyone began * Abimelech. Ju 9:27
were * about—well, I stole it!" Ju 17:2
came out of the village * them. 2Sa 16:5
this Benjaminite is merely * me. 2Sa 16:11
a nearby hillside, * as he went and 2Sa 16:13
accuse him of * God and the king. 1Ki 21:10
accused him of * God and the king; 1Ki 21:13
Let those who are experts at * Job 3:8
town and spend their time * me. Ps 35:16
insults and * God, for "No one Ps 59:7
They are proud, * liars. Ps 59:12,13
my face while * in their hearts! Ps 62:3,4
Don't overlook the * of these Ps 74:23
now don't you bless him. * is as Ps 109:18
for he is * you in his heart. Pro 26:24,25,26
You may hear your servant * you! Ecc 7:21,22
curse of God is * you, for your Mal 3:9
Their mouths are full of * and Rom 3:14
hatred, *, and dirty language. Col 3:8
And so blessing and * come Jas 3:10

CURTAIN
down to form a * across the front Ex 26:9
Hang the * from the hooks. Ex 26:33
Behind this * place the Ark Ex 26:33
God's laws. The * will separate the Ex 26:33
tent, make another * from Ex 26:36
Hang up this * on five acacia Ex 26:37
be 22½ feet of *, held up by three Ex 27:14,15
a thirty-foot-wide *, made of Ex 27:16
75 feet wide, with * walls 7½ feet Ex 27:18
The * for the door of the Ex 35:10-19
He attached the * at the entrance Ex 40:28
the * for the Tabernacle entrance. Num 4:25
fence, and the * across the Num 4:26
You stretched out the starry * of Ps 104:1
a * and makes his tent from them. Is 40:22
And look! The * secluding the Mt 27:51
And the * Mk 15:38
Then there was a * and behind Heb 9:3
and behind the * was a room called Heb 9:3
us by tearing the *—his human Heb 10:20

CURTAIN-DOOR
The * of the Tabernacle; Ex 39:33-40
tent, and hang the * at the Ex 40:8
and set up the * at the entrance of Ex 40:33

CURTAINS
* made from fine-twined linen. Ex 27:9,10
On the south side the * will Ex 27:9,10
post holders. The * will be held up Ex 27:9,10
court—150 feet of * held up by Ex 27:11
"They will carry the * of the Num 4:25
behind the sacred * of heaven, Heb 6:19

CURTLY
and then Solomon * dismissed him. 1Ki 1:53
Jesus * commanded the demon to Mk 1:25

CURVES
Straighten the *! Lk 3:5

CUSH
entire length of the land of *. Gen 2:13
The sons of Ham were:*, Gen 10:6
The sons of * were:Seba, Havilah, Gen 10:7
Or, "the son of *." Gen 10:8f
of * was Nimrod, who became the Gen 10:8
she came was sometimes called *. Num 12:1f
were also known as *, so it is Num 12:1f
Then Joab said to a man from *, 2Sa 18:21
got there ahead of the man from *. 2Sa 18:23
Then the man from * arrived and 2Sa 18:31
*, Misream, Canaan, and 1Ch 1:5-9
The sons of * were: 1Ch 1:5-9
Another of the sons of * was 1Ch 1:10
Come, all of you from * and Put Jer 46:9
The land of * has been ravished. Eze 30:4
ravished. For * and Put and Lud, Eze 30:5
Peras, * and Put shall join you Eze 38:5

CUSHAN
I see the people of * and of Hab 3:7

CUSHAN-RISHATHAIM
* of eastern Syria conquer them. Ju 3:8
the army of King *, the Lord helped Ju 3:10

CUSHI
Shelemiah, son of *) to ask Baruch Jer 36:14,15
To: Zephaniah (son of *, grandson Zep 1:1

CUSHION
of the boat with his head on a *. Mk 4:38

CUSHITE
Moses because his wife was a * Num 12:1
Literally, "because of the * Num 12:1f
or (if she was a * from Ethiopia) Num 12:1f

CUSTODIAL
they also did the * work and 1Ch 23:28

CUSTODIAN
He was the chief * of the Temple. 1Ch 9:10,11
been appointed as * of the Temple Neh 13:4

CUSTODY
were placed in the * of an officer Act 27:1
kept in protective *, so to speak, Gal 3:23

CUSTOM
(The * was that the stone was Gen 29:3
"It's not our * to marry off a Gen 29:26
And after that it became a * in Ju 11:39
village, as was the * of the day. Ju 14:10,11
This refers to the * of the day. Ru 1:11f
In those days it was the * in Ru 4:7
This was an approved * for those 1Sa 1:11f
as was the * in those days for 2Sa 13:17,18
and, as was their *, cut themselves 1Ki 18:28
pillar, as was the * at times of 2Ki 11:13,14
At that time David began the * of 1Ch 16:7
as was his * with all the 1Ch 20:3
vast tribute, *, and toll. Ez 4:20
and Asaph that the * began of Neh 12:46
began this annual *, as a reminder Est 9:23
of sorrow (as is their heathen *). Jer 16:6
their traditional * of fasting and Zec 7:3
Now the governor's * was to Mt 27:15
Now, it was Pilate's * to release Mk 15:6
washing required by Jewish *. Lk 11:37,38
Implied by ancient *. Lk 12:53f
The * of the period was to Jn 13:23f
singled out in the * of that time. Jn 13:26f
But you have a * of asking me to Jn 18:39
as is the Jewish * of burial. Jn 19:40
Gate—as was his * every day. Act 3:2
the ancient Jewish * of Act 15:1
As was Paul's *, he went there Act 17:2
Jewish *, for he had taken a vow. Act 18:18
approve of this * for the Hebrew Act 21:24
to every Jewish law and *. Php 3:5

CUSTOMARY
More literally, "* marriage Ex 22:16f
following the * procedures that Lev 5:10
its * grain and drink offerings; Num 29:33
the * grain and drink offerings. Num 29:37
He must give the * double Deu 21:17
his * place beside the entrance. 1Sa 1:9
At the * time for offering the 1Ki 18:36
suffering. (The * pomp and ceremony 2Ch 21:19
You refused me the * kiss of Lk 7:45
CUSTOMER
She was their biggest * for gold Rev 18:12
CUSTOMERS
and their *, and knocked over the Mk 11:15
CUSTOMS
practice any of these horrible *. Lev 18:29,30
You must not follow the * of the Lev 20:23
* of the nations now living there. Deu 18:9
in their loathsome *, thus sinning Deu 20:18
evil * of the nations around them. Ju 2:19
the heathen * of the nations around 2Ki 16:3
They had followed the evil * of 2Ki 17:8
the religious * of the nations from 2Ki 17:33
from their immoral * and joined the Ez 6:21,22
up the horrible * of the heathen Ez 9:1
* and laws which were worthless. Eze 20:25
the pagan * of verses 18 and 26. Eze 20:25f
to change all laws, morals, and *. Dan 7:25
who follow heathen * and who rob Zep 1:9
disciples follow our age-old *? Mk 7:5
all the Jewish * and ceremonies. Act 15:5
the Jewish traditions and *. Act 21:20
against our Jewish *, and that you Act 21:21
these Jewish * at all—except for Act 21:25
Jewish laws and * very carefully. Act 22:3
an expert on Jewish laws and *. Act 26:3
to obedience to Jewish laws and *. Act 26:5
violated the * of our ancestors. Act 28:17
we follow Jewish * if we have faith Rom 4:16
worry about the Jewish laws and * Rom 7:6
Jewish laws and *, but that is not Rom 10:3
Don't copy the behavior and * of Rom 12:2
who follow Jewish * and ceremonies 1Co 9:20
CUT
slay them and to * them apart down Gen 15:10
of his penis shall be * off. Gen 17:11
shall be * off from his people; Gen 17:14
from outside—and * off their Gen 17:23
a flint knife and * off the Ex 4:25,26
I will * them apart with my sword Ex 15:9
upon the altar. * up the ram and Ex 29:17
and * down their shameful idols. Ex 34:13
he can * and set stones like a Ex 35:33
thin plates and * it into wire Ex 39:3
and scarlet cloth * from Ex 39:4,5
anyway, shall be * off from his Lev 7:20
offering, shall be * off from his Lev 7:21
then he shall * it out from the Lev 13:56
You shall not * yourselves nor Lev 19:28
that man and * him off from all his Lev 20:3
and his family and * him off, along Lev 20:5
* that person off from his people. Lev 20:6
* off from the people of Israel. Lev 20:17
hair or beards, nor * their flesh. Lev 21:5
idols, and I will * down your Lev 26:30
time he must never * his hair, for Num 6:5
Eshcol where they * down a single Num 13:23
first grain that is * each year. Num 15:19,20,21
be * off from among his people. Num 15:30
soul shall be utterly * off; Num 15:31f
the obelisks and * up the shameful Deu 7:5
Lord told me to * two more stone Deu 10:1
shameful images, * down the metal Deu 12:3
of God, never * yourselves [as the Deu 14:1
just don't * down the trees. Deu 20:19
But you may * down trees that Deu 20:20
or his penis * off, he shall not Deu 23:1
hand shall be * off without pity. Deu 25:12
and * them down from the rear. Jos 10:19
and * off his thumbs and big toes. Ju 1:4,5,6
it down, and to * down the wooden Ju 6:25
groups * them down in the fields. Ju 9:44
So each of them quickly * a Ju 9:49
Your son's hair must never be *, Ju 13:5
"My hair has never been *," he Ju 16:16,17
If my hair were *, my strength Ju 16:16,17
in a barber and * off his hair. Ju 16:19
took a knife and * her body into Ju 19:29
So I * her body into twelve Ju 20:6
has been * off, and is gone. Ju 21:6
and his hair shall never be *." 1Sa 1:11
and hands had been * off and were 1Sa 5:4
Saul the choicest * of meat, the 1Sa 9:23
He took two oxen and * them into 1Sa 11:7
will kill you and * off your head; 1Sa 17:46
with it, and then * off his head. 1Sa 17:50,51
It is the hem of your robe! I * 1Sa 24:11
They * off Saul's head and 1Sa 31:9
murdered him and * off his head. 2Sa 4:6,7
and they did. They * off their 2Sa 4:12
their beards and * their robes off 2Sa 10:4
such praise. He * his hair only 2Sa 14:26
Then Ahima-az took a short * 2Sa 18:23
advice, and they * off Sheba's head 2Sa 20:22
of Lebanon to * cedar timber for 1Ki 5:6
can * timber like you Sidonians!" 1Ki 5:6
expensive stones, * to measure. 1Ki 7:9
walls were also * to measure, and 1Ki 7:11
* down and burned at Kidron Brook. 1Ki 15:13
to * off all trade with Jerusalem. 1Ki 15:17
one they wish and * it into pieces 1Ki 18:23
was their custom, * themselves with 1Ki 18:28
upon the altar and * the young bull 1Ki 18:33
place, and Elisha * a stick and 2Ki 6:6
I have * down the tallest cedars 2Ki 19:23
He smashed the obelisks and * 2Ki 23:14
and they * apart all the gold 2Ki 24:13
Saul's armor and * off his head; 1Ch 10:9
and he * down the army of the 1Ch 14:16
Asherah-idol; he * down the idol 2Ch 15:16
in isolation, * off from his people 2Ch 26:21
block them, and to * off the brook 2Ch 32:4
they did the whole thing—* the Neh 3:3
So the people went out and * Neh 8:16
to wither, even before it is *. Job 8:11-13
for a tree—if it's * down it Job 14:7
others, * off like heads of grain. Job 24:24
and * off your river of blessings. Ps 30:6,7
their posterity shall be * off. Ps 37:38
Let death seize them and * them Ps 55:15
They * me down with sharpened Ps 64:3
"I will * off the strength of Ps 75:10
So he * their lives short and Ps 78:33
Your terrors have * me off. Ps 88:16
You have * haughty Egypt Ps 89:10
Jehovah our God will * them off. Ps 94:23
He has * me down in middle life, Ps 102:23
brass and * apart their iron bars. Ps 107:16
he has done, and * off his name Ps 109:15
that made you * yourself in two? Ps 114:5
flying above me I will * them off. Ps 118:11
* me down with all their lies. Ps 119:78
Though my back is * to ribbons Ps 129:3,4
and kind to me, * off all my Ps 143:12
Literally, "shall be * off from Pro 2:22f
They have * themselves off from Is 1:4
THE LORD OF Hosts will * off Is 3:1
He built a watchtower and * a Is 5:2
be like a tree * down, whose stump Is 6:13
The sycamore trees are * down, Is 9:8,9,10
He, the Mighty One, will * down Is 10:34
will be * off, chopped down like Is 11:1
How you are * down to the Is 14:12
armies, and will * off his children Is 14:22
in sorrow and * off their beards. Is 15:2
The enemy war-lords have * down Is 16:8
grapes, he will * you off as though Is 18:5
* down and tossed in the fire. Is 33:12
of the west. I * down the tallest Is 37:24
it is * short as when a weaver Is 38:12
the rock from which you were *! Is 51:1
your sins have * you off from God. Is 59:2
has said to them, * down her trees Jer 6:6
and foolish. They * down a tree and Jer 10:2,3
friends shall not * themselves nor Jer 16:6
will be * down by the fierceness of Jer 25:37
contract I will * you apart just as Jer 34:18,19
apart just as you * apart the calf Jer 34:18,19
their clothes and * themselves, and Jer 41:5
The numberless soldiers * down Jer 46:22,23
"Come," they say, "we will * Jer 48:2,3,4
Moab is ended—her horns are * off; Jer 48:25
For the destroyer has * off your Jer 48:32
Literally, "those who * the Jer 49:32f
the thread of your life is *. Jer 51:13
and you shall be * off from among Eze 13:9
I will * off its branches and let Eze 17:9
you, and * off your nose and ears; Eze 23:25
I will * you off from being a Eze 25:7
I, myself, will * her down. Eze 31:11
her land and * her down and leave Eze 31:12
They won't * wood from the fields Eze 39:10
sacrifices were * up and prepared. Eze 40:41
But as you watched, a Rock was * Dan 2:34
of the Rock * from the mountain Dan 2:45
"He shouted, '* down the tree; Dan 4:14
and saying, '* down the tree and Dan 4:23
They have * themselves off from Hos 8:4
off their fruit and * their roots. Amo 2:9
The horns of the altar will be * Amo 3:14
I will * you down to size among Ob 1:2
you will be * off forever. Ob 1:10
you and * off all your visions; Mic 3:6
and * your chains of slavery. Mic 6:4
He is * off forever; Nah 1:15
the sword will * you down; Nah 3:15
Stagger and fall! You * down the Hab 2:17
of Lebanon—now you will be * down! Hab 2:17
"I have * off many nations, Zep 3:6
God's sword will * his arm and Zec 11:17
of Israel will be * off and die, Zec 13:8
May the Lord * off from his Mal 2:12
sin, * it off and throw it away. Mt 5:3
sin, * it off and throw it away. Mt 18:
of him, and others * branches from Mt 21:
to the prison to * off John's head Mk 6:2
"If your hand does wrong, * it Mk 9:43,4
carries you toward evil, * it off! Mk 9:45,4
sever your roots and * you down. Lk 3:
Jesus * him short. Lk 4:3
he told his gardener to * it down. Lk 13:
if not, I'll * it down.' Lk 13:
servant, and * off his right ear. Lk 22:5
ear Peter had * off—asked, "Didn't Jn 18:26
So the soldiers * the ropes Act 27:32
for those who * their bodies in Rom 2:29
you don't, you too will be * off. Rom 11:22
she should * off all her hair. 1Co 11:6
But I will do it to * out the 2Co 11:12
who want you to * yourselves by Gal 5:12
circumcised would * themselves off Gal 5:12
desires were not yet * away. Col 2:13
at and their backs * open with Heb 11:36
your sickle now to * off the Rev 14:18
CUTH
those from * worshiped their god 2Ki 17:30
CUTHAH
from Babylon, *, Avva, Hamath, and 2Ki 17:24
CUTS
brought the fatty * of meat from Gen 4:4
He * one down 1Sa 2:7
* him off and takes away his life? Job 27:8
feared, for he * down princes and Ps 76:12
a woodsman's axe * down the forest Is 10:34
it is placed. He * down cedars, he Is 44:14
I, the Lord, who * down the high Eze 17:24
and all the most tender *. Eze 24:4
* or scars—for a sin offering. Eze 43:22
Evidently self-inflicted *, as Zec 13:6f
CUTTER-LOCUSTS
After the * finish eating your Joe 1:4
CUTTING
and for * down the Asherah idol." Ju 6:30
builders in * the timber and making 1Ki 5:18
Jordan, they began * down trees; 2Ki 6:4
their beards and * their robes off 1Ch 19:4
and we will begin * wood from the 2Ch 2:16
of Canaan, * off its food supply. Ps 105:16
Some people like to make * Pro 12:18
is as foolish as * off your feet Pro 26:6
For the time has come for the * Eze 7:25
screaming and * himself with sharp Mk 5:5
Priest's servant, * off his ear. Mk 14:47
They finally decided to try. * Act 27:40
dealings, justly * them short." Rom 9:28
For it isn't the * of our bodies Php 3:3
sharpest dagger, * swift and deep Heb 4:12
CYCLONE
Disaster strikes like a * and the Pro 10:25
of the * and the raging storms; Nah 1:3
CYMBALS
for joy with tambourines and *. 1Sa 18:6
tambourines, castanets, and *. 2Sa 6:5
tambourines, *, and trumpets. 1Ch 13:8
upon psaltries, harps, and *. 1Ch 15:16
were chosen to sound the bronze *; 1Ch 15:19
the crashing of *, and loud playing 1Ch 15:28
of this detail, sounded the *. 1Ch 16:5
They used their trumpets and * 1Ch 16:42
of zithers, harps, and *. 1Ch 25:1
playing of *, harps, and zithers; 1Ch 25:6,7
played the *, lyres, and harps. 2Ch 5:11,12
the clashing of *, and the loud 2Ch 5:13,14
using *, psalteries, and harps. 2Ch 29:25,26
with music and * day after day. 2Ch 30:21
crashed their * to praise the Lord Ez 3:10
*, psaltries, and harps. Neh 12:27
Praise him with the *, yes, loud Ps 150:5
the cymbals, yes, loud clanging *. Ps 150:5
CYPRESS
I can supply both cedar and *. 1Ki 5:8
as much cedar and * timber as he 1Ki 5:10
the floors were made of * boards. 1Ki 6:15
folding doors of * wood, and each 1Ki 6:34
all the cedar and * lumber and gold 1Ki 9:11,12
and choicest * tree and have 2Ki 19:23
was paneled with * wood, plated 2Ch 3:5
cedars and choicest * trees. Is 37:24
*, fir and pine—on barren land. Is 41:19
he selects the * and the oak, he Is 44:14
The walls of your cabin are of * Eze 27:6
no * had branches equal to it; Eze 31:8
Weep, O * trees, for all the Zec 11:2
CYPRUS
shall come from the coasts of *, Num 24:23,24
The rumors that you heard in * Is 23:1
Even if you flee to *, you will Is 23:12
to the west to the island of *; Jer 2:10,11
from the southern coast of *. Eze 27:6
and scarlet dyes from eastern *. Eze 27:7
Or, from *. Dan 11:30,31f
of Levi, from the island of *). Act 4:36
far as Phoenicia, *, and Antioch, Act 11:19

YPRUS Con't)
to Antioch from * and Cyrene also Act 11:20
to Seleucia and then sailed for *. Act 13:4
him and sailed for *, while Paul Act 15:39
We sighted the island of *, Act 21:3
*, one of the early believers; Act 21:16
we sailed north of * between the Act 27:4
"we sailed under the lee of *." Act 27:4f

YRENE
across a man from *, in Mt 27:32
Simon of *, who was coming in Mk 15:21
death, Simon of *, who was just Lk 23:26
Phrygia, Pamphylia, Egypt, the * Act 2:10
by Jews from *, Alexandria in Act 6:9
from Cyprus and * also gave their Act 11:20
Lucius (from *), Manaen (the Act 13:1

YRIA
To: That dear woman *, one of 2Jn 1:1

YRUS
But in the first year of King * 2Ch 36:22,23
up the spirit of * to make this 2Ch 36:22,23
the reign of King * of Persia, the Ez 1:1
by giving King * the desire to Ez 1:1
"*, King of Persia, hereby Ez 1:2
King * himself donated the gold Ez 1:7
The items * donated included: Ez 1:9,10
to Joppa, for King * had included Ez 3:7
just as King * has commanded." Ez 4:3
to tell lies about them to King *. Ez 4:4,5
"But they insist that King * of Ez 5:13
and they say King * returned the Ez 5:14
* appointed as governor of Judah. Ez 5:14
King * ever made such a decree; Ez 5:17
the reign of King *, a decree has Ez 6:3
God and decreed by *, Darius, and Ez 6:14
when * captured the city. Is 21:5f
Doubtless * the Great of Persia. Is 41:2f
wait for word of *' new campaigns. Is 41:5
But I have stirred up (*) from Is 41:25
Not *, as in chapter 41, but Is 42:1f
Egypt and Ethiopia and Seba [to * Is 43:3
When I say of *, Is 44:28
many years before * began his Is 44:28f
THIS IS JEHOVAH'S message to *, Is 45:1
I will go before you, *, and Is 45:2
I have raised up * Is 45:13
distant future, as well as to *. Is 45:13f
nations that escape from *' hand. Is 45:20
concerning * would come true? Is 45:21
they save their worshipers from *? Is 46:1
the east—that man * from far away. Is 46:11
told you this: "The Lord loves *. Is 48:14
I have called *; Is 48:15
The troops of * the Great entered Jer 25:12f
* Cyrus is God's Jer 51:20
" * was used of God to Jer 51:20f
and does not confine himself to *. Jer 51:26f
first year of the reign of King *. Dan 1:21
whose first great ruler was *. Dan 2:39f
and in the reign of * the Persian. Dan 6:28
of the reign of *, king of Persia, Dan 10:1

D
(*) One might even say that Levi Heb 7:9

DABBESHETH
near Mareal and * until it reached Jos 19:11

DABERATH
and from there to * and Japhia; Jos 19:12
Kishion, *, Jarmuth, and Engannim. Jos 21:28,29
gave them Kedesh, *, Ramoth, and 1Ch 6:72

DADDY
old enough to say '*' or 'Mommy,' Is 8:4

DAGGER
a double-edged * eighteen inches Ju 3:16
the double-bladed * strapped Ju 3:21
The hilt of the * disappeared Ju 3:22,23
Leaving the * there, Ehud locked Ju 3:22,23
but then he pulled out a * and 2Sa 3:27
with a * strapped to his side. 2Sa 20:8,9,10
slipped the * from its sheath. 2Sa 20:8,9,10
Amasa didn't notice the * in his 2Sa 20:8,9,10
than the sharpest *, cutting swift Heb 4:12

DAGGERS
Then he took three * and plunged 2Sa 18:14
were sweet, but underneath were *. Ps 55:21

DAGON
god * and excitedly praised him. Ju 16:23,24
idol * in the city of Ashdod. 1Sa 5:1
the next morning, * had fallen with 1Sa 5:3
the priests of * nor his worshipers 1Sa 5:5
of the temple of * in Ashdod. 1Sa 5:5
all perish along with our god *." 1Sa 5:7

DAGON'S
his head to the wall of * temple. 1Ch 10:10

DAILY
"Fulfill your * quota just as Ex 5:13
refrain from doing our * tasks. Ex 16:23
Six days a week are for your * Ex 20:9
"This shall be a perpetual * Ex 29:42
and lay the * burnt offering on it, Lev 6:12
the fat of the * peace offering. Lev 6:12
sweet incense, the * grain Num 4:16
to the regular * burnt offering and Num 28:15
to the usual * sacrifices. Num 28:23
to the regular * burnt offerings Num 28:31
to the regular * burnt sacrifices, Num 29:6
to the regular * burnt sacrifices, Num 29:11
to the regular * burnt sacrifice Num 29:16
to the regular * burnt sacrifice, Num 29:19
And in addition to the regular * Num 29:22
to the regular * sacrifices. Num 29:25
to the usual * sacrifices. Num 29:28
In addition to the usual * Num 29:31
to the regular * sacrifices. Num 29:34
to the regular * sacrifices. Num 29:38
The * food requirements for the 1Ki 4:22
in accordance with our * needs. 1Ki 8:59
The king also gave him a * cash 2Ki 25:30
Six guards were assigned * to 1Ch 26:17
of animals for the * morning and 2Ch 31:3
people brought a * supply of food Neh 12:47
He came * to the court of the Est 2:11
enjoyed them more than my * food. Job 23:12
How long must I be hiding * Ps 13:2
He who * bears our burdens also Ps 68:19
are, and of your constant, * care. Ps 71:15
in my house. My * task will be to Ps 101:8
on you to give them * food. Ps 104:27
he watches for me * at my gates, or Pro 8:34
to cover his * needs until the day Jer 52:34
no more important than any * task. Eze 22:26
Memphis will be in * terror. Eze 30:16
to the Lord. This * offering will Eze 45:23
every morning for the * sacrifice. Eze 46:14,15
by canceling the * sacrifices Dan 8:11
the * sacrifice is restored again? Dan 8:13
putting a stop to the * Dan 11:30,31
"From the time the * sacrifice Dan 12:11
I was with you teaching * in the Mt 26:55
All mankind scratches for its * Lk 12:30
went about their * business—eating Lk 17:28
After that he taught * in the Lk 19:47
three o'clock * prayer meeting. Act 3:1
much food, in the * distribution, Act 6:1
So the church grew * in faith Act 16:5
and spoke * in the public square to Act 17:17
of Tyrannus and preached there *. Act 19:9
even thank him for all his * care. Rom 1:21
our * problems and in our praying. Rom 8:26
He gave you his rules for * life Rom 9:4
it is a fact that I face death *; 1Co 15:31
that your * lives should not 1Th 2:12
please God in your * living, for 1Th 4:1
He never needs the * blood of Heb 7:27

DAINTIES
what they do, sharing their *. Ps 141:4

DAINTIEST
care for even the * dessert. Job 33:20

DAINTY
What * morsels rumors are. Pro 18:8
Gossip is a * morsel eaten with Pro 26:22
"The * luxuries and splendor Rev 18:14

DAIRY
fruit and steal your * cattle. Eze 25:4

DALES
and mountains, * and valleys, and Eze 36:4
and mountains, * and valleys of Eze 36:6

DALMANUTHA
and came to the region of *. Mk 8:10

DALMATIA
has gone to Galatia, Titus to *. 2Ti 4:10

DALPHON
Parshandatha, *, Aspatha, Poratha, Est 9:7-10

DAM
held back by a *, and will pile up Jos 3:13,14
piling up as though against a *! Jos 3:15,16
like water bursting through a *!" 1Ch 14:11
They * up streams of water and Job 28:11
it is water over the *; Ecc 1:12-15

DAMAGE
be incalculable * to the king that Est 7:4
heal Jerusalem's * and give her Jer 33:6
exceed the actual * done to Tyre by Eze 26:14f
great spiritual * to a brother with 1Co 8:11
but what enormous * it can do. Jas 3:5
Literally, "do not * the oil and Rev 6:6f

DAMAGES
silver pieces as * for what I did, Gen 20:16
shall pay full * to the owner of Ex 21:34
must pay for all * by giving the Ex 22:5

DAMARIS
and a woman named *, and others. Act 17:34

DAMASCUS
to Hobah, north of *, and Gen 14:15
Or, "Eliezer of *." Gen 15:2,3f
Syrians from * when they came to 2Sa 8:5
army garrisons in *, and the 2Sa 8:6
fled with him to * (where he later 1Ki 11:24
to take to *, to King Ben-hadad of 1Ki 15:18
the desert road to *, and when you 1Ki 19:15
*, as my father did in Samaria." 1Ki 20:34
Pharpar River of * better than all 2Ki 5:12
Afterwards Elisha went to * (the 2Ki 8:7
how he recovered * and Hamath 2Ki 14:28
So the Assyrians attacked *, the 2Ki 16:9
King Ahaz now went to * to meet 2Ki 16:10
saw the altar that was at *." 2Ki 16:10f
his return from *, inaugurated it 2Ki 16:11,12
When the Syrians arrived from * 1Ch 18:5
troops in *, the Syrian capital. 1Ch 18:6
of Syria, at *, with this message: 2Ch 16:2
of booty to the king of *. 2Ch 24:23
large numbers of his people to *. 2Ch 28:5
of the people of * who had defeated 2Ch 28:23
tower of Lebanon overlooking *. Sol 7:4
not succeed, for * will remain the Is 7:8
will invade both * and Samaria and Is 8:4
destroy Samaria just as we did *. Is 10:9
THIS IS GOD'S message to *, Is 17:1
Look, * is gone! Is 17:1
and the power of * will end, and Is 17:3
That is how it will be in * and Is 17:6
like that of women in labor.* Jer 49:22
a raging storm. * has become Jer 49:24
at the edge of * that shall burn up Jer 49:27
and with honey, oil and balm. * Eze 27:18
the border between * and Hamath, Eze 47:16
to the north and * to the south. Eze 47:17
the border between * to the south Eze 48:1
The Lord says, "The people of * Amo 1:3
the gates of *, and kill her people Amo 1:5
far to the east of *," says the Amo 5:25,26,27
of Hadrach and *, for the Lord is Zec 9:1
"Doomed is Hamath, near *, and Zec 9:2
to synagogues in *, requiring their Act 9:2
As he was nearing * on this Act 9:3
He had to be led into * and was Act 9:8,9
Now there was in * a believer Act 9:10
to arrest every believer in *!" Act 9:14
He stayed with the believers in * Act 9:19
preaching, and the * Jews couldn't Act 9:22
Lord on the way to *, what the Lord Act 9:27
Jewish leaders in *, with Act 22:5
"As I was on the road, nearing * Act 22:6
up and go into *, and there you Act 22:10
to be led into * by my companions. Act 22:11
by all the Jews of *, came to me, Act 22:12
spoke to him [there on the * road Act 23:9
"I was on such a mission to *, Act 26:12
I preached first to those in *, Act 26:20
For instance, in * the governor 2Co 11:32
then came back to the city of *. Gal 1:17

DAMMED
great wealth. He * up the Upper 2Ch 32:30

DAMNABLE
cunning and deadly and * it is. Rom 7:13

DAMNATION
O Israel, the day of your * Eze 7:7
But the * of those who say such Rom 3:8

DAMNED
this godless nation, doomed and *; Is 10:5,6
City of Murder, doomed and * Eze 22:3
and will never be * for his sins, Jn 5:24
forever * if that would save you. Rom 9:1

DAMNING
women who are * the souls of my Eze 13:18

DAN
the retiring army as far as *. Gen 14:14
Rachel named him * (meaning Gen 30:6
Rachel's servant-girl:*, Naphtali. Gen 35:25
* and his son: Hushim. Gen 46:23,24,25
"* shall govern his people like Gen 49:16
*, Naphtali,Gad, Asher. Ex 1:1
tribe of *) to be his assistant; Ex 31:6
of Ahisamach, of the tribe of *. Ex 35:34
of Ahisamach of the tribe of *); Ex 38:23
of Dibri of the tribe of *. Lev 24:11
* -Ahiezer (son of Num 1:2-15
* -62,700 Num 1:20-46
Tribe: * Asher Naphtali Num 2:3-31
next to * Num 2:3-31
of the tribe of * and his offerings Num 7:66-71
of the tribe of * under the Num 10:25
of Gemalli, from the tribe of *; Num 13:3-15
The tribe of *: 64,400. Num 26:42,43
named after Shuham, the son of *. Num 26:42,43
* Bukki (son of Jogli) Num 34:16-28
Asher, Zebulun, *, and Naphtali Deu 27:13
Of the tribe of *, Moses said: Deu 33:22
"* is like a lion's cub Deu 33:22
out across Gilead as far as *: Deu 34:1
The Land Given to the Tribe of *: Jos 19:40
to be assigned its land was *. Jos 19:40
so the tribe of * captured the city Jos 19:47,48
and they called the city "*," Jos 19:47,48
*, and the half-tribe of Manasseh. Jos 21:5
were given by the tribe of *: Jos 21:23,24
As for the tribe of *, the Ju 1:34
And why did * remain with his Ju 5:17
*, who lived in the city of Zorah. Ju 13:2,3
of the tribe of *, located between Ju 13:25
The tribe of * was trying to find Ju 18:1
So the men of * chose five army Ju 18:2
* set out from Zorah and Eshta-ol. Ju 18:11

(DAN Con't)
"The Camp of *"), then they went Ju 18:12
the men of * demanded. Ju 18:23
mister," the men of * replied. Ju 18:25
So the men of * kept going. Ju 18:26
of * arrived at the city of Laish. Ju 18:27
Then the people of the tribe of * Ju 18:28
The city was named "*" after Ju 18:29
by the tribe of * as long as the Ju 18:31
They came from as far away as * Ju 20:1
And all Israel from * to 1Sa 3:20
all the way from * to Beer-sheba, 2Sa 3:9,10
as far away as * and Beer-sheba, so 2Sa 17:11
in Bethel and the other in *. 1Ki 12:29
and he destroyed Ijon, *, 1Ki 15:20
at Bethel and *—this was the great 2Ki 10:29
Issachar, Zebulun, *, Joseph, 1Ch 2:1
From the tribe of * there were 1Ch 12:24-37
Literally, "from Beer-sheba to * 1Ch 21:2f
Over *, Azarel (son of Jeroham). 1Ch 27:16-22
a Jewish woman from * in Israel; 2Ch 2:14
cities of Ijon, *, Abel-maim and 2Ch 16:4
Israel, from * to Beer-sheba, 2Ch 30:5
From * and from Mount Ephraim Jer 4:15
all the way from * in the north." Jer 8:16f
is to get. For *: From the Eze 48:1
named for Joseph, Benjamin and *. Eze 48:32
idols of Samaria, *, and Beersheba Amo 8:14

DAN-JAAN
and to * and around to Sidon; 2Sa 24:6

DAN'S
So the total on * side of the camp Num 2:3-31
lies south of * and has the same Eze 48:2

DANCE
Then they began to * around the 1Ki 18:26
A time to *; Ecc 3:4
King Solomon: "Because you * so Sol 6:13
Literally, "as upon a * before Sol 6:13f
the demons will come there to *. Is 13:21
But instead, you sing and * and Is 22:13
You will again be happy and * Jer 31:4
The young girls will * for joy, Jer 31:13
the young no longer * and sing. Lam 5:14
ended; our * has turned to death. Lam 5:15
performed a * that greatly pleased Mt 14:6
flute for you and you didn't *; Lk 7:32f
when he returned home, he heard * Lk 15:25
*" in worship of the golden calf. 1Co 10:7

DANCED
And David * before the Lord with 2Sa 6:14
Then David and all the people * 1Ch 13:8
came in and * before them and Mk 6:22,23

DANCES
a timbrel and led the women in *. Ex 15:20
come out for their *, rush out and Ju 21:21
honor at their *, singing, 'Saul 1Sa 21:11
about in their *: 'Saul has slain 1Sa 29:5

DANCING
the calf and the *, and in terrible Ex 32:19
on a tambourine and * for joy. Ju 11:34
were singing and * for joy with 1Sa 18:6
and drinking and * with joy because 1Sa 30:16
leaping and * before the Lord; 2Sa 6:16
David retorted, "I was * before 2Sa 6:21
and saw him * like a madman. 1Ch 15:29
spend their time singing and *. Job 21:12,13
Praise his name with *, Ps 149:3

DANDLED
on her hips and * on her knees. Is 66:12

DANGER
Lot, despite the * they all faced Gen 13:7
and is in great * because he has Lev 22:16
Aaron was in great * because the Deu 9:20
me from every *, I decree that 1Ki 1:29
I, the governor, run away from *? Neh 6:11
yourselves are in * of punishment Job 19:29
lure you away from * into a wide Job 36:16
strength, my shield from every *. Ps 28:7
have faithfully rescued me from *. Ps 71:15
pull back your foot from *. Pro 4:27
of * and to give you a good life. Pro 6:23
God rescues good men from * while Pro 11:8
wise man is cautious and avoids *; Pro 14:16
all blind to every *. Is 56:10
and give no warning when * comes. Is 56:10
have made? When * comes, let them Jer 2:28
streets without * to our lives. Lam 4:18
But they will be in constant *, Dan 11:33
horsemen can't outrun the * then. Amo 2:15
to live beyond the reach of *. Hab 2:9
you are in * of judgment! Mt 5:22
idiot, you are in * of being Mt 5:22
you are in * of the fires of hell. Mt 5:22
For you will be in great *. Mk 13:9
them, and they were in real *. Lk 8:23
Only at night is there * of a Jn 11:10
heard about his *, they took him to Act 9:30
for we are in * of being called Act 19:40
have faced grave * from the plots Act 20:19
penniless, or in *, or threatened Rom 8:35
your eyes open for spiritual *; 1Co 16:13
Yes, we live under constant * to 2Co 4:11
often in great * from flooded 2Co 11:26
how terrible our * if we refuse to Heb 12:25
distance, fearing * to themselves, Rev 18:15

DANGEROUS
are becoming * to us because there Ex 1:9
I will chase away the * animals. Lev 26:6
multiply too quickly and become *. Deu 7:22
with the * snakes and scorpions, Deu 8:15
It's too *." Ju 19:20
leave you alone. * animals will be Job 5:23
It is * and sinful to rush into Pro 19:2
The king's anger is as * as a Pro 19:12
A prostitute is a * trap; Pro 22:14
Jealousy is more * and cruel than Pro 27:4
A wicked ruler is as * to the Pro 28:15
Fear of man is a * trap, but to Pro 29:25
Egypt is a * ally. Is 36:6
"When I send an invasion of * Eze 14:15
and drive away the * animals from Eze 34:25
shepherding a whirlwind—a * game! Hos 12:1
and were so * that no one could go Mt 8:28
You are a * trap to me. Mt 16:23
"Am I some * criminal," he Mt 26:55
Jesus asked them, "Am I some * Mk 14:48
The weather was becoming * for Act 27:9
Watch out for those wicked men—* Php 3:2

DANGERS
more, nor fear the * of the day; Ps 91:5
nor will there be any other *; Is 35:9
great * to our lives at present. 1Co 7:26
I have faced grave * from mobs in 2Co 11:26

DANGLED
as he * alive from the oak. 2Sa 18:14

DANGLING
His mule went on, leaving him * 2Sa 18:9
me up and leave me * in the air; Ps 140:5

DANIEL
The second was *, whose mother was 1Ch 3:1
From the clan of Ithamar—*; Ez 8:2-14
Obadiah, *, Ginnethon, Neh 10:1
feast are seen in *, chapter 5, as Is 21:5f
event is further described in * 5. Jer 25:12f
"mortal man." In * 7:13, the Eze 2:1f
If Noah, * and Job were here Eze 14:14
though Noah, * and Job were living Eze 14:20
You are wiser than *, for no Eze 28:2,3
*, Hananiah, Misha-el, and Dan 1:6
follows:* was called Belteshazzar; Dan 1:7
But * made up his mind not to eat Dan 1:8
appreciation for *, and sympathy Dan 1:9
* talked it over with the steward Dan 1:11
to look after *, Hananiah, Dan 1:11
of the ten days, * and his three Dan 1:15
and God gave to * special ability Dan 1:17
him as much as *, Hananiah, Dan 1:18,19
* held this appointment as the Dan 1:21
of Babylon. And * and his Dan 2:13
came to kill them, * handled the Dan 2:14
So * went in to see the king. Dan 2:16
told * what the king had dreamed. Dan 2:19
Then * praised the God of heaven, Dan 2:19
Then * went in to see Ari-och, Dan 2:24
Then Ari-och hurried * in to the Dan 2:25
The king said to *, "Is this Dan 2:26
* replied, "No wise man, Dan 2:27
the ground before * and worshiped Dan 2:46
"Truly, O *," the king said, Dan 2:47
Then the king made * very great; Dan 2:48
of Babylon; * served as chief Dan 2:49
At last * came in—the man I Dan 4:8
Then * Dan 4:19
Literally, "*, whose name was Dan 4:19f
* replied: "Oh, that the events Dan 4:19
Call for this man, *—or Dan 5:12
So * was rushed in to see the Dan 5:13
him, "Are you the * that King Dan 5:13
* answered, "Keep your gifts, or Dan 5:17
Then at Belshazzar's command, * Dan 5:29
three presidents (* was one of Dan 6:2
* soon proved himself more Dan 6:3
fault in the way * was handling his Dan 6:4
But though * knew about it, he Dan 6:10
"That fellow *, one of the Jewish Dan 6:13
the law, and determined to save *. Dan 6:14
to get * out of this predicament. Dan 6:14
one could rescue * from the lions. Dan 6:17
in anguish, "O *, servant of the Dan 6:20
It was *! Dan 6:21
that * be lifted from the den. Dan 6:23
who had accused *, and throw them Dan 6:24
of * in every part of my kingdom. Dan 6:25,26
it is he who delivered * from the Dan 6:27
So * prospered in the reign of Dan 6:28
Babylonian empire, * had a dream Dan 7:1
by all I had seen (* wrote in his Dan 7:15
tell * the meaning of his dream." Dan 8:16
of his reign, I, *, learned from Dan 9:2
and said to me, "*, I am here to Dan 9:22
king of Persia, * (also called Dan 10:1
When this vision came to me (* Dan 10:2
I, *, alone saw this great Dan 10
And I heard his voice—"O *, Dan 10:1
be frightened, *, for your request Dan 10:1
"But *, keep this prophecy a Dan 12
Then I, *, looked and saw two men Dan 12
But he said, "Go now, *, for Dan 12
(told about by * Mt 24:1
* 9:27, 11:31, 12:11. Mt 24:1
3½ years, as in * 12:7. Rev 11:
3½ years, as in * 12:7. Rev 11:

DANIEL'S
But he was alarmed by * Dan 1:1
Then, at * request, the king Dan 2:4
and Abednego as * assistants, to be Dan 2:4
Then the men thronged to * house Dan 6:1
gave the order for * arrest, and he Dan 6:1

DANNAH
Shamir, Jattir, Socoh, *, Jos 15:48-6

DAPPLED-GREYS
white horses and the fourth by *. Zec 6:
while the * will go south." Zec 6:

DARA
Calcol, and *. 1Ch 2:

DARDA
Calcol, and *, the sons of Mahol; 1Ki 4:3

DARE
as a lion—who will * to rouse him? Gen 49:
"How * you demand a mortgage as Neh 5:
"Who would * touch you?" Est 7:
innocent, I * not think of it. Job 9:2
"How * you go on persecuting me, Job 19:2
back and did not * to tell you what Job 32:
With your wisdom, would we then * Job 37:19,2
HOW * YOU tell me, "Flee Ps 11:
"How * you grind my people in Is 3:1
and * the Lord to punish them. Is 5:1
Will they * tell Pharaoh about Is 19:1
Who will * to fight against me Is 50:
would * to come unless invited. Jer 30:2
How * you come to ask my help? Eze 20:
* not refuse to proclaim it. Amo 3:
* not show themselves outside Mic 1:1
and those who * God to punish them Mal 3:14,1
The other believers didn't * Act 5:1
through me. I * not judge how Rom 15:1
We * to say these good things 2Co 3:4
Oh, don't worry, I wouldn't * say 2Co 10:1
God forbid that anyone should * Gal 2:1
than we would ever * to ask or even Eph 3:2
body, did not * to accuse even Jud 1:9

DARED
"Since I have * to speak to God, Gen 18:31
And after that no one * to attack Jos 10:21
* to die upon the fields of Ju 5:18
who * to stand against you." 2Sa 18:28
help but no one * to rescue them; Ps 18:41
And after that no one * ask him Mt 22:46
And after that, no one * ask Mk 12:34
at a distance and * not even lift Lk 18:13
questions, for they * ask no more! Lk 20:40
and none of us * ask him if he Jn 21:12
Moses shook with terror and * Act 7:32

DARES
Who * arouse him? Num 24:3-9
who can stop him? Who * to ask Job 9:12
soon be gone. He * not go out into Job 15:22
No one * to stir him up, let Job 41:10
* come within reach of his jaws? Job 41:13
no one * even to travel through? Jer 9:12
of yours who * to plot against Nah 1:11
Who * accuse us whom God has Rom 8:33

DARING
grandson of Jehu), * him to 2Ki 14:8
I'm not strong and * like that! 2Co 11:21
proud and willful, * even to scoff 2Pe 2:10

DARIUS
until King * took the throne. Ez 4:4,5
of the reign of King * of Persia. Ez 4:24
while King * looked into the matter Ez 5:5
other officials sent to King *: Ez 5:6
"To King *: Ez 5:7
SO KING * issued orders that a Ez 6:1
So King * sent this message Ez 6:6
I, *, have issued this decree; Ez 6:12
once with the command of King *. Ez 6:13
decreed by Cyrus, *, and Ez 6:14
sixth year of the reign of King *. Ez 6:15
the reign of King * of Persia, in Neh 12:22
king, was killed, and * the Mede Dan 5:31
This * is not to be confused with Dan 5:31f
be confused with * the Persian, Dan 5:31f
* DIVIDED THE kingdom into 120 Dan 6:1
and say, "King *, live forever! Dan 6:6
So King * signed the law. Dan 6:9
Afterward King * wrote this Dan 6:25,26
in the reign of *, and in the reign Dan 6:28
of King *, the son of Ahasuerus. Dan 9:1
son of Ahasuerus. (* was a Mede but Dan 9:1
and help * the Mede in the first Dan 11:1
year of the reign of King * I. Hag 1:1
year of King *' reign, and Hag 1:14,15

DARIUS Con't)
the reign of King *, this message Hag 2:10
year of the reign of King *. Zec 1:1
the reign of King *, another Zec 1:7
year of the reign of King *. Zec 7:1

DARK
of God brooding over the * vapors. Gen 1:2
"over the *, gaseous mass." Gen 1:2f
and his face grew * with fury. Gen 4:5
"Why is your face so * with Gen 4:6
As the sun went down and it was * Gen 15:17
night, when it was *, Laban took Gen 29:23
"God has removed the * slur Gen 30:23,24
in the form of a * cloud, so that Ex 19:9
(also called Jebus) before *. Ju 19:10
He walked upon * clouds. 2Sa 22:10
return— a land as * as midnight, a Job 10:22
brightest light is * as midnight.' Job 10:22
light, even the * shadow of death. Job 12:22
labors with its * details, and Ps 7:14
They lurk in * alleys of the Ps 10:8
dense clouds * as murky waters. Ps 18:11
Even when walking through the * Ps 23:4
Make their path * and slippery Ps 35:6
heart, his * and evil deeds. Ps 53:1
be afraid of the * any more, nor Ps 91:5
ways to walk down * and evil paths, Pro 2:11,12,13
man gropes and stumbles in the *. Pro 4:19
directed into the * corners of your Pro 6:23
The sinner's road is * and Pro 13:9
that obligation and that * battle. Ecc 8:8
The Girl: "I am * but beautiful, Sol 1:5
tanned as the * tents of Kedar." Sol 1:5
is so *—the sun has tanned me. Sol 1:6
trouble and anguish and * despair. Is 8:22
in the * concerning what they do! Is 29:15
I form the light and make the *. Is 45:7
in some * corner so that no one can Is 45:19
your "fate" shall be a * one; Is 65:12
And all the heavens were *. Jer 4:23
and fall upon the * mountains; Jer 13:16
Therefore their paths will be * Jer 23:12
they will be chased down * and Jer 23:12
He buried me in * places, like Lam 3:6
Don't be dismayed by their * Eze 2:6
be a * day for Tehaphnehes too; Eze 30:18
Tehaphnehes too; a * cloud will Eze 30:18
bright stars will be * above you. Eze 32:8
in that * and cloudy day. Eze 34:12
his face became * with anger at Dan 3:19
or a man in a * room who leans Amo 5:19
Yes, that will be a * and Amo 5:20
down into the * hold of the ship to Jon 1:3
within, with no * corners, then Lk 11:36
have said in the * shall be heard Lk 12:3
AFTER * ONE night a Jewish Jn 3:1
a wrong step, because of the *." Jn 11:10
to shine in this * world, so that Jn 12:46
MORNING, while it was still *, Jn 20:1
minds became * and confused. Rom 1:21
of God in a * world full of people Php 2:15
you are not in the * about these 1Th 5:4
shining into * corners, their words 2Pe 1:19
would be * and difficult. 2Pe 1:19
and the sun became * like black Rev 6:12
*, dark will be her nights; Rev 18:23
Dark, * will be her nights; Rev 18:23

DARKEN
veil the heavens and * the stars. Eze 32:7
and * the earth in the daytime. Amo 8:9

DARKENED
the sun so that the land was *; Ex 10:15
The sun and moon will be * and Joe 3:15
the sun will be *, and the moon Mt 24:29
was blighted and *, and a third of Rev 8:12
sun and air were * by the smoke. Rev 9:2

DARKER
His eyes are * than wine and his Gen 49:12

DARKEST
You have thrust me down to the * Ps 88:6
as though it were the * night! Is 59:10
in Jerusalem's * corners to find Zep 1:12

DARKNESS
Or, "over the cloud of *," or, Gen 1:2f
or, "over the * and waters," or Gen 1:2f
and divided the light from the *. Gen 1:4,5
and then there was * again. Gen 1:4,5
and the * "nighttime." Gen 1:4,5
to divide the light from the *. Gen 1:18
foreboding, *, and horror. Gen 15:12
to heaven, and * without a ray of Ex 10:21
there was thick * over all the land Ex 10:22
of fire, it gave * to the Egyptians Ex 14:20
into the deep * where God was. Ex 20:21
by black clouds and deep *. Deu 4:11
thick * that engulfed Mount Sinai. Deu 5:22
voice from the *, and saw the Deu 5:23
just as the blind man gropes in *. Deu 28:29
trembling hearts, *, and bodies Deu 28:65
* between them and the Egyptians; Jos 24:7
down through the * to the outposts Ju 7:11
the wicked shall be silenced in *. 1Sa 2:9
* surrounded him, 2Sa 22:12
You make my * bright. 2Sa 22:29
that he would live in the thick *; 1Ki 8:12,13
that he would live in the thick *, 2Ch 6:1
city be shut as * fell on Friday Neh 13:19
Literally, "a day of *." Job 3:4f
to God, shrouded in eternal *. Job 3:4
Yes, let the * claim it for its Job 3:5
for the land of * and the shadow of Job 10:20,21
* will be as bright as morning! Job 11:17
He floods the * with light, even Job 12:22
He dares not go out into the *, Job 15:22
No, * shall overtake him forever; Job 15:30
"If I die, I go out into *, and Job 17:13,14
There will be * in every home Job 18:6
*, and chased out of the world. Job 18:18
my path and turned my light to *. Job 19:8
will be lost in deepest *. Job 20:26
fears, and * and waves of horror. Job 22:10,11
can he judge through the thick *? Job 22:13
terrified me with * all around me, Job 23:16,17
thick, impenetrable * everywhere. Job 23:16,17
with the terrors of the *. Job 24:17
Men know how to put light into * Job 28:3,4
and I walked safely through the *; Job 29:3
I waited for the light. * came. Job 30:26
he sees them all. No * is thick Job 34:22
clouds and thick *, and barred Job 38:8,9
Or tell me about the *. Job 38:19
give me light in my * lest I die. Ps 13:3
thick * was beneath his feet. Ps 18:9
He enshrouded himself with *, Ps 18:11
The Lord my God has made my * Ps 18:28
and sending us into * and death. Ps 44:19
else, and enters eternal *. Ps 49:19
disappear; let *, blindness and Ps 69:23
For the land is full of * and Ps 74:20
Because you are in *, all the Ps 82:5
Can the * speak of your Ps 88:12
There is only * everywhere. Ps 88:18
nor dread the plagues of *, nor Ps 91:6
Clouds and * surround him. Ps 97:2
He sends the night and *, when Ps 104:20
and he sent thick * through the Ps 105:28
Who are these who sit in *, in Ps 107:10
He led them from the * and Ps 107:14
When * overtakes him, light will Ps 112:4
If I try to hide in the *, the Ps 139:11
For even * cannot hide from God; Ps 139:12
* and light are both alike to you. Ps 139:12
They force me to live in the * Ps 143:3
just as light is better than *; Ecc 2:13,14
futile and end in *, without even a Ecc 6:4
Over all Israel lies a pall of * Is 5:30
will be thrust out into the *." Is 8:22
NEVERTHELESS, THAT TIME of * Is 9:1
The people who walk in * shall Is 9:2
and * the blind will see my plans. Is 29:18
who sit in prison * and despair. Is 42:7
He will make the * bright before Is 42:16
hidden in the *, secret riches; Is 45:3
Sit in * and silence, O Babylon; Is 47:5
to the prisoners of *, 'Come out! Is 49:8,9
I am the one who sends the * out Is 50:3
If such men walk in *, without Is 50:10
shine out from the *, and the Is 58:10
darkness, and the * around you Is 58:10
No wonder you are in * when you Is 59:9
from you. * as black as night Is 60:2
Have I been to them a land of * Jer 2:31
deep, impenetrable * to fall upon Jer 13:16
you will find only terrible *. Jer 13:16
your homes shall lie in silent *. Jer 25:10
He has brought me into deepest * Lam 3:2
I went out into the * with my Eze 12:7
Yes, * will be everywhere across Eze 32:8
and * is no obstacle to him. Dan 2:22
It is a day of * and gloom, of Joe 2:2
of black clouds and thick *. Joe 2:2
"The sun will be turned into * Joe 2:31
he turns the morning to * and Amo 4:13
Orion, who turns * into morning, Amo 5:8
and prosperity, but * and doom! Amo 5:18
How terrible the * will be for Amo 5:18
people in utter spiritual *, Jon 4:11
all your visions; * will cover you, Mic 3:6
When I sit in *, the Lord himself Mic 7:8
God will bring me out of my * Mic 7:9
and desolation, of *, gloom, Zep 1:15
sat in * have seen a great Light; Mt 4:15,16
you are in deep spiritual *. Mt 6:23
And oh, how deep that * can be! Mt 6:23
be cast into outer *, into the Mt 8:12
out into the outer * where there is Mt 22:13
out into outer *: there shall be Mt 25:30
was covered with * for three Mt 27:45
About noon, * fell across the Mk 15:33
those who sit in * and death's Lk 1:79
the light and plunges you into *. Lk 11:34
By now it was noon, and * fell Lk 23:44
shines through the *—and the Jn 1:5
the * can never extinguish it. Jn 1:5
but they loved the * more than the Jn 3:19
they wanted to sin in the *. Jn 3:20
But as * fell and Jesus still Jn 6:17
through the *, for living light Jn 8:12
to go before the * falls, for then Jn 12:35
me will no longer wander in the *. Jn 12:46
Instantly mist and * fell upon Act 13:11
of in Satan's *, so that they may Act 26:18
As the * gave way to the early Act 27:33
men who are lost in * to God. Rom 2:19
So quit the evil deeds of * and Rom 13:12,13
be light in the *," has made us 2Co 4:6
How can light live with *? 2Co 6:14
Their closed hearts are full of * Eph 4:17,18
heart was full of *, now it is full Eph 5:8
of evil and *, but instead, rebuke Eph 5:11
of * which the ungodly do. Eph 5:12
princes of * who rule this world; Eph 6:12
us out of the * and gloom of Col 1:13
and do not belong to * and night. 1Th 5:5
fire, gloom, * and a terrible Heb 12:18
of the * into his wonderful light. 1Pe 2:9
and * until the judgment day. 2Pe 2:4
doomed to the eternal pits of *. 2Pe 2:17
Light and in him is no * at all. 1Jn 1:5
spiritual * and sin, we are lying. 1Jn 1:6
one another, the * in our lives 1Jn 2:8
his fellow man, is still in *. 1Jn 2:9
stumbling around in * and sin. 1Jn 2:10
in spiritual * and doesn't know 1Jn 2:11
is going, for the * had made him 1Jn 2:11
*, waiting for the judgment day. Jud 1:6
* that God has prepared for them. Jud 1:13
and the nighttime * deepened. Rev 8:12
his kingdom was plunged into *. Rev 16:10

DARKON
Peruda, Jaalah, *, Giddel, Ez 2:55,56,57
Jaala, *, Giddel, Neh 7:57,58,59

DARLING
"Come to bed with me, my *." 2Sa 13:11
How sweet is your love, my *, my Sol 4:10
"My * bride is like a private Sol 4:12
here in my garden, my *, my bride! Sol 5:1
'Open to me, my *, my lover, my Sol 5:2
is still my son, my * child. Jer 31:20

DART
nor spear nor * nor pointed shaft. Job 41:26

DARTED
The living beings * to and fro, Eze 1:14

DARTING
the squares, * like lightning, Nah 2:4

DARTS
Will his hide be hurt by *, or Job 41:7

DASH
the young men, * their babies 2Ki 8:12
Wear fine clothes—with a * of Ecc 9:8
upon you and * you to the ground. Is 28:2
and made a * for it across the Jer 52:7

DASHED
my head and * them to the ground! Deu 9:17
water there, their hopes are *. Job 6:19-21
And so my hopes in you are *—you Job 6:19-21
He has taken me by the neck and * Job 16:12
Their little children will be * Is 13:16
But Zedekiah's hopes were *. Jer 21:1f
even mothers and children were * Hos 10:14
army, her babies * to death against Hos 13:16
her babies were * to death Nah 3:10
enemies' advance will all be *. Zec 9:5

DASHES
It * the enemy to pieces. Ex 15:6
control of him it * him to the Mk 9:18

DASHING
blue, * about on their horses. Eze 23:6

DASTARDLY
don't do such a * act," he begged, Ju 19:23

DATE
selected as the * of the annual Ex 12:42
The * of his death was July 15, Num 33:38,39
(a * he decided upon himself), 1Ki 12:32,33
at the earlier *, and there wasn't 2Ch 30:2,3
The completion * was February 18 Ez 6:15
year was the * indicated. Est 3:7
"write down this *, for today the Eze 24:2
to bring his accounts up to *. Mt 18:23
But no one knows the * and hour Mt 24:36
know the * or moment of my return. Mt 25:13
December 25 was the usual * for Jn 10:22,23f
for the old one is out of * now Heb 8:13

DATES
* appointed each year in March; Ex 34:18
* and it was recorded as law. Est 9:32
are like its clusters of *. Sol 7:7
"The Father sets those *," he Act 1:7

DATHAN
conspired with * and Abiram (the Num 16:1
Then Moses summoned * and Num 16:11,12
tents of Korah, *, and Abiram." Num 16:23,24
to the tents of * and Abiram, Num 16:25

(DATHAN Con't)
the tents of Korah, *, and Abiram. Num 16:27
and Abiram. And * and Abiram came Num 16:27
of Nemu-el, Abiram, and *. Num 26:5-11
and Dathan. This * and Abiram were Num 26:5-11
They weren't there when * and Deu 11:6
*, Abiram and his friends; Ps 106:17

DATING
A papyrus * from the 5th century Jer 7:18f

DAUGHTER
who was the * of their brother Gen 11:29
"Whose * are you, miss?" Gen 24:23
"my master's brother's *." Gen 24:48f
Rebekah, the * of Bethuel the Gen 25:20
Judith, * of Be-eri the Hethite; Gen 26:34
and he also married Basemath, * Gen 26:34
and * of Ishmael, Abraham's son. Gen 28:9
Look, there comes his * Rachel Gen 29:6
was his cousin—the * of his Gen 29:10
off a younger * ahead of her Gen 29:26
birth to a * and named her Dinah. Gen 30:21
ONE DAY DINAH, Leah's *, went out Gen 34:1
in love with your *, and longs for Gen 34:8
Adah (* of Elon the Hethite), Gen 36:2,3
Oholibamah (* of Anah and Gen 36:2,3
Literally, "the * of Ishmael." Gen 36:2,3f
—she was a * of Ishmael—the sister Gen 36:2,3
wife Oholibamah (* of Anah):The Gen 36:18,19
King Hadad's wife was Mehetabel, * Gen 36:31-39
a Canaanite girl—the * of Shua. Gen 38:2
named Asenath, * of Potiphera, Gen 41:45
by Asenath, the * of Potiphera, Gen 41:50
including their * Dinah, born to Gen 46:15
was Asenath, the * of Potiphera, Gen 46:19-22
Aaron married Elisheba, the * of Ex 6:23
shall your son, *, or Ex 20:10
"If a man sells his * as a Ex 21:7
but must treat her as a *. Ex 21:9
whether the * of his father or his Lev 18:9
granddaughter—the * of either your Lev 18:10
*—for she is a close relative. Lev 18:10
father's wife's *; Lev 18:11
a woman and her * or granddaughter, Lev 18:17
whether the * of his father or of Lev 20:17
son, *, brother, or unmarried Lev 21:2,3
you, am holy. The * of any priest Lev 21:9
If a priest's * is married Lev 22:12
* of Dibri of the tribe of Dan. Lev 24:11
* of Reuel (Exodus 2:21); Num 12:1f
The girl's name was Cozbi, * of Num 25:15
Asher also had a * named Serah. Num 26:44-47
While Levi was in Egypt, a *, Num 26:58,59
And if he has no *, it shall Num 27:9
and his * who is living at home. Num 30:16
a brother, son, *, or beloved wife Deu 13:6,7
them, 'I gave my * to this man to Deu 22:16
her beloved husband, son, and *. Deu 28:56,57
he would give his * Achsah to be Jos 15:16
have my * Achsah as his wife!" Ju 1:12
When Jephthah returned home his * Ju 11:34
"Alas, my *!" Ju 11:35
lament the fate of Jephthah's *. Ju 11:40
Here, take my virgin * and this Ju 19:24
Naomi said, "All right, dear *. Ru 2:2
Saul's wife was Ahino-am, the * 1Sa 14:50,51
to marry Saul's *, Saul wanted to 1Sa 17:55f
my oldest * Merab as your wife. 1Sa 18:17
In the meantime Saul's * Michal 1Sa 18:20
I will give you my youngest *." 1Sa 18:21
dowry to marry the * of a king?" 1Sa 18:23
Michal, Saul's *, to marry a man 1Sa 25:44
the * of King Talmai of Geshur. 2Sa 3:3
me my wife Michal, Saul's *." 2Sa 3:13
Michal, Saul's *, watched from a 2Sa 6:16
* of Eliam and the wife of Uriah. 2Sa 11:3
it in his arms like a baby *. 2Sa 12:3
He had three sons and one *, 2Sa 14:27
was Abigal, the * of Nahash, who 2Sa 17:25
* Merab, the wife of Adri-el. 2Sa 21:8
married Solomon's *, the princess 1Ki 4:8-19
for Pharaoh's *—one of his wives. 1Ki 7:8
the city to his * as dowry—she was 1Ki 9:16
King Solomon moved Pharaoh's * 1Ki 9:24
was Maacah, the * of Abishalom. 1Ki 15:1
was Maacah, the * of Abishalom. 1Ki 15:10
Jezebel, the * of King Ethbaal of 1Ki 16:31
His mother was Azubah, the * of 1Ki 22:42
for she is the * of a king." 2Ki 9:34
(for she was a * of King Jehoram, 2Ki 11:2,3
your * to be a wife for my son.' 2Ki 14:9
Mother's name: Jerusha (* of 2Ki 15:32,33
His mother's name: Abi (* of 2Ki 18:1
* of Zion isn't afraid of you! 2Ki 19:21
afraid of you! The * of Jerusalem 2Ki 19:21
His mother's name: Meshullemeth (* 2Ki 21:19,20
Name of his mother: Jedidah (* of 2Ki 22:1
to burn his son or * to death as a 2Ki 23:10
His mother's name: Hamutal (the * 2Ki 23:31,32
His mother's name: Zebidah (* of 2Ki 23:36,37
Name of his mother: Nehushta (* of 2Ki 24:8,9
His mother's name: Hamutal (* of 2Ki 24:18,19
and Esau's * was named Timna. 1Ch 1:38,39
was Mehetabel, the * of Matred and 1Ch 1:50
Hezron married Machir's * at the 1Ch 2:21
Caleb also had a *, whose name 1Ch 2:48,49
the * of King Talmai of Geshur. 1Ch 3:2
(the * of Ammi-el) became the 1Ch 3:5
David also had a * Tamar. 1Ch 3:9
Jushab-hesed, Shelomith (a *). 1Ch 3:19,20
(his *),Penuel (the ancestor of 1Ch 4:3-4
wife Michal, the * of King Saul, 1Ch 15:29
(she was Pharaoh's *) from the City 2Ch 8:11
She was the * of David's son 2Ch 11:18
the * of David's brother Eliab. 2Ch 11:18
Later he married Maacah, the * of 2Ch 11:20
His mother's name was Micaiah (* 2Ch 13:1
with [the * of 2Ch 18:1
name was Azubah, the * of Shilhi. 2Ch 20:31
Literally, "the king's *," i.e. 2Ch 22:11f
King Jehoram's *, verse 11. 2Ch 22:11f
She was a * of King Jehoram, and 2Ch 22:11
your * in marriage to my son.' 2Ch 25:18
His mother was Jerushah, * of 2Ch 27:1
was Abijah, the * of Zechariah. 2Ch 29:1
* of Meshullam (son of Berechiah). Neh 6:18
His uncle's *. Est 2:7f
family and raised as his own *. Est 2:7
Literally, "Esther, the * of Est 2:15f
Meanwhile, Queen Esther (* of Est 9:29-31
Literally, "in the gates of the * Ps 9:14f
"I advise you, O *, not to fret Ps 45:10,11
Literally, "The king's *." Ps 45:13f
dishonored virgin, * of Sidon, will Is 23:12
helpless virgin * of Zion—laughs at Is 37:22
honor are ended. O * of Chaldea, Is 47:1
your neck, O captive * of Zion. Is 52:2
will you vacillate, O wayward *? Jer 31:22
for medicine, O virgin * of Egypt! Jer 46:11
Weep, * of Rabbah! Jer 49:3
O wicked *, you trusted in your Jer 49:4
His mother's name was Hamutal (* Jer 52:1
" 'Like mother, like *'—that is Eze 16:44
and the king of Egypt. The * of Dan 11:6
Ptolemy II of Egypt gave his * Dan 11:6f
king, giving him a * in marriage, Dan 11:17
So Hosea married Gomer, * of Hos 1:3
had another child—this one a *. Hos 1:6
Rise, thresh, O * of Zion; Mic 4:13
father; the * defies her mother; Mic 7:6
Sing, O * of Zion; Zep 3:14
all your heart, O * of Jerusalem. Zep 3:14
"My little * has just died," he Mt 9:18
"*," he said, "all is well! Mt 9:22
his father, and a * against her Mt 10:35
or if you love your son or * more Mt 10:37
Herod, Herodias' * performed a Mt 14:6
For my * has a demon within her, Mt 15:22
And her * was healed right Mt 15:28
with him to heal his little *. Mk 5:23
And he said to her, "*, your Mk 5:34
was too late—his * was dead and Mk 5:35
Then Herodias' * came in and Mk 6:22,23
She was the * of Phanuel, of the Lk 2:36,37
"*," he said to her, "your Lk 8:48
mother and * will disagree; Lk 12:53
him, Pharaoh's * found him and Act 7:21

DAUGHTER-IN-LAW
child), and his * Sarai, and left Gen 11:31
Then Judah told Tamar, his *, Gen 38:11
of course that she was his own *. Gen 38:16
that Tamar, his *, was pregnant, Gen 38:24
"You may not marry your *—your Lev 18:15
with his *, both shall be executed: Lev 20:12
Parents kept a widowed * in the Ru 1:11f
for he is the son of your * who Ru 4:15
When Eli's *, Phinehas's wife, 1Sa 4:19
a *, a half sister—this is common. Eze 22:11
her mother, and a * against her Mt 10:35
will be spurned by her *." Lk 12:53

DAUGHTER'S
"Do not violate your * sanctity Lev 19:29
Ephraim's * name was Sheerah. 1Ch 7:24

DAUGHTERS
and *, and died at the age of 930. Gen 5:3,4,5
and *, and died at the age of 912. Gen 5:6,7,8
and *, and died at the age of 905. Gen 5:9,10,11
and *, and died at the age of 910. Gen 5:12,13,14
and *, and died at the age of 895. Gen 5:15,16,17
and *, and died at the age of 962. Gen 5:18,19,20
with God, and produced sons and *; Gen 5:21-24
and *, and died at the age of 969. Gen 5:25,26,27
and *, and died at the age of 777. Gen 5:28-31
of Seth, and "* of men" to the Gen 6:1f
years, and had many sons and *. Gen 11:10,11
years, and had many sons and *. Gen 11:12,13
that, and had many sons and *. Gen 11:14,15
and had many sons and *. Gen 11:16,17
and had many sons and *. Gen 11:18,19
after that, with many sons and *. Gen 11:20,21
afterwards, with many sons and *. Gen 11:22,23
afterwards, and had sons and *. Gen 11:24,25
Look—I have two virgin *, and Gen 19:8
sons, *, or anyone else. Gen 19:12
So Lot rushed out to tell his *' Gen 19:14
wife and your two * who are here Gen 19:15
his wife and two * and rushed them Gen 19:16
in the mountains with his two *. Gen 19:30
Literally, "* of the Gen 24:37f
Laban's *. Gen 28:2
Now Laban had two *, Leah, the Gen 29:16
"Are my * prisoners, captured in Gen 31:26
take his * from me by force.' Gen 31:31
*, and six years to get the flock! Gen 31:41
women are my *, and these children Gen 31:43
So how could I harm my own * and Gen 31:43
And if you are harsh to my *, or Gen 31:50
and kissed his * and grandchildren, Gen 31:55
us and to let your * marry our Gen 34:9,10
our * as wives for your young men. Gen 34:9,10
sons and *, grandsons and Gen 46:7
one of Pharaoh's *, came down to Ex 2:5
girls who were * of the priest of Ex 2:16
You will clothe your sons and * Ex 3:22
married one of the * of Puti-el, Ex 6:25
"We will go with our sons and *, Ex 10:9
they have sons or *, the wife and Ex 21:4
And you would accept their *, Ex 34:16
to your sons and * for your food. Lev 10:14
your own sons and *, and I will Lev 26:29
your families, sons and * alike. Num 18:11
And his * are captured Num 21:27-30
Here are the names of his *: Num 26:28-37
ONE DAY THE * of Zelophehad came Num 27:1
"The * of Zelophehad are correct. Num 27:6,7
shall be passed on to his *. Num 27:8
our brother Zelophehad to his *. Num 36:1
concerning the * of Zelophehad: Num 36:6
The * of Zelophehad did as the Num 36:10
sons, *, servants, oxen, donkeys, Deu 5:14
* marry their sons and daughters. Deu 7:3
daughters marry their sons and *. Deu 7:3
with your sons and * and servants; Deu 12:12
sons and * before their gods. Deu 12:31
and * are taken away as slaves. Deu 28:32
Your sons and * will be snatched Deu 28:41
your own sons and * in the terrible Deu 28:53
His sons and * were insulting him. Deu 32:19
his sons, his *, his oxen, donkeys, Jos 7:24
He had only five * whose names Jos 17:3
He had thirty sons and thirty *. Ju 12:9,10
He married his * to men outside Ju 12:9,10
never to let their * marry a man Ju 21:1
we will not give them our *?" Ju 21:7
But we can't give them our own * Ju 21:18
let them have your *, for we didn't Ju 21:22
* to them without being guilty.' Ju 21:22
No, my *, return to your Ru 1:12
No, of course not, my *; Ru 1:13
gave Hannah three sons and two *. 1Sa 2:21
He will take your * from you and 1Sa 8:13
and two *, Merab and Michal. 1Sa 14:49
him one of his * for a wife, and 1Sa 17:25
and had many sons and *. 2Sa 5:13
days for virgin * of the king. 2Sa 13:17,18
your *, your wives and concubines; 2Sa 19:5
Egypt, and married one of his *. 1Ki 3:1
*), whose area was Naphtali; 1Ki 4:8-19
he even married one of Ahab's *. 2Ki 8:18
their own sons and * to death on 2Ki 17:17
sons, although he had several *. 1Ch 2:34,35
He gave one of his * to be the 1Ch 2:34,35
sons and six *, but none of his 1Ch 4:27
had only *. 1Ch 7:15
the father of many sons and *. 1Ch 14:3
any sons, and his * were married to 1Ch 23:22
with fourteen sons and three *. 1Ch 25:4,5
twenty-eight sons and sixty *). 2Ch 11:21
had twenty-two sons and sixteen *. 2Ch 13:21
married one of the * of Ahab, and 2Ch 21:6
for him, and he had sons and *. 2Ch 24:3
and our sons and * and wives are in 2Ch 29:9
married one of the * of Barzillai Ez 2:61
You told us not to let our * Ez 9:12
sons marry their *, and not to help Ez 9:12
his * repaired the next section. Neh 3:12
sold some of our *, and we are Neh 5:5
married one of the * of Barzillai Neh 7:63
wives and sons and * who were old Neh 10:28
We also agreed not to let our * Neh 10:30
*, and was immensely wealthy, Job 1:2,3
Job's sons and * were dining at the Job 1:12,13
"Your sons and * were feasting in Job 1:18
seven more sons and three more *. Job 42:13,14
These were the names of his *: Job 42:13,14
girls as lovely as the * of Job; Job 42:15
Sons and *, come and listen and Ps 34:11
Kings' * are among your Ps 45:9
* of graceful beauty like the Ps 144:12-15
sons and as many * and lives to be Ecc 6:3
I will bring my sons and * back Is 43:6
and your * on their shoulders. Is 49:22
receive from having sons and *. Is 56:5
For your sons and * are coming Is 60:4

DAUGHTERS Con't)

*—squandered on priests and idols. Jer 3:24
little sons and * as sacrifices to Jer 7:31
Teach your * to wail and your Jer 9:20
Husbands, wives, sons and *—all Jer 14:16
our wives or our sons or * either. Jer 35:8
of the king's * and of the people Jer 41:10
the king's * and all those whom Jer 43:6
and * are taken away as slaves. Jer 48:46
for my sons and * are taken far Lam 1:18
And you took my sons and * you Eze 16:20
living with her * north of you; Eze 16:46
is Sodom and her *, in the south. Eze 16:46
Sodom and her * have never been as Eze 16:48
been as wicked as you and your *. Eze 16:48
them your *, for you to rule over. Eze 16:61
them, and they bore me sons and *. Eze 23:4,5
sons and * and burn their homes. Eze 23:47
And your sons and * in Judea Eze 24:20,21
sons and their *— on that day a Eze 24:25
* will be taken away as captives. Eze 30:18
There your * turn to prostitution Hos 4:13
Your sons and * will prophesy; Joe 2:28
I will sell your sons and * to Joe 3:8
and your sons and * will be killed Amo 7:17
said to them, "* of Jerusalem, Lk 23:28
and your sons and * shall prophesy, Act 2:17
* who had the gift of prophecy. Act 21:9
and you will be my sons and *." 2Co 6:18
good * and doing what is right; 1Pe 3:6

DAUGHTERS-IN-LAW

to Israel with her *, for she had Ru 1:6,7
said to her two *, "Why don't you Ru 1:8

DAVID

Jesse and grandfather of King *. Ru 4:16,17
Salmon, Boaz, Obed, Jesse, *. Ru 4:18-22
So as * stood there among his 1Sa 16:13
he send his son * the shepherd. 1Sa 16:19
sending not only * but a young goat 1Sa 16:20
From the instant he saw *, Saul 1Sa 16:21
him; and * became his bodyguard. 1Sa 16:21
"Please let * join my staff, for I 1Sa 16:22
God troubled Saul, * would play 1Sa 16:23
and frightened. * (the son of 1Sa 17:12
the Philistines. * was the 1Sa 17:14,15
One day Jesse said to *, "Take 1Sa 17:17
So * left the sheep with another 1Sa 17:20
against army. * left his luggage 1Sa 17:22
* talked to some others standing 1Sa 17:26
* talking like that, he was angry. 1Sa 17:28
"What have I done now?" * 1Sa 17:29
realized what * meant, someone told 1Sa 17:31
"Don't worry about a thing," * 1Sa 17:32
But * persisted. 1Sa 17:34
Then Saul gave * his own armor—a 1Sa 17:38,39
a coat of mail. * put it on, 1Sa 17:38,39
Goliath walked out towards * 1Sa 17:41,42
"Am I a dog," he roared at *, 1Sa 17:43
And he cursed * by the names of 1Sa 17:43
* shouted in reply, "You come to 1Sa 17:45
As Goliath approached, * ran out 1Sa 17:48,49
to the ground. So * conquered the 1Sa 17:50,51
(Later * took Goliath's head to 1Sa 17:54
As Saul was watching * go out to 1Sa 17:55
Since * was, if successful, 1Sa 17:55f
so that he didn't recognize *. 1Sa 17:55f
After * had killed Goliath, Abner 1Sa 17:57
And * replied, "His name is Jesse 1Sa 17:58
conversation with *, David met 1Sa 18:1
with David, * met Jonathan, the 1Sa 18:1
King Saul now kept * at Jerusalem 1Sa 18:4
home after * had killed Goliath. 1Sa 18:6
and * his ten thousands!" 1Sa 18:7
"They credit * with ten 1Sa 18:8
Saul kept a jealous watch on *. 1Sa 18:9
like a madman. * began to soothe 1Sa 18:10
hurled it at *, intending to pin 1Sa 18:11,12
But * jumped aside and escaped. 1Sa 18:11,12
had left him and was now with *. 1Sa 18:11,12
But the controversy put * more 1Sa 18:13
* continued to succeed in 1Sa 18:14
One day Saul said to *, "I am 1Sa 18:17
king's son-in-law?" * exclaimed. 1Sa 18:18
in love with *, and Saul was 1Sa 18:20
But to * he said, "You can be my 1Sa 18:21
confidentially to * that the king 1Sa 18:22
But * replied, "How can a poor 1Sa 18:23
told them, "Tell * that the only 1Sa 18:25
* would be killed in the fight. 1Sa 18:25
* was delighted to accept the 1Sa 18:26
the Lord was with * and how 1Sa 18:28
army attacked, * was more 1Sa 18:30
his son Jonathan to assassinate *. 1Sa 19:1
friendship with *, told him what 1Sa 19:1
he spoke well of * and begged him 1Sa 19:4
begged him not to be against *. 1Sa 19:4
Afterwards Jonathan called * and 1Sa 19:7
Then he took * to Saul and 1Sa 19:7
after that and * led his troops 1Sa 19:8
home, listening to * playing the 1Sa 19:9,10
it at * in an attempt to kill him. 1Sa 19:9,10
to kill him. But * dodged out of 1Sa 19:9,10
to arrest * and take him to Saul, 1Sa 19:14
In that way * got away and went 1Sa 19:18
So Samuel took * with him to live 1Sa 19:18
reached Saul that * was at Naioth 1Sa 19:19
"Where are Samuel and *?" 1Sa 19:22
* NOW FLED from Naioth in Ramah, 1Sa 20:1
don't know about it!" * fumed. 1Sa 20:3
And * replied, "Tomorrow is the 1Sa 20:5
Then * asked, "How will I know 1Sa 20:10
Then Jonathan told *, "I promise 1Sa 20:12
with the family of *, and David 1Sa 20:16
of David, and * swore to it with a 1Sa 20:16
But Jonathan made * swear to it 1Sa 20:17
So * hid himself in the field. 1Sa 20:24,25
so that * was ceremonially impure. 1Sa 20:26
"Why hasn't * been here for dinner 1Sa 20:27
it when he said that * must die. 1Sa 20:33
shameful behavior toward *. 1Sa 20:34
only Jonathan and * knew. 1Sa 20:39
As soon as he was gone, * came 1Sa 20:41
cheeks until * could weep no more. 1Sa 20:41
Literally, "* . . . 1Sa 20:41f
other and wept until * exceeded." 1Sa 20:41f
At last Jonathan said to *, 1Sa 20:42
So they parted, * going away 1Sa 20:42
* WENT TO the city of Nob to see 1Sa 21:1
me on a private matter," * lied. 1Sa 21:2
"Rest assured," * replied. 1Sa 21:5
* asked Ahimelech if he had a 1Sa 21:8
without a weapon!" * explained. 1Sa 21:8
"Just the thing!" * replied. 1Sa 21:9
Then * hurried on, for he was 1Sa 21:10
and * his ten thousands'?" 1Sa 21:11
* heard these comments and was 1Sa 21:12
SO * LEFT Gath and escaped to the 1Sa 22:1
discontented—until * was the leader 1Sa 22:2
(Later * went to Mizpeh in Moab 1Sa 22:3
protection until * knew what God 1Sa 22:3
when * was living in the cave. 1Sa 22:4
One day the prophet Gad told * to 1Sa 22:5
So * went to the forest of Hereth. 1Sa 22:5
"Has * promised you fields and 1Sa 22:7
My own son—encouraging * to come 1Sa 22:8
* talking to Ahimelech the priest. 1Sa 22:9,10
to find out what * should do, and 1Sa 22:9,10
"Why have you and * conspired 1Sa 22:13
as faithful as * your son-in-law? 1Sa 22:14
allies and conspirators with *; 1Sa 22:17
Ahimelech, escaped and fled to *. 1Sa 22:20
done, * exclaimed, "I knew it! 1Sa 22:22
ONE DAY NEWS came to * that the 1Sa 23:1
* asked the Lord, "Shall I go 1Sa 23:2
* asked the Lord again, and the 1Sa 23:4
to Keilah with *, taking his ephod 1Sa 23:6
get answers for * from the Lord. 1Sa 23:6
Saul soon learned that * was at 1Sa 23:7
Keilah and besiege * and his men. 1Sa 23:8
and his men. But * learned of 1Sa 23:9
"O Lord God of Israel," * said, 1Sa 23:10
betray me to Saul?" * persisted. 1Sa 23:12
So * and his men—about six 1Sa 23:13
Word soon reached Saul that * had 1Sa 23:13
there after all. * now lived in 1Sa 23:14,15
Jonathan now went to find *; 1Sa 23:16
of friendship; and * stayed at 1Sa 23:18
in Gibe-ah and betrayed * to him. 1Sa 23:19
But when * heard that Saul was on 1Sa 23:24,25
He and * were now on opposite 1Sa 23:26
began to close in, * tried his best 1Sa 23:26
the place where * was camped has 1Sa 23:28
Rock of Escape!" * then went to 1Sa 23:29
he was told that * had gone into 1Sa 24:1
as it happened, * and his men were 1Sa 24:3
Then * crept forward and 1Sa 24:4
These words of * persuaded his 1Sa 24:7,8
gone on his way, * came out and 1Sa 24:7,8
And when Saul looked around, * 1Sa 24:7,8
"Is it really you, my son *?" 1Sa 24:15
And he said to *, "You are a 1Sa 24:17
So * promised, and Saul went 1Sa 24:22
went home, but * and his men went 1Sa 24:22
Meanwhile * went down to the 1Sa 25:1
When * heard that Nabal was 1Sa 25:4
"Who is this fellow *?" 1Sa 25:10
started off with * and two hundred 1Sa 25:13
told Abigail, "* sent men from the 1Sa 25:14
she met * coming towards her. 1Sa 25:20
* had been saying to himself, "A 1Sa 25:21
When Abigail saw *, she quickly 1Sa 25:23
* replied to Abigail, "Bless the 1Sa 25:32
Then * accepted her gifts and 1Sa 25:35
with * until the next morning. 1Sa 25:36
When * heard that Nabal was dead, 1Sa 25:39
Then * wasted no time in sending 1Sa 25:39
and followed the men back to *. 1Sa 25:42
* also married Ahino-am from 1Sa 25:43
to tell him that * had returned to 1Sa 26:1
wilderness where * was hiding, but 1Sa 26:3,4
was hiding, but * knew of Saul's 1Sa 26:3,4
* slipped over to Saul's camp one 1Sa 26:5,6,7
there with me?" * asked Ahimelech 1Sa 26:5,6,7
replied. So * and Abishai went to 1Sa 26:5,6,7
sure," Abishai whispered to *. 1Sa 26:8
"No," * said. 1Sa 26:9
So * took the spear and jug of 1Sa 26:12
Then * shouted down to Abner and 1Sa 26:14
fellow, aren't you?" * taunted. 1Sa 26:15
said, "Is that you, my son *?" 1Sa 26:17,18
And * replied, "Yes, sir, it is. 1Sa 26:17,18
"Here is your spear, sir," * 1Sa 26:22
And Saul said to *, "Blessings 1Sa 26:25
"Blessings on you, my son *. 1Sa 26:25
Then * went away and Saul returned 1Sa 26:25
BUT * KEPT thinking to himself, 1Sa 27:1
So * took his six hundred men and 1Sa 27:2,3
Word soon reached Saul that * 1Sa 27:4
One day * said to Achish, "My 1Sa 27:5
And * would reply, "Against the 1Sa 27:10
Achish believed * and thought 1Sa 27:12
King Achish said to * and his men. 1Sa 28:1
"Good," * agreed. 1Sa 28:2
you and given it to your rival, *. 1Sa 28:17
and companies, * and his men 1Sa 29:2
them, "This is *, the runaway 1Sa 29:3
and * his ten thousands!' 1Sa 29:5
So Achish finally summoned * and 1Sa 29:6
this treatment?" * demanded. 1Sa 29:8
So * headed back into the land of 1Sa 29:11
THREE DAYS LATER, when * and his 1Sa 30:1
and children. As * and his men 1Sa 30:3
been captured.) * was seriously 1Sa 30:6
But * took strength from the Lord. 1Sa 30:6
* asked the Lord, "Shall I chase 1Sa 30:8
So * and his six hundred men set 1Sa 30:9,10
in a field and brought him to *. 1Sa 30:11,12
do you come from?" * asked him. 1Sa 30:13
me where they went?" * asked. 1Sa 30:15
the men of Judah. * and his men 1Sa 30:17
fled on camels. * got back 1Sa 30:18,19
and * rescued his two wives. 1Sa 30:18,19
they told *. 1Sa 30:20
to go on, * greeted them joyfully. 1Sa 30:21
But * said, "No, my brothers! 1Sa 30:23
From then on * made this a law 1Sa 30:25
where * and his men had been: 1Sa 30:27-31
SAUL WAS DEAD and * had returned 2Sa 1:1
He fell to the ground before * in 2Sa 1:1
"Where do you come from?" * 2Sa 1:3
"What happened?" * demanded. 2Sa 1:4
field and thought * would reward 2Sa 1:10f
* and his men tore their clothes 2Sa 1:11
Then * said to the young man who 2Sa 1:13
God's chosen king?" * demanded. 2Sa 1:14
"You die self-condemned," * 2Sa 1:16
Then * composed a dirge for Saul 2Sa 1:17,18
* THEN ASKED the Lord, "Shall I 2Sa 2:1
So * and his wives—Ahino-am from 2Sa 2:2
of Judah came to * and crowned him 2Sa 2:4
When * heard that the men of 2Sa 2:4
meanwhile, * was reigning in 2Sa 2:10,11
and the forces of *. 2Sa 2:17
the followers of Saul and of *. 2Sa 3:1
Several sons were born to * while 2Sa 3:2
betraying you to *, is this my 2Sa 3:8
*, just as the Lord predicted." 2Sa 3:9,10
Then Abner sent messengers to * 2Sa 3:12
"All right," * replied, "but I 2Sa 3:13
daughter." * then sent this 2Sa 3:14
they had wanted * as their king. 2Sa 3:17
"For the Lord has said, 'It is * 2Sa 3:18
and reported to * his progress with 2Sa 3:19
* entertained them with a feast. 2Sa 3:20
As Abner left, he promised *, 2Sa 3:21
So * let Abner return in safety. 2Sa 3:21
them; but * knew nothing about it. 2Sa 3:26
When * heard about it he 2Sa 3:28
Then * said to Joab and to all 2Sa 3:31
And King * accompanied the bier 2Sa 3:31
again for him. * had refused to 2Sa 3:35,36
of supper. But * vowed that he 2Sa 3:35,36
And * said to his people, "A 2Sa 3:38
They presented the head to * at 2Sa 4:8
But * replied, "I swear by the 2Sa 4:9
So * ordered his young men to 2Sa 4:12
of Israel came to * at Hebron and 2Sa 5:1
So * made a contract before the 2Sa 5:3
* now led his troops to Jerusalem 2Sa 5:6
were safe. But * and his troops 2Sa 5:7
of Zion, now called the City of *. 2Sa 5:7
the city reached *, he told his 2Sa 5:8
So * made the stronghold of Zion 2Sa 5:9
the City of *) his headquarters. 2Sa 5:9
city center. So * became greater 2Sa 5:10
masons to build a palace for *. 2Sa 5:11
palace for David. * now realized 2Sa 5:12
to Jerusalem, * married additional 2Sa 5:13
When the Philistines heard that * 2Sa 5:17
capture him; but * was told that 2Sa 5:17
Then * asked the Lord, "Shall I 2Sa 5:19
So * went out and fought with 2Sa 5:20
At that time * and his troops 2Sa 5:21

(DAVID Con't)
When * asked the Lord what to do, 2Sa 5:23
So * did as the Lord had 2Sa 5:25
THEN * MOBILIZED thirty thousand 2Sa 6:1
was followed by * and the other 2Sa 6:5
beside the Ark. * was angry at 2Sa 6:8
* was now afraid of the Lord and 2Sa 6:9
into the City of *, but carried it 2Sa 6:10
When * heard this, he brought the 2Sa 6:12
of * with a great celebration. 2Sa 6:12
a fat lamb. And * danced before 2Sa 6:14
Literally, "* was girded with a 2Sa 6:14f
and saw King * leaping and dancing 2Sa 6:16
tent which * had prepared for it; 2Sa 6:17
* returned to bless his family. 2Sa 6:20
* retorted, "I was dancing 2Sa 6:21
nations, * said to Nathan the 2Sa 7:2
"Tell my servant * not to do it! 2Sa 7:5
this message to * from the Lord of 2Sa 7:8
So Nathan went back to * and told 2Sa 7:17
Then * went into the Tabernacle 2Sa 7:18
AFTER THIS * subdued and humbled 2Sa 8:1
regain his power. * captured 2Sa 8:4
help Hadadezer. * placed several 2Sa 8:6
he turned. * brought the gold 2Sa 8:7
He gave * presents made from 2Sa 8:10
gold, and bronze. * dedicated all 2Sa 8:11,12
So * became very famous. 2Sa 8:13
* reigned with justice over 2Sa 8:15
ONE DAY * began wondering if any 2Sa 9:1
So King * sent for 2Sa 9:5,6
But * said, "Don't be afraid! 2Sa 9:7
with King *, as though he were one 2Sa 9:10,11
respect for him," * said, 2Sa 10:2
kind to me." So * sent ambassadors 2Sa 10:2
honor your father! * has sent them 2Sa 10:3
When * heard what had happened 2Sa 10:5
they had angered *, so they hired 2Sa 10:6
When * heard about this, he sent 2Sa 10:7,8
When * heard what was happening, 2Sa 10:17
to * and became his servants. 2Sa 10:19
when wars begin, * sent Joab and 2Sa 11:1
Rabbah. But * stayed in Jerusalem. 2Sa 11:1
Then * sent for her and when she 2Sa 11:4
So * dispatched a memo to Joab: 2Sa 11:6
When he arrived, * asked him 2Sa 11:7
When * heard what Uriah had done, 2Sa 11:10
"Well, stay here tonight," * 2Sa 11:12
the palace. * invited him to 2Sa 11:13
Finally the next morning * wrote 2Sa 11:14
When Joab sent a report to * of 2Sa 11:18
and gave the report to *. 2Sa 11:22
not to be discouraged," * said. 2Sa 11:25
mourning was over, * sent for her 2Sa 11:27
displeased with what * had done. 2Sa 11:27
Nathan to tell * this story: 2Sa 12:1
* was furious. 2Sa 12:5
Then Nathan said to *, "You are 2Sa 12:7
the Lord," * confessed to Nathan. 2Sa 12:13
deathly sick. * begged him to 2Sa 12:16
But when * saw them whispering, 2Sa 12:19
Then * got up off the ground, 2Sa 12:20
* replied, "I fasted and wept 2Sa 12:22
Then * comforted Bath-sheba; 2Sa 12:24
the prophet. * nicknamed the baby 2Sa 12:25
Joab sent messengers to tell *, 2Sa 12:26,27
So * led his army to Rabbah and 2Sa 12:29,30
to Jerusalem, and * took the king 2Sa 12:29,30
Ammonites. Then * and the army 2Sa 12:31
for him to eat. * agreed, and sent 2Sa 13:7
When King * heard what had 2Sa 13:21-24
the report reached *: "Absalom has 2Sa 13:29,30
Meanwhile *, now reconciled to 2Sa 13:37,38,39
Then at last * summoned Absalom, 2Sa 14:33
before the king, and * kissed him. 2Sa 14:33
to tell King *, "All Israel has 2Sa 15:13
palace in order. * paused at the 2Sa 15:17,18
So * replied, "All right, come 2Sa 15:22
"If the Lord sees fit," * said, 2Sa 15:25,26
* walked up the road that led to 2Sa 15:30
When someone told * that 2Sa 15:31
backing Absalom, * prayed, "O 2Sa 15:31
worshiped God, * found Hushai the 2Sa 15:32
But * told him, "If you go with 2Sa 15:33,34
* WAS JUST past the top of the 2Sa 16:1
As * and his party passed 2Sa 16:5
he shouted at *. 2Sa 16:7,8
So * and his men continued on, 2Sa 16:13
* and tossing dust into the air. 2Sa 16:13
the way to treat your friend *?" 2Sa 16:17
told him to, just as * had; 2Sa 16:23
men to start out after * tonight. 2Sa 17:1
And if * has escaped into some 2Sa 17:13
"Find * and urge him not to stay 2Sa 17:16
they were to take to King *. 2Sa 17:17
*, and he told Absalom about it. 2Sa 17:18
the well and hurried on to King *. 2Sa 17:21
and killed. So * and all the 2Sa 17:22
* soon arrived at Mahanaim. 2Sa 17:24
When * arrived at Mahanaim, he 2Sa 17:27
* NOW APPOINTED regimental 2Sa 18:1

me run to King * with the good news 2Sa 18:19
man from Cush. * was sitting at 2Sa 18:24
He shouted the news down to *, 2Sa 18:25
Let's ask * to return and be our 2Sa 19:8,9,10
Then * sent Zadok and Abiathar 2Sa 19:11,12
men of Judah to welcome King *. 2Sa 19:16
"Don't talk to me like that!" * 2Sa 19:22
"All right," * replied. 2Sa 19:29
and after * had kissed and 2Sa 19:39
"We want nothing to do with *. 2Sa 20:1
and deserted * and followed Sheba! 2Sa 20:2
Then * said to Abishai, "That 2Sa 20:6
are for *, come and follow Joab." 2Sa 20:11
who has revolted against King *. 2Sa 20:21
three years, and * spent much time 2Sa 21:1
So King * summoned the 2Sa 21:2
* asked them, "What can I do for 2Sa 21:3
"What can I do, then?" * asked. 2Sa 21:4
When * learned what she had 2Sa 21:11
with Israel, and * and his men were 2Sa 21:15
* became weak and exhausted. 2Sa 21:15
in on * and was about to kill him. 2Sa 21:16
* SANG THIS song to the Lord after 2Sa 22:1
To * and his family, 2Sa 22:51
THESE ARE THE last words of *: 2Sa 23:1
"*, the son of Jesse, speaks. 2Sa 23:1
*, the man to whom God gave such 2Sa 23:1
*, the anointed of the God of 2Sa 23:1
*, sweet psalmist of Israel: 2Sa 23:1
men who, with *, held back the 2Sa 23:9
One time when * was living in the 2Sa 23:13
to visit him. * was in the 2Sa 23:14
* remarked, "How thirsty I am 2Sa 23:15
from the well and brought it to *. 2Sa 23:16
* made him chief of his bodyguard. 2Sa 23:23
Israel, and * was moved to harm 2Sa 24:1
The Lord said to Gad, "Tell * 2Sa 24:12
So Gad came to * and asked him, 2Sa 24:13
"This is a hard decision," * 2Sa 24:14
When * saw the angel, he said to 2Sa 24:17
That day Gad came to * and said 2Sa 24:18
So * went to do what the Lord 2Sa 24:19
And * replied, "To buy your 2Sa 24:21
So * paid him 2Sa 24:24
and the oxen. And * built an altar 2Sa 24:25
IN HIS OLD age King * was confined 1Ki 1:1
Now his father, King *, had 1Ki 1:6
loyal to King * and refused to 1Ki 1:8
other sons of King *—and all the 1Ki 1:9
lord * doesn't even know about it? 1Ki 1:11
Go at once to King * and ask 1Ki 1:13
"Call Bath-sheba," * said. 1Ki 1:28
"Our lord King * has declared 1Ki 1:43
King *, saying, 'May God bless you 1Ki 1:46,47
Then * died and was buried in 1Ki 2:10
new king, replacing his father *; 1Ki 2:12
of my father * and this kingdom he 1Ki 2:23,24
the Lord declare * and his 1Ki 2:33
you did to my father, King *? 1Ki 2:44
in the City of * until he could 1Ki 3:1
kind to my father * because he was 1Ki 3:6
of my father *, but I am as a 1Ki 3:7
my laws as your father * did." 1Ki 3:14
a great admirer of *, so when he 1Ki 5:1
His father *, Solomon pointed out 1Ki 5:2,3
"Praise God for giving * a wise 1Ki 5:7
I told your father * I would do: I 1Ki 6:11,12
for that purpose by his father *. 1Ki 7:51
the City of *, to the Temple. 1Ki 8:1
promised my father *: for he said 1Ki 8:15
This man was my father, *. 1Ki 8:17
my father *, who was your servant; 1Ki 8:24
* and to his people Israel. 1Ki 8:66
as your father * did, always 1Ki 9:4
your father * when I told him, 'One 1Ki 9:5
from the City of *—the old sector 1Ki 9:24
the Lord as his father * had done. 1Ki 11:4
the Lord as his father * did. 1Ki 11:6
of your father *, I won't do this 1Ki 11:12,13
Years before, when * had been in 1Ki 11:15
Egypt, heard that * and Joab were 1Ki 11:21
king) when * destroyed Zobah. 1Ki 11:24
for the sake of my servant * and 1Ki 11:32
instructions as his father * did. 1Ki 11:33
for the sake of my servant *, my 1Ki 11:34
the descendants of * will continue 1Ki 11:36
* did, then I will bless you; 1Ki 11:38
once made this same promise to *. 1Ki 11:38
of *—though not forever. 1Ki 11:39
in the city of his father *; 1Ki 11:43
with * and all his relatives! 1Ki 12:16,17
the dynasty of * to this day. 1Ki 12:19
the kingship of the family of *. 1Ki 12:20
a descendant of * as their king. 1Ki 12:26
the family line of *, and he shall 1Ki 13:2
from the family of * and gave it to 1Ki 14:8
commandments as my servant * did. 1Ki 14:8
descendants. For * had obeyed God 1Ki 15:5
the Lord like his ancestor King *. 1Ki 15:11
the city of his forefather *; 1Ki 22:50
his servant * that he would watch 2Ki 8:19

of *—the old section of Jerusalem. 2Ki 8:24,25
that had belonged to King *. 2Ki 11:10
not quite like his ancestor *; 2Ki 14:3
City of * section of Jerusalem. 2Ki 14:20
*, and his son Jotham became king. 2Ki 15:7
City of * section of Jerusalem. 2Ki 15:38
the Lord as his ancestor * had; 2Ki 16:2
in the City of * sector of 2Ki 16:20
the kingdom of * and chose Jeroboam 2Ki 17:21
to that of his ancestor *). 2Ki 18:1
and for the sake of my servant *.' 2Ki 19:34
of his ancestor * has heard his 2Ki 20:5
for the sake of my servant *." 2Ki 20:6
Lord had spoken to * and Solomon 2Ki 21:7
*, obeying the Lord completely 2Ki 22:1
was Ozem, and his seventh was *. 1Ch 2:15
* also had nine other sons: 1Ch 3:6-8
* also had a daughter Tamar. 1Ch 3:9
their control until the time of *. 1Ch 4:31
King * appointed songleaders and 1Ch 6:31
At the time of King *, the total 1Ch 7:2
of King *, numbered 36,000 troops; 1Ch 7:4
At the time of * there were 1Ch 7:9
warriors at the time of King *. 1Ch 7:11
were appointed by * and Samuel 1Ch 9:22
kingdom to *, the son of Jesse. 1Ch 10:14
of Israel went to * at Hebron and 1Ch 11:1
So * made a contract with them 1Ch 11:3
Then * and the leaders went to 1Ch 11:4
enter the city. So * captured the 1Ch 11:5,6
called the City of *, and said to 1Ch 11:5,6
of David's army. * lived in the 1Ch 11:7
Jerusalem is called the City of *. 1Ch 11:7
of Jerusalem. And * became more 1Ch 11:9
of Israel to make * their king, as 1Ch 11:10
He was with * in the battle 1Ch 11:13
went to * while he was hiding in 1Ch 11:15
of Rephaim, and * was in the 1Ch 11:16
Bethlehem. * wanted a drink from 1Ch 11:17
well, and brought it back to *. 1Ch 11:18,19
among The Thirty. * made him 1Ch 11:24,25
who joined * at Ziklag while he was 1Ch 12:1
also went to * in the wilderness. 1Ch 12:8-13
Others came to * from Benjamin 1Ch 12:16
and Judah. * went out to meet them 1Ch 12:17
"We are yours, *; 1Ch 12:18
So * let them join him, and he 1Ch 12:18
army and joined * just as he was 1Ch 12:19
to let * and his men go with them. 1Ch 12:19
were afraid that * and his men 1Ch 12:19
to * as he was en route to Ziklag: 1Ch 12:20
and they assisted * when he fought 1Ch 12:21
More men joined * almost every 1Ch 12:22
recruits who joined * at Hebron. 1Ch 12:23
They were all anxious to see * 1Ch 12:23
purpose of helping * become king. 1Ch 12:24-37
armed and totally loyal to *. 1Ch 12:24-37
of making * the king of Israel. 1Ch 12:38
They feasted and drank with * 1Ch 12:39
AFTER * HAD consulted with all of 1Ch 13:1
with him. So * summoned the people 1Ch 13:5
Then * and all Israel went to 1Ch 13:6
Then * and all the people danced 1Ch 13:8
there before God. * was angry at 1Ch 13:11
Now * was afraid of God and 1Ch 13:12
of bringing it to the City of *. 1Ch 13:13
cedar lumber. * now realized why 1Ch 14:2
After * moved to Jerusalem, he 1Ch 14:3
When the Philistines heard that * 1Ch 14:8
capture him. But * learned that 1Ch 14:8
of Rephaim, and * asked the Lord, 1Ch 14:10
but * ordered them burned. 1Ch 14:12
and again * asked God what to do. 1Ch 14:14
So * did as the Lord commanded 1Ch 14:16
* NOW BUILT several palaces for 1Ch 15:1
Then * summoned all Israel to 1Ch 15:3
Then * called for Zadok and 1Ch 15:11
King * also ordered the Levite 1Ch 15:16
Then * and the elders of Israel 1Ch 15:25
and seven lambs. *, the Levites 1Ch 15:27
robes. * also wore a linen ephod. 1Ch 15:27
a deep disgust for * as she watched 1Ch 15:29
the Tabernacle. * had prepared for 1Ch 16:1
of these offerings * blessed the 1Ch 16:2
At that time * began the custom 1Ch 16:7
* arranged for Asaph and his 1Ch 16:37
to be active. * left Zadok the 1Ch 16:39
commanded Israel. * also appointed 1Ch 16:41
their homes, and * returned to 1Ch 16:43
AFTER * HAD been living in his new 1Ch 17:1
give my servant * this message: 1Ch 17:4
"Tell my servant *, 'The Lord of 1Ch 17:7
So Nathan told King * everything 1Ch 17:15
Then King * went in and sat 1Ch 17:16
* FINALLY SUBDUED the Philistines 1Ch 18:1
Euphrates River. * captured a 1Ch 18:4
King Hadadezer, * killed twenty-two 1Ch 18:5
And the Lord gave * victory 1Ch 18:6
learned that King * had destroyed 1Ch 18:9
congratulate King * on his success 1Ch 18:10
King * dedicated these gifts to 1Ch 18:11

(DAVID Con't)
large sums of money annually to *. 1Ch 18:13
Lord gave * victory after victory. 1Ch 18:13
after victory. * reigned over all 1Ch 18:14
Then * declared, "I am going to 1Ch 19:2,3
So * sent a message of sympathy to 1Ch 19:2,3
fool yourself that * has sent these 1Ch 19:2,3
then he sent them back to * in 1Ch 19:4
When * heard what had happened, 1Ch 19:5
When * learned of this, he sent 1Ch 19:8
When this news reached *, he 1Ch 19:17,18
But the Syrians again fled from * 1Ch 19:17,18
to King * and became his subjects. 1Ch 19:19
Meanwhile, * had stayed in 1Ch 20:1
When * arrived on the scene, he 1Ch 20:2
pounds! * also took great amounts 1Ch 20:2
peoples. Then * and all his army 1Ch 20:3
were killed by * and his soldiers. 1Ch 20:8
he made * decide to take a census. 1Ch 21:1
But * said to God, "I am the one 1Ch 21:8
"Go and tell *, 'The Lord has 1Ch 21:10,11
to make," * replied, "but let me 1Ch 21:13
When * saw the angel of the 1Ch 21:16
And * said to God, "I am the one 1Ch 21:17
Gad to instruct * to build an altar 1Ch 21:18
the Jebusite. So * went to see 1Ch 21:19,20
bowed to the ground before King *. 1Ch 21:21
* said to Ornan, "Let me buy 1Ch 21:22
it as you wish," Ornan said to *. 1Ch 21:23
So * paid Ornan $4,300 in gold, 1Ch 21:25
and when * saw that the Lord had 1Ch 21:28
of Gibeon, but * didn't have time 1Ch 21:30
THEN * SAID, "Right here at 1Ch 22:1
* now drafted all the resident 1Ch 22:2
great rafts of cedar logs to *. 1Ch 22:4
and tender," * said, "and the 1Ch 22:5
So * collected the construction 1Ch 22:5
build it myself," * told him, 1Ch 22:7
Then * ordered all the leaders of 1Ch 22:17
BY THIS TIME * was an old, old 1Ch 23:1
at the Temple," * instructed, 1Ch 23:4,5
Then * divided them into three 1Ch 23:6
the Temple. For * said, "The Lord 1Ch 23:25
things * did before his death. 1Ch 23:27
left to carry on. * consulted with 1Ch 24:3
presence of King *, Zadok, 1Ch 24:31
* AND THE officials of the 1Ch 25:1
the Lord by King * and the other 1Ch 26:26
Elihu (a brother of King *); 1Ch 27:16-22
When * took his census he didn't 1Ch 27:23
put into the annals of King *. 1Ch 27:24
* NOW SUMMONED all of his 1Ch 28:1
Then * turned to Solomon and 1Ch 28:8
Then * gave Solomon the blueprint 1Ch 28:11
For the Holy Spirit had given * 1Ch 28:12
* weighed out enough gold and 1Ch 28:14
this blueprint," * told Solomon, 1Ch 28:19
THEN KING * turned to the entire 1Ch 29:1
King * was moved with deep joy. 1Ch 29:9
whole assembly, * expressed his 1Ch 29:10
Then * said to all the people, 1Ch 29:20
him as co-regent" (with King *). 1Ch 29:22f
take the throne of his father *; 1Ch 29:23
* was king of the land of Israel 1Ch 29:26,27
Detailed biographies of King * 1Ch 29:29
built by King * for the Ark of God 2Ch 1:4
good to my father *, and now you 2Ch 1:8
your promise to * my father and 2Ch 1:9
* when he was building his palace. 2Ch 2:3
who were selected by my father *. 2Ch 2:7
who has given to * such a wise, 2Ch 2:12
by my lord *, your father. 2Ch 2:14
as his father * had done) and found 2Ch 2:17
father, King *, and where the 2Ch 3:1
Jebusite had been. * had selected 2Ch 3:1
to the Lord by his father, King *. 2Ch 5:1
City of *, also known as Zion, 2Ch 5:2
to my father * and has now 2Ch 6:4
as that city, and * as that king.' 2Ch 6:5,6
"My father * wanted to build 2Ch 6:7
kept your promise to my father *, 2Ch 6:15
Literally, "* your servant." 2Ch 6:15f
Oh, remember your love for * and 2Ch 6:42
that King * himself had made and 2Ch 7:6
been so good to * and Solomon and 2Ch 7:10
me as your father * did, then I 2Ch 7:17
from the City of * sector of 2Ch 8:11
chart prepared by his father *; 2Ch 8:14
"Forget * and his dynasty!" 2Ch 10:16
by a descendant of * to this day. 2Ch 10:19
King * and King Solomon had done. 2Ch 11:17
in the way of * and Solomon." 2Ch 11:17f
that is led by a descendant of *? 2Ch 13:8
end the dynasty of *, for he had 2Ch 21:7
a covenant with * always to have 2Ch 21:7
of your ancestor * says that 2Ch 21:12
descendant of King * shall be our 2Ch 23:2,3
These had once belonged to King * 2Ch 23:9
the Levite clans that King * had. 2Ch 23:18
He was buried in the City of * 2Ch 24:16
him in the City of *, but not in 2Ch 24:25
king, unlike his ancestor King *. 2Ch 28:1
the directions of * and the 2Ch 29:25,26
of the psalms of * and of the 2Ch 29:30
in the City of *, and manufactured 2Ch 32:5
the City of * sector in Jerusalem. 2Ch 32:30
where God had told * and his son 2Ch 33:7
of the City of * and the wall from 2Ch 33:14
example of his ancestor King *. 2Ch 34:2
for the God of his ancestor *; 2Ch 34:3
organized by King * of Israel and 2Ch 35:4,5
earlier by King *, Asaph, Heman, 2Ch 35:15
in the manner ordained by King *. Ez 3:10
From the subclan of * of the clan Ez 8:2-14
first instituted by King *. Ez 8:20
City of * section of Jerusalem. Neh 3:15
He was appointed by King *, Neh 11:22,23
as commanded by *, the man of God. Neh 12:24
musical instruments of King *. Neh 12:35,36
the castle to the old City of *; Neh 12:37
the laws of * and his son Solomon. Neh 12:45
(It was in the days of * and Neh 12:46
A Psalm of * when he fled from his Ps 3:1
This song of * was written at a Ps 18:1
had come to inform * of God's Ps 51:1
Written by * to protest against Ps 52:1
Written by * at the time the men Ps 54:1
Written by * at the time King Saul Ps 59:1
Written by * at the time he was at Ps 60:1
A Psalm of * when he was hiding in Ps 63:1
(This ends the psalms of *, son Ps 72:20
He chose his servant *, taking Ps 78:70
God presented * to his people as Ps 78:71,72
with my chosen servant *. Ps 89:3,4
who was sent to anoint * as king. Ps 89:19f
be the king— he is my servant *! Ps 89:20
For I have sworn to * (and a Ps 89:35,36
to * with a faithful pledge? Ps 89:49
Do not reject your servant *—the Ps 132:10
the dynasty of * shall never end. Ps 132:12
servant * from the fatal sword. Ps 144:10
of *, King of Jerusalem." Ecc 1:1f
as the tower of *, jeweled with a Sol 4:4
said, O House of *, you aren't Is 7:13
from the throne of his father *. Is 9:7
THE ROYAL LINE of * Is 11:1
the city of *. Is 29:1
and in memory of my servant *." Is 37:35
of your forefather * hears you Is 38:5
and love that I had for King *. Is 55:3
covenant with *, here remembered. Is 55:3f
be descendants of * sitting on the Jer 17:25
the throne of * or rule in Judah. Jer 22:30
Lord their God, and * their King, Jer 30:9
true vine from the roots of *." Jer 33:15f
*, the man after God's own heart. Jer 33:15f
of *, and he shall rule justly. Jer 33:15
that from then on, * shall forever Jer 33:17
my covenant with *, my servant, be Jer 33:20,21
the descendants of * my servant and Jer 33:22
the Jews, or * my servant, or Jer 33:25,26
upon the throne of *. Jer 36:30
all my people, even my Servant, *. Eze 34:23
and my Servant * shall be a Prince Eze 34:24
"And *, my Servant—the Eze 37:24
And my Servant *, their Messiah, Eze 37:25
Literally, "to *, their king." Hos 3:5f
Christ was "the greater *." Hos 3:5f
as great musicians as King * was. Amo 6:5
the City of *, which is now lying Amo 9:11
the royal line of * won't be filled Zec 12:7
them will be as mighty as King *! Zec 12:8
of King * and of Abraham: Mt 1:1
Jesse was the father of King *. Mt 1:6
of King David. * was the father of Mt 1:6
Abraham unto * are fourteen." Mt 1:17f
from Abraham to King *; Mt 1:17
"Joseph, son of *," the angel Mt 1:20
Son of King *, have mercy on us." Mt 9:27
read what King * did when he and Mt 12:3
Literally, "the Son of *." Mt 12:23f
bless the Son of *," they were Mt 21:15
"The son of *," they replied. Mt 22:42
"Then why does *, speaking under Mt 22:43
"For * said, Mt 22:43
Since * called him 'Lord,' how Mt 22:45
the time King * and his companions Mk 2:25,26
Son of *, have mercy on me!" Mk 10:47
"O Son of *, have mercy on me!" Mk 10:48
must be a descendant of King *? Mk 12:35
King David? For * himself said—and Mk 12:36
Since * called him his Lord, Mk 12:37
Joseph, a descendant of King *. Lk 1:27
him the throne of his ancestor *. Lk 1:32
of his servant *, just as he Lk 1:69
Literally, "in the City of *." Lk 2:11f
Nathan's father was *; Lk 3:23-38
Haven't you ever read what King * Lk 6:3
Son of *, have mercy on me!" Lk 18:38
"Son of *, have mercy on me!" Lk 18:39
said to be a descendant of King *? Lk 20:41
King David? For * himself wrote in Lk 20:42,43
the royal line of *, in Bethlehem, Jn 7:41,42
the village where * was born." Jn 7:41,42
Spirit, speaking through King *. Act 1:16
"King * quoted Jesus as Act 2:25
"Dear brothers, think! * wasn't Act 2:29
sit on David's throne. * was Act 2:31
"[No, * was not speaking of Act 2:34
our ancestor King *, your servant, Act 4:25,26
and used until the time of King *. Act 7:45
"God blessed * greatly, and Act 7:46
David greatly, and * asked for the Act 7:46
replaced him with * as king, a man Act 13:22
whom God said, '* (son of Jesse) is Act 13:22
the wonderful thing I promised *.' Act 13:34
This was not a reference to *, Act 13:36
David, for after * had served his Act 13:36
renew the broken contract with *, Act 15:16
tabernacle of * which is fallen." Act 15:16f
King * spoke of this, describing Rom 4:6
King * spoke of this same thing Rom 11:9
No, for in the book of Psalms * Heb 2:6
He announced this through King * Heb 4:7
and Jephthah and * and Samuel and Heb 11:32
and has the key of * to open what Rev 3:7
Judah, the Root of *, has Rev 5:5

DAVID'S
brought and poured it upon * head; 1Sa 16:13
But when * oldest brother, Eliab, 1Sa 17:28
officers. So * name became very 1Sa 18:30
Saul sent troops to watch * 1Sa 19:11
Saul, but * place was empty. 1Sa 20:24,25
me that my own son is on * side. 1Sa 22:8
But * men said, "We're afraid 1Sa 23:3
"Now's your time!" * men 1Sa 24:4
The young men gave * message to 1Sa 25:9
So * messengers returned and told 1Sa 25:12
was * reply as he strapped on 1Sa 25:13
at them. But * men were very good 1Sa 25:15,16
had forced * wife Michal, Saul's 1Sa 25:44
Saul recognized * voice and said, 1Sa 26:17,18
weep no more. (* two wives, 1Sa 30:5
But some of the ruffians among * 1Sa 30:22
led * troops out to meet them. 2Sa 2:13
Saul and of David. * position now 2Sa 3:1
Joab and some of * troops returned 2Sa 3:22
understood from * actions that he 2Sa 3:37
spared to become * servants—they 2Sa 8:2
the Syrians became * subjects and 2Sa 8:6
Hamath heard about * victory over 2Sa 8:9
and * sons were his assistants. 2Sa 8:18
So Hanun took * men and shaved 2Sa 10:4
* aides were afraid to tell him. 2Sa 12:18
PRINCE ABSALOM, * son, had a 2Sa 13:1
(the son of * brother Shime-ah). 2Sa 13:3
(the son of * brother Shime-ah) 2Sa 13:32,33
Hebron was King * first capital, 2Sa 15:9f
* counselors who lived in Giloh. 2Sa 15:12
was * instant response to his 2Sa 15:14
Then, following * instructions, 2Sa 15:25,26
So * friend Hushai returned to 2Sa 15:37
When * friend, Hushai the 2Sa 16:16
troops were beaten back by * men. 2Sa 18:7
upon some of * men and as he fled 2Sa 18:9
One of * men saw him and told 2Sa 18:10
Ira the Jairite was * personal 2Sa 20:26
THERE WAS A famine during * reign 2Sa 21:1
After that * men declared, "You 2Sa 21:17
defied Israel, and * nephew 2Sa 21:20,21
of * brother Shime-i—killed him. 2Sa 21:20,21
Gath, and were killed by * troops. 2Sa 21:22
most heroic men in * army: the 2Sa 23:8
taken the census, * conscience 2Sa 24:10
Gad, who was * contact with God. 2Sa 24:11
At about that time, * son 1Ki 1:5
Shime-i, Rei, and * army chiefs. 1Ki 1:8
Benaiah, and * bodyguard took 1Ki 1:38
Gihon, riding on King * own mule. 1Ki 1:38
AS THE TIME of King * death 1Ki 2:1
and may one of * descendants always 1Ki 2:45
all of his father * instructions 1Ki 3:3
he learned that * son Solomon was 1Ki 5:1
of one tribe, for * sake and for 1Ki 11:12,13
not right with God, as King * was. 1Ki 15:3
sin, the Lord remembered * love 1Ki 15:4
Literally, "for * sake." 1Ki 15:4f
and did not end the line of * 1Ki 15:4
KING * OLDEST son was Amnon, who 1Ch 3:1
he became the general of * army. 1Ch 11:5,6
of the bravest of * warriors (who 1Ch 11:10
three greatest heroes among * men. 1Ch 11:11
Other famous warriors among * 1Ch 11:26-47
to help build * palace and he 1Ch 14:1
Gibeon to Gezer. * fame spread 1Ch 14:17
in Jerusalem, * wife Michal, the 1Ch 15:29
* sons were his chief aides. 1Ch 18:17
But when * ambassadors arrived, 1Ch 19:2,3
So King Hanun insulted King * 1Ch 19:4
but he was killed by * nephew 1Ch 20:6,7
the son of * brother Shimea. 1Ch 20:6,7
Then the Lord said to Gad, * 1Ch 21:9
the fortieth year of King * reign. 1Ch 26:31,32

(DAVID'S Con't)
officers in * army. 1Ch 27:5,6
These men were King * overseers. 1Ch 27:31
sons was Jonathan, * uncle, a wise 1Ch 27:32
they crowned King * son Solomon 1Ch 29:22
KING * SON Solomon was now the 2Ch 1:1
not live in King * palace, for the 2Ch 8:11
in any way from * instructions 2Ch 8:15
She was the daughter of * son 2Ch 11:18
the daughter of * brother Eliab. 2Ch 11:18
Israel swore that * descendants 2Ch 13:5
a mere servant of * son, and was a 2Ch 13:6
just as his ancestor * had been. 2Ch 29:2
the days of King * son Solomon. 2Ch 30:26
Literally, "* soul." Ps 132:1f
shout for joy. * power shall grow, Ps 132:17
of King Solomon of Israel, * son: Pro 1:1
of Jerusalem, King * son, "The Ecc 1:1
is, "the Heir of * royal line." Is 11:10f
God will establish * throne Is 16:4,5
king sitting on * throne, and the Jer 13:13
of Judah, sitting on * throne; Jer 22:2
kings to sit on * throne, and there Jer 22:4
Branch upon King * throne. Jer 23:5,6
king who sits on * throne—and make Jer 29:16,17
The Messiah, * greater Son, whom Jer 30:9f
shall prosper as in * reign; Jer 30:20
and fourteen from King * time to Mt 1:17
mercy on me, O Lord, King * Son! Mt 15:22
King * Son, have mercy on us!" Mt 20:30
"God bless King * Son!" Mt 21:9
of our father * kingdom . . ." Mk 11:10
in Judea, King * ancient Lk 2:4
Nathan's father was David;* father Lk 3:23-38
Messiah be both * son and David's Lk 20:44
son and * God at the same time?" Lk 20:44
King * prediction of this Act 1:20
oath that one of * own descendants Act 2:30
sit on * throne. Act 2:30
And it is one of King * Act 13:23
into King * royal family line; Rom 1:3
a Man, born into King * family; 2Ti 2:8
I am both * Root and his Rev 22:16

DAVIDÇ
who created the royal dynasty of * Is 11:10

DAWN
At * the next morning the angels Gen 19:15
a Man wrestled with him until *. Gen 32:22,23,24
said, "Let me go, for it is *." Gen 32:26
The brothers were up at * and on Gen 44:3
night there. At * the next morning Jos 6:12,13,14
for six days. At * of the seventh Jos 6:15
Finally, just at *, they let her Ju 19:25
all on the other bank before *. 2Sa 17:22
morning,' and then I toss till *. Job 7:4
it won't last. At * he seems so Job 8:16
* to kill the poor and needy; Job 24:14,15
caused the * to rise in the east? Job 38:12
Have you ever robbed the * in Job 38:14
Let us greet the * with song! Ps 57:8
The * and sunset shout for joy! Ps 65:8
on the Lord. At * they slink back Ps 104:22
We will meet the * with song. Ps 108:2
than sentinels long for the *. Ps 130:6
God's favor; the * gives way to Pro 4:18
She gets up before * to prepare Pro 31:15
And you will waken at * with the Ecc 12:4
Before the * comes and the Sol 2:17
'arising as the *, fair as the Sol 6:10
but by * her enemies are dead. Is 17:14
my warnings will finally * on you. Is 28:19
* or the rain of early spring." Hos 6:3
you rise at * to carry out your Mic 2:1
time, who by * have left no trace Zep 3:3
from * to dusk and dusk to dawn." Zep 3:7
from dawn to dusk and dusk to *." Zep 3:7
*, you will deny me three times!" Mt 26:34
early * or late daybreak. Mk 13:35,36,37
and heaven's * is about to break Lk 1:78
all night. At * we saw a man Jn 21:4
At *, the jail was in great Act 12:18
was * when he finally left them! Act 20:10,11,12
the light will * in your souls and 2Pe 1:19

DAWNED
And * upon us from Mount Seir; Deu 33:2

DAWNING
"Your judgment day is * now. Is 21:12
as the new day was *, Mary Mt 28:1

DAWNS
Until the morning * and the Sol 4:6
the day of your damnation *; Eze 7:7
the morning *, for your Eze 7:10,11

DAY
Together they formed the first *. Gen 1:4,5
one * (or, 'period of time')." Gen 1:4,5f
This all happened on the second * Gen 1:7,8
second * (or, 'period of time')." Gen 1:7,8f
This all occurred on the third * Gen 1:13
third * (or, 'period of time')." Gen 1:13f
to identify the * and the night; Gen 1:14,15
preside over the * and the smaller Gen 1:16
preside over the * and night, and Gen 1:18
This all happened on the fourth *. Gen 1:19
fourth * (or, 'period of time')." Gen 1:19f
That ended the fifth *. Gen 1:23
fifth * (or, 'period of time')." Gen 1:23f
This ended the sixth *. Gen 1:31
sixth * (or, 'period of time')." Gen 1:31f
So on the seventh *, having Gen 2:2
the seventh * and declared it holy, Gen 2:3
because it was the * when he ceased Gen 2:3
to master it, until your dying *. Gen 3:19
One * Cain suggested to his Gen 4:8
One * Lamech said to Adah and Gen 4:23
God from the * of his creation. Gen 5:1
FINALLY THE * came when the Lord Gen 7:1
the boat that very * with his wife Gen 7:13
Literally, "on the first * of the Gen 8:5f
month, the first * of the month." Gen 8:13f
winter and summer, * and night." Gen 8:22
he made wine. One * as he was drunk Gen 9:20,21
So that * Jehovah made this Gen 15:18
on the eighth * after birth. Gen 17:12
Then, that very *, Abraham took Gen 17:23
Both were circumcised the same *, Gen 17:24-27
daughters. One * the older girl Gen 19:31
and Shur. One *, when visiting the Gen 20:1
On the third * of the journey Gen 22:4
still goes by that name to this *. Gen 22:14
in every way. One * Abraham said Gen 24:2
One * Jacob was cooking stew when Gen 25:29
One * Isaac had visitors from Gen 26:26
That very same * Isaac's servants Gen 26:32
and is called that to this *. Gen 26:33
ONE *, IN Isaac's old age when he Gen 27:1
and expect to die 'most any *. Gen 27:2,3,4
of both of you in one *?" Gen 27:45
if you stop so early in the *!" Gen 29:7
said to him one *, "Just because Gen 29:15
One * during the wheat harvest, Gen 30:14
So that very * Laban went out and Gen 30:35,36
So one * Jacob sent for Rachel Gen 31:4
So one * while Laban was out Gen 31:17-20
Literally, "stolen by * or by Gen 31:39f
heat of the *, and through the cold Gen 31:40
started back to Seir that same *. Gen 33:16
ONE * DINAH, Leah's daughter, went Gen 34:1
my prayers in the * of my distress, Gen 35:3
grave, and it is there to this *. Gen 35:20
So one * Jacob gave him a special Gen 37:3
One * Joseph's brothers took Gen 37:12
One * at about this time Gen 39:7
her suggestions * after day, even Gen 39:10
day after *, even though he refused Gen 39:10
Then one * as he was in the Gen 39:11
The third * Joseph said to them, Gen 42:18
ONE * NOT long after this, word Gen 48:1
So Jacob blessed the boys that * Gen 48:20
One *, many years later Ex 2:11
The next * as he was out visiting Ex 2:13
ONE * AS Moses was tending the Ex 3:1
That same * Pharaoh sent this Ex 5:6
the very next *, and it did. Ex 9:5
without hail that * was the land of Ex 9:26
wind to blow all that * and night; Ex 10:13
"The * you do, you shall die." Ex 10:28
Annually, on the tenth * of this Ex 12:3,4
of the fourteenth * of this month, Ex 12:6
Don't eat any of it the next *; Ex 12:10
On the first * of the Ex 12:16
on the seventh *, there will be Ex 12:16
today as the * when I brought you Ex 12:17
celebrate this * annually, Ex 12:17
of the fourteenth * of the month Ex 12:18
the twenty-first * of the month. Ex 12:18
it was on the last * of the 430th Ex 12:40,41
That very * the Lord brought out Ex 12:51
"This is a * to remember Ex 13:3
forever—the * of leaving Egypt and Ex 13:3
Mark this * of your exodus, at Ex 13:4,5
Literally, "the tenth * of Ex 13:4,5f
Then, on the seventh *, a great Ex 13:6,7
So they could travel either by * Ex 13:21
Thus Jehovah saved Israel that * Ex 14:30
on the fifteenth * of the second Ex 16:1
Everyone can go out each * and Ex 16:4
on the sixth * of each week." Ex 16:5
On the sixth * they gathered Ex 16:22
tomorrow as a * of seriousness and Ex 16:23
be none there for you on that *." Ex 16:26
much on the sixth *, so that there Ex 16:28,29
* as a day of Sabbath rest; Ex 16:28,29
day as a * of Sabbath rest; Ex 16:28,29
up food from the ground that *." Ex 16:28,29
people rested on the seventh *. Ex 16:30
The next * Moses sat as usual to Ex 18:13
all * long to get your help?" Ex 18:14
Then, the * after tomorrow, I Ex 19:11
On the morning of the third * Ex 19:16
observe the Sabbath as a holy *. Ex 20:8
but the seventh * is a day of Ex 20:10
seventh day is a * of Sabbath rest Ex 20:10
On that * you are to do no work Ex 20:1
in them, and rested the seventh *; Ex 20:1
so he blessed the Sabbath * and Ex 20:1
me on the eighth *, after leaving Ex 22:3
the seventh * he called to Moses Ex 24:1
room, tending it * and night before Ex 27:2
Every * you shall sacrifice a Ex 29:3
it to God every * for seven days. Ex 29:3
"Each * offer two yearling lambs Ex 29:3
rest on my Sabbath *, for the Ex 31:12,1
work on that * shall be killed. Ex 31:14,1
for the seventh * is a special day Ex 31:1
day is a special * of solemn rest, Ex 31:1
seventh *, and was refreshed." Ex 31:1
three thousand men died that *. Ex 32:2
The next * Moses said to the Ex 32:3
the seventh * is a day of solemn Ex 35:2
the seventh day is a * of solemn Ex 35:2
* to be used to worship Jehovah; Ex 35:2
anyone working on that * must Ex 35:2
the fires in your homes that *." Ex 35:3
on the first * of the first month. Ex 40:2
On the first * of the first Ex 40:17
have it— on the * he is found Lev 6:4,5
and on the same * he shall bring Lev 6:4,5
to Moses, "On the * Aaron and his Lev 6:19,20
on the * of their anointing. Lev 6:22,23
be eaten that same *, and none left Lev 7:15
none left to be eaten the next *. Lev 7:15
is not eaten the * it is sacrificed Lev 7:16
may be eaten the next *. Lev 7:16
until the third * shall be burned. Lev 7:17,18
*, the Lord will not accept it; Lev 7:17,18
For on the * the Lord anointed Lev 7:36
he had done that * had been Lev 8:34
* and night for seven days. Lev 8:35
ON THE EIGHTH * (of the Lev 9:1
offering on such a * as this, would Lev 10:19
On the eighth *, her son must be Lev 12:3
on the seventh *, the priest will Lev 13:5
Again on the seventh * the Lev 13:6
examine him again the seventh *. Lev 13:27
examined again on the seventh *. Lev 13:32
on the seventh *, and if the spot Lev 13:34
look at it again on the seventh *. Lev 13:51
on the seventh * the spot has not Lev 13:53
The seventh * he shall again Lev 14:9
"The next *, the eighth day, he Lev 14:10
"The next day, the eighth *, he Lev 14:10
on the eighth *, for his ceremony Lev 14:23
the seventh * to look at it again. Lev 14:39
On the eighth * he shall take Lev 15:14
"On the eighth *, she shall take Lev 15:29
on the twenty-fifth * of September Lev 16:29,30
Literally, "on the tenth * of the Lev 16:29,30f
but must spend the * in Lev 16:29,30
for this is the * commemorating Lev 16:29,30
spend the * in quiet humility; Lev 16:31
Eat it the same * you offer it, or Lev 19:6
it, or the next * at the latest; Lev 19:6
any remaining until the third * Lev 19:6
eaten on the third * is repulsive Lev 19:7
If you eat it on the third * you Lev 19:8
from the eighth * onward it is Lev 22:26,27
*, whether she is a cow or ewe. Lev 22:28
animal the same * it is slain. Lev 22:29,30
none of it for the following *. Lev 22:29,30
—the seventh * of every week—which Lev 23:3
Literally, "on the fourteenth * Lev 23:5f
the * following the Passover. Lev 23:6
On the first * of this festival, Lev 23:7
on the seventh * of the festival. Lev 23:8
priest on the * after the Sabbath. Lev 23:9,10,11
That same * you shall sacrifice Lev 23:12
That * shall be announced as a Lev 23:21
don't do any work that *. Lev 23:21
Literally, "the first * of the Lev 23:23,24f
Don't do any work on the * of Lev 23:25
"The * of Atonement follows nine Lev 23:26,27
Literally, "on the tenth * of the Lev 23:26,27f
Don't do any work that *, for it Lev 23:28
it is a special * for making Lev 23:28
Anyone who does not spend the * Lev 23:29
who does any kind of work that *. Lev 23:30,31
later, on the last * of September, Lev 23:33,34
Literally, "on the fifteenth * of Lev 23:33,34f
On the first * there will be a Lev 23:35
don't do any hard work that *. Lev 23:35
The eighth * requires another Lev 23:36
"This last * of September, at Lev 23:39
On the first *, take boughs of Lev 23:40
"Every Sabbath * the High Priest Lev 24:5-8
Out in the camp one *, a young Lev 24:10
"Every fiftieth year, on the * Lev 25:9
Literally, "the tenth * of the Lev 25:9f
IT WAS ON the fifteenth * of April Num 1:1
Literally, "on the first * of the Num 1:1f
On the same * Num 1:17,18,19
Literally, "on the first * of the Num 1:17,18,19f
From the * I killed all the Num 3:13
The next *, the eighth day, he Num 6:10

(DAY Con't)

The next day, the eighth *, he	Num 6:10
And he must renew his vows that *	Num 6:11
the * he finished setting it up.	Num 7:1
gifts on the * the altar was	Num 7:10
on a different * for the dedication	Num 7:11
brought his gift the first *.	Num 7:12
The next * Nethanel, the son of	Num 7:18-23
had presented on the previous *.	Num 7:18-23
On the third * Eliab, the son of	Num 7:24-29
On the fourth * the gifts were	Num 7:30-35
On the fifth * came Shelumi-el,	Num 7:36-41
The next * it was Eliasaph's	Num 7:42-47
On the seventh *, Elishama, the	Num 7:48-53
eighth * with the same offerings.	Num 7:54-59
On the ninth * it was Abidan the	Num 7:60-65
brought his gifts on the tenth *.	Num 7:66-71
on the eleventh *—the same gifts	Num 7:72-77
On the twelfth * came Ahira, son	Num 7:78-83
So, beginning the * the altar was	Num 7:84,85,86
fourteenth * of this first month,	Num 9:2,3
Note: The 14th * of the first	Num 9:2,3f
to our first * of April.	Num 9:2,3f
on the fourteenth * of the second	Num 9:11
On the * the Tabernacle was	Num 9:15
next morning. But * or night, when	Num 9:20,21
twentieth * of the second month	Num 10:11
One * Moses said to his	Num 10:29
is gone, and * after day we have to	Num 11:6
* we have to face this manna!"	Num 11:6
not for just a * or two, or five	Num 11:19,20
As far as one could walk in a *	Num 11:31
quail all that * and through the	Num 11:32
the night and all the next * too!	Num 11:32
ONE * MIRIAM and Aaron were	Num 12:1
lead and protect us * and night.	Num 14:14
year for each *, bearing the burden	Num 14:34,35
One * while the people of Israel	Num 15:32
gathering wood on the Sabbath *.	Num 15:32
ONE * KORAH (son of Izhar,	Num 16:1
died the previous * with Korah).	Num 16:49
went in the next *, he found that	Num 17:8
this on the third *, he will	Num 19:12
defiled even after the seventh *.	Num 19:12
from the Lord that *, as a warning	Num 26:5-11
ONE * THE daughters of Zelophehad	Num 27:1
One * the Lord said to Moses,	Num 27:12
* as a regular burnt offering.	Num 28:3
"On the Sabbath *, sacrifice two	Num 28:9,10
"Also, on the first * of each	Num 28:11
"Also on the first * of each	Num 28:15
"On the fourteenth * of the	Num 28:16
On the following *, a great,	Num 28:17
On the first * of the festival a	Num 28:18
hard work shall be done on that *.	Num 28:18
On the seventh * there shall	Num 28:25
that * you may do no hard work.	Num 28:25
"On the * of First-fruits (also	Num 28:26
On that * you are to present the	Num 28:26
no hard work by anyone on that *.	Num 28:26
the Lord, shall be offered that *.	Num 28:27
on the fifteenth * of September	Num 29:1
Literally, "upon the first * of	Num 29:1f
*, and no hard work may be done.	Num 29:1
On that * you shall offer a	Num 29:2
monthly burnt offering for that *,	Num 29:6
Literally, "on the tenth * of the	Num 29:7f
This will be a * of solemn	Num 29:7
On that * you shall offer a	Num 29:8
offering of the * of Atonement	Num 29:11
[offered annually on that *	Num 29:11
Literally, "on the fifteenth * of	Num 29:12f
that * no hard work shall be done;	Num 29:12
sacrifice that *, which will give	Num 29:13
"On the second * of this	Num 29:17
"On the third * of the festival,	Num 29:20
"On the fourth * of the	Num 29:23
"On the fifth * of the festival,	Num 29:26,27
"On the sixth * of the festival,	Num 29:29
"On the seventh * of the	Num 29:32
"On the eighth * summon the	Num 29:35
you must do no hard work that *.	Num 29:35
on the first * he hears about it;	Num 30:5
nothing on the * he hears of it,	Num 30:7
it on the first * he hears of it,	Num 30:12
says nothing for a *, then he has	Num 30:14
If he waits more than a * and	Num 30:15
On the seventh * you must wash	Num 31:24
Egypt, on the first * of April,	Num 33:3,4
Literally, "on the fifteenth * of	Num 33:3,4f
the * after the night of the	Num 33:3,4
Literally, "the first * of the	Num 33:38,39f
Literally, "the first * of the	Deu 1:1f
a pillar of cloud during the *.	Deu 1:33
Tell them especially about the *	Deu 4:10
form of God that * as he spoke to	Deu 4:15
thought for the *: Jehovah is God	Deu 4:39
" 'Keep the Sabbath * holy.	Deu 5:12
but the seventh * is the Sabbath	Deu 5:14
no work shall be done that * by	Deu 5:14
if you do, it will be a sad * for	Deu 7:16
the * you left Egypt until now?	Deu 9:7
Lord from the first * I knew you.	Deu 9:24
*, just as the Lord commanded me.	Deu 10:5
against you until this very *!	Deu 11:4
His eyes are always upon it, *	Deu 11:12
day after * throughout the year!	Deu 11:12
Remember that * all the rest of	Deu 16:3
On the seventh * there shall be a	Deu 16:8
Don't do any work that *.	Deu 16:8
He must read from it every * of	Deu 17:19
You must bury him the same *, for	Deu 21:23
Pay him his wage each * before	Deu 24:14,15
That same * Moses gave this	Deu 27:11
You will live night and * in	Deu 28:66
and gold. The * that any of	Deu 29:18
nations, that * a root will be	Deu 29:18
* that you shall surely perish;	Deu 30:18
So, on that very *, Moses wrote	Deu 31:22
That same *, the Lord said to	Deu 32:48
about them every * and every night	Jos 1:8
On the third *, officers went	Jos 3:2,3,4
and it is there to this *.	Jos 4:9
It was a tremendous * for Joshua!	Jos 4:14
Literally, "The tenth * of the	Jos 4:19f
That * the entire nation crossed	Jos 4:19
to set aside a * to circumcise the	Jos 5:2,3
of the 14th * of the month.	Jos 5:10
The next * they began to eat	Jos 5:11,12
The following * no manna fell,	Jos 5:11,12
the city once a * for six days,	Jos 6:3,4
On the seventh * you are to walk	Jos 6:3,4
the city once that *, after which	Jos 6:11
At dawn of the seventh * they	Jos 6:15
there to this *, and even today	Jos 7:26
in all, was wiped out that *.	Jos 8:25
There had never been such a *	Jos 10:14
On that same * Joshua destroyed	Jos 10:28
gave it to them on the second *;	Jos 10:32
Eglon on the first * and, as at	Jos 10:34,35
among the Israelites to this *.	Jos 13:13
the people of Judah to this *.	Jos 15:63
with them that * at Shechem,	Jos 24:25
ONE * THE Angel of the Lord	Ju 2:1
by Israel that *, and the land was	Ju 3:30
One * she summoned Barak (son of	Ju 4:6
So that * the Lord used Israel	Ju 4:23
But one * the Angel of the Lord	Ju 6:11
ONE * GIDEON'S son Abimelech	Ju 9:1
The next * the men of Shechem	Ju 9:42
The battle went on all * before	Ju 9:45
Then one * the Angel of the Lord	Ju 13:2,3
birth until the * of his death!"	Ju 13:7
talked to my wife the other *?"	Ju 13:11
ONE * WHEN Samson was in Timnah,	Ju 14:1
as was the custom of the *.	Ju 14:10,11
On the fourth * they said to his	Ju 14:15
At last, on the seventh *, he	Ju 14:17
* they gave him their reply.	Ju 14:18
ONE * SAMSON went to the	Ju 16:1
She nagged at him every * until	Ju 16:16,17
One * he said to his mother,	Ju 17:2
One * a young priest	Ju 17:7,8
On the fourth * they were up	Ju 19:5
to stay one more *, as they were	Ju 19:6
So they had another * of	Ju 19:8
thousand Israelis that *.	Ju 20:21
next * to fight at the same place.	Ju 20:22,23,24
And that * they lost another	Ju 20:25
again on the third * and set	Ju 20:30
of Benjamin that *, leaving but a	Ju 20:35-39
warriors that *, leaving only six	Ju 20:46,47
This refers to the custom of the *	Ru 1:11f
One * Ruth said to Naomi,	Ru 2:2
So she worked there all *, and	Ru 2:17
ONE * NAOMI said to Ruth, "My	Ru 3:1
On the * he presented his	1Sa 1:4
One * a prophet	1Sa 2:27
Phinehas, to die on the same *!	1Sa 2:34
Israel died that * and the	1Sa 4:10
at Shiloh the same * with his	1Sa 4:12
expression of grief in that *.	1Sa 4:12f
(That is why to this * neither	1Sa 5:5
that * by the men of Beth-shemesh.	1Sa 6:15
returned to Ekron that same *.	1Sa 6:16
They also went without food all *	1Sa 7:6
One * Kish's donkeys strayed	1Sa 9:3
had told Samuel the previous *,	1Sa 9:15
prophecies came true that *.	1Sa 10:9
of Israel that *, except for Saul's	1Sa 13:22
A * OR so later, Prince Jonathan	1Sa 14:1
So the Lord saved Israel that *,	1Sa 14:23
So no one ate anything all *,	1Sa 14:24,25
who ate food that *, and everyone	1Sa 14:28
Philistines all * from Michmash to	1Sa 14:31
ONE * SAMUEL said to Saul, "I	1Sa 15:1
great power from that * onward.	1Sa 16:13
For forty days, twice a *,	1Sa 17:16
One * Jesse said to David, "Take	1Sa 17:17
The very next *, in fact, a	1Sa 18:10
One * Saul said to David, "I am	1Sa 18:17
him more with every passing *.	1Sa 18:29
But one * as Saul was sitting at	1Sa 19:9,10
and lay naked all * and all night,	1Sa 19:24
until the evening of the third *.	1Sa 20:5
or the next * at the latest, I will	1Sa 20:12
By the * after tomorrow,	1Sa 20:19
about it that *, for he supposed	1Sa 20:26
empty the next *, Saul asked	1Sa 20:27
to eat all that *, for he was hurt	1Sa 20:34
It had just been replaced that *	1Sa 21:6
One * the prophet Gad told David	1Sa 22:5
ONE * NEWS came to David that the	1Sa 23:1
of Ziph. One * near Horesh he	1Sa 23:14,15
Saul hunted him * after day, but	1Sa 23:14,15
Saul hunted him day after *, but	1Sa 23:14,15
"Today is the * the Lord was	1Sa 24:4
This very * you have seen that it	1Sa 24:9,10
in fact, * and night they were	1Sa 25:15,16
him down some *, or he will die in	1Sa 26:10
"Some * Saul is going to get me.	1Sa 27:1
One * David said to Achish, "My	1Sa 27:5
of Judah to this *), and they	1Sa 27:6
for he had eaten nothing all *.	1Sa 28:20
the entire next * until evening.	1Sa 30:17
troops died together that same *.	1Sa 31:6
The next * when the Philistines	1Sa 31:8
and fasted all * for Saul and his	2Sa 1:12
men of Israel who had died that *.	2Sa 1:12
One * General Abner led some of	2Sa 2:12
by the end of the * Abner and the	2Sa 2:17
eat anything the * of the funeral,	2Sa 3:35,36
it is still called to this *).	2Sa 6:8
ONE * DAVID began wondering if any	2Sa 9:1
Then, on the seventh *, the baby	2Sa 12:18
One * Jonadab said to Amnon,	2Sa 13:4
death, longed * after day for	2Sa 13:37,38,39
longed day after * for fellowship	2Sa 13:37,38,39
men laid down their lives that *.	2Sa 18:7
"This is not a * for execution	2Sa 19:22
the * the king left Jerusalem.	2Sa 19:24,25
bodies during the * and the wild	2Sa 21:10
In the * of my calamity,	2Sa 22:19
live to see the * when there will	2Sa 24:3
That * Gad came to David and said	2Sa 24:18
every man on earth must some * go.	1Ki 2:2
One * Adonijah the son of Haggith	1Ki 2:13
very * for this plot against me!	1Ki 2:23,24
and they remain there to this *.	1Ki 8:8
Temple night and *—this place you	1Ki 8:29
by night or by *, please listen to	1Ki 8:29
before him * and night, so that he	1Ki 8:59
they stand here * after day	1Ki 10:8
after * listening to your wisdom!	1Ki 10:8
One * as Jeroboam was leaving	1Ki 11:29
the dynasty of David to this *.	1Ki 12:19
Literally, "on the fifteenth * of	1Ki 12:32,33f
against him. One * King Elah was	1Ki 16:9
But one * the woman's son became	1Ki 17:17
That same *, while Elijah was on	1Ki 18:5
traveling all *, and sat down under	1Ki 19:4
on the seventh * the battle began.	1Ki 20:29
Syrian infantrymen that first *.	1Ki 20:29
palace. One * the king talked to	1Ki 21:2
intense as the * wore on, and King	1Ki 22:35
And sure enough, the next * at	2Ki 3:20
ONE * THE wife of one of the	2Ki 4:1
One * Elisha went to Shunem.	2Ki 4:8
One * when her child was older,	2Ki 4:18
in the land. One * as he was	2Ki 4:38
One * a man from Baal-shalishah	2Ki 4:42
One * the little girl said to her	2Ki 5:3
ONE * THE seminary students came	2Ki 6:1
One * as the king of Israel was	2Ki 6:26-30
my son one * and her son the next.	2Ki 6:26-30
him, but the next * when I said,	2Ki 6:26-30
this very *," the king vowed.	2Ki 6:31
were sold that * for one dollar,	2Ki 7:16
on the previous * when the king had	2Ki 7:17
for so little on the following *.	2Ki 7:18
But the next * Hazael took a	2Ki 8:15
its independence to this *.	2Ki 8:22
One * King Joash said to	2Ki 12:4,5
as it is called to this *.	2Ki 14:7
One * he sent a message to King	2Ki 14:8
lasted until the * of his death;	2Ki 15:5
live there, as they do to this *.	2Ki 16:6
where they remain to this *.	2Ki 17:23
And to this * their descendants	2Ki 17:41
says, 'This is a * of trouble,	2Ki 19:3
One * Hilkiah the High Priest	2Ki 22:8
the twenty-seventh * of the last	2Ki 25:27
where they remain to this *.	1Ch 5:26
annual * of Atonement for Israel.	1Ch 6:49
family was wiped out in one *.	1Ch 10:6
went back the next * to strip the	1Ch 10:8
David almost every * until he had a	1Ch 12:22
Declare each * that he is the one	1Ch 16:23
doing each * whatever needed to	1Ch 16:37
Six guards were assigned each *	1Ch 26:18
The next * they brought a	1Ch 29:21
on the seventeenth * of April in	2Ch 3:2
Look down with favor * and night	2Ch 6:20,21

(DAY Con't)

for use that * as a place of	2Ch 7:7
service was held on the eighth *.	2Ch 7:9
differed from * to day in	2Ch 8:13
from day to * in accordance with	2Ch 8:13
a descendant of David to this *.	2Ch 10:19
elite troops of Israel that *.	2Ch 13:17
hotter all that *, and King Ahab	2Ch 18:34
On the fourth * they gathered in	2Ch 20:26
But to this * Edom has been	2Ch 21:10
This went on * after day, and	2Ch 24:11
This went on day after *, and	2Ch 24:11
a leper until the * of his death	2Ch 26:21
On a single *, Pekah, the son of	2Ch 28:6
This all began on the first * of	2Ch 29:17
and by the eighth * they had	2Ch 29:17
On the first * of May the people	2Ch 30:15
music and cymbals * after day.	2Ch 30:21
music and cymbals day after *.	2Ch 30:21
One * when Hilkiah, the High	2Ch 34:14
first * of April, in Jerusalem.	2Ch 35:1
was completed in that one *.	2Ch 35:16
To this * they still sing sad	2Ch 35:24,25
specified for each * of the feast.	Ez 3:4
It was on the fifteenth * of	Ez 3:6
Literally, "the first * of the	Ez 3:6f
and olive oil each * without fail.	Ez 6:9
Literally, "the third * of the	Ez 6:15f
on the first * of April.	Ez 6:19
Literally, "the fourteenth * of	Ez 6:19f
Or, "the twelfth * of the first	Ez 8:31f
On the fourth * after our arrival	Ez 8:33
days, on the fifth * of December,	Ez 10:9
Literally, "the twentieth * of	Ez 10:9f
can be done in a * or two, for	Ez 10:13
and * for your people Israel.	Neh 1:6,7
ONE * IN April four months later,	Neh 2:1
* if they offer enough sacrifices?	Neh 4:1
* and night to protect ourselves.	Neh 4:9
duty as well as work during the *.	Neh 4:22
to them this very * and drop your	Neh 5:11
wine and $100 a * in cash, and had	Neh 5:15
required for each * were one ox,	Neh 5:18
Or, "twenty-fifth * of the month	Neh 6:15f
"Don't cry on such a * as this!	Neh 8:9
For today is a sacred * before	Neh 8:9
For this is a * of holy joy, not	Neh 8:11
The next * the clan leaders and	Neh 8:13
and on the eighth * there was a	Neh 8:18
Literally, "the twenty-fourth *"	Neh 9:1f
cloud during the * and a pillar of	Neh 9:12
led them forward * by day, and the	Neh 9:19
forward day by *, and the pillar of	Neh 9:19
holy *, we would refuse to buy it.	Neh 10:31
on that joyous *, for God had given	Neh 12:43
On that * men were appointed to	Neh 12:44
ON THAT SAME *, as the laws of	Neh 13:1
One * I was on a farm and saw	Neh 13:15
they took that * into Jerusalem.	Neh 13:15
be brought in on the Sabbath *.	Neh 13:19
On the final *, when the king was	Est 1:10
And before this * is out, the	Est 1:18
One *, as Mordecai was on duty at	Est 2:21
the others demanded * after	Est 3:3,4
the others demanded day after *	Est 3:3,4
Literally, "Then, on the 13th *	Est 3:12f
killed on the 28th * of February of	Est 3:13
their duty on the appointed *."	Est 3:14
drink for three days, night or *;	Est 4:16
ON THAT SAME * King Ahasuerus	Est 8:1
was now the 23rd * of the month of	Est 8:9,10
property. The * chosen for this	Est 8:12
was the 28th * of February!	Est 8:12
This was the same * as was set by	Est 8:12f
SO ON THE 28th * of February, the	Est 9:1
of February, the * the two decrees	Est 9:1
into effect—the * the Jews' enemies	Est 9:1
* and slaughtered their enemies.	Est 9:5
together the next * also and killed	Est 9:15
done on the 28th * of February, and	Est 9:17
and the next * they rested,	Est 9:17
enemies the second * also, and	Est 9:18
*, with feasting and gladness.	Est 9:18
Israel to this * have an annual	Est 9:19
on the second *, when they rejoice	Est 9:19
this historic * when the Jews were	Est 9:22
One * as the angels	Job 1:6
and cursed the * of his birth.	Job 3:1
"Let the * of my birth be	Job 3:2,3
Let that * be forever forgotten.	Job 3:4
Literally, "a * of darkness."	Job 3:4f
How he longs for the * to end.	Job 7:2
My life flies by—* after	Job 7:6
flies by—day after hopeless *.	Job 7:6
test him every moment of the *?	Job 7:18
They say that night is * and day	Job 17:12
They say that night is day and *	Job 17:12
spared in the * of calamity, and	Job 21:30-32
for the * and for the night.	Job 26:10
wants them to, and * and night are	Ps 1:2
They are not safe on Judgment *;	Ps 1:5
This is your Coronation *.	Ps 2:7
Literally, "This * have I	Ps 2:7f
is angry with the wicked every *.	Ps 7:11
On the * when I was weakest, they	Ps 18:18
craftsmanship. * and night they	Ps 19:2
IN YOUR * of trouble, may the Lord	Ps 20:1
to my groans? * and night I keep	Ps 22:2
his presence every * of my life,	Ps 27:4
frustration. All * and all night	Ps 32:4
water on a sunny * until I finally	Ps 32:4
I will praise you all * long.	Ps 35:28
knows their judgment * is coming.	Ps 37:12,13
* by day the Lord observes the	Ps 37:18
Day by * the Lord observes the	Ps 37:18
stand before him? * and night I	Ps 42:3
Yet * by day the Lord also pours	Ps 42:8
Yet day by * the Lord also pours	Ps 42:8
people of our *, will shower you	Ps 45:12
"Your sons will some * be kings	Ps 45:16
deed—it haunts me * and night.	Ps 51:3
walls night and * against invaders,	Ps 55:10
LORD, HAVE MERCY on me; all *	Ps 56:1
The very * I call for help, the	Ps 56:9
of safety in the * of my distress.	Ps 59:16
you every *, and you have given	Ps 61:5
my vow of praising you each *.	Ps 61:8
and joy there was that *!	Ps 66:6
protector. All * long I'll praise	Ps 71:8
I will talk to others all * long	Ps 71:24
will bless him all * long.	Ps 72:15
and woe—every * and all day long!	Ps 73:14
and woe—every day and all * long!	Ps 73:14
Then one * I went into God's	Ps 73:17
* and night alike belong to you;	Ps 74:16
hurled against you all * long.	Ps 74:22
and fled when the * of battle came,	Ps 78:9
A single * spent in your Temple	Ps 84:10
have wept before you * and night.	Ps 88:1
weeping. Each * I beg your help;	Ps 88:9
will keep on pleading * by day.	Ps 88:13
will keep on pleading day by *.	Ps 88:13
They flow around me all * long.	Ps 88:17
They rejoice all * long in your	Ps 89:16
nor fear the dangers of the *;	Ps 91:5
A song to sing on the Lord's *	Ps 92:1
Literally, "for the Sabbath *."	Ps 92:1f
Bless his name. Each * tell	Ps 96:2
My enemies taunt me * after day	Ps 102:8
My enemies taunt me day after *	Ps 102:8
In that * of your power your	Ps 110:3
renewed * by day like morning dew.	Ps 110:3
renewed day by * like morning dew.	Ps 110:3
many kings in the * of his anger.	Ps 110:5
This is the * the Lord has made.	Ps 118:24
I think about them all * long.	Ps 119:97
* because of your wonderful laws.	Ps 119:164
He protects you * and night.	Ps 121:6
sun to rule the *, for his	Ps 136:8
did on that * when the armies of	Ps 137:7
the night shines as bright as *.	Ps 139:12
and scheduled each * of my life	Ps 139:16
Every * was recorded in your	Ps 139:16
a * your thoughts turn towards me.	Ps 139:17,18
and stir up trouble all * long.	Ps 140:2
your name each * and forever.	Ps 145:1
Some * you'll be in trouble, and	Pro 1:26
done their evil deed for the *.	Pro 4:16
Every * and all night long their	Pro 6:22
guide you into the new *.	Pro 6:22
on you in his * of vengeance.	Pro 6:34
of my house one *, and saw a	Pro 7:6
me; this * have I paid my vows."	Pro 7:14f
the hours of your * more profitable	Pro 9:11
for God adds hours to each *;	Pro 10:27
won't help you on Judgment *;	Pro 11:4
* along with argument and strife.	Pro 17:1
against the * of battle."	Pro 21:31f
is as refreshing as a cool *	Pro 25:13
A constant dripping on a rainy *	Pro 27:15
The * one dies is better than the	Ecc 7:1
is better than the * he is born!	Ecc 7:1
to prevent his * of death, for	Ecc 8:8
activity, * and night.	Ecc 8:16,17
rejoice in every * of life, but let	Ecc 11:8
wedding *, his day of gladness."	Sol 3:11
wedding day, his * of gladness."	Sol 3:11
majesty, for the * is coming when	Is 2:11
On that * the Lord of Hosts will	Is 2:12
be crushed before the Lord that *.	Is 2:16
throughout the *, and clouds of	Is 4:5
In that * the haughty shall be	Is 5:15
In that * the Lord will take	Is 7:20
In that glorious * of peace	Is 9:5
Therefore the Lord, in one *,	Is 9:14,15
visit you in that * when I send	Is 10:3
On that * God will end the	Is 10:27
Nob for the remainder of that *.	Is 10:32
In that * the wolf and the lamb	Is 11:6
In that * he who created the	Is 11:10
ON THAT * you will say, "Praise	Is 12:1
In that wonderful * you will say,	Is 12:4
For see, the * of the Lord is	Is 13:9
* of his wrath and fierce anger.	Is 13:9
In that wonderful * when the Lord	Is 14:3
for help in that *, neither will	Is 17:8
a pleasant summer * or a lovely	Is 18:4
In that * the Egyptians will be	Is 19:16
In that * the Lord will make	Is 19:21
In that * Egypt and Iraq	Is 19:23
he shouted, "Sir, * after day and	Is 21:8,9
"Sir, day after * and night after	Is 21:8,9
"Your judgment * is dawning now.	Is 21:12
Oh, what a * of crushing	Is 22:5
What a * of confusion and terror	Is 22:5
forgiven you until the * you die.	Is 22:14
On that * the Lord will punish	Is 24:21
In that * the people will	Is 25:9
What a * of rejoicing!	Is 25:9
In that * the whole land of Judah	Is 26:1
IN THAT * the Lord will take his	Is 27:1
In that * [of Israel's freedom	Is 27:2
every * I'll water them, and day	Is 27:3
every day I'll water them, and *	Is 27:3
In that * the great trumpet will	Is 27:13
In that * the deaf will hear the	Is 29:18
In that * when God steps in to	Is 30:25
I know the glorious * will come	Is 31:7
Be our strength each * and our	Is 33:2
For it is the * of vengeance,	Is 34:8
"This is a * of trouble and	Is 37:3
And one * while he was	Is 37:38
In one short * my life hangs by a	Is 38:12
Every * of my life from now on I	Is 38:20
Which can predict a single *	Is 43:9
some * honor me before the world.	Is 43:21
measure in one *: widowhood and the	Is 47:9
and fear their anger all * long?	Is 51:13
constantly blasphemed, * by day.	Is 52:5
constantly blasphemed, day by *.	Is 52:5
the people of that * realized it	Is 53:8
But in that coming *, no weapon	Is 54:17
They come to the Temple every *	Is 58:2
you shall be as bright as *.	Is 58:10
business on that *, but enjoying	Is 58:13
as the Lord's holy *, and honoring	Is 58:13
my glorious Temple in that *.	Is 60:7
* of his wrath to their enemies.	Is 61:2
cry to God all * and all night for	Is 62:6,7
them all * long—have rebelled;	Is 65:2
and thoughts. All * long they	Is 65:3
They stifle me. * in and day	Is 65:5
Day in and * out they infuriate	Is 65:5
For in one *, suddenly, a nation,	Is 66:7,8
In that *, says the Lord, the	Jer 4:9
Ever since the * your fathers	Jer 7:25
them my prophets, * after day.	Jer 7:25
them my prophets, day after *.	Jer 7:25
I would sob * and night for the	Jer 9:1
this *: Obey my every command!	Jer 11:7
this: Night and * my eyes shall	Jer 14:17
is gone down while it is yet *.	Jer 15:9
But there will come a glorious *,	Jer 16:14,15
my Refuge in the * of trouble,	Jer 16:19
work on the Sabbath * but make it	Jer 17:21,22
Sabbath day but make it a holy *.	Jer 17:21,22
on the Sabbath * and keep it	Jer 17:24
The * is coming, says the Lord,	Jer 19:6
The next * when Pashhur finally	Jer 20:3
Yet, cursed be the * that I was	Jer 20:14
Terrify him all * long with	Jer 20:16
In that * people will no longer	Jer 23:7
so that from that * until this they	Jer 25:18
On that * those the Lord has	Jer 25:33
ON A DECEMBER * in that same	Jer 28:1
terror such as in that coming *?	Jer 30:7
For on that *, says the Lord of	Jer 30:8
But in that coming *, all who are	Jer 30:16
The * shall come when watchmen on	Jer 31:6
The * will come, says the Lord,	Jer 31:31
still remembered to this *.	Jer 32:20
refused to return; * after day,	Jer 32:33
day after *, year after year, I	Jer 32:33
too, for some * I will restore	Jer 32:44
Yes, the * will come, says the	Jer 33:14
In that * the people of Judah	Jer 33:16
covenant with the * and with the	Jer 33:20,21
the night so that * and night don't	Jer 33:20,21
of night and *, of earth and sky.	Jer 33:25,26
Temple on the next * of Fasting,	Jer 36:6
for on that * people will be there	Jer 36:6
This occurred on the * of	Jer 36:9
the services at the Temple that *.	Jer 36:9
fresh bread every * as long as	Jer 37:21
One * King Zedekiah sent for	Jer 38:14
yard until the * that Jerusalem was	Jer 38:28
The next *, before the outside	Jer 41:4
there is desolation until this *.	Jer 44:6
For this is the * of the Lord	Jer 46:10
a * of vengeance upon his enemies.	Jer 46:10
run, for it is the * of great	Jer 46:20,21
in one *, says the Lord of Hosts.	Jer 49:26
and now your * of reckoning has	Jer 50:31

(DAY Con't)	
against her in her * of trouble.	Jer 51:2
on the tenth * of the tenth month,	Jer 52:4
Then finally, on the ninth * of	Jer 52:6
On the tenth * of the fifth month	Jer 52:12
needs until the * of his death.	Jer 52:34
me in the * of his fierce wrath.	Lam 1:12
and desolate the whole * through.	Lam 1:13
In his * of awesome fury he has	Lam 2:1
no rest from weeping * or night.	Lam 2:18
in the * of your anger none	Lam 2:22
He has turned against me. * and	Lam 3:3
My own people laugh at me; all *	Lam 3:14
begins afresh each *.	Lam 3:23
My eyes flow * and night with	Lam 3:48,49
One * late in June, when I was	Eze 1:1
and doom. Each * you lie there	Eze 4:4,5
Each * will represent one year.	Eze 4:6
ounces at a time, one meal a *.	Eze 4:10
And use one quart of water a *;	Eze 4:11
Each * take flour from the	Eze 4:12
O Israel, the * of your	Eze 7:7
the time has come; the * of	Eze 7:7
It is a * of shouts of anguish,	Eze 7:7
it. The * of judgment has come;	Eze 7:10,11
"Yes, the time has come; the *	Eze 7:12
have no value in that * of wrath.	Eze 7:19
On that * when you were born, you	Eze 16:5
Judah too will prosper in that *.	Eze 16:55
And I gave them the Sabbath—a *	Eze 20:12
rest every seventh *—as a symbol	Eze 20:12
your final * of reckoning is here.	Eze 21:25
for when the * of final reckoning	Eze 21:29
Now comes your * of doom.	Eze 22:4
you be then, in my * of reckoning?	Eze 22:14
of Israel: In the * of my	Eze 22:24
On the same * they defiled my	Eze 23:38
even that same * they actually came	Eze 23:39
ONE * LATE in December of the	Eze 24:1
"Son of dust, on the * I finish	Eze 24:25
on that * a refugee from Jerusalem	Eze 24:26
And on the * of his arrival,	Eze 24:27
Lord on the first * of the month,	Eze 26:1
sea on the * of your vast ruin.	Eze 27:27
They were given to you on the *	Eze 28:13
you did from the * you were created	Eze 28:15
And the * will come when I will	Eze 29:21
for the terrible * is almost here;	Eze 30:2,3
is almost here; the * of the Lord;	Eze 30:2,3
the day of the Lord; a * of	Eze 30:2,3
a day of clouds and gloom; a * of	Eze 30:2,3
be a dark * for Tehaphnehes too;	Eze 30:18
their lives on the * of your fall.	Eze 32:10
on the fifteenth * of the month."	Eze 32:17f
in that dark and cloudy *.	Eze 34:12
in the land of Israel on that *.	Eze 38:19
That * of judgment will come;	Eze 39:8
for Israel on that * when I	Eze 39:13
"The second *, sacrifice a young	Eze 43:22
"Every * for seven days a male	Eze 43:25
Do this each * for seven days to	Eze 43:26
On the eighth *, and on each day	Eze 43:27
On the eighth day, and on each *	Eze 43:27
the Sabbath is kept a sacred *.	Eze 44:24
The first * he returns to work	Eze 44:27
God says: On each New Year's *	Eze 45:18
Do this also on the seventh * of	Eze 45:20
"On the fourteenth * of the same	Eze 45:21
On the * of Passover the prince	Eze 45:22
given each * for a sin offering.	Eze 45:23
three times a *, just as he always	Dan 6:10
of his God three times a *."	Dan 6:13
He spent the rest of the * trying	Dan 6:14
Then one * early in April, as I	Dan 10:4
the very first * you began to fast	Dan 10:12
that very * I was sent here to	Dan 10:12
and remain until the 1335th *!	Dan 12:12
in that * her people will be too	Hos 1:10
what a * that will be—the day	Hos 1:11
what a day that will be—the *	Hos 1:11
Literally, "the * of Jezreel	Hos 1:11f
as naked as the * she was born, and	Hos 1:3
In that coming *, says the Lord,	Hos 1:16
In that *, says the Lord, I will	Hos 1:21,22
Israel: When your * of punishment	Hos 5:9
you as surely as * follows night.	Hos 6:5
has come; the * of recompense is	Hos 9:7
Yes, it will be a sad * when I	Hos 9:12
Alas, this terrible * of	Joe 1:15
Or, "the * of the Lord."	Joe 1:15f
in fear, for the * of the Lord's	Joe 2:1
It is a * of darkness and gloom,	Joe 2:2
his orders. The * of judgment	Joe 2:11
terrible * of the Lord shall come.	Joe 2:31
For the * of the Lord is near, in	Joe 3:14
of Tekoa. All * long he sat on the	Amo 1:1
One *, in a vision, God told him	Amo 1:2
and run for their lives that *."	Amo 2:16
"On the same * that I punish	Amo 3:14
into morning, and * into night, who	Amo 5:8
in the dread * of your punishment.	Amo 5:13
You say, 'If only the * of the	Amo 5:18
For that * will not be light and	Amo 5:18
In that * you will be as a man	Amo 5:19
be a dark and hopeless * for you.	Amo 5:20
you bring the * of Judgment near.	Amo 6:3
bitter, bitter will be that *.	Amo 8:10
In that * not one wise man	Ob 1:8
in the * of his misfortune;	Ob 1:12
* of his calamity and looted him.	Ob 1:13
But the very first * when Jonah	Jon 3:4,5
upon you, and your * will end.	Mic 3:6
In that coming *, the Lord says	Mic 4:6
But your judgment * is coming	Mic 7:4
O Judah, proclaim a * of	Nah 1:15
will not be overdue a single *!	Hab 2:3
I will quietly wait for the * of	Hab 3:16
For the awesome * of his Judgment	Zep 1:7
"On that * of Judgment I will	Zep 1:8
"That terrible * is near.	Zep 1:14
Swiftly it comes—a * when strong	Zep 1:14
It is a * of the wrath of God	Zep 1:15
it is a * of terrible distress	Zep 1:15
and anguish, a * of ruin and	Zep 1:15
you in that * of the Lord's wrath.	Zep 1:18
terrible * of his wrath begins.	Zep 2:2
from his wrath in that * of doom.	Zep 2:3
he does no wrong. * by day his	Zep 3:5
Day by * his justice is more	Zep 3:5
On that * the announcement to	Zep 3:16
today, this 24th * of the month,	Hag 2:18,19
"The 24th * of Kislev."	Hag 2:18,19f
this * onward, I will bless you.	Hag 2:18,19
From this * I will bless you."	Hag 2:18,19
Haggai from the Lord that same *:	Hag 2:20
will some * be so full of people	Zec 2:4
sins of this land in a single *.	Zec 3:9
The same * they arrive, meet them	Zec 6:10,11
who will some * come from distant	Zec 6:15
his people in that *, as a Shepherd	Zec 9:16,17
"In that *," says the Lord, "I	Zec 12:4
"In that * I will make the clans	Zec 12:6
"In that * I will get rid of every	Zec 13:2
WATCH, FOR THE * of the Lord is	Zec 14:1
On that * the Lord will gather	Zec 14:1
That * his feet will stand upon	Zec 14:4
yet there will be continuous *!	Zec 14:7
There will be no normal * and	Zec 14:7
In that * there shall be one	Zec 14:9
In that * the bells on the horses	Zec 14:20
that * when I make up my jewels.	Mal 3:17
declares, "the * of judgment is	Mal 4:1
One * as he was walking along the	Mt 4:18
ONE * AS the crowds were	Mt 5:1
Live one * at a time.	Mt 6:34
Literally, "sufficient unto the *	Mt 6:34f
Literally, "in that *."	Mt 7:22f
One * the disciples of John the	Mt 9:14
off at Judgment * than they.	Mt 10:15
off on the Judgment * than you!	Mt 11:22
off at the Judgment * than you."	Mt 11:24
was walking one * through some	Mt 12:1
the Jewish * of worship, and his	Mt 12:1
by healing on the Sabbath *?"	Mt 12:10
you work to rescue it that *?	Mt 12:11
* for every idle word you speak.	Mt 12:36
One * some of the Jewish leaders,	Mt 12:38
LATER THAT SAME *, Jesus left the	Mt 13:1
in the crowd that *, besides all	Mt 14:21
ONE * THE Pharisees and Sadducees	Mt 16:1
foul weather all *—but you can't	Mt 16:2,3
One * while they were still in	Mt 17:22,23
and on the third * afterwards I	Mt 17:22,23
He agreed to pay them $20 a *	Mt 20:2
was right at the end of the *.	Mt 20:4
all * in the scorching heat.'	Mt 20:11,12
Didn't you agree to work all *	Mt 20:13
* I will rise to life again."	Mt 20:19
out the merchants the * before.	Mt 21:23
But that same * some of the	Mt 22:23
know what * your Lord is coming.	Mt 24:42
to feed my children * by day?	Mt 24:45
to feed my children day by *?	Mt 24:45
On the first * of the Passover	Mt 26:17
again until the * I drink it new	Mt 26:29
The next *—at the close of the	Mt 27:62
first * of the Passover ceremonies	Mt 27:62
until the third *, to prevent his	Mt 27:64
as the new * was dawning, Mary	Mt 28:1
believed by them to this very *.	Mt 28:15
Then one * Jesus came from	Mk 1:9
One * as Jesus was walking along	Mk 1:16
religion. One * some people came to	Mk 2:18
But some * he will be taken away	Mk 2:20
Another time, on a Sabbath * as	Mk 2:23
Or is this a * for doing harm?	Mk 3:4
Is it a * to save lives or to	Mk 3:4
many healings that * and as a	Mk 3:10
control him. All * long and	Mk 5:5
ONE * SOME Jewish religious	Mk 7:1
ONE * ABOUT this time as another	Mk 8:1
in the crowd that * and when the	Mk 8:8,9
Or, "is growing weaker * by	Mk 9:18f
Or, "is growing weaker day by *	Mk 9:18f
John, told him one *, "Teacher, we	Mk 9:38
*, and exclaimed, "Look, Teacher!	Mk 11:21
the Temple that *, one of his	Mk 13:1
knows the * or hour when these	Mk 13:32
On the first * of the Passover,	Mk 14:12
the Passover, the * the lambs were	Mk 14:12
the * I drink a different kind	Mk 14:25
oriental greeting, even to this *.	Mk 14:44f
I was there teaching every *.	Mk 14:49
This all happened the * before	Mk 15:42,43
Later that *	Mk 16:12
One * as Zacharias was going	Lk 1:8,9
That * a man named Simeon, a	Lk 2:25
him to go to the Temple that *;	Lk 2:27
also there in the Temple that *.	Lk 2:36,37
there night and *, worshiping God	Lk 2:36,37
miss him the first *, for they	Lk 2:43
Then one *, after the crowds	Lk 3:21
the synagogue that *, he went to	Lk 4:38
ONE * AS he was preaching on the	Lk 5:1
One * in a certain village he was	Lk 5:12
One * while he was teaching, some	Lk 5:17
that *, since it was the Sabbath.	Lk 6:7
on the Sabbath *, or to do harm?	Lk 6:9
One * soon afterwards he went out	Lk 6:12
The report of what he did that *	Lk 7:17
One * he gave this illustration	Lk 8:4
One * about that time, as he and	Lk 8:22
ONE * JESUS called together his	Lk 9:1
One * as he was alone, praying,	Lk 9:18
him every * and keep close to me!	Lk 9:23
The next * as they descended from	Lk 9:37
One * he sent messengers ahead to	Lk 9:52
such a city on the Judgment *.	Lk 10:12
on the Judgment * than you.	Lk 10:14
One * an expert on Moses' laws	Lk 10:25
The next * he handed the	Lk 10:35
Give us our food * by day.	Lk 11:3
Give us our food day by *.	Lk 11:3
"And at the Judgment * the Queen	Lk 11:31
Will it add a single * to your	Lk 12:25
all you need from * to day if you	Lk 12:31
need from day to * if you will make	Lk 12:31
had healed her on the Sabbath *.	Lk 13:14
it is the Sabbath *, to free this	Lk 13:16
and the third * I will reach my	Lk 13:32
today, tomorrow, and the next *!	Lk 13:33
a man on the Sabbath *, or not?"	Lk 14:3
lived each * in mirth and luxury.	Lk 16:19
and luxury. One * Lazarus, a	Lk 16:20
Jesus said one * to his disciples,	Lk 17:1
you seven times a * and each time	Lk 17:4
One * the apostles said to the	Lk 17:5
One * the Pharisees asked Jesus,	Lk 17:20
*, but I won't be here," he said.	Lk 17:22
as the people were in Noah's *.	Lk 17:26
right up to the * when Noah went	Lk 17:27
"Those away from home that *	Lk 17:31
ONE * JESUS told his disciples a	Lk 18:1
who plead with him * and night?	Lk 18:7
One * some mothers brought their	Lk 18:15
And the third * I will rise	Lk 18:33
Every * Jesus went to the Temple	Lk 21:37,38
Now the * of the Passover	Lk 22:7
I was there every *.	Lk 22:53
That * Herod and Pilate—enemies	Lk 23:12
* of preparation for the Sabbath.	Lk 23:54
* as required by the Jewish law.	Lk 23:56
he would rise again the third *?"	Lk 24:6,7
That same *, Sunday, two of	Lk 24:13
from the dead on the third *;	Lk 24:46
The next * John saw Jesus coming	Jn 1:29
The following * as John was	Jn 1:35
The next * Jesus decided to go to	Jn 1:43
water there. One * someone began	Jn 3:25
this long trip out here every *."	Jn 4:15
Give us free bread every *, like	Jn 6:30,31
that bread every * of our lives!"	Jn 6:34
to eternal life at the Last *.	Jn 6:39
should raise him at the Last *."	Jn 6:40
and at the Last * I will cause all	Jn 6:44
I will raise him at the Last *.	Jn 6:54
On the last *, the climax of the	Jn 7:37
Abraham rejoiced to see my *.	Jn 8:56
* when all work was forbidden.	Jn 9:14f
of daylight every *, and during	Jn 11:9
else does, on Resurrection *."	Jn 11:24
The Passover, a Jewish holy *,	Jn 11:55
The next *, the news that Jesus	Jn 12:12
be judged at the * of Judgment by	Jn 12:48
of Passover * that it would be his	Jn 13:1
I am doing it; some * you will."	Jn 13:7
now and some * shall be in you.	Jn 14:17
It was now about noon of the *	Jn 19:14
there the next *, which was the	Jn 19:31
Literally, "on the first * of the	Jn 20:1f
heaven, and some *, just as he	Act 1:11
During this time, on a * when	Act 1:15
by John until the * he was taken	Act 1:21,22

(DAY Con't)
* of Pentecost had now arrived. Act 2:1
met together that *, suddenly Act 2:1
in Jerusalem that * for the Act 2:5
awesome * of the Lord arrives. Act 2:20
at the Temple each *, met in small Act 2:46
to them, and each * God added to Act 2:47
Gate—as was his custom every *. Act 3:2
The next * it happened that the Act 4:5
And every *, in the Temple and Act 5:42
But one * some of the men from Act 6:9
"One * as he was nearing his Act 7:23
"The next * he visited them Act 7:26
began that *, sweeping over the Act 8:1
gates of the city * and night Act 9:24
The next *, as they were nearing Act 10:9,10
The next * he went with them, Act 10:23
the following *, and Cornelius was Act 10:24
"One * in Joppa," he said, Act 11:5
and when the * arrived he put on Act 12:21
and Paul. One * as these men were Act 13:2
Literally, "This * have I Act 13:32,33f
something in your *—something that Act 13:41
the synagogue that *, they asked Act 13:42
The next * he left with Barnabas Act 14:20
the church that * as they read it. Act 15:31
and the next * on to Neapolis, and Act 16:11
One * as we were going down to Act 16:16
This went on * after day until Act 16:18
This went on day after * until Act 16:18
They searched the Scriptures * by Act 17:11
Scriptures day by * to check up on Act 17:11
For he has set a * for justly Act 17:31
and preached boldly each Sabbath * Act 19:8
Literally, "the first * of the Act 20:7f
next *, he talked until midnight! Act 20:7
the next * we passed Chios; Act 20:15
and a * later we arrived at Act 20:15
know that from the * I set foot in Act 20:18
and * and my many tears for you. Act 20:31
The next * we reached Rhodes and Act 21:1
believers, but stayed only one *. Act 21:7
The second * Paul took us with Act 21:18
and the next * went with the men to Act 21:26,27
city earlier that *, they had seen Act 21:29
"One * after my return to Act 22:17,18
The next * the commander freed Act 22:30
following * opened Paul's trial. Act 25:6
* and ordered Paul brought in. Act 25:17
So the next *, after the king and Act 25:23
* to attain this same hope I have! Act 26:7
priests, when one * about noon, Act 26:13
The next * when we docked at Act 27:3
like a perfect * for the trip; Act 27:13
The next * as the seas grew Act 27:18
The following * they threw out Act 27:19
When it was *, they didn't Act 27:39
to Rhegium; a * later a south wind Act 28:13
so the following * we arrived at Act 28:13
So a time was set and on that * Act 28:23
I pray for you. * and night I bring Rom 1:9
stand before God at Judgment * Rom 1:20
for there is going to come a * of Rom 2:5
they do it. The * will surely come Rom 2:16
for that future * when God will Rom 8:19
For on that * thorns and Rom 8:20,21
anxiously for that * when God will Rom 8:23
moment of the *—we are like sheep Rom 8:36
* and night because of you. Rom 9:1
And so it is to this very *. Rom 11:8
rebels, but some * they, too, will Rom 11:31
The night is far gone, the * of Rom 13:12,13
for every * alike belongs to God. Rom 14:5
guilt on that * when he returns. 1Co 1:8
Christ's Judgment * to see what 1Co 3:13
Don't you know that some * we 1Co 6:2
because some * God will do away 1Co 6:13
and 23,000 fell dead in one *. 1Co 10:8
come back to life again some *. 1Co 15:20
the dead will some * rise again? 1Co 15:29
some * have a body like Christ's. 1Co 15:49
On every Lord's * each of you 1Co 16:2
be of you on that * when our Lord 2Co 1:13,14
in the Lord is growing every *. 2Co 4:16
eagerly to the * when we shall have 2Co 5:2
I helped you on a * when 2Co 6:2
all night and the whole next *. 2Co 11:25
sealed unto the * of redemption." Eph 4:30f
on that * when salvation from sin Eph 4:30
that * when Jesus Christ returns. Php 1:6
toward that * when I will finally Php 3:12
that very first * you heard it and Col 1:6
Night and * we toiled and sweated 1Th 2:9
For night and * we pray on and 1Th 3:10
guiltless on that * when our Lord 1Th 3:13
no one knows. That * of the Lord 1Th 5:2
when that * of the Lord comes. 1Th 5:4
light and of the *, and do not 1Th 5:5
until that * when our Lord Jesus 1Th 5:23
* of the Lord has already begun. 2Th 2:1
For that * will not come until two 2Th 2:3
we worked hard * and night for 2Th 3:8
* will reveal the terrible truth. 1Ti 5:24
I pray for you every *, and many 2Ti 1:3
him until the * of his return. 2Ti 1:12
at the * of Christ's return. 2Ti 1:18
remember that some * we are going 2Ti 2:12
this forever. Some * their deceit 2Ti 3:9
will some * judge the living and 2Ti 4:1
me on that great * of his return. 2Ti 4:8
God-fearing lives * after day, Tit 2:12
lives day after *, looking forward Tit 2:12
Literally, "this * I have Heb 1:5,6f
clothes, and some * you will fold Heb 1:12
these things every * while there is Heb 3:13
on the seventh * of creation, Heb 4:4
to the * of Christ's resurrection. Heb 5:5f
for he said, "The * will come when Heb 8:8
fathers on the * when I took them Heb 8:9
before the altar * after day Heb 10:11
altar day after * offering Heb 10:11
now that the * of his coming back Heb 10:25
And it was a happy * for him Jas 1:18
on that coming * of judgment. Jas 5:3
that coming last * for all to see. 1Pe 1:5
and honor on the * of his return. 1Pe 1:7
* when it will be displayed. 1Pe 4:13
and darkness until the judgment *. 2Pe 2:4
everywhere around him * after day. 2Pe 2:7,8
everywhere around him day after *. 2Pe 2:7,8
the * of final judgment comes. 2Pe 2:9
For they live in evil pleasures * 2Pe 2:13
in evil pleasures day after *. 2Pe 2:13
since the first * of creation." 2Pe 3:4
at the judgment *, when all ungodly 2Pe 3:7
friends, that a * or a thousand 2Pe 3:8
to repent. The * of the Lord is 2Pe 3:10
forward to that * and hurry it 2Pe 3:12
hurry it along—the * when God will 2Pe 3:12
embarrassed at the * of judgment, 1Jn 4:17
waiting for the judgment *. Jud 1:6
It was the Lord's * and I was Rev 1:10
covered with eyes. * after day and Rev 4:8
Day after * and night after night Rev 4:8
because the great * of their anger Rev 6:17
him * and night in his temple. Rev 7:15
year and month and * and hour, and Rev 9:15
world from this * to eternity." Rev 11:15f
them * and night before our God. Rev 12:10
have no relief * or night, for they Rev 14:11
coming Judgment * of God Almighty. Rev 16:14
her in a single *, and she shall be Rev 18:8
* and night forever and ever. Rev 20:10
they stay open all * long—and Rev 21:25

DAY'S

sample of the first * harvest; Ex 23:19
troops died in that * battle. Ju 20:44
the joy of that * wonderful victory 2Sa 19:2
the priests in each * duties; 2Ch 8:14
the * work for her servant girls. Pro 31:15
hasn't done a * work in his life; Ecc 2:20-23
the payment for a * labor; Mt 20:2f
the equivalent of a modern * wage. Lk 10:35f
a denarius being a full * wage. Jn 6:7f
him, too, for each * problems; Col 2:6

DAYBREAK

up early, before *, for he had said Ru 3:14
him there. At * the next morning, 1Sa 9:26,27
all night and reached Hebron at *. 2Sa 2:32
gloom, shout abroad when * comes. Mt 10:27
was up long before * and went out Mk 1:35
at midnight, early dawn or late *. Mk 13:35,36,37
all night. At * he called together Lk 6:13
Early the next morning at * the Lk 22:66
the Temple about *, and immediately Act 5:21

DAYLIGHT

But if it happens in the *, it Ex 22:3
the Lord in broad *, so that his Num 25:4
soon as it is *, storm the city. Ju 9:33
grope like blind men in the *; Job 5:14
Have you ever told the * to Job 38:13
along in broad *, yes, even at Is 59:10
Go in the * so they can see, for Eze 12:3
during the * so they can watch. Eze 12:4
outside in the *—all I could take Eze 12:7
stumble in broad * as well as in Hos 4:5
twelve hours of * every day, and Jn 11:9
from the stern and prayed for *. Act 27:29
as we who live in the * should! Rom 13:12,13
stars, so that the * was dimmed by Rev 8:12

DAYS

earth, and mark the * and years." Gen 1:14,15
In those *, and even afterwards, Gen 6:4
begin forty * and nights of rain; Gen 7:4
and seventeen * old, the rain came Gen 7:10,11,12
the earth for forty * and nights. Gen 7:10,11,12
For forty * the roaring floods Gen 7:17
the water covered the earth 150 *. Gen 7:24
receded until, 150 * after it Gen 8:3,4
After another forty *, Noah Gen 8:6
Seven * later Noah released the Gen 8:10
Twenty-nine * after that, Gen 8:13
Eight * after he was born, Gen 21:4,
at least another ten * or so!" Gen 24:5
a few *, he was so much in love. Gen 29:2
to take them three *' distance, and Gen 30:35,3
learn of their flight for three *. Gen 31:2
seven * later, at Mount Gilead. Gen 31:2
But three * later, when their Gen 34:2
A few * later Israel called for Gen 37:13,1
"The three branches mean three * Gen 40:1
Within three * Pharaoh is going Gen 40:1
"The three baskets mean three * Gen 40:18,1
"Three * from now Pharaoh will Gen 40:18,1
Pharaoh's birthday came three * Gen 40:2
them all into jail for three *. Gen 42:1
to happen to you in the * to come. Gen 49:
required forty *, with a period of Gen 50:
of national mourning of seventy *. Gen 50:
us to go three *' journey into the Ex 3:1
"We must take a three *' trip Ex 5:
over all the land for three *. Ex 10:2
celebration shall last seven *. Ex 12:1
during the seven * of the Ex 12:1
* except the preparation of food. Ex 12:1
For these seven * there must be Ex 12:1
Again I repeat, during those * Ex 12:2
For seven * you shall eat only Ex 13:6,
"During those celebration * each Ex 13:
Egypt after three *, but to keep on Ex 14:
were there three * without water. Ex 15:22
Gather the food for six *, but Ex 16:26
there will be enough for two *? Ex 16:28,29
appearance two * from now, and do Ex 19:15
a holy day. Six * a week are for Ex 20:9
For in six * the Lord made the Ex 20:11
for a couple of *, then the man Ex 21:21
it with its mother for seven *. Ex 22:30
"Work six * only, and rest the Ex 23:12
when for seven * you are not to eat Ex 23:15
full quota of the * of your life. Ex 23:26
and the cloud covered it six *; Ex 24:16
for forty * and forty nights. Ex 24:18
clothes for seven * before Ex 29:30
shall go on for seven *. Ex 29:35
it to God every day for seven *. Ex 29:37
Work six * only, for the seventh Ex 31:16
For in six * the Lord made heaven Ex 31:17
Bread for seven *, just as I Ex 34:18
six *, and rest on the seventh. Ex 34:21
the Lord for forty * and forty Ex 34:28
"Work six * only; Ex 35:2
entrance for seven *, after which Lev 8:33
be completed—for it takes seven *. Lev 8:33
day and night for seven *. Lev 8:35
defiled for seven *, and under the Lev 12:2
next thirty-three *, while she is Lev 12:4
Then for a further sixty-six * Lev 12:5
"When these * of purification Lev 12:6
shall quarantine him for seven *. Lev 13:4
must quarantine him seven * more. Lev 13:5
shall quarantine him for seven *. Lev 13:21
him for seven *, and examine him Lev 13:26
for seven *, and examined again on Lev 13:31
him for another seven *. Lev 13:33
it away for seven * and look at it Lev 13:50
then isolated for seven more *. Lev 13:54
stay outside his tent for seven *. Lev 14:8
house for seven *, and return the Lev 14:38
for seven * afterwards, and during Lev 15:19
defiled for seven *, and every bed Lev 15:24
Seven * after the menstruating Lev 15:28
mother for seven *, but from the Lev 22:26,27
are always * of solemn rest in Lev 23:3
On each of the intervening * you Lev 23:8
Pentecost: Fifty * later you shall Lev 23:15,16
of Atonement follows nine * later: Lev 23:26,27
Tabernacles: Five * later, on the Lev 23:33,34
before the Lord for seven *. Lev 23:33,34
On each of the seven * of the Lev 23:36
regular weekly * of holy rest. Lev 23:38
the first and last * of the Lev 23:39
the festival are * of solemn rest. Lev 23:39
the Lord your God for seven *. Lev 23:40
During those seven *, all of you Lev 23:42
him, then seven * later he shall Num 6:9
grow again. The * of his vow that Num 6:12
those presented on the previous *. Num 7:24-29
as those given on the previous *. Num 7:30-35
those presented on the previous *. Num 7:48-53
same as those on the previous *. Num 7:66-71
But if it stayed only a few *, Num 9:19
then they remained only a few *; Num 9:19
the Tabernacle two *, a month, or a Num 9:22
They traveled for three * after Num 10:33
face she would be defiled seven *. Num 12:14
the camp for seven *, and after Num 12:14
the camp for seven *, and the Num 12:15
Forty * later they returned from Num 13:25
the land for forty *, you must Num 14:34,35
defiled for seven *, and must Num 19:11
third and seventh * with water [run Num 19:12
time, shall be defiled seven *. Num 19:14

(DAYS Con't)
he shall be defiled seven *. Num 19:16
place on the third and seventh *; Num 19:19
they mourned for him for thirty *. Num 20:29
each of the seven * of the feast; Num 28:24
"Ten * later Num 29:7
"Five * later Num 29:12
the camp for seven *, all of you Num 31:19
on the third and seventh *. Num 31:19
and on for three * into the Etham Num 33:8
takes only eleven * to travel by Deu 1:1
In earlier * the Horites lived Deu 2:12
But your * there will be brief; Deu 4:26
When those bitter * have come Deu 4:30
Work the other six *, but the Deu 5:13
I was there for forty * and forty Deu 9:9
At the end of those forty * and Deu 9:10,11
Then, for another forty * and Deu 9:18
him for forty * and nights when the Deu 9:25
the Lord for forty * and nights the Deu 10:10
Eat unleavened bread for seven * Deu 16:3
For seven * no trace of yeast Deu 16:4
For the following six * you Deu 16:8
observed for seven * at the end of Deu 16:13
* of siege that lie ahead. Deu 28:53
life and the length of your *. Deu 30:20
and in the * to come evil will Deu 31:29
Remember the * of long ago! Deu 32:7
match the length of your *! Deu 33:25
thirty * on the plains of Moab. Deu 34:8
"In three * we will go across Jos 1:10,11
"Hide there for three * until Jos 2:16
stayed there three *, until the men Jos 2:22
for a few * before crossing. Jos 3:1
once a day for six *, followed by Jos 6:3,4
followed this pattern for six *. Jos 6:12,13,14
Three * later the facts came Jos 9:16
reached their cities in three *. Jos 9:17
In the * of Shamgar and of Jael, Ju 5:6
went away for four * each year to Ju 11:40
during these seven * of the Ju 14:12
Three * later they were still Ju 14:14
(For in those * Israel had no Ju 17:6
so he stayed three *, and they all Ju 19:4
of God was in Bethel in those *. Ju 20:27,28
just as on the previous *. Ju 20:35-39
in Israel in those *, because the Ju 21:15
in Israel in those *, and every man Ju 21:25
In those * it was the custom in Ru 4:7
one of them will live out his *. 1Sa 2:32
very rare in those *, but one 1Sa 3:1
and the Amorites in those *. 1Sa 7:14
(In those * prophets were called 1Sa 9:9,10,11
* ago, for they have been found. 1Sa 9:20
wait there seven * for me, for I 1Sa 10:8
"Give us seven * to see if we 1Sa 11:3
to wait seven * for his arrival, 1Sa 13:8
of Israel in those *, for the 1Sa 13:19
For forty *, twice a day, 1Sa 17:16
* who run away from their masters. 1Sa 25:10
for about ten *, then died, for 1Sa 25:37,38
THREE * LATER, when David and his 1Sa 30:1
or drink for three * and nights, so 1Sa 30:11,12
three * ago because I was sick. 1Sa 30:13
at Jabesh and fasted for seven *. 1Sa 31:13
Three * later a man arrived from 2Sa 1:1
custom in those * for virgin 2Sa 13:17,18
* and to report back at that time. 2Sa 20:4
the three * he had been given. 2Sa 20:5
task in nine months and twenty *. 2Sa 24:8
or to submit to three * of plague? 2Sa 24:13
and it lasted for three *. 2Sa 24:15
When it was three * old, this 1Ki 3:17,18
for fourteen *, and a great crowd 1Ki 8:65
Jerusalem in those *, and cedar was 1Ki 10:27
"Give me three * to think this 1Ki 12:5
returned three * later, the new 1Ki 12:12
toward Jehovah all his *." 1Ki 15:14f
But Zimri lasted only seven *; 1Ki 16:15,16
to travel forty * and forty nights 1Ki 19:8
other for seven *, and on the 1Ki 20:29
from the * of his father Asa. 1Ki 22:46
for three *, but didn't find him. 2Ki 2:17
the wilderness for seven *; 2Ki 3:9
again as they had in former *. 2Ki 13:5
In those * bandit gangs of 2Ki 13:20,21
In those * the Lord caused King 2Ki 15:37
I will heal him, and three * from 2Ki 20:5
Temple again three * from now." 2Ki 20:8
that since the * of the judges of 2Ki 23:22
In those * King Neco of Egypt 2Ki 23:29
were 212 doorkeepers in those *. 1Ch 9:22
to time, for seven * at a time. 1Ch 9:25
mourned and fasted for seven *. 1Ch 10:12
David for three *, for preparations 1Ch 12:39
Israel, or three * of deadly plague 1Ch 21:12
before us; our * on earth are like 1Ch 29:15
For the next seven *, they 2Ch 7:8
to count for much in those *! 2Ch 9:20
in three * for his decision. 2Ch 10:5
returned in three * to hear King 2Ch 10:12
them three * to cart it all away! 2Ch 20:25
which took eight * to clean up, so 2Ch 29:17
job was completed in sixteen *. 2Ch 29:17
for seven * with great joy. 2Ch 30:21
So, for seven * the observance 2Ch 30:22
observance for another seven *. 2Ch 30:23
the * of King David's son Solomon. 2Ch 30:26
Bread for the next seven *. 2Ch 35:17
months and ten *, and it was an 2Ch 36:9
of Unleavened Bread for seven *. Ez 6:21,22
there for three * while I went over Ez 8:15
within three * and that the leaders Ez 10:7,8
Within three *, on the fifth day Ez 10:9
to eat for several *, for I spent Neh 1:4
Three * after my arrival at Neh 2:11,12
of all kinds of wines every ten *. Neh 5:18
A few * later I went to visit Neh 6:10
—just fifty-two * after we had Neh 6:15
During those fifty-two * many Neh 6:17
huts for the seven * of the feast, Neh 8:17
carried out since the * of Joshua. Neh 8:17
each of the seven * of the feast, Neh 8:18
ancestors from the * when the kings Neh 9:32
of Persia, in the * of Eliashib, Neh 12:22
* of Johanan, the son of Eliashib. Neh 12:23
(It was in the * of David and Neh 12:46
So now, in the * of Zerubbabel Neh 12:47
evil * upon us and upon our city? Neh 13:18
alike—for seven * of revelry, held Est 1:5
do not eat or drink for three *, Est 4:16
THREE * LATER Esther put on her Est 5:1
on the last * of the month, to Est 9:21
* at the appointed time each year. Est 9:27
confirm these two * annually as the Est 9:29-31
lasted several *—Job would summon Job 1:5
silently for seven * and nights, no Job 2:13
the * of the month of that year. Job 3:6
alone for these few remaining *. Job 7:16
so little; our * here on earth are Job 8:9
"HOW FRAIL IS man, how few his *, Job 14:1
are good * they will soon be gone. Job 15:21
My good * are in the past. Job 17:11
"Those were the * when I went Job 29:7
Depression haunts my * Job 30:16
his request; the * of his life Ps 21:4
and filled my * with frustration. Ps 32:3
Literally, "knows the * of the Ps 37:18f
My * are filled with anguish. Ps 38:5,6
Temple on festival *, singing with Ps 42:4,5
you did in the * of long ago. Ps 44:1
the Temple of the Lord on holy *. Ps 55:14
will not live out half their *. Ps 55:23
Literally, "to the * of the Ps 61:6f
I keep thinking of the good old * Ps 77:5
be as endless as the * of heaven. Ps 89:29
All our * are filled with Ps 90:9
Teach us to number our * and Ps 90:12
for my * disappear like smoke. Ps 102:3,4
in middle life, shortening my *. Ps 102:23
and that our * are few and brief, Ps 103:15
months, and the sun to mark the *. Ps 104:19
I have known from earliest * Ps 119:152
miracles you did in * of long ago. Ps 143:5
For man is but a breath; his * Ps 144:4
and won't return for several *." Pro 7:20
Literally, "prolongs *." Pro 10:27f
For they spend their * plotting Pro 24:2
die, and in the * to come both will Ecc 2:16
all his hard work? * full of sorrow Ecc 2:20-23
In these few * of our empty Ecc 6:12
say how one's * can best be spent? Ecc 6:12
Don't long for "the good old * Ecc 7:10
good lives—their * shall pass away Ecc 8:13
the fleeting * of life, for the Ecc 9:9
for in the * ahead you yourself Ecc 11:2
and Jerusalem in the * ahead. Is 1:1
and your special * for fasting—even Is 1:12,13
In the last * Jerusalem and the Is 2:2
For in those * the world will Is 2:3
In those * a man will say to his Is 3:6
In those * flocks will feed Is 5:17
Babylon's * are numbered; Is 13:22
of Egypt in those *, and a monument Is 19:19
Then, in the * of another king, Is 23:15,16
the happy * are ended. Is 24:8
sunlight brighter than seven *! Is 30:26
In those * the ungodly, the Is 32:5
desert will rejoice in those *; Is 35:1
tell her that her sad * are gone. Is 40:2
what will happen in the * ahead! Is 41:23
is going to happen in the * ahead? Is 44:7
for your * of glory, pomp and Is 47:1
of childhood * shall slip away and Is 47:15
Rouse yourself as in the * of old Is 51:9
"He shall prolong his *." Is 53:10f
* of rest, but honors them; Is 56:2
them away from evil * ahead. Is 57:1
your * of mourning all will end. Is 60:20
Then they remembered those * of Is 63:11
And yet, the * will come Is 65:16
babies die when only a few * old; Is 65:20
In those *, when a man builds a Is 65:21,22
In those * nothing and no one Is 65:25
In those * Israel was a holy Jer 2:3
for "the good old * of long ago" Jer 3:16
Those * will not be missed or Jer 3:16
C. (the * of the Hebrew Jer 5:15f
to walk in, in the * of long ago. Jer 6:16
As a sign to them of these sad * Jer 16:8
just as on other *, then I will set Jer 17:27
the * of Hezekiah (Isaiah 36–37). Jer 21:1f
Literally, "in the latter *." Jer 23:20f
for back in the * when Micah the Jer 26:18
prophesied in the * of King Jer 26:18
In those * when you pray, I will Jer 29:12
Literally, "in the latter *." Jer 30:24f
of all I did in younger *." Jer 31:19
but wrong since their earliest *; Jer 32:30
back in the * of Josiah, and write Jer 36:2
there for several *, but Jer 37:15,16
Ten * later the Lord gave his Jer 42:7
for in those * we had plenty to Jer 44:17
But in the latter *, says the Jer 48:47
all your wise men of * gone by? Jer 49:7
But in the latter * I will bring Jer 49:39
In those *, says the Lord, no Jer 50:20
(They had been made in the * of Jer 52:20
she remembers happy bygone *. Lam 1:7
used to do on * of holy feasts! Lam 2:7
Our end is near—our * are Lam 4:18
them, overwhelmed, for seven *. Eze 3:14,15
At the end of the seven *, the Eze 3:16
Some versions read, "190 *." Eze 4:4,5f
*, to show that Israel will be Eze 4:4,5
side for forty *, to signify the Eze 4:6
completed all the * of your siege. Eze 4:8
"During the first 390 * eat Eze 4:9
in Israel—'The * as they pass make Eze 12:22
thought of those * long ago when Eze 16:22
In your proud * you held Sodom Eze 16:56
those former * when as a young girl Eze 23:21
Literally, "in the latter *," Eze 38:15,16f
"Every day for seven * a male Eze 43:25
Do this each day for seven * to Eze 43:26
he must wait seven * before he is Eze 44:26
shall be eaten during those *. Eze 45:21
On each of the seven * of the Eze 45:23
each of the seven * of the annual Eze 45:25
the six work * but open on the Eze 46:1
* of the new moon celebrations. Eze 46:1
* of the new moon celebrations. Eze 46:3
on the Sabbath * shall be six lambs Eze 46:4
Well, at the end of the ten *, Dan 1:15
Literally, "at the end of the * Dan 4:34f
In the * of your father this man Dan 5:11
has numbered the * of your reign, Dan 5:26
the next thirty * anyone who asks a Dan 6:7
or man—except you—for thirty *? Dan 6:12
and the Ancient of *—the Almighty Dan 7:9
he approached the Ancient of * Dan 7:13
the Ancient of * came and opened Dan 7:22
"But then the Ancient of * will Dan 7:26
replied, "Twenty-three hundred * Dan 8:14
happen in the last * of the coming Dan 8:19
hundred * to pass before the rights Dan 8:26
faint and was sick for several *. Dan 8:27
But for twenty-one * the mighty Dan 10:13
ministry of teaching in those *. Dan 11:33
stumble in those * and fall, but Dan 11:35
of the last * becomes the center of Dan 11:40f
worshiped, there will be 1,290 *. Dan 12:11
your full share of those last *." Dan 12:13
Literally, "at the end of the * Dan 12:13f
with joy as in * long ago in her Hos 1:15
"You must live alone for many *; Hos 3:3
In just a couple of *, Hos 6:2
Literally, "In two *." Hos 6:2f
What then will you do on holy *, Hos 9:5
on holy days, on * of feasting to Hos 9:5
first delightful * when I led you Hos 9:10
harrow. Her * of ease are gone. Hos 10:11
the fish three * and three nights. Jon 1:17
take three * to walk around it. Jon 3:3
him, "Forty * from now Nineveh Jon 3:4,5
hope for better *, but only Mic 1:12
BUT IN THE last * Mount Zion will Mic 4:1
For in those * the whole world Mic 4:2
and figs when harvest * are over. Mic 7:1
In those * ten men from ten Zec 8:23
earthquake in the * of Uzziah, king Zec 14:5
Literally, "in those *." Mt 3:1f
For forty * and forty nights he Mt 4:2
fish for three * and three nights, Mt 12:39,40
earth three * and three nights. Mt 12:39,40
with me for three * now, and have Mt 15:32
and that three * later he would be Mt 16:21
SIX * LATER Jesus took Peter, Mt 17:1
to those with babies in those *. Mt 24:19
"In fact, unless those * are Mt 24:22
of those * the sun will be Mt 24:29
celebration begins in two *, and I Mt 26:2
of God and rebuild it in three *.' Mt 26:60,61

(DAYS Con't)
it again in three *, can you? Mt 27:40
* I will come back to life again.' Mt 27:63
There, for forty *, alone except Mk 1:12,13
SEVERAL * LATER he returned to Mk 2:1
what men can do on Sabbath *!" Mk 2:28
to do kind deeds on Sabbath *? Mk 3:4
away, and as the * went by, the Mk 4:27
*, and have nothing left to eat. Mk 8:1
rise again three * afterwards. Mk 8:31
message in these * of unbelief and Mk 8:38
Six * later Jesus took Peter, Mk 9:2
killed and three * later I will Mk 9:30,31
but after three * I will come Mk 10:34
women in those *, and to mothers Mk 13:17
For those will be * of such Mk 13:19
chosen ones he will limit those *. Mk 13:20
began two * later—an annual Jewish Mk 14:1
hands and in three * I will build Mk 14:58
Temple and rebuild it in three *! Mk 15:29,30
for the remaining * of his Temple Lk 1:23
A few * later Mary hurried to the Lk 1:39,40
When the baby was eight * old, Lk 1:59
Eight * later, at the baby's Lk 2:21
Three * later they finally Lk 2:46,47
Satan tempted him for forty *. Lk 4:1
help in those * of famine, for Lk 4:25,26
and three * later I will come Lk 9:22
Eight * later he took Peter, Lk 9:28
longed for these *, to see and hear Lk 10:24
"There are six * of the week to Lk 13:14
"Those are the * to come for Lk 13:14
"A few * later this younger son Lk 15:13
as it was in the * of Lot: people Lk 17:28
ON ONE OF those * when he was Lk 20:1
For those will be * of God's Lk 21:22
Literally, "* of vengeance." Lk 21:22f
*, and those with tiny babies. Lk 21:23
true to me in these terrible *, Lk 22:28
For the * are coming when the Lk 23:29
Literally, "in these *." Lk 24:18f
happened three * ago— some women Lk 24:21
TWO * LATER Jesus' mother was a Jn 2:1
for a few * with his mother, Jn 2:12
in three * I will raise it up!" Jn 2:19
and you can do it in three *?" Jn 2:20
and he did, for two *, long Jn 4:40,41
At the end of the two *' stay he Jn 4:43,44
* and made no move to go to them. Jn 11:6
Finally, after the two *, he Jn 11:7
said, "only a few * ago the Jewish Jn 11:8
been in his tomb for four *. Jn 11:17
for he has been dead four *." Jn 11:39
Jerusalem several * early so that Jn 11:55
SIX * BEFORE the Passover Jn 12:1
Eight * later the disciples were Jn 20:26
During the forty * after his Act 1:3
the Holy Spirit in just a few * Act 1:5
meeting went on for several *. Act 1:15
came fifty * after the Passover Act 2:1f
'In the last *,' God said, 'I Act 2:17
when he was eight * old. Act 7:8
was there three *, blind, going Act 9:8,9
Damascus for a few * and went at Act 9:19
Cornelius replied, "Four * ago I Act 10:30
life again three * later and showed Act 10:40,41
to stay with them for several *. Act 10:48
the next few * by the men who had Act 13:31
In bygone * he permitted the Act 14:16
Yet only a few * later, some Jews Act 14:19
They stayed several *, Act 15:33
Several * later Paul suggested to Act 15:36
and stayed there several *. Act 16:12
Paul stayed in the city several * Act 18:18
The head was shaved thirty * Act 18:18f
to stay for a few *, but he felt Act 18:20
within the prescribed thirty *. Act 18:20f
The head was shaved thirty *. Act 18:22f
Greece and five * later arrived in Act 20:6
During our stay of several *, a Act 21:10
Literally, "the * of Act 21:26,27f
* later with the others. Act 21:26,27
The seven * were almost ended when Act 21:26,27
Literally, "before these *." Act 21:37,38f
FIVE * LATER Ananias the High Act 24:1
more than twelve * ago that I Act 24:11
A few * later Felix came with Act 24:24
THREE * AFTER Festus arrived in Act 25:1
Eight or ten * later he returned Act 25:6
A few * later King Agrippa Act 25:13
During their stay of several * Act 25:14
We had several * of rough Act 27:7,8
There we stayed for several *. Act 27:9
storm raged unabated many *, Act 27:20
and fed us for three *. Act 28:7
Syracuse, where we stayed three *. Act 28:12
us to stay with them seven *. Act 28:14
Three * after his arrival, he Act 28:17
And now in these * also he can Rom 3:26
did not in those * judge them Rom 5:13
In those * when you were slaves Rom 6:20
as special * to worship God, but Rom 14:5
If you have special * for Rom 14:6
last * as the world nears its end. 1Co 10:11
and that three * afterwards he 1Co 15:4
glory in these * when the Holy 2Co 3:8
there with him for fifteen *. Gal 1:18
* or months or seasons or years. Gal 4:10
For in those * I know you would Gal 4:15
Remember that in those * you Eph 2:12
these are difficult *. Eph 5:15,16
when I was eight * old, having been Php 3:5
who spends his * in laziness and 2Th 3:6
that in the last * it is going to 2Ti 3:1
But now in these * he has spoken Heb 1:2
those wonderful * when you first Heb 10:32
Men of God in * of old were Heb 11:2
*, as God had commanded them. Heb 11:30
last *, as a blessing to you. 1Pe 1:20
long before in the * of Noah, had 1Pe 3:20
showed me that my * here on earth 2Pe 1:13,14
too, in those *, just as there will 2Pe 2:1
that in the last * there will come 2Pe 3:3
You will be persecuted for 'ten * Rev 2:10
In those * men will try to kill Rev 9:6
two witnesses to prophesy 1,260 * Rev 11:3
and for three and a half * their Rev 11:8,9
But after three and a half *, the Rev 11:11
to take care of her for 1,260 *. Rev 12:6

DAYTIME
He called the light "*," and Gen 1:4,5
cloud during the *, and by a pillar Ex 13:21
during the *, and at night there Ex 40:38
It was always so—the * Cloud Num 9:16
It was * when they left, with Num 10:34
they see no better in the * than Job 5:14
and sleep in the *—they are not Job 24:16
In the * he led them by a cloud, Ps 78:14
* heat and from rains and storms. Is 4:6
us sunlight in the * and the moon Jer 31:35
and darken the earth in the *. Amo 8:9

DAZZLED
robes so bright their eyes were *. Lk 24:4

DAZZLING
heaven, clothed in * splendor. Job 37:22
* splendor of your presence lives. Ps 26:8
all glowing bronze, * like fire; Eze 1:27,28
and his clothing became * white. Mt 17:2
clothing became * white, far more Mk 9:3
and his clothes became * white Lk 9:29

DEACONS
one of the first seven *. Act 21:8
To: The pastors and * and all the Php 1:1
The * must be the same sort of 1Ti 3:8
Before they are asked to be * 1Ti 3:10
then they may be chosen as *. 1Ti 3:10
they do. * should have only one 1Ti 3:12
Those who do well as * will be 1Ti 3:13

DEAD
* animals floating on the water. Gen 8:7f
him, "You are a * man, for that Gen 20:3
Go and bury your *." Gen 23:11
and then I will bury my *." Gen 23:13
Go ahead and bury your *." Gen 23:14,15
law requires of a * man's brother; Gen 38:8
and one of our brothers is *." Gen 42:13
one is *, and the youngest is Gen 42:32
brother Joseph is * and he alone is Gen 42:38
And his brother is *, and he Gen 44:20
But when I am *, take me out of Gen 47:30
But now that their father was *, Gen 50:15
who wanted to kill you are *." Ex 4:19
as Moses promised—* frogs covered Ex 8:13
cattle were *, yet when he found Ex 9:7
a house where there was not one *. Ex 12:30
said, "We are as good as *." Ex 12:33
than * in the wilderness." Ex 14:12
*, washed up on the seashore. Ex 14:30
The famous Egyptian captains are * Ex 15:4
But the * man's relatives may Ex 21:30
the * animal shall belong to him. Ex 21:34
shall also own half of the * ox. Ex 21:35
in full for the * ox, and the dead Ex 21:36
ox, and the * one shall be his. Ex 21:36
as the * body of an animal Lev 5:2
or the * body of some forbidden Lev 5:2
If you do, God will strike you * Lev 10:6
meat or even touch their * bodies; Lev 11:8
meat or even touch their * bodies. Lev 11:11
"Anyone touching their * bodies Lev 11:24
Anyone touching the * body of Lev 11:27
Anyone touching their * bodies Lev 11:31
"If the * body of such an animal Lev 11:35
eats the * body of an animal that Lev 17:15
by touching a * person, unless it Lev 21:1
presence of any * person—not even Lev 21:11
And any priest who touches a * Lev 22:4
* bodies to rot among your idols; Lev 26:30
defiled by touching a * person. Num 5:1
But if the person he wronged is *, Num 5:8
"And he may not go near any * Num 6:6,7
someone fall * beside him, then Num 6:9
having touched the *, so they Num 9:6,7
of touching a * body, or if they Num 9:10
Don't let her be as one *, whose Num 12:12
But as for you, your * bodies Num 14:32
last of you lies * in the desert. Num 14:33
were struck * before the Lord. Num 14:36,37,38
the living and the *, and the Num 16:48
"We are as good as *," they Num 17:12,13
"Anyone who touches a * human Num 19:11
Anyone who touches a * person Num 19:13
*, or has touched a grave. Num 19:18
twenty years of age were now *. Num 26:64,65f
killed anyone or touched a * body. Num 31:19
will begin at the * Sea, and will Num 34:3
River, ending at the * Sea." Num 34:12
from the * man's relatives who want Num 35:12
over to the avenger of the * man. Num 35:24
them until finally all were *. Deu 2:14,15
You may not even touch the * Deu 14:8
call forth the spirits of the *. Deu 18:11
the * man's avenger, to kill him. Deu 19:12
as the son of the * brother, so Deu 25:6
But if the * man's brother Deu 25:7
have I offered any of it to the *. Deu 26:14
Your * bodies will be food to Deu 28:26
"Now that my disciple is *, [you Jos 1:2
arms when they left Egypt were *; Jos 5:6
Ai until the last person was *. Jos 8:26
time tomorrow they will all be *! Jos 11:6
relatives of the * man, who may try Jos 20:3
If a relative of the * man comes Jos 20:5
found their master * on the floor. Ju 3:25
Sisera lying there *, with the tent Ju 4:22
Lay at her feet * . Ju 5:27
But as soon as Gideon was *, the Ju 8:33
When his men saw that he was *, Ju 9:55
was no answer, for she was *; Ju 19:28
raped my wife until she was *. Ju 20:5
of the tribe of Benjamin are *?" Ju 21:16
us as well as to your * husband!" Ru 2:20
family name of her * husband." Ru 4:10
troops are * on the battlefield. 1Sa 4:17
*, her labor pains suddenly began. 1Sa 4:19
and her father-in-law were *. 1Sa 4:21,22
may God strike me * if you are 1Sa 14:44
Amalekites, until they are all *.' 1Sa 15:18
and then I will give the * bodies 1Sa 17:46
was *, they turned and ran. 1Sa 17:50,51
The bodies of the * and wounded 1Sa 17:52
need is one hundred * Philistines! 1Sa 18:25
him, "you'll be * by morning." 1Sa 19:11
Any harm to you will be over my * 1Sa 22:23
as worthless as a * dog or a flea? 1Sa 24:14
When David heard that Nabal was * 1Sa 25:39
"I've got to talk to a * man," 1Sa 28:7,8
saw that he was *, he also fell 1Sa 31:5
*, they abandoned their cities; 1Sa 31:7
out to strip the *, they found the 1Sa 31:8
SAUL WAS * and David had returned 2Sa 1:1
Thousands of men are * and 2Sa 1:4
"How do you know they are *?" 2Sa 1:5
Probably he had found Saul * upon 2Sa 1:10f
and joy lies * upon the hills; 2Sa 1:19
Stripped of their weapons, and *. 2Sa 1:27
subjects, now that Saul is *. 2Sa 2:7
the tribe of Benjamin) were *. 2Sa 2:31
told me, 'Saul is *,' thinking he 2Sa 4:10
kindness to a * dog like me?" 2Sa 9:8
charioteers * on the field, also 2Sa 10:18
and Uriah the Hittite is * too." 2Sa 11:24
was *, she mourned for him; 2Sa 11:26
when we tell him the child is *?" 2Sa 12:18
"Is the baby *?" 2Sa 12:19
but now that the baby is *, you 2Sa 12:21
why should I fast when he is *? 2Sa 12:23
Your sons aren't all *! 2Sa 13:32,33
"Why should this * dog curse my 2Sa 16:9
to the king that his son is *. 2Sa 18:20
the country, but now Absalom is *. 2Sa 19:8,9,10
may God strike me * if I do not 2Sa 19:13
criminals as soon as you are *." 1Ki 1:21
God strike me * if Adonijah does 1Ki 2:23,24
and laid her * child in my arms and 1Ki 3:20
I tried to feed my baby it was *! 1Ki 3:21
woman said, "the * one is yours 1Ki 3:22
the * child belongs to the other. 1Ki 3:23
and Joab were both *, he asked 1Ki 11:21
Sir, if I do that, I'm *!" 1Ki 18:14
word to Jezebel that Naboth was *. 1Ki 21:14
Well, you can have it now! He's * 1Ki 21:15
the Lord said, 'Their king is *; 1Ki 22:17
The king is *!" 1Ki 22:36,37
him, "The child is still *." 2Ki 4:31
child was indeed *, lying there 2Ki 4:32
and he sank down * in his chariot. 2Ki 9:24
that her son was *, she killed all 2Ki 11:1
bones, the * man revived and jumped 2Ki 13:20,21
Hamath and the * Sea, just as the 2Ki 14:25
troops, and * bodies were seen all 2Ki 19:35
*, killed himself in the same way. 1Ch 10:5
and his sons were *, they abandoned 1Ch 10:7

DEAD Con't)
look there were * bodies lying on 2Ch 20:24
because Queen Athaliah was *. 2Ch 23:21
and mother were *, and whom he had Est 2:7
fell in on them and all are *; Job 1:19
evening they are *, gone forever Job 4:20
Soon you'll look upon me *. Job 7:8
hide me with the *, and forget me Job 14:13
For when he is *, then he will Job 21:21
"The * stand naked, trembling Job 26:5,6
lest God should strike me *. Job 32:21,22
seem to think that God is *. Ps 10:4
you will not leave me among the *; Ps 16:10
I am forgotten like a * man, Ps 31:12
what they will do when I am *. Ps 41:7
even offered sacrifices to the *! Ps 106:28
and fill them with their *. Ps 110:6
nations say, "Their God is *!" Ps 115:2
The * cannot sing praises to Ps 115:17
the place of the *, you are there. Ps 139:8
from common sense will end up *! Pro 21:16
So I felt that the * were better Ecc 4:2
he would be better off born *. Ecc 6:3
forgotten all the * man's evil Ecc 8:9,10
to be a live dog than a * lion!" Ecc 9:4
But the * know nothing Ecc 9:5
* FLIES WILL cause even a bottle Ecc 10:1
—will both be *. Is 7:15,16
find out the future from the *? Is 8:19
long *, are there to see you. Is 14:9
* bodies of those slain in battle. Is 14:19
that the king who smote you is *. Is 14:29
but by dawn her enemies are *. Is 17:14
Your mighty army will be left * Is 18:6
The * Sea manuscript reads, Is 21:16f
Those we served before are * and Is 26:14
My people are like the * branches Is 27:11
Their * will be left unburied, Is 34:3
all these lay * before them. Is 37:36
For * men cannot praise you. Is 38:18
Or perhaps his meaning is, "* Is 38:18f
beneath the waves, *, their lives Is 43:17
Truth falls * in the streets, and Is 59:14
and look at the * bodies of those Is 66:24
now poised to strike them *!" Jer 4:10
* from starvation and disease. Jer 14:18
faints, for all her sons are *. Jer 15:9
and leave your * bodies for Jer 19:7
For I will fill Jerusalem with * Jer 19:12
Don't weep for the *! Jer 22:10
will not even care that he is *. Jer 22:18
He shall be buried like a * Jer 22:19
already as good as *, for I have Jer 33:5
and say, "Alas, our king is *!" Jer 34:5
I will feed your * bodies to the Jer 34:20
upon the throne of David. His * Jer 36:30
and famine until all of you are *. Jer 44:27
Your young men lie * in the Jer 49:26
her * shall lie in the streets. Jer 51:47
All my little children lie * upon Lam 2:22
in dark places, like those long *. Lam 3:6
We are orphans—our fathers *, Lam 5:3
or that I found injured or *; Eze 4:14
filled your streets with the *. Eze 11:6
Your city will lie in ruins, * Eze 26:20
ago the nether world of the *. Eze 26:20
now * at the hands of their foes. Eze 32:23
now they lie *. Eze 32:26
mountains with the *—your hills, Eze 35:8
the Travelers, east of the * Sea. Eze 39:11
the presence of a * person, unless Eze 44:25
Valley to the * Sea, where it will Eze 47:8
Fish will abound in the * Sea, Eze 47:9
the shores of the * Sea, fishing Eze 47:10
kind will fill the * Sea just as Eze 47:10
Gilead, past the * Sea to Tamar. Eze 47:18
whose bodies lie * and buried will Dan 12:2
She will gather your *; Hos 9:6
a virgin weeps whose fiancé is *. Joe 1:8
The grapevines are *; Joe 1:12
half shall be driven into the * Joe 2:20
Edom, with no respect for the *. Amo 2:1
to weeping then. * bodies will be Amo 8:3
I'd rather be * than alive [when Jon 4:3
He is *! Mic 4:9
Your finest youth lie *. Nah 2:13
the cavalry! The * are lying in the Nah 3:3
your princes lie * in the dust; Nah 3:18
someone touches a * person, and so Hag 2:13
are now long *, but remember the Zec 1:5,6
half toward the * Sea and half Zec 14:8
For they are *." Mt 2:18
trying to kill the child are *." Mt 2:20
is *, then I will follow you." Mt 8:21
* care for their own dead." Mt 8:22
dead care for their own *." Mt 8:22
out, for the little girl isn't *; Mt 9:24
Heal the sick, raise the *, cure Mt 10:8
hear, and the * raised to life; Mt 11:5
after he had risen from the *. Mt 17:9
get all the * man's property. Mt 22:24
of the *—don't you ever read the Mt 22:31
So God is not the God of the *, Mt 22:32
and Jacob, long *, were not alive Mt 22:32f
mausoleums—full of * men's bones, Mt 23:27
saw him, and fell into a * faint. Mt 28:4
has risen from the *, and that he Mt 28:7
daughter was * and there was no Mk 5:35
"The child isn't *; Mk 5:39
He has come back from the *." Mk 6:16
had risen from the *. Mk 9:9
he meant by "rising from the *." Mk 9:10
motionless, to all appearance *. Mk 9:26
ran through the crowd—"He is *." Mk 9:26
on until all were *, and still Mk 12:20,21,22
rise from the *, they won't be Mk 12:25
though * for hundreds of years, Mk 12:27
Jesus was already * so he called Mk 15:44
who had seen him alive from the *. Mk 16:14
The deaf can hear again. The * Lk 7:20,21,22
news that the little girl was *. Lk 8:49
She isn't *; Lk 8:52
for they all knew she was *. Lk 8:53
prophet risen from the *." Lk 9:8
prophets risen from the *." Lk 9:19
* care for their own dead." Lk 9:60f
dead care for their own *." Lk 9:60f
him lying half * beside the road. Lk 10:30
was * and has returned to life. Lk 15:24
and he was * and has come back to Lk 15:32
in the place of the righteous *. Lk 16:22
to them from the *, then they will Lk 16:30
though someone rises from the *.' Lk 16:31
the * man, to carry on his name. Lk 20:28
raised from the * get to heaven, Lk 20:34,35
raised up in new life from the *. Lk 20:36
means that person is alive, not *! Lk 20:37,38
*, they went home in deep sorrow. Lk 23:48
again from the * on the third day; Lk 24:46
He will even raise from the * Jn 5:21
is here, when the * shall hear my Jn 5:25
when all the * in their graves Jn 5:28
all such to rise again from the *. Jn 6:44
told them plainly, "Lazarus is *. Jn 11:14
the * and gives them life again. Jn 11:25
But Martha, the * man's sister, Jn 11:39
for he has been * four days." Jn 11:39
saw that he was * already, so they Jn 19:33
to us since his return from the *. Jn 21:14
that Jesus rose from the *. Act 2:32
denied the resurrection of the *. Act 4:1f
that Jesus had risen from the *. Act 4:2
words, he fell to the floor, *! Act 5:5
fell to the floor, *, and the young Act 5:10
that she was *, carried her out and Act 5:10
with him after he rose from the *. Act 10:40,41
be the Judge of all—living and *. Act 10:42
him out of the city, apparently *. Act 14:19
who had been *, some laughed, but Act 17:32
in the resurrection of the *!" Act 23:6
eat nor drink till he is *. Act 23:21
that the * will rise again!' Act 24:21
in the resurrection of the *? Act 26:8
to rise from the *, to bring light Act 26:23
begin swelling or suddenly fall *; Act 28:6
in the resurrection of the *. Act 28:20f
and by being raised from the * Rom 1:4
who makes the * live again and Rom 4:17
back Jesus our Lord from the *. Rom 4:24
Christ rose from the * and will Rom 6:9
old sin nature as * and Rom 6:11
and since you are "*," you are Rom 7:4
who rose from the *, so that you Rom 7:4
up Jesus from the *, lives in you, Rom 8:11
to go among the * to bring Christ Rom 10:7
him from the *, you will be saved. Rom 10:9
It will be like * people coming Rom 11:15
bodies from the * by his power just 1Co 6:14
and 23,000 fell * in one day. 1Co 10:8
rose from the *, why are some of 1Co 15:12
of you saying that * people will 1Co 15:12
*, then Christ must still be dead. 1Co 15:13
dead, then Christ must still be *. 1Co 15:13
And if he is still *, then all 1Co 15:14
* do not come back to life again. 1Co 15:15
Christ is still *, and you are 1Co 15:16
rise from the *, and has become the 1Co 15:20
is the resurrection from the *. 1Co 15:21
If the * will not come back to 1Co 15:29
the * will some day rise again? 1Co 15:29
* be brought back to life again? 1Co 15:35
us, for he can even raise the *. 2Co 1:9
Father who raised him from the *. Gal 1:1
interest in me is also long *. Gal 6:14
Christ from the * and seated him in Eph 1:20
were spiritually * and doomed by Eph 2:5
when he raised Christ from the * Eph 2:5
O sleeper, and rise up from the *; Eph 5:14
of those who are alive from the *. Php 3:11
of all those who arise from the *, Col 1:18
the firstborn from the *." Col 1:18f
God who raised Christ from the *. Col 2:12
You were * in sins, and your Col 2:13
arose from the *, now set your Col 3:1
for this world as a * person does. Col 3:3
now it is * and gone. Col 3:9
And the believers who are * will 1Th 4:16
whether we are * or alive at the 1Th 5:10
that he rose again from the *. 2Ti 2:8
of the * has already occurred; 2Ti 2:18
the living and the * when he 2Ti 4:1
you are in * earnest about it. Tit 2:7
and the resurrection of the * and Heb 6:2
person who wrote the will is *. Heb 9:16
and though Abel is long *, we can Heb 11:4
again from the * our Lord Jesus, Heb 13:20,21
faith at all—it is * and useless. Jas 2:17
Just as the body is * when there Jas 2:26
in it, so faith is * if it is not Jas 2:26
Christ rose again from the *. 1Pe 1:3
the * and gave him great glory. 1Pe 1:21
the Judge of all, living and *; 1Pe 4:5
who were *—killed by the flood 1Pe 4:6
They are not only *, but doubly Jud 1:12
dead, but doubly *, for they have Jud 1:12
"the First-born from the *." Rev 1:5f
saw him, I fell at his feet as *; Rev 1:17,18
was * and then came back to life. Rev 2:8
and I will strike her children * Rev 2:23
and active church, but you are *. Rev 3:1
or from among the * was permitted Rev 5:3
and from the * beneath the earth Rev 5:13
of the city, leaving 7,000 *. Rev 11:13
It is time to judge the *, and Rev 11:18
like the watery blood of a * man; Rev 16:3
at his reappearance after being *. Rev 17:8
(The rest of the * did not come Rev 20:5
I saw the *, great and small, Rev 20:12
And the * were judged according Rev 20:12
underworld gave up the * in them. Rev 20:13

DEADEN
earthly things; * the evil desires Col 3:5

DEADENED
for when you are * to sin you Rom 6:7

DEADLY
of God will send a * plague to Ex 9:3
And * serpents Deu 32:24
or three days of * plague as the 1Ch 21:12
* arrows made from shafts of fire. Ps 7:13
They are poisonous as * snakes, Ps 58:4,5
hand in a nest of * adders will Is 11:8
plans which end up in * actions. Is 59:5
Their weapons are *; Jer 5:16
"I will shower you with * arrows Eze 5:16
city, mistress of * charms, enticed Nah 3:4
the sting and poison of * snakes. Rom 3:13
So you can see how cunning and * Rom 7:13
my slavery to this * lower nature? Rom 7:23,24,25
ready to pour out its * poison. Jas 3:8

DEAF
"You must not curse the * nor Lev 19:14
But I am * to all their threats; Ps 38:13,14
Is God * and blind—he who makes Ps 94:9
but you yourself will be * and Ecc 12:4
In that day the * will hear the Is 29:18
and unstop the ears of the *. Is 35:5
Are you so * to the words of Is 40:21
Oh, how blind and * you are Is 42:18
as they are and * when I call Is 43:8
And he isn't getting * ! Is 59:1
They will stand in silent awe, * Mic 7:16
lepers, and the * who hear, and the Mt 11:5
the Ten Towns. A * man with a Mk 7:32
Zacharias was apparently stone * Lk 1:62f
healed. The * can hear again. Lk 7:20,21,22

DEAFNESS
he even corrects * and Mk 7:37
"O demon of * and dumbness," he Mk 9:25

DEAL
We'll * with you far worse than Gen 19:9
He will * with them personally. Deu 7:10
I will personally * with anyone Deu 18:19
enemies until you * with this sin. Jos 7:13
David to discuss a *—to surrender 2Sa 3:12
* gently with young Absalom." 2Sa 18:5
"What sort of * is this, my 1Ki 9:13
Then I called a public trial to * Neh 5:7
Why aren't you ashamed to * with Job 19:3
But I refuse even to * with Job 21:16
Come and * with all these proud Ps 10:2
But the Lord will not * gently Ps 12:3,4
Literally, "you * out the Ps 58:1f
But as for me, O Lord, * with me Ps 109:21
Literally, "* bountifully that I Ps 119:17f
Lord, * with me in Ps 119:124
fairness in every business *. Pro 16:11
Therefore God will * with them Is 5:24
you; * with them in your anger. Jer 18:23
No wonder the Lord has had to * Lam 3:34,35,36
Therefore I will * with them in Eze 8:18
will personally * with anyone in Eze 14:4
him to Babylon and * with him there Eze 17:20
to its sheath before I * with you? Eze 21:30

(DEAL Con't)
against you and * furiously with Eze 23:25
They will * with you in hatred, Eze 23:29
And I will * severely with all Zep 3:19
well enough to * with his speck! Lk 6:42
great * about the Kingdom of God. Lk 8:10
for you are a hard man to * Lk 19:21
I am afraid to come to * with you. 1Co 4:18
job to judge and * strongly with 1Co 5:12
But you yourselves must * with 1Co 5:13
God will * with that person, Gal 5:10
And because he is a man he can * Heb 5:1
but not to * again with our sins. Heb 9:28
a great * to know more about it. 1Pe 1:12

DEALERS
quarrymen, timber *, and stone 2Ki 12:11,12

DEALING
After * with him, the Israelis Num 33:41
For you are * with the one who Amo 4:13
God's power to use in * with you. 2Co 13:4
truly, * truly, living truly Eph 4:15,16
in * with the sins of the people. Heb 2:17

DEALINGS
for they had no * with anyone. Ju 18:28
All your * are crooked: you give Ps 58:1
he was just and fair in all his *. Jer 22:15
*, justly cutting them short." Rom 9:28
God and his * with you, as some of 1Co 10:10
that in all our * we have been pure 2Co 1:12
Christ is not weak in his * with 2Co 13:3
all other men in their * with God. Heb 5:1

DEALS
The remainder of 1 Chronicles * 1Ch 10:1
help me to abhor all crooked * of Ps 101:3

DEALT
God has * me bitter blows. Ru 1:20
has * to him, is not a happy one. Ecc 1:12-15
and suffering you have * to me! Lam 3:19
The Lord himself has * with Lam 4:16
never again be * a blow like this. Joe 2:27
For the old system * only with Heb 9:10

DEAR
"Let his curses be on me, * son. Gen 27:13
our * brothers the Lord killed!" Num 20:3
And Naomi said, "All right, * Ru 2:2
ONE DAY NAOMI said to Ruth, "My * Ru 3:1
"Well, what happened, *?" Ru 3:15-18
Your lips, my *, are made of Sol 4:11
all that you hold *, and I will Jer 15:7
So Jesus said it again: "* Mk 10:24
* FRIEND WHO loves God: Lk 1:1
said to her, "Martha, * friend, Lk 10:41
"* friends, don't be afraid of Lk 12:4
" 'Look, * son,' his father said Lk 15:31
so very soon. *, dear children, Jn 13:33
Dear, * children, how brief are Jn 13:33
* FRIEND WHO loves God: Act 1:1
"* brothers, think! Act 2:29
"* brothers, I realize that what Act 3:17
among yourselves, * brothers, and Act 6:3
said, "You know, * brother, how Act 21:20
* FRIENDS IN Rome: This letter is Rom 1:1
And you, * friends in Rome, are Rom 1:6,7
I want you to know, * brothers, Rom 1:13
DON'T YOU UNDERSTAND yet, * Rom 7:1
So, * brothers, you have no Rom 8:12
* BROTHERS, THE longing of my Rom 10:1
truth from God, * brothers, so that Rom 11:25
AND SO, * brothers, I plead with Rom 12:1
* friends, never avenge Rom 12:19
PHOEBE, A * Christian woman from Rom 16:1
workers, and to * Persis, who has Rom 16:12
and also his * mother who has Rom 16:13
But, * brothers, I beg you in the 1Co 1:10
and quarrels, * brothers. 1Co 1:11
Notice among yourselves, * 1Co 1:26
* BROTHERS, EVEN when I first came 1Co 2:1
* BROTHERS, I have been talking to 1Co 3:1
So, * brothers, whatever 1Co 7:24
FOR WE MUST never forget, * 1Co 10:1
against it. So, * friends, 1Co 10:14
I am so glad, * brothers, that 1Co 11:2
of the world. So, * brothers, when 1Co 11:33
* friends, even if I myself 1Co 14:6
* brothers, don't be childish in 1Co 14:20
So, my * brothers, since future 1Co 15:58
1 * FRIENDS, 2Co 1:1
and from our * brother Timothy. 2Co 1:1
I think you ought to know, * 2Co 1:8
But Titus, my * brother, wasn't 2Co 2:13
Oh, my * Corinthian friends! 2Co 6:11
promises as these, * friends, let 2Co 7:1
this to help you, * friends—to 2Co 12:19
* friends, I solemnly swear that Gal 1:11
this faith. * brothers, even in Gal 3:15
speak of God as our * Father. Gal 4:6
* brothers, please feel as I do Gal 4:12
You and I, * brothers, are the Gal 4:28
free woman's son. * brothers, we Gal 4:31
For, * brothers, you have been Gal 5:13
* BROTHERS, IF a Christian is Gal 6:1
* brothers, may the grace of our Gal 6:18
* CHRISTIAN FRIENDS at Ephesus, Eph 1:1
And I want you to know this, * Php 1:12
WHATEVER HAPPENS, * friends, be Php 3:1
No, * brothers, I am still not Php 3:13
* brothers, pattern your lives Php 3:17
* BROTHER CHRISTIANS, I love you Php 4:1
two * women, Euodias and Syntyche. Php 4:2
the kingdom of his * Son, who Col 1:13
* doctor Luke sends his love, and Col 4:14
* brothers, much beloved of God. 1Th 1:4
YOU YOURSELVES KNOW, * 1Th 2:1
Don't you remember, * brothers, 1Th 2:9
And then, * brothers, you 1Th 2:14
* brothers, after we left you and 1Th 2:17
So we are greatly comforted, * 1Th 3:7
LET ME ADD this, * brothers: You 1Th 4:1
Even so, * friends, we beg you to 1Th 4:10
And now, * brothers, I want you 1Th 4:13
about that, * brothers, for you 1Th 5:1
But, * brothers, you are not in 1Th 5:4
* brothers, honor the officers of 1Th 5:12
* brothers, warn those who are 1Th 5:14
* brothers, pray for us. 1Th 5:25
* brothers, giving thanks to God 2Th 1:3
upset and excited, * brothers, by 2Th 2:1
With all these things in mind, * 2Th 2:15
FINALLY, * BROTHERS, as I come to 2Th 3:1
Now here is a command, * 2Th 3:6
And to the rest of you I say, * 2Th 3:13
To: Timothy, my * son. 2Ti 1:2
praying for you, * Philemon, Phm 1:4
Yes, * brother, give me joy with Phm 1:20
THEREFORE, * BROTHERS whom Heb 3:1
Beware then of your own hearts, * Heb 3:12
* friends, even though I am Heb 6:9
And so, * brothers, now we may Heb 10:19
* brothers, is your life full of Jas 1:2
So don't be misled, * brothers. Jas 1:16
* brothers, don't ever forget Jas 1:19
* BROTHERS, HOW can you claim that Jas 2:1
Listen to me, * brothers: God has Jas 2:5
* brothers, what's the use of Jas 2:14
* BROTHERS, DON'T be too eager to Jas 3:1
of the same mouth. * brothers, Jas 3:10
evil about each other, * brothers. Jas 4:11
Now as for you, * brothers who Jas 5:7
But most of all, * brothers, do Jas 5:12
* brothers, if anyone has slipped Jas 5:19
* friends, God the Father chose 1Pe 1:2
* brothers, you are only visitors 1Pe 2:11
* friends, don't be bewildered or 1Pe 4:12
So, * brothers, work hard to 2Pe 1:10
THIS IS MY second letter to you, * 2Pe 3:1
But don't forget this, * friends, 2Pe 3:8
* friends, while you are waiting 2Pe 3:14
I am warning you ahead of time, * 2Pe 3:17
* brothers, I am not writing out 1Jn 2:7
* children, this world's last 1Jn 2:18
Yes, * friends, we are already 1Jn 3:2
Oh, * children, don't let anyone 1Jn 3:7
So don't be surprised, * 1Jn 3:13
* young friends, you belong to 1Jn 4:4
* friends, let us practice loving 1Jn 4:7
* friends, since God loved us as 1Jn 4:11
* children, keep away from 1Jn 5:21
To: That * woman Cyria, one of 2Jn 1:1
remind you, * friends, of the old 2Jn 1:5
To: * Gaius, whom I truly love. 3Jn 1:1
* friend, I am praying that all 3Jn 1:2
* friend, you are doing a good 3Jn 1:5
* friend, don't let this bad 3Jn 1:11
* friends, remember what the Jud 1:17
But you, * friends, must build up Jud 1:20
* Friends: Rev 1:4

DEAREST
Don't let them say, "Aha! Our * Ps 35:25
I have surrendered my * ones to Jer 12:7
* friends, when I was there with Php 2:12

DEARLY
For he loves us very *, and his Ps 117:2
The Pharisees, who * loved their Lk 16:14
himself loves you * because you Jn 16:27
Rome, are among those he * loves; Rom 1:6,7
for we know how * God loves us, and Rom 5:5
we belong to his * loved Son. Eph 1:6
We loved you *—so dearly that we 1Th 2:8
We loved you dearly—so * that we 1Th 2:8
at those who would * love to 1Jn 2:26
But, * loved friends, if our 1Jn 3:21
* LOVED FRIENDS, don't always 1Jn 4:1
he tells us that he loves us *. 1Jn 4:16
* loved friends, I had been Jud 1:3

DEATH
and was 950 years old at his *. Gen 9:29
old, so that his * occurred in the Gen 11:32f
AFTER THE * of Abram's father, God Gen 12:1
of * that engulfed the cities. Gen 19:29
* along with all your household." Gen 20:7
After Abraham's *, God poured out Gen 25:11
after his father's *, and gave them Gen 26:18
before his *, instead of Esau!" Gen 27:8,9,10
"succeeded at his * by . . ." Gen 36:31-39f
for his *, for, after all, he is Gen 37:26,27
god-like power of life and *!" Gen 41:45
us before we all starve to *." Gen 42:2
years old at the time of his *. Gen 47:28
hundred years after Joseph's *. Ex 1:8f
if we don't obey him, we face * Ex 5:3
your God to take away this *. Ex 10:17
The wail of * will resound Ex 11:6
stoned or shot to * with arrows, Ex 19:13
he dies shall surely be put to *. Ex 21:12
mother shall surely be put to *. Ex 21:15
father shall surely be put to *. Ex 21:17
"If a man beats his slave to * Ex 21:20
a man or woman to *, the ox shall Ex 21:28
"A sorceress shall be put to *. Ex 22:18
an innocent person be put to *. Ex 23:7
substitute: the * of the animal Lev 1:4
God instead of the * of the man who Lev 1:4
may lament the * of Nadab and Lev 10:6
under penalty of *, for the Lev 10:7
The penalty for intrusion is *. Lev 16:1
lived, but also after his *. Lev 18:14f
put to *, because she is not free. Lev 19:20
to put him to *, then I myself Lev 20:4
surely be put to *—for he has Lev 20:9
man and woman shall be put to *. Lev 20:10
acts is * to both parties. Lev 20:13
woman—shall surely be stoned to *. Lev 20:27
And I will put to * anyone who Lev 23:30,31
he shall surely be put to *. Lev 27:29
to be put to *, may be ransomed." Lev 27:29f
of being in the presence of *. Num 6:9
stone him to * outside the camp." Num 15:35
If these men die a natural * or Num 16:29
of Aaron's *, they mourned for him Num 20:29
just seen by the * of Cozbi." Num 25:18
a natural *, but he had no sons. Num 27:3,4
Passover—[when the * angel passed Num 28:16
The date of his * was July 15, Num 33:38,39
who want to avenge his *; Num 35:12
The avenger of his * shall Num 35:19
until the * of the High Priest. Num 35:25
until the * of the High Priest. Num 35:28
But after the * of the High Num 35:28
before the * of the High Priest. Num 35:32
him to put him to *, then the hands Deu 13:9
Stone him to * because he has Deu 13:10
that has died a natural *. Deu 14:21
the city and shall be stoned to *. Deu 17:5
However, never put a man to * on Deu 17:6
this purpose, the penalty is *. Deu 17:12
to be burned to * as a sacrifice to Deu 18:10
Anyone seeking to avenge the * Deu 19:6,7
able to avoid the * of innocent Deu 19:10
of the city shall stone him to *. Deu 21:21
a crime worthy of *, and is Deu 21:22
of the city shall stone her to *. Deu 22:21
and stoned to *—the girl because Deu 22:23,24
"Fathers shall not be put to * Deu 24:16
every man worthy of * shall be Deu 24:16
you life and *, depending on Deu 30:15
you life or *, blessing or curse. Deu 30:19
rebellious will you be after my *! Deu 31:27
I know that after my * you will Deu 31:29
the people of Israel before his *: Deu 33:1
AFTER THE * of Moses, the Lord's Jos 1:1
there are scared to * of us." Jos 2:24
stoned them to * and burned their Jos 7:25
to them, for the * was accidental. Jos 20:5
the accidental * must stay in that Jos 20:6
there until the * of the High Jos 20:6
AFTER EHUD'S * the people of Ju 4:1
of the city and scraped them to * Ju 8:16
is, "A quick * is less painful." Ju 8:21f
AFTER ABIMELECH'S *, the next Ju 10:1
At his * he was buried in one of Ju 12:7
birth until the day of his *!" Ju 13:7
the moment of his * were more than Ju 16:30
anything but * to separate us." Ru 1:17
since the * of your husband, and Ru 2:10,11
it by the jaw and club it to *. 1Sa 17:35
that I am only a step away from *! 1Sa 20:3
"Why should he be put to *?" 1Sa 20:32
Now I have caused the * of all of 1Sa 22:22
news of Saul's * to their idols and 1Sa 31:9
were together in life and in *. 2Sa 1:23
for the * of his brother Asahel. 2Sa 3:27
because of the * of their brother 2Sa 3:30
no way responsible for Abner's *. 2Sa 3:37
about Abner's * at Hebron, he was 2Sa 4:1
to Hanun about his father's *. 2Sa 10:2
like that should be put to *; 2Sa 12:5
to Amnon's *, longed day after 2Sa 13:37,38,39
it means life or *." 2Sa 15:21
could expect only * from you, but 2Sa 19:28
The waves of * surrounded me; 2Sa 22:5
By hell and *; 2Sa 22:6
But as the * angel was preparing 2Sa 24:16
AS THE TIME of King David's * 1Ki 2:1

DEATH Con't)
to arrange a bloody * for him." 1Ki 2:9
about Adonijah's * (Joab had joined 1Ki 2:28
outside the city on pain of *. 1Ki 2:36,37
there until the * of Solomon. 1Ki 11:40
a great mob stoned him to *. 1Ki 12:18
and the * of all of his family. 1Ki 13:34
that you are sending me to my *? 1Ki 18:9
outside the city and stoned to *. 1Ki 21:13
AFTER KING AHAB'S * the nation of 2Ki 1:1
They shall no longer cause * or 2Ki 2:21
but after Ahab's *, the king of 2Ki 3:5
to tell him of her husband's *. 2Ki 4:1
trampled him to * at the gate! 2Ki 7:20
face until he smothered to *. 2Ki 8:15
who don't come will be put to *." 2Ki 10:18,19
into quietness after Athaliah's *. 2Ki 11:20
After his father's * he built 2Ki 14:22
lasted until the day of his *; 2Ki 15:5
to * on the altars of Molech; 2Ki 17:17
All of this instead of *! 2Ki 18:31,32
to your plea. The * of this nation 2Ki 22:20
to * as a sacrifice to Molech. 2Ki 23:10
At the time of Hadad's *, the 1Ch 1:51-54
After Azubah's *, Caleb married 1Ch 2:19
Soon after his father Hezron's *, 1Ch 2:24
to Hanun for the * of his father. 1Ch 19:2,3
materials before his *. 1Ch 22:5
things David did before his *. 1Ch 23:27
sent word to him of Solomon's *. 2Ch 10:2,3
the people stoned him to *. 2Ch 10:18
the Syrians to * with these!" 2Ch 18:10
*, and they led him on to ruin. 2Ch 22:4
the news of her son Ahaziah's *. 2Ch 22:10
But after his * the leaders of 2Ch 24:17,18
the * of King Joash of Israel. 2Ch 25:25
After his father's *, he rebuilt 2Ch 26:2
the day of his * and lived in 2Ch 26:21
Jerusalem honored him at his *. 2Ch 32:33
its people until after your *.' 2Ch 34:28
songs about his *, for these songs 2Ch 35:24,25
immediately by *, banishment, Ez 7:26
Instantly the * veil was placed Est 7:8
For there in * the wicked cease Job 3:17
who long for *, and it won't come; Job 3:20,21
who search for * as others search Job 3:20,21
crushed to * as easily as moths! Job 4:18,19
"He will keep you from * in Job 5:20
When he sends * to snatch a man Job 9:12
and the shadow of *, never to Job 10:20,21
of the shadow of * where only Job 10:22
their only hope is *." Job 11:20
light, even the dark shadow of *. Job 12:22
anguish I eagerly await sweet *! Job 14:14
on my eyelids is the shadow of *. Job 16:16
"I AM SICK and near to *; Job 17:1
His skin is eaten by disease. * Job 18:13
escaped * by the skin of my teeth. Job 19:20
It is like poison and * to him. Job 20:16
The terrors of * are upon him. Job 20:25
their children. * consumes sinners Job 24:19
will die in war, or starve to *. Job 27:14
Everyone will cheer at his *, Job 27:23
rock, shadowed by *, men descend on Job 28:3,4
"But Destruction and * speak of Job 28:22
that your purpose for me is *. Job 30:23
and bones, and draws near to *. Job 33:22
gates of * been revealed to you? Job 38:17,18
into the dust, stone-faced in *. Job 40:13
full of the stench of sin and *. Ps 5:9
snatch me back from the jaws of *. Ps 9:13
* bound me with chains, and the Ps 18:4
the ropes that drew me on to *. Ps 18:5
you have laid me in the dust of *. Ps 22:15
Rescue me from *; Ps 22:20
the dark valley of * I will not be Ps 23:4
* itself, and here I am alive! Ps 30:3
He will keep them from * even in Ps 33:18,19
I am sinking down to *. Ps 35:12
who was sick and nearing *. Ps 35:14
them and then demanding their *. Ps 37:32
with happiness again before my *. Ps 39:13
sending us into darkness and *. Ps 44:19
For we are facing * threats Ps 44:22
* is the shepherd of all mankind. Ps 49:14
of *, for he will receive me. Ps 49:15
Don't sentence me to *. Ps 51:14,15
against me and threaten me with *. Ps 55:3
Let * seize them and cut them Ps 55:15
For you have saved me from * and Ps 56:13
they plot my * and use lies and Ps 62:3,4
He rescues us from *. Ps 68:20
lie before us in the sleep of *; Ps 76:5
But in * you are mere men. Ps 82:7
Protect me from *, for I try to Ps 86:2
of troubles, and * draws near. Ps 88:3
who condemn the innocent to *? Ps 94:21,22
were children of *—and released Ps 102:20
*, crushed by misery and slavery? Ps 107:10
of * and snapped their chains. Ps 107:14
Their appetites were gone and * Ps 107:18
from the door of *. Ps 107:20
hounded brokenhearted ones to *. Ps 109:16
about me and threaten me with *. Ps 109:20
I am slipping down the hill to *; Ps 109:22,23
* stared me in the face—I was Ps 116:3
I was facing * and then he saved Ps 116:6
He has saved me from *, my eyes Ps 116:8
the Lord is the * of his saints." Ps 116:15f
me, but not handed me over to *. Ps 118:18
I am close to * at the hands of Ps 119:107
fearing you will starve to *; Ps 127:2
They will die a violent *. Pro 1:19
For you turned away from me—to * Pro 1:32
lie along the road to * and hell. Pro 2:18
She leads you down to * and Pro 5:5
refuse me show that they love *." Pro 8:36
good man starve to *, nor will he Pro 10:3
also the godless man's *. Pro 11:10
the evil man, *. Pro 11:19
So why fear *? Pro 12:28
that seems right but ends in *. Pro 14:12
being sentenced to *, but a false Pro 14:25
its waters keep a man from *. Pro 14:27
* and a wise man will appease it. Pro 16:14
thinks is right, but it ends in *. Pro 16:25
despising them means *. Pro 19:16
who are unjustly sentenced to *; Pro 24:11,12
around firebrands, arrows and *! Pro 26:18,19
and * are alike in this: neither Pro 27:20
at the brink of *, and wine for Pro 31:6,7
money at his * that his children Ecc 6:3
Yes, a wise man thinks much of * Ecc 7:4
prostitute is more bitter than *. Ecc 7:26
prevent his day of *, for there is Ecc 8:8
is nothing but * ahead anyway. Ecc 9:2,3
do well, for in *, where you are Ecc 9:10
love is strong as * and jealousy is Sol 8:6
in the land of the shadow of *. Is 9:2
will be dashed to * against the Is 13:16
* echoes from the mountainsides. Is 22:5
of * that hangs over the earth; Is 25:7
he will swallow up * forever. Is 25:8
You have struck a bargain with *, Is 28:15
of compromise with * and the devil, Is 28:18
nobles and find them worthy of *. Is 34:11
have lovingly delivered me from *; Is 38:17
dungeon, starvation and * are not Is 51:14
trial they led him away to his *. Is 53:8
he has poured out his soul unto *. Is 53:12
behind a trail of misery and *. Is 59:7
of drought and *, where no one Jer 2:6
How long must I see war and * Jer 4:21
there they burn to * their little Jer 7:31
I will visit them with *. Jer 8:12
too. For * has crept in through Jer 9:21
in God's name on pain of *. Jer 11:21,22
who are destined for *, to death; Jer 15:2
who are destined for death, to *; Jer 15:2
at noon time I will bring * to Jer 15:8
grief for their parents' *. Jer 16:7
children starve to * and let the Jer 18:21
Take your choice of life or *! Jer 21:8
by the * blows I rain upon them." Jer 25:16
not deserve the * sentence, for he Jer 26:16
* by war and famine and disease. Jer 34:17
"On pain of *, don't tell anyone Jer 38:24
threaten you with * unless you tell Jer 38:25
slashed to * in her streets. Jer 51:4
needs until the day of his *. Jer 52:34
at home, disease and *. Lam 1:20
for food, risking * from enemies. Lam 5:9
our dance has turned to *. Lam 5:15
the penalty of *, therefore repent Eze 3:18
for his *, and punish you. Eze 3:20
* by war and famine and disease. Eze 12:16
You have led those to * who Eze 13:19
"SING THIS * dirge for the Eze 19:1
Thus they have caused your * Eze 21:29
come you will be wounded unto *. Eze 21:29
accused and sent to their *. Eze 22:9
one who has been wounded unto *. Eze 30:24
world among the denizens of *. Eze 32:18
hold you responsible for his *. Eze 33:8
pleasure in the * of the wicked; Eze 33:11
dies a natural * or that dies after Eze 44:31
stamped others to * with its feet. Dan 7:19
for at the time of Messiah's *. Dan 9:25f
my mouth, threatening you with *. Hos 6:5
children were dashed to * there. Hos 10:14
The Lord will sentence him to * Hos 12:14
Shall I redeem him from *? Hos 13:14
him from Death? O *, bring forth Hos 13:14
babies dashed to * against the Hos 13:16
The stench of * was terrible to Amo 4:10
our nation and is plotting your *. Amo 7:10
for his *, for it is not our Jon 1:14
from the depths of * I called, Jon 2:2
"I sank beneath the waves, and * Jon 2:5
and imprisoned in the land of *. Jon 2:6
me from the yawning jaws of *! Jon 2:6
For he said, "* is better than Jon 4:8
her babies were dashed to * Nah 3:10
nations, but like * and hell, they Hab 2:5
been judged and sentenced to *." Zec 5:3
I have delivered you from * in a Zec 9:11
stayed there until King Herod's *. Mt 2:15
they sat in the land of *, and Mt 4:15,16
betray brother to *, and fathers Mt 10:21
to plot Jesus' arrest and *. Mt 12:14
men to a horrible *, and lease the Mt 21:41
resurrection after *, came to him Mt 22:23
sadness to the point of * . . . Mt 26:38
that would result in a * sentence. Mt 26:59
They shouted, "*! Mt 26:65,66
They shouted, "Death!—*! Mt 26:65,66
—Death!—*!" Mt 26:65,66
government to sentence Jesus to *. Mt 27:1
against Jesus to put him to *." Mt 27:1f
release, and for Jesus' *. Mt 27:20
"She is at the point of *," he Mk 5:23
after his * and resurrection. Mk 10:1f
each other to *, fathers will Mk 13:12
Jesus secretly and put him to *. Mk 14:1
by sorrow to the point of *; Mk 14:34
be sufficient to condemn him to *. Mk 14:55
And the vote for the * sentence Mk 14:63,64
that Christ's *, for man's sin, had Mk 15:38f
army captain was sick and near *. Lk 7:2
and they were speaking of his * Lk 9:31
to wait until his father's *. Lk 9:59
who believed that * is the end of Lk 20:27
has done calls for the * penalty. Lk 23:15
no reason to sentence him to *. Lk 23:22
*, and their voices prevailed. Lk 23:23
Jesus away to his *, Simon of Lk 23:26
talking of Jesus' *, when suddenly Lk 24:14
to *, and they crucified him. Lk 24:20
already passed out of * into life. Jn 5:24
leaders were plotting his *. Jn 7:1
not *, but for the glory of God. Jn 11:4
that Jesus' * would not be for Jn 11:52
leaders began plotting Jesus' *. Jn 11:53
But my * will produce many new Jn 12:23,24
for us to put any man to *." Jn 18:31f
indicates his * by crucifixion, a Jn 18:32f
of the men broken to hasten *; Jn 19:31
of * he would die to glorify God. Jn 21:19
What sort of * will he die?" Jn 21:21
about my * and resurrection." Act 1:8
The news of his * spread rapidly Act 1:19
by since Jesus' * and resurrection, Act 2:1
the horrors of * and brought him Act 2:24
to life again, for * could not keep Act 2:24
all will be well with me in *— Act 2:26
blame for this man's * on us!" Act 5:28
after Stephen's * traveled as far Act 11:19
and sentenced to *. Act 12:19
concerning his *, he was taken from Act 13:29
at all by the ravages of *. Act 13:37
The jailer was threatened with * Act 16:23
fell three stories to his * below. Act 20:9
hounding them to *, binding and Act 22:4
worthy of imprisonment or *. Act 23:29
of *, I don't refuse to die! Act 25:10,11
is the man whose * is demanded both Act 25:24
he has done nothing worthy of *. Act 25:25
and when they were condemned to * Act 26:10
worthy of * or imprisonment." Act 26:31
loss of cargo, injuries, and *." Act 27:10
no cause for the * sentence Act 28:18
They were fully aware of God's * Rom 1:32
back to God by the * of his Son, Rom 5:10
His sin spread * throughout all Rom 5:12
the world, and * through sin." Rom 5:12f
them guilty of * for breaking his Rom 5:13
For this one man, Adam, brought * Rom 5:15
the penalty of * to many, while Rom 5:16
man, Adam, caused * to be king over Rom 5:17
brought them to *, but now God's Rom 5:21
through his * the power of your Rom 6:2,3
him in the likeness of his *." Rom 6:5f
never die again. * no longer has Rom 6:9
you are back from * and you want to Rom 6:13
You can choose sin (with *) or Rom 6:16
For the wages of sin is *, but Rom 6:23
deeds, the rotting fruit of *. Rom 7:5
in my being given the * penalty. Rom 7:10
using them to make me guilty of *. Rom 7:11
the vicious circle of sin and *. Rom 8:2
nature leads to *, because the old Rom 8:6
and thistles, sin, *, and decay Rom 8:20,21
* as they await this great event. Rom 8:22
with *, has God deserted us? Rom 8:35
be ready to face * at every moment Rom 8:36
his love. * can't, and life can't. Rom 8:38
when God will conquer sin and *. Rom 15:4
Christ and his * on the cross. 1Co 2:2
life and even * are your servants. 1Co 3:22
*, that he has died for you. 1Co 11:26
for he is trifling with the * of 1Co 11:29
* came into the world because of 1Co 15:21
wherever there is sin, * results. 1Co 15:22

(DEATH Con't)
including the last enemy—*. 1Co 15:26
our lives, facing * hour by hour? 1Co 15:30
For it is a fact that I face * 1Co 15:31
They are just human bodies at *, 1Co 15:44
* is swallowed up in victory." 1Co 15:54
O *, where then your victory? 1Co 15:55,56
For sin—the sting that causes * 1Co 15:55,56
and saved us from a terrible *; 2Co 1:10
a fearful smell of * and doom, 2Co 2:16
the Ten Commandments, ends in *; 2Co 3:6
of law that led to * began with 2Co 3:7
who is on the road to eternal *. 2Co 4:3
facing * just as Jesus did; 2Co 4:10
preaching we face *, but it has 2Co 4:12
Jesus back from * will also bring 2Co 4:14
we live close to *, but here we 2Co 6:9
have been injured but kept from *. 2Co 6:9
and does not prevent eternal *. 2Co 7:10
faced * again and again and again. 2Co 11:23
cities and from * in the deserts 2Co 11:26
treats Christ's * as meaningless. Gal 2:21
of Jesus Christ's * as clearly as Gal 3:1
on Christ's * to clear away our Gal 5:5
harvest of spiritual decay and *; Gal 6:8
By his * he ended the angry Eph 2:15
to die a criminal's * on a cross. Php 2:8
*, even the death of the cross." Php 2:8f
death, even the * of the cross." Php 2:8f
at the point of * while trying to Php 2:30
earth—for Christ's * on the cross Col 1:20
He has done this through the * Col 1:22
and then you came up out of * Col 2:12
broke the power of * and showed us 2Ti 1:10
because he suffered * for us. Heb 2:9
* for everyone in all the world. Heb 2:9
the devil who had the power of *. Heb 2:14
through fear of * have been living Heb 2:15
is exceeding sorrowful unto *." Heb 5:7f
and premature *: for an angel was Heb 5:7f
out from *, at the Resurrection. Heb 5:7f
*. And God heard his prayers Heb 5:7
were, no record of his birth or *. Heb 7:3f
the * of the person who wrote it. Heb 9:17
sprinkled [as proof of Christ's * Heb 9:18
sin is not covered by Christ's *; Heb 10:26
*, but he came back again alive! Heb 11:19
save him from the * the king Heb 11:23
terrible Angel of * could not touch Heb 11:28
faith, escaped * by the sword. Heb 11:34
loved ones back again from *. Heb 11:35
and were beaten to *, preferring to Heb 11:35
to die a shameful * on the cross Heb 12:2
to the * penalty from God. Jas 1:15
soul from *, bringing about the Jas 5:20
been saved from * and doom by the 1Pe 3:21
were punished with *, they could 1Pe 4:6
others is headed for eternal *. 1Jn 3:14
to us eternal life through his *. 1Jn 4:9
and again as he was facing * 1Jn 5:6,7,8
baptism\but also as he faced *. 1Jn 5:6,7,8
does not end in *, you should ask 1Jn 5:16
sin which ends in * and if he has 1Jn 5:16
of that one that ends in *. 1Jn 5:17
physical * or spiritual death. 1Jn 5:17f
physical death or spiritual *. 1Jn 5:17f
in spiritual * (Mark 3:29) but can 1Jn 5:17f
ends in physical * (1 Cor. 1Jn 5:17f
He was the first to rise from *, Rev 1:5
of hell and *—don't be afraid! Rev 1:17,18
even when facing * and I will give Rev 2:10
shall not be hurt by the Second *. Rev 2:11
what is left is at the point of *. Rev 3:2
wounds that once had caused his *. Rev 5:6
horse, and its rider's name was *. Rev 6:8
won't be able to—* will not come. Rev 9:6
They will long to die—but * will Rev 9:6
Their power of * was not only in Rev 9:19
to celebrate the * of the two Rev 11:10
those destined for * will be Rev 13:10
Verse 12 implies * from Rev 14:13f
Therefore the sorrows of * and Rev 18:8
For them the Second * holds no Rev 20:6
to his deeds. And * and Hell were Rev 20:14
This is the Second *—the Lake of Rev 20:14
shall be no more *, nor sorrow, nor Rev 21:4
This is the Second *." Rev 21:8

DEATH-WOUND
the Creature whose * had been Rev 13:12

DEATH'S
standing at * door, and nearing his Ecc 12:5
in darkness and * shadow, and to Lk 1:79
his son, who was now at * door. Jn 4:46,47

DEATHLY
Those who didn't die were * ill; 1Sa 5:12
made Bath-sheba's baby * sick. 2Sa 12:15
HEZEKIAH NOW BECAME * sick, and 2Ki 20:1
Hezekiah became * sick, and he 2Ch 32:24
true. * silence is everywhere. Is 23:2,3
Hezekiah became * sick and Isaiah Is 38:1

DEATHS
of their *, then so be it." Gen 43:14

virtual widowhood until their *. 2Sa 20:3
no party to the * of General Abner, 1Ki 2:32
guiltless concerning their *." 1Ki 2:33
he is responsible for their *. Eze 33:6
charge the watchman with their *. Eze 33:6
their parents and cause their *. Mt 10:21

DEBASED
"She was in fact more * than Eze 23:14,15

DEBATE
in public *, showing by the Act 18:28

DEBATERS
* of this world's great affairs? 1Co 1:20

DEBIR
King * of Eglon. Jos 10:3
Then they turned back to *, Jos 10:38
*, Anab, Judah, and Israel; Jos 11:21
The king of *; Jos 12:8-24
Valley of Achor to *, where it Jos 15:7
in the city of * (formerly called Jos 15:15
(or, *), Anab, Eshtemoh, Anim, Jos 15:48-62
Libnah, Jattir, Eshtemoa, Holon, * Jos 21:9-16
the city of * (formerly called Ju 1:11
will lead the attack against *?" Ju 1:12
Libnah, Jattir, Eshtemoa, Hilen, * 1Ch 6:58,59

DEBORAH
after this, Rebekah's old nurse * Gen 35:8
back to God, was *, a prophetess, Ju 4:4
And * marched with them. Ju 4:10
Then * said to Barak, "Now is Ju 4:14
THEN * AND Barak sang this song Ju 5:1
Until * became a mother to Israel. Ju 5:7
Awake, O *, and sing! Ju 5:12
With * and Barak. Ju 5:15

DEBORAH'S
place now called "* Palm Tree," Ju 4:5

DEBRIS
all the * from the holy place. 2Ch 29:4,5
planks and * from the broken ship. Act 27:44

DEBT
must be sold as a slave for his *. Ex 22:3
* cancellation is close at hand! Deu 15:9
garment in pledge of her *. Deu 24:17
such as being in *, or merely 1Sa 22:2
oil and pay your *, and there will 2Ki 4:7
his *, you are in serious trouble. Pro 6:1
them for their * of a piece of Amo 8:6
him sold for the *, also his wife Mt 18:25
released him and forgave his *. Mt 18:27
until the * would be paid in full. Mt 18:30
that tremendous *, just because you Mt 18:32
you owe him?' 'My * is 850 gallons Lk 16:5,6
For I owe a great * to you and Rom 1:14
Pay all your debts except the * Rom 13:8
* to the Jerusalem Christians. Rom 15:27
* to God by keeping those laws; Gal 5:4

DEBTOR
to foreclose nor a * refusing to Jer 15:10

DEBTOR'S
are thrown into a * cell, for you Mt 5:25

DEBTORS
to all enslaved *, and a time for Lev 25:10
does not crush his * with high Ps 15:5
bankers and *—none will be spared. Is 24:2
in pledge by poor *, and is no Eze 18:7
and robs his * by refusing to let Eze 18:12
in clothing stolen from their *, Amo 2:8
pledged clothing of * overnight. Amo 2:8f
"Suddenly your * will rise up in Hab 2:7
In the process, one of his * was Mt 18:24

DEBTS
of all public and private *. Lev 25:10
is to be a canceling of all *! Deu 15:1
cancel the * of our brother Jews. Neh 10:31
hard labor shall repay his *. Job 20:10
withhold repayment of your *. Pro 3:27,28
to become responsible for his *. Pro 17:18
who agrees to pay a stranger's *. Pro 27:13
was taken in payment for your *. Is 50:1
the poor who can't repay their *; Amo 2:6
Pay all your * except the debt Rom 13:8

DECAPOLIS
Or, "to visit *." Mk 5:20f

DECAY
the filth and * they found there. 2Ch 29:16
but the moral * of the wicked Pro 11:11
tongues will * in their mouths. Zec 14:12
let the body of your Holy Son *. Act 2:27
in hell and his body would not *. Act 2:31
'God will not let his Holy One *.' Act 13:35
and thistles, sin, death, and * Rom 8:20,21
which die and * are different from 1Co 15:42
harvest of spiritual * and death; Gal 6:8
beyond the reach of change and *. 1Pe 1:4

DECAYED
has *, this body shall see God! Job 19:26
and was buried, and his body *. Act 13:36

DECAYING
* corpses fertilized the soil. Ps 83:10
It is * from within; Eze 19:14

DECAYS
and its stump *, it may sprout and Job 14:8,9

DECEASED
[to deny a child to his * brother Gen 38:10
the name and inheritance of the *. Lev 18:16

DECEIT
and use lies and * to try to force Ps 62:3,4
corruption and * of every kind. Pro 8:13
a false man by * and lies. Pro 12:17
* fills hearts that are plotting Pro 12:20
for the false prophets, full of *. Jer 23:9
*, inventing everything they say. Jer 23:26
the first his method will be *; Dan 11:23
me with lies and *, but Judah still Hos 11:12
be sinners, full of lies and *. Zep 3:13
wickedness, *, lewdness, envy, Mk 7:22
Some day their * will be well 2Ti 3:9

DECEITFUL
they say is crooked and *; Ps 36:3
charges of these merciless, * men. Ps 43:1
The heart is the most * thing Jer 17:9
For you were * when you sent me Jer 42:20
their bags of false, * weights? Mic 6:11

DECEITFULNESS
Literally, "*." Heb 3:13f

DECEIVE
let him no longer * himself, for Job 15:31
But I will not allow those who * Ps 101:7
smooth taste of strong wine * you. Pro 23:31
of one who will * and fool them." Is 28:15
For these evil men * my people Eze 13:10
table, attempting to * each other. Dan 11:27
that would *, if possible, even Mk 13:22
don't let anyone * you about this: 1Jn 3:7
He will go out to * the nations Rev 20:8

DECEIVED
"Why have you * me and let my 1Sa 19:17
she screamed, "You've * me! 1Sa 28:12
O king, my servant Ziba * me. 2Sa 19:26
Deceivers and * are both his Job 12:16
"If I have lied and *— but God Job 31:5
people have been * by what you Jer 4:10
Then I said, O Lord, you * me Jer 20:7
The town of Achzib has * the Mic 1:14
ones would be *. Mt 24:24
* by Satan in the Garden of Eden. 2Co 11:3
Don't be carried away and * 2Th 2:3
themselves having been * by Satan. 2Ti 3:13
* all nations with her sorceries. Rev 18:23
that * all who had accepted the Rev 19:20

DECEIVERS
and wisdom. * and deceived are both Job 12:16

DECEIVES
Everyone * and flatters and Ps 12:2
Or, "An evil man * his neighbor Pro 16:29f

DECEIVING
worse and worse, * many, they 2Ti 3:13
a stain among you, * you by living 2Pe 2:13
or Satan, the one * the whole Rev 12:9
he was * people everywhere. Rev 13:14

DECEMBER
three days, on the fifth day of *, Ez 10:9
we began our work on * 15, and Ez 10:16-19
In * of the twentieth year of the Neh 1:1
ON A * day in that same year—the Jer 28:1
of Fasting held in * of the fifth Jer 36:9
for it was *, and cold. Jer 36:22
ONE DAY LATE in * of the ninth Eze 24:1
LATE IN * of the tenth year (of Eze 29:1
year of our exile, late in *, one Eze 33:21
In early *, in the second year of Hag 2:10
corresponds to early in our *. Hag 2:18,19f
* 25 was the usual date for this Jn 10:22,23f

DECENT
king and giving him a * burial. 2Sa 2:5
"Why can't he give us * food as Ps 78:19,20
even give him a * burial—I say that Ecc 6:3
be room enough for * burial Jer 19:11
should! Be * and true in everything Rom 13:12,13

DECEPTION
Your words are based on clever *, Job 15:4,5
how you abhor all murder and *. Ps 5:6
I hate lies and every kind of *. Pro 8:6,7
"He will be a master of *, Dan 8:25
(His wife had agreed to this *. Act 5:2
away all evil, *, envy, and fraud. 1Pe 2:2,3

DECEPTIVE
Charm can be * and beauty doesn't Pro 31:30

DECIDE
all to see and to * whose it is! Gen 31:36,37
except to * what he wanted to eat! Gen 39:6
but if you * not to trade, the Ex 13:13
him their questions to *; Ex 18:19,20
until I * what to do with you." Ex 33:5
If you * not to redeem it, then Ex 34:20
shall pay as the priest shall *. Lev 27:8
the priest will * its value and the Lev 27:14,15
and tens to * their quarrels and Deu 1:15
of entry, and to * which cities we Deu 1:22
hard for you to *—for instance, Deu 17:8
his blessings and * lawsuits and Deu 21:5
marrying her you * you don't like Deu 21:14
the sacred dice to * which section Jos 18:5,6

ECIDE Con't)
then * today whom you will obey. Jos 24:15
came to her to * their disputes. Ju 4:5
to * how to dispose of the Ark. 1Sa 5:8
heart and soul, whatever you *." 1Sa 14:7
"The Lord will * between us. 1Sa 24:12
from home and will * to return; 2Ki 19:7
he made David * to take a census. 1Ch 21:1
did * really to please the Lord. 2Ch 12:14
and help them to * justly, lest the 2Ch 19:10
political leaders to * what to do. 2Ch 28:14
* this matter for himself. Est 1:8
Will you let him * where to work? Job 39:11
* before knowing the facts! Pro 18:13
but me, and * to do what I don't Is 30:1
I bring a case before you to *. Jer 12:1
If you * to stay, then return to Jer 40:5
They will * to turn toward Eze 21:22
rich food, and * whether or not to Dan 1:13
Perhaps even yet he will * to let Joe 2:14
Perhaps even yet God will * to Jon 3:9
have authority even to * what men Mk 2:28
over you to * such things as that? Lk 12:14
A father will * one way about Lk 12:53
replied, "You * whether God wants Act 4:19
was yours to * how much to give. Act 5:4
meeting to * this question. Act 15:6
and then he would * the case. Act 24:22
I was perplexed as to how to * a Act 25:20
kind everyone must * for himself. Rom 14:5
himself who must examine me and *. 1Co 4:4
a heathen court to * the matter 1Co 6:1
to * which of you is right? 1Co 6:1
So why can't you * even these 1Co 6:2
So you should be able to * your 1Co 6:3
able to * these things for you." 1Co 6:4f
wise enough to * these arguments? 1Co 6:5
But if you men * to go ahead 1Co 7:28
He cannot * afterward to do Gal 3:15
Yes, and those who * to please 2Ti 3:12
But your job is not to * whether Jas 4:11

ECIDED
"I have * to destroy all mankind; Gen 6:12,13
We've * to ask for a treaty Gen 26:28
the distance, they * to kill him! Gen 37:18
Moses eventually * to accept Ex 2:21
sorrows, and had * to rescue them, Ex 4:31
If it is * that it was Num 35:25
I had * to scatter them to Deu 32:26
which area was * by throwing dice Jos 14:1
So we * to build the altar as a Jos 22:26,27
groups * by the way they drink. Ju 7:5,6
and they * that since his mother Ju 9:3
Once upon a time the trees * to Ju 9:8
or sons. She * to return to Israel Ru 1:6,7
slipping away, he * to sacrifice 1Sa 13:9
to you: 'I have * to settle 1Sa 15:2
So he * against taking it into 2Sa 6:10
was Haggith) * to crown himself 1Ki 1:5
she * to test him with some hard 1Ki 10:1
(a date he * upon himself), 1Ki 12:32,33
the king, they * on General Omri, 1Ki 16:15,16
We have * that you should be our 2Ki 10:5
He had * to wipe Judah out of his 2Ki 24:3,4
Finally he * to take it to the 1Ch 13:13
a dog, yet you have * to honor me! 1Ch 17:18
SOLOMON NOW * that the time had 2Ch 2:1
as yet really * to follow the God 2Ch 20:33
for God had * to punish Ahaziah 2Ch 22:7
Later on, Joash * to repair and 2Ch 24:4
own officials * to kill him for 2Ch 24:25
it was unanimously * to continue 2Ch 30:23
Hezekiah * to prepare storerooms 2Ch 31:11
of war, and it was * to plug the 2Ch 32:3
* to send you this information. Ez 4:14
and elders had * that anyone who Ez 10:7,8
then each case will be * and the Ez 10:14
Haman was furious, but * not to Est 3:5,6
sleeping and * to read awhile. Est 6:1
indeed, the Jews themselves had * Est 9:29-31
"If I * to forget my complaints Job 9:27
"I've * to forget our quarrel! Pro 7:14
So, after a lot of thinking, I * Ecc 2:3
So I * that there was nothing Ecc 2:24-26
All things are * by fate; Ecc 6:10
Then I * to spend my time having Ecc 8:15
God has rightly * to destroy his Is 10:22
Yes, it has already been * by Is 10:23
I have * to break the Assyrian Is 14:25
it was I who * all this long ago? Is 37:26
afraid and * to move to Jerusalem. Jer 35:11
it over and * to turn from his sins Eze 18:28
They * to go to the king and say, Dan 6:6
have unanimously * that you should Dan 6:7
Then the crew * to draw straws to Jon 1:7
yes, I, the Lord, for I have * to Zec 3:2
* to break the engagement but to Mt 1:19
to a king who * to bring his Mt 18:23
They * to send some of their men Mt 22:16
They talked it over and finally * Mt 27:7
called, and it was * to bribe the Mt 28:12,13
A farmer * to sow some grain. Mk 4:3
They finally * that he must be Mk 8:16
has * to wonderfully bless you! Lk 1:30
The next day Jesus * to go to Jn 1:43
Then the chief priests * to kill Jn 12:10
was furious, and * to kill them. Act 5:33
So the believers * to send Act 11:29
When she insisted they *, "It Act 12:15
They * that Barnabas was the Act 14:12
have * concerning your question. Act 15:26
the Gentiles, as * by the apostles Act 16:4
of the earth. He * beforehand which Act 17:26
The incantation they * on was Act 19:13
* to go north to Macedonia first. Act 20:3
Paul had * against stopping at Act 20:16
to kill him, I * to send him on to Act 23:30
They finally * to try. Act 27:40
their minds and * he was a god. Act 28:6
For from the very beginning God * Rom 8:29
what he had * from the beginning; Rom 9:10-13
For I * that I would speak only 1Co 2:2
I have already * what to do, just 1Co 5:3,4
came, the time God * on, he sent Gal 4:4
do for us; he * then to make us Eph 1:4
a plan he * on in mercy long ago; Eph 1:9
happen just as he * long ago. Eph 1:11
it no longer, I * to stay alone in 1Th 3:1
* to stay there for the winter. Tit 3:12

DECIDES
he * that there is leprosy there. Lev 14:36
If the man * to redeem the Lev 27:19
But if he * not to redeem the Lev 27:20
If God * to argue with him, can Job 9:3
he fears God and * against that Eze 18:14
because someone * to have them or Rom 9:16
not to marry and * that he doesn't 1Co 7:37
He alone * to save us or destroy. Jas 4:12

DECIDING
"I am their judge, * who is Ex 18:15,16
* all the people's arguments. Ps 122:5
But be sure in * these matters 1Co 7:17
gifts and powers, * which each one 1Co 12:11

DECISION
before God for a *, and the one Ex 22:9
duty at the time will make the *. Deu 17:9
the decision. His * is without Deu 17:10
to accept the * of the priest or Deu 17:12
of Israel. The * as to which tribe Jos 14:1
Ark. The * was to take it to Gath. 1Sa 5:8
in making this *, because you have 2Sa 14:13
replied. "My * is that you and 2Sa 19:29
"This is a hard *," David 2Sa 24:14
waiting for your * as to whether 1Ki 1:20
Word of the king's * spread 1Ki 3:28
"This is a terrible * to make," 1Ch 21:13
to return in three days for his *. 2Ch 10:5
*, he spoke roughly to them; 2Ch 10:12
* than what God tells you to. 2Ch 19:7
the matter and returned his *. Ez 5:5
The king agreed, confirming his * Est 3:10
This was their unanimous * at Ps 83:5
be done to them apart from his *. Ps 105:14
to find the right * every time. Pro 2:9
it is the Lord who controls its *. Pro 16:33
"The * is right; Jer 26:18
For it is my * to gather together Zep 3:8
this * of mine to bless you. Zec 8:14,15
of their * to turn their backs on Mk 1:4
Their * was to send Jesus under Mk 15:1
and the * of an honored Lk 12:53
"If the * is negative, then Lk 14:32
agreed with the * and actions of Lk 23:50,51,52
And many came to the * that he Jn 10:42
and Barnabas, to report on this *. Act 15:22
agreed on our *, to send to you Act 15:25
making known the * concerning the Act 16:4
Jews protested the *, I felt it Act 28:19
and won't, he has made a wise *. 1Co 7:37
and every * you then make will Jas 1:7,8

DECISIONS
ask for God's *," Moses told him. Ex 18:15,16
you will tell them his *, Ex 18:19,20
'When giving your *,' I told Deu 1:17
of the wisest and corrupt their *. Deu 16:19
From that time on your * should 1Sa 10:7
I don't make * the way you do! 1Sa 16:7
mountains. Your * are as full of Ps 36:6
I know, O Lord, that your * are Ps 119:75,76,77
Their * must be based upon my Eze 44:24
understand his * and his methods! Rom 11:33
in faith, not for * of scruples." Rom 14:1f

DECISIVE
For the * question is whether Mt 7:21

DECK
*—and put a door in the side. Gen 6:16

DECKED
scarlet linens, * out with gold and Rev 18:16

DECKS
and construct * and stalls Gen 6:14
and make three * inside the Gen 6:16

DECLAIMS
Micah bitterly * each town, Mic 1:11f
Micah bitterly * each town, Mic 1:11f
Micah bitterly * each town, Mic 1:11f

DECLARATION
and sent him their * of Lk 19:14

DECLARE
mountain, and to * it off limits Ex 19:23
"But if the man shall plainly *, Ex 21:5
and the priest must * him a leper. Lev 13:3
Literally, "shall * him Lev 13:3f
the priest shall * him defiled, for Lev 13:20
the priest must * him a leper. Lev 13:22
priest shall * that all is well. Lev 13:23
* that he does not have leprosy. Lev 13:28
hair develops, * him a leper. Lev 13:36
and the priest shall * him healed. Lev 13:37
cleansed, and * the leprosy gone. Lev 14:48
must without fail * war against Deu 13:15
of the city and *, 'This son of Deu 21:20
Then you shall * before the Lord Deu 26:13
gods— then I * to you this day Deu 30:18
go to the people of Israel and * Jos 9:11
God of Israel, * that although I 1Sa 2:30
and may the Lord * David and his 1Ki 2:33
* each day that he is the one who 1Ch 16:23
And I now * that I will cause 1Ch 17:10
is lying, or else * him innocent. 2Ch 6:23
We wish to * that if this city Ez 4:16
them to * an annual holiday on the Est 9:21
Those who * otherwise are my Job 27:7
And he will * to his friends, 'I Job 33:27
* that you will rescue them. Ps 31:19
O LORD, FIGHT those fighting me; * Ps 35:1
vindicate me. * me "not Ps 35:24
But as for me, I shall forever * Ps 75:9
Can those in the grave * your Ps 88:11
This I *, that he alone is my Ps 91:2
The heavens * his perfect Ps 97:6
He will * that every one of his Is 10:8
strength," the people shall *. Is 45:24
Who shall * me guilty? Is 50:9
There they shall * my glory to Is 66:19
Come, let us * in Jerusalem all Jer 51:10
you to legally * my marriage vow. Eze 16:8
for the Scriptures *, 'God will Mt 4:6
"I solemnly * that any sin of Mk 3:28
said, "I solemnly * that one of Mk 14:18
I solemnly * that I shall never Mk 14:25
But I solemnly * to you that no Lk 4:24
"The Scriptures *, 'My Temple is a Lk 19:46
"I solemnly * to you that when Lk 21:32
And I solemnly * that the time Jn 5:25
For the Scriptures * that rivers Jn 7:38
Literally, "Who can * his Act 8:33f
and acquit us—* us "not Rom 3:21,22
as the Scriptures also *. 1Co 14:34
Don't let anyone * you lost when Col 2:18
so that he could * us good in Tit 3:7
will * war against them and Rev 11:7
And I solemnly * to everyone who Rev 22:18

DECLARED
seventh day and * it holy, because Gen 2:3
I have * it. Gen 17:5
And Sarah *, "God has brought me Gen 21:6
about his neck and *, "See, I have Gen 41:41,42
And Pharaoh * to Joseph, "I, Gen 41:44
Hebrews has met with us," they *. Ex 5:3
the man shall be * a leper. Lev 13:14,15
be * fully cured of his leprosy. Lev 14:9
house will not be * contaminated if Lev 14:36
after that he shall be * Lev 17:15
lest they be * guilty and die for Lev 22:9
Israel," he *. Num 20:14
"King Sihon then * war on us and Deu 2:32
have * to be ceremonially defiled. Deu 14:3,4,5
You have * today that he is your Deu 26:17
And the Lord has * today that Deu 26:18
Then Joshua * a terrible curse Jos 6:26
Israel again. He *, "Because these Ju 2:20
The Philistine leaders * a great Ju 16:23,24
credit for your account," she *. Ju 17:3
Samuel *, "that you can never 1Sa 12:5
Saul had *, "A curse upon anyone 1Sa 14:24,25
and the people were * innocent. 1Sa 14:41
among David's men *, "They didn't 1Sa 30:22
When David heard about it he *, 2Sa 3:28
Ahithophel * for Absalom, as did 2Sa 15:12
After that David's men *, "You 2Sa 21:17
"Our lord King David has * 1Ki 1:43
Then Zimri * himself to be the 1Ki 16:10
as * by Joshua, the son of Nun. 1Ki 16:34
the Syrians have *, 'The Lord is a 1Ki 20:28
iron horns and *, "The Lord 1Ki 22:11
the nation of Moab * its 2Ki 1:1
the salt in and *, "The Lord has 2Ki 2:21
comes true. He * through his 2Ki 10:9,10
of Israel * war on Ahaz and 2Ki 16:5
Then the Lord * through the 2Ki 21:10
Lord's prophet had * would happen 2Ki 23:16
deserters who had * their 2Ki 25:11
They * war on the Hagrites, the 1Ch 5:19
harm my chosen people,' he *. 1Ch 16:22

(DECLARED Con't)
You have * that your people 1Ch 17:22
Then David *, "I am going to 1Ch 19:2,3
Lord your God is with you," he *. 1Ch 22:18
strong, and * war against the rest 2Ch 11:1
Baasha of Israel * war on him and 2Ch 16:1
of them * war on King Jehoshaphat. 2Ch 17:10
of the Meunites * war on 2Ch 20:1
his counselors and * war on King 2Ch 25:17
blessed him. He * war on the 2Ch 26:6
Uzziah, to burn incense," they *. 2Ch 26:17,18
they *. 2Ch 28:13
him, and * his son Josiah to be the 2Ch 33:25
River, and Josiah * war on him. 2Ch 35:20
Then I * a fast while we were at Ez 8:21
citizens who were * guilty: Ez 10:25
fail to keep this promise," I *. Neh 5:13
and * her queen instead of Vashti. Est 2:17
great celebration and * a holiday. Est 8:17
became Jews; they * they would Est 9:27
Ten times now you have * I am a Job 19:3
O GOD, YOU have * me perfect in Ps 4:1
So the Lord * he would destroy Ps 106:23
best to be wise. I *, "I will be Ecc 7:23
king of Babylon, has * war on us! Jer 21:1
will happen just as I have * it. Eze 39:8
as the prophets have *. Dan 9:24
throne and * war against the Dan 11:7f
turn and publicly * their hatred, Hos 9:8
And they believed him and * a Jon 3:4,5
of prayer," he *, "but you have Mt 21:13
Peter *, "If everyone else Mt 26:33
Finally two men were found who *, Mt 26:60,61
are talking about," he angrily *. Mt 26:70
"I have sinned," he *, "for I Mt 27:4
must die, as the prophets * long Mk 14:21
"for God has * through the Mk 14:27
praying," they *, "and so do the Lk 5:33
at him intently and then *, "See! Jn 1:36
and see for yourself," Philip *. Jn 1:46
this, some of them *, "This man Jn 7:40
"Our father is Abraham," they * Jn 8:39
you, a mere man, have * yourself Jn 10:33
* an angel had spoken to him. Jn 12:29
They *, "We have heard him say Act 6:14
"Never, Lord," Peter *, "I Act 10:14
from all guilt and * Act 13:39
out boldly and *, "It was Act 13:46
to their feet and * that all Act 15:5
his sins and * him "not guilty." Rom 4:3
sinner who is * "not guilty" Rom 4:6
accepted him and * him just and Rom 4:11
his sins and * him "not guilty." Rom 4:22
now that he has * us not guilty? Rom 5:9
and when we came, he * us "not Rom 8:30
I myself might be * unfit and 1Co 9:27
experience—God * him fit for heaven Gal 3:6
father Abraham was * good because Jas 2:21
God, and the Lord * him good in Jas 2:23

DECLARES
the one whom God * guilty shall pay Ex 22:9
He knows where wisdom is and * Job 28:27
For the Lord *, Ps 2:6
for all heaven * that he is just. Ps 50:6
disappear, * the Lord of Hosts. Is 17:3
THE LORD *: Jer 23:1
See, * the Lord of Hosts, the Jer 25:32
the God of Israel, *: I have Jer 28:2
The Lord * that the happy voices Jer 33:10,11
For the Lord * that from then Jer 33:17
for this, the Lord *, by destroying Jer 49:2
The Lord * that he will destroy Jer 50:40
For the Lord *, Israel shall eat Eze 4:13
* that they alone would be saved. Eze 14:18
the Lord *, "it will vanish. Nah 1:12
Therefore the Lord *: I have Zec 1:16
The Lord of Hosts * that the cities Zec 1:17
Lord of Hosts *: 'If you will Zec 3:7
the Lord of Hosts *, 'you will all Zec 3:10
The Lord of Hosts * that Zec 8:4
And the Lord of Hosts *, "In Zec 13:2
"WATCH NOW," THE Lord of Hosts * Mal 4:1
The Scripture *, 'One who eats Jn 13:18
Anyone who * himself a king is a Jn 19:12
it isn't right when God * it is!' Act 11:9
"The Holy Spirit *, 'So shall the Act 21:11
yet now God * us "not guilty" Rom 3:24
For God * sinners to be good in Rom 4:4,5
we can believe whatever God *. 1Jn 5:9
And God * that Jesus is his Son. 1Jn 5:9

DECLARING
God, the laws I am * to you today, Deu 28:1
* his independence of Judah. 2Ch 21:8
you have endorsed my work, * from Ps 9:4
Maaseiah), who are * lies to you in Jer 29:21
for God's mercy, * that all was Zec 4:7
many will come * themselves to be Mk 13:6
* that you don't even know me." Lk 22:34
from * all God's message to you. Act 20:27
Jews chimed in, * that everything Act 24:9
and worship God, * that God is 1Co 14:25

loving one another, * it is wrong. Jas 4:11
of the waters *, "You are just in Rev 16:5

DECLINING
When you fast, * your food for a Mt 6:16

DECORATE
an idol, and * it with gold and Jer 10:4
and to * your bed of prostitution. Eze 16:16

DECORATED
* with three almond flowers. Ex 25:32,33
itself will be * with four almond Ex 25:34,35
Each of the branches was * with Ex 37:19
was similarly * with almond Ex 37:20,21
was highly * with gold, and Ju 8:27f
Each capital was * with seven 1Ki 7:16-22
These crosspieces were * with 1Ki 7:27-30
and * with wreaths on each side. 1Ki 7:27-30
* on the outside with wreaths. 1Ki 7:31
fine-spun linen, * with angels. 2Ch 3:14
The pillars were * with palm tree Eze 40:16
The walls were * with carvings of Eze 41:17,18
into the nave were * with cherubim Eze 41:25
Look at the * stonework on the Mk 13:1

DECORATING
of pomegranates * the 4½-foot 2Ki 25:17
I gave you gold to use in * the Eze 7:20

DECORATIONS
The entire lampstand and its * Ex 25:31
These * and branches and the Ex 25:36
lamp-holders, and * of almond Ex 37:17
four in all. The * and branches Ex 37:22
the floral * on the base and Num 8:4
the lions and oxen were wreath *. 1Ki 7:27-30
and silver and for the artistic *. 1Ch 29:4,5
the floral *, tongs, lamp 2Ch 4:21
garden. The * were green, white, Est 1:6
were decorated with palm tree *. Eze 40:16
and the palm tree * just the same Eze 40:22
were palm tree * along the walls. Eze 40:26
It had palm tree * on the Eze 40:31
were palm tree * on its columns, Eze 40:34
it had palm tree * on the walls of Eze 40:37
and the memorial * on the walls. Lk 21:5

DECREE
behind my * to the people of Lev 17:12
And I * the punishment of all her Deu 32:35
every danger, I * that your son 1Ki 1:30
fulfilling the * of Jehovah at 1Ki 2:27
reign, issued a * that the Temple Ez 5:13
King Cyrus ever made such a *; Ez 5:17
of King Cyrus, a * has been sent Ez 6:3
Moreover, I * that you are to Ez 6:8
I, Darius, have issued this *; Ez 6:12
"I * that any Jew in my realm, Ez 7:13
king, send this * to all the Ez 7:21
I also * that no priest, Levite, Ez 7:24
When this * is published Est 1:20
of the king's *, Esther was brought Est 2:8
If it please the king, issue a * Est 3:9
and despair at the king's *; Est 4:3
copy of the king's * dooming all Est 4:8
me, send out a * reversing Haman's Est 8:5
for whatever other * Mordecai can Est 8:8f
dictated—a * to the Jews and to the Est 8:9,10
127 in all; the * was translated Est 8:9,10
This * gave the Jews everywhere Est 8:11
a copy of this *, which must be Est 8:13
The same * was also issued at Est 8:14
as the king's * arrived, the Jews Est 8:17
So the king agreed, and the * was Est 9:14
king, he issued a * causing Haman's Est 9:24,25
You are my King and my God. * Ps 44:4
it endures by your *, for Ps 119:90,91
See, here is my * all written out Is 65:6
The Lord's * of desolation Jer 4:27
because of my * against my people, Jer 4:28
This, then, is my * against my Jer 6:18,19
Therefore this is God's * of Jer 22:18
And nothing will change this *, Jer 28:14
Therefore, I make this *, that Dan 3:29
The purpose of this * is that all Dan 4:17
"Haven't you signed a *," they Dan 6:12
"Greetings! I * that everyone Dan 6:25,26

DECREED
for God has * it, and it is going Gen 41:32
as the Lord had * when he said of Num 26:64,65
For the Lord had * that this Deu 2:14,15
Lord has * disaster upon you." 1Ki 22:23
The king of Assyria then * that 2Ki 17:27,28
do these things? I * your conquest 2Ki 19:25
by God and * by Cyrus, Darius, and Ez 6:14
farms as * by the laws of Moses. Neh 12:44
Moses had * that these offerings Neh 13:5
Feast of Purim, * by both Mordecai Est 9:29-31
"Who * the boundaries of the Job 38:8,9
valleys sank to the levels you *. Ps 104:7,8
for I have * for him a mighty Son. Ps 132:17
their necks, and destroy it as *. Is 10:27
For the Lord our God has * our Jer 8:14
* such terrible things against us? Jer 16:10
for God has * holy words of Jer 23:9
This I have *, says the Lord. Jer 34:5

are under your control, as God *. Dan 2:3
For this has been * by the Dan 4:1
Most High God has *—and it will Dan 4:2
* from that time to the very end. Dan 9:2
O God our Rock, you have * the Hab 1:1
Has not the Lord * that godless Hab 2:1
I have * mercy to Joshua and his Zec 3:
the Roman Emperor, * that a census Lk 2:

DECREEING
of the empire, * that the Est 3:1
* that the Syrians should go back Amo 1:5

DECREES
The king's * were delivered to Ez 8:3
the day the two * of the king were Est 9:
Your royal * cannot be changed. Ps 93:
all your laws; your * are eternal. Ps 119:16
world by perpetual *, so that the Jer 5:2
full penalty he * against them. Jer 23:2
and announce his * from there. Mic 4:

DEDAHZUR
Gamaliel (son of *) Num 1:2-1

DEDAM
O caravans from *, you will hide Is 21:1

DEDAN
The sons of Raamah were:Sheba, *. Gen 10:7
two sons were Sheba and *. Gen 25:3
The sons of Raama were Sheba and * 1Ch 1:5-9
Jokshan's sons were Sheba and *. 1Ch 1:32
across the sea; * and Tema and Jer 25:23
parts of the desert, O people of * Jer 49:8
* was in Northern Arabia and was a Jer 49:8f
everything from Teman to *. Eze 25:13
calamus, while * brings expensive Eze 27:20
"But Sheba and * Eze 38:13

DEDAN'S
Sheba and Dedan. * sons were Gen 25:3

DEDICATE
THE LORD INSTRUCTED Moses, "* Ex 13:1
garments, and then * these men to Ex 28:41
"You may not * to the Lord the Lev 27:26
In this way you will * the Num 8:14
and someone else would * it! Deu 20:5
Spirit said, "* Barnabas and Paul Act 13:2
action was to * themselves to the 2Co 8:5

DEDICATED
handles the gifts * to Jehovah, he Lev 22:3
anointed, it was * by these gifts Num 7:84,85,86
people of Israel * the Levites, Num 8:20
for they are holy, * to the Lord. Num 16:36,37
So everything that is * to the Num 18:14,15
hands upon him and * him to his Num 27:23
For you are a holy people, * to Deu 7:6
a new house, but not yet * it? Deu 20:5
into a holy people * to himself; Deu 28:9
and iron will be * to the Lord, and Jos 6:19
will be * to God from the moment of Ju 13:7
those who were wholly * to God. 1Sa 1:11f
David * all of these to the 2Sa 8:11,12
all the vessels * for that purpose 1Ki 7:51
and all the people * the Temple by 1Ki 8:62,63
shields his grandfather had *, 1Ki 15:15
Literally, "the * objects of his 1Ki 15:15f
kings of Judah—had *, along with 2Ki 12:18
he himself had *, and all the gold 2Ki 12:18
These had been * by former kings 2Ki 23:11
King David * these gifts to the 1Ch 18:11
For these men * their war loot 1Ch 26:27
care of the items * to the Lord by 1Ch 26:28
for the gifts * by famous persons. 1Ch 28:12
in the gifts * to the Lord by his 2Ch 5:1
and all the people * the Temple by 2Ch 7:4,5
and his father had * to the Lord. 2Ch 15:18
and everything * to the worship of 2Ch 24:7,8
a tithe of the * things to give to 2Ch 31:5,6
All the * supplies were brought 2Ch 31:12,13
The Temple was then * with great Ez 6:16
Gate, hung its doors, and * it. Neh 3:1
The priests and Levites first * Neh 12:30
O my son, whom I have * to the Pro 31:2
armies has * himself to do it! Is 9:7
Who is so blind as my "* one," Is 42:19
boy, he shall be * to the Lord." Lk 2:23

DEDICATES
"If a man * any part of his Lev 27:16
If a man * his field in the Year Lev 27:17
"If a man * to the Lord a field Lev 27:22

DEDICATION
"THIS IS THE ceremony for the * Ex 29:1
of his period of special *. Num 6:21
The leaders also presented * Num 7:10
day for the * of the altar." Num 7:11
During the * celebration 100 Ez 6:17
During the * of the new Jerusalem Neh 12:27
to come to the * of his statue. Dan 3:2
at the time of the * Celebration. Jn 10:22,23

DEED
made you think of this vile *?" Gen 20:9,10
When Moses realized that his * Ex 2:14
about his evil *, and will fear Deu 13:11
But if this * takes place out in Deu 22:25,26,27
* that Gideon and his family did. Ju 8:27

(DEED Con't)
Benjamin because of this awful *. Ju 19:30
Gibe-ah for this horrible *." Ju 20:8,9,10
of God and done this horrible *? 2Sa 12:9
of this evil * of Eliashib—that he Neh 13:7
O my God, remember this good * Neh 13:14
Remember this good *, O my God! Neh 13:22
you get away with this sinful *?" Neh 13:27
For I admit my shameful *—it Ps 51:3
You boast about this evil * of Ps 52:1
Suddenly the * is done, yet they Ps 64:4
(For this good * Phineas will be Ps 106:31
done their evil * for the day. Pro 4:16
We can justify our every * but Pro 21:2
to their gods—a * so horrible I've Jer 7:31
I signed and sealed the * of Jer 32:10
Then I took the sealed * Jer 32:11
who had signed the *, and as the Jer 32:12
both this sealed * and the copy and Jer 32:14
always be remembered for this *. Mt 26:13
this woman's * will be remembered Mk 14:9
was who would do this terrible *. Jn 13:24
you mean the good * done to the Act 4:9
this good * of theirs, I will come Rom 15:28

DEEDED
the field and cave * to him by the Gen 23:19,20
Abraham * everything he owned to Gen 25:5
* it to those doleful creatures; Is 34:17

DEEDS
of these terrible * shall be Lev 18:29,30
with the evil * of those living in Lev 18:29,30
Their * Deu 32:32
the amazing * which the Lord had Jos 24:31
And he will judge your *. 1Sa 2:3
He did great * and conquered the 1Sa 14:48
You shall do heroic * and be a 1Sa 26:25
wicked men for their wicked *." 2Sa 3:39
These were some of the * that 2Sa 23:22
all of their evil *, and make their 1Ki 8:50
conquests and * and the names of 1Ki 15:23
the Lord by all his evil *. 1Ki 16:4-7
biography—his * and conquests—are 1Ki 16:4-7
The rest of the * of Jehoshaphat 1Ki 22:45
and his great *—including the pool 2Ki 20:20
saints rejoice in your kind *. 2Ch 6:41
the evil * of King Ahaz of Israel, 2Ch 28:19
The rest of Manasseh's *, and his 2Ch 33:18
very angry with them for their *. 2Ch 34:25
and his good *, and how he followed 2Ch 35:26
The rest of the * of Jehoiakim, 2Ch 36:8
of those never-to-be-forgotten *. Neh 9:10
His great *, and also the full Est 10:2
or your good * may profit him. Job 35:8
for how you hate their evil *. Ps 5:5
you men of evil *, for the Lord has Ps 6:8
world about his unforgettable *. Ps 9:11
them back for all their evil *. Ps 28:4
accusing honest men of evil *." Ps 31:18
forever urging them on to evil *. Ps 36:1
their evil * and not get caught. Ps 36:2
the good * done by godly men, Ps 37:18
to tell of all your wonderful *. Ps 40:5
Go forth to awe-inspiring *! Ps 45:4
wicked heart, his dark and evil *. Ps 53:1
He will cause the evil * of my Ps 54:5
With dread * and awesome power Ps 65:5
How awe-inspiring are your *, O Ps 66:3
Those wonderful * are constantly Ps 77:12
these glorious * of Jehovah to your Ps 78:4
When God saw their *, his wrath Ps 78:59
Lord telling about his mighty *! Ps 98:1
Think of the mighty * he did for Ps 105:5,6
Their evil * defiled them, for Ps 106:39
and for all of his wonderful *! Ps 107:8
and for all of his wonderful *! Ps 107:15
and for all of his wonderful *! Ps 107:21
and sing about his glorious *. Ps 107:22
and for all of his wonderful *! Ps 107:31
performs—* of mercy and of grace? Ps 111:4
good * will never be forgotten. Ps 112:3
His * will never be forgotten. Ps 112:9
but live to tell of all his *. Ps 118:17
against the wicked and their *. Ps 141:5
Your awe-inspiring * shall be on Ps 145:6
The Lord despises the * of the Pro 15:9,10
in thought, planning his evil *. Pro 16:30
everyone according to his *. Pro 24:11,12
These good * of hers shall bring Pro 31:31
dead man's evil *, these men were Ecc 8:9,10
your evil * are the spark that Is 1:31
Who has done such mighty *, Is 41:4
Let men cast off their wicked *; Is 55:7
plotting evil * and doing them. Is 59:4
for their evil *—fury for his foes Is 59:18
is no limit to their wicked *. Jer 5:28
thoughts and *, and are fair to Jer 7:5
and weeps over their wicked *! Jer 12:4
filled it up with all your evil *. Jer 16:18
to his *—how he has lived. Jer 17:10
Quit your evil *! Jer 22:3
all these terrible * you are doing, Jer 22:4
upon them because of their evil *. Jer 26:3
according to his life and *. Jer 32:19
me with all their evil *. Jer 32:30
be bought and sold—* signed and Jer 32:44
his previous good * won't help Eze 3:20
punishing you for all your evil *. Eze 7:8,9
Publicly denounce her terrible *. Eze 22:2
and Samaria of all their awful *. Eze 23:36
of his good * will be remembered. Eze 33:13
of you in accordance with his *." Eze 33:20
back your angry * with mine—I will Eze 35:11
they defiled it by their evil *; Eze 36:17
all his terrible *, the Enemy shall Dan 9:27
and people for all their wicked *. Hos 4:9
I have seen your evil *: Israel, Hos 5:3
Your * won't let you come to God Hos 5:4
Their sinful * give them away on Hos 7:2
you, but by your * you bring the Amo 6:3
sworn: "I won't forget your *! Amo 8:7
They go at their evil * with both Mic 7:3
turned from sin by doing worthy *. Mt 3:8
let your good * glow for all to Mt 5:15,16
DON'T do your good * publicly, to Mt 6:1
Go away, for your * are evil.' Mt 7:23
each person according to his *. Mt 16:27
to do kind * on Sabbath days? Mk 3:4
A good man produces good * from Lk 6:45
And an evil man produces evil * Lk 6:45
We deserve to die for our evil *, Lk 23:40,41
the Light, for their * were evil. Jn 3:19
good * and are acceptable to him. Act 10:35
confessed their * and brought their Act 19:18,19
their repentance by doing good *. Act 26:20
each one whatever his * deserve. Rom 2:6
is not based on our good *; Rom 3:27
Was it because of his good * that Rom 4:1
fruit, that is, good * for God. Rom 7:4
*, the rotting fruit of death. Rom 7:5
it and its evil *, you shall live. Rom 8:13
So quit the evil * of darkness Rom 13:12,13
His good * will be an honor to 2Co 9:9
* are as good as your doctrine. 2Co 9:13
seem to think my * and words are 2Co 10:2
punishment their wicked * deserve. 2Co 11:15
We never forget your loving * as 1Th 1:3
orderly, and full of good *. 1Ti 3:2
their good * aren't known until 1Ti 5:25
to them of good * of every kind. Tit 2:7
careful to do good * all the time, Tit 3:8
their sins and lawless *." Heb 10:17
in good * is not real faith. Jas 2:20
did, by his actions, his good *. Jas 2:22
the kind that results in good *. Jas 2:26
that only good * will pour forth. Jas 3:13
it is full of mercy and good *. Jas 3:17
your friendship and your loving *. 3Jn 1:6
* of the licentious Nicolaitans, Rev 2:6
"I am aware of all your good * Rev 2:19
of death. Your * are far from right Rev 3:2
for their good * follow them to Rev 14:13
For your righteous * Rev 15:3,4
to repent of all their evil *. Rev 16:11
double penalty for all her evil *. Rev 18:6
good * done by the people of God. Rev 19:8
according to the * he had done. Rev 20:12
was judged according to his *. Rev 20:13
according to the * he has done. Rev 22:12

DEEP
man to fall into a * sleep, and Gen 2:21
was going down, a * sleep fell upon Gen 15:12
(Esau begins to sob with * and Gen 27:34
* mourning by these Egyptians." Gen 50:11
their burdens, in * trouble because Ex 2:23
"I have seen the * sorrows of my Ex 3:7
into the * darkness where God was. Ex 20:21
May his miracles have a * and Deu 4:9
by black clouds and * darkness. Deu 4:11
It is a time of * thanksgiving to Deu 16:15
it * into the king's belly. Ju 3:21
There was * sadness throughout Ju 21:6
She was in * anguish and was 1Sa 1:10
"Because I am in * trouble," he 1Sa 28:15
ground before David in * respect. 2Sa 1:1
"Go into * mourning for Abner." 2Sa 3:31
* humility, bowing low before him. 2Sa 9:5,6
However, he hated him with a * 2Sa 13:21-24
in * sorrow for a long time." 2Sa 14:2,3
There was * sadness throughout 2Sa 15:23
body into a * pit in the forest and 2Sa 18:17
of the king's * grief for his son, 2Sa 19:2
victory was turned into * sadness. 2Sa 19:2
feet long and fifteen feet *. 1Ki 6:3
Its center was concave, 2¼ feet * 1Ki 7:31
and went about in * humility. 1Ki 21:27
King Saul, felt a * disgust for 1Ch 15:29
King David was moved with * joy. 1Ch 29:9
In this time of * trial, King 2Ch 28:22
a * sin before the Lord our God; 2Ch 29:6
Israel, were filled with * joy. 2Ch 30:25
So Sennacherib returned home in * 2Ch 32:21
You look like a man with * Neh 2:1
before him in * reverence whenever Est 3:2
he has sent his poisoned arrows * Job 6:4
God also destroys those in * and Job 21:25
and its * secrets explored. Job 28:3,4
for they are * within the mines. Job 28:8
of the night when * sleep falls on Job 33:15
God, look * within the hearts of Ps 7:9
He rescued me from * waters. Ps 18:16
despised my cries of * despair; Ps 22:24
overwhelmed, in * distress; Ps 25:16
SIN LURKS * in the hearts of the Ps 36:1
Your arrows have struck *; Ps 38:2
Literally, "* calls to deep at Ps 42:7f
Literally, "deep calls to * at Ps 42:7f
and the heart of everyone is *." Ps 64:6f
slopes and * within the sea! Ps 68:22
and from these * waters I am in. Ps 69:14
for I am in * trouble. Ps 69:17
But I am in * trouble. Ps 70:5
You have let me sink down * in Ps 71:20
I am in * trouble and I need his Ps 77:2
answer me, for I am * in trouble. Ps 86:1
And how * are your thoughts! Ps 92:5
a * impression on all who see it. Ps 112:6
have dug * pits for me to fall in. Ps 119:85,86
Their lies have brought me into * Ps 119:85,86
the fire, or into * pits from which Ps 140:10
deliver me from * waters, from Ps 144:7
Write them * within your heart. Pro 3:3
and space. The * fountains of the Pro 3:20
let them penetrate * within your Pro 4:21
and also keep them * within your Pro 7:3
Reverence for God gives a man * Pro 14:26
with pursed lips, * in thought, Pro 16:30
A wise man's words express * Pro 18:4
Though good advice lies * within Pro 20:5
For a prostitute is a * and Pro 23:26,27,28
wine for those in * depression. Pro 31:6,7
that has made a * impression on me Ecc 9:13
the water brooks, * and quiet. Sol 5:12
no matter how * the stain of your Is 1:18
of * oppression met his ears. Is 5:7
Literally, "let it be * as Sheol Is 7:11f
Israel will strike * terror in Is 19:17
out upon you a spirit of * sleep. Is 29:10
When you go through * waters and Is 43:2
Call on them to help you strike * Is 47:12
drink * of her glory even as an Is 66:11
striking * within your hearts. Jer 4:18
before he causes *, impenetrable Jer 13:16
its roots reaching * into the Jer 17:8
says the Lord. Go * into the Jer 49:30
For your wound is * as the sea. Lam 2:13
sent his arrows * within my heart. Lam 3:13
name, O Lord, from * within the Lam 3:55
sink * into your own heart first; Eze 3:10
with * remorse and say, Alas for Eze 6:11
Samaria did. In * anguish you will Eze 23:34
of heart and * mourning. Eze 27:31
Its roots went * into the moist Eze 31:4
for its roots went * to water. Eze 31:7
whose roots went * into the water, Eze 31:16
was 17½ feet wide and 8¾ feet *. Eze 41:2
a hallway 12¼ feet * behind it. Eze 41:3
to fall into * sin, I have raised Eze 44:12
become a river so * I wouldn't be Eze 47:5
It was too * to cross on foot. Eze 47:5
ground face downward in a * faint. Dan 10:9
a * pit to trap them at Acacia. Hos 5:2
of adultery is * within you, and Hos 5:4
wound is far too * to heal. Mic 1:9
wound—it is far too * to cure. Nah 3:19
but their guilt is *, for they Hab 1:11
In this time of our * need, begin Hab 3:2
The mighty * cried out, Hab 3:10
you are in * spiritual darkness. Mt 6:23
And oh, how * that darkness can Mt 6:23
* mourning all around the earth. Mt 24:30
don't go very *, and though at Mk 4:17
of Law, discussing * questions with Lk 2:46,47
them alone (for a * wave of fear Lk 8:37
their people would have sat in * Lk 10:13
when he saw him, he felt * pity. Lk 10:33
to this hour with * longing, Lk 22:15
dead, they went home in * sorrow. Lk 23:48
"You seem to be in a * Lk 24:17
said, "and this is a very * well! Jn 4:11
So there was a * division of Jn 9:16
Jesus was moved with * anger. Jn 11:37,38
and prayer meetings. A * sense Act 2:43
soon a * silence enveloped the Act 21:40
but there is something else * Rom 7:23,24,25
speaks to us * in our hearts, and Rom 8:16
really like, * down in our hearts. 1Co 4:5
(preaching the * truths of God) is 1Co 14:22
We are in * trouble for bringing 2Co 1:6,7
* within, you really know it too. 2Co 5:11
anxiously and with such * concern. 2Co 7:15
joy with their * poverty, and the 2Co 8:2
pray for you with * fervor and 2Co 9:14
I am anxious for you with the * 2Co 11:2

(DEEP Con't)
May your roots go down * into the Eph 3:17
how wide, how *, and how high his Eph 3:18,19
Only God knows how * is my love Php 1:8
obeying God with * reverence, Php 2:12
and because of his * love and Col 3:12
cutting swift and * into our Heb 4:12
up it causes * trouble, hurting Heb 12:15
That kind of * beauty was seen 1Pe 3:5
continue to show * love for each 1Pe 4:8
* within men's hearts, and minds; Rev 2:23

DEEPENED
and the nighttime darkness *. Rev 8:12

DEEPENS
answer me, for my depression *; Ps 143:7

DEEPER
brothers, causing even * hatred. Gen 37:5
not seem to be * than the skin, and Lev 13:4
not appear to be * than the skin, Lev 13:21
appears to be no * than the skin Lev 13:26
not seem to be * than the skin, he Lev 13:32
appears to be no * than the skin, Lev 13:34
silver buried * than the rest." Jos 7:21
And your love for me was * 2Sa 1:26
The floods have risen. * and Ps 69:1
Deeper and * I sink in the mire; Ps 69:1
go out where it is * and let down Lk 5:4
apparently not in this * sense. Jn 16:5f
you into an ever * understanding of 2Th 3:5
and understand the * things of Heb 5:14
false teaching ('* truths,' as they Rev 2:24,25

DEEPEST
son in * mourning for many weeks. Gen 37:34
"My request, my * wish, is that if Est 5:7,8
"His treasures will be lost in * Job 20:26
I will worship you with * awe. Ps 5:7
You have rescued me from * hell. Ps 86:13
your laws had been my * delight. Ps 119:92
and earth, and in the * seas. Ps 135:6
and examines * motives so he can Jer 17:10
and examines the * thoughts of Jer 20:12
He has brought me into * Lam 3:2
me a cup of * sorrows to drink. Lam 3:15
filled with horror and * distress. Mk 14:33
And the * thoughts of many hearts Lk 2:34,35
the sky, or in the * ocean—nothing Rom 8:39
shows us all of God's * secrets. 1Co 2:10
examines our hearts' * thoughts. 1Th 2:4

DEEPLY
He fell * in love with her, and Gen 34:3
by the hand, bowed * to him, and Gen 48:12,13
* against the Lord your God. Deu 20:18
him * all the rest of his life. Jos 4:14
Samuel was so * moved when he 1Sa 15:11
something is * troubling her and 2Ki 4:27
you shall be rooted * in the soil 2Ki 19:30
now we are even more * under Ez 10:10
Mordecai, she was * distressed and Est 4:4
Let him drink * of the anger of Job 21:20
Wasn't I * grieved for the needy? Job 30:25
I have thought * about all that Ecc 8:9,10
Yes, drink *!" Sol 5:1
Oh, the joy of drinking * from Is 12:3
them were counted * guilty, and Jer 2:3
the lily and root * in the soil Hos 14:5
"I have loved you very *," says Mal 1:2,3
King Herod was * disturbed by Mt 2:3
and are * concerned about them. Mt 6:31,32
don't root very *, and after a Mt 13:21
and * regretted what he had done, Mt 27:3
for he was * disturbed by their Mk 3:5
He sighed * when he heard this Mk 8:12
with indignation and * troubled. Jn 11:33
Now my soul is * troubled. Jn 12:27
Peter's moved them *, and they said Act 2:37
He was a godly man, * reverent, Act 10:2
in Athens, he was * troubled by all Act 17:16
This indicates how * the whole Act 19:20
see to it that she * respects her Eph 5:33
you will grow to love them *. 2Pe 1:7

DEEPS
fish you from the * where you are Jer 16:16

DEER
"Naphtali is a * let loose, Gen 49:21
as you do now with gazelle and *. Deu 12:15
as you do now with gazelle and *. Deu 12:20-23
The *, the gazelle, the roebuck, Deu 14:3,4,5
as anyone may eat a gazelle or *. Deu 15:22
Asahel could run like a *, and 2Sa 2:18
from time to time, *, gazelles, 1Ki 4:23
swift as * upon the mountains." 1Ch 12:8-13
AS THE * pants for water, so I Ps 42:1
yourself like a * that escapes from Pro 6:5
the gazelles and * in the park, Sol 2:7
is like a gazelle or young *. Sol 2:9
the gazelles and * of the park, not Sol 3:5
* upon the mountains of spices." Sol 8:14
own land like * chased by dogs, Is 13:14
leap up like a *, and those who Is 35:6
the farmers are afraid. The * Jer 14:5
you down like * in the forests or Jer 16:16

her princes are like starving * Lam 1:6
me the speed of a * and bring me Hab 3:19

DEFAMED
her temple and have not * her. Act 19:37

DEFAULTS
owes you money and * on the Ex 21:2f

DEFEAT
and I will cause you to * the Ex 23:31
of victory or *, but singing." Ex 32:18
You will * all of your enemies. Lev 26:8
"The Lord will * your enemies Deu 28:7
Soon after Jericho's *, Joshua Jos 7:2
and you cannot * your enemies until Jos 7:13
and no one has been able to * you. Jos 23:9
And the Lord helped them * the Ju 1:4,5,6
River, and you will * them there.' Ju 4:7
for I will cause you to * them! Ju 7:8,9
God helped Israel * King Sihon and Ju 11:21,22
that you * the men of Benjamin." Ju 20:27,28
So the Lord helped Israel * Ju 20:35-39
that he will help us * them!" 1Sa 14:10
the Lord will help us * them!" 1Sa 14:12
Will you help us * them?" 1Sa 14:37
us safe and helped us * the enemy. 1Sa 30:23
Will you * them for me?" 2Sa 5:19
For the Lord had arranged to * 2Sa 17:14
yourself, or the * of your enemies— 1Ki 3:11
and their enemies * them, hear them 1Ki 8:33,34
For after their *, Ben-hadad's 1Ki 20:23
I will help you * this vast army, 1Ki 20:28
to let the king of Moab * us." 2Ki 3:10
After their *, the Syrians 1Ch 19:16
let their enemies * them and take 2Ch 6:36
Do you really think you can * 2Ch 13:8
Don't let mere men * you!" 2Ch 14:11
king of Syria to * him and deport 2Ch 28:5
Don't let my enemies * me. Ps 31:1
permitting wrong to * right? Ps 94:20
Jews be brought to ignominious *. Ps 129:5
They keep you safe from * and Pro 3:23
your neighbor in shameful *. Pro 25:8,9,10
They cannot * me; Jer 20:11
The Babylonians shall * them and Jer 37:7
stagger out and * you and put this Jer 37:10
with your cry of despair and *; Jer 46:12
He will attack and * them. Eze 21:23
enough to * the Egyptian force. Eze 30:21f
and march against him and * him. Dan 11:7
vast forces of Syria and * them. Dan 11:10,11
armies of Egypt will go down to *. Dan 11:15
strong enough to * the 20,000 men Lk 14:31
is a real * for you as Christians. 1Co 6:7

DEFEATED
of the forces that * the army of Gen 36:31-39
request and * the Canaanites; Num 21:3
The Lord had certainly * all the Num 33:3,4
had already been * at Heshbon, and Deu 1:1
been * at Ashtaroth, near Edre-i. Deu 1:1
"The Lord will cause you to be * Deu 28:25
*, for I have given them to you! Jos 6:2
were sent—and they were soundly *. Jos 7:4
the people of Israel are being *. Jos 7:12
Joshua, "for they are already *! Jos 10:8
These forces * the Israelis and Ju 3:13
but was *, and many of the men of Ju 9:40
his land after Israel * him? Ju 11:25
And the Philistines * Israel, 1Sa 4:2
why the Lord had let them be *. 1Sa 4:3
and Israel was * again. 1Sa 4:10
Israel has been * and thousands of 1Sa 4:17
men of Israel had been * by Joab 2Sa 2:17
But David and his troops * them 2Sa 5:7
them at Baal-perazim, and * them. 2Sa 5:20
Syrians had been *, they 2Sa 10:19
was * and the army fled home. 2Ki 14:12
attacked and * King Hoshea, so 2Ki 17:3
the men of Reuben * the Hagrites in 1Ch 5:10
and all their allies were *. 1Ch 5:20
THE PHILISTINES ATTACKED and * 1Ch 10:1
of their fathers, * Israel, and 2Ch 13:18,19
Then the Lord * the Ethiopians, 2Ch 14:12
be * no matter how well you fight; 2Ch 25:8
was *, and its army fled home. 2Ch 25:22
captured the * King Amaziah of 2Ch 25:23
Damascus who had * him, for he felt 2Ch 28:23
before me and fall * at my feet. Ps 18:39
who harm the innocent shall be *. Ps 25:3
us and * us before our foes. Ps 44:10
be attacked and *, but two can Ecc 4:12
so when we have * Samaria and her Is 10:11
You shall be * by the king of Jer 37:17
and his army were * beside the Jer 46:2
and * some of their leaders. Dan 8:10
later * by the Romans at Magnesia. Dan 11:13f
King until he has * all his 1Co 15:25
This too must be * and ended. 1Co 15:26
They * him by the blood of the Rev 12:11

DEFEATING
I will get in * Pharaoh and all his Ex 14:17
shouted, "We're * them again!" Ju 20:32
of deception, * many by catching Dan 8:25

Soon after * Israel, the Assyrian Hos 1:7f
God can obey him, * sin and evil 1Jn 5:4

DEFEATS
conquer him as a king * his foes. Job 15:23,24

DEFECT
entirely without * if it is to be Lev 3:1
it must have no * and may be either Lev 3:6
* as a sin offering to the Lord. Lev 4:3
billy goat without any physical *. Lev 4:23
without * to atone for his sin. Lev 4:28
be a female without physical *. Lev 4:32
ram without *, worth whatever fine Lev 5:15
be a ram without *, and must be Lev 6:6
ram without bodily * for a burnt Lev 9:2
*, for their burnt offering. Lev 9:3
without physical *, one yearling Lev 14:10
without physical *, ten quarts of Lev 14:10
have any bodily * may not offer the Lev 21:16,17
a dwarf, or has a * in his eye, or Lev 21:20
Lord because of his physical *. Lev 21:21
altar, because of the physical *; Lev 21:23
if it is a male animal without *; Lev 22:19
Anything that has a * must not Lev 22:20
animal that has no *, or it will Lev 22:21
without * as a burnt offering. Lev 23:12
Lord, a year-old lamb without *. Num 6:14
a yearling ewe lamb without *; Num 6:14
a peace offering, a ram without * Num 6:14
*, one that has never been yoked. Num 19:1
male lambs—each without *. Num 28:3
lambs—both without * —in addition Num 28:9,10
male yearling lambs—all without *. Num 28:11
yearling male lambs—all without *. Num 28:19
you sacrifice are without *. Num 28:31
yearling male lambs—all without *. Num 29:2
lambs—each without *— and their Num 29:8
—each without *— accompanied by Num 29:13
lambs—each without *— accompanied Num 29:17
lambs—each without *— and the Num 29:20
lambs—each without *— each with Num 29:23
without *—accompanied by Num 29:26,27
lambs—each without *— along with Num 29:29
lambs—each without *— each with its Num 29:32
lambs—each without *— and the Num 29:36
animal has any * such as being lame Deu 15:21

DEFECTED
the Jews who have * to them, and Jer 38:19
those who had * to him to Babylon. Jer 39:9

DEFECTING
he was * to the Babylonians. Jer 37:13

DEFECTIVE
yourselves, for no * animal is Lev 22:25
"NEVER SACRIFICE A sick or * ox Deu 17:1

DEFECTS
a sheep or a goat, without any *. Ex 12:5
two rams with no *, and bread made Ex 29:1
only a bull with no physical *. Lev 1:2,3
*, one young bull, and two rams. Lev 23:18
goat without any *—without Eze 43:22
None are to have any * or Eze 43:25

DEFEND
fearful, Abram, for I will * you. Gen 15:1
"We'll * you with our lives." Jos 2:15
to try to help * the city, but Jos 10:33
even prepared to * themselves! Ju 18:9,10
came, for I will * and save this 2Ki 19:34
And may God use you to * the 2Ch 19:11
provinces to * themselves against Est 9:1
cheated, with no one to * them. Job 5:4
"And I cannot * myself, for you Job 9:32,33
remains no matter how I * myself; Job 16:6
he will * me. Ps 7:10
"I will arise and * the oppressed, Ps 12:5
* your people, Lord; Ps 28:9
Defend your people, Lord; * and Ps 28:9
O GOD, * me from the charges of Ps 43:1
O God, and save me! * me with Ps 54:1
you will * us from our enemies, Ps 65:5
Help him to * the poor and needy Ps 72:4
for they have no one else to * Ps 72:12
and to * the meek of the earth. Ps 76:9
Even so you saved them—to * the Ps 106:8
are like sharp arrows to * him. Ps 127:4
the godly *. Pro 12:6
You should * those who cannot Pro 31:8
Don't try to * yourself by Ecc 5:6,7
upon his thigh to * his king Sol 3:8
won't * the widows and orphans. Is 1:23
will * the poor and the exploited. Is 11:4
he will * the city and deliver it. Is 31:4,5
For my own honor I will * it, Is 37:35
I will * you, says the Lord, and Is 38:6
They must * themselves, for Jer 13:19
tried to * them from your anger. Jer 18:20
ally and has sworn to * Jerusalem! Eze 21:23
in the gap and * you from my just Eze 22:30
then he will * me from my Mic 7:9
leader to * them from their foes? Hab 1:14
He will * his people and they Zec 9:15
The Lord will * the people of Zec 12:8
the Council to * myself for Act 24:21

(DEFEND Con't)
He is given an opportunity to * Act 25:16
me here to use me to * the Truth. Php 1:16,17
power to * themselves against you. Jas 5:6
you to stoutly * the truth which Jud 1:3

DEFENDANT
If the * refuses to accept the Deu 17:12

DEFENDED
"An Egyptian * us against the Ex 2:19
The Ammonites * the gates of 2Sa 10:7,8

DEFENDER
He is my lawyer and *, and he 1Sa 24:15
God himself is the * of Ps 48:3
O God, our * and our Shield, Ps 84:9
He is your *. Ps 121:5
For the Lord is their *. Pro 22:22,23

DEFENDERS
message from the * of the city 2Sa 5:8
I will put her * to flight and Jer 50:44

DEFENDING
But the men * the village Ju 20:21
at Ramoth-gilead, * Israel against 2Ki 9:14
I would stop * myself and die. Job 13:19
For I have not finished * God! Job 36:2
for joy because you are * them. Ps 5:11
* truth, humility, and justice. Ps 45:4
laid in ruins every fort * him. Ps 89:40
always stand your ground in * him. 1Co 13:7
when I was out, * the truth and Php 1:7

DEFENDS
proves true. He * all who come to Pro 30:5

DEFENSE
* against the rest of Israel. Ju 20:14,15
had nothing to say in their own *. Neh 5:8
to unite in the * of their lives Est 8:11
as ashes. Your * of God is as Job 13:12
JOB'S FINAL *: Job 27:1
I will sign my signature to my *; Job 31:35
my * as one he listens to). Job 31:37
the heavens down and came to my *; Ps 18:9
Lift your spear in my *, for my Ps 35:3
Rock, my rescuer, * and fortress. Ps 62:2
Rock, my rescuer, * and Ps 62:6
trouble, but honesty is its own *. Pro 12:13
*, a high wall of safety. Pro 18:11
Then Jeremiah spoke in his *. Jer 26:12
worry about what to say in your *. Mk 13:11
to say in your *, for the Holy Lk 12:11
to make his *, Gallio turned to his Act 18:14
listen to me as I offer my *." Act 22:1
me confidence as I make my *. Act 24:10
presented his *: Act 26:1
arsenal—weapons of *, and weapons 2Co 6:7

DEFENSELESS
so the city was left *; Jos 8:16
Don't steal the land of * orphans Pro 23:10,11
self-control is as * as a city with Pro 25:28
ashamed and *, you will be cut Ob 1:10

DEFENSES
strengthened his * by repairing the 2Ch 32:5
have rejected us and broken our *; Ps 60:1
the strong man and levels his *. Pro 21:22
Prepare your *, Babylon! Jer 51:12
Judah has constructed great * for Hos 8:14
on the strong, breaking all *. Amo 5:9
and demolish the * of your cities. Mic 5:11
Muster your *, full force, and Nah 2:1
to the walls to set up their *. Nah 2:5
as in his other *, to his belief in Act 28:20f

DEFENSIVE
Hezekiah was seeking a * alliance Is 30:2f

DEFER
I will not * their punishment Amo 8:2

DEFERENCE
pavement. In * to the king of 2Ki 16:18
How they enjoy the * paid them Mt 23:7
their journey. In * to the Jews of Act 16:3

DEFERRED
Hope * makes the heart sick; Pro 13:12

DEFIANCE
Listen to this man's * of the 2Ki 19:16

DEFIANT
with you, you are * rebels against Deu 31:27
my ties. *, you would not obey me. Jer 2:20

DEFIED
* the armies of the living God! 1Sa 17:36
very God whom you have *. 1Sa 17:45
toes on each foot * Israel, and 2Sa 21:20,21
They * all the commandments of 2Ki 17:16
Whom have you * and blasphemed? 2Ki 19:22
a giant) * and taunted Israel; 1Ch 20:6,7
she has haughtily * the Lord, the Jer 50:29
affairs—who have * you, refusing to Dan 3:12
servants when they * the king's Dan 3:28
For you have * the Lord of Dan 5:23

DEFIES
the daughter * her mother; Mic 7:6

DEFILE
Do not * yourselves by touching Lev 11:43
therefore do not * yourselves by Lev 11:44
wife, to * yourself with her. Lev 18:20
"Do not * yourselves in any of Lev 18:24
Do not * yourselves with the evil Lev 18:29,30
"Do not * yourselves by Lev 19:31
priests never to * themselves by Lev 21:1
not ceremonially * himself as an Lev 21:4
this would * my sanctuary, for it Lev 21:23
careful not to * my holy name by Lev 22:1
wild animals, for this will * him. Lev 22:8
that they will not * the camp where Num 5:3
You shall not * the land where Num 35:34
Horeb, so do not * yourselves by Deu 4:16,17
Don't * the land the Lord your Deu 21:23
you will utterly * yourselves and Deu 31:29
altar at Bethel to * it, just as 2Ki 23:16
bones upon the altars to * them. 2Ki 23:20
spots of sin to * you, can you walk Job 11:15
come too close, you'll * me! Is 65:5
And I will * all the homes in Jer 19:13
They shall * my Temple. Eze 7:21
I will not look when they * it, Eze 7:22
so proud of, and * your Temple. Eze 7:24
And he said, "* the Temple! Eze 9:7
do not * yourselves with the Eze 20:7
Don't * yourselves with their Eze 20:18
wisdom and * your splendor! Eze 28:7
They and their kings will not * Eze 43:7
"A priest must not * himself by Eze 44:25
that he would not * himself." Dan 1:8f
to allow him not to * himself." Dan 1:8f
utterly * the sanctuary of God. Dan 9:27
"And a man and his father * the Amo 2:7
her priests * the Temple by their Zep 3:4
and * the man who says them. Mt 15:18
These are what *; Mt 15:20
in themselves for that would "*" Jn 18:28
Moreover, he was trying to * the Act 24:6

DEFILED
have * with your brother's blood. Gen 4:11
from Egypt have * themselves, and Ex 32:7
for he has * what is sacred. Lev 7:20
for he has * what is holy." Lev 7:21
bodies shall be * until the Lev 11:24
as being ceremonially *. Lev 11:25
"You are also * by touching any Lev 11:26
animal shall be * until evening. Lev 11:27
be ceremonially * until evening; Lev 11:28
bodies shall be * until evening, Lev 11:31
falls shall be *—any article of Lev 11:32
water, and is * until evening. Lev 11:32
*, and you shall smash the bowl. Lev 11:33
to cleanse the * article touches Lev 11:34
touches any food, all of it is *. Lev 11:34
Any drink which is in the * bowl Lev 11:34
oven, it is * and must be smashed. Lev 11:35
is water, that water is not *; Lev 11:36
who pulls out the carcass is *. Lev 11:36
falls upon it, the seed is *. Lev 11:38
carcass shall be * until evening. Lev 11:39
clothes and be * until evening. Lev 11:40
feet may be eaten, for it is *. Lev 11:41,42
is ceremonially * and may not be Lev 11:47
be ceremonially * for seven days, Lev 12:2
the priest must pronounce him *. Lev 13:11
shall declare him *, for leprosy Lev 13:20
* and must live outside the camp. Lev 13:46
into a * place outside the city. Lev 14:40
in a * place outside the city. Lev 14:41
it is leprosy, and the house is *. Lev 14:44
out of the city to a * place. Lev 14:45
closed shall be * until evening. Lev 14:46
is ceremonially *. Lev 15:1
is ceremonially * until evening, Lev 15:5
has sat upon while * is himself Lev 15:6
Any saddle he rides on is *. Lev 15:9
him shall be * until evening, and Lev 15:10
If the * man touches anyone Lev 15:11
himself and be * until evening. Lev 15:11
Any earthen pot touched by the * Lev 15:12
ceremonially * until evening. Lev 15:17
* until the next evening. Lev 15:18
her shall be * until evening. Lev 15:19
on during that time shall be *. Lev 15:20
be ceremonially * until evening. Lev 15:21,22,23
is ceremonially * for seven days, Lev 15:24
every bed he lies upon shall be *. Lev 15:24
that time is *, just as it would be Lev 15:26
sits on shall be *, and shall wash Lev 15:27
and bathe and be * until evening. Lev 15:27
she is no longer ceremonially *. Lev 15:28
man who is * by a genital disease Lev 15:32
because it is * by the sins of the Lev 16:16
himself and be * until evening; Lev 17:15
That entire country is * with Lev 18:25
am taking you, and the land is *. Lev 18:27
are considered ceremonially *. Lev 19:23
he has * what is his father's; Lev 20:11
is ceremonially * sacrifices the Lev 22:3
person, or who is * by a seminal Lev 22:4
is ceremonially * for any reason— Lev 22:5
priest shall be * until evening, Lev 22:6
Israel must not be * by being eaten Lev 22:15
been * by touching a dead person. Num 5:1
If she has been *, having Num 5:27
If he is * by having someone Num 6:9
later he shall shave his * head; Num 6:9
were ceremonially * by having Num 9:6,7
to come, are * at Passover time Num 9:10
"But anyone who is not *, and Num 9:13
face she would be * seven days. Num 12:14
are ceremonially * at the time. Num 18:13
ceremonially * until the evening. Num 19:7
he too shall be * until evening. Num 19:8
not ceremonially * shall gather up Num 19:9
clothes and be * until evening; Num 19:10
body shall be * for seven days, Num 19:11
be * even after the seventh day. Num 19:12
specified, has * the Tabernacle of Num 19:13
the time, shall be * seven days. Num 19:14
tent without a lid over it is *. Num 19:15
a grave, he shall be * seven days. Num 19:16
Then a person who is not * shall Num 19:18
who has been * by being in the Num 19:18
then the * person must wash his Num 19:19
"But anyone who is * and doesn't Num 19:20
for he has * the sanctuary of the Num 19:20
so he remains *. Num 19:20
water shall be * until evening. Num 19:21
And anything a * person touches Num 19:22
shall be * until evening." Num 19:22
time, and you have * yourselves by Deu 4:25
out of Egypt had * themselves, Deu 9:12
Those who are ceremonially * may Deu 12:15
are ceremonially * may eat them. Deu 12:20-23
declared to be ceremonially *. Deu 14:3,4,5
other kinds are ceremonially *. Deu 14:10
Anyone, even if ceremonially * at Deu 15:22
She has * Israel by flagrant Deu 22:21
ceremonially * because of a seminal Deu 23:9,10
her again, for she has been *; Deu 24:4
I was ceremonially * (for instance, Deu 26:14
your land is *, then join us on our Jos 22:19
then he * these places by 2Ki 23:14
was totally * by the horrible Ez 9:11
God, for they have * the priesthood Neh 13:29
Your Temple is * and Jerusalem is Ps 79:1
Their evil deeds * them, for Ps 106:39
The land is * by crime; Is 24:4,5
you haven't been * by your Jer 3:2
land was greatly polluted and *. Jer 3:9
because you have * my land with Jer 16:18
They have even * my own Temple Jer 32:34
But now you refuse and have * my Jer 34:16
* by foreigners from Babylon." Jer 51:51
and priests, who * the city by Lam 4:13
"You are *!" Lam 4:15
Israel shall eat * bread in the Eze 4:13
God, must I be * by using dung? Eze 4:14
For I have never been * before in Eze 4:14
Because you have * my Temple with Eze 5:11
And they * my Sabbaths. Eze 20:21
and * my Temple and my holiness. Eze 22:26
holy name is greatly * among them. Eze 22:26
On the same day they * my Temple Eze 23:38
of kings. You * your holiness with Eze 28:18
they * it by their evil deeds; Eze 36:17
name that you *, and the people of Eze 36:23
you are utterly *. Hos 5:3
other gods, Israel utterly *. Hos 6:10
all who eat such sacrifices are * Hos 9:4
men of Judah have * God's holy and Mal 2:11
are not * by non-kosher food. Mt 15:15
Literally, "They have not * Rev 14:4f

DEFILEMENT
* of all that was sat upon. Gen 31:35f
of ceremonial * for seven days Lev 15:19
on is in a similar state of *. Lev 15:26
the Lord, for her menstrual *. Lev 15:30
Israel from their *, lest they die Lev 15:31
is in her period of * afterwards. Lev 15:33
them and surrounded by their *. Lev 16:16
and make atonement for his *. Num 6:11
before his * no longer count. Num 6:12
upon him, so the * continues. Num 19:13
he will be out from under the *. Num 19:19
winged insects are a * to you and Deu 14:19,20
The * was probably in eating Dan 1:8f
but there is no spiritual * from Mt 15:20

DEFILES
comes out of a man * a man." Mt 15:11f
out of the man * the man." Mk 7:15,16f
* it by bringing Gentiles in!" Act 21:28
If anyone * and spoils God's 1Co 3:17

DEFILING
by unintentionally * what is holy, Lev 5:15
die because of * my Tabernacle that Lev 15:31
any female animal, thus * himself; Lev 18:23
upon themselves by * each other. Lev 20:12
blood, * everything they touch. Lam 4:14
their idols, * herself. Eze 23:7
adultery with her, * her in the bed Eze 23:17
* yourself with all their idols. Eze 23:30
to him, and by * his Temple. Dan 8:11

DEFINE
But first of all we must * among — Job 34:4
DEFINITE
back and give me a more * report. — 1Sa 23:23
I went there with * orders from — Gal 2:2
DEFINITELY
observation, for he is * diseased. — Lev 13:11
DEFLATE
O rebel lands, he will * your — Ps 66:7
DEFORMED
noticed there a man with a * hand. — Mt 12:10
noticed a man there with a * hand. — Mk 3:1
present whose right hand was *. — Lk 6:6
But he said to the man with the * — Lk 6:8
DEFORMITIES
sickness, *, cuts or scars—for a — Eze 43:22
DEFRAUD
that you won't * me or my son or my — Gen 21:23
must not steal nor lie nor *. — Lev 19:11
they fool and * each other; — Jer 9:5
and orphans, or * strangers, and do — Mal 3:5
DEFRAUDED
Have I ever * you? — 1Sa 12:3
"you have never * or oppressed us — 1Sa 12:4
princes, for they have * the poor. — Is 3:14
DEFY
great, do you, and * my power, and — Ex 9:17
will be afraid to * the court's — Deu 17:13
slaves! I * the armies of Israel! — 1Sa 17:10
* the armies of the living God?" — 1Sa 17:26
O God, proud and insolent men * — Ps 86:14
What shepherd can * me? — Jer 49:20
He will * the Most High God, and — Dan 7:25
of, Nineveh, to * the Lord? — Nah 1:9
He will * every god there is, — 2Th 2:4
DEFYING
Assyrian general * the living God, — 2Ki 19:4
rebels joined him, * Solomon's son — 2Ch 13:7
fist against God, * the Almighty, — Job 15:25,26
in Christ after * God like that. — 1Ti 1:19
each one * and insulting God. — Rev 13:1
DEGENERATE
Why have you become this * race — Jer 2:21
DEGRADE
Or, "You * yourselves through — Eze 22:10f
DEGRADED
your brother be * in your eyes. — Deu 25:1
DEGRADING
immoral lives, * their bodies and — Jud 1:8
DEGREES
* as measured on Ahaz' sun dial!" — Is 38:8
So the sun retraced ten * that it — Is 38:8
DEJECTED
This made Cain both * and very — Gen 4:5
that they looked * and sad. — Gen 40:6
You must not be * and sad!" — Neh 8:10
DELAIAH
Pelaiah, Akkub, Johanan, *, Anani. — 1Ch 3:24
Twenty-third, the group led by *; — 1Ch 24:7-18
the subclans of *, Tobiah, and — Ez 2:60
Shemaiah (son of *, who was the son — Neh 6:10
these were the subclans of *, — Neh 7:62
there, as well as * (son of — Jer 36:12
except Elnathan, * and Gemariah. — Jer 36:24,25
DELAY
"Why did you * so long?" — Num 22:37
Don't *." — 2Ch 24:5
Do not *, for we must not permit — Ez 4:22
costs without * from my taxes — Ez 6:8
Please don't *! — Ps 40:17
He will not * his help. — Ps 46:5
O Lord, don't *. — Ps 70:5
Why do you *? — Ps 74:11
How long will you *? — Ps 90:13
something, don't * in doing it, for — Ecc 5:4
Jerusalem: "Flee now, don't *!" — Jer 4:6
Lord God says, All * has ended! — Eze 12:28
Don't *—for your own sake, O my — Dan 9:19
And now, why *? — Act 22:16
should be no more *, but that when — Rev 10:6
DELAYED
"So, when the bridegroom was *, — Mt 25:5,6
His coming will not be * much — Heb 10:37
DELAYS
There will be no more *, O rebels — Eze 12:25
DELEGATES
cities, but the * made friends with — Act 12:20
of the city the * went on to — Act 15:3
voted to send * to Antioch with — Act 15:22
DELEGATION
A * from the tribe of Judah, led — Jos 14:6
First, however, they sent a * — Jos 22:13
In this * were ten high — Jos 22:14
Then Israel sent a peace * to the — Ju 21:13
Now a * of the city officials of — 2Ki 2:19
he sent a truce * of the following — 2Ki 18:18
While he was in Caesarea, a * — Act 12:20
DELIBERATE
And keep me from * wrongs; — Ps 19:13
DELIBERATELY
However, if a man * attacks — Ex 21:14
"If someone * lets his animal — Ex 22:5
"But anyone who * makes the — Num 15:30
Lord and * failed to obey his law; — Num 15:31
"You have * brought us into — Num 20:4
died since he had not killed *. — Deu 19:6,7
listen. You * sinned before my very — Is 65:12
You have * called for this — Lam 2:22
"And so the Lord * crushed us — Dan 9:14
it was someone who * touched me, — Lk 8:46
Yes, and you * destroyed God's — Act 7:53
God, they * chose to believe lies. — Rom 1:25
Instead, God has * chosen to use — 1Co 1:27
* done what they knew was wrong. — 1Ti 1:19
If anyone sins * by rejecting the — Heb 10:26
They * forget this fact: that God — 2Pe 3:5,6
are people who are * stupid, and — 2Pe 3:15,16
DELICATE
The most tender and * woman — Deu 28:56,57
You made all the *, inner parts — Ps 139:13
Cliff badgers: * little animals — Pro 30:24-28
the lovely princess, tender and *. — Is 47:1
are beautiful and *—and doomed. — Jer 6:2
DELICIOUS
the * odor and said . . ." — Gen 8:21f
Here is the * venison you wanted. — Gen 27:19
Oh, that we had some of the * — Num 11:4,5
You provide * food for me in the — Ps 23:5
as their pawn. The * food they — Pro 23:6,7,8
are in blossom. How * they smell! — Sol 2:13
of this * morsel, Jerusalem. — Is 5:14
around the world—a * feast of good — Is 25:6
A variety that produces * fruit — Mt 7:18
DELIGHT
For I was his *. — 2Sa 22:20
lord the king * in this thing?" — 2Sa 24:3f
of those of us who * to honor you. — Neh 1:11
with * when they saw her. — Est 2:15
"Then you will * yourself in the — Job 22:26
For he does not * himself in the — Job 27:10
of God: But they * in doing — Ps 1:2
Let them shout with *, "Great is — Ps 35:27
them drink from your rivers of *. — Ps 36:8
And I * to do your will, my God, — Ps 40:8
Literally, "then you will * in — Ps 51:19f
and who * in aggressive wars." — Ps 68:30f
Scatter all who * in war. — Ps 68:30
They are after my life, and * in — Ps 70:2,3
I will * in them and not forget — Ps 119:16
For your law is my *. — Ps 119:75,76,77
your laws had been my deepest *. — Ps 119:92
salvation, and your law is my *. — Ps 119:174
her love alone fill you with *. — Pro 5:19
with delight. Why * yourself with — Pro 5:20
I was his constant *, laughing — Pro 8:30
how pleasant, O love, for utter * — Sol 7:6
* will be obedience to the Lord. — Is 11:3
and * of the drunkards of Israel! — Is 28:1
the joy and * of the drunkards of — Is 28:3
my Chosen One, in whom I *. — Is 42:1
of it with * as the Lord's holy — Is 58:13
Lord will be your *, and I will see — Is 58:14
Land of God's *" and "The — Is 62:4
mourned for her. * in Jerusalem; — Is 66:11
to my sorrowing heart and * me. — Jer 15:16
you are my *." — Mk 1:11
my much loved Son, yes, my *." — Lk 3:22
and take * in honoring each other. — Rom 12:10
for the joy and * you have given us — 1Th 3:9
DELIGHTED
her father, who was * to meet him. — Ju 19:3
Saul was * when he heard about it. — 1Sa 18:20
David was * to accept the offer. — 1Sa 18:26
He was so * with her that he set — Est 2:17
Be * with the Lord. — Ps 37:4
The women of Jerusalem were * — Sol 6:9
day and are so * to hear the — Is 58:2
(This sort of reasoning * the — Mk 12:37
They were, of course, * to know — Lk 22:5
Herod was * at the opportunity — Lk 23:8
DELIGHTFUL
for I know how * they really are. — Ps 119:35
his praises! How *, and how right! — Ps 147:1
"Oh, how * you are; — Sol 7:6
those first * days when I led you — Hos 9:10
DELIGHTING
day of my life, * in his — Ps 27:4
ways, * in their sins, are cursed. — Is 66:3
DELIGHTS
the king honors those he * in." — Est 6:11
a place of safety, for he * in me. — Ps 18:19
one who claims the Lord * in him? — Ps 22:8
Lord. He * in each step they take. — Ps 37:23
Your royal husband * in your — Ps 45:10,11
Yes, happy is the man who * in — Ps 112:1
punishes a son he * in to make him — Pro 3:11,12
THE LORD HATES cheating and * in — Pro 11:1
The Lord hates the stubborn but * — Pro 11:20
God * in those who keep their — Pro 12:22
* in the prayers of his people. — Pro 15:8
the thoughts of the wicked but * — Pro 15:26
for the Lord * in you and will — Is 62:4
is my Beloved, in whom my soul *. — Mt 12:18
this world and the * of wealth, and — Mk 4:19
to God that he * in, for as part of — Eph 1:11
DELILAH
* over in the valley of Sorek. — Ju 16:4
So * begged Samson to tell her — Ju 16:6
Afterward * said to him, "You — Ju 16:10
* took new ropes and tied him — Ju 16:12
Again * exclaimed, — Ju 16:12
told me more lies!" * complained. — Ju 16:13
* realized that he had finally — Ju 16:18
cut off his hair. * began to hit — Ju 16:19
DELIRIOUS
apart by lions. *, I chattered — Is 38:14
DELIRIUM
and have * tremens, and you will — Pro 23:33
DELIVER
O Lord, please * me from — Gen 32:11
I have come to * them from the — Ex 3:8
* the regular quota of bricks." — Ex 5:18
great miracles to * them from — Ex 6:6
in order to * Israel, and all the — Ex 18:8
He will * their kings into your — Deu 7:24
bring him home and * him over to — Deu 19:12
The Lord will * over to you the — Deu 31:5
to Joab and gave it to Uriah to *. — 2Sa 11:14
If you will * him to me, we will — 2Sa 20:21
You * me from violence. — 2Sa 22:49
apart and * the timber to you. — 1Ki 5:9
I will * them all to you today. — 1Ki 20:13
you that the Lord will * you. — 2Ki 18:31,32
mother has no strength to * it. — 2Ki 19:3
* us from the king of Assyria"! — 2Ch 32:11
this, God will * the Jews from some — Est 4:14
He will * you again and again, — Job 5:19
you at the only one who can * you. — Job 36:18
your paths. You * the humble but — Ps 18:27
Literally, "* my soul from the — Ps 22:20f
Save me from them! * my life — Ps 25:20
then you can * your beloved — Ps 60:4,5
Answer us! * us! — Ps 83:1
you are so kind, O Lord, * me. — Ps 109:21
* me, O Lord, from liars. — Ps 120:2
O LORD, * me from evil men. — Ps 140:1
and rescue me; * me from deep — Ps 144:7
Save me! * me from these — Ps 144:11
them a Savior—and he shall * them. — Is 19:20
* on his promises to save you. — Is 30:3
he will defend the city and * it. — Is 31:4,5
them and * them to slaughter. — Is 34:2
Lord will * you from my armies. — Is 36:18
of yours can * Jerusalem from me? — Is 36:20
He will * you and this city from — Is 38:6
prays to it. "* me," he says. — Is 44:17
They cannot even * themselves! — Is 47:14
Have I no longer power to *? — Is 50:2
the point of birth and then not *? — Is 66:9
"I will * you." — Jer 1:19
against me, I will * your wealth — Jer 15:12,13
protect and * you, says the Lord. — Jer 15:20
Yes, I will certainly * you from — Jer 15:21
And finally I will * King — Jer 21:7
doing, then I will * this nation — Jer 22:4
your eyes, but I will * you. — Jer 39:17
you and to * you from his hand. — Jer 42:11
I will * them into the hands of — Jer 46:26
magic, for I will * my people out — Eze 13:23
and I will * you into the hands of — Eze 21:31
I will surely * you over to your — Eze 23:28
clouds, I will * her into the — Eze 31:11
And what god can * you out of my — Dan 3:15
furnace, our God is able to * us; — Dan 3:17
and he will * us out of your — Dan 3:17
sent his angel to * his trusting — Dan 3:28
you worship continually, * you." — Dan 6:16
able to * you from the lions?" — Dan 6:20
God would * us from all our foes.' — Amo 5:18
He will * us from the Assyrians — Mic 5:6
but * us from the Evil One. — Mt 6:13
I have come down to * them. — Act 7:34
Herod's intention was to * Peter — Act 12:4
Yes, and the Lord will always * — 2Ti 4:18
Only in that way could he * — Heb 2:15
DELIVERANCE
the annual celebration of God's *. — Ex 12:42
a wonderful * through me today! — Ju 15:18
He gives wonderful * to his king, — 2Sa 22:51
* has come from all our efforts. — Is 26:18
For I am offering you my *; — Is 46:13
LISTEN TO ME, all who hope for *, — Is 51:1
had in mind God's * of Jerusalem — Jer 21:1f
For my * comes from the Lord — Jon 2:9
goodness, and of * from judgment. — Jn 16:8
there is * from judgment because — Jn 16:11
DELIVERED
and blessed be God, who has * — Gen 14:19,20
and you have not * them at all!" — Ex 5:23
* me from the sword of Pharaoh"). — Ex 18:4
had * his people from all of them. — Ex 18:8
god because he * his people from — Ex 18:11
he had already * to the people and — Deu 31:9

DELIVERED Con't)
and so I * Israel from him. Jos 24:10
He has already * Sisera into your Ju 4:14
the Lord has * them to us, I will Ju 8:7
his life and * you from the Ju 9:17
"Our god has * our enemy Samson Ju 16:23,24
God has * him to me, for he has 1Sa 23:7
for when the Lord * me into your 1Sa 24:18
An Egyptian chariot * to 1Ki 10:29
from the Lord was * to King Baasha 1Ki 16:1
other nations ever * their people 2Ki 18:33
the other nations * them—such 2Ki 19:12
horses for $100, * at Jerusalem. 2Ch 1:17
and he * them all into your han[...] 2Ch 16:8
They say these items were * in[...] Ez 5:14
The king's decrees were * to h[...] Ez 8:36
Euphrates River, I * the king[...] Neh 2:9
who * them from their ene[...] Neh 9:27
in your wonderful mercy * [...]eh 9:28
as tithes was * to the Te[...] [...]h 10:38
Then he * his final pu[...] [...] 5:12
And God has * me [...] [...]6:11
when the Lord ha[...] [...]8:1
deep waters. He [...] [...]7
they trusted y[...]
Again and a[...]
and he hel[...]
ever * th[...]
yo[...]
wh[...]
B[...]
Bu[...]
Li[...]
As[...]
and [...]
Literally[...]
forgotten[...]
that we have[...]

DELIVERER
of strength and saf[...] Ps 144:2
come out of Zion a [...] Rom 11:26

DELIVERERS
villages. For * will com[...] Ob 1:21

DELIVERING
After * the money to King Eglon Ju 3:17,18,19
He punished them b[...] * them to 2Ki 17:20
am the one who is [...] this city from Is 37:30
and cry like a wo[...]an * her child. Is 42:14
heavily upon you * you to many Eze 25:7
by * you from [...]ile among them. Eze 36:23
God show his approval by * him! Mt 27:41,42,43
* both men and women to prison. Act 22:4
promising much and * nothing; 2Pe 2:17

DELIVERS
When the Lord your God * them Deu 7:2
Lord your God * into your hands. Deu 7:16
the Lord your God * your enemies to Deu 21:10
No one * from my power. Deu 32:39
and depravity. He * by distress! Job 36:15
* them from the plots of evil men. Ps 37:40
The good man's goodness * him; Pro 11:6
never end. He * his people, Dan 6:27

DELIVERY
After a very hard *, the midwife Gen 35:17
In due season the time of her * Gen 38:27
pain of her labor, awaiting her *. Rev 12:2

DELUDED
those from Memphis are utterly *. Is 19:13
The poor, * fool feeds on Is 44:20
For you have * the people with Hos 5:1

DEMAND
dowry or gift you *, I will pay Gen 34:12
you to Pharaoh, to * that he let Ex 3:10
"Pharaoh will * that you show him Ex 7:9
sent me back to * that you let his Ex 7:16
and make your * upon Pharaoh; Ex 10:1
*, and as the judges approve. Ex 21:22
be worth whatever value you *. Lev 6:6
we pay whatever you * for it. Num 20:19
"Don't * interest on loans you Deu 23:19
into the pot and * that whatever it 1Sa 2:13,14
and he would * raw meat before it 1Sa 2:15
He will * your slaves and the 1Sa 8:16
He will * a tenth of your 1Sa 8:17
Shall I not * your lives?" 2Sa 4:11
with fifty men to *, "O man of 2Ki 1:11
I will pay whatever tribute you * 2Ki 18:14
He discussed their * with the 2Ch 10:6
sent a prophet to *, "Why have you 2Ch 25:15
"How dare you * a mortgage as a Neh 5:7
and * an accounting from them? Job 14:3
How can you * purity in one born Job 14:4
for I am going to * some answers Job 38:3
Awake! * justice for me, Lord! Ps 7:6
am innocent. They * that I be Ps 69:4
our tormentors, * that we sing for Ps 137:3,4
Don't * an audience with the king Pro 25:6,7
the Lord of Hosts will * of Is 3:15
Who can * that a tyrant let his Is 49:24
I will * your blood for theirs. Eze 3:18
The governor and judge alike * Mic 7:3
If the military * that you carry Mt 5:41
chained him in prison at the * of Mt 14:3
Since you knew I would * your Mt 25:26
said to him, "I * in the name of Mt 26:63
up the mob to * the release of Mk 15:11
was afraid [you would * my profits Lk 19:21
will overflow! I * that you love Jn 15:12
give it to you. I * that you love Jn 15:17
But Paul replied, "No! I * my Act 25:10,11
Love does not * its own way. 1Co 13:5
they did not even * that Titus, Gal 2:3
was God, did not * and cling to his Php 2:6
the Pharisees who * the strictest Php 3:5
Now we beg you—yes, we * of you 1Th 4:1
I could * it of you in the name Phm 1:8,9
stupid, and always * some unusual 2Pe 3:15,16

DEMANDED
this you have done to me?" he *. Gen 12:18
is this you've done to us?" he *. Gen 20:9,10
upon Abraham and *, "Get rid of Gen 21:10
[...]aban *. Gen 31:26
[...]did you find?" he *. Gen 31:36,37
[...]irl for me," he *. Gen 34:4
[...]e you from?" he *. Gen 42:7
Gen 44:7
Gen 44:15
[...]n and *, "Why have you Ex 1:18
[...]*. Ex 2:14
[...]her *. Ex 2:20
Ex 15:24
Ex 32:21
[...]u," he *, "to make you Lev 10:17
[...]m before the Lord?" he *. Num 22:32
[...]ngel *. Num 23:11
[...]hat have you done to me?" * Num 31:15
[...]et all the women live?" he *. Num 32:6
Moses *.
Joshua strode over to him and *, Jos 5:13
Joshua *. Jos 9:8
their leaders and *, "Why have you Jos 9:22
they *. Jos 10:6
everyone *. Ju 6:29
they *. Ju 8:1
from Succoth and * that he write Ju 8:14
that big mouth of yours?" he *. Ju 9:38
back our land peaceably," he *. Ju 11:13
then they *, "Say 'Shibboleth.' Ju 12:6
the Philistines *. Ju 15:6
they * of him. Ju 15:11
to her and * that she find out from Ju 16:5
by now, the people *, "Bring out Ju 16:25,26
the young priest * when he saw Ju 18:18
the men of Dan *. Ju 18:23
"Who are you?" he *. Ru 3:9
you come here drunk?" he *. 1Sa 1:14
Saul *. 1Sa 14:19
you've done," Saul * of Jonathan. 1Sa 14:43
Samuel *. 1Sa 15:14
And it was only when my troops * 1Sa 15:21
of the people and did what they *. 1Sa 15:24
doing around here, anyway?" he *. 1Sa 17:28
Saul * of Michal. 1Sa 19:17
are Samuel and David?" he *. 1Sa 19:22
"His brother * that he be there, 1Sa 20:28,29
Jonathan *. 1Sa 20:32
Saul *. 1Sa 22:13
Abner *. 1Sa 26:14
the woman *. 1Sa 28:9
But the Philistine commanders *, 1Sa 29:3
they *. 1Sa 29:4
David *. 1Sa 29:8
David *. 2Sa 1:4
David *. 2Sa 1:14
he grabbed her and *, "Come to bed 2Sa 13:11
He shouted for his valet and *, 2Sa 13:17,18
Then Joab came to Absalom and *, 2Sa 14:31
Abishai *. 2Sa 16:9
Joab *. 2Sa 18:11
the king *. 2Sa 18:29
the king *. 2Sa 18:32
Joab *. 1Ki 1:41
sent for him and *, "Didn't I 1Ki 2:42
silver and gold, just as he *." 1Ki 20:7
Jezebel *. 1Ki 21:7
the king *. 1Ki 22:16
leave me and speak to you?" he *. 1Ki 22:24
the king *. 2Ki 1:7
Elijah *. 2Ki 1:16
*, "Which of you is the traitor? 2Ki 6:11
you are friend or foe," he *. 2Ki 9:18
He rode up to them and * in the 2Ki 9:19
and King Joram *, "Do you come as 2Ki 9:22
thistle of Lebanon * of the mighty 2Ki 14:9
The king of Assyria then * a 2Ki 18:14
They * that King Hezekiah come 2Ki 18:18
the money that the Pharaoh had *. 2Ki 23:35
and * that the entire nation obey 2Ch 14:4
"Why haven't you * that the 2Ch 24:6
a thistle * of a cedar tree, 'Give 2Ch 25:18
brave men, and * that he get out. 2Ch 26:17,18
offerings—and * that the people of 2Ch 33:16
king of Egypt, who * an annual 2Ch 36:3
in Jerusalem and *, "Who gave you Ez 5:3
And we * their names so that we Ez 5:10
So I stood up and * that the Ez 10:5
is this you are doing?" I *. Neh 5:7
governors who had * food and wine Neh 5:15
Then I * that the room be Neh 13:9
the leaders and *, "Why has the Neh 13:11
King Solomon's problem?" I *. Neh 13:26
Later, the king * a second bevy Est 2:19
the others * day after day, but Est 3:3,4
King Ahasuerus *. Est 7:5
him to act, but * better food, Ps 106:14
If only I had not * my own way! Pro 5:12
astrologers, and * that they tell Dan 2:1
in his anger, had * such a hot fire Dan 3:22
the Watchers, * by the Holy Ones. Dan 4:17
they *. Mt 15:2
the throat and * instant payment. Mt 18:28
came up to him and * to know by Mt 21:23
Pilate *. Mt 27:13
Pilate *. Mt 27:23
standing there *, "What are you Mk 11:4,5
Pilate *. Mk 15:14
it, the owners * an explanation. Lk 19:33
They * to know by what authority Lk 20:2
for the third time, he *, "Why? Lk 23:22
sentenced Jesus to die as they *. Lk 23:24
Nathanael *. Jn 1:48
*. "If you have this authority Jn 2:18
they *. Jn 5:12
they *. Jn 7:45
"Tell us who you are," they *. Jn 8:25
had been blind and *, "This man Jn 9:17
to answer the High Priest?" he *. Jn 18:22
crucified," they *, "and your Jn 18:31
Pilate *. Jn 19:10
Instead you * the release of a Act 3:14
the Council *. Act 4:7
the High Priest *. Act 5:28
man whose death is * both by the Act 25:24
sentence * by the Jewish leaders. Act 28:18
understand what the law really *. Rom 7:9
We have never * payment of any 1Co 9:12

DEMANDING
the sleeve *, "Sleep with me." Gen 39:12
just as before," they kept *. Ex 5:13
king of Egypt, * that the people be Ex 6:13
it to Pharaoh, * that the people of Ex 7:2
And now are you * the priesthood Num 16:10
home, * that she surrender them. Jos 2:3
the king of Ammon, * to know why Ju 11:12
this king you are *, but the Lord 1Sa 8:18
the king, *, "What have you done? 2Sa 3:24,25
Now the rest of the family is * 2Sa 14:7
now the creditor was * it back. 2Ki 4:1
them and then * their death. Ps 37:32
They murmured and complained, * Ps 78:18
of conduct by * his own way. Pro 18:1
came up to him *, "What's going Mk 11:27,28
They kept * an answer, so he Jn 8:7
rejected by *, 'Who made you a Act 7:35
* that he be tried by Roman law. Act 24:8
to anyone, never * my rights. 1Co 9:18
you and even * that your daily 1Th 2:11

DEMANDS
for making such unreasonable *." Ex 5:16
of the Hebrews, * that you let his Ex 9:1
him, for the Lord * that you Deu 23:21
of the Lord * to know why you are Jos 22:16
to make certain * upon Rehoboam. 1Ki 12:2,3,4
the king refused the people's *. 1Ki 12:15
led the people's * on Rehoboam: 2Ch 10:2,3
king turned down the people's *. 2Ch 10:15
God of heaven * for his Temple; Ez 7:23
and do what he *: separate Ez 10:11
God tailor his justice to your *? Job 34:33
against the innocent and * bribes. Ps 26:9,10
So he gave them their *, but Ps 106:15
Your * are just and right. Ps 119:138
see how much I really love your *. Ps 119:159
The Lord * fairness in every Pro 16:11
but one who * bribes destroys it. Pro 29:4
beneath the Lord's *, to lie face Lam 3:28
to them the sentences the law *. Eze 23:45
and all the * of the prophets stem Mt 22:40
They load you with impossible * Mt 23:4
If someone * your coat, give him Lk 6:29
religious *—demands that you Lk 11:46
religious demands—* that you Lk 11:46
Law with its rigid * and merciless Jn 1:17

(DEMANDS Con't)
And if Rome * an explanation, I Act 19:40
folk tales and the * of men who Tit 1:14
us good, as God * that we must be. Jas 1:20

DEMAS
sends his love, and so does *. Col 4:14
as you can, for * has left me. 2Ti 4:10
So do Mark, Aristarchus, * and Phm 1:24

DEMETRIUS
It began with *, a silversmith Act 19:24
defamed her. If * and the Act 19:38
Truth itself, speaks highly of *. 3Jn 1:12

DEMOLISH
man to help * Ramah and haul away 1Ki 15:22
Dig a well—and fall into it! * an Ecc 10:8,9
with sledge hammers * your forts. Eze 26:9
nations—are sent to * the land. Eze 30:11
Israel, I will * your cities and Eze 35:4,5
too—and * their ivory palaces." Amo 3:15
and * the defenses of your cities. Mic 5:11

DEMOLISHED
Josiah * the shrines on the hills 2Ki 23:19
Lord his God. He * the heathen 2Ch 14:3
a shambles and * its greatest Is 14:17
The high walls of Moab will be * Is 25:12
a man-eater. He * the palaces of Eze 19:7

DEMON
Call out the * hordes you've Is 47:12
speak because a * was inside him. Mt 9:32
So Jesus cast out the *, and Mt 9:33
by Satan, the * king!" Mt 9:34
Literally, "he has a *." Mt 11:18f
is like a man possessed by a *. Mt 12:43,44,45
For if the * leaves, it goes into Mt 12:43,44,45
Then the * finds seven other Mt 12:43,44,45
For my daughter has a * within Mt 15:22
Then Jesus rebuked the * in Mt 17:18
couldn't we cast that * out?" Mt 17:19
But this kind of * won't leave Mt 17:21
A man possessed by a * was Mk 1:23
Jesus curtly commanded the * to Mk 1:25
Then Jesus spoke to the * within Mk 5:7,8
Jesus asked, and the * replied, Mk 5:9
little girl was possessed by a *. Mk 7:25
Go on home, for the * has left Mk 7:29
in bed, and the * was gone. Mk 7:30
because he is possessed by a *. Mk 9:17
And whenever the * is in control Mk 9:18
the *, but they couldn't do it." Mk 9:18
he saw Jesus the * convulsed the Mk 9:20
small, and the * often makes him Mk 9:22
was growing he rebuked the *. Mk 9:25
"O * of deafness and dumbness," Mk 9:25
Then the * screamed terribly and Mk 9:26
couldn't we cast that * out?" Mk 9:28
man possessed by a * began shouting Lk 4:33
he told the *. Lk 4:35
The * threw the man to the Lk 4:35
Literally, "He has a *." Lk 7:33f
commanding the * to leave him. Lk 8:29
to leave him. This * had often Lk 8:29
Jesus asked the *. Lk 8:30
only son, and a * keeps seizing Lk 9:39
the * out, but they couldn't." Lk 9:40
As the boy was coming the * Lk 9:42
But Jesus ordered the * to come Lk 9:42
Once, when Jesus cast out a * Lk 11:14
"When a * is cast out of a man, Lk 11:24
along you were possessed by a *?" Jn 8:48
"No," Jesus said, "I have no * Jn 8:49
we know you are possessed by a *. Jn 8:52
Some of them said, "He has a * Jn 10:20
to us like a man possessed by a *! Jn 10:21
Can a * open the eyes of blind Jn 10:21
and spoke to the * within her. Act 16:18
man possessed by a *, the demon Act 19:15
by a demon, the * replied, "I know Act 19:15

DEMON-POSSESSED
That evening several * people Mt 8:16
is that he is * himself—possessed Mt 9:34
Then a * man—he was both blind Mt 12:22
and *, brought to him for healing; Mk 1:32,33
side of the lake a * man ran out Mk 5:1
who had been * for a long time. Lk 8:27
man who had been * sitting quietly Lk 8:35
how the * man had been healed. Lk 8:36
The man who had been * begged to Lk 8:38
river, we met a * slave girl who Act 16:16

DEMON-WORSHIP
They would not renounce their *, Rev 9:20

DEMON'S
her child from the * control. Mk 7:26
completely under the * power. Lk 8:29

DEMONS
The other so-called gods are *, 1Ch 16:26
children to the *—the idols of Ps 106:37,38
the * will come there to dance. Is 13:21
and the * will come there to rest. Is 34:14
were possessed by *, or were Mt 4:24
name to cast out * and to do many Mt 7:22
a single word, all the * fled; Mt 8:16
two men with * in them met him. Mt 8:28
distance, so the * begged, "If Mt 8:31
he can cast out * is that he is Mt 9:34
cure the lepers, and cast out *. Mt 10:8
cast out * because he is Satan, Mt 12:24
I am casting out * by invoking the Mt 12:27
But if I am casting out * by the Mt 12:28
Only then can his * be cast out! Mt 12:29
prepared for the devil and his *. Mt 25:41
you come to destroy us *? Mk 1:24
* to come out of their victims. Mk 1:34
(But he refused to allow the * to Mk 1:34
many from the power of *. Mk 1:39
And whenever those possessed by * Mk 3:11
out to preach and to cast out *. Mk 3:14,15
possessed by Satan, king of *. Mk 3:22
That's why * obey him." Mk 3:22
be bound before his * are cast out Mk 3:27
Then the * begged him again and Mk 5:10
into those hogs," the * begged. Mk 5:12
possessed by the * begged Jesus to Mk 5:18
by two, with power to cast out *. Mk 6:7
And they cast out many *, and Mk 6:13
man using your name to cast out *; Mk 9:38
from whom he had cast out seven *. Mk 16:9
to cast out *, and they shall speak Mk 16:17
words that even * obey him?" Lk 4:36
Some were possessed by *; Lk 4:41
and the * came out at his Lk 4:41
And he cast out many *. Lk 6:17,18
cast out * or whom he had healed; Lk 8:2
had cast out seven * from her), Lk 8:2
Whether the * were speaking Lk 8:30f
nearby, and the * pled with him to Lk 8:32
authority over all *—power to cast Lk 9:1
using your name to cast out *. Lk 9:49
* obey us when we use your name." Lk 10:17
thing is not that * obey you, but Lk 10:20
the king of *!" Lk 11:15
*, how can his kingdom survive? Lk 11:18
For they cast out *! Lk 11:19
But if I am casting out * Lk 11:20
gets seven other * more evil than Lk 11:26
on casting out * and doing miracles Lk 13:32
folk and those possessed by *; Act 5:16
by *, for God was with him. Act 10:38
and any * within them came out. Act 19:12
town casting out * planned to Act 19:13
to *, certainly not to God. 1Co 10:20
be partners with * when you eat the 1Co 10:20
the activity of *), hatred and Gal 5:20
Well, remember that the * believe Jas 2:19
with all the * and powers of hell. 2Pe 2:12
angel, "Release the four mighty * Rev 9:14
These miracle-working * Rev 16:14
she has become a den of *, a Rev 18:2
conversing with *, and idol Rev 21:8

DEMONSTRATE
for I wanted to * my power to you Ex 9:16
mighty miracles to * my power." Ex 11:9
Lord: "Didn't I * my power when 1Sa 2:27
And remember, you must * the 1Sa 20:14
on their heads to * their sorrow. Job 2:12
You still * your awesome power. Ps 77:14
condemned to die. * the greatness Ps 79:11
of the roaring seas * his glory. Ps 96:11
and * your power to all the world. Ps 106:8
For his miracles * his honor, Ps 111:3
"I the Lord have called you to * Is 42:6
who were to * to all the world the Is 42:22
a wall of iron. * how an enemy army Eze 4:3
when I * my glory, says the Lord. Eze 39:13
Thus I will * my glory among the Eze 39:21
O Grave, * your plagues! Hos 13:14
"But to * the power of God. Jn 9:3
baptism was to * a desire to turn Act 19:4

DEMONSTRATED
Purity is best * by generosity. Lk 11:41
the love of God * by our Lord Jesus Rom 8:39

DEMONSTRATING
I can do more miracles * my power. Ex 10:1
And praise God for * such Ez 7:28
each town, * by the use of puns Mic 1:11f
each town, * by the use of puns Mic 1:11f
each town, * by the use of puns Mic 1:11f
leave, * God's anger against it Lk 9:5

DEMONSTRATION
"Meanwhile continue your * of Eze 4:7
So now put on a *, to show them Eze 12:3
what you did was a * of what is Eze 12:11
public * of his heaven-sent power. Jn 2:11
I am glad to be a living * of 2Co 12:9

DEMONSTRATIONS
you with many * of his love! 2Sa 2:6
them some great * in the skies. Mt 16:1
And I will cause strange * in Act 2:19
*, and will do great miracles. 2Th 2:9

DEMOTED
and * him to the rank of captain. 1Sa 18:13

DEMOTING
no longer. I am * you, for you Gen 49:4

DEN
Hyenas and jackals will * within Is 13:2
Is my Temple but a * of robbers Jer 7:1
he was taken to the * of lions. Dan 6:1
placed over the mouth of the *; Dan 6:1
out to the lions' *, and called Dan 6:1
that Daniel be lifted from the *. Dan 6:2
them into the * along with their Dan 6:2
they even hit the bottom of the *. Dan 6:2
turned it into a * of thieves." Mt 21:1
turned it into a * of robbers." Mk 11:1
but you have turned it into a * Lk 19:4
they were kept from harm in a * Heb 11:3
she has become a * of demons, a Rev 18:2

DENARII
Literally, "200 *," a year's Mk 6:37
Literally, "two *," each the Lk 10:35
Literally, 200 *, a denarius being Jn 6:7

DENARIUS
Literally, "a *," the payment Mt 20:2
Literally, 200 denarii, a * being Jn 6:7
of wheat for a *, and three choenix Rev 6:6
choenix of barley for a *. . . ." Rev 6:6

DENIED
But Sarah * it. Gen 18:15
But their petition was *. Ju 11:17
not * the words of the holy God. Job 6:10
mean that I * the God of heaven. Job 31:28
so foolishly * your providence. Job 42:3
we have * the Lord our God. Is 59:13
But Peter * it loudly. Mt 26:70
Again Peter * it, this time with Mt 26:72
Peter * it. Mk 14:68
Peter * it again. Mk 14:70
Everyone * it, and Peter said, Lk 8:45
Peter * it. Lk 22:57
He * it flatly. Jn 1:20
Again Peter * it. Jn 18:27
* the resurrection of the dead. Act 4:1f
humiliation, justice was * him; Act 8:33
Paul * the charges: "I am not Act 25:8
and have not * my Name. Rev 3:8

DENIES
someone else who * it, both parties Ex 22:9
But if anyone publicly * me, I Mt 10:33

DENIZENS
The * of hell crowd to meet you Is 14:9
nether world among the * of death. Eze 32:18

DENOUNCE
How can I * Num 23:7-10
If they accept bribes to * their Job 17:5
Publicly * her terrible deeds. Eze 22:2

DENOUNCED
A people God has not *? Num 23:7-10
coming to be baptized, he * them. Mt 3:7
is that they are * everywhere!" Act 28:22

DENOUNCING
was also * the city and the nation Jer 26:20

DENS
mountains, living in caves and *. Ju 6:2
hide in the rocks or in their *. Job 37:8
*, or lie in wait in the jungle? Job 38:39,40
back into their * to rest, and men Ps 104:22
where the lions have their *, and Sol 4:8
where only jackals have their *. Jer 9:11
Judah shall become * of jackals. Jer 10:22
But Jesus said, "Foxes have * Mt 8:20
Foxes have * to live in, and Lk 9:58
mountains, hiding in * and caves. Heb 11:37,38

DENSE
* clouds dark as murky waters. Ps 18:11

DENUNCIATIONS
Then he began to pour out his * Mt 11:20

DENY
* a child to his deceased brother Gen 38:10
woman replied, "How can I * it? 2Sa 14:19
They are wealthy and need * Job 21:12,13
your ignorance to * my providence? Job 38:2
Can you * that you have claimed Eze 13:7
and prophets—can you * this, Amo 2:11
* him before my Father in heaven. Mt 10:33
of mine, let him * himself and take Mt 16:24
And if we * that God sent him, Mt 21:26
dawn, you will * me three times!" Mt 26:34
you will * me three times." Mt 26:75
you will * me three times." Mk 14:30
I'll never * you!" Mk 14:31
you will * me three times." Mk 14:72
But I will * before the angels Lk 12:9
those who * me here among men. Lk 12:9
crows, you will * me three times, Lk 22:34
you will * me three times." Lk 22:61
you will * that you even know me! Jn 13:38
"We can't * that they have done Act 4:16
To win the contest you must * 1Co 9:25
Some may * these things, but 1Ti 6:3
me, and refused to * me, even when Rev 2:13

DEPART
The scepter shall not * from Gen 49:10
Literally, "* from the peak of Sol 4:8f
For the mountains may * and the Is 54:10

DEPART Con't)
Let the farm hands all *. Jer 50:16
in Christ, never to * from him. 1Jn 2:27

DEPARTED
So Abram * as the Lord had Gen 12:4
grew hot against them, and he *. Num 12:9
for they had * from Jehovah and Ju 2:12-14
And I have not * from my God. 2Sa 22:22
For as Israel's glory *, so Is 17:3
though he has * from the city for a Jer 34:21
* honor of their shattered gods. Hos 10:5
Literally, "* from them." Act 13:13f
words, the Jews *, having much Act 28:28,29f
Literally, "the sky *." Rev 6:14f

DEPARTING
can hold back his spirit from *; Ecc 8:8

DEPARTURE
year of Abraham's * from Haran. Gen 11:32f
the night of their * from Egypt. Ex 19:1
And I set a time for my *! Neh 2:5,6

DEPEND
the Lord does not * on weapons to 1Sa 17:47
* upon the Lord alone to save us. Ps 33:20
and let your widows * upon me. Jer 49:11
the weapons you * on, and tear Mic 5:10
(For our salvation does not * on Rom 6:15
less I have, the more I * on him. 2Co 12:10
Yes, and those who * on the Gal 3:10
will not need to * on others for 1Th 4:12

DEPENDABLE
Where in all the world can * men Ps 12:1

DEPENDED
I have * upon you since birth; Ps 22:9,10,11
he can be * on to forgive us and 1Jn 1:9

DEPENDENT
food, but they are * on the Lord. Ps 104:21
* upon trade with Herod's country. Act 12:20

DEPENDENTS
with the number of their *. Gen 47:12

DEPENDING
or more families * upon the number Ex 12:21
* on whether you obey or disobey. Deu 30:15
So Judah, * upon the Lord God of 2Ch 13:18,19
I AM * on you, O Lord my God, to Ps 7:1
Take courage if you are * on the Ps 31:24
brag about * on the God of Israel. Is 48:1
good instead of by * on faith. Rom 9:32
sincere, quietly * upon the Lord 2Co 1:12
without faith, without * on him. Heb 11:6

DEPENDS
whether to share in this way * on Ex 12:3,4
he does this * on your obedience to Deu 19:9
But each of these blessings * on Deu 28:14
if my happiness * on wealth, or Job 31:25
for he * upon the steadfast love Ps 21:7
Every one of these * on you to Ps 104:27
His right to rule * upon his Pro 16:12
in this: each * on God for light. Pro 29:13
The amount * on how much the Lord 1Co 16:2
right with himself * on Php 3:9
beauty that * on jewelry, or 1Pe 3:3

DEPLETED
"His vigor is * by hunger; Job 18:12

DEPORT
shall * you from this land!" Num 24:21,22
the land and * the men of Reuben, 1Ch 5:26
to defeat him and * large numbers 2Ch 28:5
order to * all Jews from Rome. Act 18:2,3

DEPORTATION
years later, the * and exile. Zep 1:1f

DEPORTED
had been * to Babylon by King Ez 2:1
craftsmen had been * to Babylon by Jer 29:1
wicked that the Lord has * them. Eze 11:15

DEPOSE
* an entire nation just as easily. Job 34:29,30

DEPOSED
had made. He * his grandmother 1Ki 15:13
Then he was * by the king of 2Ch 36:3
That is why I have * your Is 43:28

DEPOSES
He promotes one and * another. Ps 75:6,7

DEPOSIT
to return a * on something borrowed Lev 6:2
why didn't you * the money in the Lk 19:23

DEPOSITED
and * the Urim and the Thummim Lev 8:8
which were * at the Temple treasury 1Ch 29:8

DEPOT
went to a palace * for discarded Jer 38:11

DEPRAVED
was vicious and *, he said to Noah, Gen 6:12,13
for Chemosh, the * god of Moab, and 1Ki 11:7
of Judah became as * as the heathen 1Ki 14:24
are as thoroughly * as the men of Jer 23:14
The things my people do are as * Hos 9:9
"Don't give holy things to * Mt 7:6

DEPRAVITY
after lives of dissipation and *. Job 36:14

DEPRESSED
Yet I am standing here * and Ps 42:6

DEPRESSING
It is all so pointless and *. Ecc 4:8

DEPRESSION
that filled him with * and fear. 1Sa 16:14
My heart is broken. * haunts my Job 30:16
and answer me, for my * deepens; Ps 143:7
and wine for those in deep *. Pro 31:6,7

DEPRIVE
Don't let Hezekiah * you of all Is 36:18

DEPRIVED
die, for God has * her of wisdom. Job 39:17
of the world, and * men of their Lam 3:34,35,36

DEPTH
where there was little * of earth; Mt 13:5
doesn't have much * in his life, Mt 13:21

DEPTHS
They went down into the * like a Ex 15:5
That burns to the * of the Deu 32:22
their enemies in the * of the sea; Neh 9:11
seas when they gushed from the *? Job 38:8,9
walked in the sources of their *? Job 38:16
He churns the *. Job 41:31,32
At the blast of your breath the * Ps 18:15
polluted to the * of their souls. Ps 55:15
it now, for it is shaken to its *. Ps 60:2
me shall go down to the * of hell. Ps 63:9
again, up from the * of the earth. Ps 71:20
It trembled to its *! Ps 77:16
thrust me down to the darkest *. Ps 88:6
formation of the * of the earth and Ps 95:4
heavens and sink again to the *; Ps 107:26
O LORD, FROM the * of despair I Ps 130:1
you creatures of the ocean *. Ps 148:7
by exploring the * of meaning in Pro 1:5,6
springs in the * of the oceans. Pro 8:27,28,29
The * of hell are open to God's Pro 15:11
pit of hell, down to its lowest *. Is 14:15
No one can fathom the * of his Is 40:28
Their graves are in the * of Eze 32:23
from the * of death I called, and Jon 2:2
You threw me into the ocean *; Jon 2:3
you will throw them into the * of Mic 7:19
as they call them—* of Satan, Rev 2:24,25

DEPUTIES
counselors and * have unanimously Dan 6:7

DEPUTY
in Edom at that time, only a *. 1Ki 22:47
him as my *), and I will bring them Jer 25:8,9
of Babylon, who is my *. Jer 27:6

DERANGED
for he is mentally *, and in great Mt 17:15

DERBE
Lycaonia, Lystra, *, and the Act 14:5,6
day he left with Barnabas for *. Act 14:20
PAUL AND SILAS went first to * and Act 16:1
Gaius, from *; Act 20:4

DERIDE
"BUT NOW THOSE younger than I * Job 30:1
All your enemies * you. Lam 2:16

DERIDED
his brothers *. Gen 37:8

DERISION
They laughed at him in bitter *, Mk 5:40

DESCEND
will * upon the land of Egypt." Ex 10:21
While the gentle rains * from Deu 33:28
the stairs that * from the City of Neh 3:15
by death, men * on ropes, swinging Job 28:3,4

DESCENDANT
It may be eaten by any male * of Lev 6:18
although he is a * of Aaron—he is Lev 21:21
of Kohath, and a * of Levi) Num 16:1
one who is not a * of Aaron—may Num 16:40
But the man, who was a * of 1Sa 25:3
want a * of David as their king. 1Ki 12:26
Or, "*." The subsequent usage of 1Ch 1:24-27f
could also be interpreted "*." 1Ch 1:24-27f
Another * was Zelophehad, who had 1Ch 7:15
Hashabiah, who was a * of Merari). 1Ch 9:14
of Levi: Amram; his * Shuba-el; 1Ch 24:20
and Shuba-el's * Jehdeiah; 1Ch 24:20
of Shelamoth and his * Jahath. 1Ch 24:22
Division was Dodai (a * of Ahohi). 1Ch 27:4
with Jehiel (a * of Gershom). 1Ch 29:8
ruled by a * of David to this day. 2Ch 10:19
Lord that is led by a * of David? 2Ch 13:8
"The Lord's promise—that a * of 2Ch 23:2,3
he was a very astute man and a * Ez 8:18
A priest—a * of Aaron—would be Neh 10:38
son of Mahalelel, a * of Perez); Neh 11:4,5,6
son of Mica), a * of Asaph, whose Neh 11:22,23
Pethahiah (son of Meshezabel, a * Neh 11:24
*) of David, King of Jerusalem." Ecc 1:1f
a * of King David and of Abraham: Mt 1:1
Messiah must be a * of King David? Mk 12:35
tribe of the Jews, a * of Aaron. Lk 1:5
named Joseph, a * of King David. Lk 1:27
is said to be a * of King David? Lk 20:41
myself am a Jew, a * of Abraham and Rom 11:1
I am both David's Root and his *. Rev 22:16

DESCENDANTS
"This is the roll of Adam's *." Gen 5:1f
of the * of Adam—the man who was Gen 5:1
son, had done, he cursed Ham's *: Gen 9:24,25
The Canaanites were Ham's *. Gen 9:24,25f
To the * of Shem and Japheth." Gen 9:24,25
"*." Gen 10:2f
Their * became the maritime Gen 10:5
One of the * Gen 10:8
Eventually the * of Canaan spread Gen 10:15-19
These, then, were the * of Ham, Gen 10:20
Here is a list of Shem's other * Gen 10:22
Or, "*." Gen 10:23f
These * of Joktan lived all the Gen 10:26-30
These, then, were the * of Shem, Gen 10:31
Shem's line of * included Gen 11:10,11
to give this land to your *." Gen 12:7
to give it all to you and your *. Gen 13:15
give you so many * that, like dust, Gen 13:16
if you can. Your * will be like Gen 15:5
Then Jehovah told Abram, "Your * Gen 15:13
to your * from the Wadi-el-Arish Gen 15:18
I will give you millions of * Gen 17:6
Kings shall be among your *! Gen 17:6
with him forever, and with his *. Gen 17:19
out to have godly * and a godly Gen 18:19
a nation of the * of the Gen 21:13
make a great nation from his *." Gen 21:18
and multiply your * into countless Gen 22:17
These * of yours will conquer Gen 22:17
May your *Overcome all your Gen 24:60
births, of the * of Ishmael, who Gen 25:12-15
These * of Ishmael were Gen 25:18
to you and to your *, just as I Gen 26:3
And I will cause your * to Gen 26:4
give you so many * that they will Gen 26:24
to you and to your * the mighty Gen 28:4
will give it to you and to your *. Gen 28:13
For you will have * as many as Gen 28:14
be blessed through you and your *. Gen 28:14
and to multiply my * until they Gen 32:12
many kings shall be among your *. Gen 35:11
give it to you and to your *." Gen 35:12
HERE IS A list of the * of Esau Gen 36:1
Here are the names of Esau's *, Gen 36:9
The above clans were the * of Gen 36:15,16
The following clans were the * of Gen 36:17
(All were Edomites, * of Esau. Gen 36:40-43
I will bring your * back again; Gen 46:3,4
So these * of Jacob and Leah, not Gen 46:15
sons and * of Jacob and Rachel: Gen 46:19-22
seven sons and * of Jacob and Gen 46:23,24,25
Egypt, of his own *, not counting Gen 46:26
Therefore, I will scatter their * Gen 49:7
* of Abraham, Isaac and Jacob." Gen 50:24
Meanwhile, their * were very Ex 1:7
to the * of Joseph. Ex 1:8
* back into the land of Canaan Ex 2:24
them and their * the land of Canaan Ex 6:4
"Therefore tell the * of Israel Ex 6:6
The sons of Jacob and their * had Ex 12:40,41
promised to your *, and they shall Ex 32:13
'I will give this land to your *.' Ex 33:1
* from generation to generation. Lev 10:8,9
that any of his * from generation Lev 21:16,17
* of the ancient race of giants. Num 13:33
as a spy, and his * shall have Num 14:24
the Lord and you and your *. Num 18:19
"We are the * of your brother Num 20:14
of the Ammonites to the * of Lot. Num 21:24f
his * shall be priests forever." Num 25:12,13
and Jacob, and all of their *.' Deu 1:8
giants there—the * of the Anakim!' Deu 1:28
the * of Esau who live in Seir; Deu 2:4
I have given it to the * of Lot.' Deu 2:9
the Edomites, the * of Esau, just Deu 2:12
I have given it to the * of Lot.' Deu 2:19
helped the * of Esau at Mount Seir, Deu 2:22
to bless their * that he personally Deu 4:37
and Abiram (the sons of Eliab, * Deu 11:6
and to you, their *—a wonderful Deu 11:9
any of his * for ten generations. Deu 23:2
you and your * as a warning: You Deu 28:46
that I would give it to their *. Deu 34:4
of the giants—the * of Anak who Jos 11:21
belong to you and your * forever.' Jos 14:9
Caleb drove out the * of the Jos 15:14
But since the * of Manasseh Jos 17:12
the tribe of Levi, * of Aaron). Jos 21:4
the priests—the * of Aaron, who was Jos 21:9-16
to the priests—the * of Aaron. Jos 21:19
The * of Gershon, another Jos 21:27
him many * through Isaac his son. Jos 24:3
south of Arad, the * of Moses' Ju 1:16
they were * of the three sons of Ju 1:20
Kenites were the * of Moses' Ju 4:11
You and your sons and all your * Ju 8:22
right by Gideon and all of his *. Ju 9:16
by Gideon and his *, then may you Ju 9:19
and may the * the Lord will give Ru 4:12
I will bless his *, and his 1Sa 2:35
Then all of your * shall bow 1Sa 2:36
make you and your * kings of Israel 1Sa 13:13

(DESCENDANTS Con't)
himself and his *, should he be 1Sa 20:16
family and destroy my line of *!" 1Sa 24:21
royalty for your *, for you are 1Sa 25:28
and your * shall rule this land 2Sa 7:10,11
children and their * watch their 1Ki 2:4
at Shiloh concerning the * of Eli. 1Ki 2:27
May Joab and his * be forever 1Ki 2:33
David and his * guiltless 1Ki 2:33
* always sit upon this throne." 1Ki 2:45
him: that if his * follow your ways 1Ki 8:25
I will cause your * to be the kings 1Ki 9:5
one so that the * of David will 1Ki 11:36
and your * shall rule Israel 1Ki 11:38
the * of David—though not forever. 1Ki 11:39
end the line of David's royal *. 1Ki 15:4
killed all of the * of King 1Ki 15:29
just as I did the * of Jeroboam. 1Ki 16:3
of Jeroboam's * for their sins. 1Ki 16:4-7
This destruction of the * of 1Ki 16:12
single one of your male * survive! 1Ki 21:21
I will destroy his *." 1Ki 21:29
his *, he did not destroy Judah. 2Ki 8:19
all of King Ahab's * were—for he 2Ki 8:27
this would happen to Ahab's *." 2Ki 10:9,10
So the Lord rejected all the * 2Ki 17:20
Literally, "* of Israel." 2Ki 17:20f
he gave to the * of Jacob (whose 2Ki 17:34
and power. The * of Jacob were to 2Ki 17:37
And to this day their * do the 2Ki 17:41
identification of ancestors and *. 1Ch 1:1f
These were the * of Abraham by 1Ch 1:33
The * of Salma were his son 1Ch 2:54
These are the * of King Solomon: 1Ch 3:10-14
The * of Etam:Jezreel, Ishma, 1Ch 4:3-4
The * of Recah were: 1Ch 4:11,12
Their * also lived in or near 1Ch 4:32,33
but the land belonged to the * of 1Ch 4:40,41
tents and houses of the * of Ham; 1Ch 4:40,41
Joel's * were his son Shemaiah, 1Ch 5:4
Bashan, lived the * of Gad, who 1Ch 5:11
The * of Buz, in the order of 1Ch 5:14
Amram's * included: 1Ch 6:3
But only Aaron and his * were 1Ch 6:49
The * of Aaron were: 1Ch 6:50-53
by lot to the * of Aaron, all of 1Ch 6:54
to the remaining * of Kohath, and 1Ch 6:61
Their *, at the time of King 1Ch 7:4
mighty warriors among their *; 1Ch 7:9
and their * included 17,200 1Ch 7:11
The sons of Naphtali (* of 1Ch 7:13
The tribe of Manasseh, * of 1Ch 7:29
These * of Asher were heads of 1Ch 7:40
Their * in the official genealogy 1Ch 7:40
They and their * were in charge 1Ch 9:23
From the priests—* of 1Ch 12:24-37
O * of his servant Abraham, 1Ch 16:12,13
I will cause your * to be kings of 1Ch 17:10
his * will always be kings.' 1Ch 17:14
These giants were * of the 1Ch 20:8
his sons and his * to reign over 1Ch 22:10
the priests—the * of Aaron—in the 1Ch 23:28
THE PRIESTS (THE * of Aaron) were 1Ch 24:1
then he divided Aaron's * into 1Ch 24:3
Eleazar's * were divided into 1Ch 24:4
ability among the * of Eleazar). 1Ch 24:4
These were the other * of Levi: 1Ch 24:20
Mahli's * were Eleazar, who had 1Ch 24:28
These were the * of Levi in their 1Ch 24:30
Like the * of Aaron, they were 1Ch 24:31
The line of * from Eliezer went 1Ch 26:25
Over the * of Aaron, Zadok; 1Ch 27:16-22
to him that 'your * shall always 2Ch 6:16
that you and your * will always be 2Ch 7:18
and Jebusites—the * of those 2Ch 8:7,8
swore that David's * would always 2Ch 13:5
Only the * of Aaron are our 2Ch 13:10
to the * of your friend Abraham? 2Ch 20:7
have one of his * upon the throne. 2Ch 21:7
(the * of Jeshua and Joab), 2,812; Ez 2:3-35
From the subclan of Ater (the * of Ez 2:3-35
From the * of the gatekeepers (the Ez 2:40,41,42
the * of King Solomon's officials: Ez 2:55,56,57
The Temple assistants and the * Ez 2:58
actually were * of priests or not. Ez 2:62,63
and the * of Asaph crashed their Ez 3:10
"Following is a list of the * of Neh 7:57,58,59
assistants and the * of Solomon's Neh 7:60
they actually were * of priests. Neh 7:64,65
give him and his * the land of the Neh 9:8
and the * of Solomon's servants Neh 11:3
These were the 468 stalwart * of Neh 11:4,5,6
The 968 * of Gabbai and Sallai. Neh 11:7,8,9
Literally, "to the * of Aaron the Neh 12:47f
* and to all who became Jews; Est 9:27
* shall be as numerous as grass! Job 5:25
kind to me and will be to my *. Ps 18:50
and is allied with the * of Lot. Ps 83:8
and Ammonites were among Lot's *. Ps 83:8f
to establish his * as kings forever Ps 89:3,4
his chosen ones—* of God's servant Ps 105:5,6
You also promised that if my * Ps 132:12
And your * will possess the Is 54:3
Their * shall be known and Is 61:9
There shall always be * of David Jer 17:25
None of his * shall see the good Jer 29:32
and for the good of all their *. Jer 32:39
measured, so the * of David my Jer 33:22
* of Abraham, Isaac and Jacob. Jer 33:25,26
have * who will worship me." Jer 35:18,19
lie in ruins. O * of the Anakim, Jer 47:5
to her and her * that I would bring Eze 20:5,6
of the altar—the * of Zadok—for Eze 40:46
And if his * should say, 'We Mal 1:4
for we are Jews—* of Abraham.' Mt 3:9
safe because you are * of Abraham. Lk 3:8
"But we are * of Abraham," they Jn 8:33
realize that you are * of Abraham! Jn 8:37
own * would [be the Messiah and Act 2:30
to him and his *—though as yet he Act 7:5
him that these * of his would leave Act 7:6
to free his * from slavery, the Act 7:17,18
And it is one of King David's * Act 13:23
to Abraham and his * was not Rom 4:13
would have many * and become a Rom 4:18
Isaac and Isaac's *, though Abraham Rom 9:7
And they are * of Abraham? 2Co 11:22
we are the true * of Abraham, and Gal 3:29
give Abraham a whole nation of *! Heb 11:18

DESCENDED
from Canaan * these Gen 10:15-19
Eber * from Shem, the oldest Gen 10:21
All of the men listed above * Gen 10:32
* from his wife Adah, born to her Gen 36:10,11,12
of the tribes that * from Seir, the Gen 36:20,21
* upon it in the form of fire; Ex 19:18
Then the Lord * in the form of a Ex 34:5,6
Then the Lord * in the Cloud and Num 12:5
all families * from Anak. Num 13:22
The people of Edom were * from Num 20:14f
of Israel were * from his brother Num 20:14f
whom all the nation of Israel *! Ru 4:11
* the Zorathites and Eshtaolites). 1Ch 2:53
All these are Kenites who * from 1Ch 2:55
As they * the mountainside he Mk 9:9
The next day as they * from the Lk 9:37
and a solemn fear * on the city, Act 19:17
from the smoke and * onto the earth Rev 9:3

DESCENDING
the form of a dove * on him, and a Mk 1:10
the form of a dove * from heaven Jn 1:32
the Holy Spirit * and resting upon Jn 1:33
* out of the skies from God. Rev 21:10

DESCENDS
He * from the heavens Deu 33:26
Like a vulture, the enemy * upon Hos 8:1

DESCENT
This is Ephraim's line of *: 1Ch 7:25,26,27
his royal line of * forever. 1Ch 17:12

DESCRIBE
seen many instances such as you *. Job 13:1
so that you can * these glorious Ps 78:4
Let me * for you a worthless and Pro 6:12,13
Here it is used differently to * Is 4:2,3,4f
How can we * God? Is 40:18
This change seems to * an Jer 31:33f
Your 'prophets' * false visions Eze 22:28
"Son of dust, * the Temple I Eze 43:10
to * and incredibly strong. Dan 7:7
that * what is happening now?" Mt 26:54
Jesus asked, "How can I * the Mk 4:30
a man's power to * or put in words 2Co 12:4

DESCRIBED
What happened is * in this Num 21:17,18
the situation * in Numbers 25:1-3. Num 24:25f
This is * in greater detail in Jos 10:13
and his wars are * in The Annals of 1Ki 22:45
This event is further * in Daniel Jer 25:12f
Isaiah the prophet * you very Mk 7:6,7
that I've *, you can be sure that Mk 13:29
place that I've * you can be just Lk 21:31
we have just *, is our High Priest, Heb 8:1
Holy Spirit are *, and Zechariah Rev 1:4f
city fittingly * as "Sodom" or Rev 11:8,9
* in 13:11-15 and 19:20. Rev 16:13f
are also * in 12:3, 9 and 13:1. Rev 17:3f
to him the plagues * in this book. Rev 22:18

DESCRIBES
For when he * how God appeared to Lk 20:37,38

DESCRIBING
once more began * all that was Mk 10:32
King David spoke of this, * the Rom 4:6

DESCRIPTION
It was terrible beyond *. Ex 9:24
the priest with a detailed *. 2Ki 16:10
For the Lord is great beyond *, Ps 96:4
Here is my * of Ps 144:12-15
They are proud beyond *, Pro 30:13,14
sure and certain as my * of it." Dan 2:45
This is his * of what he saw: Dan 7:1
For a * of this event, see Lk 10:13f

DESCRIPTIVE
11-19) some * phrases apply to a Eze 28:12f

DESECRATE
servants and don't * the Sabbath, Is 56:6
rob and * the Temple in Jerusalem. Dan 11:20

DESECRATED
the Sabbath to be * in this way." Neh 13:18
his people and * his Temple. Jer 51:11
For they * the tombs of the kings Amo 2:1
the Jewish laws or * the Temple or Act 25:8

DESECRATING
by * the people's sacred gifts; Lev 22:1

DESECRATION
for any * of the sanctuary," he Num 18:1
Such * of my holy name must stop! Eze 20:39

DESERT
as El-paran at the edge of the *. Gen 14:5,6
a * spring along the road to Shur. Gen 16:7
at the edge of the * near Horeb, Ex 3:1
into the * to sacrifice to him. Ex 3:18
now, between the * and the sea!' Ex 14:3
here to die in the * because there Ex 14:11
in the morning the * all around the Ex 16:13
left the Sihn *, going by easy Ex 17:1
sacrifices to God in the Sinai *. Lev 7:38
out into the * as a scapegoat. Lev 16:10
send it into the *, led by a man Lev 16:21
who took the goat out into the * Lev 16:26
You must wander in the * like Num 14:33
last of you lies dead in the *. Num 14:33
the Lord, and now he will * you." Num 14:43
Then they left the * and proceeded Num 21:17,18
overlooks the * with Mount Pisgah Num 21:20
of Mount Peor, overlooking the *. Num 23:28
great and terrible *, finally Deu 1:19,20,21
across the * toward the Red Sea.' Deu 1:40
northward toward the Moab *. Deu 2:8
the way from Negeb * in the south Jos 1:4
the cities of the eastern *. Jos 12:1
the Judean *, and the Negeb. Jos 12:8-24
For the land you gave me is a *. Jos 15:18,19
the valley of Zeboim near the *. 1Sa 13:18
of Maon in the south of the *. 1Sa 23:24,25
the rocks and wild goats of the *. 1Sa 24:2
along the road into the Gibeon *. 2Sa 2:24
the * that night and escaped. 2Sa 4:6,7
buried beside his house in the *. 1Ki 2:34
Baalath, and Tamar, a * city. 1Ki 9:17,18
"Go back by the * road to 1Ki 19:15
to the edge of the * and to the 1Ch 5:9
gave them Bezer (a * town), Jahzah, 1Ch 6:78,79
He built Tadmor in the *, and 2Ch 8:4
swept in from the *, and engulfed Job 1:19
rain, and the earth becomes a *; Job 12:15
Like the wild donkeys in the *, Job 24:5
They are sent into the * to Job 24:5
Don't * me now! Ps 35:22
Lord, don't you * me! Ps 41:10
The * nomads shall bow before him; Ps 72:9
You gave him to the * tribes to Ps 74:13,14
* years and grieved his heart. Ps 78:40
or like an owl alone in the *. Ps 102:6
Yes, as dry as any *! Ps 106:9
*, hungry and thirsty and faint. Ps 107:4
as by streams in the *. Ps 126:4
Better to live in the * than with Pro 21:19
a * without dropping any rain. Pro 25:14
HellThe barren wombA barren *Fire Pro 30:15,16
the *, leaning on her beloved?" Sol 8:5
The wild animals of the * will Is 13:21
from the terrible *, like a Is 21:1
the terrible * to Egypt—donkeys and Is 30:6
as a river in the * and as the Is 32:2
The wild animals of the * will Is 34:14
EVEN THE WILDERNESS and * will Is 35:1
the * will blossom with flowers. Is 35:1
wilderness, and streams in the *. Is 35:6
Where * jackals lived, there will Is 35:7
smooth road through the *. Is 40:3
Join in the chorus, you * Is 42:11
create rivers for them in the *! Is 43:19
springs in the *, so that my Is 43:20
the searing sun and scorching * Is 49:10
the *, they never stumbled. Is 63:13
Lord, why did your fathers * me? Jer 2:4,5
sit alone like a Bedouin in the *. Jer 3:2
wind from the * upon them—not in Jer 4:11,12
the "* wolves" shall pounce Jer 5:6
shack in the *, for they are all Jer 9:2
by the fierce winds off the *. Jer 13:24,25
O Lord, don't * us now! Jer 14:9
*, with no hope for the future; Jer 17:6
which will soon * her and fly away, Jer 17:11
Lord, don't * me now! Jer 17:17
of the nomadic tribes of the *; Jer 25:24
* them, but only to do them good. Jer 32:40
parts of the *, O people of Dedan Jer 49:8
An Arab tribe living in the * east Jer 49:28f
alone in the * without a care in Jer 49:31
a home for wild animals of the *. Jer 49:33
wilderness, a dry and * land. Jer 50:12
for the wild animals of the *. Jer 50:39
They are like cruel * ostriches, Lam 4:3,4

(DESERT Con't)
will learn not to * me and not to Eze 14:11
and utterly consume them in the *. Eze 20:13
bring you into my * judgment hall. Eze 20:35,36
tribes. This * would be traversed Eze 20:35,36f
wilderness, or a * without rain. Eze 22:24
Bedouins from the * to the east of Eze 25:4
And Bedouin tribes from the * to Eze 25:9,10
stranded in the * to die, and you Eze 29:5
east through the * and the Jordan Eze 47:8
his army will *, and many be Dan 11:26
my people are determined to * me. Hos 11:7
the Lord from the *—will blow hard Hos 13:15
you through the * forty years, to Amo 2:10
you were in the *, Israel—but Amo 5:25,26,27
across the * sands at night. Mic 1:8
off the * from the south. Zec 9:14
give it to the jackals of the *. Mal 1:2,3
is nothing to eat here in the *; Mt 14:15
the * for all this mob to eat?" Mt 15:33
*, don't bother to go and look. Mt 24:26
them, "Tonight you will all * me. Mt 26:31
Spirit urged Jesus into the *. Mk 1:12,13
alone except for * animals, he was Mk 1:12,13
food for them here in the *?" Mk 8:4
"All of you will * me," Jesus Mk 14:27
"I will never * you no matter what Mk 14:29
of Abraham from these * stones! Lk 3:8
morning he went out into the *. Lk 4:42
out into the *, completely under Lk 8:29
he went to the edge of the *, to Jn 11:54
"Forty years later, in the * Act 7:30
forty years in the *, Israel? Act 7:42
Gaza *, arriving around noon." Act 8:26
Assassins with him into the *?" Act 21:37,38
and water to drink there in the *; 1Co 10:3,4
the * while he was testing them. Heb 3:7,8
rebelled against him in the *." Heb 3:15

DESERTED
so that your roads will be *. Lev 26:22
You have * the Lord, and now he Num 14:43
You have not * your brother Jos 22:2,3
The main roads were *. Ju 5:6
plundered the * Philistine camp. 1Sa 17:53
and * David and followed Sheba! 2Sa 20:2
when all his men * him and fled, he 2Sa 23:11,12
* his post and fled the country. 1Ki 11:23
And they all * him except for the 1Ki 12:16,17
but his army * him and fled. 2Ki 8:21
Some men from Manasseh * the 1Ch 12:19
from Manasseh who * to David as he 1Ch 12:20
they turned around and * him. 2Ch 10:16
"The Lord has * me," for you Ps 31:22
Our hearts have not * you! Ps 44:18
you have become angry and * us. Ps 60:1
Have you * our army? Ps 108:11
*, their owners killed or gone." Is 5:9
and all the land of Israel lies *! Is 6:12
Or, "the lands will be * (of Is 7:15,16f
like sheep * by their shepherd. Is 13:14
The cities of Aroer are *. Is 17:2
Their largest cities will be as * Is 17:9
of the Amorites, * when the Is 17:9
be *, the crowded cities empty. Is 32:14
The land will lie * from Is 34:10
Yet they say, "My Lord * us; Is 49:14
"Has God * us?" Jer 8:19
moved away, leaving the land *. Jer 12:4
For they have * me and turned to Jer 18:15
and leave you * and uninhabited. Jer 22:6
safety, you have * them and driven Jer 23:2
went out to the * farms and Jer 40:12
The pastures of Nimrim are * now. Jer 48:34
shall become * wasteland, and all Jer 50:13
and those who had * Zedekiah and Jer 52:15
Lord are desolate, * by all but Lam 5:18
and your farmlands *, and you shall Eze 12:20
her lovers, and * me: for all these Hos 1:13
* me and turned to other gods. Hos 4:10
do, for you have * your God and Hos 9:1
But then you * me for Baal-peor, Hos 9:10
Then they will say, "We * the Hos 10:3
For you * Israel in his time of Ob 1:11
and their cities * without a single Zep 3:6
At that point, all the disciples * Mt 26:56
("My God, my God, why have you * Mk 15:34
here in this * spot," they said. Lk 9:12
disciples turned away and * him. Jn 6:66
with me—he has not * me—for I Jn 8:29
Jewish leaders had * and believed Jn 12:11
There John * Act 13:13
John had * them in Pamphylia. Act 15:38
with death, has God * us? Rom 8:35
I ASK THEN, has God rejected and * Rom 11:1
who came here from Asia have * me; 2Ti 1:15

DESERTERS
and the Jewish * who had declared 2Ki 25:11

DESERTING
imperil them by * to King Saul. 1Ch 12:19
for you worship idols there, * me. Is 57:7,8
my people for * me and for Jer 1:16

harlot, serving other gods, * me. Hos 4:12
Woe to my people for * me; Hos 7:13
Her soldiers slip away, * her; Nah 2:8

DESERTS
* as far as the Euphrates River; Ex 23:31
been cast out into * and the Job 30:3
upon the barren *, so that the Job 38:25-27
It resounds through the * and Ps 29:8
I would fly to the far off * and Ps 55:7
Or, "*." Ps 68:4f
land of the wicked into * of salt. Ps 107:34
Again, he turns * into fertile, Ps 107:35
in from the * like a cloud of smoke Sol 3:6
You too shall get your just *. Is 3:11
the *, and even down to the sea. Is 16:8
you will hide in the * of Arabia. Is 21:13
and joy! The * will become as green Is 35:2
In the * will be pools of water, Is 41:18
when he led them through the *; Is 48:21
I can turn the rivers into *, Is 50:2
again, and make her * blossom; Is 51:3
me even through the barren *. Jer 2:2
a land of * and rocks, of drought Jer 2:6
send to the east to the * of Jer 2:10,11
The deer * her fawn because Jer 14:5
Go deep into the *, O people of Jer 49:30
and give them all their just *. Eze 7:26,27
*, peopled by nomadic tribes. Eze 20:35,36f
Now you will get your just * for Hab 2:6
I see God moving across the * Hab 3:3
demon leaves, it goes into the * Mt 12:43,44,45
everyone else * you, I won't." Mt 26:33
as he was living out in the *. Lk 3:1
the *, searching there for rest; Lk 11:24
from death in the * and in the 2Co 11:26
No, I went away into the * of Gal 1:17
wandering over * and mountains, Heb 11:37,38

DESERVE
jail when I did nothing to * it." Gen 40:15
for they * their punishment. Lev 20:16
"What have I done to * this 1Sa 29:8
punishing you far less than you *! Job 11:6
the punishment they so richly *! Ps 28:4
done nothing against them to * it. Ps 38:19
me. You * honesty from the heart; Ps 51:6
the proud to the penalties they *. Ps 94:1
toward those who don't * it; Ps 103:8
He has not punished us as we * Ps 103:10
think about all the honors they *! Pro 25:27
and give them what they *! Jer 15:15
man does not * the death sentence, Jer 26:16
"What have I ever done to * Jer 37:18
You will know you don't * this Eze 16:61
again, but not because you * it; Eze 36:22
"Do you think you * credit for Lk 6:32
you are dying? We * to die for our Lk 23:40,41
each one whatever his deeds *. Rom 2:6
that he will repay those who * it. Rom 12:19
punishment their wicked deeds *. 2Co 11:15
Though I did nothing to * it, and Eph 3:8
which we don't *, comfort your 2Th 2:16
"Those who work * their pay!" 1Ti 5:18
to each of you whatever you *. Rev 2:23

DESERVED
far less than we *), and even Ez 9:13
that you gave us only what we *. Neh 9:33
have borne the blow that they *! Lam 5:7
who had received what she *. Eze 23:10
your punishment is well *. Amo 3:5
"We have gotten what we * from Zec 1:5,6
with the penalty they so richly *. Rom 1:27
not because we * it but because 2Ti 1:9

DESERVES
"What have I done that * Gen 20:9,10
"What have I done that * your Num 22:28
one whatever he *, for you know the 2Ch 6:30
far more severe than my fault *. Job 23:2
Give him the glory he *! Ps 96:8
destroy her as her wickedness *. Eze 31:11
"If anyone * your help, it is Lk 7:4
him what he justly *, but Lysias, Act 24:6
whatever he * for the good or bad 2Co 5:10

DESIGN
exact * the Lord had shown Moses. Num 8:4

DESIGNATE
at the place the Lord will *. Deu 16:15
then you must * three additional Deu 19:9
"Tell the people of Israel to * Jos 20:2

DESIGNATED
of the animals and birds God had * Gen 8:20
All was done in the order * by Ex 38:21
For I have * the breast and Lev 7:34
of Refuge shall be * for anyone to Num 35:11
leaders and I were * as judges; Ez 10:16-19
square, shall be * for the Temple. Eze 45:2

DESIGNED
this hall. (He * similar living 1Ki 7:8
who are * to be my messengers of Is 42:19

DESIGNER
as an artistic * of objects made of Ex 31:4
city whose * and builder is God. Heb 11:10

DESIGNERS
embroidery * in blue, purple, and Ex 35:35

DESIGNS
* of rosebuds and open flowers. 1Ki 6:18
2,410 silver bowls (of various *), Ez 1:9,10
goblets of many *, and there was an Est 1:7

DESIRABLE
They are more * than gold. Ps 19:10
handsome uniforms—all of them *. Eze 23:12

DESIRE
" 'You must not burn with * for Deu 5:21
my help and my * to sprout." 2Sa 23:5f
May he give us the * to do his 1Ki 8:58
His heart's * was always to obey 1Ki 14:8
It was my * to build a temple in 1Ch 28:2
your greatest * is to help your 2Ch 1:11
It was good to have the *, the 2Ch 6:8
He built to his heart's * in 2Ch 8:6
strong, God-given * to obey the 2Ch 30:12
by giving King Cyrus the * to Ez 1:1
Then God gave a great * to the Ez 1:5
Then I told them about the * God Neh 2:18
"Do not * the nighttime, with Job 36:20
May he grant you your heart's * Ps 20:4
*, everything he asks you for! Ps 21:2
And I * no one on earth as much Ps 73:25
without sexual *, standing at Ecc 12:5
is, "terrible * to sit beside my Sol 6:12f
Our hearts' * is to glorify your Is 26:8
"The Land of *" and "The City Is 62:12
return to the land of your *. Jer 22:27
I will put a * into their hearts Jer 32:40
of the wicked; I * that the wicked Eze 33:11
showing their * for foreign gods Zep 1:8f
And the Lord gave them a * to Hag 1:14,15
nations, and the * of All Nations Hag 2:7
It is my * to pay all the same; Mt 20:14
to demonstrate a * to turn from sin Act 19:4
that we must not * evil things as 1Co 10:6
hearts' * is obedience to Christ. 2Co 10:5
You should have as little * for Col 3:3
that Satan's great * was that Heb 5:7f
strong * to obey God at all times. Heb 5:7

DESIRED
took any they * to be their wives. Gen 6:1
their king, as you've so long *." 2Sa 3:21
timber as he *, and in return 1Ki 5:10
everything their evil hearts *. Is 57:17

DESIRES
following your own * and going your Num 15:39
Lord our God and * to worship these Deu 29:18
your personal * [so that you can Ru 3:10
My heart's * are broken. Job 17:11
will give you all your heart's *. Ps 37:4
with clean thoughts and right *. Ps 51:10
living according to their own *. Ps 81:12
tried to live according to your *. Ps 119:94
thanks and teach me your *. Ps 119:108
He fulfills the * of those who Ps 145:19
don't let your * get out of Pro 7:25
beloved's and I am the one he *. Sol 7:10
following your own * and pleasure, Is 58:13
stubbornly follow their evil *. Jer 3:17
its own evil * and worships idols; Jer 13:10
Your merchandise satisfied the * Eze 27:33
*—and put a new spirit within you. Eze 36:26
anyone he * to reign over them. Dan 5:21
evil thoughts and *, you are in Mt 6:23
the opinions and * of men, but Mk 12:14
put aside his own * and Lk 9:23
Your old evil * were nailed to Rom 6:6
do not give in to its sinful *. Rom 6:12
active, sinful * were at work Rom 7:5
my heart—the evil * that are hidden Rom 7:7
not have evil * in your heart." Rom 7:7
law against evil * by reminding me Rom 7:8
me that such * are wrong and Rom 7:8
kinds of forbidden * within me! Rom 7:8
old evil *, can never please God. Rom 8:8
the Lord, but your own *; 1Co 3:1
by your own *, not God's. 1Co 3:3
But remember this—the wrong * 1Co 10:13
the opposite of our natural *. Gal 5:17
their natural evil * to his cross Gal 5:24
his own wrong *, he will be Gal 6:8
prayers, *, thoughts, or hopes. Eph 3:20
from your evil *, not by a bodily Col 2:11
sinful * were not yet cut away. Col 2:13
a person's evil thoughts and *. Col 2:23
deaden the evil * lurking within Col 3:5
impurity, lust and shameful *; Col 3:5
many evil pleasures and wicked *. Tit 3:3
thoughts and * with all their Heb 4:12
a whole army of evil * within you? Jas 4:1
chasing after evil *, but will be 1Pe 4:2
put aside your own * so that you 2Pe 1:6
things, these evil *—the craze for 1Jn 2:16

DESIST
Will he beg you to * or try to Job 41:3

DESOLATE
I will make your cities *, and Lev 26:31

(DESOLATE Con't)
Yes, I will * your land; Lev 26:32
Your land shall be * and your Lev 26:33
for it will lie * all the years Lev 26:34,35
enjoy its Sabbaths as it lies *. Lev 26:43
So Ai became a * mound of Jos 8:28
So Tamar lived as a * woman in her 2Sa 13:20
cursed and become *, and because 2Ki 22:18,19
and the wastelands, * and gloomy. Job 30:3
Let their homes be * and Ps 69:25
even into the * valleys and caves Is 7:19
I will make Babylon into a * Is 14:23
Even Nimrim River is *! Is 15:6
they are left *, destroyed by the Is 24:6
"Even the most * parts of your Is 49:19
Jerusalem is a * wilderness. Is 64:10
her cities in ruins, burned and *. Jer 2:15
they are *, without a living soul. Jer 9:10
They have made it *; Jer 12:11
The whole land is * and no one Jer 12:11
land shall become *, so that all Jer 18:16
land shall become a * wasteland; Jer 25:11
they have been *, hated and cursed, Jer 25:18
and left * without a living soul. Jer 34:22
he made your land *, an incredible Jer 44:22
It shall become a * heap, and the Jer 49:2
It shall be * forever. Jer 49:33
Babylon is * among the nations! Jer 50:23
it shall lie * forever. Jer 50:39
You shall be * forever Jer 51:26
Babylon will be left * without a Jer 51:29
He has left me sick and * the Lam 1:13
claws, and left me bleeding and *. Lam 3:11
we are trapped and *, destroyed. Lam 3:47
of the Lord are *, deserted by all Lam 5:18
make your cities * from the Eze 6:14
And I will make the land * Eze 15:8
shall become a * wasteland, and the Eze 29:9
I will make Egypt *, surrounded Eze 29:12
surrounded by * nations, and her Eze 29:12
She shall be *, surrounded by Eze 30:7
surrounded by * nations, and her Eze 30:7
I will * the land and her pride, Eze 33:28
and make you *, and then you shall Eze 35:4,5
will rejoice when I make you *. Eze 35:14
must lie * for seventy years. Dan 9:2
and joy upon your * sanctuary—for Dan 9:17
be * because of its inhabitants." Mic 7:13f
a * wasteland like a wilderness. Zep 2:13
Their land became *; Zec 7:14
now your house is left to you, *. Mt 23:38
* spot, and it is getting late." Mk 6:35,36
And now—now your house is left * Lk 13:35
* with no one living in it.' Act 1:20

DESOLATED
their farms were *, their crops Eze 19:7

DESOLATION
remember the land (and its *). Lev 26:42
their * would last forever. Ps 81:15
* upon you from a distant land? Is 10:3
been your lot: * and destruction. Is 51:19
The Lord's decree of * covers Jer 4:27
For the land shall lie in *. Jer 7:34
heads in amazement at its utter *. Jer 18:16
and there is * until this day. Jer 44:6
a day of ruin and *, of darkness, Zep 1:15
will be rooted out and left in *. Zep 2:4
and salt pits and eternal *; Zep 2:9
Literally, "the abomination of * Mt 24:15f

DESPAIR
They ripped their clothing in *, Gen 44:13
his clothing in *, and summoned 2Ch 34:19
your clothing in * and wept before 2Ch 34:27
and * at the king's decree; Est 4:3
he was doomed. In * he fell upon Est 7:8
Wailing loudly in *, they tore Job 2:12
the ground or are tempted to *. Job 4:3,4
not despised my cries of deep *; Ps 22:24
I groan in *. Ps 38:8
He lifted me out of the pit of * Ps 40:2
because of all my groaning and *. Ps 102:5
O LORD, FROM the depths of * I cry Ps 130:1
So I turned in * from hard work Ecc 2:20-23
be trouble and anguish and dark *. Is 8:22
and * shall not go on forever. Is 9:1
as a sign of their * and told him Is 36:22
fainthearted, those tempted to *. Is 42:3
who sit in prison darkness and *. Is 42:7
and *, while they sing for joy. Is 65:14
You will be left in *, and cover Jer 2:37
Hear Jerusalem weeping in *. Jer 9:19
from their time of anguish and *. Jer 11:12
shouting in *, for the Lord has Jer 25:36
with your cry of * and defeat; Jer 46:12
* shall be heard around the world. Jer 50:46
see my anguish and *, for my sons Lam 1:18
upon their heads in sorrow and *. Lam 2:10
will stand helpless, weeping in *. Eze 7:26,27
utter * because of all their sins. Eze 12:19
a day of * for the nations! Eze 30:2,3
joy will be turned to cries of *. Amo 8:10
of *: "We are finished, ruined. Mic 2:4
If it seems slow, do not *, for Hab 2:3
to be filled with anguish and *. Mt 26:37

DESPAIRED
I would have * and perished Ps 119:92

DESPAIRING
Yes, you came at my * cry and Lam 3:57

DESPAIRS
my heart is broken and my soul *, Lam 1:20

DESPERATE
in a last * attempt to break 2Ki 3:26
me sink down deep in * problems. Ps 71:20
For I am overwhelmed and *, and Ps 142:3
are gone. The * refugees take only Is 15:7
* is my wound. Jer 10:19
* enough to beg me for help. Jer 11:14
*, and cover their heads in grief. Jer 14:3
Fearing for their lives, the * Jon 1:5
Then they became *. Lk 23:5

DESPERATELY
So the Philistines fought * and 1Sa 4:10
brother) fell * in love with her. 2Sa 13:1
thing there is, and * wicked. Jer 17:9
of whom you are so * afraid—to Jer 22:24,25
of my people, and * pleading with Dan 9:20

DESPERATION
I impulsively cried out in *? Job 6:25,26
Gaza will huddle in * and Ekron Zec 9:5
point of death," he said in *. Mk 5:23

DESPICABLE
I have seen their * acts right Jer 23:11
* people—even eating with them! Lk 15:2

DESPISE
for Egyptians * Hebrews and never Gen 43:32
live among you, and not * you. Lev 26:11
"How long will these people * me? Num 14:10,11
other gods and * me and break my Deu 31:20
and I will * those who despise me. 1Sa 2:30
and I will despise those who * me. 1Sa 2:30
of the Lord to * and blaspheme him, 2Sa 12:14
Oh, do not * the chastening of Job 5:17
not think of it. I * what I am. Job 9:21
and * me, a man you have made; Job 10:3
are quick to * all those in need. Job 12:5
Even young children * me. Job 19:18
They * me and won't come near Job 30:10
and yet does not * anyone! Job 36:5
to those who * God and trust in Ps 52:7
despised, but I don't * your laws. Ps 119:141
* God's Word and find yourself in Pro 13:13
to sin is to * him. Pro 14:2
Even his own neighbors * the poor Pro 14:20
To * the poor is to sin. Pro 14:21
Literally, "* him." Pro 19:7f
He will * the wisest advice. Pro 23:9
* an old mother's experience. Pro 23:22
Because you * what I tell you and Is 30:12
* the commandments of their God! Is 58:2
choosing to do what you know I *. Is 65:12
Your allies * you and will kill Jer 4:30
rebels who * me, "Don't worry! Jer 23:17
All who honored her * her now, Lam 1:8
you *, killed by the sword. Eze 31:18
be laid beside the people you *. Eze 32:19
How you * people who tell the Amo 5:10
his own name, "I * the pride and Amo 6:8
Do not * this small beginning, Zec 4:10
O priests, but you * my name." Mal 1:6
"When did we ever * your name?" Mal 1:6
about one and * the other. Lk 16:13
If you * your life down here—you Jn 12:25
Don't let anyone * or ignore him 1Co 16:11
others honor us or * us, whether 2Co 6:8
You did not * me then when I Gal 4:12

DESPISED
Esau realized that his father * Gen 28:6,7,8
For shepherds were * and hated Gen 46:34
shall inherit what you have *. Num 14:31
For he has * the commandment of Num 15:31
that these men have * the Lord." Num 16:30
And they * him and refused to 1Sa 10:27
Why, then, have you * the laws 2Sa 12:9
ancestors, and * all his warnings. 2Ki 17:15
of God and * their words, scoffing 2Ch 36:16
out, for they have * you in Neh 4:5
a man, scorned and * by my own Ps 22:6
not * my cries of deep despair; Ps 22:24
I am constantly *, mocked, Ps 44:15,16
was strong and he * his people. Ps 78:59
Thus they * their Savior who had Ps 106:21,22
and mourned and * his command. Ps 106:25
But Moab and Edom are *; Ps 108:9
I am worthless and *, but I Ps 119:141
by the reaper, * by the binder. Ps 129:6,7
but a man with a warped mind is *. Pro 12:8
fools are * for their folly. Pro 14:24
poor, he will be *, and what he Ecc 9:16
and have * the Holy One of Israel. Is 1:4
laws of God and * the Word of the Is 5:24
I am here to help you. * though Is 41:14
to the one who is *, rejected by Is 49:7
us want him. We * him and rejected Is 53:
He was * and we didn't care. Is 53:
Though once * and hated and Is 60:1
and chose what they knew I *. Is 66:
They shall be * and loathed, Jer 44:1
and * by all, says the Lord. Jer 49:1
she prays, "and see how I'm *." Lam 1:1
sisters, for they * their husbands Eze 16:4
and whose covenant he * and broke. Eze 17:1
The things of God are all *; Eze 22:
"And I * her just as I despised Eze 23:1
"And I despised her just as I * Eze 23:1
hand them out to be crushed and *. Eze 23:4
they formerly * her and treated her Eze 28:2
she *, all victims of the sword. Eze 32:2
Edom, making you small and *. Ob 1:
(But she was Syrophoenician—a "* Mk 7:2
"But a * Samaritan Lk 10:3
All Samaritans were * by Jews, Lk 10:33
And note this: some who are * Lk 13:3
This man was a * Lk 17:16
Samaritans were * by Jews as Lk 17:16
Jew would ask a "* Samaritan" for Jn 4:9
He has chosen a plan * by the 1Co 1:28
right even if we ourselves are *. 2Co 13:7
We are glad to be weak and * if 2Co 13:9
this world, being willing to be * Heb 13:1
you have * the poor man. Jas 2:6

DESPISERS
and perish, you * [of the truth Act 13:41

DESPISES
girl of mine * me, though I myself Gen 16:5
wife, and now he * her, and has Deu 22:16
" 'Cursed is anyone who * his Deu 27:16
Only a fool * his father's Pro 15:5
The Lord * the deeds of the Pro 15:9,10
Literally, "* his mother." Pro 15:20f
The Lord * those who say that bad Pro 17:15
The Lord * every kind of Pro 20:10
A man who mocks his father and * Pro 30:17
own altar, for he * the false Lam 2:7
For the son * his father; Mic 7:6

DESPISING
my laws and for * my rule. Lev 26:43
* us who are building your wall." Neh 4:5
see how all the people are * me. Ps 89:50
your life; * them means death. Pro 19:16
punish him for * the solemn oath he Eze 17:19

DESPITE
Lot, * the danger they all faced Gen 13:7
my rule. But * all they have done, Lev 26:44
the hill country, * the fact that Num 14:44
yet been cleansed * the plague that Jos 22:17,18
Gideon * all he had done for them. Ju 8:35
wicked does,' but * your 1Sa 24:13
into a pit and, * the slippery snow 2Sa 23:20
* the prophet's warning, Jeroboam 1Ki 13:33
David's was. But * Abijam's sin, 1Ki 15:4
He was as evil as Jeroboam * the 1Ki 16:4-7
"He is stirring up trouble * the 1Ki 20:7
Yes, they worshiped idols, * the 2Ki 17:12
idols * the Lord's stern warnings. 2Ki 17:15
All this * the fact that I Neh 5:17
"But * all this they were Neh 9:26
They did not worship you * the Neh 9:35
And he has kept his faith in me * Job 2:3
gives me comfort * all the Job 6:10
All this * the fact that they Job 21:14
the innocent * the bribes offered Ps 15:5
Lord, * our loyalty to you. Ps 44:17
therefore it stands unmoved * the Ps 46:5
They can't talk or see, * their Ps 115:5
faultless * their many sins. Pro 30:11,12
* all your witchcraft and magic. Is 47:9
You will not succeed * their aid. Jer 2:37
I am the Lord. * all you have Eze 16:63
by blessing you * your wickedness, Eze 20:44
all remains * the hottest fire. Eze 24:12
so merciful * our grievous sins. Dan 9:18
be rebuilt * the perilous times. Dan 9:25
But * all the miracles he had Jn 12:37
before Pilate, * Pilate's Act 3:13
slaughter; but * all this, Rom 8:37
obeyed me * the persecution, Rev 3:10

DESPOILING
Literally, "Plundering and * Is 8:1f

DESSERT
care for even the daintiest *. Job 33:20

DESSERTS
and of course I went without *. Dan 10:3

DESTINATION
his land to get to their *. Ju 11:19
the third day I will reach my *. Lk 13:32
you can send me on to my next *. 1Co 16:6

DESTINE
therefore I will "*" you to the Is 65:12

DESTINED
who are * for death, to death; Jer 15:2
is * for God's mightiest praise. Lk 1:42
And just as it is * that men die Heb 9:27
of God who are * for prison will be Rev 13:10

(DESTINED Con't)
those * for death will be killed. Rev 13:10

DESTINY
But its * is destruction!" Num 24:20
use arguing with God about your *. Ecc 6:10
of "Fate" and "*," therefore I Is 65:11
of life and controls your *! Dan 5:23

DESTITUTE
You have come to see how * the Gen 42:8,9
them this home when they were *. Ps 68:9,10
afflicted, the fatherless, the *. Ps 82:3
the prayers of the *, for he is Ps 102:17
who are helpless, poor and *. Is 58:7

DESTROY
to attack you, longing to * you. Gen 4:7
"I have decided to * all mankind; Gen 6:12,13
Yes, I will * mankind from the Gen 6:12,13
with a flood and * every living Gen 6:17
send another flood to * the earth. Gen 9:9,10,11
the floods come and * all life. Gen 9:15
the city—will you * it, and not Gen 18:24
Will you * the city for lack of Gen 18:28
And God said, "I will not * it if Gen 18:28
And God replied, "I won't * it if Gen 18:29
And God said, "Then I won't * it Gen 18:31
sake of the ten, I won't * it." Gen 18:32
For we will * the city Gen 19:13
and God has sent us to * it." Gen 19:13
for the Lord is going to * it." Gen 19:14
and won't * that little city. Gen 19:21
to * either one of us who does." Gen 31:53
his household to * the idols they Gen 35:2
You shall * your enemies. Gen 49:8
I will * Egypt with my miracles, Ex 3:20
a deadly plague to * your cattle, Ex 9:3
you going to * us completely? Ex 10:7
you and I will not * your firstborn Ex 12:13
will pass over you and not * you. Ex 12:21
and did not come in to * us.' Ex 12:27
Catch up with them, * them. Ex 15:9
themselves, lest Jehovah * them." Ex 19:22
come up here, or I will * them." Ex 19:24
And I will * those people before Ex 23:23
elders saw God, he did not * them; Ex 24:11
out against them and * them all; Ex 32:10
tempted to * you along the way." Ex 33:3
your children and * your cattle and Lev 26:22
I will * your food supply so Lev 26:26
and I will * the altars on the Lev 26:30
desolate, and * your places of Lev 26:31
I will not utterly * them and my Lev 26:44
families of Kohath * themselves! Num 4:17,18,19
I will disinherit them and * Num 14:12
so that I may instantly * them." Num 16:21
so that I can instantly * them." Num 16:45
altar, lest I * both them and you. Num 18:2,3
And * the sons of Sheth. Num 24:15-19
And shall * many cities." Num 24:15-19
Then the Lord said to Moses, "* Num 25:16,17
has used Israel to * the population Num 32:3,4
living there and * all their Num 33:52
And I will * you as I had Num 33:56
I had planned for you to * them." Num 33:56
so that he could * Sihon by the Deu 2:30
abandon you nor * you nor forget Deu 4:31
soon will, he will * the following Deu 7:1
you and he would surely * you. Deu 7:4
"You must * all the nations Deu 7:16
against those nations and * them. Deu 7:23
devouring fire to * them, so that Deu 9:3
He was ready to * you. Deu 9:8
" 'Let me alone that I may * Deu 9:13,14
the Lord was ready to * you. Deu 9:19
when the Lord was ready to * you. Deu 9:25
Lord God, don't * your own people. Deu 9:26
For if you * them the Egyptians Deu 9:28
to my pleas and didn't * you. Deu 10:10
"You must * all the heathen Deu 12:2
city and utterly * all of its Deu 13:15
save no one; * every living thing. Deu 20:16
Utterly * the Hittites, the Deu 20:17
a city, don't * the fruit trees. Deu 20:19
you are utterly to * the name of Deu 25:19
rain, and dust storms shall * you. Deu 28:24
wine, for worms will * the vines. Deu 28:39
The locusts shall * your trees Deu 28:42
lead you, and will * the nations Deu 31:3
The Lord will * the nations Deu 31:4
* them as I have commanded you. Deu 31:5
It is he who cries, '* them!' Deu 33:27
God's command to * everything Jos 7:1
or three thousand of us to * it; Jos 7:3
and * all the people living in it. Jos 9:24
"Come and help me * Gibeon," he Jos 10:4
I have given them to you to *. Jos 10:8
help you to completely * them." Jos 10:19
the Lord helped them * all their Jos 21:44
turn upon you and * you, even Jos 24:20
"then you must * all the idols you Jos 24:23
I told you to * their heathen Ju 2:2
* the nations living in your land; Ju 2:3
them out, nor let Israel * them. Ju 2:23
And you shall quickly * the Ju 6:16
of himself and * the one who broke Ju 6:31
and * the fleeing army of Midian. Ju 7:23
fail, they'll return and * us." Ju 8:6
then may Abimelech * the citizens Ju 9:20
and may they * Abimelech!" Ju 9:20
rest of us will * Gibe-ah for this Ju 20:8,9,10
to * the people of Jabesh-gilead. Ju 21:10,11,12
Then the Lord began to * the 1Sa 5:6
and * every last one of them." 1Sa 14:36
Now go and completely * the 1Sa 15:3
'Go and completely * the sinners, 1Sa 15:18
and * Keilah because I am here. 1Sa 23:10
and * my line of descendants!" 1Sa 24:21
into the city and * those 'lame' 2Sa 5:8
the way for you and will * them." 2Sa 5:24
You have done great miracles to * 2Sa 7:23
Israeli army to * the Ammonites. 2Sa 11:1
Then when we find him we can * 2Sa 17:12
Should you * what is the 2Sa 20:19
the man who did his best to * us. 2Sa 21:5,6
But you * those who are evil. 2Sa 22:27
was preparing to * Jerusalem, the 2Sa 24:16
your home and will * all of your 1Ki 14:10
who will * the family of Jeroboam. 1Ki 14:14
So now I will * you and your 1Ki 16:3
He is going to * your family as 1Ki 21:22
I will * his descendants." 1Ki 21:29
thing: he did not * the shrines on 1Ki 22:43
and * you and your fifty men!" 2Ki 1:10
and * you and your fifty men." 2Ki 1:12
Don't * us as you did the 2Ki 1:14
descendants, he did not * Judah. 2Ki 8:19
You are to * the family of Ahab; 2Ki 9:7
I will * the family of Ahab as I 2Ki 9:9
However, he didn't * the golden 2Ki 10:29
to * the dynasty of Ahab. 2Ki 10:30
Yet even so he didn't * the 2Ki 12:3
However, he didn't * the shrines 2Ki 14:4
he didn't * the shrines on the 2Ki 15:4
But he didn't * the shrines on 2Ki 15:34,35
lions among us to * us because we 2Ki 17:26
told us, 'Go and * this nation!' 2Ki 18:25
that I am going to * this city and 2Ki 22:15,16
of the Temple to * all the 2Ki 23:4
had said, "I will * Judah just as 2Ki 23:27
Judah in order to * the nation, 2Ki 24:2
go before you and * the enemy." 1Ch 14:15
And because God didn't * the 1Ch 15:26
God sent an angel to * Jerusalem; 1Ch 21:15
O Lord my God, * me and my 1Ch 21:17
but do not * your people." 1Ch 21:17
then I will * my people from this 2Ch 7:20
I will not completely * you; 2Ch 12:7
we went around and didn't * them. 2Ch 20:10
that he did not * the idol shrines 2Ch 20:33
* your nation with a great plague. 2Ch 21:14
has determined to * you because you 2Ch 25:16
was arranging to * him for 2Ch 25:20
prayer and did not * them. 2Ch 30:20
" 'Yes, the Lord will * this 2Ch 34:24
will * you, for he is with me." 2Ch 35:21
of Babylon to * them completely. 2Ch 36:17
Nebuchadnezzar * this Temple and Ez 5:12
of Jerusalem will * any king and Ez 6:12
Surely your anger will * us now Ez 9:14
around us who are trying to * us? Neh 5:9
"May God * your homes and Neh 5:13
mercy you did not * them completely Neh 9:31
the Jews, and * all of them Est 3:5,6
been sold to those who will * us. Est 7:4
Haman's order to * the Jews Est 8:5
gallows because he tried to * you. Est 8:7
their families, to * all the forces Est 8:11
had plotted to * them at the time Est 9:24,25
have made me, and yet you * me. Job 10:8
making me was to * me if I sinned; Job 10:13,14
the breath of God shall * him; Job 15:30
all the wicked shall * him. Job 20:22
merciful that he does not * us. Job 37:23
them, or the wild animals * them. Job 39:15
behalf, and won't * you as I should Job 42:8
You will * them for their lies; Ps 5:6
to let my enemies * me, crush me to Ps 7:5
The Lord will * your cities; Ps 9:6
he will * those proud liars who Ps 12:3,4
The Lord will * them and their Ps 21:9,10
When evil men come to * me, they Ps 27:2
these who are trying to * me. Ps 40:14,15
among themselves—* them with their Ps 55:9
He will * them more quickly than Ps 58:9
from these who have come to * me. Ps 59:1
Angrily * them. Ps 59:12,13
But those plotting to * me shall Ps 63:9
that came to * us have fled!" Ps 68:11,12,13
His people must * them. Ps 68:23
Help! * them! Ps 71:13
their sins and didn't * them all. Ps 78:38
a nation—we will * the very memory Ps 83:4
him, and * those who hate him. Ps 89:23
He will * them by their own Ps 94:23
So the Lord declared he would * Ps 106:23
from his wrath, and not * them. Ps 106:23
Nor did Israel * the nations in Ps 106:34
for them, they are trying to * me. Ps 109:4
For then all their efforts to * Ps 109:28
out behind his banner and * them. Ps 118:10
Yet beneath his flag I shall * Ps 118:12
* those who are trying to harm me; Ps 143:12
Evil words *. Pro 11:9
A time to *; Ecc 3:3
* your prosperity. Ecc 5:6,7
or too wise! Why * yourself? Ecc 7:15-17
he will * her armies, judges, Is 3:2
you like flies and * you, like bees Is 7:18
in one day, will * the leaders of Is 9:14,15
"We will * Calno just as we did Is 10:9
and we will * Samaria just as we Is 10:9
we will * Jerusalem with hers." Is 10:11
fire and flame that will * them. Is 10:17
The Lord will * them, soul and Is 10:18
God has rightly decided to * his Is 10:22
rise against them to * them." Is 10:25
their necks, and * it as decreed. Is 10:27
Nothing will hurt or * in all my Is 11:9
uniting forces to * them, and they Is 11:14
against Babylon to * the palaces of Is 13:2
them and will * your whole land. Is 13:5
adder, a fiery serpent to * you! Is 14:29
plunder and * the people of God. Is 17:14
has done it to * your pride and Is 23:9
merchant city, to * its strength. Is 23:11
unusual thing—to * his own people! Is 28:21
and build forts around it to * it. Is 29:3
And you will * all your silver Is 30:22
God steps in to * your enemies, he Is 30:25
He will utterly * them and Is 34:2
God is coming to * your enemies. Is 35:4
The Lord said to me, 'Go and * Is 36:10
Of course the Assyrians could * Is 37:19
my anger and not * you lest the Is 48:11
For the moth shall * them like Is 51:8
the earth and * its life, so now I Is 54:9
I have created the armies that *. Is 54:16
But I will not * them all, says Is 65:8
so I will not * all Israel, Is 65:8
tear down some and * them, and Jer 1:10
to * her and leave her cities in Jer 2:15
* Israel's glory and power. Jer 2:16
just one, I'll not * the city! Jer 5:1
rows of the vineyards and * them! Jer 5:10
north, coming to * this nation! Jer 6:1
"Let us attack by night and * Jer 6:5
Yes, I will * this Temple, as I Jer 7:13,14
"Let's * this man and all his Jer 11:19
my fists against you to * you. Jer 15:6
dear, and I will * my own people Jer 15:7
and utterly * them, and no one Jer 17:27
I will not * it as I had planned. Jer 18:8
And I myself will * you for Jer 21:14
but I will * you and leave you Jer 22:6
Why did he * such a great city?" Jer 22:8
and I will utterly * you and make Jer 25:8,9
them— then I will * this Temple as Jer 26:6
say the Lord will * this Temple Jer 26:9
Even if I utterly * the nations Jer 30:11
to * them in my furious anger. Jer 33:5
of Babylon would * this country and Jer 36:29
I will * it before your eyes, Jer 39:16
And when he comes he shall * the Jer 43:11
and causing me to * you completely Jer 44:8
and I will * every one of you! Jer 44:11
I will * this nation that I built; Jer 45:4
I will * all the nations to which Jer 46:28
exiled you, but I will not * you. Jer 46:28
it will * their cities and Jer 47:2
have been completed to * her. Jer 48:2,3,4
coalition against Edom and * her. Jer 49:14
the Lord will send him to * them. Jer 49:28
you and is preparing to * you. Jer 49:30
The Lord of Hosts says: I will * Jer 49:35
I will * her king and princes. Jer 49:38
heaps of ruins and utterly * her; Jer 50:26
The Lord declares that he will * Jer 50:40
land of the Chaldeans, and * it. Jer 51:1
to march on Babylon and * her. Jer 51:11
and see, and shall * them all. Jer 51:18
in pieces and to * many kingdoms. Jer 51:20
said that you will * Babylon so Jer 51:61,62
The Lord determined to * Lam 2:8
this remnant and * all Israel." Eze 5:4
deadly arrows of famine to * you. Eze 5:16
war upon you to * your idols. Eze 6:3
war will * those in the land of Eze 6:12
God says: I will * you for these Eze 13:8
says: Repent and * your idols, and Eze 14:6,7
* him from among my people Israel. Eze 14:9
famine to * both man and beast. Eze 14:13
and I would * the remainder of Eze 14:14
enemy to come and * everything, Eze 14:17
await Jerusalem to * all life: war, Eze 14:21

(DESTROY Con't)
was right for me to * Jerusalem. Eze 14:22
many nations—to *, and they will Eze 16:39
I will unsheath my sword and * Eze 21:3
No, I will * you in your own Eze 21:30
and they * lives for profit. Eze 22:27
of Israel: I will * my lovely, Eze 24:20,21
I will * you; Eze 25:7
The sword will * everything from Eze 25:13
* those along the sea coast. Eze 25:16
They will * the walls of Tyre Eze 26:4
First he will * your suburbs; Eze 26:8
They will * your lovely homes and Eze 26:12
"For the Lord God says: I will * Eze 26:19
When I * you and show forth my Eze 28:22
of disease and an army to *; Eze 28:23
O Egypt, and * both men and herds. Eze 29:8
and I will utterly * the land of Eze 29:10
will * the multitudes of Egypt. Eze 30:10
I will * Egypt and everything in Eze 30:12
* her as her wickedness deserves. Eze 31:11
"And when I * you, Eze 32:9
I will * you with Babylon's Eze 32:12
I will * all your flocks and Eze 32:13
And when I * Egypt and wipe out Eze 32:15
evil man will not * him if he Eze 33:12
I will * him for his sins. Eze 33:13
And I will * the powerful, fat Eze 34:15,16
with my fist and utterly * you. Eze 35:3
I will march against her and * Eze 38:11
But when you come to * the land Eze 38:18
And I will * 85 percent Eze 39:2
them and let their enemies * them. Eze 39:23
when he came to * the city. Eze 43:3
down the tree and * it, but leave Dan 4:23
ten, and will * three of them. Dan 7:24
to consume and * it until the end. Dan 7:26
he turns, he will * all who oppose Dan 8:24
Without warning he will * them. Dan 8:25
will * the city and the Temple. Dan 9:26
in great anger to * as he goes. Dan 11:44
I will * her vineyards and her Hos 1:12
and I will * all weapons, and all Hos 1:18
and I will * your mother, Israel. Hos 4:5
I will * her as a moth does Hos 5:12
My God will * the people of Hos 9:17
This is the last time I will * Hos 11:9
you, and I did not come to *. Hos 11:9
O Israel, if I * you, who can Hos 13:9
but they * it to the ground; Joe 2:3
* Ekron and the king of Ashkelon; Amo 1:8
will * all the palaces in Kerioth. Amo 2:2
And I will * their king and slay Amo 2:3
So I will * Judah with fire, and Amo 2:5
is, I am getting ready to * you. Amo 3:4
also * the idol altars at Bethel. Amo 3:14
"And I will * the beautiful Amo 3:15
for I will pass through and *. Amo 5:17
of locusts to * all the main crop Amo 7:1
and I will * the dynasty of King Amo 7:9
after them to bite and * them. Amo 9:3
armies against Edom and * her!' Ob 1:1
'I am going to * you, for your Jon 1:2
his plan to * them, and didn't Jon 3:10
for your blood, eager to * you. Mic 4:11
the Lord, I will * all the weapons Mic 5:10
to consult— and * all your idols. Mic 5:13
among you, and * the cities where Mic 5:14
of Moab, tried to * you through the Mic 6:5
example of you—I will * you. Mic 6:16
And I will * your gods and Nah 1:14
* those who are better than they? Hab 1:13
"I will * it to the ground. Zep 1:2
with my fist, and * every remnant Zep 1:4
I will * them. Zep 1:5
And I will * those who formerly Zep 1:6
The Lord will * you until not one Zep 2:5
he will * Assyria and make its Zep 2:13
thrones and * the strength of the Hag 2:22
his home and completely * it." Zec 5:4
Go ahead and * yourselves!" Zec 11:9
For my plan is to * all the Zec 12:9
like, but I will * it again,' for Mal 1:4
Fear only God who can * both soul Mt 10:28
'I am able to * the Temple of God Mt 26:60,61
You can * the Temple and build it Mt 27:40
you come to * us demons? Mk 1:24
Is it a day to save lives or to * Mk 3:4
him say, 'I will * this Temple made Mk 14:58
"Sure, you can * the Temple and Mk 15:29,30
You have come to * us. Lk 4:34
To save life, or to * it?" Lk 6:9
* men's lives, but to save them." Lk 9:55f
no moth can * them. Lk 12:33
I will do for you: * this sanctuary Jn 2:19
purpose is to steal, kill and *. Jn 10:10
of Nazareth will * the Temple, and Act 6:14
and eager to * every Christian, Act 9:1
For God says, "I will * all 1Co 1:19
spoils God's home, God will * him. 1Co 3:17
why God sent his Angel to * them. 1Co 10:10
* by his presence when he returns. 2Th 2:8
nothing can *, let us please God by Heb 12:28
He alone decides to save us or *. Jas 4:12
fact: that God did * the world with 2Pe 3:5,6
But the Son of God came to * 1Jn 3:8
and small—and to * those who have Rev 11:18
power to * the world with fire, Rev 14:18

DESTROYED
and birds. God * them all, leaving Gen 7:23
Jehovah * Sodom and Gomorrah); Gen 13:10
called Kadesh) and * the Gen 14:7
and utterly * them, along with the Gen 19:25
All the frogs will be *, except Ex 8:11
shattered and the crops were *. Ex 9:25
knocked down and * (for the barley Ex 9:31
the emmer were not *, for they were Ex 9:32
grain, are *, the one who started Ex 22:6
Literally, "shall be utterly *." Ex 22:20f
presence of the Lord and * them. Lev 10:2
contagious and must be * by fire. Lev 13:52
be desolate and your cities *. Lev 26:33
and be * among your enemies. Lev 26:38
in their sins [and be * with them Num 16:26
and the Israelis completely * Num 21:3
Hormah (meaning "Utterly *"). Num 21:3
He has * Num 21:27-30
But the Kenites shall be *, Num 24:21,22
They too must be *." Num 24:23,24
and 250 men were * by fire from Num 26:5-11
the cause of the plague that * us. Num 31:16
but Jehovah * them as the Deu 2:21
Mount Seir, for he * the Horites Deu 2:22
invaded and * the tribe of Avvim Deu 2:23
and utterly * everything, including Deu 2:33,34
We utterly * the kingdom of Deu 3:6
just as we had * King Sihon's Deu 3:6
where he * many people for Deu 4:3
shall be quickly * from the land. Deu 4:26
you will then be utterly *. Deu 4:26
he and his people were * by Moses Deu 4:44,45,46
over to you to be *, do a complete Deu 7:2
shall be punished publicly and *. Deu 7:10
them," or "He * them because he Deu 9:28
"WHEN THE LORD your God has * Deu 19:1
at last you are * because of the Deu 28:20
you until you are * from the face Deu 28:21
you until you are *—all because you Deu 28:45
around your neck until you are *! Deu 28:47,48
in this book, until you are *. Deu 28:61
in battle, but we * them, and took Deu 29:7
* by the Lord in his anger. Deu 29:23
land, just as he * Sihon and Og, Deu 31:4
from them, and they shall be *. Deu 31:17
"Israel is * by our own might; Deu 32:27
Unless the Lord had * them? Deu 32:30
[and * many sinners Deu 33:9
and completely * their people. Jos 2:10
loot, for everything is to be *. Jos 6:18
They * everything in it—men and Jos 6:21
*" or else become totally God's. Jos 7:12f
the loot were not *, for the armies Jos 8:27
had captured and * Ai and had Jos 10:1
the Lord * them with a great Jos 10:11
On that same day Joshua * the Jos 10:28
killed him and * his entire army. Jos 10:33
slopes. They * everyone in the Jos 10:40
Then he attacked and * all the Jos 11:12
all of the others were *. Jos 11:19
all and completely * their cities. Jos 11:21
whose cities were * by the Jos 12:1
of Israel had * these people, and Jos 12:6
Here is a list of the kings * by Jos 12:7
kings and their cities were *. Jos 12:8-24
land of those you have already *. Jos 23:4,5
I * them and gave you their land. Jos 24:8
against you but I * them all. Jos 24:11
until all of Sisera's army was *; Ju 4:16
he and all his people were *. Ju 4:24
nations came and * their crops and Ju 6:3,4
Then they * their foreign gods Ju 10:16
the victory. He * the Ammonites Ju 11:33
for them when we * Jabesh-gilead, Ju 21:22
They are the same gods who * the 1Sa 4:8
had * them with dreadful plagues. 1Sa 6:6
So they * their idols of Baal and 1Sa 7:4
you and your king will be *." 1Sa 12:25
Then Jonathan attacked and * the 1Sa 13:3,4
He announced that he had * the 1Sa 13:3,4
to them. They * only what was 1Sa 15:9
and we have * everything else." 1Sa 15:15
Lord has * all of your enemies." 1Sa 20:15
will be routed and * by the 1Sa 28:19
instructed him and * the 2Sa 5:25
have gone and have * your enemies. 2Sa 7:9
He also * the forces of King 2Sa 8:3
After his return he * eighteen 2Sa 8:13
be * from the face of the earth." 2Sa 14:7
your God who has * the rebels who 2Sa 18:28
And * them. 2Sa 22:38
I have * them 2Sa 22:39
I have * them all. 2Sa 22:41
became king) when David * Zobah. 1Ki 11:2
and he * Ijon, Dan, 1Ki 15:2
that the Lord had * all of 1Ki 16:4-
He even * distant relatives and 1Ki 16:1
these horns until they are *." 1Ki 22:1
to be * by the king of Moab!" 2Ki 3:1
They * the cities, threw stones 2Ki 3:2
of Ahab as I * the families of 2Ki 9:
Thus Jehu * every trace of Baal 2Ki 10:2
for the king of Syria had * the 2Ki 13:
Syria until they were entirely *; 2Ki 13:1
and they were not totally *. 2Ki 13:2
You have * Edom and are very 2Ki 14:1
Menahem * the city of Tappuah and 2Ki 15:16
which the Lord * when the people of 2Ki 16:3
their attackers until they were *. 2Ki 17:2
one whose hilltop altars you've *. 2Ki 18:22
they have completely * 2Ki 19:11
The former kings of Assyria * 2Ki 19:12
of Assyria have * all those 2Ki 19:17
they were * because they were 2Ki 19:18
wells, and I * the strength of 2Ki 19:24
which his father Hezekiah had *. 2Ki 21:3,4,5
though Jehovah had * those nations 2Ki 21:9
He also * the shrines at the 2Ki 23:8
Then the king * the altar of 2Ki 23:10
He also * the altars which 2Ki 23:12
Judah just as I have * Israel; 2Ki 23:27
in his anger, * the people of 2Ki 24:20
Bedad—the one who * the army of 1Ch 1:46
There they * the few surviving 1Ch 4:43
of the people whom God had *. 1Ch 5:25
The Lord * us before because we 1Ch 15:13
I have * your enemies, and I will 1Ch 17:8
King David had * Hadadezer's army, 1Ch 18:9
Abishai (son of Zeruiah) then * 1Ch 18:12
"If your people Israel are * 2Ch 6:24
Temple shall be * even though I 2Ch 7:20
for the Lord and his army * them 2Ch 14:13
the cities, but * the cattle tents 2Ch 14:15
took courage and * all the idols in 2Ch 15:8
Israel. They * the cities of Ijon, 2Ch 16:4
themselves, and they * each other! 2Ch 20:22
the Lord has * your work." 2Ch 20:37
for he had * the spiritual fiber 2Ch 28:19
God of their fathers and were *. 2Ch 30:7
They set to work and * the 2Ch 30:14
very person who * all the idols, 2Ch 32:12
sent an angel who * the Assyrian 2Ch 32:21
heathen nations * by the Lord when 2Ch 33:2
Hezekiah had *—the altars of Baal, 2Ch 33:3
* when Israel entered the land. 2Ch 33:9
the palaces and * all the valuable 2Ch 36:19
in fact, it was * because of its Ez 4:15
And then you * their enemies in Neh 9:11
when Jerusalem was * by King Est 2:6
that they be *, and I will pay Est 3:9
see my people butchered and *?" Est 8:6
their lives and * all their Est 9:16
they shall all be broken and *. Job 4:10
with shame, and the wicked *." Job 8:22
He has * all hope. Job 19:10
Yes, let him be * for his Job 21:20
the righteous shall see them *; Job 22:19
enemies have been * in the fire.' Job 22:20
the nations and * the wicked, Ps 9:5
them until the last of them is *. Ps 10:15
You made them turn and run; I * Ps 18:40
When you appear, they will be * Ps 21:9,10
caught in their own net, and *. Ps 35:8
For the wicked shall be *, but Ps 37:9
and you will see the wicked *. Ps 37:34
But evil men shall be *, and Ps 37:38
his sins, he is *, for he is as Ps 39:11
They will stagger backward, * by Ps 64:8
by locusts. He * their grapevines Ps 78:47
For they have * your people Ps 79:7
enemies announced and seen them *. Ps 92:11
Remember how he * our enemies. Ps 105:5,6
He * many a king who tried! Ps 105:14
and were finally * by their sin. Ps 106:43
by our enemies, * by their anger. Ps 124:2,3
discrimination—but not *! Ps 129:2
treasuries. He * the eldest child Ps 135:8
evil beast, you shall be *. Ps 137:8
who destroys you as you have * us. Ps 137:8
Let them be * by the very evil Ps 140:9
and they themselves shall be *. Pro 2:22
But he will be * suddenly, Pro 6:15
is * by lack of common sense. Pro 10:21
the evil man is * by his Pro 11:3
it is * when you are cruel. Pro 11:17
are being * by their wickedness. Pro 13:6
from harm, but cheaters will be *. Pro 28:18
will be utterly abolished and *. Is 2:18
their cities are *—without a person Is 6:11
and again and *, yet Israel will be Is 6:13
the two invading kings would be *. Is 7:14f
whole flocks and herds will be *, Is 7:21,22
'Your enemies will soon be *.' Is 8:1
"Your enemies will soon be *." Is 8:18

(DESTROYED Con't)
as he did when he * the vast host Is 9:4
down the walls and * the people and Is 10:13
who * the land of Israel. Is 10:17
glorious forest, yet it will be *. Is 10:18
The land shall be *, and all the Is 13:9
will be as utterly * as Sodom and Is 13:19
Can this be the one who * the Is 14:17
you, for you have * your nation and Is 14:20
cities of Ar and Kir will be *. Is 15:1
the remnant of Syria shall be *. Is 17:3
I see you plundered and *. Is 21:2
my people as I watch them being *. Is 22:4
oceans, for your home port is *! Is 23:14
they are left desolate, * by the Is 24:6
You came against them and * them, Is 26:14
And the Assyrians will be *, but Is 31:8
will be * and their cities laid Is 32:19
who have * everything around you Is 33:1
you, too, will be betrayed and *. Is 33:1
Lebanon has been *; Is 33:9
Assyrian kings completely * them! Is 37:12
of Assyria have * all those Is 37:18
and * their thickest forests.' Is 37:24
his people and * them in battle. Is 42:25
* Israel, leaving her to shame. Is 43:28
All my enemies shall be * like Is 50:9
For though I * you in my anger, I Is 60:10
they shall be *. Is 60:12
cities long ago *, reviving them Is 61:4
And now our enemies have * her. Is 63:18
Your holy cities are *; Is 64:10
all the things of beauty are *. Is 64:11
it—it will not be * by invading Is 65:21,22
shall be hurt or * in all my Holy Is 65:25
You have * them but they refuse Jer 5:3
of my people shall be * again. Jer 6:9
God will never let Jerusalem be *. Jer 7:4
them until I have utterly * them. Jer 9:16
for they have * Israel and made a Jer 10:25
planted the tree has ordered it *. Jer 11:17
raped and * by the invading army. Jer 13:22
to be taken up and *, then if that Jer 18:7
Let that messenger be * like the Jer 20:16
See, they are all *. Jer 22:20
they have * and scattered the very Jer 23:1
until they are * from the land of Jer 24:10
this Temple as I * the Tabernacle Jer 26:6
"What do you mean—Jerusalem * Jer 26:9
this whole city will be *. Jer 27:17
you shall be *, and all your Jer 30:16
In the past I painstakingly * Jer 31:28
never again be captured or *. Jer 31:40
are completely * and left desolate Jer 34:22
until the whole scroll was *. Jer 36:23
Even if you * the entire Jer 37:10
have been * by sword and famine." Jer 44:18
and you shall be * by war and Jer 44:27
*, and left without a soul alive. Jer 46:19
from Tyre and Sidon will be *. Jer 47:4
living along the sea must be *. Jer 47:7
Horonaim, for all Moab is being *. Jer 48:2,3,4
be *, for the Lord has said it. Jer 48:8
But now Moab is to be *; Jer 48:15
of the Arnon, that Moab is *." Jer 48:20
god Chemosh are *, and your sons Jer 48:46
Cry out, O Heshbon, for Ai is *! Jer 49:3
*—and she herself will perish too. Jer 49:9,10
Suddenly Edom shall be *, and I Jer 49:19
your entire army shall be * in Jer 49:26
are going to be * by Jer 49:28
the world that Babylon will be *; Jer 50:2
to attack her, and she shall be *. Jer 50:9
fury upon those who * his Temple. Jer 50:28
Babylon just as he * Sodom and Jer 50:40
young and old alike shall be *. Jer 51:3
If you stay, you will be * when Jer 51:6
work shall be * by fire! Jer 51:58
The Lord without mercy has * Lam 2:2
He has * her forts and palaces. Lam 2:5
and say, "We have * her at last! Lam 2:16
He has * Jerusalem without mercy Lam 2:17
we are trapped and desolate, *. Lam 3:47
all will be *. Eze 7:13
Your cities shall be * and your Eze 12:20
were desolated, their crops *; Eze 19:7
the fruit was * by fire. Eze 19:12
care for them that I * them. Eze 20:14
with the same terrors that * her. Eze 23:31
when my Temple was *, and mocked Eze 25:3
Tyre, * in the midst of the sea? Eze 27:32
a common sinner. I * you, O Eze 28:16
you are * forever." Eze 28:19
is taken away, her foundations *. Eze 30:4
Egypt on fire and * her allies. Eze 30:8
fell to Nebuchadnezzar and was *. Eze 30:20f
Her allies too are all * and Eze 31:17
to be attacked and *, and you were Eze 34:8
more will they be picked on and *. Eze 34:22
as theirs, and * you on every side Eze 36:3
cities, * and mocked by heathen Eze 36:4
up a kingdom that will never be *; Dan 2:44
* and whose power shall never end. Dan 6:25,26
up afterward and * three of the Dan 7:20
My people are * because they Hos 4:6
Israel is *; Hos 8:8
*; even mothers and children were Hos 10:14
the king of Israel shall be *. Hos 10:15
Egypt will be *, and Edom too, Joe 3:19
and all her forts shall be *. Amo 1:7
And yet you refused to come. I * Amo 4:11
of Israel will be *, and I will Amo 7:9
days from now Nineveh will be *!" Jon 3:4,5
your shelter is *, though you did Jon 4:10
crumbles and its people are *. Nah 1:5
head to toe. You * with their own Hab 3:14
fig trees are all *, and there is Hab 3:17
and Ammon will be * like Sodom and Zep 2:9
be so totally * that its site is Zep 2:15f
and Ashkelon will be completely *. Zec 9:5
You will be * as though by fire Zec 11:1
never again to be cursed and *. Zec 14:11
brother, Esau, and * Esau's Mal 1:2,3
* [for my mercy endures forever Mal 3:6
Better for part of you to be * Mt 5:29
Cities * by God for their Mt 11:21f
Cities * by God for their Mt 11:23f
out his army and * the murderers Mt 22:7
the godly men they *, and say, 'We Mt 23:29,30
Cities * by God in judgment for Lk 10:13f
and the flood came and * them all. Lk 17:27
down from heaven and * them all. Lk 17:29
listen to him shall be utterly *.' Act 3:23
Literally, "* from among the Act 3:23f
Yes, and you deliberately * Act 7:53
Then he * seven nations in Act 13:19,20
are sinful—and * sin's control over Rom 8:3
are hunted down or *, is it because Rom 8:35
the Jews would be *—all of Rom 9:29
and he * them in the wilderness. 1Co 10:5
He took this list of sins and * Col 2:14
At that time God completely * the 2Pe 2:5
and they will be * along with all 2Pe 2:12
Literally, "will be * in the 2Pe 2:12f
Those cities were * by fire and Jud 1:7

DESTROYER
not permit the * to enter . . ." Ex 12:23f
that home and not permit the * to Ex 12:23
A lion—a * of nations—stalks Jer 4:7
be destroyed; her * is on the way; Jer 48:15
For the * has cut off your Jer 48:32
THE LORD SAYS: I will stir up a * Jer 51:1
mountain, Babylon, * of the earth! Jer 51:25
Apollyon [and in English, the * Rev 9:11

DESTROYERS
them four kinds of *, says the Jer 15:3

DESTROYING
curse the earth, * all living Gen 8:21
they will finish * everything that Ex 10:4,5
could slay them, * them from off Ex 32:12
nations, * you with war as you go. Lev 26:33
of the Lord began * those at the Num 11:1
so I have stopped * all Israel as Num 25:10,11
they are * you with their wiles. Num 25:18
be responsible for * his people and Num 32:15
that time will rejoice in * you; Deu 28:63
began * the enemy from the rear. Jos 8:22
Kiriath-arba), * the cities of Ju 1:10
But instead of * them, the Ju 3:6
of grain, and * the olive trees. Ju 15:5
the Lord began * its people, young 1Sa 5:9
You are * an ancient, 2Sa 20:19
Moab, * everything as they went. 2Ki 3:24
* cities both large and small. 2Ki 18:8
After * them, he laid siege to 1Ch 20:1
and commanded the * angel, "Stop! 1Ch 21:15
hills, and * the Asherim idols. 2Ch 17:6
and Jerusalem, * the heathen altars 2Ch 34:3
he overturns them, * them, or Job 34:25
liars who are so intent upon * me. Ps 57:3
against them a band of * angels. Ps 78:49
everything green, * all the crops. Ps 105:35
while you watch, foreigners are * Is 1:7
He is * all of that vast army, Is 10:33
* nation whose land the upper Nile Is 18:2
that conquering, * nation whose Is 18:7
and chase away all those * you. Is 49:17
For suddenly the * armies will be Jer 6:26
cares. * armies plunder the land; Jer 12:12
day, all who are * you shall be Jer 30:16
you: Why are you * yourselves? Jer 44:7
earth like a flood, * every foe. Jer 46:8
For the Lord is * the Jer 47:4
Dibon, for those * Moab shall Jer 48:18
by * your city of Rabbah. Jer 49:2
With you I will crush armies, * Jer 51:21
north shall come * armies against Jer 51:48
For the Lord is * Babylon; Jer 51:55
roar in upon her. * armies come Jer 51:56
of your hands by * you, and you Eze 13:23
a terrible example of him, * him; Eze 14:8
it will devour the whole world, * Dan 7:23
from * him for this transgression. Dan 8:12
marching through Israel and * it. Dan 11:28
—my great * army that I sent Joe 2:25
Hazael's palace, * the strong Amo 1:4
back his fierce anger from * us." Jon 3:9
your plans for * these people. Jon 4:2
himself, and * his own kingdom. Mt 12:26
I have been *, of trying to be Gal 2:18
sea, * a third of all the ships; Rev 8:8,9

DESTROYS
When he * the nations in the Deu 12:29
Who * those who oppose me 2Sa 22:48
commandment and * this Temple. Ez 6:12
For he is the one who *, and Job 9:17
same to him, for he * both kinds. Job 9:22
What he * can't be rebuilt. Job 12:14
He raises up a nation and then * Job 12:23
supreme Judge? He * those who are Job 21:23,24
God also * those in deep and Job 21:25
It is a devastating fire that * Job 31:12
he publicly honors them and * the Ps 41:2
For God * the mightiest warships Ps 48:7
for he * those serving other gods. Ps 73:27
while God traps them and * them. Ps 94:12,13
Blessed is the man who * you as Ps 137:8
who love him, but * the wicked. Ps 145:20
upon you like a robber and * you; Pro 6:11
utter fool, for he * his own soul. Pro 6:32
God protects the upright but * Pro 10:29
The Lord * the possessions of the Pro 15:25
violence boomerangs and * them. Pro 21:7
but one who demands bribes * it. Pro 29:4
a bribe; it * his understanding. Ecc 7:7
and the Lord * him, his previous Eze 3:20
He furiously * their enemies. Nah 1:2
against you. He * your weapons. Nah 2:13
with strife and division * itself. Mk 3:25

DESTRUCTION
be caught in the * of the city." Gen 19:15
O Lord, please deliver me from * Gen 32:11
Then he shall order the * of the Lev 14:45
you because you are headed for *. Num 22:32
But its destiny is *!" Num 24:20
had finished the * of its enemies! Jos 10:13
instead, you have saved us from * Jos 22:31
resulted in the * of Jeroboam's 1Ki 13:34
This * of the descendants of 1Ki 16:12
Jerusalem and south of * Mountain. 2Ki 23:13
or three months of * by the enemies 1Ch 21:12
of the Lord brings * to the land. 1Ch 21:12
aside and he didn't send total *; 2Ch 12:12
treasury for the * of the Jews. Est 4:7
We are doomed to * and slaughter. Est 7:4
"But * and Death speak of Job 28:22
send my enemies to the pit of *. Ps 55:23
and down to their *: an instant Ps 73:18
is only eternal * ahead of them. Ps 92:7
Pride goes before * and Pro 16:18
Pride ends in *; Pro 18:12
with women—the royal pathway to *. Pro 31:3
you down the garden path to *. Is 3:12
down to escape the * of Jerusalem Is 4:2,3,4
with the broom of *, says the Lord Is 14:23
and Elealeh, for * has come upon Is 16:9
making it a vast wasteland of *. Is 24:1
* falls from the heavens upon you; Is 24:18
have never felt * for yourselves. Is 33:1
that land and find it worthy of *. Is 34:11
have been no need for your *. Is 48:19
been your lot: desolation and *. Is 51:19
forge and makes the weapons of *. Is 54:16
vast * on you from the north. Jer 4:6
Wave upon wave of * rolls over Jer 4:20
and even there the sword of * Jer 9:16
nor mercy spare them from utter *. Jer 13:14
Yes, bring double * upon them! Jer 17:18
it is disaster and horror and *. Jer 20:8
them and driven them to *. Jer 23:2
all the terrible * he has planned. Jer 30:24
of * shall devour all around you. Jer 46:14
north with such * that no one shall Jer 50:3
in the land, a shout of great *. Jer 50:22
The sword of * shall smite the Jer 50:35
This complete * of the city of Jer 51:26f
But the time is coming for the * Jer 51:52
Hear the cry of great * out of Jer 51:54
the city's *, and those who had Jer 52:15
laid out an unalterable line of *. Lam 2:8
deliberately called for this *; Lam 2:22
that have kept us from complete *. Lam 3:22
because of the * of my people. Lam 3:48,49
hands of cruel men skilled in *. Eze 21:31
with glee at the * of my people, Eze 25:6
in your terrible * before their Eze 38:15,16
How long until the * of the Dan 8:13
Or, consider the * of Jerusalem Dan 9:25f
is on the way. * from the Joe 1:15
violence he brings * on the strong, Amo 5:9
peace while plotting your *. Ob 1:7
The armies of * are coming; Mic 6:9
confusion, *, and terror will be Mic 7:4

(DESTRUCTION Con't)
But first comes terrible * to Mic 7:13
"the way that leads to *." Mt 7:13f
the time of its * has arrived. Lk 21:20
are fit only for *, those he has Rom 9:22
Literally, "for the * of the 1Co 5:5f
a blazing flame of * and disaster. Jas 3:6
ago and their * is on the way. 2Pe 2:3
in the same * with them." 2Pe 2:12f
themselves slaves to sin and *. 2Pe 2:19
have caused * upon the earth." Rev 11:18
pit and go to eternal *; Rev 17:8

DETACHMENTS
army into three *, and launched a 1Sa 11:11

DETAIL
to Moses were followed in every *. Lev 8:21
in *, for I am the Lord your God. Lev 18:4,5
in every *, going the whole way he Deu 5:32
This is described in greater * in Jos 10:13
completed in every * in November of 1Ki 6:38
of this *, sounded the cymbals. 1Ch 16:5
your plan in every *, for it is the 1Ch 17:2
in the smallest *, and will look 1Ch 29:19
to go over the law in greater *. Neh 8:13
Follow every * you have Est 6:10
But he knows every * of what is Job 23:10
future and tells everyone in *! Ecc 10:14
not one * will he miss; Is 34:16
* of what I have told you to do. Eze 4:3

DETAILED
the priest with a * description. 2Ki 16:10
in his place. * biographies of 1Ch 29:29

DETAILS
reported the * to his brothers, Gen 37:5
and the * of each furnishing. Ex 25:9
I'll handle all the *, for Ru 3:11
Further * of Baasha's reign are 1Ki 15:31
Additional * about King Shallum 2Ki 15:15
They saw to it that all the * 1Ch 6:49
The * of Jehoshaphat's reign from 2Ch 20:34
The other * of Uzziah's reign 2Ch 26:22
The other * of his life and 2Ch 28:26
with its dark *, and brings to Ps 7:14
More * of the feast are seen in Is 21:5f
to them the * of its Eze 43:11
anyone the * of what had happened. Lk 8:56
you are so upset over all these * Lk 10:41
But enough of such *. Heb 9:5

DETAINED
Literally, "* before the Lord." 1Sa 21:7f

DETECT
You can * them by the way they Mt 7:16

DETERMINATION
* to be wise is the first step Pro 4:7
despite Pilate's * to release him. Act 3:13

DETERMINE
The judges will * the amount. Ex 21:30
before God to * whether or not he Ex 22:8
the High Priest to * God's "yes" Ex 28:30,31f
sacred lot used to * the Lord's Lev 8:8f
and cast lots to * which is the Lev 16:8
in her hands to * whether or not Num 5:18
his wife— to * whether or not she Num 5:30
idols. * to obey only the Lord; 1Sa 7:3
to * when—at regular times each Neh 10:34
this my people and * their value. Jer 6:27
* their prophetic significance. Dan 5:8f

DETERMINED
sacrifice of a value * by Moses. Lev 5:17,18
The exact value cannot be *. Deu 22:19f
"Why is your father so * to kill 1Sa 20:1
actually he has * just the opposite 2Ch 18:22
* to beg for help from the Lord; 2Ch 20:3
of the people, he * that there 2Ch 20:21
know that God has * to destroy you 2Ch 25:16
This was because Ezra had * to Ez 7:10
action was * by throwing dice. Est 3:7
the time * by a throw of the dice; Est 9:24,25
were *, and who did the surveying? Job 38:5
This mighty King is * to give Ps 99:4
I am * to obey you until I die. Ps 119:112
I searched everywhere, * to find Ecc 7:25
Jerusalem and is * that the poor of Is 14:32
told me that he is * to crush you. Is 28:22
They are *, with faces hard as Jer 5:3
as you said—as you * it should! Jer 32:24
so I am * to be rid of it. Jer 32:31
dead, for I have * to destroy them Jer 33:5
The Lord * to destroy Jerusalem. Lam 2:8
Literally, "* . . . Dan 1:8f
the law, and * to save Daniel. Dan 6:14
because she is * to follow idols. Hos 5:11
For my people are * to desert Hos 11:7
the Jewish leaders * to kill him. Act 9:23
and when. He * their boundaries. Act 17:26

DETERMINES
everyone who * to follow the 2Ch 30:17,18,19
For a man's heart * his speech. Mt 12:34
If any of you really * to do Jn 7:17

DETERMINING
used as lots in * the will of God. 1Sa 28:5,6f

DETEST
Utterly * it, for it is a cursed Deu 7:26

DETESTABLE
guilty, for it is * to the Lord, Lev 7:17,18
both are * to the Lord your God. Deu 23:17,18
are * to the Lord your God. Deu 25:16
They made *, shameful idols and 2Ki 17:16
my land with your * idols, and Jer 16:18

DETESTED
And * them! Deu 32:19

DETOUR
travelers * on back roads. Is 33:8

DETOURS
he has filled my path with *. Lam 3:9

DEUEL
Gad -Eliasaph (son of * Num 1:2-15
* in chapter 1. Num 2:3-31f
of *, chief of the tribe of Gad. Num 7:42-47
Gad led by Eliasaph, the son of *. Num 10:20

DEUTERONOMY
See Exodus 34:1, * 10:1–4. Ex 34:28f
of the deceased. See * 25:5. Lev 18:16f
she had no children. See * 25:5. Lev 20:21f
was strong." * 2:19 indicates that Num 21:24f
See * 27:2–8. Jos 8:31f
her former husband. See * 25:5–10. Ru 1:11f
See Leviticus 19:9 and * 24:19. Ru 2:2f
* 23:3–5. Neh 13:1f
* 24:1–4. Jer 3:1f
See * 19:14; Hos 5:10f
with Sodom and Gomorrah (* 29:23). Hos 11:8f
not live by bread alone." * 8:3. Lk 4:4f
See * 18:15. Jn 1:21f

DEVASTATE
into the land to * the land, even Eze 14:15
and he will * God's people. Dan 8:24
everywhere to * the believers, even Act 8:3

DEVASTATED
was completely stripped and *. Ju 6:5
He also * the land of Moab. 2Sa 8:2
No, for he has * her enemies, Is 27:7,8
time has come for Babylon to be *. Jer 50:27
be saved, but the land would be *. Eze 14:16
The entire country would be *. Amo 1:12f

DEVASTATING
It is a * fire that destroys to Job 31:12
surrounded by * fire; Ps 50:3
Suddenly the * whirlwind of the Jer 30:23

DEVASTATION
shall see the * of the land and the Deu 29:22
you to many nations for *. Eze 25:7

DEVASTATIONS
All these * shall pursue you Deu 28:22

DEVELOP
"We can't afford to let a rift * Gen 13:8
* good judgment and common sense! Pro 4:5
And with your wisdom, * common Pro 4:7
It is pleasant to see plans *. Pro 13:19
* your business first before Pro 24:27
Call your councils of war, * your Is 8:9,10

DEVELOPED
nations that * after the flood. Gen 10:32
A fierce storm * that threatened Lk 8:23
"But a famine * in Egypt and Act 7:11
time, a big blowup * in Ephesus Act 19:23

DEVELOPING
hairs in the spot, and an ulcer *. Lev 13:9,10
that a riot was *, he sent for a Mt 27:24
and the divisions * among you, and 1Co 11:18
others and also by * their own 1Ti 3:13

DEVELOPS
hair *, declare him a leper. Lev 13:36
And patience * strength of Rom 5:4

DEVIATE
do not * from them the least Jos 23:6
Solomon did not * in any way 2Ch 8:15

DEVIL
you have sold yourself to the *. 1Ki 21:20
sold out to the * as Ahab, for his 1Ki 21:25
say, and sold yourselves to the * Is 28:15
with Death and the *, so when the Is 28:18
thistles among the wheat is the *; Mt 13:39
prepared for the * and his demons. Mt 25:41
and the * told him, "I will Lk 4:6,7
When the * had ended all the Lk 4:13
God, but then the * comes and Lk 8:12
twelve of you, and one is a *." Jn 6:70
of your father the * and you love Jn 8:44
Foreigner! *!" Jn 8:48
During supper the * had already Jn 13:1
"You son of the *, full of every Act 13:10
there be between Christ and the *? 2Co 6:15
give a mighty foothold to the *. Eph 4:27
the * who had the power of death. Heb 2:14
unspiritual, inspired by the *. Jas 3:15
Resist the * and he will flee Jas 4:7
to destroy these works of the *. 1Jn 3:8
the * cannot get his hands on him. 1Jn 5:18
to suffer—for the * will soon throw Rev 2:10
serpent called the *, or Satan, the Rev 12:9
the world, for the * has come down Rev 12:12
old Serpent, the *, Satan—and bound Rev 20:2
Then the * who had betrayed them Rev 20:10

DEVIL-INSPIRED
of teachers with * ideas. 1Ti 4:1

DEVIL'S
Idle hands are the * workshop; Pro 16:27
to knock down the * strongholds. 2Co 10:4

DEVILISH
No, it was sin, * stuff that it Rom 7:13

DEVILS
king of *." Mt 12:24
* and every kind of evil spirit. Rev 18:2

DEVISE
Mordecai can * that will offset the Est 8:8f

DEVISES
Literally, "A worthless man * Pro 16:27f

DEVOTED
crop shall be * to the Lord, and Lev 19:24
Lord as a field * to him, and it Lev 27:21
However, anything utterly * to Lev 27:28
who was a * follower of the Lord. 1Ki 18:3,4
* to the service of the Temple. 2Ch 31:17,18
Oh, for a king who is * to his Ecc 5:9
you entirely pure and * to God; 1Th 5:23

DEVOTEES
martyred among you by Satan's *. Rev 2:13

DEVOTION
absolute loyalty and exclusive *. Ex 34:14
And now, because of my * to the 1Ch 29:3
never give up your * and sacrifices Jer 44:25
at your side with such real *. 1Co 16:16
pure and simple * to our Lord, just 2Co 11:3
require strong * and are Col 2:23

DEVOUR
I will * them! Deu 32:24
Death shall * him. Job 18:13
A raging fire will * his goods, Job 20:26
For they * my people like bread Ps 53:4
Jehovah who has not let them * us. Ps 124:6
disdainful. They * the poor with Pro 30:13,14
With bared fangs they will * Is 9:11,12
of the forest, * my people. Is 56:9
The sword shall * until it is Jer 46:10
shall * all around you. Jer 46:14
War shall * her horses and Jer 50:37
famine and disease will * you. Eze 7:15
stalking prey. They * many lives; Eze 22:25
whole earth will * you until they Eze 32:4
and wild animals to * you. Eze 39:4
to it, "Get up! * many people!" Dan 7:5
it will * the whole world, Dan 7:23
and like a lion I will * you. Hos 13:8
You * them, flog them, break Mic 3:3
preparations, the fire will * you; Nah 3:15

DEVOURED
And * Num 21:27-30
All who found them * them and Jer 50:7
of its branches and * its fruit." Eze 19:14f
strong. It * some of its victims by Dan 7:7
They will be * like first-ripe Nah 3:12
For the whole land will be * by Zep 1:18
All the earth shall be * with the Zep 3:8

DEVOURING
He is a * fire, a jealous God. Deu 4:24
go before you as a * fire to Deu 9:3
of the flesh he is *—the flesh of Deu 28:55
and with * flames and tornados and Is 30:30
is coming, and is * the land and Jer 8:16
waters and was * the entire land. Amo 7:4

DEVOURS
that prowls. He * his enemies in Gen 49:27
My sword * the flesh and blood Deu 32:40,41
Literally, "the sword * now one 2Sa 11:25f
the sword of the Lord * from one Jer 12:12
ancestral home—and * the land from Jer 48:45
is a land that * her people!' Eze 36:13

DEVOUT
He was a good man, very *, filled Lk 2:25
Literally, "* men." Act 8:2f
the Jews and the * Gentiles, and Act 17:17

DEW
around the camp was wet with *; Ex 16:13
and when the * disappeared later Ex 16:14
The manna fell with the * during Num 11:9
Like the gentle rain and *, Deu 32:2
but the ground was covered with *! Ju 6:40
Let there be no * nor rain upon 2Sa 1:21
won't be any * or rain for several 1Ki 17:1
did prospered; the * lay all night Job 29:19
Where does * come from? Job 38:28
renewed day by day like morning *. Ps 110:3
refreshing as the * on Mount Ps 133:3
as refreshing as the * on grass. Pro 19:12
the night and am covered with *.' Sol 5:2
life will fall like * upon them! Is 26:19
Let him be wet with the * of Dan 4:23
your back wet with * from heaven. Dan 4:25
cows, and his body was wet with *; Dan 4:33
was wet with the * of heaven, until Dan 5:21
moisture and for *—and the whole Hos 1:21,22
clouds, and disappears like *. Hos 6:4

DEW Con't)
morning mist, like * that quickly Hos 13:3
I will refresh Israel like the * Hos 14:5
like a gentle * or the welcome Mic 5:7
DEWS
Let the * of heaven drench him Dan 4:15
DIADEM
glory, the * of beauty to his Is 28:5
DIAGRAM
See * 4, page 000. Eze 40:6f
See * 5, page 000. Eze 40:28f
See * 6, page 000. Eze 43:13f
See * 7, page 000. Eze 47:13f
See * 7, page 000. Eze 48:8f
DIAGRAMS
See * 1, 2, 3, pages 000, 000, and Eze 40:5f
DIAL
as measured on Ahaz' sun *!" Is 38:8
DIALECT
(in their local *, of course), Act 14:11
DIALECTS
in its own languages and *; Est 3:12
the languages and * of all the Est 8:9,10
DIAMOND
an emerald, a sapphire, and a *. Ex 28:18
an emerald, a sapphire, and a *. Ex 39:11
an iron pen or * point upon their Jer 17:1
stone—ruby, topaz, *, chrysolite, Eze 28:13
from a glittering *, or from a Rev 4:3
DIANA
shrines of the Greek goddess *. Act 19:24
the great goddess * will lose its Act 19:27
and that *—this magnificent goddess Act 19:27
"Great is * of the Ephesians!" Act 19:28
"Great is * of the Ephesians! Act 19:34
Great is * of the Ephesians!" Act 19:34
of the religion of the great *, Act 19:35
DIBLAIM
Gomer, daughter of *, and she Hos 1:3
DIBON
As far as *, Nophah, and Medeba. Num 21:27-30
*, Jazer, Nimrah, Heshbon, Elealeh, Num 32:3,4
*, Ataroth, Aroer, Num 32:34,35,36
the tableland of Medeba to *; Jos 13:9
on the plain—*, Bamoth-baal, Jos 13:17
Kiriath-arba, *, Jekabzeel (and Neh 11:25-30
Your people in * go mourning to Is 15:2
The stream near * will run red Is 15:9
but I am not through with * yet! Is 15:9
dust, O people of *, for those Jer 48:18
Moab shall shatter * too, and tear Jer 48:18
Mepha-ath, and * and Nebo and Jer 48:22
DIBON-GAD
From there they went to *, and Num 33:45
DIBRI
daughter of * of the tribe of Dan. Lev 24:11
DICE
by throwing * before the Lord, and Jos 14:1
throw the sacred * to decide which Jos 18:5,6
by the throw of the sacred *. Jos 18:8
by the toss of the sacred *. Jos 21:8
"cast lots," a form of *. Neh 10:34f
was determined by throwing *. Est 3:7
determined by a throw of the *; Est 9:24,25
*" in Persian is "pur." Est 9:26
themselves by a toss of the *. Ps 22:18
Literally, "cast * into the Pro 16:33f
the soldiers threw * to divide up Mt 27:35
him—and threw * for his clothes. Mk 15:24
Probably by throwing * or Lk 1:8,9f
throwing * for each piece. Lk 23:34
"Let's throw * to see who gets Jn 19:23,24
"cast lots," or, "threw *." Act 1:26f
DICTATE
Did Jeremiah himself * them to Jer 36:17
and * to strong nations far away. Mic 4:3
DICTATED
secretaries and * letters to the Est 3:12
wrote as Mordecai *—a decree to the Est 8:9,10
and as Jeremiah *, Baruch wrote Jer 36:4
that Jeremiah had * them to him Jer 36:18
another scroll and * again to Jer 36:32
* this sentence to me: "Blessed Rev 19:9
DICTATING
as Jeremiah was * them to him: Jer 45:1
DICTATOR
king or ruler or * or leader. Eph 1:21
DIE
fruit, you will be doomed to *." Gen 2:16,17
or even touch it, or we will *." Gen 3:2,3
"You'll not *! Gen 3:4
All will *. Gen 6:17
and reptiles I have made will *." Gen 7:4
Man-killing animals must *, and Gen 9:5,6
(But you will * in peace, at a Gen 15:15
here on the plain or you will *." Gen 19:17
"I don't want to watch him *," Gen 21:16
this man or his wife shall *." Gen 26:11
and expect to * 'most any day. Gen 27:2,3,4
before I *." Gen 27:2,3,4
I'd rather * than see Jacob marry Gen 27:46
"Give me children or I'll *," Gen 30:1
Let him *! Gen 31:32
are driven too hard, they will *. Gen 33:13
that way he'll * without our Gen 37:21,22
"I will * in mourning for my Gen 37:35
And now we are going to * because Gen 42:22
should happen to him, I would *." Gen 42:38
otherwise we will all * of Gen 43:8
any one of us, let that one *. Gen 44:9
father, for his father would *.' Gen 44:22
him, I shall * with sorrow.' Gen 44:29
is not with us, our father will *; Gen 44:31
I will go and see him before I * Gen 45:28
but you shall * in Egypt with Gen 46:3,4
"Now let me *, for I have seen you Gen 46:30
for why should we *?" Gen 47:15
Why should we *? Gen 47:19
near for him to *, he called for Gen 47:29
"I am about to *, but God will be Gen 48:21
he told them, "Soon I will *. Gen 49:29,30
"Soon I will *," Joseph told Gen 50:24
The fish will * and the river Ex 7:18
the frogs will * at the time you Ex 8:9
fields will * beneath the hail!" Ex 9:19
"The day you do, you shall *." Ex 10:28
And all the oldest sons shall * Ex 11:5
nor shall any of their animals *. Ex 11:7
us out here to * in the desert Ex 14:11
"Must we * of thirst?" Ex 15:24
Why did you bring us here to *, Ex 17:3
whoever does shall *— no hand Ex 19:12
try to see God, for they will *. Ex 19:21
bed, but doesn't *, if later he is Ex 21:18
However, if the slave does not * Ex 21:21
Holy Place, so that he will not *. Ex 28:35
Place, lest they be guilty and *. Ex 28:43
before doing so, or they will *. Ex 30:20
does not obey this command must *; Ex 31:14,15
anyone working on that day must * Ex 35:2
them, "you will *—this is what the Lev 8:35
into the Tabernacle, lest you *; Lev 10:8,9
lest they * because of defiling my Lev 15:31
thus he will not *. Lev 16:13
both the man and the woman must * Lev 20:11
bear their sin and * childless. Lev 20:20
and * for violating these rules. Lev 22:9
must pay the penalty: he must *. Lev 24:15,16
He must *. Lev 24:15,16
and whoever kills a man must *. Lev 24:21
they will * beneath your swords. Lev 26:7
to * may pay a fine instead; Lev 27:29
touch the holy items, lest they *. Num 4:15
that they will not * when they Num 4:17,18,19
the sacred objects there and *." Num 4:20
all * here in this wilderness! Num 14:29
shall * here in this wilderness.' Num 14:34,35
and * in his sin." Num 15:31
"The man must *—all the people Num 15:35
If these men * a natural death Num 16:29
to perform these duties shall *." Num 18:7
lest they be judged guilty and *. Num 18:22
they were common, lest you *." Num 18:32
come for Aaron to *—for he shall Num 20:24
and Aaron shall * there." Num 20:26
to * here in the wilderness?" Num 21:5
If only I could * as happy as an Num 23:7-10
shall * in the wilderness." Num 26:64,65
seen it, you shall * as Aaron your Num 27:13
idolatry, and then you must *." Num 31:1
murder, and the murderer shall *. Num 35:17
no man shall * with only one Num 35:30
of murder, he must *—no ransom may Num 35:31
said would * in the wilderness. Deu 1:39
I must * here on this side of the Deu 4:21,22
a man may speak to God and not *; Deu 5:24
but we will surely * if he Deu 5:25
fire on the mountain, lest you *. Deu 18:16
his message is from me, shall *. Deu 18:20
a message from other gods must *.' Deu 18:20
You might * in battle and someone Deu 20:6
For you might * in the battle, Deu 20:7
the country, only the man shall *. Deu 22:25,26,27
the kidnapper must *, in order to Deu 24:7
time has come when you must *. Deu 31:14
shall * and join your ancestors. Deu 31:16
the land you must * and join your Deu 32:50
against your commands, he shall *. Jos 1:17,18
oldest son would *, and when the Jos 6:26
set up, his youngest son would *. Jos 6:26
of all the earth—I am going to *. Jos 23:14
Dared to * upon the fields of Ju 5:18
You shall not *." Ju 6:23
"He must * for insulting the Ju 6:30
You are the ones who should * for Ju 6:31
"We will *," Manoah cried out Ju 13:22
Must I now * of thirst, and fall Ju 15:18
"Let me * with the Ju 16:30
anyone who refused to come must *. Ju 21:5
I want to * where you die, and Ru 1:17
I want to die where you *, and Ru 1:17
Every member will * before his 1Sa 2:31
and their children shall * by the 1Sa 2:33
Phinehas, to * on the same day! 1Sa 2:34
country, lest the entire city *. 1Sa 5:11
Those who didn't * were deathly 1Sa 5:12
"Pray for us lest we *!" 1Sa 12:19
son Jonathan, he shall surely *!" 1Sa 14:39
but now I must *." 1Sa 14:43
Saul said, "you must *; 1Sa 14:44
who saved Israel today, shall *? 1Sa 14:45
Amalekites or else * with them. 1Sa 15:6
it when he said that David must *. 1Sa 20:33
"You shall *, Ahimelech, along 1Sa 22:16
he will * in battle or of old age. 1Sa 26:10
ought to * for your carelessness. 1Sa 26:16
Must I * on foreign soil, far 1Sa 26:20
"You * self-condemned," David 2Sa 1:16
or be sterile, or * of starvation, 2Sa 3:29
For when you *, I will put one 2Sa 7:12
back and leave him there to *! 2Sa 11:15
you, and you won't * for this sin. 2Sa 12:13
him, so your child shall *." 2Sa 12:14
All of us must * eventually; 2Sa 14:14
otherwise he will *, and his 2Sa 17:16
and half of us *, it will make no 2Sa 18:3
not Shime-i *, for he cursed the 2Sa 19:21
Then let me return again to * in 2Sa 19:37
but if he does not, he shall *." 1Ki 1:52
to do—don't let him * in peace. 1Ki 2:6
Adonijah does not * this very day 1Ki 2:23,24
"No," he said, "I'll * here." 1Ki 2:30
you go beyond Kidron Brook, you *; 1Ki 2:36,37
of God to stay in Jerusalem or *? 1Ki 2:42
his sons, "When I *, bury me in 1Ki 13:31
of your family who * in the city 1Ki 14:11
and those who * in the field shall 1Ki 14:11
into the city, the child will *. 1Ki 14:12
Those of your family who * in 1Ki 16:4-7
and those who * in the fields will 1Ki 16:4-7
son and I must * of starvation." 1Ki 17:12
bush and prayed that he might *. 1Ki 19:4
I've got to * sometime, and it 1Ki 19:4
if he gets away, you must *, or 1Ki 20:39
man I said must *, now you must die 1Ki 20:42
die, now you must * in his place, 1Ki 20:42
The members of your family who * 1Ki 21:24
dogs and those who * in the country 1Ki 21:24
to go and * at Ramoth-gilead?' 1Ki 22:20
he will surely *.' 2Ki 1:4,5
you will surely *.' 2Ki 1:6
you will surely *." 2Ki 1:16
"Why sit here until we *?" 2Ki 7:3
here and * with the rest of us!" 2Ki 7:13
shown me that he will surely *!" 2Ki 8:10
prepare to *," Isaiah told him. 2Ki 20:1
until after you *—you will not see 2Ki 22:20
is over and you *, I will place one 1Ch 17:11
to do this must *—whether old or 2Ch 15:13
fathers shall not * for the 2Ch 25:4
staying there—to * by famine and 2Ch 32:11
them to * in the wilderness! Neh 9:19
is doomed to * unless the king Est 4:11
but you and your relatives will *; Est 4:14
I shall have nothing when I *. Job 1:21
Curse him and *." Job 2:9
"Why didn't I * at birth? Job 3:11
relief when at last they *! Job 3:22
They * beneath the hand of God. Job 4:9
out. They * and no one cares. Job 4:21
They * in helpless frustration, Job 5:2
I long for most—to * beneath his Job 6:8,9
How can I be patient till I *? Job 6:11
so those who * shall go away Job 7:9
I would rather * of Job 7:15
in the dust and *, and when you Job 7:21
Why didn't you let me * at birth? Job 10:18
All wisdom will * with you! Job 12:2
would stop defending myself and *. Job 13:19
"If I *, I go out into darkness, Job 17:13,14
He shall * from the roots up, Job 18:16
to life when anyone else would *. Job 24:22,23
until I * I will vow my Job 27:5
will * in war, or starve to death. Job 27:14
"I thought, 'Surely I shall * Job 29:18
wife, then may I *, and may my Job 31:10
Do not make him *, for I have Job 33:23,24
He did not let me *. Job 33:28
In a moment they *, and at Job 34:20
in battle and * because of their Job 36:12
They * young after lives of Job 36:14
though they *, for God has Job 39:16
For if I * I cannot give you Ps 6:5
let him *. Ps 7:16
me light in my darkness lest I *. Ps 13:3
to *—shall worship him. Ps 22:29
me, I might as well give up and *. Ps 28:1
at my fall—let them *. Ps 35:19
but those cursed by him shall *. Ps 37:22
he soon * and be forgotten!" Ps 41:5
He will be our guide until we *. Ps 48:14
You must * like all the rest! Ps 49:10
But man with all his pomp must * Ps 49:12

(DIE Con't)
though after they * they will be Ps 49:13
is gone when they *; Ps 49:14
For when they * they carry Ps 49:17
must * like any animal. Ps 49:20
and as those who * at birth, who Ps 58:8
They are doomed to * by the Ps 63:10
and those condemned to *. Ps 79:11
fall as any prince—for all must *. Ps 82:7
Make their mighty nobles * as Ps 83:11
let all their princes * like Ps 83:11
They have left me here to *, Ps 88:5
I have been sickly and ready to *. Ps 88:15
All will *. Ps 89:48
fall. We * beneath your anger; Ps 90:7
Don't let me * half through my Ps 102:24
they * and turn again to dust. Ps 104:29
May they *. Ps 109:12,13
he does not lightly let them *. Ps 116:15
I shall not *, but live to tell Ps 118:17
determined to obey you until I *. Ps 119:112
turn away from me or I shall *. Ps 143:7
for every man must *. Ps 146:4
They will * a violent death. Pro 1:19
He shall * because he will not Pro 5:23
a refuge when they *, but the Pro 14:32
that punishment, they will *. Pro 15:9,10
They won't * if you use a stick Pro 23:13,14
don't stand back and let them *. Pro 24:11,12
tired out, O God, and ready to *. Pro 30:2
from you before I *: First, help Pro 30:7
as the fool will *, so will I. Ecc 2:15
For the wise and fool both *, Ecc 2:16
A time to be born, a time to *; Ecc 3:2
breathe the same air, and both *. Ecc 3:19
and they * and others get it all! Ecc 6:2
For you are going to * and it is Ecc 7:2
some of the good * young and some Ecc 7:15-17
Why should you * before your Ecc 7:15-17
at least know that they will *! Ecc 9:5
the * is cast, for there it lies. Ecc 11:3
Their husbands shall * in Is 3:25,26
common people will * of thirst. Is 5:13
everything will *. Is 19:7
difference, for tomorrow we *." Is 22:13
forgiven you until the day you *. Is 22:14
there you will *, O glorious Is 22:18
in order, for you are going to *; Is 38:1
Anyone opposing you will *. Is 41:11
of the earth shall * like flies. Is 51:6
my righteous rule will never * Is 51:6
the godly * before their time and Is 57:1
For the godly who * shall rest Is 57:2
No longer will babies * when only Is 65:20
Only sinners will * that young! Is 65:20
me, for their worm shall never *; Is 66:24
They shall * beneath my anger. Jer 6:15
shall long to *, rather than live Jer 8:3
fruit trees will *, and all the Jer 8:13
"Why should we wait here to *? Jer 8:14
shall bite you and you will *. Jer 8:17
it in your anger, for I would *. Jer 10:24
And so their young men shall * in Jer 11:21,22
famine they themselves shall *! Jer 14:15
those who must * by the sword, to Jer 15:2
shall * from terrible diseases. Jer 16:4
They shall * from war and famine, Jer 16:4
Both great and small shall * in Jer 16:6
Let their men * in epidemics and Jer 18:21
and their youths * in battle! Jer 18:21
* by the swords of their enemies. Jer 20:4
in Babylon and * there—you and Jer 20:6
and both men and animals shall *. Jer 21:6
Stay here in Jerusalem and * Jer 21:9
He shall * in a distant land Jer 22:12
and you shall * in a foreign land. Jer 22:26
"This man should *!" Jer 26:11
from this land to *—you and all Jer 27:15
the Lord says you must *. Jer 28:16
For everyone shall * for his own Jer 31:30
there for many years until you *. Jer 32:5
but that you will * quietly among Jer 34:5
that dungeon, for I'll * there." Jer 37:20
in Jerusalem would * by sword, Jer 38:2
said: "Sir, this fellow must *. Jer 38:4
He will * of hunger, for almost Jer 38:9
house, for you would * there." Jer 38:26
Yes, you will * from sword, Jer 42:17
that you will * by sword, famine Jer 42:22
and many shall * of plague. Jer 43:11
all shall *, from the least to Jer 44:12
will fall in the streets and *; Jer 50:30
she shall *, says the Lord. Jer 51:53
Shall priests and prophets * Lam 2:20
those who * of slow starvation. Lam 4:9
life—they will * in their sins, but Eze 3:18
repent, they will * in their sins, Eze 3:19
help him—he shall * in his sin. Eze 3:20
One-third of you will * from Eze 5:12
and any who remain will * by Eze 6:12
All your boasting will * away, Eze 7:10,11
and he shall * there. Eze 12:13
those to death who should not *! Eze 13:19
a field and left to *, unwanted. Eze 16:5
my fury against you will * away; Eze 16:42
and let its leaves wither and *. Eze 17:9
Lord, the king of Israel shall *. Eze 17:16
shall * in Babylon, where the Eze 17:16
a man's own sins that he will *. Eze 18:4
He shall surely *, and it is his Eze 18:13
and obeys my laws—he shall not * Eze 18:17
But his father shall * for his Eze 18:18
he shall surely live and not *. Eze 18:21
think I like to see the wicked *? Eze 18:23
and he shall * for his sins. Eze 18:24
shall surely live—he shall not *. Eze 18:28
For why will you *, O Israel? Eze 18:31
I do not enjoy seeing you *, the Eze 18:32
tree will *, green and dry alike. Eze 20:47
All alike shall *. Eze 21:12
Suddenly, she will *. Eze 24:16
hell and you shall * as those Eze 28:8
You will * like an outcast at Eze 28:10
in the desert to *, and you won't Eze 29:5
and Bubastis shall * by the sword Eze 30:17
you stranded on the land to *. Eze 32:4
The Egyptians will * with the Eze 32:20
They will * in their sins, but I Eze 33:6
'O wicked man, you will *!' Eze 33:8
wicked person will * in his sins, Eze 33:8
doesn't, he will * in his sin, and Eze 33:9
for why will you *, O Israel? Eze 33:11
the wicked he will * and then he Eze 33:14
He shall not *. Eze 33:15
man turns to evil, he shall *. Eze 33:18
in the ruins shall * by the sword. Eze 33:27
and caves shall * of disease. Eze 33:27
armies will * upon the mountains. Eze 39:4
they would not * with the others. Dan 2:18
were willing to * rather than serve Dan 3:28
reign, he will * mysteriously, Dan 11:20
to waste away and * of thirst as in Hos 1:3
all living things grow sick and *; Hos 4:3
they shall * in shame, because Hos 4:19
your children will * at birth, or Hos 9:11
dry away, and he will * of thirst. Hos 13:15
wastelands where they will *; Joe 2:20
She is left alone to *." Amo 5:2
You yourself will * in a heathen Amo 7:17
touch us,' will * by the sword. Amo 9:10
"don't make us * for this man's Jon 1:14
he grew faint and wished to *. Jon 4:8
for me to be angry enough to *!" Jon 4:9
even if the flocks * in the Hab 3:17
all your loan sharks—all will *. Zep 1:11
If you *, you die; Zec 11:9
If you die, you *; Zec 11:9
'You must *,' they will tell him, Zec 13:3
of Israel will be cut off and *, Zec 13:8
was, 'If you kill, you must *.' Mt 5:21
who reviles his parents must *.' Mt 15:4
and they will condemn me to *. Mt 20:18
For I must * Mt 26:24
"I would * first!" Mt 26:35
been condemned to *, changed his Mt 27:3
his father or mother must *. Mk 7:10
sentence me to * and hand me over Mk 10:33
must *, as the prophets declared Mk 14:21
"Not even if I have to * with Mk 14:31
that he would not * until he had Lk 2:26
"Lord," he said, "now I can * Lk 2:29,30,31
right now will not * until you have Lk 9:27
Tonight you *. Lk 12:20
instead of waiting until you *!' Lk 15:12
lest they come here when they *.' Lk 16:28
And they never * again; Lk 20:36
must *. It is part of God's plan. Lk 22:22
you, and even to * with you." Lk 22:33
So Pilate sentenced Jesus to * as Lk 23:24
We deserve to * for our evil Lk 23:40,41
must suffer and * and rise again Lk 24:46
forever, and not * as your fathers Jn 6:58
and you will search for me, and * Jn 8:21
said that you will * in your sins; Jn 8:24
of God, you will * in your sins." Jn 8:24
one who obeys me shall ever *!" Jn 8:51
"Let's go too—and * with him." Jn 11:16
let this one man * for the Jn 11:50
This prophecy that Jesus should * Jn 11:51
"I must fall and * like a kernel Jn 12:23,24
Unless I * I will be alone—a Jn 12:23,24
to indicate how he was going to *. Jn 12:33
* -asked the crowd Jn 12:34
would live forever and never *. Jn 12:34
Why are you saying he will *? Jn 12:34
he asked, "for I am ready to * Jn 13:37
Jesus answered, "* for me? Jn 13:38
that one should * for all." Jn 18:14
laws he ought to * because he Jn 19:7
death he would * to glorify God. Jn 21:19
What sort of death will he *?" Jn 21:21
that that disciple wouldn't *! Jn 21:23
back to life again, no more to *. Act 13:34
but also to * for the sake of the Act 21:13
of death, I don't refuse to *! Act 25:10,11
* unless everyone stays aboard." Act 27:31
expect anyone to * for us, though, Rom 5:7
sending Christ to * for us while we Rom 5:8
began to grow old and *, Rom 5:12
the dead and will never * again. Rom 6:9
law and was a sinner, doomed to *. Rom 7:9
your body will * because of sin; Rom 8:10
again after you *, by means of this Rom 8:11
be sick again and will never *. Rom 8:23
who loved us enough to * for us. Rom 8:37
or * as we ourselves might choose. Rom 14:7
both while we live and when we *. Rom 14:9
But did I, Paul, * for your sins? 1Co 1:13
In fact, I would rather * of 1Co 9:15
again after we *, then we might as 1Co 15:32
For tomorrow we *, and that ends 1Co 15:32
bodies which * and decay are 1Co 15:42
life again, for they will never *. 1Co 15:42
us for they become sick and *; 1Co 15:43
we shall not all *, but we shall 1Co 15:51
bodies that will never, never *; 1Co 15:52
have now that can *, must be 1Co 15:53
We felt we were doomed to * and 2Co 1:9
must obey every law of God or *; 2Co 3:6
taken down—when we * and leave 2Co 5:1
quite content to *, for then we 2Co 5:8
forever and I live and * with you. 2Co 7:3
there was no need for Christ to *. Gal 2:21
sending Jesus Christ to * for us. Eph 1:5
I live or whether I must *. Php 1:20
which is better, to live or *! Php 1:22
* a criminal's death on a cross. Php 2:8
is, if I am to * for you—even then Php 2:17
means to suffer and to * with him. Php 3:10
away a single penny when we *. 1Ti 6:7
alone can never *, who lives in 1Ti 6:16
when we suffer and * for Christ it 2Ti 2:11
being could he * and in dying break Heb 2:14
* on the cross for all mankind. Heb 5:7f
that Christ should * prematurely, Heb 5:7f
himself to God to * for our sins—he Heb 9:14
would have had to * again and Heb 9:26
destined that men * only once, and Heb 9:27
Christ came to * on the cross. Heb 10:4f
* away, no matter what happens. Heb 10:35
the harlot did not * with all the Heb 11:31
preferring to * rather than turn Heb 11:35
He was willing to * a shameful Heb 12:2
touched the mountain it must *. Heb 12:20
They will soon * and leave behind Jas 1:10,11
his son Isaac to * on the altar? Jas 2:21
are numbered, and I am soon to *. 2Pe 1:13,14
God and will * under his curse. Jud 1:11
to rise from death, to * no more. Rev 1:5
rose to * again. Rev 1:5f
implies "to * no more." Rev 1:5f
They will long to *—but death Rev 9:6
refusing to worship it must *! Rev 13:15
Literally, "those who * in the Rev 14:13f

DIED

and * at the age of 930. Gen 5:3,4,5
and * at the age of 912. Gen 5:6,7,8
and * at the age of 905. Gen 5:9,10,11
and * at the age of 910. Gen 5:12,13,14
and * at the age of 895. Gen 5:15,16,17
and * at the age of 962. Gen 5:18,19,20
and * at the age of 969. Gen 5:25,26,27
and * at the age of 777. Gen 5:28-31
But Haran * young, in the land Gen 11:28
And there Terah * at the age of Gen 11:32
says that Terah * when he was 145 Gen 11:32f
* in Hebron in the land of Canaan; Gen 23:1
Then Abraham *, at the ripe old Gen 25:7,8
Ishmael finally * at the age of Gen 25:17
old nurse Deborah * and was buried Gen 35:8
breath (for she *) she named him Gen 35:18
So Rachel *, and was buried near Gen 35:19
Isaac * soon afterwards, at the Gen 35:28,29
process of time Judah's wife *. Gen 38:12
Er and Onan * while still in Gen 46:8-14
For your mother Rachel * after Gen 48:7
the bed, breathed his last, and *. Gen 49:33
"Before he *, your father Gen 50:16,17
was 110 years old when he *. Gen 50:22
So Joseph * at the age of 110, Gen 50:26
*, ending that generation. Ex 1:6
years later the king of Egypt *. Ex 2:23
The fish * and the water became Ex 7:21
three thousand men * that day. Ex 32:28
AFTER AARON'S TWO sons * before Lev 16:1
Except when the brother * and left Lev 18:16f
*, as Jehovah had commanded Moses. Lev 24:23
But Nadab and Abihu * before the Num 3:4
"We wish we had * in Egypt," Num 14:2
14,700 people had * (in addition to Num 16:49
* the previous day with Korah). Num 16:49
battle, or who has * in any other Num 19:16
where Miriam * and was buried. Num 20:1

(DIED Con't)
"Would that we too had * with our Num 20:3
and Aaron * on the top of the Num 20:28
many of them were bitten and *. Num 21:6
after 24,000 people had already *. Num 25:9
Onan who * in the land of Canaan: Num 26:19-22
But Nadab and Abihu * when they Num 26:61
counted then had *, as the Lord Num 26:64,65
"Our father * in the Num 27:3,4
until all that evil generation *. Num 32:13
into the mountain, and there he *. Num 33:38,39
old enough to bear arms, had *. Deu 2:14,15
where Aaron * and was buried. Deu 10:6
"Don't eat anything that has * a Deu 14:21
he should not have * since he had Deu 19:6,7
* in Mount Hor and joined them. Deu 32:50
of the Lord, * in the land of Moab Deu 34:5
Moses was 120 years old when he * Deu 34:7
generation had * during the years Jos 5:4,5
and many others * while being Jos 7:5
in a trap and all of them *; Jos 8:22
in fact, more men * from the hail Jos 10:11
Soon after this he * at the age Jos 24:29
Eleazar, the son of Aaron, also * Jos 24:33
AFTER JOSHUA *, the nation of Ju 1:1
taken to Jerusalem, and * there. Ju 1:7
Joshua, the man of God, * at the Ju 2:7-9
But finally all that generation * Ju 2:10
But when the judge *, the people Ju 2:19
unconquered by Joshua when he *. Ju 2:21
But when Othni-el *, the people Ju 3:11
and so he *, for he was fast Ju 4:21
Gideon finally *, an old, old Ju 8:32
So all the people inside *, about Ju 9:49
him with his sword, and he *. Ju 9:54
When he *, he was buried in Ju 10:2
When Jair * he was buried in Ju 10:5
of Ephraim * there at that time. Ju 12:6
he *, and was buried at Bethlehem. Ju 12:9,10
Then he * and was buried in Ju 12:15
so that about thirty of them *. Ju 20:31
troops * in that day's battle. Ju 20:44
there, Elimelech * and Naomi was Ru 1:3
But later, both men *, so that Ru 1:4,5
Thirty thousand men of Israel * 1Sa 4:10
and he * (for he was old and fat). 1Sa 4:18
Just before she *, the women who 1Sa 4:20
SHORTLY AFTERWARDS, SAMUEL * 1Sa 25:1
Literally, "his heart * within 1Sa 25:37,38f
for about ten days, then *, for 1Sa 25:37,38
(Meanwhile, Samuel had * and all 1Sa 28:3
upon his sword and * with him. 1Sa 31:5
troops * together that same day. 1Sa 31:6
men of Israel who had * that day. 2Sa 1:12
through with his sword and he *. 2Sa 1:15
For there the mighty Saul has *; 2Sa 1:21
side, so that all of them *. 2Sa 2:16
He stumbled to the ground and * 2Sa 2:23
"Should Abner have * like a 2Sa 3:33,34
so he * there beside the Ark. 2Sa 6:7
* and his son Hanun replaced him. 2Sa 10:1
on the seventh day, the baby *. 2Sa 12:18
so he * and was buried beside his 2Sa 17:23
If only I could have * for you! 2Sa 18:33
of us had *, you would be happy. 2Sa 19:6
to strike again, and he * there. 2Sa 20:8,9,10
So all seven of them * together 2Sa 21:9
had * in battle on Mount Gilboa. 2Sa 21:12,13,14
of fame to replace those who *. 2Sa 23:24-39f
and seventy thousand men * 2Sa 24:15
Then David * and was buried in 1Ki 2:10
But her baby * during the night 1Ki 3:19
soldiers who had * in battle, the 1Ki 11:15
years, and then * and was buried 1Ki 11:43
and the child * just as she 1Ki 14:17
*, his son Nadab took the throne. 1Ki 14:20
When Rehoboam *—his mother was 1Ki 14:31
When he * he was buried in 1Ki 15:8
and when he * he was buried in the 1Ki 15:24
it over him and * in the flames. 1Ki 16:18
When Omri * he was buried in 1Ki 16:28
his oldest son, Abiram, *; 1Ki 16:34
gates, his youngest son, Segub, *. 1Ki 16:34
the woman's son became sick and *. 1Ki 17:17
Finally, toward evening, he *. 1Ki 22:35
When King Jehoshaphat * he was 1Ki 22:50
So Ahaziah * as the Lord had 2Ki 1:17
some money when he *, and now the 2Ki 4:1
but around noontime he *. 2Ki 4:20
kill us, we would have * anyway." 2Ki 7:4
of Judah. He * and was buried in 2Ki 8:24,25
on as far as Megiddo, but * there. 2Ki 9:27
When Jehu *, he was buried in 2Ki 10:35
Jehoahaz * and was buried in 2Ki 13:9,10
Joash * and was buried in 2Ki 13:13
So Elisha * and was buried. 2Ki 13:20,21
Then King Hazael of Syria *, and 2Ki 13:24
When Joash *, he was buried in 2Ki 14:16
When Jeroboam II * he was buried 2Ki 14:29
When Azariah *, he was buried 2Ki 15:7
When he *, his son Pekahiah 2Ki 15:22
When Jotham * he was buried with 2Ki 15:38
When Ahaz * he was buried in the 2Ki 16:20
When he *, his son Manasseh 2Ki 20:21
When he * he was buried in the 2Ki 21:18
Jehoahaz to Egypt, where he *. 2Ki 23:34
When he *, his son Jehoiachin 2Ki 24:6
they were put to the sword and *. 2Ki 25:21
When Bela *, Jobab the son of 1Ch 1:44
When Jobab *, Husham from the 1Ch 1:45
When Husham *, Hadad the son of 1Ch 1:46
When Hadad *, Samlah from the 1Ch 1:47
When Samlah *, Shaul from the 1Ch 1:48
When Shaul *, Baal-hanan the son 1Ch 1:49
When Baal-hanan *, Hadad became 1Ch 1:50
Seled * without children, but 1Ch 2:30
Jether * without children, but 1Ch 2:32
of the enemy also * in the battle, 1Ch 5:22
So Saul and his three sons * 1Ch 10:6
Saul * for his disobedience to 1Ch 10:13
And so he * there before God. 1Ch 13:10
WHEN KING NAHASH of Ammon *, 1Ch 19:1
and 70,000 men * as a result. 1Ch 21:14
Eleazar * without any sons, and 1Ch 23:22
of Aaron, but they * before their 1Ch 24:1
in Jerusalem. He * at an old age, 1Ch 29:28
Then he * and was buried in 2Ch 9:31
When Rehoboam * he was buried in 2Ch 12:16
the Lord struck him and he *. 2Ch 13:20
So he * in the forty-first year 2Ch 16:13,14
sank into the western skies, he *. 2Ch 18:34
WHEN JEHOSHAPHAT *, he was 2Ch 21:1
and he * in terrible suffering. 2Ch 21:19
eight years, and * unmourned. 2Ch 21:20
Zechariah's last words as he * 2Ch 24:22
When Joash *, his son Amaziah 2Ch 24:27
When Uzziah *, he was buried in 2Ch 26:23
When he *, he was buried in 2Ch 27:9
When King Ahaz *, he was buried 2Ch 28:27
When Hezekiah * he was buried in 2Ch 32:33
When Manasseh * he was buried 2Ch 33:20,21
him back to Jerusalem where he *. 2Ch 35:24,25
For if only I had * at birth, Job 3:13
Then at last he *, an old, old Job 42:17
Their cattle * in the fields, Ps 78:48
and their girls * before they were Ps 78:63
and their widows * before they Ps 78:64
I would have * unless the Lord Ps 94:17
Men have * for saying the wrong Pro 18:21
THE YEAR KING Uzziah * I saw the Is 6:1
came to me the year King Ahaz *: Is 14:28
Others * that you might live; Is 43:4
oh, that I had * at birth. Jer 15:10
Oh, that I had * within my Jer 20:17
two months later Hananiah *. Jer 28:17
and pull Jeremiah out before he *. Jer 38:10
the year King Josiah *. Jer 47:1f
Our fathers sinned but * before Lam 5:7
any animal that * of sickness or Eze 4:14
(son of Benaiah) suddenly *. Eze 11:13
and in the evening my wife *. Eze 24:18
sorrow, as if your only son had *; Amo 8:10
so that it withered away and *. Jon 4:7
to be angry because the plant *?" Jon 4:9
him as for an oldest child who *. Zec 12:10
When Herod *, an angel of the Mt 2:19
"My little daughter has just * Mt 9:18
*, for they had so little root. Mt 13:6
said that if a man * without Mt 22:24
married and then *, without Mt 22:25
This brother also * without Mt 22:26
And then she also *. Mt 22:27
for foreigners who * in Jerusalem. Mt 27:7
dismissed his spirit, and *. Mt 27:50
who had * came back to life again. Mt 27:52
the hot sun and * because the roots Mk 4:5,6
and *, and left no children. Mk 12:20,21,22
he * too, and left no children. Mk 12:20,21,22
married her, and * without Mk 12:20,21,22
and last of all, the woman * too. Mk 12:20,21,22
just as he told you before he *!' Mk 16:7
The boy who had * was the only Lk 7:12
and * for lack of moisture. Lk 8:6
Then, as the voice * away, Jesus Lk 9:36
when his father *, collect the Lk 9:59f
eighteen men who * when the Tower Lk 13:4
Finally the beggar * and was Lk 16:22
The rich man also * and was Lk 16:22
The oldest married and then * Lk 20:29
married the widow and he, too, *. Lk 20:30
her and *, leaving no children. Lk 20:31
Finally the woman * also. Lk 20:32
you," and with those words he *. Lk 23:46
bread from the skies, they all *. Jn 6:48-51
mightiest prophets *, and yet you Jn 8:52
than our father Abraham, who *? Jn 8:53
greater than the prophets, who *? Jn 8:53
But Jesus meant Lazarus had *. Jn 11:12,13
here, my brother wouldn't have *. Jn 11:21
for he * and was buried, and his Act 2:29
*, and his followers scattered. Act 5:37
in Syria, until his father *. Act 7:4
where he *, and all his sons. Act 7:15
and with that, he *. Act 7:60
this time she became ill and *. Act 9:37
with maggots and *—because he Act 12:23
will of God, he * and was buried, Act 13:36
who *, but Paul insists is alive! Act 25:19
from the dead. He * for our sins Rom 4:25
the right time and * for us sinners Rom 5:6
So when their bodies * it was Rom 5:14
by baptism when he *, and when God Rom 6:4
of him, and so you * with him, so Rom 6:5
with him, so to speak, when he * Rom 6:5
nature "*" with Christ, we know Rom 6:8
over him. He * once for all to end Rom 6:10
but you "*," as it were, with Rom 7:4
because you "*" while in their Rom 7:6
For he is the one who * for us Rom 8:34
Jesus Christ when he * for us. Rom 8:39
has * to make them right with God. Rom 10:3
Christ * and rose again for this Rom 14:9
ruin someone for whom Christ *. Rom 14:15
lost, when they hear that Jesus * 1Co 1:18
conscience for whom Christ *. 1Co 8:11
did, and * from snake bites. 1Co 10:9
death, that he has * for you. 1Co 11:26
and sick, and some have even *. 1Co 11:30
to me, that Christ * for our sins 1Co 15:3
alive, though some have * by now. 1Co 15:6
Christians who have * are lost! 1Co 15:18
and all the Christians who have * 1Co 15:52
Since we believe that Christ * 2Co 5:13,14
* to the old life we used to live. 2Co 5:13,14
used to live. He * for all so that 2Co 5:15
who * and rose again for them. 2Co 5:15
His weak, human body * on the 2Co 13:4
Jesus Christ. He * for our sins Gal 1:4
I through the law * unto the law, Gal 2:19f
Gentiles, for he * to annul that Eph 2:15
the church when he * for her, to Eph 5:25
in fact, he almost *. Php 2:27
News that Jesus * for you, and Col 1:23
old, evil nature * with him and was Col 2:12
Since you *, as it were, with Col 2:20
believe that Jesus * and then came 1Th 4:14
him all the Christians who have *. 1Th 4:14
Jesus Christ; he * for us so that 1Th 5:10
the living God who * for all, and 1Ti 4:9,10
husbands have *, if they don't have 1Ti 5:3
Jesus Christ. He * under God's Tit 2:14
He is the one who * to cleanse us Heb 1:3
as a result * in the wilderness. Heb 3:17
He was never born and he never * Heb 7:3
the older ones * off, the system Heb 7:23
For Christ * to rescue them from Heb 9:15
so also Christ * only once as an Heb 9:28
I have mentioned * without ever Heb 11:13
He believed that if Isaac * God Heb 11:19
Some * by stoning and some by Heb 11:37,38
That is why Jesus suffered and * Heb 13:12
own body when he * on the cross, so 1Pe 2:24
Christ also suffered. He * once 1Pe 3:18
But though his body *, his spirit 1Pe 3:18
Christ * to wash away our sins. 1Jn 1:9
and the voice before he *. 1Jn 5:6,7,8
the Living One who *, who is now Rev 1:17,18
on the earth and many people *. Rev 8:11
everything in all the oceans *. Rev 16:3
The scarlet animal that * is the Rev 17:11

DIES
he * shall surely be put to death. Ex 21:12
and she *, he shall be executed. Ex 21:23
another, and it *, then the two Ex 21:35
for him, and it *, or is hurt, or Ex 22:10
The fat of an animal that * of Lev 7:24
permitted to eat * of disease, Lev 11:39
of an animal that * of itself, or Lev 17:15
However, if your wife *, then it Lev 18:18
He may not eat any animal that * Lev 22:8
comes close to the Tabernacle *. Num 17:12,13
"When a man * in a tent, these Num 19:14
you, that if a man * and has no Num 27:8
so that he *, he is a murderer; Num 35:21
enemy—yet the man *, then the Num 35:22,23
divorces her, or *, the former Deu 24:3
"If a man's brother * without a Deu 25:5
few moments of relief before he *. , Job 14:6
But when a man * and is buried, Job 14:10
"If a man *, shall he live Job 14:14
Before he *, all this futility Job 15:32
yet in the end he * like everyone Ps 49:19
When an evil man *, his hopes Pro 11:7
When a good man *, he leaves an Pro 13:22
but when a sinner *, his wealth Pro 13:22
when courage *, what hope is left? Pro 18:14
The day one * is better than the Ecc 7:1
the grass that * away, and all his Is 40:6
will not weep for him when he *. Jer 22:18
The one who sins is the one who *. Eze 18:20
begins sinning and * in his sins, Eze 18:26
he * for the evil he has done. Eze 18:26
if he * the fault is his own. Eze 33:4

(DIES Con't)
or animal that * a natural death or Eze 44:31
death or that * after being Eze 44:31
the worm never *, and the fire Mk 9:48
own the farm when his father *. Mk 12:7
that when a man * without children, Mk 12:19
all the land when his father *. Lk 20:14
that if a man * without children, Lk 20:28
come now before my child *." Jn 4:49
the stones at her until she *. Jn 8:7
me, even though he * like anyone Jn 11:25
that when a person * the law no Rom 7:1
But if he *, she is no longer Rom 7:2
is perfectly all right after he *. Rom 7:3
if her husband *, then she may 1Co 7:39
Everyone * because all of us are 1Co 15:22
a plant unless it "*" first. 1Co 15:36
that if a father * and leaves great Gal 4:1
Christian when he * so that when it 1Th 4:13
ages, the unseen one who never *; 1Ti 1:17
Now, if someone * and leaves a Heb 9:16
people when he *—no one gets Heb 9:16

DIET
* of only vegetables and water; Dan 1:12
not to let them continue their *. Dan 1:13

DIETARY
See the * laws Ezekiel here refers Eze 4:14f

DIFFER
And the stars * from each other 1Co 15:41
Commentators * widely in their 1Jn 5:17f

DIFFERED
The number of sacrifices * from 2Ch 8:13

DIFFERENCE
to teach them the * between what is Lev 10:10
For it makes no * to him how many 1Sa 14:6
it will make no * to them—they will 2Sa 18:3
well and know the * between what is 1Ki 3:9
Don't I know the * between right Job 6:30
and provoke God—it makes no *! Job 12:6
soul and meditate upon the * now. Ps 77:6
come and go but it makes no *. Ecc 1:3-7
merry, for it makes no * to God! Ecc 9:7
the *, for tomorrow we die." Is 22:13
There is a * between chaff and Jer 23:28
my people the * between right and Eze 22:26
The only * was that it had eight Eze 40:31
"He shall teach my people the * Eze 44:23
But it will make no *, for Dan 11:27
But what's the *? Hos 10:3
Then you will see the * between Mal 3:18
the * the next time I am here.' Lk 10:35
*, for the world can't hate you; Jn 7:6
And what a * between man's sin Rom 5:15
that it makes no * to the Lord Rom 15:1
For it doesn't make any * at all 1Co 7:19
But it makes a lot of * whether 1Co 7:19
It makes no * who worked the 1Co 15:11
What's the *? 1Co 15:32
leaders made no * to me, for all Gal 2:6
(And there is this further *. Gal 3:19
It doesn't make any * now Gal 6:15
to see clearly the * between right Php 1:10
the * between right and wrong. Heb 5:12,13
the * between true and false. 1Jn 2:21

DIFFERENT
down and give them * languages, so Gen 11:7
But it will be very * in the Ex 8:22
and that we are * from any other Ex 33:16
mate your cattle with a * kind; Lev 19:19
his gift on a * day for the Num 7:11
"* trumpet blasts will be Num 10:5,6,7
But my servant Caleb is a * kind Num 14:24
will feel and act like a * person. 1Sa 10:6
matter before you in a * light. 2Sa 14:20
Why would you be any *? 2Ki 19:11
* language groups), and Joktan. 1Ch 1:19
Apparently a * Sheshan than in 1Ch 2:34,35f
their laws are * from those of any Est 3:8
But for sinners, what a * story! Ps 1:4
It would be *, Lord, if I were Ps 7:3
But the good man—what a * story! Ps 37:37
"If their messages are * than Is 8:20
will be no * than she was before; Is 23:17
Do you think you will be any *? Is 37:11
* to happen—Israel shall seek him! Jer 31:22
I will prepare a * kind of feast Jer 51:39
So you are * from other Eze 16:33,34
the water, each * from the other. Dan 7:3
it will be a very * story from Dan 11:29
But all is * now, because you Hag 2:15
"But it is all so * now!" Zec 8:11
In those days ten men from ten * Zec 8:23
how are you * from anyone else? Mt 5:47
with thistles. * kinds of fruit Mt 7:17
leaders of two * parties. Mt 16:1f
But among you it is quite *. Mt 20:26
but among you it is *. Mk 10:43
until the day I drink a * kind Mk 14:25
"You're * from most. Jn 2:10
But now God has shown us a * way Rom 3:21,22
into effect a * plan to save us. Rom 8:3
but be a new and * person with a Rom 12:2
for we each have * work to do. Rom 12:4,5
Don't criticize him for having * Rom 14:1
life aren't anything new and *. 1Co 10:13
There are * kinds of service to 1Co 12:5
are hundreds of * languages in the 1Co 14:10
* from the seed you first planted. 1Co 15:37
it to have; a * kind of plant grows 1Co 15:38
And just as there are * kinds of 1Co 15:39
also there are * kinds of flesh. 1Co 15:39
fish, and birds are all *. 1Co 15:39
in heaven have bodies far * from 1Co 15:40
of their bodies is * from the 1Co 15:40
die and decay are * from the bodies 1Co 15:42
the Lord commends him, that's *! 2Co 10:18
we preach, or a * spirit than the 2Co 11:4
or shows you a * way to be saved. 2Co 11:4
Five * times the Jews gave me 2Co 11:24
Three * times I begged God to 2Co 12:8
you are already following a * Gal 1:6
How * from this way of faith Gal 3:12
this would be a * way of gaining Gal 3:18
had to give us a * way to get out Gal 3:21,22
changed into new and * people. Gal 6:15
told us something *, or has Eph 4:14
Yes, you must be a new and * Eph 4:24
Anyone who says anything * is 1Ti 6:4
LONG AGO GOD spoke in many * Heb 1:1
sent them safely away by a * road. Jas 2:25
something quite * from what he 2Pe 3:15,16
of your first love (how * now! Rev 2:5

DIFFERENTLY
Here it is used * to describe Is 4:2,3,4f
like myself. How * I feel now! 2Co 5:16

DIFFICULT
Bring me any cases too * for you, Deu 1:17
nothing was too * for him, for 1Ki 10:3
they were already having a * time. Neh 5:18
Wisdom is far away; and very * Ecc 7:24
to tribes with strange, * tongues. Eze 3:6
"You say, 'Oh, it's too * to Mal 1:13
that made it * to keep the ship on Act 27:4
these are * days. Eph 5:15,16
to be very * to be a Christian. 2Ti 3:1
otherwise would be dark and *. 2Pe 1:19

DIFFICULTIES
A prudent man foresees the * Pro 22:3
and hardships, persecutions and *; 2Co 12:10
life full of * and temptations? Jas 1:2

DIFFICULTY
for three years without *; 2Ch 11:17
When you go through rivers of *, Is 43:2
its site is with * discovered." Zep 2:15f
wind with great * and moving slowly Act 27:7,8
where with great * we hoisted Act 27:16
in helping me in my present *. Php 4:14

DIG
wells you didn't *, and vineyards Deu 6:10,11,12
movement he must * a hole with the Deu 23:13
refine gold, to * iron from the Job 28:2
* a well—and fall into it! Ecc 10:8,9
and people, and * out their bones Jer 8:2
"Now * into the wall," he said. Eze 8:8
to distant lands. * a tunnel Eze 12:5
"Though they * down to Sheol, I Amo 9:2
to go out and * ditches, and I'm Lk 16:3

DIGEST
you couldn't * anything stronger. 1Co 3:2
for food and stomachs to * it. 1Co 6:13

DIGESTIVE
through the * tract and out again? Mt 15:17
passes through the * system." Mk 7:19

DIGGING
—in the well they had been *. Gen 26:32
her hands * into the threshold. Ju 19:27

DIGNIFIED
love to parade in * robes and to be Lk 20:46

DIGNITY
that will lend * to his work. Ex 28:2
and will make you walk with *. Lev 26:13
She is a woman of strength and *, Pro 31:25
given their rightful place of *! Ecc 10:6

DIGS
"If a man * a well and doesn't Ex 21:33

DIKLAH
Hadoram, Uzal, *, Obal, Abima-el, Gen 10:26-30
Hadoram, Uzal, *, Ebal, Abima-el, 1Ch 1:20-23

DILEAN
Zenan, Hadashah, Migdal-gad, *, Jos 15:37-44

DILIGENCE
let it be obeyed with all *." Ez 6:12

DILIGENT
hunting, but the * man makes good Pro 12:27
while the * are prospering. Pro 13:4

DILL
A sledge is never used on *, but Is 28:27

DILUTED
Once so pure, but now * like Is 1:22

DILUTING
ideas, for fear of * the mighty 1Co 1:17

DIM
My eyes are * with weeping and I Job 17:7
My eyes are growing old and * Ps 6:7
My eyes grow * with weeping. Ps 88:9
My eyes grow * with longing for Ps 119:123
moon and stars are * to your old Ecc 12:2
* when poverty stalks the land. Is 17:4
our eyes grow *. Lam 5:17
the sun will grow * and the moon Mk 13:24
Let their eyes be *," he said, Rom 11:10
laws gave only a * foretaste of the Heb 10:1

DIME
words of fools are a * a dozen. Pro 10:20

DIMENSIONS
identical in all *, and each was 1Ki 6:23-28
He jotted down its * and made a 2Ki 16:10
Do you know how its * were Job 38:5
its other *—1,500 miles each way. Rev 21:16

DIMLY
nor quench the * burning flame. Is 42:3
Literally, "He will not burn * or Is 42:4f

DIMMED
the daylight was * by a third, and Rev 8:12

DIMMER
spots are growing *, this is not Lev 13:39

DIMNAH
Jokne-am, Kartah, *, and Nahalal. Jos 21:34,35

DIMONAH
Kabzeel, Eder, Jagur, Kinah, *, Jos 15:21-32

DINAH
to a daughter and named her *. Gen 30:21
ONE DAY *, Leah's daughter, went Gen 34:1
much in love with *, and could, he Gen 34:18,19
They rescued * from Shechem's Gen 34:26
their daughter *, born to Jacob in Gen 46:15

DINAH'S
Then Shechem addressed * father Gen 34:11
they made, two of * brothers, Gen 34:25

DINE
wine and * and sleep with my wife? 2Sa 11:11

DINHABAH
King Bela (son of Beor), from * in Gen 36:31-39
Beor), who lived in the city of *. 1Ch 1:43

DINING
* service was made of solid gold. 1Ki 10:21
and daughters were * at the oldest Job 1:12,13
WHEN * WITH a rich man, Pro 23:1
Why are yours wining and *?" Lk 5:33

DINNER
for * either yesterday or today?" 1Sa 20:27
David invited him to * and got 2Sa 11:13
passed that way, he stopped for *. 2Ki 4:8
There they sit around the * table Ps 128:3
Gedaliah invited them to *. Jer 41:1
palace and went to bed without *. Dan 6:18
were eating * [at Matthew's house Mt 9:10
a great wedding * for his son. Mt 22:1
got up and prepared * for them! Mk 1:31
sinners to be his * guests so that Mk 2:15
over the big * she was preparing. Lk 10:40
who came to the * were trying to Lk 14:7
"When you put on a *," he said, Lk 14:12
guests home for * or, if they need Rom 12:13
asks you out to *, go ahead; 1Co 10:27

DIONYSIUS
Among them was *, a member of the Act 17:34

DIOTREPHES
this, but proud *, who loves to 3Jn 1:9

DIP
branches and * them into the lamb's Ex 12:22
and shall * his finger in the Lev 4:6
and shall * his finger in the Lev 4:17
left hand, and * his right finger Lev 14:16
bowl, and * the cedar wood, hyssop Lev 14:51,52
branches and * them into the water Num 19:18
here if only to * the tip of his Lk 16:24
When this was done he said, "* Jn 2:7,8
shall * the sop and give it him." Jn 13:26f

DIPHATH
Ashkenaz, *, and Togarmah. 1Ch 1:5-9

DIPLOMACY
in international * at this time. Is 36:11f

DIPPED
for him, and he * his finger in it Lev 9:9
living, shall be * in the blood, Lev 14:6
parched grain and * her morsels of Ru 2:14f
so he * a stick into a honeycomb, 1Sa 14:27
Jordan River and * himself seven 2Ki 5:14
took a blanket and * it in water 2Ki 8:15
Literally, "he that * his hand Mt 26:23f
often * into them for his own use! Jn 12:6
giving the bread * in the sauce." Jn 13:26
And when he had * it, he gave it Jn 13:26
He was clothed with garments * Rev 19:13

DIRECT
that was the most * route from Ex 13:17,18
You and Aaron are to * the Num 1:2-15
at the * command of the Lord. 2Ki 24:3,4
cause it to strike as you * it? Job 38:35
first, and he will * you and crown Pro 3:6
plans—counting on God to * us. Pro 16:9
At whom did you * your violence Is 37:23
and I will * all his paths. Is 45:13

(DIRECT Con't)
violate the * commandments of God? Mt 15:3
you nullify the * command of God to Mt 15:5,6
and others will * you and take you Jn 21:18
a country that God would * him to. Act 7:3
These are not * commands from the 1Co 7:12
sent out by the * command of God 1Ti 1:1
Noah's belief in God was in * Heb 11:7

DIRECTED
master's son, as Jehovah has *." Gen 24:51
thread, just as God had * Moses. Ex 39:4,5
priest, as the Lord had * Moses. Num 31:41
the priest was * by the Lord to go Num 33:38,39
which the Lord our God had * us. Deu 1:19,20,21
So he * one of his officials to 2Ki 8:6
Then, as * by the laws of Moses, 2Ch 35:13
I also * that the guards be Neh 7:3
The lightning bolts are * by his Job 37:12
The steps of good men are * by Ps 37:23
is a beam of light * into the dark Pro 6:23
The upright are * by their Pro 11:5
the potters as the Lord * me." Mt 27:10
* by the Holy Spirit they went to Act 13:4

DIRECTING
Since the Lord is * our steps, Pro 20:24
such mighty deeds, * the affairs of Is 41:4
as beacon lights, * men who are Rom 2:19

DIRECTION
that the trend and * of men's lives Gen 6:5
can see in every *, for I am going Gen 13:14
border in the * of Assyria). Gen 25:18
in a day in any *, there were quail Num 11:31
in the * of the Red Sea." Num 14:25
in the * of Zin. Num 34:4
walls for 1500 feet in each *. Num 35:4
look out in every *, and there you Deu 3:27
in upon the city from every *." Jos 6:5
In the other *, the boundary Jos 19:12
army out in every * against Moab, 1Sa 14:47
It was flowing from the * of 2Ki 3:20
Under the * of Heman, the king's 1Ch 25:4,5
all were under the * of their 1Ch 25:6,7
to obey the Lord's * as commanded 2Ch 30:12
were under the * of Zerubbabel (son Ez 3:8
* of Jezrahiah the choirmaster. Neh 12:42
lightning flashes out in every *. Job 37:3
I thought about the wrong * in Ps 119:59,60
in every *: One tenth of one per Ecc 7:27,28
when they changed * but could go in Eze 10:9-13
"437½ feet" in every *. Eze 48:17f
strong winds blowing from every *. Dan 7:2
Jesus said, "At God's * I have Jn 10:32
with God's * and help, and 1Co 7:17
Under his * the whole body is Eph 4:15,16

DIRECTIONS
Hike in all * and explore the Gen 13:17
God's * and laws. Ex 24:7
These were the Lord's * to Moses Ex 30:34
They are to follow exactly the * Ex 31:11
for Jehovah's * to Moses were Lev 8:21
Thus the Lord's * to Moses were Num 16:40
in order to get * from the Lord. Num 27:21
In accordance with the Lord's *, Num 31:47
God, following his * in every Deu 5:32
you by following the Lord's *. Deu 21:9
but scatter before you in seven *! Deu 28:7
They have received their * from Deu 33:3
with the Lord's * to Moses. Jos 14:5
began to melt away in all *. 1Sa 14:16
by following these * and had it 2Ki 16:11,12
in the Temple at the Lord's *. 2Ki 24:13
This was in accordance with the * 2Ch 29:25,26
places, following * issued 2Ch 35:15
walk in opposite * along the top of Neh 12:31,32
They come at me from all *. Job 30:14
see in all * everything was ruins. Jer 4:23
From all * I will bring calamity Jer 49:32
* without having to face around. Eze 1:17
forward in each of four *; Eze 10:9-13
Write out all the * and the rules Eze 43:11
pointing in four *. Dan 8:8
NOW HERE ARE the * about the 1Co 16:1
these are the same * I gave to the 1Co 16:1
us, for whatever * God might give 2Co 8:5
HERE ARE MY *: Pray much for 1Ti 2:1

DIRECTLY
* to us, or it will kill us." Ex 20:19
will be * responsible to Aaron's Num 4:28
had come * from the mouth of God. 2Sa 16:23
and Heman reported * to the king. 1Ch 25:6,7
were supplied * from there, so 2Ch 31:16
I would have gone * from the womb Job 10:19
Oh, how I long to speak * to the Job 13:3
Go over and speak * to the king of Jer 22:1
palace official, * above the room Jer 35:4
* in line for royal succession. Dan 11:21
God was speaking * to you when he Mt 22:31
personally, or speaking to you *. Jn 5:37
for you can go * to the Father and Jn 16:23
I can tell you this * from the 1Th 4:15
in the thunder. * in front of his Rev 4:5
i.e., * in front, not to one Rev 7:17f

DIRECTOR
was the first * of this division in 1Ch 9:20
Asaph was the * of this choral 1Ch 16:7
(A note to the choir *: When Hab 3:19

DIRECTORS
of having choir * to lead the Neh 12:46

DIRECTS
whatever the Lord * me to say." Num 22:8
For he * the snow, the showers, Job 37:6
so the Lord * the king's thoughts. Pro 21:1

DIRGE
Then David composed a * for Saul 2Sa 1:17,18
"SING THIS DEATH * for the Eze 19:1
you, singing this *: 'O mighty Eze 26:17
"Son of dust, sing this sad * Eze 27:2
you and mock your * of despair: Mic 2:4
by some to mean a mournful *. Hab 3:1f
we sang a * and you didn't Lk 7:32f

DIRT
clothes torn and * on his head. 1Sa 4:12
torn and with * on his head as a 2Sa 1:1
and sprinkled * in their hair. Neh 9:1
the poor from the *, and the hungry Ps 113:7
them like * beneath his feet. Is 10:5,6
but always churns up mire and *. Is 57:20
he has rolled me in ashes and *. Lam 3:16
They simply heap up * against Hab 1:10
silver is like * to her, and fine Zec 9:3
like * under foot, like garbage. 1Co 4:13

DIRTIED
* by his contacts with the world. Jas 1:27

DIRTIEST
and he can bleach the * garments! Mal 3:2

DIRTY
It is better to get your hands * Pro 12:9
she is tossed away like * rags. Lam 1:8
*—full of greed and wickedness! Lk 11:39
any such things. * stories, foul Eph 5:4
hatred, cursing, and * language. Col 3:8
They have * minds, warped and 2Ti 3:8
for his * mind and rebellious heart Tit 1:15
disgrace like the * foam left along Jud 1:13

DIRTY-MINDED
called us to be * and full of lust, 1Th 4:7

DISABLED
that is blind or * or mutilated, or Lev 22:22
and some are * by men, and some Mt 19:12

DISADVANTAGE
be much to your *, for the Jews Ez 4:13

DISAGREE
mother and daughter will *; Lk 12:53
You *? 1Co 14:36
things, and if you * on some point, Php 3:15
* with them where they are wrong. Tit 1:9

DISAGREEMENT
Her father must state his * on Num 30:5
pledge, his * makes it void, and Num 30:8
Their * over this was so sharp Act 15:39

DISAGREEMENTS
to resolve any * among my people. Eze 44:24

DISAGREES
hating anyone who * with them. Rom 3:15
But if anyone still *—well, we 1Co 14:38
Or, "If he *, ignore his 1Co 14:38f

DISAPPEAR
floods began to *, for the Gen 8:1
to cause the swarms of flies to *. Ex 8:29
to *, so that not one remained. Ex 8:31,32
* just because he had no son? Num 27:3,4
oil, calves, and lambs will all *. Deu 28:51
and you shall * from the land. Deu 28:63
Would *. Deu 32:26
eyes, and you will * from this good Jos 23:13
shall * like stones from a sling! 1Sa 25:29
before I * into the wilderness." 2Sa 15:28
Let the stars of the night *. Job 3:9
My years * like swift ships, Job 9:26
"Mountains wear away and *. Job 14:18,19
For all he counted on will *, Job 15:32
His home shall * beneath a fiery Job 18:15
sipping it slowly, lest it *. Job 20:13
His wealth will * beneath the Job 20:28
"But how quickly they * from the Job 24:18
all life would * and mankind would Job 34:15
even the memory of them will *. Ps 9:6
they fade away like grass and *. Ps 37:2
while and the wicked shall *. Ps 37:10
like grass, and * like smoke. Ps 37:20
Let them * like water into Ps 58:7
turn to ashes and their peace *; Ps 69:22
soon they *, and we are gone. Ps 90:10
for my days * like smoke. Ps 102:3,4
For riches can * as though they Pro 23:4,5
and tensions * when gossip stops. Pro 26:20
Riches can * fast. Pro 27:23,24
The strongest among you will * Is 1:31
They will * like straw on fire. Is 5:24
*, declares the Lord of Hosts. Is 17:3
lands * and never will be rebuilt. Is 25:2
you can't understand, will *. Is 33:19
will melt away and * just like a Is 34:4
slip away and *, unable to help. Is 47:15
the skies shall * like smoke, the Is 51:6
sorrow and mourning will all *. Is 51:11
who wither like the grass and *? Is 51:12
and the hills *, but my kindness Is 54:10
it will never *. Is 56:5
Violence will * out of your Is 60:18
with a name that shall never *. Is 66:22
Their figs and grapes will *, Jer 8:13
* like that of women in labor. Jer 49:22
all strength will *. Eze 21:7
have trouble on the way, and *. Dan 11:19
and even the fish begin to *. Hos 4:3
they and all their wealth will *. Hos 5:7
As for Samaria, her king shall * Hos 10:7
They shall * like morning mist, Hos 13:3
Our food will * before our eyes; Joe 1:16
yes, drink and stagger back and * Ob 1:16
will flee away and *, like locusts Nah 3:17
even the memory of them will *. Zep 1:4
"Heaven and earth will *, but my Mt 24:35
Heaven and earth shall *, but my Mk 13:31
Your treasures there will never * Lk 12:33
command—will all *, and the world Rom 8:20,21
knowledge—these gifts will *. 1Co 13:8
come to an end, and they will *. 1Co 13:10
They will * into nothingness, Heb 1:11
bodies will * in fire, and the 2Pe 3:10
bodies will melt and * in flames. 2Pe 3:12
stone, and she shall * forever. Rev 18:21

DISAPPEARED
with God, he *, for God took him! Gen 5:21-24
and what he received for us has *. Gen 31:15
and when the dew * later in the Ex 16:14
the ground, the food melted and *. Ex 16:21
and * into the cloud at the top. Ex 24:15
And Moses * into the Ex 24:18
brought us here from Egypt has *; Ex 32:1
The hilt of the dagger * beneath Ju 3:22,23
they looked for him, he had *! 1Sa 10:21
* in the forest than were killed. 2Sa 18:8
something else, the prisoner *!" 1Ki 20:40
As they * from sight he tore his 2Ki 2:12
My hopes have *. Job 17:11
was in the distant past and *. Ecc 3:15
And now all your allies have * Jer 22:22
men and animals alike have *. Jer 32:43
for all their wealth has *. Jer 48:36
years later and the nation *. Hos 4:19f
The good men have * from the Mic 7:1
And then the angel *. Lk 1:38
they were going, their leprosy *. Lk 17:14
And at that moment he *! Lk 24:31
o'clock his fever suddenly *!" Jn 4:52
and Jesus had * into the crowd. Jn 5:13
into the sky and * into a cloud, Act 1:9
all it contained * into heaven. Act 11:10
lash him, quickly * when they heard Act 22:29
each other has *, for both of us Eph 2:16
And the starry heavens * Rev 6:14
the present earth and sky had *. Rev 21:1

DISAPPEARING
GODLY men are fast *. Ps 12:1

DISAPPEARS
a person whose leprosy *: Lev 14:1
and snow, but in hot weather, *. Job 6:15-18
But when he *, he isn't even Job 8:18
of a passing cloud, he quickly *. Job 14:2
a lake, as a river * in drought, so Job 14:11,12
Wealth from gambling quickly *; Pro 13:11
morning clouds, and * like dew. Hos 6:4
Your income *, as though you were Hag 1:6
And instantly the leprosy *. Mt 8:3
a heavenly reward that never *. 1Co 9:25
in our lives * and the new light of 1Jn 2:8

DISAPPOINT
pride in you—and you didn't * me. 2Co 7:14
never * those who trust in him." 1Pe 2:6

DISAPPOINTED
How have we * you?" 1Ki 11:22
they were never * when they Ps 22:5
you will be *, humiliated and Is 30:3
call them gods will be greatly *; Is 42:17
All who worship idols shall be * Is 45:16
they shall never be * in their Is 45:17
great shall be * and humbled; Mt 23:12
fruit on it, but he was always *. Lk 13:6
believe in him will never be *." Rom 9:33
believes in Christ will ever be *. Rom 10:11

DISAPPOINTMENT
weep in bitter *, for Assyria has Is 33:7
Then I wept with * Rev 5:4

DISAPPROVAL
"Your approval or * means Jn 5:41,42
punished enough by your united *. 2Co 2:5,6

DISARM
I will * all peoples of the Zec 9:10

DISARRAY
hair grow in wild *, and cover his Lev 13:45

DISASTER
for I fear * in the mountain. Gen 19:18,19,20

(DISASTER Con't)
Otherwise, * will surely — Gen 41:36
* and then lead my people out. — Ex 7:4
send just one more * on Pharaoh and — Ex 11:1
that would be an utter * to you." — Ex 23:33
* to this entire nation!" — Num 32:15
If it isn't, * will fall upon the — Jos 6:18
thereby saving Israel from *. — Ju 3:31
didn't realize the impending *. — Ju 20:34
he could bring * upon Absalom! — 2Sa 17:14
example and proverb of sudden *. — 1Ki 9:7
me, I will bring * upon your home — 1Ki 14:10
—the man who brought this * upon — 1Ki 18:17
the Lord has decreed * upon you." — 1Ki 22:23
enough, he had saved him from *. — 2Ki 6:10
Why provoke * for both yourself — 2Ki 14:10
This * came upon the nation of — 2Ki 17:7
and keep me from all evil and *!" — 1Ch 4:10
THEN SATAN BROUGHT * upon — 1Ch 21:1
So the ships met * and never — 2Ch 20:37
him, and that * could come only to — Ez 8:22
moment, but then comes sudden *. — Job 5:3
or they may fail and face *, but — Job 14:20,21
came to * because of their sins. — Job 21:28
gave them years of terror and *. — Ps 78:33
from defeat and * and from — Pro 3:23
you need not be afraid of * or — Pro 3:24,25,26
* strikes like a cyclone and the — Pro 10:25
The unjust tyrant will reap * and — Pro 22:8
them to sudden *, and who knows — Pro 24:21,22
when the wicked meet *, good men — Pro 28:28
* is roaring down upon you from — Is 21:1
Who has brought this * on Tyre, — Is 23:8
That is why * shall overtake you — Is 47:11
* on disaster shall befall you. — Jer 6:9
Disaster on * shall befall you. — Jer 6:9
'We are ruined! * has befallen — Jer 9:19
I will bring a great * upon them. — Jer 11:23
always it is * and horror and — Jer 20:8
I will send * upon the leaders of — Jer 23:1
shocked at the * that befalls you. — Jer 25:11
has brought this * on this land, — Jer 40:2,3
Sodom, where utter * struck in a — Lam 4:6
woe upon woe, * upon disaster! — Eze 7:26,27
woe upon woe, disaster upon *! — Eze 7:26,27
has there been a * like what — Dan 9:12
people experience * such as this. — Joe 2:26
For I, the Lord, am sending * — Amo 3:6
Is a yet future * foretold here? — Zec 13:8f
all of a sudden, * will fall upon — 1Th 5:3
flame of destruction and *. — Jas 3:6
the result is * for them. — 2Pe 3:15,16

DISASTERS
and great * come upon them, then — Deu 31:21
It is clear that these * befell — 2Ki 24:3,4
of darkness, nor * in the morning. — Ps 91:6

DISBAND
Tell them to * and go home, for — 1Ki 12:23,24

DISBANDED
When Joshua finally * the armies — Ju 2:6
* and returned to their homes. — Ju 9:55

DISBELIEF
inside he was laughing in *! — Gen 17:17
show the others, they stared in *! — Num 17:9
will mock, or shake his head in *. — Zep 2:15
to the sin and * of the rest of the — Heb 11:7

DISC
For sharpening a *, 60Ç — 1Sa 13:21

DISCARD
and I will * my chosen city of — 2Ki 23:27
me and absolutely * your idols, — Jer 4:1

DISCARDED
dead man, like a broken and * pot. — Ps 31:12
Silver," and I have * them. — Jer 6:30
This man Coniah is like a *, — Jer 22:28
a palace depot for * supplies where — Jer 38:11
some old rags and * garments which — Jer 38:11
speak of) a 'stone * by the — Act 4:11
No, God has not * his own people — Rom 11:2,3
have long since * the Jewish laws; — Gal 2:14

DISCERN
of God and can * good from evil. — 2Sa 14:17
Literally, "can I * between good — 2Sa 19:35f
as those who can * the difference — 1Jn 2:21

DISCERNMENT
better insight and *, and are — Pro 2:3,4,5
to apply these verses with *. — Eze 28:12f

DISCHARGE
Or if he touches human * of any — Lev 5:3
"Any man who has a genital * — Lev 15:1
not only while the * is active, but — Lev 15:3
"When the * stops, he shall — Lev 15:13
Lord for the man because of his *. — Lev 15:15
if you do this, you will * your — 2Ch 19:10
for there is no * from that — Ecc 8:8

DISCHARGED
he shall be * from the priesthood. — Lev 22:3
Then you will have * your duty to — Num 32:22

DISCIPLE
So Moses, the * of the Lord, died — Deu 34:5
Moses, the Lord's *, God spoke to — Jos 1:1
"Now that my * is dead, [you are — Jos 1:2
instructed his * Moses to conquer — Jos 9:24
Lord had commanded his * Moses; — Jos 11:15
"You have done as the Lord's * — Jos 22:2,3
"Come and be my *," Jesus said — Mt 9:9
"Come be my *." — Mk 2:14
each * to place before the people. — Mk 6:41
There's that * of Jesus!" — Mk 14:69
His * John came to him and — Lk 9:49
him and to be his *, the man — Lk 9:59
life—otherwise he cannot be my *. — Lk 14:26
And no one can be my * who does — Lk 14:27
So no one can become my * unless — Lk 14:33
*, but we are disciples of Moses. — Jn 9:28
but his other * with that name) — Jn 14:22
So that other * was permitted — Jn 18:15
Then the other * spoke to the — Jn 18:16
Literally, "standing by the * — Jn 19:26f
Literally, "to the *." — Jn 19:27f
had been a secret * of Jesus for — Jn 19:38
Literally, "the other * whom — Jn 20:2f
Literally, "Peter and the other * — Jn 20:3,4f
Literally, "the other * also, who — Jn 20:3,4f
Literally, "that * therefore whom — Jn 21:7f
Peter turned around and saw the * — Jn 21:20
that that * wouldn't die! — Jn 21:23
I am that *! — Jn 21:24

DISCIPLES
hillside with his * and sat down — Mt 5:1
he instructed his * to get ready to — Mt 8:18
Another of his * said, "Sir, — Mt 8:21
across the lake with his *. — Mt 8:23
The * went to him and wakened — Mt 8:25
calm. The * just sat there, awed! — Mt 8:27
Later, as Jesus and his * were — Mt 9:10
One day the * of John the Baptist — Mt 9:14
"Why don't your * fast as we do — Mt 9:14
As Jesus and the * were going to — Mt 9:19
are so few," he told his *. — Mt 9:37
JESUS CALLED HIS twelve * to him, — Mt 10:1
are the names of his twelve *: — Mt 10:2,3,4
to his twelve *, he went off — Mt 11:1
so he sent his * to ask Jesus, — Mt 11:2
When John's * had gone, Jesus — Mt 11:7
some grainfields with his *. — Mt 12:1
of worship, and his * were hungry; — Mt 12:1
"Your * are breaking the law. — Mt 12:2
He pointed to his *. — Mt 12:49
His * came and asked him, "Why — Mt 13:10
the house. His * asked him to — Mt 13:36
law who are now my * have double — Mt 13:52
Then John's * came for his body — Mt 14:12
That evening the * came to him — Mt 14:15
the * to place before the people. — Mt 14:19
Jesus told his * to get into their — Mt 14:22
on the lake the * were in trouble. — Mt 14:23,24
"Why do your * disobey the — Mt 15:2
Then the * came and told him, — Mt 15:12
Then his * urged him to send her — Mt 15:23
Then Jesus called his * to him — Mt 15:32
The * replied, "And where would — Mt 15:33
* who presented them to the crowd. — Mt 15:36
Arriving across the lake, the * — Mt 16:5
*, "Who are the people saying I — Mt 16:13
Then he warned the * against — Mt 16:20
plainly to his * about going to — Mt 16:21
Then Jesus said to the *, "If — Mt 16:24
At this the * fell face downward — Mt 17:6
His * asked, "Why do the Jewish — Mt 17:10
Then the * realized he was — Mt 17:13
so I brought him to your *, but — Mt 17:16
Afterwards the * asked Jesus — Mt 17:19
And the *' hearts were filled — Mt 17:22,23
ABOUT THAT TIME the * came to — Mt 18:1
Jesus' * then said to him, "If — Mt 19:10
But the * scolded those who — Mt 19:13
Then Jesus said to his *, "It is — Mt 19:23
This remark confounded the *. — Mt 19:25
you my * shall certainly sit on — Mt 19:28
he took the twelve * aside, and — Mt 20:17
The other ten * were indignant — Mt 20:24
As Jesus and the * left the city — Mt 20:29
AS JESUS AND the * approached — Mt 21:1
The two * did as Jesus said, and — Mt 21:6
The * were utterly amazed and — Mt 21:20
crowds, and to his *, "You would — Mt 23:1
grounds, his * came along and — Mt 24:1
the * asked him later, as he — Mt 24:3
talk with his *, he told them, — Mt 26:1
The * were indignant. — Mt 26:8,9
Jewish home, the * came to Jesus — Mt 26:17
meal with my * at your house.' — Mt 26:18
So the * did as he told — Mt 26:19
and gave it to the * and said, — Mt 26:26
And all the other * said the same — Mt 26:35
Then he returned to the three * — Mt 26:40
Then he came to the * and said, — Mt 26:45
At that point, all the * deserted — Mt 26:56
you are one of his *, for we can — Mt 26:73
to prevent his * from coming and — Mt 27:64
and tell his * that he has risen — Mt 28:7
rushed to find the * to give them — Mt 28:8
asleep when Jesus' * came during — Mt 28:12,13
Then the eleven * left for — Mt 28:16
He told his *, "I have been — Mt 28:18
Therefore go and make * in — Mt 28:19
teach these new * to obey all the — Mt 28:20
he and his * went over to Simon and — Mk 1:29,30
they could meet Jesus and his *. — Mk 2:15
they said to his *, "How can he — Mk 2:16
John's * and the Jewish leaders — Mk 2:18
why his * didn't do this too. — Mk 2:18
as Jesus and his * were walking — Mk 2:23
the fields, the * were breaking off — Mk 2:23
Meanwhile, Jesus and his * — Mk 3:7,8
He instructed his * to bring — Mk 3:9
and with his other *, they asked — Mk 4:10
was alone with his *, he would — Mk 4:34
Jesus said to his *, "Let's cross — Mk 4:35
His * said to him, "All this — Mk 5:31
and his three *, he went into the — Mk 5:40
his * to Nazareth, his home town. — Mk 6:1
And he called his twelve * — Mk 6:7
So the * went out, telling — Mk 6:12
When John's * heard what had — Mk 6:29
Late in the afternoon his * came — Mk 6:35,36
instructed his * to get back into — Mk 6:45
During the night, as the * in — Mk 6:47
that some of his * failed to follow — Mk 7:2
your * follow our age-old customs? — Mk 7:5
crowds, and his * asked him what he — Mk 7:17
Jesus called his * to discuss the — Mk 8:1
his * scoffed. — Mk 8:4
pieces and passed them to his *; — Mk 8:6
and the * placed them before the — Mk 8:6
and told the * to serve them. — Mk 8:7
a boat with his * and came to the — Mk 8:10
But the * had forgotten to stock — Mk 8:14
the * asked each other. — Mk 8:16
Jesus and his * now left Galilee — Mk 8:27
the Baptist," the * replied, "and — Mk 8:28
Jesus turned and looked at his * — Mk 8:33
Then he called his * and the — Mk 8:34
JESUS WENT ON to say to his *, — Mk 9:1
the other nine *, as some Jewish — Mk 9:14
So I begged your * to cast out — Mk 9:18
Jesus said [to his * — Mk 9:19
the house with his *, they asked — Mk 9:28
time with his *, teaching them. — Mk 9:30,31
One of his *, John, told him one — Mk 9:38
was alone with his * in the house, — Mk 10:10
to bless them, the * shooed them — Mk 10:13
with his * and said to them, "Let — Mk 10:14
and said to his *, "It's almost — Mk 10:23
The * were incredulous! — Mk 10:26
and the other * had left behind. — Mk 10:28
and as the * were following they — Mk 10:32
When the other * discovered what — Mk 10:41
Jesus sent two of his * on ahead. — Mk 11:1
to Jesus and the * threw their — Mk 11:7
out to Bethany with the twelve *. — Mk 11:11
And the * heard him say it. — Mk 11:14
Next morning, as the * passed — Mk 11:20
In reply Jesus said to the *, — Mk 11:22,23
He called his * to him and — Mk 12:43,44
day, one of his * said, "Teacher, — Mk 13:1
Then Judas Iscariot, one of his * — Mk 14:10
sacrificed, his * asked him where — Mk 14:12
So the two * went on ahead into — Mk 14:16
with the other *, and as they were — Mk 14:17
he instructed his *, "Sit here, — Mk 14:32
Then he returned to the three * — Mk 14:37
Judas (one of his *) arrived with a — Mk 14:43
Meanwhile, all his * had fled. — Mk 14:50
message to his * including Peter: — Mk 16:7
She found the * wet-eyed with — Mk 16:10,11
* as they were eating together. — Mk 16:14
And the * went everywhere — Mk 16:20
early * and other eyewitnesses. — Lk 1:1,2
him, "Come and be one of my *!" — Lk 5:27
bitterly to Jesus' * about his — Lk 5:30
was that Jesus' * were feasting — Lk 5:33
"John the Baptist's * are — Lk 5:33
so do the * of the Pharisees. — Lk 5:33
ONE SABBATH AS Jesus and his * — Lk 6:1
illegal! Your * are harvesting — Lk 6:2
to be the inner circle of his *. — Lk 6:13
Then he turned to his * and said, — Lk 6:20
went with his * to the village of — Lk 7:11
The * of John the Baptist soon — Lk 7:18
he sent two of his * to Jesus to — Lk 7:19
The two * found Jesus while he — Lk 7:20,21,22
and took his twelve * with him. — Lk 8:1
to the support of Jesus and his *. — Lk 8:3
as he and his * were out in a boat, — Lk 8:22
all twelve of the * came and urged — Lk 9:12
for his * to set before the crowd. — Lk 9:16
praying, with his * nearby, he came — Lk 9:18
Jesus was there alone with his *. — Lk 9:36
I begged your * to cast the — Lk 9:40
people," Jesus said [to his * — Lk 9:41
Jesus said to his *, "Listen to — Lk 9:43

(DISCIPLES Con't)
But the * didn't know what he Lk 9:45
THE LORD NOW chose seventy other * Lk 10:1
Then he said to the *, "Those Lk 10:16
When the seventy * returned, they Lk 10:17
Then, turning to the twelve *, he Lk 10:23
As Jesus and the * continued on Lk 10:38
one of his * came to him as he Lk 11:1
just as John taught one to his * Lk 11:1
He turned now to his * and warned Lk 12:1
Then turning to his * he said, Lk 12:22
JESUS NOW TOLD this story to his * Lk 16:1
one day to his *, "but woe to the Lk 17:1
again about this with his *. Lk 17:22
the * asked. Lk 17:37
ONE DAY JESUS told his * a story Lk 18:1
But the * told them to go away. Lk 18:15
and said to the *, "Let the little Lk 18:16,17
then said to his *, "How hard it Lk 18:24
walking along ahead of his *. Lk 19:28
he sent two * ahead, with Lk 19:29
And the * simply replied, "The Lk 19:34
he turned to his * and said, Lk 20:45
Some of his * began talking about Lk 21:5
one of the twelve *, and he went Lk 22:3
eat the Passover meal with his *.' Lk 22:11
Then the * wondered among Lk 22:23
Then, accompanied by the *, he Lk 22:39
returned to the *—only to find them Lk 22:45
led by Judas, one of his twelve *. Lk 22:47
When the other * saw what was Lk 22:49
*, for both are from Galilee." Lk 22:59
to tell his eleven *—and everyone Lk 24:9
where the eleven * and the other Lk 24:33,34
two of his *, Jesus walked by. Jn 1:35
Then John's two * turned and Jn 1:37
Jesus and his * were invited too. Jn 2:2
And his * believed that he really Jn 2:11
Literally, "His * believed on Jn 2:11f
with his mother, brothers, and *. Jn 2:12
Then his * remembered this Jn 2:17
to life again, the * remembered his Jn 2:22
Afterwards Jesus and his * left Jn 3:22
with John's *, telling them that Jn 3:25
and to become his *—(though Jesus Jn 4:1
them, but his * did)— he left Jn 4:1
at the time as his * had gone into Jn 4:8
Just then his * arrived. Jn 4:27
Meanwhile, the * were urging Jn 4:31
the * asked each other. Jn 4:33
sat down with his * around him, he Jn 6:2-5
*, "so that nothing is wasted." Jn 6:12
That evening his * went down to Jn 6:16
For they knew that he and his * Jn 6:22,23
and that the * had gone off in Jn 6:22,23
there, nor his *, they got into the Jn 6:24
Even his * said, "This is very Jn 6:60
himself that his * were complaining Jn 6:61
At this point many of his * Jn 6:66
"You are truly my * if you live as Jn 8:30,31
"Master," his * asked him, Jn 9:2
Do you want to become his * Jn 9:27
disciple, but we are * of Moses. Jn 9:28
to his *, "Let's go to Judea." Jn 11:7
But his * objected. Jn 11:8
The *, thinking Jesus meant Jn 11:12,13
said to his fellow *, "Let's go Jn 11:16
and stayed there with his *. Jn 11:54
But Judas Iscariot, one of his * Jn 12:4
in charge of the *' funds and often Jn 12:6
(His * didn't realize at the time Jn 12:16
want to be my *, tell them to Jn 12:26
And how he loved his *! Jn 13:1
began to wash the *' feet and to Jn 13:5
The * looked at each other, Jn 13:22
to the world that you are my *." Jn 13:35
* and not to the world at large?" Jn 14:22
My true * produce bountiful Jn 15:8
some of his * asked. Jn 16:17,18
his * said, "and not in riddles. Jn 16:29
and these * know you sent me. Jn 17:25
ravine with his * and entered a Jn 18:1
gone there many times with his *. Jn 18:2
did another of the * who was Jn 18:15
"Aren't you one of Jesus' *?" Jn 18:17
"Aren't you one of his *?" Jn 18:25
Literally, "the *." Jn 20:10f
Mary Magdalene found the * and Jn 20:18
That evening the * were meeting Jn 20:19
One of the *, Thomas, "The Jn 20:24
Eight days later the * were Jn 20:26
Jesus' * saw him do many other Jn 20:30,31
the * beside the Lake of Galilee. Jn 21:1
and two other *. Jn 21:2
languages being spoken by the *. Act 2:6
So the two * were brought in Act 4:7
found the other * and told them Act 4:23
roughed up the *) and brought them Act 5:26,27
He drew away some people as *, Act 5:37
* increased vastly in Jerusalem; Act 6:7
Literally, "the *." Act 13:52f
and making many *, they returned Act 14:21
Ephesus, where he found several *. Act 19:1
Paul wanted to go in, but the * Act 19:30
Paul sent for the *, preached a Act 20:1
These * warned Paul—the Holy Act 21:4
Some * from Caesarea accompanied Act 21:16
just as the other * do, and as the 1Co 9:5
and gave it to his * and said, 1Co 11:24
The name given to Jesus' twelve *, 1Co 15:5f
can boast that you are their *. Gal 6:13

DISCIPLINE
my *, disregarding my laws. Ps 50:17
If you refuse to * your son, it Pro 13:24
* your son in his early years Pro 19:18
your children; * won't hurt them! Pro 23:13,14
* your son and he will give you Pro 29:17
mere words are not enough—* is Pro 29:19
O Lord, your * is good and leads Is 38:16
man to be under *, for it causes Lam 3:27
up with the loving * the Lord Eph 6:4
I continually * and punish Rev 3:19

DISCIPLINED
David, had never * him at any 1Ki 1:6

DISCLAIM
Don't try to * responsibility by Pro 24:11,12

DISCLOSED
Have been *." Rev 15:3,4

DISCONTENT
This added to the * of the people Num 11:4,5
evil he can do, and stirring up *. Pro 6:14
there were rumblings of *. Act 6:1

DISCONTENTED
in debt, or merely *—until David 1Sa 22:2

DISCONTINUED
of the attack, he * building the 1Ki 15:21
was happening, he * building Ramah 2Ch 16:5

DISCORD
witnessSowing * among brothers Pro 6:16-19
Accepting them might cause * in Rom 14:1f

DISCOURAGE
"Are you trying to * the rest Num 32:7
residents tried to * and frighten Ez 4:4,5
prophets who have tried to * me." Neh 6:14

DISCOURAGED
might become * by having to fight Ex 13:17,18
The people were very *; Num 21:4
of Eshcol, they * the people from Num 32:9
to Joshua, "Don't be afraid or *; Jos 8:1
"Don't ever be afraid or *," Jos 10:25
the people and * them from entering Jos 14:8
"Well, tell Joab not to be *," 2Sa 11:25
he is weary and *, and he and his 2Sa 17:2,3
get *, for you will be rewarded." 2Ch 15:7
Don't be afraid or *! 2Ch 20:17
When they were *, I smiled and Job 29:24
Let all who are * take heart. Ps 34:2
Why be * and sad? Ps 42:4,5
But O my soul, don't be *. Ps 42:11
O my soul, why be so gloomy and *? Ps 43:5
I am completely *—I lie in the Ps 119:25
*, frustrated, and angry. Ecc 5:17
These statements are Solomon's * Ecc 9:5f
These statements are Solomon's * Ecc 9:5f
These statements are Solomon's * Ecc 9:10f
news bring cheer to all * ones. Is 35:3
Your lies have * the righteous, Eze 13:22
remnant, small, * as you are—but it Zec 8:6
So don't be afraid or *! Zec 8:13
so bitter and * that he won't be 2Co 2:7
those who are * refreshed us by the 2Co 7:6
if we don't get * and give up. Gal 6:9
they become * and quit trying. Col 3:21
Don't be * when he has to show Heb 12:5

DISCOURAGEMENT
In my * I thought, "They are Ps 116:10,11
griping brings *. Pro 15:4

DISCOURAGING
I have will be given to him—how *! Ecc 2:19

DISCOVER
send out spies to * the best route Deu 1:22
to * the best way to attack us." Jos 2:3
were terrified to * that their city Ju 20:40,41
is very crafty. * his hiding 1Sa 23:23
ostensibly to * whose sins had 1Ki 21:9f
ancient records to * what a Ez 4:15
of Babylon to * whether King Cyrus Ez 5:17
birds in the sky cannot * it. Job 28:21
to * knowledge and understanding. Pro 8:12
king's privilege to * and invent. Pro 25:2,3
Those who believe him * that God Jn 3:33,34
You can quickly * that it was no Act 24:11
and you will * that I have never Act 24:12
and * what he wants you to do. 2Pe 1:5

DISCOVERED
was * in the land of Babylon, Gen 11:2
(This is the boy who * a hot Gen 36:24
and * that it had been burned! Lev 10:16
"Anyone who is * to have leprosy Lev 13:45
"If a man is * committing Deu 22:22
to stir, someone * that the altar Ju 6:28
and so his secret was not *. Ju 16:9
to Mizpah, and * that no one had Ju 21:8,9
And he has * the man he wants and 1Sa 13:14
they * that it was only an idol! 1Sa 19:16
And the Lord did, and they * 2Ki 6:20
power, but this treachery was *. 2Ki 17:4
"I have * a scroll in the Temple, 2Ki 22:8
which had been * in the Temple. 2Ki 23:1
all of whom were * hiding in the 2Ki 25:19
When she * how wise he really 2Ch 9:3
scroll, and how Hilkiah had * it. 2Ch 34:18
were * and copied by the aides of Pro 25:1
in the universe. I * that the lot Ecc 1:12-15
and said: I have * a conspiracy Jer 11:9
special counselors * in the city, Jer 52:24,25
to a land I had * and explored for Eze 20:5,6
its site is with difficulty *." Zep 2:15f
a treasure a man * in a field. Mt 13:44
choice pearls. He * a real Mt 13:46
the disciples * they had forgotten Mt 16:5
When the other disciples * what Mk 10:41
Three days later they finally * Lk 2:46,47
Mary has * it—and I won't take it Lk 10:42
for Syria when he * a plot by the Act 20:3
I soon * it was something about Act 23:29

DISCOVERS
the wrong road and * his mistake, Jer 8:4,5

DISCOVERY
His greatness is beyond *! Ps 145:3

DISCREDIT
Are you going to * my justice Job 40:8
And the Council could hardly * Act 4:14

DISCRETION
and it is at your * that men are 1Ch 29:12
A beautiful woman lacking * and Pro 11:22

DISCRIMINATED
widows were being * against, that Act 6:1

DISCRIMINATION
never-ending *—but not destroyed! Ps 129:2
A typical case of * (cf. Lk 9:53f
greatly reduced the * against us. Act 24:2

DISCS
their plowshares, *, axes, or 1Sa 13:20

DISCUSS
Ramah to * the matter with Samuel. 1Sa 8:4
to David to * a deal—to surrender 2Sa 3:12
If you were, then we could * it Job 9:32,33
fear you, and we will * your laws. Ps 119:79
* the matter with him privately. Pro 25:8,9,10
They stopped at Mizpah to * their Jer 40:12
High Priest, to * ways of Mt 26:4
met again to * how to induce the Mt 27:1
to * plans for killing Jesus. Mk 3:6
Jesus called his disciples to * Mk 8:1
Court—met to * their next steps. Mk 15:1
a truce team to * terms of peace. Lk 14:32
to come and * the situation. Lk 16:5,6
Temple guards to * the best way to Lk 22:4
a council to * the situation. Jn 11:47
ask you," i.e., * what is true. Jn 16:30f
thoughts, or to * them with him, or 1Co 2:16

DISCUSSED
As they * who should be Gen 41:38
and their leaders * why the Lord 1Sa 4:3
his decision. He * their demand 2Ch 10:6
tell them what we *, just say that Jer 38:25
hour, and was being * everywhere. Lk 3:15
he had previously * with them. Act 1:4
Paul and Barnabas argued and * Act 15:2
* Paul's case with the king. Act 25:14

DISCUSSING
at the city gates, * various issues Ju 9:35
While they were still * it with Est 6:14
they began * what had happened. Mk 1:27
Jesus realized what they were * Mk 8:17
were you * out on the road?" Mk 9:33
On the way they were * how they Mk 16:3
teachers of Law, * deep questions Lk 2:46,47
his counselors and * whether his Lk 14:31
him why, or what they had been *. Jn 4:27
their time * the latest new ideas! Act 17:21

DISCUSSION
Meanwhile, there was much * and 2Sa 19:8,9,10
After much * they sent them back, 1Ch 12:19
A friendly * is as stimulating as Pro 27:17
listening to the * realized that Mk 12:28
"You seem to be in a deep * Lk 24:17
There was a lot of * about him Jn 7:12
At the meeting, after long *, Act 15:7
There was no further *, and Act 15:12
That ended Paul's * with them, Act 17:33
synagogue for a * with the Jews. Act 18:19
*, for they are subordinate to men 1Co 14:34
It allows * and is willing to Jas 3:17

DISCUSSIONS
what wonderful * as we walked Ps 55:14
He went to the synagogue for * Act 17:17
Steer clear of foolish * which 2Ti 2:16

DISDAINFUL
beyond description, arrogant, *. Pro 30:13,14

DISEASE
that dies of *, or is attacked and Lev 7:24

(DISEASE Con't)
to eat dies of *, anyone touching Lev 11:39
the marks of the * have become Lev 13:6
As long as the * lasts, he is Lev 13:46
man who is defiled by a genital * Lev 15:32
or any other skin *, must not be Lev 22:22
*, for she is responsible." Num 5:31
*, then Jehovah has not sent me. Num 16:29
He will send * among you until Deu 28:21
Burning fever, and fatal *. Deu 32:24
caused by plant * or locusts or 1Ki 8:37
plagues, or crop *, or attacks of 2Ch 6:28
such as war, *, or famine—we can 2Ch 20:9
* and your bowels will rot away." 2Ch 21:15
down with the incurable bowel *. 2Ch 21:18
His skin is eaten by *. Job 18:13
to the grave by * and plague, with Job 27:15
friends stay away, fearing my *. Ps 38:11
Literally, "*." Pro 5:11f
in return is war and famine and *. Jer 14:12
those dead from starvation and *. Jer 14:18
by starvation and *—or go out and Jer 21:9
and famine and * among them until Jer 24:10
I will send war, famine and * Jer 27:8
war and famine and *, which the Jer 27:13
the city by sword, famine and *. Jer 32:24
famine and *, but I will bring my Jer 32:36
of death by war and famine and *. Jer 34:17
starvation or *, but anyone Jer 38:2
will die from sword, famine and *. Jer 42:17
sword, famine and * in Egypt, where Jer 42:22
Jerusalem, by sword, famine and *. Jer 44:13
at home, * and death. Lam 1:20
of you will die from famine and *; Eze 5:12
and your families; * and war will Eze 5:17
perish from war and famine and *. Eze 6:11
* will strike down those in exile; Eze 6:12
If you stay inside, famine and * Eze 7:15
death by war and famine and *. Eze 12:16
an epidemic of * into the land, and Eze 14:19
I will send an epidemic of * and Eze 28:23
forts and caves shall die of *. Eze 33:27
I will fight you with sword, *, Eze 38:22
every kind of sickness and *. Mt 4:23
heal every kind of sickness and *. Mt 10:1
go in peace, healed of your *." Mk 5:34
clear me of every trace of my *." Lk 5:12
handicapped by a * of the eyes. Gal 4:15f
and famine and * and wild animals. Rev 6:8

DISEASED
for he is definitely *. Lev 13:11
In his old age his feet became *, 1Ki 15:23
became seriously * in his feet but 2Ch 16:12
and my whole body is *. Ps 38:7
One day Lazarus, a * beggar, was Lk 16:20

DISEASES
you suffer the * I send on the Ex 15:26
* of Egypt you remember so well; Deu 7:15
He will bring upon you all the * Deu 28:60
* the Lord will have sent upon it. Deu 29:22
shall die from terrible *. Jer 16:4
our sicknesses and bore our *." Mt 8:17
* were, brought them to Jesus; Lk 4:40
and to be healed of their *. Lk 5:15
of their various *—healing the lame Lk 7:20,21,22
cast them out—and to heal all *. Lk 9:1

DISEMBARKED
their wives all *, along with all Gen 8:18,19

DISFIGURED
and bloodied, so * one would Is 52:14,15

DISGRACE
It would be a * for her to marry Gen 34:14
of you as a * upon all Israel!" 1Sa 11:2
make it a public horror and *. 2Ch 7:20
and rid ourselves of this *!" Neh 2:17
Don't * me, Lord, by not Ps 31:17
to destroy me. * these scoffers Ps 40:14,15
Cover them with failure and * Ps 71:13
Utterly * them until they Ps 83:16
Clothe them with *. Ps 109:29
For now I must face public *." Pro 5:14
Wounds and constant * are his Pro 6:33
you will end in poverty and *; Pro 13:18
Sin brings *. Pro 18:3
father or mother is a public *. Pro 19:26
be left to them is shame and *. Is 3:24
one—you who * your nation! Is 22:18
Do not * yourself and the throne Jer 14:21
glory of God for the * of idols. Hos 4:7
he didn't want to publicly * her. Mt 1:19
away my * of having no children!" Lk 1:25
They are a * and a stain among 2Pe 2:13
them is shame and * like the dirty Jud 1:13

DISGRACED
be * in man, wholly evil as he is. Gen 6:3
Meanwhile, Ahithophel—publicly * 2Sa 17:23
and *, just as we are today. Ez 9:7
terror-stricken, and *. Ps 6:10
will ever be * for trusting him. Ps 25:3
me have been * and dishonored. Ps 71:24
his time and publicly * him. Ps 89:45
Let those who worship idols be * Ps 97:7
Then I will not be *, for I will Ps 119:6
Let the proud be *, for they have Ps 119:78
the end of the line, publicly *! Pro 25:6,7
humiliated and *, for he can't Is 30:3
She sits childless now, *, for Jer 15:9
from you shall be * and shamed; Jer 17:13
her god Marduk will be utterly *! Jer 50:2
Don't let them be * by the taunts Joe 2:17

DISGRACEFUL
that. It's *, that sort of talk. Mic 2:6

DISGRACES
around with prostitutes * him. Pro 29:3

DISGRACING
at home, to avoid * the church and 1Co 11:22

DISGUISE
with a veil to * herself, and sat Gen 38:14
Jeroboam told his wife, "* 1Ki 14:2
over his eyes to * himself. 1Ki 20:38
"I'll * myself so that no one will 2Ch 18:29
glory, taking the * of a slave and Php 2:7

DISGUISED
one at Endor. Saul * himself by 1Sa 28:7,8
So Ahab went into the battle * in 1Ki 22:30
teachers who come * as harmless Mt 7:15
And I saw three evil spirits * Rev 16:13

DISGUST
in anger and * he shouted, "I Num 24:10
of horror and * to the Lord, and it Deu 18:12
and exclaimed in *, "How glorious 2Sa 6:20
back in * to their own land. 2Ki 3:27
Saul, felt a deep * for David as 1Ch 15:29
them in *," the Lord God says. Ps 95:10
You will be received with * and Jer 42:18

DISGUSTED
And I am * about this, that I Ecc 2:18
from which you turned away, *. Eze 23:22

DISGUSTEDLY
feet, remarking *, "What a Ex 4:25,26

DISGUSTING
shall be a * sight to all mankind. Is 66:24

DISGUSTS
Pride * the Lord. Pro 16:5

DISH
father's favorite * from them. Gen 27:8,9,10
favorite * and brings it to him. Gen 27:31
* and turns it upside down to dry. 2Ki 21:13
his food from his * to his mouth! Pro 26:15
will smash you like a broken *; Is 30:14
is like a discarded, broken *. Jer 22:28
his hand with me in the *." Mt 26:23f

DISHAN
tribe of Ezer,The tribe of *. Gen 36:20,21
The children of *:Uz, Aran. Gen 36:28,29,30
*; and Esau's daughter was named 1Ch 1:38,39

DISHAN'S
* sons were Uz and Aran. 1Ch 1:42

DISHEARTEN
trying to frighten and * them. 2Ch 32:18

DISHES
And make golden *, spoons, Ex 25:29
bowls, flagons, *, and spoons to be Ex 37:15,16
and place the *, spoons, bowls, Num 4:7
of silver and gold *, beautiful 1Ki 10:25
soon the golden * taken from the Jer 27:16
that the golden * still here in the Jer 27:18
bring slaves and bronze *, while Eze 27:13
gold and silver * and for many Dan 11:8
of cleansing for pots, pans and *. Mk 7:4
In a wealthy home there are * 2Ti 2:20
The expensive * are used for 2Ti 2:20
like one of these * made of purest 2Ti 2:21

DISHEVEL
"Wear mourning clothes, and * 2Sa 14:2,3

DISHEVELED
to look wan and * so people will Mt 6:16

DISHON
Anah,The tribe of *,The tribe of Gen 36:20,21
The children of Anah:*, Gen 36:25
The children of *:Hemdan, Gen 36:26
Lotan, Shobal, Zibeon, Anah, *, 1Ch 1:38,39
Anah's son was *: 1Ch 1:41
The sons of *: Hamran, Eshban, 1Ch 1:41

DISHONEST
* money brings grief to all the Pro 15:27
great wealth gotten by * means. Pro 16:8
and *. Pro 19:1
it is better to be poor than *. Pro 19:22
* gain will never last, so why Pro 21:6
halt to your * gain and bloodshed. Eze 22:13
from * scales—they love to cheat. Hos 12:7
* TAX COLLECTORS and other Lk 15:1
the accountant was thoroughly *. Lk 16:1
one immoral or *—but only those Rev 21:27

DISHONESTY
who do not practice * and lying. Ps 24:4
But my * made me miserable and Ps 32:3
and * are entrenched in the heart Ps 55:10
evil man is destroyed by his *. Pro 11:3
Lord loathes all cheating and *. Pro 20:23
reign if he hates * and bribes. Pro 28:16
full of selfish greed and all *! Jer 22:17
they commit adultery and love *. Jer 23:14
this world are more clever [in *! Lk 16:8
as a sinner if my * brought him Rom 3:7
Be done with * and jealousy and 1Pe 2:1

DISHONOR
shall not * and profane his name; Lev 21:6
for that would * his great name. 1Sa 12:22
a day of trouble, insult, and *. 2Ki 19:3
* those who are trying to kill me. Ps 35:4
Bare them to *. Ps 35:26
tossed us aside in *, and have not Ps 44:9
and how they so shamefully * me. Ps 69:19
allow our enemies to * your name? Ps 74:9,10
Instead of shame and *, you Is 61:7
We lie in shame and in *, for we Jer 3:25
"But you * it, saying that my Mal 1:12
For I honor my Father—and you * Jn 8:49
worthy to suffer * for his name. Act 5:41
but you * him by breaking them. Rom 2:23

DISHONORABLY
and Hamor, acting * because of what Gen 34:13

DISHONORED
their sister had been * there. Gen 34:27
one of my wives and thus * me. Gen 49:4
For you * me among the people of Deu 32:51
but since he * his father by 1Ch 5:1
advantage of and * in this way, we Ez 4:14
*, terror-stricken, and disgraced. Ps 6:10
hurt me have been disgraced and *. Ps 71:24
He says, "Never again, O * Is 23:12
You will be * among the nations, Eze 22:16

DISHONORS
praying or preaching, he * Christ. 1Co 11:4
on her head * her husband [for her 1Co 11:5

DISINHERIT
I will * them and destroy them Num 14:12

DISINHERITED
* and excommunicated from Israel. Ez 10:7,8

DISLIKE
or unjustly attacking those I *. Ps 7:4
Quarreling, harsh words, and * of Eph 4:31

DISLIKED
shame among the nations, * by all. Ps 44:14

DISLIKES
the likes and * of her husband. 1Co 7:34
of Christ but * his fellow man, is 1Jn 2:9
For he who * his brother is 1Jn 2:11

DISLOYALTY
driven us because of our * to you. Dan 9:7

DISMANTLE
therefore God will * them like Ps 28:5
to bring out its tools to * you. Jer 22:7

DISMANTLED
Then the king * the wheeled 2Ki 16:17
walls of Jerusalem *, from the gate 2Ch 25:23
The Babylonians * the two large Jer 52:17

DISMAY
I am terrified, blinded with *. Is 21:3
and shrink back in horror and *. Jer 2:12
the people will drink it with *. Eze 4:16
their clothing in * and ran out Act 14:14

DISMAYED
this, they were * and frightened. 1Sa 17:11
So do not be * when evil men Ps 49:16
And so God's people are * and Ps 73:10
Then how * the Philistines Is 20:5,6
Do not be *. Is 41:10
God helps me, I will not be *; Is 50:7
don't be *, O Israel; Jer 30:10
to your own land, don't be *; Jer 46:27
Don't be * by their dark scowls. Eze 2:6
They watch *.' Eze 26:18
But do not be *, for here is Rev 13:10

DISMISS
* ALL THE charges against me, Ps 26:1

DISMISSAL
by giving her a letter of *.' Mt 5:31
writing her a letter of *?" Mt 19:7
is write his wife a letter of *." Mk 10:4

DISMISSED
The king immediately * all those Ju 3:17,18,19
and then Solomon curtly * him. 1Ki 1:53
Then Jesus shouted out again, * Mt 27:50
loud cry, and * his spirit. Mk 15:37
cross saw how he * his spirit, he Mk 15:39
in order, for you are to be *.' Lk 16:2
bowed his head and * his spirit. Jn 19:30
Then he * them, and they Act 19:41

DISMOUNTED
Rebekah noticed him and quickly *. Gen 24:64
piece of land. She * from her Ju 1:14
* and bowed low before him. 1Sa 25:23

DISOBEDIENCE
Saul died for his * to the Lord 1Ch 10:13
We know our *; Is 59:13
will come against you for your *; Hos 10:10
Temple by their * to God's laws. Zep 3:4
Literally, "shut up all unto *." Rom 11:32f
them of their * and guilt instead Heb 10:3

DISOBEDIENT
you have been * to his clear 1Ki 13:21,22

(DISOBEDIENT Con't)
were * and rebelled against you. Neh 9:26
* minds to the wisdom of faith." Lk 1:17
the * to the wisdom of the just." Lk 1:17f
not * to that vision from heaven! Act 26:19
being * to their parents. Rom 1:30
Literally, "*, obstinate." Rom 10:21f
sneering at God, * to their 2Ti 3:2
being wild or * to their parents. Tit 1:6
They are rotten and *, worthless Tit 1:16
Once we, too, were foolish and *; Tit 3:3

DISOBEY
"And if you still * me, I will Lev 26:18
Lord your God and begin to * him. Deu 8:11
on whether you obey or *. Deu 30:15
bring evil upon you if you * him. Jos 23:15,16
will begin to * their husbands when Est 1:17
refused to yield and * your laws. Ps 119:87
They try to make me *, but I have Ps 119:157
For the king punishes those who * Ecc 8:2,3
that they wanted above all to *. Jer 31:33f
And now the people * more and Hos 13:2
"Why do your disciples * the Mt 15:2
everybody to * the Jewish laws. Act 21:28
He is very hard on those who *, Rom 11:22
careful not to * God as the Heb 4:11

DISOBEYED
"Why have you * my command and let Ex 1:18
for the Lord's treasury was *. Jos 7:1
Israel has sinned and * my Jos 7:10,11
"You have * the commandment of 1Sa 13:13
"Yes, I have * your instructions 1Sa 15:24
prophet who * the Lord's command; 1Ki 13:26
time he continually * the Lord. 1Ki 15:34
his covenant and * all the laws 2Ki 18:12
Land and * as their fathers had. Ps 78:57
I weep because your laws are *. Ps 119:136
"O Lord our God, we have * you; Dan 9:10
All Israel has *; Dan 9:11
that the astrologers had * him. Mt 2:16
since they themselves had never * Rom 5:14
sinners because he * God, and Rom 5:19
For some people have * their 1Ti 1:19
speaking to all those who * him. Heb 3:18
they * God and failed to enter. Heb 4:6
and like Korah, they have * God Jud 1:11

DISOBEYING
and is guilty of * one of God's Lev 4:22
Now you are * the Lord's orders Num 14:41
why you are * his commandments. 2Ch 24:20
"Why are you * the king's Est 3:3,4
And anyone * will be thrown to Dan 6:12
Keep *—your sins are mounting up. Amo 4:4
in addition to * their Sabbath Jn 5:18
rules he is not * the rules of men 1Th 4:8
been punished for * them, what Heb 2:2

DISOBEYS
Anyone who * this rule at any Ex 12:15
"Anyone who * some law of God Lev 5:17,18

DISORDER
be * and every other kind of evil. Jas 3:16

DISORDERLY
likes things to be * and upset. 1Co 14:33

DISOWN
Even if Abraham and Jacob would * Is 63:16
How can you * your God like Jer 2:32
us, for he cannot * us who are part 2Ti 2:13

DISPARAGING
a * nickname—for Jeconiah and Jer 22:24,25f

DISPATCH
received the *, his hands fell Jer 50:43

DISPATCHED
The dove which Noah next * would Gen 8:7f
that evening. He * a police Jos 2:3
So David * a memo to Joab: "Send 2Sa 11:6
and trouble. He * against them a Ps 78:49

DISPENSES
earth and * justice for the world. Job 34:13

DISPERSE
and * the armies of your enemy. Zep 3:15

DISPERSED
*), and Joktan (Peleg's brother). Gen 10:25
Later they were * among the Ps 105:13
his followers were harmlessly *. Act 5:36
he dismissed them, and they *. Act 19:41

DISPERSES
As a cloud * and vanishes, so Job 7:9

DISPERSING
scatter them, * them to the ends of Eze 20:23,24

DISPIRITED
they were too * after the tragic Ex 6:8,9

DISPLACE
as Israel would * the peoples of Deu 2:12
the Lord your God will * them. Deu 18:12
nations you will *, and when you Deu 19:1

DISPLACED
driven out and * by the Edomites, Deu 2:12

DISPLAY
power I will * through you. Ex 34:10
Egypt with a great * of power. Deu 4:37
out with a great * of miracles. Deu 5:15
* the special sacrificial bread, 2Ch 2:4
a tremendous * of the wealth and Est 1:4
they are a marvelous * of his Ps 19:1
Summon your might; * your Ps 68:28
* your power and radiant glory. Ps 80:1
fields, for they * his greatness. Ps 96:12
A wise man doesn't * his Pro 12:23
for the Lord will * his glory Is 35:2
They will be as jewels to *, as Is 49:18
from Egypt in a great * of power. Dan 9:15
saw this * of the power of God. Lk 9:43
be killed, put on * at the end of a 1Co 4:9

DISPLAYED
of the Presence is *, and place the Num 4:7
you * in rescuing your people. Num 14:13
of God was *, the lampstands (five 1Ki 7:48
then they * them throughout the 1Ch 10:9
the Red Sea. You * great miracles Neh 9:10
Literally, "that it may be * Ps 60:4,5f
and God openly * to the whole world Col 2:15
that coming day when it will be *. 1Pe 4:13

DISPLAYING
very purpose of * the awesome power Rom 9:17

DISPLAYS
but a fool * his foolishness. Pro 12:23
The Holy Spirit * God's power 1Co 12:7

DISPLEASE
back from all that might * him. Php 2:12

DISPLEASED
But Joseph was upset and * when Gen 48:17
Moses too was highly *. Num 11:10
But the Lord was very * with what 2Sa 11:27
And God, too, was * with the 1Ch 21:7
* with you and stop punishing him! Pro 24:18
the evil and was * to find no steps Is 59:15
Literally, "Was the Lord * Hab 3:8,9f
Were you * with them? Hab 3:8,9
was only a little * with my people, Zec 1:15
he was very much * with his Mk 10:14
But the crowds were *. Lk 19:7
He was highly * with the people Act 12:20

DISPLEASURE
Don't fear their *, for you are Deu 1:17
the world shall hide before his * Jer 10:10

DISPOSE
to decide how to * of the Ark. 1Sa 5:8

DISPOSED
Or, "were * to," or, "ordained Act 13:48f

DISPOSES
Man proposes, but God *. Pro 19:21

DISPOSSESS
* the nations on the other side. Deu 9:1
She shall * those who Jer 49:2
yet the Lord will * her, and hurl Zec 9:4

DISPOSSESSED
shall live in them and not be *. Ps 69:35
She shall dispossess those who * Jer 49:2
and lame and *— and make them Mic 4:6

DISPUTE
parties to the * shall come before Ex 22:9
and cases of * were brought to him 1Sa 7:16
Does the clay * with him who Is 45:9

DISPUTES
to me with their *, to ask for Ex 18:15,16
of God to their particular *." Ex 18:15,16
came to her to decide their *. Ju 4:5
ends arguments and settles * Pro 18:18
Lord will settle international *; Is 2:4

DISQUALIFIED
rules or is * and wins no prize. 2Ti 2:5

DISREGARD
wrong, and they * my Sabbaths, so Eze 22:26
right for a man to * his needy Mk 7:11
they are likely to * their vow to 1Ti 5:11

DISREGARDED
way my enemies have * your laws. Ps 119:139

DISREGARDING
refused my discipline, * my laws. Ps 50:17

DISREPAIR
reign the Temple was still in *. 2Ki 12:6

DISRESPECTFULLY
* against these evil Mighty Ones. 2Pe 2:11

DISROBED
"But I said, 'I have *. Sol 5:3

DISSATISFIED
done, that you are * with him?" Num 16:11,12

DISSENTING
having much * among themselves." Act 28:28,29f

DISSIPATION
They die young after lives of * Job 36:14

DISSOLVE
whirlwind and * me in the storm. Job 30:22
Let them be as snails that * Ps 58:8

DISSOLVES
when wet, the salt * and drains Lk 14:34f

DISSUADED
he wouldn't be *, we gave up and Act 21:14

DISTANCE
Abraham saw the place in the *. Gen 22:4
He saw in the * three flocks of Gen 29:2
them three days' *, and Jacob Gen 30:35,36
itself, separated by a * between. Gen 32:16
THEN, FAR IN the *, Jacob saw Esau Gen 33:1
the *, they decided to kill him! Gen 37:18
them in the *, probably Ishmaelite Gen 37:25
were just a short * from Ephrath, Gen 48:7
* to see what would happen to him. Ex 2:4
them far in the *, speeding after Ex 14:10
and they stood at a *, shaking Ex 20:18
As the people stood in the *, Ex 20:21
Moses are to worship at a *. Ex 24:1
a short * east of Moab, and from Num 21:11
desert with Mount Pisgah in the *. Num 21:20
you will see the land in the *. Deu 3:27
They lived a great * from their Ju 18:7
When they were quite a * from Ju 18:22
camp until they were at a safe *. 1Sa 26:13
young prophets watched from a *. 2Ki 2:6,7
saw her in the * and said to 2Ki 4:25
a * of about six hundred feet. 2Ki 14:13
has seen these things from a *. Job 36:25
her prey, from a very great *. Job 39:29
Even my own family stands at a *. Ps 38:11
but proud men must keep their *. Ps 138:6
square, with a * of 8¾ feet along Eze 40:7-12
guardrooms; this * was 43¾ feet. Eze 40:13
the same * as the passageway did. Eze 40:18
and found that the * was 175 Eze 40:19
inner court. The * between the two Eze 40:23
And the * between the passageways Eze 40:27
was feeding in the *, so the Mt 8:30
for him were watching from a *. Mt 27:55
some of them have come a long *." Mk 8:3
watching from a *—Mary Magdalene, Mk 15:40
And while he was still a long * Lk 15:20
Lazarus in the far * with Abraham. Lk 16:23
lepers stood at a *, crying out, Lk 17:12
stood at a * and dared not even Lk 18:13
and Peter followed at a *. Lk 22:54
Galilee, stood in the * watching. Lk 23:49
* I frankly don't know what to do. Gal 4:20
shall stand at a *, fearing danger Rev 18:15

DISTANT
be dragged away to * lands as Lev 26:36
Far down the * trail, Num 24:15-19
apply only to * cities, not to Deu 20:15
"The Lord will bring a * nation Deu 28:49
that pass by from * lands shall see Deu 29:22
far heavens, so * that you can't Deu 30:12
to scatter them to * lands, Deu 32:26
have come from a * land to ask for Jos 9:6
"We are from a very * country; Jos 9:9
you lived in a * land, when you Jos 9:22
name and come from * lands to 1Ki 8:41,42
He even destroyed * relatives and 1Ki 16:11
Philistines as far * as Gaza and 2Ki 18:8
lived in Aroer and as far * as 1Ch 5:7,8
and come from * lands to worship 2Ch 6:32
Simeon, even to * Naphtali, and did 2Ch 34:6
exile as slaves in * lands, but you Neh 5:8
angry—on and on to * generations? Ps 85:5
and Tyre, or even * Ethiopia, Ps 87:4
away to * lands as exiles. Ps 106:27
Ephrathah, then in the * Ps 132:6
Then you won't need to go to a * Pro 27:10
brought by ship from * ports. Pro 31:14
was in the * past and disappeared. Ecc 3:15
desolation upon you from a * land? Is 10:3
and all the * coastal lands. Is 11:11
as deserted as the * wooded hills Is 17:9
you away into a *, barren land; Is 22:18
Tyre, returning home from * lands! Is 23:1
the colonists you sent to * lands! Is 23:7
Yet [the * time will come when Is 23:18
Beautiful palaces in * lands Is 25:2
trees on the * mountain tops. Is 30:17
nor until even * lands beyond the Is 42:4
Sing, all you who live in * lands Is 42:10
* future, as well as to Cyrus. Is 45:13f
not in the * future, but right Is 46:13
for his foes in * lands. Is 59:18
coming home to you from * lands. Is 60:4
is coming from a * land and they Jer 4:16
See, I will bring a * nation Jer 5:15
my people: (Listen to it, * lands; Jer 6:18,19
world, to be strangers in * lands; Jer 9:16
slaves to your enemies in * lands. Jer 17:4
captive: He shall die in a * land Jer 22:12
will be exiled to * lands. Jer 22:28
home again from * lands, and your Jer 30:10
you from the * land of the enemy. Jer 31:16
bring your children from a * land. Jer 46:27
shall be taken away to * lands! Jer 48:7
Yes, come against her from * Jer 50:26
far away as slaves to * lands. Lam 1:18
They flee to * lands and wander Lam 4:15
begin their long march to * lands. Eze 12:4
"You even sent away to * lands Eze 23:40
back again from * lands where I Eze 28:25
the * nations you have never seen. Eze 32:9
* north, as well as many others. Eze 38:6
to action. In * years you will Eze 38:8

(DISTANT Con't)
This will happen in the * Eze 38:15,16
bringing you from the * north. Eze 39:2
They have gone as slaves to * Mic 1:16
and from * hills and mountains. Mic 7:12
proudly forward from a * land; Hab 1:8
some day come from * lands to Zec 6:15
for she came from a * land to Mt 12:42
not to send them to some * land. Mk 5:10
took a trip to a * land, and there Lk 15:13
called away to the * capital of the Lk 19:12
* land to live for several years. Lk 20:9
and even to those in * lands!" Act 2:39
them in * cities in foreign lands. Act 26:11

DISTILLS
vapor and then * it into rain, Job 36:27

DISTINCT
And prefer to remain * Num 23:7-10

DISTINCTION
for I will make a * between your Ex 8:23
* between Egyptians and Israelis.' Ex 11:7
God who has made a * between you Lev 20:24
"You shall therefore make a * Lev 20:25
without * as to age or rank. 1Ch 24:31
of Zeruiah, and anyone else of * 1Ch 26:28
The Hebrew text makes no * between Jon 3:3f
name, a name of * among all the Zep 3:20
He made no * between them and Act 15:9

DISTINCTIONS
These are the * between what is Lev 11:47

DISTINGUISH
be able to * good from evil!" Gen 3:5
be necessary to * between the Num 10:5,6,7
He shows how to * right from Pro 2:9
God says, I will * lambs from kids Eze 34:17

DISTINGUISHED
of even more * ambassadors than the Num 22:15
Jabez was more * than any of his 1Ch 4:9

DISTINGUISHING
carefully, * the true from false. Pro 20:8

DISTORT
Some of you yourselves will * Act 20:30

DISTORTED
You have * the covenant of Levi, Mal 2:8

DISTRACT
to * your attention from him. 1Co 7:35

DISTRACTED
lets himself be * from the work I Lk 9:62

DISTRACTING
"* the people from their work? Ex 5:4,5

DISTRAUGHT
When the woman saw how * he was, 1Sa 28:21

DISTRESS
in the day of my *, and was with me Gen 35:3
and the awful * caused by your Deu 28:56,57
them save you in your hour of *!" Ju 10:14
your family will be in * and need. 1Sa 2:32
I called upon the Lord in my *, 2Sa 22:7
the Hebrew word meaning "*." 1Ch 4:9f
Jabez, means * 1Ch 4:9
of Israel in their *, and searched 2Ch 15:4
He lives in fear, *, and anguish. Job 15:23,24
He delivers by *! Job 36:15
have always cared for me in my *; Ps 4:1
In my * I screamed to the Lord Ps 18:6
helpless, overwhelmed, in deep *; Ps 25:16
of safety in the day of my *. Ps 59:16
for rebels there is famine and *. Ps 68:6
away from me in this time of my *. Ps 102:2
to their cries and heeded their *; Ps 106:44
In my * I prayed to the Lord and Ps 118:5
In my * and anguish, your Ps 119:143
by anguish and *, then I will not Pro 1:27
knowledge only increases *. Ecc 1:16-18
Lord, in their * they sought for Is 26:16
them and refuse to notice their *. Jer 18:17
surrounded me with anguish and *. Lam 3:5
of sorrow and *, just as your Eze 23:33
in that terrible time of his *. Ob 1:14
it is a day of terrible * and Zep 1:15
pass safely through the sea of *, Zec 10:11
filled with horror and deepest *. Mk 14:33
For there will be great * upon Lk 21:23
Paul, in great *, turned and spoke Act 16:18
Yet this short time of * will 2Co 4:17

DISTRESSED
because he was so * at what the 1Ch 21:6
she was deeply * and sent clothing Est 4:4
I am too * even to pray! Ps 77:4
but I was greatly * by the dream Dan 8:27

DISTRIBUTE
harvest and * it to his favorites. 1Sa 8:15
and righteousness are mine to *. Pro 8:18
tribes of Israel. * the land as an Eze 47:22
servants who * God's blessings by 1Co 4:1

DISTRIBUTED
already mentioned * captured stores 2Ch 28:15
Shecaniah. They * the gifts to the 2Ch 31:14,15
is *, the most sacred land of all. Eze 48:12

DISTRIBUTES
when he * his sorrows and anger. Job 21:17

DISTRIBUTING
of * the offerings to the priests. 2Ch 31:14,15

DISTRIBUTION
So the * of the land was in Jos 14:5
they were not included in this *. 2Ch 31:16
handled the * throughout all Judah, 2Ch 31:20
honest * to their fellow-Levites. Neh 13:13
Where is the path to the * point Job 38:24
apostles for * to those in need. Act 4:37
*, as the widows who spoke Hebrew. Act 6:1

DISTRICT
one of these cities in each *; Deu 19:2,3
*, repaired the Fountain Gate. Neh 3:15
the mayor of half the Beth-zur *; Neh 3:16
of half the Keilah *, who Neh 3:17
building of the wall in his own *. Neh 3:17
of the other half of the Keilah *. Neh 3:18
the administrative * of Nineveh Jon 3:3f

DISTRICTS
Egypt into five administrative *, Gen 41:34,35
and let the officials of these * Gen 41:34,35
Divide the country into three *, Deu 19:2,3

DISTRUST
message stirred up * among the Act 14:2

DISTURB
Don't * his bones." 2Ki 23:18
"Do not * the construction of the Ez 6:6
will * those waters any more. Eze 32:13

DISTURBED
"Why have you * me by bringing 1Sa 28:15
of your son's head shall be *!" 2Sa 14:11
They will not be * again; 1Ch 17:9
mercy, and all heaven is *. 2Ch 28:9
dawn in red, and * the haunts of Job 38:15
He is not * by raging rivers, Job 40:23
is sick, and I am upset and *. Ps 6:3
says, Don't be * by this speech Is 37:6
I was confused and * by all I had Dan 7:15
When I awoke, I was greatly *, Dan 7:28
King Herod was deeply * by their Mt 2:3
David," they were * and indignant Mt 21:15
for he was deeply * by their Mk 3:5
Herod was * whenever he talked Mk 6:20
Confused and *, Mary tried to Lk 1:29
time to time and * the water, and Jn 5:4
came over to them, very * that Act 4:2
you shouldn't be * no matter what Act 19:36

DISTURBING
now they are here * our city," Act 17:6
Or, "Would that those * you would Gal 5:12f

DISUNITY
backs, filled with conceit and *. 2Co 12:20

DITCH
evaporated all the water in the *! 1Ki 18:38
plunge me into the * and mud; Job 9:31
an irrigation *, with lush, green Eze 19:10
and both will fall into a *." Mt 15:13,14
He will fall into a * and pull Lk 6:39

DITCHES
into irrigation *, so the Lord Pro 21:1
the fields; the * will be parched Is 19:5
dig *, and I'm too proud to beg. Lk 16:3

DIVERSE
Literally, "* weights and diverse Pro 20:10f
Literally, "diverse weights and * Pro 20:10f
Literally, "* weights . . . Pro 20:23f

DIVERTED
hands, lest it be * to care for 2Ki 12:8

DIVIDE
there be a dome to * the waters." Gen 1:6f
to * the light from the darkness. Gen 1:18
halves, but not to * the birds. Gen 15:10
Let Pharaoh * Egypt into five Gen 41:34,35
And * the captured booty." Ex 15:9
the live ox and * the price between Ex 21:35
Then the Lord told Moses to * the Num 26:52,53
then * it into two parts. Num 31:27
instructed you to * the land by lot Num 36:1
flee to safety. * the country into Deu 19:2,3
territory when you * the land among Jos 13:2-7
so that I can * it for you. Jos 18:4
to * the land among the tribes. Jos 19:51
There the Lord told him, "* them Ju 7:5,6
* the land equally between you." 2Sa 19:29
Then he said, "* the living 1Ki 3:25
yours nor mine; * it between us!" 1Ki 3:26
and shall * his silver among them. Job 27:17
they * my clothes among Ps 22:18
You commanded the Red Sea to *, Ps 106:9
later. * your gifts among many, Ecc 11:2
sending a mighty wind to * it Is 11:15
"whose land the rivers *." Is 18:2f
land the rivers *, will bring gifts Is 18:7
* your pastures for their flocks. Jer 6:3
"WHEN YOU * the land among the Eze 45:1
"* the land within these Eze 47:21
* up his clothes among themselves. Mt 27:35
to * my father's estate with me." Lk 12:13
his father agreed to * his Lk 15:12
of one another and * up into 1Co 3:3
but you should * with them. 2Co 8:14

DIVIDED
and * the light from the darkness. Gen 1:4,5
afterwards the river * into four Gen 2:10
Then he * out the ewes from Gen 30:39,40
with fear. He * his household, Gen 32:7
The waters *! Ex 15:8
the plains, * by tribal areas. Num 24:2
when it was * among the tribes. Num 26:62
of land will be * by lot among the Num 33:54
"It is to be * up among the nine Num 34:13
When God * up the world among the Deu 32:8
living among them—* into two Jos 8:33
That was how Moses * the land Jos 13:32
they were told and * the entire Jos 18:9
So all the land was * among the Jos 19:49
And I have * to you the land of Jos 23:4,5
'There is much loot to be *, Ju 5:30
He * the three hundred men into Ju 7:16
plans, so he had * his men into Ju 9:43
arrived, having * his army into 1Sa 11:11
land of Moab. He * his victims by 2Sa 8:2
and the river * and they went 2Ki 2:8
(which means "*," for it was 1Ch 1:19
of the earth were * into different 1Ch 1:19
* into the families of his sons: 1Ch 6:25,26,27
and behind him, he * his army and 1Ch 19:10
Then David * them into three main 1Ch 23:6
were still further * into six 1Ch 23:8,9
then he * Aaron's descendants 1Ch 24:3
Eleazar's descendants were * 1Ch 24:4
THE ISRAELI ARMY was * into twelve 1Ch 27:1
and Levites were * into their Ez 6:18
deeds. You * the sea for your Neh 9:11
of the wall and * them into two Neh 12:31,32
* the Red Sea with your strength; Ps 74:13,14
For he * the sea before them and Ps 78:13
Their treasure will be * by the Is 33:23
the deserts; he * the rock, and Is 48:21
Where is he whose mighty power * Is 63:12
no longer shall they be * into Eze 37:22
later on, this kingdom will be *. Dan 2:41,42
"Parsin means '*'—your kingdom Dan 5:28
kingdom will be * and given to the Dan 5:28
DARIUS * THE kingdom into 120 Dan 6:1
break apart and be * into four Dan 11:4
"They * up my people as their Joe 3:3
will be killed and your land * up. Amo 7:17
and * Jerusalem among them by lot; Ob 1:11
the loot *, the women raped; Zec 14:1
"A * kingdom ends in ruin. Mt 12:25
A city or home * against itself Mt 12:25
God for them, and * them into Mt 15:36
A kingdom * against itself will Mk 3:24
So the crowd was * about him. Jn 7:43
* in their opinions about him. Jn 10:19
that says,"They * my clothes among Jn 19:23,24
* in their opinion about them. Act 14:4
This * the Council right down the Act 23:7
His interests are *. 1Co 7:34

DIVIDES
and in the evening * the spoil." Gen 49:27
*. And this is the message sent Is 18:2

DIVIDING
So God made the sky, * the Gen 1:7,8
to handle the * up of the land: Num 34:16-28
* of the land among the tribes." Num 34:29
* the land among the tribes. Jos 11:23
* it to young and old alike. 2Ch 31:14,15
women of Israel are * the booty. Ps 68:11,12,13
* up the plunder they have won. Is 9:3
Here are the instructions for * Eze 47:13
of authority and * the land to them Dan 11:39
the nations and * up my land. Joe 3:2
$1,000 to the last—* it in Mt 25:15
and * with those in need. Act 2:45
than Apollos, and * the church. 1Co 3:4

DIVINATION
Literally, "I have learned by * Gen 30:27f
was used only for purposes of *. 2Ki 16:15
will call his magicians to use *; Eze 21:21
A very common type of * by which Eze 21:21f

DIVINE
full of words with no * authority. Jer 5:13
temple, without a * law to govern Lam 2:9
* knowledge and understanding. Dan 5:12
them what to do. "* Truth" comes Hos 4:12
was born—a child of * beauty. Act 7:20

DIVINERS
their priests and * and asked them, 1Sa 6:2
how could the * make this Eze 21:23

DIVISION
Peleg (meaning "*," for during Gen 10:25
will not be a * of the income; Ex 21:36
the Kohath * of the Levite tribe. Num 4:1
of the Gershonite * of the tribe of Num 4:21,22,23
of the Merari * of the Levite Num 4:29
The Merari * will also report to Num 4:33
of the Kohath *, including all of Num 4:34
of the Gershon * totaled 2,630. Num 4:38-41
And of the Merari *, 3,200. Num 4:42-45
to the Gershon * for their use, Num 7:7

DIVISION Con't)
to the Merari *, which was under Num 7:8
to the Kohath *, for they were Num 7:9
of the Kohath * (of the tribe of Jos 21:4
of the Kohath * were given ten Jos 21:5
The Gershon * received thirteen Jos 21:6
The Merari * received twelve Jos 21:7
of the Kohath * of the Levites. Jos 21:9-16
of the Kohath * received four Jos 21:20,21,22
remainder of the Kohath * was ten. Jos 21:26
Gershon, another * of the Levites, Jos 21:27
were assigned to the * of Gershon. Jos 21:33
Levites—the Merari *—were given Jos 21:34,35
So the Merari * of the Levites Jos 21:40
of this * in ancient times. 1Ch 9:20
Gershom *, the 1Ch 23:6
Kohath * and the 1Ch 23:6
Merari *. 1Ch 23:6
The * of Kohath was subdivided 1Ch 23:12
officials of the Temple in each *. 1Ch 24:5
Two groups from the * of Eleazar 1Ch 24:6
and one from the * of Ithamar were 1Ch 24:6
the Asaph * of the Korah clan. 1Ch 26:1
The commander of the First * was 1Ch 27:2,3
The commander of the Second * was 1Ch 27:4
The commander of the Third * was 1Ch 27:5,6
succeeded him as * commander. 1Ch 27:5,6
The commander of the Fourth * was 1Ch 27:7
The commander of the Fifth * was 1Ch 27:8
The commander of the Sixth * was 1Ch 27:9
The commander of the Seventh * 1Ch 27:10
The commander of the Eighth * was 1Ch 27:11
The commander of the Ninth * was 1Ch 27:12
The commander of the Tenth * was 1Ch 27:13
The commander of the Eleventh * 1Ch 27:14
The commander of the Twelfth * 1Ch 27:15
known since the * of Solomon's Is 7:17
A home filled with strife and * Mk 3:25
* of the Temple service corps. Lk 1:5
the Temple—for his * was on duty Lk 1:8,9
Rather, strife and *! Lk 12:51
So there was a deep * of Jn 9:16

DIVISIONS
Gershon and Merari * of the tribe Num 10:17
* so that I can divide it for you. Jos 18:4
into three main * named after the 1Ch 23:6
two * named after Aaron's sons, 1Ch 24:1
The * of the Temple guards were 1Ch 26:12
He was in charge of the * named 1Ch 26:23,24
of the twelve army *, the other 1Ch 28:1
Stay away from those who cause * Rom 16:17
meetings, and the * developing 1Co 11:18
If anyone is causing * among Tit 3:10

DIVORCE
his wife and he may never * her. Deu 22:19
he may never * her. Deu 22:28,29
For we agree before our God to * Ez 10:3
(they vowed to * their wives and Ez 10:16-19
says he hates * and cruel men. Mal 2:16
his wife, he can * her merely by Mt 5:31
"Do you permit *?" Mt 19:3
And no man may * what God has Mt 19:5,6
say a man may * his wife by merely Mt 19:7
asked him, "Do you permit *?" Mk 10:2
"What did Moses say about *?" Mk 10:3
And the husband must not * his 1Co 7:11
he must not leave her or * her. 1Co 7:12

DIVORCED
shall not marry a * woman, for he Lev 21:7
woman who is *, nor a prostitute. Lev 21:14,15
But if she is a widow or * and Lev 22:13
or is *, she must fulfill her vow. Num 30:9
that he has * her, give her the Deu 24:1
Shaharaim * his wives 1Ch 8:8,9,10
Is your mother gone because I * Is 50:1
she saw that I * faithless Israel. Jer 3:8
he may not marry a * woman. Eze 44:22
"And the man who marries a * Mt 19:9f
a * woman commits adultery." Lk 16:18

DIVORCES
husband also * her, or dies, the Deu 24:3
that if a man * a woman who then Jer 3:1
But I say that a man who * his Mt 5:32
that anyone who * his wife, except Mt 19:9
He told them, "When a man * his Mk 10:11
And if a wife * her husband and Mk 10:12
"So anyone who * his wife and Lk 16:18

DIVORCING
your treachery in * your wives who Mal 2:14
there be no * of your wives. Mal 2:16

DIZAHAB
Tophel, Laban, Hazeroth, and *. Deu 1:1

DOCKED
The next day when we * at Sidon, Act 27:3

DOCTOR
who are well don't need a *! Mt 9:12
need the *, not healthy ones! Mk 2:17
a *, not those in good health. Lk 5:31
Dear * Luke sends his love, and Col 4:14

DOCTORS
with the problem, but to the *. 2Ch 16:12
You are * who don't know what Job 13:4
much from many * through the years Mk 5:26
had spent everything she had on * Lk 8:43,44

DOCTRINE
your deeds are as good as your *. 2Co 9:13
will be wrong *, envy, murder, Gal 5:20
men who are teaching such wrong *. 1Ti 1:3,4

DOCTRINES
women and teach them their new *. 2Ti 3:6

DOCUMENTS
archives, where * were stored. Ez 6:1

DODAI
was * (a descendant of Ahohi). 1Ch 27:4

DODANIM
Javan:Elishah, Tarshish,Kittim, *. Gen 10:4

DODAVAHU
Then Eliezer, son of * from 2Ch 20:37

DODGED
But David * out of the way and 1Sa 19:9,10

DODO
(son of Puah and grandson of *). Ju 10:1
son of * and grandson of Ahohi. 2Sa 23:9
Elhanan (son of *) from Bethlehem; 2Sa 23:24-39
the son of *, a member of the 1Ch 11:12
Elhanan, the son of * from 1Ch 11:26-47

DOE
a loving hind and a pleasant *." Pro 5:19f

DOEG
(Incidentally, * the Edomite, 1Sa 21:7
Then * the Edomite, who was 1Sa 22:9,10
Then the king said to *, "You do 1Sa 22:18
So * turned on them and killed 1Sa 22:18
When I saw * there, I knew he 1Sa 22:22
against his enemy * (1 Samuel 22), Ps 52:1

DOG
" 'But not a * shall move his Ex 11:7
"Am I a *," he roared at David, 1Sa 17:43
worthless as a dead * or a flea? 1Sa 24:14
"Am I a Judean * to be kicked 2Sa 3:8
kindness to a dead * like me?" 2Sa 9:8
"Why should this dead * curse my 2Sa 16:9
"Am I a *?" 2Ki 8:13
You know that I am but a *, yet 1Ch 17:18
one from the power of the *!" Ps 22:20f
As a * returns to his vomit, so a Pro 26:11
"It is better to be a live * Ecc 9:4
God as putting a * or the blood of Is 66:3
saying that "A * comes back to 2Pe 2:22

DOG'S
Yanking a * ears is no more Pro 26:17

DOGS
Leave its carcass for the * to Ex 22:31
to their mouths and lap it like *. Ju 7:5,6
shall be eaten by *, and those who 1Ki 14:11
will be eaten by *, and those who 1Ki 16:4-7
Because you have done this, * 1Ki 21:19
told me that the * of Jezreel shall 1Ki 21:23
shall be eaten by * and those who 1Ki 21:24
bathed, * came and licked the 1Ki 22:38
(son of Ahijah). * shall eat 2Ki 9:10
He told Elijah the prophet that * 2Ki 9:36
whose fathers are less than my *. Job 30:1
men, circles me like a pack of *; Ps 22:16
around like * that prowl the city. Ps 59:6
like * and searching for food. Ps 59:14,15
with their blood; * will eat them. Ps 68:23
good, but trouble * the wicked. Pro 15:6
deer chased by *, wandering like Is 13:14
And they are as greedy as *, Is 56:11
sword to kill, the * to tear, and Jer 15:3
and throw it to the *," he said. Mt 15:26
food and throw it to the *." Mk 7:27
man's table, the * would come and Lk 16:21
men—dangerous *, I call them—who Php 3:2

DOINGS
About his mighty *. 1Ch 16:8
Literally, "Proclaim his * among Is 12:4f
Are your *, Rev 15:3,4

DOLED
pittance has been * out to you. Lev 26:26

DOLEFUL
deeded it to those * creatures; Is 34:17

DOLLAR
His payment shall be half a *. Ex 30:13
the servant said, "I have a *! 1Sa 9:8
the markets of Samaria for a *!" 2Ki 7:1
one *, just as the Lord had said! 2Ki 7:16

DOLLARS
to sixty shall pay twenty-five *; Lev 27:3
to sixty shall pay fifteen *; Lev 27:4
five to twenty shall pay ten *; Lev 27:5
a girl, five *. Lev 27:5
paid for him two and a half *; Lev 27:6
a girl, one and a half *. Lev 27:6
shall pay seven and a half *; Lev 27:7
a woman, five *. Lev 27:7
sowing is valued at twenty-five *. Lev 27:16
the number of Levites, pay five * Num 3:47,48
* made for each firstborn child. Num 18:16
and fine him one hundred * Deu 22:19
* for this job," they promised. Ju 16:5
"That thousand * you thought was Ju 17:2
I will give you ten * a year plus Ju 17:10,11
"For a million * I wouldn't do 2Sa 18:12
sold for fifty * and a pint of 2Ki 6:25
of dove's dung brought three *! 2Ki 6:25
of over a million * in gold, and 2Ch 9:9
Solomon received a billion * 2Ch 9:13,14
for a couple of * and eight Hos 3:2

DOLPHIN
and sandals made of * hide. Eze 16:9,10

DOMAIN
to meet you as you enter their *. Is 14:9

DOME
Literally, "Let there be a * to Gen 1:6f

DOMESTIC
from among all the * and wild Gen 3:14
kind of animal—* and wild—and Gen 7:14,15
perished—birds, * and wild animals, Gen 7:21
flocks and other * animals, as they Lev 27:32
and a large number of * fowls; Neh 5:18
of his palace and * affairs), Lk 8:3

DOMESTICATED
for food, wild or *, or the dead Lev 5:2

DOMINATES
that the Most High * the kingdoms Dan 4:17
the Most High God * the kingdoms of Dan 4:25

DOMINION
His * extended over all the 1Ki 4:24
He conquered the * of King 1Ch 18:3
power and * forever and ever. 1Ti 6:16

DOMINIONS
throughout his *, but this will Dan 11:24

DON
to mount them—* your helmets, Jer 46:4

DONATED
Moses gave them the materials * Ex 36:3
bronze mirrors * by the women who Ex 38:8
and gold vessels he himself had *. 1Ki 15:15
* 7,700 rams and 7,700 male goats. 2Ch 17:11
and the princes * 1,000 young 2Ch 30:24
King Cyrus himself * the gold Ez 1:7
The items Cyrus * included: Ez 1:9,10
of grain shall be * to the priests Eze 44:30

DONATES
"If someone * his home to the Lev 27:14,15

DONATIONS
that no more * were needed. Ex 36:4-7
and thigh as * from the people of Lev 7:34

DONKEY
altar, saddled his *, and took with Gen 22:3
"Stay here with the *," Abraham Gen 22:5
and put them on a *, and returned Ex 4:20
A firstborn * may be purchased Ex 13:13
to trade, the * shall be killed. Ex 13:13
it, and an ox or a * falls into it, Ex 21:33
a live ox or * or sheep or whatever Ex 22:4
"In every case in which an ox, * Ex 22:9
neighbor to keep a *, ox, sheep, or Ex 22:10
an enemy's ox or * that has strayed Ex 23:4
trying to get his * onto its feet Ex 23:5
The firstborn colt of a * may be Ex 34:20
so much as a * from them, and have Num 16:15
his * and started off with them. Num 22:21
along, Balaam's * suddenly saw the Num 22:22,23
When the * saw him standing Num 22:25
that the * couldn't get by at all. Num 22:26
Then the Lord caused the * to Num 22:28
the * asked. Num 22:30
"Why did you beat your * those Num 22:32
Three times the * saw me and Num 22:33
to get an ox or * onto its feet Deu 22:4
"Don't plow with an ox and a * Deu 22:10
She got off her * to speak to Jos 15:18,19
She dismounted from her * to Ju 1:14
and an extra *, went to see her to Ju 19:3
king—whose ox or * have I stolen? 1Sa 12:3
a young goat and a * carrying a 1Sa 16:20
the trail on her *, she met David 1Sa 25:20
mounted her *, and followed the men 1Sa 25:42
advice—saddled his *, went to his 2Sa 17:23
I told him, 'Saddle my * so that 2Sa 19:26
he saddled a * and went to Gath to 1Ki 2:40
"Quick, saddle the *," the old 1Ki 13:13
And when they had saddled the * 1Ki 13:13
the prophet's *, and the prophet 1Ki 13:23
* and the lion standing beside it. 1Ki 13:24,25
said to his sons, "Saddle my *!" 1Ki 13:27
and the * and lion were still 1Ki 13:28
eaten the body nor attacked the *. 1Ki 13:28
the body upon the * and took it 1Ki 13:29
the servants and a * so that I can 2Ki 4:22
So she saddled the * and said to 2Ki 4:24
I was mounted on my * and the Neh 2:11,12
* couldn't get through the rubble. Neh 2:14,15
Guide a horse with a whip, a * Pro 26:3
Even the animals—the * and the Is 1:3
You are a wild *, sniffing the Jer 2:24
He shall be buried like a dead * Jer 22:19
"you will see a * tied there, with Mt 21:2
Then he put the man on his * and Lk 10:34
look for a * tied beside the road. Lk 19:30

(DONKEY Con't)
Jesus rode along on a young *, Jn 12:14
course when his * spoke to him with 2Pe 2:16

DONKEY-LOADS
He sent his father ten * of the Gen 45:23

DONKEY'S
Then he picked up a * jawbone Ju 15:15
All with a * jaw! Ju 15:16,17
All with a * jaw!" Ju 15:16,17
so he threw her across the * back Ju 19:28
long while even a * head sold for 2Ki 6:25
* colt is likely to be born a man! Job 11:12
Yet he is lowly, riding on a * Zec 9:9
her, riding humbly on a * colt!" Mt 21:5
you meekly, sitting on a * colt!" Jn 12:15

DONKEYS
her—sheep, oxen, *, men and women Gen 12:16
and many slaves and camels and *. Gen 24:35
with many servants, camels, and *. Gen 30:43
now I own oxen, *, sheep, and many Gen 32:5
bulls,20 female *,10 male Gen 32:13,14,15
female donkeys,10 male *. Gen 32:13,14,15
and herds and *—everything they Gen 34:28
he was grazing his father's *. Gen 36:24
So they loaded up their * with Gen 42:26
grain to feed the *, there was his Gen 42:27
Load your * with the best Gen 43:11
seize us as slaves, with our *." Gen 43:18
and their * were fed. Gen 43:24
on their way with their loaded *. Gen 44:3
backs of their * and opened them. Gen 44:11
* again, and returned to the city. Gen 44:13
of Egypt, and ten * loaded with Gen 45:23
flocks, herds, and * of Egypt were Gen 47:17
*, camels, flocks, and herds. Ex 9:3
*, or anything else he has." Ex 20:17
this is to give your oxen and * a Ex 23:12
*, and flocks kept by the army. Num 31:28
61,000 *; Num 31:32-35
30,500 * (of which 61 were given Num 31:36-40
oxen,30,500 *, and16,000 girls Num 31:42-46
servants, oxen, *, or cattle; Deu 5:14
*, nor anything else he owns.' Deu 5:21
The same applies to *, clothing, Deu 22:3
of the meat. Your * will be driven Deu 28:31
sheep; *—everything. Jos 6:21
his oxen, *, sheep, his tent, and Jos 7:24
on their *, old, patched wineskins Jos 9:3,4,5
Those who ride on white * Ju 5:10
away all their sheep, oxen, and *. Ju 6:3,4
together on thirty *, and they Ju 10:4
grandsons, who rode on seventy *. Ju 12:14
fodder for our *, and plenty of Ju 19:19
He fed their * while they rested, Ju 19:21
One day Kish's * strayed away, so 1Sa 9:3
about us than about the *!" 1Sa 9:5
he can tell us where the * are." 1Sa 9:6
And don't worry about those * 1Sa 9:20
they will tell you that the * 1Sa 10:2
the *, but we couldn't find them; 1Sa 10:14
"He said the * had been found!" 1Sa 10:16
oxen, sheep, camels, and *.' 1Sa 15:3
also all the oxen, *, and sheep. 1Sa 22:19
fig cakes, and packed them onto *. 1Sa 25:18
the sheep, oxen, *, camels, and 1Sa 27:9
He was leading two * loaded with 2Sa 16:1
And Ziba replied, "The * are for 2Sa 16:2
horses, *, and everything else. 2Ki 7:7
The horses and * were tethered 2Ki 7:10
2,000 *, and 100,000 captives. 1Ch 5:21
on *, camels, mules, and oxen. 1Ch 12:40
from Meronoth had charge of the *. 1Ch 27:30
sick and old on *, and took them 2Ch 28:15
mules, 435 camels, and 6,720 *. Ez 2:66,67
mules, 435 camels, and 6,720 *. Neh 7:68,69
and loading their * with wine, Neh 13:15
*, and employed many servants. Job 1:2,3
plowing, with the * feeding beside Job 1:14,15
When wild * bray, it is because Job 6:5,6,7
and even the * of the poor and Job 24:3
Like the wild * in the desert, Job 24:5
"Who makes the wild * wild? Job 39:5
teams of oxen, and 1,000 female *. Job 42:12
There the wild * quench their Ps 104:11
When he sees riders in pairs on * Is 21:6,7
desert to Egypt—* and camels laden Is 30:6
The oxen and young * that till Is 30:24
Wild herds of * and goats will Is 32:14
The wild * stand upon the bare Jer 14:6
and he lived among the wild *; Dan 5:21
mules, camels, *, and all the other Zec 14:15

DONOR
be changed; the * may neither Lev 27:10

DOOM
for I know you can * me in an Gen 44:18
They have caused their own *." Lev 20:27
it, for then your * is sealed. Deu 7:26
Their * is sealed. Deu 32:35
paths of the godless lead to *. Ps 1:6
I have heard the * of my enemies Ps 92:11
a dwindling nation is his *. Pro 14:28
to the wicked, "Your * is sure. Is 3:11
Then I said, "My * is sealed, Is 6:5
of Amoz) concerning Babylon's *. Is 13:1
her time of * will soon be here. Is 13:22
them and lead them off to their *. Is 30:28
swift chariots of * to pour out the Is 66:15
he will pronounce their *. Jer 4:11,12
Ephraim your * has been announced. Jer 4:15
Their claims of * will fall upon Jer 5:13
But your * is certain. Jer 5:31
has decreed our * and given us a Jer 8:14
* and give you life and joy again? Jer 11:15
have heard the news of their *. Jer 49:23
promises of * he made so long ago. Lam 2:17
sing with glee, preparing my *. Lam 3:63
sorrows and pronouncements of *. Eze 2:9,10
for 390 years by captivity and *. Eze 4:4,5
This will prophesy her *. Eze 4:7
your final * is waiting. Eze 7:5,6
not save the people from their *. Eze 14:16
And the Lord God says: Your * is Eze 21:7
Now comes your day of *. Eze 22:4
them at that time of Egypt's *. Eze 30:9
Yet your * is the pit; Eze 32:19
your jaws and pull you to your *. Eze 38:4
will seal his own *, for he shall Dan 8:25
Fools! Your * is sealed, for you Hos 4:14
my prophets to warn you of your *; Hos 6:5
worshiped Baal and sealed his *. Hos 13:1
valley for the verdict of their *! Joe 3:14
THIS IS your *! Amo 3:1
The Lord God has sounded your *—I Amo 3:8
prosperity, but darkness and *! Amo 5:18
its *, and everyone will mourn. Amo 8:8
*, as I told you to before!" Jon 3:1
the impending * of Nineveh: Nah 1:1
from his wrath in that day of *. Zep 2:3
a public announcement of your *. Lk 10:11
"There is no eternal * awaiting Jn 3:18
for all of them end in eternal *. Rom 6:21
Didn't the law cause my *? Rom 7:13
smell of death and *, while to 2Co 2:16
If the plan that leads to * was 2Co 3:9
out from under the * of that Gal 3:13
* by the resurrection of Christ; 1Pe 3:21
reign, he, too, will go to his *. Rev 17:11
all liars—their * is in the Lake Rev 21:8

DOOMED
its fruit, you will be * to die." Gen 2:16,17
to him, you are * to death along Gen 20:7
raped her, and we would be *." Gen 26:10
that those whom you curse are *." Num 22:5,6
For they are * with you to eat 2Ki 18:27
his summons is * to die unless the Est 4:11
We are * to destruction and Est 7:4
Esther, for he knew that he was *. Est 7:7
O enemies of mine, you are * Ps 9:6
They are *, for God has rejected Ps 53:5
They are * to die by the sword, Ps 63:10
The men who enter them are *. Pro 2:19
The wicked man is * by his own Pro 5:22
They have * themselves. Is 3:9
this godless nation, * and damned; Is 10:5,6
Weep, Philistine cities—you are *. Is 14:31
All your nation is *. Is 14:31
upon Edom, the people I have *. Is 34:5
Woe, woe upon us, for we are *. Jer 4:13
are beautiful and delicate—and *. Jer 6:2
those * to starvation, to famine; Jer 15:2
I don't want them *! Jer 17:16
be heard again in this * land. Jer 33:10,11
animal and city is *—will once more Jer 33:12
her choicest youth are * to Jer 48:15
"We are surrounded and *!" Jer 49:29
We are *. Lam 4:18
City of Murder, * and Eze 22:3
for all are * and they will land in Eze 31:14
of the royal family: You are *! Hos 5:1
all are *. Hos 9:12
I have seen the sons of Israel *. Hos 9:13
Ephraim is *. Hos 9:16
"* is Hamath, near Damascus, and Zec 9:2
their enemy is *. Zec 10:5
filled with civil war is *; Lk 11:17
law and was a sinner, * to die. Rom 7:9
of this world, who are * to fall. 1Co 2:6
We felt we were * to die and saw 2Co 1:9
YOU WERE under God's curse, * Eph 2:1
dead and * by our sins, he gave us Eph 2:5
Isaac was * to death, but he came Heb 11:19
and are * and cursed. 2Pe 2:14
They are * to the eternal pits of 2Pe 2:17

DOOMING
the king's decree * all Jews, and Est 4:8

DOOMS
from them. He * the great men of Is 40:23

DOOR
deck—and put a * in the side. Gen 6:16
closed the * and shut them in. Gen 7:16
Noah opened the * to look, and Gen 8:13
from the tent * behind him. Gen 18:10
them, shutting the * behind him. Gen 19:
Lot and began breaking down the *. Gen 19:
in and bolted the *, and Gen 19:1
so that they couldn't find the *. Gen 19:1
side-frames of the * of every home Ex 12:
home and on the panel above the *. Ex 12:
lintel above the * and against the Ex 12:2
at the top of the * and on the two Ex 12:2
Or, "He will pause at the * of Ex 12:23
"As a screen for the * of the Ex 26:3
at the * of the Tabernacle. Ex 29:3
offering at the * of the Tabernacle Ex 29:4
* while the Lord spoke with Moses. Ex 33:
The curtain for the * of the Ex 35:10-1
it at the * of the Tabernacle. Lev 3:
He shall bring it to the * of Lev 4:
She must take them to the * of the Lev 12:
Then bring the Levites to the * Num 8:
at the * of the Tabernacle. Num 25:
his ear into the *, and after that Deu 15:1
the girl to the * of her father's Deu 22:2
And when they opened the *, they Ju 3:2
"Stand in the * of the tent," Ju 4:2
beating at the * and yelling at the Ju 19:2
She fell down at the * of the Ju 19:2
When her husband opened the * to Ju 19:2
in front of the * with her hands Ju 19:2
out and lock the * behind her." 2Sa 13:17,1
wood, and each * was hinged to fold 1Ki 6:3
So when Ahijah heard her at the * 1Ki 14:
walked through the * of her home. 1Ki 14:1
sons and shut the * behind you. 2Ki 4:
bed of the prophet and shut the *; 2Ki 4:2
He went in and shut the * behind 2Ki 4:3
stood at the * of Elisha's home. 2Ki 5:
When he arrives, shut the * and 2Ki 6:3
Then he opened the * and ran. 2Ki 9:1
the priests at the * of the Temple 2Ki 22:3,4
and Je-iel, the * keepers. 1Ch 15:1
Temple, the main *, and the inner 2Ch 4:2
and nailed the * of the Temple shut 2Ch 28:2
point opposite the * of Eliashib's Neh 3:2
and bolt the *," he exclaimed, Neh 6:1
Has he slammed the * in anger on Ps 77:
from the * of death. Ps 107:2
road, and at the * of every house. Pro 8:
She sits at the * of her house Pro 9:14
He sticks to his bed like a * to Pro 26:14
at death's *, and nearing his Ecc 12:
he was knocking at my bedroom *. Sol 5:2
* and my heart was moved for him. Sol 5:4
and if she is a * we will enclose Sol 8:9
the * of the Temple to hold court. Jer 26:1
near the * of the New Gate. Jer 36:1
Then he brought me to the * of Eze 8:7
I did, and uncovered a * to a Eze 8:8
and there at the *, between the Eze 8:16
went over to the * of the Temple. Eze 10:4
moved from the * of the Temple and Eze 10:18
and needy suffered outside her *. Eze 16:49
But a * led from its entry hall Eze 40:38
* faced north and the other south. Eze 41:11
The space above the * leading Eze 41:17,18
And there was a * from the outer Eze 42:12
and put it on the * posts of the Eze 45:19
After that, using the * through Eze 46:19,20
THEN HE BROUGHT me back to the * Eze 47:1
could to the open * of the flaming Dan 3:26
of Troubles into a * of Hope. Hos 1:15
and shut the * behind you and pray Mt 6:6
Knock, and the * will be opened. Mt 7:7
If only you will knock, the * Mt 7:8
feast, and the * was locked. Mt 25:10
calling, 'Sir, open the * for us!' Mt 25:11
gathered outside the * to watch. Mk 1:32,33
more, not even outside the *. Mk 2:2
near, that I am right at the *. Mk 13:29
me to get up. The * is locked for Lk 11:7
knock and the * will be opened. Lk 11:9
and the * is opened to everyone Lk 11:10
ready to open the * and let him in Lk 12:36
And he replied, "The * to heaven Lk 13:24,25
locked the *, it will be too late. Lk 13:24,25
'Lord, open the * for us,' he will Lk 13:24,25
beggar, was laid at his *. Lk 16:20
his son, who was now at death's *. Jn 4:46,47
a heavy stone rolled across its *. Jn 11:37,38
Just outside that * are the young Act 5:9
He knocked at the * in the gate, Act 12:13
*, their surprise knew no bounds. Act 12:16
* of faith to the Gentiles too. Act 14:27
and lived next * to the synagogue. Act 18:7
can be laid at my *, for I didn't Act 20:26
* for me to preach and teach here. 1Co 16:9
Therefore I have opened a * to Rev 3:8
I have been standing at the * and Rev 3:20
him and opens the *, I will come in Rev 3:20
THEN AS I looked, I saw a * Rev 4:1

DOORFRAMES
into its * and ceilings. Jer 22:13

DOORKEEPERS
entrance. The * put all of the 2Ki 12:9

(DOORKEEPERS Con't)
There were 212 * in those days. 1Ch 9:22
DOORMAN
I would rather be a * of the Ps 84:10
of Shallum), who was the temple *. Jer 35:4
DOORPOSTS
have placed on the * will be proof Ex 12:13
write them on the * of your house! Deu 6:9
Then he made square * of olive 1Ki 6:33
and from the * he had overlaid with 2Ki 18:16
There were square * at the doors Eze 41:21
the blood on the * of their homes, Heb 11:28
DOORS
in their tent * watching until he Ex 33:8
from their tent *, bowing low to Ex 33:10
around their tent * weeping, and Num 11:10
Write them upon the * of your Deu 11:20
Ehud locked the * behind him and Ju 3:22,23
and saw that the * were locked, Ju 3:24
then opened the * of the Temple as 1Sa 3:15
He scratched on the * and let his 1Sa 21:13
its two olive-wood * were carved 1Ki 6:32
There were two folding * of 1Ki 6:34
carved on these * and carefully 1Ki 6:35
the hinges of the * to the Most 1Ki 7:50
the main entrance * of the Temple. 1Ki 7:50
from the Temple *, and from the 2Ki 18:16
* in the gates and for the clamps; 1Ch 22:3
All the walls, beams, *, and 2Ch 3:7
the * of these courts with bronze. 2Ch 4:9
and the inner * to the Holy of 2Ch 4:22
* of the Temple and repaired them. 2Ch 29:3
backs on it. The * have been shut 2Ch 29:7
hung its *, and dedicated it. Neh 3:1
*, and made the bolts and bars. Neh 3:3
They laid the beams, set up the * Neh 3:6
Gate, hung the *, and installed the Neh 3:13
it, he hung the * and installed the Neh 3:14
it, hung its *, and installed its Neh 3:15
yet hung all the * of the gates— Neh 6:1
we had hung the * in the gates and Neh 7:1
but have opened my * to all)— or Job 31:32
fruits are at our *, the new as Sol 7:13
home, my people, and lock the *! Is 26:20
Behind closed * you set your Is 57:7,8
about you at the *, saying, 'Come Eze 33:30
the outside * of the guardrooms; Eze 40:13
inner court. Two * opened from the Eze 41:11
doorposts at the * of the nave, and Eze 41:21
Holies had double *, each with two Eze 41:23
sections. The * leading into the Eze 41:25
* of the building facing north. Eze 42:4
and *—they were identical units. Eze 42:11
construction—its * and Eze 43:11
the ravens will croak from her *. Zep 2:14
OPEN YOUR *, O Lebanon, to Zec 11:1
who would shut the * and refuse Mal 1:10
whatever * you lock on earth Mt 16:19
and whatever * you open on earth Mt 16:19
return is near, even at the *. Mt 24:33
behind locked *, in fear of the Jn 20:19
was with them. The * were locked; Jn 20:26
"The jail * were locked, and the Act 5:23
all the * flew open—and the chains Act 16:26
to see the prison * wide open, and Act 16:27
the * of welcome were wide open. 2Co 6:2
DOORWAY
cut off and were lying in the *; 1Sa 5:4
The * to the inner sanctuary was 1Ki 6:31
to her as she stood in the *. 2Ki 4:15,16
Even the * of the Temple, the 2Ch 4:22
room, but not from the outside *. 2Ch 5:9
was a 10½-foot * opening into a Eze 40:7-12
to the * to the entry hall inside. Eze 40:22
the pillars that formed its *. Eze 41:1
3½ feet thick; its * was 10½ feet Eze 41:3
DOORWAYS
Each of the * and windows had a 1Ki 7:5
DOPHKAH
Next was *, and then Alush; Num 33:12
DOR
mountain areas of *, on the west; Jos 11:1
The king of * in the city of Jos 12:8-24
Ible-am, *, En-dor, Taanach, Jos 17:11
Taanach, *, Ibleam, Megiddo, with Ju 1:27
whose area was the highlands of *; 1Ki 4:8-19
Taanach, Megiddo, and *. 1Ch 7:29
DORCAS
was a woman named * ("Gazelle"), Act 9:36
took him upstairs where * lay. Act 9:39
garments * had made for them. Act 9:39
the body he said, "Get up, *," Act 9:40
DORMITORY
you can see, our * is too small. 2Ki 6:1
DOSE
it is a bitter * of your own Jer 4:18
a strong * of alchemy and magic! Dan 1:3,4f
DOTHAN
say they were going to *." Gen 37:17
So Joseph followed them to * Gen 37:17
came back, "Elisha is at *." 2Ki 6:13

DOTTED
Four Living Beings, * front and Rev 4:6
DOUBLE
be erased. The * dream gives Gen 41:32
The double dream gives * impact, Gen 41:32
Take * money so that you can pay Gen 43:12
So they took the gifts and * Gen 43:15
he shall pay * value as his fine. Ex 22:4
thief shall pay * if he is found. Ex 22:7
guilty shall pay * to the other. Ex 22:9
He must give the customary * Deu 21:17
* walls near the king's garden. 2Ki 25:4,5
you shall have a * portion of Is 61:7
Yes, bring * destruction upon Jer 17:18
Holy of Holies had * doors, each Eze 41:23
my disciples have * treasures—from Mt 13:52
who had been bent * for eighteen Lk 13:11
ordered him bound with * chains. Act 21:33
that I could be a * blessing to you 2Co 1:15,16
* penalty for all her evil deeds. Rev 18:6
DOUBLE-BLADED
pulled out the * dagger strapped Ju 3:21
and a sharp, * sword in his mouth, Rev 1:16
who wields the sharp and * sword. Rev 2:12
DOUBLE-CHAINED
he was asleep, * between two Act 12:6
DOUBLE-EDGED
he made himself a * dagger eighteen Ju 3:16
And take a * sword to execute his Ps 149:6,7
is left to you, sharp as a * Pro 5:4
DOUBLED
square, * over to form a pouch; Ex 39:9
$2,000 to use, and I have * it.' Mt 25:22
DOUBLY
And I will punish you * for all Jer 16:18
They are not only dead, but * Jud 1:12
DOUBT
Joseph is without * torn in Gen 37:33
Don't even *!' Deu 1:19,20,21
if there is no * it is true, Deu 17:4
Your lives will hang in *. Deu 28:66
Banish fear and *! Jos 1:9
Let him alone, for no * the Lord 2Sa 16:11
there's not a shadow of a * that 1Ki 20:25
But no * you gave men of Job 22:8
are those who don't * me.' Mt 11:6
"Why did you * me?" Mt 14:31
faith, and don't *, you can do Mt 21:21
you really believe and have no *! Mk 11:22,23
you will know it beyond all *. Lk 17:24
"Why do you * that it is really Lk 24:38
undecided, filled with joy and *. Lk 24:41
And you no * know that Jesus of Act 10:38
But there could be no * about Act 10:46,47
to each other, "A murderer, no *! Act 28:4
very nicely, no *, but the other 1Co 14:17
God's house. No * you already know Eph 3:2,3
now they can know without * that Heb 6:18
There is no longer any room for * Heb 10:23
say without any * or fear, "The Heb 13:6
Be merciful to those who *. Jud 1:22
DOUBTED
For there your fathers * me, Ps 95:9
But Abraham never *. Rom 4:20
DOUBTERS
provide clothing for you, you *? Lk 12:28
DOUBTFUL
to tell you, for a * mind will be Jas 1:6
DOUBTLESS
* to tell them that a messenger Gen 24:28f
and never returned—* torn to pieces Gen 44:28
its people * very proud of him. 2Sa 15:9f
God is * punishing you far less Job 11:6
* Cyrus the Great of Persia. Is 41:2f
King Zedekiah * had in mind God's Jer 21:1f
not have life." *, the reference Eze 20:25f
* Alexander the Great. Dan 11:3f
DOUBTS
Lord, when * fill my mind, when Ps 94:19
things others have no * about." Rom 14:1f
considerate of the * and fears of Rom 15:1
DOUGH
them their bread * without yeast, Ex 12:34
* they had brought along. Ex 12:39
* and baked unleavened bread. 1Sa 28:24
he could watch her mix some *; 2Sa 13:8
the women knead * and make cakes to Jer 7:18
he kneads the * and waits for it to Hos 7:4
permeates every part of the *." Mt 13:33
become as evident as yeast in *. Lk 12:2
It is like yeast kneaded into *, Lk 13:20,21
DOVE
on the water. The * which Noah next Gen 8:7f
Meanwhile he sent out a * to see Gen 8:8
ground, but the * found no place Gen 8:9
and drew the * back into the boat. Gen 8:9
Noah released the * again, and Gen 8:10
A week later he released the * Gen 8:12
Oh, for wings like a *, to fly Ps 55:6
"My * is hiding behind some Sol 2:14
lover, my lovely *,' he said, 'for Sol 5:2

but you, my *, my perfect one, Sol 6:9
a swallow and mourned like a *; Is 38:14
Ephraim is a silly, witless *, Hos 7:11
coming down in the form of a *. Mt 3:16
in the form of a * descending on Mk 1:10
in the form of a * settled upon Lk 3:22
in the form of a * descending from Jn 1:32
DOVE'S
of * dung brought three dollars! 2Ki 6:25
DOVES
covered all over as wings cover *! Ps 68:11,12,13
Your eyes are soft as *'. Sol 1:15
Your eyes are those of *. Sol 4:1
His eyes are like * beside the Sol 5:12
moan with mournful cries like *. Is 59:11
to Israel, like * to their nests? Is 60:8
in the caves like * that nest in Jer 48:28
lonely as mourning * hiding on the Eze 7:16
Egypt—like * flying from Assyria. Hos 11:11
listen to them mourn like *, and Nah 2:7
as serpents and harmless as *. Mt 10:16
and the stalls of those selling *. Mt 21:12
of those selling *, and stopped Mk 11:15
cattle, sheep, and * for Jn 2:14
to the men selling *, he told them, Jn 2:16
DOWNCAST
Theirs was no * look of Ps 34:5
Why then be *? Ps 42:4,5
DOWNFALL
will live to see the tyrant's *. Pro 29:16
own household will bring his *; Dan 11:26
as a sign of their *, but for you Php 1:28
(Satan's * is an example. 1Ti 3:6
DOWNHILL
decay of the wicked drives it *. Pro 11:11
DOWNSTAIRS
Then Elijah took him * and gave 1Ki 17:23
DOWNTRODDEN
O Lord, don't let your * people Ps 74:21
see, that the * shall be freed from Lk 4:18,19
DOWNWARD
Abram fell face * in the dust Gen 17:2,3,4
Then Moses and Aaron fell face * Num 14:5
he fell face * to the ground. Num 16:4
But Moses and Aaron fell face * Num 16:22
But Moses and Aaron fell face * Num 16:45
they fell face * before the Lord; Num 20:6
Manoah and his wife fell face * Ju 13:20
she fell face * on the floor in 2Sa 14:4
We lie face * in the dust. Ps 44:25
his enemies shall fall face * in Ps 72:9
of animals goes * into dust? Ecc 3:21
away to follow his own * road. Ecc 7:29
to lie face * in the dust; Lam 3:29
And when I saw it, I fell face * Eze 1:27,28
Then I fainted, lying face * on Dan 8:18
the ground face * in a deep faint. Dan 10:9
At this the disciples fell face * Mt 17:6
and fell face * on the ground, and Mt 26:39
before him, face * in the dust, Lk 5:12
of Jesus, face * in the dust, Lk 17:16
DOWRY
No matter what * or gift you Gen 34:12
with her, he must pay the usual * Ex 22:16
family find enough * to marry the 1Sa 18:23
that the only * I need is one 1Sa 18:25
*—she was one of Solomon's wives. 1Ki 9:16
DOZEN
the words of fools are a dime a *. Pro 10:20
If you try once you must try a * Pro 19:19
and then, a * years later, the Zep 1:1f
DRAFT
of Levi from the *, and do not Num 1:47,48,49
in charge of the *) to conscript 1Ki 12:18
sent Hadoram to * forced labor from 2Ch 10:18
DRAFTABLE
So the total number of the * men Num 26:51
DRAFTED
man is not to be * into the army Deu 24:5
who had been * into the Philistine 1Sa 14:21
Then Solomon * thirty thousand 1Ki 5:13
David now * all the resident 1Ch 22:2
to which men were * under quotas 2Ch 26:11
DRAG
to kill him, * him even from my Ex 21:14
can take ropes and * the walls of 2Sa 17:13
and maul me and * me away with no Ps 7:2
your home, and * you away from the Ps 52:5
Evil men have tried to * me into Ps 119:61
Woe to those who * their sins Is 5:18
Lord, * them off like helpless Jer 12:3
into your jaws and * you out onto Eze 29:4
they will * the last of you away Amo 4:2
pick on you and * you into court? Jas 2:6
DRAGGED
cause them to be * away to distant Lev 26:36
he was * away and killed. Ju 12:6
stare at him, they * him off the 2Sa 20:12
and he was * outside the city and 1Ki 21:13
So they slaughtered them all and * 2Ki 10:25
the inner temple, * out the pillar 2Ki 10:26

(DRAGGED Con't)
So they * her to the palace 2Ki 11:16
like a dead donkey—* out of Jer 22:19
children will be * away as slaves! Jer 49:20
shall be * away as slaves; Jer 50:45
her virgins have been * away. Lam 1:4
He has * me into the underbrush Lam 3:11
you will be * out and slaughtered. Eze 11:7
on their hooks and * out in their Hab 1:15
So they * him out of the Mt 21:39
You will be * before the courts, Mk 13:9
So they * him out of the Lk 20:15
and you will be * into synagogues Lk 21:12
So Simon Peter went out and * Jn 21:11
their shouts, and * him out of the Act 7:58
stoned Paul and * him out of the Act 14:19
they grabbed Paul and Silas and * Act 16:19
Not finding them there, they * Act 17:6
by some of the Jews and * forward. Act 19:33
Paul was * out of the Temple, and Act 21:30

DRAGGING
withered old man, * himself along: Ecc 12:5
private homes and * out men and Act 8:3
the amphitheater, * along Gaius and Act 19:29

DRAGON
serpent, the * of the sea. Is 27:1
"The Reluctant *," Is 30:7
you slew Egypt, the * of the Nile. Is 51:9
Literally, "Rahab, the *." Is 51:9f
of Egypt—mighty * lying in the Eze 29:3
Suddenly a red * appeared, with Rev 12:3
* and his hosts of fallen angels. Rev 12:7
And the * lost the battle and Rev 12:8
This great *—the ancient serpent Rev 12:9
And when the * found himself cast Rev 12:13
the *, for three and a half years. Rev 12:14
Then the furious * set out to Rev 12:17
And the * gave him his own power Rev 13:2
They worshiped the * for giving Rev 13:4
Then the * encouraged the Rev 13:5
in heaven. The * gave him power to Rev 13:7
the mouth of the *, the Creature, Rev 16:13
The *—Satan—and the Creature from Rev 17:3f
He seized the *—that old Rev 20:2

DRAGON'S
but a fearsome voice like the *. Rev 13:11

DRAGS
as shards; he * across the ground Job 41:30
is too late and he * you into court Mt 5:25
When the net is full, he * it up Mt 13:47,48

DRAIN
not destroy you. * the lamb's Ex 12:22
here to kill and * them, and not to 1Sa 14:34
They must * that cup to the Ps 75:8
In deep anguish you will * that Eze 23:34

DRAINED
their life-blood has been * off. Gen 9:4
be * out at the side of the altar. Lev 1:15,16,17
be * out at the base of the altar; Lev 5:9
My strength has * away like Ps 22:14
my years are shortened, * away Ps 31:9,10

DRAINS
salt dissolves and * out, leaving a Lk 14:34f

DRANK
so he ate and * and went on about Gen 25:34
and they ate and * in preparation Gen 26:30
that time he neither ate nor *. Ex 34:28
and the people and their cattle * Num 20:11
They * the sparkling wine. Deu 32:14
Only three hundred of the men * Ju 7:5,6
all the others * with their Ju 7:5,6
spirit was revived as he *. Ju 15:19
ate some food and * some water at 1Ki 13:19
evening, and he * from the brook. 1Ki 17:6
So he ate and * and lay down 1Ki 19:6
So he got up and ate and *, and 1Ki 19:8
They feasted and * with David 1Ch 12:39
Then they feasted and * before 1Ch 29:22
kings and princes * of the cup so Jer 25:18
people—they too * from that Jer 25:19,20
* from this cup of God's wrath. Jer 25:26
which she * was full and large. Eze 23:32
and concubines * toasts from them Dan 5:2,3,4
your heads. You * my cup of Ob 1:16
and they all * from it. Mk 14:23
They ate and * and Lk 17:27
to us who ate and * with him after Act 10:40,41
* the water that Christ gave them. 1Co 10:3,4
Literally, "For they * of a 1Co 10:3,4f

DRAPE
goat skins, and the entrance *; Ex 39:33-40

DRAPED
of salvation and * about me the Is 61:10
heavens shall be * with black, Jer 4:28

DRAPERIES
formed by eleven * made of goats' Ex 36:14,15
Bezalel coupled five of these * Ex 36:16
loops so that the * were firmly Ex 36:18

DRAPERY
Then he made a * for the entrance Ex 36:37
This * was connected by five Ex 36:38
The * covering the entrance to Ex 38:18

DRAPES
The * for the walls of the court; Ex 35:10-19
* for the entrance to the court; Ex 35:10-19
it consisted of * woven from Ex 38:9
posts to hold *, with bases of Ex 38:10
the walls were made from * Ex 38:12
The * at either side of the Ex 38:14,15
All the * making up the walls of Ex 38:16
hold up the * were solid silver. Ex 38:17
the same as the * composing the Ex 38:18
supporting the * enclosing the Ex 38:29
The * for the walls of the court Ex 39:33-40
The bases and the * at the gate of Ex 39:33-40
Set up the * at the entrance of Ex 40:5
its entry *, the drapes covering Num 3:25-30
entry drapes, the * covering the Num 3:25-30
They are also to carry the * Num 4:26

DRAW
village were coming to * water. Gen 24:11
village are coming out to * water. Gen 24:13
Then she said, "I'll * water Gen 24:19
who comes out to * water, "Please Gen 24:43
Hebrew word meaning "to * out." Ex 2:10f
"to * out") because she had Ex 2:10
of Midian came to * water and fill Ex 2:16
* for the smaller sections." Num 26:55,56
he has tried to * you away from the Deu 13:10
The Lord says, 'I will * them to Ju 4:7
girls going out to * water and 1Sa 9:9,10,11
Then Saul said, "Now * lots 1Sa 14:42
and gives me strength to * an iron Ps 18:34
heart, the wise man will * it out. Pro 20:5
it before you and * a map of the Eze 4:1
Jerusalem on it. * a picture of Eze 4:1
In the hope that they would * Eze 20:26
shall suddenly * their swords Eze 28:7
Then the crew decided to * straws Jon 1:7
When you came to * fifty gallons Hag 2:16,17
Soon a Samaritan woman came to * Jn 4:7
I will * everyone to me." Jn 12:32
So we did, and couldn't * in Jn 21:6
truth in order to * a following. Act 20:30
not reach out to me and * me in. 2Co 6:12
him and * up nourishment from him. Col 2:7
God, and now we may * near to him. Heb 7:19
No, and you can't * fresh water Jas 3:12
And when you * close to God, God Jas 4:8
to God, God will * close to you. Jas 4:8

DRAWING
I will give you a * of the Ex 25:9
have a lottery, * for the larger Num 26:55,56
similar—"* straws" would be a Lk 1:8,9f
celebration was * near—the Jewish Lk 22:1
his coming back again is * near. Heb 10:25

DRAWN
she had * him out of the water. Ex 2:10
wagons, each * by two oxen—a wagon Num 7:3
in the road with a * sword. Num 22:22,23
the roadway with * sword, and he Num 22:31
listen—if you are * away to worship Deu 30:17
appeared nearby with a * sword. Jos 5:13
and Benjamin was * away from the Ju 20:31
them and be * away from the town. Ju 20:32
a chariot of fire, * by horses of 2Ki 2:11
Lots were then * to assign land 1Ch 6:61
with his sword *, pointing toward 1Ch 21:16
* sword of the angel of Jehovah. 1Ch 21:30
strung their bows, * their arrows Ps 11:2
They have fled from * swords and Is 21:15
with lovingkindness I have * you Jer 31:3
sword is * from its sheath; Eze 21:28
is * against the land of Egypt. Eze 32:20
She will be * down to judgment. Eze 32:20
They will rule Assyria with * Mic 5:6
the armies * up against her, and Zec 12:4
of Remembrance * up in which he Mal 3:16
to Jerusalem, * there irresistibly Act 20:22

DRAWS
and bones, and * near to death. Job 33:22
eternity. He * up the water vapor Job 36:27
of troubles, and death * near. Ps 88:3
the day * near. Eze 7:12
Father who sent me * him to me, and Jn 6:44

DREAD
Terror and * have overcome them. Ex 15:16
of you, and * your arrival.' Deu 2:25
will send fear and * ahead of you Deu 11:25
that I * more than anything else. Job 31:23
and friends. They * meeting me and Ps 31:11
With * deeds and awesome power Ps 65:5
stand in * and awe of him. Ps 89:7
of the day; nor * the plagues of Ps 91:6
gone, for the * of them was great. Ps 105:38
nor live in * of what may happen. Ps 112:7
How I * being mocked for obeying, Ps 119:39
Will you be in constant * of Is 51:13
in the * day of your punishment. Amo 5:13
were filled with sorrow and *. Mt 17:22,23
were filled with terror and *. Mk 10:32
hearts were full of * and fear. 2Co 7:5
lives as slaves to constant *. Heb 2:1
all * of what he might do to us. 1Jn 4:1

DREADFUL
I am going to do all of the * 1Sa 3:1
had destroyed them with * plagues. 1Sa 6:
Then out of the * silence came Job 4:1
"God is powerful and *. Job 25:
I will bring you to a * end; Eze 26:2
their heads, for your fate is *; Eze 27:3
of the ocean, too * to describe and Dan 7:

DREAM
came to him in a * and told him, Gen 20:
season, I had a *, and saw that the Gen 31:1
Then, in my *, the Angel of God Gen 31:1
God appeared to Laban in a *. Gen 31:2
One night Joseph had a * and Gen 37:
And they hated him both for the * Gen 37:
Then he had another * and told it Gen 37:
"Listen to my latest *," he Gen 37:
One night each of them had a *. Gen 40:
The wine taster told his * first. Gen 40:9,1
"In my *," he said, "I saw a Gen 40:9,1
"I know what the * means," Gen 40:1
saw that the first * had such a Gen 40:1
he told his * to Joseph, too. Gen 40:1
"In my *," he said, "there were Gen 40:1
asleep again and had a second *. Gen 41:
again and realized it was all a *. Gen 41:
and I each had a * one night. Gen 41:1
"I had a * last night," Pharaoh Gen 41:1
So Pharaoh told him the *. Gen 41:1
"A little later I had another *. Gen 41:2
The double * gives double Gen 41:3
"I had this strange *," he was Ju 7:12,1
"Your * can mean only one thing! Ju 7:1
When Gideon heard the * and the Ju 7:1
The Lord appeared to him in a * 1Ki 3:
up and realized it had been a *. 1Ki 3:1
He will fade like a *. Job 20:
Their present life is only a *! Ps 73:2
one awakens from a * of things that Ps 73:2
and vanish as quickly as a *. Ps 90:5,6
to Jerusalem, it was like a *! Ps 126:
my heart awakened in a *. Sol 5:2
Jerusalem will vanish like a *! Is 29:7
your enemies will * of victorious Is 29:8
to lie there, love to sleep, to *. Is 56:10
"Listen to the * I had from God Jer 23:25
worse, he couldn't remember his *! Dan 2:
they tell him what his * had been. Dan 2:1
"Sir, tell us the * and then we Dan 2:4
the * is gone—I can't remember it. Dan 2:5
what the * was and what it means. Dan 2:6
tell you what the * means unless Dan 2:7
befalls me that the * foretells. Dan 2:8,9
But if you don't tell me the *, Dan 2:8,9
can tell you your *, and they are Dan 2:11
you the * and what it means." Dan 2:16
of the king's *, and the Dan 2:23
who will tell you your *!" Dan 2:25
Can you tell me what my * was and Dan 2:26
* what will happen in the future. Dan 2:28
This was your *: Dan 2:28
secret of your *, for God showed it Dan 2:30
"That was the *; Dan 2:36
of your * is as sure and certain as Dan 2:45
a * that greatly frightened me. Dan 4:5
the meaning of my *, but when they Dan 4:6
the *, they couldn't interpret it. Dan 4:7
holy gods, and I told him the *. Dan 4:8
Tell me what my * means: Dan 4:9
"O Belteshazzar, that was my *; Dan 4:18
aghast at the meaning of the *. Dan 4:19
in this * would happen to your Dan 4:19
Twelve months after this *, he Dan 4:29
had a * and he wrote it down. Dan 7:1
In my * I saw a great storm on a Dan 7:2
Then, as I watched in my *, a Dan 7:7
That was the end of the *. Dan 7:28
another * similar to the first. Dan 8:1
Daniel the meaning of his *." Dan 8:16
the * and did not understand it. Dan 8:27
a vision and many a parable and *. Hos 12:10
your old men will * dreams, and Joe 2:28
he fell into a *, and saw an angel Mt 1:20
in a * to go home another way. Mt 2:12
Lord appeared to Joseph in a *. Mt 2:13
Lord appeared in a * to Joseph in Mt 2:19
Then, in another *, he was warned Mt 2:22
"Or what king would ever * of Lk 14:31
and your old men * dreams. Act 2:17
thought it was a * or vision, and Act 12:9
In his * he saw a man over in Act 16:9
on some mere human whim or *. Gal 1:11
to ask or even * of—infinitely Eph 3:20

DREAMED
For who would have * that I Gen 21:7
to sleep, and * that a staircase Gen 28:12
later, Pharaoh * that he was Gen 41:1
of all the things he * of—none Job 20:20
can tell others what they have *! Dan 2:10

DREAMED Con't)
told Daniel what the king had *. Dan 2:19
"You * of coming events. Dan 2:29

DREAMER
What a *! Pro 18:11
And say this to Shemaiah the *: Jer 29:24
the name of which means "*." Jer 29:24f
was, "He's a *," or, "He's Act 17:18

DREAMERS
fortune-tellers, *, mediums and Jer 27:9

DREAMING
destroy your prosperity. * Ecc 5:6,7
mere * of nice things is foolish; Ecc 6:9
Then as I lay there *, I saw one Dan 4:13

DREAMS
what will become of all his *!" Gen 37:19,20
And they replied, "We both had * Gen 40:8
"Interpreting * is God's Gen 40:8
as to what the * might mean; Gen 41:8
could suggest what his * meant. Gen 41:8
We told the * to a young Hebrew Gen 41:12
and he told us what our * meant. Gen 41:12
you can interpret *, and that is Gen 41:15
"Both * mean the same thing," Gen 41:25
the meaning of the * to you, you Gen 41:39
Then Joseph remembered the * of Gen 42:8,9
communicate by visions and *; Num 12:6
the future by *, and if his Deu 13:1
him, either by *, or by Urim, 1Sa 28:5,6
and won't reply by prophets or *; 1Sa 28:15
and again, in *, in visions of the Job 33:15
but when * come true at last, Pro 13:12
As a hungry man * of eating, but Is 29:8
as a thirsty man * of drinking, but Is 29:8
By telling these false * they Jer 23:27
tell their * and let my true Jer 23:28
Their made-up * are flippant Jer 23:32
Don't listen to the * that they Jer 29:8
the meanings of * and visions. Dan 1:17
He can interpret *, explain Dan 5:12
your old men will dream *, and Joe 2:28
visions, and your old men dream *. Act 2:17
visions, *, and even face to face Heb 1:1

DREGS
They must drain that cup to the * Ps 75:8
You have drunk to the * the cup Is 51:17

DRENCH
And I will * the earth with your Eze 32:6
Let the dews of heaven * him and Dan 4:15

DRESS
Next, * his sons in their robes, Ex 29:8
A lazy man won't even * the game Pro 12:27
Get up and * and go out and tell Jer 1:17
will seek to hide her wedding *? Jer 2:32
As the lowliest of slaves would *. Jn 13:4f

DRESSED
bringing the * kids, which she Gen 27:14
his authority, and * him in Gen 41:41,42
They replied, "They were * just Ju 8:18
of wine, five * sheep, two bushels 1Sa 25:18
kings, who were * in their royal 1Ki 22:10
leader were all * in linen robes. 1Ch 15:27
sons and brothers, * in finespun 2Ch 5:11,12
willingly, * in holy altar robes. Ps 110:3
saucy and pert, and * seductively. Pro 7:10
Shall I get * again? Sol 5:3
older priests—all * in sackcloth—to Is 37:2
it means, will be * in purple robes Dan 5:7
a man * as a prince in a palace? Mt 11:8
palace guard, * him in a purple Mk 15:16,17
Did you find him * in expensive Lk 7:25
"Be prepared—all * and ready— Lk 12:35
Then the angel told him, "Get * Act 12:8
If a man comes into your church * Jas 2:2
in who is poor and * in threadbare Jas 2:2
The armies of heaven, * in Rev 19:14

DRESSES
lingerie, beautiful * and veils. Is 3:23

DRESSING
* according to his instructions. Est 2:15

DREW
So Noah held out his hand and * Gen 8:9
and * water and filled the jug. Gen 24:45
first, but he * back his hand and Gen 38:29
As the time * near for him to Gen 47:29
told him; "he * water for us and Ex 2:19
animals, and * it off into basins. Ex 24:6
yourself," he * off his sandal. Ru 4:8
a great ceremony, * water from the 1Sa 7:6
He * me out from the waters; 2Sa 22:17
ranks and * water from the well and 2Sa 23:16
Then Jehu * his bow with his full 2Ki 9:24
Then Jeroboam * Israel away from 2Ki 17:21
Philistine camp, * some water from 1Ch 11:18,19
the ropes that * me on to death. Ps 18:5
and * me out of my great trials. Ps 18:16
and Jonah * the short one. Jon 1:7
Soldiers * straws to see who Nah 3:10
As the time * near for his return Lk 9:51
Then Simon Peter * a sword and Jn 18:10
Then they * straws, Act 1:26
of Galilee. He * away some people Act 5:37
"As the time * near when God Act 7:17,18
he * his sword to kill himself. Act 16:27
His tail * along behind him a Rev 12:4

DRIBLETS
portioned out in *, and the people Eze 4:16

DRIED
Tell them how the Lord our God * Jos 4:23
that the Lord had * up the Jordan Jos 5:1
But after awhile the brook * up, 1Ki 17:7
to boil some * figs and to make a 2Ki 20:7
my strength has * up like Ps 22:15
and then you * a path for them Ps 74:15
The grassy banks are * up and the Is 15:6
But they are as useless as * Is 47:14
the mighty God who * up the sea, Is 51:10
Lord of Hosts, who * a path for you Is 51:15
pastures are * up—for the prophets Jer 23:10
* human dung as fuel, and eat it. Eze 4:12
The roots of Israel are * up; Hos 9:16
the grain has * up in the fields. Joe 1:17
*, and all the shepherds mourned. Amo 1:2
Euphrates and it * up so that the Rev 16:12

DRIED-OUT
heap of * bones—all hope is gone.' Eze 37:11

DRIED-UP
These men are as useless as * 2Pe 2:17

DRIES
He * up rivers, and turns the Ps 107:33
dew that quickly * away, like chaff Hos 13:3

DRIFT
heard, or we may * away from them. Heb 2:1

DRILL
They * tunnels in the rocks and Job 28:10

DRINK
the canteen and gave the lad a *. Gen 21:19
one of them for a * and she says, Gen 24:14
the servant asked her for a *. Gen 24:17
lowered the jug for him to *. Gen 24:18
"Please give me a * of water!" Gen 24:43
said to her, 'Please give me a *.' Gen 24:45
so that I could *, and told me, Gen 24:46
see them when they came to *; Gen 30:38
it, and gave it to him to *." Gen 40:11
will be unwilling to * it." Ex 7:18
that the Egyptians couldn't * it; Ex 7:21
they couldn't * from the river. Ex 7:24
they couldn't * the water because Ex 15:23
meal offerings, or * offerings. Ex 30:9
down to feast and * at a wild Ex 32:6
water and made the people * it. Ex 32:20
Aaron, "Never * wine or strong Lev 10:8,9
wine or strong * when you go into Lev 10:8,9
it is defiled. Any * which is in Lev 11:34
Also offer a * offering Lev 23:13
(When he requires the woman to * Num 5:24
require the woman to * the water. Num 5:26
Lord, taste strong * or wine or Num 6:3,4
grain offering and * offerings. Num 6:15
along with the * offering. Num 6:17
Nazirite may again * wine, for he Num 6:20
pints of wine for a * offering. Num 15:5
pints of wine for a * offering. Num 15:7
quarts of wine for the * offering. Num 15:10
grain offering and * offering, and Num 15:23,24
There was not enough water to * Num 20:2
isn't even water enough to *!" Num 20:5
we won't even * water from your Num 20:17
and will not even * your water Num 20:19
and nothing to *, and we hate this Num 21:5
your vineyards or * your water." Num 21:22
Along with it shall be the * Num 28:7
grain offering and * offering. Num 28:8
oil, and the usual * offering. Num 28:9,10
shall be a * offering—six pints of Num 28:14
burnt offering and its * offering. Num 28:15
grain offerings and * offerings. Num 28:31
offerings and * offerings, as Num 29:6
grain offerings, and * offerings. Num 29:11
grain offerings and * offerings. Num 29:16
grain offerings and * offerings. Num 29:18
and * offering for a sin offering. Num 29:19
* offering with each sacrifice. Num 29:21
grain offering and * offering. Num 29:22
grain offering and * offering; Num 29:24
usual grain and * offerings) in Num 29:25
grain offerings and * offerings; Num 29:26,27
usual grain and * offerings, as a Num 29:28
their usual grain and * offerings. Num 29:30
and * offerings as a sin offering. Num 29:31
customary grain and * offerings; Num 29:33
usual grain and * offerings, in Num 29:34
customary grain and * offerings. Num 29:37
usual grain and * offerings for a Num 29:38
* offerings, or peace offerings." Num 29:39
was no water for the people to *). Num 33:14
bite we eat and everything we *; Deu 2:28
I didn't even take a * of water. Deu 9:9
or some strong *, to feast there Deu 14:26
eat the grapes or * the wine, for Deu 28:39
wine and strong *, is so that you Deu 29:6
They * the wine of serpent venom. Deu 32:33
groups decided by the way they *. Ju 7:5,6
Don't * any wine or beer, and Ju 13:4
And he told me not to * any wine Ju 13:7
or raisins, or * any wine or beer, Ju 13:13,14
anything to eat or * for three days 1Sa 30:11,12
and let it * from his own cup; 2Sa 12:3
But he refused to * it! 2Sa 23:16
nor would I eat or * even water 1Ki 13:8
to eat anything or * any water 1Ki 13:9
or to * any water at Bethel. 1Ki 13:16,17
the Jordan River. * from the brook 1Ki 17:4
Give them food and * and send 2Ki 6:22
offering, poured a * offering over 2Ki 16:13
including their * offerings. 2Ki 16:15
excrement and * their own urine!" 2Ki 18:27
David wanted a * from the 1Ch 11:17
But he refused to * it! 1Ch 11:18,19
"God forbid that I should * it! 1Ch 11:18,19
they also offered * offerings and 1Ch 29:21
and the usual * offering with each, 2Ch 29:35
offerings, and * offerings, all of Ez 7:17
Temple and refused all food and *; Ez 10:6
do not eat or * for three days, Est 4:16
eat and * with great merriment. Job 1:4
there to *, and so they perish. Job 6:15-18
Let him * deeply of the anger of Job 21:20
He is my food and *, my highest Ps 16:5
* from your rivers of delight. Ps 36:8
and confused, and * it all in. Ps 73:10
that no one could *, and how he Ps 78:44
My tears run down into my * Ps 102:9,10
water for all the animals to *. Ps 104:11
They eat and * wickedness and Pro 4:17
* from your own well, my son—be Pro 5:15
come to wisdom's banquet and * Pro 9:5
Let's go and have another *!" Pro 23:35
thirsty, give him something to *! Pro 25:21,22
O Lemuel, to * wine and whiskey. Pro 31:4
For if they * they may forget Pro 31:5
Let them * to forget their Pro 31:6,7
to try the road of *, while still Ecc 2:3
enjoy his food and *, and his job. Ecc 2:24-26
he should eat and * and enjoy the Ecc 3:13
a man to eat well, * a good glass Ecc 5:18
a man should eat, *, and be merry, Ecc 8:15
So go ahead, eat, *, and be Ecc 9:7
they feast and *, and then only to Ecc 10:16,17
honey. I * my wine with my milk." Sol 5:1
lover and beloved, eat and *! Sol 5:1
eat and drink! Yes, * deeply!" Sol 5:1
I would give you spiced wine to * Sol 8:2
dance and play, and feast and *. Is 22:13
"Let us eat, *, and be merry," Is 22:13
strong * turns bitter in the Is 24:9
own dung and * his own urine." Is 36:12
water gushed out for them to *. Is 48:21
you shall * no more of my fury; Is 51:22
Come and *—even if you have no Is 55:1
shall * the wine you pressed. Is 62:9
you shall be thirsty while they * Is 65:13
Delight in Jerusalem; * deep of Is 66:11
to * because of all our sins. Jer 8:14
and give them poison to *. Jer 9:15
and give them poison to *. Jer 23:15
to whom I send you * from it. Jer 25:15
They shall * from it and reel, Jer 25:16
all the nations * from it—every Jer 25:17
of Israel, says, * from this cup of Jer 25:27
Lord of Hosts says you must * it! Jer 25:28
rooms and offer them a * of wine. Jer 35:2
to have a *, but they refused. Jer 35:5
"We don't *, for Jonadab our Jer 35:6
of us should ever *, neither we nor Jer 35:6
We have never had a * of wine Jer 35:8
They don't *, because their Jer 35:14
You must * this cup of judgment! Jer 49:12
made the whole earth * and go mad. Jer 51:7
and make them * until they fall Jer 51:39
me a cup of deepest sorrows to *. Lam 3:15
We must even pay for water to *; Lam 5:4
the people will * it with dismay. Eze 4:16
out their * offerings to them! Eze 20:27,28
all they have to * is water that Eze 34:19
Come, eat the flesh and * the Eze 39:17
of mighty men and * the blood of Eze 39:18
* blood until you are drunk; Eze 39:19
No priest may * wine before Eze 44:21
meal offerings, * offerings and Eze 45:17
by urging them to * your wine, and Amo 2:12
who never have enough to *! Amo 4:1
journey for a * of water to a city Amo 4:8
are building, nor * the wine from Amo 5:11
You * wine by the bucketful and Amo 6:6
eat their crops and * their wine. Amo 9:14
round about will * it, too; Ob 1:16
it, too; yes, * and stagger back Ob 1:16
at all, nor even * any water. Jon 3:7
joys of wine and *"—that is the Mic 2:11
replaced by shame. * down God's Hab 2:16
They will never * wine from the Zep 1:13

(DRINK Con't)
enough to eat or *, and not enough Hag 1:6
about things—food, *, and clothes. Mt 6:25
doesn't even * wine and often goes Mt 11:18
feast and *, and you complain Mt 11:19
"Are you able to * from the Mt 20:22
cup I am about to * from?" Mt 20:22
"You shall indeed * from it," Mt 20:23
and give you anything to *? Mt 25:37
wouldn't give me anything to *; Mt 25:42
said, "Each one * from it, for Mt 26:27
Mark my words—I will not * this Mt 26:29
until the day I * it new with you Mt 26:29
I * it all, your will be done." Mt 26:42
gave him drugged wine to *; Mt 27:34
stick and held it up to him to *. Mt 27:48
Are you able to * from the bitter Mk 10:38
cup of sorrow I must * from? Mk 10:38
"You shall indeed * from my cup Mk 10:39
until the day I * a different kind Mk 14:25
Literally, "* it new." Mk 14:25f
and if they * anything poisonous, Mk 16:18
But I eat my food and * my wine, Lk 7:34
Literally, "Eat, *, and be Lk 12:19f
about food—what to eat and *; Lk 12:29
For I will not * wine again Lk 22:18
and * at my table in that Kingdom; Lk 22:30
by offering him a *—of sour wine. Lk 23:36
and Jesus asked her for a *. Jn 4:7
and * his blood, you cannot have Jn 6:53
eat my flesh and * my blood has Jn 6:54
food, and my blood is the true *. Jn 6:55
thirsty, let him come to me and *. Jn 7:37
Shall I not * from the cup the Jn 18:11
nor * until they had killed Paul! Act 23:12,13
neither eat nor * till he is dead. Act 23:21
him something to * and you will be Rom 12:20
not what we eat or * but stirring Rom 14:17
allowed to * some of the milk? 1Co 9:7
same supernatural food and *." 1Co 10:3,4f
water to * there in the desert; 1Co 10:3,4
down to eat and * and then got up 1Co 10:7
it, that all who * it are sharing 1Co 10:16
You cannot * from the cup at the 1Co 10:21
has too much to * and gets drunk. 1Co 11:21
of me whenever you * it." 1Co 11:25
eat this bread and * this cup you 1Co 11:26
time: let us eat, *, and be merry. 1Co 15:32
Don't * too much wine, for many Eph 5:18
what you eat or *, or for not Col 2:16
You are like babies who can * Heb 5:12,13
foods to eat and *, rules for Heb 9:10
* the wine of the anger of God; Rev 14:10
let him come and * the Water of Rev 22:17

DRINKER
He must not be a * or 1Ti 3:3

DRINKERS
They must not be heavy * and must 1Ti 3:8
not heavy *, not gossipers, but 1Ti 3:11
must not be heavy *, but they Tit 2:3

DRINKING
had finished *, he produced a Gen 24:22
personal silver * cup, which he Gen 44:5
river bank to get * water, for they Ex 7:24
eating bread nor * water, for you Deu 9:18
no sound, thought she had been *. 1Sa 1:12,13
fields, eating and * and dancing 1Sa 30:16
and they are feasting and * with 1Ki 1:25
as they were * in their tents. 1Ki 20:12
kings were still * themselves 1Ki 20:16
another, eating, * wine, and 2Ki 7:8
The only restriction on the * Est 1:8
sat down for a * spree as the city Est 3:15
and sinful, * in sin as a sponge Job 15:16
off your feet and * poison! Pro 26:6
to go on long * bouts that last Is 5:11
when it comes to *, and boast about Is 5:22
Oh, the joy of * deeply from the Is 12:3
man dreams of *, but is still faint Is 29:8
You are stupid—and not from *, Is 29:9
While Belshazzar was * he was Dan 5:2,3,4
Suddenly, as they were * from Dan 5:5
have been * wine from them while Dan 5:23
finish up their * bouts, and off Hos 4:18
'a glutton and a * man, and hang Mt 11:19
* in the sights around him. Mk 8:25
But no one after * the old wine Lk 5:39
place, eating and * without Lk 10:7
spend his time at * parties and in Lk 12:45
and *, buying and selling, farming Lk 17:28
carousing and *, and occupied with Lk 21:34,35
thirsty again after * this water. Jn 4:13
eating meat or * wine or doing Rom 14:21
blessing upon our * from the cup of 1Co 10:16
of God, even your eating and *. 1Co 10:31
Can't you do your eating and * at 1Co 11:22
the bread and * from the cup. 1Co 11:28
and * God's judgment upon himself; 1Co 11:29
should completely give up * wine. 1Ti 5:23
wild parties, * bouts, and the 1Pe 4:3

DRINKS
he also * the wine Jacob brings Gen 27:25
yellow marble. * were served in Est 1:7
he *, or the rich food he eats. Ps 109:18
them for food and * and clothes." Hos 1:5
he makes a fool of himself and * Hos 7:5
And he *! Lk 7:34
Everyone who eats my flesh and * Jn 6:56
this bread and * from this cup of 1Co 11:27
For if he eats the bread and * 1Co 11:29

DRIP
"Sweet wine will * from the Joe 3:18
hills of Israel will * sweet wine! Amo 9:13

DRIPPED
it and my hands * with perfume, my Sol 5:5

DRIPPING
They are sweeter than honey * Ps 19:10
wife annoys like constant *. Pro 19:13
A constant * on a rainy day and a Pro 27:15

DRIVE
He instructed his servants to * Gen 32:16
but will * them out of his land! Ex 6:1
and I will send hornets to * out Ex 23:28
But I will * them out a little Ex 23:30
you will * them out ahead of you. Ex 23:31
before you to * out the Canaanites, Ex 33:2
then I will * out from before you Ex 34:11
For I will * out the nations from Ex 34:24
that I can * them out of my land; Num 22:5,6
Canaan, you must * out all the Num 33:52
But if you refuse to * out the Num 33:55
to * out those who hide from you! Deu 7:20
conquer them and * them out. Deu 9:3
will * them out from before you! Deu 9:5
then the Lord will * out all the Deu 11:23
without fail, * out the Canaanites, Jos 3:10
I am ready to * these people out Jos 13:2-7
I shall * them out of the land." Jos 14:12
of Judah could not * out the Jos 15:63
Manasseh could not * out the people Jos 17:12
And I'm sure you can * out the Jos 17:16,17,18
Lord your God will * out all the Jos 23:4,5
ahead of you to * out the two kings Jos 24:12
The tribe of Manasseh failed to * Ju 1:27
nor did the tribe of Asher * out Ju 1:31,32
Naphtali did not * out the people Ju 1:33
I will no longer * out the nations Ju 2:21
land and did not * them out, nor Ju 2:23
O our God, didn't you * out the 2Ch 20:7
Chase them away! * them off like Ps 68:2
punishment will * it out of him. Pro 22:15
A murderer's conscience will * Pro 28:17
Syrians * the chariots; Is 22:6,7
"Yes, I will * you out of Is 22:19
of Babylon, I will * you out of Jer 27:10
them, I must * you from this land Jer 27:15
For all your neighbors shall * Jer 49:5
with them, and * away the dangerous Eze 34:25
and gold and * away their cattle Eze 38:13
I will turn you and * you toward Eze 39:2
I will * them from my land Hos 9:15
and began to * out the merchants Mk 11:15
Who gave you the authority to * Mk 11:27,28
and began to * out the merchants Lk 19:45

DRIVEN
are * too hard, they will die. Gen 33:13
And they were * out from Ex 10:11
chariots * by Egyptian officers. Ex 14:7
The sound of a leaf * in the wind Lev 26:36
until the Lord has * out his Num 32:21
but they were * out and displaced Deu 2:12
Your donkeys will be * away as Deu 28:31
the Lord your God will have * you. Deu 30:1
had attacked them and * them out. Jos 13:12
of Israel had not * out the Jos 13:13
Gezer were never * out, so they Jos 16:10
He has * out great, strong Jos 23:9
* me out of my father's house? Ju 11:7
they had not yet * out the people Ju 18:1
For you have * me out of my home 1Sa 26:19
It was * by Abinadab's sons, 2Sa 6:3
And you have * away the priests 2Ch 13:9
of Chaldeans have * off your camels Job 1:17
He will be * out from the Job 18:18
Are they * before the wind like Job 21:18
having been * from civilization. Job 30:5
* from one kingdom to another; Ps 105:13
seeks what has been * away." Ecc 3:15f
* away like chaff before the wind. Is 29:5
flood-tide * by Jehovah's breath. Is 59:19
them and * them to destruction. Jer 23:2
for they shall be * out of their Eze 12:11
wherever you have * us because of Dan 9:7
He was * off by special Hos 1:7f
half shall be * into the Dead Sea Joe 2:20
You have * out the widows from Mic 2:9
authority he had * out the Lk 20:2
afraid of being * across to the Act 27:17
and were thus * before the wind. Act 27:17
as we were being * to and fro on Act 27:27
knew they would soon be * ashore; Act 27:29
rocks and be * up onto the beach. Act 27:39
a poisonous snake, * out by the Act 28:3
They stop at nothing, being * by Eph 4:19
persecuted us and * us out. 1Th 2:15
that is * and tossed by the wind; Jas 1:6
To: The Jewish Christians * out of 1Pe 1:1
they are as unstable as clouds * 2Pe 2:17

DRIVER
to each *, with the same message. Gen 32:19
he groaned to his chariot *. 1Ki 22:34
he groaned to the * of his chariot, 2Ch 18:33

DRIVERS
the camel * to wash their feet. Gen 24:32
So he hired chariots and * and 1Ki 1:5
and chariot *, and resort cities 1Ki 9:19
and want no * shouting at them! Job 39:7

DRIVES
decay of the wicked * it downhill. Pro 11:11

DRIVING
He told the men * the first Gen 32:17
the towns and * out the Amorites. Num 21:31,32
"It must be Jehu, for he is * so 2Ki 9:20
miracles in * out the nations from 1Ch 17:21
the * force of envy and jealousy! Ecc 4:4
men who are like a * rain that Is 25:4
me from the north, * before it a Eze 1:4

DROMEDARIES
* used in the king's service. Est 8:9,10
converge upon you, * from Midian Is 60:6

DROOP
my spirits *, yet God remains! Ps 73:26

DROOPS
is like a flower that * and falls; 1Pe 1:24

DROP
For the trees will * their fruit Deu 28:40
of barley and * them on purpose for Ru 2:16
and * your claims against them." Neh 5:11
and made them * their victims. Job 29:17
who fights at the * of a hat, the Is 29:21
him—they are but a * in the bucket, Is 40:15
there is not a * of water left. Lam 4:3,4
lick the inside to get every *. Eze 23:34
will * off sharply, says the Lord. Eze 36:14
mighty men will * their weapons and Amo 2:16
and never took a * of liquor all Lk 7:33
to the last * of anger in the cup Rev 16:19

DROPLETS
* of gum from the bark of a tree. Num 11:7
like lightning across the vapor *. Job 41:18

DROPPED
pick up the grains * by the Ru 2:7
have evidently * out in copying, 1Sa 13:1f
but she fell and * him as she was 2Sa 4:4
as the crowds * in their money. Mk 12:41
Then a poor widow came and * in Mk 12:42
Then a poor widow came by and * Lk 21:2
instead you have * back to the Heb 5:12,13

DROPPING
over a desert without * any rain. Pro 25:14
gold and silver is * fast, yet it Jas 5:3

DROPS
and squeezed out the last *. Is 51:17
enthusiasm fades, and he * out. Mt 13:21
blood, with great * falling to the Lk 22:44
sweating of great * of blood? Heb 5:7f
until you sweat great * of blood. Heb 12:4

DROPSY
present who was suffering from *. Lk 14:1

DROSS
When you remove * from silver, Pro 25:4,5
All is *. Jer 6:29
They are the *, compounded from Eze 22:18,19,20
you are worthless *, I will bring Eze 22:18,19,20
watch as the * is burned away. Mal 3:3

DROUGHT
disappears in *, so a man lies down Job 14:11,12
Death consumes sinners as * and Job 24:19
left desolate, destroyed by the *. Is 24:6
and rocks, of * and death, where no Jer 2:6
nor worried by long months of *. Jer 17:8
a land riddled with famine and *. Hos 1:3
In fact, I have called for a * Hag 1:11
highlands, too; a * to wither the Hag 1:11
other crops, a * to starve both you Hag 1:11

DROUGHTTIME
speak as those in * long for rain. Job 29:23

DROVE
his intentions. He * the flocks Gen 31:17-20
conquered it, and * out the Num 32:39
of power. He * away other nations Deu 4:38
Caleb * out the descendants of Jos 15:14
It was the Lord who * out the Jos 24:18
so Caleb * out the inhabitants of Ju 1:20
as he slept, she * the peg through Ju 4:21
cruel to you, and * out your Ju 6:9
time, and Zebul * Gaal and his Ju 9:41
herds and * them on ahead of them. 1Sa 30:20
* out to make room for his people. 1Ki 14:24
fire, appeared and * between them, 2Ki 2:11
for Syria; he * out the Jews and 2Ki 16:6
Uzza and Ahio * the oxen. 1Ch 13:7
from the city. He * the people 1Ch 20:3
Sabeans raided us, * away the Job 1:14,15

DROVE Con't)
told us how you * the heathen Ps 44:1
made for them. He * out the Ps 78:55
his enemies and * them back and Ps 78:66
a tender vine and * away the Ps 80:8
Or, "and the guardian cherub * Eze 28:16f
I killed your lads in war and * Amo 4:10
Jesus went into the Temple, * out Mt 21:12
them all out, and * out the sheep Jn 2:15
And he * them out of the Act 18:16

DROVES
These enemy hordes arrived on * Ju 6:5
Vast * of camels will converge Is 60:6

DROWN
love, neither can the floods * it. Sol 8:7
of difficulty, you will not *! Is 43:2
care that we are all about to *?" Mk 4:38

DROWNED
but the Lord * them in the sea. Ex 14:27
The horse and rider have been * in Ex 15:21
chariots—how he * them in the Red Deu 11:4
covered the road and * their foes; Ps 106:11
We would have * beneath the Ps 124:4,5
forever— but * Pharaoh's army in Ps 136:15
* the Egyptian armies in the sea. Is 10:26
sweep it away, and you will be *. Is 28:17
a cliff and * in the water below. Mt 8:32
hillside into the lake and *. Mk 5:13
into the lake below, where they *. Lk 8:33
them tried it, they all were *. Heb 11:29

DROWNING
* them in the sea. Ex 15:4
in upon the Egyptians, * them. Jos 24:7
their ears, and * out his voice Act 7:57
from * in that terrible flood. 1Pe 3:20

DROWSY
been very * and had fallen asleep. Lk 9:32

DRUDGERY
them from the * and humiliation Ex 3:17

DRUGGED
soldiers gave him * wine to drink; Mt 27:34
Wine * with bitter herbs was Mk 15:23

DRUMS
Sing, accompanied by *; Ps 81:2
accompanied by * and lyre. Ps 149:3

DRUNK
One day as he was * and lay naked Gen 9:20,21
So they got him * that night, Gen 19:33
So they got him * again that Gen 19:35
And have * the blood of the Num 23:18-24
My arrows shall be * with blood! Deu 32:40,41
Half * by now, the people Ju 16:25,26
"Must you come here *?" 1Sa 1:14
she replied, "I'm not *! 1Sa 1:15,16
He was roaring *, so she didn't 1Sa 25:36
him to dinner and got him *; 2Sa 11:13
*, then, at my signal, kill him! 2Sa 13:28
and have eaten and * water in the 1Ki 13:21,22
One day King Elah was half * at 1Ki 16:9
themselves *, the first of Ahab's 1Ki 20:16
feeling high, half * from wine, he Est 1:10
are already * in the morning. Ecc 10:16,17
of men lying * in the streets! Is 28:1
* with rivers of their own blood. Is 49:26
You have * enough from the cup of Is 51:17
You have * to the dregs the cup Is 51:17
not from being *)— this is what Is 51:21
let's all get *. Is 56:12
until you are * and vomit and fall Jer 25:27
it is sated, yes, * with your Jer 46:10
I will make * her princes, wise Jer 51:57
drink blood until you are *; Eze 39:19
birthday, the princes get him *; Hos 7:5
girl for wine enough to get *. Joe 3:3
and getting *, your Lord will Mt 24:49
"They're *, that's all!" Act 2:13
of you are saying these men are *! Act 2:15
People don't get * by 9 A.M. Act 2:15
and getting * or in adultery and Rom 13:12,13
has too much to drink and gets *. 1Co 11:21
and the time when people get *. 1Th 5:7
sin, lust, getting *, wild parties, 1Pe 4:3
* by the wine of her immorality." Rev 17:2
I could see that she was *—drunk Rev 17:6
I could see that she was drunk—* Rev 17:6
For all the nations have * the Rev 18:3

DRUNKARD
he is a worthless *.' Deu 21:20
than a thorn in the hand of a *. Pro 26:9
make Egypt stagger like a sick *. Is 19:14
The world staggers like a *; Is 24:20
and stagger as a * does from wine, Jer 23:9
and fall like a *, for she has Jer 48:26
You will reel like a * beneath Eze 23:33
like a * and hide herself in fear. Nah 3:11
idols, or is a *, or abusive. 1Co 5:11

DRUNKARDS
of the town and the song of the *. Ps 69:12
They reel and stagger like * and Ps 107:27
don't carouse with * and Pro 23:19,20,21
and delight of the * of Israel! Is 28:1
and delight of the * of Israel—will Is 28:3
men and * from the wilderness, who Eze 23:42
Wake up and weep, you *, for all Joe 1:5
and stagger like * beneath your Hab 2:15
people, *, slanderers, or robbers. 1Co 6:9,10
they must not be * or fighters or Tit 1:7

DRUNKEN
When Noah awoke from his * Gen 9:24,25
think that I am just some * bum!" 1Sa 1:15,16
late at night—woe to you * bums. Is 5:11
up, and all her * throngs. Is 5:14
In their * feasts, the men of Jer 51:38
of *, lying prophet that you like! Mic 2:11

DRUNKENLY
them reel * down the street! Pro 20:1

DRUNKENNESS
parties and in *— well, his master Lk 12:45
envy, murder, *, wild parties, and Gal 5:21

DRUNKS
But Jerusalem is now led by *! Is 28:7

DRUSILLA
later Felix came with *, his legal Act 24:24

DRY
so that the * land will emerge." Gen 1:9,10
Then God named the * land Gen 1:9,10
breathed and lived upon * land. Gen 7:22
until the earth was *. Gen 8:7
if it could find * ground, but the Gen 8:8
Then at last the earth was *. Gen 8:14
pour it upon the * land, and it Ex 4:9
shall walk through on * ground! Ex 14:16
through the sea on * ground! Ex 14:22
scraped along the * ground. Ex 14:25
walked through on * land, and the Ex 14:29
Israel walked through on * land. Ex 15:19
with olive oil or *, are the common Lev 7:10
where it was so hot and *. Deu 8:15
The land will become as * as Deu 28:24
the Ark stood on * ground in the Jos 3:17
the Jordan River on * ground! Jos 4:22
it * until we were all across! Jos 4:23
wineskins and *, moldy bread. Jos 9:3,4,5
now as you see, it is * and moldy; Jos 9:12
and the ground is *, I will know Ju 6:37
the fleece remain * while the Ju 6:39
that night the fleece stayed *, Ju 6:40
with grain on it to * in the sun; 2Sa 17:19
and they went across on * ground! 2Ki 2:8
"The Lord says to fill this * 2Ki 3:16
and turns it upside down to *. 2Ki 21:13
they could go through on * land! Neh 9:11
Will you chase *, useless straws? Job 13:25
pot that is fired by * rushes. Job 41:20
oceans back to let * land appear. Ps 24:2
The rivers of God will not run *! Ps 65:9
He made a * road through the sea Ps 66:6
my throat is * and hoarse; Ps 69:3
through the * and barren land; Ps 105:41
a * road across its bottom. Ps 106:9
Yes, as * as any desert! Ps 106:9
A * CRUST eaten in peace is better Pro 17:1
The Lord will * a path through Is 11:15
the ditches will be parched and * Is 19:5
As a hot, * land is cooled by Is 25:5
flow across the *, parched ground. Is 41:18
He will * up the rivers and Is 42:15
to the rivers and say, "Be *!" Is 44:27
they shall be *. Is 44:27
can rebuke the sea and make it *! Is 50:2
a root in * and sterile ground. Is 53:2
the forests and boil the oceans *. Is 64:2
the wells, but the wells are *. Jer 14:3
flood, sometimes as * as a bone." Jer 15:17,18
crags of Mount Hermon never run *. Jer 18:14
wilderness, a * and desert land. Jer 50:12
I will * up her river, her water Jer 51:36
in ruins—she is a * wilderness Jer 51:43
it is * and hard and withered. Lam 4:8
tree wither and the * tree grow. Eze 17:24
where the ground is hard and *. Eze 19:13
tree will die, green and * alike. Eze 20:47
I will * up the Nile and sell Eze 30:12
full of old, * bones that were Eze 37:1
bones and say: "O * bones, listen Eze 37:4
for both liquid and * measure. Eze 45:11
of a homer) for * measure, and the Eze 45:11
the strength of Judah like * rot. Hos 5:12
in that * and thirsty land Hos 13:5
hard upon him and * up his land. Hos 13:15
* away, and he will die of thirst. Hos 13:15
The creeks are * and the pastures Joe 1:20
Water will fill the * stream beds Joe 3:18
field, another was * and withered. Amo 4:7
sets the * fields of Edom aflame. Ob 1:18
oceans and rivers become * sand; Nah 1:4
too, and the * land— I will shake Hag 2:6
The Nile will become *—the rule Zec 10:11
what will happen when it is *?" Lk 23:31f
the ground is a * little seed of 1Co 15:37
as though they were on * ground. Heb 11:29
when it becomes all brown and *. 1Pe 1:24
blowing over * land without giving Jud 1:12

DRYING
all that night, * the sea bottom. Ex 14:21
To cure them by *. Num 11:32f
piles of flax that were * there. Jos 2:6
be filled with nets * in the sun. Eze 47:10

DUE
Literally, "when life would be* Gen 18:10f
In * season the time of her Gen 38:27
there). In * season Joseph and Ex 1:6
If something is * them, don't Lev 19:13
"You shall give * honor and Lev 19:32
The glory * his name! 1Ch 16:29
given what was * them, so they and Neh 13:10
his pathway and in * season he will Ps 37:34
of peace offerings were * from me; Pro 7:14f
I said to myself, "In * season Ecc 3:17
that which is * you, which I have Jer 13:24,25
and is giving Babylon all her *. Jer 51:56
the tithes and offerings * to me. Mal 3:8
he had paid every last penny *. Mt 18:34
was mutual, * to historic reasons. Lk 10:33f
to all those to whom it is *. Rom 13:7
For in * season Christ will be 1Ti 6:15

DUFFLE
don't even carry a * bag with Mt 10:10
without money, * bag, or extra Lk 22:35
"But now," he said, "take a * Lk 22:36

DUG
earth—all those * by the servants Gen 26:15
His shepherds also * a new well Gen 26:19
Isaac's men then * another well, Gen 26:21
Abandoning that one, he * again, Gen 26:22
there, and his servants * a well. Gen 26:25
Then the Egyptians * wells along Ex 7:24
This is a wellThe leaders *. Num 21:17,18
Then he * a trench about three 1Ki 18:32
east wind? Who * the valleys for Job 38:25-27
pitfalls they have * for others; Ps 9:15
for me and * a pitfall in my path. Ps 35:7
Literally, "my ears you have *." Ps 40:6f
They have * a pitfall in my path. Ps 57:6
* deep pits for me to fall in. Ps 119:85,86
"You boast of wells you've * in Is 37:25
And I did; I * it out of the Jer 13:7
for they have * a pit for me to Jer 18:22
* through the wall with my hands. Eze 12:7
and Tabor, and * a deep pit to Hos 5:2
the $1,000 * a hole in the ground Mt 25:18
the crowd, so they * through the Mk 2:4
wall around it and * a pit for Mk 12:1

DULCIMER
sackbut, psaltry, *, and every Dan 3:5f
sackbut, psaltry, *, and every Dan 3:7f
sackbut, psaltry, *, and every Dan 3:10f

DULL
For we are too * to know! Job 37:19,20
Their minds are * and stupid, Ps 119:70
A * axe requires great strength; Ecc 10:10
what they mean.' * their Is 6:10
they are *, retarded children who Jer 4:22
are *, and they have Mt 13:15
become spiritually * and Heb 6:12

DULLED
The silversmith is * by the Jer 51:17

DULY
This was all * recorded in the Est 2:23

DUMAH
Mishma, *,Massa, Hadad, Gen 25:12-15
Giloh, Arab, *, Eshan, Janim, Jos 15:48-62
Mibsam, Mishma, *, Massa, Hadad, 1Ch 1:28-31
Literally, "*." Is 21:11f

DUMB
like animals to you, stupid and *? Job 18:3
a machine call its inventor *? Is 29:16
her shearers is *, so he stood Is 53:7
I stand amazed, silent, * with Jer 8:21

DUMBEST
Ask the * beast—he knows that it Job 12:7,8,9

DUMBFOUNDED
they shall stand *, speechless in Is 52:14,15
began, will be * at his Rev 17:8
Literally, "* at the ruler who Rev 17:8f

DUMBNESS
"O demon of deafness and *," he Mk 9:25

DUMP
*, and sets them among princes! Ps 113:7
will * the bodies in that valley. Jer 7:32
on the garbage * beyond the gate! Jer 22:19
graveyard and ash * in the valley Jer 31:40
lovely homes and * your stones and Eze 26:12

DUMPED
and the scrapings * in a defiled Lev 14:41
and * them outside the city. 2Ch 33:15
The cistern where Ishmael * the Jer 41:9
born, you were * out into a field Eze 16:5

DUMPS
through the garbage * for bread. Lam 1:19

DUNG
the skin and the *, outside the Ex 29:14
with its hide and *, was burned Lev 8:17

(DUNG Con't)
hide, meat, blood, and *. Num 19:5
of dove's * brought three dollars! 2Ki 6:25
and over to the * Gate to see the Neh 2:13
1,500 feet of wall to the * Gate. Neh 3:13
The * Gate was repaired by Neh 3:14
right toward the * Gate consisted Neh 12:31,32
forever, cast away like his own *. Job 20:7
own * and drink his own urine." Is 36:12
scattered like * upon the ground. Jer 8:2
dried human * as fuel, and eat it. Eze 4:12
God, must I be defiled by using *? Eze 4:14
use cow * instead of human dung." Eze 4:15
use cow dung instead of human *." Eze 4:15
me, and throw you out like *. Mal 2:3

DUNGEON
He was brought hastily from the * Gen 41:14
son of the captive in the *; Ex 12:29
imprisoned in a * until they are Is 24:22
shall be released; *, starvation Is 51:14
was imprisoned in the * beneath Jer 32:2
and put into the * under the house Jer 37:15,16
to that *, for I'll die there." Jer 37:20
be returned to the *, but be placed Jer 37:21
you back to the * in Jonathan's Jer 38:26
into the inner * and clamped their Act 16:24
and ran to the * and fell down Act 16:29

DUNGEONS
and others were chained in *. Heb 11:36

DUPING
said, "No, he's * the public." Jn 7:12

DURA
of *, in the province of Babylon; Dan 3:1

DURATION
* of his reign: 16 years, in 2Ki 15:32,33
* of reign: 16 years, in Jerusalem 2Ki 16:1
* of his reign: 31 years in 2Ki 22:1
to live for the * of the feast. Neh 8:15

DURING
It was * his lifetime that men Gen 4:26
Peleg (meaning "Division," for * Gen 10:25
One day * the wheat harvest, Gen 30:14
But * the night he got up and Gen 32:22,23,24
crops everywhere. * those years, Gen 41:48
* this time before the arrival of Gen 41:50
grow to seven, * which there will Gen 45:6
his father Isaac. * the night God Gen 46:2
they were under. * his visit he saw Ex 2:11
for three days. * all that time Ex 10:23
rule at any time * the seven days Ex 12:15
in your homes; * that time anyone Ex 12:19
Again I repeat, * those days you Ex 12:20
* the night and said, "Leave us; Ex 12:31
Now remember, * the annual Ex 13:3
"* those celebration days each Ex 13:8
a pillar of cloud * the daytime, Ex 13:21
and lie fallow * the seventh year, Ex 23:11
"Even * plowing and harvest Ex 34:21
the Tabernacle * the daytime, and Ex 40:38
as * her monthly periods. Lev 12:2
last two weeks, * which time she Lev 12:5
restrictions as * menstruation. Lev 12:5
seven days. If * that time the Lev 13:22
afterwards, and * that time anyone Lev 15:19
on * that time shall be defiled. Lev 15:20
with her * this time is Lev 15:24
irregular time * the month, the Lev 15:25
she lies upon * that time is Lev 15:26
as it would be * her normal Lev 15:26
with a woman * her period of Lev 20:18
The sacrifices made * the Lev 23:38
to generation. * those seven days, Lev 23:42
* the fight the Egyptian man's son Lev 24:11
your crops, but * the seventh year Lev 25:4
your vineyards * that entire year. Lev 25:4
Yes, * the Year of Jubilee Lev 25:13
is sold or bought * the preceding Lev 25:14,15,16
right of redemption * that time. Lev 25:29
not thereafter, * the entire period Num 6:3,4
near any dead body * the entire Num 6:6,7
Sinai peninsula, * the first month Num 9:1
stayed only * the night and moved Num 9:20,21
The manna fell with the dew * Num 11:9
the people, and * that day you may Num 28:25
This occurred * the fortieth year Num 33:38,39
and a pillar of cloud * the day. Deu 1:33
the Passover * the month of April, Deu 16:1
a seminal emission * the night must Deu 23:9,10
will be the hunger * the siege and Deu 28:56,57
had died * the years in the Jos 5:4,5
the Passover * the evening of the Jos 5:10
were killed * the attack, and many Jos 7:5
* the battle the five kings Jos 10:16
* the attack on Lachish, King Jos 10:33
* this period Joshua routed all Jos 11:21
has done for you * my lifetime. Jos 23:3
* the night, with the Midianites Ju 7:8,9
years—all * Gideon's lifetime. Ju 8:28
leading citizens. * the harvest Ju 9:27
"If you solve my riddle * these Ju 14:12
LATER ON, * the wheat harvest, Ju 15:1
had killed * his entire lifetime. Ju 16:30
and Chilion. * the time of their Ru 1:3
twenty years, and * that time all 1Sa 7:2
of the year, * the wheat harvest; 1Sa 12:17
not only to me * my own lifetime, 1Sa 20:14
They stayed in Moab * the entire 1Sa 22:4
him went across * the night and 2Sa 17:22
than were killed. * the battle 2Sa 18:9
them will remain here * the night; 2Sa 19:7
king and his army * their exile in 2Sa 19:31,32
THERE WAS A famine * David's reign 2Sa 21:1
at their bodies * the day and the 2Sa 21:10
Later, * a war with the 2Sa 21:18
from Harar. Once * a Philistine 2Sa 23:11,12
Ark of the Lord * my father's 1Ki 2:26
But her baby died * the night 1Ki 3:19
month of October. * the 1Ki 8:3,4
At the end of the twenty years * 1Ki 9:10
destroyed Zobah. * Solomon's 1Ki 11:25
Ammonite woman.) * his reign the 1Ki 14:22
Judah in Jerusalem * the eighteenth 1Ki 15:1
For David had obeyed God * his 1Ki 15:5
the Hittite. * Abijam's reign 1Ki 15:6
Israel in Tirzah, * the third year 1Ki 15:28
began reigning * the twenty-sixth 1Ki 16:8
(This occurred * the 1Ki 16:10
(It was * his reign that Hiel, a 1Ki 16:34
do what I promised * his lifetime; 1Ki 21:29
and Israel. But * the third year, 1Ki 22:2
had become king * the fourth year 1Ki 22:41
It was * the seventeenth year of 1Ki 22:51
reign over Israel * the eighteenth 2Ki 3:1
had been harvested * her absence. 2Ki 8:6
began his reign * the fifth year of 2Ki 8:16
* Jehoram's reign, the people in 2Ki 8:20
became the new king * the twelfth 2Ki 8:24,25
reign over Israel * the 2Ki 13:1
oppressed Israel * the entire reign 2Ki 13:22
* THE SECOND year of the reign of 2Ki 14:1
II had become king * the fifteenth 2Ki 14:23
It was * his reign that King 2Ki 15:29
It was * King Jotham's reign that 2Ki 15:34,35
It was * the fourth year of his 2Ki 18:9
Three years later (* the sixth 2Ki 18:10
Later, * the fourteenth year of 2Ki 18:13
* the remainder of my own life!" 2Ki 20:19
* THE REIGN of King Jehoiakim, 2Ki 24:1
* his reign the armies of King 2Ki 24:10
Nebuchadnezzar himself arrived * 2Ki 24:11
in Babylon * the eighth year of 2Ki 24:12
This occurred * the first year of 2Ki 25:27
for it was * his lifetime that the 1Ch 1:19
to King Jeconiah * the years that 1Ch 3:17,18
of Ham. So * the reign of King 1Ch 4:40,41
* the reign of King Saul, the men 1Ch 5:10
They crossed the Jordan River * 1Ch 12:15
surrendered. * another war with 1Ch 20:5
a weaver's beam! * another battle, 1Ch 20:6,7
died as a result. * the plague God 1Ch 21:15
quietness to Israel * his reign. 1Ch 22:9
* the ninth month of each year. 1Ch 27:12
* the eleventh month of each year. 1Ch 27:14
* the twelfth month of each year. 1Ch 27:15
seven of them * his reign in 1Ch 29:26,27
near the king. * Solomon's reign, 2Ch 1:15
difficulty; for * those years there 2Ch 11:17
regained his power * Abijah's 2Ch 13:20
It was * this visit that Ahaziah 2Ch 22:7
the Lord all * the lifetime of 2Ch 24:2
continually * the lifetime of 2Ch 24:14
upon them * Hezekiah's lifetime. 2Ch 32:26
* the eighteenth year of his 2Ch 34:8
* THE FIRST year of the reign of Ez 1:1
* THE MONTH of September everyone Ez 3:1
This went on * his entire reign Ez 4:4,5
thing * the reign of Ar-ta-xerxes. Ez 4:7
Cyrus of Babylon, * the first year Ez 5:13
all the people. * the dedication Ez 6:17
* the reign of King Ar-ta-xerxes Ez 7:1
* the reign of King Ar-ta-xerxes: Ez 8:1
I stole out * the night, taking Neh 2:11,12
duty as well as work * the day. Neh 4:22
during the day. * this period none Neh 4:23
help of our God. * those fifty-two Neh 6:17
Judah. But * the month of Neh 7:73
live in tents * the Festival of Neh 8:14
a pillar of cloud * the day and a Neh 9:12
helped them * the service. Neh 12:9
was compiled * the reign of King Neh 12:22
helped them * the ceremonies of Neh 12:24
* the dedication of the new Neh 12:27
* the wine course the king said Est 5:6
Again, * the wine course, the Est 7:2
the visions he saw * the reigns of Is 1:1
* THE REIGN of Ahaz (the son of Is 7:1
autumn morning * harvest time. Is 18:4
At least there will be peace * my Is 39:8
cities left behind * the exile, and Is 54:3
on you as I have * this exile. Is 54:9
refuses to work * my Sabbath days Is 56:2
Others came * the reign of Jer 1:3
to me * the reign of King Josiah: Jer 3:6
Lord to Jeremiah * the fourth year Jer 25:1
from the Lord * the first year of Jer 26:1
lost, they fled * the night, going Jer 39:4
* the fourth year of Zedekiah's Jer 51:59
fled from the city * the night, Jer 52:7
fifth month * the nineteenth year Jer 52:12
"* the first 390 days eat bread Eze 4:9
* the daylight so they can watch. Eze 12:4
lie with any woman * the time of Eze 18:6
also * the reign of Manasseh. Eze 23:16f
to Egypt for help * the reigns of Eze 23:17f
i.e., * the reign of Josiah. Eze 23:19,20f
me * those thirteen years at Tyre, Eze 29:20
yeast shall be eaten * those days. Eze 45:21
"Early in October, * each of the Eze 45:25
shall be closed * the six work days Eze 46:1
to sacrifice * the religious Eze 46:9
his own kitchen * their three-year Dan 1:5
"* the reigns of those kings, Dan 2:44
in Jerusalem * Nebuchadnezzar's Dan 5:2,3,4
ONE NIGHT * the first year of Dan 7:1
of 1,000,000 Jews * the following Dan 9:25f
But * a crisis he will take over Dan 11:21
son of Beeri, * the reigns of these Hos 1:1
were assassinated * Hosea's Hos 7:7f
assassinated * her last tempestuous Hos 13:11f
town of Moresheth * the reigns of Mic 1:1
When: * the reign of Josiah (son Zep 1:1
The prophet Jeremiah was active * Zep 1:1f
and mourning * the month of August Zec 7:3
and your priests, '* those seventy Zec 7:5
Judea, * the reign of King Herod. Mt 2:1
"But not * the Passover Mt 26:5
prisoner each year * the Passover Mt 27:15
* the night and stole his body. Mt 28:12,13
hills to pray. * the night, as the Mk 6:47
"But we can't do it * the Mk 14:2
Simon the leper; * supper a woman Mk 14:3
for murder * an insurrection. Mk 15:7
as they always did * that part of Lk 1:10
remember that * your lifetime you Lk 16:25
* the walk down the road. Lk 24:32
The wine supply ran out * the Jn 2:3
observed * every human birth. Jn 3:5f
every day, and * every hour of it a Jn 11:9
to his Father. * supper the devil Jn 13:1
none missing. * my time here I Jn 17:12
the Holy Spirit. * the forty days Act 1:3
for several days. * this time, on a Act 1:15
people of Israel. * this visit he Act 7:24
were sacrificing * those forty Act 7:42
to murder him. So * the night some Act 9:25
from Jerusalem * the persecution Act 11:19
* this time some prophets came Act 11:27
(This was fulfilled * the reign Act 11:28
he arrested Peter * the Passover Act 12:3
And he was seen many times * the Act 13:31
* our stay of several days, a man Act 21:10
for a visit with Festus. * their Act 25:14
his will are yours * this time of 1Co 1:7
Women should be silent * the 1Co 14:34
you have earned * the week, and use 1Co 16:2
and * the time we were with you. 2Th 2:15
and many times * the long nights I 2Ti 1:3
would not occur * their lifetime, 1Pe 1:12
but long years later, * yours. 1Pe 1:12
no rain will fall * the three and a Rev 11:6

DUSK
They left the city at * as the Jos 2:5
more fierce than wolves at *. Hab 1:8
from dawn to * and dusk to dawn." Zep 3:7
from dawn to dusk and * to dawn." Zep 3:7

DUST
body from the * of the ground Gen 2:7
You shall grovel in the * as long Gen 3:14
like *, they can't be counted! Gen 13:16
in the * as God talked with him. Gen 17:2,3,4
Lord, though I am but * and ashes. Gen 18:27
have descendants as many as *! Gen 28:14
to strike the * with his rod, and Ex 8:16
It will spread like fine * over Ex 9:9
*, for the blood is the life. Lev 17:13
and mix into it * from the floor of Num 5:17
They are as numerous as *! Num 23:7-10
it into fine *, and threw it into Deu 9:21
The land will become as dry as * Deu 28:24
and * storms shall destroy you. Deu 28:24
Crawling in the *. Deu 32:24
evening, with * on their heads. Jos 7:6
"You have brought me to the *. Ju 11:35
He lifts the poor from the *— 1Sa 2:8
David and tossing * into the air. 2Sa 16:13
I beat them into *; 2Sa 22:43
Like * along the streets. 2Sa 22:43
the ground with his face in the *. 2Sa 24:20
"I lifted you out of the *," 1Ki 16:2
the stones, the *, and even 1Ki 18:38
turn Samaria into handfuls of *!" 1Ki 20:10
they were * beneath his feet. 2Ki 13:7
it and beat it to * and threw the 2Ki 23:6

DUST Con't)
dust and threw the * on the graves 2Ki 23:6
He crushed the stones to * and 2Ki 23:15
But now he crushed them into *, 2Ki 23:19
people as the earth is full of *! 2Ch 1:9
ground into * and scattered over 2Ch 34:4
robes and threw * into the air and Job 2:12
less men made of *, who are crushed Job 4:18,19
lie down in the * and die, and when Job 7:21
that I'm made of *—will you change Job 10:9
change me back again to * so soon? Job 10:9
and have laid all hope in the *. Job 16:15
We shall rest together in the * Job 17:16
man, his bones shall lie in the *. Job 20:11
*, both eaten by the same worms. Job 21:26
money like *, with closets jammed Job 27:16
sapphires and gold *— treasures Job 28:6
I have become as * and ashes. Job 30:19
and mankind would turn again to *. Job 34:15
when everything is * and clods? Job 38:37,38
the earth, to warm them in the *. Job 39:14
Knock them into the *, Job 40:13
myself and repent in * and ashes.' Job 42:6
and trample my life in the *. Ps 7:5
So I crushed them fine as * and Ps 18:42
have laid me in the * of death. Ps 22:15
How can my * in the grave speak Ps 30:9
We lie face downward in the *. Ps 44:25
Bring them to the *, O Lord our Ps 59:11
shall fall face downward in the *. Ps 72:9
birds as thick as *, clouds of them Ps 78:27
for we are brought low to the *. Ps 79:8
O my God, blow them away like *; Ps 83:13
have thrown his crown in the *. Ps 89:39
speak, and man turns back to *. Ps 90:3
every grain of * in her streets. Ps 102:14
For he knows we are but *, and Ps 103:14
they die and turn again to *. Ps 104:29
discouraged—I lie in the *. Ps 119:25
but brings the wicked into the *. Ps 147:6
All go to one place—the * from Ecc 3:20
of animals goes downward into *? Ecc 3:21
and the * returns to the earth Ecc 12:7
haughty and bring them to the *. Is 2:12
will lie in the *, and the Lord Is 2:17
my people in the * like that?" Is 3:15
shall be brought down to the *; Is 5:15
like whirling * before a storm. Is 17:13
be demolished and brought to *. Is 25:12
brings the haughty city to the *; Is 26:5
Those who dwell in the * shall Is 26:19
in the bucket, * on the scales. Is 40:15
unconquered, come sit in the *. Is 47:1
and lick the * from off your feet; Is 49:23
* and walked upon your backs." Is 51:23
Rise from the *, Jerusalem; Is 52:2
Literally, "* (i.e. Is 65:25f
and sit in the *, for your glorious Jer 13:18
as the east wind scatters *; Jer 18:17
and sit in the *, O people of Jer 48:18
Israel lies in the * of the earth, Lam 2:1
He has brought the kingdom to *, Lam 2:2
they throw * upon their heads in Lam 2:10
to lie face downward in the *; Lam 3:29
SAID to me: "Stand up, son of *, Eze 2:1
"Son of *," he said, "I am Eze 2:3
"Son of *, don't be afraid of Eze 2:6
Listen, son of *, to what I say Eze 2:8
AND HE SAID to me: "Son of *, eat Eze 3:1
Then he said: "Son of *, I am Eze 3:10
Then he added: "Son of *, let Eze 3:17
"Son of *, I have appointed you Eze 3:17
"AND NOW, SON of *, take a large Eze 4:1
Then he told me, "Son of *, Eze 4:16
"SON OF *, take a sharp sword and Eze 5:1
"Son of *, look over toward the Eze 6:2
He said to me, "Son of *, look Eze 8:5
And he said: "Son of *, do you Eze 8:6
to me: "Son of *, have you seen Eze 8:12
to me, "Son of *, these are the Eze 11:1
Therefore, son of *, prophesy Eze 11:4
"Son of *, the remnant left in Eze 11:15
"Son of *," he said, "you live Eze 12:2
"Son of *, these rebels, the Eze 12:9
"Son of *, tremble as you eat Eze 12:18
"Son of *, what is that proverb Eze 12:22
"Son of *, the people of Israel Eze 12:27
"Son of *, prophesy against the Eze 13:2,3
"Son of *, speak out against the Eze 13:17
"Son of *, these men worship Eze 14:3
"Son of *, when the people of Eze 14:13
"Son of *, what good are vines Eze 15:2
"Son of *," he said, "speak to Eze 16:2
"Son of *, give this riddle to Eze 17:2
"Son of *, say to the elders of Eze 20:3
Judge them, son of *; Eze 20:4
"Son of *, tell them that the Eze 20:27,28
"Son of *, look toward Jerusalem Eze 20:46
"Son of *, face toward Jerusalem Eze 21:2
son of *, in your bitter anguish; Eze 21:6
"Son of *, tell them this: A Eze 21:9,10,11
Son of *, with sobbing, beat Eze 21:12
"Son of *, make a map and on it Eze 21:19,20
"Son of *, prophesy to the Eze 21:28
"Son of *, indict Jerusalem as Eze 22:2
"Son of *, the people of Israel Eze 22:18,19,20
"Son of *, say to the people of Eze 22:24
"Son of *, there were two Eze 23:2,3
"Son of *, you must accuse Eze 23:36
"Son of *," he said, "write Eze 24:2
"Son of *, I am going to take Eze 24:16
"Son of *, on the day I finish Eze 24:25
"Son of *, look toward the land Eze 25:2
"Son of *, Tyre has rejoiced Eze 26:2
the city with *, and your walls Eze 26:10
and even your * into the sea. Eze 26:12
"Son of *, sing this sad dirge Eze 27:2
and casting * upon their heads and Eze 27:30
"Son of *, say to the prince of Eze 28:2,3
"Son of *, weep for the king of Eze 28:12
"Son of *, look toward the city Eze 28:21
"Son of *, face toward Egypt and Eze 29:2
"Son of *, the army of King Eze 29:18
"Son of *, prophesy and say: The Eze 30:2,3
"Son of *, I have broken the arm Eze 30:21
"Son of *, tell Pharaoh, king of Eze 31:2,3
"Son of *, mourn for Pharaoh, Eze 32:2
"Son of *, weep for the people Eze 32:18
"Son of *, tell your people: Eze 33:2
"So with you, son of *. Eze 33:7
"Son of *, the scattered Eze 33:24
"Son of *, your people are Eze 33:30
"Son of *, prophesy against the Eze 34:2
"Son of *, face toward Mount Eze 35:2
"SON OF *, prophesy to Israel's Eze 36:1
"Son of *, when the people of Eze 36:17
"Son of *, can these bones become Eze 37:3
"Son of *, face northward Eze 38:2,3
"SON OF *, prophesy this also Eze 39:1
"And now, son of *, call all the Eze 39:17
He said to me: "Son of *, watch Eze 40:4
before him with my face in the *. Eze 43:3
"Son of *, this is the place of Eze 43:7
"Son of *, describe the Temple I Eze 43:10
"Son of *, the Lord God says: Eze 43:18
the ground with my face in the *. Eze 44:4
"Son of *, notice carefully; Eze 44:5
and push them into the *!" Dan 4:37
They trample the poor in the * Amo 2:7
In Beth-le-aphrah roll in the * Mic 1:10
clouds are billowing * beneath Nah 1:3
your princes lie dead in the *; Nah 3:18
out into the * and your bodies will Zep 1:17
and fine gold like * in the Zec 9:3
into the * beneath their feet. Zec 10:5
you—shake off the * of that place Mt 10:14
his face in the *, and said, 'Oh, Mt 18:26
falls on will be scattered as *." Mt 21:44
the * from your feet as you leave; Mk 6:11
in the *, begging to be healed. Lk 5:12
water to wash the * from my feet, Lk 7:44
by shaking its * from your feet Lk 9:5
say, 'We wipe the * of your town Lk 10:11
downward in the *, thanking him for Lk 17:16
it falls will be crushed to *." Lk 20:18
wrote in the * with his finger. Jn 8:6
and wrote some more in the *. Jn 8:8
But they shook off the * of Act 13:51
Paul shook off the * from his robe Act 18:6
air and tossed up handfuls of * Act 22:23
Adam was made from the * of the 1Co 15:47
Adam's, made of *, but all who 1Co 15:48
And they will throw * on their Rev 18:19

DUTIES
are for your daily * and your Ex 20:9
Your * will be to arbitrate for Lev 10:10
perform the sacred * at the Num 3:7,8,9
carry out the * of the priesthood; Num 3:10
These are their sacred *: Num 4:4
These will be their *: Num 4:24
"Assign * to each man by name. Num 4:32
out the sacred * required of the Num 8:19
with various light * in the Num 8:25,26
sacred * in the Tabernacle itself. Num 18:2,3
perform the sacred * within the Num 18:5
to perform these * shall die." Num 18:7
Their * are explained in chapter Jos 3:12f
the rights and * of a king were; 1Sa 10:25
Their * included sacrificing 1Ch 6:49
out the Temple * as originally 1Ch 24:19
assigned to their * by coin-toss 1Ch 24:31
without regard to their normal *. 2Ch 5:11,12
the priests in each day's *; 2Ch 8:14
don't neglect your * any longer, 2Ch 29:11
* as required in the law of God. 2Ch 31:4
priests in their *, and encouraged 2Ch 35:2
restored them to their proper *. Neh 13:11
with joy, and return him to his *. Job 33:26
may forget their * and be unable to Pro 31:5
to perform his Temple * again. Eze 44:26
and performed my * for the king, Dan 8:27
Temple * and then returned home. Lk 1:23
taxes and import * gladly, obey Rom 13:7

DUTIFUL
man spares an obedient and * son. Mal 3:17

DUTY
Even the priests on * Ex 19:22
his sons, to be worn when on *. Ex 39:41
not leave the sanctuary [when on * Lev 21:12
discharged your * to the Lord and Num 32:22
the chief judge on * at the time Deu 17:9
on * before the Lord at the time. Deu 19:17
refuses to do his * in this matter, Deu 25:7
to the priest on * and say to him, Deu 26:2,3
let him do his *; Ru 3:13
(The priests on * at that time 1Sa 1:3
those who are on * on the Sabbath 2Ki 11:5
who were going off * on the Sabbath 2Ki 11:9
who were coming on *, and he armed 2Ki 11:9
Temple and were on * at all hours. 1Ch 9:33,34
They were assigned guard * at 1Ch 26:13
for active * one month each year. 1Ch 27:1
on * the first month of each year. 1Ch 27:2,3
* the second month of each year. 1Ch 27:4
His 24,000 men were on * the 1Ch 27:5,6
He had 24,000 men on * the fourth 1Ch 27:7
on * the fifth month of each year. 1Ch 27:8
he had 24,000 men on * the sixth 1Ch 27:9
* the seventh month of each year. 1Ch 27:10
* the eighth month of each year. 1Ch 27:11
on * the tenth month of each year. 1Ch 27:13
with 24,000 men on * during the 1Ch 27:14
24,000 men on * during the twelfth 1Ch 27:15
at their posts of *, and the 2Ch 7:6
to their posts of * he followed the 2Ch 8:14
who come off * on the Sabbath will 2Ch 23:4
and Levites on * may enter the 2Ch 23:5,6
arriving for * that Sabbath, and a 2Ch 23:8
and were going off *—for Jehoiada 2Ch 23:8
However, the priests on * at the 2Ch 31:16
by the Levites on guard * there. 2Ch 34:9
their posts of *, for their meals 2Ch 35:15
* as well as work during the day. Neh 4:22
while the guards were still on *. Neh 7:3
they must be on * at regular times, Neh 7:3
One day, as Mordecai was on * at Est 2:21
do their * on the appointed day." Est 3:14
"Who is on * in the outer Est 6:4
your *, even when it's unpleasant. Ecc 8:2,3
for this is the entire * of man. Ecc 12:13
no wool while on * in the inner Eze 44:17
how the priests on * in the Temple Mt 12:5
division was on * that week—the Lk 1:8,9
Your * is to come and preach the Lk 9:60
he knew his * he refused to do it. Lk 12:47
For you have simply done your * Lk 17:10
do, but it is our * to God, because 2Th 1:3
will be doing your * as a worthy 1Ti 4:6

DWARF
back, or is a *, or has a defect in Lev 21:20

DWELL
"Zebulun shall * on the shores Gen 49:13
you build me a house to * in?" 2Sa 7:5f
Literally, "shall * in the Pro 2:21f
Those who * in the dust shall Is 26:19
Such as these shall * on high. Is 33:16
with contrite, humble spirits *; Is 57:15
and lovely, and * on the fine, good Php 4:8

DWELLERS
And you, too, * in the mountain Is 42:11
And city * and farmers and Jer 31:24

DWELLING
Tabernacle, the * place of God, Ex 26:6
and oil in the * of the wise." Pro 21:20f
are part of this * place of God. Eph 2:22

DWELLS
So Israel * safely, Deu 33:28
"wherein righteousness *." 2Pe 3:13f

DWINDLE
Don't * away! Jer 29:6

DWINDLED
Israel's population *, Ju 5:7

DWINDLING
glory; a * nation is his doom. Pro 14:28

DYED
and six feet wide, * blue, purple, Ex 26:1
of rams' skins, * red, and over Ex 26:14
and ram skins * red, and Ex 35:23
* red, and tanned goat skins. Ex 36:19
rams' skins * red, the specially Ex 39:33-40

DYES
and scarlet * from eastern Cyprus. Eze 27:7
They bring emeralds, purple *, Eze 27:16

DYING
to master it, until your * day. Gen 3:19
Esau: "When a man is * of Gen 25:32
Egyptians began *, but not one of Ex 9:6
and he is an expert in the * of 2Ch 2:14
a very old age, finally * at 130. 2Ch 24:15
The bones of the * cry from the Job 24:12
ten thousand are * around me, the Ps 91:7
live, yes, even with my * breath. Ps 146:2
his beauty fades like * flowers. Is 40:6

(DYING Con't)
into deserts, covered with * fish. Is 50:2
sins that he was * for—that he was Is 53:8
"Why do you insist on *—you and Jer 27:13
are fainting and * in the streets. Lam 2:11
wind touches it, * in the same Eze 17:10
many of them * by fire and sword, Dan 11:33
the fig trees are *; Joe 1:12
not care for the * ones, nor look Zec 11:16
And even the two robbers * with Mk 15:32
*, a little girl twelve years old. Lk 8:42
spare, and here I am, * of hunger! Lk 15:17
you even fear God when you are *? Lk 23:40,41
you will keep a man from *! Jn 8:52
couldn't he keep Lazarus from *?" Jn 11:37,38
Christ has done in * for our Rom 5:11
he will make your * bodies live Rom 8:11
Living or * we follow the Lord. Rom 14:8
So when we preach about Christ * 1Co 1:23
weakness—Christ * on the cross—is 1Co 1:25
Yes, they are weak, * bodies now, 1Co 15:43
Jesus Christ within our * bodies. 2Co 4:11
Though our bodies are *, our 2Co 4:16
of * and having no bodies at all. 2Co 5:4
so that these * bodies will, as it 2Co 5:4
on it of Christ * on the cross. Gal 3:1
and *—well, that's better yet! Php 1:21
this privilege of * for you. Php 2:18
he will take these * bodies of ours Php 3:21
he die and in * break the power of Heb 2:14
power of sin forever by * for us. Heb 9:26
* for us once and for all. Heb 10:10
took him away to heaven without *; Heb 11:5
he was old and *, blessed each of Heb 11:21
with my own eyes I saw Christ * 1Pe 5:1
from Christ's example in * for us. 1Jn 3:16

DYNASTY
forever, but now your * must end; 1Sa 13:14
Saul's * became weaker and weaker. 2Sa 3:1
speak of giving me an eternal *! 2Sa 7:19
have established my * before you. 2Sa 7:26
am the first of a * which will rule 2Sa 7:27
May our * continue on and on 2Sa 7:29
of Israel—my * will never end. 1Ki 2:4
the * of David to this day. 1Ki 12:19
to destroy the * of Ahab. 2Ki 10:30
a * that will rule Israel forever; 1Ch 28:4
"Forget David and his *!" 2Ch 10:16
to end the * of David, for he had 2Ch 21:7
appointed to end the * of Ahab. 2Ch 22:7
lie), that his * will go on Ps 89:35,36
the * of David shall never end. Ps 132:12
25th Ethiopian * would soon arise. Is 7:18f
who created the royal * of DavidÇ Is 11:10
25th Egyptian * (730–660 B.C.). Is 18:1f
* against Sennacherib of Assyria. Is 30:2f
Jehu's * to avenge the murders Hos 1:4,5
* of King Jeroboam by the sword." Amo 7:9
"I have ordered an end to your *; Nah 1:14

DYSENTERY
father was ill with fever and *. Act 28:8

E
(*) If the Jewish priests and Heb 7:11

EACH
Bring in a pair of * kind of bird Gen 6:19,20
too—a pair of *, except those kinds Gen 7:2
of * of them, and seven pairs Gen 7:2
lands, * with a separate language. Gen 10:5
understand * other's words!" Gen 11:7
were fighting * other inside her! Gen 25:22
they were up, they * took solemn Gen 26:31
we are out of * other's sight. Gen 31:49
them on ahead, * group of animals Gen 32:16
* driver, with the same message. Gen 32:19
of Edom, * giving its name to the Gen 36:40-43
One night * of them had a dream. Gen 40:5
and I * had a dream one night. Gen 41:11
to put * brother's payment at the Gen 42:25
Trembling, they exclaimed to * Gen 42:28
at the top of * was the money paid Gen 42:35
He told * of them where to sit, Gen 43:33
manager to fill * of their sacks Gen 44:1
into the mouth of * man's sack the Gen 44:1
And he did the same with * of Gen 45:15
and he gave * of them new Gen 45:22
and they fell into * other's arms Gen 46:29
of Israel bless * other by saying, Gen 48:20
In due season Joseph and * of Ex 1:6
and they greeted * other warmly. Ex 4:27
Israel) * family shall get a lamb Ex 12:3,4
this event * year (this is a Ex 12:14
You shall, all of you who eat * Ex 12:46
* year, when Jehovah brings you Ex 13:4,5
"During those celebration days * Ex 13:8
with walls of water on * side; Ex 14:21
Everyone can go out * day and Ex 16:4
on the sixth day of * week." Ex 16:5
asked * other, "What is it?" Ex 16:15
for * person in his home." Ex 16:16
no lack! * home had just enough. Ex 16:18
* home according to its need; Ex 16:21
and they stood on * side, holding Ex 17:12
they asked about * other's health Ex 18:7
* other, from morning to evening. Ex 18:13
one judge for * 1000 people; Ex 18:21
him, * in charge of a hundred; Ex 18:21
and under * of them will be two Ex 18:21
be two judges, * responsible for Ex 18:21
fifty people; and * of these will Ex 18:21
him, * counseling ten persons. Ex 18:21
between them—and * shall also own Ex 21:35
shall be returned for * stolen ox. Ex 22:1
sheep returned for * sheep stolen. Ex 22:1
At these three times * year, Ex 23:17
"As you reap * of your crops, Ex 23:19
and the details of * furnishing. Ex 25:9
corners, two rings on * side. Ex 25:12
the mercy place, one at * end. Ex 25:19
be facing * other, looking down Ex 25:20
going out from * side of the center Ex 25:32,33
the center shaft, * branch Ex 25:32,33
placed between * set of branches; Ex 25:34,35
end to end for * side of the tent, Ex 26:3
two long pieces, one for * side. Ex 26:3
There are to be fifty loops on * Ex 26:4,5
on each side, opposite * other. Ex 26:4,5
these tarpaulins, * forty-five feet Ex 26:7,8
along the edges of * of these two Ex 26:10,11
from acacia wood, * frame-piece Ex 26:15,16
with grooves on * side to mortise Ex 26:17
bases under * piece of the frame. Ex 26:18,19
for * frame, one under each edge. Ex 26:21
for each frame, one under * edge. Ex 26:21
and two frames at * corner. Ex 26:23
frames—two bases under * frame. Ex 26:25
bars on * side of the Tabernacle. Ex 26:26,27
the room from * other on the outer Ex 26:35
and a bronze socket for * pillar. Ex 26:37
a metal ring at * corner, and fit Ex 27:4
the rings at * side of the altar. Ex 27:7
feet. On * side of the entrance Ex 27:14,15
Six names shall be on * stone, Ex 28:10
in gold settings. * stone will Ex 28:21
One end of * cord is attached to Ex 28:22,23,24
"* day offer two yearling lambs Ex 29:38
Beneath the molding, on * of two Ex 30:4
on the altar, and * evening when Ex 30:8
people of Israel, * man who is Ex 30:11,12
same amounts of *, using the usual Ex 30:34
dates appointed * year in March; Ex 34:18
Festival. On * of these three Ex 34:23
your God those three times * year. Ex 34:24
of the first of * year's crop to Ex 34:26
gifts were received * morning. Ex 36:3
two long sheets, * loop being Ex 36:11,12
along the end of *, and fifty Ex 36:17
were firmly attached to * other. Ex 36:18
The height of * frame was Ex 36:21
width 2¼ feet. * frame had two Ex 36:22
silver bases. * frame was connected Ex 36:24
silver bases, two for * frame. Ex 36:25,26
frames, plus another at * corner. Ex 36:28
were linked to * other at both top Ex 36:29
beneath them, two for * frame. Ex 36:30
five for * side of the Tabernacle. Ex 36:31,32
the frames, along * side, running Ex 36:33
its four feet, two rings at * end. Ex 37:3
The cherubim faced * other, with Ex 37:9
six branches, three from * side. Ex 37:18
from each side. * of the branches Ex 37:19
stem beneath * pair of branches; Ex 37:20,21
Two gold rings were placed on * Ex 37:27
Four rings were cast for * side Ex 38:5
22½ feet wide, * with three posts Ex 38:14,15
linen. * post had a bronze base, Ex 38:17
for * socket. The silver left Ex 38:27
at the top of * shoulder strap of Ex 39:15-18
put on fresh wood * morning, and Lev 6:12
on * item in it, sanctifying them. Lev 8:10
he burned * part upon the altar. Lev 9:13
* year, because of their sins." Lev 16:34
themselves by defiling * other. Lev 20:12
which are to be observed * year: Lev 23:4
the festival. On * of the Lev 23:8
work that day. On * of the seven Lev 23:36
Holy of Holies. * morning and Lev 24:3,4
using a fifth of a bushel for * Lev 24:5-8
shall be sprinkled along * row. Lev 24:5-8
shall stumble over * other in Lev 26:37
by leaders from * tribe:" Num 1:2-15
come and register, * man Num 1:17,18,19
be executed. * tribe of Israel Num 1:52
Moses and Aaron: "* tribe will Num 2:1
When traveling, * tribe stayed Num 2:3-31
own flag, just as * was separate Num 2:3-31
up their camps, * tribe under its Num 2:34
Levi, indicating * person's clan; Num 3:14,15
and older, and register * name. Num 3:40
for * one to Aaron and his Num 3:47,48
and point out what * is to carry. Num 4:17,18,19
"Assign duties to * man by name. Num 4:32
MOSES ANOINTED AND sanctified * Num 7:1
covered wagons, * drawn by two Num 7:3
two leaders and an ox for * one; Num 7:3
The Lord said to Moses, "Let * Num 7:11
12 silver platters (* weighing Num 7:84,85,86
12 silver bowls (* weighing about Num 7:84,85,86
the beginning of * month to rejoice Num 10:10
send one leader from * tribe. Num 13:2
years—a year for * day, bearing the Num 14:34,35
herds of cattle. * Num 15:3,4
is to accompany * sacrificial bull, Num 15:11,12
Lord a sample of * year's new Num 15:19,20,21
first grain that is cut * year. Num 15:19,20,21
a censer for * man, 250 in all; Num 16:17
of Israel that * of their tribal Num 17:1
to the people, and * of the twelve Num 17:6
in disbelief! Then * man except Num 17:9
made for * firstborn child. Num 18:16
a ram were sacrificed on * altar. Num 23:2
a young bull and a ram on *." Num 23:3,4
a young bull and a ram on * altar. Num 23:14
out how many of * tribe and clan Num 26:2
male lambs—* without defect. Num 28:3
Two of them shall be offered * Num 28:3
strong wine with * lamb, poured out Num 28:7
"Also, on the first day of * Num 28:11
as a grain offering with * bull; Num 28:12
and for * lamb, three quarts of Num 28:13
Along with * sacrifice shall be Num 28:14
pints of wine with * bull, four Num 28:14
* month throughout the year. Num 28:14
"Also on the first day of * Num 28:15
the first month of * year, you Num 28:16
With * bull there shall be a Num 28:20,21
and with * of the seven lambs Num 28:20,21
* of the seven days of the feast; Num 28:24
with oil with * bull, six quarts Num 28:28,29
quarts with * of the seven lambs. Num 28:28,29
* year; there shall be a solemn Num 29:1
quarts with * of the seven lambs. Num 29:3,4
male lambs—* without defect— and Num 29:8
and three with * of the seven Num 29:9,10
yearling lambs —* without defect— Num 29:13
for * of the thirteen young bulls; Num 29:14
six quarts for * of the two rams; Num 29:14
and three quarts for * of the Num 29:15
yearling lambs—* without defect— Num 29:17
yearling lambs—* without defect— Num 29:20
drink offering with * sacrifice. Num 29:21
yearling lambs—* without defect— Num 29:23
without defect— * with its Num 29:24
yearling lambs—* without Num 29:26,27
yearling lambs—* without defect— Num 29:29
yearling lambs—* without defect— Num 29:32
without defect— * with its Num 29:33
yearling lambs—* without defect— Num 29:36
Conscript 1,000 men from * Num 31:4,5
from * tribe, as listed below: Num 34:16-28
for 1500 feet in * direction. Num 35:4
So choose some men from * tribe Deu 1:13
twelve spies, one from * tribe. Deu 1:23
these laws to * one of you from the Deu 5:22
listen closely to * command and be Deu 6:3
your God * year at his sanctuary. Deu 15:20
* city before the Lord your God. Deu 16:8
"On * of these occasions bring a Deu 16:16
one of these cities in * district; Deu 19:2,3
outside the camp. * man must have Deu 23:13
Pay him his wage * day before Deu 24:14,15
the first sample from * annual Deu 26:2,3
upper hand. But * of these Deu 28:14
He gave * of them a supervising Deu 32:8
from * tribe, for a special task. Jos 3:12
task, one from * tribe, each to Jos 4:2,3
from each tribe, * to take a stone Jos 4:2,3
where the Ark is. * of you is to Jos 4:5
one for * of the twelve tribes. Jos 4:5
river—one for * tribe, just as the Jos 4:8
ahead of the Ark, * carrying a Jos 6:3,4
Tell the people, '* of you must Jos 7:13
families, and then * member of the Jos 7:14
altar * of the Ten Commandments. Jos 8:32
* of the five kings, killing them. Jos 10:26
Select three men from * tribe Jos 18:4
will be assigned to * tribe. Jos 18:5,6
listing the cities in * section. Jos 18:9
which tribe should have * section: Jos 18:10
* of their surrounding villages. Jos 19:15,16
sixteen cities in all, * with its Jos 19:17-23
Israel, one from * of the ten Jos 22:14
ten tribes, and * a clan leader. Jos 22:14
to defeat you. * one of you has Jos 23:10
and the Jebusites. * in turn fought Jos 24:11
God's commands. * judge rescued Ju 2:18
* man receives a girl or two; Ju 5:30
groups and gave * man a trumpet and Ju 7:16
and killing * other from one end of Ju 7:22
told his men. So * of them quickly Ju 9:49
the leaders of Gilead asked * Ju 10:18
away for four days * year to lament Ju 11:40
with a torch between * pair. Ju 15:4
"* of us will give you a thousand Ju 16:5

(EACH Con't)
one piece to * tribe of Israel. Ju 19:29
* year Elkanah and his families 1Sa 1:3
* year his mother made a little 1Sa 2:19
brought to him in * of those three 1Sa 7:16
Then he brought * family of the 1Sa 10:21
killing * other, and there was 1Sa 14:20
and Israelis faced * other on 1Sa 17:3
facing * other, army against army. 1Sa 17:21
our promises to * other, for he has 1Sa 20:23
and they kissed * other and wept 1Sa 20:41f
we have entrusted * other and each 1Sa 20:42
each other and * other's children 1Sa 20:42
they sat facing * other on opposite 2Sa 2:13
* side to fight in mortal combat. 2Sa 2:15
in mortal combat. * one grabbed 2Sa 2:16
began to fight * other, and by the 2Sa 2:17
continue to kill * other forever? 2Sa 2:26
guilty ones. May * of his children 2Sa 3:29
Two-thirds of * row, as measured 2Sa 8:2
paid him tribute * year. 2Sa 8:2
six fingers on * hand and six toes 2Sa 21:20,21
and six toes on * foot defied 2Sa 21:20,21
all his ways; keep * of his 1Ki 2:3
living child, and * says that the 1Ki 3:23
give half to * of these women!" 1Ki 3:25
court—one man from * 1Ki 4:7
king's household. * of them 1Ki 4:7
and safety; and * family had its 1Ki 4:25
charioteers. * month the tax 1Ki 4:27
a month, so that * man was a month 1Ki 5:14
was an annex on * side of the 1Ki 6:10
by cedar timbers. * story of the 1Ki 6:10
made from olive wood, * fifteen 1Ki 6:23-28
* other at the center of the room; 1Ki 6:23-28
of the room; * wing was 7½ feet 1Ki 6:23-28
each wing was 7½ feet long, so * 1Ki 6:23-28
and * was overlaid with gold. 1Ki 6:23-28
cypress wood, and * door was hinged 1Ki 6:34
facing * other from three walls. 1Ki 7:3,4
from three walls. * of the 1Ki 7:5
bronze pillars, * twenty-seven feet 1Ki 7:15
* 7½ feet high, and 6 feet wide. 1Ki 7:16-22
and 6 feet wide. * capital was 1Ki 7:16-22
* 6 feet square and 4½ feet high. 1Ki 7:27-30
decorations. * of these movable 1Ki 7:27-30
axles, and at * corner of the 1Ki 7:27-30
decorated with wreaths on * side. 1Ki 7:27-30
The top of * stand was a round 1Ki 7:31
There were supports at * of the 1Ki 7:34
tip of * stand, banded with lugs. 1Ki 7:35
for * was cast from the same mold. 1Ki 7:37
on the stands. * vat was six feet 1Ki 7:38
A capital at the top of * pillar; 1Ki 7:41-46
bases of the capitals of * pillar; 1Ki 7:41-46
* of these was made of solid gold. 1Ki 7:50
for you know * heart. 1Ki 8:39
* year Solomon received gold 1Ki 10:14
$6,000 went into * piece) and three 1Ki 10:16,17
($1,800 worth of gold in *). 1Ki 10:16,17
and a lion standing on * side. 1Ki 10:19
And there were two lions on * 1Ki 10:20
the horses were valued at $150 *. 1Ki 10:29
him bread and meat * morning and 1Ki 17:6
two caves—fifty in *—and had fed 1Ki 18:3,4
So they did, * going alone. 1Ki 18:6
to find you. And * time when he was 1Ki 18:10
* of the tribes of Israel, 1Ki 18:31
Literally, "* of the tribes of 1Ki 18:31f
the attack. * one killed a Syrian 1Ki 20:20
The two armies camped opposite * 1Ki 20:29
have attacked and killed * other! 2Ki 3:23
they asked * other. 2Ki 7:3
Finally they said to * other, 2Ki 7:9
After they had greeted * other, 2Ki 10:15
used to invade the land * spring. 2Ki 13:20,21
rich, assessing * one $2,000 in the 2Ki 15:19,20
were so heavy. * pillar was 2Ki 25:17
* of these men had a great 1Ch 5:24
the surrounding pastureland of *. 1Ch 6:73
and Jazer, * with their surrounding 1Ch 6:81
The sons of Tola, * of whom was 1Ch 7:2
They were assigned to * of the 1Ch 9:24
they opened the gates * morning. 1Ch 9:27
* Sabbath. 1Ch 9:32
* was a high-ranking officer of 1Ch 12:20
* famous in his respective clan. 1Ch 12:24-37
Literally, "to * Israelite." 1Ch 16:3f
Declare * day that he is the one 1Ch 16:23
doing * day whatever needed to be 1Ch 16:37
to the Lord * morning and evening 1Ch 16:40
six fingers on * hand and six toes 1Ch 20:6,7
and six toes on * foot (his father 1Ch 20:6,7
and measures. * morning and 1Ch 23:30
of the Temple in * division. 1Ch 24:5
Ithamar were assigned to * task. 1Ch 24:6
* group carried out the Temple 1Ch 24:19
to the Lord; * one—288 of them in 1Ch 25:6,7
and two to * of the storehouses. 1Ch 26:17
Six guards were assigned * day 1Ch 26:18
twelve regiments, * with 24,000 1Ch 27:1
for active duty one month * year. 1Ch 27:1
on duty the first month of * year. 1Ch 27:2,3
duty the second month of * year. 1Ch 27:4
on duty the third month of * year. 1Ch 27:5,6
duty the fourth month of * year. 1Ch 27:7
on duty the fifth month of * year. 1Ch 27:8
on duty the sixth month of * year. 1Ch 27:9
duty the seventh month of * year. 1Ch 27:10
duty the eighth month of * year. 1Ch 27:11
during the ninth month of * year. 1Ch 27:12
on duty the tenth month of * year. 1Ch 27:13
the eleventh month of * year. 1Ch 27:14
the twelfth month of * year. 1Ch 27:15
and he gave specifications for * 1Ch 28:13
and lamps, * according to its use. 1Ch 28:15
sold for $400 * and horses for 2Ch 1:17
and sacrifice burnt offerings * 2Ch 2:4
the Temple, five against * wall; 2Ch 4:7
* wall on the right and left. 2Ch 4:8
forgive, and give * one whatever he 2Ch 6:30
the priests in * day's duties; 2Ch 8:14
worth of gold * year from the kings 2Ch 9:13,14
200 large shields, * worth 2Ch 9:15
smaller shields, * worth $140,000. 2Ch 9:16
also gold armrests, * flanked by 2Ch 9:18
Gold lions also stood at * side 2Ch 9:19
also stood at each side of * step. 2Ch 9:19
into his heart. * brought him 2Ch 9:24
in * case that comes before you. 2Ch 19:6
and they destroyed * other! 2Ch 20:22
job, they turned against * other! 2Ch 20:23
Their father had given * of them 2Ch 21:3,4
were made. * of the three leaders 2Ch 23:8
to * clan from Judah and Benjamin. 2Ch 25:5,6
with *, and many peace offerings. 2Ch 29:35
was appointed in * of the cities of 2Ch 31:19
his son Solomon. * corps will 2Ch 35:4,5
the carcasses for * tribe to 2Ch 35:12
and * gave as much as he could. Ez 2:69
specified for * day of the feast. Ez 3:4
and olive oil * day without fail. Ez 6:9
A receipt was given for * item, Ez 8:34
of his city; then * case will be Ez 10:14
* of these men had heathen wives, Ez 10:44
the Horse Gate, * one doing the Neh 3:28
So I placed armed guards from * Neh 4:13
so widely from * other, that when Neh 4:19
The provisions required for * Neh 5:18
and * time I gave the same reply. Neh 6:4
times, and that * homeowner who Neh 7:3
Ezra read from the scroll on * Neh 8:18
regular times * year—the families Neh 10:34
certain that * knew his work. Neh 13:30
We will appoint agents in * Est 2:3
to the king's bed, * would be given Est 2:12,13,14
Then, as * girl's turn came for Est 2:12,13,14
the empire, to * province in its Est 3:12
rejoice and send gifts to * other. Est 9:19
days at the appointed time * year. Est 9:27
Every year when * of Job's sons Job 1:4
a burnt offering for * of them. Job 1:5
got in touch with * other and Job 2:11
He hurls * at its target. Job 36:32
upon him. And * of them brought him Job 42:11
fruit * season without fail. Ps 1:3
anyone but you. * morning I will Ps 5:3
You have noted * evil act. Ps 10:14
"Praise the Lord, * one of you Ps 22:23
him," I will say. "* of you Ps 22:23
Now I say that * believer should Ps 32:6
But the Lord helps him in * and Ps 34:19
He delights in * step they take. Ps 37:23
But as for me, I will sing * Ps 59:16
my vow of praising you * day. Ps 61:8
kind and rewards * one of us Ps 62:12
They encourage * other to do Ps 64:5
You see them all and know what * Ps 69:19
In this way * generation has Ps 78:7
in * Egyptian family—he who was Ps 78:51
the land, and gave * tribe of Ps 78:55
in strength and * of them is Ps 84:7
covered over * one, so that all Ps 85:2
All the nations—and you made * Ps 86:9
My eyes grow dim with weeping. * Ps 88:9
Bless his name. * day tell Ps 96:2
and on to * succeeding generation. Ps 100:5
listening for * of his commands. Ps 103:20
oldest child in * Egyptian home, Ps 105:36
for * of your commands. Ps 119:131
wonder, for * of them is just. Ps 119:172
eldest child in * Egyptian home, Ps 135:8
born and scheduled * day of my life Ps 139:16
bless your name * day and forever. Ps 145:1
discovery! Let * generation tell Ps 145:4
Reverence for God adds hours to * Pro 10:27
Crooks are jealous of * other's Pro 12:12
good men long to help * other. Pro 12:12
a wise son considers * Pro 15:5
times, will * time rise again? Pro 24:15,16
this: * depends on God for light. Pro 29:13
gain warmth from * other, but how Ecc 4:11
it was known long ago what * man Ecc 6:10
made men upright, * has turned away Ecc 7:29
the power of injuring * other. Ecc 8:9,10
There is risk in * stroke of your Ecc 10:8,9
bodyguards. * one has his sword Sol 3:8
thousand pieces of silver from *. Sol 8:11
will fight over * of them and say, Is 4:1
for the fire. * fights against his Is 9:19,20
they will not fight * other any Is 11:13
fighting against * other—brother Is 19:2
* in its own section of his land? Is 28:25
down * mountain and every hill. Is 30:25
Be our strength * day and our Is 33:2
will scream at * other, and the Is 34:14
will come, * one with its mate. Is 34:15
and I will let you * have your own Is 36:16
See, his reward is with him, to * Is 40:10
leads his sheep, calling * by its Is 40:26
mobilize for war. * man encourages Is 41:6
own interest, * trying to get as Is 56:11
lusty stallions, * neighing for his Jer 5:8
Strip the branches from * vine, Jer 5:10
gives them rain * year in spring Jer 5:23,24
for as a grape-gatherer checks * Jer 6:9
at God's appointed time * year; Jer 8:7
they fool and defraud * other; Jer 9:5
They wouldn't even listen. * Jer 11:8
again, * man to his inheritance. Jer 12:15
against * other, says the Lord. Jer 13:14
idols beneath * tree, high in the Jer 17:2,3
so he can give to * person his Jer 17:10
out, and then at * of the other Jer 17:19
messages from * other—these Jer 23:30,31
You can ask * other, "What is Jer 23:35
refused to hear. * time the Jer 25:5
across * other and fall together. Jer 46:12
of Babylon fight against * other. Jer 51:46
For the pillars were * Jer 52:21
The top 7½ feet of * column had Jer 52:22
begins afresh * day. Lam 3:23
men, except that * had four faces Eze 1:6
And beneath * of their wings I Eze 1:8
* had the face of a man [in front Eze 1:10
back of his head! * had two pairs Eze 1:11
living beings on * side, and the Eze 1:11
them, one wheel belonging to *. Eze 1:15
polished amber and * wheel was Eze 1:16
* being's wings stretched Eze 1:23
* had two wings covering his body. Eze 1:23
touched against * other, and the Eze 3:13
"There is special meaning in * Eze 4:3
and doom. * day you lie there Eze 4:4,5
* day will represent one year. Eze 4:6
don't use more than that. * day Eze 4:12
mountains, * weeping for his sins. Eze 7:16
the pictures. * of them held a Eze 8:11
north gate, * one with his sword. Eze 9:2
out his hand (for * cherub had, Eze 10:7,8
* of the four cherubim had a Eze 10:9-13
them called, for * one had a second Eze 10:9-13
forward in * of four directions; Eze 10:9-13
faces looked. * of the four wheels Eze 10:9-13
rims and spokes. * of the four Eze 10:14
I knew they were the same, for * Eze 10:21
I will judge * of you, O Israel, Eze 18:30
* according to your own actions. Eze 18:30
But I will judge * of you in Eze 33:20
that I have heard * evil word you Eze 35:12
and the bones of * body came Eze 37:7
to * other as they used to be. Eze 37:7
were three guardrooms on * side; Eze 40:7-12
on each side; * of these rooms was Eze 40:7-12
the pillars on * side of the porch Eze 40:14
guardrooms on * side, and all the Eze 40:21
on the walls of * side of the Eze 40:37
to the altar; on * side of the Eze 40:39
Outside the entry hall, on * Eze 40:40
pillars, * of them 8¾ feet thick. Eze 40:48,49
* room was seven feet wide. Eze 41:5
with thirty rooms in * tier. Eze 41:6
wall for support. * tier was wider Eze 41:7
of cherubim, * with two faces, and Eze 41:17,18
* with two swinging sections. Eze 41:24
875 feet long on * side, with a Eze 42:16-20
Do this * day for seven days to Eze 43:26
On the eighth day, and on * day Eze 43:27
The first samples of * harvest of Eze 44:30
* side of the holy lands and city; Eze 45:7
giving a portion to * tribe. Eze 45:8
from * 200 sheep in all your Eze 45:15
"The Lord God says: On * New Eze 45:18
of Israel. On * of the seven days Eze 45:23
A young goat will also be given * Eze 45:23
bushel for * bullock and ram; Eze 45:24
gallons to go with * bushel. Eze 45:24
"Early in October, during * of Eze 45:25
is willing for, to go with * lamb. Eze 46:5
olive oil for * bushel of flour. Eze 46:5
to give. With * bushel he is to Eze 46:7
is willing to give with * lamb; Eze 46:11
and 1½ gallons of oil with * Eze 46:11

(EACH Con't)
“* morning a yearling lamb must Eze 46:13
must be a meal offering * morning— Eze 46:14,15
and led me to * of the four corners Eze 46:21,22
I saw that in * corner there was Eze 46:21,22
Otherwise, * tribe will have an Eze 47:14
and the territory * is to get. Eze 48:1
miles square on * side of the Eze 48:21,22
to * tribe, says the Lord God. Eze 48:29
“* city gate will be named in Eze 48:30,31
long talks with * of them, and none Dan 1:18,19
alliances with * other through Dan 2:43
120 provinces, * under a governor. Dan 6:1
water, * different from the other. Dan 7:3
holy angels talking to * other. Dan 8:13
will be plotting against * other Dan 11:27
attempting to deceive * other. Dan 11:27
on * bank of a river. Dan 12:5
not to fear * other any more; Hos 1:18
do * year at the Tabernacle Feast. Hos 12:9
They never crowd * other. Joe 2:8
They never crowd each other. * Joe 2:8
Sacrifice * morning and bring Amo 4:4
Micah bitterly declaims * town, Mic 1:11f
Micah bitterly declaims * town, Mic 1:11f
Micah bitterly declaims * town, Mic 1:11f
nations shall no longer fight * Mic 4:3
shall worship him, * in his own Zep 2:11
and companions will kill * other. Hag 2:22
bay and white, * with its rider. Zec 1:8
and prosperity and * of you will Zec 3:10
one on * side of the reservoir. Zec 4:3
two olive trees on * side of the Zec 4:11
month of August * year, as they had Zec 7:3
plotting evil against * other. Zec 7:10
two mercies for * of your woes! Zec 9:12
and people. * family will go into Zec 12:12,13,14
* other in hand-to-hand combat. Zec 14:13
go up to Jerusalem * year to Zec 14:16
And yet we are faithless to * Mal 2:10
spoke often of him to * other. Mal 3:16
* person according to his deeds. Mt 16:27
o'clock were paid, * received $20. Mt 20:9
are tyrants and * minor official Mt 20:25
had been the wife of * of them. Mt 22:26
will rise against * other and there Mt 24:7
sin and betray and hate * other. Mt 24:10
and * one asked, “Am I the one?” Mt 26:22
them and said, “* one drink from Mt 26:27
these always contradicted * other. Mt 26:60,61
Jewish prisoner * year during the Mt 27:15
being sealed at * end with clay. Mt 27:66f
“Stay at one home in * Mk 6:10
* were sitting on the green grass. Mk 6:39,40
bread and fish to * disciple to Mk 6:41
the disciples asked * other. Mk 8:16
here, one for * of you .” Mk 9:5
Live in peace with * other.” Mk 9:50
had been the wife of * of them?” Mk 12:23
war against * other, and there will Mk 13:8
“Brothers will betray * other to Mk 13:12
but they contradicted * other. Mk 14:56
Jewish prisoner * year at Passover Mk 15:6
said to * other, “Come on! Lk 2:15
which they attended * year. Lk 2:41,42
Be a guest in only one home at * Lk 9:4
of about fifty *,” Jesus replied. Lk 9:14
Literally, “two denarii,” * the Lk 10:35f
He knew the thoughts of * of Lk 11:17
about and crushing * other. Lk 12:1
“So he invited * one who owed Lk 16:5,6
lived * day in mirth and luxury. Lk 16:19
times a day and * time turns again Lk 17:4
and gave them * $2,000 to invest Lk 19:13
the other, until * of the seven had Lk 20:31
to hear him. And * evening he Lk 21:37,38
throwing dice for * piece. Lk 23:34
They began telling * other how Lk 24:32
twenty to thirty gallons *. Jn 2:6
in heaven appoints * man's work. Jn 3:27
the disciples asked * other. Jn 4:33
For you gladly honor * other, but Jn 5:44
with * other about what he meant. Jn 6:52
blind beggar asked * other, “Is Jn 9:8
they asked * other. Jn 11:47
* other, “What do you think? Jn 11:56
Then the Pharisees said to * Jn 12:19
you ought to wash * other's feet. Jn 13:14
I know so well * one of you I Jn 13:18
The disciples looked at * Jn 13:22
to you now—love * other just as Jn 13:34
Your strong love for * other Jn 13:35
I demand that you love * other Jn 15:12
I demand that you love * other, Jn 15:17
will be scattered, * one returning Jn 16:32
He gives eternal life to * one Jn 17:2
from prison * year at Passover. Jn 18:39
four piles, one for * of them. Jn 19:23,24
they asked * other. Act 2:12
And Peter replied, “* one of you Act 2:38
For Christ promised him to * one Act 2:39
everything with * other, selling Act 2:44
at the Temple * day, met in small Act 2:46
to them, and * day God added to Act 2:47
they asked * other. Act 4:16
* giving as much as he could. Act 11:29
grow in love for God and * other. Act 14:22
Turkey, and visit * city where they Act 15:36
* Sabbath found Paul at the Act 18:4
and preached boldly * Sabbath day Act 19:8
* other, “A murderer, no doubt! Act 28:4
good report, and for * one of you. Rom 1:8
by yours: * of us will be a Rom 1:11,12
things with * other's bodies. Rom 1:24
indulged in sex sin with * other. Rom 1:26
with lust for * other, men doing Rom 1:27
He will give * one whatever his Rom 2:6
us trust God more * time we use it Rom 5:4
within easy reach of * of us; Rom 10:8
As God's messenger I give * of Rom 12:3
we * have different work to do. Rom 12:4,5
So we belong to * other, and each Rom 12:4,5
So we belong to each other, and * Rom 12:4,5
God has given * of us the ability Rom 12:6
Love * other with brotherly Rom 12:10
take delight in honoring * other. Rom 12:10
Remember, * of us will stand Rom 14:10
Yes, * of us will give an Rom 14:12
So don't criticize * other any Rom 14:13
and try to build * other up. Rom 14:19
harmony with * other—each with the Rom 15:5
with each other—* with the attitude Rom 15:5
So, warmly welcome * other into Rom 15:7
God, and we can refresh * other. Rom 15:32
Shake hands warmly with * other. Rom 16:16
Why, we're just God's servants, * 1Co 3:5
same aim, though * of us will be 1Co 3:8
of material * builder has used. 1Co 3:13
see exactly what * one of us is 1Co 4:5
At that time God will give to * 1Co 4:5
to be married, * man having his own 1Co 7:2
his own wife, and * woman having 1Co 7:2
refuse these rights to * other. 1Co 7:5
plan men and women need * other. 1Co 11:11
service—wait for * other; 1Co 11:33
Spirit gives to * of you, for I 1Co 12:1
power through * of us as a means of 1Co 12:7
which * one of us should have. 1Co 12:11
of Christ. * of us is a part of 1Co 12:13
put * part just where he wants it. 1Co 12:18
the same care for * other that they 1Co 12:25
body of Christ and * one of you is 1Co 12:27
unless * note is sounded clearly. 1Co 14:7
will rise again. *, however, in 1Co 15:23
plant grows from * kind of seed. 1Co 15:38
And the stars differ from * other 1Co 15:41
Just as * of us now has a body 1Co 15:49
On every Lord's Day * of you 1Co 16:2
And give * other a loving 1Co 16:20
* one of you, and give you peace. 2Co 1:2
bare—before him. * of us will 2Co 5:10
In this way * will have as much 2Co 8:14
our eagerness to help * other. 2Co 8:19
themselves with * other, and 2Co 10:12
* time he said, “No. 2Co 12:9
and walk in * other's steps, doing 2Co 12:18
and envying * other, and being 2Co 12:20
being angry with * other, and 2Co 12:20
things about * other and whispering 2Co 12:20
whispering behind * other's backs, 2Co 12:20
Greet * other warmly in the Lord. 2Co 13:12
same God gave us * our special Gal 2:7,8,9
God's promises against * other? Gal 3:21,22
freedom to love and serve * other. Gal 5:13
Beware of ruining * other. Gal 5:15
fighting * other to win control Gal 5:17
Share * other's troubles and Gal 6:2
someone else. * of us must bear Gal 6:5
been opposed to * other and made Eph 2:15
our anger against * other has Eph 2:16
with him and with * other by the Eph 2:22
Be patient with * other, making Eph 4:2
allowance for * other's faults Eph 4:2
However, Christ has given * of Eph 4:7
perfectly, and * part in its own Eph 4:15,16
Stop lying to * other; Eph 4:25
we are parts of * other and when we Eph 4:25
* other we are hurting ourselves. Eph 4:25
Instead, be kind to * other, Eph 4:32
Instead, remind * other of God's Eph 5:4
Talk with * other much about the Eph 5:19
Honor Christ by submitting to * Eph 5:21
will pay you for * good thing you Eph 6:8
Christ will give * of you his Php 1:2
as Christians cheering * other up? Php 2:1
happy by loving * other and Php 2:2
with * other, working together with Php 2:2
will share my joy with * of you. Php 2:17
news that came to * of you and is Col 1:23
We want to be able to present * Col 1:28
Christ has done for * of them. Col 1:28
him, too, for * day's problems; Col 2:6
Don't tell lies to * other; Col 3:
teach them to * other and sing Col 3:1
and overflow to * other and to 1Th 3:1
sexual sin so that * of you will 1Th 4:3,
So comfort and encourage * other 1Th 4:1
So encourage * other to build 1Th 5:1
other to build * other up, just as 1Th 5:1
to * other and to everyone else. 1Th 5:1
of your growing love for * other. 2Th 1:
your tears as we left * other. 2Ti 1:
the sin of anger with * other. 2Ti 2:1
to help strengthen * of its Tit 1:
assigned such gifts to * of us. Heb 2:
Speak to * other about these Heb 3:1
in the Holy of Holies * year. Heb 9:2
us, let us outdo * other in being Heb 10:2
kind to * other and in doing good. Heb 10:2
encourage and warn * other, Heb 10:2
and dying, blessed * of Joseph's Heb 11:2
Look after * other so that not Heb 12:1
CONTINUE TO LOVE * other with true Heb 13:
evil about * other, dear brothers. Jas 4:1
Don't grumble about * other, Jas 5:
* other so that you may be healed. Jas 5:1
you really do love * other warmly, 1Pe 1:22
of sympathy toward * other, loving 1Pe 3:8
show deep love for * other, for 1Pe 4:8
Or, “love overlooks * other's 1Pe 4:8
God has given * of you some 1Pe 4:10
be sure to use them to help * 1Pe 4:10
And all of you serve * other with 1Pe 5:5
Give * other the handshake of 1Pe 5:14
give this same faith to * of us. 2Pe 1:1
and joy with * other, and the blood 1Jn 1:7
us practice loving * other, for 1Jn 4:7
surely ought to love * other too. 1Jn 4:11
God, when we love * other God lives 1Jn 4:12
the very first to love * other. 2Jn 1:6
and please give * of the folks 3Jn 1:15
by God to oversee * local church. Rev 1:20f
and I will give to * a white Rev 2:17
I will give to * of you whatever Rev 2:23
though in flight. * of these Rev 4:8
before the Lamb, * with a harp and Rev 5:8
White robes were given to * of Rev 6:11
give presents to * other and throw Rev 11:10
And written on * head were Rev 13:1
* one defying and insulting God. Rev 13:1
Beings handed * of them a golden Rev 15:7
in The Books, * according to the Rev 20:12
the dead in them. * was judged Rev 20:13
There were three gates on * Rev 21:13
dimensions—1,500 miles * way. Rev 21:16
—* gate from a single pearl! Rev 21:21
On * side of the river grew Trees Rev 22:2
fruit, with a fresh crop * month; Rev 22:2
say, ‘Come.’ Let * one who hears Rev 22:17

EAGER
angry about Balaam's * attitude, Num 22:22,23
encouraged and be * to attack!” Ju 7:11
The Lord is * to cause this to 2Ki 19:31
Uzziah was always * to please God. 2Ch 26:5
They are like lions * to tear me Ps 17:12
Everyone is * to help a youth Ecc 4:15
I remember how * you were to please Jer 2:2
a prostitute, so * for sin that you Eze 16:31
for your blood, * to destroy you. Mic 4:11
to come soon, and * to know whether Lk 3:15
For they were * to find some Lk 6:7
And now * multitudes are pressing Lk 16:16
were all the more * to kill him Jn 5:18
every breath and * to destroy every Act 9:1
is * to leave, it is permitted. 1Co 7:15
do it, but others are * for it. 2Co 8:8
If you are really * to give, 2Co 8:12
for he is very * to see you! 2Co 8:17
For I know how * you are to do 2Co 9:2
poor, and I, too, was * for that. Gal 2:10
Slaves, obey your masters; be * Eph 6:5
For I live in * expectation and Php 1:20
What I am * for is that all the 1Ti 1:5
Christ and become * followers of 1Ti 4:1
DEAR BROTHERS, DON'T be too * to Jas 3:1
you are * to serve the Lord. 1Pe 5:2

EAGERLY
the king * inquired. Num 23:17
will look forward * to finishing 1Ch 29:19
my anguish I * await sweet death! Job 14:14
They waited * with open mouths. Job 29:23
personally was * expecting the Mk 15:42,43
The lame man looked at them *, Act 3:5
That is why we look forward * to 2Co 5:2
show that they are * looking 2Ti 4:8
* looking forward to receiving it. Tit 3:7
* and patiently waiting for him. Heb 9:28
when you don't * join them any more 1Pe 4:4

EAGERNESS
evil* to do wrongA false Pro 6:16-19
and show our * to help each other. 2Co 8:19
told him all about your * to help. 2Co 8:22
impure thoughts, * for lustful Gal 5:19

EAGLE
The *, the metire, the osprey, Lev 11:13-19
The *, the vulture, Deu 14:11-18
swooping down upon you like an *; Deu 28:49
Even as an * overspreads her Deu 32:11
the * that swoops upon its prey. Job 9:26
Is it at your command that the * Job 39:27
How an * glides through the sky. Pro 30:18,19
of an * at the back of his head! Eze 1:10
"A great * with broad wings full Eze 17:3,4
turned toward the * and produced Eze 17:6
full-feathered * came along, this Eze 17:7
and the fourth, the form of an *, Rev 4:7
As I watched, I saw a solitary * Rev 8:13
those of a great *, to fly into the Rev 12:14
EAGLE'S
to myself as though on * wings. Ex 19:4
prey can see, no * eye observe— Job 28:7
My youth is renewed like the *! Ps 103:5
and the fourth, an *. Eze 10:14
like a lion, but it had * wings! Dan 7:4
EAGLES
They were swifter than *, stronger 2Sa 1:23
shall mount up with wings like *; Is 40:31
his steeds are swifter than *. Jer 4:13
the peaks with the *, I will bring Jer 49:16
enemies are swifter than the *; Lam 4:19
what this riddle of the * means? Eze 17:12,13
of Babylon [the first of the two * Eze 17:12,13
'his hair grew as long as *' Dan 4:33
Though you soar as high as *, Ob 1:4
distant land; like * they come Hab 1:8
EAR
publicly bore his * with an awl, Ex 21:6
tip of the right * of Aaron and his Ex 29:19,20
from a fresh *, crush and roast Lev 2:14
of Aaron's right * and the thumb of Lev 8:23
tip of the right * of the man being Lev 14:14
of the man's right * and the thumb Lev 14:17
of the man's right *—the man on Lev 14:25
of the man's right *, and upon the Lev 14:28
awl and pierce his * into the door, Deu 15:17
as though whispered in my *. Job 4:12
murder has an open * to those who Ps 9:12
Bend down your * and listen to my Ps 71:2
down your * and listen as I plead. Ps 80:1
Bend down your * and give me Ps 102:2
"O my God, bend down your * and Dan 9:18
mouth two legs and a piece of *. Amo 3:12
* of the High Priest's servant. Mt 26:51
servant, cutting off his *. Mk 14:47
servant, and cut off his right *. Lk 22:50
man's * had been and restored it. Lk 22:51
off the right * of Malchus, the Jn 18:10
of the man whose * Peter had cut Jn 18:26
if you heard an * say, "I am not 1Co 12:16
I am only an *, and not an eye"? 1Co 12:16
*, how could you smell anything? 1Co 12:17
EARLIER
go to meet the Lord as he had *. Num 24:1
Forty years *, at the time of the Num 26:64,65f
them Emim. In * days the Horites Deu 2:12
thirty-eight years * were old Deu 2:14,15
men were here *, but I didn't know Jos 2:4
came from what had * been given to Jos 19:9
Samuel had told Saul * to wait 1Sa 13:8
sanctified at the * date, and there 2Ch 30:2,3
He now rebuilt what * kings of 2Ch 34:10,11
issued centuries * by King David, 2Ch 35:15
patriarchs), and * kingdoms had Jer 5:15f
I had seen in the * vision, flew Dan 9:21
fathers were! The * prophets pled Zec 1:4
So when the men hired * came to Mt 20:10
I didn't tell you * because I was Jn 16:4
(For down in the city * that Act 21:29
EARLIEST
evil from his * youth, and even Gen 8:21
THESE ARE THE * generations of 1Ch 1:1
sinners, lying from their * words! Ps 58:3
helped me from my * childhood—and I Ps 71:17
Satisfy us in our * youth Ps 90:14
From my * youth I have tried to Ps 119:52
I have known from * days that Ps 119:152
PERSECUTED FROM MY * youth Ps 129:1
are, rebels from * childhood, Is 48:8
but wrong since their * days; Jer 32:30
From her * history Moab has lived Jer 48:11
my livelihood from my * youth.' Zec 13:5
my laws from * time, yet you may Mal 3:7
from my * childhood in Tarsus Act 26:4
Since * times men have seen the Rom 1:20
been taught his laws from * youth. Rom 2:18
EARLY
you can get up as * as you like Gen 19:2
That morning Abraham was up * and Gen 19:27
The king was up * the next Gen 20:8
So Abraham got up * the next Gen 21:14
The next morning Abraham got up * Gen 22:3
overnight. But * the next morning Gen 24:54
he got up very * and set his stone Gen 28:18
if you stop so * in the day!" Gen 29:7
Laban was up * the next morning Gen 31:55
Moses, "Get up * in the morning Ex 8:20
to Moses, "Get up * in the morning Ex 9:13
But in the * morning Jehovah Ex 14:24
Moses wrote down the laws; and * Ex 24:4
So they were up * the next Ex 32:6
ones, and was up * and climbed Ex 34:4
They were up * the next morning, Num 14:40
to send both the * and late rains Deu 11:14
* THE NEXT morning Joshua and all Jos 3:1
So, * the next morning, Joshua Jos 7:16
camp at Jericho. * the next Jos 8:10
valley, went out * the next morning Jos 8:14
out who did it! * the next Ju 6:28
his army got an * start and went as Ju 7:1
On the fourth day they were up *, Ju 19:5
The next morning they were up * Ju 19:8
can get up * and be on your way." Ju 19:9
So the entire army left * the Ju 20:19,20
The next morning they were up * Ju 21:4
morning and was up *, before Ru 3:14
The entire family was up * the 1Sa 1:19,20
But * the next morning Saul 1Sa 11:11
Lord all night. * the next morning 1Sa 15:12
* the next morning with the gifts. 1Sa 17:20
Now get up * in the morning and 1Sa 29:10
He got up * every morning and 2Sa 15:2
frontier. But * the next morning 2Ki 3:22
servant got up * the next morning 2Ki 6:15
* in his reign war broke out 2Ch 13:1
of his father's * years, and did 2Ch 17:3
* the next morning, the army of 2Ch 20:20
* the next morning, King Hezekiah 2Ch 29:20
It was an evil reign like the * 2Ch 33:22
We worked * and late, from Neh 4:20,21
finally finished in * September Neh 6:15
read from * morning until noon. Neh 8:1
them, getting up * in the morning Job 1:5
* dawn to kill the poor and needy; Job 24:14,15
yes, in my * years, when the Job 29:4
Literally, "*." Ps 90:14f
I am obeying." * in the morning, Ps 119:147
work so hard from * morning until Ps 127:2
Discipline your son in his * Pro 19:18
to a friend too * in the morning, Pro 27:14
Let us get up * and go out to Sol 7:12
Woe to you who get up * in the Is 5:11
away as an * fig is hungrily Is 28:4
like a garden in * spring, full of Is 61:11
Babylonian soil as * as 3000 B.C. Jer 5:15f
it, rising up * and calling, but Jer 7:13,14
This is apparently an * message to Jer 35:1f
* IN APRIL of the twenty-fifth Eze 40:1
"* in October, during each of Eze 45:25
Very * the next morning he Dan 6:19
Then one day * in April, as I was Dan 10:4
of dawn or the rain of * spring." Hos 6:3
How satisfying, like the * figs Hos 9:10
* fig, however much I long for it! Mic 7:1
so they all gathered in * Hag 1:14,15
IN * OCTOBER of the same year, the Hag 2:1
In * December, in the second year Hag 2:10
This corresponds to * in our Hag 2:18,19f
the prophet) in * November of the Zec 1:1
his Spirit through the * prophets. Zec 7:12
an estate went out * one morning to Mt 20:1
* ON SUNDAY morning, as the new Mt 28:1
was too * in the season for fruit. Mk 11:13
These herald only the * stages of Mk 13:8
midnight, * dawn or late Mk 13:35,36,37
* IN THE morning the chief Mk 15:1
* the following morning, just at Mk 16:1
It was * on Sunday morning when Mk 16:9
among us from the * disciples and Lk 1:1,2
* the next morning he went out Lk 4:42
* in the morning to hear him. Lk 21:37,38
* the next morning at daybreak Lk 22:66
BUT VERY * on Sunday morning they Lk 24:1
were at his tomb * this morning and Lk 24:22,23
of Olives, but * the next morning Jn 8:2
several days * so that they could Jn 11:55
in the * hours of the morning. Jn 18:28
* SUNDAY Jn 20:1
It's much too * for that! Act 2:15
Cyprus, one of the * believers; Act 21:16
As the darkness gave way to the * Act 27:33
EARN
fairly and give them what they *. Is 58:6
to God a tenth of everything I *.' Lk 18:12
about doing, to * our salvation? Rom 3:27
But didn't he * his right to Rom 4:4,5
if a person could * it by being Rom 4:4,5
with our hands to * our living. 1Co 4:12
much the Lord has helped you *. 1Co 16:2
and sweated to * enough to live on 1Th 2:9
to work, and * their own living. 2Th 3:12
EARNED
and children—for I * them from Gen 30:26
It was by such feats that he * a 2Sa 23:18,19
and strangers take all he has *. Ps 109:11
You have * the full reward of Hos 10:13
Jacob fled to Syria and * a wife Hos 12:12
with it and soon * another $5,000. Mt 25:16
work, too, and * another $2,000. Mt 25:17
you would rob me of what I *, Mt 25:24,25
it to the man who * the most.' Lk 19:24
and * much money for her masters. Act 16:16
free—it isn't free when it is *. Rom 11:6
from what you have * during the 1Co 16:2
salvation can be * by being Gal 2:5
EARNEST
years there was an * effort to obey 2Ch 11:17
and you must listen to my * cry! Ps 17:1
seek me, if you look for me in *. Jer 29:13
And my * prayer went to you in Jon 2:7
they began to worship him in *. Hag 1:12
were you really in * about leaving Zec 7:5
the Passover. But * prayer was Act 12:5
but became * and sincere, and very 2Co 7:11
experience to be an * Christian. 2Co 8:22
They must be *, wholehearted 1Ti 3:9
that you are in dead * about it. Tit 2:7
may be healed. The * prayer of a Jas 5:16
Therefore be *, thoughtful men of 1Pe 4:7
EARNESTLY
my requests before you, praying *. Ps 5:3
behind him; how * they turned Ps 78:34
search for you; * I seek for God; Is 26:9
So I * pleaded with the Lord God Dan 9:3
Jesus instructed them very * not Mk 5:43
So they began pleading * with Lk 7:4
more earnestly. * last he stood up Lk 22:45
am telling you so * is this: Unless Jn 3:5
"How * I tell you this—anyone Jn 6:47
* for all Christians everywhere. Eph 6:18
He is always * praying for you, Col 4:12
yet when he prayed * that no rain Jas 5:17

EARNEST[illegible]
I prayed [illegible] utmost *, Ps 35:13
I am praying with great *; Ps 119:145
With all the * I have I say: Mt 5:18
I tell you in all *, they have Mt 6:2
Jesus replied, "With all the * I Jn 3:3
"With all the * I possess I tell Jn 6:53
With all the * I have I tell you Jn 8:51
EARNING
of them * your two daughters, and Gen 31:41
EARNINGS
offering from the * of a prostitute Deu 23:17,18
The good man's * advance the Pro 10:16
EARRING
he produced a quarter-ounce gold * Gen 24:22
EARRINGS
idols and their *, and he buried Gen 35:4
"Give me your golden *," Aaron Ex 32:2,3
told them, 'Bring me your gold *.' Ex 32:24
of gold, jewelry—*, rings from Ex 35:22
anklets, rings, *, and necklaces. Num 31:50
Give me all the * collected from Ju 8:23,24
Ishmaelites, all wore golden *. Ju 8:23,24
in the gold * he had gathered. Ju 8:25
We shall make you golden * and Sol 1:11
headbands, *, and perfumes; Is 3:20
she put on her * and jewels and Hos 1:13
EARS
of their right *, upon their right Lev 8:24
or eyes that see or * that hear! Deu 29:4
My cry reached his *. 2Sa 22:7
May your eyes be open and your * 1Ki 8:52
and Judah that the * of those who 2Ki 21:12
He opens their * in times like Job 33:16
my cry reached his *. Ps 18:6
Literally, "my * you have dug." Ps 40:6f
* to the most expert of charmers. Ps 58:4,5
Open your * to what I am saying. Ps 78:1
and blind—he who makes * and eyes? Ps 94:9
eyes and * that cannot hear; Ps 135:17
He who shuts his * to the cries Pro 21:13
Yanking a dog's * is no more Pro 26:17
your * open and your mouth shut! Ecc 5:1
of deep oppression met his *. Is 5:7
fate—with my own * I heard him say, Is 5:9
close their * and shut their eyes. Is 6:10
and unstop the * of the deaf. Is 35:5
Come to me with your * wide open. Is 55:3
do not see and the * that do not Jer 5:21
Their * are closed and they Jer 6:10
terrible that the * of those who Jer 19:3
"You have heard with your own * Jer 26:11
two more for your *, and a lovely Eze 16:12
you, and cut off your nose and *; Eze 23:25
use your eyes and * Eze 44:5
are mere noise to my *. Amo 5:23
their * to keep from hearing me. Zec 7:11
What I whisper in your *, Mt 10:27
If you have *, listen!" Mt 13:9
and heavy, and their * Mt 13:15
and your *, for they hear. Mt 13:16
Let those with *, listen! Mt 13:43
If you have *, listen!" Mk 4:9
If you have *, listen! Mk 4:23

(EARS Con't)
"If any man has * to hear, let Mk 7:15,16f
into the man's *, then spat and Mk 7:33
Why don't you open your * and Mk 8:18
has listening *, use them now!" Lk 8:8
but he has open * to those who Jn 9:31
hands over their *, and drowning Act 7:57
ringing in their *: "The Holy Act 28:25
too fat and your * don't listen and Act 28:27
their eyes and * so that they do Rom 11:8
Their cries have reached the * of Jas 5:4
sink into the * of anyone who Rev 2:7

EARTH
the heavens and the *, the earth Gen 1:1
the heavens and the earth, the * Gen 1:2
Then God named the dry land * Gen 1:9,10
And he said, "Let the * burst Gen 1:11,12
give light to the * and to identify Gen 1:14,15
*, and mark the days and years." Gen 1:14,15
down upon the *—the larger one, the Gen 1:16
sky to light the *, and to preside Gen 1:17
Fill the *!" Gen 1:21,22
And God said, "Let the * bring Gen 1:24
all life upon the * and in the Gen 1:26
and fill the * and subdue it; Gen 1:28
throughout the *, and all the fruit Gen 1:29
NOW AT LAST the heavens and * were Gen 2:1
and * which the Lord God made. Gen 2:4
up across the * at first, for the Gen 2:5
of the whole *—to be cursed. Gen 3:14
a tramp upon the *, wandering from Gen 4:12
explosion took place upon the *. Gen 6:1
looked upon the beautiful * women Gen 6:1
the * all mankind that I created. Gen 6:7
man living on the * at that time. Gen 6:9,10
rapidly across the *, and, as seen Gen 6:11
for the * is filled with crime Gen 6:12,13
I will destroy mankind from the *. Gen 6:12,13
I am going to cover the * with a Gen 6:17
the people of the *, I consider you Gen 7:1
the * for forty days and nights. Gen 7:10,11,12
lifting the boat high above the *. Gen 7:17
And all living things upon the * Gen 7:21
All existence on the * was Gen 7:23
And the water covered the * 150 Gen 7:24
until the * was dry. Gen 8:7
Then at last the * was dry. Gen 8:14
again curse the *, destroying all Gen 8:21
As long as the * remains, there Gen 8:22
children and to repopulate the *. Gen 9:1
repopulate the * and subdue it." Gen 9:7
another flood to destroy the *. Gen 9:9,10,11
of time, to you and to all the *. Gen 9:13
When I send clouds over the *, Gen 9:14
to every living being on the *." Gen 9:16,17
came all the nations of the *. Gen 9:19
God scattered them all over the *; Gen 11:8
them across the face of the *. Gen 11:9
heaven and *, be upon you, Abram; Gen 14:19,20
of heaven and *, that I will not Gen 14:22
for all the nations of the *. Gen 18:18
Should not the Judge of all the * Gen 18:25
the nations of the *—all because Gen 22:18
God of heaven and *, that you will Gen 24:3
to all the nations of the *. Gen 26:4
up his wells with *—all those dug Gen 26:15
good smell of the * and fields that Gen 27:27,28,29
reached from * to heaven, and he Gen 28:12
and all the nations of the * will Gen 28:14
him, with their faces to the *. Gen 42:6
above and of the * Gen 49:25
God of all the *, for I will make Ex 8:22
is no other God in all the *. Ex 9:14
my power to you and to all the *. Ex 9:16
This will prove to you that the * Ex 9:29
the face of the * and blotted out Ex 10:15
hand and the * swallowed them. Ex 15:12
among all the nations of the *; Ex 19:5
for all the * is mine. Ex 19:5
in heaven or * or in the sea." Ex 20:4f
made the heaven, *, and sea, and Ex 20:11
for me must be simple altars of *. Ex 20:24
made heaven and *, and rested on Ex 31:17
them from off the face of the *"? Ex 32:12
people upon the face of the *?" Ex 33:16
in all the *, and all the people of Ex 34:10
things that crawl upon the *. Lev 11:44
among all animal life upon the *. Lev 11:47
as iron, and your * as bronze. Lev 26:19
Moses was the humblest man on *. Num 12:3,4
true that all the * shall be filled Num 14:20,21
into Sheol and the * closed upon Num 16:33
that the * would swallow them too. Num 16:34
downward to the * before the Lord. Num 16:45
the face of the * and are headed Num 22:5,6
But the * opened and swallowed Num 26:5-11
the whole * tremble with fear Deu 2:25
all of heaven or * can do what you Deu 3:23,24,25
sin, heaven and * are witnesses Deu 4:26
man upon the *, search from one end Deu 4:32
great pillar of fire upon the *; Deu 4:36
heaven and down here upon the *; Deu 4:39
wipe you off the face of the *. Deu 6:15
whole * to be his own chosen ones. Deu 7:6
above all the nations of the *; Deu 7:14
names from the face of the *. Deu 7:24
hearts and souls? * and highest Deu 10:14
of Reuben) sinned, and the * Deu 11:6
is sky above the *, you and your Deu 11:21
pour the blood out upon the *. Deu 12:24,25
other nation on the face of the *. Deu 14:2
and the * beneath will be as iron. Deu 28:23
among all the nations of the *. Deu 28:25
one end of the * to the other. Deu 28:64
at the ends of the *, he will go Deu 30:4
"I call heaven and * to witness Deu 30:19
and * to witness against them. Deu 31:28
"LISTEN, O HEAVENS and *! Deu 32:1
Consuming the * and all of its Deu 32:22
And of the * that lies below. Deu 33:13
Of the * and its fullness, Deu 33:16
*, will lead you across the river! Jos 3:11
the nations of the * will realize Jos 4:24
of all the *—I am going to die. Jos 23:14
The * trembled Ju 5:4
and the scum of the *, mobilized Ju 12:4
For all the * is the Lord's 1Sa 2:8
He judges throughout the *. 1Sa 2:10
I'll pin him to the * with 1Sa 26:8
up out of the *," she said. 1Sa 28:13
What other nation in all the * 2Sa 7:23
before the Lord on the bare *. 2Sa 12:16
from the face of the *." 2Sa 14:7
torn clothing and * upon his head. 2Sa 15:32
Then the * shook and trembled; 2Sa 22:8
the heavens down and came to *; 2Sa 22:10
The * was radiant with his 2Sa 22:13
Springs forth upon the *; 2Sa 23:4
"I am going where every man on * 1Ki 2:2
a lovely home on *, a place for you 1Ki 8:12,13
you in heaven or *, for you are 1Ki 8:22,23
that God would really live on *? 1Ki 8:27
And all the nations of the * will 1Ki 8:43
and all the * will know that this 1Ki 8:43
* to be your own special people." 1Ki 8:53
May people all over the * know 1Ki 8:60
wiser than all the kings of the *. 1Ki 10:23
on * from end to end to find you. 1Ki 18:10
two mule-loads of * to take back 2Ki 5:17
God of all the kingdoms of the *. 2Ki 19:15
You created the heavens and the * 2Ki 19:15
then all the kingdoms of the * 2Ki 19:19
the people of the * were divided 1Ch 1:19
is seen throughout the *. 1Ch 16:14
Sing to the Lord, O *, 1Ch 16:23
O people of all nations of the *, 1Ch 16:28
Tremble before him, all the *! 1Ch 16:30
Let the heavens be glad, the * 1Ch 16:31
For he comes to judge the *. 1Ch 16:33
as great as the greatest of the *. 1Ch 17:8
" 'When your time here on * is 1Ch 17:11
in all the * is like Israel? 1Ch 17:21
between heaven and * with his sword 1Ch 21:16
Everything in the heavens and * 1Ch 29:11
our days on * are like a shadow, 1Ch 29:15
people as the * is full of dust! 2Ch 1:9
heavens and the * and who has given 2Ch 2:12
like you in all of heaven and *. 2Ch 6:14
really live upon the * with men? 2Ch 6:18
Then all the peoples of the * 2Ch 6:33
than any other king in all the *. 2Ch 9:22
across the whole *, looking for 2Ch 16:9
*—you are so powerful, so mighty. 2Ch 20:6
his face to the *, and all the 2Ch 20:18
"All the kingdoms of the * have 2Ch 36:22,23
God of heaven and * and we are Ez 5:11
the heavens, the * and the seas, Neh 9:6
replied, "From patroling the *." Job 1:7
He is the finest man in all the * Job 1:8
"From patroling the *," Satan Job 2:2
man in all the *—a good man who Job 2:3
the air and put * on their heads to Job 2:12
He sends the rain upon the * to Job 5:10
our days here on * are as Job 8:9
And others spring up from the * Job 8:19
He shakes the * to its Job 9:6
The whole * is in the hands of Job 9:24
His Spirit is broader than the * Job 11:9
or let the * teach you, or the Job 12:7,8,9
He withholds the rain, and the * Job 12:15
grown old in the *, and its stump Job 14:8,9
What man in all the * can be as Job 15:14
O *, do not conceal my blood. Job 16:18
existence will perish from the *; Job 18:17
he will stand upon the * at last. Job 19:25
placed upon the *, the triumph of Job 20:4
* will give testimony against him. Job 20:27
him as the soft * covers him. Job 21:33
disappear from the face of the *. Job 24:18
light shines down on all the *. Job 25:3
Who in all the * can boast that Job 25:4
and hangs the * upon nothing. Job 26:7
the * and melt copper from stone. Job 28
be sunk into the *, and the earth Job 28:3
the earth, and the * searched and Job 28:3
*, while underneath there is fire. Job 28
whole *, under all the heavens. Job 28:23,2
authority over the * and dispenses Job 34:1
and storm to fall upon the *. Job 37:
he commands throughout the *. Job 37:1
I laid the foundations of the *? Job 38:
*, to end the night's wickedness? Job 38:1
you realize the extent of the *? Job 38:17,1
how the heavens influence the *? Job 38:3
the *, to warm them in the dust. Job 39:1
He paws the * and rejoices in Job 39:21-2
else so fearless anywhere on *. Job 41:3
O kings and rulers of the *, Ps 2:1
the * and overflows the heavens. Ps 8:
glory of your name fills the *. Ps 8:
everything that happens here on *. Ps 11:
Then the * rocked and reeled, Ps 18:
his mouth, setting fire to the *; Ps 18:
The whole * shall see it and Ps 22:2
THE * BELONGS to God! Ps 24:
his children shall inherit the *. Ps 25:1
* is filled with his tender love. Ps 33:
the memory of evil men from the *. Ps 34:1
his equal in all of heaven and *? Ps 35:1
shall inherit the *, but those Ps 37:2
how brief my time on * will be. Ps 39:4
the *, as all my fathers were. Ps 39:1
the nations of the * will praise Ps 45:1
God speaks, the * melts in Ps 46:6
end throughout the *, breaking and Ps 46:9
he is the great King of all the * Ps 47:2
our King, the King of all the *. Ps 47:6,7
joy of all the *, the residence of Ps 48:2
The kings of the * have arrived Ps 48:4
is known throughout the *, O God. Ps 48:10
of it in all the * to buy eternal Ps 49:8,9
To heaven and * he shouts, Ps 50:4
Show your glory high above the *. Ps 57:5
your glory shine throughout the *. Ps 57:11
a God who judges justly here on *. Ps 58:11
the *, I will cry to you for help. Ps 61:2
In the farthest corners of the * Ps 65:8
He waters the * to make it Ps 65:9
He prepares the * for his people Ps 65:9
Showers soften the *, melting the Ps 65:10
SING TO THE Lord, all the *! Ps 66:1
All the * shall worship you and Ps 66:4
How everyone throughout the * Ps 67:3
May all the peoples of the * give Ps 67:5
For the * has yielded abundant Ps 67:6,7
* trembled and the heavens shook. Ps 68:8
The kings of the * are bringing Ps 68:29
O kingdoms of the *—sing praises to Ps 68:32
Praise him, all heaven and *! Ps 69:34
up from the depths of the *. Ps 71:20
showers that water the *! Ps 72:6
River to the ends of the *. Ps 72:8
Let the whole * be filled with Ps 72:19
their words strut through the *. Ps 73:9
And I desire no one on * as much Ps 73:25
as your home on *! Ps 74:2
Though the * shakes and all its Ps 75:3
nowhere on *, but only from God. Ps 75:6,7
out upon the wicked of the *. Ps 75:8
from heaven; the * trembles and Ps 76:8
and to defend the meek of the *. Ps 76:9
things to the kings of the *. Ps 76:12
world! The * trembled and shook. Ps 77:18
enduring as the heavens and the *. Ps 78:69
Literally, "of the *." Ps 82:5f
Stand up, O God, and judge the *. Ps 82:8
in supreme charge of all the *. Ps 83:18
Truth rises from the * and Ps 85:11
the mightiest king in all the *. Ps 89:27
before the * was formed, you are Ps 90:2
Arise and judge the *; Ps 94:1
the * and the mightiest mountains; Ps 95:4
glorious acts throughout the *. Ps 96:3
Let the * tremble before him. Ps 96:9
Let the heavens be glad, the * Ps 96:11
the Lord is coming to judge the *; Ps 96:13
Let all the * rejoice! Ps 97:1
world. The * sees and trembles. Ps 97:4
wax before the Lord of all the *. Ps 97:5
over the entire * and are far Ps 97:8,9
The whole * has seen God's Ps 98:2,3
That is why the * breaks out in Ps 98:4
Let the * and all those living on Ps 98:7
Let the whole * shake. Ps 99:1
supreme above all rulers of the *. Ps 99:2
WITH JOY before the Lord, O *! Ps 100:1
and many rulers throughout the * Ps 102:21,22
foundations of the *, and made the Ps 102:25
height of the heavens above the *. Ps 103:11
of the * to form the seas. Ps 104:3
You clothed the * with floods of Ps 104:6
would never again cover the *. Ps 104:9
and fills the * with fruit. Ps 104:13

(EARTH Con't)
all! The * is full of your riches. Ps 104:24
replenish all the living of the *. Ps 104:30
The * trembles at his glance; Ps 104:32
Because of this the * opened and Ps 106:17
the farthest corners of the *. Ps 107:3
It towers above the *. Ps 108:5
him are the heavens and the *; Ps 113:6
Tremble, O *, at the presence of Ps 114:7
and * will personally bless you! Ps 115:15
he has given the * to all mankind. Ps 115:16
sing praises to Jehovah here on *, Ps 115:17
Yes, in his presence—here on *! Ps 116:9
him, all the peoples of the *. Ps 117:1
I am but a pilgrim here on *: Ps 119:19
O Lord, the * is full of your Ps 119:64
like the * you created; Ps 119:90,91
the Lord who made heaven and *. Ps 124:8
in God's permanent home here on *. Ps 132:7
Lord who made heaven and *. Ps 134:3
and *, and in the deepest seas. Ps 135:6
throughout the * and sends the Ps 135:7
planted the water within the *, Ps 136:6
Or, "who separated the * from the Ps 136:6f
Every king in all the * shall Ps 138:4
and cleaves the *, our bones are Ps 141:6,7f
God who made both * and heaven, the Ps 146:6
and hurls the hail upon the *. Ps 147:17
And praise him down here on *, Ps 148:7
greater than all of * and heaven. Ps 148:13
The Lord's wisdom founded the *; Pro 3:19
The deep fountains of the * were Pro 3:20
I existed before the * began. Pro 8:23
forth their waters onto the *; Pro 8:24
* and fields, and high plateaus. Pro 8:26
blueprint for the * and oceans. Pro 8:27,28,29
godly shall be rewarded here on *; Pro 11:31
goals are at the ends of the *! Pro 17:24
the size of the *, or all that goes Pro 25:2,3
that make the * tremble—no, four Pro 30:21,22,23
monarchs in the *—no, four: Pro 30:29,30,31
Literally, "but the * remains Ecc 1:3-7f
throughout the * justice is giving Ecc 3:16
throughout the *—the tears of the Ecc 4:1
evil and crime throughout the *. Ecc 4:3
piece of foolishness around the *. Ecc 4:7
on *, so let your words be few. Ecc 5:1
man in all the * who is always good Ecc 7:20
here upon the *: Providence seems Ecc 8:14
better in all the * than that a man Ecc 8:15
across the *—ceaseless activity, Ecc 8:16,17
in anything here on * any more. Ecc 9:6
Again I looked throughout the * Ecc 9:11
and the dust returns to the * as Ecc 12:7
Listen, O heaven and *, to what Is 1:2
to shake up the *, his enemies will Is 2:19
when he rises to terrify the *. Is 2:21
be alone in the midst of the *! Is 5:8
at the ends of the *, and they will Is 5:26
the whole * is filled with his Is 6:3
you like, in heaven or on *." Is 7:11
sea, so shall the * be full of the Is 11:9
Israelites from the ends of the *. Is 11:12
anger, and the * will move from its Is 13:13
But at last the whole * is at Is 14:7
* and the kingdoms of the world? Is 14:16
This is my plan for the whole * Is 14:26
he shakes the kingdoms of the *; Is 23:11
them over the face of the *. Is 24:1
of its people. The * languishes, Is 24:4,5
the ends of the *, singing glory to Is 24:15,16
beneath you. The * has broken down Is 24:19
the sins of the * are very great. Is 24:20
proud rulers of the nations on *. Is 24:21
of death that hangs over the *; Is 25:7
in judgment on the * to punish it Is 26:9
people of the * for their sins. Is 26:21
their sins. The * will no longer Is 26:21
fill the whole * with her fruit! Is 27:6
from the * where you lie buried. Is 29:4
AND listen, O nations of the *; Is 34:1
God of all the kingdoms of the *. Is 37:16,17
You alone made heaven and *. Is 37:16,17
kingdoms of the * will know that Is 37:20
weight of all the * and weighs the Is 40:12
sits above the circle of the *. Is 40:22
the *, never grows faint or weary? Is 40:28
the ends of the * and said that you Is 41:9
throughout the *, nor until even Is 42:4
and created the * and everything in Is 42:5
the farthest corners of the *. Is 43:6
Shout, O *; Is 44:23
By myself I made the * and Is 44:24
sprout up together from the *. Is 45:8
I have made the * and created Is 45:12
the heavens and * and put Is 45:18
all of heaven and * do I compare? Is 46:5
laid the foundations of the *; Is 48:13
shout to the ends of the * that Is 48:20
shout, O *. Is 49:13
They shall bow to the * before Is 49:23
and watch the * beneath, for the Is 51:6
like smoke, the * shall wear out Is 51:6
of the * shall die like flies. Is 51:6
the skies and made the *. Is 51:13
in place and molded all the *. Is 51:16
the ends of the * shall see the Is 52:10
of Israel, the God of all the *. Is 54:5
flood to cover the * and destroy Is 54:9
higher than the *, so are my ways Is 55:9
to water the *, and cause the grain Is 55:10
the peoples of the *, but the glory Is 60:2
and admired throughout the *. Is 62:6,7
heavens and a new *—so wonderful Is 65:17
HEAVEN IS MY throne and the * is Is 66:1
My hand has made both * and Is 66:2
As surely as my new heavens and * Is 66:22
people left. The * shall mourn, Jer 4:28
listen to it, all the *! Jer 6:18,19
Among all the wise men of the * Jer 10:7
The whole * shall tremble at his Jer 10:10
the heavens and *, shall vanish Jer 10:11
vanish from the *, but our God Jer 10:11
our God formed the * by his power Jer 10:12
He causes mist to rise upon the * Jer 10:13
themselves to the * and a great cry Jer 14:2
they are registered for * and not Jer 17:13
Jerusalem off the *, so that Jer 19:8
O *, earth, earth! Jer 22:29
O earth, *, earth! Jer 22:29
O earth, earth, *! Jer 22:29
everywhere throughout the *. Jer 23:5,6
everywhere in all of heaven and *? Jer 23:24
nation of the *, and they shall be Jer 24:9
all the peoples of the *." Jer 25:29
against all those living on the *. Jer 25:30
ends of the *, for the Lord has a Jer 25:31
the farthest corners of the *. Jer 25:32
the * from one end to the other. Jer 25:33
they shall fertilize the *. Jer 25:33
word in every nation of the *. Jer 26:6
I have made the * and all mankind Jer 27:5
foundations of the * explored, will Jer 31:37
You have made the heavens and * Jer 32:17
*—Jehovah is his name—says this: Jer 33:2
before all the nations of the *! Jer 33:9
of night and day, of * and sky. Jer 33:25,26
of all the nations of the *. Jer 44:8
it will cover the * like a flood, Jer 46:8
of your shame. The * is filled with Jer 46:12
The * shakes with the noise of Jer 49:21
the *, lies broken and shattered. Jer 50:23
The whole * shall shake at Jer 50:46
made the whole * drink and go mad. Jer 51:7
God made the * by his power and Jer 51:15
Babylon, destroyer of the *! Jer 51:25
Babylon, lauded by all the *! Jer 51:41
Heaven and * shall rejoice, for Jer 51:48
in the dust of the *, cast from the Lam 2:1
World,' and 'Joy of All the *'?" Lam 2:15
wipe them off the *, beneath the Lam 3:66
Not a king in all the *—no one Lam 4:12
our own against any nation on *! Lam 4:20
choicest spot on *, because they Eze 20:15
to the ends of the * because they Eze 20:23,24
Kings at the ends of the * Eze 27:33
to ashes upon the * in the sight of Eze 28:18
carrying heavy basketfuls of *); Eze 29:18
roots went deep into the moist *. Eze 31:4
of the whole * will devour you Eze 32:4
And I will drench the * with Eze 32:6
the face of the *, and there was no Eze 34:6
the whole * revolves around them!' Eze 38:12
walls shall crumble to the *. Eze 38:20
mountain that covered the whole *. Dan 2:35
your rule to the ends of the *. Dan 4:22
the roots in the * surrounded by Dan 4:23
All the people of the * are Dan 4:35
here among the inhabitants of *. Dan 4:35
great miracles in heaven and *; Dan 6:27
kings who will someday rule the *. Dan 7:17
that will rule the *. Dan 7:23
* in answer to its cry for rain. Hos 1:21,22
Then the * can answer the parched Hos 1:21,22
the windows. The * quakes before Joe 2:10
symbols in the * and sky—blood and Joe 2:30
and the * and sky begin to shake. Joe 3:16
"Of all the peoples of the *, I Amo 3:2
and darken the * in the daytime. Amo 8:9
heavens, the first floor on the *. Amo 9:6
heaven, who made the * and sea." Jon 1:9,10
to *, walking on the mountaintops. Mic 1:3
the Lord, the Lord of all the *. Mic 4:13
men have disappeared from the *; Mic 7:1
hills melt; the * crumbles and its Nah 1:5
never again will you rule the *. Nah 2:13
"and now all the * will see your Nah 3:5
the sun comes up and warms the *. Nah 3:17
come when all the * is filled, as Hab 2:14
let all the * be silent before Hab 2:20
splendor fills the * and sky; Hab 3:3
and the * is full of his praise! Hab 3:3
for a moment, gazing at the *. Hab 3:6
You ribboned the * with rivers." Hab 3:8,9f
forth upon the * at your command! Hab 3:8,9
kingdoms of the *, and pour out my Zep 3:8
All the * shall be devoured with Zep 3:8
the peoples of the *, and they will Zep 3:20
the heavens and *—and the oceans, Hag 2:6
heavens and the *, and to Hag 2:21
them to patrol the * for him." Zec 1:10
the whole *, and everywhere there Zec 1:11
for he has come to * from heaven, Zec 2:13
assist the Lord of all the *." Zec 4:14
before the Lord of all the *; Zec 6:5
the *, so the Lord said, "Go. Zec 6:7
all peoples of the *, including my Zec 9:10
the river to the ends of the *. Zec 9:10
battle, the Ruler over all the *. Zec 10:4
foundation of the *, and formed the Zec 12:1
the nations of the * unite in an Zec 12:3
Lord shall be King over all the *. Zec 14:9
And if you say 'By the *!' Mt 5:35
it is a sacred vow, for the * is Mt 5:35
May your will be done here on *, Mt 6:10
treasures here on * where they can Mt 6:19
have the authority on * to Mt 9:5,6
I came to bring peace to the *! Mt 10:34
Lord of heaven and *, thank you for Mt 11:25
shall be in the heart of the * Mt 12:39,40
where there was little depth of *; Mt 13:5
whatever doors you lock on * Mt 16:19
and whatever doors you open on * Mt 16:19
you bind on * is bound in heaven, Mt 18:18
free on * will be freed in heaven. Mt 18:18
agree down here on * concerning Mt 18:19
anyone here on * as 'Father,' for Mt 23:9
kingdoms of the * will rise against Mt 24:7
the * will be convulsed. Mt 24:29
be deep mourning all around the *. Mt 24:30
farthest ends of the * and heaven. Mt 24:31
"Heaven and * will disappear, Mt 24:35
so I hid your money in the * and Mt 25:24,25
That afternoon, the whole * Mt 27:45
and the * shook, and rocks broke, Mt 27:51
all authority in heaven and *. Mt 28:18
to *, and that a special Mk 1:2
have the authority on * to Mk 2:9,10,11
"All these will be his here on *, Mk 10:30
of the * lord it over the people; Mk 10:42
a soul in all the * will survive. Mk 13:20
farthest bounds of * and heaven. Mk 13:27
Heaven and * shall disappear, Mk 13:31
to * in the clouds of heaven." Mk 14:62
"and peace on * for all those Lk 2:14
have the authority on * to Lk 5:23,24
Lord of heaven and *, for hiding Lk 10:21
me here on * as your Friend. Lk 12:8
rich on * but not in heaven." Lk 12:21
bring fire to the *, and, oh, that Lk 12:49
have come to give peace to the *? Lk 12:51
and unshakable as heaven and *. Lk 16:17
Your enemies will pile up * Lk 19:43
for people here on *, but when Lk 20:34,35
the land," or, "upon the *." Lk 21:23f
and down here on * the nations Lk 21:25
coming upon the *, for the Lk 21:26
Then the peoples of the * shall Lk 21:27
And though all heaven and * Lk 21:33
and lived here on * among us and Jn 1:14
have come to * and will return to Jn 3:13
I am of the *, and my Jn 3:31
is limited to the things of *. Jn 3:31
never been slaves to any man on *! Jn 8:33
falls into the furrows of the *. Jn 12:23,24
* before returning to his Father. Jn 13:1
Here on * you will have many Jn 16:33
every man and woman in all the *. Jn 17:2
Christ, the one you sent to *! Jn 17:3
I brought glory to you here on * Jn 17:4
I came down to * from you, and they Jn 17:8
to the ends of the *, about my Act 1:8
heavens and on the *—blood and fire Act 2:19
"O Lord, Creator of heaven and * Act 4:24
The kings of the * unite to fight Act 4:25,26
prophets, 'and * is my footstool. Act 7:48,49
Didn't I make both heaven and * Act 7:50
For his life is taken from the * Act 8:33
Literally, "upon the *." Act 11:28f
corners of the * to my salvation.' Act 13:47
* and sea and everything in them. Act 14:15
Lord of heaven and *, he doesn't Act 17:24
nations across the face of the *. Act 17:26
men have seen the * and sky and all Rom 1:20
to give the whole * to Abraham and Rom 4:13
published abroad in all the *." Rom 9:17f
sentence upon the *, quickly ending Rom 9:28
been told to the ends of the *. Rom 10:18
comes from here on *, and not the 1Co 2:6
down here on * easily enough. 1Co 6:3
gods, both in heaven and on *. 1Co 8:5
For the * and every good thing 1Co 10:26
all of heaven and *, but didn't 1Co 13:1

(EARTH Con't)
the dust of the *, but Christ came 1Co 15:47
heaven or on *—to be with him in Eph 1:10
some down here on *— that out of Eph 3:14,15
down to the lowest parts of the *. Eph 4:9
will be staying on * a little Php 1:25
in heaven and on * and under the Php 2:10
and under the *, and every tongue Php 2:10
about is this life here on *. Php 3:19
in heaven and *, the things we can Col 1:16
in heaven and on *—for Christ's Col 1:20
and remain on the * will be caught 1Th 4:17
who came to * as a man, was proved 1Ti 3:16
Son came to *—God said, "Let all Heb 1:5,6
you made the *, and the heavens are Heb 1:10
Yet while Christ was here on * he Heb 5:7
if he were here on * he wouldn't Heb 8:4
was a sacred tent down here on *. Heb 9:1
tent down here on *, and everything Heb 9:23
down here on * offers animal blood Heb 9:25
agreed that this * was not their Heb 11:13
fathers here on *, though they Heb 12:9
voice shook the *, but, "Next Heb 12:26
the *, but the heavens too." Heb 12:26
your years here on * having fun, Jas 5:5
by heaven or * or anything else; Jas 5:12
my days here on * are numbered, and 2Pe 1:13,14
the face of the *, making them an 2Pe 2:6
to form the * and surround it. 2Pe 3:5,6
And God has commanded that the * 2Pe 3:7
in fire, and the * and everything 2Pe 3:10
heavens and a new * afterwards, 2Pe 3:13
Christ came to * as a human being 2Jn 1:7
than any king in all the *. Rev 1:5
But no one in all heaven or * Rev 5:3
they shall reign upon the *." Rev 5:10
in heaven and *, and from the dead Rev 5:13
dead beneath the * and in the sea, Rev 5:13
peace and bring anarchy to the *; Rev 6:4
one-fourth of the *, to kill with Rev 6:8
the * for what they've done to us? Rev 6:10
against those living on the *?" Rev 6:10
martyred on the * and joined them. Rev 6:11
heaven appeared to be falling to * Rev 6:13
stars of heaven fell to the *." Rev 6:13f
The kings of the *, and world Rev 6:15
corners of the *, holding back the Rev 7:1
to injure * and sea, "Wait! Rev 7:2
yet—hurt neither * nor sea nor Rev 7:3
and threw it down upon the *; Rev 8:5
blood were thrown down upon the *. Rev 8:7
One-third of the * was set on Rev 8:7
on the * and many people died. Rev 8:11
the people of the * because of the Rev 8:13
who was fallen to * from heaven, Rev 9:1
descended onto the * and were given Rev 9:3
left foot on the *, and gave a Rev 10:2
in it and the * and all that it Rev 10:6
before the God of all the *. Rev 11:4
upon the * as often as they wish. Rev 11:6
caused destruction upon the *." Rev 11:18
stars, which he plunged to the *. Rev 12:4
down onto the * with all his army. Rev 12:9
from heaven onto *—he accused them Rev 12:10
cast down to *, he persecuted the Rev 12:13
but the * helped her by opening Rev 12:16
the * for forty-two months. Rev 13:5
up out of the *, with two little Rev 13:11
fire flame down to * from the skies Rev 13:13
who had been redeemed from the *. Rev 14:3
the men on the * as a consecrated Rev 14:4
preach to those on *—to every Rev 14:6
*, the sea and all its sources." Rev 14:7
the harvest is ripe on the *." Rev 14:15
sickle over the *, and the harvest Rev 14:16
the vines of the *, for they are Rev 14:18
his sickle on the * and loaded the Rev 14:19
to carry down to * the seven last Rev 15:1
of the wrath of God upon the *." Rev 16:1
his flask over the *, and horrible, Rev 16:2
their blood poured out upon the *; Rev 16:6
the people of the * have been made Rev 17:2
and the people of *, whose names Rev 17:8
rules over the kings of the *." Rev 17:18
* grew bright with his splendor. Rev 18:1
The rulers of * have enjoyed Rev 18:3
The merchants of the * will weep Rev 18:11
who corrupted the * with her sin; Rev 19:2
governments of the * and their Rev 19:19
broad plain of the * and surround Rev 20:9
whose face the * and sky fled away, Rev 20:11
and the * and the underworld gave Rev 20:13
THEN I SAW a new * (with no Rev 21:1
and a new sky, for the present * Rev 21:1
the nations of the *, and the Rev 21:24

EARTH'S
World leaders and * mightiest Is 14:9
who live in * remotest corners! Is 42:10
the north and from * farthest ends, Jer 31:8

EARTHEN
evening. Any * pot touched by the Lev 15:12
rain that melts down an * wall. Is 25:4
up an * bank against its walls. Is 37:33

EARTHENWARE
an * pot held above running water. Lev 14:5
fresh water in an * bowl, and dip Lev 14:50
of the gold—are treated as * pots. Lam 4:2

EARTHLY
* man will terrify them no longer. Ps 10:18
only concern is * gain—these men Ps 17:13,14
to be ransomed by mere * wealth. Ps 49:8,9
these years of my * pilgrimage. Ps 119:54
they are based upon this * life. Pro 11:7
down here for all your * toil. Ecc 9:9
the heel of * rulers: "Kings shall Is 49:7
any * process could ever make it! Mk 9:3
have no * home at all." Lk 9:58
answered, "I am not an * king. Jn 18:36
from all these * prides and fears. 1Co 7:23
he has to think about his * 1Co 7:33
In the same way, our * bodies 1Co 15:42
my brothers: an * body made of 1Co 15:50
For our * bodies, the ones we 1Co 15:53
These * bodies make us groan and 2Co 5:4
we spend in these * bodies is time 2Co 5:6
things he has done in his * body. 2Co 5:10
Away then with sinful, * things; Col 3:5
always obey your * masters, not Col 3:22
those offered by the * priests. Heb 8:4
with a mere * model of the real Heb 8:5
It was not in the * place of Heb 9:24
Our * fathers trained us for a Heb 12:10
to Moses, the * messenger, how Heb 12:25
Such things are *, unspiritual, Jas 3:15

EARTHQUAKE
mountain shook with a violent *. Ex 19:18
And just then there was a great * 1Sa 14:15
After the wind, there was an *, 1Ki 19:11
but the Lord was not in the *. 1Ki 19:11
And after the *, there was a 1Ki 19:12
is this going to start an *? Job 18:4
thunder, *, whirlwind and fire. Is 29:6
by the sound of a great *. Eze 3:12
me the sound of a great *." Eze 3:12f
of Israel—two years before the *. Amo 1:2
ago from the * in the days of Zec 14:5
by the * and all that happened. Mt 27:54
Suddenly there was a great *; Mt 28:2
suddenly there was a great *; Act 16:26
seal, and there was a vast *; Rev 6:12
and there was a terrible *. Rev 8:5
will be a terrible * that levels a Rev 11:13
world was shaken by a mighty *. Rev 11:19
and there was a great * of a Rev 16:18

EARTHQUAKES
be famines and * in many places. Mt 24:7
be * in many lands, and famines. Mk 13:8
will be great *, and famines in Lk 21:11

EASE
will be no life of * and luxury, Gen 27:39,40
At * beside his harbors? Ju 5:17
There even prisoners are at *, Job 3:18
a finger—theirs is a life of *; Ps 73:12
women who loll around in lazy *; Is 32:9
Tremble, O women of *; Is 32:11
kingdom, living at *, bragging as Is 47:8
Her days of * are gone. Hos 10:11
sitting around at *, for I was only Zec 1:15
"The world will be at * Mt 24:37,38
living in careless *, carousing and Lk 21:34,35
welcome and set his mind at *. 2Co 7:13

EASIER
That way it will be * for you Ex 18:22
it is simply a way of * 1Ch 1:1f
they said. "Be * on us than he 2Ch 10:4
"Shall I be * on them than my 2Ch 10:8,9
going to be tougher on you, not *! 2Ch 10:11
I say it again—it is * for a Mt 19:24
It is * for a camel to go Mk 10:25
It is * for a camel to go Lk 18:25

EASILY
He won't be fooled that *. Gen 27:11,12
* as though it were a young goat! Ju 14:6
But we can beat them * on the 1Ki 20:23
crushed to death as * as moths! Job 4:18,19
depose an entire nation just as *. Job 34:29,30
I am shaken off from life as * as Ps 109:22,23
* to the man with common sense. Pro 14:6
man starts fights as * as a match Pro 26:21
nation, its government topples *; Pro 28:2
cord is not * broken. Ecc 4:12
streams that can * be crossed. Is 11:15
Bread grain is * crushed, so he Is 28:28
It will pull out * enough—it Eze 17:9
He is not * angered; Joe 2:13
I knew how * you could cancel Jon 4:2
and he does not * forgive. Nah 1:3
Then you can take him *." Mk 14:44
down here on earth * enough. 1Co 6:3
I can't * stop when I want to. 1Co 6:12
bother them *, I don't act as 1Co 9:22

EAST
in Eden, to the *, and placed in Gen 2:8
to the * of the city of Asher. Gen 2:1
angels at the * of the garden of Gen 3:2
in the land of Nod, * of Eden. Gen 4:1
on the west and Ai on the *. Gen 12:
over there to the *, then I'll stay Gen 13:
I'll go over there to the *." Gen 13:
Jordan valley to the * of them. Gen 13:1
off into the *, away from Isaac. Gen 25:
They will cover the land from * Gen 28:14
arriving in the land of the *. Gen 29:
and withered by the * wind. Gen 41:
Jehovah caused an * wind to blow Ex 10:13
and when it was morning, the * Ex 10:13
and a strong * wind blew all that Ex 14:21
ten sockets. The * side will also Ex 27:13
and rods. The * side was also Ex 38:13
throw them on the * side of the Lev 1:15,16,17
the ancient Near *, the word Lev 2:13,
finger upon the * side of the mercy Lev 16:14
* side of the Tabernacle Num 2:3-31
The area * of the Tabernacle was Num 3:38
camped on the * side of the Num 10:5,6,7
a short distance * of Moab, and Num 21:11
of Moab and camped * of the Jordan Num 22:1
have it on this side, on the *." Num 32:19
on to Riblah at the * side of Ain. Num 34:10,11
land on the * side of the Jordan, Num 34:14,15
on the * side of the Jordan River. Num 35:13,14
of Moab, * of the Jordan River. Deu 1:1
of the Amorites * of the Jordan Deu 3:8
apart three cities * of the Jordan Deu 4:41
they were camped * of the Jordan Deu 4:44,45,46
two Amorite kings * of the Jordan. Deu 4:47
and all the Arabah * of the Deu 4:49
River in the *, including all the Jos 1:4
here on the * side of the Jordan Jos 1:12,13
on the * side of the Jordan." Jos 1:15
two Amorite kings * of the Jordan, Jos 2:10
on the city of Ai, * of Bethel. Jos 7:2
The kings of Canaan, both * and Jos 11:1
the kings on the * side of the Jos 12:1
Bashan in the *, and on the west, Jos 12:5
inheritance on the * side of the Jos 13:8
then the border turned * from the Jos 13:27,28
divided the land * of the Jordan Jos 13:32
on the * side of the Jordan River. Jos 14:3,4
at the Sea, ran * past Michmethath, Jos 16:5,6
[on the * side of the Jordan River Jos 17:1
which is * of Shechem. Jos 17:7
and * of the sea went to Manasseh. Jos 17:10
have land on the * side of the Jos 18:7
reached the brook * of Jeokne-am. Jos 19:11
boundary line went * to the border Jos 19:12
then it continued * of Jos 19:13
turned * toward Beth-dagon, and Jos 19:27
It then passed to the * of Kabul, Jos 19:27
with the Jordan River at the *. Jos 19:34
purpose on the * side of the Jordan Jos 20:8
lived * of the Euphrates River; Jos 24:2
nations of the * were crowded Ju 7:12,13
of the allied armies of the *; Ju 8:10
the caravan route * of Nobah and Ju 8:11
These attacks took place * of the Ju 10:7,8
army of Benjamin * of Gibe-ah, and Ju 20:43
Bethel, along the * side of the Ju 21:19
and they camped at Michmash * of 1Sa 13:5
all the way to Shur, * of Egypt. 1Sa 15:7
the *, including those in Egypt. 1Ki 4:30
west, three south, and three *. 1Ki 7:25
"Go to the * and hide by Cherith 1Ki 17:3
Brook at a place * of where it 1Ki 17:3
of the country * of the Jordan 2Ki 10:32,33
on the hills * of Jerusalem and 2Ki 23:13
traveled to the * side of Gedor 1Ch 4:34-39
towns, on the * by Naaran, on the 1Ch 7:28
sides: *, west, north, and south. 1Ch 9:24
on both the * and west banks. 1Ch 12:15
troops from * of the Euphrates 1Ch 19:16
The responsibility of the * gate 1Ch 26:14,15
daily to the * gate, four to the 1Ch 26:17
west, three south, and three *. 2Ch 4:4
at the * side of the altar. 2Ch 5:11,12
at the open space * of the Temple, 2Ch 29:4,5
gatekeeper at the * Gate, was put 2Ch 31:14,15
wall as far as the * Water Gate and Neh 3:26
the gatekeeper of the * Gate. Neh 3:29
went to the Water Gate on the *. Neh 12:37
of the night. The * wind carries Job 27:21
caused the dawn to rise in the *? Job 38:12
Where is the home of the * wind? Job 38:24
all mankind from * to west! Ps 50:1
And he led forth the * wind and Ps 78:26
from us as the * is from the west. Ps 103:12
from the * who practice magic and Is 2:6
* and the Philistines on the west. Is 9:11,12
their land on the * and on the Is 11:14
in the * will respond with praise. Is 24:15,16
blown away in a storm from the *. Is 27:7,8
a revolt in the * against Is 39:1f
stirred up this one from the *, Is 41:2
up (Cyrus) from the north and *; Is 41:25

(EAST Con't)
I will gather you from * and Is 43:5
all the world from * to west will Is 45:6
*—that man Cyrus from far away. Is 46:11
the name of God from west to *. Is 59:19
send to the * to the deserts of Jer 2:10,11
as the * wind scatters dust; Jer 18:17
by the * gate of the city. Jer 19:1
Gate on the * side of the city; Jer 31:40
and in the cities * of the Jer 33:13
in the desert * of Palestine. Jer 49:28f
Wherever you look—*, west, north or Eze 7:2
facing *, worshiping the sun! Eze 8:16
them to the * gate of the Temple. Eze 10:19
me over to the * gate of the Eze 11:1
above the mountain on the * side. Eze 11:23
when the * wind touches it, dying Eze 17:10
by a strong wind from the *; Eze 19:12
to the * of you overrun your land. Eze 25:4
the desert to the * will pour in Eze 25:9,10
the Travelers, * of the Dead Sea. Eze 39:11
same as for the * passageway—87½ Eze 40:21
just the same as on the * side. Eze 40:22
just as at the *, if one walked Eze 40:23
The inner court at the * of the Eze 41:14
court to these rooms from the *. Eze 42:9,10
at the *. Eze 42:12
me out through the * passageway to Eze 42:15
the outer wall leading to the *. Eze 43:1
God of Israel appeared from the *. Eze 43:2
On the * side are steps to climb Eze 43:17
took me 1,500 feet * along the Eze 47:3
He told me: "This river flows * Eze 47:8
the same * and west boundaries. Eze 48:2
lines on the * and the west. Eze 48:3
boundaries on the * and the west. Eze 48:5,6,7
Outside the city, stretching * Eze 48:18
same borders on * and west, while Eze 48:27,28
On the * side, with its 1½-mile Eze 48:32
the south and *, and warred against Dan 8:9
"But then news from the * and Dan 11:44
brothers, but the * wind—a wind of Hos 13:15
you far to the * of Damascus," Amo 5:25,26,27
five miles * of Petra, in Edom. Ob 1:8f
on the * side of the city, and he Jon 4:5
a scorching * wind to blow on Jon 4:8
had mastered most of the Near *. Hab 1:6f
my people from * and west, wherever Zec 8:7
of Olives, to the * of Jerusalem, Zec 14:4
running from * to west, for half Zec 14:4
the sky from * to west, so shall my Mt 24:27
the area * of the Jordan River. Mk 10:1
coming from the *, carrying the Rev 7:2
the kings from the * could march Rev 16:12
side—north, south, *, and west. Rev 21:13

EASTERN
Mesha to the * hills of Sephar. Gen 10:26-30
From the * mountains. Num 23:7-10
And the land on the * side shall Num 32:22
"The * border will be from Num 34:10,11
the * edge of the city of Jericho; Jos 4:19
the cities of the * desert. Jos 12:1
The * boundary extended along the Jos 15:5
* boundary began at Ataroth-addar. Jos 16:5,6
of Asher and the * boundary was the Jos 17:10
The * border was the Jordan Jos 18:20
of * Syria conquer them. Ju 3:8
traveled along the * border until Ju 11:18
"Open that * window," he 2Ki 13:16,17
They escaped into * Turkey—the 2Ki 19:37
tents on the * edge of Gilead. 1Ch 5:10
responsible for the * royal gate. 1Ch 9:17,18
(and in many * lands today) only Is 47:2f
In * Babylonia. Jer 50:21f
I will open up the * flank of Moab, Eze 25:9,10
and scarlet dyes from * Cyprus. Eze 27:7
flounders in the heavy * gale, Eze 27:26
that goes through the * wall. Eze 40:6
As I followed, he left the * Eze 40:20
the court to the * entrance of the Eze 40:32
Temple through the * passageway. Eze 43:4
* passageway, but it was closed. Eze 44:1
in length, and its * and western Eze 45:7
the inner wall's * entrance shall Eze 46:1
Lord, the inner * gate shall be Eze 46:12
The * passageway was closed. Eze 47:2f
and around to the * entrance, Eze 47:2
south side [of the * passageway Eze 47:2
"The * border will run south Eze 47:18
Those are the * and western Eze 48:1
same * and western boundary lines. Eze 48:4
It has the same * and western Eze 48:8
clear out to the * and western Eze 48:21,22
Israel, from its * border clear Eze 48:23
these same * and western borders. Eze 48:24
on the * outskirts of Jerusalem. Zec 14:5f
astrologers from * lands arrived in Mt 2:1
star in far-off * lands, and have Mt 2:2
still used among men in * lands. Mt 26:49f
greeting among men in * lands. Lk 22:47f

EASTWARD
grew and spread *, a plain was Gen 11:2
and will proceed * to Mount Hor, Num 34:7,8,9
and * into the valley of Mizpah; Jos 11:8
his animals * to the edge of the 1Ch 5:9
I saw a stream flowing * from Eze 47:1

EASY
going by * stages to Rephidim. Ex 17:1
be * to conquer the whole area. Deu 1:41
weapons within * reach beside them, Neh 4:17
the good man's path is *! Pro 15:19
The lizards: they are * to catch Pro 30:24-28
and were such * prey for you. Is 37:27
out the grain—an * job she loves. Hos 10:11
Israel would be an * prey. Hab 3:14
multitudes who choose its * way. Mt 7:13
come back on you. Go * on others; Lk 6:37
Now take it *! Lk 12:19
because it is * to understand: just Rom 6:19
within * reach of each of us; Rom 10:8
should have an * time of it at your 2Co 8:13
a godly life is not an * matter. 1Ti 3:16
Some of his comments are not * to 2Pe 3:15,16

EAT
warning: "You may * any fruit in Gen 2:16,17
If you * its fruit, you will be Gen 2:16,17
God says you mustn't * any of Gen 3:1
"Of course we may * it," the Gen 3:2,3
the garden that we are not to *. Gen 3:2,3
God says we mustn't * it or even Gen 3:2,3
the instant you * it you will Gen 3:5
you, and you shall * its grasses. Gen 3:18
But never * animals unless their Gen 9:4
and a bite to * to strengthen you. Gen 18:5
"I don't want to * until I have Gen 24:33
it here for me to *, and I will Gen 27:2,3,4
Sit up and * it, so that you will Gen 27:19
and I will * it and bless you with Gen 27:25
Sit up and * it so that you can Gen 27:31
still do not * the sciatic muscle Gen 32:32
to decide what he wanted to *! Gen 39:6
will be enough to * when the seven Gen 41:36
men will * with me this noon. Gen 43:16
"Let's *," he said. Gen 43:31
Hebrews and never * with them. Gen 43:32
other food, to * on his journey. Gen 45:23
* everything the hail has left." Ex 10:12
Everyone shall * roast lamb that Ex 12:8
Don't * any of it the next day; Ex 12:10
"* it with your traveling Ex 12:11
in your hands; * it hurriedly. Ex 12:11
* only bread made without yeast. Ex 12:15
not * anything made with yeast; Ex 12:20
When they stopped to *, they Ex 12:39
No foreigners shall * the lamb, Ex 12:43
* it if he has been circumcised. Ex 12:44
foreigner may not * of it. Ex 12:45
You shall, all of you who * each Ex 12:46
who eat each lamb, * it together in Ex 12:46
person shall ever * the lamb. Ex 12:48
For seven days you shall * only Ex 13:6,7
For there we had plenty to *. Ex 16:3
The Lord will give you meat to * Ex 16:7,8,9
food Jehovah has given you to *. Ex 16:15
where there were crops to *. Ex 16:35
people—do not * any animal that has Ex 22:31
its carcass for the dogs to *. Ex 22:31
you are not to * bread with yeast, Ex 23:15
Aaron and his sons shall * the Ex 29:32
They alone shall * those items Ex 29:33
The ordinary people shall not * Ex 29:33
shall * neither fat nor blood." Lev 3:17
the priests may * these offerings Lev 6:18
the ceremony shall * it in the Lev 6:26
the priests may * this offering, Lev 6:29
priests may then * the carcass, and Lev 7:6
of Israel never to * fat, whether Lev 7:23
"Never * blood, whether of birds Lev 7:26,27
Tabernacle, and * it along with the Lev 8:31
in it, and * it beside the altar. Lev 10:12
therefore you must * it in the Lev 10:13
You may not * their meat or even Lev 11:8
"As to fish, you may * whatever Lev 11:9
You mustn't * their meat or even Lev 11:11
these are the ones you may not *: Lev 11:13-19
are permitted to * dies of disease, Lev 11:39
living among them, may * blood. Lev 17:12
of Israel never to * it, for the Lev 17:14
will be accepted: * it the same Lev 19:6
If you * it on the third day you Lev 19:8
trees, do not * the first three Lev 19:23
You must not * meat with Lev 19:26
to * and those you may not eat. Lev 20:25
to eat and those you may not *. Lev 20:25
a running sore may * the holy Lev 22:4
and shall not * of the holy Lev 22:6
again and may * the holy food, for Lev 22:7
He may not * any animal that Lev 22:8
"No one may * of the holy Lev 22:10
a hired servant, may * this food. Lev 22:10
that slave may * it, and any slave Lev 22:11
born in his household may * it. Lev 22:11
may not * the sacred offerings. Lev 22:12
may * of her father's food again. Lev 22:13
priestly families may * this food. Lev 22:13
"If someone should * of the holy Lev 22:14
done you must not * any of the Lev 23:14
and you can * your fill in safety. Lev 25:19
'What shall we * the seventh year, Lev 25:20
You shall * your fill, and live Lev 26:4,5
for your enemies will * them. Lev 26:16
You shall * your own sons and Lev 26:29
He may * nothing that comes from Num 6:3,4
* the Passover lamb that night. Num 9:6,7
They are to * the lamb at that Num 9:11
they shall have meat to *. Num 11:18
You shall * it, not for just a Num 11:18
they are but bread for us to *! Num 14:9
your families may * these unless Num 18:11
Your families may * these unless Num 18:13
their families may * it in their Num 18:31
"There is nothing to * here, and Num 21:5
"This mob will * us like an ox Num 22:4
And shall * up the nations that Num 24:3-9
bite we * and everything we drink; Deu 2:28
see nor hear nor * nor smell. Deu 4:28
plenty to * and be fully content. Deu 11:15
However, the meat you * may be Deu 12:15
gazelle and deer. * as much of this Deu 12:15
defiled may * it, too. Deu 12:15
you are not to * the blood—pour it Deu 12:16
* them before the Lord your God. Deu 12:18
ceremonially defiled may * them. Deu 12:20-23
is never to * the blood, for the Deu 12:20-23
not * the life with the meat. Deu 12:20-23
altar, and you will * the meat. Deu 12:26,27
"You are not to * any animal I Deu 14:3,4,5
These are the animals you may *: Deu 14:3,4,5
So you may not * the camel, the Deu 14:7
"You may * any bird except the Deu 14:11-18
"Don't * anything that has died Deu 14:21
a foreigner among you may * it. Deu 14:21
to him, but don't * it yourself, Deu 14:21
Bring this tithe to * before the Deu 14:23
that they can * and be satisfied; Deu 14:29
your family shall * these animals Deu 15:20
at the time, may * it, just as Deu 15:22
as anyone may * a gazelle or deer. Deu 15:22
But don't * the blood; Deu 15:23
at his sanctuary. * the sacrifice Deu 16:3
unleavened bread. * unleavened Deu 16:3
Roast the lamb and * it, then Deu 16:7
shall * no bread made with yeast. Deu 16:8
and someone else would * it! Deu 20:6
trees. * all the fruit you wish; Deu 20:19
"You may * your fill of the Deu 23:24
grain—you may * a few handfuls of Deu 23:25
someone else will * the fruit of Deu 28:30
even heard of will * the crops you Deu 28:33
for the locusts will * your crops. Deu 28:38
but you won't * the grapes or drink Deu 28:39
They will * you out of house and Deu 28:51
You will even * the flesh of Deu 28:53
she herself can * them: so terrible Deu 28:56,57
The next day they began to * Jos 5:11,12
leaving nothing to *, and taking Ju 6:3,4
* any food that isn't kosher. Ju 13:4
beer, and not to * food that isn't Ju 13:7
She must not * grapes or raisins, Ju 13:13,14
or * anything that isn't kosher." Ju 13:13,14
we can get you something to *." Ju 13:15
"but I'll not * anything. Ju 13:16
to her, "Come and * with us." Ru 2:14
more than she could *. Ru 2:14
her cry so much she couldn't *. 1Sa 1:7
so that I will have enough to *.' 1Sa 2:36
the guests can't * until he 1Sa 9:12,13
ahead of me and we'll * together; 1Sa 9:19
"Go ahead and * it," Samuel 1Sa 9:24
been allowed to * freely from the 1Sa 14:30
sit down to * until he arrives." 1Sa 16:10,11
king sat down to * at his usual 1Sa 20:24,25
and refused to * all that day, for 1Sa 20:34
Now, what is there to *? 1Sa 21:3
you something to * so you'll regain 1Sa 28:22
He had not had anything to * or 1Sa 30:11,12
David had refused to * anything 2Sa 3:35,36
But David vowed that he would * 2Sa 3:35,36
and * with them, but he refused. 2Sa 12:17
living, you wept and refused to *; 2Sa 12:21
a little something for him to *. 2Sa 13:6
tray before him, he refused to *! 2Sa 13:9
fruit are for the young men to *; 2Sa 16:2
all those who * at your own table! 2Sa 19:28
nor would I * or drink even water 1Ki 13:8
orders not to * anything or drink 1Ki 13:9
"Come home with me and *." 1Ki 13:15
for I am not allowed to * 1Ki 13:16,17
Drink from the brook and * what 1Ki 17:4
son continued to * from her supply 1Ki 17:15
him and told him to get up and *! 1Ki 19:5
said, "Get up and * some more, for 1Ki 19:7
He refused to * and went to bed 1Ki 21:4
"Get up and * and don't worry 1Ki 21:7

(EAT Con't)
invited him in to *, and 2Ki 4:8
Go ahead and *!" 2Ki 4:41
proposed that we * my son one day 2Ki 6:26-30
so we can * him,' she hid him." 2Ki 6:26-30
Dogs shall * Ahab's wife Jezebel 2Ki 9:10
that dogs would * her flesh and 2Ki 9:36
For they are doomed with you to * 2Ki 18:27
my people will * the volunteer 2Ki 19:29
locust swarms to * up all of your 2Ch 7:13
were permitted to * the Passover 2Ch 30:17,18,19
them out to the people to *. 2Ch 35:13
even allow them to * the priests' Ez 2:62,63
In fact, I refused to * for Neh 1:4
So the people went away to * a Neh 8:12
do not * or drink for three days, Est 4:16
On these occasions they would * Job 1:4
I cannot * for sighing; Job 3:24
They * what they find that grows Job 24:6
They * roots and leaves, having Job 30:4
They * my people like bread and Ps 14:4
shall * and be satisfied; Ps 22:26
I refused to *; Ps 35:13
dogs will * them. Ps 68:23
him to the desert tribes to *! Ps 74:13,14
me. I * ashes instead of bread. Ps 102:9,10
That is why you must * the Pro 1:31
of life to those who * her fruit; Pro 3:18
They * and drink wickedness and Pro 4:17
to get your hands dirty—and *, Pro 12:9
while the evil man lives to *. Pro 13:25
It is better to * soup with Pro 15:17
cold, you won't * at the harvest. Pro 20:4
and there will be plenty to *! Pro 20:13
Don't * too much of it, or it Pro 25:16
Just as it is harmful to * too Pro 25:27
but if he is hungry, he'll * Pro 27:7
A workman may * from the orchard Pro 27:18
For who can * or enjoy apart from Ecc 2:24-26
and second, that he should * and Ecc 3:13
it is for a man to * well, drink a Ecc 5:18
that a man should *, drink, and be Ecc 8:15
So go ahead, *, drink, and be Ecc 9:7
and his fruit is lovely to *. Sol 2:3
and * its choicest fruits." Sol 4:16
and * my honeycomb with my honey. Sol 5:1
lover and beloved, * and drink! Sol 5:1
and (is old enough to) * curds Is 7:15,16f
Finally they will even * their Is 9:19,20
lions will * grass like the cows. Is 11:7
birds and wild animals to *; Is 18:6
to * . . . . Quick, quick, grab Is 21:5
"Let us *, drink, and be Is 22:13
the ground will * grain, its chaff Is 30:24
that he will * his own dung and Is 36:12
the worm shall * them like wool; Is 51:8
* pork and other forbidden foods. Is 65:4
starve, but my servants shall *; Is 65:13
vineyards and * the fruit Is 65:21,22
the lion shall * straw as the ox Is 65:25
fruitful land, to * of its bounty Jer 2:7
And they shall * your harvest Jer 5:17
*, but there is none to be found. Jer 14:6
even * a meal with them. Jer 16:8
* their own children and friends. Jer 19:9
spoiled and moldy—too rotten to *. Jer 24:2
like rotting figs, too bad to *. Jer 29:16,17
we will be here to * the fruit from Jer 29:28
and * from your own gardens there. Jer 31:5
Literally, "The fathers * the Jer 31:29f
* and we were well off and happy! Jer 44:17
Shall mothers * their little Lam 2:20
He has made me * gravel and Lam 3:16
Those who used to * fastidiously Lam 4:5
Open your mouth and * what I give Eze 2:8
me: "Son of dust, * what I am Eze 3:1
I am giving you—* this scroll! Eze 3:1
"* it all," he said. Eze 3:3
"During the first 390 days * Eze 4:9
human dung as fuel, and * it. Eze 4:12
Israel shall * defiled bread in the Eze 4:13
Fathers will * their own sons, Eze 5:10
and sons will * their fathers; Eze 5:10
"Son of dust, tremble as you * Eze 12:18
evil! You * meat with the blood; Eze 33:25
the sheep? You * the best food and Eze 34:3
take away their right to *. Eze 34:9,10
they are food for us to *!' Eze 35:12
Come, * the flesh and drink the Eze 39:17
drink the blood! * the flesh of Eze 39:18
to the Lord shall * of the most Eze 42:13
Priests may never * meat from Eze 44:31
up his mind not to * the food and Dan 1:8
to * other things instead. Dan 1:8
fruit, enough for everyone to *. Dan 4:12
him * grass with the wild animals! Dan 4:15
fruit for all to *, the wild Dan 4:21
For seven years let him * grass Dan 4:23
the fields, and to * grass like the Dan 4:32
wild animals will * their fruit. Hos 1:12
They will * and still be hungry. Hos 4:10
if it has any, foreigners will * Hos 8:7
all who * such sacrifices are Hos 9:4
They may * this food to feed Hos 9:4
loosened his muzzle so he could *. Hos 11:4
and gardens and * their crops and Amo 9:14
even the animals, * anything at Jon 3:7
You will * but never have Mic 6:14
Not a cluster to *, not a single Mic 7:1
that * up everything before them. Nah 3:15
You have scarcely enough to * or Hag 1:6
instead, he will * the fat ones, Zec 11:16
important than what to * and wear. Mt 6:25
They don't worry about what to * Mt 6:26
then for them to refuse to *. Mt 9:15
nothing to * here in the desert; Mt 14:15
handwashing before they *." Mt 15:2
that anything you * passes through Mt 15:17
to * the crumbs that fall." Mt 15:27
now, and have nothing left to *; Mt 15:32
desert for all this mob to *?" Mt 15:33
shall we plan to * the Passover?" Mt 26:17
come, and I will * the Passover Mt 26:18
and * it, for this is my body." Mt 26:26
stand it, to * with such scum?" Mk 2:16
refuse to * at the wedding feast? Mk 2:19
only priests were allowed to *? Mk 2:25,26
he couldn't even find time to *. Mk 3:20
them to give her something to *. Mk 5:43
that they scarcely had time to *. Mk 6:31
is nothing to * here in this Mk 6:35,36
will never * until they have Mk 7:3
For they * without first Mk 7:5
harmed by what you *, but by what Mk 7:15,16
"Can't you see that what you * Mk 7:18
Literally, "Let the children * Mk 7:27f
days, and have nothing left to *. Mk 8:1
* the traditional Passover supper. Mk 14:12
us, where we will * the Passover Mk 14:14
said, "* it—this is my body." Mk 14:22
then they won't want to *." Lk 5:35
But I * my food and drink my Lk 7:34
As they sat down to *, a woman Lk 7:36
"Give her something to *!" Lk 8:55
"For there is nothing to * here Lk 9:12
I've nothing to give him to *.' Lk 11:5,6
he sat down to * without first Lk 11:37,38
Literally, "*, drink, and be Lk 12:19f
food to * or clothes to wear. Lk 12:22
about food—what to * and drink; Lk 12:29
and serve them as they sit and *! Lk 12:37
just sit down and *, but first Lk 17:7,8,9
room where he can * the Passover Lk 22:11
anxious to * this Passover meal Lk 22:15
now that I won't * it again until Lk 22:16
you. * it in remembrance of me." Lk 22:19
you the right to * and drink at my Lk 22:30
As they sat down to *, he asked Lk 24:30
you have anything here to *?" Lk 24:41
disciples were urging Jesus to *. Jn 4:31
this man give us his flesh to *?" Jn 6:52
you * the flesh of the Messiah Jn 6:53
But anyone who does * my flesh Jn 6:54
be allowed to * the Passover lamb. Jn 18:28
kill and * any of them you wish." Act 10:13
and birds [which we are not to * Act 11:6
'Kill and * whatever you wish.' Act 11:7
them about: not to * food offered Act 21:25
to idols, not to * unbled meat from Act 21:25
a curse neither to * nor drink Act 23:12,13
* nor drink till he is dead. Act 23:21
light, Paul begged everyone to *. Act 27:33
"Please * something now for Act 27:34
whether or not to * meat that has Rom 14:2
meat at all and * vegetables rather Rom 14:2
rather than * that kind of meat. Rom 14:2
it is all right to * such meat must Rom 14:3
by what you *, you are not acting Rom 14:15
in love if you go ahead and * it. Rom 14:15
is not what we * or drink but Rom 14:17
* it if it makes another stumble. Rom 14:20
Don't even * lunch with such a 1Co 5:11
But that doesn't mean we should * 1Co 6:13
Should we * meat that has been 1Co 8:4
So when they * such food it 1Co 8:7
care whether we * it or not. 1Co 8:8
We are no worse off if we don't * 1Co 8:8
your freedom to * it, lest you 1Co 8:9
it is wrong to * this food will see 1Co 8:10
sin, I'll not * any of it as long 1Co 8:13
have the right to * some of it? 1Co 9:7
God sent them food to * and water 1Co 10:3,4
people sat down to * and drink and 1Co 10:7
from the loaf to * there together, 1Co 10:16
there are, we all * from the same 1Co 10:17
And the Jewish people, all who * 1Co 10:18
demons when you * the same food, 1Co 10:20
You cannot * bread both at the 1Co 10:21
You are certainly free to * food 1Co 10:23
it's not against God's laws to * 1Co 10:23
if you want to. * whatever is on 1Co 10:27
idols, then don't * it for the sake 1Co 10:28
When you come together to *, it 1Co 11:
and said, "Take this and * it. 1Co 11:
For every time you * this 1Co 11:
hungry he should * at home so that 1Co 11:
let us *, drink, and be merry. 1Co 15:
to harvest and *, will give you 2Co 9:
me food to * and a place to stay. 2Co 12:
came, he wouldn't * with the Gal 2:
you for what you * or drink, or for Col 2:
who does not work shall not *." 2Th 3:
and wrong to * meat, even though 1Ti 4
good, and we may * it gladly if we 1Ti 4
him * as he goes along!" 1Ti 5:
You will never be able to * Heb 5:
foods to * and drink, rules for Heb 9:
stay warm and * hearty," and Jas 2:
you, and * your flesh like fire. Jas 5
cries for milk. * God's Word—read 1Pe 2:2,
victorious shall * of the hidden Rev 2:1
immorality and to * meat that has Rev 2:2
"Yes, take it and * it," he Rev 10:
* the baby as soon as it was born. Rev 12:
Come and * the flesh of kings, Rev 19:1
* the fruit from the Tree of Life. Rev 22:1

EATEN
"Have you * fruit from the tree Gen 3:1
these young men of mine have *; Gen 14:2
and I have already * it and blessed Gen 27:3
A leafy plant * by peasant women Gen 30:14
that a wild animal has * him. Gen 37:19,2
A wild animal has * him. Gen 37:3
Use the blood of the lamb * in Ex 12:
The meat must not be * raw or Ex 12:
if all is not * that night, burn Ex 12:1
yeast may be * from the evening of Ex 12:1
and its flesh not *, but the owner Ex 21:2
it shall not be *, for it is Ex 29:3
it shall be * without yeast in Lev 6:1
It may be * by any male Lev 6:1
none of it shall be *." Lev 6:22,2
No sin offering may be * by the Lev 6:3
and it must be * in a holy place, Lev 7:
its meat is to be * that same day, Lev 7:1
none left to be * the next day. Lev 7:1
that is not * the day it is Lev 7:1
sacrificed may be * the next day. Lev 7:1
For if any of it is * on the Lev 7:17,1
shall not be *, but burned; Lev 7:1
and as for the meat that may be * Lev 7:1
eaten, it may be * only by a person Lev 7:1
for other purposes, but never *. Lev 7:2
him, may be * in any holy place. Lev 10:1
"Why haven't you * the sin Lev 10:1
* it there, as I ordered you." Lev 10:1
"but if I had * the sin offering Lev 10:1
that the following may not be *: Lev 11:4-
legs must not be *, with the Lev 11:2
and grasshoppers—may be *. Lev 11:21,22
that crawl shall not be *. Lev 11:41,42
feet may be *, for it is defiled. Lev 11:41,42
clean and may be *, and what is Lev 11:47
and may not be *, among all animal Lev 11:47
For any of it * on the third day Lev 19:7
defiled by being * by unauthorized Lev 22:15
he has * the sacred offerings; Lev 22:16
The bread shall be * by Aaron Lev 24:9
They are to be * only in a most Num 18:10
Until they have * what they Num 23:18-24
when you have * until you can hold Deu 6:10,11,12
When you have * your fill, bless Deu 8:10
of the offerings may be * at home. Deu 12:17
the cud may be *, but if the Deu 14:6
have both, it may not be *. Deu 14:7
Pigs may not be * because, Deu 14:8
with fins and scales may be *; Deu 14:9
to you and may not be *. Deu 14:19,20
"The Passover is not to be * in Deu 16:5
It must be * at the place the Deu 16:6
but not yet * any of its fruit? Deu 20:6
* the honey he felt much better. 1Sa 14:27
I have * this little bit of honey. 1Sa 14:29
for he had * nothing all day. 1Sa 28:20
here, and have * and drunk water in 1Ki 13:21,22
the lion had not * the body nor 1Ki 13:28
the city shall be * by dogs, and 1Ki 14:11
in the field shall be * by birds.' 1Ki 14:11
the city will be * by dogs, and 1Ki 16:4-7
fields will be * by the birds." 1Ki 16:4-7
the city shall be * by dogs and 1Ki 21:24
country shall be * by vultures." 1Ki 21:24
But after the men had * a bite 2Ki 4:40
The last food in the city was * 2Ki 25:3
His skin is * by disease. Job 18:13
"But suddenly the food he has * Job 20:14
dust, both * by the same worms. Job 21:26
A DRY CRUST * in peace is better Pro 17:1
They are * with great relish! Pro 18:8
Gossip is a dainty morsel * with Pro 26:22
out by ravens and * by vultures. Pro 30:17
like old clothes * up by moths! Is 50:9
Their harvests will not be * by Is 65:23

EATEN Con't)
of Babylon, has * and crushed us Jer 51:34,35
cooked and * their own children; Lam 4:10
now I have never * any animal that Eze 4:14
and I have never * any of the Eze 4:14
with great care and * fearfully. Eze 4:16
Literally, "The fathers have * Eze 18:2f
fields shall be * by wild animals, Eze 33:27
shall be * during those days. Eze 45:21
But when you had * and were Hos 13:6
no bread made with yeast was *. Mk 14:1
and * with the unleavened bread. Lk 22:7
As soon as Judas had * it, Satan Jn 13:27
in all my life * such creatures, Act 10:14
'For I have never yet * anything Act 11:8
No one had * for a long time, but Act 27:21
food was made to be * and used up. Col 2:22
EATER
came out of the *, and sweetness Ju 14:14
EATING
I have chosen for * and for Gen 7:2
animals—those for * and sacrifice, Gen 7:8,9
told that they would be * there. Gen 43:25
lion that has finished * its prey. Gen 49:9
Also, anyone * its meat or Lev 11:40
hateful to me by * any animal or Lev 20:25
in the right way, * the sacrificial Lev 22:29,30
But as everyone began * the Num 11:33
the Lord, neither * bread nor Deu 9:18
honey with him, * as he went, and Ju 14:9
"Why aren't you *? 1Sa 1:8
against the Lord by * blood. 1Sa 14:33
against the Lord by * the blood." 1Sa 14:34
across the fields, * and drinking 1Sa 30:16
your mourning and are * again." 2Sa 12:21
wild animals from * them at night. 2Sa 21:10
"Why aren't you *? 1Ki 21:5
after another, *, drinking wine, 2Ki 7:8
We have been * from these stores 2Ch 31:10
I gag at the thought of * it! Job 6:5,6,7
But they had hardly finished *, Ps 78:30
happy is the man who keeps on * Pro 3:18
while *, when your teeth are gone! Ecc 12:4
As a hungry man dreams of *, but Is 29:8
sins—the person * sour grapes is Jer 31:30
While they were *, Ishmael and Jer 41:2
yourself by * the food brought to Eze 24:22
was probably in * pork or other Dan 1:8f
* the food supplied by the king! Dan 1:15
like an animal, * grass like a cow, Dan 4:25
finish * your crops, the Joe 1:4
with luxury, * the meat of the Amo 6:4
were * dinner [at Matthew's house Mt 9:10
heads of wheat and * the grain. Mt 12:1
made unholy by * non-kosher food! Mt 15:11
defilement from * without first Mt 15:20
While he was *, a woman came in Mt 26:7
That evening as he sat * with the Mt 26:20,21
As they were *, Jesus took a Mt 26:26
saw him * with these men of ill Mk 2:16
heads of wheat and * the grain. Mk 2:23
the usual Jewish rituals before *. Mk 7:2
around the table *, Jesus said, "I Mk 14:18
of you who is here * with me." Mk 14:18
one of you twelve * with me now. Mk 14:20
As they were *, Jesus took bread Mk 14:22
disciples as they were * together. Mk 16:14
his * with such notorious sinners. Lk 5:30
in their hands and * the grains. Lk 6:1
stay in one place, * and drinking Lk 10:7
people—even * with them! Lk 15:2
daily business—* and drinking, Lk 17:28
Anyone * this Bread shall live Jn 6:48-51
to refrain from * meat sacrificed Act 15:20
and also from * unbled meat of Act 15:20
to abstain from * food offered to Act 15:27,28,29
better and began *, all two Act 27:36
After *, the crew lightened the Act 27:38
law against * the forbidden fruit, Rom 5:14
really wrong with * meat that has Rom 14:14
Don't let your * ruin someone for Rom 14:15
to do is to quit * meat or drinking Rom 14:21
instance, take the matter of *. 1Co 6:13
Don't think of * as important, 1Co 6:13
NEXT IS YOUR question about * food 1Co 8:1
food will see you * at a temple 1Co 8:10
So if * meat offered to idols is 1Co 8:13
ox to keep it from * when it is 1Co 9:9
having a bad conscience over * it. 1Co 10:27
of God, even your * and drinking. 1Co 10:31
Supper you are *, but your own. 1Co 11:20
Can't you do your * and drinking 1Co 11:22
carefully before * the bread and 1Co 11:28
it means, he is * and drinking 1Co 11:29
yourselves before * you will not 1Co 11:31
such rules as not *, tasting, or Col 2:21
rules about * certain foods—a Heb 13:9
EATS
bad, what if he * the fruit of the Gen 3:22
takes it over to him and Isaac *; Gen 27:25
during that time anyone who * Ex 12:19
and the priest who * it shall be Lev 7:17,18
who * it must answer for his sin. Lev 7:17,18
unclean but * the thanksgiving Lev 7:20
or beast, and then * the peace Lev 7:21
Anyone who * fat from an Lev 7:25
Anyone who lies down or * in the Lev 14:47
you, who * blood in any form. Lev 17:10
Therefore, anyone who * blood Lev 17:14
or foreigner—who * the dead body of Lev 17:15
an ox * grass," they exclaimed. Num 22:4
upon anyone who * anything before 1Sa 14:24,25
I made you! He * grass like an ox. Job 40:15
of an ox that * grass, to the Ps 106:19,20
he drinks, or the rich food he *. Ps 109:18
The good man * to live, while the Pro 13:25
well whether he * little or much, Ecc 5:12
He goes right on and *. Is 31:4,5
sacrifices that she * with blood. Zec 9:7
his supper before he * his own. Lk 17:7,8,9
eternal life to everyone who * it. Jn 6:48-51
Everyone who * my flesh and Jn 6:56
and anyone who * this Bread shall Jn 6:58
declares, 'One who * supper with me Jn 13:18
So is the person who * meat that Rom 14:6
So if anyone * this bread and 1Co 11:27
For if he * the bread and drinks 1Co 11:29
EAVESDROP
Don't *! Ecc 7:21,22
EBAL
Manahath, *,Shepho, Onam. Gen 36:23
Gerizim, and a curse from Mount *! Deu 11:29
(Gerizim and * are mountains Deu 11:30
on the other side, at Mount *. Deu 27:2,3,4
upon Mount * to proclaim a curse. Deu 27:13
Mount *, as Moses had commanded Jos 8:30
Lord had said concerning Mount *. Jos 8:31
and half at the foot of Mount *. Jos 8:33
Uzal, Diklah, *, Abima-el, Sheba, 1Ch 1:20-23
Manahath, *, Shephi, and Onam. 1Ch 1:40
EBB
and your life shall * away; Lev 26:16
He will watch their power * away, Deu 32:36
joy has reached its lowest *; Is 24:11
Their lives * away like those Lam 2:12
EBBING
They say my life is * out—a Ps 88:4
EBED
At that time Gaal (the son of *) Ju 9:26
"Gaal, son of *, and his relatives Ju 9:31
From the clan of Adin—* (son of Ez 8:2-14
EBED-MELECH
When * the Ethiopian, an Jer 38:7
on a rope. * called down to Jer 38:12
"Send this word to * the Jer 39:16
EBEDMELECH
Then the king commanded * to take Jer 38:10
he died. So * took thirty men and Jer 38:11
EBENEZER
near *, the Philistines at Aphek. 1Sa 4:1
battleground at * to the temple of 1Sa 5:1
and named it * (meaning, "the 1Sa 7:12
EBER
* descended from Shem, the oldest Gen 10:21
Shelah, and Shelah's son was *. Gen 10:24
Two sons were born to *: Gen 10:25
old when his son * was born, living Gen 11:14,15
* was thirty-four years old when Gen 11:16,17
And shall oppress both * and Num 24:23,24
Shelah's son *. 1Ch 1:18
* had two sons: Peleg (which 1Ch 1:19
The son of Shelah was *, 1Ch 1:24-27
The son of * was Peleg, 1Ch 1:24-27
Sheba, Jorai, Jacan, Zia, and *. 1Ch 5:13
*, Misham, 1Ch 8:12
Ishpan, *, Eliel, Abdon, Zichri, 1Ch 8:22-25
*, leader of the Amok clan; Neh 12:12-21
Peleg's father was *; Lk 3:23-38
EBER'S
Peleg's father was Eber;* father Lk 3:23-38
EBEZ
Rabbith, Kishion, *, Remeth, Jos 19:17-23
EBIASAPH
Elkanah, *, Assir, Tahath, Uriel, 1Ch 6:22,23,24
Tahath, Assir, *, Korah, Izhar, 1Ch 6:33-38
back through Kore and * to Korah. 1Ch 9:19
EBONY
giving payment in * and ivory. Eze 27:15
EBRON
east of Kabul, *, Rehob, Hammon, Jos 19:28
ECBATANA
at *, in the province of Media. Ez 6:2
ECHO
Her streets * with the sounds of Jer 6:7
in the ceilings * what they say. Hab 2:11
ECHOES
The voice of the Lord * from the Ps 29:3
of death * from the mountainsides. Is 22:5
It is his voice that * in the Jer 10:13
ECONOMICALLY
their cities were * dependent upon Act 12:20
ECONOMY
the * of Judah remained strong. 2Ch 12:12
birth rate and the expanding *, Is 29:23
EDEN
a garden in *, to the east, and Gen 2:8
A river from the land of * Gen 2:10
in the Garden of * as its gardener, Gen 2:15
from the Garden of *, and sent him Gen 3:23
of the garden of *, with a flaming Gen 3:24
in the land of Nod, east of *. Gen 4:16
section was like the Garden of *, Gen 13:10
and * in the land of Telassar? 2Ki 19:12
of Zimmah) and * (son of Joah). 2Ch 29:12,13,14
His faithful assistants were *, 2Ch 31:14,15
or the people of * in Telassar? Is 37:12
as beautiful as the Garden of *. Is 51:3
Haran and Canneh, *, Asshur and Eze 27:23
You were in *, the garden of Eze 28:13
envy of all the other trees of *. Eze 31:9
proud trees of *, the choicest and Eze 31:16
of *—the nations of the world. Eze 31:18
by Satan in the Garden of *. 2Co 11:3
EDEN'S
land has become like * garden! Eze 36:35
land lies fair as * Garden in all Joe 2:3
EDER
and camped beyond the Tower of *. Gen 35:21
Kabzeel, *, Jagur, Kinah, Dimonah, Jos 15:21-32
Zebadiah, Arad, *, Michael, 1Ch 8:15,16
Mushi's sons were Mahli, *, and 1Ch 23:23
The sons of Mushi were Mahli, *, 1Ch 24:30
EDGE
El-paran at the * of the desert. Gen 14:5,6
the reeds along the river's *. Ex 2:3
Midian, out at the * of the desert Ex 3:1
Etham at the * of the wilderness. Ex 13:20
wide around the * of the top, and a Ex 25:25
for each frame, one under each *. Ex 26:21
the outer top * of the chestpiece. Ex 28:22,23,24
front * of the ephod at the sash. Ex 28:27
The bottom * of the ephod shall Ex 28:33,34
a golden molding all around the *. Ex 37:11
ran a gold molding around the *. Ex 37:26
set at the lower * of the Ex 39:19
the * so that it would not tear. Ex 39:23
to the bottom * of the robe; Ex 39:24
along the bottom * of the skirt, Ex 39:25,26
alternating all around the *. Ex 39:25,26
Etham (at the * of the wilderness), Num 33:5,6
Kadesh to Mount Hor (at the * Num 33:15-37
of Zin, along the * of Edom. Num 34:3
southern * of the Promised Land. Deu 1:1f
to Gilead—from the * of the Arnon Deu 2:35,36
from Aroer at the * of the Arnon Deu 4:48
around the * of the flat rooftop to Deu 22:8
to stop at the * of the river." Jos 3:8
at the river's *, suddenly, far up Jos 3:13,14
eastern * of the city of Jericho; Jos 4:19
* of a valley north of the city. Jos 8:11,12,13
from Aroer, on the * of the Arnon Jos 12:2
from Aroer, on the * of the valley Jos 13:9
from Aroer on the * of the valley Jos 13:16
at the northern * of the Negeb. Jos 15:1
ran from the * of Kiriath-baal, Jos 18:15
along the north * of the Arabah. Jos 18:18
was buried at the * of his property Ju 2:7-9
the outer * of the camp of Midian. Ju 7:19,20
"I live on the far * of the Ju 19:18
him to the * of the city. 1Sa 9:26,27
were camped at the * of Gibe-ah, 1Sa 14:2
near the south * of the field and 1Sa 20:41
the road at the * of the wilderness 1Sa 26:3,4
David paused at the * of the 2Sa 15:17,18
When the lepers arrived at the * 2Ki 7:8
eastward to the * of the desert and 1Ch 5:9
tents on the eastern * of Gilead. 1Ch 5:10
close to the * of the cliff! Ps 73:2
sliding over the * of the cliff and Ps 73:18
vinegar that sets the teeth on *. Pro 10:26
children's teeth are set on *." Jer 31:29f
the one whose teeth are set on *. Jer 31:30
And I will start a fire at the * Jer 49:27
children's teeth are set on *." Eze 18:2f
8¾ feet out to the * of the Eze 41:9
rim around its *, and it extends Eze 43:13
over to the * of the courtyard. Mk 14:68
took him to the * of the hill on Lk 4:29
at the water's * while the Lk 5:2
But the instant she touched the * Lk 8:43,44
you from here is stopped at its *; Lk 16:26
he went to the * of the desert, Jn 11:54
EDGES
Use loops at the * to join these Ex 26:4,5
Use fifty loops along the * of Ex 26:10,11
to the front * of the two settings Ex 28:25
lower, inside * of the chestpiece; Ex 28:26
looped along the * of these two Ex 36:11,12
around the * of the table, with a Ex 37:12
or clip the * of your beard, as the Lev 19:27
filled with eyes around their *. Eze 1:18
with a 10½-inch curb around the *. Eze 43:17
EDIBLE
and sorts out the * ones into Mt 13:47,48

EDICT
THEN GOD ISSUED this *: Ex 20:1
you issue a royal *, a law of the Est 1:19
"A copy of this *," the letter Est 3:14
The * went out by the king's Est 3:15
EDOM
"*," which means "Red Stuff." Gen 25:30
brother Esau in *, in the land of Gen 32:3
of Esau (also called *): Gen 36:1
of the kings of * (before Israel Gen 36:31-39
(son of Beor), from Dinhabah in *. Gen 36:31-39
the sub-tribes of *, each giving Gen 36:40-43
The leaders of * are appalled, Ex 15:15
to the king of *: "We are the Num 20:14
The people of * were descended Num 20:14f
But the king of * said, "Stay Num 20:18
But the king of * was adamant. Num 20:20
Because * refused to allow Num 20:21,22
of the land of *, "The time has Num 20:23
order to go around the land of *. Num 21:4
Israel shall possess all * and Num 24:15-19
(at the edge of the land of *). Num 33:15-37
of Zin, along the edge of *. Num 34:3
"So we passed through * where Deu 2:8
northern border of *, crossed the Jos 15:1
borders of * in the Negeb, namely: Jos 15:21-32
Out across the fields of *, Ju 5:4
to the king of * asking permission Ju 11:17
"Finally they went around * and Ju 11:18
Moab, Ammon, *, the kings of Zobah, 1Sa 14:47
throughout *, so that the entire 2Sa 8:14
Sea in the land of *, where he 1Ki 9:26
—Moab, Ammon, *, Sidon, and from 1Ki 11:1
a member of the royal family of *. 1Ki 11:14
David had been in * with Joab to 1Ki 11:15
for permission to return to *. 1Ki 11:21
(There was no king in * at that 1Ki 22:47
of *," Jehoram replied. 2Ki 3:6,7,8
by troops from *, moved along a 2Ki 3:9
and * went to consult Elisha. 2Ki 3:12
the direction of *, and soon there 2Ki 3:20
to break through to the king of *; 2Ki 3:26
the people in * revolted from Judah 2Ki 8:20
surrounded by the army of *. 2Ki 8:21
him and fled. So * has maintained 2Ki 8:22
You have destroyed * and are 2Ki 14:10
of the kings of * who reigned 1Ch 1:43
death, the kings of * were: 1Ch 1:51-54
the nations of *, Moab, Ammon, 1Ch 18:11
He put garrisons in * and forced 1Ch 18:13
and Eloth, in *, to launch a fleet 2Ch 8:17,18
At that time the king of * 2Ch 21:8
Nevertheless * . . . 2Ch 21:9f
But to this day * has been 2Ch 21:10
your conquest of *, but my advice 2Ch 25:19
him for worshiping the gods of *. 2Ch 25:20
his war against the armies of *. 2Ch 28:16
of Edom. For * was invading Judah 2Ch 28:16
men of * in the Valley of Salt. Ps 60:1
my lowly servant, and * my slave. Ps 60:8
But Moab and * are despised; Ps 108:9
upon * I cast my shoe." Ps 108:9f
Who else can lead me into *? Ps 108:10
nations of * and Moab and Ammon. Is 11:14
This is God's message to *: Is 21:11
upon *, the people I have doomed. Is 34:5
great sacrifice in * and make a Is 34:6
for what * has done to Israel. Is 34:8
The streams of * will be filled Is 34:9
This judgment on * will never Is 34:10
WHO IS THIS who comes from *, from Is 63:1
the nations of *, Moab and Ammon; Jer 25:21
to the kings of *, Moab, Ammon, Jer 27:3
Ammonites and in * and the other Jer 40:11
for when I punish *, I will Jer 49:8
The Lord says to *: If the Jer 49:12
against * and destroy her. Jer 49:14
The fate of * will be horrible; Jer 49:17
Suddenly * shall be destroyed, Jer 49:19
do this to * and also the people of Jer 49:20
Do you rejoice, O people of *, in Lam 4:21
who is scorned—by * and all her Eze 16:57
the people of * have sinned so Eze 25:12
I will smash * with my fist and Eze 25:13
ebony and ivory. * sends her Eze 27:16
"* is there with her kings and Eze 32:29
Mount Seir and all who live in *! Eze 35:15
especially *, for grabbing my land Eze 36:5
Moab, *, and most of Ammon will Dan 11:41
Egypt will be destroyed, and * Joe 3:19
selling them as slaves in *. Amo 1:6
and led him into slavery to *. Amo 1:9
The Lord says, "* has sinned Amo 1:11
Teman was in the north of *, and Amo 1:12f
*, with no respect for the dead. Amo 2:1
what is left of *, and of all the Amo 9:12
the future of the land of *. Ob 1:1
armies against * and destroy her!' Ob 1:1
*, making you small and despised. Ob 1:2
* was noted for her wise men; Ob 1:8f
five miles east of Petra, in *. Ob 1:8f
will be left in all of *! Ob 1:8
For I will fill the wise men of * Ob 1:8
sets the dry fields of * aflame. Ob 1:18
occupy the hill country of *; Ob 1:19
come to Jerusalem and rule all *. Ob 1:21
EDOM'S
in triumph into * strong cities? Ps 60:9,10
shakes with the noise of * fall; Jer 49:21
will end at last, but * never. Lam 4:22
EDOMITE
(Incidentally, Doeg the *, Saul's 1Sa 21:7
Then Doeg the *, who was standing 1Sa 22:9,10
So the Lord caused Hadad the * to 1Ki 11:14
EDOMITES
the *, born to him in Mount Seir: Gen 36:9
(All were *, descendants of Esau. Gen 36:40-43
their brothers the *, the Deu 2:4
* will be nervous, so be careful. Deu 2:4
displaced by the *, the descendants Deu 2:12
pass through. The * at Seir Deu 2:29
But don't look down on the * and Deu 23:7
the Egyptians; the * are your Deu 23:7
he destroyed eighteen thousand * 2Sa 8:13
ten thousand * in Salt Valley; 2Ki 14:7
thousand * in the Valley of Salt. 1Ch 18:12
and forced the * to pay large sums 1Ch 18:13
struck down the *. . . 2Ch 21:9f
slaughter of the *, he brought with 2Ch 25:14
and * and Moabites and Hagrites; Ps 83:6
forget what these * did on that day Ps 137:7
Egyptians, *, Ammonites, Moabites, Jer 9:25,26
the Ammonites, says the Lord.The * Jer 49:6
the * the person of my choice. Jer 49:19
EDRE-I
met them with his army at *. Num 21:33
defeated at Ashtaroth, near *. Deu 1:1
his army and attacked us at *. Deu 3:1
as the cities of Salecah and *. Deu 3:10
at Ashtaroth and *: He ruled a Jos 12:4
had reigned in Ashtaroth and *. Jos 13:12
of Ashtaroth and * were given to Jos 13:31
Hazor, Kedesh, *, Enhazor, Yiron, Jos 19:35-39
EDUCATE
to pay tuition to * a rebel who has Pro 17:16
EDUCATED
a wise counselor and an * man. 1Ch 27:32
I am better * than any of the kings Ecc 1:16-18
in Cilicia, but * here in Jerusalem Act 22:3
yes, to the * and uneducated Rom 1:14
EDUCATION
a nationwide religious * program. 2Ch 17:7,8,9
and * shall be vastly increased!" Dan 12:4
or race or * or social position is Col 3:11
EFFECT
the Lord to Moses were put into *. Num 1:54
instructions were put into *. Num 5:4
remains in *, and he is Num 6:6,7
and permanent * upon your lives! Deu 4:9
(for these laws don't go into * Deu 12:9
it is no longer in *, and I no Ju 2:3
he put the plan into immediate *. Est 2:4
to be put into *—the day the Jews' Est 9:1
me with great power and *. Job 30:21
what * will it have upon him? Job 35:6
An undeserved curse has no *. Pro 26:2
me with great *, to the people in Act 1:8
* a different plan to save us. Rom 8:3
And so, in *, you have broken 1Co 1:13
but they have no * when it comes to Col 2:23
a powerful * upon you, for the Holy 1Th 1:5
The will goes into * only after Heb 9:17
first agreement could go into *. Heb 9:18
EFFECTIVE
sense is more * than a hundred Pro 17:10
EFFECTIVELY
I dare not judge how * he has Rom 15:18
EFFECTS
be free from the * of this bitter Num 5:19
EFFICIENTLY
could administer the kingdom *. Dan 6:2
EFFORT
Why have you made no * to recover Ju 11:26
was an earnest * to obey the Lord 2Ch 11:17
an all-out * against Greece. Dan 11:2f
And the Lord honored this * so Act 11:21
anger, constant * to get the best Gal 5:20
woman in an * to get rid of her; Rev 12:15
EFFORTS
For then all their * to destroy Ps 109:28
you and crown your * with success. Pro 3:6
tears hers down by her own *. Pro 14:1
he inherits all my *, free of Ecc 2:20-23
has come from all our *. Is 26:18
will gain nothing by all your *. Is 33:11
But their * were in vain. Mk 14:55
faith is being helped by their *. 1Ti 6:2
EGG
white of an *—my appetite is gone Job 6:5,6,7
If he asks for an *, do you give Lk 11:12
EGGS
are young ones or * in it with the Deu 22:6
She lays her * on top of the Job 39:14
a farmer gathers *, and no one can Is 10:14
nest and lay her * and hatch her Is 34:15
EGLAH
and Ithream was born to *. 2Sa 3:5
Ithream, the son of his wife *. 1Ch 3:3
EGLATH
His people flee to Zoar and *. Is 15:5
EGLATH-SHELISHIYAH
from Zoar to Horonaim and to *. Jer 48:34
EGLON
King Debir of *. Jos 10:3
Hebron, Jarmuth, Lachish, and *. Jos 10:22,23
The Israeli army then captured * Jos 10:34,35
After leaving * they went to Jos 10:36
The king of *; Jos 12:8-24
Lachish, Bozkath, *, Cabbon, Jos 15:37-44
so God helped King * of Moab to Ju 3:12
to pay crushing taxes to King *. Ju 3:14
* (who, by the way, was very fat! Ju 3:17,18,19
King * stood up at once to receive Ju 3:20
EGYPT
Abram went on down to * to live. Gen 12:10
the borders of *, he asked Sarai Gen 12:11,12,13
in * everyone spoke of her beauty. Gen 12:14
SO THEY LEFT * and traveled north Gen 13:1
countryside around Zoar in *. Gen 13:10
Literally, "River of *," at the Gen 15:18f
for him with a girl from *. Gen 21:20,21
and told him, "Don't go to *. Gen 26:2
and herbs from Gilead to *. Gen 37:25
and they took him along to *. Gen 37:28
Meanwhile, in *, the traders sold Gen 37:36
of the Pharaoh—the king of *. Gen 37:36
WHEN JOSEPH ARRIVED in * as a Gen 39:1
staff of Pharaoh, the king of *. Gen 39:1
that the king of * became angry Gen 40:1
and sages of * and told them about Gen 41:8
specimens in all the land of *. Gen 41:19
going to do here in the land of *. Gen 41:25
throughout all the land of *; Gen 41:29
the wisest man in * and put him in Gen 41:33
Let Pharaoh divide * into five Gen 41:34,35
throughout all the land of *. Gen 41:40
in charge of all the land of *." Gen 41:41,42
"I, the king of *, swear that you Gen 41:44
charge over all the land of *." Gen 41:44
famous throughout the land of *. Gen 41:45
*, storing them in nearby cities. Gen 41:48
too, but in * there was plenty of Gen 41:54
to * to buy grain from Joseph. Gen 41:56,57
grain available in * he said to his Gen 42:1
there is grain available in *. Gen 42:2
brothers went down to * to buy Gen 42:3
sons arrived in * along with many Gen 42:5
governor of all *, and in charge of Gen 42:6
not going to leave * until this Gen 42:15
had brought from * was almost gone, Gen 43:2
to *, and stood before Joseph. Gen 43:15
our first trip to * to buy food, Gen 43:20
your brother whom you sold into *! Gen 45:4
ruler of all the land of *. Gen 45:8
me chief of all the land of *. Gen 45:9
in *, and how everyone obeys me. Gen 45:13
and come here to * to live. Gen 45:18
best territory in the land of *. Gen 45:18
take wagons from * to carry their Gen 45:19
of all the land of * is yours." Gen 45:20
the good things of *, and ten Gen 45:23
is ruler over all the land of *!" Gen 45:26
Don't be afraid to go down to *, Gen 46:3,4
down with you into * and I will Gen 46:3,4
but you shall die in * with Gen 46:3,4
brought him to *, along with their Gen 46:5
and came to *—Jacob and all his Gen 46:6
who went with him into *: Gen 46:8-14
Canaan, before Israel went to *). Gen 46:8-14
in the land of *, were Manasseh and Gen 46:19-22
of those going to *, of his own Gen 46:26
there in * totaled seventy. Gen 46:27
and hated in other parts of *. Gen 46:34
We have come to live here in *, Gen 47:4
Give them the best land of *. Gen 47:5,6
the best land of *—the land of Gen 47:11
of * and Canaan were starving. Gen 47:13
all the money in * and Canaan in Gen 47:14
of * were in Pharaoh's possession. Gen 47:17
all the land of * for Pharaoh; Gen 47:20
Thus all the people of * became Gen 47:21
the land of *—and it is still the Gen 47:26
land of Goshen in *, and soon the Gen 47:27
last request: do not bury me in *. Gen 47:29
take me out of * and bury me beside Gen 47:30
in the land of * before I arrived, Gen 48:5
whom God has given me here in *." Gen 48:9
Then Joseph returned to * with Gen 50:14
families continued to live in *. Gen 50:22
of this land of * and take you back Gen 50:24
body was placed in a coffin in *. Gen 50:26
accompanied him to *, with their Ex 1:1
throne of * who felt no obligation Ex 1:8

EGYPT Con't)
Then Pharaoh, the king of *, Ex 1:15,16
Several years later the king of * Ex 2:23
of my people in *, and have heard Ex 3:7
take them out of * into a good Ex 3:8
let you lead my people out of *." Ex 3:10
the people out of *, you shall Ex 3:12
is happening to them there in *. Ex 3:16
you to the king of * and tell him, Ex 3:18
"But I know that the king of * Ex 3:19
I will destroy * with my Ex 3:20
daughters with the best of *!" Ex 3:22
back to * and visit my relatives. Ex 4:18
to return to *, for all those who Ex 4:19
to the land of *, holding tightly Ex 4:20
you arrive back in * you are to go Ex 4:21
So Moses and Aaron returned to * Ex 4:29
Pharaoh, king of *, demanding that Ex 6:13
out of the land of *," and who Ex 6:26
of Israel be allowed to leave *. Ex 7:2
my miracles in the land of *. Ex 7:3
so I will crush * with a final Ex 7:4
magicians of *—and they were able Ex 7:11
the waters of *: all its rivers, Ex 7:19
blood throughout the land of *. Ex 7:21
But then the magicians of * used Ex 7:22
Every home in * will be filled Ex 8:3,4
and pools of *, so that there will Ex 8:5
throughout all the land of *." Ex 8:16
send swarms of flies throughout *. Ex 8:21
palace and in every home in *. Ex 8:24
will affect only the cattle of *; Ex 9:4
all the land of * and cause boils Ex 9:9
animals alike throughout all *. Ex 9:10
never been since * was founded! Ex 9:18
throughout all *, upon the people, Ex 9:22
Never in all the history of * had Ex 9:24
like that. All * lay in ruins. Ex 9:25
The only spot in all * without Ex 9:26
incredible things I am doing in *! Ex 10:2
and all the houses of * Ex 10:6
Never in the history of * has Ex 10:6
even yet that all * lies in ruins? Ex 10:7
over the land of * to bring Ex 10:12
land of * from border to border; Ex 10:14
throughout all the land of *. Ex 10:15
one locust in all the land of *! Ex 10:19
will descend upon the land of *." Ex 10:21
man in the land of * and was Ex 11:3
midnight I will pass through *. Ex 11:4
in every family in *, from the Ex 11:5
throughout the entire land of *; Ex 11:6
the land of * tonight and kill all Ex 12:12
in all the land of *, and execute Ex 12:12
the gods of *—for I am Jehovah. Ex 12:12
when I smite the land of *. Ex 12:13
brought you out of the land of *; Ex 12:17
in the land of *, from Pharaoh's Ex 12:29
people of * got up in the night; Ex 12:30
all the land of *, for there was Ex 12:30
were pushed out of * and didn't Ex 12:39
had lived in * 430 years, and it Ex 12:40,41
his people out from the land of *; Ex 12:42
from the land of *, wave after wave Ex 12:51
from the land of *, all of the Ex 12:51f
day of leaving * and your slavery; Ex 13:3
Lord did for you when you left *. Ex 13:8
us out of * from our slavery. Ex 13:14
of *, both of men and animals; Ex 13:15
us out of * with great power." Ex 13:16
route from * to the Promised Land. Ex 13:17,18
even though they had left * armed; Ex 13:17,18
he thought they might return to * Ex 13:17,18
out of *—as he was sure God would. Ex 13:19
When word reached the king of * Ex 14:5
to return to * after three days, Ex 14:5
much of the wealth of * with them. Ex 14:8
not enough graves for us in *? Ex 14:11
Why did you make us leave *? Ex 14:11
And all * shall know that I am Ex 14:18
the second month after leaving *. Ex 16:1
"Oh, that we were back in *," Ex 16:3
brought you out of the land of *. Ex 16:6
when he brought them from *. Ex 16:32
did you ever take us out of *? Ex 17:3
Lord had brought them out of *. Ex 18:1
about his bringing them out of *. Ex 18:9
night of their departure from *. Ex 19:1
you from your slavery in *. Ex 20:2
were foreigners in the land of *. Ex 22:21
own experience in the land of *. Ex 23:9
in March, the month you left *; Ex 23:15
I brought them out of * so that I Ex 29:46
us here from * has disappeared; Ex 32:1
god that brought you out of *!" Ex 32:4
you brought from * have defiled Ex 32:7
that brought you out of *.' Ex 32:8
from the land of * with such great Ex 32:11
fellow Moses who led us out of *.' Ex 32:23
you brought from * to the land I Ex 33:1
that was the month you left *. Ex 34:18
of the land of * to be your God. Lev 11:45
the people of * where you lived so Lev 18:3
were foreigners in the land of *. Lev 19:34
brought you from the land of *. Lev 19:35,36
you from * to be my own people! Lev 22:32,33
I rescued you from *, and caused Lev 23:43
out of the land of * to give you Lev 25:38
of *, and you are my servants; Lev 25:42
I brought them from the land of * Lev 25:55
out of the land of *, with the Lev 26:13
forefathers out of * as all the Lev 26:45
the Israelis left * that the Lord Num 1:1
the second year after leaving *: Num 9:1
second year of Israel's leaving *; Num 10:11
to long for the good things of *. Num 11:4,5
enjoyed so much in *, and the Num 11:4,5
you left behind in *, and he is Num 11:18
you, and you have wept for *.' Num 11:19,20
who had lusted for meat and for *. Num 11:34
in *). Then they came to what is Num 13:22
"We wish we had died in *," they Num 14:2
get out of here and return to *!" Num 14:3
a leader to take us back to *!" Num 14:4
from when we left * until now." Num 14:19
I did both in * and in the Num 14:22
brought you out of the land of *; Num 15:41
us out of lovely * to kill us here Num 16:13
Why did you ever make us leave * Num 20:5
went down to visit * and stayed Num 20:15
brought us out of *, and now we are Num 20:16
* to die here in the wilderness?" Num 21:5
has arrived from *, and they cover Num 22:5,6
of people from * has arrived at his Num 22:11
God has brought them out of *. Num 23:18-24
God has brought them from *. Num 24:3-9
While Levi was in *, a daughter, Num 26:58,59
in *, leaving them unharmed Num 28:16
had rescued from *, no one over Num 32:10,11
Moses and Aaron led them out of *. Num 33:1
They left the city of Rameses, * Num 33:3,4
all the gods of * that night! Num 33:3,4
the people of Israel had left *. Num 33:38,39
Literally, "the brook of *." Num 34:5f
us here from * to be slaughtered by Deu 1:27
just as you saw him do in *. Deu 1:30
you from prison—*—to be his special Deu 4:20
in *, right before your very eyes. Deu 4:34
* with a great display of power. Deu 4:37
when they left *, and as they were Deu 4:44,45,46
who rescued you from slavery in *. Deu 5:6
you were slaves in *, and the Lord Deu 5:15
land of *, the land of slavery. Deu 6:10,11,12
slaves in *, and the Lord brought Deu 6:21
brought us out of * with great Deu 6:21
* and Pharaoh and all his people. Deu 6:22
He brought us out of * so that Deu 6:23
out of slavery in * with such Deu 7:8
of * you remember so well; Deu 7:15
Pharaoh and to all the land of *. Deu 7:18
he used to bring you out of *? Deu 7:19
of your slavery in the land of *. Deu 8:14
from the day you left * until now? Deu 9:7
I had led out of * had defiled Deu 9:12
saved from * by your mighty power Deu 9:26
you brought from * by your great Deu 9:29
were foreigners in the land of *. Deu 10:19
went down into * there were only Deu 10:22
miracles he did in * against Deu 11:3
to the armies of * and to their Deu 11:4
like the land of * where you have Deu 11:10
out of slavery in the land of *. Deu 13:5
land of *, the place of slavery. Deu 13:10
in the land of * and the Lord your Deu 15:15
God brought you out of * by night. Deu 16:1
you ate as you escaped from *. Deu 16:3
you that you left * in such a hurry Deu 16:3
Literally, "For you left * in Deu 16:3f
You were a slave in *, so be sure Deu 16:12
send his men to * to raise horses Deu 17:16
you, 'Never return to * again.' Deu 17:16
who brought you safely out of *! Deu 20:1
and water when you came out of *; Deu 23:4
came with you from * may enter the Deu 23:8
Miriam as you were coming from *. Deu 24:9
you were slaves in *, and that the Deu 24:18
in the land of *—that is why I am Deu 24:22
did to you as you came from *. Deu 25:17
Arameans who went to * for refuge. Deu 26:5
They were few in number, but in * Deu 26:5
brought us out of * with mighty Deu 26:8
the diseases of * which you feared Deu 28:60
send you back to * in ships, a Deu 28:68
and his people in the land of *. Deu 29:2,3
in the land of *, and how as we Deu 29:16
brought them out of the land of *. Deu 29:25
entire court in *, and before the Deu 34:11,12
Red Sea for you when you left *! Jos 2:10
when Israel left * all of the men Jos 5:4,5
arms when they left * were dead; Jos 5:6
Literally, "the shame of *." Jos 5:8,9f
all that he did in *, and what you Jos 9:9
from the brook of * to the southern Jos 13:2-7
the Brook of *, and along that to Jos 15:2,3,4
villages as far as the Brook of *; Jos 15:47
of the Brook of * on the south, to Jos 15:47
and his children went into *. Jos 24:4
to bring terrible plagues upon *; Jos 24:5
the Euphrates River and in *. Jos 24:14
their slavery in the land of *. Jos 24:17
when they left *, were buried in Jos 24:32
brought you out of * into this land Ju 2:1
God who had brought them out of *. Ju 2:12-14
out of slavery in *, and rescued Ju 6:8
as when God brought them out of *? Ju 6:13
Israel from * (much on Gideon's Ju 6:16f
when the Israelis came from *; Ju 11:13
their journey from * after crossing Ju 11:16
Israel left *," everyone said. Ju 19:30
people of Israel were slaves in *? 1Sa 2:27
Ever since I brought them from * 1Sa 8:8
brought you from * and rescued you 1Sa 10:18,19
ancestors out of the land of *. 1Sa 12:6
"When the Israelites were in * 1Sa 12:8
territory when Israel came from *. 1Sa 15:2
of the land of *," he explained. 1Sa 15:6
all the way to Shur, east of *. 1Sa 15:7
to * ever since ancient times. 1Sa 27:8
time I brought Israel out of *. 2Sa 7:6
to destroy * and its gods. 2Sa 7:23
the king of *, and married one of 1Ki 3:1
and down to the borders of *. 1Ki 4:21
of the East, including those in *. 1Ki 4:30
of Israel left their slavery in *. 1Ki 6:1
of Israel after they left *. 1Ki 8:9
my people from *, I didn't appoint 1Ki 8:16
them out of the land of *." 1Ki 8:21
out of the land of *, you told your 1Ki 8:53
brought them out of the land of *; 1Ki 9:9
Gezer was the city the king of * 1Ki 9:16
to him from * and southern Turkey, 1Ki 10:28
who took him to * (he was a very 1Ki 11:16,17,18
them to *, and Pharaoh had given 1Ki 11:16,17,18
When Hadad, there in *, heard 1Ki 11:21
to King Shishak of * and stayed 1Ki 11:40
Jeroboam, who was still in * 1Ki 12:2,3,4
return from *, he was asked to come 1Ki 12:20
you from your captivity in *!" 1Ki 12:28
King Shishak of * attacked and 1Ki 14:25
asking King So of * to help him 2Ki 17:4
safely out of their slavery in *. 2Ki 17:7
out of the land of * with such 2Ki 17:35,36
will give you more than words? *? 2Ki 18:20,21
If you lean on *, you will find 2Ki 18:20,21
Even if * supplies you with 2Ki 18:24
of * just by walking by!" 2Ki 19:24
brought their ancestors from *." 2Ki 21:15
In those days King Neco of * 2Ki 23:29
Then he took King Jehoahaz to *, 2Ki 23:34
area claimed by *—all of Judah from 2Ki 24:7
Brook of * to the Euphrates River. 2Ki 24:7
fled in panic to *, for they were 2Ki 25:26
of *—to the entrance of Hamath." 1Ch 13:5f
time I brought Israel out of *. 1Ch 17:5
redeemed it from * so that the 1Ch 17:21
Solomon sent horse-traders to * 2Ch 1:16
of Israel as they were leaving *. 2Ch 5:10
from the land of *, chosen a city 2Ch 6:5,6
to the brook of * at the other. 2Ch 7:8
out of the land of *, and they 2Ch 7:22
as far away as the border of *. 2Ch 9:26
to him from * and other countries. 2Ch 9:28
He was in * at the time, where he 2Ch 10:2,3
As a result, King Shishak of * 2Ch 12:2
So King Shishak of * conquered 2Ch 12:9
when Israel left *, so we went 2Ch 20:10
to *, for he was very powerful. 2Ch 26:8
Afterwards King Neco of * led 2Ch 35:20
by the king of *, who demanded an 2Ch 36:3
The king of * now appointed 2Ch 36:4
Jehoahaz was taken to * as a 2Ch 36:4
our ancestors in *, and you heard Neh 9:9
take them back into slavery in *! Neh 9:17
He brought us out of *!' Neh 9:18
delight in war. * will send gifts Ps 68:31
them, and for their fathers in *. Ps 78:11,12
the frogs had covered all of *! Ps 78:45
You brought us from * as though Ps 80:8
of his war against * where we were Ps 81:5
brought you out of the land of *. Ps 81:10
the names of * and Babylonia, Ps 87:4
You have cut haughty * Ps 89:10
as a slave to * to save his people Ps 105:17
Then Jacob (Israel) arrived in * Ps 105:23
of terror upon the land of *. Ps 105:27
from one end of * to the other. Ps 105:31
*, loaded with silver and gold; Ps 105:37
among them then. * was glad when Ps 105:38
your miracles in *, and soon forgot Ps 106:7
miracles in * and at the Sea. Ps 106:21,22
escaped from *, from that land of Ps 114:1
He did great miracles in * Ps 135:9
the firstborn of *, for his Ps 136:10

(EGYPT Con't)
imported from *, perfumed with Pro 7:16,17
whistle for the army of Upper *, Is 7:18
of the streams of *" refers to Is 7:18f
refers to Upper * where the Is 7:18f
Upper and Lower *, Ethiopia, Elam, Is 11:11
Literally, "the Sea of *." Is 11:15f
ago when they returned from *. Is 11:16
THIS IS GOD'S message concerning * Is 19:1
Look, the Lord is coming against * Is 19:1
the idols of * tremble; Is 19:1
I will hand over * to a hard, Is 19:4
of * is utterly stupid and wrong. Is 19:11
what the Lord is going to do to *. Is 19:12
* with their foolish counsel. Is 19:13
they make * stagger like a sick Is 19:14
a sick drunkard. * cannot be saved Is 19:15
of the cities of * will follow the Is 19:18
in the heart of * in those days, Is 19:19
The Lord will smite * and then Is 19:22
In that day * and Iraq Is 19:23
For the Lord will bless * and Is 19:25
He will say, "Blessed be *, my Is 19:25
I will bring upon * and Ethiopia. Is 20:3
uncovered, to the shame of *. Is 20:4
and their "glorious ally," *! Is 20:5,6
to *, what chance have we?" Is 20:5,6
ocean, from * and along the Nile. Is 23:2,3
When * hears the news, there Is 23:5
Assyria and *, will be rescued and Is 27:13
have gone down to * to find aid and Is 30:2
terrible desert to *—donkeys and Is 30:6
* will give you nothing in return! Is 30:6
of mine concerning *, so that it Is 30:8
"We will get our help from *; Is 30:16
WOE TO THOSE who run to * for Is 31:1
that the king of * will help you. Is 36:4
me! * is a dangerous ally. Is 36:6
For you'll get no help from *. Is 36:8,9
land, and * with all its armies is Is 37:25
I gave * and Ethiopia and Seba Is 43:3
the mighty army of * with all its Is 43:17
slew *, the dragon of the Nile. Is 51:9
without cause by * and Assyria, and Is 52:4
his people out of * and they cried Is 63:11
them safely out of * and led them Jer 2:6
I see the armies of * rising Jer 2:16
alliances with * and with Assyria? Jer 2:18
new friends in * will forsake you Jer 2:36
who fled to * continued to worship Jer 7:18f
found at Hermopolis in *, Jer 7:18f
fathers when I led them out of *. Jer 7:22
your fathers left * until now, I Jer 7:25
out of slavery in * that if they Jer 11:4
them out of *—and have kept on Jer 11:7
brought you out from slavery in *. Jer 16:14,15
*. Jer 22:12f
they took back to * with them. Jer 22:13f
from the land of *," but they Jer 23:7
those too who live in *. Jer 24:8
I went to *, and Pharaoh and his Jer 25:19,20
heard about it and fled to *. Jer 26:21
(son of Achbor) to * along with Jer 26:22
who escaped from *, to whom I Jer 31:2
out of the land of *—a contract Jer 31:32
in the land of *—things still Jer 32:20
"You brought Israel out of * Jer 32:21
them from their slavery in *. Jer 34:13
Pharaoh Hophra of * appeared at the Jer 37:5
is about to return in flight to *! Jer 37:7
to prepare to leave for *. Jer 41:16,17
insist on going to * where you Jer 42:13,14
insist on going to *, the war and Jer 42:15
who insists on going to live in *. Jer 42:17
out on you when you enter *. Jer 42:18
of Judah, do not go to *!" Jer 42:19
in *, where you insist on going." Jer 42:22
you to tell us not to go to *! Jer 43:2,3
started off for * with Johanan and Jer 43:5
And so they arrived in * at the Jer 43:7
here to *, for he is my servant. Jer 43:10
the land of *, killing all those I Jer 43:11
of the gods of * and burn the idols Jer 43:12
the land of * as a shepherd picks Jer 43:12
the temples of the gods of *." Jer 43:13
in the north of * in the cities of Jer 44:1
and throughout southern * as well: Jer 44:1
worshiped here in *, burning Jer 44:8
here to * and I will consume them. Jer 44:12
They shall fall here in *, killed Jer 44:12
I will punish them in * just as Jer 44:13
in southern *) answered Jeremiah: Jer 44:15
of Judah who are here in *! Jer 44:24
in the land of *: I have sworn by Jer 44:26
on living in *—shall find out who Jer 44:28
Hophra, or Apries, ruled * from Jer 44:30f
king of *, over to those Jer 44:30
This message was given against * Jer 46:2
Necho, king of *, and his army were Jer 46:2
chariots and mighty soldiers of *! Jer 46:9
medicine, O virgin daughter of *! Jer 46:11
king of Babylon, to attack *: Jer 46:13
Shout it out in *; Jer 46:14
is coming against * who is as tall Jer 46:18
you citizens of *, for the city of Jer 46:19
a soul alive. * is sleek as a Jer 46:20,21
for *, a time of great punishment. Jer 46:20,21
a serpent gliding away, * flees; Jer 46:22,23
of its trees. * is as helpless as Jer 46:24
and all the other gods of *. Jer 46:25
The reference is to * and Israel's Lam 1:2f
The reference is probably to *. Lam 1:19f
The reference is probably to *. Lam 4:17f
We beg for bread from *, and Lam 5:6
And you added lustful * to your Eze 16:26
ambassadors to * to seek for a Eze 17:15
and brought him in chains to *. Eze 19:4
myself to her in *, I swore to her Eze 20:5,6
bring them out of * to a land I had Eze 20:5,6
idols, nor forsake the gods of *. Eze 20:8
them while they are still in *. Eze 20:8
So I brought my people out of * Eze 20:9,10
bring them out of * would say that Eze 20:14
power in bringing them out of *. Eze 20:22
after I brought you out of *. Eze 20:35,36
girls became prostitutes in *. Eze 23:2,3
For when she left *, she did not Eze 23:8
in Judah looked to * for help Eze 23:17f
when she was a prostitute in *. Eze 23:19,20
your virginity to those from *. Eze 23:21
brought from the land of *; Eze 23:27
you will no more long for * and Eze 23:27
"Son of dust, face toward * and Eze 29:2
Pharaoh, king of *—mighty dragon Eze 29:3
*, and destroy both men and herds. Eze 29:8
The land of * shall become a Eze 29:9
the land of *, from Migdol to Eze 29:10
I will make * desolate, Eze 29:12
the fortunes of * and bring her Eze 29:14
in southern * where they were born, Eze 29:14
never again will * be great Eze 29:15
no longer expect any help from *. Eze 29:16
Lord was giving * to him to make up Eze 29:18f
give the land of * to Eze 29:19
him the land of * for his salary, Eze 29:20
Lord was giving * to him to make up Eze 29:20f
and * shall know I am the Lord." Eze 29:21
A sword shall fall on *; Eze 30:4
when I have set * on fire and Eze 30:8
will destroy the multitudes of *. Eze 30:10
They shall war against * and Eze 30:11
I will destroy * and everything Eze 30:12
And I will smash the idols of * Eze 30:13
and there will be no king in *; Eze 30:13
fortress of *, and I will stamp out Eze 30:15
Yes, I will set fire to *, Eze 30:16
break the power of * it will be a Eze 30:18
And so I will greatly punish * Eze 30:19
of Pharaoh, king of *, and it has Eze 30:21
Pharaoh, king of *, and I will Eze 30:22
Pharaoh, king of *, and he shall Eze 30:24
*, Egypt shall know I am the Lord. Eze 30:25
Egypt, * shall know I am the Lord. Eze 30:25
Pharaoh, king of *, and all his Eze 31:2,3
"But * Eze 31:10
"O *, you are great and glorious Eze 31:18
Pharaoh, king of *, and say to him: Eze 32:2
It will smash the pride of * and Eze 32:12
Therefore the waters of * will Eze 32:14
And when I destroy * and wipe Eze 32:15
Yes, cry for the sorrows of *. Eze 32:16
for the people of * and for the Eze 32:18
is as beautiful as you, O *? Eze 32:19
is drawn against the land of *. Eze 32:20
of the Brook of * (Wadi el-Arish) Eze 47:19
the Brook of * (Wadi el-Arish) to Eze 48:27,28
were Ptolemy I of *, Seleucus of Dan 8:8f
* in a great display of power. Dan 9:15
One of them, the king of *, Dan 11:5
Seleucid wars between * and Syria. Dan 11:6f
and the king of *. Dan 11:6
The daughter of the king of * Dan 11:6
Ptolemy II of * gave his daughter Dan 11:6f
the king of *, and of her Dan 11:6
takes over as king of *, he will Dan 11:7
When he returns again to * he Dan 11:8
will invade * briefly, but will Dan 11:9
into *, to a fortress there. Dan 11:10,11
Then the king of *, Dan 11:10,11
join him in a crusade against *. Dan 11:14
fortified city of * and capture it, Dan 11:15
of * will go down to defeat. Dan 11:15
for conquering all *: he too will Dan 11:17
and raise a great army against *; Dan 11:25
against Egypt; and *, too, will Dan 11:25
will escape, but * and many other Dan 11:42
the treasures of *, and the Libyans Dan 11:43
had freed her from captivity in *. Hos 1:15
calling to *, flying to Assyria. Hos 7:11
And all * will laugh at them. Hos 7:16
they shall return to *. Hos 8:13
you will be carried off to * and Hos 9:3
possessions left behind? * will! Hos 9:6
as a son and brought him out of *. Hos 11:1
But my people shall return to * Hos 11:5
*—like doves flying from Assyria. Hos 11:11
For she has given gifts to * and Hos 12:1
from slavery in *, and I am the one Hos 12:9
his people out of * by a prophet, Hos 12:13
since I brought you out from *. Hos 13:4
Acacia Valley. * will be Joe 3:19
must go back to * as slaves, for Amo 1:5f
And I brought you out from * and Amo 2:10
entire family I brought from *: Amo 3:1
plagues like those of * long ago. Amo 4:10
It rises like the river Nile in * Amo 9:5
brought you out of *, done as much Amo 9:7
For I brought you out of *, and Mic 6:4
Assyria to *, and from Egypt to the Mic 7:12
to Egypt, and from * to the Mic 7:12
I brought you out of slavery in *. Mic 7:15
Ethiopia and the whole land of * Nah 3:9
'For I promised when you left * Hag 2:5
I will bring them back from * Zec 10:10
Or, "the Sea of *," referring to Zec 10:11f
and * over my people will end." Zec 10:11
But if * refuses to come, God Zec 14:18
And so * and the other nations Zec 14:19
"Get up and flee to * with the Mt 2:13
night he left for * with Mary and Mt 2:14
"I have called my Son from *." Mt 2:15
dream to Joseph in *, and told him, Mt 2:19
Phrygia, Pamphylia, *, the Act 2:10
Alexandria in *, and the Turkish Act 6:9
and sold him to be a slave in *. Act 7:9
favor before Pharaoh, king of *. Act 7:10
governor over all *, as well as Act 7:10
"But a famine developed in * and Act 7:11
grain in *, so he sent his sons Act 7:12
to *, seventy-five persons in all. Act 7:14
So Jacob came to *, where he Act 7:15
people greatly multiplied in *; Act 7:17,18
in * and have heard their cries. Act 7:34
Come, I will send you to *.' Act 7:34
he led them out of * and through Act 7:36
Moses and wanted to return to *. Act 7:39
Moses, who brought us out of *.' Act 7:40
honored them in * by gloriously Act 13:17
in Ephesus from Alexandria in *. Act 18:24
While he was in *, someone had Act 18:25,26
Pharaoh, king of *, was an Rom 9:17
him the kingdom of * for the very Rom 9:17
out of * with Moses their leader. Heb 3:16
to lead them out of the land of *; Heb 8:9
the people of Israel out of *; Heb 11:22
the treasures of *, for he was Heb 11:26
left the land of * and wasn't Heb 11:27
out of the land of *, and then Jud 1:5
as "Sodom" or "*")—the very Rev 11:8,9

EGYPT'S
by the pick of * chariot corps—600 Ex 14:7
with treasure to pay for * aid. Is 30:6
For * promises are worthless! Is 30:7
Your sails are made of * finest Eze 27:7
"For the Lord says: All * allies Eze 30:6
them at that time of * doom. Eze 30:9

EGYPTIAN
So Sarai took her maid, an * girl Gen 16:1
and the * girl Hagar—teasing Gen 21:9
and Hagar the *, Sarah's slave Gen 25:12-15
northeast of the * border in the Gen 25:18
(meaning "* Mourners") for they Gen 50:11
They are not slow like the * Ex 1:19
During his visit he saw an * Ex 2:11
* and hid his body in the sand. Ex 2:12
me as you did that * yesterday?" Ex 2:14
"An * defended us against the Ex 2:19
her * master's wife and neighbors. Ex 3:22
and to all the * people, and prove Ex 9:14
locust plague in all * history; Ex 10:14
to ask their * neighbors for costly Ex 11:2
officials and the * people alike. Ex 11:3
chariots driven by * officers. Ex 14:7
and the * army overtook the Ex 14:9
As the * army approached, the Ex 14:10
The famous * captains are dead Ex 15:4
father was an *, got into a fight Lev 24:10
During the fight the * man's son Lev 24:11
"He will send upon you * boils, Deu 28:27
Along the way they found an * 1Sa 30:11,12
"I am an *—the servant of an 1Sa 30:13
he killed an * warrior who was 2Sa 23:21
brought out from the * furnace. 1Ki 8:51
prices. An * chariot delivered to 1Ki 10:29
girls besides the * princess. 1Ki 11:1
* Pharaoh is totally unreliable! 2Ki 18:20,21
Or, "on the steps of Ahaz." * 2Ki 20:11f
$230,000. The * king then chose 2Ki 23:34
(The * Pharaoh never returned 2Ki 24:7
the wife of Jarha, his * servant. 1Ch 2:34,35
Mered married Bithi-ah, an * 1Ch 4:17
Once he killed an * who was 1Ch 11:23
At that time * chariots sold for 2Ch 1:17

EGYPTIAN Con't)
in each * family—he who was the Ps 78:51
child in each * home, their pride Ps 105:36
child in each * home, along with Ps 135:8
drowned the * armies in the sea. Is 10:26
25th * Dynasty (730–660 B.C.). Is 18:1f
Euphrates River to the * boundary. Is 27:12
with Ethiopia's * dynasty against Is 30:2f
over the * army at Carchemish. Jer 36:1f
But look! The * army flees in Jer 46:5
It is the * army, boasting that Jer 46:8
by the * army. Jer 47:1
with the * gods, for I am the Lord Eze 20:7
long enough to defeat the * force. Eze 30:21f
now ascended the * throne and Dan 11:7f
alliance with the * king, giving Dan 11:17
Call together the Assyrian and * Amo 3:9
During this visit he saw an * Act 7:24
So Moses killed the *. Act 7:24
as you killed that * yesterday?' Act 7:28
"Aren't you that * who led a Act 21:37,38
There our officer found an * Act 27:6

EGYPTIAN'S
he wrenched the spear from the * 2Sa 23:21

EGYPTIANS
"and when the * see you they will Gen 12:11,12,13
sister, then the * will treat me Gen 12:11,12,13
sold grain to the * and to those Gen 41:56,57
table, and the * at still another; Gen 43:32
still another; for * despise Gen 43:32
all the * sold him their fields Gen 47:20
very deep mourning by these *." Gen 50:11
So the * made slaves of them and Ex 1:11
But the more the * mistreated Ex 1:12
to multiply! The * became alarmed, Ex 1:12
them from the * and to take them Ex 3:8
the * have oppressed them with. Ex 3:9
And I will see to it that the * Ex 3:21
the *, and I remember my promise. Ex 6:5
who has rescued them from the *. Ex 6:7
people out. The * will find out Ex 7:5
* will be unwilling to drink it." Ex 7:18
foul that the * couldn't drink it; Ex 7:21
Then the * dug wells along the Ex 7:24
covering the * and their animals. Ex 8:17
are hated by the *, and if we do Ex 8:26
the cattle of the * began dying, Ex 9:6
Some of the *, terrified by this Ex 9:20
I made of the *, and how I proved Ex 10:2
(For God caused the * to be very Ex 11:3
between * and Israelis.' Ex 11:7
through the land and kill the *; Ex 12:23
of Israel, though he killed the *; Ex 12:27
And the * were urgent upon the Ex 12:33
said and asked the * for silver and Ex 12:35
favor with the *, so that they gave Ex 12:36
And the * were practically Ex 12:36
* shall know that I am the Lord." Ex 14:4
* than dead in the wilderness." Ex 14:12
you today. The * you are looking Ex 14:13
the hearts of the * and they will Ex 14:17
the people of Israel and the *. Ex 14:20
darkness to the * but light to the Ex 14:20
So the * couldn't find the Ex 14:20
Then the * followed them between Ex 14:23
the *, and began to harass them. Ex 14:24
"Let's get out of here," the * Ex 14:25
come back over the * and their Ex 14:26
morning light. The * tried to flee, Ex 14:27
saved Israel that day from the *; Ex 14:30
* dead, washed up on the seashore. Ex 14:30
them against the *, they were Ex 14:31
I send on the *, for I am the Lord Ex 15:26
to Pharaoh and the * in order to Ex 18:8
saved you from the * and from Ex 18:10
from the proud and cruel *." Ex 18:11
what I did to the *, and how I Ex 19:4
Do you want the * to say, 'God Ex 32:12
oldest sons of the *, I took for Num 3:13
I killed all the firstborn *. Num 8:17
Then the * who had come with them Num 11:4,5
"But what will the * think when Num 14:13
long, and became slaves of the *. Num 20:15
along by the * who were burying all Num 33:3,4
For if you destroy them the * Deu 9:28
down on the Edomites and the * Deu 23:7
and you lived among the *. Deu 23:7
The grandchildren of the * who Deu 23:8
nation. The * mistreated us and we Deu 26:6,7
before the *, and has brought us Deu 26:8
the Red Sea, the * chased after Jos 24:6
darkness between them and the *; Jos 24:7
in upon the *, drowning them. Jos 24:7
you from the * and from all who Ju 6:9
save you from the *, the Amorites, Ju 10:11
who destroyed the * with plagues 1Sa 4:8
as Pharaoh and the * were. 1Sa 6:6
you from the * and from all of the 1Sa 10:18,19
* to attack us," they cried out. 2Ki 7:6
of infantrymen—*, Libyans, Sukkiim, 2Ch 12:3
Moabites, *, and Amorites. Ez 9:1
brutally the * were treating them; Neh 9:10
he sent upon the * in Tanis Ps 78:43
did not spare the *' lives, but Ps 78:50
At that point God turned the * Ps 105:25
you just as the * did long ago. Is 10:24
the hearts of the * melt with Is 19:1
In that day the * will be as weak Is 19:16
will make himself known to the *. Is 19:21
For the * will turn to the Lord Is 19:22
a highway, and the * and the Iraqi Is 19:23
will take away the * and Ethiopians Is 20:4
For these * are mere men, not Is 31:3
Jehovah says: The *, Ethiopians Is 45:14
not in spirit—the *, Edomites, Jer 9:25,26
He was chosen by the * to replace Jer 22:13f
from Jerusalem to fight the *. Jer 37:5
you have,' they'll say, 'those *. Jer 38:21,22
concerning foreign nations.The * Jer 46:1
Buckle on your armor, you * and Jer 46:3
my name, lest the * laugh at Eze 20:9,10
right before the *' eyes, and led Eze 20:9,10
youth, when the * poured out their Eze 23:8
wasteland, and the * will know that Eze 29:9
I will exile the * to other Eze 29:12
he will bring the * home again from Eze 29:13
And I will banish the * to many Eze 30:23
I will scatter the * among the Eze 30:26
you despise. The * will die with Eze 32:20
the wisdom of the *, and he became Act 7:22
homes, as he did among the *. Heb 11:28
But when the * chasing them tried Heb 11:29

EHI
*, Rosh, Muppim, Gen 46:19-22

EHUD
them a savior, * (son of Gera, a Ju 3:15
was left-handed. * was the man Ju 3:15
interview. * walked over to him as Ju 3:20
it, whereupon * reached beneath Ju 3:21
Leaving the dagger there, * Ju 3:22,23
Meanwhile * had escaped past the Ju 3:26
The next judge after * was Ju 3:31
Jeush, Benjamin, *, Chenaanah, 1Ch 7:10
The sons of *, chiefs of the 1Ch 8:6,7

EHUD'S
AFTER * DEATH the people of Israel Ju 4:1

EIGHT
was gone. * more weeks went by. Gen 8:14
"Laughter!"). * days after he Gen 21:4,5
Nahor, had borne him * sons. Gen 22:20-23
So, in all, there will be * Ex 26:25
were a total of * frames with Ex 36:30
four wagons and * oxen were given Num 7:8
you must sacrifice * young bulls, Num 29:29
They were under his rule for * Ju 3:8
He was Israel's judge for * Ju 12:14
He once killed * hundred men in 2Sa 23:8
reigned in Jerusalem for * years. 2Ki 8:17
and Ithamar's into * (for there was 1Ch 24:4
he reigned * years, in Jerusalem. 2Ch 21:5
* years, and died unmourned. 2Ch 21:20
court, which took * days to clean 2Ch 29:17
JOSIAH WAS ONLY * years old when 2Ch 34:1
Jehoiachin was * years old when 2Ch 36:9
to seven, yes, even to *." Ecc 11:2f
Meanwhile Ishmael escaped with * Jer 41:15
at the rate of * ounces at a time, Eze 4:10
was that it had * steps leading up Eze 40:31
but there were * steps instead of Eze 40:34
and there were * steps leading up Eze 40:37
So, in all, there were * tables, Eze 40:41
for a couple of dollars and * Hos 3:2
were only about * miles in Jon 3:3f
over us, * princes to lead us. Mic 5:5
When the baby was * days old, all Lk 1:59
* days later, at the baby's Lk 2:21
* days later he took Peter, Lk 9:28
* days later the disciples were Jn 20:26
when he was * days old. Act 7:8
and bedridden for * years. Act 9:33
* or ten days later he returned Act 25:6
when I was * days old, having been Php 3:5
Yet only * persons were saved 1Pe 3:20

EIGHTEEN
the ship, * inches below the roof; Gen 6:16
It is to be * inches square and Ex 30:2
the choicest of spices—* pounds Ex 30:22,23
It was * inches square and three Ex 37:25
For the next * years the Ju 3:14
dagger * inches long and hid it in Ju 3:16
This went on for * years. Ju 10:9
And that day they lost another * Ju 20:25
of them there. * thousand of the Ju 20:44
After his return he destroyed * 2Sa 8:13
feet high and * feet around, with 1Ki 7:15
then destroyed * thousand Edomites 1Ch 18:12
Meshelemiah's * sons and 1Ch 26:9
concubines (he had * wives and 2Ch 11:21
with * of his sons and brothers; Ez 8:18
feet high and * feet in Jer 52:21
was a low barrier * inches high and Eze 40:7-12
inches high and * inches wide. Eze 40:7-12
"And what about the * men who Lk 13:4
bent double for * years and was Lk 13:11
Satan has held her for * years?" Lk 13:16

EIGHTEEN-INCH
Or, an * pillar in front of (or Eze 40:7-12f

EIGHTEENTH
during the * year of Jeroboam's 1Ki 15:1
Israel during the * year of the 2Ki 3:1
In the * year of his reign, King 2Ki 22:3,4
This Passover was in the * year 2Ki 23:23
*, the group led by Happizzez; 1Ch 24:7-18
*, Hanani and twelve of his sons 1Ch 25:9-31
Jerusalem, in the * year of the 2Ch 13:1
During the * year of his reign, 2Ch 34:8
This all happened in the * year 2Ch 35:19
* year of Nebuchadnezzar's reign). Jer 32:1

EIGHTH
on the * day after birth. Gen 17:12
it to me on the * day, after Ex 22:30
ON THE * day (of the consecration Lev 9:1
On the * day, her son must be Lev 12:3
"The next day, the * day, he Lev 14:10
Tabernacle on the * day, for his Lev 14:23
On the * day he shall take two Lev 15:14
"On the * day, she shall take Lev 15:29
days, but from the * day onward it Lev 22:26,27
to the Lord. The * day requires Lev 23:36
of the * year are harvested!' Lev 25:21,22
The next day, the * day, he must Num 6:10
the * day with the same offerings. Num 7:54-59
"On the * day summon the people Num 29:35
* month" of the Hebrew calendar. 1Ki 12:32,33f
* year of Nebuchadnezzar's reign. 2Ki 24:12
Johanan was * in command; 1Ch 12:8-13
*, the group led by Ahijah; 1Ch 24:7-18
*, Jeshaiah and twelve of his 1Ch 25:9-31
Pe-ullethai (the *). 1Ch 26:4,5
The commander of the * Division 1Ch 27:11
on duty the * month of each year. 1Ch 27:11
service was held on the * day. 2Ch 7:9
April, and by the * day they had 2Ch 29:17
years old, in the * year of his 2Ch 34:3
feast, and on the * day there was a Neh 8:18
On the * day, and on each day Eze 43:27
that died is the * king, having Rev 17:11
The * with beryl; Rev 21:18,19,20

EIGHTY
Moses was * years old and Aaron Ex 7:7
was at peace for the next * years. Ju 3:30
He was very old now, about *, and 2Sa 19:31,32
I am * years old today, and life 2Sa 19:35
laborers, * thousand stonecutters 1Ki 5:15
the building with * of his men and 2Ki 10:24
in after him with * other priests, 2Ch 26:17,18
And some may even live to *. Ps 90:10
all queens, and * concubines, and Sol 6:8
had happened, * men approached Jer 41:5

EIGHTY-FIVE
and today I am * years old. Jos 14:10
and killed them, * priests in all, 1Sa 22:18
* priests and their families. Ps 52:1

EIGHTY-FOUR
been a widow for * years following Lk 2:36,37

EIGHTY-SEVEN
and so also * times throughout Eze 2:1f

EIGHTY-SIX
(Abram was * years old at this Gen 16:16

EIGHTY-THREE
old and Aaron * at this time of Ex 7:7

EJECTED
of Israel were * from the Lord's Jer 52:3

EKER
Maaz, Jamin, and *. 1Ch 2:27

EKRON
to the southern boundary of *; Jos 13:2-7
Ashkelon, Gath, *. Jos 13:2-7
the hill north of *, where it bent Jos 15:10,11
all the towns and villages of *. Jos 15:45
From * the boundary extended to Jos 15:46
Elon, Timnah, *, Eltekeh, Jos 19:41-46
Ashkelon, and *, with their Ju 1:18
So they sent the Ark to *, but 1Sa 5:10
when the people of * saw it coming 1Sa 5:10
they returned to * that same day. 1Sa 6:16
Gaza, Ashkelon, Gath, and *. 1Sa 6:17
The Israeli cities between * and 1Sa 7:14
as far as Gath and the gates of *. 1Sa 17:52
* to ask whether he would recover. 2Ki 1:2
the god of *, to ask whether the 2Ki 1:3
of Baal-zebub, the god of *. 2Ki 1:6
*, to ask about your sickness?" 2Ki 1:16
Ashkelon, Gaza, *, and what remains Jer 25:19,20
* and the king of Ashkelon; Amo 1:8
Gaza, Ashkelon, Ashdod, *—these Zep 2:4
in desperation and * will shake Zec 9:5
the Philistines of * will Zec 9:7

EL-ARISH
(Wadi *) to the Mediterranean. Eze 47:19
(Wadi *) to the Mediterranean. Eze 48:27,28

EL-ELOHE-ISRAEL
and called it "*," "The Altar to Gen 33:20

EL-KANAH
son of Asa, son of *, who lived in 1Ch 9:15,16
EL-PARAN
as * at the edge of the desert. Gen 14:5,6
ELA
Shime-i (son of *), whose area was 1Ki 4:8-19
ELABORATE
tied down by an * one-piece woven Ex 39:4,5
ELAH
clan of *,The clan of Pinon,The Gen 36:40-43
a buildup of forces at * Valley. 1Sa 17:2
were camped at the valley of *. 1Sa 17:19
you killed in the valley of *. 1Sa 21:9
*, Baasha's son, began reigning 1Ki 16:8
One day King * was half drunk at 1Ki 16:9
the sins of Baasha and his son *; 1Ki 16:13
Then Hoshea (the son of *) 2Ki 15:30
Father's name: * 2Ki 17:1
Hoshea (son of *), who had been the 2Ki 18:1
Oholibamah, Chief *, Chief Pinon, 1Ch 1:51-54
*, Naam. 1Ch 4:15
The sons of * included Kenaz. 1Ch 4:15
* (the son of Uzzi, the son of 1Ch 9:7,8
ELAH'S
The rest of the history of * 1Ki 16:14
ELAM
* Asshur,Arpachshad, Lud, Aram. Gen 10:22
Ched-or-laomer, king of *, and Gen 14:1
*, Asshur, 1Ch 1:17
*, Anthothijah, Iphdeiah, Penuel. 1Ch 8:22-25
* (the fifth), 1Ch 26:2,3
From the subclan of *, 1,254; Ez 2:3-35
From the subclan of *, 1,254; Ez 2:3-35
From the clan of *—Jeshaiah (son Ez 8:2-14
of the clan of *) said to me, "We Ez 10:2
From the clan of *: Ez 10:26
From the subclan of *, 1,254; Neh 7:8-38
From the subclan of *, 1,254; Neh 7:8-38
Parosh, Pahath-moab, *, Zattu, Neh 10:14-27
* and Ezer. Neh 12:42
Egypt, Ethiopia, *, Babylonia, Is 11:11
and all the kings of Zimri, * Jer 25:25
It shall be desolate forever.* Jer 49:33
God's message against * Jer 49:34
the army of *, and I will scatter Jer 49:35
the people of * to the four winds; Jer 49:36
great evil upon *, says the Lord, Jer 49:37
And I will set my throne in *, Jer 49:38
"Great kings of * lie there with Eze 32:24
in the province of *, standing Dan 8:2
ELAMITES
and destroyed. * and Medes will Is 21:2
mountainsides. * are the archers; Is 22:6,7
Here we are—Parthians, Medes, *, Act 2:9
ELASAH
Ishmael, Nethanel, Jozabad, *. Ez 10:22
He sent the letter with * (son Jer 29:3
ELATH
that goes south to * and Deu 2:8
built * and restored it to Judah. 2Ki 14:22
recovered the city of * for Syria; 2Ki 16:6
ELBOW
the table, leaning on the left *. Jn 13:23f
ELBOWS
sprinkled their arms to the *, Mk 7:3
ELDAAH
Epher, Hanoch, Abida, and *. Gen 25:4
Ephah, Epher, Hanoch, Abida, and * 1Ch 1:33
ELDAD
But two of the seventy—* and Num 11:26
ELDER
leader" or "presiding *." 1Ti 3:1f
I, too, am an *; 1Pe 5:1
FROM: JOHN, THE old * of the 2Jn 1:1
FROM: JOHN, THE *. 3Jn 1:1
ELDERLY
to the *, in the fear of God. Lev 19:32
ELDERS
"Call together all the * of Ex 3:16
The * of the people of Ex 3:18
and summoned the * of the people of Ex 4:29
Then the * believed that God had Ex 4:31
THIS PRESENTATION to the *, Ex 5:1
Then Moses called for all the * Ex 12:21
Moses, "Take the * of Israel with Ex 17:5,6
and seventy of the * of Israel. Ex 24:1
and seventy of the * of Israel went Ex 24:9
Yet, even though the * saw God, Ex 24:11
He told the *, "Stay here and Ex 24:14
Literally, "*." Lev 4:15f
sons and the * of Israel, and told Lev 9:1
and he gathered the seventy * and Num 11:24
and put it upon the seventy *; Num 11:25
to the camp with the * of Israel. Num 11:30
of Refuge, the * of his home town Deu 19:12
the murder, the * and judges shall Deu 21:2
Then the * of that city shall Deu 21:3
him before the * of the city and Deu 21:19
go to the city * and say to them, Deu 25:7
The * of the city will then Deu 25:8
presence of the *, pull his sandal Deu 25:9
THEN MOSES AND the * of Israel Deu 27:1
of the laws to the * of Israel. Deu 31:9
Now summon all the * and Deu 31:28
Joshua and the * of Israel tore Jos 7:6
accompanied by the * of Israel, Jos 8:10
the *, officers, judges, and the Jos 8:33
So our * and our people Jos 9:11
of Israel—the *, judges, and Jos 23:2
*, officers, and judges. Jos 24:1
replied the * of Jabesh. 1Sa 11:3
at Bethlehem, the * of the city 1Sa 16:4
of the loot to the * of Judah. 1Sa 30:26
The gifts were sent to the * in 1Sa 30:27-31
Absalom and all the * of Israel 2Sa 17:4
to say to the * of Judah, "Why are 2Sa 19:11,12
anything more," the * advised. 1Ki 20:8
a meeting with the * of Israel when 2Ki 6:32
Elisha said to the *, "This 2Ki 6:32
THEN THE KING sent for the * and 2Ki 23:1
Then David and the * of Israel 1Ch 15:25
he and the * of Israel clothed 1Ch 21:16
Then the king summoned all the * 2Ch 34:29
leaders and the * of Israel at Ez 8:29
the leaders and * had decided that Ez 10:7,8
with the * and judges of his city; Ez 10:14
orators, and the insight of the *. Job 12:20
took my place among the honored *. Job 29:7
The princes and * of Judah, and Ps 68:27
judges, prophets, *, army Is 3:2
wrath will be the * and the Is 3:14
sight of all the * of his people. Is 24:23
Take some of the * of the people Jer 19:1
it to the Jewish * and priests and Jer 29:1
Nor could my priests and *—they Lam 1:19
The * of Jerusalem sit upon the Lam 2:10
and * who stayed true to God. Lam 4:16
the priests and * and the kings and Eze 7:26,27
as I was talking with the * of Eze 8:1
Seventy * of Israel were Eze 8:11
you seen what the * of Israel are Eze 8:12
began by killing the seventy *. Eze 9:6
THEN SOME OF the * of Israel Eze 14:1
some of the * of Israel came to ask Eze 20:1
"Son of dust, say to the * of Eze 20:3
Gather the * and all the people Joe 1:14
Bring everyone—the *, the Joe 2:16
Literally, "of the *, and chief Mt 16:21f
be rejected by the * and the Chief Mk 8:31
Literally, "scribes and *." Mk 11:27,28f
the chief priests, * and teachers Mk 15:1
respected Jewish * to ask him to Lk 7:3
Jewish leaders—the *, chief Lk 9:22
leaders and * of our nation, if Act 4:8
Literally, "the * and the Act 6:12f
the * of the church in Jerusalem. Act 11:30
also appointed * in every church Act 14:23
and * there about this question. Act 15:2
the apostles and * were present—and Act 15:4
So the apostles and church * set Act 15:6
Then the apostles and * and the Act 15:22
"From: The apostles, * and Act 15:23
the apostles and * in Jerusalem. Act 16:4
a message to the * of the church at Act 20:17
PARTING FROM the Ephesian *, Act 21:1
and the * of the Jerusalem church. Act 21:18
chief priests and * and told them Act 23:14
Literally, '*.' Act 24:1f
prophets when the * of the church 1Ti 4:14
More literally, "*." Tit 1:5f
More literally, "*." Tit 1:7f
He should call for the * of the Jas 5:14
AND NOW, A word to you * of the 1Pe 5:1
Fellow *, this is my plea to you: 1Pe 5:1
twenty-four * sitting on them; Rev 4:4
the twenty-four * fell down before Rev 4:10
But one of the twenty-four * said Rev 5:5
the twenty-four *, in front of the Rev 5:6
the twenty-four * fell down before Rev 5:8
Beings and the *: "The Lamb is Rev 5:11
And the twenty-four * fell down Rev 5:14
and around the * and the four Rev 7:11
Then one of the twenty-four * Rev 7:13
And the twenty-four * sitting on Rev 11:16
Beings and the twenty-four *; Rev 14:3
Then the twenty-four * and four Rev 19:4
ELDEST
"Israel is my * son, and I have Ex 4:22
now see, I will slay your * son." Ex 4:23
* sons are always bought back.' Ex 13:15
census of all the * sons in Israel Num 3:40
for the * sons of Israel; Num 3:41
So Moses took a census of the * Num 3:42
total number of * sons a month old Num 3:43
* sons of the people of Israel; Num 3:45
To redeem the 273 * sons in Num 3:46
money for the 273 * sons of Israel Num 3:49
place of all the * sons of Israel. Num 8:18
(Reuben was Israel's * son. Num 26:5-11
burying all their * sons, killed by Num 33:3,4
Then he killed the * son Ps 78:51
He destroyed the * child in each Ps 135:8
beginning with the *, until only Jn 8:9
ELDEST-SON
* rights to his younger brother. Gen 25:33
ELE-AD
Ezer, *. 1Ch 7:20,21
* and Ezer attempted to rustle 1Ch 7:20,21
ELE-ASAH
Helez's son was *; 1Ch 2:39
ELE-ASAH'S
Helez's son was Ele-asah; * son 1Ch 2:40
ELEADAH
Shuthelah, Bered, Tahath, *, 1Ch 7:20,21
ELEALEH
Heshbon, *, Sebam, Nebo, and Beon. Num 32:3,4
Heshbon, *, Num 32:37,38
of Heshbon and * are heard far Is 15:4
for Heshbon and *, for destruction Is 16:9
clear across to * and to Jahaz; Jer 48:34
ELEASAH
Raphah, *, Azel. 1Ch 8:37
of Bine-a, Rephaiah, *, and Azel. 1Ch 9:43
ELEAZAR
were:Nadab, Abihu,*, Ithamar. Ex 6:23
Aaron's son * married one of the Ex 6:25
Aaron and his sons * and Ithamar, Lev 10:6
who were left, * and Ithamar, Lev 10:12
about this with * and Ithamar, the Lev 10:16
Nadab (his oldest), Abihu, *, Num 3:2
this left only * and Ithamar to Num 3:4
(Note: *, Aaron's son, shall be Num 3:31-35
"Aaron's son * shall be Num 4:16
to Moses, "Tell * the son of Aaron Num 16:36,37
So * the priest took the 250 Num 16:39
Give her to * the priest and he Num 19:1
as he watches. * shall take some Num 19:4
blood, and dung. * shall take Num 19:6
Now take Aaron and his son * and Num 20:25
him and put them on * his son; Num 20:26
Aaron and put them on his son *; Num 20:28
Moses and * returned, and when Num 20:28
When Phinehas (son of * and Num 25:7
"Phinehas (son of * and grandson Num 25:10,11
to Moses and to * (son of Aaron the Num 26:1
So Moses and * issued census Num 26:3,4
born Nadab, Abihu, *, and Ithamar. Num 26:60
by Moses and * the priest, in the Num 26:63
petition to Moses, * the priest, Num 27:1
and take him to * the priest, and Num 27:19
to consult with * the priest in Num 27:21
The Lord will speak to * through Num 27:21
of the Urim, and * will pass on Num 27:21
and took Joshua to * the priest. Num 27:22
Phinehas (son of * the priest) Num 31:6
to Moses and * the priest, and to Num 31:12
Moses and * the priest and all Num 31:13
Then * the priest said to the men Num 31:21
Moses, "You and * the priest and Num 31:26
Give this share to * the priest Num 31:29
So Moses and * the priest did as Num 31:31
was given to * the priest, as the Num 31:41
Moses and * the priest received Num 31:51,52
So they came to Moses and * the Num 32:2
by saying to *, Joshua, and the Num 32:28
up of the land: * the priest, Num 34:16-28
His son * became the next priest. Deu 10:6
* the priest, Joshua, and the Jos 14:1
These women came to * the priest Jos 17:4
* the priest, Joshua, and the Jos 19:51
to consult with * the priest and Jos 21:1
Phinehas, the son of * the priest. Jos 22:13
*, the son of Aaron, also died; Jos 24:33
Phinehas, the son of * and Ju 20:27,28
and installed his son * to be in 1Sa 7:1
Next in rank was *, the son of 2Sa 23:9
Nadab, Abihu, *, Ithamar. 1Ch 6:3
*, the father of 1Ch 6:4-15
*, Phinehas, Abishua, 1Ch 6:50-53
Phinehas, the son of *, was the 1Ch 9:20
The second of The Top Three was * 1Ch 11:12
* and Kish. 1Ch 23:21
Eleazar and Kish. * died without 1Ch 23:22
* and 1Ch 24:1
so only * and Ithamar were left 1Ch 24:1
represented the * clan, and with 1Ch 24:3
among the descendants of *). 1Ch 24:4
Two groups from the division of * 1Ch 24:6
Mahli's descendants were *, who 1Ch 24:28
Phinehas was the son of *; Ez 7:1
* was the son of Aaron, the chief Ez 7:1
Uriah the priest), * (son of Ez 8:33
Izziah, Malchijah, Mijamin, *, Ez 10:25
Ma-aseiah, Shemaiah, *, Neh 12:42
Eliud was the father of *; Mt 1:15
* was the father of Matthan; Mt 1:15
ELEAZAR'S
at various times. * descendants 1Ch 24:4
ELEAZER
sons Nadab, Abihu, *, and Ithamar, Ex 28:1
ELECT
"Let's * a leader to take us Num 14:4
the trees decided to * a king. Ju 9:8

(ELECT Con't)
and they will * you as their king, 2Sa 3:21
Literally, "the *." Mt 24:22f
Literally, "the *." Mt 24:24f
Literally, "* of God." Mk 13:22f
That is why Christ did not * Heb 5:5

ELECTED
These were the tribal leaders * Num 1:16
* by a convocation of the leaders Deu 33:5
Apparently new names were * to 2Sa 23:24-39f
* to the wise men's hall of fame. Pro 15:31,32
and they * the following: Act 6:5
In fact, this man was * by the 2Co 8:19

ELECTRIFIED
of the city was * by these Act 21:30

ELECTRONS
the reference is to atoms, *, etc. Heb 11:3f

ELEVATED
will be on an * site, covering the Zec 14:10

ELEVATION
Literally, "the * of the holy Lev 22:12f

ELEVEN
two concubines and * children, Gen 32:22,23,24
"The sun, moon, and * stars Gen 37:9
There are to be * of these Ex 26:7,8
layer formed by * draperies made of Ex 36:14,15
festival, offer * young bulls, two Num 29:20
it takes only * days to travel by Deu 1:1
with * other teams ahead of him; 1Ki 19:19
he reigned * years, in Jerusalem; 2Ch 36:5
he reigned * years, in Jerusalem. 2Ch 36:11
he reigned * years in Jerusalem. Jer 52:1
Then, * years later, he took 832 Jer 52:29
Then the * disciples left for Mt 28:16
Still later he appeared to the * Mk 16:14
to tell his * disciples—and Lk 24:9
where the * disciples and the other Lk 24:33,34
an apostle with the other *. Act 1:26
forward with the * apostles, and Act 2:14

ELEVENTH
his gifts on the * day—the same Num 7:72-77
first day of the * month" (of the Deu 1:1f
of the * year of his reign. 1Ki 6:38
Literally, "*." 2Ki 9:29f
The siege continued into the * 2Ki 25:2
Machbannai was * in command. 1Ch 12:8-13
*, the group led by Eliashib; 1Ch 24:7-18
*, Azarel and twelve of his sons 1Ch 25:9-31
The commander of the * Division 1Ch 27:14
during the * month of each year. 1Ch 27:14
until July of the * year of the Jer 1:3
the month, in the * year (after Eze 26:1
of March of the * year of King Eze 30:20
IN MID-MAY OF the * year of King Eze 31:1
In the * Eze 33:21
The * with jacinth; Rev 21:18,19,20

ELHANAN
at the same place, * killed the 2Sa 21:19
* (son of Dodo) from Bethlehem; 2Sa 23:24-39
*, the son of Dodo from Bethlehem; 1Ch 11:26-47
the Philistines, * (the son of 1Ch 20:5

ELI
two sons of *—Hophni and Phinehas. 1Sa 1:3
to the Tabernacle. * the priest was 1Sa 1:9
* noticed her mouth moving as she 1Sa 1:12,13
"In that case," * said, "cheer 1Sa 1:17
they took the child to *. 1Sa 1:25
for he assisted * the priest. 1Sa 2:11
Now the sons of * were evil men 1Sa 2:12
Before they returned home * 1Sa 2:20
* was now very old, but he was 1Sa 2:22
you are doing," * told his sons. 1Sa 2:23,24,25
came to * and gave him this 1Sa 2:27
helping the Lord by assisting *. 1Sa 3:1
one night after * had gone to bed 1Sa 3:2,3
He jumped up and ran to *. 1Sa 3:4,5
"I didn't call you," * said. 1Sa 3:4,5
Samuel jumped up and ran to *. 1Sa 3:6
didn't call you, my son," * said. 1Sa 3:6
Samuel jumped up and ran to *. 1Sa 3:8
Then * realized it was the Lord 1Sa 3:8
dreadful things I warned * about. 1Sa 3:12
that the sins of * and of his sons 1Sa 3:14
* what the Lord had said to him. 1Sa 3:15
said to him. But * called him. 1Sa 3:16,17
"It is the Lord's will," * 1Sa 3:18
*, accompanied it into the battle. 1Sa 4:4
* was waiting beside the road to 1Sa 4:13
is all the noise about?" * asked. 1Sa 4:14
* and told him what had happened. 1Sa 4:14
had happened. (* was ninety-eight 1Sa 4:15
today," he told *, "and Israel 1Sa 4:16
to the Ark, * fell backward from 1Sa 4:18
great-grandson of *, the priest of 1Sa 14:3
concerning the descendants of *. 1Ki 2:27
Jesus shouted, "*, Eli, lama Mt 27:46
shouted, "Eli, *, lama Mt 27:46
"*, Eli, lama sabachthani? Mk 15:34
"Eli, *, lama sabachthani?" Mk 15:34

ELI-E-HO-ENAI
From the clan of Pahath-moab—* Ez 8:2-14

ELI-ENAI
Jakim, Zichri, Zabdi, *, 1Ch 8:19,20,21

ELI-O-ENAI
*, Hizkiah, Azrikam. 1Ch 3:23
* had seven sons: 1Ch 3:24
Joel, Jehu, *, Ja-akobah, 1Ch 4:34-39
Zemirah, Joash, Eliezer, *, Omri, 1Ch 7:8
*, Ma-aseiah, Ishmael, Nethanel, Ez 10:22
*, Eliashib, Mattaniah, Jeremoth, Ez 10:27
Micaiah, *, Zechariah, Neh 12:40,41

ELI'S
it brought up be given to * sons. 1Sa 2:13,14
When * daughter-in-law, 1Sa 4:19

ELIAB
Zebulun -* (son of Helon Num 1:2-15
Leader: son of Zuar) * Num 2:3-31
On the third day *, the son of Num 7:24-29
led by *, the son of Helon. Num 10:16
(the sons of *) and On (the son of Num 16:1
of *), but they refused to come. Num 16:11,12
(In the sub-clan of *—who was one Num 26:5-11
Abiram (the sons of *, descendants Deu 11:6
took one look at * and thought, 1Sa 16:6
The three oldest—*, Abinadab, 1Sa 17:13
oldest brother, *, heard David 1Sa 17:28
Jesse's first son was *, his 1Ch 2:13
Elkanah, Zophai, Nahath, *, 1Ch 6:25,26,27
* was third in command; 1Ch 12:8-13
Jehiel, Unni, *, Benaiah, 1Ch 15:18
Jehiel, Unni, *, Ma-aseiah, and 1Ch 15:20
*, Benaiah, Obed-edom, and Je-iel; 1Ch 16:5
the daughter of David's brother *. 2Ch 11:18

ELIADA
Japhia, Elishama, *, Eliphelet. 2Sa 5:14,15,16
Elishama, *, and Eliphelet. 1Ch 3:6-8
the command of *, a great general. 2Ch 17:17

ELIAHBA
* from Sha-albon; 2Sa 23:24-39
* from Sha-albon; 1Ch 11:26-47

ELIAKAM
men: *, his business manager; 2Ki 18:18

ELIAKIM
Then *, Shebnah, and Joah said to 2Ki 18:26
Then * (son of Hilkiah) the 2Ki 18:37
Then he told *, Shebnah, and 2Ki 19:2
The Egyptian king then chose *, 2Ki 23:34
The king of Egypt now appointed * 2Ch 36:4
*, Ma-aseiah, Miniamin, Neh 12:40,41
call my servant *, the son of Is 22:20
Then *, Hilkiah's son, who was Is 36:3
Then * and Shebna and Joah said Is 36:11
Then * (son of Hilkiah), the Is 36:22
Meanwhile he sent * his prime Is 37:2
Abiud was the father of *; Mt 1:13
Eliakim; * was the father of Azor; Mt 1:13
Jonam's father was *; Lk 3:23-38

ELIAKIM'S
(* name was changed to Jehoiakim. 2Ch 36:4
Jonam's father was Eliakim;* Lk 3:23-38

ELIAM
of * and the wife of Uriah. 2Sa 11:3
* (the son of Ahithophel) from 2Sa 23:24-39

ELIASAPH
Gad -* (son of Deuel) Num 1:2-15
Gad * (son of Reuel) Num 2:3-31
and the tribe of Gad led by *, Num 10:20

ELIASAPH'S
The next day it was * turn, son Num 7:42-47

ELIASHIB
Hodaviah, *, Pelaiah, Akkub, 1Ch 3:24
Eleventh, the group led by *; 1Ch 24:7-18
Of the singers, there was *. Ez 10:24
Eli-o-enai, *, Mattaniah, Ez 10:27
Vaniah, Meremoth, *, Mattaniah, Ez 10:34-42
THEN * THE High Priest and the Neh 3:1
to the home of * the High Priest. Neh 3:20
Joiakim was the father of *; Neh 12:10,11
* was the father of Joiada; Neh 12:10,11
in the days of *, Joiada, Johanan, Neh 12:22
the days of Johanan, the son of *. Neh 12:23
Before this had happened, * the Neh 13:4
this evil deed of *—that he had Neh 13:7
(the son of * the High Priest) was Neh 13:28

ELIASHIB'S
* house to the side of the house. Neh 3:21

ELIATHAH
Hananiah, Hanani, *, Geddalti, 1Ch 25:4,5
Twentieth, * and twelve of his 1Ch 25:9-31

ELIDAD
* (son of Chislon) Num 34:16-28

ELIE-HO-ENAI
* (the seventh). 1Ch 26:2,3

ELIEL
Epher, Ishi, *, Azri-el, Jeremiah, 1Ch 5:24
III, Jeroham, *, Toah, Zuph, 1Ch 6:33-38
*, Adaiah, Beraiah, Shimrath. 1Ch 8:19,20,21
Ishpan, Eber, *, Abdon, Zichri, 1Ch 8:22-25
* from Mahavi; 1Ch 11:26-47
*; Obed; Ja-asiel from Mezoba. 1Ch 11:26-47
* was seventh in command; 1Ch 12:8-13
of Hebron; with * as their leader; 1Ch 15:4-10
Joel, Shemaiah, *, and Amminadab. 1Ch 15:11
*, Ismachiah, Mahath, Benaiah. 2Ch 31:12,13

ELIEZER
Or, "* of Damascus." Gen 15:2,3f
land") and * (meaning "God is my Ex 18:4
Zemirah, Joash, *, Eli-o-enai, 1Ch 7:8
Benaiah, and *—all of whom were 1Ch 15:24
* were included with the tribe of 1Ch 23:14,15
The line of descendants from * 1Ch 26:25
Over Reuben, * (son of Zichri); 1Ch 27:16-22
Then *, son of Dodavahu from 2Ch 20:37
So I sent for *, Ari-el, Ez 8:16
Ma-aseiah, *, Ez 10:16-19
Petha-haiah, Judah, *. Ez 10:23
*, Isshijah, Malchijah, Shemaiah, Ez 10:31,32
Joshua's father was *; Lk 3:23-38

ELIEZER'S
by Shebuel, and * only son, 1Ch 23:17
Joshua's father was Eliezer;* Lk 3:23-38

ELIGIBLE
and fifty who are * for the sacred Num 4:21,22,23
are * for the Tabernacle service. Num 4:29
of age who were * for the Num 4:35
old and who were * for the Num 4:46,47,48

ELIHOREPH
* and Ahijah (sons of Shisha) were 1Ki 4:1

ELIHU
His grandfather was *, 1Sa 1:1
Michael, Jozabad, *, Zillethai. 1Ch 12:20
Their brave brothers, * and 1Ch 26:6,7
Over Judah, * (a brother of King 1Ch 27:16-22
Then * (son of Barachel, the Job 32:2
condemned him. * had waited until Job 32:4
* CONTINUED: Job 34:1
* CONTINUED: Job 35:1
* CONTINUED: Job 36:1

ELIJAH
THEN *, THE prophet 1Ki 17:1
Then the Lord said to *, "Go to 1Ki 17:2
But * said to her, "Don't be 1Ki 17:13
So she did as * said, and she and 1Ki 17:15
said, and she and * and her son 1Ki 17:15
the Lord had promised through *! 1Ki 17:16
"Give him to me," * replied. 1Ki 17:19
Then * took him downstairs and 1Ki 17:23
the Lord said to *, "Go and tell 1Ki 18:1
So * went to tell him. 1Ki 18:2
That same day, while * was on the 1Ki 18:5
Suddenly Obadiah saw * coming 1Ki 18:7
"Is it really you, my lord *?" 1Ki 18:7
"Yes, it is," * replied. 1Ki 18:8
And each time when he was told '* 1Ki 18:10
say, 'Go and tell him * is here'! 1Ki 18:11
'Go tell the king that * is here'! 1Ki 18:14
But * said, "I swear by the Lord 1Ki 18:15
went to tell Ahab that * had come; 1Ki 18:16
about yourself," * answered. 1Ki 18:18
Then * talked to them. 1Ki 18:21
Then * spoke again. 1Ki 18:22
Then * turned to the prophets of 1Ki 18:25
About noontime, * began mocking 1Ki 18:27
Then * called to the people, 1Ki 18:30
evening sacrifice, * walked up to 1Ki 18:36
Then * told them to grab the 1Ki 18:40
So they seized them all, and * 1Ki 18:40
Then * said to Ahab, "Go and 1Ki 18:41
So Ahab prepared a feast. But * 1Ki 18:42
He did, but returned to * and told 1Ki 18:43
Then * told him, "Go again, and 1Ki 18:43
Then * shouted, "Hurry to Ahab 1Ki 18:44
strength to * so that he was able 1Ki 18:46
Queen Jezebel what * had done, and 1Ki 19:1
this message to *: "You killed my 1Ki 19:2
So * fled for his life; 1Ki 19:3
"What are you doing here, *?" 1Ki 19:9
And as * stood there the Lord 1Ki 19:11
When * heard it, he wrapped his 1Ki 19:13
said, "Why are you here, *?" 1Ki 19:13
So * went and found Elisha who 1Ki 19:19
the last team. * went over to him 1Ki 19:19
and ran after * and said to him, 1Ki 19:20
* replied, "Go on back! 1Ki 19:20
Then he went with *, as his 1Ki 19:21
But the Lord said to *, "Go to 1Ki 21:17
Ahab exclaimed to *. 1Ki 21:20
"Yes," * answered, "I have come 1Ki 21:20
Then another message came to *: 1Ki 21:28
left alive by * at Carmel, though 1Ki 22:6f
But an angel of the Lord told * 2Ki 1:3
Literally, "* the Tishbite." 2Ki 1:3f
When * told the messengers this, 2Ki 1:4,5
"It was * the prophet!" 2Ki 1:8
But * replied, "If I am a man of 2Ki 1:10
* replied, "If I am a man of 2Ki 1:12
his knees before * and pleaded with 2Ki 1:13
Lord said to *, "Don't be afraid. 2Ki 1:15
Go with him." So * went to the 2Ki 1:15
about your sickness?" * demanded. 2Ki 1:16
predicted through *, and his 2Ki 1:17
the Lord to take * to heaven—by 2Ki 2:1
of a whirlwind! * said to Elisha as 2Ki 2:1

(ELIJAH Con't)
to take * away from you today?" 2Ki 2:3
Then * said to Elisha, "Please 2Ki 2:4
Then * said to Elisha, "Please 2Ki 2:6,7
Then * folded his cloak together 2Ki 2:8
on the other side * said to Elisha, 2Ki 2:9
asked a hard thing," * replied. 2Ki 2:10
them, and * was carried by a 2Ki 2:11
"Where is the Lord God of *?" 2Ki 2:13,14
spirit of * rests upon Elisha!" 2Ki 2:15
He told * the prophet that dogs 2Ki 9:36
He declared through his servant * 2Ki 10:9,10
relatives, just as *, speaking for 2Ki 10:17
Athaliah, Jaareshiah, *, Zichri. 1Ch 8:26,27
Then * the prophet wrote him this 2Ch 21:12
Ma-aseiah, *, Shemaiah, Ez 10:21
Abdi, Jeremoth, *. Ez 10:26
what I mean, he is *, the one the Mt 11:14
some, *; Mt 16:14
Suddenly Moses and * appeared and Mt 17:3
and one for Moses and one for *." Mt 17:4
leaders insist * must return before Mt 17:10
Literally, "that * must come Mt 17:10f
"They are right. * must come and Mt 17:11
and thought he was calling for *. Mt 27:47
Let's see whether * will come and Mt 27:49
Others thought Jesus was * the Mk 6:15
others say you are * or some other Mk 8:28
Then * and Moses appeared and Mk 9:4
and Moses and * were gone, and only Mk 9:8
spoke of, that * must return Mk 9:11
Jesus agreed that * must come Mk 9:12,13
he was calling for the prophet *. Mk 15:34f
he was calling for the prophet *. Mk 15:35
"Let's see if * will come and Mk 15:36
spirit and power like *, the Lk 1:17
For example, remember how * the Lk 4:25,26
land; yet * was not sent to them. Lk 4:25,26
and others, "It is * or some Lk 9:8
him, "or perhaps * or one of the Lk 9:19
talking with him—Moses and *! Lk 9:30
As Moses and * were starting to Lk 9:33
and one for Moses and one for *!" Lk 9:33
"Are you *?" Jn 1:21
the Messiah or * or the Prophet, Jn 1:24,25
say about this? * the prophet was Rom 11:2,3
down God's altars; * claimed that Rom 11:2,3
results. * was as completely human Jas 5:17

ELIJAH'S
And the Lord heard * prayer; 1Ki 17:22
Then he picked up * cloak and 2Ki 2:13,14
Then he added, "He was * 2Ki 3:11

ELIKA
* from Harod; 2Sa 23:24-39

ELIM
And they came to * where there Ex 15:27
NOW THEY LEFT * and journeyed on Ex 16:1
Sihn Wilderness, between * and Mt. Ex 16:1
Leaving Marah, they came to *, Num 33:9
Leaving *, they camped beside the Num 33:10

ELIMELECH
a man named *, from Bethlehem, Ru 1:1
residence there, * died and Naomi Ru 1:3
the property of *, Chilion, and Ru 4:9

ELIMELECH'S
She is selling our brother * Ru 4:3

ELIMINATES
his perfect love for us * all 1Jn 4:18

ELIMINATING
of the plain, * all life—people, Gen 19:25

ELIPHAL
* (son of Ur); 1Ch 11:26-47

ELIPHAZ
Esau and Adah had a son named *. Gen 36:4
wife Adah, born to her son * Gen 36:10,11,12
(born to Timna, *' concubine). Gen 36:10,11,12
the descendants of *, the oldest Gen 36:15,16
*, Reuel, Jeush, Jalam, and Korah. 1Ch 1:35
The sons of *: 1Ch 1:36
Their names were * the Temanite, Job 2:11
A REPLY TO Job from * the Job 4:1
THE ANSWER OF * the Temanite: Job 15:1
ANOTHER ADDRESS FROM *: Job 22:1
Job, he said to * the Temanite: Job 42:7
So * the Temanite, and Bildad the Job 42:9
Edom was noted for her wise men; * Ob 1:8f

ELIPHELEHU
Mattithiah, *, Mikneiah, Obed-edom 1Ch 15:18
Mattithiah, *, Mikneiah, 1Ch 15:21

ELIPHELET
Japhia, Elishama, Eliada, *. 2Sa 5:14,15,16
* (son of Ahasbai) from Maacah; 2Sa 23:24-39
Ibhar, Elishama, *, Nogah, Nepheg, 1Ch 3:6-8
Japhia, Elishama, Eliada, and *. 1Ch 3:6-8
*, the third. 1Ch 8:39
Japhia, Elishama, Beeliada, *. 1Ch 14:4-7
From the clan of Adonikam—*, Ez 8:2-14
Mattenai, Matattah, Zabad, *, Ez 10:33

ELISAPH
* (son of Lael) Num 3:16-24

ELISHA
Israel, and anoint * (the son of 1Ki 19:16
escape Jehu shall be killed by *! 1Ki 19:17
So Elijah went and found * who 1Ki 19:19
* left the oxen standing there 1Ki 19:20
* then returned to his oxen, 1Ki 19:21
Elijah said to * as they left 2Ki 2:1
But * replied, "I swear to God 2Ki 2:1
them and asked *, "Did you know 2Ki 2:3
"Quiet!" * snapped. 2Ki 2:3
Then Elijah said to *, "Please 2Ki 2:4
But * replied again, "I swear to 2Ki 2:4
Seminary came to * and asked him, 2Ki 2:5
Then Elijah said to *, "Please 2Ki 2:6,7
But * replied as before, "I swear 2Ki 2:6,7
Elijah said to *, "What wish shall 2Ki 2:9
And * replied, "Please grant me 2Ki 2:9
* saw it and cried out, "My 2Ki 2:12
And the water parted and * went 2Ki 2:13,14
spirit of Elijah rests upon *!" 2Ki 2:15
"No," * said, "don't bother." 2Ki 2:16
* was still at Jericho when they 2Ki 2:18
officials of Jericho visited *. 2Ki 2:19
The water was purified, just as * 2Ki 2:22
"* is here," one of the king of 2Ki 3:11
Judah, and Edom went to consult *. 2Ki 3:12
"I want no part of you," * 2Ki 3:13
Jehoshaphat of Judah," * replied. 2Ki 3:14
the message of the Lord came to *: 2Ki 3:15
students came to * to tell him of 2Ki 4:1
"What shall I do?" * asked. 2Ki 4:2
One day * went to Shunem. 2Ki 4:8
"Call her back again," * told 2Ki 4:15,16
year, just as * had predicted. 2Ki 4:17
As she approached Mount Carmel, * 2Ki 4:25
But when she came to * at the 2Ki 4:27
you." So * returned with her. 2Ki 4:30
He returned to meet * and told 2Ki 4:31
When * arrived, the child was 2Ki 4:32
* now returned to Gilgal, but 2Ki 4:38
"Bring me some meal," * said. 2Ki 4:41
brought * a sack of fresh corn 2Ki 4:42
of his harvest. * told Gehazi to 2Ki 4:42
But * said, "Go ahead, for the 2Ki 4:43
But when * the prophet heard 2Ki 5:8
of Elisha's home. * sent a 2Ki 5:10
But * replied, "I swear by 2Ki 5:16
"All right," * said. 2Ki 5:19
arrived at the hill where * lived, 2Ki 5:24
When he went in to his master, * 2Ki 5:25
But * asked him, "Don't you 2Ki 5:26
students came to * and told him, 2Ki 6:1
him the place, and * cut a stick 2Ki 6:6
"Grab it," * said to him; 2Ki 6:7
Immediately * warned the king of 2Ki 6:9
The king sent a scout to see if * 2Ki 6:10
replied. "*, the prophet, tells 2Ki 6:12
And the report came back, "* is 2Ki 6:13
he cried out to *. 2Ki 6:15
"Don't be afraid!" * told him. 2Ki 6:16
Then * prayed, "Lord, open his 2Ki 6:17
upon them, * prayed, "Lord, please 2Ki 6:18
Then * went out and told them, 2Ki 6:19
As soon as they arrived * prayed, 2Ki 6:20
*, "Oh, sir, shall I kill them? 2Ki 6:21
"Of course not!" * told him. 2Ki 6:22
* this very day," the king vowed. 2Ki 6:31
* was sitting in his house at a 2Ki 6:32
messenger arrived * said to the 2Ki 6:32
While * was still saying this, 2Ki 6:33
* REPLIED, "THE Lord says that by 2Ki 7:1
But * replied, "You will see it 2Ki 7:2
This is what * had predicted on 2Ki 7:17
* HAD TOLD the woman whose son he 2Ki 8:1
of the great things * has done." 2Ki 8:4
the time when * brought a little 2Ki 8:5
very one * brought back to life!" 2Ki 8:5
Afterwards * went to Damascus 2Ki 8:7
as presents for * and said to him, 2Ki 8:8,9
And * replied, "Tell him, 'Yes.' 2Ki 8:10
* stared at Hazael until he 2Ki 8:11
and then * started crying. 2Ki 8:11
* replied, "I know the terrible 2Ki 8:12
But * replied, "The Lord has 2Ki 8:13
MEANWHILE * HAD summoned one 2Ki 9:1
When * was in his last illness, 2Ki 13:14
* told him, "Get a bow and some 2Ki 13:15
upon the bow, and * laid his own 2Ki 13:16,17
"Shoot!" * commanded, and he 2Ki 13:16,17
Then * proclaimed, "This is the 2Ki 13:16,17
So * died and was buried. 2Ki 13:20,21
threw his body into the tomb of *. 2Ki 13:20,21
Or think of the prophet *, who Lk 4:27

ELISHA'S
and stood at the door of * home. 2Ki 5:9
But Gehazi, * servant, said to 2Ki 5:20
with Gehazi, * servant, and saying, 2Ki 8:4
And as soon as the body touched * 2Ki 13:20,21

ELISHAH
The sons of Javan:*, Gen 10:4
*, Tarshish, Kittim, and Rodanim. 1Ch 1:5-9

ELISHAMA
* (son of Ammihud) Num 1:2-15
Leader: * (son of Ammihud Num 2:3-31
On the seventh day, *, the son of Num 7:48-53
led by *, the son of Ammihud; Num 10:22
Japhia, *, Eliada, Eliphelet. 2Sa 5:14,15,16
Jekamiah's son was *. 1Ch 2:41
Ibhar, *, Eliphelet, Nogah, 1Ch 3:6-8
Japhia, *, Eliada, and Eliphelet. 1Ch 3:6-8
*, the father of 1Ch 7:25,26,27
Japhia, *, Beeliada, Eliphelet. 1Ch 14:4-7
also the priests, * and Jehoram. 2Ch 17:7,8,9
were meeting. * (the scribe) was Jer 36:12
in the room of * the scribe and Jer 36:20
Jehudi brought it from * the Jer 36:21
Nethaniah, son of *), who was a Jer 41:1

ELISHAPHAT
of Adaiah), and * (son of Zichri). 2Ch 23:1

ELISHEBA
Aaron married *, the daughter of Ex 6:23

ELISHU-A
Solomon, Ibhar, *, Nepheg, Japhia, 2Sa 5:14,15,16
Solomon, Ibhar, *, Elpelet, Nogah, 1Ch 14:4-7

ELITE
So Saul took his * corps of 1Sa 26:2
Sheba with an * guard from Joab's 2Sa 20:7
* troops of Israel that day. 2Ch 13:17
of 307,500 men, all * troops. 2Ch 26:13

ELIUD
Achim was the father of *; Mt 1:14
* was the father of Eleazar; Mt 1:15

ELIZABETH
(His wife * was, like himself, a Lk 1:5
Zacharias and * were godly Lk 1:6
But they had no children, for * Lk 1:7
your wife * will bear you a son! Lk 1:13
Soon afterwards * his wife Lk 1:24
*—'the barren one,' they called Lk 1:36
where Zacharias lived, to visit *. Lk 1:39,40
Mary stayed with * about three Lk 1:56
But * said, "No! Lk 1:60

ELIZABETH'S
Mary's greeting, * child leaped Lk 1:41
By now * waiting was over, for Lk 1:57

ELIZAPHAN
* (son of Uzziel) Num 3:25-30
Zebulun * (son of Parnach Num 34:16-28
200 from the subclan of *; 1Ch 15:4-10
From the * clan, Shimri and 2Ch 29:12,13,14

ELIZUR
Reuben -* (son of Num 1:2-15
* (son of Shedeur) Num 2:3-31
were presented by *, son of Num 7:30-35
of Reuben, with * the son of Num 10:18

ELKANAH
The sons of Korah:Assir, *, Ex 6:24
THIS IS THE story of *, a man of 1Sa 1:1
Each year * and his families 1Sa 1:3
his sacrifice, * would celebrate 1Sa 1:4
"What's the matter, Hannah?" * 1Sa 1:8
to Ramah, and when * slept with 1Sa 1:19,20
The next year * and Peninnah and 1Sa 1:21,22
you think best," * agreed. 1Sa 1:23
Eli would bless * and Hannah and 1Sa 2:20
*, Ebiasaph, Assir, Tahath, Uriel, 1Ch 6:22,23,24
The subclan of * was further 1Ch 6:25,26,27
Amasai, Ahimoth, *, Zophai, 1Ch 6:25,26,27
Jeroham, *. 1Ch 6:25,26,27
Joel, Samuel, * III, Jeroham, 1Ch 6:33-38
Eliel, Toah, Zuph, * II, Mahath, 1Ch 6:33-38
Mahath, Amasai, * I, Joel, Azariah, 1Ch 6:33-38
Shephatiah from Haruph; *, 1Ch 12:3-7
Berechiah and * were guards for 1Ch 15:23
the king's second-in-command *. 2Ch 28:7

ELKOSH
who lived in *, concerning the Nah 1:1

ELLASAR
Arioch, king of *, Gen 14:1

ELMADAM
Cosam's father was *; Lk 3:23-38

ELMADAM'S
Cosam's father was Elmadam;* Lk 3:23-38

ELNA-AM
Jeribai and Joshaviah (sons of *); 1Ch 11:26-47

ELNATHAN
of *, a citizen of Jerusalem) 2Ki 24:8,9
Ari-el, Shemaiah, *, Jarib, Ez 8:16
Elnathan, Jarib, *, Nathan, Ez 8:16
I also sent for Joiarib and *, Ez 8:16
Then King Jehoiakim sent * (son Jer 26:22
(son of Shamaiah), * (son of Jer 36:12
And no one protested except *, Jer 36:24,25

ELOI
first two words ("*, Eloi") and Mk 15:34f
two words ("Eloi, *") and thought Mk 15:34f

ELON
daughter of * the Hethite. Gen 26:34
Adah (daughter of * the Hethite), Gen 36:2,3
Zebulun and his sons: Sered, *, Gen 46:8-14
named after their ancestor *. Num 26:26,27
Aijalon, Ithlah, *, Timnah, Ekron, Jos 19:41-46
The next judge was * from Ju 12:11,12

ELON-BETH-HANAN
Sha-albim, Beth-shemesh, and *; 1Ki 4:8-19

ELONITES
The *, named after their ancestor Num 26:26,27
ELOTH
Ezion-geber near * on the Red Sea 1Ki 9:26
of Ezion-geber and *, in Edom, to 2Ch 8:17,18
of * and restored it to Judah. 2Ch 26:2
ELPAAL
*. 1Ch 8:11
The sons of * were: 1Ch 8:12
The sons of * also included: 1Ch 8:17,18
ELPAAL'S
* sons also included: 1Ch 8:14
ELPELET
Ibhar, Elishu-a, *, Nogah, Nepheg, 1Ch 14:4-7
ELSE'S
nor with anyone * wife, to Lev 18:20
It is the same with someone * Deu 23:25
* house (though it is all he has); Mic 2:2
in someone * eye—his little fault Lk 6:41
about being in someone * field. 2Co 10:16
ELSEWHERE
born in the same house or *. Lev 18:9
and * throughout the land. 1Ki 9:19
ELTEKE
*, Gibbethon, Aijalon, and Jos 21:23,24
ELTEKEH
Timnah, Ekron, *, Gibbethon, Jos 19:41-46
ELTEKON
Beth-anoth, *, Kiriath-baal (also Jos 15:48-62
ELTOLAD
Baalah, Iim, Ezem, *, Chesil, Jos 15:21-32
Balah, Ezem, *, Bethul, Hormah, Jos 19:2-7
ELUL
day of the month *." Neh 6:15f
ELUZAI
Jozabad from Gederah; *; 1Ch 12:3-7
ELYMAS
But the sorcerer, * (his name in Act 13:8
ELZABAD
* was ninth in command; 1Ch 12:8-13
Obed, *. 1Ch 26:6,7
ELZAPHAN
The sons of Uzziel:Misha-el, *, Ex 6:22
ELZAPHON
for Misha-el and *, Aaron's Lev 10:4
EMASCULATED
"born eunuchs," or, "born *." Mt 19:12f
EMBALM
his morticians to * the body. Gen 50:2
spices and ointments to * him; Lk 23:56
EMBALMED
of 110, and they * him, and his Gen 50:26
EMBALMING
the body. The * process required Gen 50:3
went out and purchased * spices. Mk 16:1
hundred pounds of * ointment made Jn 19:39
EMBARRASS
would * you no end when sober. Pro 23:33
The bodies we have now * us for 1Co 15:43
lives should not * God, but bring 1Th 2:12
EMBARRASSED
neither of them was * or ashamed. Gen 2:25
of their nakedness, and were *. Gen 3:7
for the men were very * over 2Sa 10:5
until he was *, and finally said, 2Ki 2:17
*, and then Elisha started crying. 2Ki 8:11
a message to his * emissaries, 1Ch 19:5
you, and be * at their puny might. Mic 7:16
sorry, but he was * to break his Mk 6:26
And you, *, will have to take Lk 14:9
so we will not be ashamed and * 1Jn 4:17
EMBARRASSMENT
compensate for any * and to settle Gen 20:16
stood before the Lord in great *; Ez 9:5
don't let * stand in the way. Pro 6:3
brothers turn away from him in *; Pro 19:7
EMBASSY
entertained the * from Babylon Eze 23:16f
EMBERS
Literally, "like hot * to coals Pro 26:21f
EMBITTER
Don't let your suffering * you at Job 36:18
EMBITTERED
God who has * my soul, that as Job 27:2
EMBRACE
and tender * Pro 5:19
and his right hand would * me. Sol 8:3
EMBRACED
to meet him and * him Gen 33:4
Then, weeping with joy, he * Gen 45:14
to him and he kissed and * them. Gen 48:10
and * Mt 26:49
he exclaimed, and * him with a Mk 14:45
and ran and * him and kissed him. Lk 15:20
wept aloud as they * him in Act 20:37
EMBRACES
and with his right hand he * me. Sol 2:6
EMBRACING
prostitutes, * what isn't yours? Pro 5:20
EMBROIDERED
scarlet, with cherubim * on them. Ex 26:1
with cherubim * into the cloth. Ex 26:31
from skillfully * blue, purple, and Ex 26:36
of beautifully * blue, purple, and Ex 27:16
the ephod shall be * with blue, Ex 28:33,34
and make him an * sash. Ex 28:39
cherubim skillfully * upon them. Ex 36:8,9
cherubim skillfully * into it. Ex 36:35
* with blue, purple, and scarlet. Ex 36:37
linen, beautifully * with blue, Ex 38:18
these were made of linen cloth, * Ex 39:24
was beautifully * with blue, Ex 39:28,29
Literally, "* work." Ps 45:14f
linens and silk, *, and sandals Eze 16:9,10
silk and linen and beautifully *. Eze 16:13
You used the beautifully * Eze 16:18
on a beautifully * bed and put my Eze 23:41
EMBROIDERING
weaving, and at * blue, purple, and Ex 38:23
EMBROIDERY
carpenters, * designers in blue, Ex 35:35
purple dyes, *, fine linen, and Eze 27:16
trade—blue cloth, * and Eze 27:24
EMEK-KEZIZ
Jericho, Beth-hoglah, *, Jos 18:21-28
EMERALD
an * shall be in the first row. Ex 28:17
The second row will be an *, a Ex 28:18
in the second row were an *, a Ex 39:11
carbuncle, and *—all in beautiful Eze 28:13
like an * encircled his throne. Rev 4:3
The fourth with *; Rev 21:18,19,20
EMERALDS
They bring *, purple dyes, Eze 27:16
EMERGE
so that the dry land will *." Gen 1:9,10
EMERGENCY
and lowered the * boat as though Act 27:30
EMERGES
the new order that * will not Eze 21:27
EMIM
The * in the plain of Kiriathaim; Gen 14:5,6
"(The * used to live in that Deu 2:10
both the * and the Anakim are Deu 2:11
but the Moabites call them *. Deu 2:11
EMISSARIES
to his embarrassed *, telling them 1Ch 19:5
EMISSION
or by a seminal *; Lev 15:32
by a seminal *, or who touches any Lev 22:4
of a seminal * during the night Deu 23:9,10
EMMANUEL
'*" (meaning "God is with us").' Mt 1:23
EMMAUS
*, seven miles out of Jerusalem. Lk 24:13
By this time they were nearing * Lk 24:28
Then the two from * told their Lk 24:35
EMMER
the wheat and the * were not Ex 9:32
EMPEROR
of King Ahasuerus, * of vast Est 1:1
to which the * invited all his Est 1:1
and appointed by the Babylonian *. Jer 41:18
the Assyrian * Sennacherib invaded Hos 1:7f
the Roman *, decreed that a census Lk 2:1
of the reign of * Tiberius Caesar, Lk 3:1
He said, "Then give the * all Lk 20:25
of a hearing before the * himself. Act 25:10,11
arrange to get him to the *." Act 25:21
But what shall I write the *? Act 25:26
a prisoner to the * without any Act 25:27
EMPEROR'S
But when they conveyed the * Est 1:12
They replied, "The *." Mk 12:16
replied, "Caesar's—the Roman *." Lk 20:24
EMPHASIZE
bold enough to * some of these Rom 15:15,16
EMPHATICALLY
"I say * that anyone who listens Jn 5:24
EMPIRE
The heart of his * included Gen 10:10
Calah), the main city of the *. Gen 10:11,12
throughout his * (he also put it Ez 1:1
gave me my vast *, has now given me Ez 1:2
this part of your * beyond the Ez 4:16
of the wealth and glory of his *. Est 1:4
official and citizen of your *. Est 1:16
throughout your * will hear what Est 1:18
girls in the * and bring them to Est 2:2
in the * next to the king himself. Est 3:1
throughout the *, to each province Est 3:12
provinces of the *, decreeing that Est 3:13
and cities of the *, so that the Est 9:28
of Solomon's * into Israel and Is 7:17
disaster on Tyre, * builder and top Is 23:8
put an end to the * of Babylonia. Is 48:14
The old Babylonian * lasted from Jer 5:15f
The Medo-Persian *, whose first Dan 2:39f
This * will be inferior to yours. Dan 2:39
The Greek *, founded by Alexander Dan 2:39f
Apparently the Roman *. Dan 2:40f
provinces of his *, to come to the Dan 3:2
and as the capital of my *." Dan 4:30
* as his administrative officer. Dan 6:3
addressed to everyone in his *: Dan 6:25,26
the Babylonian *, Daniel had a Dan 7:1
believed to be a revived Roman *. Dan 7:23f
kings that will rise out of his *; Dan 7:24
capitals of the * at this time. Dan 8:2f
that the Grecian * will break into Dan 8:22
For his * will be torn apart and Dan 11:4
of so vast an *, a city of sixty Zep 2:15f
capital of the * to be crowned king Lk 19:12
EMPLOYED
and * twelve thousand charioteers. 1Ki 4:26
donkeys, and * many servants. Job 1:2,3
a silversmith who * many craftsmen Act 19:24
with others * in related trades, Act 19:25
EMPLOYEE
A faithful * is as refreshing as Pro 25:13
EMPLOYEES
* first instituted by King David. Ez 8:20
He laid out his *' work for them Mk 13:34
EMPLOYER
*, lest he curse you for your sin. Pro 30:10
"So his * called him in and Lk 16:2
owed money to his * to come and Lk 16:5,6
EMPLOYERS
A lazy fellow is a pain to his * Pro 10:26
EMPLOYMENT
need other * but could apply 2Ch 31:4
EMPOWER
God shall * his right hand and he Is 45:1
EMPOWERED
And if I am * by Satan, what Lk 11:19
EMPOWERING
against himself by * me to cast out Lk 11:18
EMPTIED
So she * the jug into the Gen 24:20
As they * out the sacks, there at Gen 42:35
the house to be * before he Lev 14:36
The land will be completely * Is 24:3
crushed us and * out our strength; Jer 51:34,35
branches that * oil into golden Zec 4:12
angels, who had * the flasks Rev 21:9
EMPTIES
the Jordan River * into the Salt Jos 15:5
EMPTINESS
these years are often * and pain; Ps 90:10
than nothing—mere * and froth. Is 40:17
hunger pangs and * will still Mic 6:14
EMPTY
So the boat was soon *. Gen 8:18,19
* well—there was no water in it. Gen 37:24
Salt Sea until the riverbed was *. Jos 3:15,16
the Lord has brought me home *; Ru 1:21
when your place at the table is *. 1Sa 20:18
Saul, but David's place was *. 1Sa 20:24,25
But when his place was still * 1Sa 20:27
God stretches out heaven over * Job 26:7
Is it an *, futile life you give Ps 89:47
An * stable stays clean—but there Pro 14:4
is no income from an * stable. Pro 14:4
is ruin in a flood of * words; Ecc 5:6,7
In these few days of our * Ecc 6:12
will be silent and *, houses Is 27:10
be deserted, the crowded cities *. Is 32:14
your idols are all as * as the Is 41:29
be lived in, not to be an * chaos. Is 45:18
is silent and * when I come home? Is 50:2
If you don't listen, I will * the Jer 6:8
an * cistern in the prison yard. Jer 38:6
Cook the meat well and then * the Eze 24:10
Now set it * on the coals to Eze 24:11
lay * as a barren wilderness; Eze 36:34
strip all around is to be left *. Eze 45:2
the barns and granaries are *; Joe 1:17
people of God lies * and broken Nah 2:2
Soon the city is an * shambles; Nah 2:10
cattle barns are *, yet I will Hab 3:17
finds the man's heart clean but *! Mt 12:43,44,45
sent the rich away with * hands. Lk 1:53
He noticed two * boats standing Lk 5:2
But *, since the person is neutral Lk 11:25f
in and saw the * linen wrappings; Lk 24:12
as well be talking to an * room. 1Co 14:9
in God is *, worthless, hopeless; 1Co 15:14
go your ways and * out the seven Rev 16:1
EMPTY-HANDED
you will by no means go out *! Ex 3:21
him, and don't send him away *! Deu 15:13
And did not return from battle *. 2Sa 1:22
up the man and sent him back *. Mk 12:3
beat him up and sent him back *. Lk 20:10
EMPTYING
See how he is * out all its Is 24:1
EN
Upon Jacob's arrival at Bethel, * Gen 35:9
David as he was * route to Ziklag: 1Ch 12:20
EN-DOR
Ible-am, Dor, *, Taanach, Megiddo Jos 17:11
EN-EGLAIM
all the way from En-gedi to *. Eze 47:10

EN-GANNIM
Eshtaol, Zorah, Ashnah, Zanoah, *, Jos 15:33-36
Ebez, Remeth, *, En-haddah, Jos 19:17-23
EN-GEDI
Nibshan, The City of Salt, and *. Jos 15:48-62
all the way from * to En-eglaim. Eze 47:10
EN-HADDAH
Remeth, En-gannim, *, Beth-pazzez, Jos 19:17-23
EN-RIMMON
Sharuhen, *, Ether, and Ashan. Jos 19:2-7
*, Zorah, Jarmuth, Neh 11:25-30
EN-ROGEL
springs at En-shemesh and on to *. Jos 15:7
lived, and continued down to *. Jos 18:16
From * the boundary proceeded Jos 18:17
been staying at * so as not to be 2Sa 17:17
But a boy saw them leaving * to 2Sa 17:18
Adonijah went to * where he 1Ki 1:9
EN-SHEMESH
springs at * and on to En-rogel. Jos 15:7
northeast to * and on to Geliloth Jos 18:17
ENACTED
The tax law * by Moses the 2Ch 24:6
ENAIM
*, which is on the way to Timnah. Gen 38:14
ENAM
Tappu-ah, *, Jarmuth, Adullam, Jos 15:33-36
ENAN
Ahira (son of *) Num 1:2-15
Ahira (son of *) Num 2:3-31
came Ahira, son of *, chief of the Num 7:78-83
led by Ahira, the son of *. Num 10:27
ENCAMP
know how we are to * in the Num 10:31f
ENCAMPED
* on the borders of your land. Num 20:16
ENCAMPMENT
So he led them to the Amalekite * 1Sa 30:16
ENCAMPMENTS
Literally, "Two *." Gen 32:1f
They will set up their * among Eze 25:4
ENCHANTED
* by the fragrance of my perfume. Sol 1:12
ENCIRCLE
My enemies * me with murder in Ps 17:9
your walls and * you and close in Lk 19:43
ENCIRCLED
They * the army of Benjamin east Ju 20:43
like an emerald * his throne. Rev 4:3
ENCLOSE
The veil to * the Holy Place; Ex 35:10-19
and install the veil to * the Ark Ex 40:3
and if she is a door we will * Sol 8:9
ENCLOSED
the Tabernacle, * with curtains Ex 27:9,10
long by 52½ feet wide, * by walls. Eze 46:21,22
ENCLOSING
the drapes * the court, and for all Ex 38:29
ENCLOSURE
Then he erected the * surrounding Ex 40:33
at the entrance of the *. Ex 40:33
ENCOMPASS
or, "a woman shall * a man." Jer 31:22f
ENCOUNTER
He also had an * with some of the Act 17:18
ENCOUNTERED
Putting to sea from there, we * Act 27:4
ENCOURAGE
lead the people. * him as he Deu 1:38
you, and then * him, for he shall Deu 3:28
Why did you * him to revolt 1Sa 22:13
of Ephraim to * them to worship the 2Ch 19:4
He worked very hard to * respect 2Ch 31:21
or, in his lovingkindness, to *. Job 37:13
They * each other to do evil. Ps 64:5
my heart is heavy with sorrow; * Ps 119:28
you answer me, and * me by giving Ps 138:3
But men who * the upright to do Pro 28:10
ones. * those who are afraid. Is 35:4
He will * the fainthearted, those Is 42:3
dishonesty. They * and compliment Jer 23:14
women who * your husbands to rob Amo 4:1
Cilicia, to * the churches there. Act 15:40,41
us patience and to * us, so that we Rom 15:4
to visit you and * you to complete 2Co 8:6
Our responsibility is to * the 2Co 13:8
you are, and to comfort and * you. Col 4:8
your faith and * you, and to keep 1Th 3:2,3
So comfort and * each other with 1Th 4:18
of his return. So * each other to 1Th 5:11
Teach these truths, Timothy, and * 1Ti 6:2
when they need it, * them to do 2Ti 4:2
these things and * your people to Tit 2:15
people do, but * and warn each Heb 10:25
will lift you up, * and help you. Jas 4:10
Don't * him in any way. 2Jn 1:10
Let this * God's people to Rev 14:12
ENCOURAGED
You will be greatly * and be Ju 7:11
he met him at Horesh and * him in 1Sa 23:16
his old age. They * him to worship 1Ki 11:4
* him to do every sort of evil. 1Ki 21:25
like Jeroboam, he * the people to 2Ki 13:11
son of Nebat), he * Israel in the 2Ki 15:9
warriors (who also * the leaders of 1Ch 11:10
instead who * the people to worship 2Ch 11:15
his mother * him in doing wrong. 2Ch 22:3
and * them with this address: 2Ch 32:6
This greatly * them. 2Ch 32:8
evil reign, for he * his people to 2Ch 33:2
and sorcerers, and * every sort of 2Ch 33:6
But Manasseh * the people of 2Ch 33:9
their duties, and * them to begin 2Ch 35:2
they were greatly * by the Ez 6:14
and have * those who are weak or Job 4:3,4
And how you have * me in my great Job 26:2
I smiled and that * them, and Job 29:24
This is a fact, but not to be *! Pro 17:8f
And you have * the wicked by Eze 13:22
But because they * the people to Eze 44:12
and joy, and * the believers to Act 11:23
each other. They * them to continue Act 14:22
and the believers * him in this. Act 18:27
with you but to be * by yours: Each Rom 1:11,12
and * others to do them, too. Rom 1:32
will learn and be * and helped. 1Co 14:31
You have greatly * me; 2Co 7:4
urged Titus, who * your giving in 2Co 8:6
and me and * us to keep right on Gal 2:7,8,9
and you should feel honored and *. Eph 3:13
how we are and be * by his report. Eph 6:22
Somehow my patience has * them Php 1:14
that you will be * and knit Col 2:2
he visited me and * me often. 2Ti 1:16
I hope I have * you by this 1Pe 5:12
Then the Dragon * the Creature to Rev 13:5
ENCOURAGEMENT
Aaron's *, and much to the Ex 32:25
of good will, and * to confirm Est 9:29-31
but a word of * does wonders! Pro 12:25
steadiness, and * help you to live Rom 15:5
been a wonderful * to me, as I am 1Co 16:18
our sympathy and *, we can pass on 2Co 1:3,4
shower us with his comfort and *. 2Co 1:5
In addition to the * you gave us 2Co 7:13
ENCOURAGES
Each man * his neighbor and Is 41:6
ENCOURAGING
My own son—* David to come and 1Sa 22:8
* them to begin building again! Ez 5:1
king's provinces, * them to Est 9:21
not important, and * people to Mal 1:12
all the believers, * them and Act 18:23
your brother by * him to do 1Co 8:12
the Lord, * and comforting them. 1Co 14:3
(that is, * the activity of Gal 5:20
—pleading with you, * you and even 1Th 2:11
forgotten the * words God spoke to Heb 12:5
and * them to go to idol feasts. Rev 2:14
ENCRUSTED
his body is bright ivory * with Sol 5:14
END
promise until the * of time, to you Gen 9:13
them, and at the * they will come Gen 15:14
our clan will not come to an *." Gen 19:32
down at the * of his field. Gen 23:9
the cave at the * of the field, and Gen 23:17,18
years of plenty came to an *. Gen 41:53
out a way to put an * to this. Ex 1:10
Beg God to * this terrifying Ex 9:28
of your exodus, at the * of March Ex 13:4,5
the * of six years as the men are. Ex 21:7
at the * of the harvest season. Ex 23:16
the mercy place, one at each *. Ex 25:19
Join five sheets * to end for Ex 26:3
Join five sheets end to * for Ex 26:3
frames on that * of the building Ex 26:25
from * to end of the Tabernacle. Ex 26:28
from end to * of the Tabernacle. Ex 26:28
of pure gold. One * of each cord is Ex 28:22,23,24
and forth from one * of the camp to Ex 32:27
were attached * to end, then five Ex 36:10
attached end to *, then five others Ex 36:10
loops along the * of each, and Ex 36:17
of acacia wood standing on *. Ex 36:20
running from one * to the other. Ex 36:33
four feet, two rings at each *. Ex 37:3
At the * of that time, on the Lev 13:5
be celebrated at the * of March. Lev 23:5
September, at the * of your Lev 23:39
those at the far * of the camp. Num 11:1
Oh, that my * might be Num 23:7-10
search from one * of the heavens to Deu 4:32
At the * of those forty days and Deu 9:10,11
"AT THE * of every seventh year Deu 15:1
free him at the * of the sixth year Deu 15:12
seven days at the * of the harvest Deu 16:13
one * of the earth to the other. Deu 28:64
the people at the * of every Deu 31:10,11
called Gilgal (meaning, "to *" Jos 5:8,9
* of the Valley of Rephaim. Jos 15:8
southern * of the Jordan River. Jos 18:19
other from one * of the camp to the Ju 7:22
Your actions at the * of the Ju 8:2,3
them until the * of the barley Ru 2:23
I will put an * to your family, 1Sa 2:31
but now your dynasty must *; 1Sa 13:14
a little bit on the * of a stick; 1Sa 14:43
other, and by the * of the day 2Sa 2:17
with the butt * of his spear. 2Sa 2:23
would * our existence in Israel. 2Sa 14:15,16
people from one * of the nation to 2Sa 24:2
country from one * to the other to 1Ki 1:3,4
of Israel—my dynasty will never *. 1Ki 2:4
room at the far * of the Temple—the 1Ki 6:16
one * of the land to the other. 1Ki 8:65
At the * of the twenty years 1Ki 9:10
family who will come to a quiet *. 1Ki 14:13
and did not * the line of David's 1Ki 15:4
earth from * to end to find you. 1Ki 18:10
earth from end to * to find you. 1Ki 18:10
he was at the * of the line with 1Ki 19:19
of Baal from one * to the other. 2Ki 10:20,21
filled from one * to the other with 2Ki 21:16
Within the Temple, at one *, was 2Ch 3:8
as Hamath at one * of the country 2Ch 7:8
would * in triumph for the king. 2Ch 18:12
of Ziz at the * of the valley that 2Ch 20:16
was unwilling to * the dynasty of 2Ch 21:7
In the process of time, at the * 2Ch 21:19
to * the dynasty of Ahab. 2Ch 22:7
the Ahava River at the * of March Ez 8:31
From one * to the other it is Ez 9:11
my face—my hair stood up on *. Job 4:15
How he longs for the day to *. Job 7:2
How he grinds on to the * of the Job 7:2
little, you would * with much. Job 8:7
against God, to * my sadness and be Job 9:27
they are prosperous to the *. Job 21:12,13
Will this put an * to your Job 36:19
to * the night's wickedness? Job 38:13
So the Lord blessed Job at the * Job 42:12
before them all. * all wickedness, Ps 7:9
the heavens from * to end, and Ps 19:6
from end to *, and nothing can hide Ps 19:6
Put an * to their arrogance, Ps 38:16
one * of the country to the other. Ps 44:1
and causes wars to * throughout the Ps 46:9
yet in the * he dies like everyone Ps 49:19
Do as you promised and put an * Ps 54:5
But in the *, you brought us into Ps 66:12
of peace to the * of time. Ps 72:7
an instant * to all their Ps 73:19
who can say when it all will *? Ps 74:9,10
my covenant with him will never * Ps 89:28
will continue to the * of time. Ps 89:35,36
are God without beginning or *. Ps 90:2
joy to the * of our lives. Ps 90:14
forever, and your years never *. Ps 102:27
from one * of Egypt to the other. Ps 105:31
and are at their wit's *. Ps 107:27
dynasty of David shall never *. Ps 132:12
Literally, "But in the * she is Pro 5:4f
Proud men * in shame, but the Pro 11:2
will * in poverty and disgrace; Pro 13:18
If you love sleep, you will * in Pro 20:13
from common sense will * up dead! Pro 21:16
and his reign of terror shall *. Pro 22:8
the rich shall * in poverty. Pro 22:16
For in the * it bites like a Pro 23:32
embarrass you no * when sober. Pro 23:33
and who knows where it all will *? Pro 24:21,22
* of the line, publicly disgraced! Pro 25:6,7
the poor will * up in the hands of Pro 28:8
In the *, people appreciate Pro 28:23
of God's work from beginning to *. Ecc 3:11
then be futile and * in darkness, Ecc 6:4
there is no * of opinions ready to Ecc 12:12
and all military training will *. Is 2:4
You will find him at the * of the Is 7:3
submerging it from * to end." Is 8:7,8
submerging it from end to *." Is 8:7,8
peaceful government will never *. Is 9:7
against you will *, and then it Is 10:25
On that day God will * the Is 10:27
between Israel and Judah will *; Is 11:13
weeping, from one * to the other. Is 15:8
of Damascus will *, and the remnant Is 17:3
the nations she enslaved will *. Is 21:2
the mighty tribe of Kedar, will * Is 21:16
He will * their pride and all Is 25:11
stand until the * of time, forever Is 30:8
judgment on Edom will never *. Is 34:10
*, Queen Kingdom of the world. Is 47:7
He will use him to put an * to Is 48:14
rule will never die nor *. Is 51:6
which * up in deadly actions. Is 59:5
out of your land—all war will *. Is 60:18
your days of mourning all will *. Is 60:20
come to an evil *, says Jehovah. Is 66:17
Yet for years on * my people have Jer 2:32
I will * the happy singing and Jer 7:34
one * of the nation to the other; Jer 12:12

(END Con't)
very eyes, I will * all laughter in Jer 16:9
riches and at the * of his life Jer 17:11
If you put an * to all these Jer 22:4
the earth from one * to the other. Jer 25:33
This very year your life will * Jer 28:16
by you, and I will * your slavery Jer 29:14
that your sorrow should never *! Jer 30:15
the land from * to end with all its Jer 48:45
* with all its rebellious people. Jer 48:45
of commerce, your * has come; Jer 51:13
I thought, This is the *! Lam 3:54
* is near—our days are numbered. Lam 4:18
will * at last, but Edom's never. Lam 4:22
At the * of the seven days, the Eze 3:16
I will finish you. The * has come; Eze 7:5,6
at the south * of the Temple when Eze 10:3
I will put an * to this proverb and Eze 12:23
other gods and * your payments to Eze 16:40,41
my jealousy against you will *, Eze 16:42
I will bring you to a dreadful * Eze 26:21
says that at the * of the forty Eze 29:13
at the * of a 13-year siege Eze 29:18f
at the * of a 13-year siege Eze 29:20f
the pride of her power shall *. Eze 30:6
and her power shall come to an *. Eze 33:28
in a mighty battle of the * times. Eze 38:2,3f
necessarily mean "the * times." Eze 38:15,16f
At the * of the seven months, Eze 39:14
God says, I will * the captivity of Eze 39:25
Beyond this hall, at the inner * Eze 40:7-12
87½ feet from one * to the other. Eze 40:15
inner room at the * of the nave and Eze 41:3
But a wall extended from the * of Eze 42:7,8
wall at the other * while the Eze 46:2
There, at the extreme west * of Eze 46:19,20
then, at the * of this trial Dan 1:13
Well, at the * of the ten days, Dan 1:15
come to an *, another world power Dan 2:39
"At the * of seven years Dan 4:34
Literally, "at the * of the Dan 4:34f
and whose power shall never *. Dan 6:25,26
power is eternal—it will never *; Dan 7:14
But in the * the people of the Dan 7:18
and destroy it until the *. Dan 7:26
That was the * of the dream. Dan 7:28
place until the * times come." Dan 8:17
"Toward the * of their kingdoms, Dan 8:23
at the * of human history. Dan 8:23f
the Lord God [to * our captivity Dan 9:3
from that time to the very *. Dan 9:26
the Jews, at the * times—for the Dan 10:14
until the final * of all their Dan 11:35
"Then at the time of the *, Dan 11:40
until the * times, when travel and Dan 12:4
it be until all these terrors *?" Dan 12:6
not * until three and a half years Dan 12:7
the holy people comes to an *." Dan 12:7f
until the time of the *. Dan 12:9
"But go on now to the * of your Dan 12:13
Literally, "at the * of the Dan 12:13f
in fact, I will put an * to Hos 1:4,5
I will put an * to all her joys, Hos 1:11
all weapons, and all wars will *. Hos 1:18
to his blessings, in the * times. Hos 3:5
suddenly your revelry will *. Amo 6:7
for the Sabbath to * and the Amo 8:5
time will scarcely * before the Amo 9:13
upon you, and your day will *. Mic 3:6
each other, for all war will *. Mic 4:3
I will put an * to all Mic 5:12
no * of getting rich by cheating? Mic 6:10
to nothing at the *, and what Mic 6:14
have ordered an * to your dynasty; Nah 1:14
There seems to be no * of Nah 2:9
I will put an * to their Zep 1:4
and Egypt over my people will *." Zec 10:11
That was the * of the agreement. Zec 11:11
In the *, those who survive the Zec 14:16
endure to the * shall be saved. Mt 10:22
He will * all conflict with his Mt 12:20
the harvest is the * of the Mt 13:39
shall it be at the * of the world: Mt 13:40
it will be at the * of the world Mt 13:49
was right at the * of the day. Mt 20:4
return, and the * of the world?" Mt 24:3
these must come, but the * is not Mt 24:6
But those enduring to the * Mt 24:13
then, finally, the * will come. Mt 24:14
"From the four winds, from one * Mt 24:31f
the * will be—not even the angels. Mt 24:36
being sealed at each * with clay. Mt 27:66f
even to the * of the world." Mt 28:20
But all who endure to the * Mk 13:13
that will signal the * of the age. Mk 13:30
his Kingdom shall never *!" Lk 1:33
day raced from * to end of Judea Lk 7:17
raced from end to * of Judea and Lk 7:17
But this would imply the * Lk 16:9f
that death is the * of existence, Lk 20:27
True, wars must come, but the * Lk 21:9
things happen, the * of this age Lk 21:32
Emmaus and the * of their journey. Lk 24:28
At the * of the two days' stay he Jn 4:43,44
falls and all work comes to an *. Jn 9:4
next and where all this would *! Act 5:24
* your opposition to the Lord? Act 13:10
At the * of the week when we Act 21:5
to * all God's anger against us. Rom 3:25
his laws we always * up under his Rom 4:15
He died once for all to * sin's Rom 6:10
for all of them * in eternal doom. Rom 6:21
to say before I * this letter. Rom 16:17
right up to the * that you will be 1Co 1:8
at the very * of the line, like 1Co 4:9
on display at the * of a victor's 1Co 4:9
days as the world nears its *. 1Co 10:11
to an *, but love goes on forever. 1Co 13:8
to an *, and they will disappear. 1Co 13:10
After that the * will come when 1Co 15:24
In the * they will get every bit 2Co 11:15
will never see the * of it or fully Eph 3:18,19
to reach the * of the race and Php 3:14
as I come to the * of this letter I 2Th 3:1
as I do at the * of all my letters, 2Th 3:17
Put an * to their myths and 1Ti 1:3,4
and your years will never *." Heb 1:12
firm to the *, and our joy and our Heb 3:6
For if we are faithful to the *, Heb 3:14
flowing from a life that cannot *. Heb 7:16
He came once for all, at the * of Heb 9:26
as he neared the * of his life, Heb 11:22
you, they will * up praising God 1Pe 2:12
The * of the world is coming 1Pe 4:7
will be a swift and terrible *. 2Pe 2:1
that the * of the world is near. 1Jn 2:18
way that does not * in death, you 1Jn 5:16
terrible * of those who fall away. 1Jn 5:17f
to the very * keeps on doing things Rev 2:26
remain firm to the * in obedience Rev 14:12
of human history has come to an *. Rev 16:17f
When the thousand years *, Satan Rev 20:7
and the Z—the Beginning and the *. Rev 21:6
and the *, the First and Last. Rev 22:13

END-TIME
this is not the signal of the *. Mk 13:7
nation before the * finally comes. Mk 13:10

ENDANGER
His words * him. Pro 18:6,7
to be like them and * your soul. Pro 22:24,25

ENDANGERED
presence among them has * them! Is 8:14,15

ENDED
That * the fifth day. Gen 1:23
every way. This * the sixth day. Gen 1:31
again after the flood has *. Gen 7:3
and that * the building of the Gen 11:8
That * the conversation and God Gen 17:22
purification are * (the following Lev 12:6
AFTER THE PLAGUE had *, Jehovah Num 26:1
"Today I have * your shame of not Jos 5:8,9
fierce anger of the Lord was *. Jos 7:26
of Zin, and * at the northern edge Jos 15:1
and * at the Mediterranean Sea. Jos 15:10,11
and * at the Jordan River. Jos 16:7
Beth-hoglah, and * at the north bay Jos 18:19
and * at the Valley of Iphtahel. Jos 19:14
The boundary of Issachar * at the Jos 19:17-23
answered prayer and * the famine. 2Sa 21:12,13,14
After the famine *, she returned 2Ki 8:3
At last the celebration * and the 1Ch 16:43
is now *," Hezekiah said. 2Ch 29:31
So the work * until the second Ez 4:24
be opened until the Sabbath had *; Neh 13:19
When these birthday parties * Job 1:5
Job's words are *. Job 31:40
days of the past, long since *. Ps 77:5
your blazing anger, is now *. Ps 85:3
You have * his splendor and Ps 89:44
all he planned for himself is *. Ps 146:4
But even so, his anger is not *; Is 5:25
I have * all their harvest joys. Is 16:10
of Moab shall be *, and few of all Is 16:13,14
the harvest is *, two or three in Is 17:6
the happy days are *. Is 24:8
of glory, pomp and honor are *. Is 47:1
of slavery are *, I will punish Jer 25:12
The strength of Moab is *—her Jer 48:25
The joy of our hearts has *; Lam 5:15
And so * the vision of my visit Eze 11:24
Lord God says, All delay has *! Eze 12:28
of your reign, and they are *. Dan 5:26
all joy and gladness will be * in Joe 1:16
are *. They will be changed to Zec 8:19
The time for sleep has *! Mk 14:41
when the Sabbath *, Mary Magdalene Mk 16:1
When the devil had * all the Lk 4:13
And that * their questions, for Lk 20:40
Jesus' trial before Caiaphas * in Jn 18:28
That * Paul's discussion with Act 17:33
ceremonies *, we boarded ship at Act 20:6
The seven days were almost * when Act 21:26,27
This too must be defeated and *. 1Co 15:26
By his death he * the angry Eph 2:15
And so the feud * at last at the Eph 2:16
rules that * when Christ came. Col 2:17
plan finally * in good, for he is Jas 5:11
until the thousand years had *. Rev 20:5

ENDING
brothers died, * that generation. Ex 1:6
Jordan River, * at the Dead Sea." Num 34:12
Beth-horon and * at the village of Jos 18:14
and Lakkum, * at the Jordan River. Jos 19:33
the Lord by * my prayers for you; 1Sa 12:23
and * his insults to Israel?" 1Sa 17:26
were successfully * their siege of 2Sa 12:26,27
us and kill us, thus * our work. Neh 4:11
For him there is a happy *. Ps 37:37
oracle—* the Northern kingdom. Is 7:8f
the earth, quickly * his dealings, Rom 9:28
up arguments * in jealousy and 1Ti 6:4
the Beginning and the * of all Rev 1:8

ENDLESS
Your sins are *! Job 22:5
their * evil thoughts and plans. Ps 64:6
his throne will be as * as the Ps 89:29
in an * stream of prostitution. Eze 16:25
Glad News of the * treasures Eph 3:8
and ever through * ages because of Eph 3:21
favor with an * chain of angels 1Ti 1:3,4

ENDLESSLY
I said that makes you speak so *? Job 16:3
You have murdered * and filled Eze 11:6

ENDOR
to do, and they found one at *. 1Sa 28:7,8
to your enemies at *, whose Ps 83:10

ENDORSE
his name alone to * your promises. Deu 6:13
and refused to * Adonijah were the 1Ki 1:8
SON, IF YOU * a note for someone Pro 6:1

ENDORSED
you have * my work, declaring Ps 9:4
God publicly * Jesus of Nazareth Act 2:22

ENDOWED
You have * him with eternal Ps 21:6

ENDS
the two * of the lid of the Ark. Ex 25:18
The other * of the two cords are Ex 28:25
at the two * of the golden lid. Ex 37:7
seven lamps at the * of the Ex 37:23,24
Though you are at the * of the Deu 30:4
so long that their * could be seen 2Ch 5:9
me there until your anger *; Job 14:13
to spread to the * of the earth, to Job 38:13
flatteries to gain their wicked *. Ps 5:9
And all his busy rushing * in Ps 39:5,6
far away at the * of the earth, I Ps 61:2
River to the * of the earth. Ps 72:8
(This * the psalms of David, son Ps 72:20
For your kingdom never *. Ps 145:13
His breathing stops, life *, and Ps 146:4
that seems right but * in death. Pro 14:12
When the laughter *, the grief Pro 14:13
is right, but it * in death. Pro 16:25
goals are at the * of the earth! Pro 17:24
Pride * in destruction; Pro 18:12
humility * in honor. Pro 18:12
* arguments and settles disputes Pro 18:18
Pride * in a fall, while humility Pro 29:23
to those at the * of the earth, and Is 5:26
from the * of the earth. Is 11:12
their wits' * to know what to do; Is 19:3
the Lord from the * of the earth, Is 24:15,16
you back from the * of the earth Is 41:9
shout to the * of the earth that Is 48:20
the nations; the * of the earth Is 52:10
reach the farthest * of the earth, Jer 25:31
earth's farthest *, not forgetting Jer 31:8
the prophecy concerning Moab *. Jer 48:47
(This * Jeremiah's messages. Jer 51:64
of hope: his compassion never *. Lam 3:22
them to the * of the earth because Eze 20:23,24
Kings at the * of the earth Eze 27:33
your rule to the * of the earth. Dan 4:22
the river to the * of the earth. Zec 9:10
Or, "to the * of the land" of Zec 9:10f
"A divided kingdom * in ruin. Mt 12:25
* of the earth and heaven. Mt 24:31
"After the tribulation *, then Mk 13:24
triumph * in God's good time. Lk 21:24
the summer * four months from now? Jn 4:35
and to the * of the earth, about my Act 1:8
his laws. He * all of that. Rom 10:4
been told to the * of the earth. Rom 10:18
begins and * with you Corinthians? 1Co 14:36
For tomorrow we die, and that * 1Co 15:32
the Ten Commandments, * in death; 2Co 3:6
that * with a promise. Eph 6:2
the oath * all argument about it. Heb 6:16
But there is that one sin which * 1Jn 5:16
I am speaking of that one that * 1Jn 5:17
* in physical death (1 Cor. 1Jn 5:17f
One terror now *, but there are Rev 9:12

ENDURANCE
opportunity for * and confidence. Rev 13:10

ENDURE
"I can't * this," she exclaimed. Gen 25:22
will be able to * the pressures, Ex 18:23
For how can I * it, to see my Est 8:6
Your fame will * to every Ps 102:12
are written in the Book will * it. Dan 12:1
Who can * it? Joe 2:11
Who can * his coming? Mal 3:2
But all of you who * to the end Mt 10:22
But all who * to the end without Mk 13:13
will give you the strength to *. 2Co 1:6,7
We patiently * suffering and 2Co 6:4
God's people to * patiently every Rev 14:12

ENDURES
Your throne, O God, * forever. Ps 45:6
Literally, "his righteousness * Ps 112:3f
Literally, "his righteousness * Ps 112:9f
us very dearly, and his truth * Ps 117:2
you created; it * by your decree, Ps 119:90,91
O Jehovah, your name * forever; Ps 135:13
For he is good and his mercy * Jer 33:10,11
they learned, that God's Word *! Zec 1:5,6
destroyed [for my mercy * forever Mal 3:6

ENDURING
* as the heavens and the earth. Ps 78:69
your truth is as * as the Ps 89:2
But those * to the end shall be Mt 24:13

ENEMIES
the woman will be *, as will all of Gen 3:15
delivered your * over to you." Gen 14:19,20
will conquer their *, and be a Gen 22:17
descendantsOvercome all your *." Gen 24:60
You shall destroy your *. Gen 49:8
He devours his * in the morning, Gen 49:27
they will join our * and fight Ex 1:10
then I will be an enemy to your *. Ex 23:22
amusement of their *— he stood at Ex 32:25
You will chase your *; Lev 26:7
You will defeat all of your *. Lev 26:8
in vain, for your * will eat them. Lev 26:16
you will be conquered by your *. Lev 26:25
your land; your * shall live in it, Lev 26:32
no power to stand before their *. Lev 26:37
and be destroyed among your *. Lev 26:38
them into the land of their *. Lev 26:40,41
war against your *, God will hear Num 10:9
save you from your * when you sound Num 10:9
O Lord, and scatter your *; Num 10:35
*, for the Lord is not with you. Num 14:42
"I told you to curse my *, and Num 23:11
you to curse my * and instead you Num 24:10
They shall overcome their *. Num 24:15-19
has driven out his *, then, when Num 32:21
be struck down before their *.' Deu 1:42
throw out all the * living in your Deu 6:19
he will give them all to your *! Deu 7:15
safe from all your *, then you Deu 12:10
you against your *, and he will Deu 20:4
They aren't * who need to be Deu 20:19
God delivers your * to you, and Deu 21:10
cause your * to fall before you; Deu 23:14
rest from all your * in the Deu 25:19
"The Lord will defeat your * Deu 28:7
you to be defeated by your *. Deu 28:25
before your * in utter confusion; Deu 28:25
sheep will be given to your *. Deu 28:31
slaves to your * because of your Deu 28:47,48
The Lord will send your * against Deu 28:47,48
caused by your * at your gates. Deu 28:56,57
yourselves to your * as slaves—but Deu 28:68
them against your *—against those Deu 30:7,8
Outside, the *' sword— Deu 32:25
'My * will boast, Deu 32:27
the punishment of all her *: Deu 32:35
And hurl my punishments upon my *! Deu 32:40,41
Taking vengeance on his *, Deu 32:40,41
Fight for him against his *." Deu 33:7
Crush those who are their *; Deu 33:11
He thrusts out your * before you; Deu 33:27
Your * shall bow low before you, Deu 33:29
that Israel has fled from her *! Jos 7:8
from their *—for they are cursed. Jos 7:12
* until you deal with this sin. Jos 7:13
finished the destruction of its *! Jos 10:13
to do this to all of your *." Jos 10:25
helped them destroy all their *. Jos 21:44
against their * and when Joshua was Jos 23:1
* and has given you their land. Jos 23:3
us from our * when we passed Jos 24:17
the mercy of their *, for they had Ju 2:12-14
*, the Lord blocked their path. Ju 2:15
judges to save them from their *. Ju 2:16
Israel from their * throughout his Ju 2:18
in conquering their *: Ju 3:1
*, the Moabites, at your mercy!" Ju 3:28
Against his *.' Ju 5:23
O Lord, may all your * Ju 5:31
the Lord let their * harass them. Ju 6:1
and drove out your * from before Ju 6:9
from all their * on every side. Ju 8:34
save us once more from our *." Ju 10:15
over your *, the Ammonites. Ju 11:36
was finally conquered by its *. Ju 18:30
Now I have an answer for my *, 1Sa 2:1
will surely save us from our *." 1Sa 4:3
then told their *, "We surrender. 1Sa 11:10
will only rescue us from our *.' 1Sa 12:10
I have full revenge on my *." 1Sa 14:24,25
found among our *, think how many 1Sa 14:30
Vengeance on my * is all I 1Sa 18:25
has destroyed all of your *." 1Sa 20:15
* shall be as cursed as Nabal is. 1Sa 25:26
But the lives of your * shall 1Sa 25:29
"Why can't I fight your *?" 1Sa 29:8
the Lord's *," he wrote them. 1Sa 30:26
and from all their other *.' 2Sa 3:18
saved me from my *, that when 2Sa 4:9
"He burst through my * like a 2Sa 5:20
gone and have destroyed your *. 2Sa 7:9
him, for Hadadezer and Toi were *. 2Sa 8:10
the *' best men were fighting; 2Sa 11:16
opportunity to the * of the Lord to 2Sa 12:14
your * be as that young man is!" 2Sa 18:32
"For he saved us from our *, the 2Sa 19:8,9,10
Saul and from all his other *: 2Sa 22:1
For saving me from all my *. 2Sa 22:3
He will save me from all my *. 2Sa 22:4
And routed his *. 2Sa 22:15
He saved me from powerful *, 2Sa 22:18
I have chased my * 2Sa 22:38
You have made my * 2Sa 22:41
And rescues me from my *. 2Sa 22:49
months before your *, or to submit 2Sa 24:13
the defeat of your *— yes, I'll 1Ki 3:11
I have no foreign * or internal 1Ki 5:4
sin and their * defeat them, hear 1Ki 8:33,34
or if Israel's * besiege one of her 1Ki 8:37
against their * and they pray to 1Ki 8:44
them and let their * lead them away 1Ki 8:46
Another of Solomon's * whom God 1Ki 11:23
and Hadad were his *, for they 1Ki 11:25
but his * sent assassins and 2Ki 14:19
he will save you from all your * 2Ki 17:39
I will hand them over to their *. 2Ki 21:14
to betray me to my * when I am 1Ch 12:17
to sweep away my * like water 1Ch 14:11
I have destroyed your *, and I 1Ch 17:8
I will subdue all of your *. 1Ch 17:10
For Hadadezer and Tou had been * 1Ch 18:10
destruction by the * of Israel, or 1Ch 21:12
his * in the surrounding lands. 1Ch 22:9
me to curse your *, and you haven't 2Ch 1:11
before their * because they have 2Ch 6:24
if your people's * are in the land 2Ch 6:28
to fight their *, and they pray 2Ch 6:34
and you let their * defeat them and 2Ch 6:36
marvelous rescue from their *. 2Ch 20:27
fought against the * of Israel, the 2Ch 20:29
WHEN THE * of Judah and Benjamin Ez 4:1
situation, our * did not force us Ez 5:5
us from the * along the way. Ez 8:22
from * and bandits along the way. Ez 8:31
Meanwhile, our * were planning Neh 4:11
for a visit, our * tried to talk Neh 4:12
Our * learned that we knew of Neh 4:15
Don't we have enough * among the Neh 5:9
the rest of our * found out that we Neh 6:1
When our * and the surrounding Neh 6:16
And then you destroyed their * in Neh 9:11
So you gave them to their *. Neh 9:27
who delivered them from their *. Neh 9:27
more you let their * conquer them. Neh 9:28
and prepared to overcome their *. Est 8:13
day the Jews' * had hoped to Est 9:1
day and slaughtered their *. Est 9:5
all their *, killing 75,000 of Est 9:16
on killing their * the second day Est 9:18
saved from their *, when their Est 9:22
and anguish. His * conquer him as a Job 15:23,24
they slap my cheek. My * gather Job 16:10
'the last of our * have been Job 22:20
declare otherwise are my wicked *. Job 27:7
made against me by my *. Job 31:35
I have so many *. Ps 3:1
And now, although ten thousand * Ps 3:6
otherwise my * will conquer me. Ps 5:8
with grief because of all my *. Ps 6:7
All my * shall be suddenly Ps 6:10
for you to let my * destroy me, Ps 7:5
anger against the anger of my *. Ps 7:6
example shame and silence your *! Ps 8:2
My * will fall back and perish in Ps 9:3
* of mine, you are doomed forever. Ps 9:6
do, and their * fall before them. Ps 10:5
Don't let my * say, "We have Ps 13:4
My * encircle me with murder in Ps 17:9
from his many *, including Saul. Ps 18:1
Lord—and I am saved from all my *! Ps 18:3
of lightning and routed all my *. Ps 18:14
I chased my *; Ps 18:37
for the battle. My * quail before Ps 18:39
He rescues me from my *; Ps 18:48
find your *, all who hate you. Ps 21:8
I am surrounded by fearsome *, Ps 22:12
for me in the presence of my *. Ps 23:5
Don't let my * succeed. Ps 25:2
See how many * I have and how Ps 25:19
rock out of reach of all my *. Ps 27:6
I am surrounded by waiting *. Ps 27:11
for you have saved me from my *. Ps 30:1
Don't let my * defeat me. Ps 31:1
Pull me from the trap my * have Ps 31:4
I am scorned by all my * and Ps 31:11
about me, the slanders of my *. Ps 31:13
Don't let my * rejoice over me in Ps 35:24
These * of God will wither like Ps 37:20
Meanwhile my * are trying to kill Ps 38:12
But my * persecute with vigor, Ps 38:19
and destroys the power of their *. Ps 41:2
But my * say, "May he soon Ps 41:5
haven't let my * triumph over me. Ps 41:11
and all the while my * taunt me. Ps 42:3
suffer these attacks from my *?" Ps 42:9
I mourn at the oppression of my *? Ps 43:2
name that we tread down our *; Ps 44:5
our foes. Our * have invaded our Ps 44:10
and cursed by my vengeful *. Ps 44:15,16
In your *' hearts; Ps 45:5
come, even though surrounded by *! Ps 49:5
the bones of these, your *. Ps 53:5
of my * to boomerang upon them. Ps 54:5
trouble, and triumphed over my *. Ps 54:7
My * shout against me and Ps 55:3
O Lord, make these * begin to Ps 55:9
He will send my * to the pit of Ps 55:23
tide of battle turns. My * flee! Ps 56:9
My * have set a trap for me. Ps 57:6
O MY GOD, save me from my *. Ps 59:1
see my wish come true upon my *. Ps 59:10
Yes, Lord, help us against our * Ps 60:11
where my * can never reach me. Ps 61:3
you will defend us from our *, Ps 65:5
No wonder your * surrender! Ps 66:3
O GOD, and scatter all your *! Ps 68:1
God scattered their * like Ps 68:14
But he will crush his *, for Ps 68:21
"Come," to all his people's *; Ps 68:22
Rebuke our *, O Lord. Ps 68:30
your cause, your * insult me even Ps 69:9
Ransom me from all my *. Ps 69:18
Save me from my *, for you are Ps 71:2
is failing. My * are whispering, Ps 71:10
and disgrace—these * of mine. Ps 71:13
before him; his * shall fall face Ps 72:9
allow our * to dishonor your name? Ps 74:9,10
Lord, see how these * scoff at Ps 74:18
and state your case against our *. Ps 74:22
the cursing of these * of yours; Ps 74:23
he breaks the weapons of our *. Ps 76:3
The mightiest of our * are Ps 76:5
he had rescued them from their *; Ps 78:42
upon their * and overwhelmed them. Ps 78:53
he routed his * and drove them Ps 78:66
are chopped and burned by our *. Ps 80:16
quickly then I would subdue her *! Ps 81:14
tumult and commotion of your *? Ps 83:2
as you did to your * at Endor, Ps 83:10
to pieces. Your * are scattered Ps 89:10
him strong. His * shall not outwit Ps 89:22
You have strengthened his * Ps 89:42
Your * joke about me, the one Ps 89:51
while his *—all evil-doers—shall Ps 92:9
I have heard the doom of my * Ps 92:11
respite from our * while God traps Ps 94:12,13
My * taunt me day after day and Ps 102:8
Remember how he destroyed our *. Ps 105:5,6
you rescued them from their *. Ps 106:10
them and oppressed by their *. Ps 106:41,42
* who captured them to pity them. Ps 106:46
he has saved you from your *. Ps 107:2
Oh, help us fight against our *, Ps 108:12
punishment upon my * who tell lies Ps 109:20
hungry to save them from their *. Ps 109:31
will subdue your * and make them Ps 110:1
to rule over your *. Ps 110:2
They make me wiser than my *, Ps 119:98
to death at the hands of my *; Ps 119:107
safe above the heads of all my *; Ps 119:117
*, for I have done what is right; Ps 119:121
my * have disregarded your laws. Ps 119:139
My * are so many. Ps 119:157
our *, destroyed by their anger. Ps 124:2,3
he needs when arguing with his *. Ps 127:5
speak with their * in the gate." Ps 127:5f
not destroyed! My * have never been Ps 129:2
I'll clothe his * with shame, Ps 132:18
to strike their *, for his Ps 136:11,12
who were their *, for his Ps 136:18
your fist against my angry *! Ps 138:7
Yes, I hate them, for your * are Ps 139:22
for your enemies are my * too. Ps 139:22

ENEMIES Con't)

the traps my * have set for me.	Ps 142:3
My * chased and caught me.	Ps 143:3
Save me from my *, O Lord, I run	Ps 143:9
me, cut off all my * and destroy	Ps 143:12
upon your *, and scatter them.	Ps 144:6
waters, from the power of my *.	Ps 144:7
Deliver me from these *, these	Ps 144:11
all *, and blessed your children.	Ps 147:13
worst * to be at peace with him.	Pro 16:7
me, you will be killed by your *;	Is 1:20
pour out my anger on you, my *!	Is 1:24
up the earth, his * will crawl with	Is 2:19
crush your * as I have said.	Is 7:11
'Your * will soon be destroyed.'	Is 8:1
our *,	Is 8:9,10
Listen to me, all you * of ours:	Is 8:9,10
"Your * will soon be destroyed."	Is 8:18
Or, "Rezin's *," in some ancient	Is 9:11,12f
* against you—the Syrians on the	Is 9:11,12
enslaved—Israel shall rule her *!	Is 14:2
hide them from our *!	Is 16:4,5
but by dawn her * are dead.	Is 17:14
by the fire reserved for your *.	Is 26:11
wrath against your * has passed.	Is 26:20
I'll watch to keep all * away.	Is 27:3
up, unless these * of mine	Is 27:4,5
as much as he has punished her *?	Is 27:7,8
No, for he has devastated her *,	Is 27:7,8
perish among their *, Assyria and	Is 27:13
and trampled beneath the *' feet.	Is 28:3
But suddenly your ruthless * will	Is 29:5
wakes up, so your * will dream of	Is 29:8
swiftness of your * chasing you!	Is 30:16
in to destroy your *, he will give	Is 30:25
arm upon his * with angry	Is 30:30
and save us. The *' sails hang	Is 33:23
God is coming to destroy your *.	Is 35:4
See, all your angry * lie	Is 41:11
to tear all * apart, making chaff	Is 41:15
* shall come and be your slaves.	Is 49:18
people, and your * who enslaved you	Is 49:19
I will feed your * with their	Is 49:26
Where are my *?	Is 50:8
All my * shall be destroyed like	Is 50:9
fair. Your * will stay far away;	Is 54:14
He will repay his * for their	Is 59:18
the day of his wrath to their *.	Is 61:2
never again give you to your *;	Is 62:8
In my wrath I have trodden my *	Is 63:3
And now our * have destroyed her.	Is 63:18
then your * would learn the	Is 64:2
* will not confiscate it.	Is 65:21,22
will not be eaten by their *;	Is 65:23
Lord taking vengeance upon his *.	Is 66:6
people, and his wrath upon his *.	Is 66:14
the blast of the *' trumpets and	Jer 4:19
trumpets and the *' battle cries.	Jer 4:19
Their * shall live in their	Jer 6:12
the fury of your * to burn you up	Jer 11:16
my dearest ones to their *.	Jer 12:7
you to spare these * of mine."	Jer 15:11
I will have your * take you as	Jer 15:14
treasures to your * as the price	Jer 17:2,3
slaves to your * in distant lands.	Jer 17:4
* as the east wind scatters dust;	Jer 18:17
I will see to it that your * lay	Jer 19:9
them die by the swords of their *.	Jer 20:4
And I will let your * loot	Jer 20:5
In fact, I will bring your *	Jer 21:3,4
by your *, killed by starvation and	Jer 21:9
and all your * shall be slaves.	Jer 30:16
the city will belong to our *."	Jer 32:25
I will give you to your * and	Jer 34:20
a day of vengeance upon his *.	Jer 46:10
knocked him down before your *.	Jer 46:15
will cause her * to wipe her out.	Jer 49:37
*' arrows go straight to the mark;	Jer 50:9
their own lands as the * advance.	Jer 50:16
to explode his wrath upon his *.	Jer 50:25
be filled with *, like fields	Jer 51:14
All her friends are now her *.	Lam 1:2
Her * prosper, for the Lord has	Lam 1:5
Her * have plundered her	Lam 1:10
my strength and gave me to my *;	Lam 1:14
All my * have heard my troubles	Lam 1:21
palaces to their *, who carouse in	Lam 2:7
All your * deride you.	Lam 2:16
and caused her * to rejoice over	Lam 2:17
girls, killed by the *' swords.	Lam 2:21
All our * have spoken out	Lam 3:46
My *, whom I have never harmed,	Lam 3:52
We are doomed. Our * are swifter	Lam 4:19
for food, risking death from *.	Lam 5:9
Israel against her *—by	Eze 13:5
to your *, to those you loathe.	Eze 23:28
For their * will stone them and	Eze 23:47
"Your * have sneered at you and	Eze 36:2
them and let their * destroy them.	Eze 39:23
the lands of their *—and my glory	Eze 39:27
your *, my lord, and not to you!	Dan 4:19
thousands of his * killed, but his	Dan 11:12
free her from her * without any	Hos 1:7
and now her * will chase her.	Hos 8:3
their * will crash through their	Hos 11:6
I shall roar as a lion [at their *	Hos 11:10
You are the * of everything good;	Amo 5:12
and everything in it to her *."	Amo 6:8
you were as one of his *.	Ob 1:11
them to their * in that terrible	Ob 1:14
will be a prize to your *.	Mic 1:15
Then your * will taunt you and	Mic 2:4
free you from the grip of your *.	Mic 4:10
together the * of his people like	Mic 4:12
people to their * until the time of	Mic 5:3
all her * will be wiped out.	Mic 5:9
Yes, a man's * will be found in	Mic 7:6
then he will defend me from my *,	Mic 7:9
He furiously destroys their *.	Nah 1:2
But he sweeps away his * with an	Nah 1:8
He tosses his * into the fire	Nah 1:10
You crushed your * to feed your	Nah 2:12
sold herself to the * of God.	Nah 3:4
wealth, but your * swarm like	Nah 3:16
Jerusalem's * have done to her.	Zec 8:2
the *' advance will all be dashed.	Zec 9:5
go out against his * like a	Zec 9:14
will subdue their *, treading them	Zec 9:15
grinding their *' faces into the	Zec 10:5
of Judah, but blind all her *.	Zec 12:4
your friends and hate your *.'	Mt 5:43
But I say: Love your *!	Mt 5:44
* will be right in his own home!	Mt 10:36
I put your * beneath your feet.'	Mt 22:44
Jesus' * watched him closely.	Mk 3:2
Then turning to his * he asked,	Mk 3:4
I make your * your footstool.'	Mk 12:36
from our *, from all who hate us.	Lk 1:71
freed from our *, and by making us	Lk 1:74
At this, the * of Jesus were	Lk 6:11
Love your *.	Lk 6:27
"Love your *!	Lk 6:35
This shamed his *.	Lk 13:17
And now about these * of mine	Lk 19:27
Your * will pile up earth	Lk 19:43
within you; your * will not leave	Lk 19:44
place your * beneath your feet."	Lk 20:42,43
That day Herod and Pilate—*	Lk 23:12
your * into complete subjection.'	Act 2:35
And since, when we were his *,	Rom 5:10
Now many of the Jews are * of the	Rom 11:28
put down all * of every kind.	1Co 15:24
defeated all his *, including the	1Co 15:25
against all his *, then he, the Son	1Co 15:28
happening, but there are many *.	1Co 16:9
* that mark me as his slave.	Gal 6:17
you were * of God's children and	Eph 2:12
no matter what your * may do.	Php 1:28
really * of the cross of Christ.	Php 3:18
You were his * and hated him and	Col 1:21
though we were surrounded by *.	1Th 2:2
all your * beneath your feet"?	Heb 1:13
his * to be laid under his feet.	Heb 10:13
which will consume all his *.	Heb 10:27
wife who loves her husband's *.	Jas 4:4
friends with God's *—the evil	Jas 4:4
in a cloud as their * watch.	Rev 11:12

ENEMY

It dashes the * to pieces.	Ex 15:6
The * said, "I will chase after	Ex 15:9
will kill you with * armies, so	Ex 22:24
If you see your * trying to get	Ex 23:5
I will be an * to your enemies.	Ex 23:22
that you are captives in * lands.	Lev 26:34,35
Those left shall pine away in *	Lev 26:39
the * was already conquered!	Num 21:34
wanting to harm an *—yet the man	Num 35:22,23
the territory of * nations.	Deu 29:16
How could one single * chase a	Deu 32:30
The heads of the *	Deu 32:40,41
destroying the * from the rear.	Jos 8:22
and took the * armies by surprise.	Jos 10:9
And as the * was racing down the	Jos 10:11
* and cut them down from the rear.	Jos 10:19
so not one * troop survived the	Jos 11:8
For the Lord made the * kings	Jos 11:20
a thousand of the *, for the Lord	Jos 23:10
of the * were slain at Bezek.	Ju 1:4,5,6
Then the Lord threw the * into a	Ju 4:15
Barak and his men chased the *	Ju 4:16
Of the horsehoofs of the *!	Ju 5:22
These * hordes arrived on droves	Ju 6:5
to the outposts of the * camp.	Ju 7:11
as the whole vast * army began	Ju 7:21
Lord caused the * troops to begin	Ju 7:22
tired, but still chasing the *.	Ju 8:4
Lord helped me to conquer the *.	Ju 12:3
"Our god has delivered our *	Ju 16:23,24
the vast mass of * troops, they	1Sa 13:6
him how many * troops there are!"	1Sa 14:6
deceived me and let my * escape?"	1Sa 19:17
would let his * get away when he	1Sa 24:19
"God has put your * within your	1Sa 26:8
left you and has become your *?	1Sa 28:16
safe and helped us defeat the *.	1Sa 30:23
* chariots closing in upon him.	2Sa 1:6
your * Saul who tried to kill you.	2Sa 4:8
"The * came out against us," he	2Sa 11:23
saved him from his * Absalom."	2Sa 18:19
hundred of the * singlehanded and	2Sa 23:18,19
"Do you see all these * forces?	1Ki 20:13
"So my * has found me!"	1Ki 21:20
A great number of the * also	1Ch 5:22
go before you and destroy the *."	1Ch 14:15
When Joab realized that the *	1Ch 19:10
engaged the * troops in battle.	1Ch 19:17,18
with the * before and behind them.	2Ch 13:13,14
a single one of the * had escaped.	2Ch 20:24
that the * wouldn't recognize him.	2Ch 35:22
was from God. The * archers struck	2Ch 35:23
"This wicked Haman is our *."	Est 7:6
the Jews' *, to Queen Esther.	Est 8:1
(son of Hammedatha), the Jews' *—	Est 9:7-10
the Agagite), the * of all the	Est 9:24,25
Why hand me over to my *?	Job 13:24
He has good cause for fear—his *	Job 18:11
he counts me as an *.	Job 19:11
at harm to an *— (but actually I	Job 31:29
and so to count you as his *.	Job 33:10
How long shall my * have the	Ps 13:2
He delivered me from my strong *	Ps 18:17
of death. The *, this gang of evil	Ps 22:16
me over to my *, but have given me	Ps 31:8
against his * Doeg (1 Samuel 22),	Ps 52:1
It was not an * who taunted	Ps 55:12
all day long the * troops press	Ps 56:1
a Rock where no * can reach me.	Ps 62:7
The Lord speaks. The * flees.	Ps 68:11,12,13
the * has done to your sanctuary.	Ps 74:3
he surrendered his glory into *	Ps 78:61
and animals. The * has butchered	Ps 79:3
O my *, but the Lord helped me.	Ps 118:13
No * attacking the walls, but	Ps 144:12-15
Do not rejoice when your * meets	Pro 24:17
If your * is hungry, give him	Pro 25:21,22
are better than kisses from an *!	Pro 27:6
But the * stops at Nob for the	Is 10:32
will cut down the * as a woodsman's	Is 10:34
See the flags waving as their *	Is 13:2
at Sibmah. The * war-lords have cut	Is 16:8
"the great power of their *,	Is 21:16
knock it down! The * will come like	Is 28:17
when the terrible * floods in, you	Is 28:18
I will be your *.	Is 29:3
* runs at the sound of your voice.	Is 33:3
of protection, and no * can cross.	Is 33:21
That is why he became their * and	Is 63:10
their doom. The * shall roll down	Jer 4:13
nations that the * is coming from a	Jer 4:16
For the * is everywhere, ready to	Jer 6:25
THEN, SAYS THE Lord, the * shall	Jer 8:1
army, for the * is coming, and is	Jer 8:16
For I will send these * troops	Jer 8:17
closed their gates against the *.	Jer 13:19
and treasures as spoil to the *.	Jer 15:12,13
I will be its * and not its	Jer 21:10
cruelly, as though I were your *;	Jer 30:14
from the distant land of the *.	Jer 31:16
siege guns of the *, yet the	Jer 33:4
The arrows of the * shall strike	Jer 51:3
before her mocking * struck her	Lam 1:7
my plight. The * has triumphed."	Lam 1:9
his protection as the * attacks.	Lam 2:3
his people as though he were an *.	Lam 2:4
has vanquished Israel like an *.	Lam 2:5
upon the streets before the *.	Lam 2:22
have believed an * could enter	Lam 4:12
the city, and * camps around it,	Eze 4:1
Demonstrate how an * army will	Eze 4:3
will be slaughtered by the *;	Eze 5:12
sword of the * chasing after you.	Eze 5:12
the sword of the * will slay you;	Eze 5:17
there stands the * to kill you.	Eze 7:15
the armies of the * to come and	Eze 14:17
the terrible waves of * attack.	Eze 26:19
wise as God, an * army, the terror	Eze 28:7
"The Lord God says: I am your *,	Eze 28:22
says: I am your *, Pharaoh, king of	Eze 29:3
But if the watchman sees the *	Eze 33:6
deeds, the * shall utterly defile	Dan 9:27
the * for their insolence to me.	Hos 7:16
Like a vulture, the * descends	Hos 8:1
Lord God says, "an * is coming!	Amo 3:11
MOBILIZE! THE * lays siege to	Mic 5:1
against me, O my *, for though I	Mic 7:8
Then my * will see that God is	Mic 7:10
For this * from Nineveh will	Nah 1:15
You are already surrounded by *	Nah 2:1
watch for the * attack to begin!	Nah 2:1
The river gates are open! The *	Nah 2:6
the * and set on fire and burned.	Nah 3:13
cut you down; the * will consume	Nah 3:15
*, whose homes will be ransacked;	Zep 1:13

(ENEMY Con't)
and disperse the armies of your *. Zep 3:15
their * is doomed. Zec 10:5
the other animals in the * camp. Zec 14:15
quickly with your * before it is Mt 5:25
but one night as he slept, his * Mt 13:25
" 'An * has done it,' he Mt 13:28
to Satan. The * who sowed the Mt 13:39
the power of the *, and to walk Lk 10:19
then while the * troops are still Lk 14:32
brutally killed by * weapons, or Lk 21:24
and villainy, * of all that is Act 13:10
Instead, feed your * if he is Rom 12:20
including the last *—death. 1Co 15:26
that "our former * is now Gal 1:23
And now have I become your * Gal 4:16
to resist the * whenever he Eph 6:13
Don't think of him as an *, but 2Th 3:15
this world—makes you an * of God? Jas 4:4
attacks from Satan, your great *. 1Pe 5:8

ENEMY'S
"If you come upon an * ox or Ex 23:4

ENERGETIC
The workmen were * under the 2Ch 34:12
She is *, a hard worker, and Pro 31:17

ENERGIES
He now turned his * to 2Ch 8:2
their time and * were devoted to 2Ch 31:17,18
am bringing all my * to bear on Php 3:13

ENERGY
forward with great * and success. Ez 5:8
*, and are a feather in your cap. Pro 3:22
You spend your time and * in Is 59:5
No, spend your * seeking the Jn 6:27
mighty * is at work within me. Col 1:29
Spend your time and * in the 1Ti 4:7
Do it with all the strength and * 1Pe 4:11

ENFORCED
the Lord must be * so that the 2Ch 24:6
The law is not * and there is no Hab 1:4

ENFORCES
dreadful. He * peace in heaven. Job 25:2

ENGAGE
sent one group to * the Syrians. 1Ch 19:10
from Jerusalem to * Pharaoh's army Jer 37:11

ENGAGED
who is not * to anyone, and Ex 22:16
girl who is * to be married, they Lev 19:20
Has anyone just become *? Deu 20:7
If a girl who is * is seduced Deu 22:23,24
a girl who is not *, and is caught Deu 22:28,29
which was then * in attacking the 1Ki 16:15,16
and * the enemy troops in battle. 1Ch 19:17,18
was * to be married to Joseph. Mt 1:18
to a virgin, Mary, * to be married Lk 1:27

ENGAGEMENT
And if he arranges an * between Ex 21:9
decided to break the * but to do Mt 1:19

ENGANNIM
Kishion, Daberath, Jarmuth, and *. Jos 21:28,29

ENGEDI
went to live in the caves of *. 1Sa 23:29
had gone into the wilderness of *; 1Sa 24:1
Hazazon-tamar" (also called *). 2Ch 20:2
of flowers in the gardens of *. Sol 1:14

ENGINES
And he produced * of war 2Ch 26:15

ENGLISH
An example in * might be, Gen 30:6f
for speaking in plain, simple * 1Co 14:7
Apollyon [and in *, the Destroyer Rev 9:11

ENGRAVE
Take two onyx stones, and * on Ex 28:9
of pure gold and * on it, just as Ex 28:36
beside, and I will * this Zec 3:9
and I will * its inscription." Zec 3:9f

ENGRAVED
the Ten Commandments * on them. Ex 25:16
stone tablets * with God's laws. Ex 26:33
will be * upon it like a seal. Ex 28:21
the stones were * with the names of Ex 39:6,7
as initials are * upon a ring. Ex 39:6,7
The stones were * like a seal, Ex 39:14
of the turban, * with the words, Ex 39:30
Ten Commandments * on them, and Ex 40:20
by wreaths were * on the borders of 1Ki 7:36
and * with palm trees and chains. 2Ch 3:5
gold, with angels * on the walls. 2Ch 3:7
the stone will be * a new name that Rev 2:17

ENGRAVER
He is an * besides, and an 2Ch 2:14

ENGRAVERS
and skilled * to work beside the 2Ch 2:7

ENGRAVING
When * these names, use the same Ex 28:11
also an expert at *, weaving, and Ex 38:23

ENGULF
Their fury and hatred rise to * Ps 55:3

ENGULFED
of death that * the cities. Gen 19:29
thick darkness that * Mount Sinai. Deu 5:22
the desert, and * the house so that Job 1:19
For a crime wave has * Job 24:2
and when you are * by anguish and Pro 1:27
You have * us by your anger, Lam 3:43

ENGULFS
wave after wave * me. Ps 88:7

ENHANCE
she wished, to * her beauty. Est 2:12,13,14

ENHAZOR
Kedesh, Edre-i, *, Yiron, Jos 19:35-39

ENJOIN
commandments I * on you today." Deu 27:1f

ENJOY
the rest for the animals to *. Ex 23:11
appreciate and *— for in this way Lev 17:5
appreciate and *— instead of the Lev 17:6
land will rest and * its Sabbaths! Lev 26:34,35
For the land shall * its Lev 26:43
the Lord will appreciate and *. Num 29:2
your children will * the good life Deu 11:21
to Ahab, "Go and * a good meal! 1Ki 18:41
for you * good men. 1Ch 29:17
He shall not * the goods he Job 20:17
again be able to * his family. Job 21:21
How I * your commands! Ps 119:47
May you live to * your Ps 128:6
for they thoroughly * their sins. Pro 2:14
only good men * life to the full; Pro 2:21
The wicked * fellowship with Pro 17:4
liars * liars. Pro 17:4
Some men * cheating, but the cake Pro 20:17
don't even * their company. Pro 24:1
When you * becoming wise, there Pro 24:13,14
merry; * yourself to the full." Ecc 2:1
* his food and drink, and his job. Ecc 2:24-26
For who can eat or * apart from Ecc 2:24-26
to * himself as long as he can; Ecc 3:12
eat and drink and * the fruits of Ecc 3:13
back to life to * what will be in Ecc 3:22
the future, so let them * it now. Ecc 3:22
in life, and * his work whatever Ecc 5:18
Lord, and the good health to * it. Ecc 5:19,20
to enjoy it. To * your work and to Ecc 5:19,20
them the health to * it, and they Ecc 6:2
facts of nature. * prosperity Ecc 7:14
to be young! * every minute of it! Ecc 11:9
you'll no longer * living. Ecc 12:1
will long * their hard-won gains. Is 65:21,22
For he does not * afflicting men Lam 3:33
I do not * seeing you die, the Eze 18:32
says, since you * blood so much, I Eze 35:6
let them * the fertile pastures Mic 7:14
Then once more the Lord will * Mal 3:4
How they * the deference paid Mt 23:7
those who * listening to sermons, Lk 8:13
feel secure or * God's blessing. Rom 3:17
given his wonderful new life to *. Rom 6:4
from sin which God's children *. Rom 8:20,21
* the company of ordinary folks. Rom 12:16
and don't make plans to * evil. Rom 13:14
without stopping to * them; 1Co 7:31
to the Lord and is yours to *. 1Co 10:26
for the food and * it, why let 1Co 10:30
We own nothing, and yet we * 2Co 6:10
He must * having guests in his 1Ti 3:2
to * and be thankful for. 1Ti 4:3
love them and * being with them. 2Ti 1:7
Have faith and love, and * the 2Ti 2:22
They must * having guests in Tit 1:8
if your aim is to * the evil Jas 4:4
things the godless *—sex sin, lust, 1Pe 4:3
is for you to * other people and to 2Pe 1:7
in life is to * themselves in every Jud 1:18

ENJOYABLE
Kind words are like honey—* and Pro 16:24
Being punished isn't * while it Heb 12:11

ENJOYED
and after he has * it he will bless Gen 27:8,9,10
delicious fish we * so much in Num 11:4,5
so they ate and were full and * Neh 9:25
* her, and called for her by name. Est 2:12,13,14
"He * the taste of his Job 20:12
* them more than my daily food. Job 23:12
he and his sons and cattle *?" Jn 4:12
what freedom we * in Christ Jesus, Gal 2:4
The rulers of earth have * Rev 18:3
immoral acts and * her favors, will Rev 18:9

ENJOYING
I've been * are all because of your Gen 30:27
on that day, but * the Sabbath and Is 58:13
the Truth, and * their sins. 2Th 2:12
* the fleeting pleasures of sin. Heb 11:24,25

ENJOYMENT
music is being played for your *. Ps 45:8
I have forgotten what * is. Lam 3:17
gives us all we need for our *. 1Ti 6:17

ENJOYS
he loves you and * your pleasant Deu 15:16
Lord who * helping his child!" Ps 35:27
For Jehovah * his people; Ps 149:4,5
If a man * folly, something is Pro 15:21
Everyone * giving good advice, Pro 15:
truth—he * his sinning too much. Pro 19:2

ENLARGE
before you and * your boundaries. Ex 34:2
husband stayed! * your house; Is 54
For in their wars in Gilead to * Amo 1:
Literally, "* their Mt 23:

ENLARGED
And I will set your * boundaries Ex 23:3
work among you will be greatly *. 2Co 10:1

ENLARGES
"If, when the Lord * your Deu 12:20-2
"If the Lord * your boundaries Deu 19:

ENLIGHTENED
How you have * my stupidity! Job 26:

ENLIGHTENMENT
you are filled with * and wisdom. Dan 5:1

ENLIST
to * mercenary troops, chariots, 1Ch 19:

ENLISTED
the one who has * you in his army. 2Ti 2:

ENLISTING
Otherwise I fear that after * 1Co 9:2

ENMISHPAT
Then they swung around to * Gen 14:

ENMITY
his attitude of * against Christ is 1Jn 4:

ENOCH
him with a baby son named *; Gen 4:1
he named it *, after his son. Gen 4:1
* was the father Gen 4:1
years old when his son * was born. Gen 5:18,19,2
*: Enoch was sixty-five years old Gen 5:21-2
Enoch: * was sixty-five years old Gen 5:21-2
*, Methuselah, Lamech, Noah, 1Ch 1:
Methuselah's father was *; Lk 3:23-3
* trusted God too, and that is Heb 11:
how pleased he was with *. Heb 11:
*, who lived seven generations Jud 1:1

ENOCH'S
Methuselah's father was Enoch;* Lk 3:23-3

ENORMOUS
forbidden, for it is an * sin. Lev 18:2
land become full of * wickedness. Lev 19:2
and the work ahead of him is *; 1Ch 29:
limbs, and throughout his * frame. Job 41:12
Then frogs invaded in * numbers; Ps 105:3
Then once again * crops will Is 32:15
The weight of the two * pillars Jer 52:2
healed them all. * crowds followed Mt 4:25
but what * damage it can do. Jas 3:5

ENORMOUSLY
and your wealth has increased *; Gen 30:3

ENOS
Cainan's father was *; Lk 3:23-38
Cainan's father was Enos;*' father Lk 3:23-38

ENOSH
up, he had a son and named him *. Gen 4:26
years old when his son * was born. Gen 5:6,7,8
*: Enosh was ninety years old Gen 5:9,10,11
Enosh: * was ninety years old Gen 5:9,10,11
Adam, Seth, *, Kenan, Mahalalel, 1Ch 1:1

ENOUGH
And sure *, when they arrived Gen 12:14
Use your best flour, and make * Gen 18:6
camels, too, until they have *!" Gen 24:19
to the camels until they had *. Gen 24:20
And sure *, she had twins. Gen 25:24
Well of Room * for Us at Last!" Gen 26:22
"Wasn't it * to steal my husband? Gen 30:15
generous to me and I have *." Gen 33:11
For the land is large * to hold Gen 34:21
(For there was not land * to Gen 36:6,7,8
son Shelah was old * to marry her. Gen 38:11
that there will be * to eat when Gen 41:36
And sure *, for the next seven Gen 41:47
"Fair *," the man replied, Gen 44:10
And sure *, when Pharaoh heard Ex 2:15
don't have * to do or else they Ex 5:7,8
"You don't have * work, or else Ex 5:17
were not * graves for us in Egypt? Ex 14:11
there was just * for everyone—three Ex 16:18
Each home had just *. Ex 16:18
that there will be * for two days? Ex 16:28,29
pouring out, * for everyone!" Ex 17:5,6
has increased * to fill the land. Ex 23:30
have more than * materials on hand Ex 36:4-7
gets together * money, then he may Lev 25:26
oven will be large * to bake all Lev 26:26
flocks and herds it won't be *! Num 11:22
He wasn't strong * to bring them Num 14:16
have had * of your presumption; Num 16:3
There was not * water to drink Num 20:2
Why, there isn't even water * to Num 20:5
water from a rock, * for all the Num 20:8
And sure *, Israel was Num 21:35
us, 'You have stayed here long *. Deu 1:6
One look was * to convince us Deu 1:24,25
" 'You have stayed here long *. Deu 2:3
were old * to bear arms, had died. Deu 2:14,15
* olive oil to anoint yourselves! Deu 28:40

ENOUGH Con't)
who had been old * to bear arms had Jos 5:4,5
who had been old * to bear arms Jos 5:6
became strong *, they forced the Jos 17:13
is not large * for you," Joshua Jos 17:15
have been kind * to give me land in Ju 1:15
"when there is * light, we'll find Ju 16:2
in the area strong * to try it. Ju 18:7
but there were not * of these Ju 21:14
we didn't find * wives for them Ju 21:22
so that I will have * to eat.' 1Sa 2:36
And sure *, the cows went 1Sa 6:12
have mourned long * for Saul, for I 1Sa 16:1
family find * dowry to marry the 1Sa 18:23
We already have * of them around 1Sa 21:14,15
that is why I have been bold * to 2Sa 7:27
and if that had not been *, I 2Sa 12:8
"* of this nonsense," Joab 2Sa 18:14
and sure *, they turned his heart 1Ki 11:3
And as though that were not *, 1Ki 16:31
be * food for you and your son. 1Ki 17:13
see if we can find * grass to save 1Ki 18:5
And sure *, the sky was soon 1Ki 18:45
"I've had *," he told the Lord. 1Ki 19:4
the food gave him * strength to 1Ki 19:8
And sure *, as he turned to go 1Ki 20:36
me: 'Isn't killing Naboth bad *? 1Ki 21:19
water—and only * to keep him alive 1Ki 22:27
And sure *! 2Ki 2:22
And sure *, the next day at about 2Ki 3:20
and there will be * money left for 2Ki 4:7
And sure *, there was, just as 2Ki 4:44
*, he had saved him from disaster. 2Ki 6:10
It is *!" 1Ch 21:15
David weighed out * gold and 1Ch 28:14
He also weighed out * silver for 1Ch 28:15
for building it—* gold, silver, 1Ch 29:2
heaven would be beautiful *! 2Ch 2:6
"You'll find out soon *," 2Ch 18:24
We are in * trouble with God as 2Ch 28:13
April, because not * priests were 2Ch 30:2,3
wasn't * time to get notices out. 2Ch 30:2,3
a day if they offer * sacrifices? Neh 4:1
slavery to get * money to live. Neh 5:5
Don't we have * enemies among the Neh 5:9
And all who were old * to Neh 8:1
who were old * to understand, had Neh 10:28
there would be * money to care for Neh 10:32
Wasn't it * that your fathers Neh 13:18
and sure *, Job 1:12,13
let me alone—even long * to spit? Job 7:19
* to keep soul and body together. Job 24:5
No darkness is thick * to hide Job 34:22
you shout loudly * against God, he Job 36:19
Who is wise * to number all the Job 38:37,38
For you alone are strong *. Ps 31:4
strength is not * to save anyone. Ps 33:16,17
even in famine, they will have *. Ps 37:19
I can never thank you *! Ps 44:8
There is not * of it in all the Ps 49:8,9
old * to sing their wedding songs. Ps 78:63
Who can ever praise him half *? Ps 106:2
but I have sense * to follow you. Ps 119:70
and never has * of lust and shame. Pro 9:13
"but the wicked never get *." Pro 13:25f
But one calamity is * to lay you Pro 24:15,16
pleasant *, but don't believe him; Pro 26:24,25,26
then there will be lamb's wool * Pro 27:25,26,27
and goat's milk * for food for all Pro 27:25,26,27
mere words are not *—discipline Pro 29:19
Give me just * to satisfy my Pro 30:8
loves money shall never have *. Ecc 5:10
for food, and never seem to get *. Ecc 6:7,8
Oh, my people, haven't you had * Is 1:5,6
this child was old * to talk (verse Is 7:14f
shall know (is old *) to refuse the Is 7:15,16f
and (is old * to) eat curds and Is 7:15,16f
child is even old * to say 'Daddy' Is 8:4
his food, but will never have *. Is 9:19,20
children, barely old * to talk? Is 28:9
we've heard more than * about Is 30:10,11
Not a piece will be left large * Is 30:14
it will give you * seed for a small Is 37:30
a sacrifice large * to honor him, Is 40:16
its animals * to offer to our God. Is 40:16
You have drunk * from the cup of Is 51:17
They are smart * at doing wrong, Jer 4:22
won't be room * for all the graves Jer 7:32
Who is wise * to understand all Jer 9:12
desperate * to beg me for help. Jer 11:14
won't be room * for decent burial Jer 19:11
who lives close * to God to hear Jer 23:18
Has even one of them cared * to Jer 23:18
And sure *, two months later Jer 28:17
And sure *, it wasn't long before Jer 38:27
Don't I have troubles * already? Jer 45:3
I will punish you, but only * to Jer 46:28
Aren't the Jews * to fill them Jer 49:1
So I looked and, sure *, north Eze 8:5
you tell us that it wasn't good *? Eze 13:12
you were old * for marriage; Eze 16:8
Wasn't it * that you should be a Eze 16:20
you can never find * new gods. Eze 16:28
It will pull out easily *—it Eze 17:9
no search will be * to find you, Eze 26:21
never again will Egypt be great * Eze 29:15
* to defeat the Egyptian force. Eze 30:21f
it strong * to hold a sword again. Eze 30:21
fuel—* to last them seven years. Eze 39:9
That is *! Eze 44:28
sensible, and have * poise to look Dan 1:3,4
with fruit, * for everyone to eat. Dan 4:12
girl for wine * to get drunk. Joe 3:3
won't be fast * to flee, and even Amo 2:15
who never have * to drink! Amo 4:1
had rain, but there wasn't ever *. Amo 4:8
For how can I thank you * for all Jon 2:9
it is right for me to be angry * Jon 4:9
You will eat but never have *; Mic 6:14
not get * to anoint Mic 6:15
my people, I have punished you *! Nah 1:12
You have scarcely * to eat or Hag 1:6
not * clothes to keep you warm. Hag 1:6
it is big * for all the people!" Zec 2:2
she won't have room * for all! Zec 2:4
You have been listening long *! Zec 8:9
there will be food * in my Temple; Mal 3:10
won't have room * to take it in! Mal 3:10
Your word is *. Mt 5:37
about having * food and clothing. Mt 6:31,32
is broad, and its gate is wide * Mt 7:13
will be taken from them. Time * Mt 9:15
the plants sprang up quickly * in Mt 13:5
he owned to get * money to buy the Mt 13:44
where would we get * here in the Mt 15:33
of them were wise * to fill their Mt 25:2,3,4
the others replied, 'We haven't *. Mt 25:9
"They can guard it safely *." Mt 27:65
It grew up quickly *, but soon Mk 4:5,6
No one was strong * to control Mk 5:3,4
And sure *, as soon as she had Mk 5:29
is willing *, the body is weak." Mk 14:38
That isn't *. Lk 3:8
think themselves already good *." Lk 5:32
see well * to deal with his speck! Lk 6:42
go and buy * for this whole mob?" Lk 9:13
keep knocking long * he will get up Lk 11:8
Then I'll have room *. Lk 12:18
* stored away for years to come. Lk 12:19
* food to eat or clothes to wear. Lk 12:22
You interpret the sky well *, but Lk 12:56
he has * money to pay the bills? Lk 14:28
10,000 is strong * to defeat the Lk 14:31
men have food * and to spare, and Lk 15:17
would be large * to uproot that Lk 17:6
they said, 'he has * already!' Lk 19:25
said, and sure *, as they were Lk 19:33
*! he said Lk 22:38
to see, and sure *, Jesus' body was Lk 24:24
Your miracles are proof * of Jn 3:1
Or, "Physical birth is not *. Jn 3:5f
and he did, for two days, long * Jn 4:40,41
though you readily * receive those Jn 5:43
He is old * to speak for himself. Jn 9:21
for you get * hate from the world! Jn 15:18
If you do this, it is *. Act 15:27,28,29
to quiet them down * to speak. Act 19:35
—not by "being good *" and Rom 3:21,22
who are "good *," then you are Rom 4:14
who loved us * to die for us. Rom 8:37
themselves good * to gain God's Rom 10:3
it is not by their being good *. Rom 11:6
Who knows * to be his counselor Rom 11:34
the Lord * to induce him to act? Rom 11:35
* to receive a message from God. Rom 12:6
But even so I have been bold * Rom 15:15,16
even * clothes to keep us warm. 1Co 4:11
down here on earth easily *. 1Co 6:3
wise * to decide these arguments? 1Co 6:5
Then he will become bold * to do 1Co 8:10
one doesn't get * and goes hungry 1Co 11:21
He has been punished * by your 2Co 2:5,6
he that gathered little had *." 2Co 8:15
will not only be * for your own 2Co 9:8
letters are bold * when he is far 2Co 10:1
* clothing to keep me warm. 2Co 11:27
Do you love me * to want to help Php 2:1
by being good * or by obeying God's Php 3:9
Pray that I will be bold * to Col 4:4
sweated to earn * to live on so 1Th 2:9
How can we thank God * for you 1Th 3:9
for * money to pay your bills. 1Th 4:12
if we have * food and clothing. 1Ti 6:8
we were good * to be saved, but Tit 3:5
milk, not old * for solid food. Heb 5:12,13
mercy seat. But * of such details. Heb 9:5
one offering would have been *; Heb 10:2
So you see, it isn't * just to Jas 2:17
hold that "only believing" is *? Jas 2:19
You have had * in the past of 1Pe 4:3
be good, and even that is not *. 2Pe 1:5
and of adultery they never have *. 2Pe 2:14
has money * to live well, and sees 1Jn 3:17

ENRAGED
For the Lord is * against the Is 34:2

ENRICH
* your lives and make you wise; Col 3:16

ENRICHED
ours and the land will be *. Gen 34:23
He * you 2Sa 1:24
he has * your whole life. 1Co 1:5

ENROLLED
Literally, "* as a widow." 1Ti 5:9f

ENSHRINED
be the place for my name to be *. 1Ki 11:36
Wisdom is * in the hearts of men Pro 14:33

ENSHROUDED
wings of wind. He * himself with Ps 18:11

ENSLAVE
he will * them and plunder them Is 10:5,6
great kings shall * the Chaldeans, Jer 25:14
king of Babylon will not * you. Jer 27:9
violence, so I will * her people. Eze 7:23

ENSLAVED
the land to all * debtors, and a Lev 25:10
them, and they are * and afflicted, Job 36:8
they hated and * them. Ps 105:25
Those enslaving Israel will be * Is 14:2
of all the nations she * will end. Is 21:2
for they are robbed, *, Is 42:22
who * you shall be far away. Is 49:19
Why are my people * again, and Is 52:5
had captured and * Jeconiah (son of Jer 24:1
just as they * my people; Jer 25:14
Her kings and princes are * in Lam 2:9
I find myself still * to sin. Rom 7:23,24,25

ENSLAVES
the nation that * them, and at the Gen 15:14
the nation that * them,' God told Act 7:7
the law where sin * you, but you Rom 6:14

ENSLAVING
Those * Israel will be Is 14:2

ENSUES
the battle that *, and you will Job 41:8

ENSURE
* his having a long, good reign. Deu 17:20
Can you * the proper sequence of Job 38:32
Will this * your entry into an Lk 16:9

ENTER
permit the Destroyer to * . " Ex 12:23f
to * and kill your firstborn. Ex 12:23
past the altar to * the Tabernacle, Ex 40:32
Moses was not able to * because Ex 40:35
sacred, nor * the Tabernacle. Lev 12:4
Aaron not to * into the Holy Place Lev 16:1
"When you * the land and have Lev 19:23
and his sons will * the Tabernacle Num 4:5
Otherwise they must never * the Num 4:20
me, shall * the Promised Land. Num 14:30
of Nun) are permitted to * it. Num 14:30
Levites shall not * the sanctuary, Num 18:22
If you attempt to * my land I Num 20:18
he shall not * the land I have Num 20:24
shall not * the Promised Land! Deu 1:37
our God had forbidden us to *. Deu 2:37
want to live and * into and possess Deu 4:1
the land you are to * and possess. Deu 5:33
Lord told you to * the land he had Deu 9:23
the land you are about to *. Deu 11:8
For the land you are about to * Deu 11:10
off, he shall not * the sanctuary. Deu 23:1
A bastard may not * the Deu 23:2
Moabite may ever * the sanctuary, Deu 23:3
may * the sanctuary of the Lord. Deu 23:8
* his house to get his security. Deu 24:10
you are about to * and possess. Deu 28:21
You are standing here to * into Deu 29:12
I know now, even before they * Deu 31:21
Israel, but you will not * it." Deu 32:52
seen it, but you will not * it." Deu 34:4
wouldn't let them * the land he had Jos 5:6
your ambush and * the city, for the Jos 8:7
is that he shall not * this city. 2Ki 19:32
refused to let them * the city. 1Ch 11:5,6
And now, O Lord God, arise and * 2Ch 6:41
so that the priests couldn't *! 2Ch 7:1
of the Lord leave me and * you?" 2Ch 18:23
on duty may * the Temple itself, 2Ch 23:5,6
to * in mourning clothes. Est 4:2
The Lord is my fort where I can * Ps 18:2
of the Lord and * where he lives? Ps 24:3
hangouts and refuse to * them. Ps 26:5
as they * in the palace gates! Ps 45:15
to be able to * your courtyard and Ps 84:2
they would never * the Promised Ps 95:11
Literally, "* his courts." Ps 96:8f
* his courts with praise. Ps 100:4
They refused to * the Promised Ps 106:24
the Lord, and the godly * there. Ps 118:20
Arise, O Lord, and * your Temple Ps 132:8
For wisdom and truth will * the Pro 2:10
The men who * them are doomed. Pro 2:19
AS YOU * the Temple, keep your Ecc 5:1

(ENTER Con't)
to meet you as you * their domain. Is 14:9
all may * in who love the Lord. Is 26:2
armies shall not * Jerusalem, nor Is 37:33
not * this city, says the Lord. Is 37:34
now I must * the gates of Sheol. Is 38:10
God—will no longer * your gates. Is 52:1
Babylonians will *, and the men of Jer 33:5
out on you when you * Egypt. Jer 42:18
you had forbidden even to *. Lam 1:10
could * through Jerusalem's gates! Lam 4:12
They shall not * Israel, but I Eze 20:38
among you shall * my sanctuary if Eze 44:9
They shall * my sanctuary and Eze 44:16
clothing when they * the passageway Eze 44:17
The prince shall * the outside Eze 46:2
The prince shall * and leave Eze 46:10
up for him to * and he shall offer Eze 46:12
And he will also * 'The Glorious Dan 11:16
He will * the richest areas of Dan 11:24
* the gates of the land of Nimrod. Mic 5:6
Whenever you * a city or Mt 10:11
and all * the man and live in him. Mt 12:43,44,45
Better to * heaven crippled than Mt 18:8
Better to * heaven with one eye Mt 18:9
man to * the Kingdom of God!" Mt 19:24
"Just as you *," he said, "you Mt 21:2
For you won't let others * the Mt 23:13,14
couldn't publicly * a city Mk 1:45
of this child and * him no more!" Mk 9:25
Better * the Kingdom of God half Mk 9:47
to * the Kingdom of God. Mk 10:24
man to * the Kingdom of God." Mk 10:25
"and just as you * you will see a Mk 11:2
to * the inner sanctuary and burn Lk 1:8,9
him to let them * into the pigs. Lk 8:32
to you when you * it, turn around Lk 9:5
"Whenever you * a home, give it Lk 10:5
"When you * a village, don't Lk 10:7
itself, and they all * the man. Lk 11:26
give light to all who * the room. Lk 11:33
many will try to * but when the Lk 13:24,25
the rich to * the Kingdom of God! Lk 18:24
man to * the Kingdom of God." Lk 18:25
"As soon as you * Jerusalem, Lk 22:10
Literally, "that you * not into Lk 22:40f
and the Spirit, he cannot * the Jn 3:5
that they must * into the Kingdom Act 14:22
that all may * his place of rest—we Heb 4:1
God can * into his place of rest. Heb 4:3
"They shall never * my rest." Heb 4:5
disobeyed God and failed to *. Heb 4:6
first failure to *, saying in the Heb 4:7
heaven for you to * into the 2Pe 1:11
* them and they will stand up! Rev 11:11
to * into their full reward. Rev 14:13
and no one could * until the Rev 15:8
have the right to * in through the Rev 22:14

ENTERED
took their swords, * the city Gen 34:25
He was thirty years old as he * Gen 41:46
And I * into a solemn covenant Ex 6:4
distance, Moses * into the deep Ex 20:21
As he *, the pillar of cloud Ex 33:9
people * the Tabernacle." Num 8:19
into the land he * as a spy, and Num 14:24
Israel had not yet * and conquered Jos 18:1
Then the five spies * the shrine Ju 18:17
as she * and bowed low to her. 1Ki 2:19
the side rooms was * from the right 1Ki 6:8
When Jehu * the gate of the 2Ki 9:31
the people of Israel * the land. 2Ki 16:3
the people of Israel * the land. 2Ki 21:9
Then they * into a contract to 2Ch 15:12
God, for they had * into it with 2Ch 15:15
the people of Israel * the land. 2Ch 33:2
destroyed when Israel * the land. 2Ch 33:9
and * again at the Valley Gate. Neh 2:14,15
royal robes and * the inner court Est 5:1
The troops of Cyrus the Great * Jer 25:12f
And the Spirit * into me as he Eze 2:2
Then the Spirit * into me and set Eze 3:24
the underworld who * long ago the Eze 26:20
the God of Israel, * here and so it Eze 44:2
* the city and began reigning at Dan 5:31
day when Jonah * the city and began Jon 3:4,5
The enemy has *! Nah 2:6
"Heaven can be * only through Mt 7:13
And they came out of the men and * Mt 8:32
of Jerusalem was stirred as he *. Mt 21:10
out of the man and * the hogs, and Mk 5:13
And so he * Jerusalem and went Mk 11:11
So they * the tomb—and there on Mk 16:5
When I * your home, you didn't Lk 7:44
and as they * a village there, ten Lk 17:12
and as they * they were to look for Lk 19:30
Then he * the Temple and began to Lk 19:45
Then Satan * into Judas Iscariot, Lk 22:3
had eaten it, Satan * into him. Jn 13:27
and * a grove of olive trees. Jn 18:1
As Peter * his home, Cornelius Act 10:25
When Adam sinned, sin * the Rom 5:12
Literally, "Sin * into the world, Rom 5:12f
that is in you, that * into you 2Ti 1:6
Christ has already * there. Heb 4:10
For Christ has * into heaven Heb 9:24

ENTERING
Anyone * the house while it is Lev 14:46
conditions for his * there: He must Lev 16:3
soon be *, where you will live. Deu 6:1
them from * the Promised Land. Jos 14:8
and as they were * the gates they 1Sa 9:14
to be seen * and leaving the city. 2Sa 17:17
unauthorized person * the Temple. 2Ch 23:7
Lord his God by * the forbidden 2Ch 26:16
They turned back from * the Ps 78:57
clothes before * the parts of the Eze 42:14
invading armies from * Israel. Zec 9:8
* the house where the baby and Mt 2:11
before * his time of glory?" Lk 24:26
By Jewish law, * the house of a Jn 18:28f
believers, even * private homes and Act 8:3
him not to risk his life by *. Act 19:31

ENTERPRISE
Any * is built by wise planning, Pro 24:3,4

ENTERS
when Aaron * to make atonement in Lev 16:17
Everyone who * the tent, and those Num 19:14
of where it * the Jordan River. 1Ki 17:3
left side as one * the city gate. 2Ki 23:8
else, and * eternal darkness. Ps 49:19
to work and * the inner court and Eze 44:27
At the house he *, tell the man Mk 14:14
Follow him into the house he *, Lk 22:10

ENTERTAINED
and David * them with a feast. 2Sa 3:20
This occurred when Hezekiah * the Eze 23:16f
* angels without realizing it! Heb 13:2

ENTERTAINING
You are very * to them, like Eze 33:32

ENTERTAINMENT
tasty, and * is not much fun; 2Sa 19:35
He refused his usual * and didn't Dan 6:18

ENTHRONED
heaven who is * above the angels. 1Sa 4:4
of heaven * above the cherubim. 2Sa 6:1
the Lord God * above the angels. 1Ch 13:6
choice, and I have * him in Ps 2:6
O God * above the cherubim, bend Ps 80:1
He is * upon the cherubim. Ps 99:1
Who can be compared with God * on Ps 113:5
O GOD * in heaven, I lift my eyes Ps 123:1
God of Israel * above the cherubim, Is 37:16,17
shall be * beside Almighty God." Lk 22:69

ENTHUSIASM
the Lord with true *, and that you 1Sa 12:20
Lord with great *, accompanied by 1Ch 13:8
fathers. The * continued, so it 2Ch 30:23
his * fades, and he drops out. Mt 13:21
I know what * they have for the Rom 10:2
so much *, so much love for us. 2Co 8:7
In fact, it was this * of yours 2Co 9:2
hearts and real * for doing kind Tit 2:14

ENTHUSIASTIC
and courageous, fearless and *! 1Ch 22:13
and are * about asking King Rezin Is 8:6
were so * about Jesus' teaching. Mk 11:18
The crowd was excited and *, but Lk 11:14
* about one and despise the other. Lk 16:13
They were so * about it that we 2Co 8:6
Let your * idea at the start be 2Co 8:11
become * about the things of God. Rev 3:19

ENTHUSIASTICALLY
Cling to him and serve him *." Jos 22:5
man who * served the Lord. 2Ch 22:9
So he was preaching boldly and * Act 18:25,26
in your work but serve the Lord *. Rom 12:11
ball rolling so *, you should carry 2Co 8:11

ENTICE
"Then the Lord said, 'Who will * 1Ki 22:20

ENTICED
Lord, and Manasseh * them to do 2Ki 21:9
has been secretly *, and I have Job 31:27
of deadly charms, * the nations Nah 3:4

ENTICEMENT
their eyes to all * to do wrong. Is 33:15

ENTIRELY
Stay away from the mountain * Ex 19:13
the animal must be * without defect Lev 3:1
These offerings shall be * burned Lev 6:22,23
That carcass must be * burned Lev 6:30
was made * of beaten gold. Num 8:4
lost their nerve * and tried to 1Sa 13:6
were constructed * from huge, 1Ki 7:9
Syria until they were * destroyed; 2Ki 13:19
Yes, I'll tell you things * new, Is 48:8
last of the food * gone, the Jer 52:6
he seemed to be * flame, and there Eze 1:27,28
his feet washed to be * clean. Jn 13:10
In this way he was being * fair, Rom 3:25
life, leaving * behind us the 1Co 5:8
you * pure and devoted to God; 1Th 5:23
themselves to be * trustworthy. Tit 2:1
someone, you have * broken God's Jas 2:1

ENTRAILS
and wash off the * and the legs; Ex 29:1
all the fat on the *, the two Lev 4:
fat covering the *, the fatty mass Lev 8:15,1
closed over it as the * oozed out. Ju 3:22,2

ENTRANCE
guard the * to the Tree of Life. Gen 3:2
angels came to the * of the city of Gen 19:
This is the awesome * to Gen 28:16,1
the road at the * to the village of Gen 38:1
road at the * of the village?" Gen 38:2
As they arrived at the * to the Gen 43:1
On each side of the * there will Ex 27:14,1
"The * to the court will be a Ex 27:1
bring it to the * of the Ex 29:3,
Aaron and his sons there at the *. Ex 29:3,
Lord, at the * of the Tabernacle. Ex 29:1
stood at the camp * and shouted, Ex 32:2
watching until he reached its *. Ex 33:8
Drapes for the * to the court; Ex 35:10-1
Then he made a drapery for the * Ex 36:3
at the * to the Tabernacle. Ex 38:8
either side of the * were 22½ feet Ex 38:14,1
The drapery covering the * to the Ex 38:18
the posts at the * to the Ex 38:29
goat skins, and the * drape; Ex 39:33-40
Set up the drapes at the * of the Ex 40:
burnt offerings in front of the *. Ex 40:6
at the * to the courtyard. Ex 40:8
his sons to the * of the Tabernacle Ex 40:12
He attached the curtain at the * Ex 40:28
offerings near the *, and offered Ex 40:29
at the * of the enclosure. Ex 40:33
Bring the animal to the * of the Lev 1:2,3
altar at the * of the Tabernacle. Lev 1:5
it at the * of the Tabernacle; Lev 3:7,8
it at the * of the Tabernacle. Lev 3:13
at the * to the Tabernacle. Lev 4:7
altar, at the * to the Tabernacle. Lev 4:18
his sons to the * of the Lev 8:1
the meat at the * of the Lev 8:31
the Tabernacle * for seven days, Lev 8:33
to stay at the * of the Tabernacle Lev 8:35
things to the * of the Tabernacle, Lev 9:5
Lord at the * of the Tabernacle. Lev 14:11
the priest at the * of the Lev 14:23
the Lord at the * of the Lev 15:14
the priest at the * of the Lev 15:29
the Lord at the * of the Lev 16:7
the priest at the * of the Lev 17:5
of the Lord at the * of the Lev 17:6
other than at the * of the Lev 17:8,9
Lord at the * of the Tabernacle; Lev 19:21
the screen at the * of the Num 3:25-30
the curtain for the Tabernacle *. Num 4:25
curtain across the * to the Num 4:26
priest at the * of the Tabernacle. Num 6:10
he must go to the * of the Num 6:13
This shall be done at the * of Num 6:18
gather at the * of the Tabernacle. Num 10:3
stood at the * of the Tabernacle. Num 12:5
and stood at the * of the Num 16:18
and stood at the * of the Num 16:43,44
Moses at the * of the Tabernacle; Num 16:50
and went to the * of the Num 20:6
came to the * of the Tabernacle to Num 27:1
at the Tabernacle *, and said to Deu 31:15
to the * of Hamath in the north; Jos 13:2-7
the * of the Tabernacle at Shiloh. Jos 19:51
the * passage through the wall. Ju 1:24
Baal-hermon to the * of Hamath. Ju 3:1
his customary place beside the *. 1Sa 1:9
at the * to the Tabernacle. 1Sa 2:22
the * to the Most Holy Place. 1Ki 6:21,22
wood for the * to the Temple. 1Ki 6:33
Hiram set these pillars at the * 1Ki 7:16-22
the main * doors of the Temple. 1Ki 7:50
chariot to the * of the city! 1Ki 18:46
and stood at the * of the cave. 1Ki 19:13
two heaps at the * of the city 2Ki 10:8
side of the altar at the Temple *. 2Ki 12:9
between the Temple * and the new 2Ki 16:14
the shrines at the * of the palace 2Ki 23:8
located near the * of the Temple, 2Ki 23:11
of the * to the Tabernacle. 1Ch 9:21
of Egypt—to the * of Hamath." 1Ch 13:5f
Across the * to this room he 2Ch 3:14
will stay at the * as guards. 2Ch 23:4
his pillar at the *, with the army 2Ch 23:12
Go over to the * of the Temple of Jer 7:2
him at the side * of the Temple. Jer 38:14
stones at the * of Pharaoh's palace Jer 43:9
that stood at the * of the Temple, Jer 52:17
Jerusalem, to the * of the north Eze 8:3
gate, in the *, stood the idol. Eze 8:5
had rested and stood above the * Eze 9:3
steps into the * and he measured Eze 40:6
The full length of the * passage Eze 40:15
in the exit and in the * halls. Eze 40:16

NTRANCE Con't)
Its guardrooms, pillars and * and Eze 40:29,30
to the eastern * of the inner wall, Eze 40:32
Its guardrooms, pillars and * Eze 40:33
of seven going up to the *. Eze 40:34
eight steps leading up to the *. Eze 40:37
*, there were two more tables. Eze 40:40
the northern *, facing south, and Eze 40:44
the southern *, facing north. Eze 40:44
the inner southern * is for the Eze 40:46
Then he brought me to the * hall Eze 40:48,49
8¾ feet thick. The * was 24½ feet Eze 40:48,49
They were 10½ feet square. The * Eze 41:2
the columns at the * and found them Eze 41:3
and on the canopy over the *. Eze 41:26
And there was an * from the Eze 42:9,10
wall's eastern * shall be closed Eze 46:1
return back to the *, which shall Eze 46:2
led me through the * to the block Eze 46:19,20
and around to the eastern *, Eze 47:2
stone across the * as he left. Mt 27:60
rolled a stone in front of the *. Mk 15:46
aside the huge stone from the *. Mk 16:3
moved away and the * was open! Mk 16:4
the * had been rolled aside. Lk 24:2
stone was rolled aside from the *. Jn 20:1

NTRANCES
and stood at the * of their tents Num 16:27
and *—and everything about it. Eze 43:11

NTREAT
with gifts and * your favors." Ps 45:12

NTREATED
from Pharaoh and * the Lord, and Ex 10:18

NTRENCHED
are * in the heart of the city. Ps 55:10

NTRUST
up for the future. * it to some Is 8:16
"And now I * you to God and his Act 20:32

NTRUSTED
the valuables were * shall be Ex 22:8
return something * to him, or by Lev 6:2
up, for we have * each other and 1Sa 20:42
the Korahite) was * with making the 1Ch 9:31
"Everything has been * to me by Mt 11:27
The man to whom he had * the Mt 25:20
you be * with money of your own? Lk 16:12
with the little I * to you, and as Lk 19:17
do these things that God * to you. 1Ti 6:20

ENTRY
its coverings, its * drapes, the Num 3:25-30
the best route of *, and to decide Deu 1:22
he slept at the * to the palace. 2Sa 11:13
the * hall of the passage; Eze 40:6
There were windows, an * hall Eze 40:22
the doorway to the * hall inside. Eze 40:22
Here at the north *, just as at Eze 40:23
as the others did, and an * hall. Eze 40:25
the windows along its walls and *. Eze 40:29,30
along the walls and in the * hall; Eze 40:33
feet wide. Its * hall faced the Eze 40:34
pillars and * hall of this Eze 40:36
of 43¾ feet. Its * hall faced Eze 40:37
But a door led from its * hall Eze 40:38
on each side of the * hall of Eze 40:39
Outside the * hall, on each side Eze 40:40
the walls of the * hall, and on the Eze 40:43
Thus the * hall was 35 feet wide Eze 40:48,49
of Holies and the * hall were Eze 41:15,16
a wooden canopy over the * hall. Eze 41:25
both sides of the * hall, the Eze 41:26
the * hall of the passage." Eze 44:3
walls at the * of the inner court. Eze 45:19
enter the outside * hall of the Eze 46:2
"The prince shall go in at the * Eze 46:8
Will this ensure your * into an Lk 16:9

ENVELOPED
soon a deep silence * the crowd, Act 21:40
union with Christ are * by him. Gal 3:27

ENVIABLE
"How * the man whom God Job 5:17

ENVIED
How greatly to be * are those Ps 65:4
because they * Jesus' popularity. Mk 15:10
"Blessed, and to be *," he Rom 4:7
*, for God will reward you for it. 1Pe 3:14

ENVIOUS
barren, became * of her sister. Gen 30:1
"You must not be * of your Ex 20:17
Don't be * of evil men who Ps 37:7
For I was * of the prosperity of Ps 73:3
They were * of Moses; Ps 106:16
never jealous or *, never boastful 1Co 13:4

ENVOY
Now the Assyrian * left Jerusalem Is 37:8,9

ENVOYS
this and took the * from Babylon on Is 39:2

ENVY
man's wife, nor * him for his home, Deu 5:21
You will * the prosperity I will 1Sa 2:32
NEVER * THE wicked! Ps 37:1
Well may you look with * at Mount Ps 68:15,16
Don't * violent men. Pro 3:31
Don't * evil men but continue to Pro 23:17,18
DON'T * GODLESS men; Pro 24:1
Don't * the wicked. Pro 24:19,20
driving force of * and jealousy! Ecc 4:4
* of all the other trees of Eden. Eze 31:9
all your acts of * and of hate. Eze 35:11
Jesus out of * because of his Mt 27:18
deceit, lewdness, *, slander, Mk 7:22
of greed and hate, *, murder, Rom 1:29
wrong doctrine, *, murder, Gal 5:21
were full of resentment and *. Tit 3:3
all evil, deception, *, and fraud. 1Pe 2:2,3

ENVYING
hating, *—is long gone, and they Ecc 9:6
quarreling, and * each other, and 2Co 12:20

EPAENETUS
Greet my good friend *. Rom 16:5

EPAPHRAS
*, our much-loved fellow worker, Col 1:7
*, from your city, a servant of Col 4:12
* my fellow prisoner, who is also Phm 1:23

EPAPHRODITUS
I ought to send * back to you. Php 2:25
the gifts you sent me when * came. Php 4:18

EPHAH
Midian's sons were *, Epher, Gen 25:4
*, Epher, Hanoch, Abida, and 1Ch 1:33
Caleb's concubine * bore him 1Ch 2:46
Regem, Jotham, Geshan, Pelet, *, 1Ch 2:47
and Sheba and *, too, bringing gold Is 60:6
Smaller units shall be the * Eze 45:11
Literally, one *. Eze 46:7f
Literally, one *. Eze 46:7f

EPHAI
the sons of * (the Netophathite), Jer 40:8

EPHER
Midian's sons were Ephah, *, Gen 25:4
Ephah, *, Hanoch, Abida, and 1Ch 1:33
Mered, *, Jalon. 1Ch 4:17
*, Ishi, Eliel, Azri-el, Jeremiah, 1Ch 5:24

EPHES-DAMMIM
Socoh in Judah and Azekah in *. 1Sa 17:1

EPHESIAN
AFTER PARTING FROM the * elders, Act 21:1

EPHESIANS
Implied in * 4:8. Ps 68:18f
See * 6:12. Mt 24:29f
See 2 Corinthians 4:4, and * Jn 12:31f
"Great is Diana of the *!" Act 19:28
hours: "Great is Diana of the *! Act 19:34
Great is Diana of the *!" Act 19:34

EPHESUS
Arriving at the port of *, he Act 18:19
But he promised to return to * Act 18:21
in * from Alexandria in Egypt. Act 18:24
and arrived in *, where he found Act 19:1
*, to Jews and Greeks alike; Act 19:17
in * concerning the Christians. Act 19:23
not only here in *, but throughout Act 19:26
"Men of *," he said, "everyone Act 19:35
knows that * is the center Act 19:35
stopping at * this time, as he was Act 20:16
of the church at * asking them to Act 20:17
from * in Turkey, and assumed Act 21:29
men of *—if it was only for what I 1Co 15:32
I will be staying here at * 1Co 16:8
DEAR CHRISTIAN FRIENDS at *, Eph 1:1
stay there in * and try to stop the 1Ti 1:3,4
you how much he helped me at *. 2Ti 1:18
is gone too, as I sent him to *. 2Ti 4:12
to the church in *, the one in Rev 1:11
of the church at * and tell him Rev 2:1

EPHLAL
Zabad's son was *; 1Ch 2:37

EPHLAL'S
Zabad's son was Ephlal; * son 1Ch 2:37

EPHOD
in the * and in the breastplate. Ex 25:1
shall make: a chestpiece, an *, Ex 28:4
"The * shall be made by the most Ex 28:5,6
shoulders of the *, as memorial Ex 28:12
clasps on the shoulder of the *. Ex 28:13,14
linen as you did in the *. Ex 28:15
chestpiece to the * by means of two Ex 28:22,23,24
stones on the shoulder of the *. Ex 28:25
front edge of the * at the sash. Ex 28:27
of the * by means of blue ribbons; Ex 28:28
from coming loose from the *. Ex 28:28
"The * shall be made of blue Ex 28:30,31
The bottom edge of the * shall Ex 28:33,34
Aaron shall wear the * whenever Ex 28:35
and the tunic, *, chestpiece, and Ex 29:5
be used for the * and chestpiece. Ex 35:5-9
used for the * and the chestpiece; Ex 35:27
to Moses. The * was made from this Ex 39:2
The * was held together by Ex 39:4,5
shoulder straps of the *, were Ex 39:6,7
just like the *, made from the Ex 39:8
[To attach the chestpiece to the * Ex 39:15-18
strap of the *, and from these gold Ex 39:15-18
on the under side, next to the *. Ex 39:19
straps of the *, close to where the Ex 39:20
close to where the * joined its Ex 39:20
woven sash of the * by tying the Ex 39:21
of the *, with a blue ribbon. Ex 39:21
The main part of the * was woven, Ex 39:22
Hanniel (son of *) Num 34:16-28
Gideon made an * Ju 8:27
An * was usually a linen pouch Ju 8:27f
In this case the * evidently was Ju 8:27f
also an * and some teraphim, and he Ju 17:4,5
in there with an *, some teraphim, Ju 18:14
idols, the *, and the teraphim. Ju 18:17
*, the teraphim, and the idols. Ju 18:20
Literally, "wore a linen *." 1Sa 2:18f
Literally, "wear an *." 1Sa 2:28f
Literally, "behind the *." 1Sa 21:9f
David, taking his * with him to get 1Sa 23:6
to bring the * and to ask the Lord 1Sa 23:9
the priest, "Bring me the *!" 1Sa 30:7
was girded with a linen *." 2Sa 6:14f
David also wore a linen *. 1Ch 15:27

EPHOD-JACKET
* with its beautifully woven belt. Lev 8:7

EPHRAIM
The second boy was named * Gen 41:52
were Manasseh and * (their mother Gen 46:19-22
and *, he went to visit him. Gen 48:1
two sons of yours, * and Manasseh, Gen 48:5
knees—* at Israel's left hand and Gen 48:12,13
upon the head of *, the younger Gen 48:14
as prosperous as * and Manasseh.' Gen 48:20
(Note that he put * before Gen 48:20
* (son of Joseph) Num 1:2-15
Joseph: * (son of Joseph) Num 1:20-46
Tribe: * Num 2:3-31
Next to * Next to Num 2:3-31
So the total on the * side of the Num 2:3-31
of the tribe of *, brought his Num 7:48-53
Next in line was the tribe of * Num 10:22
of Nun, from the half-tribe of *; Num 13:3-15
32,500 in the half-tribe of *; Num 26:28-37
the half-tribe of * included the Num 26:28-37
clans, named after the sons of *: Num 26:28-37
* Kemuel (son of Shiptan) Num 34:16-28
my blessing on the multitudes of * Deu 33:17
and there is * and Manasseh; Deu 34:2
Manasseh and *, and the Levites Jos 14:3,4
(* and the half-tribe of Manasseh): Jos 16:1
The Land Given to the Tribe of *: Jos 16:5,6
Sea. * was also given some of the Jos 16:9
as slaves among the people of *. Jos 16:10
land, belonged to the tribe of *. Jos 17:8
to the tribe of *, though they were Jos 17:9
was assigned to *, and the land Jos 17:10
"If the hill country of * is not Jos 17:15
in the hill country of *; Jos 19:50
Shechem, in the hill country of * Jos 20:7
the territories of *, Dan, and the Jos 21:5
pasturelands from the tribe of *: Jos 21:20,21,22
hill country of *, on the north Jos 24:30
hill country of *, at Gibe-ah, the Jos 24:33
still live among the tribe of *. Ju 1:29
of *, north of Mount Gaash. Ju 2:7-9
hill country of *, he blew a Ju 3:27
Bethel, in the hill country of *; Ju 4:5
They came from * and Benjamin, Ju 5:13,14
hill country of * summoning troops Ju 7:24
BUT THE TRIBAL leaders of * were Ju 8:1
the last grapes of * better than Ju 8:2,3f
Shamir in the hill country of *. Ju 10:1
also in Judah, Benjamin, and *. Ju 10:9
THEN THE TRIBE of * mobilized its Ju 12:1
at the taunt of * that the men of Ju 12:4
army and attacked the army of *. Ju 12:4
behind the army of *, and whenever Ju 12:5
a fugitive from * tried to cross Ju 12:5
you a member of the tribe of *?" Ju 12:5
So forty-two thousand people of * Ju 12:6
in Pirathon, in *, in the hill Ju 12:15
IN THE HILL country of * lived a Ju 17:1
in that area of *, looking for a Ju 17:7,8
Arriving in the hill country of * Ju 18:2
on up into the hill country of *. Ju 18:13
hill country of *, who brought home Ju 19:1
hill country of *, but was living Ju 19:16
"I live on the far edge of the * Ju 19:18
of the tribe of * who lived in 1Sa 1:1
in the hills of *. 1Sa 1:1
hill country of *, the land of 1Sa 9:4
Ashuri, Jezreel, *, the tribe of 2Sa 2:9
at Baal-hazor in *, Absalom invited 2Sa 13:21-24
in the forest of *, and the 2Sa 18:6
hill country of *, who has revolted 2Sa 20:21
was the hill country of *; 1Ki 4:8-19
from the city of Zeredah in *; 1Ki 11:26
of *, and it became his capital. 1Ki 12:25
from the hills of * have just 2Ki 5:22
from the Gate of * to the Corner 2Ki 14:13
The tribe of * gave these Cities 1Ch 6:66-69
Shechem, in Mount *; 1Ch 6:66-69

(EPHRAIM Con't)
The sons of *: 1Ch 7:20,21
Their father * mourned for them 1Ch 7:22
Judah, Benjamin, *, and Manasseh 1Ch 9:3
From the tribe of *, 20,800 mighty 1Ch 12:24-37
from Pelona in *, with 24,000 men 1Ch 27:10
from Pirathon in *, with 24,000 men 1Ch 27:14
Over *, Hoshea (son of Azaziah); 1Ch 27:16-22
hill country of *, King Abijah 2Ch 13:4
hill country of *, and he rebuilt 2Ch 15:8
the territories of *, Manasseh, and 2Ch 15:9
* that his father had conquered. 2Ch 17:2
hill country of * to encourage them 2Ch 19:4
them home again to *, which made 2Ch 25:10
the gate of * to the Corner Gate. 2Ch 25:23
great warrior from *, killed the 2Ch 28:7
Some of the top leaders of * also 2Ch 28:12
of Israel, Judah, *, and Manasseh, 2Ch 30:1
to city throughout * and Manasseh 2Ch 30:10
arriving from *, Manasseh, 2Ch 30:17,18,19
Judah, Benjamin, *, and Manasseh 2Ch 31:1
of Manasseh, *, and Simeon, even to 2Ch 34:6
from Manasseh, *, and other parts 2Ch 34:9
Gate, or at the * Gate Plaza. Neh 8:16
then from the * Gate to the Old Neh 12:39
kings, and * great warriors. Ps 60:6,7
The people of *, though fully Ps 78:9
the tribe of *, and chose the Ps 78:67
glory. Let *, Benjamin and Ps 80:2
the land of * is the helmet on my Ps 108:8
And within sixty-five years *, Is 7:8
Samaria, the capital of "*," Is 7:8f
Samaria is the capital of * Is 7:9
Manasseh against * and Ephraim Is 9:21
Manasseh against Ephraim and * Is 9:21
From Dan and from Mount * your Jer 4:15
your brothers, the people of *. Jer 7:15
on the hills of * will call out and Jer 31:6
Israel, and * is my oldest child. Jer 31:9
And the Lord replies: * is still Jer 31:20
more on Mount * and Mount Gilead. Jer 50:19
tribe of Joseph (* and Manesseh Eze 47:13
Next, to the south, is *, and Eze 48:5,6,7
a waterfall, and * will be crushed Hos 5:11
When * and Judah see how sick Hos 5:13
how sick they are, * will turn to Hos 5:13
I will tear * and Judah as a lion Hos 5:14
O * and Judah, what shall I do Hos 6:4
thing in Israel—* chasing other Hos 6:10
* is a silly, witless dove, Hos 7:11
wonderful king! * has built many Hos 8:11
leaders are rebels. * is doomed. Hos 9:16
great king there. * will be laughed Hos 10:6
* is accustomed to treading out Hos 10:11
Oh, how can I give you up, my *? Hos 11:8
is the last time I will destroy *. Hos 11:9
cheat. * boasts, "I am so rich! Hos 12:8
* has bitterly provoked the Lord. Hos 12:14
O *! Hos 14:8
the fields of * and Samaria. Ob 1:19
Judah, you are my bow! *, you Zec 9:13
to the village of *, and stayed Jn 11:54
Literally, "fugitives of *." Ju 12:4f

EPHRAIM'S
* and Manasseh's portion from you. Gen 48:6
had laid his right hand on * head; Gen 48:17
birth of his son * children, and Gen 50:23
* daughter's name was Sheerah. 1Ch 7:24
This is * line of descent: 1Ch 7:25,26,27
I have heard * groans: "You have Jer 31:18
don't know it. * hair is turning Hos 7:9
in my wrath. * sins are Hos 13:12

EPHRATH
traveled on toward * (Bethlehem). Gen 35:16
road to * (also called Bethlehem). Gen 35:19
distance from *, and I buried her Gen 48:7
*, who presented him with a son, 1Ch 2:19

EPHRATHAH
Caleb married *, his father's 1Ch 2:24
and *) were 1Ch 2:50
the oldest son of *, who was the 1Ch 4:3-4
"Lo, we heard of it in *." Ps 132:6f
*, then in the distant Ps 132:6
O Bethlehem *, you are but a Mic 5:2

EPHRATHITES
Literally, "They were * from Ru 1:1f

EPHRON
so kind as to ask *, Zohar's son, Gen 23:8
* was sitting there among the Gen 23:10
and replied to *, as all listened: Gen 23:13
of silver," * said, "but what is Gen 23:14,15
So Abraham paid * the price he Gen 23:16
had purchased from * the son of Gen 25:9,10
* the Hethite for a burial ground. Gen 49:29,30
of * the Hethite, close to Mamre. Gen 50:12,13
cities of Mount * before it turned Jos 15:9
over Mount * to the spring of Jos 18:15
Jeshanah, *, and their suburbs. 2Ch 13:18,19

EPHRON'S
This is the land he bought: * Gen 23:17,18

EPICUREAN
of the * and Stoic philosophers. Act 17:18

EPIDEMIC
are struck by an * or plague—or 1Ki 8:37
or if I send an * among you, then 2Ch 7:13
fury by sending an * of disease Eze 14:19
I will send an * of disease and Eze 28:23

EPIDEMICS
Let their men die in * and their Jer 18:21
in many lands, and *, and Lk 21:11

EPIPHANES
by Antiochus IV *, with a further Dan 8:9f
to Antiochus * and future further Dan 8:23f
This may refer to Antiochus IV * Dan 11:21f

EPOCH
has happened." An * of human Rev 16:17f

EQUAL
or vineyard an * amount of the best Ex 22:5
all are * before the Lord. Num 15:15,16
There isn't his * in all of 1Sa 10:24
a reputation * to The Three, though 2Sa 23:18,19
men are without * as lumbermen, and 2Ch 2:8
Where is his * in all of heaven Ps 35:10
we'll split with you in * Pro 1:14
one among them all, without an *! Sol 6:9
sin is * to the sin of Sodom; Is 3:9
Who is my *?" Is 40:25
weigh the hair into three * parts. Eze 5:1
no cypress had branches * to it; Eze 31:8
Fifty shekels shall always * one Eze 45:12
each tribe will have an * share. Eze 47:14
and *," says the Lord of Hosts. Zec 13:7
thereby making himself * with God. Jn 5:18

EQUALED
miracles which have never been *. Deu 34:11,12
to compare; none * it in beauty. Eze 31:8

EQUALLED
be * by your realistic action now. 2Co 8:11

EQUALLY
with it, or you will be * guilty. Lev 19:17
divide the land * between you." 2Sa 19:29
and he is * available to all. Col 3:11
of this verse are * possible. 1Jn 5:6,7,8f

EQUALS
Whom can you find who * me? Is 46:5

EQUATED
lamps are * with the one Spirit. Rev 4:5f
the seven eyes are * with the seven Rev 5:6f

EQUINOX
at about the time of the autumn *. Act 27:9f

EQUIP
our Lord Jesus, * you with all you Heb 13:20,21

EQUIPMENT
its *, and for the holy garments. Ex 35:21
all of the * needed for their use; Num 3:36,37
have a spade as part of his *; Deu 23:13
make his weapons and chariot *. 1Sa 8:12
and those who guard the *." 1Sa 30:24
of clothing and * all the way to 2Ki 7:15
to destroy all the * used in the 2Ki 23:4
Bread of the Presence and its *. 2Ch 29:18
the treas ures—the * and money and Ez 8:28
they are storing some of their * Is 10:28,29
big crew or a lot of * to do that. Eze 17:9

EQUIPPED
troops * with shields and spears. 1Ch 12:24-37
* with every kind of weapon. 1Ch 12:24-37
* with light shields and spears. 2Ch 14:8
Benjamin supplied 200,000 men * 2Ch 17:17
arrived with a mob * with swords Mk 14:43
It is that God's people will be * Eph 4:12
fully * to do good to everyone. 2Ti 3:17

EQUIVALENT
* to our "He got religion." 1Sa 10:12f
This paraphrase is the modern * 1Sa 20:30f
* to $20 in modern times, or L7. Mt 20:2f
straws" would be a modern *. Lk 1:8,9f
each the * of a modern day's wage. Lk 10:35f
* of this idea, otherwise obscure. Jn 16:26f

ER
three sons, *, Onan, and Shelah. Gen 38:3,4,5
*, who was named by his father. Gen 38:3,4,5
When his oldest son * grew up, Gen 38:6
named Tamar. But * was a wicked Gen 38:7
Judah and his sons: *, Onan, Gen 46:8-14
Zerah (however, * and Onan died Gen 46:8-14
not including * and Onan who died Num 26:19-22
*, Onan, and Shelah. 1Ch 2:3
But the oldest son, *, was so 1Ch 2:3
* (the father of Lecah), 1Ch 4:21-22
Elmadam's father was *; Lk 3:23-38

ER'S
Then Judah said to * brother, Gen 38:8
Then * widow, Tamar, and her 1Ch 2:4
Elmadam's father was Er;* father Lk 3:23-38

ERAN
ancestor *, a son of Shuthelah. Num 26:28-37

ERASE
and you will * their names from the Deu 7:24
Don't keep looking at my sins—* Ps 51:9
and I will not * his name from the Rev 3:5

ERASED
of the good years will be *. Gen 41:31
Go and beg to have your name *. Pro 6:3

ERASTUS
Timothy and *, on ahead to Greece Act 19:22
here in his home. *, the city Rom 16:23
of Onesiphorus. * stayed at 2Ti 4:20

ERECH
included Babel, *, Accad, and Gen 10:10
the men of * and Susa, and men Ez 4:8,9

ERECT
are you to * shameful images beside Deu 16:21
to Mount Carmel to * a monument to 1Sa 15:12

ERECTED
And there he * an altar and Gen 33:20
And Jacob * an altar there and Gen 35:7
Moses always * the sacred tent Ex 33:7
Moses * it by setting its frames Ex 40:18
Then he * the enclosure Ex 40:33
(The Tabernacle was already * in Num 10:21
So a tent was * on the roof of 2Sa 16:22
of Judah, and * fortresses and 2Ch 27:4
battle cry and * their idols to Ps 74:4
the totem poles * by their kings. Eze 43:7
* by their kings, and I will live Eze 43:9
future, when it is * for the Eze 43:18
the golden statue you have *." Dan 3:18

ERECTING
They made him angry by * idols Ps 78:58

ERECTS
the statues and idols she *. Hos 10:1

ERI
Ezbon, *, Arodi, and Areli. Gen 46:16,17
named after their ancestor *. Num 26:15-18

ERITES
The *, named after their ancestor Num 26:15-18

ERODE
they can * away or may be stolen. Mt 6:19

ERRAND
Laban said, "tell us your *." Gen 24:33
And he sent you on an * and told 1Sa 15:18
I have sent him on this * and I Is 48:15
when the Lord has sent it on an *? Jer 47:7

ERRONEOUSLY
the Negro, as was once * supposed. Gen 9:18f

ERROR
Their fatal * is not clearly Lev 10:1f
realize their *, they must offer Num 15:23,24
for it was an *, and they have Num 15:25
in such * and forgiveness. Num 15:26
"If the * is made by a single Num 15:27
Those in * will believe the Is 29:24
has sinned through * or ignorance, Eze 45:20
But Jesus said, "Your * is Mt 22:29
You have made a serious *." Mk 12:27

ERRORS
connected with any * regarding the Ex 28:37,38
of his sins and *, including a list 2Ch 33:19
making stupid * and mistakes. Is 28:7

ERUPTED
the leprosy has * and spread all Lev 13:12

ESAR-HADDON
* of Assyria brought us here." Ez 4:2
Ararat, and * his son became king. Is 37:38

ESÁRHADDON
his son * became the new king. 2Ki 19:37

ESAU
So they called him "*." Gen 25:25
As the boys grew, * became a Gen 25:27
Isaac's favorite was *, because Gen 25:28
cooking stew when * arrived home Gen 25:29
*: "Boy, am I starved! Gen 25:30
*: "When a man is dying of Gen 25:32
And * vowed, thereby selling all Gen 25:33
Then Jacob gave * bread, peas, Gen 25:34
Literally, "thus did * consider Gen 25:34f
*, at the age of forty, married a Gen 26:34
he called for * his oldest son. Gen 27:1
*: "Yes, father?" Gen 27:1
So when * left for the field to Gen 27:5
before his death, instead of *!" Gen 27:8,9,10
Think how hairy * is, and how Gen 27:11,12
Who is it, my son—* or Jacob?" Gen 27:18
Jacob: "It's *, your oldest son. Gen 27:19
you, and be sure it really is *!" Gen 27:21
Isaac: "Are you really *?" Gen 27:24
leaves the room, * arrives, coming Gen 27:30
*: "Here I am, father, with the Gen 27:31
*: "Why, it's me, of course! Gen 27:32
Esau: "Why, it's me, of course! * Gen 27:32
(* begins to sob with deep and Gen 27:34
*: "O my father, bless me, bless Gen 27:34
*: (bitterly) "No wonder they Gen 27:36
*: "Not one blessing left for Gen 27:38
as * weeps.) Gen 27:38
So * hated Jacob because of what Gen 27:41
life was being threatened by *. Gen 27:42
* realized that his father Gen 28:6,7,8
Paddan-aram. So * went to his Gen 28:9
to his brother * in Edom, in the Gen 32:3
with the news that * was on the way Gen 32:6
for he said, "If * attacks one Gen 32:8
hand of my brother *, for I am Gen 32:11

SAU Con't)
or his brother *:200 nanny Gen 32:13,14,15
hat when they met * and he asked, Gen 32:17
re a present for his master *! Gen 32:18
was to appease * with the presents Gen 32:20
aw * coming with his 400 men. Gen 33:1
And then * ran to meet him and Gen 33:4
Then * looked at the women and Gen 33:5
nerds I met as I came?" * asked. Gen 33:8
"Brother, I have plenty," * Gen 33:9
and finally * accepted them. Gen 33:11
'Well, let's be going," * said. Gen 33:12
'Well," * said, "at least let Gen 33:15
So * started back to Seir that Gen 33:16
you fled from your brother *." Gen 35:1
to him when he was fleeing from *. Gen 35:7
And his sons * and Jacob buried Gen 35:28,29
of * (also called Edom): Gen 36:1
* married three local girls from Gen 36:2,3
* and Adah had a son named Gen 36:4
son named Eliphaz. * and Basemath Gen 36:4
* and Oholibamah had sons named Gen 36:5
All these sons were born to * in Gen 36:5
Then * took his wives, children, Gen 36:6,7,8
* also had grandchildren from his Gen 36:13,14
the oldest son of * and Adah. Gen 36:15,16
of Reuel, born to * and his wife Gen 36:17
after the sons of * and his wife Gen 36:18,19
the sub-tribes of *, living in the Gen 36:40-43
were Edomites, descendants of *. Gen 36:40-43
descended from *, while the people Num 20:14f
descendants of * who live in Seir; Deu 2:4
the descendants of *, just as Deu 2:12
the descendants of * at Mount Seir, Deu 2:22
whom I gave him, were Jacob and *. Jos 24:4
Jacob and Esau. To * I gave the Jos 24:4
* and Israel. 1Ch 1:34
The sons of *: 1Ch 1:35
The sons of * 1Ch 1:38,39
bare the land of *, and there will Jer 49:9,10
very own brother, *, and destroyed Mal 1:2,3
God told her that *, the child born Rom 9:10-13
chose to bless Jacob, but not *." Rom 9:10-13
to his two sons, Jacob and *. Heb 11:20
about God as * did: he traded his Heb 12:16

SAU'S
was born with his hand on * heel! Gen 25:26
Then she took * best Gen 27:15
is Jacob's, but the hands are *!" Gen 27:22
Here are the names of * Gen 36:9
* grandchildren Gen 36:15,16
Dishan; and * daughter was named 1Ch 1:38,39
and destroyed * mountains and Mal 1:2,3

SCAPE
and their wives, to * the flood. Gen 7:7
"And don't look back. * to the Gen 19:17
group, perhaps the other can *." Gen 32:8
us and * out of the country." Ex 1:10
You will not * punishment if you Ex 20:7
"* to the mountains," she told Jos 2:16
fighting men, letting not one *. Ju 3:29
deceived me and let my enemy *?" 1Sa 19:17
tell you, so you can * and live. 1Sa 20:13
his best to *, but it was no use. 1Sa 23:26
been called, "The Rock of *!" 1Sa 23:28
"Don't let a single one *," he 1Ki 18:40
* Jehu shall be killed by Elisha! 1Ki 19:17
"don't let anyone * to Jezreel to 2Ki 9:15
you let anyone *, you'll pay for it 2Ki 10:24
Don't let a single one *." 2Ki 10:25
had gone to * from King Solomon. 2Ch 10:2,3
some will *. 2Ch 12:7
you think you will * there in the Est 4:13
the wicked shall find no way to *; Job 11:20
closes in on a man, there is no *. Job 12:14
day of calamity, and allowed to *. Job 21:30-32
The good man does not * all Ps 34:19
deep pits from which they can't *. Ps 140:10
into their own snares, while I *. Ps 141:10
May it please God that you * from Ecc 7:26
written down to * the destruction Is 4:2,3,4
those who * and those who remain. Is 15:9
a pit, and if you * from the pit Is 24:18
nations that * from Cyrus' hand. Is 45:20
"those who *" means survivors of Is 66:19f
who *, as missionaries to the Is 66:19
upon them and they shall not *. Jer 11:11
nothing shall *. Jer 12:12
Wherever you run to * my Jer 16:16
You cannot *! Jer 25:28
no place to hide, no way to *. Jer 25:35
You shall not *; Jer 34:3
army and you will not *." Jer 38:18
Babylonians, and you will not *. Jer 38:23
None of you will * from the evil Jer 42:17
Not one of them shall * from my Jer 44:14
their coming and * from the others Jer 44:14
remnant) shall * my wrath, but all Jer 44:28
The swift will not *, nor the Jer 46:6
they will * back to their own Jer 50:28
the city so that none can *. Jer 50:29
All the * routes are blocked; Jer 51:32
I cannot *; Lam 3:7
a few of my people *—to be Eze 6:8
Any who * will be lonely as Eze 7:16
to it that if they * from one fire, Eze 15:7
therefore he shall not *. Eze 17:18
try to * and all those who return. Eze 35:7
most of Ammon will *, but Egypt Dan 11:41
even in Jerusalem some will *, Joe 2:32
Though they run, they will not *; Amo 9:1
and killed those trying to *; Ob 1:14
will become a refuge, a way of *. Ob 1:17
There is no *, though you Nah 3:15
again. *, escape to Zion now!' Zec 2:6,7
Escape, * to Zion now!' Zec 2:6,7
You will * through that valley, Zec 14:5
Yes, you will * as your people Zec 14:5
"Who said that you could * the Mt 3:7
How shall you * the judgment of Mt 23:33
You are trying to * hell without Lk 3:7
Let those in Jerusalem try to *, Lk 21:21
any of them swim ashore and *. Act 27:42
with no way of *, Christ came at Rom 5:6
He will show you how to * 1Co 10:13
the way of * is open to all who Gal 3:21,22
their senses and * from Satan's 2Ti 2:26
think that we can * if we are Heb 2:3
of Israel did not * when they Heb 12:25
No woman can * their sinful 2Pe 2:14

ESCAPED
One of the men who * came and Gen 14:13
everything that * the hail. Ex 10:4,5
bread you ate as you * from Egypt. Deu 16:3
not one man survived or *. Jos 8:22
* and hid in a cave at Makkedah. Jos 10:16
King Adoni-bezek *, but the Ju 1:4,5,6
and * across an upstairs porch. Ju 3:22,23
Meanwhile Ehud had * past the Ju 3:26
from his chariot and * on foot. Ju 4:15
Meanwhile, Sisera had * to the Ju 4:17
youngest, Jotham, who * and hid. Ju 9:5
Then Jotham * and lived in Beer Ju 9:21
hundred men who * to the rock of Ju 20:46,47
* to the land of Gad and Gilead. 1Sa 13:7
But David jumped aside and *. 1Sa 18:11,12
SO DAVID LEFT Gath and * to the 1Sa 22:1
of Ahimelech, * and fled to David. 1Sa 22:20
that David had *, so he didn't go 1Sa 23:13
No one * except four hundred 1Sa 30:17
the desert that night and *. 2Sa 4:6,7
And if David has * into some 2Sa 17:13
Meanwhile, they * to Bahurim 2Sa 17:18
slaves * to King Achish of Gath. 1Ki 2:39
But King Rehoboam * by chariot 1Ki 12:18
and a few others * on horses. 1Ki 20:20
of you who have * the ravages of 2Ki 19:30
killed him. They * into eastern 2Ki 19:37
the king of Syria has * from you. 2Ch 16:7
a single one of the enemy had *. 2Ch 20:24
his youngest son, Jehoahaz, *. 2Ch 21:17
to us who have * from the power of 2Ch 30:6
and I alone have * to tell you." Job 1:16
and I alone have * to tell you." Job 1:17
and I alone * to tell you." Job 1:19
I am skin and bones and have * Job 19:20
I could have hidden and *. Ps 55:12
LONG AGO WHEN the Israelis * from Ps 114:1
We have * with our lives as a Ps 124:7
then they * into the land of Is 37:38
as I did those who * from Egypt, to Jer 31:2
Meanwhile Ishmael * with eight of Jer 41:15
Go, you who * the sword! Jer 51:50
in the day of your anger none * Lam 2:22
one of those who * from Jerusalem Eze 33:21
to grab him, he *, though his Mk 14:51,52
threatened with death if they *, Act 16:23
the prisoners had *, he drew his Act 16:27
So everyone * safely ashore! Act 27:44
Though he * the sea, justice will Act 28:4
Some, through their faith, * Heb 11:34
just * from such wicked living. 2Pe 2:18
And when a person has * from the 2Pe 2:20

ESCAPES
"If a slave * from his master, Deu 23:15,16
Anyone who * from Hazael shall 1Ki 19:17
not even this little remnant *. Ez 9:14
like a deer that * from a hunter, Pro 6:5
a trap and he who * from the trap Jer 48:44
not one thing *. Joe 2:3

ESCAPING
Midianites from * by going across. Ju 7:24
a man * through a wall of flames. 1Co 3:15

ESCORT
under armed *—Abram, his wife, and Gen 12:20
him and * him across the river! 2Sa 19:15

ESCORTED
and all the people * the king from 2Ch 23:20
congregation had * them out of the Act 15:3

ESCORTS
Then their * returned to Samaria. 2Ch 28:15

ESEB
*. Gen 26:20f

ESHAN
Arab, Dumah, *, Janim, Jos 15:48-62

ESHBAAL
Jonathan, Malchishua, Abinadab, *. 1Ch 8:33
Malchishua, Abinadab, and *. 1Ch 9:39

ESHBAN
The children of Dishon:Hemdan,* Gen 36:26
The sons of Dishon: Hamran, *, 1Ch 1:41

ESHCOL
of * and Aner, Abram's allies). Gen 14:13
Aner, *, and Mamre, my allies." Gen 14:24
as the Valley of * where they cut Num 13:23
named the valley "*" at that time Num 13:24
from the valley of *, they Num 32:9
to the Valley of *, and returned Deu 1:24,25

ESHEK
Azel's brother * had three sons: 1Ch 8:39

ESHTA-OL
Zorah, *, Ir-shemesh, Sha-alabbin, Jos 19:41-46
between the cities of Zorah and *. Ju 13:25
between Zorah and *, where his Ju 16:31
of Zorah and * as scouts to go and Ju 18:2
to their people in Zorah and *. Ju 18:8
of Dan set out from Zorah and *. Ju 18:11

ESHTAOL
*, Zorah, Ashnah, Zanoah, Jos 15:33-36

ESHTAOLITES
descended the Zorathites and *). 1Ch 2:53

ESHTEMOA
Libnah, Jattir, *, Holon, Debir, Jos 21:9-16
Aroer, Siphmoth, *, Racal, the 1Sa 30:27-31
ancestor of *. 1Ch 4:17
the father of * the Maacathite. 1Ch 4:19
Libnah, Jattir, *, Hilen, Debir, 1Ch 6:58,59

ESHTEMOA'S
* wife was a Jewess; 1Ch 4:18

ESHTEMOH
(or, Debir), Anab, *, Anim, Goshen, Jos 15:48-62

ESHTON
the father of *; 1Ch 4:11,12
* was the father of Bethrapha, 1Ch 4:11,12

ESLI
Nahum's father was *; Lk 3:23-38

ESLI'S
Nahum's father was Esli;* father Lk 3:23-38

ESPECIALLY
Tell them * about the day you Deu 4:10
on the other side, * at Jericho. Jos 2:1
Probably King Saul was * worried, 1Sa 17:11f
from the Lord, * in his old age. 1Ki 11:4
He was * guilty because he 1Ki 21:26
He stood on a wooden stand made * Neh 8:1
of the land, * in Jerusalem, Neh 8:15
unless he had * enjoyed her, and Est 2:12,13,14
I'll keep quiet, * when the Ps 39:1
I need your help, * in my own home, Ps 101:2
* if they are trying to bribe him! Pro 21:27
so he was * interested in Is 39:1f
I have measured out * for you. Jer 13:24,25
these nations, * Edom, for grabbing Eze 36:5
opposed to God, * in a mighty Eze 38:2,3f
(For the Jews, * the Pharisees, Mk 7:3
everyone else, * like that tax Lk 18:11
things for others, * for the poor. Act 9:36
you all, and * you, King Agrippa, Act 25:26
someone else may be * good at 1Co 12:8
Yes, we are * glad to have some 1Co 12:23
Spirit gives, and * the gift of 1Co 14:1
He is * interested, as he looks 2Co 8:22
sincere hearts, * if they aren't Gal 4:18
God had * promised he would come. Gal 4:23
and * to our Christian brothers. Gal 6:10
remembered to you, * those who work Php 4:22
they need help, * those living in 1Ti 5:8
appreciated, * those who work hard 1Ti 5:17
I taught you, * concerning the 2Ti 1:13
the books, but * the parchments. 2Ti 4:13
this is * true among those who Tit 1:10
better—a beloved brother, * to me. Phm 1:16
warn each other, * now that the day Heb 10:25
holds us back, and * those sins Heb 12:1
it that way. I * need your prayers Heb 13:19
He is * hard on those who follow 2Pe 2:10

ESSENCE
perfume made from * of nard, and Jn 12:3

ESTABLISH
Jachin means "to *," and Boaz 1Ki 7:16-22f
and you may * trading posts in 1Ki 20:34
temple, and I will * his royal line 1Ch 17:12
But justify me publicly; * my Ps 7:7,8
I have taken an oath to * his Ps 89:3,4
is past, God will * David's throne Is 16:4,5
His name means, "The Lord will * Jer 22:24,25f
I will * an everlasting covenant Eze 16:59,60

ESTABLISHED
symptoms, it is an * case of Lev 13:11
Has he not * you and made you Deu 32:6
for they * their camp at the Jos 11:5
when you have * Israel as your 2Sa 7:26
and have * my dynasty before you. 2Sa 7:26
had become solidly * as king, he 2Ch 21:3,4

(ESTABLISHED Con't)
When he was well * as the new 2Ch 25:3
* it and examined it thoroughly. Job 28:27
God has * Jerusalem forever. Ps 48:8
Literally, "The world is * . Ps 93:1f
your throne is *." Ps 93:1f
Jehovah has * your throne Ps 110:2
he * them forever and forever. Ps 148:6
his understanding * all the Pro 3:19
"I was there when he * the Pro 8:27,28,29
He * this principle. Pro 16:11
Literally, "for the throne is * Pro 16:12f
Literally, "shall be * as the Is 2:2f
and * his reputation forever? Is 63:12
their nations shall be * before Jer 30:20
I will wipe out what I *. Jer 45:4
* and set in motion by my blood. 1Co 11:25

ESTABLISHES
unless a fair trial * his guilt. Num 35:12
no rest until he * Jerusalem and Is 62:6,7

ESTATE
He was buried on his own * at Jos 24:30
not get any of our father's *." Ju 11:1
complicate his * for the Ru 4:6f
Ahasuerus gave the * of Haman, the Est 8:1
to be in charge of Haman's *. Est 8:2
May creditors seize his entire * Ps 109:11
wicked sons and share their *. Pro 17:2
"The owner of an * went out Mt 20:1
'Here comes the heir to this *; Mt 21:38
to divide my father's * with me." Lk 12:13
my share of your * now, instead of Lk 15:12
we landed was an * belonging to Act 28:7

ESTATES
all the family * sold to others Lev 25:10
of the laborers on the king's *. 1Ch 27:26
You name your * after yourselves Ps 49:11
Your homes are built on great * Is 5:8

ESTEEM
for to be held in loving * is Pro 22:1

ESTEEMED
* above his brothers; Deu 33:24

ESTHER
Hadassah (also called *), whose Est 2:7
the king's decree, * was brought to Est 2:8
in the harem. * hadn't told anyone Est 2:10
harem to ask about * and to find Est 2:11
Literally, "*, the daughter of Est 2:15f
they saw her. So * was taken to Est 2:16
Well, the king loved * more than Est 2:17
Or, "When * and the other girls Est 2:19f
* still hadn't told anyone she Est 2:20
to Queen *, who told the king, Est 2:22
Then * sent for Hathach, one of Est 4:5
him to show it to * and to tell her Est 4:8
So Hathach returned to * with Est 4:9
message. * told Hathach to go back Est 4:10
This was Mordecai's reply to *: Est 4:13
Then * said to tell Mordecai: Est 4:15
So Mordecai did as * told him to. Est 4:17
THREE DAYS LATER * put on her Est 5:1
And when he saw Queen * standing Est 5:2
* approached and touched its tip. Est 5:2
her, "What do you wish, Queen *? Est 5:3
And * replied, "If it please Est 5:4
the king said to *, "Now tell me Est 5:6
* replied, "My request, my Est 5:7,8
line: "Yes, and * the queen Est 5:12
to the banquet * had prepared. Est 6:14
"What is your petition, Queen *? Est 7:2
And at last Queen * replied, "If Est 7:3
* replied, "This wicked Haman is Est 7:6
*, for he knew that he was doomed. Est 7:7
couch where Queen * was reclining, Est 7:8
the Jews' enemy, to Queen *. Est 8:1
the king, for * had told the king Est 8:1
and * appointed Mordecai to be Est 8:2
And now once more * came before Est 8:3
held out the golden scepter to *. Est 8:4
said to Queen * and Mordecai the Est 8:7
"I have given * the palace of Est 8:7
Shushan, he called for Queen *. Est 9:12
And * said, "If it please Your Est 9:13
Meanwhile, Queen * (daughter of Est 9:29-31
Mordecai the Jew and by Queen *; Est 9:29-31
So the commandment of * Est 9:32

ESTHER'S
When it was * Est 2:15
When * maids and eunuchs came and Est 4:4
So Hathach gave * message to Est 4:12
So the king and Haman came to * Est 5:5
SO THE KING and Haman came to * Est 7:1

ESTIMATE
then the whole * shall stand; Lev 27:17
the priest shall * the value until Lev 27:23
pay the priest's * of its worth, Lev 27:27
It was impossible to * the 2Ki 25:16
Be honest in your * of yourselves, Rom 12:3

ESTIMATED
give that * value to the Lord, and Lev 27:23
Their value was * at $25,000, Ju 8:26
Then he * the pillars on each Eze 40:14
(Someone * the value of the books Act 19:18,19
there were an "* 200,000,000 armed Rev 9:16f

ESTIMATES
first getting * and then checking Lk 14:28

ESTIMATING
your towers and * how much they Is 33:18
They had no way of * it. Jer 52:20

ESTIMATIONS
Literally, "and all your * shall Lev 27:25f

ETAM
live in a cave in the rock of *. Ju 15:8
at the cave in the rock of *. Ju 15:11
The descendants of *:Jezreel, 1Ch 4:3-4
*, Ain, Rimmon, Tochen, and Ashan; 1Ch 4:32,33
Bethlehem, *, Tekoa, 2Ch 11:5-10

ETC
(besides the jewelry, clothing, *. Num 31:32-35
2:23, *. Zec 4:6f
"I was the God of Abraham, *." Mt 22:32f
8:36, 56, 58, *. Jn 10:25f
is to atoms, electrons, *. Heb 11:3f
his own free will he gave us, *." Jas 1:18f
8:14, 1 Corinthians 9:5, *. 1Pe 5:13f
Others (Lazarus, *. Rev 1:5f
expositors (Origen, Jerome, *. Rev 1:20f

ETERNAL
and remember my * promise to every Gen 9:16,17
proud, * monument to themselves. Gen 11:3,4
the * God [to witness the covenant Gen 21:33
(This is my * name, to be used Ex 3:15
shall place this * flame in the Ex 27:21
It is an * symbol of the Ex 31:17
olive oil for an * flame in the Lev 24:1
It will be an * flame before the Lev 24:3,4
The * God is your Refuge, Deu 33:27
reward you with * royalty for your 1Sa 25:28
speak of giving me an * dynasty! 2Sa 7:19
His agreement is *, final, sealed. 2Sa 23:5
And may this bring * honor to 1Ch 17:24
Lord, it is an * blessing!" 1Ch 17:27
to God, shrouded in * darkness. Job 3:4
them upon *, kingly thrones. Job 36:7
pleasures of your own * presence. Ps 16:11
God's laws are pure, *, just. Ps 19:9
You have endowed him with * Ps 21:6
and gives them * rewards. Ps 37:18
So if you want an * home, leave Ps 37:27
the earth to buy * life for just Ps 49:8,9
else, and enters * darkness. Ps 49:19
and your * plan for all mankind. Ps 67:2
back and sent them to * shame. Ps 78:66
It shall be * as the moon, my Ps 89:37
only * destruction ahead of them. Ps 92:7
honor, majesty, and * goodness. Ps 111:3
Your justice is * for your laws Ps 119:142
your decrees are *. Ps 119:160
And God has pronounced this * Ps 133:3
as an * gift to his people Israel. Ps 135:12
The hope of good men is * Pro 10:28
saved by Jehovah with * salvation; Is 45:17
But our refuge is your throne, *, Jer 17:12
and her cities shall be * wastes. Jer 49:13
the Lord with an * pledge that will Jer 50:5
His power is *—it will never end; Dan 7:14
One, you who are *—is your plan in Hab 1:12
and salt pits and * desolation; Zep 2:9
the whole world—and lose * life? Mt 16:26
compared with the value of * life? Mt 16:26
what must I do to have * life?" Mt 19:16
in return, and shall have * life. Mt 19:29
ones, into the * fire prepared for Mt 25:41
"And they shall go away into * Mt 25:46
It is an * sin." Mk 3:29
to come he shall have * life. Mk 10:30
* fire and store away the grain." Lk 3:17
those without * life concern Lk 9:60
you into the * tabernacles!" Lk 16:9f
* life in the world to come." Lk 18:30
began to cry. "* peace was within Lk 19:42
he didn't make. * life is in him, Jn 1:4
believes in me will have * life. Jn 3:15
shall not perish but have * life. Jn 3:16
"There is no * doom awaiting Jn 3:18
Son—to save them have * life; Jn 3:36
them forever with * life." Jn 4:14
will be gathering * souls into the Jn 4:36
who sent me has * life, and will Jn 5:24
who have done good, to * life; Jn 5:29
you believe they give you * life. Jn 5:39
that I can give you this life *! Jn 5:40
the * life that I, the Messiah, Jn 6:27
them to * life at the Last Day. Jn 6:39
on him should have * life—that I Jn 6:40
believes in me already has * life! Jn 6:47
But the Bread from heaven gives * Jn 6:48-51
you cannot have * life within you. Jn 6:53
drink my blood has * life, and I Jn 6:54
Only the Holy Spirit gives * Jn 6:63
words that give * life, and we Jn 6:68
I give them * life and they Jn 10:28
He is given * life for believing Jn 11:26
will exchange it for * glory. Jn 12:25
his instructions lead to * life; Jn 12:50
He gives * life to each one you Jn 17:2
And this is the way to have * Jn 17:3
to him and receiving * life!" Act 11:18
unworthy of * life—well, we will Act 13:46
* life, believed. Act 13:48
angels or even * spirit within us, Act 23:8
his existence and great * power. Rom 1:20
He will give * life to those who Rom 2:7
glory and honor and * life that Rom 2:7
and resulting in * life through Rom 5:21
do, for all of them end in * doom. Rom 6:21
gift of God is * life through Jesus Rom 6:23
far greater, for it is *. 2Co 3:11
one who is on the road to * death. 2Co 4:3
it has resulted in * life for you. 2Co 4:12
our * home in heaven with Jesus. 2Co 5:6
received * life from him—might live 2Co 5:15
away from sin and seek * life. 2Co 7:10
and does not prevent * death. 2Co 7:10
* life he gives through Christ; Gal 1:6
Christ has given * life don't need Gal 5:6
he has given you * life with him. Php 1:28
Their future is * loss, for Php 3:19
Hold tightly to the * life which 1Ti 6:12
about the * life he has promised 2Ti 1:1
salvation and * glory in Christ 2Ti 2:10
that they can have * life, which Tit 1:1
For the free gift of * salvation Tit 2:11
the wealth of the * life he gives Tit 3:7
the Giver of * salvation to all Heb 5:9
of the dead and * judgment. Heb 6:2
made sure of our * salvation. Heb 9:12
For by the help of the * Holy Heb 9:14
Now we live in the hope of * life 1Pe 1:3
the priceless gift of * life; 1Pe 1:4
Christ, will give you his * glory. 1Pe 5:10
to enter into the * kingdom of our 2Pe 1:11
They are doomed to the * pits of 2Pe 2:17
I am speaking of Christ, who is * 1Jn 1:2
who know the * God, and to you 1Jn 2:14
has promised us this: * life. 1Jn 2:25
from hell and given * life. 1Jn 3:14
for others is headed for * death. 1Jn 3:14
to murder has * life within. 1Jn 3:15
to us * life through his death. 1Jn 4:9
That he has given us * life, and 1Jn 5:11
that you may know you have * life. 1Jn 5:13
and he is * Life. 1Jn 5:20
Wait patiently for the * life Jud 1:21
worshiped him, the * Living One, Rev 4:10
the * plan and knowledge of God. Rev 13:8f
pit and go to * destruction; Rev 17:8

ETERNALLY
And may you be * honored when 2Sa 7:26
and you could live on them *. Ps 49:11

ETERNITY
will continue his kingdom into *. 2Sa 7:13
It sweeps him into *. Job 27:21
at his death, and boo him into *. Job 27:23
No one can begin to understand *. Job 36:26
on into everlasting * ahead. Ps 41:13
their happiness, an * of terror. Ps 73:19
on his throne, from now until *!" Ps 89:3,4
But though God has planted * in Ecc 3:11
also remember that * is far longer, Ecc 11:8
From * to eternity I am God. Is 43:13
From eternity to * I am God. Is 43:13
in their God through all *. Is 45:17
one who inhabits *, the Holy One, Is 57:15
to God through all the ages of *. Gal 1:5
is the only safe investment for *! 1Ti 6:19
the world from this day to *." Rev 11:15f

ETHAM
Leaving Succoth, they camped in * Ex 13:20
stayed in Succoth, * (at the edge Num 33:5,6
* wilderness, camping at Marah. Num 33:8

ETHAN
He was wiser than * the Ezrahite 1Ki 4:31
*, Heman, 1Ch 2:6
Zerah, Adaiah, *, Zimmah, Shime-i, 1Ch 6:39-43
Heman's second assistant was *, a 1Ch 6:44-47
of Berechiah), and * (son of 1Ch 15:17
Heman, Asaph, and * were chosen 1Ch 15:19

ETHAN'S
* son was Azariah. 1Ch 2:8

ETHBAAL
daughter of King * of the 1Ki 16:31

ETHER
Makkedah, Libnah, *, Ashan, Iphtah, Jos 15:37-44
Sharuhen, En-rimmon, *, and Ashan. Jos 19:2-7

ETHIOPIA
But areas of * and Babylon were Num 12:1f
from *) because of her color. Num 12:1f
of * was coming to attack him. 2Ki 19:9
troops from * with 300 chariots, 2Ch 14:9,10
stretching from India to *. Est 1:1
from India to *, 127 in all; Est 8:9,10
Topaz from * cannot purchase it, Job 28:19

ETHIOPIA Con't)
precious metals. * will stretch out Ps 68:31
or even distant *, someone boasts Ps 87:4
and Lower Egypt, *, Elam, Is 11:11
"land beyond the rivers of *." Is 18:1f
of Ethiopia." * was the seat of Is 18:1f
I will bring upon Egypt and *. Is 20:3
crown prince of *, was leading an Is 37:8,9
I gave Egypt and * and Seba [to Is 43:3
as far south as the border of *. Eze 29:10
by the river? * and the whole land Nah 3:9
the rivers of * will come with Zep 3:10
the Treasurer of *, a eunuch of Act 8:27

ETHIOPIA'S
will be, who counted on "* Is 20:5,6
alliance with * Egyptian dynasty Is 30:2f

ETHIOPIAN
and the entire * army was wiped out 2Ch 14:13
25th * Dynasty would soon arise. Is 7:18f
Can the * change the color of his Jer 13:23
When Ebed-melech the *, an Jer 38:7
to Ebed-melech the *: The Lord of Jer 39:16

ETHIOPIANS
Libyans, Sukkiim, and *. 2Ch 12:3
Then the Lord defeated the *, and 2Ch 14:12
of Judah triumphed as the * fled. 2Ch 14:12
happened to the * and Libyans and 2Ch 16:8
next to the * to attack Jehoram. 2Ch 21:16
the Egyptians and * as prisoners, Is 20:4
Jehovah says: The Egyptians, * Is 45:14
to bring panic to the *; Eze 30:9
and * shall be his servants. Dan 11:43
you any more to me than the * are? Amo 9:7
You *, too, will be slain by his Zep 2:12

ETHKAZIN
of Gath-hepher, *, and Rimmon and Jos 19:13

ETHNAN
bore him Zereth, Izhar, and *. 1Ch 4:7

ETHNI
Malchijah, *, Zerah, Adaiah, Ethan, 1Ch 6:39-43

EUBULUS
before winter. * sends you 2Ti 4:21

EUNICE
* and your grandmother Lois do; 2Ti 1:5

EUNUCH
quarters of Nathan-melech the *. 2Ki 23:11
Hegai, the * in charge, will see Est 2:3
of Hegai, the * in charge of the Est 2:15
Literally, "his chief *." Dan 1:3,4f
of Ethiopia, a * of great authority Act 8:27
The * asked Philip, "Was Isaiah Act 8:34
of water, and the * said, "Look! Act 8:36
And the * replied, "I believe Act 8:37
Philip, and the * never saw him Act 8:39

EUNUCHS
And two or three * looked out 2Ki 9:32
away and made into * who will serve 2Ki 20:18
he told the seven * who were his Est 1:10
of the king's *, and lived there Est 2:12,13,14
two of the king's *, Bigthan and Est 2:21
When Esther's maids and * came Est 4:4
one of the king's * who had been Est 4:5
two of the king's *, watchmen at Est 6:1
slaves, yes, *, in the palace of Is 39:7
And this is for the * too. Is 56:3
For I say this to the * who keep Is 56:4
the chief of the *, and Jer 39:13
*, to prepare to leave for Egypt. Jer 41:16,17
Literally, "born *," or, "born Mt 19:12f

EUODIAS
two dear women, * and Syntyche. Php 4:2

EUPHRATES
And the fourth is the *. Gen 2:14
to the * River. Gen 15:18
and crossed the * River and headed Gen 31:21
deserts as far as the * River; Ex 23:31
land of Pethor, near the * River. Num 22:5,6
Mediterranean Sea to the * River. Deu 1:7
* River to the Mediterranean Sea. Deu 11:24
in the west to the * River in the Jos 1:4
Nahor, lived east of the * River; Jos 24:2
beyond the * River and in Egypt. Jos 24:14
beyond the * or the gods of the Jos 24:15
in a battle at the * River, for 2Sa 8:3
the other side of the * River. 2Sa 10:15,16
area from the * River to the land 1Ki 4:21
the * River, from Tiphsah to Gaza. 1Ki 4:24
them beyond the * River, for they 1Ki 14:15
of Assyria at the * River, and King 2Ki 23:29
the Brook of Egypt to the * River. 2Ki 24:7
desert and to the * River, for 1Ch 5:9
his grip along the * River. 1Ch 18:3
from east of the * River, led 1Ch 19:16
kingdoms from the * River to the 2Ch 9:26
at Carchemish on the * River, 2Ch 35:20
lands west of the * River. Ez 4:10
subjects west of the * River. Ez 4:11
*, for it will be lost to you." Ez 4:16
the area west of the * River: Ez 4:17
land beyond the * River and have Ez 4:20
lands west of the *, and Ez 5:3
the other officials west of the *: Ez 6:6
west of the * River: 'You are to Ez 7:21
the people west of the * River; Ez 7:25
west of the * River, and of course Ez 8:36
west of the * River instructing Neh 2:7
west of the * River, I delivered Neh 2:9
* River to the ends of the earth. Ps 72:8
Mediterranean Sea to the * River. Ps 80:11
He will hold sway from the * Ps 89:25
my people with * mighty flood; Is 8:7,8
and wave his hand over the *, Is 11:15
* River to the Egyptian boundary. Is 27:12
out to the * River and hide it in a Jer 13:4
beside the * River by Jer 46:2
In the north, by the river *, Jer 46:6
north country beside the river *! Jer 46:10
throw it into the * River, and Jer 51:63
from Egypt to the *, from sea to Mic 7:12
held bound at the great River * Rev 9:14
the great River * and it dried up Rev 16:12

EUTYCHUS
a young man named *, sitting on the Act 20:9

EVADE
but sinners don't * her snares. Ecc 7:26
No, you shall not * punishment. Jer 25:29

EVALUATE
that I could * all these things. Ecc 2:9

EVALUATING
So stop * Christians by what the 2Co 5:16

EVANGELIST
*, one of the first seven deacons. Act 21:8

EVAPORATED
even * all the water in the ditch! 1Ki 18:38
My strength * like water on a Ps 32:4

EVAPORATES
As water * from a lake, as a Job 14:11,12

EVE
The man named his wife * (meaning Gen 3:20
Hebrew word for * sounds similar to Gen 3:20f
intercourse with * his wife, and Gen 4:1
Later on * gave birth to another Gen 4:25
for, as * put it, "God has Gen 4:25
benefit, but * was made for Adam. 1Co 11:9
our Lord, just as * was deceived by 2Co 11:3
first, and afterwards he made *. 1Ti 2:13
but *, and sin was the result. 1Ti 2:14

EVE'S
was not made for * benefit, but Eve 1Co 11:9

EVENING
Literally, "And there was * and Gen 1:4,5f
Literally, "There was * and there Gen 1:7,8f
Literally, "And there was * and Gen 1:13f
Literally, "And there was * and Gen 1:19f
Literally, "And there was * and Gen 1:23f
Literally, "And there was * and Gen 1:31f
That * they heard the sound of Gen 3:8
this time, towards *, the bird Gen 8:11
That * as the sun was going down, Gen 15:12
THAT * THE two angels came to the Gen 19:1
It was *, and the women of the Gen 24:11
One * as he was taking a walk out Gen 24:63
That * as Jacob was coming home Gen 30:16
and in the * divides the spoil." Gen 49:27
"On the * of the fourteenth day Ex 12:6
be eaten from the * of the Ex 12:18
month until the * of the Ex 12:18
told them, "This * you will Ex 16:6
the *, and bread in the morning. Ex 16:7,8,9
Tell them, 'In the * you will Ex 16:11,12
That * vast numbers of quail Ex 16:13
each other, from morning to *. Ex 18:13
morning and the other in the *. Ex 29:39
Offer the other lamb in the *, Ex 29:41
altar, and each * when he lights Ex 30:8
in the morning and half in the *. Lev 6:19,20
defiled until the *, and must wash Lev 11:24
animal shall be defiled until *. Lev 11:27
be ceremonially defiled until *; Lev 11:28
be defiled until *, and anything Lev 11:31
water, and is defiled until *. Lev 11:32
carcass shall be defiled until *. Lev 11:39
clothes and be defiled until *. Lev 11:40
closed shall be defiled until *. Lev 14:46
defiled until *, and must wash his Lev 15:5
unclean until *, and must wash his Lev 15:6
unclean until *, and must wash his Lev 15:8
be defiled until *, and must wash Lev 15:10
himself and be defiled until *. Lev 15:11
bath and be unclean until the *. Lev 15:16
ceremonially defiled until *. Lev 15:17
defiled until the next *. Lev 15:18
her shall be defiled until *. Lev 15:19
be ceremonially defiled until *. Lev 15:21,22,23
and bathe and be defiled until *. Lev 15:27
himself and be defiled until *; Lev 17:15
be defiled until *, and shall not Lev 22:6
until after he has bathed that *. Lev 22:6
on the previous * and goes on until Lev 23:32
and goes on until the next *. Lev 23:32
Each morning and * Aaron shall Lev 24:3,4
beginning in the *. Num 9:2,3
would begin on the * of the Num 9:4,5
second month, beginning in the *. Num 9:11
and that * the Cloud changed to Num 9:15
ceremonially defiled until the *. Num 19:7
he too shall be defiled until *. Num 19:8
clothes and be defiled until *; Num 19:10
himself, and that * he will be out Num 19:19
water shall be defiled until *. Num 19:21
shall be defiled until *." Num 19:22
the morning, the other in the *. Num 28:4
Offer the second lamb in the * Num 28:8
* just as the sun goes down. Deu 16:6
and stay outside until the *; Deu 23:11
And in the * you will say, 'Oh, Deu 28:67
had arrived in the city that *. Jos 2:2
and arrived that * at the banks of Jos 3:1
* of the 14th day of the month. Jos 5:10
until *, with dust on their heads. Jos 7:6
Ai on a tree until *, but as the Jos 8:29
hanged them on five trees until *. Jos 10:26
today and leave sometime this *." Ju 19:8
have a pleasant * together and Ju 19:9
"We arrived one * at Gibe-ah, a Ju 20:4
the Lord until * and asked him, Ju 20:22,23,24
and fasted until *, offering burnt Ju 20:26
God until *, weeping bitterly. Ju 21:2
day, and in the * when she had Ru 2:17
One * after supper, when they 1Sa 1:9
anything before *—before I have 1Sa 14:24,25
That * 1Sa 14:32
a day, morning and * the Philistine 1Sa 17:16
until the * of the third day. 1Sa 20:5
and the entire next day until *. 1Sa 30:17
unusual beauty taking her * bath. 2Sa 11:2
*, and he drank from the brook. 1Ki 17:6
the time of the * sacrifice, but 1Ki 18:29
for offering the * sacrifice, 1Ki 18:36
Finally, toward *, he died. 1Ki 22:35
So that * they went out to the 2Ki 7:5
offering, the * grain offering, the 2Ki 16:15
each morning and * upon the altar 1Ch 16:40
Each morning and * they stood 1Ch 23:30
each morning and *, and on the 2Ch 2:4
every morning and *—burnt offerings 2Ch 13:11
daily morning and * burnt 2Ch 31:3
Passover lambs were slain that *. 2Ch 35:1
and * burnt offerings to the Lord; Ez 3:3
the time of the * burnt offering. Ez 9:4
apartment in the * and the next Est 2:12,13,14
Late that *, when the king was Est 9:11
morning, but by * they are dead, Job 4:20
men. At * they come to spy, Ps 59:6
men slink back at *, and prowl the Ps 59:14,15
before the * shadows fall. Ps 90:5,6
* rejoice in all his faithfulness. Ps 92:2
passing swiftly as the * shadows. Ps 102:11
until the * shadows fall again. Ps 104:23
Regard my prayer as my * Ps 141:2
In the * Israel waits in terror, Is 17:14
rages, until the * shadows fall. Jer 6:4
exile—and in the * I dug through Eze 12:7
and in the * my wife died. Eze 24:18
me the previous *, and he had Eze 33:22
which shall not be closed until *. Eze 46:2
In the * the men came again to Dan 6:15
at the time of the * sacrifice, Dan 9:21
ravenous wolves at * time, who by Zep 3:3
* time it will still be light. Zec 14:7
That * several demon-possessed Mt 8:16
That * the disciples came to him Mt 14:15
"At five o'clock that * he was Mt 20:6
"That * he told the paymaster to Mt 20:8
That * as he sat eating with the Mt 26:20,21
When * came, a rich man from Mt 27:57
of sick folk that * and ordered Mk 1:34
As * fell, Jesus said to his Mk 4:35
after the miracle the * before! Mk 6:52
That * as usual they left the Mk 11:19
will come, at *, at midnight, Mk 13:35,36,37
eat the Passover supper this *!' Mk 14:14
In the * Jesus arrived with the Mk 14:17
THE NEXT *, when the Sabbath Mk 16:1
But when he didn't show up that * Lk 2:44
As the sun went down that *, all Lk 4:40
And each * he returned to spend Lk 21:37,38
that afternoon until the *. Jn 1:39
That * his disciples went down to Jn 6:16
JESUS KNEW ON the * of Passover Jn 13:1
That * the disciples were meeting Jn 20:19
already *, jailed them overnight. Act 4:3
morning and went on into the *! Act 28:23

EVENINGS
fell on Friday * and not be opened Neh 13:19
hundred mornings and *." Dan 8:14f
Literally, "The vision of the * Dan 8:26f

EVENT
"You shall celebrate this * each Ex 12:14
of this * you are to use no yeast; Ex 13:3
"So celebrate the * annually in Ex 13:10
is to be an annual * at the regular Ex 23:15
This shall be a regular, annual * Ex 30:10

(EVENT Con't)
It would be an annual * from Est 9:28
This * is further described in Jer 25:12f
This * occurred six years after Jer 51:59f
In any *, he represents the Eze 38:2,3f
to that final * in history. Dan 8:19
* was fulfilled in 168–167 B.C. Dan 11:30,31f
For a description of this *, see Lk 10:13f
death as they await this great *. Rom 8:22

EVENTS
Here is a summary of the * in the Gen 2:4
with fear at this turn of *. Jos 7:5
In the * that followed, both Ju 9:24
wars and the other * of his 1Ki 14:19
The other * in Rehoboam's reign 1Ki 14:29
deals with * preceding chapter 9. 1Ch 10:1
of all these *, and sent letters to Est 9:20
* are a sealed book to them. Is 29:11
(* told about in chapter 39. Jer 52:1
World * are under his control. Dan 2:21
"You dreamed of coming *. Dan 2:29
Daniel replied: "Oh, that the * Dan 4:19
that the * you have seen in your Dan 8:17
It concerned * certain to happen Dan 10:1
This chapter predicts the * of the Nah 2:1f
"What * will signal your return, Mt 24:3
"Yes, these are the * that will Mk 13:30
"Then there will be strange * in Lk 21:25
when you see the * taking place Lk 21:31
I saw these * and have recorded Jn 21:24
if all the other * in Jesus' life Jn 21:25
I am sure these * are all familiar Act 26:26
speaks of future * with as much Rom 4:17
to write down the * which, since 1Pe 1:11

EVENTUALLY
* the descendants of Canaan spread Gen 10:15-19
Then, *, Ex 1:8
Moses * decided to accept Reuel's Ex 2:21
Moses, and * it was kept in the Ark Ex 16:34
He returned home, and * had Ju 8:30
All of us must die *; 2Sa 14:14
* the Lord struck him and he died. 2Ch 13:20
* the record was found in the Ez 6:2
several days, but * King Zedekiah Jer 37:17
and robbed. * these pressures will Dan 11:34
but * she got on his nerves. Lk 18:4,5
"However, God promised that * the Act 7:5

EVER
that I would * have a baby? Gen 21:7
Then if you * find any white Gen 30:33
below Bethel. And * after it was Gen 35:8
she exclaimed. And * after he Gen 38:29
he said, 'Don't * come back again Gen 43:3,4,5
"Why did you * tell him you had Gen 43:6
Why did you * send me, if you Ex 5:22
do this to them? * since I gave Ex 5:23
and don't let me * see you again," Ex 10:28
person shall * eat the lamb. Ex 12:48
did you * take us out of Egypt? Ex 17:3
with us, who will * know that I and Ex 33:16
the fire stopped. * after, the Num 11:3
Why did you * make us leave Num 20:5
"Have I * done anything like Num 22:30
Has he * promised, Num 23:18-24
years of age would * see the land Num 32:10,11
Where else will you * find Deu 4:34
'How can we * conquer these nations Deu 7:17
"If you * hear it said about one Deu 13:12,13,14
"No Ammonite or Moabite may * Deu 23:3
And * afterwards his house Deu 25:10
Every commandment Moses had * Jos 8:35
"Don't * be afraid or Jos 10:25
Has there * been a time when you Ju 10:12
was the last they * saw of him. Ju 13:21
called "Jawbone Hill" * since. Ju 15:16,17
"I don't think anyone could * Ju 16:6
she has been at it * since except Ru 2:7
king any longer. * since I brought 1Sa 8:8
Have I * defrauded you? 1Sa 12:3
Have I * oppressed you? 1Sa 12:3
Have I * taken a bribe? 1Sa 12:3
"I am sorry that I * made Saul 1Sa 15:11
he had * made Saul king of Israel. 1Sa 15:35
more than * in the public eye. 1Sa 18:13
For not one of you has * told me 1Sa 22:8
the Philistines. * since that time 1Sa 23:28
to Egypt * since ancient times. 1Sa 27:8
finest men I've * met, and I think 1Sa 29:6
The place has been known * since 2Sa 2:16
can I * bring the Ark home?" 2Sa 6:9
My home has been a tent * since 2Sa 7:6
Have I * asked them, 'Why haven't 2Sa 7:7
Absalom has been plotting this * 2Sa 13:32,33
have * been in your entire life." 2Sa 19:7
else has * had or ever will have! 1Ki 3:12
else has ever had or * will have! 1Ki 3:12
everything she had * heard about 1Ki 10:4
than anything I've * heard of ! 1Ki 10:7
King Solomon had * received. 1Ki 10:10
more priests than * from the common 1Ki 13:33
the other nations * delivered their 2Ki 18:33
What god has * been able to save 2Ki 18:35
have angered me * since I brought 2Ki 21:15
that no one could * again use it to 2Ki 23:10
And they have lived there * 1Ch 4:43
it * since Saul became king." 1Ch 13:3
I * get the Ark of God home?" 1Ch 13:12
as Baal-perazim * since (meaning, 1Ch 14:11
praise your name for * and ever! 1Ch 29:10
praise your name for ever and *! 1Ch 29:10
other king has * had before you! 2Ch 1:12
But who can * build him a worthy 2Ch 2:6
than I could * have imagined. 2Ch 9:6
of any nation has * yet been able 2Ch 32:15
by Moses—I won't * again exile 2Ch 33:8
we have sacrificed to him * since Ez 4:2
been working on it * since, though Ez 5:16
King Cyrus * made such a decree; Ez 5:17
with me—* took off our clothes. Neh 4:23
"What reward did we * give Est 6:3
Have you * known a truly good and Job 4:7,8
Have I * asked you for one Job 6:22
Have I * asked your help? Job 6:23
Who has * opposed him Job 9:4
Won't you * stop your flow of Job 16:3
"Don't you realize that * since Job 20:4
his family will * see him again. Job 20:9
How did you * think of all these Job 26:4
No wild animal has * walked upon Job 28:8
my servants have * gone hungry— Job 31:31
"Have you * once commanded the Job 38:12
Have you * told the daylight to Job 38:13
Have you * robed the dawn in Job 38:14
Have you * seen them giving birth Job 39:1
"I am nothing—how could I * find Job 40:4
out their names forever and *. Ps 9:5
God nor man can * keep them Ps 10:6
But how can I * know what sins Ps 19:12
* be disgraced for trusting him. Ps 25:3
My eyes are * looking to the Lord Ps 25:15
us, and we are * in your thoughts. Ps 40:5
(but how could you * forget them! Ps 42:4,5
God is our God forever and *. Ps 48:14
* more bold in their wickedness." Ps 52:7
in the mercy of God forever and *. Ps 52:8
forever and * for your punishment. Ps 52:9
can they * be really happy again. Ps 53:6
their hearts could * wish for! Ps 73:7
nor * have an idol in your home. Ps 81:9
FOREVER AND * I will sing about Ps 89:1
Who can * list the glorious Ps 106:2
Who can * praise him half enough? Ps 106:2
for I am * thinking of your rules. Ps 119:99
* get an answer to his prayers? Ps 130:3,4
you search for me * so anxiously. Pro 1:28
None of these men will * be the Pro 2:19
don't * trust yourself. Pro 3:4,5
Keep these thoughts * in mind; Pro 4:21
Who can * say, "I have cleansed Pro 20:9
in this: neither is * satisfied. Pro 27:20
Don't * put your trust in him! Is 2:22
from * sitting on his throne. Is 14:22
to you than his father * was! Is 14:29
who has * looked to her for help. Is 36:6
Have any other nation's gods * Is 36:18
which one has * delivered their Is 36:20
Has he * needed anyone's advice? Is 40:14
I, Israel's God, will not * Is 41:17
Which of all their idols * has Is 43:9
What idol * told you they would Is 45:21
which one has * told you this: Is 48:14
upon my palm and * before me is a Is 49:16
and orthodox Christianity * since. Is 52:13f
See if anyone there has * heard Jer 2:10,11
that cannot * be washed away. Jer 2:22
* find her help and her salvation. Jer 3:23
her sickness and wounds are * Jer 6:7
of forward. * since the day your Jer 7:25
one has * heard of such a thing! Jer 18:13
Why was I * born? Jer 20:18
his children shall * sit upon the Jer 22:30
when has there * been a time of Jer 30:7
than it has * been before. Jer 33:10,11
none of us should * drink, neither Jer 35:6
all the evil I have * threatened. Jer 35:17
"What have I * done to deserve Jer 37:18
any of your fathers have * known. Jer 44:2,3
and happy! But * since we quit Jer 44:18
No one will * brag of Moab any Jer 48:2,3,4
thought no one could * harm you. Jer 49:4
No one shall * live there again. Jer 49:33
In all the world has there * been Lam 2:13
than I have * done before or will Eze 5:9
done before or will * do again. Eze 5:9
O evil prophets, what have you * Eze 13:5
and became more beautiful than *. Eze 16:13
world was there * such a wondrous Eze 27:32
special land shall * be sold or Eze 48:14
of God forever and *, for he alone Dan 2:20
no one will * conquer it. Dan 2:44
he reigns forever and *. Dan 4:3
lives for-ever and *, that they Dan 12:7
O Israel, * since that awful Hos 10:9
and have been * since I brought you Hos 13:4
history, have you * heard of such a Joe 1:2
rain, but there wasn't * enough. Amo 4:8
"Who can * reach us way up Ob 1:3
How shall I * again see your holy Jon 2:4
God forever and *, even though all Mic 4:5
* return, for crime was rampant. Zec 8:10
"When did we * despise your Mal 1:6
When have we * done a thing like Mal 1:7
When did we * rob you?' Mal 3:8
all the reward they will * get. Mt 6:2
is all the reward they will * get. Mt 6:5
the only reward they will * get. Mt 6:16
narrow, and only a few * find it. Mt 7:14
"Truly, of all men * born, none Mt 11:11
If * you were willing to Mt 11:15
"Haven't you * read what King Mt 12:3
And haven't you * read in the Mt 12:5
Won't you * understand? Mt 16:9
"Didn't you * read the Mt 21:16
them, "Didn't you * read in the Mt 21:42
you * read the Scriptures? Mt 22:31
Don't * let anyone call you Mt 23:8
we * see you hungry and feed you? Mt 25:37
When did we * see you sick or in Mt 25:39
'Lord, when did we * see you Mt 25:44
But Jesus replied, "Didn't you * Mk 2:25,26
the Good News will * know what it Mk 8:35
earthly process could * make it! Mk 9:3
that no one has * given up Mk 10:29
creation, nor will * be again. Mk 13:19
how they could * roll aside the Mk 16:3
most joyful news * announced, and Lk 2:10
Haven't you * read what King Lk 6:3
"Who * heard of someone Lk 8:16
him and hardly * leaves him alone. Lk 9:39
"Or what king would * dream of Lk 14:31
of them would * do such a thing. Lk 22:23
No one has * actually seen God, Jn 1:18
who told me everything I * did! Jn 4:28,29
"He told me everything I * did!" Jn 4:39
No one coming to me will * be Jn 6:35
one who obeys me shall * die!" Jn 8:51
before Abraham was * born!" Jn 8:58
he was more frightened than *. Jn 19:8
the Kingdom will * see me again. Act 20:25
How could he * condemn anyone? Rom 3:6
No one has * really followed Rom 3:11
No one can * be made right in Rom 3:20
and trust grew * stronger, and he Rom 4:20
What can we * say to such Rom 8:31
If God is on our side, who can * Rom 8:31
Who then can * keep Christ's love Rom 8:35
can * separate us from his love. Rom 8:38
ocean—nothing will * be able to Rom 8:39
no one had * loved them before. Rom 9:25
a small number would * be saved. Rom 9:27
in Christ will * be disappointed. Rom 10:11
And who could * offer to the Rom 11:35
I don't remember * baptizing 1Co 1:16
can * brag in the presence of God. 1Co 1:29
no mere man has * seen, heard or 1Co 2:9
And no one can * lay any other 1Co 3:11
And have you * heard of a farmer 1Co 9:7
born from women * since, and both 1Co 11:12
do for the Lord is * wasted as it 1Co 15:58
blessing upon us forever and *! 2Co 4:17
the Lord, which is * present in our 2Co 5:11
that no one will * be offended or 2Co 6:3
He loves you more than * when he 2Co 7:15
and *, knows I tell the truth. 2Co 11:31
For no one will * be saved by Gal 2:16
that no one can * win God's favor Gal 3:11
at Ephesus, * loyal to the Lord: Eph 1:1
That is why, * since I heard of Eph 1:15
favor have we * been saved— and Eph 2:5
more than we would * dare to ask or Eph 3:20
glory forever and * through endless Eph 3:21
so that, whether I * see you again Php 1:27
Yet if anyone * had reason to Php 3:4
So I was a real Jew if there * Php 3:5
Not that I was * in need, for I Php 4:11
our Father be glory forever and *. Php 4:20
and have been * since the Gospel Col 1:5
has given you. So * since we first Col 1:9
are as strong as *, and that you 1Th 3:6
May the Lord bring you into an * 2Th 3:5
and honor to God forever and *. 1Ti 1:17
No mere man has * seen him, nor 1Ti 6:16
man has ever seen him, nor * will. 1Ti 6:16
power and dominion forever and *. 1Ti 6:16
still trusting him as much as *. 2Ti 1:5
Don't * forget the wonderful fact 2Ti 2:8
To God be the glory forever and * 2Ti 4:18
O God, will last forever and *; Heb 1:8
And did God * say to an angel, as Heb 1:13
again, * since the world began. Heb 9:26
Don't * forget those wonderful Heb 10:32
died without * receiving all that Heb 11:13
To him be glory forever and *. Heb 13:20,21

EVER Con't)
Dear brothers, don't * forget Jas 1:19
When will you * learn that Jas 2:20
be glory and power forever and *. 1Pe 4:11
and make you stronger than *. 1Pe 5:10
over all things, forever and *. 1Pe 5:11
in Scripture was * thought up by 2Pe 1:20,21
love within us grows * stronger. 1Jn 4:12
a Christian * sin in such a way? 1Jn 5:17f
up your lives * more strongly upon Jud 1:20
lives forever and *, the Rev 4:9
and to the Lamb forever and *." Rev 5:13
lives forever and *, who created Rev 10:6
through the ages * since it was Rev 10:7
and he shall reign forever and * Rev 11:15
rises forever and *, and they will Rev 14:11
No industry of any kind will * Rev 18:22
in a window will * be seen again. Rev 18:23
day and night forever and *. Rev 20:10
they shall reign forever and *. Rev 22:5
EVER-BRIGHTENING
in the * light of God's favor; Pro 4:18
EVER-EXPANDING
His *, peaceful government Is 9:7
EVER-FLOWING
path for them across the * Jordan. Ps 74:15
garden, like an * spring. Is 58:11
EVER-INCREASING
me and pour out an * volume of Job 10:17
EVER-LIVING
the glorious, * God, they took wood Rom 1:23
Christ, God's * Message to men. 1Pe 1:23
EVER-WIDENING
God's message was preached in * Act 6:7
EVERGREEN
I am like an * tree, yielding my Hos 14:8
EVERLASTING
as participants in my * covenant. Gen 17:13
children, for an * possession.' Gen 48:4
the utmost bounds of the * hills. Gen 49:26
This shall be an * law for you, Lev 16:34
in memory of his * covenant with Lev 24:5-8
And of the * hills. Deu 33:15
And underneath are the * arms. Deu 33:27
An * covenant with me; 2Sa 23:5
With an * promise: 1Ch 16:17
he lives from * to everlasting. Neh 9:5
he lives from everlasting to *. Neh 9:5
"I will reveal the * purposes of Ps 2:7
Their hearts shall rejoice with * Ps 22:26
eyes of * love and kindness. Ps 25:6,7
who exists from * ages past—and on Ps 41:13
past—and on into * eternity ahead. Ps 41:13
God himself—God from * ages Ps 55:19
The * mountains cannot compare Ps 76:4
times, from the * past. Ps 93:1
the Lord is from * to everlasting, Ps 103:17,18
to *, to those who reverence him; Ps 103:17,18
of Israel, from * to everlasting. Ps 106:48
of Israel, from everlasting to *. Ps 106:48
lead me along the path of * life. Ps 139:24
and nearing his * home as the Ecc 12:5
God," "The * Father," "The Is 9:6
of God and broken his * commands. Is 24:4,5
Lord Jehovah is your * strength. Is 26:4
of this all-consuming, * Fire?" Is 33:14
Zion, singing the songs of * joy. Is 35:10
Don't you know by now that the * Is 40:28
filled with joy and * gladness; Is 51:11
but with * love I will have pity Is 54:8
I am ready to make an * covenant Is 55:3
an * sign [of God's power and love Is 55:13
that I will give them is an * one; Is 56:5
God will be your * light, and he Is 60:19
the Lord will be your * light; Is 60:20
portion of prosperity and * joy. Is 61:7
and make an * covenant with them. Is 61:8
God, the living God, the * King. Jer 10:10
the land of Chaldea an * waste. Jer 25:12
you, O my people, with an * love; Jer 31:3
And I will make an * covenant Jer 32:40
I will establish an * covenant Eze 16:59,60
of peace with them, an * pact. Eze 37:26
for sure that his kingdom is *; Dan 4:3
rule is *, his kingdom evermore. Dan 4:34
then the kingdom of * Dan 9:24
rise up, some to * life and some to Dan 12:2
and some to shame and * contempt. Dan 12:2
who is alive from * ages past! Mic 5:2
scattering the * mountains and Hab 3:6
but the righteous into * life." Mt 25:46
entry into an * home in heaven? Lk 16:9
you include holiness and * life. Rom 6:22
were, be swallowed up by * life. 2Co 5:4
he will reap the * life which the Gal 6:8
They will be punished in * hell, 2Th 1:9
us and given us * comfort and hope 2Th 2:16
that they, too, can have * life. 1Ti 1:16
Unto him be honor and * power and 1Ti 6:16
of * life through trusting him. 2Ti 1:10
we are looking forward to our * Heb 13:14
of the sheep by an * agreement Heb 13:20,21
of them is the * gloom and darkness Jud 1:13
with mighty shouts of * joy. Jud 1:24,25
Give to him * glory! Rev 1:6
carrying the * Good News to preach Rev 14:6
EVERMORE
is everlasting, his kingdom *. Dan 4:34
To him be glory *. Rom 11:36
his they are and his they * shall Jud 1:24,25
all that is or was or * shall be Rev 3:14
EVERY
burst forth with * sort of grass Gen 1:11,12
be filled with birds of * kind." Gen 1:20
sea creatures, and * sort of fish Gen 1:21,22
sort of fish and * kind of bird. Gen 1:21,22
earth bring forth * kind of Gen 1:24
reptiles and wildlife of * kind." Gen 1:24
and it was excellent in * way. Gen 1:31
from the soil * kind of animal and Gen 2:19,20
very image of his father in * way. Gen 5:3,4,5
flood and destroy * living Gen 6:17
Bring a pair of * animal—a male Gen 6:19,20
of * kind of bird. Gen 7:3
Thus there will be * kind of life Gen 7:3
boat were pairs of * kind of Gen 7:14,15
reptiles and birds of * sort. Gen 7:14,15
to you and to * being, that never Gen 9:15
to * living being on the earth." Gen 9:16,17
as you can see in * direction, for Gen 13:14
that * male among you shall be Gen 17:9,10
this covenant. * male shall be Gen 17:12
This applies to * foreign-born Gen 17:12
his son and * other male—born in Gen 17:23
man, and God blessed him in * way. Gen 24:1
shapely, and in * way a beauty. Gen 29:17
You made me pay for * animal Gen 31:39
I'll tell you what we'll do—if * Gen 34:15
one condition—that * one of us men Gen 34:22
and sensitive to * move they made, Gen 34:25
and slaughtered * man there, Gen 34:25
children, and wealth of * kind. Gen 34:29
* kernel well formed and plump. Gen 41:5
out empty-handed! * woman will ask Ex 3:22
into your beds! * home in Egypt Ex 8:3,4
frogs in * corner of the land." Ex 8:5
palace and in * home in Egypt. Ex 8:24
the fields, for * man and animal Ex 9:19
and they ate * bit of vegetation Ex 10:15
sons shall die in * family in Ex 11:5
of the door of * home and on the Ex 12:7
of Israel, and * firstborn male Ex 13:1
blot out * trace of Amalek." Ex 17:14
"In * case in which an ox, Ex 22:9
times each year, * man in Israel Ex 23:17
to obey * one of these rules." Ex 24:7
for seven days. * day you shall Ex 29:36
it to God * day for seven days. Ex 29:37
"* morning when Aaron trims the Ex 30:7
"* firstborn male Ex 34:19
gold objects of * kind. Ex 35:22
So the people of Israel—* man Ex 35:29
in fact, he has * needed skill. Ex 35:33
"* offering must be seasoned Lev 2:13
out thoroughly. * male among the Lev 6:29
Moses were followed in * detail. Lev 8:21
be broken, and * wooden utensil Lev 15:12
seven days, and * bed he lies upon Lev 15:24
for the life of * bird and animal Lev 17:14
Literally, "* creature." Lev 17:14f
crop—don't strip * last piece of Lev 19:10
—the seventh day of * week—which Lev 23:3
of solemn rest in * home, times for Lev 23:3
"* Sabbath day the High Priest Lev 24:5-8
before the Lord * seventh year. Lev 25:1
"* fiftieth year, on the Day of Lev 25:8
"In * contract of sale there Lev 25:24
you didn't give it * seventh year Lev 26:34,35
And the Lord owns * tenth animal Lev 27:32
count * male down to one month Num 3:14,15
oxen—a wagon for * two leaders and Num 7:3
We would have to catch * fish in Num 11:22
I, Jehovah, have spoken. * one of Num 14:34,35
wine, grain, and * other crop. Num 18:13
From * other nation. Num 23:7-10
a young bull and ram on * altar. Num 23:30
with trumpets blaring. And * man Num 31:7
His share is one out of * five Num 31:28
the inheritance of * tribe is to Num 36:7
some from * tribe, and appointed Deu 1:15
quarrels and assist them in * way. Deu 1:15
and blessed you * step of the way Deu 2:7
but will purchase * bite we eat and Deu 2:28
can look out in * direction, and Deu 3:27
his directions in * detail, going Deu 5:32
comes by obeying * command of God. Deu 8:3
to be above * other nation, as is Deu 10:15
and obey * one of his commands. Deu 11:1
tithe all of your crops * year. Deu 14:22
"* third year you are to use Deu 14:28
"AT THE END of * seventh year Deu 15:1
of all debts! * creditor shall Deu 15:2
"* man in Israel shall appear Deu 16:16
They will administer justice in * Deu 16:18
He must read from it * day of his Deu 17:19
and the stomach of * ox or sheep Deu 18:3
to you, kill * male in the city; Deu 20:13
destroy * living thing. Deu 20:16
"* new house must have a Deu 22:8
after * bowel movement he must Deu 23:13
of their fathers; * man worthy of Deu 24:16
"* third year is a year of Deu 26:12
to give you fine crops * season. Deu 28:12
The Lord will bring upon you * Deu 28:61
at the end of * seventh year—the Deu 31:10,11
And preserves him from * harm." Deu 33:12
obey to the letter * law Moses gave Jos 1:7
careful to obey * one of them you Jos 1:7
think about them * day and every Jos 1:8
them every day and * night so that Jos 1:8
then move in upon the city from * Jos 6:5
city from * side and captured it! Jos 6:20
of God's laws. * commandment Moses Jos 8:35
city and its king. * last person Jos 10:30
those kingdoms.) * person there Jos 11:11
their enemies. * good thing the Jos 21:45
and have obeyed * order I have Jos 22:2,3
you—* order of the Lord your God. Jos 22:2,3
who live around you on * side. Ju 6:10
from all their enemies on * side. Ju 8:34
She nagged at him * day until he Ju 16:16,17
get angry and kill * one of you." Ju 18:25
burned down * city and village in Ju 20:48
in those days, and * man did Ju 21:25
her barrenness. * year it was the 1Sa 1:7
* member will die before his time. 1Sa 2:31
the right eye of * one of you as a 1Sa 11:2
and destroy * last one of them." 1Sa 14:36
army out in * direction against 1Sa 14:47
hate him more with * passing day. 1Sa 18:29
* inch of the entire land!" 1Sa 23:23
trees and playing * sort of musical 2Sa 6:5
He got up early * morning and 2Sa 15:2
he sent spies to * part of Israel 2Sa 15:10
as David had; for * word Ahithophel 2Sa 16:23
until * stone is torn down." 2Sa 17:13
helped them in * way they could. 2Sa 19:18
For you watch their * move. 2Sa 22:28
rescued me from * danger, I decree 1Ki 1:29
"I am going where * man on earth 1Ki 2:2
has given Israel peace on * side; 1Ki 5:4
was completed in * detail in 1Ki 6:38
Listen to * plea of the people 1Ki 8:30
gave him the right answers * time. 1Ki 10:3
Hiram's, and once * three years a 1Ki 10:22
* male in the entire country. 1Ki 11:15
Literally, "* male, both bond and 1Ki 14:10f
and idols on * high hill and under 1Ki 14:23
high hill and under * green tree. 1Ki 14:23
all Judah, asking * able-bodied man 1Ki 15:22
"We must check * stream and brook 1Ki 18:5
king has searched * nation and 1Ki 18:10
they have killed * one of your 1Ki 19:14
him to do * sort of evil. 1Ki 21:25
they mobilized * man who could 2Ki 3:21
threw stones on * good piece of 2Ki 3:25
Soon * container was full to the 2Ki 4:6
healed of * trace of his leprosy! 2Ki 5:10
wiped out—* male, no matter who. 2Ki 9:8
See to it that * one of them 2Ki 10:18,19
"Be sure that * worshiper wears 2Ki 10:22
Thus Jehu destroyed * trace of 2Ki 10:28
* hill and under every green tree; 2Ki 17:10
every hill and under * green tree; 2Ki 17:10
and wizards, and * kind of idol 2Ki 23:24
THE FAMILY TREE of * person in 1Ch 9:1
More men joined David almost * 1Ch 12:22
equipped with * kind of weapon. 1Ch 12:24-37
then he gave * person present 1Ch 16:3
out your plan in * detail, for it 1Ch 17:2
him a large sum of money * year. 1Ch 18:2
him large amounts of money * year. 1Ch 18:6
over * generation of Israel.' 1Ch 22:10
and craftsmen of * kind. 1Ch 22:15
Now try with * fiber of your 1Ch 22:19
you to search out * commandment of 1Ch 28:8
for the Lord sees * heart and 1Ch 28:9
understands and knows * thought. 1Ch 28:9
"* part of this blueprint," 1Ch 28:19
Others with skills of * kind will 1Ch 28:21
Using * resource at my command, 1Ch 29:2
is— listen to * individual's 2Ch 6:29
I will listen, wide awake, to * 2Ch 7:15
in those days! * three years the 2Ch 9:21
Kings from * nation came to 2Ch 9:23
in armories in * city as a further 2Ch 11:12
leaders from * part of the nation 2Ch 12:5
to the Lord * morning and 2Ch 13:11
The golden lampstand is lighted * 2Ch 13:11
from * one of Judah's cities. 2Ch 14:5
Problems troubled the nation on * 2Ch 15:5
"He does it * time. 2Ch 18:17
As the people from * part of 2Ch 20:13

(EVERY Con't)
Seir and killed * one of them. 2Ch 20:23
the hills and under * green tree. 2Ch 28:4
gods in * corner of Jerusalem. 2Ch 28:24
And he did the same in * city of 2Ch 28:25
So the people from * part of 2Ch 29:31
and encouraged * sort of evil, 2Ch 33:6
of all kinds of wines * ten days. Neh 5:18
people in * corner of the land; Neh 9:22
us until now. * time you punished Neh 9:33
not to do any work * seventh year Neh 10:31
the first part of * crop to the Neh 10:35
the first offerings of * harvest. Neh 13:31
them in from * part of Media-Persia Est 1:1
only the king but * official and Est 1:16
out, the wife of * one of us Est 1:18
stressing that * man should rule Est 1:22
as law in * province, and made Est 3:14
Follow * detail you have Est 6:10
And in * city and province, as Est 8:17
celebrated by * family throughout Est 9:28
* year when each of Job's sons Job 1:4
Must you be his inquisitor * Job 7:18
and test him * moment of the day? Job 7:18
He will supply your * need Job 12:6
For the soul of * living thing Job 12:10
prison and shut me in on * side. Job 13:27,28
life, and notice * mistake I make. Job 14:16
Torrents tear away the soil. So * Job 14:18,19
There will be darkness in * home Job 18:6
There is a booby-trap in * path Job 18:10
He has broken me down on * side, Job 19:10
Because he stole at * Job 20:21
Their homes are safe from * Job 21:9
wicked get away with it * time. Job 21:17
But he knows * detail of what is Job 23:10
among them. * house built by the Job 27:18
He sees everything I do, and * Job 31:4
say, 'and watches * move I make.' Job 33:11
flashes out in * direction. Job 37:3
there they search for * blade of Job 39:8
me on * side, I am not afraid. Ps 3:6
silly idols, when * claim that's Ps 4:2
I am worn out with pain; * night Ps 6:6
he is angry with the wicked * day. Ps 7:11
they prowl on * side and vileness Ps 12:8
knows, for he watches my * step. Ps 18:24
How perfect in * way! Ps 18:30
You gave me victory in * battle. Ps 18:43,44,45
I can count * bone in my body. Ps 22:17
the people of * nation shall Ps 22:27
And when we obey him, * path he Ps 25:10
in his presence * day of my life, Ps 27:4
strength, my shield from * danger. Ps 28:7
You are my hiding place from * Ps 32:7
His intentions are the same for * Ps 33:11
Lord helps him in each and * one. Ps 34:19
Lord shall be given * blessing. Ps 37:9
shall be given * blessing, and Ps 37:11
he will honor you with * blessing, Ps 37:34
You hear my * sigh. Ps 38:9
Yes, he knows the secrets of * Ps 44:21
breaking and burning * weapon. Ps 46:9
I will be honored by * nation in Ps 46:10
You have recorded * one in your Ps 56:8
you * day, and you have given me Ps 61:5
He watches * movement of the Ps 66:7
and woe—* day and all day long! Ps 73:14
"Let's wipe out * trace of Ps 74:8
Will your jealousy burn till * Ps 79:5
people Israel, invading * home. Ps 79:7
You will receive * blessing you Ps 81:10
will go there. May * fiber of my Ps 86:11
in ruins * fort defending him. Ps 89:40
For he rescues you from * trap, Ps 91:3
* morning tell him, "Thank you Ps 92:2
kindness," and * evening rejoice Ps 92:2
* nation sees his glory. Ps 97:6
gods—for * god must bow to him! Ps 97:7
and revealed it to * nation by Ps 98:2,3
* kind, to have no part in them. Ps 101:3
and stay away from * evil. Ps 101:4
Your fame will endure to * Ps 102:12
For your people love * stone in Ps 102:14
* grain of dust in her streets. Ps 102:14
of * kind, both great and small. Ps 104:25
play in the sea. * one of these Ps 104:27
around the world, in * nation. Ps 108:3
Keep me far from * wrong; Ps 119:29,30
Help me to love your * wish; Ps 119:80
Your faithfulness extends to * Ps 119:90,91
no wonder I hate * false teaching. Ps 119:104
the finest gold. * law of God is Ps 119:128
I hate * other way. Ps 119:128
as watchmen in the Temple * night. Ps 134:1
your fame is known to * Ps 135:13
He gives food to * living thing, Ps 136:25
* king in all the earth shall Ps 138:4
When far away you know my * Ps 139:2
* moment, you know where I am. Ps 139:3
* day was recorded in your Book! Ps 139:16
to the brim with crops of * kind. Ps 144:12-15
deeds shall be on * tongue; Ps 145:6
and thirst of * living thing. Ps 145:16
leaders fail; for * man must die. Ps 146:4
He is the God who keeps * Ps 146:6
your God is King in * generation! Ps 146:10
live—how to act in * circumstance, Pro 1:2
* YOUNG MAN who listens to me and Pro 2:1
For the Lord grants wisdom! His * Pro 2:6
to find the right decision * time. Pro 2:9
of their advice. * day and all Pro 6:22
* corner for men to be her lovers. Pro 7:11,12
city gates and at * fork in the Pro 8:1
road, and at the door of * house. Pro 8:1
hate lies and * kind of deception. Pro 8:6,7
corruption and deceit of * kind. Pro 8:13
Knowing God results in * other Pro 9:10
Before * man there lies a wide Pro 14:12
The Lord demands fairness in * Pro 16:11
Before * man there lies a wide Pro 16:25
better than steak * day along with Pro 17:1
THE SELFISH MAN quarrels against * Pro 18:1
The Lord despises * kind of Pro 20:10
We can justify our * deed but God Pro 21:2
* word of God proves true. Pro 30:5
be surprised! For * official is Ecc 5:8
Tackle * task that comes along, Ecc 7:18
researching in * direction: One Ecc 7:27,28
let him rejoice in * day of life, Ecc 11:8
Enjoy * minute of it! Ecc 11:9
* hidden thing, good or bad. Ecc 12:14
* other spice that can be bought? Sol 3:6
my love, in * part of you. Sol 4:7
and perfume from * other incense Sol 4:13,14
aloes, and * other lovely spice. Sol 4:13,14
sweet, lovable in * way. Sol 5:16
and hills, and * high tower and Is 2:15
all Jerusalem—over * home and all Is 4:5
He will declare that * one of Is 10:8
* home comes the sound of weeping. Is 15:3
The city lies in chaos; * home Is 24:10
fruitful vines; * day I'll water Is 27:3
down each mountain and * hill. Is 30:25
day will come when * one of you Is 31:7
The Lord healed me! * day of my Is 38:20
whom victory meets at * step? Is 41:2
and forests, yes, and * tree; Is 44:23
it is true—that * knee in all the Is 45:23
bow to me, and * tongue shall swear Is 45:23
the guilt and sins of * one of us! Is 53:6
justice against * courtroom lie. Is 54:17
all blind to * danger. Is 56:10
himself from * possible source. Is 56:11
the shade of * tree, and slay your Is 57:5
They come to the Temple * day and Is 58:2
to satisfy your * need, and you Is 60:16
his messengers to * land and said, Is 62:11
your brethren from * nation as a Is 66:20
not obey me. On * hill and under Jer 2:20
On every hill and under * tree Jer 2:20
to other men at * chance, so Israel Jer 3:6
* hill, beneath every shady tree. Jer 3:6
every hill, beneath * shady tree. Jer 3:6
by worshiping idols under * tree; Jer 3:13
suddenly, in a moment, * house is Jer 4:20
RUN UP AND down through * street Jer 5:1
Search * square, and if you find Jer 5:1
we are terrorized at * turn. Jer 6:25
until this day: Obey my * command! Jer 11:7
are along * street in Jerusalem. Jer 11:13
Literally, "that * bottle shall Jer 13:12f
watching you and I see * sin. Jer 16:17
Yet on * side I hear their Jer 20:10
faithfully proclaim my * word. Jer 23:28
I will make them repulsive to * Jer 24:9
it—* nation God had sent me to; Jer 25:17
word in * nation of the earth. Jer 26:6
He gave me * word of all that I Jer 26:12
and upon * person living in it; Jer 26:15
sent me to speak * word that you Jer 26:15
and all mankind and * animal;' Jer 27:5
has promised to * nation that will Jer 27:13
And in * nation where I place Jer 29:18
This land—though * man and Jer 33:12
I told them that * Hebrew slave Jer 34:14
your father in * respect, he shall Jer 35:18,19
and write down * one of them. Jer 36:2
of fresh bread * day as long as Jer 37:21
That is the fate awaiting * one Jer 42:17
and I will destroy * one of you! Jer 44:11
them on * side, says the Lord. Jer 46:5
like a flood, destroying * foe. Jer 46:8
Crying and sorrow will be in * Jer 48:38
Shout against her from * side. Jer 50:15
they shall come from * side to Jer 51:2
Messengers from * side come Jer 51:31
has destroyed * home in Israel. Lam 2:2
In his wrath he has broken * Lam 2:2
has broken every fortress, * wall. Lam 2:2
their wings. And * time they Eze 1:25
until * bit of bread is gone. Eze 5:16
and altars on * hill and mountain Eze 6:13
mountain and under * green tree and Eze 6:13
you think—* thought that comes into Eze 11:5
* trace of all this idol worship. Eze 11:18
pass make liars out of * prophet.' Eze 12:22
to * man who came along. Eze 16:15
and idol altars on * street, and Eze 16:24
your beauty to * man who came by, Eze 16:25
your brothels, on * street. Eze 16:31
Animals of * sort will gather Eze 17:22,23
its branches will shelter * kind Eze 17:22,23
him, coming from * side, and Eze 19:8
I said to them: Get rid of * idol; Eze 20:7
day of rest * seventh day—as a Eze 20:12
* high hill and under every tree! Eze 20:27,28
every high hill and under * tree! Eze 20:27,28
O forest, and * tree will die, Eze 20:47
all strength will disappear. * Eze 21:7
for a sword glitters at * gate; Eze 21:15
"* leader in Israel who lives Eze 22:6
to their death. * mountain top is Eze 22:9
Her name was known to * woman in Eze 23:10
They will surround you on * side Eze 23:24
lick the inside to get * drop. Eze 23:34
Horsemen will occupy * street in Eze 26:11
Ships come from * land with all Eze 27:9
was bejeweled with * precious Eze 28:13
your streets by troops on * side. Eze 28:23
They have become a prey to * Eze 34:5
destroyed you on * side and sent Eze 36:3
I will summon * kind of terror Eze 38:21
"* day for seven days a male Eze 43:25
or barley for * sixty you reap; Eze 45:13
* morning for the daily sacrifice. Eze 46:14,15
Year of Release (* seventh year) Eze 46:17
Fish of * kind will fill the Dead Eze 47:10
There will be a new crop * Eze 47:12
Literally, "437½ feet" in * Eze 48:17f
and * other sort of instrument." Dan 3:5f
and * other sort of instrument." Dan 3:7f
and * other sort of instrument." Dan 3:10f
sent to people of * language in Dan 4:1
language in * nation of the world: Dan 4:1
whose * act is right and good; Dan 4:37
of Daniel in * part of my kingdom. Dan 6:25,26
winds blowing from * direction. Dan 7:2
of * language must obey him. Dan 7:14
Then * nation under heaven, and Dan 7:27
and our rulers. * curse against us Dan 9:13
to be greater than * god there is, Dan 11:36
And yet * one of your people Dan 12:1
and practice * kind of sin. Hos 6:9
deeds give them away on * side; Hos 7:2
other gods on * threshing floor. Hos 9:1
blocked them at * turn and publicly Hos 9:8
them and follows them on * side! Joe 2:3
winds, and knows your * thought; Amo 4:13
in all the streets and * road. Amo 5:16
and crying in * vineyard, for I Amo 5:17
would be left! * nook and cranny Ob 1:6
and * treasure found and taken. Ob 1:6
children of * God-given right. Mic 2:9
murder and sin of * kind— you Mic 3:10
fist, and destroy * remnant of Zep 1:4
into the home of * thief and Zec 5:4
and showers. * field will become a Zec 10:1
I will get rid of * vestige of idol Zec 13:2
In fact, * container in Zec 14:21
"* time you say, 'Don't bother Mal 1:7
from his covenant * last man, Mal 2:12
them to kill * baby boy two years Mt 2:16
and, in fact, from * section of Mt 3:5
to chop down * unproductive tree. Mt 3:10
* word of God is what we need." Mt 4:4
And he healed * kind of sickness Mt 4:23
I have I say: * law in the Book Mt 5:18
your Father who knows * secret. Mt 6:18
people of * sort of illness. Mt 9:35
* kind of sickness and disease. Mt 10:1
his face, into * city and place Mt 11:1f
justify your * inconsistency!" Mt 11:19
Day for * idle word you speak. Mt 12:36
permeates * part of the dough." Mt 13:33
out of the Kingdom * temptation and Mt 13:41
of * kind, valuable and worthless. Mt 13:47,48
Jesus replied, "* plant not Mt 15:13,14
he had paid * last penny due. Mt 18:34
"I've always obeyed * one of Mt 19:20
you should obey their * whim! Mt 23:3
with * sort of hypocrisy and sin. Mt 23:28
was purged from * Jewish home, the Mt 26:17
that * kind of food is kosher. Mk 7:19
be made known in * nation before Mk 13:10
I was there teaching * day. Mk 14:49
her old age! For * promise from Lk 1:37
cut you down. Yes, * tree that does Lk 3:9
there in the synagogue * Saturday. Lk 4:31
touch of his hands healed * one! Lk 4:40
me of * trace of my disease." Lk 5:12
men showed up from * village in all Lk 5:17
grass, moved by * breath of wind? Lk 7:24

(EVERY Con't)
him * day and keep close to me! Lk 9:23
"Yes, * man is a fool who gets Lk 12:21
a lamp and look in * corner of the Lk 15:8
house and sweep * nook and cranny Lk 15:8
"I've obeyed * one of these laws Lk 18:21
hung on * word he said. Lk 19:48
* day Jesus went to the Temple to Lk 21:37,38
I was there * day. Lk 22:53
observed during * human birth. Jn 3:5f
this long trip out here * day." Jn 4:15
Give us free bread * day, like Jn 6:30,31
that bread * day of our lives!" Jn 6:34
judgment in * respect, for I have Jn 8:16
are slaves of sin, * one of you. Jn 8:34
but the Son has * right there is! Jn 8:35
hours of daylight * day, and during Jn 11:9
day, and during * hour of it a man Jn 11:9
He lops off * branch that Jn 15:2
* man and woman in all the earth. Jn 17:2
they said, "you know * heart; Act 1:24,25
Gate—as was his custom * day. Act 3:2
"Samuel and * prophet since have Act 3:24
and * one of them was healed. Act 5:16
for his name. And * day, in the Act 5:42
News there and in * city along the Act 8:40
BUT PAUL, THREATENING with * Act 9:1
eager to destroy * Christian, went Act 9:1
arrest * believer in Damascus!" Act 9:14
favorites! In * nation he has Act 10:35
the devil, full of * sort of Act 13:10
prophets' words read * Sabbath. Act 13:27
elders in * church and prayed for Act 14:23
synagogues in * city on every Act 15:21
* Sabbath for many generations." Act 15:21
now and visit * city wherein we Act 15:36f
chains of * prisoner fell off ! Act 16:26
and satisfies * need there is. Act 17:25
* synagogue who believed on you. Act 22:19
So God let them go ahead into * Rom 1:24
Their lives became full of * Rom 1:29
* one has turned away; Rom 3:12
God will accept all people in * Rom 4:17
completely to God—* part of you—for Rom 6:13
to face death at * moment of the Rom 8:36
it, and it takes * one of us to Rom 12:4,5
for * day alike belongs to God. Rom 14:5
says the Lord, "* knee shall bow Rom 14:11
me and * tongue confess to God." Rom 14:11
Help her in * way you can, for Rom 16:1
Now you have * grace and 1Co 1:7
and blessing; * spiritual gift and 1Co 1:7
Then * workman who has built on 1Co 3:14
So use * part of your body to 1Co 6:20
the goal with purpose in * step. 1Co 9:26
avoid idol-worship of * kind. 1Co 10:14
For the earth and * good thing 1Co 10:26
For * time you eat this bread 1Co 11:26
and could speak in * language there 1Co 13:1
put down all enemies of * kind. 1Co 15:24
heaven above. * human being has a 1Co 15:48
in Galatia). On * Lord's Day each 1Co 16:2
the source of * mercy, and the one 2Co 1:3,4
must obey * law of God or die; 2Co 3:6
We are pressed on * side by 2Co 4:8
in the Lord is growing * day. 2Co 4:16
realizing that * moment we spend in 2Co 5:6
hardship and trouble of * kind. 2Co 6:4
outside, trouble was on * hand 2Co 7:5
will reap much. * one must make up 2Co 9:7
These weapons can break down * 2Co 10:5
against God and * wall that can be 2Co 10:5
weapons against * rebel who remains 2Co 10:6
you—but I shall make good * claim. 2Co 10:8
I promise this with * ounce of 2Co 11:10
In the end they will get * bit of 2Co 11:15
certainly gave you * proof that I 2Co 12:12
bless those in * nation who trust Gal 3:8,9
* law of God, without one slip. Gal 3:12
obey * other Jewish law or perish. Gal 5:3
leading in * part of our lives. Gal 5:25
blessed us with * blessing in Eph 1:3
within us, doing * wicked thing Eph 2:3
household with * other Christian. Eph 2:19
and living through * part of us. Eph 4:6
—and so become more and more in * Eph 4:15,16
be wise: make the most of * Eph 5:15,16
So use * piece of God's armor to Eph 6:13
with God. In * battle you will Eph 6:16
which is above * other name, that Php 2:9
the name of Jesus * knee shall bow Php 2:10
the earth, and * tongue shall Php 2:11
to * Jewish law and custom. Php 3:5
and I tried to obey * Jewish rule Php 3:6
of contentment in * situation, Php 4:12
with authority over * other power. Col 2:10
and faultless toward * one of you. 1Th 2:10
Keep away from * kind of evil. 1Th 5:22
Jesus Christ be with you, * one. 1Th 5:28
He will defy * god there is, and 2Th 2:4
is, and tear down * other object of 2Th 2:4
in * good thing you say and do. 2Th 2:17
from satanic attacks of * kind. 2Th 3:3
harming them in * way I could. 1Ti 1:13
I pray for you * day, and many 2Ti 1:3
Literally, "* Scripture." 2Ti 3:16f
well prepared at * point, fully 2Ti 3:17
in * city who would follow the Tit 1:5
to them of good deeds of * kind. Tit 2:7
as one who has * right to do so. Tit 2:15
about these things * day while Heb 3:13
And since * high priest is Heb 8:3
by the wind; and * decision you Jas 1:7,8
And the person who keeps * law of Jas 2:10
who has broken * law there is. Jas 2:10
over himself in * other way. Jas 3:1
and poisons * part of the body. Jas 3:6
Men have trained, or can train, * Jas 3:7
that lives and * kind of reptile Jas 3:7
disorder and * other kind of evil. Jas 3:16
satisfying your * whim, and now Jas 5:5
For the Lord's sake, obey * law 1Pe 2:13
who will do * wrong they can think 2Pe 3:3
his Son cleanses us from * sin. 1Jn 1:7
us and to cleanse us from * wrong. 1Jn 1:9
against God, for * sin is done 1Jn 3:4
hard at all; for * child of God 1Jn 5:4
him. * wrong is a sin, of course. 1Jn 5:17
and then killed * one of them who Jud 1:5
full of lust of * kind including Jud 1:7
in * evil way imaginable. Jud 1:18
their sins. Hate * trace of their Jud 1:23
by clouds; and * eye shall see Rev 1:7
to the churches: * one who is Rev 2:17
"To * one who overcomes—who to Rev 2:26
I will let * one who conquers Rev 3:21
of God, sent out into * part of Rev 5:6
from * nation as gifts for God. Rev 5:9
taken away; and * mountain and Rev 6:14
blood, and to send * kind of plague Rev 11:6
those on earth—to * nation, tribe, Rev 14:6
endure patiently * trial and Rev 14:12
of people of * race and nation. Rev 17:15
devils and * kind of evil spirit. Rev 18:2
Literally, "of * foul and hateful Rev 18:2f
and scarlet; and * kind of perfumed Rev 18:12
on * side. But fire from God in Rev 20:9

EVERYBODY
this law. * must rest as you do. Deu 5:14
the palace where * could see it, 2Sa 16:22
baptizing too, and * is going over Jn 3:26
Then the meeting broke up and * Jn 7:53
and * in Jerusalem knows about it. Act 4:16
* to disobey the Jewish laws. Act 21:28
* here sends greetings. Tit 3:15

EVERYDAY
Dear brothers, even in * life a Gal 3:15

EVERYONE
and a tramp; and * who sees me will Gen 4:14
to tell * that she was his sister! Gen 12:11,12,13
in Egypt * spoke of her beauty. Gen 12:14
He will be against *, and Gen 16:9-12
* will feel the same towards him. Gen 16:9-12
as to * born in your household. Gen 17:12
here in Egypt, and how * obeys me. Gen 45:13
in that home. * shall eat roast Ex 12:8
heaven for them. * can go out each Ex 16:4
Jehovah has said for * to gather Ex 16:16
enough for *—three quarts apiece; Ex 16:18
come pouring out, enough for *!" Ex 17:5,6
you left Egypt; * must bring me a Ex 23:15
of Israel that * who wants to may Ex 25:1
the camp, and * who wanted to Ex 33:7
nation, and * will be forgiven. Lev 4:20
Year of Jubilee * shall return home Lev 25:13
But as * began eating the meat, Num 11:33
than anyone else; * in Israel has Num 16:3
they whined. "* who even comes Num 17:12,13
regulations: * who enters the tent, Num 19:14
Blessed is * who blesses you, O Num 24:3-9
And curses shall fall upon * who Num 24:3-9
way as you do now, * doing whatever Deu 12:8
released * from his obligation. Deu 15:2
Then * will hear about what Deu 17:13
will be reasonably close to *; Deu 19:6,7
"We are all afraid of you; * is Jos 2:9
and when * was over, the people Jos 4:11
day, after which * returned to the Jos 6:11
previously, "Kill * except Rahab Jos 6:17
the prostitute and * with her." Jos 6:22
and finished off * left inside. Jos 8:24
and killed its king and * in it. Jos 10:28
they killed * in the city. Jos 10:34,35
And they killed * just as they Jos 10:39
They destroyed * in the land, Jos 10:40
large monument for * to see, in the Jos 22:10
"Who did this?" * demanded. Ju 6:29
out a sheet for * to throw in the Ju 8:25
robbed * else who passed that way. Ju 9:25
and * began cursing Abimelech. Ju 9:27
to tell * that you predicted it!" Ju 13:17
had no king, so * did whatever he Ju 17:6
and noticed how secure * felt. Ju 18:7
since Israel left Egypt," * said. Ju 19:30
* in it, and set it on fire. Ju 20:35-39
the details, for * knows what a Ru 3:11
their plight, * broke into tears. 1Sa 11:4
Why is * crying?" 1Sa 11:5
* was weary and faint as a result. 1Sa 14:28
the Amalekites, but killed * else. 1Sa 15:8
King Agag but killed * else. 1Sa 15:20
By the day after tomorrow, * 1Sa 20:19
died there, and * stopped when they 2Sa 2:23
funeral, and now * begged him to 2Sa 3:35,36
gave a present to *—men and women 2Sa 6:19
When it was all over, and * had 2Sa 6:19
over Israel and was fair to *. 2Sa 8:15
"* get out of here," he told his 2Sa 13:9
the road until * had passed. 2Sa 15:24
into a panic and * will run away; 2Sa 17:2,3
your troops and * will start 2Sa 17:9
that he was there, * went to him. 2Sa 19:8,9,10
it seemed as if * in Judah had come 2Sa 19:15
With the body out of the way, * 2Sa 20:13
* expected me to be the next king. 1Ki 2:15
heap of ruins, and * passing by 1Ki 9:8
him as king. Then * clapped and 2Ki 11:12
trumpeters; and * was rejoicing and 2Ki 11:13,14
and the people. * went over to the 2Ki 11:18
So * was happy, and the city 2Ki 11:20
of their fathers: * must pay the 2Ki 14:6
For you require * to worship at 2Ki 18:22
consent, for * agreed with him. 1Ch 13:4
Tell * about his miracles. 1Ch 16:24
to your name as * realizes that you 1Ch 17:24
of Gershom). * was excited and 1Ch 29:9
* but the king of Israel!" 2Ch 18:30
at the Lower Gate. * else must stay 2Ch 23:5,6
No, * must pay for his own sins. 2Ch 25:4
Throughout the entire ceremony * 2Ch 29:28
Manasseh, inviting * to come to the 2Ch 30:1
Dan to Beer-sheba, inviting *. 2Ch 30:5
good Lord pardon * who 2Ch 30:17,18,19
And he required * in Jerusalem 2Ch 34:32
* present in Jerusalem took part 2Ch 35:17
DURING THE MONTH of September * Ez 3:1
Then * in our party sacrificed Ez 8:35
and Jerusalem that * should appear Ez 10:7,8
trials for us. * who has a heathen Ez 10:14
I told * living outside the Neh 4:22
that * could see him as he read. Neh 8:1
until noon. * stood up as he opened Neh 8:1
feast, and * was filled with joy! Neh 8:17
* worshiped the Lord their God. Neh 9:3
* decide this matter for himself. Est 1:8
generous gifts to * and making Est 2:18
He longs to flee from God. * Job 27:23
and renewed. * listened to me and Job 29:21
Surely * knows that God doesn't Job 34:10
he is so famous. * has seen these Job 36:25
But make * rejoice who puts his Ps 5:11
my heart, and tell * about the Ps 9:1
* deceives and flatters and lies. Ps 12:2
He is a shield for * who hides Ps 18:30
by all mankind. * who sees me Ps 22:7
Let * in all the world—men, women Ps 33:8
reverence him; for * who does this Ps 34:9
Try to live in peace with *; Ps 34:14
will redeem them; * who takes Ps 34:22
And I will tell * how great and Ps 35:28
Your innocence will be clear to *. Ps 37:6
I have told * the Good News that Ps 40:9
* who loves him and his salvation. Ps 40:16
COME, *, AND clap for joy! Ps 47:1
LISTEN, *! Ps 49:1
end he dies like * else, and enters Ps 49:19
your mercies—for * knows what a Ps 52:9
Then at last * will know that the Ps 58:11
and the heart of * is deep." Ps 64:6f
Then * shall stand in awe and Ps 64:9
acts of God shall startle *. Ps 65:8
Let * bless God and sing his Ps 66:8
all mankind. How * throughout the Ps 67:3
Literally, "* submitting himself Ps 68:30f
I will tell * how good you are, Ps 71:15
I tell * that you alone are just Ps 71:16
with problems like * else, so Ps 73:5
and I will tell * about the Ps 73:28
God. Let * bring him presents. Ps 76:11
defending him. * who comes along Ps 89:41
the earth. Tell * about the amazing Ps 96:3
Sing his praises and tell * Ps 105:2
to the Lord, praising him to *. Ps 109:30
Cause * to praise your Ps 115:1
your greatness. * will tell about Ps 145:7
He is good to *, and his Ps 145:9
courts, and to * in all the land: Pro 1:21
because * knows his reputation." Pro 11:9f
* admires a man with good sense, Pro 12:8
* enjoys giving good advice, and Pro 15:23
An evil man is suspicious of * Pro 17:20
who is generous; * is his friend! Pro 19:6
And he will reward * according to Pro 24:11,12

(EVERYONE Con't)
When the godly are successful, * Pro 28:12
When the wicked succeed, * is Pro 28:12
born in poverty. * is eager to Ecc 4:15
the other—so that * will realize Ecc 7:14
The same providence confronts *, Ecc 9:2,3
the future and tells * in detail! Ecc 10:14
* can see how much he loves me. Sol 2:4
"Come," * will say, "let us go Is 2:3
will prevail—* stepping on someone Is 3:5
of milk, and * left will live on Is 7:21,22
lowest depths. * there will stare Is 14:16
Where is * going? Is 22:1
wondrous feast for * around the Is 25:6
Open the gates to *, for all Is 26:2
you ask advice from * but me, and Is 30:1
outstanding men! * will recognize Is 32:6
That is the experience of * who Is 36:6
hills and making * in Judah worship Is 36:7
"My master wants * in Jerusalem to Is 36:12
under siege until * is so hungry Is 36:12
crushed * who has opposed them. Is 37:11
barren land. * will see this Is 41:20
and spirit to * in all the world, Is 42:5
You cheat and shortchange *. Is 59:6
warn * that a powerful army is on Jer 6:1
I will fill * living in this land Jer 13:13
reassuring * that all was well, Jer 14:18
the earth, so that * going by will Jer 19:8
priests and to * in Jerusalem. Jer 29:25
For * shall die for his own Jer 31:30
know the Lord. For *, both great Jer 31:34
* according to his life and deeds. Jer 32:19
had ordered * to free his Hebrew Jer 34:9
the people— that * remaining in Jer 38:2
and had not exiled * to Babylon, Jer 40:7
be sacked until * is sated with Jer 50:10
nations and before * traveling past Eze 5:14
awesome example to *, for all to Eze 5:15
* whose forehead isn't marked. Eze 9:5
wipe out * left in Israel?" Eze 9:8
going to kill * in all Israel?" Eze 11:13
personally punish *, whether people Eze 14:6,7
is what * will say of you. Eze 16:44
kind of bird. And * shall know Eze 17:24
crops destroyed; * in the land Eze 19:7
into the hearts of * are now dead Eze 32:23
crops, and * will live in safety. Eze 34:27
and * will know I am the Lord." Eze 36:37,38
bury the bodies. * in Israel will Eze 39:13
miles for a city open to * in Eze 45:6
began to play, *—whatever his Dan 3:7
made a law that * must fall down Dan 3:10
be seen by * in all the world. Dan 4:10,11
with fruit, enough for * to eat. Dan 4:12
addressed to * in his empire: Dan 6:25,26
I decree that * shall tremble and Dan 6:25,26
* knows that it is yours. Dan 9:18
Listen, you aged men of Israel! * Joe 1:2
holy mountain! Let * tremble in Joe 2:1
Bring *—the elders, the Joe 2:16
"* who calls upon the name of Joe 2:32
awaits its doom, and * will mourn. Amo 8:8
from the king on down, * put on Jon 3:4,5
drink any water. * must wear Jon 3:8
to God, and let * turn from his Jon 3:8
* will live quietly in his own Mic 4:4
And he knows * who trusts in him! Nah 1:7
powers, and * shall worship him, Zep 2:11
animals to live! * passing that way Zep 2:15
"Why is * saying it is not the Hag 1:2
Priest and * left in the land: Hag 2:2
of every thief and * who swears Zec 5:4
to be merciful and kind to *. Zec 7:8,9
Live at peace with *. Zec 8:16
eats with blood. * left will Zec 9:7
like lost sheep; * attacks them, Zec 10:2
synagogues where * can see them. Mt 6:5
opened. For * who asks, receives. Mt 7:8
their deaths. * shall hate you Mt 10:22
and astonished * with his wisdom Mt 13:53,54
the people. And * ate until full! Mt 14:20
around, telling * to bring in their Mt 14:35
to the crowd. And * ate until Mt 15:37,38
"Not * can accept this Mt 19:11
notify * that it was time to come. Mt 22:3
corners and invite * you see.' Mt 22:9
* is as the angels in heaven. Mt 22:30
Peter declared, "If * else Mt 26:33
telling * he came back to life! Mt 27:64
said, "and will proclaim that * Mk 1:3
told him, "* is asking for you." Mk 1:36,37
is healed, so that * will have Mk 1:43,44
news as they ran. * rushed out to Mk 5:14
were telling * about it, and the Mk 5:16
and began to tell * about the great Mk 5:20
* they met to turn from sin. Mk 6:12
to him, and * begged Jesus to lay Mk 7:32
Literally, "For * shall be salted Mk 9:49f
and stopped * from bringing in Mk 11:16
and to have * bow to them as they Mk 12:38
to be killed. And * will hate you Mk 13:13
my message to you and to * else." Mk 13:35,36,37
the Good News to *, everywhere. Mk 16:15
had been to her, and * rejoiced. Lk 1:58
Judean hills. And * who heard Lk 1:66
* was required to return to his Lk 2:3
ever announced, and it is for *! Lk 2:10
The shepherds told * what had Lk 2:17
God and telling * in Jerusalem who Lk 2:38
them and amazing * with his Lk 2:46,47
* was expecting the Messiah to Lk 3:15
in the synagogues; * praised him. Lk 4:15
sat down, while * in the synagogue Lk 4:20
"Please heal her," * begged. Lk 4:38
"This will prove to * that you Lk 5:14
And immediately, as * watched, Lk 5:25
praising God! * present was Lk 5:26
and stand here where * can see." Lk 6:8
And he cast out many demons. * Lk 6:19
been healed. And * begged Jesus to Lk 8:37
* about Jesus' mighty miracle. Lk 8:39
* denied it, and Peter said, Lk 8:45
Then he sent them away to tell * Lk 9:2
the crowd. And * ate and ate; Lk 9:17
be opened. * who asks, receives; Lk 11:10
and the door is opened to * who Lk 11:10
* as you walk through the markets! Lk 11:43
"* would be ready for him if Lk 12:39
you talking just to us or to *?" Lk 12:41
other guests. For * who tries to Lk 14:11
And then how * would laugh! Lk 14:29
man who had great contempt for *. Lk 18:2
their virtue and scorned * else: Lk 18:9
not a sinner like * else, Lk 18:11
"Yes," Jesus replied, "and * Lk 18:29
be killed. And * will hate you Lk 21:17
* else—what had happened. Lk 24:9
shine on * coming into the world. Jn 1:9
afterwards, when * is full and Jn 2:10
the Light to let * see that they Jn 3:21
that man so that * will go to him. Jn 3:28
village and told *, "Come and meet Jn 4:28,29
his Son, so that * will honor the Jn 5:23
"Tell * to sit down," Jesus Jn 6:10
the fish. And * ate until full! Jn 6:11
Father's will that * who sees his Jn 6:40
eternal life to * who eats it. Jn 6:48-51
the true drink. * who eats my Jn 6:56
be given to * believing in him; Jn 7:39
"Yes," Martha said, "when * Jn 11:24
I will draw * to me." Jn 12:32
that isn't true of * here." Jn 13:10
And you also must tell * about Jn 15:27
their heads. And * present was Act 2:4
"Therefore I clearly state to * Act 2:36
to Peter and John! * stood there Act 3:11
a riot. For * was praising God for Act 4:21
owned was his own; * was sharing. Act 4:32
the floor, dead! * was terrified, Act 5:5
who are well thought of by *; Act 6:3
At this point * in the Council Act 6:15
in Jerusalem, and * except the Act 8:1
synagogue to tell * there the Good Act 9:20
him, saying that * who believes in Act 10:43
inside to tell * that Peter was Act 12:14
the need for * in Israel to turn Act 13:24
for your sins! * who trusts in him Act 13:39
discussion, and * now listened as Act 15:12
they left, for * knew that his Act 16:3
now he commands * to put away idols Act 17:30
two years, so that * in the Turkish Act 19:10
with confusion. * rushed to the Act 19:29
"Men of Ephesus," he said, "* Act 19:35
"Then * will know that you Act 21:24
facts to *, both great and small. Act 26:22
both you and * here in this Act 26:29
all die unless * stays aboard." Act 27:31
light, Paul begged * to eat. Act 27:33
Suddenly * felt better and began Act 27:36
ship. So * escaped safely ashore! Act 27:44
debt to you and to * else, both to Rom 1:14
alone, but now * is invited to come Rom 1:16
For God treats * the same. Rom 2:11
secret lives of *, their inmost Rom 2:16
Though * else in the world is a Rom 3:4
And not * born into a Jewish Rom 9:6
kind to us so that * can see how Rom 9:23,24
of them—just as * in the cities of Rom 9:29
But not * who hears the Good News Rom 10:16
Do things in such a way that * Rom 12:17
Be at peace with *, just as much Rom 12:18
serving you. Pay * whatever he Rom 13:7
On questions of this kind * must Rom 14:5
you Gentiles, let * praise him." Rom 15:11
by them. But * knows that you Rom 16:19
the light so that * can see exactly 1Co 4:5
our hearts. Then * will know why we 1Co 4:5
* IS TALKING about the terrible 1Co 5:1
I wish * could get along without 1Co 7:7
On this question * feels that 1Co 8:1
In a race, * runs but only one 1Co 9:24
I try to please * in everything I 1Co 10:33
services. * keeps telling me about 1Co 11:18
For I am told that * hastily 1Co 11:21
Is * an apostle? 1Co 12:29
Of course not. Is * a preacher? 1Co 12:29
Are all teachers? Does * have the 1Co 12:29
do miracles? Can * heal the sick? 1Co 12:30
you can tell * afterwards what you 1Co 14:5
language that * understands. 1Co 14:15
the other, and * will learn and be 1Co 14:31
from the dead. * dies because all 1Co 15:22
and we have told * how faithful 2Co 1:20
in your hearts, * can see that we 2Co 3:2
our weak bodies. * can see that the 2Co 4:7
of urging * to come into his favor 2Co 5:18
but I want * else to know it too. 2Co 8:21
I will tell * in Greece about it! 2Co 11:10
"Cursed is * who at any time Gal 3:10
the feeling that * else is wrong Gal 5:20
Let * be sure that he is doing Gal 6:4
always be kind to *, and especially Gal 6:10
God's anger just like * else. Eph 2:3
telling * about this plan of his; Eph 3:7
and to explain to * that God is Eph 3:9
Christ. For * around here, Php 1:13
interest in you; * else seems to Php 2:21
I say it again, rejoice! Let * Php 4:5
will have the right answer for *. Col 4:6
each other and to * else, just as 1Th 3:12
and be patient with *. 1Th 5:14
good to each other and to * else. 1Th 5:15
Then * will be praising the name 2Th 1:12
and will trick * with strange 2Th 2:9
men, for not * loves the Lord. 2Th 3:2
how I long that * should know it, 1Ti 1:15
an example to show * how patient he 1Ti 1:16
This is the truth and * should 1Ti 4:9,10
and make sure * learns them well. 1Ti 4:11
your tasks so that * may notice 1Ti 4:15
She must be well thought of by * 1Ti 5:10
lead sinful lives and * knows it. 1Ti 5:24
In the same way, * knows how, 1Ti 5:25
be well known to *, as was the sin 2Ti 3:9
fully equipped to do good to *. 2Ti 3:17
here to help me. * had run away. 2Ti 4:16
and permits me to tell it to *. Tit 1:3
is now being offered to *; Tit 2:11
death for * in all the world. Heb 2:9
He knows about *, everywhere. Heb 4:13
Abraham, and as * knows, a person Heb 7:7
the Lord,' because *, great and Heb 8:11
Now you can have real love for * 1Pe 1:22
Show respect for *. 1Pe 2:17
and be at peace with * so that he 2Pe 3:14
he really is. And * who really 1Jn 3:3
as does * else in the church. 2Jn 1:1
far from God. But *, including 3Jn 1:12
the churches: To * who is Rev 2:7
Let * who can hear, listen to Rev 2:11
"Let * who can hear, listen to Rev 2:17
they are worthy. * who conquers Rev 3:5
upon the world to test * alive. Rev 3:10
discipline and punish * I love; Rev 3:19
And then I heard * in heaven and Rev 5:13
And great fear will fall on *. Rev 11:11
7,000 dead. Then * left will, in Rev 11:13
the skies while * was watching. Rev 13:13
He required *—great and small, Rev 13:16
sores broke out on * who had the Rev 16:2
with its fire. * was burned by Rev 16:9
Life—as a gift! * who conquers Rev 21:7
with me, to repay * according to Rev 22:12
And I solemnly declare to * who Rev 22:18

EVERYONE'S
he was becoming * favorite (and he 1Sa 2:26
of paper and to * surprise wrote, Lk 1:63
them—much to * joy—that the Act 15:3
builder has used. * work will be 1Co 3:13

EVERYTHING
every living being—* in which there Gen 6:17
And Noah did * as God Gen 6:22
So Noah did * the Lord commanded Gen 7:5
and all mankind— * that breathed Gen 7:22
and recovered *—the loot that had Gen 14:16
have a son to inherit * you own." Gen 15:4
and that * they do is wicked. Gen 18:20
that God helps you in * you do; Gen 21:22
of the best of * his master owned, Gen 24:10
my master has given him * he owns. Gen 24:36
Abraham deeded * he owned to Gen 25:5
back a tenth of * you give me!" Gen 28:22
Jehovah has blessed you from * I Gen 30:30
"He owes * he owns to our father. Gen 31:1
took * he owned and started out to Gen 31:17-20
and have searched through *. Gen 31:36,37
Now put * I stole out here in Gen 31:36,37
herds and donkeys—* they could lay Gen 34:28
so that * he did succeeded. Gen 39:2
responsibility over * he owned. Gen 39:6
me with * in the entire household; Gen 39:8
took care of *, and the Lord was Gen 39:23

(EVERYTHING Con't)

so that * ran smoothly and well.	Gen 39:23
dreams meant. And * happened just	Gen 41:13
too! * has been against me."	Gen 42:36
flocks and herds and * they own.'	Gen 46:32
of * you get belongs to Pharaoh.	Gen 47:24
Tell Aaron * I say to you, and	Ex 7:2
All Egypt lay in ruins. * left	Ex 9:25
* that escaped the hail.	Ex 10:4,5
"We will take * with us;	Ex 10:9
and eat * the hail has left."	Ex 10:12
stripped of * they owned!	Ex 12:36
Jethro was very happy about *	Ex 18:9
certainly do * he asks of us."	Ex 19:8
and sea, and * in them, and rested	Ex 20:11
"Be sure that * you make follows	Ex 25:40
firmly, and overlay * with bronze.	Ex 27:2
the Tabernacle and * it contains.	Ex 31:3
the Tabernacle and * in it, upon	Ex 40:9
and * will be normal again.	Lev 13:6
it, so that * in the house will not	Lev 14:36
period, and * she sits on is in a	Lev 15:26
Tabernacle and * in it will be his	Num 4:16
pegs, cords, and * else connected	Num 4:32
and his sons; * was done just as	Num 8:22
swallows them and * that belongs to	Num 16:30
with them, and * they owned.	Num 16:32
at the time. So * that is	Num 18:14,15
your garments and * made of	Num 31:20
every bite we eat and * we drink;	Deu 2:28
*, including the women and babies.	Deu 2:33,34
We conquered * from Aroer to	Deu 2:35,36
You must actively obey him in *	Deu 6:17
that food isn't *, and that real	Deu 8:3
the Lord your God in * you do.	Deu 12:18
you in * you do because of this!	Deu 15:10
and have done * you commanded me.	Deu 26:14
and prosper * you do when you	Deu 28:8
He will bless * you do;	Deu 28:12
and a failure in * you do, until at	Deu 28:20
thirsty, naked, and in want of *.	Deu 28:47,48
that you will prosper in * you do.	Deu 29:9
The Lord your God will prosper *	Deu 30:9
* he does is just and fair.	Deu 32:4
will be successful in * you do.	Jos 1:7
Don't take any loot, for * is to	Jos 6:18
They destroyed * in it—men and	Jos 6:21
donkeys—*.	Jos 6:21
the city and * in it except that	Jos 6:24
God's command to destroy * except	Jos 7:1
fire, along with * he has, for he	Jos 7:15
his tent, and * he had, and brought	Jos 7:24
stone has heard * the Lord said, so	Jos 24:27
* collapsed.	Ju 5:8
this time he has told me *."	Ju 16:18
She told Naomi * and gave her the	Ru 3:15-18
Tell me *.	1Sa 3:16,17
her told her that * was all right	1Sa 4:20
because * he says comes true;	1Sa 9:6
—*, in fact, that appealed to them.	1Sa 15:9
and we have destroyed * else."	1Sa 15:15
David continued to succeed in *	1Sa 18:14
then I'll tell you * I can find	1Sa 19:3
Then he took David to Saul and *	1Sa 19:7
he always tells me * he's going to	1Sa 20:2
family and multiply * you own.	1Sa 25:6
you will recover * that was taken	1Sa 30:8
David got back * they had taken.	1Sa 30:18,19
May God curse me if I don't do *	2Sa 3:9,10
as * else he did pleased them!	2Sa 3:35,36
and told him * the Lord had said.	2Sa 7:17
And now, in addition to * else,	2Sa 7:19
master's grandson * that belonged	2Sa 9:9
and you know * that happens!"	2Sa 14:20
Ziba, "I give you * he owns."	2Sa 16:4
come and confirm * you've said."	1Ki 1:14
in * you do, wherever you turn.	1Ki 2:3
"* was going well for me," he	1Ki 2:15
But the tables are turned, and *	1Ki 2:15
to do his will in *, and to obey	1Ki 8:58
She soon realized that * she had	1Ki 10:4
She exclaimed to him, "* I heard	1Ki 10:6
Solomon gave her * she asked him	1Ki 10:13
"* is wonderful," he replied,	1Ki 11:22
palace and stole *, including all	1Ki 14:26
'I will give you * you asked for	1Ki 20:9
Moab, destroying * as they went.	2Ki 3:24
"Yes," she told Gehazi, "* is	2Ki 4:26
"Is * all right?"	2Ki 5:21
horses, donkeys, and * else.	2Ki 7:7
to see to it that * she had owned	2Ki 8:6
fellow want? Is * all right?"	2Ki 9:11
The Lord has done that, for * he	2Ki 10:9,10
For he followed the Lord in *,	2Ki 18:6
with him and prospered * he did.	2Ki 18:7
they have completely destroyed *.	2Ki 19:11
I know * about you.	2Ki 19:27
to please you in * I do ."	2Ki 20:3
aromatic oils, the armory—*.	2Ki 20:13
And Hezekiah replied, "*.	2Ki 20:15
will come when * in this palace	2Ki 20:17
and to do * the book commanded.	2Ki 23:3
They found good pastures, and *	1Ch 4:40,41
Let the countryside and * in it	1Ch 16:32
So Nathan told King David * the	1Ch 17:15
I have now collected * that is	1Ch 28:2
He will see to it that * is	1Ch 28:20
and majesty. * in the heavens and	1Ch 29:11
you as being in control of *.	1Ch 29:11
anything to you? * we have has come	1Ch 29:14
he could explain * to her.	2Ch 9:2
to the king, "* I heard about you	2Ch 9:5
to him, plus * else she asked for!	2Ch 9:12
above * else, and they found him!	2Ch 15:15
Believe his prophets, and * will	2Ch 20:20
and carried away * of value in the	2Ch 21:17
gates kept out * that was not	2Ch 23:19
the Temple, and * dedicated to the	2Ch 24:7,8
For when you do, * you try fails.	2Ch 24:20
oil, money, and * else—a tithe of	2Ch 31:5,6
* was laid out in great piles.	2Ch 31:5,6
He prospered in * he did.	2Ch 32:30
When * was organized, and the	2Ch 35:10
then they told him * I had said;	Neh 6:19
earth and the seas, and * in them.	Neh 9:6
Levites a tenth of * our land	Neh 10:37
You have prospered * he does—look	Job 1:10
The Lord gave me * I had, and	Job 1:21
web. * he counts on will collapse.	Job 8:14
for he knows * you've done.	Job 11:6
"Yes, I realize you know *!	Job 12:2
"Look, * the wicked touch has	Job 21:16
the earth. * they own is cursed.	Job 24:18
For * I did prospered;	Job 29:19
They block my road and do * they	Job 30:13
He sees * I do, and every step I	Job 31:4
wind is blowing and * is still?	Job 37:16,17
heaven, when * is dust and clods?	Job 38:37,38
I owe no one anything. * under	Job 41:11
delight in doing * God wants them	Ps 1:2
You have put him in charge of *	Ps 8:6
you made; * is put under his	Ps 8:6
Yet there is success in * they	Ps 10:5
He closely watches * that happens	Ps 11:4
heart's desire, * he asks you for!	Ps 21:2
is my Shepherd, I have * I need!	Ps 23:1
THE EARTH BELONGS to God! * in	Ps 24:1
* he does is worthy of our trust.	Ps 33:4
and closely watches * they do.	Ps 33:13,14,15
for everyone who does this has *	Ps 34:9
strips them bare of * they own.	Ps 35:26
not get caught. * they say is	Ps 36:3
Commit * you do to the Lord.	Ps 37:5
the world is mine, and * in it.	Ps 50:12
Praise him, all the seas and * in	Ps 69:34
These fat cats have * their	Ps 73:7
their victory. * lies in shambles	Ps 74:5,6
Make them failures in * they do;	Ps 83:17
world, *—for you created them all.	Ps 89:11
He knows *—doesn't he also know	Ps 94:10
Fairness is the touchstone of *	Ps 99:4
from there he rules over * there	Ps 103:19
Let * everywhere bless the Lord.	Ps 103:22
* green, destroying all the crops.	Ps 105:35
Make them fail in * they do.	Ps 109:29
I will pay * I vowed to the Lord.	Ps 116:18,19
it endures by your decree, for *	Ps 119:90,91
to apply your rules to * I do.	Ps 119:125
You know this because * I do is	Ps 119:168
my heart and know * about me.	Ps 139:1
is intertwined with * he does.	Ps 145:9
The Lord is fair in * he does,	Ps 145:17
heaven, the seas and * in them.	Ps 146:6
Let * he has made give praise to	Ps 148:5
Let * alive give praises to the	Ps 150:6
just and fair in * they did.	Pro 1:3
* they do is crooked and wrong.	Pro 2:15
don't ever trust yourself. In *	Pro 3:6
For they influence * else in your	Pro 4:23
and he weighs carefully * you do.	Pro 5:21
* in his house to pay it back.	Pro 6:31
for you. * I say is right and true,	Pro 8:6,7
Only a fool blurts out * he	Pro 10:14
but the wicked shall lose *.	Pro 10:30
to hold on too tightly and lose *.	Pro 11:24,25
strength and tears down * he does.	Pro 12:4
man makes good use of * he finds.	Pro 12:27
A quick retort can ruin *.	Pro 13:3
When a man is gloomy, * seems to	Pro 15:15
when he is cheerful, * seems	Pro 15:15
The Lord has made * for his own	Pro 16:4
* that happens along the way?	Pro 20:24
Why risk * you own?	Pro 22:26,27
is the rule for * she says.	Pro 31:26
is worthwhile; * is futile.	Ecc 1:2
to the sea.... * is unutterably	Ecc 1:8-11
about * in the universe.	Ecc 1:12-15
But as I looked at * I had tried,	Ecc 2:11
THERE IS A right time for *:	Ecc 3:1
* is appropriate in its own time.	Ecc 3:11
* man does, both good and bad."	Ecc 3:17
that they can have * they want, but	Ecc 6:2
In this silly life I have seen *,	Ecc 7:15-17
time and a way for *, though man's	Ecc 8:6,7
(Of course, only God can see *,	Ecc 8:16,17
man who says he knows *, doesn't!	Ecc 8:16,17
happiness, and money gives *!	Ecc 10:19
longer, and that * down here is	Ecc 11:8
take in *, but realize that you	Ecc 11:9
must account to God for * you do.	Ecc 11:9
For God will judge us for * we	Ecc 12:14
If a man tried to buy it with *	Sol 8:7
and plundering * they see.	Is 1:7
—and use it on you to shave off *	Is 7:20
All crops will perish; * will	Is 19:7
to the ground, and * it supports	Is 22:25
* is lost, abandoned and confused.	Is 24:19
He tells us * over and over	Is 28:10
who have destroyed * around you	Is 33:1
let the world and * in it hear my	Is 34:1
tried to obey you in * you said?"	Is 38:3
to them all his treasures—*.	Is 39:2
"I showed them * I own, all my	Is 39:4
"The time is coming when * you	Is 39:6
the earth and * in it, and gives	Is 42:5
carved idols. * I prophesied came	Is 42:9
By myself I made the earth and *	Is 44:24
and earth and put * in place, and	Is 45:18
doing * their evil hearts desired.	Is 57:17
* you do is filled with sin;	Is 59:6
we have seen * our fathers	Jer 3:24
see in all directions * was ruins.	Jer 4:23
Tell them * that I will do to	Jer 7:27
the land and * in it—the cities and	Jer 8:16
that * would be all right."	Jer 20:6
that will burn up * in its path."	Jer 21:14
They are making up * they say.	Jer 23:16
of deceit, inventing * they say.	Jer 23:26
message, saying * the Lord had told	Jer 26:7,8
I hope the Lord will do * you say	Jer 28:6
I know, for I have seen * they	Jer 29:23
and disease. * has happened just as	Jer 32:24
have fully obeyed * that Jonadab	Jer 35:10
Get another scroll and write *	Jer 36:28
destroy this country and * in it.	Jer 36:29
do to this city * I threatened;	Jer 39:16
For if we obey him, * will turn	Jer 42:6
their cities and * in them.	Jer 47:2
thieves don't take *, but I will	Jer 49:9,10
that will burn * around them.	Jer 50:32
For he made * there is, and	Jer 51:19
taking * precious she owns.	Lam 1:10
with blood, defiling * they touch.	Lam 4:14
Yes, I know it is, for I know *	Eze 11:5
And I told the exiles * the Lord	Eze 11:25
come and destroy *, even if these	Eze 14:17
slaves, and * left will be burned.	Eze 23:25
The sword will destroy * from	Eze 25:13
the heart of the seas! * is lost.	Eze 27:27
* she has, for his army.	Eze 29:19
I will destroy Egypt and * in it,	Eze 30:12
Egypt and wipe out * she has, then	Eze 32:15
will come; * will happen just as I	Eze 39:8
and take to heart * I show you, for	Eze 40:4
and entrances—and * about it.	Eze 43:11
fresh and pure. * touching the	Eze 47:9
Wherever this water flows, * will	Eze 47:9
world, destroying * before it.	Dan 7:23
The ram butted * out of its way	Dan 8:4
he is fair in * he does, but we	Dan 9:14
accomplish * he sets out to do.	Dan 11:3
You are the enemies of * good;	Amo 5:12
I will turn over this city and *	Amo 6:8
They ate * in sight.	Amo 7:2
you—for they would not take *!	Ob 1:5
locusts that eat up * before them.	Nah 3:15
"I will sweep away * in all your	Zep 1:2
for * that they can get.	Zep 3:3
cattle, and ruin * you have worked	Hag 1:11
sacrifices, but * else that you did	Hag 2:14
And so * you did went wrong.	Hag 2:15
"* has been entrusted to me by	Mt 11:27
In his excitement, he sold * he	Mt 13:44
sold * he owned to purchase it!	Mt 13:46
Elijah must come and set * in	Mt 17:11
* you say by these witnesses.	Mt 18:16
wife and children and * he had.	Mt 18:25
go and sell * you have and give the	Mt 19:21
But with God, * is possible."	Mt 19:26
to him, "We left * to follow you.	Mt 19:27
to tell them, '* is ready and the	Mt 22:4
give God * that belongs to God."	Mt 22:21
"* they do is done for show.	Mt 23:5
swearing by it and * on it, and	Mt 23:20
ones in charge of * I own!	Mt 24:47
for you and * will be all right."	Mt 28:14
Again and again they said, "* he	Mk 7:37
and he saw * clearly, drinking in	Mk 8:25
But with God * is possible."	Mk 10:27
"We've given up * to follow	Mk 10:28
He looked around carefully at *	Mk 11:11
it to him. But * that belongs to	Mk 12:17
the city and found * as Jesus had	Mk 14:16

(EVERYTHING Con't)
"Father, Father," he said, "* Mk 14:36
wants. May * you said come true." Lk 1:38
they left * and went with him. Lk 5:11
So Levi left *, sprang up and Lk 5:28
that someday * [in men's hearts Lk 8:17
she had spent * she had on doctors Lk 8:43,44
I am the Agent of my Father in * Lk 10:22
up and give you * you want—just Lk 11:8
overflowing—he couldn't get * in. Lk 12:17
very close, and * I have is yours. Lk 15:31
lifetime you had * you wanted, and Lk 16:25
They ate and drank and married—* Lk 17:27
give to God a tenth of * I earn.' Lk 18:12
as she is, has given * she has." Lk 21:4
the city and found * just as Jesus Lk 22:13
Yes, * written about me by the Lk 22:37
telling you that * written about me Lk 24:44
He created * there is—nothing Jn 1:3
and God has given him * there is. Jn 3:35
does, he will explain * to us." Jn 4:25
a man who told me * I ever did! Jn 4:28,29
"He told me * I ever did!" Jn 4:39
Son, and tells him * he is doing; Jn 5:20
had given him * and that he had Jn 13:1
your coming. When * is ready, then Jn 14:2,3
you of * I myself have told you. Jn 14:26
told you * the Father told me. Jn 15:15
that you know * and don't need Jn 16:30
earth by doing * you told me to. Jn 17:4
Now they know that * I have is a Jn 17:7
back to me with * else of yours, Jn 17:10
Jesus knew that * was now Jn 19:28
and shared * with each other, Act 2:44
Listen carefully to * he tells Act 3:21,22
and of the sea and * in them— you Act 4:24
and earth and sea and * in them. Act 14:15
"He made the world and * in it, Act 17:24
life and breath to *, and satisfies Act 17:25
some another—* was in confusion. Act 19:32
to honor God in * I did, just as Act 22:3
that * Tertullus said was true. Act 24:9
the Jewish law and * written in the Act 24:14
* their evil minds could think of. Rom 1:28
loaded with lies. * they say has in Rom 3:13
so * began to grow old and die, Rom 5:12
he also surely give us * else? Rom 8:32
who trust in him * they are trying Rom 10:4
act? For * comes from God alone. Rom 11:36
from God alone. * lives by his Rom 11:36
his power, and * is for his glory. Rom 11:36
Be decent and true in * you do so Rom 13:12,13
has insight into *, and that 1Co 2:15
For God has already given you * 1Co 3:21
who made * and gives us life. 1Co 8:6
let someone spoil * just because he 1Co 10:30
It is because you must do * for 1Co 10:31
I try to please everyone in * I 1Co 10:33
and doing * I taught you. 1Co 11:2
the future, knew * about 1Co 13:2
everything about *, but didn't love 1Co 13:2
If I gave * I have to poor 1Co 13:3
then I will see * clearly, just as 1Co 13:12
will be pricked by * he hears. 1Co 14:24
language, but * that is done must 1Co 14:26
however, be sure that * is done 1Co 14:40
* else will be utterly supreme. 1Co 15:28
tomorrow we die, and that ends *! 1Co 15:32
and do * you can to help them as 1Co 16:16
for then we put * into the hands of 2Co 1:9
him always in * we do, whether we 2Co 5:9
In fact, in * we do we try to 2Co 6:4
own nothing, and yet we enjoy *. 2Co 6:10
us turn away from * wrong, whether 2Co 7:1
You have done * you could to make 2Co 7:11
you by giving you * you need and 2Co 9:8
slaves and take * you have, and 2Co 11:19,20
he actually owns * his father had. Gal 4:1
And since we are his sons, * he Gal 4:7
Author and Giver of * everywhere. Eph 1:23
FOLLOW GOD'S EXAMPLE in * you Eph 5:1
Always give thanks for * to our Eph 5:20
your husbands in *, just as the Eph 5:24
dear brothers: * that has happened Php 1:12
In * you do, stay away from Php 2:14
have this sorrow on top of * else. Php 2:27
Yes, * else is worthless when Php 3:8
Now I have given up * else—I Php 3:10
instead, pray about *; Php 4:6
live on almost nothing or with *. Php 4:12
for I can do * God asks me to Php 4:13
Creator who made * in heaven and Col 1:16
his power that holds * together. Col 1:17
so that he is first in *; Col 1:18
cleared a path for * to come to Col 1:20
so you have * when you have Col 2:10
you know his will in * you do. Col 4:12
"All is well, * is quiet and 1Th 5:3
but test * that is said to be sure 1Th 5:21
but faithful in * they do. 1Ti 3:11
thankful for. For * God made is 1Ti 4:4
for he fought against * we said. 2Ti 4:15
sees goodness and purity in *; Tit 1:15
finds evil in *, for his dirty mind Tit 1:15
doing * with love and patience. Tit 2:2
quiet and respectful in * they do. Tit 2:3
of every kind. Let * you do reflect Tit 2:7
the winter. Do * you can to help Tit 3:13
see that they are given * they Tit 3:13
whom he has given *, and through Heb 1:2
he made the world and * there is. Heb 1:2
in complete charge of * there is. Heb 2:8
that God, who made * for his own Heb 2:10
build houses, but only God made *. Heb 3:4
everywhere. * about us is bare and Heb 4:13
agreement almost * was cleansed by Heb 9:22
here on earth, and * in it—all Heb 9:23
live by faith, trusting him in *. Heb 10:38
he will sift out * without solid Heb 12:27
greatly bless him in * he does. Jas 1:25
But be holy now in * you do, 1Pe 1:15
with perfect justice for * you do; 1Pe 1:17
and watching * that concerns you. 1Pe 5:7
his great power, * you need for 2Pe 1:3
close attention to * they have 2Pe 1:19
can remember * has remained exactly 2Pe 3:4
and * on it will be burned up. 2Pe 3:10
And so since * around us is going 2Pe 3:11
ambition to buy * that appeals to 1Jn 2:16
for he knows * we do. 1Jn 3:20
always believe * you hear just 1Jn 4:1
Christ and * he heard and saw. Rev 1:2
say, "Write down * you see, and Rev 1:11
"You say, 'I am rich, with * I Rev 3:17
created heaven and * in it and the Rev 10:6
man; and * in all the oceans died. Rev 16:3

EVERYWHERE
well watered * (this was before Gen 13:10
years there were bumper crops *. Gen 41:47
severe in Canaan as it was * else. Gen 42:5
So the people scattered * to Ex 5:12
specify, * except in the river." Ex 8:9
Then Moses searched * for the Lev 10:16
Olive trees will be growing *, Deu 28:40
To push against the nations *; Deu 33:17
* along the road without success. Jos 2:22
and his name became famous *. Jos 6:27
and Beersheba, and * between, and Ju 20:1
and there was weeping *. 1Sa 5:12
there was terrible confusion *. 1Sa 14:20
was the great topic *. 2Sa 19:8,9,10
Edom, and soon there was water *. 2Ki 3:20
troops, horses, and chariots *. 2Ki 6:15
of fire * upon the mountain! 2Ki 6:17
David's fame spread *, and the 1Ch 14:17
And I have been with you * 1Ch 17:8
And the Lord gave David victory * 1Ch 18:6
Crime was on the increase *. 2Ch 15:5
He did this * throughout the 2Ch 34:7
"Geshem tells me that * he goes Neh 6:5,6
For women * will begin to Est 1:17
kingdom, husbands *, whatever their Est 1:20
This decree gave the Jews * Est 8:11
must be recognized * as law, must Est 8:13
and gladness, and were honored *. Est 8:16
I see them *. Job 17:2
thick, impenetrable darkness *. Job 23:16,17
all men * may recognize his power. Job 37:7
No wonder men * fear him! Job 37:24
of my enemies. * I looked I was Ps 31:13
unmoved despite the turmoil *. Ps 46:5
He is highly honored *. Ps 47:9
You are praised * for the Ps 48:10
Yes, kings from *! Ps 72:11
helping me * throughout the land. Ps 74:12
There is only darkness *. Ps 88:18
Sing it * around the world! Ps 96:1
Let everything * bless the Lord. Ps 103:22
is seen * throughout the land. Ps 105:7
Good men * will see it and be Ps 107:42
I will praise you * around the Ps 108:3
His children shall be honored *, Ps 112:2
PRAISE THE LORD, all nations *. Ps 117:1
attacking the walls, but peace *. Ps 144:12-15
call on all men * to bless his holy Ps 145:21
The Lord is watching * and keeps Pro 15:3
Fools start fights * while wise Pro 29:8
I have seen *—savings are put into Ecc 5:13,14
which I have seen *— God has given Ecc 6:1
I searched *, determined to find Ecc 7:25
work which God gives to mankind *. Ecc 8:15
that was going on * across the Ecc 8:16,17
that reaches * around the world. Is 14:26
Lying *, slain by plague Is 22:2
Deathly silence is *. Is 23:2,3
still prevails and treachery is *. Is 24:15,16
filth is *. Is 28:8
it to, and prosper * I send it. Is 55:11
of young plants springing up *. Is 61:11
For the enemy is *, ready to Jer 6:25
is only trouble and terror *. Jer 14:19
For I am hated * I go. Jer 15:10
to prevail * throughout the earth. Jer 23:5,6
Am I not * in all of heaven and Jer 23:24
And yet, O people *, behold and Lam 1:18
lewdness is *. Eze 22:9
racketeers and extortioners are *. Eze 22:12
But just persons * will judge Eze 23:45
Yes, darkness will be * across Eze 32:8
scattered * across the ground. Eze 37:1
There is violence *, with one Hos 4:2
They look * except to heaven, to Hos 7:16
Sorrow and sadness are *. Joe 1:10
together and come, all nations *. Joe 3:11
yourselves and crow about it *! Amo 4:5
Dead bodies will be scattered *. Amo 8:3
Men will wander * from sea to Amo 8:12
heaps of bodies, *. Nah 3:3
bewitching people *. Nah 3:4
and violence in cities *. Hab 2:17
* there is prosperity and peace." Zec 1:11
that see * around the world." Zec 4:10
* throughout the land." Zec 5:6
foes, leaving horrible carnage *. Zec 9:15
Jewish synagogues, * preaching the Mt 4:23
prophet is honored * except in his Mt 13:57
Sin will be rampant * and will Mt 24:12
And people from * came to him Mk 1:45
prophet is honored * except in his Mk 6:4
his miracles were talked about *. Mk 6:14
the Good News to everyone, *. Mk 16:15
And the disciples went * Mk 16:20
frantic, searching for you *." Lk 2:48
hour, and was being discussed *. Lk 3:15
The crowds searched * for him and Lk 4:42
the government * he goes, all over Lk 23:5
* except in his own country!" Jn 4:43,44
a wild man, going * to devastate Act 8:3
who had fled Jerusalem went * Act 8:4
the Good News * and to testify that Act 10:42
he saw * throughout the city. Act 17:16
You are to take his message *, Act 22:15
to make Christians * curse Christ. Act 26:11
with all people * whose sins are Act 26:18
is that they are denounced *!" Act 28:22
to tell all people * the great Rom 1:5
this warm love * within us because Rom 5:5
is being preached *, so that people Rom 16:25,26,27
And to: All Christians *—whoever 1Co 1:2
helping and serving Christians *. 1Co 16:15
for you, that I do * else in all 2Co 12:13
those * who are really God's own. Gal 6:16
for Christians *, I have never Eph 1:15
Author and Giver of everything *. Eph 1:23
fill all things * with himself, Eph 4:10
earnestly for all Christians *. Eph 6:18
he will use to conquer all else *. Php 3:21
and changing lives *, just as it Col 1:6
So * we go we talk about Christ Col 1:28
from you to others *, far beyond 1Th 1:8
* as it did when it came to you. 2Th 3:1
So I want men * to pray with 1Ti 2:8
accepted by men * and was received 1Ti 3:16
tell men and women * about the 2Ti 1:1
Rome he searched * trying to find 2Ti 1:17
He knows about everyone, *. Heb 4:13
To: Jewish Christians scattered *. Jas 1:1
Love Christians *. 1Pe 2:17
he saw * around him day after day. 2Pe 2:7,8
To: Christians *—beloved of God Jud 1:1
war and killing broke out *. Rev 6:4
holiday—people * will rejoice and Rev 11:10
he was deceiving people *. Rev 13:14
Idol Worship * around the World." Rev 17:5
the Lamb are worshiped in it *. Rev 21:22

EVI
Rekem, Zur, Hur, and Reba.* Num 31:8
Rekem, Zur, Hur, and Reba.* Jos 13:21

EVICTED
may they be * from the ruins of Ps 109:9,10

EVICTING
you are * widows from their homes. Mt 23:13,14

EVIDENCE
is insufficient *, or whether Deu 17:8
are to clarify the * for them and 2Ch 19:10
them all together as * against me. Job 14:17
judges refuse to listen to the *? Ps 82:2
weighs all the * carefully, Pro 20:8
appearance, false *, or hearsay, Is 11:3
at that time, as * of the covenant Act 7:8
it will stand as * against you, and Jas 5:3

EVIDENT
to him, "It is * that God helps Gen 21:22
every other nation, as is * today. Deu 10:15
as is * today. 2Ch 6:15
futility will become * to him. Job 15:32
real poverty is * to the poor. Pro 28:11
For her wickedness is * to Eze 24:7
* to all the nations when I do it. Eze 39:27
Day by day his justice is more *, Zep 3:5
It will become as * as yeast in Lk 12:2
It will be as * as the lightning Lk 17:24
And this trend is * not only here Act 19:26

EVIDENTLY

These were * additional to the Jos 8:11,12,13f
In this case the ephod * was Ju 8:27f
the numbers have * dropped out in 1Sa 13:1f
He was * lying. 2Sa 1:10f
These were * the 400 Asherah 1Ki 22:6f
and Jeconiah) * did not qualify as Jer 36:30f
This passage * refers to the Zec 2:8f
* self-inflicted cuts, as Zec 13:6f
And what was the result? * not Rom 6:21

EVIL

able to distinguish good from *!" Gen 3:5
in man, wholly * as he is. Gen 6:3
when the * beings from the spirit Gen 6:4
*, he was sorry he had made them. Gen 6:5
is always toward * from his Gen 8:21
are utterly *, and that everything Gen 18:20
the * we did to him," they said. Gen 50:15
us for the great * we did to you. Gen 50:16,17
what you meant for *, for he Gen 50:20
Do not cooperate with an * man by Ex 23:1
"Don't join mobs intent on *. Ex 23:2,3
falsely charging anyone with *; Ex 23:7
* example of these heathen people; Ex 23:24
Turn away from this terrible * Ex 32:12
soon be following their * ways. Ex 34:12
people's sacrificing to * spirits Lev 17:7
with the * deeds of those living in Lev 18:29,30
with her mother, it is a great *. Lev 20:14
When at last their * hearts are Lev 26:40,41
and bring us here to this * place? Num 20:5
until all that * generation died. Num 32:13
and follow * ways, you shall Deu 8:19
destroy this *, stubborn people!' Deu 9:13,14
clear out the * from among you. Deu 13:5
hear about his * deed, and will Deu 13:11
In this way you will purge all * Deu 17:7
or call on the * spirits for aid, Deu 18:10
all do these * things, but the Lord Deu 18:14
In this way you will purge out * Deu 19:19
put away this * from among you, and Deu 21:21
and such * must be cleansed from Deu 22:21
in this way * will be cleansed Deu 22:22
camps must stay away from all *. Deu 23:9,10
to purge the * from among you. Deu 24:7
and in the days to come * will Deu 31:29
is *, making him very angry." Deu 31:29
* upon you if you disobey him. Jos 23:15,16
They stubbornly returned to the * Ju 2:19
Israel were very * in God's sight, Ju 3:7
so it became an * deed that Gideon Ju 8:27
Give up these * men from the Ju 20:13
them and purge Israel of her *." Ju 20:13
Now the sons of Eli were * men 1Sa 2:12
who brought this great * upon us; 1Sa 6:9
and the * spirit would go away. 1Sa 16:23
for you have repaid me good for *. 1Sa 24:17
God and can discern good from *. 2Sa 14:17
Floods of * burst upon me; 2Sa 22:5
But you destroy those who are *. 2Sa 22:27
for all of their * deeds, and make 1Ki 8:50
has brought this * upon them.' 1Ki 9:9
did not turn away from his * ways; 1Ki 13:33
But you have done more * than 1Ki 14:9
He followed the * paths of 1Ki 15:34
but you have walked in the * 1Ki 16:2
the Lord by all his * deeds. 1Ki 16:4-7
He was as * as Jeroboam despite 1Ki 16:4-7
is * in the sight of the Lord." 1Ki 21:20f
him to do every sort of *. 1Ki 21:25
He was a very * man, but not as 2Ki 3:2
He was an * king, just as all of 2Ki 8:27
But he was an * king, and he 2Ki 13:2
following the * ways of Jeroboam; 2Ki 13:6
But he was an * man, for, like 2Ki 13:11
But he was as * as Jeroboam I 2Ki 14:24
But Zechariah was an * king in 2Ki 15:9
But Menahem was an * king. 2Ki 15:18
But Pekahiah was an * king, and 2Ki 15:24
who led Israel down that * trail. 2Ki 15:24
Pekah, too, was an * king, and he 2Ki 15:28
Character of his reign: * 2Ki 16:1
Character of his reign: *—but not 2Ki 17:1
They had followed the * customs 2Ki 17:8
had done many * things, and the 2Ki 17:11
Judah to turn from their * ways; 2Ki 17:13
magic and sold themselves to *. 2Ki 17:17
they too walked in the same * 2Ki 17:19
quit doing the * things that 2Ki 17:22
and I also know the * things you 2Ki 19:27
Character of his reign: * 2Ki 21:1
was an * man, in God's opinion. 2Ki 21:6
to do even more * than the 2Ki 21:9
nations for their * ways when the 2Ki 21:9
has done these * things and is even 2Ki 21:11
I will bring such * upon Jerusalem 2Ki 21:12
For they have done great * and 2Ki 21:15
Character of his reign: * 2Ki 21:19,20
He did all the * things his 2Ki 21:21
will not see the * which I will 2Ki 22:20
the * goddess of the Sidonians; 2Ki 23:13
and for Chemosh, the * god of 2Ki 23:13
and for Milcom, the * god of the 2Ki 23:13
Character of his reign: *, like 2Ki 23:31,32
Character of his reign: *, like 2Ki 23:36,37
Character of his reign: *, like 2Ki 24:18,19
keep me from all * and disaster!" 1Ch 4:10
But he was an * king, for he 2Ch 12:14
never prophesies anything but *! 2Ch 18:6,7
anything but * against me." 2Ch 18:17
was one constant binge of doing *. 2Ch 21:6
you have been as * as the kings 2Ch 21:13
He, too, walked in the * ways of 2Ch 22:3
Yes, he was as * as Ahab, for 2Ch 22:4
Following their * advice, Ahaziah 2Ch 22:5
But he was an * king, unlike his 2Ch 28:1
* deeds of King Ahaz of Israel, 2Ch 28:19
But it was an * reign, for he 2Ch 33:2
of *, making the Lord very angry. 2Ch 33:6
to do even more * than the nations 2Ch 33:9
It was an * reign like the early 2Ch 33:22
send the promised * upon this city 2Ch 34:28
but his reign was an * one. 2Ch 36:5
and all the * he did, are written 2Ch 36:8
and it was an * reign as far as the 2Ch 36:9
His reign, too, was * so far as 2Ch 36:12
rebellious and * city; Ez 4:12
"What you are doing is very *," Neh 5:9
forget all the * of Tobiah, Neh 6:14
learned of this * deed of Neh 13:7
* days upon us and upon our city? Neh 13:18
feared God and stayed away from *. Job 1:1
will have nothing to do with *." Job 1:8
God and turns away from all *. Job 2:3
again, so that no * can touch you. Job 5:19
Innocent or *, it is all the Job 9:22
all these * things against him. Job 15:13
truth, that the * man is usually Job 21:30-32
*, my tongue shall speak no lies. Job 27:4
They are * men. Job 27:7
"The * man may accumulate money Job 27:16
to forsake * is real Job 28:28
for good to come, * came instead. Job 30:26
much time with * men, for he said, Job 34:7,8
enough to hide * men from his eyes, Job 34:22
Or, 'We know not what * we have Job 34:32
Turn back from *, for it was to Job 36:21
of * that God sent this suffering. Job 36:21
that what he does is absurd or *? Job 36:23
who do not follow * men's advice, Ps 1:1
for how you hate their * deeds. Ps 5:5
Go, leave me now, you men of * Ps 6:8
if I were doing * things— if I Ps 7:3
I were paying back * for good or Ps 7:4
The wicked man conceives an * Ps 7:14
Pour upon these men the * they Ps 10:2
men brag of all their * lusts; Ps 10:3
always boasting of their * plans. Ps 10:7
You have noted each * act. Ps 10:14
from the reach of * men, although Ps 12:7
that is warped and * and cannot Ps 14:1
gone along with cruel and * men. Ps 17:4
not punish those who run from *. Ps 18:25
The enemy, this gang of * men, Ps 22:16
See these men of * gloat and Ps 22:17
life from all these * men. Ps 22:20
When * men come to destroy me, Ps 27:2
pay them back for all their * Ps 28:4
accusing honest men of * deeds." Ps 31:18
memory of * men from the earth. Ps 34:16
These * men swear to a lie. Ps 35:11
forever urging them on to * deeds. Ps 36:1
their * deeds and not get caught. Ps 36:2
to hatch their * plots, instead of Ps 36:4
Don't be envious of * men who Ps 37:7
* men take aim to slay the poor; Ps 37:14
than to own an * man's wealth; Ps 37:16
for the strength of * men shall Ps 37:17
enough. But * men shall perish. Ps 37:20
like smoke. * men borrow and Ps 37:21
home, leave your *, low-down ways Ps 37:27
* men spy on the godly, waiting Ps 37:32
will not let these * men succeed, Ps 37:33
a proud and * man, towering like a Ps 37:35,36
happy ending. But * men shall be Ps 37:38
them from the plots of * men. Ps 37:40
They repay me * for good and Ps 38:20
of all the * you have sent. Ps 44:13
those who are * will be the slaves Ps 49:14
So do not be dismayed when * men Ps 49:16
But God says to * men: Recite my Ps 50:16
your time with * and immoral men. Ps 50:18
You boast about this * deed of Ps 52:1
a tack in plotting your * tricks. Ps 52:2
heart, his dark and * deeds. Ps 53:1
He will cause the * deeds of my Ps 54:5
Do not spare these *, Ps 59:5
Let these * men slink back at Ps 59:14,15
They encourage each other to do *. Ps 64:5
endless * thoughts and plans. Ps 64:6
about the future of these * men. Ps 73:17
of * men," says the Lord, Ps 75:10
and needy from the grasp of * men. Ps 82:4
Replace the * years with good. Ps 90:15
me, the * will not touch me. Ps 91:7
How then can * overtake me or Ps 91:10
How these men of * boast! Ps 94:4
God has made the sins of * men Ps 94:23
The Lord loves those who hate *; Ps 97:10
and stay away from every *. Ps 101:4
and learned their * ways, Ps 106:35
Their * deeds defiled them, for Ps 106:39
while * men are stricken silent. Ps 107:42
They return * for good, and Ps 109:5
Think constantly about the * Ps 109:15
be overthrown by * circumstances. Ps 112:6
*, and walking only in his paths. Ps 119:3
back to you. * men have tried to Ps 119:61
walk the paths of * for I will Ps 119:101
For these * men have violated Ps 119:126
that I will not be overcome by *. Ps 119:133
me from the oppression of * men; Ps 119:134
He keeps you from all *, and Ps 121:7
but lead * men to execution. Ps 125:5
that * men had bound me with. Ps 129:3,4
O Babylon, * beast, you shall be Ps 137:8
O LORD, DELIVER me from * men. Ps 140:1
very * they have planned for me. Ps 140:9
Take away my lust for * things; Ps 141:4
to stay away from * men who want Pro 2:11,12,13
walk down dark and * paths, and Pro 2:11,12,13
* men lose the good things they Pro 2:22
the Lord, and turn your back on *; Pro 3:7,8
else, for * men don't sleep until Pro 4:16
done their * deed for the day. Pro 4:16
while the * man gropes and Pro 4:19
of all the * he can do, and Pro 6:14
*Eagerness to do wrongA false Pro 6:16-19
There is nothing of * in it. Pro 8:8
and fears God, he will hate *. Pro 8:13
an * man inwardly curses his luck. Pro 10:6
the * man is filled with curses. Pro 10:11
The * man squanders his on sin. Pro 10:16
the hopes of * men are all in Pro 10:28
his honesty; the * man is destroyed Pro 11:3
* man's treachery is his undoing. Pro 11:6
When an * man dies, his hopes Pro 11:7
* words destroy. Pro 11:9
The * man gets rich for the Pro 11:18
The good man finds life; the * Pro 11:19
You can be very sure that the * Pro 11:21
if you search for * you will find Pro 11:27
* man's mind is crammed with lies. Pro 12:5
hearts that are plotting for *; Pro 12:20
life, while * men are being Pro 13:6
Be with * men and become evil. Pro 13:20
Be with evil men and become *. Pro 13:20
while the * man lives to eat. Pro 13:25
* men shall bow before the godly. Pro 14:19
Those who plot * shall wander Pro 14:22
eye on both the * and the good. Pro 15:3
he speaks; the * man pours out his Pro 15:28
the evil man pours out his * Pro 15:28
* is avoided by reverence for God. Pro 16:6
horrible thing for a king to do *. Pro 16:12
of the godly leads away from *; Pro 16:17
An * man sows strife; Pro 16:28
Or, "An * man deceives his Pro 16:29f
in thought, planning his * deeds. Pro 16:30
If you repay * for good, a curse Pro 17:13
An * man is suspicious of Pro 17:20
Don't repay * for evil. Pro 20:22
Don't repay evil for *. Pro 20:22
Punishment that hurts chases * Pro 20:30
Pride, lust, and * actions Pro 21:4
An * man lives an evil life; Pro 21:8
An evil man lives an * life; Pro 21:8
An * man loves to harm others; Pro 21:10
God loathes the gifts of * men, Pro 21:27
An * man is stubborn, but a godly Pro 21:29
Don't associate with * men; Pro 23:6,7,8
Don't envy * men but continue to Pro 23:17,18
To plan * is as wrong as doing Pro 24:8
O * man, leave the upright man Pro 24:15,16
For the * man has no future; Pro 24:19,20
To obey the law is to fight *. Pro 28:4
* men don't understand the Pro 28:5
Trying to get rich quick is * and Pro 28:22
Flattery is a trap; * men are Pro 29:5,6
proud or plotting *, don't brag Pro 30:32
* and crime throughout the earth. Ecc 4:3
YES, BUT THERE is a very serious * Ecc 6:1
all the dead man's * deeds, these Ecc 8:9,10
a fool's heart leads him to do *. Ecc 10:2
There is another * I have seen as Ecc 10:5
youth before the * years come—when Ecc 12:1
Their fathers before them were * Is 1:4
quit your * ways. Is 1:16
straw; your * deeds are the spark Is 1:31
* spirits, as the Philistines do. Is 2:6
the * and to choose the good . Is 7:15,16f
Because of all your * boasting, O Is 10:16
its *, the wicked for their sin; Is 13:11

(EVIL Con't)
power, and broken your * rule." Is 14:5
all her * ways around the world. Is 23:17
with grief, for * still prevails Is 24:15,16
their pride and all their * works. Is 25:11
all those plotting * will be Is 29:20
he will send great * on his people Is 31:2
them for the * they have done, and Is 31:2
Everyone will recognize an * man Is 32:6
The smooth tricks of * men will Is 32:7
Listen to me, you stubborn, * Is 46:12
and had never spoken an * word. Is 53:9
them away from * days ahead. Is 57:1
everything their * hearts desired. Is 57:17
Because you are living in * Is 58:3
you spend your time plotting * Is 59:4
energy in spinning * plans which Is 59:5
Your feet run to do * and rush Is 59:7
It is because of all this * that Is 59:9
The Lord saw all the * and was Is 59:15
enemies for their * deeds—fury for Is 59:18
they follow their own * paths and Is 65:2
caves to worship * spirits, and Is 65:4
and forget the * that you did. Is 65:16
come to an * end, says Jehovah. Is 66:17
* fell on anyone who touched them. Jer 2:3
my inheritance into an * thing. Jer 2:7
For my people have done two * Jer 2:13
You will see what an *, bitter Jer 2:19
this degenerate race of * men? Jer 2:21
them a land of darkness and of *? Jer 2:31
on doing all the * that you can. Jer 3:4,5
stubbornly follow their * desires. Jer 3:17
by casting out your * thoughts. Jer 4:14
bother us! No * will come upon us! Jer 5:12
their homes are full of * plots. Jer 5:27
* shepherds shall surround you. Jer 6:3
She spouts * like a fountain! Jer 6:7
I will bring * upon this people; Jer 6:18,19
full of * talk against the Lord? Jer 6:28
if you quit your * ways I will let Jer 7:3
back to all these * things again? Jer 7:10
For I see all the * going on in Jer 7:11
of all this * you have done. Jer 7:13,14
their own stubborn, * thoughts. Jer 7:24
And those of this * nation who Jer 8:3
* path, even though I warn them. Jer 8:4,5
idols and strange * rites?" Jer 8:19
"They pile * upon evil, lie upon Jer 9:6
"They pile evil upon *, lie upon Jer 9:6
plans and showed me their * plots. Jer 11:18
Why are * men so happy? Jer 12:1
his court and all his * priests? Jer 12:5
says this to the * nations, the Jer 12:14
This * nation refuses to listen Jer 13:10
own * desires and worships idols; Jer 13:10
to doing * now start being good. Jer 13:23
now I will remember all the * you Jer 14:10
back to me from all their * ways. Jer 15:7
You follow * to your hearts' Jer 16:12
it up with all your * deeds. Jer 16:18
as though their * were laws Jer 17:1
renounces its * ways, I will not Jer 18:8
mind and turns to * and refuses to Jer 18:10
I am planning * against you now Jer 18:11
turn back from your * paths and Jer 18:11
Should they repay * for good? Jer 18:20
bring terrible * upon this place, Jer 19:3
towns all the * I have promised, Jer 19:15
of all the * you are doing. Jer 21:12
Quit your * deeds! Jer 22:3
for the * you have done to them. Jer 23:2
* and their power is used wrongly. Jer 23:10
For I will bring * upon them and Jer 23:12
were unbelievably *, for they Jer 23:13
who are doing *, instead of turning Jer 23:14
turn my people from their * ways. Jer 23:22
Turn from the * road you are Jer 25:5
from the * things you are doing. Jer 25:5
all the * that has come your way. Jer 25:7
Weep and moan, O * shepherds; Jer 25:34
turn from their * ways, and then I Jer 26:3
them because of their * deeds. Jer 26:3
good and not for *, to give you a Jer 29:11
proverbial of all *, so that Jer 29:22
all this terrible * upon them. Jer 32:23
me with all their * deeds. Jer 32:30
What an incredible *, causing Jer 32:35
all the * I have ever threatened. Jer 35:17
turn from their * ways and ask the Jer 36:7
upon them all the * I promised—upon Jer 36:31
have done a very * thing in putting Jer 38:9
the * I will bring upon you there. Jer 42:17
bear all the * things you were Jer 44:22
I will see to it that * befalls Jer 44:27
For though I will bring great * Jer 45:5
will bring great * upon Elam, says Jer 49:37
for all the * they have done to my Jer 51:24
of the * I am bringing upon her.' Jer 51:64
well for all the * they have done. Lam 3:64
with idols and * sacrifices, Eze 5:11
Alas for all the * we have done! Eze 6:11
you for all your * deeds. Eze 7:8,9
do to them the * they have done, Eze 7:26,27
* that will come upon Jerusalem." Eze 12:6
your walls! O * prophets, what Eze 13:5
For these * men deceive my Eze 13:10
"Tell these * builders that Eze 13:11
False prophets and hypocrites—* Eze 14:10
me by all these * things you do, I Eze 16:43
shame all the * you have done; Eze 16:61
he dies for the * he has done. Eze 18:26
because of the * you have done. Eze 20:43
* prince of Israel, your final Eze 21:25
her into the * clutches of the Eze 23:9
for all the * you have done. Eze 24:23
turn from his * ways and live. Eze 33:11
and the sins of an * man will not Eze 33:12
not doing *—he shall surely live. Eze 33:15
good man turns to *, he shall die. Eze 33:18
You are powerless, for you do *! Eze 33:25
"Is it a small thing to you, O * Eze 34:18
I have heard each * word you spoke Eze 35:12
they defiled it by their * deeds; Eze 36:17
them for the * way they lived. Eze 36:19
For at that time an * thought Eze 38:10
and * triumphed and prospered. Dan 8:12
be poured out upon this * One." Dan 9:27
days the mighty * Spirit who Dan 10:13
power will be an * man not directly Dan 11:21
I have seen your * deeds: Israel, Hos 5:3
heathen, picking up their * ways; Hos 7:8
I will punish her for all her * Hos 7:12
O * men, you make "justice" a Amo 5:7
Be good, flee *—and live! Amo 5:14
Hate * and love the good; Amo 5:15
they receive * and not good." Amo 9:4
turn from his * ways, from his Jon 3:8
a stop to their * ways, he Jon 3:10
I will reward your * with evil; Mic 2:3
I will reward your evil with *; Mic 2:3
ones who hate good and love *; Mic 3:2
They go at their * deeds with Mic 7:3
all the * they have done to me. Mic 7:9
getting rich by * means, attempting Hab 2:9
with * gain of violence and fraud. Zep 1:9
continue all their * ways from dawn Zep 3:7
up and accuse these * nations. Zep 3:8
attitudes and * hearts—and not only Hag 2:14
to turn from all their * ways. Zec 1:4
plotting * against each other. Zec 7:10
leaders—all these * shepherds—for Zec 11:3
And I got rid of their three * Zec 11:8
And you claim this isn't *? Mal 1:8
By saying that * is good, that it Mal 2:17
For those who do * shall Mal 3:14,15
to both the * and the good, and Mt 5:45
but deliver us from the * One. Mt 6:13
Or, "from *." Mt 6:13f
is clouded with * thoughts and Mt 6:23
unto the day is the * thereof." Mt 6:34f
Go away, for your deeds are *.' Mt 7:23
are you thinking such * thoughts? Mt 9:4
to cast out * spirits and to heal Mt 10:1
How could * men like you speak Mt 12:34
But Jesus replied, "Only an *, Mt 12:39,40
to God from all their * ways. Mt 12:41
"This * nation is like a man Mt 12:43,44,45
other spirits more * than itself, Mt 12:43,44,45
Literally, "the *." Mt 13:19f
and all who are *, and throw them Mt 13:41
out again? But * words come from Mt 15:18
But evil words come from an * Mt 15:18
For from the heart come * Mt 15:19
This *, unbelieving nation is Mt 16:4
of your hard and * hearts, but it Mt 19:8
meaning: "Surely * men and Mt 21:31
very * men and prostitutes did. Mt 21:32
up the full measure of their *. Mt 23:32
"But if you are * and say to Mt 24:48
am betrayed into the hands of * Mt 26:45
At that the * spirit screamed Mk 1:26
"Why, even * spirits obey his Mk 1:27
said, "Come out, you * spirit." Mk 5:7,8
Then the * spirits came out of Mk 5:13
men's hearts, come * thoughts of Mk 7:21
"will be able to speak * of me." Mk 9:39f
If your foot carries you toward * Mk 9:45,46
"He was counted among * men." Mk 15:28
And an * man produces evil deeds Lk 6:45
And an evil man produces * deeds Lk 6:45
blind and casting out * spirits. Lk 7:20,21,22
other demons more * than itself, Lk 11:26
are * times, with evil people. Lk 11:29,30
are evil times, with * people. Lk 11:29,30
leave your * ways and turn to God? Lk 13:3
but God knows your * hearts. Lk 16:15
said, "If even an * judge can be Lk 18:6
skies—warnings, * omens and Lk 21:25
We deserve to die for our * Lk 23:40,41
into the power of * men and be Lk 24:6,7
the Light, for their deeds were *. Jn 3:19
and those who have continued in * Jn 5:2
because I accuse it of sin and *. Jn 7:
love to do the * things he does. Jn 8:4
we know Jesus is an * person." Jn 9:2
Well, God doesn't listen to * Jn 9:3
* prince of this world approaches. Jn 14:3
Many * spirits were cast out, Act 8:
yet forgive your * thoughts— for I Act 8:2
all sorts of * things about them. Act 14:
speak * of any of your rulers.' Act 23:
all sinful, * men who push away the Rom 1:1
them do all these * things, so that Rom 1:2
their * minds could think of. Rom 1:2
of God and walk in * ways—God's Rom 2:
speaks * of God because of you. Rom 2:2
of doing all these * things; Rom 3:1
Your old * desires were nailed Rom 6.
that these laws of God are *? Rom 7:
in my heart—the * desires that are Rom 7:
have * desires in your heart." Rom 7:
this law against * desires by Rom 7:
good laws for its own * purposes. Rom 7:1
that makes me do these * things. Rom 7:1
sin still has me in its * grasp. Rom 7:2
obey the old * nature within us. Rom 8:
* desires, can never please God. Rom 8:
and its * deeds, you shall live. Rom 8:1
Never pay back * for evil. Rom 12:1
Never pay back evil for *. Rom 12:1
Don't let * get the upper hand Rom 12:2
hand but conquer * by doing good. Rom 12:2
but those doing * will always Rom 13:
So quit the * deeds of darkness Rom 13:12,1
and don't make plans to enjoy *. Rom 13:1
We have replied quietly when * 1Co 4:1
you, something so * that even the 1Co 5:
Remove this * cancer—this wicked 1Co 5:
I said not to mix with * people. 1Co 5:
we must not desire * things as they 1Co 10:
to know whether * spirits are 1Co 12:1
comes to planning *, but be men of 1Co 14:2
Satan, who is the god of this * 2Co 4:4
at all times, not to hope for *. 2Co 13:
this * world in which we live. Gal 1:4
you and cast an * spell upon you? Gal 3:1
things your * nature wants you to. Gal 5:16
For we naturally love to do * Gal 5:17
will produce these * results: Gal 5:19
their natural * desires to his Gal 5:24
planting seeds of * and he will Gal 6:8
expressing the * within us, doing Eph 2:3
our * thoughts might lead us into. Eph 2:3
being born with * natures, and were Eph 2:3
their * minds and reckless lusts. Eph 4:19
throw off your old * nature—the old Eph 4:22
a partner in your * ways—rotten Eph 4:22
pleasures of * and darkness, but Eph 5:11
without bodies—the * rulers of the Eph 6:12
beings and great * princes of Eph 6:12
from him by your * thoughts and Col 1:21
you free from your * desires, not Col 2:11
see how your old, * nature died Col 2:12
a person's * thoughts and desires. Col 2:23
deaden the * desires lurking Col 3:5
motives or * purposes in mind; 1Th 2:3
See that no one pays back * for 1Th 5:15
pays back evil for *, but always 1Th 5:15
Keep away from every kind of *. 1Th 5:22
of the clutches of * men, for not 2Th 3:2
accusations, and * suspicions. 1Ti 6:4
Run from all these * things and 1Ti 6:11
that gives you the * thoughts that 2Ti 2:22
In fact, * men and false 2Ti 3:13
me from all * and will bring me 2Ti 4:18
but a person whose own heart is * Tit 1:15
untrusting finds * in everything, Tit 1:15
go around speaking * of others and Tit 2:3
They must not speak * of anyone, Tit 3:2
* pleasures and wicked desires. Tit 3:3
they, too, are * and unbelieving Heb 3:12
man's own * thoughts and wishes. Jas 1:14
These * thoughts lead to evil Jas 1:15
These evil thoughts lead to * Jas 1:15
and every other kind of *. Jas 3:16
army of * desires within you? Jas 4:1
God's enemies—the * pleasures of Jas 4:4
is to enjoy the * pleasure of the Jas 4:4
stand against all such * longings. Jas 4:6
Don't criticize and speak * about Jas 4:11
* because you knew no better. 1Pe 1:14
all *, deception, envy, and fraud. 1Pe 2:2,3
the * pleasures of this world; 1Pe 2:11
Don't repay * for evil. 1Pe 3:9
Don't repay evil for *. 1Pe 3:9
Turn away from * and do good. 1Pe 3:11
is hard against those who do *. 1Pe 3:12
you, calling you * names, they will 1Pe 3:16
life chasing after * desires, but 1Pe 4:2
in the past of the * things the 1Pe 4:3
Many will follow their * 2Pe 2:2
follow their own *, lustful 2Pe 2:10

EVIL Con't)
against these * Mighty Ones. 2Pe 2:11
For they live in * pleasures day 2Pe 2:13
Stop loving this * world and all 1Jn 2:15
things, these * desires—the craze 1Jn 2:16
They are from this * world 1Jn 2:16
away, and these *, forbidden things 1Jn 2:17
* teacher in this wicked world. 1Jn 4:4
defeating sin and * pleasure by 1Jn 5:4
and those who continue in * prove 3Jn 1:11
on living their *, immoral lives, Jud 1:8
church, they are * smears among Jud 1:12
doing whatever * they feel like; Jud 1:16
in every * way imaginable. Jud 1:18
they love the * things of the Jud 1:19
of Life—worshiped the * Creature. Rev 13:8
over the * Creature and his statue Rev 15:2
to repent of all their * deeds.. Rev 16:11
And I saw three * spirits Rev 16:13
devils and every kind of * spirit. Rev 18:2
penalty for all her * deeds. Rev 18:6
Then I saw the * Creature Rev 19:19
And the * Creature was captured, Rev 19:20
miracles when the * Creature was Rev 19:20
had accepted the * Creature's mark, Rev 19:20
Both of them—the * Creature and Rev 19:20
Nothing * will be permitted in Rev 21:27
be nothing in the city which is *; Rev 22:3

EVIL-DOERS
You stand up to punish the * and Ps 76:9
enemies—all *—shall be scattered. Ps 92:9
but it is a calamity to *. Pro 21:15

EVIL-HEARTED
No * men may walk upon it. Is 35:8
within him. An * man is filled with Mt 12:35
forgiven and said, 'You * wretch! Mt 18:32

EVIL-MERODACH
of the reign of King * of Babylon. 2Ki 25:27
king of Judah, *, who became king Jer 52:31

EVIL-MINDED
* men will be infuriated when Ps 112:10
Begone, you * men. Ps 119:115
the * only wants to fight. Pro 13:2
them and make them * and finally 1Ti 6:9

EVILDOERS
away a good man, nor prosper *. Job 8:20
humble when * are oppressing them. Ps 14:6

EVILS
I will heap * upon them Deu 32:23
as long as the * of your mother 2Ki 9:22
caused by the * of King Manasseh. 2Ki 23:26
all the * stated in the contract. Jer 11:8
these terrors and * upon them, so Jer 32:42
"But I will show you greater * Eze 8:15
yourselves for all the * you did. Eze 36:31
all the * he predicted—all have Dan 9:13
these further * I have spoken of. Amo 4:12
* surely will not come our way." Mic 2:6
upon the world for all its *. Mt 18:7
from the * of their nation. Act 2:40
for many * lie along that path; Eph 5:18

EWE
But when he took seven * lambs Gen 21:28,29
or *, billy goat or nanny goat. Lev 3:6
day, whether she is a cow or *. Lev 22:28
a yearling * lamb without defect; Num 6:14

EWE-LAMB
one yearling * without physical Lev 14:10

EWES
Then he divided out the * from Gen 30:39,40
I cared for your * and nanny goats Gen 31:38
billy goats,200 *,20 rams,30 milk Gen 32:13,14,15
from following the * with lambs; Ps 78:71,72
as freshly washed *, perfectly Sol 6:6
and gently lead the * with young. Is 40:11

EX-WIFE
brother Philip's *, because John Mt 14:3

EXACT
The * measure is not known. Ex 16:16f
The * weight is not known. Ex 25:39f
The * weight cannot be Ex 30:22,23f
The * weight cannot be Ex 38:27f
* design the Lord had shown Moses. Num 8:4
The * value cannot be Deu 22:19f
but no one knows the * place. Deu 34:6
out from them the * time when they Mt 2:7
if they knew the * hour of his Lk 12:39
was constructed in * accordance Act 7:44
Christ is the * likeness of the Col 1:15
Literally, "he"; the * Rev 19:9f

EXACTLY
godly and wicked * the same! Gen 18:25
Rebekah: "Now do * as I tell you. Gen 27:8,9,10
They are to follow * the Ex 31:11
to be injured in * the same way: Lev 24:19
They were * the same as Nahshon Num 7:18-23
vow must do * as he has promised. Num 30:1
of sinners doing * the same thing! Num 32:14
your instructions *," the people Num 32:25
and do * what God said not to?" 1Sa 15:19
of your son Solomon—do * as I say! 1Ki 1:12
"Wasn't this * King Solomon's Neh 13:26
Then I would tell him * what I Job 31:37
And today I have told you * Jer 42:21
And you are * like your sisters, Eze 16:45
And you have done * as you Dan 9:12
"The king will do * as he Dan 11:36
it: "This is * what I thought Jon 4:2
Remember, your Father knows * Mt 6:7,8
"We have * five small loaves of Mt 14:17
For you are * like your ancestors Lk 11:47
That's * how I'll be toward you! Lk 19:22
This is * what Isaiah the Jn 12:38
It stays * as it is." Jn 19:22
everyone can see * what each one of 1Co 4:5
Many others have faced * the same 1Co 10:13
He always does * what he says. 2Co 1:19
This is * what happened—I am not Gal 1:20
All must be treated * the same. 1Ti 5:21
He is, therefore, * the kind of Heb 7:26
him to follow * the pattern of the Heb 8:5
has remained * as it was since the 2Pe 3:4
for its height was * the same as Rev 21:16

EXALT
He is my father's God—I will * Ex 15:2
the Lord together, and * his name. Ps 34:3
Israel. * the Lord our holy God! Ps 99:5
* the Lord our God, and worship Ps 99:9
If you * wisdom, she will exalt Pro 4:8,9
If you exalt wisdom, she will * Pro 4:8,9

EXALTED
It is no longer 'Abram' ('* Gen 17:5
Their kingdom is *. Num 24:3-9
Lord, be * above the highest Ps 57:5
Yes, be *, O God, above the Ps 57:11
continues forever, * in the Ps 92:8
Literally, "You have * your Word Ps 138:2f
the Lord alone will be *. Is 2:11
and the Lord alone will be *. Is 2:17
but the Lord of Hosts is * above Is 5:16
he shall be highly *. Is 52:13
Now the poor are *, and the rich Eze 21:26
who humble themselves shall be *. Mt 23:12
their thrones and * the lowly. Lk 1:52
Will you be * to heaven? Lk 10:15
Then, with mighty power, God * Act 5:31

EXALTS
Godliness * a nation, but sin is Pro 14:34
the high trees and * the low, that Eze 17:24

EXAMINATION
man must go to the priest for *. Lev 13:19
But if the priest's * reveals Lev 13:31

EXAMINE
the priest will * him again, and if Lev 13:5
the priest will * him, and if the Lev 13:6
then the priest must * the spot. Lev 13:25
and * him again the seventh day. Lev 13:27
or chin, the priest must * him; Lev 13:29,30
the priest must * him again and, Lev 13:36
In that case the priest shall * Lev 13:43
shall go out of the camp to * him. Lev 14:3
hearts of men and * all their Ps 7:9
Let us * ourselves instead, and Lam 3:40
King Agrippa, to * him and then Act 25:26
It is the Lord himself who must * 1Co 4:4
That is why a man should * 1Co 11:28
But if you carefully * yourselves 1Co 11:31

EXAMINED
of his sons for the spot to be *. Lev 13:3
the priest to be *, he must come Lev 13:7
to the priest to be * again. Lev 13:16,17
and * again on the seventh day. Lev 13:32
He shall be * again on the Lev 13:34
be taken to the priest to be *. Lev 13:49
and when he has * me, he will Job 23:10
He established it and * it Job 28:27
O LORD, YOU have * my heart and Ps 139:1
you needs to have his head *! Is 41:24
right over to the priest to be *; Mt 8:4
"Go and be * immediately by the Mk 1:43,44
and be * by the Jewish priest. Lk 5:14
I have * him thoroughly on this Lk 23:14
you have carefully * the claims of Rev 2:2

EXAMINES
"But if when he * it again on Lev 13:53
then the priest who * him shall Lev 14:11
emptied before he * it, so that Lev 14:36
He searches all hearts and * Jer 17:10
are righteous and * the deepest Jer 20:12
for we serve God alone, who * our 1Th 2:4
be ashamed when God * your work. 2Ti 2:15

EXAMINING
be identified by * their fruit. Mt 7:17
accusations by * him yourself." Act 24:8

EXAMPLE
a Hebrew pun. An * in English might Gen 30:6f
evil * of these heathen people; Ex 23:24
ever find another * of God's Deu 4:34
their * in worshiping their gods. Deu 12:30
living there. For *, any Israeli Deu 18:10
"Here is an * of the purpose of Deu 19:4
Abimelech's *, the bundles were Ju 9:49
to Israel—another * of the way the 2Sa 8:14
* and proverb of sudden disaster. 1Ki 9:7
continued in the * of Jeroboam I 2Ki 15:28
This is just another * of how the 1Ch 18:13
Now then, who will follow my *? 1Ch 29:4,5
He followed the generally good * 2Ch 27:2
For he followed the * of the 2Ch 28:2
good * of his ancestor King David. 2Ch 34:2
May their * shame and silence Ps 8:2
and others will learn from his *. Pro 19:25
So here, too, we see an * of Ecc 2:24-26
Here is an * of serious punning Is 5:7f
"So I will make a public * of Eze 5:14
and an awesome * to everyone, for Eze 5:15
terrible * of him, destroying him; Eze 14:8
Ezekiel is an * to you, the Lord Eze 24:24
you are an * of horror; Eze 28:19
the south began to follow your *. Mic 1:13
the only * you follow is that of Mic 6:16
* of you—I will destroy you. Mic 6:16
He also used this *: Mt 13:33
else, don't follow their *. Mt 23:3
And this is only one *. Mk 7:12,13
home town! For *, remember how Lk 4:25,26
and I'm following his *." Jn 5:17
were, you would follow his good *. Jn 8:39
I have given you an * to follow: Jn 13:15
And I was a constant * to you in Act 20:35
They can see from his * that it Rom 4:12
Pharaoh, king of Egypt, was an * Rom 9:17
So I beg you to follow my *, and 1Co 4:16
AND YOU SHOULD follow my *, just 1Co 11:1
following Peter's *, though they Gal 2:13
FOLLOW GOD'S * in everything you Eph 5:1
following the * of Christ who loved Eph 5:2
Or, "your lives should be an *." Eph 5:10f
notice who else lives up to my *. Php 3:17
Then you yourselves became an * 1Th 1:7
This is only one * of the fair, 2Th 1:5
our *: you never saw us loafing; 2Th 3:7
could use me as an * to show 1Ti 1:16
(Satan's downfall is an *. 1Ti 3:6
no one else will follow his *. 1Ti 5:20
must be an * to them of good deeds Tit 2:7
to follow the * of those who Heb 6:12
prostitute, is another * of this. Jas 2:25
Job is an * of a man who Jas 5:11
who suffered for you, is your *. 1Pe 2:21
them by your good *, and when the 1Pe 5:3
making them an * for all the 2Pe 2:6
from Christ's * in dying for us. 1Jn 3:16
Dear friend, don't let this bad * 3Jn 1:11
For they follow the * of Cain who Jud 1:11

EXAMPLES
and mention * of your power. Ps 145:11
This is but one of many * of laws Mk 7:4
and myself as * to illustrate what 1Co 4:6
to them as *—as object lessons to 1Co 10:11
or the harp—are * of the need for 1Co 14:7
* of those who belong to the Lord. 2Co 8:23
point to us as * of how very, very Eph 2:7
and Alexander are two * of this. 1Ti 1:20
For * of patience in suffering, Jas 5:10

EXAMS
*, as he had been ordered to do. Dan 1:18,19

EXCAVATORS
* at the site of ancient Mizpah. Jer 41:9f

EXCEED
verses 12 and 14 * the actual Eze 26:14f

EXCEEDED
other and wept until David *." 1Sa 20:41f
Apparently Jehu in his zeal * the 2Ki 10:11f

EXCEEDING
altar of God my * joy, and praise Ps 43:4
soul is * sorrowful unto death." Heb 5:7f

EXCEEDINGLY
After this the altar shall be * Ex 29:37
Literally, "lusted *." Ps 106:14f

EXCEL
as weavers—they * in all the crafts Ex 35:35

EXCELLED
In fact, his wisdom * that of 1Ki 4:30

EXCELLENCY
his glory there, the * of our God. Is 35:2
"To: His *, Governor Felix. Act 23:26
"Your *, you have given quietness Act 24:2

EXCELLENT
made, and it was * in every way. Gen 1:31
He is your * sword! Deu 33:29
These men, all of whom had * 1Ch 26:31,32
to the Levites of their * music. 2Ch 30:22
These men had an * reputation, Neh 13:13
"*!" Est 6:10
Literally, "most * Theophilus." Lk 1:1f
"I am not insane, Most * Festus. Act 26:25
world, and all are * for those who 1Co 14:10

EXCEPT
in the garden * fruit from the Tree Gen 2:16,17
pair of each, * those kinds I have Gen 7:2
In fact, * for the grace of Gen 31:42
I owned nothing * a walking Gen 32:10

(EXCEPT Con't)
by their mother, * for Er, who was Gen 38:3,4,5
* to decide what he wanted to eat! Gen 39:6
nothing from me * you yourself Gen 39:9
the man replied, "* that only the Gen 44:10
of all the crops * those produced Gen 47:26
let you go * under heavy pressure. Ex 3:19
everywhere * in the river." Ex 8:9
destroyed, * those in the river." Ex 8:11
days * the preparation of food. Ex 12:16
males to the Lord—* that all the Ex 13:15
will be innocent * that he must pay Ex 21:19
All of you * Moses are to worship Ex 24:1
an ox, lamb, or goat anywhere * Lev 17:3,4
* when the brother died and left Lev 18:16f
has slept with you * your husband, Num 5:19
Then each man * Aaron claimed his Num 17:9
are yours, * for the sample Num 18:9
* what God tells me to say; Num 22:38
* what Jehovah tells me to?" Num 23:12
be made for murder * by the Num 35:33
their fathers, * Caleb (the son of Deu 1:36
We left nothing alive * the Deu 2:35,36
God require of you * to listen Deu 10:12,13
"You may eat any bird * the Deu 14:11-18
"Let there be complete silence * Jos 6:10
"Kill everyone * Rahab the Jos 6:17
everything in it * that the silver Jos 6:24
destroy everything * that which was Jos 7:1
or escaped, * for the king of Ai, Jos 8:23
the five armies * for a tiny Jos 10:20
built on mounds * for Hazor. Jos 11:13
treaty * the Hivites of Gibeon; Jos 11:19
no land at all, * cities in which Jos 14:3,4
* for this man and his family. Ju 1:25
his half-brothers, * for the Ju 9:5
at it ever since * for a few Ru 2:7
day, * for Saul's and Jonathan's. 1Sa 13:22
No one escaped * four hundred 1Sa 30:17
horses * for one hundred teams. 2Sa 8:4
He left no one behind * ten of 2Sa 15:16
So all * Judah and Benjamin 2Sa 20:2
instructions * that he continued to 1Ki 3:3
Ark at that time * the two stone 1Ki 8:9
finally killed all * Hadad and a 1Ki 11:16,17,18
And they all deserted him * for 1Ki 12:16,17
his entire life * for the affair 1Ki 15:5
every one of your prophets * me; 1Ki 19:14
fight no one * King Ahab himself. 1Ki 22:31
bother with you * for the presence 2Ki 3:14
"Nothing at all, * a jar of olive 2Ki 4:2
God in all the world * in Israel; 2Ki 5:15
to any other God * the Lord. 2Ki 5:17
his children, * for his year-old 2Ki 11:2,3
no one * the Levites may carry 1Ch 15:2
the chariot teams * a hundred that 1Ch 18:4
Nothing was in the Ark * the two 2Ch 5:10
* what the Lord tells you to?" 2Ch 18:15
None of his sons, however, * for 2Ch 22:9
and killed all the farmhands * me. Job 1:14,15
to God * in times of crisis. Job 27:10
For who is God * our Lord? Ps 18:31
I have no hope * in you. Ps 25:5
Nothing is perfect * your words. Ps 119:96
of wealth—* perhaps to watch it as Ecc 5:11
Don't fear anything * the Lord Is 8:13
bare of people * for a few of the Is 17:6
And no one protested * Elnathan, Jer 36:24,25
from my wrath * those who repent of Jer 44:14
looked like men, * that each had Eze 1:6
No one * the gods can tell you Dan 2:11
or worship any god * their own. Dan 3:28
of God or man—* from you, Your Dan 6:7
God or man—* you—for thirty days? Dan 6:12
constantly aflame—* while he kneads Hos 7:4
They look everywhere * to heaven, Hos 7:16
divorces his wife, * for Mt 5:32
you are hungry, * your Father who Mt 6:18
be forgiven—all * one: speaking Mt 12:31,32
and none will be given * what Mt 12:39,40
honored everywhere * in his own Mt 13:57
will be given * the miracle that Mt 16:4
divorces his wife, * for Mt 19:9
There, for forty days, alone * Mk 1:12,13
home * Peter and James and John. Mk 5:37
honored everywhere * in his home Mk 6:4
among them * to place his hands on Mk 6:5
nothing with them * their walking Mk 6:8,9
left upon another, * as ruins." Mk 13:2
All, that is, * the Pharisees Lk 7:30
into the room * Peter, James, John, Lk 8:51
and no one really knows the Son * Lk 10:22
knows the Father * the Son and Lk 10:22
God to be killed * in Jerusalem! Lk 13:33
everywhere * in his own country!" Jn 4:43,44
No one can get to the Father * by Jn 14:6
not one perished, * the son of Jn 17:12
and everyone * the apostles fled Act 8:1
our Jewish laws, * that we should Act 15:20
not knowing what awaits me, * Act 20:23
customs at all—* for the ones we Act 21:25
found in me, * that I said one Act 24:21
Literally, "* it be for this one Act 24:21f
I teach nothing * what the Act 26:22
as I am, * for these chains." Act 26:29
body like ours—* that ours are Rom 8:3
another place that * for God's Rom 9:29
Pay all your debts * the debt of Rom 13:8
any of you * Crispus and Gaius. 1Co 1:14
like, * that person himself. 1Co 2:11
God's thoughts * God's own Spirit. 1Co 2:11
as much as I can, * of course that 1Co 9:21
by his Father; *, of course, Christ 1Co 15:27
have come up * for some so-called Gal 2:4
else is wrong * those in your own Gal 5:20
about anything * the cross of our Gal 6:14
ours (* that his was sinless). Heb 5:7f
before the flood * Noah, the one 2Pe 2:5
win this battle * by believing that 1Jn 5:5
else knows * the one receiving it. Rev 2:17
and no one could sing this song * Rev 14:3

EXCEPTION
with the * of those that jump; Lev 11:21,22
However, there is one *—if the Lev 22:11
"There is one *: The homes of Lev 25:32
Lord, with the * that he did not 2Ch 20:33
The only * to this rule would be 1Co 7:5

EXCEPTIONS
The only * were Caleb (son of Num 26:64,65
The only * were Caleb (son of Num 32:12
"With certain *, Deu 14:19,20

EXCESS
all the * crops of the next seven Gen 41:34,35
273 eldest sons in * of the number Num 3:46
in * of the number of Levites. Num 3:49

EXCESSIVELY
Lord, neither shall he be * rich. Deu 17:17

EXCHANGE
and Canaan in * for grain, and he Gen 47:14
I will trade you food in *." Gen 47:16
cattle to Joseph in * for food. Gen 47:17
Lord in * for a lamb or baby goat; Ex 13:13
The Levites are mine in * for Num 3:13
Israel to him in * for becoming 2Sa 3:12
In * for the gifts from the queen 1Ki 10:13
give "justice" in * for bribes. Ps 58:1
in * for his protection against Is 28:15
in * for your freedom, as your Is 43:3
I will * your brass for gold, Is 60:17
will * it for eternal glory. Jn 12:25
Then, in *, he poured God's 2Co 5:21

EXCHANGED
Or, probably better, "They * wine Eze 27:19f
it must always be * for twenty Eze 45:12
against me. They * the glory of God Hos 4:7
After greetings were *, Paul Act 21:19

EXCHANGING
After * greetings with the Ru 2:4,5

EXCITE
the Lord began to * him whenever he Ju 13:25

EXCITED
Everyone was * and happy for 1Ch 29:9
come, they were * and happy and Mk 14:11
The crowd was * and enthusiastic, Lk 11:14
Please don't be upset and *, dear 2Th 2:1

EXCITEDLY
their god Dagon and * praised him. Ju 16:23,24
Naomi cried *. Ru 2:20
were talking *, and those with Mt 15:31
they asked *. Mk 1:27

EXCITEMENT
today, and life has lost its *. 2Sa 19:35
Why all the *?" 1Ki 19:20
They went across on foot. What * Ps 66:6
DON'T LET THE * of being young Ecc 12:1
In his *, he sold everything he Mt 13:44
to his house in great * and joy. Lk 19:6
he was filled with * and joy, and Act 11:23

EXCITING
the godly man's life is *. Pro 14:14
and your kisses as * as the best Sol 7:9
contact with the * things the world 1Co 7:31

EXCLAIM
laws they will *, 'What other Deu 4:6
Elkanah would *. 1Sa 1:8
They will *, 'The Lord of heaven 1Ch 17:24
"Why don't people * to their Job 34:31
May they constantly *, "How Ps 40:16
*, "What a wonderful God he is!" Ps 70:4
or the pot *, "How clumsy can Is 45:9

EXCLAIMED
Adam *. Gen 2:23
of it," the king *, "and I have Gen 21:26
her mother and brother *. Gen 24:55
"I can't endure this," she *. Gen 25:22
Abimelech called for Isaac and *, Gen 26:9
Abimelech *. Gen 26:10
"God lives here!" he * in Gen 28:16,17
own flesh and blood," Laban *. Gen 29:14
or I'll die," she * to Jacob. Gen 30:1
When he saw them he *, "God Gen 32:1
*, "Wonderful—another boy!" Gen 35:17
that master-dreamer," they *. Gen 37:19,2
Judah *. Gen 38:2
she *. Gen 38:2
"No, no," they *. Gen 42:1
"Look," he * to his brothers, Gen 42:2
Trembling, they * to each other, Gen 42:2
Then Jacob *, "You have bereaved Gen 42:3
Moses *. Ex 3:1
of God," they * to Pharaoh. Ex 8:1
his father-in-law *. Ex 18:1
The people *, "O Israel, this is Ex 32:
shouting, he * to Moses, "It Ex 32:1
like an ox eats grass," they *. Num 22:
the king * to Balaam. Num 23:2
Gideon *. Ju 8:1
they *. Ju 9:1
When Gaal saw them, he * to Ju 9:3
Jephthah *. Ju 11:
soon as she had tied him up she *, Ju 16:
Again Delilah *, Ju 16:1
me now," Micah *, "because now I Ju 17:1
Naomi *. Ru 2:1
Naomi *. Ru 2:2
God for a girl like you!" he *. Ru 3:1
she *, and went happily back, 1Sa 1:1
happening, they *, "We can't keep 1Sa 5:
heard about it, they *, "What? 1Sa 10:1
*, "How can this man save us?" 1Sa 10:2
Then the people * to Samuel, 1Sa 11:1
Samuel *. 1Sa 13:1
me," Jonathan * to his bodyguard, 1Sa 14:1
Jonathan *. 1Sa 14:2
"I can hardly move!" he *, and 1Sa 17:38,3
David *. 1Sa 18:1
they *. 1Sa 19:24
"What have I done?" he *. 1Sa 20:1
Jonathan *. 1Sa 20:9
Saul * when he heard the news. 1Sa 22:7
had done, David *, "I knew it! 1Sa 22:22
"Good!" he *. 1Sa 23:7
they *. 2Sa 4:8
"The Lord did it!" he *. 2Sa 5:20
to meet him and * in disgust, "How 2Sa 6:20
to a dead dog like me?" he *. 2Sa 9:8
"Long live the king!" he *. 2Sa 16:16
David *. 2Sa 19:22
"No, my God," he *, "I cannot 2Sa 23:17
and *, "Oh, thank you, sir. 1Ki 1:31
She * to him, "Everything I 1Ki 10:6
had happened he *, "It is the 1Ki 13:26
Ahab * when he saw him. 1Ki 18:17
Ahab * to Elijah. 1Ki 21:20
the king *. 2Ki 1:8
had happened, they *, "The spirit 2Ki 2:15
they *. 2Ki 3:23
"O man of God," she *, "don't 2Ki 4:15,16
Gehazi *. 2Ki 4:43
troops to seize him," the king *. 2Ki 6:13
Gehazi *. 2Ki 8:5
the watchman *. 2Ki 9:20
or six times," he *, "for then 2Ki 13:19
the secretary and *, "I have 2Ki 22:8
they *. 2Ch 7:3
Finally she * to the king, 2Ch 9:5
their sins and *, "The Lord is 2Ch 12:6
Jehoshaphat *. 2Ch 18:6,7
the king of Israel * to 2Ch 18:17
you, O king Jehoshaphat!" he *. 2Ch 20:15
Jehoiada *. 2Ch 23:2,3
"Look!" he *. 2Ch 28:9
Hilkiah * to Shaphan, the 2Ch 34:15,16
the battle," he * to his aides. 2Ch 35:23
you are doing is very evil," I *. Neh 5:9
the door," he *, "for they are Neh 6:10
And all the other girls * with Est 2:15
he *, "and also Haman's ten sons. Est 9:12
in amazement and * to his advisors, Dan 3:24
This man is saying he is God!" * Mt 9:3
seen anything like this," they *. Mt 9:33
they *. Mt 12:23
" 'An enemy has done it,' he *. Mt 13:28
the people *. Mt 13:55
they *. Mt 14:17
they *. Mt 14:33
"You hypocrites!" he *. Mt 22:18
*, "Surely this was God's Son." Mt 27:54
they all *. Mk 2:12
Peter *. Mk 9:5
day, and *, "Look, Teacher! Mk 11:21
"Master!" he *, and embraced Mk 14:45
his spirit, he *, "Truly, this was Mk 15:39
with grief and * that she had seen Mk 16:10,11
"How kind the Lord is," she *, Lk 1:25
She gave a glad cry and * to Lk 1:42
they *. Lk 1:61
of the Law * among themselves. Lk 5:21
crowd, and they * with praises to Lk 7:16
and finally *, 'I know—I'll tear Lk 12:18
table with Jesus *, "What a Lk 14:15
Those who heard him say this *, Lk 18:26
the king *. Lk 19:17

(EXCLAIMED Con't)
they *. Lk 21:7
they *, "Master, shall we fight? Lk 22:49
"Nazareth!" * Nathanael. Jn 1:46
they *. Jn 2:20
"Born again!" * Nicodemus. Jn 3:4
had happened, they *, "Surely, he Jn 6:14
they *. Jn 6:42
the man *. Jn 9:27
Simon Peter *, "Then wash my Jn 13:9
of spirit and *, "Yes, it is Jn 13:21
Pilate *. Jn 18:38
she *. Jn 20:16
they *. Act 2:7
power too," he *, "so that when I Act 8:19
"Pray for me," Simon *, "that Act 8:24
"But Lord," * Ananias, "I have Act 9:13
they *. Rev 13:4

EXCLAIMING
grave, *, "Alas, my brother!" 1Ki 13:30
the matter by *, "Yes, your 1Ki 20:33
Meanwhile, as they were * over all Lk 9:43
chest in sorrow, *, 'God, be Lk 18:13
and in the sea, *, "The blessing Rev 5:13

EXCLUDE
hate you and * you and insult you Lk 6:22

EXCLUDED
So Miriam was * from the camp for Num 12:15
and who is to be * from it. Eze 44:5
the Jews and * the Gentiles, for he Eph 2:15

EXCLUSIVE
absolute loyalty and * devotion. Ex 34:14

EXCLUSIVELY
You belong * to the Lord your Deu 14:2

EXCOMMUNICATE
I will * him from his people. Lev 17:10
it, then the church should * him. Mt 18:17
would * them from the synagogue; Jn 12:42

EXCOMMUNICATED
shall be * from Israel. Ex 12:15
* from the congregation of Israel. Ex 12:19
who is not a priest shall be *.' Ex 30:33
it for himself shall be *." Ex 30:38
Anyone who does shall be * from Lev 7:26,27
and shall be * from his nation. Lev 17:3,4
to the Lord, shall be *. Lev 17:8,9
anyone who eats blood must be *. Lev 17:14
deeds shall be * from this nation. Lev 18:29,30
shall be * from Jehovah's people. Lev 19:8
both shall be *, for he has Lev 20:18
sin shall be * from his people. Lev 23:29
time, shall be * from the people of Num 9:13
Lord, and shall be * from Israel. Num 19:13
himself shall be *, for he has Num 19:20
be disinherited and * from Israel. Ez 10:7,8
Jesus was the Messiah would be *. Jn 9:22,23
For you will be * from the Jn 16:2

EXCREMENT
with the spade and cover the *. Deu 23:13
own * and drink their own urine!" 2Ki 18:27

EXCUSE
for giving them an * to kill us." Ex 5:21
"A man's poverty is no * for Ex 23:6
He is only trying to get an * to 2Ki 5:7
which was the * he had given them. Est 3:3,4
waiting for an * to accuse them and Ps 37:32
men who use any * to be unfair. Is 29:21
again, and oppressed without *? Is 52:5
But now they have no * for their Jn 15:22
So they will have no * [when they Rom 1:20
Or, "They have no * for saying Rom 1:20f
not one of them has any *; Rom 3:19
those who try to * these sins, for Eph 5:6
that is no * for slowing down; 1Ti 6:2

EXCUSED
to inspect it, and asked to be *. Lk 14:18

EXCUSES
for this sin. * might even be Pro 6:30
The lazy man is full of *. Pro 22:13
But they all began making *. Lk 14:18
accuses them, or sometimes * them. Rom 2:12-15

EXCUSING
Corinth who were * their sins. 1Co 6:12f

EXECUTE
land of Egypt, and * judgment upon Ex 12:12
then all the people are to * him Lev 24:13,14
"* all the tribal leaders of Num 25:4
So Moses ordered the judges to * Num 25:5
his horrible suggestion. * him! Deu 13:9
so that we can * them and purge Ju 20:13
guilty of murder, let him * me." 2Sa 14:32
So King Solomon sent Benaiah to * 1Ki 2:25
Solomon, he sent Benaiah to * him. 1Ki 2:29
Then take him out and * him." 1Ki 21:10
"May God kill me if I don't * 2Ki 6:31
* his punishment upon the nations. Ps 149:6,7
chains, and * their sentences. Ps 149:9
to Nebuchadnezzar to * publicly. Jer 29:21
I will * terrible vengeance upon Eze 25:17
to * all the wise men of Babylon. Dan 2:12
been ordered to * the wise men of Dan 2:24
command to * the family of Ahab. Hos 1:4,5f
them in and * them before me.' Lk 19:27
They found no just cause to * Act 13:28
"For the Lord will * his Rom 9:28

EXECUTED
was *, and impaled on a pole." Gen 41:13
he ordered Moses arrested and *. Ex 2:15
woman and she dies, he shall be *. Ex 21:23
an animal shall certainly be *. Ex 22:19
other god than Jehovah shall be *. Ex 22:20
both shall be *: they have brought Lev 20:12
shall be * and the animal killed. Lev 20:15
"Also, all murderers must be *. Lev 24:17
else touching it shall be *. Num 1:51
assume this office shall be *." Num 3:10
into the Tabernacle, was to be *. Num 3:38
he must be *, Num 15:31
and the murderer must be *. Num 35:16
and the murderer shall be * by Num 35:21
"All murderers must be *, but Num 35:30
you astray must be *, for he has Deu 13:5
he imposes is to be fully *. Deu 17:11
of death, and is * and then hanged Deu 21:22
shall be * for his own crime. Deu 24:16
replied, "No one will be * today; 1Sa 11:13
dead if you are not * for this." 1Sa 14:44
the mediums and fortune-tellers *. 1Sa 28:9
to be * for murdering his brother. 2Sa 14:7
to see Israelites * in revenge." 2Sa 21:4
be arrested and * as criminals as 1Ki 1:21
King David. He * the male 1Ki 15:12
at Bethel. He * the priests of the 2Ki 23:20
him * in the court of the Temple. 2Ch 24:21
In that way God * judgment upon 2Ch 24:24
the new king, he * the men who had 2Ch 25:3
until Phineas * those whose sins Ps 106:30
I was amazed and appalled. So I * Is 63:5
went north have * my judgment and Zec 6:8
were led out to be * with him at a Lk 23:32,33
The night before he was to be *, Act 12:6
they even * the Lord Jesus; 1Th 2:15

EXECUTING
land of Egypt. By * him you will Deu 13:5

EXECUTION
except by the * of the murderer. Num 35:33
"This is not a day for * but for 2Sa 19:22
but lead evil men to *. Ps 125:5
As they were on the way to the * Mt 27:32
taken out to the * grounds and Lk 17:37f
concerning the method of his *. Jn 18:32
the Jews for * after the Passover. Act 12:4

EXECUTIONER
of the palace guard, the chief *. Gen 37:36
king's bodyguard and his chief *. Gen 39:1
of the guard, who was the chief *. Gen 40:1
It is ready now to hand to the *. Eze 21:9,10,11
But when Ari-och, the chief *, Dan 2:14

EXECUTIONERS
his people and has chosen their *. Zep 1:7
The official witnesses—the *—took Act 7:58

EXECUTIONS
unit handling the * saw what had Lk 23:47

EXECUTIVE
Mikloth was his * officer. 1Ch 27:4

EXEMPT
said to Moses, "* the entire tribe Num 1:47,48,49

EXEMPTED
Levites, who were * by Jehovah's Num 2:32,33
will be * from paying taxes!" 1Sa 17:25

EXERCISE
to the youth of Israel to * faith Ju 3:1
the * of keeping spiritually fit. 1Ti 4:7
Bodily * is all right, but 1Ti 4:8
but spiritual * is much more 1Ti 4:8
for all you do. So * yourself 1Ti 4:8

EXERCISED
the Dragon's. He * all the Rev 13:12

EXHAUST
aren't satisfied to * my patience; Is 7:13
you * the Lord's as well! Is 7:13

EXHAUSTED
Esau arrived home * from the hunt. Gen 25:29
the men were too * to cross, but 1Sa 30:9,10
who had been too * to go on, David 1Sa 30:21
battle, David became weak and *. 2Sa 21:15
I am * and crushed; Ps 38:8
Lord, don't hit me anymore—I am * Ps 39:10
I have wept until I am *; Ps 69:3
in the smoke, * with waiting. Ps 119:83
chronic rebellion was finally *. Is 6:10f
will run until *, fleeing back to Is 13:14
Even the youths shall be *, and Is 40:30
Tell me why your patience is *! Mic 6:3
to find them asleep, * from grief. Lk 22:45

EXHAUSTING
go on forever, and become very *! Ecc 12:12

EXHAUSTION
mobs, worked to *, stayed awake 2Co 6:5

EXHIBITS
He made permanent * in the 1Ki 15:15
This honors the Lord, and * his Ps 92:15

EXILE
"He will * you and the king you Deu 28:36
and while in * you shall worship Deu 28:36
to bring your son back from his *. 2Sa 14:14
guest in Israel, a foreigner in *. 2Sa 15:19,20
army during their * in Mahanaim, 2Sa 19:31,32
Hagrites until the time of the *. 1Ch 5:22
Jehozadak (who went into * when 1Ch 6:4-15
if in that land of * they turn to 2Ch 6:37,38
won't ever again * Israel from this 2Ch 33:8
and * the people to Babylonia.' Ez 5:12
to return to Jerusalem from our *. Ez 9:8
our punishment in * because of our Ez 9:13
to Jerusalem from their * here?" Neh 1:2
have returned from * as slaves in Neh 5:8
Therefore I will send you into * Is 5:13
The generations born in * shall Is 49:20
into *, leaving me here alone. Is 49:21
I sold you into * I asked no fee Is 52:3
behind during the *, and rule the Is 54:3
on you as I have during this *. Is 54:9
from their * in the north, to the Jer 3:18
And I will send you into *, just Jer 7:15
will be shamed by * for this sin, Jer 8:9
ruler before the * of 597 B.C. Jer 21:1f
and your children from their *. Jer 30:10
As you travel into *, set up road Jer 31:21
get ready to leave for *, you Jer 46:19
shall have the pouring out of *! Jer 48:11
and * to Babylon along with Jer 51:59
So it was that Judah's * was Jer 52:27
Now she sits in * far away. Lam 1:3
Israel's * for her sins will end Lam 4:22
to your people in *, and whether or Eze 3:11
Gentile lands to which I * them!" Eze 4:13
will strike down those in *; Eze 6:12
Babylon, to the Jews in * there. Eze 11:24
I could take into *—and in the Eze 12:7
their homes and sent away into *. Eze 12:11
the countries where they are in *. Eze 20:38
you back from *, and the nations Eze 20:41
I will * the Egyptians to other Eze 29:12
year of our *, late in December, Eze 33:21
delivering you from * among them. Eze 36:23
the years of * lay empty as a Eze 36:34
your graves of * and cause you to Eze 37:12
was sent away to *—it was Eze 39:23
them away to *, and responsible for Eze 39:28
year of our *—the fourteenth year Eze 40:1
they will return from * together; Hos 1:11
lands, I will send her off to *. Hos 8:10
Her people will return from * Hos 14:7
For she sent my people into *, Amo 1:6
princes will go into * together." Amo 1:15
be carried off to *, and those of Amo 5:5
far away into * and slavery." Amo 7:11
slaves in *, far from their land.' Amo 7:17
Though they volunteer for *, I Amo 9:4
will lead you out of * and bring Mic 2:13
you will be sent far away into * Mic 4:10
then at last the * remnants of Mic 5:3
later, the deportation and *. Zep 1:1f
seventy years of * when you fasted Zec 7:5
at the time of the * to Babylon). Mt 1:11
After the *: Mt 1:12
from King David's time to the *; Mt 1:17
and fourteen from the * to Mt 1:17

EXILED
who was * from his brothers. Gen 49:26
of Israel were * to Assyria. 2Ki 17:6
that one of the * priests from 2Ki 17:27,28
So Judah was * from its land. 2Ki 25:21
in the land and would not be *. 2Ki 25:24
captured in war and * to Manahath. 1Ch 8:6,7
Judah was * to Babylon because the 1Ch 9:1
though you are * to the farthest Neh 1:9
Judah after being * by King Neh 7:6
and had been * to Babylon along Est 2:6
He and his children will be * to Jer 22:28
to which he had * them." Jer 23:8
king of Judah, and * him to Babylon Jer 24:1
Babylon, when he * all the Jer 27:19,20,21
* to Babylon, says the Lord. Jer 28:4
has * to Babylon from Jerusalem: Jer 29:4
who were not * to Babylon, and on Jer 29:16,17
you and you shall be * to Babylon. Jer 34:3
along with all the * people of Jer 40:1
and had not * everyone to Babylon, Jer 40:7
* you, but I will not destroy you. Jer 46:28
Milcom shall be * along with his Jer 49:3
they shall be * to countries Jer 49:36
Then when they are * among the Eze 6:9
them what being * will be like. Eze 12:3
broad river and he * the top men of Eze 17:12,13
And I * them to many lands; Eze 36:19
Those * in Asia Minor shall Ob 1:20
gold from the Jews * in Babylon. Zec 6:10,11
I was on the island of Patmos, * Rev 1:9

EXILES
that they will not be forever *." 2Sa 14:14f
were all taken as * to Babylon. 2Ki 25:11

(EXILES Con't)
And all the Jewish * Ez 1:6
of the * returning to Judah. Ez 1:8
HERE IS THE list of the Jewish * Ez 2:1
heard that the * had returned and Ez 4:1
of the sin of the returned *. Ez 10:6
away to distant lands as *. Ps 106:27
He brought the * back from the Ps 107:3
JEHOVAH BROUGHT back his * to Ps 126:1
Jerusalem and bringing back the *. Ps 147:2
represent the * sent to Babylon. Jer 24:4,5
Send an open letter to all the * Jer 29:31
you over all the world as *. Jer 34:17
shall help your * as they flee. Jer 49:5
with the Jewish * beside the Chebar Eze 1:1
Jewish * beside the Chebar River. Eze 3:14,15
about your brother *: 'It is Eze 11:15
"But tell the * that the Lord Eze 11:16
And I told the * everything the Eze 11:25
to join you as * in Babylon, you Eze 14:22
The Israeli * shall return and Ob 1:20
I will give glory to my former *, Zep 3:19
Note: They were among the * who Hag 1:1f
says the Lord to all his * there; Zec 2:6,7
or sent away as * and captives to Lk 21:24

EXILING
but a little, * her far from her Is 27:7,8

EXIST
How do you know it didn't * long Ecc 1:8-11
am the God' of those who don't *! Mk 12:27
gods that did not even *. Gal 4:8
will ever again * there, and there Rev 18:22

EXISTED
From ages past, I am. I * before Pro 8:23
BEFORE ANYTHING ELSE *, Jn 1:1
I am—for he * long before I did!' Jn 1:15
is coming, who * long before me!' Jn 1:30
* before God made anything at all, Col 1:15

EXISTENCE
dry land. All * on the earth was Gen 7:23
And vow by my *, Deu 32:40,41
who would end our * in Israel. 2Sa 14:15,16
have been spared this miserable *. Job 10:19
"All memory of his * will perish Job 18:17
destroy the very memory of her *. Ps 83:4
even knowing its *, yet that is Ecc 6:5
is the end of *, that there is no Lk 20:27
* before Abraham was ever born!" Jn 8:58
of his * and great eternal power. Rom 1:20

EXISTS
God of Israel, who * from Ps 41:13
is—nothing * that he didn't make. Jn 1:3

EXIT
Then Joseph made a hasty *, Gen 43:30
The windows were also in the * Eze 40:16
and entrance and * hall were Eze 40:29,30

EXITS
width and the same * and doors—they Eze 42:11

EXODUS
and herds—a vast * of cattle. Ex 12:38
Mark this day of your *, at the Ex 13:4,5
grandfather of Bezalel (* 31:1,2). Ex 17:10f
See * 3:14. Ex 33:19f
Implied. See * 34:1, Deuteronomy Ex 34:28f
daughter of Reuel (* 2:21); Num 12:1f
name is used here as in * 3:14. Ju 6:16f
the will of God. See * 28:30. 1Sa 28:5,6f
See * 12:22, Hebrews 9:18-22. Ps 51:7f
* 17:7. Ps 95:8f
* from Kir and now were free. Amo 1:5f
of debtors overnight. See * 22:26. Amo 2:8f
The price of a slave. See * 21:32 Zec 11:12f
in the book of * about Moses and Mk 12:26

EXPANDING
birth rate and the * economy, Is 29:23

EXPECT
now, and * to die 'most any day. Gen 27:2,3,4
how can I * Pharaoh to? Ex 6:12
"Do you * me to believe that?" Ju 11:9
I and all my relatives could * 2Sa 19:28
"Why should I * any help from 2Ki 6:33
saying this—in fact, I * him to. Job 13:15
bodyguards, for I * you to protect Ps 25:21
Don't be upset. * God to act! Ps 42:11
They * to get away with it. Ps 56:7
but I * your help, for you have Ps 119:81
who * him to be loving and kind. Ps 147:11
so how can the wicked * a long, Pro 10:27
while the wicked can * only wrath. Pro 11:23
will * you to treat him as a son! Pro 29:21
fear God you can * his blessing. Ecc 7:18
yourselves. You * others to respect Is 33:1
Then I said, "But what can we * Jer 5:4
them, but don't * them to listen. Jer 7:27
but don't * them to respond. Jer 7:27
And yet you * him to fulfill your Eze 13:6
"Israel will no longer * any Eze 29:16
certainly can't * me to believe Dan 2:8,9
Do you really * him to listen? Mic 3:4
what did you * him to be like? Mt 11:7
miracles do you * the Messiah to do Jn 7:31
you * me to become a Christian?" Act 26:28
we really wouldn't * anyone to die Rom 5:7
* some share of the harvest. 1Co 9:10
in him, always * the best of him, 1Co 13:7
yes, and we * him to do it again 2Co 1:10
Shall we not * far greater glory 2Co 3:8
that you really * him to tell you, Jas 1:6
with faith, don't * the Lord to Jas 1:7,8

EXPECTANT
Woe to * mothers in those days, Lk 21:23

EXPECTANTLY
No wonder I wait * for each of Ps 119:131
That is why I wait *, trusting Ps 130:5
will look forward * to the time Rom 15:4

EXPECTATION
For I live in eager * and hope Php 1:20

EXPECTATIONS
*, and how the mountains quaked! Is 64:3

EXPECTED
forces * from Bethel (verse 17). Jos 8:11,12,13f
everyone * me to be the next king. 1Ki 2:15
and talk to me! I * him to wave his 2Ki 5:11
me is death. I * my fall to be Job 30:24
not at all the sweet ones he *. Is 5:2
acreage! He * them to yield a crop Is 5:7
instead. He * righteousness, but Is 5:7
are in darkness when you * light. Is 59:9
We * peace, but no peace came; Jer 8:15
The nation we * most to help us Lam 4:17
Before, when you * a Hag 2:16,17
will come when least *." Lk 12:40

EXPECTING
I am * the Lord to rescue me Ps 27:13
I will keep on * you to help me. Ps 71:14
But if he sins, * his past Eze 33:13
be * much from him, your God. Hos 12:6
Or were you * to see a man Mt 11:8
was eagerly * the arrival of God's Mk 15:42,43
and constantly * the Messiah Lk 2:25
Everyone was * the Messiah to Lk 3:15
"or are you * us to go and buy Lk 9:13
was a godly man who had been * Lk 23:50,51,52
is the Prophet we have been *!" Jn 6:14
looked at them eagerly, * a gift. Act 3:5
They are out there now, * you to Act 23:21
time we've been *, when his glory Tit 2:13

EXPEDITION
they are on an *, and since they 1Sa 21:5

EXPEL
that they must * all lepers from Num 5:1
I will never again * them from this 2Ki 21:8

EXPELLED
Thus God * him, and placed Gen 3:24
immediately * from the assembly. Neh 13:3
to obey me will be * again and Jer 12:17
They had been * from Italy as a Act 18:2,3

EXPELLING
land, and * them from their homes. Eze 45:9

EXPEND
So at last I will * my fury on Eze 6:12

EXPENDITURES
their *, for they were honest men. 2Ki 22:7

EXPENSE
his wealth is at our father's *." Gen 31:1
me wealthy at your father's *. Gen 31:9
be very gracious to him [at your * Ex 22:27
*, they shall know I am the Lord. Eze 34:27
You made yourselves rich at his * Ob 1:13
Or, "at his own *." Act 28:30f
Good News without * to anyone, 1Co 9:18
time of it at your *, but you 2Co 8:13

EXPENSES
healed, and pay any medical *. Ex 21:19
the operating * of the Temple. 1Ch 26:27
toward the * of those who do, and Ez 1:4
All * will be paid by the king. Ez 6:4
the * involved in this purge." Est 3:9
in the army has to pay his own *? 1Co 9:7
on so that our * would not be a 1Th 2:9

EXPENSIVE
of stone—a very * job—for the 1Ki 5:17
huge, * stones, cut to measure. 1Ki 7:9
He gave him two * robes, tied up 2Ki 5:23
on the road! And * cedar lumber was 2Ch 1:15
valuable than the most * perfume. Ecc 7:1
The man too poor to buy * gods Is 40:20
Keep your * perfumes! Jer 6:20
brings * saddlecloths for riding. Eze 27:20
a bottle of very * perfume, and Mt 26:7
a beautiful flask of * perfume. Mk 14:3
Did you find him dressed in * Lk 7:25
flask filled with * perfume. Lk 7:37
he brings out the less * brands. Jn 2:10
wood and clay. The * dishes are 2Ti 2:20
church dressed in * clothes and Jas 2:2
goods and most * wooden carvings, Rev 18:12

EXPERIENCE
known from past * to gore, and its Ex 21:36
remember your own * in the land Ex 23:9
who was punished? * teaches that it Job 4:7,8
I have found from * that all of Job 5:27
teach you. The * of others will Job 8:10
you from my own *, confirmed by the Job 15:17-19
confirmed by the * of wise men who Job 15:17-19
You have let me * the joys of Ps 16:11
your own way, and * the full Pro 1:31
of old men, their *. Pro 20:29
don't despise an old mother's *. Pro 23:22
so that I could * the only Ecc 2:3
That is the * of everyone who has Is 36:6
he wrote this poem about his *: Is 38:9
you won't * any peace, either. Is 59:8
to describe an * very much like, if Jer 31:33f
Never again will my people * Joe 2:26
My similar * will prove that God Lk 11:29,30
having to * these horrors." Lk 21:36
world about this * and about the Act 26:16
from your own * how his ways will Rom 12:2
from our personal * how God will 2Co 1:6,7
from * to be an earnest Christian. 2Co 8:22
That * is something worth 2Co 12:5
Abraham had the same *—God Gal 3:6
and to * this love for Eph 3:18,19
know Christ and to * the mighty Php 3:10
If you do this you will * God's Php 4:7
will have the rich * of knowing Col 2:2
had to learn from * what it was Heb 5:8
perfect in this * that Jesus became Heb 5:9
I will not * sorrow.' Rev 18:7

EXPERIENCED
who are wise, *, and understanding, Deu 1:13
who have never * the Lord's Deu 11:2
who had not * the wars of Canaan. Ju 3:1
thousand men, all * swordsmen. Ju 20:25
King Hiram supplied * sailors to 1Ki 9:27,28
These ships, with King Hiram's * 2Ch 8:17,18
100,000 * mercenaries from Israel. 2Ch 25:5,6
created, and you are so very *! Job 38:21
Literally, "when I learn (have *) Ps 119:7f
swordsmen and * bodyguards. Sol 3:8
and because of what he has *, my Is 53:11
The most * harlot could learn a Jer 2:33
land has * God's blessing upon it. Heb 6:7
them, having never * its power. 1Pe 2:15

EXPERIENCES
of Jonah, whose * proved to the Lk 11:29,30
What were his * concerning this Rom 4:1
I will say this: because these * 2Co 12:7
from his * we can see how the Jas 5:11

EXPERIMENT
demons planned to * by using the Act 19:13

EXPERT
of Paran, and became an * archer. Gen 21:20,21
and also an * at engraving, Ex 38:23
were * marksmen with their bows. 1Ch 8:40
All of them were * archers and 1Ch 12:2
They are * gold and silver 1Ch 22:16
and he is an * in the dying of 2Ch 2:14
ears to the most * of charmers. Ps 58:4,5
purple robes that * tailors make. Jer 10:9
One day an * on Moses' laws came Lk 10:25
"Sir," said an * in religious Lk 11:45
named Gamaliel (an * on religious Act 5:34
an * on Jewish laws and customs. Act 26:3
taught me how to be an * builder. 1Co 3:10

EXPERTS
who are known as *, so that they Ex 31:6
They were * with both shield and 1Ch 12:8-13
Let those who are * at cursing Job 3:8
Then he added, "Those * in Mt 13:52
"Woe to you * in religion! Lk 11:52
The Pharisees and legal * were Lk 11:53,54
and legal * standing around, Lk 14:3
leaders and the * on Jewish law Lk 15:2
remarked some of the * in the Lk 20:39
"Beware of these * in religion, Lk 20:46

EXPIRED
So, before the time limit *, he 1Sa 18:26
This interval had now almost *. Dan 9:2f

EXPLAIN
each year you must * to your Ex 13:8
city council and * what happened, Jos 20:4
which he could not * to her." 1Ki 10:3f
he could * everything to her. 2Ch 9:2
And tomorrow I will * what this Est 5:7,8
Yet it is so hard to * it—this Ps 73:16
is the Lord's messenger to * it? Jer 9:12
people of Israel. * that what you Eze 12:11
have done, then * to them the Eze 43:11
He can interpret dreams, * Dan 5:12
I will * mysteries hidden since Mt 13:34,35
His disciples asked him to * to Mt 13:36
Then Peter asked Jesus to * what Mt 15:15
he would * his meaning to them. Mk 4:34
he will * everything to us." Jn 4:25
(I should * that all the Act 17:21
to * the Holy Spirit's facts. 1Co 2:13
I say this to * to you how I Eph 3:4
and to * to everyone that God is Eph 3:9
the Lord, and as I * to them that Eph 6:19
If you * this to the others you 1Ti 4:6
Until I get there, read and * 1Ti 4:13

XPLAIN Con't)
we must * all that we have done. Heb 4:13
heaven to * the vision's meaning. Rev 1:1

XPLAINED
"I am Abraham's servant," he *. Gen 24:34
crying! He * about being her Gen 29:12,13
Rachel *, "but I'm pregnant." Gen 31:35
and Aaron and * their problem and Num 9:6,7
toward me," he frantically *. Num 22:5,6
* to him what Balak wanted. Num 22:7
they *. Num 32:16
"They are spies," he *. Jos 2:3
Their duties are * in chapter 4, Jos 3:12f
Then Joshua * again the purpose Jos 4:21
"This is the plan," he * to Jos 8:5
for, as he had * to them, the Lord Jos 13:33
Then he * his plan. Ju 7:17
hated her," he *, "so I married Ju 15:2
out of the land of Egypt," he *. 1Sa 15:6
David *. 1Sa 21:8
garden," the king *, "because 1Ki 21:2
so spread out," I * to them, "and Neh 4:19
and * the meaning of the passage Neh 8:7,8
God's people, as * by the parallel Is 4:2,3,4f
So Baruch * that Jeremiah had Jer 36:18
these things, and he * them to me. Dan 7:16
Then he * to them that only they Mt 13:11
What was in Peter's mind is not *. Mt 17:4f
Then Jesus * his meaning: "Surely Mt 21:31
with them and * the Scriptures Lk 24:32
Then Jesus *: "My nourishment Jn 4:34
he meant, so he * it to them. Jn 10:7
In another Psalm he * more Act 13:35
met with him and * what had Act 18:25,26
Literally, "* to him the way of Act 18:25,26f
tales when we * to you the power of 2Pe 1:16

XPLAINING
from the Lord, * why he was holding Jer 14:1
the Scriptures, * what the passages Lk 24:27
to the people, * the prophecies Act 17:3
So the officer did, *, "Paul, Act 23:18
blessings by * God's secrets. 1Co 4:1

EXPLAINS
This * why a man leaves his Gen 2:24

EXPLANATION
The other * of this confusing 1Sa 17:55f
"Now here is the * of the story Mt 13:18
it, the owners demanded an *. Lk 19:33
And if Rome demands an *, I won't Act 19:40
But some readers may prefer the * Heb 5:7f

EXPLODE
to * his wrath upon his enemies. Jer 50:25

EXPLODED
Peter *. Mk 14:31

EXPLOIT
have just begun to * their Gen 11:6
"You must not * widows or Ex 22:22

EXPLOITED
will defend the poor and the *. Is 11:4

EXPLOITING
Income from * the poor will end Pro 28:8
* orphans, widows and foreigners. Jer 7:6

EXPLORE
Hike in all directions and * the Gen 13:17

EXPLORED
searched and its deep secrets *. Job 28:3,4
"Have you * the springs from Job 38:16
THIS, TOO, I carefully *—that Ecc 9:1
of the earth *, will I consider Jer 31:37
had discovered and * for them—a Eze 20:5,6

EXPLORING
become leaders by * the depths of Pro 1:5,6

EXPLOSION
NOW A POPULATION * took place Gen 6:1
This was the beginning of an * of Gen 11:6f
veritable population * among them. Gen 47:27
population * so that they soon Ex 1:7
a population * for his people. 1Ch 27:23
You caused a population * among Neh 9:23

EXPLOSIVELY
Israel multiplied *, until they Ps 105:24

EXPORTS
from the * of his merchants. 2Ch 9:13,14

EXPOSE
at the middle to * their buttocks; 1Ch 19:4
He will * their nakedness for all Is 3:17
strip off your robe; * yourself Is 47:2
I myself will * you to utter Jer 13:26
I will * you to the war you have Eze 11:8
Now I will * her nakedness in Hos 1:10
but instead, rebuke and * them. Eph 5:11
But when you * them, the light Eph 5:13

EXPOSED
looked today! He * himself to the 2Sa 6:20
had * and frustrated their plan. Neh 4:15
how Mordecai had * the plot of Est 6:1
The bodies of your people lie * Ps 79:2
lies are soon *. Pro 12:19
evil men will be *, as will all the Is 32:7
has been * to all the world, and Eze 16:57
shall be * to all the world. Eze 23:29
to the ground and * you helpless Eze 28:17
Now your sins will be * for all Ob 1:10
birds came and ate it as it lay *. Lk 8:5
be * and they would be punished. Jn 3:20
And since Fair Havens was an * Act 27:12
the stern was * to the violence of Act 27:41
bodies will be * in the streets of Rev 11:8,9

EXPOSING
is the Lord's searchlight * his Pro 20:27
and her forts, * their foundations, Mic 1:6
* us for what we really are. Heb 4:12

EXPOSITORS
Some * (Origen, Jerome, etc. Rev 1:20f

EXPOSURE
only a northwest and southwest *. Act 27:12

EXPRESS
gods, violating his * command. Deu 29:26
Now then, sons of Israel, * your Ju 20:7
So David sent ambassadors to * 2Sa 10:2
were sent for the * purpose of 1Ch 12:24-37
Ah, let me * my anguish. Job 7:11
me awhile and let me * my opinion. Job 32:10
I WANT to * publicly before his Ps 111:1
Literally, "* his opinion." Pro 18:2f
A wise man's words * deep streams Pro 18:4
and who can * the wickedness of Act 8:33
for women to * their opinions in 1Co 14:35
As the Scriptures * it, "See, I 1Pe 2:6

EXPRESSED
and * interest in his problem. 2Sa 15:2
assembly, David * his praises to 1Ch 29:10
no end of opinions ready to be *. Ecc 12:12
the meaning * in the paraphrase. Dan 8:26f
shepherds' story * astonishment, Lk 2:18
that it cannot be * in words. Rom 8:26

EXPRESSING
* grief for their parents' death. Jer 16:7
are, our lives * the evil within Eph 2:3

EXPRESSION
believe that the * "sons of God" Gen 6:1f
This was a common * of grief in 1Sa 4:12f
This was an * of surprise 1Sa 10:12f
trust in him are blessed beyond *. Ps 112:1
the only true * of David, the man Jer 33:15f
in the Hebrew * used here. Jer 36:30f
Aramaic * is used for the Messiah Eze 2:1f
latter days," an * which does not, Eze 38:15,16f
a noble, pious * in public, but God Lk 16:15
God's personal * of himself to Jn 1:1f
God's personal * of himself to Jn 1:14f
As used here the * therefore Rev 1:5f

EXPRESSLY
which the Lord had * forbidden, Ju 2:11
* prohibited in verses 8 and 9. 1Co 6:12f

EXQUISITE
and also does * work with brass and 2Ch 2:14
of life and the * pleasures of your Ps 16:11
and brought an * flask filled with Lk 7:37

EXTEND
Their pasturelands shall * Num 35:4
* congratulations and good wishes. 1Ki 5:1
be rich, or to * his possessions. Job 15:29

EXTENDED
From there he * his reign to Gen 10:11,12
The Israeli territory now * all Jos 11:17
His kingdom * from Aroer, on the Jos 12:2
* as far as the borders of Ammon. Jos 13:10
Their land * from Aroer on the Jos 13:16
It also * from Heshbon to Jos 13:26
Their territory * north from Jos 13:30
The eastern boundary * along the Jos 15:5
From there the border * to the Jos 15:7
From there the border * from the Jos 15:9
From Ekron the boundary * to the Jos 15:46
This boundary * from the Jordan Jos 16:1
tribe of Manasseh * southward from Jos 17:7
in Zaanannim, and * across to Jos 19:33
His dominion * over all the 1Ki 4:24
City of David. He * the city out 1Ch 11:8
You have * your boundaries out Eze 27:4
pavement." It * out from the walls Eze 40:18
Its walls * up on either side to Eze 40:48,49
* out 10½ feet onto the terrace. Eze 41:8
But a wall * from the end of the Eze 42:7,8
So Jesus launched into an * Mk 13:5

EXTENDING
with his borders * to Sidon. Gen 49:13
received the area * from the Jabbok Deu 3:16
and across there, Judah, * to the Deu 34:2
and on the west, * to the boundary Jos 12:5
* as far as the Lake of Galilee; Jos 13:27,28
of the wall * from a point opposite Neh 3:21
tiers of rooms, * the entire Eze 42:4
of this area, * clear out to the Eze 48:21,22
of Simeon, also * out to these same Eze 48:24
Then comes Zebulun, also * all Eze 48:26

EXTENDS
Your faithfulness * to every Ps 119:90,91
For though his power * to Zoan Is 30:4
its edge, and it * twenty-one Eze 43:13
The entire platform * out from Eze 43:17
Benjamin's section * across the Eze 48:23

EXTENSIVE
program was also *, and he had a 2Ch 17:13
and also did * rebuilding of the 2Ch 27:3
large city, with * suburbs—so large Jon 3:3

EXTENT
When the Lord God saw the * of Gen 6:5
will realize the * of your 1Sa 12:17
Do you realize the * of the Job 38:17,18
to see the * of ruin in your land. Eze 36:34
So, to the fullest * of my Rom 1:15
all could see the * of their Rom 5:20
me, as you already are to some *; 2Co 1:13,14
forgiven (to the * that this 2Co 2:10

EXTERMINATE
for even a moment, I would * you. Ex 33:5
the tribe of Judah * the people of Ju 1:19
The tribe of Benjamin failed to * Ju 1:21
But Jehu's plan was to * them. 2Ki 10:18,19
I scatter you, I will not * you; Jer 30:11

EXTERMINATED
Josiah also * the mediums and 2Ki 23:24

EXTERMINATION
by Haman for the * of the Jews. Est 8:12f

EXTERNAL
There were * wars, and internal 2Ch 15:6

EXTINGUISH
the darkness can never * it. Jn 1:5

EXTOL
"Fear God," he shouted, "and * Rev 14:7

EXTORT
they seize treasures and * Eze 22:25
needy and cruelly * from aliens. Eze 22:29
John replied, "Don't * money by Lk 3:14

EXTORTED
Menahem * the money from the 2Ki 15:19,20
* from the helpless peasants. Is 3:14

EXTORTION
Don't become rich by * and Ps 62:10,11
wealthy through * and violence; Mic 6:12
for your oppression and *!' Hab 2:6
inside is foul with * and greed. Mt 23:25

EXTORTIONERS
racketeers and * are everywhere. Eze 22:12

EXTRA
broken nose or any * fingers or Lev 21:18
there shall be an * burnt offering Num 28:11
also sacrifice an * sin offering Num 29:34
a servant and an * donkey, went to Ju 19:3
there were * sacrifices on the 2Ch 8:13
what he owes with some * besides. Ps 37:21
Unless you have the * cash on Pro 22:26,27
"A little * sleep, Pro 24:32,33
"You have some * clothing, so you Is 3:6
I have no * food or clothes. Is 3:7
Whenever the prince offers an * Eze 46:12
proper forms and give * offerings. Amo 4:5
a duffle bag with * clothes and Mt 10:10
money, not even an * pair of shoes Mk 6:8,9
For they gave a little of their * Mk 12:43,44
If you have * food, give it away Lk 3:11
Not even an * coat. Lk 9:3
bag, or even an * pair of shoes. Lk 10:4
duffle bag, or * clothing, how did Lk 22:35
However, marriage will bring * 1Co 7:28
in such a way that * honor and care 1Co 12:24

EXTRACT
struggle to * a living from it. Gen 3:17

EXTRAVAGANCE
Showing wealth and *. Gen 49:11f

EXTREME
There, at the * west end of these Eze 46:19,20

EXULT
No wonder I *! Ps 60:6,7
All who trust in him *, while Ps 63:11
But may the godly man *. Ps 68:3
be allowed to triumph and *? Ps 94:3
no wonder I *! Ps 108:7
O people of Jerusalem, * in your Ps 149:2
evil paths, and * in doing wrong, Pro 2:14
shall * in the Holy One of Israel. Is 29:19
let no other nation * with pride Eze 31:14

EXULTATION
Those who rule them shout in *, Is 52:5

EXULTED
wiped them out. He *, "God has 1Ch 14:11
they *. Lk 19:38

EXULTING
No, it is the Lord himself * over Zep 3:17,18

EXULTS
How he * in your salvation. Ps 21:1

EYE
"If her * is injured, injure Ex 21:24
his slave in the *, whether man or Ex 21:26
or woman, and the * is blinded, Ex 21:26
shall go free because of his *. Ex 21:26
a defect in his *, or has pimples Lev 21:20
* for eye, tooth for tooth. Lev 24:20
eye for *, tooth for tooth. Lev 24:20
Life for life, * for eye, tooth Deu 19:21
Life for life, eye for *, tooth Deu 19:21

(EYE Con't)
they were the apple of his *. Deu 32:10
out the right * of every one of you 1Sa 11:2
more than ever in the public *. 1Sa 18:13
see, no eagle's * observe— for Job 28:7
as you would the pupil of your *; Ps 17:8
Literally, "wink with the *." Ps 35:19f
He keeps his * upon you as you Ps 121:8
* on both the evil and the good. Pro 15:3
shall have his * plucked out by Pro 30:17
sticks his finger in Jehovah's *! Zec 2:8
and pierce through his right *; Zec 11:17
useless and his right * blinded." Zec 11:17
with lust in his * has already Mt 5:28
So if your *—even if it is your Mt 5:29
Literally, "your right *." Mt 5:29f
* causes you to lust Mt 5:29
*, he must pay with his own eye. Mt 5:38
eye, he must pay with his own *. Mt 5:38
Literally, "an * for an eye and a Mt 5:38f
Literally, "an eye for an * and a Mt 5:38f
"If your * is pure, there will Mt 6:22
But if your * is clouded with Mt 6:23
a speck in the * of a brother when Mt 7:3
speck out of your *,' when you Mt 7:4
And if your * causes you to sin, Mt 18:9
Better to enter heaven with one * Mt 18:9
to go through the * of a needle Mt 19:24
"And if your * is sinful, gouge Mk 9:47
to go through the * of a needle Mk 10:25
someone else's *—his little fault Lk 6:41
that speck in your *,' when you Lk 6:42
A pure * lets sunshine into your Lk 11:34
A lustful * shuts out the light Lk 11:34
to go through the * of a needle Lk 18:25
staying out of the public *. Jn 7:10
I am only an ear, and not an *"? 1Co 12:16
Suppose the whole body were an * 1Co 12:17
The * can never say to the hand, 1Co 12:21
*, when the last trumpet is blown. 1Co 15:52
power, with God's * upon us. 2Co 2:17
and every * shall see him—yes, Rev 1:7

EYE-TO-EYE
will see * with me on these things, Php 3:15

EYEBROWS
head, beard, and *, and wash his Lev 14:9

EYELIDS
she painted her * and fixed her 2Ki 9:30
on my * is the shadow of death. Job 16:16
painted your *, and put on your Eze 23:40

EYES
will open your * to make you aware Gen 2:16,17
like him, for your * will be Gen 3:5
Then God opened her * and she saw Gen 21:19
Leah had lovely *, but Rachel Gen 29:17
wife began making * at Joseph, and Gen 39:7
and had him bound before their *. Gen 42:24
His * are darker than wine and Gen 49:12
before their *, they will kill us. Ex 8:26
before Pharaoh's *, the Lord Ex 11:10
Lord's * from all of your sins. Lev 16:29,30
fever; your * shall be consumed and Lev 26:16
and you will serve as * for us." Num 10:31f
and did not sanctify me in the * Num 20:12
Then the Lord opened Balaam's * Num 22:31
The man whose * are open says, Num 24:3-9
I fell, and my * were opened: Num 24:3-9
Whose * are open! Num 24:15-19
He fell, and his * were opened: Num 24:15-19
right before the * of Moses and all Num 25:6
your * and thorns in your sides. Num 33:55
Egypt, right before your very *. Deu 4:34
is right and good in the Lord's *. Deu 6:18
We saw it all with our own *. Deu 6:22
it with their own *—and the mighty Deu 7:19
I smashed them before your *! Deu 9:17
cares for! His * are always upon Deu 11:12
to your forehead between your *! Deu 11:18
If you do what is right in the * Deu 12:28
is right in the * of the Lord. Deu 13:18
For bribes blind the * of the Deu 16:19
blood, neither have our * seen it. Deu 21:7
brother be degraded in your *. Deu 25:1
before your *, but you won't get a Deu 28:31
"You have seen with your own * Deu 29:2,3
or * that see or ears that hear! Deu 29:4
The Lord made him great in the * Jos 4:14
right before our *, and then kept Jos 4:23
a thorn in your *, and you will Jos 23:13
before the * of Israel, as we Jos 24:17
and gouged out his * and took him Ju 16:21
loss of at least one of my *." Ju 16:28
seemed right in his own *. Ju 17:6
very great in the * of the Lord; 1Sa 2:17
ruddy-faced, and with pleasant *. 1Sa 16:12
May your * be open and your ears 1Ki 8:52
over his * to disguise himself. 1Ki 20:38
bandage from his *, and the king 1Ki 20:41
mouth, and his * upon the child's 2Ki 4:34
upon the child's *, and his hands 2Ki 4:34
seven times and opened his *! 2Ki 4:35
open his * and let him see!" 2Ki 6:17
the young man's * so that he could 2Ki 6:17
open their * and let them see." 2Ki 6:20
Open your *, O Lord, and see. 2Ki 19:16
his sons were killed before his *; 2Ki 25:7
then his * were put out and he 2Ki 25:7
home forever; my * and my heart 2Ch 7:16
got here and saw it with my own *. 2Ch 9:6
For the * of the Lord search 2Ch 16:9
in the palace, before my very *?" Est 7:8
man be truly good in the * of God? Job 9:2
God blinds the * of the judges Job 9:24
Literally, "Have you the * of Job 10:4-7f
You claim you are pure in the * Job 11:4
by your anger, with flashing *? Job 15:12
in the dust. My * are red with Job 16:16
they spit in my face. My * are Job 17:7
For it is hid from the * of all Job 28:21
I served as * for the blind and Job 29:15
"I MADE A covenant with my * not Job 31:1
lusted for what my * have seen, or Job 31:7,8
evil men from his *, so there is Job 34:22
droplets. His * glow like sparks. Job 41:18
declared me perfect in your *; Ps 4:1
with tears. My * are growing old Ps 6:7
me with murder in their *. Ps 17:9
Look at me instead through * of Ps 25:6,7
through * of everlasting love and Ps 25:6,7
My * are ever looking to the Lord Ps 25:15
My * are red from weeping; Ps 31:9,10
But the * of the Lord are Ps 33:18,19
For the * of the Lord are Ps 34:15
"With our own * we saw him do Ps 35:21
my throat is dry and hoarse; my * Ps 69:3
out. My * grow dim with weeping. Ps 88:9
and blind—he who makes ears and *? Ps 94:9
see, despite their * and mouths! Ps 115:5
He has saved me from death, my * Ps 116:8
Open my * to see wonderful Ps 119:18
promised it. My * are straining to Ps 119:82
oppress me! My * grow dim with Ps 119:123
in heaven, I lift my * to you. Ps 123:1
servant keeps his * upon his master Ps 123:2
* and ears that cannot hear; Ps 135:16
their loads. The * of all mankind Ps 145:15
and opens the * of the blind; Ps 146:8
"For you closed your * to the Pro 1:29
with * and feet and fingers. Pro 6:12,13
smoke in their * or vinegar that Pro 10:26
Who is the man with bloodshot * Pro 23:29,30
Literally, "a man's *." Pro 27:20f
who close their * to poverty. Pro 28:27
dim to your old *, and there is no Ecc 12:2
Your * are soft as doves'. Sol 1:15
Your * are those of doves. Sol 4:1
one glance of your *, by a single Sol 4:9
raven hair. His * are like doves Sol 5:12
Look the other way, for your * Sol 6:5
ivory tower, your * as limpid pools Sol 7:4
have found favor in my lover's *. Sol 8:10
with wanton * that rove among the Is 3:16
wise and shrewd in their own *! Is 5:21
close their ears and shut their *. Is 6:10
the pavement right before their *; Is 13:16
He has closed the * of your Is 29:10
own * you will see your Teacher. Is 30:20
Then at last the * of Israel Is 32:3
* to all enticement to do wrong. Is 33:15
Your * will see the King in his Is 33:17
he will open the * of the blind, Is 35:5
like a dove; my * grew weary of Is 38:14
in his * they are less than Is 40:17
You will open the * of the Is 42:7
God has shut their * so that they Is 44:18
right before their * they see the Is 52:8
before the * of all the nations; Is 52:10
In God's * Is 53:2
But in our * there was no Is 53:2
Lift up your * and see! Is 60:4
Your * will shine with joy, your Is 60:5
has glorified you in the * of all. Is 60:9
and to open the * of the blind. Is 61:1
before my very *, choosing to do Is 65:12
wrong before my *, and chose what Is 66:4
and brighten your * with mascara? Jer 4:30
with the * that do not see and the Jer 5:21
but a den of robbers in your *? Jer 7:11
before my very *, says the Lord. Jer 7:30
OH, THAT MY * were a fountain of Jer 9:1
Let the tears flow from your *. Jer 9:17,18
of your pride. My * will overflow Jer 13:17
They strain their * looking for Jer 14:6
my * shall overflow with tears; Jer 14:17
before your very *, I will end all Jer 16:9
for your * are open to all the Jer 32:19
Then he gouged out Zedekiah's * Jer 39:7
I will destroy it before your *, Jer 39:16
before your * I will repay Jer 51:24
believe its * at Babylon's fall! Jer 51:41
killed before his *, and then his Jer 52:10
and then his * were gouged out and Jer 52:11
With our own * we've seen her Lam 2:16
My * flow day and night with Lam 3:48,49
faint and weary; our * grow dim. Lam 5:17
filled with * around their edges. Eze 1:18
* that long for other gods. Eze 6:9
I will turn my * away and show Eze 7:4
*, including the rims and spokes. Eze 10:9-13
may not see the land with his *." Eze 12:12f
the fact that his * were put out Eze 12:12f
may not see the land with his *." Eze 12:13f
the fact that his * were put out Eze 12:13f
see with your own * how wicked they Eze 14:22
you before the * of many women. Eze 16:40,41
the Egyptians' *, and led them into Eze 20:9,10
I will be honored before their * Eze 36:23
before their *, so that all the Eze 38:15,16
use your * and ears. Eze 44:5
this little horn had a man's * Dan 7:8
horn with the *, and the loud, Dan 7:20
horn between its *, rushed Dan 8:5
Open your * and see our Dan 9:18
and his * were pools of fire; Dan 10:5,6
food will disappear before our *; Joe 1:16
"The * of the Lord God are Amo 9:8
Now with my own * I see them Mic 7:10
your very *," says the Lord. Zep 3:20
beginning, for the * of the Lord Zec 4:10
represent the * of the Lord that Zec 4:10
their * will shrivel in their Zec 14:12
O Israel, lift your * to see what Mal 1:5
in the * of all the people; Mal 2:9
this happen right before their *. Mt 9:8
Then he touched their * and said, Mt 9:29
closed their * in sleep, Mt 13:15
But blessed are your *, for they Mt 13:16
pity for them and touched their *. Mt 20:34
for their * were heavy, so he went Mt 26:43
'Your * are to see with—why Mk 8:18
*, and laid his hands over them. Mk 8:23
over the man's * again and as the Mk 8:25
than have two * and see the fires Mk 9:47
Your * light up your inward Lk 11:34
not even lift his * to heaven as he Lk 18:13
so bright their * were dazzled. Lk 24:4
* were opened—they recognized him! Lk 24:31
the blind man's *, and told him, Jn 9:6
it over my * and told me to go to Jn 9:11
the mud over his *, and when it was Jn 9:15
your *—who do you say he is?" Jn 9:17
open the * of someone born blind. Jn 9:32
Can a demon open the * of blind Jn 10:21
Tears came to Jesus' *. Jn 11:35
had come true before their *. Jn 12:16
has blinded their * and hardened Jn 12:40
As they were straining their * Act 1:10
fell from his *) Paul could see, Act 9:18
and she opened her *! Act 9:40
to open their * to their true Act 26:18
have closed your * against Act 28:27
* of the others have been blinded. Rom 11:7
shutting their * and ears so that Rom 11:8
Let their * be dim," he said, Rom 11:10
But God has opened the * of 1Co 1:24
seen Jesus our Lord with my own *. 1Co 9:1
protect from the * of others those 1Co 12:23
Keep your * open for spiritual 1Co 16:13
* and given them to replace mine Gal 4:15
handicapped by a disease of the *. Gal 4:15f
us holy in his *, without a single Eph 1:4
with tears in my *, there are many Php 3:18
us good in God's *—all because of Tit 3:7
all-seeing * of our living God; Heb 4:13
Keep your * on Jesus, our leader Heb 12:2
with my own * I saw Christ dying 1Pe 5:1
My own * have seen his splendor 2Pe 1:16
own * and listened to him speak. 1Jn 1:1
seen with our own * and now tell 1Jn 4:14
with his own *—the piercing of Rev 1:7f
* penetrated like flames of fire. Rev 1:14
Son of God, whose * penetrate like Rev 2:18
* and give you back your sight. Rev 3:18
and back with *, stood at the Rev 4:6
their wings were covered with *. Rev 4:8
He had seven horns and seven *, Rev 5:6
where the seven * are equated with Rev 5:6f
makes war. His * were like flames, Rev 19:12
tears from their *, and there shall Rev 21:4

EYESIGHT
he died, yet his * was perfect and Deu 34:7
If you have good * and good Pro 20:12

EYEWITNESS
and there is no * to report just Ex 22:10

EYEWITNESSES
the early disciples and other *. Lk 1:1,2

EZBAI
Naarai (son of *); 1Ch 11:26-47

EZBON
*, Eri, Arodi, and Areli. Gen 46:16,17
*, Uzzi, Uzziel, Jerimoth, Iri. 1Ch 7:7

EZEKIEL
at the time of Jeremiah and *. Jer 49:8f

(EZEKIEL Con't)
* was a priest (the son of Buzi) Eze 1:1
times throughout the book of *. Eze 2:1f
See the dietary laws * here refers Eze 4:14f
See * 1:10. Eze 10:14f
you have done. * is an example to Eze 24:24
This is what * means by the first Eze 30:21f
See * 18:14. Tammuz-Adonis, a Dan 11:37f
this event, see *, chapters 26-28. Lk 10:13f

EZEM
Baalah, Iim, *, Eltolad, Chesil, Jos 15:21-32
Balah, *, Eltolad, Bethul, Hormah, Jos 19:2-7
Bilhah, *, Tolad, Bethuel, 1Ch 4:29

EZER
tribe of *,The tribe of Dishan. Gen 36:20,21
The children of *:Bilhan, Zaavan, Gen 36:27
*, and 1Ch 1:38,39
The sons of *: Bilhan, Zaavan, 1Ch 1:42
Gedor),* (the ancestor of Hushah), 1Ch 4:3-4
*, Ele-ad. 1Ch 7:20,21
Ele-ad and * attempted to rustle 1Ch 7:20,21
* was the chief; 1Ch 12:8-13
were led by * (son of Jeshua), the Neh 3:19
Elam and *. Neh 12:42

EZI-ON-GEBER
south to Elath and *, and traveling Deu 2:8

EZION-GEBER
From Abronah to *; Num 33:15-37
From * to Kadesh (in the Num 33:15-37
King Solomon had a shipyard in * 1Ki 9:26
for they were wrecked at *. 1Ki 22:48
seaport towns of * and Eloth, in 2Ch 8:17,18
They made ships in * to sail to 2Ch 20:36

EZNITE
known also as Adino, the *. 2Sa 23:8

EZRA
HERE IS THE genealogy of *, who Ez 7:1
* was the son of Seriah; Ez 7:1
As a Jewish religious leader, * Ez 7:6
This was because * had Ez 7:10
this letter to * the priest, the Ez 7:11
"To: *, the priest, the teacher Ez 7:12
'You are to give * whatever he Ez 7:21
"And you, *, are to use the Ez 7:25
the remainder of the book, is *. Ez 7:28f
Then I, * the priest, arose and Ez 10:10
Gate and requested *, their Neh 8:1
So * the priest brought out to Neh 8:1
Then * blessed the Lord, the Neh 8:6
As * read from the scroll, Neh 8:7,8
Then * the priest, and I as Neh 8:9
Levites met with * to go over the Neh 8:13
days of Joshua.) * read from the Neh 8:18
Then * prayed, "You alone are Neh 9:6
Seraiah, Jeremiah, *, Amariah, Neh 12:1
Meshullam, leader of the * clan; Neh 12:12-21
governor, and when * was the priest Neh 12:26
Hoshaiah, Azariah, *, Meshullam, Neh 12:33
* the priest led this procession. Neh 12:35,36
mentioned in *, Haggai, and Dan 5:31f

EZRAH'S
* sons were:Jether, 1Ch 4:17

EZRAHITE
He was wiser than Ethan the * 1Ki 4:31

EZRI
* (son of Chelub) was manager of 1Ch 27:26

FABLED
heard of Solomon's * wisdom, she 2Ch 9:1

FABLES
Put an end to their myths and *, 1Ti 1:3,4

FABRIC
linen garment or *, or in a piece Lev 13:47,48
burn the clothing, *, linen or Lev 13:52

FABRICS
They bring choice * to Eze 27:24

FACE
and his * grew dark with fury. Gen 4:5
"Why is your * so dark with Gen 4:6
blot out from the * of the earth. Gen 6:7
them across the * of the earth. Gen 11:9
Abram fell * downward in the Gen 17:2,3,4
So she covered her * with her Gen 24:65
before meeting him * to face! Gen 32:20
before meeting him face to *! Gen 32:20
"Peniel" ("The * of God"), for Gen 32:30
"I have seen God * to face, and Gen 32:30
to *, and yet my life is spared." Gen 32:30
* as one sees the face of God." Gen 33:10f
face as one sees the * of God." Gen 33:10f
since her * was veiled. Gen 38:15
Then he washed his * and came Gen 43:31
(Moses covered his * with his Ex 3:6
if we don't obey him, we * death Ex 5:3
For the locusts covered the * of Ex 10:15
them from off the * of the earth'? Ex 32:12
spoke to Moses * to face, as a man Ex 33:11
*, as a man speaks to his friend. Ex 33:11
people upon the * of the earth?" Ex 33:16
the glory of my *, for man may not Ex 33:20
shall see my back, but not my *." Ex 33:23
tablets that his * glowed from Ex 34:29
radiance upon his *, Aaron and the Ex 34:30
them, he put a veil over his *; Ex 34:33
the people would see his * aglow. Ex 34:35
"And I will turn my * against Lev 17:10
myself will set my * against that Lev 20:5
"I will set my * against anyone Lev 20:6
I will set my * against you and Lev 26:17
may the Lord's * radiate with joy Num 6:24,25,26
day we have to * this manna!" Num 11:6
With him I speak * to face! Num 12:7,8
With him I speak face to *! Num 12:7,8
*.she would be defiled seven days. Num 12:14
Then Moses and Aaron fell * Num 14:5
that you talk with her * to face. Num 14:14
that you talk with her face to *. Num 14:14
he fell * downward to the ground. Num 16:4
But Moses and Aaron fell * Num 16:22
But Moses and Aaron fell * Num 16:45
fell * downward before the Lord; Num 20:6
and they cover the * of the earth Num 22:5,6
He spoke with you * to face from Deu 5:4
He spoke with you face to * from Deu 5:4
wipe you off the * of the earth. Deu 6:15
the people on the * of the whole Deu 7:6
names from the * of the earth. Deu 7:24
nation on the * of the earth. Deu 14:2
from his foot and spit in his *. Deu 25:9
at Mount Ebal. * the stones with a Deu 27:2,3,4
destroyed from the * of the land Deu 28:21
them, hiding my * from them, and Deu 31:17
With savage arm and * and head. Deu 33:20
the Lord talked to him * to face. Deu 34:10
the Lord talked to him face to *. Deu 34:10
to Joshua, "Get up off your *! Jos 7:10,11
the Angel of the Lord * to face!" Ju 6:22
the Angel of the Lord face to *!" Ju 6:22
Manoah and his wife fell * Ju 13:20
to * anything like this before! 1Sa 4:7
fallen with his * to the ground 1Sa 5:3
idol had fallen * down before the 1Sa 5:4
judge by a man's * or height, for 1Sa 16:7
ranks to * the forces of Israel. 1Sa 17:4-7
man fell on his * to the ground. 1Sa 17:48,49
I could never * your brother Joab 2Sa 2:22
the king, she fell * downward on 2Sa 14:4
from the * of the earth." 2Sa 14:7
He bowed low with his * to the 2Sa 18:28
The king covered his * with his 2Sa 19:4
they came * to face with Amasa. 2Sa 20:8,9,10
they came face to * with Amasa. 2Sa 20:8,9,10
the ground with his * in the dust. 2Sa 24:20
live in—and as I * toward the 1Ki 8:29
they * this place to pray; 1Ki 8:30
knees, with his * between his 1Ki 18:42
it, he wrapped his * in his scarf 1Ki 19:13
to bed with his * to the wall! 1Ki 21:4
over and slapped Micaiah on the *. 1Ki 22:24
Lay the staff upon the child's * 2Ki 4:29
child's *, but nothing happened. 2Ki 4:31
* until he smothered to death. 2Ki 8:15
Hezekiah turned his * to the 2Ki 20:2
The names in bold * type are 1Ch 1:1f
appeared in bold * type. 1Ch 1:5-9f
And seek his * untiringly. 1Ch 16:11
to you as I * toward this place. 2Ch 6:20,21
to you again, and * toward this 2Ch 6:37,38
* away from me, your anointed one. 2Ch 6:42
and slapped him across the *. 2Ch 18:23
ground with his * to the earth, and 2Ch 20:18
* from you if you return to him." 2Ch 30:9
I blush to lift up my * to you, Ez 9:6
veil was placed over Haman's *. Est 7:8
see him curse you to your *!" Job 1:11
and he will curse you to your *!" Job 2:4,5
my *—my hair stood up on end. Job 4:15
Would I lie to your *? Job 6:28
am willing to * the consequences. Job 13:13
only then will I be able to * Job 13:20
or they may fail and * disaster, Job 14:20,21
they spit in my *. Job 17:6
disappear from the * of the earth. Job 24:18
and don't mind spitting in my *. Job 30:10
my servants, how could I * God? Job 31:14
Rather that than * the judgment Job 31:23
And he will slap them in the *, Ps 3:7
of your * shine down upon us. Ps 4:6
the godly shall see his *. Ps 11:7
Or, "His * shines down in mercy Ps 11:7f
for I will see you * to face. Ps 17:15
for I will see you face to *. Ps 17:15
Then, Lord, you turned your * Ps 30:6,7
sorrow always stares me in the *. Ps 38:17
We lie * downward in the dust. Ps 44:25
They are so friendly to my * Ps 62:3,4
let your * beam with joy as you Ps 67:1
his enemies shall fall * downward Ps 72:9
Literally, "Cause your * to shine Ps 80:3f
Literally, "Cause your * to shine Ps 80:7f
Look down on us, your * aglow Ps 80:19
* because you help and comfort me. Ps 86:17
Why are you turning your * from Ps 88:14
afraid, but can calmly * his foes. Ps 112:8
Death stared me in the *—I was Ps 116:3
in heaven. I * your Temple as I Ps 138:2
about some problems they will *. Pro 1:4
For now I must * public Pro 5:14
fool falls flat on his *. Pro 10:8
to fool himself and won't * facts. Pro 14:8
A happy * means a glad heart; Pro 15:13
a sad * means a breaking heart. Pro 15:13
A mirror reflects a man's *, but Pro 27:19
Wisdom lights up a man's *, Ecc 8:1
voice and see your handsome *. Sol 2:14
Your hair falls across your * Sol 4:1
falls across your *, is like a Sol 6:5
them over the * of the earth. Is 24:1
his * to the wall and prayed: Is 38:2
a man to carve a * on it, and Is 40:20
hide from shame—they spit in my *. Is 50:6
therefore, I have set my * like Is 50:7
I turned my * a little while; Is 54:8
he has turned his * away from you Is 59:2
insult me to my * by worshiping Is 65:3
in the land! * the awful sins that Jer 2:23
and cover your * with your hands, Jer 2:37
For I have set my * against this Jer 21:10
is fury in my * and I will destroy Jer 44:11
She groans and hides her *. Lam 1:8
and refused to * the fact that Lam 1:9
to lie * downward in the dust; Lam 3:29
Each had the * of a man [in Eze 1:10
with a lion's * on the right Eze 1:10
and the * of an ox on his left Eze 1:10
left side, and the * of an eagle at Eze 1:10
without having to * around. Eze 1:17
And when I saw it, I fell * Eze 1:27,28
And I fell to the ground on my *. Eze 3:23
I fell to the ground on my * and Eze 9:8
Literally, "cherub's *." Eze 10:14f
Then I fell to the ground on my * Eze 11:13
muffle your * and don't gaze Eze 12:6
*, for he won't be able to see. Eze 12:12
"Son of dust, * toward Jerusalem Eze 21:2
the great massacre they *! Eze 21:14
"Son of dust, * toward Egypt and Eze 29:2
hills and over the * of the earth, Eze 34:6
"Son of dust, * toward Mount Eze 35:2
"Son of dust, * northward Eze 38:2,3
Therefore I turned my * away from Eze 39:23
I turned my * away and punished Eze 39:24
And I will never hide my * from Eze 39:29
I saw a man whose * shone like Eze 40:3
the cherubim. One *—that of a Eze 41:19,20
and the other *—that of a young Eze 41:19,20
before him with my * in the dust. Eze 43:3
the ground with my * in the dust. Eze 44:4
with fury and his * became dark Dan 3:19
they wrote. His * blanched with Dan 5:6
hysterical; his * reflected the Dan 5:9
disturbed, and my * was pale with Dan 7:28
fell down with my * to the ground. Dan 8:17
Then I fainted, lying * downward Dan 8:18
Let your * shine again with peace Dan 9:17
From his * came blinding flashes Dan 10:5,6
ground * downward in a deep faint. Dan 10:9
He met God there at Bethel * to Hos 12:4
met God there at Bethel face to *. Hos 12:4
the Judge of Israel on the *. Mic 5:1
apart, to * their sorrow alone. Zec 12:12,13,14
and two before his *, into every Mt 11:1f
so that his * shone like the sun Mt 17:2
At this the disciples fell * Mt 17:6
the king, his * in the dust, and Mt 18:26
a little, and fell * downward on Mt 26:39
Then they spat in his * and Mt 26:67
sat on it. His * shone like Mt 28:3
Suddenly his * began to shine with Mk 9:2
Then the man's * fell, and he Mk 10:22
to hammer his * with their fists. Mk 14:65
ground before him, * downward in Lk 5:12
And as he was praying, his * Lk 9:29
appearance of his * changed." Lk 9:29f
corners, then your * will be Lk 11:36
in front of Jesus, * downward in Lk 17:16
an inch in the * of what others Lk 20:21
his * muffled in a head swath. Jn 11:44
* become as radiant as an angel's! Act 6:15
nations across the * of the earth. Act 17:26
* to face with his accusers. Act 25:16
face to * with his accusers. Act 25:16
They tried at first to * back to Act 27:14,15
must be ready to * death at every Rom 8:36
you didn't have to * right now. 1Co 7:28
in his completeness, * to face. 1Co 13:12
in his completeness, face to *. 1Co 13:12
For it is a fact that I * death 1Co 15:31
not bear to look at Moses' *. 2Co 3:7
law to obey, his * shone out with 2Co 3:7
shone from Moses' * is worth 2Co 3:10
a veil over his * so that the 2Co 3:13
Not only Moses' * was veiled, but 2Co 3:14
is seen in the * of Jesus Christ. 2Co 4:6

(FACE Con't)
Because of our preaching we * 2Co 4:12
on airs, and slap you in the *. 2Co 11:19,20
dreams, and even * to face Heb 1:1
dreams, and even face to * Heb 1:1
You have not had to stand * to Heb 12:18
to stand face to * with terror, Heb 12:18
man looking at his * in a mirror; Jas 1:23
but the Lord's * is hard against 1Pe 3:12
that they must * the Judge of all, 1Pe 4:5
them off the * of the earth, making 2Pe 2:6
judgment, but can * him with 1Jn 4:17
and his * shone like the power of Rev 1:16
the third had the * of a man; Rev 4:7
hide us from the * of the one Rev 6:16
and falling * down before the Rev 7:11
over his head; his * shone like the Rev 10:1
it, from whose * the earth and sky Rev 20:11
And they shall see his *; Rev 22:4

FACED
Lot, despite the danger they all * Gen 13:7
The cherubim * each other, with Ex 37:9
and Israelis * each other on 1Sa 17:3
Then the king turned around and * 1Ki 8:14
we are * with any calamity such as 2Ch 20:9
him as he read. He * the square in Neh 8:1
is speaking), and * with Ps 129:2
When he * them he said, "Oh, Jer 41:6
Its entry hall * the outer court Eze 40:34
Its entry hall * toward the Eze 40:37
one door * north and the other Eze 41:11
inner wing that * the Temple court, Eze 42:7,8
of sacred chambers that * north. Eze 46:19,20
tears—and have * grave danger from Act 20:19
Many others have * exactly the 1Co 10:13
put in jail, * angry mobs, worked 2Co 6:5
* death again and again and again. 2Co 11:23
I have * grave dangers from mobs 2Co 11:26
baptism but also as he * death. 1Jn 5:6,7,8

FACES
him, with their * to the earth. Gen 42:6
they fell to their * upon the 1Ki 18:39
with their * toward the ground. Neh 8:6
They mask their * so no one will Job 24:14,15
The very look on their * gives Is 3:9
their wings they covered their *; Is 6:2
city reflect upon your pallid *. Is 13:8
Who is it you mock, making * and Is 57:4
They are determined, with * hard Jer 5:3
stream down their *, and I will Jer 31:9
but now their * are as black as Lam 4:8
had four * and two pairs of wings! Eze 1:6
of the four ways their * looked. Eze 10:9-13
*—the first was that of an ox; Eze 10:14
for each had four * and four Eze 10:21
Their * too were identical to Eze 10:22
identical to the * of those I had Eze 10:22
afraid and look on with twisted *. Eze 27:35
each with two *, and of palm trees Eze 41:17,18
their * grow pale with fright. Joe 2:6
will cover your * in shame, and Mic 3:7
their enemies' * into the dust Zec 10:5
spread on your * the manure of Mal 2:3
sadness written across their *. Lk 24:17
marries. She * the same problem. 1Co 7:34
have no veil over our *; 2Co 3:18
lies with straight * and do it so 1Ti 4:2
and their * looked like men's. Rev 9:7

FACETS
stone with seven * I have set Zec 3:9f

FACING
of Mach-pelah, * Mamre—the field Gen 49:29,30
angels—shall be * each other, Ex 25:20
rear of the building, * westward. Ex 26:26,27
* each other, army against army. 1Sa 17:21
where they sat * each other on 2Sa 2:13
* each other from three walls. 1Ki 7:3,4
to tail, three * north, three west, 1Ki 7:25
They stood on the floor * the 2Ch 3:11,12,13
to tail, three * north, three west, 2Ch 4:4
For we are * death threats Ps 44:22
I was * death and then he saved Ps 116:6
Lord, * east, worshiping the sun! Eze 8:16
northern entrance, * south, and one Eze 40:44
the southern entrance, * north. Eze 40:44
stood on the west, * the Temple Eze 41:12
the doors of the building * north. Eze 42:4
rooms * the Temple yard are holy; Eze 42:13
better off than * the punishment in Lk 17:2,3
We Christians are * great dangers 1Co 7:26
our lives, * death hour by hour? 1Co 15:30
* death just as Jesus did; 2Co 4:10
and again as he was * death 1Jn 5:6,7,8
Remain faithful even when * Rev 2:10

FACT
mighty nation. In * you shall be Gen 17:2,3,4
harmed you, and in *, have done Gen 26:29
ten times! In *, except for the Gen 31:42
chief jailer. In *, the jailer Gen 39:22
skinny and bony—in *, I've never Gen 41:19
let you go; in *, he will be so Ex 11:1
"You are witnesses to the * that Ex 20:22
to confirm the *, and shall not be Ex 22:13
in *, he has every needed skill. Ex 35:33
anointing oil—in *, the supervision Num 4:16
despite the * that neither the Ark Num 14:44
This * is mentioned in The Book Num 21:14
and Aaron, and in * challenged the Num 26:5-11
way to Azekah; in *, more men died Jos 10:11
* had vowed that he would do it. Ju 2:15
in *, that appealed to them. 1Sa 15:9
The very next day, in *, a 1Sa 18:10
harm from them; in *, day and night 1Sa 25:15,16
As a matter of *, I have a favor 1Ki 2:14
interests. In *, his wisdom 1Ki 4:30
precious gems; in *, it was the 1Ki 10:10
despite the * that the Lord had 1Ki 16:4-7
despite the * that I have already 1Ki 20:7
prophets, but the * of the matter 1Ki 22:23
God of Israel. In *, none of the 2Ki 18:5
king of Israel. In *, all of Israel 1Ch 12:38
no other God. In *, we have never 1Ch 17:20
destruction; in *, even after 2Ch 12:12
idols; in *, he compelled his 2Ch 21:11
rushed him out; in *, he himself 2Ch 26:20
in the past; in *, it was destroyed Ez 4:15
many kings; in *, rebellion and Ez 4:19
down and cried. In *, I refused to Neh 1:4
All this despite the * that I Neh 5:17
He was, in *, the richest Job 1:2,3
in me despite the * that you Job 2:3
criticisms are not based on *. Job 6:25,26
saying this—in *, I expect him to. Job 13:15
"The * of the matter is that God Job 19:6
All this despite the * that they Job 21:14
to get it, but, in *, it is not to Job 28:13
and happiness! In *, the Lord gave Job 42:10
learn this great *: that a life of Pro 4:11
This is a *, but not to be Pro 17:8f
ideas. In *, he looks for them. Pro 18:15
as being rich; in *, it is better. Ecc 7:11
including the * that some of the Ecc 7:15-17
They ignore the * that it was I, Jer 2:6
Lord God says. In *, faithless Jer 3:11
besieging you. In *, I will bring Jer 21:3,4
to face the * that punishment was Lam 1:9
Apparently a reference to the * Eze 12:12f
Apparently a reference to the * Eze 12:13f
"She was in * more debased than Eze 23:14,15
he committed; in *, I will put an Hos 1:4,5
This illustrates the * that Hos 3:4
had a reason? The * is, I am Amo 3:4
scant crops. In *, I have called Hag 1:11
the altar. In *, every container Zec 14:21
Valley, and, in *, from every Mt 3:5
to the crowds. In *, because the Mt 13:34,35
And, in *, he has already come, Mt 17:12
"In *, unless those days are Mt 24:22
The chief priests and, in *, the Mt 26:59
In *, he taught only by Mk 4:34
no better but, in *, was worse. Mk 5:26
And he could hardly accept the * Mk 6:6
that he had, in *, already come! Mk 9:12,13
The officer confirmed the *, and Mk 15:45
than mine; in *, I am not even Lk 3:16
about the * that they won't repay. Lk 6:35
This illustrates the * that Lk 8:17
fine crops. In *, his barns were Lk 12:17
a witness to the * that Jesus Jn 1:6,7
is based on this *: that the Light Jn 3:19
time is coming, in *, it is here, Jn 5:25
their witness is accepted as *. Jn 8:17
proved by the * that I have told Jn 15:15
But the * of the matter is that Jn 16:7
"But the time is coming—in *, Jn 16:32
witnesses of this *, for after you Act 3:15
he could do—in *, the Samaritan Act 8:9,10,11
confirmed the * that he accepts Act 15:8
And this * of Gentile conversion Act 15:15
in confusion. In *, most of them Act 19:32
Since this is an indisputable *, Act 19:36
give the Jews? In *, those heathen Rom 2:27
has any excuse; in *, all the world Rom 3:19
Just the opposite! In *, only Rom 3:31
But the * of the matter is this: Rom 4:15
worry about the * that he was too Rom 4:19
It seems to be a * of life that Rom 7:21
Just the * that they come from Rom 9:7
Egypt, was an example of this *. Rom 9:17
of each of us; in *, it is as near Rom 10:8
understand. In * that is the very Rom 15:22
*, they risked their lives for me; Rom 16:4
your own way? In *, you are acting 1Co 3:3
to start now. In *, I would rather 1Co 9:15
a * for all the angels to notice 1Co 11:10
him of the * that he is a sinner, 1Co 14:24
But the * is that Christ did 1Co 15:20
For it is a * that I face death 1Co 15:31
with God. In *, that first glory 2Co 3:10
on the Lord. In *, in everything 2Co 6:4
the churches. In *, this man was 2Co 8:19
a year ago. In *, it was this 2Co 9:2
same to God.) In *, when Peter, Gal 2:7,8,9
offend anyone. The * that I am Gal 5:11
for doing it, the * remains that Php 1:18
But the * is that I can be of Php 1:24
And he surely was; in *, he Php 2:27
and, in *, Christ himself is the Col 1:15
being in jail. In *, when he came 2Ti 1:17
Don't ever forget the wonderful * 2Ti 2:8
as shown by the * that he rose 2Ti 2:8
who hate him. In *, evil men and 2Ti 3:13
the truth and the * that you are in Tit 2:7
you owe me! The * is, you even owe Phm 1:19
as proved by the * that his name Heb 1:4
for worship. In * we can say that Heb 9:22
and the stars—in *, all things—were Heb 11:3
They deliberately forget this *: 2Pe 3:5,6
is: Remember this *—which you know Jud 1:5
as it was long; in * it was in the Rev 21:16

FACTS
the * to see if the rumor is true. Deu 13:12,13,14
Three days later the * came Jos 9:16
"Let's get the * straight: both of 1Ki 3:23
(These * are recorded in their 1Ch 4:32,33
scoff at wisdom and fight the *? Pro 1:22
your eyes to the * and did not Pro 1:29
to fool himself and won't face *. Pro 14:8
A rebel doesn't care about the *. Pro 18:2
—to decide before knowing the *! Pro 18:13
Get the * at any price, and hold Pro 23:23
by keeping abreast of the *. Pro 24:3,4
Don't fight the * of nature. Ecc 7:13
Why fight the *? Jer 32:5
These are the * concerning the Mt 1:18
an appendix giving additional *. Mk 16:9f
on me without knowing the *. Jn 8:15
to tell these * to everyone, both Act 26:22
to explain the Holy Spirit's *. 1Co 2:13
of these great *, and command them 2Ti 2:14
will let me—about * you already 2Pe 3:1
you already know: * you learned 2Pe 3:1

FADE
people would not see the glory *. Ex 34:33f
He will * like a dream. Job 20:8
Soon they * away like grass and Ps 37:2
sun and moon will seem to * away. Is 24:23
The grass withers, the flowers * Is 40:8
Like autumn leaves we *, wither Is 64:6
of Bashan and Carmel * away; Nah 1:4
and moon began to *, obscured by Hab 3:11
could not see the glory * away. 2Co 3:13
life they gave you will * away. 1Pe 1:23
Yes, our natural lives will * as 1Pe 1:24

FADED
that the spot has * after the Lev 13:56
So if the old system that * into 2Co 3:11

FADES
his beauty * like dying flowers. Is 40:6
The grass withers, the flower * Is 40:7
Antiochus IV * from view and the Dan 11:40f
enthusiasm *, and he drops out. Mt 13:21
that quickly *," given to the 1Co 9:25f
its beauty and * away, Jas 1:10,11

FADING
the skin and is *, the priest shall Lev 13:26
the skin, and is *, it is simply a Lev 13:28
Woe to her * beauty, the crowning Is 28:1
Once glorious, her * beauty Is 28:4
the brightness was already * away. 2Co 3:7
And this world is * away, and 1Jn 2:17

FAIL
* to sleep with her as his wife. Ex 21:10
without * be stoned by his peers. Lev 20:1
future generations * to carry out Num 15:22
they shall be guilty if they *. Num 18:23
you must without * declare war Deu 13:15
He will neither * you nor forsake Deu 31:6
he will not * nor forsake you." Deu 31:8
I will not abandon you or * to Jos 1:5
he will, without *, drive out the Jos 3:10
If we feed you and you *, they'll Ju 8:6
Hezekiah will *, too," he wrote. 2Ch 32:17
and olive oil each day without *. Ez 6:9
livelihood if you * to keep this Neh 5:13
they declared they would never * Est 9:27
or they may * and face disaster, Job 14:20,21
fruit each season without *. Ps 1:3
Don't * me, Lord, for I am Ps 25:2
from them, nor let my promise *. Ps 89:33
to destroy me will *, and I shall Ps 109:28
Make them * in everything they Ps 109:29
the harp. If I * to love her more Ps 137:5,6
their greatest leaders *; Ps 146:3
Don't * to correct your children; Pro 23:13,14
to get rich quick will quickly *. Pro 28:20
years, without *, the glory of Moab Is 16:13,14
* to rise and flood the fields; Is 19:5
or cotton, for the crops will *. Is 19:9
grape harvest will *, the wine will Is 24:7
All will * together. Is 31:3
For the crops of fruit will *; Is 32:10
They will try, but they will *. Jer 1:19

(FAIL Con't)
your businesses shall * and all Jer 25:10
mightiest warriors * with fear like Jer 48:41
even her water supply will *. Jer 50:38
mighty army shall * to help Israel Eze 17:17
a new crop every month—without *! Eze 47:12
But the plan will *. Dan 11:17
My mercies never *. Hos 14:8
But sinners trying it will *. Hos 14:9
The archer's aim will *, the Amo 2:15
all your counterstrategy will *. Ob 1:7
and *; Hab 2:4
all *, and the fields lie barren; Hab 3:17
that when it shall * you, they Lk 16:9f
faith should not completely *. Lk 22:32
Literally, "* not." Lk 22:32f
for we always * to keep them. Rom 4:15
Oh, Timothy, don't * to do these 1Ti 6:20
* to find God's best blessings. Heb 12:15
never * you nor forsake you." Heb 13:5
made you, for he will never * you. 1Pe 4:19

FAILED
secret arts, but this time they *. Ex 8:18
deliberately * to obey his law; Num 15:31
though they * in their attempt to Ju 1:19
The tribe of Benjamin * to Ju 1:21
The tribe of Manasseh * to drive Ju 1:27
"You * to help us in our time of Ju 12:2
not one word has * of all the 1Ki 8:56
but he *. 2Ki 3:26
* to conquer a nation we attacked? 2Ch 32:13
the other nations * to save their 2Ch 32:17
My relatives have * me; Job 19:14
Has his promise *? Ps 77:8
Never let it be said that God * Ps 119:116
even the springtime rains have *. Jer 3:3
Yet you have * me in my time of Jer 15:17,18
men of my kingdom have * me. Dan 4:18
balances and have * the test. Dan 5:27
of his disciples * to follow the Mk 7:2
Even Christ's resurrection * to Lk 16:31f
to outwit him before the people *; Lk 20:26
Well then, has God * to fulfill Rom 9:6
they disobeyed God and * to enter. Heb 4:6
offered, but these * to cleanse the Heb 9:9

FAILING
that his father was * rapidly. Gen 48:1
he will realize his * strength. Job 18:7
He restores my * health. Ps 23:2,3
me now when my strength is *. Ps 71:9
by trying—and *—to obey the laws. Gal 2:19
verge of * to get there after all. Heb 4:1
of Israel did, thus * to get in. Heb 4:11
Or, "I will keep you from * in Rev 3:10f

FAILS
If he * in any of these three Ex 21:11
when you do, everything you try *. 2Ch 24:20
strength *, and I am going blind. Ps 38:10
My health *; Ps 73:26
But anyone who * to go after 2Pe 1:9

FAILURE
You will be confused and a * in Deu 28:20
because of your * to praise God for Deu 28:47,48
Curse it for its * to shut my Job 3:10
of your sin, your * to speak Job 42:8
these scoffers with their utter *! Ps 40:14,15
Cover them with * and Ps 71:13
I am a symbol of * to all Ps 109:25
of their * to obey God's laws. Rom 5:20
after man's first * to enter, Heb 4:7

FAILURES
There were crop * in all the Gen 41:54
Make them * in everything they Ps 83:17
I will abolish crop * and famine. Eze 36:29
by the use of puns their *. Mic 1:11f
by the use of puns their *. Mic 1:11f
by the use of puns their *. Mic 1:11f

FAINT
those who were * and weary and Deu 25:18
was weary and * as a result. 1Sa 14:28
Aijalon, growing more and more *. 1Sa 14:31
He was also * with hunger, for he 1Sa 28:20
wilderness for any who become *." 2Sa 16:2
strikes, you * and are broken. Job 4:5
When my heart is * and Ps 61:2
I long, yes, * with longing to be Ps 84:2
desert, hungry and thirsty and *. Ps 107:5
I * for your salvation; Ps 119:81
sick and weak and *, covered with Is 1:5,6
to a child. I * when I hear what Is 21:3
but is still * from thirst when he Is 29:8
the earth, never grows * or weary? Is 40:28
they shall walk and not *. Is 40:31
hungry and thirsty, weak and *. Is 44:12
sighs are many and my heart is *. Lam 1:22
plead for your children as they * Lam 2:19
Our hearts are * and weary; Lam 5:17
Every spirit will *; Eze 21:7
Then I grew * and was sick for Dan 8:27
ground face downward in a deep *. Dan 10:9
alike will grow * and weary, Amo 8:13

until he grew * and wished to die. Jon 4:8
or they will * along the road." Mt 15:32
saw him, and fell into a dead *. Mt 28:4
them, they will * along the road! Mk 8:3

FAINTED
For your sons have * and lie in Is 51:20
Then I *, lying face downward on Dan 8:18

FAINTER
have become * and have not spread, Lev 13:6

FAINTHEARTED
He will encourage the *, those Is 42:3
you from becoming * in all the 1Th 3:2,3
keep from becoming * and weary, Heb 12:3

FAINTING
"One should be kind to a * Job 6:14
God has given me a * heart; Job 23:16,17
are * and dying in the streets. Lam 2:11

FAINTS
and *, for all her sons are dead. Jer 15:9

FAIR
the Judge of all the earth be *?" Gen 18:25
"* enough," the man replied, Gen 44:10
they must always be perfectly *. Lev 19:15
years, a * price shall be arrived Lev 25:14,15,16
a * trial establishes his guilt. Num 35:12
to be perfectly * at all times, Deu 1:16
be * to great and small alike. Deu 1:17
* as these I am giving you today? Deu 4:8
Everything he does is just and *. Deu 32:4
This is only * after the way I Jos 2:12,13
But if you have not been * to Ju 9:20
over Israel and was * to everyone. 2Sa 8:15
what was just and * in the sight of 2Ch 31:20
us you were being perfectly *; Neh 9:33
with sympathy. * and honest men Job 23:7
even strangers received a * trial. Job 29:16
God is a judge who is perfectly * Ps 7:11
me, Lord, for you are always *. Ps 17:2
and * and knows right from wrong. Ps 37:30,31
Give * judgment to the poor man, Ps 82:3
to those who are * to others and Ps 106:3
I've been perfectly *. Ps 119:121
just and your punishments are *. Ps 119:137
for your laws are perfectly *. Ps 119:142
Your laws are always *; Ps 119:144
The Lord is * in everything he Ps 145:17
just and * in everything they did. Pro 1:3
Literally, "a * garland and Pro 1:7,8,9f
his people are truthful and *. Pro 16:13
If a king is kind, honest and *, Pro 20:28
and * than when we give him gifts. Pro 21:3
his reign will be just and *. Pro 25:4,5
A king who is * to the poor shall Pro 29:14
my love, my * one, and come away. Sol 2:10
Arise, my love, my * one, and Sol 2:13
as the dawn, * as the moon, pure as Sol 6:10
Learn to do good, to be * and to Is 1:17
Once "The City of * Play," but Is 1:21
who are honest and *, who reject Is 33:15
your troubles and isn't being *? Is 40:27
trapped, * game for all, with no Is 42:22
a government that is just and *. Is 54:14
BE JUST AND * to all, the Lord God Is 56:1
No one cares about being * and Is 59:4
you can find one * and honest man! Jer 5:1
and deeds, and are * to others, Jer 7:5
Because he was just and * in all Jer 22:15
and is honest and * when judging Eze 18:8
adultery, and is * to those who Eze 18:16
you say: 'The Lord isn't being *!' Eze 18:25
and does what is * and right— if Eze 33:14
are saying the Lord isn't *. Eze 33:17
The trouble is they aren't *. Eze 33:17
what's * and just, he shall live. Eze 33:19
you are saying the Lord isn't *. Eze 33:20
Always be * and honest. Eze 45:9
he is * in everything he does, Dan 9:14
Ahead of them the land lies * as Joe 2:3
"Righteousness" and "* play" Amo 5:7
all it is: to be * and just and Mic 6:8
"Tell them to be honest and * Zec 7:8,9
your part: Tell the truth. Be *. Zec 8:16
tonight means * weather tomorrow; Mt 16:2,3
And my judgment is absolutely * Jn 5:30
* Havens, near the city of Lasea. Act 27:7,8
And since * Havens was an Act 27:12
place and not left * Havens—you Act 27:21
Is it *, then, for him to punish Rom 3:5
was being entirely *, even though Rom 3:25
be just and * to all your slaves. Col 4:1
one example of the *, just way God 2Th 1:5
They must be sensible men, and *. Tit 1:8

FAIR-MINDED
my former self. * men are Job 17:8
The Lord says: Be *. Jer 22:3
not one * man is left. Mic 7:1

FAIREST
You are the * of all; Ps 45:2
Jerusalem; the * city of Israel Lam 2:1

FAIRLY
could discuss it *, but there is no Job 9:32,33

it that you are finally treated *. Ps 48:11
He will judge all nations *. Ps 96:10
he will judge the nations * and Ps 96:13
man who conducts his business *. Ps 112:5
the king to judge the people *; Pro 16:10
* and give them what they earn. Is 58:6
hands of God who always judges *. 1Pe 2:23

FAIRNESS
For the Lord loves justice and * Ps 37:28
them with complete *, for all Ps 50:6
know the meaning of the word! *? Ps 58:1
to give justice. * is the Ps 99:4
Therefore in * renew my life, for Ps 119:40,41,42
The Lord demands * in every Pro 16:11
right to rule depends upon his *. Pro 16:12
He will rule with perfect * and Is 9:7
For he will be clothed with * Is 11:5
the righteous man; * is unknown. Is 59:14

FAIRY
But the story sounded like a * Lk 24:11
been telling you * tales when we 2Pe 1:16

FAITH
him righteous on account of his *. Gen 15:6
LATER ON, GOD tested Abraham's [* Gen 22:1
judges, but broke * with Jehovah by Ju 2:17
away from the true * of their Ju 2:17
the youth of Israel to exercise * Ju 3:1
encouraged him in his * in God. 1Sa 23:16
And he has kept his * in me Job 2:3
None who have * in God will ever Ps 25:3
I tested your * at Meribah, when Ps 81:7
have abandoned their fathers' *. Dan 11:30,31
* with the wife of your youth. Mal 2:15
care for you, O men of little *? Mt 6:30
"I haven't seen * like this in all Mt 8:10
answered, "O you men of little *! Mt 8:26
When Jesus saw their *, he said Mt 9:2
is well! Your * has healed you." Mt 9:22
of your * it will happen." Mt 9:29
"O man of little *," Jesus Mt 14:31
told her, "your * is large, and Mt 15:28
told them, "O men of little *! Mt 16:8
"Because of your little *," Mt 17:20
"For if you had * even as small Mt 17:20
who trusts in me to lose his *, Mt 18:6
if you have *, and don't doubt, you Mt 21:21
things—justice and mercy and *. Mt 23:23
your * has made you well; Mk 5:34
"Oh, what tiny * you have; Mk 9:19
is possible if you have *." Mk 9:23
instantly replied, "I do have *; Mk 9:24
in me to lose *—it would be better Mk 9:42
Your * has healed you." Mk 10:52
"If you only have * in God—this is Mk 11:22,23
minds to the wisdom of *." Lk 1:17
Seeing their *, Jesus said to the Lk 5:20
I met a man with * like this." Lk 7:9
who does not lose his * in me.' Lk 7:23
the woman, "Your * has saved you; Lk 7:50
words but whose * afterwards is Lk 8:14
asked them, "Where is your *?" Lk 8:25
to her, "your * has healed you. Lk 8:48
to the Lord, "We need more *; Lk 17:5
"If your * were only the size of Lk 17:6
go; your * has made you well." Lk 17:19
I find who have * [and are praying Lk 18:8
have their kind of * will never get Lk 18:16,17
seeing! Your * has healed you." Lk 18:42
your * should not completely fail. Lk 22:32
build up the * of your brothers." Lk 22:32
he was before. * in Jesus' Act 3:16
Faith in Jesus' name—* given us Act 3:16
Stephen (a man unusually full of * Act 6:5
*, who had become a Christian). Act 6:5
Stephen, the man so full of * Act 6:8
the Holy Spirit and strong in *. Act 11:24
realized he had * to be healed. Act 14:9
to continue in the * in spite of Act 14:22
the door of * to the Gentiles too. Act 14:27
through *, just as he did ours. Act 15:9
believers, strengthening their *. Act 15:32
So the church grew daily in * Act 16:5
* in our Lord Jesus Christ. Act 20:21
able to build your * and give you Act 20:32
told them about * in Christ Jesus. Act 24:24
who are set apart by * in me.' Act 26:18
For your * in God is becoming Rom 1:8
so that I can impart to you the * Rom 1:11,12
that is, *." Rom 1:11,12f
only to share my * with you but to Rom 1:11,12
* and trust in Christ to save us. Rom 1:17
from start to finish by *. Rom 1:17
God is revealed from * to faith." Rom 1:17f
God is revealed from faith to *." Rom 1:17f
"our breaking * with God is good, Rom 3:5
He used Christ's blood and our * Rom 3:25
Christ has done and our * in him. Rom 3:27
by * in Christ and not by the Rom 3:28
are acquitted if they have *. Rom 3:30
Well then, if we are saved by *, Rom 3:31
this question of being saved by *? Rom 4:1

(FAITH Con't)

sight if they have * in Christ to	Rom 4:4,5
Literally, "* is reckoned for	Rom 4:4,5f
to those who have * in Christ but	Rom 4:9
these blessings through his *.	Rom 4:9
Was it by * alone?	Rom 4:9
of his *, that he was circumcised.	Rom 4:11
already had * and that God had	Rom 4:11
are justified by God through *.	Rom 4:11
favor with God by * alone, before	Rom 4:12
to those who have * are	Rom 4:14
are meaningless, and * is foolish.	Rom 4:14
given to us by *, as a free gift;	Rom 4:16
customs if we have * like	Rom 4:16
it comes to these matters of *.	Rom 4:16
And because his * was strong, he	Rom 4:19
He believed God, for his * and	Rom 4:20
And because of Abraham's * God	Rom 4:22
through his *—wasn't just for	Rom 4:23
in God's sight by * in his	Rom 5:1
For because of our *, he has	Rom 5:2
hope and * are strong and steady.	Rom 5:4
And in the same way—by our *	Rom 8:26
to be acquitted by *, even though	Rom 9:30
good instead of by depending on *.	Rom 9:32
that comes through * says, "You	Rom 10:6
his *, confirming his salvation.	Rom 10:10
Yet * comes from listening to	Rom 10:17
by how much * God has given you.	Rom 12:3
often as your * is strong enough to	Rom 12:6
you, even though his * is weak.	Rom 14:1
that is weak in *, not for	Rom 14:1f
but the * of others is weaker;	Rom 14:2
don't flaunt your * in front of	Rom 14:22
upsetting people's *, teaching	Rom 16:17
have * in Christ and obey him.	Rom 16:25,26,27
I wanted your * to stand firmly	1Co 2:5
Literally, "*."	1Co 8:9f
He gives special * to another,	1Co 12:9
Even if I had the gift of * so	1Co 13:2
things that remain—*, hope, and	1Co 13:13
do now, for your * is squarely	1Co 15:1
much to help your *, for it is	2Co 1:24
have so much *, so many good	2Co 8:7
Instead, we hope that your * will	2Co 10:15
the very * he tried to wreck."	Gal 1:23
laws, but only by * in Jesus Christ	Gal 2:16
by God because of *—and not because	Gal 2:16
Wouldn't we need to say that * in	Gal 2:17
men of * who truly trust in God.	Gal 3:7
Gentiles also, through their *.	Gal 3:8,9
can be right in his sight is by *.	Gal 3:11
from this way of * is the way of	Gal 3:12
Holy Spirit through this *.	Gal 3:14
to save through *—and God wrote	Gal 3:17
The only way out is through * in	Gal 3:21,22
standing with God through our *.	Gal 3:24
of God through * in Jesus Christ,	Gal 3:26
to God because of our *.	Gal 4:31
for all we need is * working	Gal 5:6
* in the cross of Christ alone.	Gal 5:11
of your strong * in the Lord Jesus	Eph 1:15
only one Lord, one *, one baptism,	Eph 4:5
In every battle you will need *	Eph 6:16
and love, with * from God the	Eph 6:23
grow and become happy in your *;	Php 1:25
out over your * which I am offering	Php 2:17
on *—counting on Christ alone.	Php 3:9
of your strong * in Christ.	Col 2:5
Don't let others spoil your * and	Col 2:8
and your strong * and steady	1Th 1:3
us about your remarkable * in God.	1Th 1:8
to strengthen your * and encourage	1Th 3:2,3
whether your * was still strong.	1Th 3:5
news that your * and love are as	1Th 3:6
cracks there may yet be in your *.	1Th 3:10
by the armor of * and love, and	1Th 5:8
wonderful way your * has grown, and	2Th 1:3
and complete * in God, in spite of	2Th 1:4
—rewarding your * with his power.	2Th 1:11
people accept God's plan of *.	1Ti 1:3,4
will be clean and their * strong.	1Ti 1:5
Cling tightly to your * in	1Ti 1:19
they lost their * in Christ after	1Ti 1:19
God's plan of salvation through *.	1Ti 2:7
is the hidden Source of their *.	1Ti 3:9
who is fed by * and by the true	1Ti 4:6
your *, and your clean thoughts.	1Ti 4:12
a brother in the * is being helped	1Ti 6:2
them through * in Jesus Christ.	2Ti 1:1
concerning the * and love Christ	2Ti 1:13
weak to have any * left, he remains	2Ti 2:13
and they have weakened the * of	2Ti 2:18
to do right. Have * and love, and	2Ti 2:22
turned against the Christian *.	2Ti 3:8
You know my * in Christ and how I	2Ti 3:10
I have been sent to bring * to	Tit 1:1
them strong in the *, and to stop	Tit 1:13
that the Christian * can't be	Tit 2:5
as you share your * with others it	Phm 1:6
and the High Priest of our *.	Heb 3:1
They didn't mix it with *.	Heb 4:2
about the necessity of * in God;	Heb 6:1
of their strong * and patience.	Heb 6:12
And those whose * has made them	Heb 10:38
by *, trusting him in everything.	Heb 10:38
No, our * in him assures our	Heb 10:39
WHAT IS *?	Heb 11:1
of old were famous for their *.	Heb 11:2
By *—by believing God—we know	Heb 11:3
It was by * that Abel obeyed God	Heb 11:4
*, without depending on him.	Heb 11:6
because of his * he became one of	Heb 11:7
Sarah, too, had *, and because of	Heb 11:11
These men of * I have mentioned	Heb 11:13
It was by * that Isaac knew God	Heb 11:20
By * Jacob, when he was old and	Heb 11:21
And it was by * that Joseph, as	Heb 11:22
Moses' parents had * too.	Heb 11:23
It was by * that Moses, when he	Heb 11:24,25
It was * that brought the walls	Heb 11:30
them. By *—because she believed in	Heb 11:31
the stories of the * of Gideon and	Heb 11:32
Some, through their *, escaped	Heb 11:34
And some women, through *,	Heb 11:35
renounce their *, then were killed	Heb 11:37,38
And these men of *, though they	Heb 11:39
crowd of men of * watching us from	Heb 12:1
If you don't ask with *, don't	Jas 1:7,8
to be rich in *, and the Kingdom of	Jas 2:5
that you have * and are Christians	Jas 2:14
Will that kind of * save anyone?	Jas 2:14
it isn't enough just to have *.	Jas 2:17
that you have it. * that doesn't	Jas 2:17
* at all—it is dead and useless.	Jas 2:17
God is by * alone, plus nothing;	Jas 2:18
prove whether you have * or not;	Jas 2:18
but anyone can see that I have *	Jas 2:18
God wants you to? * that does not	Jas 2:20
in good deeds is not real *.	Jas 2:20
told him to; his * was made	Jas 2:22
spirit in it, so * is dead if it is	Jas 2:26
if offered in *, will heal him, for	Jas 5:15
only to test your *, to see whether	1Pe 1:7
it—and your * is far more precious	1Pe 1:7
so if your * remains strong after	1Pe 1:7
Now your * and hope can rest in	1Pe 1:21
All of you who have our kind of *.	2Pe 1:1
kind of faith. The * I speak of is	2Pe 1:1
to give this same * to each of us.	2Pe 1:1
these gifts, you need more than *;	2Pe 1:5
these additions to * is blind	2Pe 1:9
of our holy *, learning to pray in	Jud 1:20
also I know your love and * and	Rev 2:19
who die in the * of Jesus."	Rev 14:13f
who testify of their * in Jesus.	Rev 19:10

FAITHFUL

But all of you who were * to the	Deu 4:4
your God is the * God who for a	Deu 7:9
He is *, without sin.	Deu 32:4
"Then I will raise up a * priest	1Sa 2:35
is as * as David your son-in-law?	1Sa 22:14
their step and are * to God, one of	1Ki 2:4
and true and * to you, and obeyed	1Ki 3:6
for they were honest and * men.	2Ki 12:15
you have tried to be * to God."	2Ch 19:3
only a * few had been doing it in	2Ch 30:5f
the priests. His * assistants were	2Ch 31:14,15
fortress—a very * man who revered	Neh 7:2
When he was * to you, you made a	Neh 9:8
it, commends the * followers of the	Ps 15:4
moon, my * witness in the sky!"	Ps 89:37
promised to David with a * pledge?	Ps 89:49
They will shelter you. His *	Ps 91:4
the Lord, and exhibits his * care.	Ps 92:15
of those who are * to his covenant	Ps 103:17,18
This was done to make them * and	Ps 105:45
answer my plea, because you are *	Ps 143:1
my son—be * and true to your wife.	Pro 5:15
A * employee is as refreshing as	Pro 25:13
Jerusalem, once my * wife!	Is 1:21
of Justice," and "The * Town."	Is 1:26
For the Lord is * to his	Is 30:18
he, the * Lord, the Holy One of	Is 49:7
He was * and honest, and made no	Dan 6:4
of all your * mercies, Lord, please	Dan 9:16
in God and is * to the Holy One.	Hos 11:12
be called 'The * City,' and 'The	Zec 8:3
who have been * to you through the	Mal 2:14
"Are you a wise and * servant of	Mt 24:45
I will put such * ones in charge	Mt 24:47
'You have been * in handling this	Mt 25:21
'You are a good and * servant.	Mt 25:23
You have been * over this small	Mt 25:23
talking to any *, sensible man	Lk 12:42,43,44
And if you are not * with other	Lk 16:12
You have been * with the little I	Lk 19:17
"If you agree that I am * to the	Act 16:15
and we have told everyone how *	2Co 1:20
you and me into * Christians and	2Co 1:21
loved brother and * helper in the	Eph 6:21
To: The * Christian	Col 1:2
He is Jesus Christ's * slave,	Col 1:7
I am also sending Onesimus, a *	Col 4:9
But the Lord is *;	2Th 3:3
the strength to be * to him, even	1Ti 1:12
but * in everything they do.	1Ti 3:11
left, he remains * to us and will	2Ti 2:13
our merciful and * High Priest	Heb 2:17
merciful to us and * to God in	Heb 2:17
For Jesus was * to God who	Heb 3:2
But Christ, God's * Son, is in	Heb 3:6
For if we are * to the end,	Heb 3:14
in my opinion, a very * brother.	1Pe 5:12
Remain * even when facing death	Rev 2:10
when Antipas, my * witness, was	Rev 2:13
the * and true Witness [of all	Rev 3:14
for being * in their witnessing.	Rev 6:9
the called and chosen and * ones.	Rev 17:14
horse was named "* and True"—the	Rev 19:11

FAITHFULLY

Jacob replied, "You know how *	Gen 30:29
you have * rescued me from danger.	Ps 71:15
I will * reward my people for	Is 61:8
* proclaim my every word.	Jer 23:28
I have * passed them on to you,	Jer 25:2,3
and find you * doing your work.	Mt 24:46
also * served in God's house.	Heb 3:2
and from Jesus Christ who *	Rev 1:5

FAITHFULNESS

your * to your husbands and to me.	Ru 1:8
and tell the world about your *?	Ps 30:9
Your * reaches beyond the clouds.	Ps 36:5
only hope is in your love and *.	Ps 40:11
me, because of his love and his *.	Ps 57:3
Your * is higher than the skies.	Ps 57:10
telling of your * to all your	Ps 71:22
Can they proclaim your *?	Ps 88:11
will praise you for your *.	Ps 89:5
you? * is your very character.	Ps 89:8
evening rejoice in all his *.	Ps 92:2
and kind, and his * goes on and on	Ps 100:5
heavens. Your * reaches the skies.	Ps 108:4
Your * extends to every	Ps 119:90,91
and your *, for your promises are	Ps 138:2
Literally, "answer me in * and	Ps 143:1f
One generation makes known your *	Is 38:19
Great is his *;	Lam 3:23
I will betroth you to me in *	Hos 1:20
There is no *, no kindness, no	Hos 4:1
Or, "shall live by his *."	Hab 2:4f
*, gentleness and self-control;	Gal 5:22

FAITHLESS

For they are a stubborn, *	Deu 32:20
Judah and had been * to the Lord.	2Ch 28:19
And her * sister Judah saw the	Jer 3:7
she saw that I divorced * Israel.	Jer 3:8
Then, afterwards, this * one	Jer 3:10
In fact, * Israel is less guilty	Jer 3:11
you have been like a * wife who	Jer 3:20
The beautiful and * city,	Nah 3:4
And yet we are * to each other,	Mal 2:10
"Only an evil, * nation would ask	Mt 12:39,40
"Oh, you stubborn, * people!	Mt 17:17
"O you stubborn * people,"	Lk 9:41
Don't be * any longer.	Jn 20:27

FAITHLESSNESS

will pay for your *, until the last	Num 14:33
apostasy, your * to me, and your	Jer 13:27
of idolatry and *, and my love will	Hos 14:4

FAKE

you ask in * surprise.	Mal 2:17
a * prophet named Bar-Jesus.	Act 13:6,7

FAKED

was only *, the Lord God says.	Jer 3:10

FAKES

by God or whether they are *?	1Co 12:3

FAKING

They thought he was *!	Act 9:26

FAL

Babylon is *	Rev 14:8

FALCON

The * (all kinds), the kite,	Lev 11:13-19
The * (any variety),	Deu 14:11-18

FALL

caused the man to * into a deep	Gen 2:21
the tent, let it * across their	Gen 9:23
cause the hail to * throughout all	Ex 9:22
"The terror of the Lord shall *	Ex 23:27
the grapes that * to the ground.	Lev 19:10
they shall * when no one is	Lev 26:36
by having someone * dead beside	Num 6:9
* into the camp and all around it!	Num 11:31
bodies shall * in this wilderness.	Num 14:32
will never again * upon any of the	Num 18:5
blessings * on those whom you	Num 22:5,6
And curses shall * upon everyone	Num 24:3-9
your enemies to * before you;	Deu 23:14
My words shall * upon you	Deu 32:2
the walls of the city will * down;	Jos 6:5
If it isn't, disaster will * upon	Jos 6:18
Must I now die of thirst, and *	Ju 15:18
was broken by the * and he died	1Sa 4:18

(FALL Con't)
a few of your men *, there will be 2Sa 17:9
it is better to * into the hand of 2Sa 24:14
"Where did it *?" 2Ki 6:6
calamity will certainly * upon us; 2Ki 7:9
"but let me * into the hands of 1Ch 21:13
the Lord did not * upon them during 2Ch 32:26
May their scoffing * back upon Neh 4:4
disappear, and * to the ground Job 15:33
I expected my * to be broken, Job 30:24
and storm to * upon the earth. Job 37:6
the rain to * upon the barren Job 38:25-27
rejoice with trembling. * down Ps 2:12
let them * beneath the weight of Ps 5:10
let him * into his own trap. Ps 7:15
My enemies will * back and perish Ps 9:3
The nations * into the pitfalls Ps 9:15
and their enemies * before them. Ps 10:5
and * beneath their blows. Ps 10:10
I never need to stumble or to *. Ps 16:8
My enemies quail before me and * Ps 18:39
he will never stumble, never *; Ps 21:7
me, they will stumble and *! Ps 27:2
Don't let me * into their hands! Ps 27:12
at my *—let them die. Ps 35:19
If they * it isn't fatal, for Ps 37:24
Literally, "I am ready to *." Ps 38:17f
They * before you. Ps 45:5
unheard-of terror will * on them. Ps 53:5
not permit the godly to slip or *. Ps 55:22
his enemies shall * face downward Ps 72:9
He caused the birds to * to the Ps 78:28
You will * as any prince—for all Ps 82:7
before the evening shadows *. Ps 90:5,6
Though a thousand * at my side, Ps 91:7
so that it would never * apart. Ps 104:5
until the evening shadows * again. Ps 104:23
have dug deep pits for me to * in. Ps 119:85,86
never let me stumble, slip or *. Ps 121:3,4
Let burning coals * down upon Ps 140:10
Let them * into their own Ps 141:10
cause someone to stumble and *. Pro 4:16
house, lest you * to her Pro 5:9
but a crook will slip and *. Pro 10:9
the wicked shall * beneath their Pro 11:5
letting the wicked * into it. Pro 11:8
the wicked plunge ahead—and *. Pro 12:26
and haughtiness before a *. Pro 16:18
Pride ends in a *, while humility Pro 29:23
See the way God does things and * Ecc 7:13
Dig a well—and * into it! Ecc 10:8,9
stones will * and crush you! Ecc 10:8,9
their well-set hair will all * Is 3:24
Babylon will *, and the groaning Is 21:2
It will come out and * to the Is 22:25
it supports will * with it, for the Is 22:25
in terror you will * into a pit, Is 24:18
For God's light of life will * Is 26:19
will stumble and * and be broken, Is 28:13
will stumble and * among those they Is 31:3
and the stars will * as leaves, as Is 34:4
watch, for it will * upon Edom, the Is 34:5
grain this *, still it will give Is 37:30
thing in place so it won't * over! Is 41:7
An idol to * down before and Is 44:15
Should I * down before a chunk of Is 44:19
in chains, and * down on their Is 45:14
from such a *, how can they save Is 46:1
Then they * down and worship it! Is 46:6
them * into your hands, O Babylon. Is 47:6
stagger and * to the ground." Is 63:6
leaves we fade, wither and *. Is 64:6
Their claims of doom will * upon Jer 5:13
year in spring and * and sends the Jer 5:23,24
until the evening shadows *. Jer 6:4
After the * of Jerusalem the Jer 7:18f
so that it won't * over, and there Jer 10:4
If you stumble and * on open Jer 12:5
darkness to * upon you so that you Jer 13:16
and * upon the dark mountains; Jer 13:16
terror to * upon them suddenly. Jer 15:8
a pit for me to * in, and they have Jer 18:22
and treacherous trails, and *. Jer 23:12
and vomit and * and rise no more, Jer 25:27
they shall * like fragile women. Jer 25:34
city that it will * to the king of Jer 32:36
They shall * here in Egypt, Jer 44:12
across each other and * together. Jer 46:12
Vast multitudes * in heaps. Jer 46:16
Let her stagger and * like a Jer 48:26
her, and were happy at her *. Jer 48:27
He who flees shall * in a trap Jer 48:44
shakes with the noise of Edom's *; Jer 49:21
Her young men will * in the Jer 50:30
will stumble and * and no one will Jer 50:32
shake at Babylon's *, and her cry Jer 50:46
They shall * down slain in the Jer 51:4
drink until they * unconscious to Jer 51:39
believe its eyes at Babylon's *! Jer 51:41
Kings and priests together * Lam 2:6
our own eyes we've seen her *." Lam 2:16
O walls of Jerusalem, let tears * Lam 2:18
builders that their wall will *. Eze 13:11
Yes, it will surely *. Eze 13:13
wall, and it will * on you and Eze 13:14
fire, they will * into another; Eze 15:7
fell upon her will * upon you—and Eze 23:32
the * of Jerusalem, saying, 'Ha! Eze 26:2
country will shake with your *; Eze 26:15
How the islands tremble at your *! Eze 26:18
A sword shall * on Egypt; Eze 30:4
allies shall *, and the pride of Eze 30:6
of Pharaoh * useless to his sides. Eze 30:25
the sound of her *, for I threw her Eze 31:16
their lives on the day of your *. Eze 32:10
For I have caused my terror to * Eze 32:32
will * upon the open fields; Eze 39:5
causing Israel to * into deep sin, Eze 44:12
*, and there will always be fruit. Eze 47:12
strikes up, you are to * flat on Dan 3:5
that everyone must * down and Dan 3:10
When the music plays, if you * Dan 3:15
his government shall never *. Dan 7:14
in those days and *, but this will Dan 11:35
when thrown or allowed to *. Hos 4:12f
of guilt, and Judah, too, shall *. Hos 5:5
to * upon them and crush them. Hos 10:8
your forts will *, just as at Hos 10:14
be cut off and * to the ground. Amo 3:14
shall * and never rise again." Amo 8:14
The Lord's vengeance will soon * Ob 1:15
for though I *, I will rise again! Mic 7:8
to their feet, and * again. Nah 3:3
All your forts will *. Nah 3:12
figs that * into the mouths of Nah 3:12
Stagger and *! Hab 2:16
I will let them * into the clutches Zec 11:6
it will * with a mighty crash." Mt 7:27
Two for a penny?) can * to the Mt 10:29
and both will * into a ditch." Mt 15:13,14
to eat the crumbs that *." Mt 15:27
many of you shall * back into sin Mt 24:10
Literally, "the stars shall * Mt 24:29f
to * from the heavens, and the Mt 24:29
of him they would * down before him Mk 3:11
often makes him * into the fire or Mk 9:22
'Rise up and * into the Mk 11:22,23
will *—the heavens will convulse. Mk 13:25
He will * into a ditch and pull Lk 6:39
Pray God that you will not * when Lk 22:46
the mountains to * on them and Lk 23:30
and that "I must * and die like a Jn 12:23,24
shadow would * across some of them Act 5:15
which those should rise and *, and when. Act 17:26
the ropes and let the boat * off. Act 27:32
begin swelling or suddenly * dead; Act 28:6
Yes, all have sinned; all * Rom 3:23
on them and * back upon their heads Rom 11:9
this world, who are doomed to *. 1Co 2:6
you might * back into sin. 1Co 7:2
For you too may * into sin. 1Co 10:12
bare and he will * down on his 1Co 14:25
Let God's curses * on anyone, Gal 1:8
let God's curse * upon him. Gal 1:9
of his plan I * down on my knees Eph 3:14,15
disaster will * upon them as 1Th 5:3
soon, and pride comes before a *. 1Ti 3:6
It is a fearful thing to * Heb 10:31
and lame, will not * and hurt Heb 12:13
that no rain would *, none fell for Jas 5:17
the Rock that will make them *." 1Pe 2:8
must follow—that they will *. 1Pe 2:8
you will never stumble or * away. 2Pe 1:10
terrible end of those who * away. 1Jn 5:17f
the Israelites to * by lust. Rev 2:6f
are lying) to * at your feet and Rev 3:9
to crush them. "* on us," they Rev 6:16
that no rain will * during the Rev 11:6
And great fear will * on Rev 11:11

FALLEN
fields, nor pick up the * grain; Lev 23:22
from your * foes,"—for the troops Ju 8:23,24
found her there, * down in front of Ju 19:27
morning, Dagon had * with his face 1Sa 5:3
idol had * face down before the Ark 1Sa 5:4
Michal had * in love with David, 1Sa 18:20
Mighty heroes have *. 2Sa 1:19
These mighty heroes have * in the 2Sa 1:25
The mighty ones have *, 2Sa 1:27
a great man has * today in Israel; 2Sa 3:38
They have * beneath my feet. 2Sa 22:39
Israel's new king, Ahaziah, had * 2Ki 1:2
fire of God has * from heaven and Job 1:16
I am like a *, rotten tree, like Job 13:27,28
* unto me in pleasant places." Ps 16:6f
They have *. Ps 36:12
They themselves have * into it! Ps 57:6
The Lord lifts the * and those Ps 145:14
you as clean as freshly * snow. Is 1:18
salvation and lie * and crushed Is 8:14,15
How you are * from heaven, O Is 14:12
out, "Babylon is *, is fallen; Is 21:8,9
out, "Babylon is fallen, is *; Is 21:8,9
will punish the * angels in the Is 24:21
will strip the * army of Assyria! Is 33:4
they will get from your * city. Is 33:18
your breath. I've * in love with Jer 2:25
to it that they lie among the *. Jer 8:12
My people have * Jer 12:9
Later, when Jerusalem has *, Jer 23:20
they have stumbled and *. Jer 46:6
Her cities are *; Jer 48:41
Her walls have *. Jer 50:15
now, suddenly Babylon too has *. Jer 51:8
How Babylon is *—great Babylon, Jer 51:41
the wall of Babylon has *. Jer 51:44
The crown is * from our head. Lam 5:16
Literally, "no lot has * upon Eze 24:6f
has been broken, and I have * Eze 26:2
and leave her * on the ground. Eze 31:12
and not as the * lords who are Eze 32:27
to tell me, "The city has *!" Eze 33:21
And after that kingdom has *, yet Dan 2:39
and most beautiful of them are *. Zec 11:2
been very drowsy and had * asleep. Lk 9:32
tabernacle of David which is *." Act 15:16f
Literally, "a star * from Rev 9:1f
who was * to earth from heaven, Rev 9:1
Literally, "(*) angels." Rev 9:14f
Dragon and his hosts of * angels. Rev 12:7
is fal en, is *—that great Rev 14:8
Five have already *, the sixth Rev 17:10
the Great is *, is fallen; Rev 18:2
the Great is fallen, is *; Rev 18:2

FALLING
anyone from * off and bringing Deu 22:8
before the king, * down at his feet Est 8:3
who are weak or *, or lie crushed Job 4:3,4
them from * into some trap. Job 33:17,18
keeping me from slipping and *. Ps 26:12
of heights and of *—a white-haired, Ecc 12:5
* down upon them! Sol 1:10
The gods are * out onto the Is 46:1
But now it was mildewed and * Jer 13:7
her tears * down upon his feet; Lk 7:38
"I saw Satan * from heaven as a Lk 10:18
with great drops * to the ground as Lk 22:44
his treachery and * headlong there, Act 1:18
us from constant * into sin and Tit 2:14
from slipping and * away, and to Jud 1:24,25
heaven appeared to be * to earth Rev 6:13
Living Beings, and * face down Rev 7:11

FALLOW
land rest and lie * during the Ex 23:11
* before the Lord, uncultivated. Lev 25:4

FALLS
heels, so that the rider * off. Gen 49:17
an ox or a donkey * into it, the Ex 21:33
which the carcass * shall be Lev 11:32
If it * into a pottery bowl, Lev 11:33
If the body * into a spring or Lev 11:36
* upon it, the seed is defiled. Lev 11:38
just as one who * stretches out his Job 30:24
when deep sleep * on men as they Job 33:15
fool * flat on his face. Pro 10:8
gladness when he *— for the Lord Pro 24:17
If one *, the other pulls him Ecc 4:10
but if a man * when he is alone, Ecc 4:10
when a tree *, whether south or Ecc 11:3
Your hair * across your face like Sol 4:1
Your hair, as it * across your Sol 6:5
* from the heavens upon you; Is 24:18
in a storm. It * and will not rise Is 24:20
a bulging wall that bursts and *; Is 30:13
a carved idol! He * down before it Is 44:17
Truth * dead in the streets, and Is 59:14
a person *, he jumps up again; Jer 8:4,5
And when the wall *, the people Eze 13:12
until the flesh * off the bones. Eze 24:5
anger of the Lord * and the Zep 2:2
* into the fire or into the water; Mt 17:15
shall be broken, but those it * Mt 21:44
"If your cow * into a pit, don't Lk 14:5
and those on whom it * will be Lk 20:18
your children * on the Sabbath, you Jn 7:21,22,23
* and all work comes to an end. Jn 9:4
* into the furrows of the earth. Jn 12:23,24
the darkness *, for then it will be Jn 12:35
over his own "wisdom" and *. 1Co 3:19
* without my longing to help him? 2Co 11:29
like a flower that droops and *; 1Pe 1:24

FALSE
Or, "You must not give * Ex 20:16f
stand something you know is *. Ex 23:1
sin of worshiping * gods, and that Ex 23:33
If anyone gives * witness, Deu 19:16
You shall not show pity to a * Deu 19:21
"Go to the * prophets of your 2Ki 3:13
But it is * to say he doesn't Job 35:13
and it is even more * to say Job 35:14,15
claim that's made for them is *?" Ps 4:2
they are * and hypocritical. Ps 26:4
no wonder I hate every * teaching. Ps 119:104

(FALSE Con't)
swear to the truth of what is *. Ps 144:8
to do wrongA * witnessSowing Pro 6:16-19
a * man by deceit and lies. Pro 12:17
lies; a * witness always lies. Pro 14:5
but a * witness is a traitor. Pro 14:25
Punish * witnesses. Pro 19:5
A * witness shall be punished and Pro 19:9
WINE GIVES * courage; Pro 20:1
distinguishing the true from *. Pro 20:8
weights * scales." Pro 20:23f
A * witness must be punished; Pro 21:28
by appearance, * evidence, or Is 11:3
what liars all * prophets are, by Is 44:25
and to stop making * accusations Is 58:9
surely they will not be * Is 63:8
are ruled by * prophets, and my Jer 5:31
put your trust in * gods, I will Jer 13:24,25
My heart is broken for the * Jer 23:9
Don't listen to these * prophets Jer 23:16
By telling these * dreams they Jer 23:27
Let these * prophets tell their Jer 23:28
And as for the * prophets and Jer 23:34
the priests and * prophets and all Jer 26:7,8
Then the priests and the * Jer 26:11
to the priests and * prophets, Jer 26:16
"Do not listen to your * Jer 27:9
Don't listen to the * prophets Jer 27:14
(son of Azzur), a * prophet from Jer 28:1
Then Hananiah, the * prophet, Jer 28:10
to Hananiah, the * prophet, Jer 28:15
Don't let the * prophets and Jer 29:8
But now, because you accept the * Jer 29:15
this about your * prophets, Ahab Jer 29:21
* prophet Jeremiah of Anathoth? Jer 29:27
"We will not listen to your * Jer 44:16
are *—her helplessness is great. Jer 48:30
Moab's worshiping * gods and Jer 48:35
for their help. * hope—they could Lam 1:19
the * "worship" of his people; Lam 2:7
foolish things, * to the core. Lam 2:14
becomes of all the * predictions of Eze 12:24
against the * prophets of Israel Eze 13:2,3
And if one of the * prophets Eze 14:9
my people Israel. * prophets and Eze 14:10
Your magicians and * prophets Eze 21:29
Your 'prophets' describe * Eze 22:28
visions and speak * messages they Eze 22:28
guard as they bask in * security. Dan 8:25
so will your * "prophets" too; Hos 4:5
The hearts of her people are * Hos 10:2
the pride and * glory of Israel, Amo 6:8
(Those who worship * gods have Jon 2:8
the other way! You * prophets! Mic 3:5
bags of *, deceitful weights? Mic 6:11
them all to worship her * gods, Nah 3:4
be forgotten. All * prophets and Zec 13:2
if anyone begins * prophecy again, Zec 13:3
cuts, as practiced by * prophets. Zec 13:6f
This is a * prophet who is lying Zec 13:6f
"Beware of * teachers who come Mt 7:15
And many * prophets will appear Mt 24:11
believe it. For * Christs shall Mt 24:24
shall arise, and * prophets, and Mt 24:24
who agreed to be * witnesses, these Mt 26:60,61
For there will be many * Mk 13:22
false Messiahs and * prophets who Mk 13:22
Many * witnesses volunteered, Mk 14:56
by the crowds—for * prophets have Lk 6:26
after I leave you, * teachers, like Act 20:29
to be like those * teachers of 2Co 3:1
there—* ones, really—who came to Gal 2:4
Those * teachers who are so Gal 4:17
preaching with any * motives or 1Th 2:3
In fact, evil men and * teachers 2Ti 3:13
BUT THERE WERE * prophets, too, in 2Pe 2:1
will be * teachers among you. 2Pe 2:1
than these * teachers, never speak 2Pe 2:11
But * teachers are fools—no 2Pe 2:12
the difference between true and *. 1Jn 2:21
For there are many * teachers 1Jn 4:1
Watch out for the * leaders—and 2Jn 1:7
Yet these * teachers carelessly Jud 1:8
not followed this * teaching Rev 2:24,25
the Creature, and his * Prophet. Rev 16:13
for the worship of * gods. Rev 19:2f
and with him the * Prophet, Rev 19:20
Creature and his * Prophet—were Rev 19:20
the Creature and * Prophet are, and Rev 20:10

FALSEHOOD
nor use it to swear to a *. Ex 20:7
You must not swear to a *, thus Lev 19:12
How I hate all * but how I love Ps 119:163
Or, "with cords of *." Is 5:18f
for believing *, refusing the 2Th 2:12
No * can be charged against them; Rev 14:5

FALSELY
may have been * claiming her Gen 31:35f
of the Lord your God to swear *." Ex 20:7f
"Keep far away from * charging Ex 23:7
Don't * accuse your neighbor of Lev 19:16
But any prophet who * claims Deu 18:20
has * accused a virgin of Israel. Deu 22:19
Never * accuse a man to his Pro 30:10
Prisoners are * accused and sent Eze 22:9
who swears * by my name," says the Zec 5:4
of themselves for * accusing you 1Pe 3:16

FALTER
many people will * because of the Lk 21:26

FAME
have heard your * will say, 'The Num 14:15
of * to replace those who died. 2Sa 23:24-39f
Literally, "heard of the * of 1Ki 10:1f
David's * spread everywhere, and 1Ch 14:17
will hear of your * and will 2Ch 6:33
to him, and his * spread even to 2Ch 26:8
palace and his * was known Est 9:4
You have given him * and honor. Ps 21:5
* will endure to every generation. Ps 102:12
* is known to every generation. Ps 135:13
you are on the road to *. Pro 13:18
to the wise men's hall of *. Pro 15:31,32
would learn the reason for your *! Is 64:2
not heard my * nor seen my glory. Is 66:19
We have heard the * of their Jer 6:24
You have been fooled by your * Jer 49:16
spread his * all over the town. Mt 9:31

FAMED
Among them are the * Anak giants, Deu 9:1
This was part of the * "law of Est 8:8f
All the * treasures of the city, Jer 20:5
Even her * mercenaries have Jer 46:20,21

FAMILIAR
if they are not * with the laws Ez 7:25
Since the writing was in * Dan 5:8f
events are all * to him, for they Act 26:26

FAMILIES
THESE ARE THE * of Shem, Ham, and Gen 10:1
of the native * of the land of Gen 36:20,21
go on home with grain for your *; Gen 42:19
grain for your * and go on home, Gen 42:33
keep you and your * alive, so that Gen 45:7
* and come here to Egypt to live. Gen 45:18
people—his brothers and their *. Gen 50:8
take care of you and your *." Gen 50:21
* continued to live in Egypt. Gen 50:22
Egypt, with their *:Reuben, Simeon, Ex 1:1
The above are the * of the Ex 6:19
These are the * within the clan of Ex 6:24
and the * within the clans. Ex 6:25
way depends on the size of the *). Ex 12:3,4
for one or more * depending upon Ex 12:21
of persons in the *, and kill the Ex 12:21
the priestly * may eat this food. Lev 22:13
bread available for ten entire *; Lev 26:26
* of Kohath destroy themselves! Num 4:17,18,19
Moses heard all the * standing Num 11:10
all * descended from Anak. Num 13:22
their tents and * and the friends Num 16:32
your *, sons and daughters alike. Num 18:11
For all the members of your * may Num 18:11
other crop. Your * may eat these Num 18:13
they are for you and your * as Num 18:19
Aaron and his sons and their * Num 18:31
* of Nemu-el, Abiram, and Dathan. Num 26:5-11
These are the * of the tribe of Num 26:58,59
here for our *, to keep them safe Num 32:17
cities for your * and sheepfolds Num 32:24
There you and your * shall feast Deu 12:7
and sisters, and all their *. Jos 2:12,13
and the clan must come by its *, Jos 7:14
Then the * of that clan were Jos 7:17
Literally, "according to its *." Jos 13:15f
Literally, "according to its *." Jos 13:24f
Literally, "according to its *." Jos 13:29f
assigned to the * of the tribe of Jos 18:11
The other * of the Kohath Jos 21:5
The other * of the Kohath Jos 21:20,21,22
Each year Elkanah and his * 1Sa 1:3
of all the * of the tribe! 1Sa 9:21
the priests' *—men, women, 1Sa 22:19
men and their * to live at Gath 1Sa 27:2,3
happened to their *, they wept 1Sa 30:3
The men recovered their * and all 1Sa 30:18,19
and their * all moved to Hebron. 2Sa 2:3
men and their * went along. 2Sa 15:22
as I destroyed the * of Jeroboam 2Ki 9:9
The * of Kiriath-jearim were the 1Ch 2:53
they also included the * of the 1Ch 2:55
The * of the linen workers who 1Ch 4:21-22
brothers had large *—they all had 1Ch 4:27
divided into the * of his sons: 1Ch 6:25,26,27
The * of the subclan of Samuel 1Ch 6:28
war from these * totaled 22,600. 1Ch 7:2
All of these * lived together near 1Ch 8:30,31,32
former cities were * from the 1Ch 9:2
Then some * from the tribes of 1Ch 9:3
They and their * were all trained 1Ch 25:6,7
of their *, for it was all done by 1Ch 26:13
* of Judah, my father's family; 1Ch 28:4
them back to their * in Jericho, 2Ch 28:15
on duty at the Temple and their * 2Ch 31:16
was given to all * of properly 2Ch 31:17,18
From the * of Jedaiah of the Ez 2:36-39
From the * of Jeshua and Kedmi-el Ez 2:40,41,42
gatekeepers (the * of Shallum, Ez 2:40,41,42
The following * of the Temple Ez 2:43-54
fight for your friends, your *, Neh 4:14
What was happening was that * Neh 5:2,3,4
From the * of Jeshua and Joab of Neh 7:8-38
each year—the * of the priests, Neh 10:34
lives and their *, to destroy all Est 8:11
eighty-five priests and their *. Ps 52:1
He gives * to the lonely, and Ps 68:6
But our * will continue; Ps 102:28
They raise big * there, and many Ps 107:38
them and their * for saying this. Jer 23:34
the Lord, all the * of Israel shall Jer 31:1
Go to the settlement where the * Jer 35:2
all the Rechab *—to the Temple, Jer 35:3
a lesson from the * of Rechab? Jer 35:13
or obey. The * of Rechab have Jer 35:16
you and kill you and your *; Eze 5:17
who live among you with their *. Eze 47:22
From now on * will be split Lk 12:52
all his brothers' * to come to Act 7:14
should have happy, obedient *. 1Ti 3:12
Already whole * have been turned Tit 1:11

FAMILY
boat with all your *, for among all Gen 7:1
that our * line will continue." Gen 19:34
a permanent cemetery for my *." Gen 23:9
the * of my master's relatives." Gen 24:27
*, and to bring back a girl from Gen 24:38
my relatives, from my brother's *. Gen 24:40
Then I asked her, 'Whose * are Gen 24:47
path to find a girl from the * Gen 24:48
Uncle Ishmael's * and married two Gen 28:9
than to someone outside the *." Gen 29:19
should I provide for my own *?" Gen 30:30
Jacob now arranged his * into a Gen 33:2
camped on from the * of Hamor, Gen 33:19
many weeks. His * all tried to Gen 37:35
Joseph thus married into a * of Gen 41:45f
us about our *," they told him. Gen 43:7
married and had a *, and a baby Ex 2:1
As Moses and his * were traveling Ex 4:24
shall die in every * in Egypt, from Ex 11:5
of Israel) each * shall get a lamb Ex 12:3,4
(or, if a * is small, let it Ex 12:3,4
small * in the neighborhood; Ex 12:3,4
Hur was a man of Judah, of the * Ex 17:10f
to you and your *, for the Lord has Lev 10:15
atonement for himself and his *. Lev 16:6
himself and his *, he shall take a Lev 16:11
that man and his * and cut him off, Lev 20:5
It shall be a year when all the * Lev 25:10
home to his original * possession; Lev 25:13
to his own * and possessions. Lev 25:41
to the foreigner's *, he may be Lev 25:47
is not part of his * possession, Lev 27:22
war, indicating their tribe and *. Num 1:2-15
his tribe and *, as the Lord had Num 1:17,18,19
your sons and your * are Num 18:1
Instead, you and your * shall Deu 15:20
it for food for your * at home. Deu 15:22
Lord with your * and household. Deu 16:11
together with your * and servants. Deu 16:14
must not marry outside the *; Deu 25:5
Celebrate with your * and with Deu 26:11
you—man or woman, * or tribe of Deu 29:18
* aren't harmed," they promised. Jos 2:14
the guilty * must come one by one. Jos 7:14
and the * of Zabdi was indicated. Jos 7:17
Zabdi's * was brought man by Jos 7:18
But as for me and my *, we will Jos 24:15
and that of his * if he would show Ju 1:24
except for this man and his *. Ju 1:25
I save Israel? My * is the poorest Ju 6:15
thought of in the entire *!" Ju 6:15
best ox to the * altar of Baal, and Ju 6:25
deed that Gideon and his * did. Ju 8:27
kindness to the * of Gideon despite Ju 8:35
priests. This * continued as Ju 18:30
in the * by marrying her off to a Ru 1:11f
the * name of her dead husband." Ru 4:10
This is the * tree of Boaz, Ru 4:18-22
The entire * was up early the 1Sa 1:19,20
I will put an end to your *, so 1Sa 2:31
* will be in distress and need. 1Sa 2:32
and his * shall be priests to my 1Sa 2:35
him and his entire * with 1Sa 3:13
in Israel, and my * is the least 1Sa 9:21
Then he brought each * of the 1Sa 10:21
the * of the Matrites was chosen. 1Sa 10:21
and his whole * will be exempted 1Sa 17:25
what sort of * does this young 1Sa 17:55
wanted to know more about his *! 1Sa 17:55f
"My father's * is nothing!" 1Sa 18:18
me from an unknown * find enough 1Sa 18:23
Bethlehem for an annual * reunion. 1Sa 20:6
covenant with the * of David, and 1Sa 20:16
* celebration," Jonathan replied. 1Sa 20:28,29

(FAMILY Con't)
and all his * and all the other 1Sa 22:11,12
accuse me and my * in this matter, 1Sa 22:15
along with your entire *!" 1Sa 22:16
death of all of your father's *. 1Sa 22:22
will not kill my * and destroy my 1Sa 24:21
buried him in his * plot at Ramah. 1Sa 25:1
* and multiply everything you own. 1Sa 25:6
and his whole *—he's such a 1Sa 25:17
Joab and his * are the guilty 2Sa 3:29
upon Saul and upon his entire *!" 2Sa 4:8
David returned to bless his *. 2Sa 6:20
father and his * and who appointed 2Sa 6:21
Your * shall rule my kingdom 2Sa 7:16
promised concerning me and my *. 2Sa 7:25
Bless me and my * forever! 2Sa 7:29
if any of Saul's * was still 2Sa 9:1
"Is anyone left from Saul's *? 2Sa 9:3
to Saul and his *," he said. 2Sa 9:9
him, to produce food for his *; 2Sa 9:10,11
threat in your * from this time on, 2Sa 12:10
since it's all in the * anyway. 2Sa 13:20
Now the rest of the * is 2Sa 14:7
son of Gera, a member of Saul's *. 2Sa 16:5
for murdering King Saul and his *; 2Sa 16:7,8
of Saul and his *, for they 2Sa 21:1
To David and his *, 2Sa 22:51
And it is my * 2Sa 23:5
be only against me and my *." 2Sa 24:17
from me and from my father's *. 1Ki 2:31
and each * had its own home and 1Ki 4:25
* and give it to someone else. 1Ki 11:11
a member of the royal * of Edom. 1Ki 11:14
Let Rehoboam be king of his own * 1Ki 12:16,17
the kingship of the * of David. 1Ki 12:20
be born into the * line of David, 1Ki 13:2
and the death of all of his *. 1Ki 13:34
away from the * of David and gave 1Ki 14:8
I will sweep away your * as a 1Ki 14:10
I vow that those of your * who 1Ki 14:11
* who will come to a quiet end. 1Ki 14:13
sees in the entire * of Jeroboam. 1Ki 14:13
will destroy the * of Jeroboam. 1Ki 14:14
one of the royal * was left, just 1Ki 15:29
you and your *, just as I did the 1Ki 16:3
Those of your * who die in the 1Ki 16:4-7
to Baasha and his * because he had 1Ki 16:4-7
*—leaving not a single male child. 1Ki 16:11
"For you and your * have refused 1Ki 18:18
That land has been in my * for 1Ki 21:3
He is going to destroy your * as 1Ki 21:22
as he did the * of King Jeroboam 1Ki 21:22
Jeroboam and the * of King Baasha, 1Ki 21:22
The members of your * who die in 1Ki 21:24
life, "Take your * and move to 2Ki 8:1
So the woman took her * and lived 2Ki 8:2
You are to destroy the * of 2Ki 9:7
The entire * of Ahab must be 2Ki 9:8
I will destroy the * of Ahab as 2Ki 9:9
the members of the * of Ahab who 2Ki 10:11
the founder of the * of Rechab. 1Ch 2:55
THE * TREE of every person in 1Ch 9:1
One * was that of Uthai (the son 1Ch 9:4
The Shilonites were another * to 1Ch 9:5
the entire * was wiped out in one 1Ch 10:6
members of his * were officers of 1Ch 12:24-37
there with the * of Obed-edom for 1Ch 13:14
the Lord blessed him and his *. 1Ch 13:14
* that you have given me all this? 1Ch 17:16
destroy me and my *, but do not 1Ch 21:17
all my father's * to begin a 1Ch 28:4
families of Judah, my father's *; 1Ch 28:4
Ahab, for Ahab's * became his 2Ch 22:4
and killing the * and friends of 2Ch 22:8
and took her * name)—also returned Ez 2:61
guards from each * in the cleared Neh 4:13
From the * of Hezekiah of the Neh 7:8-38
From the * of Jeshua of the Neh 7:39-42
From the * of Kadmi-el of the Neh 7:43,44,45
and took her * name), whose Neh 7:63
their * inheritance was located. Neh 11:20
* and raised as his own daughter. Est 2:7
by every * throughout the Est 9:28
He had a large * of seven sons Job 1:2,3
forever from their * and their Job 7:10
me down, and taken away my *. Job 16:7
Neither his friends nor his * Job 20:9
again be able to enjoy his *. Job 21:21
Even my own * stands at a Ps 38:11
in each Egyptian *—he who was the Ps 78:51
But he rejected Joseph's *, the Ps 78:67
May his * name be blotted out in Ps 109:12,13
her a beloved member of your *. Pro 7:4
world and all his * of mankind! Pro 8:31
The fool who provokes his * to Pro 11:29
grief to all the *, but hating Pro 15:27
* forever—so watch your business Pro 27:23,24
you and on your nation and your *. Is 7:17
will be an honor to his * name." Is 22:23,24
for you are Abraham's *, and he Is 41:8
The smallest * shall multiply Is 60:22
own *, have turned against you. Jer 12:6
you and all your * and household Jer 20:6
on the throne: His * will not weep Jer 22:18
I will punish him and his *. Jer 29:32
Jerahmeel (a member of the royal * Jer 36:26
punish him and his * and his Jer 36:31
Malchiah, a member of the royal *. Jer 38:6
you and your * shall live and the Jer 38:17
of the royal * and one of the Jer 41:1
a member of the royal * [Zedekiah Eze 17:12,13
At that time the Zadok * of the Eze 43:19
men of the royal * and nobility of Dan 1:3,4
command to execute the * of Ahab. Hos 1:4,5f
of the royal *: You are doomed! Hos 5:1
the entire * I brought from Egypt: Amo 3:1
I do not come from a * of Amo 7:14
and people. Each * will go into Zec 12:12,13,14
Well, we had among us a * of Mt 22:25
his relatives and by his own *." Mk 6:4
I should help my own *—the Jews. Mk 7:27
Jesus sent him home to his *. Mk 8:26
"There is no one in all your * Lk 1:61
"Go back to your *," he told Lk 8:39
We know of a * of seven Lk 20:29
I have kept safe within your * Jn 17:12
he and all his * were baptized. Act 16:33
into King David's royal * line; Rom 1:3
the bosom of his *, and calling to Rom 8:15
into a Jewish * is truly a Jew! Rom 9:6
from his Jewish *) and will love Rom 9:25
and a member of Benjamin's *. Rom 11:1
Oh, yes, and I baptized the * 1Co 1:16
Otherwise, if the * separates, 1Co 7:14
whereas a united * may, in God's 1Co 7:14
you remember Stephanas and his *? 1Co 16:15
us into his own * by sending Jesus Eph 1:5
Gentiles by making us all one *, Eph 2:14
of God's very own *, citizens of Eph 2:19
is when all of his *—Jews and Eph 3:10
of all the great * of God—some of Eph 3:14,15
of the old original Benjamin *. Php 3:5
He must have a well-behaved *, 1Ti 3:4
his own little * behave, how can he 1Ti 3:5
living in his own *, has no right 1Ti 5:8
and all his *, because he visited 2Ti 1:16
a Man, born into King David's *; 2Ti 2:8
based on * lines was canceled Heb 7:18
he built the ark and saved his *. Heb 11:7
you don't really belong in his *. Heb 12:8
the first children in his new *. Jas 1:18
we are now members of God's own *. 1Pe 1:3
like one big happy *, full of 1Pe 3:8
being in Christ's * and being 1Pe 4:16
up for God, and his * of seven. 2Pe 2:5
born into God's * does not make a 1Jn 3:9
shows that he is not in God's *; 1Jn 3:10
part of God's * makes a practice of 1Jn 5:18

FAMINE
time a terrible * in the land: and Gen 12:10
NOW A SEVERE * overshadowed the Gen 26:1
be seven years of * following the Gen 41:27
be seven years of * so great that Gen 41:30
out; * will consume the land. Gen 41:30
the land. The * will be so Gen 41:31
when the seven years of * come. Gen 41:36
the first of the * years, two sons Gen 41:50
Then the seven years of * began, Gen 41:54
So now, with severe * all over Gen 41:56,57
buy food, for the * was as severe Gen 42:5
the * has made our land." Gen 42:8,9
terrible * throughout the land. Gen 43:1
These two years of * will grow Gen 45:6
still five years of * ahead of us. Gen 45:11,12
Canaan—the * is very bitter there. Gen 47:4
dependents. The * became worse and Gen 47:13
because the * was so severe. Gen 47:20
left the country because of a * Ru 1:1
THERE WAS A * during David's reign 2Sa 21:1
Then the Lord said, "The * is 2Sa 21:1
answered prayer and ended the *. 2Sa 21:12,13,14
seven years of * across the land, 2Sa 24:13
"If there is a * in the land 1Ki 8:37
Meanwhile the * had become very 1Ki 18:2
whose sins had caused the *. 1Ki 21:9f
but there was a * in the land. 2Ki 4:38
As a result there was a great * 2Ki 6:25
has called down a * on Israel that 2Ki 8:1
After the * ended, she returned 2Ki 8:3
You may have three years of *, 1Ch 21:12
"If there is a * in the land, or 2Ch 6:28
war, disease, or *—we can stand 2Ch 20:9
there—to die by * and thirst—while 2Ch 32:11
you from death in *, and from the Job 5:20
"You shall laugh at war and *; Job 5:22
They are gaunt with * and have Job 30:3
from death even in times of *! Ps 33:18,19
even in *, they will have enough. Ps 37:19
But for rebels there is * and Ps 68:6
He called for a * on the land of Ps 105:16
wipe you out with * and the sword. Is 14:30
destruction. Yes, * and the sword. Is 51:19
There will be neither * nor war! Jer 5:12
return is war and * and disease. Jer 14:12
well—that no war or * will come. Jer 14:13
who say no war shall come nor *. Jer 14:15
By war and * they themselves Jer 14:15
Jerusalem, victims of * and war; Jer 14:16
those doomed to starvation, to *; Jer 15:2
They shall die from war and *, Jer 16:4
And I will send massacre and * Jer 24:10
I will send war, * and disease Jer 27:8
Why should you choose war and * Jer 27:13
warning of war, * and plague. Jer 28:8
I will send war, * and plague upon Jer 29:16,17
the city by sword, * and disease. Jer 32:24
through warfare, * and disease, Jer 32:36
of death by war and * and disease. Jer 34:17
the war and * you fear will follow Jer 42:16
Yes, you will die from sword, * Jer 42:17
will die by sword, * and disease in Jer 42:22
in Egypt, killed by * and sword; Jer 44:12
by sword, * and disease. Jer 44:13
been destroyed by sword and *." Jer 44:18
and * until all of you are dead. Jer 44:27
month, when the * in the city was Jer 52:6
Our skin was black from *. Lam 5:10
One-third of you will die from * Eze 5:12
deadly arrows of * to destroy you. Eze 5:16
destroy you. The * will become more Eze 5:16
And not only * will come, but Eze 5:17
perish from war and * and disease. Eze 6:11
and any who remain will die by * Eze 6:12
If you stay inside, * and disease Eze 7:15
death by war and * and disease. Eze 12:16
* to destroy both man and beast. Eze 14:13
war, *, ferocious beasts, plague. Eze 14:21
will abolish crop failures and *. Eze 36:29
a land riddled with * and drought. Hos 1:3
I will send a * on the land—not a Amo 8:11
on the land—not a * of bread or Amo 8:11
in those days of *, for there had Lk 4:25,26
was gone a great * swept over the Lk 15:14
"But a * developed in Egypt and Act 7:11
that a great * was coming upon the Act 11:28
* and disease and wild animals. Rev 6:8
and mourning and * shall overtake Rev 18:8

FAMINES
to scoff at your land for its *. Eze 36:30
* and earthquakes in many places. Mt 24:7
earthquakes in many lands, and *. Mk 13:8
earthquakes, and * in many lands, Lk 21:11

FAMOUS
and make your name *, and you will Gen 12:2
Or, "I will make your name so * Gen 12:2f
So Joseph became * throughout the Gen 41:45
The * Egyptian captains are dead Ex 15:4
and his name became * everywhere. Jos 6:27
may he be * in Israel. Ru 4:14
So David's name became very * 1Sa 18:30
of the most * men in the world! 2Sa 7:9
So David became very *. 2Sa 8:13
The most * of the hilltop 1Ki 3:4
be as rich and * as you for the 1Ki 3:13
and he was * among all the 1Ki 4:31
And David became more and more * 1Ch 11:9
He was the chief and the most * 1Ch 11:21
Kabzeel, killed the two * giants 1Ch 11:22
he was very * among The Thirty. 1Ch 11:24,25
Other * warriors among David's 1Ch 11:26-47
THESE ARE THE names of the * 1Ch 12:1
each * in his respective clan. 1Ch 12:24-37
structure, * and glorious 1Ch 22:5
there were many * men and high 1Ch 24:5
the gifts dedicated by * persons. 1Ch 28:12
a master crafts-man—my * Huramabi! 2Ch 2:13
Instead of its being *, all who 2Ch 7:21
So he became very *, for the Lord 2Ch 26:15
mighty works for which he is so *. Job 36:24
The Lord is * for the way he Ps 9:16
you, Lord, are a * King forever. Ps 102:12
and killed * kings who were their Ps 136:18
better to be slow-tempered than *; Pro 16:32
men are not necessarily *; Ecc 9:11
women in labor. O * city, city of Jer 49:25
your *, huge pillars will topple. Eze 26:11
and Samaria, so * and popular among Amo 6:1
"You can't be * when you hide Jn 7:4
They want to become * as 1Ti 1:7
Men of God in days of old were * Heb 11:2

FANCY
plain robes and thirty * robes. Ju 14:12
So great will he * himself to be Dan 8:25
of the harp, and * yourselves to be Amo 6:5
of their jewels or * clothes. 1Ti 2:9,10
"All the * things you loved so Rev 18:14

FANGS
the * of the wicked are broken. Job 5:16
I knocked out the * of the Job 29:17
O God, break off their *. Ps 58:6
With bared * they will devour Is 9:11,12

FANTASTIC
for I know what * blessings fall Num 22:5,6

(FANTASTIC Con't)
By his * powers in nature he Job 36:31

FAR

Abram, "Look as * as you can see Gen 13:14
The Horites in Mount Seir, as * as Gen 14:5,6
the retiring army as * as Dan. Gen 14:14
We'll deal with you * worse than Gen 19:9
And when God sent me traveling * Gen 20:13
who will come so * from home?" Gen 24:5
THEN, * IN the distance, Jacob saw Gen 33:1
household went as * as Succoth. Gen 33:17
his brother's. So * as the Lord Gen 38:10
punish you? As * as I am Gen 50:20
"but don't go too * away. Ex 8:28
of Israel saw them * in the Ex 14:10
"Keep * away from falsely Ex 23:7
as * as the Euphrates River; Ex 23:31
he called it) * outside the camp, Ex 33:7
those at the * end of the camp. Num 11:1
The load is * too heavy! Num 11:14
all around it! As * as one could Num 11:31
you into a nation * greater and Num 14:12
Then they moved to the * side of Num 21:13
* as the borders of the Ammonites; Num 21:24
As * as Dibon, Nophah, and Num 21:27-30
* down the distant trail, Num 24:15-19
Beth-jeshimoth as * as Num 33:49
the countryside as * away as Gaza. Deu 2:23
and Bashan as * as the cities of Deu 3:10
flames shot * into the sky, Deu 4:11
There, * away, you will worship Deu 4:28
nations greater by * than you, and Deu 4:38
altar is too * away from you, then Deu 12:20-23
sanctuary is so * away that it Deu 14:24
chariots, an army * greater than Deu 20:1
for these laws are not in the * Deu 30:12
the ocean, so * that no one can Deu 30:13
out across Gilead as * as Dan: Deu 34:1
edge, suddenly, * up the river at Jos 3:15,16
men of Ai as * as the quarries. Jos 7:5
Mediterranean as * north as the Jos 9:1
of Merom as * as one could see; Jos 11:4
who chased them as * as Great Sidon Jos 11:8
River valley as * north as the Jos 12:3
and as * south as the Salt Sea Jos 12:3
as * as the borders of Ammon. Jos 13:10
Ammon as * as Aroer near Rabbah. Jos 13:25
as * as the Lake of Galilee; Jos 13:27,28
as * as the Brook of Egypt; Jos 15:47
the Japhletites as * as Lower Jos 16:1
the brook and as * west as the Jos 17:10
The cities as * south as Jos 19:8
and ran as * as Zebulun in the Jos 19:27
both of us have.' * be it from us Jos 22:29
various places as * away as the Oak Ju 4:11
the chariots as * as Ju 4:16
the countryside as * away as Gaza, Ju 6:3,4
went as * as the spring of Harod. Ju 7:1
night to places as * away as Ju 7:22
and as * away as Vineyard Meadow. Ju 11:33
for they were too * away from Ju 18:28
Levi living on the * side of the Ju 19:1
left, getting as * as Jerusalem Ju 19:10
"I live on the * edge of the Ju 19:18
They came from as * away as Dan Ju 20:1
* as the border of Beth-shemesh. 1Sa 6:12
"As for me, * be it from me that 1Sa 12:23
to high heaven as * as the 1Sa 13:3,4
today, shall die? * from it! 1Sa 14:45
Obedience is * better than 1Sa 15:22
* as Gath and the gates of Ekron. 1Sa 17:52
Must I die on foreign soil, * 1Sa 26:20
But Achish insisted, "As * as 1Sa 29:9
* as Behurim, weeping as he went. 2Sa 3:16
Such generosity is * beyond any 2Sa 7:19
them from as * away as Dan and 2Sa 17:11
"No," he replied, "I am * too 2Sa 19:34
south to Judah as * as Beer-sheba. 2Sa 24:7
inner room at the * end of the 1Ki 6:16
land, whether * or near, and they 1Ki 8:46
Your wisdom and prosperity are * 1Ki 10:7
He was able to go on as * as 2Ki 9:27
Arnon as * as Gilead and Bashan. 2Ki 10:32,33
the Philistines as * distant as 2Ki 18:8
"From * away in Babylon," 2Ki 20:14
as * away as Geba and Beersheba. 2Ki 23:8
some were as * away as Baal. 1Ch 4:32,33
lived in Aroer and as * distant 1Ch 5:7,8
who were spread as * as Salecah. 1Ch 5:11
as * as Ayyah and its towns. 1Ch 7:28
People from nearby and from as * 1Ch 12:40
of Zobah (as * as Hamath) at the 1Ch 18:3
nation near or *, and if in that 2Ch 6:36
they arrived from as * away as 2Ch 7:8
Your wisdom is * greater than I 2Ch 9:6
as * away as the border of Egypt. 2Ch 9:26
They chased them as * as Gerar, 2Ch 14:13
the wilderness, as * as they could 2Ch 20:24
a good king so * as the Lord's 2Ch 26:4
and Manasseh and as * as Zebulun. 2Ch 30:10
us who is * greater than he is! 2Ch 32:7
as * as the Lord was concerned. 2Ch 36:9
His reign, too, was evil so * as 2Ch 36:12
stubborn man so * as obeying the 2Ch 36:13
that could be heard from * away! Ez 3:13
have been punished * less than we Ez 9:13
the wall as * as the Tower of the Neh 3:1
he built as * as the royal Neh 3:16
the wall as * as the East Water Neh 3:26
repaired as * as the Temple Neh 3:31
It is * greater than we can think Neh 9:5
of Jerusalem was heard * away! Neh 12:43
the Jews near and *, throughout all Est 9:20
God is doubtless punishing you * Job 11:6
and my punishment * more severe Job 23:2
Wisdom is * more valuable than Job 28:17
its price is * above rubies. Job 28:18
and said, 'Thus * and no farther Job 38:11
He smells the battle when * Job 39:25
things * too wonderful for me. Job 42:3
have given me is * greater than Ps 4:7
ARE you standing aloof and * away? Ps 10:1
for problems * too big for me to Ps 40:12
parents in your homeland * away. Ps 45:10,11
For a soul is * too precious to Ps 49:8,9
How you love wickedness—* more Ps 52:3
I would fly to the * off deserts Ps 55:7
For wherever I am, though * away Ps 61:2
the world and * away upon the sea. Ps 65:5
their hearts were * away. Ps 78:37
and heart were * away from me. Ps 95:10
* greater than these other gods. Ps 97:8,9
He has removed our sins as * Ps 103:12
His glory is * more vast than Ps 108:5
his glory is * greater than the Ps 113:4
on high? * below him are the Ps 113:6
Keep me * from every wrong; Ps 119:29,30
The wicked are * from salvation Ps 119:155
is greater * than any other god. Ps 135:5
* away you know my every thought. Ps 139:2
His glory is * greater than all Ps 148:13
Don't do it, son! Stay * from men Pro 1:15
For such wisdom is * more Pro 3:13,14,15
Stay * from her. Pro 4:24
Their counsel will keep you * Pro 6:24
My instruction is * more Pro 8:10
For the value of wisdom is * Pro 8:11
The Lord is * from the wicked, Pro 15:29
Good sense is * more valuable Pro 20:15
Good news from * away is like Pro 25:25
She works * into the night! Pro 31:18
It is * better not to say you'll Ecc 5:5
who is wise lives a * better life. Ecc 6:7,8
Wisdom is * away, and very Ecc 7:24
that eternity is * longer, and that Ecc 11:8
you into exile * away because you Is 5:13
to the nations * away, whistling to Is 5:26
to other countries * away, and all Is 6:12
whose idols were * greater than Is 10:10
them here, from countries * away. Is 13:5
of Assembly * away in the north. Is 14:13
are heard * away, even in Jahaz. Is 15:4
their armies spread out as * as Is 16:8
nation feared * and wide, a Is 18:2
terror to all both * and near, that Is 18:7
merchandise from * across the Is 23:2,3
exiling her * from her own land as Is 27:7,8
The bed you have made is * too Is 28:20
I have done, O nations * away! Is 33:13
the highlands of heaven * away. Is 33:17
"From * away in Babylon," Is 39:3
east—that man Cyrus from * away. Is 46:11
shall return from * away, from Is 49:12
who enslaved you shall be * away. Is 49:19
* behind you—it is unclean to you. Is 52:11
Your enemies will stay * away; Is 54:14
my walls —a name * greater than the Is 56:5
You have traveled *, even to hell Is 57:9
and *, for I will heal them all. Is 57:19
home again from * away, bringing Is 60:9
can't do that! I'm * too young! Jer 1:6
Why is she captured and led * Jer 2:14
backs on God and wandered * away. Jer 3:21
their land and as * as I could see Jer 4:23
loved to wander * from me and have Jer 14:10
* and near, one after the other; Jer 25:26
and send you * away to perish. Jer 27:10
for I will save you from * away Jer 46:27
Her crying will be heard as * Jer 48:2,3,4
of the land of Moab, * and near. Jer 48:24
is heard as * away as the Red Sea. Jer 49:21
and return to Jerusalem * away! Jer 51:50
Now she sits in exile * away. Lam 1:3
and taken * away as slaves. Lam 1:5
My Comforter is * away—he who Lam 1:16
* away as slaves to distant lands. Lam 1:18
Those killed by the sword are * Lam 4:9
in a very short time you * Eze 16:47
You have worshiped idols * more Eze 16:51
others and noticed from * away. Eze 19:11
For those * stronger than you Eze 21:9,10,11
Near and * they will mock you, a Eze 22:5
* south as the border of Ethiopia. Eze 29:10
until they're scattered * away. Eze 34:21
Come from * and near to the Eze 39:17
It was * more brutal and vicious Dan 7:7
scattered near and * wherever you Dan 9:7
* richer than the others. Dan 11:2
army * greater than the one he Dan 11:13
He went * beyond God's command to Hos 1:4,5f
may Judah stay * from such a life. Hos 4:15
but her sins were * too great—no Hos 7:1
they applied to someone * away. Hos 8:12
There, * from home, you are not Hos 9:4
* away and rest beneath my shadow. Hos 14:7
the north and send them * away; Joe 2:20
took them * from their own land. Joe 3:6
sell them to the Sabeans * away. Joe 3:8
Announce this * and wide: Get Joe 3:9
kill her people as * away as the Amo 1:5
captivity with you * to the east of Amo 5:25,26,27
* away into exile and slavery." Amo 7:11
in exile, * from their land.' Amo 7:17
* better it would be for you if Ob 1:5
took him * away to foreign lands; Ob 1:12
strip as * north as Zarephath. Ob 1:20
for my people's wound is * too Mic 1:9
land and sent us * away, and given Mic 2:4
dictate to strong nations * away. Mic 4:3
you will be sent * away into Mic 4:10
wound—it is * too deep to cure. Nah 3:19
for the wicked * outnumber the Hab 1:4
We are wicked, but they * more! Hab 1:13
Those who live * beyond the Zep 3:10
them * beyond my intentions. Zec 1:15
have come from so * away represent Zec 6:15
power goes * beyond our borders!" Mal 1:5
From now on, as * as we're Mal 3:14,15
but someone else is coming, * Mt 3:11
miracles spread * beyond the Mt 4:24
be healed from as * away as Syria. Mt 4:24
body—and they are * more important Mt 6:25
And you are * more valuable to Mt 6:26
me, but their hearts are * away. Mt 15:8
and it would go * away. Mt 17:20
I am betrayed. * better for that Mt 26:24
Meanwhile, Peter was following * Mt 26:58
"Someone is coming soon who is * Mk 1:7
from as * away as Tyre and Sidon. Mk 3:7,8
had spread * and wide and vast Mk 3:7,8
When Jesus was still * out on the Mk 5:6
dazzling white, * more glorious Mk 9:3
And I know it is * more Mk 12:33
not * from the Kingdom of God." Mk 12:34
break out near and *, but this is Mk 13:7
Peter followed * behind and then Mk 14:54
has * higher authority than mine; Lk 3:16
and from as * north as the Lk 6:17,18
but one * greater than Solomon is Lk 11:31
and someone * greater than Jonah Lk 11:32
Never fear, you are * more Lk 12:7
For life consists of * more than Lk 12:23
And you are * more valuable to Lk 12:24
follower must love me * more than Lk 14:26
troops are still * away, he will Lk 14:32
in the * distance with Abraham. Lk 16:23
neck, he would be * better off than Lk 17:2,3
who is greater by * than I am—for Jn 1:15
said, 'Soon a man * greater than I Jn 1:30
and the Son will do * more Jn 5:20
David was looking * into the Act 2:31
captivity * away beyond Babylon.' Act 7:43
death traveled as * as Phoenicia, Act 11:19
he is not * from any one of us. Act 17:27
with him, going as * as Turkey; Act 20:4
send you * away to the Gentiles!' Act 22:21
So as * as I was concerned, the Rom 7:10
and through so * as my old sinful Rom 7:18
I love to do God's will so * as Rom 7:22
of you, a Jew so * as his human Rom 9:5
you who were so * away from Rom 11:24
that he will be * more ready to put Rom 11:24
The night is * gone, the day of Rom 13:12,13
plan of God is * wiser than the 1Co 1:25
cross—is * stronger than any man. 1Co 1:25
your thrones, leaving us * behind! 1Co 4:8
It would be * more honoring to 1Co 6:7
my thoughts grew * beyond those of 1Co 13:11
in heaven have bodies * different 1Co 15:40
how * you would go in obeying me. 2Co 2:9
Well, when I got as * as the city 2Co 2:12
sweet perfume. As * as God is 2Co 2:15
Shall we not expect * greater 2Co 3:8
is certainly * greater, for it is 2Co 3:11
they could afford, but * more; 2Co 8:3
enough when he is * away, but when 2Co 10:1
We are not going too * when we 2Co 10:14
cities that are * beyond you, where 2Co 10:16
But I have served him * more! 2Co 11:23
hand in heaven, *, far above any Eph 1:21
in heaven, far, * above any other Eph 1:21
Yes, his honor is * more glorious Eph 1:21
you once were * away from God, now Eph 2:13

FAR Con't)
who were very * away from him, and Eph 2:17
us is able to do * more than we Eph 3:20
heights of heaven, * down to the Eph 4:9
they are * away from the life of Eph 4:17,18
further, going so * as actually to Php 2:8
do because you were * away. Php 2:30
peace, which is * more wonderful Php 4:7
who were once so * away from God. Col 1:21
For though I am * away from you Col 2:5
others everywhere, * beyond your 1Th 1:8
worthless so * as doing anything Tit 1:16
Thus he became * greater than the Heb 1:4
his Father, is * greater than the Heb 1:4
But Jesus has * more glory than Heb 3:3
he isn't very * along in the Heb 5:12,13
But now we have a * better hope, Heb 7:19
The sacrifice he offers is * Heb 8:4
rewarded with a * more important Heb 8:6
* more wonderful promises. Heb 8:6
with * more precious offerings. Heb 9:23
system in favor of a * better one. Heb 10:9
leave home and go * away to another Heb 11:8
happened, for as * as Abraham was Heb 11:19
your faith is * more precious to 1Pe 1:7
the Lord, and are * greater in 2Pe 2:11
Why, as * back as anyone can 2Pe 3:4
prove that they are * from God. 3Jn 1:11
He is * greater than any king in Rev 1:5
Your deeds are * from right in Rev 3:2
They will stand * off, trembling Rev 18:10

FAR-OFF
in this * land, to his brother's Gen 24:38
I am like a vulture in a * Ps 102:6
LISTEN TO ME, all of you in * Is 49:1
* foreign nations and their kings; Is 52:14,15
are enslaved in * lands, without a Lam 2:9
I am not sending you to some * Eze 3:5
"Your army includes men from * Eze 27:10
a whirlwind among the * nations. Zec 7:14
for we have seen his star in * Mt 2:2

FARCE
It is all a *. Jer 3:23
Their worship is a *, for they Mk 7:6,7

FAREWELL
a chance to have a * party, with Gen 31:27
Or, "say * to me forever!" Ex 12:32f
Give him a large * present from Deu 15:14
this was his final * to Galilee. Mk 10:1f
Literally, "bid them * at home." Lk 9:61f
If you do this, it is enough. * Act 15:27,28,29
preached a * message to them, said Act 20:1
embraced him in *, sorrowing most Act 20:37
Christ be with your spirit.*,Paul 2Ti 4:22

FAREWELLS
us where we prayed and said our *. Act 21:5

FARM
nor was there anyone to * the Gen 2:5
sent him out to * the ground from Gen 3:23
Lord a gift of his * produce, and Gen 4:3
me from my * and from you, and made Gen 4:14
a nation-wide * program. Gen 41:33
take it to your * and keep it there Deu 22:2
on the * of Joash the Abiezrite. Ju 6:11
servants are to * the land for him, 2Sa 9:10,11
people were left to * the land. 2Ki 25:12
One day I was on a * and saw some Neh 13:15
A poor man's * may have good Pro 13:23
each have your own * and garden and Is 36:16
country and * the land as usual." Jer 27:11
ask you to buy the * he owns in Jer 32:6,7
Let the * hands all depart. Jer 50:16
go out and work on the * today.' Mt 21:28
to his *, another to his store; Mt 22:5
Then he leased the * to tenant Mk 12:1
own the * when his father dies. Mk 12:7
him—and then the * will be ours!' Mk 12:7
* that produced fine crops. Lk 12:16
of his men to the * to collect his Lk 20:10

FARMER
a shepherd, while Cain was a *. Gen 4:2
Noah became a * and planted a Gen 9:20,21
destroyed, and a * will be Is 7:21,22
up kingdoms as a * gathers eggs, Is 10:14
a * always plow and never sow? Is 28:23,24
teacher and gives the * wisdom. Is 28:29
seed for the * and bread for the Is 55:10
end before the * starts again to Amo 9:13
I am a *. Zec 13:5
"A * was sowing grain in his Mt 13:2,3
I told about the * planting grain: Mt 13:18
a * sowing good seed in his field; Mt 13:24
am the * who sows the choice Mt 13:37
"Listen! A * decided to sow some Mk 4:3
"The * I talked about is anyone Mk 4:14
"A * sowed his field, and went Mk 4:26
and then the * came at once with Mk 4:29
"A * went out to his field to Lk 8:5
He persuaded a local * to hire Lk 15:15
And have you ever heard of a * 1Co 9:7
will get little. A * who plants 2Co 9:6
For God, who gives seed to the * 2Co 9:10
Work hard, like a * who gets 2Ti 2:6
be patient, like a * who waits Jas 5:7

FARMER'S
"The * men came and told him, Mt 13:27
When a * land has had many Heb 6:7

FARMERS
and sixty *, all of whom were 2Ki 25:19
they were killed by the local *. 1Ch 7:20,21
rented out to some * there, the Sol 8:11
lack of rain; the * are afraid. Jer 14:4
And city dwellers and * and Jer 31:24
* and oxen, captains and rulers; Jer 51:23
Well may you * stand so shocked Joe 1:11
Call for the * to weep with you, Amo 5:16
vineyard to some * on a sharecrop Mt 21:33
to the * to collect his share. Mt 21:34
But the * attacked his men, beat Mt 21:35
"But when these * saw the son Mt 21:38
you think he will do to those *?" Mt 21:40
they were the * in his story— they Mt 21:45
* and moved to another country. Mk 12:1
But the * beat up the man and Mk 12:3
"But when the * saw him coming Mk 12:7
were the wicked * in his story. Mk 12:12
it out to some *, and went away to Lk 20:9

FARMHANDS
and killed all the * except me. Job 1:14,15

FARMING
the hard work of * this ground Gen 5:28-31
and selling, * and building— until Lk 17:28

FARMLAND
around it—are like *, redeemable at Lev 25:31
will not be given * like the other Lev 25:33

FARMLANDS
destroyed and your * deserted, and Eze 12:20

FARMS
on your own *, just as you do now Deu 12:20-23
clothing and olive * and vineyards 2Ki 5:26
soil and had many * and vineyards, 2Ch 26:10
* as decreed by the laws of Moses. Neh 12:44
services had returned to their *. Neh 13:10
for the abandoned * of Heshbon and Is 16:8
those bountiful * of yours that Is 32:12
their wives and their * to others; Jer 8:10
*, but always to live in tents; Jer 35:7
or owned * or planted crops. Jer 35:9
to the deserted * and gathered a Jer 40:12
their * were desolated, their Eze 19:7
and to the ruined * and the Eze 36:4
on your * and your vineyards; Amo 4:9
and on the nearby *, for the Mt 2:16
villages and * and buy themselves Mk 6:35,36
and out on the *—they laid the sick Mk 6:56
villages and *, to find food and Lk 9:12

FARTHER
of the Lord moved * down the road Num 22:26
But if I tell him, 'Go *—the 1Sa 20:22
'Thus far and no * shall you come, Job 38:11
flee to Heshbon, unable to go *. Jer 48:45
A little * up the beach he saw Mt 4:21
A little * up the beach, he saw Mk 1:19
been to go still *, preaching where Rom 15:20

FARTHEST
and have conquered the * borders. 2Ki 19:23
are exiled to the * corners of the Neh 1:9
In the * corners of the earth Ps 65:8
Tell the * islands to be glad. Ps 97:1
from the * corners of the earth. Ps 107:3
winds to the * oceans, even there Ps 139:9
the Creator of the * parts of the Is 40:28
from the * corners of the earth. Is 43:6
will reach the * ends of the earth, Jer 25:31
the * corners of the earth. Jer 25:32
and from earth's * ends, not Jer 31:8
You rule the * provinces, and Dan 2:38
will begin at the * gate of Zep 1:10
them waste to their * borders; Zep 3:6
* ends of the earth and heaven. Mt 24:31
the * bounds of earth and heaven. Mk 13:27
lead them from the * corners of the Act 13:47

FASHION
him in friendly *. Mt 26:49

FAST
and so he died, for he was * Ju 4:21
You'd better think *, for there 1Sa 25:17
But why should I * when he is 2Sa 12:23
Then I declared a * while we were Ez 8:21
the Jews of Shushan and * for me; Est 4:16
GODLY men are * disappearing. Ps 12:1
I mourn and * before the Lord! Ps 69:10
Hold her * and she will lead you Pro 4:8,9
Riches can disappear *. Pro 27:23,24
Land that sends ambassadors in * Is 18:2
No, the kind of * I want is that Is 58:6
When they *, I will not pay any Jer 14:12
Calamity is coming * to Moab. Jer 48:16
day you began to * before the Lord Dan 10:12
Announce a *; Joe 1:14
tiny horses, and they run as *. Joe 2:4
Call a * and gather all the Joe 2:15
runners won't be * enough to flee, Amo 2:15
believed him and declared a *; Jon 3:4,5
When you *, declining your food Mt 6:16
But when you *, put on festive Mt 6:17
your disciples * as we do and as Mt 9:14
the news of his arrival spread *. Mk 7:24
mob arrested Jesus and held him *. Mk 14:46
Jesus asked, "Do happy men *? Lk 5:34
before—became * friends. Lk 23:12
window sill, went * asleep and fell Act 20:9
Literally, "because the * was now Act 27:9f
The bow of the ship stuck *, Act 27:41
silver is dropping *, yet it will Jas 5:3

FASTED
the Lord and * until evening, Ju 20:26
at Jabesh and * for seven days. 1Sa 31:13
They mourned and wept and * all 2Sa 1:12
David replied, "I * and wept 2Sa 12:22
put on rags, *, slept in sackcloth, 1Ki 21:27
and mourned and * for seven days. 1Ch 10:12
So we * and begged God to take Ez 8:23
this time they * and clothed Neh 9:1
"We have * before you," they Is 58:3
As I prayed, I *, and wore rough Dan 9:3
of exile when you * and mourned in Zec 7:5
leaders sometimes *, that is, went Mk 2:18

FASTEN
golden clasps to * the loops Ex 26:6
in gold settings. * the two stones Ex 28:12
together, and then * the thing in Is 41:7
and silver and * it securely in Jer 10:4
Make a yoke and * it on your neck Jer 27:2

FASTENED
young goats, and * a strip of the Gen 27:16
There were four golden rings * Ex 37:3
was * to the wall of Beth-shan. 1Sa 31:10
They * his armor to the walls of 1Ch 10:10
and blue, * with purple ribbons Est 1:6
Literally, "* with cords of fine Est 1:6f
to be so firmly * to the wall! Is 22:25
he has * me with heavy chains. Lam 3:7
four inches long, * along the walls Eze 40:43
A signboard was * to the cross Mk 15:26
the heat, * itself onto his hand! Act 28:3

FASTER
power spread even * and vast crowds Lk 5:15

FASTIDIOUSLY
Those who used to eat * are Lam 4:5

FASTING
Or, "in *." Lev 16:31f
together for * and prayer. 1Ki 21:9
among the Jews, *, weeping, and Est 4:3
of their national * and prayer. Est 9:29-31
My knees are weak from * and I Ps 109:24
special days for *—even your most Is 1:12,13
even while you are *, and you keep Is 58:3
Look, what good is * when you Is 58:4
This kind of * will never get you Is 58:4
Is this what you call *? Is 58:5
on the next Day of *, for on that Jer 36:6
This occurred on the Day of * Jer 36:9
Come with *, weeping, mourning. Joe 2:12
custom of * and mourning during the Zec 7:3
"And now about *. Mt 6:16
"And *" is added in some Mk 9:29f
God by praying and often *. Lk 2:36,37
were feasting instead of *. Lk 5:33
worshiping and * the Holy Spirit Act 13:2
So after more * and prayer, Act 13:3
for them with *, turning them over Act 14:23

FASTS
"The traditional * and times of Zec 8:19

FAT
and selected a * calf and told a Gen 18:7
seven sleek, * cows came up out of Gen 41:2
over and stood beside the * cows. Gen 41:3
Then the skinny cows ate the * Gen 41:4
suddenly, seven *, healthy-looking Gen 41:18
ate up the seven * ones that had Gen 41:20
heads swallowed up the * ones! Gen 41:24
The seven * cows (and also the Gen 41:26
also the seven *, well-formed heads Gen 41:26
You shall live off the * of the Gen 45:18
no sacrificial * shall be left Ex 23:18
Then take all the * that covers Ex 29:13
kidneys, and the * on them, and Ex 29:13
"Then take the * of the ram, Ex 29:22
ram, including the * tail and the Ex 29:22
fat tail and the * that covers the Ex 29:22
kidneys and the * surrounding them, Ex 29:22
and its head and * upon the wood. Lev 1:8
the head and the *, on top of the Lev 1:12
the Lord the * that covers the Lev 3:3,4,5
upon the altar the *, the tail Lev 3:9,10,11
the backbone, the * covering the Lev 3:9,10,11
to the Lord, the * which covers the Lev 3:14
All the * is Jehovah's. Lev 3:15,16
shall eat neither * nor blood." Lev 3:17
Then he shall take all the * on Lev 4:8
All the * shall be removed and Lev 4:19
All the * shall be burned upon Lev 4:26

(FAT Con't)
as if it were the * of the Lev 4:26
All the * shall be taken off, Lev 4:31
of the altar. The * shall be used Lev 4:35
lamb—the priest shall burn the * Lev 4:35
the * of the daily peace offering. Lev 6:12
the altar all its *, including the Lev 7:3
the tail, the * that covers the Lev 7:3
never to eat *, whether from oxen, Lev 7:23
or goats. The * of an animal that Lev 7:24
Anyone who eats * from an Lev 7:25
offering of the * and breast, which Lev 7:30
Then the priest shall burn the * Lev 7:31
He took all the * covering the Lev 8:15,16
kidneys and their *, and burned Lev 8:15,16
the pieces, the head and the *. Lev 8:20
Then he took the *, the tail, the Lev 8:25
fat, the tail, the * upon the inner Lev 8:25
kidneys with their *, and the right Lev 8:25
upon the altar the *, kidneys, and Lev 9:10
Then he collected the * of the Lev 9:19
ox and the ram—the * from their Lev 9:19
tails and the * covering the inner Lev 9:19
bladders. The * was placed upon Lev 9:20
burnt offering and * on the altar; Lev 9:24
offered when the * was burned, and Lev 10:15
altar the * for the sin offering. Lev 16:25
and to burn the * as a savor the Lev 17:5
and to burn the * as a savor the Lev 17:6
altar, and their * shall be burned Num 18:17
they have become * and prosperous, Deu 31:20
Yes, * and bloated; Deu 32:15
To whom they sacrificed their * Deu 32:38
(who, by the way, was very *! Ju 3:17,18,19
the flesh, and the * closed over it Ju 3:22,23
of burning the * on the altar had 1Sa 2:15
you want, but the * must first be 1Sa 2:16
they have become * from the best of 1Sa 2:29
he died (for he was old and *). 1Sa 4:18
offering the * of rams to him. 1Sa 15:22
sacrifice an ox and a * lamb. 2Sa 6:13
sheep, oxen, and * young goats at 1Ki 1:9
sacrificing oxen, * goats, and many 1Ki 1:19
oxen and * goats and many sheep, 1Ki 1:25
offerings, and the * of the peace 1Ki 8:64
the * of the burnt offerings. 2Ch 35:14
were one ox, six * sheep, and a Neh 5:18
You gave them a large, * land, Neh 9:35
I was not * and lazy, yet Job 3:26
"This wicked man is * and rich, Job 15:27,28
wealthy, *, and prosperous; Job 21:23,24
is hard and firm, not soft and *. Job 41:23
these * he-goats, rams and calves. Ps 66:15
They grow sleek and *. Ps 73:4
These * cats have everything Ps 73:7
I don't want your * rams; Is 1:11
Calves and * cattle will be safe Is 11:6
and the soil made rich with *. Is 34:7
pleased me with the sacrificial *. Is 43:24
my people, and are * as cows that Jer 50:11
destroy the powerful, * shepherds; Eze 34:15,16
between these * shepherds and their Eze 34:20
the goats and the * young bulls of Eze 39:18
me my food, the * and the blood. Eze 44:7
me to offer the * and blood of the Eze 44:15
LISTEN TO ME, you "* cows" of Amo 4:1
instead, he will eat the * ones, Zec 11:16
For their hearts are * Mt 13:15
gave a little of their extra *, Mk 12:43,44
They are * and prosperous now, Lk 6:25
hearts are too * and your ears Act 28:27
whim, and now your * hearts are Jas 5:5

FATAL
to remind you of this * night. Ex 12:14
Their * error is not clearly Lev 10:1f
Burning fever, and * disease. Deu 32:24
this turned out to be a * mistake; 2Ch 22:7
to oppose him will be *." Est 6:13
If they fall it isn't *, for the Ps 37:24
"It's *, whatever it is," they Ps 41:8
taunts pierce me like a * wound; Ps 42:10
protects you from the * plague. Ps 91:3
servant David from the * sword. Ps 144:10
watching me, waiting for a * slip. Jer 20:10
he has sinned that one * sin. 1Jn 5:16
that struck and bit with * wounds. Rev 9:19
the * wound was healed! Rev 13:3
* wine of her intense immorality. Rev 18:3

FATALLY
their arrows and * wounded him. 2Ch 35:23
was crushed and * wounded, so that Rom 6:6
Creature, who was * wounded and Rev 13:14

FATE
That will be your *, too, if you Deu 8:20
And so she did, bewailing her * Ju 11:38
the * of Jephthah's daughter. Ju 11:40
alike will be horrified by his *. Job 18:20
"This is the * awaiting the Job 27:13
this is the * of all the nations Ps 9:17
And I said: This is my *, that Ps 77:10
tongue, what shall be your *? Ps 120:3
Such is the * of all who live by Pro 1:19
knowing the * awaiting it there. Pro 7:23
All things are decided by *; Ecc 6:10
It seems so unfair, that one * Ecc 9:2,3
sworn your awful *—with my own ears Is 5:9
O poor Anathoth, what a * is Is 10:30
weep for the * of Nebo and Medeba; Is 15:2
the * of those who do them harm. Is 47:7
and death are not your *. Is 51:14
worship gods of "*" and Is 65:11
your "*" shall be a dark one; Is 65:12
their * and future in the stars! Jer 10:2,3
severely that your * will horrify Jer 15:4
of the awful * awaiting them, Jer 23:9
Their * shall become proverbial Jer 29:22
you and left you to your *!' Jer 38:21,22
That is the * awaiting every one Jer 42:17
The * of Edom will be horrible; Jer 49:17
one will be left to bewail your *. Eze 7:10,11
heads, for your * is dreadful; Eze 27:36
know you are appalled at your *; Eze 28:19
This is the * of Pharaoh and all Eze 31:18
their * is the same as that of Eze 32:24
rejoiced at Israel's fearful *. Eze 35:15
That will be your *, too, you Hos 10:15
no one anywhere regrets your *! Nah 3:7
All who hear your * will clap Nah 3:19
This is the * of that vast, Zep 2:15
THIS IS THE * of Israel, as Zec 12:1
student shares his teacher's *. Mt 10:25
Your words now reflect your * Mt 12:37
you have abandoned it to its *." Mk 6:11
of the fearful * they see coming Lk 21:26
our backs on God and sealed our *. Heb 10:39
what terrible * awaits those who 1Pe 4:17
punishment. The * of such people Jud 1:4
you, O heaven, rejoice over her *; Rev 18:20

FATHER
a man leaves his * and mother and Gen 2:24
Enoch was the * Gen 4:18
Irad was the * Gen 4:18
Mehujael was the * Gen 4:18
Methusael was the * Gen 4:18
Literally, "He was the * of all Gen 4:21f
Literally, "He was the * of all Gen 4:22f
very image of his * in every way. Gen 5:3,4,5
tent, Ham, the * of Canaan, saw Gen 9:22
fall across their * to cover his Gen 9:23
Or, "*." Gen 10:13,14f
and he was also the * of Heth; Gen 10:15-19
Joktan was the * Gen 10:26-30
and was survived by his *. Gen 11:28
AFTER THE DEATH of Abram's *, Gen 12:1
to become the * of a great nation; Gen 12:2
In fact you shall be the * of not Gen 17:2,3,4
'Abram' ('Exalted *'), but Gen 17:5
but 'Abraham' ('* of Nations')—for Gen 17:5
"Me, be a *?" Gen 17:17
that our * would let us marry. Gen 19:31
And our * will soon be too old Gen 19:31
had sexual intercourse with her *; Gen 19:33
"I slept with my * last night. Gen 19:34
became pregnant from their *. Gen 19:36
the same *)—and I married her. Gen 20:11,12
"*," Isaac asked, "we have the Gen 22:7
oldest,Kemuel (* of Aram),Chesed, Gen 22:20-23
Jidlaph,Bethuel (* of Rebekah). Gen 22:20-23
* was Bethuel the son of Nahor Gen 24:15,16
"Would your * have any room to Gen 24:23
"My * is Bethuel, the son of Gen 24:24
And she told me, 'Nahor's. My * Gen 24:47
just as I promised Abraham your *. Gen 26:3
by the servants of his * Abraham. Gen 26:15
the wells of his * Abraham, the Gen 26:18
before, when his * had named them. Gen 26:18
"I am the God of Abraham your * Gen 26:24
Esau: "Yes, *?" Gen 27:1
his * had said to his brother. Gen 27:6,7
Then take it to your *, and after Gen 27:8,9,10
What if my * feels me? Gen 27:11,12
the room where his * was lying. Gen 27:18
Jacob: "*?" Gen 27:18
(Jacob goes over to his *. Gen 27:22
Esau: "Here I am, *, with the Gen 27:31
Esau: "O my *, bless me, bless me Gen 27:34
for me? O my *, bless me too." Gen 27:38
He said to himself, "My * will Gen 27:41
Literally, "your mother's *." Gen 28:2f
Esau realized that his * despised Gen 28:6,7,8
and that his * and mother had sent Gen 28:6,7,8
of Abraham, and of your * Isaac. Gen 28:13
back safely to my *, then I will Gen 28:21
She quickly ran and told her *, Gen 29:12,13
So he told her *, "I'll work for Gen 29:18
owes everything he owns to our *. Gen 31:1
"Your * has turned against me," Gen 31:5
worked for your *, but he has been Gen 31:6
given you from our * were legally Gen 31:16
his * Isaac in the land of Canaan. Gen 31:17-20
the God of your * appeared to me Gen 31:29
"Forgive my not getting up, *," Gen 31:35
God of Isaac, my *—you would have Gen 31:4
and of their *, to destroy either Gen 31:5
mighty God of his * Isaac, to Gen 31:5
and of my * Isaac—O Jehovah who Gen 32:
*, for 100 pieces of silver. Gen 33:1
Then he spoke to his * about it. Gen 34:
Hamor, Shechem's *, went to talk Gen 34:6,
Then Shechem addressed Dinah's * Gen 34:1
but his * called him "Benjamin" Gen 35:1
last to Isaac his * at Mamre in Gen 35:2
of Canaan, where his * had lived. Gen 37:
But Joseph reported to his * some Gen 37:
This time he told his * as Gen 37:1
but his * rebuked him. Gen 37:1
affair, but his * gave it quite a Gen 37:1
a well and tell * that a wild Gen 37:19,2
out later and return him to his *. Gen 37:21,2
* and asked him to identify it. Gen 37:3
Their * recognized it at once. Gen 37:3
for Er, who was named by his *. Gen 38:3,4,
stick is the * of my child. Gen 38:2
our * is in the land of Canaan. Gen 42:1
is there with our *, and one of our Gen 42:1
So they came to their * Jacob Gen 42:2
twelve brothers, sons of one *; Gen 42:3
with our * in the land of Canaan.' Gen 42:3
gripped them, as it did their *. Gen 42:3
Then Reuben said to his *, "Kill Gen 42:3
almost gone, their * said to them, Gen 43:2
"He wanted to know whether our * Gen 43:7
Judah said to his *, "Send the Gen 43:8
So their * Israel finally said to Gen 43:11
"And how is your *—the old man Gen 43:27
of you can go on home to your *." Gen 44:17
"Sir, you asked us if we had a * Gen 44:19
'Yes, we have a *, an old man, and Gen 44:20
and his * loves him very much.' Gen 44:20
his *, for his father would die.' Gen 44:22
his father, for his * would die.' Gen 44:22
So we returned to our * and Gen 44:24
"Then my * said to us, 'You know Gen 44:27
if I go back to my * and the lad is Gen 44:30
is not with us, our * will die; Gen 44:31
Sir, I pledged my * that I would Gen 44:32
For how shall I return to my * Gen 44:34
"Is my * still alive?" Gen 45:3
"Hurry, return to my * and tell Gen 45:9
Tell our * about all my Gen 45:13
and to bring your * and all of Gen 45:18
ones, and to bring your * here. Gen 45:19
He sent his * ten donkey-loads Gen 45:23
land of Canaan, to Jacob their *. Gen 45:25
there to the God of his * Isaac. Gen 46:1
replied, "the God of your *. Gen 46:3,4
given to Leah by her *, Laban. Gen 46:18
given to Rachel by her *, Laban: Gen 46:23,24,25
Goshen to meet his * and they fell Gen 46:29
"My * and my brothers are here Gen 47:1
Then Joseph brought his * Jacob Gen 47:7
of Rameses—to his * and brothers, Gen 47:11
that his * was failing rapidly. Gen 48:1
he saw that his * had laid his Gen 48:17
"No, *," he said. Gen 48:18
But his * refused. Gen 48:19
listen to Israel your *. Gen 49:2
* blessed his twelve sons with. Gen 49:28
"that Joseph's * made Joseph swear Gen 50:5
to permit me to go and bury my *; Gen 50:5
"Go and bury your *, as you Gen 50:6
of lamentation for Joseph's *. Gen 50:10
him to the funeral of his *. Gen 50:14
But now that their * was dead, Gen 50:15
he died, your * instructed us to Gen 50:16,17
We servants of the God of your * Gen 50:16,17
When they returned to their * Ex 2:18
their * demanded. Ex 2:20
"Honor your * and mother, that Ex 20:12
"Anyone who strikes his * or Ex 21:15
or * shall surely be put to death. Ex 21:17
But if her * utterly refuses to Ex 22:17
as you did their *, that they may Ex 40:15
A girl may not marry her *; Lev 18:7
daughter of his * or his mother, Lev 18:9
is so closely related to your *; Lev 18:12
"Anyone who curses his * or Lev 20:9
daughter of his * or of his mother, Lev 20:17
of his *—for they are near of kin; Lev 20:19
relative—a mother, *, son, Lev 21:2,3
person—not even his * or mother. Lev 21:11
he must not be the * of children of Lev 21:14,15
and whose * was an Egyptian, got Lev 24:10
Ithamar to assist their * Aaron. Num 3:4
his *, mother, brother, or sister; Num 6:6,7
Am I their *? Num 11:12
to Moses, "If her * had but spit Num 12:14
his son Zelophehad was their *. Num 27:1
"Our * died in the wilderness," Num 27:3,4
Why should the name of our * Num 27:3,4
given to their * if he had lived. Num 27:6,7
home, and her * hears that she has Num 30:4
But if her * refuses to let her Num 30:5

FATHER Con't)

invalid. Her * must state his Num 30:5
her * would not let her do it. Num 30:5
wife and between a * and his Num 30:16
just as a * cares for his child!' Deu 1:31
" 'Honor your * and mother Deu 5:16
her * and mother for a full month. Deu 21:13
of the wife his * doesn't love. Deu 21:17
will not obey his * or mother, even Deu 21:18
him, then his * and mother shall Deu 21:19
then the girl's * and mother shall Deu 22:15
"Her * shall tell them, 'I gave Deu 22:16
to be given to the girl's *, for Deu 22:19
Literally, "shall pay her * fifty Deu 22:28,29f
to the girl's * and marry her; Deu 22:28,29
since she belonged to his *. Deu 22:30
who despises his * or mother.' Deu 27:16
wives, for she belongs to his *.' Deu 27:20
Is not God your *? Deu 32:6
(Ask your * and the aged men; Deu 32:7
along with my * and mother, my Jos 2:12,13
relatives—your *, mother, brothers, Jos 2:17,18
along with her *, mother, brothers, Jos 6:23
had been named after Anak's *. Jos 15:13
him to ask her * for an additional Jos 15:18,19
son who was the * of Gilead) had Jos 17:1
(Arba was the * of Anak)—although Jos 21:9-16
Terah the * of Abraham and Nahor, Jos 24:2
But I took your * Abraham from Jos 24:3
she urged him to ask her * for an Ju 1:14
sepulcher of his * Joash in Ophrah, Ju 8:32
For my * fought for you and Ju 9:17
a prostitute. His * (whose name was Ju 11:1
And she said, "*, you must do Ju 11:36
Then she returned to her *, who Ju 11:39
home he told his * and mother that Ju 14:2
But Samson told his *, "She is Ju 14:3
His * and mother didn't realize Ju 14:4
But he didn't tell his * or Ju 14:6
some of it to his * and mother. Ju 14:9
As his * was making final Ju 14:10,11
"I haven't even told it to my * Ju 14:16
to live with his * and mother. Ju 14:19
but her * wouldn't let him in. Ju 15:1
* gave her to another man." Ju 15:6
and her * and burned them alive. Ju 15:6
where his *, Manoah, was buried. Ju 16:31
*, who was delighted to meet him. Ju 19:3
to meet him. Her * urged him to Ju 19:4
but the girl's * insisted on their Ju 19:5
again the girl's * pleaded, "Stay Ju 19:8
how you left your * and mother in Ru 2:10,11
He was the * of Jesse and Ru 4:16,17
listen to their *, for the Lord was 1Sa 2:23,24,25
but they were not like their *, 1Sa 8:3
by now my * will be more worried 1Sa 9:5
and that your * is worried about 1Sa 10:2
added, "With a * like his?" 1Sa 10:12
But he didn't tell his * that 1Sa 14:1
Then someone told him that his * 1Sa 14:28
(Abner's *, Ner, and Saul's 1Sa 14:50,51
and Saul's *, Kish, were brothers; 1Sa 14:50,51
to help his * with the sheep. 1Sa 17:14,15
"Tell me about your *, my boy," 1Sa 17:58
told him what his * was planning. 1Sa 19:2
I'll ask my * to go out there 1Sa 19:3
as Jonathan and his * were 1Sa 19:4
"Why is your * so determined to 1Sa 20:1
"Your * knows perfectly well 1Sa 20:3
been with your * for this occasion, 1Sa 20:5
If your * asks where I am, tell 1Sa 20:6
*, but don't betray me to him!" 1Sa 20:8
my * was planning to kill you?" 1Sa 20:9
whether or not your * is angry?" 1Sa 20:10
I will talk to my * about you and 1Sa 20:12
you as he used to be with my *. 1Sa 20:13
realized that his * really meant it 1Sa 20:33
the king for his * and mother to 1Sa 22:3
him. "My * will never find you! 1Sa 23:17
to you, as my * is well aware." 1Sa 23:17
and buried him beside his *; 2Sa 2:32
you and for your * by not betraying 2Sa 3:8
me above your * and his family and 2Sa 6:21
I will be his * and he shall be 2Sa 7:14
of my vow to your * Jonathan. 2Sa 9:7
"because his * Nahash was always 2Sa 10:2
men aren't here to honor your *! 2Sa 10:3
when your * comes to see you, ask 2Sa 13:5
invited his * and all his brothers 2Sa 13:21-24
his grandfather—his mother's *. 2Sa 13:37,38,39f
will counsel you as I did your *.' 2Sa 15:33,34
back the kingdom of my *, Saul.' 2Sa 16:3
I helped your * and now I will 2Sa 16:19
You know your * and his men; 2Sa 17:8
And your * is an old soldier and 2Sa 17:8
a mighty man your * is and how 2Sa 17:10
died and was buried beside his *. 2Sa 17:23
second cousin; his * was Ithra, an 2Sa 17:25
where my * and mother are buried. 2Sa 19:37
in the grave of Saul's *, Kish. 2Sa 21:12,13,14
king in place of his aged *. 1Ki 1:5

Now his *, King David, had never 1Ki 1:6
new king, replacing his * David; 1Ki 2:12
the throne of my * David and this 1Ki 2:23,24
For my * was no party to the 1Ki 2:32
you did to my *, King David? 1Ki 2:44
all of his * David's instructions 1Ki 3:3
kind to my * David because he was 1Ki 3:6
king instead of my * David, but I 1Ki 3:7
my laws as your * David did." 1Ki 3:14
to build. His * David, Solomon 1Ki 5:2,3
instructed my * that I should do. 1Ki 5:5
what I told your * David I would 1Ki 6:11,12
Naphtali, and his * had been a 1Ki 7:14
for that purpose by his * David. 1Ki 7:51
he promised my * David: for he 1Ki 8:15
This man was my *, David. 1Ki 8:17
for I have followed my * as king 1Ki 8:20
my * David, who was your servant; 1Ki 8:24
and truth as your * David did, 1Ki 9:4
as I promised your * David when I 1Ki 9:5
the Lord as his * David had done. 1Ki 11:4
the Lord as his * David did. 1Ki 11:6
However, for the sake of your * 1Ki 11:12,13
of this city his * had built. 1Ki 11:27,28
instructions as his * David did. 1Ki 11:33
buried in the city of his * David; 1Ki 11:43
"Your * was a hard master," they 1Ki 12:2,3,4
who had counseled his * Solomon. 1Ki 12:6
'If you think my * was hard on you, 1Ki 12:10
Yes, my * was harsh, but I'll be 1Ki 12:11
even harsher! My * used whips on 1Ki 12:11
a sinner as his * was, and his 1Ki 15:3
all the idols his * had made. 1Ki 15:12
like his *, he worshiped many 1Ki 15:26
even more wicked than his * Omri; 1Ki 16:30
say good-bye to my * and mother, 1Ki 19:20
the cities my * took from your 1Ki 20:34
took from your *, and you may 1Ki 20:34
as my * did in Samaria." 1Ki 20:34
He did as his * Asa had done, 1Ki 22:43
from the days of his * Asa. 1Ki 22:46
footsteps of his * and mother and 1Ki 22:52,53
saw it and cried out, "My *! 2Ki 2:12
and cried out, "My father! My *! 2Ki 2:12
as wicked as his * and mother had 2Ki 3:2
to Baal that his * had made. 2Ki 3:2
prophets of your * and mother!" 2Ki 3:13
out to visit his *, who was working 2Ki 4:18
in pain. His * said to one of the 2Ki 4:19
along behind his * Ahab, the Lord 2Ki 9:25
of King Jehoram, Ahaziah's *). 2Ki 11:2,3
"My *! 2Ki 13:14
"My father! My *! 2Ki 13:14
that his * had lost to Ben-hadad. 2Ki 13:25
was as good a king as his * Joash. 2Ki 14:3
men who had assassinated his *; 2Ki 14:5
Name of his *: Amaziah, the 2Ki 15:1
Lord just as his * Amaziah had. 2Ki 15:3
Name of his *: Jeroboam 2Ki 15:8
Like his * Uzziah, 2Ki 15:34,35
his * Hezekiah had destroyed. 2Ki 21:3,4,5
He did all the evil things his * 2Ki 21:21
Ram was the * of Amminadab, and 1Ch 2:10
* of Nahshon, a leader of Israel. 1Ch 2:10
Nahshon was the * of Salma, and 1Ch 2:11
and Salma was the * of Boaz. 1Ch 2:11
Boaz was the * of Obed, and Obed 1Ch 2:12
Obed, and Obed was the * of Jesse. 1Ch 2:12
(Machir was also the * of Gilead. 1Ch 2:21
Segub was the * of Jair, who 1Ch 2:22
Soon after his * Hezron's death, 1Ch 2:24
birth to Ashhur, the * of Tekoa. 1Ch 2:24
he was the * of Ziph, who was 1Ch 2:42
of Ziph, who was * of Mareshah, who 1Ch 2:42
of Mareshah, who was the * of 1Ch 2:42
Shema was the * of Raham, who was 1Ch 2:44
Raham, who was the * of Jorke-am. 1Ch 2:44
Rekem was the * of 1Ch 2:44
Shammai's son was Maon, the * of 1Ch 2:45
Shaaph (the * of Madmannah), and 1Ch 2:48,49
* of Machbenah and of Gibe-a). 1Ch 2:48,49
Shobal (the * of Kiriath-jearim), 1Ch 2:50
Salma (the * of Bethlehem), and 1Ch 2:51
and Hareph (the * of Beth-gader). 1Ch 2:51
Pedaiah was the * of 1Ch 3:19,20
Shobal's son Re-aiah was the * of 1Ch 4:2
who was the * of Bethlehem. 1Ch 4:3-4
Ashhur, the * of Tekoa, had two 1Ch 4:5
Koz was the * of Anub and 1Ch 4:8
whose son was Mahir, the * of 1Ch 4:11,12
Eshton was the * of Bethrapha, 1Ch 4:11,12
Tehinnah was the * of Irnahash. 1Ch 4:11,12
Meonothai was the * of Ophrah; 1Ch 4:14
Seraiah was the * of Joab, the 1Ch 4:14
One of her sons was the * of 1Ch 4:19
the * of Eshtemoa the Maacathite. 1Ch 4:19
Er (the * of Lecah), 1Ch 4:21-22
Laadah (the * of Mareshah), 1Ch 4:21-22
* of Zaccur and grandfather of 1Ch 4:26
he dishonored his * by sleeping 1Ch 5:1
Eleazar, the * of 1Ch 6:4-15

Phinehas, the * of 1Ch 6:4-15
Abishua, the * of 1Ch 6:4-15
Bukki, the * of 1Ch 6:4-15
Uzzi, the * of 1Ch 6:4-15
Zerahiah, the * of 1Ch 6:4-15
Meraioth, the * of 1Ch 6:4-15
Amariah, the * of 1Ch 6:4-15
Ahitub, the * of 1Ch 6:4-15
Zadok, the * of 1Ch 6:4-15
Ahima-az, the * of 1Ch 6:4-15
Azariah, the * of 1Ch 6:4-15
Johanan, the * of 1Ch 6:4-15
Temple at Jerusalem), the * of 1Ch 6:4-15
Amariah, the * of 1Ch 6:4-15
Ahitub, the * of 1Ch 6:4-15
Zadok, the * of 1Ch 6:4-15
Shallum, the * of 1Ch 6:4-15
Hilkiah, the * of 1Ch 6:4-15
Azariah, the * of 1Ch 6:4-15
Seraiah, the * of 1Ch 6:4-15
Machir (who became the * of 1Ch 7:14
Their * Ephraim mourned for them 1Ch 7:22
Rephah, the * of 1Ch 7:25,26,27
Resheph, the * of 1Ch 7:25,26,27
Telah, the * of 1Ch 7:25,26,27
Tahan, the * of 1Ch 7:25,26,27
Ladan, the * of 1Ch 7:25,26,27
Ammihud, the * of 1Ch 7:25,26,27
Elishama, the * of 1Ch 7:25,26,27
Nun, the * of 1Ch 7:25,26,27
Heber, Malchi-el (the * of 1Ch 7:31
Gera (also called Heglam), the * 1Ch 8:6,7
Je-iel, the * of Gibeon, lived at 1Ch 8:29
Mikloth who was the * of Shimeah. 1Ch 8:30,31,32
Ner was the * of Kish, and Kish 1Ch 8:33
Kish, and Kish was the * of Saul; 1Ch 8:33
Ahaz was the * of Jehoaddah, 1Ch 8:36
Jehoaddah was the * of: 1Ch 8:36
Moza was the * of Bine-a, whose 1Ch 8:37
Ner was the * of Kish, 1Ch 9:39
Kish was the * of Saul, 1Ch 9:39
Saul was the * of Jonathan, 1Ch 9:39
Jonathan was the * of 1Ch 9:40
was the * of Micah; 1Ch 9:40
Micah was the * of Pithon, 1Ch 9:41
Ahaz was the * of Jarah; 1Ch 9:42
Jarah was the * of Alemeth, 1Ch 9:42
Zimri was the * of Moza. 1Ch 9:42
Moza was the * of Bine-a, 1Ch 9:43
Benaiah, whose * was a mighty 1Ch 11:22
the * of many sons and daughters. 1Ch 14:3
I will be his *, and he shall be 1Ch 17:13
kind things his * did for me." 1Ch 19:2,3
to Hanun for the death of his *. 1Ch 19:2,3
sent these men to honor your *! 1Ch 19:2,3
on each foot (his * was also a 1Ch 20:6,7
as my own son and I will be his *; 1Ch 22:10
their * did and had no children; 1Ch 24:1
direction of their * as they 1Ch 25:6,7
him as my son and I will be his *. 1Ch 28:6
Lord God of our * Israel, praise 1Ch 29:10
to take the throne of his * David; 1Ch 29:23
wealth and honor than his *. 1Ch 29:25
and good to my * David, and now you 2Ch 1:8
to David my * and have made me king 2Ch 1:9
who were selected by my * David. 2Ch 2:7
his * is from here in Tyre. 2Ch 2:14
by my lord David, your *. 2Ch 2:14
(just as his * David had done) and 2Ch 2:17
to Solomon's *, King David, and 2Ch 3:1
to the Lord by his *, King David. 2Ch 5:1
personally to my * David and has 2Ch 6:4
"My * David wanted to build this 2Ch 6:7
kept your promise to my * David, 2Ch 6:15
follow me as your * David did, 2Ch 7:17
chart prepared by his * David; 2Ch 8:14
"Your * was a hard master," 2Ch 10:4
who had counseled his * Solomon. 2Ch 10:6
be easier on them than my * was?" 2Ch 10:8,9
"Tell them, 'If you think my * 2Ch 10:10
not easier! My * used whips on you, 2Ch 10:11
"My * gave you heavy burdens but 2Ch 10:14
he told them. "My * punished 2Ch 10:14
his * had dedicated to the Lord. 2Ch 15:18
was between your * and my father. 2Ch 16:3
was between your father and my *. 2Ch 16:3
Ephraim that his * had conquered. 2Ch 17:2
good king, just as his * Asa was. 2Ch 20:32
Their * had given each of them 2Ch 21:3,4
good ways of your * Jehoshaphat, 2Ch 21:12
men who had assassinated his *. 2Ch 25:3
footsteps of his * Amaziah, and 2Ch 26:4
example of his * Uzziah—who had, 2Ch 27:2
heathen altars his * Hezekiah had 2Ch 33:3
the early years of his * Manasseh; 2Ch 33:22
all the idols just as his * had. 2Ch 33:22
But he didn't change as his * had. 2Ch 33:23
Jeshua was the * of Joiakim; Neh 12:10,11
Joiakim was the * of Eliashib; Neh 12:10,11
Eliashib was the * of Joiada; Neh 12:10,11
Joiada was the * of Jonathan; Neh 12:10,11

(FATHER Con't)

Jonathan was the * of Jaddu-a.	Neh 12:10,11
Esther), whose * and mother were	Est 2:7
he was her cousin and foster *.	Est 8:1
aged men much older than your *!	Job 15:10
call the grave my *, and the worm	Job 17:13,14
I was as a * to the poor, and	Job 29:16
"Has the rain a *?	Job 38:28
and their * put them into his	Job 42:15
For if my * and mother should	Ps 27:10
some day be kings like their *.	Ps 45:16
He is a * to the fatherless;	Ps 68:5
to me, 'You are my *, my God, and	Ps 89:26
He is like a * to us, tender and	Ps 103:13
Punish the sins of his * and	Ps 109:14
Listen to your * and mother.	Pro 1:7,8,9
Just as a * punishes a son he	Pro 3:11,12
to me as you would to your *.	Pro 4:1
child, and the companion of my *.	Pro 4:3
Young man, obey your * and your	Pro 6:20
A sensible son gladdens his *.	Pro 15:20
A child's glory is his *.	Pro 17:6
It's no fun to be a rebel's *.	Pro 17:21
* and a bitter blow to his mother.	Pro 17:25
a calamity to his *, and a nagging	Pro 19:13
A * can give his sons homes and	Pro 19:14
A son who mistreats his * or	Pro 19:26
heritage to have an honest *.	Pro 20:7
man who curses his * or mother.	Pro 20:20
you can get. The * of a godly man	Pro 23:24,25
lawless gang is a shame to his *.	Pro 28:7
A wise son makes his * happy, but	Pro 29:3
There are those who curse their *	Pro 30:11,12
A man who mocks his * and	Pro 30:17
*," "The Prince of Peace."	Is 9:6
from the throne of his * David.	Is 9:7
to you than his * ever was!	Is 14:29
and he will be a * to the people of	Is 22:21
who squalls to his * and mother,	Is 45:10
I promised to Jacob, your *.	Is 58:14
Surely you are still our *!	Is 63:16
*, our Redeemer from ages past.	Is 63:16
And yet, O Lord, you are our *.	Is 64:8
wooden post their *, and for their	Jer 2:26,27
And yet you say to me, "O *,	Jer 3:4,5
your calling me "*," and thought	Jer 3:19
my * the news that a son was born.	Jer 20:15
his * King Josiah, and was taken	Jer 22:11
Why did your * Josiah reign so	Jer 22:15
who succeeded his * Josiah on the	Jer 22:18
For I am a * to Israel, and	Jer 31:9
for Jonadab our * (son of Rechab)	Jer 35:6
that Jonadab our * commanded us.	Jer 35:10
because their * told them not to.	Jer 35:14
have obeyed their * completely, but	Jer 35:16
have obeyed your * in every	Jer 35:18,19
of Canaan—your * must have been an	Eze 16:3
a Hittite and your * an Amorite.	Eze 16:45
But his * shall die for his own	Eze 18:18
sins, nor the * for his son's.	Eze 18:20
the land I gave their * Jacob.	Eze 28:25
unless it is his *, mother, child,	Eze 44:25
Nabonidus his *, who was out of	Dan 5:7f
In the days of your * this man	Dan 5:11
your *"—the Aramaic word for	Dan 5:11f
Aramaic word for "*" can also	Dan 5:11f
but those of her *, the king of	Dan 11:6
"And a man and his * defile the	Amo 2:7
For the son despises his *;	Mic 7:6
us, as you promised our * Abraham!	Mic 7:20
own * and mother will slay him!	Zec 13:3
for you by loving your *, Jacob.	Mal 1:2,3
"A son honors his *, a servant	Mal 1:6
I am your * and Master, yet you	Mal 1:6
* Levi," says the Lord of Hosts.	Mal 2:4
We are children of the same *,	Mal 2:10
Abraham was the * of Isaac;	Mt 1:2
Isaac was the * of Jacob;	Mt 1:2
Jacob was the * of Judah and his	Mt 1:2
Judah was the * of Perez and	Mt 1:3
Perez was the * of Hezron;	Mt 1:3
Hezron was the * of Aram;	Mt 1:3
Aram was the * of Amminadab;	Mt 1:4
Amminadab was the * of Nahshon;	Mt 1:4
Nahshon was the * of Salmon;	Mt 1:4
Salmon was the * of Boaz (Rahab	Mt 1:5
Boaz was the * of Obed (Ruth was	Mt 1:5
Obed was the * of Jesse;	Mt 1:5
Jesse was the * of King David.	Mt 1:6
David was the * of Solomon (his	Mt 1:6
Solomon was the * of Rehoboam;	Mt 1:7
Rehoboam was the * of Abijah;	Mt 1:7
Abijah was the * of Asa;	Mt 1:7
Asa was the * of Jehoshaphat;	Mt 1:8
Jehoshaphat was the * of Joram;	Mt 1:8
Joram was the * of Uzziah;	Mt 1:8
Uzziah was the * of Jotham;	Mt 1:9
Jotham was the * of Ahaz;	Mt 1:9
Ahaz was the * of Hezekiah;	Mt 1:9
Hezekiah was the * of Manasseh;	Mt 1:10
Manasseh was the * of Amos;	Mt 1:10

Amos was the * of Josiah;	Mt 1:10
Josiah was the * of Jechoniah and	Mt 1:11
Jechoniah was the * of Shealtiel;	Mt 1:12
Shealtiel was the * of	Mt 1:12
Zerubbabel was the * of Abiud;	Mt 1:13
Abiud was the * of Eliakim;	Mt 1:13
Eliakim was the * of Azor;	Mt 1:13
Azor was the * of Zadok;	Mt 1:14
Zadok was the * of Achim;	Mt 1:14
Achim was the * of Eliud;	Mt 1:14
Eliud was the * of Eleazar;	Mt 1:15
Eleazar was the * of Matthan;	Mt 1:15
Matthan was the * of Jacob;	Mt 1:15
Jacob was the * of Joseph (who	Mt 1:16
* Zebedee, mending their nets;	Mt 4:21
their * behind, went with him.	Mt 4:22
they will praise your heavenly *.	Mt 5:15,16
as true sons of your * in heaven.	Mt 5:45
as your * in heaven is perfect.	Mt 5:48
the reward from your * in heaven.	Mt 6:1
And your * who knows all secrets	Mt 6:4
and pray to your * secretly, and	Mt 6:6
secretly, and your *, who knows	Mt 6:6
Remember, your * knows exactly	Mt 6:7,8
"Pray along these lines: 'Our *	Mt 6:9
Your heavenly * will forgive	Mt 6:14,15
your * who knows every secret.	Mt 6:18
your heavenly * feeds them.	Mt 6:26
But your heavenly * already knows	Mt 6:31,32
If a child asks his * for a loaf	Mt 7:9
won't your * in heaven even more	Mt 7:11
whether they obey my * in heaven.	Mt 7:21
"Sir, when my * is dead, then I	Mt 8:21
"Let me first go and bury my *."	Mt 8:21f
heavenly * speaking through you!	Mt 10:20
ground without your * knowing it.	Mt 10:29
my friend before my * in heaven.	Mt 10:32
deny him before my * in heaven.	Mt 10:33
a man against his *, and a daughter	Mt 10:35
If you love your * and mother	Mt 10:37
this prayer: "O *, Lord of heaven	Mt 11:25
Yes, *, for it pleased you to do	Mt 11:26
has been entrusted to me by my *.	Mt 11:27
Only the * knows the Son, and the	Mt 11:27
the Son, and the * is known only by	Mt 11:27
who obeys my * in heaven is my	Mt 12:50
law is 'Honor your * and mother;	Mt 15:4
not planted by my * shall be rooted	Mt 15:13,14
said, "for my * in heaven has	Mt 16:17
in the glory of my * and judge each	Mt 16:27
to my *.	Mt 18:10
my * in heaven will do it for you.	Mt 18:19
So shall my heavenly * do to you	Mt 18:35
should leave his * and mother, and	Mt 19:5,6
lie, honor your * and mother, and	Mt 19:19
sisters, *, mother, wife,	Mt 19:29
for the persons my * selects."	Mt 20:23
Then the * told the youngest,	Mt 21:30
of the two was obeying his *?"	Mt 21:31
here on earth as '*,' for only God	Mt 23:9
Only the * knows.	Mt 24:36
blessed of my *, into the Kingdom	Mt 25:34
on the ground, and prayed, "My *!	Mt 26:39
he left them and prayed, "My *!	Mt 26:42
I could ask my * for thousands of	Mt 26:53
the name of the * and of the Son	Mt 28:19
they left their * Zebedee in the	Mk 1:20
the little girl's * and mother and	Mk 5:40
God: 'Honor your * and mother.'	Mk 7:10
against his * or mother must die.	Mk 7:10
of my *, with the holy angels."	Mk 8:38
Jesus asked the *.	Mk 9:21
The * instantly replied, "I do	Mk 9:24
is welcoming my * who sent me!"	Mk 9:37
therefore a man is to leave his *	Mk 10:6,7
respect your * and mother."	Mk 10:19
sisters, mother, *, children, or	Mk 10:29
of our * David's kingdom . "	Mk 11:10
so that your * in heaven will	Mk 11:25
neither will your * who is in	Mk 11:26,f
will own the farm when his * dies.	Mk 12:7
only the * knows.	Mk 13:32
"*, Father," he said,	Mk 14:36
"Father, *," he said,	Mk 14:36
(Simon is the * of Alexander and	Mk 15:21
would be Zacharias, after his *.	Lk 1:59
So they asked the baby's *,	Lk 1:62
Then his * Zacharias was filled	Lk 1:67
this to us? Your * and I have been	Lk 2:48
Joseph's * was Heli;	Lk 3:23-38
Heli's * was Matthat;	Lk 3:23-38
Matthat's * was Levi;	Lk 3:23-38
Levi's * was Melchi;	Lk 3:23-38
Melchi's * was Jannai;	Lk 3:23-38
Jannai's * was Joseph;	Lk 3:23-38
Joseph's * was Mattathias;	Lk 3:23-38
Mattathias' * was Amos;	Lk 3:23-38
father was Amos;Amos' * was Nahum;	Lk 3:23-38
Nahum's * was Esli;	Lk 3:23-38
Esli's * was Naggai;	Lk 3:23-38
Naggai's * was Maath;	Lk 3:23-38

Maath's * was Mattathias;	Lk 3:23-38
Mattathias' * was Semein;	Lk 3:23-38
Semein's * was Josech;	Lk 3:23-38
Josech's * was Joda;	Lk 3:23-38
Joda's * was Joanan;	Lk 3:23-38
Joanan's * was Rhesa;	Lk 3:23-38
Rhesa's * was Zerubbabel;	Lk 3:23-38
Zerubbabel's * was Shealtiel;	Lk 3:23-38
Shealtiel's * was Neri;	Lk 3:23-38
Neri's * was Melchi;	Lk 3:23-38
Melchi's * was Addi;	Lk 3:23-38
Addi's * was Cosam;	Lk 3:23-38
Cosam's * was Elmadam;	Lk 3:23-38
Elmadam's * was Er;	Lk 3:23-38
Elmadam's father was Er;Er's * was	Lk 3:23-38
Joshua's * was Eliezer;	Lk 3:23-38
Eliezer's * was Jorim;	Lk 3:23-38
Jorim's * was Matthat;	Lk 3:23-38
Matthat's * was Levi;	Lk 3:23-38
Levi's * was Simeon;	Lk 3:23-38
Simeon's * was Judah;	Lk 3:23-38
Judah's * was Joseph;	Lk 3:23-38
Joseph's * was Jonam;	Lk 3:23-38
Jonam's * was Eliakim;	Lk 3:23-38
Eliakim's * was Melea;	Lk 3:23-38
Melea's * was Menna;	Lk 3:23-38
Menna's * was Mattatha;	Lk 3:23-38
Mattatha's * was Nathan;	Lk 3:23-38
Nathan's * was David;	Lk 3:23-38
David's * was Jesse;	Lk 3:23-38
Jesse's * was Obed;	Lk 3:23-38
Obed's * was Boaz;	Lk 3:23-38
Obed's father was Boaz;Boaz' * was	Lk 3:23-38
Salmon's * was Nahshon;	Lk 3:23-38
Nahshon's * was Amminadab;	Lk 3:23-38
Amminadab's * was Admin;	Lk 3:23-38
Admin's * was Arni;	Lk 3:23-38
Arni's * was Hezron;	Lk 3:23-38
Hezron's * was Perez;	Lk 3:23-38
Perez' * was Judah;	Lk 3:23-38
Judah's * was Jacob;	Lk 3:23-38
Jacob's * was Isaac;	Lk 3:23-38
Isaac's * was Abraham;	Lk 3:23-38
Abraham's * was Terah;	Lk 3:23-38
Terah's * was Nahor;	Lk 3:23-38
Nahor's * was Serug;	Lk 3:23-38
Serug's * was Reu;	Lk 3:23-38
Serug's father was Reu;Reu's * was	Lk 3:23-38
Peleg's * was Eber;	Lk 3:23-38
Eber's * was Shelah;	Lk 3:23-38
Shelah's * was Cainan;	Lk 3:23-38
Cainan's * was Arphaxad;	Lk 3:23-38
Arphaxad's * was Shem;	Lk 3:23-38
Shem's * was Noah;	Lk 3:23-38
Noah's * was Lamech;	Lk 3:23-38
Lamech's * was Methuselah;	Lk 3:23-38
Methuselah's * was Enoch;	Lk 3:23-38
Enoch's * was Jared;	Lk 3:23-38
Jared's * was Mahalaleel;	Lk 3:23-38
Mahalaleel's * was Cainan;	Lk 3:23-38
Cainan's * was Enos;	Lk 3:23-38
Cainan's father was Enos;Enos' *	Lk 3:23-38
Seth's * was Adam;	Lk 3:23-38
Adam's * was God.	Lk 3:23-38
as much compassion as your * does.	Lk 6:36
"She's gone," he told her *;	Lk 8:49
said to the *, "Don't be afraid!	Lk 8:50
the little girl's * and mother.	Lk 8:51
the glory of the * and the holy	Lk 9:26
boy and handed him over to his *.	Lk 9:42
to go and bury my *,' "—perhaps	Lk 9:59f
could, when his * died, collect the	Lk 9:59f
"I praise you, O *, Lord of heaven	Lk 10:21
Yes, thank you, *, for that is	Lk 10:21
I am the Agent of my * in	Lk 10:22
the Son except the *, and no one	Lk 10:22
really knows the * except the Son	Lk 10:22
he taught them: "*, may your name	Lk 11:2
that your heavenly * will do at	Lk 11:13
your heavenly * knows your needs.	Lk 12:30
For it gives your * great	Lk 12:32
A * will decide one way about me;	Lk 12:53
not hate his * and mother."	Lk 14:26f
he does his own *, mother, wife,	Lk 14:26
When the younger told his *, 'I	Lk 15:12
you die!' his * agreed to divide	Lk 15:12
I will go home to my * and say,	Lk 15:18
father and say, "*, I have sinned	Lk 15:18
"So he returned home to his *.	Lk 15:20
distance away, his * saw him	Lk 15:20
"His son said to him, '*, I have	Lk 15:21
"But his * said to the slaves,	Lk 15:22
told, 'and your * has killed the	Lk 15:27
go in. His * came out and begged	Lk 15:28
" 'Look, dear son,' his * said	Lk 15:31
" '* Abraham,' he shouted, 'have	Lk 16:24
"Then the rich man said, 'O *	Lk 16:27
"The rich man replied, 'No, *	Lk 16:30
all the land when his * dies.	Lk 20:14
and because my * has granted me	Lk 22:29
this prayer: "*, if you are	Lk 22:41,42

ATHER Con't)
"*, forgive these people," Lk 23:34
Then Jesus shouted, "*, I commit Lk 23:46
iterally, "the promise of my * Lk 24:49f
upon you, just as my * promised. Lk 24:49
of the only Son of the heavenly *! Jn 1:14
* and has told us all about him. Jn 1:18
or limit. The * loves this man Jn 3:35
he * here or in Jerusalem. Jn 4:21-24
as we should. The * wants this kind Jn 4:21-24
Then the * realized it was the Jn 4:53
But Jesus replied, "My * Jn 5:17
Literally, "My * works even Jn 5:17f
of God as his *, thereby making Jn 5:18
He does only what he sees the * Jn 5:19
For the * loves the Son, and Jn 5:20
he wants to, just as the * does. Jn 5:21
And the * leaves all judgment of Jn 5:22
the Son, just as they honor the *. Jn 5:23
are certainly not honoring the *. Jn 5:23
shall live. The * has life in Jn 5:26
judgment without consulting the *. Jn 5:30
is to the witness of his *. Jn 5:32,33f
assigned me by the *, and they Jn 5:36
they prove that the * has sent me. Jn 5:36
And the * himself has also Jn 5:37
representing my * and you refuse to Jn 5:43
you of this to the *—Moses will! Jn 5:45
For God the * has sent me for Jn 6:27
didn't give it to them. My * did. Jn 6:32
to me—those the * has given me—and Jn 6:37
whose * and mother we know. Jn 6:42
to me unless the * who sent me Jn 6:44
Those the * speaks to, who learn Jn 6:45
the *, for only I have seen him. Jn 6:46
of the living * who sent me, and in Jn 6:57
unless the * attracts him to me." Jn 6:65
I have with me the * who sent me. Jn 8:16
Well, I am one witness, and my * Jn 8:18
"Where is your *?" Jn 8:19
am, so you don't know who my * is. Jn 8:19
Literally, "the *." Jn 8:27f
have spoken what the * taught me. Jn 8:28
what I saw when I was with my *. Jn 8:38
following the advice of your *." Jn 8:38
"Our * is Abraham," they Jn 8:39
No, you are obeying your real * Jn 8:41
true * is God himself." Jn 8:41
children of your * the devil and Jn 8:44
for he is the * of liars. Jn 8:44
Anyone whose * is God listens Jn 8:47
For I honor my *—and you dishonor Jn 8:49
So you are greater than our * Jn 8:53
But it is my *—and you claim him Jn 8:54
Your * Abraham rejoiced to see Jn 8:56
* knows me and I know the Father; Jn 10:15
Father knows me and I know the *; Jn 10:15
"The * loves me because I lay Jn 10:17
For the * has given me this Jn 10:18
miracles I do in the name of my *. Jn 10:25
from me, for my * has given them Jn 10:29
I and the * are one." Jn 10:30
the * says, 'I am the Son of God'? Jn 10:34,35,36
* is in me, and I in the Father." Jn 10:38
Father is in me, and I in the *." Jn 10:38
"*, thank you for hearing me. Jn 11:41
And if they follow me, the * will Jn 12:26
Shall I pray, '*, save me from Jn 12:27
why I came! *, bring glory and Jn 12:28
you what the * said to tell you. Jn 12:49
earth before returning to his *. Jn 13:1
Jesus knew that the * had given Jn 13:1
is to welcome the * who sent me." Jn 13:20
up there where my * lives, and I am Jn 14:2,3
No one can get to the * except by Jn 14:6
you would have known who my * is. Jn 14:7
Philip said, "Sir, show us the * Jn 14:8
who has seen me has seen the *! Jn 14:9
in the * and the Father is in me? Jn 14:10
in the Father and the * is in me? Jn 14:10
but are from my * who lives in me. Jn 14:10
in the * and the Father is in me. Jn 14:11
in the Father and the * is in me. Jn 14:11
I am going to be with the *. Jn 14:12,13
praise to the * because of what I, Jn 14:12,13
and I will ask the * and he will Jn 14:15,16
my *, and you in me, and I in you. Jn 14:20
and because he loves me, my * Jn 14:21
and obey me. The * will love them Jn 14:23
It is the answer given by the * Jn 14:24
But when the * sends the Jn 14:26
the *, who is greater than I am. Jn 14:28
freely do what the * requires of me Jn 14:31
world will know that I love the *. Jn 14:31
"I AM THE true Vine, and my * is Jn 15:1
This brings great glory to my *. Jn 15:8
"I have loved you even as the * Jn 15:9
I obey my * and live in his love. Jn 15:10
told you everything the * told me. Jn 15:15
ask for from the *, using my name, Jn 15:16
hating me is also hating my *. Jn 15:23
they hated both of us—me and my *. Jn 15:24
He will come to you from the * Jn 15:26
they have never known the * or me. Jn 16:3
* and you shall see me no more; Jn 16:10
is this about 'going to the *'? Jn 16:17,18
go directly to the * and ask him, Jn 16:23
'tell you plainly all about the *. Jn 16:25
And I won't need to ask the * to Jn 16:26
requests, for the * himself loves Jn 16:27
believe that I came from the *. Jn 16:27
Yes, I came from the * into the Jn 16:28
the world and return to the *." Jn 16:28
be alone, for the * is with me. Jn 16:32
and said, "*, the time has come. Jn 17:1
And now, *, reveal my glory as I Jn 17:5
to you. Holy *, keep them in your Jn 17:11
as you and I are, *—that just as Jn 17:21
as you love me. *, I want them Jn 17:24
"O righteous *, the world Jn 17:25
from the cup the * has given me?" Jn 18:11
I haven't yet ascended to the *. Jn 20:17
I ascend to my * and your Father, Jn 20:17
and your *, my God and your God." Jn 20:17
and said, "As the * has sent me, Jn 20:21
"The * sets those dates," he Act 1:7
And just as promised, the * gave Act 2:33
Haran, in Syria, until his * died. Act 7:4
Isaac became the * of Jacob, and Act 7:8
and Jacob was the * of the twelve Act 7:8
Then Joseph sent for his * Jacob Act 7:14
the sons of Hamor, Shechem's *. Act 7:16
Jewess but his * a Greek. Act 16:1
knew that his * was a Greek [and Act 16:3
As it happened, Publius' * was Act 28:8
* and from Jesus Christ our Lord. Rom 1:6,7
So Abraham is the spiritual * of Rom 4:11
also the spiritual * of those Jews Rom 4:12
for Abraham is the * of us all when Rom 4:16
Abraham the * of many nations. Rom 4:17
too old to be a *, at the age of Rom 4:19
and when God the *, with glorious Rom 6:4
and calling to him, "*, Father." Rom 8:15
and calling to him, "Father, *." Rom 8:15
And the * who knows all hearts Rom 8:27
the * of our Lord Jesus Christ. Rom 15:6
May God our * and the Lord Jesus 1Co 1:3
that you have only me as your *. 1Co 4:15
God, the *, who created all things 1Co 8:6
over to God the *, having put down 1Co 15:24
has been given to Christ by his *; 1Co 15:27
not rule over the * himself, who 1Co 15:27
May God our * and the Lord Jesus 2Co 1:2
we have—he is the * of our Lord 2Co 1:3,4
you, and be a * to you, and you 2Co 6:18
who sinned, or his * 2Co 7:12
God, the * of our Lord Jesus 2Co 11:31
* who raised him from the dead. Gal 1:1
* and from the Lord Jesus Christ. Gal 1:3
just as God our * planned, and Gal 1:4
BUT REMEMBER THIS, that if a * Gal 4:1
owns everything his * had. Gal 4:1
he reaches whatever age his * set. Gal 4:2
speak of God as our dear *. Gal 4:6
our * and Jesus Christ our Lord. Eph 1:2
How we praise God, the * of our Eph 1:3
God, the glorious * of our Lord Eph 1:16,17
come to God the * with the Holy Eph 2:18
and pray to the * of all the great Eph 3:14,15
the same God and * who is over us Eph 4:6
a much loved child imitates his *. Eph 5:1
to our God and * in the name of our Eph 5:20
man must leave his * and mother Eph 5:31
Honor your * and mother. Eph 6:2
if you honor your * and mother, Eph 6:3
the * and the Lord Jesus Christ. Eph 6:23
Yes, I pray that God our * and Php 1:2
Lord, to the glory of God the *. Php 2:11
Now unto God our * be glory Php 4:20
May God our * shower you with Col 1:2
thanks to God the * of our Lord Col 1:3
thankful to the * who has made us Col 1:12
God the * to give him your thanks. Col 3:17
belong to God the * and the Lord 1Th 1:1
*, and from Jesus Christ our Lord. 1Th 1:1
to our God and * about you, and 1Th 1:3
We talked to you as a * to his 1Th 2:11
May God our * himself and our 1Th 3:11
holy by God our *, so that you may 1Th 3:13
* and in the Lord Jesus Christ. 2Th 1:1
May God the * and the Lord Jesus 2Th 1:2
and God our *, who has loved us and 2Th 2:16
May God our * and Jesus Christ 1Ti 1:2
just as though he were your own *. 1Ti 5:1
May God the * and Christ Jesus 2Ti 1:2
May God the * and Christ Jesus our Tit 1:4
May God our * and the Lord Jesus Phm 1:3
on to him from his *, is far Heb 1:4
"I am his * and he is my Son." Heb 1:5,6
Jesus, now have the same * he has. Heb 2:11
about God my *, and together we Heb 2:12
the * of a great nation of people. Heb 6:14
Melchizedek had no * or mother Heb 7:3
who Melchizedek's * or mother were, Heb 7:3f
loving * does for his children. Heb 12:7
that even our * Abraham was Jas 2:21
our heavenly *, and sometimes it Jas 3:9
Dear friends, God the * chose you 1Pe 1:2
All honor to God, the God and * 1Pe 1:3
And remember that your heavenly * 1Pe 1:17
next to God the *, with all the 1Pe 3:22
with honor given him by God his *; 2Pe 1:17,18
He was with the * and then was 1Jn 1:2
* and with Jesus Christ his Son. 1Jn 1:3
to plead for you before the *. 1Jn 2:1
have learned to know God our *. 1Jn 2:13
in God the * and in his Son. 1Jn 2:22
Son, can't have God the * either. 1Jn 2:23
God's Son, has God the * also. 1Jn 2:23
with both God the * and his Son. 1Jn 2:24
SEE HOW VERY much our heavenly * 1Jn 3:1
And all who love the * love his 1Jn 5:1
forever, God the * and Jesus 2Jn 1:3
Then you will have both the * and 2Jn 1:9
and made us priests of God his *. Rev 1:6
of iron just as my * gave me the Rev 2:27
* and his angels that he is mine. Rev 3:5
my place with my * on his throne Rev 3:21

FATHER-IN-LAW
Tamar that her * had left for the Gen 38:13
message to her *: "The man who Gen 38:25
high nobility, his * being a major Gen 41:45f
tending the flock of his * Jethro, Ex 3:1
Moses' * goes under two names in Ex 3:1f
talked it over with Jethro, his *. Ex 4:18
SOON REACHED Jethro, Moses' * Ex 18:1
"Jethro, your *, has come to Ex 18:5,6
Moses went out to meet his * and Ex 18:7
Moses related to his * all that Ex 18:8
When Moses' * saw how much time Ex 18:14
his * exclaimed. Ex 18:17
Soon afterwards Moses let his * Ex 18:27
of Moses' *—members of the Kenite Ju 1:16
of Moses' * Hobab—had moved away Ju 4:11
refused, but his * kept urging him Ju 19:7
* said, "Look, it's getting late. Ju 19:9
her husband and * were dead, her 1Sa 4:19
her husband and her * were dead. 1Sa 4:21,22
Then Er's widow, Tamar, and her * 1Ch 2:4
to him because his * was Shecaniah Neh 6:18
him to Annas, the * of Caiaphas, Jn 18:13

FATHER-IN-LAW'S
Moses listened to his * advice, Ex 18:24

FATHER'S
of Canaan, saw his * nakedness and Gen 9:22
Literally, "go into my * house." Gen 24:38f
filled after his * death, and gave Gen 26:18
your * favorite dish from them. Gen 27:8,9,10
prepared in his * favorite way. Gen 27:14
He also has prepared his * Gen 27:31
with his * blessing, to get a wife Gen 28:6,7,8
arrived with her * sheep, for she Gen 29:9
her cousin on her * side, and that Gen 29:12,13
All his wealth is at our * Gen 31:1
made me wealthy at your * expense. Gen 31:9
* wealth will come to us anyway! Gen 31:14
Rachel stole her * household gods Gen 31:21
with Bilhah, his * concubine, and Gen 35:22
he was grazing his * donkeys. Gen 36:24
the sons of his * wives Bilhah and Gen 37:2
was to shepherd his * flocks. Gen 37:2
noticed their * partiality, and Gen 37:4
took their * flocks to Shechem to Gen 37:12
and for the loss of his * home). Gen 41:51
us—seeing that our * life is bound Gen 44:30
Your * sons shall bow before you. Gen 49:8
JOSEPH THREW HIMSELF upon his * Gen 50:1
water troughs for their * flocks. Ex 2:16
married Jochebed, his * sister; Ex 6:20
He is my * God—I will exalt him. Ex 15:2
and require that a * sins be Ex 34:7
any other of his * wives, nor his Lev 18:8
* wife's daughter; Lev 18:11
nor your aunt—your * Lev 18:12
nor your aunt—the wife of your * Lev 18:14
If a man sleeps with his * wife, Lev 20:11
he has defiled what is his *; Lev 20:11
thus violating her * holiness as Lev 21:9
home to her * household, she may Lev 22:13
she may eat of her * food again. Lev 22:13
you punish the * fault in the Num 14:17,18
along with our * brothers." Num 27:3,4
at home in her * home, and her Num 30:3
the curse of a * sins upon even the Deu 5:9,10
to the door of her * home where the Deu 22:21
A man shall not sleep with his * Deu 22:30
Literally, "his * wife." Deu 22:30f
with one of his * wives, for she Deu 27:20
to hitch his * best ox to the Ju 6:25
members of his * household, and for Ju 6:27
He took them to his * home at Ju 9:5
"You'll not get any of our * Ju 11:1
So Jephthah fled from his * home Ju 11:3

(FATHER'S Con't)
have driven me out of my * house? Ju 11:7
down your * house with you in it. Ju 14:15
returned to her * home in Ju 19:2
His * name was Jeroham, 1Sa 1:1
had not heard his * command; 1Sa 14:27
"When I am taking care of my * 1Sa 17:34
David exclaimed. "My * family 1Sa 18:18
* shameful behavior toward David. 1Sa 20:34
the death of all of your * family. 1Sa 22:22
to Hanun about his * death. 2Sa 10:2
sleep with your * wives, for he has 2Sa 16:21
the tent to lie with his * wives. 2Sa 16:22
the Lord during my * reign, and you 1Ki 2:26
from me and from my * family. 1Ki 2:31
After his * death he built Elath 2Ki 14:22
* name: Jabesh 2Ki 15:13
* name: King Menahem 2Ki 15:23
* name: Remaliah 2Ki 15:27
* name: King Uzziah 2Ki 15:32,33
* name: Jotham 2Ki 16:1
* name: Elah 2Ki 17:1
* name: Ahaz 2Ki 18:1
Ephrathah, his * widow, and she 1Ch 2:24
with one of his * wives, his 1Ch 5:1
from among all my * family to begin 1Ch 28:4
families of Judah, my * family; 1Ch 28:4
become king in my * place, and I 2Ch 6:10
finger is thicker than my * loins! 2Ch 10:10
footsteps of his * early years, and 2Ch 17:3
of his * God—quite unlike the 2Ch 17:4
advisors after his * death, and 2Ch 22:4
nor the children for the * sins. 2Ch 25:4
After his * death, he rebuilt 2Ch 26:2
A WISE YOUTH accepts his * rebuke; Pro 13:1
Only a fool despises his * Pro 15:5
Listen to your * advice and Pro 23:22
a friend—either yours or your *. Pro 27:10
who sees all his * wickedness, so Eze 18:14
not die because of his * sins; Eze 18:17
'Doesn't the son pay for his * Eze 18:19
punished for his * sins, nor the Eze 18:20
as the sun in their * Kingdom. Mt 13:43
Just so, it is not my * will Mt 18:14
it new with you in my * Kingdom." Mt 26:29
at the Temple, in my * House?" Lk 2:49
wanted to wait until his * death. Lk 9:59
to divide my * estate with me." Lk 12:13
send him to my * home— for I have Lk 16:27
Don't turn my * House into a Jn 2:16
For it is my * will that Jn 6:40
All the * glory is mine; Jn 16:15
fulfillment of the * promise, a Act 1:4
is living in sin with his * wife. 1Co 5:1
also under his * orders, so that 1Co 15:28
pay for their * and mother's 2Co 12:14
from God the * point of view, is Jas 1:27
* Name written on their foreheads. Rev 14:1

FATHERLESS
be widows and your children *. Ex 22:24
He gives justice to the * and Deu 10:18
"God saves the * and the poor Job 5:15
of the poor and * are taken. Job 24:3
"The wicked snatch * children Job 24:9
the * who had no one to help them. Job 29:12
He is a father to the *; Ps 68:5
afflicted, the *, the destitute. Ps 82:3
May his children become * and Ps 109:9,10
let no one pity his * children. Ps 109:12,13
help the poor, the *, and widows. Is 1:17
rob the widows and * children. Is 10:2
(But I will preserve your * Jer 49:11
for in you alone, O Lord, the * Hos 14:3

FATHERS
*, and to your relatives there; Gen 31:3
of my * has come and spoken to me. Gen 31:5
the God of your *, must have put it Gen 43:23
* have been for many generations.' Gen 46:34
God, the God of my * Abraham and Gen 48:15
names of my * Abraham and Isaac; Gen 48:16
to Canaan, the land of your *. Gen 48:21
May the God of your *, the Gen 49:25
You must bury me with my * in the Gen 49:29,30
I am the God of your *—the God Ex 3:6
them that their *' God has sent me, Ex 3:13
he promised your *, a land 'flowing Ex 13:4,5
"The God of my * was my helper, Ex 18:4
replace their *, they shall be Lev 6:22,23
your mothers and *, and obey my Lev 19:1
the same sins as those of their *. Lev 26:39
*' sins of treachery against me. Lev 26:40,41
the same kind of thing your * did! Num 32:8
had promised their *, except Caleb Deu 1:34,35
as the God of your * promised you. Deu 6:3
tender love, he made with your *. Deu 7:12
he promised your * to give you. Deu 7:13
promised to your * by the Lord. Deu 8:1
to the land I promised their *. Deu 10:11
And yet he rejoiced in your * Deu 10:15
Literally, "your *." Deu 11:21f
of your *, has given you forever: Deu 12:1
"* shall not be put to death for Deu 24:16
the sons for the sins of their *; Deu 24:16
over you as he did over your *. Deu 30:9
Even his own children, brothers, * Deu 33:9
grown up to take their *' places. Jos 5:7
the Lord which our * made, Jos 22:28
who rescued our * from their Jos 24:17
And when their * and brothers Ju 21:22
the Lord with our *, at the time 1Ki 8:21
which you have given to their *. 1Ki 8:33,34
land which you have given their *. 1Ki 8:40
have given their *, and toward this 1Ki 8:48
you brought our * out of the land 1Ki 8:53
be with us as he was with our *; 1Ki 8:57
buried in the grave of your *." 1Ki 13:21,22
good land of their * and scatter 1Ki 14:15
"Let us be allies just as our * 1Ki 15:19
"I am no better than my *." 1Ki 19:4f
The city * followed the queen's 1Ki 21:11
law of Moses that * shall not be 2Ki 14:6
the sins of their *: everyone must 2Ki 14:6
them from this land of their *." 2Ki 21:8
not true to the God of their *; 1Ch 5:25
God of our * see and judge you." 1Ch 12:17
get to know the God of your *. 1Ch 28:9
the land as our * were before us; 1Ch 29:15
"O Lord God of our *: Abraham, 1Ch 29:18
this land you gave to their *. 2Ch 6:25
land which you gave to our *." 2Ch 6:31f
you gave their *, and this city and 2Ch 6:37,38
Lord God of their *, the God who 2Ch 7:22
of their *, and sacrifice to him. 2Ch 11:16
*, for you will not succeed!" 2Ch 13:12
Lord God of their *, defeated 2Ch 13:18,19
Lord God of their *, and agreed 2Ch 15:12
"O Lord God of our *—the only 2Ch 20:6
away from the Lord God of his *. 2Ch 21:10
of Moses, that the * shall not die 2Ch 25:4
away from the Lord God of their *. 2Ch 28:6
"The Lord God of your * was 2Ch 28:9
angering the Lord God of his *. 2Ch 28:25
For our * have committed a deep 2Ch 29:6
see us today. Our * have been 2Ch 29:9
Do not be like your * and 2Ch 30:7
God of their * and were destroyed. 2Ch 30:7
Lord God of his *, even though 2Ch 30:17,18,19
sins to the Lord God of their *. 2Ch 30:22
Jehovah the God of their * sent 2Ch 36:15
to the Lord God of our *. Ez 8:28
Lord God of your * and do what he Ez 10:11
to rebuild the city of my *!" Neh 2:4
Wasn't it enough that your * did Neh 13:18
thing from their *—our ancestors to Job 15:17-19
men whose * are less than my dogs. Job 30:1
The praises of our * surrounded Ps 22:3,4
the earth, as all my * were. Ps 39:12
and commanded our * to teach them Ps 78:5
to be as their * were—stubborn, Ps 78:8
them, and for their * in Egypt. Ps 78:11,12
Land and disobeyed as their * had. Ps 78:57
For there your * doubted me, Ps 95:9
Both we and our * have sinned so Ps 106:6
Then our * joined the worshipers Ps 106:28
Their * before them were evil Is 1:4
*—will be carried off to Babylon. Is 39:6
Temple where our * praised you is Is 64:11
for those of their * too, says the Is 65:7
Lord, why did your * desert me? Jer 2:4,5
their * as an inheritance forever. Jer 3:18
everything our * had—flocks and Jer 3:24
for we and our * have sinned from Jer 3:25
* and sons shall be frustrated; Jer 6:21
I gave to your * to keep forever. Jer 7:7
place I gave to you and to your *. Jer 7:13,14
wood and the * build fires, and the Jer 7:18
* when I led them out of Egypt. Jer 7:22
Ever since the day your * left Jer 7:25
even than their * were. Jer 7:26
of Baal, as their * told them to. Jer 9:14
with their *—and cursed is the man Jer 11:1
that your * made with God, and do Jer 11:6
For I solemnly said to your * Jer 11:7
But your * didn't do it. Jer 11:8
the sins of their *, refusing to Jer 11:10
The agreement I made with their * Jer 11:10
And I will smash * and sons Jer 13:14
wickedness, and that of our * too. Jer 14:20
their mothers and *, shall die Jer 16:3
this: Because your * forsook me. Jer 16:11
have been worse than your * were! Jer 16:12
you nor your * have been before, Jer 16:13
to this same land I gave your *. Jer 16:14,15
you saying, "Our * have been Jer 16:19
I gave this commandment to your * Jer 17:21,22
same way as their * did, who turned Jer 23:27
city I gave to you and your *. Jer 23:38,39
I gave to them and to their *." Jer 24:10
this land that I gave to their *; Jer 30:3
pay for their *' sins." Jer 31:29
Literally, "The * eat the sour Jer 31:29f
I made with their * when I took Jer 31:32
children suffer for their *' sins; Jer 32:18
you promised their * long ago—a Jer 32:22
Our * came and conquered it and Jer 32:23
just as they did for your *. Jer 34:5
I made a covenant with your * long Jer 34:13
the land I gave to you and your *. Jer 35:15
nor any of your * have ever known. Jer 44:2,3
the sins of your *, and the sins of Jer 44:9
I gave you and your * before you. Jer 44:10
as we and our * before us, and our Jer 44:17
that you and your * and your kings Jer 44:21
go rushing by; * flee without a Jer 47:3
of justice, the hope of their *." Jer 50:7
We are orphans—our * dead, our Lam 5:3
Our * sinned but died before the Lam 5:7
They and their * have kept on Eze 2:3
ever do again. * will eat their Eze 5:10
sons, and sons will eat their *; Eze 5:10
are punished for their *' sins? Eze 18:2
Literally, "The * have eaten sour Eze 18:2f
are mine to judge—* and sons Eze 18:4
the times of their * until now. Eze 20:4
Don't follow your *' footsteps. Eze 20:18
and longed for their *' idols. Eze 20:23,24
God says: Your * continued to Eze 20:27,28
just as your * did, and keep on Eze 20:30
*, you will know I am the Lord. Eze 20:42
bent on murder. * and mothers are Eze 22:7
with their *' wives and lie with Eze 22:10
land which I gave your * long ago. Eze 36:28
Israel where their * lived, the Eze 37:25
*, and you shall inherit it now. Eze 47:14
you, O God of my *, for you have Dan 2:23
and princes and * are weighted down Dan 9:8
who have abandoned their *' faith. Dan 11:30,31
the gods of his *, nor for the god Dan 11:37
—a god his * never knew—and lavish Dan 11:38
Israel doomed. The * are forced to Hos 9:13
hearts and sinned as their * did. Amo 2:4
Hosts was very angry with your *. Zec 1:2
Don't be like your * were! Zec 1:4
Your * and their prophets are now Zec 1:5,6
Your * would not listen to this Zec 7:11
I would when your * angered me and Zec 8:14,15
violating the covenant of our *! Mal 2:10
* shall betray their own children. Mt 10:21
killed by your * and lay flowers on Mt 23:29,30
never have acted as our * did.' Mt 23:29,30
other to death, * will betray their Mk 13:12
the hearts of the * to the Lk 1:17f
For he promised our *—Abraham Lk 1:55
"You men who are *—if your boy Lk 11:11
You agree with your * that what Lk 11:48
day, like our * had while they Jn 6:30,31
When your * in the wilderness ate Jn 6:48-51
not die as your * did—though they Jn 6:58
Literally, "our *." Act 7:12f
"But our * rejected Moses and Act 7:39
But your * did, and so do you! Act 7:51
we nor our * were able to bear? Act 15:10
"BROTHERS AND *, listen to me as Act 22:1
'The God of our * has chosen you to Act 22:14
Great men of God were your *, Rom 9:5
always obey your * and mothers, for Col 3:20
pleases the Lord. *, don't scold Col 3:21
their * and mothers, and murder. 1Ti 1:9
He is my *' God, and mine, and my 2Ti 1:3
ways to our * through the prophets Heb 1:1
I gave to their * on the day when I Heb 8:9
need it, as other * punish their Heb 12:8
Since we respect our * here on Heb 12:9
Our earthly * trained us for a Heb 12:10
heaven which your * tried to take, 1Pe 1:18
And so I say to you * who know 1Jn 2:14

FATHOM
No one can * the depths of his Is 40:28

FATHOMLESS
His mind is *—what can you know Job 11:8

FATTEN
This will * your purses in Lk 12:33

FATTENED
a flock being * for the butcher. Zec 11:4

FATTENING
The woman had been * a calf, so 1Sa 28:24
10 oxen from the * pens, 20 1Ki 4:23
the calf we have in the * pen. Lk 15:23
the calf we were * and has prepared Lk 15:27

FATTENS
get good food that * up the soul! Is 55:2

FATTEST
and oxen and the * of the 1Sa 15:9

FATTY
Abel brought the * cuts of meat Gen 4:4
the entrails, the * mass above the Lev 8:15,16

FAULT
said to Abram, "It's all your *. Gen 16:5
that isn't our *—it is the fault of Ex 5:16
fault—it is the * of your Ex 5:16
"I finally see my *," he Ex 9:27
must die, for it is their own *. Lev 20:11
the father's * in the children to Num 14:17,18

AULT Con't)
)ne * in him since he arrived." 1Sa 29:3
'ind * with me about some woman? 2Sa 3:8
and it will be your own *." 1Ki 2:36,37
'Well, it's your own *," the 1Ki 20:40
nore severe than my * deserves. Job 23:2
:o find a single *, and so to count Job 33:10
ı hollow mockery, and a serious *. Ecc 6:2
surely die, and it is his own *. Eze 18:13
f he dies the * is his own. Eze 33:4
and wouldn't listen; the * is his. Eze 33:5
searching for some * in the way Dan 6:4
and it is all your *, you priests, Hos 4:6
for it is not our *—you have sent Jon 1:14
and confront him with his *. Mt 18:15
ın someone else's eye—his little * Lk 6:41
don't find * with those who do. Rom 14:3
no one can find * with us and blame 2Co 6:3
no one should find * with the way 2Co 8:20
without a single *—we who stand Eph 1:4
being holy and without a single *. Eph 5:27
no one can find * with you from now 1Ti 6:14
But God himself found * with the Heb 8:8
without a single sin or *. Heb 9:14
pure and without *, from God the Jas 1:27

AULTLESS
He is as * as heaven is high—but Job 11:8
* despite their many sins. Pro 30:11,12
and * toward every one of you. 1Th 2:10

AULTS
For he knows perfectly all the * Job 11:11
Cleanse me from these hidden *. Ps 19:12
and wearied me with all your *. Is 43:24
whitewash it and cover up its *?' Eze 13:12
in addition to all your other *. Eze 16:43
Each of us must bear some * and Gal 6:5
other's * because of your love. Eph 4:2
too eager to tell others their *, Jas 3:1
Admit your * to one another and Jas 5:16
love makes up for many of your *. 1Pe 4:8
overlooks each other's many *." 1Pe 4:8f

AUSSET
—Jamieson, * and Brown Zep 2:15f

AVOR
are my gifts, to curry your *!" Gen 33:8
him * with the chief jailer. Gen 39:21
are back in his *, and mention me Gen 40:14
And the Lord gave the Israelis * Ex 12:36
your testimony in * of a man just Ex 23:2,3
and that I have found * before Ex 33:12
people have found * with you, and Ex 33:16
certainly found * with me, and you Ex 33:17
that I have found * in your sight, Ex 34:9
his *, and give you his peace.' Num 6:24,25,26
'never * a man because he is rich; Deu 1:17
And with the * of God who appeared Deu 33:16
asked him for this *—that his 2Sa 13:6
As a matter of fact, I have a * 1Ki 2:14
But now I have just a small * to 1Ki 2:16
So she went to ask the * of King 1Ki 2:19
Look down with * day and night 2Ch 6:20,21
king for a great *—put it into his Neh 1:11
me with your royal *, send me to Neh 2:4
I have won your *, O king, and if Est 7:3
This at least will be in my *, Job 13:16
peace at last! His * will surround Job 22:21
His anger lasts a moment; his * Ps 30:5
The Lord has shown me his *. Ps 30:6,7
Let your * shine again upon your Ps 31:16
Lord, restore us again to your *. Ps 60:1
Send me a sign of your *. Ps 86:17
Our power is based on your *! Ps 89:17
our God * us and give us success. Ps 90:17
If you want * with both God and Pro 3:4,5
ever-brightening light of God's *; Pro 4:18
for good you will find God's *; Pro 11:27
It is wrong for a judge to * the Pro 18:5
no one knows whether he will * Ecc 9:1
and I have found * in my lover's Sol 8:10
the time of God's * to them has Is 61:2
The context seems to * the Is 66:19f
and you will be overcome by my * Eze 16:61
anyone who asks a * of God or Dan 6:7
But he will turn again and * you Zec 1:3
should he show you any * at all? Mal 1:9
Jesus and respectfully asked a *. Mt 20:20
consequences, without fear or *. Mt 22:16
"we want you to do us a *." Mk 10:35
apart, three in * of me, and two Lk 12:52
* before Pharaoh, king of Egypt. Act 7:10
wanted to gain * with the Jews, he Act 24:27
you know right from wrong and * Rom 2:18
for Abraham found * with God by Rom 4:12
are free under God's * and mercy. Rom 6:14
to gain God's * by keeping the Rom 10:3
the * of God they are looking for. Rom 11:7
May the love and * of the Lord 1Co 16:23
his * and be reconciled to him. 2Co 5:18
never find God's * by trying—and Gal 2:19
can ever win God's * by trying to Gal 3:11
of gaining God's * than Abraham's Gal 3:18
You are trying to find * with Gal 4:10
* are not doing it for your good. Gal 4:17
Anyone trying to find * with God Gal 5:3
to us and his * that he has poured Eph 1:6
by his undeserved * have we ever Eph 2:5
of showing God's * to you Gentiles, Eph 3:2,3
doing himself a * and loving Eph 5:28
saved by finding * with an endless 1Ti 1:3,4
Now I want to ask a * of you. Phm 1:8,9
He cancels the first system in * Heb 10:9
you * the rich and fawn over them; Jas 2:9

FAVORABLE
to be very * to the people of Ex 11:3
to give them a * reply and treat 2Ch 10:7
a * reading," the man ventured. 2Ch 18:12
the kings of Persia to be * to us. Ez 9:9
Will he never again be *? Ps 77:7
request has come at a * time. Is 49:8,9
The whole city was * to them, and Act 2:47
came to me at a * time, when the 2Co 6:2

FAVORED
menu for her, * her for the beauty Est 2:9
you smiled upon them and * them. Ps 44:3
said, "Congratulations, * lady! Lk 1:28
to Mary, "You are * by God above Lk 1:42
Jewish laws which * the Jews and Eph 2:15

FAVORITE
Isaac's * was Esau, because of Gen 25:28
home, and Rebekah's * was Jacob. Gen 25:28
your father's * dish from them. Gen 27:8,9,10
prepared in his father's * way. Gen 27:14
* dish and brings it to him. Gen 27:31
became quite a * with him. Gen 39:4
"Asher is a * son, Deu 33:24
everyone's * (and he was a favorite 1Sa 2:26
he was a * of the Lord's, too! 1Sa 2:26
Maacah's son Abijah was his *, 2Ch 11:22
As a man would lead his * ox, Hos 11:4

FAVORITES
and distribute it to his *. 1Sa 8:15
* break the law without rebuke." Mal 2:9
the Jews are not God's only *! Act 10:34
saying: that you must not have *. 1Co 4:6
Master they do, and he has no *. Eph 6:9
* who can get away with shirking. Col 3:25
you pray has no * when he judges. 1Pe 1:17

FAVORITISM
glory, if you show * to rich people Jas 2:1

FAVORS
with gifts and entreat your *." Ps 45:12
shower special * on the wicked? Ps 82:2
Many * are showered on those who Pro 16:15
Many beg * from a man who is Pro 19:6
don't long for their * and gifts. Pro 23:6,7,8
O God, I beg two * from you Pro 30:7
like—and I will grant you no *! Jer 16:13
there, asking * of his God. Dan 6:11
He is asking * of his God three Dan 6:13
And I will not give special * to Hos 1:4
church's verdict * you, but he Mt 18:17
and enjoyed her *, will mourn for Rev 18:9

FAWN
Don't * on the judge, but ask the Pro 29:26
The deer deserts her * because Jer 14:5
(And yet you * upon the Lord and Mic 3:11
favor the rich and * over them; Jas 2:9

FAWNED
She * over her Assyrian neighbors, Eze 23:12

FAWNS
let loose, producing lovely *. Gen 49:21
Your breasts are like twin * of Sol 4:5
Your two breasts are like two *, Sol 7:3

FEAR
And I will put the * of you into Gen 3:15
for I * disaster in the mountain. Gen 19:18,19,20
And great * swept through the Gen 20:8
he said. "* not, for I am with you Gen 26:24
Jacob was frantic with *. Gen 32:7
to do this, for * God would kill Gen 38:11
go with them, for * some harm might Gen 42:4
* has gripped the people of Phi- Ex 15:14
the people of Canaan melt with *. Ex 15:15
at a distance, shaking with *. Ex 20:18
blind man as he walks. * your God; Lev 19:14
to the elderly, in the * of God. Lev 19:32
"You must * your God and not Lev 25:17,18
in your home. * your God and let Lev 25:36
or treated harshly; * your God. Lev 25:43
you will go to sleep without *. Lev 26:6
they will live in constant *. Lev 26:36
do not * the people of the land. Num 14:9
by striking * into the hearts of Num 14:36,37,38
The Lord told Moses not to * Num 21:34
Don't * their displeasure, for Deu 1:17
earth tremble with * because of Deu 2:25
might against the people you *. Deu 7:19
Walk in his ways and * him. Deu 8:6
You must * the Lord your God Deu 10:20
your God will send * and dread Deu 11:25
deed, and will * such wickedness as Deu 13:11
You have nothing to * from him. Deu 18:22
with no respect or * of God. Deu 25:18
blindness, *, and panic upon you. Deu 28:28
bodies wasted from sorrow and *. Deu 28:65
You will live night and day in *, Deu 28:66
Banish * and doubt! Jos 1:9
and they were paralyzed with *. Jos 5:1
with * at this turn of events. Jos 7:5
and because we * that in the future Jos 22:24,25
But he did it at night for * of Ju 6:27
and for * of the men of the city; Ju 6:27
for * of his brother Abimelech. Ju 9:21
* was sweeping across the city. 1Sa 5:11
"Now if you will * and worship 1Sa 12:14
with * at what awaited them. 1Sa 13:7
allow them for * of their making 1Sa 13:19
filled him with depression and *. 1Sa 16:14
home without *, for he would not 1Sa 25:35
was frantic with * and asked the 1Sa 28:5,6
was paralyzed with *, and his 2Sa 4:1
Mephibosheth arrived in great * 2Sa 9:5,6
lions, will be paralyzed with *; 2Sa 17:10
Who rules in the * of God. 2Sa 23:3
will know and * your name just as 1Ki 8:43
caused all the nations to * him. 1Ch 14:17
Then the * of the Lord fell upon 2Ch 17:10
the * of God, with honest hearts. 2Ch 19:9
the * of God fell upon them. 2Ch 20:29
of the others who * our God. Ez 10:3
"Should you not walk in the * of Neh 5:9
the Jews for * of Mordecai; Est 9:3
Suddenly, * gripped me; Job 4:14
no need to * the future. Job 5:21
me without the slightest * of God. Job 6:14
Then I could speak without * to Job 9:35
steadily forward to God without *. Job 11:15
Have you no * of God? Job 15:4,5
He lives in *, distress, and Job 15:23,24
He has good cause for *—his Job 18:11
*, and God does not punish them. Job 21:9
to * the Lord is true wisdom; Job 28:28
No wonder men everywhere * him! Job 37:24
them and fills them with *. Ps 2:5
Serve the Lord with reverent *; Ps 2:11
Make them tremble in *; Ps 9:20
must * and reverence his name. Ps 22:23
whom shall I *? Ps 27:1
me, my heart shall know no *! Ps 27:3
women and children—* the Lord and Ps 33:8
over those who * him, who rely upon Ps 33:18,19
They have no * of God to hold Ps 36:1
And so we need not * even if the Ps 46:2
is no need to * when times of Ps 49:5
Stark * overpowers me. Ps 55:4
For they refuse to * him or even Ps 55:19
Frantic * grips me. Ps 57:6
this nation to tremble in *; Ps 60:2
Why then should I be tense with * Ps 62:2
tense with * when troubles come? Ps 62:6
Which of us can * you as he Ps 90:11
nor * the dangers of the day; Ps 91:5
toward those who * and honor him is Ps 103:11
For all who * God and trust in Ps 112:1
He does not * bad news, nor live Ps 112:7
All those who * and trust in you Ps 119:74
me, who trust and * you, and we Ps 119:79
I tremble in * of you; Ps 119:120
I tremble in fear of you; I * Ps 119:120
I am paralyzed with *. Ps 143:4
on guard you can sleep without *; Pro 3:24,25,26
blackmail, or to * of vengeance Pro 5:9f
For the reverence and * of God Pro 9:10
So why * death? Pro 12:28
* of man is a dangerous trap, but Pro 29:25
She has no * of winter for her Pro 31:21
dignity, and has no * of old age. Pro 31:25
man should * the all-powerful God. Ecc 3:14
of empty words; * God instead. Ecc 5:6,7
* God you can expect his blessing. Ecc 7:18
that those who * God will be better Ecc 8:12
shadows because they don't * God. Ecc 8:13
Here is my final conclusion: * Ecc 12:13
will crawl with * into the holes in Is 2:19
trembled with * as the trees of a Is 7:2
the two kings you * so much—the Is 7:15,16
Don't * anything except the Lord Is 8:13
If you * him, you need fear Is 8:13
If you fear him, you need * Is 8:13
Geba. * strikes the city of Ramah; Is 10:28,29
and of the * of the Lord. Is 11:2
Your arms lie paralyzed with *; Is 13:7
and are afraid. * grips you with Is 13:8
from sorrow and *, from slavery and Is 14:3
of the Egyptians melt with *. Is 19:1
women, cowering in * beneath the Is 19:16
I am gripped by awful *. Is 21:4
will shake with * before you; Is 25:3
longer pale with *, or be ashamed. Is 29:22
then they will * and rejoice in Is 29:23
among my people shake with *. Is 33:14
Tell them, "Be strong, * not, Is 35:4
the sea watch in * and wait for Is 41:5

(FEAR Con't)
away. * not, for I am with you. Is 41:10
Despised though you are, * not, Is 41:14
will turn to cries of *. Is 43:14
So what right have you to * mere Is 51:12
And yet you have no * of God, Is 51:13
and * their anger all day long? Is 51:13
* not; you will no longer live in Is 54:4
gentle, that you have no * of me? Is 57:11
God, all you who * him, and tremble Is 66:5
and the princes will tremble in *; Jer 4:9
they have no respect or * for me. Jer 5:23,24
Who would not * you, O King of Jer 10:7
I awake with * and stagger as a Jer 23:9
"There is only * and trembling. Jer 30:5
of * or anger at what he had done. Jer 36:24,25
be killed by those you * so much. Jer 39:17
Don't * the king of Babylon any Jer 42:11
war and famine you * will follow Jer 42:16
make her afraid. * not, O Jacob, Jer 46:28
warriors fail with * like women in Jer 48:41
against the Lord. * and traps and Jer 48:43
are stricken with *, for they have Jer 49:23
turn to flee. *, anguish and sorrow Jer 49:24
We are filled with *, for we are Lam 3:47
cry and told me not to *. Lam 3:57
So don't be afraid of them, or * Eze 3:9
The people will tremble with *, Eze 7:26,27
boldest heart will melt with *; Eze 21:7
with * at what they have seen. Eze 26:16
I made the nations shake with * Eze 31:16
and awoke trembling with *. Dan 2:1
Tell me, for I * some tragedy Dan 2:1
His face blanched with *, and Dan 5:6
world trembled before him in *. Dan 5:19
shall tremble and * before the God Dan 6:25,26
stood up, still trembling with *. Dan 10:11
not to * each other any more; Hos 1:18
*, for he was a mighty prince; Hos 13:1
Let everyone tremble in *, for Joe 2:1
* grips the waiting people; Joe 2:6
* not, my people; Joe 2:21
alarm has sounded—listen and *! Amo 3:6
The Lion has roared—tremble in *. Amo 3:8
with the * of its inhabitants to Mic 1:11f
with the * of its inhabitants to Mic 1:11f
with the * of its inhabitants to Mic 1:11f
for there will be nothing to *. Mic 4:4
They will * him; Mic 7:17
a drunkard and hide herself in *. Nah 3:11
Cushan and of Midian in mortal *. Hab 3:7
my lips quiver with *. Hab 3:16
will be over—you need * no more. Zep 3:15
it happen and be filled with *; Zec 9:5
Cry in *, you oaks of Bashan, as Zec 11:2
* me," says the Lord of Hosts. Mal 3:5
"But for you who * my name, the Mal 4:2
A chill of * swept through the Mt 9:8
touch your souls! * only God who Mt 10:28
consequences, without * or favor. Mt 22:16
The guards shook with * when Mt 28:4
Their problem was their * of Mk 11:18
to touch him for * of a mob. Mk 12:12
was gripped with awe and *. Lk 5:26
A great * swept the crowd, and Lk 7:16
with awe and * of him and said to Lk 8:25
wave of * had swept over them). Lk 8:37
But I'll tell you whom to *—fear Lk 12:5
But I'll tell you whom to fear—* Lk 12:5
Never *, you are far more Lk 12:7
" 'I * neither God nor man,' he Lk 18:4,5
"Don't you even * God when you Lk 23:40,41
that Light for * their sins would Jn 3:20
him in public for * of reprisals Jn 7:13
They said this in * of the Jewish Jn 9:22,23
because of their * that the Jn 12:42
of Jesus for * of the Jewish Jn 19:38
locked doors, in * of the Jewish Jn 20:19
how to walk in the * of the Lord Act 9:31
Trembling with *, the jailer Act 16:29
and a solemn * descended on the Act 19:17
doing evil will always * him. Rom 13:3
ideas, for * of diluting the mighty 1Co 1:17
of any kind for * that, if we did, 1Co 9:12
Otherwise I * that after 1Co 9:27
It is because of this solemn * of 2Co 5:11
in the wholesome * of God, giving 2Co 7:1
hearts were full of dread and *. 2Co 7:5
or seasons or years. I * for you. Gal 4:11
to have lost their * of chains! Php 1:14
for * some might be saved; 1Th 2:16
those who through * of death have Heb 2:15
to tremble with * because some of Heb 4:1
that he shook with terrible *. Heb 12:21
hearts, and with holy * and awe. Heb 12:28
any doubt or *, "The Lord is my Heb 13:6
freedom from all anxiety and *. 1Pe 1:2
so act in reverent * of him from 1Pe 1:17
Love Christians everywhere. * God 1Pe 2:17
then you will not need to * 1Pe 3:6
future to look back upon and *. 2Pe 2:6
We need have no * of someone who 1Jn 4:18
If we are afraid, it is for * of 1Jn 4:18
without * of God's punishment. Jud 1:4
And great * will fall on Rev 11:11
alike, all who * your Name, both Rev 11:18
"* God," he shouted, "and Rev 14:7
Who shall not *, Rev 15:3,4
trembling with * and crying out, Rev 18:10
small and great, who * him." Rev 19:5

FEARED
For he * for his life if he Gen 26:7
But the midwives * God and Ex 1:17
do to you what you *: You will all Num 14:28
How I * for you—for the Lord was Deu 9:19
of Egypt which you * so much, and Deu 28:60
So we * for our lives because of Jos 9:24
for they all * Saul's curse. 1Sa 14:26
Then many who * the God of Ez 9:4
* what the Jews might do to them. Est 8:17
tried, for they were greatly *. Est 9:1
man who * God and stayed away Job 1:1
What I always * has happened to Job 3:25
No wonder you are greatly *! Ps 76:7
He should be reverenced and *, Ps 76:11
the Red Sea saw you, how it *! Ps 77:16
and supple nation * far and wide, a Is 18:2
the things they *, for when I Is 66:4
Isn't such a God to be * and Jer 5:22
have so greatly *, says the Lord Eze 11:8
Then those who * and loved the Mal 3:16
names of those who * him and loved Mal 3:16
riot—a possibility they greatly *. Lk 22:2
to the judges, who * for their Act 16:38
* we would never live through it. 2Co 1:8

FEARFUL
*, Abram, for I will defend you. Gen 15:1
Afterwards Lot left Zoar, * of Gen 19:30
the glorious and * name of Jehovah Deu 28:58,59
on, for he was * of Saul, and went 1Sa 21:10
for they were * for their lives. 1Ki 1:49,50
for the people were * of attack. Ez 3:3
He flashed his * arrows of Ps 18:14
their waves arise in * storms; Ps 89:9
You rejoiced at Israel's * fate. Eze 35:15
the * things you are going to do. Hab 3:2
asked them, "Why were you so *? Mk 4:40
because of the * fate they see Lk 21:26
be like cringing, * slaves, but we Rom 8:15
saved, we seem a * smell of death 2Co 2:16
It is a * thing to fall into Heb 10:31

FEARFULLY
out with great care and eaten *. Eze 4:16

FEARING
at their screams, * that the earth Num 16:34
to hide my sins, * the crowd and Job 31:34
of trusting and * the Lord. Ps 34:11
friends stay away, * my disease. Ps 38:11
night, * you will starve to death; Ps 127:2
instead of * the Assyrians. Is 10:20
to the bottom. * for their lives, Jon 1:5
Finally the commander, * they Act 23:10
Literally, "* lest they should be Act 27:17f
driven ashore; and * rocks along Act 27:29
But I am frightened, * that in 2Co 11:3
at a distance, * danger to Rev 18:15

FEARLESS
Be strong and courageous, * and 1Ch 22:13
assistants. "Be * in your stand 2Ch 19:11
There is nothing else so * Job 41:33
They want reputations as * Php 1:15
Jesus who gave a * testimony before 1Ti 6:13

FEARLESSLY
on those who rebuke sin *. Pro 24:25
the Lord your God, * forsaking him, Jer 2:19
of the Lord, * announcing God's Mic 3:8
of serving God *, freed from our Lk 1:74
Now we can come * right into Eph 3:12
the Good News *, no matter what Php 1:28

FEARS
man who * God and will have Job 1:8
good man who * God and turns away Job 2:3
traps and sudden *, and darkness Job 22:10,11
of you who * him," I will say. Ps 22:23
Where is the man who * the Lord? Ps 25:12
He freed me from all my *. Ps 34:4
Anyone is my brother who * and Ps 119:63
If anyone respects and * God, he Pro 8:13
The wicked man's * will all come Pro 10:24
but a woman who * and reverences Pro 31:30
Who among you * the Lord and Is 50:10
so that he * God and decides Eze 18:14
love away. Our * for today, our Rom 8:38
of the doubts and * of others—of Rom 15:1
all these earthly prides and *. 1Co 7:23

FEARSOME
I am surrounded by * enemies, Ps 22:12
the * news that God has given me. Eze 21:7
but a * voice like the Dragon's. Rev 13:11

FEAST
and he set a great * before them, Gen 19:3
So Isaac prepared a great * for Gen 26:30
companions to a *, and afterwards Gen 31:54
them home and prepare a big *." Gen 43:16
religious *, to worship me there.' Ex 5:1
great * to the Lord shall be held. Ex 13:6,7
there will be a * to Jehovah!" Ex 32:5
afterwards they sat down to * and Ex 32:6
"Be sure to celebrate the * of Ex 34:18
Or, "* of Tabernacles." Lev 23:33,34f
This seven-day annual * is a law Lev 23:41
each of the seven days of the *; Num 28:24
families shall * before the Lord Deu 12:7
the Levites to * with you, for they Deu 12:12
strong drink, to * there before the Deu 14:26
"This * will be held at the Deu 16:15
Afterwards, go and * on all the Deu 26:11
upon it also, and * there with Deu 27:7
During the harvest * at Shechem Ju 9:27
After the *, when they had 1Sa 9:25
David entertained them with a *. 2Sa 3:20
to a * to celebrate the occasion. 2Sa 13:21-24
So Ahab prepared a *. 1Ki 18:42
and they all had a great *. 1Ki 19:21
So the king made a great * for 2Ki 6:23
of sheep and oxen for the *. 2Ch 18:2
followed by the * of Unleavened 2Ch 35:17
And they celebrated the * of Ez 3:4
specified for each day of the *. Ez 3:4
ate the Passover * and celebrated Ez 6:21,22
and celebrated the * of Unleavened Ez 6:21,22
to live for the duration of the *. Neh 8:15
seven days of the *, and everyone Neh 8:17
seven days of the *, and on the Neh 8:18
his annual * of Purim. Est 9:29-31
annually as the * of Purim, decreed Est 9:29-31
hard before they * and drink, and Ecc 10:16,17
More details of the * are seen in Is 21:5f
dance and play, and * and drink. Is 22:13
spread a wondrous * for everyone Is 25:6
world—a delicious * of good food, Is 25:6
I will * the priests with the Jer 31:14
different kind of * for them, and Jer 51:39
the mountains to * before the idols Eze 18:6
the mountains to * before the idols Eze 18:15
for a mighty sacrificial *. Eze 39:17
young bulls of Bashan for my *! Eze 39:18
this is the sacrificial * I have Eze 39:19
prepared for you. * at my banquet Eze 39:20
Feast at my banquet table—* on Eze 39:20
to * there before the Lord. Eze 44:3
It will be a seven-day *. Eze 45:21
seven days of the * he shall Eze 45:23
days of the annual *, he shall Eze 45:25
* where the wine flowed freely. Dan 5:1
brought in to the *, and when they Dan 5:2,3,4
do each year at the Tabernacle *. Hos 12:9
Literally, "the * of Zec 14:16f
* and drink, and you complain Mt 11:19
'The wedding * is ready, and the Mt 22:8
*, and the door was locked. Mt 25:10
refuse to eat at the wedding *? Mk 2:19
Lord's return from the wedding *. Lk 12:36
to a wedding *, don't always head Lk 14:8
* and sent out many invitations. Lk 14:16
We must celebrate with a *, for Lk 15:23
prepared a great * to celebrate his Lk 15:27
goat for a * with my friends. Lk 15:29
them at the * one (prisoner)." Lk 23:17,f
the * of the Jews, was at hand." Jn 6:2-5f
"I go not up (yet) unto this *." Jn 7:8f
Literally, "*." Act 18:21f
So let us * upon him and grow 1Co 5:8
Let us * instead upon the pure 1Co 5:8
to the wedding * of the Lamb." Rev 19:9

FEASTED
They * and drank with David for 1Ch 12:39
Then they * and drank before the 1Ch 29:22
arrived and * with him in his home, Job 42:11

FEASTING
So they had another day of *. Ju 19:8
and they are * and drinking with 1Ki 1:25
their victory with * and gladness. Est 9:17
the next day, with * and gladness. Est 9:18
to celebrate with *, gladness, and Est 9:22
and daughters were * in their Job 1:18
in the garden, * there on pork and Is 66:17
days, on days of * to the Lord, Hos 9:5
were * instead of fasting. Lk 5:33

FEASTS
Or, "* you must celebrate." Ex 23:14f
only attending the *, but also Num 25:2
of your annual *, and are in Num 29:39
* as required in the law of God. 2Ch 31:3
regular annual * of the Lord. Ez 3:5
new moon *, and the annual feasts. Neh 10:33
new moon feasts, and the annual *. Neh 10:33
in the night when holy * are held; Is 30:29
the people in their merry *. Jer 15:17,18
any more in their * and Jer 16:8
the marriage *, the songs of Jer 16:9
your gladness and your wedding *; Jer 25:10
In their drunken *, the men of Jer 51:38

FEASTS Con't)
come to celebrate the Temple *; Lam 1:4
their holy * and Sabbaths. Lam 2:6
used to do on days of holy *! Lam 2:7
of the religious *, the new moon Eze 45:17
the religious *, they must go out Eze 46:9
"To summarize: At the special * Eze 46:11
her parties, holidays, and *. Hos 1:11
At their religious * they lounge Amo 2:8
religious * and solemn assemblies. Amo 5:21
And even now in your holy * to Zec 7:6
holidays and * or new moon Col 2:16
* as though they were honest men. 2Pe 2:13
you at the love * of the church, Jud 1:12
encouraging them to go to idol *. Rev 2:14

FEATHER
energy, and are a * in your cap. Pro 3:22
They serve you—it is a * in your Eze 27:10
that will be a * in our caps 2Co 13:7

FEATHERBRAINED
They are * and give no warning Is 56:10

FEATHERS
the crop and the * and throw them Lev 1:15,16,17
of many-colored * came to Lebanon Eze 17:3,4
as long as eagles' *, and his nails Dan 4:33

FEATS
It was by such * that he earned a 2Sa 23:18,19

FEBRUARY
The speech was given on * 15, Deu 1:1
The completion date was * 18 Ez 6:15
of Ahasuerus, and * of the Est 3:7
on the 28th day of * of the Est 3:13
Ahasuerus was the 28th day of *! Est 8:12
SO ON THE 28th day of *, the day Est 9:1
on the 28th day of *, and the next Est 9:17
On * 25, of the 37th year of the Jer 52:31
The following *, still in the Zec 1:7

FED
and their donkeys were *. Gen 43:24
bread the Lord had * them with in Ex 16:32
However, he shall be * with the Lev 21:22
from the rock! He * you with manna Deu 8:16
so that they will be well *. Deu 26:12
manner and have * them the scraps Ju 1:7
home with him. He * their donkeys Ju 19:21
Those who were starving are *. 1Sa 2:5
pet and he * it from his own plate 2Sa 12:3
Barzillai, who had * the king and 2Sa 19:31,32
hasn't * us or given us gifts!" 2Sa 19:42
had * them with bread and water. 1Ki 18:3,4
and * them with bread and water? 1Ki 18:13
that I regularly * 150 Jewish Neh 5:17
You have * us with sorrow and Ps 80:5
water, and rivers * by springs Is 41:18
keep him warm and * and well Is 44:16
You shall be * with the treasures Is 61:6
not gods at all. I * my people Jer 5:7
rich, and well * and well groomed, Jer 5:28
new clothes and * him from the Jer 52:33
* yourselves and let them starve; Eze 34:8
So after that the steward * them Dan 1:16
and all the world was * from it. Dan 4:12
I myself have stooped and * him. Hos 11:4
"Union," and I * the flock as I Zec 11:7
at all the 5,000 I * with five Mt 16:9
Don't you remember the 4,000 I * Mt 16:10
For I was hungry and you * me; Mt 25:35
"What about the 5,000 men I * Mk 8:19
"And when I * the 4,000 with Mk 8:20
with me because I * you, not Jn 6:26
He welcomed us courteously and * Act 28:7
you still have to be * on milk. 1Co 3:2
pastor who is * by faith and by the 1Ti 4:6

FEDERAL
Without making a * case of it, Job 34:24

FEDERATION
of the * of all those kingdoms. Jos 11:10

FEE
included in the original rental *. Ex 22:15
I asked no * from your oppressors; Is 52:3

FEEBLE
"What does this bunch of poor, * Neh 4:1
there were no sick and * folk Ps 105:37
Damascus has become * and all Jer 49:24
All hands shall be *, and all Eze 7:17
even the old and *, as well as the Nah 2:11

FEEBLENESS
blindness and great * be theirs. Ps 69:23

FEEBLER
them, but didn't with the * ones. Gen 30:42

FEED
the camels, and * for them, and Gen 24:32
get some grain to * the donkeys, Gen 42:27
Do not let the flocks or herds * Ex 34:3
If we * you and you fail, they'll Ju 8:6
in my bedroom and * it to me." 2Sa 13:10
I tried to * my baby it was dead! 1Ki 3:21
I have commanded them to * you." 1Ki 17:4
There is a widow there who will * 1Ki 17:8,9
fellow in jail and * him with bread 1Ki 22:27
Elisha told Gehazi to use it to * 2Ki 4:42
Gehazi exclaimed. "* one 2Ki 4:43
in prison and * him with bread and 2Ch 18:26
Worms shall * sweetly on him. Job 24:20
your wings. You * them with Ps 36:8
us, and the wild animals * on us. Ps 80:13
But he would * you with the Ps 81:16
at his command to * the cattle, and Ps 104:14
You open wide your hand to * them Ps 104:28
lazy they won't even * themselves! Pro 19:24
* your sheep and their lambs. Sol 1:8
he loves me. Oh, * me with your Sol 2:5
In those days flocks will * Is 5:17
He will * his flock like a Is 40:11
I will * your enemies with their Is 49:26
* the hungry! Is 58:10
they shall * your flocks and plow Is 61:5
The wolf and lamb shall * Is 65:25
says: Lo, I will * them with Jer 9:15
and wild animals to * upon. Jer 19:7
Hosts says: I will * them with Jer 23:15
I will * your dead bodies to the Jer 34:20
fat as cows that * in lush Jer 50:11
her own land, to * in the fields of Jer 50:19
Even the jackals * their young, Lam 4:3,4
It will neither satisfy nor * Eze 7:19
the shepherds who * themselves Eze 34:2
Shouldn't shepherds * the sheep? Eze 34:2
I will take away their right to * Eze 34:9,10
Israel, and I will * them upon the Eze 34:13
* in luscious mountain pastures. Eze 34:14
I will * them, yes—feed them Eze 34:15,16
I will feed them, yes—* them Eze 34:15,16
He shall * them and be a Shepherd Eze 34:23
They may eat this food to * Hos 9:4
And he shall stand and * his Mic 5:4
You crushed your enemies to * Nah 2:12
broken bones, nor * the healthy Zec 11:16
that bread won't * men's souls: Mt 4:4
for those you help should * and Mt 10:10
isn't necessary—you * them!" Mt 14:16
to * my children day by day? Mt 24:45
we ever see you hungry and * you? Mt 25:37
was hungry and you wouldn't * me; Mt 25:42
But Jesus said, "You * them." Mk 6:37
But Jesus replied, "'You * Lk 9:13
farmer to hire him to * his pigs. Lk 15:15
buy bread to * all these people?" Jn 6:2-5
"Then * my lambs," Jesus told Jn 21:15
Jesus said, "Then * my little Jn 21:17
Be sure that you * and shepherd Act 20:28
Instead, * your enemy if he is Rom 12:20
I have had to * you with milk 1Co 3:2
to ask you to * us, but we wanted 2Th 3:9
plea to you: * the flock of God; 1Pe 5:2
the throne will * them and be Rev 7:17

FEEDING
go hungry and then * you with Deu 8:3
with the donkeys * beside them, Job 1:14,15
Will he stay beside your * crib? Job 39:9
the land and prosper, * in safety. Ps 37:3
taking him from * sheep, and from Ps 78:70
He is * among the lilies! Sol 2:16
of a gazelle, * among the lilies. Sol 4:5
A herd of pigs was * in the Mt 8:30
them home without * them, they will Mk 8:3
A herd of pigs was * on the Lk 8:32
of * the other servants. Lk 12:42,43,44
* the swine looked good to him. Lk 15:16
administering a * program," they Act 6:2
* and caring for her own children. 1Th 2:7
* them patiently with God's Word. 2Ti 4:2

FEEDS
science * upon itself and grows. Gen 11:6f
you'll feel better if she * you." 2Sa 13:5
pastures. He * the wild animals Ps 147:9
while the mocker * on trash. Pro 15:14
man, the one who * the poor. Pro 22:9
The poor, deluded fool * on Is 44:20
rob them, but * the hungry and Eze 18:16
the olive oil that * the lamps, Zec 4:2
your heavenly Father * them. Mt 6:26
along all right—for God * them. Lk 12:24

FEEL
will * the same towards him. Gen 16:9-12
I want to * you, and be sure it Gen 27:21
my husband will * affection for me, Gen 29:34
But see here—though you * you Gen 31:30
he had no son? We * that we should Num 27:3,4
you would never * that it was your Deu 8:17
slave you must not * bad, for Deu 15:18
He doesn't * honored by such Deu 17:1
* and act like a different person. 1Sa 10:6
See how much better I * now that 1Sa 14:29
and Saul would * better, and the 1Sa 16:23
Tell him you'll * better if she 2Sa 13:5
this, making us * ashamed, as 2Sa 19:5
* is the will of your God. Ez 7:18
You have tried to make me * Job 20:3
Let him * the penalty himself. Job 21:19
We * his presence in the thunder. Job 36:33
See my sorrows; * my pain; Ps 25:18
a cooking pot can * the blazing Ps 58:9
What awe we *, kneeling here Ps 68:35
in her walls and * sympathy for Ps 102:14
This will make him * ashamed of Pro 25:21,22
and mother, and * themselves Pro 30:11,12
people * it is safe to do wrong. Ecc 8:11
First to * his wrath will be the Is 3:14
at last you shall * my wrath. Jer 10:18
How will you * when I set your Jer 13:21
Who will * sorry for you, Jer 15:5
But you too will * the awful Lam 4:21
Then the Lord said, "You * sorry Jon 4:10
And why shouldn't I * sorry for Jon 4:11
so people will * sorry for them. Mt 6:16
lad had begun to * better, and they Jn 4:52
God, and perhaps * their way toward Act 17:27
* secure or enjoy God's blessing. Rom 3:17
loves us, and we * this warm love Rom 5:5
not * proud and start bragging. Rom 11:25
In other words, he will * Rom 12:20
who * these things are wrong. Rom 15:1
do this, for they * that they owe a Rom 15:27
from there, they * that the least Rom 15:27
makes us * important, what is 1Co 8:1
churches * the same way about it. 1Co 11:16
But I suppose you * this is 1Co 11:19
If Timothy comes make him * at 1Co 16:10
How differently I * now! 2Co 5:16
Yet I don't * that these 2Co 11:5
and I do not * his sadness? 2Co 11:29
Do you * Christ's presence and 2Co 13:5
Dear brothers, please * as I do Gal 4:12
should * honored and encouraged. Eph 3:13
and may you be able to * and Eph 3:18,19
How natural it is that I should * Php 1:7
down here and so I * certain I will Php 1:25
and I * sure you are still 2Ti 1:5
They do whatever they * like; 2Pe 2:12
consciences and * that we have done 1Jn 3:20
Lord will surely * it even more, 1Jn 3:20
do whatever they * like, thereby Jud 1:10
doing whatever evil they * like; Jud 1:16

FEELING
this is your * in the matter, be so Gen 23:8
prevent him from * that he is Deu 17:20
their own altars, * that this 2Ch 34:5
for the king was * very generous. Est 1:7
when the king was * high, half Est 1:10
by Jews, and the * was mutual, due Lk 10:33f
for us with such * that it cannot Rom 8:26
In this case his * about it is 1Co 10:29
deep fervor and * because of the 2Co 9:14
criticisms, the * that everyone Gal 5:20
their * of guilt would be gone. Heb 10:2

FEELINGS
His thoughts and * became those Dan 5:21
I have told you all my *; 2Co 6:11
which lead to jealousy and hard *. Gal 5:26
SO GET RID of your * of hatred. 1Pe 2:1

FEELS
What if my father * me? Gen 27:11,12
goes over to his father. He * him! Gen 27:22
make the vow, or * that the Num 30:5
know at once how he * about you. 1Sa 20:12
defend them. He * pity for the Ps 72:13
Show him how it *! Ps 109:6
starves, but * that it is better to Ecc 4:5,6
from what he * is right is sin. Rom 14:23
But if anyone * he ought to marry 1Co 7:36
On this question everyone * that 1Co 8:1
the time he still * it is wrong. 1Co 8:10

FEET
Make it 450 * long, 75 feet Gen 6:15
Make it 450 feet long, 75 * Gen 6:15
long, 75 feet wide, and 45 * high. Gen 6:15
twenty-two * and more above the Gen 7:20
to refresh your *, and a bite to Gen 18:3,4
the camel drivers to wash their *. Gen 24:32
given water to refresh their *; Gen 43:24
son, who played at his *. Gen 50:23
it against Moses' *, remarking Ex 4:25,26
donkey onto its * beneath a heavy Ex 23:5
under his * there seemed to be a Ex 24:10
make an Ark 3¾ * long, 2¼ feet Ex 25:10
long, 2¼ * wide, and 2¼ feet high. Ex 25:10
gold, 3¾ * long and 2¼ feet wide. Ex 25:17
gold, 3¾ feet long and 2¼ * wide. Ex 25:17
acacia wood three * long, 1½ feet Ex 25:23
long, 1½ * wide, and 2¼ feet high. Ex 25:23
long, 1½ feet wide, and 2¼ * high. Ex 25:23
linen, forty-two * long and six Ex 26:1
feet long and six * wide, dyed Ex 26:1
* across and six feet wide. Ex 26:7,8
feet across and six * wide. Ex 26:7,8
being fifteen * high and 2¼ feet Ex 26:15,16
feet high and 2¼ * wide, standing Ex 26:15,16
7½ * wide, and three feet high. Ex 27:1
7½ feet wide, and three * high. Ex 27:1
stretch for 150 *, and be held up Ex 27:9,10
of the court—150 * of curtains held Ex 27:11
be seventy-five * wide, with ten Ex 27:12

(FEET Con't)
side will also be seventy-five *. Ex 27:13
there will be 22½ * of curtain, Ex 27:14,15
court will be 150 * long, and 75 Ex 27:18
feet long, and 75 * wide, with Ex 27:18
curtain walls 7½ * high, made from Ex 27:18
and the big toes of their right *; Ex 29:19,20
square and three * high, with horns Ex 30:2
their hands and * there, when they Ex 30:19
* long and six feet wide). Ex 36:14,15
feet long and six * wide). Ex 36:14,15
fifteen * and the width 2¼ feet. Ex 36:21
fifteen feet and the width 2¼ *. Ex 36:21
wood and was 3¾ * long, 2¼ feet Ex 37:1
long, 2¼ * wide, and 2¼ feet high. Ex 37:1
long, 2¼ feet wide, and 2¼ * high. Ex 37:1
its four *, two rings at each end. Ex 37:3
it was 3¾ * long and 2¼ feet Ex 37:6
it was 3¾ feet long and 2¼ * Ex 37:6
acacia wood, three * long, 1½ feet Ex 37:10
long, 1½ * wide and 2¼ feet high. Ex 37:10
long, 1½ feet wide and 2¼ * high. Ex 37:10
square and three * high, with its Ex 37:25
it was 7½ * square at the top, Ex 38:1
square at the top, and 4½ * high. Ex 38:1
The south wall was 150 * long; Ex 38:9
The north wall was also 150 * Ex 38:11
The west side was seventy-five * Ex 38:12
side was also seventy-five * wide. Ex 38:13
entrance were 22½ * wide, each with Ex 38:14,15
It was thirty * long and 7½ feet Ex 38:18
It was thirty feet long and 7½ * Ex 38:18
washed their hands and * there. Ex 40:31
the big toes of their right *. Lev 8:24
have four * are forbidden to you. Lev 11:23
your * or crawl upon the ground: Lev 11:29,30
No crawling thing with many * may Lev 11:41,42
three or four * above the ground. Num 11:31
with them, three * thick!" Num 11:31f
for 1500 * in each direction. Num 35:4
Thus there will be 3000 * Num 35:5
a half * long by six feet wide. Deu 3:11
a half feet long by six * wide. Deu 3:11
old, and your * haven't been Deu 8:4
or donkey onto its * when it has Deu 22:4
much as touch her * to the Deu 28:56,57
He bathes his * in soothing olive Deu 33:24
water with their *, the river will Jos 3:13,14
river and as the * of the priests Jos 3:13,14
put their * on the kings' necks. Jos 10:24
And he lay at her *, Ju 5:27
the cover off his * and lie down Ru 3:4
covering off his * and lay there. Ru 3:6,7
There was a woman lying at his *! Ru 3:8
So she lay at his * until the Ru 3:14
a man, measuring over nine * tall! 1Sa 17:4-7
Your * were not tied— 2Sa 3:33,34
They cut off their hands and * 2Sa 4:12
like marching * in the tops of the 2Sa 5:24
was lame in both *) moved to 2Sa 9:13
His head was covered and his * 2Sa 15:30
He had not washed his * or 2Sa 19:24,25
You have made wide steps for my * 2Sa 22:37
They have fallen beneath my *. 2Sa 22:39
The Temple was ninety * long, 1Ki 6:2
* wide, and forty-five feet high. 1Ki 6:2
feet wide, and forty-five * high. 1Ki 6:2
* long and fifteen feet deep. 1Ki 6:3
feet long and fifteen * deep. 1Ki 6:3
floor being 7½ * wide, the second 1Ki 6:6
the second floor 9 * wide, and the 1Ki 6:6
and the upper floor 10½ * wide. 1Ki 6:6
Each story of the annex was 7½ * 1Ki 6:10
Most Holy Place—was sixty * long. 1Ki 6:17
was thirty * long, thirty feet 1Ki 6:20
* wide, and thirty feet high. 1Ki 6:20
feet wide, and thirty * high. 1Ki 6:20
olive wood, each fifteen * high. 1Ki 6:23-28
each wing was 7½ * long, so each 1Ki 6:23-28
* from wing tip to wing tip. 1Ki 6:23-28
It was huge—measuring 150 * long, 1Ki 7:2
long, 75 * wide, and 45 feet high. 1Ki 7:2
long, 75 feet wide, and 45 * high. 1Ki 7:2
It was seventy-five * long and 1Ki 7:6
and forty-five * wide, with a porch 1Ki 7:6
were twelve to fifteen * across. 1Ki 7:10
each twenty-seven * high and 1Ki 7:15
high and eighteen * around, with 1Ki 7:15
each 7½ * high, and 6 feet wide. 1Ki 7:16-22
each 7½ feet high, and 6 * wide. 1Ki 7:16-22
bronze tank, 7½ * high and 15 feet 1Ki 7:23
high and 15 * from brim to brim; 1Ki 7:23
to brim; 45 * in circumference. 1Ki 7:23
each 6 * square and 4½ feet high. 1Ki 7:27-30
each 6 feet square and 4½ * high. 1Ki 7:27-30
stand was a round piece 1½ * high. 1Ki 7:31
Its center was concave, 2¼ * 1Ki 7:31
Each vat was six * square and 1Ki 7:38
In his old age his * became 1Ki 15:23
he dug a trench about three * wide 1Ki 18:32
him and caught hold of his *. 2Ki 4:27
She fell to the floor at his * 2Ki 4:37
her skull, her *, and her hands. 2Ki 9:35
they were dust beneath his *. 2Ki 13:7
man revived and jumped to his *! 2Ki 13:20,21
a distance of about six hundred *. 2Ki 14:13
Each pillar was twenty-seven * 2Ki 25:17
seven and one-half * tall, whose 1Ch 11:23
The foundation was ninety * long 2Ch 3:3
feet long and thirty * wide. 2Ch 3:3
The roof was 180 * high. 2Ch 3:4
Holy of Holies—thirty * square. 2Ch 3:8
two pillars 52½ * high, topped by a 2Ch 3:15
altar thirty * long, thirty feet 2Ch 4:1
* wide, and fifteen feet high. 2Ch 4:1
feet wide, and fifteen * high. 2Ch 4:1
fifteen * across from rim to rim. 2Ch 4:2
The rim stood 7½ * above the 2Ch 4:2
and was forty-five * around. 2Ch 4:2
7½ * square and 4½ feet high. 2Ch 6:12,13
7½ feet square and 4½ * high. 2Ch 6:12,13
diseased in his * but he didn't go 2Ch 16:12
The height will be ninety * and Ez 6:3
and the width will be ninety *. Ez 6:3
then they repaired the 1,500 * of Neh 3:13
wear out and their * didn't swell! Neh 9:21
The king jumped to his * and Est 7:7
down at his * and begging him with Est 8:3
for the blind and * for the lame. Job 29:15
'And he puts my * in the Job 33:11
down before his Son and kiss his * Ps 2:12
and evil men. My * have not Ps 17:5
thick darkness was beneath his *. Ps 18:9
my * so that I need never slip. Ps 18:36
I placed my * upon their necks. Ps 18:38
me and fall defeated at my *. Ps 18:39
they have pierced my hands and *. Ps 22:16
mire, and set my * on a hard, firm Ps 40:2
from death and my * from slipping, Ps 56:13
And he holds our * to the path. Ps 66:9
Cover your * with their blood; Ps 68:23
the cliff ! My * were slipping Ps 73:2
even trample them beneath your *! Ps 91:13
Bow low before his *. Ps 99:5
There in prison they hurt his * Ps 105:18
smell, nor use their hands or *! Ps 115:7
from tears, my * from stumbling. Ps 116:8
with eyes and * and fingers. Pro 6:12,13
hot coals and not blister his *? Pro 6:28
off your * and drinking poison! Pro 26:6
I have washed my *, and should I Sol 5:3
your tripping *, O queenly maiden. Sol 7:1
their *, and with two they flew. Is 6:2
them like dirt beneath his *. Is 10:5,6
beneath his * and left to rot. Is 25:10
trampled beneath the enemies' *. Is 28:3
down beneath your *, as grass upon Is 37:27
and lick the dust from off your *; Is 49:23
mountains are the * of those who Is 52:7
Your * run to do evil and rush Is 59:7
They will kiss your *! Is 60:14
each twenty-seven * high and Jer 52:21
high and eighteen * in Jer 52:21
The top 7½ * of each column had Jer 52:22
beneath your * the lowly of the Lam 3:34,35,36
our necks beneath the victors' *; Lam 5:5
of men, but their * were cloven Eze 1:7
*, and shone like burnished brass. Eze 1:7
as he spoke, and set me on my *. Eze 2:2
into me and set me on my *. Eze 3:24
your hands and stamp your *." Eze 6:11f
don't bare your head nor *, and Eze 24:17
Your head and * shall not be Eze 24:23
and muddy the rest with your *? Eze 34:18
stick, which was 10½ * long. Eze 40:5
He told me, "This wall is 10½ * Eze 40:5
is 10½ feet high and 10½ * wide." Eze 40:5
it was 10½ * wide. Eze 40:6
each of these rooms was 10½ * Eze 40:7-12
8¾ * along the wall between them. Eze 40:7-12
22¾ * wide and 17½ feet long. Eze 40:7-12
22¾ feet wide and 17½ * long. Eze 40:7-12
this distance was 43¾ *. Eze 40:13
the porch to be about 100 * high. Eze 40:14
87½ * from one end to the other. Eze 40:15
found that the distance was 175 *. Eze 40:19
passageway—87½ * long and 43¾ feet Eze 40:21
feet long and 43¾ * from side to Eze 40:21
the two passageways was 175 *. Eze 40:23
And like the others, it was 87½ * Eze 40:25
was 87½ feet long and 43¾ * wide. Eze 40:25
between the passageways was 175 *. Eze 40:27
it were 37½ * by 8¾ feet broad." Eze 40:28f
it were 37½ feet by 8¾ * broad." Eze 40:28f
37½ * long and 8¾ feet broad." Eze 40:29,30f
37½ feet long and 8¾ * broad." Eze 40:29,30f
was 87½ * long by 43¾ feet wide. Eze 40:29,30
was 87½ feet long by 43¾ * wide. Eze 40:29,30
and it was 87½ * long by 43¾ feet Eze 40:33
and it was 87½ feet long by 43¾ * Eze 40:33
of 87½ * and a width of 43¾ feet. Eze 40:36
of 87½ feet and a width of 43¾ *. Eze 40:36
These tables were about 2⅝ * Eze 40:42
2⅝ feet square and 1¾ * high. Eze 40:42
and found it to be 175 * square, Eze 40:47
pillars, each of them 8¾ * thick. Eze 40:48,49
The entrance was 24½ * wide with Eze 40:48,49
Thus the entry hall was 35 * wide Eze 40:48,49
was 35 feet wide and 19¼ * long. Eze 40:48,49
They were 10½ * square. Eze 41:1
The entrance hall was 17½ * wide Eze 41:2
was 17½ feet wide and 8¾ * deep. Eze 41:2
The nave itself was seventy * Eze 41:2
feet long by thirty-five *. Eze 41:2
and found them to be 3½ * thick; Eze 41:3
its doorway was 10½ * wide, with Eze 41:3
a hallway 12¼ * deep behind it. Eze 41:3
The inner room was thirty-five * Eze 41:4
that it was 10½ * thick, with a row Eze 41:5
Each room was seven * wide. Eze 41:5
out 10½ * onto the terrace. Eze 41:8
these rooms was 8¾ * thick, leaving Eze 41:9
a free space of 8¾ * out to the Eze 41:9
Thirty-five * away from the Eze 41:10
terrace yard, which was 8¾ * wide; Eze 41:11
122½ * wide by 157½ feet long. Eze 41:12
122½ feet wide by 157½ * long. Eze 41:12
Its walls were 8¾ * thick. Eze 41:12
The area was 175 * square. Eze 41:13
was also 175 * wide, and so was Eze 41:14
This altar was 3½ * square, and Eze 41:22
was 3½ feet square, and 5¼ * high; Eze 41:22
was 175 * long by 87½ feet wide. Eze 42:2
was 175 feet long by 87½ * wide. Eze 42:2
court, were 87½ * long—only half as Eze 42:7,8
court, which was 175 * long. Eze 42:7,8
of a square, 875 * long on each Eze 42:16-20
is a stone platform 3½ * high. Eze 43:14
on all sides, and seven * high. Eze 43:14
rises seven *, and this is the top Eze 43:15
the altar is twenty-one * square. Eze 43:16
The platform beneath it is 24½ * Eze 43:17
"A section of this land, 875 * Eze 45:2
was a room 70 * long by 52½ feet Eze 46:21,22
by 52½ * wide, enclosed by walls. Eze 46:21,22
he took me 1,500 * east along the Eze 47:3
He measured off another 1,500 * Eze 47:4
Fifteen hundred * after that it Eze 47:5
Another 1,500 * and it had become Eze 47:5
Literally, "437½ *" in every Eze 48:17f
its * part iron and part clay. Dan 2:33
and crushed the * of iron and clay, Dan 2:34
conquering. The * and toes you Dan 2:41,42
statue ninety * high and nine feet Dan 3:1
feet high and nine * wide and set Dan 3:1
the ground, on two *, like a man; Dan 7:4
others it crushed beneath its *. Dan 7:7
others to death with its *. Dan 7:19
a touch, and helped me to my *. Dan 8:18
his arms and * shone like Dan 10:5,6
* again, to live in his kindness! Hos 6:2
underneath his *: Jehovah, the Amo 4:13
They melt beneath his *, and Mic 1:4
tread our sins beneath your *; Mic 7:19
are billowing dust beneath his *! Nah 1:3
to their *, and fall again. Nah 3:3
with walls 100 * high and so thick Zep 2:15f
"It appears to be about thirty * Zec 5:2
feet long and fifteen * wide!" Zec 5:2
treading them beneath their *. Zec 9:15
into the dust beneath their *. Zec 10:5
ones, even tearing off their *. Zec 11:16
That day his * will stand upon Zec 14:4
place from your * as you leave. Mt 10:14
with both of your hands and *. Mt 18:8
put your enemies beneath your *.' Mt 22:44
holding his * and worshiping him. Mt 28:9
And Levi jumped to his * and went Mk 2:14
* and told him what she had done. Mk 5:33
the dust from your * as you leave; Mk 6:11
your * for the sake of tradition. Mk 7:9
and fell at his *, and pled with Mk 7:25
helped him to his * and he stood up Mk 9:27
have two * that carry you to hell. Mk 9:45,46
man jumped to his *, picked up his Lk 5:25
behind him at his *, weeping, with Lk 7:38
her tears falling down upon his *; Lk 7:38
the dust from my *, but she has Lk 7:44
she has kissed my * again and again Lk 7:45
covered my * with rare perfume. Lk 7:46
at Jesus' *, clothed and sane! Lk 8:35
down at Jesus' * and begged him to Lk 8:41
by shaking its dust from your * Lk 9:5
your town from our * as a public Lk 10:11
your enemies beneath your *." Lk 20:42,43
Look at my *! Lk 24:39
his *. Lk 24:40
* and wiped them with her hair? Jn 11:1
fell down at his *, saying, "Sir, Jn 11:32
anointed Jesus' * with it and wiped Jn 12:3
the disciples' * and to wipe them Jn 13:5
be washing our * like this!" Jn 13:6
"you shall never wash my *!" Jn 13:8

(FEET Con't)
and head as well—not just my *!" Jn 13:9
his * washed to be entirely clean. Jn 13:10
After washing their * he put on Jn 13:12
have washed your *, you ought to Jn 13:14
you ought to wash each other's *. Jn 13:14
to the beach, about 300 * away. Jn 21:8
the hand and pulled him to his *. Act 3:7,8
And as he did, the man's * and Act 3:7,8
the * of a young man named Paul. Act 7:58
the dust of their * against the Act 13:51
man with crippled * who had been Act 14:8
and the man leaped to his * and Act 14:10
stood to their * and declared that Act 15:5
clamped their * into the stocks. Act 16:24
bound his own * and hands with it Act 21:11
Gamaliel, at whose * I learned to Act 22:3
They sounded, and found 120 * of Act 27:28
again, and found only ninety *. Act 27:28
beautiful are the * of those who Rom 10:15
soon crush Satan under your *. Rom 16:20
The head can't say to the *, 1Co 12:21
from under the * of those who boast 2Co 11:12
things under his * and made him the Eph 1:22
all your enemies beneath your *"? Heb 1:13
enemies to be laid under his *. Heb 10:13
around our * and trip us up; Heb 12:1
path for your * so that those who Heb 12:13
of fire. His * gleamed like Rev 1:15
When I saw him, I fell at his * Rev 1:17,18
whose * are like glowing brass. Rev 2:18
to fall at your * and acknowledge Rev 3:9
sun and his * flashed with fire. Rev 10:1
moon beneath her *, and a crown of Rev 12:1
had bear's * and a lion's mouth! Rev 13:2
Then I fell down at his * to Rev 19:10
them to be 216 * across (the angel Rev 21:17

FELIX
get him safely to Governor *." Act 23:23,24
"To: His Excellency, Governor *. Act 23:26
*, who knew Christians didn't go Act 24:22
A few days later * came with Act 24:24
judgment to come, * was terrified. Act 24:25
* was succeeded by Porcius Festus. Act 24:27
And because * wanted to gain Act 24:27
"whose case was left for me by *. Act 25:14

FELL
down, a deep sleep * upon Abram, Gen 15:12
Abram * face downward in the Gen 17:2,3,4
* to his knees before Jehovah. Gen 24:52
and raped her. He * deeply in love Gen 34:3
Soon he * asleep again and had a Gen 41:5
they * to the ground before him. Gen 44:14
father and they * into each other's Gen 46:29
Then his brothers came and * down Gen 50:18
Moses * down before the Lord and Ex 34:8
all shouted and * flat upon the Lev 9:24
The manna * with the dew during Num 11:9
Then Moses and Aaron * face Num 14:5
he * face downward to the ground. Num 16:4
But Moses and Aaron * face Num 16:22
But Moses and Aaron * face Num 16:45
* face downward before the Lord; Num 20:6
* flat on the ground before him. Num 22:31
I *, and my eyes were opened: Num 24:3-9
He *, and his eyes were opened: Num 24:15-19
That is why I * down before him Deu 9:25
The following day no manna *, and Jos 5:11,12
Joshua * to the ground before him Jos 5:14
crumbled and * before them, and the Jos 6:20
Manoah and his wife * face Ju 13:20
like thread and * from his wrists! Ju 15:14
Later on he * in love with a girl Ju 16:4
let her go. She * down at the door Ju 19:26
to the Ark, Eli * backward from his 1Sa 4:18
the Philistines * back as Jonathan 1Sa 14:13
The stone sank in, and the man * 1Sa 17:48,49
Saul now * full length upon the 1Sa 28:20
his own sword and * upon the point 1Sa 31:3,4
was dead, he also * upon his sword 1Sa 31:5
of mourning. He * to the ground 2Sa 1:1
troops then * to two brothers, 2Sa 4:2,3
and fled, but she * and dropped him 2Sa 4:4
Mephibosheth * to the ground 2Sa 9:8
* desperately in love with her. 2Sa 13:1
and * prostrate to the ground. 2Sa 13:31
the king, she * face downward on 2Sa 14:4
Joab * to the ground before the 2Sa 14:22
crossing, Shime-i * down before 2Sa 19:18
came forward and * flat on the 2Sa 24:20
and * to the ground before him. 1Ki 18:7
saw it, they * to their faces upon 1Ki 18:39
but the wall * on them and killed 1Ki 20:30
time the captain * to his knees 2Ki 1:13
but even that finally * to them. 2Ki 3:25
the mountain she * to the ground 2Ki 4:27
She * to the floor at his feet 2Ki 4:37
his axhead * into the river. 2Ki 6:5
reign, Samaria * and the people of 2Ki 17:6
King Hoshea of Israel) Samaria *. 2Ki 18:10
own sword and * against its point; 1Ch 10:4
* to the ground before the Lord. 1Ch 21:16
and now they * flat on the 2Ch 7:3
Then the fear of the Lord * upon 2Ch 17:10
Then King Jehoshaphat * to the 2Ch 20:18
the fear of God * upon them. 2Ch 20:29
then I * to my knees and lifted Ez 9:5
shut as darkness * on Friday Neh 13:19
city * into confusion and panic. Est 3:15
In despair he * upon the couch Est 7:8
* in on them and all are dead; Job 1:19
and * down upon the ground before Job 1:20
God of Jacob, steeds and riders *. Ps 76:6
and fire * from heaven to Ps 106:18
hard labor; they * and none could Ps 107:12
of "Ephraim," * to the Assyrian Is 7:8f
The city * to the Medes and Is 21:6,7f
evil * on anyone who touched them. Jer 2:3
wall, and the city *, and all the Jer 39:2
boiled forth and * as fire upon the Jer 44:6
his hands * helpless at his sides; Jer 50:43
and walls * down before him. Lam 2:8
before the hand of judgment *. Lam 5:7
And when I saw it, I * face Eze 1:27,28
And I * to the ground on my face. Eze 3:23
power of the Lord God * upon me. Eze 8:1
I was alone. I * to the ground on Eze 9:8
Then I * to the ground on my face Eze 11:13
Samaria, for she * in love with Eze 23:14,15
Yes, the terrors that * upon her Eze 23:32
the year Jerusalem * to Eze 30:20f
the year Jerusalem *. Eze 31:1f
"The Lord God says: When she * I Eze 31:15
And I * down before him with my Eze 43:3
of the Lord, and I * to the ground Eze 44:4
Then Nebuchadnezzar * to the Dan 2:46
—* to the ground and worshiped the Dan 3:7
and Abednego * down bound into the Dan 3:23
At his whim they rose or *. Dan 5:19
* down with my face to the ground. Dan 8:17
Then he spoke to me, and I * to Dan 10:9
While rain * on one field, Amo 4:7
Yet Thebes * and her people were Nah 3:10
considering this, he * into a Mt 1:20
one sheep, and it * into a well on Mt 12:11
the ground, some * beside a path, Mt 13:4
And some * on rocky soil where Mt 13:5
Other seeds * among thorns, and Mt 13:7
But some * on good soil, and Mt 13:8
some of the seeds * represents the Mt 13:19
Night *, and out on the lake the Mt 14:23,24
At this the disciples * face Mt 17:6
"But the man * down before the Mt 18:26
"The man * down before him and Mt 18:29
He went forward a little, and * Mt 26:39
saw him, and * into a dead faint. Mt 28:4
And they * to the ground before Mt 28:9
field, some of it * on a path, and Mk 4:4
Some * on thin soil with Mk 4:5,6
Other seeds * among thorns that Mk 4:7
But some of the seeds * into Mk 4:8
some of the seed *, represents the Mk 4:15
As evening *, Jesus said to his Mk 4:35
And the wind *, and there was a Mk 4:39
meet him, and * down before him. Mk 5:6
Jairus, came and * down before him, Mk 5:22
to her, came and * at his feet and Mk 5:33
now she came and * at his feet, Mk 7:25
horribly, and he * to the ground Mk 9:20
Then the man's face *, and he Mk 10:22
He went on a little further and * Mk 14:35
About noon, darkness * across the Mk 15:33
week—the honor * to him by lot Lk 1:8,9
Wonder * upon the whole Lk 1:65
words that * from his lips. Lk 4:22
had happened, he * to his knees Lk 5:8
When he saw Jesus he * to the Lk 5:12
ground, some of it * on a footpath Lk 8:5
Other seed * on shallow soil Lk 8:6
Still other * on fertile soil; Lk 8:8
The hard path where some seed * Lk 8:12
he shrieked and * to the ground Lk 8:28
mountainside and * over a cliff Lk 8:33
came and * down at Jesus' feet and Lk 8:41
to tremble and * to her knees Lk 8:47
the Tower of Siloam * on them? Lk 13:4
He * flat on the ground in Lk 17:16
darkness * across the whole land Lk 23:44
But as darkness * and Jesus Jn 6:17
Jesus was, she * down at his feet, Jn 11:32
And as he said it, they all * Jn 18:6
words, he * to the floor, dead! Act 5:5
Instantly she * to the floor, Act 5:10
And he * to his knees, Act 7:60
down upon him! He * to the ground Act 9:4
as though scales * from his eyes) Act 9:18
prepared, he * into a trance. Act 10:9,10
home, Cornelius * to the floor Act 10:25
Spirit * upon all those listening! Act 10:44
the Holy Spirit * on them, just as Act 11:15
as he * on us at the beginning! Act 11:15
And the chains * off his Act 12:7
Instantly mist and darkness * upon Act 13:11
of every prisoner * off ! Act 16:26
and * down before Paul and Silas. Act 16:29
image * down to us from heaven. Act 19:35
fast asleep and * three stories to Act 20:9
And I * to the ground and heard Act 22:7
in the Temple, I * into a trance Act 22:17,18
We all * down, and I heard a Act 26:14
and 23,000 * dead in one day. 1Co 10:8
would fall, none * for the next Jas 5:17
son of Beor, who * in love with the 2Pe 2:15
When I saw him, I * at his feet Rev 1:17,18
twenty-four Elders * down before Rev 4:10
twenty-four Elders * down before Rev 5:8
And the twenty-four Elders * Rev 5:14
Literally, "the stars of heaven * Rev 6:13f
great flaming star * from heaven Rev 8:10
the world * in heaps of rubble; Rev 16:19
a hundred pounds * from the sky Rev 16:21
In one moment her judgment *." Rev 18:10
four Living Beings * down and Rev 19:4
Then I * down at his feet to Rev 19:10
these things, and * down to worship Rev 22:8

FELLED
the wells, and * the fruit trees; 2Ki 3:25
you watch the thickest forests *. Zec 11:2

FELLOW
We let this * settle among us and Gen 19:9
"Do you know a * there named Gen 29:5
to a young Hebrew * there who was a Gen 41:12
THERE WERE AT this time a Hebrew * Ex 2:1
out to visit his * Hebrews and saw Ex 2:11
lead us, for this * Moses who Ex 32:1
* Moses who led us out of Egypt.' Ex 32:23
"If a * Israelite becomes poor Lev 25:39
have led their * citizens astray Deu 13:12,13,14
he holds against a * Israelite, for Deu 15:2
he is better than his * citizens. Deu 17:20
man, whether a * Israelite or a Deu 24:14,15
There he captured a young * from Ju 8:14
instead to the * who had been best Ju 14:20
he knew a young * in Bethlehem, the 1Sa 16:18
does this young * come from?" 1Sa 17:55
As long as that * is alive, 1Sa 20:31
the Philistine—the * you killed in 1Sa 21:9
Should such a * as this be my 1Sa 21:14,15
"Who is this * David?" 1Sa 25:10
of good it did us to help this *. 1Sa 25:21
"Well, Abner, you're a great *, 1Sa 26:15
to Abishai, "That * Sheba is going 2Sa 20:6
says to put this * in jail and feed 1Ki 22:27
"Who was this *?" 2Ki 1:7
have let this * get away without 2Ki 5:20
him, "What did that crazy * want? 2Ki 9:11
for Asaph and his * Levites to 1Ch 16:37
says to put this * in prison and 2Ch 18:26
They in turn summoned their * 2Ch 29:15
Jozadak) with his * priests, and Ez 3:1
their * priests and the Levites. Ez 3:8
one of my * Jews named Hanani came Neh 1:2
Bakbukiah and Unno, their * Neh 12:9
lesson from the ants, you lazy *. Pro 6:6
A lazy * is a pain to his Pro 10:26
A lazy * has trouble all through Pro 15:19
of a certain lazy * and saw that it Pro 24:30,31
and said: "Sir, this * must die. Jer 38:4
Then they told the king, "That * Dan 6:13
and set the little * down among Mt 18:2
oppressing your * servants, Mt 24:49
That night Levi invited his * tax Mk 2:15
"You lucky *," Mk 10:49
"I don't even know this * you Mk 14:71
"Who does this * think he is?" Lk 5:21
Many of Levi's * tax collectors Lk 5:29
And so the poor * is seven times Lk 11:26
" 'See that * there?' Lk 14:30
our chance! This * will inherit all Lk 20:14
"I know this * is one of Jesus' Lk 22:59
him: "This * has been leading our Lk 23:2
this the same *—that beggar?" Jn 9:8
Some of them said, "Then this * Jn 9:16
but as for this *, we don't know Jn 9:29
said to his * disciples, "Let's go Jn 11:16
But some said, "This * healed a Jn 11:37,38
Some time ago there was that * Act 5:36
him say that this * Jesus of Act 6:14
shouted, "Away with such a *! Act 22:22
Let's please the other *, not Rom 15:1
They have been my * workers in Rom 16:3
our * worker, and beloved Stachys. Rom 16:9
Try to think of the other *, too, 1Co 10:24
So, my * believers, long to be 1Co 14:39
*, that Paul, and he fooled us. 2Co 12:16
and the rest of my * workers whose Php 4:3
Epaphras, our much-loved * Col 1:7
our brother and * worker, God's 1Th 3:2,3
To: Philemon, our much loved * Phm 1:1
Epaphras my * prisoner, who is Phm 1:23
Demas and Luke, my * workers. Phm 1:24
when he returns. * elders, this is 1Pe 5:1
his * man, is still in darkness. 1Jn 2:9

(FELLOW Con't)
But whoever loves his * man is 1Jn 2:10
It is I, your brother John, a * Rev 1:9
other brothers, * servants of Rev 6:11

FELLOW-BELIEVERS
They wrote to their * there, Act 18:27

FELLOW-CLANSMEN
Their * helped them during the Neh 12:24

FELLOW-HEBREW
"If you lend money to a needy *, Ex 22:25

FELLOW-JEWS
to our * without any interest. Neh 5:10

FELLOW-LEVITES
an honest distribution to their *. Neh 13:13

FELLOW-PRIESTS
* to minister to the Lord there. 1Ch 16:39

FELLOW-WORKER
Timothy my *, and Lucius and Rom 16:21

FELLOWS
"Please, *," he begged, Gen 19:7
"What do you * think I should 2Ch 10:8,9
with the worthless * of the town Ps 35:16
with the other * who ate the king's Dan 1:13
"They protested, 'Those * worked Mt 20:11,12
some worthless * from the streets Act 17:5
other marvelous * have that I don't 2Co 12:11

FELLOWSHIP
300 years in * with God, and Gen 5:21-24
day for * with his son Absalom. 2Sa 13:37,38,39
I do not have * with tricky, Ps 26:4
What * we had, what wonderful Ps 55:14
The wicked enjoy * with others Pro 17:4
only of the food and * and fun. Zec 7:6
Lord Jesus, and there was warm * Act 4:33
forever in unbroken * with God. Rom 6:10
this man from the * of the church 1Co 5:5
you may share the * and the joys we 1Jn 1:3
we have wonderful * and joy with 1Jn 1:7
and brought us into * with God; 1Jn 2:2
always be in close * with both God 1Jn 2:24
stay in happy * with the Lord so 1Jn 2:28
in and * with him and he with me. Rev 3:20

FELLOWSHIPED
"You * with Gentiles and even Act 11:3

FELT
and could, he * sure, sell the idea Gen 34:18,19
of Egypt who * no obligation Ex 1:8
The reason was that God * the Ex 13:17,18
who * called to the work to begin. Ex 36:1
race of giants. We * like Num 13:33
I reported what I * was the Jos 14:7
Abimelech * close kinship there. Ju 9:2f
and noticed how secure everyone *. Ju 18:7
property. I * that I should speak Ru 4:4
eaten the honey he * much better. 1Sa 14:27
And toward whom have you * so 2Ki 19:22
of King Saul, * a deep disgust for 1Ch 15:29
but then he * such compassion 1Ch 21:15
him, for he * that since these gods 2Ch 28:23
But in Judah the entire nation * 2Ch 30:12
up on end. I * the spirit's Job 4:16
of God was * in my home; Job 29:4
will no more be * than a thorn in Pro 26:9
So I * that the dead were better Ecc 4:2
fun, because I * that there was Ecc 8:15
* destruction for yourselves. Is 33:1
You * secure in all your Is 47:10
the terror he *, and his officers Dan 5:9
and I * my strength returning. Dan 10:18
these words, I * stronger and said Dan 10:19
And what pity he * for the Mt 9:36
Jesus * genuine love for this man Mk 10:21
as they left Bethany, he * hungry. Mk 11:12
* healing power go out from me." Lk 8:46
when he saw him, he * deep pity. Lk 10:33
their hearts had * strangely warm Lk 24:32
* that what he owned was his own; Act 4:32
he * that he had no time to lose. Act 18:20
Afterwards, Paul * impelled by Act 19:21
Suddenly everyone * better and Act 27:36
the decision, I * it necessary, Act 28:19
That is why I * fine so long as I Rom 7:9
through it. We * we were doomed to 2Co 1:9
me greatest joy. I * sure that your 2Co 2:3
kind of sorrow you *, the kind of 2Co 7:9
spirit that we * together then? Gal 4:15
of God is, and * the mighty powers Heb 6:5
us because we have * his love and 1Jn 4:16

FEMALE
male and a *—into the boat with Gen 6:19,20
Literally, "the male and *." Gen 7:3f
and *, just as God commanded Noah. Gen 7:8,9
Two by two they came, male and * Gen 7:16
a three-year-old * goat, a Gen 15:9
* donkeys,10 male donkeys. Gen 32:13,14,15
slave is male or *—that man shall Ex 21:20
whether male or *, the slave's Ex 21:32
of male and * genital organs. Ex 34:13f
either a male or *—ram or ewe, Lev 3:6
be a * without physical defect. Lev 4:32
to the Lord, a * lamb or goat, and Lev 5:6
* animal, thus defiling himself; Lev 18:23
a one-year-old * goat for a sin Num 15:27
not one of you, whether male or * Deu 7:14
and two * bears came out of the 2Ki 2:24
teams of oxen, 500 * donkeys, and Job 1:2,3
of oxen, and 1,000 * donkeys. Job 42:12
* camel, seeking for a male! Jer 2:23

FEMALES
spotted, and the * that were Gen 30:35,36

FENCE
covering the * surrounding the Num 3:25-30
the courtyard *, and the curtain Num 4:26
for the courtyard * with their Num 4:32
But I will * her in with Hos 1:6

FENCES
I will tear down the * and let Is 5:5

FEROCIOUS
iron bars. How * he is among all Job 40:19
war, famine, * beasts, plague. Eze 14:21
Lord roared—like a * lion from his Amo 1:2

FERRET
My daily task will be to * out Ps 101:8

FERRIED
men from Judah had * him and his 2Sa 19:41

FERRYING
They all worked hard * the 2Sa 19:18

FERTILE
Lot took a long look at the * Gen 13:10
cause you to be * and to multiply Gen 35:11
*, increasing rapidly in numbers; Ex 1:7
and whether the land is * or Num 13:19
It is very *, a land 'flowing Num 14:8
Where is the * land of wonderful Num 20:5
He will make you * and give Deu 7:13
God gave them * hilltops, Deu 32:13
Rolling, * fields, Deu 32:13
taking—a broad, *, wonderful Ju 18:9,10
into your home, as * as Rachel and Ru 4:11
hillsides and in the * valleys. 2Ch 26:10
fortified cities and * land; Neh 9:25
He waters the earth to make it * Ps 65:9
Again, he turns deserts into *, Ps 107:35
has a vineyard on a very * hill. Is 5:1
as well as to all your * acres. Is 7:19
No one will go to the * Is 7:25
surrounded by a * valley will Is 28:4
field again, a lush and * forest. Is 29:17
The * valleys were wilderness and Jer 4:26
You are proud of your * valleys, Jer 49:4
in * ground beside a broad river, Eze 17:5
and planted it in * ground beside a Eze 17:12,13
where the land is * and good. Eze 34:13
* soil of their own land again." Hos 1:11
let them enjoy the * pastures of Mic 7:14
the ground will be *, with plenty Zec 8:12
Still other fell on * soil; Lk 8:8
a * farm that produced fine crops. Lk 12:16

FERTILITY
fertile and give * to your ground Deu 7:13
Curses upon the * of your cattle Deu 28:15-19
Tammuz, the god of *, because, Eze 8:14f
and * had vanished with him. Eze 8:14f

FERTILIZE
the ground to rot and * the soil. Jer 16:4
they shall * the earth. Jer 25:33

FERTILIZED
whose decaying corpses * the soil. Ps 83:10

FERTILIZER
special attention and plenty of *. Lk 13:8
is fit for nothing—not even for *. Lk 14:35

FERVENT
Paul became more and more * in Act 9:22

FERVOR
for you with deep * and feeling 2Co 9:14

FESTERING
My wounds are * and full of pus. Ps 38:5,6

FESTIVAL
festivals: the * of Weeks, the Ex 34:22
of Weeks, the * of the First Wheat, Ex 34:22
First Wheat, and the Harvest *. Ex 34:22
"The * of Unleavened Bread: This Lev 23:6
On the first day of this *, you Lev 23:7
same on the seventh day of the *. Lev 23:8
"The * of First Fruits: When you Lev 23:9,10,11
"The * of Pentecost: Fifty days Lev 23:15,16
"The * of Trumpets: Lev 23:23,24
"The * of Tabernacles: Five days Lev 23:33,34
is the * of Shelters Lev 23:33,34
seven days of the * you are to Lev 23:36
this seven-day * before the Lord. Lev 23:39
of the * are days of solemn rest. Lev 23:39
joyous seven-day * will begin, but Num 28:17
On the first day of the * a holy Num 28:18
(also called the * of Weeks, or Num 28:26
THE * OF Trumpets shall be Num 29:1
of a seven-day * before the Lord. Num 29:12
of this seven-day * you shall Num 29:17
"On the third day of the *, Num 29:20
"On the fourth day of the *, you Num 29:23
"On the fifth day of the *, Num 29:26,27
"On the sixth day of the *, you Num 29:29
"On the seventh day of the *, Num 29:32
shall be another * before the Lord Deu 16:10
your God called the * of Weeks. Deu 16:10
"Another celebration, the * of Deu 16:13
The * of Unleavened Bread, Deu 16:16
The * of Weeks, Deu 16:16
The * of Shelters. Deu 16:16
of Release—at the * of Tabernacles, Deu 31:10,11
declared a great * to celebrate the Ju 16:23,24
annual religious * held in the Ju 21:19
* in the month of October. 1Ki 8:2
annual Tabernacle * would be held 1Ki 12:32,33
to the annual * at Jerusalem; 1Ki 12:32,33
at the annual * of Tabernacles. 2Ch 5:3
the Tabernacle *, with large crowds 2Ch 7:8
celebration, the * of Weeks, and 2Ch 8:13
Weeks, and the * of Tabernacles. 2Ch 8:13
tents during the * of Tabernacles Neh 8:14
to the Temple on * days, singing Ps 42:4,5
*, which they attended each year. Lk 2:41,42
near—the Jewish * when only bread Lk 22:1
Then, midway through the *, Jesus Jn 7:14

FESTIVALS
annual religious *: the Festival of Ex 34:22
several annual * of the Lord—times Lev 23:1
These are the holy * which are Lev 23:4
the regular annual *—sacred Lev 23:37
These annual * are in addition Lev 23:38
The sacrifices made during the * Lev 23:38
So Moses announced these annual * Lev 23:44
at your annual * and at the Num 10:10
any of the annual *—must be Num 15:3,4
year at the sanctuary for these *. Deu 16:16
celebrations, and at all the *. 1Ch 23:31
regular * of the Lord our God. 2Ch 2:4
on new moon *, and at the three 2Ch 8:13
the three annual *—the Passover 2Ch 8:13
monthly new moon *, and for the 2Ch 31:3
And in the * they'll sing, "All Ps 87:7
your time at funerals than at *. Ecc 7:2
at all the sacred *, and they shall Eze 44:24
feasts and sacred * the meal Eze 46:11
They will be changed to joyous * Zec 8:19
the synagogues and at religious *! Lk 20:46

FESTIVE
also removed the * passageway he 2Ki 16:18
eat a * meal and to send presents; Neh 8:12
gave me gay and * garments to Ps 30:11
But when you fast, put on * Mt 6:17

FESTIVITIES
invited your sons to attend the *. 1Ki 1:25
During the * the priests carried 1Ki 8:3,4
ran out during the *, and Jesus' Jn 2:3

FESTUS
Felix was succeeded by Porcius *. Act 24:27
THREE DAYS AFTER * arrived in Act 25:1
But * replied that since Paul Act 25:4
Then *, anxious to please the Act 25:9
* conferred with his advisors and Act 25:12
for a visit with *. Act 25:13
of several days * discussed Paul's Act 25:14
And * replied, "You Act 25:22
city, * ordered Paul brought in. Act 25:23
Then * addressed the audience: Act 25:24
Suddenly * shouted, "Paul, you Act 26:24
am not insane, Most Excellent *. Act 26:25
And Agrippa said to *, "He could Act 26:32

FETTERS
hurt his feet with *, and placed Ps 105:18

FEUD
And so the * ended at last at the Eph 2:16

FEVER
with tuberculosis and burning *; Lev 26:16
He will send tuberculosis, *, Deu 28:22
Burning *, and fatal disease. Deu 32:24
My bones burn with *. Job 30:30
was in bed with a high *. Mt 8:14
touched her hand, the * left her; Mt 8:15
sick in bed with a high *. Mk 1:29,30
her to sit up, the * suddenly left, Mk 1:31
very sick with a high *. Lk 4:38
he spoke to the *, rebuking it, and Lk 4:39
his * suddenly disappeared!" Jn 4:52
was ill with * and dysentery. Act 28:8

FEVERISH
But all your * plans will not Is 22:9,10,11

FEW
But they seemed to him but a * Gen 29:20
We are so * that they will come Gen 34:30
them there. A * days later Israel Gen 37:13,14
if * years, the price will be low; Lev 25:14,15,16
passed and only a * remain until Lev 25:52
But if it stayed only a * days, Num 9:19
then they remained only a * days; Num 9:19
wept, "Oh, for a * bites of meat! Num 11:4,5
are strong or weak, many or *; Num 13:18
and you will be but * in number. Deu 4:27
may eat a * handfuls of it, but Deu 23:25
They were * in number, but in Deu 26:5
There will be * of you left, Deu 28:62
for a * days before crossing. Jos 3:1

(FEW Con't)
get wives for the * who remain, Ju 21:7
since except for a * minutes' rest Ru 2:7
and attacks and a * of your men 2Sa 17:9
except Hadad and a * royal 1Ki 11:16,17,18
I was just gathering a * sticks 1Ki 17:12
and a * others escaped on horses. 1Ki 20:20
and forth in the house a * times; 2Ki 4:35
Oh, pray for the * of us who are 2Ki 19:4
Then I will reject even those * 2Ki 21:14
There they destroyed the * 1Ch 4:43
When Israel was * in number—oh, 1Ch 16:19
Israel was few in number—oh, so *— 1Ch 16:19
King Ahab of Israel. A * years 2Ch 18:2
A * months later the Syrian army 2Ch 24:23
But there were too * priests to 2Ch 29:34
only a faithful * had been doing 2Ch 30:5f
have permitted a * of us to return Ez 9:8
taking only a * men with me; Neh 2:11,12
A * days later I went to visit Neh 6:10
and only a * houses were Neh 7:4
them and punched a * of them and Neh 13:25
Oh, let me alone for these * Job 7:16
Well, I know a * things Job 12:3
"HOW FRAIL IS man, how * his Job 14:1
and let him have a * moments of Job 14:6
you give me so * steps upon the Job 14:16
days and recognize how * they are; Ps 90:12
that our days are * and brief, like Ps 103:15
when they were but * in number, Ps 105:12
in number, very *, and were only Ps 105:12
Let his years be * and brief; Ps 109:8
Plans go wrong with too * Pro 15:22
The man of * words and settled Pro 17:27,28
on earth, so let your words be *. Ecc 5:1
In these * days of our empty Ecc 6:12
city with only a * people living in Ecc 9:14
teeth will be too * to do their Ecc 12:3
in to save a * of us, we would have Is 1:9
AT THAT TIME so * men will be left Is 4:1
Only a * from all that mighty Is 10:19
so * a child could count them! Is 10:19
shore, yet only a * of them will be Is 10:22
of the rich. * will live when I Is 13:12
be ended, and * of all its people Is 16:13,14
Oh, a very * of her people will Is 17:6
be left, just as a * stray olives Is 17:6
for a * of the poor who remain. Is 17:6
Only a * of its stalwart archers Is 21:17
the drought. * will be left alive. Is 24:6
and incense have been very *! Is 43:23
You worry at being so small and * Is 51:1
BUT, OH, HOW * believe it! Is 53:1
babies die when only a * days old; Is 65:20
But leave a scattered * to live. Jer 5:10
Even the * who remain in Israel Jer 6:9
the morale of the * soldiers we Jer 38:4
of Judah he left a * people, the Jer 39:10
heard that a * people were still Jer 40:11
grapes leave a * for the poor, and Jer 49:9,10
then take a * hairs out and Eze 5:4
"But I will let a * of my people Eze 6:8
But I will spare a * of them Eze 12:16
For the sake of a * paltry Eze 13:19
"A * years later the Syrian king Dan 11:13
If there are as * as ten of them Amo 6:9
Priest, and the * people remaining Hag 1:12
though you are * and weak.' Zec 4:6
From the * that are left, their Zec 10:8
narrow, and only a * ever find it. Mt 7:14
are so *," he told his disciples. Mt 9:37
And so he did only a * great Mt 13:58
of bread and a * small fish!" Mt 15:34
For many are called, but * are Mt 22:14
on a * sick people and heal them. Mk 6:5
the people. A * small fish were Mk 8:7
A * days later Mary hurried to Lk 1:39,40
so plentiful and the workers so *. Lk 10:2
is here [and * pay any attention Lk 11:31
him, "Will only a * be saved?" Lk 13:23
A * minutes later some Pharisees Lk 13:31
"A * days later this younger son Lk 15:13
Only a * would welcome and Jn 1:11,12
Capernaum for a * days with his Jn 2:12
how * believe what he tells them! Jn 3:32
"Master," they said, "only a * Jn 11:8
the Holy Spirit in just a * Act 1:5
in Damascus for a * days and went Act 9:19
during the next * days by the men Act 13:31
Yet only a * days later, some Act 14:19
* joined him and became believers. Act 17:34
They asked him to stay for a * Act 18:20
who led a rebellion a * years ago Act 21:37,38
"Pretend you want to ask a * Act 23:15
A * days later Felix came with Act 24:24
A * days later King Agrippa Act 25:13
there are a * being saved as a Rom 11:5
are looking for. A * have—the ones Rom 11:7
brothers, that * of you who follow 1Co 1:26
Lord best, with as * other things 1Co 7:35
A farmer who plants just a * 2Co 9:6
He had said just a * moments Heb 5:7f
trained us for a * brief years, Heb 12:10
"And yet I have a * things Rev 2:14

FEWER
the smaller tribes will give *." Num 35:8
all had * children than was normal 1Ch 4:27

FIANCÉ
as a virgin weeps whose * is dead. Joe 1:8
Then Joseph, her *, Mt 1:19

FIANCÉE
someone else would marry your *. Deu 20:7
the virginity of another man's *. Deu 22:23,24
"Someone else will marry your *; Deu 28:30
He took with him Mary, his *, Lk 2:5

FIANCÉS
his daughters' *, "Quick, get out Gen 19:14

FIBER
Now try with every * of your 1Ch 22:19
the spiritual * of Judah and had 2Ch 28:19
May every * of my being unite in Ps 86:11

FICTIONS
play" are meaningless * to you! Amo 5:7

FIDDLING
But Saul, who was * with his 1Sa 18:10

FIELD
down at the end of his *. Gen 23:9
cave and the * without any charge. Gen 23:11
*, and then I will bury my dead." Gen 23:13
bought: Ephron's * at Mach-pelah, Gen 23:17,18
*, and all the trees in the field. Gen 23:17,18
field, and all the trees in the *. Gen 23:17,18
there, in the * and cave deeded to Gen 23:19,20
near Mamre, in the * Abraham had Gen 25:9,10
So when Esau left for the * to Gen 27:5
an open *, waiting to be watered. Gen 29:2
growing in a * and brought them Gen 30:14
to come out to the * where he was Gen 31:4
"We were out in the * binding Gen 37:7
"We found this in the *," they Gen 37:32
in the cave in the * of Mach-pelah, Gen 49:29,30
facing Mamre—the * Abraham Gen 49:29,30
had bought in the * of Ephron the Gen 50:12,13
into another man's * to graze, he Ex 22:5
the owner of the * or vineyard an Ex 22:5
"If the * is being burned off Ex 22:6
goes into another * so that the Ex 22:6
in the *, it is not contaminated; Lev 11:37
living bird fly into the open *. Lev 14:7
into an open * outside the city. Lev 14:53
don't sow your * with two kinds Lev 19:19
For six years you may sow your * Lev 25:3
any part of his * to the Lord, Lev 27:16
If a man dedicates his * in the Lev 27:17
to redeem the *, he shall pay Lev 27:19
and the * will be his again. Lev 27:19
not to redeem the *, or if he has Lev 27:20
if he has sold the * to someone Lev 27:20
to the Lord as a * devoted to him, Lev 27:21
to the Lord a * he has bought, but Lev 27:22
of Jubilee the * shall return to Lev 27:24
"If someone out in a * touches Num 19:16
She bolted off the road into a *, Num 22:22,23
found lying in a * and no one has Deu 21:1
hear and rescue her out in the *. Deu 22:25,26,27
the *, don't go back after it. Deu 24:19
Blessings in the *; Deu 28:2-6
additional * as a wedding present. Jos 15:18,19
wife as she was sitting in the *. Ju 13:9
And as it happened, the * where Ru 2:3
that the owner of the * was Boaz. Ru 2:19
until the entire * is harvested." Ru 2:21
safer there than in any other *!" Ru 2:22
The cart came into the * of a man 1Sa 6:14
still be seen in the * of Joshua. 1Sa 6:18
Saul was plowing in the *, and 1Sa 11:5
I'll hide in the * and stay there 1Sa 20:5
"Come out to the * with me," 1Sa 20:11
So David hid himself in the *. 1Sa 20:24,25
went out into the * and took a 1Sa 20:35
south edge of the * and they sadly 1Sa 20:41
in a * and brought him to David. 1Sa 30:11,12
and wounded on the *, and Saul and 2Sa 1:4
Saul dead upon the * and thought 2Sa 1:10f
been known ever since as Sword *. 2Sa 2:16
dead on the *, also forty thousand 2Sa 10:18
a fight out in the *, and since no 2Sa 14:5,6
to that barley * of Joab's next to 2Sa 14:30
your servants set my * on fire?" 2Sa 14:31
a * and threw a garment over him. 2Sa 20:12
at the center of a * of lentils and 2Sa 23:11,12
were alone in the *, Ahijah tore 1Ki 11:29
in the * shall be eaten by birds.' 1Ki 14:11
who was plowing a * with eleven 1Ki 19:19
went out into the * to gather 2Ki 4:39
They met him at the * of Naboth, 2Ki 9:21
him into the * of Naboth, for once 2Ki 9:25
So throw him out on Naboth's *, 2Ki 9:26
manure upon the *, so that no one 2Ki 9:36
Assyria sent his * marshal, his 2Ki 18:17
highway beside the * where cloth 2Ki 18:17
was in a barley * and had begun to 1Ch 11:13
the middle of the *, and recovered 1Ch 11:14
forces were out in the *. 1Ch 19:9
up in the open *, then leave their Job 39:4
For all the animals of * and Ps 50:10,11
I walked by the * of a certain Pro 24:30,31
She goes out to inspect a *, and Pro 31:16
shanty in the * when the harvest Is 1:8
leads down to the bleaching *. Is 7:3
left dead on the * for the mountain Is 18:6
will be a fruitful * again, a lush Is 29:17
the * where cloth is bleached. Is 36:2
the trees of the *—all the world Is 55:12
Come, wild animals of the *; Is 56:9
Even the grass of the * groans Jer 12:4
like an open * and this city of Jer 26:18
"Buy my * in Anathoth, in the Jer 32:8
So I bought the *, paying Hanamel Jer 32:9
And yet you say to buy the * Jer 32:25
a * and left to die, unwanted. Eze 16:5
Thrive like a plant in the *!' Eze 16:6,7
tall tree out in a *, growing Dan 4:10,11
grass with the animals of the *.' Dan 4:23
weeds in the furrows of the *. Hos 10:4
furrows in a *—are used for Hos 12:11
sweeping across a *, and like a Joe 2:5
While rain fell on one *, another Amo 4:7
and become an open *, her streets Mic 1:6
a *, and become a heap of rubble; Mic 3:12
Every * will become a lush Zec 10:1
Look at the * lilies! Mt 6:28
farmer sowing good seed in his *; Mt 13:24
him, 'Sir, the * where you planted Mt 13:27
tiny mustard seed planted in a *. Mt 13:31,32
choice seed. The * is the world, Mt 13:38
treasure a man discovered in a *. Mt 13:44
the *—and get the treasure, too! Mt 13:44
to hire workers for his harvest *. Mt 20:1
to buy a certain * where the clay Mt 27:7
still called "The * of Blood." Mt 27:8
and purchased a * from the potters Mt 27:10
As he scattered it across his *, Mk 4:3
"A farmer sowed his *, and went Mk 4:26
"A farmer went out to his * to Lk 8:5
you are like hidden graves in a *. Lk 11:44
One said he had just bought a * Lk 14:18
He bought a * with the money he Act 1:18
named the place 'The * of Blood.' Act 1:19
He was one of those who sold a * Act 4:37
about being in someone else's *. 2Co 10:16
Hear the cries of the * workers Jas 5:4

FIELDED
Judah, led by King Abijah, * 2Ch 13:3

FIELDS
"Let's go out into the *." Gen 4:8
a walk out in the *, meditating, he Gen 24:63
through the * to meet us?" Gen 24:65
out into the * and get me some Gen 27:2,3,4
and * that Jehovah has blessed. Gen 27:27,28,29
the *, Leah went out to meet him. Gen 30:16
were out in the * herding cattle, Gen 34:5
came in from the *, too shocked and Gen 34:6,7
and outside in the *, and took all Gen 34:28
noticed him wandering in the *. Gen 37:15
sold him their * because the famine Gen 47:20
and hard in the * and to carry Ex 1:13,14
Bring in your cattle from the *, Ex 9:19
the * will die beneath the hail!" Ex 9:19
cattle and slaves in from the *; Ex 9:20
Everything left in the *, men and Ex 9:25
in the open *, and to cause them to Lev 17:5
out in the *. Lev 17:7
corners of your *, and don't pick Lev 19:9
*, nor pick up the fallen grain; Lev 23:22
crops that grow wild in the *. Lev 25:12
cities, and the surrounding *. Lev 25:33
to sell the * of common land Lev 25:34
or inherited *—shall not be sold or Lev 27:28
nor given us * and vineyards. Num 16:14
*, nor through your vineyards; Num 20:17
We won't trample your * or touch Num 21:22
Balaam into the * of Zophim at the Num 23:14
off into the * on either side. Deu 2:27
herds to work your *, and do not Deu 15:19
Curses in the *; Deu 28:15-19
Rolling, fertile *, Deu 32:13
gardens and grain * which they Jos 5:11,12
Anak)—although the * beyond the Jos 21:9-16
Out across the * of Edom, Ju 5:4
Dared to die upon the * of battle. Ju 5:18
an army and hide out in the *; Ju 9:32
into three groups hiding in the *. Ju 9:43
two groups cut them down in the *. Ju 9:44
run through the * of the Ju 15:5
way home from his work in the *. Ju 19:16
held in the * of Shiloh, between Ju 21:19
go out into the * of some kind man Ru 2:2
think of going to any other *. Ru 2:8,9
plow in the royal *, and harvest 1Sa 8:12
the best of your * and vineyards 1Sa 8:14
"But he's out in the * watching 1Sa 16:10,11
find a hiding place out in the *. 1Sa 19:2

(FIELDS Con't)
“Has David promised you * and 1Sa 22:7
They were spread out across the * 1Sa 30:16
Tob, and Maacah fought in the *. 2Sa 10:7,8
out to fight the Syrians in the *. 2Sa 10:9
out in open *, and should I go home 2Sa 11:11
* will be eaten by the birds.” 1Ki 16:4-7
have hidden in the *, thinking that 2Ki 7:12
all burned in the * of the Kidron 2Ki 23:4
of Midian in the * of Moab—became 1Ch 1:46
(although the * and suburbs were 1Ch 6:55,56,57
the brook running through the *. 2Ch 32:4
or mortgage their *, vineyards, and Neh 5:2,3,4
them, for our *, too, are mortgaged Neh 5:5
Restore their *, vineyards, Neh 5:11
and its nearby *, Azekah Neh 11:25-30
earth to water the *, and gives Job 5:10
the dew lay all night upon my * Job 29:19
* of slaughtered, wicked men. Ps 58:10
of people as the * are of grass. Ps 72:16
Their cattle died in the *, Ps 78:48
Praise him for the growing *, Ps 96:12
to sow their * and plant their Ps 107:37
by the thousands out in our *. Ps 144:12-15
earth and *, and high plateaus. Pro 8:26
the * and stay in the villages. Sol 7:11
grain * in the Valley of Rephaim. Is 17:5
will fail to rise and flood the *; Is 19:5
Just as locusts strip the * and Is 33:4
The wild animals in the * will Is 43:20
thirst and for your parched *. Is 44:3
your * and tend your vineyards. Is 61:5
homes and take their * and wives. Jer 6:12
Don't go out to the *! Jer 6:25
across the * like manure, like Jer 9:22
worship in the * and on the hills. Jer 13:27
If I go out in the *, there lie Jer 14:18
so shall all the * out to the brook Jer 31:40
houses and vineyards and *.” Jer 32:15
* will again be bought and sold Jer 32:43
Yes, * shall once again be Jer 32:44
the * toward the Jordan valley. Jer 39:4
and gave them * and vineyards. Jer 39:10
to feed in the * of Carmel and Jer 50:19
with enemies, like * filled with Jer 51:14
it across the *, toward Arabah. Jer 52:7
Zedekiah in some * near Jericho—for Jer 52:8
Those living in the open * shall Eze 33:27
Their fruit trees and * will Eze 34:27
fruit trees and *, and never again Eze 36:30
will fall upon the open *; Eze 39:5
They won't cut wood from the * or Eze 39:10
widely in many *, are well Dan 1:3,4
will live in the * like an animal, Dan 4:25
the animals in the *, and to eat Dan 4:32
out of his palace into the *. Dan 5:21
of God. The * are bare of crops. Joe 1:10
the grain has dried up in the *. Joe 1:17
sets the dry * of Edom aflame. Ob 1:18
the * of Ephraim and Samaria. Ob 1:19
leave this city and live in the *; Mic 4:10
all fail, and the * lie barren; Hab 3:17
even if the flocks die in the * Hab 3:17
more workers for his harvest *.” Mt 9:38
farmer was sowing grain in his *. Mt 13:2,3
them also into his *, telling them Mt 20:4
the others in my *,' he told them. Mt 20:7
Those in the * should not return Mt 24:18
together in the *, and one will be Mt 24:40
through the *, the disciples were Mk 2:23
down leafy branches from the *. Mk 11:8
If you are out in the *, don't Mk 13:15,16
were in the * outside the village, Lk 2:8
again to their * and flocks, Lk 2:20
older son was in the * working; Lk 15:25
those in the * must not return to Lk 17:31
working side by side in the *.” Lk 17:35,36
Look around you! Vast * of human Jn 4:35
abandon their children in the *. Act 7:19

FIERCE
said, “I am in a * contest with my Gen 30:8
anger, for it is * and cruel. Gen 49:7
Turn back from your * wrath. Ex 32:12
his * anger against their sins.” Num 1:53
so that his * anger will turn away Num 25:4
will turn from his * anger and be Deu 13:17
a nation of * and angry men who Deu 28:50
And so the * anger of the Lord Jos 7:26
Jonathan left the table in * 1Sa 20:34
* anger of the Lord is upon you.” 2Ch 28:11
* anger will turn away from us. 2Ch 29:10
* anger will turn away from you. 2Ch 30:8
cleared up and the * wrath of our Ez 10:14
Though they are * as young Job 4:10
And then in * fury he rebukes Ps 2:5
For he was angry. * flames Ps 18:8
in the * fire of your presence. Ps 21:9,10
I am surrounded by * Ps 57:4
Your * wrath has overwhelmed me. Ps 88:16
frightened by the * anger of those Is 7:4
day of his wrath and * anger. Is 13:9
in my wrath and * anger, and the Is 13:13
These *, violent people, with a Is 33:19
hearts, for the * anger of the Lord Jer 4:8
Lord, and crushed by his * anger. Jer 4:26
* anger of the Lord is upon them. Jer 12:13
by the * winds off the desert. Jer 13:24,25
of the * anger of the Lord. Jer 25:38
the world. My * anger will bring Jer 49:37
save yourselves from the * anger Jer 51:45
to me in the day of his * wrath. Lam 1:12
Go after them in * pursuit and Lam 3:66
like silver in * heat, and you will Eze 22:22
as much as my * anger tells me to. Hos 11:9
The storm was too * to fight Jon 1:13
his * anger from destroying us.” Jon 3:9
They are a * people, more fierce Hab 1:8
They are a fierce people, more * Hab 1:8
before the * anger of the Lord Zep 2:2
began to rise. A * storm developed Lk 8:23

FIERCELY
and javelin. * he paws the ground Job 39:24
The bellows blow *; Jer 6:29
on they plied him * with a host of Lk 11:53,54

FIERCENESS
consume them with the * of your Ps 69:24
He loosed on them the * of his Ps 78:49
by the * of the anger of the Lord. Jer 25:37
The Lord will not call off the * Jer 30:24
of the wine of the * of his wrath. Rev 16:19
* of the wrath of Almighty God. Rev 19:15

FIERCER
Israel will be even * this time. Num 32:14

FIERCEST
his * anger has been poured out. Lam 4:11
my * anger and wrath upon them. Zep 3:8

FIERY
Literally, “Make a * serpent.” Num 21:8f
beneath a * barrage of brimstone. Job 18:15
Chase them with your * storms, Ps 83:15
adder, a * serpent to destroy you! Is 14:29
He sat upon a * throne brought in Dan 7:9
* arrows aimed at you by Satan. Eph 6:16
den of lions, and in a * furnace. Heb 11:34
the test tube of * trials, it will 1Pe 1:7
you go through the * trials ahead, 1Pe 4:12

FIERY-RED
their riders wore * breastplates, Rev 9:17,18

FIFTEEN
frame-piece being * feet high and Ex 26:15,16
The height of each frame was * Ex 36:21
to sixty shall pay * dollars; Lev 27:4
* thousand troops were in Karkor. Ju 8:10
Ziba, who had * sons and twenty 2Sa 9:10,11
Ziba's * sons and twenty servants; 2Sa 19:17
thirty feet long and * feet deep. 1Ki 6:3
made from olive wood, each * feet 1Ki 6:23-28
* feet from wing tip to wing tip. 1Ki 6:23-28
were twelve to * feet across. 1Ki 7:10
Amaziah lived * years longer than 2Ki 14:17
I will add * years to his life 2Ki 20:6
thirty feet wide, and * feet high. 2Ch 4:1
* feet across from rim to rim. 2Ch 4:2
Judah lived on for * years after 2Ch 25:25
will let you live * more years. Is 38:5
up to my knees. * hundred feet Eze 47:5
feet long and * feet wide!” Zec 5:2
stayed there with him for * days. Gal 1:18

FIFTEENTH
Sinai, arriving there on the * Ex 16:1
Literally, “on the * day of the Lev 23:33,34f
IT WAS ON the * day of April Num 1:1
on the * day of September Num 29:1
Literally, “on the * day of the Num 29:12f
Literally, “on the * day of the Num 33:3,4f
Literally, “on the * day of the 1Ki 12:32,33f
king during the * year of the reign 2Ki 14:23
*, the group led by Bilgah; 1Ch 24:7-18
*, Jeremoth and twelve of his sons 1Ch 25:9-31
in June of the * year of King Asa's 2Ch 15:10
It was on the * day of September Ez 3:6
year, on the * day of the month.” Eze 32:17f
IN THE * year of the reign of Lk 3:1

FIFTH
That ended the * day. Gen 1:23
a * day (or, ‘period of time’).” Gen 1:23f
and gave birth to her * son. Gen 30:17
a * of all the crops . ” Gen 41:34,35f
And when you harvest it, a * of Gen 47:24
Finally, in the * year, the crop Lev 19:25
consisting of a * of a bushel of Lev 23:13
Bake this bread from a * of a Lev 23:17
using a * of a bushel for each. Lev 24:5-8
he must add a * to its value. Lev 27:31
On the * day came Shelumi-el, the Num 7:36-41
“On the * day of the festival, Num 29:26,27
first day of the * month” (of the Num 33:38,39f
The * tribe to be assigned its Jos 19:24,25,26
So his mother took a * of it to a Ju 17:4,5
In the * year of Rehoboam's 1Ki 14:25
reign during the * year of the 2Ki 8:16
was Nethanel, his * was Raddai, 1Ch 2:14
The * was Shephatiah, the son of 1Ch 3:3
the fourth, Rapha, the *. 1Ch 8:1
Jeremiah was * in command; 1Ch 12:8-13
*, the group led by Malchijah; 1Ch 24:7-18
*, Nethaniah and twelve of his 1Ch 25:9-31
Elam (the *), 1Ch 26:2,3
Nethanel (the *), 1Ch 26:4,5
The commander of the * Division 1Ch 27:8
on duty the * month of each year. 1Ch 27:8
Jerusalem in the * year of King 2Ch 12:2
Within three days, on the * day Ez 10:9
same reply. The * time, Neh 6:5,6
in December of the * year of the Jer 36:9
On the tenth day of the * month Jer 52:12
in this instance, * removed. Dan 5:11f
Literally, “fourth, *, seventh, Zec 8:19f
And when he broke open the * Rev 6:9
THEN THE * angel blew his trumpet Rev 9:1
Then the * angel poured out his Rev 16:10
The * with sardonyx; Rev 21:18,19,20

FIFTIES
hundreds, *, and tens. Ex 18:25
hundreds, *, and tens to decide Deu 1:15

FIFTIETH
“Every * year, on the Day of Lev 25:8
For the * year shall be holy, a Lev 25:10

FIFTY
Suppose you find * godly people Gen 18:24
And God replied, “If I find * Gen 18:26
for the affairs of * people; Ex 18:21
There are to be * loops on each Ex 26:4,5
Then make * golden clasps to Ex 26:6
Use * loops along the edges of Ex 26:10,11
together with * bronze clasps. Ex 26:10,11
long roof-sheets. * blue ribbons Ex 36:11,12
Then * clasps of gold were made Ex 36:13
Then he made * loops along the Ex 36:17
end of each, and * small bronze Ex 36:18
“The Festival of Pentecost: * Lev 23:15,16
ages thirty to * who are able to Num 4:3
ages of thirty and * who are Num 4:21,22,23
men from thirty to * who are Num 4:29
the men thirty to * years of age Num 4:35
who were thirty to * years old Num 4:46,47,48
and are to retire at the age of *. Num 8:23,24
Two hundred and * popular Num 16:2
pay her father * of silver.” Deu 22:28,29f
* footmen to run ahead of him. 2Sa 15:1
Literally, “paid him * shekels of 2Sa 24:24f
and recruited * men to run down the 1Ki 1:5
them in two caves—* in each—and had 1Ki 18:3,4
with * soldiers to arrest him. 2Ki 1:9
and destroy you and your * men!” 2Ki 1:10
captain with * men to demand, “O 2Ki 1:11
and destroy you and your * men.” 2Ki 1:12
Once more the king sent * men, 2Ki 1:13
lives of these, your * servants. 2Ki 1:13
Jordan River as * of the young 2Ki 2:6,7
say the word and * of our best 2Ki 2:16
Then * men searched for three 2Ki 2:17
head sold for * dollars and a pint 2Ki 6:25
Jehoahaz's army to * mounted 2Ki 13:7
against him with * men from Gilead, 2Ki 15:25
also, two hundred * of them were 2Ch 8:10
and, ten shekels at ten shekels! * Eze 45:12
When you came to draw * gallons Hag 2:16,17
the country and walked the * miles Mt 15:21
colorful groups of * or a hundred Mk 6:39,40
About * miles away. Mk 7:24f
of about * each,” Jesus replied. Lk 9:14
“You aren't even * years old—sure, Jn 8:57
This annual celebration came * Act 2:1f

FIFTY-CENT
came from the * head tax collected Ex 38:25,26

FIFTY-FIVE
he reigned * years, in Jerusalem. 2Ch 33:1

FIFTY-ONE
* years before this prophecy. Nah 3:8f

FIFTY-THREE
See 1 Kings 15:22. * cisterns have Jer 41:9f

FIFTY-TWO
In all, he reigned * years, in 2Ch 26:3
—just * days after we had begun! Neh 6:15
During those * days many letters Neh 6:17

FIG
So they strung * leaves together Gen 3:7
of grape vines, * trees, Deu 8:8
“Then they said to the * tree, Ju 9:10
“But the * tree also refused. Ju 9:11
and two hundred * cakes, and packed 1Sa 25:18
gave him part of a * cake, two 1Sa 30:11,12
of bread, some * bars, and a jar of 1Ki 14:3
Vast supplies of flour, * cakes, 1Ch 12:40
myrtle, palm, and * trees and to Neh 8:15
Their grape vines and * trees Ps 105:33
Literally, “The * tree puts forth Sol 2:13f
away as an early * is hungrily Is 28:4
the bark from the * trees, leaving Joe 1:7
The grapevines are dead; the * Joe 1:12
their fruit; the * trees and grape Joe 2:22
*, however much I long for it! Mic 7:1

(FIG Con't)
Even though the * trees are all Hab 3:17
noticed a * tree beside the road. Mt 21:19
the * tree withered up. Mt 21:19
the * tree wither so quickly?" Mt 21:20
"Now learn a lesson from the * Mt 24:32
A little way off he noticed a * Mk 11:13
passed the * tree he had cursed, Mk 11:20
* tree you cursed has withered!" Mk 11:21
"Now, here is a lesson from a * Mk 13:28
"A man planted a * tree in his Lk 13:6
and there hasn't been a single *!' Lk 13:7
the * tree, or any other tree. Lk 21:29
* tree before Philip found you." Jn 1:48
I had seen you under the * tree? Jn 1:50
Can you pick olives from a * Jas 3:12
—like green fruit from * trees Rev 6:13

FIGHT
but again there was a * over it. Gen 26:21
our enemies and * against us and Ex 1:10
by having to * their way through, Ex 13:17,18
The Lord will * for you, and you Ex 14:14
of Amalek came to * against the Ex 17:8
to * the army of Amalek. Ex 17:9
went out to * the army of Amalek. Ex 17:10
a * with one of the men of Israel. Lev 24:10
During the * the Egyptian man's Lev 24:11
and he will * for you with his Deu 1:30
We will go into the land and * Deu 1:41
on up into the hill country to *. Deu 1:43
Don't start a *! Deu 2:5
So the Lord helped us * against Deu 3:3
the Lord your God will * for you.' Deu 3:22
afraid as you go out to * today! Deu 20:3
He will * for you against your Deu 20:4
"As you approach a city to * Deu 20:10
* for him against his enemies." Deu 33:7
No one has any * left in him Jos 2:11
will come out to * as they did Jos 8:5
their armies to * for their lives Jos 9:1
kings want to * the Israelis Jos 11:20
and * as well as I could then! Jos 14:11
Lead them to Mount Tabor, to * Ju 4:7
I can't let all of you * the Ju 7:2
remained who were willing to *. Ju 7:3
'We * for God and for Gideon!' Ju 7:18
went out to * the Midianites?" Ju 8:1
up an army and come on out and *!' Ju 9:29
Go on out and *!" Ju 9:38
us to help you * against Ammon? Ju 12:1
Is that anything for you to * us Ju 12:3
him, "Shall we * further against Ju 20:22,23,24
next day to * at the same place. Ju 20:22,23,24
go out again and * against our Ju 20:27,28
Those who * against the Lord 1Sa 2:10
the wilderness. * as you never 1Sa 4:9
if they say, 'Come on up and *!' 1Sa 14:10
and we'll show you how to *!" 1Sa 14:12
Send me a man who will * with 1Sa 17:10
Saul's army to * the Philistines. 1Sa 17:13
"How can a kid like you * with a 1Sa 17:33
David go out to * Goliath, he asked 1Sa 17:55
David would be killed in the *. 1Sa 18:25
to * the whole Philistine army!" 1Sa 23:3
and returned to * the Philistines. 1Sa 23:28
"Come and help us *," King 1Sa 28:1
"Why can't I * your enemies?" 1Sa 29:8
each side to * in mortal combat. 2Sa 2:15
The two armies then began to * 2Sa 2:17
to Jerusalem to * against the 2Sa 5:6
I go out and * against them? 2Sa 5:19
he would have to * on two fronts, 2Sa 10:9
to * the Syrians in the fields. 2Sa 10:9
* harder next time, and conquer 2Sa 11:25
my two sons had a * out in the 2Sa 14:5,6
that they must not * against their 1Ki 12:23,24
will * against them in the plains; 1Ki 20:25
* no one except King Ahab himself. 1Ki 22:31
Will you help me * him?" 2Ki 3:6,7,8
man who could *, old and young, and 2Ki 3:21
and prepare to * for his throne. 2Ki 10:2,3
his army and come out and *. 2Ki 14:8
him to help him * the attacking 2Ki 16:7
"If I go out and * them, will you 1Ch 14:10
at your command to * their enemies, 2Ch 6:34
" 'The Lord says, Do not * 2Ch 11:4
and refused to * against Jeroboam. 2Ch 11:4
O people of Israel, do not * 2Ch 13:12
in his chariot, to * the Syrians, 2Ch 18:34
But you will not need to *! 2Ch 20:17
defeated no matter how well you *; 2Ch 25:8
our God to * our battles for us!" 2Ch 32:8
a * with you, O king of Judah! 2Ch 35:21
I have come only to * the king of 2Ch 35:21
and glorious; * for your friends, Neh 4:14
and God will * for us." Neh 4:19
Why should you * against him Job 33:13
Now get ready to *, for I am Job 38:3
O LORD, * those fighting me; Ps 35:1
Don't give victory to those who * Ps 35:19
So many are proud to * against Ps 56:1
Oh, help us * against our Ps 108:12
to hate and * me, yet they do! Ps 109:3
scoff at wisdom and * the facts? Pro 1:22
the evil-minded only wants to *. Pro 13:2
Sinners love to *; Pro 17:19
for a man to stay out of a *. Pro 20:3
To obey the law is to * evil. Pro 28:4
Don't * the facts of nature. Ecc 7:13
seven women will * over each of Is 4:1
Then we'll * our way into Is 7:6
they will not * each other any Is 11:13
will come and * upon Mount Zion. Is 31:4,5
Assyria, came to * against the Is 36:1
for I will * those who fight you, Is 49:25
for I will fight those who * you, Is 49:25
Who will dare to * against me Is 50:8
If any nation comes to * you, it Is 54:15
For I will not * against you Is 57:16
They will * against you like a Jer 15:20
and I myself will * against you, Jer 21:5
I will * against this city of Jer 21:13
until you die. Why * the facts? Jer 32:5
and they will * against it and Jer 34:22
from Jerusalem to * the Egyptians. Jer 37:5
Yes, prepare to * with Babylon, Jer 50:14
mightiest soldiers no longer *; Jer 51:30
of Babylon * against each other. Jer 51:46
to * against Nebuchadnezzar. Eze 17:15
God, and you will * against Eze 38:21
I will * you with sword, Eze 38:22
I will go again to * my way back, Dan 10:20,21
will stand up [and * for you in Dan 12:1
The storm was too fierce to * Jon 1:13
nations shall no longer * each Mic 4:3
nations, full of * and boldness, Nah 2:11
men who love to argue and to *. Hab 1:3
shall lead his people as they *! Zec 9:14
The Lord is with them as they *; Zec 10:5
the nations to * Jerusalem; Zec 14:1
war, to * against those nations. Zec 14:3
the Lord, and will * against each Zec 14:13
He does not * nor shout; Mt 12:19
exclaimed, "Master, shall we *? Lk 22:49
The kings of the earth unite to * Act 4:25,26
punish those who * against the Rom 2:8
mind and wins the * and makes Rom 7:23,24,25
purpose in every step. I * to win. 1Co 9:26
We are in this * together. Php 1:30
my command to you: * well in the 1Ti 1:18
patient and gentle. * on for God. 1Ti 6:12
And these teachers * truth just 2Ti 3:8
a * to take it away from them. Jas 4:2
they are not for you, for they * 1Pe 2:11
already won your * with those who 1Jn 4:4
But who could possibly * and win 1Jn 5:5
you suddenly and * against them Rev 2:16
"Who is able to * against him?" Rev 13:4
The Dragon gave him power to * Rev 13:7
Literally, "It was permitted to * Rev 13:7f
their armies to * against the one Rev 19:19

FIGHTERS
its men were known as hard *. Jos 10:2
selected the best * in his army, 2Sa 10:9
they must not be drunkards or * Tit 1:7

FIGHTING
"This * between our men has got Gen 13:8
were * each other inside her! Gen 25:22
again, he saw two of them *. Ex 2:13
"Jehovah is * for them and Ex 14:25
"If two men are *, and one hits Ex 21:18
"If two men are *, and in the Ex 21:22
go across and do all the *?" Num 32:6
"If two men are * and the wife Deu 25:11
But the Lord was * for Israel. Jos 10:14
of Israel was * for his people. Jos 10:42
* men, letting not one escape. Ju 3:29
summoning their * forces, and all Ju 6:35
troops to begin * and killing each Ju 7:22
soldier by * the Lord's battles." 1Sa 18:17
for you are * his battles; 1Sa 25:28
that the enemies' best men were *; 2Sa 11:16
the Israelis were * at Gath, a 2Sa 21:20,21
for God was * against them. 1Ch 5:22
pressed with heavy * all around 1Ch 10:3
were officers of the * priests. 1Ch 12:24-37
wars, and internal * of city 2Ch 15:6
Seir to begin * among themselves, 2Ch 20:22
strong horn of a mighty * bull. Ps 18:2
O LORD, FIGHT those * me; Ps 35:1
are * me, yet he will rescue me. Ps 55:18
be rid of tension, * and quarrels. Pro 22:10
Who is always * and quarreling? Pro 23:29,30
Greed causes *; Pro 28:25
else, neighbors * neighbors, youths Is 3:5
I will set them to * against Is 19:2
And all the nations * Jerusalem Is 29:7
when you keep on * and quarreling? Is 58:4
All Judah will be * at Zec 14:14
out Satan, he is * himself, and Mt 12:26
risen and they were * heavy seas. Mt 14:23,24
And if Satan is * against Mk 3:26
that Satan is * against himself by Lk 11:18
yourselves * even against God." Act 5:39
again and saw two men of Israel *. Act 7:26
and shouldn't be * like this! Act 7:26
*, lying, bitterness, and gossip. Rom 1:29
and lust, or *, or jealousy. Rom 13:12,13
And what value was there in * 1Co 15:32
us are constantly * each other to Gal 5:17
hatred and *, jealousy and anger, Gal 5:20
For we are not * against people Eph 6:12
come for me to stop * and rest. 2Ti 4:7
took from the kings he had been *. Heb 7:4
If you do, you will be * against Jas 4:11

FIGHTS
pasture. So * broke out between Gen 13:7
the Lord your God * for you, just Jos 23:10
Don't get into needless *. Pro 3:30
A quick-tempered man starts *; Pro 15:18
A fool gets into constant *. Pro 18:6,7
A quarrelsome man starts * as Pro 26:21
Fools start * everywhere while Pro 29:8
A hot-tempered man starts * and Pro 29:22
Each * against his brother to Is 9:19,20
violent man who * at the drop of a Is 29:21
Woe to the man who * with his Is 45:9
WHAT IS CAUSING the quarrels and * Jas 4:1

FIGS
samples of the pomegranates and *. Num 13:23
crops—the *, vines, and Num 20:5
to boil some dried * and to make a 2Ki 20:7
with wine, grapes, *, and all sorts Neh 13:15
"The fig tree puts forth its *." Sol 2:13f
an ointment of * and spread it over Is 38:21
yes, and your grapes and *; Jer 5:17
Their * and grapes will Jer 8:13
I saw two baskets of * placed in Jer 24:2
just-ripened *, but in the other Jer 24:2
in the other the * were spoiled and Jer 24:2
I replied, "*, some very good and Jer 24:3
Then the Lord said: "The good * Jer 24:4,5
"But the rotten * represent Jer 24:8
I will treat them like spoiled *, Jer 24:8
like rotting *, too bad to eat. Jer 29:16,17
How satisfying, like the early * Hos 9:10
the locusts ate your * and olive Amo 4:9
and * when harvest days are over. Mic 7:1
like first-ripe * that fall into Nah 3:12
the grapes and * and pomegranates Hag 2:18,19
thorn bushes or * with thistles. Mt 7:16
any *, but there were only leaves. Mt 21:19
see if he could find any * on it. Mk 11:13
fruit it produces. * never grow on Lk 6:44
If we get * next year, fine; Lk 13:9
fig tree, or * from a grape vine? Jas 3:12

FIGURE
Let's * out a way to put an end Ex 1:10
Name your own *! Num 22:16,17
the total census * of the people of Num 26:62
were still trying to * it out. Ju 14:14
The total population * which he 1Ch 21:5
of wood and carves the * of a man. Is 44:13
stops to think or * out, "Why, Is 44:19
historical * like Nebuchadnezzar. Eze 38:2,3f
If this is a literal *, it is no Rev 9:16f

FIGURED
"Well," Abraham said, "I * Gen 20:11,12

FIGURES
The above * are approximate. Lev 27:3f
So these are the census * as Num 26:63
* of angels, palm trees, and open 1Ki 6:29
Benjamin in his * because he was so 1Ch 21:6

FILE
from the rank and * of the 1Ki 12:31

FILED
The Lord has * a lawsuit against Hos 4:1

FILIGREE
and a jasper—all set in gold *. Ex 39:13

FILL
numbers increase. * the earth!" Gen 1:21,22
and * the earth and subdue it; Gen 1:28
Come, let's * him with wine and Gen 19:32
Let's * him with wine again Gen 19:34
his servants to * the men's sacks Gen 42:25
manager to * each of their sacks Gen 44:1
to draw water and * the water Ex 2:16
They will * your ovens and your Ex 8:3,4
They will * your palace, and the Ex 10:6
increased enough to * the land. Ex 23:30
the altar, and * it with water. Ex 30:17,18
the altar, and * it with water. Ex 40:7
of the Lord, and * his hands with Lev 16:12
and you can eat your * in safety. Lev 25:19
You shall eat your *, and live Lev 26:4,5
When you have eaten your *, Deu 8:10
"You may eat your * of the Deu 23:24
"* four barrels with water," he 1Ki 18:33
"The Lord says to * this dry 2Ki 3:16
He will yet * your mouth with Job 8:21
Just as he is about to * his Job 20:23
defending them. * all who love you Ps 5:11
Though sins * our hearts, you Ps 65:3

(FILL Con't)
* the followers of God with joy. Ps 70:4
The people ate their *. Ps 78:29
swarms of flies to * the land, and Ps 78:45
wide and see if I won't * it. Ps 81:10
Lord, when doubts * my mind, when Ps 94:19
and * them with their dead. Ps 110:6
them and will let them * my life. Ps 119:48
For we have had our * of contempt Ps 123:3,4
and he will * your barns with wheat Pro 3:9,10
away, for they * you with living Pro 3:22
Let her love alone * you with Pro 5:19
Come on, let's take our * of Pro 7:18
wealthy. I * their treasuries. Pro 8:21
shall have his * of bread." Pro 12:11f
for as the waters * the sea, so Is 11:9
the shields. They * your choicest Is 22:6,7
* the whole earth with her fruit! Is 27:6
bodies will * the land, and the Is 34:3
Their howls will * the night. Is 34:14
the desert. * the valleys; Is 40:4
And the joy of the Lord shall * Is 41:16
bruise him and * him with grief. Is 53:10
I will * everyone living in this Jer 13:13
For I will * Jerusalem with dead Jer 19:12
has slain shall * the earth from Jer 25:33
Aren't the Jews enough to * them Jer 49:1
the Temple! * its courts with the Eze 9:7
the fire to boil. * it with Eze 24:4
and * the valleys with your bones. Eze 32:5
I will * your mountains with the Eze 35:8
the flocks that * Jerusalem's Eze 36:37,38
Fish of every kind will * the Eze 47:10
Water will * the dry stream beds Joe 3:18
For I will * the wise men of Edom Ob 1:8
unfairness, and * Jerusalem with Mic 3:10
as the waters * the sea, with an Hab 2:14
rob and kill to * their masters' Zep 1:9
and I will * it with splendor." Hag 2:7f
Temple, and I will * this place Hag 2:7
wise enough to * their lamps with Mt 25:2,3,4
Level the mountains! * up the Lk 3:5
to * them to the brim with water. Jn 2:7,8
to * our hearts with his love. Rom 5:5
poor, for I do not * my sermons 1Co 1:17
to * our bodies with himself. 1Co 6:13
up, that he might * all things Eph 4:10
Literally, "that he might * all Eph 4:10f
and * you with his great peace. Col 1:2
Let heaven * your thoughts; Col 3:2
see you again, to * up any little 1Th 3:10

FILLED
be * with birds of every kind." Gen 1:20
for the earth is * with crime Gen 6:12,13
NOW WAR * the land— Gen 14:1
shoulder and * it at the spring. Gen 24:15,16
and drew water and * the jug. Gen 24:45
So they * up his wells with Gen 26:15
Philistines had * after his Gen 26:18
* with the Spirit of God." Gen 41:38
They were * with terror. Gen 42:28
he saw the wagons * with food that Gen 45:27
and they * the land of Goshen. Ex 1:7
Every home in Egypt will be * Ex 8:3,4
and * the nation's homes. Ex 8:13
Your homes will be * with them Ex 8:21
Judah), and have * him with the Ex 31:3
God has * them both with Ex 35:35
and the altar, and * it with water Ex 40:30
and the glory of the Lord * it. Ex 40:34
of the Lord * the Tabernacle. Ex 40:35
your souls and be * with remorse; Lev 23:32
one pound, both * with grain Num 7:13
the earth shall be * with the glory Num 14:20,21
give me a palace * with silver and Num 22:18
gave me a palace * with silver and Num 24:13
was completely * with people. Ju 16:27
* him with depression and fear. 1Sa 16:14
and she was * with contempt for 2Sa 6:16
off the altar and * the trench. 1Ki 18:35
forces that * the countryside! 1Ki 20:27
me a new bowl * with salt." 2Ki 2:20
valley will be * with water, and 2Ki 3:17
them aside as they are *!" 2Ki 4:4
her, and she * one after another! 2Ki 4:5
and they all came and * the 2Ki 10:20,21
Now the land of Israel was * with 2Ki 17:5
And Jerusalem was * from one end 2Ki 21:16
for he had * Jerusalem with blood, 2Ki 24:3,4
as a bright cloud, * the Temple so 2Ch 5:13,14
And the glory of the Lord * the 2Ch 7:1
from Israel, were * with deep joy. 2Ch 30:25
From one end to the other it is * Ez 9:11
and everyone was * with joy! Neh 8:17
streets * with shouting people. Est 8:15
the Jews were * with joy and had a Est 8:17
"My skin is * with worms and Job 7:5
"My life passes swiftly away, * Job 9:25
count. I am * with frustration. Job 10:15
Yet they forgot that he had * Job 22:18
My weary nights are * with pain Job 30:17
Their hearts are * to the brim Ps 5:9
Their tongues are * with Ps 5:9
My mind is * with apprehension Ps 6:3
I will be glad, yes, * with joy Ps 9:2
gods shall all be * with sorrow; Ps 16:4
Heart, body, and soul are * with Ps 16:9
men whom you have * with your Ps 17:13,14
and * my days with frustration. Ps 32:3
the earth is * with his tender Ps 33:5
they come together in meetings * Ps 35:15
My days are * with anguish. Ps 38:5,6
Let me recover and be * with Ps 39:13
Your words are * with grace; Ps 45:2
they are * with panic like a Ps 48:6
Literally, "Your right hand is * Ps 48:10f
they are wise and * with insight. Ps 49:3
heart, O God, * with clean thoughts Ps 51:10
The pastures are * with flocks Ps 65:13
Let the whole earth be * with his Ps 72:19
When I saw this, what turmoil * Ps 73:21
Then my nights were * with Ps 77:6
and we took root and * the land. Ps 80:9
our land will be * with his Ps 85:9
All our days are * with sighing. Ps 90:9
heart was so * with turmoil? Ps 132:1
Their mouths are * with lies; Ps 144:8
of the evil man is * with curses. Pro 10:11
A good man's mind is * with Pro 12:5
A youngster's heart is * with Pro 22:15
Whose heart is * with anguish and Pro 23:29,30
is lovely as a goblet * with wine. Sol 7:2
They have * their barns with Is 3:14
the Temple was * with his glory. Is 6:1
the whole earth is * with his Is 6:3
entire sanctuary was * with smoke. Is 6:4
to the sea, will be * with glory. Is 9:1
again be great, * with joy like Is 9:3
The meek will be * with fresh Is 29:19
His lips are * with fury; Is 30:27
The streams of Edom will be * Is 34:9
They cannot be * with hope and Is 38:18
to Jerusalem, * with joy and Is 51:11
Everything you do is * with sin; Is 59:6
shall again be * with flocks, and Is 65:10
land is once more * with people, Jer 3:16
bottle shall be * with wine." Jer 13:12f
* it up with all your evil deeds. Jer 16:18
they have * this place with the Jer 19:4
hand this wine cup * to the brim Jer 25:15
The cities will be * with joy Jer 30:19
The earth is * with your cry of Jer 46:12
is * with sin against the Holy Jer 51:5
cities shall be * with enemies, Jer 51:14
like fields * with locusts in a Jer 51:14
great monster and * his belly with Jer 51:34,35
mourn, no longer * with joyous Lam 1:4
he has * my path with detours. Lam 3:9
He has * me with bitterness, and Lam 3:15
We are * with fear, for we are Lam 3:47
Our homes, our nation, now are * Lam 5:2
* with eyes around their edges. Eze 1:18
lives are * with sin will recover. Eze 7:13
Jerusalem is * with violence, so Eze 7:23
And the cloud of glory * the Eze 10:3
The Temple was * with the cloud Eze 10:4
of the Temple was * with the Eze 10:4
and * your streets with the dead. Eze 11:6
it into a city * with merchants. Eze 17:3,4
you do, all is * with sin. Eze 21:24
Every mountain top is * with Eze 22:9
your island warehouse is * to the Eze 27:25
Your great wealth * you with Eze 28:16
Your heart was * with pride Eze 28:17
* with those the sword has killed. Eze 35:8
will be rebuilt and * with people. Eze 36:10
again you will be * with homes. Eze 36:11
and walled and * with people!' Eze 36:35
that are now * with people Eze 38:12
and the glory of the Lord * the Eze 43:5
glory of the Lord * the Temple of Eze 44:4
The shores will be * with nets Eze 47:10
Then Nebuchadnezzar was * with Dan 3:19
his mind is * with divine knowledge Dan 5:12
* with enlightenment and wisdom. Dan 5:14
they were suddenly * with Dan 10:7
and defeat them. * with pride Dan 11:12
it is * with sadness, and all Hos 4:3
luxuriant vine all * with fruit! Hos 10:1
home, for you have * it with sin Mic 2:10
But as for me, I am * with power, Mic 3:8
your wives, and * your city and Nah 2:12
Merchants, numerous as stars, * Nah 3:16
You have * the countryside with Hab 2:8
all the earth is *, as the waters Hab 2:14
it into pockets * with holes! Hag 1:6
to Jerusalem * with mercy; Zec 1:16
is a bushel basket * with the sin Zec 5:6
the plain were * with people, the Zec 7:7
be * with boys and girls at play. Zec 8:5
see it happen and be * with fear; Zec 9:5
be * with pride at their success. Zec 12:7
all Jerusalem was * with rumors. Mt 2:3
An evil-hearted man is * with Mt 12:35
were * with sorrow and dread. Mt 17:22,23
"Then the king was * with pity Mt 18:27
and the banquet hall was * with Mt 22:10
to be * with anguish and despair. Mt 26:37
One of them ran and * a sponge Mt 27:48
but also * with joy, and rushed to Mt 28:8
By sunset the courtyard was * Mk 1:32,33
A home * with strife and Mk 3:25
And they were * with awe and said Mk 4:41
they were * with terror and dread. Mk 10:32
and began to be * with horror and Mk 14:33
got a sponge and * it with sour Mk 15:36
he will be * with the Holy Spirit, Lk 1:15
she was * with the Holy Spirit. Lk 1:41
Then his father Zacharias was * Lk 1:67
He was a good man, very devout, * Lk 2:25
both boats were * with fish and on Lk 5:7
flask * with expensive perfume. Lk 7:37
And they were * with awe and fear Lk 8:25
the man was * with thousands Lk 8:30
The home was * with mourning Lk 8:52
Then he was * with the joy of the Lk 10:21
* with civil war is doomed; Lk 11:17
so is a home * with argument and Lk 11:17
If you are * with light within, Lk 11:36
coming, and was * with loving pity Lk 15:20
undecided, * with joy and doubt. Lk 24:41
to Jerusalem * with mighty joy, Lk 24:52
I am * with joy at his success. Jn 3:29
And twelve baskets were * with Jn 6:13
And the house was * with Jn 12:3
so that you will be * with my joy. Jn 15:11
Instead you are only * with Jn 16:6
that they would be * with my joy. Jn 17:13
above them and it * the house where Act 2:2
And everyone present was * with Act 2:4
'No wonder my heart is * with joy Act 2:26
Then Peter, * with the Holy Act 4:8
and they were all * with the Holy Act 4:31
"Ananias, Satan has * your heart. Act 5:3
"And instead you have * all Act 5:28
so that you may be * with the Holy Act 9:17
The room was * with weeping Act 9:39
was doing, he was * with excitement Act 11:23
so that he was * with maggots and Act 12:23
Then Paul, * with the Holy Act 13:9
were * with joy and with the Holy Act 13:52
the city was * with confusion. Act 19:29
us "not guilty," * us with Rom 8:30
who are * with the Spirit. 1Co 3:1
loving and * with the Holy Spirit. 2Co 6:6
* with conceit and disunity. 2Co 12:20
you will finally be * with Christ. Gal 4:19
which is his body, * with himself, Eph 1:23
And so at last you will be * up Eph 3:18,19
point of being * full with Christ. Eph 4:13
that path; be * instead with the Eph 5:18
that you will be * with his mighty, Col 1:11
and you are * with God through your Col 2:10
there will be * with love that 1Ti 1:5
let your hearts be * with God alone Jas 4:8
and golden vials * with incense—the Rev 5:8
Then the angel * the censer with Rev 8:5
a golden flask * with the terrible Rev 15:7
The temple was * with smoke from Rev 15:8
It was * with the glory of God, Rev 21:11

FILLING
from the city was * the sky, and Jos 8:20,21
the Lord is * the entire building! 1Ki 8:11
your being, * your life with joy. Pro 2:10
to you, * you with futile hopes. Jer 23:16
gushing blood, * the ravines to the Eze 32:6
in their steps, * up the full Mt 23:32
God, * us with God's goodness. Rom 4:25

FILLS
a bright cloud * the Temple! 1Ki 8:10
but * me with bitter sorrows. Job 9:18
* his hands with lightning bolts. Job 36:32
rebukes them and * them with fear. Ps 2:5
glory of your name * all the earth Ps 8:1
glory of your name * the earth. Ps 8:9
He * me with strength and Ps 18:32
He * my life with good things! Ps 103:5
and * the earth with fruit. Ps 104:13
and * the hungry soul with good. Ps 107:9
your nation, and * your barns with Ps 147:14
Deceit * hearts that are plotting Pro 12:20
for evil; joy * hearts that are Pro 12:20
Like a bird that * her nest with Jer 17:11
them that wickedness * this land. Jer 23:15
His brilliant splendor * the Hab 3:3
his glory * the heavens, and the Hab 3:3
* you with power from heaven." Lk 24:49

FILLY
What a lovely * Sol 1:9

FILTH
the * and decay they found there. 2Ch 29:16
* by the horrors and the fire. Is 4:2,3,4
with vomit; * is everywhere. Is 28:8

(FILTH Con't)
I will cover you with * and show Nah 3:6
their garments with the world's *; Rev 3:4

FILTHINESS
will be clean—your * will be washed Eze 36:25

FILTHY
less * than you consider me to be! Job 9:31
they are * with sin—corrupt and Ps 53:3
like * things you hate to touch. Is 30:22
and your fingers are * with sin. Is 59:3
we find they are but * rags. Is 64:6
Literally, "* as a menstruating Is 64:6f
Let her be thrown out like * Lam 1:17
What a * heart you have, says Eze 16:30
Because I see your * sins, your Eze 16:36
of Idols, * and foul— you are Eze 22:3
corruption of your * lewdness, of Eze 24:13
refused, remain * until my fury has Eze 24:13
worship was as foul as * rags. Eze 36:17
WOE TO *, sinful Jerusalem, city Zep 3:1
Joshua's clothing was * as he Zec 3:3
there, "Remove his * clothing." Zec 3:4
Their talk is foul and * like the Rom 3:13
don't touch their * things, and I 2Co 6:17

FILTHY-MOUTHED
for they are all *, wicked liars. Is 9:17

FINAL
so I will crush Egypt with a * Ex 7:4
Here is the * tabulation: Num 1:20-46
sons, who had the * responsibility Num 3:38
As his father was making * Ju 14:10,11
His agreement is eternal, *, 2Sa 23:5
upon Israel; the * total was never 1Ch 27:24
at the other. A * religious 2Ch 7:9
to be the court of * appeal in 2Ch 19:11
of * appeal in all civil cases; 2Ch 19:11
was his * word to them. 2Ch 19:11
On the * day, when the king was Est 1:10
Then he delivered his * punch Est 5:12
JOB'S * DEFENSE: Job 27:1
your fist and give them a * blow. Ps 74:11
WE CAN MAKE our plans, but the * Pro 16:1
God does is *—nothing can be added Ecc 3:14
Here is my * conclusion: fear God Ecc 12:13
to the * restoration under Christ. Jer 30:21f
The end has come; your * doom is Eze 7:5,6
evil prince of Israel, your * day Eze 21:25
when the day of * reckoning has Eze 21:29
to that * event in history. Dan 8:19
pure until the * end of all their Dan 11:35
all conflict with his * victory, Mt 12:20
was his * farewell to Galilee. Mk 10:1f
heaven until the * recovery of all Act 3:21,22
left with this * word from Paul Act 28:25
but even that isn't * proof. 1Co 4:4
I will write these * words of 1Co 16:21
until the day of * judgment comes. 2Pe 2:9

FINALLY
* THE DAY came when the Lord said Gen 7:1
until * the water covered all Gen 7:19
in Haran—and * arrived in Canaan. Gen 12:5
*, Abraham said, "Oh, let not Gen 18:32
Ishmael * died at the age of Gen 25:17
local residents * left him alone. Gen 26:22
Isaac sniffs his clothes, and * Gen 27:26
but you will * shake loose from him Gen 27:39,40
JACOB TRAVELED ON, * arriving in Gen 29:1
so much in love. * the time came Gen 29:21
Laban * caught up with Jacob Gen 31:25
* he went into Rachel's tent. Gen 31:33
and bowed, and * Rachel and Joseph Gen 33:7
So Jacob insisted, and * Esau Gen 33:11
not attacked. * they arrived at Gen 35:6
the midwife * exclaimed, Gen 35:17
So their father Israel * said to Gen 43:11
who * found their tongues! Gen 45:15
* see my fault," he confessed. Ex 9:27
Moses' arms * became too tired Ex 17:12
your crops. And, *, the Pilgrimage Ex 23:16
But * the workmen all left their Ex 36:4-7
commanded Moses. * they made the Ex 39:30
then be pronounced * cleansed. Lev 14:20
in praise to him. *, in the fifth Lev 19:25
over that, and * a covering of Num 4:8
spread over them. *, the carrying Num 4:14
without yeast; and * the grain Num 6:17
your children * live in the land I Num 15:1
when the land is * subdued before Num 32:22
Mount Nebo, and * to the plains of Num 33:48
terrible desert, * arriving among Deu 1:19,20,21
years to * get across Zered Brook Deu 2:14,15
them until * all were dead. Deu 2:14,15
times, you will * return to the Deu 4:30
Joshua and the other leaders * Jos 9:14,15
So the land * rested from its Jos 11:23
Azmon, until it * reached the Brook Jos 15:2,3,4
"* I brought you into the land Jos 24:8
When Joshua * disbanded the Ju 2:6
But * all that generation died; Ju 2:10
* they begged the Lord for help. Ju 4:2,3
everyone demanded. * they Ju 6:29
Gideon * died, an old, old man, Ju 8:32
"Then all the trees * turned to Ju 9:14
before Abimelech * captured the Ju 9:45
eighteen years. * the Israelis Ju 10:10
"* they went around Edom and Ju 11:18
It was then that Manoah * Ju 13:21
longer and * told her his secret. Ju 16:16,17
Delilah realized that he had * Ju 16:18
was * conquered by its enemies. Ju 18:30
urging him until * he gave in. Ju 19:7
*, just at dawn, they let her go. Ju 19:25
of justice. * the leaders of 1Sa 8:4
them anywhere. *, after searching 1Sa 9:5
was chosen. And *, the sacred lot 1Sa 10:21
the Israelis. * even the men 1Sa 14:22
When Samuel * found him, Saul 1Sa 15:13
"I have sinned," Saul * 1Sa 15:24
So Samuel * agreed and went with 1Sa 15:31
* THE LORD said to Samuel, "You 1Sa 16:1
When it was * realized what 1Sa 17:31
Saul * consented, "All right, go 1Sa 17:37
now with David. * Saul banned him 1Sa 18:13
* Saul agreed, and vowed, "As 1Sa 19:6
* King Achish said to his men, 1Sa 21:14,15
then I will * be safe again." 1Sa 27:1
* the woman said, "Well, whom do 1Sa 28:11
the woman until he * yielded and 1Sa 28:23
So Achish * summoned David and 1Sa 29:6
WHEN THE LORD * sent peace upon 2Sa 7:1
* the next morning David wrote a 2Sa 11:14
the matter until * the king agreed, 2Sa 13:27
think best," the king * replied. 2Sa 18:4
And Joab * said, "All right, go 2Sa 18:23
Abishag, from Shunam, was * 1Ki 1:3,4
When the Temple was * finished, 1Ki 7:51
this, but they * killed all except 1Ki 11:16,17,18
and when he * completed it by 1Ki 16:34
*, the seventh time, his servant 1Ki 18:44
*, toward evening, he died. 1Ki 22:35
* said, "All right, go ahead." 2Ki 2:17
Carmel and * returned to Samaria. 2Ki 2:25
the fruit trees; *, only Fort 2Ki 3:25
but even that * fell to them. 2Ki 3:25
and hiding it. * they said to each 2Ki 7:9
private chaplains. *, no one was 2Ki 10:11
at Samaria. * the Lord reduced 2Ki 13:7
city of Israel. *, in the ninth 2Ki 17:6
until the Lord * swept them away, 2Ki 17:23
them. * he returned to Jerusalem. 2Ki 23:20
So the Lord *, in his anger, 2Ki 24:20
its villages, and * by Shechem and 1Ch 7:28
* he decided to take it to the 1Ch 13:13
DAVID * SUBDUED the Philistines 1Ch 18:1
gold and silver. *, he weighed out 1Ch 28:18
* THE ACTUAL construction of the 2Ch 3:1
SO THE TEMPLE was * finished. 2Ch 5:1
* she exclaimed to the king, 2Ch 9:5
before * returning to Jerusalem. 2Ch 14:15
suggestions, but * a spirit stepped 2Ch 18:19,20
So the work went forward, and * 2Ch 24:13
He lived to a very old age, * 2Ch 24:15
Zechariah, and * King Joash himself 2Ch 24:21
Jerusalem. But * Hezekiah and the 2Ch 32:26
At that point Manasseh * realized 2Ch 33:13
but his reign was an evil one. * 2Ch 36:6
The Temple was * finished, as had Ez 6:14
* I stood before the Lord in Ez 9:5
The wall was * finished in early Neh 6:15
he still refused. * they spoke to Est 3:3,4
"Yet, *, the innocent shall come Job 17:8
sunny day until I * admitted all Ps 32:5
it that you are * treated fairly. Ps 48:11
until God's time * came—how God Ps 105:19
Then they * sang his praise. Ps 106:12
and were * destroyed by their sin. Ps 106:43
then these men will * listen to Ps 141:6,7
* have nothing worthwhile left. Pro 11:29
The wicked will * lose; Pro 21:18
the righteous will * win. Pro 21:18
Be patient and you will * win, Pro 25:15
* come to light for all to see. Pro 26:24,25,26
A bitter woman when she * Pro 30:21,22,23
chronic rebellion was * exhausted. Is 6:10f
When they * stop plundering, the Is 7:21,22
never have enough. * they will even Is 9:19,20
of my warnings will * dawn on you. Is 28:19
Does he not * plant his many Is 28:25
them when they are * desperate Jer 11:14
The next day when Pashhur * Jer 20:3
shall die. And * I will deliver Jer 21:7
of the world. And *, the king of Jer 25:26
Then *, on the ninth day of the Jer 52:6
for this hour and it is * here! Lam 2:16
And so the land will * be Eze 39:15,16
and Hamath, and * to Eze 47:16
The steward * agreed to the test. Dan 1:14
of the dream. * the king said to Dan 4:19
years until you * realize that God Dan 4:32
in Samaria are * rescued—all they Amo 3:12
When the crowd was * outside, Mt 9:25
So they * replied, "We don't Mt 21:27
were the same. * the owner sent Mt 21:37
and then, *, the end will come. Mt 24:14
* two men were found who declared, Mt 26:60,61
They talked it over and * decided Mt 27:7
formed and * the grain ripened, Mk 4:28
Herodias' chance * came. Mk 6:21
each other. They * decided that he Mk 8:16
only son. He * sent him, thinking Mk 12:6
before the end-time * comes. Mk 13:10
* some men stood up to lie about Mk 14:57
When they * tired of their sport, Mk 15:20
When they * realized who he was, Mk 16:13
When he * came out, he couldn't Lk 1:22
that the Messiah had * arrived. Lk 2:38
Three days later they * Lk 2:46,47
him and when they * found him they Lk 4:42
his problem, and * exclaimed, 'I Lk 12:18
disappointed. * he told his Lk 13:7
"When he * came to his senses, Lk 15:17
his open sores. * the beggar died Lk 16:22
* they replied, "We don't know!" Lk 20:7
children. * the woman died also. Lk 20:32
staring at him. * she spoke: "This Lk 22:56
to go to them. *, after the two Jn 11:7
saw it happen, * believed on him. Jn 11:45
"Do you * believe this?" Jn 16:31
them further, and * let them go Act 4:21
name of Jesus, and * let them go. Act 5:40
Peter * realized what had Act 12:11
When they * went out and opened Act 12:16
island until * they reached Paphos Act 13:6,7
* they returned by ship to Act 14:26
at length, and * the believers sent Act 15:2
and * reached Philippi, a Roman Act 16:12
it was dawn when he * left them! Act 20:10,11,12
this way and that. * the commander, Act 23:10
ARRANGEMENTS WERE * made to Act 27:1
sailing, and * neared Cnidus; Act 27:7,8
We * sailed behind a small island Act 27:16
a long time, but * Paul called the Act 27:21
They * decided to try. Act 27:40
Or, "that I will * succeed in Rom 1:10f
we use it until * our hope and Rom 5:4
When Christ has * won the battle 1Co 15:28
years later that I * went to Gal 1:18
you will * be filled with Christ. Gal 4:19
until * we all believe alike Eph 4:13
task within you is * finished on Php 1:6
day when I will * be all that Php 3:12
*, WHEN I could stand it no 1Th 3:1
*, DEAR BROTHERS, as I come to the 2Th 3:1
and * send them to hell itself. 1Ti 6:9
trying to find me, and * did. 2Ti 1:17
get in, for God * said, "They Heb 4:5
patiently until * God gave him a Heb 6:15
For when your patience is * in Jas 1:4
the Lord's plan * ended in good, Jas 5:11
They were * told that these 1Pe 1:12
to like them, and * you will grow 2Pe 1:7
of his Christ are * here; Rev 12:10

FINANCIAL
full, the king's * secretary and 2Ki 12:10
was the chief * officer in charge 1Ch 27:25
As to the * arrangements, I will 2Ch 2:10

FIND
to see if it could * dry ground, Gen 8:8
Suppose you * fifty godly people Gen 18:24
And God replied, "If I * fifty Gen 18:26
destroy it if I * forty-five." Gen 18:28
so that they couldn't * the door. Gen 19:11
and * a wife for him there." Gen 24:4
"But suppose I can't * a girl Gen 24:5
see to it that you * a girl from Gen 24:7
'But suppose I can't * a girl Gen 24:39
successful. Yes, * a girl from Gen 24:40
path to * a girl from the family Gen 24:48
Isaac: "How were you able to * Gen 27:20
Then if you ever * any white Gen 30:33
If you * a single thing we've Gen 31:32
the concubines, but didn't * them. Gen 31:33
thoroughly, he didn't * them. Gen 31:34
"What did you *?" Gen 31:36,37
her, but Hirah couldn't * her! Gen 38:20
him he couldn't * her anywhere, and Gen 38:22
My suggestion is that you * the Gen 41:33
Then we'll * out whether your Gen 42:16
is the way I will * out if you are Gen 42:33
If you * his cup with any one of Gen 44:9
"Shall I go and * one of the Ex 2:7
Go and * it wherever you can; Ex 5:10,11
The Egyptians will * out that I Ex 7:5
are going to * out that I am God. Ex 7:17
So the Egyptians couldn't * the Ex 14:20
"* some capable, godly, honest Ex 18:21
himself if he can * the money. Lev 25:49
until they could * out the Lord's Num 15:34
* out whom the Lord has chosen. Num 16:6,7
so that I can * out whether the Num 22:19
old or older, to * out how many of Num 26:2
God, and you shall * him when you Deu 4:29
to see if you can * anything like Deu 4:32

(FIND Con't)

Where else will you ever *	Deu 4:34
and testing you to * out how you	Deu 8:2
wherever you * them—high in the	Deu 12:2
For the Lord is testing you to *	Deu 13:3
If you * that it is, that it is	Deu 13:12,13,14
clothing, or anything else you *.	Deu 22:3
nations you shall * no rest, but	Deu 28:65
he will go and * you and bring you	Deu 30:4
light, we'll * him and kill him."	Ju 16:2
demanded that she * out from Samson	Ju 16:5
The tribe of Dan was trying to *	Ju 18:1
"What did you *?"	Ju 18:8
for we didn't * enough wives for	Ju 21:22
time that I try to * a husband for	Ru 3:1
but couldn't * them anywhere.	1Sa 9:4
let's go and * him and perhaps he	1Sa 9:6
is asking, 'How am I to * my son?'	1Sa 10:2
donkeys, but we couldn't * them;	1Sa 10:14
"* out who isn't here," Saul	1Sa 14:17
We must * out what sin was	1Sa 14:38
morning he went out to * Saul.	1Sa 15:12
to Bethlehem and * a man named	1Sa 16:1
"We'll * a good harpist to play	1Sa 16:15,16
"All right," Saul said. "* me	1Sa 16:17
to the ranks to * his brothers.	1Sa 17:22
"Well, * out!"	1Sa 17:56
an unknown family * enough dowry to	1Sa 18:23
him, "you must * a hiding place	1Sa 19:2
tell you everything I can * out."	1Sa 19:3
* the arrows as I shoot them."	1Sa 20:36
Ahimelech consulted the Lord to *	1Sa 22:9,10
but the Lord didn't let him * him.	1Sa 23:14,15
(Prince Jonathan now went to *	1Sa 23:16
"My father will never * you!	1Sa 23:17
area at all, I'll * him if I have	1Sa 23:23
aides to try to * a medium so that	1Sa 28:7,8
* fault with me about some woman?	2Sa 3:8
He sent to * out who she was and	2Sa 11:3
life if you will * a way to bring	2Sa 14:14
and Jonathan to * me and tell me	2Sa 15:35,36
Then when we * him we can	2Sa 17:12
he told them. "* David and	2Sa 17:16
would certainly * out who did it),	2Sa 18:13
told him, "is to * a young virgin	1Ki 1:2
to the other to * the most	1Ki 1:3,4
to see if we can * enough grass to	1Ki 18:5
on earth from end to end to * you.	1Ki 18:10
and can't * you, he will kill me;	1Ki 18:12
Then summon Naboth, and * two	1Ki 21:10
question when you * yourself hiding	1Ki 22:25
for three days, but didn't * him.	2Ki 2:17
If so, we can * out what to do!"	2Ki 3:11
party went back to * the prophet;	2Ki 5:15
"Go and * out where he is, and	2Ki 6:13
oil with you, and * Jehu (the son	2Ki 9:2
Jezreel himself to * King Joram,	2Ki 9:16
"Send out a rider and * out if he	2Ki 9:17
If you lean on Egypt, you will *	2Ki 18:20,21
to * Huldah the prophetess.	2Ki 22:14
If you seek him, you will * him;	1Ch 28:9
you look for him, you will * him.	2Ch 15:2
"You'll * out soon enough,"	2Ch 18:24
You will * them coming up the	2Ch 20:16
of Assyria come and * water?"	2Ch 32:4
from Babylon to * out about the	2Ch 32:31
be consulted, to * out from God	Ez 2:62,63
normal there! I *, moreover, that	Ez 4:20
been consulted to * out from God	Neh 7:64,65
so that they could * their way.	Neh 9:12
"Let us go and * the most	Est 2:2
* out what was happening to her.	Est 2:11
to Mordecai and * out what the	Est 4:5
But the wicked shall * no way to	Job 11:20
Be careful that he doesn't * out	Job 13:9
for I do not * a wise man among	Job 17:10
Can anyone * any?	Job 17:15
Oh, that I knew where to *	Job 23:3
seek him there, and cannot * him.	Job 23:8
the North, but cannot * him there;	Job 23:9
nor can I * him in the South;	Job 23:9
They eat what they * that grows	Job 24:6
to * that all his wealth is gone.	Job 27:19
"They know how to * sapphires	Job 28:6
to * wisdom and understanding.	Job 28:12
I must speak to * relief, so let	Job 32:20
comb to try to * a single fault,	Job 33:10
Can you * its boundaries, or go	Job 38:20
"I am nothing—how could I ever *	Job 40:4
them down—somehow they'll * a way!	Ps 10:6
LORD, WHO MAY go and * refuge and	Ps 15:1
Your hand, O Lord, will * your	Ps 21:8
all who seek the Lord shall * him	Ps 22:26
when I am trying to * you.	Ps 27:9
before the largest crowd I can *.	Ps 35:18
I searched but could not * him!	Ps 37:35,36
How constantly I * myself upon	Ps 38:17
Where can I * him to come and	Ps 42:2
(And let the nations * out too	Ps 59:12,13
How I long to * you!	Ps 63:1
the rocks and * protection there.	Ps 104:18
I have tried my best to *	Ps 119:10
come and * me for I have not	Ps 119:176
Point out anything you * in me	Ps 139:24
* the right decision every time.	Pro 2:9
If you want to * the road to	Pro 7:27
search for me shall surely * me.	Pro 8:17
If you search for good you will *	Pro 11:27
if you search for evil you will *	Pro 11:27
Despise God's Word and * yourself	Pro 13:13
If you can * a truly good wife,	Pro 31:10
Then I tried to * fulfillment by	Ecc 2:4,5,6
A time to *;	Ecc 3:6
over, but doesn't *	Ecc 6:6
far away, and very difficult to *.	Ecc 7:24
determined to * wisdom and the	Ecc 7:25
The wise man will * a time and a	Ecc 8:5
look for him but couldn't * him.	Sol 3:1
I searched for him but couldn't *	Sol 5:6
Jerusalem, if you * my beloved one,	Sol 5:8
We will help you * him."	Sol 6:1
You will * him at the end of the	Is 7:3
So why are you trying to * out	Is 8:19
Can the living * out the future	Is 8:19
will * a refuge within her walls.	Is 14:32
They are the best you can *, but	Is 19:13
to Cyprus, you will * no rest."	Is 23:12
is gone. If I * thorns and briars	Is 27:4,5
down to Egypt to * aid and have put	Is 30:2
and * it worthy of destruction.	Is 34:11
He will test its nobles and *	Is 34:11
like that will * a tree free from	Is 40:20
Whom can you * who equals me?	Is 46:5
Seek the Lord while you can *	Is 55:6
itself, to * new gods to love.	Is 57:9
to * no steps taken against sin.	Is 59:15
we * they are but filthy rags.	Is 64:6
What sin did they * in me that	Jer 2:4,5
and see if you can * another nation	Jer 2:10,11
ever * her help and her salvation.	Jer 3:23
you can * one fair and honest man!	Jer 5:1
Search every square, and if you *	Jer 5:1
Travel there, and you will * rest	Jer 6:16
you will * only terrible darkness.	Jer 13:16
I will * you and punish you.	Jer 16:16
And you will * no place to hide,	Jer 25:35
children, and then * mates for them	Jer 29:6
You will * me when you seek me,	Jer 29:13
"Where shall we * peace?"	Jer 30:5
told Nebuzaradan to * Jeremiah.	Jer 39:11,12
in Egypt—shall * out who tells the	Jer 44:28
of my own sighing and I * no rest.	Jer 45:3
flee to the mountains they * us.	Lam 4:19
it seems that you can never *	Eze 16:28
no search will be enough to *	Eze 26:21
to * her there with them in hell.	Eze 31:16
be comforted to * that he is not	Eze 32:31
I will search and * my sheep.	Eze 34:11
I will * my sheep and rescue them	Eze 34:12
But they couldn't * anything to	Dan 6:4
search for them but not * them.	Hos 1:7
and off they go to * some whores.	Hos 4:18
be too late—they will not * him.	Hos 5:6
to his God, nor even try to * him.	Hos 7:10
O Lord, the fatherless * mercy."	Hos 14:3
going there, but will not * it.	Amo 8:12
It is as hard to * an honest man	Mic 7:1
darkest corners to * and punish	Zep 1:12
"Oh, to * one priest among you	Mal 1:10
And when you * him, come back and	Mt 2:8
Better that than * yourself in	Mt 5:30
Seek, and you will *.	Mt 7:7
narrow, and only a few ever * it.	Mt 7:14
you shall * rest for your souls;	Mt 11:29,30
birds can come and * shelter."	Mt 13:31,32
his life for me shall * it again.	Mt 16:25
You will * a coin to cover the	Mt 17:26,27
they could *, good and bad alike;	Mt 22:10
Keep only these and you will *	Mt 22:40
* you faithfully doing your work.	Mt 24:46
joy, and rushed to * the disciples	Mt 28:8
Jesus had said they would * him.	Mt 28:16
others went out to * him, and told	Mk 1:36,37
he couldn't even * time to eat.	Mk 3:20
"Go and * out."	Mk 6:38
"Are we supposed to * food for	Mk 8:4
see if he could * any figs on it.	Mk 11:13
Don't let me * you sleeping.	Mk 13:35,36,37
were trying to * something against	Mk 14:55
his people how to * salvation	Lk 1:77
You will * a baby wrapped in a	Lk 2:12
and when they couldn't * him,	Lk 2:45
For they were eager to * some	Lk 6:7
"Did you * him weak as grass,	Lk 7:24
Did you * him dressed in	Lk 7:25
But did you * a prophet?	Lk 7:26
years, and could * no cure (though	Lk 8:43,44
* food and lodging for the night.	Lk 9:12
all who seek, *;	Lk 11:10
to see if he could * any fruit on	Lk 13:6
urge anyone you * to come, so that	Lk 14:23
return, how many will I * who	Lk 18:8
the poor, and if I * I have	Lk 19:8
the money, to * out what they had	Lk 19:15
were trying to * some way to get	Lk 19:47
don't let me * you living in	Lk 21:34,35
murder, trying to * a way to kill	Lk 22:2
and John ahead to * a place to	Lk 22:8
disciples—only to * them asleep,	Lk 22:45
on this point and * him innocent.	Lk 23:14
people! You * it so hard to believe	Lk 24:25
Andrew then went to * his brother	Jn 1:41
They were surprised to * him	Jn 4:27
Then the man went to * the Jewish	Jn 5:15
The Jewish leaders tried to *	Jn 7:11
You will search for me but not *	Jn 7:34
not being able to * him, and, 'You	Jn 7:36
not * a home within your hearts.	Jn 8:37
in and out and * green pastures.	Jn 10:9
be too late for you to * your way.	Jn 12:35
clearly that I * him not guilty."	Jn 19:4
said. "I * him not guilty."	Jn 19:6
But go * my brothers and tell	Jn 20:17
them, lest you * yourselves	Act 5:39
Street and * the house of a man	Act 9:11
Now send some men to Joppa to *	Act 10:5,6
to Joppa to * Simon Peter!	Act 11:13
so that Gentiles, too, will *	Act 15:17
way toward him and * him—though he	Act 17:27
When he couldn't * out anything	Act 21:34
a man as you could * for obeying	Act 22:12
He wanted to * out why the crowd	Act 22:24
them to try to * out what the	Act 22:30
to try to * out what he had done.	Act 23:28
You can * out the truth of our	Act 24:8
will * it through trusting God."	Rom 1:17
I * myself still enslaved to sin.	Rom 7:23,24,25
the Holy Spirit * themselves doing	Rom 8:5
There God says that he will *	Rom 9:25
the heavens to * Christ and bring	Rom 10:6
don't * fault with those who do.	Rom 14:3
world would never * God through	1Co 1:21
me, and then I'll * out whether	1Co 4:19
is like, I try to * common ground	1Co 9:22
You will * the answer in your own	1Co 15:36
so that I could * out how far you	2Co 2:9
on to Macedonia to try to * him.	2Co 2:13
so that no one can * fault with us	2Co 6:3
that no one should * fault with the	2Co 8:20
with me, only to * that you still	2Co 9:4
won't like what I *, and then you	2Co 12:20
I am afraid that I will * you	2Co 12:20
save us and then * that we are	Gal 2:17
that I could never * God's favor by	Gal 2:19
will * it through trusting God."	Gal 3:11
You are trying to * favor with	Gal 4:10
* out what those laws really mean?	Gal 4:21
Anyone trying to * favor with God	Gal 5:3
but try to * out and do whatever	Eph 5:17
just as soon as I * out what is	Php 2:23
life again, and to * out what it	Php 3:10
wherever we go we * people telling	1Th 1:8
I sent Timothy to * out whether	1Th 3:5
so that no one can * fault with you	1Ti 6:14
trying to * me, and finally did.	2Ti 1:17
brothers, lest you * that they,	Heb 3:12
his mercy and to * grace to help us	Heb 4:16
fail to * God's best blessings.	Heb 12:15
and the way to * out if their	1Jn 4:2
So you can * out how much you	1Jn 5:2
us understand and * the true God.	1Jn 5:20
How happy I am to * some of your	2Jn 1:4
us, but now I * I must write of	Jud 1:3
And as for others, help them to *	Jud 1:23

FINDING

neighbor, or by * a lost article	Lev 6:3
that you aren't * God's blessings;	Is 59:9
before searched for me are * me.	Is 65:1
they left without * out the truth,	Jer 38:27
for a while, seeking rest but *	Mt 12:43,44,45
on looking and you will keep on *;	Lk 11:9
for rest; but * none, it returns to	Lk 11:24
Not * them there, they dragged	Act 17:6
or kept back from * the Lord by the	2Co 6:3
be built to keep men from * him.	2Co 10:5
of being saved by * favor with an	1Ti 1:3,4

FINDS

will be very happy when he * you.	Ex 4:14
If he * these symptoms, it is an	Lev 13:11
If he * greenish or reddish	Lev 14:37
and the avenger * him outside and	Num 35:27
then if he * that I am guilty of	2Sa 14:32
like one who * a great treasure.	Ps 119:162
Literally, "the man that *	Pro 3:13,14,15f
For whoever * me finds life and	Pro 8:35
For whoever finds me * life and	Pro 8:35
The good man * life;	Pro 11:19
makes good use of everything he *.	Pro 12:27
A mocker never * the wisdom he	Pro 14:6
The man who * a wife finds a good	Pro 18:22
The man who finds a wife * a good	Pro 18:22
* life, righteousness and honor.	Pro 21:21
How a ship * its way across the	Pro 30:18,19

FINDS Con't)
all her life. She * wool and flax Pro 31:13
Anyone who seeks, *. Mt 7:8
So it returns and * the man's Mt 12:43,44,45
Then the demon * seven other Mt 12:43,44,45
And if he * it, he will rejoice Mt 18:13
it left, and * that its former Lk 11:25
If his master returns and * that Lk 12:42,43,44
nook and cranny until she * it? Lk 15:8
it, "The man who * life will find Rom 1:17
He likes harmony, and he * it in 1Co 14:33
it, "The man who * life will find Gal 3:11
and untrusting * evil in Tit 1:15

FINE
Leah replied, "That's * with us! Gen 31:14
"we'll get along just *. Gen 33:15
The land of Goshen will be *. Gen 47:5,6
It will spread like * dust over Ex 9:9
accept a * instead, if they wish. Ex 21:30
it, he shall pay a * of five to Ex 22:1
For sheep, the * shall be four to Ex 22:1
shall pay double value as his *. Ex 22:4
Beat some of it very * and put Ex 30:36
threads into * linen cloth. Ex 38:23
Lord is to bring * flour and is to Lev 2:1
of * flour mixed with olive oil. Lev 2:7
a tenth of a bushel of * flour. Lev 5:11
without defect, worth whatever * Lev 5:15
a twenty percent *, and give it to Lev 6:4,5
of a bushel of * flour, half to be Lev 6:19,20
and only three quarts of * white Lev 14:21
beaten into * powder, and bring it Lev 16:12
of * flour containing yeast. Lev 23:17
courts to die may pay a * instead; Lev 27:29
pancakes made of * flour mixed Num 6:15
of * flour mixed with oil. Num 7:13
grain offering of * flour mingled Num 8:8
three quarts of * flour mixed with Num 15:3,4
use six quarts of * flour mixed Num 15:6
of nine quarts of * flour mixed Num 15:8,9
of six quarts of * flour mixed with Num 28:9,10
quarts of * flour mixed with oil; Num 28:20,21
shall be three quarts of * flour. Num 28:20,21
of nine quarts of * flour mixed Num 28:28,29
of nine quarts of * flour mingled Num 29:3,4
Nine quarts of * flour mixed with Num 29:9,10
quarts of * flour mingled with oil Num 29:14
and have built * homes to live in, Deu 8:12,13
you are such *, upright people that Deu 9:5
and ground it into * dust, and Deu 9:21
and * him one hundred dollars Deu 22:19
caught in the act, he must pay a * Deu 22:28,29
to give you * crops every season. Deu 28:12
"*," said the tribes of Joseph, Jos 17:16,17,18
him, and if he will marry you, *; Ru 3:13
"*!" 1Sa 14:7
* -his men replied 1Sa 14:36
He was a * looking boy, 1Sa 16:12
If he says, '*!' 1Sa 20:7
With * clothing and golden 2Sa 1:24
195 bushels of * flour, 390 bushels 1Ki 4:22
"*," Jehoshaphat said. 2Ki 3:12
told Gehazi, "everything is *." 2Ki 4:26
supplies such as * flour, wine, 1Ch 9:29
of * linen and purple thread." Est 1:6f
an outer cloak of * linen and Est 8:15
for jewels mounted in * gold. Job 28:17
So I crushed them * as dust and Ps 18:42
a * gold ring in a pig's snout. Pro 11:22
How short-sighted to * the godly Pro 17:26
"There are many * women in the Pro 31:29
Praise her for the many * things Pro 31:31
Wear * clothes—with a dash of Ecc 9:8
for good food and * clothes for the Is 23:18
it looks so *, but it is so weak Is 28:17
"It's coming along *. Is 41:7
of the sea? Like * stallions racing Is 63:13
They will tear out all of your * Jer 22:7
with bitterness. '* friends you Jer 38:21,22
to come with me to Babylon, *; Jer 40:4
it—the * flour and oil and honey I Eze 16:19
those handsome young men on * Eze 23:12
dyes, embroidery, * linen, and Eze 27:16
"Beautiful girls and * young men Amo 8:13
Your only concern is your own * Hag 1:9
giving you these * new clothes." Zec 3:4
dirt to her, and * gold like dust Zec 9:3
of gold and silver and * clothing. Zec 14:14
man who promises a * ram from his Mal 1:14
they get along *, as soon as Mk 4:17
farm that produced * crops. Lk 12:16
If we get figs next year, *; Lk 13:9
*! the King exclaimed Lk 19:17
"*," they replied. Lk 22:35
for money or * clothing— you know Act 20:33
That is why I felt * so long as I Rom 7:9
gave him such a * welcome and set 2Co 7:13
It is a * thing when people are Gal 4:18
on the *, good things in others. Php 4:8
a man who builds a * house gets Heb 3:3
Well, Moses did a * job working Heb 3:5
away, and your * clothes are Jas 5:2
wine, olive oil, and * flour; Rev 18:13
of linens." (* linen represents Rev 19:8

FINE-SPUN
* linen, decorated with angels. 2Ch 3:14

FINE-TOOTHED
You say God is using a * comb Job 33:10

FINE-TWINED
scarlet cloth, * linen, goat's Ex 25:1
colored sheets of * linen, Ex 26:1
scarlet cloth, the * linen, with Ex 26:31
blue, purple, and scarlet * linen. Ex 26:36
with curtains made from * linen. Ex 27:9,10
and scarlet * linen, and attached Ex 27:16
7½ feet high, made from * linen. Ex 27:18
and scarlet threads of * linen. Ex 28:5,6
blue, purple, and scarlet * linen. Ex 28:8
* linen as you did in the ephod. Ex 28:15
"Weave Aaron's tunic from * Ex 28:39
made of * linen or of goat's hair; Ex 35:5-9
from the * linen or goats' hair; Ex 35:23
and * linen, and brought them in. Ex 35:25
drapes woven from * linen thread. Ex 38:9
the court were woven of * linen. Ex 38:16
court was made of * linen, Ex 38:18
too, woven from * linen thread. Ex 39:2
cloth cut from * linen thread, just Ex 39:4,5
and his sons from * linen thread. Ex 39:27

FINED
her shall be * whatever amount the Ex 21:22
But even so, he is * seven times Pro 6:31

FINELY
be made with * ground wheat flour. Ex 29:2
three quarts of * ground flour Ex 29:40
must be made from * ground flour, Lev 2:4
shall be made of * ground flour Lev 2:5
a handful of the * ground flour Lev 6:15
ten quarts of * ground flour mixed Lev 14:10
of a bushel of * ground flour mixed Lev 23:13
be baked from * ground flour, using Lev 24:5-8
of three quarts of * ground flour Num 28:5
nine quarts of * ground flour mixed Num 28:12
and six quarts of * ground flour Num 28:12
three quarts of * ground flour Num 28:13

FINELY-TWINED
ten sheets from * blue, purple, and Ex 36:8,9

FINES
by all your taxes, *, and usury; Amo 5:11

FINESPUN
it was woven from * linen, Ex 36:37
dressed in * linen robes and 2Ch 5:11,12

FINEST
you choose the * of our sepulchres, Gen 23:5,6
can give me your * blessings!" Gen 27:31
gold, and the * of clothes from her Ex 3:22
made from the * gold, blue, purple, Ex 39:8
And the * of the wheat; Deu 32:14
With the * of mountain crops Deu 33:15
slaves and the * of your youth and 1Sa 8:16
are some of the * men I've ever 1Sa 29:6
This too was overlaid with the * 2Ch 3:8
He is the * man in all the Job 1:8
"He is the * man in all the Job 2:3
jewelry of * gold from Ophir. Ps 45:9
the * of Israel's young men. Ps 78:31
commandments more than the * gold. Ps 119:127
barns with plenty of the * wheat. Ps 147:14
your wine vats with the * wines. Pro 3:9,10
colored sheets of * linen imported Pro 7:16,17
She also upholsters with * Pro 31:22
an apple tree, the * in the orchard Sol 2:3
of * gold, like cedars of Lebanon; Sol 5:15
land, the * in the world. Jer 3:19
them to kill their * youth. Lam 2:4
HOW THE * gold has lost its Lam 4:1
The cream of our youth—the * of Lam 4:2
the * specimens of men; Lam 4:7
You ate the * foods and became Eze 16:13
will take the * and most tender Eze 17:22,23
offerings and the * of your gifts. Eze 20:40
and put on your * jewels for them. Eze 23:40
You are like a ship built of * Eze 27:5
Your sails are made of Egypt's * Eze 27:7
in beautiful settings of * gold. Eze 28:13
food and wear the * clothes, but Eze 34:3
and unused. Your * youth lie dead. Nah 2:13
Bring the * robe in the house and Lk 15:22
the * calf we have on the place.' Lk 15:30
stones, pearls, * linens, purple Rev 18:12
a woman clothed in * purple and Rev 18:16
and whitest and * of linens." Rev 19:8
heaven, dressed in * linen, white Rev 19:14

FINGER
ring on Joseph's * as a token of Gen 41:41,42
"This is the * of God," they Ex 8:19
and you won't need to lift a *!" Ex 14:14
it on with your *, and pour the Ex 29:12
were written with the * of God. Ex 31:18
and shall dip his * in the blood Lev 4:6
and shall dip his * in the blood Lev 4:17
place it with his * upon the horns Lev 4:25
the blood with his * and smear it Lev 4:30
the blood with his * and smear it Lev 4:34
the blood with his * upon the four Lev 8:15,16
and he dipped his * in it and Lev 9:9
and dip his right * into it, and Lev 14:16
his * seven times before the Lord. Lev 14:16
and with his right * he is to Lev 14:27
it with his * upon the east side of Lev 16:14
times with his *, thus cleansing it Lev 16:19
her blood upon his * and sprinkle Num 19:4
Tie them on your *, wear them on Deu 6:8
Tell them, 'My little * is 2Ch 10:10
from his * and giving it to Haman, Est 3:10
they never have to lift a * Ps 73:12
around your * so you won't forget. Pro 6:21
no one can move a * or open his Is 10:14
Don't point your * at someone Hos 4:4
Look, priest, I am pointing my * Hos 4:4
refusing to lift a * to help him Ob 1:11
you like a signet ring upon my *; Hag 2:23
you sticks his * in Jehovah's eye! Zec 2:8
shall arise and point her * at Lk 11:31
And a jeweled ring for his *; Lk 15:22
dip the tip of his * in water and Lk 16:24
and wrote in the dust with his *. Jn 8:6
"Put your * into my hands. Jn 20:27

FINGERS
rings from their *, necklaces—and Ex 35:22
nose or any extra * or toes, or Lev 21:18
a giant with six * on each hand and 2Sa 21:20,21
a giant with six * on each hand and 1Ch 20:6,7
the work of your *—the moon and the Ps 8:3
friends with eyes and feet and *. Pro 6:12,13
Literally, "Bind them upon your * Pro 7:3f
it as it runs through your *! Ecc 5:11
with perfume, my * with lovely Sol 5:5
and your * are filthy with sin. Is 59:3
"But now I snap my * and call a Eze 22:13
cups, they saw the * of a man's Dan 5:5
The king himself saw the * as Dan 5:5
And so God sent those * to write Dan 5:24,25
away and put their * in their ears Zec 7:11
crowd and put his * into the man's Mk 7:33
hands—and put my * into them—and Jn 20:25
gold rings on his *, and at the Jas 2:2

FINISH
to see if she would * the job, Gen 24:21
and they will * destroying Ex 10:4,5
of the army and * the job, so that 2Sa 12:28
until he could * building his 1Ki 3:1
this Temple and * these walls?" Ez 5:3
like a lion and quickly * me off. Job 10:16
never been able to * me off! Ps 129:2
you can't * and go down before your Pro 25:8,9,10
wild animals to * up what's left. Jer 15:3
blow after another I will * you. Eze 7:5,6
my fury and let it * its work of Eze 7:8,9
I didn't * them off in the Eze 20:17
"Son of dust, on the day I * Eze 24:25
The men of Israel * up their Hos 4:18
After the cutter-locusts * Joe 1:4
And Zerubbabel will * building Zec 4:7
"Get on with the job and * it! Zec 8:9
from start to * by faith. Rom 1:17
for others—never * paying that! Rom 13:8
I want to suggest that you * what 2Co 8:10
I am helping to * up the remainder Col 1:24

FINISHED
So on the seventh day, having * Gen 2:2
* his conversation with Abraham. Gen 18:33
the camels had * drinking, he Gen 24:22
* giving you all I am promising." Gen 28:15
Judah is a young lion that has * Gen 49:9
Then, when Jacob had * his Gen 49:33
When the Ark is *, place inside Ex 25:16
Then, as God * speaking with Ex 31:18
When Moses had * speaking with Ex 34:33
piece of workmanship when *. Ex 39:3
the Tabernacle was *, following all Ex 39:32
So at last Moses * the work. Ex 40:33
When Aaron and his sons have * Num 4:15
on the day he * setting it up. Num 7:1
He had hardly * speaking the Num 16:31
You are *, Num 21:27-30
but when they * their survey and Num 32:9
When the officers have * saying Deu 20:9
When Moses had * writing down all Deu 31:24
When the army of Israel had * Jos 8:24
and * off everyone left inside. Jos 8:24
* the destruction of its enemies! Jos 10:13
tears as the Angel * speaking; Ju 2:4
see you until he has * his supper. Ru 3:3
After Boaz had * a good meal, he Ru 3:6,7
When Saul had * prophesying he 1Sa 10:13
AFTER KING SAUL had * his 1Sa 18:1
surrounded Absalom and * him off. 2Sa 18:15
At last the Temple was *. 1Ki 6:14
When the Temple was finally *, 1Ki 7:51
As he * this prayer, he rose from 1Ki 8:54,55
WHEN SOLOMON HAD * building the 1Ki 9:1
As soon as he had * sacrificing 2Ki 10:25

(FINISHED Con't)
but he never * it, for the anger of 1Ch 27:24
it that everything is * correctly. 1Ch 28:20
SO THE TEMPLE was finally *. 2Ch 5:1
AS SOLOMON * praying, fire flashed 2Ch 7:1
So Solomon * building the Temple 2Ch 7:11
And when they had * that job, 2Ch 20:23
When all was *, the remaining 2Ch 24:14
until the work was *—and until more 2Ch 29:34
and the walls *, you might as well Ez 4:16
The Temple was finally *, as had Ez 6:14
on December 15, and * by March 15. Ez 10:16-19
The wall was finally * in early Neh 6:15
AFTER THE WALL was * and we had Neh 7:1
Before this man *, still another Job 1:17
For I have not * defending God! Job 36:2
After the Lord had * speaking Job 42:7
But they had hardly * eating, Ps 78:30
They had almost * me off, yet I Ps 119:87
Yes, we have * off many a Is 10:10
Few will live when I have * up Is 13:12
And when my sword has * its work Is 34:5
"The harvest is *; Jer 8:20
again and *, says the Lord. Jer 12:17
When Jeremiah had * his message, Jer 26:7,8
wrath until it has * all the Jer 30:24
When all was *, Jeremiah said to Jer 36:5
By the time he * they were badly Jer 36:16
And whenever Jehudi * reading Jer 36:23
WHEN JEREMIAH HAD * giving this Jer 43:1
Then, when you have * reading Jer 51:63
north or south—your land is *. Eze 7:2
* the work you gave me to do." Eze 9:11
sheath again until its work is *. Eze 21:5
When he had * making these Eze 42:15
When you have * this cleansing Eze 43:23
of despair: "We are *, ruined. Mic 2:4
NINEVEH, YOU ARE *! Nah 2:1
Lord's Temple is *, and from this Hag 2:18,19
that await you when it's *. Zec 8:9
WHEN JESUS HAD * giving these Mt 11:1
When Jesus had * giving these Mt 13:53,54
AFTER JESUS HAD * this address, he Mt 19:1
WHEN JESUS HAD * this talk with Mt 26:1
When the Lord Jesus had * talking Mk 16:19
When he had * speaking, he said Lk 5:4
WHEN JESUS HAD * his sermon he Lk 7:1
came to him as he * and said, Lk 11:1
ran out of money before it was *!' Lk 14:30
but by the time they were * it Lk 23:56
WHEN JESUS HAD * saying all these Jn 17:1
everything was now *, and to Jn 19:28
it, he said, "It is *," and Jn 19:30
soon as they had * their business, Act 12:25
When they had *, James took the Act 15:13
When he had * speaking, he knelt Act 20:36
you is finally * on that day when Php 1:6
* all that he had planned to make. Heb 4:4
for he * all sacrifices, once and Heb 7:27
so that we can be * with sin and 1Pe 2:24
at last God's anger will be *. Rev 15:1
in heaven, saying, "It is *!" Rev 16:17
until the thousand years were *. Rev 20:3
is trustworthy and true: It is *! Rev 21:6

FINISHING
But just as he was *, Samuel 1Sa 13:10
just as they were * their banquet. 1Ki 1:41
After * the meal, the old man 1Ki 13:23
forward eagerly to * the building 1Ch 29:19
* is better than starting! Ecc 7:8
who sent me, and from * his work. Jn 4:34
As John was * his work he asked, Act 13:25

FINS
eat whatever has * and scales, Lev 11:9
* or scales is forbidden to you. Lev 11:12
"Only sea animals with * and Deu 14:9

FIR
Also send me cedar trees, * 2Ch 2:8
of the woods—the * trees and cedars Is 14:8
* and pine—on barren land. Is 41:19
Where once were thorns, * trees Is 55:13
ship built of finest * from Senir. Eze 27:5

FIRE
Then the Lord rained down * and Gen 19:24
chopped wood for a * upon the Gen 22:3
and the flint for striking a *. Gen 22:6
flint to make the *, but where is Gen 22:7
ready for the *, and then tied Gen 22:9
to him as a flame of * in a bush. Ex 3:2
the bush was on * and that it Ex 3:2
and by a pillar of * at night. Ex 13:21
The cloud and * were never out Ex 13:22
to a pillar of *, it gave darkness Ex 14:20
from the cloud of * upon the array Ex 14:24
consumed them as * consumes straw. Ex 15:7
upon it in the form of *; Ex 19:18
burned off and the * gets out of Ex 22:6
the * shall make full restitution. Ex 22:6
top looked like a raging *. Ex 24:17
carcass-hooks, and * pans are all Ex 27:3
down into the * box, resting it Ex 27:5
melted it in the *, and when the Ex 32:20
I threw them into the *, and Ex 32:24
basins, meat hooks, and * pans. Ex 38:3
about halfway up [in the * box Ex 38:4
at night there was * in the cloud Ex 40:38
and build a wood * upon the altar, Lev 1:6,7
altar, an offering made by *." Lev 2:2f
burned there on a wood *. Lev 4:11,12
sacrifice made to Jehovah by *; Lev 4:35
offering to Jehovah made by *; Lev 5:12
with the altar * kept burning. Lev 6:9
Meanwhile, the * on the altar Lev 6:12
offering. The * must be kept Lev 6:13
offerings made by * to the Lord." Lev 6:18
burned with * before the Lord. Lev 6:30
sacrificed by * to the Lord shall Lev 7:25
Then * came from the Lord and Lev 9:24
placed unholy * in their censers, Lev 10:1
incense on the *, and offered the Lev 10:1
Or, "placed * in their censers Lev 10:1f
and offered unholy * .I.I." Lev 10:1f
them! So * blazed forth from the Lev 10:2
the terrible * the Lord has sent. Lev 10:6
offerings to Jehovah made by *; Lev 10:13
and must be destroyed by *. Lev 13:52
by * to the Lord their God. Lev 21:6
to offer the * sacrifices to the Lev 21:21
as a sacrifice by * to the Lord. Lev 22:26,27
make an offering by * to the Lord. Lev 23:8
to be offered by * to the Lord; Lev 23:13
All are * offerings, very Lev 23:18
a sacrifice by * to the Lord. Lev 23:25
offer sacrifices by * to the Lord. Lev 23:26,27
an offering by * to the Lord. Lev 23:36
be an offering by * to the Lord. Lev 23:36
to the Lord are to be made by *. Lev 23:37
offering made by * to the Lord, in Lev 24:5-8
For these are offerings made by * Lev 24:9
of Sinai when they used unholy *. Num 3:4
be put in the * under the peace Num 6:18
the appearance of *, and stayed Num 9:15
to the appearance of * at night. Num 9:16
complaints, so the * of the Lord Num 11:1
he prayed for them the * stopped. Num 11:2
because the * from the Lord Num 11:3
of cloud and * standing above us, Num 14:14
other offering by *, their Num 15:3,4
This shall be offered by * as a Num 15:10
Lord with sacrifices offered by *; Num 15:13,14
sacrifice made by * before the Num 15:25
Then * came forth from Jehovah Num 16:35
to pull those censers from the *; Num 16:36,37
and place * in it from the altar; Num 16:46
shall be burned as a * offering; Num 18:17
For a * has flamed forth Num 21:27-30
and 250 men were destroyed by * Num 26:5-11
offered unholy * before the Lord. Num 26:61
"When you make offerings by *, Num 28:3
an offering made by * to the Lord. Num 28:6
the Lord, an offering made by *. Num 28:8
be presented by *, and will please Num 28:13
be passed through * in order to be Num 31:23
by a pillar of * at night and a Deu 1:33
and the mountain burned with *; Deu 4:11
the Lord spoke to you from the *; Deu 4:12
to you from the * at Mount Horeb, Deu 4:15
He is a devouring *, a jealous Deu 4:24
it from *, as you did, and lived! Deu 4:33
great pillar of * upon the earth; Deu 4:36
words from the center of the *. Deu 4:36
of the *, there at the mountain. Deu 5:4
were afraid of the * and did not go Deu 5:5
the heart of the *, surrounded by Deu 5:22
saw the terrible * at the top of Deu 5:23
his voice from the heart of the *. Deu 5:24
This awesome * will consume us. Deu 5:25
from the heart of the *, and live? Deu 5:26,27
you as a devouring * to destroy Deu 9:3
the heart of the * on the mountain Deu 10:4
* on the mountain, lest you die. Deu 18:16
For my anger has kindled a * Deu 32:22
And setting its mountains on *. Deu 32:22
And with flaming * at his right Deu 33:2
be burned with *, along with Jos 7:15
Set the city on *, as the Lord Jos 8:8
into the city and set it on *. Jos 8:19
its people, setting the city on *. Ju 1:8
his staff, and * flamed up from the Ju 6:21
as wood for the * on the altar." Ju 6:26
If you refuse, let * flame forth Ju 9:15
walls of the fort and set on *. Ju 9:49
the Angel ascended in the * Ju 13:20
tow snaps when it touches the *." Ju 16:9f
everyone in it, and set it on *. Ju 20:35-39
their city was on *, and that they Ju 20:40,41
of the cart for a * and killed the 1Sa 6:14
"Go and set * to that barley field 2Sa 14:30
your servants set my field on *?" 2Sa 14:31
* leaped from his mouth 2Sa 22:9
Setting * to the world. 2Sa 22:9
wood to build a * on the altar. 2Sa 24:22
he sacrificed by * to the 1Ki 10:
putting any * under the wood; 1Ki 18:2
Lord's altar, with no * under it. 1Ki 18:2
answers by sending * to light the 1Ki 18:24
but don't put any * under the 1Ki 18:2
Then, suddenly, * flashed down 1Ki 18:38
there was a *, but the Lord was not 1Ki 19:12
but the Lord was not in the *. 1Ki 19:12
And after the *, there was the 1Ki 19:12
to build a * to roast their flesh. 1Ki 19:21
a man of God, let * come down from 2Ki 1:10
a man of God, let * come down from 2Ki 1:12
And again the * from God burned 2Ki 1:12
a chariot of *, drawn by horses of 2Ki 2:11
drawn by horses of *, appeared and 2Ki 2:11
see horses of * and chariots of 2Ki 6:17
of * everywhere upon the mountain! 2Ki 6:17
for wood for the * and use the 1Ch 21:23
by sending down * from heaven to 1Ch 21:26
AS SOLOMON FINISHED praying, * 2Ch 7:1
children in the *, just like the 2Ch 28:3
and a pillar of * at night so that Neh 9:12
and the pillar of * showed them the Neh 9:19
bad news: "The * of God has fallen Job 1:16
as flames shoot upwards from a *. Job 5:7
God's * consumes them with all Job 15:34
A raging * will devour his goods, Job 20:26
have been destroyed in the *.' Job 22:20
while underneath there is *. Job 28:5
It is a devastating * that Job 31:12
His eyes glow like sparks. * Job 41:19
arrows made from shafts of *. Ps 7:13
He will rain down * and Ps 11:6
his mouth, setting * to the earth; Ps 18:8
Literally, "coals of *." Ps 18:12f
oh, the *! Ps 18:13
in the fierce * of your presence. Ps 21:9,10
surrounded by devastating *; Ps 50:3
blazing * of thorns beneath it. Ps 58:9
You have purified us with *, Ps 66:10
We went through * and flood. Ps 66:12
melt them like wax in *! Ps 68:2
the sanctuary on *, and razed it to Ps 74:7
and at night by a pillar of *. Ps 78:14
and was angry; the * of his wrath Ps 78:21
Their young men were killed by * Ps 78:63
* that roars across a mountain. Ps 83:14
long will your wrath burn like *? Ps 89:46
of his throne. * goes forth before Ps 97:3
his messengers—his servants of *! Ps 104:4
his friends; and * fell from Ps 106:18
them into the *, or into deep pits Ps 140:10
ocean depths. Let * and hail, Ps 148:8
Can a man hold * against his Pro 6:27
his lips there is a scorching *." Pro 16:27f
Silver and gold are purified by * Pro 17:3
* goes out for lack of fuel, and Pro 26:20
embers to coals and wood to *." Pro 26:21f
sets * to paper. Pro 26:21
barren wombA barren desert* Pro 30:15,16
gone as paper in *, and it is silly Ecc 7:6
It flashes *, the very flame of Sol 8:6
sets the straw on *, and no one Is 1:31
filth by the horrors and the *. Is 4:2,3,4
day, and clouds of * at night, Is 4:5
will disappear like straw on *. Is 5:24
The land is blackened by that *, Is 9:19,20
The people are fuel for the *. Is 9:19,20
will be the * and flame that will Is 10:17
were when God sent * from heaven; Is 13:19
the * reserved for your enemies. Is 26:11
earthquake, whirlwind and *. Is 29:6
his words consume like *. Is 30:27
The breath of the Lord, like * Is 30:33
a volcano, will set it all on *. Is 30:33
Your own breath will turn to * Is 33:11
cut down and tossed in the *. Is 33:12
all-consuming, Everlasting *?" Is 33:14
the ground will be covered with *. Is 34:9
and thrown their gods into the *; Is 37:19
Yet, though set on * and burned, Is 42:25
When you walk through the * of Is 43:2
the wood to make a * to warm Is 44:15
as dried grass burning in the *. Is 47:14
Theirs is no * to sit beside to Is 47:14
The consuming * of your glory Is 64:2
will come with * and with swift Is 66:15
his hot rebuke with flames of *. Is 66:15
the world by * and by his sword, Is 66:16
their * shall not be quenched, Is 66:24
one will be able to put the * out. Jer 4:4
them into raging * and burn up Jer 5:14
the refining * grows hotter, but Jer 6:29
No matter how hot the *, they Jer 6:29
by the unquenchable * of my anger. Jer 7:20
like *, and it shall consume you. Jer 15:14
For you have kindled a * of my Jer 17:4
then I will set * to these gates. Jer 17:27
these gates. The * shall spread to Jer 17:27
my heart is like * that burns in my Jer 20:9
you like a * no man can quench. Jer 21:12

FIRE Con't)
I will light a * in the forests Jer 21:14
beams and throw them on the *. Jer 22:7
Does not my word burn like *? Jer 23:29
come in and set * to the city and Jer 32:29
in which a * was burning." Jer 36:22f
throw it into the *, until the Jer 36:23
He will set * to the temples of Jer 43:12
forth and fell as * upon the cities Jer 44:6
But a * comes from Jer 48:45
And I will start a * at the edge Jer 49:27
Lord will light a * in the cities Jer 50:32
work shall be destroyed by *! Jer 51:58
He has sent * from heaven that Lam 1:13
land of Israel like a raging *. Lam 2:3
His fury is poured out like * Lam 2:4
He started a * in Jerusalem that Lam 4:11
cloud glowing with *, with a mass Eze 1:4
* inside that flashed continually; Eze 1:4
and in the * there was something Eze 1:4
bright coals of * or brilliant Eze 1:13
glowing bronze, dazzling like *; Eze 1:27,28
bake it over a *, using dried human Eze 4:12
them into the *, for a fire shall Eze 5:4
the fire, for a * shall come from Eze 5:4
his waist down, he was made of *; Eze 8:2
and after being put in the *! Eze 15:5,6
*, they will fall into another; Eze 15:7
the fruit was destroyed by *. Eze 19:12
Literally, "A * is gone out of Eze 19:14f
I will set you on *, O forest, Eze 20:47
that I, the Lord, have set the *. Eze 20:48
and blow upon the * of my wrath Eze 21:31
You are the fuel for the *; Eze 21:32
I will blow the * of my wrath Eze 22:21
I will consume you with the * of Eze 22:31
a pot of water on the * to boil. Eze 24:3
fuel on the * beneath the pot. Eze 24:5
let the * roar and the pot boil. Eze 24:10
all remains despite the hottest *. Eze 24:12
You walked among the stones of *. Eze 28:14
from the midst of the stones of *. Eze 28:16
the midst of the stones of *." Eze 28:16f
therefore I brought forth * from Eze 28:18
Literally, "I brought * from the Eze 28:18f
on * and destroyed her allies. Eze 30:8
Yes, I will set * to Egypt, Eze 30:16
great hailstones, * and brimstone! Eze 38:22
And I will rain down * on Magog Eze 39:6
and throw them into the *. Dan 3:20
such a hot * in the furnace, the Dan 3:22
around in the *, and they aren't Dan 3:25
So they stepped out of the *. Dan 3:26
and saw that the * hadn't touched Dan 3:27
river of * flowed from before him. Dan 7:10
and his eyes were pools of *; Dan 10:5,6
of them dying by * and sword, or Dan 11:33
it flames forth like raging *. Hos 7:6
Therefore, I will send down * Hos 8:14
of the world! * goes before them Joe 2:3
or the roar of * sweeping across a Joe 2:5
and * and pillars of smoke. Joe 2:30
So I will set * to King Hazael's Amo 1:4
So I will set * to the walls of Amo 1:7
So I will set * to the walls of Amo 1:10
So I will set * to Teman, and it Amo 1:12
"So I will set * to the walls of Amo 1:14
Now in return I will send * upon Amo 2:2
So I will destroy Judah with *, Amo 2:5
firebrands snatched away from *. Amo 4:11
he will sweep like * through Israel Amo 5:6
* he had prepared to punish them; Amo 7:4
Israel will be a * that sets the Ob 1:18
*, like water pouring down a hill. Mic 1:4
His fury is like *; Nah 1:6
He tosses his enemies into the * Nah 1:10
the enemy and set on * and burned. Nah 3:13
the * will devour you; Nah 3:15
devoured by the * of his jealousy. Zep 1:18
with the * of my jealousy. Zep 3:8
will be a wall of * protecting them Zec 2:5
a brand plucked out of the *?" Zec 3:2f
stick pulled out of the *." Zec 3:2
and she shall be set on * and Zec 9:4
by * raging through your forests. Zec 11:1
like a little * that sets the Zec 12:6
remain through the * and make them Zec 13:9
are refined and purified by *. Zec 13:9
For he is like a blazing * Mal 3:2
Or, "in the Holy Spirit and in * Mt 3:11f
the Holy Spirit and with *. Mt 3:11
*, and storing away the grain." Mt 3:12
Literally, "the hell of *." Mt 5:22f
chopped down and thrown on the *. Mt 7:19
casting the wicked into the *; Mt 13:50
into the * or into the water; Mt 17:15
into the eternal * prepared for the Mt 25:41
the * or into water to kill him. Mk 9:22
dies, and the * never goes out— Mk 9:48
out— where all are salted with *. Mk 9:49
everyone shall be salted with *." Mk 9:49f
beside a * among the servants. Mk 14:54
Peter warming himself at the *. Mk 14:66,67
around the * began saying to Peter, Mk 14:70
down and thrown into the *." Lk 3:9
He will baptize you with *—with Lk 3:16
* and store away the grain." Lk 3:17
shall we order * down from heaven Lk 9:54
"I have come to bring * to the Lk 12:49
left Sodom. Then * and brimstone Lk 17:29
The soldiers lit a * in the Lk 22:55
* they had made, for it was cold. Jn 18:18
standing by the *, he was asked Jn 18:25
we saw that a * was kindled and Jn 21:9
or tongues of * appeared and Act 2:3
and * and clouds of smoke; Act 2:19
to him in a flame of * in a bush. Act 7:30
to lay on the *, a poisonous snake, Act 28:3
snake into the * and was unharmed. Act 28:5
coals of * on his head." Rom 12:20
be put through the * so that all 1Co 3:13
heaven in flaming * with his mighty 2Th 1:7
and as servants made of flaming *; Heb 1:7
terror, flaming *, gloom, darkness Heb 12:18
For our God is a consuming *. Heb 12:29
A great forest can be set on * by Jas 3:5
And the tongue is a flame of *. Jas 3:6
And the tongue is set on * by Jas 3:6
you, and eat your flesh like *. Jas 5:3
It is being tested as * tests 1Pe 1:7
will disappear in *, and the earth 2Pe 3:10
set the heavens on *, and the 2Pe 3:12
Those cities were destroyed by * Jud 1:7
eyes penetrated like flames of * Rev 1:14
like flames of *, whose feet are Rev 2:18
gold purified by *—only then will Rev 3:18
the censer with * from the altar Rev 8:5
and hail and * mixed with blood Rev 8:7
earth was set on * so that Rev 8:7
and smoke and * and flaming sulphur Rev 9:17,18
sun and his feet flashed with *. Rev 10:1
of * shooting from their mouths. Rev 11:5
such as making * flame down to Rev 13:13
And they will be tormented with * Rev 14:10
power to destroy the world with *, Rev 14:18
Literally, "who has power over * Rev 14:18f
to be an ocean of * and glass, and Rev 15:2
it to scorch all men with its *. Rev 16:8
leave her naked and ravaged by *. Rev 17:16
shall be utterly consumed by *; Rev 18:8
Lake of * that burns with sulphur. Rev 19:20
on every side. But * from God in Rev 20:9
be thrown into the Lake of * Rev 20:10
were thrown into the Lake of * Rev 20:14
is the Second Death—the Lake of *. Rev 20:14
he was thrown into the Lake of *. Rev 20:15
that burns with * and sulphur. Rev 21:8

FIRE-CLOUD
Sometimes the * stayed only Num 9:20,21

FIRE-COVERED
spoken from the * mountain while Deu 9:10,11

FIRE-POT
saw a smoking * and a flaming torch Gen 15:17

FIREBRANDS
around *, arrows and death! Pro 26:18,19
those left are like half-burned * Amo 4:11

FIRED
King Jeroboam had * them, telling 2Ch 11:13,14
pot that is * by dry rushes. Job 41:20

FIRELIGHT
in the * and began staring at him. Lk 22:56

FIREPANS
upon the cloth—the *, hooks, Num 4:14
basins, spoons, *, the hinges of 1Ki 7:50
the pots, shovels, *, snuffers, 2Ki 25:14,15
and *—all were made of pure gold. 2Ch 4:22
He also took the * and the solid Jer 52:19

FIREPLACE
the time, sitting in front of a *, Jer 36:22

FIRES
Don't even light the * in your Ex 35:3
I mused, the hotter the * inside. Ps 39:2,3
your own * and not from God's; Is 50:11
the fathers build *, and the women Jer 7:18
in the * of strange altars? Eze 16:21
need nothing else for their *. Eze 39:10
are in danger of the * of hell. Mt 5:22
unquenchable * of hell with two! Mk 9:43,44
eyes and see the * of hell, where Mk 9:47

FIREWOOD
a bundle of *, and placed it upon Ju 9:47,48

FIRM
As soon as he had a * grip on the 2Ki 14:5
a child's, * and youthful again. Job 33:25
His flesh is hard and *, not Job 41:23
a man shall stand * forever. Ps 15:5
we will arise to stand * and Ps 20:8
my feet on a hard, * path and Ps 40:2
*, for I have set them in place!" Ps 75:3
and goodness, and stand * forever. Ps 111:8
your Word stands * in heaven. Ps 119:89
A good man has * footing, but a Pro 10:9
Stone in Zion—a *, tested, precious Is 28:16
*, for it is strongly built. Lk 6:47,48
For if you stand *, you will win Lk 21:19
it steadfast and *, strong in the Col 1:23
brothers, stand * and keep a strong 2Th 2:15
But God's truth stands * like a 2Ti 2:19
—if we keep up our courage * to Heb 3:6
tired hands, stand * on your shaky Heb 12:12
Stand * when he attacks. 1Pe 5:9
is from the one who stands *, Rev 3:14
saints who remain * to the end in Rev 14:12

FIRMAMENT
Literally, "in the * of his Ps 150:1f
Literally, "from above the *, Eze 1:25f

FIRMLY
altar, attach them *, and overlay Ex 27:2
were * attached to each other. Ex 36:18
The godly shall be * planted in Ps 37:29
but I am * anchored to your laws. Ps 119:61
to be so * fastened to the wall! Is 22:25
I will * plant them there upon Amo 9:15
our ancestors; I * believe in the Act 24:14
faith to stand * upon God, not on 1Co 2:5
you if you still * believe it, 1Co 15:2
up, and set you * in place, and 1Pe 5:10
help you to stand * in his love. 1Pe 5:12
hold to it * and turn to me Rev 3:3

FIRS
their nests, the storks in the *. Ps 104:17
shaded by the cedar trees and *." Sol 1:17
forests of * and pines, and box Is 60:13

FIRST
and the earth, the earth was at * Gen 1:2
Together they formed the * day. Gen 1:4,5
the earth at *, for the Lord God Gen 2:5
He became the * of the cattlemen Gen 4:20
Jubal, the * musician—the inventor Gen 4:21
He opened the * foundry Gen 4:22
lifetime that men * began to call Gen 4:26
Or, "This man was the * to invoke Gen 4:26f
Literally, "on the * day of the Gen 8:5f
601st year, in the * month, the Gen 8:13f
month, the * day of the month." Gen 8:13f
who became the * of the kings. Gen 10:8
* arrived in the land of Canaan. Gen 16:2,3
"This is the * I've heard of Gen 21:26
I know that God is * in your Gen 22:12
had twins. The * was born so Gen 25:25
Laban went * into Jacob's tent to Gen 31:33
He told the men driving the * Gen 32:17
(before Israel had her * king): Gen 36:31-39
child who appeared *, but he drew Gen 38:28
was actually the * to be born. Gen 38:29
The wine taster told his dream *. Gen 40:9,10
baker saw that the * dream had such Gen 40:16
that had come out *, and Gen 41:20
the arrival of the * of the famine Gen 41:50
"O sir, after our * trip to Egypt Gen 43:20
sea, and you shall be * no longer. Gen 49:4
"If they don't believe the * Ex 4:8
month will be the * and most Ex 12:2
On the * day of the celebration, Ex 12:16
"The * is the Pilgrimage of Ex 23:15
bring to me the * of your crops. Ex 23:16
sample of the * day's harvest; Ex 23:19
an emerald shall be in the * row. Ex 28:17
tablets like the * ones and I will Ex 34:1
of stone like the * ones, and was Ex 34:4
* Wheat, and the Harvest Festival. Ex 34:22
the best of the * of each year's Ex 34:26
The skilled weavers * made ten Ex 36:8,9
In the * row were a sardius, a Ex 39:10
on the * day of the first month. Ex 40:2
on the first day of the * month. Ex 40:2
On the * day of the first month, Ex 40:17
On the first day of the * month, Ex 40:17
legs shall * be washed with water. Lev 1:13
"If you are offering from the * Lev 2:14
is handed to him *, wringing its Lev 5:8
for himself *, and then for the Lev 9:7
anyone without * rinsing his hands, Lev 15:11
burnt offering. * he shall present Lev 16:6
do not eat the * three crops, for Lev 19:23
day of the * month" (of the Hebrew Lev 23:5f
On the * day of this festival, Lev 23:7
"The Festival of * Fruits: When Lev 23:9,10,11
you and reap your * harvest, bring Lev 23:9,10,11
harvest, bring the * sheaf of the Lev 23:9,10,11
* sampling of your later crops. Lev 23:17
Literally, "as * fruits to the Lev 23:17f
* sampling of your later crops. Lev 23:20
Literally, "the * day of the Lev 23:23,24f
On the * day there will be a Lev 23:35
Remember that the * and last days Lev 23:39
On the * day, take boughs of Lev 23:40
if he does, both the * and the Lev 27:10
Literally, "on the * day of the Num 1:1f
Literally, "on the * day of the Num 1:17,18,19f
the Tabernacle * and take down the Num 4:5
before the Lord: * the sin offering Num 6:16
Judah, brought his gift the * day. Num 7:12

(FIRST Con't)
during the * month of the second Num 9:1
fourteenth day of this * month, Num 9:2,3
Note: The 14th day of the * month Num 9:2,3f
to our * day of April. Num 9:2,3f
of the Tabernacle shall leave *; Num 10:5,6,7
This was their * journey after Num 10:13
(The * of the grapes were being Num 13:20
Going northward, they passed * Num 13:22
the * grain that is cut each year. Num 15:19,20,21
Literally, "the * month." Num 20:1f
my own people. But *, let me tell Num 24:14
"Amalek was the * of the nations, Num 24:20
at the time of the * census, they Num 26:64,65f
"Also, on the * day of each Num 28:11
"Also on the * day of each month Num 28:15
"On the fourteenth day of the * Num 28:16
On the * day of the festival a Num 28:18
are to present the * of the new Num 28:26
Literally, "upon the * day of the Num 29:1f
on the * day he hears about it; Num 30:5
to allow it on the * day he hears Num 30:12
of Israel. But *, the Lord gets a Num 31:28
inheritance. But * we will need to Num 32:17
Egypt, on the * day of April, Num 33:3,4
day of the * month" (of the Hebrew Num 33:3,4f
Literally, "the * day of the Num 33:38,39f
large half-circle, * going south Num 34:10,11
permanently as it was * allotted. Num 36:7
Literally, "the * day of the Deu 1:1f
"But they replied, "* let's send Deu 1:22
which cities we should capture *.' Deu 1:22
at bedtime and the * thing in the Deu 6:7
Lord from the * day I knew you. Deu 9:24
tablets like the * ones, and to Deu 10:1
tablets like the * two, and took Deu 10:3
just as I had the *, and the Lord Deu 10:10
Your own hand shall be the * upon Deu 13:9
foreign gods, * check the facts to Deu 13:12,13,14
always to put God * in your lives. Deu 14:23
Literally, "Abib"—the * month of Deu 16:1f
* check the rumor very carefully; Deu 17:4
The witnesses shall throw the * Deu 17:7
to the Lord—the * of the grain, the Deu 18:4
against it, * offer it a truce. Deu 20:10
with her. The * son she bears to Deu 25:6
the * sample from each annual Deu 26:2,3
you a token of the * of the crops Deu 26:10
tenth day of the * month" (of the Jos 4:19f
Eglon on the * day and, as at Jos 10:34,35
* to receive their assignment Jos 21:9-16
brother tribes. *, however, they Jos 22:13
should be the * to go to war Ju 1:1
was with them. * they sent scouts, Ju 1:22,23
But if you are afraid, * go down Ju 7:10
for us when you * went out to fight Ju 8:1
to elect a king. * they asked the Ju 9:8
home in peace, the * person coming Ju 11:30,31
Ammonites. But * let me go up into Ju 11:37
They camped * at a place west of Ju 18:12
on their having breakfast *. Ju 19:5
a good time. At * the man refused, Ju 19:7
Bethel * to ask counsel from God. Ju 20:18
replied, "Judah shall go *." Ju 20:18
You have the * right to purchase Ru 4:4
but the fat must * be burned," [as 1Sa 2:16
up his court * at Bethel, then 1Sa 7:16
built an altar to the Lord—his *. 1Sa 14:35
priest said, "Let's ask God *." 1Sa 14:36
as your wife. But * you must prove 1Sa 18:17
This was certainly not the * 1Sa 22:15
that I am the * of a dynasty which 2Sa 7:27
Hebron was King David's * capital, 2Sa 15:9f
would be the * to accuse me." 2Sa 18:13
"The * man looks like Ahima-az, 2Sa 18:27
today, the very * person in all the 2Sa 19:20
And, remember, we were the * to 2Sa 19:43
David's army: the * was 2Sa 23:8
people of Israel. * they crossed 2Sa 24:5
"No," the * woman said, "the 1Ki 3:22
second time (the * time had been at 1Ki 9:2,3
at Bethel on the * of November 1Ki 12:32,33
worshiping Baal. * he built a 1Ki 16:32
bake me a little loaf of bread *; 1Ki 17:13
"You *," he said, "for there 1Ki 18:25
and said to him, "* let me go and 1Ki 19:20
you asked for the * time, but your 1Ki 20:9
"Shall we attack *?" 1Ki 20:14
drunk, the * of Ahab's troops 1Ki 20:16
Syrian infantrymen that * day. 1Ki 20:29
ask the Lord *, to be sure of what 1Ki 22:5
from the * grain of his harvest. 2Ki 4:42
the Lord when they * arrived, the 2Ki 17:25
This occurred during the * year of 2Ki 25:27
Jesse's * son was Eliab, his 1Ch 2:13
Bela, the *,Ashbel, the 1Ch 8:1
Ulam, the *, 1Ch 8:39
The * to return and live again in 1Ch 9:2
Eleazar, was the * director of this 1Ch 9:20
to his men, "The * man to kill a 1Ch 11:5,6
Zeruiah, was the *, so he became 1Ch 11:5,6
*, the group led by Jehoiarib; 1Ch 24:7-18
The * toss indicated Joseph of 1Ch 25:9-31
The commander of the * Division 1Ch 27:2,3
on duty the * month of each year. 1Ch 27:2,3
the land for the * ten years of his 2Ch 14:1
let's check with the Lord *." 2Ch 18:3,4,5
reign from * to last are written in 2Ch 20:34
reign from * to last are recorded 2Ch 26:22
In the very * month of the first 2Ch 29:3
In the very first month of the * 2Ch 29:3
This all began on the * day of 2Ch 29:17
On the * day of May the people 2Ch 30:15
with the * of their crops and 2Ch 31:5,6
great heaps. The * of these tithes 2Ch 31:7,8
the * day of April, in Jerusalem. 2Ch 35:1
your ancestors, as * organized by 2Ch 35:4,5
But in the * year of King Cyrus 2Ch 36:22,23
DURING THE * year of the reign of Ez 1:1
Literally, "the * day of the Ez 3:6f
during the * year of his reign, Ez 5:13
This is what it said: "In this * Ez 6:3
celebrated on the * day of April. Ez 6:19
* month" of the Hebrew calendar. Ez 6:19f
* instituted by King David. Ez 8:20
Or, "the twelfth day of the * Ez 8:31f
* triumphed over us until now. Neh 9:32
to bring the * part of every crop Neh 10:35
contributions, the * of our fruit, Neh 10:37
* of the new wine and olive oil. Neh 10:37
The priests and Levites * Neh 12:30
the * offerings of every harvest. Neh 13:31
The king was furious, but * Est 1:13-15
13th day of the * month . " Est 3:12f
after being * proclaimed in the Est 3:15
*, without actually canceling it. Est 8:8f
ever since man was * placed upon Job 20:4
what is right. But * of all we must Job 34:4
* the Ark was in Ps 132:6
How does a man become wise? The * Pro 1:7,8,9
In everything you do, put God *, Pro 3:6
by giving him the * part of all Pro 3:9,10
Determination to be wise is the * Pro 4:7
man; *, he is a constant liar; Pro 6:12,13
Develop your business * before Pro 24:27
*, help me never to tell a lie. Pro 30:8
So I conclude that, *, there is Ecc 3:12
dawn with the * note of the birds; Ecc 12:4
his people! * to feel his wrath Is 3:14
It is I, the Lord, the * and Is 41:4
I was the * to tell Jerusalem, Is 41:27
From the very * your ancestors Is 43:27
who says it—I am the * and Last; Is 44:6
I am the *; Is 48:12
The * of these messages came to Jer 1:1
holy people, the * of my children. Jer 2:3
* here, then there, you flit Jer 2:36
woman giving birth to her * child; Jer 4:31
Go to Shiloh, the city I * Jer 7:12
of Jerusalem, * at the gate where Jer 17:19
Lord during the * year of the reign Jer 26:1
you the * right to purchase it." Jer 32:8
Begin with the * message back in Jer 36:2
"But *, tell us how you got Jer 36:17
* the king of Assyria ate them up; Jer 50:17
the * rumor of approaching forces. Jer 51:46
sink deep into your own heart *; Eze 3:10
there, just as in my * vision! Eze 3:23
"During the * 390 days eat bread Eze 4:9
faces—the * was that of an ox; Eze 10:14
When I * saw you, your umbilical Eze 16:4
you anymore. But *, because you Eze 16:43
Babylon [the * of the two eagles Eze 17:12,13
the Lord on the * day of the month, Eze 26:1
* he will destroy your suburbs; Eze 26:8
means by the * "broken arm." Eze 30:21f
ministering must * be removed, for Eze 42:14
the other visions, * by the Chebar Eze 43:3
on all sides. The * stage of the Eze 43:14
duties again. The * day he returns Eze 44:27
the priests'. The * of the Eze 44:30
the priests. The * samples of each Eze 44:30
Israel, you shall * give a section Eze 45:1
April was the * month of the Eze 45:18f
the same size and shape as the *. Eze 48:13
* year of the reign of King Cyrus. Dan 1:21
The Medo-Persian Empire, whose * Dan 2:39f
ONE NIGHT DURING the * year of Dan 7:1
the other. The * was like a lion, Dan 7:4
and three of the * ones were yanked Dan 7:8
another dream similar to the *. Dan 8:1
growing slowly at *, soon became Dan 8:9
must * go by." Dan 8:14
the * great king of that country. Dan 8:21
none of them as great as the *. Dan 8:22
IT WAS NOW the * year of the reign Dan 9:1
In that * year of his reign, I, Dan 9:2
answered the very * day you began Dan 10:12
Mede in the * year of his reign. Dan 11:1
From the * his method will be Dan 11:23
with great riches, * marching Dan 11:28
story from those * two occasions. Dan 11:29
Here is the * message: Hos 1:2
I remember those * delightful days Hos 9:10
figs of summer in their * season! Hos 9:10
"But always, * of all, I warn Amo 3:
Therefore you will be the * to Amo 6:7
up after the * mowing, which went Amo 7:1
heavens, the * floor on the earth. Amo 9:6
But the very * day when Jonah Jon 3:4,5
and you * told me to come here. Jon 4:2
for you were the * of the cities of Mic 1:13
But * comes terrible destruction Mic 7:13
than the splendor of the * one! Hag 2:8,9
of brass. The * chariot was pulled Zec 6:2
them out of slavery the * time. Zec 10:11f
the rest of Judah *, before Zec 12:7
time when they * saw the star. Mt 2:7
told him the star * appeared to Mt 2:16
if you give him * place in your Mt 6:33
Hypocrite! * get rid of the Mt 7:5
Or, "Let me * go and bury my Mt 8:21f
kingdom without * binding Satan. Mt 12:29
eating without * going through the Mt 15:20
"that Elijah must come *." Mt 17:10f
the mouth of the * fish you catch. Mt 17:26,27
But many who are * now will be Mt 19:30
who are last now will be * then." Mt 19:30
beginning with the last men *. Mt 20:8
shall be *, and the first, last." Mt 20:16
shall be first, and the *, last." Mt 20:16
one question *," Jesus replied. Mt 21:24
They replied, "The *, of Mt 21:31
brothers. The * of these men Mt 22:25
This is the * and greatest Mt 22:38,39
Blind Pharisees! * cleanse the Mt 23:26
On the * day of the Passover Mt 26:17
"It is the one I served *. Mt 26:23
"I would die *!" Mt 26:35
and crucify. But * they took him Mt 27:27
* day of the Passover ceremonies Mt 27:62
be worse off than we were at *." Mt 27:64
would arrive * to prepare the world Mk 1:2
and though at * they get along Mk 4:17
the seeds grow. * a leaf-blade Mk 4:28
For they eat without * performing Mk 7:5
Jesus told her, "* I should help Mk 7:27
"Let the children eat *." Mk 7:27f
back to the village *," he said. Mk 8:26
Elijah must come * and prepare the Mk 9:12,13
For from the very * he made man Mk 10:6,7
But when you are praying, * Mk 11:25
And the Good News must * be made Mk 13:10
On the * day of the Passover, the Mk 14:12
misunderstood his * two words Mk 15:34f
to life, and the * person who saw Mk 16:9
recognize him at * because he had Mk 16:12
accounts from * to last and after Lk 1:3
and she gave birth to her * Lk 2:7
"If a woman's * child is a boy, he Lk 2:23
His parents didn't miss him the * Lk 2:43
to be baptized! * go and prove by Lk 3:8
Hypocrite! * get rid of the Lk 6:42
again from the time I * came in. Lk 7:45
'Lord, suffer me * to go and bury Lk 9:59f
I will come, but * let me ask Lk 9:61
to eat without * performing the Lk 11:37,38
For none of those I invited * Lk 14:24
a building without * getting Lk 14:28
to war without * sitting down with Lk 14:31
disciple unless he * sits down and Lk 14:33
He asked the * one, 'How much do Lk 16:5,6
down and eat, but * prepares his Lk 17:7,8,9
the skies. But * I must suffer Lk 17:25
"The * man reported a tremendous Lk 19:16
God and the * cause of all things; Jn 1:1f
God and the * cause of all things; Jn 1:14f
uses the best wine *, and Jn 2:10
Galilee was Jesus' * public Jn 2:11
the water, and the * person to step Jn 5:4
never sinned may throw the *!" Jn 8:7
place where John was * baptizing. Jn 10:40
and tied him. * they took him to Jn 18:13
Literally, "on the * day of the Jn 20:1f
other disciple also, who came *." Jn 20:3,4f
outran Peter and got there *, Jn 20:3,4
In my * letter Act 1:1
from our * association with the Act 1:21,22
again, he sent him * of all to you Act 3:26
were * called "Christians." Act 11:26
They passed the * and second Act 12:10
God should be given * to you Jews. Act 13:46
about the time God * visited the Act 15:14
PAUL AND SILAS went * to Derbe and Act 16:1
to go north to Macedonia *. Act 20:3
Literally, "the * day of the Act 20:7f
one of the * seven deacons. Act 21:8
I preached * to those in Act 26:20
suffer, and be the * to rise from Act 26:23
They tried at * to face back to Act 27:14,15
to me in the * place and not left Act 27:21
the island. Our * stop was Act 28:12
Let me say * of all that wherever Rom 1:8

(FIRST Con't)
This message was preached * to Rom 1:16
* of all, God trusted them with Rom 3:2
be the *, with many brothers. Rom 8:29
the child born *, would be a Rom 9:10-13
put there in the * place, he won't Rom 11:21
who were there in the * place? Rom 11:24
for two reasons: *, to keep from Rom 13:5
is nearer now than when we * Rom 13:11
He was the very * person to Rom 16:5
DEAR BROTHERS, EVEN when I * 1Co 2:1
but only one person gets * prize. 1Co 9:24
is the woman. The * man didn't 1Co 11:8
but the * woman came out of man. 1Co 11:8
And Adam, the * man, was not 1Co 11:9
For although the * woman came 1Co 11:12
*, however, let me tell you about 1Co 12:31
should be the * to realize that 1Co 14:37
really believed it in the * place. 1Co 15:2
you right from the * what had been 1Co 15:3
and has become the * of millions 1Co 15:20
in his own turn: Christ rose *; 1Co 15:23
into a plant unless it "dies" *. 1Co 15:36
from the seed you * planted. 1Co 15:37
The Scriptures tell us that the * 1Co 15:45
*, then, we have these human 1Co 15:46
been to Macedonia *, but I will be 1Co 16:5
They were the * to become 1Co 16:15
to him, and as the * installment of 2Co 1:22
In fact, that * glory as it 2Co 3:10
hopes, for their * action was to 2Co 8:5
your giving in the * place, to 2Co 8:6
were not only the * to propose this 2Co 8:10
this idea, but the * to begin doing 2Co 8:10
after I have * used them on you 2Co 10:6
for we were the * to come to you 2Co 10:14
For when he * arrived he ate Gal 2:12
life in the * place, why do you Gal 3:3
me then when I * preached to you, Gal 4:12
I was sick when I * brought you the Gal 4:13
who were the * to trust in Christ. Eph 1:12
This means that he had * come Eph 4:9
This is the * of God's Ten Eph 6:2
the time you * heard it until now. Php 1:5
As you well know, when I * Php 4:15
the Gospel * was preached to you. Col 1:5
yours that very * day you heard it Col 1:6
So ever since we * heard about Col 1:9
so that he is * in everything; Col 1:18
be the * to rise to meet the Lord. 1Th 4:16
two things happen: *, there will be 2Th 2:3
the very * to give you salvation, 2Th 2:13
to be among the * to believe." 2Th 2:13f
pray for us. Pray * that the Lord's 2Th 3:1
Because God made Adam *, and 1Ti 2:13
they broke their * promise. 1Ti 5:12
For the love of money is the * 1Ti 6:10
The * time I was brought before 2Ti 4:16
be given a * and second warning. Tit 3:10
as we did when we * became Heb 3:14
those who had the * chance, for Heb 4:6
years after man's * failure to Heb 4:7
very * principles in God's Word. Heb 5:12,13
those * lessons about Christ. Heb 6:1
(a) Even Abraham, the * and most Heb 7:4
did, to cover over * their own sins Heb 7:27
NOW IN THAT * agreement between Heb 9:1
two rooms. The * one contained the Heb 9:1
in and out of the * room whenever Heb 9:6
before even the * agreement Heb 9:18
He cancels the * system in favor Heb 10:9
they broke their * agreement: I Heb 10:16
when you * learned about Christ. Heb 10:32
turn * this way, and then that. Jas 1:7,8
the * children in his new family. Jas 1:18
water bubble out * with fresh water Jas 3:11
from heaven is * of all pure and Jas 3:17
begin * among God's own children. 1Pe 4:17
*, I want to remind you that in 2Pe 3:3
was since the * day of creation." 2Pe 3:4
who since he * began to sin has 1Jn 3:8
test it * to see if it really is. 1Jn 4:1
as a result of his loving us *. 1Jn 4:19
the very * to love each other. 2Jn 1:6
He was the * to rise from death, Rev 1:5
these are the * and last letters Rev 1:8f
"I am A and Z, the * and Last!" Rev 1:11
Though I am the * and Last, the Rev 1:17,18
you don't love me as at *! Rev 2:4
of your * love (how different now! Rev 2:5
him who is the * and Last, who was Rev 2:8
what you heard and believed at *; Rev 3:3
four sides. The * of these Living Rev 4:7
AS I WATCHED, the Lamb broke the * Rev 6:1
The * angel blew his trumpet, and Rev 8:7
he said. "At * it will taste like Rev 10:9
* Creature was there to watch him. Rev 13:14
statue of the * Creature, who was Rev 13:14
So the * angel left the temple Rev 16:2
This is the * Resurrection. Rev 20:5
who share in the * Resurrection. Rev 20:6
The * layer Rev 21:18,19,20
and the End, the * and Last. Rev 22:13

FIRST-BORN
to you, my * son, Gen 27:2,3,4
Literally, "the * from the Rev 1:5f

FIRST-FRUITS
"On the Day of * (also called Num 28:26
Literally, "the * of them that 1Co 15:20f

FIRST-OF-THE-HARVEST
"Yours also are the * gifts the Num 18:12
this as your * offering to him of Num 18:27
the tithes, and * offerings, and to Neh 12:44

FIRST-RIPE
The first of the * fruits and Eze 44:30
They will be devoured like * figs Nah 3:12

FIRSTBORN
and even the * of the animals. Ex 11:5
oldest sons and * male animals in Ex 12:12
not destroy your * children when I Ex 12:13
to enter and kill your *. Ex 12:23
killed all the * sons in the land Ex 12:29
also all the * of the cattle. Ex 12:29
"Dedicate to me all of the * sons Ex 13:1
Literally, "all the *." Ex 13:1f
of Israel, and every * male Ex 13:1
now living, all * sons and Ex 13:12
firstborn sons and * male animals Ex 13:12
them to him. A * donkey may be Ex 13:13
However, you must buy back your * Ex 13:13
killed all the * males throughout Ex 13:15
that is why we now give all the * Ex 13:15
"As to the * of the oxen and the Ex 22:30
"Every * male Ex 34:19
and goats. The * colt of a donkey Ex 34:20
to the Lord the * of any ox or Lev 27:26
But if it is the * of an animal Lev 27:27
for myself all the * in Israel of Num 3:13
* cattle of the whole nation." Num 3:41
* cattle of the people of Israel; Num 3:45
place of all the * children of the Num 8:16
For all the * among the people Num 8:17
I killed all the * Egyptians. Num 8:17
including the * sons of the people Num 18:14,15
and the * of their animals. Num 18:14,15
never accept the * sons, nor the Num 18:16
sons, nor the * of any animals that Num 18:16
dollars made for each * child. Num 18:16
"However, the * of cows, sheep, Num 18:17
offerings of the * animals of your Deu 12:6
olive oil, nor the * of your flocks Deu 12:17
the * of your flocks and herds. Deu 14:23
for God all the * males from your Deu 15:19
Do not use the * of your herds to Deu 15:19
do not shear the * of your flocks Deu 15:19
However, if this * animal has Deu 15:21
the rights of a * son, even though Deu 21:17
Sidon (his *) and Heth. 1Ch 1:13-16
sons and the * of all our cattle, Neh 10:36
Literally, "all the *." Ps 78:51f
"I will treat him as my * son, Ps 89:27
along with the * of the flocks. Ps 135:8
Praise the God who smote the * Ps 136:10
They burnt their * children as Eze 20:26
Literally, "he is the * of all Col 1:15f
Beginning, the * from the dead." Col 1:18f
time—when his * Son came to Heb 1:5,6

FIRSTFRUITS
Literally, "the * of his Jer 2:3f

FIRSTHAND
to show you, *, how you should work 2Th 3:9

FISH
waters teem with * and other life, Gen 1:20
sort of * and every kind of bird. Gen 1:21,22
you are masters of the * and Gen 1:28
and birds and * will be afraid of Gen 9:2,3
to blood! The * will die and the Ex 7:18
to blood. The * died and the water Ex 7:21
resembling animals, birds, or *. Ex 20:4
"As to *, you may eat whatever Lev 11:9
of the delicious * we enjoyed so Num 11:4,5
We would have to catch every * in Num 11:22
runs along the ground, or a *. Deu 4:18
whether of birds, animals, or *. Deu 5:8
birds, snakes, *, and trees—from 1Ki 4:33
and then to the * Gate, and around 2Ch 33:14
The * Gate was built by the sons Neh 3:3
Gate, passed the * Gate and the Neh 12:39
Tyre bringing in * and all sorts of Neh 13:16
teach you, or the * of the sea. Job 12:7,8,9
*, and all the life in the sea. Ps 8:8
water into blood, poisoning the *. Ps 105:29
He is like a * caught in a net, Ecc 9:12
those who * with hooks and those Is 19:8
deserts, covered with dying *. Is 50:2
many fishermen to * you from the Jer 16:16
with * sticking to your scales. Eze 29:4
you and all the * stranded in the Eze 29:5
river shall live. * will abound in Eze 47:9
drying in the sun. * of every kind Eze 47:10
and even the * begin to disappear. Hos 4:3
for a great * to swallow Jonah. Jon 1:17
And Jonah was inside the * three Jon 1:17
Lord his God from inside the *: Jon 2:1
And the Lord ordered the * to Jon 2:10
Are we but *, to be caught and Hab 1:14
and the * in the sea will perish. Zep 1:3
how to * for the souls of men!" Mt 4:19
If he asks for *, will he be Mt 7:10
For as Jonah was in the great * Mt 12:39,40
and gathers in * of every kind, Mt 13:47,48
small loaves of bread and two *!" Mt 14:17
loaves and two *, looked up into Mt 14:19
of bread and a few small *!" Mt 15:34
loaves and the *, and gave thanks Mt 15:36
mouth of the first * you catch. Mt 17:26,27
five loaves of bread and two *. Mk 6:38
He took the five loaves and two * Mk 6:41
of the bread and * to each disciple Mk 6:41
A few small * were found, too, Mk 8:7
and you will catch a lot of *!" Lk 5:4
* and on the verge of sinking. Lk 5:7
of bread and two * among the lot of Lk 9:13
loaves and two * and looked up into Lk 9:16
If he asks for *, do you give him Lk 11:11
*, and he ate it as they watched! Lk 24:42
barley loaves and a couple of *! Jn 6:8,9
he did the same with the *. Jn 6:11
He called, "Any *, boys?" Jn 21:5
of the *, there were so many! Jn 21:6
was kindled and * were frying over Jn 21:9
"Bring some of the * you've just Jn 21:10
his count there were 153 large *; Jn 21:11
around serving us the bread and *. Jn 21:13
Humans, animals, *, and birds are 1Co 15:39
of reptile and *, but no human Jas 3:7
and a third of the * were killed. Rev 8:8,9

FISH-MONGERS
partners sell him to the *? Job 41:6

FISHERMAN
illustrated by a *—he casts a net Mt 13:47,48

FISHERMEN
everything will die. The * will Is 19:8
Now I am sending for many * to Jer 16:16
a place for * to spread their nets, Eze 26:5
a place for * to spread their Eze 26:14
will live. * will stand along the Eze 47:10
a net, for they were commercial *. Mt 4:18
nets, for they were commercial *. Mk 1:16
And I will make you * for the Mk 1:17
while the * washed their nets. Lk 5:2

FISHHOOKS
drag the last of you away with *! Amo 4:2

FISHING
to play with? Do * partners sell Job 41:6
of the Dead Sea, * all the way from Eze 47:10
* with a net, for they were Mt 4:18
his brother Andrew * with nets, for Mk 1:16
From now on you'll be * for the Lk 5:10
Simon Peter said, "I'm going * Jn 21:3

FISSURE
them, and a great * swallowed them Num 16:32

FIST
stone or with his * and injures him Ex 21:18
him with his * so that he dies, he Num 35:21
and shook his * at him. 1Ki 13:4
he clenches his * against God, Job 15:25,26
Unleash your * and give them a Ps 74:11
power and upraised * to strike Ps 136:11,12
You will clench your * against my Ps 138:7
be satisfied—his * will still be Is 9:11,12
satisfied, but his * is still Is 9:17
satisfied, but my * will still be Is 10:4
He shakes his * at Jerusalem on Is 10:32
beneath the upraised * of God. Is 19:16
not look to see your upraised *. Is 26:11
When the Lord clenches his * Is 31:3
crush them with my * and break off Eze 14:13
I have crushed you with my *; Eze 16:27
I will rule you with an iron * Eze 20:33
smash Edom with my * and wipe out Eze 25:13
I will shake my * over the land of Eze 25:16
with my * and utterly destroy you. Eze 35:3
Jerusalem with my *, and destroy Zep 1:4
" 'I will smash them with my * Zec 2:9
Literally, "to wash with the *." Mk 7:3f
there struck Jesus with his *. Jn 18:22

FISTS
Who else holds the wind in his *, Pro 30:4
and shake their * at heaven and Is 8:21
Therefore I will clench my * Jer 15:6
to hammer his face with their *. Mk 14:65
* on him as they led him away. Mk 14:65
hit him with their * and asked, Lk 22:63,64
and struck him with their *. Jn 19:3

FIT
as you see *," Abram replied. Gen 16:6
His brothers were * to be tied Gen 37:11
produce rich foods, * for kings! Gen 49:20
with gold, and * the poles into the Ex 25:13,14
for the frames to * into—two bases Ex 26:18,19
each corner, and * the grating Ex 27:5
it is not a * burnt offering for Lev 22:22

(FIT Con't)
In a great * of temper Balaam Num 22:27
"If the Lord sees *," David 2Sa 15:25,26
of whom were strong and * for war. 2Ki 24:16
is not * for the Kingdom of God." Lk 9:62
Flavorless salt is * for Lk 14:35
I am not even * to be his slave." Jn 1:27
* in with it, just as I don't. Jn 17:14
He isn't * to live!" Act 22:22
those who are * only for Rom 9:22
declared him * for heaven only Gal 3:6
who has made us * to share all the Col 1:12
exercise of keeping spiritually *. 1Ti 4:7
Leader, one * to bring them into Heb 2:10
WIVES, * IN with your husbands' 1Pe 3:1

FITS
Wear my yoke—for it * Mt 11:29,30

FITTED
up by twenty posts * into bronze Ex 27:11
his bow and * it with deadly Ps 7:13
But the Holy Spirit has * us all 1Co 12:13
the whole body is * together Eph 4:15,16
* in with their husbands' plans. 1Pe 3:5

FITTING
* into twenty bronze post holders. Ex 27:9,10
bottoms * into forty silver bases. Ex 36:24
* the size of its territory to its Jos 13:15
love God and are * into his plans. Rom 8:28

FITTINGLY
(the city * described as "Sodom" Rev 11:8,9

FIVE
Sea Valley (four kings against *). Gen 14:8,9
destroy the city for lack of *?" Gen 18:28
Let Pharaoh divide Egypt into * Gen 41:34,35
to Benjamin—* times as much as to Gen 43:34
* years of famine ahead of us. Gen 45:11,12
Benjamin he gave * changes of Gen 45:22
He took * of his brothers with Gen 47:2
and each of these will have * Ex 18:21
pay a fine of * to one—five oxen Ex 22:1
of five to one—* oxen shall be Ex 22:1
Join * sheets end to end for Ex 26:3
Connect * of these tarpaulins Ex 26:9
across the frames, * bars on each Ex 26:26,27
Tabernacle. Also * bars for the Ex 26:26,27
Hang up this curtain on * acacia Ex 26:37
Literally, "* hundred shekels." Ex 30:22,23f
upon them. * of these sheets were Ex 36:10
end to end, then * others similarly Ex 36:10
Bezalel coupled * of these Ex 36:16
Then he made * sets of bars from Ex 36:31,32
* for each side of the Tabernacle. Ex 36:31,32
The middle bar of the * was Ex 36:33
This drapery was connected by * Ex 36:38
by five hooks to * posts. Ex 36:38
their * bases were molded from Ex 36:38
"The Festival of Tabernacles: * Lev 23:33,34
your swords. * of you will chase a Lev 26:8
a boy from * to twenty shall pay Lev 27:5
a girl, * dollars. Lev 27:5
A boy one month to * years old Lev 27:6
a woman, * dollars. Lev 27:7
number of Levites, pay * dollars Num 3:47,48
Literally, "* shekels apiece by Num 3:47,48f
two oxen, * rams, five male goats, Num 7:17
oxen, five rams, * male goats, and Num 7:17
goats, and * male yearling lambs. Num 7:17
two, or * or ten or even twenty! Num 11:19,20
"* days later Num 29:12
Among those killed were all * of Num 31:8
His share is one out of every * Num 31:28
That night Joshua sent another * Jos 8:11,12,13
Perhaps the additional * thousand Jos 8:11,12,13f
So these * Amorite kings combined Jos 10:5
During the battle the * kings Jos 10:16
and wiped out the * armies except Jos 10:20
to bring out the * kings—of Jos 10:22,23
each of the * kings, killing them. Jos 10:26
He then hanged them on * trees Jos 10:26
* cities of the Philistines: Jos 13:2-7
He had only * daughters whose Jos 17:3
Moses, these * women were given an Jos 17:5,6
along with their * great-uncles, Jos 17:5,6
The Philistines (* cities), Ju 3:1
of Sorek. The * heads of the Ju 16:5
sent for the * Philistine leaders. Ju 16:18
with people. The * Philistine Ju 16:27
So the men of Dan chose * army Ju 18:2
So the * men went on to the town Ju 18:7
the * spies told the others. Ju 18:14
So the * men went over to the Ju 18:15,16
Then the * spies entered the Ju 18:17
of Rimmon, but * thousand were Ju 20:45
the mayors of the * cities of the 1Sa 5:8
And they were told, "Send * gold 1Sa 6:4,5
by the plague, and * gold models of 1Sa 6:4,5
After the * Philistine mayors had 1Sa 6:16
same day. The * gold models of 1Sa 6:17
controlled by the * capitals. 1Sa 6:18
Then he picked up * smooth 1Sa 17:40
Give me * loaves of bread, or 1Sa 21:3
barrels of wine, * dressed sheep, 1Sa 25:18
she took along * of her serving 1Sa 25:42
He was * years old at the time 2Sa 4:4
He also gave them the * adopted 2Sa 21:8
above the other, * to a tier, 1Ki 7:3,4
gallons of water. * of these vats 1Ki 7:39
on the left and * on the right-hand 1Ki 7:39
the lampstands (* on the 1Ki 7:49
side and * on the left, in front of 1Ki 7:49
Let them take * of the remaining 2Ki 7:13
struck the floor * or six times," 2Ki 13:19
officer, * of the king's 2Ki 25:19
So Judah had * sons. 1Ch 2:4
Later, * hundred of these 1Ch 4:42
among whose * sons were Michael, 1Ch 7:3
for all * of them had several 1Ch 7:4
These * mighty warriors were 1Ch 7:7
wing of a cherub, * cubits long." 2Ch 3:11,12,13f
The walls of the tank were * 2Ch 4:5
the offerings, * to the right of 2Ch 4:6
the huge tank and * to the left. 2Ch 4:6
the Temple, * against each wall; 2Ch 4:7
tables and placed * against each 2Ch 4:8
or * out on the tips of the limbs. Is 17:6
At that time * of the cities of Is 19:18
a thousand of you! * of them will Is 30:17
he took 832 more; * years after Jer 52:30
gerahs, no less; * shekels shall be Eze 45:12
five shekels shall be valued at * Eze 45:12
* miles east of Petra, in Edom. Ob 1:8f
"We have exactly * small loaves Mt 14:17
and he took the * loaves and two Mt 14:19
5,000 I fed with * loaves, and the Mt 16:9
"At * o'clock that evening he Mt 20:6
When the men hired at * o'clock Mt 20:9
But only * of them were wise Mt 25:2,3,4
other * were foolish and forgot. Mt 25:2,3,4
Then the * who hadn't any oil Mt 25:7,8
"Later, when the other * Mt 25:11
* loaves of bread and two fish. Mk 6:38
He took the * loaves and two fish Mk 6:41
men I fed with * loaves of bread? Mk 8:19
went into seclusion for * months. Lk 1:24
"Why, we have only * loaves of Lk 9:13
Jesus took the * loaves and two Lk 9:16
"What is the price of * Lk 12:6
he had just bought * pair of oxen Lk 14:19
home— for I have * brothers—to Lk 16:28
gain—* times the original amount. Lk 19:18
'You can be governor over * Lk 19:19
"For you have had * husbands, Jn 4:17,18
Pool, with * covered platforms or Jn 5:2
"There's a youngster here with * Jn 6:8,9
Greece and * days later arrived in Act 20:6
* DAYS LATER Ananias the High Act 24:1
the * books of Moses and the books Act 28:23
much rather speak * words that 1Co 14:19
seen by more than * hundred 1Co 15:6
again and again. * different times 2Co 11:24
torture them for * months with Rev 9:5
for * months, was in their tails. Rev 9:10
seven kings. * have already fallen, Rev 17:10

FIVE-OUNCE
and two * golden bracelets for Gen 24:22

FIVE-SIDED
sanctuary was a * opening, and its 1Ki 6:31

FIX
one more thing: * your thoughts on Php 4:8
for the way they * their hair or 1Ti 2:9,10

FIXED
* her hair and sat at a window. 2Ki 9:30

FIXING
some down for stone for * walls. Is 22:9,10,11

FLAG
(meaning "Jehovah is my *"). Ex 17:15,16
camping area with its own *. Num 1:52
under its own *, just as each was Num 2:3-31
grouped behind its *, and led by Num 10:14
Then came the * of the camp of Num 10:18
Ephraim behind its *, led by Num 10:22
headed by the * of the tribe of Dan Num 10:25
but with his * flying above me I Ps 118:11
Yet beneath his * I shall destroy Ps 118:12
He will raise a * among the Is 11:12
When I raise my battle * upon the Is 18:3
boulders, raise the * of Israel." Is 62:10

FLAGONS
dishes, spoons, pitchers, and *; Ex 25:29
he made the bowls, *, dishes, and Ex 37:15,16

FLAGPOLE
with its * and tribal banner; Num 2:1

FLAGRANT
She has defiled Israel by * Deu 22:21

FLAGS
of your victory, * flying with Ps 20:5
See the * waving as their enemy Is 13:2
battle * of Israel, says the Lord. Is 31:9

FLAIL
but it is beaten softly with a *. Is 28:27

FLAILING
in just a little while the * will Jer 51:33

FLAKES
it left tiny * of something as Ex 16:14

FLAME
to him as a * of fire in a bush. Ex 3:2
And my anger shall * out against Ex 22:24
place this eternal * in the outer Ex 27:21
oil for an eternal * in the Lev 24:1
It will be an eternal * before Lev 24:3,4
Then my anger will * out against Deu 31:17
would * out against Israel again. Ju 2:20
If you refuse, let fire * forth Ju 9:15
the perpetual * has been put out, 2Ch 29:7
And your bright * shall be put Job 18:5
the mountains burst into * at his Ps 104:32
of * at night to give them light. Ps 105:39
blaze against me like a roaring *. Ps 118:12
It flashes fire, the very * of Sol 8:6
Many waters cannot quench the * Sol 8:7
fire and * that will destroy them. Is 10:17
For the * of God burns brightly Is 31:9
nor quench the dimly burning *. Is 42:3
to be entirely *, and there was a Eze 1:27,28
to him in a * of fire in a bush. Act 7:30
into * the strength and boldness 2Ti 1:6
And the tongue is a * of fire. Jas 3:6
* of destruction and disaster. Jas 3:6
as making fire * down to earth from Rev 13:13

FLAMED
For a fire has * forth Num 21:27-30
So the anger of the Lord * out Ju 2:12-14
Then the anger of the Lord * out Ju 3:8
staff, and fire * up from the rock Ju 6:21

FLAMES
burned with fire; * shot far into Deu 4:11
thing, for as the * from the altar Ju 13:20
it over him and died in the *. 1Ki 16:18
as * shoot upwards from a fire. Job 5:7
the * shall burn up all he has. Job 15:30
coals—* leap from his mouth. Job 41:21
Fierce * leaped from his mouth, Ps 18:8
and the * will consume the Is 9:18
helpless, as the * of the burning Is 13:8
and with devouring * and tornados Is 30:30
up—the * will not consume you. Is 43:2
and his hot rebuke with * of fire. Is 66:15
be able to put out the raging *. Jer 17:27
coals from the * between the Eze 10:7,8
The terrible * will not be Eze 20:47
the furnace, the * leaped out and Dan 3:22
down bound into the roaring *. Dan 3:23
they aren't even hurt by the *! Dan 3:25
it * forth like raging fire. Hos 7:6
They burst into * like straw. Nah 1:10
for I am in anguish in these *.' Lk 16:24
Then, what looked like * or Act 2:3
man escaping through a wall of *. 1Co 3:15
will melt and disappear in *. 2Pe 3:12
as from the very * of hell itself. Jud 1:23
eyes penetrated like * of fire. Rev 1:14
penetrate like * of fire, whose Rev 2:18
His eyes were like *, and on his Rev 19:12

FLAMING
of Eden, with a * sword to guard Gen 3:24
fire-pot and a * torch that passed Gen 15:17
down fire and * tar from heaven Gen 19:24
And with * fire at his right hand. Deu 33:2
and holding the * torches in their Ju 7:19,20
be thrown into a * furnace." Dan 3:6
will be thrown into a * furnace. Dan 3:11
into a * furnace within the hour. Dan 3:15
If we are thrown into the * Dan 3:17
open door of the * furnace and Dan 3:26
brought in on * wheels, and a Dan 7:9
from heaven in * fire with his 2Th 1:7
and as servants made of * fire; Heb 1:7
face with terror, * fire, gloom, Heb 12:18
blew, and a great * star fell from Rev 8:10
smoke and fire and * sulphur Rev 9:17,18

FLANK
up the eastern * of Moab, wiping Eze 25:9,10

FLANKED
also gold armrests, each * by a 2Ch 9:18

FLAPS
"The ostrich * her wings Job 39:13

FLARE
rages and scoffs, and tempers *. Pro 29:9

FLARED
"Am I God?" he *. Gen 30:2
His anger * out against them Num 11:1
Then the anger of the Lord * out 2Sa 6:7
ONCE AGAIN THE anger of the Lord * 2Sa 24:1
The two * capitals on the tops of 2Ch 4:12-16

FLARING
7½-foot capital * out to the roof. 2Ch 3:15
* out like the cup of a lily. 2Ch 4:5

FLASH
to * forth from the clouds? Job 37:15
Shields * red in the sunlight! Nah 2:3
From his hands * rays of Hab 3:4
from heaven as a * of lightning! Lk 10:18
God in heaven will * down on the Rev 20:9

FLASHED
Then, suddenly, fire * down from 1Ki 18:38
praying, fire * down from heaven 2Ch 7:1
oh, the fire! He * his fearful Ps 18:14
Your lightning *. Ps 77:17
of fire inside that * continually; Eze 1:4
it was from these the lightning *. Eze 1:13
Suddenly Jesus' words * through Mk 14:72
Great bursts of light * forth Rev 4:3
rumbled, lightning *, and there was Rev 8:5
the sun and his feet * with fire. Rev 10:1
Lightning * and thunder crashed Rev 11:19
and rolled, and lightning *; Rev 16:18
glory of God, and * and glowed like Rev 21:11

FLASHES
* out in every direction. Job 37:3
His lightning * out across the Ps 97:4
* overwhelmed the nation. Ps 105:32
* fire, the very flame of Jehovah. Sol 8:6
my burning fury * out upon you like Jer 21:12
every gate; it * like lightning; Eze 21:15
and polished and * like lightning. Eze 21:28
From his face came blinding * Dan 10:5,6
For as the lightning * across Mt 24:27
lightning that * across the skies. Lk 17:24

FLASHING
away by your anger, with * eyes? Job 15:12
him, or the * spear and javelin. Job 39:21-23
See the * swords and glittering Nah 3:3
the * of your glittering spear. Hab 3:11

FLASHLIGHT
Your words are a * to light the Ps 119:105

FLASK
THEN SAMUEL TOOK a * of olive oil 1Sa 10:1
At Gihon, Zadok took a * of 1Ki 1:39
been poured from * to flask, and is Jer 48:11
to *, and is fragrant and smooth. Jer 48:11
beautiful * of expensive perfume. Mk 14:3
* filled with expensive perfume. Lk 7:37
of them a golden * filled with the Rev 15:7
and poured out his * over the Rev 16:2
The second angel poured out his * Rev 16:3
The third angel poured out his * Rev 16:4
poured out his * upon the sun, Rev 16:8
poured out his * upon the throne of Rev 16:10
The sixth angel poured out his * Rev 16:12
poured out his * into the air; Rev 16:17

FLASKS
out the seven * of the wrath of God Rev 16:1
had emptied the * containing the Rev 21:9

FLAT
*, and tasted like honey bread. Ex 16:31
* upon the ground before the Lord. Lev 9:24
fell * on the ground before him. Num 22:31
the edge of the * rooftop to Deu 22:8
It hit our tent and knocked it * Ju 7:12,13
forward and fell * on the ground 2Sa 24:20
the * cakes for grain offerings. 1Ch 9:31
and now they fell * on the 2Ch 7:3
fool falls * on his face. Pro 10:8
strikes up, you are to fall * on Dan 3:5
which, being *, were used as Mt 24:17f
He fell * on the ground in Lk 17:16
the * roof of his house to pray. Act 10:9,10

FLATLY
later someone else * stated, "I Lk 22:59
He denied it *. Jn 1:20

FLATTEN
For it will * out before him! Zec 4:7

FLATTENED
and mountains * out, and there was Rev 16:20

FLATTER
and don't make me * anyone. Job 32:21,22
try to * you from your intentions? Job 41:3
He will * those who hate the Dan 11:32

FLATTERIES
Their tongues are filled with * Ps 5:9
from prostitutes with all their *. Pro 6:24

FLATTERS
Everyone deceives and * and Ps 12:2

FLATTERY
a man from the * of prostitutes; Pro 2:16,17
smooth * is her stock in trade. Pro 5:3
from listening to her *. Pro 7:5
He couldn't resist her *. Pro 7:21
* is a form of hatred and wounds Pro 26:28
appreciate frankness more than *. Pro 28:23
* is a trap; Pro 29:5,6
the kingdom by * and intrigue. Dan 11:21
to please you by sweet talk and *; Gal 1:10
to win you with *, as you very well 1Th 2:5

FLAUNT
their idols to * their victory. Ps 74:4
don't * your faith in front of Rom 14:22

FLAUNTED
because she * herself before them Eze 23:18

FLAVOR
If you lose your *, what will Mt 5:13
So don't lose your *! Mk 9:50

FLAVORLESS
* salt is fit for nothing—not Lk 14:35

FLAX
All the * and barley were Ex 9:31
was ripe, and the * was in bloom), Ex 9:31
piles of * that were drying there. Jos 2:6
She finds wool and * and busily Pro 31:13
The weavers will have no * or Is 19:9

FLEA
as worthless as a dead dog or a *? 1Sa 24:14

FLEAS
a shepherd picks * from his cloak! Jer 43:12

FLED
Sodom and Gomorrah *, some slipped Gen 14:10
the remainder * to the mountains. Gen 14:10
on camels, and * without telling Gen 31:17-20
So he * with all of his Gen 31:21
you * from your brother Esau." Gen 35:1
holding it as he * from the house. Gen 39:12
he had *, she began screaming; Gen 39:13
He *, leaving his jacket behind!" Gen 39:18
All of the people of Israel * at Num 16:34
His sons have *, Num 21:27-30
Israel has * from her enemies! Jos 7:8
Joshua and the Israeli army * Jos 8:15
other, and they * into the night to Ju 7:22
The two kings *, but Gideon Ju 8:12
entire population * into it, Ju 9:51
So Jephthah * from his father's Ju 11:3
The rest of the army * into the Ju 20:45
the remainder * to their tents. 1Sa 4:10
out of the way and * into the 1Sa 19:9,10
DAVID NOW * from Naioth in Ramah, 1Sa 20:1
Ahimelech, escaped and * to David. 1Sa 22:20
that David had * to Gath, so he 1Sa 27:4
hundred young men who * on camels. 1Sa 30:17
and the Israelis * from them and 1Sa 31:1
their comrades had * and that Saul 1Sa 31:7
man replied, "Our entire army *. 2Sa 1:4
even though they * to Gittaim, 2Sa 4:2,3
grabbed him and *, but she fell and 2Sa 4:4
Taking his head with them, they * 2Sa 4:6,7
But again the Syrians * from the 2Sa 10:18
king jumped on their mules and *. 2Sa 13:29,30
Absalom * to King Talmai of 2Sa 13:37,38,39
some of David's men and as he * 2Sa 18:9
And the army of Israel * to their 2Sa 18:17
the rest of the Israeli army *. 2Sa 23:9
deserted him and *, he stood alone 2Sa 23:11,12
the banquet table and * in panic; 1Ki 1:49,50
I * from your brother Absalom. 1Ki 2:7
his post and * the country. 1Ki 11:23
of bandits—men who * with him to 1Ki 11:24
Jeroboam, but he * to King Shishak 1Ki 11:40
Egypt where he had * from King 1Ki 12:2,3,4
by chariot and * to Jerusalem. 1Ki 12:18
So Elijah * for his life; 1Ki 19:3
entire Syrian army panicked and *. 1Ki 20:20
The rest * behind the walls of 1Ki 20:30
Ben-hadad * into the city and hid 1Ki 20:30
and the army of Moab *. 2Ki 3:24
So they panicked and * into the 2Ki 7:7
but his army deserted him and *. 2Ki 8:21
around and *, shouting to King 2Ki 9:23
* along the road to Beth-haggan. 2Ki 9:27
was defeated and the army * home. 2Ki 14:12
in Jerusalem, and he * to Lachish; 2Ki 14:19
the inner wall and * out toward the 2Ki 25:4,5
guerrilla leaders * in panic to 2Ki 25:26
who turned and * and were 1Ch 10:1
they abandoned their cities and *. 1Ch 10:7
and the Syrians turned and *. 1Ch 19:14
retreating, they * into the city. 1Ch 19:15
But the Syrians again * from 1Ch 19:17,18
his chariot and * to Jerusalem. 2Ch 10:18
nation (they had * to Jerusalem for 2Ch 12:5
triumphed as the Ethiopians *. 2Ch 14:12
was defeated, and its army * home. 2Ch 25:22
and how he * to Lachish—but they 2Ch 25:27
A Psalm of David when he * from Ps 3:1
that came to destroy us have *!" Ps 68:11,12,13
their backs and * when the day of Ps 78:9
They have * from drawn swords Is 21:15
All my sleep has * because of my Is 38:15
the birds of the heavens had * Jer 4:25
abandoned—all have * in terror. Jer 4:29
the refugees who * to Egypt Jer 7:18f
All have *. Jer 9:10
Uriah heard about it and * to Jer 26:21
was lost, they * during the night, Jer 39:4
many places to which they had *. Jer 40:12
where they had *, now started off Jer 43:5
Why has Apis, your bull god, * Jer 46:15
all the soldiers * from the city Jer 52:7
Jacob * to Syria and earned a Hos 12:12
a single word, all the demons *; Mt 8:16
The herdsmen * to the nearest Mt 8:33
the disciples deserted him and *. Mt 26:56
The herdsmen * to the nearby Mk 5:14
all his disciples had *. Mk 14:50
The women * from the tomb, Mk 16:8
"At this, Moses * the country, Act 7:29
apostles * into Judea and Samaria. Act 8:1
who had * Jerusalem went Act 8:4
Meanwhile, the believers who * Act 11:19
stone them, they * for their lives, Act 14:5,6
up, so that they * out of his house Act 19:16
The woman * into the wilderness, Rev 12:6
the earth and sky * away, but they Rev 20:11

FLEE
"* for your lives," the angels Gen 19:17
such mercy, let me * to that little Gen 19:18,19,20
"* to your Uncle Laban in Haran. Gen 27:43
The Egyptians tried to *, but the Ex 14:27
and they will * before you. Ex 23:27
you will * before your attackers; Lev 26:17
You will * to your cities, and I Lev 26:25
let them * before you." Num 10:35
for anyone to * into if he has Num 35:11
killed someone could * for safety. Deu 4:42
kills someone may * to safety. Deu 19:2,3
neighbor, he may * to one of those Deu 19:5
gloriously, but * before your Deu 28:25
"Then we must * at once or it 2Sa 15:14
the land, or to * for three months 2Sa 24:13
He longs to * from God. Job 27:22
Arrows cannot make him *. Job 41:27,28
HOW DARE YOU tell me, "* Ps 11:1
Literally, "* as a bird." Ps 11:1f
"What can the righteous do but * Ps 11:3
They will turn and * when they Ps 21:12
I would * to some refuge from Ps 55:8
My enemies *! Ps 56:9
THE WICKED * when no one is Pro 28:1
and the shadows * away, come to me, Sol 2:17
and the shadows * away, I will go Sol 4:6
His people * to Zoar and Eglath. Is 15:5
and * across the Brook of Willows. Is 15:7
They will *, scattered like chaff Is 17:13
All your leaders *; Is 22:3
be great sorrow. * to Tarshish, Is 23:6
Even if you * to Cyprus, you will Is 23:12
When you * in terror you will Is 24:18
They will panic and *, and the Is 31:8
with terror and * when they see the Is 31:9
When you stand up, the nations *. Is 33:3
"Run for your lives! * to the Jer 4:5
Jerusalem: "* now, don't delay!" Jer 4:6
All the cities * in terror at the Jer 4:29
the bushes and * to the mountains. Jer 4:29
for your lives! * from Jerusalem! Jer 6:1
fathers * without a backward Jer 47:3
the city below. * for your lives; Jer 48:6
shout to those who * from Moab, Jer 48:19
O people of Moab, * from your Jer 48:28
They * to Heshbon, unable to go Jer 48:45
shall help your exiles as they *. Jer 49:5
in all of Teman? * to the remotest Jer 49:8
and all her people turn to *. Jer 49:24
* for your lives, says the Lord. Jer 49:30
gone—both men and animals shall *. Jer 50:3
But now, * from Babylon, the land Jer 50:8
But my people will *; Jer 50:28
* from Babylon! Jer 51:6
O my people, * from Babylon; Jer 51:45
Don't stand and watch—* while you Jer 51:50
They * to distant lands and Lam 4:15
if we * to the mountains they Lam 4:19
be fast enough to *, and even the Amo 2:15
Be good, * evil—and live! Amo 5:14
you prophet, you! * to the land of Amo 7:12
Use your swiftest chariots and *, Mic 1:13
all of them will * away and Nah 3:17
" 'Come, * from the land of the Zec 2:6,7
"Get up and * to Egypt with the Mt 2:13
in one city, * to the next! Mt 10:23
then those in Judea must * into Mt 24:16
go inside to pack before they *. Mt 24:17
—reader, pay attention!—*, if you Mk 13:14
Then let the people of Judea * Lk 21:21
Now all those who * to him to Heb 6:18
Resist the devil and he will * Jas 4:7
long to die—but death will * away! Rev 9:6

FLEECE
and of the * at shearing time. Deu 18:4
the morning, the * is wet and the Ju 6:37
he pressed the * together and wrung Ju 6:38
this time let the * remain dry Ju 6:39
that night the * stayed dry, but Ju 6:40
him clothing, or * from my sheep to Job 31:19,20

FLEEING
and pursued the * army to Hobah, Gen 14:15
to him when he was * from Esau. Gen 35:7
will send them * as though chased Lev 26:36
flight, as though * in battle, with Lev 26:37
and destroy the * army of Midian. Ju 7:23
make me sin by * to the Temple; Neh 6:12,13
of Madmenah, all *, and the Is 10:31
until exhausted, * back to their Is 13:14

FLEES
him, and then * into one of the Deu 19:11
The enemy *. Ps 68:11,12,13
The Egyptian army * in terror; Jer 46:5
a serpent gliding away, Egypt *; Jer 46:22,23

(FLEES Con't)
He who * shall fall in a trap Jer 48:44

FLEET
Edom, where he built a * of ships. 1Ki 9:26
King Solomon's merchant * was in 1Ki 10:22
* presented to him by King Hiram. 2Ch 8:17,18

FLEETING
love through the * days of life, Ecc 9:9
enjoying the * pleasures of sin. Heb 11:24,25

FLESH
is part of my own bone and *! Gen 2:23
Literally, "one *." Gen 2:24f
"Just think, my very own * and Gen 29:14
will come and pick off your *!" Gen 40:18,19
be stoned and its * not eaten, but Ex 21:28
But if there is raw * anywhere, Lev 13:14,15
It is proved by the raw *. Lev 13:14,15
But if the raw * later changes Lev 13:16,17
Literally, "an issue out of his * Lev 15:1f
For the life of the * is in the Lev 17:11
he has cursed his own * and blood. Lev 20:9
hair or beards, nor cut their *. Lev 21:5
You will even eat the * of your Deu 28:53
a share of the * he is Deu 28:55
is devouring—the * of his own Deu 28:55
My sword devours the * and blood Deu 32:40,41
* of their wounds had been healed. Jos 5:8,9
beneath the *, and the fat closed Ju 3:22,23
and tear your * with the thorns and Ju 8:7
me, your own * and blood!" Ju 9:2
and while the * of the sacrificed 1Sa 2:13,14
and I'll give your * to the birds 1Sa 17:44
own tribe, my own * and blood!" 2Sa 19:11,12
to build a fire to roast their *. 1Ki 19:21
And his * became as healthy as a 2Ki 5:14
made of sackcloth next to his *. 2Ki 6:26-30
dogs would eat her * and that her 2Ki 9:36
Literally, "your bone and *." 1Ch 11:1f
Is my * made of brass? Job 6:12
My * breaks open, full of pus. Job 7:5
"Have you the eyes of *?" Job 10:4-7f
You gave me skin and * and knit Job 10:11
me and angrily tears at my *; Job 16:9
Or, "then even without my * I Job 19:26f
he goes. His * is hard and firm, Job 41:23
your sacrifices of * and blood. Ps 50:13
Their horses are puny *, not Is 31:3
it is gorged with * as though Is 34:6
with their own * and they shall be Is 49:26
to pick the * from their corpses. Jer 12:9
city the caldron and we the *." Eze 11:3f
are the * and this is the Eze 11:7f
Boil the meat well, until the * Eze 24:5
hills with your * and fill the Eze 32:5
Literally, "hearts of *," in Eze 36:26f
I will replace the * and muscles Eze 37:6
the muscles and * formed over the Eze 37:8
Come, eat the * and drink the Eze 39:17
Eat the * of mighty men and Eze 39:18
Gorge yourselves with * until Eze 39:19
room where the * of the sacrifices Eze 40:38
* of the offering was to be laid. Eze 40:43
corpses, their * rotting away; Zec 14:12
this Bread is my * given to Jn 6:48-51
"How can this man give us his * Jn 6:52
you eat the * of the Messiah Jn 6:53
But anyone who does eat my * and Jn 6:54
For my * is the true food, and Jn 6:55
Everyone who eats my * and Jn 6:56
Literally, "the * profits Jn 6:63f
"for the destruction of the *." 1Co 5:5f
there are different kinds of *. 1Co 15:39
body made of * and blood cannot get 1Co 15:50
been a thorn in my *, a messenger 2Co 12:7
people made of * and blood, but Eph 6:12
beings—made of * and blood—he Heb 2:14
blood—he became * and blood too by Heb 2:14
you, and eat your * like fire. Jas 5:3
Come and eat the * of kings, and Rev 19:18
heaven were gorged with their *. Rev 19:21

FLESHHOOK
a three-pronged * into the pot and 1Sa 2:13,14

FLESHHOOKS
The pots, shovels, and *. 2Ch 4:12-16

FLEW
a raven that * back and forth Gen 8:7
Jacob * into a rage. Gen 30:2
they * upon the spoils of battle 1Sa 14:32
the wall. He * into a rage, and Neh 4:1
their feet, and with two they *. Is 6:2
Then one of the seraphs * over to Is 6:6
to wing, and they * straight Eze 1:9
When the four living beings * Eze 1:19,20,21
When they * upwards, the wheels Eze 1:19,20,21
And as they *, their wings Eze 1:24
and stayed beside them as they *. Eze 10:15,16
And as I watched, the cherubim * Eze 10:19
earlier vision, * swiftly to me at Dan 9:21
* off with it, high in the sky. Zec 5:9
all the doors * open—and the chains Act 16:26

FLICKERING
met was lighted with many * lamps; Act 20:8

FLIES
send swarms of * throughout Egypt. Ex 8:21
Israelis live. No * will be there; Ex 8:22
terrible swarms of * in Pharaoh's Ex 8:24
the swarms of * to disappear. Ex 8:29
the Lord to get rid of the *. Ex 8:30
and the axe head * off the handle Deu 19:5
My life * by—day after hopeless Job 7:6
vast swarms of * to fill the land, Ps 78:45
When Moses spoke, the * and Ps 105:31
How swiftly his word *. Ps 147:15
DEAD * WILL cause even a bottle of Ecc 10:1
down upon you like * and destroy Is 7:18
of the earth shall die like *. Is 51:6
But as she *, I throw my net Hos 7:12
The glory of Israel * away like Hos 9:11

FLIGHT
Laban didn't learn of their * Gen 31:22
over each other in *, as though Lev 26:37
you left Egypt in hurried *." Deu 16:3f
And two put ten thousand to *, Deu 32:30
Each one of you has put to * a Jos 23:10
and put to * their entire army. 1Sa 19:8
another * of stairs led from the 1Ki 6:8
is about to return in * to Egypt! Jer 37:7
I will put her defenders to * and Jer 50:44
warriors will stumble in *. Amo 2:14
And pray that your * will not be Mt 24:20
And pray that your * will not be Mk 13:18
wings spread out as though in *. Rev 4:7

FLIMSY
My people build a * wall and Eze 13:10

FLING
For suddenly I'll * you from Jer 10:18

FLINT
and the * for striking a fire. Gen 22:6
the wood and the * to make the Gen 22:7
Then Zipporah his wife took a * Ex 4:25,26
* knives for this purpose. Jos 5:2,3
set my face like * to do his will, Is 50:7
their hearts like *, afraid to hear Zec 7:12

FLINTY
Or, "oil from * rocks." Deu 32:13f
Men know how to tear apart * Job 28:9
streams to burst from * rock. Ps 114:8

FLIPPANT
Their made-up dreams are * Jer 23:32

FLIT
First here, then there, you * Jer 2:36

FLITTING
or swallow * through the sky. Pro 26:2

FLOAT
We will * them along the coast to 1Ki 5:9

FLOATED
ground, the boat * safely upon it; Gen 7:18
axhead rose to the surface and *! 2Ki 6:6
mountains and * along the coast of Ez 3:7

FLOATING
of dead animals * on the water. Gen 8:7f
not alight on such * carrion, and Gen 8:7f

FLOATS
it to you in log * across the sea 2Ch 2:16

FLOCK
stone and watered his uncle's *. Gen 29:10
or sheep in my *, you will know Gen 30:33
out and formed a * for Jacob of all Gen 30:35,36
stayed and cared for Laban's *. Gen 30:35,36
and Jacob added them to his *. Gen 30:39,40
ewes from Laban's * and segregated Gen 30:39,40
then all the * produced speckled; Gen 31:8
mating with the * were streaked, Gen 31:10
you to reduce the count of your *? Gen 31:39
and six years to get the *! Gen 31:41
goat from my *," he promised. Gen 38:17
ONE DAY AS Moses was tending the * Ex 3:1
be my own little * from among all Ex 19:5
from the herd or *, whether to Lev 22:21
present from your *, your olive Deu 15:14
a lamb from the *, I go after it 1Sa 17:34
that road like a * of sheep, with Ps 77:20
own people like a *, guiding them Ps 78:52
Israel who leads Israel like a *; Ps 80:1
are you leading your * today? Sol 1:7
the trail of my * to the Sol 1:8
his * and to gather the lilies. Sol 6:2
He pastures his * among the Sol 6:3
face, is like a * of goats frisking Sol 6:5
He will feed his * like a Is 40:11
* shall be carried away as slaves. Jer 13:17
Where is your *, Jerusalem, Jer 13:20
your beautiful * I gave you to Jer 13:20
Instead of leading my * to Jer 23:2
the remnant of my * from wherever I Jer 23:3
them as a shepherd does his *. Jer 31:10
sheep from the *, and heap fuel on Eze 24:5
you abandoned my *, leaving them to Eze 34:8
for what has happened to my *. Eze 34:9,10
right to feed the *—and take away Eze 34:9,10
I will save my * from being taken Eze 34:9,10
like a shepherd looking for his *. Eze 34:12
"And as for you, O my *—my Eze 34:17
All that's left for my * is what Eze 34:19
my sick and hungry * until they're Eze 34:21
So I myself will save my *; Eze 34:22
You are my *, the sheep of my Eze 34:31
and a perfect ram from the *. Eze 43:23
and a ram from the * shall be Eze 43:25
Like a * of birds, they will Hos 11:11
in a fold, like a * in a pasture—a Mic 2:12
And he shall stand and feed his * Mic 5:4
lead your *; Mic 7:14
arrived to help his * of Judah. Zec 10:3
* being fattened for the butcher. Zec 11:4
the * as I had been told to do. Zec 11:7
who doesn't care for the *. Zec 11:17
fine ram from his *, and Mal 1:14
sheep of the * will be scattered. Mt 26:31
to him than a whole * of sparrows. Lk 12:7
"So don't be afraid, little *. Lk 12:32
leaps on them and scatters the *. Jn 10:12
and there will be one * with one Jn 10:16
because you are not part of my *. Jn 10:26
and shepherd God's *—his church, Act 20:28
among you, not sparing the *. Act 20:29
What shepherd takes care of a * 1Co 9:7
him without freedom to lead his *. 1Ti 3:7
plea to you: Feed the * of God; 1Pe 5:2

FLOCKED
his arrival, they * to see him and Jn 12:9

FLOCKS
Lot with all their * and herds. Gen 13:6
He went there with his * and Gen 13:11
God has given him * of sheep and Gen 24:35
He had large * of sheep and Gen 26:14
Go out to the * and bring me two Gen 27:8,9,10
He saw in the distance three * Gen 29:2
until all the * were there. Gen 29:3
"Why don't you water the * so Gen 29:7
until all the * and shepherds are Gen 29:8
how your * and herds have grown. Gen 30:29
Let me go out among your * today Gen 30:31,32
so that the * would see them when Gen 30:38
So the * mated before the Gen 30:39,40
Thus he built his * from Laban's. Gen 30:39,40
As a result, Jacob's * increased Gen 30:43
*, to talk things over with them. Gen 31:4
He drove the * before him—Jacob's Gen 31:17-20
before him—Jacob's * he had gotten Gen 31:17-20
*, whether I could help it or not. Gen 31:39
mine, and these * and all that you Gen 31:43
along with the * and herds and Gen 32:7
"And what were all the * and Gen 33:8
are small, and the * and herds have Gen 33:13
with pens for his * and herds. Gen 33:17
They confiscated all the * and Gen 34:28
cattle and *—all the wealth he had Gen 36:6,7,8
was to shepherd his father's *. Gen 37:2
* to Shechem to graze them there. Gen 37:12
are over in Shechem grazing the *. Gen 37:13,14
with the *, and bring me word." Gen 37:13,14
"For my brothers and their *," Gen 37:16
flourished and his * multiplied. Gen 39:5
your * and herds, and all that you Gen 45:10
with them their * and herds and Gen 46:32
their * and herds and possessions. Gen 47:1
no pasture for our * in Canaan—the Gen 47:4
put them in charge of my *, too." Gen 47:5,6
Soon all the horses, *, herds, Gen 47:17
* and herds in the land of Goshen. Gen 50:8
troughs for their father's *. Ex 2:16
the shepherds and watered their *. Ex 2:17
the * watered so quickly today?" Ex 2:18
water for us and watered the *." Ex 2:19
donkeys, camels, *, and herds. Ex 9:3
none of the Israeli herds and * Ex 9:4
* and herds," Moses replied. Ex 10:9
let your * and herds stay here; Ex 10:24
"we must take our * and herds for Ex 10:25
lambs from your *, a lamb for one Ex 12:21
Take your * and herds and be Ex 12:32
and there were * and herds—a vast Ex 12:38
Do not let the * or herds feed Ex 34:3
use animals from your herds and *. Lev 1:2,3
of your herds and * and other Lev 27:32
If we butcher all our * and Num 11:22
animal from their * of sheep and Num 15:3,4
of us, along with our * and herds. Num 20:4
the cattle and * and a lot of Num 31:9,10,11
donkeys, and * kept by the army. Num 31:28
all the captives, *, and cattle Num 31:30
Gad (who had large * of sheep) Num 32:1
sheep country, ideal for our *. Num 32:3,4
sheepfolds for our * and cities for Num 32:16
"Our children, wives, *, and Num 32:26
cattle, *, and other livestock. Num 35:3
olives, and great * of cattle, Deu 7:13
in, and when your * and herds have Deu 8:12,13
animals of your * and herds. Deu 12:6
firstborn of your * and herds, nor Deu 12:17
you, then your * and herds may be Deu 12:20-23
the firstborn of your * and herds. Deu 14:23
males from your * and herds. Deu 15:19

(FLOCKS Con't)
of your * of sheep and goats. Deu 15:19
Large * and herds; Deu 28:2-6
fertility of your cattle and *; Deu 28:15-19
He will demand a tenth of your * 1Sa 8:17
We protected his * in the 1Sa 25:21
His troops rounded up all the * 1Sa 30:20
* of sheep and herds of goats; 2Sa 12:1
lamb from his own * for food for 2Sa 12:4
like two little * of baby goats in 1Ki 20:27
in search of pasture for their *: 1Ch 4:34-39
* of sheep and goats he purchased; 2Ch 32:28,29
and *, just as the law requires; Neh 10:36
are moved, * of sheep are stolen, Job 24:2
The pastures are filled with * Ps 65:13
along with the firstborn of the *. Ps 135:8
Know the state of your * and your Pro 27:23,24
I also bred great herds and *, Ecc 2:7,8
among the * of your companions." Sol 1:7
your face like * of goats that Sol 4:1
In those days * will feed among Is 5:17
whole * and herds will be Is 7:21,22
up, and their * and herds will Is 32:20
of God. The * of Kedar shall be Is 60:7
they shall feed your * and plow Is 61:5
be filled with *, and the valley of Is 65:10
our fathers had—* and herds and Jer 3:24
bread, and your * of sheep and Jer 5:17
divide your pastures for their *. Jer 6:3
Therefore they perish and their * Jer 10:21
given him all your * and herds. Jer 28:14
oil, and the healthy * and herds. Jer 31:12
Once again their * will prosper Jer 33:13
Their * and their tents will be Jer 49:29
shepherds and *, farmers and oxen, Jer 51:23
land where * of sheep can graze. Eze 25:5
her people, her cattle and her *. Eze 25:13
* and herds gave birth to young. Eze 31:6
I will destroy all your * and Eze 32:13
themselves instead of their *. Eze 34:2
but you let your * starve. Eze 34:3
Not only the people, but your * Eze 36:11
them like the * that fill Eze 36:37,38
* in Israel, give him one sheep. Eze 45:15
come with their * and herds to Hos 5:6
"Let the * and herds forget Joe 2:22
caring for the * and told me, 'Go Amo 7:15
even if the * die in the fields Hab 3:17
guarding their * of sheep. Lk 2:8
their fields and *, praising God Lk 2:20

FLOG
You devour them, * them, break Mic 3:3
* me with their whips and kill me; Mk 10:34

FLOGGED
and had him * and put into the Jer 37:15,16
And he ordered Jesus * with a Mk 15:15

FLOOD
the earth with a * and destroy Gen 6:17
to keep them alive through the *. Gen 6:19,20
again after the * has ended. Gen 7:3
He was 600 years old when the * Gen 7:6
and their wives, to escape the *. Gen 7:7
So the * gradually receded Gen 8:3,4
another * to destroy the earth. Gen 9:9,10,11
years after the *, and was 950 Gen 9:28
were born to them after the *. Gen 10:1
that developed after the *. Gen 10:32
the * when Shem was 100 years old; Gen 11:10,11
my enemies like a raging *." 2Sa 5:20
At the *, the Lord showed his Ps 29:10
They are like a *, higher than my Ps 38:3,4
We went through fire and *. Ps 66:12
* of these men's fury and pride. Ps 124:4,5
* sweeping away their last hope. Pro 28:3
is ruin in a * of empty words; Ecc 5:6,7
people with Euphrates' mighty *; Is 8:7,8
against them. This * will overflow Is 8:7,8
fail to rise and * the fields; Is 19:5
The enemy will come like a * and Is 28:17
Again and again that * will come Is 28:19
the waters of a * to cover the Is 54:9
a *, sometimes as dry as a bone." Jer 15:17,18
* time, overflowing all the land? Jer 46:7
like a *, destroying every foe. Jer 46:8
The Lord says: A * is coming from Jer 47:2
and with a great * of anger and Eze 13:13
as with a *, and war and its Dan 9:26
"I want to see a mighty * of Amo 5:24
enemies with an overwhelming *; Nah 1:8
before the sudden coming of the *; Mt 24:37,38
happen until the * actually arrived Mt 24:39
the * came and destroyed them all. Lk 17:27
living light will * your path." Jn 8:12
then no sign of a *, and wasting no Heb 11:7
from drowning in that terrible *. 1Pe 3:20
who were dead—killed by the * 1Pe 4:6
times before the * except Noah, the 2Pe 2:5
of ungodly men with the vast *. 2Pe 2:5
with a mighty *, long after he had 2Pe 3:5,6
mouth a vast * of water gushed out Rev 12:15
its mouth and swallowing the *! Rev 12:16

FLOOD-TIDE
For he will come like a * driven Is 59:19

FLOODED
great danger from * rivers, and 2Co 11:26
hearts will be * with light so that Eph 1:18

FLOODING
its seasonal * and conquered the 1Ch 12:15

FLOODLIGHT
though a * is beamed upon you." Lk 11:36

FLOODS
For forty days the roaring * Gen 7:17
waters, and the * began to Gen 8:1
the * come and destroy all life. Gen 9:15
* of evil burst upon me; 2Sa 22:5
as a brook; it * when there is ice Job 6:15-18
he sends the storms, and * the Job 12:15
the strong. He * the darkness with Job 12:22
chains, and the * of ungodliness Ps 18:4
gone over me, and * of sorrow pour Ps 42:7
SAVE ME, O my God. The * have Ps 69:1
Don't let the * overwhelm me, or Ps 69:15
You clothed the earth with * of Ps 104:6
love, neither can the * drown it. Sol 8:7
the terrible enemy * in, you will Is 28:18
His wrath pours out like * upon Is 30:28
torrential *, great hailstones, Eze 38:22
I sank down into the * of waters Jon 2:3
torrents, and the * rise and the Mt 7:25
For when the rains and * come, Mt 7:27
When the * sweep down against Lk 6:49

FLOODTIME
at *, toss about, and sink again. Amo 8:8

FLOODWATERS
When the * rise and break against Lk 6:47,48

FLOOR
dust from the * of the Tabernacle. Num 5:17
your threshing *, and must be Num 15:19,20,21
own threshing * and wine press. Num 18:30
found their master dead on the *. Ju 3:25
on the threshing * tonight, and if, Ju 6:37
at the threshing * of Nacon, the 2Sa 6:6
downward on the * in front of him, 2Sa 14:4
He was by the threshing * of 2Sa 24:16
* of Araunah the Jebusite." 2Sa 24:18
buy your threshing *, so that I can 2Sa 24:21
for the threshing * and the oxen. 2Sa 24:24
high, the lower * being 7½ feet 1Ki 6:6
wide, the second * 9 feet wide, and 1Ki 6:6
and the upper * 10½ feet wide. 1Ki 6:6
The bottom * of the side rooms 1Ki 6:8
stairs going up to the second *; 1Ki 6:8
The entire inside, from * to 1Ki 6:15
paneled from the * to the ceiling 1Ki 6:16
Temple, and the * of both rooms 1Ki 6:30
cedar from the * to the rafters. 1Ki 7:7
threshing * near the city gate. 1Ki 22:10
She fell to the * at his feet and 2Ki 4:37
and strike them against the *." 2Ki 13:18
up and struck the * three times. 2Ki 13:18
"You should have struck the * 2Ki 13:19
They stood on the * facing the 2Ch 3:11,12,13
The rim stood 7½ feet above the * 2Ch 4:2
away like sweepings from the *. Ps 18:42
great threshing * that reaches all Is 27:12
like the wheat upon a threshing *; Jer 51:33
unconscious to the *, to sleep Jer 51:39
the Temple led up from * to floor. Eze 41:7
the Temple led up from floor to *. Eze 41:7
were set back from the ground *. Eze 42:6
other gods on every threshing *. Hos 9:1
heavens, the first * on the earth. Amo 9:6
that rise from off the ocean *. Jon 2:6
*, helpless before Israel. Mic 4:12
the money onto the * of the Temple Mt 27:5
the man to the * as the crowd Lk 4:35
Her sister Mary sat on the *, Lk 10:39
* and turning over their tables! Jn 2:15
words, he fell to the *, dead! Act 5:5
Instantly she fell to the *, Act 5:10
to the * before him in worship. Act 10:25
had finished, James took the *. Act 15:13
or else sit on the *"—well, Jas 2:3

FLOORBOARDS
his wound running down onto the *. 1Ki 22:35

FLOORS
at Keilah robbing the threshing *. 1Sa 23:1
the * were made of cypress boards. 1Ki 6:15
The threshing * will pile high Joe 2:24

FLORAL
The lampstand, including the * Num 8:4
lampstands, the * decorations, 2Ch 4:21

FLOUNDERS
Your mighty vessel * in the heavy Eze 27:26

FLOUR
Use your best *, and make enough Gen 18:6
made with finely ground wheat *. Ex 29:2
of finely ground * mixed with 2½ Ex 29:40
along with * and the wine libation Ex 29:41
is to bring fine * and is to pour Lev 2:1
The remainder of the * is to be Lev 2:3
from finely ground *, baked with Lev 2:4
of finely ground * without yeast, Lev 2:5
of fine * mixed with olive oil. Lev 2:7
no yeast with your offerings of *; Lev 2:11
a tenth of a bushel of fine *. Lev 5:11
The rest of the * shall belong to Lev 5:13
the finely ground * with the olive Lev 6:15
remainder of the * will belong to Lev 6:16
a bushel of fine *, half to be Lev 6:19,20
batter of * mixed with olive oil. Lev 7:12
offering—* mingled with olive oil. Lev 9:4
of finely ground * mixed with olive Lev 14:10
of fine white *, mixed with olive Lev 14:21
of finely ground * mixed with olive Lev 23:13
bushel of fine * containing yeast. Lev 23:17
from finely ground *, using a fifth Lev 24:5-8
pancakes made of fine * mixed Num 6:15
of fine * mixed with oil. Num 7:13
offering of fine * mingled with Num 8:8
crushed it into * or pounded it in Num 11:8
quarts of fine * mixed with three Num 15:3,4
six quarts of fine * mixed with Num 15:6
quarts of fine * mixed with three Num 15:8,9
loaf, using coarse * from the first Num 15:19,20,21
* mixed with three pints of oil. Num 28:5
six quarts of fine * mixed with Num 28:9,10
of finely ground * mixed with oil Num 28:12
and six quarts of finely ground * Num 28:12
of finely ground * mixed with oil Num 28:13
quarts of fine * mixed with oil; Num 28:20,21
shall be three quarts of fine *. Num 28:20,21
quarts of fine * mixed with oil Num 28:28,29
quarts of fine * mingled with oil Num 29:3,4
Nine quarts of fine * mixed with Num 29:9,10
quarts of fine * mingled with oil Num 29:14
bread from a bushel of *. Ju 6:19
and a bushel of * and some wine. 1Sa 1:24
wheat and barley *, parched grain, 2Sa 17:28,29
bushels of fine *, 390 bushels of 1Ki 4:22
And I have only a handful of * 1Ki 17:12
be plenty of * and oil left in your 1Ki 17:14
from her supply of * and oil as 1Ki 17:15
two gallons of * or four gallons of 2Ki 7:1
two gallons of * and four gallons 2Ki 7:16
told the king that * and barley 2Ki 7:18
fine *, wine, incense, and spices. 1Ch 9:29
Vast supplies of *, fig cakes, 1Ch 12:40
the Presence, the * for the grain 1Ch 23:29
eat bread made of * mixed from Eze 4:9
Mix the various kinds of * Eze 4:9
Each day take * from the barrel Eze 4:12
* and oil and honey I gave you; Eze 16:19
of one bushel of * to go with the Eze 46:5
of olive oil for each bushel of *. Eze 46:5
of * for a meal offering. Eze 46:7
of *. With the lamb, he is to Eze 46:7
bushel of * with half a gallon of Eze 46:14,15
and bake the * of the flour Eze 46:19,20
of the * offerings into bread. Eze 46:19,20
She takes a measure of * and Mt 13:33
$20, or three pounds of barley *, Rev 6:6
wine, olive oil, and fine *; Rev 18:13

FLOURISH
May the mountains and hills * in Ps 72:3
May all good men * in his reign, Ps 72:7
the wicked * like weeds, there is Ps 92:7
But the godly shall * like palm Ps 92:12
Trust in God and * as a tree! Pro 11:28
the work of the godly will *. Pro 14:11
your own soil and * and multiply. Is 37:31
But the sins of Gilgal * just Hos 12:11
and grape vines will * once more. Joe 2:22
make the young men and girls *; Zec 9:16,17

FLOURISHED
crops * and his flocks multiplied. Gen 39:5
where Baal-worship * (Hosea 4:15; Hos 9:15f

FLOURISHING
They are tall and *. Ps 104:16
Arabia and was a * caravan city at Jer 49:8f

FLOUT
the prayers of men who * the law. Pro 28:9

FLOUTED
husbands and * the laws of God. Pro 2:16,17
we have * all the laws you gave Dan 9:10

FLOW
"If the menstrual * continues Lev 15:25
let his spittle * down his beard, 1Sa 21:13
Won't you ever stop your * of Job 16:3
They * around me all day long. Ps 88:17
Be sensible and turn off the *! Pro 10:19
and people from many lands will * Is 2:2
My tears shall * for Heshbon and Is 16:9
mountains will * with their blood. Is 34:3
* across the dry, parched ground. Is 41:18
the world will * to you, bringing Is 60:5
the riches of the Gentiles will * Is 66:12
Let the tears * from your eyes. Jer 9:17,18
tears * down my cheeks. Lam 1:16
My eyes * day and night with Lam 3:48,49
be as clear and * as smoothly as Eze 32:14
and the hills shall * with milk. Joe 3:18
his feet, and * into the valleys Mic 1:4

(FLOW Con't)
Life-giving waters will * out Zec 14:8
"Priests' lips should * with the Mal 2:7
living water shall * from the Jn 7:38

FLOWED
places and * across the land. Gen 2:6
A river from the land of Eden * Gen 2:10
and forth, and the wine * freely! Gen 43:34
And the water below that point * Jos 3:15,16
that "* with milk and honey." Jos 5:6
god, the wine * freely and everyone Ju 9:27
blood has * like water. Ps 79:3
The water * above my head. Lam 3:54
feast where the wine * freely. Dan 5:1
a river of fire * from before him. Dan 7:10
spear, and blood and water * out. Jn 19:34
city, and blood * out in a stream Rev 14:20

FLOWER
also, there will be one * above Ex 25:34,35
almond blossoms, a * on the stem Ex 37:20,21
also a * below the bottom pair Ex 37:20,21
for a moment like a *—and withers; Job 14:2
Literally, "shall cast off his * Job 15:33f
the pomegranates are in *. Sol 7:12
of kingdoms, the * of Chaldean Is 13:19
The grass withers, the * fades Is 40:7
He has killed off the * of your Jer 9:21
be gone, like a * that has lost its Jas 1:10,11
All our greatness is like a * 1Pe 1:24

FLOWERS
of the grain and *, blessings Gen 49:26
decorated with three almond *. Ex 25:32,33
with four almond *—one placed Ex 25:34,35
of almond * were all of one piece. Ex 37:17
designs of rosebuds and open *. 1Ki 6:18
trees, and open * were carved on 1Ki 6:29
open *, all overlaid with gold. 1Ki 6:32
Angels, palm trees, and open * 1Ki 6:35
Holy Place), the *, lamps, tongs, 1Ki 7:49
like grass, like *, blown by the Ps 103:15
of * in the gardens of Engedi. Sol 1:14
and gone. The * are springing up Sol 2:12
Their roots will rot and their * Is 5:24
the desert will blossom with *. Is 35:1
of * and singing and joy! Is 35:2
all his beauty fades like dying *. Is 40:6
The grass withers, the * fade, Is 40:8
so wonderfully for * that are here Mt 6:30
fathers and lay * on the graves of Mt 23:29,30
clothing for the * that are here Lk 12:28
them cartloads of * and prepared to Act 14:13
used for holding *, and another to Rom 9:21

FLOWING
land, a land '* with milk and Ex 3:8
a land "* with milk and honey." Ex 3:17
a land '* with milk and honey.' Ex 13:4,5
It is a land '* with milk and Ex 33:3
It is a land '* with milk and Lev 20:24
land '* with milk and honey.' Num 13:27
It is very fertile, a land '* Num 14:8
a glorious land '* with milk and Deu 6:3
a land '* with milk and honey'! Deu 11:9
land "* with milk and honey!" Deu 26:9
make it a land "* with milk and Deu 26:15
Land—a land '* with milk and Deu 27:2,3,4
ancestors—a land '* with milk and Deu 31:20
river will stop * as though held Jos 3:13,14
River stopped * when the Ark of God Jos 4:7
It was * from the direction of 2Ki 3:20
And then the oil stopped *! 2Ki 4:6
There is a river of joy * through Ps 46:4
Streams poured from the rock, * Ps 78:16
streams of water * down each Is 30:25
Then you would have had peace * Is 48:18
It will be like offerings * into Is 66:20
The cold, * streams from the Jer 18:14
them—a good land, * as it were with Eze 20:5,6
and * turbans on their heads. Eze 23:14,15
I saw a stream * eastward from Eze 47:1
I saw the stream * along on the Eze 47:2
by the river * from the Temple. Eze 47:12
All his * springs and green oases Hos 13:15
* into them through seven tubes. Zec 4:2
the Mediterranean, * continuously Zec 14:8
* from a life that cannot end. Heb 7:16
clear as crystal, * from the throne Rev 22:1

FLOWS
the Tigris, which * to the east of Gen 2:14
Smoke * from his nostrils, like Job 41:20
the Jordan River * and where Mount Ps 42:6
and * again to the sea Ecc 1:3-7
you a land that "* with milk and Jer 11:5
land that '* with milk and honey.' Jer 32:22
He told me: "This river * east Eze 47:8
Wherever this water *, everything Eze 47:9

FLUNG
suddenly the Lord * a terrific wind Jon 1:4
his old coat and *, it aside, jumped Mk 10:50

FLUTE
of the harp and *. Gen 4:21
a timbrel, a *, and a harp, and 1Sa 10:5
Literally, "the cornet, *, harp, Dan 3:5f
Literally, "the cornet, *, harp, Dan 3:7f
Literally, "the cornet, *, harp, Dan 3:10f
Literally, "We played the * for Lk 7:32f
Even musical instruments—the *, 1Co 14:7
the tune the * is playing unless 1Co 14:7

FLUTIST
heart, as when a * leads a pilgrim Is 30:29

FLY
All other things that * and have Lev 11:23
living bird * into the open field. Lev 14:7
let the live bird * away into an Lev 14:53
me, letting * their arrows, so that Job 16:13
Oh, for wings like a dove, to * Ps 55:6
I would * to the far off deserts Ps 55:7
that * when iron strikes iron. Pro 27:17
sparks * from their horses' Is 5:28
Together they will * against the Is 11:14
And who are these who * like a Is 60:8
desert her and * away, so is the Jer 17:11
that she could * away, for her Jer 48:9
The one who will come will * as Jer 49:22
it could no longer *, and it was Dan 7:4
His arrows shall * like Zec 9:14
a great eagle, to * into the Rev 12:14

FLYING
"* insects with four legs must Lev 11:20
there were quail * three or four Num 11:31
victory, flags * with praise to God Ps 20:5
but with his flag * above me I Ps 118:11
He was as a bird * into a snare, Pro 7:23
calling to Egypt, * to Assyria. Hos 7:11
Egypt—like doves * from Assyria. Hos 11:11
saw a scroll * through the air. Zec 5:1
"A * scroll!" Zec 5:2
Then I saw two women * toward us, Zec 5:9
a solitary eagle * through the Rev 8:13
And I saw another angel * through Rev 14:6

FOAM
Let the oceans roar and *; Ps 46:3
and makes him * at the mouth and Mk 9:18
like the dirty * left along the Jud 1:13

FOAMING
writhing and * at the mouth. Mk 9:20

FOAMS
so that he * at the mouth; Lk 9:39

FODDER
though we have * for our donkeys, Ju 19:19
will not be born to be cannon *. Is 65:23

FOE
demanded, "Are you friend or *?" Jos 5:13
and harassing the *, Joshua prayed Jos 10:12
or *," King Joram shouted back. 2Ki 9:17
are friend or *," he demanded. 2Ki 9:18
as though I were an implacable *; Jer 30:14
like a flood, destroying every *. Jer 46:8

FOES
from your fallen *,"—for the Ju 8:23,24
Jonathan slew their strongest *, 2Sa 1:22
him as a king defeats his *. Job 15:23,24
seeking your help against their *. Ps 17:7
a great Rock of safety from my *. Ps 31:2
us and defeated us before our *. Ps 44:10
He who abandoned us to our *! Ps 60:9,10
for he will trample down our *. Ps 60:12
soon my hands would be upon her *! Ps 81:14
before him and burns up all his *. Ps 97:3
the road and drowned their *; Ps 106:11
For he treads down our *. Ps 108:13
afraid, but can calmly face his *. Ps 112:8
And saved us from our *, for his Ps 136:24
Do not turn us over to our *. Is 16:3
full of fury toward his *. Is 42:13
for his * in distant lands. Is 59:18
In my fury I trampled my *. Is 63:3
to keep on running from their *. Lam 1:6
"Let her neighbors be her *! Lam 1:17
You have seen the plots my * Lam 3:60
now dead at the hands of their *. Eze 32:23
would deliver us from all our *.' Amo 5:18
She will stand up to her *; Mic 5:9
to defend them from their *? Hab 1:14
They will slaughter their *, Zec 9:15

FOG
as the morning *—now you see it; Jas 4:14

FOLD
was hinged to * back upon itself. 1Ki 6:34
into their own *, and they shall be Jer 23:3
stalking the sheep in the *. Jer 49:19
remember how to get back to the *. Jer 50:6
like sheep in a *, like a flock in Mic 2:12
other sheep, too, in another *. Jn 10:16
will * them up and replace them. Heb 1:12

FOLDED
Then Elijah * his cloak together 2Ki 2:8

FOLDING
There were two * doors of 1Ki 6:34
A little * of the hands to rest" Pro 24:32,33

FOLDS
two * of cloth, forming a pouch. Ex 28:16
his animals, and * for the great 2Ch 32:28,29
of shepherd camps and * for sheep. Zep 2:6

FOLIAGE
green * because of all the water. Eze 19:10

FOLK
when all the forest * come out. Ps 104:20
there were no sick and feeble * Ps 105:37
for joy, and men *—old and Jer 31:13
so that sick * were soon coming to Mt 4:24
numbers of sick * that evening and Mk 1:34
were godly *, careful to obey all Lk 1:6
* and those possessed by demons; Act 5:16
to Jewish * tales and the demands Tit 1:14

FOLKS
The girl ran home to tell her *, Gen 24:28
Moreover, we invite you * to Gen 34:9,10
You have made even the old * Is 47:6
* to him on mats and stretchers. Mk 6:55
Crowds of sick *—lame, blind, or Jn 5:3
enjoy the company of ordinary *. Rom 12:16
give each of the * there a special 3Jn 1:15

FOLLIES
bring up all the * of my youth. Job 13:26

FOLLOW
to * Abraham's instructions. Gen 24:9
of us and we'll * at our own pace Gen 33:14
Tried to * through the sea; Ex 15:19
will * my instructions or not. Ex 16:4
If you * this advice, and if the Ex 18:23
and you must not * the evil example Ex 23:24
They are to * exactly the Ex 31:11
He shall * the same procedure as Lev 4:20
You must not * the customs of Lev 20:23
Warn the priests to * these Lev 22:9
They will * his instructions and Num 3:7,8,9
Be sure to * all of my Num 9:2,3
of it, and must * all the regular Num 9:12
* all these same instructions. Num 9:14
If you * these instructions the Num 18:5
"We will * your instructions Num 32:25
will do— we will * the Lord fully Num 32:32
From Azmon the boundary will * Num 34:5
gods instead, and * evil ways, you Deu 8:19
will live, don't * their example Deu 12:30
His sons will then * him upon the Deu 17:20
"Be very careful to * the Deu 24:8
your God and to * his paths and to Deu 30:16
Israel began to * foreign gods, Deu 32:16
* them. You have never before Jos 3:2,3,4
Love the Lord and * his plan for Jos 22:5
"But be very sure to * all the Jos 23:6
worship them. But * the Lord your Jos 23:8
"* me," he told them, "for the Ju 3:28
to * Saul and Samuel to battle!" 1Sa 11:7
you and your king * the Lord your 1Sa 12:14
her young men, "and I will *." 1Sa 25:19
"Should we * Ahithophel's 2Sa 17:6
are for David, come and * Joab." 2Sa 20:11
Obey the laws of God and * all 1Ki 2:3
a long life if you * me and obey my 1Ki 3:14
I tell you to and * all of my 1Ki 6:11,12
if his descendants * your ways and 1Ki 8:25
them, help them to * the good ways 1Ki 8:35,36
and refused to * the Lord as his 1Ki 11:6
"If the Lord is God, * him! 1Ki 18:21
But if Baal is God, then * him!" 1Ki 18:21
This isn't the right city! * me 2Ki 6:19
for his master will soon * him." 2Ki 6:32
But Jehu didn't * the Lord God of 2Ki 10:31
But he did not * the Lord as his 2Ki 16:2
But they continued to * the 2Ki 17:33
them today—they * their former 2Ki 17:34
Israel will only * the instructions 2Ki 21:8
For Josiah wanted to * all the 2Ki 23:24
good judgment to * all his laws 1Ch 22:12
Now then, who will * my example? 1Ch 29:4,5
"As for yourself, if you * me as 2Ch 7:17
but if you don't * me, if you 2Ch 7:19
we are careful to * the 2Ch 13:11
He continually tried to * the 2Ch 20:32
to * the God of their ancestors. 2Ch 20:33
to * the path of the Lord his God. 2Ch 27:6
who determines to * the Lord 2Ch 30:17,18,19
to the Lord to * his commandments 2Ch 34:31
people who come. * all of the 2Ch 35:6
for he refused to * him. 2Ch 36:13
we will * your commands, and the Ez 10:3
the Chancellery. * every detail you Est 6:10
should choose to * what is right. Job 34:4
OH, THE JOYS of those who do not * Ps 1:1
about ways to * him more closely. Ps 1:2
Those who * other gods shall be Ps 10:16
no one can * me in and slay me. Ps 18:2
Their honors will not * them. Ps 49:17
of your wings. I * close behind Ps 63:8
They refused to * his ways. Ps 78:10
and refused to * his commands. Ps 78:56
Oh, that Israel would * me, Ps 81:13
above all else to * your steps. Ps 84:5
for I try to * all your laws. Ps 86:2
This makes us * his paths, and Ps 94:12,13
HAPPY ARE ALL who perfectly * the Ps 119:1

(FOLLOW Con't)
how I want to * them consistently. Ps 119:5
I cling to your commands and * Ps 119:31
* your laws even more closely. Ps 119:32
now I closely * all you say. Ps 119:67
make me * your lead. Ps 119:68
but I have sense enough to * you. Ps 119:70
I have chosen to * your will. Ps 119:173
You both precede and * me, and Ps 139:5
* the steps of the godly instead, Pro 2:20
life, closely * my instructions. Pro 3:1
"If you * them," he said, "you Pro 4:4
* MY ADVICE, my son; Pro 7:1
Those who love and * me are Pro 8:21
are all who * my instructions. Pro 8:32
Listen to this wise advice; * it Pro 22:17,18,19
but those who * the Lord are much Pro 28:5
away to * his own downward road. Ecc 7:29
in all the world, * the trail of my Sol 1:8
of Egypt will * the Lord of Hosts Is 19:18
They shall * you as prisoners in Is 45:14
along the paths that you should *. Is 48:17
We, who left God's paths to * our Is 53:6
and those who * you won't Is 59:8
do good, who * godly ways. Is 64:5
rebelled; they * their own evil Is 65:2
confess that you refused to * me. Jer 3:13
stubbornly * their evil desires. Jer 3:17
they no longer * God nor ask his Jer 10:21
have not tried to * in my paths. Jer 14:10
fathers were! You * evil to your Jer 16:12
liars, and if you * their advice Jer 27:10
to obey you or to * your laws; Jer 32:23
you fear will * close behind you Jer 42:16
return to me, or * the laws I gave Jer 44:10
the other men: "* him through the Eze 9:5
Don't * your fathers' footsteps. Eze 20:18
I am the Lord your God. * my laws; Eze 20:19
king of Babylon to *—one to Eze 21:19,20
and then * the course of the Brook Eze 47:19
she is determined to * idols. Hos 5:11
mighty army and they * his orders. Joe 2:11
cities of Judah to * Israel in her Mic 1:13
the south began to * your example. Mic 1:13
(Therefore we will * the Lord Mic 4:5
the only example you * is that of Mic 6:16
They '* the Lord,' but worship Zep 1:5
Yes, I will punish those who * Zep 1:9
'If you will * the paths I set for Zec 3:7
by white horses will * it there, Zec 6:6
instructions and * them are wise, Mt 7:24
said to him, "Teacher, I will * Mt 8:19
is dead, then I will * you." Mt 8:21
But Jesus told him, "* me now! Mt 8:22
up your cross and * me, you are not Mt 10:38
and take up his cross and * me. Mt 16:24
and come, * me." Mt 19:21
"We left everything to * you. Mt 19:27
children, or property, to * me, Mt 19:29
else, don't * their example. Mt 23:3
called out to them, "Come, * me! Mk 1:17
failed to * the usual Jewish Mk 7:2
and still *, such as their ceremony Mk 7:4
disciples * our age-old customs? Mk 7:5
your cross, and * me closely. Mk 8:34
in heaven—and come, * me." Mk 10:21
"We've given up everything to * Mk 10:28
carrying a pitcher of water. * him. Mk 14:13
who wants to * me must put aside Lk 9:23
* you no matter where you go." Lk 9:57
"If a town welcomes you, * these Lk 10:8,9
not carry his own cross and * me. Lk 14:27
you in heaven—and come, * me." Lk 18:22
but the end won't * immediately— Lk 21:9
pitcher of water. * him into the Lk 22:10
to *, carrying Jesus' cross. Lk 23:26
So if you * me, you won't be Jn 8:12
you would * his good example. Jn 8:39
and they * him, for they Jn 10:4
They won't * a stranger but will Jn 10:5
and I know them, and they * me. Jn 10:27
whole nation will * him—and then Jn 11:48
them to come and * me, for my Jn 12:26
And if they * me, the Father will Jn 12:26
I have given you an example to * Jn 13:15
but you will * me later." Jn 13:36
Then Jesus told him, "* me." Jn 21:19
what is that to you? You * me." Jn 21:22
"Now put on your coat and * Act 12:8
and required to * all the Jewish Act 15:5
must continue to * the Jewish Act 21:20
asking them to * these Jewish Act 21:25
feet I learned to * our Jewish laws Act 22:3
to as a sect; I * that system of Act 24:14
If you * through with that idea Rom 3:8
whether or not we * Jewish customs Rom 4:16
God's laws if we * after the Holy Rom 8:4
but those who * after the Holy Rom 8:5
obey God, and punishment will *. Rom 13:2
Living or dying we * the Lord. Rom 14:8
few of you who * Christ have big 1Co 1:26
So I beg you to * my example, 1Co 4:16
When I am with Gentiles who * 1Co 9:20
That is the plan I *, too. 1Co 10:33
AND YOU SHOULD * my example, just 1Co 11:1
my example, just as I * Christ's. 1Co 11:1
Please * their instructions and 1Co 16:16
He is glad to * my suggestion 2Co 8:17
possibly could to * all the old, Gal 1:14
and the Jews, who try to * that Gal 4:24,25
But when you * your own wrong Gal 5:19
power, let us * the Holy Spirit's Gal 5:25
Instead, we will lovingly * the Eph 4:15,16
* GOD'S EXAMPLE in everything you Eph 5:1
so careful to * my instructions. Php 2:12
and does not * the ideal of hard 2Th 3:6
that you ought to * our example: 2Th 3:7
let them * the way you teach and 1Ti 4:12
no one else will * his example. 1Ti 5:20
you in his army. * the Lord's 2Ti 2:5
* their own misguided ideas. 2Ti 4:4
in every city who would * the Tit 1:5
the paths I wanted them to *." Heb 3:10
will be anxious to * the example of Heb 6:12
the priests still * the old Jewish Heb 8:4
God warned him to * exactly the Heb 8:5
so that those who * you, though Heb 12:13
must *—that they will fall. 1Pe 2:8
is your example. * in his steps: 1Pe 2:21
You younger men, * the leadership 1Pe 5:5
Many will * their evil teaching 2Pe 2:2
hard on those who * their own evil, 2Pe 2:10
you. * only what is good. 3Jn 1:11
For they * the example of Cain Jud 1:11
for their good deeds * them to Rev 14:13

FOLLOWED

So Jacob * his mother's Gen 27:14
So Joseph * them to Dothan and Gen 37:17
So the people of Israel * all of Ex 12:50
in his chariot, * by the pick of Ex 14:7
Then the Egyptians * them Ex 14:23
advice, and * this suggestion. Ex 18:24
party, * by sexual immorality. Ex 32:6
So the people of Israel * all the Ex 39:42
to Moses were * in every detail. Lev 8:21
"When you have * the Lord's Lev 9:6
And Aaron * all these Lev 16:35
the people broke camp and *. Num 9:20,21
* from generation to generation. Num 10:8
wilderness, and * the Cloud until Num 10:12
Dathan and Abiram, * closely by the Num 16:25
the Jazer area; he * up with an Num 21:31,32
Balak * his instructions, and a Num 23:2
"These are the very ones who * Num 31:16
wholeheartedly * the Lord and urged Num 32:12
he had wholly * the Lord, would Deu 1:36
and is to be * to the letter. Deu 17:10
They * in your steps, O Lord. Deu 33:3
obeyed him, and * the commandments Deu 34:9
day for six days, * by seven Jos 6:3,4
the procession * by seven priests Jos 6:6-9
the Ark, * by a rearguard. Jos 6:6-9
They * this pattern for six days. Jos 6:12,13,14
But since I had * the Lord my Jos 14:8
he had * the Lord God of Israel. Jos 14:13,14
went from Tappu-ah, and * along Jos 16:8
border of Manasseh * the north bank Jos 17:9
So he * her into the tent and Ju 4:22
The people gladly *! Ju 5:2
When Gideon had * these Ju 6:20
In the events that *, both Ju 9:24
that night and * her Ru 3:6,7
until he has * through on this. Ru 3:15-18
and the Philistine mayors * them 1Sa 6:12
forsaken me and * other gods. 1Sa 8:8
But Saul * them there. 1Sa 23:24,25
and * the men back to David. 1Sa 25:42
all of Israel, and it is still *. 1Sa 30:25
He * along behind her as far as 2Sa 3:16
in front, and was * by David and 2Sa 6:5
and deserted David and * Sheba! 2Sa 20:2
(Solomon loved the Lord and * all 1Ki 3:3
for I have * my father as king of 1Ki 8:20
He has not * my paths and has not 1Ki 11:33
and * that of the young men; 1Ki 12:13,14
the Lord. He * the evil paths of 1Ki 15:34
half * Tibni, the son of Ginath. 1Ki 16:21
The city fathers * the queen's 1Ki 21:11
good king, for he * in the 1Ki 22:52,53
messenger arrived [* by the king 2Ki 6:33
They * a trail of clothing and 2Ki 7:15
So the officers * Jehoiada's 2Ki 11:9
evil king, and he * the wicked 2Ki 13:2
he * the Lord. 2Ki 15:34,35
They had * the evil customs of 2Ki 17:8
For he * the Lord in everything, 2Ki 18:6
for he * in the steps of his 2Ki 22:1
ancestors have * your commands." 2Ki 22:12,13
Lord and * all the laws of Moses; 2Ki 23:25
Joel was the greatest and was * 1Ch 5:12
servant of God were strictly *. 1Ch 6:49
oldest son was named Abdon, * by: 1Ch 8:30,31,32
posts of duty he * the 2Ch 8:14
* the counsel of the younger ones. 2Ch 10:14
and the people * him in this sin. 2Ch 12:1
because he * in the good footsteps 2Ch 17:3
He boldly * the paths of 2Ch 17:6
you have not * in the good ways of 2Ch 21:12
their children but * the command of 2Ch 25:4
Jerusalem. He * in the footsteps 2Ch 26:4
And as long as the king * the 2Ch 26:5
of Zadok. He * the generally good 2Ch 27:2
For he * the example of the 2Ch 28:2
as he carefully * the good example 2Ch 34:2
and this was * by the Feast of 2Ch 35:17
deeds, and how he * the laws of the 2Ch 35:26
You warned us that only if we * Ez 9:12
So this was the plan that was *: Ez 10:16-19
So we circled the city, and I * Neh 2:14,15
good sense, so he * Memucan's Est 1:21
with oil of myrrh, * by six months Est 2:12,13,14
I have * your commands and have Ps 17:4
For I have * his commands and Ps 18:21
they turned around and * him! Ps 78:34
they * him, not with their hearts; Ps 78:36
cloud and they * his instructions. Ps 99:7
In the years that *, the people Ps 105:24
* his instructions and he sent Ps 105:28
her flattery. He * her as an ox Pro 7:22
course again and * the path of Ecc 2:3
you loved me and * me even through Jer 2:2
They wouldn't even listen. Each * Jer 11:8
You have * in your sister's Eze 23:31
As I *, he left the eastern Eze 40:20
under King Josiah * about ten years Zep 1:1f
who strictly * the letter of the Mt 3:7f
Enormous crowds * him wherever Mt 4:25
LARGE CROWDS * Jesus as he came Mt 8:1
two blind men * along behind, Mt 9:27
and * by land from many villages. Mt 14:13
Vast crowds * him, and he healed Mt 19:2
they could see, and * him. Mt 20:34
type among the crowds that * him. Mk 2:15
to the beach, * by a huge crowd Mk 3:7,8
behind (though other boats *). Mk 4:36
see, and * Jesus down the road! Mk 10:52
Peter * far behind and then Mk 14:54
miracles that * their messages. Mk 16:20
out where he was going, and *. Lk 9:11
have left our homes and * you." Lk 18:28
see, and * Jesus, praising God. Lk 18:43
and Peter * at a distance. Lk 22:54
the women who had * him down from Lk 23:49
women from Galilee * and saw it Lk 23:55
two disciples turned and * Jesus. Jn 1:37
And many * him. Jn 10:41
so they * her. Jn 11:31
Simon Peter * along behind, as Jn 18:15
and were * by Samuel the prophet. Act 13:19,20
at the synagogue * Paul and Act 13:43
her masters. She * along behind us Act 16:17
accusations and a great riot *. Act 21:30
No one has ever really * God's Rom 3:11
* them, and the Rock was Christ." 1Co 10:3,4f
You know what I was like when I * Gal 1:13
by the true teaching you have *. 1Ti 4:6
who have not * this false teaching Rev 2:24,25
And there * after him another Rev 6:8
miracle and * the Creature in awe. Rev 13:3
Then another angel * him through Rev 14:8
Then a third angel * them Rev 14:9
and clean, * him on white horses. Rev 19:14

FOLLOWER

who was a devoted * of the Lord. 1Ki 18:3,4
wants to be a * of mine, let him Mt 16:24
"If any of you wants to be my * Mk 8:34
be my * must love me far more than Lk 14:26
are saying, "I am a * of Paul"; 1Co 1:12

FOLLOWERS

*, living off the land as bandits. Ju 11:3
the * of Saul and of David. 2Sa 3:1
leader among the * of Saul. 2Sa 3:6
(The * of wicked Athaliah had 2Ch 24:7,8
the faithful * of the Lord, keeps a Ps 15:4
The * of God will see it happen. Ps 52:6
But fill the * of God with joy. Ps 70:4
with a mere handful of *, he will Dan 11:23
because you are my *—wonderful! Mt 5:11
one of Jesus' *, went to Pilate Mt 27:57
governors and kings of being my *. Mk 13:9
women who were his * had ministered Mk 15:41
together his * and chose twelve of Lk 6:13
by many of his * who, in turn, were Lk 6:17,18
by Satan, what about your own *? Lk 11:19
* for saying things like that!" Lk 19:39
two of Jesus' * were walking to the Lk 24:13
our group of his * were at his tomb Lk 24:22,23
and the other * of Jesus greeted Lk 24:33,34
Jesus about his * and what he had Jn 18:19
If I were, my * would have fought Jn 18:36
All who love the truth are my * Jn 18:37
his * were harmlessly dispersed. Act 5:36
he also died, and his * scattered. Act 5:37

(FOLLOWERS Con't)
* so bitterly in Jerusalem?" Act 9:21
do many horrible things to the * Act 26:9
alone are the true * of Christ. 1Co 1:12
sea and cloud!—as * of Moses—their 1Co 10:2
So you became our * and the 1Th 1:6
wholehearted * of Christ who is the 1Ti 3:9
and become eager * of teachers with 1Ti 4:1
Balaamites; * of the man who Rev 2:6f
of these very same * of Balaam Rev 2:15
along with all her immoral *, Rev 2:22

FOLLOWING
* tribes at the places indicated: Gen 14:5,6
back as she was * along behind him, Gen 19:26
The * clans were the descendants Gen 36:17
* the seven years of prosperity. Gen 41:27
The * week(continued in next Ex 7:25
before them the * conditions, to Ex 15:25
to obey him, * all my instructions, Ex 23:22
will soon be * their evil ways. Ex 34:12
be kept over until the * morning. Ex 34:25
was finished, * all of the Lord's Ex 39:32
before the Lord, * all the Ex 40:25
of Israel journeyed onward, * it. Ex 40:36
him to give the * instructions to Lev 1:2,3
a burnt offering, * the customary Lev 5:10
This means that the * may not be Lev 11:4-7
are ended (the * instructions are Lev 12:6
Leave none of it for the * day. Lev 22:29,30
beginning the day * the Passover. Lev 23:6
the * instructions to Moses. Num 1:1
* Jehovah's instructions to Moses. Num 8:20
laws instead of * your own desires Num 15:39
He issued the * command to Moses: Num 25:4
In this tribe were the * clans, Num 26:5-11
In this tribe were the * clans, Num 26:12-14
In this tribe were the * clans Num 26:15-18
In this tribe were the * clans Num 26:19-22
In this tribe were the * clans Num 26:23-25
In this tribe were the * clans Num 26:26,27
Manasseh was the * clan of Num 26:28-37
included the * clans, named after Num 26:28-37
In this tribe were the * clans Num 26:38-41
In this tribe were the * clans Num 26:44-47
In this tribe were the * clans, Num 26:48-50
before them by * my instructions Num 27:14
On the * day, a great, joyous Num 28:17
of Reuben built the * cities: Num 32:37,38
the Lord your God, * his directions Deu 5:32
will destroy the * seven nations, Deu 7:1
may eat any bird except the *: Deu 14:11-18
For the * six days you shall eat Deu 16:8
you by * the Lord's directions. Deu 21:9
bread. The * day no manna fell, and Jos 5:11,12
urgent messages to the * kings: Jos 11:1
Moses had assigned the * area to Jos 13:15
Moses had assigned the * territory Jos 13:29
The * cities situated in the Jos 15:33-36
was also given the * cities which Jos 17:11
Its boundaries included the * Jos 19:17-23
The * four cities and Jos 21:23,24
to the town where, * Abimelech's Ju 9:49
the elders in the * cities where 1Sa 30:27-31
IN THE SPRING of the * year, at 2Sa 11:1
Then, * David's instructions, 2Sa 15:25,26
suggested. The * year he called up 1Ki 20:26
had a baby boy the * year, just as 2Ki 4:17
sell for so little on the * day. 2Ki 7:18
have done well in * my instructions 2Ki 10:30
But they continued to sin, * the 2Ki 13:6
to the gods, * the heathen customs 2Ki 16:3
just like it by * these directions 2Ki 16:11,12
drew Israel away from * the Lord. 2Ki 17:21
delegation of the * men: Eliakam, 2Ki 18:18
For we have not been * the 2Ki 22:12,13
to in the * verse or verses. 1Ch 1:1f
chiefs of their clans were the *: 1Ch 5:24
and the * Cities of Refuge with 1Ch 6:58,59
The * Cities of Refuge and their 1Ch 6:70
controlled the * cities and their 1Ch 7:29
The * men were chosen as their 1Ch 15:18
THE * SPRING (spring was the 1Ch 20:1
Carefully * God's instructions, 2Ch 4:7
* their evil advice, Ahaziah made 2Ch 22:5
brother Shime-i and the * aides: 2Ch 31:12,13
in their places, * directions 2Ch 35:15
concerned. The * spring he was 2Ch 36:10
The * families of the Temple Ez 2:43-54
* is the letter which governor Ez 5:6
* is the list of priests who had Ez 10:16-19
"The * is a list of the names of Neh 7:6
"Of the Temple assistants, the * Neh 7:46-56
"* is a list of the descendants Neh 7:57,58,59
* is a list of the names of the Neh 11:3
The * were the clan leaders of Neh 12:12-21
for she was still * Mordecai's Est 2:20
the * year was the date indicated. Est 3:7
of February of the * year, and Est 3:13
"I have stayed in God's paths, * Job 23:11
For they turned aside from * Job 34:27
sinned by turning back from * him. Ps 18:21
and from * the ewes with lambs; Ps 78:71,72
By reading your Word and * its Ps 119:9
what you do, not * your own desires Is 58:13
they wanted to, * their own Jer 7:24
THE * MESSAGE came to Jeremiah Jer 32:1
That is why the Lord gave the * Jer 34:12
The Lord gave the * message to Jer 39:15
I saw the way she was going, * Eze 23:13
world. * it, the fourth kingdom Dan 2:40
Jews during the * three and a half Dan 9:25f
you listing the * charges: There is Hos 4:1
The * February, still in the Zec 1:7
the synagogue, with many * him. Mt 12:15
And you are * in their steps, Mt 23:32
Meanwhile, Peter was * far to Mt 26:58
and as the disciples were * they Mk 10:32
left town, a great crowd was *. Mk 10:46
a young man * along behind, clothed Mk 14:51,52
Early the * morning, just at Mk 16:1
The * month God sent the angel Lk 1:26
years * seven years of marriage. Lk 2:36,37
Great crowds were * him. Lk 14:25
The * day as John was standing Jn 1:35
looked around and saw them *. Jn 1:38
and I'm * his example." Jn 5:17
were * him wherever he went, to Jn 6:2-5
But you are * the advice of your Jn 8:38
Jesus loved *, the one who had Jn 21:20
But God, * his prearranged plan, Act 2:23
assembly, and they elected the *: Act 6:5
baptized and began * Philip Act 8:13
They arrived in Caesarea the * Act 10:24
So Peter left the cell, * the Act 12:9
was offering. The * week almost Act 13:44
the truth in order to draw a *. Act 20:30
in the * address to the governor: Act 24:2
and the * day opened Paul's trial. Act 25:6
overboard. The * day they threw Act 27:19
blowing, so the * day we arrived at Act 28:13
that please God. * after the Holy Rom 8:6
and peace, but * after the old Rom 8:6
selves, bent on * their old evil Rom 8:8
For if you keep on * it you are Rom 8:13
I have been * the plan spoken of Rom 15:21
* the Lord, but your own desires; 1Co 3:1
So don't be proud of * the wise 1Co 3:21
you are already * a different Gal 1:6
hypocrites too, * Peter's example, Gal 2:13
and weren't * the truth of the Gal 2:14
to hold you back from * the truth? Gal 5:7
Be full of love for others, * Eph 5:2
set you free from * the world's Col 2:20
—why do you keep right on * them Col 2:20
Women of that kind are forever * 2Ti 3:7
same, you will be * in her steps 1Pe 3:6
as they should, * the Truth, 2Jn 1:4
* the Lamb wherever he goes. Rev 14:4
But cowards who turn back from * Rev 21:8

FOLLOWS
you make * the pattern I am showing Ex 25:40
"The Day of Atonement * nine Lev 23:26,27
combined offerings were as *: Num 7:84,85,86
Israel as *: "O Israel, listen! Deu 27:9
and addressed them as *: Jos 22:2,3
Then Joshua addressed them as *: Jos 24:2
* the instructions I gave her. Ju 13:13,14
(The schedule of charges was as *: 1Sa 13:21
generations of Aaron were as *: 1Ch 6:4-15
the assembled men of Israel as *: 1Ch 13:2
of the tribes of Israel were as *: 1Ch 27:16-22
them and addressed them as *: 1Ch 28:2
precedes and * him as the soft Job 21:33
he who * that path is safe. Pro 16:17
Lord and the judgment that * sin. Jer 5:5
listen to me, and * its own evil Jer 13:10
This message, in point of time, * Jer 45:1f
tribes are as *: Benjamin's section Eze 48:23
and then * the Brook of Egypt (Wadi Eze 48:27,28
*:Daniel was called Belteshazzar; Dan 1:7
This translation * the Greek Hos 4:18f
you as surely as day * night. Hos 6:5
Fire goes before them and * them Joe 2:3
plague * close behind. Hab 3:5
The translation here * the Syriac Zec 11:13f
addressed them as *: "Anyone who Lk 14:25
stood up and addressed them as *: Act 1:15
he addressed his colleagues as *: Act 5:35
addressed them as *: "Brothers, Act 15:7
Hill forum, addressed them as *: Act 17:22
trades, and addressed them as *: Act 19:25
he addressed them in Hebrew as *: Act 21:40
leaders and spoke to them as *: Act 28:17
an athlete either * the rules or is 2Ti 2:5
is past, but the third quickly *: Rev 11:14

FOLLY
do not this *." 2Sa 13:12f
Such is the * of these men, Ps 49:13
be led away into incredible *. Pro 5:23
The simpleton is crowned with *; Pro 14:18
fools are despised for their *. Pro 14:24
If a man enjoys *, something is Pro 15:21
it, but a fool's burden is his *. Pro 16:22
cubs than a fool caught in his *. Pro 17:12
to a fool as his * requires." Pro 26:4,5f
vomit, so a fool repeats his *. Pro 26:11
the path of *, so that I could Ecc 2:3
of wisdom and *, and anyone else Ecc 2:12
the wickedness of *, and that Ecc 7:25
slander, pride, and all other *. Mk 7:22

FOMENT
has attempted to * rebellion Deu 13:5

FOND
staff, for I am very * of him." 1Sa 16:22
Although Jesus was very * of Jn 11:5

FONDEST
your * wish will be fulfilled!" 1Sa 23:20

FOOD
all the fruit trees for your *. Gen 1:29
animals and birds for their *." Gen 1:30
Store away in the boat all the * Gen 6:21
yours to use for *, in addition to Gen 9:2,3
their wealth and *, and went on Gen 14:11
morning, prepared * for the Gen 21:14
of straw and * for the camels, and Gen 24:25
Jacob carried the platter of * Gen 27:18
and give me * and clothes, and Gen 28:20
touched one ram of yours for *. Gen 31:38
They pleaded with Pharaoh for *, Gen 41:55
many lands to buy *, for the famine Gen 42:5
"We have come to buy *. Gen 42:10
again and buy us a little *." Gen 43:2
to Egypt to buy *, as we were Gen 43:20
Their * was served to them from Gen 43:34
buy us a little *,' we replied, Gen 44:25
of other *, to eat on his journey. Gen 45:23
wagons filled with * that Joseph Gen 45:27
And Joseph furnished * to them Gen 47:12
came to Joseph crying again for *. Gen 47:15
I will trade you * in exchange." Gen 47:16
to Joseph in exchange for *. Gen 47:17
We will trade ourselves for *, Gen 47:19
they were assigned * from Pharaoh Gen 47:22
seed, and as * for yourselves and Gen 47:24
days except the preparation of *. Ex 12:16
rain down * from heaven for them. Ex 16:4
and gather as much * as he needs. Ex 16:4
And Moses told them, "It is the * Ex 16:15
So they gathered the * morning Ex 16:21
the * melted and disappeared. Ex 16:21
And the next morning the * was Ex 16:24
Moses said, "This is your * for Ex 16:25
will be no * on the ground today. Ex 16:25
Gather the * for six days, but Ex 16:26
anyway to gather *, even though it Ex 16:27
up * from the ground that day." Ex 16:28,29
And the * became known as Ex 16:31
may not reduce her * or clothing, Ex 21:10
then I will bless you with * and Ex 23:25
to Aaron and his sons as their *; Lev 2:3
forbidden for *, wild or Lev 5:2
to Aaron and his sons for their *; Lev 6:16
the atonement ceremony, for his *. Lev 7:7
grain offering—the * that remains Lev 10:12
sons and daughters for your *. Lev 10:14
may be used for * include any Lev 11:2,3
on paws is forbidden to you as *. Lev 11:27
any *, all of it is defiled. Lev 11:34
kind permitted for *, and shall Lev 14:4
to the priest for *, as in the case Lev 14:13
kind permitted for *, must pour out Lev 17:13
be unfit to make * offerings by Lev 21:6
be fed with the * of the priests Lev 21:22
*, for it is his source of life. Lev 22:7
a hired servant, may eat this *. Lev 22:10
may eat of her father's * again. Lev 22:13
priestly families may eat this *. Lev 22:13
will be given to the priests as *. Lev 23:20
That year your * shall be the Lev 25:12
I will destroy your * supply so Lev 26:26
that I do not permit for *. Num 18:16
for you and your families as *; Num 18:19
my *, and are a pleasure to me; Num 28:1
Pay them for whatever * or water Deu 2:6
We will not steal * as we go, Deu 2:28
you with manna, a * previously Deu 8:3
you realize that * isn't Deu 8:3
it is a land where * is Deu 8:9
and gives them * and clothing. Deu 10:18
Instead, use it for * for your Deu 15:22
trees that aren't valuable for *. Deu 20:20
welcome you with * and water when Deu 23:4
of money, *, or anything else. Deu 23:19
Your dead bodies will be * to Deu 28:26
*, though you did not plant them.' Jos 24:13
He asked the men of Succoth for *. Ju 8:5
* there, but got the same answer. Ju 8:8
refused to give us * when we were Ju 8:15
don't eat any * that isn't kosher. Ju 13:4
and not to eat * that isn't kosher, Ju 13:7
This was his riddle: "* came out Ju 14:14
of * and wine for ourselves." Ju 19:19
line to bring us *, and the rest of Ju 20:8,9,10

(FOOD Con't)
his reapers and he gave her *, Ru 2:14
her morsels of * in the wine." Ru 2:14f
him, begging for money and *. 1Sa 2:36
They also went without * all day 1Sa 7:6
"Even our * is gone and we don't 1Sa 9:7
he arrives and blesses the *." 1Sa 9:12,13
anyone who ate * that day, and 1Sa 14:28
freely from the * they found among 1Sa 14:30
carrying a load of * and wine. 1Sa 16:20
So, since there was no other * 1Sa 21:6
and then gave him * and the sword 1Sa 22:9,10
"Why did you give him * and a 1Sa 22:13
him, to produce * for his family; 2Sa 9:10,11
his own flocks for * for the 2Sa 12:4
and went without * and lay all 2Sa 12:16
come and prepare some * for you. 2Sa 13:5
and prepare some * for him. 2Sa 13:7
"Now bring me the * again here in 2Sa 13:10
* and wine are no longer tasty, 2Sa 19:35
for requisitioning * from the 1Ki 4:7
The daily * requirements for the 1Ki 4:22
* for King Solomon and his court; 1Ki 4:27
You can pay me with * for my 1Ki 5:9
had given them homes and *. 1Ki 11:16,17,18
and rest awhile and have some *; 1Ki 13:7
me and give you * and water." 1Ki 13:18
prophet ate some * and drank some 1Ki 13:19
be enough * for you and your son. 1Ki 17:13
and drank, and the * gave him 1Ki 19:8
"How much * do you have in the 2Ki 4:2
Give them * and drink and send 2Ki 6:22
"I have neither * nor wine to 2Ki 6:26-30
The last * in the city was eaten 2Ki 25:3
Naphtali brought * on donkeys, 1Ch 12:40
how wonderful the * at his tables, 2Ch 9:4
them with *, olive oil, and wine. 2Ch 11:11
should go without * for a time, in 2Ch 20:3
gave them shoes, *, and wine, and 2Ch 28:15
these stores of * for many weeks, 2Ch 31:10
A regular * allotment was given 2Ch 31:17,18
priests to issue * and other 2Ch 31:19
priests' share of * from the Ez 2:62,63
them with *, wine, and olive oil. Ez 3:7
and refused all * and drink; Ez 10:6
out of money for * had to sell Neh 5:2,3,4
who had demanded * and wine and Neh 5:15
priests' share of * from the Neh 7:64,65
a daily supply of * for the members Neh 12:47
as others search for * or money? Job 3:20,21
oxen do not low when they have *; Job 6:5,6,7
when there is no salt in his *. Job 6:5,6,7
can taste good *, so my mind tastes Job 12:11
He wanders around begging for *. Job 15:23,24
"But suddenly the * he has eaten Job 20:14
enjoyed them more than my daily *. Job 23:12
search for * for their children. Job 24:5
carry * while they are starving. Job 24:10
"Men know how to obtain * from Job 28:5
weep, or refused * to hungry Job 31:17
and appetite for * and doesn't care Job 33:20
taste we want in *, and we should Job 34:3
giving them * in abundance. Job 36:31
The mountains offer their best * Job 40:20
He is my * and drink, my highest Ps 16:5
You provide delicious * for me in Ps 23:5
like dogs and searching for *. Ps 59:14,15
sword, to become the * of jackals. Ps 63:10
me! For * they gave me poison; Ps 69:21
other * than God was giving them. Ps 78:18
"Why can't he give us decent * Ps 78:19,20
and rained down manna for their *. Ps 78:24
They ate angel's *! Ps 78:25
exposed—* for birds and animals. Ps 79:2
is withered. My * is tasteless, and Ps 102:3,4
roar for their *, but they are Ps 104:21
on you to give them daily *. Ps 104:27
Canaan, cutting off its * supply. Ps 105:16
to act, but demanded better *, Ps 106:14
he drinks, or the rich * he eats. Ps 109:18
He gives * to those who trust Ps 111:5
and satisfy her poor with *. Ps 132:15
He gives * to every living thing, Ps 136:25
you give them their * as they Ps 145:15
oppressed, and * to the hungry. Ps 146:7
the young ravens cry to him for *. Ps 147:9
gathering * for the winter. Pro 6:8
she had plenty of * on hand, left Pro 7:14f
Literally, "*." Pro 9:17f
The delicious * they serve will Pro 23:6,7,8
your enemy is hungry, give him *! Pro 25:21,22
his * from his dish to his mouth! Pro 26:15
milk enough for * for all your Pro 27:25,26,27
but store up * for the winter. Pro 30:24-28
his * and drink, and his job. Ecc 2:24-26
*, and never seem to get enough. Ecc 6:7,8
and Judah's * and water supplies Is 3:1
I have no extra * or clothes. Is 3:7
We will furnish our own * and Is 4:1
his *, but will never have enough. Is 9:19,20
They load the tables with *; Is 21:5
O people of Tema, bring * and Is 21:14
but used for good * and fine Is 23:18
feast of good *, with clear, Is 25:6
of safety; * will be supplied to Is 33:16
good * that fattens up the soul! Is 55:2
I want you to share your * with Is 58:7
shall be the serpent's *." Is 65:25f
my people shall be * for the birds Jer 7:33
they are * to my hungry soul. Jer 15:16
the city until all * is gone, and Jer 19:9
some * and money and let him go. Jer 40:5
the last of the * entirely gone, Jer 52:6
for * to give a little strength. Lam 1:11
"Mamma, Mamma, we want *," they Lam 2:12
now scratch in garbage pits for *. Lam 4:5
for *, risking death from enemies. Lam 5:9
shall ration their * with utmost Eze 12:19
break off their * supply and send Eze 14:13
and too much *, while the poor and Eze 16:49
robber, but gives * to the hungry Eze 18:7
don't accept the * brought to you Eze 24:17
by eating the * brought to you by Eze 24:22
* to the wild animals and birds. Eze 29:5
You eat the best * and wear the Eze 34:3
from being taken for their *. Eze 34:9,10
they are * for us to eat!' Eze 35:12
me my *, the fat and the blood. Eze 44:7
"Their * shall be the gifts and Eze 44:29
The fruit will be for * and the Eze 47:12
them the best of * and wine from Dan 1:5
not to eat the * and wine given to Dan 1:8
the king's rich *, and decide Dan 1:13
eating the * supplied by the king! Dan 1:15
for * and drinks and clothes." Hos 1:5
and live there on scraps of *. Hos 9:3
it is polluted, just as * of Hos 9:4
They may eat this * to feed Hos 9:4
* will disappear before our eyes; Joe 1:16
you will have all the * you want. Joe 2:26
shows it is ready for its *. Amo 3:4
those who give you *, and threaten Mic 3:5
of the * and fellowship and fun. Zec 7:6
will be * enough in my Temple; Mal 3:10
his * was locusts and wild honey. Mt 3:4
Then Satan tempted him to get * Mt 4:3
Give us our * again today, as Mt 6:11
When you fast, declining your * Mt 6:16
things—*, drink, and clothes. Mt 6:25
reap or store up *—for your Mt 6:26
having enough * and clothing. Mt 6:31,32
without * while he is with them?" Mt 9:15
*, and you say, 'He's crazy.' Mt 11:18
to the villages and buy some *." Mt 14:15
unholy by eating non-kosher *! Mt 15:11
are not defiled by non-kosher *. Mt 15:15
Jesus asked them, "How much * do Mt 15:34
they had forgotten to bring any *. Mt 16:5
you so worried about having no *? Mt 16:8
even think I was talking about *? Mt 16:11
have prayed and gone without *." Mt 17:21
locusts and wild honey were his * Mk 1:6
* as part of their religion. Mk 2:18
[Besides, going without * is Mk 2:21
walking sticks—no *, no knapsack, Mk 6:8,9
themselves some *, for there is Mk 6:35,36
to buy * for all this crowd!" Mk 6:37
"How much * do we have?" Mk 6:38
to heaven, gave thanks for the *. Mk 6:41
in this way before touching any *. Mk 7:4
your soul? For * doesn't come in Mk 7:19
that every kind of * is kosher. Mk 7:19
* and throw it to the dogs." Mk 7:27
the people ran out of * again. Mk 8:1
"Are we supposed to find * for Mk 8:4
to stock up on * before they left, Mk 8:14
If you have extra *, give it away Lk 3:11
going without *, and praying," Lk 5:33
used to go without * and never took Lk 7:33
But I eat my * and drink my Lk 7:34
a beggar's bag, nor *, nor money. Lk 9:3
find * and lodging for the night. Lk 9:12
Give us our * day by day. Lk 11:3
* to eat or clothes to wear. Lk 12:22
of far more than * and clothes. Lk 12:23
store away their *, and yet they Lk 12:24
And don't worry about *—what to Lk 12:29
the hired men have * enough and to Lk 15:17
I go without * twice a week, and I Lk 18:12
blessing on the * and then took a Lk 24:30
into the village to buy some *. Jn 4:8
"No," he said, "I have some * Jn 4:32
about perishable things like *. Jn 6:27
For my flesh is the true *, and Jn 6:55
go and pay for the * or to give Jn 13:29
given as much *, in the daily Act 6:1
When their * was gone, Jacob Act 7:11
without * and water all that time. Act 9:8,9
birds [forbidden to the Jews for * Act 10:12
and giving you * and gladness." Act 14:17
from eating * offered to idols and Act 15:27,28,29
about: not to eat * offered to Act 21:25
"You haven't touched * for two Act 27:33
"Let their good * and other Rom 11:9
and not with solid *, because you 1Co 3:2
have all the spiritual * you need. 1Co 4:8
for * and stomachs to digest it. 1Co 6:13
do away with both stomachs and *. 1Co 6:13
about eating * that has been 1Co 8:1
have believed that * offered to the 1Co 8:7
So when they eat such * it 1Co 8:7
wrong to eat this * will see you 1Co 8:10
return, for mere * and clothing? 1Co 9:11
* brought there as gifts to him? 1Co 9:13
get a share of the * that is 1Co 9:13
same supernatural * and drink." 1Co 10:3,4f
God sent them * to eat and water 1Co 10:3,4
those who offer * to these idols 1Co 10:20
you eat the same *, along with the 1Co 10:20
You are certainly free to eat * 1Co 10:23
If I can thank God for the * and 1Co 10:30
gobbles all the * he can without 1Co 11:21
who are poor and can bring no *? 1Co 11:22
of watching, and gone without *. 2Co 6:5
thirsty and have gone without *; 2Co 11:27
me * to eat and a place to stay. 2Co 12:13
*—it's the other way around; 2Co 12:14
parents supply * for their 2Co 12:14
teachings, for * was made to be Col 2:22
we never accepted * from anyone 2Th 3:8
if we have enough * and clothing. 1Ti 6:8
milk, not old enough for solid *. Heb 5:12,13
solid spiritual * and understand Heb 5:14
who is in need of * and clothing, Jas 2:15
or *, what good does that do? Jas 2:16
and take neither *, clothing, 3Jn 1:7

FOODS

"Asher shall produce rich *, fit Gen 49:20
they are forbidden * for you. Lev 11:8
saw the wonderful * on his table, 1Ki 10:5
feed you with the choicest *. Ps 81:16
She buys imported *, brought by Pro 31:14
eat pork and other forbidden *. Is 65:4
You ate the finest * and became Eze 16:13
or other * outlawed in Leviticus. Dan 1:8f
without the rich * and wines! Dan 1:16
or even touching certain *? Col 2:21
rituals—what * to eat and drink, Heb 9:10
eating certain *—a method which, by Heb 13:9

FOODSTUFFS

Why spend your money on * that Is 55:2

FOOL

He'll think I'm making a * of Gen 27:11,12
Whom are you trying to *? Num 16:14
you have made me look like a *!" Num 22:29
"You *!" 1Sa 13:13
He is a *—just like his name 1Sa 25:25
I have been a *, and very, very 1Sa 26:21
"Should Abner have died like a * 2Sa 3:33,34
So I am willing to act like a * 2Sa 6:21
'Don't let King Hezekiah * you. 2Ki 18:29
Don't let him * you into 2Ki 18:30
him, "Don't * yourself that David 1Ch 19:2,3
What a * you have been! 2Ch 16:9
Don't let Hezekiah * you! 2Ch 32:15
Or do you think you can * God as Job 13:9
"Who are you trying to *? Job 18:2
you, Job, are speaking like a *. Job 34:34,35
Job, you have spoken like a *." Job 35:16
THAT MAN IS a * who says to Ps 14:1
ONLY A * would say to himself, Ps 53:1
them! No * can comprehend this: Ps 92:6
*, for he destroys his own soul. Pro 6:32
* falls flat on his face. Pro 10:8
Only a * blurts out everything he Pro 10:14
to slander is to be a *. Pro 10:18
The * who provokes his family to Pro 11:29
only a * idles away his time. Pro 12:11
A * thinks he needs no advice, Pro 12:15
A * is quick-tempered; Pro 12:16
but a * displays his foolishness. Pro 12:23
A wise man thinks ahead; a * Pro 13:16
The wise man looks ahead. The * Pro 14:8
The fool attempts to * himself Pro 14:8
avoids danger; a * plunges ahead Pro 14:16
A short-tempered man is a *. Pro 14:17
Only a * despises his father's Pro 15:5
cubs than a * caught in his folly. Pro 17:12
therefore, even a * is thought to Pro 17:27,28
A * gets into constant fights. Pro 18:6,7
Literally, "a *." Pro 19:1f
It doesn't seem right for a * to Pro 19:10
Literally, "Reply to a * as his Pro 26:4,5f
In the mouth of a * a proverb Pro 26:7
vomit, so a * repeats his folly. Pro 26:11
There is one thing worse than a * Pro 26:12
A man is a * to trust Pro 28:26
There's no use arguing with a *. Pro 29:9
There is more hope for a * than Pro 29:20
If you have been a * by being Pro 30:32
man sees, while the * is blind. Ecc 2:13,14
just as the * will die, so will I. Ecc 2:15
For the wise and * both die, and Ecc 2:16

(FOOL Con't)
my son will be a wise man or a *? Ecc 2:19
the wind. The * won't work and Ecc 4:5,6
Don't be a * who doesn't even Ecc 5:1
a * makes you a blabbermouth. Ecc 5:1
death, while the * thinks only of Ecc 7:4
man than to be praised by a *! Ecc 7:5
The wise man is turned into a * Ecc 7:7
quick-tempered—that is being a *. Ecc 7:9
be too wicked either—don't be a *! Ecc 7:15-17
You can identify a * just by the Ecc 10:3
sheer madness. A * knows all about Ecc 10:14
to happen? A * is so upset by a Ecc 10:15
one who will deceive and * them." Is 28:15
hypocrites will * no one at all. Is 32:6
says you are a * to think that the Is 36:4
"Don't let Hezekiah * Is 36:14
God you trust in * you by promising Is 37:10
Who but a * would make his own Is 44:10
The poor, deluded * feeds on Is 44:20
make a * of you in front of them. Jer 1:17
Don't * yourselves! Jer 7:8
With practiced tongues they * Jer 9:5
of his life become a poor old *. Jer 17:11
who are there among you * you. Jer 29:8
Don't * yourselves that the Jer 37:9
he makes a * of himself and Hos 7:5
Don't * yourselves! Ob 1:3
to try to * the people then. Zec 13:4
"Who are you trying to * with Mt 22:18
them, "Don't let anyone * you. Mt 24:4
"But God said to him, '*! Lk 12:20
"Yes, every man is a * who gets Lk 12:21
all aside and be a * rather than 1Co 3:18
Don't * yourselves. 1Co 6:9,10
me as I keep on talking like a *. 2Co 11:1
witless man, a *—while I also boast 2Co 11:16
I am acting like a brainless *. 2Co 11:17
* again—I can boast about it, too. 2Co 11:21
and would be no * in doing it, but 2Co 12:6
You have made me act like a * 2Co 12:11
may * you with smooth talk. Col 2:4
He will completely * those who 2Th 2:10
So don't * yourselves. Jas 1:22
that they tremble in terror! *! Jas 2:20
that he could not * the nations any Rev 20:3

FOOL'S
A * fun is being bad; Pro 10:23
it, but a * burden is his folly. Pro 16:22
men, but a * goals are at the ends Pro 17:24
For a * compliment is as quickly Ecc 7:6
a * heart leads him to do evil. Ecc 10:2
but a * speech brings him to ruin. Ecc 10:12,13

FOOLED
He won't be * that easily. Gen 27:11,12
"Don't be * by that god you 2Ki 19:10
But don't be * by those who lie Jer 7:4
send him, and has * you into Jer 29:31
You have been * by your fame and Jer 49:16
penalty. Sin * me by taking the Rom 7:11
people are often * by them. Rom 16:18
Don't be * by those who say such 1Co 15:33
they are "phonies" who have * 2Co 11:13
fellow, that Paul, and he * us. 2Co 12:16
you are being * by those who Gal 1:7
Don't be * by those who try to Eph 5:6
And it was not Adam who was * by 1Ti 2:14

FOOLING
"The man wasn't * one bit when he Gen 43:3,4,5
They are only * themselves. Ps 119:118
says, "I was just *," is like a Pro 26:18,19
and that I wasn't * when I told Eze 6:10
Stop * yourselves. 1Co 3:18
are not interested in * anyone. 2Co 4:2
to stoop to this, he is * himself. Gal 6:3
tongue is just * himself, and his Jas 1:26
sin, we are only * ourselves, and 1Jn 1:8

FOOLISH
* vow he has taken, he is guilty. Lev 5:4
"If she takes a vow or makes a * Num 30:6
accept her vow or * pledge, his Num 30:8
O * people, Deu 32:6
To the * Gentile nations of the Deu 32:21
*, without understanding. Deu 32:28
to look even more * than this, but 2Sa 6:22
"Don't be *! 2Sa 13:12
give Absalom * advice!" 2Sa 15:31
Please forgive this * wickedness 2Sa 24:10
yet you give us all this * talk. Job 15:2
"Let him no longer trust in * Job 15:31
ever stop your flow of * words? Job 16:3
lease on life than *, stupid men. Ps 49:10
But you are so * and so Ps 82:5
are just as * as their idols are. Ps 115:8
"How * and naive you are! Pro 8:4,5
understanding. O * ones, let me Pro 8:4,5
To quarrel with a neighbor is *; Pro 11:12
her house, while a * woman tears Pro 14:1
A rebel's * talk should prick his Pro 14:3
It is * and rash to make a Pro 20:25
but the * man spends whatever he Pro 21:20
and you will say *, silly things Pro 23:33
a rebel, don't use * arguments as Pro 26:4,5
or you will become as * as he is! Pro 26:4,5
a message is as * as cutting off Pro 26:6
Yanking a dog's ears is no more * Pro 26:17
hard to be wise instead of * Ecc 1:16-18
to wise and * alike—just as the Ecc 2:13,14
This is not only *, but unfair. Ecc 2:20-23
and * king who refuses all advice. Ecc 4:13
mere dreaming of nice things is * Ecc 6:9
For I have seen * men given great Ecc 10:6
Since he begins with a * premise, Ecc 10:12,13
Weak as women! * as little Is 3:12
ruined Egypt with their * counsel. Is 19:13
They are a * nation, a witless, Is 27:11
See, they are all *, worthless Is 41:29
Listen, O *, senseless people—you Jer 5:21
Their ways are futile and *. Jer 10:2,3
idols are altogether stupid and *. Jer 10:8
But * men without knowledge of Jer 10:14
Jacob is not like these * idols. Jer 10:16
fathers have been *, for they have Jer 16:19
deserted me and turned to * idols. Jer 18:15
many * things, false to the core. Lam 2:14
after idols has made them *. Hos 4:12
in the womb—how stubborn! how *! Hos 13:13
What a * lie that they could Hab 2:18
lush pasture. How * to ask the Zec 10:2
you have said, 'It is * to Mal 3:14,15
the Lord your God to a * test!" Mt 4:7
ignore them are *, like a man who Mt 7:26
the other five were * and forgot. Mt 25:2,3,4
the Lord your God to a * test.' Lk 4:12
"You are such *, foolish people! Lk 24:25
"You are such foolish, * people! Lk 24:25
the Lord, and the * nations plan Act 4:25,26
worship of these * things and to Act 14:15
The result was that their * minds Rom 1:21
are meaningless, and faith is *. Rom 4:14
to the * heathen nations. Rom 10:19
it is wrong and * to go to all that Rom 14:5
I know very well how * it sounds 1Co 1:18
God has made them all look *, and 1Co 1:20
which the world calls * and silly. 1Co 1:21
It seems * to the Jews because 1Co 1:22
and it is * to the Gentiles 1Co 1:22
This so-called "*" plan of God 1Co 1:25
world considers * and of little 1Co 1:27
They sound * to him, because only 1Co 2:14
and how * and futile it is. 1Co 3:20
Religion has made us *, you say, 1Co 4:10
it all and don't say they are *; 1Co 9:22
and you are very * to keep on 1Co 15:17
What a * question! 1Co 15:36
THIS BOASTING IS all so *, but let 2Co 12:1
OH, * GALATIANS! Gal 3:1
Don't waste time arguing over * 1Ti 4:7
Keep out of * arguments with 1Ti 6:20
Steer clear of * discussions 2Ti 2:16
get involved in * arguments which 2Ti 2:23
But this is * talk; Tit 1:10
Once we, too, were * and Tit 3:3
though they are * and ignorant, for Heb 5:1

FOOLISHLY
It isn't right to speak so *. Job 15:3
You ask who it is who has so * Job 42:3
for he became angry and spoke *. Ps 106:33
an example of * chasing the wind. Ecc 2:24-26
silence those who * condemn the 1Pe 2:15

FOOLISHNESS
In their * they worshiped heathen 2Ki 17:15
Leave behind your * and begin to Pro 9:6
but a fool displays his *. Pro 12:23
a rebellious teacher spouts *. Pro 15:2
* and then blame it on the Lord! Pro 19:3
* though you crush him to powder. Pro 27:22
It is all *, chasing the wind. Ecc 1:12-15
of more value than *, just as light Ecc 2:13,14
all is *, chasing the wind. Ecc 2:17
But this, too, is *, chasing the Ecc 4:4
piece of * around the earth. Ecc 4:7
So again, it is all *, chasing Ecc 4:16
Dreaming instead of doing is *, Ecc 5:6,7
have enough. The * of thinking that Ecc 5:10
of folly, and that * is madness. Ecc 7:25
The Lord has sent a spirit of * Is 19:14
"Until my people leave their *, Jer 4:22
they speak * concocted out of Jer 14:14
The Lord replied: "Stop this * Jer 15:19
wisdom of this world is * to God. 1Co 3:19
their time arguing and talking *. 1Ti 1:6
further about the * of trying to be Heb 6:1

FOOLS
Tell them what * I made of the Ex 10:2
we were * to do such a thing. Num 12:11
one of the greatest * in Israel. 2Sa 13:13
"He makes * of counselors and Job 12:17
but they are useless, stupid *. Job 30:2
turned out to be *, yes, children Job 30:8
WHAT * Ps 2:1
for even * will mock me then. Ps 39:8
*! Is God deaf and blind- Ps 94:8
Others, the *, were ill because Ps 107:17
Only * refuse to be taught. Pro 1:7,8,9
"How long will you go on being * Pro 1:22
own complacency will kill you. *! Pro 1:32
but * are promoted to shame! Pro 3:35
the words of * are a dime a dozen. Pro 10:20
That is why * refuse to give them Pro 13:19
for advice, stay away from *. Pro 14:7
Or, "* make a mock at sin." Pro 14:9f
* are despised for their folly. Pro 14:24
loudly before * will hear it. Pro 14:33
to brawls; what * men are to let it Pro 20:1
Only * insist on quarreling. Pro 20:3
HONOR DOESN'T GO with * any more Pro 26:1
* start fights everywhere while Pro 29:8
it, for God has no pleasure in *. Ecc 5:4
Wise men and * alike spend their Ecc 6:7,8
than the shout of a king of *. Ecc 9:17
Can't you see what * your rulers Is 3:12
What * the counselors of Zoan Is 19:11
from Zoan are also *, and those Is 19:13
their wisest counselors as *." Is 29:14
What * they are who manufacture Is 44:9
they should, and make them into *. Is 44:25
Cyrus' hand. What * they are who Is 45:20
them into * who worship idols? Jer 2:4,5
wise counselors shall become *! Jer 50:36
harlots and temple prostitutes. *! Hos 4:14
And Gilead, too, is full of * Hos 12:11
could help! What * you were to Hab 2:18
her, and make * of them, for I will Zec 12:4
Blind *! Mt 23:17
of greed and wickedness! *! Lk 11:40
God, they became utter * instead. Rom 1:22
Or, "were confused *." Rom 1:31f
you listen gladly to those *; 2Co 11:19,20
Don't be *; Eph 5:15,16
But false teachers are *—no 2Pe 2:12

FOOT
women and children, going on *. Ex 12:37
then gather at the * of the Ex 19:13
stood at the * of the mountain. Ex 19:17
and so on—hand for hand, * for Ex 21:24
for hand, foot for *, burn for Ex 21:24
an altar at the * of the mountain, Ex 24:4
broken at the * of the mountain. Ex 32:19
upon the big toe of his right *. Lev 8:23
body from head to * wherever he Lev 13:12
upon the big toe of his right *. Lev 14:14
toe of his right *—just as he did Lev 14:17
and on the big toe of his right *. Lev 14:25
toe of his right *, just as he did Lev 14:28
or has a broken * or hand, or has Lev 21:19
Balaam's * in the process. Num 22:25
camped at the * of Mount Migdol). Num 33:7
While they were at the * of Mount Num 33:38,39
days to travel by * from Mount Deu 1:1
You stood at the * of the Deu 4:11
There at the * of the mountain Deu 18:16
tooth, hand for hand, * for foot; Deu 19:21
tooth, hand for hand, foot for *; Deu 19:21
from his * and spit in his face. Deu 25:9
you with boils from head to *. Deu 28:35
standing at the * of Mount Gerizim Jos 8:33
and half at the * of Mount Ebal. Jos 8:33
Lebanon, at the * of Mount Hermon. Jos 11:17
from his chariot and escaped on *. Ju 4:15
six toes on each * defied Israel, 2Sa 21:20,21
six toes on each * (his father was 1Ch 20:6,7
the others were on *, and we went Neh 2:11,12
case of boils from head to *. Job 2:7
They went across on *. Ps 66:6
pull back your * from danger. Pro 4:27
from head to *, but an evil man Pro 10:6
You keep putting your * in your Pro 10:19
or trying to run on a broken *. Pro 25:19
From head to * you are sick and Is 1:5,6
It was too deep to cross on *. Eze 47:5
So if your hand or * causes you Mt 18:8
'Bind him hand and * and throw him Mt 22:13
If your * carries you toward Mk 9:45,46
is left at the * of the table! Lk 14:9
"Do this instead—start at the *; Lk 14:10
at the head and * of the place Jn 20:12
from the day I set * in Turkey Act 20:18
like dirt under *, like garbage. 1Co 4:13
If the * says, "I am not a part 1Co 12:15
He set his right * on the sea and Rev 10:2
sea and his left * on the earth, Rev 10:2

FOOTHOLD
you give a mighty * to the devil. Eph 4:27

FOOTING
A good man has firm *, but a Pro 10:9

FOOTMEN
hired fifty * to run ahead of him. 2Sa 15:1
the streets before him as royal *. 1Ki 1:5

FOOTNOTE
the book of Luke; see * chapter Act 1:1f

FOOTPATH
fell on a * and was trampled on; Lk 8:5

FOOTPRINTS
sinners, tracked with * of blood. Hos 6:8
FOOTSTEPS
he followed in the * of his father 1Ki 22:52,53
in the good * of his father's early 2Ch 17:3
He followed in the * of his 2Ch 26:4
Don't follow your fathers' *. Eze 20:18
in your sister's *, so I will Eze 23:31
FOOTSTOOL
Literally, "a *." 1Ch 28:2f
It had six gold steps and a * of 2Ch 9:18
we will worship at his *." Ps 132:7f
the earth is my *: What Temple can Is 66:1
Literally, "*." Lam 2:1f
my throne, and my *, where I shall Eze 43:7
vow, for the earth is his *. Mt 5:35
until I make your enemies your *.' Mk 12:36
his prophets, 'and earth is my *. Act 7:48,49
FOR-EVER
by him who lives * and ever, that Dan 12:7
FORASMUCH
Literally, "* as I have seen your Gen 33:10f
FORBADE
but the more he * them, the more Mk 7:36
FORBID
But God * that I should kill the 1Sa 26:11
"God * that I should drink it! 1Ch 11:18,19
(God * that I should say a Job 22:18
But Gedaliah said, "I * you to Jer 40:16
"Heaven *, sir," he said. Mt 16:22
"Don't * him!" Mk 9:39
and that you * the circumcision of Act 21:21
gently and not to * any of his Act 24:23
God *! Rom 3:6
had ruined us? God * that anyone Gal 2:17
As for me, God * that I should Gal 6:14
FORBIDDEN
And murder is *. Gen 9:5,6
body of an animal * for food, wild Lev 5:2
dead body of some * insect—is Lev 5:2
they are * foods for you. Lev 11:8
creatures are strictly * to you. Lev 11:10
have fins or scales is * to you. Lev 11:12
and have four feet are * to you. Lev 11:23
walks on paws is * to you as food. Lev 11:27
for it is * to you. Lev 11:28
"These are the * small animals Lev 11:29,30
"Homosexuality is absolutely *, Lev 18:22
*, though the land teem with them. Lev 20:25
reptile or other * thing, or who Lev 22:5
protested at being * from offering Num 9:6,7
our God had * us to enter. Deu 2:37
Lord your God has utterly * this. Deu 4:23
I have strictly *— first check the Deu 17:2,3
Lord had expressly *, including the Ju 2:11
by entering the * sanctuary of the 2Ch 26:16
and then, though it is strictly * Est 4:16
they eat pork and other * foods. Is 65:4
and mouse and all * meat—they will Is 66:17
you had * even to enter. Lam 1:10
holy day when all work was *. Jn 9:14f
and birds [* to the Jews for food Act 10:12
see Leviticus 11 for the * list. Act 10:12f
they are * by our Jewish laws." Act 10:14
anything * by our Jewish laws!' Act 11:8
eating the * fruit, as Adam had. Rom 5:14
all kinds of * desires within me! Rom 7:8
and these evil, * things will go 1Jn 2:17
FORBIDS
the kinds of animals our law *." Eze 4:14
FORCE
take his daughters from me by *.' Gen 31:31
and * them to let my people go." Ex 7:5
to the frontier with a great *. Num 20:20
you must not * him to return; Deu 23:15,16
This arrangement is still in * at Jos 9:27
did * them to leave the country. Ju 1:28
them, routing their entire *. Ju 8:12
to me now or I'll take it by *." 1Sa 2:16
from you and * them to cook and 1Sa 8:13
now today should I * you to wander 2Sa 15:19,20
so that you will have a huge *. 2Sa 17:11
special troops—to * the rest of 1Ki 12:21
He built up a huge * of 1,400 2Ch 1:14
This required a * of 70,000 2Ch 2:2
The work * was made up of all Ez 3:8
enemies did not * us to stop Ez 5:5
to try to * me from the throne. Ps 62:3,4
the ground. They * me to live in Ps 143:3
driving * of envy and jealousy! Ecc 4:4
Why will you * me to whip you Is 1:5,6
See, I will * you from your land Jer 12:14
and * Nebuchadnezzar to withdraw Jer 21:1
enough to defeat the Egyptian *. Eze 30:21f
ruled them with * and cruelty. Eze 34:4
never take anyone's property by *. Eze 46:18
Muster your defenses, full *, and Nah 2:1
I am raising a new * on the Hab 1:6
men of violence take it by *." Mt 11:12f
its * in even the smallest point. Lk 16:17
to take him by * and make him their Jn 6:15
away from them by * and bring him Act 23:10
Don't * anyone to give more than 2Co 9:7
* yourself to obey Jewish laws. Gal 5:18
than himself to * him to do what he Heb 6:16
"Note this: I will * those Rev 3:9
FORCED
"For he must be * to let my Ex 6:1
enough, they * the Canaanites to Jos 17:13
Dan, the Amorites * them into the Ju 1:34
they will be * to plow in the 1Sa 8:12
King Saul, meanwhile, had * 1Sa 25:44
entire nation was * to pay tribute 2Sa 8:14
was stronger than she, he * her. 2Sa 13:14
Adoram was in charge of the * 2Sa 20:24
So Solomon * Abiathar to give up 1Ki 2:27
Solomon had conscripted * labor 1Ki 9:15
here,' King Ahab * the king of that 1Ki 18:10
He was * to watch as his sons 2Ki 25:7
So the Syrians, too, were * to 1Ch 18:6
He put garrisons in Edom and * 1Ch 18:13
Hadoram to draft * labor from the 2Ch 10:18
and * the Jews to stop building. Ez 4:23
clothing, and are * to carry food Job 24:10
They are * to press out the Job 24:11
lest the godly be * to do wrong. Ps 125:3
just as Judah will be * from hers; Jer 12:14
your great palace with * labor. Jer 22:13
They even * Jeremiah and Baruch Jer 43:6
immigrants and visitors are * to Eze 22:7
You will be * out of the palace Dan 4:32
The fathers are * to lead their Hos 9:13
* him to carry Jesus' cross. Mt 27:32
the country, was * to follow, Lk 23:26
the battle and was * from heaven. Rev 12:8
FORCES
the leader of the * that defeated Gen 36:31-39
us and mobilized his * at Jahaz. Deu 2:32
* expected from Bethel (verse 17). Jos 8:11,12,13f
when he led the * of Israel against Ju 3:10
These * defeated the Israelis and Ju 3:13
*, and all of them responded. Ju 6:35
all the allied * of Midian!" Ju 7:14
this, he led his * to Mount Zalmon Ju 9:47,48
"Who will lead our * against the Ju 10:18
of the Israeli * at Mizpah soon Ju 20:3
the Israeli * retreated and Ju 20:31
but a tiny remnant of their *. Ju 20:35-39
a buildup of * at Elah Valley. 1Sa 17:2
ranks to face the * of Israel. 1Sa 17:4-7
and Philistine * stood facing each 1Sa 17:21
and the * of David. 2Sa 2:17
He also destroyed the * of King 2Sa 8:3
of all of Hadadezer's *. 2Sa 10:15,16
When Joab's * arrived, they 2Sa 20:15
Solomon conscripted his labor * 1Ki 9:20,21
who were overseers of the labor *. 1Ki 9:23
"Do you see all these enemy *? 1Ki 20:13
* that filled the countryside! 1Ki 20:27
our * at ÇÇ" (naming the place). 2Ki 6:8
the * of King Hazael of Syria. 2Ki 9:14
When the Israeli guerrilla * 2Ki 25:23
mobilized their * to capture him. 1Ch 14:8
These * camped at Medeba where 1Ch 19:7
Meanwhile, the mercenary * were 1Ch 19:9
that the enemy * were both in front 1Ch 19:10
* with him against Ramoth-gilead. 2Ch 18:2
to destroy all the * opposed to Est 8:11
captain of his *, slaughtered Ps 60:1
the west, uniting * to destroy Is 11:14
to withdraw his *." Jer 21:1
captains of his *, and for all the Jer 42:8
the first rumor of approaching *. Jer 51:46
might of the * opposed to God, Eze 38:2,3f
vast * of Syria and defeat them. Dan 11:10,11
you in heaven against satanic * Dan 12:1
These two * within us are Gal 5:17
FORCING
more bitter still, * them to toil Ex 1:13,14
lands, but you are * them right Neh 5:8
all these nations, * them into Jer 28:14
they broke, * me to reject them, Jer 31:32
against our race, * parents to Act 7:19
FORD
at the Jabbok *, then returned Gen 32:22,23,24
I will stop at the * of the 2Sa 15:28
the * of the Jordan River tonight. 2Sa 17:16
FORDING
seek them at the * points of Jer 22:20
FORDS
to seize the * of the Jordan River Ju 3:28
who seized the * of the Jordan Ju 7:24
He captured the * of the Jordan Ju 12:5
are left at the * of the Arnon Is 16:2
FOREBEARS
me—all your * transgressed my law. Is 43:27
FOREBODING
terrible *, darkness, and horror. Gen 15:12
FORECLOSE
I am neither a creditor soon to * Jer 15:10
FORECLOSED
the poor and * their homes; Job 20:19
FOREFATHER
the city of his * David; 1Ki 22:50
Lord God of your * David hears you Is 38:5
FOREFATHERS
For I brought their * out of Lev 26:45
of long ago. Our * have told us how Ps 44:1
nor their * nor the kings of Judah Jer 19:4
FOREGO
All such shameful methods we *. 2Co 4:2
FOREHEAD
upon your hands or your *. Ex 13:9
it upon his *, and thus bear the Ex 28:37,38
a bald *, but this is not leprosy. Lev 13:41
thereof or in the * thereof." Lev 13:55f
wear them on your *, and write Deu 6:8
them to your * between your eyes! Deu 11:18
and hit the Philistine in the *. 1Sa 17:48,49
appeared in his *! 2Ch 26:19
I have made your * as hard as Eze 3:9
everyone whose * isn't marked. Eze 9:5
on the right hand or on the *. Rev 13:16
his mark on the * or the hand, Rev 14:9
was written on her *: "Babylon the Rev 17:5
A name was written on his *, Rev 19:12
FOREHEADS
ownership were placed upon your *. Ex 13:16
put a mark on the * of the men who Eze 9:4
God upon the * of his servants." Rev 7:3
have the mark of God on their *. Rev 9:4
Father's Name written on their *. Rev 14:1
mark on their * or their hands. Rev 20:4
name shall be written on their *. Rev 22:4
FOREIGN
slaves in a * land for 400 years. Gen 15:13
"Here I am, a visitor in a * Gen 23:4
our rights to those of * women; Gen 31:15
"I am a stranger in a * land." Ex 2:22
wandering in a * land") and Ex 18:3
slaves from the * nations living Lev 25:44
and worship these * gods, do not Deu 13:6,7
that they worship * gods, first Deu 13:12,13,14
to help them. A * nation you have Deu 28:33
* gods in the Promised Land. Deu 31:16
And they lived without * gods, Deu 32:12
Israel began to follow * gods, Deu 32:16
Then they destroyed their * gods Ju 10:16
* gods and your Ashtaroth idols. 1Sa 7:3
Must I die on * soil, far from 1Sa 26:20
I have no * enemies or internal 1Ki 5:4
captives to some * land, whether 1Ki 8:46
temples for these * wives to use 1Ki 11:8
Thus even in a * land he could 2Ki 5:17f
$50,000 in * currency; 1Ch 29:6,7
captives to some * nation near or 2Ch 6:36
the Levites, the * residents, and 2Ch 30:25
He also removed the * gods from 2Ch 33:15
become captives in a * land! Neh 4:4
was led into idolatry by * women. Neh 13:26
where we were slaves on * soil. Ps 81:5
Literally, "There shall no * god Ps 81:9f
from that land of * tongue, then Ps 114:1
far-off * nations and their kings; Is 52:14,15
my power by conquering * nations. Is 55:4
never again shall * soldiers come Is 62:8
yourself to a host of * gods; Jer 3:20
Many * rulers have ravaged my Jer 12:10
chase you into a * land where Jer 16:13
and you shall die in a * land. Jer 22:26
* population living in his land. Jer 25:19,20
to Jeremiah concerning * nations. Jer 46:1
She has seen * nations violate Lam 1:10
to some far-off * land where you Eze 3:5
cut her down. A * army (from Eze 31:12
Worshiping * gods has sapped Hos 7:9
the time will come when no * Joe 3:17
they took him far away to * lands; Ob 1:12
showing their desire for * gods Zep 1:8f
foreign gods and * ways, and their Zep 1:8f
all those gods of * powers, and Zep 2:11
from many * cities to attend these Zec 8:20,21
keep them away; no * oppressors Zec 9:8
land and live in a * country and Act 7:6
"He's pushing some * religion." Act 17:18
them in distant cities in * lands. Act 26:11
who have that gift of * speech? 1Co 12:30
lands to speak in * languages to 1Co 14:21
FOREIGN-BORN
This applies to every * slave as Gen 17:12
FOREIGNER
Gershom (meaning "*"), for he Ex 2:22
A hired servant or a visiting * Ex 12:45
Gershom (meaning "*," for Moses Ex 18:3
you know what it's like to be a * Ex 23:9
the land or are a * living among Lev 16:29,30
an Israelite or a * living among Lev 17:8,9
an Israelite or a * living among Lev 17:10
they, nor any * living among them, Lev 17:12
an Israelite or a * living among Lev 17:13
"And anyone—native born or *—who Lev 17:15
an Israelite or a * living among Lev 20:1
this law applies to the * as well Lev 24:15,16

(FOREIGNER Con't)
same law for the * as for the — Lev 24:22
"If a * living among you becomes — Lev 25:47
himself to the * or to the — Lev 25:47
If he sells himself to a *, the — Lev 25:53
a foreigner, the * must treat him — Lev 25:53
And if a * is living among you — Num 9:14
native-born or *, and this shall be — Num 15:15,16
shall the * be before Jehovah." — Num 15:15,16f
Israeli or a *, is blaspheming — Num 15:30
However, a * among you may eat — Deu 14:21
He must be an Israelite, not a *. — Deu 17:15
You may take interest from a *, — Deu 23:20
or a * living in your town. — Deu 24:14,15
the *, the orphan, and the widow.' — Deu 27:19
"You must know I am only a *." — Ru 2:10,11
a guest in Israel, a * in exile. — 2Sa 15:19,20
I am like a * to them. — Job 19:15
He will not be a *. — Jer 30:21
"The Lord God says: No * of all — Eze 44:9
* from the land of Sidon. — Lk 4:25,26
Does only this * return to give — Lk 17:18
"You Samaritan! *! — Jn 8:48

FOREIGNER'S
or to the * family, he may be — Lev 25:47

FOREIGNERS
where we now are *, for God has — Gen 28:4
These same rules apply to * who — Ex 12:19
the Passover. No * shall eat the — Ex 12:43
"As to *, if they are living — Ex 12:48
and to * living among you." — Ex 12:49
to sell her to *, since he has — Ex 21:8
remember, you yourselves were * — Ex 22:21
"Do not oppress *; — Ex 23:9
Israel and to * living among you. — Lev 18:26
"Do not take advantage of * in — Lev 19:33
too were * in the land of Egypt. — Lev 19:34
sacrifices made by * among you as — Lev 22:25
leave it for the poor and for * — Lev 23:22
and any * living among you. — Lev 25:6,7
children of the * living among you, — Lev 25:45
Israelis and to * living among you — Num 15:13,14
including the * living among them, — Num 15:26
* who are living among you. — Num 15:29
and any * living among them. — Num 19:10
but also for * and travelers. — Num 35:15
fair at all times, even to *! — Deu 1:16
or cattle; even * living among you — Deu 5:14
He loves * and gives them food — Deu 10:18
(You too must love *, for you — Deu 10:19
were * in the land of Egypt. — Deu 10:19
among you, or to *, or to widows — Deu 14:29
(This release does not apply to *. — Deu 15:3
Levites, *, widows, and orphans. — Deu 16:11
the Levites, *, orphans, and widows — Deu 16:14
trees and vines. * living among — Deu 28:43
your wives and the * that are among — Deu 29:11
to come and the * that pass by from — Deu 29:22
children, and * living among you—to — Deu 31:12
judges, and the * living among — Jos 8:33
* who lived among the Israelis. — Jos 8:35
of Refuge were for * living in — Jos 20:9
* shall serve me — 2Sa 22:44
"And when * hear of your great — 1Ki 8:41,42
But these * also worshiped their — 2Ki 17:29
a census of all * in the country — 2Ch 2:17
"And when * hear of your power, — 2Ch 6:32
separated themselves from all *. — Neh 9:1
was read, all the * were — Neh 13:3
So I purged out the *, and — Neh 13:30
and bow before me. * who have — Ps 18:43,44,45
and you become a slave of *. — Pro 5:10
while you watch, * are destroying — Is 1:7
you welcome * from the East who — Is 2:6
* who speak strange gibberish! — Is 28:11
* will come and build your — Is 60:10
* shall be your servants; — Is 61:5
now you must be slaves to * in — Jer 5:19
exploiting orphans, widows and *. — Jer 7:6
their chains, and * shall no longer — Jer 30:8
been defiled by * from Babylon." — Jer 51:51
—* you had forbidden even to enter. — Lam 1:10
and wander there among the *; — Lam 4:15
our nation, now are filled with *. — Lam 5:2
I will give it to * and to — Eze 7:21
hand you over to * who will carry — Eze 11:9
of Israel or the * living among — Eze 14:6,7
like an outcast at the hands of *. — Eze 28:10
in it, using * to do it. — Eze 30:12
* to take charge of my sanctuary. — Eze 44:8
and for the * who live among you — Eze 47:22
their parents are *—are to be — Eze 47:22
if it has any, * will eat it. — Hos 8:7
and orphans, * and poor people, and — Zec 7:10
"* will take over the city of — Zec 9:6
where so many * live—there the — Mt 4:15,16
people, or against conquered *?" — Mt 17:25
"Against the *," Peter replied. — Mt 17:26,27
for * who died in Jerusalem. — Mt 27:7
as well as the * in Athens seemed — Act 17:21
to God and * to heaven, but you are — Eph 2:19

FOREMAN
he said to his *, "Hey, who's that — Ru 2:4,5
And the * replied, "It's that — Ru 2:6

FOREMEN
These * went to Pharaoh and — Ex 5:15
Then the * saw that they were — Ex 5:19
and thirty-three hundred *. — 1Ki 5:16
in the hills, and 3,600 *. — 2Ch 2:2
80,000 as loggers and 3,600 as *. — 2Ch 2:18

FORESAIL
raised the * and headed ashore. — Act 27:40

FORESEES
A prudent man * the difficulties — Pro 22:3

FORESHADOW
and * what happened to the island — Eze 26:14f

FORESHADOWED
that the events * in this dream — Dan 4:19

FORESKIN
* of his penis shall be cut off. — Gen 17:11
and cut off the * of her young — Ex 4:25,26
remove the * of your hearts." — Jer 4:4f

FORESKINS
*, just as God had told him to. — Gen 17:23
was named "The Hill of the *." — Jos 5:2,3
Literally, "one hundred * of the — 1Sa 18:25f
presented their * to King Saul. — 1Sa 18:27

FOREST
man goes into the * with his — Deu 19:5
may clear out the * land where the — Jos 17:15
the ground in the *, for they all — 1Sa 14:24,25
So David went to the * of Hereth. — 1Sa 22:5
So the battle began in the * of — 2Sa 18:6
in the * than were killed. — 2Sa 18:8
a deep pit in the * and piled a — 2Sa 18:17
the Hall of the * of Lebanon. — 1Ki 7:2
in the Hall of the * of Lebanon. — 1Ki 10:16,17
in the Hall of the * of Lebanon his — 1Ki 10:21
The king placed these in the * of — 2Ch 9:16
in the * of Lebanon Room. — 2Ch 9:20
of the king's *, instructing him to — Neh 2:8
animals of field and * are mine! — Ps 50:10,11
like a * chopped to the ground. — Ps 74:5,6
The boar from the * roots around — Ps 80:13
the wind— as a * fire that roars — Ps 83:14
Let the trees of the * rustle — Ps 96:12
when all the * folk come out. — Ps 104:20
the trees of a * shake in a storm. — Is 7:2
*, yet it will be destroyed. — Is 10:18
cuts down the * trees in Lebanon. — Is 10:34
field again, a lush and fertile *. — Is 29:17
the * to be nourished by the rain. — Is 44:14
come, wild animals of the *, — Is 56:9
fury of the "lion from the *"; — Jer 5:6
like a lion of the *, so I have — Jer 12:8
of stone, and a * shall grow at the — Jer 26:18
who clear a * of its trees. — Jer 46:22,23
what good are vines from the *? — Eze 15:2
the vines of the *—useless before — Eze 15:5,6
it and the * lands of the Negeb. — Eze 20:46
I will set you on fire, O *, and — Eze 20:47
thick branches and * shade, with — Eze 31:2,3
fire that sets the * aflame—like a — Zec 12:6
A great * can be set on fire by — Jas 3:5

FORESTS
have the mountain *," Joshua — Jos 17:16,17,18
trees from the * of Lebanon, for — 2Ch 2:8
It strips the * bare. — Ps 29:9
melting in the * of Zalmon. — Ps 68:14
and the flames will consume the * — Is 9:18
and destroyed their thickest *.' — Is 37:24
All of Lebanon's * do not — Is 40:16
and *, yes, and every tree; — Is 44:23
will be yours—the * of firs and — Is 60:13
the * and boil the oceans dry. — Is 64:2
like deer in the * or mountain — Jer 16:16
I will light a fire in the * that — Jer 21:14
Gilead and the green * of Lebanon; — Jer 22:6
from the fields or *, for these — Eze 39:10
fragrant as the * of Lebanon. — Hos 14:6
the green * of Lebanon wilt. — Nah 1:4
You cut down the * of — Hab 2:17
by fire raging through your *. — Zec 11:1
you watch the thickest * felled. — Zec 11:2

FORETASTE
within us as a * of future glory, — Rom 8:23
gave only a dim * of the good — Heb 10:1

FORETELL
one who claims to * the future by — Deu 13:1

FORETELLS
So a prophet who * peace has the — Jer 28:9
befalls me that the dream *. — Dan 2:8,9

FORETOLD
come, just as all the prophets *. — Ps 40:7
idols ever has * such things? — Is 43:9
Is a yet future disaster * here? — Zec 13:8f
son of hell, as the Scriptures *. — Jn 17:12
But now as the prophets * and as — Rom 16:25,26,27
the grave just as the prophets *. — 1Co 15:4

FOREVER
of the Tree of Life and lives *?" — Gen 3:22
So the Lord God banished him * — Gen 3:23
for you, even if you toil on it *! — Gen 4:12
Spirit must not * be disgraced in — Gen 6:3
to give you this land *." — Gen 15:7
after generation, *, for it shall — Gen 17:7,8
land of Canaan to you and them, *. — Gen 17:7,8
him *, and with his descendants. — Gen 17:19
you, then let me bear the blame *. — Gen 43:9
will be slaves * to your master." — Gen 44:9
to you, I shall bear the blame *.' — Gen 44:32
Or, "say farewell to me *!" — Ex 12:32f
a day to remember *—the day of — Ex 13:3
Jehovah shall reign * and — Ex 15:18
Jehovah shall reign forever and * — Ex 15:18
a museum specimen *, so that later — Ex 16:32
to be remembered *, and announce to — Ex 17:14
after that he will be a slave *. — Ex 21:6
They will then be priests *; — Ex 29:9
the covenant between me and you *; — Ex 31:12,13
and they shall inherit it *.' — Ex 32:13
children shall * be my priests." — Ex 40:15
it is their right * throughout — Lev 7:36
From now on and *, if a priest — Lev 22:3
* from generation to generation; — Num 15:15,16
descendants shall be priests *." — Num 25:12,13
it, it shall belong to Israel *.' — Deu 2:31
that you will live * in the land — Deu 4:40
of your fathers, has given you *: — Deu 12:1
well with you and your children *. — Deu 12:28
That city shall * remain a — Deu 13:16
that he shall be your slave *. — Deu 15:17
for us and our children to obey *. — Deu 29:29
Let Reuben live * — Deu 33:6
all of you will worship him *." — Jos 4:24
to you and your descendants *.' — Jos 14:9
Put away * the idols which your — Jos 24:14
of Israel will not be lost *. — Ju 21:17
shall be priests to my kings *. — 1Sa 2:35
*, but now your dynasty must end; — 1Sa 13:13
"The Lord is our mediator *." — 1Sa 20:23f
children into God's hands *." — 1Sa 20:42
to stay here and serve me *!" — 1Sa 27:12
continue to kill each other *? — 2Sa 2:26
family shall rule my kingdom *.' — 2Sa 7:16
people *, and you became our God. — 2Sa 7:24
which will rule your people *; — 2Sa 7:27
Bless me and my family *! — 2Sa 7:29
that they will not be * exiles." — 2Sa 14:14f
David and his family, *. — 2Sa 22:51
May my lord the king live *!" — 1Ki 1:31
his descendants be * guilty of — 1Ki 2:33
a place for you to live *." — 1Ki 8:12,13
built and have put my name here *. — 1Ki 9:2,3
kings of Israel *, just as I — 1Ki 9:5
descendants shall rule Israel *. — 1Ki 11:38
descendants of David—though not *. — 1Ki 11:39
well, you can be their king *." — 1Ki 12:7
and your children's children *." — 2Ki 5:27
will place my name * in this — 2Ki 21:7
they are to minister to him *." — 1Ch 15:2
Remember his covenant *— — 1Ch 16:15
His love and his kindness go on *. — 1Ch 16:34
* and forevermore." — 1Ch 16:36
his royal line of descent *. — 1Ch 17:12
kingdom of Israel *—and his — 1Ch 17:14
*, and you have become their God. — 1Ch 17:22
upon my children *, for when you — 1Ch 17:27
a dynasty that will rule Israel *; — 1Ch 28:4
I will make his kingdom last *.' — 1Ch 28:7
it to your children to rule *. — 1Ch 28:8
His lovingkindness lasts *!" — 2Ch 5:13,14
for you, O Lord, to live in *!" — 2Ch 6:1
Then they will reverence you *, — 2Ch 6:31
Lovingkindness Is *," using the — 2Ch 7:6
and sanctified it to be my home *; — 2Ch 7:16
to be a great, strong nation *." — 2Ch 9:8
And didn't you give this land * — 2Ch 20:7
Lovingkindness Is *" as they — 2Ch 20:21
he has sanctified *, and worship — 2Ch 30:8
said that he would be honored *. — 2Ch 33:4,5
to be honored * above all the other — 2Ch 33:7
mercy toward Israel will last *." — Ez 3:11
nation and * leave that prosperity — Ez 9:12
Literally, "Let the king live * — Neh 2:3f
with him to * give him and his — Neh 9:8
them completely or abandon them *. — Neh 9:31
Queen Vashti be * banished from — Est 1:19
Let that day be * forgotten. — Job 3:4
are dead, gone * with hardly a — Job 4:20
die shall go away *— gone forever — Job 7:9
forever— gone * from their family — Job 7:10
No, darkness shall overtake him *; — Job 15:30
with an iron pen in the rock *. — Job 19:23,24
*, cast away like his own dung. — Job 20:7
of their lives washed out *? — Job 22:15,16
of men, will you * turn my glory — Ps 4:2
out their names * and ever. — Ps 9:5
enemies of mine, you are doomed *. — Ps 9:6
But the Lord lives on *; — Ps 9:7,8
the needy shall not be ignored *; — Ps 9:18
The Lord is King * and forever. — Ps 10:16
The Lord is King forever and *. — Ps 10:16

'OREVER Con't)
O Lord, we know that you will * Ps 12:7
LONG WILL you forget me, Lord? *? Ps 13:1
him—such a man shall stand firm *. Ps 15:5
of his life stretch on and on *. Ps 21:4
will live with you * in your home. Ps 23:6
and carry them * in your arms. Ps 28:9
my prosperity I said, "This is *; Ps 30:6,7
I will keep on thanking you *! Ps 30:12
him, but his own plan stands *. Ps 33:11
* urging them on to evil deeds. Ps 36:1
They will be kept safe *; Ps 37:28
in the land, and live there *. Ps 37:29
you have admitted me * to your Ps 41:12
Are we cast off *? Ps 44:23
God himself is blessing you *. Ps 45:2
Your throne, O God, endures *. Ps 45:6
of the earth will praise you *." Ps 45:17
God has established Jerusalem *. Ps 48:8
For this great God is our God * Ps 48:14
lands could be * yours, and you Ps 49:11
Don't toss me aside, banished * Ps 51:11
I trust in the mercy of God * and Ps 52:8
O Lord, I will praise you * and Ps 52:9
I shall live * in your Ps 61:4
I shall live before the Lord *. Ps 61:7
of his great power he rules *. Ps 66:7
where God has chosen to live *. Ps 68:15,16
continue in the skies! Yes, *! Ps 72:5
His name will be honored *; Ps 72:17
Blessed be his glorious name *! Ps 72:19
he is mine *! Ps 73:26
O GOD, WHY have you cast us away * Ps 74:1
you let them get away with this *? Ps 74:9,10
But as for me, I shall * declare Ps 75:9
Has the Lord rejected me *? Ps 77:7
Is his lovingkindness gone *? Ps 77:8
long will you be angry with us? *? Ps 79:5
will thank you * and forever, Ps 79:13
you forever and *, praising your Ps 79:13
their desolation would last *. Ps 81:15
I will give glory to your name *, Ps 86:12
* AND EVER I will sing about the Ps 89:1
Your love and kindness are *; Ps 89:2
as kings * on his throne, from now Ps 89:3,4
I will love him *, and be kind Ps 89:28
dynasty will go on *, and his Ps 89:35,36
Will you hide yourself from me *? Ps 89:46
No man can live *. Ps 89:48
And yet—blessed be the Lord *! Ps 89:52
But the Lord continues *, Ps 92:8
Holiness is * the keynote of your Ps 93:5
you, Lord, are a famous King *. Ps 102:12
"O God, you live * and forever! Ps 102:24
"O God, you live forever and *! Ps 102:24
shall perish, but you go on *. Ps 102:26
You are *, and your years never Ps 102:27
a grudge, nor remains angry *. Ps 103:9
blown by the wind and gone *. Ps 103:16
Praise God *! Ps 104:31
Your love for us continues on *. Ps 106:1
deed Phineas will be remembered *. Ps 106:31
vow, that you are a priest * like Ps 110:4
and goodness, and stand firm *. Ps 111:8
Praise his name *. Ps 111:10
"his righteousness endures *." Ps 112:3f
"his righteousness endures *." Ps 112:9f
Blessed is his name * and Ps 113:2
Blessed is his name forever and *. Ps 113:2
We praise him *! Ps 115:18
my bonds and I will serve you *. Ps 116:16
His lovingkindness is *. Ps 118:1
"His lovingkindness is *." Ps 118:2
"His lovingkindness is *." Ps 118:3
"His lovingkindness is *." Ps 118:4
For his lovingkindness is *. Ps 118:29
on obeying you * and forever, free Ps 119:44,45,46
you forever and *, free within the Ps 119:44,45,46
*, O Lord, your Word stands firm Ps 119:89
laws are my joyous treasure *. Ps 119:111
O Jehovah, your name endures *; Ps 135:13
his lovingkindness continues *. Ps 136:1
his lovingkindness continues *. Ps 136:2
his lovingkindness continues *. Ps 136:3
his lovingkindness continues *. Ps 136:4
his lovingkindness continues *. Ps 136:5
his lovingkindness continues *. Ps 136:6
continues *: the sun to rule the Ps 136:7
his lovingkindness continues *; Ps 136:8
his lovingkindness continues *. Ps 136:9
continues *. Ps 136:10
continues *. Ps 136:11,12
continues *, and led them safely Ps 136:13
continues *— but drowned Pharaoh's Ps 136:14
continues *. Ps 136:15
his lovingkindness continues *. Ps 136:16
continues *, and killed famous Ps 136:17
continues *: Sihon, king of Ps 136:18
continues *— and Og, king of Ps 136:19
continues *. Ps 136:20
Israel as a gift *, for his Ps 136:21
continues *; Ps 136:21
his lovingkindness continues *. Ps 136:22
his lovingkindness continues *. Ps 136:23
his lovingkindness continues *. Ps 136:24
his lovingkindness continues *. Ps 136:25
his lovingkindness continues *. Ps 136:26
lovingkindness, Lord, continues *. Ps 138:8
bless your name each day and *. Ps 145:1
bless his holy name * and forever. Ps 145:21
bless his holy name forever and *. Ps 145:21
The Lord will reign *. Ps 146:10
he established them * and Ps 148:6
he established them forever and *. Ps 148:6
wicked man's riches continue *. Pro 10:3
but the good man's reward lasts *. Pro 11:18
evil man will not go unpunished *. Pro 11:21
family *—so watch your business Pro 27:23,24
* craving more: no, three things! Pro 30:15,16
"but the earth remains *." Ecc 1:3-7f
Studying them can go on *, and Ecc 12:12
Must you * rebel? Is 1:5,6
and despair shall not go on *. Is 9:1
David's throne *, and on that Is 16:4,5
in the wine presses has ceased *. Is 16:10
he will swallow up death *. Is 25:8
and take away * all insults and Is 25:8
Is he * harrowing the soil and Is 28:23,24
the end of time, * and forever, as Is 30:8
time, forever and *, as an Is 30:8
and confidence will reign * more. Is 32:17
Its smoke will rise up *. Is 34:10
they shall possess it *, from Is 34:17
and all sighing will be gone *; Is 35:10
Word of our God shall stand *." Is 40:8
But my salvation lasts *; Is 51:6
mercy shall last *, and my Is 51:8
you *, nor always show my wrath; Is 57:16
and their children's children *." Is 59:21
will be beautiful *, a joy for all Is 60:15
They will possess their land *, Is 60:21
and established his reputation *? Is 63:12
us, Lord, nor * remember our sins. Is 64:9
rejoice * in my creation. Is 65:18
I will not be * angry with you. Jer 3:12
their fathers as an inheritance *. Jer 3:18
I gave to your fathers to keep *. Jer 7:7
I would weep *; Jer 9:1
his name will be * forgotten." Jer 11:19
of my anger that shall burn *. Jer 17:4
good times pass him by *. Jer 17:6
then this nation shall continue *. Jer 17:25
and this city shall remain *. Jer 17:25
shall have a stigma upon them *. Jer 20:11
to you and to your ancestors *. Jer 25:5
make you a byword of contempt *. Jer 25:8,9
them away * for their sins! Jer 31:37
mind to worship me *, for their own Jer 32:39
is good and his mercy endures *!" Jer 33:10,11
on, David shall * have an heir Jer 33:17
neither we nor our children *. Jer 35:6
It shall be desolate *. Jer 49:33
it shall lie desolate *. Jer 50:39
You shall be desolate * Jer 51:26
floor, to sleep *, never to waken Jer 51:39
and it will be abandoned *.' Jer 51:61,62
the Lord will not abandon him *. Lam 3:31
O Lord, * you remain the same! Lam 5:19
Why do you forget us *? Lam 5:20
covenant with you *, and you will Eze 16:59,60
you have * perished.' Eze 27:36
you are destroyed *." Eze 28:19
You will be abandoned *; Eze 35:9
Messiah, shall be their Prince *. Eze 37:25
and put my Temple among them *. Eze 37:26
among the people of Israel *. Eze 43:7
and I will live among them *. Eze 43:9
his sons, it will belong to him *. Eze 46:16
be the name of God * and ever, for Dan 2:20
it shall stand *, indestructible. Dan 2:44
he reigns * and ever. Dan 4:3
him who lives *, whose rule is Dan 4:34
and say, "King Darius, live *! Dan 6:6
"Your Majesty, live *!" Dan 6:21
of the world * and forever." Dan 7:18
of the world forever and *." Dan 7:18
they shall rule all things *, and Dan 7:27
will glitter like stars *. Dan 12:3
and I will bind you to me * with Hos 1:19
for my anger will be * gone! Hos 14:4
Jerusalem shall be mine *; Joe 3:17
"But Israel will prosper *, and Joe 3:20
you will be cut off *. Ob 1:10
the Lord our God * and ever, even Mic 4:5
be their King from Mount Zion *. Mic 4:7
He is cut off *; Nah 1:15
Must I * see this sin and Hab 1:3
you let them get away with this *? Hab 1:17
Will they succeed * in their Hab 1:17
destroyed [for my mercy endures * Mal 3:6
and the power and the glory *. Mt 6:13f
and be * united to his wife. Mt 19:5,6
disappear, but my words remain *. Mt 24:35
Better live * with one hand than Mk 9:43,44
Better be lame and live * than Mk 9:45,46
but my words stand sure *. Mk 13:31
And he shall reign over Israel * Lk 1:33
* shall call me blest of God. Lk 1:48
be merciful to them *." Lk 1:55
ready to stand in his presence *. Lk 1:75
need to do to live * in heaven?" Lk 10:25
such hypocrisy cannot be hidden *. Lk 12:1
away, yet my words remain * true. Lk 21:33
them * with eternal life." Jn 4:14
eating this Bread shall live *; Jn 6:48-51
Bread shall live *, and not die as Jn 6:58
would live * and never die. Jn 12:34
Must you * resist the Holy Act 7:51
* in unbroken fellowship with God. Rom 6:10
* damned if that would save you. Rom 9:1
Praise God *! Rom 9:5
bent-backed * with a heavy load." Rom 11:10
has rejected his Jewish people *? Rom 11:11
* through Jesus Christ our Lord. Rom 16:25,26,27
to an end, but love goes on *. 1Co 13:8
are not the right kind to live *. 1Co 15:50
cannot perish but will live *. 1Co 15:53
blessing upon us * and ever! 2Co 4:17
but the joys to come will last *. 2Co 4:18
* and I live and die with you. 2Co 7:3
deeds will be an honor to him *." 2Co 9:9
is to be praised * and ever, knows 2Co 11:31
message, let him be * cursed. Gal 1:8
earth—to be with him in Christ, *. Eph 1:10
curse, doomed * for your sins. Eph 2:1
May he be given glory * and ever Eph 3:21
be like children, * changing our Eph 4:14
our Father be glory * and ever. Php 4:20
in the air and remain with him *. 1Th 4:17
can live with him *, whether we are 1Th 5:10
everlasting hell, * separated from 2Th 1:9
But we must * give thanks to God 2Th 2:13
Glory and honor to God * and 1Ti 1:17
power and dominion * and ever. 1Ti 6:16
Women of that kind are * 2Ti 3:7
won't get away with all this *. 2Ti 3:9
To God be the glory * and ever. 2Ti 4:18
he can be yours *, no longer only Phm 1:15
O God, will last * and ever; Heb 1:8
but you will remain *. Heb 1:11
to be a priest *, with the same Heb 5:6
that of the Son of God—a priest *. Heb 7:3
* with the rank of Melchizedek." Heb 7:17
*, with the rank of Melchizedek." Heb 7:21
can guarantee * the success of this Heb 7:22
But Jesus lives * and continues Heb 7:24
Since he will live *, he will Heb 7:25
his oath his Son who is perfect *. Heb 7:28
date now and has been put aside *. Heb 8:13
may come and have * all the wonders Heb 9:15
power of sin * by dying for us. Heb 9:26
which * took those sins away. Heb 10:4f
offering he made * perfect in the Heb 10:14
Now, when sins have once been * Heb 10:18
things that would be yours *. Heb 10:34
the same yesterday, today, and *. Heb 13:8
To him be glory * and ever. Heb 13:20,21
shines * without change or shadow. Jas 1:17
This new one will last *, for it 1Pe 1:23
the Word of the Lord will last *. 1Pe 1:25
him be glory and power * and ever. 1Pe 4:11
power over all things, * and ever. 1Pe 5:11
doing the will of God will live *. 1Jn 2:17
And the Holy Spirit, * truthful, 1Jn 5:6,7,8
is in our hearts *, God the Father 2Jn 1:2
He rules *! Rev 1:6
throne, who lives * and ever, the Rev 4:9
and to the Lamb * and ever." Rev 5:13
be to our God * and forever. Rev 7:12
be to our God forever and *. Rev 7:12
by him who lives * and ever, who Rev 10:6
and he shall reign * and ever." Rev 11:15
torture rises * and ever, and they Rev 14:11
God who lives * and forever. Rev 15:7
God who lives forever and *. Rev 15:7
They are gone *." Rev 18:14
stone, and she shall disappear *. Rev 18:21
burning ascends * and forever!" Rev 19:3
burning ascends forever and *!" Rev 19:3
day and night * and ever. Rev 20:10
All of that has gone *." Rev 21:4
and they shall reign * and ever. Rev 22:5
Blessed * are all who are Rev 22:14

FOREVERMORE
Forever and *." 1Ch 16:36
even life *. Ps 133:3
that will be ours *, made for us by 2Co 5:1
splendid honor, both now and *. 2Pe 3:18
who is now alive *, who has the Rev 1:17,18

FORFEIT
being a priest, I would * my life. Neh 6:11

FORFEITED
shamed your name and * your lives. Hab 2:10

FORFEITING
world when it means * one's self? Lk 9:25
FORGAVE
And you * me! Ps 32:5
Yet he was merciful and * their Ps 78:38
You answered them and * their Ps 99:8
and released him and * his debt. Mt 18:27
Here I * you all that tremendous Mt 18:32
back, so he kindly * them both, Lk 7:42
faith God * his sins and declared Rom 4:22
his blood and * us all our sins. Col 1:14
of Christ, for he * all your sins, Col 2:13
Remember, the Lord * you, so you Col 3:13
FORGE
The metalsmith stands at his * Is 44:12
coals beneath the * and makes the Is 54:16
FORGED
Then he * a huge round tank 2Ch 4:2
FORGET
GOD DIDN'T * about Noah and all Gen 8:1
(meaning "Made to *"—what he Gen 41:51
For don't * that this nation is Ex 33:13
Be very careful never to * what Deu 4:9
destroy you nor * the promises he Deu 4:31
beware lest you * the Lord who Deu 6:10,11,12
When you are full, don't * to be Deu 6:13
you don't * the Lord your God and Deu 8:11
become proud, and * the Lord your Deu 8:14
Beware that you don't * the God Deu 8:15
"But if you * about the Lord Deu 8:19
"Don't you remember (oh, never * Deu 9:7
not to * about the Levites. Deu 12:19
"Don't * to share your income Deu 14:27
And don't * to include the local Deu 16:11
And don't * to include the Deu 16:14
your harvest, you * to bring in a Deu 24:19
"You must never * what the Deu 25:17
Never * this. Deu 25:19
They will * about me and break Deu 31:16
forgive me and * the terrible thing 2Sa 19:19
* the covenant I made with you; 2Ki 17:38
"* David and his dynasty!" 2Ch 10:16
you might as well * about this part Ez 4:16
"O my God," I prayed, "don't * Neh 6:14
deed and do not * all that I have Neh 13:14
Even when I try to * my misery Job 7:13,14
those who * God have no hope. Job 8:11-13
"If I decided to * my complaints Job 9:27
Only then can you * your misery. Job 11:16
* me there until your anger ends; Job 14:13
sinner's own mother shall * him. Job 24:20
Don't * the poor or anyone else Ps 10:12
HOW LONG WILL you * me, Lord? Ps 13:1
(but how could you ever * them! Ps 42:4,5
my people soon * such lessons—but Ps 59:11
and not * his glorious miracles. Ps 78:7
the Lord and not * the glorious Ps 103:2
Who can * the wonders he Ps 111:4
I will delight in them and not * Ps 119:16
May I never * your words; Ps 119:43
Never * your promises to me your Ps 119:49,50
If I * you, O Jerusalem, let my Ps 137:5,6
hand * its skill upon the harp. Ps 137:5,6
O Jehovah, do not * what these Ps 137:7
MY SON, NEVER * the things I've Pro 3:1
Never * to be truthful and kind. Pro 3:3
He told me never to * his words. Pro 4:4
Literally, "* not nor turn from Pro 4:5f
don't * them, for they will lead Pro 4:13
to me, and never * what I'm about Pro 5:7
around your finger so you won't *. Pro 6:21
"I've decided to * our quarrel! Pro 7:14
For if they drink they may * Pro 31:5
Let them drink to * their poverty Pro 31:6,7
cause you to * about your Creator. Ecc 12:1
tell us lies. * all this gloom; Is 30:10,11
And don't * what happened to the Is 37:13
But * all that—it is nothing Is 43:18
I made you, and I will not * to Is 44:21
"Don't * this, O guilty ones. Is 46:8
And don't * the many times I Is 46:9
Can a mother * her little child Is 49:15
that should be, I will not * you. Is 49:15
anger and * the evil that you did. Is 65:16
Can a girl * her jewels? Jer 2:32
Surely you will just * it?" Jer 3:4,5
Oh, that I could go away and * Jer 9:2
Their youths do not * to sin, Jer 17:2,3
get my people to * me in the same Jer 23:27
I will forgive and * their sins. Jer 31:34
Jeremiah concluded: "Never * the Jer 42:19
For I can never * these awful Lam 3:20
Why do you * us forever? Lam 5:20
O Israel, I will cause you to * Hos 1:17
will "*" to bless your children. Hos 4:6
But never *—I will settle up with Hos 5:2
The Lord does not *. Hos 9:9
"Let the flocks and herds * Joe 2:22
and again, and I will not * it. Amo 1:3
and again, and I will not * it. Amo 1:6
and again and I will not * it. Amo 1:9
and again, and I will not * it. Amo 1:11
and again, and I will not * it. Amo 1:13
and again, and I will not * it. Amo 2:1
and again, and I will not * it. Amo 2:4
and again, and I will not * it. Amo 2:6
has sworn: "I won't * your deeds! Amo 8:7
at once to try to make them * it. Mk 4:15
Never * how close you were to the Lk 10:11
you completely * about justice and Lk 11:42
Yet God does not * a single one Lk 12:6
FOR WE MUST never *, dear 1Co 10:1
Never * that once you were Eph 2:11
tell God your needs and don't * Php 4:6
Don't * to pray for us too, that Col 4:3
We never * your loving deeds as 1Th 1:3
Don't ever * the wonderful fact 2Ti 2:8
Never * the warning, "Today if Heb 3:15
How can he * your hard work for Heb 6:10
work for him, or * the way you used Heb 6:10
Don't ever * those wonderful days Heb 10:32
Don't * to be kind to strangers, Heb 13:2
Don't * about those in jail. Heb 13:3
Don't * to do good and to share Heb 13:16
Dear brothers, don't ever * that Jas 1:19
They deliberately * this fact: 2Pe 3:5,6
But don't * this, dear friends, 2Pe 3:8
And don't * the cities of Sodom Jud 1:7
FORGETFULNESS
condition caused *, so that he 1Sa 17:55f
Can anyone in the Land of * talk Ps 88:12
FORGETS
and he * what you have done. Gen 27:45
in the dust. She * that someone Job 39:15
pass he never * his promise, his Ps 105:8,9
he never * his promises. Ps 111:5
Love * mistakes; Pro 17:9
FORGETTING
* it was God who had given them Deu 32:18
of all the nations * the Lord. Ps 9:17
farthest ends, not * their blind Jer 31:8
about their * to bring bread. Mk 8:16
on this one thing: * the past and Php 3:13
FORGING
* instruments of bronze and iron. Gen 4:22
FORGIVE
"* my not getting up, father," Gen 31:35
us to tell you to * us for the Gen 50:16,17
of your father beg you to * us." Gen 50:16,17
and against you. * my sin only Ex 10:17
Yet now if you will only * their Ex 32:32
steadfast love. * us, even though Num 14:17,18
and then Jehovah will * her Num 30:5
it void, and Jehovah will * her. Num 30:8
is void and Jehovah will * her. Num 30:12
O Lord, * your people Israel Deu 21:8
an innocent man. * us the guilt of Deu 21:8
he will not * your rebellion and Jos 24:19
your young men. * me for my 1Sa 25:28
the king, please * me and forget 2Sa 19:19
Please * this foolish wickedness 2Sa 24:10
you live, and when you hear, *. 1Ki 8:30
from heaven and * them if they turn 1Ki 8:33,34
from heaven and * them when they 1Ki 8:35,36
from heaven and * and answer all 1Ki 8:39
"* your people for all of their 1Ki 8:50
Please * me, for I realize now 1Ch 21:8
from heaven, and when you hear, *. 2Ch 6:20,21
from heaven and * their sins and 2Ch 6:25
from heaven and * the sins of your 2Ch 6:27
you live, and *, and give each one 2Ch 6:30
their hearts to * them, then hear 2Ch 6:37,38
and help them and * your people who 2Ch 6:39
* their sins and heal their land. 2Ch 7:14
year and to * and cancel the debts Neh 10:31
and to refuse to * my iniquity. Job 10:13,14
feel my pain; * my sins. Ps 25:18
Good News that you * men's sins. Ps 40:9
fill our hearts, you * them all. Ps 65:3
Oh, save us and * our sins. Ps 79:9
so good and kind, so ready to *; Ps 86:5
But you *! Ps 130:3,4
God will not * you for this sin. Is 2:9
* them their sins and bless them. Is 33:24
Don't * them, don't blot out Jer 18:23
I will * and forget their sins. Jer 31:34
And then I can * them." Jer 36:3
ask the Lord to * them before it is Jer 36:7
in shame when I * you all that you Eze 16:63
O Lord, *. Dan 9:19
mercy upon Israel, to * her again. Hos 1:6
I WANTED TO * Israel, but her sins Hos 7:1
Lord God, please * your people! Amo 7:2
Then would he * your sins? Mic 6:7
and he does not easily *. Nah 1:3
'Those Whom God Does Not *.' Mal 1:4
"Come and I will * you. Mal 3:7
as usual, and * us our sins, just Mt 6:12
Your heavenly Father will * you Mt 6:14,15
you * those who sin against you; Mt 6:14,15
but if you refuse to * them, he Mt 6:14,15
forgive them, he will not * you. Mt 6:14,15
have the authority on earth to * Mt 9:5,
I * a brother who sins against me? Mt 18:2
refuse to truly * your brothers." Mt 18:3
It is poured out to * the sins of Mt 26:2
on sin, so that God could * them. Mk 1:
For only God can * sins." Mk 2:
have the authority on earth to * Mk 2:9,10,1
are praying, first * anyone you are Mk 11:2
heaven will * you your sins too." Mk 11:2
if you do not *, neither will your Mk 11:26,
is in heaven * your trespasses." Mk 11:26,
Who but God can * sins?" Lk 5:2
have the authority on earth to * Lk 5:23,24
day by day. And * our sins—for we Lk 11:4
he sins, and * him if he is sorry. Lk 17:2,3
and asks forgiveness, * him." Lk 17:4
"Father, * these people," Jesus Lk 23:34
If you * anyone's sins, they are Jn 20:23
If you refuse to * them, they are Jn 20:23
Perhaps God will yet * your evil Act 8:22
Now it is time to * him and 2Co 2:7
When you * anyone, I do too. 2Co 2:10
Please * me for this wrong! 2Co 12:13
Be gentle and ready to *; Col 3:13
forgave you, so you must * others. Col 3:13
by some sin, the Lord will * him. Jas 5:15
he can be depended on to * us and 1Jn 1:9
should ask God to * him and God 1Jn 5:16
FORGIVEN
the people will be accepted and *. Ex 28:37,38
nation, and everyone will be *. Lev 4:20
his sin, and he shall be *. Lev 4:26
for that man, and he shall be *. Lev 4:31
the man, and his sin shall be *. Lev 4:35
his sin and he shall be *. Lev 5:10
of this kind, and he shall be *. Lev 5:13
guilt offering, and he shall be *. Lev 5:16
so that he will be * for whatever Lev 5:17,18
the Lord, and he shall be *." Lev 6:7
committed, and it shall be * him. Lev 19:22
just as you have * them all the Num 14:19
of Israel and they shall be *; Num 15:25
All the people shall be *, Num 15:26
the Lord, and he shall be *. Num 15:28
* by sacrifices and offerings." 1Sa 3:14
but the Lord has * you, and you 2Sa 12:13
FOR those whose guilt has been *! Ps 32:1
them, while there is time to be *. Ps 32:6
Lord takes care of those he has *. Ps 37:17
of Israel, and * the sins of Ps 85:2
Your sins are all *." Is 6:7
be * you until the day you die. Is 22:14
you have * all my sins. Is 38:17
just as we have * those who have Mt 6:12
For I have * your sins!" Mt 9:2
or any other sin, can be *—all Mt 12:31,32
shall never be *, either in this Mt 12:31,32
him the man he had * and said, 'You Mt 18:32
man, "Son, your sins are *!" Mk 2:5
be *, even blasphemy against me; Mk 3:28
the Holy Spirit can never be *. Mk 3:29
to God, or be * for their sins.' Mk 4:11,12
from their sins, in order to be *. Lk 3:3
"My friend, your sins are *!" Lk 5:20
many—are *, for she loved me much; Lk 7:47
but one who is * little, shows Lk 7:47
said to her, "Your sins are *." Lk 7:48
* those who sinned against us. Lk 11:4
may be *—while those who speak Lk 12:10
the Holy Spirit shall never be *. Lk 12:10
not the Pharisee, returned home *! Lk 18:14
forgive anyone's sins, they are *. Jn 20:23
and for their sins to be *. Act 5:31
their sins * through his name." Act 10:43
you how to have your sins *." Act 16:17
sins are * and put out of sight. Rom 4:7
He is the one who has * us and Rom 8:33
And whatever I have * (to the 2Co 2:10
just as God has * you because you Eph 4:32
plan we have been * and made clean Heb 10:10
once been forever * and forgotten, Heb 10:18
* in the name of Jesus our Savior. 1Jn 2:12
FORGIVENESS
be able to obtain his * for you." Ex 32:30
is involved in such error and *. Num 15:26
But you are a God of *, always Neh 9:17
eyes of mercy and *, through eyes Ps 25:6,7
For God's * does not come that Ps 49:7
Then I will sing of your *, Ps 51:14,15
of this promise of *, for we must Is 43:26
rains he sends are tokens of *. Joe 2:23
of repentance for the * of sins." Mk 1:4f
salvation through * of their sins. Lk 1:77
again and asks *, forgive him." Lk 17:4
* of sins for all who turn to me. Lk 24:47
among us and was full of loving * Jn 1:14
brought us loving * as well. Jn 1:17
Christ for the * of your sins; Act 2:38
In this man Jesus, there is * for Act 13:38
they may receive * for their sins Act 26:18
between man's sin and God's *! Rom 5:15

ORGIVENESS Con't)
* to many through God's mercy. Rom 5:15
* and acquittal are kings of life Rom 5:17
us more and more kindness and *? Rom 6:1
A further reason for * is to 2Co 2:11
of blood there is no * of sins. Heb 9:22
the truth of *, this sin is not Heb 10:26
about the * of his many sins. Jas 5:20
and he is the * 1Jn 2:2

ORGIVES
He * all my sins. Ps 103:3
which graciously * instead of Heb 12:24

ORGIVING
to many thousands by * their sins; Ex 34:7
Literally, "* iniquity and Ex 34:7f
by * our sins and showing us Num 14:17,18
Plead your case for my * you. Is 43:26
true and yet * them their sins!" Zec 8:8
he is, going around * sins?" Lk 7:49
we see God's abounding grace * us. Rom 5:20
tenderhearted, * one another, just Eph 4:32

ORGOT
ran, and * to take his jacket." Gen 39:14,15
however, promptly * all about Gen 40:23
But they soon * about the Lord 1Sa 12:9
Yet they * that he had filled Job 22:18
And they * about the wonderful Ps 78:11,12
They * his power and love, and Ps 78:42
they * the plagues he sent upon Ps 78:43
in Egypt, and soon * your many acts Ps 106:7
Yet how quickly they * again! Ps 106:13
Land" or the "Land that God *." Is 62:4
people living here * the Lord their Jer 22:9
then you became proud and * me. Hos 13:6
the other five were foolish and *. Mt 25:2,3,4
never * the horror of it. Rev 1:7f

FORGOTTEN
will be * and wiped out; Gen 41:30
so that his name will not be *. Deu 25:6
I have not violated or * any of Deu 26:13
Have you * about the time he 1Sa 19:5
Let that day be forever *. Job 3:4
I am * like a dead man, like a Ps 31:12
say, "May he soon die and be *!" Ps 41:5
of you who have * God, before I Ps 50:22
Has he * to be kind to one so Ps 77:9
his good deeds will never be *. Ps 112:3
His deeds will never be *. Ps 112:9
days to come both will be long *. Ecc 2:16
cemetery, having * all the dead Ecc 8:9,10
For seventy years Tyre will be *. Is 23:15,16
them, and they are long *. Is 26:14
he has * us." Is 49:14
Maker—you have * him, the one who Is 51:13
end my people have * me—the most Jer 2:32
that his name will be forever *." Jer 11:19
Have you * the sins of your Jer 44:9
I have * what enjoyment is. Lam 3:17
the Lord, and he has not * it. Lam 3:42
All his past sins will be *, and Eze 18:22
* and he shall die for his sins. Eze 18:24
Because you have * me and turned Eze 23:35
Since you have * my laws, I will Hos 4:6
but they have * their Maker. Hos 8:14
My people have * what it means Amo 3:10
the names of the idols will be *. Zec 13:2
they had * to bring any food. Mt 16:5
because they had * to bring bread. Mt 16:7
But the disciples had * to stock Mk 8:14
He has not * his promise to be Lk 1:54
rapturous joy and the pain is *. Jn 16:21
all around the world—will be *!" Act 19:27
forgiven and *, there is no need to Heb 10:18
And have you quite * the Heb 12:5
and has * that God delivered him 2Pe 1:9

FORK
gates and at every * in the road, Pro 8:1
* where he made the wrong turn. Jer 8:4,5
And put a signpost at the * in Eze 21:19,20
stands at a *, uncertain whether to Eze 21:21

FORM
to * the sky above and the oceans Gen 1:6
who will * many nations! Gen 17:6
come to you in the * of a dark Ex 19:9
upon it in the * of fire; Ex 19:18
will hang down to * a curtain Ex 26:9
Twenty of these frames will * Ex 26:18,19
tooled it into the * of a calf. Ex 32:4
Then the Lord descended in the * Ex 34:5,6
* the ceiling of the Tabernacle. Ex 36:13
square, doubled over to * a pouch; Ex 39:9
it—it is a * of grain offering. Lev 2:6
you, who eats blood in any *. Lev 17:10
And he shall see the very * of Num 12:7,8
You didn't see the * of God that Deu 4:15
God—an idol in any *, whether of a Deu 4:16,17
it is in the * of money, food, or Deu 23:19
Ahaziah is an alternate * of the 2Ki 8:24,25f
$2,000 in the * of a special tax. 2Ki 15:19,20
were made in the * of miniature 2Ki 20:11f
You Levites, * a bodyguard for 2Ch 23:7
to his people. * yourselves into 2Ch 35:4,5
Literally, "cast lots," a * of Neh 10:34f
in the * of remission of taxes. Est 2:18
of the earth to * the seas. Ps 104:3
gushed out to * a river through the Ps 105:41
Flattery is a * of hatred and Pro 26:28
Mobs * in the streets, crying Is 24:11
I alone am God. I * the light Is 45:7
the nations to * a coalition Jer 49:14
on either side to * two pillars, Eze 40:48,49
He found that it was in the * of Eze 42:16-20
Egypt: he too will * an alliance Dan 11:17
came to Micah in the * of visions. Mic 1:1
allow sin in any *, stand idly by Hab 1:13
coming down in the * of a dove. Mt 3:16
Holy Spirit in the * of a dove Mk 1:10
Holy Spirit in the * of a dove Lk 3:22
beginning to * in the west, you Lk 12:54
Holy Spirit in the * of a dove Jn 1:32
to * a mob and start a riot. Act 17:5
for the world in its present * 1Co 7:31
Literally, "having a * of 2Ti 3:5f
too by being born in human *; Heb 2:14
Abraham in human *, or simply that Heb 7:3f
to * the earth and surround it. 2Pe 3:5,6
Greek * of "Balaamites." Rev 2:15f
Beings was in the * of a lion; Rev 4:7
and the fourth, the * of an Rev 4:7
in fact it was in the * of a Rev 21:16

FORMAL
And Hiram and Solomon made a * 1Ki 5:12

FORMALLY
* vow to carry out their promises. Neh 5:12

FORMATION
in their usual battle *. Ju 20:30
He controls the * of the depths Ps 95:4

FORMED
Together they * the first day. Gen 1:4,5
The time came when the Lord God * Gen 2:7
in the garden the man he had *. Gen 2:8
So the Lord God * from the Gen 2:19,20
Laban went out and * a flock for Gen 30:35,36
every kernel well * and plump. Gen 41:5
was a second layer * by eleven Ex 36:14,15
Soon a great, sullen mob *; Num 16:42
A great mob *, and they held a Num 20:2
ring * by the slumbering soldiers. 1Sa 26:5,6,7
whom were priests—* a bugle corps 1Ch 15:24
These officers, fully armed, * a 2Ch 23:10
The priests * a trumpet corps. 2Ch 29:25,26
the Levites were * into service 2Ch 35:10
*, and all the galaxies of stars. Ps 33:6
He * the mountains by his mighty Ps 65:6
the earth was *, you are God Ps 90:2
He made the sea and * the land; Ps 95:5
for they are * from truth and Ps 111:8
I was being * in utter seclusion! Ps 139:15
The Lord * me in the beginning, Pro 8:22
the heavens and * the great springs Pro 8:27,28,29
royal secretary, * a truce team and Is 36:3
Lord—the Lord who * me from my Is 49:5
We are all * by your hand. Is 64:8
were * within your mother's womb; Jer 1:5
but our God * the earth by his Jer 10:12
muscles and flesh * over the bones, Eze 37:8
the pillars that * its doorway. Eze 41:1
be * between the king of Syria Dan 11:6
* with skill by the hands of men. Hos 13:2
with the one who * the mountains Amo 4:13
* the spirit of man within him: Zec 12:1
the wheat-heads * and finally the Mk 4:28
cloud * above them; Lk 9:34
A mob was quickly * against Paul Act 16:22

FORMER
the wine taster to his * position; Gen 40:21
ambassadors than the * group. Num 22:15
and all of the * kingdom of King Deu 3:13
her, or dies, the * husband may Deu 24:4
all of Bashan, the * kingdom of Jos 13:30
younger brother of her * husband. Ru 1:11f
again as they had in * days. 2Ki 13:5
of his father: Amaziah, the * king 2Ki 15:1
follow their * practices instead of 2Ki 17:34
of Telassar? The * kings of Assyria 2Ki 19:12
of Joshua, the * mayor of 2Ki 23:8
These had been dedicated by * 2Ki 23:11
again in their * cities were 1Ch 9:2
Let it be rebuilt on its * site, Ez 6:6
a contrast to the * governors who Neh 5:15
I am but a shadow of my * self. Job 17:7
sisters, and * friends arrived and Job 42:11
down to us from * generations. Ps 78:2,3
not hold us guilty for our * sins! Ps 79:8
in proportion to our * misery! Ps 90:15
* guests are now citizens of hell. Pro 9:18
happened in those * times, and in Ecc 1:8-11
The context seems to favor the *. Is 66:19f
Egypt and Israel's other * allies. Lam 1:2f
Our * servants have become our Lam 5:8
And thus you celebrated those * Eze 23:21
by Antiochus II's * wife Laodice, Dan 11:7f
return it to its * glory, and Amo 9:11
I will give glory to my * exiles, Zep 3:19
will grow again to * size. Zec 10:8
its * home is all swept and clean. Lk 11:25
those who sinned in * times. Rom 3:25
This plan was hidden in * times, 1Co 2:7
saying, that "our * enemy is now Gal 1:23
Of course, your * friends will be 1Pe 4:4

FORMERLY
(This was the land * occupied by Deu 4:44,45,46
Debir (* called Kiriath-sepher). Jos 15:15
in Hebron (* called Kiriath-arba), Ju 1:10
Debir (* called Kiriath-sepher). Ju 1:11
city of Bethel, * known as Luz, and Ju 1:22,23
though they * despised her and Eze 28:24
And I will destroy those who * Zep 1:6
A man named Simon had * been a Act 8:9,10,11

FORMING
side of the tent, * two long Ex 26:3
of two folds of cloth, * a pouch. Ex 28:16
attached, * two long roof-sheets. Ex 36:10
* a dry road across its bottom. Ps 106:9
But the jar that he was * didn't Jer 18:4
themselves by * alliances with each Dan 2:43

FORMS
with him who * it, saying, "Stop, Is 45:9
four strange * appeared that looked Eze 1:5
them were other * that glowed like Eze 1:13
Go through all your proper * and Amo 4:5

FORNICATION
wife, except for *, causes her to Mt 5:32
*, theft, lying and slander. Mt 15:19
wife, except for *, and marries Mt 19:9
to idols, from all *, and also from Act 15:20
and, of course, from *. Act 15:27,28,29
animals, and not to commit *." Act 21:25
Literally, "have committed * with Rev 18:3f
Literally, "*," the word used Rev 19:2f

FORSAKE
He will neither fail you nor * Deu 31:6
he will not fail nor * you." Deu 31:8
* the Lord and worship other gods! Jos 24:16
If you * him and worship other Jos 24:20
of Israel and never * them." 1Ki 6:13
may he never * us. 1Ki 8:57
but if you * him, he will 1Ch 28:9
he will not * you. 1Ch 28:20
But if you * him, he will forsake 2Ch 15:2
But if you forsake him, he will * 2Ch 15:2
to * evil is real understanding.' Job 28:28
Don't * me, O God of my Ps 27:9
the Lord * a man who loves him; Ps 37:25
Don't * me now when my strength Ps 71:9
I am old and gray, don't * me. Ps 71:18
and we will never * you again. Ps 80:18
If his children * my laws and Ps 89:30,31,32
The Lord will not * his people, Ps 94:14
Oh, don't * me and let me slip Ps 119:8
Literally, "Oh, * me not Ps 119:8f
I, Israel's God, will not ever * Is 41:17
He will not * them. Is 42:16
will * you as Assyria did before. Jer 2:36
Why do you * us for so long? Lam 5:20
idols, nor * the gods of Egypt. Eze 20:8
How can I * you like Admah and Hos 11:8
that all must * their sins and turn Act 26:20
never, never fail you nor * you." Heb 13:5

FORSAKEN
you and have * you as our God and Ju 10:10
* me and followed other gods. 1Sa 8:8
For Solomon has * me and 1Ki 11:33
says, 'You have * me, so I have 2Ch 12:5
me, so I have * you and abandoned 2Ch 12:5
is our God and we have not * him. 2Ch 13:10
but you have * him. 2Ch 13:11
You have * the Lord, and now he 2Ch 24:20
the Lord, and now he has * you." 2Ch 24:20
* the Lord God of their ancestors. 2Ch 24:24
For my people have * me and have 2Ch 34:25
come only to those who had * him! Ez 8:22
"Why has the Temple been *?" Neh 13:11
my friends have all * me. Job 19:14
For you have never yet * those Ps 9:10
MY GOD, MY God, why have you * Ps 22:1
I cry, "why have you * me? Ps 42:9
are whispering, "God has * him! Ps 71:11
rest of you have * the Lord and his Is 65:11
things: They have * me, the Jer 2:13
for the Lord has rejected and * Jer 7:29
"my people have * my commandments Jer 9:13
You have * me and turned your Jer 15:6
for they have * the Lord, the Jer 17:13
For Israel has * me and turned Jer 19:4
city of joy, how you are * now! Jer 49:25
For the Lord of Hosts has not * Jer 51:5
God, my God, why have you * me?" Mt 27:46

FORSAKES
But if he confesses and * them, Pro 28:13

FORSAKING
because of the sin of * him. Deu 28:20
God, fearlessly * him, says the Jer 2:19

(FORSAKING Con't)
by * your promise to bless us! Jer 14:21

FORSOOK
Then, in plenty, they * their God. Deu 32:15
this: Because your fathers * me. Jer 16:11

FORT
took refuge in the * next to the Ju 9:46
walls of the * and set on fire. Ju 9:49
However, there was a * inside Ju 9:51
his palace, * Millo, the wall of 1Ki 9:15
Then he built * Millo. 1Ki 9:24
was rebuilding * Millo, repairing 1Ki 11:27,28
finally, only * Kir-hareseth was 2Ki 3:25
He also reinforced * Millo in the 2Ch 32:5
The Lord is my * where I can Ps 18:2
protects me like the walls of a *! Ps 31:21
in ruins every * defending him. Ps 89:40
Literally, "castle," or "*." Act 21:34f

FORTH
the earth burst * with every sort Gen 1:11,12
the earth bring * every kind of Gen 1:24
waters burst * upon the earth for Gen 7:10,11,12
a raven that flew back and * Gen 8:7
and *, and the wine flowed freely! Gen 43:34
You sent * your anger, and it Ex 15:7
and go back and * from one end of Ex 32:27
blood back and * upon the altar. Lev 1:11
procedures that have been set *; Lev 5:10
back and * upon the altar. Lev 7:2
blood back and * upon the altar. Lev 8:19
back and * upon the altar. Lev 8:24
it back and * upon the altar; Lev 9:12
it back and * upon the altar. Lev 9:18
So fire blazed * from the Lev 10:2
it all back and * before the Lord Num 6:20
be waved back and * before the Num 15:19,20,21
Then fire came * from Jehovah Num 16:35
For a fire has flamed * Num 21:27-30
us wander back and * in the Num 32:13
or call * the spirits of the dead. Deu 18:11
in this book) broke * upon them. Deu 29:27
traveled back and * across the Jos 5:6
If you refuse, let fire flame * Ju 9:15
He went back and * to Bethlehem 1Sa 17:14,15
The argument continued back and *, 2Sa 19:43
He shot * his arrows of lightning 2Sa 22:15
Springs * upon the earth; 2Sa 23:4
And so they argued back and * 1Ki 3:22
They used to run back and * from 1Ki 9:27,28
and * in the house a few times; 2Ki 4:35
search back and * across the whole 2Ch 16:9
carry it back and * upon your 2Ch 35:3
went back and * between Tobiah and Neh 6:17
on ropes, swinging back and *. Job 28:3,4
Literally, "He brings * to the Job 28:11f
and they send * his lightning. Job 37:11
to flash * from the clouds? Job 37:15
of God breaking * upon us from Job 37:22
Literally, "going * from his Ps 19:5f
Go * to awe-inspiring deeds! Ps 45:4
burst * to give your people water; Ps 74:15
And he led * the east wind and Ps 78:26
But he led * his own people like Ps 78:52
Fire goes * before him and burns Ps 97:3
Literally, "The Lord will send * Ps 110:2f
* their waters onto the earth; Pro 8:24
Who else but God goes back and * Pro 30:4
back and *, getting nowhere. Ecc 1:3-7
Literally, "The fig tree puts * Sol 2:13f
There the mandrakes give * their Sol 7:13
freely back and * between their Is 19:23
they poured * a whispered prayer. Is 26:16
Springs will burst * in the Is 35:6
I called * the mighty army of Is 43:17
break * into song, O mountains Is 44:23
Break * with song, O mountains, Is 49:13
until she shines * in his Is 62:1
OH, THAT YOU would burst * from Is 64:1
and anger boiled * and fell as fire Jer 44:6
God has broken * in fury upon those Jer 50:28
* branches and bearing fruit. Eze 17:22,23
therefore I brought * fire from Eze 28:18
When I destroy you and show * my Eze 28:22
it flames * like raging fire. Hos 7:6
O Death, bring * your terrors for Hos 13:14
will burst * from the Temple of the Joe 3:18
night, who calls * the water from Amo 5:8
meaning "to go *," here Mic 1:11f
meaning "to go *," here Mic 1:11f
meaning "to go *," here Mic 1:11f
who is in travail has brought *." Mic 5:3f
Then springs burst * upon the Hab 3:8,9
Literally, "He will bring * the Zec 4:7f
to patrol back and * across the Zec 6:7
Literally, "bringing * the Mt 21:43f
And I shall send * my angels Mt 24:31
back and * to me, the Messiah." Jn 1:51
Sea, and back and * through the Act 7:36
Literally, "stretched * his Act 26:1f
argued back and * among themselves, Act 28:25
to show * the power of Jesus Christ 2Co 4:11

that only good deeds will pour *. Jas 3:13
Great bursts of light flashed * Rev 4:3

FORTHRIGHT
Literally, "If you are * men." Gen 42:19f

FORTIETH
This occurred during the * year Num 33:38,39
the * year of King David's reign. 1Ch 26:31,32
"One day as he was nearing his * Act 7:23

FORTIFICATIONS
by adding to the *, and 2Ch 32:5
are blocked; the * are burning and Jer 51:32
break down your * you are so proud Eze 7:24
her, and hurl her * into the sea; Zec 9:4

FORTIFIED
they are villages or are *; Num 13:19
their cities are * and very large; Num 13:28
They were all * cities with Num 32:34,35,36
managed to reach their * cities. Jos 10:20
Ramah and the * city of Tyre and Jos 19:29
at the east. The * cities included Jos 19:35-39
cities, both the * cities and the 1Sa 6:18
* city where we can't reach him." 2Sa 20:6
those that are *—and ruin all the 2Ki 3:19
and a * city and an armory." 2Ki 10:2,3
of the watchman to the * cities." 2Ki 18:8f
all the * cities of Judah. 2Ki 18:13
conquest of all those * cities! 2Ki 19:25
centers. He * the cities of upper 2Ch 8:5
in Jerusalem and * these cities of 2Ch 11:5-10
other sons in the * cities 2Ch 11:23
He quickly conquered Judah's * 2Ch 12:4
in all of the * cities of Judah, in 2Ch 17:2
* cities throughout the nation. 2Ch 17:19
of some of the * cities of Judah. 2Ch 21:3,4
He built * towers in Jerusalem at 2Ch 26:9
laid siege to the * cities, 2Ch 32:1
in all of the * cities of Judah. 2Ch 33:14
Your people captured * cities Neh 9:25
to conquer these * cities? Ps 108:10
For he has * your gates against Ps 147:13
brother than to capture a * city. Pro 18:19
You are strong like a * city that Jer 1:18
Flee to the * cities!" Jer 4:5
King Asa when he * Mizpah to Jer 41:9
and lay siege to a * city of Egypt Dan 11:15

FORTIFY
"Let us build and * cities now, 2Ch 14:7

FORTIFYING
settlement without * walls around Lev 25:31

FORTRESS
My * and my Savior. 2Sa 22:2
God is my strong *; 2Sa 22:33
King Baasha built the * city of 1Ki 15:17
So David captured the * of Zion, 1Ch 11:5,6
David lived in the * and that is 1Ch 11:7
out around the * while Joab rebuilt 1Ch 11:8
war on him and built the * 2Ch 16:1
the gates of the * near the Temple, Neh 2:8
commander of the *—a very faithful Neh 7:2
making her home in her mountain *. Job 39:28
Yes, you are my Rock and my *; Ps 31:3
Rock, my rescuer, defense and *. Ps 62:2
defense and *—why then should I be Ps 62:6
The Lord my God is my *—the Ps 94:21,22
he is my *, my tower of strength Ps 144:2
is a strong *. Pro 18:10
will be their * of safety; Is 33:16
O Lord, my Strength and *, my Jer 16:19
he has broken every *, every wall. Lam 2:2
the strongest * of Egypt, and I Eze 30:15
Israel into Egypt, to a * there. Dan 11:10,11
of these he will worship the * god Dan 11:38
the strong * of Ben-hadad. Amo 1:4

FORTRESSES
cities, villages, and * of Israel. 1Ch 27:25
strong, and built * and supply 2Ch 17:12
* and towers on the wooded hills. 2Ch 27:4
Literally, "the god of *." Dan 11:38f
success against the strongest *. Dan 11:39
those palaces and burn those *. Hos 8:14
and trap them in their own *. Hos 11:6
their * to meet the Lord our God. Mic 7:17

FORTS
will burn their *, kill the young 2Ki 8:12
strengthened the *, and manned them 2Ch 11:11
He also constructed * in the 2Ch 26:10
The strongest * are turned to Is 25:2
build * around it to destroy it. Is 29:3
will grow in its *, and it will Is 34:13
The city of Kiriathaim and its * Jer 48:1
and built * around it, and laid Jer 52:4
He has destroyed her * and Lam 2:5
He has built * against me and Lam 3:5
sledge hammers demolish your *. Eze 26:9
* and caves shall die of disease. Eze 33:27
and all your * will fall, just as Hos 10:14
and all her * shall be destroyed. Amo 1:7
burn down all his * and palaces." Amo 1:10
burn down all the * of Bozrah." Amo 1:12
burn down their * and palaces; Amo 1:14
all Jerusalem's palaces and *." Amo 2:5
will shatter their * and plunder Amo 3:1
her wall and her *, exposing their Mic 1:
All your * will fall. Nah 3:1
Strengthen the *! Nah 3:1
and princes, and scorn their *. Hab 1:1

FORTUNATE
And most * of all are those who Ecc 4:
a farmer will be * to have a cow Is 7:21,2
"Humble men are very *!" Mt 5:
Those who mourn are *! Mt 5:4
The meek and lowly are *! Mt 5:
children will be counted * indeed. Lk 23:2
"I am *, King Agrippa," he Act 26:

FORTUNATUS
I am so glad that Stephanas, *, 1Co 16:17

FORTUNE
of cattle, and a * in silver and Gen 24:35
cup, which he uses for * telling? Gen 44:5
nor use * telling or witchcraft. Lev 19:26
for aid, or be a * teller, or be a Deu 18:10
A * can be made from cheating, Pro 20:21
a * and given it to the poor." Mt 26:8,9
"It would take a * Mk 6:37
that perfume for a * and given the Mk 14:4,5
replied, "It would take a * Jn 6:7
"That perfume was worth a *. Jn 12:5

FORTUNE-TELLER
"for a * that I consulted Gen 30:27
girl who was a *, and earned much Act 16:16

FORTUNE-TELLERS
all of the mediums and * executed. 1Sa 28:9
they consulted * and used magic 2Ki 17:17
too, and * and sorcerers, and 2Ch 33:6
false prophets, *, dreamers, Jer 27:9
astrologers, *, and wizards—and I Dan 4:7
will be no more * to consult— and Mic 5:12
like that! *' predictions are all a Zec 10:2
All false prophets and * will be Zec 13:2

FORTUNE-TELLING
magic and used *, and patronized 2Ki 21:6

FORTUNES
You have restored the * Ps 85:1
Literally, "Restore our *, Ps 126:4f
and restore your *, and gather you Jer 29:14
I will restore the * of my people, Jer 30:3
and restore your *, Jerusalem will Jer 30:18
and Israel and restore their *. Jer 33:7
* of the Ammonites, says the Lord. Jer 49:6
I will restore the * of Sodom and Eze 16:53
And I will restore the * of Eze 29:14
and restore their *, for I am Eze 39:25
I will restore the * of my Amo 9:14
I restore your * before your very Zep 3:20

FORTY
begin * days and nights of rain; Gen 7:4
the earth for * days and nights. Gen 7:10,11,12
For * days the roaring floods Gen 7:17
After another * days, Noah opened Gen 8:6
"Suppose there are only *?" Gen 18:29
won't destroy it if there are *." Gen 18:29
Isaac was * years old when he Gen 25:20
Esau, at the age of *, married a Gen 26:34
The embalming process required * Gen 50:3
ate the manna * years until they Ex 16:35
there for * days and forty nights. Ex 24:18
there for forty days and * nights. Ex 24:18
sacred tent, with * silver bases Ex 26:18,19
with their * silver bases, two Ex 26:21
with the Lord for * days and forty Ex 34:28
for forty days and * nights, and in Ex 34:28
fitting into * silver bases. Ex 36:24
Tabernacle, with * silver bases, Ex 36:25,26
* days later they returned from Num 13:25
desert like nomads for * years. Num 14:33
in the land for * days, you must Num 14:34,35
the wilderness for * years—a year Num 14:34,35
* years earlier, at the time of Num 26:64,65f
the wilderness for * years until Num 32:13
* years after the people of Deu 1:1
"It was * years ago, at Mount Deu 1:6
way for all these * years as you Deu 2:7
for all those * years, humbling you Deu 8:2
For all these * years your Deu 8:4
I was there for * days and forty Deu 9:9
I was there for forty days and * Deu 9:9
At the end of those * days and Deu 9:10,11
Then, for another * days and Deu 9:18
before him for * days and nights Deu 9:25
the Lord for * days and nights the Deu 10:10
with up to * stripes in proportion Deu 25:1
but no more than * stripes may be Deu 25:1
that hear! For * years God has led Deu 29:5
instructed, and * thousand Jos 4:12,13
thing the Lord did * years ago Jos 4:23
the wilderness for * years until Jos 5:6
"I was * years old at the time, Jos 14:7
Then, for * years under Othni-el, Ju 3:11
Among * thousand men of Israel, Ju 5:8
was peace in the land for * years. Ju 5:31
was at peace for * years—all during Ju 8:28
He had * sons and thirty Ju 12:14

FORTY Con't)
them in subjection for * years. Ju 13:1
He had judged Israel for * years. 1Sa 4:18
the sheep. For * days, twice a 1Sa 17:16
Ish-bosheth was * years old at 2Sa 2:10,11
so he reigned for * years 2Sa 5:4,5
on the field, also * thousand 2Sa 10:18
He had reigned over Israel for * 1Ki 2:11
Solomon owned * thousand chariot 1Ki 4:26
He ruled in Jerusalem for * 1Ki 11:42
strength to travel * days and forty 1Ki 19:8
forty days and * nights to Mount 1Ki 19:8
So Hazael took * camel-loads of 2Ki 8:8,9
He reigned in Jerusalem for * 2Ki 12:1
and * thousand of their troops. 1Ch 19:17,18
of the land of Israel for * years; 1Ch 29:26,27
over all of Israel for * years. 2Ch 9:30
he reigned * years, in Jerusalem. 2Ch 24:1
their thirst. For * years you Neh 9:21
"For * years I watched them in Ps 95:10
right side for * days, to signify Eze 4:6
of Ethiopia. For * years not a Eze 29:11
lie as wastelands for * years. Eze 29:12
at the end of the * years he will Eze 29:13
through the desert * years, to Amo 2:10
"You sacrificed to me for * Amo 5:25,26,27
around him, "* days from now Jon 3:4,5
by Satan. For * days and forty Mt 4:2
For forty days and * nights he Mt 4:2
There, for * days, alone except Mk 1:12,13
Satan tempted him for * days. Lk 4:1
During the * days after his Act 1:3
man who had been lame for * years. Act 4:22
"* years later, in the desert Act 7:30
the wilderness for * years. Act 7:36
* years in the desert, Israel? Act 7:42
And he nursed them through * Act 13:18
Benjamin, who reigned for * years. Act 13:21
The next morning some * or more Act 23:12,13
There are more than * men hiding Act 23:21
But God was patient with them * Heb 3:9
God angry for all those * years? Heb 3:17

FORTY-EIGHT
In all, there shall be * cities Num 35:7
given to the Levites came to *. Jos 21:41,42

FORTY-FIRST
So he died in the * year of his 2Ch 16:13,14

FORTY-FIVE
Suppose there are only *? Gen 18:28
will not destroy it if I find *." Gen 18:28
* feet across and six feet wide. Ex 26:7,8
* feet long and six feet wide). Ex 36:14,15
well for all these * years since Jos 14:10
thirty feet wide, and * feet high. 1Ki 6:2
There were * windows in the 1Ki 7:3,4
feet long and * feet wide, with a 1Ki 7:6
the floor, and was * feet around. 2Ch 4:2

FORTY-NINE
the preceding * years, a fair price Lev 25:14,15,16
It will be * years plus 434 years Dan 9:25

FORTY-ONE
He was * years old when he began 1Ki 14:21
over Israel, and reigned * years. 1Ki 15:10
Jeroboam's reign lasted * years. 2Ki 14:23
king at the age of *, and his 2Ch 12:13

FORTY-SIX
"It took * years to build this Jn 2:20

FORTY-THREE
About * miles from Rome. Act 28:15f

FORTY-TWO
fine-twined linen, * feet long and Ex 26:1
safe, and * other cities besides. Num 35:6
and killed. So * thousand people of Ju 12:6
of the woods and killed * of them. 2Ki 2:24
cistern and killed all * of them. 2Ki 10:14
Literally, "* years old"; 2Ch 22:2f
the Holy City for * months. Rev 11:2
to control the earth for * months. Rev 13:5

FORTYFOUR
Judah also received these * Jos 15:48-62

FORUM
But they invited him to the * at Act 17:19
Hill *, addressed them as follows: Act 17:22
and came to meet us at the * Act 28:15

FORWARD
Then the concubines came * with Gen 33:6
Then Judah stepped * and said, Gen 44:18
get the people moving! *, march! Ex 14:15
that they reflect their light *. Ex 25:37
they will throw their light *." Num 8:2
As the Ark was carried *, Moses Num 10:35
"Aaron and Miriam, step *," he Num 12:5
to put yourselves *, claiming that Num 16:3
* and walk in front of Samuel. 1Sa 16:8
Then David crept * and quietly 1Sa 24:4
As he stepped * to greet Amasa, 2Sa 20:8,9,10
him, he came * and fell flat on the 2Sa 24:20
Then the men of Israel moved * 2Ki 3:24
the sundial to go * ten points or 2Ki 20:9
"The shadow always moves *," 2Ki 20:10
and will look * eagerly to 1Ch 29:19
a spirit stepped * before the Lord 2Ch 18:19,20
So the work went *, and finally 2Ch 24:13
* and sanctified themselves. 2Ch 30:24
The work is going * with great Ez 5:8
The pillar of cloud led them * Neh 9:19
That is all he can look * to! Job 8:19
steadily * to God without fear. Job 11:15
righteous shall move onward and *; Job 17:9
Have you made him able to leap * Job 39:20
ground and rushes * into battle Job 39:24
as an athlete looking * to a race! Ps 19:5
let others step * to replace him. Ps 109:8
The good man can look * to Pro 11:23
your godliness will lead you *, Is 58:8
I looked * to your calling me Jer 3:19
They went backward instead of *. Jer 7:24
flew straight * without turning. Eze 1:9
went they went, going straight * Eze 1:12
living beings flew *, the wheels Eze 1:19,20,21
the wheels moved * with them. Eze 1:19,20,21
the cherubim could go straight * Eze 10:9-13
Straight * they march, never Joe 2:7
chariots moving * side by side, Nah 2:3
the chariots rush * against her, Nah 3:2
Their cavalry move proudly * from Hab 1:8
prophets looked * [to the Messiah Mt 11:13
He went * a little, and fell face Mt 26:39
Then the Sadducees stepped *—a Mk 12:18
and he said, "I have looked * Lk 22:15
Stepping * to meet them he asked, Jn 18:4,5
Then Peter stepped * with the Act 2:14
by some of the Jews and dragged *. Act 19:33
When Tertullus was called *, he Act 24:2
I am looking * to the fulfillment Act 26:6
For he was looking * to the time Rom 3:25
and joyfully look * to actually Rom 5:2
And trusting means looking * to Rom 8:24
that we will look * expectantly to Rom 15:4
I am looking * to seeing him 1Co 16:11
us, but we look * to the joys in 2Co 4:18
That is why we look * eagerly to 2Co 5:2
Now we look * with confidence to 2Co 5:6
you were looking * to my visit, and 2Co 7:7
as he looks * to this trip, because 2Co 8:22
Scriptures looked * to this time Gal 3:8,9
past and looking * to what lies Php 3:13
and we are looking * to his Php 3:20
And you are looking * to the Col 1:5
and steady looking * to the return 1Th 1:3
you are looking * to the return of 1Th 1:10
* to his coming back again. 2Ti 4:8
day, looking * to that wonderful Tit 2:13
eagerly looking * to receiving it. Tit 3:7
Now we can look * to the Heb 10:23
There will be nothing to look * Heb 10:27
* to their real home in heaven. Heb 11:14
for he was looking * to the great Heb 11:26
we are looking * to our Heb 13:14
So now you can look * soberly 1Pe 1:13
You should look * to that day 2Pe 3:12
But we are looking * to God's 2Pe 3:13
to push himself * as the leader of 3Jn 1:9
He stepped * and took the scroll Rev 5:7

FOSTER
he was her cousin and * father. Est 8:1

FOSTER-BROTHER
(the * of King Herod), and Paul. Act 13:1

FOUGHT
Goiim * against Bera Gen 14:2
people of Israel * against Jehovah, Num 20:13
Remember that they * with you Deu 25:18
Then he * against the people Jos 15:15
He has * for you against your Jos 23:3
and they * against you, but I Jos 24:8
The men of Jericho * against you, Jos 24:11
Each in turn * against you but I Jos 24:11
Afterward the army of Judah * Ju 1:9
Simeon's and they * the Canaanites Ju 1:17
The kings of Canaan * in Taanach Ju 5:19
* Sisera. Ju 5:20
For my father * for you and Ju 9:17
the battle and * with Abimelech, Ju 9:39
So the Philistines * desperately 1Sa 4:10
The Israelis * constantly with 1Sa 14:52
So David went out and * with them 2Sa 5:20
Tob, and Maacah * in the fields. 2Sa 10:7,8
David when he * against the Amalek 1Ch 12:21
too, that Solomon * against the 2Ch 8:3
Lord himself had * against the 2Ch 20:29
You have actually * against us Ps 44:10
and personally * against them. Is 63:10
he ruled, came and * against Jer 34:1
for you have * against the Lord. Jer 50:24
of Babylon * hard against Tyre. Eze 29:18
He * against the people of God Dan 8:10
when he became a man, he even * Hos 12:3
on all the people who * Jerusalem. Zec 14:12
would have * when I was arrested by Jn 18:36
and Jambres * against Moses. 2Ti 3:8
I have * long and hard for my 2Ti 4:7
he * against everything we said. 2Ti 4:15
under his command * the Dragon and Rev 12:7

FOUL
water became so * that the Ex 7:21
Idols, filthy and *— you are Eze 22:3
to me their worship was as * as Eze 36:17
and soon you were as * as they. Hos 9:10
red sky in the morning means * Mt 16:2,3
is * with extortion and greed. Mt 23:25
Their talk is * and filthy like Rom 3:13
Dirty stories, * talk and coarse Eph 5:4
you by living in * sin on the side 2Pe 2:13
Literally, "of every * and Rev 18:2f

FOUL-MOUTHED
sealed, for I am a * sinner, a Is 6:5
a member of a sinful, * race; Is 6:5

FOULED
channels * with rotting reeds. Is 19:6
to drink is water that you've *. Eze 34:19

FOULNESS
I will save them from all this *. Eze 37:23
bones, and of * and corruption. Mt 23:27

FOUND
where nuggets of pure gold are *, Gen 2:11,12
but the dove * no place to light, Gen 8:9
The Angel of the Lord * her Gen 16:7
suppose only thirty are * there?" Gen 18:30
Suppose only ten are *?" Gen 18:32
* a gushing underground spring. Gen 26:19
him, "We have * water" —in the Gen 26:32
at sundown, he * a rock for a Gen 28:11
harvest, Reuben * some mandrakes Gen 30:14
some mandrakes my son has *!" Gen 30:16
them to Dothan and * them there. Gen 37:17
"We * this in the field," they Gen 37:32
Now he left the room and * a Gen 42:24
we * in the mouth of our sacks? Gen 44:8
And the cup was * in Benjamin's! Gen 44:12
he in whose sack the cup was *." Gen 44:16
who finally * their tongues! Gen 45:15
dead, yet when he * out that it was Ex 9:7
thief shall pay double if he is *. Ex 22:7
But if no thief is *, then the Ex 22:8
believes he has * it in the Ex 22:9
and that I have * favor before Ex 33:12
and my people have * favor with Ex 33:16
you have certainly * favor with me, Ex 33:17
true that I have * favor in your Ex 34:9
on the day he is * guilty of any Lev 6:4,5
and yellow hair is * in the sore, Lev 13:29,30
black hairs are * in the spot, then Lev 13:37
commanded, and * the total number Num 3:43
* that the total number was 2,750. Num 4:36
leaders of Israel * that the total Num 4:46,47,48
of the cluster of grapes they *! Num 13:24
the next day, he * that Aaron's Num 17:8
commanders, and * its total value Num 31:51,52
a murder victim is * lying in a Deu 21:1
The young men * her and rescued Jos 6:23
Achan was * to be the guilty one. Jos 7:18
They ran to the tent and * the Jos 7:22
that they had been *, he issued a Jos 10:17
that as spies we * the Anakim Jos 14:12
* their master dead on the floor. Ju 3:25
into the tent and * Sisera lying Ju 4:22
Not a weapon could be *! Ju 5:8
happen if they * out who did it! Ju 6:27
quickly ran and * her husband and Ju 13:10
with the girl and * her to be just Ju 14:7
And he * a swarm of bees in it, Ju 14:8
have * the answer to my riddle!" Ju 14:18
be on his way, he * her there, Ju 19:27
field where she * herself belonged Ru 2:3
and * the relative he had Ru 4:1
days ago, for they have been *. 1Sa 9:20
donkeys have been * and that your 1Sa 10:2
"He said the donkeys had been * 1Sa 10:16
So they * him and brought him 1Sa 10:23
He counted them in Bezek and * 1Sa 11:8
still with him, he * that there 1Sa 13:15
And when they had checked, they * 1Sa 14:17
to the battle and * the Philistines 1Sa 14:20
even though they * honeycomb on 1Sa 14:24,25
from the food they * among our 1Sa 14:30
When Samuel finally * him, Saul 1Sa 15:13
Naioth in Ramah, and * Jonathan. 1Sa 20:1
When she arrived home she * that 1Sa 25:36
to Saul's camp and * him asleep, 1Sa 26:5,6,7
to do, and they * one at Endor. 1Sa 28:7,8
and I've never * one fault in him 1Sa 29:3
of Ziklag, they * that the 1Sa 30:1
Along the way they * an Egyptian 1Sa 30:11,12
the dead, they * the bodies of Saul 1Sa 31:8
Probably he had * Saul dead upon 2Sa 1:10f
to come back. They * him at the 2Sa 3:26
When she * that he had gotten 2Sa 11:5
God, David * Hushai the Archite 2Sa 15:32
And when he had * his slaves, he 1Ki 2:40
* him sitting under an oak tree. 1Ki 13:14
He * the prophet's body lying in 1Ki 13:28
cities he built—is * in The Annals 1Ki 15:23
So Elijah went and * Elisha who 1Ki 19:19

(FOUND Con't)
"So my enemy has * me!" 1Ki 21:20
Literally, "I have * you because 1Ki 21:20f
* him sitting on top of a hill. 2Ki 1:9
Four chariot-horses were * and 2Ki 7:14
Ramoth-gilead, he * Jehu sitting 2Ki 9:5
to bury her, they * only her skull, 2Ki 9:35
reign is * in The Annals of the 2Ki 15:11
mentioned the scroll * by Hilkiah. 2Ki 22:9,10
the priest had * in the Temple. 2Ki 23:24
They * good pastures, and 1Ch 4:40,41
It was Machir who * wives for 1Ch 7:15
* the bodies of Saul and his sons. 1Ch 10:8
* that there were 153,600 of them. 2Ch 2:17
everything else, and they * him! 2Ch 15:15
for Ahaziah, they * him hiding in 2Ch 22:9
Then he took a census and * that 2Ch 25:5,6
the filth and decay they * there. 2Ch 29:16
at the gates, he * an old scroll 2Ch 34:14
"See what I have * in the 2Ch 34:15,16
of God that was * in the Temple. 2Ch 34:30
and have indeed * that Jerusalem Ez 4:19
Eventually the record was * in Ez 6:2
and I * that not one Levite had Ez 8:15
it to them and * it to total Ez 8:26,27
of our enemies * out that we had Neh 6:1
For I had * the record of the Neh 7:5
read, the people * a statement Neh 13:1
men * guilty, and impaled alive. Est 2:23
city square, and * Mordecai just Est 4:6
I have * from experience that Job 5:27
is not to be * among the living. Job 28:13
Where can it be *? Job 28:20
where it is to be *, for he looks Job 28:23,24
Do not make him die, for I have * Job 33:23,24
the world can dependable men be *? Ps 12:1
in the night and * nothing amiss Ps 17:3
they were * even in the king's Ps 105:30
Excuses might even be * for a Pro 6:30
rebuke you, and you be * a liar. Pro 30:6
yet are * even in king's palaces! Pro 30:24-28
But I * that this, too, was Ecc 2:1
I even * great pleasure in hard Ecc 2:10
And I * that though God has made Ecc 7:29
afterwards that I * him and held Sol 3:4
The guards * me and struck and Sol 5:7
and I have * favor in my lover's Sol 8:10
justice, but * bloodshed instead. Is 5:7
The guilty will be *. Is 26:21
affliction, but * no silver there. Is 48:10
Joy and gladness will be * there, Is 51:3
for just as good grapes are * Is 65:8
5th century B.C., * at Hermopolis Jer 7:18f
to eat, but there is none to be *. Jer 14:6
I did as he told me, and * the Jer 18:3
Yes, says the Lord, I will be * Jer 29:14
There he * some old rags and Jer 38:11
All who * them devoured them and Jer 50:7
no sin shall be * in Israel or in Jer 50:20
other men of importance * hiding. Jer 52:24,25
or that I * injured or dead; Eze 4:14
my just attacks, but I * not one. Eze 22:30
that time when wrong was * in you. Eze 28:15
and * that the distance was 175 Eze 40:19
its passageway and * they were just Eze 40:24
He measured this passageway and * Eze 40:28
and * it to be 175 feet square, Eze 40:47
and * them to be 3½ feet thick; Eze 41:3
of the Temple and * that it was 10½ Eze 41:5
Temple area. He * that it was in Eze 42:16-20
judgment, the king * these young Dan 1:20
and said, "I've * one of the Dan 2:25
this man was * to be as full of Dan 5:11
Daniel's house and * him praying Dan 6:11
And not a scratch was * on him, Dan 6:23
one honest man is * among you? Hos 8:5
and every treasure * and taken. Ob 1:6
he * a ship leaving for Tarshish. Jon 1:3
Yes, a man's enemies will be * in Mic 7:6
where can one be * who has not Nah 3:19
of Jerusalem have * strength in the Zec 12:5
at this meeting he * out from Mt 2:7
three disciples and * them asleep. Mt 26:40
He returned to them again and * Mt 26:43
But even though they * many who Mt 26:60,61
Finally two men were * who Mt 26:60,61
home, where they * Simon's Mk 1:29,30
A few small fish were *, too, so Mk 8:7
the mountain they * a great crowd Mk 9:14
Off went the two men and * the Mk 11:4,5
into the city and * everything as Mk 14:16
three disciples and * them asleep. Mk 14:37
Again he returned to them and * Mk 14:40
This statement is * in only some Mk 14:68f
Verses 9 through 20 are not * in Mk 16:9f
seven demons. She * the disciples Mk 16:10,11
They ran to the village and * Lk 2:16
home where he * Simon's Lk 4:38
when they finally * him they begged Lk 4:42
* the slave completely healed. Lk 7:10
The two disciples * Jesus while Lk 7:20,21,22
Men who live in luxury are * in Lk 7:25
But the crowds * out where he Lk 9:11
for the lost one until you * it? Lk 15:3,4
you because your lost sheep was *. Lk 15:6
He was lost and is *.' Lk 15:24
He was lost and is *!' Lk 15:32
They * the colt as Jesus said, Lk 19:32
They went off to the city and * Lk 22:13
I have * no reason to sentence Lk 23:22
to the tomb— and * that the huge Lk 24:2
him, "We have * the Messiah!" Jn 1:41
go to Galilee. He * Philip and told Jn 1:43
told him, "We have * the Messiah! Jn 1:45
fig tree before Philip * you." Jn 1:48
This man went over to Cana, * Jn 4:46,47
But afterwards Jesus * him in Jn 5:14
When they arrived and * him, they Jn 6:25
had happened, he * the man and Jn 9:35
to the tomb and * that the stone Jn 20:1
She ran and * Simon Peter and me Jn 20:2
Mary Magdalene * the disciples Jn 20:18
Peter and John * the other Act 4:23
Pharaoh's daughter * him and Act 7:21
Meanwhile, Philip * himself at Act 8:40
any believers he * there, both men Act 9:2
ground, he * that he was blind. Act 9:8,9
So Ananias went over and * Paul Act 9:17
by Cornelius had * the house and Act 10:17
When he * him, he brought him Act 11:26
When Herod sent for him and * Act 12:19
They * no just cause to execute Act 13:28
Each Sabbath * Paul at the Act 18:4
where he * several disciples. Act 19:1
We went ashore, * the local Act 21:4
any Christians I * to Jerusalem in Act 22:5
For we have * him to be a Act 24:5
their Council * in me, except that Act 24:20
There our officer * an Egyptian Act 27:6
They sounded, and * 120 feet of Act 27:28
again, and * only ninety feet. Act 27:28
where we * some believers! Act 28:14
me, for they * no cause for the Act 28:18
will punish sin wherever it is *. Rom 2:12-15
them, for Abraham * favor with God Rom 4:12
that God would be * by people who Rom 10:20
the Jews have not * the favor of Rom 11:7
And now that you have * God (or Gal 4:9
now that God has * you) how can it Gal 4:9
else—I have * it to be the only way Php 3:10
me, and they never * the paths I Heb 3:10
But God himself * fault with the Heb 8:8
You have * out how they lie. Rev 2:2
And when the Dragon * himself Rev 12:13
away, but they * no place to hide. Rev 20:11
And if anyone's name was not * Rev 20:15
When he measured it, he * it was Rev 21:16
of the walls and * them to be 216 Rev 21:17

FOUNDATION
that when the * was laid, the Jos 6:26
job—for the * of the Temple. 1Ki 5:17
The * of the Temple was laid in 1Ki 6:37
to measure. The * stones were 1Ki 7:10
The * was ninety feet long and 2Ch 3:3
building the * of the Temple. Ez 3:6
When the builders completed the * Ez 3:10
the * of the Temple had been laid. Ez 3:11
huge stones in the *, topped with a Ez 6:4
justice are the * of his throne. Ps 97:2
I am placing a * Stone in Zion—a Is 28:16
to check the * wall you built; Is 28:17
rebuild you on a * of sapphires and Is 54:11
like a word for "*," which had Mic 1:11f
like a word for "*," which had Mic 1:11f
like a word for "*," which had Mic 1:11f
as the * of the Lord's Temple is Hag 2:18,19
He will be the * Stone of the Zec 3:9
"Zerubbabel laid the * of this Zec 4:9
For since you began laying the * Zec 8:9
and laid the * of the earth, and Zec 12:1
* laid upon the underlying rock. Lk 6:47,48
who builds a house without a *. Lk 6:49
the * before running out of funds. Lk 14:29
I have laid the * and Apollos has 1Co 3:10
But he who builds on the * must 1Co 3:10
lay any other real * than that one 1Co 3:11
can be used to build on that *. 1Co 3:12
has built on the * with the right 1Co 3:14
What a * you stand on now: the Eph 2:20
and are the * for a godly life. 1Ti 6:3
It is a * stone with these words 2Ti 2:19
* of Rock upon which God builds; 1Pe 2:4
strongly upon the * of our holy Jud 1:20
The walls had twelve * stones, Rev 21:14
of * stones inlaid with gems: Rev 21:18,19,20

FOUNDATIONS
The * of the heavens quaked 2Sa 22:8
When he laid the *, his oldest 1Ki 16:34
have repaired the * of the Temple. Ez 4:12
the * of the Temple at Jerusalem; Ez 5:16
It is to be rebuilt, and the * Ez 6:3
the corner to the * of the upper Neh 3:25
He shakes the earth to its *. Job 9:6
in youth, and the * of their lives Job 22:15,16
when I laid the * of the earth? Job 38:4
What supports its *, and who Job 38:6,7
Literally, "If the * have been Ps 11:3f
in darkness, all the * of society Ps 82:5
In ages past you laid the * of Ps 102:25
It shook the Temple to its *, and Is 6:4
It was my hand that laid the * Is 48:13
measured and the * of the earth Jer 31:37
that burned it down to its *. Lam 4:11
Her wealth is taken away, her * Eze 30:4
exposing their *, and pour their Mic 1:6
their walls. The * of Beth-ezel Mic 1:11
the prison was shaken to its *, Act 16:26
without solid *, so that only Heb 12:27

FOUNDED
so when Cain * a city, he named Gen 4:17
has never been since Egypt was *! Ex 9:18
been * seven years before Tanis Num 13:22
times) was * about 1720 B.C. Num 13:22f
clans, * by Simeon's sons: Num 26:12-14
clans * by the sons of Gad: Num 26:15-18
moved to Syria and * a city there, Ju 1:26
Literally, "He has * it upon the Ps 24:2f
Your throne is * on two strong Ps 89:14,15
The Lord's wisdom * the earth; Pro 3:19
Tell them that the Lord has * Is 14:32
The Greek Empire, * by Alexander Dan 2:39f

FOUNDER
the * of the family of Rechab. 1Ch 2:55
the * of our Jewish nation. Rom 4:1

FOUNDERS
of his became the * of twelve Gen 25:16

FOUNDING
for you from the * of the world. Mt 25:34
servants from the * of the world— Lk 11:50
the * of the world in the slain Rev 13:8
slain before the * of the world." Rev 13:8f

FOUNDRY
He opened the first * Gen 4:22
had been a * worker from Tyre. 1Ki 7:14

FOUNDRYMEN
and to * who made articles of 2Ch 24:12

FOUNTAIN
is a fruitful tree beside a *. Gen 49:22
Then we went to the * Gate and Neh 2:14,15
district, repaired the * Gate. Neh 3:15
When they arrived at the * Gate Neh 12:37
For you are the * of life; Ps 36:9
the Lord, who is Israel's *. Ps 68:26
Reverence for the Lord is a * of Pro 14:27
Wisdom is a * of life to those Pro 16:22
a * or muddying a spring. Pro 25:26
is broken at the *, and the wheel Ecc 12:6
one else can have, a * of my own. Sol 4:12
You are a garden *, a well of Sol 4:15
deeply from the * of Salvation!" Is 12:3
me, the * of Life-giving Water; Jer 2:13
She spouts evil like a *! Jer 6:7
OH, THAT MY eyes were a * of Jer 9:1
the Lord, the * of living waters. Jer 17:13
of Judah, and a * will burst forth Joe 3:18
"AT THAT TIME a * will be opened Zec 13:1
and Jerusalem, a * to cleanse them Zec 13:1
discover that God is a * of truth. Jn 3:33,34

FOUNTAINS
The deep * of the earth were Pro 3:20
I will give them * of water in Is 41:18

FOUR
the river divided into * branches. Gen 2:10
Sea Valley (* kings against five). Gen 14:8,9
After * generations they will Gen 15:16
He also had * other children from Gen 22:24
to Pharaoh. Keep * parts for Gen 47:24
This incident occurred about * Ex 1:8f
For sheep, the fine shall be * to Ex 22:1
be four to one—* sheep returned for Ex 22:1
Cast * rings of gold for it and Ex 25:12
attach them to the * lower corners, Ex 25:12
Put a molding * inches wide Ex 25:25
Make * golden rings and put the Ex 25:26,27
of the * legs, close to the top; Ex 25:26,27
be decorated with * almond Ex 25:34,35
Hang this upon * acacia pillars Ex 26:32
with gold, with * golden hooks. Ex 26:32
The pillars are to rest in * Ex 26:32
Make horns for the * corners of Ex 27:2
and attached to * posts imbedded in Ex 27:16
posts imbedded in their * sockets. Ex 27:16
Attach to it * rows of stones: A Ex 28:17
The veil was then attached to * Ex 36:36
hooks set into * posts of acacia Ex 36:36
gold and set into * silver bases. Ex 36:36
There were * golden rings Ex 37:3
its * feet, two rings at each end. Ex 37:3
A rim * inches high was Ex 37:12
Then he cast * rings of gold and Ex 37:13
them into the * table legs, close Ex 37:13
and above the top pair, * in all. Ex 37:20,21
There were * horns at the four Ex 38:2

FOUR Con't)
There were four horns at the * Ex 38:2
* rings were cast for each Ex 38:5
It was supported by * posts, Ex 38:19
four posts, with * bronze bases, Ex 38:19
there were * rows of stones Ex 39:10
finger upon the * horns of the Lev 8:15,16
"Flying insects with * legs must Lev 11:20
have * feet are forbidden to you. Lev 11:23
The responsibility of these * Num 3:31-35
Two wagons and * oxen were given Num 7:7
their use, and * wagons and eight Num 7:8
weighing about * ounces apiece); Num 7:84,85,86
three or * feet above the ground. Num 11:31
flour mixed with * pints of oil, Num 15:6
pints of oil, and * pints of wine Num 15:7
with each bull, * pints for a ram, Num 28:14
"You must sew tassels on the * Deu 22:12
* cities and their pasturelands: Jos 21:17,18
of the Kohath division received * Jos 21:20,21,22
The following * cities and Jos 21:23,24
The tribe of Issachar gave * Jos 21:28,29
The tribe of Asher gave * cities Jos 21:30,31
* cities by the tribe of Zebulun: Jos 21:34,35
Gad gave them * cities with Jos 21:38,39
and split into * groups, stationing Ju 9:34
went away for * days each year to Ju 11:40
and was there about * months. Ju 19:2
where they lived for * months. Ju 20:46,47
There were * hundred of these, Ju 21:10,11,12
Rimmon Rock. The * hundred girls Ju 21:14
killing * thousand of them. 1Sa 4:2
the leader of about * hundred men. 1Sa 22:2
on his own. * hundred of them 1Sa 25:13
for a year and * months. 1Sa 27:7
the other * hundred kept going. 1Sa 30:9,10
No one escaped except * hundred 1Sa 30:17
he shall repay * lambs to the 2Sa 12:6
After * years, Absalom said to 2Sa 15:7,8
These * were from the tribe of 2Sa 21:22
upon * rows of cedar pillars. 1Ki 7:2
lattices and * hundred pomegranates 1Ki 7:16-22
The sides of the tank were * 1Ki 7:26
movable stands had * bronze wheels 1Ki 7:27-30
The stands rode on * wheels which 1Ki 7:32
at each of the * corners of the 1Ki 7:34
* hundred pomegranates in two rows 1Ki 7:41-46
"Fill * barrels with water," he 1Ki 18:33
So King Ahab summoned his * 1Ki 22:6
of flour or * gallons of barley 2Ki 7:1
Now there were * lepers sitting 2Ki 7:3
* chariot-horses were found and 2Ki 7:14
of flour and * gallons of barley 2Ki 7:16
to each of the * sides: east, west, 1Ch 9:24
The * head gatekeepers, all 1Ch 9:26
and his * sons ran and hid. 1Ch 21:19,20
and judges, * thousand will be 1Ch 23:4,5
temple guards, and * thousand will 1Ch 23:4,5
* sons: Jahath was greatest, Zizah 1Ch 23:10,11
* groups named after his sons 1Ch 23:12
to the east gate, * to the north 1Ch 26:17
to the north gate, * to the south 1Ch 26:17
to the west gate, * to the upper 1Ch 26:18
Then the * men already mentioned 2Ch 28:15
David; and * years later he began 2Ch 34:3
ONE DAY IN April * months later, Neh 2:1
* times they sent the same Neh 6:4
more: no, three things! no, *! Pro 30:15,16
for me to understand—no, *! Pro 30:18,19
tremble—no, * it cannot stand: Pro 30:21,22,23
There are * things that are small Pro 30:24-28
monarchs in the earth—no, *: Pro 30:29,30,31
highest branches, * or five out on Is 17:6
I will appoint over them * kinds Jer 15:3
reading three or * columns, the Jer 36:23
the people of Elam to the * winds; Jer 49:36
of the cloud, * strange forms Eze 1:5
* faces and two pairs of wings! Eze 1:6
The * living beings were joined Eze 1:9
all of this, I saw * wheels on the Eze 1:15
They could go in any of the * Eze 1:17
face around. The * wheels had rims Eze 1:18
When the * living beings flew Eze 1:19,20,21
For the spirit of the * living Eze 1:19,20,21
Each of the * cherubim had a Eze 10:9-13
forward in each of * directions; Eze 10:9-13
of the * ways their faces looked. Eze 10:9-13
Each of the * wheels was covered Eze 10:9-13
Each of the * cherubim had four Eze 10:14
Each of the four cherubim had * Eze 10:14
for each had * faces and four Eze 10:21
had four faces and * wings, with Eze 10:21
and guards to the * winds and send Eze 12:14
"And the Lord says: * great Eze 14:21
will be scattered to the * winds. Eze 17:21
Come from the * winds, O Spirit, Eze 37:9
were eight tables, * inside and Eze 40:41
four inside and * outside, where Eze 40:41
There were also * stone tables Eze 40:42
There were hooks, three or * Eze 40:43
of the altar, with * horns Eze 43:15
smear it on the * horns of the Eze 43:20
altar and on the * corners of the Eze 43:20
and upon the * corners of the base Eze 45:19
of the * corners of the court. Eze 46:21,22
and Azariah were * of the young men Dan 1:6
God gave these * youths great Dan 1:17
"I see * men, unbound, walking Dan 3:25
Then * huge animals came up out Dan 7:3
of birds, and it had * heads! Dan 7:6
"These * huge animals," he Dan 7:17
said, "represent * kings who will Dan 7:17
its place grew * good-sized horns Dan 8:8
The * principal successors of Dan 8:8f
pointing in * directions. Dan 8:8
break off, and * smaller horns Dan 8:22
will break into * sections with Dan 8:22
four sections with * kings, none of Dan 8:22
be divided into * weaker nations, Dan 11:4
reigns of these * kings of Judah: Hos 1:1
Then I looked and saw * animal Zec 1:18
He replied, "They represent the * Zec 1:19
Then the Lord showed me * Zec 1:20
take hold of the * horns that Zec 1:21
THEN I LOOKED up again and saw * Zec 6:1
He replied, "These are the * Zec 6:5
was one of * "kings" over the Mt 14:1f
About * o'clock in the morning Mt 14:25
"From the * winds, from one end Mt 24:31f
the Word to them. * men arrived Mk 2:3
giving him back * times as much!" Lk 19:8
him from about * o'clock that Jn 1:39
the summer ends * months from now? Jn 4:35
They were three or * miles out Jn 6:18,19
been in his tomb for * days. Jn 11:17
for he has been dead * days." Jn 11:39
* piles, one for each of them. Jn 19:23,24
sheet, suspended by its * Act 10:11
Cornelius replied, "* days ago I Act 10:30
by its * corners from the sky. Act 11:5
The * messengers went at once to Act 15:30
He had * unmarried Act 21:9
"We suggest this: We have * men Act 21:23
they threw out * anchors from the Act 27:29
or changed * hundred and thirty Gal 3:17
shiny crystal sea. * Living Beings, Rev 4:6
stood at the throne's * sides. Rev 4:6
And the * Living Beings kept Rev 5:14
Then one of the * Living Beings, Rev 6:1
And a voice from among the * Rev 6:6
THEN I SAW * angels standing at Rev 7:1
standing at the * corners of the Rev 7:1
holding back the * winds from Rev 7:1
And he shouted out to those * Rev 7:2
the Elders and the * Living Beings, Rev 7:11
speaking from the * horns of the Rev 9:13
"Release the * mighty demons Rev 9:14
God and before the * Living Beings Rev 14:3
And one of the * Living Beings Rev 15:7
Then the twenty-four Elders and * Rev 19:4

FOUR-INCH-THICK
feet around, with * walls. 1Ki 7:15

FOUR-WHEELED
Then he made ten * movable 1Ki 7:27-30

FOURTEEN
Yes, twenty years—* of them Gen 31:41
were these * sons and descendants Gen 46:19-22
two rams, and * male yearling lambs Num 29:13
quarts for each of the * lambs. Num 29:15
two rams, and * male yearling Num 29:17
bulls, two rams, * male yearling Num 29:20
two rams, and * male yearling Num 29:23
two rams, and * male yearling Num 29:26,27
two rams, and * male yearling Num 29:29
two rams, and * male yearling Num 29:32
In all, there were * of these Jos 15:33-36
The celebration lasted for * 1Ki 8:65
(For God had honored him with * 1Ch 25:4,5
He married * wives and had 2Ch 13:21
And the prince shall provide * Eze 45:24
from Abraham unto David are *." Mt 1:17f
* of the generations from Abraham Mt 1:17
to King David; and * from King Mt 1:17
and * from the exile to Christ. Mt 1:17
* years ago I 2Co 12:2,3
THEN * YEARS later I went back to Gal 2:1

FOURTEENTH
"On the evening of the * day of Ex 12:6
the evening of the * day of the Ex 12:18
Literally, "on the * day of the Lev 23:5f
on the * day of this first month, Num 9:2,3
the evening of the *, there in the Num 9:4,5
later, on the * day of the second Num 9:11
"On the * day of the first month Num 28:16
Later, during the * year of the 2Ki 18:13
*, the group led by Jeshebe-ab; 1Ch 24:7-18
*, Mattithiah and twelve of his 1Ch 25:9-31
Literally, "the * day of the Ez 6:19f
SO IN THE * year of King Is 36:1
of our exile—the * year after Eze 40:1
"On the * day of the same month, Eze 45:21
About midnight on the * night of Act 27:27

FOURTH
This all happened on the * day. Gen 1:19
a * day (or, 'period of time')." Gen 1:19f
And the * is the Euphrates. Gen 2:14
an amethyst. The * row will be an Ex 28:20
In the * row, a beryl, an onyx, Ex 39:13
And the * year the entire crop Lev 19:24
On the * day the gifts were Num 7:30-35
to the third and * generation. Num 14:17,18
"On the * day of the festival, Num 29:23
even the third and * generation of Deu 5:9,10
The * tribe to be assigned its Jos 19:17-23
On the * day they said to his new Ju 14:15
On the * day they were up early, Ju 19:5
of Geshur. The * was Adonijah, who 2Sa 3:4
IT WAS IN the spring of the * year 1Ki 6:1
of May in the * year of Solomon's 1Ki 6:37
king during the * year of the reign 1Ki 22:41
It was during the * year of his 2Ki 18:9
was Shimea, his * was Nethanel, 1Ch 2:14
The * was Adonijah, the son of 1Ch 3:2
the *,Rapha, the fifth. 1Ch 8:1
Mishmannah was * in command; 1Ch 12:8-13
was third, and Jekameam was *. 1Ch 23:19
*, the group led by Se-orim; 1Ch 24:7-18
Jekameam, his * son. 1Ch 24:23
The *, Izri and twelve of his sons 1Ch 25:9-31
Jathni-el (the *), 1Ch 26:2,3
Sacar (the *), 1Ch 26:4,5
Zechariah, the *. 1Ch 26:11
The commander of the * Division 1Ch 27:7
He had 24,000 men on duty the * 1Ch 27:7
* year of King Solomon's reign. 2Ch 3:2
On the * day they gathered in 2Ch 20:26
On the * day after our arrival Ez 8:33
during the * year of the reign of Jer 25:1
that same year—the * year of the Jer 28:1
IN THE * year Jer 36:1
Jeremiah gave to Baruch in the * Jer 45:1
of Babylon, in the * year of the Jer 46:2
During the * year of Zedekiah's Jer 51:59
ninth day of the * month, when the Jer 52:6
and the *, an eagle's. Eze 10:14
Following it, the * kingdom Dan 2:40
And the * looks like a god!" Dan 3:25
in my dream, a * animal rose up out Dan 7:7
As I watched, the brutal * animal Dan 7:11
Then I asked about the * animal, Dan 7:19
"This * animal," he told me, Dan 7:23
he told me, "is the * world power Dan 7:23
reign, to be succeeded by a *, Dan 11:2
horses and the * by dappled-greys. Zec 6:3
November of the * year of the reign Zec 7:1
Literally, "*, fifth, seventh, Zec 8:19f
and the *, the form of an eagle, Rev 4:7
And when the * seal was broken, I Rev 6:7
the * Living Being say, "Come!" Rev 6:7
The * angel blew his trumpet and Rev 8:12
Then the * angel poured out his Rev 16:8
The * with emerald; Rev 21:18,19,20

FOWL
gazelles, roebucks, and plump *. 1Ki 4:23

FOWLS
and a large number of domestic *; Neh 5:18

FOX
"If even a * walked along the top Neh 4:3
Jesus replied, "Go tell that * Lk 13:32

FOXES
three hundred * and tied their Ju 15:4
and let the * run through the Ju 15:5
"The little * are ruining the Sol 2:15
as * for rebuilding your walls! Eze 13:4
But Jesus said, "* have dens and Mt 8:20
to lay my head. * have dens to live Lk 9:58

FRACTURE
the same way: * for fracture, eye Lev 24:20
*, eye for eye, tooth for tooth. Lev 24:20

FRAGILE
Your defense of God is as * as a Job 13:12
the wicked is as * as a spider web, Job 27:18
is as * as a moth-infested cloth; Ps 39:11
And so it is with * man. Is 40:7
they shall fall like * women. Jer 25:34
And the peace I give isn't * like Jn 14:27

FRAGRANCE
that is a pleasing * to the Lord. Num 15:7
fire as a pleasing * to the Lord. Num 15:10
enchanted by the * of my perfume. Sol 1:12
give forth their * and the rarest Sol 7:13
they have no sweet * for me. Jer 6:20
And the house was filled with *. Jn 12:3
a sweet, wholesome * in our lives. 2Co 2:15
It is the * of Christ within us, 2Co 2:15

FRAGRANT
oil and for the * incense, onyx Ex 25:1
as a * burnt offering to him. Ex 29:25
a * burnt offering to the Lord. Ex 29:41
offered as a * odor, an offering Num 28:6
It too is a * odor to the Lord, Num 28:8
he guides us on is * with his Ps 25:10
as precious as the * anointing oil Ps 133:2

(FRAGRANT Con't)
than wine. How * your cologne, and Sol 1:3
* than all the richest spices. Sol 4:10
throughout with * cedar and painted Jer 22:14
to flask, and is * and smooth. Jer 48:11
* as the forests of Lebanon. Hos 14:6
be as * as the wines of Lebanon. Hos 14:7
you up as a * sacrifice to God; Rom 15:15,16

FRAIL
"HOW * IS man, how few his days, Job 14:1
Must you be so harsh with * men, Job 14:3
Proud man! * as breath! Ps 39:5,6
yes, man is * as breath. Ps 39:11
Puny man! * as his breath! Is 2:22
Christ's body, being human, was * Heb 5:7f

FRAME
bases under each piece of the *. Ex 26:18,19
for each *, one under each edge. Ex 26:21
the frames—two bases under each *. Ex 26:25
The height of each * was fifteen Ex 36:21
Each * had two clasps joining it Ex 36:22
silver bases. Each * was connected Ex 36:24
silver bases, two for each *. Ex 36:25,26
beneath them, two for each *. Ex 36:30
shall be placed upon a carrying *. Num 4:10
and placed on the carrying *. Num 4:12
and windows had a square *. 1Ki 7:5
and throughout his enormous *. Job 41:12

FRAME-PIECE
acacia wood, each * being fifteen Ex 26:15,16

FRAMES
Twenty of these * will form the Ex 26:18,19
bases for the * to fit into—two Ex 26:18,19
be twenty of these *, with their Ex 26:20
*, and two frames at each corner. Ex 26:22
frames, and two * at each corner. Ex 26:23
These corner * will be connected Ex 26:24
will be eight * on that end of the Ex 26:25
the *—two bases under each frame. Ex 26:25
to run across the *, five bars on Ex 26:26,27
The middle bar, halfway up the * Ex 26:28
Overlay the * with gold, and Ex 26:29
*, bars, pillars, and bases; Ex 35:10-19
* of acacia wood standing on end. Ex 36:20
There were twenty * on the south Ex 36:23
There were also twenty * on the Ex 36:25,26
*, plus another at each corner. Ex 36:27
These *, including those at the Ex 36:29
a total of eight * with sixteen Ex 36:30
wood to tie the * together along Ex 36:31,32
was halfway up the *, along each Ex 36:33
to the other. The * and bars were Ex 36:34
The bases for the * of the Ex 38:27
clasps; *; Ex 39:33-40
it by setting its * into their Ex 40:18
the * of the Tabernacle building; Num 3:36,37
are to carry the * of the Num 4:30,31
the bases, the * for the courtyard Num 4:32

FRAMEUP
that this was a *, backed by the Mk 15:10

FRAMEWORK
"The * of the sacred tent shall Ex 26:15,16
coverings over the *, and put on Ex 40:19

FRANK
answered, and a * account of his 2Ch 33:19
Let me be *, lest God should Job 32:21,22
It is an honor to receive a * Pro 24:26

FRANKINCENSE
galbanum, and pure *, weighing out Ex 30:34
for each. Pure * shall be sprinkled Lev 24:5-8
without oil or * mingled with Num 5:15
grain offerings, *, bowls, and Neh 13:5
bowls, the grain offerings, and *. Neh 13:9
of myrrh and * and every other Sol 3:6
of myrrh and to the hill of *. Sol 4:6
and gave him gold, * and myrrh. Mt 2:11
ointment and *, wine, olive oil, Rev 18:13

FRANKLY
He talked about it quite * with Mk 8:32
I speak * for I am sure these Act 26:26
I * don't know what to do. Gal 4:20

FRANKNESS
In the end, people appreciate * Pro 28:23

FRANTIC
Jacob was * with fear. Gen 32:7
he was * with fear and asked the 1Sa 28:5,6
a trap for me. * fear grips me. Ps 57:6
Listen to the * cries of the Jer 25:36
at one another in * terror, and to Eze 4:17
Your father and I have been *, Lk 2:48
this, they were *, wondering what Act 5:24

FRANTICALLY
toward me," he * explained. Num 22:5,6
head on a cushion. * they wakened Mk 4:38

FRAUD
full of profanity and lies and *. Ps 10:7
making profit by *, who hold back Is 33:15
you take it by * and threats and Mic 2:2
with evil gain of violence and *. Zep 1:9
all evil, deception, envy, and *. 1Pe 2:2,3

FRAUDS
most pious meetings—all are *! Is 1:12,13

trust instead in * and lies and Is 30:12
what they make are *, gods without Jer 10:14

FRAY
of mail, so that it will not *. Ex 28:32

FREE
one—* and untamed as a wild ass! Gen 16:9-12
of my people, I give it to you *. Gen 23:11
then you are * from this oath; Gen 24:8
shake loose from him and be *." Gen 27:39,40
and the rest of you can go *." Gen 44:10
from slavery, and make them *. Ex 6:6
and he shall go out by himself *. Ex 21:4
rather not go *,' then his master Ex 21:5
shall go * because of his eye. Ex 21:26
let him go * to pay for the tooth. Ex 21:27
washing his clothes, he is *. Lev 13:34
to death, because she is not *. Lev 19:20
is a spontaneous * will offering— Lev 22:17,18
be offered as a * will offering, Lev 22:23
that year shall be * to all—for Lev 25:6,7
your husband, be * from the effects Num 5:19
or woman, you must * him at the end Deu 15:12
But when you * a slave you must Deu 15:18
must let her go *—you may not sell Deu 21:14
for a year he shall be * to be at Deu 24:5
Both slave and *. Deu 32:36
But then he is * to return to his Jos 20:6
I brought my people out as * men. Jos 24:5
I'll just shake myself *." Ju 16:20
some kind man to glean the * grain Ru 2:2
He set me * and rescued me, 2Sa 22:20
"every male, both bond and *." 1Ki 14:10f
to help him shake * of Assyria's 2Ki 17:4
They were * from other 1Ch 9:33,34
is * at last from his master. Job 3:19
Let me be * to speak out of the Job 7:11
'Set him *. Job 33:23,24
they say, "and * ourselves from Ps 2:3
Only then can I be * of guilt and Ps 19:13
He gave * course to his anger Ps 78:50
I will * your hands from their Ps 81:6
* the city of God from their grip. Ps 101:8
king sent for him and set him *. Ps 105:20
now they are always * to come to Ps 111:9
* within the limits of your laws. Ps 119:44,45,46
The snare is broken and we are *! Ps 124:7
the poor, and let the rich go *. Pro 24:23
he inherits all my efforts, * of Ecc 2:20-23
the wicked go * and putting Is 5:23
will find a tree * from rot and Is 40:20
have paid the price to set you *. Is 44:22
He shall restore my city and * my Is 45:13
Yet even now, be * from your Is 48:20
of wine and milk—it's all *! Is 55:1
say, "At last we are * from God; Jer 2:31
as we want to, * from any Jer 18:12
my own people, so should you go *? Jer 25:29
everyone to * his Hebrew slaves, Jer 34:9
think you will be * from war and Jer 42:13,14
my people * like birds from cages. Eze 13:20
thick, leaving a * space of 8¾ feet Eze 41:9
seventh year) when he is set *; Eze 46:17
I will personally * her from her Hos 1:7
least she will be * of the burden Hos 8:10
and no one shall set them *. Hos 11:7
exodus from Kir and now were *. Amo 1:5f
But there I will rescue you and * Mic 4:10
use any of them * of charge to boil Zec 14:21
And you will go *, leaping with Mal 4:2
Jesus said, "the citizens are *! Mt 17:26,27
and whatever you * on earth will be Mt 18:18
you won't be * again until the last Lk 12:59
Sabbath day, to * this Jewish woman Lk 13:16
Give us * bread every day, like Jn 6:30,31
and the truth will set you *." Jn 8:32
What do you mean, 'set *'?" Jn 8:33
So if the Son sets you *, you Jn 8:36
you will indeed be *— (Yes, I Jn 8:36
The Greek here is a very * Jn 12:40f
you going to * Israel [from Rome Act 1:6
to Abraham to * his descendants Act 7:17,18
by the * gift of the Lord Jesus?" Act 15:11
told Paul they were * to leave. Act 16:36
"He could be set * if he hadn't Act 26:32
*, and say that they are innocent? Rom 3:26
then it wouldn't be *—but it is! Rom 4:4,5
given to us by faith, as a * gift; Rom 4:16
are * under God's favor and mercy. Rom 6:14
And now you are * from your old Rom 6:18
But now you are * from the power Rom 6:22
is death, but the * gift of God is Rom 6:23
Who will * me from my slavery Rom 7:23,24,25
He has set me *. Rom 7:23,24,25
For in that case the * gift would Rom 11:6
*—it isn't free when it is earned. Rom 11:6
free—it isn't * when it is earned. Rom 11:6
will be counted * from all sin and 1Co 1:8
Or, "to * us from slavery to 1Co 1:30f
the wonderful * gifts of grace and 1Co 2:12
you get a chance to be *, take it. 1Co 7:21
you * from the awful power of sin; 1Co 7:22
you and you are *, remember that 1Co 7:22
belong to him—be * now from all 1Co 7:23
as * as possible for the Lord; 1Co 7:29
In all you do, I want you to be * 1Co 7:32
services of my own * will, then the 1Co 9:17
You are certainly * to eat food 1Co 10:23
some are slaves and some are *. 1Co 12:13
or slaves or * men or even merely Gal 3:28
for I am as * from these chains as Gal 4:12
along with the * woman's son. Gal 4:30
children of the * woman, acceptable Gal 4:31
SO CHRIST HAS made us *. Gal 5:1
Now make sure that you stay * and Gal 5:1
are never * from their pressures. Gal 5:17
do, whether you are slave or *. Eph 6:8
Christ he set you * from your evil Col 2:11
this has set you * from following Col 2:20
lifted up to God, * from sin and 1Ti 2:8
For the * gift of eternal Tit 2:11
from God and be *—trusting that Heb 11:35
Literally, "Of his own * will he Jas 1:18f
into God's law for * men, he will Jas 1:25
You are * from the law, but that 1Pe 2:16
mean you are * to do wrong. 1Pe 2:16
Live as those who are * to do 1Pe 2:16
Do what you like, be *." 2Pe 2:19
us and who set us * from our sins Rev 1:5
small, slave and *, hid themselves Rev 6:15
poor, slave and *—to be tattooed Rev 13:16
great and small, slave and *." Rev 19:18

FREE-WILL
a vow, or a * offering, or a Num 15:3,4
with vows, or as * offerings, burnt Num 29:39
your vows, your * offerings, and Deu 12:6
At that time bring to him a * Deu 16:10
had been given as * offerings to Ez 8:28

FREEBORN
and one from his * wife. Gal 4:22
But the baby of the * wife was Gal 4:23

FREED
then you are * from your promise.' Gen 24:41
six years and be * in the seventh Ex 21:2
afterwards, only he shall be *; Ex 21:3
be * with him at the same time. Ex 21:3
she shall not be * at the end of Ex 21:7
and he shall be * from his sin, and Lev 5:6
children shall be * at that time. Lev 25:54
When it is * in the Year of Lev 27:21
wine, for he is * from his vow. Num 6:20
and be * from his painful grip. Job 6:8,9
me! He * me from all my fears. Ps 34:4
O Lord, you have * me from my Ps 116:16
and most terrible shall all be *; Is 49:25
of Judah had * all the slaves in Jer 34:8
king's command and * their slaves, Jer 34:10
must be * after serving six years. Jer 34:14
commanded you, and * your slaves. Jer 34:15
see that they are * to live again Jer 50:34
had * her from captivity in Egypt. Hos 1:15
free on earth will be * in heaven. Mt 18:18
God fearlessly, * from our enemies, Lk 1:74
shall be * from their oppressors, Lk 4:18,19
You didn't want him *—this holy, Act 3:14
As soon as they were *, Peter and Act 4:23
Everyone who trusts in him is * Act 13:39
The next day the commander * him Act 22:30
to sin you are * from all its Rom 6:7
Christ Jesus—has * me from the Rom 8:2

FREEDMEN
cult of "The *" started an Act 6:9

FREEDOM
* from their harsh taskmasters. Ex 3:7
need pay nothing to regain his *. Ex 21:2
yet redeemed, nor given her *." Lev 19:20f
The price of his * shall be in Lev 25:50
In that day [of Israel's * Is 27:2
in exchange for your *, as your Is 43:3
I am giving you your *!' Is 49:8,9
in the glorious * from sin which Rom 8:20,21
But be careful not to use your * 1Co 8:9
he is there is * [from trying to be 2Co 3:17
on us and see what * we enjoyed in Gal 2:4
as a Jew, to buy * for us who were Gal 4:5
who has called you to * in Christ. Gal 5:8
have been given *: not freedom to Gal 5:13
given freedom: not * to do wrong, Gal 5:13
* to love and serve each other. Gal 5:13
who bought our * with his blood Col 1:14
him without * to lead his flock. 1Ti 3:7
others were promised * if they Heb 11:37,38
* from all anxiety and fear. 1Pe 1:2
who offer this "*" from law are 2Pe 2:19

FREELY
and forth, and the wine flowed *! Gen 43:34
may leave * without any payment. Ex 21:11
Israel was joining * in the worship Num 25:3
the wine flowed * and everyone Ju 9:27
allowed to eat * from the food they 1Sa 14:30
where they could * worship the Lord 2Ch 11:16
Let me complain *. Job 10:1
refuge in him will be * pardoned. Ps 34:22

(FREELY Con't)
Iraqi will move * back and forth Is 19:23
to attack them *, for they have Jer 50:7
feast where the wine flowed *. Dan 5:1
Give as * as you have received! Mt 10:8
me, but I will * do what the Jn 14:31
kindness * takes away our sins. Rom 3:24
many, while Christ * takes away Rom 5:16
yet I have * and happily become a 1Co 9:19
enough to tell it * and fully, and Col 4:4

FREES
He reduces kings to slaves and * Job 12:18
He * us! Ps 68:20
to the hungry. He * the prisoners, Ps 146:7
His sacrifice * us from the worry Heb 9:14

FREEWILL
their * offerings to him. Ex 35:29
the Lord, nor your * offerings, nor Deu 12:17
and a * offering for the Temple." Ez 1:4

FREEZE
and even the widest torrents *. Job 37:10

FREEZING
I have seen anyone * and not given Job 31:19,20
Who can stand before his * cold? Ps 147:17

FREIGHTERS
King Jehoshaphat built great * to 1Ki 22:48

FREQUENT
the * puns in the prophetic books. Jer 29:24f
In the Hebrew, there is * word Mic 1:11f
In the Hebrew, there is * word Mic 1:11f
In the Hebrew, there is * word Mic 1:11f
Those in * contact with the 1Co 7:31

FREQUENTLY
southward to the Negeb, pausing *. Gen 12:9
city came to him * to appeal for Lk 18:3

FRESH
How lovely and * looking it was! Gen 3:6
Then Jacob took * shoots from Gen 30:37
and to put on * clothing. Gen 35:2
the kernels from a * ear, crush and Lev 2:14
The priest shall put on * wood Lev 6:12
after the * plastering, then he Lev 14:48
of the birds over * water in an Lev 14:50
killed over the * water, and shall Lev 14:51,52
yourselves—neither * kernels nor Lev 23:14
it with * oil and trim the wicks. Lev 24:3,4
or wine or even * wine, grape Num 6:3,4
carried out. Two * cows were 1Sa 6:10
replaced that day with * bread. 1Sa 21:6
brought Elisha a sack of * corn 2Ki 4:42
Literally, "* grain." 2Ki 4:42f
me and bring * armies against me. Job 10:17
and watered them. * honors were Job 29:20
Literally, "anointed with * Ps 92:10f
The meek will be filled with * Is 29:19
In one basket there were *, Jer 24:2
a small loaf of * bread every day Jer 37:21
waters and make them * and pure. Eze 47:8
Its leaves were * and green, and Dan 4:12
to see, with its * green leaves, Dan 4:21
to present any * revelation. Mt 7:29f
they thought up a * question of Mt 22:34,35
New wine needs * wineskins." Mk 2:22
seems to want the * and the new. Lk 5:39
* newness in all you do and think. Rom 12:2
who lives in the * newness of life Php 3:11
like a breath of * air, and he was 2Ti 1:16
This is the *, new, life-giving Heb 10:20
out first with * water and then Jas 3:11
No, and you can't draw * water Jas 3:12
fruit, with a * crop each month; Rev 22:2

FRESH-BAKED
its rich aroma, and some * bread. Gen 27:17

FRESHLY
with * baked unleavened bread. Gen 19:3
Your teeth are white as * washed Sol 6:6
you as clean as * fallen snow. Is 1:18

FRET
Don't * and worry—it only leads Ps 37:8
O daughter, not to * about your Ps 45:10,11

FRIDAY
darkness fell on * evenings and not Neh 13:19
This was done late on * Lk 23:54

FRIED
baked, *, or grilled—you are to Lev 2:8
sacrifice is baked, *, or grilled. Lev 7:9
like pancakes * in vegetable oil. Num 11:8
* or mixed with olive oil); 1Ch 23:29

FRIEND
him, "Come and stay with us, *; Gen 24:31
Judah and his * Hirah, the Gen 38:12
Judah asked his * Hirah the Gen 38:20
to face, as a man speaks to his *. Ex 33:11
You say you are my *, Ex 33:12
favor with me, and you are my *." Ex 33:17
or closest *, even a brother, son, Deu 13:6,7
demanded, "Are you * or foe?" Jos 5:13
He and his * Zebul should be our Ju 9:28
But Amnon had a very crafty * 2Sa 13:3
So David's * Hushai returned to 2Sa 15:37
When David's *, Hushai the 2Sa 16:16
"Is this the way to treat your * 2Sa 16:17
personal priest and special *; 1Ki 4:1
find out if he is * or foe," King 2Ki 9:17
you are * or foe," he demanded. 2Ki 9:18
"Do you come as a *, Jehu?" 2Ki 9:22
who were burying a * spied these 2Ki 13:20,21
the descendants of your * Abraham? 2Ch 20:7
was also a good * of Tobiah, had Neh 13:4
was a * at court for all of them. Est 10:3
kind to a fainting *, but you have Job 6:14
a helpless orphan, or selling a *. Job 6:27
not as a stranger, but as a *! Job 19:27
for him as a *, to show him what is Job 33:23,24
it were my mother, * or brother who Ps 35:14
Even my best * has turned against Ps 41:9
He is a * of mine! Ps 54:4
myself, my companion and my *. Ps 55:13
This * of mine betrayed me—I who Ps 55:20
Lover, *, acquaintance —all are Ps 88:18
A true * is always loyal, and a Pro 17:17
but there is a * who sticks closer Pro 18:24
everyone is his *! Pro 19:6
grace and truth is the king's *. Pro 22:11
Wounds from a * are better than Pro 27:6
Never abandon a *—either yours or Pro 27:10
greeting to a * too early in the Pro 27:14
Jerusalem, is my beloved, my *." Sol 5:16
Abraham's family, and he was my *. Is 41:8
Father, you have always been my *; Jer 3:4,5
I will be its enemy and not its * Jer 21:10
your best *—not even your wife! Mic 7:5
say, 'Please be my *, for I know Zec 8:23
into a brawl at the home of a *!' Zec 13:6
If you call your * an idiot, you Mt 5:22
remember that a * has something Mt 5:23
Should you say, '*, let me help Mt 7:4
me as his *, I will openly Mt 10:32
my * before my father in heaven. Mt 10:32
" '*,' he answered one of them, Mt 20:13
" '*,' he asked, 'how does it Mt 22:12
Jesus said, "My *, go ahead and Mt 26:50
DEAR * WHO loves God: Lk 1:1
"My *, your sins are forgiven!" Lk 5:20
Literally, "is a * of tax Lk 7:34f
said to her, "Martha, dear *, Lk 10:41
You would shout up to him, 'A * Lk 11:5,6
won't do it as a *, if you keep Lk 11:8
me here on earth as your *. Lk 12:8
say to myself, "*, you have enough Lk 12:19
come and say, '*, we have a better Lk 14:10
*, is the man who will betray me. Lk 22:21
I am the Bridegroom's *, and I am Jn 3:29
your good * is very, very sick." Jn 11:3
Then he said, "Our * Lazarus Jn 11:11
being his closest *, Simon Peter Jn 13:23
man, you are no * of Caesar's. Jn 19:12
there beside me, his close *, Jn 19:26
replied, "You know I am your *." Jn 21:15
said, "you know I am your *." Jn 21:16
son of John, are you even my *?" Jn 21:17
DEAR * WHO loves God: Act 1:1
Greet my good * Epaenetus. Rom 16:5
is a special * of yours or not. 1Ti 5:21
that I am your * even though I am 2Ti 1:8
If I am really your *, give him Phm 1:17
to speak to his * or neighbor or Heb 8:11
to appear now before God as our *. Heb 9:24
If you have a * who is in need Jas 2:15
was even called "the * of God." Jas 2:23
you cannot also be a * of God. Jas 4:4
Dear *, I am praying that all is 3Jn 1:2
Dear *, you are doing a good work 3Jn 1:5
Dear *, don't let this bad 3Jn 1:11

FRIEND'S
you went to a * house at midnight, Lk 11:5,6

FRIENDLINESS
"What do you know about *? 2Ki 9:19
him with a great show of *. Mk 14:45

FRIENDLY
you will be on * terms with my Gen 21:23
"This is obviously no * visit, Gen 26:27
hoping that you will be * to us." Gen 32:5
hoped, "he will be * to us." Gen 32:20
relief it is to see your * smile! Gen 33:10
If you become * with them and one Ex 34:15
will become * with King Rehoboam; 1Ki 12:27
their intentions were * or not. 2Ki 9:19
For they had not been * to the Neh 13:2
They act so * when they come Ps 41:6
They are so * to my face while Ps 62:3,4
* suggestions are as pleasant as Pro 27:9
A * discussion is as stimulating Pro 27:17
If you are * only to your Mt 5:47
to stay, be *, and if it turns out Mt 10:12
him in * fashion. Mt 26:49
him on the cheek in * greeting. Lk 22:47
she gave a * welcome to the spies. Heb 11:31

FRIENDS
"but what is that between *? Gen 23:14,15
"Those men are our *," they Gen 34:21
your brothers, *, and neighbors.' Ex 32:27
before the Lord with all your *; Num 16:16
families and the * who were Num 16:32
roam with my girl * for two months, Ju 11:37
fate with her * for two months. Ju 11:38
groves and give them to his *. 1Sa 8:14
When his * heard about it, they 1Sa 10:11
Pharaoh's closest *, and he gave 1Ki 11:19
heard about the plans from his *. 1Ki 12:2,3,4
destroyed distant relatives and *. 1Ki 16:11
pans from your * and neighbors!" 2Ki 4:3
room away from his *, and pour the 2Ki 9:2
Jehu went back to his * and one 2Ki 9:11
personal *, and private chaplains. 2Ki 10:11
all of Ahab's * and relatives, just 2Ki 10:17
have come to help me, we are *; 1Ch 12:17
Meanwhile, * of Jeroboam (son of 2Ch 10:2,3
the family and * of Ahab, he met 2Ch 22:8
* and the Samaritan army officers. Neh 4:1
fight for your *, your families, Neh 4:14
They were his personal * as well Est 1:13-15
together his * and Zeresh his wife, Est 5:10
wife and all his *, "get ready a Est 5:14
wife and all his * what had Est 6:13
When three of Job's * heard of Job 2:11
there on high. My * scoff at me, Job 16:20
*, their children shall go blind. Job 17:5
sent away my brothers, and my *. Job 19:13
me; my * have all forsaken me. Job 19:14
"My best * abhor me. Job 19:19
"Oh, my *, pity me, for the Job 19:21
Neither his * nor his family Job 20:9
money to needy * unless they gave Job 22:6
with Job's three * because they had Job 32:3
And he will declare to his *, 'I Job 33:27
answer you, and all your * too. Job 35:4
and with your two *, for you have Job 42:7
Then, when Job prayed for his *, Job 42:10
and former * arrived and feasted Job 42:11
glory by praising you before my *. Ps 6:5
can I praise you then to all my *? Ps 30:9
even more by my neighbors and *. Ps 31:11
My loved ones and * stay away, Ps 38:11
I mention among my * the names of Ps 87:4
You have made my * to loathe me, Ps 88:8
Dathan, Abiram and his *; Ps 106:17
brothers and my * who live here; Ps 122:8
* with eyes and feet and fingers. Pro 6:12,13
The good man asks advice from *; Pro 12:26
while the rich have many "*." Pro 14:20
gossip separates the best of *. Pro 16:28
about them parts the best of *. Pro 17:9
There are "*" who pretend to be Pro 18:24
who pretend to be *, but there is a Pro 18:24
A wealthy man has many "*"; Pro 19:4
how much more his *! Pro 19:7
you what loyal * they are, but are Pro 20:6
shown by the kind of * he chooses. Pro 27:19
and as their * returned from the Ecc 8:9,10
Never again will I see my * in Is 38:11
And all your * of childhood days Is 47:15
but it's all no good—your new * Jer 2:36
neighbors and * shall collapse Jer 6:21
and their * shall not cut Jer 16:6
to eat their own children and *. Jer 19:9
you and all your *, and you will Jer 20:4
Even those who were my * are Jer 20:10
all your * are taken off as Jer 22:22
'Fine * you have,' they'll say, Jer 38:21,22
O * of Moab, weep for her and Jer 48:17
All her * are now her enemies. Lam 1:2
brought to you by consoling *." Eze 24:17
brought to you by sympathetic *. Eze 24:22
with all her *, to lie there beside Eze 32:21
and his three * looked healthier Dan 1:15
The only * she has are those she Hos 8:9
But though she hires "*" from Hos 8:10
Your trusted * will set traps for Ob 1:7
of Job's three *, was from Teman, Ob 1:8f
People will write their * in Zec 8:20,21
I received in the house of my *." Zec 13:6f
"There is a saying, 'Love your * Mt 5:43
only to your *, how are you Mt 5:47
"Should the bridegroom's * mourn Mt 9:15
to their little *, 'We played Mt 11:16
did when he and his * were hungry? Mt 12:3
"Then the man's * went to the Mt 18:31
Jesus replied, "Do * of the Mk 2:19
When his * heard what was Mk 3:21
"Go home to your *," he told Mk 5:19
the relatives and * came for the Lk 1:59
with * among the other travelers. Lk 2:44
him among their relatives and *; Lk 2:44
captain sent some * to say, "Sir, Lk 7:6,7,8
And when the captain's * returned Lk 7:10
complain to their *, 'You don't Lk 7:32
And has the lowest sort of *!' Lk 7:34
"Dear *, don't be afraid of Lk 12:4
"don't invite *, brothers, Lk 14:12
call together your * and neighbors Lk 15:6
And then won't she call in her * Lk 15:9
young goat for a feast with my *. Lk 15:29

(FRIENDS Con't)
And then I'll have plenty of * to — Lk 16:4
to yourselves * by means of the — Lk 16:9f
relatives, and * will betray you — Lk 21:16
before—became fast *. — Lk 23:12
Meanwhile, Jesus' *, including — Lk 23:49
A bridegroom's * rejoice with — Jn 3:29
"They were close *," the Jewish — Jn 11:36
lays down his life for his *; — Jn 15:13
and you are my * if you obey me. — Jn 15:14
now you are my *, proved by the — Jn 15:15
his relatives and * among the — Act 5:17
ill and died. Her * prepared her — Act 9:37
and close * to meet Peter. — Act 10:24
the delegates made * with Blastus, — Act 12:20
of the province, * of Paul, also — Act 19:31
forbid any of his * from visiting — Act 24:23
* and receive their hospitality. — Act 27:3
DEAR * IN Rome: This letter is — Rom 1:1
And you, dear * in Rome, are — Rom 1:6,7
brag that you are his special *. — Rom 2:17
his *, and he is living within us! — Rom 5:10
for our sins—making us * of God. — Rom 5:11
Dear *, never avenge yourselves. — Rom 12:19
So, dear *, carefully avoid — 1Co 10:14
Dear *, even if I myself should — 1Co 14:6
All the * here have asked me to — 1Co 16:20
1 DEAR *, — 2Co 1:1
Oh, my dear Corinthian *! — 2Co 6:11
as these, dear *, let us turn away — 2Co 7:1
boasted to the * in Macedonia that — 2Co 9:2
to help you, dear *—to build you up — 2Co 12:19
Dear *, I solemnly swear that the — Gal 1:11
But afterwards when some Jewish * — Gal 2:12
Listen to me, you * who think you — Gal 4:21
DEAR CHRISTIAN * at Ephesus, ever — Eph 1:1
Dearest *, when I was there with — Php 2:12
WHATEVER HAPPENS, DEAR *, be — Php 3:1
My beloved *, stay true to the — Php 4:1
help, quarrel no more—be * again. — Php 4:2
he has brought you back as his *. — Col 1:21
for my many other * who have never — Col 2:1
to the Christian * at Laodicea, and — Col 4:15
* so that you would give us money! — 1Th 2:5
Even so, dear *, we beg you to — 1Th 4:10
They will betray their *; — 2Ti 3:4
to all of the Christian * there. — Tit 3:15
Dear *, even though I am talking — Heb 6:9
Don't you realize that making * — Jas 4:4
Dear *, God the Father chose you — 1Pe 1:2
Of course, your former * will be — 1Pe 4:4
Dear *, don't be bewildered or — 1Pe 4:12
But don't forget this, dear *, — 2Pe 3:8
Dear *, while you are waiting for — 2Pe 3:14
So if we say we are his *, but — 1Jn 1:6
Yes, dear *, we are already — 1Jn 3:2
So don't be surprised, dear *, — 1Jn 3:13
But, dearly loved *, if our — 1Jn 3:21
DEARLY LOVED *, don't always — 1Jn 4:1
Dear young *, you belong to God — 1Jn 4:4
Dear *, let us practice loving — 1Jn 4:7
Dear *, since God loved us as — 1Jn 4:11
remind you, dear *, of the old rule — 2Jn 1:5
So good-bye for now. * here send — 3Jn 1:15
Dearly loved *, I had been — Jud 1:3
Dear *, remember what the — Jud 1:17
But you, dear *, must build up — Jud 1:20
Dear *: — Rev 1:4

FRIENDSHIP
of his close * with David, told — 1Sa 19:1
well about our *, so he has said to — 1Sa 20:3
of them renewed their pact of *; — 1Sa 23:18
Jehu replied, "How can there be * — 2Ki 9:22
am going to show * to Hanun because — 1Ch 19:2,3
the * of God was felt in my home; — Job 29:4
* with God is reserved for those — Ps 25:14
but he gives his * to the godly. — Pro 3:32
It is harder to win back the * of — Pro 18:19
Egypt and Iraq because of their * — Is 19:25
way, to buy * through cheating? — Lk 16:9
this wonderful * with his Son, even — 1Co 1:9
and the Holy Spirit's * be yours. — 2Co 13:14
of your * and your loving deeds. — 3Jn 1:6

FRIENDSHIPS
homes and make * with silly, — 2Ti 3:6

FRIGHT
army began to run away in *. — 1Sa 17:24
with * because of Samuel's words. — 1Sa 28:20
Then Haman grew pale with * before — Est 7:6
armies and we are weak with *. — Jer 6:24
weak with fright. * and pain have — Jer 6:24
as your pilots scream with *. — Eze 27:28
face was pale with *, but I told no — Dan 7:28
and I grew pale and weak with *. — Dan 10:8
their faces grow pale with *. — Joe 2:6

FRIGHTEN
If you are, go home before you * — Deu 20:8
trying to * and dishearten them. — 2Ch 32:18
to discourage and * them by sending — Ez 4:4,5
many threatening letters to * me. — Neh 6:19
For the policeman does not * — Rom 13:3

FRIGHTENED
Esau, for I am *—terribly afraid — Gen 32:11
I was as * of you as though — Gen 33:10
They were badly * when they saw — Gen 43:18
dead, Joseph's brothers were *. — Gen 50:15
that his deed was known, he was *. — Ex 2:14
they were terribly *, and cried out — Ex 14:10
land have * us with their report. — Deu 1:28
greater than yours, don't be *! — Deu 20:1
now their allies, he was very *. — Jos 10:2
who went with us * the people and — Jos 14:8
of your men who are timid and *." — Ju 7:3
The Israelis were badly * when — 1Sa 7:7
"Don't be *," Samuel reassured — 1Sa 12:20
this, they were dismayed and *. — 1Sa 17:11
"Don't be *!" — 1Sa 28:13
and his people too were badly *. — 2Sa 4:1
But they were too * to do it. — 2Ki 10:4
Don't be * by the size of the — 1Ch 28:20
* and couldn't stand up to them. — 2Ch 13:7
I was badly *, but I replied, — Neh 2:1
it, they were * and humiliated, and — Neh 6:16
Even I am * when I see myself. — Job 21:6
You need not be * of me. — Job 33:7
me in the face—I was * and sad. — Ps 116:3
"Tell him he needn't be * by the — Is 7:4
He will not be * away! — Is 31:4,5
Don't be * by predictions such as — Jer 10:2,3
he finished they were badly *. — Jer 36:16
have become like * calves. — Jer 46:20,21
don't be * even though their — Eze 2:6
I had a dream that greatly * me. — Dan 4:5
don't be so pale and * over this. — Dan 5:10
But as he approached, I was too * — Dan 8:17
Then he said, "Don't be *, — Dan 10:12
The men were terribly * when they — Jon 1:9,10
But on the way he was * to learn — Mt 2:22
Why are you so *?" — Mt 8:26
to the ground, terribly *. — Mt 17:6
were terribly * by the earthquake — Mt 27:54
"Don't be *!" — Mt 28:5
the tomb, badly *, but also filled — Mt 28:8
Jesus said to them, "Don't be *! — Mt 28:10
and perfectly sane, they were *. — Mk 5:15
Then the * woman, trembling at — Mk 5:33
say and they were all terribly *. — Mk 9:6
and bewildered, too * to talk. — Mk 16:8
"Don't be *, Mary," the angel — Lk 1:30
They were badly *, but the angel — Lk 2:9
And the whole crowd was badly *. — Lk 8:35
group was terribly *, thinking they — Lk 24:37
"Why are you *?" — Lk 24:38
this, he was more * than ever. — Jn 19:8
the commander was * because he had — Act 22:29
You became * about what had — 2Co 7:11
But I am *, fearing that in some — 2Co 11:3
comfort those who are *; — 1Th 5:14
Moses himself was so * at the — Heb 12:21

FRIGHTENING
and the long, * trumpet blast; — Ex 20:18
So now they live in * ravines, — Job 30:6
It is * even to think about it! — Job 41:9
brilliantly, * and terrible. — Dan 2:31
When I saw this * vision my — Dan 10:8

FRINGES
and by lengthening the memorial * — Mt 23:5
least touch the * of his clothes; — Mk 6:56

FRISK
* across the slopes of Gilead. — Sol 4:1

FRISKING
goats * down the slopes of Gilead. — Sol 6:5

FRO
and you will be tossed to and * — Deu 28:25
to and * over the other trees?' — Ju 9:9
to and *, swift as lightning. — Eze 1:14
driven to and * on the Adriatic — Act 27:27

FROGS
vast hordes of * across your land — Ex 8:2
* in every corner of the land." — Ex 8:5
Aaron did, and * covered the — Ex 8:6
caused * to come up upon the land. — Ex 8:7
God to take the * away, and I will — Ex 8:8
will pray that the * will die at — Ex 8:9
All the * will be destroyed, — Ex 8:11
Lord concerning the * he had sent. — Ex 8:12
promised—dead * covered the — Ex 8:13
But when Pharaoh saw that the * — Ex 8:15
the * had covered all of Egypt! — Ps 78:45
Then * invaded in enormous — Ps 105:30
disguised as * leap from the mouth — Rev 16:13

FRONDS
fruit, and palm *, and the boughs — Lev 23:40

FRONT
as we are must present a united *! — Gen 13:8
stole out here in * of us, before — Gen 31:36,37
across the * of the sacred tent. — Ex 26:9
and a 1½-foot length at the *. — Ex 26:13
It will consist of two pieces, * — Ex 28:7
attached to the * edges of the two — Ex 28:25
* edge of the ephod at the sash. — Ex 28:27
ribbon to the * of Aaron's turban. — Ex 28:37,38
put some of it in * of the Ark — Ex 30:36
him, and passed in * of him and — Ex 34:5,6
to wear on the * of the turban, — Ex 39:30
for the incense in * of the Ark. — Ex 40:5
offerings in * of the entrance. — Ex 40:6
before the Lord in * of the veil — Lev 4:6
before the Lord, in * of the veil. — Lev 4:17
"Aaron's sons shall stand in * of — Lev 6:14
plate at its *—the holy crown—as — Lev 8:9
If the hair is gone from the * — Lev 13:41
and then seven times in * of it. — Lev 16:14
of mercy and in * of it, just as he — Lev 16:15
the Lord in * of the Tabernacle. — Num 7:3
with the Ark at the * of the — Num 10:33
I meet with you, in * of the Ark. — Num 17:4
towards the * of the Tabernacle. — Num 19:4
nor shave the * halves of your — Deu 14:1
laid it on the ground in * of him. — Jos 7:23
threw it in * of the city gate. — Jos 8:29
Only the altar in * of the — Jos 22:29
goods at the * of the column. — Ju 18:21
fallen down in * of the door with — Ju 19:27
The crag on the north was in * — 1Sa 14:5
the southern one was in * of Geba. — 1Sa 14:5
forward and walk in * of Samuel. — 1Sa 16:8
three arrows in * of the pile as — 1Sa 20:20
Ahio was walking in *, and was — 2Sa 6:4
put Uriah at the * of the hottest — 2Sa 11:15
* of him, and cried out, "O king! — 2Sa 14:4
All along the * of the Temple — 1Ki 6:3
with a porch in * covered by a — 1Ki 7:6
on the left, in * of the Most Holy — 1Ki 7:49
the court in * of the Temple for — 1Ki 8:64
stood across the * of the — 2Ki 11:11
priest of Baal, in * of the altar. — 2Ki 11:18
altar from the * of the Temple (it — 2Ki 16:14
He stood beside the pillar in * — 2Ki 23:3
were both in * and behind him, he — 1Ch 19:10
still stood in * of the old — 2Ch 1:5,6
At the * of the Temple were two — 2Ch 3:15
the pillars at the * of the Temple, — 2Ch 3:17
in * of the altar of the Lord. — 2Ch 6:12,13
in * of the porch of the Temple. — 2Ch 8:12
of the Lord in * of the Temple. — 2Ch 15:8
to the other in * of the Temple and — 2Ch 23:10
AS I LAY on the ground in * of the — Ez 10:1
at the plaza in * of the Water Gate — Neh 8:1
He faced the square in * of the — Neh 8:1
sitting there in * of the king's — Est 5:13
and protect me by standing in *. — Ps 35:2
singers in *, musicians behind, — Ps 68:25
make a fool of you in * of them. — Jer 1:17
he stopped in * of the Temple of — Jer 19:14
in * of the Temple in Jerusalem. — Jer 24:2
Stand out in * of the Temple of — Jer 26:2
to Hananiah, in * of all the — Jer 28:5
time, sitting in * of a fireplace, — Jer 36:22
Each had the face of a man [in * — Eze 1:10
their children in * of their idols, — Eze 23:39
between them. In * of these rooms — Eze 40:7-12
Or, an eighteen-inch pillar in * — Eze 40:7-12f
inner court [in * of the Temple — Eze 40:47
standing in * of the Temple. — Eze 40:47
the nave, and in * of the Holy of — Eze 41:21
passageway to the * of the Temple. — Eze 44:4
the Lord in * of this passageway on — Eze 46:3
was standing in * of me—or at least — Dan 8:15
to back down in * of his guests, he — Mt 14:9
Jesus was there in * of them! — Mt 28:9
Once a leper came and knelt in * — Mk 1:40
right down in * of Jesus. — Mk 2:4
stand in * of the congregation. — Mk 3:3
break his oath in * of his guests. — Mk 6:26
A heavy veil hung in * of the room — Mk 15:38f
a stone in * of the entrance. — Mk 15:46
sleeping mat, right in * of Jesus. — Lk 5:18,19
Thus you will be honored in * of — Lk 14:10
on the ground in * of Jesus, face — Lk 17:16
her out in * of the staring crowd. — Jn 8:3
in * of the crowd with the woman. — Jn 8:9
don't flaunt your faith in * of — Rom 14:22
brother in * of unbelievers. — 1Co 6:6
I said to Peter in * of all the — Gal 2:14
be rebuked in * of the whole church — 1Ti 5:20
is right there in * of him, how can — 1Jn 4:20
Directly in * of his throne were — Rev 4:5
Four Living Beings, dotted * and — Rev 4:6
Elders, in * of the throne and the — Rev 5:6
I looked, and there in * of me — Rev 6:2
standing in * of the throne and — Rev 7:9
For the Lamb standing in * of — Rev 7:17
directly in *, not to one side. — Rev 7:17f
new song in * of the throne of God — Rev 14:3

FRONTAL
replied, "Don't make a * attack. — 2Sa 5:23

FRONTIER
to the * with a great force. — Num 20:20
was the Ammonite *) to the middle — Deu 3:16
themselves along their *. — 2Ki 3:21
wiping out her * cities, the glory — Eze 25:9,10

FRONTIERS
is yours. Your * will stretch from — Deu 11:24

FRONTS
to fight on two *, he selected the — 2Sa 10:9
FROST
is the mother of the ice and *? — Job 38:29
would think the sea was made of *! — Job 41:31,32
and scatters the * upon the ground, — Ps 147:16
FROSTY
to the hot sun and * nights, and I — Jer 36:30
FROTH
He leaves a shining wake of * — Job 41:31,32
than nothing—mere emptiness and *. — Is 40:17
FROWN
May they perish at your *. — Ps 80:16
FRUIT
plant, and * trees with seeds — Gen 1:11,12
seeds inside the *, so that these — Gen 1:11,12
and all the * trees for your food. — Gen 1:29
trees producing the choicest of *. — Gen 2:9
"You may eat any * in the garden — Gen 2:16,17
the garden except * from the Tree — Gen 2:16,17
Conscience—for its * will open your — Gen 2:16,17
If you eat its *, you will be — Gen 2:16,17
"None of the * in the garden? — Gen 3:1
"It's only the * from the tree — Gen 3:2,3
So she ate some of the * and gave — Gen 3:6
"Have you eaten * from the tree — Gen 3:11
wife and ate the * when I told you — Gen 3:17
if he eats the * of the Tree of — Gen 3:22
last piece of * from the vines, and — Lev 19:10
all kinds of * trees, do not eat — Lev 19:23
Literally, "you shall count the * — Lev 19:23f
take boughs of * trees laden with — Lev 23:40
trees laden with *, and palm — Lev 23:40
with * long after the normal time! — Lev 26:4,5
its crops, nor your trees their *. — Lev 26:20
or *, is the Lord's, and is holy. — Lev 27:30
to buy back this * or grain, he — Lev 27:31
the * they had brought with them. — Num 13:26
Here is some * we have brought — Num 13:27
with samples of the local *. — Deu 1:24,25
but not yet eaten any of its *? — Deu 20:6
a city, don't destroy the * trees. — Deu 20:19
Eat all the * you wish; — Deu 20:19
fulness of the * be consecrated." — Deu 22:9f
Blessings of * and bread; — Deu 28:2-6
Curses on your * and bread; — Deu 28:15-19
someone else will eat the * of — Deu 28:30
For the trees will drop their * — Deu 28:40
will grow bitter and poisonous *. — Deu 29:18
sweetness and * just to lift my — Ju 9:11
* are for the young men to eat; — 2Sa 16:2
the wells, and felled the * trees; — 2Ki 3:25
in the soil and bear * for God. — 2Ki 19:30
oliveyards and many, many * trees; — Neh 9:25
or from our * and olive trees. — Neh 10:35
the first of our *, and the first — Neh 10:37
I stole the * it bears, or if I — Job 31:38,39
* each season without fail. — Ps 1:3
may there be * like that of — Ps 72:16
produce * and be vital and green. — Ps 92:14
and fills the earth with *. — Ps 104:13
and there are * trees, vegetables — Ps 104:14
and hills, the * trees and cedars, — Ps 148:9
eat the bitter * of having your own — Pro 1:31
of life to those who eat her *; — Pro 3:18
*, and all who win souls are wise. — Pro 11:30
Literally, "Give her of the * of — Pro 31:31f
shade and his * is lovely to eat. — Sol 2:3
lovely orchard bearing precious *, — Sol 4:13,14
lushest bounty and its richest *. — Is 4:2,3,4
phrase, "* of the land." — Is 4:2,3,4f
fill the whole earth with her *! — Is 27:6
For the crops of * will fail; — Is 32:10
leaves, as ripe * from the trees. — Is 34:4
it out and it always produces *. — Is 55:11
and eat the * themselves—their — Is 65:21,22
it will be the * of their own — Jer 6:18,19
disappear, their * trees will die, — Jer 8:13
to see and full of good *; — Jer 11:16
on producing all its luscious *. — Jer 17:8
we should plant * trees, for we — Jer 29:28
be here to eat the * from them for — Jer 29:28
vine, producing leaves and *. — Eze 17:8
forth branches and bearing *. — Eze 17:22,23
east; the * was destroyed by fire. — Eze 19:12
its branches and devoured its *." — Eze 19:14f
They will harvest all your * and — Eze 25:4
Their * trees and fields will — Eze 34:27
There will be heavy crops of * to — Eze 36:8
harvests from your * trees and — Eze 36:30
All kinds of * trees will grow — Eze 47:12
fall, and there will always be *. — Eze 47:12
the Temple. The * will be for food — Eze 47:12
*, enough for everyone to eat. — Dan 4:12
off its leaves, and scatter its *. — Dan 4:14
loaded with * for all to eat, the — Dan 4:21
wild animals will eat their *. — Hos 1:12
she shall bear no more *. — Hos 9:16
luxuriant vine all filled with *! — Hos 10:1
my * to you throughout the year. — Hos 14:8
The trees will bear their *; — Joe 2:22
But I lopped off their * and cut — Amo 2:9
I am just a herdsman and * — Amo 7:14
a vision, a basket full of ripe *. — Amo 8:1
"A basket full of ripe *." — Amo 8:2
Then the Lord said, "This * — Amo 8:2
of all their *—for at least the — Ob 1:5
blossom left nor *, and though the — Hab 3:17
will be weighted down with *; — Zec 8:12
you can identify a tree by its *. — Mt 7:16
Different kinds of * trees can — Mt 7:17
identified by examining their *. — Mt 7:17
* never produces an inedible kind. — Mt 7:18
the inedible * are chopped down and — Mt 7:19
is by the kind of * produced. — Mt 7:20
"A tree is identified by its *. — Mt 12:33
a select variety produces good *; — Mt 12:33
to it, "Never bear * again!" — Mt 21:19
was too early in the season for *. — Mk 11:13
"You shall never bear * again!" — Mk 11:14
not produce good * will be chopped — Lk 3:9
produce scrub * nor do trees from — Lk 6:43
from poor stock produce choice *. — Lk 6:43
by the kind of * it produces. — Lk 6:44
he could find any * on it, but he — Lk 13:6
that bear * for even larger crops. — Jn 15:2
For a branch can't produce * when — Jn 15:4
shall produce a large crop of *. — Jn 15:5
and produce lovely * always, so — Jn 15:16
the forbidden *, as Adam had. — Rom 5:14
*, that is, good deeds for God. — Rom 7:4
deeds, the rotting * of death. — Rom 7:5
more and more * from your harvest. — 2Co 9:10
this kind of * in us: love, joy, — Gal 5:22
producing the good * that comes — Heb 6:9
They are like * trees without any — Jud 1:12
without any * at picking time. — Jud 1:12
I will give * from the Tree of Life — Rev 2:7
—like green * from fig trees — Rev 6:13
*, with a fresh crop each month; — Rev 22:2
eat the * from the Tree of Life. — Rev 22:14
FRUITFUL
Ephraim (meaning "*"—"For God — Gen 41:52
God has made me * in this land of — Gen 41:52
"Joseph is a * tree beside a — Gen 49:22
And * gardens by the riverside; — Num 24:3-9
of mine be as gentle and * as the — Ps 72:6
the years of your life more *." — Pro 9:11
I, the Lord, will tend the * — Is 27:3
Lebanon will be a * field again, a — Is 29:17
for those * vines of other years. — Is 32:12
And I brought them into a * — Jer 2:7
beloved to me as * Gilead and the — Jer 22:6
and they shall be * and increase. — Jer 23:3
Joy and gladness are gone from * — Jer 48:33
He was called the most * of all — Hos 13:15
Nor can you be * apart from me. — Jn 15:4
And they will be living a * — 1Ti 6:19
that their lives will be *. — Tit 3:14
and become * and useful to our Lord — 2Pe 1:8
FRUITS
of plants and * they came from." — Gen 1:11,12
"The Festival of First *: When — Lev 23:9,10,11
Literally, "as first * to the — Lev.23:17f
* of all my hard work to others. — Ecc 2:18
and enjoy the * of his labors, for — Ecc 3:13
garden and eat its choicest *." — Sol 4:16
and the rarest * are at our doors, — Sol 7:13
upon their summer * and harvests. — Is 16:9
Harvest the grapes and summer * — Jer 40:10
your grapes and summer *. — Jer 48:32
The first of the first-ripe * — Eze 44:30
Literally, "bringing forth the * — Mt 21:43f
FRUSTRATE
Then you can * and counter — 2Sa 15:33,34
for God has power to help or to * — 2Ch 25:8
FRUSTRATED
God had exposed and * their plan. — Neh 4:15
discouraged, *, and angry. — Ecc 5:17
fathers and sons shall be *; — Jer 6:21
FRUSTRATES
"He * the plans of crafty men. — Job 5:12
FRUSTRATION
at his clothes in anguish and *. — Gen 37:29
life of uselessness and *? — Job 3:23
They die in helpless *, overcome — Job 5:2
of *, these long and weary nights. — Job 7:3
I am filled with *. — Job 10:15
and filled my days with *. — Ps 32:3
"This is a day of trouble and * — Is 37:3
FRUSTRATIONS
A rebel's * are heavier than sand — Pro 27:3
FRYING
* over it, and there was bread. — Jn 21:9
FUEL
Fire goes out for lack of *, and — Pro 26:20
The people are * for the fire. — Is 9:19,20
contain sufficient * to consume a — Is 40:16
to drink; our * is sold to us at — Lam 5:4
dried human dung as *, and eat it. — Eze 4:12
All they are good for is *—and — Eze 15:4
You are the * for the fire; — Eze 21:32
* on the fire beneath the pot. — Eze 24:5
I will pile on the * beneath her. — Eze 24:9
*—enough to last them seven years. — Eze 39:9
FUGITIVE
From now on you will be a * and a — Gen 4:12
you, and made me a * and a tramp; — Gen 4:14
and whenever a * from Ephraim tried — Ju 12:5
FUGITIVES
Literally, "* of Ephraim" — Ju 12:4f
If you let Moab's * settle among — Is 16:4,5
food and water to these weary *! — Is 21:14
FULFILL
The taskmasters were brutal. "* — Ex 5:13
his sin, and need not * the vow. — Lev 5:6
it is to * a promise or is a — Lev 22:17,18
flock, whether to * a vow or as a — Lev 22:21
you, and * my covenant with you. — Lev 26:9
in the ocean to * your promise!" — Num 11:22
or a sacrifice to * a vow, or a — Num 15:3,4
is divorced, she must * her vow. — Num 30:9
* his promise to your ancestors. — Deu 8:18
your offerings to * your vows, your — Deu 12:6
that you promptly * your vows; — Deu 23:21
on weapons to * his plans—he works — 1Sa 17:47
If so, I want to * a sacred vow — 2Sa 9:3
told him, "go and * your vow." — 2Sa 15:9
then the Lord will * the promise he — 1Ki 2:4
and now, O Lord God of Israel, * — 1Ki 8:25
Yes, O God of Israel, * this — 1Ki 8:26
this in order to * his promise to — 1Ki 12:15
Israel, please * this promise too. — 2Ch 6:17
do it in order to * his prediction — 2Ch 10:15
will * all your promises to him. — Job 22:27
desire and * all your plans. — Ps 20:4
I will publicly * my vows in the — Ps 22:25
silent praise, and thus * our vow. — Ps 65:1
* all your vows that you have — Ps 76:11
longing for you to * your wonderful — Ps 119:123
to * my righteous purpose, and I — Is 45:13
And yet you expect him to * your — Eze 13:6
fury upon them and * my anger — Eze 20:8
they shall * my requirements. — Eze 44:16
you always * your promises of — Dan 9:4
Literally, "in order to * the — Dan 11:14f
and did not * the vision. — Amo 7:3
I will surely * my promises. — Jon 2:9
This will * God's message — Mt 1:22
Literally, "to * all — Mt 3:15f
No, I came to * them, and to make — Mt 5:17
vows to God, but must * them all.' — Mt 5:33
This was done to * the ancient — Mt 21:4
But this is all happening to * — Mt 26:56
to * the prophecies about me." — Mk 14:49
finished, and to * the Scriptures — Jn 19:28
when God would * his promise to — Act 7:17,18
Well then, has God failed to * — Rom 9:6
Pilate, that you * all he has told — 1Ti 6:14
FULFILLED
through whom my promise will be *. — Gen 21:12
"I have * my contract," Jacob — Gen 29:21
"Why haven't you * your quotas — Ex 5:14
The days of his vow that were * — Num 6:12
and your fondest wish will be *!" — 1Sa 23:20
Today you have * your promise to — 1Ki 8:24
"Blessed be the Lord who has * — 1Ki 8:56
the Lord * his warning by causing — 1Ki 13:26
of Samaria shall surely be *." — 1Ki 13:32
For you have * your promise to — 2Ch 1:9
now * the promise he made to him. — 2Ch 6:4
This also * the prediction of — 2Ch 36:22,23
the Lord * Jeremiah's prophecy — Ez 1:1
wish against him will soon be *!" — Ps 35:25
I want your promises *. — Ps 50:14,15
* when Cyrus captured the city. — Is 21:5f
and seen them *, but you refuse to — Is 48:6
He has * the promises of doom he — Lam 2:17
for all these prophecies to be *.' — Eze 12:23
my judgments will be *!" — Eze 21:7
same hour this prophecy was *. — Dan 4:33
seem to have been * many years — Dan 11:6f
This event was * in 168–167 B.C. — Dan 11:30,31f
when the vision will be *. — Hab 2:3
This * the prophet's prediction, — Mt 2:15
This brutal action of Herod's * — Mt 2:17
in Nazareth. This * the prediction — Mt 2:23
This * Isaiah's prophecy: — Mt 4:14
This * the prophecy of Isaiah, — Mt 8:17
This * the prophecy of Isaiah — Mt 12:17
laws and are * if you obey them. — Mt 22:40
the Scriptures be * that describe — Mt 26:54
This * the prophecy of Jeremiah — Mt 27:9
And so the Scripture was * that — Mk 15:28
When Jesus' parents had * all the — Lk 2:39
the prophets will be abundantly *. — Lk 21:22
This has * what the prophets — Jn 15:25
This * Jesus' prediction — Jn 18:32
This * the Scripture that — Jn 19:23,24
(This was * during the reign of — Act 11:28
* prophecy by killing Jesus; — Act 13:27
When they had * all the — Act 13:29
servants the prophets—would be *. — Rev 10:7

(FULFILLED Con't)
that the words of God will be *. Rev 17:17

FULFILLING
the Lord, thereby * the decree of 1Ki 2:27
* my vow of praising you each day. Ps 61:8
to every nation by * his promise to Ps 98:2,3
While they were * their orders, I Eze 9:8
will join them, thus * prophecy, Dan 11:14
on a young donkey, * the prophecy Jn 12:14
But God was * the prophecies Act 3:18
laws, * all his requirements. Rom 13:8

FULFILLMENT
giving and normal * of your vows. Lev 23:38
See 1 Kings 16:34 for the * of Jos 6:26f
to the Lord in * of a vow I made to 2Sa 15:7,8
Then I tried to find * by Ecc 2:4,5,6
was a further * of this prophecy, Is 7:14f
night for the * of his promises. Is 62:6,7
no strong branch remains. The * Eze 19:14
with a further * of this prophecy Dan 8:9f
and future further * by the Dan 8:23f
For their future * see verse 27 Dan 9:25f
a partial * of this prophecy. Dan 9:25f
end times—for the * of this Dan 10:14
But a further * may lie in the Dan 11:32f
that this was a * of prophecy; Jn 12:16
The soldiers did this in * of Jn 19:36,37
came upon them in * of the Father's Act 1:4
forward to the * of God's promise Act 26:6
for the time of * is near. Rev 22:10

FULFILLS
him sincerely. He * the desires of Ps 145:19
murderer and who * none of his Eze 18:10
"This * the prophecy of Isaiah: Mt 13:14
He carries out and * all of 2Co 1:20

FULL
As it happened, the valley was * Gen 14:10
I will of course pay the * price Gen 23:9
Let me pay the * price of the Gen 23:13
all seven heads were plump and *. Gen 41:22
the granaries were * to Gen 41:49
and when they looked, it was * of Ex 16:20
the well shall pay * damages to the Ex 21:34
ox shall pay in * for the dead ox, Ex 21:36
he must make * restitution; Ex 22:3
the fire shall make * restitution. Ex 22:6
* quota of the days of your life. Ex 23:26
take a censer * of live coals from Lev 16:12
become * of enormous wickedness. Lev 19:29
volumes—and give * measure, for I Lev 19:35,36
to redeem it, with * right of Lev 25:29
his sin and make * repayment for Num 5:7
"The land is * of warriors, the Num 13:32
"They know * well the power you Num 14:13
shall have their * share in it. Num 14:24
you great cities * of good Deu 6:10,11,12
When you are *, don't forget to Deu 6:13
For when you have become * and Deu 8:12,13
write "Paid in *" on any Deu 15:2
father and mother for a * month. Deu 21:13
be a * sister or a half-sister.' Deu 27:22
Joshua (son of Nun) was * of the Deu 34:9
I went out * and the Lord has Ru 1:21
I have * revenge on my enemies." 1Sa 14:24,25
Agag arrived all * of smiles, 1Sa 15:32
Saul now fell * length upon the 1Sa 28:20
built along the * length of both 1Ki 6:5
Soon every container was * to 2Ki 4:6
Then Jehu drew his bow with his * 2Ki 9:24
Whenever the chest became *, the 2Ki 12:10
arrow, * of victory over Syria; 2Ki 13:16,17
from you at its * price; 1Ch 21:22
"I will buy it for the * price; 1Ch 21:24
over a nation as * of people as the 2Ch 1:9
people as the earth is * of dust! 2Ch 1:9
his stewards in * regalia, and saw 2Ch 9:4
on thrones in * regalia at an open 2Ch 18:9
leading them, * of joy that the 2Ch 20:27
Jehoram attacked him with his * 2Ch 21:9
it in the chest until it was *. 2Ch 24:10
For the Lord your God is * of 2Ch 30:9
you are to pay the * construction Ez 6:8
But now I told them, "You know * Neh 2:17
angry, and * of love and mercy; Neh 9:17
they took over houses * of good Neh 9:25
so they ate and were * and Neh 9:25
throwing her * support behind Est 9:29-31
His great deeds, and also the * Est 10:2
castles are * of rich treasures. Job 3:14,15
My flesh breaks open, * of pus. Job 7:5
know * well I've not committed? Job 10:4-7
few his days, how * of trouble! Job 14:1
closets jammed * of clothing— yes, Job 27:16
as * of cracks as a leafy booth! Job 27:18
calamity, knowing * well that I Job 30:13
I know * well that Almighty God Job 31:2,3
For I am pent up and * of words, Job 32:18
them their * share of punishment. Job 36:6
Their suggestions are * of the Ps 5:9
Their mouths are * of profanity Ps 10:7
So powerful is his voice; so * Ps 29:4
Your decisions are as * of wisdom Ps 36:6
My wounds are festering and * of Ps 38:5,6
King, for I am as * of words as the Ps 45:1
life, as rich and * as those of Ps 61:6
may the cities be as * of people Ps 72:16
For the land is * of darkness and Ps 74:20
celebrations at * moon, new moon Ps 81:3
They are * of craftiness and Ps 83:3
to forgive; so * of mercy for all Ps 86:5
in getting angry, * of constant Ps 86:15
for my life is * of troubles, and Ps 88:3
I will satisfy him with a * life Ps 91:16
he is slow to get angry and * of Ps 103:8
The earth is * of your riches. Ps 104:24
He has paid a * ransom for his Ps 111:9
them and give them my * respect. Ps 119:15
O Lord, the earth is * of your Ps 119:64
man who has his quiver * of them. Ps 127:5
Barns * to the brim with crops of Ps 144:12-15
slow to get angry, * of love. Ps 145:8
he does, and * of kindness. Ps 145:17
and experience the * terrors of the Pro 1:31
only good men enjoy life to the *; Pro 2:21
want attacks you in * armor. Pro 6:11
Next, his heart is * of Pro 6:14
He has taken a wallet * of money Pro 7:20
The good man's life is * of Pro 13:9
The lazy man is * of excuses. Pro 22:13
seems tasteless to a man who is *; Pro 27:7
the sea is never *, and the water Ecc 1:3-7
enjoy yourself to the *." Ecc 2:1
hard work? Days * of sorrow and Ecc 2:20-23
and idols—the land is * of them! Is 2:8
be * of the knowledge of the Lord. Is 11:9
* of swamps and marshes. Is 14:23
hustling port was * of ships from Is 23:2,3
among them will be * of sense and Is 32:4
his treasure house * of silver, Is 39:2
joy of the Lord shall fill you *; Is 41:16
He will see * justice given to Is 42:3
* of fury toward his foes. Is 42:13
But now he will give * vent to Is 42:14
in one moment, in * measure in one Is 47:9
afflicted ones—* of troubles and in Is 51:21
and make them * of joy within my Is 56:7
high, and get your * share of the Is 58:14
in early spring, * of young plants Is 61:11
I will pay them back in *. Is 65:7
I see * well what they are Is 66:18
and Judah are * of treachery Jer 5:11
"are windbags * of words with no Jer 5:13
Like a coop * of chickens their Jer 5:27
their homes are * of evil plots. Jer 5:27
For all this I am * of the wrath Jer 6:11
* of evil talk against the Lord? Jer 6:28
great and your name is * of power. Jer 10:6
to see and * of good fruit; Jer 11:16
All your jugs will be * of wine. Jer 13:12
any restraint, * of stubbornness Jer 18:12
You are * of selfish greed and Jer 22:17
the false prophets, * of deceit. Jer 23:9
For the land is * of adultery Jer 23:10
penalty in * for all their sins. Jer 23:12
* penalty he decrees against them. Jer 23:20
Because the whole land is * of Jer 50:38
May she be paid in * for all our Jer 51:34,35
I saw that it was * of warnings and Eze 2:9,10
I will repay you in *, and you Eze 7:4
the land is * of bloody crimes. Eze 7:23
all the land is * of murder and Eze 9:9
with broad wings * of many-colored Eze 17:3,4
given them, a land * of milk and Eze 20:15
I have heaped upon you the * Eze 22:31
which she drank was * and large. Eze 23:32
You will suffer the * penalty, Eze 23:49
cedar of Lebanon, * of thick Eze 31:2,3
you until they are glutted and *. Eze 32:4
God says, I am * of fury because Eze 36:6
Lord to a valley * of old, dry Eze 37:1
feet high. The * length of the Eze 40:15
with its branches * of birds— that Dan 4:21
was found to be as * of wisdom and Dan 5:11
so much and are * of wickedness, Dan 9:15
in mourning for three * weeks. Dan 10:2
your * share of those last days." Dan 12:13
You have earned the * reward of Hos 10:13
And Gilead, too, is * of fools Hos 12:11
he is * of kindness, and anxious Joe 2:13
Tread the winepress, for it is * Joe 3:13
"Their beautiful homes are * of Amo 3:10
vision, a basket * of ripe fruit. Amo 8:1
I replied, "A basket * of ripe Amo 8:2
to get angry, and * of kindness; Jon 4:2
He will prosecute them to the *. Mic 6:2
The homes of the wicked are * of Mic 6:10
Muster your defenses, * force, Nah 2:1
of the nations, * of fight and Nah 2:11
WOE TO NINEVEH, City of Blood, * Nah 3:1
and the earth is * of his praise! Hab 3:3
They will not be sinners, * of Zep 3:13
some day be so * of people that she Zec 2:4
choice seed is * of thistles!' Mt 13:27
When the net is *, he drags it up Mt 13:47,48
And everyone ate until *! Mt 14:20
And everyone ate until *—4,000 Mt 15:37,38
until the debt would be paid in *. Mt 18:30
mausoleums—* of dead men's bones, Mt 23:27
up the * measure of their evil. Mt 23:32
and soon it was so * of visitors Mk 3:20
* of water and about to sink. Mk 4:37
until they were *, and afterwards Mk 8:8,9
a fig tree in * leaf, so he went Mk 11:13
surely give him their * respect. Mk 12:6
THEN JESUS, * of the Holy Spirit, Lk 4:1
Then Jesus returned to Galilee, * Lk 4:14
were so * that they began to tear! Lk 5:6
to their own kind for * return! Lk 6:34
Your gift will return to you in * Lk 6:38
dirty—* of greed and wickedness! Lk 11:39
In fact, his barns were * to Lk 12:17
the last penny is paid in *." Lk 12:59
come, so that the house will be *. Lk 14:23
us and was * of loving forgiveness Jn 1:14
when everyone is * and doesn't Jn 2:10
a denarius being a * day's wage. Jn 6:7f
And everyone ate until *! Jn 6:11
claiming it was the * price. Act 5:2
When you claimed this was the * Act 5:3
men, wise and * of the Holy Spirit, Act 6:3
Stephen (a man unusually * of Act 6:5
Stephen, the man so * of faith Act 6:8
Literally, "* of grace and Act 6:8f
But Stephen, * of the Holy Act 7:55
Barnabas was a kindly person, * Act 11:24
stayed there for a * year, teaching Act 11:26
son of the devil, * of every sort Act 13:10
Paul spent his * time preaching and Act 18:5
I know * well that after I leave Act 20:29
Their lives became * of every Rom 1:29
are * of all knowledge and truth. Rom 2:20
Their mouths are * of cursing and Rom 3:14
will give us our * rights as his Rom 8:23
* of peace as you believe in him. Rom 15:13
In this way I have preached the * Rom 15:19
a * understanding of the truth; 1Co 1:5
the Lord knows * well how the human 1Co 3:20
You are * and spiritually 1Co 4:8
no longer has * right to her own 1Co 7:4
no longer has * right to his own 1Co 7:4
but they will be * of glory when 1Co 15:43
again they will be * of strength. 1Co 15:43
into nothing was * of heavenly 2Co 3:11
within us, our hearts were * of 2Co 7:5
You know how * of love and 2Co 8:9
all the others, * of sin, obeying Eph 2:2
will have their * share with the Eph 3:6
of being filled * with Christ. Eph 4:13
healthy and growing and * of love. Eph 4:15,16
Their closed hearts are * of Eph 4:17,18
and through, * of lust and sham. Eph 4:22
his father. Be * of love for Eph 5:2
For though once your heart was * Eph 5:8
now it is * of light from the Lord, Eph 5:8
be a long life, * of blessing. Eph 6:3
All my prayers for you are * of Php 1:3
you, my heart is * of joy, because Php 1:4
in a dark world * of people who are Php 2:15
Always be * of joy in the Lord; Php 4:4
whether it be a * stomach or Php 4:12
happens—always * of the joy of the Col 1:11
you your * portion of all he owns. Col 3:24
gave you great and * assurance that 1Th 1:5
dirty-minded and * of lust, but to 1Th 4:7
you will not be * of sorrow, as 1Th 4:13
as Satan's tool, * of satanic 2Th 2:9
* of the love of Christ Jesus. 1Ti 1:14
he alone is God, and * of wisdom. 1Ti 1:17
orderly, and * of good deeds. 1Ti 3:2
Our lives were * of resentment Tit 3:3
Then God, * of this anger against Heb 3:11
So there is a * complete rest Heb 4:9
For whatever God says to us is * Heb 4:12
that you will get your * reward. Heb 6:11
Dear brothers, is your life * of Jas 1:2
is finally in * bloom, then you Jas 1:4
in character, * and complete. Jas 1:4
It is * of wickedness, and Jas 3:6
pure and * of quiet gentleness. Jas 3:17
it is * of mercy and good deeds. Jas 3:17
he is * of tenderness and mercy. Jas 5:11
big happy family, * of sympathy 1Pe 3:8
our God, who is * of kindness 1Pe 5:10
will be * of joy, and so will we. 1Jn 1:4
See to it that you win your * 2Jn 1:8
towns, all * of lust of every kind Jud 1:7
to enter into their * reward. Rev 14:13
a golden goblet * of obscenities. Rev 17:4

FULL-BREASTED
and * Sol 8:10

FULL-FEATHERED
broad-winged, * eagle came along, Eze 17:7

FULL-FORMED
* and your pubic hair had grown; Eze 16:6,7

FULL-GROWN
and all become * in the Lord—yes, Eph 4:13
FULLEST
So, to the * extent of my Rom 1:15
each of you his * blessings, and Php 1:2
FULLNESS
Of the earth and its *, Deu 33:16
is to give life in all its *. Jn 10:10
us with wonderful *—and all because Tit 3:6
Long to grow up into the * of 1Pe 2:2,3
FULLY
for you know how * I have paid for Gen 30:26
though he was * grown, she laid Gen 38:14
and the Lord will be * pleased. Lev 2:2
will be * appreciated by the Lord. Lev 2:9
declared * cured of his leprosy. Lev 14:9
They are * responsible for the Num 4:26
kind of man—he has obeyed me *. Num 14:24
follow the Lord * armed into Num 32:32
plenty to eat and be * content. Deu 11:15
he imposes is to be * executed. Deu 17:11
"IF YOU * obey all of these Deu 28:1
but your troops, * armed, must lead Jos 1:14
To this they * agreed, and Jos 1:16
of Manasseh—* armed as Moses had Jos 4:12,13
they were * armed and totally 1Ch 12:24-37
These officers, * armed, formed 2Ch 23:10
apply themselves * to their duties 2Ch 31:4
and we will * cooperate." Ez 10:4
heaven, I will be * satisfied, for Ps 17:15
At last I shall be * satisfied; Ps 63:5
The people of Ephraim, though * Ps 78:9
The Lord is * aware of how Ps 94:11
I fed my people until they were * Jer 5:7
people, * armed, mounted for war. Jer 6:23
in tents and have * obeyed Jer 35:10
They are * armed for slaughter; Jer 50:42
you * ready for the battle. Jer 50:42
them, and I will * repay them for Eze 9:10
I will repay them * for their Eze 11:21
you do, I will * repay you for all Eze 16:43
great army * prepared for attack. Eze 23:24
For you will be * repaid for all Eze 23:49
you a mighty host, all * armed. Eze 38:4
them into the furnace, * clothed. Dan 3:21
and oil, to * satisfy your need. Joe 2:19
Then the Lord will go out * armed Zec 14:3
man sitting there, * clothed and Mk 5:15
strong and * armed, guards his Lk 11:21
But it is true—I know him and * Jn 8:55
Jesus * realized all that was Jn 18:4,5
he explained more *, saying, 'God Act 13:35
"I will hear your case * when Act 23:35
They were * aware of God's death Rom 1:32
That's why it * satisfies all of Rom 13:10
Or, "I have * accomplished my Rom 15:19f
believe in Christ and * trust him. Gal 3:5
of it or * know or understand it. Eph 3:18,19
if you * obey the truth you have. Php 3:16
the only condition is that you * Col 1:23
tell it freely and *, and make it Col 4:4
* equipped to do good to everyone. 2Ti 3:17
with true hearts * trusting him to Heb 10:22
the prophets did not * understand. 1Pe 1:10
that we are not * convinced that he 1Jn 4:18
I am * aware that you live in Rev 2:13
and they will be * protected from Rev 7:16
they are * ripe for judgment." Rev 14:18
FULLY-EQUIPPED
will return with a * army far Dan 11:13
FULNESS
Literally, "Lest the * of the Deu 22:9f
FUMED
David *. 1Sa 20:3
FUMES
of smoke and *, as from a furnace, Gen 19:28
FUN
whether in innocent * or Gen 21:9f
a man, and maimed oxen just for *. Gen 49:6
to him, "You are making * of me! Ju 16:10
"You've made * of me three times Ju 16:15
so we can have some * with him!" Ju 16:25,26
Samson and making * of him. Ju 16:27
and entertainment is not much *; 2Sa 19:35
* of him because of his bald head. 2Ki 2:23
A fool's * is being bad; Pro 10:23
a wise man's * is being wise! Pro 10:23
It's no * to be a rebel's father. Pro 17:21
my time having *, because I felt Ecc 8:15
having your own * and business on Is 58:13
take their part in all the *; Jer 31:13
'Come on, let's have some *! Eze 33:30
of the food and fellowship and *. Zec 7:6
on earth having *, satisfying your Jas 5:5
FUND
a special repair * that would not 2Ki 12:8
for the building *, so that we can 2Ch 24:5
FUNDS
These * are to be used primarily Ez 7:17
* from the royal treasury. Ez 7:20
before running out of *. Lk 14:29

of the disciples' * and often Jn 12:6
FUNERAL
great and solemn * service, with a Gen 50:10
him to the * of his father. Gen 50:14
in connection with * rites; Lev 19:28
just attended a *, and were Num 9:6,7
gathered for his * and buried him 1Sa 25:1
the day of the *, and now everyone 2Sa 3:35,36
of incense for him at his *. 2Ch 16:13,14
and ceremony was omitted at his *. 2Ch 21:19
A great * procession precedes Job 21:33
and song. The * pyre has long been Is 30:33
You will wear * clothes and shave Amo 8:10
and heard the * music, he said, Mt 9:23
we played * but you weren't sad.' Mt 11:17
at his heels. A * procession was Lk 7:12
don't like it if we play "*" '! Lk 7:32
FUNERALS
front halves of your heads for *. Deu 14:1
your time at * than at festivals. Ecc 7:2
FUR
think he was wearing a * coat! Gen 25:25
FURIOUS
heard his wife's story, he was *. Gen 39:19
what Gaal was saying, he was *. Ju 9:30
Then Jephthah, * at the taunt of Ju 12:4
But he was * about it and Ju 14:19
Samson was *. Ju 15:3
Abner of this, Abner was *. 2Sa 3:8
David was *. 2Sa 12:5
made me * with your gold calves. 1Ki 14:9
Uzziah was *, and refused to set 2Ch 26:19
being repaired, they became *. Neh 4:7
The king was *, but first Est 1:12
Haman was *, but decided not to Est 3:5,6
or trembling before him, he was *. Est 5:9
husband will be * in his jealousy, Pro 6:34
See, the Lord is sending a * Jer 23:19
you have gone ahead and made me * Jer 25:7
to destroy them in my * anger. Jer 33:5
an entire nation in * rebuke. Eze 5:15
They will carry out my * Eze 25:14
Upon hearing this, the king was * Dan 2:12
turn away your * anger from Dan 9:16
Herod was * when he learned that Mt 2:16
and legal experts were *; Lk 11:53,54
At this, the Council was *, and Act 5:33
out why the crowd had become so *! Act 22:24
Then the * Dragon set out to Rev 12:17
FURIOUSLY
be Jehu, for he is driving so *." 2Ki 9:20
you and deal * with you, and cut Eze 23:25
rushed * at the two-horned ram. Dan 8:6
them. He * destroys their enemies. Nah 1:2
concerned—yes, * angry—because of Zec 8:2
FURNACE
a *, rising from the cities there. Gen 19:28
the sky as from a *, and the whole Ex 19:18
brought out from the Egyptian *. 1Ki 8:51
who repaired the * Tower in Neh 3:11
I refined you in the * of Is 48:10
be thrown into a flaming *." Dan 3:6
will be thrown into a flaming *. Dan 3:11
into a flaming * within the hour. Dan 3:15
*, our God is able to deliver us; Dan 3:17
He commanded that the * be heated Dan 3:19
them into the *, fully clothed. Dan 3:21
a hot fire in the *, the flames Dan 3:22
we throw three men into the *?" Dan 3:24
of the flaming * and yelled: Dan 3:26
Their hearts blaze like a * with Hos 7:6
is coming, burning like a *. Mal 4:1
them into the * and burn them. Mt 13:42
a den of lions, and in a fiery *. Heb 11:34
from some huge *, and the sun and Rev 9:2
FURNACES
We walked from the Tower of * to Neh 12:38
FURNISH
to * you with no more straw. Ex 5:10,11
you must always * us with servants Jos 9:23
ride horses, we'll * the horses! 2Ki 18:23
We will * our own food and Is 4:1
drunken bums. You * lovely music Is 5:12
be required to * the people with Eze 45:17
FURNISHED
And Joseph * food to them in Gen 47:12
and gold he had * for the 1Ki 9:11,12
FURNISHING
plan, and the details of each *. Ex 25:9
and * the Tabernacle." Ex 36:1
their wrists and * them with magic Eze 13:18
FURNISHINGS
all the * of the Tabernacle; Ex 31:7
They are in charge of all the * Num 3:7,8,9
* in the Forest of Lebanon Room. 2Ch 9:20
FURNITURE
*; clasps; Ex 39:33-40
and all the *, to hallow it; Ex 40:9
All the utensils and * used in 1Ki 7:48
for the *, the items in the 1Ch 9:29
FURROWS
He waters the * with abundant Ps 65:10

weeds in the * of the field. Hos 10:4
Row on row of altars—like * in a Hos 12:11
falls into the * of the earth. Jn 12:23,24
FURTHER
he said, "please don't go any *. Gen 18:3,4
me go on and speak * to the Lord, Gen 18:27
Then Abraham went * with his Gen 18:29
Then Moses gave them this * Ex 16:32
went into Moses' tent to talk *. Ex 18:7
The Lord then gave these * Ex 31:12,13
THEN THE LORD gave these * Lev 4:1
Then for a * sixty-six days she Lev 12:5
be quarantined for * observation, Lev 13:11
it there is no * trouble, it can be Lev 13:58
of Israel these * instructions: Lev 15:1
THE LORD GAVE Moses these * Lev 20:1
THE LORD GAVE these * instructions Num 2:1
THESE ARE * instructions from the Num 5:1
THE LORD GAVE Moses these * Num 6:1
he must bring any * offering he Num 6:21
if there were any * complaints Num 17:10
this would ward off * catastrophe Num 17:10
The Lord gave these * Num 18:8
it must then be * purified with Num 31:23
This is what the Lord has * Num 36:6
these * instructions to obey: Deu 27:1
* against our brother Benjamin?" Ju 20:22,23,24
I will give you * instructions 1Sa 10:8
his men went even * into the 1Sa 23:24,25
"There is no * news to send." 2Sa 18:22
to the king for * instructions. 1Ki 2:30
fulfill your * promise to him: that 1Ki 8:25
* details of Baasha's reign are 1Ki 15:31
to this * word from the Lord. 1Ki 22:19
The subclan of Elkanah was * 1Ch 6:25,26,27
These subdivisions were still * 1Ch 23:8,9
carry out your * promise to him 2Ch 6:16
every city as a * safety measure. 2Ch 11:12
Then Hezekiah * strengthened his 2Ch 32:5
Then I pressed *. Neh 5:9
We * agreed that if the heathen Neh 10:31
It * stated that a copy of this Est 8:13
THE * REPLY of Bildad the Shuhite: Job 18:1
THE * REPLY of Bildad the Shuhite: Job 25:1
THE THREE MEN refused to reply * Job 32:1
that they had no * reply, he spoke Job 32:5
there baffled, with no * replies. Job 32:15
sent this * message to King Ahaz: Is 7:10
that there was a * fulfillment of Is 7:14f
This event is * described in Jer 25:12f
THIS * MESSAGE came to me from Eze 7:1
Then this * message came to me Eze 28:11
Then this * word came to me from Eze 36:16
Epiphanes, with a * fulfillment of Dan 8:9f
and future * fulfillment by the Dan 8:23f
of * punishment upon Jerusalem Dan 9:24
But a * fulfillment may lie in Dan 11:32f
these * evils I have spoken of. Amo 4:12
nation would ask for * proof; Mt 12:39,40
heavens, but no * proof will be Mt 16:4
He went on a little * and fell to Mk 14:35
left him without hurting him *. Lk 4:35
To * illustrate the point, he told Lk 15:10
chosen apostles * instructions from Act 1:1
Moreover, he * stated, 'God spoke Act 2:34
threatened them *, and finally let Act 4:21
and await my * instructions." Act 9:6
* meeting to decide this question. Act 15:6
There was no * discussion, and Act 15:12
trying to go * up the coast to Act 27:12
lightened the ship * by throwing Act 27:38
for your good. A * reason for 2Co 2:11
(And there is this * difference. Gal 3:19
And he humbled himself even *, Php 2:8
very lives were * proof to you of 1Th 1:5
Surely we don't need to speak * Heb 6:1
you don't need * instruction Heb 6:2
And your * reward for trusting 1Pe 1:9
I will ask nothing * of you; Rev 2:24,25
must prophesy * about many peoples, Rev 10:11
FURTHERMORE
*, the same Lord God of the Is 22:15,16
God. *, six months ago your Aunt Lk 1:36
he with us. And *, we have seen 1Jn 4:14
FURY
and his face grew dark with *. Gen 4:5
your brother's * is spent, and he Gen 27:44
So he attacked them with great * Ju 15:8
He has destroyed all hope. His * Job 19:11
And then in fierce * he rebukes Ps 2:5
Their * and hatred rise to engulf Ps 55:3
Pour out your * upon them; Ps 69:24
flood of these men's * and pride. Ps 124:4,5
The king's * is like that of a Pro 20:2
His lips are filled with *; Is 30:27
his * is against their armies. Is 34:2
full of * toward his foes. Is 42:13
poured out such * and wrath on his Is 42:25
from the cup of the * of the Lord. Is 51:17
The Lord has poured out his * and Is 51:20
you shall drink no more of my *; Is 51:22

(FURY Con't)
robes of vengeance and of godly *. Is 59:17
* for his foes in distant lands. Is 59:18
In my * I trampled my foes. Is 63:3
to pour out the * of his anger and Is 66:15
* of the "lion from the forest"; Jer 5:6
my anger, yes, my * on this Jer 7:20
Pour out your * on the nations Jer 10:25
but now he has sent the * of your Jer 11:16
before my burning * flashes out Jer 21:12
the brim with my *, and make all Jer 25:15
So I took the cup of * from the Jer 25:17
of the Lord roars with *; Jer 30:23
other gods, causing my * to rise! Jer 32:29
where in my * I will scatter them. Jer 32:37
as my anger and * were poured out Jer 42:18
And so my * and anger boiled Jer 44:6
says: There is * in my face and I Jer 44:11
broken forth in * upon those who Jer 50:28
In his day of awesome * he has Lam 2:1
finest youth. His * is poured out Lam 2:4
So at last I will expend my * on Eze 6:12
Soon I will pour out my * and Eze 7:8,9
me and arousing my * against them? Eze 8:17
I will deal with them in *. Eze 8:18
Will your * against Jerusalem Eze 9:8
"And when I pour out my * by Eze 14:19
"Then at last my * against you Eze 16:42
But the vine was uprooted in * Eze 19:12
I will pour out my * upon them and Eze 20:8
I will pour out my * upon them and Eze 20:13
my * upon you in the wilderness. Eze 20:21
They roused my * as they offered Eze 20:27,28
With might and * I will bring Eze 20:34
Jerusalem and satisfy my *." Eze 21:17
I will pour out my * upon you Eze 21:31
filthy until my * has accomplished Eze 24:13
And I will pour out my * upon Eze 30:15
says, I am full of * because you Eze 36:6
so I poured out my * upon them. Eze 36:18
land of Israel, my * will rise! Eze 38:18
was filled with * and his face Dan 3:19
the strength and * of a whirlwind; Dan 11:40
have made. My * burns against you. Hos 8:5
an angry God? His * is like fire; Nah 1:6
These remarks stung them to *; Lk 4:28
the crowds to * against Stephen, Act 6:12
were stung to * by Stephen's Act 7:54
right to show his * and power Rom 9:22
hurt without my * rising against 2Co 11:29

FUSED
thus he * us together to become Eph 2:15

FUSS
Why make such a * over having no 1Sa 1:8
you make a lot of * over the rich Jas 2:3

FUTILE
Man's * wrath will bring you Ps 76:10
Is it an empty, * life you give Ps 89:47
of how limited and * the thoughts Ps 94:11
everything is *. Ecc 1:2
But I found that this, too, was *. Ecc 2:1
I realized that even wisdom is *. Ecc 2:15
in the long run, it is all so *. Ecc 4:5,6
would then be * and end in Ecc 6:4
down here is * in comparison. Ecc 11:8
All is *, says the Preacher; Ecc 12:8
utterly *. Ecc 12:8
Their ways are * and foolish. Jer 10:2,3
to you, filling you with * hopes. Jer 23:16
and how foolish and * it is. 1Co 3:20

FUTILITY
Before he dies, all this * will Job 15:32

FUTURE
"And in the *, when your Ex 13:14
"If by mistake you or * Num 15:22
I see in the * of Israel, Num 24:15-19
"In the *, when your children Deu 4:25
with them in the *, and with their Deu 5:29
to foretell the * by dreams, and Deu 13:1
* generations of Israel as well. Deu 29:14,15
so that in the *, when your Jos 4:6
stones: "In the *," he said, Jos 4:21
fear that in the * your children Jos 22:24,25
you have promised to do in the *! 1Ch 17:17
are speaking of * generations of my 1Ch 17:17
no need to fear the *. Job 5:21
has a wonderful * ahead of him. Ps 37:37
about the * of these evil men. Ps 73:17
I am recording this so that * Ps 102:18
The wise man saves for the *, Pro 21:20
have a wonderful * ahead of you. Pro 23:17,18
A bright * lies ahead! Pro 24:13,14
For the evil man has no *; Pro 24:19,20
times, and in the * generations no Ecc 1:8-11
the *, so let them enjoy it now. Ecc 3:22
best for the * after he is gone? Ecc 6:12
For who knows the *? Ecc 6:12
A fool knows all about the * and Ecc 10:14
Lord, and seal it up for the *. Is 8:16
to godly men of * generations. Is 8:16
to find out the * by consulting Is 8:19
Can the living find out the * Is 8:19
yet in the * these very lands, Is 9:1
so all of these * events are a Is 29:11
blessedness of the * life for those Is 38:18f
gone by, or what the * holds. Is 41:22
I will tell you the * before it Is 42:9
distant *, as well as to Cyrus. Is 45:13f
what was going to happen in the *. Is 46:9
not in the distant *, but right Is 46:13
try to tell you what the * holds. Is 47:13
what was going to happen in the *. Is 48:3
their fate and * in the stars! Jer 10:2,3
desert, with no hope for the *; Jer 17:6
evil, to give you a * and a hope. Jer 29:11
There is hope for your *, says Jer 31:17
* these papers will be valuable. Jer 32:15
My children have no *; Lam 1:16
This will happen in the distant * Eze 38:15,16
to be made in the *, when it is Eze 43:18
dream what will happen in the *. Dan 2:28
will happen in the *, and this Dan 2:45
Probably the * Antichrist of 2 Dan 7:24f
this prophecy indicated for the *; Dan 8:9f
Epiphanes and * further fulfillment Dan 8:23f
For their * fulfillment see verse Dan 9:25f
to happen in the *: times of great Dan 10:1
is written in the 'Book of the *.' Dan 10:20,21
I will show you what the * holds. Dan 11:2
fulfillment may lie in the *. Dan 11:32f
Obadiah the * of the land of Edom. Ob 1:1
'The * splendor of this Temple Hag 2:8,9
Is a yet * disaster foretold Zec 13:8f
And in the * you will see me, the Mt 26:64
He will tell you about the *. Jn 16:13
but also for the * believers who Jn 17:20
David was looking far into the * Act 2:31
and speaks of * events with as much Rom 4:17
hopefully for that * day when God Rom 8:19
as a foretaste of * glory, also Rom 8:23
of the present and all of the *. 1Co 3:22
to happen in the *, knew everything 1Co 13:2
So, my dear brothers, since * 1Co 15:58
the * he has called you to share. Eph 1:18
called to the same glorious *. Eph 4:4
Their * is eternal loss, for Php 3:19
And the * world we are talking Heb 2:5
warning about the *, Noah believed Heb 11:7
God would give * blessings to his Heb 11:20
the * to look back upon and fear. 2Pe 2:6
THIS BOOK UNVEILS some of the * Rev 1:1
of life—an unending, glorious *. Rev 2:10
you what must happen in the *!" Rev 4:1
of 6,000,000,000 in the near *. Rev 9:16f
prophets what the * holds, has sent Rev 22:6,7

GAAL
At that time * (the son of Ebed) Ju 9:26
"Who is Abimelech," * shouted, Ju 9:28
what * was saying, he was furious. Ju 9:30
telling him, "*, son of Ebed, and Ju 9:31
The next morning as * sat at the Ju 9:35
When * saw them, he exclaimed to Ju 9:36
"No, look over there," * said. Ju 9:37
So * led the men of Shechem into Ju 9:39
and Zebul drove * and his relatives Ju 9:41

GAASH
north side of the mountains of *. Jos 24:30
of Ephraim, north of Mount *. Ju 2:7-9
Hiddai from the brooks of *; 2Sa 23:24-39
Hurai from near the brooks of *; 1Ch 11:26-47

GABA
Gibeon, *, Anathoth, and Almon. Jos 21:17,18

GABBAI
The 968 descendants of * and Neh 11:7,8,9

GABBATHA
The Pavement, but in Hebrew, *." Jn 19:13f

GABRIEL
the river, "*, tell Daniel the Dan 8:16
So * started toward me. Dan 8:17
holy mountain, *, whom I had seen Dan 9:21
Then the angel said, "I am *! Lk 1:19
God sent the angel * to Nazareth, a Lk 1:26
* appeared to her and said, Lk 1:28

GAD
Leah named him * (meaning "My Gen 30:11
Leah's servant-girl:*, Asher. Gen 35:26
* and his sons: Ziphion, Haggi, Gen 46:16,17
shall stamp upon *, but he shall Gen 49:19
Dan, Naphtali,*, Asher. Ex 1:1
* -Eliasaph (son of Num 1:2-15
* -45,650 Num 1:20-46
* Eliasaph (son of Reuel) Num 2:3-31
of Deuel, chief of the tribe of *. Num 7:42-47
and the tribe of * led by Num 10:20
son of Machi, from the tribe of *. Num 13:3-15
The tribe of *: 40,500. Num 26:15-18
clans founded by the sons of *: Num 26:15-18
of Reuben and * (who had large Num 32:1
people of * and Reuben replied. Num 32:25
of the tribes of * and Reuben who Num 32:29
The tribes of * and Reuben said Num 32:31
the tribes of *, Reuben, and the Num 32:33
The people of * built these Num 32:34,35,36
of Reuben and * and the half-tribe Num 34:14,15
*, and the half-tribe of Manasseh. Deu 3:12
To the tribes of Reuben and * I Deu 3:12
The tribes of Reuben and * Deu 3:16
of Reuben and * and the half-tribe Deu 3:18
in Gilead, for the tribe of *; Deu 4:43
tribes of Reuben, *, Asher, Deu 27:13
of Reuben and * and to the Deu 29:8
Concerning the tribe of *, Moses Deu 33:20
"A blessing upon those who help * Deu 33:20
tribes of Reuben, *, and the Jos 1:12,13
The troops of Reuben, *, and the Jos 4:12,13
of Reuben and *, had already Jos 13:8
The Land Given to the Tribe of *: Jos 13:24
* in proportion to its population. Jos 13:24
And of course the tribes of * and Jos 18:7
the territory of the tribe of *; Jos 20:8
tribes of Reuben, *, and Zebulun. Jos 21:7
* gave them four cities with Jos 21:38,39
tribes of Reuben, *, and the Jos 22:1
So the troops of Reuben, *, and Jos 22:9
tribes of Reuben, *, and Manasseh. Jos 22:13
*, and the half-tribe of Manasseh, Jos 22:15
people of Reuben, *, and the Jos 22:21
tribes of Reuben, *, and Manasseh, Jos 22:30
more of war against Reuben and *. Jos 22:33
The people of Reuben and * named Jos 22:34
to the land of * and Gilead. 1Sa 13:7
One day the prophet * told David 1Sa 22:5
Bani from *; 2Sa 23:24-39
of the valley of *, near Jazer; 2Sa 24:5
to the prophet *, who was David's 2Sa 24:11
The Lord said to *, "Tell David 2Sa 24:11
So * came to David and asked him, 2Sa 24:13
That day * came to David and said 2Sa 24:18
as all of Gilead, *, and Reuben; 2Ki 10:32,33
Benjamin, Naphtali, *, Asher. 1Ch 2:1
the descendants of *, who were 1Ch 5:11
*, and the half-tribe of Manasseh. 1Ch 5:18
*, and the half-tribe of Manasseh. 1Ch 5:26
tribes of Reuben, *, and Zebulun. 1Ch 6:63
The tribe of * gave them Ramoth 1Ch 6:80
from the tribe of * also went to 1Ch 12:8-13
of Reuben and * and the half-tribe 1Ch 12:24-37
Then the Lord said to *, David's 1Ch 21:9
Then the angel of the Lord told * 1Ch 21:18
*, and the half-tribe of Manasseh. 1Ch 26:31,32
history written by the prophet *. 1Ch 29:29
and the prophets * and Nathan—who 2Ch 29:25,26
taken over * and all its cities? Jer 49:1
Then *, with the same borders on Eze 48:27,28
named for *, Asher and Naphtali. Eze 48:34
* 12,000 Rev 7:4-8

GADARA
from the city of * came to meet Lk 8:27

GADARENES
the country of the *, two men with Mt 8:28

GADDI
*, son of Susi, from the tribe of Num 13:3-15

GADDIEL
*, son of Sodi, from the tribe of Num 13:3-15

GADFLY
as a heifer, but a * sends her Jer 46:20,21
her running—a * from the north! Jer 46:20,21

GADI
(the son of *) came to Samaria from 2Ki 15:14

GAG
I * at the thought of eating it! Job 6:5,6,7

GAHAM
Reumah:Tebah, *,Tahash, Maacah. Gen 22:24

GAHAR
Hanan, Giddel, *, Re-aiah, Rezin, Ez 2:43-54
Shalmai, Hanan, Giddel, *, Neh 7:46-56

GAIN
I have planned this to * great Ex 14:4
your animals for his personal *. 1Sa 8:16
Would it be any * to him if you Job 22:3
flatteries to * their wicked ends. Ps 5:9
concern is earthly *—these men whom Ps 17:13,14
you *, O Lord, from killing me? Ps 30:9
it will * you many honors. Pro 1:7,8,9
"all who are greedy of *." Pro 1:19f
Ill-gotten * brings no lasting Pro 10:2
such ill-gotten * will turn to Pro 20:17
Dishonest * will never last, so Pro 21:6
the same blanket * warmth from each Ecc 4:11
You Assyrians will * nothing by Is 33:11
to your dishonest * and bloodshed. Eze 22:13
your holiness with lust for *; Eze 28:18
with evil * of violence and fraud. Zep 1:9
are liars seeking their own *; Zep 3:4
What profit is there if you * Mt 16:26
a tremendous *—ten times as much as Lk 19:16
*—five times the original amount. Lk 19:18
And because Felix wanted to * Act 24:27
when we try to * God's blessing and Rom 4:15
good enough to * God's favor by Rom 10:3
but only want * for themselves. Rom 16:18
what I * in this life down here? 1Co 15:32
* of knowing Christ Jesus my Lord. Php 3:8

GAINED
and wrong use of the knowledge *. Gen 11:6f
the wealth he had * in the land of Gen 36:6,7,8
with the booty * from ransacking Deu 2:35,36
He had * his place among The 1Ch 11:20
A little, * honestly, is better Pro 16:8
nation's gods ever * victory over Is 36:18
What have you * by your alliances Jer 2:18
* from murdering and robbery! Hab 2:12
I myself have * much joy and Phm 1:7

GAINING
works hard to keep * more riches, Ecc 4:8
and what profit is there in * Lk 9:25
a different way of * God's favor Gal 3:18

GAINS
which its owner * his livelihood. Deu 24:6
He who * by oppressing the poor Pro 22:16
will long enjoy their hard-won *. Is 65:21,22
godless nations' * will turn to Hab 2:13
man benefit if he * the whole world Mk 8:36

GAIUS
dragging along * and Aristarchus, Act 19:29
from Thessalonica; *, from Derbe; Act 20:4
brother. * says to say "hello" Rom 16:23
any of you except Crispus and *. 1Co 1:14
To: Dear *, whom I truly love. 3Jn 1:1

GALAL
Bakbakkar, Heresh, *, 1Ch 9:15,16
son of *, son of Jeduthun). 1Ch 9:15,16
of Shammua, son of *, son of Neh 11:15,16,17

GALATIA
Phrygia and *, because the Holy Act 16:6
going through * and Phrygia Act 18:23
I gave to the churches in *). 1Co 16:1
To: The churches of *. Gal 1:1
* was a province in what is now Gal 1:1f
Crescens has gone to *, Titus to 2Ti 4:10
throughout Pontus, *, Cappadocia, 1Pe 1:1

GALATIANS
OH, FOOLISH *! Gal 3:1

GALAXIES
formed, and all the * of stars. Ps 33:6

GALBANUM
onycha, *, and pure frankincense, Ex 30:34

GALE
flounders in the heavy eastern *, Eze 27:26
But soon a * swept down upon Jn 6:18,19
and let the ship run before the *. Act 27:14,15

GALEED
language, and "*" in Jacob's. Gen 31:47,48

GALILEAN
Literally, "with Jesus the *." Mt 26:69f
for we can tell by your * Mt 26:73
They and many other * women who Mk 15:41
from the * village of Nazareth. Lk 2:4
"Is he then a *?" Lk 23:6
"Are you a wretched * too? Jn 7:52

GALILEANS
But the * welcomed him with Jn 4:45

GALILEE
tip of the Sea of *, and then Num 34:10,11
western shores of the Lake of *; Jos 12:3
extending as far as the Lake of *; Jos 13:27,28
* in the hill country of Naphtali; Jos 20:7
Kedesh, in * (a City of Refuge), Jos 21:32
in the land of * to King Hiram of 1Ki 9:11,12
*, and all the land of Naphtali; 2Ki 15:29
them Kedesh in *, Hammon, and 1Ch 6:76
these very lands, * and Northern Is 9:1
great city north of the Sea of *; Jer 49:30f
tip of the Sea of *, and down along Eze 47:18
* instead, and lived in Nazareth. Mt 2:22
Then Jesus went from * to the Mt 3:13
to Nazareth in *; Mt 4:12,13
*, close to Zebulun and Naphtali. Mt 4:12,13
River, and Upper * where so many Mt 4:15,16
beside the Lake of *, he saw two Mt 4:18
Jesus traveled all through * Mt 4:23
the borders of * so that sick folk Mt 4:24
went—people from *, and the Ten Mt 4:25
to his home town, Nazareth in *, Mt 13:53,54
sovereignty being * and Peraea. Mt 14:1f
to the Sea of *, and climbed a hill Mt 15:29
they were still in *, Jesus told Mt 17:22,23
address, he left * and circled back Mt 19:1
prophet from Nazareth up in *." Mt 21:11
go to *, and meet you there." Mt 26:32
for both of you are from *." Mt 26:69
had come down from * with Jesus to Mt 27:55
is going to * to meet them there. Mt 28:7
at once for *, to meet me there." Mt 28:10
disciples left for *, going to the Mt 28:16
from Nazareth in *, and was Mk 1:9
Jesus went to * to preach God's Mk 1:14
of the Sea of *, he saw Simon and Mk 1:16
through that entire area of *. Mk 1:28
the province of *, preaching in the Mk 1:39
from all over *, Judea, Jerusalem, Mk 3:7,8
and the leading citizens of *. Mk 6:21
Then he left * and went to the Mk 7:24
Sea of * by way of the Ten Towns. Mk 7:31
disciples now left * and went out Mk 8:27
traveled through * where he tried Mk 9:30,31
this was his final farewell to *. Mk 10:1f
will go to * and meet you there." Mk 14:28
one of them, for you are from *!" Mk 14:70
when he was up in *, and had come Mk 15:41
'Jesus is going ahead of you to *. Mk 16:7
a village in *, to a virgin, Mary, Lk 1:26
returned home to Nazareth in *. Lk 2:39
Herod, over *; Lk 3:1
Herod, governor of *, for marrying Lk 3:19,20
Then Jesus returned to *, full of Lk 4:14
a city in *, and preached there in Lk 4:31
village in all * and Judea, as well Lk 5:17
of the cities and villages of * Lk 8:1
country across the lake from *. Lk 8:26
some Jews from * as they were Lk 13:1
sinners than other men from *?" Lk 13:2
the border between * and Samaria, Lk 17:11
disciples, for both are from *." Lk 22:59
over Judea, from * to Jerusalem!" Lk 23:5
* was under Herod's jurisdiction; Lk 23:7
*, stood in the distance watching. Lk 23:49
the women from * followed and saw Lk 23:55
you back in *—that the Messiah Lk 24:6,7
next day Jesus decided to go to *. Jn 1:43
village of Cana in *, and Jesus Jn 2:1
This miracle at Cana in * was Jn 2:11
and returned to the province of *. Jn 4:3
two days' stay he went on into *. Jn 4:43,44
journey through * he arrived at the Jn 4:46,47
from Judea and was traveling in *. Jn 4:46,47
in * after coming from Judea. Jn 4:54
over the Sea of *, also known as Jn 6:1
AFTER THIS, JESUS went to *, going Jn 7:1
So he remained in *. Jn 7:9
Will the Messiah come from *? Jn 7:41,42
prophets will come from *!" Jn 7:52
disciples beside the Lake of *. Jn 21:1
Cana in *, my brother James and I Jn 21:2
and said, "Men of *, why are you Act 1:11
"For these men are all from *, Act 2:7
taxation, there was Judas of *. Act 5:37
throughout Judea, * and Samaria, Act 9:31
with John the Baptist in *. Act 10:36,37
to Jerusalem from *—these men have Act 13:31

GALL
parts, also the * bladder and two Ex 29:13
insides, also the * bladder and the Ex 29:22
on them, and the * bladder. Lev 3:3,4,5
on them, and the * bladder, as a Lev 3:9,10,11
on them, and the * bladder. Lev 3:15,16
on them, and the * bladder, and Lev 4:9
loin-fat, and the * bladder—all Lev 7:4
inner organs, the * bladder, the Lev 8:25
fat, kidneys, and * bladder from Lev 9:10
the kidneys and * bladders. Lev 9:19
point comes out from his *. Job 20:25
Literally, "the * of Act 8:23f

GALLIM
* named Palti (the son of Laish). 1Sa 25:44
scream in terror, O people of *. Is 10:30

GALLIO
But when * became governor of Act 18:12
make his defense, * turned to his Act 18:14
But * couldn't have cared less. Act 18:17

GALLON
had a twelve thousand * capacity. 1Ki 7:26
will not produce a * of juice! Is 5:10
bushel of flour with half a * of Eze 46:14,15

GALLONS
and 1½ * of olive oil. Ex 30:24
and 96 * of pure olive oil. 1Ki 5:11
and contained 240 * of water. 1Ki 7:38
time tomorrow two * of flour or 2Ki 7:1
of flour or four * of barley grain 2Ki 7:1
So it was true that two * of 2Ki 7:16
of flour and four * of barley were 2Ki 7:16
1,225 bushels of wheat; 990 * of Ez 7:22
scales, honest bushels, honest * Eze 45:10
and twenty-one * of olive oil—1½ Eze 45:24
oil—1½ * to go with each bushel. Eze 45:24
And he shall bring 1½ * of olive Eze 46:5
he is to bring 1½ * of olive oil. Eze 46:7
and 1½ * of oil with each bushel. Eze 46:11
When you came to draw fifty * Hag 2:16,17
'My debt is 850 * of olive oil,' Lk 16:5,6
perhaps twenty to thirty * each. Jn 2:6

GALLOP
as the horses * through your broken Eze 26:10

GALLOPING
and a loud * of horses and the 2Ki 7:6

GALLOWS
a * on which he will be hanged; Ez 6:11
a 75-foot-high *, and in the Est 5:14
and he ordered the * built. Est 5:14
from the * he was building. Est 6:4
ordered a 75-foot * constructed, to Est 7:9
* because he tried to destroy you. Est 8:7
ten sons be hanged upon the *." Est 9:13
and his sons were hanged on the *. Est 9:24,25

GAMAD
towers are manned by men from *. Eze 27:11

GAMALIEL
* (son of Dedahzur) Num 1:2-15
Leader: Elishama * Num 2:3-31
*, son of Pedahzur, prince of the Num 7:54-59
led by * the son of Pedahzur; Num 10:23
a Pharisee named * (an expert on Act 5:34
in Jerusalem under *, at whose feet Act 22:3

GAMBLED
And the soldiers * for his Lk 23:34

GAMBLING
Wealth from * quickly disappears; Pro 13:11

GAME
A lazy man won't even dress the * Pro 12:27
trapped, fair * for all, with no Is 42:22
pasture—helpless * too weak to keep Lam 1:6
a whirlwind—a dangerous *! Hos 12:1
They make a * of luring unstable 2Pe 2:14

GAMUL
Twenty-second, the group led by *; 1Ch 24:7-18

GANG
to the occasion, a * of sex Ju 19:22
and give it to a * who suddenly 1Sa 25:11
He had become the leader of a * 1Ki 11:24
Then a whole * of worthless 2Ch 13:7
The enemy, this * of evil men, Ps 22:16
* is a shame to his father. Pro 28:7
Play," but now a * of murderers. Is 1:21
to * up at the city's brothels. Jer 5:7

GANGS
In those days bandit * of Moabites 2Ki 13:20,21
wicked men, these * of criminals. Ps 64:1
Her citizens are * of robbers, Hos 6:9

GAP
could stand in the * and defend you Eze 22:30

GAPING
These 'comforters' have * jaws Job 16:10
hooting from the * windows; Zep 2:14

GARAGED
the chariots were *, though some, 2Ch 1:14

GARB
replace his prison *, and for as 2Ki 25:29

GARBAGE
hungry from the * dump, and sets Ps 113:7
on the * dump beyond the gate! Jer 22:19
through the * dumps for bread. Lam 1:19
You have made us as refuse and * Lam 3:45
now scratch in * pits for food. Lam 4:5
and another to throw * into? Rom 9:21
are like dirt under foot, like *. 1Co 4:13
in the kitchen or to put * in. 2Ti 2:20

GARDEN
Then the Lord God planted a * in Gen 2:8
in the * the man he had formed. Gen 2:8
trees there in the *, trees Gen 2:9
At the center of the * he placed Gen 2:9
flowed through the * to water it; Gen 2:10
the man in the * of Eden as its Gen 2:15
any fruit in the * except fruit Gen 2:16,17
"None of the fruit in the *? Gen 3:1
of the * that we are not to eat. Gen 3:2,3
of the Lord God walking in the *; Gen 3:8
forever from the * of Eden, and Gen 3:23
at the east of the * of Eden, with Gen 3:24
the whole section was like the * Gen 13:10
Literally, "the * of Jehovah." Gen 13:10f
family had its own home and *. 1Ki 4:25
"I want it for a *," the king 1Ki 21:2
was buried in the * of his palace 2Ki 21:18
in a crypt in the * of Uzza, and 2Ki 21:26
double walls near the king's *. 2Ki 25:4,5
to the king's * and the stairs that Neh 3:15
in the courtyard of the palace *. Est 1:5
into the palace * as Haman stood up Est 7:7
king returned from the palace *. Est 7:8
his branches spread across the *. Job 8:16
the Lord's own *, and are under his Ps 92:13
is like a private *, a spring that Sol 4:12
You are a * fountain, a well of Sol 4:15
come, south wind, blow upon my * Sol 4:16
Let him come into his * and eat Sol 4:16
KING SOLOMON: "I am here in my *, Sol 5:1
gone down to his *, to his spice Sol 6:2
tree or a * without water. Is 1:30
Leading you down the * path to Is 3:12
your own farm and * and water, Is 36:16
as beautiful as the * of Eden. Is 51:3
*, like an ever-flowing spring. Is 58:11
tree, or like a * in early spring, Is 61:11
a tree in the *, feasting there on Is 66:17
like a helpless scarecrow in a *! Jer 10:5
be like a watered *, and all their Jer 31:12
back of the palace * and across the Jer 39:4
of leaves and branches in a *! Lam 2:6
You were in Eden, the * of God; Eze 28:13
than any other in the * of God; Eze 31:8
land has become like Eden's *! Eze 36:35
holy grounds, is * area belonging Eze 48:18
They will be a watered * and Hos 14:7
fair as Eden's * in all its beauty, Joe 2:3

(GARDEN Con't)
mint leaf in your *, but ignore the Mt 23:23
Then Jesus brought them to a * Mt 26:36
grove called the * of Gethsemane, Mk 14:32
a fig tree in his * and came again Lk 13:6
tiny mustard seed planted in a *; Lk 13:19
Literally "a *." Jn 19:41f
made the * grow in your hearts. 1Co 3:6
You are God's *, not ours; 1Co 3:9
find the answer in your own *! 1Co 15:36
by Satan in the * of Eden. 2Co 11:3
underwent in the *, that caused Heb 5:7f

GARDENER
as its *, to tend and care for it. Gen 2:15
Finally he told his * to cut it Lk 13:7
one more chance,' the * answered. Lk 13:8
true Vine, and my Father is the *. Jn 15:1
She thought he was the *. Jn 20:15

GARDENING
their pottery, *, and planting; 1Ch 4:23

GARDENS
And fruitful * by the riverside; Num 24:3-9
to eat from the * and grain fields Jos 5:11,12
homes, vineyards, *, parks and Ecc 2:4,5,6
of flowers in the * of Engedi. Sol 1:14
"O my beloved, living in the *, Sol 8:13
where once the * grew, for thorns Is 7:25
idols in many * and burning incense Is 65:3
and eat from your own * there. Jer 31:5
near the king's * (for the city was Jer 52:7
vineyards and * and eat their crops Amo 9:14
and the * began to grow again. Jas 5:18

GAREB
* from Ithra; 2Sa 23:24-39
* from Ithra; 1Ch 11:26-47
and from the Hill of * at the Jer 31:38,39

GARLAND
Literally, "a fair * and Pro 1:7,8,9f

GARLIC
and melons, leeks, onions, and *! Num 11:4,5

GARMENT
a woolen or linen * or fabric, or Lev 13:47,48
it out from the * or leather goods Lev 13:56
leprosy in a * or anything made of Lev 13:59
may appear: in a * or in a house, Lev 14:55
And they shall spread the * Deu 22:17,18
a widow's * in pledge of her debt. Deu 24:17
a field and threw a * over him. 2Sa 20:12
wear out like a *, and the people Is 51:6
"And who would patch an old * Mt 9:16
and put his own * on him again, and Mt 27:31
It is like patching an old * Mk 2:21
* to make a patch for an old one. Lk 5:36
Not only will the new * be Lk 5:36
but the old * will look worse with Lk 5:36

GARMENTS
with * made from skins of animals. Gen 3:21
Then Israel tore his * and put on Gen 37:34
to God—beautiful * that will lend Ex 28:2
to make the * that will set him Ex 28:3
They shall also make special * Ex 28:4
sons with these *, and then Ex 28:41
"These sacred * of Aaron shall Ex 29:29
the beautifully made, holy * for Ex 31:10
priest, and the * for his sons, so Ex 31:10
The holy * for Aaron the priest, Ex 35:10-19
its equipment, and for the holy *. Ex 35:21
made beautiful * of blue, purple, Ex 39:1
and scarlet cloth—* to be used Ex 39:1
for Aaron's sacred *, in accordance Ex 39:1
tailored * to be worn while Ex 39:41
and the holy * for Aaron the priest Ex 39:41
and clothe Aaron with the holy * Ex 40:13
his linen outer * and clean out the Lev 6:10
with their *, the anointing oil, Lev 8:1
take off the linen * he wore when Lev 16:23
on the holy linen *, and make Lev 16:32
the special *—must not let his hair Lev 21:10
Aaron's priestly * from him and put Num 20:26
the priestly * from Aaron and put Num 20:28
to purify all your * and everything Num 31:20
in sanctified * and singing the 2Ch 20:21
loaded with money, *, and jewels 2Ch 20:25
and turn, and my * bind about me. Job 30:18
before him clothed in sacred *. Ps 29:2
me gay and festive * to rejoice in Ps 30:11
She makes belted linen * to sell Pro 31:24
the scent of your * is like the Sol 4:11
moth shall destroy them like *; Is 51:8
For he has clothed me with * of Is 61:10
with his magnificent * of crimson? Is 63:1
rags and discarded * which he took Jer 38:11
Put on * of mourning; Jer 49:3
and beautiful * and sit on the Eze 26:16
robed in linen *, with a belt of Dan 10:5,6
at your hearts and not your *." Joe 2:13
* worn at times of mourning. Jon 3:4,5
and he can bleach the dirtiest *! Mal 3:2
and threw their * over the colt Mt 21:7
they put his * into four piles, one Jn 19:23,24
other * Dorcas had made for them. Act 9:39
all these rotten * of anger, Col 3:8
their * with the world's filth; Rev 3:4
And to purchase from me white *, Rev 3:18
He was clothed with * dipped in Rev 19:13

GARMITE
of Keilah the *, and another was 1Ch 4:19

GARRISON
the oak beside the * at Shechem, Ju 9:6
where the * of the Philistines is. 1Sa 10:5
the * of the Philistines at Geba. 1Sa 13:3,4
the Philistine * and warned his 1Sa 13:3,4
to the * of the Philistines." 1Sa 14:1
To reach the Philistine *, 1Sa 14:4
then he placed a * of his troops 1Ch 18:6
of the Roman * that all Jerusalem Act 21:31
commander of the *, came and took Act 24:7
of Lysias, the * commander, and Act 24:22

GARRISONS
David placed several army * in 2Sa 8:6
and then placed * throughout Edom, 2Sa 8:14
He put * in Edom and forced the 1Ch 18:13
He placed * in all of the 2Ch 17:2

GASEOUS
even, "over the dark, * mass." Gen 1:2f

GASP
who pass by will * and shake their Jer 18:16
going by will * with astonishment Jer 19:8
be appalled, and * at the sight. Jer 49:17

GASPING
it is the cry of my people * for Jer 4:31

GATAM
Teman, Omar, Zepho, *, Kenaz, Gen 36:10,11,12
clan of *,The clan of Amalek. Gen 36:15,16
Teman, Omar, Zephi, *, Kenaz, 1Ch 1:36

GATE
of the men of Heth at the city *. Gen 23:17,18
Literally, "came into the * of Gen 34:20f
The bases and the drapes at the * Ex 39:33-40
threw it in front of the city *. Jos 8:29
wounded all the way to the city *. Ju 9:40
Abimelech stormed the city * to Ju 9:44
night at the city * to capture him Ju 16:2
just outside the *, they talked to Ju 18:15,16
Literally, "the *" of the city, Ru 4:1f
seat beside the * and his neck was 1Sa 4:18
aside at the city * as if to speak 2Sa 3:27
and went out to the * of the city; 2Sa 15:2
So he stood at the * of the city 2Sa 18:4
David was sitting at the * of 2Sa 18:24
over the *, crying as he went. 2Sa 18:33
(The well was near the city *. 2Sa 23:15
threshing floor near the city *. 1Ki 22:10
the traffic at the *, but he was 2Ki 7:17
trampled him to death at the *! 2Ki 7:20
When Jehu entered the * of the 2Ki 9:31
of the city *, and to leave them 2Ki 10:8
its wall from the * of Ephraim to 2Ki 14:13
to the Corner *, a distance of 2Ki 14:13
that the upper * of the Temple of 2Ki 15:34,35
side as one enters the city *. 2Ki 23:8
Arabah through a * that lay between 2Ki 25:4,5
for the eastern royal *. 1Ch 9:17,18
well beside the *, and when he 1Ch 11:17
The responsibility of the east * 1Ch 26:14,15
of the north * to his son 1Ch 26:14,15
of the south * to Obed-edom and 1Ch 26:14,15
of the west * and the 1Ch 26:16
the Shallecheth * on the upper 1Ch 26:16
daily to the east *, four to the 1Ch 26:17
four to the north *, four to the 1Ch 26:17
four to the south *, and two to 1Ch 26:17
day to the west *, four to the 1Ch 26:18
near the Samaria *, and all the 2Ch 18:9
a third will be at the Lower *. 2Ch 23:5,6
way from the Upper * to the palace, 2Ch 23:20
made and set outside the Temple *. 2Ch 24:7,8
* of Ephraim to the Corner Gate. 2Ch 25:23
gate of Ephraim to the Corner *. 2Ch 25:23
at the Corner *, and the Valley 2Ch 26:9
*, and at the turning of the wall. 2Ch 26:9
He built the Upper * of the 2Ch 27:3
at the East *, was put in charge of 2Ch 31:14,15
then to the Fish *, and around 2Ch 33:14
through the Valley * toward the Neh 2:13
over to the Dung * to see the Neh 2:13
Then we went to the Fountain * Neh 2:14,15
and entered again at the Valley *. Neh 2:14,15
then they rebuilt the Sheep *, Neh 3:1
The Fish * was built by the sons Neh 3:3
The Old * was repaired by Joiada Neh 3:6
built the Valley *, hung the doors, Neh 3:13
1,500 feet of wall to the Dung *. Neh 3:13
The Dung * was repaired by Neh 3:14
district, repaired the Fountain *. Neh 3:15
Water * and the Projecting Tower. Neh 3:26
beyond the Horse *, each one doing Neh 3:28
the gatekeeper of the East *. Neh 3:29
Guild Hall, opposite the Muster *; Neh 3:31
from that corner to the Sheep *. Neh 3:32
front of the Water * and requested Neh 8:1
front of the Water *, and read from Neh 8:1
*, or at the Ephraim Gate Plaza. Neh 8:16
Gate, or at the Ephraim * Plaza. Neh 8:16
toward the Dung * consisted of half Neh 12:31,32
at the Fountain * they went Neh 12:37
then they went to the Water * on Neh 12:37
from the Ephraim * to the Old Gate, Neh 12:39
Gate to the Old *, passed the Fish Neh 12:39
passed the Fish * and the Tower of Neh 12:39
the * of the Tower of the Hundred; Neh 12:39
* and stopped at the Prison Gate. Neh 12:39
Gate and stopped at the Prison *. Neh 12:39
at the palace *—became angry at the Est 2:21
Then he stood outside the * of Est 4:2
there at the *, not standing up or Est 5:9
king's *, refusing to bow to me." Est 5:13
out to the city * and took my place Job 29:7
with their enemies in the *." Ps 127:5f
Heshbon by the * of Bath-rabbim. Sol 7:4
first at the * where the king goes Jer 17:19
by the east * of the city. Jer 19:1
at Benjamin * near the Temple. Jer 20:2
on the garbage dump beyond the *! Jer 22:19
to the Corner * at the northwest; Jer 31:38,39
* on the east side of the city; Jer 31:40
near the door of the New *. Jer 36:10
the Benjamin *, a sentry arrested Jer 37:13
rushed out to the * of Benjamin Jer 38:8
sat in triumph at the middle *. Jer 39:3
out through the * between the two Jer 39:4
going out by the * between the two Jer 52:7
of the north *, where the large Eze 8:3
north of the altar *, in the Eze 8:5
He brought me to the north * of Eze 8:14
north *, each one with his sword. Eze 9:2
them to the east * of the Temple. Eze 10:19
over to the east * of the Temple, Eze 11:1
for a sword glitters at every *; Eze 21:15
Literally, "the * of the Eze 26:2f
standing beside the Temple *, Eze 40:3
to the south * and measured the Eze 40:24
to the north * of the inner wall, Eze 40:35
the inner northern * is for the Eze 40:45
"This * shall remain closed; Eze 44:2
the inner eastern * shall be opened Eze 46:12
"Each city * will be named in Eze 48:30,31
at the farthest * of Jerusalem, Zep 1:10
will reach across to the city *. Zec 14:5
the way from the * of Benjamin over Zec 14:10
site of the old *, then to the Zec 14:10
then to the Corner *, and from the Zec 14:10
entered only through the narrow *! Mt 7:13
is broad, and its * is wide Mt 7:13
Later, out by the *, another girl Mt 26:71
as he approached the village *. Lk 7:12
near the Sheep *, was Bethesda Jn 5:2
walk through the * into a Jn 10:1
a shepherd comes through the *. Jn 10:2
The gatekeeper opens the * for Jn 10:3
"I am the * for the sheep," he Jn 10:7
Yes, I am the *. Jn 10:9
Those who come in by way of the * Jn 10:9
while Peter stood outside the *. Jn 18:16
at the *, and she let Peter in. Jn 18:16
beside the Temple *—the one called Act 3:2
*—as was his custom every day. Act 3:2
at The Beautiful *, they were Act 3:10
outside at the *, inquiring Act 10:17
before the prison *, when suddenly Act 12:6
came to the iron * to the street, Act 12:10
He knocked at the door in the *, Act 12:13
—each * from a single pearl! Rev 21:21

GATEKEEPER
Shallum (the chief *), Akkub, 1Ch 9:17,18
who was the * at the East Gate, was 2Ch 31:14,15
choir member, *, Temple attendant, Ez 7:24
the * of the East Gate. Neh 3:29
the * to watch for his return. Mk 13:34
the gate. The * opens the gate for Jn 10:3

GATEKEEPERS
The * were Shallum (the chief 1Ch 9:17,18
The four head *, all Levites, 1Ch 9:26
and he assigned the * to their 2Ch 8:14
prophet. The * guarded the gates, 2Ch 35:15
From the descendants of the * (the Ez 2:40,41,42
and the singers, the *, the Ez 2:70
Levites, singers, *, and Temple Ez 7:7,8,9
Of the *, Shallum, Telem, and Uri. Ez 10:24
had appointed the *, singers, and Neh 7:1
(all of whom were *), 138. Neh 7:43,44,45
The priests, the Levites, the *, Neh 7:73
the Levites; the *; Neh 10:28
the *, and the choir singers. Neh 10:39,40
There were also 172 *, led by Neh 11:19
The * who had charge of the Neh 12:25
of the singers and *, who assisted Neh 12:45
the choir, the *, and the Levites. Neh 12:47
members of the choir, and the *. Neh 13:5

GATEMEN
They may be Temple guards and *; Eze 44:11

GATEPOSTS
two *, right out of the ground. Ju 16:3

GATES

with high walls and barred *. Deu 3:5
and upon your *, so that as long Deu 11:20
and opens its * to you, then all Deu 20:11
taken outside the * and stoned to Deu 22:23,24
caused by your enemies at your *. Deu 28:56,57
dusk as the city * were about to Jos 2:5
meanwhile, the city * were kept Jos 2:7
THE * OF Jericho were kept tightly Jos 6:1
die, and when the * were set up, Jos 6:26
the city * were left wide open. Jos 8:17
this does not mean via the city *. Ju 1:24f
Marched through the *! Ju 5:11
sat at the city *, discussing Ju 9:35
it, barricaded the *, and climbed Ju 9:51
out to the city * and lifted them, Ju 16:3
He lives just inside the city *. 1Sa 9:12,13
were entering the * they saw Samuel 1Sa 9:14
as far as Gath and the * of Ekron. 1Sa 17:52
The Ammonites defended the * of 2Sa 10:7,8
back to the city *, the men on the 2Sa 11:23
sat at the city *, and as the news 2Sa 19:8,9,10
sixty walled cities with bronze *; 1Ki 4:8-19
*, his youngest son, Segub, died. 1Ki 16:34
As he arrived at the * of the 1Ki 17:10
lepers sitting outside the city *. 2Ki 7:3
they opened the * each morning. 1Ch 9:27
at the * of the city of Medeba. 1Ch 19:9
doors in the * and for the clamps; 1Ch 22:3
at the various * without regard to 1Ch 26:13
walls and installing barred *. 2Ch 8:5
the gatekeepers to their *. 2Ch 8:14
walls and * to protect himself: 2Ch 11:5-10
with walls, towers, *, and bars." 2Ch 14:7
The guards at the Temple * kept 2Ch 23:19
at the Temple * by the Levites on 2Ch 34:9
collected at the *, he found an old 2Ch 34:14
The gatekeepers guarded the *, 2Ch 35:15
torn down, and the * are burned." Neh 1:3
and the * have been burned down." Neh 2:3
beams and for the * of the fortress Neh 2:8
see the broken walls and burned *. Neh 2:13
it lies in ruins and its * are Neh 2:17
the doors of the *— they sent me a Neh 6:1
the doors in the * and had Neh 7:1
open the Jerusalem * until well Neh 7:3
collection centers at the * were: Neh 12:25
the people, the *, and the wall. Neh 12:30
commanded that the * of the city be Neh 13:19
to guard the * so that no Neh 13:19
and to guard the * in order to Neh 13:22
outside the palace *, and heard Est 4:6
at the palace *, who had plotted to Est 6:1
Has the location of the * of Job 38:17,18
Literally, "in the * of the Ps 9:14f
* and rejoice that you have Ps 9:14
Open up, O ancient *, and let the Ps 24:7
Yes, open wide the * and let the Ps 24:9
as they enter in the palace *! Ps 45:15
Go through his open * with great Ps 100:4
For he broke down their prison * Ps 107:16
Open the * of the Temple Ps 118:19
Literally, "the * of Ps 118:19f
Those * are the way into the Ps 118:20
beside the city *, deciding all the Ps 122:5
For he has fortified your * Ps 147:13
She is standing at the city * and Pro 8:1
for me daily at my *, or waits for Pro 8:34
her works praise her in the *." Pro 31:31f
valleys and crowd against your *. Is 22:6,7
The city is left in ruins; its * Is 24:12
Open the * to everyone, for Is 26:2
to the last before your *. Is 28:6
open the * and come out, and I Is 36:16
march outside its *, nor build up Is 37:33
now I must enter the * of Sheol. Is 38:10
God shall open the * of Babylon Is 45:1
to him; the * shall not be shut Is 45:1
the city * of brass and iron bars. Is 45:2
God—will no longer enter your *. Is 52:1
your * and walls of shining gems. Is 54:12
Your * will stay wide open Is 60:11
and your * "Praise." Is 60:18
thrones at the * of the city and Jer 1:15
iron pillar and heavy * of brass. Jer 1:18
closed their * against the enemy. Jer 13:19
I will sift you at the * of your Jer 15:7
and stand in the * of Jerusalem, Jer 17:19
each of the other *, and say to Jer 17:19
through these * of Jerusalem, just Jer 17:27
then I will set fire to these *. Jer 17:27
they need neither walls nor *. Jer 49:31
houses and broken down the city *. Jer 51:30
and her high * shall be burned; Jer 51:58
the city * are silent, her Lam 1:4
Jerusalem's * are useless. Lam 2:9
could enter through Jerusalem's *! Lam 4:12
men sit no longer in the city *; Lam 5:14
the *, shouting for the kill; Eze 21:22
*, pulling chariots behind them. Eze 26:10
will be three *, one named for Eze 48:30,31
1½-mile wall, the * will be named Eze 48:32
* of Simeon, Issachar and Zebulun; Eze 48:33
through their * and trap them in Hos 11:6
that locked the * of Damascus, and Amo 1:5
at Jerusalem's * to punish her. Mic 1:9
you through the * of your cities of Mic 2:13
enter the * of the land of Nimrod. Mic 5:6
The river * are open! Nah 2:6
as women. The * of your land will Nah 3:13
The city * were closed on the Mt 24:20f
slipped inside the * of the High Mk 14:54
get within the Kingdom's *." Lk 18:16,17
night, opened the * of the jail and Act 5:19
opened the *, no one was there!" Act 5:23
were watching the * of the city day Act 9:24
at the city * before the crowds. Act 14:13
the * were closed behind him. Act 21:30
guards at the city * to catch me; 2Co 11:32
And God will open wide the * of 2Pe 1:11
twelve * guarded by twelve angels. Rev 21:12
of Israel were written on the *. Rev 21:12
There were three * on each Rev 21:13
the city and its * and walls. Rev 21:15
The twelve * were made of pearls Rev 21:21
glory to it. Its * never close; Rev 21:25
in through the * of the city, and Rev 22:14

GATEWAY

He stayed that night at the * of 2Sa 11:9
But the * to Life is small, and Mt 7:14

GATH

remained in Gaza, *, and Ashdod. Jos 11:22
Gaza, Ashdod, Ashkelon, * Jos 13:2-7
The decision was to take it to *. 1Sa 5:8
But when the Ark arrived at *, 1Sa 5:9
Gaza, Ashkelon, *, and Ekron. 1Sa 6:17
between Ekron and *, which had been 1Sa 7:14
champion from *, came out of the 1Sa 17:4-7
far as * and the gates of Ekron. 1Sa 17:52
and went to King Achish of *. 1Sa 21:10
SO DAVID LEFT * and escaped to the 1Sa 22:1
to live at * under the protection 1Sa 27:2,3
to *, so he quit hunting for him. 1Sa 27:4
alive to come to * and tell where 1Sa 27:11
Hide it from the cities of * and 2Sa 1:20
of Obed-edom, who had come from *. 2Sa 6:10
conquering *, their largest city. 2Sa 8:1
come with him from *, and the 2Sa 15:17,18
Literally, "slew Goliath of *." 2Sa 21:19f
were fighting at *, a giant with 2Sa 21:20,21
tribe of giants in *, and were 2Sa 21:22
escaped to King Achish of *. 1Ki 2:39
and went to * to visit the king. 1Ki 2:40
and had gone to * and returned, he 1Ki 2:41
to war against * and captured it; 2Ki 12:17
rustle cattle at *, but they were 1Ch 7:20,21
chased out the inhabitants of *. 1Ch 8:13
* and its surrounding towns. 1Ch 18:1
During another battle, at *, a 1Ch 20:6,7
of the giants of *, and they were 1Ch 20:8
*, Mareshah, Ziph, 2Ch 11:5-10
the city of * and broke down its 2Ch 26:6
to * in the Philistines' land. Amo 6:2
Woe to the city of *. Mic 1:10
of *; there is no hope of saving Mic 1:14

GATH-HEPHER

then it continued east of *, Jos 19:13
of Amittai) the prophet from *. 2Ki 14:25

GATH-RIMMON

Jehud, Bene-berak, *, Me-jarkon, Jos 19:41-46
Elteke, Gibbethon, Aijalon, and *. Jos 21:23,24
of Taanach and * with their Jos 21:25
Aijalon; *. 1Ch 6:66-69

GATHER

told his men to * stones and make a Gen 31:46
of these districts * into the royal Gen 41:34,35
sons and said, "* around me and I Gen 49:1
scattered everywhere to * straw. Ex 5:12
and * as much food as he needs. Ex 16:4
Tell them to * twice as much as Ex 16:5
for everyone to * as much as is Ex 16:16
the ground today. * the food for Ex 16:26
went out anyway to * food, even Ex 16:27
* at the foot of the mountain!" Ex 19:13
you shall * the people for worship, Lev 23:7
don't * the grapes for yourself; Lev 25:5
In it you shall not sow, nor * Lev 25:11
that they are to * at the entrance Num 10:3
defiled shall * up the ashes of the Num 19:9
people to come and * at the rock; Num 20:10
you and come and * you out of all Deu 30:3
* at the village well Ju 5:11
boy with him to * his arrows. 1Sa 20:35
into the field to * vegetables and 2Ki 4:39
of $1,500,000. To * this amount, 2Ki 18:15
in action and to * the booty from 1Ch 10:8
"Go and * together all the Jews Est 4:16
My enemies * themselves against Job 16:10
Demand justice for me, Lord! * Ps 7:7,8
For they * with the worthless Ps 35:16
he shouts, "* together my own Ps 50:5
You supply it, and they * it. Ps 104:28
And when you * up their breath, Ps 104:29
my bride! I * my myrrh with my Sol 5:1
his flock and to * the lilies. Sol 6:2
he will * the scattered Is 11:12
when the Lord will * them together Is 27:12
I will * you from east and west, Is 43:5
* the nations together! Is 43:9
* together and come, you nations Is 45:20
great compassion I will * you. Is 54:7
so I will * together all nations Is 66:18
Watch how the children * wood and Jer 7:18
the young men * no more in the Jer 9:21
And I will * together the Jer 23:3
to me, I will * together all the Jer 25:8,9
No one shall mourn for them nor * Jer 25:33
your fortunes, and * you out of the Jer 29:14
his people will * them back Jer 31:10
Those who * grapes leave a few Jer 49:9,10
there, and I will * you back from Eze 11:17
to do: I will * together all your Eze 16:37
Animals of every sort will * Eze 17:22,23
For I will * them back again from Eze 28:25
and say to them: * together for a Eze 39:17
She will * your dead; Hos 9:6
I will * the armies of the Hos 10:10
call a solemn meeting. * the Joe 1:14
Call a fast and * all the people Joe 2:15
Lord, "I will * the armies of the Joe 3:2
Let the weak be strong. * Joe 3:11
when I will * you—all that are Mic 2:12
when the Lord will * together the Mic 4:12
there is no shepherd now to * Nah 3:18
* TOGETHER AND pray, you Zep 2:1
For it is my decision to * Zep 3:8
"At that time, I will * you Zep 3:20
On that day the Lord will * Zec 14:1
For where two or three * Mt 18:20
How often I have wanted to * your Mt 23:37
is, there the vultures will *. Mt 24:28
and they shall * my chosen ones Mt 24:31
crowds began to * again, and soon Mk 3:20
out the angels to * together my Mk 13:27
How often I have wanted to * your Lk 13:34
the body is, the vultures *!" Lk 17:37
"Now * the scraps," Jesus told Jn 6:12
A crowd began to * and soon the Act 19:29
So, dear brothers, when you * 1Co 11:33
is ripe he will * us all together Eph 1:10
of the world to * them for battle Rev 16:14
the birds, "Come! * together for Rev 19:17
of the world and * them together, Rev 20:8

GATHERED

beneath the sky be * into oceans so Gen 1:9,10
Literally, "and was * to his Gen 25:17f
your sheaves all * around it and Gen 37:7
had arrived, he * his strength and Gen 48:2
of Israel went out and * it. Ex 16:17
those who * a lot had nothing Ex 16:18
those who * little had no lack! Ex 16:18
So they * the food morning by Ex 16:21
On the sixth day they * twice as Ex 16:22
Assembly is to be * together, you Num 10:5,6,7f
The people * it from the ground Num 11:8
and he * the seventy elders and Num 11:24
The least anyone * was 100 Num 11:32
them—all Israel * at Shiloh to set Jos 18:1
in the gold earrings he had *. Ju 8:25
of sex perverts * around the house Ju 19:22
So they * there and, in a great 1Sa 7:6
So the boy quickly * up the 1Sa 20:38
and all Israel * for his funeral 1Sa 25:1
the ground—it can't be * up again. 2Sa 14:14
and all the people * before the 1Ki 8:5
the crowd that had * around them. 2Ki 10:9,10
and Judah * there at the Temple so 2Ki 23:1
I have also * timber and stone 1Ch 22:14
my command, I have * as much as I 1Ch 29:2
that we have * to build a temple 1Ch 29:16
among them as they * at the new 2Ch 20:5
On the fourth day they * in the 2Ch 20:26
to the people * on the walls of the 2Ch 32:18
* around and cried with me. Ez 10:1
went on home and * together his Est 5:10
contrary—the Jews * in their cities Est 9:1
Then the Jews at Shushan * Est 9:15
provinces had * together and stood Est 9:16
Literally, "quickly *." Pro 20:21f
and the mountain grasses are * in. Pro 27:25,26,27
of riches and * up kingdoms as a Is 10:14
Their bones shall not be * up Jer 8:2
the crowd that had *, "The Lord Jer 28:11
deserted farms and * a great Jer 40:12
to the crowds that * around him, Jon 3:4,5
True, many nations have * Mic 4:11
"I have * your wounded and taken Zep 3:17,18
so they all * in early September Hag 1:14,15
where an immense crowd soon *. Mt 13:2,3
And all the nations shall be * Mt 25:32
and as the crowds * before Mt 27:17
* outside the door to watch. Mk 1:32,33
to the crowds that * around him. Mk 2:13

(GATHERED Con't)
ONCE AGAIN AN immense crowd * Mk 4:1
And a large crowd soon * where Mk 5:15
crowd * around him on the shore. Mk 5:21
great crowd *, the people ran out Mk 8:1
and other Jewish leaders soon *. Mk 14:53
of God's Kingdom), * his courage Mk 15:42,43
A crowd soon *, and he sat down Jn 8:2
withers, and is * into a pile with Jn 15:6
many were * for a prayer meeting. Act 12:12
we * for a communion service, Act 20:7
from Jerusalem * around, hurling Act 25:7
As Paul * an armful of sticks to Act 28:3
"He that * much had nothing left 2Co 8:15
and he that * little had enough." 2Co 8:15
our being * together to meet him? 2Th 2:1
He has * us into his kingdom and Rev 1:6
And you have * them into a Rev 5:10
earth, and the harvest was * in. Rev 14:16
And they * all the armies of the Rev 16:16

GATHERERS
Literally, "is a friend of tax * Lk 7:34f

GATHERING
caught * wood on the Sabbath day. Num 15:32
shall be a quiet * of the people of Deu 16:8
that a crowd was * around to stare 2Sa 20:12
the city he saw a widow * sticks; 1Ki 17:10
I was just * a few sticks to cook 1Ki 17:12
all summer, * food for the winter. Pro 6:8
A time for * stones; Ecc 3:5
"For the Lord God says: I am * Eze 37:21
ONE DAY AS the crowds were *, he Mt 5:1
didn't sow, and * where you didn't Mt 25:24,25f
all the Jewish leaders were *. Mt 26:57
crowd that was * to hear him—while Lk 8:4
* the Twelve around him he told Lk 18:31
the crowds began * early in the Lk 21:37,38
wages and will be * eternal souls Jn 4:36
lake, crowds began * on the shore Jn 6:22,23
the * of countless happy angels; Heb 12:22
Then I saw the Evil Creature * Rev 19:19

GATHERINGS
streets, upon the * of young men, Jer 6:11

GATHERS
And the one who * up the ashes Num 19:10
as a farmer * eggs, and no one can Is 10:14
into the water and * in fish of Mt 13:47,48
together as a hen * her chicks Mt 23:37

GAUNT
They are * with famine and have Job 30:3

GAUZE
and veils of shimmering *. Is 3:19

GAVE
But the Lord God * the man this Gen 2:16,17
of the fruit and * some to her Gen 3:6
was the woman you * me who brought Gen 3:12
she conceived and * birth to a son, Gen 4:1
Later on Eve * birth to another Gen 4:25
Then Pharaoh * Abram many gifts Gen 12:16
Then Abram * Melchizedek a tenth Gen 14:19,20
is rich because of what I * him!' Gen 14:23
named Hagar, and * her to Abram to Gen 16:2,3
though I myself * her the privilege Gen 16:5
So Hagar * Abram a son, and Abram Gen 16:15
men and women—and * them to Gen 20:14
pregnant and * Abraham a baby son Gen 21:1
and Abraham * a party to Gen 21:8
so she refilled the canteen and * Gen 21:19
Then Abraham * sheep and oxen to Gen 21:27
Laban, and Laban * him straw to bed Gen 24:32
was very old, she * birth to my Gen 24:36
So I * her the ring and the Gen 24:47
and he * many valuable presents Gen 24:53
however, he * gifts to the sons Gen 25:6
Then Jacob * Esau bread, peas, Gen 25:34
death, and * them the same names Gen 26:18
then she * him the meat, with Gen 27:17
(And Laban * to Leah a servant Gen 29:24
Then Laban * him Rachel, too. Gen 29:28
And Laban * to Rachel a servant Gen 29:29
So she * him Bilhah to be his Gen 30:4
again and * Jacob a second son. Gen 30:7
anymore, she * her servant-girl Gen 30:9
and * birth to her fifth son. Gen 30:17
Afterwards she * birth to a Gen 30:21
For she became pregnant and * Gen 30:23,24
black sheep. He * them to Jacob's Gen 30:35,36
Jacob * the same instructions to Gen 32:19
So they * Jacob all their idols Gen 35:4
the land I * to Abraham and Isaac. Gen 35:12
So one day Jacob * him a special Gen 37:3
but his father * it quite a bit of Gen 37:11
So he * them to her and she let Gen 38:18
So Potiphar * Joseph the Gen 39:6
it, and * it to him to drink." Gen 40:11
Pharaoh also * Joseph the chariot Gen 41:43
Pharaoh * him a name meaning "He Gen 41:45
And he * him a wife, a girl named Gen 41:45
grain, but also * secret Gen 42:25
He also * them provisions for Gen 42:25
When Joseph came home they * him Gen 43:26
his own table. He * the largest Gen 43:34
So Joseph * them wagons, as Gen 45:21
journey, and he * each of them new Gen 45:22
to Benjamin he * five changes of Gen 45:22
he * them children of their own. Ex 1:21
them, and Reuel * him one of the Ex 2:21
Ever since I * Pharaoh your Ex 5:23
And the Lord * the Israelis Ex 12:36
they * them whatever they wanted. Ex 12:36
pillar of fire, it * darkness to Ex 14:20
Then Moses * them this further Ex 16:32
But if his master * him a wife Ex 21:4
exactly the directions I * you." Ex 31:11
The Lord then * these further Ex 31:12,13
on Mount Sinai, he * him the two Ex 31:18
to him, and he * them the Ex 34:32
Moses * them the materials Ex 36:3
THEN THE LORD * these further Lev 4:1
AND THE LORD * Moses these Lev 14:1
that the Lord * to Moses. Lev 16:35
THE LORD * to Moses these Lev 17:1
THE LORD * Moses these further Lev 20:1
So Moses * these instructions to Lev 21:24
Sinai, the Lord * him these Lev 25:1
that Jehovah * to the people of Lev 26:46
the Lord * to Moses for the people Lev 27:34
THE LORD * these further Num 2:1
And Moses * it to Aaron and his Num 3:51
THE LORD * Moses these further Num 6:1
JEHOVAH * THESE instructions to Num 9:1
So Moses * the instructions to Num 17:6
The Lord * these further Num 18:8
and sheep, and * animals to Balaam Num 22:40
Then the Lord * Balaam a Num 23:5
that even if you * me a palace Num 24:13
But not before Balaam * insidious Num 24:25f
THE LORD * Moses these Num 28:1
So Moses * all of these Num 29:40
the Lord * Moses concerning Num 30:16
directions, Moses * two percent of Num 31:47
So Moses * his approval by saying Num 32:28
So Moses * Gilead to the Num 32:40
which the Lord * to the people of Num 36:13
And I * them other instructions Deu 1:18
Lord our God * all of them to us. Deu 2:35,36
"At that time I * the conquered Deu 3:12
Reuben and Gad I * the area Deu 3:12
Then I * Gilead to the clan of Deu 3:15
far than you, and * you their land Deu 4:38
he * you at that time, Deu 5:22
stone tablets and * them to me. Deu 5:22
dry. He * you water from the rock! Deu 8:15
nights the Lord * me the contract, Deu 9:10,11
on them and * them to me. Deu 10:4
tell them, 'I * my daughter to this Deu 22:16
elders of Israel * the people these Deu 27:1
That same day Moses * this charge Deu 27:11
your ancestors * a second thought; Deu 28:36
their land and * it to the tribes Deu 29:8
to the people and * them to the Deu 31:9
Moses also * copies of the laws Deu 31:9
He * each of them a supervising Deu 32:8
God * them fertile hilltops, Deu 32:13
He * them milk and meat— Deu 32:14
the man of God, * to the people of Deu 33:1
every law Moses * you, for if you Jos 1:7
the priests and * them their Jos 6:6-9
There, too, the Lord * them the Jos 10:30
And the Lord * it to them on the Jos 10:32
And the Lord * all that vast Jos 11:8
and he * it to the people of Jos 11:23
people, and Moses * the land to the Jos 12:6
So Joshua blessed him and * him Jos 14:13,14
For the land you * me is a Jos 15:18,19
Then he * her the upper and Jos 15:18,19
and the nation of Israel * a Jos 19:49
The tribes of Judah and Simeon * Jos 21:9-16
The tribe of Benjamin * them Jos 21:17,18
The half-tribe of Manasseh * the Jos 21:25
The tribe of Issachar * four Jos 21:28,29
The tribe of Asher * four cities Jos 21:30,31
The tribe of Naphtali *: Jos 21:32
Reuben * them: Jos 21:36,37
Gad * them four cities with Jos 21:38,39
So in this way the Lord * to Jos 21:43
And the Lord * them peace, just Jos 21:44
of the commandments Moses * you. Jos 22:5
land of Canaan and * him many Jos 24:3
Isaac's children, whom I * him, Jos 24:4
To Esau I * the area around Mount Jos 24:4
them and * you their land. Jos 24:8
you victory! I * you land you had Jos 24:13
are now living. I * you vineyards Jos 24:13
So Caleb * her the upper and lower Ju 1:15
to the Lord, he * them Caleb's Ju 3:9
So she * him some milk and Ju 4:19
And she * him milk in a beautiful Ju 5:25
before you, and * you their land. Ju 6:9
three groups and * each man a Ju 7:16
They * him money from the temple Ju 9:4
the Amorites and * it to Israel. Ju 11:23
and the Lord * him the victory. Ju 11:3
follows the instructions I * her. Ju 13:13,1
as he went, and * some of it to his Ju 14:
* the answer to the young men. Ju 14:1
day they * him their reply. Ju 14:1
clothing, and * it to the young men Ju 14:1
father * her to another man." Ju 15:
urging him until finally he * in. Ju 19:
his reapers and he * her food, Ru 2:1
into the city and * it to her Ru 2:1
She told Naomi everything and * Ru 3:15-1
with her, the Lord * her a son. Ru 4:1
And the Lord * Hannah three sons 1Sa 2:2
came to Eli and * him this 1Sa 2:27
started to go, God * him a new 1Sa 10:9
at Mizpah, and * them this message 1Sa 10:18,19
came upon him and * him great power 1Sa 16:13
Then Saul * David his own armor—a 1Sa 17:38,39
Then the Israelis * a great shout 1Sa 17:52
So Saul * Michal to him. 1Sa 18:27
Then Jonathan * his bow and 1Sa 20:40
the priest * him the holy bread—the 1Sa 21:6
do, and then * him food and the 1Sa 22:9,10
The young men * David's message 1Sa 25:9
So Achish * him Ziklag (which 1Sa 27:6
nights, so they * him part of a fig 1Sa 30:11,12
and * him their pledge of loyalty. 2Sa 5:1
of heaven, and * a present to 2Sa 6:19
So the Lord * him victories 2Sa 8:6
were enemies. He * David presents 2Sa 8:10
Joab and * it to Uriah to deliver. 2Sa 11:14
and * the report to David. 2Sa 11:22
and she * birth to his son. 2Sa 11:27
power of Saul. I * you his palace 2Sa 12:8
she conceived and * birth to a son 2Sa 12:24
But he * them the two sons of 2Sa 21:8
He also * them the five adopted 2Sa 21:8
The God above all gods * out a 2Sa 22:14
David, the man to whom God * such 2Sa 23:1
and the Lord * him a great 2Sa 23:10
and God * him a great victory. 2Sa 23:11,12
of the deeds that * Benaiah almost 2Sa 23:22
* this charge to his son Solomon: 1Ki 2:1
the promise he * me, that if my 1Ki 2:4
God * Solomon great wisdom and 1Ki 4:29
So the Lord * great wisdom to 1Ki 5:12
the palace, he * twenty cities in 1Ki 9:11,12
him, for the Lord * him the right 1Ki 10:3
he * you to them as their king! 1Ki 10:9
Then she * the king a gift of 1Ki 10:10
King Solomon * her everything she 1Ki 10:13
friends, and he * him a wife—the 1Ki 11:19
Then he * this proof that his 1Ki 13:3
"Even if you * me half your 1Ki 13:8
and an angel * me a message from 1Ki 13:18
of David and * it to you, but you 1Ki 14:8
of the palace, and * them to his 1Ki 15:18
and * him to his mother. 1Ki 17:23
and the Lord * special strength to 1Ki 18:46
and the food * him enough strength 1Ki 19:8
see King Ahab and * him this 1Ki 20:13
insisted. He * him two expensive 2Ki 5:23
in two bags, and * them to two of 2Ki 5:23
Then he * them their 2Ki 11:5
upon his head and * him a copy of 2Ki 11:12
it into bags, and * it to the 2Ki 12:11,12
the laws he * to the descendants of 2Ki 17:34
and * it all to the Assyrian king. 2Ki 18:16
the instructions I * them through 2Ki 21:8
He * the scroll to Shaphan to 2Ki 22:8
She * them this message from 2Ki 22:15,16
kindly and * him preferential 2Ki 25:28
The king also * him a daily cash 2Ki 25:30
widow, and she * birth to Ashhur, 1Ch 2:24
daughters. He * one of his 1Ch 2:34,35
The tribe of Ephraim * these 1Ch 6:66-69
The tribe of Issachar * them 1Ch 6:72
The tribe of Asher * them Abdon, 1Ch 6:74
The tribe of Naphtali * them 1Ch 6:76
The tribe of Zebulun * Rimmono 1Ch 6:77
tribe of Reuben * them Bezer (a 1Ch 6:78,79
The tribe of Gad * them Ramoth in 1Ch 6:80
So the Lord killed him and * the 1Ch 10:14
then he * every person present 1Ch 16:3
And the Lord * David victory 1Ch 18:6
* David victory after victory. 1Ch 18:13
figure which he * came to 1,100,000 1Ch 21:5
which he * to Israel through Moses, 1Ch 22:13
What a blessing God * him with all 1Ch 26:4,5
Then David * Solomon the 1Ch 28:11
He also * Solomon his plans for 1Ch 28:12
and he * specifications for each 1Ch 28:13
And the Lord * him great 1Ch 29:25
And he * them names: Jachin (the 2Ch 3:17
this land you * to their fathers. 2Ch 6:25
land which you * to our fathers." 2Ch 6:31f
this land you * their fathers, and 2Ch 6:37,38
She * the king a gift of over a 2Ch 9:9
King Solomon * the Queen of Sheba 2Ch 9:12
"My father * you heavy burdens 2Ch 10:14
and Benjamin, and * them large 2Ch 11:23

(GAVE Con't)

That is why God * his kingdom	2Ch 14:5
And he * them peace throughout	2Ch 15:15
and * up his plan to attack Judah.	2Ch 16:5
and King Ahab * a great party for	2Ch 18:2
However, he * the kingship to	2Ch 21:3,4
and * them these instructions:	2Ch 24:5
The king and Jehoiada * the	2Ch 24:12
who needed it, and * them shoes,	2Ch 28:15
King Hezekiah * the people 1,000	2Ch 30:24
land which I * your ancestors."	2Ch 33:8
Hilkiah * the scroll to	2Ch 34:15,16
of the Temple, * the priests 2,600	2Ch 35:8
and Jozabad—* 5,000 sheep and goats	2Ch 35:9
who * him messages from the Lord.	2Ch 36:12
God of heaven who * me my vast	Ez 1:2
Then God * a great desire to the	Ez 1:5
who chose to remain in Persia *	Ez 1:6
and each * as much as he could.	Ez 2:69
Then all the people * a great	Ez 3:11
demanded, "Who * you permission to	Ez 5:3
for the Lord * them a good trip.	Ez 7:7,8,9
I weighed the money as I * it to	Ez 8:26,27
* us through your servant Moses.	Neh 1:6,7
and each time I * the same reply.	Neh 6:4
and Levites, I * the	Neh 7:2
Some of their leaders * gifts for	Neh 7:70
The governor * $5,000 in gold, 50	Neh 7:70
The other leaders * a total of	Neh 7:71
and the common people * $100,000	Neh 7:72
from heaven and * them good laws	Neh 9:13
"You * them bread from heaven	Neh 9:15
So you * them to their enemies.	Neh 9:27
you * us only what we deserved.	Neh 9:33
upon them. You * them a large, fat	Neh 9:35
which you * to our ancestors!	Neh 9:36
The Levites, in turn, * a portion	Neh 12:47
When it was all over, the king *	Est 1:5
Queen Vashti * a party for the	Est 1:9
beauty treatments, * her seven	Est 2:9
as her maids, and * her the most	Est 2:9
Mordecai also * Hathach a copy	Est 4:8
So Hathach * Esther's message to	Est 4:12
ON THAT SAME day King Ahasuerus *	Est 8:1
from Haman—and * it to Mordecai,	Est 8:2
This decree * the Jews	Est 8:11
The Lord * me everything I had,	Job 1:21
like cheese. You * me skin and	Job 10:11
and sinews. You * me life and were	Job 10:12
unless they * you all their	Job 22:6
But no doubt you * men of	Job 22:8
In fact, the Lord * him twice as	Job 42:10
God also * him seven more sons	Job 42:13,14
You * me victory in every battle.	Ps 18:43,44,45
you, and you * me my health again.	Ps 30:2
of mourning and * me gay and	Ps 30:11
from this land and * it all to us,	Ps 44:1
lived, for you * them this home	Ps 68:9,10
For food they * me poison;	Ps 69:21
* him to the desert tribes to eat!	Ps 74:13,14
For he * his laws to Israel, and	Ps 78:5
food. He * them bread from heaven!	Ps 78:24
They ate angel's food! He * them	Ps 78:25
The people ate their fill. He *	Ps 78:29
lives short and * them years of	Ps 78:33
He * their crops to caterpillars.	Ps 78:46
angels. He * free course to his	Ps 78:50
the land, and * each tribe of	Ps 78:55
of Israel. He * them as reminders	Ps 81:5
burning sun, and * them a pillar of	Ps 105:39
* them manna—bread from heaven.	Ps 105:40
He * them the lands of the	Ps 105:44
So he * them their demands, but	Ps 106:15
The punishment you * me was the	Ps 119:71,72
and the kings of Canaan— and *	Ps 135:12
continues forever. God * the	Ps 136:21
of the seas and * them his	Pro 8:27,28,29
God who * them to you.	Pro 20:12
spirit returns to God who * it.	Ecc 12:7
where your mother * birth to you in	Sol 8:5
and to cure the wounds he * them.	Is 30:26
That it was I who * you all this	Is 37:26
* him this message from the Lord:	Is 38:1
as he * her punishment before.	Is 40:2
he * before the worlds began?	Is 40:21
Not one * any answer when I	Is 41:28
One of Israel. I * Egypt and	Is 43:3
your search, but you never * up.	Is 57:10
How is it that you * not even a	Is 57:11
Spirit of the Lord * them rest.	Is 63:14
Thus he * himself a magnificent	Is 63:14
to the land I * their fathers as an	Jer 3:18
rejected him and * yourselves to	Jer 5:19
* to your fathers to keep forever.	Jer 7:7
I * to you and to your fathers.	Jer 7:13,14
the land God * his people Israel:	Jer 12:14
your beautiful flock I * you to	Jer 13:20
this same land I * your fathers.	Jer 16:14,15
it a holy day. I * this commandment	Jer 17:21,22
to speak for me; I * them no	Jer 23:21
city I * to you and your fathers.	Jer 23:38,39
Lord * me this vision.	Jer 24:1
* to them and to their fathers."	Jer 24:10
which the Lord * to you and to your	Jer 25:5
and this city. He * me every word	Jer 26:12
Soon afterwards, the Lord * this	Jer 28:12
Then the Lord * this message to	Jer 29:30
land that I * to their fathers;	Jer 30:3
and terror. You * Israel this land	Jer 32:22
That is why the Lord * the	Jer 34:12
THIS IS THE message the Lord *	Jer 35:1
Then the Lord * this message to	Jer 35:12
land I * to you and your fathers.	Jer 35:15
Lord * this message to Jeremiah:	Jer 36:1
and * them fields and vineyards.	Jer 39:10
The Lord * the following message	Jer 39:15
Then Nebuzaradan * Jeremiah some	Jer 40:5
Ten days later the Lord * his	Jer 42:7
THIS IS THE message God * to	Jer 44:1
* you and your fathers before you.	Jer 44:10
Jeremiah * to Baruch in the	Jer 45:1
Then God * Jeremiah this message	Jer 46:13
above— and * the scroll to Seraiah	Jer 51:61,62
to him and * him preference over	Jer 52:32
in Babylon, and * him new clothes	Jer 52:33
He sapped my strength and * me to	Lam 1:14
for your sin. I * you gold to use	Eze 7:20
the work you * me to do."	Eze 9:11
had taken place, I * you beautiful	Eze 16:9,10
dolphin hide. I * you lovely	Eze 16:11
gifts I * you, says the Lord God.	Eze 16:14
and you * yourself as a	Eze 16:15
You used the lovely things I *	Eze 16:16
silver ornaments I * to you and	Eze 16:17
I * you—to cover your idols!	Eze 16:18
flour and oil and honey I * you;	Eze 16:19
the king lives who * him his power,	Eze 17:16
Then the Lord * me this message:	Eze 20:2
There I * them my laws so they	Eze 20:11
And I * them the Sabbath—a day	Eze 20:12
Literally, "* them."	Eze 20:25f
with the very gifts I * them.	Eze 20:26
instead of me, and * her love to	Eze 23:4,5
them and * herself to their lust.	Eze 23:18
a young girl you * your virginity	Eze 23:21
the land I * their father Jacob.	Eze 28:25
It grew luxuriantly and *	Eze 31:4
flocks and herds * birth to young.	Eze 31:6
that I * it, it was the envy of all	Eze 31:9
which I * your fathers long ago.	Eze 36:28
the land I * my servant Jacob.	Eze 37:25
You have not kept the laws I *	Eze 44:8
Lord * him victory over Jehoiakim.	Dan 1:1
However, their superintendent *	Dan 1:7
God * these four youths great	Dan 1:17
the time, and God * to Daniel	Dan 1:17
very great; he * him many costly	Dan 2:48
Then the king * promotions to	Dan 3:30
and his legs * way beneath him.	Dan 5:6
the Most High God * Nebuchadnezzar,	Dan 5:18
and honor. He * him such majesty	Dan 5:19
So at last the king * the order	Dan 6:16
all the laws you * us through your	Dan 9:10
Ptolemy II of Egypt * his	Dan 11:6f
and this time * birth to a son.	Hos 1:8
It was I who * her all the gold	Hos 1:8
and the clothes I * her to cover	Hos 1:9
claims her lovers * her—and let	Hos 1:12
Even if I * her ten thousand	Hos 8:12
them save you! I * you kings in my	Hos 13:11
of slavery. I * you Moses, Aaron,	Mic 6:4
THIS IS THE vision God * to Nahum,	Nah 1:1
And the Lord * them a desire	Hag 1:14,15
So they * him one.	Zec 3:5,6
to honor those who * it—Heldai,	Zec 6:14
to the laws I * your father Levi,"	Mal 2:4
"Remember to obey the laws I *	Mal 4:4
their presents and * him gold,	Mt 2:11
to him, and * them authority to	Mt 10:1
loaves apart and * them to the	Mt 14:19
But Jesus * her no reply—not even	Mt 15:23
and the fish, and * thanks to God	Mt 15:36
into pieces, and * them to the	Mt 15:36
"He * $5,000 to one, $2,000 to	Mt 25:15
report, 'Sir, you * me $2,000 to	Mt 25:22
I was thirsty and you * me water;	Mt 25:35
And they * him thirty silver	Mt 26:15
broke it apart and * it to the	Mt 26:26
And he took a cup of wine and *	Mt 26:27
thanks for it and * it to them and	Mt 26:27
whipped Jesus, he * him to the	Mt 27:26
* him drugged wine to drink;	Mt 27:34
It * a terrible scream, shrieking,	Mk 5:7,8
And Jesus * them permission.	Mk 5:13
It was Herod's birthday and he *	Mk 6:21
on a tray, and * it to the girl and	Mk 6:28
to heaven, * thanks for the food.	Mk 6:41
into pieces, he * some of the bread	Mk 6:41
For instance, Moses * you this	Mk 7:10
going on here? Who * you the	Mk 11:27,28
* to the people at that time:	Mk 12:1
"Teacher, Moses * us a law that	Mk 12:19
For they * a little of their	Mk 12:43,44
while she * up her last penny."	Mk 12:43,44
it in pieces and * it to them and	Mk 14:22
Then he took a cup of wine and *	Mk 14:23
to God for it and * it to them;	Mk 14:23
She * a glad cry and exclaimed to	Lk 1:42
Holy Spirit and * this prophecy:	Lk 1:67
and she * birth to her first	Lk 2:7
And Jesus * him back to his	Lk 7:15
One day he * this illustration to	Lk 8:4
apostles and * them authority over	Lk 9:1
up into the sky and * thanks;	Lk 9:16
He * them strict orders not to	Lk 9:21
and the breasts that * you suck!"	Lk 11:27
Then he * an illustration: "A	Lk 12:16
of the table, he * them this	Lk 14:7
And no one * him anything.	Lk 15:16
and in all that time you never *	Lk 15:29
to whom he * this illustration.	Lk 16:31f
ten assistants and * them each	Lk 19:13
Then he * them this illustration:	Lk 21:29
broke it apart and * it to them,	Lk 22:19
After supper he * them another	Lk 22:20
They * him a piece of broiled	Lk 24:42
But to all who received him, he *	Jn 1:11,12
For Moses * us only the Law with	Jn 1:17
world so much that he * his only	Jn 3:16
ground Jacob * to his son Joseph.	Jn 4:5,6
Then Jesus took the loaves and *	Jn 6:11
As the Scriptures say, 'Moses *	Jn 6:30,31
And when he had dipped it, he * it	Jn 13:26
by means of the commands I * you.	Jn 15:3
world, but then you * them to me.	Jn 17:6
yours, and you * them to me;	Jn 17:6
on to them the commands you * me;	Jn 17:8
all of these you * me.	Jn 17:12
them the glory you * me—the	Jn 17:22
see my glory. You * me the glory	Jn 17:24
one of those you * me"	Jn 18:9
but Jesus * no answer.	Jn 19:9
Then Pilate * Jesus to them to be	Jn 19:16
Then she * them his message.	Jn 20:18
for the Holy Spirit * them this	Act 2:4
the Father * him the authority to	Act 2:33
is the promise God * to Abraham.	Act 3:25
of Israel, but * him no property	Act 7:5
"God also * Abraham the ceremony	Act 7:8
his anguish, and * him favor before	Act 7:10
God also * Joseph unusual wisdom,	Act 7:10
and the Angel who * them the Law of	Act 7:38
away from them and * them up, and	Act 7:42
she sat up! He * her his hand and	Act 9:41
household. He * generously to	Act 10:2
And since it was God who *	Act 11:17
the same gift he * us when we	Act 11:17
and Cyrene also * their message	Act 11:20
At its conclusion the people *	Act 12:22
in Canaan, and * Israel their land	Act 13:19,20
a king, and God * them Saul (son of	Act 13:21
Spirit, just as he * him to us.	Act 15:8
Christians and * them the letter.	Act 15:30
And God * Paul the power to do	Act 19:11
be dissuaded, we * up and said,	Act 21:14
and * him their story about Paul.	Act 25:2
Jewish leaders * me their side of	Act 25:15
couldn't, so they * up and let the	Act 27:14,15
As the darkness * way to the	Act 27:33
Then he took some hardtack and *	Act 27:35
The Romans * me a trial and	Act 28:18
So it was that when they * God up	Rom 1:28
him, God * them up to doing	Rom 1:28
God because he * his laws to you;	Rom 2:17
Christ's goodness, * us right	Rom 8:30
own Son for us but * him up for us	Rom 8:32
to bless you. He * you his rules	Rom 9:4
He let you worship him, and * you	Rom 9:4
and * himself to purchase our	1Co 1:30
Holy Spirit God * you, and that he	1Co 6:19
For in the law God * to Moses he	1Co 9:9
the water that Christ * them.	1Co 10:3,4
he broke it and * it to his	1Co 11:24
If I * everything I have to poor	1Co 13:3
who * him this power to rule.	1Co 15:27
I * to the churches in Galatia).	1Co 16:1
of Troas, the Lord * me tremendous	2Co 2:12
For as he * them God's law to	2Co 3:7
encouragement you * us by your	2Co 7:13
joy when you * him such a fine	2Co 7:13
They * not only what they could	2Co 8:3
Five different times the Jews *	2Co 11:24
When I was there I certainly *	2Co 12:12
And they * glory to God	Gal 1:24
the same God * us each our special	Gal 2:7,8,9
who loved me and * himself for me.	Gal 2:20
Jewish laws never * you spiritual	Gal 3:3
Now, God * some promises to	Gal 3:16
when God * the Ten Commandments.	Gal 3:17
difference. God * his laws to	Gal 3:19
who then * them to the people;	Gal 3:19
but when God * his promise to	Gal 3:20
* the Ten Commandments to Moses.	Gal 4:24,25

(GAVE Con't)
sins, he * us back our lives again Eph 2:5
Satan, he * generous gifts to men. Eph 4:8
who loved you and * himself to God Eph 5:2
the church. (He * his very life to Eph 5:23
of heaven and * him a name which is Php 2:9
Then he * you a share in the very Col 2:13
the Holy Spirit * you great and 1Th 1:5
welcome you * us, and how you 1Th 1:9
Yet God * us the courage to 1Th 2:2
dearly that we * you not only God's 1Th 2:8
* you from the Lord Jesus himself. 1Th 4:1
there with you we * you this rule: 2Th 3:10
proper time God * to the world. 1Ti 2:6
even though God * these things to 1Ti 4:3
Christ Jesus who * a fearless 1Ti 6:13
But the Lord stood with me and * 2Ti 4:17
follow the instructions I * you. Tit 1:5
am I and the children God * me." Heb 2:13
once * way to them and sinned. Heb 4:15
until finally God * him a son, Heb 6:15
battle and * it to Melchizedek. Heb 7:2
chosen people, * Melchizedek a Heb 7:4
like the old one I * to their Heb 8:9
Christ willingly * himself to God Heb 9:14
THE OLD SYSTEM of Jewish laws * Heb 10:1
There he * his own blood which Heb 10:4f
But Christ * himself to God for Heb 10:12
to whom God * the same promise. Heb 11:9
that God, who * her his promise, Heb 11:11
* a friendly welcome to the spies. Heb 11:31
Sinai when God * them his laws. Heb 12:18
his own free will he * us, etc." Jas 1:18f
when he * us our new lives, Jas 1:18
the dead and * him great glory. 1Pe 1:21
life they * you will fade away. 1Pe 1:23
who * them true messages from God. 2Pe 1:20,21
the old rule God * us right from 2Jn 1:5
truth which God *, once for all, to Jud 1:3
to idols. I * her time to change Rev 2:21
* me the authority to rule them; Rev 2:27
And when the Living Beings * Rev 4:9
on the earth, and * a great Rev 10:3
in my mouth but it * me a stomach Rev 10:10
it was born. She * birth to a boy Rev 12:5
And the Dragon * him his own Rev 13:2
the Lord; and * him authority to Rev 13:5
The Dragon * him power to fight Rev 13:7
He * a mighty shout, "Babylon Rev 18:2
underworld * up the dead in them. Rev 20:13

GAY
and gave me * and festive garments Ps 30:11

GAZA
the way to Gerar, in the * strip; Gen 10:15-19
the countryside as far away as *. Deu 2:23
to *, and from Goshen to Gibeon. Jos 10:41
remained in *, Gath, and Ashdod. Jos 11:22
*, Ashdad, Ashdelon, Gath Jos 13:2-7
its villages, and * with its Jos 15:47
the cities of *, Ashkelon, and Ju 1:18
as far away as *, leaving nothing Ju 6:3,4
Philistine city of * and spent the Ju 16:1
and took him to *, where he was Ju 16:21
*, Ashkelon, Gath, and Ekron. 1Sa 6:17
River, from Tiphsah to *. 1Ki 4:24
as far distant as * and its 2Ki 18:8
cities: Ashkelon, *, Ekron, and Jer 25:19,20
of *, before the city was captured Jer 47:1
The cities of * and Ashkelon Jer 47:5
The Lord says, "* has sinned Amo 1:6
to the walls of *, and all her Amo 1:7
*, Ashkelon, Ashdod, Ekron—these Zep 2:4
filled with fear; * will huddle in Zec 9:5
all be dashed. * will be conquered, Zec 9:5
* Desert, arriving around noon." Act 8:26

GAZE
all the men could * upon her Est 1:11
Turn away your angry * and let Job 14:6
neither can we * at the terrible Job 37:22
they * at their bountiful crops. Ps 4:7
your searching *, for how you hate Ps 5:5
wicked to lower their insolent *, Ps 75:4
muffle your face and don't * Eze 12:6
before the curious * of kings. Eze 28:17
will crowd around to * at them. Rev 11:8,9

GAZED
* out across Gilead as far as Dan: Deu 34:1
the synagogue * at him intently. Lk 4:20
the Holy Spirit, * steadily upward Act 7:55

GAZELLE
as you do now with * and deer. Deu 12:15
as you do now with * and deer. Deu 12:20-23
The deer, the *, the roebuck, Deu 14:3,4,5
as anyone may eat a * or deer. Deu 15:22
My beloved is like a * or young Sol 2:9
and be like a * or a young stag on Sol 2:17
of a *, feeding among the lilies. Sol 4:5
Literally, "twins of a *." Sol 7:3f
and be like a * or young deer upon Sol 8:14
named Dorcas ("*"), a believer Act 9:36

GAZELLES
deer, *, roebucks, and plump fowl. 1Ki 4:23
adjure you by the * and deer in the Sol 2:7
Jerusalem, by the * and deer of the Sol 3:5

GAZES
The Lord * down upon mankind Ps 33:13,14,15

GAZEZ
Haran, Moza, and *; 1Ch 2:46
Haran had a son named *. 1Ch 2:46

GAZING
he stands still for a moment, * Hab 3:6
had been blind were * about them! Mt 15:31
* INTENTLY AT the Council, Paul Act 23:1

GAZZAM
Rezin, Nekoda, *, Uzza, Paseah, Ez 2:43-54
*, Uzza, Paseah, Besai, Neh 7:46-56

GEAR
remained behind to guard their *. 1Sa 25:13
longer be the issuing of battle *; Is 9:5
their * for a mile, carry it two. Mt 5:41

GEBA
Ophni, *, Gibeon, Ramah, Be-eroth, Jos 18:21-28
in ambush west of * jumped up from Ju 20:33
garrison of the Philistines at *. 1Sa 13:3,4
camp in * in the land of Benjamin; 1Sa 13:16
southern one was in front of *. 1Sa 14:5
all the way from * to Gezer. 2Sa 5:25
build the city of * in Benjamin and 1Ki 15:22
as far away as * and Beersheba. 2Ki 23:8
pastures—including *, Alemeth, and 1Ch 6:60
subclans living at *, were captured 1Ch 8:6,7
to build * and Mizpah instead. 2Ch 16:6
From the subclans of Ramah and *, Ez 2:3-35
From the subclans of Ramah and *, Neh 7:8-38
*, Michmash, Aija, Bethel (and its Neh 11:31-35
and the area of * and Azmaveth, for Neh 12:29
they are staying overnight at *. Is 10:28,29
All the land from * (the Zec 14:10

GEBAL
Men from * helped Solomon's and 1Ki 5:18
people from the lands of *, Ps 83:7
Wise old craftsmen from * do the Eze 27:9

GEBALITES
The land of the * on the coast Jos 13:2-7

GEBER
* (son of Uri), whose area was 1Ki 4:8-19

GEBIM
of * are preparing to run. Is 10:31

GECKO
The great lizard, the *, Lev 11:29,30

GEDALIAH
appointed * (the son of Ahikam and 2Ki 25:22
had appointed * as governor, some 2Ki 25:23
* vowed that if they would give 2Ki 25:24
ten men and killed * and his 2Ki 25:25
were his six sons: *, Zeri, 1Ch 25:3
The second, *, along with twelve 1Ch 25:9-31
Jarib, *. Ez 10:16-19
of Mattan) and * (son of Pashhur) Jer 38:1
into the care of * (son of Ahikam, Jer 39:14
then return to *, who has been Jer 40:5
So Jeremiah returned to * and Jer 40:6
had appointed * as governor over Jer 40:7
they came to see * at Mizpah, Jer 40:8
their men. And * assured them that Jer 40:9
all away, and that * was the Jer 40:11
their plans with * and then went Jer 40:12
to Mizpah to warn * that Baalis, Jer 40:13,14
him. But * wouldn't believe them. Jer 40:13,14
had a private conference with *. Jer 40:15
But * said, "I forbid you to do Jer 40:16
ten men. * invited them to dinner. Jer 41:1
out their swords and killed *. Jer 41:2
who were in Mizpah with *. Jer 41:3
and see what has happened to *!" Jer 41:6
Ishmael had killed * the governor, Jer 41:18
of the guard, had left with *. Jer 43:6
Cushi, grandson of *, Zep 1:1

GEDALIAH'S
been left under * care in Mizpah by Jer 41:10

GEDDALTI
Hanani, Eliathah, *, Romamti-ezer, 1Ch 25:4,5

GEDER
The king of *; Jos 12:8-24

GEDERA
Baal-hanan from * was 1Ch 27:28

GEDERAH
Adithaim, *, and Gederothaim. Jos 15:33-36
Jozabad from *; 1Ch 12:3-7

GEDEROTH
Lahmam, Chitlish, *, Beth-dagon, Jos 15:37-44
Aijalon, *, Soco, Timnah, and Gimzo 2Ch 28:17,18

GEDEROTHAIM
Adithaim, Gederah, and *. Jos 15:33-36

GEDOR
Halhul, Beth-zur, *, Maarath, Jos 15:48-62
*),Ezer (the ancestor of Hushah), 1Ch 4:3-4
the east side of * Valley in search 1Ch 4:34-39
Zur, Kish, Baal, Nadab, *, Ahio, 1Ch 8:30,31,32
Ner, Nadab, *, Ahio, Zechariah, 1Ch 9:35,36,37
Zebadiah (sons of Jeroham from *). 1Ch 12:3-7

GEDORITES
the *, Socoites, and Zanoahites. 1Ch 4:18

GEHAZI
to his servant *, "Tell the woman 2Ki 4:11,12
When she came, he said to *, 2Ki 4:13
he asked * afterwards. 2Ki 4:14
and said to *, "Look, that woman 2Ki 4:25
"Yes," she told *, "everything 2Ki 4:26
hold of his feet. * began to push 2Ki 4:27
Then he said to *, "Quick, take 2Ki 4:29
* went on ahead and laid the 2Ki 4:31
Then the prophet summoned *. 2Ki 4:36
he said to *, "Make some stew for 2Ki 4:38
Elisha told * to use it to feed 2Ki 4:42
"What?" * exclaimed. 2Ki 4:43
But *, Elisha's servant, said to 2Ki 5:20
So * caught up with him. 2Ki 5:21
his servants to carry back with *. 2Ki 5:23
* took the bags from the servants 2Ki 5:24
him, "Where have you been, *?" 2Ki 5:25
And * walked from the room a 2Ki 5:27
was talking with *, Elisha's 2Ki 8:4
And * was telling the king 2Ki 8:5
"Oh, sir!" * exclaimed. 2Ki 8:5

GELILOTH
and on to * (which is opposite the Jos 18:17

GEM
*, crystal clear like jasper. Rev 21:11

GEMALLI
Ammiel, son of *, from the tribe Num 13:3-15

GEMARIAH
of Shaphan) and * (son of Hilkiah) Jer 29:3
Baruch went to the office of * Jer 36:10
When Micaiah (son of *, son of Jer 36:11
(son of Achbor), * (son of Jer 36:12
except Elnathan, Delaiah and *. Jer 36:24,25

GEMS
*—and placed it on his own head. 2Sa 12:29,30
quantity of spices and precious *; 1Ki 10:10
great supply of algum trees and *. 1Ki 10:11
It was made of gold inlaid with * 1Ch 20:2
she is worth more than precious *! Pro 31:10
your gates and walls of shining *. Is 54:12
gold and precious * and pearls, and Rev 17:4
foundation stones inlaid with *: Rev 21:18,19,20

GENEALOGICAL
the seer, and in The * Register. 2Ch 12:15
The priests were listed in the * 2Ch 31:17,18
A * record of the heads of the Neh 12:22

GENEALOGIES
facts are recorded in their *. 1Ch 4:32,33
were recorded in the official *). 1Ch 7:7
the basis of their *, and they were 1Ch 9:22
and were selected by their *. 1Ch 9:33,34
However, they had lost their * Ez 2:59
But they too had lost their *, Ez 2:62,63
THESE ARE THE names and * of the Ez 8:1
the record of the * of those who Neh 7:5
But they had lost their * and Neh 7:61
name), whose * had been lost. Neh 7:64,65

GENEALOGY
So the official * doesn't name 1Ch 5:1
were included in the official *: 1Ch 5:7,8
in the official * at the time of 1Ch 5:17
his * was traced back through: 1Ch 6:33-38
was his colleague Asaph, whose * 1Ch 6:39-43
all included in the official *. 1Ch 7:5
* numbered 36,000 men of war. 1Ch 7:40
HERE IS THE * of Ezra, who Ez 7:1

GENERAL
* superintendent of the project. Ex 35:30,31
Moreover, this is a * law among Num 27:8
The * law against adultery Deu 22:30f
under * Sisera's command. Ju 4:7
When * Sisera was told that Ju 4:12
at a * assembly of all the people. Ju 11:11
by Sisera, the * of King Hazor's 1Sa 12:9
asked Abner, the * of his army, 1Sa 17:55
by the army and * public alike. 1Sa 18:5
King Saul and * Abner were 1Sa 26:5,6,7
One day * Abner led some of 2Sa 2:12
Mahanaim, and * Joab (the son of 2Sa 2:13
to everyone. The * of his army was 2Sa 8:16
cavalrymen, including * Shobach. 2Sa 10:18
the armies and the * and his 2Sa 11:11
WHEN * JOAB realized how much the 2Sa 14:1
Absalom had appointed Amasa as * 2Sa 17:25
He took * Joab and Abiathar the 1Ki 1:7
Abiathar the priest and * Joab. 1Ki 1:19
He also invited * Joab and 1Ki 1:25
He and Abiathar the priest and * 1Ki 2:22
to the deaths of * Abner, 1Ki 2:32
of Israel, and * Amasa, 1Ki 2:32
A * manager supervised these 1Ki 4:8-19
Adoniram was the * superintendent 1Ki 5:14
Then * Zimri, who had charge of 1Ki 16:9
they decided on * Omri, 1Ki 16:15,16
half the people were loyal to * 1Ki 16:21
* Omri won and Tibni was killed; 1Ki 16:22
king or to the * of the army?" 2Ki 4:13
the commanding * of his army, 2Ki 15:25
Then the Assyrian * sent this 2Ki 18:19
But the Assyrian * replied, "Has 2Ki 18:27

GENERAL Con't)
him what the Assyrian * had said. 2Ki 18:37
heard the Assyrian * defying the 2Ki 19:4
Then the Assyrian * returned to 2Ki 19:8
* Nebuzaradan, the captain of the 2Ki 25:8
The * took Seraiah, the chief 2Ki 25:18
were taken by * Nebuzaradan to the 2Ki 25:20
he became the * of David's army. 1Ch 11:5,6
Naharai from Be-eroth—he was * 1Ch 11:26-47
under the leadership of * Zerah. 2Ch 14:9,10
troops were there under * Adnah. 2Ch 17:14,15
the command of Eliada, a great *. 2Ch 17:17
and was, in *, a good king so far 2Ch 26:4
The commander-in-chief was * 2Ch 26:11
to assist the people in a * way. Eze 44:14
But a * will stop him and cause Dan 11:18
to the * public, but to us who ate Act 10:40,41
they called a * meeting of the Act 15:30

GENERAL-IN-CHIEF
And the * of his army was his 1Sa 14:50,51
secretary of the * of the Jewish Jer 52:24,25

GENERALLY
* speaking, Jotham was a good 2Ki 15:34,35
He followed the * good example 2Ch 27:2

GENERALS
Oreb and Zeeb, the two * of Ju 7:25
Zeeb, the * of the army of Midian! Ju 8:2,3
Top Three, plus * Joab, Abishai, 2Sa 23:24-39f
my two *, Abner and Amasa. 1Ki 2:5
time replace the kings with *! 1Ki 20:24
the Philistine * refused to let 1Ch 12:19
as the officers and * of the army. 1Ch 26:26
army with all its officers and *! 2Ch 32:21
And he stationed his army * in 2Ch 33:14
Even their * will quake with Is 31:9
Amasis, one of his * who had Jer 44:30f
Medes and their *, and the armies Jer 51:28
kings, and captains, and great *; Rev 19:18

GENERATION
between us * after generation, Gen 17:7,8
generation after *, forever, for it Gen 17:7,8
his brothers died, ending that *. Ex 1:6
day annually, * after generation. Ex 12:17
day annually, generation after *. Ex 12:17
sacred place from * to generation. Ex 16:33
sacred place from generation to *. Ex 16:33
with Amalek * after generation." Ex 17:15,16
with Amalek generation after *." Ex 17:15,16
succeeds him, from * to generation, Ex 29:29
to *, for his anointing ceremony. Ex 29:29
shall go on from * to generation. Ex 30:8
shall go on from generation to *. Ex 30:8
annual event from * to generation, Ex 30:10
from generation to *, for this is Ex 30:10
his sons from * to generation." Ex 30:21
his sons from generation to *." Ex 30:21
be permanent from * to generation: Ex 40:15
from generation to *: all their Ex 40:15
any priest, * after generation. Lev 6:18
any priest, generation after *. Lev 6:18
descendants from * to generation. Lev 10:8,9
descendants from generation to *. Lev 10:8,9
law for you, from * to generation. Lev 17:7
law for you, from generation to *. Lev 17:7
descendants from * to generation Lev 21:16,17
from generation to * who have any Lev 21:16,17
be honored from * to generation. Lev 23:21
be honored from generation to *. Lev 23:21
This is a law of Israel from * to Lev 23:30,31
of Israel from generation to *. Lev 23:30,31
is a law from * to generation. Lev 23:41
is a law from generation to *. Lev 23:41
people of Israel, * after Lev 23:43
generation after *, that I rescued Lev 23:43
the Lord from * to generation. Lev 24:3,4
the Lord from generation to *. Lev 24:3,4
be followed from * to generation. Num 10:8
be followed from generation to *. Num 10:8
to the third and fourth *. Num 14:17,18
true forever from * to generation; Num 15:15,16
true forever from generation to *; Num 15:15,16
be observed from * to generation. Num 15:19,20,21
be observed from generation to *. Num 15:19,20,21
regulation from * to generation) Num 15:37,38
from generation to *) and to attach Num 15:37,38
years until all that evil * died. Num 32:13
all Israel from * to generation. Num 35:29
all Israel from generation to *. Num 35:29
in that entire * would live to see Deu 1:34,35
But as for you of the older *, Deu 1:40
third and fourth * of the children Deu 5:9,10
to the Lord from * to generation. Deu 18:5
to the Lord from generation to *. Deu 18:5
sanctuary, even after the tenth *. Deu 23:3
(For this song will live from * Deu 31:21
will live from generation to *. Deu 31:21
They are a stubborn, twisted *. Deu 32:5
they are a stubborn, faithless *. Deu 32:20
that entire * had died during the Jos 5:4,5
the old men of his * were still Ju 2:7-9
But finally all that * died; Ju 2:10
and the next * did not worship Ju 2:10
to test the new * of Israel who had Ju 3:1
a test to the new * of Israel, to Ju 3:4
to reign over every * of Israel.' 1Ch 22:10
annual event from * to generation, Est 9:28
from generation to *, celebrated by Est 9:28
are the same for every *. Ps 33:11
Give me time to tell this new * Ps 71:18
Thus his laws pass down from * to Ps 78:6
pass down from generation to *. Ps 78:6
In this way each * has been able Ps 78:7
greatness from * to generation. Ps 79:13
greatness from generation to *. Ps 79:13
on and on to each succeeding *. Ps 100:5
Your fame will endure to every *. Ps 102:12
But our families will continue; * Ps 102:28
generation after * will be Ps 102:28
name be blotted out in a single *. Ps 109:12,13
*, like the earth you created; Ps 119:90,91
your fame is known to every *. Ps 135:13
Let each * tell its children Ps 145:4
You rule * after generation. Ps 145:13
You rule generation after *. Ps 145:13
your God is King in every *! Ps 146:10
But, then, the younger * grows up Ecc 4:16
Babylon will never rise again. * Is 13:20
Generation after * will come and Is 13:20
The land will lie deserted from * Is 34:10
lie deserted from generation to *; Is 34:10
it forever, from * to generation. Is 34:17
it forever, from generation to *. Is 34:17
as I do today. One * makes known Is 38:19
my salvation from * to generation. Is 51:8
my salvation from generation to *. Is 51:8
that neither this * nor their Jer 19:4
Your throne continues from * to Lam 5:19
continues from generation to *. Lam 5:19
pass the awful story down from * Joe 1:3
story down from generation to *. Joe 1:3
upon the heads of this very *. Mt 23:36
place, this * shall pass away." Mt 24:34f
Literally, "Why does this * seek Mk 8:12f
Literally, "O unbelieving *." Mk 9:19f
Literally, "of this *." Mk 13:30f
girl, and now * after generation Lk 1:48
generation after * forever shall Lk 1:48
His mercy goes on from * to Lk 1:50
to *, to all who reverence him. Lk 1:50
her finger at this *, condemning Lk 11:31
"And you of this * will be held Lk 11:50
Or, "this *." Lk 21:32f
wickedness of the people of his *? Act 8:33
"Who can declare his *." Act 8:33f
had served his * according to the Act 13:36

GENERATIONS
Noah, through many *, living in the Gen 10:32
After four * they will return Gen 15:16
our fathers have been for many *.' Gen 46:34
name, to be used throughout all *. Ex 3:15
Literally, "according to their * Ex 6:16f
Literally, "according to their * Ex 6:19f
so that later * could see the bread Ex 16:32
and grandsons, and even later *." Ex 34:7
forever throughout all their *." Lev 7:36
This ceremony, in later *, shall Lev 16:32
Literally, "these are the * of Num 3:2f
now or in the * to come, are Num 9:10
"If by mistake you or future * Num 15:22
to a thousand * of those who love Deu 5:9,10
their children throughout all *! Deu 5:29
who for a thousand * keeps his Deu 7:9
any of his descendants for ten *. Deu 23:2
all future * of Israel as well. Deu 29:14,15
Then your children and the * to Deu 29:22
rule this land for * to come! 2Sa 7:10,11
has been in my family for *." 1Ki 21:3
THESE ARE THE earliest * of 1Ch 1:1
in the order of their *, were: 1Ch 5:14
* of Aaron were as follows: 1Ch 6:4-15
To a thousand *: 1Ch 16:15
* of my children being kings too! 1Ch 17:17
of the Lord; * yet unborn shall Ps 22:31
your name to be honored in all *; Ps 45:17
of many *, all packed into one. Ps 61:6
handed down to us from former *. Ps 78:2,3
angry—on and on to distant *? Ps 85:5
LORD, THROUGH ALL the * you have Ps 90:1
so that future * will also praise Ps 102:18
Though a thousand * pass he Ps 105:8,9
* come and go but it makes no Ecc 1:3-7
and in the future * no one will Ecc 1:8-11
on down to godly men of future *. Is 8:16
of * of mankind as they march by? Is 41:4
In Jehovah all the * of Israel Is 45:25
be far away. The * born in exile Is 49:20
a joy for all the * of the world, Is 60:15
they have lain there many *. Is 61:4
their grandchildren, for all *. Eze 37:25
throughout the * of the world! Joe 2:2
Jerusalem will thrive as * pass. Joe 3:20
Literally, "So all the * from Mt 1:17f
fourteen of the * from Abraham to Mt 1:17
on every Sabbath for many *." Act 15:21
for centuries and * past, but now Col 1:26,27
Enoch, who lived seven * after Jud 1:14

GENEROSITY
dynasty! Such * is far beyond any 2Sa 7:19
Purity is best demonstrated by * Lk 11:41

GENEROUS
For God has been very * to me and Gen 33:11
to, all those with * hearts, may Ex 35:5-9
of Assyria to be * to Israel and to Ez 6:21,22
for the king was feeling very *. Est 1:7
servants, giving * gifts to Est 2:18
are able to be * with their gifts Ps 37:26
goes well for the * man who Ps 112:5
beg favors from a man who is *; Pro 19:6
Happy is the * man, the one who Pro 22:9
spoken of as *, outstanding men! Is 32:5
But good men will be * to others Is 32:8
an infant at a mother's * breasts. Is 66:11
If God has given you money, be * Rom 12:8
because of your * gifts to 2Co 9:13
Satan, he gave * gifts to men. Eph 4:8
them on their way with a * gift. 3Jn 1:6

GENEROUSLY
immediately and * with the first of 2Ch 31:5,6
were able to give * toward the Ez 2:68
He gives * to those in need. Ps 112:9
She sews for the poor, and * Pro 31:19,20
GIVE *, FOR your gifts will return Ecc 11:1
He gave * to charity and was a Act 10:2
the same Lord who * gives his Rom 10:12
godly man gives * to the poor. 2Co 9:9
than I need! I am * supplied with Php 4:18

GENESIS
Implied. See * 20:12. Gen 11:29f
This is more consistent with * Gen 11:32f
with the book of * and going right Lk 24:27
* 17:17. Rom 4:19f
* 2:21–22. 1Co 11:8f

GENITAL
of male and female * organs. Ex 34:13f
"Any man who has a * discharge Lev 15:1
man who is defiled by a * disease Lev 15:32

GENITALS
An animal that has injured * Lev 22:24

GENNESARET
They landed at *. Mt 14:34
When they arrived at * on the Mk 6:53
the shore of Lake *, great crowds Lk 5:1

GENTILE
because she was a * or (if she was Num 12:1f
To the foolish * nations of the Deu 32:21
O * nations, Deu 32:40,41
holy throne. The * rulers of the Ps 47:9
Let the * converts chant, Ps 118:4
* lands to which I exile them!" Eze 4:13
will soon fall upon all * nations. Ob 1:15
you as the * and the publican." Mt 18:17f
Syrophoenician—a "despised *!" Mk 7:26
* triumph ends in God's good time. Lk 21:24
of a * was a serious offense. Jn 18:28f
Nicolaus of Antioch (a * convert Act 6:5
against the * nations, this Act 7:45
to come into a * home like this. Act 10:28
declared that all * converts must Act 15:5
And this fact of * conversion Act 15:15
"To: The * brothers in Antioch, Act 15:23
he stayed with Titus Justus, a * Act 18:7
"As for the * Christians, we Act 21:25
had seen him with Trophimus, a * Act 21:29
I have among the other * churches. Rom 1:13
Jew and * are the same in this Rom 10:12
them: so are all the * churches. Rom 16:4
be circumcised, though he was a *. Gal 2:3
he ate with the * Christians [who Gal 2:12
by birth, not mere * sinners, and Gal 2:15

GENTILES
He gave them the lands of the *, Ps 105:44
a signal to the * and they shall Is 49:22
And my blessings are for *, too, Is 56:3
As for the *, the outsiders who Is 56:6
the riches of the * will flow to Is 66:12
shall declare my glory to the *. Is 66:19
by the * from morning till night. Mal 1:11
be mightily revered among the *." Mal 1:14
And I tell you this, that many * Mt 8:11
"Don't go to the * or the Mt 10:5
lost sheep of Israel—not the *." Mt 15:24
I will be handed over to the * Lk 18:32
down by the * until the period of Lk 21:24
lands, or maybe even to the *! Jn 7:35
Spirit would be given to * too! Act 10:45
that * also were being converted! Act 11:1
"You fellowshiped with * and Act 11:3
not to worry about their being *! Act 11:12
God who gave these * the same gift Act 11:17
has given to the *, too, the Act 11:18
of these * became believers. Act 11:21
also all of you * here who Act 13:26
And many Jews and godly * who Act 13:43

(GENTILES Con't)
life—well, we will offer it to *. Act 13:46
you a light to the *, to lead them Act 13:47
When the * heard this, they were Act 13:48
many—both Jews and *—believed. Act 14:1
distrust among the * against Paul Act 14:2
to incite a mob of *, Jews, and Act 14:5,6
the door of faith to the * too. Act 14:27
the *, too, were being converted. Act 15:3
Good News to the *, so that they Act 15:7
that he accepts * by giving them Act 15:8
by burdening the * with a yoke that Act 15:10
had done through them among the *. Act 15:12
first visited the * to take from Act 15:14
so that *, too, will find the Act 15:17
insist that the * who turn to God Act 15:19
concerning the *, as decided by the Act 16:4
and the devout *, and spoke daily Act 17:17
now on I will preach to the *." Act 18:6
for Jews and * alike—the necessity Act 20:21
among the * through his work. Act 21:19
and defiles it by bringing * in!" Act 21:28
will send you far away to the *!' Act 22:21
both your own people and the *. Act 26:17
to send you to the * to open their Act 26:17
and also to the * that all must Act 26:20
bring light to Jews and * alike." Act 26:23
* too, and they will accept it." Act 28:28,29
Literally, "among the *." Rom 1:13f
and * alike who keep on sinning. Rom 2:9
whether they are Jews or *. Rom 2:10
are sinners, whether Jews or *. Rom 3:9
No, the *, too, may come to him Rom 3:29
all, whether Jews or *, are Rom 3:30
we are Jews or *, and to be kind to Rom 9:23,24
God has given the * the opportunity Rom 9:30
available to the *, and then the Rom 11:11
as a special messenger to you *. Rom 11:13
them want what you * have and in Rom 11:14
And you * who were branches from, Rom 11:17
until all of you * have come to Rom 11:25
God's giving his gifts to you *. Rom 11:28
came also that the * might be saved Rom 15:9
the *, and sing to your name." Rom 15:9
"Be glad, O you *, along with his Rom 15:10
you *, let everyone praise him." Rom 15:11
and he will be King over the *; Rom 15:12
So I pray for you * that God who Rom 15:13
Christ to you *, bringing you the Rom 15:15,16
has used me to win the * to God. Rom 15:18
* from the church in Jerusalem. Rom 15:27
Literally, "For if the * have Rom 15:27f
salvation for you *, kept secret Rom 16:25,26,27
and it is foolish to the * 1Co 1:22
and the * say it's all nonsense. 1Co 1:23
both Jews and *, to see that Christ 1Co 1:24
When I am with * who follow 1Co 9:20
they are Jews or * or Christians. 1Co 10:32
Some of us are Jews, some are *, 1Co 12:13
well as from the hands of the *. 2Co 11:26
I could go to the * and show them Gal 1:16
message I was preaching to the *. Gal 2:2
me in winning the *, just as Peter Gal 2:7,8,9
preaching to the * while they Gal 2:7,8,9
eat with the * anymore because he Gal 2:12
trying to make these * obey them? Gal 2:14
the * also, through their faith. Gal 3:8,9
Now God can bless the *, too, Gal 3:14
Before you * knew God you were Gal 4:8
you * by making us all one family, Eph 2:14
and excluded the *, for he died to Eph 2:15
of peace to you * who were very far Eph 2:17
Now all of us, whether Jews or * Eph 2:18
you * are a part of God's house. Eph 3:1
God's favor to you *, as I briefly Eph 3:2,3
of his, that the *, too, are Eph 3:2,3
secret: that the * will have their Eph 3:6
joy of telling the * the Glad News Eph 3:8
the Savior of the * too, just as he Eph 3:9
family—Jews and * alike—are seen to Eph 3:10
his salvation is for the * too. Eph 6:19
to tell his secret plan to you *. Col 1:25
of his plan are for you * too. Col 1:26,27
* for fear some might be saved; 1Th 2:16
this truth to the *, and to show 1Ti 2:7
to preach to the * and teach them. 2Ti 1:11

GENTLE
Like the * rain and dew, Deu 32:2
While the * rains descend from Deu 33:28
was the sound of a * whisper. 1Ki 19:12
of mine be as * and fruitful as Ps 72:6
But you are merciful and *, Ps 86:15
* words cause life and health; Pro 15:4
are planning to refuse my * care Is 8:6
He will be *—he will not shout Is 42:2
flowing like a * river, and great Is 48:18
Is it because I've been too *, Is 57:11
but please be *. Jer 10:24
Israel, the Lord will be very *. Joe 3:16
the world like a * dew or the Mic 5:7
for I am * and humble, and you Mt 11:29,30
Be humble and *. Eph 4:2
Be * and ready to forgive; Col 3:13
But we were as * among you as a 1Th 2:7
but he must be * and kind, and not 1Ti 3:3
others, and to be patient and *. 1Ti 6:11
they must be *, patient teachers 2Ti 2:24
be * and truly courteous to all. Tit 3:2
lasting charm of a * and quiet 1Pe 3:4
do it in a * and respectful way. 1Pe 3:15

GENTLEMEN
"*: Greetings! Ez 4:18
I beg you, *, stop this business Neh 5:10
He tried to be a peacemaker. '*,' Act 7:26
"*, this business is our income. Act 19:25

GENTLENESS
Your * has made me great. 2Sa 22:36
Is his * too rough? Job 15:11
me; your * has made me great. Ps 18:35
I come with quiet love and *? 1Co 4:21
faithfulness, * and self-control; Gal 5:23
of all pure and full of quiet *. Jas 3:17

GENTLY
sake, deal * with young Absalom." 2Sa 18:5
But the Lord will not deal * with Ps 12:3,4
and * lead the ewes with young. Is 40:11
to the Lord, transporting them * Is 66:20
to treat him * and not to forbid Act 24:23
*, as Christ himself would do. 2Co 10:1
are godly should * and humbly help Gal 6:1
a man he can deal * with other men, Heb 5:1

GENUBATH
She presented him with a son, *, 1Ki 11:20

GENUINE
have a * priest working for me!" Ju 17:13
Jesus felt * love for this man as Mk 10:21

GEOGRAPHICAL
languages, and * locations. Gen 10:31

GERA
Ashbel, *, Naaman, Gen 46:19-22
Ehud (son of *, a Benjaminite), who Ju 3:15
It was Shime-i, the son of *, a 2Sa 16:5
Then Shime-i (the son of * the 2Sa 19:16
of * the Benjaminite from Bahurim? 1Ki 2:8
Addar, *, Abihud, Abishua, Naaman, 1Ch 8:3,4,5
Ahoah, *, Shephuphan, Huram. 1Ch 8:3,4,5
* (also called Heglam), the father 1Ch 8:6,7

GERAHS
shekel is twenty *], half a shekel Ex 30:13f
twenty * shall be the shekel." Lev 27:25f
(The shekel is twenty *. Num 3:47,48f
exchanged for twenty *, no less; Eze 45:12

GERAR
the way to *, in the Gaza strip; Gen 10:15-19
the city of *, he remarked that Gen 20:1
to the city of * where Abimelech, Gen 26:1
So Isaac stayed in *. Gen 26:6
So Isaac moved to * Valley and Gen 26:17
dug a new well in * Valley, and Gen 26:19
One day Isaac had visitors from * Gen 26:26
They chased them as far as *, 2Ch 14:13
While they were at * they 2Ch 14:14

GERASENE
other side, in the * country across Lk 8:26

GERAZIM
claim it is here [at Mount * Jn 4:20

GERIZIM
*, and a curse from Mount Ebal! Deu 11:29
from Mount Ebal! (* and Ebal are Deu 11:30
stand upon Mount * to proclaim a Deu 27:12
the foot of Mount * and half at the Jos 8:33
the top of Mount * and shouted Ju 9:7

GERSHOM
They had a baby named * (meaning Ex 2:22
Moses' two sons, * (meaning Ex 18:3
(son of * and grandson of Moses! Ju 18:30
*, Kohath, Merari. 1Ch 6:1
*, Kohath, Merari. 1Ch 6:16
The sons of * were:Libni, 1Ch 6:17
In the * clan: 1Ch 6:19,20,21
Zimmah, Shime-i, Jahath, *, Levi. 1Ch 6:39-43
The subclans of the * clan 1Ch 6:62
to the clan of * by the half-tribe 1Ch 6:71
130 from the clan of *; 1Ch 15:4-10
* division, the 1Ch 23:6
Subdivisions of the * corps were 1Ch 23:7
* and 1Ch 23:14,15
from the clan of * included 1Ch 26:20,21,22
Shebuel, son of * and grandson 1Ch 26:23,24
with Jehiel (a descendant of *). 1Ch 29:8
From the clan of Phinehas—*; Ez 8:2-14

GERSHOM'S
tribe of Levi. * sons were led by 1Ch 23:16

GERSHON
Levi and his sons: *, Kohath, Gen 46:8-14
*, Kohath, Merari. Ex 6:16
The sons of * were:Libni, Ex 6:17
Levi's son * Num 3:16-24
A similar census of the * Num 4:38-41
were given to the * division for Num 7:7
and the men of the * and Merari Num 10:17
named after their ancestor *. Num 26:57
of Manasseh. The * division Jos 21:6
The descendants of *, another Jos 21:27
assigned to the division of *. Jos 21:33
From the * clan, Joah (son of 2Ch 29:12,13,14

GERSHON-ITES
to them, but the * will be Num 4:28

GERSHONITE
a census of the * division of the Num 4:21,22,23

GERSHONITES
may assign the *' tasks to them, Num 4:27
The *, named after their ancestor Num 26:57

GERUTH
to the village of * Chimham, near Jer 41:16,17

GESHAN
Regem, Jotham, *, Pelet, Ephah, 1Ch 2:47

GESHEM
and Tobiah and * the Arab heard of Neh 2:19
WHEN SANBALLAT, TOBIAH, * the Neh 6:1
"* tells me that everywhere he Neh 6:5,6

GESHUR
of the kingdoms of * and Ma-acah. Jos 12:5
the daughter of King Talmai of *. 2Sa 3:3
Absalom fled to King Talmai of * 2Sa 13:37,38,39
Then Joab went to * and brought 2Sa 14:23
* if he didn't intend to see me. 2Sa 14:32
him while I was at *—that if he 2Sa 15:7,8
of Gilead. But * and Aram wrested 1Ch 2:23
the daughter of King Talmai of *. 1Ch 3:2

GESHURITES
borders of the * and Ma-acthites. Deu 3:14
The land of the *; Jos 13:2-7
the territory of the * and the Jos 13:11
not driven out the * or the Jos 13:13
time raiding the *, the Girzites, 1Sa 27:8

GESTURE
in a * of offering to the Lord. Ex 29:24
the Lord in a * of offering; Ex 29:26
to the Lord by a * of waving it Lev 7:14
* of waving them before the altar. Lev 8:27
the Lord as a * of offering it to Lev 9:21
to the Lord by the * of waving it Lev 10:14
the Lord by the * of waving them. Lev 10:15
* of waving them before the altar. Lev 14:12
as a * of offering to the Lord. Lev 14:24
the Lord in a * of offering, and it Lev 23:9,10,11
the Lord in a * of offering. Lev 23:17
the Lord in a * of offering; Num 6:20
and Aaron, with a * of offering, Num 8:11
to the Lord in a * of offering. Num 8:21
in a * of offering to the Lord. Num 15:19,20,21
to the Lord by the * of waving them Num 18:8
to me by the * of waving them Num 18:11
the * of waving before the altar. Num 18:18
to the Lord by the * of waving Num 18:24
the * of waving before the altar. Num 18:25,26
the * of waving before the altar. Num 31:29
presented by the * of waving before Deu 12:6
the king of Syria as a * of peace, Dan 11:6

GESTURES
realized from his * that he must Lk 1:22
father, talking to him by *. Lk 1:62
So Paul, with many *, Act 26:1

GETHER
were:Uz, Hul, *, Mash. Gen 10:23
Arpachshad, Lud, Aram, Uz, Hul, *, 1Ch 1:17

GETHSEMANE
to a garden grove, *, and told them Mt 26:36
the Garden of *, and he instructed Mk 14:32
anguished cry in * ("Let this cup Heb 5:7f

GETTING
of her lying down or * up again. Gen 19:33
that she wasn't * pregnant anymore, Gen 30:9
"Forgive my not * up, father," Gen 31:35
Go and see how they are * along, Gen 37:13,14
He asked how they had been * Gen 43:27
What are we * into? Deu 1:28
would know what they are * into! Deu 32:29
of Shechem from * back in, while Ju 9:44
and asked him how he was * along. Ju 18:15,16
said, "Look, it's * late. Ju 19:9
so they left, * as far as Jerusalem Ju 19:10
His servant said to him, "It's * Ju 19:11
in two ways—he was * taller, and he 1Sa 2:26
and see how the boys are * along; 1Sa 17:18
Quickly * ready, she took along 1Sa 25:42
and the army were * along and how 2Sa 11:7
* there just as Absalom arrived. 2Sa 15:37
the ringleader in * the people to 1Ki 12:2,3,4
about * back her house and land. 2Ki 8:3
all be spent on * the Temple into 2Ki 12:7
"How are they * along?" Neh 1:2
and sanctify them, * up early in Job 1:5
"What is this you are doing, * Job 15:12
their time just * barely enough to Job 24:5
prevent you from * into a life of Job 36:21
you even keep me from * into Ps 32:7
for my pursuers are * very close. Ps 35:3
Lord, slow in * angry, full of Ps 86:15
back and forth, * nowhere. Ecc 1:3-7
And he isn't * deaf! Is 59:1
that Israel knows is * caught. Jer 2:26,27

(GETTING Con't)
Then tell them: You're * the Jer 13:13
The fact is, I am * ready to Amo 3:4
For it was * worse and worse. Jon 1:11
be no end of * rich by cheating? Mic 6:10
He is slow in * angry, but when Nah 1:3
"Woe to you for * rich by evil Hab 2:9
partying and * drunk, your Lord Mt 24:49
When Pilate saw that he wasn't * Mt 27:24
desolate spot, and it is * late." Mk 6:35,36
don't worry about * them back. Lk 6:30
on asking and you will keep on *; Lk 11:9
without first * estimates and then Lk 14:28
night with them, as it was * late. Lk 24:29
"That means he is * better!" Jn 11:12,13
but just as I was * started with my Act 11:15
how the new converts were * along. Act 15:36
and, as a result, * paid within Rom 1:27
looking forward to * something we Rom 8:24
wild parties and * drunk or in Rom 13:12,13
them—whose idea in * out the Gospel 2Co 2:17
and I was * hungry I still didn't 2Co 11:8,9
the churches are * along: Who 2Co 11:28
You were * along so well. Gal 5:7
you all about how I am * along. Eph 6:21
a great boost in * out the Good Php 1:12
about you and how you are * along. Php 2:19
because you are * along so well, Col 2:5
will tell you how I am * along. Col 4:7
* into other people's business. 1Ti 5:13
for when Moses was * ready to Heb 8:5
sin, lust, * drunk, wild parties, 1Pe 4:3
and are really * along quite well! 2Pe 1:12
they are * to know him better. 1Jn 4:7

GEUEL
*, son of Machi, from the tribe of Num 13:3-15

GEZER
King Horam of * arrived with his Jos 10:33
The king of *; Jos 12:8-24
then to * and on over to the Jos 16:1
The Canaanites living in * were Jos 16:10
Shechem (a City of Refuge), *, Jos 21:20,21,22
of the Canaanites living in *; Ju 1:29
all the way from Geba to *. 2Sa 5:25
cities of Hazor, Megiddo, and *. 1Ki 9:15
and Gezer. * was the city the king 1Ki 9:16
So now Solomon rebuilt * along 1Ki 9:17,18
*; Jokme-am; 1Ch 6:66-69
on the west by * and its villages, 1Ch 7:28
all the way from Gibeon to *. 1Ch 14:16
the Philistines again, at *. 1Ch 20:4

GHOST
Your voice will whisper like a * Is 29:4
The cities of Judah shall be * Jer 9:11
for they thought he was a *. Mt 14:26
it was a *, for they all saw him. Mk 6:49
thinking they were seeing a *! Lk 24:37
and make sure that I am not a *! Lk 24:39

GHOSTS
not a ghost! For * don't have Lk 24:39

GIAH
at Ammah Hill near *, along the 2Sa 2:24

GIANT
was the last of the * Rephaim. Deu 3:11
He was a * of a man, measuring 1Sa 17:4-7
the Philistine * strutted before 1Sa 17:16
he saw Goliath the * step out from 1Sa 17:23
"Have you seen the *?" 1Sa 17:25
* with a sling and a stone. 1Sa 17:50,51
Ishbi-benob, a * whose speartip 2Sa 21:16
Hushathite killed Saph, another *. 2Sa 21:18
at Gath, a * with six fingers on 2Sa 21:20,21
of the sons of the *, Sippai, and 1Ch 20:4
the brother of Goliath the *; 1Ch 20:5
battle, at Gath, a * with six 1Ch 20:6,7
a *) defied and taunted Israel; 1Ch 20:6,7
me, running upon me like a *. Job 16:14
strong as the * bulls from Bashan. Ps 22:12
It splits the * trees of Lebanon. Ps 29:5,6

GIANTS
children became *, of whom so many Gen 6:4
and what's more, we saw Anakim * Num 13:28
of the ancient race of *. Num 13:33
They have even seen * there—the Deu 1:28
tribe, tall as the * of Anakim; Deu 2:10
Among them are the famed Anak *, Deu 9:1
routed all of the *—the descendants Jos 11:21
from the tribe of * in Gath, and 2Sa 21:22
Benaiah killed two *, 2Sa 23:20
Kabzeel, killed the two famous * 1Ch 11:22
These * were descendants of the 1Ch 20:8
descendants of the * of Gath, and 1Ch 20:8

GIBBAR
From the subclan of *, 95; Ez 2:3-35

GIBBERISH
foreigners who speak strange *! Is 28:11

GIBBETHON
Ekron, Eltekeh, *, Baalath, Jehud, Jos 19:41-46
Elteke, *, Aijalon, and Jos 21:23,24
siege to the Philistine city of *. 1Ki 15:27
Philistine city of *, heard that 1Ki 16:15,16
So Omri led the army of * to 1Ki 16:17

GIBE-A
father of Machbenah and of *). 1Ch 2:48,49

GIBE-AH
Zanoah, Kain, *, Timnah, Halhul, Jos 15:48-62
Jerusalem), *, and Kiriath-jearim. Jos 18:21-28
of Ephraim, at *, the city which Jos 24:33
go on to *, or possibly Ramah." Ju 19:12,13
as they came to *, a village of the Ju 19:14
was living now in *, even though it Ju 19:16
"We arrived one evening at *, a Ju 20:4
"That night the men of * Ju 20:5
we have punished the village of *. Ju 20:8,9,10
* for this horrible deed." Ju 20:8,9,10
from the city of * so that we can Ju 20:13
of them arrived in * to join the Ju 20:14,15
*, to attack the men of Benjamin. Ju 20:19,20
between Bethel and *, so that about Ju 20:31
*, and killed most of them there. Ju 20:43
to his home at *, a band of men 1Sa 10:26
When a messenger came to *, 1Sa 11:4
son, in * in the land of Benjamin. 1Sa 13:2
went to * in the land of Benjamin. 1Sa 13:15
at the edge of *, around the 1Sa 14:2
Saul's lookouts in * saw a 1Sa 14:16
to Ramah, and Saul returned to *. 1Sa 15:34
He was in * at the time, sitting 1Sa 22:6
in * and betrayed David to him. 1Sa 23:19
back to Saul at * to tell him that 1Sa 26:1
Ittai (son of Ribai) from *, of 2Sa 23:24-39
of Ribai) a Benjaminite from *; 1Ch 11:26-47
Ahi-ezer, son of Shemaah from *. 1Ch 12:3-7

GIBEAH
Micaiah (daughter of Uriel of *). 2Ch 13:1
all the people of *—the city of Is 10:28,29
Warn with trumpet blasts in * and Hos 5:8
as depraved as what they did in * Hos 9:9
ever since that awful night in *, Hos 10:9
that the men of * were wiped out? Hos 10:9

GIBEATH-ELOHIM
After that you will come to *, 1Sa 10:5

GIBEON
But when the people of * heard Jos 9:3,4,5
(The names of the cities were *, Jos 9:17
how the people of * had made peace Jos 10:1
frightened. For * was a great Jos 10:2
"Come and help me destroy *," Jos 10:4
armies for a united attack on *. Jos 10:5
The men of * hurriedly sent Jos 10:6
left Gilgal and went to rescue *. Jos 10:7
numbers of them at * and chased the Jos 10:10
stand still over *, and let the Jos 10:12
to Gaza, and from Goshen to *. Jos 10:41
treaty except the Hivites of *; Jos 11:19
Ophni, Geba, *, Ramah, Be-eroth, Jos 18:21-28
*, Gaba, Anathoth, and Almon. Jos 21:17,18
troops to * from Mahanaim, and 2Sa 2:12
They met at the pool of *, where 2Sa 2:13
along the road into the * desert. 2Sa 2:24
brother Asahel at the battle of *. 2Sa 3:30
the great stone in *, they came 2Sa 20:8,9,10
in *, the city of King Saul." 2Sa 21:5,6
The men of * impaled them in the 2Sa 21:9
altars was at * and now the king 1Ki 3:4
had been at *) and said to him, 1Ki 9:2,3
Je-iel, the father of *, lived at 1Ch 8:29
the father of Gibeon, lived at *; 1Ch 8:29
wife was Maacah) lived in *. 1Ch 9:35,36,37
*, Abdon (the oldest), Zur, Kish, 1Ch 9:35,36,37
Ishmaiah from * (a brave warrior 1Ch 12:3-7
all the way from * to Gezer. 1Ch 14:16
hill of * continued to be active. 1Ch 16:39
on the hill of *, but David didn't 1Ch 21:29
the army officers and judges to * 2Ch 1:2,3
Next to them were Melatiah from *; Neh 3:7
and men from * and Mizpah, who Neh 3:7
From the subclan of *, 95; Neh 7:8-38
Mount Perazim and *, to do a Is 28:21
false prophet from *, addressed me Jer 28:1
up with him at the pool near *. Jer 41:12

GIBEONITES
family, for they murdered the *." 2Sa 21:1
So King David summoned the *. 2Sa 21:2
won't do it," the * replied, "and 2Sa 21:4

GIDDALTI
Twenty-second, * and twelve of his 1Ch 25:9-31

GIDDEL
Shamlai, Hanan, *, Gahar, Re-aiah, Ez 2:43-54
Jaalah, Darkon, *, Shephatiah, Ez 2:55,56,57
Shalmai, Hanan, *, Gahar, Neh 7:46-56
Jaala, Darkon, *, Neh 7:57,58,59

GIDEON
Joash's son, *, had been Ju 6:11
"Stranger," * replied, "if the Ju 6:13
But * replied, "Sir, how can I Ju 6:15
God is telling * that the same Ju 6:16f
* replied, "If it is really true Ju 6:17
* hurried home and roasted a Ju 6:19
When * had followed these Ju 6:20
When * realized that it had Ju 6:22
And * built an altar there and Ju 6:24
That night the Lord told * to Ju 6:25
So * took ten of his servants and Ju 6:27
that it was *, the son of Joash. Ju 6:29
From then on * was called Ju 6:32
the Lord came upon *, and he blew a Ju 6:34
Then * said to God, "If you are Ju 6:36
Then * said to the Lord, "Please Ju 6:39
JERUBBAAL (THAT IS, *—his other Ju 7:1
The Lord then said to *, "There Ju 7:2
But the Lord told *, "There are Ju 7:4
So * assembled them at the water. Ju 7:5,6
the Lord told *. Ju 7:7
So after * had collected all the Ju 7:8,9
the Lord said to *, "Get up! Ju 7:8,9
even to count! * crept up to one of Ju 7:12,13
only one thing! *, the son of Ju 7:14
When * heard the dream and the Ju 7:15
'We fight for God and for *!' Ju 7:18
of guards when * and the hundred Ju 7:19,20
"For the Lord and for *!" Ju 7:19,20
Then * sent for the troops of Ju 7:23
army of Midian. * also sent Ju 7:24
and Zeeb across the Jordan to *. Ju 7:25
were violently angry with *. Ju 8:1
But * replied, "God let you Ju 8:2,3
* now crossed the Jordan River Ju 8:4
Then * warned them, "When the Ju 8:7
Then * circled around by the Ju 8:11
The two kings fled, but * chased Ju 8:12
Later, * returned by way of Ju 8:13
Then * asked King Zebah and King Ju 8:18
been my brothers!" * exclaimed. Ju 8:19
Then Zebah and Zalmunna said to * Ju 8:21
So * killed them and took the Ju 8:21
Now the men of Israel said to *, Ju 8:22
But * replied, "I will not be Ju 8:23,24
camels' necks. * made an ephod Ju 8:27
deed that * and his family did. Ju 8:27
named Abimelech. * finally died, Ju 8:32
But as soon as * was dead, the Ju 8:33
to the family of * despite all he Ju 8:35
by * and all of his descendants. Ju 9:16
have done right by * and his Ju 9:19
not been fair to *, then may Ju 9:20
Then the Lord sent *, Barak, 1Sa 12:11
like the time when * triumphed over Is 10:26
of the faith of * and Barak and Heb 11:32

GIDEON'S
Egypt (much on * mind: see verse Ju 6:16f
forty years—all during * lifetime. Ju 8:28
ONE DAY * son Abimelech visited Ju 9:1
by seventy kings—* seventy sons—or Ju 9:2
Of all of * wives, only Ju 9:2f
him in butchering * seventy sons Ju 9:24
sin of murdering * seventy sons. Ju 9:56,57
So the curse of Jotham, * son, Ju 9:56,57
the Midianites by * little band. Is 9:4

GIDEONI
Abidan (son of *) Num 1:2-15
Abidan (son of *) Num 2:3-31
Abidan the son of *, chief of the Num 7:60-65
led by Abidan the son of *. Num 10:24

GIDOM
way, and two thousand more near *. Ju 20:45

GIFT
brought the Lord a * of his farm Gen 4:3
"They are my * to you as a public Gen 21:30
No matter what dowry or * you Gen 34:12
special *—a brightly-colored coat. Gen 37:3
appear before me without a *. Ex 34:20
will accept your * for the Lord. Lev 1:2,3
be accepted by the Lord as your *. Lev 23:9,10,11
of Israel bring a * to the Lord it Num 5:9,10
of them bring his * on a different Num 7:11
brought his * the first day. Num 7:12
to the Lord as a * from the entire Num 8:11
just as any other * to the Lord is Num 8:13
as a * to Aaron and his sons. Num 8:19
They are a * to you from the Num 18:6
is your special * of service. Num 18:7
occasions bring a * to the Lord. Deu 16:16
say to him, 'This * is my Deu 26:2,3
What sort of * shall we send with 1Sa 6:2
"Yes, send it back with a *," 1Sa 6:3
"No, I will not have it as a *. 2Sa 24:24
Then she gave the king a * of 1Ki 10:10
the largest single * of spices King 1Ki 10:10
Take him a * of ten loaves of 1Ki 14:3
or some special *, use it to pay 2Ki 12:4,5
him off with a * of $2,000,000, so 2Ki 15:19,20
She gave the king a * of over a 2Ch 9:9
good, is this some great * to him? Job 35:7
And each of them brought him a * Job 42:11
Children are a * from God; Ps 127:3
an eternal * to his people Israel. Ps 135:12
to Israel as a * forever, for his Ps 136:21
yes, a permanent * to his Ps 136:22
man is silenced by giving him a *! Pro 21:14
One who doesn't give the * he Pro 25:14
life—that is indeed a * from God. Ecc 5:19,20
who accompany the * to Jerusalem Is 16:3

(GIFT Con't)
and perfume to Molech as your *. Is 57:9
every nation as a * to the Lord, Is 66:20
the prince gives a * of land to one Eze 46:16
But if he gives a * of land to Eze 46:17
boasting then of his prophetic *! Zec 13:4
bring that kind of *, why should he Mal 1:9
When you give a * to a beggar, Mt 6:2
For which is greater, the * on Mt 23:19
itself that sanctifies the *? Mt 23:19
you will get! Your * will return to Lk 6:38
what a wonderful * God has for you, Jn 4:10
will never receive this *. Jn 6:63
"I am leaving you with a *—peace Jn 14:27
I have is a * from you, for I have Jn 17:7
receive this *, the Holy Spirit. Act 2:38
at them eagerly, expecting a *. Act 3:5
thinking God's * can be bought! Act 8:20
amazed that the * of the Holy Act 10:45
Gentiles the same * he gave us when Act 11:17
by the free * of the Lord Jesus?" Act 15:11
daughters who had the * of Act 21:9
who also had the * of prophecy, Act 21:10
Literally, "some spiritual * Rom 1:11,12f
No, for being saved is a *; Rom 4:4,5
given to us by faith, as a free *; Rom 4:16
will take God's * of forgiveness Rom 5:17
but the free * of God is eternal Rom 6:23
For in that case the free * would Rom 11:6
If your * is that of serving Rom 12:7
* to the Jewish Christians there. Rom 15:25
spiritual * of the Gospel from Rom 15:27
every spiritual * and power for 1Co 1:7
God gives some the * of a husband 1Co 7:7
he gives the * of being able to 1Co 7:7
is his * from the same Spirit. 1Co 12:8
Those who have the * of healing, 1Co 12:28
who have that * of foreign speech? 1Co 12:30
IF I HAD the * of being able to 1Co 13:1
If I had the * of prophecy and 1Co 13:2
Even if I had the * of faith so 1Co 13:2
and especially the * of prophecy, 1Co 14:1
But if your * is that of being 1Co 14:2
I wish you all had the * of 1Co 14:5
If someone is given the * of 1Co 14:13
pray also for the * of knowing what 1Co 14:13
*, while all the others listen. 1Co 14:29,30
In this way all who have the * 1Co 14:31
You who claim to have the * of 1Co 14:37
send your loving * with a letter to 1Co 16:3
me to take the * to Jerusalem. 2Co 8:19
way we are handling this large *. 2Co 8:20
me to see that the * you promised 2Co 9:5
I want it to be a real * and not 2Co 9:5
Thank God for his Son—his * too 2Co 9:15
Macedonia brought me another *. 2Co 11:8,9
it too is a * from God. Eph 2:8
to others he has given the * of Eph 4:11
still others have a * for caring Eph 4:11
Literally, "stir up the * of 2Ti 1:6f
For the Holy Spirit, God's *, 2Ti 1:7
you received as a * from the Holy 2Ti 1:14
For the free * of eternal Tit 2:11
and along with this * comes the Tit 2:12
and proved it by accepting his *; Heb 11:4
comes as a * from God, not from Heb 13:9
for that is the * God has promised Jas 2:5
the priceless * of eternal life; 1Pe 1:4
on their way with a generous *. 3Jn 1:6
of the Water of Life—as a *! Rev 21:6

GIFTED
him and Oholiab * teachers of their Ex 35:34
"And some who are most * in the Dan 11:35
and Silas, both being * speakers, Act 15:32
of those most * is still so poor. 1Co 13:9

GIFTS
Then Pharaoh gave Abram many * Gen 12:16
however, he gave * to the sons Gen 25:6
Zebulun (meaning "*"), for she Gen 30:20
given me good * for my husband. Gen 30:20
And Jacob replied, "They are my * Gen 33:8
Please take my *. Gen 33:11
Take them to the man as *—balm, Gen 43:11
So they took the * and double Gen 43:15
load you down with * when you Ex 3:21
to their tents to prepare their *. Ex 35:20
* were received each morning. Ex 36:3
The people brought * of 3,140 Ex 38:24
desecrating the people's sacred *; Lev 22:1
or handles the * dedicated to Lev 22:3
"Accept their *," the Lord told Num 7:4,5
dedication * on the day the altar Num 7:10
brought his * and offerings. Num 7:18-23
On the fourth day the * were Num 7:30-35
of Reuben; his * and offerings were Num 7:30-35
tribe of Simeon, with the same *. Num 7:36-41
He, too, offered the same * and Num 7:42-47
brought his *, the same as those Num 7:48-53
Benjamin, with his *, the same as Num 7:60-65
brought his * on the tenth day. Num 7:66-71
Asher, brought his * on the Num 7:72-77
* and offerings as the others. Num 7:72-77
dedicated by these * from the Num 7:84,85,86
priests all the * which are brought Num 18:8
All other * presented to me by Num 18:11
* the people bring as offerings to Num 18:12
not treat the holy * of the people Num 18:32
Only your * to the Lord, and the Deu 12:26,27
He doesn't feel honored by such * Deu 17:1
With the choicest * of heaven Deu 33:13
May he be blessed with the best * Deu 33:16
Many * for me.' Ju 5:30
If you send these * and then 1Sa 6:4,5
to the Lord were * from the mayors 1Sa 6:17
early the next morning with the *. 1Sa 17:20
Then David accepted her * and 1Sa 25:35
wrote them. The * were sent to the 1Sa 30:27-31
hasn't fed us or given us *!" 2Sa 19:42
In exchange for the * from the 1Ki 10:13
So Naaman started out, taking * of 2Ki 5:5
now please accept my *." 2Ki 5:15
get away without taking his *. 2Ki 5:20
him with many * of gold, silver, 1Ch 18:10
King David dedicated these * to 1Ch 18:11
the care of the * brought to the 1Ch 26:20,21,22
to care for the * given to the Lord 1Ch 26:26
who brought * to the Lord. 1Ch 26:28
the * dedicated by famous persons. 1Ch 28:12
their * willingly and joyously. 1Ch 29:17
Then Solomon brought in the * 2Ch 5:1
the Queen of Sheba * of the same 2Ch 9:12
of them valuable * of money and 2Ch 21:3,4
sheep were brought as holy *. 2Ch 29:32,33
They distributed the * to the 2Ch 31:14,15
nations, and many * for the Lord 2Ch 32:23
system for * for the Temple. 2Ch 34:9
guard duty there. * were brought by 2Ch 34:9
as well as * for the Temple. Ez 1:6
to present these * to Shesh-bazzar, Ez 1:8
The total value of their * Ez 2:69
Some of their leaders gave * for Neh 7:70
giving generous * to everyone and Est 2:18
rejoice and send * to each other. Est 9:19
and the giving of * this historic Est 9:22
with pleasure the * you have given Ps 20:3
with their * and loans to others, Ps 37:26
with * and entreat your favors." Ps 45:12
He receives * for Ps 68:18
* to your temple in Jerusalem. Ps 68:29
Egypt will send * of precious Ps 68:31
from Seba—all will bring their *. Ps 72:10
to distribute. My * are better Pro 8:19
The Lord hates the * of the Pro 15:8
and fair than when we give him *. Pro 21:3
God loathes the * of evil men, Pro 21:27
don't long for their favors and * Pro 23:6,7,8
labors, for these are * from God. Ecc 3:13
GIVE GENEROUSLY, FOR your * will Ecc 11:1
Divide your * among many, Ecc 11:2
divide, will bring * to the Lord of Is 18:7
you and will bring you many *." Is 62:11
* I gave you, says the Lord God. Eze 16:14
services—men pay with many *. Eze 16:33,34
But not you, you give them *, Eze 16:33,34
with the very * I gave them. Eze 20:26
For when you offer * to them and Eze 20:31
don't bring your * to me as well! Eze 20:39
and the finest of your * Eze 20:40
"Their food shall be the * and Eze 44:29
fruits and all the * for the Lord Eze 44:30
Only * to his sons are permanent. Eze 46:17
you many wonderful * and honors if Dan 2:6
he gave him many costly *, and Dan 2:48
Daniel answered, "Keep your *, Dan 5:17
knew—and lavish on him costly *! Dan 11:38
and her orchards—* she claims her Hos 1:12
gods and offered them choice *." Hos 3:1
For she has given * to Egypt and Hos 12:1
built with the * of worshipers, Mic 1:7
Jedaiah will bring * of silver and Zec 6:10,11
Accept their * and make from them Zec 6:10,11
sometime—give him * like that—and Mal 1:8
how to give good * to your Mt 7:11
* to those who ask him for them? Mt 7:11
and your * I want—I want you to be Mt 9:13
the * on the altar' is binding! Mt 23:18
their * into the collection box. Lk 21:1
consigning their * to Barnabas and Act 11:30
days before such * and sacrifices Act 18:18f
days before such * and sacrifices Act 18:22f
or bringing him * to make his stay Act 24:23
a result we were showered with *, Act 28:10
giving his * to you Gentiles. Rom 11:28
For God's * and his call can Rom 11:29
* God was merciful to you instead. Rom 11:30
all the wonderful * he has given 1Co 1:4
the wonderful free * of grace and 1Co 2:12
In telling you about these * we 1Co 2:13
food brought there as * to him? 1Co 9:13
gives all these * and powers, 1Co 12:11
the more important of these *. 1Co 12:31
All the special * and powers from 1Co 13:8
knowledge—these * will disappear. 1Co 13:8
with our special *, and the 1Co 13:9
inadequate special * will come to 1Co 13:10
to have special * from the Holy 1Co 14:12
doesn't have these *, comes to 1Co 14:23
give rich spiritual * to others. 2Co 6:10
who receive your * should have an 2Co 8:13
when we take your * to those who 2Co 9:11
a result of your *—those in need 2Co 9:12
of your generous * to themselves 2Co 9:13
each our special *—they shook hands Gal 2:7,8,9
we have become * to God that he Eph 1:11
out of his rich storehouse of *. Eph 4:7
Satan, he gave generous * to men. Eph 4:8
But though I appreciate your *, Php 4:17
supplied with the * you sent me Php 4:18
heart be your rich * from God our 1Th 1:1
yes, God has assigned such * to Heb 2:4
He presents their * to God and Heb 5:1
about baptism and spiritual * Heb 6:2
by law to give * to help their Heb 7:5
appointed to offer * and Heb 8:3
For under the old system, * and Heb 9:9
But to obtain these *, you need 2Pe 1:5
poor, your * and service to them; Rev 2:19
from every nation as * for God. Rev 5:9

GIGANTIC
Can you spread out the * mirror Job 37:18

GIHON
is called the *, crossing the Gen 2:13
Solomon and my officers to *. 1Ki 1:33
took Solomon to *, riding on King 1Ki 1:38
own mule. At *, Zadok took a flask 1Ki 1:39
"The king sent him to * with 1Ki 1:44,45
Upper Spring of * and brought the 2Ch 32:30
of the Spring of * in the Kidron 2Ch 33:14
which leads from * Spring to the Is 7:3

GILALAI
*, Maai, Nethanel, Neh 12:35,36

GILBOA
the armies of Israel were at *. 1Sa 28:4
slaughtered wholesale on Mount *. 1Sa 31:1
and his three sons on Mount *. 1Sa 31:8
"Because I was on Mount * and 2Sa 1:6
O Mount *, 2Sa 1:21
had died in battle on Mount *. 2Sa 21:12,13,14
on the slopes of Mount *. 1Ch 10:1

GILEAD
and headed for the territory of *. Gen 31:21
them seven days later, at Mount *. Gen 31:23
spices, and herbs from * to Egypt. Gen 37:25
named after their ancestor *. Num 26:28-37
Manasseh's son * was their Num 27:1
land of Jazar and *, the tribes of Num 32:1
stay here in the cities of *. Num 32:26
you must give them the land of *; Num 32:29
Manasseh went to * and conquered Num 32:39
So Moses gave * to the Num 32:40
of the towns in *, and changed the Num 32:41
of the sub-clan of * (of the clan Num 36:1
from Aroer to *—from the edge of Deu 2:35,36
and all of * and Bashan as far as Deu 3:10
of Mount *, including its cities. Deu 3:12
the remainder of * and all of the Deu 3:13
Then I gave * to the clan of Deu 3:15
Jabbok River in * (which was the Deu 3:16
Ramoth, in *, for the tribe of Deu 4:43
gazed out across * as far as Dan: Deu 34:1
present area of *, which lies north Jos 12:2
northern half of * where the Jos 12:5
It included *; Jos 13:11
all the cities of * and half of the Jos 13:25
Half of * and King Og's royal Jos 13:31
was the father of *) had already Jos 17:1
given the land of * and Bashan [on Jos 17:1
(grandson of *, great-grandson of Jos 17:3
to the land of * and Bashan across Jos 17:5,6
Ramoth of *, in the territory of Jos 20:8
River to their own homeland of *. Jos 22:9
in the land of * they said to the Jos 22:15
Why did * remain across the Ju 5:17
Jair, a man from *, who judged Ju 10:3
in the land of * which are still Ju 10:4
(that is, in *), and also in Ju 10:7,8
were mobilized in * at that time, Ju 10:17
the leaders of * asked each Ju 10:18
from the land of *, but his mother Ju 11:1
His father (whose name was *) had Ju 11:1
The leaders of * sent for Ju 11:5
we will make you the king of *." Ju 11:8
across the land of * and Manasseh, Ju 11:29
*, and attacked the army of Ammon. Ju 11:29
the men of * were mere outcasts Ju 12:4
the * guards challenged him. Ju 12:5
buried in one of the cities of *. Ju 12:7
the Jordan in the land of *. Ju 20:1
escaped to the land of Gad and *. 1Sa 13:7
His territory included *, 2Sa 2:9
army now camped in the land of *. 2Sa 17:26
then they went to * in the land 2Sa 24:6
Jair (the son of Manasseh) in *; 1Ki 4:8-19

(GILEAD Con't)
whose area was *, including the 1Ki 4:8-19
from Tishbe in *, told King Ahab, 1Ki 17:1
well as all of *, Gad, and Reuben; 2Ki 10:32,33
the Arnon as far as * and Bashan. 2Ki 10:32,33
fifty men from *, and assassinated 2Ki 15:25
Kedesh, Hazor, *, Galilee, and all 2Ki 15:29
(Machir was also the father of *. 1Ch 2:21
cities in the land of *. 1Ch 2:22
were many cattle in the land of *. 1Ch 5:9
tents on the eastern edge of *. 1Ch 5:10
Jahdo, Jeshishai, Michael, *, 1Ch 5:14
The clan lived in and around * 1Ch 5:16
them Ramoth in *, Mahanaim, 1Ch 6:80
Machir (who became the father of * 1Ch 7:14
So these were the sons of *, the 1Ch 7:17
at Jazer in * in the fortieth year 1Ch 26:31,32
in *, Iddo (son of Zechariah); 1Ch 27:16-22
"Shechem, Succoth, *, Ps 60:6,7
Succoth Valley. "* is mine to Ps 108:8
that frisk across the slopes of *. Sol 4:1
frisking down the slopes of *. Sol 6:5
Is there no medicine in *? Jer 8:22
to me as fruitful * and the green Jer 22:6
Go up to * for medicine, O Jer 46:11
more on Mount Ephraim and Mount *. Jer 50:19
*, past the Dead Sea to Tamar. Eze 47:18
you refused my love. * is a city Hos 6:8
who invaded * around 740 B.C. Hos 10:14f
And *, too, is full of fools Hos 12:11
my people in * as grain is threshed Amo 1:3
For in their wars in * to enlarge Amo 1:13
of Benjamin shall possess *. Ob 1:19
Bashan and * as they did long ago. Mic 7:14
them in Israel—in * and Lebanon; Zec 10:10

GILEADITE
and Barzillai (a * of Rogelim). 2Sa 17:27
to the sons of Barzillai the *. 1Ki 2:7
of Barzillai the * and took her Ez 2:61
of Barzillai the * and took her Neh 7:63

GILEADITES
Machirites was the *, named after Num 26:28-37
The tribes of the *: Num 26:28-37

GILGAL
*, where the oaks of Moreh are. Deu 11:30
and camped in * at the eastern edge Jos 4:19
was called * (meaning, "to end" Jos 5:8,9
While they were camped at * on Jos 5:10
camp of Israel at *, they told Jos 9:6
sent messengers to Joshua at *. Jos 10:6
left * and went to rescue Gibeon. Jos 10:7
Joshua traveled all night from * Jos 10:9
the Israeli army returned to *. Jos 10:15
army returned to their camp at *. Jos 10:43
The king of Goiim in *; Jos 12:8-24
led by Caleb, came to Joshua in *. Jos 14:6
northwest toward *, opposite the Jos 15:7
coming from *, and announced to the Ju 2:1
at the quarries of *, he sent his Ju 3:17,18,19
at Bethel, then *, and then Mizpah, 1Sa 7:16
Go to * and wait there seven 1Sa 10:8
let us all go to * and reconfirm 1Sa 11:14
So they went to * and in a solemn 1Sa 11:15
mobilized again and joined at *. 1Sa 13:3,4
Meanwhile, Saul stayed at *, and 1Sa 13:7
Samuel then left * and went to 1Sa 13:15
and had then gone on to *. 1Sa 15:12
in pieces before the Lord at *. 1Sa 15:33
Judah had come to * to meet him and 2Sa 19:15
The king then went on to *, 2Sa 19:40
as they left *, "Stay here, for 2Ki 2:1
Elisha now returned to *, but 2Ki 4:38
worship me at * and at Bethel. Hos 4:15
All their wickedness began at *; Hos 9:15
*, the town where Baal-worship Hos 9:15f
But the sins of * flourish just Hos 12:11
to idols at Bethel and *. Amo 4:4
idols of Bethel, *, or Beer-sheba; Amo 5:5
for the people of * will be Amo 5:5
*, and how I blessed you there? Mic 6:5

GILO
(the son of Ahithophel) from *; 2Sa 23:24-39

GILOH
Goshen, Holon, *, Arab, Dumah, Jos 15:48-62
David's counselors who lived in *. 2Sa 15:12

GIMARAYA
as Mushki, Tabal, *, Tegerama, Eze 38:2,3f

GIMZO
Soco, Timnah, and * with their 2Ch 28:17,18

GINATH
half followed Tibni, the son of *. 1Ki 16:21

GINNETHOI
*, Abijah, Mijamin, Neh 12:1

GINNETHON
Obadiah, Daniel, *, Neh 10:1
Meshullam, leader of the * clan; Neh 12:12-21

GIRDED
Literally, "David was * with a 2Sa 6:14f

GIRDERS
was supported by * and not attached Eze 41:6
was not built with * as those in Eze 42:6

GIRGASHITES
Amorites, *,Hivites, Arkites, Gen 10:15-19
Canaanites, *, Jebusites." Gen 15:19,20,21
The Hittites, the *, Deu 7:1
Perizzites, *, Amorites, and Jos 3:10
*, the Hivites, and the Jebusites. Jos 24:11
Amorites, *, Hivites, Arkites, 1Ch 1:13-16
Perizzites, Jebusites, and *; Neh 9:8

GIRL
maid, an Egyptian * named Hagar, Gen 16:1
with my servant *, and her children Gen 16:2,3
For now this servant * of mine Gen 16:5
* as you see fit," Abram replied. Gen 16:6
One day the older * said to her Gen 19:31
and the older * went in and had Gen 19:33
and the younger * went in and lay Gen 19:35
and the Egyptian * Hagar—teasing Gen 21:9
rid of that slave * and her son. Gen 21:10
for him with a * from Egypt. Gen 21:20,21
"But suppose I can't find a * Gen 24:5
* from there to be my son's wife. Gen 24:7
about this, a beautiful young * Gen 24:15,16
The * ran home to tell her folks, Gen 24:28
family, and to bring back a * Gen 24:38
'But suppose I can't find a * Gen 24:39
Yes, find a * from among my Gen 24:40
I will say to some * who comes Gen 24:43
Let that * be the one you have Gen 24:44
path to find a * from the family Gen 24:48
* and ask her what she thinks." Gen 24:57
Sarah's slave *:Nebaioth, Kedar, Gen 25:12-15
forty, married a * named Judith, Gen 26:34
a Canaanite *, and that Jacob had Gen 28:6,7,8
servant *, Zilpah, to be her maid. Gen 29:24
servant *, Bilhah, to be her maid. Gen 29:29
"Get this * for me," he Gen 34:4
give me the * as my wife." Gen 34:12
Canaanite *—the daughter of Shua. Gen 38:2
for him to marry a * named Tamar. Gen 38:6
And he gave him a wife, a * named Gen 41:45
mother was a * from Canaan). Gen 46:8-14
Hebrew fellow and * of the tribe of Ex 2:1
So the little * rushed home and Ex 2:8
if the ox gores a boy or a *. Ex 21:31
"If a man seduces a * Ex 22:16
"When a baby * is born, the Lev 12:5
baby is a boy or *), she must bring Lev 12:6
A * may not marry her father; Lev 18:7
* who is engaged to be married, Lev 19:20
ten dollars; a *, five dollars. Lev 27:5
a *, one and a half dollars. Lev 27:6
a Midianite * into the camp, right Num 25:6
tent, where he had taken the *. Num 25:8
with the Midianite * was Zimri, son Num 25:14
and she is still a * at home in her Num 30:3
a beautiful * you want as your Deu 21:11
"If a man marries a *, then Deu 22:13,14
shall take the * to the door of her Deu 22:21
If a * who is engaged is seduced Deu 22:23,24
to death—the * because she didn't Deu 22:23,24
man shall die. The * is as Deu 22:25,26,27
If a man rapes a * who is not Deu 22:28,29
Each man receives a * or two; Ju 5:30
and roam with my * friends for two Ju 11:37
certain Philistine *, and when he Ju 14:1
"Why don't you marry a Jewish * Ju 14:3
Isn't there one * among all the Ju 14:3
he talked with the * and found her Ju 14:7
came and got the * and her father Ju 15:6
Samson stayed in bed with the * Ju 16:3
Later on he fell in love with a * Ju 16:4
who brought home a * from Bethlehem Ju 19:1
"Hey, who's that * over there?" Ru 2:4,5
"It's that * from the land of Moab Ru 2:6
"Thank God for a * like you!" Ru 3:10
concubines, a * named Rizpah. 2Sa 3:7
Tamar, who was a very beautiful *. 2Sa 14:27
made for a servant * to carry to 2Sa 17:17
most beautiful * in all the land. 1Ki 1:3,4
was a little * who had been given 2Ki 5:2
One day the little * said to her 2Ki 5:3
king what the little * had said. 2Ki 5:4
by Bath-shua, a * from Canaan: 1Ch 2:3
after that, the * who pleases you Est 2:4
not to look with lust upon a *. Job 31:1
master or a slave * watches her Ps 123:2
of this wayward *, a prostitute. Pro 7:8,9
of love between a man and a *. Pro 30:18,19
a * will let herself be seduced." Pro 30:18,19f
A servant * who marries her Pro 30:21,22,23
composed by King Solomon:The *: Sol 1:1
The *: "The king has brought me Sol 1:4
The *: "I am dark but beautiful, Sol 1:4
The *: "Don't look down on me, Sol 1:5
The *: "Tell me, O one I love, Sol 1:6
The *: "The king lies on his Sol 1:11
THE *: "I am the rose of Sharon, Sol 2:1
The *: "My lover is an apple Sol 2:2
The *: "Ah, I hear him—my Sol 2:7
THE *: "One night my lover was Sol 3:1
The *: "Go out and see King Sol 3:10
The *: "Come, north wind, Sol 4:15
The *: "One night as I was Sol 5:1
The *: "My beloved one is tanned Sol 5:9
The *: "He has gone down to his Sol 6:1
The *: "I went down into the Sol 6:10
The *: "Why should you seek a Sol 6:13
The *: "I am my beloved's and I Sol 7:9
THE *: "Oh, if only you were my Sol 8:1
The *: "Seal me in your heart Sol 8:5
The *: "We have a little sister Sol 8:7
The *: "I am slim, tall, Sol 8:9
Can a * forget her jewels? Jer 2:32
Helpless as a *, you are Jer 6:2
Egypt is as helpless as a * Jer 46:24
The older * was named Oholah; Eze 23:4,5
when as a young * you gave your Eze 23:21
"Go and marry a * who is a Hos 1:2
* for wine enough to get drunk. Joe 3:3
out, for the little * isn't dead; Mt 9:24
where the little * was lying and Mt 9:25
urging, the * asked for John the Mt 14:8
the *, who took it to her mother. Mt 14:11
in the courtyard a * came over and Mt 26:69
Later, out by the gate, another * Mt 26:71
said to her, "Get up, little *!" Mk 5:41,42
* and she took it to her mother. Mk 6:28
little * was possessed by a demon. Mk 7:25
that I have healed your little *. Mk 7:29
home, her little * was lying Mk 7:30
his lowly servant *, and now Lk 1:48
a little * twelve years old. Lk 8:42
news that the little * was dead. Lk 8:49
and called, "Get up, little *!" Lk 8:54
A servant * noticed him in the Lk 22:56
spoke to the * watching at the Jn 18:16
let Peter in. The * asked Peter, Jn 18:17
a * named Rhoda came to open it. Act 12:13
slave * who was a fortune-teller, Act 16:16
husband: for a * who marries no 1Co 7:4
and if a * gets married in times 1Co 7:28
It is the same with a * who 1Co 7:34
She faces the same problem. A * 1Co 7:34

GIRL'S
The older * baby was named Moab; Gen 19:37
The name of the younger * baby Gen 19:38
of Simeon. The * name was Cozbi, Num 25:15
her,' then the * father and mother Deu 22:15
to be given to the * father, for Deu 22:19
to the * father and marry her; Deu 22:28,29
chosen his slave * son, Abimelech, Ju 9:18
to leave, but the * father insisted Ju 19:5
and again the * father pleaded, Ju 19:8
Then the * husband pushed her out Ju 19:25
Then, as each * turn came for Est 2:12,13,14
taking the little * father and Mk 5:40
the little * father and mother. Lk 8:51

GIRLS
And so it was that both * became Gen 19:36
these local *, these Canaanites. Gen 24:3
spring, and the * of the village Gen 24:13
Isaac marry one of the local *, Gen 24:37
So Rebekah and her servant * Gen 24:61
sick and tired of these local *. Gen 27:46
marry one of these Canaanite *. Gen 28:1
despised the local *, and that his Gen 28:6,7,8
the neighborhood *, but when Gen 34:1
Esau married three local * from Gen 36:2,3
were born, but to let the * live. Ex 1:15,16
But the *, he said, could live. Ex 1:22
a well, seven * who were daughters Ex 2:16
But the shepherds chased the * Ex 2:17
of the *, Zipporah, as his wife. Ex 2:21
all did—men and women, boys and *. Ex 32:2,3
parties with the local Moabite *. Num 25:1
These * also invited them to Num 25:2
Only the little * may live; Num 31:18
and 32,000 young *. Num 31:32-35
16,000 * (of whom 32 went to the Num 31:36-40
oxen,30,500 donkeys, and16,000 * Num 31:42-46
allotted. The * throughout the Num 36:8
These *, Mahlah, Tirzah, Hoglah, Num 36:11,12
Shall terrorize young men and * Deu 32:25
Israel took their * as wives, and Ju 3:6
the Israeli * married their men. Ju 3:6
that the young * went away for Ju 11:40
in thirty * to marry his sons. Ju 12:9,10
The four hundred * were given to Ju 21:14
enough of these * for all of them. Ju 21:14
and when the * of Shiloh come out Ju 21:21
and kidnapped the * who took part Ju 21:23
married * of Moab, Orpah and Ruth. Ru 1:4,5
Stay with his * right through the Ru 2:22
saw some young * going out to draw 1Sa 9:9,10,11
of her serving * as attendants, 1Sa 25:42
He exposed himself to the * along 2Sa 6:20
by the * of whom you spoke!" 2Sa 6:22
to her, for the * and young men 2Sa 13:2
SOLOMON MARRIED many other * 1Ki 11:1
He also had two * (by the same 1Ch 2:16
killing even young * and old men. 2Ch 36:17
The men of Israel had married * Ez 9:2

(GIRLS Con't)
let our sons marry non-Jewish *. Neh 10:30
the most beautiful * in the empire Est 2:2
along with many other young *. Est 2:8
gave her seven * from the palace as Est 2:9
concerning these * were that before Est 2:12,13,14
And all the other * exclaimed Est 2:15
more than any of the other *. Est 2:17
a second bevy of beautiful *. Est 2:19
Or, "When Esther and the other * Est 2:19f
him to your little * to play with? Job 41:5
were no other * as lovely as the Job 42:15
* playing the timbrels in between. Ps 68:25
by fire and their * died before Ps 78:63
these * have abandoned their Pro 2:16,17
the day's work for her servant *. Pro 31:15
No wonder all the young * love Sol 1:3
No wonder all the young * love Sol 1:4
but beautiful, O * of Jerusalem, Sol 1:5
look down on me, you city *, Sol 1:6
as compared with any other *." Sol 2:2
he embraces me. O * of Jerusalem, Sol 2:7
love from the * of Jerusalem!' Sol 3:10
and masters, slave * and Is 24:2
their boys and * shall starve. Jer 11:21,22
The young * will dance for joy, Jer 31:13
*, killed by the enemies' swords. Lam 2:21
to the young * of Jerusalem. Lam 3:51
and the * in Judah's cities. Lam 5:11
*, women and little children; Eze 9:6
* became prostitutes in Egypt. Eze 23:2,3
"Beautiful * and fine young men Amo 8:13
be filled with boys and * at play. Zec 8:5
make the young men and * flourish; Zec 9:16,17
"All the * jumped up and trimmed Mt 25:7,8
What about * who are not yet 1Co 7:25
mothers, and the * as your sisters, 1Ti 5:2
younger boys and * because you, 1Jn 2:13

GIRZITES
Geshurites, the *, and the 1Sa 27:8

GISHPA
Ziha and *) all lived in Ophel. Neh 11:21

GITTAIM
even though they fled to *, 2Sa 4:2,3
* is not in Benjamin. 2Sa 4:2,3f
Hazor, Ramah, *, Hadid, Zeboim, Neh 11:31-35

GITTITE
and a third under Ittai, the *. 2Sa 18:2
the brother of Goliath the *, 2Sa 21:19
of Obed-edom the * instead of 1Ch 13:13

GITTITES
way—six hundred * who had come 2Sa 15:17,18
of the six hundred *, and said to 2Sa 15:19,20

GIVE
in the sky to * light to the earth Gen 1:14,15
you, for I will * seven times your Gen 4:15
I will * him 120 years to mend Gen 6:3
Come, let us go down and * them Gen 11:7
* this land to your descendants." Gen 12:7
for I am going to * it all to you Gen 13:15
And I am going to * you so many Gen 13:16
told him, "Just * me back my Gen 14:21
have eaten; but * a share of the Gen 14:24
And I will * you great Gen 15:1
to * you this land forever." Gen 15:7
sure that you will * it to me?" Gen 15:8
And I * to them these nations: Gen 15:19,20,21
I will * you millions of Gen 17:6
And I will * all this land of Gen 17:7,8
And I will bless her and * you a Gen 17:16
I will * you and Sarah a son!" Gen 18:10
I will * you the cave and the Gen 23:11
of my people, I * it to you free. Gen 23:11
to * me and my children this land. Gen 24:7
"Please * me a drink of water!" Gen 24:43
I said to her, 'Please * me a Gen 24:45
Isaac pleaded with Jehovah to * Gen 25:21
Esau: "Boy, am I starved! * me a Gen 25:30
you, and I will * all this land to Gen 26:3
And I will * them all of these Gen 26:4
you, and will * you so many Gen 26:24
* you the blessings that belong Gen 27:2,3,4
May God always * you plenty of Gen 27:27,28,29
can * me your finest blessings!" Gen 27:31
wine—what is there left to *?" Gen 27:37
God Almighty bless you and * you Gen 28:2
I will * it to you and to your Gen 28:13
this journey and * me food and Gen 28:20
and I will * you back a tenth of Gen 28:22
a tenth of everything you * me!" Gen 28:22
you'll * me Rachel as my wife." Gen 29:18
"I'd rather * her to you than to Gen 29:19
"Now * me my wife, so that I can Gen 29:21
of her sister. "* me children or Gen 30:1
Rachel begged Leah to * some of Gen 30:14
for she said, "May Jehovah * Gen 30:23,24
sheep. * them to me as my wages. Gen 30:31,32
"Don't * him your blessing and Gen 31:24
Why didn't you * me a chance to Gen 31:27
I'll * it back without question." Gen 31:32
sons, and we will * our daughters Gen 34:9,10
"I will * whatever you require. Gen 34:11
* me the girl as my wife." Gen 34:12
Yes, I will * it to you and to Gen 35:12
"What pledge will you * me, so Gen 38:17
to * her to my son Shelah." Gen 38:26
out of prison and * you back your Gen 40:13
and I'm going to * you an Gen 42:18
say, then I will * you back your Gen 42:34
May God Almighty * you mercy Gen 43:14
* them the best land of Egypt. Gen 47:5,6
they said, "but * us bread; Gen 47:15
replied, "* me your livestock. Gen 47:16
nation and I will * this land of Gen 48:4
to him. * us your permission.' Ex 3:18
So I will * him all the pressure Ex 3:20
Israel: "Don't * the people any Ex 5:7,8
under its terms I promised to * Ex 6:4
to * to Abraham, Isaac, and Jacob. Ex 6:8,9
Go in and * Pharaoh the message I Ex 6:28,29
and this will * me the opportunity Ex 11:9
that the Lord will * you, just as Ex 12:25
and oh, * me a blessing Ex 12:32
Lord, and you shall * them to him. Ex 13:12
that is why we now * all the Ex 13:15
The Lord will * you meat to eat Ex 16:7,8,9
to Moses. "* us water!" Ex 17:2
Now listen, and let me * you a Ex 18:19,20
"* these instructions to the Ex 19:2,3
land the Lord your God will * you. Ex 20:12
Or, "You must not * false Ex 20:16f
him, then he shall * for the Ex 21:30f
for my help, I will surely * it. Ex 22:23
and the sheep, * it to me on the Ex 22:30
this is to * your oxen and Ex 23:12
and remain until I * you the laws Ex 24:12
I will * you a drawing of the Ex 25:9
of stone I will * you, with the Ten Ex 25:16
Testimony which I shall * you." Ex 25:16f
tablets of stone I shall * you. Ex 25:21
to * them honor and respect. Ex 28:40
"* the breast and thigh of the Ex 29:27
is numbered shall * a ransom to the Ex 30:11,12
birthday shall * this offering. Ex 30:14
The rich shall not * more and Ex 30:15
the poor shall not * less, for it Ex 30:15
"* me your golden earrings," Ex 32:2,3
heaven, and I will * them all of Ex 32:13
now he will * you a great Ex 32:29
for I said, 'I will * this land Ex 33:1
go with you and * you success." Ex 33:14
commanded him to * the following Lev 1:2,3
for burnt offerings * much Lev 1:13
"WHEN ANYONE WANTS to * an Lev 3:1
And it will * the Lord much Lev 3:3,4,5
"ANYONE REFUSING TO * testimony Lev 5:1
and * it to the one he has harmed; Lev 6:4,5
Then the Lord said to Moses, "* Lev 6:9
Israel * these portions to them; Lev 7:36
THE LORD TOLD Moses to * these Lev 12:1
LORD TOLD Moses and Aaron to * Lev 15:1
and * them to the priest. Lev 15:14
"You shall not * any of your Lev 18:21
and a woman must never * herself Lev 18:23
"You shall * due honor and Lev 19:32
and volumes—and * full measure, for Lev 19:35,36
Literally, "that the land I * you Lev 20:22f
I will * it to you to possess it. Lev 20:24
in the land I will * you and reap Lev 23:9,10,11
land I am going to * you, you must Lev 25:1
Remember—no interest; and * him Lev 25:37
land of Egypt to * you the land of Lev 25:38
I will * you regular rains, and Lev 26:4,5
land, for I will * you peace, and Lev 26:6
rest you didn't * it every seventh Lev 26:34,35
a special vow to * himself to the Lev 27:1
the Lord, he shall * these payments Lev 27:1
shall immediately * that estimated Lev 27:23
Now the Lord said to Moses, "* Num 3:45
of Israel; and * me the cattle of Num 3:45
that they are to * this special Num 6:22,23
his favor, and * you his peace.' Num 6:24,25,26
of the Tabernacle. * them to the Num 7:4,5
And I will * the Levites as a Num 8:19
pick on me, to * me the burden of a Num 11:11
For they weep to me saying, '* us Num 11:13
and he is going to * you meat. Num 11:18
into the land and * it to us. Num 14:8
land he swore he would * them.' Num 14:16
THE LORD TOLD Moses to * these Num 15:1
land I am going to * them, and Num 15:1
that I am going to * them, they Num 15:17,18
the Levites to * to the Lord a Num 18:25,26
* the best tenth to the priests. Num 18:32
never been yoked. * her to Eleazar Num 19:1
You will * them water from a Num 20:8
people, and I will * them water." Num 21:16
"If he were to * me a palace Num 22:18
said I would * you great honors?" Num 22:37
the Tabernacle to * a petition to Num 27:1
are correct. * them land along with Num 27:6,7
with their uncles; * them the Num 27:6,7
Publicly * him your authority so Num 27:20
continue to * them guidance." Num 27:21
instructions to * to the people of Num 28:1
day, which will * much pleasure to Num 29:13
five hundred. * this share to Num 31:29
must * them the land of Gilead; Num 32:29
of Israel to * to the Levites as Num 35:2
"You shall * the Levites the six Num 35:6
many cities will * several to the Num 35:8
the smaller tribes will * fewer." Num 35:8
Moses, "and to * the inheritance Num 36:1
I will * the land to the Deu 1:39
and I will not * you even a tiny Deu 2:5
will not * you any of their land; Deu 2:9
will not * you any of their land. Deu 2:19
to * you the land of King Sihon; Deu 2:31
If you obey them they will * you Deu 4:6
me, and I will * you all my Deu 5:31
"THE LORD YOUR God told me to * Deu 6:1
so that he could * us this land he Deu 6:23
He will make you fertile and * Deu 7:13
he promised your fathers to * you. Deu 7:13
he will * them all to your Deu 7:15
the commandments I * you today. Deu 8:1
I am going to * you today, so that Deu 11:8
that I am going to * you today, and Deu 11:13
He will * you lush pastureland Deu 11:15
the commandments I * you, loving Deu 11:22
of rest the Lord will * to you). Deu 12:9
you have vowed to * the Lord, nor Deu 12:17
Obey all the commandments I * Deu 12:32
You may * it or sell it to him, Deu 14:21
welfare programs: * it to the Deu 14:29
land the Lord will * you, there are Deu 15:7
empty-handed! * him a large Deu 15:14
gift to the Lord. * as you are Deu 16:17
Lord your God will * you, and have Deu 17:14
And any prophet who claims to * a Deu 18:20
and he will * you the victory!' Deu 20:4
love, he may not * a larger Deu 21:16
He must * the customary double Deu 21:17
for it, and then * it to him. Deu 22:2
has divorced her, * her the letter, Deu 24:1
That year you are to * all your Deu 26:12
"The Lord will * you an Deu 28:11
to * you fine crops every season. Deu 28:12
He will refuse to * them a share Deu 28:55
but the Lord will * you trembling Deu 28:65
you do and * you many children and Deu 30:9
I can * him his instructions." Deu 31:14
"* to godly Levi Deu 33:8
I would * it to their descendants. Deu 34:4
God is going to * my country to Jos 2:9
"The Lord will certainly * us Jos 2:24
Joshua, "I will * you great honor, Jos 3:7
and said, "* me your commands." Jos 5:14
Then, when they * one long, loud Jos 6:5
the people are to * a mighty shout Jos 6:5
Joshua said to Achan, "My son, * Jos 7:19
for the Lord will * it to you. Jos 8:7
Ai, for I will * you the city." Jos 8:18
So I'm asking that you * me the Jos 14:12
Caleb said that he would * his Jos 15:16
And she replied, "* me another Jos 15:18,19
desert. * us some springs, too!" Jos 15:18,19
* him a place to live among them. Jos 20:4
"The Lord instructed Moses to * Jos 21:2
And I will * them a great Ju 1:2
kind enough to * me land in the Ju 1:15
* us springs of water too." Ju 1:15
For God wanted to * opportunity Ju 3:1
"Please * me some water," he Ju 4:19
and you refused to * us food when Ju 8:15
However, I have one request. * me Ju 8:23,24
"* us back our land peaceably," Ju 11:13
to us again and * us more Ju 13:8
the child you are going to * us." Ju 13:8
So Manoah asked him, "Can you * Ju 13:12
he said, "I'll * you thirty plain Ju 14:12
then you must * the robes to me!" Ju 14:13
"Each of us will * you a thousand Ju 16:5
"I am going to * it to the Lord Ju 17:3
I will * you ten dollars a year Ju 17:10,11
your mind and * me your counsel!" Ju 20:7
done among you? * up these evil Ju 20:13
in order to * the ambush more room Ju 20:35-39
will not * them our daughters?" Ju 21:7
But we can't * them our own Ju 21:18
can * Naomi an heir by marrying me Ru 3:10
the Lord will * you from this young Ru 4:12
much, he could * her only one 1Sa 1:5
so she had no children to * 1Sa 1:5
my prayer and * me a son, then I 1Sa 1:11
a son, then I will * him back to 1Sa 1:11
I asked him to * me this child, 1Sa 1:27
"No, * it to me now or I'll take 1Sa 2:16
and ask God to * them other 1Sa 2:20
prosperity I will * my people, but 1Sa 2:32
'Please,' they will say, '* me a 1Sa 2:36
Then the Lord began to * messages 1Sa 3:21,4:1
"* us a king like all the other 1Sa 8:5

(GIVE Con't)
groves and * them to his friends. 1Sa 8:14
as they say and * them a king." 1Sa 8:22
we don't have a thing to * him." 1Sa 9:7
I will * you further instructions 1Sa 10:8
"* us seven days to see if we 1Sa 11:3
to your brothers. * this cheese to 1Sa 17:18
And the king will * him one of 1Sa 17:25
"Come over here and I'll * your 1Sa 17:44
and then I will * the dead bodies 1Sa 17:46
He will * you to us!" 1Sa 17:47
"I am ready to * you my oldest 1Sa 18:17
will * you my youngest daughter." 1Sa 18:21
Now, what is there to eat? * me 1Sa 21:3
David replied. "* it to me!" 1Sa 21:9
"Why did you * him food and a 1Sa 22:13
and * me a more definite report. 1Sa 23:23
men to Carmel to * him this 1Sa 25:5
Please * us a present of whatever 1Sa 25:8
my shearers and * it to a gang who 1Sa 25:11
Now do what I say, and let me * 1Sa 28:22
not kill me or * me back to my 1Sa 30:15
any of the loot. * them their wives 1Sa 30:22
to Beer-sheba, and * it to David, 2Sa 3:9,10
to Ish-bosheth: "* me back my wife 2Sa 3:14
ahead, for I will * them to you." 2Sa 5:19
"Now go and * this message to 2Sa 7:8
I will * your wives to another 2Sa 12:11
Yes, the king will * us peace 2Sa 14:17
me, and I would * him justice!" 2Sa 15:4
* Absalom foolish advice!" 2Sa 15:31
"I * you everything he owns." 2Sa 16:4
"NOW," AHITHOPHEL SAID, "* me 2Sa 17:1
heard the king * them this charge. 2Sa 18:5
"* him all of it," Mephibosheth 2Sa 19:30
good things you want to * him." 2Sa 19:37
For we always * wise counsel. 2Sa 20:18
"Well, then," they replied, "* 2Sa 21:5,6
No wonder I * thanks to you, O 2Sa 22:50
that I will * him three choices." 2Sa 24:12
me know what answer to * to God." 2Sa 24:13
I will * it all to you, and may 2Sa 24:23
and ask him to * me Abishag, the 1Ki 2:17
"If I were to * him Abishag, I 1Ki 2:22
So Solomon forced Abiathar to * 1Ki 2:27
people to count! * me an 1Ki 3:9
I'll * you what you asked for! 1Ki 3:12
I will * you a wiser mind than 1Ki 3:12
And I will also * you what you 1Ki 3:13
And I will * you a long life if 1Ki 3:14
* half to each of these women!" 1Ki 3:25
* her the child—don't kill him!" 1Ki 3:26
Then the king said, "* the baby 1Ki 3:27
for the Lord to * him peace. 1Ki 5:2,3
May he * us the desire to do his 1Ki 8:58
And you * your people a just, 1Ki 10:9
family and * it to someone else. 1Ki 11:11
and * ten of the tribes to you! 1Ki 11:31
and * ten of the tribes to you. 1Ki 11:35
Israel, and * you absolute power. 1Ki 11:37
"* me three days to think this 1Ki 12:5
And they replied, "If you * them 1Ki 12:7
and I'll * you a reward because 1Ki 13:7
me and * you food and water." 1Ki 13:18
sad news for you. * your husband 1Ki 14:7
"* him to me," Elijah replied. 1Ki 17:19
must not only * me your silver, 1Ki 20:5,6
"Don't * him anything more," 1Ki 20:8
the king, 'I will * you everything 1Ki 20:9
the one you lost; * us the same 1Ki 20:25
possession of it. * him this 1Ki 21:19
Am I God, that I can kill and * 2Ki 5:7
But please * me two mule-loads of 2Ki 5:17
and two suits to * to them." 2Ki 5:22
"Do we kill prisoners of war? * 2Ki 6:22
neither food nor wine to * you. 2Ki 6:26-30
"Then * me your hand," Jehu 2Ki 10:15
cedar tree, '* your daughter to be 2Ki 14:9
But which of your allies will * 2Ki 18:20,21
"All right, the Lord will * you 2Ki 20:9
to the Temple to * instruction to 2Ki 22:3,4
come to worship. * this money to 2Ki 22:5,6
that if they would * themselves up 2Ki 25:24
it was for a special reason—to * 1Ch 14:2
them, will you * me the victory?" 1Ch 14:10
"Oh, * thanks to the Lord and 1Ch 16:8
'I will * you the land of Canaan 1Ch 16:18
Oh, * thanks to the Lord, for he 1Ch 16:34
chosen by name to * thanks to the 1Ch 16:41
Nathan, "Go and * my servant 1Ch 17:4
And I will * a permanent home to 1Ch 17:9
offering. I * it all to you." 1Ch 21:23
I cannot take what is yours and * 1Ch 21:24
But I will * you a son,' he told 1Ch 22:9
peace, for I will * him peace with 1Ch 22:9
and I will * peace and quietness to 1Ch 22:9
And may the Lord * you the good 1Ch 22:12
Who will * himself and all that 1Ch 29:4,5
be permitted to * anything to you? 1Ch 29:14
only * you what is yours already! 1Ch 29:14
never changes. * my son Solomon a 1Ch 29:19
"* praise to the Lord your God!" 1Ch 29:20
and I will * it to you!" 2Ch 1:7
full of dust! Now * me wisdom and 2Ch 1:10
their sins and * them back this 2Ch 6:25
and forgive, and * each one 2Ch 6:30
from heaven and * them success. 2Ch 6:35
How he must love Israel to * them 2Ch 9:8
"you will have to * them a 2Ch 10:7
but I will * you heavier!" 2Ch 10:14
God will * you a great victory!" 2Ch 18:3,4,5
with them and * the king a 2Ch 18:12
you and help you * justice in each 2Ch 19:6
Be very much afraid to * any 2Ch 19:7
And didn't you * this land 2Ch 20:7
to * you much more than this!" 2Ch 25:9
of a cedar tree, '* your daughter 2Ch 25:18
* thanks and praise to the Lord. 2Ch 31:2
things to * to the Lord and piled 2Ch 31:5,6
were able to * generously toward Ez 2:68
your territory. * the priests in Ez 6:9
God of heaven; and * them wheat, Ez 6:9
River: 'You are to * Ezra whatever Ez 7:21
and we prayed that he would * us Ez 8:21
what hope can we have if you * us Ez 9:15
please the king, * me letters to Neh 2:7
instructing him to * me timber for Neh 2:8
him to forever * him and his Neh 9:8
the land you had sworn to * them; Neh 9:15
We agreed to * to God our oldest Neh 10:36
I will * it to you, even if it is Est 5:3
want, and I will * it to you, even Est 5:6
"What reward did we ever * Est 6:3
Whatever it is, I will * it to Est 7:2
"A man will * anything to save Job 2:4,5
is only going to * him a hopeless Job 3:23
of life—months is all you * him! Job 14:5
So * him a little rest, won't you? Job 14:6
But now, instead, you * me so Job 14:16
you * us all this foolish talk. Job 15:2
* birth only to wickedness." Job 15:35
wealth will * him no joy. Job 20:18
will * testimony against him. Job 20:27
If you * up your lust for money, Job 22:24
And don't * me that line about Job 32:13
No, I will * my answer too. Job 32:17
relief, so let me * my answers. Job 32:20
* account to you of what he does? Job 33:13
I will * you many illustrations Job 36:3
YOU KNOW how mountain goats * Job 39:1
bow themselves to * birth to their Job 39:2,3
Let me ask you a question, and * Job 40:7
splendor. * vent to your anger. Job 40:11
like a bird, or * him to your Job 41:5
"Only ask, and I will * you Ps 2:8
For if I die I cannot * you Ps 6:5
grave, who shall * you thanks?" Ps 6:5f
Answer me, O Lord my God; * me Ps 13:3
You * blessings to the pure but Ps 18:26
us wise, and * us joy and light. Ps 19:7,8
* success to those who obey them. Ps 19:11
* victory to our king, O Lord; Ps 20:9
Don't * them victory over me. Ps 25:2
me, I might as well * up and die. Ps 28:1
to murder them. * them the Ps 28:4
He will * his people strength. Ps 29:11
of his; * thanks to his holy name. Ps 30:4
Don't * victory to those who Ps 35:19
Bare them to dishonor. But * Ps 35:27
Then he will * you all your Ps 37:4
Only you can * us the victory Ps 44:7
you, and you can * me glory. Ps 50:14,15
Oh, * me this wisdom. Ps 51:6
me, * me back my joy again. Ps 51:8
* your burdens to the Lord. Ps 55:22
are crooked: you * "justice" in Ps 58:1
You will * me Ps 61:6
and will * true justice to their Ps 67:4
of the earth * thanks to you. Ps 67:5
do not * them the joys of life Ps 69:28
don't forsake me. * me time to tell Ps 71:18
You will * me greater honor than Ps 71:21
Help him to * justice to your Ps 72:2
Unleash your fist and * them a Ps 74:11
forth to * your people water; Ps 74:15
insulted. * cause for these poor Ps 74:21
Your mighty miracles * proof that Ps 75:1
refusing to * their hearts to God. Ps 78:8
the wilderness to * them plenty of Ps 78:15
"Why can't he * us decent food Ps 78:19,20
while I * you stern warnings. Ps 81:8
on the wicked? * fair judgment to Ps 82:3
in constant hope. * me happiness, Ps 86:4
I will * glory to your name Ps 86:12
Is it an empty, futile life you * Ps 89:47
end of our lives. * us gladness in Ps 90:15
our God favor us and * us success. Ps 90:17
and * him my salvation." Ps 91:16
and * me renewed hope and cheer. Ps 94:19
sing to the Lord! * a joyous shout Ps 95:1
* him the glory he deserves! Ps 96:8
Literally, "* glory to his holy Ps 97:12f
King is determined to * justice. Ps 99:4
enter his courts with praise. * Ps 100:4
Bend down your ear and * me Ps 102:2
They * water for all the animals Ps 104:11
skin, and bread to * him strength. Ps 104:15
on you to * them daily food. Ps 104:27
Israel: "I will * you the land of Ps 105:10,11
of flame at night to * them light. Ps 105:39
receive the glory you * to them. Ps 106:5
He has promised to * us all the Ps 108:7
"Gilead is mine to * to you," Ps 108:8
Who but God can * me strength to Ps 108:10
But I will * repeated thanks to Ps 109:30
—I will go in and * him my thanks. Ps 118:19
Save us. * us success. Ps 118:25
* you this thanks and this praise. Ps 118:27,28
this praise. Oh, * thanks to the Ps 118:29
I will meditate upon them and * Ps 119:15
Now * me your instructions. Ps 119:26
* me strength in all my troubles; Ps 119:49,50
At midnight I will rise to * my Ps 119:62
You made my body, Lord; now * me Ps 119:73
And since only your rules can * Ps 119:104
of my enemies; oh, * me back my Ps 119:107
not * up obedience to your laws. Ps 119:109
therefore * me common sense to Ps 119:125
Yes, rescue me and * me back my Ps 119:154
oh, * me back my life again. Ps 119:156
your demands. Now * me back my life Ps 119:159
O Lord, listen to my prayers; * Ps 119:169
OH, * THANKS to the Lord, for he Ps 136:1
* thanks to the God of gods, for Ps 136:2
forever. * thanks to the Lord of Ps 136:3
forever. Oh, * thanks to the God Ps 136:26
the earth shall * you thanks, O Ps 138:4
* them their food as they need it. Ps 145:15
Let everything he has made * Ps 148:5
Let everything alive * praises to Ps 150:6
your honor, and * the remainder of Pro 5:9
danger and to * you a good life. Pro 6:23
Let me * you understanding. Pro 8:4,5
"I, Wisdom, * good advice and Pro 8:14,15
It is possible to * away and Pro 11:24,25
That is why fools refuse to * Pro 13:19
Only the good can * good advice. Pro 15:7
reports * happiness and health. Pro 15:30
Ability to * wise advice Pro 18:20
A father can * his sons homes and Pro 19:14
can * them understanding wives. Pro 19:14
and fair than when we * him gifts. Pro 21:3
to get, while the godly love to *! Pro 21:25,26
son is! So * your parents joy! Pro 23:24,25
One who doesn't * the gift he Pro 25:14
If your enemy is hungry, * him Pro 25:21,22
If he is thirsty, * him something Pro 25:21,22
If you * to the poor, your needs Pro 28:27
Discipline your son and he will * Pro 29:17
Second, * me neither poverty nor Pro 30:8
nor riches! * me just enough to Pro 30:8
and be unable to * justice to those Pro 31:5
Literally, "* her of the fruit of Pro 31:31f
but he doesn't * them the health to Ecc 6:2
can't even * him a decent burial—I Ecc 6:3
* GENEROUSLY, FOR your gifts will Ecc 11:1
Literally, "* a portion to seven, Ecc 11:2f
And there I will * you my love. Sol 7:12
There the mandrakes * forth Sol 7:13
I would * you spiced wine to Sol 8:2
silver and I will * two hundred Sol 8:12
And afterwards I will * you good Is 1:26
Why did my vineyard * me wild Is 5:4
of the son I am going to * you. Is 8:1
plead for advice and help. "* Is 16:3
know the Lord and * their Is 19:21
so that I can * you better news. Is 21:12
I will * him responsibility over Is 22:22
her businesses will * their Is 23:18
God does not * them a rough and Is 26:7
He will * a longing for justice Is 28:6
When you * it to one who can Is 29:11
When you * it to another, he Is 29:12
will * you nothing in return! Is 30:6
they will * us swift horses for Is 30:16
Though he * you the bread of Is 30:20
enemies, he will * you streams of Is 30:25
If you do, he will * you 2,000 Is 36:8,9
offer to you: * me a present as a Is 36:16
labor trying to * birth, and the Is 37:3
still it will * you enough seed for Is 37:30
sign will the Lord * me to prove Is 38:22
and the Lord will * her twice as Is 40:2
be his teacher or * him counsel? Is 40:13
and the young men will all * up. Is 40:30
I will * them fountains of water Is 41:18
name, and I will * him victory over Is 41:25
That is my name, and I will not * Is 42:8
He will * a great shout and Is 42:13
But now he will * full vent to Is 42:14
For I will * you abundant water Is 44:3
he is trusting what can never * Is 44:20
I make wise men * opposite advice Is 44:25

(GIVE Con't)

And I will * you treasures	Is 45:3
me for what I didn't plan to *!	Is 45:19
harm and * you as a token and	Is 49:8,9
"See, I will * a signal to the	Is 49:22
nor turn away. I * my back to the	Is 50:6
Therefore I will * him the	Is 53:12
that don't * you strength?	Is 55:2
with you, to * you all the	Is 55:3
his laws: I will * them—in my	Is 56:5
For the name that I will * them	Is 56:5
They are featherbrained and * no	Is 56:10
and I refresh the humble and *	Is 57:15
fairly and * them what they earn.	Is 58:6
the sun or moon to * you light, for	Is 60:19
Israel he will *:Beauty for ashes;	Is 61:3
you who pray, and * God no rest	Is 62:6,7
never again * you to your enemies;	Is 62:8
But I will not * you up—I will	Jer 2:9
And I will * you leaders after	Jer 3:15
I planned to * you part of this	Jer 3:19
Yet the priests and prophets *	Jer 6:14
of the Lord and * this message to	Jer 7:2
Once again * them this message	Jer 8:4,5
I will * their wives and their	Jer 8:10
They * useless medicine for my	Jer 8:11
and * them poison to drink.	Jer 9:15
from Uphaz, and * them to skillful	Jer 10:9
I want to * you a land that	Jer 11:5
doom and * you life and joy again?	Jer 11:15
O LORD, YOU always * me justice	Jer 12:1
But in their hearts they * no	Jer 12:2
he has spoken. * glory to the Lord	Jer 13:16
What I will * them in return is	Jer 14:12
to speak or * them any message.	Jer 14:14
What heathen god can * us rain?	Jer 14:22
and * them what they deserve!	Jer 15:15
And so I will * all your	Jer 17:2,3
motives so he can * to each person	Jer 17:10
who persecute me, but * me peace.	Jer 17:18
to them whatever words I * you.	Jer 19:1
I have to * them your messages	Jer 20:7
Quick! * justice to these you	Jer 21:12
and once more * kings to sit on	Jer 22:4
pull you off and * you to those who	Jer 22:24,25
and * them poison to drink.	Jer 23:15
I will * them hearts that	Jer 24:7
Judah. * them the entire message;	Jer 26:2
and I * these things of mine to	Jer 27:5
to * you a future and a hope.	Jer 29:11
Do men * birth?	Jer 30:6
I will * you back your health	Jer 30:17
ones, those ready to * birth.	Jer 31:8
Yes, I will * this city to the	Jer 32:28
And I will * them one heart and	Jer 32:39
and * her prosperity and peace.	Jer 33:6
to me, and it will * me joy and be	Jer 33:9
says this: I will * this city to	Jer 34:2
I will * you to your enemies and	Jer 34:20
kill Jeremiah or * him to the men	Jer 38:16
"Look after him well and * him	Jer 39:11,12
punishment I have had to * to you.	Jer 42:10
you will never * up your devotion	Jer 44:25
And this is the proof I * you	Jer 44:29
Weep for her; * her medicine;	Jer 51:8
to Jeremiah to * to Seraiah (son of	Jer 51:59
there was no one to * her aid.	Lam 1:7
for food to * a little strength.	Lam 1:11
you like a river; * yourselves no	Lam 2:18
bread but no one can * them any.	Lam 4:3,4
That is our only hope! * us back	Lam 5:21
But I am sending you to * them my	Eze 2:4
You must * them my messages	Eze 2:7
Open your mouth and eat what I *	Eze 2:8
Then go and * its message to the	Eze 3:1
But whenever I * you a message,	Eze 3:27
I will * it to foreigners and to	Eze 7:21
and * them all their just deserts.	Eze 7:26,27
* you the land of Israel again.	Eze 11:17
I will * you one heart and a new	Eze 11:19
of stone and * you tender hearts of	Eze 11:19
stop saying it. * them this one	Eze 12:23
that came to me to * to them:	Eze 14:2
But not you, you * them gifts,	Eze 16:33,34
I will * you to your	Eze 16:39
"Son of dust, * this riddle to	Eze 17:2
gifts to them and * your little	Eze 20:31
says, I will not * you any message,	Eze 20:31
And I will * it all to him.	Eze 21:27
she longed to * herself to the men	Eze 23:16
And now * this parable to these	Eze 24:3
God says, I will * the land of	Eze 29:19
moon shall not * you her light.	Eze 32:7
Yes, I will * them good pasture	Eze 34:14
"I will * them bumper crops."	Eze 34:29f
so much, I will * you a blood	Eze 35:6
And I will * you a new heart—I	Eze 36:26
a new heart—I will * you new and	Eze 36:26
sin and * you new hearts of love.	Eze 36:26
I will * you huge harvests from	Eze 36:30
I will * you to the vultures and	Eze 39:4
weapons will * them all they need.	Eze 39:10
you shall first * a section of it	Eze 45:1
"This is the tax you must * to	Eze 45:13
flocks in Israel, * him one sheep.	Eze 45:15
to *. With each bushel he is to	Eze 46:7
is willing to * with each lamb;	Eze 46:11
oath of truth to * the land to your	Eze 47:14
But I will * you many wonderful	Dan 2:6
to see the king. "* me a little	Dan 2:16
I'll * you one more chance.	Dan 3:15
your gifts, or * them to someone	Dan 5:17
out, roots and all, to * it room;	Dan 7:8
And I will not * special favors	Hos 1:4
will no longer * her rich harvests	Hos 1:9
There I will * back her	Hos 1:15
Their sinful deeds * them away on	Hos 7:2
to * yourselves to other gods,	Hos 9:10
I will ask for wombs that don't *	Hos 9:14
But the more wealth I * her, the	Hos 10:1
the richer the harvests I * her,	Hos 10:1
Oh, how can I * you up, my	Hos 11:8
is time. * me all your hearts.	Joe 2:12
let you alone and * you a blessing	Joe 2:14
Perhaps he will * you so much	Joe 2:14
And I will * you back the crops	Joe 2:25
forms and * extra offerings.	Amo 4:5
of Nineveh, and * them this	Jon 1:2
she promised help she cannot *.	Mic 1:14
to those who * you food, and	Mic 3:5
I will * you horns of iron and	Mic 4:13
and you will * their wealth as	Mic 4:13
I'll * to those who conquer you!	Mic 6:14
answer God will * to my complaint.	Hab 2:1
My legs * way beneath me and I	Hab 3:16
and he will * me the speed of a	Hab 3:19
He will * you victory.	Zep 3:17,18
I will * glory to my former	Zep 3:19
home again, and * you a good name,	Zep 3:20
And here I will * peace,'	Hag 2:8,9
* me my pay, whatever I am worth;	Zec 11:12
how I will * this nation a shepherd	Zec 11:16
The Lord will * victory to the	Zec 12:7
* it to the jackals of the desert.	Mal 1:2,3
governor sometime—* him gifts like	Mal 1:8
your ways and * glory to my name,	Mal 2:1
these laws was to * him life and	Mal 2:5
She shall * birth to a Son, and	Mt 1:23
"I'll * it all to you," he	Mt 4:9
taken from you, * your coat too.	Mt 5:40
carry it two. * to those who ask,	Mt 5:42
When you * a gift to a beggar,	Mt 6:2
it is in heaven. * us our food	Mt 6:11
them, and he will * them to you if	Mt 6:33
them to you if you * him first	Mt 6:33
"Don't * holy things to depraved	Mt 7:6
Don't * pearls to swine!	Mt 7:6
men know how to * good gifts to	Mt 7:11
more certainly * good gifts to	Mt 7:11
* as freely as you have received!	Mt 10:8
a godly home, * it your blessing;	Mt 10:13
This will * you the opportunity	Mt 10:18
but if you * it up for me, you	Mt 10:39
you * even a cup of cold water to a	Mt 10:42
Then * him this message,	Mt 11:6
Come to me and I will * you	Mt 11:28
for I * you only light burdens."	Mt 11:29,30
that you must * account on Judgment	Mt 12:36
to * her anything she wanted.	Mt 14:7
in need, you may * their support	Mt 15:5,6
And I will * you the keys of the	Mt 16:19
begged him to * him a little time.	Mt 18:29
you have and * the money to the	Mt 19:21
is it against the law to * away	Mt 20:15
* my life as a ransom for many."	Mt 20:28
will * God his share of the crop.	Mt 21:43
"Well, then," he said, "* it to	Mt 22:21
if it is his, and * God everything	Mt 22:21
* light, and the stars will seem	Mt 24:29
* you many more responsibilities.	Mt 25:21
so now I will * you much more.'	Mt 25:23
* it to the man with the $10,000.	Mt 25:28
Or thirsty and * you anything to	Mt 25:37
thirsty, and you wouldn't * me	Mt 25:42
to * them the angel's message.	Mt 28:8
towns as well, and * my message to	Mk 1:38
them to * her something to eat.	Mk 5:43
kingdom, and I will * it to you!"	Mk 6:22,23
"go and sell all you have and *	Mk 10:21
* my life as a ransom for many."	Mk 10:45
surely * him their full respect.	Mk 12:6
said, "if it is his, * it to him.	Mk 12:17
Now go and * this message to his	Mk 16:7
And the Lord God shall * him the	Lk 1:32
break upon us, to * light to those	Lk 1:79
he replied, "* one to the poor.	Lk 3:11
If you have extra food, * it away	Lk 3:11
told him, "I will * you all these	Lk 4:6,7
they are mine to * to anyone I	Lk 4:6,7
God is ready to * blessings to all	Lk 4:18,19
If someone demands your coat, *	Lk 6:29
shirt besides. * what you have to	Lk 6:30
For if you *, you will get!	Lk 6:38
Whatever measure you use to *	Lk 6:38
up! "* her something to eat!"	Lk 8:55
"Whenever you enter a home, * it	Lk 10:5
send your Kingdom soon. * us our	Lk 11:3
and I've nothing to * him to eat.'	Lk 11:5,6
he will get up and * you everything	Lk 11:8
for bread, do you * him a stone?	Lk 11:11
If he asks for fish, do you * him	Lk 11:11
If he asks for an egg, do you *	Lk 11:12
like yourselves * children what	Lk 11:13
least as much, and * the Holy	Lk 11:13
but the only proof I will *	Lk 11:29,30
* light to all who enter the room.	Lk 11:33
Holy Spirit will * you the right	Lk 12:12
He will always * you all you	Lk 12:31
happiness to * you the Kingdom.	Lk 12:32
Sell what you have and * to	Lk 12:33
"Do you think I have come to *	Lk 12:51
" '* it one more chance,' the	Lk 13:8
year, and I'll * it special	Lk 13:8
return to * glory to God?"	Lk 17:18
God will surely * justice to his	Lk 18:7
a week, and I * to God a tenth of	Lk 18:12
"Sell all you have and * the	Lk 18:22
from now on I will * half my wealth	Lk 19:8
away from him and * it to the man	Lk 19:24
He said, "Then * the emperor all	Lk 20:25
* to God all that is his!"	Lk 20:25
you, for I will * you the right	Lk 21:15
Tell us, so we can * an answer to	Jn 1:22
"But the water I * them," he	Jn 4:14
said, "* me some of that water!	Jn 4:15
believe they * you eternal life.	Jn 5:39
I can * you this life eternal!	Jn 5:40
can * you. For God the Father has	Jn 6:27
are the Messiah. * us free bread	Jn 6:30,31
Jesus said, "Moses didn't * it	Jn 6:32
"Sir," they said, "* us that	Jn 6:34
"How can this man * us his flesh	Jn 6:52
You alone have the words that *	Jn 6:68
in the world, I * it my light."	Jn 9:5
and told him, "* the glory to God,	Jn 9:24
into the world to * sight to those	Jn 9:39
My purpose is to * life in all	Jn 10:10
they follow me. I * them eternal	Jn 10:28
for this will * you another	Jn 11:15
shall dip the sop and * it him."	Jn 13:26f
or to * some money to the poor.	Jn 13:29
And God shall * me his own	Jn 13:32
Father and he will * you another	Jn 14:15,16
And the peace I * isn't fragile	Jn 14:27
my name, he will * it to you.	Jn 15:16
him, and he will * you what you ask	Jn 16:23
he can * the glory back to you.	Jn 17:1
'You will * me back my life, and	Act 2:28
back my life, and * me wonderful	Act 2:28
But I'll * you something else!	Act 3:6
apostles to * to others in need.	Act 4:34,35
was yours to decide how much to *.	Act 5:4
for us come and * it!"	Act 13:15
your faith and * you all the	Act 20:32
blessed to * than to receive.'	Act 20:35
you when you * them my message.'	Act 22:17,18
mounted cavalry. * Paul a horse to	Act 23:23,24
But lest I bore you, kindly * me	Act 24:4
* you time to turn from your sin?	Rom 2:4
He will * each one whatever his	Rom 2:6
He will * eternal life to those	Rom 2:7
laws, won't God * them all the	Rom 2:26
honors he planned to * the Jews?	Rom 2:26
God * this blessing to Abraham?	Rom 4:10
God's promise to * the whole earth	Rom 4:13
that he would * him a son who would	Rom 4:18
do not * in to its sinful	Rom 6:12
for sinning; but * yourselves	Rom 6:13
lives in you will * you life, for	Rom 8:10f
to the glory he will * us later.	Rom 8:18
day when God will * us our full	Rom 8:23
also surely * us everything else?	Rom 8:32
I will * you and Sarah a son."	Rom 9:9
[that God would * his salvation to	Rom 10:19
with you to * your bodies to God.	Rom 12:1
As God's messenger I * each of	Rom 12:3
If he is thirsty * him something	Rom 12:20
over you, and * honor and respect	Rom 13:7
* A WARM welcome to any brother	Rom 14:1
Yes, each of us will * an	Rom 14:12
might be saved and * glory to God	Rom 15:9
return is to * some material aid.	Rom 15:27
* me a great blessing for you.	Rom 15:29
Please * my greetings to all	Rom 16:5
Please * them my greetings.	Rom 16:7
greet him for me. And * my best	Rom 16:10
And please * my greetings to	Rom 16:14
are with them. * my love to	Rom 16:15
Lord Jesus Christ * you all of his	1Co 1:3
At that time God will * to each	1Co 4:5
But if you * yourself to the	1Co 6:17
of your body to * glory back to	1Co 6:20
The man should * his wife all	1Co 7:3

(GIVE Con't)
so that they can * themselves more 1Co 7:5
and clothing? You * them to others 1Co 9:12
Lord would * me a special reward; 1Co 9:17
the ability to * wise advice; 1Co 12:8
Does God * all of us the ability 1Co 12:30
the help you aren't here to * me. 1Co 16:17
you for them. And * each other a 1Co 16:20
each one of you, and * you peace. 2Co 1:2
He will * you the strength to 2Co 1:6,7
of all that he is going to * us. 2Co 1:22
who ought to * me greatest joy. 2Co 2:3
and so we never * up. 2Co 4:1
do, but we don't * up and quit. 2Co 4:8
That is why we never * up. 2Co 4:16
We are poor, but we * rich 2Co 6:10
God might * to them through us. 2Co 8:5
If you are really eager to *, 2Co 8:12
important how much you have to *. 2Co 8:12
God wants you to * what you have, 2Co 8:12
But remember this—if you * 2Co 9:6
mind as to how much he should *. 2Co 9:7
Don't force anyone to * more than 2Co 9:7
left over to * joyfully to others. 2Co 9:8
and eat, will * you more and more 2Co 9:10
so that you can * away more and 2Co 9:10
Yes, God will * you much so that 2Co 9:11
so that you can * away much, and 2Co 9:11
didn't ask you to * me food to eat 2Co 12:13
I am glad to * you myself and 2Co 12:15
I will * you all the proof you 2Co 13:3
I ask you again, does God * you Gal 3:5
God gave his laws to angels to * Gal 3:19
not have had to * us a different Gal 3:21,22
Christ came to * us right standing Gal 3:24
For I am going to * you many Gal 4:27
we don't get discouraged and * up. Gal 6:9
praise God and * glory to him for Eph 1:12
will * us all that he promised; Eph 1:14
Jesus Christ, to * you wisdom to Eph 1:16,17
resources he will * you the mighty Eph 3:16
for when you are angry you * a Eph 4:27
so he can * to others in need. Eph 4:28
and what will * them a blessing. Eph 4:29
and Christ shall * you light." Eph 5:14
Always * thanks for everything Eph 5:20
so that he could * her to Eph 5:27
be eager to * them your very Eph 6:5
and ask God to * me the right words Eph 6:19
May God * peace to you, my Eph 6:23
Jesus Christ will * each of you his Php 1:2
But if living will * me more Php 1:22
make you glad and * you reason to Php 1:26
the Father to * him your thanks. Col 3:17
too, that God will * us many Col 4:3
He and Tychicus will * you all Col 4:9
And as I said before, * Mark a Col 4:10
Please * my greeting to the Col 4:15
so that you would * us money! 1Th 2:5
Think highly of them and * them 1Th 5:13
Lord Jesus Christ * you rich 2Th 1:2
God will * you rest along with us 2Th 1:7
But we must forever * thanks to 2Th 2:13
the very first to * you salvation, 2Th 2:13
May the Lord of peace himself * 2Th 3:16
and mercy and * you great peace of 1Ti 1:2
I had to * them over to Satan to 1Ti 1:20
mercy upon them; * thanks for all 1Ti 2:1
completely * up drinking wine. 1Ti 5:23
works and should * happily to those 1Ti 6:18
will * you strength in suffering. 2Ti 1:8
May the Lord * him a special 2Ti 1:18
But if we * up when we suffer, 2Ti 2:12
and never * in to others; 2Ti 3:3
Judge, will * me on that great day 2Ti 4:8
* you his blessings and his peace. Tit 1:4
* you his blessings and his peace. Phm 1:3
If I am really your friend, * him Phm 1:17
welcome you would * to me if I were Phm 1:17
Yes, dear brother, * me joy with Phm 1:20
and again, and * him a son and make Heb 6:14
doubt that he will * them the Heb 6:18
required by law to * gifts to help Heb 7:5
I have come to * my life." Heb 10:9
promised to * him, Abraham obeyed. Heb 11:8
had promised to * Abraham a whole Heb 11:18
knew God would * future blessings Heb 11:20
great reward that God would * him. Heb 11:26
well they do this. * them reason to Heb 13:17
him to see you. * my greetings to Heb 13:24,25
is always ready to * a bountiful Jas 1:5
Lord to * you any solid answer. Jas 1:7,8
Happy is the man who doesn't * in Jas 1:12
the rich man and * him the best Jas 2:3
and then don't * him clothes or Jas 2:16
only what will * you pleasure. Jas 4:3
So * yourselves humbly to God. Jas 4:7
in heaven would * a great deal to 1Pe 1:12
will * you his eternal glory. 1Pe 5:10
so does my son Mark. * each 1Pe 5:14
* this same faith to each of us. 2Pe 1:1
better, he will * you, through his 2Pe 1:3
us, and to * us his own character. 2Pe 1:4
him and God will * him life, unless 1Jn 5:16
love, and please * each of the 3Jn 1:15
in his mercy is going to * you. Jud 1:21
* to him everlasting glory! Rev 1:6
victorious, I will * fruit from the Rev 2:7
death and I will * you the crown of Rev 2:10
and I will * to each a white Rev 2:17
I will * to each of you whatever Rev 2:23
will * power over the nations. Rev 2:26
And I will * you the Morning Rev 2:28
eyes and * you back your sight. Rev 3:18
and asked him to * me the scroll. Rev 10:9
And I will * power to my two Rev 11:3
will rejoice and * presents to each Rev 11:10
* glory to the God of heaven. Rev 11:13
saying, "We * thanks, Lord God Rev 11:17
she was about to * birth to her Rev 12:4
He was permitted to * breath to Rev 13:15
mind and attitude to * him glory. Rev 16:9
mutually agree to * their authority Rev 17:17
to you, and more—* double penalty Rev 18:6
for others—* twice as much to her. Rev 18:6
I will * to the thirsty the Rev 21:6

GIVEN
I have * you the seed-bearing Gen 1:29
And I've * all the grass and Gen 1:30
Abram: "I have * this land to your Gen 15:18
"Since the Lord has * me no Gen 16:2,3
Yet I have * Abraham a child in Gen 21:7
God has * him flocks of sheep and Gen 24:35
has * him everything he owns. Gen 24:36
master, and have * him yourself and Gen 27:37
for God has * it to Abraham." Gen 28:4
and so he has * me another son." Gen 29:33
since I have * him three sons!" Gen 29:34
The name * is a Hebrew pun. Gen 30:6f
said, "God has * me justice, and Gen 30:6
heard my plea and * me a son." Gen 30:6
* me good gifts for my husband. Gen 30:20
me, for I have * him six sons." Gen 30:20
The riches God has * you from Gen 31:16
These names were * to them by Gen 38:3,4,5
the pledges he had * her, but Hirah Gen 38:20
and * water to refresh their feet; Gen 43:24
But when they had * him Joseph's Gen 45:27
* to Leah by her father, Laban. Gen 46:18
* to Rachel by her father, Laban: Gen 46:23,24,25
whom God has * me here in Egypt." Gen 48:9
And I have * the choice land of Gen 48:22
and Levi were not * land holdings, Gen 49:7f
"Pharaoh has * orders to furnish Ex 5:10,11
"We are * no straw and told to Ex 5:16
No straw will be * you, and you Ex 5:18
the message I have * you." Ex 6:28,29
the food Jehovah has * you to eat. Ex 16:15
For the Lord has * you the Ex 16:28,29
master shall be * thirty pieces of Ex 21:32
and regulations God had * him; Ex 24:3
Instruct those to whom I have * Ex 28:3
moreover, I have * special skill Ex 31:6
laws that I have * you, for they Ex 34:27
Lord had * him upon the mountain. Ex 34:32
God had * him, and the people Ex 34:34
assist in the work * to them by the Ex 35:29
is to be an ox * as a burnt Lev 1:2,3
the flour is to be * to Aaron and Lev 2:3
I have * to the priests this Lev 6:17
carcass shall be * to the priest Lev 7:7
shall also be * the animal's hide. Lev 7:8
the Lord shall be * whatever Lev 7:9
the sacrifices * to the Lord as Lev 7:11
then it shall be * to the assisting Lev 7:14
be * to the officiating priest. Lev 7:32,33
* this portion of the sacrifice. Lev 7:34
offerings, and * to all who have Lev 7:35
these instructions were * to Lev 7:38
with the instructions God had *. Lev 9:16
Jehovah has * through Moses." Lev 10:11
holy, and God has * it to you to Lev 10:17
shall then be * to the priest for Lev 14:13
which I have * you, and I place Lev 14:33,34
That is why these laws are *. Lev 14:57
blood, and I have * you the blood Lev 17:11
yet redeemed, nor * her freedom." Lev 19:20f
be * to the Lord in praise to him. Lev 19:24
because he has * his child to Lev 20:3
and animals I have * you permission Lev 20:25
will be * to the priests as food. Lev 23:20
for the Levites will not be * Lev 25:33
is vowed to be * to the Lord as a Lev 27:9
Lord as a sacrifice, it must be *. Lev 27:9
But if the animal * to the Lord Lev 27:11,12
else [and has * to the Lord his Lev 27:20
and it shall be * to the priests. Lev 27:21
The tenth * to the Lord shall Lev 27:33
been * to the Lord in their place. Num 3:49
made, it must be * to the priest, Num 5:8
Two wagons and four oxen were * Num 7:7
eight oxen were * to the Merari Num 7:8
or teams was * to the Kohath Num 7:9
as those * on the previous days. Num 7:30-35
to the Lord is * to the priests! Num 8:13
for the Lord has * wonderful Num 10:29
Is that why you have * me the job Num 11:12
which the Lord has * you over the Num 15:22
* this task to only you Levites? Num 16:10
nor * us fields and vineyards. Num 16:14
to Aaron: "I have * the priests Num 18:8
Yes, I have * to you all of Num 18:19
shall be * to Aaron the priest. Num 18:28,29
the land I have * the people of Num 20:24
tribes to be * more land, the Num 26:54
the Levites were * no land when it Num 26:62
We feel that we should be * Num 27:3,4
* to their father if he had lived. Num 27:6,7
I have * to the people of Israel. Num 27:12
Jehovah has * Moses: 'Anything Num 31:21
to be * to the people of Israel. Num 31:27
are * to the people of Israel. Num 31:30
So the half * to the army Num 31:36-40
337,500 sheep (of which 675 were * Num 31:36-40
36,000 oxen (of which 72 were * to Num 31:36-40
30,500 donkeys (of which 61 were * Num 31:36-40
All of the Lord's portion was * Num 31:41
the land that the Lord has * them? Num 32:7
I have * the land to you; Num 33:53
You will be * land in proportion Num 33:54
pastureland * to the Levites. Num 35:7
The speech was * on February 15, Deu 1:1
'The Lord God has * us this land. Deu 1:19,20,21
land the Lord our God had * us. Deu 1:24,25
For I have * them all the Mount Deu 2:5
I have * it to the descendants of Deu 2:9
I have * it to the descendants of Deu 2:19
land the Lord our God has * us.' Deu 2:29
the Lord had * them the land, they Deu 3:18
the Lord has * you, caring for your Deu 3:19
after the Lord has * victory to the Deu 3:20
Lord your God has * them across the Deu 3:20
possess the land * you by the Lord Deu 4:1
He has * them to me to pass on to Deu 4:5
he has * you as your inheritance. Deu 4:21,22
to all these laws God has * you; Deu 5:1
"The Lord has * these laws to Deu 5:22
and when he has * you great cities Deu 6:10,11,12
which the Lord our God has * us?' Deu 6:20
for the good land he has * you. Deu 8:10
the land he had * you, you rebelled Deu 9:23
he had * you from the heart of the Deu 10:4
the good land the Lord has * you. Deu 11:17
your fathers, has * you forever: Deu 12:1
the Lord has * you, you must Deu 13:12,13,14
* property like the other tribes. Deu 18:1
must be * to the priests. Deu 18:3
He shall be * his share of the Deu 18:8
Lord who has * him the message; Deu 18:22
When the Lord your God has * it Deu 20:13
land the Lord your God has * you. Deu 21:23
to be * to the girl's father, for Deu 22:19
into the army nor * any other Deu 24:5
for I have * him rules and Deu 24:8
"Justice must be * to migrants Deu 24:17
that is why I have * you this Deu 24:18
stripes may be * lest the Deu 25:1
Lord your God has * you rest from Deu 25:19
to this place and * us this land Deu 26:9
from the ground you have * me.' Deu 26:10
all the good things he has * you. Deu 26:11
your God, 'I have * all of my Deu 26:13
the land you have * us, as you Deu 26:15
these commandments I have * you." Deu 27:10
way from the laws I have * you; Deu 28:14
Your sheep will be * to your Deu 28:31
God for all that he has * you. Deu 28:47,48
But even yet the Lord hasn't * Deu 29:4
I have * you today, then the Lord Deu 30:2
Forgetting it was God who had * Deu 32:18
the laws I have * you today, and Deu 32:46
The laws I have * Deu 33:4
that the Lord had * to Moses. Deu 34:9
in the land which God has * us!" Jos 1:10,11
Lord your God has * you a homeland Jos 1:12,13
which had been * to Joshua by Jos 4:10
for I have * them to you! Jos 6:2
The Lord has * us the city!" Jos 6:16
I have * the king of Ai and all Jos 8:1
* long before by Moses. Jos 8:33
Moses had ever * was read before Jos 8:35
I have * them to you to destroy. Jos 10:8
None of the cities was * a peace Jos 11:19
The Land * to the Tribe of Levi: Jos 13:14
instead, they were * the offerings Jos 13:14
The Land * to the Tribe of Jos 13:15
The Land * to the Tribe of Gad: Jos 13:24
The Land * to the Half-Tribe of Jos 13:29
and Edre-i were * to half of the Jos 13:31
But Moses had * no land to the Jos 13:33
(Moses had already * land to the Jos 14:3,4
the Levites were * no land at all, Jos 14:3,4
The Land * to Caleb: Jos 14:6

(GIVEN Con't)
THE LAND * to the Tribe of Judah Jos 15:1
The Land * to Caleb: Jos 15:13
so he was * the city of Arba (also Jos 15:13
the lowlands were also * to Judah: Jos 15:33-36
The Land * to the Tribe of Jos 16:5,6
Ephraim was also * some of the Jos 16:9
THE LAND * to the Half-tribe of Jos 17:1
had already been * the land of Jos 17:1
was * to the clans of Abiezer, Jos 17:2
five women were * an inheritance Jos 17:5,6
Manasseh was also * the following Jos 17:11
"Why have you * us only one Jos 17:14
has * us such large populations?" Jos 17:14
the land God had * them—all Israel Jos 18:1
the Lord your God has * to you? Jos 18:3
The Land * to the Tribe of Jos 18:11
land * to the tribe of Benjamin: Jos 18:21-28
were * to the tribe of Benjamin. Jos 18:21-28
THE LAND * to the Tribe of Jos 19:1
also * to the tribe of Simeon. Jos 19:8
had earlier been * to Judah, for Jos 19:9
The Land * to the Tribe of Jos 19:10
The Land * to the Tribe of Jos 19:17-23
The Land * to the Tribe of Asher: Jos 19:24,25,26
The Land * to the Tribe of Jos 19:32
The Land * to the Tribe of Dan: Jos 19:40
So they were * some of the Jos 21:3
These were * to some of the Jos 21:4
division were * ten cities from the Jos 21:5
These cities were * by the tribes Jos 21:6
* to Caleb, the son of Jephunneh; Jos 21:9-16
So in all, thirteen cities were * Jos 21:19
were * by the tribe of Dan: Jos 21:23,24
and pasturelands * to the remainder Jos 21:26
division—were * four cities by the Jos 21:34,35
was * twelve cities in all. Jos 21:40
and pasturelands * to the Levites Jos 21:41,42
every order I have * you—every Jos 22:2,3
And now the Lord our God has * Jos 22:4
So go home now to the land * you Jos 22:4
of the tribe was * land on the west Jos 22:7,8
when the Lord had * success to the Jos 23:1
enemies and has * you their land. Jos 23:3
which the Lord your God has * you. Jos 23:13
as the Lord has * you the good Jos 23:15,16
land which the Lord has * you. Jos 23:15,16
had been * to his son Phinehas. Jos 24:33
The city of Hebron was * to Caleb Ju 1:20
Lord had * to them through Moses. Ju 3:4
seventy sons were * their just Ju 9:24
Lord, for he has * you a great Ju 11:36
said, "You have * Israel such a Ju 15:18
For God has * it to us!" Ju 18:9,10
The four hundred girls were * to Ju 21:14
you couldn't have * your daughters Ju 21:22
has * you this little grandson; Ru 4:14
child, and he has * me my request; 1Sa 1:27
it brought up be * to Eli's sons. 1Sa 2:13,14
this one they had * to the Lord. 1Sa 2:20
I have * you a king. 1Sa 12:1
you today and has * it to a 1Sa 15:28
you and * it to your rival, David. 1Sa 28:17
Today the Lord has * you revenge 2Sa 4:8
"I have * your master's grandson 2Sa 9:9
would have * you much, much more. 2Sa 12:8
But you have * great opportunity 2Sa 12:14
Lord has * it to your son Absalom! 2Sa 16:7,8
Literally, "* you ten pieces of 2Sa 18:11f
hasn't fed us or * us gifts!" 2Sa 19:42
than the three days he had been *. 2Sa 20:5
You have * me the shield of your 2Sa 22:36
For you have * me strength for 2Sa 22:40
living God who has * me the throne 1Ki 2:23,24
wanted, and it would be * to him! 1Ki 3:5
the great wisdom God had * him. 1Ki 3:28
has * Israel peace on every side; 1Ki 5:4
which you have * to their fathers. 1Ki 8:33,34
land which you have * your people. 1Ki 8:35,36
which you have * their fathers. 1Ki 8:40
which you have * their fathers, and 1Ki 8:48
and * rest to his people Israel; 1Ki 8:56
he has * our ancestors. 1Ki 8:58
this land which I have * them. 1Ki 9:7
later he had * the city to his 1Ki 9:16
Pharaoh had * them homes and 1Ki 11:16,17,18
For the Lord has * me strict 1Ki 13:9
I have * her my instructions." 1Ki 17:8,9
been * to Naaman's wife as a maid. 2Ki 5:2
sin offerings was * to the priests 2Ki 12:16
which he had * to their ancestors 2Ki 17:13
all the laws * to them by Moses the 2Ki 18:12
"Collect the money * to the 2Ki 22:3,4
Jehoiachin was * civilian 2Ki 25:29
was * to his half brother, Joseph. 1Ch 5:1
and suburbs were * to Caleb the son 1Ch 6:55,56,57
and Anathoth—were * to the priests 1Ch 6:60
pasturelands were * to the subclans 1Ch 6:70
and pastureland * to the clan of 1Ch 6:71
Lord our God has * his approval, 1Ch 13:2
These are the names of those * 1Ch 16:4
that you have * me all this? 1Ch 17:16
O Lord, you have * me these 1Ch 17:19
"He has * you peace with the 1Ch 22:18
God of Israel has * us peace, and 1Ch 23:25
were * charge of the storehouses); 1Ch 26:14,15
by Ahijah, were * the care of the 1Ch 26:20,21,22
care for the gifts * to the Lord by 1Ch 26:26
sons—the Lord has * me many 1Ch 28:5
For the Holy Spirit had * David 1Ch 28:12
Solomon, "was * to me in writing 1Ch 28:19
men are made great and * strength. 1Ch 29:12
and now you have * me the kingdom— 2Ch 1:8
earth and who has * to David such a 2Ch 2:12
which you have * to your people as 2Ch 6:27
the laws I have * you, and worship 2Ch 7:19
mine which I have * them, and this 2Ch 7:20
Hiram of Tyre had * to him, and he 2Ch 8:2
with the instructions Moses had *; 2Ch 8:13
of your land which you have * us. 2Ch 20:11
that the Lord had * them this 2Ch 20:27
quiet, for his God had * him rest. 2Ch 20:30
Their father had * each of them 2Ch 21:3,4
Even so, Ahaziah was * a royal 2Ch 22:9
So even though Ahaz had * him 2Ch 28:21
law to be * to the Lord their God. 2Ch 31:5,6
A regular food allotment was * to 2Ch 31:17,18
for God had * him great wealth. 2Ch 32:28,29
and instructions * to you by 2Ch 33:8
be the laws of God as * to Moses! 2Ch 34:14
earth have been * to me by the Lord 2Ch 36:22,23
empire, has now * me the Ez 1:2
entire project was * to Jeshua, Ez 3:9
We asked the leaders, 'Who has * Ez 5:9
had * to the people of Israel. Ez 7:6
the wisdom God has * you to select Ez 7:25
I was * great status because the Ez 7:28
which had been * as free-will Ez 8:28
A receipt was * for each item, Ez 8:34
But now we have been * a moment Ez 9:8
You have * us a moment of joy and Ez 9:8
They have even * us their Ez 9:9
of God which he had * to Moses. Neh 8:1
God had * us cause for great joy. Neh 12:43
had not been * what was due them, Neh 13:10
see that they are * beauty Est 2:3
bed, each would be * six months of Est 2:12,13,14
Ahasuerus, she was * her choice of Est 2:12,13,14
was the excuse he had * them. Est 3:3,4
* to those who killed them. Est 3:13
the king had * him, and how he had Est 5:11
the Jew, "I have * Esther the Est 8:7
and the honors * him by the king, Est 10:2
light and life be * to those in Job 3:20,21
"This truth was * me in secret, Job 4:12
alone the land was *—and they have Job 15:17-19
God has * me a fainting heart; Job 23:16,17
Fresh honors were constantly * Job 29:20
freezing and not * him clothing, or Job 31:19,20
You should be * the maximum Job 34:36
and * understanding to the mind?" Job 38:36f
and * them salt plains to live in. Job 39:6
"Have you * the horse strength, Job 39:19
Yes, the gladness you have * me Ps 4:7
He sees that I am * pleasant Ps 16:6
You have * me your salvation as Ps 18:35
the gifts you have * him, your Ps 20:3
For you have * him his heart's Ps 21:2
You have * him fame and honor. Ps 21:5
You have * him the unquenchable Ps 21:6
my enemy, but have * me open ground Ps 31:8
Lord shall be * every blessing. Ps 37:9
the Lord shall be * every blessing, Ps 37:11
He has * me a new song to sing, Ps 40:3
Many blessings are * to those Ps 40:4
But may the joy of the Lord be * Ps 40:16
Has * you more gladness Ps 45:7
But you have * us a banner to Ps 60:4,5
you every day, and you have * me Ps 61:5
and to him will be * the gold of Ps 72:15
For God has * us these times of Ps 81:4
One of Israel, has * us our king. Ps 89:18
Seventy years are * us! Ps 90:10
God has * sacred promises; Ps 108:7
he has * the earth to all mankind. Ps 115:16
and now he has * me the victory. Ps 118:14
You have * us your laws to obey— Ps 119:4
will be * wisdom and good sense. Pro 2:1
wisdom will be * you, and knowledge Pro 2:3,4,5
You will be * the sense to stay Pro 2:11,12,13
be * renewed health and vitality. Pro 3:7,8
shall be * a worthwhile reward. Pro 28:10
And yet all I have will be * to Ecc 2:19
of work God has * to mankind. Ecc 3:10
God has * to some men very great Ecc 6:2
seen foolish men * great authority, Ecc 10:6
* their rightful place of dignity! Ecc 10:6
I have * you the story of God's Is 5:7
I and the children God has * me Is 8:18
unto us a Son is *; Is 9:6
No monument will be * you, for Is 14:20
God has * him victory over many Is 41:2
He will see full justice * to all Is 42:3
you, for I have * you to my people Is 42:6
Israel, who has * me the strength Is 49:5
yourself, 'Who has * me all these? Is 49:21
The Lord God has * me his words Is 50:4
This is the blessing I have * Is 54:17
The flocks of Kedar shall be * Is 60:7
And yet my people have * up their Jer 2:10,11
has left me and * herself to Jer 3:8
you have gone off and * yourself Jer 3:20
our doom and * us a cup of poison Jer 8:14
It is your message I've * them, Jer 17:16
and help were * the poor and the Jer 22:16
the laws I have * you, and if you Jer 26:4
So now I have * all your Jer 27:6
* him all your flocks and herds. Jer 28:14
For I have * rest to the weary Jer 31:25
Then after I had * the papers to Jer 32:16
and that he be * a small loaf of Jer 37:21
be brought out and * to the Jer 38:21,22
the warning I have * you today. Jer 42:19
alike, who had * him that answer: Jer 44:20
HERE ARE THE messages * to Jer 46:1
This message was * against Egypt Jer 46:2
do the work that God has * them! Jer 48:10
And he was * a regular allowance Jer 52:34
he has * their palaces to their Lam 2:7
bitterness, and * me a cup of Lam 3:15
those to whom I have * the city! Eze 9:1
counsel being * out in this city. Eze 11:1
Now the Lord has * us their Eze 11:15
the Lord has * them his messages. Eze 13:17
on to the items * to him in pledge Eze 18:7
what they have * him in pledge, and Eze 18:12
the land I had * them, a land full Eze 20:15
fearsome news that God has * me. Eze 21:7
be inhabited or be * beauty here in Eze 26:20
HERE IS ANOTHER message * to me Eze 28:1
They were * to you on the day you Eze 28:13
buried, for I have * you as food to Eze 29:5
Yes, I have * him the land of Eze 29:20
be * a bullock for a sin offering. Eze 43:19
A young goat will also be * each Eze 45:23
shall be * two sections. Eze 47:13
All these immigrants are to be * Eze 47:23
"The sections * to the remaining Eze 48:23
and wine * to them by the king. Dan 1:8
Now as it happened, God had * Dan 1:9
for you have * me wisdom and Dan 2:23
God of heaven has * you your Dan 2:37
and * to the Medes and Persians." Dan 5:28
and a man's mind was * to it. Dan 7:4
And great power was * to it over Dan 7:6
He was * the ruling power and Dan 7:14
shall be * to the people of God; Dan 7:27
began praying, a command was *. Dan 9:23
from the time the command is * to Dan 9:25
be torn apart and * to others. Dan 11:4
of Egypt will be * in marriage to Dan 11:6
He has * all! Hos 1:21,22
For she has * gifts to Egypt and Hos 12:1
upon the land that I have * them; Amo 9:15
and * what is ours to others." Mic 2:4
is no justice * in the courts, for Hab 1:4
from the Lord were * to Zechariah Zec 1:1
Governor of Judah, who was * the Zec 4:6f
all these blessings will be * to Zec 8:12
* through the prophet Malachi: Mal 1:1
at the rules he has * you to obey. Mal 1:13
Kingdom of Heaven is * to them. Mt 5:3
"Ask, and you will be * what you Mt 7:7
will he be * a stone instead? Mt 7:9
will he be * a poisonous snake? Mt 7:10
for you will be * the right words Mt 10:19
* the same reward a prophet gets. Mt 10:41
will be * a reward like theirs. Mt 10:41
and none will be * except what Mt 12:39,40
has will more be *," he told them, Mt 13:12,13
on a tray and * to the girl, who Mt 14:11
proof will be * except the miracle Mt 16:4
away from you, and * to a nation Mt 21:43
Have I * you the task of managing Mt 24:45
well what he is * shall be given Mt 25:29
is given shall be * more, and he Mt 25:29
a fortune and * it to the poor." Mt 26:8,9
"I have been * all authority in Mt 28:18
all the commands I have * you; Mt 28:20
To him who has shall be *; Mk 4:25
For I have * to God what I could Mk 7:11
God what I could have * to you.' Mk 7:11
the table are * some scraps from Mk 7:28
"We've * up everything to follow Mk 10:28
no one has ever * up anything—home, Mk 10:29
who won't be * back, a hundred Mk 10:30
belongs to God must be * to God!" Mk 12:17
poor widow has * more than all Mk 12:43,44
and * the money to the poor!" Mk 14:4,5
that is why he has * you this Lk 1:45
Jesus, the name * him by the angel Lk 2:21
I have seen the Savior you have * Lk 2:29,30,31
measure what is * back to you." Lk 6:38

(GIVEN Con't)
has, to him shall be * more; Lk 8:18
And I have * you authority over Lk 10:19
to whom much is *, for their Lk 12:48
men to whom he had * the money, to Lk 19:15
"God has * us a King!" Lk 19:38
poor widow has * more than all the Lk 21:3
For they have * a little of what Lk 21:4
is, has * everything she has." Lk 21:4
and when he had * thanks for it, he Lk 22:17
"This is my body, * for you. Lk 22:19
God has * him everything there is. Jn 3:35
the Father has * me—and I will Jn 6:37
all those he has * me, but that I Jn 6:39
this Bread is my flesh * to Jn 6:48-51
be * to everyone believing in him; Jn 7:39
but the Spirit had not yet been * Jn 7:39
For the Father has * me this Jn 10:18
for my Father has * them to me, Jn 10:29
He is * eternal life for Jn 11:26
and the money * to the poor." Jn 12:5
Jesus knew that the Father had * Jn 13:1
I have * you an example to Jn 13:15
It is the answer * by the Father Jn 14:24
For you have * him authority Jn 17:2
life to each one you have * him. Jn 17:2
* me because they belong to you. Jn 17:9
and you have * them back to me Jn 17:10
those you have * me—so that they Jn 17:11
name those whom you have * me." Jn 17:12f
I have * them your commands. Jn 17:14
"I have * them the glory you Jn 17:22
me—these you've * me—so that they Jn 17:24
and Pharisees had * Judas a squad Jn 18:3
the cup the Father has * me?" Jn 18:11
it were * to you from above. Jn 19:11
I saw all this myself and have * Jn 19:35
And again, 'Let his work be * to Act 1:20
Faith in Jesus' name—faith * us Act 3:16
is * by God to all who obey him." Act 5:32
were not being * as much food, in Act 6:1
Holy Spirit was * when the apostles Act 8:18
Spirit would be * to Gentiles too! Act 10:45
"Yes," they said, "God has * Act 11:18
God should be * first to you Jews. Act 13:46
were * to God at the Temple. Act 18:18f
were * to God at the Temple. Act 18:22f
"Your Excellency, you have * Act 24:2
"We would have * him what he Act 24:6
He is * an opportunity to defend Act 25:16
well aware, I was * a thorough Act 26:4
After all, salvation is not * to Rom 2:12-15
It is * to those who do not work Rom 4:4,5
Is this blessing * only to those Rom 4:9
the blessing also * to those who do Rom 4:9
So God's blessings are * to us by Rom 4:16
us because God has * us the Holy Rom 5:5
he had not yet * his laws to them, Rom 5:13
The Ten Commandments were * so Rom 5:20
* his wonderful new life to enjoy. Rom 6:4
in my being * the death penalty. Rom 7:10
has already * you righteousness." Rom 8:10f
* us right standing with himself. Rom 8:33
God has * you so much, but still Rom 9:4
blessings are not * just because Rom 9:16
They are * because God takes pity Rom 9:16
For God told him he had * him the Rom 9:17
Just this, that God has * the Rom 9:30
For God has * them all up to sin Rom 11:32
by how much faith God has * you. Rom 12:3
God has * each of us the ability Rom 12:6
So if God has * you the ability Rom 12:6
If God has * you money, be Rom 12:8
If God has * you administrative Rom 12:8
your love for me—* to you by the Rom 15:30
gifts he has * you, now that you 1Co 1:4
for him and has * you a full 1Co 1:5
And God has actually * us his 1Co 2:12
and blessing that God has * us. 1Co 2:12
the very words * to us by the Holy 1Co 2:13
For God has already * you 1Co 3:21
He has * you Paul and Apollos 1Co 3:22
He has * you the whole world to 1Co 3:22
He has * you all of the present 1Co 3:22
do you have that God hasn't * you? 1Co 4:7
God has * us an appetite for food 1Co 6:13
his kindness has * me wisdom that 1Co 7:25
In the same way the Lord has * 1Co 9:14
picked me out and * me this sacred 1Co 9:17
quickly fades," * to the winners 1Co 9:25f
and when he had * thanks to God 1Co 11:24
This is my body, which is * 1Co 11:24
either, are * power to understand 1Co 12:10
all been * that same Holy Spirit. 1Co 12:13
honor and care are * to those parts 1Co 12:24
If someone is * the gift of 1Co 14:13
God has * him, or speak in an 1Co 14:26
The name * to Jesus' twelve 1Co 15:5f
been * to Christ by his Father; 1Co 15:27
that God who has * him the victory 1Co 15:28
Adam, was * a natural, human body 1Co 15:45
but we shall all be * new bodies! 1Co 15:51
help and comfort God has * us. 2Co 1:3,4
of ownership—and * us his Holy 2Co 1:22
his mercy, who has * us this 2Co 4:1
he has * us his Holy Spirit. 2Co 5:5
And God has * us the privilege of 2Co 5:18
he has * us to tell others. 2Co 5:19
to God that he has * Titus the same 2Co 8:16
if it were being * under pressure. 2Co 9:5
so I was * a physical condition 2Co 12:7
which he has * me, not to punish 2Co 13:10
Well then, why were the laws *? Gal 3:19
the promise was *, to show men how Gal 3:19
eyes and * them to replace mine Gal 4:15
And we to whom Christ has * Gal 5:6
you have been * freedom: not Gal 5:13
are Christ's have been * to him! Eph 1:18
* us new lives from Christ Jesus; Eph 2:10
know that God has * me this special Eph 3:2,3
God has * me the wonderful Eph 3:7
and he has * me his power and Eph 3:7
May he be * glory forever and Eph 3:21
However, Christ has * each of us Eph 4:7
Some of us have been * special Eph 4:11
to others he has * the gift of Eph 4:11
* themselves over to impure ways. Eph 4:19
has * you eternal life with him. Php 1:28
For to you has been * the Php 1:29
Now I have * up everything Php 3:10
which the Holy Spirit has * you. Col 1:8
by God who has * you this new kind Col 3:12
have * us in our praying for you? 1Th 3:9
has loved us and * us everlasting 2Th 2:16
dear brothers, * in the name of our 2Th 3:6
they should be * other jobs in the 1Ti 3:10
abilities God has * you through his 1Ti 4:14
life which God has * you, and which 1Ti 6:12
others whatever God has * them. 1Ti 6:18
* him until the day of his return. 2Ti 1:12
was * to us by inspiration from 2Ti 3:16
be * a first and second warning. Tit 3:10
see that they are * everything Tit 3:13
Son to whom he has * everything, Heb 1:2
and today I have * you the honor Heb 1:5,6
save us—has been * to us just as it Heb 4:2
He has * us both his promise and Heb 6:18
Moses had never * them that work. Heb 7:12,13,14
* the place of honor in heaven. Heb 7:26
of things to be * away to certain Heb 9:16
For after Moses had * the people Heb 9:19
to obey the laws * by Moses was Heb 10:28
When they saw that God had * them Heb 11:23
Others were * great power in Heb 11:34
mercy that has * us the privilege 1Pe 1:3
part of the work God has * you. 1Pe 2:21
God has * each of you some 1Pe 4:10
letter for I have * you a true 1Pe 5:12
power he has * us all the other 2Pe 1:4
honor * him by God his Father; 2Pe 1:17,18
commandments that were * to him. 2Pe 2:21
This is the message God has * us 1Jn 1:5
from hell and * eternal life. 1Jn 3:14
Spirit he has * us tells us so. 1Jn 3:24
That he has * us eternal life, 1Jn 5:11
May you be * more and more of Jud 1:2
salvation God has * us, but now I Jud 1:3
Its rider was * a long sword and Rev 6:4
They were * control of one-fourth Rev 6:8
White robes were * to each of Rev 6:11
who had been * power to injure Rev 7:2
How many were * this mark? Rev 7:4-8
and they were * seven trumpets. Rev 8:2
of incense was * to him to mix with Rev 8:3
* the key to the bottomless pit. Rev 9:1
* power to sting like scorpions. Rev 9:3
power to hurt, * to them for five Rev 9:10
NOW I WAS * a measuring stick and Rev 11:1
who had * birth to the child. Rev 12:13
But she was * two wings like Rev 12:14
For at last God has * judgment Rev 18:20
who had been * the right to judge. Rev 20:4

GIVER
and * of everything everywhere. Eph 1:23
Jesus became the * of eternal Heb 5:9

GIVERS
* are the ones God prizes. 2Co 9:7

GIVES
and he * Jacob his blessings): Gen 27:23
The double dream * double Gen 41:32
"If someone * money or goods to Ex 22:7
Lord your God who * you power to Deu 8:18
no bribes. He * justice to the Deu 10:18
He loves foreigners and * them Deu 10:18
Land, and the Lord * you rest and Deu 12:10
ancestors, and * you all the land Deu 19:8
If anyone * false witness, Deu 19:16
If the man is poor and * you his Deu 24:12,13
your god Chemosh * you, and we will Ju 11:24
whatever Jehovah our God * us! Ju 11:24
The Lord * life. 1Sa 2:6
He * mighty strength to his King, 1Sa 2:10
And * great glory to his anointed 1Sa 2:10
The Lord * his own reward for 1Sa 26:23
* up and quits hunting for me; 1Sa 27:1
I'm the one who * the orders 2Sa 13:28
He * me skill in war 2Sa 22:35
He * wonderful deliverance to his 2Sa 22:51
their gods, but none * them aid. Job 5:1
the fields, and * prosperity to Job 5:11
This, at least, * me comfort Job 6:10
This thought * me hope, so that Job 14:14
would die. God * them confidence Job 24:22,23
breath of the Almighty * me life. Job 33:4
like that, and * them wisdom and Job 33:16
God my Maker who * songs in the Job 35:9,10
his blessings, but * them their Job 36:6
"Who * intuition and instinct? Job 38:36
What joys he * to all his people. Ps 3:8
me; he * me wisdom in the night. Ps 16:7
wherever I go. He * me the Ps 18:33
He prepares me for battle and * Ps 18:34
for you are the God who * me Ps 25:5
* victory to his anointed king. Ps 28:8
* attention when they cry to him. Ps 34:15
and * them eternal rewards. Ps 37:18
and pray to God who * me life. Ps 42:8
the fatherless; he * justice to the Ps 68:5
He * families to the lonely, and Ps 68:6
burdens also * us our salvation. Ps 68:19
The God of Israel * strength and Ps 68:35
He * us grace and glory. Ps 84:11
his paths, and * us respite from Ps 94:12,13
He * justice throughout Israel. Ps 99:4
the eagle's! He * justice to all Ps 103:6
who are godly and * them many Ps 107:41
He * food to those who trust him; Ps 111:5
He * generously to those in need. Ps 112:9
among princes! He * children to Ps 113:9
He * food to every living thing, Ps 136:25
No one * me a passing thought. Ps 142:4
* me strength and skill in battle. Ps 144:1
promise, and * justice to the poor Ps 146:7
Wisdom *:A long, good Pro 3:16,17
he * his friendship to the godly. Pro 3:32
the dawn * way to morning Pro 4:18
A godly man * good advice, but a Pro 10:21
The good man * wise advice, but Pro 10:31
Telling the truth * a man great Pro 12:14
Reverence for God * a man deep Pro 14:26
Reverence for God * life, Pro 19:23
WINE * FALSE courage; Pro 20:1
A just king * stability to his Pro 29:4
and generously * to the needy. Pro 31:19,20
For God * those who please him Ecc 2:24-26
and * it to those who please him. Ecc 2:24-26
Just as being too busy * you Ecc 5:1
on his past, for God * him joy. Ecc 5:19,20
realize that God * one as well as Ecc 7:14
which God * to mankind everywhere. Ecc 8:15
for the wife God * you is your best Ecc 9:9
A party * laughter, and wine Ecc 10:19
laughter, and wine * happiness, and Ecc 10:19
happiness, and money * everything! Ecc 10:19
The very look on their faces * Is 3:9
day when the Lord * his people rest Is 14:3
teacher and * the farmer wisdom. Is 28:29
understanding. He * power to the Is 40:29
in it, and * life and breath and Is 42:5
He who * me justice is near. Is 50:8
you and * you all this joy. Is 51:12
Like a wanton wife who * herself Jer 3:6
Though I am the one who * them Jer 5:23,24
The Lord who * us sunlight in the Jer 31:35
"for the law * you the first right Jer 32:8
for the Lord God * just punishment Jer 51:56
Although God * him grief, yet he Lam 3:32
the false prophets * him a message Eze 14:9
is no robber, but * food to the Eze 18:7
and right— if he * back the Eze 33:15
Whatever anyone * to the Lord Eze 44:29
If the prince * a gift of land to Eze 46:16
But if he * a gift of land to Eze 46:17
If he * property to his sons, it Eze 46:18
their thrones. He * wise men their Dan 2:21
of the world, and * them to anyone Dan 4:17
and * power to anyone he chooses. Dan 4:25
and * them to anyone he chooses." Dan 4:32
the God who * you the breath of Dan 5:23
And if she * birth, I will slay Hos 9:16
For he * his sunlight to both the Mt 5:45
And anyone who * up his home, Mt 19:29
If anyone so much as * you a cup Mk 9:41
For it * your Father great Lk 12:32
man whose master * him the Lk 12:42,43,44
this life * light to all mankind. Jn 1:4
Spirit * new life from heaven; Jn 3:6
and he * life to the world." Jn 6:33
But the Bread from heaven * Jn 6:48-51
Only the Holy Spirit * eternal Jn 6:63
the dead and * them life again. Jn 11:25
like the peace the world *. Jn 14:27
born—her anguish * place to Jn 16:21

(GIVES Con't)
all the earth. He * eternal life to Jn 17:2
He himself * life and breath to Act 17:25
years, and this * me confidence as Act 24:10
sins and * glorious life instead. Rom 5:16
all God * to his Son Jesus is now Rom 8:17
that Christ * to those who trust in Rom 10:4
who generously * his riches to all Rom 10:12
May God who * patience, Rom 15:5
that God who * you hope will keep Rom 15:13
And now may our God, who * peace, Rom 15:33
all the same. God * some the gift 1Co 7:7
and others he * the gift of being 1Co 7:7
who made everything and * us life. 1Co 8:6
the Holy Spirit * to each of you, 1Co 12:1
Now God * us many kinds of 1Co 12:4
To one person the Spirit * the 1Co 12:8
same Spirit. He * special faith to 1Co 12:9
heal the sick. He * power for 1Co 12:10
and preach. He * someone else the 1Co 12:10
Holy Spirit who * all these gifts 1Co 12:11
the Holy Spirit *, and especially 1Co 14:1
then God * it a beautiful new 1Co 15:38
* us spiritual, heavenly bodies. 1Co 15:46
in the new way, the Holy Spirit * 2Co 3:6
The Lord is the Spirit who * 2Co 3:17
the Lord, but this * us constant 2Co 4:11
man * generously to the poor. 2Co 9:9
For God, who * seed to the farmer 2Co 9:10
eternal life he * through Christ; Gal 1:6
life which the Holy Spirit * him. Gal 6:8
Why is it that he * us these Eph 4:12
who * me the strength and power. Php 4:13
we live for, that * us hope and joy 1Th 2:19
God who * his Holy Spirit to you. 1Th 4:8
I command you before God who * 1Ti 6:13
who always richly * us all we need 1Ti 6:17
the strength Christ Jesus * you. 2Ti 2:1
Run from anything that * you the 2Ti 2:22
eternal life he * us, and we are Tit 3:7
But he * us more and more Jas 4:6
As the Scripture says, God * Jas 4:6
spirits, for God * special 1Pe 5:5
Christ our God and Savior * to us. 2Pe 1:1
*, and we shall share his kingdom! Rev 1:9

GIVING
* knowledge of Good and Bad. Gen 2:9
confused them by * them many Gen 11:9
the new possessions I am * you." Gen 13:17
"Look," he said, "I am * your Gen 20:16
* you all I am promising." Gen 28:15
* my slave-girl to my husband." Gen 30:18
her prayers by * her a child. Gen 30:22
of Edom, each * its name to the Gen 36:40-43
Joseph, never * him a thought. Gen 40:23
for * them an excuse to kill us." Ex 5:21
"Don't they realize that I am * Ex 16:28,29
for all damages by * the owner of Ex 22:5
"You must be prompt in * me the Ex 22:29
with you in * you these laws." Ex 24:8
the Spirit of God, * him great Ex 31:3
redeemed by * a lamb in its place. Ex 34:20
to your regular * and normal Lev 23:38
his mind about * it to the Lord, Lev 27:10
Canaan—the land I am * to Israel; Num 13:2
of Canaan (I am * you the entire Num 34:1
Then Moses replied publicly, * Num 36:5
I am * all of it to you! Deu 1:8
'When * your decisions,' I told Deu 1:17
to the land the Lord was * them. Deu 3:18
as fair as these I am * you today? Deu 4:8
land the Lord your God is * you." Deu 4:40
life in the land he is * you. Deu 5:16
them in the land I am * to them.' Deu 5:31
commandments I am * you today. Deu 6:6
commandments I am * you today. Deu 7:11
your God is not * you this good Deu 9:6
commandments I am * you today, Deu 10:12,13
"I am * you the choice today Deu 11:26
God which I am * you today, and a Deu 11:27
in the land the Lord is * you. Deu 11:31
all the laws I am * you today. Deu 11:32
which I am * you today, and if you Deu 13:18
is * you if you obey this command. Deu 15:4,5
your God that I am * you today. Deu 15:4,5
That is why I am * you this Deu 15:15
cities the Lord your God is * you. Deu 16:18
which the Lord your God is * you. Deu 16:20
commandments I am * you Deu 19:9
Lord your God is * you, remember Deu 19:14
land the Lord your God is * you. Deu 24:4
is why I am * you this command. Deu 24:22
land the Lord your God is * you. Deu 25:13,14,15
the Lord your God is * you today. Deu 26:16
land the Lord your God is * you. Deu 28:8
your God that I am * you today, he Deu 28:13
these laws I am * you today, then Deu 28:15-19
By * my affections Deu 32:21
I am * to the people of Israel. Deu 32:49
you the land I am * the people of Deu 32:52
through the camp * these Jos 3:2,3,4
people by * them good crops again. Ru 1:6,7
happy occasion by * presents to 1Sa 1:4
and now I am * him to the Lord 1Sa 1:28
And now they are * you the same 1Sa 8:8
sealed the pact by * him his robe, 1Sa 18:4
king and * him a decent burial. 2Sa 2:5
speak of * me an eternal dynasty! 2Sa 7:19
I would be * him the kingdom too! 1Ki 2:22
him by * him a son to succeed him. 1Ki 3:6
"Praise God for * David a wise 1Ki 5:7
before the Ark by * constant praise 1Ch 16:4
Under Jeduthun, who led in * 1Ch 25:3
of God, I am * all of my own 1Ch 29:3
people— yes, I am * you the wisdom 2Ch 1:12
And I am also * you such riches, 2Ch 1:12
by * King Cyrus the desire to Ez 1:1
other items we are * you for the Ez 7:19
of our God and in * us Jerusalem as Ez 9:9
you did not stop * them bread from Neh 9:20
the wall, * thanks as they went. Neh 12:31,32
and servants, * generous gifts to Est 2:18
from his finger and * it to Haman, Est 3:10
Now the king is * permission Est 8:8f
gladness, and the * of gifts this Est 9:22
people, * them food in abundance. Job 36:31
Have you ever seen them * birth Job 39:1
Today I am * you your glory.' Ps 2:7
Never stop * your salvation Ps 36:10
other food than God was * them. Ps 78:18
Israel from * them his blessings. Ps 78:41
with your lovingkindness, * us Ps 90:14
to his people by * them the land of Ps 111:6
as I worship, * thanks to you for Ps 138:2
me by * me the strength I need. Ps 138:3
Honor the Lord by * him the first Pro 3:9,10
Everyone enjoys * good advice, Pro 15:23
An angry man is silenced by * him Pro 21:14
* preferred treatment to rich Pro 28:21
earth justice is * way to crime and Ecc 3:16
And why is he * up so much now? Ecc 4:8
of a woman * birth to a child. Is 21:3
We suffered as a woman * birth, Is 26:17
ostriches too, for * them water in Is 43:20
out! I am * you your freedom!' Is 49:8,9
This is adultery, for you are * Is 57:7,8
woman * birth to her first child; Jer 4:31
I am tired of always * you Jer 15:6
If we kill Jeremiah for * us the Jer 26:19
WHEN JEREMIAH HAD finished * this Jer 43:1
women in the pains of * birth. Jer 48:41
and is * Babylon all her due. Jer 51:56
what I am * you—eat this scroll! Eze 3:1
* off a greenish-yellow glow. Eze 10:9-13
* payment in ebony and ivory. Eze 27:15
so the Lord was * Egypt to him to Eze 29:18f
so the Lord was * Egypt to him to Eze 29:20f
people, * a portion to each tribe. Eze 45:8
always had, * thanks to his God. Dan 6:10
his people, * them worldwide powers Dan 7:22
the Egyptian king, * him a daughter Dan 11:17
to quit * herself to others. Hos 1:2
heaven and * you such scant crops. Hag 1:10
Notice, I am * you this promise Hag 2:18,19
am * you these fine new clothes." Zec 3:4
and instead of * you blessings as I Mal 2:1
by * her a letter of dismissal.' Mt 5:31
How they praised God for * such Mt 9:8
WHEN JESUS HAD finished * these Mt 11:1
When Jesus had finished * these Mt 13:53,54
"How about * you the 'King of Mk 15:9
an appendix * additional facts. Mk 16:9f
(As he was * this illustration Lk 8:8
* him back four times as much!" Lk 19:8
* the bread dipped in the sauce." Jn 13:26
"And so I am * a new commandment Jn 13:34
to heaven after * his chosen Act 1:1
Judea, each * as much as he could. Act 11:29
instead of * the glory to God. Act 12:23
* them power to do great miracles. Act 14:3
and * you food and gladness." Act 14:17
Gentiles by * them the Holy Spirit, Act 15:8
rules instead, * us right standing Rom 5:21
control over us by * himself as a Rom 8:3
to wake them up by * his salvation Rom 10:19
God's * his gifts to you Gentiles. Rom 11:28
with one voice, * glory to God, the Rom 15:6
* her a warm Christian welcome. Rom 16:1
and I think I am * you counsel 1Co 7:40
who claim to be * God's messages—or 1Co 12:10
can understand the praise I am *; 1Co 14:15
How can they join you in * thanks 1Co 14:16
You will be * thanks very 1Co 14:17
he is, * glory to his name. 2Co 1:20
when the Holy Spirit is * life? 2Co 3:8
No, I am * you some good 2Co 5:12
of God, * ourselves to him alone. 2Co 7:1
been an overflow of * to others. 2Co 8:2
encouraged your * in the first 2Co 8:6
your share in this ministry of *. 2Co 8:6
also in the spirit of cheerful *. 2Co 8:7
I am not * you an order; 2Co 8:8
just as gladly, * whatever you can 2Co 8:11
it up to you by * you everything 2Co 9:8
One way was by * them his laws to Gal 4:24,25
my partners in * and receiving. Php 4:15
we always begin by * thanks to God Col 1:3
going to pay you, * you your full Col 3:24
Dear brothers, * thanks to God 2Th 1:3
messengers, and * me the strength 1Ti 1:12
by * his life for all mankind. 1Ti 2:6
away our sins and * us the new joy Tit 3:5
miracles and by * certain special Heb 2:4
* more time for sinners to repent. 2Pe 3:9
He is * us time to get his 2Pe 3:15,16
dry land without * rain, promising Jud 1:12
* probability to the paraphrase; Rev 1:4f
They worshiped the Dragon for * Rev 13:4
They will all sign a treaty * Rev 17:13

GIZON
of Hashem from *; 1Ch 11:26-47

GLAD
rewarded him for his '* tidings.' 2Sa 4:10
"I'm * to see you, my brother," 2Sa 20:8,9,10
his reply and was * that Solomon 1Ki 3:10
'I am * you want to do it,' he 1Ki 8:18
Let the heavens be *, the earth 1Ch 16:31
the people were *, and brought the 2Ch 24:10
I will be *, yes, filled with Ps 9:2
The Lord is good and * to teach Ps 25:8
that I might sing * praises to the Ps 30:12
that I am in trouble they are *; Ps 35:15
hate me and are * that I am lying Ps 41:6
What a joyful, * procession as Ps 45:15
the Lord! How * the nations will Ps 67:4
No wonder they will be so *! Ps 69:32
No wonder I am *! Ps 92:4
Let the heavens be *, the earth Ps 96:11
Tell the farthest islands to be * Ps 97:1
Lord, and are * that you reign in Ps 97:8,9
wine to make him *, and olive oil Ps 104:15
Egypt was * when they were gone, Ps 105:38
will see it and be *, while evil Ps 107:42
We will rejoice and be * in it. Ps 118:24
I WAS * for the suggestion of Ps 122:1
The wise man is * to be Pro 10:8
A happy face means a * heart; Pro 15:13
are successful, everyone is *. Pro 28:12
about the old ones anymore. Be *; Is 65:18
Rejoice with Jerusalem; be * with Is 66:10
Though you were *, O Chaldeans, Jer 50:11
are * to see what you have done. Lam 1:21
The king is * about their Hos 7:3
Fear not, my people; be * now and Joe 2:21
child, would that make him *? Mic 6:7
the mountains with * news: "The Nah 1:15
shout, O Israel; be * and rejoice Zep 3:14
the mercies of the Lord and be *. Zec 10:7
Be very *! Mt 5:12
She gave a * cry and exclaimed to Lk 1:42
He knew I was coming and was *." Jn 8:56
And for your sake, I am * I Jn 11:15
* and rejoiced in Paul's message; Act 13:48
bring * tidings of good things." Rom 10:15
Be * for all God is planning for Rom 12:12
in these affairs, God will be *; Rom 14:18
And in another place, "Be *, O Rom 15:10
They were very * to do this, for Rom 15:27
be * to tell you what I think. 1Co 7:25
I am so *, dear brothers, that 1Co 11:2
Yes, we are especially * to have 1Co 12:23
is honored, all the parts are *. 1Co 12:26
It is never * about injustice, 1Co 13:6
I am so * that Stephanas, 1Co 16:17
We are so * that we can say with 2Co 1:12
Now I am * I sent it, not 2Co 7:9
He is * to follow my suggestion 2Co 8:17
Those you help will be * not 2Co 9:13
Now I am * to boast about how 2Co 12:9
weak I am; I am * to be a living 2Co 12:9
I am * to give you myself and 2Co 12:15
We are * to be weak and despised 2Co 13:9
the Gentiles the * News of the Eph 3:8
assured of his * welcome when we Eph 3:12
is being preached and I am *. Php 1:18
I am going to keep on being *, Php 1:19
my staying will make you * and Php 1:26
Then when Christ returns how * I Php 2:16
then I will be *, and will share my Php 2:17
DEAR friends, be * in the Lord. Php 3:1
can praise God for and be * about. Php 4:8
and I am *, for I am helping to Col 1:24
on ahead and were *, for they Heb 11:13
world should be *, for he is great Jas 1:9
But a rich man should be * that Jas 1:10,11
and humbly be * for the wonderful Jas 1:21
So be truly *! 1Pe 1:6
Instead, be really *—because 1Pe 4:13
loving deeds. I am * when you send 3Jn 1:6
citizens of heaven, rejoice! Be *! Rev 12:12
Let us be * and rejoice and Rev 19:7

GLADDENS
A sensible son * his father. Pro 15:20

GLADLY
Hamor and Shechem * agreed, and Gen 34:18,19
"We will * be the serfs of Gen 47:25
Some other women * used their Ex 35:26
The people * followed! Ju 5:2
* -they replied Ju 8:25
Asaph, which they * did, and bowed 2Ch 29:30
if you did, how * I would do it! Ps 51:16
* I bring my sacrifices to you; Ps 54:6
Obey him *; Ps 100:2
But those doing right come * to Jn 3:21
For you * honor each other, but Jn 5:44
God listens * to the words of God. Jn 8:47
and * listened to the message. Act 17:11
and import duties *, obey those Rom 13:7
completion just as *, giving 2Co 8:11
you listen * to those fools; 2Co 11:19,20
I know you would * have taken out Gal 4:15
and we may eat it * if we are 1Ti 4:4
him, and he will * tell you, for he Jas 1:5
patient and godly, * letting God 2Pe 1:6

GLADNESS
Use the trumpets in times of *, Num 10:10
Strength and * walk beside him. 1Ch 16:27
And the Jews had joy and *, and Est 8:16
their victory with feasting and *. Est 9:17
the next day, with feasting and *. Est 9:18
with feasting, *, and the giving of Est 9:22
was turned to * and their mourning Est 9:22
The voice of joy and * has Job 30:31
Yes, the * you have given me is Ps 4:7
his people. What * when the Lord Ps 14:7
Has given you more * Ps 45:7
Give us * in proportion to our Ps 90:15
Let there be no * when he falls— Pro 24:17
his wedding day, his day of *." Sol 3:11
Gone now is the *, gone the joy Is 16:10
joy has reached its lowest ebb; * Is 24:11
his people will have * of heart, Is 30:29
only joy and * will be there. Is 35:10
Joy and * will be found there, Is 51:3
filled with joy and everlasting *; Is 51:11
your * and your wedding feasts; Jer 25:10
Joy and * are gone from fruitful Jer 48:33
all joy and * will be ended in Joe 1:16
will rejoice over you in great *; Zep 3:17,18
have great joy and * at his birth, Lk 1:14
crops and giving you food and *." Act 14:17
work hard and with * all the Eph 6:6,7
* upon you than on anyone else." Heb 1:9

GLAMOR
God, being blinded by the * Heb 3:13

GLANCE
Humiliate the haughty with a *; Job 40:12
The earth trembles at his *; Ps 104:32
I am overcome by one * of your Sol 4:9
soldiers run without a backward *. Jer 46:5
fathers flee without a backward * Jer 47:3
a * and rush to tell the others. Hab 2:2

GLANCED
She * over her shoulder and saw Jn 20:14

GLANCES
crowds to catch the * of the men. Is 3:16

GLARED
the Holy Spirit, * angrily at the Act 13:9

GLASS
far more valuable than gold and *. Job 28:17
well, drink a good * of wine, Ecc 5:18
Then he took a * of wine, and Lk 22:17
gave them another * of wine, Lk 22:20
the ocean became as smooth as *. Rev 7:1
ocean of fire and *, and on it Rev 15:2
was pure, transparent gold like *! Rev 21:18,19,20
pure, transparent gold, like *. Rev 21:21

GLAZE
pretty * covers a common clay pot. Pro 26:23

GLEAMED
His feet * like burnished Rev 1:15

GLEAMING
like lightning, * like torches. Nah 2:4

GLEAN
don't * the vines after they are Deu 24:21
some kind man to * the free grain Ru 2:2
"Stay right here with us to *; Ru 2:8,9
men to let her * right among the Ru 2:15
to *, and not to make any remarks. Ru 2:16
"Where in the world did you * Ru 2:19
* the vineyards of the wicked. Job 24:6

GLEANED
had *, it came to a whole bushel! Ru 2:17
So Ruth did, and * with them Ru 2:23
in Israel shall be * again, the Jer 6:9

GLEANINGS
at least the * would be left! Ob 1:5

GLEE
the Philistines shouted with *; Ju 15:14
their hands in *, and the hills Ps 98:8,9
sing with *, preparing my doom. Lam 3:63
and cheered with * at the Eze 25:6

GLIDE
We * along the tides of time as Ps 90:5,6
where winged sailboats * along Is 18:1

GLIDES
How an eagle * through the sky. Pro 30:18,19

GLIDING
he pierces the swiftly * serpent. Job 26:13
Silent as a serpent * away, Jer 46:22,23

GLIMPSE
eyes for another *, suddenly two Act 1:10

GLITTER
will * like stars forever. Dan 12:3

GLITTERING
* point comes out from his gall. Job 20:25
"Against you also my * sword is Eze 21:28
See their * chariots moving Nah 2:3
See the flashing swords and * Nah 3:3
and the flashing of your * spear. Hab 3:11
They shall shine in his land as * Zec 9:16,17
from him as from a * diamond, or Rev 4:3

GLITTERS
for a sword * at every gate; Eze 21:15

GLOAT
Don't let them * that I am Ps 13:4
See these men of evil * and Ps 22:17
these who * when I am cast down! Ps 38:16

GLOATED
they * as they saw him there in Ju 16:23,24
You should not have * when they Ob 1:12

GLOATING
* over their nakedness and shame. Hab 2:15

GLOOM
with apprehension and with *. Ps 6:3
the cloud of *, the pall of death Is 25:7
and out of their * and darkness the Is 29:18
Forget all this *; Is 30:10,11
wonder you are walking in the *. Is 59:9
a day of clouds and *; Eze 30:2,3
It is a day of darkness and *, of Joe 2:2
of darkness, *, clouds, blackness, Zep 1:15
"What I tell you now in the *, Mt 10:27
the darkness and * of Satan's Col 1:13
flaming fire, *, darkness and a Heb 12:18
of laughter, and * instead of joy. Jas 4:9
is the everlasting * and darkness Jud 1:13

GLOOMY
He always has something * to say. 1Ki 22:8
the wastelands, desolate and *. Job 30:3
here depressed and *, but I will Ps 42:6
O my soul, why be so * and Ps 43:5
The sinner's road is dark and *. Pro 13:9
When a man is *, everything seems Pro 15:15
is under a cloud—*, discouraged, Ecc 5:17
hell, chained in * caves and 2Pe 2:4

GLORIES
I will constantly speak of his * Ps 34:1
worship you and sing of your *. Ps 66:4
receive me into the * of heaven! Ps 73:24
to bring us into the * of heaven. 1Co 2:7
with him and share in all his *. Col 3:4
Or, "the * of the unseen world." 2Pe 2:10f

GLORIFIED
will be * before all the people.' Lev 10:3
my Temple where my name will be *; 2Ch 6:5,6
redeemed Jacob and is * in Israel! Is 44:23
I, the Lord your God, have * you. Is 55:5
has * you in the eyes of all. Is 60:9
then God will be *. Rom 15:7
and the more the Lord is *. 2Co 4:15
that God will be * through Jesus 1Pe 4:11

GLORIFY
Israel rebelled, you did not * me Num 27:14
Instead, * him for his mighty Job 36:24
* YOUR NAME, not ours, O Lord! Ps 115:1
ruthless nations will obey and * Is 25:3
Our hearts' desire is to * your Is 26:8
Let the western coastlands * the Is 42:12
will reverence and * the name of Is 59:19
* my glorious Temple in that day. Is 60:7
will come to me and * my name. Jer 4:2
praise and * and honor the King of Dan 4:37
of death he would die to * God. Jn 21:19
This will * the Lord and show our 2Co 8:19
give you reason to * Christ Jesus Php 1:26
And * your Name? Rev 15:3,4

GLORIOUS
Abraham, even the * God of Isaac, Gen 31:42
Your right hand, O Lord, is * in Ex 15:6
Who is * in holiness like him? Ex 15:11
about the * miracles he did. Deu 4:9
great nation in a * land 'flowing Deu 6:3
your mighty power and * strength. Deu 9:26
reverence to the * and fearful name Deu 28:58,59
How * he is! Deu 32:3
he was almost too * to look at. Ju 13:6
* the king of Israel looked today! 2Sa 6:20
He rode upon the *— 2Sa 22:11
his troops to many * victories. 2Ki 5:1
when you did * miracles in driving 1Ch 17:21
famous and * throughout the world; 1Ch 22:5
and praise your * name, but who am 1Ch 29:13
It will be a * victory!" 2Ch 18:14
the Lord who is great and *; Neh 4:14
Praise his * name! Neh 9:5
you have a * reputation because Neh 9:10
What a * hope! Job 19:27
God is so * that even the moon Job 25:5
His voice is * in the thunder. Job 37:5
O Lord, for all your * power. Ps 21:13
Now many will hear of the * Ps 40:3
Who else can do such * things? Ps 40:5
O GOD, WE have heard of the * Ps 44:1
So *, so majestic! Ps 45:3
Come, see the * things that our Ps 46:8
What a * sight! Ps 48:2
of the earth the * acts of God Ps 65:8
Sing of his * name! Ps 66:2
Come, see the * things God has Ps 66:5
What a * Lord! Ps 68:19
Blessed be his * name forever! Ps 72:19
can describe these * deeds of Ps 78:4
God and not forget his * miracles. Ps 78:7
hand is lifted high in * strength. Ps 89:13
let our children see * things, Ps 90:16
Publish his * acts throughout the Ps 96:3
that God alone is * and strong. Ps 96:7
the * things he does for me. Ps 103:2
THANK THE LORD for all the * Ps 105:1
Who can ever list the * miracles Ps 106:2
to the * presence of God himself. Ps 106:19,20
and sing about his * deeds. Ps 107:22
arm of the Lord has done * things! Ps 118:15,16
Yes, * things! Ps 126:3
shame, but he shall be a * King." Ps 132:18
about Jehovah's * ways, for his Ps 138:5
This is too *, too wonderful to Ps 139:6
I remember the * miracles you did Ps 143:5
children what * things he does. Ps 145:4
in terror from his * majesty, for Is 2:10
covering the * Land, protecting it Is 4:5
In that * day of peace there Is 9:5
Assyria's vast army is like a * Is 10:18
where he lives will be a * place. Is 11:10
And so Babylon, the most * of Is 13:19
and their "* ally," Egypt! Is 20:5,6
there you will die, O * one—you Is 22:18
Once *, her fading beauty Is 28:4
I know the * day will come when Is 31:7
and unmoved. The * Lord will be to Is 33:21
his law and made it truly *. Is 42:21
Prepare a * highway for my Is 57:14
shed his own * light upon you. Is 58:8
glorify my * Temple in that day. Is 60:7
My Temple will be *. Is 60:13
Lord" and "The * Mountain of the Is 60:14
and is * in his salvation. Is 62:1
and see us from your holy, * home; Is 63:15
up their * God for silly idols! Jer 2:10,11
the dust, for your * crowns are Jer 13:18
But there will come a * day, says Jer 16:14,15
your throne, eternal, high and *. Jer 17:12
your architects have made you *. Eze 27:4
"O Egypt, you are great and * Eze 31:18
for it will be a * victory for Eze 39:13
Literally, "the * land." Dan 8:9f
And he will also enter 'The * Dan 11:16
as it was before? How * it was! Hag 2:3
I will make them strong and * Zec 10:3
* Jordan valley lies in ruins. Zec 11:3
shall sit upon my * throne in the Mt 19:28
sins and act on this * news!" Mk 1:15
white, far more * than any earthly Mk 9:3
the prophet of the * God, for you Lk 1:76
splendid in appearance, * to see; Lk 9:31
We had thought he was the * Lk 24:21
is saying these * things about me. Jn 8:54
you gave me—the * unity of being Jn 17:22
reply: "The * God appeared to our Act 7:2
of worshiping the *, ever-living Rom 1:23
all fall short of God's * ideal; Rom 3:23
sins and gives * life instead. Rom 5:16
the Father, with * power, brought Rom 6:4
will share in the * freedom from Rom 8:20,21
would hear about God's * name. Rom 9:17
leads to doom was *, much more 2Co 3:9
much more * is the plan that makes 2Co 3:9
unable to see the * light of the 2Co 4:4
Everyone can see that the * power 2Co 4:7
reason for us to praise our * God. Eph 1:14
asking God, the * Father of our Eph 1:16,17
Yes, his honor is far more * than Eph 1:21
that out of his *, unlimited Eph 3:16
been called to the same * future. Eph 4:4
to himself as a * church without a Eph 5:27
change them into * bodies like his Php 3:21
with his mighty, * strength so that Col 1:11
contradict the * Good News of our 1Ti 1:10,11
I heard that *, majestic voice 2Pe 1:17,18
daring even to scoff at the * Ones 2Pe 2:10
them, even scoffing at the * Ones. Jud 1:8
perfect, into his * presence with Jud 1:24,25
of life—an unending, * future. Rev 2:10
It was a * sight, beautiful as a Rev 21:2

GLORIOUSLY
the Lord, for he has triumphed *; Ex 15:1

(GLORIOUSLY Con't)
the Lord, for he has triumphed *. Ex 15:21
You will march out to battle *, Deu 28:25
in Zion and rule * in Jerusalem, in Is 24:23
them in Egypt by * leading them out Act 13:17

GLORY
great honor and * over Pharaoh and Ex 14:4
you will see more of his *; Ex 16:7,8,9
appeared the awesome * of Jehovah. Ex 16:10
And the * of the Lord rested Ex 24:16
awesome sight: the * of the Lord on Ex 24:17
shall be sanctified by my *. Ex 29:43
Then Moses asked to see God's *. Ex 33:18
But you may not see the * of my Ex 33:20
And when my * goes by, I will Ex 33:22
people would not see the * fade. Ex 34:33f
and the * of the Lord filled it. Ex 40:34
there, and the * of the Lord filled Ex 40:35
his * will appear to you." Lev 9:6
and the * of the Lord appeared to Lev 9:23
Then the * of the Lord appeared, Num 14:10,11
be filled with the * of the Lord, Num 14:20,21
who has seen my * and the miracles Num 14:22
Then the * of Jehovah appeared to Num 16:19
awesome * of the Lord was seen. Num 16:42
and the * of Jehovah appeared to Num 20:6
has shown us his * and greatness; Deu 5:24
"My son, give * to the God of Jos 7:19
And gives great * to his anointed 1Sa 2:10
For Israel's * is gone." 1Sa 4:21,22
(Ichabod means "there is no * 1Sa 4:21,22
And he who is the * of Israel is 1Sa 15:29
in order to bring * to your name. 2Sa 7:23
because the * of the Lord is 1Ki 8:11
content with your * and stay home! 2Ki 14:10
And it will all be done for the * 2Ki 20:6
* in his holy name; 1Ch 16:10
Show his * to the nations! 1Ch 16:24
Ascribe great strength and * to 1Ch 16:28
The * due his name! 1Ch 16:29
Yours is the mighty power and * 1Ch 29:11
And at that moment the * of the 2Ch 5:13,14
And the * of the Lord filled the 2Ch 7:1
of the wealth and * of his empire. Est 1:4
He has stripped me of my * and Job 19:9
Today I am giving you your *.' Ps 2:7
my shield, my *, and my only hope. Ps 3:3
forever turn my * into shame by Ps 4:2
For if I die I cannot give you * Ps 6:5
O LORD OUR God, the majesty and * Ps 8:1
and placed a crown of * and honor Ps 8:5
* of your name fills the earth. Ps 8:9
THE HEAVENS ARE telling the * of Ps 19:1
gates, and let the King of * in. Ps 24:7
Who is this King of *? Ps 24:8
gates and let the King of * in. Ps 24:9
Who is this King of *? Ps 24:10
incomparable perfections and *. Ps 27:4
praise his * and his strength. Ps 29:1
Praise him for his majestic *, Ps 29:2
majestic glory, the * of his name. Ps 29:2
The God of * thunders through the Ps 29:3
"*, glory to the Lord." Ps 29:9
"Glory, * to the Lord." Ps 29:9
We have heard of the city's * Ps 48:8
rescue you, and you can give me *. Ps 50:14,15
Show your * high above the earth. Ps 57:5
May your * shine throughout the Ps 57:11
Literally, "*." Ps 62:7f
your strength and *, for your love Ps 63:2
whole earth be filled with his *. Ps 72:19
cannot compare with you in *! Ps 76:4
futile wrath will bring you *. Ps 76:10
he surrendered his * into enemy Ps 78:61
Display your power and radiant *. Ps 80:1
He gives us grace and *. Ps 84:11
land will be filled with his *. Ps 85:9
I will give * to your name Ps 86:12
You are their strength. What *! Ps 89:17
belongs, let your * shine out. Ps 94:1
Give him the * he deserves! Ps 96:8
roaring seas demonstrate his *. Ps 96:11
every nation sees his *. Ps 97:6
Literally, "give * to his holy Ps 97:12f
on it shout, "* to the Lord." Ps 98:7
before the Lord, before his *. Ps 102:15
He will appear in his *! Ps 102:16
his miracles. * in the Lord; Ps 105:3
receive the * you give to them. Ps 106:5
the skies. His * is far more vast Ps 108:5
* is far greater than the heavens. Ps 113:4
ways, for his * is very great. Ps 138:5
Lord, saving me will bring * to Ps 143:11
I will meditate about your *, Ps 145:5
together about the * of your Ps 145:11
the majesty and * of your reign. Ps 145:12
For he alone is worthy. His * is Ps 148:13
He is the * of his people. Ps 149:9
growing population is a king's *; Pro 14:28
White hair is a crown of * and is Pro 16:31
grandchildren are his crowning *. Pro 17:6
A child's * is his father. Pro 17:6
The * of young men is their Pro 20:29
All the * of mankind will bow Is 2:17
because of the * of his majesty. Is 2:19
the Lord and the * of his majesty Is 2:21
they offend his *. Is 3:8
the Temple was filled with his *. Is 6:1
earth is filled with his *." Is 6:3
to the sea, will be filled with *. Is 9:1
lie in stately * in their graves, Is 14:18
without fail, the * of Moab shall Is 16:13,14
For as Israel's * departed, so Is 17:3
Yes, the * of Israel will be Is 17:4
singing * to the Righteous One! Is 24:15,16
his people. Such * there will be Is 24:23
the crowning * of a nation of men Is 28:1
be their crowning *, the diadem of Is 28:5
for the Lord will display his * Is 35:2
in the road. The * of the Lord Is 40:5
you shall * in the God of Israel. Is 41:16
will not give my * to anyone else; Is 42:8
to all the world the * of his law; Is 42:22
for I have made them for my *; Is 43:7
and Israel, who is my *. Is 46:13
for your days of *, pomp and Is 47:1
I will not let them have my *. Is 48:11
God, and you shall bring me *." Is 49:3
you, and the * of the Lord will Is 58:8
For the * of the Lord is Is 60:1
* of the Lord will shine from you. Is 60:2
to see the * of the Lord upon you. Is 60:3
they shall be destroyed. The * Is 60:13
light, and he will be your *. Is 60:19
this will bring me *. Is 60:21
and graceful oaks for his own *. Is 61:3
and shall * in their riches. Is 61:6
Kings shall be blinded by your *; Is 62:2
The consuming fire of your * Is 64:2
my name. "* to God," they scoff. Is 66:5
drink deep of her * even as an Is 66:11
where they shall see my *. Is 66:18
not heard my fame nor seen my *. Is 66:19
There they shall declare my * to Is 66:19
destroy Israel's * and power. Jer 2:16
Give * to the Lord your God Jer 13:16
the throne of your * by forsaking Jer 14:21
earth and not for *, for they have Jer 17:13
of praise and * to me before all Jer 33:9
Come down from your * and sit in Jer 48:18
Our * is gone. Lam 5:16
That was the way the * of the Eze 1:27,28
me up and the * of the Lord began Eze 3:12
and oh, I saw the * of the Lord Eze 3:23
Suddenly the * of the God of Eze 8:4
And the * of the God of Israel Eze 9:3
And the cloud of * filled the Eze 10:3
Then the * of the Lord rose from Eze 10:4
with the cloud of *, and the court Eze 10:4
brightness of the * of the Lord. Eze 10:4
Then the * of the Lord moved from Eze 10:18
And the * of the God of Israel Eze 10:19
them, and the * of the God of Eze 11:22
Then the * of the Lord rose from Eze 11:23
hearts and their * and joys—their Eze 24:25
cities, the * of the Eze 25:9,10
upon the walls, perfecting your *. Eze 27:11
cause the ancient * of Israel to Eze 29:21
I demonstrate my *, says the Lord. Eze 39:13
Thus I will demonstrate my * Eze 39:21
enemies—and my * shall be evident Eze 39:27
And suddenly the * of the God of Eze 43:2
landscape lighted up with his *. Eze 43:2
And the * of the Lord came into Eze 43:4
and the * of the Lord filled the Eze 43:5
I looked and saw that the * of Eze 44:4
kingdom, power, strength and *. Dan 2:37
so did my honor and * and kingdom. Dan 4:36
and majesty and * and honor. Dan 5:18
and took away his *, and he was Dan 5:20
ruling power and * over all the Dan 7:14
sanctuary—for your own *, Lord. Dan 9:17
They exchanged the * of God for Hos 4:7
foul as they. The * of Israel Hos 9:11
pride and false * of Israel, and Amo 6:8
it to its former *, and Israel Amo 9:11
an awareness of the * of the Lord. Hab 2:14
Soon your own * will be replaced Hab 2:16
earth and sky; his * fills the Hab 3:3
I will give * to my former Zep 3:19
there in my *," says the Lord. Hag 1:8
my *,' says the Lord of Hosts. Hag 2:7
he will be the * of the city. Zec 2:5
"The Lord of * has sent me Zec 2:8
your ways and give * to my name, Mal 2:1
of the world and all their *. Mt 4:8
and the power and the * forever. Mt 6:13f
Yet King Solomon in all his * Mt 6:29
my angels in the * of my Father and Mt 16:27
of heaven, with power and great *. Mt 24:30
shall come in my *, and all the Mt 25:31
I shall sit upon my throne of *. Mt 25:31
I return in the * of my Father, Mk 8:38
to shine with *, and his clothing Mk 9:2
the clouds with great power and *. Mk 13:26
bright with the * of the Lord. Lk 2:9
"* to God in the highest Lk 2:14
be the * of your people Israel!" Lk 2:32
kingdoms and their *—for they are Lk 4:6,7
come in my * and in the glory of Lk 9:26
come in my glory and in the * of Lk 9:26
brightness and *, and the two men Lk 9:32
Solomon in all his * was not robed Lk 12:27
"* to God, I'm healed!" Lk 17:15
return to give * to God?" Lk 17:18
Let all heaven rejoice! * to God Lk 19:38
in a cloud with power and great *. Lk 21:27
before entering his time of *?" Lk 24:26
And some of us have seen his * Jn 1:14
—the * of the only Son of the Jn 1:14
yet returned to his * in heaven. Jn 7:39
him, "Give the * to God, not to Jn 9:24
not death, but for the * of God. Jn 11:4
I, the Son of God, will receive * Jn 11:4
but after Jesus returned to his * Jn 12:16
to return to his * in heaven, and Jn 12:23,24
will exchange it for eternal *. Jn 12:25
Father, bring * and honor to Jn 12:28
seen a vision of the Messiah's *. Jn 12:41
time has come; the * of God will Jn 13:31
And God shall give me his own *, Jn 13:32
This brings great * to my Father. Jn 15:8
great honor by showing you my *. Jn 16:14
All the Father's * is mine; Jn 16:15
I say that he will show you my *. Jn 16:15
Reveal the * of your Son so that Jn 17:1
he can give the * back to you. Jn 17:1
I brought * to you here on earth Jn 17:4
And now, Father, reveal my * as Jn 17:5
your presence, the * we shared Jn 17:5
of yours, and so they are my *! Jn 17:10
"I have given them the * you Jn 17:22
me—so that they can see my *. Jn 17:24
You gave me the * because you Jn 17:24
who has brought * to his servant Act 3:13
heaven and saw the * of God and Act 7:55
instead of giving the * to God. Act 12:23
* and honor and eternal life that Rom 2:7
But there will be * and honor Rom 2:10
brought him * by pointing up his Rom 3:7
But if we are to share his *, we Rom 8:17
to the * he will give us later. Rom 8:18
of future *, also groan to be Rom 8:23
himself, and promised us his *. Rom 8:30
a bright cloud of * and told you Rom 9:4
the riches of his * into, whether Rom 9:23,24
can see how very great his * is. Rom 9:23,24
and everything is for his *. Rom 11:36
To him be * evermore. Rom 11:36
one voice, giving * to God, the Rom 15:6
* to God for his mercies to them. Rom 15:9
is wise, be the * forever through Rom 16:25,26,27
have crucified the Lord of *. 1Co 2:8
Literally, "Let no one * in 1Co 3:21f
* back to God, because he owns it. 1Co 6:20
everything for the * of God, even 1Co 10:31
God's * is man made in his image, 1Co 11:7
image, and man's * is the woman. 1Co 11:7
the beauty and the * of their 1Co 15:40
from the beauty and the * of ours. 1Co 15:40
The sun has one kind of * while 1Co 15:41
but they will be full of * when 1Co 15:43
he is, giving * to his name. 2Co 1:20
began with such * that people could 2Co 3:7
out with the very * of God—though 2Co 3:7
expect far greater * in these days 2Co 3:8
In fact, that first * as it 2Co 3:10
* of the new agreement. 2Co 3:10
full of heavenly *, the glory of 2Co 3:11
glory, the * of God's new plan for 2Co 3:11
Since we know that this new * 2Co 3:12
could not see the * fade away. 2Co 3:13
reflect the * of the Lord. 2Co 3:18
about the * of Christ, who is God. 2Co 4:4
brightness of his * that is seen in 2Co 4:6
If so, it is to bring * to God. 2Co 5:13,14
is to use such weakness for his *. 2Co 12:5
we live. All * to God through all Gal 1:5
And they gave * to God because Gal 1:24
God and give * to him for doing Eph 1:12
the grave into * along with Christ, Eph 2:6
Now * be to God who by his mighty Eph 3:20
May he be given * forever and Eph 3:21
much praise and * to the Lord. Php 1:11
mighty power and *, taking the Php 2:7
Lord, to the * of God the Father. Php 2:11
We Christians * in what Christ Php 3:3
from his riches in *, because of Php 4:19
Now unto God our Father be * Php 4:20
by Christ for his own use and *. Col 1:16
and the riches and * of his plan Col 1:26,27
hearts is your only hope of *. Col 1:26,27
into his kingdom to share his *. 1Th 2:12

(GLORY Con't)
never to see the * of his power, 2Th 1:9
and your greatest * will be that 2Th 1:12
in the * of our Lord Jesus Christ. 2Th 2:14
everlasting life. * and honor to 1Ti 1:17
up again to his * in heaven. 1Ti 3:16
and eternal * in Christ Jesus to 2Ti 2:10
To God be the * forever and ever. 2Ti 4:18
when his * shall be seen—the glory Tit 2:13
shall be seen—the * of our great Tit 2:13
God's Son shines out with God's * Heb 1:3
have crowned him with * and honor. Heb 2:7
now by God with * and honor because Heb 2:9
for his own *, should allow Jesus Heb 2:10
But Jesus has far more * than Heb 3:3
guardians of God's *—with their Heb 9:5
others of the * of his name. Heb 13:15
To him be * forever and ever. Heb 13:20,21
the Lord of *, if you show Jas 2:1
much praise and * and honor on the 1Pe 1:7
and his great * afterwards. 1Pe 1:11
the dead and gave him great *. 1Pe 1:21
be * and power forever and ever. 1Pe 4:11
joy of sharing his * in that coming 1Pe 4:13
will come upon you with great *. 1Pe 4:14
Or, "the * of the Spirit of God 1Pe 4:14f
and I, too, will share his * and 1Pe 5:1
share in his * and honor. 1Pe 5:4
will give you his eternal *. 1Pe 5:10
* and his own goodness with us! 2Pe 1:3
splendor and his *: I was there on 2Pe 1:16
To him be all * and splendid 2Pe 3:18
And now—all * to him who alone is Jud 1:24,25
Give to him everlasting *! Rev 1:6
him in * at the Transfiguration. Rev 1:13f
in heaven and saw—oh, the * of it! Rev 4:2
And when the Living Beings gave * Rev 4:9
to receive the * and the honor and Rev 4:11
and the *, and the blessing." Rev 5:12
the honor and the * and the power Rev 5:13
"Blessing, and *, and wisdom, Rev 7:12
give * to the God of heaven. Rev 11:13
with smoke from his * and power; Rev 15:8
mind and attitude to give him *. Rev 16:9
It was filled with the * of God, Rev 21:11
light it, for the * of God and of Rev 21:23
will come and bring their * to it. Rev 21:24
And the * and honor of all the Rev 21:26

GLORY-LIGHT
God's * shines from the beautiful Ps 50:2

GLOVES
And she made him a pair of * Gen 27:16

GLOW
His eyes * like sparks. Job 41:18
giving off a greenish-yellow *. Eze 10:9-13
let your good deeds * for all to Mt 5:15,16

GLOWED
that his face * from being in the Ex 34:29
other forms that * like bright Eze 1:13
and flashed and * like a precious Rev 21:11

GLOWING
arrows and burned with * coals. Ps 120:4
it a huge cloud * with fire, with a Eze 1:4
all * bronze, dazzling like fire; Eze 1:27,28
and there was a * halo like a Eze 1:27,28
take a handful of * coals and Eze 10:2
me wisdom and * health, and now, Dan 2:23
his waist, and *, lustrous skin! Dan 10:5,6
* in the night for all to see. Mt 5:14
fire, whose feet are like * brass. Rev 2:18
and a rainbow * like an emerald Rev 4:3

GLUTTED
you until they are * and full. Eze 32:4
until you are *, drink blood until Eze 39:19

GLUTTON
that I am 'a * and a drinking man, Mt 11:19
and you say, 'What a * Jesus is! Lk 7:34

GLUTTONS
with drunkards and *, for they are Pro 23:19,20,21

GNASH
they will * their teeth in anger Ps 112:10

GNASHED
he has * upon me with his teeth, Job 16:9

GNASHING
There shall be weeping and * of Mt 13:42
there shall be weeping and * of Mt 13:50
there is weeping and * of teeth.' Mt 22:13
there will be weeping and * of Mt 24:51
shall be weeping and * of teeth.' Mt 25:30
great weeping and * of teeth as you Lk 13:28

GNAT
You strain out a * and swallow a Mt 23:24

GNAW
animals will * bones all winter. Is 18:6

GNAWED
And his subjects * their tongues Rev 16:10

GNAWING
were relentlessly * at my bones. Job 30:17

GO-BETWEEN
Moses was the *—the mediator Act 7:38

GO-BETWEENS
without angels or Moses as *. Gal 3:20

GOAD
with an ox *, thereby saving Israel Ju 3:31
For sharpening an ox *, 30Ç) 1Sa 13:21

GOADS
The wise man's words are like * Ecc 12:11

GOAH
across to * on the southeast. Jer 31:38,39

GOAL
whose only * in life is money. Ps 10:3
So I run straight to the * with 1Co 9:26
do not have. Our * is to measure up 2Co 10:13

GOALS
Have two *: wisdom—that is, Pro 3:21
* are at the ends of the earth! Pro 17:24

GOAT
female *, a three-year-old ram, a Gen 15:9
Then the brothers killed a * and Gen 37:31
"I'll send you a young * from my Gen 38:17
to take the young * back to her, Gen 38:20
can also mean "kid"—a baby *. Ex 12:3,4f
sheep or a *, without any defects. Ex 12:5
in exchange for a lamb or baby *; Ex 13:13
"Do not boil a young * in its Ex 23:19
You must not cook a young * in Ex 34:26
dyed red, and tanned * skins. Ex 36:19
* skins, and the entrance drape; Ex 39:33-40
is a sheep or a *, it too must be a Lev 1:10
"If a * or sheep is used as a Lev 3:6
or ewe, billy * or nanny goat. Lev 3:6
or ewe, billy goat or nanny *. Lev 3:6
"If anyone brings a * as his Lev 3:12
* without any physical defect. Lev 4:23
sacrifice a nanny * without defect Lev 4:28
a female lamb or *, and the priest Lev 5:6
"to select a male * for their sin Lev 9:3
he killed the * and offered it in Lev 9:15
everywhere for the * of the sin Lev 10:16
The * allotted to the Lord shall Lev 16:9
The other * shall be kept alive Lev 16:10
sin offering *, and bring its blood Lev 16:15
young bull and the * on the horns Lev 16:18
bring the live * and, laying both Lev 16:20
the head of the * and send it into Lev 16:21
So the * shall carry all the Lev 16:22
"(The man who took the * out Lev 16:26
And the young bull and the * Lev 16:27
an ox, lamb, or * anywhere except Lev 17:3,4
be a young bull or a sheep or a *. Lev 22:19
bullock, sheep, or * is born, it Lev 22:26,27
And you shall offer one male * Lev 23:19
a male * for a sin offering; Num 7:16
bull, ram, lamb, or young *. Num 15:11,12
and one male * for a sin offering. Num 15:23,24
female * for a sin offering, and Num 15:27
* for a sin offering to the Lord. Num 28:15
You must also offer a male * as Num 28:22
Also offer one male * to make Num 28:30
shall be a male * sacrificed as a Num 29:5
one male * for a sin offering. Num 29:11
There must also be a male * Num 29:16
sacrifice a male * with its Num 29:19
sacrifice a male * for a sin Num 29:22
also a male * as a sin offering Num 29:25
also sacrifice a male * with the Num 29:28
sacrifice a male * and the usual Num 29:31
of one male *, with the usual grain Num 29:34
Sacrifice also one male * with Num 29:38
The ox, the sheep, the *, Deu 14:3,4,5
The wild *, the ibex, Deu 14:3,4,5
"You must not boil a young * in Deu 14:21
roasted a young *, and baked some Ju 6:19
Then Manoah took a young * and a Ju 13:19
as though it were a young *! Ju 14:6
took a young * as a present to his Ju 15:1
David but a young * and a donkey 1Sa 16:20
of a mountain * upon the crags. Ps 18:33
a young male * without any Eze 43:22
seven days a male *, a bullock and Eze 43:25
A young * will also be given each Eze 45:23
suddenly a buck * appeared from the Dan 8:5
the ground. This *, which had one Dan 8:5
and the buck * knocked him down and Dan 8:7
the shaggy-haired * is the Dan 8:21
* for a feast with my friends. Lk 15:29

GOAT-SKINS
ram's skins, *, acacia wood, olive Ex 25:1

GOAT'S
fine-twined linen, * hair, red-dyed Ex 25:1
is made of * hair tarpaulins. Ex 26:7,8
of fine-twined linen or of * hair; Ex 35:5-9
of leather, * hair, or wood." Num 31:20
its head on a pillow of * hair. 1Sa 19:13
for clothing, and * milk enough Pro 27:25,26,27

GOATS
of sheep and *, great herds of Gen 26:14
bring me two young *, and I'll Gen 27:8,9,10
Go out and get the *." Gen 27:13
skin of the young *, and fastened a Gen 27:16
and remove all the * that are Gen 30:31,32
find any white * or sheep in my Gen 30:33
of all the male * that were ringed Gen 30:35,36
nanny * with streaked, speckled, Gen 31:12
ewes and nanny * so that they Gen 31:38
Esau:200 nanny *,20 billy Gen 32:13,14,15
goats,20 billy *,200 ewes,20 Gen 32:13,14,15
is mine—cattle, sheep, and *. Ex 34:19
the fine-twined linen or *' hair; Ex 35:23
to spin the *' hair into cloth. Ex 35:26
draperies made of *' hair Ex 36:14,15
whether from oxen, sheep, or *. Lev 7:23
bring him two male * for their sin Lev 16:5
Then he shall bring the two * Lev 16:7
*, and five male yearling lambs. Num 7:17
12 yearling male * (with the grain Num 7:87
12 male *. Num 7:87
60 rams, 60 male *, Num 7:88
*, or from their herds of cattle. Num 15:3,4
or * may not be bought back; Num 18:17
cattle, sheep, and * when you Deu 7:13
of your flocks of sheep and *. Deu 15:19
Choice Bashan rams, and *— Deu 32:14
three young *, another will have 1Sa 10:3
rocks and wild * of the desert. 1Sa 24:2
and a thousand *, and was at his 1Sa 25:2
you are shearing your sheep and *. 1Sa 25:7
flocks of sheep and herds of *; 2Sa 12:1
Like mountain * upon the rocks. 2Sa 22:34
young * at the Serpent's Stone. 1Ki 1:9
oxen, fat *, and many sheep and has 1Ki 1:19
oxen and fat * and many sheep, and 1Ki 1:25
oxen and 120,000 sheep and *! 1Ki 8:62,63
flocks of baby * in comparison to 1Ki 20:27
carved statues of * and calves 2Ch 11:15
7,700 rams and 7,700 male *. 2Ch 17:11
and seven male * for a sin offering 2Ch 29:21
The male * for the sin offering 2Ch 29:23
of sheep and * he purchased; 2Ch 32:28,29
lambs and young * for the people's 2Ch 35:7
2,600 sheep and *, and 300 oxen as 2Ch 35:8
5,000 sheep and * and 500 oxen to 2Ch 35:9
and twelve male * were presented Ez 6:17
and twelve * as a sin offering. Ez 8:35
"DO YOU KNOW how mountain * give Job 39:1
and * that I really want from you. Ps 50:9
for the wild *, and rock-badgers Ps 104:18
like flocks of * that frisk across Sol 4:1
is like a flock of * frisking down Sol 6:5
cattle, sheep and * will graze Is 7:25
leopard and * will be at peace. Is 11:6
Wild herds of donkeys and * will Is 32:14
slaying lambs and * for sacrifice. Is 34:6
as wild * caught in a net. Is 51:20
mountain * on inaccessible crags. Jer 16:16
to the slaughter, like rams and *. Jer 51:40
bring you lambs and rams and *. Eze 27:21
from kids and rams from billy *! Eze 34:17
the lambs, the * and the fat young Eze 39:18
I will punish them—these *. Zec 10:3
the sheep from the *, and place Mt 25:32
right hand, and the * at my left. Mt 25:33
flock of sheep and * and isn't 1Co 9:7
but it was not the blood of * and Heb 9:12
blood of bulls and * and the ashes Heb 9:13
of calves and *, along with water, Heb 9:19
and * really to take away sins. Heb 10:4
The blood of bulls and * merely Heb 10:4f
blood of bulls and * cannot satisfy Heb 10:5
skins of sheep and *, wandering Heb 11:37,38

GOATSKIN
the veil with * leather, cover the Num 4:6
a covering of * leather on top of Num 4:8
be covered with * leather, and the Num 4:10
with a covering of * leather, and Num 4:11
covered with * leather, and placed Num 4:12
a cover of * leather will be spread Num 4:14
its coverings, the * leather roof, Num 4:25

GOATSKINS
and over them a top layer of *. Ex 26:14
skins and specially treated *; Ex 35:5-9
dyed red, and specially treated *. Ex 35:23
leather, cover the * with a blue Num 4:6

GOB
the Philistines at *, Sibbecai the 2Sa 21:18

GOBBLED
fig is hungrily snatched and * up! Is 28:4

GOBBLES
everyone hastily * all the food he 1Co 11:21

GOBLET
its brim was shaped like a *, and 1Ki 7:26
Your navel is lovely as a * Sol 7:2
a golden * full of obscenities. Rev 17:4

GOBLETS
Drinks were served in golden * Est 1:7

GOD
WHEN * BEGAN creating Gen 1:1
Or, "In the beginning * created Gen 1:1f
with the Spirit of * brooding Gen 1:2
* said, "Let there be light." Gen 1:3
And light appeared. And * was Gen 1:4,5
And * said, "Let the vapors Gen 1:6
So * made the sky, dividing Gen 1:7,8
Then * said, "Let the water Gen 1:9,10

(GOD Con't)

And so it was. Then * named the	Gen 1:9,10
And * was pleased.	Gen 1:9,10
And so it was, and * was	Gen 1:11,12
Then * said, "Let there be	Gen 1:14,15
And so it was. For * made two	Gen 1:16
he also made the stars. And *	Gen 1:17
the darkness. And * was pleased.	Gen 1:18
Then * said, "Let the waters	Gen 1:20
So * created great sea	Gen 1:21,22
kind of bird. And * looked at them	Gen 1:21,22
And * said, "Let the earth bring	Gen 1:24
And so it was. * made all	Gen 1:25
and reptiles. And * was pleased	Gen 1:25
Then * said, "Let us make a man	Gen 1:26
So * made man like his Maker.	Gen 1:27
Like * did God make man;	Gen 1:27
Like God did * make man;	Gen 1:27
And * blessed them and told them,	Gen 1:28
Then * looked over all that he	Gen 1:31
finished his task, * ceased from	Gen 2:2
been doing, and * blessed the	Gen 2:3
and earth which the Lord * made.	Gen 2:4
the Lord * hadn't sent any rain;	Gen 2:5
The time came when the Lord *	Gen 2:7
Then the Lord * planted a garden	Gen 2:8
The Lord * planted all sorts of	Gen 2:9
The Lord * placed the man in the	Gen 2:15
But the Lord * gave the man this	Gen 2:16,17
And the Lord * said, "It isn't	Gen 2:18
So the Lord * formed from the	Gen 2:19,20
Then the Lord * caused the man	Gen 2:21
the creatures the Lord * had made.	Gen 3:1
in the garden? * says you mustn't	Gen 3:1
we are not to eat. * says we	Gen 3:2,3
"You'll not die! * knows very	Gen 3:5
the Lord * walking in the garden;	Gen 3:8
The Lord * called to Adam, "Why	Gen 3:9
the Lord * asked.	Gen 3:11
Then the Lord * asked the woman,	Gen 3:13
So the Lord * said to the	Gen 3:14
Then * said to the woman, "You	Gen 3:16
And to Adam, * said, "Because	Gen 3:17
and the Lord * clothed Adam and	Gen 3:21
So the Lord * banished him	Gen 3:23
Thus * expelled him, and placed	Gen 3:24
for, as Eve put it, "* has	Gen 4:25
Literally, "In the likeness of *	Gen 5:1f
* from the day of his creation.	Gen 5:1
of his creation. * created man and	Gen 5:2
in fellowship with *, and produced	Gen 5:21-24
touch with *, he disappeared, for	Gen 5:21-24
he disappeared, for * took him!	Gen 5:21-24
this ground which * has cursed."	Gen 5:28-31
Literally, "sons of *" used here	Gen 6:1f
"sons of *" refers to the "godly	Gen 6:1f
When the Lord * saw the extent	Gen 6:5
and, as seen by *, the world was	Gen 6:11
As * observed how bad it was, and	Gen 6:12,13
And Noah did everything as *	Gen 6:22
female, just as * commanded Noah.	Gen 7:8,9
female, just as * had commanded.	Gen 7:16
Then the Lord *	Gen 7:16
and birds. * destroyed them all,	Gen 7:23
* DIDN'T FORGET about Noah and all	Gen 8:1
Then * told Noah, "You may all	Gen 8:15,16
animals and birds * had designated	Gen 8:20
ritually approved by *.	Gen 8:20f
* BLESSED NOAH and his sons and	Gen 9:1
be afraid of you," * told him;	Gen 9:2,3
a man is to kill one made like *.	Gen 9:5,6
Then * told Noah and his sons,	Gen 9:8
"* bless Shem,	Gen 9:26,27
Or, "Blessed be Jehovah, the * of	Gen 9:26,27f
* bless Japheth,	Gen 9:26,27
was a mighty hunter, blessed of *,	Gen 10:9
mighty hunter, blessed of *."	Gen 10:9
But when * came down to see the	Gen 11:5
So, in that way, * scattered them	Gen 11:8
of Abram's father, * told him,	Gen 12:1
a priest of the * of Highest	Gen 14:18
"The blessing of the supreme *,	Gen 14:19,20
and blessed be *, who has	Gen 14:19,20
the supreme *, Creator of heaven	Gen 14:22
Then * brought Abram outside	Gen 15:5
And Abram believed *;	Gen 15:6
And Abram believed God; then *	Gen 15:6
name him Ishmael ('* hears'),	Gen 16:9-12
because * has heard your woes.	Gen 16:9-12
to her—as "the * who looked upon	Gen 16:13
"I saw * and lived to tell it."	Gen 16:13
years old, * appeared to him and	Gen 17:1
in the dust as * talked with him.	Gen 17:2,3,4
"What's more," * told him, "I	Gen 17:5
* and the God of your posterity.	Gen 17:7,8
God and the * of your posterity.	Gen 17:7,8
And I will be your *.	Gen 17:7,8
"Your part of the contract," *	Gen 17:9,10
Then * added, "Regarding Sarai	Gen 17:15
And Abraham said to *, "Yes, do	Gen 17:18
"No," * replied, "that isn't	Gen 17:19
That ended the conversation and *	Gen 17:22
just as * had told him to.	Gen 17:23
Then * said to Abraham, "Why did	Gen 18:13
Is anything too hard for *?	Gen 18:14
my plan from Abraham?" * asked.	Gen 18:17
And * replied, "If I find fifty	Gen 18:26
And * said, "I will not destroy	Gen 18:28
And * replied, "I won't destroy	Gen 18:29
And * replied, "I won't do it if	Gen 18:30
dared to speak to *, let me	Gen 18:31
And * said, "Then I won't destroy	Gen 18:31
And * said, "Then, for the sake	Gen 18:32
and * has sent us to destroy it."	Gen 19:13
cities there. So * heeded	Gen 19:29
But that night * came to him in a	Gen 20:3
And when * sent me traveling far	Gen 20:13
Then Abraham prayed, asking * to	Gen 20:17
children; for * had stricken all	Gen 20:18
THEN * DID as he had promised, and	Gen 21:1
old age, at the time * had said;	Gen 21:1
circumcised him, as * required.	Gen 21:4,5
And Sarah declared, "* has	Gen 21:6
But * told Abraham, "Don't be	Gen 21:12
Then * answered the lad's cries,	Gen 21:17
and the Angel of * called to Hagar	Gen 21:17
Don't be afraid! For * has heard	Gen 21:17
Then * opened her eyes and she	Gen 21:19
lad a drink. And * blessed the boy	Gen 21:20,21
* helps you in everything you do;	Gen 21:22
Eternal * [to witness the covenant	Gen 21:33
LATER ON, * tested Abraham's	Gen 22:1
"Abraham!" * called.	Gen 22:1
place where * had told him to go.	Gen 22:3
"* will see to it, my son,"	Gen 22:8
at the place where * had told	Gen 22:9
At that moment the Angel of *	Gen 22:11
"for I know that * is first in	Gen 22:12
Then the Angel of * called again	Gen 22:15
an honored prince of * among us;	Gen 23:5,6
and * blessed him in every way.	Gen 24:1
"Swear by Jehovah, the * of	Gen 24:3
For the Lord * of heaven told me	Gen 24:7
"O Jehovah, the * of my	Gen 24:12
"Thank you, Lord * of my master	Gen 24:27
of his land. * has given him flocks	Gen 24:35
'O Jehovah, the * of my master	Gen 24:42
Jehovah, the * of my master	Gen 24:48
After Abraham's death, * poured	Gen 25:11
Jacob: "Well then, vow to * that	Gen 25:33
"I am the * of Abraham your	Gen 26:24
Jacob: "Because Jehovah your *	Gen 27:20
has blessed. May * always give	Gen 27:27,28,29
Laban's daughters. * Almighty	Gen 28:2
many tribes! May * pass on to you	Gen 28:4
for * has given it to Abraham."	Gen 28:4
of * going up and down upon it.	Gen 28:12
he said, "the * of Abraham, and of	Gen 28:13
Then Jacob woke up. "* lives	Gen 28:16,17
Bethel ("House of *"), though the	Gen 28:19
And Jacob vowed this vow to *:	Gen 28:20
vow to God: "If * will help and	Gen 28:20
I will choose Jehovah as my *!	Gen 28:21
Reuben (meaning "* has noticed my	Gen 29:32
"Am I *?"	Gen 30:2
"Justice"), for she said, "*	Gen 30:6
So he did. And * answered her	Gen 30:17
for she said, "* has repaid me for	Gen 30:18
for she said, "* has given me good	Gen 30:20
Then * remembered about Rachel's	Gen 30:22
birth to a son. "* has removed the	Gen 30:23,24
"and now the * of my fathers has	Gen 31:5
and again. But * has not permitted	Gen 31:7
In this way * has made me	Gen 31:9
the Angel of * called to me and	Gen 31:11
'I am the * you met at Bethel,'	Gen 31:13
The riches * has given you from	Gen 31:16
So go ahead and do whatever * has	Gen 31:16
That night * appeared to Laban	Gen 31:24
I could crush you, but the * of	Gen 31:29
for the grace of *—the God of my	Gen 31:42
grace of God—the * of my	Gen 31:42
even the glorious * of Isaac, my	Gen 31:42
to my name. But * has seen your	Gen 31:42
I won't know, but * will see it.	Gen 31:50
I call upon the * of Abraham and	Gen 31:53
before the mighty * of his father	Gen 31:53
a sacrifice to * there at the top	Gen 31:54
And the angels of * came to meet	Gen 32:1
he exclaimed, "* lives here!"	Gen 32:1
Then Jacob prayed, "O * of	Gen 32:9
Israel—one who has power with *.	Gen 32:28
*, you shall prevail with men."	Gen 32:28
("The Face of *"), for he said,	Gen 32:30
"I have seen * face to face, and	Gen 32:30
of you as though approaching *!	Gen 33:10
face as one sees the face of *."	Gen 33:10f
Please take my gifts. For * has	Gen 33:11
"The Altar to the * of Israel."	Gen 33:20
settle there," * said to Jacob,	Gen 35:1
to worship the * who appeared to	Gen 35:1
altar there to the * who answered	Gen 35:3
And the terror of * was upon all	Gen 35:5
the * who met me here at Bethel"	Gen 35:7
Literally, "The * of Bethel."	Gen 35:7f
at Bethel that * appeared to him	Gen 35:7
from Paddan-aram, * appeared to him	Gen 35:9
blessed him. And * said to him,	Gen 35:10
('One who prevails with *').	Gen 35:10
I am * Almighty," the Lord said	Gen 35:11
place where * had appeared to him;	Gen 35:13,14
as an offering to *, and then	Gen 35:13,14
Bethel ("House of *"), because	Gen 35:15
because * had spoken to him there.	Gen 35:15
do this, for fear * would kill him,	Gen 38:11
It would be a great sin against *	Gen 39:9
* will tell you what it means!"	Gen 41:16
told Pharaoh. "* was telling you	Gen 41:25
"So * has showed you what he is	Gen 41:28
to happen, for * has decreed it,	Gen 41:32
filled with the Spirit of *."	Gen 41:38
to him, "Since * has revealed the	Gen 41:39
Or, "* (or Pharaoh) says 'He is	Gen 41:45f
of the sun * Re of Heliopolis.	Gen 41:50
he meant was that * had made up to	Gen 41:51
"Fruitful"—"For * has made me	Gen 41:52
is this that * has done to us?"	Gen 42:28
and go. May * Almighty give you	Gen 43:14
"your *, even the God of your	Gen 43:23
"your God, even the * of your	Gen 43:23
How are you, my son? * be	Gen 43:29
How can we prove our innocence? *	Gen 44:16
you did this to me, for * did it!	Gen 45:5
nor harvest. * has sent me here to	Gen 45:7
Yes, it was * who sent me here,	Gen 45:8
son Joseph says, "* has made me	Gen 45:9
to the * of his father Isaac.	Gen 46:1
During the night * spoke to him	Gen 46:2
"I am *," the voice replied,	Gen 46:3,4
replied, "the * of your father.	Gen 46:3,4
"* Almighty appeared to me at Luz	Gen 48:3
* has given me here in Egypt."	Gen 48:9
you again, but now * has let me see	Gen 48:11
blessing: "May *, the God of my	Gen 48:15
"May God, the * of my fathers	Gen 48:15
and Isaac, the * who has shepherded	Gen 48:15
other by saying, '* make you as	Gen 48:20
about to die, but * will be with	Gen 48:21
May the * of your fathers, the	Gen 49:25
We servants of the * of your	Gen 50:16,17
Am I *, to judge and punish you?	Gen 50:19
As far as I am concerned, *	Gen 50:20
brothers, "but * will surely come	Gen 50:24
But the midwives feared * and	Ex 1:17
And * blessed the midwives.	Ex 1:20
midwives revered *, he gave them	Ex 1:21
the mountain of *, suddenly the	Ex 3:1
Then * called out to him,	Ex 3:3,4
"Don't come any closer," * told	Ex 3:5
I am the * of your fathers—the	Ex 3:6
* of Abraham, Isaac, and Jacob."	Ex 3:6
for he was afraid to look at *.	Ex 3:6
Then * told him, "I will	Ex 3:12
* here upon this mountain!"	Ex 3:12
their fathers' * has sent me, they	Ex 3:13
'Which * are you talking about?'	Ex 3:13
" 'The Sovereign *,' "	Ex 3:14
Or, "the Living *."	Ex 3:14f
the * of your ancestors Abraham,	Ex 3:15
of Israel," * instructed him,	Ex 3:16
him, 'Jehovah, the * of the	Ex 3:18
that Jehovah, the * of their	Ex 4:5
And you will be as * to him,	Ex 4:16
tightly to the "rod of *"!	Ex 4:20
Then * let him alone.	Ex 4:25,26
the mountain of *, and met Moses	Ex 4:27
Moses told Aaron what * had said	Ex 4:28
Then the elders believed that *	Ex 4:31
from Jehovah, the * of Israel.	Ex 5:1
"The * of the Hebrews has met	Ex 5:3
sacrifice there to Jehovah our *;	Ex 5:3
and sacrificing to their *.	Ex 5:7,8
"May * judge you for making us	Ex 5:21
I am Jehovah, the Almighty * who	Ex 6:2,3
them as my people and be their *.	Ex 6:7
I am Jehovah their * who has	Ex 6:7
So Moses told the people what *	Ex 6:8,9
that I am indeed * when I show them	Ex 7:5
to prove that * has sent you;	Ex 7:9
Say to him, 'Jehovah, the * of	Ex 7:16
are going to find out that I am *.	Ex 7:17
"Plead with * to take the frogs	Ex 8:8
is no one like the Lord our *.	Ex 8:10
So Moses and Aaron did as *	Ex 8:17
"This is the finger of *," they	Ex 8:19
that I am the Lord * of all the	Ex 8:22
*, but do it here in the land.	Ex 8:25
Our sacrifices to * are hated by	Ex 8:26
our *, as he commanded us."	Ex 8:27
Now, hurry and plead with * for	Ex 8:28
him, 'Jehovah, the * of the	Ex 9:1
If you refuse, the power of *	Ex 9:3
him, 'Jehovah the * of the Hebrews	Ex 9:13

(GOD Con't)
is no other * in all the earth. Ex 9:14
all along. Beg * to end this Ex 9:28
"Jehovah, the * of the Hebrews, Ex 10:3
go and serve Jehovah their *!" Ex 10:7
go and serve Jehovah your *!" Ex 10:8
"In the name of * I will not let Ex 10:10
Jehovah your * and against you. Ex 10:16
your * to take away this death. Ex 10:17
burnt offerings to Jehovah our *. Ex 10:25
for the Lord our *, and we do not Ex 10:26
(For * caused the Egyptians to be Ex 11:3
the lamb so that * will pass over Ex 12:21
* did not lead them through the Ex 13:17,18
The reason was that * felt the Ex 13:17,18
Instead, * led them along a route Ex 13:17,18
Israel vow before * that they would Ex 13:19
with them when * led them out of Ex 13:19
of Egypt—as he was sure * would. Ex 13:19
Then the Angel of *, who was Ex 14:19
He is my *, and I will praise him. Ex 15:2
He is my father's *—I will exalt Ex 15:2
But * blew with his wind, and the Ex 15:10
A wonder-working *? Ex 15:11
of the Lord your *, and obey it, Ex 15:26
know that I am Jehovah your *.' Ex 16:11,12
against * and tempted him to slay Ex 17:7
with the rod of * in my hand!" Ex 17:9
wonderful things * had done for his Ex 18:1
Eliezer (meaning "* is my help," Ex 18:4
his birth, "The * of my fathers Ex 18:4
Literally, "the mountain of * Ex 18:5,6f
than any other * because he Ex 18:11
offering and sacrifices for *." Ex 18:12f
to *, and afterwards Aaron and Ex 18:12
I apply the laws of * to their Ex 18:15,16
of advice, and * will bless you: Be Ex 18:19,20
before *—bringing him their Ex 18:19,20
to meet with *, and from somewhere Ex 19:2,3
mountain * called to him and said, Ex 19:2,3
of priests to *, a holy nation.' Ex 19:6
the camp to meet *, and they stood Ex 19:17
spoke and * thundered his reply. Ex 19:19
mountain, and Moses ascended to *. Ex 19:20
try to see *, for they will die. Ex 19:21
because it is reserved for *." Ex 19:23
and told them what * had said. Ex 19:25
THEN * ISSUED this edict: Ex 20:1
"I am Jehovah your * who Ex 20:2
"You may worship no other * than Ex 20:3
for I, the Lord your *, am very Ex 20:5
your affection with any other *! Ex 20:5
of Jehovah your * irreverently, Ex 20:7
Lord your * to swear falsely." Ex 20:7f
rest before the Lord your *. Ex 20:10
the Lord your * will give you. Ex 20:12
"You tell us what * says and we Ex 20:19
but don't let * speak directly to Ex 20:19
told them, "for * has come in this Ex 20:20
the deep darkness where * was. Ex 20:21
act of *—and not intentional, then Ex 21:13
be brought before * to determine Ex 22:8
shall come before * for a decision, Ex 22:9
and the one whom * declares guilty Ex 22:9
* than Jehovah shall be executed. Ex 22:20
"You shall not blaspheme *, nor Ex 22:28
mention the name of any other *. Ex 23:13
shall appear before the Lord *. Ex 23:17
into the house of Jehovah thy *." Ex 23:19f
to the Lord your *. Ex 23:19
"You shall serve the Lord your * Ex 23:25
and regulations * had given him; Ex 24:3
And they saw the * of Israel; Ex 24:10
Yet, even though the elders saw * Ex 24:11
went up into the mountain of *. Ex 24:13
place of *, becomes a single unit. Ex 26:6
his separation to *—beautiful Ex 28:2
it to * every day for seven days. Ex 29:37
it shall be set apart for *. Ex 29:37
and be their *, and they shall Ex 29:45
know that I am the Lord their *. Ex 29:46
I am Jehovah their *. Ex 29:46
Or, "shall be set apart for *," Ex 30:29f
with the Spirit of *, giving him Ex 31:3
Then, as * finished speaking with Ex 31:18
were written with the finger of *. Ex 31:18
said, "make us a * to lead us, for Ex 32:1
* that brought you out of Egypt!" Ex 32:4
'This is your *, O Israel, that Ex 32:8
But Moses begged * not to do it. Ex 32:11
Egyptians to say, '* tricked them Ex 32:12
stone tablets. (* himself had Ex 32:16
They said to me, 'Make us a * to Ex 32:23
He told them, "Jehovah the * of Ex 32:27
for Meeting with *," he called it) Ex 33:7
and gracious *," he said, "slow Ex 34:5,6
for he is a * who claims absolute Ex 34:14
* those three times each year. Ex 34:24
the Tabernacle of the Lord your *. Ex 34:26
At that time * Ex 34:28
from being in the presence of *. Ex 34:29
instructions * had given him, and Ex 34:34
until he returned to speak with *. Ex 34:35
construct what * has commanded us: Ex 35:10-19
needed skill. And * has made him Ex 35:34
tribe of Dan.) * has filled them Ex 35:35
just as * had directed Moses. Ex 39:4,5
be accepted by * instead of the Lev 1:4
some law of * without realizing it Lev 5:17,18
to * in the Sinai desert. Lev 7:38
with the instructions * had given. Lev 9:16
If you do, * will strike you dead Lev 10:6
is most holy, and * has given it to Lev 10:17
"I am the Lord your *. Lev 11:44
of the land of Egypt to be your *. Lev 11:45
"I am Jehovah your *, so don't Lev 18:1
detail, for I am the Lord your *. Lev 18:4,5
never profane the name of your *, Lev 18:21
For I am Jehovah your *." Lev 18:29,30
I, the Lord your *, am holy. Lev 19:1
law, for I am the Lord your *. Lev 19:1
idols, for I am Jehovah your *. Lev 19:3,4
through, for I am Jehovah your *. Lev 19:10
name of your *, for I am Jehovah. Lev 19:12
Fear your *; Lev 19:14
"I am Jehovah your *! Lev 19:26
wizards, for I am Jehovah your *. Lev 19:31
to the elderly, in the fear of *. Lev 19:32
I am Jehovah your *. Lev 19:34
I am Jehovah your * who brought you Lev 19:35,36
be holy, for I am the Lord your *. Lev 20:7
I am the Lord your * who has Lev 20:24
They shall be holy unto their *, Lev 21:6
by fire to the Lord their *. Lev 21:6
woman, for he is a holy man of *. Lev 21:7
to offer the sacrifices of your *; Lev 21:8
oil of his * is upon him; Lev 21:12
may not offer the sacrifices to *. Lev 21:16,17
sacrificed to *, both from the holy Lev 21:22
I am Jehovah your *! Lev 23:22
atonement before the Lord your *. Lev 23:28
the Lord your * for seven days. Lev 23:40
I am Jehovah your *." Lev 23:43
law of *, and are most holy." Lev 24:9
cursed *, Lev 24:11
who curses his * must pay the Lev 24:15,16
for I am Jehovah your *." Lev 24:22
"You must fear your * and not Lev 25:17,18
Fear your * and let your brother Lev 25:36
For I, the Lord your *, brought Lev 25:38
land of Canaan, and to be your *. Lev 25:38
fear your *. Lev 25:43
I am the Lord your *. Lev 25:55
stones, for I am the Lord your *. Lev 26:1
*, and you shall be my people. Lev 26:12
For I am the Lord your * who Lev 26:13
them, for I am Jehovah their *. Lev 26:44
to their ancestors, to be their *. Lev 26:45
under the ban of * to be put to Lev 27:29f
to speak with *, he heard the Voice Num 7:89
your enemies, * will hear you and Num 10:9
offerings. And * will be reminded Num 10:10
For I am Jehovah, your *." Num 10:10
he shall see the very form of *! Num 12:7,8
"Heal her, O *, I beg you!" Num 12:13
remind you to be holy to your *. Num 15:40
For I am Jehovah your * who Num 15:41
yes, I am the Lord, your *." Num 15:41
to you that the * of Israel has Num 16:8,9
the Lord. "O *, the God of all Num 16:22
"O God, the * of all mankind," Num 16:22
the wrath of * will never again Num 18:5
they began to murmur against * Num 21:5
indicates that * had promised the Num 21:24f
That night * came to Balaam and Num 22:9
"Don't do it!" * told him. Num 22:12
to the command of the Lord my *. Num 22:18
That night * told Balaam, "Get Num 22:20
with them. But * was angry about Num 22:22,23
Literally, "* was angry because Num 22:22,23f
except what * tells me to say; Num 22:38
height, and * met him there. Num 23:3,4
What * has not cursed? Num 23:7-10
A people * has not denounced? Num 23:7-10
* is not a man, that he should Num 23:18-24
For * has blessed them, Num 23:18-24
Jehovah their * is with them. Num 23:18-24
* has brought them out of Egypt. Num 23:18-24
'What wonders * has done for Num 23:18-24
Perhaps it will please * to let Num 23:27
Then the Spirit of * came upon Num 24:2
'I have listened to the word of *, Num 24:3-9
I have seen what * Almighty showed Num 24:3-9
* has brought them from Egypt. Num 24:3-9
He hears the words of * Num 24:15-19
He sees what Almighty * has shown Num 24:15-19
"Alas, who can live when * does Num 24:23,24
worship of Baal, the * of Moab; Num 25:3
his zeal for his *, and because he Num 25:12,13
the very authority of *! Num 26:5-11
"O Jehovah, the * of the spirits Num 27:16
If you turn away from * like Num 32:15
all the laws * had commanded him to Deu 1:1
that Jehovah our * told us, 'You Deu 1:6
you are judging in the place of *. Deu 1:17
the Lord our * had directed us. Deu 1:19,20,21
Lord * has given us this land. Deu 1:19,20,21
land the Lord our * had given us. Deu 1:24,25
The Lord * is your leader, and Deu 1:30
the Lord our * who had led them Deu 1:32
as the Lord our * has told us to.' Deu 1:41
The Lord your * has watched over Deu 2:7
land the Lord our * has given us.' Deu 2:29
Jehovah your * made him obstinate, Deu 2:30
But the Lord our * crushed him, Deu 2:33,34
Lord our * gave all of them to us. Deu 2:35,36
our * had forbidden us to enter. Deu 2:37
land the Lord your * has given them Deu 3:20
* has done to those two kings. Deu 3:21
Lord your * will fight for you.' Deu 3:22
made this plea to *: 'O Lord God, Deu 3:23,24,25
to God: 'O Lord *, please let me Deu 3:23,24,25
for what * in all of heaven or Deu 3:23,24,25
by the Lord * of your ancestors. Deu 4:1
for they are from the Lord your *. Deu 4:2
Lord your * are still alive today. Deu 4:4
They are from the Lord our *. Deu 4:5
or small, has * among them, as the Deu 4:7
as the Lord our * is here among us Deu 4:7
you have seen * doing for you. Deu 4:9
You didn't see the form of * that Deu 4:15
make a statue of *—an idol in any Deu 4:16,17
the Lord your * has made with you! Deu 4:23
your * has utterly forbidden this. Deu 4:23
is a devouring fire, a jealous *. Deu 4:24
and the Lord your * is very angry Deu 4:25
for Jehovah your *, and you shall Deu 4:29
* and listen to what he tells you. Deu 4:30
For the Lord your * is Deu 4:31
to the time when * created man upon Deu 4:32
heard the voice of * speaking to it Deu 4:33
Yet that is what the Lord your * Deu 4:34
that Jehovah is *, and that there Deu 4:35
day: Jehovah is * both in heaven Deu 4:39
and there is no * other than him! Deu 4:39
the Lord your * is giving you." Deu 4:40
to all these laws * has given you; Deu 5:1
"The Lord our * made a contract Deu 5:2,3
" 'I am Jehovah your * who Deu 5:6
" 'Never worship any * but me. Deu 5:7
any way, for I am the Lord your *. Deu 5:9,10
I am a jealous *, and I will Deu 5:9,10
of the Lord your * to misuse it." Deu 5:11f
is the Sabbath of the Lord your *; Deu 5:14
and the Lord your * brought you out Deu 5:15
a commandment of the Lord your *); Deu 5:16
the Lord our * has shown us his Deu 5:24
a man may speak to * and not die; Deu 5:24
of the living * speaking from the Deu 5:26,27
You go and listen to all that * Deu 5:26,27
of the Lord your *, following his Deu 5:32
"THE LORD YOUR * told me to give Deu 6:1
the Lord your * by obeying all of Deu 6:2
* of your fathers promised you. Deu 6:3
Jehovah is our *, Jehovah alone. Deu 6:4
"When the Lord your * has Deu 6:10,11,12
for Jehovah your * who lives among Deu 6:15
you is a jealous *, and his anger Deu 6:15
the Lord our * has given us? Deu 6:20
all the laws of the Lord our *.' Deu 6:25
When the Lord your * delivers Deu 7:2
dedicated to the Lord your *. Deu 7:6
that the Lord your * is the Deu 7:9
is the faithful * who for a Deu 7:9
the Lord your * will keep his part Deu 7:12
your * delivers into your hands. Deu 7:16
what the Lord your * did to Pharaoh Deu 7:18
of Almighty * which he used to Deu 7:19
Well, the Lord your * will use Deu 7:19
Moreover, the Lord your * will Deu 7:20
for the Lord your * is among you, Deu 7:21
and he is a great and awesome *. Deu 7:21
it is horrible to the Lord your *. Deu 7:25
by obeying every command of *. Deu 8:3
the laws of the Lord your *. Deu 8:6
For the Lord your * is bringing Deu 8:7
the Lord your * for the good land Deu 8:10
you don't forget the Lord your * Deu 8:11
the Lord your * who brought you out Deu 8:14
don't forget the * who led you Deu 8:15
is the Lord your * who gives you Deu 8:18
the Lord your * and worship other Deu 8:19
if you don't obey the Lord your *. Deu 8:20
But the Lord your * will go Deu 9:3
Jehovah your * is not giving you Deu 9:6
made the Lord your * out in the Deu 9:7
from the laws of *, and had made an Deu 9:12
inscribed with the laws of *. Deu 9:15
sin against the Lord your *. Deu 9:16
"I prayed to him, 'O Lord *, Deu 9:26
to return to * on the mountain. Deu 10:1
tablets up on the mountain to *. Deu 10:3
does the Lord your * require of you Deu 10:12,13

(GOD Con't)

heaven belong to the Lord your *.	Deu 10:14
"Jehovah your * is God of gods	Deu 10:17
"Jehovah your God is * of gods	Deu 10:17
He is the great and mighty *, the	Deu 10:17
mighty God, the * of terror who	Deu 10:17
You must fear the Lord your *	Deu 10:20
and he is your *, the one who has	Deu 10:21
now the Lord your * has made you as	Deu 10:22
"YOU MUST LOVE the Lord your *	Deu 11:1
They didn't see what * did to	Deu 11:4
Lord your * personally cares for!	Deu 11:12
love the Lord your * with all your	Deu 11:13
turn from * to worship other gods.	Deu 11:16
the Lord your *, walking in all his	Deu 11:22
for the Lord your * will send fear	Deu 11:25
of the Lord your * which I am	Deu 11:27
When the Lord your * brings you	Deu 11:29
which Jehovah, the * of your	Deu 12:1
sacrifices to your * just anywhere,	Deu 12:4,5
the Lord your *, and shall rejoice	Deu 12:7
eat them before the Lord your *.	Deu 12:18
Rejoice before the Lord your * in	Deu 12:18
upon the altar of the Lord your *.	Deu 12:26,27
of the Lord your *, all will go	Deu 12:28
insult the Lord your * like that!	Deu 12:31
You must never worship any * but	Deu 13:4
the Lord your * who brought you out	Deu 13:5
from the Lord your * who brought	Deu 13:10
burnt offering to Jehovah your *.	Deu 13:16
Of course, the Lord your * will	Deu 13:18
"SINCE YOU ARE the people of *,	Deu 14:1
to the Lord your *, and he has	Deu 14:2
you are holy to the Lord your *.	Deu 14:21
the Lord your * at the place he	Deu 14:23
to put * first in your lives.	Deu 14:23
the Lord your *, and to rejoice	Deu 14:26
and then Jehovah your * will	Deu 14:29
your * that I am giving you today.	Deu 15:4,5
the Lord your * has blessed you.	Deu 15:14
and the Lord your * rescued you!	Deu 15:15
And the Lord your * will prosper	Deu 15:18
"You shall set aside for * all	Deu 15:19
your * each year at his sanctuary.	Deu 15:20
for that was when Jehovah your *	Deu 16:1
the Lord your * at his sanctuary.	Deu 16:2
each city before the Lord your *.	Deu 16:8
* called the Festival of Weeks.	Deu 16:10
the Lord your * three times a year	Deu 16:16
the Lord your * is giving you.	Deu 16:18
the Lord your * is giving you.	Deu 16:20
the altar of the Lord your *.	Deu 16:21
ox or sheep to the Lord your *.	Deu 17:1
your covenant with * by worshiping	Deu 17:2,3
of the Lord your *, to the priests	Deu 17:8
judge appointed by * for this	Deu 17:12
land the Lord your * will give you,	Deu 17:14
man the Lord your * shall choose.	Deu 17:15
* by obeying all of his commands.	Deu 17:19
For the Lord your * has chosen	Deu 18:5
Lord your * will displace them.	Deu 18:12
before the Lord your *.	Deu 18:13
but the Lord your * will not permit	Deu 18:14
begged of * at Mount Horeb.	Deu 18:16
voice of * again, or see the	Deu 18:16
"WHEN THE LORD your * has	Deu 19:1
the Lord your * and walking his	Deu 19:9
land the Lord your * is giving you,	Deu 19:14
The Lord your * is with you—the	Deu 20:1
with you—the same * who brought you	Deu 20:1
For the Lord your * is going	Deu 20:4
When the Lord your * has given	Deu 20:13
commandment of the Lord your *.	Deu 20:17
deeply against the Lord your *.	Deu 20:18
(for the Lord your * has chosen	Deu 21:5
and the Lord your * delivers your	Deu 21:10
hanging on a tree is cursed of *.	Deu 21:23
the Lord your * has given you.	Deu 21:23
is abhorrent to the Lord your *.	Deu 22:5
are detestable to the Lord your *.	Deu 23:17,18
the Lord your * won't bless you	Deu 23:20
you have vowed to the Lord your *.	Deu 23:23
the Lord your * is giving you.	Deu 24:4
what the Lord your * did to Miriam	Deu 24:9
and the Lord your * will count it	Deu 24:12,13
that the Lord your * rescued you;	Deu 24:18
then the Lord your * will bless	Deu 24:19
the Lord your * is giving you.	Deu 25:13,14,15
are detestable to the Lord your *.	Deu 25:16
with no respect or fear of *.	Deu 25:18
Therefore, when the Lord your *	Deu 25:19
that the Lord my * has brought me	Deu 26:2,3
the Lord your *, 'My ancestors were	Deu 26:5
us and we cried to the Lord *.	Deu 26:6,7
the Lord your *, and worship him.	Deu 26:10
the Lord your *, 'I have given all	Deu 26:13
I have obeyed the Lord my * and	Deu 26:14
Lord your * is giving you today.	Deu 26:16
that he is your *, and you have	Deu 26:17
the Lord your *, as he requires."	Deu 26:19
and then write the laws of * in	Deu 27:2,3,4
an altar there to the Lord your *.	Deu 27:5,6
offerings to the Lord your *.	Deu 27:5,6
great joy before the Lord your *.	Deu 27:7
of the Lord your *, so today you	Deu 27:9
" 'The curse of * be upon anyone	Deu 27:15
of the Lord your *, the laws I am	Deu 28:1
to you today, * will transform you	Deu 28:1
the Lord your * is giving you.	Deu 28:8
of the Lord your * that I am giving	Deu 28:13
to the Lord your * and won't obey	Deu 28:15-19
to listen to the Lord your *.	Deu 28:45
* for all that he has given you.	Deu 28:47,48
of Jehovah your *, then Jehovah	Deu 28:58,59
do not listen to the Lord your *.	Deu 28:62
For forty years * has led you	Deu 29:5
* who has been caring for you.	Deu 29:6
the Lord your *, along with your	Deu 29:10
with Jehovah your *, a contract he	Deu 29:12
that he is your *, just as he	Deu 29:13
from the Lord our * and desires to	Deu 29:18
by Jehovah, the * of their	Deu 29:25
the Lord your * has not revealed to	Deu 29:29
Lord your * will have driven you.	Deu 30:1
to the Lord your *, and you and	Deu 30:2
then the Lord your * will rescue	Deu 30:3
love the Lord your * with all your	Deu 30:6
the Lord your * will take his	Deu 30:7,8
The Lord your * will prosper	Deu 30:9
* with all your hearts and souls.	Deu 30:10
love the Lord your * and to follow	Deu 30:16
that the Lord your * will bless you	Deu 30:16
Choose to love the Lord your *	Deu 30:20
For the Lord your * will be with	Deu 31:6
hear the laws of * and to learn his	Deu 31:12
the Lord your * and obey his laws.	Deu 31:12
the Lord your * as long as you live	Deu 31:13
say, '* is no longer among us!'	Deu 31:17
turn away from * and his commands;	Deu 31:29
Is not * your Father?	Deu 32:6
When * divided up the world among	Deu 32:8
* protected them in the howling	Deu 32:10
* gave them fertile hilltops,	Deu 32:13
in plenty, they forsook their *.	Deu 32:15
Forgetting it was * who had given	Deu 32:18
* saw what they were doing,	Deu 32:19
Then * will ask,	Deu 32:37
Don't you see that I alone am *?	Deu 32:39
Moses, the man of *, gave to the	Deu 33:1
"He is beloved of *	Deu 33:12
* surrounds him with his loving	Deu 33:12
"May his land be blessed by *	Deu 33:13
And with the favor of * who	Deu 33:16
There is none like the * of	Deu 33:26
The eternal * is your Refuge,	Deu 33:27
Lord's disciple, * spoke to Moses'	Jos 1:1
For remember, the Lord your * is	Jos 1:9
the land which * has given us!"	Jos 1:10,11
"The Lord your * has given you a	Jos 1:12,13
may the Lord your * be with you as	Jos 1:17,18
well that your * is going to give	Jos 2:9
that, for your * is the supreme God	Jos 2:11
God is the supreme * of heaven, not	Jos 2:11
of heaven, not just an ordinary *.	Jos 2:11
name of your * that when Jericho is	Jos 2:12,13
the priests carrying the Ark of *,	Jos 3:2,3,4
to what the Lord your * has said.	Jos 3:9
that the living * is among you and	Jos 3:10
The Ark of *, who is Lord of the	Jos 3:11
when the Ark of * went across!'	Jos 4:7
Tell them how the Lord our *	Jos 4:23
is the mighty *, and so that all of	Jos 4:24
for the Lord your * of Israel says	Jos 7:13
give glory to the * of Israel and	Jos 7:19
against the Lord, the * of Israel.	Jos 7:20
altar to the Lord * of Israel at	Jos 8:30
of the Lord your * and of all that	Jos 9:9
Israel had made before the Lord *.	Jos 9:18
before the Lord * of Israel that we	Jos 9:19
water for the service of our *."	Jos 9:23
just as the Lord * of Israel had	Jos 10:40
for the Lord * of Israel was	Jos 10:42
the Lord * was their inheritance.	Jos 13:33
the Lord my *, Moses told me, 'The	Jos 14:8
had followed the Lord * of Israel.	Jos 14:13,14
conquered the land * had given	Jos 18:1
the Lord your * has given to you?	Jos 18:3
order of the Lord your *.	Jos 22:2,3
And now the Lord our * has given	Jos 22:4
against the * of Israel by turning	Jos 22:16
to the only true altar of our *.	Jos 22:19
"We swear by Jehovah, the * of	Jos 22:22,23
the curse of * be on us if we did.	Jos 22:22,23
to worship the Lord * of Israel?	Jos 22:24,25
have no part in the Lord our *.'	Jos 22:26,27
with * that both of us have.'	Jos 22:28
and praised * and spoke no more of	Jos 22:33
them that Jehovah is our *, too."	Jos 22:34
that the Lord your * has done for	Jos 23:3
for the Lord your * will drive out	Jos 23:4,5
But follow the Lord your * just	Jos 23:8
for the Lord your * fights for you,	Jos 23:10
that the Lord your * will no longer	Jos 23:13
the Lord your * has given you.	Jos 23:13
and presented themselves before *.	Jos 24:1
"The Lord * of Israel says, 'Your	Jos 24:2
For the Lord our * is the one	Jos 24:17
He is the * who did mighty	Jos 24:17
the Lord, for he alone is our *."	Jos 24:18
*, for he is holy and jealous;	Jos 24:19
must obey the Lord * of Israel."	Jos 24:23
contract between themselves and *.	Jos 24:25
of the laws of *, and took a huge	Jos 24:26
"Now * has paid me back."	Ju 1:7
Joshua, the man of *, died at	Ju 2:7-9
Jehovah as their *, and did not	Ju 2:10
They abandoned Jehovah, the *	Ju 2:12-14
ancestors—the * who had brought	Ju 2:12-14
of Canaan. For * wanted to give	Ju 3:1
Jehovah their * and worshiped Baal	Ju 3:7
sinful ways, so * helped King Eglon	Ju 3:12
him, "It is a message from *!"	Ju 3:20
the people back to *, was Deborah,	Ju 4:4
to her speak to them about *."	Ju 4:5f
to him, "The Lord * of Israel has	Ju 4:6
The * of Israel.	Ju 5:3
At the presence of the * of	Ju 5:5
this: "The Lord * of Israel	Ju 6:8
is the Lord your *, and that you	Ju 6:10
when * brought them out of Egypt?	Ju 6:13
as in Exodus 3:14. * is telling	Ju 6:16f
"Alas, O Lord *, for I have seen	Ju 6:22
for the Lord your *, built here on	Ju 6:26
What an insult to a *!	Ju 6:31
If Baal is really a *, let him	Ju 6:31
Then Gideon said to *, "If you	Ju 6:36
was just stand there worshiping *!	Ju 7:15
'We fight for * and for Gideon!'	Ju 7:18
But Gideon replied, "* let you	Ju 8:2,3
the Lord as their *, though he had	Ju 8:34
oil that blesses * and man, just to	Ju 9:9
that cheers both * and man, just to	Ju 9:13
Three years later * stirred up	Ju 9:22,23
of the local *, the wine flowed	Ju 9:27
Thus * punished both Abimelech	Ju 9:56,57
you as our * and have worshiped	Ju 10:10
But the Lord our * helped Israel	Ju 11:21,22
"So you see, it was the Lord *	Ju 11:23
You keep whatever your * Chemosh	Ju 11:24
whatever Jehovah our * gives us!	Ju 11:24
the Lord that if * would help	Ju 11:30,31
of * from the time of his birth;	Ju 13:5
"A man from * appeared to me and I	Ju 13:6
be dedicated to * from the moment	Ju 13:7
let the man from * come back to us	Ju 13:8
and the Angel of * appeared once	Ju 13:9
his wife, "for we have seen *!"	Ju 13:22
the request, for * was setting a	Ju 14:4
to * since before my birth.	Ju 16:16,17
* Dagon and excitedly praised him.	Ju 16:23,24
"Our * has delivered our enemy	Ju 16:23,24
"* bless you for confessing it,"	Ju 17:2
they said, "ask * whether or not	Ju 18:5
Come on, let's go! For * has	Ju 18:9,10
first to ask counsel from *.	Ju 20:18
(The Ark of * was in Bethel in	Ju 20:27,28
* until evening, weeping bitterly.	Ju 21:2
"O Lord * of Israel," they	Ju 21:3
does this shall be cursed of *."	Ju 21:18
and your * shall be my God;	Ru 1:16
and your God shall be my *;	Ru 1:16
* has dealt me bitter blows.	Ru 1:20
May the Lord * of Israel, under	Ru 2:12
a man like that! * has continued	Ru 2:20
"Thank * for a girl like you!"	Ru 3:10
who were wholly dedicated to *.	1Sa 1:11f
"asked of *") because, as she	1Sa 1:19,20
There is no other *,	1Sa 2:2
Nor any Rock like our *.	1Sa 2:2
and Hannah and ask * to give them	1Sa 2:20
Literally, "man of *."	1Sa 2:27f
"Therefore, I, the Lord * of	1Sa 2:30
*, and he doesn't stop them.	1Sa 3:13
And may * punish you if you hide	1Sa 3:16,17
"* has come into their camp!"	1Sa 4:7
And the Ark of * was captured	1Sa 4:11
for the safety of the Ark of *.	1Sa 4:13
because the Ark of * had been	1Sa 4:21,22
captured Ark of * from the	1Sa 5:1
the * of Israel here any longer.	1Sa 5:7
perish along with our * Dagon."	1Sa 5:7
* of Israel here to kill us too!"	1Sa 5:10
shall we do about the Ark of *?	1Sa 6:2
you will know * didn't send the	1Sa 6:3
then praise the * of Israel	1Sa 6:4,5
stop persecuting you and your *.	1Sa 6:4,5
Israel go until * had destroyed	1Sa 6:6
Place the Ark of * on the cart	1Sa 6:8
know that it was * who brought this	1Sa 6:9
and was not sent by * at all."	1Sa 6:9
The gold rats were to placate *	1Sa 6:18
before Jehovah, this holy *?"	1Sa 6:20
"Plead with * to save us!"	1Sa 7:8

GOD Con't)
worship * at the altar at Bethel; 1Sa 10:3
and started to go, * gave him a new 1Sa 10:9
at the Hill of * they saw the 1Sa 10:10
and the Spirit of * came upon him, 1Sa 10:10
from the Lord *: "I brought you 1Sa 10:18,19
Then the Spirit of * came 1Sa 11:6
he announced. And * caused the 1Sa 11:7
the Lord their *, so he let them be 1Sa 12:9
But the Lord your * was already 1Sa 12:12
your *, then all will be well. 1Sa 12:14
commandment of the Lord your *. 1Sa 13:13
"Bring the Ark of *," Saul 1Sa 14:18
What does * say?" 1Sa 14:19
But the priest said, "Let's ask * 1Sa 14:36
So Saul asked *, "Shall we go 1Sa 14:37
I vow by the name of the * who 1Sa 14:39
Then Saul said, "O Lord * of 1Sa 14:41
O Lord *, show us who is 1Sa 14:41
must die; may * strike me dead if 1Sa 14:44
We vow by the life of * that not 1Sa 14:45
* to do a mighty miracle today." 1Sa 14:45
of Israel because * told me to. 1Sa 15:1
when he heard what * was saying, 1Sa 15:11
sacrifice them to the Lord your *; 1Sa 15:15
* made you king of Israel. 1Sa 15:17
do exactly what * said not to?" 1Sa 15:19
me to worship the Lord your *." 1Sa 15:30
spirit from * troubled Saul, David 1Sa 16:23
defy the armies of the living *?" 1Sa 17:26
defied the armies of the living *! 1Sa 17:36
very * whom you have defied. 1Sa 17:45
know that there is a * in Israel! 1Sa 17:46
spirit from * overwhelmed Saul, and 1Sa 18:10
the Spirit of * came upon them and 1Sa 19:20
the Spirit of * came upon Saul, and 1Sa 19:23
by the Lord * of Israel that about 1Sa 20:12
what * was going to do for him. 1Sa 22:3
and a sword and talk to * for him? 1Sa 22:13
time I had consulted * for him! 1Sa 22:15
"We've got him now! * has 1Sa 23:7
"O Lord * of Israel," David 1Sa 23:10
O Lord * of Israel, please tell 1Sa 23:11
encouraged him in his faith in *. 1Sa 23:16
message: "May * prosper you and 1Sa 25:6
men who come from * knows where." 1Sa 25:11f
is insults. May * curse me if even 1Sa 25:22
by the life of *, and by your own 1Sa 25:26
of the Lord your *, just as though 1Sa 25:29
"Bless the Lord * of Israel who 1Sa 25:32
Thank * for your good sense! 1Sa 25:33
For I swear by the Lord, the * 1Sa 25:34
"Praise the Lord! * has paid back 1Sa 25:39
"* has put your enemy within 1Sa 26:8
Surely * will strike him down 1Sa 26:10
of old age. But * forbid that I 1Sa 26:11
a man, then may he be cursed by *. 1Sa 26:19
lots in determining the will of *. 1Sa 28:5,6f
war with us, and * has left me and 1Sa 28:15
as perfect as an angel of *. 1Sa 29:9
Joab shouted back, "I swear by * 2Sa 2:27
some woman? May * curse me if I 2Sa 3:9,10
the Lord * of heaven was with him. 2Sa 5:10
was because * wanted to pour out 2Sa 5:12
the Ark of * is out in a tent!" 2Sa 7:2
prayed, "O Lord *, why have you 2Sa 7:18
Oh, Lord *! 2Sa 7:19
How great you are, Lord *! 2Sa 7:22
heard of any other * like you. 2Sa 7:22
And there is no other *. 2Sa 7:22
forever, and you became our *. 2Sa 7:24
"And now, Lord *, do as you have 2Sa 7:25
O Lord of heaven, * of Israel, that 2Sa 7:27
For you are indeed *, and your 2Sa 7:28
for you, Lord *, have promised 2Sa 7:29
people and the cities of our *. 2Sa 10:12
"I swear by the living *," he 2Sa 12:5
The Lord * of Israel says, 'I 2Sa 12:7
of * and done this horrible deed? 2Sa 12:9
swear to me by * that you won't let 2Sa 14:11
"I vow by *," he replied, "that 2Sa 14:11
all the people of * as you have 2Sa 14:13
up again. But * will bless you with 2Sa 14:14
Or, "* does not sweep life away, 2Sa 14:14f
* and can discern good from evil. 2Sa 14:17
from evil. May * be with you." 2Sa 14:17
as an angel of *, and you know 2Sa 14:20
But Ittai replied, "I vow by * 2Sa 15:21
of the Covenant of * and set it 2Sa 15:24
carried the Ark of * back into the 2Sa 15:29
people worshiped *, David found 2Sa 15:32
come directly from the mouth of *. 2Sa 16:23
be the Lord your * who has 2Sa 18:28
are my nephew, may * strike me dead 2Sa 19:13
of *, so do what you think best. 2Sa 19:27
induce you to ask * to bless us?" 2Sa 21:3
Then at last * answered prayer 2Sa 21:12,13,14
I will hide in *, 2Sa 22:3
The * above all gods gave out a 2Sa 22:14
And I have not departed from my * 2Sa 22:22
As for *, his way is perfect; 2Sa 22:31
Our Lord alone is *; 2Sa 22:32
"Who is a rock save our *?" 2Sa 22:32f
* is my strong fortress; 2Sa 22:33
They cried to *, 2Sa 22:42
Blessed be * 2Sa 22:48
David, the man to whom * gave such 2Sa 23:1
David, the anointed of the * of 2Sa 23:1
Who rules in the fear of *. 2Sa 23:3
Yes, * has made 2Sa 23:5
and * gave him a great victory. 2Sa 23:11,12
"No, my *," he exclaimed, "I 2Sa 23:17
But Joab replied, "* grant that 2Sa 24:3
who was David's contact with *. 2Sa 24:11
know what answer to give to *." 2Sa 24:13
Lord * accept your sacrifice." 2Sa 24:23
to the Lord my * burnt offerings 2Sa 24:24
by the Lord your * that my son 1Ki 1:17
before by the Lord * of Israel." 1Ki 1:30
Praise *!" 1Ki 1:36
with you, and may * make Solomon's 1Ki 1:37
saying, 'May * bless you even more 1Ki 1:46,47
personally! May * make Solomon's 1Ki 1:46,47
be the Lord * of Israel who has 1Ki 1:48
Obey the laws of * and follow 1Ki 2:3
are faithful to *, one of them 1Ki 2:4
great oath, "May * strike me dead 1Ki 2:23,24
I swear it by the living * who 1Ki 2:23,24
of * to stay in Jerusalem or die? 1Ki 2:42
O Lord my *, now you have made 1Ki 3:7
the great wisdom * had given him. 1Ki 3:28
* gave Solomon great wisdom and 1Ki 4:29
"the Lord my * has given Israel 1Ki 5:4
for the Lord my *, just as he 1Ki 5:5
"Praise * for giving David a 1Ki 5:7
of the Presence of * was displayed, 1Ki 7:48
"Blessed be the Lord * of 1Ki 8:15
for the Lord * of Israel, but the 1Ki 8:17
built for the Lord * of Israel. 1Ki 8:20
and said, "O Lord * of Israel, 1Ki 8:22,23
there is no * like you in heaven or 1Ki 8:22,23
and now, O Lord * of Israel, 1Ki 8:25
Yes, O * of Israel, fulfill this 1Ki 8:26
"But is it possible that * would 1Ki 8:27
And yet, O Lord my *, you have 1Ki 8:28
and confess that you are their *. 1Ki 8:33,34
May the Lord our * be with us as 1Ki 8:57
that the Lord is *, and that there 1Ki 8:60
that there is no other * at all. 1Ki 8:60
lives before the Lord our *; 1Ki 8:61
the Lord their * who brought them 1Ki 9:9
Blessed be the Lord your * who 1Ki 10:9
the horrible * of the Ammonites. 1Ki 11:5
the depraved * of Moab, and another 1Ki 11:7
vile * of the Ammonites. 1Ki 11:7
in the Lord * of Israel who had 1Ki 11:9,10
enemies whom * raised to power was 1Ki 11:23
for the Lord * of Israel says, 'I 1Ki 11:31
and Chemosh, the * of Moab; 1Ki 11:33
and Milcom, the * of the 1Ki 11:33
their king. But * sent this 1Ki 12:22
Jerusalem, which * had ordained. 1Ki 12:32,33f
* had been speaking through him. 1Ki 13:5
your * to restore my arm again." 1Ki 13:6
from the Lord * of Israel: 'I 1Ki 14:7
which the Lord * of Israel sees in 1Ki 14:13
right with *, as King David's was. 1Ki 15:3
For David had obeyed * during 1Ki 15:5
angered the Lord * of Israel by 1Ki 15:30
same sin. So * was very angry. 1Ki 16:26
to anger the Lord * of Israel than 1Ki 16:33
surely as the Lord * of Israel 1Ki 17:1
Israel lives—the * whom I worship 1Ki 17:1
by the Lord your * that I haven't a 1Ki 17:12
For the Lord * of Israel says 1Ki 17:14
"O man of *," she cried, "what 1Ki 17:18
Lord, "O Lord my *, why have you 1Ki 17:20
Lord, "O Lord my *, please let 1Ki 17:21
For I swear by * that the king 1Ki 18:10
swear by the Lord * of the armies 1Ki 18:15
"If the Lord is *, follow him! 1Ki 18:21
But if Baal is *, then follow 1Ki 18:21
Then pray to your *, and I will 1Ki 18:24
and the * who answers by sending 1Ki 18:24
to light the wood is the true *!" 1Ki 18:24
and prepare it and call to your *; 1Ki 18:25
catch the attention of your *! 1Ki 18:27
prayed, "O Lord * of Abraham, 1Ki 18:36
that you are the * of Israel and 1Ki 18:36
know that you are * and that you 1Ki 18:37
ground shouting, "Jehovah is *! 1Ki 18:39
Jehovah is *!" 1Ki 18:39
of *, where he lived in a cave. 1Ki 19:8
for the Lord * of the heavens; 1Ki 19:10
hard for the Lord * of the armies 1Ki 19:14
Israeli * is a god of the hills; 1Ki 20:23
Israeli God is a * of the hills; 1Ki 20:23
'The Lord is a * of the hills and 1Ki 20:28
him of cursing * and the king. 1Ki 21:10
him of cursing * and the king; 1Ki 21:13
for * will help you conquer it." 1Ki 22:6
So Ahaziah made the Lord * of 1Ki 22:52,53
the temple of the * Baal-zebub at 2Ki 1:2
true that there is no * in Israel? 2Ki 1:3
to Baal-zebub, the * of Ekron, to 2Ki 1:3
of Baal-zebub, the * of Ekron. 2Ki 1:6
Is it because there is no * in 2Ki 1:6
to him, "O man of *, the king has 2Ki 1:9
"If I am a man of *, let fire come 2Ki 1:10
demand, "O man of *, the king says 2Ki 1:11
"If I am a man of *, let fire come 2Ki 1:12
And again the fire from * 2Ki 1:12
him, "O man of *, please spare my 2Ki 1:13
to Baal-zebub, the * of Ekron, to 2Ki 1:16
"Is it because there is no * in 2Ki 1:16
But Elisha replied, "I swear to * 2Ki 2:1
to * that I won't leave you." 2Ki 2:4
to * that I won't leave you." 2Ki 2:6,7
"Where is the Lord * of Elijah?" 2Ki 2:13,14
"I swear by the Lord * that I 2Ki 3:14
He was a man who had loved *, she 2Ki 4:1
"O man of *," she exclaimed, 2Ki 4:15,16
said, "I swear to * that I won't 2Ki 4:30
*, that I can kill and give life? 2Ki 5:7
prophet of * here in Israel." 2Ki 5:8
of the Lord his *, and heal me! 2Ki 5:11
that there is no * in all the world 2Ki 5:15
* that I will not accept them." 2Ki 5:16
to any other * except the Lord. 2Ki 5:17
the temple of the * Rimmon to 2Ki 5:18
"May * kill me if I don't 2Ki 6:31
to the man of * and tell him to ask 2Ki 8:8,9
Nevertheless, because * had 2Ki 8:19
said, "The Lord * of Israel says, 2Ki 9:6
But Jehu didn't follow the Lord * 2Ki 10:31
destroyed. For * pitied them, and 2Ki 13:23
just as the Lord * of Israel had 2Ki 14:25
the Lord their * who had brought 2Ki 17:7
to believe in the Lord their *. 2Ki 17:14
of the Lord their * and made two 2Ki 17:16
commandments of the Lord their *; 2Ki 17:19
the laws of the * of the land, and 2Ki 17:26
the laws of the * of the land. 2Ki 17:27,28
idols of their * Succoth-benoth; 2Ki 17:30
those from Cuth worshiped their * 2Ki 17:30
For * had said, "You must never 2Ki 17:38
strongly in the Lord * of Israel. 2Ki 18:5
him were as close to * as he was. 2Ki 18:5
to the Lord their * or to do what 2Ki 18:12
What * has ever been able to 2Ki 18:35
Yet perhaps the Lord your * has 2Ki 19:4
the living *, and will rebuke him. 2Ki 19:4
"Don't be fooled by that * you 2Ki 19:10
"O Lord * of Israel, sitting on 2Ki 19:15
you alone are the * of all the 2Ki 19:15
man's defiance of the living *. 2Ki 19:16
O Lord our *, we plead with you 2Ki 19:19
will know that you alone are *." 2Ki 19:19
"The Lord * of Israel says, 'I 2Ki 19:20
in the soil and bear fruit for *. 2Ki 19:30
the temple of his * Nisroch, his 2Ki 19:37
him that the Lord * of his ancestor 2Ki 20:5
Heathen altars to the sun *, moon 2Ki 21:3,4,5
the sun god, moon *, and the gods 2Ki 21:3,4,5
the idolatry which * hated and into 2Ki 21:16
on the Lord * of his ancestors. 2Ki 21:22
message from the Lord * of Israel: 2Ki 22:15,16
kings of Judah to the sun *. 2Ki 23:11
and for Chemosh, the evil * of 2Ki 23:13
and for Milcom, the evil * of the 2Ki 23:13
* in The Book of the Covenant. 2Ki 23:21
the man who robbed * and was such a 1Ch 2:7
who prayed to the * of Israel, 1Ch 4:10
And * granted him his request. 1Ch 4:10
They cried out to * to help 1Ch 5:20
for * was fighting against them. 1Ch 5:22
But they were not true to the * 1Ch 5:25
the people whom * had destroyed. 1Ch 5:25
had destroyed. So * caused King 1Ch 5:26
choirs to praise * in the 1Ch 6:31
of * were strictly followed. 1Ch 6:49
treasuries in the Tabernacle of *. 1Ch 9:26
And the Lord your * has told you, 1Ch 11:2
"* forbid that I should drink it! 1Ch 11:18,19
then may the * of our fathers see 1Ch 12:17
For your * is with you." 1Ch 12:18
a tremendous army—the army of *. 1Ch 12:22
since the Lord our * has given his 1Ch 13:2
the Ark of our *, for we have been 1Ch 13:3
* was brought from Kiriath-jearim. 1Ch 13:5
Lord * enthroned above the angels. 1Ch 13:6
And so he died there before *. 1Ch 13:10
Now David was afraid of * and 1Ch 13:12
I ever get the Ark of * home?" 1Ch 13:12
He exulted, "* has used me to 1Ch 14:11
again David asked * what to do. 1Ch 14:14
to attack, for * will go before you 1Ch 14:15
house the Ark of *, and issued 1Ch 15:1
may carry it, for * has chosen them 1Ch 15:2
of Jehovah, the * of Israel, to the 1Ch 15:12
Ark of Jehovah, the * of Israel. 1Ch 15:14
And because * didn't destroy the 1Ch 15:26
SO THE ARK of * was brought into 1Ch 16:1

(GOD Con't)
and peace offerings before *. 1Ch 16:1
thanks to the Lord * of Israel and 1Ch 16:4
He is the Lord our *! 1Ch 16:14
* didn't let anyone harm them. 1Ch 16:21
Cry out to him, 'Oh, save us, * 1Ch 16:35
Blessed be Jehovah, * of Israel, 1Ch 16:36
singers with loud praises to *. 1Ch 16:42
of * is out there in a tent!" 1Ch 17:1
But that same night * said to 1Ch 17:3
"Who am I, O Lord *, and what is 1Ch 17:16
For now, O Lord *, you are 1Ch 17:17
one like you—there is no other *. 1Ch 17:20
even heard of another * like you! 1Ch 17:20
and you have become their *. 1Ch 17:22
heaven is indeed the * of Israel!' 1Ch 17:24
this to me. * himself has promised 1Ch 17:26
people and the cities of our *. 1Ch 19:13
made him do. And *, too, was 1Ch 21:7
But David said to *, "I am the 1Ch 21:8
During the plague * sent an 1Ch 21:15
And David said to *, "I am the 1Ch 21:17
O Lord my *, destroy me and my 1Ch 21:17
a temple for the Lord * of Israel. 1Ch 22:6
"The Lord your * is with you," 1Ch 22:18
obey the Lord your *, and you will 1Ch 22:19
As for Moses, the man of *, his 1Ch 23:14,15
For David said, "The Lord * of 1Ch 23:25
by * through their ancestor Aaron. 1Ch 24:19
Mahazi-oth. (For * had honored him 1Ch 25:4,5
What a blessing * gave him with 1Ch 26:4,5
anger of * broke out upon Israel; 1Ch 27:24
rest—a place for our * to live in. 1Ch 28:2
the building, but * has told me, 1Ch 28:3
"Nevertheless, the Lord * of 1Ch 28:4
the people of *, and in the sight 1Ch 28:8
the sight of our *, I am 1Ch 28:8
get to know the * of your fathers. 1Ch 28:9
for the Lord my * is with you; 1Ch 28:20
son Solomon, whom * has chosen to 1Ch 29:1
is for the Lord * himself! 1Ch 29:1
to the Temple of *, I am giving all 1Ch 29:3
the Lord: "O Lord * of our father 1Ch 29:10
O our *, we thank you and praise 1Ch 29:13
O Lord our *, all of this 1Ch 29:16
I know, my *, that you test men 1Ch 29:17
"O Lord * of our fathers: 1Ch 29:18
good heart toward *, so that he 1Ch 29:19
praise to the Lord your *!" 1Ch 29:20
their priest. So * appointed 1Ch 29:23
* had made him a powerful monarch. 2Ch 1:1
for the Ark of * when he removed it 2Ch 1:4
That night * appeared to Solomon 2Ch 1:7
Solomon replied, "O *, you have 2Ch 1:8
* replied, "Because your 2Ch 1:11
Lord my *," Solomon told Hiram. 2Ch 2:4
spices before *, and display the 2Ch 2:4
festivals of the Lord our *. 2Ch 2:4
Lord our God. For * wants Israel 2Ch 2:4
a great *, greater than any other. 2Ch 2:5
allowed to build a temple for *? 2Ch 2:6
Blessed be the Lord * of Israel 2Ch 2:12
"Blessed be the Lord * of 2Ch 6:4
to them, "—the * who talked 2Ch 6:4
Name of the Lord * of Israel, and 2Ch 6:10
"O Lord * of Israel, there is no 2Ch 6:14
there is no * like you in all of 2Ch 6:14
You are the * who keeps his kind 2Ch 6:14
And now, O * of Israel, carry 2Ch 6:16
Yes, Lord * of Israel, please 2Ch 6:17
But will * really live upon the 2Ch 6:18
will heed my prayers, O Lord my *! 2Ch 6:19
claim you as our *, and turn from 2Ch 6:26
"Yes, O my *, be wide awake and 2Ch 6:40
And now, O Lord *, arise and 2Ch 6:41
Let your priests, O Lord *, be 2Ch 6:41
O Lord *, do not ignore me—do 2Ch 6:42
abandoned the Lord * of their 2Ch 7:22
their fathers, the * who brought 2Ch 7:22
Blessed be the Lord your *! 2Ch 9:8
wisdom * had put into his heart. 2Ch 9:23
people's demands. (* caused him to 2Ch 10:15
idols instead of *, and to 2Ch 11:15
worship the Lord * of their 2Ch 11:16
the city * had chosen as his 2Ch 12:13
Don't you realize that the Lord * 2Ch 13:5
* and we have not forsaken him. 2Ch 13:10
instructions of the Lord our *; 2Ch 13:11
So you see, * is with us; 2Ch 13:12
against the Lord * of your fathers, 2Ch 13:12
And as they shouted, * used King 2Ch 13:15,16
upon the Lord * of their fathers, 2Ch 13:18,19
careful to obey the Lord his *. 2Ch 14:2
of the Lord * of their ancestors. 2Ch 14:4
That is why * gave his kingdom 2Ch 14:5
"O Lord," he cried out to *, 2Ch 14:11
Oh, help us, Lord our *! 2Ch 14:11
THEN THE SPIRIT of * came upon 2Ch 15:1
worshiped the true *, and have not 2Ch 15:3
again to the Lord * of Israel in 2Ch 15:4
against * there was no peace. 2Ch 15:5
against city, for * was plaguing 2Ch 15:6
this message from *, he took 2Ch 15:8
the Lord * was with King Asa). 2Ch 15:9
only the Lord * of their fathers, 2Ch 15:12
oath of loyalty to * with trumpets 2Ch 15:14
this covenant with *, for they had 2Ch 15:15
before * throughout his lifetime. 2Ch 15:17
in the Lord your *, the army of the 2Ch 16:7
of his father's *—quite unlike the 2Ch 17:4
the paths of *—even knocking down 2Ch 17:6
* will give you a great victory!" 2Ch 18:3,4,5
But Micaiah replied, "I vow by * 2Ch 18:13
* says is what I will say." 2Ch 18:13
have tried to be faithful to *." 2Ch 19:3
worship the * of their ancestors. 2Ch 19:4
have not appointed you—* has; 2Ch 19:6
decision than what * tells you to. 2Ch 19:7
the fear of *, with honest hearts. 2Ch 19:9
and ordinances of *, you are to 2Ch 19:10
of * come down upon you and them; 2Ch 19:10
And may * use you to defend the 2Ch 19:11
and intercession before *. 2Ch 20:3
"O Lord * of our fathers—the 2Ch 20:6
fathers—the only * in all the 2Ch 20:6
O our *, didn't you drive out 2Ch 20:7
O our *, won't you stop them? 2Ch 20:12
rescue operation * will perform for 2Ch 20:17
to praise the Lord * of Israel with 2Ch 20:19
"Believe in the Lord your *, and 2Ch 20:20
the fear of * fell upon them. 2Ch 20:29
for his * had given him rest. 2Ch 20:30
follow the * of their ancestors. 2Ch 20:33
from the Lord * of his fathers. 2Ch 21:10
letter: "The Lord * of your 2Ch 21:12
fatal mistake; for * had decided to 2Ch 22:7
law of *, and proclaimed him king. 2Ch 23:11
to the worship of * had been 2Ch 24:7,8
of * had assessed upon Israel. 2Ch 24:9
Israel, for *, and for the Temple. 2Ch 24:16
the Temple of the * of their 2Ch 24:17,18
So the wrath of * came down upon 2Ch 24:17,18
Jerusalem again. * sent prophets 2Ch 24:19
Then the Spirit of * came upon 2Ch 24:20
he said to them, "* wants to know 2Ch 24:20
the Lord * of their ancestors. 2Ch 24:24
In that way * executed judgment 2Ch 24:24
you fight; for * has power to help 2Ch 25:8
"I know that * has determined to 2Ch 25:16
listen, for * was arranging to 2Ch 25:20
turning away from *, and how his 2Ch 25:27
was always eager to please *. 2Ch 26:5
had special revelations from *. 2Ch 26:5
the paths of *, he prospered, for 2Ch 26:5
he prospered, for * blessed him. 2Ch 26:5
country. * helped him not only 2Ch 26:7
He sinned against the Lord his * 2Ch 26:16
follow the path of the Lord his *. 2Ch 27:6
That is why the Lord * allowed 2Ch 28:5
from the Lord * of their fathers. 2Ch 28:6
"The Lord * of your fathers was 2Ch 28:9
own sins against the Lord your *? 2Ch 28:10
We are in enough trouble with * 2Ch 28:13
the Lord * of his fathers. 2Ch 28:25
Temple of the Lord * of your 2Ch 29:4,5
a deep sin before the Lord our *; 2Ch 29:6
with the Lord * of Israel so that 2Ch 29:10
* had accomplished so quickly. 2Ch 29:36
"Come back to the Lord * of 2Ch 30:6
against the Lord * of their fathers 2Ch 30:7
the Lord your * so that his fierce 2Ch 30:8
For the Lord your * is full of 2Ch 30:9
turned to * and came to Jerusalem. 2Ch 30:11
by the law of Moses the man of *; 2Ch 30:16
to follow the Lord * of his 2Ch 30:17,18,19
to the Lord * of their fathers. 2Ch 30:22
as required in the law of *. 2Ch 31:3
as required in the law of *. 2Ch 31:4
to be given to the Lord their *. 2Ch 31:5,6
in the sight of the Lord his *. 2Ch 31:20
* to fight our battles for us!" 2Ch 32:8
"the Lord our * will deliver us 2Ch 32:11
What makes you think your * can 2Ch 32:14
I say it again—no * of any nation 2Ch 32:15
how much less your *!' 2Ch 32:15
mocked the Lord * and God's servant 2Ch 32:16
scorning the Lord * of Israel. 2Ch 32:17
my hand, and the * of Hezekiah will 2Ch 32:17
talked about the * of Jerusalem 2Ch 32:19
out in prayer to * in heaven, and 2Ch 32:20
the temple of his *, some of his 2Ch 32:21
so the anger of * was upon him and 2Ch 32:25
and he acquired many towns, for * 2Ch 32:28,29
his being healed, * left him to 2Ch 32:31
the very Temple of *, where God had 2Ch 33:7
of God, where * had told David and 2Ch 33:7
his people. So * sent the Assyrian 2Ch 33:11
cried out humbly to * for help. 2Ch 33:12
that the Lord was really *! 2Ch 33:13
worship the Lord * of Israel. 2Ch 33:16
but only to the Lord their *. 2Ch 33:17
and his prayer to *, and God's 2Ch 33:18
His prayer, and the way * 2Ch 33:19
for the * of his ancestor David; 2Ch 34:3
the laws of * as given to Moses! 2Ch 34:14
These are the laws of *!" 2Ch 34:15,16
"The Lord * of Israel says, Tell 2Ch 34:23
Tell him, the Lord * of Israel 2Ch 34:26
yourself before * when you heard my 2Ch 34:27
of * that was found in the Temple. 2Ch 34:30
pact with *, and all of them did. 2Ch 34:32
them to worship Jehovah their *. 2Ch 34:33
Jehovah, the * of their ancestors. 2Ch 34:33
Leave me alone! * has told me to 2Ch 35:21
Don't meddle with * or he will 2Ch 35:21
that Neco's message was from *. 2Ch 35:22
obeying the Lord * of Israel was 2Ch 36:13
Jehovah the * of their fathers 2Ch 36:15
messengers of * and despised their 2Ch 36:16
to me by the Lord * of heaven, and 2Ch 36:22,23
that Jehovah, the * of heaven who Ez 1:2
the * of Israel and of Jerusalem. Ez 1:3
Then * gave a great desire to the Ez 1:5
to find out from * whether they Ez 2:62,63
the altar of the * of Israel; Ez 3:1
the laws of Moses, the man of *. Ez 3:1
and thanks to *, singing this song: Ez 3:11
shout, praising * because the Ez 3:11
interested in your * as you are; Ez 4:2
The Temple of the * of Israel Ez 4:3
messages from the * of Israel to Ez 5:1
Temple of the great * of Judah. Ez 5:8
servants of the * of heaven and Ez 5:11
angered the * of heaven, and he Ez 5:12
of * be built there as before. Ez 5:15
the Temple of * at Jerusalem where Ez 6:3
from the Temple of * by Ez 6:5
offerings to the * of heaven; Ez 6:9
sacrifices to the * of heaven, and Ez 6:10
of rubble. The * who has chosen Ez 6:12
been commanded by * and decreed by Ez 6:14
to do the work of * as instructed Ez 6:18
Israelis in worshiping the Lord *. Ez 6:21,22
for the Lord his * was blessing Ez 7:6
of the laws of the * of heaven. Ez 7:12
as an offering to the * of Israel. Ez 7:15
feel is the will of your *. Ez 7:18
the Temple of your * at Jerusalem. Ez 7:19
of the laws of the * of heaven), Ez 7:21
and whatever else the * of Ez 7:23
to use the wisdom * has given you Ez 7:25
of your *, you are to teach them. Ez 7:25
the law of your * and the law of Ez 7:26
Well, praise the Lord * of our Ez 7:27
And praise * for demonstrating Ez 7:28
because the Lord my * was with me; Ez 7:28
for the Temple of * at Jerusalem. Ez 8:17
God at Jerusalem. And * was good! Ez 8:18
of Israel. * also sent Hashabiah; Ez 8:19
humble ourselves before our *; Ez 8:21
the king that our * would protect Ez 8:22
So we fasted and begged * to Ez 8:23
had presented to the Temple of *. Ez 8:25
to the Lord * of our fathers. Ez 8:28
to Jerusalem; and * protected us Ez 8:31
offerings to the * of Israel—twelve Ez 8:35
the rebuilding of the Temple of *. Ez 8:36
So the holy people of * were Ez 9:2
Then many who feared the * of Ez 9:4
cried out, "O my *, I am ashamed; Ez 9:6
the Temple of our * and in giving Ez 9:9
"And now, O *, what can we say Ez 9:10
O Lord * of Israel, you are a Ez 9:15
God of Israel, you are a just *; Ez 9:15
sin against our *, for we have Ez 10:2
For we agree before our * to Ez 10:3
of the others who fear our *. Ez 10:3
We will obey the laws of *. Ez 10:3
Confess your sin to the Lord * Ez 10:11
* will be turned away from us." Ez 10:14
time in prayer to the * of heaven. Neh 1:4
"O Lord *," I cried out; Neh 1:5
"O great and awesome * who keeps Neh 1:5
With a quick prayer to the * of Neh 2:4
for * was being gracious to me. Neh 2:8
which * had put into my heart. Neh 2:11,12
about the desire * had put into my Neh 2:18
But I replied, "The * of heaven Neh 2:20
O Lord *, for we are being mocked. Neh 4:4
But we prayed to our * and Neh 4:9
plot, and that * had exposed and Neh 4:15
I am; and * will fight for us." Neh 4:19
you not walk in the fear of our *? Neh 5:9
And I invoked the curse of * Neh 5:13
"May * destroy your homes and Neh 5:13
but I obeyed * and did not act Neh 5:15
O my *, please keep in mind all Neh 5:19
(O Lord *, please strengthen Neh 6:9
he was receiving a message from *. Neh 6:10
Then I realized that * had not Neh 6:12,13
"O my *," I prayed, "don't Neh 6:14
been done with the help of our *. Neh 6:16
* more than most people do. Neh 7:2

GOD Con't)

to find out from * whether or not Neh 7:64,65
of * which he had given to Moses. Neh 8:1
Lord, the great *, and all the Neh 8:6
the Lord your *— it is a time to Neh 8:9
The laws of * were read aloud to Neh 9:3
worshiped the Lord their *. Neh 9:3
the Lord * with songs of joy. Neh 9:4
the Lord your *, for he lives from Neh 9:5
Ezra prayed, "You alone are *. Neh 9:6
"You are the Lord * who chose Neh 9:7
But you are a * of forgiveness, Neh 9:17
and proclaimed, 'This is our *! Neh 9:18
What a gracious and merciful * Neh 9:31
"And now, O great and awesome *, Neh 9:32
of the land in order to serve *. Neh 10:28
the curse of * unless we obeyed Neh 10:29
to care for the Temple of our *; Neh 10:32
We agreed to give to * our oldest Neh 10:36
minister in the Temple of our *. Neh 10:36
the Temple of our *—the best of our Neh 10:37
to neglect the Temple of our *. Neh 10:39,40
commanded by David, the man of *. Neh 12:24
joyous day, for * had given us Neh 12:43
them in worshiping * and performing Neh 12:45
hymns of praise and thanks to *. Neh 12:46
them—although * turned the curse Neh 13:2
O my *, remember this good deed Neh 13:14
Remember this good deed, O my *! Neh 13:22
and they vowed before * that they Neh 13:25
with him, and * loved him and made Neh 13:26
Remember them, O my *, for they Neh 13:29
Remember me, my *, with your Neh 13:31
a time like this, * will deliver Est 4:14
can say but that * has brought you Est 4:14
man who feared * and stayed away Job 1:1
have sinned and turned away from * Job 1:5
Literally, "have cursed *." Job 1:5f
Literally, "the sons of *." Job 1:6f
man who fears * and will have Job 1:8
"The fire of * has fallen from Job 1:16
down upon the ground before *. Job 1:20
this, Job did not sin or revile *. Job 1:22
Literally, "sons of *." Job 2:1f
* and turns away from all evil. Job 2:3
when * has done all this to you? Job 2:9
* and never anything unpleasant?" Job 2:10
Let it be lost even to *, Job 3:4
to be born if * is only going to Job 3:23
many a troubled soul to trust in * Job 4:3,4
in * still be your confidence? Job 4:6
Shouldn't you believe that * will Job 4:6
They die beneath the hand of *. Job 4:9
" 'Is mere man more just than *? Job 4:17
"If * cannot trust his own Job 4:18,19
Those who turn from * may be Job 5:3
Go to * and confess your sins Job 5:8
Literally, "I would seek *, and Job 5:8f
to * would I commit my cause." Job 5:8f
"* saves the fatherless and the Job 5:15
"How enviable the man whom * Job 5:17
"Oh, that * would grant the Job 6:8,9
denied the words of the holy *. Job 6:10
without the slightest fear of *. Job 6:14
"O *, am I some monster, that Job 7:12
"Has my sin harmed you, O *, Job 7:20
Does * twist justice? Job 8:3
begged Almighty * for them— if you Job 8:5
those who forget * have no hope. Job 8:11-13
A man without * is trusting in a Job 8:14
"But look! * will not cast away Job 8:20
be truly good in the eyes of *? Job 9:2
eyes of God? If * decides to argue Job 9:3
For * is so wise and so mighty. Job 9:4
"And * does not abate his anger. Job 9:13
*, or even reason with him? Job 9:14
Even if I were perfect, * would Job 9:20
of the wicked. * blinds the eyes of Job 9:24
complaints against *, to end my Job 9:27
O *, but will condemn me. Job 9:28
I will say to *, 'Don't just Job 10:2
When you mock *, shouldn't Job 11:3
you are pure in the eyes of *! Job 11:4
Oh, that * would speak and tell Job 11:5
Listen! * is doubtless punishing Job 11:6
know the mind and purposes of *? Job 11:7
"Before you turn to * and Job 11:13,14
forward to * without fear. Job 11:15
I, the man who begged * for Job 12:4
God for help, and * answered him, Job 12:4
Go ahead and provoke *—it makes Job 12:6
*, and the breath of all mankind. Job 12:10
I want to talk this over with * Job 13:3
"Must you go on 'speaking for *' Job 13:7
Does * want your help if you are Job 13:8
Or do you think you can fool * as Job 13:9
Your defense of * is as fragile Job 13:12
I really think. * may kill me for Job 13:15
"O *, there are two things I beg Job 13:20
Have you no fear of *? Job 15:4,5
you heard the secret counsel of *? Job 15:7,8
And you turn against * and say Job 15:13
Why, * doesn't even trust the Job 15:15
his fist against *, defying the Job 15:25,26
the breath of * shall destroy Job 15:30
to speak. For * has ground me Job 16:7
away my family. O *, you have Job 16:8
say, of my sins. * hates me and Job 16:9
against me. And * has delivered me Job 16:11
out my tears to *, pleading that Job 16:20
But you, O *, have kept them back Job 17:3,4
sinners, to those rejecting *." Job 18:21
the matter is that * has overthrown Job 19:6
I shriek, but get no justice. * Job 19:8
angry hand of * has touched me. Job 19:21
Why must you persecute me as * Job 19:22
decayed, this body shall see *! Job 19:26
without my flesh I shall see *." Job 19:26f
* won't let him keep it down. Job 20:15
* will rain down wrath upon him. Job 20:23
disappear beneath the wrath of *. Job 20:28
man, for * prepares it for him." Job 20:29
"I am complaining about *, Job 21:4
fear, and * does not punish them. Job 21:9
that they ordered * away and wanted Job 21:14
" 'Who is Almighty *?' Job 21:15
They never have trouble, and * Job 21:17
" 'Well,' you say, 'at least * Job 21:19
But I say that * should punish Job 21:19
"But who can rebuke *, the Job 21:22
and prosperous; * also destroys Job 21:25
"Is mere man of any worth to *? Job 22:2
"* is so great—higher than the Job 22:12
For they said to *, 'Go away, Job 22:17
For they said to God, 'Go away, *! Job 22:17
What can you do for us?' (* Job 22:18
"Quit quarreling with *! Job 22:21
If you return to * and put right Job 22:23
in the Lord, and look up to *. Job 22:26
Oh, that I knew where to find * Job 23:3
* has given me a fainting heart; Job 23:16,17
"WHY DOESN'T * open the court and Job 24:1
the wounded cry for help; yet * Job 24:12
it seems as though * preserves Job 24:22,23
else would die. * gives them Job 24:22,23
"* is powerful and dreadful. Job 25:2
How can mere man stand before * Job 25:4
that he is clean? * is so glorious Job 25:5
* in the place where they go. Job 26:5,6
where they go. * stretches out Job 26:7
"I vow by the living *, who has Job 27:2
even the Almighty * who has Job 27:2
I have breath from *, my lips Job 27:3
the godless when * cuts him off and Job 27:8
Will * listen to his cry when Job 27:9
to * except in times of crisis. Job 27:10
"I will teach you about *— but Job 27:11
* shall hurl at him unsparingly. Job 27:22
He longs to flee from *. Job 27:22
about it! And * surely knows where Job 28:23,24
years gone by when * took care of Job 29:2
of * was felt in my home; Job 29:4
* has placed my life in jeopardy. Job 30:11
me. * has thrown me into the mud. Job 30:19
"I cry to you, O *, but you Job 30:20
I know full well that Almighty * Job 31:2,3
and deceived— but * knows that I Job 31:6
my servants, how could I face *? Job 31:14
me about it? For * made me, and Job 31:15
than face the judgment sent by *; Job 31:23
For if the majesty of * opposes Job 31:23
that I denied the * of heaven. Job 31:28
acknowledge that * had just cause Job 32:2
line about 'only * can convince the Job 32:13
Let me be frank, lest * should Job 32:21,22
For the Spirit of * has made me, Job 33:4
between you and * and to be both Job 33:6
You say * is using a Job 33:10
sinned by speaking of * that way. Job 33:12
way. For * is greater than man. Job 33:12
"For * speaks again and again, Job 33:14
"Or, * sends sickness and pain, Job 33:19
right, then * pities him and says, Job 33:23,24
And when he prays to *, God will Job 33:26
And when he prays to God, * will Job 33:26
'I sinned, but * let me go. Job 33:27
"Yes, * often does these things Job 33:29
am innocent, but * says I'm not. Job 34:5
waste time trying to please *?' Job 34:9
Surely everyone knows that * Job 34:10
this: * is never wicked or unjust. Job 34:12
for the world. If * were to Job 34:14
Could * govern if he hated Job 34:17
Are you going to condemn this * Job 34:18
"For * carefully watches the Job 34:21
is called before * in judgment. Job 34:23
case of it, * simply shatters the Job 34:24
to come to the attention of *. Job 34:28
exclaim to their *, 'We have Job 34:31
"Must * tailor his justice to Job 34:33
way you have talked about *. Job 34:36
off before * than if I had'? Job 35:2,3
and knock * from his throne? Job 35:6
yet none of them cry to *, Job 35:9,10
asking, 'Where is * my Maker who Job 35:9,10
I have not finished defending *! Job 36:2
"* is almighty and yet does not Job 36:5
lead you into scoffing at *! Job 36:18
*, he will be ashamed and repent? Job 36:19
evil that * sent this suffering. Job 36:21
"Look, * is all-powerful. Job 36:22
"* is so great that we cannot Job 36:26
from the north, the cold. * Job 37:10
the wonderful miracles of *. Job 37:14
Do you know how * controls all Job 37:15
of us how we should approach *. Job 37:19,20
majesty of * breaking forth upon us Job 37:22
young cry out to * as they try to Job 38:41
for * has deprived her of wisdom. Job 39:17
Then Job replied to *: Job 40:2
Are you as strong as *, and can Job 40:9
THEN JOB REPLIED TO *: Job 42:1
* also gave him seven more sons Job 42:13,14
at the things of *: But they Ps 1:1
doing everything * wants them to, Ps 1:2
that men should try to outwit *! Ps 2:1
from all this slavery to *." Ps 2:3
But * in heaven merely laughs! Ps 2:4
purposes of *, for the Lord has Ps 2:7
So many say that * will never Ps 3:2
Save me, O my *!" Ps 3:7
For salvation comes from *. Ps 3:8
O *, YOU have declared me perfect Ps 4:1
Literally, "* of my Ps 4:1f
The Lord * asks, "Sons of men, Ps 4:2
Many say that * will never help Ps 4:6
listen to my plea, O * my King, Ps 5:1
ends. O *, hold them responsible. Ps 5:10
hereafter for those who love *. Ps 6:5f
* will turn them back in shame. Ps 6:10
AM DEPENDING on you, O Lord my * Ps 7:1
and bless all who truly worship *; Ps 7:9
for you, the righteous *, look Ps 7:9
* is my shield; Ps 7:10
* is a judge who is perfectly Ps 7:11
O LORD OUR *, the majesty and Ps 8:1
Or, "only a little lower than * Ps 8:5f
praises, O Lord * above all gods. Ps 9:2
to the * who lives in Jerusalem. Ps 9:11
they revile * and congratulate Ps 10:3
seem to think that * is dead. Ps 10:4
Literally, "that there is no *." Ps 10:4f
They boast that neither * nor Ps 10:6
their blows. "* isn't watching," Ps 10:11
O Lord, arise! O *, crush them! Ps 10:12
get away with this contempt for *? Ps 10:13
For they think that * will never Ps 10:13
from ambush at the people of *. Ps 11:2
For * is good, and he loves Ps 11:7
Answer me, O Lord my *; Ps 13:3
to himself, "There is no *!" Ps 14:1
are wise, who want to please *. Ps 14:2
Terror shall grip them, for * is Ps 14:5
already here, that * would come Ps 14:7
SAVE ME, O *, because I have come Ps 16:1
I know you will answer me, O *! Ps 17:6
the heavens; the * above all gods Ps 18:13
The Lord my * has made my Ps 18:28
What a * he is! Ps 18:30
For who is * except our Lord? Ps 18:31
* is alive! Ps 18:46
He is the * who pays back those Ps 18:47
ARE telling the glory of *; Ps 19:1
they keep on telling about *. Ps 19:2
the heavens where * placed it and Ps 19:3,4
May the * of Jacob keep you from Ps 20:1
with praise to * for all that he Ps 20:5
"* save the king"—I know he Ps 20:6
our boast is in the Lord our *. Ps 20:7
of the * who is above all gods. Ps 21:7
MY *, MY God, why have you Ps 22:1
MY GOD, MY *, why have you Ps 22:1
We'll believe it when we see * Ps 22:8
you have always been my *. Ps 22:9,10,11
O Lord, don't stay away. O * my Ps 22:19
* will answer me and rescue me. Ps 22:21
THE EARTH BELONGS to *! Ps 24:1
right standing with *. Ps 24:5f
lives by * himself, their Savior. Ps 24:5
Lord and worship the * of Jacob. Ps 24:6
None who have faith in * will Ps 25:3
for you are the * who gives me Ps 25:5
fears the Lord? * will teach him Ps 25:12
Friendship with * is reserved for Ps 25:14
I am confident that * will save Ps 27:3
The one thing I want from *, the Ps 27:4
Don't forsake me, O * of my Ps 27:9
They care nothing for * or what Ps 28:5
therefore * will dismantle them Ps 28:5
the clouds. The * of glory thunders Ps 29:3
O Lord my *, I pleaded with you, Ps 30:2
O Lord my *, I will keep on Ps 30:12
Rescue me because you are the * Ps 31:1

(GOD Con't)
You have rescued me, O * who keeps Ps 31:5,6
I said, "You alone are my *; Ps 31:14,15
and * has cleared their record. Ps 32:1
his sins to * when he is aware of Ps 32:6
Blessed is the nation whose * is Ps 33:12
Oh, put * to the test and see how Ps 34:8
and every one. * even protects him Ps 34:20
earnestness, but * did not listen. Ps 35:13
Rise up, O Lord my *; Ps 35:23
They have no fear of * to hold Ps 36:1
is your constant love, O *! Ps 36:7
These enemies of * will wither Ps 37:20
I am waiting for you, O Lord my *. Ps 38:15
and pled with *: Lord, help me to Ps 39:2,3
I WAITED PATIENTLY for * to help Ps 40:1
song to sing, of praises to our *. Ps 40:3
O Lord my *, many and many a time Ps 40:5
do your will, my *, for your law is Ps 40:8
exclaim, "How great * is!" Ps 40:16
now! O my *, you are my helper. Ps 40:17
* BLESSES THOSE who are kind to Ps 41:1
Bless the Lord, the * of Israel, Ps 41:13
for water, so I long for you, O *. Ps 42:1
I thirst for *, the living God. Ps 42:2
I thirst for God, the living *. Ps 42:2
"Where is this * of yours?" Ps 42:3
Hope in *! Ps 42:4,5
and pray to * who gives me life. Ps 42:8
"O * my Rock," I cry, "why Ps 42:9
"Where is that * of yours?" Ps 42:10
Expect * to act! Ps 42:11
He is my *! Ps 42:11
O *, DEFEND me from the charges of Ps 43:1
For you are *, my only place of Ps 43:2
go to the altar of * my exceeding Ps 43:4
him with my harp. O *—my God! Ps 43:4
O God—my *! Ps 43:4
Trust in *! Ps 43:5
for he is my *! Ps 43:5
O *, WE have heard of the glorious Ps 44:1
You are my King and my *. Ps 44:4
My constant boast is *. Ps 44:8
worshiping our *, and were Ps 44:20
idols, would * not know it? Ps 44:21
* himself is blessing you forever. Ps 45:2
Your throne, O *, endures Ps 45:6
Therefore *, your God, Ps 45:7
Therefore God, your *, Ps 45:7
* IS OUR refuge and strength, a Ps 46:1
the City of our *—the sacred home Ps 46:4
home of the * above all gods. Ps 46:4
* himself is living in that City; Ps 46:5
in anger—but when * speaks, the Ps 46:6
He, the * of Jacob, has come to Ps 46:7
things that our * does, how he Ps 46:8
Know that I am *! Ps 46:10
He, the * of Jacob, has come to Ps 46:11
For the Lord, the * above all Ps 47:2
* has ascended with a mighty Ps 47:5
Sing out your praises to our *, Ps 47:6,7
the * of Abraham—for the battle Ps 47:9
* himself is the defender of Ps 48:3
Literally, "* has made himself Ps 48:3f
in travail! For * destroys the Ps 48:7
city of our *, the Commander of the Ps 48:8
it for ourselves! * has established Ps 48:8
known throughout the earth, O *. Ps 48:10
O people of Judah, rejoice! For * Ps 48:11
For this great * is our God Ps 48:14
For this great God is our * Ps 48:14
But as for me, * will redeem my Ps 49:15
THE MIGHTY *, the Lord, has Ps 50:1
me." * will judge them with Ps 50:6
For I am your *. Ps 50:7
But * says to evil men: Recite my Ps 50:16
who have forgotten *, before I tear Ps 50:22
O LOVING AND kind *, have mercy. Ps 51:1
clean heart, O *, filled with clean Ps 51:10
O my *, you alone can rescue me. Ps 51:14,15
heart, O *, you will not ignore. Ps 51:17
lovingkindness of * continually." Ps 52:1f
But * will strike you down and Ps 52:5
The followers of * will see it Ps 52:6
those who despise * and trust in Ps 52:7
I trust in the mercy of * forever Ps 52:8
knows what a merciful * you are. Ps 52:9
say to himself, "There is no *." Ps 53:1
* looks down from heaven, Ps 53:2
does right and really seeks for *. Ps 53:2
bread and refuse to come to *. Ps 53:4
will fall on them. * will scatter Ps 53:5
They are doomed, for * has Ps 53:5
Oh, that * would come from Zion Ps 53:6
O *, and save me! Ps 54:1
nothing for * are seeking my life. Ps 54:3
But * is my helper. Ps 54:4
an end to these wicked men, O *. Ps 54:5
* has rescued me from all my Ps 54:7
LISTEN TO MY prayer, O *; Ps 55:1
and night, pleading aloud with *; Ps 55:17
will rescue me. * himself—God from Ps 55:19
God himself—* from everlasting Ps 55:19
I will trust the promises of *. Ps 56:3,4
This one thing I know: * is for Ps 56:9
I am trusting *—oh, praise his Ps 56:10,11
O *, HAVE pity, for I am trusting Ps 57:1
I will cry to the * of heaven Ps 57:2
O *, my heart is quiet and Ps 57:7
Yes, be exalted, O *, above the Ps 57:11
O *, break off their fangs. Ps 58:6
see the sun. * will sweep away Ps 58:9
* who judges justly here on earth. Ps 58:11
O MY *, save me from my enemies. Ps 59:1
(And O Jehovah, * of heaven's Ps 59:5
heaven's armies, * of Israel, arise Ps 59:5
and cursing *, for "No one will Ps 59:7
O * my Strength! Ps 59:9
of safety. My * is changeless in Ps 59:10
find out too that * rules in Israel Ps 59:12,13
tower of safety, my * of mercy. Ps 59:17
O *, YOU have rejected us and Ps 60:1
us. * has promised to help us. Ps 60:6,7
into Edom's strong cities? * will! Ps 60:9,10
O *, LISTEN to me! Ps 61:1
For you have heard my vows, O *, Ps 61:5
come from * alone. Ps 62:7
O *, MY God! Ps 63:1
O GOD, MY *! Ps 63:1
will rejoice in *. Ps 63:11
But * himself will shoot them Ps 64:7
greatness of the miracles of *; Ps 64:9
O * IN Zion, we wait before you in Ps 65:1
O * who saves us. Ps 65:5
acts of * shall startle everyone. Ps 65:8
The rivers of * will not run dry! Ps 65:9
awe-inspiring are your deeds, O *! Ps 66:3
Come, see the glorious things * Ps 66:5
Let everyone bless * and sing his Ps 66:8
Blessed be * who didn't turn away Ps 66:20
O *, IN mercy bless us; Ps 67:1
Praise *, O world! Ps 67:5
abundant harvests. *, even our own Ps 67:6,7
God, even our own *, will bless Ps 67:6,7
ARISE, O *, and scatter all your Ps 68:1
perish at the presence of *. Ps 68:2
O *, when you led your people Ps 68:7
before you—the * of Israel. Ps 68:8
*, to refresh it in its weariness! Ps 68:9,10
cover doves! * scattered their Ps 68:14
* has chosen to live forever. Ps 68:15,16
rebels. * will live among us here. Ps 68:18
The procession of * my King moves Ps 68:24
display your strength, O *, for Ps 68:28
out her hands to * in adoration. Ps 68:31
Power belongs to *! Ps 68:34
the sanctuary. The * of Israel Ps 68:35
Blessed be *! Ps 68:35
SAVE ME, O my *. Ps 69:1
weeping, waiting for my * to act. Ps 69:3
O *, you know so well how stupid Ps 69:5
O Lord * of the armies of Ps 69:6
trust in you. O * of Israel, don't Ps 69:6
My zeal for * and his work Ps 69:9
But rescue me, O *, from my Ps 69:29
Then I will praise * with my Ps 69:30
The humble shall see their * at Ps 69:32
All who seek for * shall live in Ps 69:32
them! For * will save Jerusalem; Ps 69:35
RESCUE ME, O *! Ps 70:1
But fill the followers of * with Ps 70:4
"What a wonderful * he is!" Ps 70:4
Rescue me, O *, from these Ps 71:4
and honor you, O *, for all that Ps 71:8
My enemies are whispering, "* Ps 71:11
him now!" O *, don't stay away! Ps 71:12
in the strength of the Lord *. Ps 71:16
just and good. O *, you have Ps 71:17
Where is there another * like Ps 71:19
O *, HELP the king to judge as you Ps 72:1
Blessed be Jehovah *, the God of Ps 72:18
Blessed be Jehovah God, the * of Ps 72:18
HOW GOOD * is to Israel—to those Ps 73:1
They scoff at * and threaten his Ps 73:8
"Does * realize what is going Ps 73:11
are on—suddenly * will send them Ps 73:18
seem like an animal to you, O *. Ps 73:22
my spirits droop, yet * remains! Ps 73:26
But those refusing to worship * Ps 73:27
O *, WHY have you cast us away Ps 74:1
out every trace of *," they said, Ps 74:8
How long, O *, will you allow our Ps 74:9,10
* is my King from ages past; Ps 74:12
Arise, O *, and state your case Ps 74:22
nowhere on earth, but only from *. Ps 75:6,7
the praises of the * of Jacob. Ps 75:9
When you rebuked them, * of Ps 76:6
Who can stand before an angry *? Ps 76:7
you have made to Jehovah your *. Ps 76:11
I think of * and moan, Ps 77:3
of * have changed to hate. Ps 77:10
O *, your ways are holy. Ps 77:13
You are the * of miracles and Ps 77:14
its hope anew on * and not forget Ps 78:7
to give their hearts to *. Ps 78:8
wonderful miracles * had done for Ps 78:11,12
the * who is above all gods. Ps 78:17
other food than * was giving them. Ps 78:18
They even spoke against * Ps 78:19,20
didn't believe in * or trust in him Ps 78:22
Then they remembered that * was Ps 78:35
Savior was the * above all gods. Ps 78:35
away and tempted * to kill them, Ps 78:41
against the * above all gods, and Ps 78:56
When * saw their deeds, his wrath Ps 78:59
ewes with lambs; * presented David Ps 78:71,72
O *, YOUR land has been conquered Ps 79:1
Help us, * of our salvation! Ps 79:9
to scoff, "Where is their *?" Ps 79:10
like a flock; O * enthroned above Ps 80:1
Turn us again to yourself, O *. Ps 80:3
O Jehovah, * of heaven's armies, Ps 80:4
Turn us again to yourself, O * of Ps 80:7
Literally, "the cedars of *." Ps 80:10f
Come back, we beg of you, O * of Ps 80:14
Turn us again to yourself, O * of Ps 80:19
Sing to Israel's *! Ps 81:1
* has given us these times of joy; Ps 81:4
worship any other *, nor ever have Ps 81:9
shall no foreign * be in you." Ps 81:9f
For it was I, Jehovah your *, Ps 81:10
* STANDS UP to open heaven's Ps 82:1
Stand up, O *, and judge the Ps 82:8
O *, DON'T sit idly by, silent and Ps 83:1
against Almighty *— these Ps 83:5
own use these pasturelands of *!" Ps 83:12
O my *, blow them away like dust; Ps 83:13
Jehovah, are the * above all gods Ps 83:18
and come near to the Living *. Ps 84:2
heaven's armies, my King and my *! Ps 84:3
O Jehovah, * of the heavenly Ps 84:8
Listen, * of Israel. Ps 84:8
Listen, God of Israel. O *, our Ps 84:9
of my * than live in palaces Ps 84:10
For Jehovah * is our Light and Ps 84:11
Listen closely to my prayer, O *. Ps 86:6
gods is there a * like you? Ps 86:8
You alone are *. Ps 86:10
O *, proud and insolent men defy Ps 86:14
the city of *, the city he loves Ps 87:1
O city of *, what wondrous tales Ps 87:3
For the * above all gods will Ps 87:5
O JEHOVAH, * of my salvation, I Ps 88:1
The Lord * says, Ps 89:3,4
of heaven can be compared with *? Ps 89:6
my *, and my Rock of Salvation.' Ps 89:26
David (and a holy * can never lie), Ps 89:35,36
A prayer of Moses, the man of *. Ps 90:1
are * without beginning or end. Ps 90:2
* favor us and give us success. Ps 90:17
by the * who is above all gods. Ps 91:1
he is my *, and I am trusting Ps 91:2
I choose the * above all gods to Ps 91:9
to the * who is above all gods. Ps 92:1
LORD *, TO whom vengeance belongs, Ps 94:1
Literally, "the * of Jacob." Ps 94:6,7f
Fools! Is * deaf and blind—he Ps 94:9
* traps them and destroys them. Ps 94:12,13
The Lord my * is my fortress—the Ps 94:21,22
where I can hide. * has made the Ps 94:23
Jehovah our * will cut them off. Ps 94:23
For the Lord is a great *, the Ps 95:3
Lord our Maker, for he is our *. Ps 95:7
in disgust," the Lord * says. Ps 95:10
idols, but our * made the heavens! Ps 96:5
* alone is glorious and strong. Ps 96:7
gods—for every * must bow to him! Ps 97:7
him, our holy *. Ps 97:12
to *, and sings for utter joy! Ps 98:4
Exalt the Lord our holy *! Ps 99:5
O Jehovah our *! Ps 99:8
Exalt the Lord our *, and worship Ps 99:9
what this means—the Lord is *! Ps 100:3
the city of * from their grip. Ps 101:8
Tell them that * looked down Ps 102:19
But I cried to him, "O *, you Ps 102:24
I BLESS THE holy name of * with Ps 103:1
I BLESS THE Lord: O Lord my *, how Ps 104:1
Praise * forever! Ps 104:31
I will praise * to my last Ps 104:33
O worshipers of *, rejoice. Ps 105:3
He is the Lord our *. Ps 105:7
came—how * tested his patience! Ps 105:19
At that point * turned the Ps 105:25
But * sent Moses as his Ps 105:26
list the glorious miracles of *? Ps 106:2
by * as his priest. Ps 106:16
glorious presence of * himself. Ps 106:19,20
people and their * and begged him Ps 106:23
At Meribah, too, Israel angered * Ps 106:32
in the land as * had told them to, Ps 106:34
idols, and were led away from *. Ps 106:36
was adultery in the sight of *. Ps 106:39

(GOD Con't)
O Lord *, save us! Ps 106:47
Blessed be the Lord, the * of Ps 106:48
him who is the * above all gods. Ps 107:11
observe the power of * in action. Ps 107:24
and sorrow. For * pours contempt Ps 107:40
O *, MY heart is ready to praise Ps 108:1
* has given sacred promises; Ps 108:7
Who but * can give me strength to Ps 108:10
But with the help of * we shall Ps 108:13
O * OF my praise, don't stand Ps 109:1
Help me, O Lord my *! Ps 109:26
Melchizedek. * stands beside you Ps 110:5
to * for his mighty miracles. Ps 111:1
to begin is by reverence for *. Ps 111:10
For all who fear * and trust in Ps 112:1
Who can be compared with * Ps 113:5
of the Lord, the * of Jacob. Ps 114:7
nations say, "Their * is dead!" Ps 115:2
Literally, "Where is their *?" Ps 115:2f
So merciful, this * of ours! Ps 116:5
Jehovah * is our light. Ps 118:27,28
for you are my *, and I shall give Ps 118:27,28
perfectly follow the laws of *. Ps 119:1
Happy are all who search for *, Ps 119:2
to *, but I stand unmoved. Ps 119:51
Never let it be said that * Ps 119:116
Every law of * is right, Ps 119:128
IN MY TROUBLES I pled with * to Ps 120:1
O * ENTHRONED in heaven, I lift my Ps 123:1
We look to Jehovah our * for his Ps 123:2
to death; for * wants his loved Ps 127:2
Children are a gift from *; Ps 127:3
And may * bless Israel! Ps 128:6
* to help, for he has promised. Ps 130:5
of Israel. And * has pronounced Ps 133:3
is greater far than any other *. Ps 135:5
Give thanks to the * of gods, for Ps 136:2
Praise the * who smote the Ps 136:10
continues forever. * gave the Ps 136:21
Oh, give thanks to the * of Ps 136:26
I can never get away from my *! Ps 139:7
even darkness cannot hide from *; Ps 139:12
Search me, O *, and know my Ps 139:23
* and my shield—hear me as I pray! Ps 140:6,7,8
I look to you for help, O Lord *. Ps 141:8
HOW I PLEAD with *, how I implore Ps 142:1
to do your will, for you are my *. Ps 143:10
I will sing you a new song, O *, Ps 144:9
happy land where Jehovah is *: Ps 144:12-15
Yes, happy are those whose * is Ps 144:12-15
I WILL PRAISE you, my * and King, Ps 145:1
man who has the * of Jacob as his Ps 146:5
is in the Lord his *— the God who Ps 146:5
Lord his God— the * who made both Ps 146:6
He is the * who keeps every Ps 146:6
your * is King in every Ps 146:10
sing praises to our *, Ps 147:7
Praise your *, O Zion! Ps 147:12
you, and knowledge of * himself; Pro 2:3,4,5
and flouted the laws of *. Pro 2:16,17
If you want favor with both * Pro 3:4,5
In everything you do, put * Pro 3:6
not resent it when * chastens and Pro 3:11,12
The curse of * is on the wicked, Pro 3:33
isn't yours? For * is closely Pro 5:21
If anyone respects and fears *, Pro 8:13
Yes, I was born before * made Pro 8:26
For the reverence and fear of * Pro 9:10
Knowing * results in every other Pro 9:10
Reverence for * adds hours to Pro 10:27
* protects the upright but Pro 10:29
* rescues good men from danger Pro 11:8
be very sure that * will rescue the Pro 11:21
Trust in * and flourish as a Pro 11:28
* delights in those who keep Pro 12:22
To do right honors *; Pro 14:2
Reverence for * gives a man deep Pro 14:26
poor is insulting * who made them. Pro 14:31
To help the poor is to honor *. Pro 14:31
with reverence for *, than great Pro 15:16
is avoided by reverence for *. Pro 16:6
When a man is trying to please *, Pro 16:7
to please God, * makes even his Pro 16:7
plans—counting on * to direct us. Pro 16:9
* will help the king to judge the Pro 16:10
* blesses those who obey him; Pro 16:20
by fire, but * purifies hearts. Pro 17:3
Mocking the poor is mocking the * Pro 17:5
Man proposes, but * disposes. Pro 19:21
Reverence for * gives life, Pro 19:23
* who gave them to you. Pro 20:12
* puts out the light of the man Pro 20:20
deed but * looks at our motives. Pro 21:2
* is more pleased when we are Pro 21:3
* loathes the gifts of evil men, Pro 21:27
but victory comes from *. Pro 21:31
those cursed of * are caught in Pro 22:14
know about it. For *, who knows all Pro 24:11,12
of himself, and * will reward you. Pro 25:21,22
* doesn't listen to the prayers Pro 28:9
Blessed is the man who reveres *, Pro 28:14
trusting * leads to prosperity. Pro 28:25
this: each depends on * for light. Pro 29:13
Where there is ignorance of *, Pro 29:18
but to trust in * means safety. Pro 29:25
I am tired out, O *, and ready to Pro 30:2
let alone *. Pro 30:3
Who else but * goes back and Pro 30:4
Who but * has created the world? Pro 30:4
Every word of * proves true. Pro 30:5
O *, I beg two favors from you Pro 30:7
I may become content without *. Pro 30:9
* shall be greatly praised. Pro 31:30
lot of man, which * has dealt to Ecc 1:12-15
pleasure is from the hand of *. Ecc 2:24-26
from him? For * gives those who Ecc 2:24-26
becomes wealthy, * takes the wealth Ecc 2:24-26
of work * has given to mankind. Ecc 3:10
But though * has planted eternity Ecc 3:11
for these are gifts from *. Ecc 3:13
And I know this, that whatever * Ecc 3:14
should fear the all-powerful *. Ecc 3:14
has been before; * brings to pass Ecc 3:15
Literally, "* seeks what has been Ecc 3:15f
"In due season * will judge Ecc 3:17
And then I realized that * is Ecc 3:18
rash promises to *, for he is in Ecc 5:1
So when you talk to * and vow to Ecc 5:4
for * has no pleasure in fools. Ecc 5:4
the messenger from * that it was Ecc 5:6,7
That would make * very angry; Ecc 5:6,7
of empty words; fear * instead. Ecc 5:6,7
life—that is indeed a gift from *. Ecc 5:19,20
on his past, for * gives him joy. Ecc 5:19,20
seen everywhere— * has given to Ecc 6:2
So there's no use arguing with * Ecc 6:10
See the way * does things and Ecc 7:13
realize that * gives one as well as Ecc 7:14
* you can expect his blessing. Ecc 7:18
May it please * that you escape Ecc 7:26
And I found that though * has Ecc 7:29
Because * does not punish Ecc 8:11
those who fear * will be better Ecc 8:12
shadows because they don't fear *. Ecc 8:13
* gives to mankind everywhere. Ecc 8:15
(Of course, only * can see Ecc 8:16,17
for it makes no difference to *! Ecc 9:7
life, for the wife * gives you is Ecc 9:9
to * for everything you do. Ecc 11:9
spirit returns to * who gave it. Ecc 12:7
conclusion: fear * and obey his Ecc 12:13
duty of man. For * will judge us Ecc 12:14
In these messages * showed him Is 1:1
to the Temple of the * of Israel; Is 2:3
bow before them; * will not forgive Is 2:9
Therefore * will deal with them Is 5:24
away the laws of * and despised the Is 5:24
"But the Lord * says, This plan Is 7:7
(meaning, "* is with us"). Is 7:14
us, and perish! For * is with us. Is 8:9,10
a traitor for staying true to *. Is 8:12
I and the children * has given Is 8:18
Why not ask your *? Is 8:19
words against the Word of *!" Is 8:20
and curse their King and their *. Is 8:21
have won. For * will break the Is 9:4
"The Mighty *," "The Everlasting Is 9:6
strike them down. *, the Light and Is 10:17
them will return to the mighty *. Is 10:21
at that time; * has rightly decided Is 10:22
Lord * of Hosts to consume them. Is 10:23
Therefore the Lord * of Hosts Is 10:24
Oreb or the time * drowned the Is 10:26
On that day * will end the Is 10:27
See, * has come to save me! Is 12:2
THIS IS THE vision * showed Isaiah Is 13:1
were when * sent fire from heaven; Is 13:19
Literally, "the stars of *." Is 14:13f
The Lord, the * of battle, has Is 14:27
hide them from our enemies! * Is 16:4,5
terror is past, * will establish Is 16:4,5
Then at last they will think of * Is 17:7
turned from the * who can save Is 17:10
upon a beach, * will silence them. Is 17:13
and destroy the people of *. Is 17:14
* will watch quietly from his Is 18:4
beneath the upraised fist of *. Is 19:16
they will make promises to * and Is 19:21
and they shall worship the same *. Is 19:23
horror of it all! * is telling me Is 21:2
I faint when I hear what * is Is 21:3
Hosts, the * of Israel, has said. Is 21:10
Turn again to *, so that I can Is 21:12
The Lord, the * of Israel, has Is 21:17
the Lord * of heaven's armies! Is 22:5
* has removed his protecting Is 22:8
*, who lets this come upon you. Is 22:9,10,11
The Lord * of Hosts called you Is 22:12
Furthermore, the same Lord * of Is 22:15,16
the laws of * and broken his Is 24:4,5
Therefore the curse of * is upon Is 24:6
the majesty of *, and those in the Is 24:14
your name, for you are my *; Is 25:1
The Lord * will wipe away all Is 25:8
"This is our *, in whom we trust, Is 25:9
and left to rot. * will push them Is 25:11
Trust in the Lord * always, for Is 26:4
uphill and rough! * does not give Is 26:7
earnestly I seek for *; Is 26:9
O Lord our *, once we worshiped Is 26:13
who belong to * shall live again. Is 26:19
Has * punished Israel as much as Is 27:7,8
And why did * do it? Is 27:9
people, for they turn away from *. Is 27:11
is punishment! So * will punish Is 28:11
But the Lord * says, See, I am Is 28:16
for the Lord * of Hosts has plainly Is 28:22
He knows just what to do, for * Is 28:26
their plans from *, who try to keep Is 29:15
what they do! "* can't see us," Is 29:15
crashing down. * will smash you Is 30:14
For the Lord *, the Holy One of Is 30:15
Then * will bless you with rain Is 30:23
In that day when * steps in to Is 30:25
But the people of * will sing a Is 30:29
for Molech, the Assyrian *; Is 30:33
Egyptians are mere men, not *! Is 31:3
wicked rebels, come, return to *. Is 31:6
The "sword of *" will smite Is 31:8
For the flame of * burns brightly Is 31:9
of Israel will open wide to *; Is 32:3
Their lies about * and their Is 32:6
be blessed of * for all they do. Is 32:8
* will greatly bless his people. Is 32:20
and knowledge and reverence for *. Is 33:6
a place where * is worshiped, a Is 33:20
be divided by the people of *; Is 33:23
and ravens. For * will observe that Is 34:11
there, the excellency of our *. Is 35:2
fear not, for your * is coming to Is 35:4
it. * will walk there with you; Is 35:8
are trusting in the Lord our *!' Is 36:7
And do you think this * of yours Is 36:20
But perhaps the Lord your * Is 37:4
as he scoffed at the Living *. Is 37:4
Surely * won't let him get away Is 37:4
Surely * will rebuke him for Is 37:4
"Don't let this * you trust in Is 37:10
"O Lord of Hosts, * of Israel Is 37:16,17
you alone are * of all the kingdoms Is 37:16,17
for he has mocked the Living *. Is 37:16,17
O Lord our *, save us so that Is 37:20
that you are *, and you alone." Is 37:20
"The Lord * of Israel says, This Is 37:21
Then * said to Hezekiah, "Here Is 37:30
of Nisroch his *, his sons Is 37:38
that the Lord * of your forefather Is 38:5
up for help. 'O *,' I cried, 'I am Is 38:14
who trust in * (Isaiah 57:1,2). Is 38:18f
COMFORT my people, says your *. Is 40:1
fades beneath the breath of *. Is 40:7
of our * shall stand forever." Is 40:8
of Judah, "Your * is coming!" Is 40:9
Yes, the Lord * is coming with Is 40:10
animals enough to offer to our *. Is 40:16
How can we describe *? Is 40:18
his *—a god that cannot even move! Is 40:20
his god—a * that cannot even move! Is 40:20
Are you so deaf to the words of * Is 40:21
It is * who sits above the Is 40:22
so * does with stars and planets! Is 40:26
the everlasting *, the Creator of Is 40:28
Who, indeed, but the Lord? * has Is 41:2
I am your *. Is 41:10
the Lord your *—and I say to you, Is 41:13
you shall glory in the * of Is 41:16
I, Israel's *, will not ever Is 41:17
* who did it, Israel's Holy One. Is 41:20
do! says *, the King of Israel. Is 41:21
The Lord * who created the Is 42:5
blind and deaf you are towards *! Is 42:18
That is why * poured out such Is 42:25
it is *, wanting them to repent. Is 42:25
For I am the Lord your *, your Is 43:3
All who claim me as their * will Is 43:7
confess that only * can prophesy. Is 43:9
to understand that I alone am *. Is 43:10
There is no other *; Is 43:10
From eternity to eternity I am * Is 43:13
* or the honored name of Israel. Is 44:5
there is no other *. Is 44:6
witnesses —is there any other *? Is 44:8
would make his own *—an idol that Is 44:10
claim that they have made a *. Is 44:11
a *—a god for men to worship! Is 44:15
a god—a * for men to worship! Is 44:15
he makes his *: a carved idol! Is 44:17
"You are my *!" Is 44:17
Such stupidity and ignorance! * Is 44:18
How can the rest of it be a *? Is 44:19
many lands. * shall empower his Is 45:1
of mighty kings. * shall open the Is 45:1

(GOD Con't)
the Lord, the * of Israel, the one Is 45:3
there is no other *. Is 45:5
will know there is no other *. Is 45:6
I alone am *. Is 45:6
only * there is, is your God!" Is 45:14
only God there is, is your *!" Is 45:14
Truly, O * of Israel, Savior, you Is 45:15
in their * through all eternity. Is 45:17
Who but * has said that these Is 45:21
For there is no other * but me—a Is 45:21
just * and a Savior—no, not one! Is 45:21
For I am *; Is 45:22
I will be your * through all Is 46:4
your wealth and make a * from it! Is 46:6
For I am *—I only—and there is no Is 46:9
You say, "I alone am *! Is 47:8
depending on the * of Israel. Is 48:1
I alone am *. Is 48:12
And now the Lord * and his Spirit Is 48:16
I am the Lord your *, who punishes Is 48:17
me by my name. * will make my Is 49:2
with *, and you shall bring me Is 49:3
Yet I leave it all with * for my Is 49:4
The Lord * says, "See, I will Is 49:22
The Lord * has given me his words Is 50:4
The Lord * has spoken to me and Is 50:5
Because the Lord * helps me, I Is 50:7
See, the Lord * is for me! Is 50:9
Lord, let them rely upon their *. Is 50:10
today, the mighty * who dried up Is 51:10
And yet you have no fear of *, Is 51:13
For I am the Lord your *, the Is 51:15
the Lord your * who cares for his Is 51:22
yourselves with strength [from * Is 52:1
for sinners—those who turn from * Is 52:1
news that the * of Israel reigns. Is 52:7
* bring his people home again. Is 52:8
shall see the salvation of our *. Is 52:10
you, and he, the * of Israel, will Is 52:12
To whom will * reveal his saving Is 53:1
from *, for his own sins! Is 53:4
our own. Yet * laid on him the Is 53:6
righteous before *, for he shall Is 53:11
and he pled with * for sinners. Is 53:12
of Israel, the * of all the earth. Is 54:5
Lord your *, have glorified you. Is 55:5
*, for he will abundantly pardon! Is 55:7
AND fair to all, the Lord * says. Is 56:1
For the Lord * who brings back Is 56:8
No one seems to realize that * is Is 57:1
There is no peace, says my *, Is 57:21
the commandments of their *! Is 58:2
If you do these things, * will Is 58:8
your sins have cut you off from *. Is 59:2
You look for * to keep you, but Is 59:11
*, and testify against you. Is 59:12
we have denied the Lord our *. Is 59:13
the name of * from west to east. Is 59:19
incense to add to the praise of *. Is 60:6
for the Lord your * will be your Is 60:19
THE SPIRIT OF the Lord * is upon Is 61:1
For * has planted them like strong Is 61:3
of the Lord, ministers of our *. Is 61:6
they are a people * has blessed. Is 61:9
Let me tell you how happy * has Is 61:10
or to cry out to * on her behalf Is 62:1
* will confer on you a new name. Is 62:2
or the "Land that * Forgot." Is 62:4
a virgin; and * will rejoice over Is 62:5
on your walls who shall cry to * Is 62:6,7
who pray, and give * no rest until Is 62:6,7
you shall keep it, praising *. Is 62:9
I, the Lord your *, am coming to Is 62:11
and "The City * Has Blessed." Is 62:12
tell of the lovingkindnesses of *. Is 63:7
Where is the * who sent his Holy Is 63:11
destroyed her. O *, why do you Is 63:19
or heard of such a * as ours, who Is 64:4
Therefore the Lord * says, You Is 65:13
for the Lord * will slay you and Is 65:15
shall swear by the * of Truth; Is 65:16
* will not accept their offerings. Is 66:3
ox on the altar of *, it is no more Is 66:3
is as loathsome to * as putting a Is 66:3
Hear the words of *, all you who Is 66:5
"Glory to *," they scoff. Is 66:5
asks the Lord your *. Is 66:9
the good hand of * upon his people, Is 66:14
"O Lord *," I said, "I can't Jer 1:6
their glorious * for silly idols! Jer 2:10,11
the Lord your * when he wanted to Jer 2:17
the Lord your *, fearlessly Jer 2:19
says the Lord, the * of Hosts. Jer 2:19
always before me, the Lord * says. Jer 2:22
*: Have I been unjust to Israel? Jer 2:31
say, "At last we are free from *; Jer 2:31
How can you disown your * like Jer 2:32
haven't done a thing to anger *. Jer 2:35
was only faked, the Lord * says. Jer 3:10
the Lord your * and committed Jer 3:13
backs on * and wandered far away. Jer 3:21
come, for you are the Lord our *. Jer 3:22
Only in the Lord our * can Israel Jer 3:23
childhood against the Lord our *; Jer 3:25
alone, the living *, and begin to Jer 4:2
They don't know the ways of *. Jer 5:4
too had utterly rejected their *. Jer 5:5
Therefore this is what the Lord * Jer 5:14
the Lord * asks. Jer 5:22
Isn't such a * to be feared and Jer 5:22
the Lord * asks. Jer 5:29
The word of * has angered them; Jer 6:10
of the wrath of * against them. Jer 6:11
The Lord * says, See the armies Jer 6:22
listen to this message from *. Jer 7:2
The Lord of Hosts, the * of Jer 7:3
the Lord is here, * will never let Jer 7:4
So the Lord * says, I will pour Jer 7:20
The Lord of Hosts, the * of Jer 7:21
your * and you shall be my people; Jer 7:23
its *, and refuses to be taught. Jer 7:28
They don't accept the laws of *. Jer 8:7
For the Lord our * has decreed Jer 8:14
"Has * deserted us?" Jer 8:19
Why doesn't * do something? Jer 8:22
Lord of Hosts, the * of Israel, Jer 9:15
Listen to the words of *, O Jer 9:20
there stands their * like a Jer 10:5
Don't be afraid of such a * for Jer 10:5
O Lord, there is no other * like Jer 10:6
But the Lord is the only true *, Jer 10:10
living *, the everlasting King. Jer 10:10
earth, but our * formed the earth Jer 10:12
of * bow before their idols. Jer 10:14
But the * of Jacob is not like Jer 10:16
they no longer follow * nor ask Jer 10:21
be mine and I would be their *. Jer 11:4
fathers made with *, and do all the Jer 11:6
They say, "Thank *!" Jer 12:2
Judge them, O *! Jer 12:3
Yet the people say, "* won't Jer 12:4
the land * gave his people Israel: Jer 12:14
claim me as their * instead of Baal Jer 12:16
Tell them this: The Lord * of Jer 13:12
Give glory to the Lord your * Jer 13:16
Then I said, O Lord *, their Jer 14:13
What heathen * can give us rain? Jer 14:22
Who but you alone, O Lord our *, Jer 14:22
I sit alone beneath the hand of * Jer 15:17,18
ON YET ANOTHER occasion * spoke Jer 16:1
For the Lord of Hosts, the * of Jer 16:9
our sin against the Lord our *?" Jer 16:10
will be that * is bringing his Jer 16:14,15
Can men make *? Jer 16:20
at last that I alone am *. Jer 16:21
and turns his heart away from *. Jer 17:5
*, why don't they come true?" Jer 17:15
whatever of doing what * says. Jer 18:12
The Lord of Hosts, the * of Jer 19:3
Lord of Hosts, the * of Israel, Jer 19:15
which * overthrew without mercy. Jer 20:16
tell him the Lord * of Israel says, Jer 21:3,4
this message from *, O king of Jer 22:2
the Lord their * and violated his Jer 22:9
That is why * blessed him. Jer 22:15
is how a man lives close to *. Jer 22:16
for * has decreed holy words of Jer 23:9
and the curse of * is on it. Jer 23:10
to * to hear what he is saying? Jer 23:18
Am I a * who is only in one Jer 23:23
had from * last night," they say. Jer 23:25
say, "This message is from *!" Jer 23:30,31
sad news from *," I will punish Jer 23:34
from *" that I didn't speak. Jer 23:36
sad news from *," when I have Jer 23:38,39
then I, the Lord *, will unburden Jer 23:38,39
I will be their *, for they shall Jer 24:7
Judah, until now, * has been Jer 25:2,3
through the years, * has sent you Jer 25:4
And now the Lord * of Hosts says, Jer 25:8,9
For the Lord * said to me: "Take Jer 25:15
it—every nation * had sent me to; Jer 25:17
Lord of Hosts, the * of Israel, Jer 25:27
the Lord your *, he will cancel all Jer 26:13
in the name of the Lord our *." Jer 26:16
the people that * said: 'This hill Jer 26:18
us the messages of *, who knows Jer 26:19
who knows what * will do to us!" Jer 26:19
Lord of Hosts, the * of Israel, Jer 27:4
"The Lord of Hosts, the * of Jer 28:2
prove that * has really sent him. Jer 28:9
known that he really is from *." Jer 28:9
The Lord of Hosts, the * of Jer 28:14
The Lord of Hosts, the * of Jer 29:4
The Lord of Hosts, the * of Jer 29:8
Therefore listen to the word of * Jer 29:20
The Lord of Hosts, the * of Jer 29:21
The Lord of Hosts, the * of Jer 29:25
The Lord * of Israel says, Write Jer 30:2
before. Yet * will rescue them! Jer 30:7
their *, and David their King, Jer 30:9
whom * has raised up for them. Jer 30:9
be my people and I will be your *. Jer 30:2
go up to Zion to the Lord our *." Jer 31:
for you alone are the Lord, my *. Jer 31:1
I turned away from * but I was Jer 31:1
The Lord of Hosts, the * of Jer 31:2
my people and I will be their *. Jer 31:3
"The Lord of Hosts, * of Israel, Jer 32:1
For the Lord of Hosts, * of Jer 32:1
"O Lord *! Jer 32:1
you are the great and mighty *, Jer 32:1
I am the Lord, the * of all Jer 32:2
Now therefore the Lord * of Jer 32:3
my people and I will be their *. Jer 32:3
king of Judah: * says you won't be Jer 34:4
The Lord, the * of Israel, says: Jer 34:1
The Lord of Hosts, the * of Jer 35:1
Therefore the Lord * of Hosts, Jer 35:1
God of Hosts, the * of Israel, Jer 35:1
Lord of Hosts, the * of Israel, Jer 35:18,1
these curses of * have been Jer 36:7
the messages from *, he went down Jer 36:1
"The Lord, the * of Israel, Jer 37:7
before Almighty * his Creator that Jer 38:16
"The Lord, the * of Hosts, the God Jer 38:17
God of Hosts, the * of Israel, Jer 38:17
Lord of Hosts, the * of Israel, Jer 39:16
"The Lord your * has brought this Jer 40:2,3
to the Lord your *, for as you know Jer 42:2
Beg the Lord your * to show us Jer 42:3
"May the curse of * be on us if we Jer 42:5
obey the Lord our *, to whom we Jer 42:6
to the Lord, the * of Israel, with Jer 42:9
Lord of Hosts, the * of Israel, Jer 42:15
"For the Lord of Hosts, the * of Jer 42:18
us what * says and we will do it!' Jer 42:20
this message from * to all the Jer 43:1
The Lord our * hasn't told you to Jer 43:2,3
Lord of Hosts, the * of Israel, Jer 43:10
THIS IS THE message * gave to Jer 44:1
The Lord of Hosts, the * of Jer 44:2,3
And now the Lord, the * of Hosts, Jer 44:7
God of Hosts, the * of Israel, asks Jer 44:7
Lord of Hosts, the * of Israel, Jer 44:11
to your false 'Messages from *'! Jer 44:16
The Lord of Hosts, the * of Jer 44:25
saying, 'O Lord our *, help us!' Jer 44:26
O Baruch, the Lord * of Israel Jer 45:2
day of the Lord * of Hosts, a day Jer 46:10
for the Lord * of Hosts will Jer 46:10
Then * gave Jeremiah this message Jer 46:13
Why has Apis, your bull *, fled Jer 46:15
The Lord of Hosts, the * of Jer 46:25
will punish Amon, * of Thebes, and Jer 46:25
the * of Israel, against Moab: Jer 48:1
shall perish. Your * Chemosh, with Jer 48:7
do the work that * has given them! Jer 48:10
the people of the * Chemosh are Jer 48:46
hedges, for your * Milcom shall be Jer 49:3
you, says the Lord * of Hosts. Jer 49:5
be destroyed; her * Marduk will be Jer 50:2
and seeking the Lord their *. Jer 50:4
the Lord, the * of justice, the Jer 50:7
Lord of Hosts, the * of Israel, Jer 50:18
work of the Lord, the * of Hosts. Jer 50:25
how the Lord their * has broken Jer 50:28
kings called by * from many lands. Jer 50:41
He is still their *, but the land Jer 51:5
be destroyed when * takes his Jer 51:6
for * is judging her from heaven. Jer 51:9
all the Lord our * has done. Jer 51:10
* made the earth by his power and Jer 51:15
And the time is coming when * Jer 51:18
But the * of Israel is no idol! Jer 51:19
Cyrus was used of * to conquer Jer 51:20f
For the Lord of Hosts, the * of Jer 51:33
And I will punish Bel, the * of Jer 51:44
for the Lord * gives just Jer 51:56
terrible things * had scheduled Jer 51:60
the enemy attacks. * burns across Lam 2:3
in the night and cry to your *. Lam 2:19
Although * gives him grief, yet Lam 3:32
gates! Yet * permitted it because Lam 4:13
and elders who stayed true to *. Lam 4:16
to me and I saw visions from *. Eze 1:1
like the voice of *, or like the Eze 1:24
messages of the Lord *. Eze 2:4
This is what the Lord * says!" Eze 3:11
I was helpless in the hand of *, Eze 3:22
to them: The Lord * says, Let Eze 3:27
Then I said, "O Lord *, must I Eze 4:14
The Lord * says, "This Eze 5:5,6,7
Therefore the Lord * says, I, Eze 5:8
of the Lord * against you and Eze 6:3
that I alone am *, and that I Eze 6:10
"The Lord * says: Raise your Eze 6:11
will realize that I alone am *. Eze 6:13
MESSAGE came to me from *: Eze 7:1
The Lord * says: "With one blow Eze 7:5,6
for the wrath of * is on the land. Eze 7:12
will be gone, for * has spoken Eze 7:13

(GOD Con't)

power of the Lord * fell upon me.	Eze 8:1
Suddenly the glory of the * of	Eze 8:4
The women wept for Tammuz, the *	Eze 8:14f
their *.	Eze 8:14
And the glory of the * of Israel	Eze 9:3
my face and cried out: "O Lord *!	Eze 9:8
voice of Almighty * when he speaks	Eze 10:5
And the glory of the * of Israel	Eze 10:19
seen beneath the * of Israel beside	Eze 10:20
"Therefore the Lord * says: You	Eze 11:7
says the Lord *, and I will take	Eze 11:8
out: "O Lord *, are you going to	Eze 11:13
that the Lord * says: Although I	Eze 11:16
hearts of love for *, so that you	Eze 11:19
my people, and I will be your *.	Eze 11:20
for their sins," the Lord * says.	Eze 11:21
the * of Israel stood above them.	Eze 11:22
Afterwards the Spirit of *	Eze 11:24
Tell them the Lord * says it is	Eze 12:10
people, the Lord * says that the	Eze 12:19
The Lord * says, I will put an	Eze 12:23
says the Lord *.	Eze 12:25
Lord * says, All delay has ended!	Eze 12:28
you said, 'My message is from *!'	Eze 13:6
is from God!' * did not send you.	Eze 13:6
message is from *,' when I never	Eze 13:7
"Therefore the Lord * says: I	Eze 13:8
people by saying, '* will send	Eze 13:10
The Lord * says: I will sweep it	Eze 13:13
is no peace, says the Lord *.	Eze 13:16
Tell them the Lord * says: Woe	Eze 13:18
Tell them, the Lord * says: I	Eze 14:4
them that the Lord * says: Repent	Eze 14:6,7
but to be my people and I their *.	Eze 14:11
of Israel, says the Lord *.	Eze 14:14
here, the Lord * swears that it	Eze 14:16
the land, the Lord * declares that	Eze 14:18
there, the Lord * says that only	Eze 14:20
"This is what I mean, the Lord *	Eze 15:5,6
worship idols," says the Lord *.	Eze 15:8
Tell her, the Lord * says: You	Eze 16:3
their backs to all knowledge of *.	Eze 16:3f
gifts I gave you, says the Lord *.	Eze 16:14
you, says the Lord *— you built a	Eze 16:23
*, to do such things as these;	Eze 16:30
"The Lord * says: Because I see	Eze 16:36
"As I live, the Lord * says,	Eze 16:48
"For the Lord * says: I will	Eze 16:59,60
you have done, says the Lord *."	Eze 16:63
"The Lord * asks: Shall I let	Eze 17:9
"The Lord * says: As I live,	Eze 17:19
"The Lord * says: I, myself,	Eze 17:22,23
As I live, says the Lord *, you	Eze 18:3
obey the laws of *, but worships	Eze 18:11
so that he fears * and decides	Eze 18:14
seeing you die, the Lord * says.	Eze 18:32
Israel: The Lord * says: How dare	Eze 20:3
Tell them the Lord * says: When	Eze 20:5,6
gods, for I am the Lord your *.	Eze 20:7
laugh at Israel's * who couldn't	Eze 20:9,10
idols, for I am the Lord your *.	Eze 20:19
that I am the Lord your *.	Eze 20:20
that I alone am *, I let them	Eze 20:26
them that the Lord * says: Your	Eze 20:27,28
"The Lord * wants to know	Eze 20:30
As I live, the Lord * says, I	Eze 20:31
"O Israel, the Lord * says: If	Eze 20:39
Then I said, "O Lord *, they say	Eze 20:49
fearsome news that * has given me.	Eze 21:7
And the Lord * says: Your doom is	Eze 21:7
this message came to me from *:	Eze 21:8
the Lord * asks.	Eze 21:13
"The Lord * says: Again and	Eze 21:24
jeweled crown, the Lord * says.	Eze 21:26
The things of * are all	Eze 22:8
and my commands, the Lord * says.	Eze 22:12
Therefore the Lord * says:	Eze 22:18,19,20
To them the things of * are no	Eze 22:26
claim are from *, when he hasn't	Eze 22:28
And so the Lord * says: I will	Eze 22:31
"And now the Lord * says that he	Eze 23:22
For the Lord * says: I will	Eze 23:28
"The Lord * says: Bring an army	Eze 23:46
you will know that I alone am *."	Eze 23:49
tell them the Lord * says: Put a	Eze 24:3
"For the Lord * says: Woe to	Eze 24:6
example to you, the Lord * says.	Eze 24:24
Listen to what the Lord * says.	Eze 25:3
"For the Lord * says: Because	Eze 25:6
"And the Lord * says: Because	Eze 25:8
"And the Lord * says: Because	Eze 25:12
"And the Lord * says: Because	Eze 25:15
"Therefore the Lord * says: I	Eze 26:3
I have spoken it, says the Lord *.	Eze 26:5
"For the Lord * says: I will	Eze 26:7
"For the Lord * says: I will	Eze 26:19
of the world, the Lord * speaks.	Eze 27:3
of Tyre: The Lord * says: You are	Eze 28:2,3
you think you are *, sitting on the	Eze 28:2,3
on the throne of a * on your island	Eze 28:2,3
a man, and not a *, though you	Eze 28:2,3
you boast yourself to be like *.	Eze 28:2,3
"Therefore the Lord * says:	Eze 28:6
you are as wise as *, an enemy	Eze 28:6
Then will you boast as a *?	Eze 28:9
you will be no *, but merely man!	Eze 28:9
For I have spoken it, the Lord *	Eze 28:10
Tell him, the Lord * says: You	Eze 28:12
You were in Eden, the garden of *;	Eze 28:13
access to the holy mountain of *.	Eze 28:14
of * like a common sinner.	Eze 28:16
"The Lord * says: I am your	Eze 28:22
know I am the Lord their *."	Eze 28:26
Tell them that the Lord * says:	Eze 29:3
Therefore the Lord * says: I	Eze 29:8
"But the Lord * says that at the	Eze 29:13
will know that I alone am *."	Eze 29:16
Therefore, the Lord * says, I	Eze 29:19
and say: The Lord * says, Weep, for	Eze 30:2,3
"For the Lord * says:	Eze 30:10
For, the Lord * says, I am	Eze 30:22
than any other in the garden of *;	Eze 31:8
and arrogant, the Lord * says.	Eze 31:10
"The Lord * says: When she fell	Eze 31:15
"The Lord * says: I will send a	Eze 32:3
"For the Lord * says: The sword	Eze 32:11
as olive oil, the Lord * says.	Eze 32:14
his army slain, says the Lord *.	Eze 32:31
says the Lord *, I have no pleasure	Eze 33:11
But the Lord * says: You are	Eze 33:25
"Tell them: The Lord * says: As	Eze 33:27
to them: The Lord * says to you:	Eze 34:2
"As I live, says the Lord *, you	Eze 34:8
"For the Lord * says: I will	Eze 34:11
down in peace, the Lord * says.	Eze 34:15,16
people—the Lord * says, I will	Eze 34:17
"Therefore the Lord * says: I	Eze 34:20
will be their *, and my Servant	Eze 34:24
I, the Lord their *, am with them,	Eze 34:30
are my people, says the Lord *.	Eze 34:30
You are my men and I am your *,	Eze 34:31
"The Lord * says: I am against	Eze 35:3
As I live, the Lord * says,	Eze 35:6
What do we care that * is there!'	Eze 35:10
Therefore as I live, the Lord *	Eze 35:11
hear the word of the Lord *.	Eze 36:4
Israel: The Lord * says, I am full	Eze 36:6
"The Lord * says: Now the other	Eze 36:13
of sinners, the Lord * says."	Eze 36:15
are the people of * and he couldn't	Eze 36:20
Israel: The Lord * says, I am	Eze 36:22
be my people and I will be your *.	Eze 36:28
"The Lord * says: When I cleanse	Eze 36:33
"The Lord * says: I am ready to	Eze 36:37,38
of *, for the Lord God says, See!	Eze 37:4
of God, for the Lord * says, See!	Eze 37:5
So I spoke these words from *,	Eze 37:7
say: "The Lord * says: Come from	Eze 37:9
But tell them, the Lord * says:	Eze 37:12
doing), the Lord * says: I will	Eze 37:18,19,20
"For the Lord * says: I am	Eze 37:21
truly be my people and I their *.	Eze 37:23
Yes, I will be their * and they	Eze 37:27
forces opposed to *, especially in	Eze 38:2,3f
Tell him that the Lord * says: I	Eze 38:2,3
"The Lord * says to Gog: When my	Eze 38:14
the nations will know that I am *.	Eze 38:15,16
"The Lord * says: You are the	Eze 38:17
you, says the Lord *, and you will	Eze 38:21
I have done, and know that I am *!	Eze 38:23
for I have spoken, the Lord *	Eze 39:5
valiant warriors, says the Lord *.	Eze 39:20
will know I am the Lord their *.	Eze 39:22
in treachery against their *.	Eze 39:23
"But now, the Lord * says, I	Eze 39:25
am the Lord their *—responsible for	Eze 39:28
upon them, says the Lord *."	Eze 39:29
And suddenly the glory of the *	Eze 43:2
"Son of dust, the Lord * says:	Eze 43:18
accept you, says the Lord *."	Eze 43:27
for the Lord, the * of Israel,	Eze 44:2
Israel, The Lord * says: O Israel,	Eze 44:6
have no heart for *—when you offer	Eze 44:7
"The Lord * says: No foreigner	Eze 44:9
strayed away from * to idols must	Eze 44:10
*, that they must be punished.	Eze 44:12
the sacrifices, says the Lord *.	Eze 44:15
for himself, the Lord * says.	Eze 44:27
For the Lord * says to the	Eze 45:9
who bring them, says the Lord *.	Eze 45:15
"The Lord * says: On each New	Eze 45:18
"THE LORD * says, the inner	Eze 46:1
"The Lord * says: If the prince	Eze 46:16
"The Lord * says:	Eze 47:13
to each tribe, says the Lord *.	Eze 48:29
the city will be 'The City of *.'	Eze 48:35
from the Temple of *, and placed	Dan 1:1
of his * in the land of Shinar.	Dan 1:1
Now as it happened, * had given	Dan 1:9
* gave these four youths great	Dan 1:17
of the time, and * gave to Daniel	Dan 1:17
They asked the * of heaven to	Dan 2:18
And that night in a vision *	Dan 2:19
Then Daniel praised the * of	Dan 2:19
be the name of * forever and ever,	Dan 2:20
I thank and praise you, O * of	Dan 2:23
but there is a * in heaven who	Dan 2:28
of your dream, for * showed it to	Dan 2:30
kings, for the * of heaven has	Dan 2:37
under your control, as * decreed.	Dan 2:38
those kings, the * of heaven will	Dan 2:44
"Thus the great * has shown what	Dan 2:45
king said, "your * is the God of	Dan 2:47
"your God is the * of gods, Ruler	Dan 2:47
And what * can deliver you out of	Dan 3:15
our * is able to deliver us;	Dan 3:17
And the fourth looks like a *!"	Dan 3:25
servants of the Most High *!	Dan 3:26
"Blessed be the * of Shadrach,	Dan 3:28
or worship any * except their own.	Dan 3:28
who speaks a word against the *	Dan 3:29
For no other * can do what this	Dan 3:29
that the Most High * did to me.	Dan 4:2
after my *—the man in whom is the	Dan 4:8
"Your Majesty, the Most High *	Dan 4:24
that the Most High * dominates the	Dan 4:25
Perhaps even yet * will spare	Dan 4:27
realize that * parcels out the	Dan 4:32
the Most High * and honored him who	Dan 4:34
as though he were himself a *.	Dan 5:11
Your Majesty, the Most High *	Dan 5:18
hardened in pride, * removed him	Dan 5:20
But you have not praised the *	Dan 5:23
And so * sent those fingers to	Dan 5:24,25
"Mene means 'numbered'—* has	Dan 5:26
asks a favor of * or man—except	Dan 6:7
had, giving thanks to his *.	Dan 6:10
there, asking favors of his *.	Dan 6:11
petitions to any * or man—except	Dan 6:12
He is asking favors of his *	Dan 6:13
to him, "May your *, whom you	Dan 6:16
of the Living *, was your God, whom	Dan 6:20
God, was your *, whom you worship	Dan 6:20
"My * has sent his angel," he	Dan 6:22
for I am innocent before *, nor,	Dan 6:22
him, because he believed in his *.	Dan 6:23
fear before the * of Daniel in	Dan 6:25,26
For his * is the living,	Dan 6:25,26
living, unchanging * whose kingdom	Dan 6:25,26
Almighty *—sat down to judge.	Dan 7:9
against Almighty *, and the	Dan 7:11
of the Most High * shall rule the	Dan 7:18
He will defy the Most High *,	Dan 7:25
shall be given to the people of *;	Dan 7:27
He fought against the people of *	Dan 8:10
by the hand of *, though no human	Dan 8:25
with the Lord * [to end our	Dan 9:3
"you are a great and awesome *;	Dan 9:4
"But the Lord our * is merciful,	Dan 9:9
"O Lord our *, we have disobeyed	Dan 9:10
And so the awesome curse of * has	Dan 9:11
the Lord our * by turning from our	Dan 9:13
O Lord our *, you brought	Dan 9:15
"O our *, hear your servant's	Dan 9:17
"O my *, bend down your ear and	Dan 9:18
own sake, O my *, because your	Dan 9:19
with the Lord my * for Jerusalem,	Dan 9:20
it was, for * loves you very much.	Dan 9:23
utterly defile the sanctuary of *.	Dan 9:27
greatly beloved of *," he said,	Dan 10:11
you, for * has sent me to you."	Dan 10:11
* loves you very much," he said;	Dan 10:19
those who hate the things of *,	Dan 11:32
But the people who know their *	Dan 11:32
in the things of * will stumble in	Dan 11:35
greater than every * there is, even	Dan 11:36
blaspheming the * of gods, and	Dan 11:36
nor for the * beloved of women,	Dan 11:37
Tammuz-Adonis, a Babylonian *.	Dan 11:37f
nor any other *, for he will	Dan 11:37
he will worship the Fortress *	Dan 11:38
Literally, "the * of	Dan 11:38f
—a * his fathers never knew—and	Dan 11:38
wise—the people of *—shall shine as	Dan 12:3
a daughter. And * said to Hosea,	Hos 1:6
to a son. And * said, "Call him	Hos 1:9
is not mine and I am not her *.	Hos 1:9
sons, children of the Living *.'	Hos 1:10
be—the day when * will sow his	Hos 1:11
"the day of Jezreel ('* sows')";	Hos 1:11f
now * will have mercy upon her!	Hos 1:11
used in worshiping Baal, her *!	Hos 1:8
used in reference to the true *.	Hos 1:16f
sing together that "* sows!"	Hos 1:21,22
will reply, "You are our *!"	Hos 1:23
*, and to the Messiah, their King,	Hos 3:5
no knowledge of * in your land.	Hos 4:1
They exchanged the glory of * for	Hos 4:7
let you come to * again, for the	Hos 5:4
to sacrifice to *, but it will be	Hos 5:6
yet he doesn't return to his *,	Hos 7:10
to heaven, to the Most High *.	Hos 7:16

(GOD Con't)

upon the people of * because they Hos 8:1
"Help us, for you are our *!" Hos 8:2
It is not *! Hos 8:6
have deserted your * and sacrificed Hos 9:1
stay here in this land of *; Hos 9:3
pour out wine for sacrifice to *. Hos 9:4
but may not offer it to *. Hos 9:4
only hatred for those who love *. Hos 9:7
Baal-peor, the * of Peor, a city Hos 9:10f
monarchy, hated of *, was Hos 9:15f
My * will destroy the people of Hos 9:17
of her people are false toward *. Hos 10:2
must be punished. * will break down Hos 10:2
For I am * and not man; Hos 11:9
* and is faithful to the Holy One. Hos 11:12
a man, he even fought with *. Hos 12:3
He met * there at Bethel face to Hos 12:4
face to face. * spoke to him— the Hos 12:4
to him— the Lord, the * of Hosts; Hos 12:5
Oh, come back to *. Hos 12:6
expecting much from him, your *. Hos 12:6
I am the same Lord, the same *, Hos 12:9
I alone am *, your Lord, and have Hos 13:4
You have no * but me, for there Hos 13:4
for she rebelled against her *. Hos 13:16
to the Lord, your *, for you have Hos 14:1
crying of these ministers of *. Joe 1:9
O ministers of my *, lie all Joe 1:13
your *, and weep before him there. Joe 1:14
be ended in the Temple of our *. Joe 1:16
Return to the Lord your *, for Joe 2:13
The priests, the ministers of *, Joe 2:17
"Spare your people, O our *; Joe 2:17
say, 'Where is this * of theirs? Joe 2:17
rejoice in the Lord your *! Joe 2:23
that I alone am the Lord, your *. Joe 2:27
your * in Zion, my holy mountain. Joe 3:17
One day, in a vision, * told him Amo 1:2
laws of *, refusing to obey him. Amo 2:4
The Lord * has spoken. Amo 2:16
The Lord * has sounded your Amo 3:8
Therefore," the Lord * says, Amo 3:11
says the Lord, the * of Hosts: Amo 3:13
The Lord * has sworn by his Amo 4:2
Prepare to meet your * in Amo 4:12
the * of Hosts, is his name." Amo 4:13
For the Lord * says, "The Amo 5:3
Then the Lord * of Hosts will Amo 5:14
Perhaps even yet the Lord * of Amo 5:15
Therefore the Lord * of Hosts Amo 5:16
here, for then * would deliver us Amo 5:18
in Kaiwan, your * of the stars, Amo 5:25,26,27
says the Lord, the * of Hosts. Amo 5:25,26,27
Jehovah, the Lord * of Hosts, has Amo 6:8
says the Lord, the * of Hosts. Amo 6:14
THIS IS WHAT the Lord * showed me Amo 7:1
Then I said, "O Lord *, please Amo 7:2
Then the Lord * showed me a great Amo 7:4
Then I said, "O Lord *, please Amo 7:5
THEN THE LORD * showed me, in a Amo 8:1
says the Lord *, "when I will send Amo 8:11
thirsting for the Word of *. Amo 8:13
The Lord * of Hosts touches the Amo 9:5
"The eyes of the Lord * are Amo 9:8
sinners who say, '* will not touch Amo 9:10
up again," says the Lord your *. Amo 9:15
In a vision the Lord * showed Ob 1:1
he said, "that * has sent an Ob 1:1
Get up and cry to your *, and see Jon 1:6
I worship Jehovah, the * of Jon 1:9,10
a prayer to Jehovah, Jonah's *. Jon 1:14
Lord his * from inside the fish: Jon 2:1
But, O Lord my *, you have Jon 2:6
cry mightily to *, and let everyone Jon 3:8
Perhaps even yet * will decide to Jon 3:9
And when * saw that they had put Jon 3:10
For I knew you were a gracious *, Jon 4:2
But * also prepared a worm! Jon 4:7
Then, when the sun was hot, * Jon 4:8
And * said to Jonah, "Is it Jon 4:9
But the Lord * says, I will Mic 2:3
finished, ruined. * has confiscated Mic 2:4
you, with never a word from *. Mic 3:6
your messages were not from *. Mic 3:7
see the Temple of the * of Israel; Mic 4:2
the Lord our * forever and ever, Mic 4:5
ages past! * will abandon his Mic 5:3
of the Lord his *, and his people Mic 5:4
and to walk humbly with your *. Mic 6:8
How could * be just while saying Mic 6:11
I wait for * to save me; Mic 7:7
have done to me. * will bring me Mic 7:9
Then my enemy will see that * is Mic 7:10
me, "Where is that * of yours?" Mic 7:10
Your cities, people of *, will be Mic 7:11
fortresses to meet the Lord our *. Mic 7:17
Where is another * like you, who Mic 7:18
THIS IS THE vision * gave to Nah 1:1
* is jealous over those he loves; Nah 1:2
Who can stand before an angry *? Nah 1:6
For the land of the people of * Nah 2:2
sold herself to the enemies of *. Nah 3:4
Habakkuk in a vision from *: Hab 1:1
O Lord my *, my Holy One, you who Hab 1:12
Surely not! O * our Rock, you Hab 1:12
* will give to my complaint. Hab 2:1
Can images speak for *? Hab 2:19
I see * moving across the deserts Hab 3:3
What a wonderful * he is! Hab 3:3
I will be happy in the * of my Hab 3:18
The Lord * is my Strength, and Hab 3:19
indifferent to *, thinking he will Zep 1:12
It is a day of the wrath of * Zep 1:15
For the Lord * will visit his Zep 2:7
the Lord of Hosts, * of Israel, Zep 2:9
listen even to the voice of *. Zep 3:2
trust the Lord, nor seek for *. Zep 3:2
asking me to be their * again. Zep 3:10
For the Lord your * has arrived Zep 3:17,18
message from the Lord their *; Hag 1:12
Peace with * through Christ who, Hag 2:8,9f
"Come, return to me," the Lord * Zec 1:4
we deserved from *," they said. Zec 1:5,6
the Holy Land, for * shall once Zec 2:11,12
are from *, the Lord of Hosts. Zec 4:9
been from *, the Lord of Hosts. Zec 6:15
commandments of the Lord your *." Zec 6:15
holy feasts to *, you don't think Zec 7:6
the words that *, the Lord of Zec 7:12
wrath came down on them from *. Zec 7:12
I will be their *, just and true Zec 8:8
Literally, "I will be their * in Zec 8:8f
for I know that * is with you.' Zec 8:23
Everyone left will worship * and Zec 9:7
the Lord * shall sound the Zec 9:14
The Lord their * will save his Zec 9:16,17
warriors for *, grinding their Zec 10:5
their *, will hear their cries. Zec 10:6
remember me and return again to *; Zec 10:9
through when * brought them out of Zec 10:11f
Then said the Lord my * to me, Zec 11:4
'Thank *, now I am rich!' Zec 11:5
realized that * was telling them Zec 11:11
in the Lord of Hosts, their *.' Zec 12:5
And the royal line will be as *, Zec 12:8
will say, 'The Lord is our *.' Zec 13:9
and the Lord my * shall come, and Zec 14:5
But if Egypt refuses to come, * Zec 14:18
'Those Whom * Does Not Forgive.' Mal 1:4
* is doing all around the world; Mal 1:5
very valuable to offer to *!' Mal 1:7
" '* have mercy on us,' you Mal 1:9
you recite; '* be gracious to us!' Mal 1:9
lame and sick—as offerings to *! Mal 1:13
a sick one to sacrifice to *. Mal 1:14
the knowledge of * so the people Mal 2:7
all created by the same *. Mal 2:10
"Why has * abandoned us?" Mal 2:14
For the Lord, the * of Israel, Mal 2:16
Or by saying that * won't punish Mal 2:17
the ministers of *, refining them Mal 3:3
their work for * with pure hearts. Mal 3:3
"Will a man rob *? Mal 3:8
And so the awesome curse of * is Mal 3:9
foolish to worship * and obey him. Mal 3:14,15
and those who dare * to punish them Mal 3:14,15
(meaning "* is with us").' Mt 1:23
to Herod, for * had warned them in Mt 2:12
turn to *. Mt 3:2
escape the coming wrath of *? Mt 3:7
That proves nothing. * can Mt 3:9
Literally, "* is able of these Mt 3:9f
saw the Spirit of * coming down in Mt 3:16
you are the Son of *," he said. Mt 4:3
every word of * is what we need." Mt 4:4
"and prove you are the Son of *; Mt 4:6
for the Scriptures declare, '* Mt 4:6
Lord your * to a foolish test!" Mt 4:7
say, 'Worship only the Lord * Mt 4:10
sin, and turn to *, for the Kingdom Mt 4:17
are pure, for they shall see *. Mt 5:8
shall be called the sons of *. Mt 5:9
a sacrifice to *, and suddenly Mt 5:23
and offer your sacrifice to *. Mt 5:24
to *, but must fulfill them all.' Mt 5:33
is a sacred vow to *, for the Mt 5:34
"You cannot serve two masters: * Mt 6:24
And if * cares so wonderfully Mt 6:30
about tomorrow. * will take care of Mt 6:34
do you want with us, O Son of *? Mt 8:29
This man is saying he is *!" Mt 9:3
How they praised * for giving Mt 9:8
the self-righteous, back to *." Mt 9:13
Fear only * who can destroy both Mt 10:28
they are welcoming * who sent me. Mt 10:40
he is a man of *, you will be given Mt 10:41
Or a prophet of *? Mt 11:9
because they hadn't turned to *. Mt 11:20
Cities destroyed by * for their Mt 11:21f
Cities destroyed by * for their Mt 11:23f
by the Spirit of *, then the Mt 12:28
of * has arrived among you. Mt 12:28
to * from all their evil ways. Mt 12:41
and understand and turn to * Mt 13:16
and he does less and less for *. Mt 13:22
"You really are the Son of *!" Mt 14:33
the direct commandments of *? Mt 15:3
Literally, "to *." Mt 15:5,6f
direct command of * to honor and Mt 15:5,6
laws instead of those from *.' Mt 15:9
and praised the * of Israel. Mt 15:31
and gave thanks to * for them, and Mt 15:36
the Son of the living *." Mt 16:16
"* has blessed you, Simon, son Mt 16:17
you turn to * from your sins and Mt 18:3
at the beginning * created man and Mt 19:4
And no man may divorce what * has Mt 19:5,6
what * had originally intended. Mt 19:8
"Only those whom * helps. Mt 19:11
you are calling me *," Jesus Mt 19:17
"for * alone is truly good. Mt 19:17
man to enter the Kingdom of *!" Mt 19:24
But with *, everything is Mt 19:26
"* bless King David's Son!" Mt 21:9
"Praise * in highest heaven!" Mt 21:9
Temple shouting, "* bless the Son Mt 21:15
the Baptist sent from *, or not?" Mt 21:25
"If we say, 'From *,' " they Mt 21:25
And if we deny that * sent him, Mt 21:26
repent and turn to *, and you Mt 21:32
the Kingdom of * shall be taken Mt 21:43
will give * his share of the crop. Mt 21:43
is his, and give * everything that Mt 22:21
everything that belongs to *." Mt 22:21
Don't you realize that * was Mt 22:31
* of Abraham, Isaac, and Jacob'? Mt 22:32
and Jacob'? So * is not the God of Mt 22:32
So God is not the * of the dead, Mt 22:32
in the presence of *, then God Mt 22:32f
of God, then * would have said, "I Mt 22:32f
"I was the * of Abraham, etc." Mt 22:32f
the Lord your * with all your Mt 22:37
'* said to my Lord, Sit at my Mt 22:44
For only * is your Rabbi and all Mt 23:8
'Father,' for only * in heaven Mt 23:9
by it, and by * who lives in it. Mt 23:21
Throne of * and by God himself. Mt 23:22
Throne of God and by * himself. Mt 23:22
stones all those * sends to her! Mt 23:37
the one sent to you from *." Mt 23:39
that * will smite the Shepherd, Mt 26:31
* and rebuild it in three days.' Mt 26:60,61
name of the living * that you tell Mt 26:63
to be the Messiah, the Son of *." Mt 26:63
sitting at the right hand of * Mt 26:64
cross if you are the Son of *!" Mt 27:40
He trusted *—let God show his Mt 27:41,42,43
He trusted God—let * show his Mt 27:41,42,43
which means, "My *, my God, why Mt 27:46
my *, why have you forsaken me?" Mt 27:46
Jesus the Messiah, the Son of *. Mk 1:1
prophet Isaiah, * announced that he Mk 1:2
sin, so that * could forgive them. Mk 1:4
who you are—the holy Son of *!" Mk 1:24
Does he think he is *? Mk 2:7
For only * can forgive sins." Mk 2:7
Then how they praised *. Mk 2:12
into the house of *—Abiathar was Mk 2:25,26
"You are the Son of *!" Mk 3:11
the Kingdom of * that are hidden to Mk 4:11,12
*, or be forgiven for their sins.' Mk 4:11,12
harvest for *—thirty, sixty, or Mk 4:20
what the Kingdom of * is like: Mk 4:26
can I describe the Kingdom of *? Mk 4:30
me, Jesus, Son of the Most High *? Mk 5:7,8
things * has done for you; Mk 5:19
they claim that * commands the Mk 7:6,7
*: 'Honor your father and mother.' Mk 7:10
For I have given to * what I Mk 7:11
And so you break the law of * Mk 7:12,13
you and make you unfit for *." Mk 7:23
loaves, thanked * for them, broke Mk 8:6
of * arrive in great power!" Mk 9:1
Better enter the Kingdom of * Mk 9:47
And no man may separate what * Mk 10:9
of * belongs to such as they. Mk 10:14
refuses to come to * as a little Mk 10:15
"Only * is truly good! Mk 10:18
to get into the Kingdom of *!" Mk 10:23
to enter the Kingdom of *. Mk 10:24
man to enter the Kingdom of *." Mk 10:25
*, it is utterly impossible. Mk 10:27
But with * everything is Mk 10:27
"Praise * for him who comes in Mk 11:9
"Praise * for the return of our Mk 11:10
only have faith in *—this is the Mk 11:22,23
Was he sent by *, or not? Mk 11:30
"If we reply that * sent him, Mk 11:31
But if we say * didn't send Mk 11:32
but sincerely teach the ways of *. Mk 12:14
But everything that belongs to * Mk 12:17
to God must be given to *!" Mk 12:17

(GOD Con't)	
and don't know the power of *.	Mk 12:24
the burning bush? * said to Moses,	Mk 12:26
God said to Moses, 'I am the * of	Mk 12:26
and I am the * of Isaac, and I am	Mk 12:26
Isaac, and I am the * of Jacob.'	Mk 12:26
"* was telling Moses that these	Mk 12:27
the *' of those who don't exist!	Mk 12:27
The Lord our * is the one and	Mk 12:29
our God is the one and only *.	Mk 12:29
there is only one * and no other.	Mk 12:32
not far from the Kingdom of *."	Mk 12:34
when he said it—"* said to my Lord,	Mk 12:36
Just say what * tells you to.	Mk 13:11
Literally, "elect of *."	Mk 13:22f
to * for it and gave it to them;	Mk 14:23
the new agreement between * and	Mk 14:24
in the Kingdom of *."	Mk 14:25
told them, "for * has declared	Mk 14:27
you the Messiah, the Son of *?"	Mk 14:61
sitting at the right hand of *,	Mk 14:62
("My *, my God, why have you	Mk 15:34
("My God, my *, why have you	Mk 15:34
a place reserved by * for himself;	Mk 15:38f
opened up access to the holy *.	Mk 15:38f
"Truly, this was the Son of *!"	Mk 15:39
DEAR FRIEND WHO loves *:	Lk 1:1
name means "one who loves *."	Lk 1:1f
to tell you that * has heard your	Lk 1:13
a Jew to turn to the Lord his *.	Lk 1:16
I stand in the very presence of *	Lk 1:19
The following month * sent the	Lk 1:26
told her, "for * has decided to	Lk 1:30
and shall be called the Son of *.	Lk 1:32
And the Lord * shall give him the	Lk 1:32
power of * shall overshadow you;	Lk 1:35
will be utterly holy—the Son of *.	Lk 1:35
For every promise from * shall	Lk 1:37
are favored by * above all other	Lk 1:42
You believed that * would do	Lk 1:45
How I rejoice in * my Savior!	Lk 1:47
forever shall call me blest of *.	Lk 1:48
again, and he began praising *.	Lk 1:64
"Praise the Lord, the * of	Lk 1:68
of serving * fearlessly, freed from	Lk 1:74
of the glorious *, for you will	Lk 1:76
the mercy of our * is very tender,	Lk 1:78
The little boy greatly loved *	Lk 1:80
armies of heaven—praising *:	Lk 2:13
"Glory to * in the highest	Lk 2:14
flocks, praising * for the visit of	Lk 2:20
for in these laws * had said,	Lk 2:23
the child in his arms, praising *.	Lk 2:28
* by praying and often fasting.	Lk 2:36,37
began thanking * and telling	Lk 2:38
of the Law of * they returned home	Lk 2:39
* poured out his blessings on him.	Lk 2:40
wise, and was loved by * and man.	Lk 2:52
message came from * to John (the	Lk 3:1
they had turned to * and away from	Lk 3:3
shall see the Savior sent from *.'	Lk 3:6
hell without truly turning to *!	Lk 3:7
That isn't enough. * can produce	Lk 3:8
Adam's father was *.	Lk 3:23-38
must worship *, and him alone.	Lk 4:8
you are the Son of *, jump off!	Lk 4:9,10,11
For the Scriptures say that *	Lk 4:9,10,11
Lord your * to a foolish test.'	Lk 4:12
and that * is ready to give	Lk 4:18,19
who you are—the Holy Son of *."	Lk 4:34
"You are the Son of *."	Lk 4:41
of the Kingdom of * in other places	Lk 4:43
on him to listen to the Word of *.	Lk 5:1
Who but * can forgive sins?"	Lk 5:21
his mat and went home praising *!	Lk 5:25
And they praised *, remarking	Lk 5:26
for the Kingdom of * is yours!	Lk 6:20
acting as sons of *: for he is kind	Lk 6:35
with praises to *, "A mighty	Lk 7:16
the hand of * at work today."	Lk 7:16
Kingdom of * is greater than he."	Lk 7:28
no prophet, for if * had really	Lk 7:39
of the Kingdom of *, and took his	Lk 8:1
He replied, "* has granted you	Lk 8:10
great deal about the Kingdom of *.	Lk 8:10
hear the words of *, but then the	Lk 8:12
the message of * and obey it."	Lk 8:21
me, Jesus, Son of * Most High?	Lk 8:28
thing * has done for you."	Lk 8:39
Kingdom of * and to heal the sick.	Lk 9:2
* and curing those who were ill.	Lk 9:11
"The Messiah—the Christ of *!"	Lk 9:20
you have seen the Kingdom of *."	Lk 9:27
this display of the power of *.	Lk 9:43
me is caring for * who sent me.	Lk 9:48
Kingdom of * to all the world."	Lk 9:60
is not fit for the Kingdom of *."	Lk 9:62
of * is very near you now.'	Lk 10:8,9
you were to the Kingdom of *!'	Lk 10:11
Cities destroyed by * in judgment	Lk 10:13f
me are rejecting * who sent me."	Lk 10:16
love the Lord your * with all your	Lk 10:27
of power from *, it proves that the	Lk 11:20
that the Kingdom of * has arrived.	Lk 11:20
called out, "* bless your	Lk 11:27
of * and put it into practice."	Lk 11:28
of Nineveh that * had sent him.	Lk 11:29,30
* has sent me to these people.	Lk 11:29,30
Didn't * make the inside as well	Lk 11:40
about justice and the love of *.	Lk 11:42
"This is what * says about you:	Lk 11:49
whom to fear—fear * who has the	Lk 12:5
Not much more than that. Yet *	Lk 12:6
"But * said to him, 'Fool!	Lk 12:20
along all right—for * feeds them.	Lk 12:24
And if * provides clothing for	Lk 12:28
don't worry at all that * will	Lk 12:29
Kingdom of * your primary concern.	Lk 12:31
your evil ways and turn to *?	Lk 13:3
How she praised and thanked *!	Lk 13:13
*: "What is the Kingdom like?"	Lk 13:18
the Kingdom of *— for people will	Lk 13:28
for a prophet of * to be killed	Lk 13:33
of the godly, * will reward you for	Lk 14:14
be to get into the Kingdom of *!"	Lk 14:15
who returns to * than over	Lk 15:7
of * when one sinner repents."	Lk 15:10
You cannot serve both * and	Lk 16:13
but * knows your evil hearts.	Lk 16:15
an abomination in the sight of *.	Lk 16:15
the Kingdom of * would come soon.	Lk 16:16
"Glory to *, I'm healed!"	Lk 17:15
return to give glory to *?"	Lk 17:18
will the Kingdom of * begin?"	Lk 17:20
"The Kingdom of * isn't ushered in	Lk 17:20
For the Kingdom of * is within	Lk 17:21
[as indifferent to the things of *	Lk 17:26
" 'I fear neither * nor man,' he	Lk 18:4,5
you think that * will surely give	Lk 18:7
prayer: 'Thank *, I am not a sinner	Lk 18:11
* a tenth of everything I earn.'	Lk 18:12
'*, be merciful to me, a sinner.'	Lk 18:13
For the Kingdom of * belongs to	Lk 18:16,17
"Only * is truly good, and no	Lk 18:19
rich to enter the Kingdom of *!	Lk 18:24
man to enter the Kingdom of *."	Lk 18:25
He replied, "* can do what men	Lk 18:27
of the Kingdom of *, will be	Lk 18:29
and followed Jesus, praising *.	Lk 18:43
who saw it happen praised * too.	Lk 18:43
of * would begin right away.	Lk 19:11
along, praising * for all the	Lk 19:36,37
"* has given us a King!"	Lk 19:38
Glory to * in the highest	Lk 19:38
the opportunity * offered you."	Lk 19:44
"Was John sent by *, or was he	Lk 20:4
was not sent from *, the people	Lk 20:6
think, but teach the ways of *.	Lk 20:21
give to * all that is his!"	Lk 20:25
and are sons of *, for they are	Lk 20:36
For when he describes how *	Lk 20:37,38
bush, he speaks of * as 'the God of	Lk 20:37,38
of God as 'the * of Abraham, the	Lk 20:37,38
* of Isaac, and the God of Jacob.'	Lk 20:37,38
God of Isaac, and the * of Jacob.'	Lk 20:37,38
"He had been that person's *."	Lk 20:37,38f
some person's * means that person	Lk 20:37,38
book of Psalms: '* said to my Lord,	Lk 20:42,43
and David's * at the same time?"	Lk 20:44
that the Kingdom of * is near.	Lk 21:31
occurred in the Kingdom of *."	Lk 22:16
until the Kingdom of * has come."	Lk 22:18
and when he had thanked * for it,	Lk 22:19
There he told them, "Pray *	Lk 22:40
"Get up! Pray * that you will	Lk 22:46
be enthroned beside Almighty *."	Lk 22:69
you claim you are the Son of *?"	Lk 22:70
"Don't you even fear * when you	Lk 23:40,41
with awe before * and said,	Lk 23:47
him, for * kept them from it.	Lk 24:16
highly regarded by both * and man.	Lk 24:19
in the Temple, praising *.	Lk 24:53
and power of * and the first cause	Jn 1:1f
with *. He has always	Jn 1:1
been alive and is himself *.	Jn 1:1
* sent John the Baptist as a	Jn 1:6,7
the right to become children of *.	Jn 1:11,12
or plan—but from the will of *.	Jn 1:13
and power of * and the first cause	Jn 1:14f
No one has ever actually seen *,	Jn 1:18
There is the Lamb of * who takes	Jn 1:29
"but at the time * sent me to	Jn 1:33
testify that he is the Son of *."	Jn 1:34
There is the Lamb of *!"	Jn 1:36
the Son of *—the King of Israel!"	Jn 1:49
and the angels of * coming back and	Jn 1:51
authority from *, show us a miracle	Jn 2:18
that * has sent you to teach us.	Jn 3:1
never get into the Kingdom of *."	Jn 3:3
he cannot enter the Kingdom of *.	Jn 3:5
eternal life. For * loved the	Jn 3:16
Or, "the unique Son of *."	Jn 3:16f
eternal life. * did not send his	Jn 3:17
Or, "the unique Son of *."	Jn 3:18f
Son of *.	Jn 3:18
are doing what * wants them to."	Jn 3:21
John replied, "* in heaven	Jn 3:27
that * is a fountain of truth.	Jn 3:33,34
For this one—sent by *—speaks	Jn 3:33,34
he is his Son, and * has given him	Jn 3:35
wrath of * remains upon them."	Jn 3:36
a wonderful gift * has for you, and	Jn 4:10
Spirit's help? For * is Spirit, and	Jn 4:21-24
doing the will of * who sent me,	Jn 4:34
he had spoken of * as his Father,	Jn 5:18
making himself equal with *.	Jn 5:18
and believes in * who sent me has	Jn 5:24
*—and those who listen shall live.	Jn 5:25
to the will of * who sent me and is	Jn 5:30
honor that comes from the only *!	Jn 5:44
and gave thanks to * and passed	Jn 6:11
can give you. For * the Father	Jn 6:27
should we do to satisfy *?"	Jn 6:28
is the will of *, that you believe	Jn 6:29
one sent by * from heaven, and he	Jn 6:33
to do the will of * who sent me,	Jn 6:38
And this is the will of *, that	Jn 6:39
'They shall all be taught of *.'	Jn 6:45
know you are the holy Son of *."	Jn 6:69
but those of * who sent me.	Jn 7:16
is from * or is merely my own.	Jn 7:17
of *, you will die in your sins."	Jn 8:24
he was talking to them about *.	Jn 8:27
told you the truth I heard from *.	Jn 8:40
true Father is * himself."	Jn 8:41
me, for I have come to you from *.	Jn 8:42
Anyone whose Father is * listens	Jn 8:47
listens gladly to the words of *.	Jn 8:47
make myself great, * wants this for	Jn 8:50
claim him as your *—who is saying	Jn 8:54
to demonstrate the power of *.	Jn 9:3
Jesus is not from *, because he is	Jn 9:16
sent from *," the man replied.	Jn 9:17
the glory to *, not to Jesus, for	Jn 9:24
We know * has spoken to Moses,	Jn 9:29
Well, * doesn't listen to evil	Jn 9:31
If this man were not from *, he	Jn 9:33
have declared yourself to be *."	Jn 10:33
the message of * came, do you call	Jn 10:34,35,36
Father says, 'I am the Son of *'?	Jn 10:34,35,36
me unless I do miracles of *.	Jn 10:37
not death, but for the glory of *.	Jn 11:4
I, the Son of *, will receive	Jn 11:4
for I know that * will bring my	Jn 11:22
the Son of *, the one we have so	Jn 11:27
miracle from * if you believe?"	Jn 11:40
of * scattered around the world.	Jn 11:52
* bless the King of Israel!	Jn 12:13
for as Isaiah also said: "*	Jn 12:40
of men more than the praise of *.	Jn 12:43
me, you are really trusting *.	Jn 12:44
from * and would return to God.	Jn 13:1
from God and would return to *.	Jn 13:1
the glory of * will soon surround	Jn 13:31
surround me—and * shall receive	Jn 13:31
to me. And * shall give me his own	Jn 13:32
You are trusting *, now trust in	Jn 14:1
for they don't know * who sent me.	Jn 15:21
think they are doing * a service.	Jn 16:2
we believe that you came from *."	Jn 16:30
you, the only true *, and Jesus	Jn 17:3
he called himself the Son of *."	Jn 19:7
your Father, my * and your God."	Jn 20:17
your Father, my God and your *."	Jn 20:17
"My Lord and my *!"	Jn 20:28
the Son of *, and that believing in	Jn 20:30,31
death he would die to glorify *.	Jn 21:19
DEAR FRIEND WHO loves *:	Act 1:1
to them about the Kingdom of *.	Act 1:3
about the mighty miracles of *!"	Act 2:11
the last days,' * said, 'I will	Act 2:17
"O men of Israel, listen! *	Act 2:22
well know. But *, following his	Act 2:23
Then * released him from the	Act 2:24
But he was a prophet, and knew *	Act 2:30
honor in heaven, next to *.	Act 2:33
Moreover, he further stated, "*	Act 2:34
in Israel that * has made this	Act 2:36
sin, return to *, and be baptized	Act 2:38
by the Lord our *, and to your	Act 2:39
joy and thankfulness, praising *.	Act 2:47
them, and each day * added to them	Act 2:47
and praising *, he went into the	Act 3:7,8
heard him praising *, and realized	Act 3:9
For it is the * of Abraham,	Act 3:13
* brought him back to life again.	Act 3:15
*—has caused this perfect healing.	Act 3:16
your leaders. But * was fulfilling	Act 3:18
and attitude to * and turn to him	Act 3:19
ago, 'The Lord * will raise up a	Act 3:21,22
is the promise * gave to Abraham.	Act 3:25
And as soon as * had brought his	Act 3:26
* raised back to life again.	Act 4:10

(GOD Con't)

decide whether * wants us to obey	Act 4:19
For everyone was praising * for	Act 4:21
little plots against Almighty *?	Act 4:25,26
against the anointed Son of *!'	Act 4:25,26
You weren't lying to us, but to *	Act 5:4
"We must obey * rather than men.	Act 5:29
than men. The * of our ancestors	Act 5:30
Then, with mighty power, *	Act 5:31
given by * to all who obey him."	Act 5:32
But if it is of *, you will not	Act 5:39
fighting even against *."	Act 5:39
rejoicing that * had counted them	Act 5:41
Stephen curse Moses, and even *.	Act 6:11
"The glorious * appeared to our	Act 7:2
that * would direct him to.	Act 7:3
father died. Then * brought him	Act 7:4
"However, * promised that	Act 7:5
no children! But * also told him	Act 7:6
enslaves them,' * told him, 'and	Act 7:7
"* also gave Abraham the	Act 7:8
* and the people of Abraham.	Act 7:8
in Egypt. But * was with him, and	Act 7:9
king of Egypt. * also gave Joseph	Act 7:10
"As the time drew near when *	Act 7:17,18
would realize that * had sent him	Act 7:25
to him, 'I am the * of your	Act 7:32
And so * sent back the same man	Act 7:35
people of Israel, '* will raise up	Act 7:37
*—the Living Word—on Mount Sinai.	Act 7:38
"Then * turned away from them	Act 7:42
the Lord * asks, 'Was it to me you	Act 7:42
and the star * Kaiway, and in all	Act 7:43
"* blessed David greatly, and	Act 7:46
Temple for the * of Jacob.	Act 7:46
However, * doesn't live in	Act 7:48,49
saw the glory of * and Jesus	Act 7:55
standing beside *, at his right	Act 7:56
of * which is called great."	Act 8:9,10,11f
words concerning the Kingdom of *;	Act 8:12
your heart is not right before *.	Act 8:21
Perhaps * will yet forgive your	Act 8:22
Jesus Christ is the Son of *."	Act 8:37
he is indeed the Son of *!	Act 9:20
an angel of * coming toward him.	Act 10:3
have not gone unnoticed by *!	Act 10:4
spoke again, "Don't contradict *!	Act 10:15
tell him what * wanted him to do.	Act 10:22
I'm not a *!"	Act 10:26
like this. But * has shown me in a	Act 10:28
charities have been noticed by *!	Act 10:31
is peace with * through Jesus, the	Act 10:36,37
was anointed by * with the Holy	Act 10:38
by demons, for * was with him.	Act 10:38
on a cross. But * brought him back	Act 10:40,41
certain witnesses * had selected	Act 10:40,41
is ordained of * to be the Judge of	Act 10:42
in tongues and praising *.	Act 10:46,47
right when * declares it is!'	Act 11:9
And since it was * who gave	Act 11:17
and they began praising *!	Act 11:18
"Yes," they said, "* has given	Act 11:18
wonderful things * was doing, he	Act 11:23
was going up to * from the Church	Act 12:5
voice of a * and not of a man!"	Act 12:22
instead of giving the glory to *.	Act 12:23
to hear their message from *.	Act 13:6,7
And now * has laid his hand of	Act 13:11
here who reverence *, [let me begin	Act 13:16
"The * of this nation Israel	Act 13:17
for a king, and * gave them Saul	Act 13:21
forty years. But * removed him and	Act 13:22
a man about whom * said, 'David	Act 13:22
in Israel to turn from sin to *.	Act 13:24
*—this salvation is for all of us!	Act 13:26
"But * brought him back to life	Act 13:30
own time, in that * brought Jesus	Act 13:32,33
"For * had promised to bring him	Act 13:34
fully, saying, '* will not let his	Act 13:35
to the will of *, he died and was	Act 13:36
—someone * brought back to life,	Act 13:37
accept the mercies * was offering.	Act 13:43
to hear them preach the Word of *.	Act 13:44
Good News from * should be given	Act 13:46
was the Greek * Jupiter, and that	Act 14:12
to the living * who made heaven and	Act 14:15
grow in love for * and each other.	Act 14:22
of * through many tribulations.	Act 14:22
to * for the work now completed.	Act 14:26
trip, telling how * had opened the	Act 14:27
reported on what * had been doing	Act 15:4
you all know that * chose me from	Act 15:7
could believe. *, who knows men's	Act 15:8
going to correct * by burdening the	Act 15:10
about the miracles * had done	Act 15:12
you about the time * first visited	Act 15:14
who turn to * must obey our Jewish	Act 15:19
only conclude that * was sending us	Act 16:10
She was already a worshiper of *	Act 16:14
are servants of * and they have	Act 16:17
on it—'To the Unknown *.'	Act 17:23
should seek after *, and perhaps	Act 17:27
says it, 'We are the sons of *.'	Act 17:28
shouldn't think of * as an idol	Act 17:29
from stone. * tolerated man's past	Act 17:30
who worshiped * and lived next	Act 18:7
a half, teaching the truths of *.	Act 18:11
men to worship * in ways that are	Act 18:13
were given to * at the Temple.	Act 18:18f
to Ephesus later if * permitted;	Act 18:21
were given to * at the Temple.	Act 18:22f
the way of * more accurately."	Act 18:25,26f
greatly used of * to strengthen the	Act 18:27
turn from sin to * and that those	Act 19:4
"concerning the Kingdom of *."	Act 19:8f
message. And * gave Paul the power	Act 19:11
from sin to * through faith in our	Act 20:21
"And now I entrust you to * and	Act 20:32
the many things * had accomplished	Act 21:19
They praised * but then said,	Act 21:20
I became very anxious to honor *	Act 22:3
"Then he told me, 'The * of our	Act 22:14
vision of * saying to me, 'Hurry!	Act 22:17,18
"But * said to me, 'Leave	Act 22:21
before * in all good conscience!"	Act 23:1
Paul said to him, "* shall slap	Act 23:3
of serving the * of our ancestors;	Act 24:14
clear conscience before * and man.	Act 24:16
and to offer a sacrifice to *.	Act 24:17
to you that * can bring men back to	Act 26:8
in the light of * instead of in	Act 26:18
sins and turn to *—and prove their	Act 26:20
to kill me, but * protected me so	Act 26:22
And Paul replied, "Would to *	Act 26:29
an angel of the * to whom I belong	Act 27:23
What's more, * has granted your	Act 27:24
For I believe *!	Act 27:25
and gave thanks to * before them	Act 27:35
minds and decided he was a *.	Act 28:6
When Paul saw them, he thanked *	Act 28:15
the Kingdom of * and taught them	Act 28:23
salvation from * is available to	Act 28:28,29
* and about the Lord Jesus Christ;	Act 28:31
the mighty Son of *, with the holy	Rom 1:4
with the holy nature of * himself.	Rom 1:4
the kindness of * has been poured	Rom 1:5
the great things * has done for	Rom 1:5
be yours from * our Father and from	Rom 1:6,7
For your faith in * is becoming	Rom 1:8
How I thank * through Jesus	Rom 1:8
* knows how often I pray for you.	Rom 1:9
for is the opportunity, * willing,	Rom 1:10
Literally, "in the will of *."	Rom 1:10f
to come to * in this same way.	Rom 1:16
This Good News tells us that *	Rom 1:17
righteousness of * is revealed from	Rom 1:17f
will find it through trusting *."	Rom 1:17
But * shows his anger from heaven	Rom 1:18
For the truth about * is known	Rom 1:19
* has put this knowledge in	Rom 1:19
and sky and all * made, and have	Rom 1:20
stand before * at Judgment Day	Rom 1:20
excuse for saying there is no *."	Rom 1:20f
ideas of what * was like and what	Rom 1:21
to be wise without *, they became	Rom 1:22
ever-living *, they took wood and	Rom 1:23
So * let them go ahead into every	Rom 1:24
the truth about *, they	Rom 1:25
So they prayed to the things *	Rom 1:25
blessed * who made these things.	Rom 1:25
That is why * let go of them and	Rom 1:26
So it was that when they gave *	Rom 1:28
acknowledge him, * gave them up to	Rom 1:28
haters of *, insolent, proud	Rom 1:30
And we know that *, in justice,	Rom 2:2
Do you think that * will judge	Rom 2:3
day of wrath when * will be the	Rom 2:5
who patiently do the will of *,	Rom 2:7
the truth of * and walk in evil	Rom 2:8
peace from * for all who obey him,	Rom 2:10
For * treats everyone the same.	Rom 2:11
excuses them. And * will punish the	Rom 2:12-15
* because he gave his laws to you;	Rom 2:17
You are so sure of the way to *	Rom 2:19
men who are lost in darkness to *.	Rom 2:19
the affairs of *, for you really	Rom 2:20
then make money your * instead.	Rom 2:22
speaks evil of * because of you.	Rom 2:24
God's laws, won't * give them all	Rom 2:26
know so much about * and have his	Rom 2:27
whose heart is right with *.	Rom 2:29
with God. For * is not looking for	Rom 2:29
from *, even if not from you.	Rom 2:29
special benefits for them from *?	Rom 3:1
First of all, * trusted them with	Rom 3:2
their promises to *, does that mean	Rom 3:3
mean * will break his promises?	Rom 3:3
in the world is a liar, * is not.	Rom 3:4
faith with * is good, our sins	Rom 3:5
* is when they see how bad we are.	Rom 3:5
way some people talk.) * forbid!	Rom 3:6
Then what kind of * would he be,	Rom 3:6
we are, the better * likes it!	Rom 3:
They care nothing about * nor	Rom 3:1
So the judgment of * lies very	Rom 3:1
and guilty before Almighty *.	Rom 3:1
But now * has shown us a	Rom 3:21,2
Literally, "A righteousness of *	Rom 3:21,22
it long ago). Now * says he will	Rom 3:21,2
yet now * declares us "not	Rom 3:2
For * sent Christ Jesus to take	Rom 3:2
But isn't this unfair for * to let	Rom 3:2
And does * save only the Jews in	Rom 3:2
manner. * treats us all the same;	Rom 3:3
good deeds that * accepted him?	Rom 4:
Abraham believed *, and that is why	Rom 4:
and that is why * canceled his sins	Rom 4:
work for it. For * declares sinners	Rom 4:4,
by *. "Blessed, and to be	Rom 4:6
* give this blessing to Abraham?	Rom 4:1
It wasn't until later on, after *	Rom 4:11
had faith and that * had already	Rom 4:11
are justified by * through faith.	Rom 4:11
found favor with * by faith alone,	Rom 4:12
he trusted * to keep his promise.	Rom 4:13
when they say that * made Abraham	Rom 4:17
of many nations. * will accept all	Rom 4:17
nation who trust * as Abraham did.	Rom 4:17
And this promise is from *	Rom 4:17
So, when * told Abraham that he	Rom 4:18
Abraham believed * even though such	Rom 4:18
He believed *, for his faith and	Rom 4:20
and he praised * for this blessing	Rom 4:20
He was completely sure that *	Rom 4:21
And because of Abraham's faith *	Rom 4:22
assuring us that * will accept us	Rom 4:24
the promises of * who brought back	Rom 4:24
*, filling us with God's goodness.	Rom 4:25
* has had in mind for us to be.	Rom 5:2
and helps us trust * more each time	Rom 5:4
we know how dearly * loves us, and	Rom 5:5
within us because * has given us	Rom 5:5
possible. But * showed his great	Rom 5:8
brought back to * by the death of	Rom 5:10
relationship with *—all because of	Rom 5:11
our sins—making us friends of *.	Rom 5:11
Adam until Moses, * did not in	Rom 5:13
with *, so that they can live.	Rom 5:18
he disobeyed *, and Christ caused	Rom 5:19
acceptable to * because he obeyed.	Rom 5:19
standing with * and resulting in	Rom 5:21
on sinning so that * can keep on	Rom 6:1
he died, and when * the Father,	Rom 6:4
in unbroken fellowship with *.	Rom 6:10
be alive to *, alert to him,	Rom 6:11
completely to *—every part of	Rom 6:13
in the hands of *, to be used for	Rom 6:13
Thank * that though you once	Rom 6:17
to which * has committed you.	Rom 6:17
and are slaves of *, and his	Rom 6:22
the free gift of * is eternal life	Rom 6:23
fruit, that is, good deeds for *.	Rom 7:4
to do whatever * said not to, and	Rom 7:5
and now you can really serve *;	Rom 7:6
that these laws of * are evil?	Rom 7:7
the good laws of * and using them	Rom 7:11
Thank *!	Rom 7:23,24,25
Literally, "I thank * through	Rom 7:23,24,25f
commandments of *, because we can't	Rom 8:3
keep them, but * put into effect a	Rom 8:3
doing those things that please *.	Rom 8:5
nature within us is against *.	Rom 8:7
evil desires, can never please *.	Rom 8:8
the Spirit of * living in you.	Rom 8:9
And if the Spirit of *, who	Rom 8:11
the Spirit of * are sons of God.	Rom 8:14
the Spirit of God are sons of *.	Rom 8:14
treasures—for all * gives to his	Rom 8:17
* will resurrect his children.	Rom 8:19
the revelation of the sons of *."	Rom 8:19f
for that day when * will give us	Rom 8:23
But if we must keep trusting *	Rom 8:25
* and are fitting into his plans.	Rom 8:28
For from the very beginning *	Rom 8:29
as these? If * is on our side, who	Rom 8:31
Who dares accuse us whom * has	Rom 8:33
has chosen for his own? Will *?	Rom 8:33
honor next to *, pleading for us	Rom 8:34
with death, has * deserted us?	Rom 8:35
from the love of * demonstrated by	Rom 8:39
would save you. * has given you so	Rom 9:4
Great men of * were your	Rom 9:5
Praise * forever!	Rom 9:5
Well then, has * failed to	Rom 9:6
are children of *, but only those	Rom 9:8
For * had promised, "Next year I	Rom 9:9
him twin children, * told her that	Rom 9:10-13
And * said this before the	Rom 9:10-13
This proves that * was doing what	Rom 9:10-13
of what * wanted and chose.	Rom 9:10-13
Was * being unfair?	Rom 9:14
Of course not. For * had said to	Rom 9:15
They are given because * takes	Rom 9:16

(GOD Con't)

of this fact. For * told him he had	Rom 9:17
awesome power of * against him: so	Rom 9:17
So you see, * is kind to some	Rom 9:18
Well then, why does * blame them	Rom 9:19
Who are you to criticize *?	Rom 9:20
Does not * have a perfect right	Rom 9:22
There * says that he will find	Rom 9:25
called "sons of the Living *."	Rom 9:26
Just this, that * has given the	Rom 9:30
had not been really seeking *.	Rom 9:30
to get right with * by keeping his	Rom 9:31
stumbling stone. * warned them of	Rom 9:33
of *, but it is misdirected zeal.	Rom 10:2
died to make them right with *.	Rom 10:3
own heart that * has raised him	Rom 10:9
that a man becomes right with *;	Rom 10:10
of peace with * and bring glad	Rom 10:15
And did they understand [that *	Rom 10:19
the time of Moses, * had said that	Rom 10:19
said boldly that * would be found	Rom 10:20
I ASK THEN, has * rejected and	Rom 11:1
No, * has not discarded his own	Rom 11:2,3
was complaining to * about the	Rom 11:2,3
the Jews, telling * how they had	Rom 11:2,3
who still loved *, and now they	Rom 11:2,3
And do you remember how *	Rom 11:4
how God replied? * said, "No, you	Rom 11:4
the Jews have turned away from *;	Rom 11:5
favor of * they are looking for.	Rom 11:7
A few have—the ones * has picked	Rom 11:7
when they say that * has put them	Rom 11:8
is well between themselves and *.	Rom 11:9
Does this mean that * has	Rom 11:11
As you know, * has appointed me	Rom 11:13
Christians! When * turned away from	Rom 11:15
the blessing * has promised Abraham	Rom 11:17
didn't believe *, and you are there	Rom 11:20
For if * did not spare the	Rom 11:21
Notice how * is both kind and	Rom 11:22
and come back to *, God will graft	Rom 11:23
come back to God, * will graft them	Rom 11:23
For if * was willing to take you	Rom 11:24
this truth from *, dear brothers,	Rom 11:25
still beloved of * because of his	Rom 11:28
Once you were rebels against *,	Rom 11:30
* was merciful to you instead.	Rom 11:30
For * has given them all up to sin	Rom 11:32
Oh, what a wonderful * we have!	Rom 11:33
For everything comes from *	Rom 11:36
you to give your bodies to *.	Rom 12:1
by how much faith * has given you.	Rom 12:3
* has given each of us the	Rom 12:6
So if * has given you the ability	Rom 12:6
to receive a message from *.	Rom 12:6
and helpful. If * has given you	Rom 12:8
others with it. If * has given you	Rom 12:8
Be glad for all * is planning for	Rom 12:12
pray that * will bless him.	Rom 12:14
Leave that to *, for he has said	Rom 12:19
OBEY THE GOVERNMENT, for * is	Rom 13:1
that * has not placed in power.	Rom 13:1
*, and punishment will follow.	Rom 13:2
The policeman is sent by * to	Rom 13:4
He is sent by * for that very	Rom 13:4
those who do. For * has accepted	Rom 14:3
or wrong. And * is able to make	Rom 14:4
days to worship *, but others say	Rom 14:5
for every day alike belongs to *.	Rom 14:5
before the Judgment Seat of *.	Rom 14:10
and every tongue confess to *."	Rom 14:11
give an account of himself to *.	Rom 14:12
in these affairs, * will be glad;	Rom 14:18
Don't undo the work of * for a	Rom 14:20
when * will conquer sin and death.	Rom 15:4
May * who gives patience,	Rom 15:5
giving glory to *, the Father of	Rom 15:6
you; then * will be glorified.	Rom 15:7
came to show that * is true to his	Rom 15:8
to * for his mercies to them.	Rom 15:9
So I pray for you Gentiles that *	Rom 15:13
I pray that * will help you	Rom 15:13
up as a fragrant sacrifice to *;	Rom 15:15,16
used me to win the Gentiles to *.	Rom 15:18
*—all by the Holy Spirit's power.	Rom 15:19
*, and we can refresh each other.	Rom 15:32
And now may our *, who gives	Rom 15:33
of any wrong. The * of peace will	Rom 16:20
I commit you to *, who is able to	Rom 16:25,26,27
foretold and as * commands, this	Rom 16:25,26,27
and obey him. To *, who alone is	Rom 16:25,26,27
FROM: PAUL, CHOSEN by * to be	1Co 1:1
invited by * to be his people and	1Co 1:2
May * our Father and the Lord	1Co 1:3
I can never stop thanking * for	1Co 1:4
when he returns. * will surely do	1Co 1:9
message as the very power of *.	1Co 1:18
power of God. For * says, "I will	1Co 1:19
great affairs? * has made them all	1Co 1:20
nonsense. For * in his wisdom saw	1Co 1:21
would never find * through human	1Co 1:21
all nonsense. But * has opened the	1Co 1:24
mighty power of * to save them;	1Co 1:24
plan of * is far wiser than the	1Co 1:25
wisest man, and * in his	1Co 1:25
Instead, * has deliberately	1Co 1:27
ever brag in the presence of *.	1Co 1:29
For it is from * alone that you	1Co 1:30
one who made us acceptable to *;	1Co 1:30
Or, "he brought us near to *."	1Co 1:30f
them that the message was from *.	1Co 2:4
upon *, not on man's great ideas.	1Co 2:5
they are from *, telling of God's	1Co 2:7
wonderful things * has ready for	1Co 2:9
things because * has sent his	1Co 2:10
own Spirit. And * has actually	1Co 2:12
and blessing that * has given us.	1Co 2:12
thoughts from *, which the Holy	1Co 2:14
to move the hands of * by prayer.	1Co 2:16
it, but it was *, not we, who made	1Co 3:6
important, but * is important	1Co 3:7
*, in his kindness, has taught me	1Co 3:10
are the house of *, and that the	1Co 3:16
of * lives among you in his house?	1Co 3:16
God's home, * will destroy him.	1Co 3:17
of this world is foolishness to *.	1Co 3:19
As it says in the book of Job, *	1Co 3:19
For * has already given you	1Co 3:21
At that time * will give to each	1Co 4:5
What do you have that * hasn't	1Co 4:7
And if all you have is from *,	1Co 4:7
Sometimes I think * has put us	1Co 4:9
The Kingdom of * is not just	1Co 4:20
in these ways. * alone is the	1Co 5:13
have no share in the Kingdom of *?	1Co 6:9,10
are set apart for *, and he has	1Co 6:11
Spirit of our * have done for you.	1Co 6:11
matter of eating. * has given us an	1Co 6:13
because some day * will do away	1Co 6:13
with himself. And * is going to	1Co 6:14
a part of her? For * tells us in	1Co 6:16
of the Holy Spirit * gave you, and	1Co 6:19
to you. For * has bought you with	1Co 6:20
back to *, because he owns it.	1Co 6:20
But we are not all the same. *	1Co 7:7
other stay, for * wants his	1Co 7:15
you are living as * intended,	1Co 7:17
situation * has put you into.	1Co 7:17
* and keeping God's commandments.	1Co 7:19
he was doing when * called him.	1Co 7:20
But the person who truly loves *	1Co 8:3
is not really a *, and that there	1Co 8:4
there is only one *, and no other.	1Co 8:4
there is only one *, the Father,	1Co 8:6
Just remember that * doesn't	1Co 8:8
For in the law * gave to Moses	1Co 9:9
Do you suppose * was thinking	1Co 9:9
Don't you realize that * told	1Co 9:13
at the altar of * get a share of	1Co 9:13
the situation, for * has picked me	1Co 9:17
long ago. * guided them by sending	1Co 10:1
* sent them food to eat and water	1Co 10:3,4
them did not obey *, and he	1Co 10:5
And don't murmur against * and	1Co 10:10
* sent his Angel to destroy them.	1Co 10:10
You can trust * to keep the	1Co 10:13
to demons, certainly not to *.	1Co 10:20
If I can thank * for the food	1Co 10:30
*, even your eating and drinking.	1Co 10:31
and Christ is responsible to *.	1Co 11:3
women come from * their Creator.	1Co 11:12
given thanks to * for it, he broke	1Co 11:24
agreement between * and you that	1Co 11:25
messages from the Spirit of *.	1Co 12:3
by * or whether they are fakes?	1Co 12:3
of the Spirit of * can curse Jesus,	1Co 12:3
Now * gives us many kinds of	1Co 12:4
of service to *, but it is the same	1Co 12:5
There are many ways in which *	1Co 12:6
but it is the same * who does the	1Co 12:6
the Spirit of * who is speaking.	1Co 12:10
But that isn't the way * has made	1Co 12:18
special care. So * has put the body	1Co 12:24
Of course not. Does * give all of	1Co 12:30
and powers from * will someday come	1Co 13:8
a little about * now, as if we were	1Co 13:12
as * sees into my heart right now.	1Co 13:12
able to preach the messages of *.	1Co 14:1
will be talking to * but not to	1Co 14:2
the messages of *, is helping	1Co 14:3
messages from *, helps the entire	1Co 14:4
But if I speak plainly what * has	1Co 14:6
for if you praise and thank *	1Co 14:16
you be praising * along with you?	1Co 14:16
I thank * that I "speak in	1Co 14:18
Scriptures that * would send men	1Co 14:21
the deep truths of *) is what the	1Co 14:22
knees and worship *, declaring that	1Co 14:25
that * is really there among you.	1Co 14:25
information * has given him, or	1Co 14:26
themselves and to * in the unknown	1Co 14:28
has a message from * has the power	1Co 14:32
* is not one who likes things to	1Co 14:33
the way I treated the church of *.	1Co 15:9
it is all because * poured out such	1Co 15:10
but * working in me, to bless me.	1Co 15:10
* is empty, worthless, hopeless;	1Co 15:14
we have said that * raised Christ	1Co 15:15
keep on trusting * to save you, and	1Co 15:17
kingdom over to * the Father,	1Co 15:24
he, the Son of *, will put himself	1Co 15:28
orders, so that * who has given him	1Co 15:28
all and have never really known *.	1Co 15:34
are some who know nothing of *."	1Co 15:34f
planting, then * gives it a	1Co 15:38
and later on * gives us spiritual,	1Co 15:46
How we thank * for all of this!	1Co 15:57
* to be Jesus Christ's messenger;	2Co 1:1
May * our Father and the Lord	2Co 1:2
What a wonderful * we have—he is	2Co 1:3,4
help and comfort * has given us.	2Co 1:3,4
But in our trouble * had	2Co 1:6,7
experience how * will tenderly	2Co 1:6,7
into the hands of *, who alone	2Co 1:9
praise will go to * from you who	2Co 1:11
As surely as * is true, I am not	2Co 1:18
about Jesus Christ the Son of *.	2Co 1:19
It is this * who has made you	2Co 1:21
I call upon this * to witness	2Co 1:23
But thanks be to *!	2Co 2:14
As far as * is concerned there	2Co 2:15
integrity, sent by *, speaking with	2Co 2:17
but by the Spirit of the living *;	2Co 3:3
our great trust in * through	2Co 3:4
power and success comes from *.	2Co 3:5
must obey every law of * or die;	2Co 3:6
the very glory of *—though the	2Co 3:7
plan that makes men right with *.	2Co 3:9
be saved by keeping the laws of *	2Co 3:17
IT IS * himself, in his mercy, who	2Co 4:1
We stand in the presence of * as	2Co 4:2
Satan, who is the * of this evil	2Co 4:4
the glory of Christ, who is *.	2Co 4:4
Literally, "who is the image of *	2Co 4:4f
done for us. For *, who said,	2Co 4:6
must be from * and is not our own.	2Co 4:7
We are hunted down, but * never	2Co 4:9
believe [trusting * to care for us	2Co 4:13
We know that the same * who	2Co 4:14
* himself, and not by human hands.	2Co 5:1
This is what * has prepared for	2Co 5:5
to win others. * knows our hearts,	2Co 5:11
If so, it is to bring glory to *.	2Co 5:13,14
All these new things are from *	2Co 5:18
Jesus did. And * has given us the	2Co 5:18
to him. For * was in Christ,	2Co 5:19
We are Christ's ambassadors. *	2Co 5:20
he offers you—be reconciled to *.	2Co 5:20
to God. For * took the sinless	2Co 5:21
the righteousness of * in him."	2Co 5:21f
kindness. For * says, "Your cry	2Co 6:2
Right now * is ready to welcome	2Co 6:2
that we are true ministers of *.	2Co 6:4
ignores us, but we are known to *;	2Co 6:9
do the people of * have in common	2Co 6:14
home of the living *, and God has	2Co 6:16
living God, and * has said of you,	2Co 6:16
* and they shall be my people."	2Co 6:16
*, giving ourselves to him alone.	2Co 7:1
Then * who cheers those who are	2Co 7:6
because the pain turned you to *.	2Co 7:9
the kind of sorrow * wants his	2Co 7:9
harshness. For * sometimes uses	2Co 7:10
NOW I WANT to tell you what * in	2Co 8:1
* might give to them through us.	2Co 8:5
you have to give. * wants you to	2Co 8:12
I am thankful to * that he has	2Co 8:16
this large gift. * knows we are	2Co 8:21
givers are the ones * prizes.	2Co 9:7
ones God prizes. * is able to make	2Co 9:8
For *, who gives seed to the	2Co 9:10
Yes, * will give you much so that	2Co 9:11
and praise to * for your help.	2Co 9:11
they overflow with thanks to *.	2Co 9:12
they will praise * for this proof	2Co 9:13
grace of * shown through you.	2Co 9:14
Thank * for his Son—his Gift too	2Co 9:15
argument against * and every wall	2Co 10:5
bring them back to *, and change	2Co 10:5
deep concern of * himself—anxious	2Co 11:2
"messengers from *," as they call	2Co 11:5
Because I don't love you? * knows	2Co 11:11
* never sent those men at all;	2Co 11:13
how weak I am. *, the Father of	2Co 11:31
know; only * can answer that.	2Co 12:2,3
I am and how great * is to use such	2Co 12:5
so tremendous, * was afraid I might	2Co 12:7
Three different times I begged *	2Co 12:8
sent to you by * himself: for I	2Co 12:12
I tell you, with * listening as I	2Co 12:19
that when I come * will humble me	2Co 12:21
he lives by the mighty power of *.	2Co 13:4
And may the * of love and peace be	2Co 13:11

(GOD Con't)

himself, and from * the Father who	Gal 1:1
be yours from * the Father and from	Gal 1:3
He died for our sins just as *	Gal 1:4
All glory to * through all the	Gal 1:5
away so soon from * who, in his	Gal 1:6
no, I am trying to please *.	Gal 1:10
For even before I was born * had	Gal 1:15
this in the very presence of *.	Gal 1:20
And they gave glory to *	Gal 1:24
orders from * to confer with the	Gal 2:2
to me, for all are the same to *.	Gal 2:6
saw how greatly * had used me in	Gal 2:7,8,9
Jews—for the same * gave us each	Gal 2:7,8,9
become right with * by obeying our	Gal 2:16
be accepted by * because of	Gal 2:16
had ruined us? * forbid that anyone	Gal 2:17
* comes by believing in Christ.	Gal 2:19
law, that I might live unto *."	Gal 2:19f
in the Son of *, who loved me and	Gal 2:20
I ask you again, does * give you	Gal 3:5
Abraham had the same experience—*	Gal 3:6
men of faith who truly trust in *.	Gal 3:7
to this time when * would save the	Gal 3:8,9
their faith. * told Abraham about	Gal 3:8,9
laws, because * has said that the	Gal 3:11
will find it through trusting *."	Gal 3:11
every law of *, without one slip.	Gal 3:12
Now * can bless the Gentiles,	Gal 3:14
Now, * gave some promises to	Gal 3:16
through faith—and * wrote this	Gal 3:17
when * gave the Ten Commandments.	Gal 3:17
difference. * gave his laws to	Gal 3:19
but when * gave his promise to	Gal 3:20
by his laws, then * would not have	Gal 3:21,22
standing with * through our faith.	Gal 3:24
For now we are all children of *	Gal 3:26
came, the time * decided on, he	Gal 4:4
And because we are his sons *	Gal 4:6
speak of * as our dear Father.	Gal 4:6
us, for that is the way * planned.	Gal 4:7
Before you Gentiles knew * you	Gal 4:8
And now that you have found *	Gal 4:9
say, now that * has found you) how	Gal 4:9
to find favor with * by what you do	Gal 4:10
*, or even Jesus Christ himself.	Gal 4:14
born only after * had especially	Gal 4:23
trying to please * by trying to	Gal 4:24,25
* promised, just as Isaac was.	Gal 4:28
But the Scriptures say that *	Gal 4:30
to * because of our faith.	Gal 4:31
*, then Christ cannot save you.	Gal 5:2
to find favor with * by being	Gal 5:3
debt to * by keeping those laws;	Gal 5:4
our sins and make us right with *.	Gal 5:5
It certainly isn't * who has	Gal 5:8
these things. * will deal with that	Gal 5:10
will not inherit the kingdom of *.	Gal 5:21
taught the Word of * should help	Gal 6:6
remember that you can't ignore *	Gal 6:7
As for me, * forbid that I should	Gal 6:14
* to be Jesus Christ's messenger.	Eph 1:1
sent to you from * our Father and	Eph 1:2
How we praise *, the Father of	Eph 1:3
he made the world, * chose us to be	Eph 1:4
Now all praise to * for his	Eph 1:6
* has told us his secret reason	Eph 1:9
become gifts to * that he delights	Eph 1:11
we should praise * and give glory	Eph 1:12
upon us means that * has already	Eph 1:14
for us to praise our glorious *.	Eph 1:14
never stopped thanking * for you.	Eph 1:16,17
constantly, asking *, the glorious	Eph 1:16,17
I want you to realize that * has	Eph 1:18
to come. And * has put all things	Eph 1:22
But * is so rich in mercy;	Eph 2:4
And now * can always point to us	Eph 2:7
it too is a gift from *.	Eph 2:8
It is * himself who has made us	Eph 2:10
You were lost, without *, without	Eph 2:12
were far away from *, now you have	Eph 2:13
of us have been reconciled to *.	Eph 2:16
may come to * the Father with the	Eph 2:18
strangers to * and foreigners to	Eph 2:19
constantly growing temple for *.	Eph 2:21
part of this dwelling place of *.	Eph 2:22
No doubt you already know that *	Eph 3:2,3
one of my letters. * himself showed	Eph 3:2,3
In olden times * did not share	Eph 3:5
done for them. * has given me the	Eph 3:7
to everyone that * is the Savior of	Eph 3:9
great family of *—some of them	Eph 3:14,15
will be filled up with * himself.	Eph 3:18,19
Now glory be to * who by his	Eph 3:20
all have the same * and Father who	Eph 4:6
teaching them in the ways of *.	Eph 4:11
from the life of * because they	Eph 4:17,18
another, just as * has forgiven you	Eph 4:32
gave himself to * as a sacrifice to	Eph 5:2
your sins. And * was pleased, for	Eph 5:2
of Christ and of * will never	Eph 5:5
things of this life more than *.	Eph 5:5
* is upon all those who do them.	Eph 5:6
That is why * says in the	Eph 5:14
everything to our * and Father in	Eph 5:20
to do because * has placed them in	Eph 6:1
will of * with all your hearts.	Eph 6:6,7
the Good News of peace with *.	Eph 6:15
the Spirit—which is the Word of *.	Eph 6:17
Pray all the time. Ask * for	Eph 6:18
Pray for me, too, and ask * to	Eph 6:19
for preaching this message from *.	Eph 6:20
May * give peace to you, my	Eph 6:23
with faith from * the Father and	Eph 6:23
May * bless you all.	Php 1:2
Yes, I pray that * our Father and	Php 1:2
for you are full of praise to *!	Php 1:3
And I am sure that * who began	Php 1:6
the blessings of *, both when I was	Php 1:7
Only * knows how deep is my love	Php 1:8
you are a child of *, for this will	Php 1:11
jealous of the way * has used me.	Php 1:15
a clear sign from * that he is with	Php 1:28
who, though he was *, did not	Php 2:6
to his rights as *, but laid aside	Php 2:6
Yet it was because of this that *	Php 2:9
to the glory of * the Father.	Php 2:11
saved, obeying * with deep	Php 2:12
him. For * is at work within you,	Php 2:13
as children of * in a dark world	Php 2:15
am offering up to * as a	Php 2:17
in fact, he almost died. But *	Php 2:27
that makes us children of *;	Php 3:3
prize for which * is calling us up	Php 3:14
I believe that * will make it plain	Php 3:15
loss, for their * is their	Php 3:19
everything; tell * your needs and	Php 4:6
Think about all you can praise *	Php 4:8
the * of peace will be with you.	Php 4:9
for I can do everything * asks	Php 4:13
sacrifice that pleases * well.	Php 4:18
Now unto * our Father be glory	Php 4:20
FROM: PAUL, CHOSEN by * to be	Col 1:1
May * our Father shower you with	Col 1:2
giving thanks to * the Father of	Col 1:3
praying and asking * to help you	Col 1:9
to know * better and better.	Col 1:10
exact likeness of the unseen *.	Col 1:15
He existed before * made anything	Col 1:15
everything; for * wanted all of	Col 1:19
his Son did that * cleared a path	Col 1:20
peace with * for all by his blood.	Col 1:20
who were once so far away from *.	Col 1:21
very presence of *, and you are	Col 1:22
* has sent me to help his church	Col 1:25
each one to *, perfect because of	Col 1:28
This is what I have asked of *	Col 2:2
For in Christ there is all of *	Col 2:9
* through your union with Christ.	Col 2:10
* who raised Christ from the dead.	Col 2:12
In this way * took away Satan's	Col 2:15
you of sin, and * openly displayed	Col 2:15
nourishment and strength from *.	Col 2:19
* in the place of honor and power.	Col 3:1
is in heaven with Christ and *	Col 3:3
Since you have been chosen by *	Col 3:12
the presence of * the Father to	Col 3:17
for us too, that * will give us	Col 4:3
for you, asking * to make you	Col 4:12
you who belong to * the Father and	1Th 1:1
rich gifts from * our Father, and	1Th 1:1
We always thank * for you and	1Th 1:2
as we talk to our * and Father	1Th 1:3
We know that * has chosen you,	1Th 1:4
dear brothers, much beloved of *.	1Th 1:4
about your remarkable faith in *.	1Th 1:8
from your idols to * so that now	1Th 1:9
and true * only is your Master.	1Th 1:9
heaven—Jesus, whom * brought back	1Th 1:10
there. Yet * gave us the courage to	1Th 2:2
For we speak as messengers from *	1Th 2:4
for we serve * alone, who	1Th 2:4
well know, and * knows we were not	1Th 2:5
witnesses—as is *—that we have been	1Th 2:10
not embarrass *, but bring joy to	1Th 2:12
And we will never stop thanking *	1Th 2:13
the very Word of *—which, of	1Th 2:13
They are against both * and man,	1Th 2:15
But the anger of * has caught up	1Th 2:16
How can we thank * enough for you	1Th 3:9
on for you, asking * to let us see	1Th 3:10
your faith. May * our Father	1Th 3:11
and holy by * our Father, so that	1Th 3:13
know how to please * in your daily	1Th 4:1
that ideal. For * wants you to be	1Th 4:3,4
their ignorance of * and his ways.	1Th 4:5
you before. For * has not called	1Th 4:7
of men but of * who gives his Holy	1Th 4:8
I'm sure! For * himself is teaching	1Th 4:9
Jesus returns, * will bring back	1Th 4:14
and the great trumpet-call of *.	1Th 4:16
For * has not chosen to pour out	1Th 5:9
May the * of peace himself make	1Th 5:23
entirely pure and devoted to *;	1Th 5:23
comes back again. *, who called	1Th 5:24
safe in * our Father and in the	2Th 1:1
May * the Father and the Lord	2Th 1:2
Dear brothers, giving thanks to *	2Th 1:3
it is our duty to *, because of the	2Th 1:3
complete faith in *, in spite of	2Th 1:4
the fair, just way * does things,	2Th 1:5
who are suffering, * will give you	2Th 1:7
not wish to know *, and who refuse	2Th 1:8
for you that our * will make you	2Th 1:11
The tender mercy of our * and of	2Th 1:12
messages from * about this, or	2Th 2:1
rebellion against *, and then the	2Th 2:3
He will defy every * there is,	2Th 2:4
He will go in and sit as * in the	2Th 2:4
in the temple of *, claiming that	2Th 2:4
claiming that he himself is *.	2Th 2:4
it save them, so * will allow them	2Th 2:11
give thanks to * for you, our	2Th 2:13
the Lord, because * chose from the	2Th 2:13
Or, "because * chose you to be	2Th 2:13f
Christ himself and * our Father,	2Th 2:16
of the love of * and of the	2Th 3:5
direct command of * our Savior and	1Ti 1:1
of the Lord. May * our Father and	1Ti 1:2
leading up to *—wild ideas that	1Ti 1:3,4
are good when used as * intended.	1Ti 1:8
not made for us, whom * has saved;	1Ti 1:9
they are for sinners who hate *,	1Ti 1:9
blessed *, whose messenger I am.	1Ti 1:10,11
way I could. But * had mercy on me	1Ti 1:13
of them all. But * had mercy on me	1Ti 1:16
Glory and honor to * forever and	1Ti 1:17
he alone is *, and full of	1Ti 1:17
Christ after defying * like that.	1Ti 1:19
This is good and pleases * our	1Ti 2:3
this truth: That * is on one side	1Ti 2:5
proper time * gave to the world.	1Ti 2:6
hands lifted up to *, free from sin	1Ti 2:8
Because * made Adam first, and	1Ti 2:13
the result. So * sent pain and	1Ti 2:15
of the living *, which contains and	1Ti 3:15
and holds high the truth of *.	1Ti 3:15
meat, even though * gave these	1Ti 4:3
For everything * made is good,	1Ti 4:4
it, and if we ask * to bless it,	1Ti 4:5
good by the Word of * and prayer.	1Ti 4:5
is in the living * who died for	1Ti 4:9,10
Be sure to use the abilities *	1Ti 4:14
Stay true to what is right and *	1Ti 4:16
This is something that pleases *	1Ti 5:4
are looking to * for his help and	1Ti 5:5
in the presence of * and the Lord	1Ti 5:21
Don't let the name of * or his	1Ti 6:1
turned away from * because of their	1Ti 6:10
Fight on for *.	1Ti 6:12
eternal life which * has given you,	1Ti 6:12
I command you before * who gives	1Ti 6:13
and only Almighty *, the King of	1Ti 6:15
be in the living * who always	1Ti 6:17
others whatever * has given them.	1Ti 6:18
things that * entrusted to you.	1Ti 6:20
thing in life—they don't know *.	1Ti 6:21
sent out by * to tell men and women	2Ti 1:1
To: Timothy, my dear son. May *	2Ti 1:2
How I thank * for you, Timothy.	2Ti 1:3
I beg my * to bless you richly.	2Ti 1:3
He is my fathers' *, and mine,	2Ti 1:3
"stir up the gift of *."	2Ti 1:6f
trusting him. And * has chosen me	2Ti 1:11
and that he was *, as shown by	2Ti 2:8
But the Word of * is not chained,	2Ti 2:9
Jesus to those * has chosen.	2Ti 2:10
Work hard so * can say to you,	2Ti 2:15
ashamed when * examines your work.	2Ti 2:15
can begin doing the will of *.	2Ti 2:26
sneering at *, disobedient to their	2Ti 3:2
prefer good times to worshiping *.	2Ti 3:4
inspiration from * and is useful to	2Ti 3:16
urge you before * and before Christ	2Ti 4:1
preach the Word of * urgently at	2Ti 4:2
* be the glory forever and ever.	2Ti 4:18
FROM: PAUL, THE slave of * and the	Tit 1:1
faith to those * has chosen and to	Tit 1:1
life, which * promised them before	Tit 1:1
By command of * our Savior I have	Tit 1:3
May * the Father and Christ Jesus	Tit 1:4
turned away from the grace of *.	Tit 1:11
Such persons claim they know *,	Tit 1:16
to believe in our Savior and *.	Tit 2:10
realization that * wants us to turn	Tit 2:12
great * and Savior Jesus Christ.	Tit 2:13
and love of * our Savior to appear,	Tit 3:4
May * our Father and the Lord	Phm 1:3
I always thank * when I am	Phm 1:4
I am hoping that * will answer your	Phm 1:22
LONG AGO * spoke in many different	Heb 1:1
Son is and does marks him as *.	Heb 1:3
beside the great * of heaven.	Heb 1:3

GOD Con't)

his name "Son of *," which was	Heb 1:4
the angels. For * never said to	Heb 1:5,6
But * said it about Jesus.	Heb 1:5,6
Son came to earth—* said, "Let all	Heb 1:5,6
all the angels of * worship him."	Heb 1:5,6
* speaks of his angels as	Heb 1:7
O *, will last forever and ever;	Heb 1:8
and hate wrong; so *, even your	Heb 1:9
so God, even your *, has poured	Heb 1:9
* also called him "Lord" when	Heb 1:10
And did * ever say to an angel,	Heb 1:13
* always has shown us that these	Heb 2:4
who believe; yes, * has assigned	Heb 2:4
David says to *, "What is mere man	Heb 2:6
now by * with glory and honor	Heb 2:9
and proper that *, who made	Heb 2:10
my brothers about * my Father, and	Heb 2:12
in * along with my brothers."	Heb 2:13
am I and the children * gave me."	Heb 2:13
High Priest before *, a Priest who	Heb 2:17
us and faithful to * in dealing	Heb 2:17
DEAR BROTHERS whom *	Heb 3:1
For Jesus was faithful to * who	Heb 3:2
but only * made everything.	Heb 3:4
testing them. But * was patient	Heb 3:9
"But," * says, "I was very	Heb 3:10
Then *, full of this anger	Heb 3:11
you away from the living *.	Heb 3:12
*, being blinded by the glamor	Heb 3:13
the end, trusting * just as we did	Heb 3:14
And who was it who made * angry	Heb 3:17
And to whom was * speaking when	Heb 3:18
message that * wants to save us—has	Heb 4:2
For only we who believe * can	Heb 4:3
it is written that * rested on the	Heb 4:4
Even so they didn't get in, for *	Heb 4:5
disobeyed * and failed to enter.	Heb 4:6
If that were what * meant, he	Heb 4:8
still waiting for the people of *.	Heb 4:9
just as * did after the creation.	Heb 4:10
not to disobey * as the children of	Heb 4:11
For whatever * says to us is full	Heb 4:12
all-seeing eyes of our living *;	Heb 4:13
But Jesus the Son of * is our	Heb 4:14
the very throne of * and stay there	Heb 4:16
men in their dealings with *.	Heb 5:1
He presents their gifts to * and	Heb 5:1
He has to be called by * for this	Heb 5:4
in the same way * chose Aaron.	Heb 5:4
no, he was chosen by *.	Heb 5:5
no, he was chosen by God. * said	Heb 5:5
And another time * said to	Heb 5:6
he pleaded with *, praying with	Heb 5:7
of blood? But * graciously heard	Heb 5:7f
death. And * heard his prayers	Heb 5:7
desire to obey * at all times.	Heb 5:7
For remember that * has chosen	Heb 5:10
about the necessity of faith in *;	Heb 6:1
good the Word of * is, and felt the	Heb 6:5
and then have turned against *.	Heb 6:6
nailed the Son of * to the cross	Heb 6:6
salvation. For * is not unfair.	Heb 6:10
receive all that * has promised	Heb 6:12
to Abraham: * took an oath in his	Heb 6:13
until finally * gave him a son,	Heb 6:15
about it. * also bound himself	Heb 6:17
is impossible for * to tell a lie.	Heb 6:18
they hear such assurances from *;	Heb 6:18
connecting us with * himself behind	Heb 6:19
also a priest of the Most High *.	Heb 7:1
of the Son of *—a priest forever.	Heb 7:3
us, why then did * need to send	Heb 7:11
And when * sends a new kind of	Heb 7:12,13,14
made anyone really right with *.	Heb 7:19
us acceptable to *, and now we may	Heb 7:19
* took an oath that Christ would	Heb 7:20
all who come to * through him.	Heb 7:25
be there to remind * that he has	Heb 7:25
wrong, but later * appointed by his	Heb 7:28
greatest honor next to * himself.	Heb 8:1
the tabernacle, * warned him to	Heb 8:5
on to us from * contains far more	Heb 8:6
replace it. But * himself found	Heb 8:8
* and they shall be my people.	Heb 8:10
* speaks of these new promises,	Heb 8:13
agreement between * and his people	Heb 9:1
as an offering to * to cover his	Heb 9:7
us want to serve the living *.	Heb 9:14
gave himself to * to die for our	Heb 9:14
the wonders * has promised them.	Heb 9:15
between you and *, the agreement	Heb 9:20
* commanded me to make with you."	Heb 9:20
appear now before * as our Friend.	Heb 9:24
the world, "O *, the blood of	Heb 10:5
But Christ gave himself to * for	Heb 10:12
in the sight of * all those whom he	Heb 10:14
of Holies where * is, because of	Heb 10:19
us into the holy presence of *.	Heb 10:20
us go right in, to * himself, with	Heb 10:22
the salvation * has promised us.	Heb 10:23
the Son of * and treated his	Heb 10:29
into the hands of the living *.	Heb 10:31
Otherwise, if they shrink back, *	Heb 10:38
backs on * and sealed our fate.	Heb 10:39
Men of * in days of old were	Heb 11:2
By faith—by believing *—we know	Heb 11:3
that Abel obeyed * and brought an	Heb 11:4
* more than Cain's offering did.	Heb 11:4
offering did. * accepted Abel and	Heb 11:4
lessons from him about trusting *.	Heb 11:4
Enoch trusted * too, and that is	Heb 11:5
and that is why * took him away to	Heb 11:5
suddenly he was gone because *	Heb 11:5
Before this happened * had said	Heb 11:5
You can never please * without	Heb 11:6
Anyone who wants to come to *	Heb 11:6
that there is a * and that he	Heb 11:6
Noah was another who trusted *.	Heb 11:7
Noah's belief in * was in direct	Heb 11:7
one of those whom * has accepted.	Heb 11:7
Abraham trusted *, and when God	Heb 11:8
Abraham trusted God, and when *	Heb 11:8
to whom * gave the same promise.	Heb 11:9
waiting for * to bring him to that	Heb 11:10
whose designer and builder is *.	Heb 11:10
she realized that *, who gave her	Heb 11:11
all that * had promised them;	Heb 11:13
And now * is not ashamed to be	Heb 11:16
to be called their *, for he has	Heb 11:16
While * was testing him, Abraham	Heb 11:17
still trusted in * and his	Heb 11:17
through whom * had promised to give	Heb 11:18
He believed that if Isaac died *	Heb 11:19
that Isaac knew * would give future	Heb 11:20
spoke of * bringing the people of	Heb 11:22
When they saw that * had given	Heb 11:23
they trusted that * would save him	Heb 11:23
reward that * would give him.	Heb 11:26
And it was because he trusted *	Heb 11:27
could see * right there with him.	Heb 11:27
And it was because he believed *	Heb 11:28
to kill a lamb as * had told them	Heb 11:28
The people of Israel trusted *	Heb 11:29
days, as * had commanded them.	Heb 11:30
she believed in * and his	Heb 11:31
refused to obey *, for she gave a	Heb 11:31
These people all trusted * and	Heb 11:33
received what * had promised them;	Heb 11:33
But others trusted * and were	Heb 11:35
than turn from * and be	Heb 11:35
they trusted * and won his	Heb 11:39
all that * had promised them;	Heb 11:39
them; for * wanted them to wait	Heb 11:40
race that * has set before us.	Heb 12:1
place of honor by the throne of *.	Heb 12:2
words * spoke to you, his child?	Heb 12:5
Let * train you, for he is doing	Heb 12:7
corrected? If * doesn't punish you	Heb 12:8
careless about * as Esau did: he	Heb 12:16
Sinai when * gave them his laws.	Heb 12:18
people begged * to stop speaking.	Heb 12:19
city of the living *, the heavenly	Heb 12:22
and to * who is Judge of all;	Heb 12:23
to * who speaks to us from heaven!	Heb 12:25
let us please * by serving him with	Heb 12:28
For our * is a consuming fire.	Heb 12:29
and be pure; for * will surely	Heb 13:4
what you have. For * has said, "I	Heb 13:5
who have taught you the Word of *.	Heb 13:7
as a gift from *, not from	Heb 13:9
of praise to * by telling others of	Heb 13:15
your souls, and * will judge them	Heb 13:17
And now may the * of peace, who	Heb 13:20,21
agreement between * and you, signed	Heb 13:20,21
FROM: JAMES, A servant of * and of	Jas 1:1
If you want to know what * wants	Jas 1:5
* has promised those who love him.	Jas 1:12
wrong it is never * who is tempting	Jas 1:13
tempting him, for * never wants to	Jas 1:13
to the death penalty from *.	Jas 1:15
comes to us from *, the Creator of	Jas 1:17
as * demands that we must be.	Jas 1:20
what it says, and * will greatly	Jas 1:25
fault, from * the Father's point of	Jas 1:27
Listen to me, dear brothers: *	Jas 2:5
that is the gift * has promised to	Jas 2:5
keeps every law of *, but makes one	Jas 2:10
For the * who said you must not	Jas 2:11
"Well, good-bye and * bless you;	Jas 2:16
* is by faith alone, plus nothing;	Jas 2:18
Believing in one *?	Jas 2:19
without doing what * wants you to?	Jas 2:20
willing to obey *, even if it meant	Jas 2:21
You see, he was trusting * so	Jas 2:22
to do whatever * told him to;	Jas 2:22
Abraham trusted *, and the Lord	Jas 2:23
even called "the friend of *."	Jas 2:23
against men who are made like *.	Jas 3:9
is that you don't ask * for it.	Jas 4:2
world—makes you an enemy of *?	Jas 4:4
you cannot also be a friend of *.	Jas 4:4
Holy Spirit, whom * has placed	Jas 4:5
As the Scripture says, * gives	Jas 4:6
So give yourselves humbly to *.	Jas 4:7
And when you draw close to *,	Jas 4:8
to God, * will draw close to you.	Jas 4:8
be filled with * alone to make them	Jas 4:8
self-confidence never pleases *.	Jas 4:16
slipped away from * and no longer	Jas 5:19
brings him back to * will have	Jas 5:20
Dear friends, * the Father chose	1Pe 1:2
to please him. May * bless you	1Pe 1:2
All honor to *, the God and	1Pe 1:3
All honor to God, the * and	1Pe 1:3
the dead. And * has reserved for	1Pe 1:4
and decay. And *, in his mighty	1Pe 1:5
more precious to * than mere gold;	1Pe 1:7
Obey * because you are his	1Pe 1:14
get to heaven. * paid a ransom to	1Pe 1:18
the sinless, spotless Lamb of *.	1Pe 1:19
Lamb of God. * chose him for this	1Pe 1:20
trust can be in * who raised Christ	1Pe 1:21
of Rock upon which * builds;	1Pe 2:4
very precious to * who has chosen	1Pe 2:4
—and offer to * those things that	1Pe 2:5
been chosen by * himself—you are	1Pe 2:9
show to others how * called you out	1Pe 2:9
end up praising * for your good	1Pe 2:12
Fear * and honor the government.	1Pe 2:17
the blows, * is well pleased.	1Pe 2:20
part of the work * has given you.	1Pe 2:21
of * who always judges fairly.	1Pe 2:23
wandered away from *, but now you	1Pe 2:25
spirit which is so precious to *.	1Pe 3:4
old, who trusted * and fitted in	1Pe 3:5
and * will bless us for it.	1Pe 3:9
for * will reward you for it.	1Pe 3:14
Remember, if * wants you to	1Pe 3:17
might bring us safely home to *.	1Pe 3:18
to listen to *, though he waited	1Pe 3:20
we are turning to * and asking him	1Pe 3:21
of honor next to * the Father, with	1Pe 3:22
be anxious to do the will of *.	1Pe 4:2
live in their spirits as * lives.	1Pe 4:6
* has given each of you some	1Pe 4:10
Then preach as though * himself	1Pe 4:11
and energy that * supplies, so that	1Pe 4:11
supplies, so that * will be	1Pe 4:11
the Spirit of * will come upon you	1Pe 4:14
Or, "the glory of the Spirit of *	1Pe 4:14f
Praise * for the privilege of	1Pe 4:16
yourself to the * who made you, for	1Pe 4:19
plea to you: Feed the flock of *;	1Pe 5:2
spirits, for * gives special	1Pe 5:5
the mighty hand of *, in his good	1Pe 5:6
little while, our *, who is full of	1Pe 5:10
statement of the way * blesses.	1Pe 5:12
our * and Savior gives to us.	2Pe 1:1
For then you must learn to know *	2Pe 1:5
letting * have his way with you.	2Pe 1:6
has forgotten that * delivered him	2Pe 1:9
are among those * has called and	2Pe 1:10
or fall away. And * will open wide	2Pe 1:11
honor given him by * his Father;	2Pe 1:17,18
gave them true messages from *.	2Pe 1:20,21
their lies about *, turning against	2Pe 2:1
of your money. But * condemned them	2Pe 2:3
on the way. For * did not spare	2Pe 2:4
up for *, and his family of seven.	2Pe 2:5
At that time * completely	2Pe 2:5
this fact: that * did destroy the	2Pe 3:5,6
surround it. And * has commanded	2Pe 3:7
along—the day when * will set the	2Pe 3:12
This one who is Life from * has	1Jn 1:2
This is the message * has given	1Jn 1:5
on to you: that * is Light and in	1Jn 1:5
[And it is perfectly proper for *	1Jn 1:9
lying and calling * a liar, for he	1Jn 1:10
good and who pleases * completely.	1Jn 2:1
brought us into fellowship with *;	1Jn 2:2
learn to love * more and more.	1Jn 2:5
have learned to know * our Father.	1Jn 2:13
know the eternal *, and to you	1Jn 2:14
that you do not really love *;	1Jn 2:15
importance—these are not from *.	1Jn 2:16
the will of * will live forever.	1Jn 2:17
in * the Father and in his Son.	1Jn 2:22
can't have * the Father either.	1Jn 2:23
God's Son, has * the Father also.	1Jn 2:23
both * the Father and his Son.	1Jn 2:24
Since we know that * is always	1Jn 2:29
people don't know *, naturally they	1Jn 3:1
are against *, for every sin is	1Jn 3:4
sin is done against the will of *.	1Jn 3:4
But the Son of * came to destroy	1Jn 3:8
of * and who belongs to Satan.	1Jn 3:10
us, * is greater than our heart."	1Jn 3:20f
And this is what * says we must	1Jn 3:23
Those who do what * says—they	1Jn 3:24
living with * and he with them.	1Jn 3:24
is a message from *: test it first	1Jn 4:1
If so, then the message is from *	1Jn 4:2

(GOD Con't)
is not from * but from one who is 1Jn 4:3
you belong to * and have already 1Jn 4:4
But we are children of *; 1Jn 4:6
talked with * will listen to us. 1Jn 4:6
a message is really from *; 1Jn 4:6
love comes from * and those who are 1Jn 4:7
the children of *, and that they 1Jn 4:7
he doesn't know *—for God is love. 1Jn 4:8
he doesn't know God—for * is love. 1Jn 4:8
* showed how much he loved us by 1Jn 4:9
not our love for *, but his love 1Jn 4:10
Dear friends, since * loved us as 1Jn 4:11
never yet seen *, when we love each 1Jn 4:12
we love each other * lives in us 1Jn 4:12
* sent his Son to be their Savior. 1Jn 4:14
is the Son of * has God living in 1Jn 4:15
the Son of God has * living in him, 1Jn 4:15
in him, and he is living with *. 1Jn 4:15
We know how much * loves us 1Jn 4:16
loves us dearly. * is love, and 1Jn 4:16
with * and God is living in him. 1Jn 4:16
with God and * is living in him. 1Jn 4:16
If anyone says "I love *," but 1Jn 4:20
he love * whom he has never seen? 1Jn 4:20
never seen? And * himself has said 1Jn 4:21
not only *, but his brother too. 1Jn 4:21
Savior—then you are a child of *. 1Jn 5:1
how much you love and obey *. 1Jn 5:2
Loving * means doing what he 1Jn 5:3
for every child of * can obey 1Jn 5:4
that Jesus is truly the Son of *? 1Jn 5:5
And we know he is, because * 1Jn 5:6,7,8
that Jesus Christ is the Son of *. 1Jn 5:6,7,8
can believe whatever * declares. 1Jn 5:9
* declares that Jesus is his Son. 1Jn 5:9
actually calling * a liar, because 1Jn 5:10
what * has said about his Son. 1Jn 5:10
And what is it that * has said? 1Jn 5:11
in the Son of * so that you may 1Jn 5:13
you should ask * to forgive him and 1Jn 5:16
to forgive him and * will give him 1Jn 5:16
we are children of * and that all 1Jn 5:19
us understand and find the true *. 1Jn 5:20
And now we are in * because we 1Jn 5:20
his Son, who is the only true *; 1Jn 5:20
hearts forever, * the Father and 2Jn 1:3
of the old rule * gave us right 2Jn 1:5
If we love *, we will do 2Jn 1:6
Christ, you will leave * behind; 2Jn 1:9
teachings, you will have * too. 2Jn 1:9
sister—another choice child of *. 2Jn 1:13
a good work for * in taking care of 3Jn 1:5
prove that they are far from *. 3Jn 1:11
of * and chosen by him. Jud 1:1
the salvation * has given us, but Jud 1:3
the truth which * gave, once for Jud 1:3
Now * has them chained up in Jud 1:6
* and will die under his curse. Jud 1:11
that * has prepared for them. Jud 1:13
rebellion against *, revealing all Jud 1:15
him who alone is *, who saves us Jud 1:24,25
* permitted him to reveal these Rev 1:1
down—the words of * and Jesus Rev 1:2
* who is, and was, and is to come! Rev 1:4
made us priests of * his Father. Rev 1:6
all things," says *, who is the Rev 1:8
the Word of *, and for telling what Rev 1:9
by * to oversee each local church. Rev 1:20f
Tree of Life in the Paradise of *. Rev 2:7
children of *—but they aren't, for Rev 2:9
from the Son of *, whose eyes Rev 2:18
"the seven spirits of *." Rev 3:1f
of * and the seven stars. Rev 3:1
far from right in the sight of *. Rev 3:2
a pillar in the temple of my *; Rev 3:12
in the city of my *—the New Rev 3:12
coming down from heaven from my *; Rev 3:12
about the things of *. Rev 3:19
"the seven spirits of *." Rev 4:5f
of *. Spread out before it was a Rev 4:5
holy, holy, Lord * Almighty—the one Rev 4:8
"the seven spirits of *"; Rev 5:6f
of *, sent out into every part of Rev 5:6
from every nation as gifts for *. Rev 5:9
and made them priests of our *; Rev 5:10
the Word of * and for being Rev 6:9
the Great Seal of the Living *. Rev 7:2
placed the Seal of * upon the Rev 7:3
comes from our * upon the throne, Rev 7:10
the throne and worshiping *. Rev 7:11
be to our * forever and forever. Rev 7:12
the throne of *, serving him day Rev 7:15
* will wipe their tears away." Rev 7:17
that stand before *, and they were Rev 8:2
ascended up to * from the altar Rev 8:4
the mark of * on their foreheads. Rev 9:4
the throne of *, saying to the Rev 9:13
still refused to worship *! Rev 9:20
the temple of *, including the Rev 11:1
the temple of *, and the altar, and Rev 11:1f
before the * of all the earth. Rev 11:4
of life from * will enter them and Rev 11:11
give glory to the * of heaven. Rev 11:13
thrones before * threw themselves Rev 11:16
give thanks, Lord * Almighty, who Rev 11:17
Then, in heaven, the temple of * Rev 11:19
caught up to * and to his throne. Rev 12:5
wilderness, where * had prepared a Rev 12:6
them day and night before our *. Rev 12:10
each one defying and insulting *. Rev 13:1
eternal plan and knowledge of *. Rev 13:8f
The people of * who are destined Rev 13:10
of the throne of * and before the Rev 14:3
offering to * and the Lamb. Rev 14:4
"Fear *," he shouted, "and Rev 14:7
drink the wine of the anger of *; Rev 14:10
All were holding harps of *, and Rev 15:2
of *, and the song of the Lamb: Rev 15:3,4
Lord * Almighty. Rev 15:3,4
* who lives forever and forever. Rev 15:7
the wrath of * upon the earth." Rev 16:1
say, "Yes, Lord * Almighty, your Rev 16:7
cursed the name of * who sent the Rev 16:9
and cursed the * of heaven for Rev 16:11
coming Judgment Day of * Almighty. Rev 16:14
* because of the terrible hail. Rev 16:21
over with blasphemies against *. Rev 17:3
by fire. For * will put a plan Rev 17:17
the words of * will be fulfilled. Rev 17:17
high as heaven and * is ready to Rev 18:5
and you, O children of * and the Rev 18:20
For at last * has given judgment Rev 18:20
Salvation is from our *. Rev 19:1
down and worshiped *, who was Rev 19:4
said, "Praise our *, all you his Rev 19:5
For the Lord our *, the Almighty, Rev 19:6
deeds done by the people of *. Rev 19:8
And he added, "* himself has Rev 19:9
"These are the true words of *." Rev 19:9f
For I am a servant of * just as Rev 19:10
his title was "The Word of *." Rev 19:13
of the wrath of Almighty *. Rev 19:15
for the supper of the Great *! Rev 19:17
the Word of *, and who had not Rev 20:4
will be priests of * and of Christ, Rev 20:6
But fire from * in heaven will Rev 20:9
and small, standing before *; Rev 20:12
coming down from * out of heaven. Rev 21:2
the home of * is now among men, and Rev 21:3
yes, * himself will be among them. Rev 21:3
add, "and be their *." Rev 21:3f
be his * and he will be my son. Rev 21:7
out of the skies from *. Rev 21:10
with the glory of *, and flashed Rev 21:11
city, for the Lord * Almighty and Rev 21:22
* and of the Lamb illuminate it. Rev 21:23
from the throne of * and the Lamb, Rev 22:1
for the throne of * and of the Rev 22:3
the Lord * will be their light; Rev 22:5
*, who tells his prophets what Rev 22:6,7
Worship * alone." Rev 22:9
strayed away from *, and the Rev 22:15
is written here, * shall add to him Rev 22:18
these prophecies, * shall take away Rev 22:19

GOD-FEARING
to them, "I am a * man and I'm Gen 42:18
and to live good, * lives day after Tit 2:12

GOD-FORSAKEN
be called "The * Land" or the Is 62:4
will say, 'This * land has become Eze 36:35

GOD-GIVEN
"ALL THE OTHER craftsmen with * Ex 36:1
him and listen to his * wisdom. 1Ki 10:24
felt a strong, * desire to obey the 2Ch 30:12
men of their * rights, and refused Lam 3:34,35,36
their children of every * right. Mic 2:9
Guard well the splendid, * 2Ti 1:14

GOD-LIKE
the * power of life and death!" Gen 41:45

GOD'S
For, as she said, "With * help, Gen 4:1
his affairs according to * will. Gen 6:9,10
swear to me by * name that you Gen 21:23
So he named the place "* Gen 32:1
"Interpreting dreams is * Gen 40:8
celebration of * deliverance. Ex 12:42
identify you as * people, just as Ex 13:16
NOW, AT * command, the people of Ex 17:1
"Are you trying to test * Ex 17:2
for * decisions," Moses told him. Ex 18:15,16
and instructing them in * ways. Ex 18:15,16
teaching them * laws, and showing Ex 18:19,20
He told them, "Get ready for * Ex 19:15
* directions and laws. Ex 24:7
tablets engraved with * laws. Ex 26:33
chestpiece to be used as * oracle; Ex 28:15
his heart (it is * oracle) when he Ex 28:29
to determine * "yes" or "no" on Ex 28:30,31f
Then Moses asked to see * glory. Ex 33:18
were stirred by * Spirit returned Ex 35:21
salt is a reminder of * covenant. Lev 2:13
disobeying one of * laws, as soon Lev 4:22
of Israel and * wrath—to protect Num 1:53
about it, and this was * reply: Num 9:9
reported * words to the people! Num 14:39
for them; for * anger has gone out Num 16:46
another example of * removing a Deu 4:34
between * blessing or God's curse! Deu 11:26
between God's blessing or * curse! Deu 11:26
man who refused * verdict, and they Deu 17:13
This regular reading of * laws Deu 17:20
turning away from * laws in the Deu 17:20
For Israel was * own personal Deu 32:9
The Levites shall teach * laws to Deu 33:10
Because he carried out * penalties Deu 33:21
And at * command he performed Deu 34:11,12
the Israelis. * command to destroy Jos 7:1
or else become totally *. Jos 7:12f
had written in the book of * laws. Jos 8:34
"You know very well that * Jos 23:14
* answer came, "Judah. Ju 1:2
they refused to obey * commands. Ju 2:17
were very evil in * sight, for they Ju 3:7
At * command they rushed into the Ju 5:15
you want * blessing, listen to me! Ju 9:7
wife according to * law, for you Ru 3:9
also known as "* Hill," where the 1Sa 10:5
for it will be * signal that he 1Sa 14:10
children into * hands forever." 1Sa 20:42
"It is a serious sin to attack * 1Sa 24:6
"If you swear by * name that you 1Sa 30:15
"Why did you kill * chosen 2Sa 1:14
you killed * appointed king." 2Sa 1:16
He is * appointed king no more. 2Sa 1:21
and even though I am * chosen 2Sa 3:39
but may I receive * rich 1Ki 2:45
have come to place * curse upon you 1Ki 21:20
to obey all of * laws and never 2Ki 17:37
obeyed all of * commands to Moses. 2Ki 18:6
was an evil man, in * opinion. 2Ki 21:6
He refused to listen to * 2Ki 21:22
with * laws written on it!" 2Ki 22:8
the entire book of * laws which had 2Ki 23:1
reason—to give joy to * people! 1Ch 14:2
for * mercies are very great." 1Ch 21:13
son to build * Temple, and a royal 2Ch 2:12
Carefully following * 2Ch 4:7
They have lived without * laws. 2Ch 15:3
have done, * wrath is upon you. 2Ch 19:2
no injustice among * judges, no 2Ch 19:7
the battle is not yours, but *! 2Ch 20:15
the Temple, as required by * laws. 2Ch 23:5,6
this was contrary to * rules. 2Ch 30:17,18,19
the Lord God and * servant 2Ch 32:16
prayer to God, and * reply through 2Ch 33:18
laws required of * people, he 2Ch 34:19
priest, the student of * commands: Ez 7:11
to take a copy of * laws to Judah Ez 7:14
for why should we risk * wrath Ez 7:23
it to * Temple in Jerusalem. Ez 8:30
more deeply under * condemnation Ez 10:10
could hear and understand * words. Neh 8:12
unless we obeyed * laws as issued Neh 10:29
* terrors are arrayed against me. Job 6:4
But true wisdom and power are *. Job 12:13
Is * comfort too little for you? Job 15:11
truly good. * fire consumes them Job 15:34
"I have stayed in * paths, Job 23:11
I have stepped off * pathway, or if Job 31:7,8
Do you—* critic—have the Job 40:2
he is among all of * creation, so Job 40:19
* laws are perfect. Ps 19:7,8
* laws are pure, eternal, just. Ps 19:9
They will receive * own goodness Ps 24:5
He shall live within * circle of Ps 25:13
For all * words are right, and Ps 33:4
Your justice is as solid as * Ps 36:6
of sin! For * forgiveness does not Ps 49:7
* glory-light shines from the Ps 50:2
to inform David of * judgment Ps 51:1
deed of yours against * people. Ps 52:1
With * help we shall do mighty Ps 60:12
And so * people are dismayed and Ps 73:10
Then one day I went into * Ps 73:17
* REPUTATION IS very great in Ps 76:1
they missed the target of * will. Ps 78:57
The whole earth has seen * Ps 98:2,3
* servant Abraham, and of Jacob. Ps 105:5,6
collar, until * time finally Ps 105:19
testing * patience to the Ps 106:14
circumstances. * constant care of Ps 112:6
became * new home and kingdom. Ps 114:2
stop me from obeying * commands. Ps 119:115
That is * reward to those who Ps 128:4
in * permanent home here on earth. Ps 132:7
* lovingkindness to Israel Ps 136:19
who turn from * ways to walk down Pro 2:11,12,13
ever-brightening light of * favor; Pro 4:18
The good shall never lose * Pro 10:30
for good you will find * favor; Pro 11:27
Despise * Word and find yourself Pro 13:13
The depths of hell are open to * Pro 15:11

(GOD'S Con't)

the final outcome is in * hands.	Pro 16:1
O my son, be wise and stay in *	Pro 23:19,20,21
It is * privilege to conceal	Pro 25:2,3
But those who use * wisdom are	Pro 28:26
and thus insult * holy name.	Pro 30:9
of * work from beginning to end.	Ecc 3:11
or taken from it; * purpose in this	Ecc 3:14
godly and wise men are in * will;	Ecc 9:1
of * truth on these points!	Ecc 9:5f
of * truth on these points!	Ecc 9:5f
of * truth on these points!	Ecc 9:10f
* ways are as mysterious as the	Ecc 11:5
They will be * holy people.	Is 4:2,3,4
to describe * people, as explained	Is 4:2,3,4f
I have given you the story of *	Is 5:7
Apparently * patience with their	Is 6:10f
a virgin birth. * sign was that	Is 7:14f
beneath it: * presence among them	Is 8:14,15
will be under * contempt and	Is 9:1
Yet even after all of this, *	Is 9:21
HERE IS * message to Moab:	Is 15:1
THIS IS * message to Damascus,	Is 17:1
armies thundering toward * land.	Is 17:12
THIS IS * message concerning	Is 19:1
THIS IS * message concerning	Is 21:1
This is * message to Edom:	Is 21:11
This is * message concerning	Is 21:13
THIS IS * message concerning	Is 22:1
THIS IS * message to Tyre:	Is 23:1
sing for joy! For * light of life	Is 26:19
And if you leave * paths and go	Is 30:21
message to Cyrus, * anointed, whom	Is 45:1
your own fires and not from *;	Is 50:11
The time will come when *	Is 51:11
his saving power? In * eyes	Is 53:2
We, who left * paths to follow	Is 53:6
and * program shall prosper in	Is 53:10
See 2 Samuel 7 for the terms of *	Is 55:3f
sign [of * power and love	Is 55:13
you aren't finding * blessings;	Is 59:9
that the time of * favor to them	Is 61:2
be "The Land of * Delight" and	Is 62:4
of old when Moses, * servant, led	Is 63:11
THESE ARE * messages to Jeremiah	Jer 1:1
possessed the Ark of * covenant.	Jer 3:16
famine nor war! * prophets," they	Jer 5:13
They all return at * appointed	Jer 8:7
in * name on pain of death.	Jer 11:21,22
had in mind * deliverance of	Jer 21:1f
Therefore this is * decree of	Jer 22:18
each other, "What is * message?	Jer 23:35
But stop using this term, "*	Jer 23:36
drank from this cup of * wrath.	Jer 25:26
If they are really * prophets,	Jer 27:18
David, the man after * own heart.	Jer 33:15f
written down all * messages as	Jer 45:1
THIS IS * message to Jeremiah	Jer 47:1
in ruins too, for * judgment has	Jer 48:21
Elam: * message against Elam	Jer 49:34
is * battleaxe and sword.	Jer 51:20
that come from the rod of * wrath.	Lam 3:1
dreaming, I saw one of * angels	Dan 4:13
"Then you saw * angel	Dan 4:23
been weighed in * balances and have	Dan 5:27
warring against * people and	Dan 7:21
* people will be helpless in his	Dan 7:25
is avenged and * people triumph?"	Dan 8:13
and he will devastate * people.	Dan 8:24
to help you understand * plans.	Dan 9:22
But in * time and plan, his	Dan 9:27
until * appointed time has come.	Dan 11:27
the Jews who were loyal to * laws.	Dan 11:32f
their trials, at * appointed time.	Dan 11:35
is up. For * plans are unshakable.	Dan 11:36
after the power of * people has	Dan 12:7
He went far beyond * command to	Hos 1:4,5f
of * angel (Isaiah 36–37).	Hos 1:7f
This is * message to you: The	Mic 3:5
announcing * punishment on Israel	Mic 3:8
O Jerusalem—the Watchtower of *	Mic 4:8
Drink down * judgment on	Hab 2:16
by their disobedience to * laws.	Zep 3:4
they learned, that * Word endures!	Zec 1:5,6
Then he said, "This is * message	Zec 4:6
thanksgiving for * mercy, declaring	Zec 4:7
the words of * curse going out over	Zec 5:3
THIS IS THE message concerning *	Zec 9:1
for the flock. * sword will cut his	Zec 11:17
so the people will learn * laws.	Mal 2:7
For you have left * paths.	Mal 2:8
Judah have defiled * holy and	Mal 2:11
by the Lord. In * wise plan, when	Mal 2:15
Messenger of * promises, to bring	Mal 3:1
difference between * treatment of	Mal 3:18
This will fulfill * message	Mt 1:22
"And even now the axe of *	Mt 3:10
But those who teach * laws and	Mt 5:19
God, for the heavens are * throne.	Mt 5:34
the people of Israel—* lost sheep.	Mt 10:6
money choke out * Word, and he does	Mt 13:22
the sky and asked * blessing on the	Mt 14:19
For instance, * law is 'Honor	Mt 15:4
point of view, and not from *."	Mt 16:23
"* Man is here!	Mt 21:9
of the Scriptures and of * power!	Mt 22:29
that to swear 'By * Temple' means	Mt 23:16
shortened for the sake of * chosen	Mt 24:22
if it were possible, even * chosen	Mt 24:24
No, nor even * Son.	Mt 24:36
Didn't he say, 'I am * Son'?"	Mt 27:41,42,43
"Surely this was * Son."	Mt 27:54
* Holy Spirit!"	Mk 1:8
Jesus went to Galilee to preach *	Mk 1:14
he announced. "* Kingdom is	Mk 1:15
Anyone who does * will is my	Mk 3:35
anyone who brings * message to	Mk 4:14
some of those who hear * message;	Mk 4:15
in and crowd out * message from	Mk 4:19
who truly accept * message and	Mk 4:20
For * sake, don't torture me!"	Mk 5:7,8
For you ignore * specific orders	Mk 7:8
You are simply rejecting * laws	Mk 7:9
point of view and not from *."	Mk 8:33
But it certainly isn't * way.	Mk 10:6,7
the beginning of * creation, nor	Mk 13:19
if possible, even * own children.	Mk 13:22
bread and asked * blessing on it	Mk 14:22
the arrival of * Kingdom), gathered	Mk 15:42,43
and sat down at * right hand.	Mk 16:19
to obey all of * laws in spirit as	Lk 1:6
destined for * mightiest praise.	Lk 1:42
he had seen him—* anointed King.	Lk 2:26
Satan said, "If you are * Son,	Lk 4:3
implore * blessing on those who	Lk 6:28
—agreed that * requirements were	Lk 7:29
They rejected * plan for them and	Lk 7:30
The seed is * message to men.	Lk 8:11
listen and believe * words but	Lk 8:14
They listen to * words and cling	Lk 8:15
demonstrating * anger against it	Lk 9:5
out in accordance with * plan.	Lk 9:31
for the murder of * servants from	Lk 11:50
in the presence of * angels if you	Lk 12:8
This may mean that * people will	Lk 17:37f
So from * point of view, all men	Lk 20:37,38
Therefore * heaviest sentence	Lk 20:47
For those will be days of *	Lk 21:22
triumph ends in * good time.	Lk 21:24
is the token of * new agreement to	Lk 22:20
It is part of * plan.	Lk 22:22
* Chosen One, the Messiah."	Lk 23:35
to eat, he asked * blessing on the	Lk 24:30
of all things; * personal	Jn 1:1f
of all things; * personal	Jn 1:14f
for * House will be my undoing."	Jn 2:17
For this one—sent by God—speaks *	Jn 3:33,34
God's words, for * Spirit is upon	Jn 3:33,34
And all who trust him—* Son—to	Jn 3:36
But if you refuse to honor * Son,	Jn 5:23
hear the voice of * Son, and shall	Jn 5:28
one sent to you with * message.	Jn 5:38
you don't have * love within you.	Jn 5:41,42
determines to do * will, then you	Jn 7:17
him, for * time had not yet come.	Jn 7:30
Jesus said, "At * direction I	Jn 10:32
Hail to * Ambassador!"	Jn 12:13
Who will accept * mighty miracles	Jn 12:38
availability of * goodness, and of	Jn 16:8
He is helping me. * mighty power	Act 2:25
and you are included in * promise	Act 3:25
and boldly preached * message.	Act 4:31
test the Spirit of * ability to	Act 5:9
* message was preached in	Act 6:7
destroyed * Laws, though you	Act 7:53
Jesus standing at * right hand.	Act 7:55
had accepted * message, they sent	Act 8:14
for thinking * gift can be bought!	Act 8:20
the Jews are not * only favorites!	Act 10:34
* Good News was spreading rapidly	Act 12:24
at the power of * message.	Act 13:12
is * promised Savior of Israel!	Act 13:23
Good News—that * promise to our	Act 13:32,33
eternal life, believed. So *	Act 13:49
But the Jews who spurned *	Act 14:2
area was stirred by * message.	Act 19:20
about * mighty kindness and love.	Act 20:24
declaring all * message to you.	Act 20:27
feed and shepherd * flock—his	Act 20:28
way to talk to * High Priest?"	Act 23:4
* promise made to our ancestors.	Act 26:6
for their sins and * inheritance	Act 26:18
sent out to preach * Good News.	Rom 1:1
* prophets in the Old Testament.	Rom 1:2
* very own—yes, his holy people.	Rom 1:6,7
May all * mercies and peace be	Rom 1:6,7
you in Rome to preach * Good News.	Rom 1:15
It is * powerful method of	Rom 1:16
us right in * sight—when we put our	Rom 1:17
turned against * natural plan for	Rom 1:26
They were fully aware of * death	Rom 1:32
walk in evil ways—* anger will be	Rom 2:8
they never had * written laws, for	Rom 2:12-15
* laws are written within them;	Rom 2:12-15
come when at * command Jesus Christ	Rom 2:16
this is all part of * great plan	Rom 2:16
You are so proud of knowing *	Rom 2:23
something if you obey * laws;	Rom 2:25
And if the heathen obey * laws,	Rom 2:26
That * words will always prove	Rom 3:4
No one has ever really followed *	Rom 3:11
feel secure or enjoy * blessing.	Rom 3:17
to keep * laws instead of doing	Rom 3:19
be made right in * sight by doing	Rom 3:20
For the more we know of * laws,	Rom 3:20
all fall short of * glorious	Rom 3:23
and to end all * anger against us.	Rom 3:25
we no longer need obey * laws?	Rom 3:31
But from * point of view Abraham	Rom 4:1
Christ to save them from * wrath.	Rom 4:4,5
It is clear, then, that * promise	Rom 4:13
Abraham obeyed * laws but because	Rom 4:13
So if you still claim that *	Rom 4:14
are saying that * promises to those	Rom 4:14
we try to gain * blessing and	Rom 4:15
So * blessings are given to us by	Rom 4:16
God, filling us with * goodness.	Rom 4:25
been made right in * sight by faith	Rom 5:1
Now he will save us from all of *	Rom 5:9
never disobeyed * special law	Rom 5:14
man's sin and * forgiveness!	Rom 5:15
to many through * mercy.	Rom 5:15
all who will take * gift of	Rom 5:17
of their failure to obey * laws.	Rom 5:20
* abounding grace forgiving us.	Rom 5:20
to death, but now * kindness rules	Rom 5:21
are free under * favor and mercy.	Rom 6:14
the law, but on receiving * grace!	Rom 6:15
For it uses * good laws for its	Rom 7:13
I love to do * will so far as my	Rom 7:22
In my mind I want to be * willing	Rom 7:23,24,25
So now we can obey * laws if we	Rom 8:4
It never did obey * laws and it	Rom 8:7
should behave like * very own	Rom 8:15
us that we really are * children.	Rom 8:16
its will at * command—will all	Rom 8:20,21
from sin which * children enjoy.	Rom 8:20,21
for us in harmony with * own will.	Rom 8:27
itself cannot keep * love away.	Rom 8:38
And so * blessings are not	Rom 9:16
would hear about * glorious name.	Rom 9:17
that except for * mercy all the	Rom 9:29
enough to gain * favor by keeping	Rom 10:3
that is not * way of salvation.	Rom 10:3
who come preaching * Good News!	Rom 10:15
Have they heard * Word?	Rom 10:18
prophets and torn down * altars;	Rom 11:2,3
of * kindness in choosing them.	Rom 11:5
And if it is by * kindness, then	Rom 11:6
want * salvation for themselves.	Rom 11:11
as a result of * offer of	Rom 11:12
the prophets are * people, their	Rom 11:16
sharing in * rich nourishment of	Rom 11:17
you are now a part of * tree;	Rom 11:18
it has resulted in * giving his	Rom 11:28
and Jacob. For * gifts and his	Rom 11:29
will share in * mercy upon you.	Rom 11:31
As * messenger I give each of you	Rom 12:3
I give each of you * warning: Be	Rom 12:3
When * children are in need, you	Rom 12:13
keep on doing * work, serving you.	Rom 13:6
be obeying all of * laws,	Rom 13:8
satisfies all of * requirements.	Rom 13:10
They are * servants, not yours.	Rom 14:4
you do, even from * point of view,	Rom 14:22
for I am, by * grace, a special	Rom 15:15,16
I love as one of * own children,	Rom 16:8
This is * plan of salvation for	Rom 16:25,26,27
Christ himself is the center of *	1Co 1:24
He showed us * plan of salvation;	1Co 1:30
ideas to tell you * message.	1Co 2:1
God, telling of * wise plan to	1Co 2:7
shows us all of * deepest secrets.	1Co 2:10
And no one can know * thoughts	1Co 2:11
thoughts except * own Spirit.	1Co 2:11
by your own desires, not *.	1Co 3:3
Why, we're just * servants, each	1Co 3:5
We are only * co-workers.	1Co 3:9
You are * garden, not ours;	1Co 3:9
you are * building, not ours.	1Co 3:9
If anyone defiles and spoils *	1Co 3:17
destroy him. For * home is holy and	1Co 3:17
belong to Christ, and Christ is *.	1Co 3:23
who distribute * blessings by	1Co 4:1
blessings by explaining * secrets.	1Co 4:1
You must not be proud of one of *	1Co 4:6
whether they really have * power.	1Co 4:19
it is living by * power.	1Co 4:20
Christ, * Lamb, has been slain	1Co 5:7
whereas a united family may, in *	1Co 7:14
in accordance with * direction and	1Co 7:17
God and keeping * commandments.	1Co 7:19
not keep anyone from doing * work.	1Co 7:30

(GOD'S Con't)
from * Spirit when I say this. 1Co 7:40
one who is open to * knowledge. 1Co 8:3
I AM AN apostle, * messenger, 1Co 9:1
I'm telling you what * law says. 1Co 9:8
it's not against * laws to eat 1Co 10:23
* glory is man made in his image, 1Co 11:7
But remember that in * plan men 1Co 11:11
drinking * judgment upon himself; 1Co 11:29
The Holy Spirit displays * power 1Co 12:7
claim to be giving * messages—or 1Co 12:10
Prophets—those who preach * Word, 1Co 12:28
preaching * messages, for that is a 1Co 14:5
of * Word—that is what you need; 1Co 14:6
is not a sign to * children 1Co 14:22
But if you prophesy, preaching * 1Co 14:24
the knowledge of * will begins and 1Co 14:36
you can preach * message plainly; 1Co 14:39
blood cannot get into * kingdom. 1Co 15:50
at all * will for him to go now; 1Co 16:12
you * comfort and salvation. 2Co 1:6,7
fulfills all of * promises, no 2Co 1:20
power, with * eye upon us. 2Co 2:17
For as he gave them * law to 2Co 3:7
of * new plan for our salvation 2Co 3:11
will result in * richest blessing 2Co 4:17
Then, in exchange, he poured * 2Co 5:21
AS * PARTNERS we beg you not to 2Co 6:1
message of * great kindness. 2Co 6:1
We have been truthful, with * 2Co 6:7
be between * temple and idols? 2Co 6:16
For you are * temple, the home of 2Co 6:16
to you, about helping * people. 2Co 9:1
I use * mighty weapons, not 2Co 10:4
Our goal is to measure up to * 2Co 10:13
because I preached * Good News to 2Co 11:7
they are doing * work in just the 2Co 11:12
are Israelites, * chosen people? 2Co 11:22
and have all of * power to use in 2Co 13:4
with you all. May * love and the 2Co 13:14
Let * curses fall on anyone, Gal 1:8
let * curse fall upon him. Gal 1:9
I could never find * favor by Gal 2:19
because he believed * promises. Gal 3:6
them are under * curse, for the Gal 3:10
written in * Book of the Law." Gal 3:10
one can ever win * favor by trying Gal 3:11
am trying to say: * promise to save Gal 3:17
way of gaining * favor than Gal 3:18
for he simply accepted * promise. Gal 3:18
they are of breaking * laws. Gal 3:19
Child to whom * promise was made. Gal 3:19
Well then, are * laws and God's Gal 3:21,22
Well then, are God's laws and * Gal 3:21,22
of * promises to him belong to us. Gal 3:29
no longer slaves, but * own sons. Gal 4:7
get to heaven by obeying * laws? Gal 4:9
of * two ways of helping people. Gal 4:24,25
you are lost from * grace. Gal 5:4
May * mercy and peace be upon all Gal 6:16
everywhere who are really * own. Gal 6:16
in, for as part of * sovereign plan Eph 1:11
decided long ago. * purpose in Eph 1:12
His presence within us is * Eph 1:14
place of honor at * right hand in Eph 1:20
ONCE YOU WERE under * curse, Eph 2:1
* anger just like everyone else. Eph 2:3
you were enemies of * children Eph 2:12
you are members of * very own Eph 2:19
citizens of * country, and you Eph 2:19
and you belong in * household with Eph 2:19
Gentiles are a part of * house. Eph 3:1
work of showing * favor to you Eph 3:2,3
the riches inherited by * sons; Eph 3:6
church, and all of * promises of Eph 3:6
right into * presence, assured of Eph 3:12
into the soil of * marvelous love; Eph 3:17
understand, as all * children Eph 3:18,19
for caring for * people as a Eph 4:11
It is that * people will be Eph 4:12
about our Savior, * Son, and all Eph 4:13
FOLLOW * EXAMPLE in everything Eph 5:1
Instead, remind each other of * Eph 5:4
and * Word; so that he could Eph 5:26
This is the first of * Ten Eph 6:2
Put on all of * armor so that Eph 6:11
So use every piece of * armor to Eph 6:13
and the breastplate of * approval. Eph 6:14
Jesus Christ. May * grace and Eph 6:24
or by obeying * laws, but by Php 3:9
to save me; for * way of making us Php 3:9
will experience * peace, which is Php 4:7
* people—in the city of Colosse. Col 1:2
about * great kindness to sinners. Col 1:6
understanding. For * secret plan, Col 2:2
that is idolatry. * terrible anger Col 3:6
watch for * answers and remember Col 4:2
May * blessings surround you. Col 4:18
to the return of * Son from 1Th 1:10
from * terrible anger against sin. 1Th 1:10
* message, but our own lives too. 1Th 2:8
we preached * Good News among you. 1Th 2:9
and fellow worker, * minister, to 1Th 3:2,3
part of * plan for us Christians. 1Th 3:2,3
And this also is * will: that you 1Th 4:6
should be among * people, I don't 1Th 4:9
for this is * will for you who 1Th 5:18
people accept * plan of faith. 1Ti 1:3,4
plead for * mercy upon them; 1Ti 2:1
absolute truth—as * minister and 1Ti 2:7
* plan of salvation through faith. 1Ti 2:7
preach * Word. 1Ti 4:13
Oh, Timothy, you are * man. 1Ti 6:11
know God. May * mercy be upon you. 1Ti 6:21
For the Holy Spirit, * gift, 2Ti 1:7
But * truth stands firm like a 2Ti 2:19
* people must not be quarrelsome; 2Ti 2:24
more likely, with * help, to turn 2Ti 2:25
you wise to accept * salvation by 2Ti 3:15
It is * way of making us well 2Ti 3:17
them patiently with * Word. 2Ti 4:2
teach them to know * truth—the kind Tit 1:1
because they are * ministers. Tit 1:7
He died under * judgment against Tit 2:14
declare us good in * eyes—all Tit 3:7
May * blessings be with you all. Tit 3:15
refreshed the hearts of * people. Phm 1:7
* Son shines out with God's Heb 1:3
God's Son shines out with * Heb 1:3
and all that * Son is and does Heb 1:3
Yes, because of * great kindness, Heb 2:9
multitudes of * people to heaven; Heb 2:10
Since we, * children, are human Heb 2:14
this Jesus who is * Messenger and Heb 3:1
also faithfully served in * house. Heb 3:2
job working in * house, but he was Heb 3:5
But Christ, * faithful Son, is Heb 3:6
is in complete charge of * house. Heb 3:6
And we Christians are * house—he Heb 3:6
if you hear * voice speaking to Heb 3:15
of, who heard * voice speaking to Heb 3:16
ALTHOUGH * PROMISE still Heb 4:1
* perfect will at the cross. Heb 5:7f
And even though Jesus was * Son, Heb 5:8
very first principles in * Word. Heb 5:12,13
deeper things of * Word until you Heb 5:14
experienced * blessing upon it. Heb 6:7
For instance, there was * promise Heb 6:13
honored of all * chosen people, Heb 7:4
for later on * people were required Heb 7:5
So we can plainly see that * Heb 7:15
Because of * oath, Christ can Heb 7:22
guardians of * glory—with their Heb 9:5
came with * new and better way. Heb 9:10
the people all of * laws, he took Heb 9:19
over the book of * laws and over Heb 9:19
highest honor at * right hand, Heb 10:12
of ours rules over * household, Heb 10:21
punishment of * awful anger which Heb 10:27
who brings * mercy to his people. Heb 10:29
on patiently doing * will if you Heb 10:36
made them good in * sight must live Heb 10:38
all things—were made at * command; Heb 11:3
When he heard * warning about the Heb 11:7
And even when he reached * Heb 11:9
ill-treatment with * people instead Heb 11:24,25
homes, so that * terrible Angel of Heb 11:28
you aren't really * son at all—that Heb 12:8
submit to * training so that we can Heb 12:9
they knew how, but * correction is Heb 12:10
fail to find * best blessings. Heb 12:15
They staggered back under * Heb 12:20
love. * grace be with you all. Heb 13:24,25
steadily into * law for free men, Jas 1:25
entirely broken * laws and stand Jas 2:11
merciful, then * mercy toward you Jas 2:13
him good in * sight, and he was Jas 2:23
are not * kind of wisdom. Jas 3:15
friends with * enemies—the evil Jas 4:4
fighting against * law of loving Jas 4:11
are now members of * own family. 1Pe 1:3
to more of * kindness to you when 1Pe 1:13
* ever-living Message to men. 1Pe 1:23
for milk. Eat * Word—read it, think 1Pe 2:2,3f
for * use in building his house. 1Pe 2:5
will not listen to * Word, nor obey 1Pe 2:8
and pure, you are * very own—all 1Pe 2:9
now you are * own. 1Pe 2:10
Once you knew very little of * 1Pe 2:10
It is * will that your good lives 1Pe 2:15
to do only * will at all times. 1Pe 2:16
in receiving * blessings, and if 1Pe 3:7
Instead, pray for * help for 1Pe 3:9
others * many kinds of blessings. 1Pe 4:10
begin first among * own children. 1Pe 4:17
according to * will, keep on doing 1Pe 4:19
Do you want more and more of * 2Pe 1:2
But we are looking forward to * 2Pe 3:13
He is * message of Life. 1Jn 1:1
in the light of * presence, just as 1Jn 1:7
He is the one who took * wrath 1Jn 2:2
are strong, with * Word in your 1Jn 2:14
believe in Christ, * Son, can't 1Jn 2:23
But he who has Christ, * Son, has 1Jn 2:23
we are already * children, right 1Jn 3:2
of * will at any time in any way. 1Jn 3:5
has been born into * family does 1Jn 3:9
because now * life is in him; 1Jn 3:9
shows that he is not in * family; 1Jn 3:10
him—how can * love be within him? 1Jn 3:17
that we are on * side, and our 1Jn 3:19
that Jesus Christ, * Son, actually 1Jn 4:2
satisfy * anger against our sins. 1Jn 4:10
Christ—that he is * Son and your 1Jn 5:1
how much you love * children—your 1Jn 5:2
So whoever has * Son has life; 1Jn 5:12
No one who has become part of * 1Jn 5:18
for Christ, * Son, holds him 1Jn 5:18
And we know that Christ, * Son, 1Jn 5:20
might take * place in your hearts. 1Jn 5:21
Cyria, one of * very own, and to 2Jn 1:1
the Truth, obeying * command. 2Jn 1:4
prove that they are * children; 3Jn 1:11
of * kindness, peace, and love. Jud 1:2
like without fear of * punishment. Jud 1:4
* love can reach and bless you. Jud 1:21
and I will write my * Name on Rev 3:12
the primeval source of * Rev 3:14
incense—the prayers of * people! Rev 5:8
the prayers of * people, to offer Rev 8:3
his trumpet, then * veiled Rev 10:7
happened at last! * salvation and Rev 12:10
who were keeping * commandments Rev 12:17
All that time he blasphemed * Rev 13:6
power to fight against * people Rev 13:7
to fight against * people." Rev 13:7f
it is poured out undiluted into * Rev 14:10
Let this encourage * people to Rev 14:12
the great winepress of * wrath. Rev 14:19
at last * anger will be finished. Rev 15:1
were remembered in * thoughts, and Rev 16:19
of * revealing himself to man. Rev 19:13f
earth and surround * people and the Rev 20:9

GODDESS
the * Asherah that stood nearby. Ju 6:25
Ashtoreth, the * of the Sidonians, 1Ki 11:5
Ashtoreth, the * of the Sidonians; 1Ki 11:33
worship the * Asherah at Samaria. 2Ki 13:6
the evil * of the Sidonians; 2Ki 23:13
* of love and war, was called. Jer 7:18f
shrines of the Greek * Diana. Act 19:24
of the great * Diana will lose its Act 19:27
magnificent * worshiped not only Act 19:27

GODHEAD
here seen as one of the *. Zec 2:8f

GODLESS
"I figured this to be a * place. Gen 20:11,12
But the * are as thorns to be 2Sa 23:6
that I am not *, to be rejected Job 13:16
For the * are barren: they can Job 15:34
come out on top, above the *; Job 17:8
the joy of the * but for a moment? Job 20:5
Though the * be proud as the Job 20:6
"But what hope has the * when Job 27:8
I knocked out the fangs of the * Job 29:17
But the * reap his anger. Job 36:13
the paths of the * lead to doom. Ps 1:6
Pour out your wrath upon the * Ps 79:6
violent, * men are trying to kill Ps 86:14
Or, "When a * man slanders his Pro 11:9f
also the * man's death. Pro 11:10
the kindness of * men is cruel. Pro 12:10
DON'T ENVY * men; Pro 24:1
man's rights; the * don't care. Pro 29:7
this * nation, doomed and damned; Is 10:5,6
He will leave * Jews in power Dan 11:30,31
Has not the Lord decreed that * Hab 2:13
Even the * do that! Lk 6:32
he said, "a very * man who had Lk 18:2
* and "unclean" by the Jews. Eph 2:11
us to turn from * living and sinful Tit 2:12
evil things the * enjoy—sex sin, 1Pe 4:3
what chance will the * have? 1Pe 4:18
I say this because some * Jud 1:4

GODLINESS
Assign me * and Integrity as my Ps 25:21
and help his son to walk in *. Ps 72:1
* exalts a nation, but sin is a Pro 14:34
He will heal you; your * will Is 58:8
because of their *, you will be Mt 10:41
and * had made this man walk? Act 3:12
themselves as a sign of *. Eph 2:11
Literally, "having a form of *." 2Ti 3:5f

GODLY
longer * in character (verse 3). Gen 6:1f
refers to the "* line" of Seth, Gen 6:1f
him out to have * descendants and a Gen 18:19
descendants and a * household—men Gen 18:19
Suppose you find fifty * people Gen 18:24
to kill the * with the wicked! Gen 18:25
Why, you would be treating * and Gen 18:25
"If I find fifty * people there, I Gen 18:26
them the principles of * living. Ex 18:19,20

(GODLY Con't)
"Find some capable, *, honest Ex 18:21
"Give to * Levi Deu 33:8
He will protect his * ones, 1Sa 2:9
* living, and was very successful. 2Ch 31:21
still trying to be * when God has Job 2:9
Why must the * wait for him in Job 24:1
they shall not stand among the *. Ps 1:5
plans and paths of * men, but the Ps 1:6
For you bless the * man, O Lord; Ps 5:12
the * shall see his face. Ps 11:7
HELP! * men are fast Ps 12:1
I want the company of the * Ps 16:3
LET ALL THE joys of the * well up Ps 33:1
plot against the *, for he knows Ps 37:12,13
have little and be * than to own an Ps 37:16
the good deeds done by * men, Ps 37:18
the children of the * go hungry. Ps 37:25
Instead, the * are able to be Ps 37:26
The * shall be firmly planted in Ps 37:29
forever. The * man is a good Ps 37:30,31
Evil men spy on the *, waiting Ps 37:32
nor let the * be condemned when Ps 37:33
The Lord saves the *! Ps 37:39
He will not permit the * to slip Ps 55:22
The * shall rejoice in the Ps 58:10
And the * shall rejoice in the Ps 64:10
But may the * man exult. Ps 68:3
But the * shall flourish like Ps 92:12
Light is sown for the * and joy Ps 97:11
May all who are * be happy in Ps 97:12
I will make the * of the land my Ps 101:6
the poor who are * and gives them Ps 107:41
are sung in the homes of the *. Ps 118:15,16
the Lord, and the * enter there. Ps 118:20
shall not rule the *, lest the Ps 125:3
lest the * be forced to do wrong. Ps 125:3
Surely the * are thanking you, Ps 140:13
Let the * smite me! Ps 141:5
can thank you. The * will rejoice Ps 142:7
honoring his * ones—the people of Ps 148:14
He grants good sense to the * Pro 2:7,8
Follow the steps of the * Pro 2:20
he gives his friendship to the *. Pro 3:32
A * man gives good advice, but a Pro 10:21
Evil words destroy. * skill Pro 11:9
The good influence of * citizens Pro 11:11
will rescue the children of the *. Pro 11:21
* men are growing a tree that Pro 11:30
Even the * shall be rewarded here Pro 11:31
only the * have that. Pro 12:3
The wicked accuse; the * defend. Pro 12:6
The wicked shall perish; the * Pro 12:7
The path of the * leads to life. Pro 12:28
his wealth is stored up for the *. Pro 13:22
The common bond of * people is Pro 14:9
the work of the * will flourish. Pro 14:11
the * man's life is exciting. Pro 14:14
Evil men shall bow before the *. Pro 14:19
The * have a refuge when they Pro 14:32
The road of the * leads upward, Pro 15:24
The path of the * leads away from Pro 16:17
and is seen most among the *. Pro 16:31
How short-sighted to fine the * Pro 17:26
is a strong fortress. The * run Pro 18:10
a good man lives a * life. Pro 21:8
The * learn by watching ruin Pro 21:12
He is greedy to get, while the * Pro 21:25,26
An evil man is stubborn, but a * Pro 21:29
brazen; the * man is thoughtful." Pro 21:29f
The father of a * man has cause Pro 23:24,25
If a * man compromises with the Pro 25:26
But the * are bold as lions! Pro 28:1
on those who lead astray the *. Pro 28:10
When the * are successful, Pro 28:12
The * pray for those who long to Pro 29:10
* and wise men are in God's will; Ecc 9:1
or irreligious, profane or *. Ecc 9:2,3
But all is well for the * man. Is 3:10
Entrust it to some * man to pass Is 8:16
to * men of future generations. Is 8:16
THE GOOD MEN perish; the * die Is 57:1
For the * who die shall rest in Is 57:2
robes of vengeance and of * fury. Is 59:17
do good, who follow * ways. Is 64:5
But we are not *; Is 64:5
good road is, the * paths you used Jer 6:16
mourning for the * King Josiah, Zec 12:11
And what does he want? * children Mal 2:15
religious are really * people. Mt 7:21
search for a * man and stay in his Mt 10:11
a * home, give it your blessing; Mt 10:13
And if you welcome good and * men Mt 10:41
Many a prophet and * man has Mt 13:17
Then the * shall shine as the Mt 13:43
people from the *, casting the Mt 13:49
the graves of the * men they Mt 23:29,30
blood of murdered * men from Mt 23:35
opened, and many * men and women Mt 27:52
Or, "a * man." Mt 27:54f
Zacharias and Elizabeth were * Lk 1:6
of the *, God will reward you for Lk 14:14
than the * Lk 16:8
He was a * man who had been Lk 23:50,51,52
Many * Jews were in Jerusalem Act 2:5
(But some * Jews Act 8:2
they were * and sympathetic Jews. Act 8:2f
He was a * man, deeply reverent, Act 10:2
servants and a * soldier, one of Act 10:7
a good and * man, well thought of Act 10:22
And many Jews and * Gentiles who Act 13:43
up both the * women and the civic Act 13:50
a large number of * Greek men, and Act 17:4
There a man named Ananias, as * Act 22:12
All of the * man's 2Co 6:7
say: "The * man gives generously 2Co 9:9
it too, and seem like * ministers. 2Co 11:15
sin, you who are * should gently Gal 6:1
and rituals of the *, for they Eph 2:11
with suggestions and * advice. Eph 6:4
our time in * living and thinking 1Ti 2:2
a * life is not an easy matter. 1Ti 3:16
are the foundation for a * life. 1Ti 6:3
Jesus by living * lives will suffer 2Ti 3:12
behavior. Your * lives will speak 1Pe 3:1
become patient and *, gladly 2Pe 1:6
within these * men who gave them 2Pe 1:20,21
holy, * lives we should be living! 2Pe 3:11

GODS
father's household * and took them Gen 31:21
the * of Egypt—for I am Jehovah. Ex 12:12
else is like the Lord among the *? Ex 15:11
"You must not worship the * of Ex 23:24
have anything to do with their *. Ex 23:32
worshiping false *, and that would Ex 23:33
have made themselves * of gold. Ex 32:31
For you must worship no other *, Ex 34:14
the harlot worshiping their *." Ex 34:15f
by sacrificing to their *. Ex 34:15
who worship other *, as wives for Ex 34:16
me by worshiping their wives' *. Ex 34:16
who turn to other * than me. Lev 20:5
you used to do in serving other *. Num 15:39
to their *, and soon the men were Num 25:2
all the * of Egypt that night! Num 33:3,4
"You must not worship the * of Deu 6:14
beginning to worship their *. Deu 7:4
pity, and do not worship their *; Deu 7:16
and worship other * instead, and Deu 8:19
"Jehovah your God is God of * Deu 10:17
turn from God to worship other *. Deu 11:16
the * of these other nations. Deu 11:28
the heathen sacrifice to their *. Deu 12:4,5
example in worshiping their *. Deu 12:30
do these nations worship their *?' Deu 12:30
sons and daughters before their *. Deu 12:31
let us worship the * of the other Deu 13:2
these foreign *, do not consent Deu 13:6,7
worship foreign *, first check the Deu 13:12,13,14
worshiping other *, the sun, moon, Deu 17:2,3
to heathen *, must be killed. Deu 18:10
a message from other * must die.' Deu 18:20
handmade * are hated by the Lord.' Deu 27:15
you must never worship other *. Deu 28:14
shall worship * of wood and stone! Deu 28:36
There you will worship heathen * Deu 28:64
known, * made of wood and stone! Deu 28:64
to worship these * of other Deu 29:18
For they worshiped other *, Deu 29:26
to worship other *— then I declare Deu 30:17
foreign * in the Promised Land. Deu 31:16
their sins in worshiping other *. Deu 31:18
and worship other * and despise me Deu 31:20
And they lived without foreign *, Deu 32:12
Israel began to follow foreign *, Deu 32:16
They sacrificed to heathen *, Deu 32:17
To new * never before worshiped. Deu 32:17
Which are not * at all. Deu 32:21
Prayers to their * are valueless. Deu 32:31
'Where are their *— Deu 32:37
Where are these * now, Deu 32:38
Let those * arise, Deu 32:38
the God of *, that we have not Jos 22:22,23
the names of their *, much less Jos 23:7
For if you worship other * he Jos 23:15,16
and they worshiped other *. Jos 24:2
Will it be the * of your Jos 24:15
Euphrates or the * of the Amorites Jos 24:15
the Lord and worship other *! Jos 24:16
and worship other *, he will turn Jos 24:20
sides, and their * will be a Ju 2:3
the worshiping of heathen *. Ju 2:11
by worshiping other * instead. Ju 2:17
They prayed to heathen * again, Ju 2:19
Israel was worshiping their *. Ju 3:6
When Israel chose new *, Ju 5:8
to worship other *, and once again Ju 6:1
not worship the * of the Amorites Ju 6:10
the heathen * Baal and Ashtaroth, Ju 10:6
Ashtaroth, and the * of Syria, Ju 10:6
abandon me and to worship other *. Ju 10:13
Go and cry to the new * you have Ju 10:14
* and worshiped only the Lord; Ju 10:16
worshiping other *, so the Lord let Ju 13:1
"You've taken away all my * and Ju 18:24
back to her people and to her *; Ru 1:15
us from these mighty * of Israel? 1Sa 4:8
They are the same * who destroyed 1Sa 4:8
* and your Ashtaroth idols. 1Sa 7:3
forsaken me and followed other *. 1Sa 8:8
Other * can't help you. 1Sa 12:21
David by the names of his *. 1Sa 17:43
sent me away to worship heathen *. 1Sa 26:19
to destroy Egypt and its *. 2Sa 7:23
The God above all * gave out a 2Sa 22:14
and worship other * and do not obey 1Ki 9:6
they worshiped other * instead. 1Ki 9:9
them started worshiping their *. 1Ki 11:2
to worship their * instead of 1Ki 11:4
and sacrificing to their *. 1Ki 11:8
against worshiping other *. 1Ki 11:9,10
from now on these will be your * 1Ki 12:28
you have made other * and have 1Ki 14:9
now I swear by the * that I am 1Ki 19:2
to Ahab: "May the * do more to me 1Ki 20:10
sacrifice to the *, following the 2Ki 16:3
worshiped other *, thus sinning 2Ki 17:7
to other * throughout the land. 2Ki 17:9
incense to the * of the very 2Ki 17:11
also worshiped their own *. 2Ki 17:29
Ashima. The * Nibhaz and Tartak 2Ki 17:31
* Adrammelech and Anammelech. 2Ki 17:31
make sacrifices to any heathen *. 2Ki 17:35,36
laws and never worship other *. 2Ki 17:37
never worship other *. 2Ki 17:38
continued to worship other *. 2Ki 17:40
Have any of the * of the other 2Ki 18:33
What happened to the * of 2Ki 18:34
Have the * of the other nations 2Ki 19:12
But they weren't * at all; 2Ki 19:18
moon god, and the * of the stars 2Ki 21:3,4,5
* and have made me very angry; 2Ki 22:17
the Temple of the * and nailed his 1Ch 10:10
is to be held in awe above all *. 1Ch 16:25
The other so-called * are demons, 1Ch 16:26
they worshiped other * instead. 2Ch 7:22
made for you—he calls them your *! 2Ch 13:8
and set them up as *, and bowed 2Ch 25:14
have you worshiped * who couldn't 2Ch 25:15
him for worshiping the * of Edom. 2Ch 25:20
He sacrificed to the * of the 2Ch 28:23
that since these * had helped the 2Ch 28:23
* in every corner of Jerusalem. 2Ch 28:24
we attacked? The * of those nations 2Ch 32:13
"The * of all the other nations 2Ch 32:17
of the heathen *—a handmade idol! 2Ch 32:19
He also removed the foreign * 2Ch 33:15
worshiped heathen *, and I am very 2Ch 34:25
placed in the temple of his own *. Ez 1:7
they turn to their *, but none Job 5:1
praises, O Lord God above all *. Ps 9:2
Those who follow other * shall be Ps 10:16
Those choosing other * shall all Ps 16:4
even speak the names of their *. Ps 16:4
the God above all * has Ps 18:13
of the God who is above all *. Ps 21:7
worship idols, those imitation *. Ps 31:5,6
home of the God above all *. Ps 46:4
all *, is awesome beyond words; Ps 47:2
he destroys those serving other *. Ps 73:27
the God who is above all *. Ps 78:17
Savior was the God above all *. Ps 78:35
the God above all *, and refused to Ps 78:56
idols and altars to other *. Ps 78:58
"He judges among the *." Ps 82:1f
I have called you all "*" and Ps 82:6
the God above all * in supreme Ps 83:18
Where among the heathen * is Ps 86:8
For the God above all * will Ps 87:5
by the God who is above all *. Ps 91:1
I choose the God above all * to Ps 91:9
to the God who is above all *. Ps 92:1
all *. He controls the formation Ps 95:3
Worship only him among the *! Ps 96:4
For the * of other nations are Ps 96:5
*—for every god must bow to him! Ps 97:7
far greater than these other *. Ps 97:8,9
him who is the God above all *. Ps 107:11
Their * are merely man-made Ps 115:4
SHALL I LOOK to the mountain * for Ps 121:1
Give thanks to the God of *, for Ps 136:2
Literally, "before the *," or Ps 138:1f
Running after other *! Is 1:21
they will cry to their * in their Is 16:12
God, once we worshiped other *; Is 26:13
Have any other nation's * ever Is 36:18
Did their * save them? Is 36:19
Where are their * now? Is 36:19
Of all the * of these lands, Is 36:20
Did their * save the cities of Is 37:12
and thrown their * into the fire; Is 37:19
for they weren't * at all, but Is 37:19
to buy expensive * like that will Is 40:20

(GODS Con't)
If you are *, tell what will Is 41:23
* will be greatly disappointed; Is 42:17
manufacture idols for their *. Is 44:9
and pray to * that cannot save! Is 45:20
* in the Babylonian pantheon. Is 46:1f
The cart is turning over! The * Is 46:1
say their * have conquered me. Is 48:11
Your * are the smooth stones in Is 57:6
itself, to find new * to love. Is 57:9
Temple and worship * of "Fate" Is 65:11
worshiping other *—yes, idols they Jer 1:16
traded in its old * for new Jer 2:10,11
though their * are nothing. Jer 2:10,11
this weary running after other *? Jer 2:25
Why don't you call on these * Jer 2:28
For you have as many * as there Jer 2:28
worshiping these other *? Jer 3:2
worshiped other * on every hill, Jer 3:6
gone to other * to worship them. Jer 3:8
yourself to a host of foreign *; Jer 3:20
* that are not gods at all. Jer 5:7
gods that are not * at all. Jer 5:7
to other * while in your land; Jer 5:19
all of those new * of yours, and Jer 7:9
* honored by the Jewish community. Jer 7:18f
to their *—a deed so horrible I've Jer 7:31
moon and stars—the * of my people! Jer 8:2
then they clothe these * in Jer 10:9
who worship other *: Your so-called Jer 10:11
Your so-called *, who have not made Jer 10:11
* without life or power in them. Jer 10:14
O my people, you have as many * Jer 11:13
unfaithful and worshiped other *. Jer 11:15
trust in false *, I will scatter Jer 13:24,25
They worshiped other * and served Jer 16:11
Can men make God? The * they Jer 16:20
The gods they made are not real * Jer 16:20
other *, causing my fury to rise! Jer 32:29
worshiping other * and that if you Jer 35:15
the temples of the * of Egypt and Jer 43:12
the temples of the * of Egypt." Jer 43:13
worshiping other *—"gods" that Jer 44:2,3
other gods—"*" that neither they Jer 44:2,3
their sacrifices to these "*." Jer 44:5
and all the other * of Egypt. Jer 46:25
* and burning incense to idols. Jer 48:35
for he calls them *, when there Jer 51:17
Your * will be shattered; Eze 6:4-7
eyes that long for other *. Eze 6:9
incense to their *—you will realize Eze 6:13
me, and sacrificed them to your *; Eze 16:20
your allies and worshiping their * Eze 16:28
you can never find enough new *. Eze 16:28
you worshiped the * of that great Eze 16:29
sacrifices to your *, this is what Eze 16:36
with other * and end your payments Eze 16:40,41
*, for I am the Lord your God. Eze 20:7
idols, nor forsake the * of Egypt. Eze 20:8
children as offerings to their *! Eze 20:26
up their sacrifices to those '*.' Eze 20:27,28
sacrifices were made to the *. Eze 20:29f
you, serving * of wood and stone. Eze 20:32
obtain information from the *. Eze 21:21f
success—that your * will save you Eze 21:29
But then Oholah turned to other * Eze 23:4,5
whose * she loved so much. Eze 23:9
no more long for Egypt and her *. Eze 23:27
by worshiping the * of other Eze 23:30
to come with other * for you to Eze 23:40
worship of other * or by worshiping Eze 43:7
to worship other *, causing Israel Eze 44:12
No one except the * can tell you Dan 2:11
God is the God of *, Ruler of Dan 2:47
to serve your * or to worship the Dan 3:12
to serve my * or to worship the Dan 3:14
serve your * or worship the golden Dan 3:18
"looks like a son of the *." Dan 3:25f
holy *, and I told him the dream. Dan 4:8
spirit of the holy * is in you and Dan 4:9
spirit of the holy * is in you." Dan 4:18
him the spirit of the holy *. Dan 5:11
the spirit of the * within you and Dan 5:14
while praising * of silver, gold, Dan 5:23
wood, and stone—* that neither see Dan 5:23
the God of *, and prospering—until Dan 11:36
He will have no regard for the * Dan 11:37
me by worshiping other *." Hos 1:2
* and offered them choice gifts." Hos 3:1
deserted me and turned to other *. Hos 4:10
serving other *, deserting me. Hos 4:12
other *, Israel utterly defiled. Hos 6:10
Worshiping foreign * has sapped Hos 7:9
His pride in other * has openly Hos 7:10
Instead, they worship heathen *, Hos 7:14
other * on every threshing floor. Hos 9:1
to give yourselves to other *, Hos 9:10
it on the altars of her heathen *; Hos 10:1
honor of their shattered *. Hos 10:5
the idols we have made 'our *'; Hos 14:3
in your heathen *—in Sakkuth Amo 5:25,26,27
shouted to their * for help and Jon 1:5
* and caused this terrible storm; Jon 1:7
(Those who worship false * have Jon 2:8
And I will destroy your * and Nah 1:14
them all to worship her false *, Nah 3:4
their power is from their *." Hab 1:11
"These are the * who make us Hab 1:16
desire for foreign * and foreign Zep 1:8f
He will starve out all those * of Zep 2:11
own Law it says that men are *!" Jn 10:34,35,36
speaks of those as * to whom the Jn 10:34,35,36
we will have * to lead us back; Act 7:40
sun, moon and stars as their *! Act 7:42
in your heathen *—Sakkuth, and the Act 7:43
men are * in human bodies!" Act 14:11
handmade * aren't gods at all. Act 19:26
handmade gods aren't * at all. Act 19:26
*, both in heaven and on earth. 1Co 8:5
really being offered to actual *. 1Co 8:7
alive and are real *, and that 1Co 10:19
* that did not even exist. Gal 4:8
for the worship of false *. Rev 19:2f

GOG
*, and his great-grandson 1Ch 5:4
of Magog, and prophesy against * Eze 38:2,3
It therefore seems that * was, or Eze 38:2,3f
But from the context * seems to Eze 38:2,3f
God says: I am against you, *. Eze 38:2,3
You are their leader, *! Eze 38:7
"The Lord God says to *: When my Eze 38:14
prophesy this also against *. Eze 39:1
I stand against you, *, leader of Eze 39:1
vast graveyard for * and his armies Eze 39:11
There * and all his armies will Eze 39:11
all shall see the punishment of * Eze 39:21
together, with * and Magog, for Rev 20:8

GOG'S
The names of * confederates Eze 38:2,3f
place to "The Valley of * Army." Eze 39:11
the Valley of * Army to bury them. Eze 39:15,16

GOIIM
Tidal, king of * Gen 14:1
The king of * in Gilgal; Jos 12:8-24

GOINGS
"For God carefully watches the * Job 34:21
comings and * and all you do—and Is 37:28
yours put up with all their * on? Jer 12:4

GOLAN
tribe of Gad; and *, in Bashan, for Deu 4:43
tribe of Gad; and * of Bashan, in Jos 20:8
*, in Bashan (a City of Refuge), Jos 21:27
*, in Bashan; 1Ch 6:71

GOLD
where nuggets of pure * are Gen 2:11,12
rich in livestock, silver, and *. Gen 13:1
produced a quarter-ounce * earring Gen 24:22
in silver and *, and many slaves Gen 24:35
set in solid * and silver for Gen 24:53
Why would we steal silver or * Gen 44:8
jewels, silver, *, and the finest Ex 3:22
for costly * and silver jewelry." Ex 11:2
and * jewelry, and for clothing. Ex 12:35
silver or * or of anything else! Ex 20:23
*, silver, bronze, blue cloth, Ex 25:1
outside with pure *, with a molding Ex 25:11
with a molding of * all around it. Ex 25:11
Cast four rings of * for it and Ex 25:12
wood overlaid with *, and fit the Ex 25:13,14
"And make a lid of pure *, 3¾ Ex 25:17
using beaten *, and place them at Ex 25:18
wings spread out above the * lid. Ex 25:20
Overlay it with pure *, and run Ex 25:24
and run a rib of * around it. Ex 25:24
of the top, and a * ridge along the Ex 25:25
from acacia wood overlaid with *. Ex 25:28
a lampstand of pure, beaten *. Ex 25:31
to be one piece of pure, beaten *. Ex 25:36
trays are to be made of pure *. Ex 25:38
Literally, "a [*] talent." Ex 25:39f
pounds of pure * for the Ex 25:39
Overlay the frames with *, and Ex 26:29
and make * rings to hold the bars; Ex 26:29
and also overlay the bars with *. Ex 26:29
with *, with four golden hooks. Ex 26:32
overlaid with *, with hooks of Ex 26:37
with hooks of *, and a bronze Ex 26:37
of *, blue, purple, and scarlet Ex 28:8
and mount the stones in * Ex 28:11
Two chains of pure, twisted * Ex 28:13,14
use the same *, blue, purple, and Ex 28:15
a jasper—all set in * settings. Ex 28:20
of two twisted cords of pure *. Ex 28:22,23,24
alternated with * bells. Ex 28:33,34
"Next, make a plate of pure * Ex 28:36
altar with pure *, and run a gold Ex 30:3
* molding around the entire altar. Ex 30:3
construct two * rings to hold the Ex 30:4
of acacia wood overlaid with *. Ex 30:5
made of *, silver, and bronze. Ex 31:4
the pure * lampstand with its Ex 31:8
Aaron melted the *, then molded Ex 32:4
them, 'Bring me your * earrings.' Ex 32:24
have made themselves gods of *. Ex 32:31
*, silver, and bronze; Ex 35:5-9
their offerings of *, Ex 35:22
* objects of every kind. Ex 35:22
from *, silver, and bronze; Ex 35:32
Then fifty clasps of * were made Ex 36:13
*, and the rings were pure gold. Ex 36:34
gold, and the rings were pure *. Ex 36:34
attached to four * hooks set into Ex 36:36
* and set into four silver bases. Ex 36:36
and rods were overlaid with *; Ex 36:38
It was plated with pure * inside Ex 37:2
of * all the way around the sides. Ex 37:2
overlaid them with *, and put the Ex 37:4
Then, from pure *, he made a lid Ex 37:6
He made two cherubim of beaten * Ex 37:7
It was overlaid with pure *, Ex 37:11
with a * molding along the rim. Ex 37:12
Then he cast four rings of * and Ex 37:13
Next, using pure *, he made the Ex 37:15,16
again using pure, beaten *. Ex 37:17
all one piece of pure, beaten *. Ex 37:22
and the ashtrays, all of pure *. Ex 37:23,24
weighed 107 pounds, all pure *. Ex 37:23,24
He overlaid it all with pure * Ex 37:26
ran a * molding around the edge. Ex 37:26
the edge. Two * rings were placed Ex 37:27
of 3,140 pounds of *, all of which Ex 38:24
Bezalel beat * into thin plates Ex 39:3
made of the same *, blue, purple, Ex 39:4,5
ephod, were set in *, and the Ex 39:6,7
from the finest *, blue, purple, Ex 39:8
a jasper—all set in * filigree. Ex 39:13
a * ring was placed at the top Ex 39:15-18
and from these * rings, two strands Ex 39:15-18
strands of twined * attached to Ex 39:15-18
gold attached to * clasps on the Ex 39:15-18
chestpiece. Two * rings were also Ex 39:19
Two other * rings were placed Ex 39:20
Bells of pure * were placed Ex 39:25,26
holy plate of pure * to wear on the Ex 39:30
The pure [* Ex 39:33-40
lampstand of pure * which stands Lev 24:3,4
cloth over the * altar, cover it Num 4:11
* box of incense which weighed Num 7:14
(so the total weight of * was Num 7:84,85,86
was made entirely of beaten *. Num 8:4
with silver and *, I could do Num 22:18
with silver and *, I could not go Num 24:13
stand heat—such as *, silver, Num 31:22
from our booty—* jewelry, Num 31:50
the silver or * they are made of. Deu 7:25
your silver and * have multiplied, Deu 8:12,13
of wood, stone, silver, and *. Deu 29:17
But all the silver and * and the Jos 6:19
the silver and * and the bronze and Jos 6:24
$200, and a bar of * worth $500. Jos 7:21
robe, the wedge of *, his sons, his Jos 7:24
*, bronze, iron, and clothing. Jos 22:7,8
in the * earrings he had gathered. Ju 8:25
decorated with *, and probably, Ju 8:27f
from the * and put it in Ophrah, Ju 8:27
And they were told, "Send five * 1Sa 6:4,5
plague, and five * models of the 1Sa 6:4,5
containing the * models of the rats 1Sa 6:8
containing the * rats and tumors 1Sa 6:11
The five * models of tumors 1Sa 6:17
and Ekron. The * rats were to 1Sa 6:18
David brought the * shields to 2Sa 8:7
made from silver, *, and bronze. 2Sa 8:10
the silver and * he had taken from 2Sa 8:11,12
made from solid * set with gems—and 2Sa 12:29,30
overlaid with pure *, and Solomon 1Ki 6:20
the cedar altar—with pure *; 1Ki 6:21,22
and he made * chains to protect 1Ki 6:21,22
and each was overlaid with *. 1Ki 6:23-28
of both rooms was overlaid with *. 1Ki 6:30
open flowers, all overlaid with *. 1Ki 6:32
and carefully overlaid with *. 1Ki 6:35
the Temple were made of solid *. 1Ki 7:48
Each of these was made of solid * 1Ki 7:50
the silver, the *, and all the 1Ki 7:51
cypress lumber and * he had 1Ki 9:11,12
For Hiram had sent * to Solomon 1Ki 9:14
Ophir, bringing * to King Solomon, 1Ki 9:27,28
carrying spices, *, and jewels; 1Ki 10:2
of $3,500,000 in *, along with a 1Ki 10:10
ships brought * to Solomon from 1Ki 10:11
Each year Solomon received * 1Ki 10:14
Solomon had some of the * beaten 1Ki 10:16,17
pieces of armor (* worth $6,000 1Ki 10:16,17
($1,800 worth of * in each). 1Ki 10:16,17
and overlaid it with pure *. 1Ki 10:18
cups were of solid *, and in the 1Ki 10:21
service was made of solid *. 1Ki 10:21
a great load of *, silver, ivory, 1Ki 10:22
of silver and * dishes, beautiful 1Ki 10:25
the king had two * calf-idols made 1Ki 12:28
me furious with your * calves. 1Ki 14:9
the * shields Solomon had made. 1Ki 14:26

(GOLD Con't)
along with the silver and * 1Ki 15:15
all the silver and * left in the 1Ki 15:18
I am sending you a present of * 1Ki 15:19
"Your silver and * are mine, as 1Ki 20:2,3
me your silver, *, wives, and 1Ki 20:5,6
and *, just as he demanded." 1Ki 20:7
freighters to sail to Ophir for *; 1Ki 22:48
in *, and ten suits of clothing. 2Ki 5:5
and * and clothing and hiding it. 2Ki 7:8
worship Jeroboam's * calves that 2Ki 10:31
buy silver cups, * snuffers, bowls, 2Ki 12:13,14
and all the * in the treasuries of 2Ki 12:18
and all the * and silver from the 2Ki 14:14
palace treasury, also the * cups. 2Ki 14:14
Ahaz took the silver and * from 2Ki 16:8
and made two calves from molten *. 2Ki 17:16
He even stripped off the * from 2Ki 18:16
had overlaid with *, and gave it 2Ki 18:16
silver, *, spices, aromatic oils, 2Ki 20:13
and they cut apart all the * 2Ki 24:13
sacrifices. The * and silver bowls, 2Ki 25:14,15
the rest of the * and silver, were 2Ki 25:14,15
He brought the * shields of King 1Ch 18:7
with many gifts of *, silver, and 1Ch 18:10
did the silver and * he took from 1Ch 18:11
It was made of * inlaid with gems 1Ch 20:2
So David paid Ornan $4,300 in *, 1Ch 21:25
hundred shekels of * by weight." 1Ch 21:25f
worth of * bullion, $2,000,000 1Ch 22:14
talents of *" and "a million 1Ch 22:14f
They are expert * and silver 1Ch 22:16
David weighed out enough * and 1Ch 28:14
specific amount of * needed for the 1Ch 28:15
He weighed out the * for the 1Ch 28:16
and for the other * tables, and he 1Ch 28:16
Then he weighed out the * for 1Ch 28:17
gold for the solid * hooks used in 1Ch 28:17
cups, and bowls of * and silver. 1Ch 28:17
out the refined * for the altar of 1Ch 28:18
and for the * angels whose wings 1Ch 28:18
building it—enough *, silver, 1Ch 29:2
worth of * from Ophir and 1Ch 29:4,5
articles made of * and silver and 1Ch 29:4,5
king pledged $145,000,000 in *; 1Ch 29:6,7
reign, silver and * were as 2Ch 1:15
and ceiling overlaid with pure *! 2Ch 3:4
plated with pure *, and engraved 2Ch 3:5
to the beauty; the *, by the way, 2Ch 3:6
were plated with *, with angels 2Ch 3:7
finest *, valued at $18,000,000. 2Ch 3:8
Twenty-six-ounce * nails were 2Ch 3:9
rooms were also plated with *. 2Ch 3:9
of angels, and plated them with *. 2Ch 3:10
he then cast ten * lampstands and 2Ch 4:7
And he molded 100 solid * bowls. 2Ch 4:8
But in the Temple only * was 2Ch 4:19
of the Presence must be made of *; 2Ch 4:19
firepans—all were made of pure *. 2Ch 4:22
to the Holy of Holies were of *. 2Ch 4:22
$13,000,000 worth of * to him! 2Ch 8:17,18
of spices, *, and jewels. 2Ch 9:1
million dollars in *, and great 2Ch 9:9
crews brought * from Ophir, also 2Ch 9:10
dollars worth of * each year from 2Ch 9:13,14
He used some of the * to make 2Ch 9:15
ivory throne overlaid with pure *. 2Ch 9:17
It had six * steps and a 2Ch 9:18
gold steps and a footstool of *; 2Ch 9:18
of gold; also * armrests, each 2Ch 9:18
each flanked by a * lion. 2Ch 9:18
by a gold lion. * lions also stood 2Ch 9:19
cups were solid *, as were all the 2Ch 9:20
to bring back *, silver, ivory, 2Ch 9:21
of silver and * bowls, clothing, 2Ch 9:24
also all of Solomon's * shields. 2Ch 12:9
cursed with those * calves you have 2Ch 13:8
the silver and * bowls which he and 2Ch 15:18
the silver and * from the Temple 2Ch 16:2
See, here is silver and * to 2Ch 16:3
it for making the * and silver 2Ch 24:14
him the Temple * and the palace 2Ch 28:21
The king took the * bowls from 2Ch 28:24
for his silver, *, precious stones, 2Ch 32:27
and for his shields and * bowls. 2Ch 32:27
King Cyrus himself donated the * Ez 1:7
1,000 * trays, Ez 1:9,10
30 bowls of solid *, Ez 1:9,10
In all there were 5,469 * and Ez 1:11
to $300,000 of *, $170,000 of Ez 2:69
Cyrus returned the * and silver Ez 5:14
And the * and silver bowls which Ez 6:5
the silver and * which we are Ez 7:15
of silver and * from the Jews and Ez 7:16
And take with you the * bowls Ez 7:19
the silver, *, the golden bowls, Ez 8:25
$3,000,000 in *; Ez 8:26,27
and twenty * bowls worth a total Ez 8:26,27
brass which were as precious as *. Ez 8:26,27
the silver, *, and other valuables Ez 8:33
of the * and silver was noted. Ez 8:34
The governor gave $5,000 in *, 50 Neh 7:70
in * and $77,000 in silver; Neh 7:71
gave $100,000 in *, $70,000 in Neh 7:72
in marble pillars. * and silver Est 1:6
the great crown of *, with an outer Est 8:15
the wicked touch has turned to *! Job 21:16
and throw your * away, then the Job 22:24
innocent—as pure as solid *! Job 23:10
silver and refine *, to dig iron Job 28:1
find sapphires and * dust— Job 28:6
up streams of water and pan the *. Job 28:11
"It cannot be bought for * or Job 28:15
nor for all the * of Ophir or Job 28:16
more valuable than * and glass. Job 28:17
for jewels mounted in fine *. Job 28:17
it, nor even the purest *. Job 28:19
him a gift of money, and a * ring. Job 42:11
They are more desirable than *. Ps 19:10
crown of purest * upon his head. Ps 21:3
jewelry of finest * from Ophir. Ps 45:9
beautiful clothing woven with *. Ps 45:13
of silver and *, covered all over Ps 68:11,12,13
and to him will be given the * of Ps 72:15
Egypt, loaded with silver and *; Ps 105:37
things of silver and of *. Ps 115:4
me than millions in silver and *! Ps 119:71,72
more than the finest *. Ps 119:127
The heathen worship idols of * Ps 135:15
more valuable than silver or *." Pro 8:10
the purest * or sterling silver! Pro 8:19
a fine * ring in a pig's snout. Pro 11:22
How much better is wisdom than *, Pro 16:16
Silver and * are purified by Pro 17:3
than * or precious jewels. Pro 20:15
is better than silver and *. Pro 22:1
The purity of silver and * can be Pro 27:21
I collected silver and * as taxes Ecc 2:7,8
its canopy *, the seat is purple; Sol 3:10
His head is purest *, and he has Sol 5:11
His arms are round bars of * set Sol 5:14
finest *, like cedars of Lebanon; Sol 5:15
of silver and *, and great numbers Is 2:7
will abandon their * and silver Is 2:20
Men will be as scarce as *—of Is 13:12
greater value than the * of Ophir. Is 13:12
of silver or * will buy them off. Is 13:17
of silver, *, spices and perfumes. Is 39:2
overlaid with *, and with silver Is 40:19
lavishly with silver and with *? Is 46:6
too, bringing * and incense to add Is 60:6
I will exchange your brass for * Is 60:17
decorate it with * and silver and Jer 10:4
from Tarshish and * from Uphaz, and Jer 10:9
jewels and * and silver of your Jer 20:5
and the solid * and silver Jer 52:19
HOW THE FINEST * has lost its Lam 4:1
*—are treated as earthenware pots. Lam 4:2
I gave you * to use in Eze 7:20
beautiful with * and silver, and Eze 16:13
You took the very jewels and * Eze 16:17
all kinds of spices, jewels and *. Eze 27:22
* and silver and many treasures. Eze 28:4
in beautiful settings of finest *. Eze 28:13
them of silver and * and drive away Eze 38:13
was made of purest *, its chest and Dan 2:32
iron, clay, brass, silver, and *; Dan 2:35
You are that head of *. Dan 2:38
the clay, the silver, and the *. Dan 2:45
reminded of the * and silver cups Dan 5:2,3,4
idols made of * and silver, brass Dan 5:2,3,4
royal honor with a * chain around Dan 5:7
gods of silver, *, brass, iron, Dan 5:23
a belt of purest * around his Dan 10:5,6
with priceless * and silver dishes Dan 11:8
It was I who gave her all the * Hos 1:8
they made from their silver and *. Hos 8:4
"You have taken my silver and * Joe 3:5
Loot the *! Nah 2:9
They are overlaid with * and Hab 2:19
Your silver and * will be of no Zep 1:18
For I have plenty of silver and * Hag 2:8,9
* from the Jews exiled in Babylon. Zec 6:10,11
a crown from the silver and *. Zec 6:10,11
to her, and fine * like dust in the Zec 9:3
make them pure, as * and silver are Zec 13:9
of * and silver and fine clothing. Zec 14:14
refining them like * or silver, so Mal 3:3
him *, frankincense and myrrh. Mt 2:11
the * in the Temple' is binding! Mt 23:16
Which is greater, the *, or the Mt 23:17
the Temple that sanctifies the *? Mt 23:17
* or silver or chipped from stone. Act 17:29
Some use * and silver and jewels; 1Co 3:12
are dishes made of * and silver as 2Ti 2:20
made of purest *—the very best in 2Ti 2:21
covered on all sides with pure *. Heb 9:4
and with valuable * rings on his Jas 2:2
The value of your * and silver Jas 5:3
as fire tests * and purifies it—and 1Pe 1:7
more precious to God than mere *; 1Pe 1:7
paid was not mere * or silver, as 1Pe 1:18
me were seven candlesticks of *. Rev 1:12
you is to buy pure * from me, gold Rev 3:18
pure gold from me, * purified by Rev 3:18
idols made of * and silver, brass, Rev 9:20
with a crown of solid * upon his Rev 14:14
jewelry made of * and precious gems Rev 17:4
customer for * and silver, precious Rev 18:12
* and precious stones and pearls! Rev 18:16
pure, transparent * like glass! Rev 21:18,19,20
pure, transparent *, like glass. Rev 21:21

GOLD-PLATED
The carrying poles were * acacia Ex 37:28

GOLDEN
and two five-ounce * bracelets Gen 24:22
placed the royal * chain about his Gen 41:41,42
Make four * rings and put the Ex 25:26,27
And make * dishes, spoons, Ex 25:29
Then make fifty * clasps to Ex 26:6
with gold, with four * hooks. Ex 26:32
mercy place—the * lid of the Ark—in Ex 26:34
and attached to * clasps on the Ex 28:13,14
is attached to * rings placed at Ex 28:22,23,24
Then make two more * rings and Ex 28:26
also make two other * rings for Ex 28:27
head the turban with the * plate. Ex 29:6
"Give me your * earrings," Ex 32:2,3
There were four * rings fastened Ex 37:3
them at the two ends of the * lid. Ex 37:7
of the * lid—it was all one piece. Ex 37:8
a * molding all around the edge. Ex 37:11
The * altar; Ex 39:33-40
"Place the * altar for the Ex 40:5
the * lid, the place of mercy. Ex 40:20
and placed the * altar in the Ex 40:26
with the sacred * plate at its Lev 8:9
two rows upon the * table that Lev 24:5-8
12 * trays (the trays weighing Num 7:84,85,86
Ishmaelites, all wore * earrings. Ju 8:23,24
containing the * rats and tumors 1Sa 6:15
With fine clothing and * 2Sa 1:24
incense to the * calf-idol, a 1Ki 13:1
However, he didn't destroy the * 2Ki 10:29
holy table. The * lampstand is 2Ch 13:11
the treasures and * bowls from the 2Ch 25:24
took some of the * bowls and other 2Ch 36:7
silver, gold, the * bowls, and the Ez 8:25
$5,000 in gold, 50 * bowls, and 530 Neh 7:70
Drinks were served in * goblets Est 1:7
the king holds out his * scepter; Est 4:11
holding out the * scepter to her. Est 5:2
held out the * scepter to Esther. Est 8:4
Timely advice is as lovely as * Pro 25:11
snaps, and the * bowl is broken, Ecc 12:6
We shall make you * earrings and Sol 1:11
silver idols and * images and cast Is 30:22
throw away his * idols and silver Is 31:7
you that soon the * dishes taken Jer 27:16
of Hosts that the * dishes still Jer 27:18
Babylon has been as a * cup in Jer 51:7
NEBUCHADNEZZAR MADE a * Dan 3:1
King Nebuchadnezzar's * statue; Dan 3:5
worship the * statue when the band Dan 3:10
worship the * statue you set up." Dan 3:12
to worship the * statue I set up? Dan 3:14
the * statue you have erected." Dan 3:18
robes, with a * chain around your Dan 5:16
in purple, and a * chain was hung Dan 5:29
I answered, "I see a * lampstand Zec 4:2
* bowls through two golden tubes. Zec 4:12
golden bowls through two * tubes. Zec 4:12
dance" in worship of the * calf. 1Co 10:7
The first one contained the * Heb 9:1
In that room there were a * Heb 9:4
and the * chest, called the ark of Heb 9:4
on them, and a * jar with some Heb 9:4
Above the * chest were statues Heb 9:5
* cover, called the mercy seat. Heb 9:5
with a * band across his chest. Rev 1:13
and the seven * candlesticks: The Rev 1:20
walks among the * candlesticks." Rev 2:1f
all were clothed in white, with * Rev 4:4
with a harp and * vials filled with Rev 5:8
Then another angel with a * Rev 8:3
the * altar before the throne. Rev 8:3
They had what looked like * Rev 9:7
four horns of the * altar that Rev 9:13
with * belts across their chests. Rev 15:6
each of them a * flask filled with Rev 15:7
a * goblet full of obscenities. Rev 17:4
The angel held in his hand a * Rev 21:15

GOLDSMITH
He is a skillful * and 2Ch 2:14
Uzziel (son of Harhaiah) was a * Neh 3:8
the carver hurries the *, and the Is 41:7
They hire a * to take your wealth Is 46:6

GOLDSMITHS
"So send me skilled craftsmen—* 2Ch 2:7
Malchijah, one of the *, Neh 3:31
The other * and merchants Neh 3:32
skillful * who make their idols; Jer 10:9

GOLGOTHA
an area known as *, that is, Mt 27:33

(GOLGOTHA Con't)
brought Jesus to a place called *. Mk 15:22
called Golgotha. (* means skull. Mk 15:22
"The Skull," in Hebrew, "*." Jn 19:17

GOLIATH
Then *, a Philistine champion 1Sa 17:4-7
with them, he saw * the giant step 1Sa 17:23
and sling, started across to *. 1Sa 17:40
to Goliath. * walked out towards 1Sa 17:41,42
and wild animals," * yelled. 1Sa 17:44
As * approached, David ran out to 1Sa 17:48,49
go out to fight *, he asked Abner, 1Sa 17:55
After David had killed *, Abner 1Sa 17:57
home after David had killed *. 1Sa 18:6
his life to kill *, and how the 1Sa 19:5
have the sword of *, the 1Sa 21:9
the sword of * the Philistine." 1Sa 22:9,10
the brother of * the Gittite, 2Sa 21:19
Literally, "slew * of Gath." 2Sa 21:19f
Lahmi, the brother of * the giant; 1Ch 20:5

GOLIATH'S
over and pulled * from its sheath 1Sa 17:50,51
(Later David took * head to 1Sa 17:54

GOMER
of Japheth were:*, Magog, Gen 10:2
The sons of *:Ashkenaz, Riphath, Gen 10:3
*, Magog, Madai, 1Ch 1:5-9
The sons of *: 1Ch 1:5-9
(Meshech, Tubal, *, Beth-togarmah) Eze 38:2,3f
and so shall * and all his hordes Eze 38:6
So Hosea married *, daughter of Hos 1:3
Soon * had another child—this one Hos 1:6
After * had weaned Lo-ruhamah, Hos 1:8

GOMORRAH
and to Sodom, *, Admah, and Gen 10:15-19
Jehovah destroyed Sodom and *); Gen 13:10
Birsha, king of *, Gen 14:2
These kings (of Sodom, *, Admah, Gen 14:3
kings of Sodom, *, Admah, Zeboiim, Gen 14:8,9
kings of Sodom and * fled, some Gen 14:10
Sodom and * and carried off all Gen 14:11
of Sodom and * are utterly evil, Gen 18:20
upon Sodom and *, and utterly Gen 19:24
plain to Sodom and * and saw Gen 19:28
like Sodom and * and Admah and Deu 29:23
They act like men of Sodom and *: Deu 32:32
wiped out as Sodom and * were. Is 1:9
of Sodom and *, as I call you now. Is 1:10
as Sodom and * were when God sent Is 13:19
as the men of Sodom and * were. Jer 23:14
as Sodom and * and their Jer 49:18
and * and their neighboring towns. Jer 50:40
Sodom and * (Deuteronomy 29:23). Hos 11:8f
your cities, as I did Sodom and *; Amo 4:11
like Sodom and *, and become a Zep 2:9
of Sodom and * will be better off Mt 10:15
cities of Sodom and * perished. Rom 9:29
of Sodom and * into heaps of ashes 2Pe 2:6
of Sodom and * and their Jud 1:7

GONE.
And now in a single hour all is * Rev 18:19

GOOD
giving knowledge of * and Bad. Gen 2:9
of right and wrong, * and bad. Gen 2:16,17
"It isn't * for man to be alone; Gen 2:18
able to distinguish * from evil!" Gen 3:5
as we are, knowing * from bad, what Gen 3:22
a * indication of the water level. Gen 8:7f
Lord Jehovah, what * are all your Gen 15:2,3
who are just and *—so that I can do Gen 18:19
"Will you kill * and bad alike? Gen 18:22,23
what * is his birthright?" Gen 25:32
have done only * to you and have Gen 26:29
like it—savory and *—and bring it Gen 27:2,3,4
of my son is the * smell of the Gen 27:27,28,29
* harvest of grain, and new wine. Gen 27:27,28,29
given me * gifts for my husband. Gen 30:20
you would do me *— I am not worthy Gen 32:9
But you promised to do me *, and Gen 32:12
"Very *," Joseph replied. Gen 37:13,14
dream had such a * meaning, he told Gen 40:16
of the * years will be erased. Gen 41:31
of the * things of Egypt, and ten Gen 45:23
When he saw how * the Gen 49:15
God turned into * what you meant Gen 50:20
of Egypt into a * land, a large Ex 3:8
Lord, I'm just not a * speaker. Ex 4:10
is a * speaker. Ex 4:14
For they said, "We are as * as Ex 12:33
and *, without maggots or odor. Ex 16:24
may have a long, * life in the land Ex 20:12
is a homonym of the word "*." Lev 2:13f
whether the vow is * or bad, when Lev 5:4
Literally, "shall make it *, life Lev 24:18f
* for bad or bad for good; Lev 27:10
good for bad or bad for *; Lev 27:10
of whether it is * or bad, and Lev 27:33
Come with us and we will do you * Num 10:29
* things the Lord does for us." Num 10:32
to long for the * things of Egypt. Num 11:4,5
"We are as * as dead," they Num 17:12,13

"This seemed like a * idea, so I Deu 1:23
it was indeed a * land the Lord our Deu 1:24,25
But nothing I said did any *. Deu 1:32
live to see the * land he had Deu 1:34,35
Promised Land—the * land beyond Deu 3:23,24,25
River into the * land he has given Deu 4:21,22
cities full of * things—cities you Deu 6:10,11,12
is right and * in the Lord's eyes. Deu 6:18
in and possess the * land which the Deu 6:18
you into a * land of brooks, pools, Deu 8:7
for the * land he has given you. Deu 8:10
would grow, and he could do you *. Deu 8:16
helped us because we are so *!' Deu 9:4
giving you this * land because you Deu 9:6
because you are *, for you are Deu 9:6
obey for your own * the Deu 10:12,13
have a long and * life in the land Deu 11:9
the * land the Lord has given you. Deu 11:17
will enjoy the * life awaiting you Deu 11:21
you with a * harvest and in so many Deu 16:15
ensure his having a long, * reign. Deu 17:20
roads to these cities in * repair. Deu 19:2,3
will have a long, * life in the Deu 25:13,14,15
all the * things he has given you. Deu 26:11
The Lord will bless you with * Deu 28:8
an abundance of * things in the Deu 28:11
and he will do you * and bless you Deu 30:5
you will not have a long, * life Deu 30:18
Every * thing the Lord had Jos 21:45
from this * land which the Lord Jos 23:13
has given you the * things he Jos 23:15,16
you out from this * land which the Jos 23:15,16
looking for a * place to live. Ju 17:7,8
as they were having such a * time. Ju 19:6
by giving them * crops again. Ru 1:6,7
"You are so * to me, and I'm not Ru 2:13
After Boaz had finished a * meal, Ru 3:6,7
same, for his sons were not * men. 1Sa 8:5
you of all the * things he has done 1Sa 12:7
things which are * and right. 1Sa 12:23
"We'll find a * harpist to play 1Sa 16:15,16
strong, and had *, solid judgment. 1Sa 16:18
* -he exclaimed 1Sa 23:7
for you have repaid me * for evil. 1Sa 24:17
But David's men were very * to 1Sa 25:15,16
* it did us to help this fellow. 1Sa 25:21
but he has repaid me bad for *. 1Sa 25:21
When the Lord has done all the * 1Sa 25:30,31
Thank God for your * sense! 1Sa 25:33
This isn't * at all! 1Sa 26:16
reward for doing * and for being 1Sa 26:23
"*," David agreed. 1Sa 28:2
bringing me * news, I killed him; 2Sa 4:10
men who kill a * man in his own 2Sa 4:11
and you have promised me these * 2Sa 7:28
God and can discern * from evil. 2Sa 14:17
David with the * news that the Lord 2Sa 18:19
"it wouldn't be * news to the king 2Sa 18:20
"He is a * man and comes with 2Sa 18:27
with * news," the king replied. 2Sa 18:27
have * news for my lord the king. 2Sa 18:31
I discern between * and bad?" 2Sa 19:35f
* things you want to give him." 2Sa 19:37
"*," the king agreed. 2Sa 19:38
He causes the * to walk a steady 2Sa 22:34
that * water in the city well!" 2Sa 23:15
to him, "for you are a * man; 1Ki 1:42
you must have * news." 1Ki 1:42
congratulations and * wishes. 1Ki 5:1
them to follow the * ways in which 1Ki 8:35,36
O my people, may you live * and 1Ki 8:61
people a just, * government!" 1Ki 10:9
and agree to be * to them and serve 1Ki 12:7
For this child is the only * 1Ki 14:13
Israel from this * land of their 1Ki 14:15
But he was not a * king; 1Ki 15:26
to Ahab, "Go and enjoy a * meal! 1Ki 18:41
he never prophesies anything *. 1Ki 22:8
He never tells me anything *. 1Ki 22:18
But he was not a * king, for he 1Ki 22:52,53
ruin all the * land with stones." 2Ki 3:19
stones on every * piece of land, 2Ki 3:25
Does she want me to put in a * 2Ki 4:13
the Temple into * condition." 2Ki 12:7
He was a * king in the Lord's 2Ki 14:3
but he was as * a king as his 2Ki 14:3
Azariah was a * king, and he 2Ki 15:3
speaking, Jotham was a * king. 2Ki 15:34,35
Character of his reign: * (similar 2Ki 18:1
and chariots, it will do no *. 2Ki 18:24
is what the Lord wants, it is *." 2Ki 20:19
Character of his reign: *; 2Ki 22:1
They found * pastures, and 1Ch 4:40,41
thanks to the Lord, for he is *; 1Ch 16:34
God himself has promised this * 1Ch 17:26
And may the Lord give you the * 1Ch 22:12
to rule this * land and leave it to 1Ch 28:8
you test men to see if they are *; 1Ch 29:17
for you enjoy * men. 1Ch 29:17
I have done all this with * 1Ch 29:17
Give my son Solomon a * heart 1Ch 29:19

been so kind and * to my father 2Ch 1:8
Their theme was "He is so *! 2Ch 5:13,14
It was * to have the desire, the 2Ch 6:8
"How * he is!" 2Ch 7:3
Lord had been so * to David and 2Ch 7:10
Judah, keep up the * work and don't 2Ch 15:7
he followed in the * footsteps of 2Ch 17:3
But there are some * things 2Ch 19:3
He was a * king, just as his 2Ch 20:32
followed in the * ways of your 2Ch 21:12
nor the * ways of King Asa, but 2Ch 21:12
maintain the Temple in * repair. 2Ch 24:5
had done so much * for Israel, for 2Ch 24:16
was, in general, a * king so far as 2Ch 26:4
He followed the generally * 2Ch 27:2
the palace treasures, it did no *. 2Ch 28:21
His reign was a * one in the 2Ch 29:2
But Hezekiah said, "May the * 2Ch 30:17,18,19
SOME TIME LATER, after this * work 2Ch 32:1
and all of the * things he did are 2Ch 32:32
His was a * reign, as he 2Ch 34:2
followed the * example of his 2Ch 34:2
that there was * progress being 2Ch 34:15,16
of Josiah, and his * deeds, and how 2Ch 35:26
this song: "He is *, and his love Ez 3:11
for the Lord gave them a * trip. Ez 7:7,8,9
And God was *! Ez 8:18
he would give us a * journey and Ez 8:21
they replied, "things are not *; Neh 1:3
They replied at once, "*! Neh 2:18
and gave them * laws and true Neh 9:13
You sent your * Spirit to Neh 9:20
they took over houses full of * Neh 9:25
and who was also a * friend of Neh 13:4
O my God, remember this * deed Neh 13:14
Remember this * deed, O my God! Neh 13:22
thought this made * sense, so he Est 1:21
with messages of * will, and Est 9:29-31
the land of Uz a man named Job—a * Job 1:1
finest man in all the earth—a * Job 1:8
in all the earth—a * man who fears Job 2:3
God will care for those who are *? Job 4:6
Have you ever known a truly * and Job 4:7,8
You shall live a long, * life; Job 5:26
For your own *, listen to my Job 5:27
a breath, and nothing * is left. Job 7:7
you were pure and *, he would hear Job 8:6
God will not cast away a * man, Job 8:20
But how can a man be truly * in Job 9:2
And if I'm *, that doesn't count. Job 10:15
Just as my mouth can taste * Job 12:11
What * do such words do? Job 15:3
are * days they will soon be gone. Job 15:21
they can produce nothing truly *. Job 15:34
you. My * days are in the past. Job 17:11
He has * cause for fear—his Job 18:11
live on to a * old age, and become Job 21:7
'Why should we obey him? What * Job 21:15
who have never known anything *. Job 21:25
Is it because you are * that he Job 22:4
filled their homes with * things. Job 22:18
with the right and the *. Job 24:13
in my nest after a long, * life.' Job 29:18
I therefore looked for * to Job 30:26
define among ourselves what is *. Job 34:4
Or if you are *, is this some Job 35:7
or your * deeds may profit him. Job 35:8
He does not ignore the * men but Job 36:7
because of their lack of * sense. Job 36:12
Clubs do no *, and he laughs at Job 41:29
back evil for * or unjustly Ps 7:4
am to the Lord because he is so *. Ps 7:17
from your throne that it is *. Ps 9:4
For God is *, and he loves Ps 11:7
in mercy and joy upon the *." Ps 11:7f
really be a * person at all. Ps 14:1
Not one is *, not one! Ps 14:3
tested me and seen that I am *. Ps 17:3
He asked for a long, * life, and Ps 21:4
The Lord is * and glad to teach Ps 25:8
He loves whatever is just and *; Ps 33:5
Lord will never lack any * thing. Ps 34:10
Do you want a long, * life? Ps 34:12
and spend your time in doing *. Ps 34:14
all who live * lives, and he gives Ps 34:15
Yes, the Lord hears the * man Ps 34:17
their sins. The * man does not Ps 34:19
meted out to those who hate the *. Ps 34:21
I do them *, but they return me Ps 35:12
of peace and doing *, but of plots Ps 35:20
everyone how great and * you are; Ps 35:28
they are no longer wise and *. Ps 36:3
Be kind and * to others; Ps 37:3
the * deeds done by godly men, Ps 37:18
But the * man returns what he Ps 37:21
The steps of * men are directed Ps 37:23
low-down ways and live * lives. Ps 37:27
The godly man is a * counselor Ps 37:30,31
But the * man—what a different Ps 37:37
For the * man—the blameless, the Ps 37:37
They repay me evil for * and Ps 38:20

(GOOD Con't)

I have told everyone the * News	Ps 40:9
I have not kept this * News	Ps 40:10
You love what is *	Ps 45:7
be the slaves of those who are *.	Ps 49:14
Literally, "Do * in your good	Ps 51:18f
Literally, "Do good in your *	Ps 51:18f
then you will rejoice in the *	Ps 51:19
love wickedness—far more than *!	Ps 52:3
Not one is *, not one!	Ps 53:3
your name, O Lord, for it is *.	Ps 54:6
will know that * is rewarded, and	Ps 58:11
us among all the * things there.	Ps 65:4
I will tell everyone how * you	Ps 71:15
that you alone are just and *.	Ps 71:16
prosperity beeause of his * reign.	Ps 72:3
May all * men flourish in his	Ps 72:7
HOW * GOD is to Israel—to those	Ps 73:1
"and increase the power of * men	Ps 75:10
I keep thinking of the * old days	Ps 77:5
He gives us grace and glory. No *	Ps 84:11
O Lord, you are so * and kind,	Ps 86:5
Replace the evil years with *.	Ps 90:15
IT IS * to say, "Thank you" to	Ps 92:1
for the godly and joy for the *.	Ps 97:11
For the Lord is always *.	Ps 100:5
Only those who are truly * shall	Ps 101:6
He fills my life with * things!	Ps 103:5
THANK YOU, Lord! How * you are!	Ps 106:1
others and are always just and *.	Ps 106:3
(For this * deed Phineas will be	Ps 106:31
Lord for being so *, for always	Ps 107:1
and fills the hungry soul with *.	Ps 107:9
and turns the * land of the wicked	Ps 107:34
much prosperity. * men everywhere	Ps 107:42
They return evil for *, and	Ps 109:5
All he does is just and *, and	Ps 111:7
everywhere, for * men's sons have a	Ps 112:2
* deeds will never be forgotten.	Ps 112:3
How kind he is! How * he is!	Ps 116:5
OH, THANK THE Lord, for he's so *!	Ps 118:1
to the Lord, for he is so *!	Ps 118:29
for your laws are right and *.	Ps 119:39
my thanks to you for your * laws.	Ps 119:62
Teach me your * paths.	Ps 119:64
Now teach me * judgment as well	Ps 119:66
You are * and do only good;	Ps 119:68
You are good and do only *;	Ps 119:68
was right and did me *.	Ps 119:75,76,77
O Lord, do * to those who are	Ps 125:4
to those who are *, whose hearts	Ps 125:4
protects a city, sentries do no *.	Ps 127:1
with their whips, the Lord is *.	Ps 129:3,4
the Lord because he is so *;	Ps 135:3
THANKS to the Lord, for he is *;	Ps 136:1
Lead me in * paths, for your	Ps 143:10
good paths, for your Spirit is *.	Ps 143:10
Everyone will tell about how *	Ps 145:7
He is * to everyone, and his	Ps 145:9
For the Lord loves * men.	Ps 146:8
YES, PRAISE the Lord! How * it is	Ps 147:1
them will stand you in * stead;	Pro 1:7,8,9
they say. "* or bad, we'll treat	Pro 1:12
will be given wisdom and * sense.	Pro 2:1
He grants * sense to the	Pro 2:7,8
only * men enjoy life to the full;	Pro 2:21
evil men lose the * things they	Pro 2:22
a reputation for * judgment and	Pro 3:4,5
and has * judgment and common	Pro 3:13,14,15
Wisdom gives:A long, *	Pro 3:16,17
* judgment and common sense!	Pro 4:5
common sense and * judgment.	Pro 4:7
and you will have a long, * life.	Pro 4:10
But the * man walks along in the	Pro 4:18
danger and to give you a * life.	Pro 6:23
My advice is wholesome and *.	Pro 8:8
Wisdom and * judgment live	Pro 8:12
"I, Wisdom, give * advice and	Pro 8:14,15
simple ones without * judgment;	Pro 9:4
teach a * man, and he will learn	Pro 9:9
The Lord will not let a * man	Pro 10:3
The * man is covered with	Pro 10:6
We all have happy memories of *	Pro 10:7
A * man has firm footing, but a	Pro 10:9
There is living truth in what a *	Pro 10:11
The * man's earnings advance the	Pro 10:16
When a * man speaks, he is worth	Pro 10:20
A godly man gives * advice, but a	Pro 10:21
and so will the * man's hopes.	Pro 10:24
But the * man has a strong	Pro 10:25
the wicked expect a long, * life?	Pro 10:27
The hope of * men is eternal	Pro 10:28
The * shall never lose God's	Pro 10:30
The * man gives wise advice, but	Pro 10:31
A * man is guided by his honesty;	Pro 11:3
The * man's goodness delivers	Pro 11:6
God rescues * men from danger	Pro 11:8
The whole city celebrates a *	Pro 11:10
The * influence of godly citizens	Pro 11:11
a man with * sense holds his	Pro 11:12
but with * counselors there is	Pro 11:14
the * man's reward lasts forever.	Pro 11:18
The * man finds life;	Pro 11:19
but delights in those who are *.	Pro 11:20
The * man can look forward to	Pro 11:23
If you search for * you will find	Pro 11:27
The Lord blesses * men and	Pro 12:2
A * man's mind is filled with	Pro 12:5
Everyone admires a man with *	Pro 12:8
A * man is concerned for the	Pro 12:10
* men long to help each other.	Pro 12:12
A * man is known by his	Pro 12:17
hearts that are planning for *!	Pro 12:20
harm befalls the *, but there is	Pro 12:21
The * man asks advice from	Pro 12:26
* use of everything he finds.	Pro 12:27
The * man wins his case by	Pro 13:2
A * man hates lies;	Pro 13:5
The * man's life is full of	Pro 13:9
A man with * sense is	Pro 13:15
When a * man dies, he leaves an	Pro 13:22
A poor man's farm may have *	Pro 13:23
The * man eats to live, while the	Pro 13:25
bond of godly people is * will.	Pro 14:9
but those who plan * shall be	Pro 14:22
the truth saves * men from being	Pro 14:25
eye on both the evil and the *.	Pro 15:3
There is treasure in being *, but	Pro 15:6
Only the * can give good advice.	Pro 15:7
Only the good can give * advice.	Pro 15:7
but loves those who try to be *.	Pro 15:9,10
life; the * man's path is easy!	Pro 15:19
Everyone enjoys giving * advice,	Pro 15:23
A * man thinks before he speaks;	Pro 15:28
Pleasant sights and * reports	Pro 15:30
Hunger is *—if it makes you work	Pro 16:26
If you repay evil for *, a curse	Pro 17:13
that bad is *, and good is bad.	Pro 17:15
that bad is good, and * is bad.	Pro 17:15
A cheerful heart does * like	Pro 17:22
to fine the godly for being *!	Pro 17:26
advice satisfies like a * meal!	Pro 18:20
who finds a wife finds a * thing;	Pro 18:22
Though * advice lies deep within	Pro 20:5
If you have * eyesight and good	Pro 20:12
If you have good eyesight and *	Pro 20:12
* sense is far more valuable than	Pro 20:15
life; a * man lives a godly life.	Pro 21:8
being a * neighbor is out of his	Pro 21:10
A * man loves justice, but it is	Pro 21:15
The man who tries to be *, loving	Pro 21:21
IF YOU MUST choose, take a * name	Pro 22:1
for it will do you *, and you can	Pro 22:17,18,19
though it all tastes so *;	Pro 23:1
bribe you, and no * is going to	Pro 23:1
to all the * sense you can get.	Pro 23:23
Don't you know that this * man,	Pro 24:15,16
* news from far away is like cold	Pro 25:25
the upright to do * shall be given	Pro 28:10
* men will be rescued from harm,	Pro 28:18
When the wicked prosper, * men go	Pro 28:28
when the wicked meet disaster, *	Pro 28:28
With * men in authority, the	Pro 29:2
evil men are caught in it, but *	Pro 29:5,6
The * man knows the poor man's	Pro 29:7
are too; but * men will live to see	Pro 29:16
The * hate the badness of the	Pro 29:27
wicked hate the goodness of the *.	Pro 29:27
If you can find a truly * wife,	Pro 31:10
These * deeds of hers shall bring	Pro 31:31
all the time; what * does it do?	Ecc 2:1
man does, both * and bad."	Ecc 3:17
Well, one thing, at least, is *:	Ecc 5:18
eat well, drink a * glass of wine,	Ecc 5:18
And, of course, it is very * if	Ecc 5:19,20
and the * health to enjoy it.	Ecc 5:19,20
A * REPUTATION is more valuable	Ecc 7:1
to die and it is a * thing to think	Ecc 7:2
only of having a * time now.	Ecc 7:4
Don't long for "the * old	Ecc 7:10
To be wise is as * as being rich;	Ecc 7:11
that some of the * die young and	Ecc 7:15-17
So don't be too * or too wise!	Ecc 7:15-17
who is always * and never sins.	Ecc 7:20
not live long, * lives—their days	Ecc 8:13
to treat some * men as though they	Ecc 8:14
wicked men as though they were *.	Ecc 8:14
everyone, whether * or bad,	Ecc 9:2,3
more careful to be *, but instead	Ecc 9:2,3
only a wise man, but a * teacher;	Ecc 12:10
every hidden thing, * or bad.	Ecc 12:14
Learn to do *, to be fair and to	Is 1:17
And afterwards I will give you *	Is 1:26
are just and *, shall be redeemed.	Is 1:27
for he alone is holy, just and *.	Is 5:16
the evil and to choose the * .	Is 7:15,16f
of the hills, but it will do no *;	Is 16:12
but used for * food and fine	Is 23:18
delicious feast of * food, with	Is 25:6
For the Lord's * hand will rest	Is 25:10
But for * men the path is not	Is 26:7
to the wicked doesn't make them *;	Is 26:10
obey him, if they were kind and *.	Is 28:12
the courts. But * men will be	Is 32:8
O Lord, your discipline is * and	Is 38:16
"Yes, now I see it all—it was *	Is 38:17
"Whatever the Lord says is *.	Is 39:8
O Crier of * News, shout to	Is 40:9
at the anvil. "*," they say.	Is 41:7
I send * times and bad.	Is 45:7
You are worthless, with nothing *	Is 48:10
you for your own * and leads you	Is 48:17
Yet it was the Lord's * plan to	Is 53:10
groceries that don't do you any *?	Is 55:2
* food that fattens up the soul!	Is 55:2
Do what's right and *, for I am	Is 56:1
THE * MEN perish;	Is 57:1
and your "* works"—none of which	Is 57:12
Look, what * is fasting when you	Is 58:4
you with all * things, and keep you	Is 58:11
lie and grumble and oppose the *.	Is 59:3
what it means to be just and *;	Is 59:8
shall want the * and hate the	Is 59:21
All your people will be *.	Is 60:21
me to bring * news to the suffering	Is 61:1
do *, who follow godly ways.	Is 64:5
for just as * grapes are found	Is 65:8
are some * grapes there!"	Is 65:8
can you build for me as * as that?	Is 66:1
All the world will see the * hand	Is 66:14
children but it did them no *;	Jer 2:30
but it's all no *—your new	Jer 2:36
wish for "the * old days of long	Jer 3:16
and begin to live *, honest, clean	Jer 4:2
otherwise the * seed will be	Jer 4:3
It will do you no *!	Jer 4:30
them of all of these * things.	Jer 5:25
Ask where the * road is, the godly	Jer 6:16
die, and all the * things I	Jer 8:13
harm nor help, nor do you any *.	Jer 10:5
to see and full of * fruit;	Jer 11:16
worked hard but it does them no *.	Jer 12:13
as this loincloth—* for nothing.	Jer 13:10
to doing evil now start being *.	Jer 13:23
* times pass him by forever.	Jer 17:6
evil against you now instead of *;	Jer 18:11
highways of *, and walk the muddy	Jer 18:15
Should they repay evil for *?	Jer 18:20
I replied, "Figs, some very * and	Jer 24:3
Then the Lord said: "The * figs	Jer 24:4,5
I have done it for their *.	Jer 24:4,5
do for you all the * things I have	Jer 29:10
They are plans for * and not for	Jer 29:11
shall see the * I have waiting for	Jer 29:32
wound and no medicine does any *.	Jer 30:13
of the Lord—the * crops, the wheat	Jer 31:12
the field—paying * money for it	Jer 32:25
for their own * and for the good of	Jer 32:39
the * of all their descendants.	Jer 32:39
them, but only to do them *.	Jer 32:40
I will rejoice to do them * and	Jer 32:41
do all the * I have promised them.	Jer 32:42
are already as * as dead, for I	Jer 33:5
world will see the * I do for my	Jer 33:9
For he is * and his mercy endures	Jer 33:10,11
Judah all the * I promised them.	Jer 33:14
long, * lives in our own land.	Jer 35:7
the Babylonians are gone for *.	Jer 37:9
it will do you no * to seek my help	Jer 44:26
watch over you, but not for *!	Jer 44:27
The Lord is wonderfully * to	Lam 3:25
It is * both to hope and wait	Lam 3:26
It is * for a young man to be	Lam 3:27
And if a * man becomes bad, and	Eze 3:20
him, his previous * deeds won't	Eze 3:20
tell us that it wasn't * enough?	Eze 13:12
it would do no *—it would not save	Eze 14:16
"Son of dust, what * are vines	Eze 15:2
All they are * for is fuel—and	Eze 15:4
it was already in * soil with	Eze 17:8
When a * man turns away from	Eze 18:26
away from being * and begins	Eze 18:26
from his sins and live a * life.	Eze 18:28
for them—a * land, flowing as it	Eze 20:5,6
your people, * and bad alike— I	Eze 21:3
For the * works of a righteous	Eze 33:12
"I have said the * man will	Eze 33:13
of his * deeds will be remembered.	Eze 33:13
to the * and shall surely live.	Eze 33:16
For again I say, when the * man	Eze 33:18
where the land is fertile and *.	Eze 34:13
Yes, I will give them * pasture	Eze 34:14
for Israel, * times will return.	Eze 36:8
to look * around the palace."	Dan 1:3,4
whose every act is right and *;	Dan 4:37
Plant the * seeds of	Hos 10:12
right, and * men walk along them.	Hos 14:9
says the Lord, "but it did no *;	Amo 4:6
are the enemies of everything *;	Amo 5:12
Be *, flee evil—and live!	Amo 5:14
Hate evil and love the *;	Amo 5:15
of justice—a torrent of doing *.	Amo 5:24
all that should be * and right.	Amo 6:12

(GOOD Con't)

they receive evil and not *."	Amo 9:4
upon him for your own * reasons."	Jon 1:14
His threats are for your *, to	Mic 2:7
ones who hate * and love evil;	Mic 3:2
Shall I say "*!"	Mic 6:11
I long for it! The * men have	Mic 7:1
The Lord is *.	Nah 1:7
and give you a * name, a name of	Zep 3:20
of the * things to come.	Zec 3:8
he walked with me, living a * and	Mal 2:6
By saying that evil is *, that it	Mal 2:17
and obey him. What * does it do to	Mal 3:14,15
God's treatment of * men and bad,	Mal 3:18
preaching the * News about the	Mt 4:23
to be just and *, for they shall be	Mt 5:6
because they are *, for the Kingdom	Mt 5:10
let your * deeds glow for all to	Mt 5:15,16
the evil and the *, and sends rain	Mt 5:45
who love you, what * is that?	Mt 5:46
DON'T do your * deeds publicly,	Mt 6:1
know how to give * gifts to your	Mt 7:11
certainly give * gifts to those who	Mt 7:11
kind can't produce what is *.	Mt 7:18
the * News about the Kingdom.	Mt 9:35
And if you welcome * and godly	Mt 10:41
preaching the * News to the poor.	Mt 11:5
Yes, it is right to do * on the	Mt 12:12
a select variety produces * fruit;	Mt 12:33
you speak what is * and right?	Mt 12:34
his speech. A * man's speech	Mt 12:35
But some fell on * soil, and	Mt 13:8
who hears the * News about the	Mt 13:19
less for God. The * ground	Mt 13:23
farmer sowing * seed in his field;	Mt 13:24
He replied, "You are * at	Mt 16:2,3
this question: "* master, what	Mt 19:16
"When you call me * you are	Mt 19:17
"for God alone is truly *.	Mt 19:17
they could find, * and bad alike;	Mt 22:10
"And the * News about the	Mt 24:14
"His master praised him for *	Mt 25:21
" '* work,' his master said.	Mt 25:23
'You are a * and faithful	Mt 25:23
"What a waste of * money," they	Mt 26:8,9
For she has done a * thing to me.	Mt 26:10
wherever the * News is preached."	Mt 26:13
message: "Leave that * man alone;	Mt 27:19
of the blood of this * man.	Mt 27:24
"* morning!"	Mt 28:9
to Galilee to preach God's * News.	Mk 1:14
the * news that he was healed;	Mk 1:45
I haven't come to tell * people	Mk 2:17
seeds fell into * soil and yielded	Mk 4:8
plant * seed within their lives.	Mk 4:14
who listen to the * News and	Mk 4:18
"But the * soil represents the	Mk 4:20
that he was a * and holy man, and	Mk 6:20
*! he said	Mk 7:29
the sake of the * News will ever	Mk 8:35
"* salt is worthless if it loses	Mk 9:50
down and asked, "* Teacher, what	Mk 10:17
"Why do you call me *?"	Mk 10:18
"Only God is truly *!	Mk 10:18
to tell others the * News, who	Mk 10:29
Literally, "Be of * cheer."	Mk 10:49f
to tell them the * News.	Mk 13:9
And the * News must first be	Mk 13:10
why berate her for doing a *	Mk 14:6
that wherever the * News is	Mk 14:9
* News to everyone, everywhere.	Mk 16:15
sent me to you with this * news!	Lk 1:19
He was a * man, very devout,	Lk 2:25
does not produce * fruit will be	Lk 3:9
the * News to the people.	Lk 3:18
he has appointed me to preach *	Lk 4:18,19
must preach the * News of the	Lk 4:43
a doctor, not those in * health.	Lk 5:31
themselves already * enough."	Lk 5:32
Is it right to do * on the	Lk 6:9
And you will be in * company—the	Lk 6:23
Love your enemies. Do * to those	Lk 6:27
And if you do * only to those	Lk 6:33
who do you *—is that so wonderful?	Lk 6:33
who can repay you, what * is that?	Lk 6:34
"Love your enemies! Do * to	Lk 6:35
sermons: "What * is it for one	Lk 6:39
"A tree from * stock doesn't	Lk 6:43
bramble bushes. A * man produces	Lk 6:45
A good man produces * deeds from	Lk 6:45
good deeds from a * heart.	Lk 6:45
And the poor are hearing the *	Lk 7:20,21,22
anyone else to believe the * News.	Lk 8:14
"But the * soil represents	Lk 8:15
the * News and healing the sick.	Lk 9:6
pretend to be * when they aren't.	Lk 12:1
of worrying? What * does it do?	Lk 12:25
that he has done a * job, there	Lk 12:42,43,44
"What * is salt that has lost	Lk 14:34
feeding the swine looked * to him.	Lk 15:16
your money for *, so that it will	Lk 16:9f
But John introduced the * News	Lk 16:16
this question: "* sir, what shall	Lk 18:18
are saying when you call me '*'?"	Lk 18:19
"Only God is truly *, and no one	Lk 18:19
'You are a * man.	Lk 19:17
and preaching the * News in the	Lk 20:1
triumph ends in God's * time.	Lk 21:24
out to preach the * News and you	Lk 22:35
"He was so * at helping	Lk 23:35
"Can anything * come from	Jn 1:46
The reapers will be paid * wages	Jn 4:36
"My Father constantly does *,	Jn 5:17
who have done *, to eternal life;	Jn 5:29
But what * is that with all this	Jn 6:8,9
sent him is a * and true person.	Jn 7:18
you would follow his * example.	Jn 8:39
"I don't know whether he is * or	Jn 9:25
"I am the * Shepherd.	Jn 10:11
"I am the Good Shepherd. The *	Jn 10:11
"I am the * Shepherd and know my	Jn 10:14
They replied, "Not for any *	Jn 10:33
* friend is very, very sick."	Jn 11:3
was having a * night's rest, said,	Jn 11:12,13
if you mean the * deed done to the	Act 4:9
preaching the * News about Jesus!	Act 8:4
to preach the * News to them too.	Act 8:25
He preached the * News there and	Act 8:40
everyone there the * News about	Act 9:20
Roman officer, a * and godly man,	Act 10:22
* deeds and are acceptable to him.	Act 10:35
heard about the * News for the	Act 10:36,37
went around doing * and healing all	Act 10:38
And he sent us to preach the *	Act 10:42
telling them the * News, but just	Act 11:15
the * News, but only to Jews.	Act 11:19
God's * News was spreading	Act 12:24
of all that is *, will you never	Act 13:10
to bring you this * News—that God's	Act 13:32,33
that this * News from God should be	Act 13:46
and preaching the * News there.	Act 14:7
We have come to bring you the *	Act 14:15
you rain and * crops and giving you	Act 14:17
After preaching the * News there	Act 14:21
ago to preach the * News to the	Act 15:7
"For it seemed * to the Holy	Act 15:27,28,29
us to preach the * News there.	Act 16:10
the * News from the Lord.	Act 16:32
telling others the * News about	Act 20:24
before God in all * conscience!"	Act 23:1
their repentance by doing * deeds.	Act 26:20
Phoenix was a * harbor with only	Act 27:12
eat something now for your own *!	Act 27:34
sent out to preach God's * News.	Rom 1:1
This * News was promised long	Rom 1:2
It is the * News about his Son,	Rom 1:3
* report, and for each one of you.	Rom 1:8
others the * News about his Son.	Rom 1:9
among you and see * results, just	Rom 1:13
in Rome to preach God's * News.	Rom 1:15
For I am not ashamed of this *	Rom 1:16
This * News tells us that God	Rom 1:17
Literally, "who patiently do *."	Rom 2:7f
Literally, "all who do *."	Rom 2:10f
faith with God is *, our sins serve	Rom 3:5
our sins serve a * purpose, for	Rom 3:5
will notice how * God is when they	Rom 3:5
"No one is *—no one in all the	Rom 3:10
—not by "being * enough" and	Rom 3:21,22
is not based on our * deeds;	Rom 3:27
and not by the * things we do.	Rom 3:28
Was it because of his * deeds	Rom 4:1
heaven by all the * things he did?	Rom 4:4,5
earn it by being *, then it	Rom 4:4,5
For God declares sinners to be *	Rom 4:4,5
him just and * in his sight—before	Rom 4:11
to those who are "* enough," then	Rom 4:14
know that they are * for us—they	Rom 5:3
Even if we were *, we really	Rom 5:7
to be used for his * purposes.	Rom 6:13
Evidently not *, since you are	Rom 6:21
you can produce * fruit, that is,	Rom 7:4
fruit, that is, * deeds for God.	Rom 7:4
was concerned, the * law which was	Rom 7:10
Sin fooled me by taking the *	Rom 7:11
law itself was wholly right and *.	Rom 7:12
How then can it be *?	Rom 7:13
* to bring about my condemnation.	Rom 7:13
For it uses God's * laws for its	Rom 7:13
The law is *, then, and the	Rom 7:14
When I want to do *, I don't;	Rom 7:19
is working for our * if we love God	Rom 8:28
had done anything either * or bad.	Rom 9:10-13
the law and being * instead of by	Rom 9:32
to make themselves * enough to gain	Rom 10:3
could be perfectly * and hold out	Rom 10:5
bring glad tidings of * things."	Rom 10:15
who come preaching God's * News!	Rom 10:15
But not everyone who hears the *	Rom 10:16
* News—the Good News about Christ.	Rom 10:17
Good News—the * News about Christ.	Rom 10:17
they are; the * News has been told	Rom 10:18
it is not by their being * enough.	Rom 11:6
said, "Let their * food and other	Rom 11:9
Let these * things boomerang on	Rom 11:9
for me so I must be pretty *."	Rom 11:19
disobey, but very * to you if you	Rom 11:22
you into his own * tree—a very	Rom 11:24
If you are a teacher, do a * job	Rom 12:7
Stand on the side of the *.	Rom 12:9
Don't try to get into the *	Rom 12:16
hand but conquer evil by doing *.	Rom 12:21
you are doing a * thing.	Rom 14:6
do what is for his * and thus build	Rom 15:1
I know that you are wise and *,	Rom 15:14
message and by the * way I have	Rom 15:19
and after we have had a * time	Rom 15:24
and completed this * deed of	Rom 15:28
Greet my * friend Epaenetus.	Rom 16:5
Then there is Apelles, a * man	Rom 16:10
They are * speakers, and	Rom 16:18
send you their * wishes.	Rom 16:21
Have I been a * servant?	1Co 4:3
someone is a * servant or not.	1Co 4:5
but some of these things aren't *	1Co 6:12
that if you do not marry, it is *.	1Co 7:1
offers should make * use of their	1Co 7:31
We have planted * spiritual seed	1Co 9:11
from preaching the * News without	1Co 9:18
For the earth and every * thing	1Co 10:26
if more harm than * is done when	1Co 11:17
someone else may be especially *	1Co 12:8
love others, what * would it do?	1Co 13:2
they can get some * out of it too.	1Co 14:5
properly in a * and orderly way.	1Co 14:40
* News I preached to you before.	1Co 15:1
and it is this * News that saves	1Co 15:2
have ourselves a * time: let us	1Co 15:32
but that was *, for then we put	2Co 1:9
us apostles to preach the * News.	2Co 1:21
authority, and for your *.	2Co 2:10
is to make a * living out of it.	2Co 2:17
By looking at the * change in	2Co 3:2
we have done a * work among you.	2Co 3:2
We dare to say these * things	2Co 3:4
[of telling his * News to others	2Co 4:1
If the * News we preach is hidden	2Co 4:3
deserves for the * or bad things he	2Co 5:10
No, I am giving you some *	2Co 5:12
It was a * kind of sorrow you	2Co 7:9
Just see how much * this grief	2Co 7:11
faith, so many * preachers, so much	2Co 8:7
of the * News in all the churches.	2Co 8:18
to the poor. His * deeds will be an	2Co 9:9
and later on, * crops to harvest	2Co 9:10
So, two * things happen as a	2Co 9:12
deeds are as * as your doctrine.	2Co 9:13
I shall make * every claim.	2Co 10:8
men who tell you how * they are!	2Co 10:12
with the * News concerning Christ.	2Co 10:14
able to preach the * News to other	2Co 10:16
I preached God's * News to you	2Co 11:7
all for Christ's *, I am quite	2Co 12:10
for your spiritual *, even though	2Co 12:15
to get back into your * graces.	2Co 12:19
I pray that you will live *	2Co 13:7
show them the * News about Jesus.	Gal 1:16
brought you the * News of Christ.	Gal 4:13
favor are not doing it for your *.	Gal 4:17
nice to you with * motives and	Gal 4:18
and the * things we want to do	Gal 5:17
but if he plants the * things of	Gal 6:8
too, who heard the * News about how	Eph 1:13
a reward for the * we have done, so	Eph 2:9
And he has brought this * News	Eph 2:17
they accept the * News about Christ	Eph 3:6
and different person, holy and *.	Eph 4:24
Say only what is * and helpful to	Eph 4:29
and worships the * things of this	Eph 5:5
only what is * and right and true.	Eph 5:9
opportunity you have for doing *.	Eph 5:15,16
pay you for each * thing you do,	Eph 6:8
the * News of peace with God.	Eph 6:15
making known the * News about	Php 1:5
God who began the * work within you	Php 1:6
May you always be doing those *,	Php 1:11
out the * News concerning Christ.	Php 1:12
are preaching the * News because	Php 1:15
remains that the * News about	Php 1:18
is all going to turn out for my *.	Php 1:19
keep on hearing * reports that you	Php 1:27
tell the * News fearlessly, no	Php 1:27
don't live to make a * impression	Php 2:3
careful to do the * things that	Php 2:12
in helping me preach the * News.	Php 2:22
you this and it is * for you to	Php 3:1
saved by being * enough or by	Php 3:9
in telling the * News to others;	Php 4:3
on what is true and right.	Php 4:8
on the fine, * things in others.	Php 4:8
The same * News that came to you	Col 1:6
one who brought you this * News.	Col 1:7
always be doing *, kind things for	Col 1:10

(GOOD Con't)
convinced of the * News that Jesus Col 1:23
doing * and obeying various rules Col 2:20
These rules may seem *, for Col 2:23
don't worship the * things of Col 3:5
Don't worry about making a * Col 3:12
to preach the * News of Christ for Col 4:3
chances to tell others the * News. Col 4:5
For when we brought you the * 1Th 1:5
preached God's * News among you. 1Th 2:9
always try to do * to each other 1Th 5:15
you as * as you wish you could be! 2Th 1:11
Through us he told you the * 2Th 2:14
in every * thing you say and do. 2Th 2:17
Those laws are * when used as 1Ti 1:8
the glorious * News of our blessed 1Ti 1:10,11
This is * and pleases God our 1Ti 2:3
for being kind and *, not for the 1Ti 2:9,10
living quiet, *, and loving lives. 1Ti 2:15
he has a * ambition. 1Ti 3:1
For a pastor must be a * man 1Ti 3:2
orderly, and full of * deeds. 1Ti 3:2
and must be a * Bible teacher. 1Ti 3:2
of *, steady men as the pastors. 1Ti 3:8
For everything God made is *, 1Ti 4:4
* by the Word of God and prayer. 1Ti 4:5
because of the * she has done. 1Ti 5:10
knows how much * some pastors do, 1Ti 5:25
sometimes their * deeds aren't 1Ti 5:25
to them the * News is just a 1Ti 6:5
are if you are happy and *. 1Ti 6:6
what is right and *, learning to 1Ti 6:11
them to use their money to do *. 1Ti 6:18
They should be rich in * works 1Ti 6:18
of suffering as a * soldier of 2Ti 2:3
Be a * workman, one who does 2Ti 2:15
sneer at those who try to be *. 2Ti 3:3
prefer * times to worshiping God. 2Ti 3:4
result of my preaching the * News. 2Ti 3:11
equipped to do * to everyone. 2Ti 3:17
He loved the * things of this 2Ti 4:10
And now in his own * time he has Tit 1:3
has revealed this * News and Tit 1:3
well thought of for their * lives; Tit 1:6
homes and must love all that is *. Tit 1:8
as doing anything * is concerned. Tit 1:16
to them of * deeds of every kind. Tit 2:7
and to live *, God-fearing lives Tit 2:12
because we were * enough to be Tit 3:5
could declare us * in God's Tit 3:7
be careful to do * deeds all the Tit 3:8
for preaching the * News about Phm 1:1
see the wealth of * things in you Phm 1:6
for preaching the * News, and you Phm 1:13
But it didn't do them any * Heb 4:2
be saved by being *, or about the Heb 6:1
understood the * News and tasted Heb 6:4
for yourself the * things of heaven Heb 6:4
and know how * the Word of God is, Heb 6:5
upon it and * crops come up, that Heb 6:7
is considered no * and is ready for Heb 6:8
are producing the * fruit that Heb 6:9
* things Christ would do for us. Heb 10:1
kind to each other and in doing *. Heb 10:24
has made them * in God's sight must Heb 10:38
to the * things of this world. Heb 11:15
ill-treated—too * for this world. Heb 11:37,38
*, that we may share his holiness. Heb 12:10
Think of all the * that has come Heb 13:7
Don't forget to do * and to Heb 13:16
But whatever is * and perfect Jas 1:17
for anger doesn't make us *, as Jas 1:20
Yes indeed, it is * when you Jas 2:8
or food, what * does that do? Jas 2:16
You must also do * to prove that Jas 2:17
show itself by * works is no faith Jas 2:17
well, I say that * works are Jas 2:18
too, for without * works you can't Jas 2:18
Faith that does not result in * Jas 2:20
was declared * because of what he Jas 2:21
did, by his actions, his * deeds. Jas 2:22
Lord declared him * in God's sight, Jas 2:23
the kind that results in * deeds. Jas 2:26
that only * deeds will pour forth. Jas 3:13
being wise and * if you are bitter Jas 3:14
it is full of mercy and * deeds. Jas 3:17
You have condemned and killed * Jas 5:6
finally ended in *, for he is full Jas 5:11
And now at last this * News has 1Pe 1:12
And his message is the * News 1Pe 1:25
Don't just pretend to be *! 1Pe 2:1
your * works when Christ returns. 1Pe 2:12
It is God's will that your * 1Pe 2:15
sin and live a * life from now on. 1Pe 2:24
in her steps like * daughters and 1Pe 3:6
If you want a happy, * life, keep 1Pe 3:10
Turn away from evil and do *. 1Pe 3:11
will hurt you for wanting to do *. 1Pe 3:13
when you have only done what is *. 1Pe 3:16
for doing * than for doing wrong! 1Pe 3:17
That is why the * News was 1Pe 4:6
lead them by your * example, and 1Pe 5:3
in his * time he will lift you up. 1Pe 5:6
and how just and * he is to give 2Pe 1:1
for living a truly * life: he even 2Pe 1:3
you must also work hard to be *, 2Pe 1:5
a strong, * life for the Lord. 2Pe 1:9
because he was a * man, sick of the 2Pe 2:7,8
"You aren't saved by being *," 2Pe 2:19
But he is waiting, for the * 2Pe 3:9
* and who pleases God completely. 1Jn 2:1
that God is always * and does only 1Jn 2:29
doing what is *, it is because you 1Jn 3:7
because you are *, even as he is. 1Jn 3:7
Dear friend, you are doing a * 3Jn 1:5
Follow only what is *. 3Jn 1:11
how many * things you are doing. Rev 2:2
about you that is *: You hate the Rev 2:6
"I am aware of all your * Rev 2:19
the everlasting * News to preach to Rev 14:6
for their * deeds follow them to Rev 14:13
(Fine linen represents the * Rev 19:8
the vile will become more vile; * Rev 22:11

GOOD-BYE
So they told her *, sending along Gen 24:59
my grandchildren and tell them *? Gen 31:28
her mother-in-law *, and returned Ru 1:14
As Saul said * and started to go, 1Sa 10:9
let me go and say * to my father 1Ki 19:20
* and get them started home. Mk 6:45
land, to say * to his relatives and Act 7:3
that and then said * to the Act 18:18
to them, said * and left for Act 20:1
Quartus, a Christian brother. *. Rom 16:24
So I said * and went right on to 2Co 2:13
*. Heb 13:24,25
him, "Well, * and God bless you; Jas 2:16
both now and forevermore. *. 2Pe 3:18
about together. So * for now. 3Jn 1:15

GOOD-FOR-NOTHING
thus they become as * as a Hos 7:8

GOOD-HEARTED
soil represents honest, * people. Lk 8:15

GOOD-LOOKING
"Pick strong, healthy, * lads," Dan 1:3,4

GOOD-SIZED
and in its place grew four * horns Dan 8:8

GOODNESS
"I will make my * pass before you, Ex 33:19
for "*" in making covenants. Lev 2:13f
The Lord rewarded me for my *, 2Sa 22:21
happy for all the * that the Lord 1Ki 8:66
great * you showered upon them. Neh 9:35
in accordance with your great *. Neh 13:22
For God is good, and he loves *; Ps 11:7
Your * and unfailing kindness Ps 23:6
They will receive God's own * Ps 24:5
I will see his * to me here in the Ps 27:13
Oh, how great is your * to those Ps 31:19
Your power and *, Lord, reach to Ps 71:19
about your justice and your *. Ps 71:24
There is nothing but * in him! Ps 92:15
He is the Lord our God. His * Ps 105:7
his honor, majesty, and eternal *. Ps 111:3
and *, and stand firm forever. Ps 111:8
The good man's * delivers him; Pro 11:6
A man's * helps him all through Pro 13:6
The wicked hate the * of the Pro 29:27
justice and * and righteousness. Is 33:5
you forward, and * will be a shield Is 58:8
I will rejoice in his great * to Is 63:7
of its bounty and *, but they made Jer 2:7
radiant over the * of the Lord—the Jer 31:12
for his own * and the wicked person Eze 18:20
he shall live because of his *. Eze 18:22
All his previous * will be Eze 18:24
expecting his past * to save him, Eze 33:13
the light, and I will see his *. Mic 7:9
"But I warn you—unless your * Mt 5:20
of God's *, and of deliverance from Jn 16:8
with God, filling us with God's *. Rom 4:25
sin you didn't bother much with *. Rom 6:20
us with Christ's *, gave us right Rom 8:30
but stirring up * and peace and joy Rom 14:17
he poured God's * into us! 2Co 5:21
kindness, *, faithfulness, Gal 5:22
other of God's * and be thankful. Eph 5:4
sees * and purity in everything; Tit 1:15
but they should be teachers of *. Tit 2:3
a life of steady *, so that only Jas 3:13
of peace and reap a harvest of *. Jas 3:18
tasted the Lord's * and kindness, 1Pe 2:2,3f
own glory and his own * with us! 2Pe 1:3
where there will be only *. 2Pe 3:13

GOODS
kinds of bakery * for Pharaoh, but Gen 40:17
"If someone gives money or * to Ex 22:7
or leather * or whatever it is in. Lev 13:56
found the stolen * hidden there Jos 7:22
* at the front of the column. Ju 18:21
of *, or imprisonment." Ez 7:26
and our * as we traveled. Ez 8:21
but they did not take their *. Est 9:16
He shall not enjoy the * he Job 20:17
A raging fire will devour his *, Job 20:26
choicest of their * to satisfy your Is 60:16
Lord, with all their household *. Jer 49:29
their * to barter for your trade. Eze 27:9
the rich variety of * you make. Eze 27:18
seize their * and make them poor?' Eze 38:13
homes with captured * and slaves. Nah 2:12
is no one left to buy their *. Rev 18:11
wood, and ivory * and most Rev 18:12

GORE
ox was known to * people in the Ex 21:29
past experience to *, and its owner Ex 21:36
Lord says you will * the Syrians to 2Ch 18:10

GORES
"If an ox * a man or woman to Ex 21:28
"The same law holds if the ox * Ex 21:31
But if the ox * a slave, whether Ex 21:32

GORGE
for my feast! * yourselves with Eze 39:19

GORGED
He will vomit the plunder he *. Job 20:15
it is * with flesh as though used Is 34:6
of heaven were * with their flesh. Rev 19:21

GORGEOUS
And Sisera will get * robes, Ju 5:30

GORGEOUSLY
to be clothed so * will hurl you Is 22:17

GORGING
and carrying on, * and stuffing Jud 1:12

GORY
Are * with blood.' Deu 32:40,41

GOSHEN
You shall live in the land of * Gen 45:10
soon arrive in *—which they did. Gen 46:28
and journeyed to * to meet his Gen 46:29
you live here in the land of *." Gen 46:34
wish to settle in the land of *." Gen 47:1
to live in the land of *." Gen 47:4
The land of * will be fine. Gen 47:5,6
So Israel lived in the land of * Gen 47:27
flocks and herds in the land of *. Gen 50:8
and they filled the land of *. Ex 1:7
land of * where the Israelis live. Ex 8:22
was the land of * where the people Ex 9:26
to Gaza, and from * to Gibeon. Jos 10:41
Negeb, the land of *, the lowlands, Jos 11:16
Eshtemoh, Anim, *, Holon, Giloh, Jos 15:48-62

GOSPEL
However, the * of Matthew (1:23) Is 7:14f
who preach the * of peace with God Rom 10:15
against the * now, but this will Rom 11:25
of the Jews are enemies of the *. Rom 11:28
bringing you the * and offering you Rom 15:15,16
accomplished my * ministry." Rom 15:19f
* of Christ all the way from Rom 15:19
gift of the * from there, they feel Rom 15:27
Lord, just as the * says, and just Rom 16:25,26,27
to baptize, but to preach the *; 1Co 1:17
when I preached the * to you. 1Co 4:15
who preach the * should be 1Co 9:14
For just preaching the * isn't 1Co 9:16
* and I can win them to Christ. 1Co 9:20
I do this to get the * to them 1Co 9:23
for preaching the * but didn't love 1Co 13:3
of what the * really is, for it has 1Co 15:1
the * to you, and you believed it. 1Co 15:11
opportunities to preach the *. 2Co 2:12
spread the * like a sweet perfume. 2Co 2:14
in getting out the * is to make a 2Co 2:17
light of the * that is shining upon 2Co 4:4
of the * and by our patience. 2Co 6:6
preaches any other * than the one Gal 1:9
the truth of the *, I said to Peter Gal 2:14
have suffered so much for the *. Gal 3:4
first brought the * to you and then Php 4:15
the * first was preached to you. Col 1:5
condemn the * without knowing what 1Pe 2:15
living by the standards of the *. 3Jn 1:3

GOSSIP
"Don't *. Lev 19:16
does not listen to *, never harms Ps 15:3
A * goes around spreading rumors, Pro 11:13
An evil man sows strife; * Pro 16:28
your secrets to a * unless you Pro 20:19
tensions disappear when * stops. Pro 26:20
* is a dainty morsel eaten with Pro 26:22
lying, bitterness, and *. Rom 1:29

GOSSIPED
Jesus, and as they * in the Temple, Jn 11:56

GOSSIPERS
drinkers, not *, but faithful in 1Ti 3:11

GOSSIPING
work, and wasting your time in *. 2Th 3:11
running around *, seeking only 1Ti 5:6
spend their time * around from 1Ti 5:13

GOTTEN
and slaves he had * in Haran—and Gen 12:5
flocks he had * there at Gen 31:17-20
tell them where he had * it. Ju 14:9

(GOTTEN Con't)
When she found that he had * her 2Sa 11:5
great wealth * by dishonest means. Pro 16:8
I have * it all by myself!" Hos 12:8
"We have * what we deserved from Zec 1:5,6
perhaps Satan had * the best of you 1Th 3:5

GOUGE
condition: I will * out the right 1Sa 11:2
—causes you to lust, * it out and Mt 5:29
sin, * it out and throw it away. Mt 18:9
"And if your eye is sinful, * it Mk 9:47

GOUGED
captured him and * out his eyes and Ju 16:21
Then he * out Zedekiah's eyes Jer 39:7
then his eyes were * out and he was Jer 52:11

GOUGES
says, 'If a man * out another's Mt 5:38

GOURDS
and came back with some wild *. 2Ki 4:39

GOVERN
"Dan shall * his people like any Gen 49:16
He will * us and lead us to 1Sa 8:20
mind so that I can * your people 1Ki 3:9
for who is able to * by himself 2Ch 1:10
other officials to * all the people Ez 7:25
Could God * if he hated justice? Job 34:17
Literally, "* the nations." Ps 67:4f
a divine law to * them, or Lam 2:9
going to judge and * the world? 1Co 6:2

GOVERNING
by the ordinances * them. Num 29:6
for wisdom in * my people, and 1Ki 3:11
responsibility of * Jerusalem to my Neh 7:2
Or, "The rules * the worship of Ps 19:9f

GOVERNMENT
for the * a portion of all the Gen 41:48
God, nor curse * officials—your Ex 22:28
give your people a just, good *!" 1Ki 10:9
fifty of them were * officials who 2Ch 8:10
He sent out top * officials as 2Ch 17:7,8,9
Ammonite who was a * official) Neh 2:10
against these rich * officials. Neh 5:7
being the chief officers of the *. Est 1:13-15
Mordecai had become a * official. Est 2:19
Will you permit a corrupt * to Ps 94:20
your protection—a * permitting Ps 94:20
a nation, its * topples easily; Pro 28:2
Israel's civil * will be in utter Is 3:8
and the * shall be upon his Is 9:6
His ever-expanding, peaceful * Is 9:7
You will live under a * that is Is 54:14
men of Israel's *, so that Israel Eze 17:12,13
and that of his *, so that no one Dan 6:17
never end; his * shall never fall. Dan 7:14
giving them worldwide powers of *. Dan 7:22
over to the Roman *, and I will be Mt 20:19
pay taxes to the Roman * or not?" Mt 22:17
* to sentence Jesus to death. Mt 27:1
violent overthrow of the Roman *), Mk 3:16-19
* requires you to." Lk 3:13
pay taxes to the Roman * or not?" Lk 20:22
taxes to the Roman * and by Lk 23:2
riots against the * everywhere he Lk 23:5
a revolt against the Roman *. Lk 23:14
against the *, and for murder. Lk 23:19
over to the Roman * to be condemned Lk 24:20
of Capernaum, a * official, whose Jn 4:46,47
us and take over the Jewish *." Jn 11:48
Jesus was setting up a rebel *. Jn 18:34f
* to nail him to the cross and Act 2:23
by the Roman * for today's riot, Act 19:40
rebellions against the Roman *. Act 24:5
or rebelled against the Roman *." Act 25:8
over to the Roman * for Act 28:17
OBEY THE *, for God is the one who Rom 13:1
There is no * anywhere that God Rom 13:1
two reasons. For * workers need to Rom 13:6
REMIND YOUR PEOPLE to obey the * Tit 3:1
every law of your *: those of the 1Pe 2:13
Fear God and honor the *. 1Pe 2:17

GOVERNMENTS
God shall rule the * of the world Dan 7:18
overthrow the * of many nations. Dan 11:41
gathering the * of the earth and Rev 19:19

GOVERNOR
Since Joseph was * of all Egypt, Gen 42:6
* over the people left in Judah. 2Ki 25:22
Gedaliah as *, some of these 2Ki 25:23
take him back to * Amon and to my 2Ch 18:25
and Ma-aseiah, * of Jerusalem, and 2Ch 34:8
Others who participated were * Ez 4:8,9
made this reply to * Rehum and Ez 4:17
But Tattenai, the * of the lands Ez 5:3
Following is the letter which * Ez 5:6
Cyrus appointed as * of Judah. Ez 5:14
to * Shethar-bozenai, and the Ez 6:6
don't molest the * of Judah and the Ez 6:7
* Tattenai, Shethar-bozenai, and Ez 6:13
years that I was * of Judah—from Neh 5:14
But I replied, "Should I, the *, Neh 6:11
for the work. The * gave $5,000 in Neh 7:70
Then Ezra the priest, and I as *, Neh 8:9
I, NEHEMIAH THE *, signed the Neh 10:1
and when I was the *, and when Ezra Neh 12:26
was briefly *, but not king. Jer 22:30f
been appointed as * of Judah by the Jer 40:5
Gedaliah as * over the poor of the Jer 40:7
Gedaliah was the *, they all began Jer 40:11
Gedaliah the *, for he had been Jer 41:18
120 provinces, each under a *. Dan 6:1
* and judge alike demand bribes. Mic 7:3
(son of She-alti-el), * of Judah; Hag 1:1
She-alti-el), the * of Judah, and Hag 1:12
Ask this question of the * and Hag 2:2
Tell Zerubbabel, the * of Judah, Hag 2:21
* of Judah, who was given the Zec 4:6f
Try it on your * sometime—give Mal 1:8
village, for a * shall rise from Mt 2:6
in chains to Pilate, the Roman *. Mt 27:2
before Pilate, the Roman *. Mt 27:11
the * asked him. Mt 27:11
So when the * asked again, Mt 27:21
"If the * hears about it," the Mt 28:14
guard to Pilate, the Roman *. Mk 15:1
when Quirinius was * of Syria. Lk 2:2
(Pilate was * over Judea at that Lk 3:1
criticized Herod, * of Galilee, for Lk 3:19,20
miracles reached Herod, the *, Lk 9:7
you shall be * of ten cities.' Lk 19:17
'You can be * over five cities.' Lk 19:19
* as reason for arrest by him. Lk 20:19
took Jesus over to Pilate, the *. Lk 23:1
to the palace of the Roman *. Jn 18:28
So Pilate, the *, went out to Jn 18:29
as the Roman *, he would be Jn 18:34f
Pontius Pilate the *, and all the Act 4:27
appointed him * over all Egypt, as Act 7:10
He had attached himself to the *, Act 13:6,7
understanding. The * invited Act 13:6,7
and urged the * to pay no attention Act 13:8
When the * saw what happened he Act 13:12
But when Gallio became * of Act 18:12
him before the * for judgment. Act 18:12
and get him safely to * Felix." Act 23:23,24
he wrote this letter to the *: Act 23:25
"To: His Excellency, * Felix. Act 23:26
Paul and the letter to the *. Act 23:33
arrive," the * told him, and Act 23:35
in the following address to the *: Act 24:2
Now it was Paul's turn. The * Act 24:10
Then the king, the *, Bernice, Act 26:30
to Publius, the * of the island. Act 28:7
For instance, in Damascus the * 2Co 11:32

GOVERNOR'S
nothing, much to the * surprise. Mt 27:14
Now the * custom was to release Mt 27:15

GOVERNORS
Then the army officers, nobles, * 2Ch 23:20
and the * of all the provinces west Ez 8:36
me letters to the * west of the Neh 2:7
the king's letters to the * there. Neh 2:9
to the former * who had demanded Neh 5:15
invited all his *, aides, and army Est 1:1
letters to the * and officials Est 3:12
to the officials, *, and princes of Est 8:9,10
the provinces—the *, officials, and Est 9:3
civil war as the * of Babylon fight Jer 51:46
all the princes, *, captains, Dan 3:2
Then the princes, *, captains, Dan 3:27
a governor. The * were accountable Dan 6:2
presidents and *, for he had great Dan 6:3
presidents and * very jealous, and Dan 6:4
We presidents, *, counselors and Dan 6:7
before * and kings for my sake. Mt 10:18
* and kings of being my followers. Mk 13:9
kings and * for my Name's sake. Lk 21:12

GOWN
made—a purple * of pure linen. Pro 31:22
I shook out the lap of my *." Neh 5:13f

GOZAN
the Habor River in *, and among the 2Ki 17:6
*, and in the cities of the Medes. 2Ki 18:11
nations as *, Haran, Rezeph, and 2Ki 19:12
Hara, and the * River, where they 1Ch 5:26
save the cities of *, Haran, or Is 37:12

GRAB
Then the Lord told him, "* it by Ex 4:4
Then Elijah told them to * the 1Ki 18:40
The men were quick to * this 1Ki 20:33
"* it," Elisha said to him; 2Ki 6:7
"* them!" 2Ki 10:14
Quick, quick, * your shields and Is 21:5
When the mob tried to * him, he Mk 14:51,52

GRABBED
she came and * him by the sleeve Gen 39:12
he jumped up, * a spear, and Num 25:7
As Samuel turned to go, Saul * at 1Sa 15:27
Each one * his opponent by the 2Sa 2:16
the child's nurse * him and fled, 2Sa 4:4
before him, he * her and demanded, 2Sa 13:11
and * him by the throat and Mt 18:28
Then the others * him. Mt 26:50
And they spat on him and * the Mt 27:30
shattered; they * Paul and Silas Act 16:19
* Sosthenes, the new leader of Act 18:17
* him, yelling, "Men of Israel! Act 21:26,27

GRABBER
called him Jacob (meaning "*"). Gen 25:26
be called Jacob ('*'), but Israel Gen 35:10

GRABBING
her husband by * the testicles of Deu 25:11
Edom, for * my land with relish, in Eze 36:5

GRABS
a bear comes and * a lamb from the 1Sa 17:34

GRACE
In fact, except for the * of Gen 31:42
speak of his glories and *. Ps 34:1
Your words are filled with *; Ps 45:2
He gives us * and glory. Ps 84:11
performs—deeds of mercy and of *? Ps 111:4
He who values * and truth is the Pro 22:11
have mercy on you through my *. Is 60:10
that all was done by * alone." Zec 4:7
naming one "*" and the other Zec 11:7
And I took my staff called "*" Zec 11:10
out the spirit of * and prayer on Zec 12:10
Literally, "*." Jn 1:14f
Literally, "great * was upon them Act 4:33f
Literally, "full of * and Act 6:8f
God's abounding * forgiving us. Rom 5:20
the law, but on receiving God's *! Rom 6:15
for I am, by God's *, a special Rom 15:15,16
May the * of our Lord Jesus Rom 16:24
Now you have every * and 1Co 1:7
free gifts of * and blessing that 1Co 2:12
such kindness and * upon me—and not 1Co 15:10
what God in his * has done for the 2Co 8:1
* of God shown through you. 2Co 9:14
May the * of our Lord Jesus 2Co 13:14
kindness and *— to reveal his Son Gal 1:15
you are lost from God's *. Gal 5:4
Dear brothers, may the * of our Gal 6:18
richness of his *—for how well he Eph 1:8
May God's * and blessing be upon Eph 6:24
you grow in his * until his task Php 1:6
turned away from the * of God. Tit 1:11
* to help us in our times of need. Heb 4:16
a quiet growth in * and character. Heb 12:11
God's * be with you all. Heb 13:24,25
May you have * and peace from God Rev 1:4

GRACEFUL
Daughters of * beauty like the Ps 144:12-15
and * oaks for his own glory. Is 61:3

GRACES
Don't try to get into the good * Rom 12:16
this to get back into your good *. 2Co 12:19

GRACIOUS
God be * to you." Gen 43:29
be very * to him [at your expense Ex 22:27
the merciful and * God," he said, Ex 34:5,6
may he be * to you, show you his Num 6:24,25,26
* to me and let the child live.' 2Sa 12:22
But the Lord was * to the people 2Ki 13:23
for God was being * to me. Neh 2:8
ready to pardon, * and merciful, Neh 9:17
What a * and merciful God you Neh 9:31
Lord, don't you desert me! Be *, Ps 41:10
Honor goes to kind and * women, Pro 11:16
* to you at the sound of your cry. Is 30:19
Perhaps the Lord will be * to us Jer 21:1
don't deserve this * act, for you Eze 16:61
away our sins; be * to us and Hos 14:2
God, for he is * and merciful. Joe 2:13
For I knew you were a * God, Jon 4:2
'God be * to us!' Mal 1:9
Let your conversation be * as Col 4:6

GRACIOUSLY
It's very nice to live * in a Jer 22:23
But God * heard and answered his Heb 5:7f
blood which * forgives instead of Heb 12:24

GRADUALLY
So the flood * receded until, Gen 8:3,4
He will do it *, and you will Deu 7:23

GRADUATED
them his counselors when they *. Dan 1:5

GRAFT
* them back into the tree again. Rom 11:23
olive tree—and * you into his own Rom 11:24

GRAFTED
say, a wild olive tree, were * in. Rom 11:17

GRAIN
There were no plants or * Gen 2:5
in addition to * and vegetables. Gen 9:2,3
times the * he sowed. Gen 26:12
good harvest of *, and new wine. Gen 27:27,28,29
him abundance of * and wine—what is Gen 27:37
This time he saw seven heads of * Gen 41:5
seven heads of * on one stalk, and Gen 41:22
heads of *) mean that there are Gen 41:26
withered heads of *) indicate that Gen 41:27
plenty of * in the storehouses. Gen 41:54
and sold * to the Egyptians and to Gen 41:56,57
to Egypt to buy * from Joseph. Gen 41:56,57

(GRAIN Con't)
JACOB HEARD that there was * Gen 42:1
I have heard that there is * Gen 42:2
went down to Egypt to buy *. Gen 42:3
of the sale of the *, it was to him Gen 42:6
"We have come to buy *." Gen 42:7
on home with * for your families; Gen 42:19
men's sacks with *, but also gave Gen 42:25
with the * and started for home. Gen 42:26
sack to get some * to feed the Gen 42:27
with me and take * for your Gen 42:33
often as you like to purchase *.' Gen 42:34
each was the money paid for the *! Gen 42:35
When the * they had brought from Gen 43:2
there that we had paid for the *. Gen 43:21
additional money to buy more *. Gen 43:22
sacks with as much * as they could Gen 44:1
sack, along with the * money. Gen 44:2
loaded with * and all kinds of Gen 45:23
in exchange for *, and he brought Gen 47:14
Here is *. Gen 47:23
blessings of the * and flowers, Gen 49:26
that the shocks of *, or the Ex 22:6
or the standing *, are destroyed, Ex 22:6
to sacrifice a * offering to the Lev 2:1
it—it is a form of * offering. Lev 2:6
are to bring this * offering to the Lev 2:8
offering, for it is a * offering. Lev 2:15
of the bruised * mixed with oil and Lev 2:16
the case with the * offering." Lev 5:13
concerning the * offering: Lev 6:14
the Lord a regular * offering—a Lev 6:19,20
the people's * offerings to the Lev 7:9
All other * offerings, whether Lev 7:10
burnt offering, * offering, sin Lev 7:37
and a ram, and a * offering—flour Lev 9:4
Then he presented the * offering, Lev 9:17
"Take the * offering—the food that Lev 10:12
And if the carcass touches * to Lev 11:37
it along with the * offering upon Lev 14:20
olive oil, for a * offering, and a Lev 14:21
along with the * offering; Lev 14:31
burnt offering. A * offering shall Lev 23:13
kernels nor bread nor parched *. Lev 23:14
of the new * of your later crops. Lev 23:15,16
fields, nor pick up the fallen *; Lev 23:22
the land, whether * or fruit, is Lev 27:30
back this fruit or *, he must add a Lev 27:31
incense, the daily * offering, and Num 4:16
and the accompanying * offering Num 6:15
and finally the * offering along Num 6:17
both filled with * offerings of Num 7:13
12 yearling male goats (with the * Num 7:87
a young bull and a * offering of Num 8:8
be accompanied by a * offering. Num 15:3,4
bull, then the * offering Num 15:8,9
the first * that is cut each year. Num 15:19,20,21
with the usual * offering and drink Num 15:23,24
law. The * offerings, the sin Num 18:9
wine, *, and every other crop. Num 18:12
offering to him of * and wine, as Num 18:27
With them shall be offered a * Num 28:5
* offering and drink offering. Num 28:8
They are to be accompanied by a * Num 28:9,10
as a * offering with each bull; Num 28:12
oil as a * offering for the ram; Num 28:12
mixed with oil for a * offering. Num 28:13
there shall be a * offering of nine Num 28:20,21
* as a grain offering to the Lord; Num 28:26
grain as a * offering to the Lord; Num 28:26
by your * offering of nine quarts Num 28:28,29
* offerings and drink offerings. Num 28:31
and enjoy. A * offering of nine Num 29:3,4
the respective * offerings and Num 29:6
their accompanying * offerings. Num 29:9,10
* offerings, and drink offerings. Num 29:11
by the usual * offerings—nine Num 29:14
* offerings and drink offerings. Num 29:16
* offerings and drink offerings. Num 29:18
its accompanying * offering and Num 29:19
and the usual * offering and drink Num 29:21
* offering and drink offering. Num 29:22
* offering and drink offering; Num 29:24
with the usual * and drink Num 29:25
* offerings and drink offerings; Num 29:26,27
with the usual * and drink Num 29:28
their usual * and drink offerings. Num 29:30
goat and the usual * and drink Num 29:31
customary * and drink offerings; Num 29:33
with the usual * and drink Num 29:34
customary * and drink offerings. Num 29:37
with the usual * and drink Num 29:38
burnt sacrifices, * offerings, Num 29:39
large crops of *, grapes, and Deu 7:13
wonderful crops of *, grapes for Deu 11:14
Neither the tithe of your * and Deu 12:17
this applies to your tithes of *, Deu 14:23
season, after the * is threshed and Deu 16:13
first of the *, the new wine, the Deu 18:4
someone else's *—you may eat a few Deu 23:25
an ox as it treads out the *. Deu 25:4
are gone. Your *, new wine, olive Deu 28:51
down to grow * for bread or grapes Deu 29:6
the gardens and * fields which they Jos 5:11,12
burnt offerings or * offerings or Jos 22:22,23
* offerings, or sacrifices. Jos 22:29
a young goat and a * offering and Ju 13:19
burning the * to the ground along Ju 15:5
*, and destroying the olive trees. Ju 15:5
and made to grind * in the prison. Ju 16:21
some kind man to glean the free * Ru 2:2
Literally, "ate the parched * and Ru 2:14f
a heap of * and went to sleep. Ru 3:6,7
bushel of roasted * and these ten 1Sa 17:17
bushels of roasted *, one hundred 1Sa 25:18
Let no crops of * grow on your 2Sa 1:21
with * on it to dry in the sun; 2Sa 17:19
flour, parched *, beans, lentils, 2Sa 17:28,29
burnt offerings, * offerings, and 1Ki 8:64
He also built cities for * 1Ki 9:19
Literally, "fresh *." 2Ki 4:42f
from the first * of his harvest. 2Ki 4:42
gallons of barley * will be sold in 2Ki 7:1
offering and a * offering, poured a 2Ki 16:13
the evening * offering, the king's 2Ki 16:15
burnt offering and * offering, and 2Ki 16:15
*, wine, olive trees, and honey. 2Ki 18:31,32
hot sun, and like * blighted before 2Ki 19:26
the flat cakes for * offerings. 1Ch 9:31
use the wheat for the * offering. 1Ch 21:23
the flour for the * offerings, and 1Ch 23:29
of their crops and *, new wine, 2Ch 31:5,6
for his *, new wine, and olive oil, 2Ch 32:28,29
oxen, rams, lambs, * offerings, and Ez 7:17
lending money and * to our Neh 5:10
should bring any * or other produce Neh 10:31
as well as * offerings and burnt Neh 10:33
best of our * crops, and other Neh 10:37
these offerings of *, new wine, and Neh 10:39,40
for storing the * offerings, Neh 13:5
of *, new wine, and olive oil. Neh 13:5
the * offerings, and frankincense. Neh 13:9
their tithes of *, new wine, and Neh 13:12
like standing *, you'll not be Job 5:26
they will loan him any money or *. Job 24:9
others, cut off like heads of *. Job 24:24
in the * from the threshing-floor? Job 39:12
and sends them rich harvests of *. Ps 65:9
the valleys are carpeted with *. Ps 65:13
every * of dust in her streets. Ps 102:14
vegetables and * for man to Ps 104:14
man who holds his * for higher Pro 11:26
their barns with * extorted from Is 3:14
* fields in the Valley of Rephaim. Is 17:5
like handpicked *, selecting them Is 27:12
his many kinds of *, each in its Is 28:25
Bread * is easily crushed, so he Is 28:28
ground will eat *, its chaff blown Is 30:24
of * and grapes, a land of plenty. Is 36:17
only volunteer * this fall, still Is 37:30
and cause the * to grow and to Is 55:10
and take away your * and wine. Is 62:8
an offering of *, it is as Is 66:3
offerings and * offerings and Jer 17:26
men to grind their * and the little Lam 5:13
of each harvest of * shall be Eze 44:30
bushels of * for the meal Eze 45:24
lamb, the * offering and the olive Eze 46:14,15
rich harvests of * in its season, Hos 1:9
parched cry of the *, the grapes, Hos 1:21,22
withered, sickly, with no *; Hos 8:7
out the *—an easy job she loves. Hos 10:11
Gone are the offerings of * and Joe 1:9
everywhere. The *, the grapes, the Joe 1:10
offerings of * and wine for you. Joe 1:13
the * has dried up in the fields. Joe 1:17
* and wine to the Lord as before! Joe 2:14
as * is threshed with iron rods. Amo 1:3
other nations as * is sifted in a Amo 9:9
a drought to wither the * and Hag 1:11
harvested your *, and before the Hag 2:18,19
The abundance of * and wine will Zec 9:16,17
the chaff from the *, burning the Mt 3:12
fire, and storing away the *." Mt 3:12
heads of wheat and eating the *. Mt 12:1
"A farmer was sowing * in his Mt 13:2,3
farmer planting *: The hard path Mt 13:18
heads of wheat and eating the *. Mk 2:23
by harvesting * on the Sabbath." Mk 2:24
A farmer decided to sow some *. Mk 4:3
plants so that they produced no *. Mk 4:7
and finally the * ripened, and Mk 4:28
He will separate chaff from *, Lk 3:17
fire and store away the *." Lk 3:17
Your disciples are harvesting *, Lk 6:2
went out to his field to sow *. Lk 8:5
* stalks were soon choked out. Lk 8:7
* in Egypt, so he sent his sons Act 7:12
*—let him eat as he goes along!" 1Ti 5:18
will be no more milling of the *. Rev 18:22

GRAINFIELDS
through some * with his disciples. Mt 12:1
through some *, they were breaking Lk 6:1

GRAINS
stray * of wheat from the ground. Lev 19:9
could pick up the * dropped by the Ru 2:7
He doesn't thresh all * the Is 28:27
in their hands and eating the *. Lk 6:1

GRANARIES
After seven years of this, the * Gen 41:49
break open her *; Jer 50:26
the barns and * are empty; Joe 1:17
souls into the * of heaven! Jn 4:36

GRAND
* Togal: 603,550 Num 1:20-46
lovely music at your * parties; Is 5:12
dew—and the whole * chorus shall Hos 1:21,22

GRANDCHILDREN
Why didn't you let me kiss my * Gen 31:28
I harm my own daughters and *? Gen 31:43
his daughters and *, and blessed Gen 31:55
Esau also had * from his wife Gen 36:13,14
Esau's * Gen 36:15,16
children, your *, your flocks and Gen 45:10
* who went with him into Egypt: Gen 46:8-14
your children and * about the Ex 10:2
upon the children, *, and Ex 20:5
Tell your children and your * Deu 4:9
your children and * are born and Deu 4:25
Egyptians. The * of the Egyptians Deu 23:8
around them, and their *, too. Job 21:8
his * and great-grandchildren too. Job 42:16
and * are rich and prosperous. Ps 17:13,14
May you live to enjoy your *! Ps 128:6
he leaves an inheritance to his *; Pro 13:22
An old man's * are his crowning Pro 17:6
mates for them and have many *. Jer 29:6
and their *, for all generations. Eze 37:25
But if they have children or *, 1Ti 5:4

GRANDDAUGHTER
Oholibamah (daughter of Anah and * Gen 36:2,3
of Matred and * of Mezahab. Gen 36:31-39
"You shall not marry your *—the Lev 18:10
her daughter or *, for they are Lev 18:17
His mother was Athaliah, the * of 2Ki 8:26
of Matred and * of Mezahab). 1Ch 1:50
His mother's name was Athaliah, * 2Ch 22:2

GRANDDAUGHTERS
and *—all his loved ones. Gen 46:7

GRANDFATHER
to the house of your * Gen 28:2
God—the God of my * Abraham, even Gen 31:42
God of Abraham my *, and of my Gen 32:9
It is the cave which my * Gen 49:32
He was the * of Bezalel (Exodus Ex 17:10f
Hepher was their *, and his son Num 27:1
He was the father of Jesse and * Ru 4:16,17
His * was Elihu, 1Sa 1:1
the land of your * Saul, and you 2Sa 9:7
King Talmai was his *—his 2Sa 13:37,38,39f
Saul was Mephibosheth's *. 2Sa 16:3f
shields his * had dedicated, 1Ki 15:15
dedicated objects of his *." 1Ki 15:15f
(the father of Zaccur and * of 1Ch 4:26

GRANDFATHER'S
the boys to their * knees—Ephraim Gen 48:12,13

GRANDLY
"The ostrich flaps her wings *, Job 39:13

GRANDMOTHER
years. (His * was Maacah, the 1Ki 15:10
He deposed his * Maacah as 1Ki 15:13
king, for their * Athaliah killed 2Ch 22:10
mother Eunice and your * Lois do; 2Ti 1:5

GRANDPARENTS
and on husbands and wives and *. Jer 6:11

GRANDSON
his son Abram, his * Lot (his son Gen 11:31
me or my son or my *, but that you Gen 21:23
(son of Uri, and * of Hur, of the Ex 31:1
son of Uri and * of Hur of the Ex 35:30,31
Bezalel (son of Uri and * of Ex 38:22
ONE DAY KORAH (son of Izhar, * of Num 16:1
of Eleazar and * of Aaron the Num 25:7
of Eleazar and * of Aaron the Num 25:10,11
For Achan (the son of Carmi, * of Jos 7:1
by man, and his * Achan was found Jos 7:18
son Zelophehad (* of Gilead, Jos 17:3
Tola (son of Puah and * of Dodo). Ju 10:1
(son of Gershom and * of Moses! Ju 18:30
and * of Aaron, was the priest. Ju 20:27,28
who has given you this little *; Ru 4:14
He was the son of Abiel, * of 1Sa 9:1
Ahitub was the * of Phinehas and 1Sa 14:3
(There was a little lame * of 2Sa 4:4
son and Saul's *. 2Sa 9:5,6
"I have given your master's * 2Sa 9:9
Now Mephibosheth, Saul's *, 2Sa 19:24,25
who was Saul's *, because of the 2Sa 21:7
the son of Dodo and * of Ahohi. 2Sa 23:9
your son, your *, and your 2Ki 10:30
Jehoahaz and the * of Jehu), daring 2Ki 14:8
that Jehu's son, *, and 2Ki 15:12
son of Ahikam and * of Shaphan) as 2Ki 25:22

(GRANDSON Con't)
Shaul's son was Shallum, his * 1Ch 4:25
his * Gog, and his great-grandson 1Ch 5:4
Shime-i's son was Micah; his * 1Ch 5:5
Bela (the son of Azaz, * of Shema, 1Ch 5:7,8
Ahi, the son of Abdi-el and * of 1Ch 5:15
Shebuel, son of Gershom and * of 1Ch 26:23,24
because he was the * of King 2Ch 22:9
(son of Jehoahaz, * of Jehu). 2Ch 25:17
the son of Levi and * of Israel. Ez 8:18
He will have neither son nor * Job 18:19
son of Jotham and * of Uzziah), Is 7:1
This man Coniah's *, Zerubbabel, Jer 22:30f
his son and his * until his time is Jer 27:7
(son of Shelemiah, * of Hananiah). Jer 37:13
To: Zephaniah (son of Cushi, * of Zep 1:1
of Berechiah, and * of Iddo the Zec 1:1
of Berechiah and * of Iddo the Zec 1:7
be treated as the * of the king, Heb 11:24,25

GRANDSONS
and daughters, * and Gen 46:7
*, and even later generations." Ex 34:7
Levi's * (clan names) Num 3:16-24
Levi's * (clan names) Num 3:25-30
Levi's * (clan names) Num 3:31-35
sons, and your * to reverence the Deu 6:2
He had forty sons and thirty *, Ju 12:14
were * of Saul by his wife Aiah. 2Sa 21:8
of Gilead, the * of Machir, and the 1Ch 7:17
These men had 150 sons and *, and 1Ch 8:40
son Micah and his * Shamir and 1Ch 24:24,25
All of these sons and * of 1Ch 26:8

GRANDSTANDS
us from the *, let us strip off Heb 12:1

GRANT
May the Lord of Israel * you your 1Sa 1:17
But Joab replied, "God * that 2Sa 24:3
I * you before I am taken away?" 2Ki 2:9
And Elisha replied, "Please * me 2Ki 2:9
for when you * a blessing, Lord, it 1Ch 17:27
included this provision in his *. Ez 3:7
me, and wants to * my request, that Est 5:7,8
"Oh, that God would * the thing Job 6:8,9
May he * you your heart's desire Ps 20:4
us, Lord, and * us your salvation. Ps 85:7
so look down in pity and * Ps 86:16
For you * victory to kings! Ps 144:10
Lord, * us peace; Is 26:12
like—and I will * you no favors! Jer 16:13
and to * them their requests. Eze 36:37,38
I, here and now, * you the right Lk 22:29
ask the Father to * you these Jn 16:26
their threats, and * to your Act 4:29
May God bless you richly and * 1Pe 1:2

GRANTED
named him Seth (meaning "*"); Gen 4:25
for, as Eve put it, "God has * Gen 4:25
life, and you've * me such mercy, Gen 19:18,19,20
For you have * me this request!" 2Sa 14:22
And God * him his request. 1Ch 4:10
and the king * his request; Ez 7:6
And the king * these requests, for Neh 2:8
It will be * to you. Est 9:12
life, and you have * his request; Ps 21:4
shall be * mercy and quietness. Pro 14:22
which he has * in accordance with Is 63:7
is large, and your request is *." Mt 15:28
He replied, "God has * you to Lk 8:10
and because my Father has * me a Lk 22:29
himself, and has * his Son to have Jn 5:26
you like, and it will be *! Jn 15:7
An appointment with Herod was *, Act 12:21
What's more, God has * your Act 27:24

GRANTING
* him favor with the chief jailer. Gen 39:21
to him, and by * us the privilege Lk 1:74

GRANTS
and making * to the provinces in Est 2:18
For the Lord * wisdom! Pro 2:6
understanding. He * good sense to Pro 2:7,8
and * loans without interest, Eze 18:8

GRAPE
It is the same with your * Lev 19:10
Literally, "until the * Lev 26:4,5f
wine, * juice, grapes, or raisins! Num 6:3,4
that comes from * vines, not even Num 6:3,4
and barley, of * vines, fig trees, Deu 8:8
in the bottom of a * press—a pit Ju 6:11
to the ground like a withered *. Job 15:33
to tread out the * juice as they Job 24:11
Their * vines and fig trees were Ps 105:33
and the * vines are in blossom. Sol 2:13
to see whether the * vines were Sol 6:11
Now may your breasts be like * Sol 7:8
cut down the best of the * vines; Is 16:8
life will go: the * harvest will Is 24:7
wine at the time of the * harvest. Hos 1:9
the fig trees and * vines will Joe 2:22
"At the time of the * harvest he Mt 21:34
pressing out the * juice, and built Mk 12:1
a fig tree, or figs from a * vine? Jas 3:12

GRAPE-GATHERER
for as a * checks each vine to Jer 6:9

GRAPE-PICKING
country. At * time he sent one of Mk 12:2

GRAPES
there were clusters of ripe *. Gen 40:9,10
so I took the * and squeezed the Gen 40:11
up the * that fall to the ground. Lev 19:10
don't gather the * for yourself; Lev 25:5
not sow, nor gather crops nor *; Lev 25:11
And * will still be ripening when Lev 26:4,5
wine, grape juice, *, or raisins! Num 6:3,4
(The first of the * were being Num 13:20
single cluster of * so large that Num 13:23
of the cluster of * they found! Num 13:24
crops of grain, *, and olives, and Deu 7:13
* for your wine, and olive oil. Deu 11:14
and the * have been pressed. Deu 16:13
the crops and the * shall be Deu 22:9
"You may eat your fill of the * Deu 23:24
It is the same for the * in your Deu 24:21
you won't eat the * or drink the Deu 28:39
grain for bread or * for wine and Deu 29:6
Literally, "*." Deu 32:32f
press—a pit where * were pressed to Ju 6:11
"Are not the last * of Ephraim Ju 8:2,3f
She must not eat * or raisins, or Ju 13:13,14
of *, and a small barrel of wine. 2Sa 16:1
donkeys with wine, *, figs, and all Neh 13:15
Catch them, for the * are all in Sol 2:15
harvest, but the * that grew were Is 5:2
give me wild * instead of sweet? Is 5:4
the treading out of the * in the Is 16:10
are ripening like *, he will cut Is 18:5
of grain and *, a land of plenty. Is 36:17
red, as from treading out the *?" Is 63:2
I have trodden my enemies like *. Is 63:3
for just as good * are found Is 65:8
are some good * there!" Is 65:8
cattle, yes, and your * and figs; Jer 5:17
Their figs and * will disappear, Jer 8:13
do who tread the juice from the *. Jer 25:30
eat the sour * and the children's Jer 31:29f
person eating sour * is the one Jer 31:30
Harvest the * and summer fruits Jer 40:10
harvest of wine * and other crops. Jer 40:12
your * and summer fruits. Jer 48:32
no one treads the * with shouts Jer 48:33
Those who gather * leave a few Jer 49:9,10
beloved city as * in a winepress. Lam 1:15
have eaten sour * and the Eze 18:2f
of the grain, the *, and the olive Hos 1:21,22
your * will blight upon the vine. Hos 9:2
and blossom like * and be as Hos 14:7
for all the * are ruined and all Joe 1:5
The grain, the *, the olive oil Joe 1:10
the terraces of * upon the hills of Amo 9:13
streets plowed up for planting *! Mic 1:6
You will trample the *, but get Mic 6:15
an honest man as * and figs when Mic 7:1
the grain and * and olives and all Hag 1:11
and before the * and figs and Hag 2:18,19
and plagues. Your * won't shrivel Mal 3:11
Figs never grow on thorns, or * Lk 6:44
the clusters of * from the vines of Rev 14:18
and loaded the * into the great Rev 14:19
And the * were trodden in the Rev 14:20

GRAPEVINE
"Then they said to the *, 'You Ju 9:12
"But the * replied, 'Shall I Ju 9:13

GRAPEVINES
He destroyed their * and their Ps 78:47
they are gone. The * are dead; Joe 1:12
Your crops will prosper; the * Zec 8:12
You need never confuse * with Mt 7:16

GRASP
from the * of these oppressors. Job 5:15
and needy from the * of evil men. Ps 82:4
sin still has me in its evil *. Rom 7:20
We aren't saved from sin's * by Rom 8:3

GRASPING
Then, * it by the wings, he shall Lev 1:15,16,17
there will be no more * traders Zec 14:21

GRASS
with every sort of * and Gen 1:11,12
And I've given all the * and Gen 1:30
river and began grazing in the *. Gen 41:2
an ox eats *," they exclaimed. Num 22:4
Like rain upon the tender *, Deu 32:2
When the tender * 2Sa 23:4
we can find enough * to save at 1Ki 18:5
They were like * shriveling 2Ki 19:26
shall be as numerous as *! Job 5:25
it is because their * is gone; Job 6:5,6,7
* without water to keep it alive. Job 8:11-13
water, and tender * springs up? Job 38:25-27
they search for every blade of *. Job 39:8
He eats * like an ox. Job 40:15
He lets me rest in the meadow * Ps 23:2,3
Soon they fade away like * and Ps 37:2
like *, and disappear like smoke. Ps 37:20
trodden down and wither like *." Ps 58:7f
rains upon the *—like showers that Ps 72:6
of people as the fields are of *. Ps 72:16
We are like * that is green in Ps 90:5,6
it is trampled like * and is Ps 102:3,4
I am withering like *, while Ps 102:11
and brief, like *, like flowers, Ps 103:15
The tender * grows up at his Ps 104:14
of an ox that eats *, to the Ps 106:19,20
May they be as * in shallow Ps 129:6,7
green * grow in mountain pastures. Ps 147:8
is as refreshing as the dew on *. Pro 19:12
here upon the *, shaded by the Sol 1:16
lions will eat * like the cows. Is 11:7
grown up with *, cows grazing Is 27:10
They were as helpless as the *, Is 37:27
your feet, as * upon the housetops, Is 37:27
"Shout that man is like the * Is 40:6
flowers. The * withers, the flower Is 40:7
fragile man. The * withers, the Is 40:8
They shall thrive like watered * Is 44:4
as dried * burning in the fire. Is 47:14
wither like the * and disappear? Is 51:12
Even the * of the field groans Jer 12:4
her fawn because there is no *. Jer 14:5
eyes looking for * to eat, but Jer 14:6
brass, surrounded by the tender *. Dan 4:15
him eat * with the wild animals! Dan 4:15
by tender *, banded with a chain of Dan 4:23
For seven years let him eat * Dan 4:23
an animal, eating * like a cow, Dan 4:25
fields, and to eat * like the cows Dan 4:32
his palace and ate * like the cows, Dan 4:33
he ate * like the cows and his Dan 5:21
to be like? * blowing in the wind? Mt 11:7
the people to sit down on the *; Mt 14:19
each were sitting on the green *. Mk 6:39,40
scraps were picked up off the *! Mk 6:43,44
"Did you find him weak as *, Lk 7:24
it poured and the * turned green Jas 5:18
lives will fade as * does when it 1Pe 1:24
were burned, and all the green *. Rev 8:7
They were told not to hurt the * Rev 9:4

GRASSES
for you, and you shall eat its *. Gen 3:18
the mountain * are gathered in. Pro 27:25,26,27

GRASSHOPPER
as a man brushes a * from his arm. Ps 109:22,23

GRASSHOPPERS
crickets, and *—may be eaten. Lev 11:21,22
We felt like * before them, they Num 13:33
below must seem to him like *! Is 40:22
though you multiply like *. Nah 3:15
together like * in the hedges in Nah 3:17

GRASSY
is desolate! The * banks are dried Is 15:6
green pastures and on the * hills. Is 49:8,9
5,000—sat down on the * slopes. Jn 6:10

GRATEFUL
Since we are * to you as our Ez 4:14
Oh, how * and thankful I am to Ps 7:17
Accept my * thanks and teach me Ps 119:108
made him comfortable and very *. Jon 4:6
And for this we are very, very * Act 24:3
be humble and *—and careful. Rom 11:20
How * I am and how I praise the Php 4:10

GRATING
Make a bronze *, with a metal Ex 27:4
and fit the * halfway down into Ex 27:5
The bronze * of the altar, and its Ex 35:10-19
Next he made a bronze * that Ex 38:4
*, to insert the carrying poles. Ex 38:5
altar, the bronze *, the altar Ex 38:29
The bronze *; Ex 39:33-40

GRAVE
*, and it is there to this day. Gen 35:20
gray hairs with sorrow to the *. Gen 44:31
*, he shall be defiled seven days. Num 19:16
dead, or has touched a *. Num 19:18
in the * of Saul's father, Kish. 2Sa 21:12,13,14
buried in the * of your fathers." 1Ki 13:21,22
He laid the body in his own *, 1Ki 13:30
the * where the prophet is buried. 1Ki 13:31
him, "It is the * of the prophet 2Ki 23:17
him in the * he had selected. 2Ki 23:30
directly from the womb to the *. Job 10:19
the * is ready to receive me. Job 17:1
and call the * my father, and the Job 17:13,14
will go down with me to the *. Job 17:16
honor guard keeps watch at his *. Job 21:30-32
down to the * by disease and Job 27:15
Literally, "In the *, who shall Ps 6:5f
your beloved one to rot in the *. Ps 16:10
the brink of the *, from death Ps 30:3
How can my dust in the * speak Ps 30:9
of lying in silence in the *. Ps 30:12
your miracles when I am in the *? Ps 88:10
Can those in the * declare your Ps 88:11
his life from the power of the *? Ps 89:48
the darkness like those in the *. Ps 143:3
prostitute is a deep and narrow *. Pro 23:26,27,28

(GRAVE Con't)
it lies in an open *, covered Is 14:19
like a criminal in a rich man's *; Is 53:9
womb, that it had been my *! Jer 20:17
had him buried in an unmarked *. Jer 26:23
Let there be no wailing at her *; Eze 24:17
They are buried in a common *, Eze 32:27
O *, demonstrate your plagues! Hos 13:14
have faced * danger from the plots Act 20:19
like the stench from an open *. Rom 3:13
"Their throat is an open *." Rom 3:13f
* just as the prophets foretold. 1Co 15:4
Christ from the *, and of course 1Co 15:15
I have faced * dangers from mobs 2Co 11:26
us up from the * into glory along Eph 2:6

GRAVECLOTH
up in the *, his face muffled in a Jn 11:44

GRAVEL
will turn to * in their mouths. Pro 20:17
He has made me eat * and broken Lam 3:16

GRAVEN
up shame-idols and * images (this 2Ch 33:19

GRAVES
were not enough * for us in Egypt? Ex 14:11
Place of the * Caused by Lust," Num 11:34
on the * of the common people. 2Ki 23:6
* in the side of the mountain. 2Ki 23:16
scattered over the * of those who 2Ch 34:4
let them lie silently in their *, Ps 31:17
glory in their *, but your body is Is 14:18
At night they go out among the * Is 65:4
enough for all the * and they will Jer 7:32
break open the * of the kings of Jer 8:1
surrounded by the * of all her Eze 32:22
Their * are in the depths of Eze 32:23
by the * of all their people. Eze 32:25
surrounded by the * of all their Eze 32:26
I will open your * of exile and Eze 37:12
lay flowers on the * of the godly Mt 23:29,30
For you are like hidden * in a Lk 11:44
the dead in their * shall hear the Jn 5:28
ahead of those who are in their *. 1Th 4:15

GRAVESIDE
and all the people wept at the *. 2Sa 3:32

GRAVESTONES
This man lived among the *, and Mk 5:3,4

GRAVEYARD
city including the * and ash dump Jer 31:40
"And I will make a vast * for Eze 39:11
man ran out from a *, just as Jesus Mk 5:1

GRAVITY
Literally, "in *." 1Ti 2:2f

GRAY
* hairs with sorrow to the grave. Gen 44:31
if the color is *, then the priest Lev 13:21
And now that I am old and *, Ps 71:18
Ephraim's hair is turning *, and Hos 7:9

GRAZE
flocks to Shechem to * them there. Gen 37:12
man's field to *, he must pay for Ex 22:5
alike shall be allowed to * there. Lev 25:6,7
for your cattle to * in, and you Deu 11:15
cattle, sheep and goats will * Is 7:25
The cows will * among bears; Is 11:7
they shall * in my pasture! Is 14:30
and goats will * upon the mountains Is 32:14
herds will * in green pastures. Is 32:20
land where flocks of sheep can *. Eze 25:5
and herds that * beside the Eze 32:13

GRAZING
so they can get back to *?" Gen 29:7
he was * his father's donkeys. Gen 36:24
are over in Shechem * the flocks. Gen 37:13,14
river and began * in the grass. Gen 41:2
and began * along the river bank. Gen 41:18
with grass, cows * through the city Is 27:10
They will be my sheep, * in Is 49:8,9
Like cattle * in the valleys, so Is 63:14
that leaps upon the * sheep. Jer 50:44

GREAT
So God created * sea Gen 1:21,22
and reproduce in * numbers." Gen 8:17
about building a * city, with a Gen 11:3,4
So they made * piles of Gen 11:3,4
become the father of a * nation; Gen 12:2
And I will give you * Gen 15:1
they will come away with * wealth. Gen 15:14
I will make you into a * nation. Gen 16:9-12
to multiply and become a * nation. Gen 17:20
him, and he set a * feast before Gen 19:3
* fear swept through the crowd. Gen 20:8
my kingdom guilty of this * sin? Gen 20:9,10
a * nation from his descendants." Gen 21:18
so that he is a * man among the Gen 24:35
He was soon a man of * wealth, Gen 26:13
sheep and goats, * herds of cattle, Gen 26:14
they will become a * nation—because Gen 26:24
So Isaac prepared a * feast for Gen 26:30
may you become a * nation of many Gen 28:2
a * nation, yes, many nations; Gen 35:11
It would be a * sin against Gen 39:9

be a period of * prosperity Gen 41:29
years of famine so * that all the Gen 41:30
that you will become a * nation. Gen 45:7
that you become a * nation there. Gen 46:3,4
'I will make you a * nation and I Gen 48:4
"Manasseh too shall become a * Gen 48:19
So Joseph went, and a * number of Gen 50:7
So a very * number of chariots, Gen 50:9
they held a very * and solemn Gen 50:10
us for the * evil we did to you. Gen 50:16,17
power and perform * miracles to Ex 6:6
They were piled into * heaps, Ex 8:14
So you still think you are so *, Ex 9:17
Moses was a very * man in the land Ex 11:3
Then, on the seventh day, a * Ex 13:6,7
us out of Egypt with * power." Ex 13:16
I have planned this to gain * Ex 14:4
O Lord, because of your * power Ex 15:16
of God, giving him * wisdom, Ex 31:3
into a * nation instead of them." Ex 32:10
such * power and mighty miracles? Ex 32:11
now he will give you a * Ex 32:29
have sinned a * sin, but I will Ex 32:30
have sinned a * sin, and have made Ex 32:31
And the Lord sent a * plague upon Ex 32:35
The * lizard, the gecko, Lev 11:29,30
with her mother, it is a * evil. Lev 20:14
guilty and is in * danger because Lev 22:16
will let loose my * anger and send Lev 26:28
and will be a * help to us. Num 10:31
Their voices rose in a * chorus Num 14:2
"Oh, please, show the * power Num 14:17,18
them, and a * fissure swallowed Num 16:32
Soon a *, sullen mob formed; Num 16:42
Moses and Aaron. A * mob formed, Num 20:2
to the frontier with a * force. Num 20:20
He promises you * honors plus any Num 22:16,17
in the road! In a * fit of temper Num 22:27
said I would give you * honors?" Num 22:37
I had planned to promote you to * Num 24:11
On the following day, a *, Num 28:17
You are a * burden for me to Deu 1:9
be fair to * and small alike. Deu 1:17
through the * and terrible desert, Deu 1:19,20,21
around in this * wilderness; Deu 2:7
For what other nation, * or Deu 4:7
And what nation, no matter how * Deu 4:8
* pillar of fire upon the earth; Deu 4:36
Egypt with a * display of power. Deu 4:37
out with a * display of miracles. Deu 5:15
you will become a * nation in a Deu 6:3
he has given you * cities full of Deu 6:10,11,12
out of Egypt with * power and Deu 6:21
you and make you into a * nation. Deu 7:13
and olives, and * flocks of cattle, Deu 7:13
and he is a * and awesome God. Deu 7:21
you through the * and terrible Deu 8:15
thus provoking him to * anger. Deu 9:18
Aaron was in * danger because Deu 9:20
your * power and your mighty arm.' Deu 9:29
He is the * and mighty God, the Deu 10:17
and make you a * nation just as he Deu 13:17
The screech owl, the * owl, Deu 14:11-18
it shall be a time of * joy. Deu 16:15
He did * and awesome miracles Deu 26:8
* joy before the Lord your God. Deu 27:7
your own eyes the * plagues and Deu 29:2,3
upon them. In * anger the Lord Deu 29:28
live and become a * nation, and so Deu 30:16
He appeared to them in a * cloud Deu 31:15
my contract, and * disasters come Deu 31:21
He did * and terrifying wonders Deu 34:11,12
"the Lord will do a * miracle." Jos 3:5
"I will give you * honor, so that Jos 3:7
The Lord made him * in the eyes Jos 4:14
to the honor of your * name?" Jos 7:9
a * heap of stones upon them. Jos 7:26
There he piled a * heap of stones Jos 8:29
For Gibeon was a * city—as great Jos 10:2
For Gibeon was a great city—as * Jos 10:2
Israel slaughtered * numbers of Jos 10:10
them with a * hailstorm that Jos 10:11
a command that a * stone be rolled Jos 10:18
and a * pile of stones was placed Jos 10:27
them as far as * Sidon and a place Jos 11:8
living there in *, walled cities, Jos 14:12
after a * hero of the Anakim. Jos 14:15
for they were * warriors. Jos 17:1
to share their * wealth with their Jos 22:7,8
He has driven out *, strong Jos 23:9
And I will give them a * Ju 1:2
Marched down against * odds. Ju 5:13,14
down the * cedars of Lebanon!' Ju 9:15
NOW JEPHTHAH WAS a * warrior Ju 11:1
he has given you a * victory over Ju 11:36
So he attacked them with * fury Ju 15:8
leaders declared a * festival to Ju 16:23,24
They lived a * distance from Ju 18:7
it on fire. The * cloud of smoke Ju 20:35-39
May you be a * and successful man Ru 4:11
And gives * glory to his anointed 1Sa 2:10

very * in the eyes of the Lord; 1Sa 2:17
a * cry arose throughout the city. 1Sa 4:13
plague, and there was a * panic. 1Sa 5:9
already begun and * fear was 1Sa 5:11
who brought this * evil upon us; 1Sa 6:9
there and, in a * ceremony, drew 1Sa 7:6
heard about the * crowds at Mizpah, 1Sa 7:7
servant into the * hall and placed 1Sa 9:22
"Now watch as the Lord does * 1Sa 12:16
that would dishonor his * name. 1Sa 12:22
And just then there was a * 1Sa 14:15
"Roll a * stone over here, and 1Sa 14:33
He did * deeds and conquered the 1Sa 14:48
him * power from that day onward. 1Sa 16:13
Then the Israelis gave a * shout 1Sa 17:52
a * victory to Israel as a result? 1Sa 19:5
and arrived at the * well in Secu. 1Sa 19:22
has done these * things for you, 1Sa 25:30,31
"Well, Abner, you're a * fellow, 1Sa 26:15
deeds and be a * conqueror." 1Sa 26:25
to his people, "A * leader and a 2Sa 3:38
* man has fallen today in Israel; 2Sa 3:38
of David with a * celebration. 2Sa 6:12
want to! How * you are, Lord God! 2Sa 7:22
You have done * miracles to 2Sa 7:23
Mephibosheth arrived in * fear 2Sa 9:5,6
But you have given * opportunity 2Sa 12:14
wall saw a * crowd coming toward 2Sa 13:34
a reputation for * wisdom and told 2Sa 14:2,3
There was a * slaughter and 2Sa 18:7
thick boughs of a * oak tree, and 2Sa 18:9
piled a * heap of stones over it. 2Sa 18:17
was the * topic everywhere. 2Sa 19:8,9,10
As they arrived at the * stone 2Sa 20:8,9,10
Your gentleness has made me *. 2Sa 22:36
and the Lord gave him a * 2Sa 23:10
and God gave him a * victory. 2Sa 23:11,12
*) than into the hands of men." 2Sa 24:14
swore with a * oath, "May God 1Ki 2:23,24
a nation so * that there are almost 1Ki 3:8
of his officials to a * banquet. 1Ki 3:15
the * wisdom God had given him. 1Ki 3:28
God gave Solomon * wisdom and 1Ki 4:29
He was a * naturalist, with 1Ki 4:33
and trees—from the * cedars of 1Ki 4:33
had always been a * admirer of 1Ki 5:1
the * nation of Israel," he said. 1Ki 5:7
So the Lord gave * wisdom to 1Ki 5:12
45 feet high. The * cedar ceiling 1Ki 7:2
cedar beams. The * Court had three 1Ki 7:12
hear of your * name and come from 1Ki 8:41,42
shall hear of your * name and 1Ki 8:41,42
days, and a * crowd came from one 1Ki 8:65
heard about his * wisdom was true. 1Ki 10:4
on his table, the * number of 1Ki 10:5
* supply of algum trees and gems. 1Ki 10:11
three years a * load of gold, 1Ki 10:22
of the earth. * men from many 1Ki 10:24
Solomon built up a * stable of 1Ki 10:26
a * mob stoned him to death. 1Ki 12:18
This was of course a * sin, for 1Ki 12:30
This was a * sin, and resulted 1Ki 13:34
He was as * a sinner as his 1Ki 15:3
Literally, "as * as would contain 1Ki 18:32f
and they all had a * feast. 1Ki 19:21
However, the * bulk of the 1Ki 20:21
army was killed in a * slaughter. 1Ki 20:21
The Lord is going to bring * 1Ki 21:21
"You will have a * victory, for 1Ki 22:15
King Jehoshaphat built * 1Ki 22:48
still clung to the * sin of 2Ki 3:3
So he was a * hero, but he was a 2Ki 5:1
you to do some * thing, wouldn't 2Ki 5:13
of Syria sent a * army with many 2Ki 6:14
So the king made a * feast for 2Ki 6:23
As a result there was a * famine 2Ki 6:25
sounds of a * army approaching. 2Ki 7:6
of the * things Elisha has done." 2Ki 8:4
a * celebration to praise him. 2Ki 10:18,19
Dan—this was the * sin of Jeroboam 2Ki 10:29
the cause of such * sin in Israel. 2Ki 10:31
he did, and his * power, and his 2Ki 14:28
and removed the * tank from the 2Ki 16:17
He made them sin a * sin, and 2Ki 17:21
staff from Lachish with a * army; 2Ki 18:17
Hezekiah: "The * King of Assyria 2Ki 18:19
"Listen to the * king of Assyria! 2Ki 18:28
shall become a * nation again; 2Ki 19:30
Hezekiah and his * deeds—including 2Ki 20:20
For they have done * evil and 2Ki 21:15
* numbers of innocent people. 2Ki 21:16
people, small and *, of Jerusalem 2Ki 23:1
not hold back his * anger against 2Ki 23:26
pillars and the * tank and its 2Ki 25:16
was Nimrod, who became a * hero. 1Ch 1:10
captives. A * number of the enemy 1Ch 5:22
Each of these men had a * 1Ch 5:24
in an office of * trust, for they 1Ch 9:26
and the Lord saved them with a * 1Ch 11:14
but he was not as * as The Three. 1Ch 11:21
He was nearly as * as The Three, 1Ch 11:24,25

(GREAT Con't)
* and brave warriors from the 1Ch 12:8-13
the Lord with * enthusiasm, 1Ch 13:8
why he had made his kingdom so *; 1Ch 14:2
the army went with * joy to the 1Ch 15:25
For the Lord is *, and should be 1Ch 16:25
Ascribe * strength and glory to 1Ch 16:28
as * as the greatest of the earth. 1Ch 17:8
For all the * things you have 1Ch 17:17
as though I were someone very *. 1Ch 17:17
me, because of your own * heart. 1Ch 17:19
And you made a * name for 1Ch 17:21
as well as a * amount of bronze 1Ch 18:8
David also took * amounts of 1Ch 20:2
for God's mercies are very *." 1Ch 21:13
iron into the * quantity of nails 1Ch 22:3
* rafts of cedar logs to David. 1Ch 22:4
many men in * wars,' he told me. 1Ch 22:8
of * authority in their clan. 1Ch 26:6,7
iron, wood, and * quantities of 1Ch 29:2
They also contributed * amounts 1Ch 29:8
men are made * and given strength. 1Ch 29:12
drank before the Lord with * joy. 1Ch 29:22
And the Lord gave him * 1Ch 29:25
a * nation as this one of yours?" 2Ch 1:10
be so * a king in all the world!" 2Ch 1:12
a * God, greater than any other. 2Ch 2:5
and Zeredah. * quantities of bronze 2Ch 4:17,18
to worship your * name, and to pray 2Ch 6:32
king, and the * building projects 2Ch 8:1
A very * retinue of aides and 2Ch 9:1
He wants them to be a *, strong 2Ch 9:8
in gold, and * quantities of spices 2Ch 9:9
tents and captured * herds of sheep 2Ch 14:15
show his * power in helping them. 2Ch 16:9
people made a very * burning of 2Ch 16:13,14
command of Eliada, a * general. 2Ch 17:17
King Ahab gave a * party for him 2Ch 18:2
aides, butchering * numbers of 2Ch 18:2
God will give you a * victory!" 2Ch 18:3,4,5
your nation with a * plague. 2Ch 21:14
A * shout went up, "Long live the 2Ch 23:11
the people in a * psalm of praise. 2Ch 23:12
and sending back * quantities of 2Ch 24:23
It was a * triumph for the tiny 2Ch 24:24
the Lord let the * army of Judah be 2Ch 24:24
off * quantities of booty. 2Ch 25:13
for he had * herds of cattle out in 2Ch 26:10
* numbers of his troops. 2Ch 28:5
Then Zichri, a * warrior from 2Ch 28:7
They had not kept it in * numbers 2Ch 30:5
for seven days with * joy. 2Ch 30:21
Everything was laid out in * 2Ch 31:5,6
Lord and piled them up in * heaps. 2Ch 31:5,6
He has a * army, but they are 2Ch 32:8
and folds for the * flocks of sheep 2Ch 32:28,29
for God had given him * wealth. 2Ch 32:28,29
was before the * change in his 2Ch 33:19
reason the Lord's * anger has been 2Ch 34:21
and all the people * and small, to 2Ch 34:30
him all the items, * and small, 2Ch 36:18
Then God gave a * desire to the Ez 1:5
Then all the people gave a * Ez 3:11
own lands by the * and noble Ez 4:10
been some very * kings in Jerusalem Ez 4:20
the Temple of the * God of Judah. Ez 5:8
The work is going forward with * Ez 5:8
ago by a * king of Israel. Ez 5:11
dedicated with * joy by the Ez 6:16
There was * joy throughout the Ez 6:21,22
I was given * status because the Ez 7:28
the Lord in * embarrassment; Ez 9:5
I cried out; "O * and awesome God Neh 1:5
you rescued by your * power. Neh 1:10
ask the king for a * favor—put it Neh 1:11
Remember the Lord who is * and Neh 4:14
ABOUT THIS TIME there was a * Neh 5:1
"I am doing a * work! Neh 6:3
Then Ezra blessed the Lord, the * Neh 8:6
it was a time of * and joyful Neh 8:12
You displayed * miracles against Neh 9:10
ways, but in your * mercy you Neh 9:19
"Then you helped them conquer * Neh 9:22
heaven, and in * mercy you sent Neh 9:27
But in your * mercy you did not Neh 9:31
"And now, O * and awesome God, Neh 9:32
as nothing to you. * trouble has Neh 9:32
* goodness you showered upon them. Neh 9:35
pleasure and are in * misery. Neh 9:37
God had given us cause for * joy. Neh 12:43
accordance with your * goodness. Neh 13:22
This was the year of the * Est 1:1
throughout your * kingdom, husbands Est 1:20
there was * mourning among the Est 4:3
and white and the * crown of gold, Est 8:15
with joy and had a * celebration Est 8:17
of the sea. His * deeds, and also Est 10:2
He was, of course, very * among Est 10:3
eat and drink with * merriment. Job 1:4
his suffering was too * for words. Job 2:13
"And how * is his might! Job 12:14
He makes it *, and then reduces Job 12:23
You think yourselves so *? Job 19:5
age, and become * and powerful. Job 21:7
at his grave. A * funeral Job 21:33
"God is so *—higher than the Job 22:12
But though they are very * now, Job 24:24
have encouraged me in my * need! Job 26:2
me with * power and effect. Job 30:21
For he doesn't care how * a man Job 34:19
and at midnight * and small shall Job 34:20
to wait for some * crime before a Job 34:23
good, is this some * gift to him? Job 35:7
"God is so * that we cannot Job 36:26
her prey, from a very * distance. Job 39:29
me and drew me out of my * trials. Ps 18:16
your gentleness has made me *. Ps 18:35
Praise him who is the * rock of Ps 18:46
and innocent of some * crime. Ps 19:13
heaven and sends * victories. Ps 20:6
Be for me a * Rock of safety from Ps 31:2
Oh, how * is your goodness to Ps 31:19
For you have stored up * Ps 31:19
Literally, "When the * waters Ps 32:6f
save a king—for * strength is not Ps 33:16,17
But give * joy to all who wish Ps 35:27
Let them shout with delight, "* Ps 35:27
And I will tell everyone how * Ps 35:28
Lord, is as * as all the heavens. Ps 36:5
time you have done * miracles for Ps 40:5
exclaim, "How * God is!" Ps 40:16
when you led a * procession to Ps 42:4,5
he is the * King of all the Ps 47:2
HOW * IS the Lord! Ps 48:1
the residence of the * King. Ps 48:2
For this * God is our God forever Ps 48:14
will be quoted as having * wisdom. Ps 49:13
a * storm rages round about him. Ps 50:3
COME WITH * power, Ps 54:1
kings, and Ephraim * warriors. Ps 60:6,7
I will praise you with * joy. Ps 63:5
deeds, O God! How * your power! Ps 66:3
Because of his * power he rules Ps 66:7
and laid * burdens on our backs. Ps 66:11
us into wealth and * abundance. Ps 66:12
let darkness, blindness and * Ps 69:23
Be to me a * protecting Rock, Ps 71:3
GOD'S REPUTATION IS very * in Ps 76:1
and praise your * and holy name. Ps 86:9
For you are *, and do great Ps 86:10
For you are great, and do * Ps 86:10
he will be * because of me. Ps 89:24
I will make him * because he Ps 91:14
For the Lord is a * God, the Ps 95:3
Lord is a great God, the * King of Ps 95:3
For the Lord is * beyond Ps 96:4
Let them reverence your * and Ps 99:3
Go through his open gates with * Ps 100:4
honor him is as * as the height of Ps 103:11
O Lord my God, how * you are! Ps 104:1
of every kind, both * and small. Ps 104:25
gone, for the dread of them was *. Ps 105:38
because of his * love, and caused Ps 106:45
For your lovingkindness is * Ps 108:4
He has shown his * power to his Ps 111:6
* and small, who reverence him. Ps 115:13
I am praying with * earnestness; Ps 119:145
Lord, how * is your mercy; Ps 119:156
* men have persecuted me, though Ps 119:161
like one who finds a * treasure. Ps 119:162
Those who love your laws have * Ps 119:165
He did * miracles in Egypt Ps 135:9
He smote * nations, slaying Ps 135:10
ways, for his glory is very *. Ps 138:5
Yet though he is so *, he Ps 138:6
* is Jehovah! Ps 145:3
them all by name. How * he is! Ps 147:5
and she will lead you to * honor; Pro 4:8,9
I would have you learn this * Pro 4:11
and formed the * springs in the Pro 8:27,28,29
and has prepared a * banquet, and Pro 9:2
Telling the truth gives a man * Pro 12:14
some poor people have * wealth! Pro 13:7
a fool plunges ahead with * Pro 14:16
* treasure and trouble with it. Pro 15:16
is better than * wealth gotten by Pro 16:8
They are eaten with * relish! Pro 18:8
a good name rather than * riches; Pro 22:1
dainty morsel eaten with * relish. Pro 26:22
by inaugurating a * public works Ecc 2:4,5,6
I also bred * herds and flocks, Ecc 2:7,8
I even found * pleasure in hard Ecc 2:10
to some men very * wealth and Ecc 6:2
is backed by * power, and no one Ecc 8:4
in it, and a * king came with his Ecc 9:14
foolish men given * authority, and Ecc 10:6
A dull axe requires * strength; Ecc 10:10
your cologne, and how * your name! Sol 1:3
and gold, and * numbers of horses Is 2:7
Small and *, all bow before Is 2:9
He is the * Prosecuting Attorney Is 3:13
Your homes are built on * estates Is 5:8
much for you. Your * and honored Is 5:13
Jerusalem. Her * and small shall be Is 5:14
In a * antiphonal chorus they Is 6:3
Assyria will come with his * army! Is 7:17
shall see a * Light—a Light that Is 9:2
For Israel will again be *, Is 9:3
We are * and wise. Is 10:13
of that vast army, * and small Is 10:33
with joy. For * and mighty is the Is 12:6
for Kir-haresh will be very *. Is 16:11
crops will fail. * men and Is 19:10
They are preparing a * banquet! Is 21:5
says the Lord, "the * power of Is 21:16
the news, there will be * sorrow. Is 23:5
he has spoken out against this * Is 23:11
the sins of the earth are very *. Is 24:20
He has made our nation very *. Is 26:15
and there from his * threshing Is 27:12
In that day the * trumpet will Is 27:13
to your judges and * courage to Is 28:6
In his wisdom, he will send * Is 31:2
The Lord is very *, and lives in Is 33:5
For the Lord will slay a * Is 34:6
with a * army from Lachish to Is 36:2
the * king, the king of Assyria: Is 36:13
Then he broke down with * sobs. Is 38:3
He dooms the * men of the world Is 40:23
Doubtless Cyrus the * of Persia. Is 41:2f
He will give a * shout and Is 42:13
and * trouble, I will be with you. Is 43:2
and * waves of righteousness. Is 48:18
blessed him, he became a * nation. Is 51:1
who is mighty and *, because he has Is 53:12
But with * compassion I will Is 54:7
and their prosperity shall be *. Is 54:13
Lord's name very * and be an Is 55:13
You worship your idols with * Is 57:5
I will rejoice in his * goodness Is 63:7
I will send * troubles upon Is 66:4
them and make them strong and *." Jer 1:10
deeply guilty, and * evil fell on Jer 2:3
I see * armies marching on Jer 2:15
promised * blessings on Jerusalem. Jer 4:10
I have heard * crying like that Jer 4:31
their rebellion against me is *. Jer 5:6
Now they are * and rich, and Jer 5:27
* nation is rising against you. Jer 6:22
No wonder my anger is *! Jer 7:18
for all of them, * and small, Jer 8:10
For you are * and your name is Jer 10:6
land and pour * troubles down; Jer 10:18
My grief is *. Jer 10:19
Hear the terrible sound of * Jer 10:22
will bring a * disaster upon them. Jer 11:23
and a * cry rises from Jerusalem. Jer 14:2
Both * and small shall die in Jer 16:6
nation strong and *, but then that Jer 18:9
The slaughter shall be so * that Jer 19:11
beside me like a * warrior, and Jer 20:11
Why did he destroy such a * Jer 22:8
for you are building your * Jer 22:13
palace does not make a * king! Jer 22:15
shall return to me with * joy. Jer 24:7
The troops of Cyrus the * entered Jer 25:12f
For many nations and * kings Jer 25:14
nation to nation—a * whirlwind of Jer 25:32
where the * Temple now stands!' Jer 26:18
"By my * power I have made the Jer 27:5
many nations and * kings shall Jer 27:7
Temple, and the * bronze basin in Jer 27:19,20,21
are so many, your guilt is so *. Jer 30:14
It is because your guilt is * Jer 30:15
with joy and * thanksgiving, and I Jer 30:19
of them a * and honored nation. Jer 30:19
It will be a * company who comes. Jer 31:8
I will lead them home with * care. Jer 31:9
For everyone, both * and small, Jer 31:34
heavens and earth by your * power; Jer 32:17
you are the * and mighty God, the Jer 32:18
You have all wisdom and do * and Jer 32:19
And you have continued to do * Jer 32:20
You have made your name very *, Jer 32:20
miracles and * power and terror. Jer 32:21
them in this land, with * joy. Jer 32:41
and gathered a * harvest of wine Jer 40:12
all the people, * and small, came Jer 42:1
all the people, * and small, and Jer 42:8
to idols (it was a * crowd of all Jer 44:15
we have been in * trouble and have Jer 44:18
I have sworn by my * name, says the Jer 44:26
Are you seeking * things for Jer 45:5
For though I will bring * evil Jer 45:5
it is the day of * calamity for Jer 46:20,21
for Egypt, a time of * punishment. Jer 46:20,21
pride of Moab, for it is very *. Jer 48:29
are false—her helplessness is *. Jer 48:30
and Judges—a * city north of the Jer 49:30f
My fierce anger will bring * Jer 49:37
up an army of * nations from the Jer 50:9
land, a shout of * destruction. Jer 50:22
See them coming! A * army from Jer 50:41

(GREAT Con't)

O wealthy port, * center of	Jer 51:13
he has swallowed us like a *	Jer 51:34,35
How Babylon is fallen—* Babylon,	Jer 51:41
this * city and all her idols;	Jer 51:47
Hear the cry of * destruction out	Jer 51:54
my mighty men. A * army has come at	Lam 1:15
* is his faithfulness;	Lam 3:23
I saw, in this vision, a * storm	Eze 1:4
by the sound of a * earthquake.	Eze 3:12
me the sound of a * earthquake."	Eze 3:12f
bared [to signify * strength and	Eze 4:7
It will be weighed out with *	Eze 4:16
green tree and * oak where they	Eze 6:13
Do you see what * sins the people	Eze 8:6
and Judah are very * and all the	Eze 9:9
will undermine it; * hailstones and	Eze 13:11
and with a * flood of anger and	Eze 13:13
"And the Lord says: Four *	Eze 14:21
Your reputation was * among the	Eze 16:14
My anger is *.	Eze 16:26
the gods of that * merchant land of	Eze 16:29
"A * eagle with broad wings full	Eze 17:3,4
But when another *,	Eze 17:7
to seek for a * army and many	Eze 17:15
and it was very *, towering above	Eze 19:11
and in * anger and with power.	Eze 20:33
see the * change in your hearts.	Eze 20:41
the * massacre they face!	Eze 21:14
* army fully prepared for attack.	Eze 23:24
a * army and cavalry and chariots.	Eze 26:7
the conquest by Alexander the *.	Eze 26:14f
attack. * seas shall swallow you.	Eze 26:19
to get * wealth—gold and silver and	Eze 28:4
to apply to Satan. * care must	Eze 28:12f
Your * wealth filled you with	Eze 28:16
and treated her with * contempt.	Eze 28:24
never again will Egypt be *	Eze 29:15
to the Ethiopians; * terror shall	Eze 30:9
as Assyria was—a * and mighty	Eze 31:2,3
All the * nations of the world	Eze 31:6
Literally, "the * waters were	Eze 31:15f
"O Egypt, you are * and glorious	Eze 31:18
a * army to catch you with my net.	Eze 32:3
"* kings of Elam lie there with	Eze 32:24
who are buried in * honor with	Eze 32:27
Saying that, you boasted *	Eze 35:13
I will honor my * name that you	Eze 36:23
they lived, and stood up—a very *	Eze 37:10
* trading centers in Arabia.	Eze 38:13f
* hailstones, fire and brimstone!	Eze 38:22
God gave these four youths *	Dan 1:17
the situation with * wisdom by	Dan 2:14
down became a * mountain that	Dan 2:35
whose first * ruler was Cyrus.	Dan 2:39f
has fallen, yet a third * power	Dan 2:39
founded by Alexander the *.	Dan 2:39f
"Thus the * God has shown what	Dan 2:45
Then the king made Daniel very *;	Dan 2:48
mystery is too * for you to solve.	Dan 4:9
For you have grown strong and *;	Dan 4:22
his officers to a * feast where the	Dan 5:1
for he had * ability, and the king	Dan 6:3
he does * miracles in heaven and	Dan 6:27
In my dream I saw a * storm on a	Dan 7:2
four heads! And * power was given	Dan 7:6
as it pleased and became very *.	Dan 8:4
of Alexander the * were Ptolemy I	Dan 8:8f
Or, "and * indignities were	Dan 8:12f
the first * king of that country.	Dan 8:21
none of them as * as the first.	Dan 8:22
* shrewdness and intelligence.	Dan 8:23
destroy them. So * will he fancy	Dan 8:25
"you are a * and awesome God;	Dan 9:4
Egypt in a * display of power.	Dan 9:15
future: times of * tribulation—wars	Dan 10:1
beside the * Tigris River, I	Dan 10:4
I, Daniel, alone saw this *	Dan 10:7
Doubtless Alexander the *.	Dan 11:3f
in * anger, will rally against	Dan 11:10,11
Filled with pride after this *	Dan 11:12
Possibly Antiochus III the *, who	Dan 11:13f
the people. With * success he will	Dan 11:24
and raise a * army against Egypt;	Dan 11:25
return home with * riches, first	Dan 11:28
shall be strong and do * things.	Dan 11:32
Claiming his help he will have *	Dan 11:39
in * anger to destroy as he goes.	Dan 11:44
Many shall be purified by *	Dan 12:10
prosper and become a * nation;	Hos 1:10
to Assyria, to the * king there,	Hos 5:13
sins were far too *—no one can even	Hos 7:1
Israel has built * palaces;	Hos 8:14
Judah has constructed * defenses	Hos 8:14
a present to the * king there.	Hos 10:6
* armies can make a nation safe!	Hos 10:13
because of your * wickedness.	Hos 10:15
like night! How *, how powerful	Joe 2:2
locusts ate!—my * destroying army	Joe 2:25
blood before the * and terrible Day	Joe 2:31
be weak, and the * ones can no	Amo 2:14

For many and * are your sins.	Amo 5:12
then go to * Hamath and down to	Amo 6:2
as * musicians as King David was.	Amo 6:5
That homes both * and small should	Amo 6:11
rejoicing in how * you are, when	Amo 6:13
Then the Lord God showed me a *	Amo 7:4
"Go to the * city of Nineveh,	Jon 1:2
the sea, causing a * storm that	Jon 1:4
Now the Lord had arranged for a *	Jon 1:17
"In my * trouble I cried to the	Jon 2:2
"Go to that * city, Nineveh," he	Jon 3:1
I feel sorry for a * city like	Jon 4:11
For your sins are very *—is there	Mic 6:10
for the * wickedness of her	Mic 7:13
Where now is that * Nineveh, lion	Nah 2:11
Note: The * Revival under King	Zep 1:1f
he has prepared a * slaughter of	Zep 1:7
were part of a * wave of immigrants	Zep 2:5f
and make its * capital Nineveh a	Zep 2:13
there is no city as * as I."	Zep 2:15
He will rejoice over you in *	Zep 3:17,18
That is why such * wrath came	Zec 7:12
are—but it is no * thing for me.	Zec 8:6
be confiscated—* quantities of gold	Zec 14:14
the Lord's * power goes far beyond	Mal 1:5
For my name shall be * among the	Mal 1:11
For I am a * King," says the	Mal 1:14
promises, to bring you * joy.	Mal 3:1
out a blessing so * you won't have	Mal 3:10
than I am, so * that I am not	Mt 3:11
in darkness have seen a * Light;	Mt 4:15,16
be * in the Kingdom of Heaven.	Mt 5:19
is the capital of the * King.	Mt 5:35
and to do many other * miracles.'	Mt 7:22
as one who had * authority, and not	Mt 7:29
problems were so * and they didn't	Mt 9:36
"The harvest is so *, and the	Mt 9:37
For as Jonah was in the * fish	Mt 12:39,40
them, "and he will have * plenty;	Mt 13:12,13
bargain—a pearl of * value—and sold	Mt 13:46
How can he be so *?"	Mt 13:56
And so he did only a few *	Mt 13:58
* demonstrations in the skies.	Mt 16:1
deranged, and in * trouble, for he	Mt 17:15
a * wedding dinner for his son.	Mt 22:1
But those who think themselves *	Mt 23:12
of heaven, with power and * glory.	Mt 24:30
arrived with a * crowd armed with	Mt 26:47
tomb, and rolled a * stone across	Mt 27:60
Suddenly there was a *	Mt 28:2
So Jesus healed * numbers of	Mk 1:34
and as a result * numbers of sick	Mk 3:10
wind fell, and there was a * calm!	Mk 4:39
* things Jesus had done for him;	Mk 5:20
that all was in * confusion, with	Mk 5:38
like the * ones of the past.	Mk 6:15
time as another * crowd gathered,	Mk 8:1
of God arrive in * power!"	Mk 9:1
they found a * crowd surrounding	Mk 9:14
the kings and * men of the earth	Mk 10:42
Whoever wants to be * among you	Mk 10:43
Later, as they left town, a *	Mk 10:46
listened to him with * interest.	Mk 12:37
For you will be in * danger.	Mk 13:9
coming in the clouds with * power	Mk 13:26
A * sadness swept over them, and	Mk 14:19
him with a * show of friendliness.	Mk 14:45
Meanwhile, a * crowd stood	Lk 1:10
You will both have * joy and	Lk 1:14
will be one of the Lord's * men.	Lk 1:15
He shall be very * and shall be	Lk 1:32
Holy One, has done * things to me.	Lk 1:49
When this * army of angels had	Lk 2:15
Lake Gennesaret, * crowds pressed	Lk 5:1
For you will have a * reward	Lk 6:23
will be very *, and you will truly	Lk 6:35
the usual * crowd at his heels.	Lk 7:11
A * fear swept the crowd, and	Lk 7:16
a * deal about the Kingdom of God.	Lk 8:10
For it gives your Father *	Lk 12:32
There will be * joy for those	Lk 12:37
"And there will be * weeping and	Lk 13:28
"A man prepared a * feast and sent	Lk 14:16
* crowds were following him.	Lk 14:25
money was gone a * famine swept	Lk 15:14
and has prepared a * feast to	Lk 15:27
And besides, there is a * chasm	Lk 16:26
who had * contempt for everyone.	Lk 18:2
his house in * excitement and joy.	Lk 19:6
long prayers with * outward piety,	Lk 20:47
and there will be * earthquakes,	Lk 21:11
For there will be * distress upon	Lk 21:23
in a cloud with power and * glory.	Lk 21:27
the kings and * men order their	Lk 22:25
Literally, "they (the kings and *	Lk 22:25f
of blood, with * drops falling to	Lk 22:44
Jesus' cross. * crowds trailed	Lk 23:27
him, he soon saw a * multitude of	Jn 6:2-5
When the people realized what a *	Jn 6:14
If you're so *, prove it to the	Jn 7:4
to make myself *, God wants this	Jn 8:50

I would be as * a liar as you!	Jn 8:55
Now Jesus was in * anguish of	Jn 13:21
God shall receive * praise because	Jn 13:31
This brings * glory to my Father.	Jn 15:8
* honor by showing you my glory.	Jn 16:14
about me with * effect, to the	Act 1:8
their meals with * joy and	Act 2:46
to your servants * boldness in	Act 4:29
Literally, "* grace was upon them	Act 4:33f
who pretended to be someone *.	Act 5:36
was * misery for our ancestors.	Act 7:11
And a * wave of persecution of	Act 8:1
came and with * sorrow buried	Act 8:2
Power of God which is called *."	Act 8:9,10,11f
Turn from this * wickedness and	Act 8:22
a eunuch of * authority under	Act 8:27
He saw the sky open, and a *	Act 10:11
the Spirit that a * famine was	Act 11:28
At dawn, the jail was in *	Act 12:18
people gave him a * ovation,	Act 12:22
them power to do * miracles.	Act 14:3
And there was * joy throughout	Act 15:31
day until Paul, in * distress,	Act 16:18
suddenly there was a * earthquake;	Act 16:26
the temple of the * goddess Diana	Act 19:27
"* is Diana of the Ephesians!"	Act 19:28
"* is Diana of the Ephesians!	Act 19:34
* is Diana of the Ephesians!"	Act 19:34
of the religion of the * Diana,	Act 19:35
accusations and a * riot followed.	Act 21:30
So a * clamor arose.	Act 23:9
the courtroom with * pomp,	Act 25:23
to everyone, both * and small.	Act 26:22
Beating into the wind with *	Act 27:7,8
Clauda, where with * difficulty we	Act 27:16
everywhere the * things God has	Rom 1:5
For I owe a * debt to you and to	Rom 1:14
his existence and * eternal power.	Rom 1:20
this is all part of God's * plan	Rom 2:16
and become a * nation, Abraham	Rom 4:18
But God showed his * love for us	Rom 5:8
death as they await this * event.	Rom 8:22
mighty promises. * men of God were	Rom 9:5
can see how very * his glory is.	Rom 9:23,24
They have stumbled over the *	Rom 9:32
I lay * stress on this and remind	Rom 11:13
God we have! How * are his wisdom	Rom 11:33
will give me a * blessing for you.	Rom 15:29
and * peace of heart and mind.	1Co 1:3
of this world's * affairs?	1Co 1:20
by the world as wise and *.	1Co 1:27
world considers *, so that no one	1Co 1:28
upon God, not on man's * ideas.	1Co 2:5
with words of * wisdom, but not the	1Co 2:6
appeals to the * men of this world,	1Co 2:6
But the * men of the world have	1Co 2:8
burns up, he will have a * loss.	1Co 3:15
though you are so *, and as though	1Co 4:7
For God has bought you with a *	1Co 6:20
* dangers to our lives at present.	1Co 7:26
there are a * many gods, both in	1Co 8:5
for causing * spiritual damage to a	1Co 8:11
to happen, and the * truths of	1Co 14:6
because of our * trust in God	2Co 3:4
we can preach with * boldness, and	2Co 3:12
thank him for his * kindness, and	2Co 4:15
message of God's * kindness.	2Co 6:1
HAVING SUCH * promises as these,	2Co 7:1
in you, and my pride in you is *.	2Co 7:4
there is nothing * about him, and	2Co 10:10
have been often in * danger from	2Co 11:26
weak I am and how * God is to use	2Co 12:5
And the * leaders of the church	Gal 2:6
(By the way, their being *	Gal 2:6
dies and leaves * wealth for his	Gal 4:1
If anyone thinks he is too * to	Gal 6:3
how incredibly * his power is to	Eph 1:19
Father of all the * family of	Eph 3:14,15
though it is so * that you will	Eph 3:18,19
satanic beings and * evil princes	Eph 6:12
me here has been a * boost in	Php 1:12
in the midst of a * and terrible	Php 1:30
Welcome him in the Lord with *	Php 2:29
and fill you with his * peace.	Col 1:2
about God's * kindness to sinners.	Col 1:6
told us about the * love for others	Col 1:8
no, you listened with * interest.	1Th 1:5
Spirit gave you * and full	1Th 1:5
and the * trumpet-call of God.	1Th 4:16
will be a time of * rebellion	2Th 2:3
and will do * miracles.	2Th 2:9
you * peace of heart and mind.	1Ti 1:2
Teach these * truths to	2Ti 2:2
preached these * truths that I am	2Ti 2:9
Remind your people of these *	2Ti 2:14
* rock, and nothing can shake it.	2Ti 2:19
me on that * day of his return.	2Ti 4:8
our * God and Savior Jesus Christ.	Tit 2:13
because of his * kindness;	Tit 3:7
honor beside the * God of heaven.	Heb 1:3
to this * salvation announced by	Heb 2:3

(GREAT Con't)
Yes, because of God's * kindness, Heb 2:9
But Jesus the Son of God is our * Heb 4:14
made that Satan's * desire was that Heb 5:7f
sweating of * drops of blood? Heb 5:7f
father of a * nation of people. Heb 6:14
after winning a * battle against Heb 7:1
See then how * this Melchizedek Heb 7:4
* and small, will know me already. Heb 8:11
And since this * High Priest of Heb 10:21
* reward that God would give him. Heb 11:26
Others were given * power in Heb 11:34
until you sweat * drops of blood. Heb 12:4
May he who became the * Shepherd Heb 13:20,21
for he is * in the Lord's sight. Jas 1:9
it can do. A * forest can be set on Jas 3:5
For see! The * Judge is coming. Jas 5:9
has * power and wonderful results. Jas 5:16
and his * glory afterwards. 1Pe 1:11
a * deal to know more about it. 1Pe 1:12
the dead and gave him * glory. 1Pe 1:21
will come upon you with * glory. 1Pe 4:14
attacks from Satan, your * enemy. 1Pe 5:8
you, through his * power, 2Pe 1:3
stored away for a * bonfire at the 2Pe 3:7
will bless us with * mercy and much 2Jn 1:3
the time of * Tribulation and Rev 3:10
sitting on it! * bursts of light Rev 4:3
and all men * and small, slave and Rev 6:15
Lamb, because the * day of their Rev 6:17
the * Seal of the Living God. Rev 7:2
a vast crowd, too * to count, from Rev 7:9
of the * Tribulation," he said; Rev 7:14
and a * quantity of incense was Rev 8:3
The third angel blew, and a * Rev 8:10
held bound at the * River Rev 9:14
earth, and gave a * shout—it was Rev 10:3
And * fear will fall on everyone. Rev 11:11
* power and have begun to reign. Rev 11:17
your Name, both * and small—and to Rev 11:18
and there was a * hailstorm and the Rev 11:19
THEN A * pageant appeared in Rev 12:1
This * Dragon—the ancient Rev 12:9
down to you in * anger, knowing Rev 12:12
like those of a * eagle, to fly Rev 12:14
power and throne and * authority. Rev 13:2
"Where is there anyone as * as Rev 13:4
* blasphemies against the Lord; Rev 13:5
world to make a * statue of the Rev 13:14
He required everyone—* and small, Rev 13:16
the roaring of a * waterfall or the Rev 14:2
en, is fallen—that * city—because Rev 14:8
the * winepress of God's wrath. Rev 14:19
"* and marvelous Rev 15:3,4
his flask upon the * River Rev 16:12
the Lord on that * coming Judgment Rev 16:14
and there was a * earthquake of a Rev 16:18
history. The * city of "Babylon" Rev 16:19
"Babylon the *, Mother of Rev 17:5
represents the * city that rules Rev 17:18
from heaven with * authority, and Rev 18:1
the * is fallen, is fallen; Rev 18:2
"Alas, that * city, so Rev 18:16
"Alas, alas, for that * city! Rev 18:19
She made us all rich from her * Rev 18:19
"Babylon, that * city, shall be Rev 18:21
He has punished the * Prostitute Rev 19:2
small and *, who fear him." Rev 19:5
of * thunder, "Praise the Lord. Rev 19:6
for the supper of the * God! Rev 19:17
and captains, and * generals; Rev 19:18
and of all humanity, both * and Rev 19:18
And I saw a * white throne and Rev 20:11
I saw the dead, * and small, Rev 20:12

GREAT-GRANDCHILDREN
and * of those who hate me; Ex 20:5
see his grandchildren and * too. Job 42:16

GREAT-GRANDFATHER
Manasseh's son Gilead was their * Num 27:1
His * was Tohu, 1Sa 1:1

GREAT-GRANDSON
of Zabdi, and * of Zerah, of the Jos 7:1
of Gilead, * of Machir, and Jos 17:3
grandson of Zeror, * of Becorath, 1Sa 9:1
Phinehas and the * of Eli, the 1Sa 14:3
* to be the kings of Israel." 2Ki 10:30
and * would be kings of Israel 2Ki 15:12
was Mibsam, and his * was 1Ch 4:25
his grandson Gog, and his * 1Ch 5:4
and his * was 1Ch 5:5
Azaz, grandson of Shema, and * of 1Ch 5:7,8
of Gedaliah, * of Amariah, and Zep 1:1

GREAT-GRANDSONS
of Machir, and the * of Manasseh. 1Ch 7:17

GREAT-GREAT-GRANDFATHER
His * was Zuph. 1Sa 1:1

GREAT-GREAT-GRANDSON
and * of Manasseh) had no sons. Jos 17:3
of Becorath, and * of Aphiah. 1Sa 9:1
of Amariah, and * of Hezekiah). Zep 1:1

GREAT-UNCLE
messenger had arrived from her *. Gen 24:28f
appointed King Jehoiachin's *, 2Ki 24:17

GREAT-UNCLES
with their five *, and the total Jos 17:5,6

GREATER
punishment is * than I can bear. Gen 4:13
brother shall become even *." Gen 48:19
I know now that the Lord is * Ex 18:11
times * punishment for your sins. Lev 26:28
* and mightier than they are!" Num 14:12
as though you were * than anyone Num 16:3
Their king will be * than Agag; Num 24:3-9
He drove away other nations * by Deu 4:38
all * and mightier than you are: Deu 7:1
Those nations are much * and more Deu 9:1
mightier and * than they are.' Deu 9:13,14
no matter how much * and stronger Deu 11:23
* than yours, don't be frightened! Deu 20:1
If you do, he will make you * Deu 26:19
This is described in * detail in Jos 10:13
Rehob, Hammon, Kanah, and * Sidon. Jos 19:28
So David became * and greater, 2Sa 5:10
So David became greater and *, 2Sa 5:10
And I will make your name * yet, 2Sa 7:9
"To reject me now is a * crime 2Sa 13:16
reign even * than yours!" 1Ki 1:37
reign even * than yours!' 1Ki 1:46,47
prosperity are far * than anything 1Ki 10:7
* value than the common sycamore! 1Ki 10:27
it won't be any * loss than if they 2Ki 7:13
he amassed even * wealth and honor 1Ch 29:25
is a great God, * than any other. 2Ch 2:5
Your wisdom is far * than I could 2Ch 9:6
with us who is far * than he is! 2Ch 32:7
to go over the law in * detail. Neh 8:13
It is far * than we can think or Neh 9:5
would pour even * sorrows upon me. Job 9:28
For God is * than man. Job 33:12
given me is far * than their joys Ps 4:7
You have no * lease on life than Ps 49:10
You will give me * honor than Ps 71:21
are far * than these other gods. Ps 97:8,9
were a * nation than their rulers. Ps 105:24
his glory is far * than the Ps 113:4
he is * far than any other god. Ps 135:5
His glory is far * than all of Ps 148:13
I have * wisdom and knowledge." Ecc 1:16-18
So I became * than any of the Ecc 2:9
idols were far * than those in Is 10:10
* power than the man who uses it? Is 10:15
Is the saw * than the man who Is 10:15
Men will be as scarce as gold—of * Is 13:12
but his son will be a * scourge Is 14:29
be made even *, for the Lord God of Is 28:22
Isn't he, the Potter, * than you, Is 29:16
walls —a name far * than the honor Is 56:5
The Messiah, David's * Son, whom Jer 30:9f
For the sin of my people is * Lam 4:6
But come, and I will show you * Eze 8:6
will show you * sins than these!" Eze 8:13
"But I will show you * evils Eze 8:15
for it will be * than theirs. Eze 16:54
But now your * wickedness has Eze 16:57
She turned to even * Eze 23:19,20
with even * honor than before. Dan 4:36
army far * than the one he lost, Dan 11:13
claiming to be * than every god Dan 11:36
boast that he is * than them all. Dan 11:37
for the Jews * than any previous Dan 12:1
Christ was "the * David." Hos 3:5f
Their love for shame is * than Hos 4:18
Once they were better and * than Amo 6:2
Temple will be * than the splendor Hag 2:8,9
time will be even * than the Zec 12:11
but someone else is coming, far * Mt 3:11
is * than that of the Pharisees Mt 5:20
A student is not * than his Mt 10:24
of Heaven will be * than he is! Mt 11:11
And truly, one is here who is * Mt 12:6
And now a * than Jonah is Mt 12:41
and now a * than Solomon is Mt 12:42
a crop many times * than the amount Mt 13:23f
service to others, the * you are. Mt 23:11
Which is *, the gold, or the Mt 23:17
For which is *, the gift on the Mt 23:19
soon who is far * than I am, so Mk 1:7
than I am, so much * that I am not Mk 1:7
No other commandments are * than Mk 12:31
their punishment will be the *." Mk 12:40
there is no one * than John. Lk 7:28
the Kingdom of God is * than he." Lk 7:28
but one far * than Solomon is Lk 11:31
and someone far * than Jonah is Lk 11:32
for their responsibility is *. Lk 12:48
be honest with * responsibilities. Lk 16:10
is coming who is * by far than I Jn 1:15
'Soon a man far * than I am is Jn 1:30
You will see * proofs than this. Jn 1:50
He must become * and greater, Jn 3:30
He must become greater and *, Jn 3:30
heaven and is * than anyone else. Jn 3:31
heard about the * crowds coming to Jn 4:1
And besides, are you * than our Jn 4:12
but I have a * witness than John. Jn 5:36
So you are * than our father Jn 8:53
And * than the prophets, who died? Jn 8:53
servant is not * than his master. Jn 13:16
done, and even * ones, because I am Jn 14:12,13
to the Father, who is * than I am. Jn 14:28
you back for * strength and Jn 15:3
'A slave isn't * than his Jn 15:20
who brought me to you have the * Jn 19:11
to us to lay no * burden of Jewish Act 15:27,28,29
in Hebrew, the silence was even *. Act 22:2
think how much * a blessing the Rom 11:12
about whether I am * than Apollos, 1Co 3:4
But shouldn't we have an even * 1Co 9:12
for that is a * and more useful 1Co 14:5
Shall we not expect far * glory 2Co 3:8
is certainly far *, for it is 2Co 3:11
Thus he became far * than the Heb 1:4
his Father, is far * than the names Heb 1:4
there was no one * to swear by, Heb 6:13
upon someone * than himself to Heb 6:16
* than the person he blesses. Heb 7:7
He went into that *, perfect Heb 9:11
be * than it would be for others. Jas 3:1
Lord, and are far * in power and 2Pe 2:11
us, God is * than our heart." 1Jn 3:20f
I could have no * joy than to 3Jn 1:4
He is far * than any king in all Rev 1:5
will continue on in * holiness." Rev 22:11

GREATEST
into the * nation in the world. Deu 28:1
one of the * fools in Israel. 2Sa 13:13
Joab (son of Zeruiah), was the *. 2Sa 23:18,19
But he was the * of The 2Sa 23:18,19
He was one of the * of The 2Sa 23:23
Joel was the * and was followed 1Ch 5:12
three * heroes among David's men. 1Ch 11:11
and the * was worth a thousand! 1Ch 12:14
as great as the * of the earth. 1Ch 17:8
his four sons: Jahath was *, Zizah 1Ch 23:10,11
God replied, "Because your * 2Ch 1:11
he had become the * man in the Est 5:11
shatters the * of men, and puts Job 34:24
he can help! The * of men, or the Ps 62:9
their * leaders fail; Ps 146:3
The Lord's blessing is our * Pro 10:22
become the world's * attraction, Is 2:2
and demolished its * cities and had Is 14:17
rare crop of * value, and though Is 17:10
bragging as the * in the Is 47:8
for Israel, the * of the nations! Jer 31:7
die, from the least to the *. Jer 44:12
be * in the Kingdom of Heaven! Mt 18:1
is the * in the Kingdom of Heaven. Mt 18:4
This is the first and * Mt 22:38,39
To be the *, be a servant. Mt 23:11
about which of them was the *! Mk 9:34
wanting to be the * must be the Mk 9:35
least here shall be * there." Mk 10:31
And whoever wants to be * of all Mk 10:44
But he will be the * joy of many Lk 2:34,35
would be * [in the coming Kingdom Lk 9:46
to measure it—the * love is shown Jn 15:13
love—and the * of these is love. 1Co 13:13
LET LOVE BE your * aim; 1Co 14:1
ones who ought to give me * joy. 2Co 2:3
really strong. Our * wish and 2Co 13:9
and your * glory will be that you 2Th 1:12
I was the * of them all. 1Ti 1:15
of * honor next to God himself. Heb 8:1
And who is the * liar? 1Jn 2:22

GREATLY
and sinned * against Jehovah. Gen 13:13
The Lord * blessed Joseph there Gen 39:2
for the Lord will * bless you in Deu 15:4,5
You will be * encouraged and be Ju 7:11
his kingdom so *—it was because God 2Sa 5:12
and he prospered *, and all 1Ch 29:23
This * encouraged them. 2Ch 32:8
and they were * encouraged by the Ez 6:14
we have sinned so * that you gave Neh 9:33
but no one tried, for they were * Est 9:1
them all. How * to be envied are Ps 65:4
No wonder you are * feared! Ps 76:7
description, and * to be praised. Ps 96:4
Great is Jehovah! * praise him! Ps 145:3
reverences God shall be * praised. Pro 31:30
And God will * bless his people. Is 32:20
them gods will be * disappointed; Is 42:17
And so the land was * polluted Jer 3:9
groans: "You have punished me *; Jer 31:18
come when I will * increase the Jer 31:27
evil, causing Judah to sin so *! Jer 32:35
war you have so * feared, says the Eze 11:8
holy name is * defiled among them. Eze 22:26
have sinned so * by avenging Eze 25:12
And so I will * punish Egypt and Eze 30:19
They shall * tremble for their Eze 32:10
I will * increase your Eze 36:10
and herds will also * multiply. Eze 36:11

(GREATLY Con't)
you have sinned *, by letting the Eze 44:6
they prospered * there in the Dan 3:30
had a dream that * frightened me. Dan 4:5
When I awoke, I was * disturbed, Dan 7:28
king, but I was * distressed by the Dan 8:27
voice—"O Daniel, * beloved of Dan 10:11
be * honored all around the world. Mic 5:4
"The Lord of Hosts says, I am * Zec 8:2
"Rejoice *, O my people! Zec 9:9
a dance that * pleased him, so he Mt 14:6
them and * pleased them all. Mk 6:22,23
The little boy * loved God Lk 1:80
custom. This * surprised his host. Lk 11:37,38
now will be * honored then; Lk 13:30
riot—a possibility they * feared. Lk 22:2
The world will * rejoice over Jn 16:20
people * multiplied in Egypt; Act 7:17,18
"God blessed David *, and David Act 7:46
in Greece, he was * used of God to Act 18:27
of the Lord Jesus was * honored. Act 19:17
us Jews and have * reduced the Act 24:2
They have cheered me * and have 1Co 16:18
You have * encouraged me; 2Co 7:4
work among you will be * enlarged. 2Co 10:15
church, saw how * God had used me Gal 2:7,8,9
been blessed so * in his preaching Gal 2:7,8,9
Yes, so much so that I * Php 3:6
So we are * comforted, dear 1Th 3:7
* bless him in everything he does. Jas 1:25
though they suffered * for it. Jas 5:11

GREATNESS
In the * of your majesty Ex 15:7
result of all the * and power you Deu 3:23,24,25
God has shown us his glory and *; Deu 5:24
seen his * and his awesome power. Deu 11:2
I will proclaim the * of the Deu 32:3
account of the * of Mordecai and Est 10:2
he merely overpower me with his *? Job 23:6
We cannot comprehend the * of his Job 37:5
the * of the miracles of God; Ps 64:9
Demonstrate the * of your power Ps 79:11
* from generation to generation. Ps 79:13
fields, for they display his *. Ps 96:12
I know the * of the Lord—that he Ps 135:5
Greatly praise him! His * is Ps 145:3
I will proclaim your *. Ps 145:6
Praise his unequaled *. Ps 150:2
In our * we have robbed their Is 10:14
contempt for all the * of mankind. Is 23:9
marching in the * of his strength? Is 63:1
to the * of his lovingkindness. Lam 3:32
Thus will I show my * and bring Eze 38:23
and great; your * reaches up to Dan 4:22
others is the measure of your *." Lk 9:48
All our * is like a flower that 1Pe 1:24
he shouted, "and extol his *. Rev 14:7

GRECIAN
meant that the * Empire will break Dan 8:22

GREECE
and Antipater of Macedonia and *. Dan 8:8f
is the nation of *, and its long Dan 8:21
and after him, the prince of *. Dan 10:20,21
an all-out effort against *. Dan 11:2f
he will plan total war against *. Dan 11:2
king will rise in *, a king who Dan 11:3
against the sons of *." Zec 9:13
over in Macedonia, *, pleading with Act 16:9
about going to *, and the believers Act 18:27
And upon his arrival in *, he was Act 18:27
to go across to * before Act 19:21
on ahead to * while he stayed Act 19:22
and left for *, preaching to the Act 20:1
He was in * three months and was Act 20:3
in northern * and five days later Act 20:6
Christians in * and they are 1Co 16:15
there in Corinth and throughout *. 2Co 1:1
will tell everyone in * about it! 2Co 11:10
to all the other Christians in *. 1Th 1:7

GREED
* causes fighting; Pro 28:25
You are full of selfish * and all Jer 22:17
In their * they have collected Hab 2:5
is foul with extortion and *. Mt 23:25
dirty—full of * and wickedness! Lk 11:39
and sin, of * and hate, envy, Rom 1:29
sex sin, impurity or * among you. Eph 5:3
These teachers in their * will 2Pe 2:3

GREEDILY
suddenly be gone, * snatched away Is 28:4

GREEDY
Then why are you so * for all 1Sa 2:29
father, for they were * for money. 1Sa 8:3
Though he was always *, now he Job 20:20
Literally, "all who are * of Pro 1:19f
He is * to get, while the godly Pro 21:25,26
And they are as * as dogs, never Is 56:11
I was angry and smote these * Is 57:17
All your * businessmen, all your Zep 1:11
sexual sin, or are * cheats and 1Co 5:10
sexual sins, or is *, or is a 1Co 5:11
Neither will thieves or * people, 1Co 6:9,10
who is impure or *, for a greedy Eph 5:5
or greedy, for a * person is really Eph 5:5
and must not be * for money. 1Ti 3:8
or fighters or * for money. Tit 1:7
They train themselves to be *; 2Pe 2:14

GREEK
in Hebrew as the * name "Jesus." Num 13:16f
The * Empire, founded by Alexander Dan 2:39f
This translation follows the * Hos 4:18f
The * word is not clear on this Mk 1:8f
The * word is not clear on this Mk 1:8f
The onlookers, who spoke * and Mk 15:34f
Philip's name was *, though he was Jn 12:21f
The * here is a very free Jn 12:40f
*, so that many people read it. Jn 19:20
Those who spoke only * complained Act 6:1
(his name in *), interfered and Act 13:8
Barnabas was the * god Jupiter, and Act 14:12
Jewess but his father a *. Act 16:1
his father was a * [and hadn't Act 16:3
number of godly * men, and also Act 17:4
* women and many men also. Act 17:12
shrines of the * goddess Diana. Act 19:24
"Do you know *?" Act 21:37,38
a * from Thessalonica, was with Act 27:2
last letters of the * alphabet. Rev 1:8f
* to Hebrew, becomes Balaamites; Rev 2:6f
Literally, "Nicolaitans," * form Rev 2:15f
not clear in the * as to whether Rev 3:10f
is Abaddon, and in *, Apollyon [and Rev 9:11

GREEK-SPEAKING
But then some * Jews with whom he Act 9:29

GREEKS
Jerusalem to the *, who took them Joe 3:6
Some * who had come to Jerusalem Jn 12:20
"If these * Jn 12:26
about the Lord Jesus to some *. Act 11:20
to convince the Jews and * alike. Act 18:4
and *—heard the Lord's message. Act 19:10
Ephesus, to Jews and * alike; Act 19:17
We are no longer Jews or * or Gal 3:28

GREEN
there remained not one * Ex 10:15
I see them spread before me as * Num 24:3-9
high hill and under every * tree. 1Ki 14:23
every hill and under every * tree; 2Ki 17:10
the hills and under every * tree. 2Ch 28:4
The decorations were *, white, Est 1:6
strong and virile, like a * plant; Job 8:16
Then he crowns it all with *, Ps 65:11,12
We are like grass that is * in Ps 90:5,6
produce fruit and be vital and *. Ps 92:14
*, destroying all the crops. Ps 105:35
* grass grow in mountain pastures. Ps 147:8
reeds. All * things along the Is 19:7
herds will graze in * pastures. Is 32:20
The deserts will become as * as Is 35:2
sheep, grazing in * pastures and on Is 49:8,9
he was like a tender * shoot, Is 53:2
The Lord used to call you his * Jer 11:16
Its leaves stay * and it goes Jer 17:8
and the * forests of Lebanon; Jer 22:6
and under every * tree and great Eze 6:13
that I make the * tree wither and Eze 17:24
ditch, with lush, * foliage because Eze 19:10
tree will die, * and dry alike. Eze 20:47
Its leaves were fresh and *, and Dan 4:12
with its fresh * leaves, loaded Dan 4:21
to lead her in * pastures. Hos 4:16
All his flowing springs and * Hos 13:15
the pastures will turn * again. Joe 2:22
the * forests of Lebanon wilt. Nah 1:4
each were sitting on the * grass. Mk 6:39,40
when the tree is *, what will Lk 23:31f
go in and out and find * pastures. Jn 10:9
And when the * shoot comes up 1Co 15:37
the grass turned * and the gardens Jas 5:18
—like * fruit from fig trees Rev 6:13
were burned, and all the * grass. Rev 8:7

GREENERY
and hills and blight their *. Is 42:15

GREENISH
and there is a * or a reddish spot Lev 13:49
If he finds * or reddish streaks Lev 14:37

GREENISH-YELLOW
chrysolite, giving off a * glow. Eze 10:9-13

GREET
bed to * him, and said to him, Gen 48:2
They will * you and offer you 1Sa 10:4
the tribe of Joseph to * you." 2Sa 19:20
of Israel were there to * him. 2Sa 19:40
As he stepped forward to * Amasa, 2Sa 20:8,9,10
his son Hadoram to * and 1Ch 18:10
Let us * the dawn with song! Ps 57:8
them, and then ran to * him. Mk 9:15
one to arrest when I go over and * Mk 14:44
home. * my good friend Epaenetus. Rom 16:5
the Lord approves; * him for me. Rom 16:10
for the Lord. * Rufus for me, whom Rom 16:13
* each other warmly in the Lord. 2Co 13:12

GREETED
* him warmly and brought him home. Gen 29:12,13
and they * each other warmly. Ex 4:27
father-in-law and * him warmly; Ex 18:7
found him, Saul * him cheerfully. 1Sa 15:13
to go on, David * them joyfully. 1Sa 30:21
in great fear and * the king in 2Sa 9:5,6
he was warmly * by Shobi (son of 2Sa 17:27
And they went to meet him and * 2Ki 2:15
After they had * each other, Jehu 2Ki 10:15
arrest the man he *, for that would Mt 26:48
When you came in and * me, the Lk 1:44
followers of Jesus * them with Lk 24:33,34
there among them, and * them. Lk 24:36
Ptolemais where we * the believers, Act 21:7

GREETING
If you shout a pleasant * to a Pro 27:14
Literally, "kissed," the * still Mt 26:49f
oriental *, even to this day. Mk 14:44f
At the sound of Mary's *, Lk 1:41
customary kiss of *, but she has Lk 7:45
him on the cheek in friendly *. Lk 22:47
This is still the traditional * Lk 22:47f
After * them, he showed them his Jn 20:19
standing among them and * them. Jn 20:26
So Paul stood, waved a * to them Act 13:16
Please give my * to the Christian Col 4:15
Here is my own * in my own Col 4:18
Now here is my * which I am 2Th 3:17
folks there a special * from me. 3Jn 1:15

GREETINGS
After exchanging * with the Ru 2:4,5
ambassadors with * and a present to 2Ki 20:12
"Sir: * from your loyal subjects Ez 4:11
"Gentlemen: *! Ez 4:18
"*! Ez 5:7
*! I want you all Dan 4:1
*! I decree that everyone Dan 6:25,26
and the respectful * from everyone Lk 11:43
in Antioch, Syria and Cilicia. *! Act 15:23
Jerusalem taking * and appreciation Act 15:33
After * were exchanged, Paul Act 21:19
Governor Felix. *! Act 23:26
Please give my * to all those who Rom 16:5
Please give them my *. Rom 16:7
And please give my * to Rom 16:14
churches here send you their *. Rom 16:16
my * too, as a Christian brother. Rom 16:22
sends you his * and so does Rom 16:23
in Asia send you their loving *. 1Co 16:19
the brothers with me send their * Php 4:21
Eubulus sends you *, and so do 2Ti 4:21
Everybody here sends *. Tit 3:15
Christ Jesus, sends you his *. Phm 1:23
Give my * to all your leaders Heb 13:24,25
scattered everywhere. *! Jas 1:1
in the Lord—sends you her *; 1Pe 5:13
* from the children of your 2Jn 1:13

GREW
and his face * dark with fury. Gen 4:5
When Seth * up, he had a son Gen 4:26
As the population * and spread Gen 11:2
Time went by and the child * and Gen 21:8
And God blessed the boy and he * Gen 21:20,21
As the boys *, Esau became a Gen 25:27
and the city that * up there was Gen 26:33
When his oldest son Er * up, Gen 38:6
As the trumpet blast * louder Ex 19:19
and the anger of the Lord * hot; Num 11:10
Then the anger of the Lord * hot Num 12:9
half brothers * up, they chased Ju 11:1
the Lord blessed him as he * up. Ju 13:24
Meanwhile Samuel * up in the 1Sa 2:21
As Samuel *, the Lord was with 1Sa 3:19
Philistines * louder and louder. 1Sa 14:19
afraid of him, and * to hate him 1Sa 18:29
Jericho until their beards * out; 2Sa 10:5
The battle * hotter and hotter 2Ch 18:34
Then Haman * pale with fright Est 7:6
within me * to the bursting point. Ps 39:2,3
the grapes that * were wild and Is 5:2
*, for thorns will cover them; Is 7:25
my eyes * weary of looking up for Is 38:14
where briars *, the myrtle trees Is 55:13
gods to love. You * weary in your Is 57:10
And you did! You * up and became Eze 16:6,7
It took root and * and became a Eze 17:6
* into a strong young lion, and Eze 19:3
moist earth. It * luxuriantly and Eze 31:4
It prospered and * long thick Eze 31:5
his hair * as long as eagles' Dan 4:33
The king * more and more Dan 5:9
its place * four good-sized horns Dan 8:8
Then I * faint and was sick for Dan 8:27
and I * pale and weak with fright. Dan 10:8
he * faint and wished to die. Jon 4:8
began to grow, the thistles * too. Mt 13:26
rock. It * up quickly enough, but Mk 4:5,6
seeds * and grew without his help. Mk 4:27
seeds grew and * without his help. Mk 4:27
and when he * up he lived out in Lk 1:80

(GREW Con't)
So Jesus * both tall and wise, Lk 2:52
this seed * and produced a crop Lk 8:8
MEANWHILE THE CROWDS * until Lk 12:1
rowed, and the sea * very rough. Jn 6:18,19
and * in strength and numbers. Act 9:31
So the church * daily in faith Act 16:5
stairs, the mob * so violent that Act 21:35
The shouting * louder and louder, Act 23:10
The next day as the seas * Act 27:18
faith and trust * ever stronger, Rom 4:20
a man my thoughts * far beyond 1Co 13:11
Moses, when he * up, refused to be Heb 11:24,25
earth * bright with his splendor. Rev 18:1
On each side of the river * Trees Rev 22:2

GREY-HAIRED
here, an old, * man who has been in 1Sa 12:2

GRIDDLE
something from the *, it shall be Lev 2:5
It shall be cooked on a *, using Lev 6:21

GRIEF
alive will live in sadness and *; 1Sa 2:33
This was a common expression of * 1Sa 4:12f
in their bitter * for their 1Sa 30:6
of the king's deep * for his son, 2Sa 19:2
up and tore his robe in * Job 1:20
I would try to take away your *. Job 16:5
"But now my * remains no matter Job 16:6
with * because of all my enemies. Ps 6:7
You know what trouble and * they Ps 10:14
I am pining away with *; Ps 31:9,10
I weep with *; Ps 119:28
When the laughter ends, the * Pro 14:13
Dishonest money brings * to all Pro 15:27
A rebellious son is a * to his Pro 17:25
the more my wisdom, the more my *; Ecc 1:16-18
Days full of sorrow and *, and Ecc 2:20-23
So banish * and pain, but Ecc 11:10
be a pile of * and incurable pain. Is 17:11
But my heart is heavy with *, for Is 24:15,16
clothes—wear sackcloth for your *. Is 32:11
acquainted with bitterest *. Is 53:3
Yet it was our * he bore, our Is 53:4
to bruise him and fill him with *. Is 53:10
you back from your *—a young wife Is 54:6
My * is beyond healing; Jer 8:18
stand amazed, silent, dumb with *. Jer 8:21
Desperate is my wound. My * is Jer 10:19
and cover their heads in *. Jer 14:3
* for their parents' death. Jer 16:7
Like a widow broken with *, she Lam 1:1
Although God gives him *, yet he Lam 3:32
sigh with * and broken heart. Eze 21:6
They shave their heads in * and Eze 27:31
* will be in many hearts among Eze 32:9
SADLY I SING this song of * for Amo 5:1
Bethel shall surely come to *." Amo 5:5
with universal *—king, prophet, Zec 12:12,13,14
wet-eyed with * and exclaimed that Mk 16:10,11
them asleep, exhausted from *. Lk 22:45
Just see how much good this * 2Co 7:11
Let there be sorrow and sincere * Jas 4:9
with anguished * because of all the Jas 5:1

GRIEF-STRICKEN
along behind, and many * women. Lk 23:27

GRIEVANCES
your imagined * against others. Job 36:17

GRIEVE
oh, how I * for you that the Lord Ru 1:13
A time to *; Ecc 3:4
an only son, and * bitterly for him Zec 12:10
within me and I * bitterly day and Rom 9:1

GRIEVED
and he was * by their misery. Ju 10:16
Wasn't I deeply * for the needy? Job 30:25
desert years and * his heart. Ps 78:40
Shouldn't I be * with them? Ps 139:21
against him and * his Holy Spirit. Is 63:10
The king was *, but because of Mt 14:9
Peter was * at the way Jesus asked Jn 21:17

GRIEVOUS
the people of Israel into * sin. 2Ki 15:18
for my people's * wounds, for they Jer 8:11
so merciful despite our * sins. Dan 9:18
greater than the * mourning for the Zec 12:11

GRIEVOUSLY
sinned against you *, yet help us Jer 14:7

GRILLED
baked, fried, or *—you are to bring Lev 2:8
sacrifice is baked, fried, or *. Lev 7:9

GRIM
truth have met together. * justice Ps 85:10

GRIND
and made to * grain in the prison. Ju 16:21
"How dare you * my people in the Is 3:15
Take heavy millstones and * the Is 47:2
They hiss and * their teeth and Lam 2:16
the young men to * their grain and Lam 5:13
and * his teeth and become rigid. Mk 9:18

GRINDING
those in deep and * poverty who Job 21:25
warriors for God, * their enemies' Zec 10:5

GRINDS
How he * on to the end of the Job 7:2
Water * the stones to sand. Job 14:18,19

GRIP
So Solomon's * upon the kingdom 1Ki 2:46
As soon as he had a firm * on the 2Ki 14:5
his * along the Euphrates River. 1Ch 18:3
and be freed from his painful *. Job 6:8,9
Terror shall * them, for God is Ps 14:5
free the city of God from their *. Ps 101:8
held the nations in your angry *. Is 14:6
you from the * of your enemies. Mic 4:10
not keep this man within its *. Act 2:24
might get such a * on me that I 1Co 6:12
to get out of the * of sin—for the Gal 3:21,22
and keep a strong * on the truth 2Th 2:15
others it will * their lives too, Phm 1:6
So take a new * with your tired Heb 12:12
he ruled them with an iron *; Rev 19:15

GRIPERS
These men are constant *, Jud 1:16

GRIPING
health; * brings discouragement. Pro 15:4

GRIPPED
Terror * them, as it did their Gen 42:35
Fear has * the people of Phi- Ex 15:14
Suddenly, fear * me; Job 4:14
my heart races; I am * by awful Is 21:4
Fright and pain have * us like Jer 6:24
Fear, anguish and sorrow have * Jer 49:24
pangs of terror * him like the Jer 50:43
and such terror * him that his Dan 5:6
Pain has * you like a woman in Mic 4:9
Amazement * the audience and Mk 1:27
Everyone present was * with awe Lk 5:26
and terror * them as it covered Lk 9:34
Awe * the people as they saw this Lk 9:43
Terror * the entire church and Act 5:11

GRIPS
When I think of it, terror * me. Job 23:15
Terror * them. Job 41:25
Frantic fear * me. Ps 57:6
are afraid. Fear * you with Is 13:8
him, and come to * with his laws: Is 56:4
Fear * the waiting people; Joe 2:6

GROAN
* beneath the power of the rich; Job 35:9,10
I am exhausted and crushed; I * Ps 38:8
For I * and weep beneath my Ps 55:2
Lest afterwards you * in anguish Pro 5:11
with the wicked in power, they *. Pro 29:2
he will * and cry like a woman Is 42:14
you will cry and * in Jer 22:23
her priests *, her virgins have Lam 1:4
Her people * and cry for bread; Lam 1:11
"Sigh and * before the people, Eze 21:6
and he shall * before the king of Eze 30:24
The cattle * with hunger; Joe 1:18
"Therefore I will make you * as Amo 2:13
Writhe and * in your terrible Mic 4:10
future glory, also * to be released Rom 8:23
These earthly bodies make us * 2Co 5:4
time to cry and * with anguished Jas 5:1

GROANED
"Kill me!" he * to his youthful Ju 9:54
him badly. He * to his armor 1Sa 31:3,4
he * to his chariot driver. 1Ki 22:34
"Get me out of here," he * to 2Ch 18:33

GROANING
The Israelis were * beneath their Ex 2:23
to pity by the * of his people Ju 2:18
because of all my * and despair. Ps 102:5
Babylon will fall, and the * of Is 21:2
* in travail together until now." Rom 8:22f

GROANINGS
And now I have heard the * of Ex 6:5

GROANS
I cannot eat for sighing; my * Job 3:24
help me or even to listen to my *? Ps 22:1
and heard the * of his people in Ps 102:20
Even the grass of the field * and Jer 12:4
I have heard Ephraim's *: "You Jer 31:18
be heard the * of the wounded. Jer 51:52
She * and hides her face. Lam 1:8
Hear my *! Lam 1:21
* that is loaded with sheaves. Amo 2:13

GROCERIES
Why pay for * that don't do you Is 55:2

GROOM
while celebrating with the *? Lk 5:34

GROOMED
well fed and well *, and there is Jer 5:28

GROOVES
upright, with * on each side to Ex 26:17

GROPE
You shall * in the bright Deu 28:29
They * like blind men in the Job 5:14
No wonder you * like blind men Is 59:10

GROPES
as the blind man * in darkness. Deu 28:29
man * and stumbles in the dark. Pro 4:19

GROPING
and *, without a guiding light. Job 12:24,25

GROSSNESS
It is because of the * of your Jer 13:22

GROTESQUE
and made it into a * parody," says Mal 2:8

GROUND
welled up from the * at certain Gen 2:6
man's body from the dust of the * Gen 2:7
Then you will return to the * Gen 3:19
For you were made from the *, and Gen 3:19
and to the * you will return." Gen 3:19
* from which he had been taken. Gen 3:23
blood calls to me from the *. Gen 4:10
banished from this * which you have Gen 4:11
this * which God has cursed." Gen 5:28-31
covering the * and lifting the boat Gen 7:17
higher above the *, the boat Gen 7:18
it could find dry *, but the dove Gen 8:8
Please sell me a piece of * for Gen 23:4
The * you are lying on is yours! Gen 28:13
Literally, "spilled it on the * Gen 38:9f
and they fell to the * before him. Gen 44:14
Ephron the Hethite for a burial *. Gen 49:29,30
*—one of his own Hebrew brothers! Ex 2:11
for you are standing on holy *. Ex 3:5
"Throw it down on the *," the Ex 4:3
the * will be covered with them. Ex 8:21
they were not yet out of the *. Ex 9:32
be able to see the *, and they will Ex 10:4,5
shall walk through on dry *! Ex 14:16
walked through the sea on dry *! Ex 14:22
chariots scraped along the dry *. Ex 14:25
as small as hoarfrost on the *. Ex 16:14
hot upon the *, the food melted and Ex 16:21
will be no food on the * today. Ex 16:25
up food from the * that day." Ex 16:28,29
be made with finely * wheat flour. Ex 29:2
quarts of finely * flour mixed with Ex 29:40
the tablets to the * as they lay Ex 32:19
metal cooled, he * it into powder Ex 32:20
made from finely * flour, baked Lev 2:4
be made of finely * flour without Lev 2:5
of the finely * flour with the Lev 6:15
flat upon the * before the Lord. Lev 9:24
your feet or crawl upon the *: Lev 11:29,30
in the water or crawls upon the *. Lev 11:46
quarts of finely * flour mixed with Lev 14:10
stray grains of wheat from the *. Lev 19:9
up the grapes that fall to the *. Lev 19:10
a bushel of finely * flour mixed Lev 23:13
baked from finely * flour, using a Lev 24:5-8
it from the * and crushed it into Num 11:8
three or four feet above the *. Num 11:31
Or, "The * was covered with them, Num 11:31f
the * before the people of Israel; Num 14:5
he fell face downward to the *. Num 16:4
downward to the * before the Lord. Num 16:22
a miracle and the * opens up and Num 16:30
the words when the * suddenly split Num 16:31
he fell flat on the * before him. Num 22:31
quarts of finely * flour mixed with Num 28:5
quarts of finely * flour mixed with Num 28:12
and six quarts of finely * flour Num 28:12
quarts of finely * flour mixed with Num 28:13
that runs along the *, or a fish. Deu 4:18
fertility to your * and to your Deu 7:13
my head and dashed them to the *! Deu 9:17
burned it and * it into fine dust, Deu 9:21
it out on the *, like water. Deu 12:16
pour it out upon the * like Deu 15:23
is lying on the *, or if you spy Deu 22:6
from the * you have given me.' Deu 26:10
her feet to the *—will refuse to Deu 28:56,57
And olive oil from stony *! Deu 32:13
Ark stood on dry * in the middle of Jos 3:17
crossed the Jordan River on dry *! Jos 4:22
Joshua fell to the * before him Jos 5:14
told him, "for this is holy *." Jos 5:15
are hidden in the * beneath my Jos 7:21
laid it on the * in front of him. Jos 7:23
in the parcel of * which Jacob had Jos 24:32
to the * in humble worship. Ju 2:19
his temples and into the *; Ju 4:21
is wet and the * is dry, I will Ju 6:37
while the * around it is wet!" Ju 6:39
but the * was covered with dew! Ju 6:40
people, and leveled it to the *. Ju 9:45
downward to the *, and that was Ju 13:20
the grain to the * along with all Ju 15:5
was lying on the * and killed a Ju 15:15
a hollow in the * and Samson's Ju 15:19
two gateposts, right out of the *. Ju 16:3
and burned the city to the *. Ju 18:27
that it almost made the * shake! 1Sa 4:5
the * before the Ark of Jehovah! 1Sa 5:3
honeycomb on the * in the forest, 1Sa 14:24,25
the man fell on his face to the *. 1Sa 17:48,49
down to the * through a window. 1Sa 19:12
spear in the * beside his head. 1Sa 26:5,6,7

GROUND Con't)
length upon the *, paralyzed with 1Sa 28:20
burned it to the *, carrying off 1Sa 30:1
He fell to the * before David in 2Sa 1:1
He stumbled to the * and died 2Sa 2:23
Mephibosheth fell to the * before 2Sa 9:8
Then David got up off the *, 2Sa 12:20
robe, and fell prostrate to the *. 2Sa 13:31
*—it can't be gathered up again. 2Sa 14:14
Joab fell to the * before the 2Sa 14:22
his face to the * and said, 2Sa 18:28
his bowels gushed out onto the *. 2Sa 20:8,9,10
snow on the *, took on a lion that 2Sa 23:20
the * with his face in the dust. 2Sa 24:20
ashes on it will spill to the *." 1Ki 13:3
once and fell to the * before him. 1Ki 18:7
the * shouting, "Jehovah is God! 1Ki 18:39
and they went across on dry *! 2Ki 2:8
she fell to the * before him and 2Ki 4:27
thistle and trod it into the *! 2Ki 14:9
but he held his * in the middle of 1Ch 11:14
pit when there was snow on the *. 1Ch 11:22
and fell to the * before the Lord. 1Ch 21:16
bowed to the * before King David. 1Ch 21:21
'You have reddened the * before 1Ch 22:8
Lord was there and it is holy *." 2Ch 8:11
fell to the * with his face to the 2Ch 20:18
lying on the *—not a single one of 2Ch 20:24
the shame-idols * into dust and 2Ch 34:4
heathen altars, * to powder the 2Ch 34:7
AS I LAY on the * in front of the Ez 10:1
with their faces toward the *. Neh 8:6
it be a * crop or from our fruit Neh 10:35
and fell down upon the * before Job 1:20
Then they sat upon the * with Job 2:13
the * or are tempted to despair. Job 4:3,4
If I start to get up off the *, Job 10:16
the storms, and floods the *. Job 12:15
to the * like a withered grape. Job 15:33
For God has * me down, and taken Job 16:7
that the * is wet from my wounds. Job 16:13
parched and barren * is satisfied Job 38:25-27
Fiercely he paws the * and Job 39:24
he drags across the * like a Job 41:30
crush me to the *, and trample my Ps 7:5
are ready to throw me to the *. Ps 17:11
I pinned them to the *; Ps 18:38
me open * in which to maneuver. Ps 31:8
In anger cast them to the *. Ps 56:7
like water into thirsty *. Ps 58:7
like a forest chopped to the *. Ps 74:5,6
it to the *—your sanctuary, Lord. Ps 74:7
to fall to the * among the tents. Ps 78:28
You cleared the * and tilled the Ps 80:9
all the trees lay broken on the * Ps 105:33
"Raze her to the *!" Ps 137:7
bones are strewn across the *, Ps 141:6,7
They have knocked me to the *. Ps 143:3
the frost upon the *, and hurls Ps 147:16
Literally, "He who tills his * Pro 12:11f
of smoke along the *, smelling of Sol 3:6
shall sit crying on the *. Is 3:25,26
a hunting * overrun by wildlife. Is 7:24
How you are cut down to the *. Is 14:12
of Babylon lie broken on the *." Is 21:8,9
and fall to the *, and everything Is 22:25
upon you and dash you to the *. Is 28:2
be hurled to the * and trampled Is 28:3
you will be trampled into the *. Is 28:18
that till the * will eat grain, its Is 30:24
the * will be covered with fire. Is 34:9
The parched * will become a Is 35:7
flow across the dry, parched *. Is 41:18
gods are falling out onto the *! Is 46:1
from a root in dry and sterile *. Is 53:2
and stay upon the * to water the Is 55:10
them stagger and fall to the *." Is 63:6
them out on the * before the sun Jer 8:2
be scattered like dung upon the *. Jer 8:2
If you stumble and fall on open * Jer 12:5
business has * to a halt; Jer 14:2
in grief. The * is parched and Jer 14:4
and lie mortally wounded on the *. Jer 14:17
* to rot and fertilize the soil. Jer 16:4
this city and burn it to the *. Jer 37:8
razed to the * and lie in ruins. Jer 47:5
be leveled to the * and her high Jer 51:58
sit upon the * in silence, clothed Lam 2:10
four wheels on the * beneath them, Eze 1:15
downward on the *, and heard the Eze 1:27,28
And I fell to the * on my face. Eze 3:23
I fell to the * on my face and Eze 9:8
Then I fell to the * on my face Eze 11:13
in fertile * beside a broad Eze 17:5
it in fertile * beside a broad Eze 17:12,13
in fury and thrown down to the *. Eze 19:12
where the * is hard and dry. Eze 19:13
and sit on the * shaking with fear Eze 26:16
I will destroy Tyre to the *. Eze 26:19
you down to the * and exposed you Eze 28:17
the slain shall cover the *. Eze 30:4
and cover the * with the slain. Eze 30:11
make his sword clatter to the *. Eze 30:22
and leave her fallen on the *. Eze 31:12
prepare the * and sow your crops. Eze 36:9
scattered everywhere across the *. Eze 37:1
were set back from the * floor. Eze 42:6
to the * with my face in the dust. Eze 44:4
It shall all be holy *. Eze 45:1
Then Nebuchadnezzar fell to the * Dan 2:46
fall flat on the * to worship King Dan 3:5
—fell to the * and worshiped the Dan 3:7
and roots in the *, banded with a Dan 4:15
and the roots were left in the *! Dan 4:26
on the *, on two feet, like a man; Dan 7:4
that it didn't even touch the *. Dan 8:5
fell down with my face to the *. Dan 8:17
lying face downward on the *. Dan 8:18
* face downward in a deep faint. Dan 10:9
* when thrown or allowed to fall. Hos 4:12f
plow the hard * of your hearts, Hos 10:12
death against the *, her pregnant Hos 13:16
The seed rots in the *; Joe 1:17
but they destroy it to the *; Joe 2:3
will be cut off and fall to the *. Amo 3:14
upon the * and cannot rise. Amo 5:2
pours it down as rain upon the *. Amo 9:6
are swept away—the very * on Mic 1:11
"I will destroy it to the *. Zep 1:2
will lie there rotting on the *." Zep 1:17
with fruit; the * will be fertile, Zec 8:12
set on fire and burned to the *. Zec 9:4
can fall to the * without your Mt 10:29
seed across the *, some fell beside Mt 13:4
he drops out. The * covered with Mt 13:22
The good * represents the heart Mt 13:23
to sit down on the *, and he took Mt 15:35
to the *, terribly frightened. Mt 17:6
dug a hole in the * and hid the Mt 25:18
on the *, and prayed, "My Father! Mt 26:39
And they fell to the * before Mt 28:9
it off the hard * and ate it. Mk 4:4
"The thorny * represents the Mk 4:18
the crowd to sit down on the *. Mk 8:6
dashes him to the * and makes him Mk 9:18
and he fell to the * writhing and Mk 9:20
and fell to the * and prayed that Mk 14:35
he fell to the * before him, face Lk 5:12
As he scattered the seed on the * Lk 8:5
The stony * represents those who Lk 8:13
and fell to the * before him, Lk 8:28
to sit down on the * in groups of Lk 9:14
knocked him to the * and threw him Lk 9:42
He fell flat on the * in front Lk 17:16
*, and your children within you; Lk 19:44
falling to the * as he prayed more Lk 22:44
of * Jacob gave to his son Joseph. Jn 4:5,6
Then he spat on the * and made Jn 9:6
they all fell backwards to the *! Jn 18:6
for you are standing on holy *. Act 7:33
and * their teeth in rage. Act 7:54
He fell to the * and heard a Act 9:4
the *, he found that he was blind. Act 9:8,9
its four corners, settle to the *. Act 10:11
And I fell to the * and heard a Act 22:7
try to find common * with him so 1Co 9:22
stand your * in defending him. 1Co 13:7
When you put a seed into the * it 1Co 15:36
For all you put into the * is a 1Co 15:37
it to cut out the * from under the 2Co 11:12
over the same old * again and Heb 6:1
Sea as though they were on dry *. Heb 11:29

GROUNDS
visited the parade * of the army of Ju 13:25
and all its public *—a canopy of Is 4:5
alongside the holy *, is garden Eze 48:18
AS JESUS WAS leaving the Temple *, Mt 24:1
to the execution * they came across Mt 27:32
to the execution * and their bodies Lk 17:37f

GROUP
*, perhaps the other can escape." Gen 32:8
on ahead, each * of animals by Gen 32:16
driving the first * that when they Gen 32:17
Also in the * were these seven Gen 46:23,24,25
This entire * of objects shall Num 4:10
ambassadors than the former *. Num 22:15
way they drink. In * 1 will be all Ju 7:5,6
it like dogs. In * 2 will be those Ju 7:5,6
As soon as I and the men in my * Ju 7:18
of this choral * of priests. 1Ch 16:7
This * included Obed-edom (the 1Ch 16:38
sent one * to engage the Syrians. 1Ch 19:10
The other *, under the command 1Ch 19:11
First, the * led by Jehoiarib; 1Ch 24:7-18
Second, the * led by Jedaiah; 1Ch 24:7-18
Third, the * led by Harim; 1Ch 24:7-18
Fourth, the * led by Se-orim; 1Ch 24:7-18
Fifth, the * led by Malchijah; 1Ch 24:7-18
Sixth, the * led by Mijamin; 1Ch 24:7-18
Seventh, the * led by Hakkoz; 1Ch 24:7-18
Eighth, the * led by Ahijah; 1Ch 24:7-18
Ninth, the * led by Jeshua; 1Ch 24:7-18
Tenth, the * led by Shecaniah; 1Ch 24:7-18
Eleventh, the * led by Eliashib; 1Ch 24:7-18
Twelfth, the * led by Jakim; 1Ch 24:7-18
Thirteenth, the * led by Huppah; 1Ch 24:7-18
Fourteenth, the * led by 1Ch 24:7-18
Fifteenth, the * led by Bilgah; 1Ch 24:7-18
Sixteenth, the * led by Immer; 1Ch 24:7-18
Seventeenth, the * led by Hezir; 1Ch 24:7-18
Eighteenth, the * led by 1Ch 24:7-18
Nineteenth, the * led by 1Ch 24:7-18
Twentieth, the * led by Jehezkel; 1Ch 24:7-18
Twenty-first, the * led by Jachin; 1Ch 24:7-18
Twenty-second, the * led by Gamul; 1Ch 24:7-18
Twenty-third, the * led by 1Ch 24:7-18
Twenty-fourth, the * led by 1Ch 24:7-18
Each * carried out the Temple 1Ch 24:19
the Rehabiah *, led by his 1Ch 24:21
the Izhar *, consisting of 1Ch 24:22
The Hebron *:Jeriah, Hebron's 1Ch 24:23
The Uzziel * was led by his son 1Ch 24:24,25
The Merari * was led by his sons: 1Ch 24:26,27
(Ja-aziah's *, led by his son 1Ch 24:26,27
Hosah, one of the Merari *, 1Ch 26:10
gate went to Shelemiah and his *; 1Ch 26:14,15
Obed-edom and his * (his sons were 1Ch 26:14,15
into an orchestral *, using 2Ch 29:25,26
And at this time another large * 2Ch 30:24
Another * returned to Jerusalem Ez 2:59
This * included the subclans of Ez 2:60
Next was a * of Levites working Neh 3:17
Another * returned to Jerusalem Neh 7:61
as they went. The * which went to Neh 12:31,32
The other *, of which I was a Neh 12:38
the tiny * shall be a mighty Is 60:22
but rather, a * of Arab tribes. Jer 49:30f
This * of structures was 175 Eze 42:2
Bethel had sent a * of men headed Zec 7:2
"Then he sent a larger * of his Mt 21:36
to, for he isn't one of our *." Mk 9:38
stepped forward—a * of men who say Mk 12:18
They are like a * of children Lk 7:32
After all, he isn't in our *." Lk 9:49
women from our * of his followers Lk 24:22,23
But the whole * was terribly Lk 24:37
A * of us were there—Simon Peter, Jn 21:2
a missionary by any * or agency. Gal 1:1
in your own little *—and there will Gal 5:20
of this special * because after 1Ti 5:11

GROUPED
the tribe of Judah * behind its Num 10:14

GROUPINGS
to their political *, languages, Gen 10:31

GROUPS
left the ark in pairs and *. Gen 8:18,19
and herds and camels, into two *; Gen 32:7
into two *, half of them standing Jos 8:33
* decided by the way they drink. Ju 7:5,6
men into three * and gave each man Ju 7:16
split into four *, stationing Ju 9:34
into three * hiding in the fields. Ju 9:43
two * cut them down in the fields. Ju 9:44
different language *), and Joktan. 1Ch 1:19
divided into six * named after the 1Ch 23:8,9
into four * named after his sons 1Ch 23:12
many * to serve at various times. 1Ch 24:3
into sixteen * and Ithamar's into 1Ch 24:4
to the various * by coin-toss 1Ch 24:5
and Levites. Two * from the 1Ch 24:6
These men were from the * of 1Ch 25:1
various * of priests and Levites; 1Ch 28:13
And these various * of priests 1Ch 28:21
and soon colorful * of fifty or a Mk 6:39,40
on the ground in * of about fifty Lk 9:14
day, met in small * in homes for Act 2:46
up into quarreling *, doesn't that 1Co 3:3
Then he took the two * that had Eph 2:15
language * throughout the world. Rev 13:7

GROVE
was living in the oak * at Mamre. Gen 18:1
them to a garden *, Gethsemane, and Mt 26:36
And now they came to an olive * Mk 14:32
and entered a * of olive trees. Jn 18:1
they arrived at the olive *. Jn 18:3
there in the olive * with Jesus?" Jn 18:26
crucifixion was near a * of trees, Jn 19:41

GROVEL
You shall * in the dust as long Gen 3:14

GROVES
your vineyards and your olive *. Ex 23:11
I gave you vineyards and olive * Jos 24:13
* and give them to his friends. 1Sa 8:14
numerous altars in the * of trees. 2Ki 16:4
in your * of "sacred" oaks. Is 1:29

GROW
It will * thorns and thistles Gen 3:18
These two years of famine will * Gen 45:6
and let his hair * in wild Lev 13:45
as willows that * by the brooks—and Lev 23:40
Any crops that do * that year Lev 25:6,7
crops that * wild in the fields. Lev 25:12
is why he must let his hair *. Num 6:5

(GROW Con't)
and let his hair begin to * again. Num 6:11
for buds will * on his rod! Num 17:5
would *, and he could do you good. Deu 8:16
you will have worked so hard to *. Deu 28:33
you settle down to * grain for Deu 29:6
will * bitter and poisonous fruit. Deu 29:18
the best of what the sun makes *; Deu 33:14
long his hair began to * again. Ju 16:22
could * up to be your husbands? Ru 1:11
would you wait for them to * up? Ru 1:13
Let no crops of grain * on your 2Sa 1:21
Hadad the Edomite to * in power. 1Ki 11:14
rain, and the crops * again!" 1Ki 17:14
And the child's body began to * 2Ki 4:34
continued to * until October. 2Ch 31:7,8
rushes without any mire to * in; Job 8:11-13
see their children * to maturity Job 21:8
then let thistles * on that land Job 31:40
Their young * up in the open Job 39:4
when evil men * rich and build Ps 49:16
They * sleek and fat. Ps 73:4
They will * constantly in Ps 84:7
My eyes * dim with weeping. Ps 88:9
* tall as the cedars of Lebanon. Ps 92:12
They will * old, like worn-out Ps 102:26
But you yourself never * old. Ps 102:27
My eyes * dim with longing for Ps 119:123
David's power shall *, for I Ps 132:17
grass * in mountain pastures. Ps 147:8
Listen, and * wise, for I speak Pro 4:1
For if I * rich, I may become Pro 30:9
which will *—perhaps it all will. Ecc 11:6
stump still lives to * again." Is 6:13
but from the stump will * a Shoot Is 11:1
and nettles will * in its forts, Is 34:13
cause the grain to * and to produce Is 55:10
were thorns, fir trees will *; Is 55:13
and a forest shall * at the top Jer 26:18
our eyes * dim. Lam 5:17
* as quickly as a willow tree. Eze 17:5
I let this tree * and prosper? Eze 17:9
tree wither and the dry tree *. Eze 17:24
"They must not let their hair * Eze 44:20
All kinds of fruit trees will * Eze 47:12
horns began to *, so that it was Dan 8:3
her—and let them * into a jungle; Hos 1:12
all living things * sick and die; Hos 4:3
And thorns and thistles will * up Hos 9:6
And if your children *, I will Hos 9:12
Thorns and thistles will * up to Hos 10:8
their faces * pale with fright. Joe 2:6
men alike will * faint and weary, Amo 8:13
for a vine to * up quickly and Jon 4:6
will * up from himself Zec 6:12
Literally, "He will * up in his Zec 6:12f
will * again to former size. Zec 10:8
When the crop began to *, the Mt 13:26
Let both * together until the Mt 13:30
For the soil made the seeds *. Mk 4:28
then the sun will * dim and the Mk 13:24
Figs never * on thorns, or grapes Lk 6:44
This seed began to *, but soon Lk 8:6
them and doesn't take root and *. Lk 8:13
* in love for God and each other. Act 14:22
and helping them * in the Lord. Act 18:23
that will help your church * Rom 1:11,12
everything began to * old and die, Rom 5:12
made the garden * in your hearts. 1Co 3:6
he is the one who makes things *. 1Co 3:7
So let us feast upon him and * 1Co 5:8
is helping others * in the Lord, 1Co 14:3
helps himself * spiritually, but 1Co 14:4
* in holiness and happiness. 1Co 14:4
ground it doesn't * into a plant 1Co 15:36
How weary we * of our present 2Co 5:2
and will make it * so that you can 2Co 9:10
your faith will * and that, still 2Co 10:15
* in Christ. 2Co 13:11
on helping you * in his grace until Php 1:6
* and become happy in your faith; Php 1:25
Let your roots * down into him Col 2:7
sinews and we * only as we get our Col 2:19
and so their sins continue to *. 1Th 2:16
make your love to * and overflow to 1Th 3:12
your patience has a chance to *. Jas 1:3
So let it *, and don't try to Jas 1:4
and the gardens began to * again. Jas 5:18
think about it—and * strong in the 1Pe 2:2,3f
Long to * up into the fullness of 1Pe 2:2,3
you will * to love them deeply. 2Pe 1:7
the more you will * strong 2Pe 1:8
mixed up too. But * in spiritual 2Pe 3:18

GROWING
* in a field and brought them to Gen 30:14
these spots are * dimmer, this is Lev 13:39
Olive trees will be * Deu 28:40
* richly month by month, Deu 33:14
"You are * old," the Lord said Jos 13:1
Little Samuel was * in two 1Sa 2:26
to Aijalon, * more and more faint. 1Sa 14:31
My eyes are * old and dim with Ps 6:7
Praise him for the * fields, for Ps 96:12
complete with their * crops; Ps 105:44
Sons vigorous and tall as * Ps 144:12-15
Godly men are * a tree that bears Pro 11:30
A * population is a king's glory; Pro 14:28
many trees were * on both sides Eze 47:7
out in a field, * higher and higher Dan 4:10,11
For the tree you saw * so tall, Dan 4:20
One of these, * slowly at first, Dan 8:9
the crowd was *, he instructed his Mt 8:18
Or, "is * weaker day by day." Mk 9:18f
When Jesus saw the crowd was * he Mk 9:25
in the Lord is * every day. 2Co 4:16
constantly * temple for God. Eph 2:21
is healthy and * and full of love. Eph 4:15,16
same time keep on * in spiritual Php 1:9
See that you go on * in the Lord, Col 2:7
of your * love for each other. 2Th 1:3

GROWL
They * over their victims like Is 5:30

GROWLED
So once more the people * and Ex 17:2
I tell you not to go?" he *. 2Ki 2:18

GROWLS
Even a young lion, when it *, Amo 3:4

GROWN
how your flocks and herds have *. Gen 30:29
he was fully *, she laid aside her Gen 38:14
of all the crops * throughout Gen 41:48
when Moses had * up and become a Ex 2:11
clothes haven't * old, and your Deu 8:4
men who had * up to take their Jos 5:7
young men with whom he had * up. 1Ki 12:8
blighted before it is half *. 2Ki 19:26
their beards had * out again. 1Ch 19:5
young men who had * up with him. 2Ch 10:8,9
Though its roots have * old in Job 14:8,9
yellow when half *, ignored by the Ps 129:6,7
abandoned, streets * up with grass, Is 27:10
you have * tired of me! Is 43:22
and your pubic hair had *; Eze 16:6,7
soil where it had * so well." Eze 17:10
For you have * strong and great; Dan 4:22
son, Isaac, was * up and married, Rom 9:10-13
how little you have * in the Lord? 1Co 3:4
way your faith has *, and because 2Th 1:3
the world have * rich from all her Rev 18:3

GROWS
science feeds upon itself and *. Gen 11:6f
But if the bright spot * no Lev 13:23
which * in cracks in the wall. 1Ki 4:33
again, and * tender, new branches. Job 14:7
They eat what they find that * Job 24:6
And by his power the sea * calm; Job 26:12
of yours; it * louder and louder. Ps 74:23
The tender grass * up at his Ps 104:14
wealth from hard work *. Pro 13:11
* up around him and rejects him! Ecc 4:16
and though it * so well that it Is 17:11
the earth, never * faint or weary? Is 40:28
all his might. He * hungry and Is 44:12
the refining fire * hotter, but Jer 6:29
take root and their business *. Jer 12:2
of plants, and * into a tree where Mt 13:31,32
of seeds, yet it * to become one of Mk 4:31,32
soon it * into a tall bush, and Lk 13:19
a different kind of plant * from 1Co 15:38
a slave until he * up, even though Gal 4:1
love within us * ever stronger. 1Jn 4:12
love * more perfect and complete; 1Jn 4:17

GROWTH
for God. For * in wisdom comes from Ps 111:10
The * of love between a man and a Pro 30:18,19
need for * in truth and holiness. Jn 17:19
as my pride in your * in the Lord. 1Co 15:31
a quiet * in grace and character. Heb 12:11

GRUDGE
Don't bear a *; Lev 19:18
He never bears a *, nor remains Ps 103:9
you are holding a * against, so Mk 11:25
don't sin by nursing your *. Eph 4:26

GRUDGES
It does not hold * and will 1Co 13:5
never hold *. Col 3:13

GRUDGINGLY
care for it willingly, not *; 1Pe 5:2

GRUMBLE
You lie and * and oppose the Is 59:3
Don't * about each other, Jas 5:9

GRUMBLED
But the people of Israel only * Num 17:12,13
they *. Ps 78:19,20
of a notorious sinner," they *. Lk 19:7

GRUMBLING
Laban's sons were *, "He owes Gen 31:1

GUARANTEE
our little ones. I * his safety. Gen 43:9
and here is my *: I will send the Is 38:7
in our hearts as * that we belong 2Co 1:22
for us and, as a *, he has given us 2Co 5:5
within us is God's * that he really Eph 1:14
Paul, personally * this by writing Phm 1:19
oath, Christ can * forever the Heb 7:22
us and we * that we have seen him; 1Jn 1:2

GUARANTEED
I have * him abundance of grain Gen 27:37

GUARANTEEING
between us, * to make you into a Gen 17:2,3,4
you hardly know, * his debt, you Pro 6:1

GUARANTEES
And he * right up to the end 1Co 1:8
that he * to bring us to himself. Eph 1:14

GUARD
a flaming sword to * the entrance Gen 3:24
palace *, the chief executioner. Gen 37:36
*, who was the chief executioner. Gen 40:1
the captain of the *, the chief Gen 41:10
the captain of the *, and he told Gen 41:12
remained behind to * their gear. 1Sa 25:13
and those who * the equipment." 1Sa 30:24
with an elite * from Joab's army 2Sa 20:7
the shields back to the * chamber. 1Ki 14:28
* and the queen's bodyguard. 2Ki 11:4
the Sabbath are to * the palace. 2Ki 11:5
shall stand * at the Temple; 2Ki 11:6,7,8
Jehoiada to the officers of the *. 2Ki 11:15
officers and the * and all the 2Ki 11:19
The captain of the * was 1Ch 26:1
They were assigned * duty at the 1Ch 26:13
12,000 cavalry to * the cities 2Ch 1:14
by the Levites on * duty there. 2Ch 34:9
"* these treasures well!" Ez 8:29
other half stood * behind them. Neh 4:16
and half the men were always on * Neh 4:20,21
could go on * duty as well as work Neh 4:22
near the wall must * the section of Neh 7:3
of my servants to * the gates so Neh 13:19
themselves and to * the gates in Neh 13:22
And an honor * keeps watch at his Job 21:30-32
No one can catch him off * or Job 40:24
and truth to * and watch over me, Ps 61:7
With them on * you can sleep Pro 3:24,25,26
Love her—she will * you. Pro 4:6
Above all else, * your Pro 4:23
Obey me and live! * my words as Pro 7:2
be on your * and don't stuff Pro 23:1
I will * and support you, for I Is 42:6
Babylonians. The * making the Jer 37:13
Literally, "the court of the *." Jer 37:21f
the captain of the *, and his men Jer 39:9
the captain of the *, and Jer 39:13
NEBUZARADAN, CAPTAIN OF the *. Jer 40:1
by Nebuzaradan, captain of the *. Jer 41:10
of the *, had left with Gedaliah. Jer 43:6
captain of the *, arrived in Jer 52:12
The captain of the * took along Jer 52:24,25
his captain of the *, and took Jer 52:30
* as they bask in false security. Dan 8:25
prince who stands * over your Dan 12:1
I appointed the prophets to * my Hos 9:8
my Temple like a * to keep invading Zec 9:8
Therefore * your passions! Mal 2:15
* them from insects and plagues. Mal 3:11
"They can * it safely enough." Mt 27:65
* to Pilate, the Roman governor. Mk 15:1
the entire palace *, dressed him in Mk 15:16,17
send his angels to * you and to Lk 4:9,10,11
under the * of sixteen soldiers. Act 12:4
others standing * before the prison Act 12:6
a member of the imperial *. Act 27:1
By traveling together we will * 2Co 8:20
longer to * us and lead us to him. Gal 3:25
So be on your *, not asleep like 1Th 5:6
he will make you strong and * you 2Th 3:3
is able to safely * all that I have 2Ti 1:12
* well the splendid, God-given 2Ti 1:14
and * your lips from telling lies. 1Pe 3:10

GUARDED
So why haven't you * your master 1Sa 26:15
supervised and * the Tabernacle. 1Ch 9:19
And Obed-edom and Jehiah * the 1Ch 15:24
The gatekeepers * the gates, and 2Ch 35:15
But we prayed to our God and * Neh 4:9
all of these you gave me. I * Jn 17:12
wanted to, though * by a soldier. Act 28:16
Until Christ came we were * by Gal 3:23
twelve gates * by twelve angels. Rev 21:12

GUARDEDLY
these matters very *, but the time Jn 16:25

GUARDHOUSE
past the *, and into the palace. 2Ki 11:19

GUARDIAN
you to be the anointed * cherub. Eze 28:14
Or, "and the * cherub drove you Eze 28:16f
your Shepherd, the * of your souls 1Pe 2:25

GUARDIANS
Samaria and to the * of Ahab's 2Ki 10:1
council and the * of Ahab's sons, 2Ki 10:5
He has to do what his * and Gal 4:2
the cherubim—the * of God's Heb 9:5

GUARDING
beside me, *, guiding all the way. Ps 23:4

(GUARDING Con't)
them and * their pathway. Pro 2:7,8
who had been * the tomb went to the Mt 28:11
village, * their flocks of sheep. Lk 2:8

GUARDPOSTS
"When we arrive at the outer * of Ju 7:17

GUARDRAIL
"Every new house must have a * Deu 22:8

GUARDROOM
passageway and along the * walls. Eze 40:16

GUARDROOMS
there were three * on each side; Eze 40:7-12
(or between) the *, projecting out Eze 40:7-12f
Beyond the * was a 10½-foot Eze 40:7-12
from the outside doors of the *; Eze 40:13
Here too there were three * on Eze 40:21
to side across the top of the *. Eze 40:21
Its *, pillars and entrance and Eze 40:29,30
the others. Its *, pillars and Eze 40:33
the others: The *, pillars and Eze 40:36

GUARDS
the cave and that * be placed there Jos 10:18
and the change of * when Gideon and Ju 7:19,20
the Gilead * challenged him. Ju 12:5
There weren't even any *, so they Ju 18:27
He shouted to his *, "Arrest 1Ki 13:4
the palace * used these instead. 1Ki 14:27
to the Temple, the * paraded before 1Ki 14:28
King David. The *, with weapons 2Ki 11:11
And Jehoiada set * at the Temple 2Ki 11:18
priests and the * of the Temple to 2Ki 23:4
Temple * to Babylon as captives. 2Ki 25:18
Berechiah and Elkanah were * for 1Ch 15:23
of their colleagues as *. 1Ch 16:38
sons were appointed as *. 1Ch 16:42
will be temple *, and four thousand 1Ch 23:4,5
THE TEMPLE * were from the Asaph 1Ch 26:1
were also appointed as Temple *: 1Ch 26:4,5
The divisions of the Temple * 1Ch 26:12
and Hosah. Six * were assigned 1Ch 26:17
storehouses. Six * were assigned 1Ch 26:18
The Temple * were chosen from 1Ch 26:19
to the Temple, the * would carry 2Ch 12:11
will stay at the entrance as *. 2Ch 23:4
Levite priests as *, and to 2Ch 23:18
they worked. The * at the Temple 2Ch 23:19
So I placed armed * from each Neh 4:13
servants, nor the * who were with Neh 4:23
while the * were still on duty. Neh 7:3
I also directed that the * be Neh 7:3
Teresh—who were * at the palace Est 2:21
joy! He * all that is mine. Ps 16:5
For the Angel of the Lord * and Ps 34:7
time King Saul set * at his home to Ps 59:1
you come and go, and always * you. Ps 121:8
was no reply. The * found me and Sol 5:7
and as the prison * watched, I Jer 32:12
three chief Temple *, one of the Jer 52:24,25
his servants and * to the four Eze 12:14
righteousness that * the land, who Eze 22:30
They may be Temple * and Eze 44:11
Only Michael, the angel who * Dan 10:20,21
the stone and posted * to protect Mt 27:66
white. The * shook with fear when Mt 28:4
strong and fully armed, * his Lk 11:21
of the Temple * to discuss the best Lk 22:4
of the Temple * and the religious Lk 22:52
Now the * in charge of Jesus Lk 22:63,64
locked, and the * were standing Act 5:23
he had the sixteen * arrested, Act 12:19
but instructed the * to treat him Act 24:23
* at the city gates to catch me; 2Co 11:32

GUDGODAH
"Then they journeyed to *, and Deu 10:7

GUERRILLA
When the Israeli * forces 2Ki 25:23
of Judah and the * leaders fled in 2Ki 25:26
of the Jewish * bands in the Jer 40:7
and the other * leaders came to Jer 40:13,14
the rest of the * leaders heard Jer 41:11
So Johanan and all the * leaders Jer 43:4

GUESS
bread, which I * you can have if 1Sa 21:4

GUEST
for the camels, and a * room." Gen 24:25
live with you as a * in your home. Lev 25:35
as a hired servant or as a *; Lev 25:40
he begged, "for he is my *. Ju 19:23
been set aside for the * of honor. 1Sa 9:23
such a fellow as this be my *?" 1Sa 21:14,15
Recently a * arrived at the home 2Sa 12:4
* in Israel, a foreigner in exile. 2Sa 15:19,20
it upstairs to the * room where he 1Ki 17:19
a beautiful * room for Tobiah. Neh 13:5
he had prepared a * room in the Neh 13:7
You have welcomed me as your *; Ps 23:5
For I am your *. Ps 39:12
home with Jesus as the * of honor. Lk 5:29
Be a * in only one home at each Lk 9:4
For I am going to be a * in your Lk 19:5
"He has gone to be the * of a Lk 19:7
you to show us the * room where he Lk 22:11
mother was a * at a wedding in the Jn 2:1
The honored * was thus singled Jn 13:26f
I am his *, and the church meets Rom 16:23
have of being a * in your homes? 1Co 9:4
Please keep a * room ready for Phm 1:22

GUESTS
to my home as my * for the night; Gen 19:2
your cattle or your house *. Ex 20:10
the old man said, "be my *; Ju 19:20
you get there; the * can't eat 1Sa 9:12,13
them above the thirty special *. 1Sa 9:22
with him as *, but they knew 2Sa 15:11
Adonijah and his * heard the 1Ki 1:41
Then Adonijah and his * jumped up 1Ki 1:49,50
Make them permanent * of the 1Ki 2:7
former * are now citizens of hell. Pro 9:18
sacrifice and sanctified his *." Zep 1:7f
notorious swindlers there as *! Mt 9:10
*, he issued the necessary orders. Mt 14:9
Many * were invited, and when Mt 22:3
"But the * he had invited merely Mt 22:5
is ready, and the * I invited Mt 22:8
banquet hall was filled with *. Mt 22:10
in to meet the * he noticed a man Mt 22:11
to be his dinner * so that they Mk 2:15
break his oath in front of his *. Mk 6:26
collectors and other * were there. Lk 5:29
Do wedding * go hungry while Lk 5:34
in front of all the other *. Lk 14:10
to notify the * that it was time Lk 14:17
and asked us to be her *. Act 16:15
on arrival we were * at the home of Act 21:16
habit of inviting * home for dinner Rom 12:13
He must enjoy having * in his 1Ti 3:2
are used for *, and the cheap ones 2Ti 2:20
They must enjoy having * in Tit 1:8

GUIDANCE
will continue to give them *." Num 27:21
and did not ask the Lord for *. 1Ch 10:14
Don't go to war without wise *; Pro 24:6
and men should come to them for *. Mal 2:7
Your '*' has caused many to Mal 2:8

GUIDE
go to the land I will * you to. Gen 12:1
a success, please * me in this way: Gen 24:42
please, if this is really so, * Ex 33:13
are going now, so they will * you. Jos 3:2,3,4
for the Lord will * you. 1Sa 10:7
then I will * you to them." 1Sa 30:15
watch over and * his descendants, 2Ki 8:19
to properly * my people— yes, I am 2Ch 1:11
of the seasons, or * the Job 38:32
the Lord) and * you along the best Ps 32:8
He will be our * until we die. Ps 48:14
your commands are my chart and *. Ps 119:19
For your laws are my *. Ps 119:66
because they are my constant *. Ps 119:98
who love you. * me with your laws Ps 119:133
your hand will * me, your strength Ps 139:10
* you into the new day. Pro 6:22
* a horse with a whip, a donkey Pro 26:3
You shall also be a light to * Is 42:6
And the Lord will * you Is 58:11
heart, who will * you with wisdom Jer 3:15
or prophetic vision to * them. Lam 2:9
You will long for a prophet to * Eze 7:26,27
a place where, my * told me, the Eze 46:19,20
to * us to the path of peace." Lk 1:79
comes, he shall * you into all Jn 16:13
You think that you can * the Rom 2:20
enough to be his counselor and *? Rom 11:34
our teacher and * until Christ came Gal 3:24
Most of all, let love * your Col 3:14

GUIDED
The Lord * them by a pillar of Ex 13:21
You have * them wonderfully Ex 15:13
to camp, and had * them by a pillar Deu 1:33
the east wind and * the south wind Ps 78:26
A good man is * by his honesty; Pro 11:3
prophet, who * and protected them. Hos 12:13
long ago. God * them by sending a 1Co 10:1
But why, you may ask, must I be * 1Co 10:29
When you are * by the Holy Gal 5:18
that you are * by wrong motives. Jas 2:4

GUIDELINES
him rules and * you must obey to Deu 24:8

GUIDES
men to assist you and be your *." Gen 33:15
him, every path he * us on is Ps 25:10
They are blind * leading the Mt 15:13,14
Blind *! Mt 23:16
Blind *! Mt 23:24
of the prophets were your *. Lk 16:16

GUIDING
from within the * cloud, there Ex 16:10
and groping, without a * light. Job 12:24,25
me, guarding, * all the way. Ps 23:4
You will keep on * me all my Ps 73:24
like a flock, * them safely through Ps 78:52
betrayed Jesus by * the mob to him, Act 1:16

GUILD
* Hall, opposite the Muster Gate; Neh 3:31

GUILT
and thus bear the * connected with Ex 28:37,38
and so brings * upon the people, he Lev 4:3
sin and bring his * offering to Lev 5:6
young pigeons as his * offering; Lev 5:7
you charge against him, as his * Lev 5:15
the ram of the * offering, and he Lev 5:16
to the priest as a * offering; Lev 5:17,18
It must be offered as a * Lev 5:19
his * offering to the Tabernacle. Lev 6:4,5
Tabernacle. His * offering shall Lev 6:6
and the entire * offering. Lev 6:17
the most holy offering for *: Lev 7:1
altar as a * offering to the Lord. Lev 7:5
offering and the * offering—the Lev 7:7
sin offering, and * offering, and Lev 7:37
the iniquity and * of the people, Lev 10:17
to the Lord as a * offering by the Lev 14:12
Tabernacle; this * offering shall Lev 14:13
blood from this * offering and Lev 14:14
with the blood of the * offering. Lev 14:17
male lamb for the * offering, to be Lev 14:21
the lamb for the * offering, and Lev 14:24
the lamb for the * offering and Lev 14:25
with the blood of the * offering. Lev 14:28
shall bring his * offering to the Lev 19:21
He shall bear his *. Lev 20:17
they shall bear their *. Lev 20:19
lamb a year old for a * offering. Num 6:12
he must bear his *. Num 9:13
offerings, and the * offerings are Num 18:9
a fair trial establishes his *. Num 35:12
Forgive us the * of this man's Deu 21:8
will put away the * from among you Deu 21:9
* to both the house and its owner. Deu 22:8
this would bring * upon the land Deu 24:4
Was our * at Peor—from which we Jos 22:17,18
"Send a * offering so that the 1Sa 6:3
"What * offering shall we 1Sa 6:4,5
Philistines as a * offering to the 1Sa 6:17
is because of the * of Saul and his 2Sa 21:1
ourselves of this * and to induce 2Sa 21:3
This will remove the * of his 1Ki 2:31
contributed for * offerings and sin 2Ki 12:16
* of their sin of idol-worship. 2Ch 34:5
* is as boundless as the heavens. Ez 9:6
* by offering rams as sacrifices): Ez 10:16-19
Stop assuming my *, for I am Job 6:29
Then prove my *! Job 19:5
Only then can I be free of * and Ps 19:13
WHAT HAPPINESS FOR those whose * Ps 32:1
All my * is gone. Ps 32:5
wash me, cleanse me from this *. Ps 51:2
common bond of rebels is their *. Pro 14:9
beneath their load of *. Is 1:4
gives them away and shows their *. Is 3:9
Yet God laid on him the * and Is 53:6
You are stained with * that Jer 2:22
Only acknowledge your *; Jer 3:13
for your sins are so many, your * Jer 30:14
It is because your * is great Jer 30:15
and again your * cries out against Eze 21:24
we pine away with *. Eze 33:10
sin offerings and * offerings to be Eze 40:39
sin offerings, and * offerings, for Eze 42:13
sin offerings and the * offerings. Eze 44:29
sin, and their * will be cleansed; Dan 9:24
of *, and Judah, too, shall fall. Hos 5:5
they admit their * and look to me Hos 5:15
Samaria must bear her *, for she Hos 13:16
not clear their oppressors of *. Joe 3:21
gone, but their * is deep, for they Hab 1:11
"But your * remains because you Jn 9:41
is freed from all * and declared Act 13:39
and * on that day when he returns. 1Co 1:8
their feeling of * would be gone. Heb 10:2
disobedience and * instead of Heb 10:3

GUILTLESS
* concerning their deaths." 1Ki 2:33
stand before him * on that day when 1Th 3:13

GUILTY
my kingdom * of this great sin? Gen 20:9,10
Why kill him and have a * Gen 37:26,27
the one who killed him is not *. Ex 22:2
and the man who kills him is *. Ex 22:3
* shall pay double to the other. Ex 22:9
Place, lest they be * and die. Ex 28:43
I refuse to clear the *, and Ex 34:7
not to do, all the people are *. Lev 4:13
it and is * of disobeying one of Lev 4:22
and doesn't realize it, he is *. Lev 4:27
what he knows about a crime is *. Lev 5:1
insect—is *, even though he wasn't Lev 5:2
kind, he becomes * as soon as he Lev 5:3
foolish vow he has taken, he is *. Lev 5:4
realizing it is * anyway, and must Lev 5:17,18
is certainly * before the Lord." Lev 5:19
day he is found * of any such sin, Lev 6:4,5
eats it shall be *, for it is Lev 7:17,18

(GUILTY Con't)
the Tabernacle is * of murder and Lev 17:3,4
third day you are *, for you Lev 19:8
with it, or you will be equally *. Lev 19:17
they be declared * and die for Lev 22:9
this law is * and is in great Lev 22:16
as to whether or not she is *. Num 5:15
bitter within her [if she is * Num 5:24
lest they be judged * and die. Num 18:22
and they shall be * if they fail. Num 18:23
You Levites will not be held * Num 18:32
Whenever anyone is judged * of Num 35:31
whether someone is * of murder when Deu 17:8
"IF A MAN is * of a crime, and Deu 25:1
tribe to which the * man belongs. Jos 7:14
Lord will point out the * clan; Jos 7:14
the * family must come one by one. Jos 7:14
Achan was found to be the * one. Jos 7:18
If a man is * of killing someone Jos 20:3
to them without being *.' Ju 21:22
Are Jonathan and I *, or is the 1Sa 14:41
O Lord God, show us who is *." 1Sa 14:41
sacred lot as the * ones, and the 1Sa 14:41
Jonathan was chosen as the * one. 1Sa 14:42
punish whichever one of us is *. 1Sa 24:15
Joab and his family are the * 2Sa 3:29
I swear that I will never be * of 2Sa 11:11
then if he finds that I am * of 2Sa 14:32
be forever * of these murders, and 1Ki 2:33
He was especially * because he 1Ki 21:26
The Levites who were *: Ez 10:23
citizens who were declared *: Ez 10:25
men found *, and impaled alive. Est 2:23
tell him boldly that I am not *. Job 9:35
me, as though I were proven *? Job 19:28
seen, or if I am * of any other Job 31:7,8
Declare me "not *," for you Ps 35:24
sinners, and they—* like me—will Ps 51:13
to leave their *, stubborn ways. Ps 68:21
Oh, do not hold us * for our Ps 79:8
judgment, let him be pronounced *. Ps 109:7
pronounced 'Not *' because this Is 6:7
murderers. The * will be found. Is 26:21
"Don't forget this, O * ones. Is 46:8
Who shall declare me *? Is 50:9
counted deeply *, and great evil Jer 2:3
is less * than treacherous Judah! Jer 3:11
are * both of murder and idolatry. Eze 22:4
They are * and must be punished. Hos 10:2
have condemned those who aren't *! Mt 12:7
you will become * of all the blood Mt 23:35
You can't come in here, * as you Lk 13:27
wouldn't be *," Jesus replied. Jn 9:41
"They would not be * if I had Jn 15:22
them they would not be counted *. Jn 15:24
them, "He is not * of any crime. Jn 18:38
clearly that I find him not *." Jn 19:4
"I find him not *." Jn 19:6
They are all * of treason, for Act 17:7
charges: "I am not *," he said. Act 25:8
You know very well I am not *. Act 25:10,11
hushed and * before Almighty God. Rom 3:19
us "not *"—if we trust Jesus Rom 3:21,22
yet now God declares us "not * Rom 3:24
sins and declared him "not *." Rom 4:3
sinner who is declared "not *" Rom 4:6
sins and declared him "not *." Rom 4:22
now that he has declared us not *? Rom 5:9
days judge them * of death for Rom 5:13
using them to make me * of death. Rom 7:11
declared us "not *," filled us Rom 8:30
manner, he is * of sin against the 1Co 11:27
* they are of breaking God's laws. Gal 3:19
slip, is just as * as the person Jas 2:10
and stand utterly * before him. Jas 2:11
the sins of all us * sinners, 1Pe 3:18

GULF
at the mouth of the Persian *. Gen 11:2f
boundary was on the * of Aqaba. Ob 1:1f
and the Persian *, who began to Hab 1:6f

GULL
The sea *, the hawk (any variety), Deu 14:11-18

GULLIBLE
You seem so *: you believe 2Co 11:4

GULP
Her nestlings * down blood, for Job 39:30

GUM
who were taking *, spices, and Gen 37:25
of * from the bark of a tree. Num 11:7

GUNI
Naphtali and his sons: Jahzeel, *, Gen 46:23,24,25
named after their ancestor *. Num 26:48-50
of *, was the leader of the clan. 1Ch 5:15
Jahzi-el, *, Jezer, Shallum. 1Ch 7:13

GUNITES
The *, named after their ancestor Num 26:48-50

GUNS
against the siege * of the enemy, Jer 33:4

GUR
the road climbs to *, near Ibleam. 2Ki 9:27

GURBAAL
with the Arabs of * and in his wars 2Ch 26:7

GUSH
So the Lord caused water to * Ju 15:19
streams that * from the mountains. Ps 104:10

GUSHED
he was told, and the water * out! Ex 17:5,6
the rock twice, and water * out; Num 20:11
his bowels * out onto the ground. 2Sa 20:8,9,10
and swords until the blood * out. 1Ki 18:28
seas when they * from the depths? Job 38:8,9
He opened up a rock, and water * Ps 105:41
he divided the rock, and water * Is 48:21
flood of water * out and swept Rev 12:15

GUSHING
ceased their *, and the torrential Gen 8:2
and found a * underground spring. Gen 26:19
* springs, valleys, and hills; Deu 8:7
water, as though * from a spring. Ps 78:15
For he caused * streams to burst Ps 114:8
earth with your * blood, filling Eze 32:6

GUSTS
them—not in little * but in a Jer 4:11,12

GUTTER
Now she lies in the * with no one Lam 1:9

GYROSCOPE
a wheel," perhaps as in a *. Eze 1:16f

H
pronounce the * and said, Ju 12:6

HA
the fall of Jerusalem, saying, '*! Eze 26:2
*! Look at you now Mk 15:29,30

HA-ELEPH
Taralah, Zela, *, Jebus (or, Jos 18:21-28

HAAHASHTARI
Ahuzzam, Hepher, Temeni, and *; 1Ch 4:6

HABAIAH
Three subclans of priests—*, Ez 2:61
named after *, Hakkoz, and Neh 7:63

HABAKKUK
prophet * in a vision from God: Hab 1:1
that * sang before the Lord: Hab 3:1
* 2:4. Rom 1:17f
As the prophet * says it, "The Gal 3:11

HABAZZINIAH
who was the son of *), and brought Jer 35:3

HABIT
And get into the * of inviting Rom 12:13

HABITATION
Literally, "in his holy *." Ps 68:5f

HABOR
the banks of the * River in Gozan, 2Ki 17:6
the banks of the * River in Gozan, 2Ki 18:11
They took them to Halah, *, Hara, 1Ch 5:26

HACHILAH
caves of Horesh on * Hill, down in 1Sa 23:19
and was hiding on * Hill. 1Sa 26:1

HACHMON
son of a man from *) was the leader 1Ch 11:11

HACHMONI
Jehiel (the son of *) was their 1Ch 27:32

HADAD
*, Tema,Jetur, Naphish, Kedemah. Gen 25:12-15
Succeeded by: King * (son of Gen 36:31-39
Succeeded by: King *, from the Gen 36:31-39
So the Lord caused * the Edomite 1Ki 11:14
apprehensive, for * was a member of 1Ki 11:14
killed all except * and a few royal 1Ki 11:16,17,18
* became one of Pharaoh's closest 1Ki 11:19
When *, there in Egypt, heard 1Ki 11:21
Rezon and * were his enemies, for 1Ki 11:25
Dumah, Massa, *, Tema, Jetur, 1Ch 1:28-31
When Husham died, * the son of 1Ch 1:46
When * died, Samlah from the city 1Ch 1:47
When Baal-hanan died, * became 1Ch 1:50

HADAD-EZER
officials of King * of Zobah who 1Ki 11:23

HADAD-RIMMON
of * in the valley of Megiddo." Zec 12:11f

HADAD'S
King * wife was Mehetabel, Gen 36:31-39
At the time of * death, the kings 1Ch 1:51-54

HADADEZER
the forces of King * (son of Rehob) 2Sa 8:3
River, for * had attempted to 2Sa 8:3
Damascus when they came to help *. 2Sa 8:5
over the army of *, he sent his 2Sa 8:9
him, for * and Toi were enemies. 2Sa 8:10
Philistines, Amalek, and King *. 2Sa 8:11,12
troops summoned by * from the other 2Sa 10:15,16
dominion of King * of Zobah (as far 1Ch 18:3
at the time * went to tighten his 1Ch 18:3
to help King *, David killed 1Ch 18:5
an alliance. For * and Tou had been 1Ch 18:10

HADADEZER'S
which King * officers had used. 2Sa 8:7
* cities of Betah and Berothai. 2Sa 8:8
of all of * forces. 2Sa 10:15,16
When * allies saw that the 2Sa 10:19
shields of King * officers to 1Ch 18:7
from * cities of Tibhath and Cun. 1Ch 18:8
had destroyed * army, he sent his 1Ch 18:9
King * commander-in-chief. 1Ch 19:16
Then King * troops surrendered 1Ch 19:19

HADASHAH
Zenan, *, Migdal-gad, Dilean, Jos 15:37-44

HADASSAH
* (also called Esther), whose Est 2:7

HADES
Literally, "into *." Lk 16:23f

HADID
From the subclans of Lod, *, and Ez 2:3-35
From the subclans of Lod, *, and Neh 7:8-38
Hazor, Ramah, Gittaim, *, Zeboim, Neh 11:31-35

HADLAI
Shallum, and Amasa the son of *. 2Ch 28:12

HADN'T
for the Lord God * sent any rain; Gen 2:5
But Abimelech * slept with her Gen 20:4
is my brother.' I * the slightest Gen 20:5
he owned. He * a worry in the world Gen 39:6
(for the Lord * yet told them where Jos 9:27
Moses * assigned any land to the Jos 13:14
"I swear that if you * killed Ju 8:19
"If you * plowed with my heifer, Ju 14:18
retirement things * been the same, 1Sa 8:5
me, and that you * arrived by the 1Sa 13:11
that even if you * spoken, we would 2Sa 2:27
of the Lord * yet been built. 1Ki 3:2
But he * listened, so now the 1Ki 11:9,10
For Jerusalem * seen a 2Ch 30:26
for I * told a soul about the Neh 2:11,12
Esther * told anyone that she Est 2:10
Esther still * told anyone she Est 2:20
saw that the fire * touched Dan 3:27
because they * turned to God. Mt 11:20
Those who * been able to say a Mt 15:31
Then the five who * any oil Mt 25:7,8
and Jesus still * come back, they Jn 6:17
If I * done such mighty miracles Jn 15:24
— for until then we * realized Jn 20:9
and yet the net * torn. Jn 21:11
Greek [and * permitted this before Act 16:3
free if he * appealed to Caesar!" Act 26:32
* I really made up my mind yet? 2Co 1:17

HADORAM
Jerah, *, Uzal, Diklah, Obal, Gen 10:26-30
Jerah, *, Uzal, Diklah, Ebal, 1Ch 1:20-23
he sent his son * to greet and 1Ch 18:10
King Rehoboam sent * to draft 2Ch 10:18

HADRACH
on the lands of * and Damascus, for Zec 9:1

HAGAB
Hagabah, Akkub, *, Shamlai, Hanan, Ez 2:43-54

HAGABA
Sia, Padon, Lebana, *, Neh 7:46-56

HAGABAH
Padon, Lebanah, *, Akkub, Hagab, Ez 2:43-54

HAGAR
girl named *, and gave her to Gen 16:1
So he slept with *, and she Gen 16:4
The Angel: "*, Sarai's maid, Gen 16:8
*: "I am running away from my Gen 16:8
* spoke of Jehovah—for it was he Gen 16:13
So * gave Abram a son, and Abram Gen 16:15
and the Egyptian girl *—teasing Gen 21:9
of God called to * from the sky, Gen 21:17
from the sky, "*, what's wrong? Gen 21:17
son of Abraham and * the Egyptian, Gen 25:12-15
is called "Mount *" by the Gal 4:24,25
slave-wife * represents Jerusalem, Gal 4:24,25

HAGAR'S
of water to * shoulders and sent Gen 21:14

HAGGAI
Judah at that time—*, and Zechariah Ez 5:1
* and Zechariah (son of Iddo). Ez 6:14
mentioned in Ezra, *, and Dan 5:31f
See * 1:6. Mic 6:14f
from the Lord. To: * the prophet, Hag 1:1
message through *, his messenger), Hag 1:13
sent them this message through *: Hag 2:1
the Lord through * the prophet: Hag 2:10
Then * asked, "But if someone Hag 2:13
* then made his meaning clear. Hag 2:14
Another message came to * from Hag 2:20
rebuilding the Temple. See * 1:1; Zec 4:6f

HAGGAI'S
* message from the Lord their God; Hag 1:12

HAGGARD
look so * morning after morning?" 2Sa 13:4

HAGGEDOLIM
assisted by Zabdiel (son of *). Neh 11:10-14

HAGGI
Gad and his sons: Ziphion, *, Gen 46:16,17
named after their ancestor *. Num 26:15-18

HAGGIAH
Uzzah, Shime-a, *, Asaiah. 1Ch 6:29,30

HAGGITES
The *, named after their ancestor Num 26:15-18

HAGGITH
was Adonijah, who was born to *. 2Sa 3:4
Adonijah (his mother was *) 1Ki 1:5
One day Adonijah the son of * 1Ki 2:13
fourth was Adonijah, the son of *. 1Ch 3:2

HAGGITH'S
you realize that * son, Adonijah, 1Ki 1:11
HAGGLES
says the buyer as he * over the Pro 20:14
HAGRI
Mibhar (son of *); 1Ch 11:26-47
HAGRITE
under the care of Jaziz the *. 1Ch 27:31
HAGRITES
defeated the * in war and moved 1Ch 5:10
They declared war on the *, the 1Ch 5:19
So the * and all their allies 1Ch 5:20
the * until the time of the exile. 1Ch 5:22
and Edomites and Moabites and *; Ps 83:6
HAGS
who have become old harlot *? Eze 23:43
HAIL
fields will die beneath the *!" Ex 9:19
and cause the * to fall throughout Ex 9:22
sent thunder and * and lightning. Ex 9:23
all Egypt without * that day was Ex 9:26
thunder and *, and I will let you Ex 9:28
and the thunder and * will stop. Ex 9:29
the thunder and * stopped, and the Ex 9:33
everything that escaped the *. Ex 10:4,5
eat everything the * has left." Ex 10:12
bit of vegetation the * had left; Ex 10:15
in fact, more men died from the * Jos 10:11
seen where * is made and stored? Job 38:22,23
and a mighty storm of *. Ps 18:12
and their sycamores with *. Ps 78:47
down murderous *, and lightning Ps 105:32
and hurls the * upon the earth. Ps 147:17
Let fire and *, snow, rain, wind Ps 148:8
a storm of * will knock it down! Is 28:17
labor with rust and mildew and *. Hag 2:16,17
him in mockery. "*, King of the Mt 27:29
Literally, "All *!" Mt 28:9f
them shouting, "* to the King!" Mk 11:9
I." "* to the King of the Mk 11:10
God bless the King of Israel! * Jn 12:13
purple. "*, 'King of the Jews!' Jn 19:3
his trumpet, and * and fire mixed Rev 8:7
God because of the terrible *. Rev 16:21
HAILSTONES
all gods has spoken—oh, the *; Ps 18:13
and terrible storms and huge *. Is 30:30
great * and mighty winds will Eze 13:11
of anger and with * of wrath. Eze 13:13
great *, fire and brimstone! Eze 38:22
from heaven; * weighing a hundred Rev 16:21
HAILSTORM
time I will send a * across the Ex 9:18
them with a great * that continued Jos 10:11
like a mighty * he will burst Is 28:2
there was a great * and the world Rev 11:19
was an incredible * from heaven; Rev 16:21
HAIR
with reddish * that one would think Gen 25:25
like the Hebrew word for "*." Gen 25:25f
linen, goat's *, red-dyed ram's Ex 25:1
is made of goat's * tarpaulins. Ex 26:7,8
fine-twined linen or of goat's *; Ex 35:5-9
the fine-twined linen or goats' *; Ex 35:23
to spin the goats' * into cloth. Ex 35:26
made of goats' * (uniformly Ex 36:14,15
not let your * hang loose as a sign Lev 10:6
If the * in this spot turns Lev 13:3
the skin, and the * in the spot has Lev 13:4
skin, and if the * at the spot has Lev 13:20
If the * in the bright spot turns Lev 13:25
skin and yellow * is found in the Lev 13:29,30
there is black * in it, then he Lev 13:31
and no yellow * has appeared, and Lev 13:32
shave off all the * around the spot Lev 13:33
* develops, declare him a leper. Lev 13:36
"If a man's * is gone, this does Lev 13:40
If the * is gone from the front Lev 13:41
and let his * grow in wild Lev 13:45
shave off all his *, and bathe Lev 14:8
shave all the * from his head, Lev 14:9
"You must not trim off your * on Lev 19:27
* or beards, nor cut their flesh. Lev 21:5
not let his * hang loose in Lev 21:10
He shall unbind her * and place Num 5:18
must never cut his *, for he is Num 6:5
that is why he must let his * Num 6:5
and let his * begin to grow again. Num 6:11
shave his long *—the sign of his Num 6:18
after which the * shall be put in Num 6:18
of leather, goat's *, or wood." Num 31:20
Your son's * must never be cut, Ju 13:5
weave my * into your loom Ju 16:13
And he woke up and yanked his * Ju 16:14
"My * has never been cut," he Ju 16:16,17
If my * were cut, my strength Ju 16:16,17
in a barber and cut off his *. Ju 16:19
But before long his * began to Ju 16:22
and his * shall never be cut." 1Sa 1:11
God that not one * on his head will 1Sa 14:45
its head on a pillow of goat's *. 1Sa 19:13
opponent by the * and thrust his 2Sa 2:16
brushed his *, changed his clothes, 2Sa 12:20
and dishevel your * as though you 2Sa 14:2,3
"that not a * of your son's head 2Sa 14:11
He cut his * only once a 2Sa 14:26
and his * caught in the branches. 2Sa 18:9
fixed her * and sat at a window. 2Ki 9:30
and pulled * from my head and beard Ez 9:3
and sprinkled dirt in their *. Neh 9:1
around and pulled out their *; Neh 13:25
my face—my * stood up on end. Job 4:15
White * is a crown of glory and Pro 16:31
your cheeks are, with your * Sol 1:10
of doves. Your * falls across your Sol 4:1
gold, and he has wavy, raven *. Sol 5:11
overcome me! Your *, as it falls Sol 6:5
behind your *. Sol 6:7
so your * is your crown. Sol 7:5
their well-set * will all fall Is 3:24
when your * is white with age. Is 46:4
who cut the corners of their *." Jer 49:32f
use balances to weigh the * into Eze 5:1
Keep just a bit of the * and tie Eze 5:3
to be a hand and took me by the *. Eze 8:3
and your pubic * had grown; Eze 16:6,7
"They must not let their * grow Eze 44:20
a * of their heads was singed; Dan 3:27
wet with dew; his * grew as long as Dan 4:33
as snow, his * like whitest wool. Dan 7:9
washed nor shaved nor combed my *. Dan 10:3
Ephraim's * is turning gray, and Hos 7:9
* and he wore a leather belt; Mt 3:4
for you can't turn one * white Mt 5:36
* and he wore a leather belt; Mk 1:6
and she wiped them off with her * Lk 7:38
tears and wiped them with her *. Lk 7:44
But not a * of your head will Lk 21:18
feet and wiped them with her *? Jn 11:1
with it and wiped them with her *. Jn 12:3
For not a * of your heads shall Act 27:34
then she should cut off all her *. 1Co 11:6
of their long *, while a man with 1Co 11:14,15
with long * tends to be ashamed. 1Co 11:14,15
way they fix their * or because of 1Ti 2:9,10
clothes, or * arrangement. 1Pe 3:3
band across his chest. His * Rev 1:14
Literally, "His head—the *—was Rev 1:14f
Their * was long like women's, Rev 9:8
HAIR'S
within a * breadth, never missing! Ju 20:16
HAIRCUTS
Regular, moderate * are all they Eze 44:20
HAIRS
gray * with sorrow to the grave. Gen 44:31
skin with white * in the spot, and Lev 13:9,10
there are no white * in this spot, Lev 13:21
there are no white * in the bright Lev 13:26
stopped and black * are found in Lev 13:37
then take a few * out and throw Eze 5:4
And the very * of your head are Mt 10:30
And he knows the number of * on Lk 12:7
HAIRY
Think how * Esau is, and how Gen 27:11,12
of gloves from the * skin of the Gen 27:16
Literally, "* ones." Lev 17:7f
"He was a * man," they replied, 2Ki 1:8
HAKKATAN
(son of *), and 110 other men; Ez 8:2-14
HAKKOZ
Seventh, the group led by *; 1Ch 24:7-18
priests—Habaiah, *, and Barzillai Ez 2:61
Meremoth (son of Uriah, son of * Neh 3:4
Meremoth (son of Uriah, son of * Neh 3:21
after Habaiah, *, and Barzillai (he Neh 7:63
HAKUPHA
Nephisim, Bakbuk, *, Harhur, Ez 2:43-54
Bakbuk, *, Harhur, Neh 7:46-56
HALAH
in the city of * and along the 2Ki 17:6
They took them to *, Habor, Hara, 1Ch 5:26
HALAK
the way from Mount *, near Seir, to Jos 11:17
Lebanon and Mount *, west of Mount Jos 12:7
HALATH
in the city of * and along the 2Ki 18:11
HALF
Israel was * blind with age, so Gen 48:10
shall also own * of the dead ox. Ex 21:35
Moses took * of the blood of Ex 24:6
The other * he splashed against Ex 24:6
His payment shall be * a dollar. Ex 30:13
Literally, "* a shekel after the Ex 30:13f
is twenty gerahs], * a shekel for Ex 30:13f
of pure myrrh; * as much of Ex 30:22,23
of fine flour, * to be offered in Lev 6:19,20
the morning and * in the evening. Lev 6:19,20
don't wear clothes made of * wool Lev 19:19
made of half wool and * linen. Lev 19:19
priestly and * ordinary." Lev 21:14,15
priestly and * ordinary." Lev 21:14,15
paid for him two and a * dollars; Lev 27:6
a girl, one and a * dollars. Lev 27:6
shall pay seven and a * dollars; Lev 27:7
body is * rotted away at birth." Num 12:12
of two and a * dollars made for Num 18:16
then divide it into two parts. * Num 31:27
and the other * is to be given to Num 31:27
So the * given to the army Num 31:36-40
The * of the booty assigned to Num 31:42-46
it from the * belonging to the Num 31:42-46
a * feet long by six feet wide. Deu 3:11
Arnon River, plus * of Mount Deu 3:12
than * the price of a hired hand! Deu 15:18
However, stay about a * mile Jos 3:2,3,4
into two groups, * of them standing Jos 8:33
and * at the foot of Mount Ebal. Jos 8:33
This includes * of the present Jos 12:2
the northern * of Gilead where the Jos 12:5
The other * of the tribe of Jos 13:8
of Gilead and * of the land of Jos 13:25
Jair in Bashan. * of Gilead and Jos 13:31
were given to * of the clan Machir, Jos 13:31
nine and a * tribes of Israel. Jos 14:1
to the two and a * tribes on the Jos 14:3,4
[The western * of the northern Jos 16:8
although the other * of the tribe Jos 22:7,8
and when these * brothers grew up, Ju 11:1
in our power!" * drunk by now, Ju 16:25,26
Then he tied up a bushel and a * Ru 3:15-18
over about * an acre of land. 1Sa 14:14
men and shaved off * their beards 2Sa 10:4
and sent them home * naked. 2Sa 10:4
And Prince Amnon (her * brother) 2Sa 13:1
in love with Tamar, my * sister." 2Sa 13:4
turn and run, and * of us die, it 2Sa 18:3
And most of Judah and * of Israel 2Sa 19:40
give * to each of these women!" 1Ki 3:25
He was * Jewish, being the son 1Ki 7:14
And really! The * had not been 1Ki 10:7
if you gave me * your palace, I 1Ki 13:8
who had charge of * the royal 1Ki 16:9
One day King Elah was * drunk at 1Ki 16:9
was split in two; * the people were 1Ki 16:21
and the other * followed Tibni, the 1Ki 16:21
blighted before it is * grown. 2Ki 19:26
of * of the Menuhoth tribe. 1Ch 2:52
Atroth-beth-joab, * the 1Ch 2:54
given to his * brother, Joseph. 1Ch 5:1
Over the other * of Manasseh, in 1Ch 27:16-22
Hur), the mayor of * of Jerusalem, Neh 3:9
He was the mayor of the other * Neh 3:12
mayor of * the Beth-zur district; Neh 3:16
the mayor of * the Keilah district, Neh 3:17
other * of the Keilah district. Neh 3:18
was completed to * its original Neh 4:6
but from then on, only * worked Neh 4:16
other * stood guard behind them. Neh 4:16
* the men were always on guard. Neh 4:20,21
Gate consisted of * of the leaders Neh 12:31,32
was feeling high, * drunk from Est 1:10
even if it is * the kingdom!" Est 5:3
even if it is * of the kingdom!" Est 5:6
even if it is * of my kingdom!" Est 7:2
Anyone even * bright will agree Job 34:34,35
will not live out * their days. Ps 55:23
Don't let me die * through my Ps 102:24
Who can ever praise him * enough? Ps 106:2
and yellow when * grown, ignored by Ps 129:6,7
with * a mind—if it is only open! Pro 8:9
"My life is but * done and I Is 38:10
has not committed * your sins. Eze 16:51
a * sister—this is common. Eze 22:11
87½ feet long—only * as long as the Eze 42:7,8
silver shekel (about * an ounce); Eze 45:12
bushel of flour with * a gallon Eze 46:14,15
his hands for three and a * years. Dan 7:25
three and a * years as at least a Dan 9:25f
people, but after * that time, he Dan 9:27
not end until three and a * years Dan 12:7
Literally, "a time, times, and * Dan 12:7f
Three and a * years (verse 7) plus Dan 12:11f
they will die; * shall be driven Joe 2:20
* a chair and a tattered pillow. Amo 3:12
the women raped; * the population Zec 14:1
as slaves, and * will be left in Zec 14:1
east to west, for * the mountain Zec 14:4
the north and * toward the south. Zec 14:4
from Jerusalem, * toward the Dead Zec 14:8
the Dead Sea and * towards the Zec 14:8
king vowed, "even * of my kingdom, Mk 6:22,23
Better enter the Kingdom of God * Mk 9:47
him lying * dead beside the road. Lk 10:30
another one for * that much!' Lk 16:5,6
now on I will give * my wealth to Lk 19:8
they walked the * mile back to Act 1:12
a *, teaching the truths of God. Act 18:11
the next three and one * years! Jas 5:17
for what seemed like * an hour. Rev 8:1
the three and a * years they Rev 11:6
the three and a * years of their Rev 11:7
and for three and a * days their Rev 11:8,9
But after three and a * days, the Rev 11:11

(HALF Con't)
Dragon, for three and a * years. Rev 12:14
"a time and times and * a time." Rev 12:14f

HALF-BAKED
as good-for-nothing as a * cake! Hos 7:8

HALF-BLIND
age when he was *, he called for Gen 27:1

HALF-BREED
Jews as being only "*" Hebrews. Lk 17:16f

HALF-BREEDS
the Samaritans "*," so the Lk 9:53f

HALF-BROTHERS
His job, along with his *, the Gen 37:2
all seventy of his *, except for Ju 9:5

HALF-BURNED
those left are like * firebrands Amo 4:11

HALF-CIRCLE
From there it will make a large * Num 34:10,11

HALF-SISTER
Meanwhile, Abram married his * Gen 11:29
at least a * (we both have the same Gen 20:11,12
nor his sister or *, whether the Lev 18:9
You may not marry a *—your Lev 18:11
she be a full sister or a *.' Deu 27:22

HALF-TRIBE
son of Nun, from the * of Num 13:3-15
(actually, the * of Manasseh); Num 13:3-15
32,500 in the * of Ephraim; Num 26:28-37
and 52,750 in the * of Manasseh. Num 26:28-37
In the * of Manasseh was the Num 26:28-37
The 32,500 registered in the * of Num 26:28-37
These women were of the * of Num 27:1
the * of Manasseh (son of Joseph). Num 32:33
and Gad and the * of Manasseh Num 34:14,15
Gad, and the * of Manasseh. Deu 3:12
its cities. The * of Manasseh Deu 3:13
and Gad and the * of Manasseh, that Deu 3:18
and Gad and to the * of Manasseh as Deu 29:8
Gad, and the * of Manasseh and Jos 1:12,13
Gad, and the * of Manasseh—fully Jos 4:12,13
of Reuben and the * of Manasseh. Jos 12:6
tribes and the * of Manasseh as I Jos 13:2-7
The Land Given to the * of Jos 13:29
territory to the * of Manasseh in Jos 13:29
(Ephraim and the * of Manasseh): Jos 16:1
territory of the * of Manasseh. Jos 16:9
THE LAND GIVEN to the * of Jos 17:1
The * of Manasseh was also given Jos 17:11
and Reuben and the * of Manasseh Jos 18:7
Dan, and the * of Manasseh. Jos 21:5
Naphtali, and the * of Manasseh. Jos 21:6
The * of Manasseh gave the cities Jos 21:25
from the * of Manasseh: Jos 21:27
Gad, and the * of Manasseh, and Jos 22:1
of Bashan to the * of Manasseh, Jos 22:7,8
Gad, and the * of Manasseh left the Jos 22:9
Gad, and the * of Manasseh, Jos 22:15
Gad, and the * of Manasseh to these Jos 22:21
Gad, and the * of Manasseh. 1Ch 5:18
The * of Manasseh spread through 1Ch 5:23
Gad, and the * of Manasseh. 1Ch 5:26
territory of the * of Manasseh. 1Ch 6:61
Kohathites by the * of Manasseh: 1Ch 6:70
Gershom by the * of Manasseh were: 1Ch 6:71
From the * of Manasseh, 18,000 1Ch 12:24-37
and Gad and the * of Manasseh 1Ch 12:24-37
Gad, and the * of Manasseh. 1Ch 26:31,32
Over the * of Manasseh, Joel (son 1Ch 27:16-22

HALFWAY
The middle bar, * up the frames, Ex 26:28
fit the grating * down into the Ex 27:5
The middle bar of the five was * Ex 36:33
ledge about * up [in the fire box Ex 38:4

HALHUL
Gibe-ah, Timnah, *, Beth-zur, Jos 15:48-62

HALI
Helkath, *, Beten, Achshaph, Jos 19:24,25,26

HALL
into the great * and placed them at 1Sa 9:22
elected to this * of fame to 2Sa 23:24-39f
the * of the Forest of Lebanon. 1Ki 7:2
windows in the *, set in three 1Ki 7:3,4
Another room was called the * of 1Ki 7:6
Room or Judgment *, where Solomon 1Ki 7:7
a courtyard behind this *. 1Ki 7:8
in the * of the Forest of Lebanon. 1Ki 10:16,17
gold, and in the * of the Forest of 1Ki 10:21
Guild *, opposite the Muster Gate; Neh 3:31
beyond the royal * of the palace, Est 5:1
to the wise men's * of fame. Pro 15:31,32
He brings me to the banquet * Sol 2:4
the upper assembly * of the Temple, Jer 36:10
you into my desert judgment *. Eze 20:35,36
the entry * of the passage; Eze 40:6
a 14-foot * with 3½-foot columns. Eze 40:7-12
Beyond this *, at the inner end Eze 40:7-12
There were windows, an entry * Eze 40:22
the doorway to the entry * inside. Eze 40:22
as the others did, and an entry *. Eze 40:25
entrance and exit * were identical Eze 40:29,30
and entrance * were the same size Eze 40:33
the walls and in the entry *; Eze 40:33
Its entry * faced the outer Eze 40:34
pillars and entry * of this Eze 40:36
Its entry * faced toward the Eze 40:37
But a door led from its entry * Eze 40:38
on each side of the entry * of Eze 40:39
Outside the entry *, on each Eze 40:40
walls of the entry *, and on the Eze 40:43
to the entrance * of the Temple. Eze 40:48,49
Thus the entry * was 35 feet wide Eze 40:48,49
The entrance * was 17½ feet wide Eze 41:2
and the entry * were paneled, and Eze 41:15,16
a wooden canopy over the entry *. Eze 41:25
sides of the entry *, the hallways Eze 41:26
the entry * of the passage." Eze 44:3
the outside entry * of the Eze 46:2
go in at the entry * of the Eze 46:8
to the banquet * and said to Dan 5:10
passing a hiring * and saw some men Mt 20:3
and the banquet * was filled with Mt 22:10
the section known as Solomon's *. Jn 10:22,23
out to Solomon's *, where he was Act 3:11
known as Solomon's *, and they did Act 5:12
at the lecture * of Tyrannus and Act 19:9

HALLELUJAH
But I will praise him. *! Ps 104:35
and obedient to his laws. *! Ps 105:45
*! Ps 106:1
all the people say, "Amen!" *! Ps 106:48
*! I want to express Ps 111:1
*! Ps 113:1
*! Praise the Lord. Ps 113:9
We praise him forever! *! Ps 115:18
*! Ps 135:1
for he lives here in Jerusalem. *! Ps 135:21
is King in every generation! *! Ps 146:10
*! Yes, praise the Lord! Ps 147:1
*! Yes, praise the Lord! Ps 147:20
*! Yes, praise the Lord! Ps 148:14
*! Yes, praise the Lord! Ps 149:1
He is the glory of his people. *! Ps 149:9
*! Yes, praise the Lord! Ps 150:1
*! Ps 150:6
of a vast crowd in heaven, "*! Rev 19:1
the throne, and said, "Amen! *! Rev 19:4

HALLOHESH
Shallum (son of *) and his Neh 3:12
Hananiah, Hasshub, *, Neh 10:14-27

HALLOW
and all the furniture, to * it; Ex 40:9
Revere me and * me, for I, the Lev 22:32,33
keep my ordinances; * my Eze 20:20

HALLOWED
Or, "* it." Ex 20:11f
I have * this Temple which you 1Ki 9:2,3
which I have * for my name and I 1Ki 9:7

HALLOWING
Literally, "* it." Lev 16:19f

HALLS
in the exit and in the entrance *. Eze 40:16
remodel your courts into true * Amo 5:15

HALLUCINATIONS
You will see * and have delirium Pro 23:33

HALLWAY
projecting out into the *. Eze 40:7-12f
with a * 12¼ feet deep behind it. Eze 41:3

HALLWAYS
entry hall, the * beside the Eze 41:26

HALO
* like a rainbow all around him. Eze 1:27,28

HALT
business has ground to a *; Jer 14:2
fingers and call a * to your Eze 22:13
He will * between Jerusalem and Dan 11:45

HALTED
Then Jesus * the crowd and Mk 5:37

HALTING
"my speech is slow and *." Ex 4:10f

HALVES
*, but not to divide the birds. Gen 15:10
between the * of the carcasses. Gen 15:17
nor shave the front * of your Deu 14:1
Literally, "like * of a Sol 4:3f
Literally, "like the * of a Sol 6:7f
its * to solemnize your vows. Jer 34:18,19

HAM
three sons, Shem, *, and Japheth. Gen 5:32
And he had three sons—Shem, *, Gen 6:9,10
*, and Japheth, and their wives. Gen 7:13
sons were Shem, *, and Japheth. Gen 9:18
Ham, and Japheth. (* is the Gen 9:18
* was not the ancestor of the Gen 9:18f
in his tent, *, the father of Gen 9:22
happened and what *, his younger Gen 9:24,25
THESE ARE THE families of Shem, *, Gen 10:1
The sons of * were:Cush, Gen 10:6
the descendants of *, spread abroad Gen 10:20
The Zuzim in *; Gen 14:5,6
Shem, *, and 1Ch 1:1
The sons of *: 1Ch 1:5-9
belonged to the descendants of *. 1Ch 4:40,41
houses of the descendants of *; 1Ch 4:40,41

HAM'S
had done, he cursed * descendants: Gen 9:24,25
The Canaanites were * Gen 9:24,25f

HAMAN
appointed * (son of Hammedatha the Est 3:1
Finally they spoke to * about it, Est 3:3,4
had given them. * was furious, but Est 3:5,6
* now approached the king about Est 3:8
his finger and giving it to *, Est 3:10
Literally, "*, son of Hammedatha Est 3:10f
* called in the king's Est 3:12
Then the king and * sat down for Est 3:15
and about the $20,000,000 * had Est 4:7
I want you and * to come to a Est 5:4
"Tell * to hurry!" Est 5:5
So the king and * came to Est 5:5
come again with * tomorrow to the Est 5:7,8
What a happy man was * as he left Est 5:9
This pleased * immensely and he Est 5:14
Now, as it happened, * had just Est 6:4
to the king, "* is out there." Est 6:5
king ordered. So * came in and the Est 6:6
* thought to himself, "Whom would Est 6:6
the king said to *. Est 6:10
So * took the robes and put them Est 6:11
* hurried home utterly humiliated. Est 6:12
When * told Zeresh his wife and Est 6:13
arrived to conduct * quickly to the Est 6:14
SO THE KING and * came to Esther's Est 7:1
Esther replied, "This wicked * Est 7:6
Then * grew pale with fright Est 7:6
palace garden as * stood up to Est 7:7
said, "Sir, * has just ordered a Est 7:9
"Hang * on it," the king Est 7:9
gave the estate of *, the Jews' Est 8:1
taken back from *—and gave it to Est 8:2
the palace of * and he has been Est 8:7
day as was set by * for the Est 8:12f
the ten sons of * (son of Est 9:7-10
of the time when * (son of Est 9:24,25

HAMAN'S
death veil was placed over * face. Est 7:8
It stands in * courtyard." Est 7:9
to be in charge of * estate. Est 8:2
to stop * plot against the Jews. Est 8:3
a decree reversing * order to Est 8:5
* message, too, had been sealed Est 8:8f
But they did not try to take * Est 9:7-10
exclaimed, "and also * ten sons. Est 9:12
today, and let * ten sons be hanged Est 9:13
hung up the bodies of * ten sons. Est 9:14
a decree causing * plot to Est 9:24,25

HAMATH
wilderness of Zin to Rehob near *. Num 13:21
to the entrance of * in the north; Jos 13:2-7
Baal-hermon to the entrance of *. Ju 3:1
When King Toi of * heard about 2Sa 8:9
of Israel between * and the Dead 2Ki 14:25
Damascus and * (which had been 2Ki 14:28
Cuthah, Avva, *, and Sepharvaim and 2Ki 17:24
and the men of * worshiped 2Ki 17:30
What happened to the gods of *, 2Ki 18:34
him at Riblah in * to prevent his 2Ki 23:33
of Egypt—to the entrance of *." 1Ch 13:5f
Zobah (as far as *) at the time 1Ch 18:3
When King Tou of * learned that 1Ch 18:9
as far away as * at one end of the 2Ch 7:8
cities in * as supply centers. 2Ch 8:4
he will say, "and * will go down Is 10:9
Elam, Babylonia, * and all the Is 11:11
what I did to * and Arpad? Is 36:19
to the king of *, to the king of Is 37:13
in the land of *, where he Jer 39:5
Damascus The cities of * and Jer 49:23
in the kingdom of *, and there Jer 52:9
Damascus and *, and finally to Eze 47:16
on the border with * to the north Eze 47:17
to the south and * to the north. Eze 48:1
then go to great * and down to Amo 6:2
all the way from * to the brook of Amo 6:14
"Doomed is *, near Damascus, and Zec 9:2

HAMATH-ZOBAH
the city of * and conquered it. 2Ch 8:3

HAMATHITES
Sinites,Arvadites, Zemarites, *. Gen 10:15-19
Arvadites, Zemarites, and *. 1Ch 1:13-16

HAMLET
a * on the eastern outskirts of Zec 14:5f

HAMMATH
Ziddim, Zer, *, Rakkath, Jos 19:35-39
who descended from *, the founder 1Ch 2:55

HAMMEDATHA
* the Agagite), as prime minister. Est 3:1
Literally, "Haman, son of * the Est 3:10f
Haman (son of *), the Jews' enemy— Est 9:7-10
when Haman (son of * the Agagite), Est 9:24,25

HAMMER
tent peg and a * and, quietly Ju 4:21
took a tent pin and a workman's * Ju 5:26
the sound of *, axe, or any other 1Ki 6:7

(HAMMER Con't)
in place with * and nails, so that Jer 10:4
Is it not like a mighty * that Jer 23:29
Babylon, the mightiest * in all Jer 50:23
to * his face with their fists. Mk 14:65

HAMMERS
with sledge * demolish your forts. Eze 26:9

HAMMOLECHETH
*, Machir's sister, bore Ishhod, 1Ch 7:18

HAMMON
*, Kanah, and Greater Sidon. Jos 19:28
Kedesh in Galilee, *, and 1Ch 6:76

HAMMOTH-DOR
(a City of Refuge), *, and Kartan. Jos 21:32

HAMMU-EL
Mishma's sons included * (the 1Ch 4:26

HAMOR
from the family of *, Shechem's Gen 33:19
son of King * the Hivite, saw her, Gen 34:2
Meanwhile King *, Shechem's Gen 34:6,7
* told Jacob, "My son Shechem is Gen 34:8
to Shechem and *, acting Gen 34:13
* and Shechem gladly agreed, and Gen 34:18,19
very popular. So * and Shechem Gen 34:20
there, including * and Shechem. Gen 34:26
for $200 from the sons of *. Jos 24:32
the sons of *, Shechem's father. Act 7:16

HAMOTH
What happened to the king of * 2Ki 19:13

HAMRAN
The sons of Dishon: *, Eshban, 1Ch 1:41

HAMSTRING
will all be dead! * their horses Jos 11:6

HAMSTRUNG
for they * the horses and burned Jos 11:9

HAMUL
sons of Perez were Hezron and *. Gen 46:8-14
named after their ancestor *. Num 26:19-22
Hezron and *. 1Ch 2:5

HAMULITES
The *, named after their ancestor Num 26:19-22

HAMUTAL
His mother's name: * (the daughter 2Ki 23:31,32
His mother's name: * (daughter of 2Ki 24:18,19
His mother's name was * (daughter Jer 52:1

HANAMEL
Your cousin * (son of Shallum) will Jer 32:6,7
anyone else. So * came, as the Jer 32:8
So I bought the field, paying * Jer 32:9
of my cousin * and the witnesses Jer 32:12

HANAN
Abdon, Zichri, *, Hananiah, Elam, 1Ch 8:22-25
Ishmael, She-ariah, Obadiah, *. 1Ch 8:38
She-ariah, Obadiah, *. 1Ch 9:44
* (son of Maacah); 1Ch 11:26-47
Hagab, Shamlai, *, Giddel, Gahar, Ez 2:43-54
Shalmai, *, Giddel, Gahar, Neh 7:46-56
Azariah, Jozabad, *, Pelaiah, and Neh 8:7,8
Pelaiah, *, Mica, Rehob, Neh 10:9-13
*, Anaiah, Hoshea, Neh 10:14-27
*, Anan, Malluch, Neh 10:14-27
and I appointed * (son of Zaccur, Neh 13:13
use of the sons of * the prophet Jer 35:4

HANANEL
of the Hundred and the Tower of *; Neh 3:1
and the Tower of *, and went on to Neh 12:39
of * at the northeast corner, Jer 31:38,39
of * to the king's wine presses. Zec 14:10

HANANI
Hananiah, *, Eliathah, Geddalti, 1Ch 25:4,5
Eighteenth, * and twelve of his 1Ch 25:9-31
About that time the prophet * 2Ch 16:7
(son of *) went out to meet him. 2Ch 19:2
of Jehu the son of *, which is 2Ch 20:34
*, Zebadiah. Ez 10:20
fellow Jews named * came to visit Neh 1:2
to my brother * and to Hananiah, Neh 7:2
Judah, and *. Neh 12:35,36

HANANIAH
*, Hashubah, Ohel, Berechiah, 1Ch 3:19,20
Zichri, Hanan, *, Elam, 1Ch 8:22-25
Shebuel, Jerimoth, *, Hanani, 1Ch 25:4,5
Sixteenth, * and twelve of his 1Ch 25:9-31
commander-in-chief was General *. 2Ch 26:11
Jeho-hanan, *, Ez 10:28
Beyond him was *, a manufacturer Neh 3:8
Next was * (son of Shelemiah); Neh 3:30
Hanani and to *, the commander of Neh 7:2
*, Hasshub, Hallohesh, Neh 10:14-27
*, leader of the Jeremiah clan; Neh 12:12-21
and * Neh 12:40,41
king of Judah—* (son of Azzur), a Jer 28:1
Then Jeremiah said to *, in front Jer 28:5
Then *, the false prophet, took Jer 28:10
and broke it. And * said again to Jer 28:11
Go and tell * that the Lord says, Jer 28:13
Then Jeremiah said to *, the Jer 28:15
prophet, "Listen, *, the Lord has Jer 28:15
enough, two months later * died. Jer 28:17
Zedekiah (son of *), and all the Jer 36:12
(son of Shelemiah, grandson of *). Jer 37:13
Daniel, *, Misha-el, and Azariah Dan 1:6
* was called Shadrach; Dan 1:7
look after Daniel, *, Misha-el, and Dan 1:11
Daniel, *, Misha-el, and Azariah. Dan 1:18,19
Then he went home and told *, Dan 2:17

HANANIAH'S
* sons were Pelatiah and Jeshaiah; 1Ch 3:21,22

HAND
So Noah held out his * and drew Gen 8:9
angels seized his * and the hands Gen 19:16
Literally, "put his * under the Gen 24:9f
born with his * on Esau's heel! Gen 25:26
destruction at the * of my brother Gen 32:11
("Son of my right *"). Gen 35:18
he drew back his * and the other Gen 38:29
wine cup in my *, so I took the Gen 40:11
Joseph took the boys by the *, Gen 48:12,13
left * and Manasseh at his right. Gen 48:12,13
so that his right * was upon the Gen 48:14
boy, and his left * was upon the Gen 48:14
his right * on Ephraim's head; Gen 48:17
"You've got your right * on the Gen 48:18
Put your right * on him!" Gen 48:18
do you have there in your *?" Ex 4:2
it became a rod in his * again! Ex 4:4
Now reach your * inside your Ex 4:6
holding in your * the rod that Ex 7:15
"Point your * toward heaven and Ex 9:22
So Moses held out his *, and the Ex 9:23
"Hold out your * over the land of Ex 10:12
"Stretch out your * again over the Ex 14:26
Your right *, O Lord, is glorious Ex 15:6
You reached out your * and the Ex 15:12
with the rod of God in my *!" Ex 17:9
whoever does shall die— no * Ex 19:13
and so on—* for hand, foot for Ex 21:24
and so on—hand for *, foot for Ex 21:24
you with my * until I have passed. Ex 33:22
Then I will remove my * and you Ex 33:23
on * now to complete the job!" Ex 36:4-7
it is to lay his * upon its head, Lev 1:4
shall lay his * upon its head and Lev 3:2
it shall lay his * upon its head Lev 3:7,8
he shall lay his * upon its head Lev 3:13
and shall lay his * upon its head Lev 4:4
He shall lay his * upon its head Lev 4:24
and there lay his * upon the head Lev 4:29
and lay his * upon its head and Lev 4:33
thumb of his right * and upon the Lev 8:23
thumb of his right *, and upon the Lev 14:14
palm of his left *, and dip his Lev 14:15
in his left * shall then be placed Lev 14:17
thumb of his right * and the big Lev 14:17
of the oil in his * shall be used Lev 14:18
thumb of his right * and on the big Lev 14:25
of his own left *, and with his Lev 14:26
olive oil from his * upon the tip Lev 14:28
thumb of his right *, and upon the Lev 14:28
The remaining oil in his * shall Lev 14:29
a broken foot or *, or has a Lev 21:19
from the woman's * and wave it Num 5:25
with money in *, and urgently Num 22:7
whether or not to * the killer over Num 35:24
Yes, the * of the Lord was Deu 2:14,15
Tie them to your * to remind you Deu 11:18
Your own * shall be the first Deu 13:9
shut your heart or * against them; Deu 15:7
debt cancellation is close at *! Deu 15:9
than half the price of a hired *! Deu 15:18
tooth, * for hand, foot for foot; Deu 19:21
tooth, hand for *, foot for foot; Deu 19:21
* shall be cut off without pity. Deu 25:12
Bring it in a basket and * it to Deu 26:2,3
* and set it before the altar. Deu 26:4
mighty miracles and a powerful *. Deu 26:8
you shall always have the upper *. Deu 28:13
but they are very close at * —in Deu 30:14
I raise my * to heaven Deu 32:40,41
with flaming fire at his right *. Deu 33:2
his strong left *, pulled out the Ju 3:21
delivered Sisera into your *!" Ju 4:14
threshing wheat by * in the bottom Ju 6:11
leading him by the *, "Place my Ju 16:25,26
and * it to the other party; Ru 4:7
to him, then his * will be as heavy 1Sa 12:15
Philistine's head still in his *. 1Sa 17:57
He had his spear in his *, and 1Sa 19:9,10
See what I have in my *? 1Sa 24:11
into your *, you didn't kill me. 1Sa 24:18
a present of whatever is at *." 1Sa 25:8
put out his * to steady the Ark. 2Sa 6:6
let him, but shook his * instead! 2Sa 15:5
his right * as though to kiss him. 2Sa 20:8,9,10
dagger in his left *, and Joab 2Sa 20:8,9,10
fingers on each * and six toes on 2Sa 21:20,21
For they tear the * that touches 2Sa 23:6
* was too tired to hold his sword; 2Sa 23:10
* and killed him with it. 2Sa 23:21
to fall into the * of the Lord (for 2Sa 24:14
so she sat at his right *. 1Ki 2:19
kingdom from the * of Solomon and 1Ki 11:31
(But the Lord's * was in it—he 1Ki 12:15
as a stable * shovels out manure. 1Ki 14:10
a man's * rising from the sea." 1Ki 18:44
I expected him to wave his * over 2Ki 5:11
"Then give me your *," Jehu 2Ki 10:15
surround the king, weapons in *, 2Ki 11:6,7,8
Then he told the king to put his * 2Ki 13:16,17
your weight and pierces your *. 2Ki 18:20,21
will * them over to their enemies. 2Ki 21:14
only a club in his * and pulled the 1Ch 11:23
out his * to steady the Ark. 1Ch 13:9
fingers on each * and six toes on 1Ch 20:6,7
writing from the * of the Lord." 1Ch 28:19
all mankind; your * controls power 1Ch 29:12
troubled the nation on every *. 2Ch 15:5
he delivered them all into your *. 2Ch 16:8
king, weapons in *, and kill any 2Ch 23:7
people from my *, and the God of 2Ch 32:17
been put into the * of the 2Ch 34:17
in his * and this is what it said: Neh 6:5,6
things from the * of God and never Job 2:10
They die beneath the * of God. Job 4:9
die beneath his *, and be freed Job 6:8,9
no one can save me from your *? Job 10:4-7
thing is in the * of God, and the Job 12:10
Yes, I will take my life in my * Job 13:14
me? Why * me over to my enemy? Job 13:24
the angry * of God has touched me. Job 19:21
and lay your * upon your mouth. Job 21:5
wicked from the * of the Almighty: Job 27:13
stretches out his * or cries for Job 30:24
them by kissing my * to them, Job 31:27
pass away, removed by no human *. Job 34:20
directed by his *, and do whatever Job 37:12
I lay my * upon my mouth in Job 40:4
shall my enemy have the upper *? Ps 13:2
Your right *, O Lord, supports Ps 18:35
Your *, O Lord, will find your Ps 21:8
Into your * I commit my spirit. Ps 31:5,6
*, safe from all conspiring men. Ps 31:20
All day and all night your * was Ps 32:4
the Lord holds them with his *. Ps 37:24
My life is no longer than my *! Ps 39:5,6
am exhausted beneath your *. Ps 39:10
Literally, "Your right * is Ps 48:10f
Bring them—submissive, tax in *. Ps 68:30
You are holding my right *! Ps 73:23
In Jehovah's * there is a cup of Ps 75:8
not one can lift a * against us. Ps 76:5
Literally, "that the right * of Ps 77:10f
"the man of your right *." Ps 80:17f
Strong is your *! Ps 89:13
Your right * is lifted high in Ps 89:13
You open wide your * to feed them Ps 104:28
"your shade at your right *." Ps 121:5f
* forget its skill upon the harp. Ps 137:5,6
your * of blessing on my head. Ps 139:5
even there your * will guide me, Ps 139:10
plenty of food on *, left from her Pro 7:14f
let your desires get out of *; Pro 7:25
on *, don't countersign a note. Pro 22:26,27
a thorn in the * of a drunkard. Pro 26:9
your mouth with your * in shame. Pro 30:32
pleasure is from the * of God. Ecc 2:24-26
A bird in the * is worth two in Ecc 6:9
On the other *, don't be too Ecc 7:15-17
His left * is under my head and Sol 2:6
with his right * he embraces me. Sol 2:6
His left * would be under my Sol 8:3
and his right * would embrace me. Sol 8:3
reached out his * to smash them. Is 5:25
his * is heavy on them still. Is 5:25
yet satisfied. His * is still heavy Is 9:21
Can a rod strike unless a * is Is 10:15
child who puts his * in a nest of Is 11:8
and wave his * over the Is 11:15
When his * moves, who can stop Is 14:27
I will * over Egypt to a hard, Is 19:4
The Lord holds out his * over Is 23:11
For the Lord's good * will rest Is 25:10
pierce your * if you lean on it. Is 36:6
you with my victorious right *. Is 41:10
Or, "with the right * of my Is 41:10f
I am holding you by your right * Is 41:13
that I'm holding in my *, a lie?" Is 44:20
God shall empower his right * and Is 45:1
nations that escape from Cyrus' *. Is 45:20
It was my * that laid the Is 48:13
the palm of my right * spread out Is 48:13
hidden me in the shadow of his *; Is 49:2
and hidden you safe within my *. Is 51:16
lifted up his *, and established Is 63:12
We are all formed by your *. Is 64:8
good as that? My * has made both Is 66:2
All the world will see the good * Is 66:14
I sit alone beneath the * of God. Jer 15:17,18
slip out of your *, and I will send Jer 17:4
As the clay is in the potter's *, Jer 18:6
potter's hand, so are you in my *. Jer 18:6
I will * over Judah to the king Jer 20:4
ring on my right *, I would pull Jer 22:24,25

(HAND Con't)
me: "Take from my * this wine cup Jer 25:15
I took them by the * to bring them Jer 31:32
Babylonians will * me over to the Jer 38:19
you and to deliver you from his *. Jer 42:11
I will lift my * against you and Jer 51:25
Day and night his * is heavy on Lam 3:3
in a moment without the * of man. Lam 4:6
before the * of judgment fell. Lam 5:7
Then I looked and saw a * holding Eze 2:9,10
but the * of the Lord was strong Eze 3:14,15
I was helpless in the * of God, Eze 3:22
He put out what seemed to be a * Eze 8:3
reached out his * (for each cherub Eze 10:7,8
from Jerusalem and * you over to Eze 11:9
and lies. My * shall be against Eze 13:9
His sword is in his *, and it Eze 21:5
It is ready now to * to the Eze 21:9,10,11
against them and * them out to be Eze 23:46
I will lay my * heavily upon you, Eze 25:7
By the * of my people, Israel, Eze 25:14
beneath her * and wrenched her Eze 29:7
Thebes shall lie in ruins by my *. Eze 30:14
and place my sword in his *. Eze 30:24
my sword into the * of the king of Eze 30:25
Now the * of the Lord had been Eze 33:22
Therefore I have sworn with * Eze 36:7
together in your * as one stick. Eze 37:17
and make them one stick in my *. Eze 37:18,19,20
was captured—the * of the Lord was Eze 40:1
holding in his * a measuring tape Eze 40:3
I have raised my * and taken oath, Eze 44:12
Literally, "his * shall attain Eze 46:7f
I promised with * raised in oath Eze 47:14
us out of your *, Your Majesty. Dan 3:17
fingers of a man's * writing on the Dan 5:5
be broken by the * of God, though Dan 8:25
But a * touched me and lifted Dan 10:10
*, only to take advantage of them. Dan 11:34
be able to rescue her from my *. Hos 1:10
a wall—and puts his * on a snake. Amo 5:19
For the Lord will remove his * Zep 3:15
man carrying a yardstick in his *. Zec 2:1
*, accusing Joshua of many things. Zec 3:1
plumbline in the * of Zerubbabel. Zec 4:10
Literally, "is at *." Mt 3:2f
Or, "is at *," or, "has Mt 4:17f
And if your *—even your right Mt 5:30
your right *—causes you to sin, cut Mt 5:30
* what your right hand is doing. Mt 6:3
hand what your right * is doing. Mt 6:3
But when Jesus touched her *, Mt 8:15
took her by the *, and she jumped Mt 9:25
Or, "at *," or, "has arrived." Mt 10:7f
there a man with a deformed *. Mt 12:10
And as he did, his * became Mt 12:13
Instantly Jesus reached out his * Mt 14:31
So if your * or foot causes you Mt 18:8
And they will * me over to the Mt 20:19
aides, 'Bind him * and foot and Mt 22:13
Sit at my right * until I put your Mt 22:44
right *, and the goats at my left. Mt 25:33
Literally, "he that dipped his * Mt 26:23f
sitting at the right * of God and Mt 26:64
stick in his right * as a scepter Mt 27:29
he took her by the * and helped her Mk 1:31
a man there with a deformed *. Mk 3:1
Would he heal the man's *? Mk 3:2
to the man, "Reach out your *." Mk 3:5
He did, and instantly his * was Mk 3:5
Taking her by the * he said to Mk 5:41,42
blind man by the * and led him out Mk 8:23
But Jesus took him by the * Mk 9:27
"If your * does wrong, cut it Mk 9:43,44
Better live forever with one * Mk 9:43,44
me to die and * me over to the Mk 10:33
sit at my right * until I make your Mk 12:36
sitting at the right * of God, Mk 14:62
and sat down at God's right *. Mk 16:19
For the * of the Lord is surely Lk 1:66
whose right * was deformed. Lk 6:6
with the deformed *, "Come and Lk 6:8
to the man, "Reach out your *." Lk 6:10
seen the * of God at work today." Lk 7:16
Then he took her by the * and Lk 8:54
sick man by the * and healed him Lk 14:4
"Sit at my right * until I place Lk 20:42,43
the feast of the Jews, was at *." Jn 6:2-5f
but no * was laid on him, for Jn 7:30
close at *, they laid him there. Jn 19:42
place my * into his side." Jn 20:25
Put your * into my side. Jn 20:27
the * and pulled him to his feet. Act 3:7,8
Jesus standing at God's right *. Act 7:55
beside God, at his right *!" Act 7:56
He gave her his * and helped her Act 9:41
And now God has laid his * of Act 13:11
to take his * and lead him. Act 13:11
Literally, "beckoning with the Act 13:16f
the boy by the *, and leading him Act 23:19
Literally, "stretched forth his * Act 26:1f
heat, fastened itself onto his *! Act 28:3
On the other *, if the Jews Rom 11:23
Don't let evil get the upper * Rom 12:21
because I am not a *," that does 1Co 12:15
The eye can never say to the *, 1Co 12:21
letter with my own *: if anyone 1Co 16:21
outside, trouble was on every * 2Co 7:5
you promised is on * and waiting. 2Co 9:5
at God's right * in heaven, far, Eph 1:20
with my own *, as I do at the end 2Th 3:17
here with my own *) but I won't Phm 1:19
I took them by the * to lead them Heb 8:9
at God's right *, waiting for his Heb 10:12
under the mighty * of God, in his 1Pe 5:6
stars in his right * and a sharp, Rev 1:16
but he laid his right * on me and Rev 1:17,18
saw in my right *, and the seven Rev 1:20
stars in his right * and walks Rev 2:1f
their leaders in his right *. Rev 2:1
AND I SAW a scroll in the right * Rev 5:1
from the right * of the one sitting Rev 5:7
a pair of balances in his *. Rev 6:5
And he held open in his * a Rev 10:2
lifted his right * to heaven, and Rev 10:5
So I took it from his *, and Rev 10:10
with a heavy *, and he was caught Rev 12:5
on the right * or on the forehead. Rev 13:16
forehead or the *, must drink the Rev 14:9
head and a sharp sickle in his *. Rev 14:14
and held in her * a golden goblet Rev 17:4
pit and a heavy chain in his *. Rev 20:1
The angel held in his * a golden Rev 21:15
and Zalmunna already in your *?" Ju 8:6f

HAND-TO-HAND
against each other in * combat. Zec 14:13

HANDCUFFS
he was put into * and shackles—as Mk 5:3,4
was—he snapped the * from his Mk 5:3,4

HANDED
In fact, the jailer soon * over Gen 39:22
whichever bird is * to him first, Lev 5:8
upon his head and * him a copy of 2Ch 23:11
You have not * me over to my Ps 31:8
history, stories * down to us from Ps 78:2,3
lives, but * them over to plagues Ps 78:50
me, but not * me over to death. Ps 118:18
And I have * over to him all your Jer 27:6
guards watched, I * the papers to Jer 32:12
and its body * over to be burned Dan 7:11
And they * him a penny. Mt 22:19
When they * it to him he asked, Mk 12:16
and * him over to be crucified. Mk 15:15
the prophet was * to him, and he Lk 4:17
He closed the book and * it back Lk 4:20
boy and * him over to his father. Lk 9:42
The next day he * the innkeeper Lk 10:35
I will be * over to the Gentiles Lk 18:32
arrested him and * him over to the Lk 24:20
in Jerusalem and * over to the Act 28:17
four Living Beings * each of them a Rev 15:7

HANDFUL
Then he is to take a *, Lev 2:2
shall take out a * as a Lev 5:12
then take out a * of the finely Lev 6:15
After taking out this *, the Lev 6:16
offering, taking a * and burning it Lev 9:17
remains after the * has been Lev 10:12
He shall take a *, representing Num 5:26
it, and burn the * upon the altar, Num 5:26
And I have only a * of flour left 1Ki 17:12
there was only a * of survivors and Jer 37:10
and take a * of glowing coals and Eze 10:2
with a mere * of followers, he Dan 11:23

HANDFULS
* of it, but don't use a sickle. Deu 23:25
turn Samaria into * of dust!" 1Ki 20:10
For the sake of a few paltry * Eze 13:19
the air and tossed up * of dust. Act 22:23

HANDICAPPED
he saw a seriously * woman who had Lk 13:11
was * by a disease of the eyes. Gal 4:15f

HANDKERCHIEFS
that even when his * or parts of Act 19:12

HANDLE
all such as * the harp and pipe." Gen 4:21f
you to try to * all by yourself. Ex 18:18
you are not to * the transaction in Ex 22:25
* the situation as outlined above. Num 5:30
shall personally * all the sacred Num 18:7
have appointed to * the dividing up Num 34:16-28
for you, and I will * them.' Deu 1:17
head flies off the * and kills the Deu 19:5
for him to *, he turned back home. Ju 18:26
my child; I'll * all the details, Ru 3:11
altar was too small to * so much. 1Ki 8:64
the giant; the * of his spear was 1Ch 20:5
Wait for the Lord to * the Pro 20:22
who * the shield and bend the bow! Jer 46:9
They will be able even to * Mk 16:18
an accountant to * his affairs, but Lk 16:1
Lord himself will * these cases." Heb 10:30

HANDLED
before because we * the matter 1Ch 15:13
In this way King Hezekiah * the 2Ch 31:20
kill them, Daniel * the situation Dan 2:14

HANDLES
by the people or * the gifts Lev 22:3

HANDLING
and incense, * all the tasks 1Ch 6:49
gold hooks used in * the 1Ch 28:17
the way Daniel was * his affairs so Dan 6:4
'You have been faithful in * this Mt 25:21
military unit * the executions saw Lk 23:47
the way we are * this large gift. 2Co 8:20

HANDMADE
* gods are hated by the Lord.' Deu 27:15
one of the heathen gods—a * idol! 2Ch 32:19
that * gods aren't gods at all. Act 19:26

HANDPICKED
one by one like * grain, selecting Is 27:12

HANDS
his hand and the * of his wife and Gen 19:16
Jacob's, but the * are Esau's!" Gen 27:22
could lay their * on, both inside Gen 34:28
out to lay his * upon the boys' Gen 48:14
his face with his *, for he was Ex 3:6
will spread out my * to the Lord, Ex 9:29
and lifted his * to heaven to the Ex 9:33
Moses, "Lift your * to heaven, and Ex 10:21
your walking sticks in your *; Ex 12:11
upon your * or your forehead. Ex 13:9
rod in his *, Israel was winning; Ex 17:11
holding up his * until sunset. Ex 17:12
shall lay their * upon its head; Ex 29:10
shall lay their * upon the head of Ex 29:15,16
* upon its head as it is killed. Ex 29:19,20
Place these in the * of Aaron and Ex 29:24
them from their * and burn them on Ex 29:25
shall wash their * and feet there, Ex 30:19
holding in his * the Ten Ex 32:15
the two stone tablets in his *. Ex 34:4
washed their * and feet there. Ex 40:31
of the nation shall lay their * Lev 4:15
it personally with his own *. Lev 7:29
sons laid their * upon its head as Lev 8:14
Aaron and his sons laid their * Lev 8:18
Aaron and his sons laid their * Lev 8:22
All this was placed in the * of Lev 8:27
Then, with * spread out towards Lev 9:22
first rinsing his *, that person Lev 15:11
Lord, and fill his * with sweet Lev 16:12
and, laying both * upon its head, Lev 16:21
him to lay their * upon his head; Lev 24:13,14
offering in her * to determine Num 5:18
and put them all into the man's *. Num 6:19
of the tribes shall lay their * Num 8:10
shall lay their * upon the heads Num 8:12
Striking his * together in anger Num 24:10
Moses laid his * upon him and Num 27:23
* of Israel, as has now been done. Deu 2:30
your God delivers into your *. Deu 7:16
kings into your *, and you will Deu 7:24
holding in my * the two tablets Deu 9:15
then the * of all the people. Deu 13:9
shall wash their * over the heifer, Deu 21:6
and say, 'Our * have not shed this Deu 21:7
His holy ones are in his *. Deu 33:3
for Moses had laid his * upon him; Deu 34:9
But now we are in your *; Jos 9:25
the water in their * to get it to Ju 7:5,6
of the men drank from their *; Ju 7:5,6
in their right *, and holding the Ju 7:19,20
in their left *, all yelling, "For Ju 7:19,20
my * against the two pillars. Ju 16:25,26
her * digging into the threshold. Ju 19:27
This time his head and * had been 1Sa 5:4
So they clambered up on their * 1Sa 14:13
they sadly shook *, tears running 1Sa 20:41
children into God's * forever." 1Sa 20:42
into your own *, I pray by the life 1Sa 25:26
who took the law into his own *! 1Sa 25:30,31
out vengeance with my own *. 1Sa 25:33
"Your * were not bound, 2Sa 3:33,34
They cut off their * and feet and 2Sa 4:12
head in her * went away crying. 2Sa 13:19
Literally, "the * of all who are 2Sa 16:21f
his face with his * and kept on 2Sa 19:4
For my * were clean; 2Sa 22:21
great) than into the * of men." 2Sa 24:14
the Lord with his * spread out 1Ki 8:22,23
his * outstretched toward heaven. 1Ki 8:54,55
and his * upon the child's hands. 2Ki 4:34
and his hands upon the child's *. 2Ki 4:34
her skull, her feet, and her *. 2Ki 9:35
go through their *, lest it be 2Ki 12:8
his own * upon the king's hands. 2Ki 13:16,17
his own hands upon the king's *. 2Ki 13:16,17
left * as readily as their right! 1Ch 12:2
me fall into the * of the Lord 1Ch 21:13
who laid their * upon them. 2Ch 29:23
and lifted my * to the Lord, and Ez 9:5
and lifted their * toward heaven; Neh 8:6

(HANDS Con't)
passes into the * of the kings whom Neh 9:37
decided not to lay * on Mordecai Est 3:5,6
The whole earth is in the * of Job 9:24
and cleanse my * with lye to make Job 9:30
stretch out your * to him, get rid Job 11:13,14
sinners, into the * of the wicked. Job 16:11
even sinners by your pure *." Job 22:30
laid their * upon their mouths. Job 29:9
He fills his * with lightning Job 36:32
"If you lay your * upon him, you Job 41:8
see how I suffer at the * of Ps 9:13
me—I who was helpless in their *. Ps 18:17
they have pierced my * and feet. Ps 22:16
Only those with pure * and Ps 24:4
I wash my * to prove my Ps 26:6
Don't let me fall into their *! Ps 27:12
Lord, I lift my * to heaven Ps 28:2
my times are in your *. Ps 31:14,15
Don't let their wicked * push me Ps 36:11
violence of your * in the land." Ps 58:1f
their weapons useless in their *. Ps 58:7
lifting up my * to you in prayer. Ps 63:4
for he holds our lives in his *. Ps 66:9
Ethiopia will stretch out her * Ps 68:31
All nature is within your *; Ps 74:17
lifting my * to heaven, pleading. Ps 77:2
his glory into enemy *. Ps 78:61
with a true heart and skillful *. Ps 78:71,72
I will free your * from their Ps 81:6
How soon my * would be upon her Ps 81:14
All nations are in your *. Ps 82:8
O Lord, I reach my pleading * to Ps 88:9
you with their * to keep you from Ps 91:12
Let the waves clap their * in Ps 98:8,9
and made the heavens with your *! Ps 102:25
smell, nor use their * or feet! Ps 115:7
I am close to death at the * of Ps 119:107
Lift your * in holiness and Ps 134:2
It is better to get your * Pro 12:9
the final outcome is in God's *. Pro 16:1
Idle * are the devil's workshop; Pro 16:27
things but his * refuse to work. Pro 21:25,26
A little folding of the * to Pro 24:32,33
onto anything with oil-slick *. Pro 27:16
the * of someone who pities them. Pro 28:8
with her own * she plants a Pro 31:16
"Give her of the fruit of her *; Pro 31:31f
I jumped up to open it and my * Sol 5:5
you pray with your * stretched out Is 1:15
for your * are those of murderers; Is 1:15
worship what their * have made! Is 17:8
He will wad you up in his * like Is 22:18
pushes down the water with his *. Is 25:11
the work of my *, in his midst." Is 29:23f
hold back their * from taking Is 33:15
the oceans in his * and measured Is 40:12
tattoo upon their * the name of God Is 44:5
me concerning the work of my *? Is 45:11
With my * I have stretched out Is 45:12
them fall into your *, O Babylon. Is 47:6
prey from the * of a mighty man? Is 49:24
take from your * the terrible cup; Is 51:22
cup into the * of those who Is 51:23
program shall prosper in his *. Is 53:10
For your * are those of Is 59:3
plant them there with my own *; Is 60:21
He will hold you aloft in his * Is 62:3
from the * of their oppressors. Is 63:4
face with your *, for the Lord has Jer 2:37
you from their ruthless *." Jer 15:21
the city into the * of King Jer 21:7
ashen-faced, * pressed against Jer 30:6
* if only you will obey the Lord; Jer 38:20
I will deliver them into the * Jer 46:26
killed—into the * of Jer 46:26
* and put on clothes of sackcloth. Jer 48:37
Let the farm * all depart. Jer 50:16
his * fell helpless at his sides; Jer 50:43
cup in the Lord's *, a cup from Jer 51:7
all her weapons break in her *, Jer 51:56
I am helpless in their *. Lam 1:14
lift up your * to him; Lam 2:19
Let us lift our hearts and * to Lam 3:41
their wings I could see human *. Eze 1:8
"The Lord God says: Raise your * Eze 6:11
Literally, "clap your * and stamp Eze 6:11f
for his sins. All * shall be Eze 7:17
looked like human *) and took some Eze 10:7,8
put them into the * of the man in Eze 10:7,8
like human * under their wings. Eze 10:21
I dug through the wall with my *. Eze 12:7
people out of your * by destroying Eze 13:23
you into the * of those who hate Eze 16:27
way: Clap your * vigorously, then Eze 21:14
with clapping * that I, the Lord, Eze 21:17
you into the * of cruel men skilled Eze 21:31
an outcast at the * of foreigners. Eze 28:10
I will strengthen the * of the Eze 30:25
her into the * of a mighty nation, Eze 31:11
now dead at the * of their foes. Eze 32:23
your * and leave you helpless. Eze 39:3
without human *—the Rock that Dan 2:45
deliver you out of my * then?" Dan 3:15
his * for three and a half years. Dan 7:25
trembling, to my * and knees. Dan 10:10
He replied, with both * lifted to Dan 12:7
you worship was made by human *! Hos 8:6
formed with skill by the * of men. Hos 13:2
their right * from their left." Jon 4:11f
deeds with both *, and how skilled Mic 7:3
will clap their * for joy, for Nah 3:19
will turn to ashes in their *? Hab 2:13
From his * flash rays of Hab 3:4
Literally, "and lifts high its * Hab 3:10f
cheat their hired *, or oppress Mal 3:5
at the * of the Jewish leaders, Mt 16:21
shall also suffer at their *." Mt 17:12
hell with both of your * and feet. Mt 18:8
to lay his * on them and pray. Mt 19:13
And he put his * on their Mt 19:15
pay me to get Jesus into your *?" Mt 26:15
am betrayed into the * of evil Mt 26:45
and washed his * before the crowd, Mt 27:24
"Please come and place your * on Mk 5:23
to place his * on a few sick people Mk 6:5
lay his * on the man and heal him. Mk 7:32
eyes, and laid his * over them. Mk 8:23
Then Jesus placed his * over the Mk 8:25
and placed his * on their heads and Mk 10:16
am betrayed into the * of wicked Mk 14:41
made with human * and in three days Mk 14:58
another, made without human *!' Mk 14:58
* on the sick and heal them." Mk 16:18
sent the rich away with empty *. Lk 1:53
and the touch of his * healed Lk 4:40
in their * and eating the grains. Lk 6:1
Look at my *! Lk 24:39
As he spoke, he held out his * Lk 24:40
to Bethany, and lifting his * to Lk 24:50
"Then wash my * and head as Jn 13:9
he showed them his * and side. Jn 20:20
nail wounds in his *—and put my Jn 20:25
"Put your finger into my *. Jn 20:27
stretch out your * and others will Jn 21:18
laid their * on them in blessing. Act 6:6
live in temples made by human *. Act 7:48,49
them from the * of angels." Act 7:53
him, putting their * over their Act 7:57
Then Peter and John laid their * Act 8:17
placed their * upon people's Act 8:18
that when I lay my * on people, Act 8:19
in and laying his * on him so that Act 9:12
Paul and laid his * on him and Act 9:17
the men laid their * on them—and Act 13:3
and human * can't minister to Act 17:25
Then, when Paul laid his * upon Act 19:6
know that these * of mine worked to Act 20:34
his own feet and * with it and Act 21:11
else they could lay their * on. Act 27:19
laying his * on him, healed him! Act 28:8
to be tools in the * of God, to be Rom 6:13
reaching out his * to the Jews, but Rom 10:21
take the law into your own *. Rom 12:19
Shake * warmly with each other. Rom 16:16
or to move the * of God by prayer. 1Co 2:16
with our * to earn our living. 1Co 4:12
and into Satan's *, to punish him, 1Co 5:5
into the * of God, who alone could 2Co 1:9
God himself, and not by human *. 2Co 5:1
as from the * of the Gentiles. 2Co 11:26
gifts—they shook * with Barnabas Gal 2:7,8,9
begin using those * of his for Eph 4:28
Shake * for me with all the 1Th 5:26
to pray with holy * lifted up to 1Ti 2:8
laid their * upon your head. 1Ti 4:14
* upon your head and blessed you. 2Ti 1:6
at the * of those who hate him. 2Ti 3:12
heavens are the work of your *. Heb 1:10
Literally, "the laying on of *." Heb 6:2f
by the Lord and not by human *. Heb 8:2
fall into the * of the living God. Heb 10:31
with your tired *, stand firm on Heb 12:12
Wash your *, you sinners, and let Jas 4:8
he left his case in the * of God 1Pe 2:23
I have touched him with my own *. 1Jn 1:1
the devil cannot get his * on him. 1Jn 5:18
with palm branches in their *. Rev 7:9
on their foreheads or their *. Rev 20:4

HANDSHAKE
And give each other a loving * 1Co 16:20
Give each other the * of 1Pe 5:14

HANDSOME
Joseph, by the way, was a very * Gen 39:6
His son Saul was the most * man 1Sa 9:2
player, but was *, brave, and 1Sa 16:18
Now no one in Israel was such a * 2Sa 14:25
He was a very * man, and was 1Ki 1:6
lovely voice and see your * face. Sol 2:14
one is tanned and *, better than Sol 5:10
and commanders, in * blue, dashing Eze 23:6
those * young men on fine steeds, Eze 23:12
* uniforms—all of them desirable. Eze 23:12
red uniforms, with * belts, and Eze 23:14,15
and all the Assyrians with them—* Eze 23:23

HANDSOMELY
"I would have rewarded you * and 2Sa 18:11

HANDWASHING
of ceremonial * before they eat." Mt 15:2
the ritual of ceremonial *!" Mt 15:20

HANDWRITING
these closing words in my own *. Gal 6:11
own *: Remember me here in jail. Col 4:18
This is in my own *. 2Th 3:17

HANES
to Zoan and *, yet it will all Is 30:4

HANG
(The sixth tarpaulin will * down Ex 26:9
into the cloth. * this upon four Ex 26:32
* the curtain from the hooks. Ex 26:33
linen. * up this curtain on five Ex 26:37
of the tent, and * the curtain-door Ex 40:8
not let your hair * loose as a sign Lev 10:6
not let his hair * loose in Lev 21:10
leaders of Israel. * them up before Num 25:4
Your lives will * in doubt. Deu 28:66
We will * them before the Lord in 2Sa 21:5,6
king to let you * Mordecai on it; Est 5:14
to ask the king to * Mordecai from Est 6:4
constructed, to * Mordecai, the man Est 7:9
"* Haman on it," the king Est 7:9
advice, who do not * around with Ps 1:1
The enemies' sails * loose on Is 33:23
The virgins of Jerusalem * their Lam 2:10
making pegs to * up pots and pans! Eze 15:3
their shields * upon your walls; Eze 27:10
Their shields * row on row upon Eze 27:11
drinking man, and * around with the Mt 11:19

HANGED
executed and then * on a tree, his Deu 21:22
Joshua * the king of Ai on a tree Jos 8:29
He then * them on five trees Jos 10:26
hands and feet and * their bodies 2Sa 4:12
affairs in order, and * himself; 2Sa 17:23
a gallows on which he will be *; Ez 6:11
Literally, "* on a tree." Est 2:23f
and he has been * upon the gallows Est 8:7
ten sons be * upon the gallows." Est 9:13
his sons were * on the gallows. Est 9:24,25
Our princes are * by their Lam 5:12
Temple and went out and * himself. Mt 27:5
"Anyone who is * on a tree is Gal 3:13

HANGING
this roof-covering * down from the Ex 26:12
pins and pegs for * the utensils on Ex 27:19
and had ripe almonds * from it! Num 17:8
* on a tree is cursed of God. Deu 21:23
this rope is * from this window and Jos 2:17,18
And she left the scarlet rope * Jos 2:21
The 400 pomegranates * from the 2Ch 4:12-16
We have put away our lyres, * Ps 137:2
One of the criminals * beside him Lk 23:39
the thick veil * in the Temple Lk 23:45
want the victims * there the next Jn 19:31
killed him by * him on a cross. Act 5:30
the island saw it * there and said Act 28:4

HANGOUTS
I hate the sinners' * and refuse Ps 26:5

HANGS
and * the earth upon nothing. Job 26:7
My life * in the balance, but I Ps 119:109
but a lad who * around with Pro 29:3
of death that * over the earth; Is 25:7
In one short day my life * by a Is 38:12
on which all hope *, the Bow that Zec 10:4

HANNAH
He had two wives, * and Peninnah. 1Sa 1:2
Peninnah had some children, but * 1Sa 1:2
but although he loved * very 1Sa 1:5
* because of her barrenness. 1Sa 1:6
"What's the matter, *?" 1Sa 1:8
* went over to the Tabernacle. 1Sa 1:9
Elkanah slept with *, the Lord 1Sa 1:19,20
Tabernacle without *, for she told 1Sa 1:21,22
"Sir, do you remember me?" * 1Sa 1:26
bless Elkanah and * and ask God to 1Sa 2:20
And the Lord gave * three sons 1Sa 2:21

HANNAH'S
THIS WAS * prayer: 1Sa 2:1

HANNATHON
of Zebulun passed * and ended at Jos 19:14

HANNIEL
Manasseh * (son of Ephod) Num 34:16-28
Arah, *, Rizia. 1Ch 7:39

HANOCH
Epher, *, Abida, and Eldaah. Gen 25:4
Reuben's sons: *, Pallu, Hezron, Gen 46:8-14
oldest son:*, Pallu,Hezron, Carmi. Ex 6:14
named after their ancestor *. Num 26:5-11
Ephah, Epher, *, Abida, and 1Ch 1:33
*, Pallu, Hezron, Carmi. 1Ch 5:3

HANOCHITES
The *, named after their ancestor Num 26:5-11

HANUN
died and his son * replaced him. 2Sa 10:1
to * about his father's death. 2Sa 10:2
So * took David's men and shaved 2Sa 10:4
his son * became the new king. 1Ch 19:1
show friendship to * because of all 1Ch 19:2,3
to * for the death of his father. 1Ch 19:2,3
So King * insulted King David's 1Ch 19:4
When King * realized his mistake 1Ch 19:6
* had recruited from his cities. 1Ch 19:7
The people from Zanoah, led by *, Neh 3:13
* (the sixth son of Zalaph); Neh 3:30
HANUN'S
But * officers told him, "These 2Sa 10:3
arrived, King * counselors warned 1Ch 19:2,3
HAPHARAIM
Jezreel, Chesulloth, Shunem, *, Jos 19:17-23
HAPHAZARDLY
shot an arrow * at the Israeli 2Ch 18:33
HAPPEN
certainly going to *, for God has Gen 41:32
it, and it is going to * soon. Gen 41:32
some harm might * to him [as it had Gen 42:4
If anything should * to him, I Gen 42:38
to * to you in the days to come. Gen 49:1
to see what would * to him. Ex 2:4
All this will * tomorrow." Ex 8:23
you do, what will * to the people? Ex 18:18
the same thing * to him as happened Num 16:40
"The same thing will * to King Num 21:34
this could not * until all the men, Deu 2:14,15
prophesies doesn't *, it is not the Deu 18:22
And then what will * to the honor Jos 7:9
for he knew what would * if they Ju 6:27
close relative. I * to know that he Ru 3:2
"This is what will * to the oxen 1Sa 11:7
as the prophet had said would *. 1Ki 13:5
had said would * when he spoke 1Ki 15:29
it will * to his sons; 1Ki 21:29
"Didn't I tell you this would *? 1Ki 22:18
just as the Lord had said would *. 1Ki 22:38
"That couldn't * if the Lord made 2Ki 7:2
"You will see it *, but you won't 2Ki 7:2
"That couldn't * even if the Lord 2Ki 7:19
"You will see it *, but you won't 2Ki 7:19
just what the Lord said would *. 2Ki 9:36
would * to Ahab's descendants." 2Ki 10:9,10
his prophets had warned would *. 2Ki 17:23
Lord is eager to cause this to *. 2Ki 19:31
would * to Jeroboam's altar. 2Ki 23:16
* here at the altar at Bethel!" 2Ki 23:17
as the Lord had said would *): 1Ch 11:10
just as the Lord had said would *. 1Ch 12:23
Whatever you wish will *! Job 22:28
I myself have seen it *: a proud Ps 37:35,36
followers of God will see it *. Ps 52:6
What marvelous miracles * to his Ps 66:5
nor live in dread of what may *. Ps 112:7
he doesn't know is going to *? Ecc 8:6,7
really know what is going to *? Ecc 10:14
what was going to * to Judah and Is 1:1
This is going to * because the Is 9:7
* to Egypt, what chance have we?" Is 20:5,6
I have caused all this to * as I Is 37:26
If you are gods, tell what will * Is 41:23
but I have told you this would *? Is 41:26
is going to * in the days ahead? Is 44:7
to * than the things they say. Is 44:25
idol ever told you they would *? Is 45:21
what was going to * in the future. Is 46:9
can tell you what is going to *. Is 46:10
what was going to * in the future. Is 48:3
my carved image commanded it to * Is 48:5
plainly what would *, so that you Is 48:16
How could this *? Jer 2:21
to *—Israel shall seek him! Jer 31:22
about what is going to * here. Jer 33:3
what is going to *, that Pharaoh's Jer 37:7
"What will * then to the Jews Jer 40:15
threatened will * to you, and that Jer 44:29
what will * to Jerusalem, for she Eze 5:5,6,7
that all this would * to them. Eze 6:10
what is going to * to them, for Eze 12:11
terrible things * to them—as they Eze 33:33
This will * in the distant Eze 38:15,16
everything will * just as I have Eze 39:8
dream what will * in the future. Dan 2:28
shown what will * in the future, Dan 2:45
worried about what will * to us. Dan 3:16
this dream would * to your enemies, Dan 4:19
it will surely *— that your people Dan 4:24
what is going to * in the last days Dan 8:19
But none of these things will * Dan 8:26
It concerned events certain to * Dan 10:1
tell you what will * to your Dan 10:14
going to * to his nation, Israel. Amo 1:2
if anything would * to the city. Jon 4:5
But these things I plan won't * Hab 2:3
But none of this will * unless Zec 6:15
"Ashkelon will see it * and be Zec 9:5
flavor, what will * to the world? Mt 5:13
this * right before their eyes. Mt 9:8
of your faith it will *." Mt 9:29
and what would * to him there—that Mt 16:21
"This is not going to * to Mt 16:22
would * to him when they arrived. Mt 20:18
'how does it * that you are here Mt 22:12
"When will this *?" Mt 24:3
to *, you can know that my Mt 24:33
what was going to * until the Mt 24:39
"Make something * in the sky. Mk 8:11
that was going to * to him when Mk 10:32
all this going to * to the Temple? Mk 13:3,4
But when these things begin to * Mk 13:9
or hour when these things will *; Mk 13:32
know when it will *, stay alert. Mk 13:33
Then those who had seen it * Lk 8:36
for something to * in the sky to Lk 11:16
And all who saw it * praised God Lk 18:43
to *, stand straight and look up! Lk 21:28
things *, the end of this age Lk 21:32
what was about to *, they Lk 22:49
what will * when it is dry?" Lk 23:31f
I saw it * to this man, and I Jn 1:34
as these that * here among men, how Jn 3:12
or something even worse may * to Jn 5:14
saw it *, finally believed on him. Jn 11:45
things before they * so that when Jn 14:29
* you will remember I warned you. Jn 16:4
to * to me, and you will weep. Jn 16:20
all that was going to * to him. Jn 18:4,5
what would * next and where all Act 5:24
terrible things won't * to me." Act 8:24
You see, this is what may *: 1Co 8:10
what is going to * in the future, 1Co 13:2
what is going to *, and the great 1Co 14:6
It will all * in a moment, in 1Co 15:52
know why things * as they do, but 2Co 4:8
So, two good things * as a 2Co 9:12
* just as he decided long ago. Eph 1:11
out what is going to * to me here. Php 2:23
WHEN IS ALL this going to *? 1Th 5:1
until two things *: first, there 2Th 2:3
things that would * later on. Heb 3:5
something we want is going to *. Heb 11:1
know what is going to * tomorrow? Jas 4:14
when and to whom all this would *. 1Pe 1:11
thing that is going to * to you. 1Pe 4:12
these things to * and for him to 2Pe 3:14
John saw this * with his own Rev 1:7f
you what must * in the future!" Rev 4:1
that will soon * when the three Rev 8:13
what is going to * to the Notorious Rev 17:1
to tell you this will * soon. Rev 22:6,7
HAPPENED
This all * on the second day. Gen 1:7,8
This all * on the fourth day. Gen 1:19
learned what had * and what Ham, Gen 9:24,25
As it *, the valley was full of Gen 14:10
This is the way it *: One hot Gen 18:1
and told them what had *. Gen 20:8
the land, as had * before, in Gen 26:1
Jacob of what had *, but his sons Gen 34:5
Now as it *, Israel loved Joseph Gen 37:3
his work—as it *, no one else was Gen 39:11
*, she was crying hysterically. Gen 39:14,15
SOME TIME LATER it so * that the Gen 40:1
And everything * just as he Gen 41:13
"This has all * because of what we Gen 42:21
and told him all that had *. Gen 42:29
Well, this is what *: A princess, Ex 2:5
The nations heard what *, and Ex 15:14
report just what * to it, then the Ex 22:10
something must have * to him." Ex 32:1
for something has * to this fellow Ex 32:23
But as it *, some of the men had Num 9:6,7
When Aaron saw what had *, he Num 12:10
as * to Korah and his associates. Num 16:40
What * is described in this Num 21:17,18
to King Og as * to King Sihon at Num 21:34
hear about what * to the man who Deu 17:13
about what * and will be afraid. Deu 21:21
"WHEN ALL THESE things have * to Deu 30:1
to Joshua all that had * to them. Jos 2:23
heard what had * to Jericho, they Jos 9:1
heard what had * to Jericho and Ai, Jos 9:3,4,5
heard what had *, he sent urgent Jos 11:1
and explain what *, and they must Jos 20:4
told them what had *, and all Jos 22:32
with us, why has all this * to us? Ju 6:13
And it * just that way! Ju 6:38
What * was this: When the people Ju 11:16
place to live. He * to stop at Ju 17:7,8
with anyone. This * in the valley Ju 18:28
and asked him just what had *. Ju 20:3
"why has this *, that now one of Ju 21:3
And as it *, the field where she Ru 2:3
"Well, what *, dear?" Ru 3:15-18
and told what had *, a great cry 1Sa 4:13
to Eli and told him what had *. 1Sa 4:14
mentioned what had * to the Ark, 1Sa 4:18
the same thing had *—the idol had 1Sa 5:4
But something had * when the 1Sa 18:6
harp, as he did whenever this *. 1Sa 18:10
and escaped. This * another time, 1Sa 18:11,12
David and told him what had *. 1Sa 19:7
When Saul heard what had *, he 1Sa 19:21
The same thing * a third time! 1Sa 19:21
that something had * so that David 1Sa 20:26
but as it *, David and his men were 1Sa 24:3
told him what had *, he had a 1Sa 25:37,38
really been. This * again and again 1Sa 27:11
realized what had * to their 1Sa 30:3
"What *?" 2Sa 1:4
When David heard what had * he 2Sa 10:5
he realized what had *. 2Sa 12:19
When King David heard what had *, 2Sa 13:21-24
tell the king what actually had *. 2Sa 18:29f
home, for what has * to Rehoboam is 1Ki 12:23,24
As it *, there was an old prophet 1Ki 13:11
When he heard what had * he 1Ki 13:26
saw what had *, they exclaimed, 2Ki 2:15
prophet what had *, he said to her, 2Ki 4:7
the child's face, but nothing *. 2Ki 4:31
disaster. This * several times. 2Ki 6:10
watchmen what had *—they had gone 2Ki 7:10
his officers, "I know what has *. 2Ki 7:12
What * to the gods of Hamath, 2Ki 18:34
What * to the king of Hamoth and 2Ki 19:13
of Arpad? What * to the kings of 2Ki 19:13
tragedy") because of what had *. 1Ch 7:23
When David heard what had *, he 1Ch 19:5
might and all that * to him and to 1Ch 29:30
Don't you remember what * to the 2Ch 16:8
And as had * before, when the 2Ch 20:29
This all * in the eighteenth 2Ch 35:19
Before this had *, Eliashib the Neh 13:4
Now, as it *, Haman had just Est 6:4
friends what had *, they said, "If Est 6:13
* in the rest of the provinces! Est 9:12
memory of what had * would never Est 9:28
What I always feared has * to Job 3:25
And all this has *, Lord, despite Ps 44:17
*, Jordan River, to your waters? Ps 114:5
that could have * to me, for it Ps 119:71,72
We don't remember what * in those Ecc 1:8-11
was one thing that * to wise and Ecc 2:13,14
What has * to your "wise Is 19:12
and told him all that had *. Is 36:22
Just remember what has * Is 37:11
And don't forget what * to the Is 37:13
A horrible thing has * in this Jer 5:30
Everything has * just as you Jer 32:24
That is why it *. Jer 40:2,3
knew what had *, eighty men Jer 41:4
and see what has * to Gedaliah!" Jer 41:6
from Moab, "What has * there?" Jer 48:19
as I see what has * to my people; Lam 2:11
saw what had * to her sister she Eze 23:11
in Babylon to tell you what has *. Eze 24:26
foreshadow what * to the island Eze 26:14f
for what has * to my flock. Eze 34:9,10
Now as it *, God had given the Dan 1:9
Ari-och told him all that had *. Dan 2:15
But all these things * to Dan 4:28
disaster like what * at Jerusalem Dan 9:12
Go over to Calneh and see what * Amo 6:2
at all of what * at Acacia and Mic 6:5
survivor to remember what *. Zep 3:6
acted, and what has * as a result! Hag 1:7
what has * to Judah and Jerusalem? Zec 1:14
This has already * twice: Two Zec 13:8f
What you have believed has *!" Mt 8:13
story of what had *, and the Mt 8:33
what * to Jonah the prophet! Mt 12:39,40
and came to tell Jesus what had *. Mt 14:12
the miracle that * to Jonah." Mt 16:4
the king and told him what had *. Mt 18:31
by the earthquake and all that *. Mt 27:54
priests and told them what had *. Mt 28:11
they began discussing what had *. Mk 1:27
Now as it * there was a huge herd Mk 5:11
Those who saw what * were Mk 5:16
of what had * to her, came and fell Mk 5:33
to tell what had *, and told them Mk 5:43
heard what had *, they came for his Mk 6:29
Now it * that a blind beggar Mk 10:46
will do when he hears what *? Mk 12:9
This all * the day before the Mk 15:42,43
* spread through the Judean hills. Lk 1:65
thing that has *, which the Lord Lk 2:15
everyone what had * and what the Lk 2:17
realized what had *, he fell to his Lk 5:8
anyone what had * and be examined Lk 5:14
what had * and saw the man who had Lk 8:35
But when Jesus heard what had *, Lk 8:50
anyone the details of what had *. Lk 8:56
When word came back of what had * Lk.9:54
remember what * to Lot's wife! Lk 17:32
another, but the same thing *; Lk 20:11
man was sent and the same thing *. Lk 20:12
and Herod * to be in Jerusalem at Lk 23:7
saw what had *, he was stricken Lk 23:47

(HAPPENED Con't)
to think what could have * to it. Lk 24:4
everyone else—what had *. Lk 24:9
home again, wondering what had *. Lk 24:12
things that * there last week." Lk 24:18
"The things that * to Jesus, the Lk 24:19
all this—which * three days ago— Lk 24:21
great miracle had *, they Jn 6:14
something that has *, their witness Jn 8:17
What had *? Jn 9:10
Now as it *, this all occurred Jn 9:14
* to make him see, or who did it. Jn 9:21
When Jesus heard what had *, he Jn 9:35
This is how it *: Jn 21:1
Olives when this *, so now they Act 1:12
by the wonderful thing that had *. Act 3:11
The next day it * that the Act 4:5
came in, not knowing what had *. Act 5:7
all others who heard what had *. Act 5:11
had * and sent them off to Joppa. Act 10:8
"This * three times before the Act 11:10
heard what had *, they sent Act 11:22
Peter finally realized what had * Act 12:11
told them what had * and how the Act 12:17
the others what *," he said—and Act 12:17
What had * to Peter? Act 12:18
When the governor saw what * he Act 13:12
square to all who * to be there. Act 17:17
As it *, a Jew named Apollos, a Act 18:24
explained what had * to Jesus since Act 18:25,26
The story of what * spread Act 19:17
As it *, Publius' father was ill Act 28:8
this blessing even before it *. Rom 4:20
that hasn't * yet, it teaches us to Rom 8:25
you Christ could do for you has *! 1Co 1:6
thing that has * there among you, 1Co 5:1
brothers, what * to our people in 1Co 10:1
Another lesson for us is what * 1Co 10:8
All these things * to them as 1Co 10:11
he was and what had * to him. 2Co 2:13
about what had *, and about your 2Co 7:7
about what had *, and longed for me 2Co 7:11
But then something *! Gal 1:15
When all this * to me I didn't go Gal 1:16
This is exactly what *—I am not Gal 1:20
that has * to me here has been a Php 1:12
But just the opposite *: those Heb 10:3
Before this * God had said Heb 11:5
and that is just about what *, Heb 11:19
And so it * just as the Jas 2:23
since then, have * to Christ: his 1Pe 1:11
the heavens, "It has * at last! Rev 12:10
Literally, "It has *." Rev 16:17f

HAPPENING
what is * to them there in Egypt. Ex 3:16
all that had been * and what the Ex 18:8
Moses what was *, and Joshua (the Num 11:27
horrible thing is * among you in Deu 13:12,13,14
saw what was * and took refuge in Ju 9:46
realized what was *, they 1Sa 5:7
to Saul what was *, that the people 1Sa 14:33
When David heard what was *, he 2Sa 10:17
but I didn't know what was *," 2Sa 18:29
what was * and told him to stop. 2Sa 24:16
heard what was *, he discontinued 2Ch 16:5
told him what was *, and what all 2Ch 18:12
What was * was that families who Neh 5:2,3,4
and to find out what was * to her. Est 2:11
tell her what was *, and that she Est 4:8
every detail of what is * to me; Job 23:10
See what is *! Ps 59:4
All who see it * will scoff at Ps 64:8
There is a strange thing * here Ecc 8:14
but it is all by chance, by * to Ecc 9:11
What is *? Is 22:1
yourself, Why is all this * to me? Jer 13:22
* to the young girls of Jerusalem. Lam 3:51
heard what was *, she rushed to the Dan 5:10
And why is this *? Mic 1:5
And even when you saw this *, you Mt 21:32
that describe what is * now?" Mt 26:54
But this is all * to fulfill the Mt 26:56
heard what was * they came to try Mk 3:21
But when Jesus saw what was * he Mk 10:14
And when you see these things * Mk 13:29
But these things are * to fulfill Mk 14:49
saw what was * and who the woman Lk 7:39
for some strange * in the skies [to Lk 11:29,30
going past, he asked what was *. Lk 18:36
things * in the heavens. Lk 21:11
"That is what is * here in this Act 4:27
didn't believe it was really *. Act 12:9
Paul saw what was * they ripped at Act 14:14
So much is *, but there are many 1Co 16:9
and cared about what was * to you. 2Co 2:4
When I saw what was * and that Gal 2:14
enjoyable while it is *—it hurts! Heb 12:11

HAPPENS
But if it * in the daylight, it Ex 22:3
say, 'This is what * to a man who Deu 25:9
See what * to them then! Deu 32:20
for what * to you unless this rope Jos 2:17,18
soon see what * to Abimelech! Ju 9:29
for whatever * now," he shouted. Ju 15:3
until we hear what *, for Boaz Ru 3:15-18
offer it to him and see what *!" 1Sa 9:8
that when that * you will not kill 1Sa 24:21
and you know everything that *!" 2Sa 14:20
go, no matter what *—whether it 2Sa 15:21
Let me know what * in Jerusalem 2Sa 15:28
something * to the animals it won't 2Ki 7:13
Yes, that is what * to sinners, Job 18:21
everything that * here on earth. Ps 11:4
PRAISE the Lord no matter what *. Ps 34:1
say, "See what * to those who Ps 52:7
no one cares a bit what * to me. Ps 142:4
everything that * along the way? Pro 20:24
for tomorrow—wait and see what *. Pro 27:1
tell you the future before it *." Is 42:9
all to see what * when the Lord Eze 5:15
What I threaten always *. Eze 12:25
And when that *, you will know I Eze 20:38
And when all this *, then they Eze 25:17
[when nothing that I told them * Jon 4:3
in his robes, and * to brush Hag 2:12
But when that *, I will take Hag 2:23
And when this * you will know my Zec 6:15
If that * we'll be worse off than Mt 27:64
with unshrunk cloth! What *? Mk 2:21
When that *, rejoice! Lk 6:23
for if that * you won't be free Lk 12:59
when it *, you will believe on me. Jn 13:19
because of all that * to me. Jn 13:31
Then, when that *, we are able Rom 5:5
no matter what * and know that all Rom 5:5
And we know that all that * to Rom 8:28
When this *, then at last this 1Co 15:54
But whatever * to me, remember Php 1:27
WHATEVER *, DEAR friends, be glad Php 3:1
no matter what *—always full of the Col 1:11
you to know what * to a Christian 1Th 4:13
so that when it *, you will not be 1Th 4:13
No matter what *, always be 1Th 5:18
you his peace no matter what *. 2Th 3:16
Lord die away, no matter what *. Heb 10:35
for when that * the Spirit of God 1Pe 4:14

HAPPIER
common sense is * than the man Pro 3:13,14,15
For I will make this land * and Jer 33:10,11
way heaven will be * over one lost Lk 15:7
But in my opinion she will be * 1Co 7:40
love, we were made * still by 2Co 7:13
How much * for me than being Php 1:23

HAPPIEST
what makes me * is the well-earned Php 4:17

HAPPILY
Then Isaac sent them * home Gen 26:31
you, and get you * married again? Ru 3:1
she exclaimed, and went * back, 1Sa 1:18
Live * with the woman you love Ecc 9:9
Work * together. Rom 12:16
of being able to stay * unmarried. 1Co 7:7
yet I have freely and * become a 1Co 9:19
* whether I have much or little. Php 4:11
and should give * to those in need, 1Ti 6:18

HAPPINESS
and their mourning into *. Est 9:22
in money, if my * depends on Job 31:25
Lord restored his wealth and *! Job 42:10
Fill all who love you with your * Ps 5:11
have endowed him with eternal *. Ps 21:6
WHAT * FOR those whose guilt has Ps 32:1
with * again before my death. Ps 39:13
their *, an eternity of terror. Ps 73:19
Give me *, O Lord, for I worship Ps 86:4
* comes to those who are fair to Ps 106:3
reward shall be prosperity and *. Ps 128:2
gain brings no lasting *; Pro 10:2
The hope of good men is eternal * Pro 10:28
look forward to *, while the wicked Pro 11:23
but hating bribes brings *. Pro 15:27
good reports give * and health. Pro 15:30
Reverence for God gives life, *, Pro 19:23
will give you * and peace of mind. Pro 29:17
the only * most men have throughout Ecc 2:3
of thinking that wealth brings *! Ecc 5:10
the hope that this * would stick Ecc 8:15
*, and money gives everything! Ecc 10:19
*, and her people shall be a joy! Is 65:18
live together in peace and *. Jer 31:24
will be radiant with health and *. Zec 9:16,17
will be a land sparkling with *. Mal 3:12
and said, "What * there is for you Lk 6:20
What * there is for you who are Lk 6:21
be satisfied! What * there is for Lk 6:21
What * it is when others hate Lk 6:22
For they have their only * down Lk 6:24
Pray for the * of those who Lk 6:28
Her parents were overcome with * Lk 8:56
For it gives your Father great * Lk 12:32
describing the * of an undeserving Rom 4:6
* or sadness or wealth should 1Co 7:30
This makes for * among the 1Co 12:25
church grow in holiness and *. 1Co 14:4
I felt sure that your * was so 2Co 2:3

HAPPIZZEZ
Eighteenth, the group led by *; 1Ch 24:7-18

HAPPY
party to celebrate the * occasion. Gen 21:8
Asher (meaning "*"), for she Gen 30:13
and Pharaoh was very * to hear Gen 45:16
will be very * when he finds you. Ex 4:14
Jethro was very * about Ex 18:9
When Aaron saw how * the people Ex 32:5
"What a * year it will be! Lev 25:11
If only I could die as * as an Num 23:7-10
This will be a * time of Deu 16:14
to be at home, * with his wife. Deu 24:5
and Manasseh, they were very *. Jos 22:30
have a long and * life together. Ju 9:19
The young priest was then quite * Ju 18:20
you with another * marriage." Ru 1:9
celebrate the * occasion by giving 1Sa 1:4
Saul and all Israel were very *. 1Sa 11:15
You were certainly * about it 1Sa 19:5
But Achish's officers weren't * 1Sa 21:11
have come at a * time of holiday. 1Sa 25:8
of us had died, you would be *. 2Sa 19:6
the people home, * for all the 1Ki 8:66
Your people are * and your 1Ki 10:8
So everyone was *, and the city 2Ki 11:20
Everyone was excited and * for 1Ch 29:9
home, joyful and * because the Lord 2Ch 7:10
All were * for this covenant 2Ch 15:15
people were very * because of what 2Ch 29:36
and did his best to make her *; Est 2:9
What a * man was Haman as he left Est 5:9
you, and bless you with a * home. Job 8:6
they have many * children, they Job 21:11
"Will the wild ox be your * Job 39:9
No wonder we are * in the Lord! Ps 33:21
For him there is a * ending. Ps 37:37
Though a man calls himself * all Ps 49:18
can they ever be really * again. Ps 53:6
cry out the * news: "The armies Ps 68:11,12,13
and my God! How * are those who Ps 84:4
* are those who are strong in the Ps 84:5
May all who are godly be * in Ps 97:12
expression. Yes, * is the man who Ps 112:1
so that she becomes a * mother. Ps 113:9
* ARE ALL who perfectly follow the Ps 119:1
the laws of God. * are all who Ps 119:2
to defend him. * is the man who Ps 127:5
sing for them the * songs of Zion! Ps 137:3,4
a truly * land where Jehovah is Ps 144:12-15
Yes, * are those whose God is Ps 144:12-15
is ended. But * is the man who has Ps 146:5
who eat her fruit; * is the man who Pro 3:18
"you will have a long and * life. Pro 4:4
And how * I was with what he Pro 8:31
to me, for how * are all who follow Pro 8:32
it—and be wise. * is the man who Pro 8:34
* IS THE man with a level-headed Pro 10:1
We all have * memories of good Pro 10:7
A * face means a glad heart; Pro 15:13
God blesses those who obey him; * Pro 16:20
* is the generous man, the one Pro 22:9
My son, how * I will be if you Pro 27:11
A wise son makes his father *, Pro 29:3
has dealt to him, is not a * one. Ecc 1:12-15
a man than to be * and to enjoy Ecc 3:12
they should be * in their work, for Ecc 3:22
in the morning. * the land whose Ecc 10:16,17
into his palace. How * we will be! Sol 1:4
of harvest. The * singing in the Is 16:10
the trouble in this busy, * city? Is 22:2
no more; the * days are ended. Is 24:8
your joyous homes and * cities Is 32:13
who bring the * news of peace and Is 52:7
Does all this make me *? Is 57:6
Let me tell you how * God has Is 61:10
they scoff. "Be * in the Lord!" Is 66:5
I will end the * singing and Jer 7:34
Why are evil men so *? Jer 12:1
in this land—the * songs, the Jer 16:9
You will again be * and dance Jer 31:4
The Lord declares that the * Jer 33:10,11
to eat and we were well off and *! Jer 44:17
her, and were * at her fall. Jer 48:27
Bashan and to be * once more on Jer 50:19
she remembers * bygone days. Lam 1:7
in a pasture—a noisy, * crowd. Mic 2:12
I will be * in the God of my Hab 3:18
exulting over you in * song: Zep 3:17,18
'May you be as prosperous and * Zec 8:13
They shall be * as with wine. Zec 10:7
"* are those who long to be just Mt 5:6
satisfied. * are the kind and Mt 5:7
be shown mercy. * are those whose Mt 5:8
shall see God. * are those who Mt 5:9
the sons of God. * are those who Mt 5:10
Be * about it! Mt 5:12
and you weren't *, so we played Mt 11:17

(HAPPY Con't)
and * and promised him a reward. Mk 14:11
Jesus asked, "Do * men fast? Lk 5:34
you will be very * for me, for now Jn 14:28
When others are *, be happy with Rom 12:15
When others are happy, be * with Rom 12:15
In this situation, * is the man Rom 14:22
hope will keep you * and full of Rom 15:13
come to you with a * heart by the Rom 15:32
This makes me very *. Rom 16:19
but send him back to me * with 1Co 16:11
I want to make you *, not sad. 2Co 1:24
sad, who is going to make me *? 2Co 2:2
* either, unless I came with joy. 2Co 2:3
you have made me so * in spite of 2Co 7:4
deep concern. How * this makes me, 2Co 7:16
good, I am quite * about "the 2Co 12:10
Be *. 2Co 13:11
Where is that * spirit that we Gal 4:15
grow and become * in your faith; Php 1:25
Then make me truly * by loving Php 2:2
For you should be * about this, Php 2:18
me * and lighten all my cares. Php 2:28
heart is with you, * because you Col 2:5
along so well, * because of your Col 2:5
helmet the * hope of salvation. 1Th 5:8
We are * to tell other churches 2Th 1:4
should have *, obedient families. 1Ti 3:12
You already are if you are * and 1Ti 6:6
see you again. How * I would be, 2Ti 1:4
Do not let this * trust in the Heb 10:35
gathering of countless * angels; Heb 12:22
Then be *, for when the way is Jas 1:2
* is the man who doesn't give in Jas 1:12
And it was a * day for him Jas 1:18
We know how * they are now Jas 5:11
and even now you are * with the 1Pe 1:8
be like one big * family, full of 1Pe 3:8
If you want a *, good life, keep 1Pe 3:10
Be * if you are cursed and 1Pe 4:14
children, stay in * fellowship with 1Jn 2:28
How * I am to find some of your 2Jn 1:4
have made me very * by telling me 3Jn 1:3
wedding bells and * voices of the Rev 18:23

HAPPY-GO-LUCKY
Being * around a person whose Pro 25:20

HAR
* Baana. Neh 10:14-27

HARA
They took them to Halah, Habor, * 1Ch 5:26

HARADAH
From Mount Shepher to *; Num 33:15-37
From * to Makheloth; Num 33:15-37

HARAN
three sons, Abram, Nahor, and *. Gen 11:26
Haran. And * had a son named Lot. Gen 11:27
named Lot. But * died young, in Gen 11:28
the daughter of their brother *; Gen 11:29
the city of * and settled there. Gen 11:31
of Abraham's departure from *. Gen 11:32f
*—and finally arrived in Canaan. Gen 12:5
"Flee to your Uncle Laban in *. Gen 27:43
Beer-sheba and journeyed toward *. Gen 28:10
"At *," they said. Gen 29:4
nations as Gozan, *, Rezeph, and 2Ki 19:12
*, Moza, and Gazez; 1Ch 2:46
Haran, Moza, and Gazez; * had a 1Ch 2:46
—Shelomoth, Haziel, and *. 1Ch 23:8,9
cities of Gozan, *, or Rezeph, or Is 37:12
jewels and gold. * and Canneh, Eze 27:23
Literally, "*," a city in the Act 7:2f
and lived in *, in Syria, until his Act 7:4

HARAN'S
Lot (his son * child), and his Gen 11:31

HARAR
Shammah, the son of Agee from *. 2Sa 23:11,12
Shammah from *; 2Sa 23:24-39
Ahiam (the son of Sharar) from *; 2Sa 23:24-39
Jonathan (son of Shagee) from *; 1Ch 11:26-47
Ahiam (son of Sacher) from *; 1Ch 11:26-47

HARASS
Egyptians, and began to * them. Ex 14:24
the Lord let their enemies * them. Ju 6:1

HARASSING
were pursuing and * the foe, Joshua Jos 10:12
So they began * Jesus as a Jn 5:16

HARBONA
Biztha, *, Bigtha, Abagtha, Zethar, Est 1:10
Then *, one of the king's aides, Est 7:9

HARBOR
sea and shall be a * for ships, Gen 49:13
and its beautiful * are ours! 2Sa 12:26,27
as he brings them safely into *! Ps 107:30
ships and trim * craft—all shall be Is 2:16
Weep for your *, for it is gone! Is 23:1
of Tarshish, for your * is gone. Is 23:10
and landed at the * of Tyre, in Act 21:3
*—a poor place to spend the Act 27:12
Phoenix was a good * with only a Act 27:12

HARBORS
At ease beside his *? Ju 5:17

HARD
us relief from the * work of Gen 5:28-31
Is anything too * for God? Gen 18:14
You know how * I've worked for Gen 31:6
careful not to be too * on Jacob!' Gen 31:29
cruelty and my * work, and that is Gen 31:42
are driven too *, they will die. Gen 33:13
After a very * delivery, the Gen 35:17
lived 130 long, * years, and I am Gen 47:9
to toil long and * in the fields Ex 1:13,14
Pharaoh's heart was still * and Ex 7:13
so Pharaoh's heart remained * and Ex 7:22
But Pharaoh's heart was * and Ex 8:19
They brought the * cases to Moses Ex 18:26
"Anyone who hits a man so * that Ex 21:12
Literally, "you shall do no * Lev 23:7f
don't do any * work that day. Lev 23:35
* work shall be done on that day. Num 28:18
that day you may do no * work. Num 28:25
there is to be no * work by Num 28:26
day, and no * work may be done. Num 29:1
that day no * work shall be done; Num 29:12
you must do no * work that day. Num 29:35
"If a case arises that is too * Deu 17:8
you will have worked so * to grow. Deu 28:33
worn out from our long, * trip." Jos 9:13
its men were known as * fighters. Jos 10:2
They all worked * ferrying the 2Sa 19:18
"This is a * decision," David 2Sa 24:14
to test him with some * questions. 1Ki 10:1
"Your father was a * master," 1Ki 12:2,3,4
* on you, well, I'll be harder! 1Ki 12:10
* for the Lord God of the heavens; 1Ki 19:10
been working very * for the Lord 1Ki 19:14
"You have asked a * thing," 2Ki 2:10
a * time at his birth (Jabez means 1Ch 4:9
Saul had been * pressed with 1Ch 10:3
"By * work I have collected 1Ch 22:14
to test him with * questions. 2Ch 9:1
"Your father was a * master," 2Ch 10:4
my father was * on you, just wait 2Ch 10:10
Joash tried * to please the Lord 2Ch 24:2
He worked very * to encourage 2Ch 31:21
Zedekiah was a * and stubborn man 2Ch 36:13
And it is raining so * that we Ez 10:13
city—for the workers worked *. Neh 4:6
A man's life is long and *, like Job 7:1
* labor shall repay his debts. Job 20:10
and turns to ice, as * as rock. Job 38:30
His flesh is * and firm, not Job 41:23
His heart is * as rock, just Job 41:24
peace with everyone; work * at it. Ps 34:14
cares for them when times are *; Ps 37:19
set my feet on a *, firm path and Ps 40:2
You have been very * on us and Ps 60:3
Yet it is so * to explain Ps 73:16
That is why he broke them with * Ps 107:12
for you to work so * from early Ps 127:2
yet they labor * all summer, Pro 6:8
Lazy men are soon poor; * workers Pro 10:4
* work means prosperity; Pro 12:11
satisfaction, and * work returns Pro 12:14
Work * and become a leader; Pro 12:24
wealth from * work grows. Pro 13:11
It is * to stop a quarrel once it Pro 17:14
WINE GIVES FALSE courage; * liquor Pro 20:1
Stay awake, work *, and there Pro 20:13
a soft tongue can break * bones. Pro 25:15
* work brings prosperity; Pro 28:19
are oppressed. * liquor is for Pro 31:6,7
She is energetic, a * worker, Pro 31:17
does a man get for all his * work? Ecc 1:3-7
So I worked * to be wise Ecc 1:16-18
I even found great pleasure in * Ecc 2:10
fruits of all my * work to others. Ecc 2:18
So I turned in despair from * Ecc 2:20-23
does a man get for all his * work? Ecc 2:20-23
What does one really get from * Ecc 3:9
by, than to work * when, in the Ecc 4:5,6
yet he works * to keep gaining more Ecc 4:8
The man who works * sleeps well Ecc 5:12
his * work has been for nothing; Ecc 5:16
you can, and when * times strike, Ecc 7:14
him in all the * work which God Ecc 8:15
whose leaders work * before they Ecc 10:16,17
I will hand over Egypt to a *, Is 19:4
I knew how * and obstinate you Is 48:4
They are determined, with faces * Jer 5:3
They are insolent as brass, * and Jer 6:28
They are * and stubborn and Jer 7:26
they have worked * but it does Jer 12:13
nothing is too * for you! Jer 32:17
is there anything too * for me? Jer 32:27
it is dry and * and withered. Lam 4:8
For the whole lot of them are *, Eze 3:7
But see, I have made you * and Eze 3:8
I have made your forehead as * Eze 3:9
where the ground is * and dry. Eze 19:13
of Babylon fought * against Tyre. Eze 29:18
them but their * hearts would not Hos 7:13
plow the * ground of your hearts, Hos 10:12
* upon him and dry up his land. Hos 13:15
It is as * to find an honest man Mic 7:1
They work so *, but all in vain! Hab 2:13
you have worked so * to get." Hag 1:11
work so * beneath a heavy yoke. Mt 11:28
grain: The * path where some of Mt 13:19
of your * and evil hearts, but it Mt 19:8
I knew you were a * man, and I was Mt 25:24,25
it off the * ground and ate it. Mk 4:4
their lives. The * pathway, where Mk 4:15
represents the * hearts of some of Mk 4:15
trouble, rowing * and struggling Mk 6:48
Are your hearts too * to take it Mk 8:17
children, how * it is for those who Mk 10:24
He must never touch wine or * Lk 1:15
"we worked * all last night and Lk 5:5
But if he works *, he may learn Lk 6:40
to men. The * path where some seed Lk 8:12
represents the * hearts of those Lk 8:12
went on a long, * journey to listen Lk 11:31
is narrow. Work * to get in, for Lk 13:24,25
years I've worked * for you and Lk 15:29
disciples, "How * it is for the Lk 18:24
that *, how can anyone be saved?" Lk 18:26
for you are a * man to deal Lk 19:21
slave,' the king roared. '*, am I? Lk 19:22
You find it so * to believe all Lk 24:25
"This is very * to understand. Jn 6:60
Literally, "It is * for you to Act 26:14f
have them or works * to get them. Rom 9:16
But the Jews, who tried so * to Rom 9:31
He is very * on those who Rom 11:22
are going through such * times. Rom 15:26
She has worked * in the church Rom 16:1
who has worked so * to help us. Rom 16:6
who has worked so * for the Lord. Rom 16:12
be rewarded for his own * work. 1Co 3:8
the result of my * work for him. 1Co 9:1
like them who work * at your side 1Co 16:16
* time we went through in Asia. 2Co 1:8
that we work so * to win others. 2Co 5:11
much trouble and * times, they have 2Co 8:2
and tried as * as I possibly could Gal 1:14
I am afraid that all my * work Gal 4:11
lead to jealousy and * feelings. Gal 5:26
I know this is * to Eph 5:32
Don't work * only when your Eph 6:6,7
looking; work * and with gladness Eph 6:6,7
humiliating and * on the body, but Col 2:23
Work * and cheerfully at all you Col 3:23
He is a * worker and serves the Col 4:7
that he has worked * for you with Col 4:13
how * we worked among you? 1Th 2:9
you), we tried * to come back to 1Th 2:17
church who work * among you and 1Th 5:12
ideal of * work we set up for you. 2Th 3:6
we worked * day and night for the 2Th 3:8
and he must be * working and 1Ti 3:2
We work * and suffer much in 1Ti 4:9,10
* at both preaching and teaching. 1Ti 5:17
CHRISTIAN SLAVES SHOULD work * 1Ti 6:1
Work *, like a farmer who gets 2Ti 2:6
service for him is *, just remember 2Ti 2:12
Work * so God can say to you, 2Ti 2:15
I have fought long and * for my 2Ti 4:7
so it's * to make you understand. Heb 5:11
How can he forget your * work for Heb 6:10
but the Lord's face is * against 1Pe 3:12
you must also work * to be good, 2Pe 1:5
So, dear brothers, work * to 2Pe 1:10
He is especially * on those who 2Pe 2:10
try * to live without sinning; 2Pe 3:14
and really, that isn't * at all; 1Jn 5:3
I have been working so * to get. 2Jn 1:8
I have watched your * work and Rev 2:2
"And now think *: his seven Rev 17:9

HARD-BURNED
So they made great piles of * Gen 11:3,4

HARD-TO-UNDERSTAND
"Why do you always use these * Mt 13:10

HARD-WON
and will long enjoy their * gains. Is 65:21,22

HARD-WORKING
Do you know a * man? Pro 22:29

HARDEN
And once again I will * Ex 14:4
I will * the hearts of the Ex 14:17
Don't * your hearts as Israel did Ps 95:8
they have done. * their hearts and Lam 3:65
to you, do not * your hearts Heb 3:15
not * your hearts against him." Heb 4:7

HARDENED
were gone, he * his heart and Ex 8:15
But Pharaoh * his heart again and Ex 8:31,32
But Jehovah * Pharaoh in his Ex 9:12
but I have * him and his Ex 10:1
But the Lord * Pharaoh's heart Ex 10:20
So the Lord * Pharaoh's heart and Ex 10:27
eyes, the Lord * his heart so that Ex 11:10
O Lord, why have you * our Is 63:17
and mind were * in pride, God Dan 5:20

HARDENED Con't)
They have * their hearts and Amo 2:4
They * their hearts like flint, Zec 7:12
their hearts were *," perhaps Mk 6:52f
has blinded their eyes and * Jn 12:40
of you will become * against God, Heb 3:13

HARDER
Fight * next time, and conquer 2Sa 11:25
was hard on you, well, I'll be *! 1Ki 12:10
It is * to win back the Pro 18:19
They tried * to row the boat Jon 1:13
for I have worked * than all the 1Co 15:10
I don't want to be * on him than 2Co 2:5,6
I have worked *, been put in 2Co 11:23
rather they should work all the * 1Ti 6:2

HARDEST
who worked the *, I or they; 1Co 15:11

HARDHEADED
you are as * as brass. Is 48:4
They will be * and never give in 2Ti 3:3

HARDHEARTED
For they are a *, stiff-necked Eze 2:4
And if you *, sinful men know Mt 7:11
a concession to your * wickedness. Mk 10:5

HARDLY
with age, so that he could * see. Gen 48:10
He had * finished speaking the Num 16:31
"I can * move!" 1Sa 17:38,39
to them, "Ahab * worshiped Baal at 2Ki 10:17
with * a thought from anyone. Job 4:20
But they had * finished eating, Ps 78:30
for someone you * know, Pro 6:1
They * get started, barely take Is 40:24
they have * done one thing you Jer 32:23
is gone and I can * breathe." Dan 10:17
And he could * accept the fact Mk 6:6
it is always hitting him and * Lk 9:39
world could * contain the books! Jn 21:25
And the Council could * Act 4:14
grudges and will * even notice when 1Co 13:5
I think you * need someone's 2Co 3:1
I can * believe it! Gal 3:4

HARDNESS
up a man's face, softening its *. Ecc 8:1
Plow up the * of your hearts; Jer 4:3

HARDSHIP
He heard us and saw our *, toil, Deu 26:6,7
and * and trouble of every kind. 2Co 6:4

HARDSHIPS
not let all the * we have gone Neh 9:32
us in our * and trials. 2Co 1:3,4
*, persecutions and difficulties; 2Co 12:10
and * you are going through. 2Th 1:4

HARDTACK
Then he took some * and gave Act 27:35

HARE
The * (because although it chews Lev 11:4-7
the camel, the *, or the coney. Deu 14:7

HAREM
and she was taken into his *. Gen 12:15
young lovelies for the royal *. Est 2:3
to the king's * at Shushan Palace, Est 2:8
for the *, was very much impressed Est 2:9
most luxurious apartment in the *. Est 2:9
the court of the * to ask about Est 2:11
* where the king's wives lived. Est 2:12,13,14
in charge of the *, dressing Est 2:15
transferred to the second *." Est 2:19f

HAREPH
and * (the father of Beth-gader). 1Ch 2:51

HARHAIAH
Uzziel (son of *) was a Neh 3:8

HARHAS
of Tikvah, son of *—who was in 2Ki 22:14

HARHUR
Bakbuk, Hakupha, *, Bazluth, Ez 2:43-54
Bakbuk, Hakupha, *, Neh 7:46-56

HARIM
Third, the group led by *; 1Ch 24:7-18
From the subclan of *, 320; Ez 2:3-35
From the subclan of *, 1,017. Ez 2:36-39
The sons of *: Ez 10:21
From the clan of *: Ez 10:31,32
Then came Malchijah (son of *) Neh 3:11
From the subclan of *, 320; Neh 7:8-38
From the subclan of *, 1,017. Neh 7:39-42
Malluch, *, Meremoth, Neh 10:1
Adna, leader of the * clan; Neh 12:12-21

HARIPH
From the subclan of *, 112; Neh 7:8-38
Hashum, Bezai, *, Neh 10:14-27

HARLOT
Literally, "they play the * Ex 34:15f
she will sing sweet songs as a * Is 23:15,16
The most experienced * could Jer 2:33
these who have become old * hags? Eze 23:43
For they have played the * Hos 4:12
return to the hire of an *." Mic 1:7f
power—Rahab the * did not die with Heb 11:31

HARLOTRIES
betrays nations with her *." Nah 3:4f

HARLOTRY
your *, your worshiping of idols. Eze 23:49
Beg her to stop her *, to quit Hos 1:2

HARLOTS
lands today) only * were permitted Is 47:2f
you offspring of adulterers and *! Is 57:3
these shameless *—with all the zest Eze 23:44
with * and temple prostitutes. Hos 4:14

HARM
Promise that you will not * us, Gen 26:29
not permitted him to do me any *! Gen 31:7
So how could I * my own daughters Gen 31:43
for fear some * might happen to him Gen 42:4
me also, and any * befalls him, I Gen 44:29
Angel who has kept me from all *. Gen 48:16
But if any * comes to the woman Ex 21:23
without wanting to * an enemy—yet Num 35:22,23
And preserves him from every *." Deu 33:12
"He's never done anything to * 1Sa 19:4
But the soldiers refused to * the 1Sa 22:17
my own life. Any * to you will be 1Sa 22:23
who say that I am trying to * you? 1Sa 24:9,10
For I said, 'I will never * 1Sa 24:9,10
I am not trying to * you and that I 1Sa 24:11
do to me, but I will never * you. 1Sa 24:12
we never suffered any * from them; 1Sa 25:15,16
and I'll no longer try to * you; 1Sa 26:21
you won't let anyone * my son. 2Sa 14:11
please don't * young Absalom.' 2Sa 18:12
David was moved to * them by taking 2Sa 24:1
protested, "what * have I done to 1Ki 18:9
great * to you and sweep you away; 1Ki 21:21
And then it didn't * them. 2Ki 4:41
God didn't let anyone * them. 1Ch 16:21
'Don't * my chosen people,' he 1Ch 16:22
any who might try to * them; Est 9:1
home and his property from all *. Job 1:10
but don't * him physically." Job 1:12,13
let you * him without any cause." Job 2:3
"If I have rejoiced at * to an Job 31:29
So many seek to * me. Ps 3:1
back those who * me and subdues the Ps 18:47
For they warn us away from * and Ps 19:11
God of Jacob keep you from all *. Ps 20:1
But all who * the innocent shall Ps 25:3
them good, but they return me *. Ps 35:12
fret and worry—it only leads to *. Ps 37:8
do *, O man with the lying tongue. Ps 52:4
All their thoughts are how to * Ps 56:5
those who are trying to * me; Ps 143:12
will lead you and save you from *; Pro 6:22
* befalls the good, but there is Pro 12:21
But to reject criticism is to * Pro 15:31,32
happiness, and protection from *. Pro 19:23
An evil man loves to * others; Pro 21:10
Good men will be rescued from *, Pro 28:18
the fate of those who do them *. Is 47:7
* and give you as a token and Is 49:8,9
They cannot * you. Jer 1:18
* nor help, nor do you any good. Jer 10:5
true to me, then I'll not * you. Jer 25:6
bless you and no one will * you. Jer 42:10
thought no one could ever * you. Jer 49:4
and will protect us from all *. Eze 11:3
couldn't keep them back from * Eze 20:9,10
he couldn't protect them from *!' Eze 36:20
people, preserving them from *; Dan 6:27
return the * to your own heads. Joe 3:4
among us. No * can come to us." Mic 3:11
Don't plot * to others; Zec 8:17
angels to keep you from *,' Mt 4:6
Or is this a day for doing *? Mk 3:4
what you eat won't * your soul? Mk 7:18
on the Sabbath day, or to do *? Lk 6:9
* these little children's souls. Lk 17:2,3
am with you and no one can * you. Act 18:10
a long time and no * came to him, Act 28:6
will not want to * or cheat him, or Rom 13:9
You may believe there is no * in Rom 14:2
for you know there is no * in it. 1Co 8:10
For it sounds as if more * than 1Co 11:17
coppersmith has done me much *. 2Ti 4:14
it only does *. Tit 3:9
they were kept from * in a den of Heb 11:33
Anyone trying to * them will be Rev 11:5

HARMED
as we have not * you, and in fact, Gen 26:29
and give it to the one he has *; Lev 6:4,5
family aren't *," they promised. Jos 2:14
But the cities were not * Jos 9:18
us, we have never * them, nor 1Sa 25:7
behaves himself, he will not be *; 1Ki 1:52
"Has my sin * you, O God, Job 7:20
will be no more * by it than by a Pro 26:2
All who * them were counted Jer 2:3
My enemies, whom I have never *, Lam 3:52
Your souls aren't * by what you Mk 7:15,16
against a man who had * her. Lk 18:3
even though I had * no one nor Act 28:17
If he has * you in any way or Phm 1:18

HARMFUL
someone is as * as hitting him with Pro 25:18
Just as it is * to eat too much Pro 25:27
confusing and useless, and even *. 2Ti 2:14

HARMING
"Anyone * this man or his wife Gen 26:11
and punish them there for * my Joe 3:2
Anyone who isn't helping me is * Mt 12:30
I hunted down his people, * them 1Ti 1:13

HARMLESS
come disguised as * sheep, but are Mt 7:15
Be as wary as serpents and * as Mt 10:16

HARMLESSLY
his followers were * dispersed. Act 5:36

HARMONY
will be peace and * in the camp." Ex 18:23
pleasant, when brothers live in *! Ps 133:1
in harmony! For * is as precious Ps 133:2
of his robe. * is as refreshing as Ps 133:3
with perfect * between the two!' Zec 6:13
for us in * with God's own will. Rom 8:27
In this way aim for * in the Rom 14:19
live in complete * with each Rom 15:5
Let there be real * so that there 1Co 1:10
children to live in peace and *. 1Co 7:15
He likes *, and he finds it in 1Co 14:33
And what * can there be between 2Co 6:15
Live in * and peace. 2Co 13:11
will stay together in perfect *. Col 3:14

HARMS
to gossip, never * his neighbor, Ps 15:3
Lord who helps one and * another. Lam 3:38
you, for he who * you sticks his Zec 2:8

HARNEPHER
Suah, *, Shual, Beri, Imrah, 1Ch 7:36,37

HARNESS
to battle! * the horses and Jer 46:4
But now I will * her to the plow Hos 10:11

HARNESSED
an ox and a donkey * together. Deu 22:10
my mare * to Pharaoh's chariot." Sol 1:9f

HAROD
went as far as the spring of *. Ju 7:1
Shammah from *: 2Sa 23:24-39
Elika from *; 2Sa 23:24-39
Shammoth from *; 1Ch 11:26-47

HAROEH
Kiriath-jearim and *, the ancestor 1Ch 2:52

HAROSHETH-HA-GOIIM
army was Sisera, who lived in *. Ju 4:2,3
from * to the Kishon River. Ju 4:13
chariots as far as *, until all of Ju 4:16

HARP
such as handle the * and pipe." Gen 4:21f
of the * and flute. Gen 4:21
with singing and orchestra and *? Gen 31:27
a *, and prophesying as they come. 1Sa 10:5
"The * music will quiet you and 1Sa 16:15,16
only a talented * player, but was 1Sa 16:18
would play the * and Saul would 1Sa 16:23
him by playing the *, as he did 1Sa 18:10
David playing the *, suddenly the 1Sa 19:9,10
praise upon the lyre and on the *. Ps 33:2
accompanied skillfully on the *; Ps 33:3
joy, and praise him with my *. Ps 43:4
Arise, O * and lyre! Ps 57:8
pluck the sweet lyre and *. Ps 81:2
from the * and lute and lyre. Ps 92:3
accompanied by music from the *. Ps 98:5
Wake up, O * and lyre! Ps 108:2
hand forget its skill upon the *. Ps 137:5,6
O God, with a ten-stringed *. Ps 144:9
the trumpet and with lute and *. Ps 150:3
The melodious chords of the * Is 24:8
Literally, "the cornet, flute, *, Dan 3:5f
Literally, "the cornet, flute, *, Dan 3:7f
Literally, "the cornet, flute, *, Dan 3:10f
the sound of the *, and fancy Amo 6:5
"Don't * on things like that. Mic 2:6
instance, or the *—are examples of 1Co 14:7
Lamb, each with a * and golden Rev 5:8

HARPERS
Literally, "* . Rev 18:22f

HARPIST
"We'll find a good * to play for 1Sa 16:15,16
"Find me a *." 1Sa 16:17

HARPISTS
Je-iel, and Azaziah were the *. 1Ch 15:21

HARPOON
by darts, or his head with a *? Job 41:7

HARPS
the Lord—lyres, *, tambourines, 2Sa 6:5
* and harpsichords for his choirs. 1Ki 10:12
and by zithers, *, tambourines, 1Ch 13:8
upon psaltries, *, and cymbals. 1Ch 15:16
an octet accompanied by *." 1Ch 15:20
(or *) set to the Sheminith." 1Ch 15:21f
loud playing on the * and zithers. 1Ch 15:28
they played the * and zithers. 1Ch 16:5
of zithers, *, and cymbals. 1Ch 25:1
of cymbals, *, and zithers; 1Ch 25:6,7
played the cymbals, lyres, and *. 2Ch 5:11,12
* and lyres for the choir. 2Ch 9:11

(HARPS Con't)
by a band of *, lyres, and trumpets 2Ch 20:28
using cymbals, psalteries, and *. 2Ch 29:25,26
cymbals, psaltries, and *. Neh 12:27
accompanied by * the answer to one Ps 49:4
to our God, accompanied by *. Ps 147:7
there be the sound of * among you. Eze 26:13
of a choir accompanied by *. Rev 14:2
All were holding * of God, and Rev 15:2

HARPSICHORDS
for harps and * for his choirs. 1Ki 10:12

HARROW
Will he pull the * for you? Job 39:10
harness her to the plow and *. Hos 10:11

HARROWING
Is he forever * the soil and Is 28:23,24

HARROWS
and iron *, and in brick kilns." 2Sa 12:31f

HARSH
And if you are * to my Gen 31:50
freedom from their * taskmasters. Ex 3:7
agreed to are too *, then her Num 30:5
Yes, my father was *, but I'll 1Ki 12:11
Must you be so * with frail men, Job 14:3
wrath, but * words cause quarrels. Pro 15:1
I come how * and rough I can be. 2Co 10:2
Quarreling, * words, and dislike Eph 4:31
not bitter against them, nor *. Col 3:19

HARSHA
Bazluth, Mehida, *, Barkos, Sisera, Ez 2:43-54
Bazlith, Mehida, *, Neh 7:46-56

HARSHER
was harsh, but I'll be even *! 1Ki 12:11

HARSHLY
as ordinary slaves, or treated *; Lev 25:43
you ashamed to deal with me so *? Job 19:3
loyal to him, but * punishes all Ps 31:23

HARSHNESS
I need not come to you with *. 2Co 7:9

HARUM
named after Aharhel, the son of *. 1Ch 4:8

HARUMAPH
Jedaiah (son of *) repaired the Neh 3:10

HARUPH
Shephatiah from *; 1Ch 12:3-7

HARUZ
(daughter of *, of Jotbah) 2Ki 21:19,20

HARVEST
was a farmer. At * time Cain Gen 4:3
be springtime and *, cold and heat, Gen 8:22
and good * of grain, and new Gen 27:27,28,29
One day during the wheat *, Gen 30:14
will be neither plowing nor *. Gen 45:6
And when you * it, a fifth of Gen 47:24
among the people * any volunteer Ex 23:11
Then there is the * Pilgrimage, Ex 23:16
at the end of the * season. Ex 23:16
sample of the first day's *; Ex 23:19
"Even during plowing and * Ex 34:21
First Wheat, and the * Festival. Ex 34:22
offerings at * time, but not as Lev 2:12
the first of your *, remove the Lev 2:14
"When you * your crops, don't Lev 19:9
reap your first *, bring the first Lev 23:9,10,11
first sheaf of the * to the priest Lev 23:9,10,11
not eat any of the * for Lev 23:14
your vineyards and * your crops, Lev 25:3
to plant or * crops that year?' Lev 25:20
Literally, "until the grape *." Lev 26:4,5f
with them when the new * is ready! Lev 26:10
the people to celebrate the new *. Num 28:26
be no rain and no *, and you will Deu 11:17
"Seven weeks after the * begins, Deu 16:9
as judged by the amount of your *. Deu 16:10
at the end of the * season, after Deu 16:13
good * and in so many other ways; Deu 16:15
shall receive the * samples brought Deu 18:4
If, when reaping your *, you Deu 24:19
*. Bring it in a basket and hand Deu 26:2,3
Now it was the * season and the Jos 3:13,14
During the * feast at Shechem Ju 9:27
LATER ON, DURING the wheat *, Ju 15:1
at the beginning of the barley *. Ru 1:22
girls right through the whole * Ru 2:22
end of the barley *, and then the Ru 2:23
and then the wheat *, too. Ru 2:23
and * his crops without pay; 1Sa 8:12
He will take a tenth of your * 1Sa 8:15
of the year, during the wheat *; 1Sa 12:17
at the beginning of the barley *. 2Sa 21:9
there through the entire * season 2Sa 21:10
The * lasted six months, from 2Sa 21:10f
down at * time to visit him. 2Sa 23:13
from the first grain of his *. 2Ki 4:42
year they will have a bountiful *. 2Ki 19:29
the first offerings of every *. Neh 13:31
sin and trouble who * the same. Job 4:7,8
than their joys at * time as they Ps 4:7
Their * was consumed by locusts. Ps 78:46
the cold, you won't eat at the *. Pro 20:4
summertime or rain with * time! Pro 26:1
A time to *; Ecc 3:2
the field when the * time is Is 1:8
Then he waited for the *, but the Is 5:2
reapers when the * time has come, Is 9:3
the gladness, gone the joy of *. Is 16:10
I have ended all their * joys. Is 16:10
the trees when the * is ended, two Is 17:6
yet you will never * it—your only Is 17:11
it—your only * will be a pile of Is 17:11
autumn morning during * time. Is 18:4
will go: the grape * will fail, the Is 24:7
fail; the * will not take place. Is 32:10
seed for a small * next year, and Is 37:30
The third * from then would yield Is 37:30f
of the Lord at * time, carried in Is 66:20
"the firstfruits of his *." Jer 2:3f
And they shall eat your * and Jer 5:17
fall and sends the * times, yet Jer 5:23,24
"The * is finished; Jer 8:20
They shall * a crop of shame, for Jer 12:13
live off the land. * the grapes and Jer 40:10
* of wine grapes and other crops. Jer 40:12
They will * all your fruit and Eze 25:4
The first samples of each * of Eze 44:30
wine at the time of the grape *. Hos 1:9
is a plentiful * of punishment Hos 6:11
work; the * is ripe and waiting. Joe 3:13
rain three months before the *. Amo 4:7
of crops, that the * time will Amo 9:13
You will plant crops but not * Mic 6:15
and figs when * days are over. Mic 7:1
You plant much but * little. Hag 1:6
"The * is so great, and the Mt 9:37
more workers for his * fields." Mt 9:38
together until the *, and I will Mt 13:30
the * is the end of the world, Mt 13:39
to hire workers for his * field. Mt 20:1
"At the time of the grape * he Mt 21:34
a plentiful * for God—thirty, Mk 4:20
the Lord of the * to send out more Lk 10:2
help you, for the * is so plentiful Lk 10:2
don't plant or * or have barns to Lk 12:24
When * time came, he sent one of Lk 20:10
work, and you received the *." Jn 4:38
plentiful * of new lives. Jn 12:23,24
should expect some share of the *. 1Co 9:10
on, good crops to * and eat, will 2Co 9:10
more and more fruit from your *. 2Co 9:10
a * of spiritual decay and death; Gal 6:8
we will reap a * of blessing if we Gal 6:9
of peace and reap a * of goodness. Jas 3:18
for his precious * to ripen. Jas 5:7
the * is ripe on the earth." Rev 14:15
earth, and the * was gathered in. Rev 14:16

HARVESTED
crops of the eighth year are *!' Lev 25:21,22
grapes were being * at that time. Num 13:20
until the entire field is *." Ru 2:21
had been * during her absence. 2Ki 8:6
you'll not be * until it's time! Job 5:26
after the hay is *, and the new Pro 27:25,26,27
abandoned as the * grain fields in Is 17:5
* your grapes and summer fruits. Jer 48:32
Ephraim's sins are * and stored Hos 13:12
before you have * your grain, and Hag 2:18,19
once with his sickle and * it." Mk 4:29

HARVESTERS
He will shout as the * do who Jer 25:30

HARVESTING
at the end of your *, is the time Lev 23:39
in charge of the *, and ask him to Mt 9:38
They are * on the Sabbath." Mt 12:2
work by * grain on the Sabbath." Mk 2:24
Your disciples are * grain, and Lk 6:2
Do you think the work of * will Jn 4:35

HARVESTS
(When you reap your *, you must Lev 23:22
to the number of * until the Lev 25:27
Their * are stolen and their Job 5:5
and sends them rich * of grain. Ps 65:9
the earth has yielded abundant *. Ps 67:6,7
upon their summer fruits and *. Is 16:9
and with wonderful * and with ample Is 30:23
are bountiful * of grain and Is 36:17
Their * will not be eaten by Is 65:23
I will give you huge * from your Eze 36:30
give her rich * of grain in its Hos 1:9
Therefore your * will be small; Hos 9:2
the richer the * I give her, the Hos 10:1
disciples produce bountiful *. Jn 15:8
of a farmer who * his crop and 1Co 9:7

HAS-BEENS
of those two *, Rezin and Pekah. Is 7:4

HASADIAH
Ohel, Berechiah, *, Jushab-hesed, 1Ch 3:19,20

HASH-BADDENAH
*, Zechariah, and Meshullam. Neh 8:1

HASHABIAH
Kishi, Abdi, Malluch, *, Amaziah, 1Ch 6:44-47
of Azrikam, son of *, who was a 1Ch 9:14
Shime-i, *, and Mattithiah. 1Ch 25:3
Twelfth, * and twelve of his sons 1Ch 25:9-31
and judges. * and 1,700 of his 1Ch 26:30
Over Levi, * (son of Kemuel); 1Ch 27:16-22
and his brothers *, Je-iel, and 2Ch 35:9
God also sent *; Ez 8:19
priests—Sherebiah, *, and ten other Ez 8:24
*, Benaiah. Ez 10:25
Then came *, the mayor of half Neh 3:17
*, Zaccur, Sherebiah, Neh 10:9-13
Azrikam, son of *, son of Bunni); Neh 11:15,16,17
of Bani, son of *, son of Neh 11:22,23
*, leader of the Hilkiah clan; Neh 12:12-21
*, Sherebiah, and Jeshua (son of Neh 12:24

HASHABNAH
*, Ma-aseiah, Ahiah, Neh 10:14-27

HASHABNEIAH
to him was Hattush (son of *). Neh 3:10
Kadmi-el, Bani, *, Sherebiah, Neh 9:5

HASHEM
of * from Gizon; 1Ch 11:26-47

HASHMONAH
From Mithkah to *; Num 33:15-37
From * to Moseroth; Num 33:15-37

HASHUBAH
Hananiah, *, Ohel, Berechiah, 1Ch 3:19,20

HASHUM
From the subclan of *, 223; Ez 2:3-35
From the clan of *: Ez 10:33
From the subclan of *, 328; Neh 7:8-38
Malchijah, *, Hash-baddenah, Neh 8:1
*, Bezai, Hariph, Neh 10:14-27

HASN'T
* he spoken through us, too?" Num 12:2
do wrong when he *, both men shall Deu 19:16
But even yet the Lord * given Deu 29:4
The reason he * let you settle Deu 29:6
"There * been such a horrible Ju 19:30
Jonathan, "Why * David been here 1Sa 20:27
We have charged him nothing—he * 2Sa 19:42
the Lord * told me what it is." 2Ki 4:27
to your master? * he sent me to the 2Ki 18:27
* done a day's work in his life; Ecc 2:20-23
The Lord our God * told you to Jer 43:2,3
* spoken one word to them at all. Eze 22:28
and there * been a single fig!' Lk 13:7
this man * done one thing wrong." Lk 23:40,41
in Jerusalem who * heard about the Lk 24:18
to do that this man * done?" Jn 7:31
citizen who * even been tried?" Act 22:25
agreed, "This man * done anything Act 26:31
for something that * happened yet, Rom 8:25
What do you have that God * given 1Co 4:7
and if he * been circumcised, he 1Co 7:18
means "Useful") * been of much Phm 1:11
* helped those who have tried it! Heb 13:9

HASRAH
(son of Tokhath, son of *). 2Ch 34:22

HASSENAAH
Gate was built by the sons of *; Neh 3:3

HASSENU-AH
was assisted by Judah, son of *. Neh 11:7,8,9

HASSENUAH
son of Hodaviah, the son of *); 1Ch 9:7,8

HASSHUB
Shemaiah (son of *, son of Azrikam, 1Ch 9:14
(son of Harim) and * (son of Neh 3:11
Benjamin, *, and Azariah (son of Neh 3:23
Hananiah, *, Hallohesh, Neh 10:14-27
Shemaiah (son of *, son of Neh 11:15,16,17

HASSOPHERETH
Sotai, *, Peruda, Jaalah, Darkon, Ez 2:55,56,57

HAST
Literally, "Thou * instructed Job 4:3,4f

HASTE
required such *, and I left in such 1Sa 21:8
away by the Syrians in their *. 2Ki 7:15
You shall not leave in *, Is 52:12
they stumble in their *, rushing Nah 2:5
of the need for * before the Jn 19:42

HASTEN
"I * to reply, for I have the Job 20:2
they can to * my calamity, knowing Job 30:13
legs of the men broken to * death; Jn 19:31

HASTILY
next morning, and * called a Gen 20:8
He was brought * from the Gen 41:14
Pharaoh * summoned Moses and Ex 8:25
Ahab left * for Jezreel, and the 1Ki 18:45
marauders so they * threw his body 2Ki 13:20,21
I spoke too * when I said, "The Ps 31:22
saw her leave so *, they assumed Jn 11:31
For I am told that everyone * 1Co 11:21

HASTY
Then Joseph made a * exit, for Gen 43:30
* speculation brings poverty. Pro 21:5

HASUPHA
Ziha, *, Tabbaoth, Keros, Siaha, Ez 2:43-54
Ziha, *, Tabbaoth, Keros, Neh 7:46-56

HAT
at the drop of a *, the man who Is 29:21
to remove his * while praying or 1Co 11:4

HAT Con't)
* is a sign of subjection to men 1Co 11:7
HATCH
your chickens before they *!" 1Ki 20:11
They lie awake at night to * Ps 36:4
lay her eggs and * her young and Is 34:15
HATCHED
young she has not * and which will Jer 17:11
HATE
honest men who * bribes, and Ex 18:21
of those who * me; Ex 20:5
"Don't * your brother. Lev 19:17
those who * you will rule you; Lev 26:17
and we * this insipid manna." Num 21:5
'The Lord must * us, bringing us Deu 1:27
of the children of those who * me; Deu 5:9,10
But those who * him shall be Deu 7:10
those who * you and persecute you. Deu 30:7,8
to me when you * me and have driven Ju 11:7
me at all; you * me, for you have Ju 14:16
* him more with every passing day. 1Sa 18:29
Israel must * him bitterly by now. 1Sa 27:12
How I * them." 2Sa 5:8
his love turned to *, and now he 2Sa 13:15
You seem to love those who * 2Sa 19:6
you, and * those who love you. 2Sa 19:6
replied, "but I * him, for he 1Ki 22:8
is one, but I * him, for he never 2Ch 18:6,7
and loving those who * the Lord?" 2Ch 19:2
on and on like this. I * my life. Job 7:16
Those who * you shall be clothed Job 8:22
For they * the noise of the city Job 39:7
for how you * their evil deeds. Ps 5:5
at the hands of those who * me. Ps 9:13
find your enemies, all who * you. Ps 21:8
have and how viciously they * me! Ps 25:19
hypocritical. I * the sinners' Ps 26:5
how you * all those who worship Ps 31:5,6
meted out to those who * the good. Ps 34:21
and continue to * me—though I have Ps 38:19
* me for standing for the right. Ps 38:20
but all the time they * me and Ps 41:6
the victory over those who * us. Ps 44:7
And * what is wrong. Ps 45:7
all those who * me without cause. Ps 69:4
Rescue me from those who * me, Ps 69:14
of those who * the Lord. Ps 73:16
of God have changed to *. Ps 77:10
Those who * the Lord would Ps 81:15
these proud men who * the Lord? Ps 83:2
When those who * me see it they Ps 86:17
him, and destroy those who * him. Ps 89:23
The Lord loves those who * evil; Ps 97:10
They have no reason to * and Ps 109:3
Let those who * me beware. Ps 118:7
These proud men who * your truth Ps 119:85,86
wonder I * every false teaching. Ps 119:104
I * those who are undecided Ps 119:113
it concerns. I * every other way. Ps 119:128
How I * all falsehood but how I Ps 119:163
here among these men who * peace. Ps 120:5,6
May all who * the Jews be brought Ps 129:5
O Lord, shouldn't I * those who Ps 139:21
shouldn't I hate those who * you? Ps 139:21
Yes, I * them, for your enemies Ps 139:22
and true, for I * lies and every Pro 8:6,7
and fears God, he will * evil. Pro 8:13
he will only * you for trying to Pro 9:7,8
To * is to be a liar; Pro 10:18
than steak with someone you *. Pro 15:17
A man with * in his heart may Pro 26:24,25,26
a thief must really * himself! Pro 29:24
The good * the badness of the Pro 29:27
The wicked * the goodness of the Pro 29:27
So now I * life because it is Ecc 2:17
to do with them. I * them all; Is 1:14
like filthy things you * to touch. Is 30:22
want the good and * the wrong—they Is 59:21
justice; I * robbery and wrong. Is 61:8
Your brethren * you and cast you Is 66:5
Do not * us, Lord, for the sake Jer 14:21
horrible thing I *, but they Jer 44:4
hands of those who * you—the Eze 16:27
Because you * my people Israel, Eze 35:4,5
all your acts of envy and of *. Eze 35:11
He will flatter those who * the Dan 11:32
there I began to * them. Hos 9:15
How you * honest judges! Amo 5:10
he is. * evil and love the good; Amo 5:15
"I * your show and pretence—your Amo 5:21
and * their beautiful homes. Amo 6:8
ones who * good and love evil; Mic 3:2
of Israel who * justice and love Mic 3:9
How I * all that sort of thing!" Zec 8:17
your friends and * your enemies.' Mt 5:43
For you will * one and love the Mt 6:24
Everyone shall * you because you Mt 10:22
sin and betray and * each other. Mt 24:10
And everyone will * you because Mk 13:13
our enemies, from all who * us. Lk 1:71
it is when others * you and exclude Lk 6:22
Do good to those who * you. Lk 6:27
* his father and mother. . . ." Lk 14:26f
You will * one and show loyalty Lk 16:13
And everyone will * you because Lk 21:17
for the world can't * you; Jn 7:7
but it does * me, because I Jn 7:7
you get enough * from the world! Jn 15:18
sin, of greed and *, envy, murder, Rom 1:29
do what I don't want to—what I *. Rom 7:15
enemies of the Gospel. They * it. Rom 11:28
really love them. * what is wrong. Rom 12:9
they are for sinners who * God, 1Ti 1:9
at the hands of those who * him. 2Ti 3:12
You love right and * wrong; Heb 1:9
into their sins. * every trace of Jud 1:23
that is good: You * the deeds of Rev 2:6
reign with him—all * the woman, and Rev 17:16
HATED
So Esau * Jacob because of what Gen 27:41
and consequently * Joseph; Gen 37:4
And they * him both for the dream Gen 37:8
and * in other parts of Egypt. Gen 46:34
Our sacrifices to God are * by Ex 8:26
done what the Lord * most, thus Deu 9:18
them because he * them: he brought Deu 9:28
handmade gods are * by the Lord.' Deu 27:15
"I really thought you * her," Ju 15:2
* her more than he had loved her. 2Sa 13:15
However, he * him with a deep 2Sa 13:21-24
From those who * me 2Sa 22:18
for they * Israel intensely. 1Ki 11:25
idolatry which God * and into which 2Ki 21:16
75,000 of those who * them; Est 9:16
Could God govern if he * Job 34:17
from those who * me—I who was Ps 18:17
I destroyed all who * me. Ps 18:40
they * and enslaved them. Ps 105:25
They were ruled by those who * Ps 106:41,42
Though once despised and * and Is 60:15
treated them as though I * them. Jer 12:8
For I am * everywhere I go. Jer 15:10
been desolate, * and cursed, just Jer 25:18
and loathed, cursed and *. Jer 44:12
and those you *—and I will make you Eze 16:37
but afterward she * them and broke Eze 23:17
12:11), and where the monarchy, * Hos 9:15f
nation—and they * me too. Zec 11:8
and killed and * all over the world Mt 24:9
Samaritans naturally * the Jews. Lk 9:53f
But some of his people * him and Lk 19:14
They * the heavenly Light Jn 3:20
But then, it * me before it hated Jn 15:18
But then, it hated me before it * Jn 15:18
* both of us—me and my Father. Jn 15:24
'They * me without reason.' Jn 15:25
Oh, how I * to write that letter! 2Co 2:4
You were his enemies and * him Col 1:21
We * others and they hated us. Tit 3:3
We hated others and they * us. Tit 3:3
HATEFUL
make yourselves * to me by eating Lev 20:25
Literally, "of every foul and * Rev 18:2f
HATER
beginning and a * of truth—there is Jn 8:44
HATERS
high among these * of the Lord, Ps 120:5,6
They were backbiters, * of God, Rom 1:30
HATES
things that he *, all in the name Deu 12:31
an obelisk, for the Lord * them! Deu 16:22
"But if anyone * his neighbor Deu 19:11
of my sins. God * me and angrily Job 16:9
test; he * those loving violence. Ps 11:5
things the Lord *—no, Pro 6:16-19
For wisdom * pride, arrogance, Pro 8:13
THE LORD * cheating and delights Pro 11:1
The Lord * the stubborn but Pro 11:20
A good man * lies; Pro 13:5
fool. He * the man who is patient. Pro 14:17
The Lord * the gifts of the Pro 15:8
men because he * to be scolded. Pro 15:12
The Lord * the thoughts of the Pro 15:26
if he * dishonesty and bribes. Pro 28:16
says he * divorce and cruel men. Mal 2:16
out of the world, and so it * you. Jn 15:19
And the world * them because they Jn 17:14
No one * his own body but Eph 5:29,30
dear friends, if the world * you. 1Jn 3:13
Anyone who * his Christian 1Jn 3:15
HATHACH
Then Esther sent for *, one of Est 4:5
like that. So * went out to the Est 4:6
Mordecai also gave * a copy of Est 4:8
her people. So * returned to Est 4:9
Esther told * to go back and say Est 4:10
So * gave Esther's message to Est 4:12
HATHATH
Othni-el's sons were * and 1Ch 4:13
HATING
but * bribes brings happiness. Pro 15:27
A time for *; Ecc 3:8
lifetimes—loving, *, envying—is Ecc 9:6
Anyone * me is also hating my Jn 15:23
Anyone hating me is also * my Jn 15:23
They are quick to kill, * anyone Rom 3:15
on * his brother, he is a liar; 1Jn 4:20
HATIPHA
Barkos, Sisera, Temah, Neziah, *. Ez 2:43-54
Neziah, *. Neh 7:46-56
HATITA
Akkub, *, and Shobai), 139. Ez 2:40,41,42
HATRED
brothers, causing even deeper *. Gen 37:5
another out of * by throwing Num 35:20
him with a deep * because of what 2Sa 13:21-24
Their fury and * rise to engulf Ps 55:3
They return evil for good, and * Ps 109:5
* stirs old quarrels, but love Pro 10:12
to be so kind, his * will finally Pro 26:24,25,26
Flattery is a form of * and Pro 26:28
*—you will be cursed and reviled. Jer 42:18
They will deal with you in *, Eze 23:29
and long-standing *, I will shake Eze 25:15
only * for those who love God. Hos 9:7
*, even in the Temple of the Lord. Hos 9:8
of demons), * and fighting, Gal 5:20
*, cursing, and dirty language. Col 3:8
selfishness and * when you trusted 1Pe 1:22
SO GET RID of your feelings of *. 1Pe 2:1
HATREDS
with all its * and wickedness. 1Co 5:8
HATTIL
*, Pochereth-hazzebaim, Ami. Ez 2:55,56,57
Shephatiah, *, Neh 7:57,58,59
HATTUSH
Shemaiah had six sons, including * 1Ch 3:21,22
David of the clan of Shecaniah—*; Ez 8:2-14
to him was * (son of Hashabneiah). Neh 3:10
Malchijah, *, Shebaniah, Neh 10:1
Malluch, *, Shecaniah, Neh 12:1
HAUGHTILY
punishes all who * reject him. Ps 31:23
for she has * defied the Lord, the Jer 50:29
HAUGHTINESS
* Pro 6:16-19
destruction and * before a fall. Pro 16:18
proud man and the * of the rich. Is 13:11
there will be no pride or * on my Zep 3:11
HAUGHTY
But you bring down the *; 2Sa 22:28
Humiliate the * with a glance; Job 40:12
These wicked men, so proud and *, Ps 10:4
but condemn the proud and * ones. Ps 18:27
You have cut * Egypt Ps 89:10
contempt upon the * and causes Ps 107:40
LORD, I AM not proud and *. Ps 131:1
Mockers are proud, * and Pro 21:24
and * and bring them to the dust. Is 2:12
Next, he will judge the * Jewish Is 3:16
In that day the * shall be Is 5:15
too—for they are proud and * men. Is 10:12
and brings the * city to the dust; Is 26:5
your arrogance and your * heart. Jer 48:29
and * after I am through with you. Mic 2:3
How he scatters the proud and * Lk 1:51
never * or selfish or rude. 1Co 13:5
himself against the proud and *. Jas 4:6
HAUL
and * away its stones and timbers. 1Ki 15:22
I will * you out, and leave you Eze 32:3
HAULED
are being * away on ox carts! Is 46:1
You will be * from your Amo 4:3
HAULING
on the Sabbath, * in sheaves, and Neh 13:15
HAUNT
it will become the * of jackals and Is 34:13
a den of demons, a * of devils and Rev 18:2
HAUNTED
The houses will be * by howling Is 13:21
a heap of ruins, * by jackals, a Jer 51:37
HAUNTS
Depression * my days. Job 30:16
and disturbed the * of wicked men Job 38:15
deed—it * me day and night. Ps 51:3
Avoid their *—turn away, go Pro 4:15
HAURAN
on the border of *. Eze 47:16
to Mount *, where it will bend Eze 47:18
HAVENS
at Fair *, near the city of Lasea. Act 27:7,8
And since Fair * was an exposed Act 27:12
and not left Fair *—you would have Act 27:21
HAVI-LAH
Abima-el, Sheba, Ophir, *, Jobab. Gen 10:26-30
HAVILAH
entire length of the land of *, Gen 2:11,12
The sons of Cush were:Seba, *, Gen 10:7
the country from * to Shur (which Gen 25:18
Amalekites from * all the way to 1Sa 15:7
Seba, *, Sabta, Raama, and 1Ch 1:5-9
Sheba, Ophir, *, and Jobab. 1Ch 1:20-23

HAVROTH-JAIR
the name of their area to *. Num 32:41
HAVVOTH-JAIR
calling it * (meaning 'Jair's Deu 3:14
HAWK
The * (all kinds), the owl, Lev 11:13-19
The sea gull, the * (any variety), Deu 14:11-18
"Do you know how a * soars and Job 39:26
HAWKS
your turtledove from the *. Ps 74:19
There the * and porcupines will Is 34:11
watching him like * to see if he Lk 14:1
HAY
A wise youth makes * while the Pro 10:5
after the * is harvested, and the Pro 27:25,26,27
and some build with sticks, and * 1Co 3:12
HAZAEL
anoint * to be king of Syria. 1Ki 19:15
Anyone who escapes from * shall 1Ki 19:17
news, he said to *, "Take a 2Ki 8:8,9
So * took forty camel-loads of the 2Ki 8:8,9
Elisha stared at * until he 2Ki 8:11
"What's the matter, sir?" * 2Ki 8:12
"Am I a dog?" * asked him. 2Ki 8:13
When * went back, the king asked 2Ki 8:14
And * replied, "He told me that 2Ki 8:14
But the next day * took a blanket 2Ki 8:15
death. And * became king instead. 2Ki 8:15
in his war against *, the king of 2Ki 8:28
the forces of King * of Syria. 2Ki 9:14
of Israel. King * conquered several 2Ki 10:32,33
About this time, King * of Syria 2Ki 12:17
and the palace, and sent it to *. 2Ki 12:18
So * called off the attack. 2Ki 12:18
allowed King * of Syria and his son 2Ki 13:3
King * of Syria had oppressed 2Ki 13:22
Then King * of Syria died, and 2Ki 13:24
King * of Syria at Ramoth-gilead. 2Ch 22:5
HAZAEL'S
So I will set fire to King * Amo 1:4
HAZAIAH
Col-hozeh, son of *, son of Adaiah, Neh 11:4,5,6
HAZAR-ENAN
on through Zedad and Ziphron to *. Num 34:7,8,9
will be from * south to Shepham, Num 34:10,11
HAZAR-ENON
Mediterranean to *, on the border Eze 47:17
run south from * to Mount Hauran, Eze 47:18
and then on to * on the border Eze 48:1
HAZAR-GADDAH
Shema, Moladah, *, Heshmon, Jos 15:21-32
HAZAR-SHUAL
Beth-pelet, *, Beer-sheba, Jos 15:21-32
Beer-sheba, Sheba, Moladah, *, Jos 19:2-7
Moladah, *, Bilhah, Ezem, Tolad, 1Ch 4:28
*, Beer-sheba (and its Neh 11:25-30
HAZAR-SUSAH
Beth-marcaboth, *, Beth-lebaoth, Jos 19:2-7
HAZAR-SUSIM
*, Beth-biri, and Sha-araim. 1Ch 4:31
HAZARADDAR
it will go to *, and on to Azmon. Num 34:4
HAZARMAVETH
Almodad, Sheleph, *, Jerah, Gen 10:26-30
Almodad, Sheleph, *, Jerah, 1Ch 1:20-23
HAZAZAN-TAMAR
and also the Amorites living in *. Gen 14:7
HAZAZON-TAMAR
It is already at *" (also called 2Ch 20:2
HAZER-HATTICON
to *, on the border of Hauran. Eze 47:16
HAZEROTH
to *, where they stayed awhile. Num 11:35
Afterwards they left * and Num 12:16
From Kibroth-hattaavah to *; Num 33:15-37
From * to Rithmah; Num 33:15-37
Tophel, Laban, *, and Dizahab. Deu 1:1
HAZIEL
—Shelomoth, *, and Haran. 1Ch 23:8,9
HAZO
of Aram),Chesed, *, Pildash, Gen 22:20-23
HAZOR
WHEN KING JABIN of * heard what Jos 11:1
captured * and killed its king. Jos 11:10
killed its king. (* had at one time Jos 11:10
built on mounds except for *. Jos 11:13
The king of *; Jos 12:8-24
Adadah, Kedesh, *, Ithnan, Ziph, Jos 15:21-32
(or, *), Amam, Shema, Moladah, Jos 15:21-32
Adamah, Ramah, *, Kedesh, Edre-i, Jos 19:35-39
by King Jabin of *, in Canaan. Ju 4:2,3
Jabin of * and the clan of Heber. Ju 4:17
cities of *, Megiddo, and Gezer. 1Ki 9:15
Janoah, Kedesh, *, Gilead, Galilee, 2Ki 15:29
*, Ramah, Gittaim, Hadid, Zeboim, Neh 11:31-35
Kedar and * Jer 49:27
and the kingdoms of *, which are Jer 49:28
into the deserts, O people of * Jer 49:30
Not the * mentioned in Joshua and Jer 49:30f
* shall be a home for wild Jer 49:33
HAZOR-HADATTAH
Telem, Be-aloth, *, Keri-oth-hezron Jos 15:21-32

HAZOR'S
general of King * army, and by the 1Sa 12:9
HAZY
Now all that I know is * and 1Co 13:12
HAZZELELPONI
Ishma, Idbash,* (his 1Ch 4:3-4
HE-GOAT
The *. Pro 30:29,30,31
HE-GOATS
and saw that the * mating with the Gen 31:10
streaked, speckled, and mottled *. Gen 31:12
you these fat *, rams and calves. Ps 66:15
HE'LL
What if my father feels me? * Gen 27:11,12
"I said to myself, '* take his Gen 31:31
that way * die without our Gen 37:21,22
on this. * settle it today." Ru 3:15-18
back to you, and * be yours for his 1Sa 1:11
So hurry, because * probably be 1Sa 9:12,13
or * be stopped by the rain!" 1Ki 18:44
to themselves; "* never know!" Ps 10:11
"* never get out of that bed!" Ps 41:8
Wisdom is too much for a rebel. * Pro 24:7
but if he is hungry, * eat Pro 27:7
Then where is he? * never come! 2Pe 3:4
HE'S
"* well and prosperous. Gen 29:6
"But * out in the fields 1Sa 16:10,11
"* never done anything to harm 1Sa 19:4
"I'm sure * not planning any 1Sa 20:2
me everything * going to do, even 1Sa 20:2
his whole family—* such a stubborn 1Sa 25:17
Saul of Israel. * been with me for 1Sa 29:3
get out of here. * not our king!" 2Sa 20:1
"See! * alive!" 1Ki 17:23
Well, you can have it now! * 1Ki 21:15
"Fine," Jehoshaphat said. "* 2Ki 3:12
OH, THANK THE Lord, for * so good! Ps 118:1
when he is alone, * in trouble. Ecc 4:10
food, and you say, '* crazy.' Mt 11:18
the people exclaimed. "* just Mt 13:55
"* out of his mind," they said. Mk 3:21
trouble is that * possessed by Mk 3:22
"* no better than we are," they Mk 6:2,3
they said. "* just a carpenter, Mk 6:2,3
they said, "come on, * calling Mk 10:49
"* quite clever at 'saving' Mk 15:31
Some said, "* a wonderful man," Jn 7:12
said, "No, * duping the public." Jn 7:12
"How can he know so much when * Jn 7:15
was, "* a dreamer," or, "He's Act 17:18
"* pushing some foreign religion." Act 17:18
"Don't worry," he said, "* all Act 20:10,11,12
HEAD
He shall strike you on your *, Gen 3:15
with * bowed, worshiping Jehovah. Gen 24:26
Then I bowed my * and worshiped Gen 24:48
children at the *, Leah and her Gen 33:2
three baskets of pastries on my *. Gen 40:16
will take off your * and impale Gen 40:18,19
hand was upon the * of Ephraim, the Gen 48:14
upon the * of Manasseh, the older. Gen 48:14
his right hand on Ephraim's *; Gen 48:17
place it on Manasseh's * instead. Gen 48:17
your right hand on the wrong *! Gen 48:18
You are the * of the list in rank Gen 49:3
blessings upon the * of Joseph who Gen 49:26
the *, legs, heart, and liver. Ex 12:9
with an opening for Aaron's *. Ex 28:32
and place on his * the turban with Ex 29:6
oil and pour it upon his *. Ex 29:7
shall lay their hands upon its *; Ex 29:10
hands upon the * of one of the rams Ex 29:15,16
place them with the * and the Ex 29:17
hands upon its * as it is killed. Ex 29:19,20
the fifty-cent * tax collected from Ex 38:25,26
of mail, for the * to go through, Ex 39:23
his hand upon its *, and it then Lev 1:4
and its * and fat upon the wood. Lev 1:8
pieces, with the * and the fat, on Lev 1:12
and wring off its *, and the blood Lev 1:15,16,17
his hand upon its * and kill it at Lev 3:2
his hand upon its * and kill it at Lev 3:7,8
his hand upon its * and kill it at Lev 3:13
his hand upon its * and kill it Lev 4:4
skin, meat, *, legs, internal Lev 4:11,12
* and kill it before the Lord. Lev 4:15
He shall lay his hand upon its * Lev 4:24
* of the sin offering and kill it. Lev 4:29
his hand upon its * and kill it Lev 4:33
not severing its * from its body. Lev 5:8
and placed on Aaron's * the Lev 8:9
oil upon Aaron's *, thus setting Lev 8:12
upon its * as Moses killed it. Lev 8:14
hands upon its *, and Moses killed Lev 8:18
the pieces, the * and the fat. Lev 8:20
sons laid their hands upon its *. Lev 8:22
including the *, and he burned each Lev 9:13
over his body from * to foot Lev 13:12
has a sore on the * or chin, the Lev 13:29,30
front part of his *, he simply has Lev 13:41

it be bald in the * thereof or in Lev 13:55f
the hair from his *, beard, and Lev 14:9
be used to anoint the man's *. Lev 14:18
be placed upon the * of the man Lev 14:29
hands upon its *, confess over it Lev 16:21
sins upon the * of the goat and Lev 16:21
him to lay their hands upon his *; Lev 24:13,14
he shall shave his defiled *; Num 6:9
After the man's * has been Num 6:19
At the * of the march was the Num 10:14
* and dashed them to the ground! Deu 9:17
wood, and the axe * flies off the Deu 19:5
She must shave her * and pare her Deu 21:12
will make you the * and not the Deu 28:13
you with boils from * to foot. Deu 28:35
They shall be the * and you shall Deu 28:44
With savage arm and face and *. Deu 33:20
Crushing his *. Ju 5:26
the tent pin through his *, Ju 5:26
my * above all the other trees?' Ju 9:11
It landed on Abimelech's *, Ju 9:53
to sleep with his * in her lap, and Ju 16:19
clothes torn and dirt on his *. 1Sa 4:12
This time his * and hands had 1Sa 5:4
And he was * and shoulders taller 1Sa 9:2
placed them at the * of the table, 1Sa 9:22
it over Saul's * and kissed him on 1Sa 10:1
* and shoulders above anyone else. 1Sa 10:23
one hair on his * will be touched, 1Sa 14:45
and poured it upon David's *; 1Sa 16:13
will kill you and cut off your *; 1Sa 17:46
with it, and then cut off his *. 1Sa 17:50,51
(Later David took Goliath's * to 1Sa 17:54
Philistine's * still in his hand. 1Sa 17:57
its * on a pillow of goat's hair. 1Sa 19:13
spear in the ground beside his *. 1Sa 26:5,6,7
of water that was beside his *? 1Sa 26:16
They cut off Saul's * and 1Sa 31:9
on his * as a sign of mourning. 2Sa 1:1
murdered him and cut off his *. 2Sa 4:6,7
Taking his * with them, they fled 2Sa 4:6,7
They presented the * to David at 2Sa 4:8
"Here is the * of Ish-bosheth, 2Sa 4:8
And they took Ish-bosheth's * and 2Sa 4:12
gems—and placed it on his own *. 2Sa 12:29,30
put ashes on her * and with her 2Sa 13:19
* in her hands went away crying. 2Sa 13:19
your son's * shall be disturbed!" 2Sa 14:11
as he went. His * was covered and 2Sa 15:30
clothing and earth upon his *. 2Sa 15:32
me go over and strike off his *!" 2Sa 16:9
his * over the wall to you." 2Sa 20:21
* and threw it out to Joab. 2Sa 20:22
As the * of the nations. 2Sa 22:44
fun of him because of his bald *. 2Ki 2:23
even a donkey's * sold for fifty 2Ki 6:25
and pour the oil over his *. 2Ki 9:3
the oil over his * and said, "The 2Ki 9:6
He instructed the * of the 2Ki 10:22
the crown upon his * and gave him a 2Ki 11:12
of whom was the * of a subclan: 1Ch 7:2
The four * gatekeepers, all 1Ch 9:26
Saul's armor and cut off his *; 1Ch 10:9
* to the wall of Dagon's temple. 1Ch 10:10
march at the * of the procession. 1Ch 15:24
of Abiathar) were the * priests; 1Ch 18:16
crown from the * of King Milcom 1Ch 20:2
and placed it upon his own *. 1Ch 20:2
the crown upon his * and handed him 2Ch 23:11
hair from my * and beard and sat Ez 9:3
crown upon her * so that all the Est 1:11
royal crown on her * and declared Est 2:17
his robe and shaved his *." Job 1:20f
case of boils from * to foot. Job 2:7
against you and shake my * at you. Job 16:4
and removed the crown from my *. Job 19:9
by darts, or his * with a harpoon? Job 41:7
You alone can lift my *, now Ps 3:3
of glory and honor upon his *. Ps 8:5
crown of purest gold upon his *. Ps 21:3
my * with oil, my cup runs over." Ps 23:5f
like a flood, higher than my *; Ps 38:3,4
solve are piled higher than my *. Ps 40:12
of Ephraim is the helmet on my *. Ps 108:8
Literally, "the * of the Ps 118:22f
over Aaron's *, and ran down onto Ps 133:2
your hand of blessing on my *. Ps 139:5
a beautiful crown upon your *. Pro 4:8,9
don't even turn your * to look. Pro 4:25
blessings from * to foot, but an Pro 10:6
Literally, "the hoary *." Pro 20:29f
His left hand is under my * and Sol 2:6
others! His * is purest gold, and Sol 5:11
would be under my * and his right Sol 8:3
Must you forever rebel? From * to Is 1:5,6
and shakes her * at you in scorn. Is 37:22
you needs to have his * examined! Is 41:24
the helmet of salvation on his *. Is 59:17
O Jerusalem, shave your * in Jer 7:29
The water flowed above my *. Lam 3:54
The crown is fallen from our *. Lam 5:16

HEAD Con't)
face on the right side [of his * Eze 1:10
of an eagle at the back of his *! Eze 1:10
human race of which he is the *. Eze 2:1f
razor to shave your * and beard; Eze 5:1
hands in horror and shake your * Eze 6:11
and a lovely tiara for your *. Eze 16:12
and beautiful crowns upon your *. Eze 23:42
don't bare your * nor feet, and Eze 24:17
Your * and feet shall not be Eze 24:23
its * high up among the clouds. Eze 31:2,3
and terrible. The * of the statue Dan 2:32
You are that * of gold. Dan 2:38
reestablished as * of my kingdom, Dan 4:36
wrapped itself around my *. Jon 2:5
over Jonah's * to shade him. Jon 4:6
beat down upon his * until he grew Jon 4:8
You crushed the * of the wicked Hab 3:13
laid bare his bones from * to toe. Hab 3:13
mock, or shake his * in disbelief. Zep 2:15
have a clean turban on his *?" Zec 3:5,6
Then put the crown on the * of Zec 6:10,11
Don't even swear 'By my *!' Mt 5:36
of my own—no place to lay my *." Mt 8:20
And the very hairs of your * are Mt 10:30
John the Baptist's * on a tray. Mt 14:8
prison, and his * was brought on a Mt 14:11
Literally, "the * of the Mt 21:42f
love to sit at the * table at Mt 23:6
perfume, and poured it over his *. Mt 26:7
and put it on his *, and placed a Mt 27:29
and beat him on the * with it. Mt 27:30
And they put a sign above his *, Mt 27:37
roof above his * and lowered the Mk 2:4
the boat with his * on a cushion. Mk 4:38
"Ask for John the Baptist's *!" Mk 6:24
him, "I want the * of John the Mk 6:25
off John's * and bring it to him. Mk 6:27
brought back his * on a tray, and Mk 6:28
for his * was seriously injured. Mk 12:4
seal, she poured it over his *. Mk 14:3
sharp thorns and put it on his *. Mk 15:16,17
And they beat him on the * Mk 15:19
above his *, announcing his crime. Mk 15:26
oil to anoint my *, but she has Lk 7:46
even own a place to lay my *. Lk 9:58
the number of hairs on your *! Lk 12:7
enter but when the * of the house Lk 13:24,25
to sit near the * of the table, he Lk 14:7
don't always * for the best seat. Lk 14:8
But not a hair of your * will Lk 21:18
his face muffled in a * swath. Jn 11:44
and * as well—not just my feet!" Jn 13:9
* and robed him in royal purple. Jn 19:2
his * and dismissed his spirit. Jn 19:30
had covered Jesus' * was rolled up Jn 20:7
sitting at the * and foot of the Jn 20:12
Literally, "became the * of the Act 4:11f
At Cenchreae, Paul had his * Act 18:18
prayer. The * was shaved thirty Act 18:18f
prayer. The * was shaved thirty Act 18:22f
and have your * shaved too—and pay Act 21:24
I had shaved my * as their laws Act 24:18
coals of fire on his *." Rom 12:20
a covering on her * dishonors her 1Co 11:5
Yes, if she refuses to wear a * 1Co 11:6
woman to have her * shaved, then 1Co 11:6
anything on his * [when worshiping, 1Co 11:7
a covering on her * as a sign that 1Co 11:10
woman to have power on (her) *." 1Co 11:10f
in public without covering her *? 1Co 11:13
The * can't say to the feet, 1Co 12:21
him the supreme * of the church— Eph 1:22
is the * of his body, the church. Eph 4:15,16
He is the * of the body made up Col 1:18
to Christ, the * to which all of us Col 2:19
laid their hands upon your *. 1Ti 4:14
hands upon your * and blessed you. 2Ti 1:6
of the king as * of the state, and 1Pe 2:13
honoring him as * of the house. 1Pe 3:6
and when the * Shepherd comes, 1Pe 5:4
Literally, "His *—the hair—was Rev 1:14f
and a crown was placed upon his *; Rev 6:2
cloud, with a rainbow over his *; Rev 10:1
a crown of twelve stars on her *. Rev 12:1
And written on each * were Rev 13:1
* and a sharp sickle in his hand. Rev 14:14
and on his * were many crowns. Rev 19:12

HEAD-HAIR
Literally, "*, beard, Is 7:20f

HEADACHE
He complained about a *, and 2Ki 4:19

HEADBANDS
chains, *, earrings, and perfumes; Is 3:20

HEADED
and * for the territory of Gilead. Gen 31:21
Next was the tribe of Simeon * Num 10:19
Last of all were the tribes * by Num 10:25
the earth and are * toward me," he Num 22:5,6
because you are * for destruction. Num 22:32
So David * back into the land of 1Sa 29:11
of Samuel were * by Samuel's 1Ch 6:28
clan of Merari were * by his sons: 1Ch 6:29,30
in which I was *, and turned around Ps 119:59,60
care is * for serious trouble. Pro 28:14
and he is * for your land. Jer 4:7
with him when he * toward the Jer 41:10
a group of men * by Sharezer, the Zec 7:2
But the crowds saw where he was * Mt 14:13
because they were * for Jerusalem. Lk 9:53
religious leaders who * the mob. Lk 22:52
into the boat and * out across the Jn 6:17
of Mysia they * north for the Act 16:7
raised the foresail and * ashore. Act 27:40
must be clean minded and level *. Tit 1:8
for others is * for eternal death. 1Jn 3:14

HEADINGS
The * identifying the speakers are Sol 1:1f

HEADLONG
and falling * there, he burst open, Act 1:18

HEADQUARTERS
called the City of David) his *. 2Sa 5:9
at Mizpah, where his * were. Jer 40:8

HEADREST
found a rock for a * and lay down Gen 28:11
and set his stone * upright as a Gen 28:18

HEADS
became the * of clans, as listed Gen 36:15,16
This time he saw seven * of grain Gen 41:5
Then, suddenly, seven more * Gen 41:6
And these thin * swallowed up Gen 41:7
up the seven plump, well-formed *! Gen 41:7
This time there were seven * of Gen 41:22
all seven * were plump and full. Gen 41:22
came seven withered, thin *. Gen 41:23
And the thin * swallowed up the Gen 41:24
fat, well-formed * of grain) mean Gen 41:26
thin and withered * of grain) Gen 41:27
upon the boys' *, so that his right Gen 48:14
and bowed their * and worshiped. Ex 4:31
These are the names of the * of Ex 6:14
The * of the clans of the tribe Ex 6:15
These are the names of the * of Ex 6:16
These are all the names of the * Ex 6:25
bowed their * and worshiped. Ex 12:27
by anointing their * with olive Ex 28:41
sashes, and place caps on their *. Ex 29:9
shall lay their hands upon the * Num 8:12
THEN THE * of the sub-clan of Num 36:1
halves of your * for funerals. Deu 14:1
The * of the enemy Deu 32:40,41
evening, with dust on their *. Jos 7:6
and the Israelis took the * of Ju 7:25
The five * of the Philistine Ju 16:5
to snap off some * of barley and Ru 2:16
him covered their * and wept as 2Sa 15:30
you hold me safe above their *. 2Sa 22:49
of Israel—the * of the tribes and 1Ki 8:1
put ropes on our * and go out to 1Ki 20:31
obey me, bring the * of your 2Ki 10:6
and their * were packed into 2Ki 10:7
told Jehu that the * of the king's 2Ki 10:8
His relatives became * of clans 1Ch 5:7,8
Their relatives, the * of the 1Ch 5:13
These descendants of Asher were * 1Ch 7:40
were the * of the musicians. 1Ch 15:17
the * of the priests and Levites. 1Ch 24:6
Then the clan leaders, the * of 1Ch 29:6,7
of Israel—the * of the tribes and 2Ch 5:2
and bowed their * and worshiped. 2Ch 29:30
higher than our * and our guilt is Ez 9:6
upon their own *, and may they Neh 4:4
A genealogical record of the * of Neh 12:22
* to demonstrate their sorrow. Job 2:12
Mankind * for sin and misery as Job 5:7
others, cut off like * of grain. Job 24:24
caused men to ride over our *." Ps 66:12f
you crushed the sea-god's *! Ps 74:13,14
they see me they shake their *. Ps 109:25
He will crush many *. Ps 110:6
Hold me safe above the * of all Ps 119:117
down upon their *, or throw them Ps 140:10
of scabs to ornament their *! Is 3:17
they shave their * in sorrow and Is 15:2
and shave your * in sorrow for your Is 22:12
crowns are removed from your *. Jer 13:18
and cover their * in grief. Jer 14:3
nor shave their * as signs of Jer 16:6
and shake their * in amazement at Jer 18:16
mankind beat their * upon the Jer 25:34
it shall burst upon the * of the Jer 30:23
They shave their * and beards in Jer 48:37
they throw dust upon their * in Lam 2:10
Jerusalem hang their * in shame. Lam 2:10
and shake their * and say, "Is Lam 2:15
the firmament, over their *." Eze 1:25f
you shall shave your * in sorrow Eze 7:18
cloud of smoke above their *. Eze 8:11
appeared in the sky above the * Eze 10:1
and flowing turbans on their *. Eze 23:14,15
their * and wallowing in ashes. Eze 27:30
They shave their * in grief and Eze 27:31
*, for your fate is dreadful; Eze 27:36
The soldiers' * were bald (from Eze 29:18
their swords beneath their *. Eze 32:27
a hair of their * was singed; Dan 3:27
those of birds, and it had four *! Dan 7:6
and return the harm to your own *. Joe 3:4
and shave your * as signs of Amo 8:10
acts will boomerang upon your *. Ob 1:15
Shave your * in sorrow. Mic 1:16
so they began breaking off * of Mt 12:1
* and blessed them before he left. Mt 19:15
the * of this very generation. Mt 23:36
their * at him and saying, "So! Mt 27:39
* of wheat and eating the grain. Mk 2:23
on their * and he blessed them. Mk 10:16
And they scratched their * in Mk 12:17
by, and wagged their * in mockery. Mk 15:29,30
breaking off the * of wheat, Lk 6:1
on their * to show their remorse. Lk 10:13
appeared and settled on their *. Act 2:3
upon people's *—he offered money to Act 8:18
be upon your own *—I am Act 18:6
hands upon their *, the Holy Spirit Act 19:6
shave their * and take some vows. Act 21:23
For not a hair of your * shall Act 27:34
able to hold our * high no matter Rom 5:5
upon their * to justly crush them. Rom 11:9
that women's * should be covered? 1Co 11:14,15
with golden crowns upon their *. Rev 4:4
crowns on their *, and their faces Rev 9:7
The horses' * looked much like Rev 9:17,18
to serpents' * that struck and bit Rev 9:19
with seven * and ten horns, and Rev 12:3
horns, and seven crowns on his *. Rev 12:3
It had seven * and ten horns, and Rev 13:1
I saw that one of his * seemed Rev 13:3
that had seven * and ten horns, Rev 17:3
"And now think hard: his seven * Rev 17:9
dust on their * in their sorrow and Rev 18:19

HEADWINDS
we encountered * that made it Act 27:4

HEAL
Lord, "* her, O God, I beg you!" Num 12:13
I wound and *— Deu 32:39
He would * him of his leprosy!" 2Ki 5:3
I want you to * him of his 2Ki 5:6
"This man sends me a leper to *! 2Ki 5:7
of the Lord his God, and * me! 2Ki 5:11
I will * him, and three days from 2Ki 20:5
that the Lord will * me and that I 2Ki 20:8
their sins and * their land. 2Ch 7:14
for I am weak. * me, for my body is Ps 6:2
"be kind and * me, for I have Ps 41:4
Lord, * it now, for it is shaken Ps 60:2
words of the wise soothe and *. Pro 12:18
A time to *; Ecc 3:3
or to turn to me to * them." Is 6:10
listen to their plea and * them. Is 19:22
the Lord begins to * his people and Is 30:26
health. Oh, * me and make me live! Is 38:16
me to prove that he will * me?" Is 38:22
they do, but I will * them anyway! Is 57:18
and far, for I will * them all. Is 57:19
He will * you; Is 58:8
and I will * you from your sins. Jer 3:22
You can't * a wound by saying Jer 6:14
We thought, Now at last he will * Jer 14:19
Lord, you alone can * me, you Jer 17:14
health again and * your wounds. Jer 30:17
come when I will * Jerusalem's Jer 33:6
Who can * you? Lam 2:13
their broken limbs and * the sick. Eze 34:15,16
Sea, where it will * the salty Eze 47:8
he who has torn us—he will * us. Hos 6:1
wound is far too deep to *. Mic 1:9
the young, nor * the broken bones, Zec 11:16
"if you want to, you can * me." Mt 8:2
to his home and * his servant boy Mt 8:5,6
said, "I will come and * him." Mt 8:7
spirits and to * every kind of Mt 10:1
* the sick, raise the dead, cure Mt 10:8
to God again, and let me * them.' Mt 13:16
Would he * the man's hand? Mk 3:2
with him to * his little daughter. Mk 5:23
on a few sick people and * them. Mk 6:5
his hands on the man and * him. Mk 7:32
and begged him to touch and * him. Mk 8:22
my son for you to *—he can't talk Mk 9:17
hands on the sick and * them." Mk 16:18
he has sent me to * the Lk 4:18,19
'Physician, * Lk 4:23
"Please * her," everyone Lk 4:38
whether he would * the man that Lk 6:7
ask him to come and * his slave. Lk 7:3
them out—and to * all diseases. Lk 9:1
Kingdom of God and to * the sick. Lk 9:2
and as you * them, say, 'The Lk 10:8,9
to see if he would * a man who was Lk 14:1
within the Law to * a man on the Lk 14:3
Jesus asked, "Didn't I * ten Lk 17:17
with him and * his son, who was now Jn 4:46,47

(HEAL Con't)
he went, to watch him * the sick. Jn 6:2-5
"How did he * you?" Jn 9:26
"He can * blind men, and yet you Jn 9:30
nor turn to me to * them." Jn 12:40
and turn to me to * you." Act 28:27
else the power to * the sick. 1Co 12:9
Can everyone * the sick? 1Co 12:30
him, calling on the Lord to * him. Jas 5:14
in faith, will * him, for the Lord Jas 5:15
and to get medicine from me to * Rev 3:18
for medicine to * the nations. Rev 22:2

HEALED
*, and pay any medical expenses. Ex 21:19
spot, then he is * and is not a Lev 13:37
the priest shall declare him *. Lev 13:37
ceremony of the one who is *. Lev 14:4
eat the holy sacrifices until *. Lev 22:4
flesh of their wounds had been *. Jos 5:8,9
a reward because you * my arm." 1Ki 13:7
"The Lord has * these waters. 2Ki 2:21
* of every trace of his leprosy! 2Ki 5:10
as a little child's, and he was *! 2Ki 5:14
of his being *, God left him to 2Ch 32:31
He spoke, and they were * Ps 107:20
The Lord * me! Is 38:20
he was lashed—and we were *! Is 53:5
perhaps she can yet be *. Jer 51:8
and he had * me so that I could Eze 33:22
Sea, for its waters will be *. Eze 47:9
marshes and swamps will not be *; Eze 47:11
And he * every kind of sickness Mt 4:23
to be * from as far away as Syria. Mt 4:24
or paralyzed—he * them all. Mt 4:24
"I want to," he says; "be *." Mt 8:3
for lepers who are *—a public Mt 8:4
'Be *,' my servant will get well! Mt 8:8,9
And the boy was * that same Mt 8:13
and all the sick were *. Mt 8:16
and go on home, for you are *." Mt 9:5,6
I only touch him, I will be *." Mt 9:21
Your faith has * you." Mt 9:22
And wherever he went he * people Mt 9:35
blind people I've *, and the lame Mt 11:5
following him. He * all the sick Mt 12:15
Jesus, and Jesus * him so that he Mt 12:22
he pitied them and * their sick. Mt 14:14
to bring in their sick to be *. Mt 14:35
his robe, and all who did were *. Mt 14:36
And her daughter was * right Mt 15:28
before Jesus, and he * them all. Mt 15:30
followed him, and he * their sick. Mt 19:2
and he * them there in the Temple. Mt 21:14
So Jesus * great numbers of sick Mk 1:34
front of him and begged to be *. Mk 1:40
him and said, "I want to! Be *!" Mk 1:41
leprosy was gone—the man was *! Mk 1:42
for a leper who is *, so that Mk 1:43,44
shout the good news that he was *; Mk 1:45
and go on home, for you are *!" Mk 2:9,10,11
did, and instantly his hand was *! Mk 3:5
touch his clothing, I will be *." Mk 5:28
go in peace, * of your disease." Mk 5:34
many demons, and * many sick Mk 6:13
and as many as touched him were * Mk 6:56
that I have * your little girl. Mk 7:29
Your faith has * you." Mk 10:52
Elisha, who * Naaman, a Syrian, Lk 4:27
and the touch of his hands * Lk 4:40
in the dust, begging to be *. Lk 5:12
said, "Of course I will. Be *." Lk 5:13
for lepers who are *," he said. Lk 5:14
and to be * of their diseases. Lk 5:15
and go on home, for you are *!" Lk 5:23,24
had come to hear him or to be *. Lk 6:17,18
are, and my servant boy will be *! Lk 7:6,7,8
So just say, 'Be *!' Lk 7:6,7,8
they found the slave completely *. Lk 7:10
The lepers are completely *. Lk 7:20,21,22
cast out demons or whom he had *; Lk 8:2
demon-possessed man had been *. Lk 8:36
who wanted to be * came up behind Lk 8:43,44
to her, "your faith has * you. Lk 8:48
to come out, and * the boy and Lk 9:42
you are * of your sickness!" Lk 13:12
had * her on the Sabbath day. Lk 13:14
hand and * him and sent him away. Lk 14:4
and show him that you are *!" Lk 17:14
shouting, "Glory to God, I'm *!" Lk 17:15
Your faith has * you." Lk 18:42
Your son is *!" Jn 4:50
had told him, "Your son is *." Jn 4:53
down into it afterwards was *). Jn 5:4
Instantly, the man was *! Jn 5:9
"The man who * me told me to," Jn 5:11
them it was Jesus who had * him. Jn 5:15
But some said, "This fellow * a Jn 11:37,38
ankle-bones were * and strengthened Act 3:7,8
"Jesus' name has * this man—and Act 3:16
and how he was *, let me clearly Act 4:9
that this man stands here *! Act 4:10
the man they had * was standing Act 4:14
and every one of them was *. Act 5:16
or lame were *, so there was much Act 8:7
Jesus Christ has * you! Act 9:34
And he was * instantly. Act 9:34
and realized he had faith to be *. Act 14:9
people, they were *, and any demons Act 19:12
laying his hands on him, * him! Act 28:8
each other so that you may be *. Jas 5:16
For his wounds have * ours! 1Pe 2:24
the fatal wound was *! Rev 13:3
had been *, whom he required all Rev 13:12

HEALING
suddenly, broken beyond hope of *. Pro 6:15
My grief is beyond *; Jer 8:18
medicines, there is no * for you. Jer 46:11
There is no * for your wound—it Nah 3:19
will rise with * in his wings. Mal 4:2
So I'll prove it to you by * this Mt 9:5,6
to work by * on the Sabbath day?" Mt 12:10
brought to him for *; Mk 1:32,33
So I'll prove it to you by * this Mk 2:9,10,11
Jesus realized at once that * Mk 5:30
And the Lord's * power was upon Lk 5:17
So I'll prove it to you by * this Lk 5:23,24
for when they did * power went out Lk 6:19
various diseases—* the lame and Lk 7:20,21,22
I felt * power go out from me." Lk 8:46
the Good News and * the sick. Lk 9:6
come for *, not on the Sabbath!" Lk 13:14
miracles of * today and tomorrow; Lk 13:32
miracles than this man's *. Jn 5:20
* a man, and you were surprised. Jn 7:21,22,23
God—has caused this perfect *. Act 3:16
discredit the * when the man they Act 4:14
miracle— the * of a man who had Act 4:22
and send your * power, and may Act 4:30
doing good and * all who were Act 10:38
Those who have the gift of *, 1Co 12:28

HEALINGS
For there had been many * that Mk 3:10

HEALS
for I am the Lord who * you." Ex 15:26
in his skin which *, but which Lev 13:18
but also for a time after it *. Lev 15:3
he wounds, he binds and * again. Job 5:18
He forgives all my sins. He * me. Ps 103:3
the exiles. He * the Ps 147:3

HEALTH
they asked about each other's * Ex 18:7
He restores my failing *. Ps 23:2,3
you, and you gave me my * again. Ps 30:2
my * is broken from sorrow. Ps 31:9,10
my * is broken beneath my sins. Ps 38:3,4
how I long for my * once more. Ps 38:9
earth as much as you! My * fails; Ps 73:26
* is broken and my heart is sick; Ps 102:3,4
used them to restore my joy and *. Ps 119:93
Now give me back my life and * Ps 119:159
be given renewed * and vitality. Pro 3:7,8
real life for you, and radiant *. Pro 4:22
Gentle words cause life and *; Pro 15:4
good reports give happiness and *. Pro 15:30
Lord, and the good * to enjoy it. Ecc 5:19,20
give them the * to enjoy it, and Ecc 6:2
is good and leads to life and *. Is 38:16
vigorous * will be yours. Is 66:14
we looked for * but there was Jer 8:15
I will give you back your * Jer 30:17
wisdom and glowing *, and now, even Dan 2:23
they will be radiant with * and Zec 9:16,17
a doctor, not those in good *. Lk 5:31

HEALTHFUL
are like honey—enjoyable and *. Pro 16:24

HEALTHIER
friends looked * and better Dan 1:15

HEALTHY
So the less * lambs were Laban's Gen 30:42
that they produced * offspring, and Gen 31:38
good crops and * cattle, and Deu 28:8
And his flesh became as * as a 2Ki 5:14
He destroys those who are *, Job 21:23,24
Then his body will become as * Job 33:25
and * as young olive trees. Ps 128:3
good things, and keep you * too; Is 58:11
oil, and the * flocks and herds. Jer 31:12
"Pick strong, *, good-looking Dan 1:3,4
nor feed the * ones, nor carry the Zec 11:16
need the doctor, not * ones! Mk 2:17
you as I would to * Christians, who 1Co 3:1
is * and growing and full of love. Eph 4:15,16
is as * as I know your soul is. 3Jn 1:2

HEALTHY-LOOKING
seven fat, * cows came up out of Gen 41:18

HEAP
stones and make a *, and Jacob and Gen 31:46
This *," Laban continued, Gen 31:51,52
I will * evils upon them Deu 32:23
a great * of stones upon them. Jos 7:26
There he piled a great * of Jos 8:29
a * of grain and went to sleep. Ru 3:6,7
piled a great * of stones over it. 2Sa 18:17
This Temple will become a * of 1Ki 9:8
and Jerusalem is a * of ruins. Ps 79:1
us scoff. They * contempt on us. Ps 79:4
is like a * of wheat set about Sol 7:2
a city—it has become a * of ruins! Is 17:1
palaces and make it a * of ruins. Is 23:13
It shall become a desolate *, and Jer 49:2
shall become a * of ruins, haunted Jer 51:37
the flock, and * fuel on the fire Eze 24:5
fuel beneath her. * on the wood; Eze 24:10
They say: 'We have become a * of Eze 37:11
collapsed into a * of iron, clay, Dan 2:35
house knocked into a * of rubble. Dan 3:29
you will become a * of rubble. Hos 5:9
crumble into a * of rubble, and Mic 1:6
a field, and become a * of rubble; Mic 3:12
They simply * up dirt against Hab 1:10
it crumbles into a * of ruins." Lk 6:49
all will become one vast * of Lk 21:6

HEAPED
* upon him, he was always cold. 1Ki 1:1
bodies shall be * in this valley. Jer 19:11
I have * upon you the full Eze 22:31
upon blessing * upon us! Jn 1:16

HEAPED-UP
you to punish you for your * sins. Hos 10:10

HEAPING
servant Hezekiah, * up insults. 2Ch 32:16
"* coals of fire on his head." Rom 12:20

HEAPS
They were piled into great *, Ex 8:14
"* upon heaps, Ju 15:16,17
"Heaps upon *, Ju 15:16,17
pile them in two * at the entrance 2Ki 10:8
Lord and piled them up in great *. 2Ch 31:5,6
in nothing. He * up riches for Ps 39:5,6
You turn mighty cities into * of Is 25:2
crush walled cities into ruined *. Is 37:26
Jerusalem into * of ruined houses Jer 9:11
razed into * of stone, and a forest Jer 26:18
they lie in * and ashes, without a Jer 44:2,3
Vast multitudes fall in *. Jer 46:16
* of ruins, cursed and mocked; Jer 49:13
and houses into * of ruins and Jer 50:26
your houses made into * of rubble! Dan 2:5
* of bodies, everywhere. Nah 3:3
and Gomorrah into * of ashes and 2Pe 2:6
the world fell in * of rubble; Rev 16:19

HEAR
All who * about this shall Gen 21:6
and Pharaoh was very happy to * Gen 45:16
see or not see, * or not hear? Ex 4:11
see or not see, hear or not *? Ex 4:11
Come now before Jehovah, and * Ex 16:7,8,9
sat as usual to * the people's Ex 18:13
themselves can * me when I talk Ex 19:9
entirely until you * a ram's horn Ex 19:13
for help, I will * and be very Ex 22:27
enemies, God will * you and save Num 10:9
think when they * about it?" Num 14:13
"Rise up, Balak, and *: Num 23:18-24
When the surrounding nations * Deu 4:6
see nor * nor eat nor smell. Deu 4:28
He let you * his voice Deu 4:36
What man can *, as we have, the Deu 5:26,27
Then all Israel will * about his Deu 13:11
"If you ever * it said about one Deu 13:12,13,14
Then everyone will * about what Deu 17:13
Then those who * about it will Deu 19:20
men of Israel will * about what Deu 21:21
* and rescue her out in the field. Deu 22:25,26,27
or eyes that see or ears that *! Deu 29:4
that you can't * the laws of God and Deu 30:12
among you—to * the laws of God and Deu 31:12
these laws will * them and learn Deu 31:13
"O Lord, * the cry of Judah Deu 33:7
nearby nations * about it, they Jos 7:9
* the stamping Ju 5:22
Why don't we * the sound of the Ju 5:28
they would like to * a riddle, they Ju 14:12
they agreed, "let's * it." Ju 14:13
patient until we * what happens, Ru 3:15-18
beside the road to * the news of 1Sa 4:13
and he would * cases there, too. 1Sa 7:17
If you * me tell him, 'They're on 1Sa 20:21
When you * a sound like marching 2Sa 5:24
"As soon as you * the 2Sa 15:10
When they * of my power. 2Sa 22:45
Solomon sat to * legal matters; 1Ki 7:7
to pray; yes, * in heaven where you 1Ki 8:30
you live, and when you *, forgive. 1Ki 8:30
he didn't do it, * him in heaven 1Ki 8:32
defeat them, * them from heaven and 1Ki 8:33,34
of their sin, * them from heaven 1Ki 8:35,36
this Temple, * them from heaven 1Ki 8:39
"And when foreigners * of your 1Ki 8:41,42
(for they shall * of your great 1Ki 8:41,42
this Temple, * them from heaven 1Ki 8:43
* their prayer and help them. 1Ki 8:45
for your name, * their prayers and 1Ki 8:49

HEAR Con't)
O Lord, * and answer them 1Ki 8:52
shouting, "O Baal, * us!" 1Ki 18:26
For I * a mighty rainstorm 1Ki 18:41
whole Syrian army * the clatter of 2Ki 7:6
on the walls will * you." 2Ki 18:26
ears of those who * about it will 2Ki 21:12
When you * a sound like marching 1Ch 14:15
May you always * and answer the 2Ch 6:20,21
this Temple; yes, * us from heaven, 2Ch 6:20,21
heaven, and when you *, forgive. 2Ch 6:20,21
this altar, then * from heaven and 2Ch 6:23
public prayers. * from heaven 2Ch 6:30
"And when foreigners * of your 2Ch 6:32
this Temple, * them from heaven 2Ch 6:33
of the earth will * of your fame 2Ch 6:33
your name, then * their prayers 2Ch 6:35
them, then * from heaven where you 2Ch 6:39
ways, I will * them from heaven and 2Ch 7:14
visit him, and to * the wisdom God 2Ch 9:23
in three days to * King Rehoboam's 2Ch 10:12
"Let's * what he has to say." 2Ch 18:6,7
and that you will * us and rescue 2Ch 20:9
love and obey him! * my prayer! Neh 1:5
O Lord, please * my prayer! Neh 1:11
Then I prayed, "* us, O Lord Neh 4:4
that when you * the trumpet blow Neh 4:19
* and understand God's words. Neh 8:12
your empire will * what the queen Est 1:18
and good, he would * your prayer, Job 8:6
my mind tastes truth when I * it. Job 12:11
what I am about to say. * me out. Job 13:17
him, and he will * you, and you Job 22:27
to God, God will * and answer and Job 33:26
I want to * it, for I am anxious Job 33:32
to say he doesn't * those cries; Job 35:13
He helps them * his instruction Job 36:10
snorting is something to *! Job 39:20
now * me as I call again. Ps 4:1
Have mercy on me. * my prayer. Ps 4:1
O LORD, * me praying; Ps 5:1
Surely you will * their cries and Ps 10:17
of joy when we * the news of your Ps 20:5
king, O Lord; oh, * our prayer. Ps 20:9
for they shall * from us about the Ps 22:30
generations yet unborn shall * Ps 22:31
your faithfulness? * me, Lord; Ps 30:10
bend low and * my whispered Ps 31:2
Let me * you say that you will Ps 35:3
once more. You * my every sigh. Ps 38:9
* my prayer, O Lord; Ps 39:12
Now many will * of the glorious Ps 40:3
when I cry to you. * me, Lord! Ps 55:2
and he will * and answer. Ps 55:17
prowl the city. I * them shouting Ps 59:7
"No one will * us," they think. Ps 59:7
O GOD, LISTEN to me! * my prayer! Ps 61:1
Come and *, all of you who Ps 66:16
time—you are bending down to *! Ps 69:13
Don't you * the tumult and Ps 83:2
the heavenly armies, * my prayer! Ps 84:8
BEND DOWN AND * my prayer, O Ps 86:1
my prayer, O God. * my urgent cry. Ps 86:6
day and night. Now * my prayers; Ps 88:2
Young and old shall * about your Ps 89:1
Blessed are those who * the Ps 89:14,15
and exult? * their insolence! Ps 94:4
Oh, that you would * him calling Ps 95:7
LORD, * MY prayer! Ps 102:1
It towers above the earth. * the Ps 108:6
Nor can they *, nor smell, nor Ps 115:6
sense you promised. * my prayers; Ps 119:170
I cry for your help: "* me! Ps 130:2
eyes and ears that cannot *; Ps 135:17
all of them shall * your voice. Ps 138:4
God and my shield—* me as I pray! Ps 140:6,7,8
"* my cry, for I am very low. Ps 142:6
* MY PRAYER, O Lord; Ps 143:1
CAN'T YOU * the voice of wisdom? Pro 8:1
loudly before fools will * it. Pro 14:33
no matter how much we *, we are Ecc 1:8-11
You may * your servant cursing Ecc 7:21,22
The Girl: "Ah, I * him—my Sol 2:8
Call to me and let me * your Sol 2:14
let me * it too. Sol 8:13
Listen to the Lord. * what he is Is 1:10
I will not *, for your hands are Is 1:15
this: 'Though you * my words Is 6:9
I don't want them to see or to * Is 6:10
* the tumult on the mountains! Is 13:4
I faint when I * what God is Is 21:3
with praise. * them singing to the Is 24:15,16
Therefore * the word of the Lord, Is 28:14
In that day the deaf will * Is 29:18
astray, you will * a Voice behind Is 30:21
and everything in it * my words. Is 34:1
the people on the wall will *." Is 36:11
Jerusalem to * this, not just you. Is 36:12
on the wall, "* the words of the Is 36:13
Listen! I * the voice of someone Is 40:3
do it; you * but you won't listen. Is 42:20
I call (although they see and *! Is 43:8
* ME, MY people: you swear Is 48:1
so delighted to * the reading of my Is 58:2
Why don't you * our prayers? Is 58:3
He can * you when you call! Is 59:1
I spoke to them, they would not *. Is 66:4
* the words of God, all you who Is 66:5
I * voices high upon the Jer 3:21
are closed and they refuse to *. Jer 6:10
but you refused to * or answer. Jer 7:13,14
listen to them or even try to *. Jer 7:26
conversation and what do I *? Jer 8:6
* Jerusalem weeping in despair. Jer 9:19
* THE WORD of the Lord, O Israel: Jer 10:1
Listen! * the terrible sound of Jer 10:22
They have made it desolate; I * Jer 12:11
to all the people: * the word of Jer 17:20
saying: * the word of the Lord. Jer 18:11
of those who * it will prickle. Jer 19:3
Yet on every side I * their Jer 20:10
O earth, earth, earth! * the word Jer 22:29
to God to * what he is saying? Jer 23:18
but you have refused to *. Jer 25:4
word of all I have for them to *. Jer 26:2
And if my officials * that I Jer 38:25
land will weep. * the clattering Jer 47:3
How it is broken! * the wails! Jer 48:39
But don't panic when you * the Jer 51:46
Listen! * the cry of great Jer 51:54
* my groans! Lam 1:21
shout, he will not * my prayers! Lam 3:8
of Israel, * the message of the Eze 6:3
they could * me if they would Eze 12:2
"O prostitute, * the word of the Eze 16:35
Prophesy to it and say: * the Eze 20:47
Let's go * him tell us what the Eze 33:30
Literally, "Come and let us * Eze 33:30f
instrument. They * what you say but Eze 33:32
"Therefore, O shepherds, * the Eze 34:7
* the word of the Lord God. Eze 36:4
I am ready to * Israel's prayers Eze 36:37,38
of the world will * what I have Eze 38:23
nor *, nor know anything at all. Dan 5:23
"O our God, * your servant's Dan 9:17
"O Lord, *; Dan 9:19
* THE WORD of the Lord, O people Hos 4:1
tremble, land of Benjamin! * Hos 5:9
the priests are starving. * the Joe 1:9
name of the Lord—he might * you." Amo 6:10
he will * me. Mic 7:7
Listen! * the crack of the whips Nah 3:2
All who * your fate will clap Nah 3:19
I tremble when I * all this; Hab 3:16
Is that a joyous choir I *? Zep 3:17,18
flint, afraid to * the words that Zec 7:12
their God, will * their cries. Zec 10:6
wealth is gone. * the young lions Zec 11:3
upon my name and I will * them; Zec 13:9
"I * Mt 3:3
the wilderness to * him preach, Mt 3:5
"But those who * my instructions Mt 7:26
*, and the dead raised to life; Mt 11:5
land to * the wisdom of Solomon; Mt 12:42
will * and see but not understand. Mt 13:12,13
'They *, but don't understand; Mt 13:14
so they won't see and * Mt 13:16
and your ears, for they *. Mt 13:16
you have seen, and * what you have Mt 13:17
Literally, "* him." Mt 17:5f
him, "Do you * what these children Mt 21:15
When you * of wars beginning, Mt 24:6
all nations will * it, and then, Mt 24:14
"Don't you * what they are Mt 27:13
to see and * John, and when they Mk 1:5
"Didn't you ever * about the time Mk 2:25,26
'Though they see and *, they will Mk 4:11,12
some of those who * God's message; Mk 4:15
of those who * the message with Mk 4:16
to put into practice what you *. Mk 4:24
"as they were able to *." Mk 4:33f
called to the crowd to come and *. Mk 7:14
"If any man has ears to *, let Mk 7:15,16f
man has ears to hear, let him *." Mk 7:15,16f
Instantly the man could * Mk 7:35
"The one that says, '*, O Israel! Mk 12:29
crowds came to * him preach and to Lk 5:15
had come to * him or to be healed. Lk 6:17,18
The deaf can * again. Lk 7:20,21,22
was gathering to * him—while many Lk 8:4
But these crowds * the words and Lk 8:10
of those who * the words of God, Lk 8:12
are all those who * the message of Lk 8:21
whom I * such strange stories?" Lk 9:9
* what you have seen and heard!" Lk 10:24
are all who * the Word of God and Lk 11:28
from the housetops for all to *! Lk 12:3
I * about your stealing from me? Lk 16:2
And when you * of wars and Lk 21:9
early in the morning to * him. Lk 21:37,38
Just as you can * the wind but Jn 3:8
the dead shall * my voice—the voice Jn 5:25
their graves shall * the voice of Jn 5:28
Why do you want to * it again? Jn 9:27
sheep * his voice and come to him; Jn 10:3
(You always * me, of course, but Jn 11:42
were stunned to * their own Act 2:6
and yet we * them speaking all the Act 2:8
And we all * these men telling in Act 2:11
And now, O Lord, * their Act 4:29
And we * that he has arrest Act 9:14
Lord, anxious to * what he has told Act 10:33
to * their message from God. Act 13:6,7
believe when you * it announced.' Act 13:41
to * them preach the Word of God. Act 13:44
things and we want to * more." Act 17:20
want to * more about this later." Act 17:32
For they will certainly * that Act 21:22
and * him speak. Act 22:14
"I will * your case fully when Act 23:35
"I'd like to * the man myself," Act 25:22
But we want to * what you Act 28:22
" 'Say to the Jews, "You will * Act 28:26
want to see and * and understand Act 28:27
I go I * you being talked about! Rom 1:8
would * about God's glorious name. Rom 9:17
And how can they * about him Rom 10:14
lost, when they * that Jesus died 1Co 1:18
were an eye—then how would you *? 1Co 12:17
for you to * it again and again. Php 3:1
suit the taste of those who * it; 1Th 2:4
If you * of people having visions 2Th 2:1
Yet we * that some of you are 2Th 3:11
really believe anything they *. 2Ti 3:5
them just what they want to *. 2Ti 4:3
sermon for all the world to *. 2Ti 4:17
to be careful to * his voice today Heb 3:7,8
"Today if you * God's voice Heb 3:15
"Today when you * him calling, do Heb 4:7
they * such assurances from God; Heb 6:18
For listen! * the cries of the Jas 5:4
Don't let me * of your suffering 1Pe 4:15
everything you * just because 1Jn 4:1
* such things about my children. 3Jn 1:4
Let everyone who can *, listen Rev 2:11
"Let everyone who can *, listen Rev 2:17
"Let all who can *, listen to Rev 2:29
"Let all who can *, listen to Rev 3:6
"Let all who can *, listen to Rev 3:13
Let those who can *, listen to Rev 3:22
neither see nor * nor walk! Rev 9:20
Anyone who can *, listen Rev 13:9

HEARD
That evening they * the sound of Gen 3:8
And Adam replied, "I * you Gen 3:10
because God has * your woes. Gen 16:9-12
Abraham, "I have * that the people Gen 18:20
For God has * the lad's cries as Gen 21:17
"This is the first I've * of Gen 21:26
wrists, and * her story, he rushed Gen 24:29,30
and as soon as he * of Jacob's Gen 29:12,13
(meaning "Jehovah *"), for she Gen 29:33
said, "Jehovah * that I was Gen 29:33
* my plea and given me a son." Gen 30:6
no longer here. I * your brothers Gen 37:17
Well, when her husband * his Gen 39:19
But I have * that you can Gen 41:15
WHEN JACOB * that there was grain Gen 42:1
I have * that there is grain Gen 42:2
and anguish and * his pleadings, Gen 42:21
His sobs could be * throughout Gen 45:2
Benjamin has * me say it) ' "for Gen 45:11,12
When Jacob * that Joseph had Gen 48:2
And sure enough, when Pharaoh * Ex 2:15
the Lord. He * their cries from Ex 2:23
in Egypt, and have * their pleas Ex 3:7
and when they * that Jehovah had Ex 4:31
And now I have * the groanings Ex 6:5
The nations * what happened, and Ex 15:14
for he has * your complaints Ex 16:7,8,9
"I have * their complaints. Ex 16:11,12
the mountain, and * the thunder and Ex 20:18
When Joshua * the noise below Ex 32:17
When the people * these stern Ex 33:4
And when Moses * that, he was Lev 10:20
and tell all who * him to lay their Lev 24:13,14
speak with God, he * the Voice Num 7:89
misfortunes, and the Lord * them. Num 11:1
Moses * all the families standing Num 11:10
Tell them, 'The Lord has * your Num 11:18
But the Lord * them. Num 12:2
nations that have * your fame will Num 14:15
For I have * all that they have Num 14:26,27
When Moses * what they were Num 16:4
to the Lord he * us and sent an Num 20:16
WHEN THE KING of Arad * that the Num 21:1
When King Balak * that Balaam Num 22:36
land of Canaan, * that the people Num 33:40
"Well, the Lord * their Deu 1:34,35
* his words but didn't see him. Deu 4:12
An entire nation * the voice of Deu 4:33
you even * his words from the Deu 4:36
But when you * the loud voice Deu 5:23

(HEARD Con't)
we have even * his voice from the Deu 5:24
to me, 'I have * what the people Deu 5:28
the Lord God. He * us and saw our Deu 26:6,7
you have not even * of will eat the Deu 28:33
For we have * how the Lord made Jos 2:10
coast—* that the Lord had dried up Jos 5:1
So when the people * the trumpet Jos 6:20
surrounding area * what had Jos 9:1
But when the people of Gibeon * Jos 9:3,4,5
we have * of the might of the Jos 9:9
king of Jerusalem, * how Joshua had Jos 10:1
WHEN KING JABIN of Hazor * what Jos 11:1
But when the rest of Israel * Jos 22:11
the high officials * this from the Jos 22:30
"You have * yourselves say it," Jos 24:22
"This stone has * everything the Jos 24:27
When Gideon * the dream and the Ju 7:15
When Jotham * about this, he Ju 9:7
mayor of the city, * what Gaal was Ju 9:30
for she had * that the Lord had Ru 1:6,7
who was pregnant, * that the Ark 1Sa 4:19
When the Philistine leaders * 1Sa 7:7
in mercy and have * their cry." 1Sa 9:16
When his friends * about it, they 1Sa 10:11
Jonathan, however, had not * his 1Sa 14:27
moved when he * what God was 1Sa 15:11
of sheep and lowing of oxen I *?" 1Sa 15:14
and the Israeli army * this, they 1Sa 17:11
And have you * about the huge 1Sa 17:25
brother, Eliab, * David talking 1Sa 17:28
was delighted when he * about it. 1Sa 18:20
When Saul * what had happened, 1Sa 19:21
David * these comments and was 1Sa 21:12
Saul exclaimed when he * the 1Sa 22:7
said, "I have * that Saul is 1Sa 23:10
Saul actually come, as I have *? 1Sa 23:11
But when David * that Saul was on 1Sa 23:24,25
When David * that Nabal was 1Sa 25:4
When David * that Nabal was dead, 1Sa 25:39
beyond the Jordan * that their 1Sa 31:7
of Jabesh-gilead * what the 1Sa 31:11
in sorrow when they * the news. 2Sa 1:11
When David * that the men of 2Sa 2:4
When David * about it he 2Sa 3:28
WHEN KING ISH-BOSHETH * about 2Sa 4:1
When the Philistines * that David 2Sa 5:17
When David * this, he brought the 2Sa 6:12
We have never * of any other god 2Sa 7:22
When King Toi of Hamath * about 2Sa 8:9
Jonathan. He * about a man named 2Sa 9:2
When David * what had happened 2Sa 10:5
When David * about this, he sent 2Sa 10:7,8
When David * what was happening, 2Sa 10:17
When David * what Uriah had done, 2Sa 11:10
When Bath-sheba * that her 2Sa 11:26
When King David * what had 2Sa 13:21-24
And all the troops * the king 2Sa 18:5
"We all * the king say to you 2Sa 18:12
As the people * of the king's 2Sa 19:2
And he * me from his Temple. 2Sa 22:7
Adonijah and his guests * the 1Ki 1:41
When Joab * about Adonijah's 1Ki 2:28
When Solomon * that Shime-i had 1Ki 2:41
my God, you have * and answered my 1Ki 8:28
"I have * your prayer. 1Ki 9:2,3
WHEN THE QUEEN of Sheba * how 1Ki 10:1
Literally, "* of the fame of 1Ki 10:1f
* about his great wisdom was true. 1Ki 10:4
"Everything I * in my own country 1Ki 10:6
than anything I've ever * of0,6!! 1Ki 10:7
When Hadad, there in Egypt, * 1Ki 11:21
from King Solomon, * about the 1Ki 12:2,3,4
When he * what had happened he 1Ki 13:26
So when Ahijah * her at the door, 1Ki 14:6
city of Gibbethon, * that Zimri had 1Ki 16:15,16
And the Lord * Elijah's prayer; 1Ki 17:22
When Elijah * it, he wrapped his 1Ki 19:13
to him, "we have * that the kings 1Ki 20:31
When Jezebel * the news, she said 1Ki 21:15
When Ahab * these prophecies, he 1Ki 21:27
the people of Moab * about the 2Ki 3:21
But when Elisha the prophet * 2Ki 5:8
When the king * this he tore his 2Ki 6:26-30
When the king * the news, he said 2Ki 8:8,9
When Jezebel * that Jehu had come 2Ki 9:30
When Athaliah * all the noise, 2Ki 11:13,14
WHEN KING HEZEKIAH * their 2Ki 19:1
Lord your God has * the Assyrian 2Ki 19:4
God of Israel says, 'I have * you! 2Ki 19:20
* his prayer and seen his tears. 2Ki 20:5
When the king * what was written 2Ki 22:11
below the mountain * that their 1Ch 10:7
of Jabesh-gilead * what the 1Ch 10:11
When the Philistines * that David 1Ch 14:8
In fact, we have never even * of 1Ch 17:20
When David * what had happened, 1Ch 19:5
told him, "I have * your prayer 2Ch 7:12
WHEN THE QUEEN of Sheba * of 2Ch 9:1
"Everything I * about you in my 2Ch 9:5
When King Asa * this message from 2Ch 15:8
Baasha of Israel * what was 2Ch 16:5
kingdoms * that the Lord himself 2Ch 20:29
them when she * the news of her son 2Ch 22:10
When Queen Athaliah * all the 2Ch 23:12
and the Lord * their prayers from 2Ch 30:27
When the king * what these laws 2Ch 34:19
God when you * my words against 2Ch 34:27
before me—I have * you, says the 2Ch 34:27
that could be * from far away! Ez 3:13
Judah and Benjamin * that the Ez 4:1
When I * this, I tore my clothing Ez 9:3
When I * this, I sat down and Neh 1:4
official) * of my arrival, they Neh 2:10
Geshem the Arab * of our plan, they Neh 2:19
and Ashdodites * that the work was Neh 4:7
I was very angry when I * this; Neh 5:6
nations * about it, they were Neh 6:16
they * the commands of the law. Neh 8:9
in Egypt, and you * their cries Neh 9:9
to you and you * them from heaven, Neh 9:27
of Jerusalem was * far away! Neh 12:43
Mordecai * about it and passed Est 2:22
and * the whole story from him; Est 4:7
When three of Job's friends * of Job 2:11
believe that he had * my cry. Job 9:16
Have you * the secret counsel of Job 15:7,8
"I have * all this before. Job 16:2
'I had * about you before, but Job 42:5
I cried out to the Lord, and he * Ps 3:4
has * my weeping and my pleading. Ps 6:8
And he * me from heaven; Ps 18:6
them. You * their cries for help Ps 22:5
When I cried to him, he * and Ps 22:24
My heart has * you say, "Come Ps 27:8
discarded pot. I * the lies about Ps 31:13
Lord—and the Lord * him and saved Ps 34:6
things I have never even * about. Ps 35:11
then he listened and * my cry. Ps 40:1
O GOD, WE have * of the glorious Ps 44:1
We have * of the city's Ps 48:8
For you have * my vows, O God, Ps 61:5
But he listened! He * my prayer! Ps 66:19
Jehovah * them and was angry; Ps 78:21
I * an unknown voice that said, Ps 81:5
I have * the doom of my enemies Ps 92:11
of Judah have * of your justice, Ps 97:8,9
in heaven, and * the groans of his Ps 102:20
Literally, "Lo, we * of it in Ps 132:6f
the turtledove is * in our land." Sol 2:12f
I * the voice of my beloved; Sol 5:2
and Judah, you have * the case! Is 5:3
my own ears I * him say, "Many a Is 5:9
Then I * the Lord asking, "Whom Is 6:8
are * far away, even in Jahaz. Is 15:4
* all along the road to Horonaim. Is 15:5
concerning which we * so much? Is 16:6
the vineyards will be * no more; Is 16:10
Then I * a Voice shout out, Is 21:8,9
The rumors that you * in Cyprus Is 23:1
harp and timbrel are * no more; Is 24:8
we've * more than enough about Is 30:10,11
voice to be * and shall crush down Is 30:30
WHEN KING HEZEKIAH * the results Is 37:1
But perhaps the Lord your God * Is 37:4
against the Lord—and I * it all! Is 37:29
When Hezekiah * this, he turned Is 38:2
for he had * that Hezekiah had Is 39:1
Have you never * nor understood? Is 40:21
You have * my predictions and Is 48:6
before, secrets you haven't *. Is 48:6
no one has seen or * of such a God Is 64:4
shall not be * there any more. Is 65:19
Who has * or seen anything as Is 66:7,8
not * my fame nor seen my glory. Is 66:19
See if anyone there has ever * so Jer 2:10,11
because I have *, O my soul, the Jer 4:19
I have * great crying like that Jer 4:31
We have * the fame of their Jer 6:24
war horses can be * all the way Jer 8:16f
they have never seen nor *; Jer 14:14
no one has ever * of such a thing! Jer 18:13
Let screaming be * from their Jer 18:22
of the Lord, * what Jeremiah was Jer 20:1
officials of Judah * what was going Jer 26:10
"You have * with your own ears Jer 26:11
word that you have * from me." Jer 26:15
and officials * what he was saying, Jer 26:21
Uriah * about it and fled to Jer 26:21
longer, for I have * your prayers Jer 31:16
I have * Ephraim's groans: "You Jer 31:18
I had * was really from the Lord. Jer 32:8
be * again in this doomed land. Jer 33:10,11
Have you * what people are Jer 33:24
son of Shaphan) * the messages from Jer 36:11
(son of Malchiah) * what Jeremiah Jer 38:1
palace official, * that Jeremiah Jer 38:7
in the countryside * that the king Jer 40:7
nearby countries * that a few Jer 40:11
guerrilla leaders * what Ishmael Jer 41:11
The nations have * of your Jer 46:12
Her crying will be * as far away Jer 48:2,3,4
We have all * of the pride of Jer 48:29
I have * this message from the Jer 49:14
the cry of the people is * as far Jer 49:21
have * the news of their doom. Jer 49:23
shall be * around the world. Jer 50:46
All through the land will be * Jer 51:52
All my enemies have * my troubles Lam 1:21
within the well, and you * me! Lam 3:56
to my pleading; you * my weeping! Lam 3:56
You have * the vile names they Lam 3:61
on the ground, and * the voice of Eze 1:27,28
Literally, "I * behind me the Eze 3:12f
Then I * the Lord tell the other Eze 9:5
be * clear out in the outer court. Eze 10:5
as I * them called, for each one Eze 10:9-13
with terror when they * him roar. Eze 19:7
be * upon the mountains of Israel. Eze 19:9
For he * the warning and Eze 33:5
And you shall know that I have * Eze 35:12
And I have * them all! Eze 35:13
And I * the Lord speaking to me Eze 43:6
But when the queen-mother * what Dan 5:10
I have * that you have the Dan 5:14
Then he * a voice! Dan 6:21
* a voice saying to it, "Get up! Dan 7:5
Then I * two of the holy angels Dan 8:13
like a man— and I * a man's voice Dan 8:16
"And then in your vision you * Dan 8:26
And I * his voice—"O Daniel, Dan 10:11
request has been * in heaven and Dan 10:12
I * what he said but I didn't Dan 12:8
have you ever * of such a thing as Joe 1:2
be * upon my holy mountain! Joe 2:1
of what he saw and *: The Lord Amo 1:2
priest of Bethel, * what Amos was Amo 7:10
frightened when they * this. Jon 1:9,10
I called, and Lord, you * me! Jon 2:2
For when the king of Nineveh * Jon 3:6
O Lord, now I have * your report, Hab 3:2
"I have * the taunts of the Zep 2:8
When Jesus * that John had been Mt 4:12,13
noisy crowds and * the funeral Mt 9:23
was now in prison, * about all the Mt 11:2
But when the Pharisees * about Mt 12:24
what you have *, but couldn't. Mt 13:17
HEROD * about Jesus, he said to Mt 14:1
As soon as Jesus * the news, he Mt 14:13
But when the young man * this, Mt 19:22
when they * what James and John had Mt 20:24
road and when they * that Jesus was Mt 20:30
miracles, and * even the little Mt 21:15
When they * that he had routed Mt 22:34,35
You have all * him say it! Mt 26:65,66
When Jesus * what they were Mk 2:17
When his friends * what was Mk 3:21
She had * all about the Mk 5:27
King Herod soon * about Jesus, Mk 6:14
When John's disciples * what had Mk 6:29
She had * about Jesus and now she Mk 7:25
He sighed deeply when he * this Mk 8:12
When Bartimaeus * that Jesus from Mk 10:47
When Jesus * him he stopped there Mk 10:49
And the disciples * him say it. Mk 11:14
Jewish leaders * what he had done Mk 11:18
When the chief priests * why he Mk 14:11
and said, "We * him say, 'I will Mk 14:58
You have * his blasphemy. Mk 14:63,64
you that God has * your prayer, and Lk 1:13
me, the instant I * your voice, my Lk 1:44
had not * what his wife had said. Lk 1:62f
And everyone who * about it Lk 1:66
All who * the shepherds' story Lk 2:18
When the captain * about Jesus, Lk 7:3
* of all that Jesus was doing. Lk 7:18
you have seen and * here today: Lk 7:20,21,22
And all who * John preach—even Lk 7:29
prostitute—* he was there and Lk 7:37
"Who ever * of someone lighting Lk 8:16
When Jesus * they were standing Lk 8:20
But when Jesus * what had Lk 8:50
hear what you have seen and *!" Lk 10:24
have said in the dark shall be * Lk 12:3
when he returned home, he * dance Lk 15:25
But when the man * this he went Lk 18:23
Those who * him say this Lk 18:26
When he * the noise of a crowd Lk 18:36
religious leaders * about this Lk 20:19
"For we ourselves have * him say Lk 22:71
Jesus, for he had * a lot about him Lk 23:8
who hasn't * about the terrible Lk 24:18
He tells what he has seen and *, Jn 3:32
the Pharisees had * about the Jn 4:1
because we have * him ourselves, Jn 4:42
son was very sick, * that Jesus had Jn 4:46,47
were surprised when they * him. Jn 7:15
When the Pharisees * that the Jn 7:32
When the crowds * him say this, Jn 7:40
"We've never * anything like Jn 7:46
Jewish leaders who * him say these Jn 8:30,31
I told you the truth I * from God. Jn 8:40
When Jesus * what had happened, Jn 9:35

(HEARD Con't)
Those who * Jesus use this Jn 10:6
But when Jesus * about it he Jn 11:4
of Jerusalem * of his arrival, they Jn 12:9
had * about this mighty miracle. Jn 12:18
When the crowd * the voice, Jn 12:29
passing on to you what he has *. Jn 16:13
I have been * by all the Jewish Jn 18:20
Ask those who * me. Jn 18:21
When Pilate * this, he was more Jn 19:8
And when they * the roaring in Act 2:6
him walking and * him praising God, Act 3:9
But many of the people who * Act 4:4
we saw Jesus do and * him say." Act 4:20
As soon as Ananias * these words, Act 5:5
others who * what had happened. Act 5:11
and the chief priests * this, Act 5:24
claiming they had * Stephen curse Act 6:11
They declared, "We have * him Act 6:14
was gone, Jacob * that there was Act 7:12
in Egypt and have * their cries. Act 7:34
back in Jerusalem * that the people Act 8:14
Philip ran over and * what he was Act 8:30
He fell to the ground and * a Act 9:4
surprise, for they * the sound of Act 9:7
Ananias, "I have * about the Act 9:13
All who * him were amazed. Act 9:21
other believers * about his danger, Act 9:30
your prayers are * and your Act 10:31
I'm sure you have * about the Act 10:36,37
for they * them speaking in Act 10:46,47
And I * a voice say, 'Kill and Act 11:7
When the others * this, all their Act 11:18
When the church at Jerusalem * Act 11:22
about, though they * the prophets' Act 13:27
When the Gentiles * this, they Act 13:48
lives when they * Paul and Silas Act 16:38
When they * Paul speak of the Act 17:32
He had never * the rest of the Act 18:25,26
were there and * him—and it was a Act 18:25,26
As soon as they * this, they were Act 19:5
and Greeks—* the Lord's message. Act 19:10
you've seen and *, this man Paul Act 19:26
(When they * him speaking in Act 22:2
And I fell to the ground and * a Act 22:7
telling what you have seen and *. Act 22:15
when they * Paul was a Roman Act 22:29
We all fell down, and I * a Act 26:14
The brothers in Rome had * we Act 28:15
They replied, "We have * nothing Act 28:21
if they have never * about him? Rom 10:14
Have they * God's Word? Rom 10:18
has never yet been *, rather than Rom 15:20
who have never * the name of Christ Rom 15:21
to those who * them that the 1Co 2:4
man has ever seen, * or even 1Co 2:9
And have you ever * of a farmer 1Co 9:7
you think if you * an ear say, "I 1Co 12:16
have never * a worse preacher!" 2Co 10:10
in paradise, and * things so 2Co 12:4
you only after you * about Christ Gal 3:2
others too, who * the Good News Eph 1:13
That is why, ever since I * of Eph 1:15
If you have really * his voice Eph 4:21
the time you first * it until now. Php 1:5
because you * that he was ill. Php 2:26
for we have * how much you trust Col 1:4
very first day you * it and Col 1:6
So ever since we first * about Col 1:9
many others have * me speak about. 2Ti 2:2
*, or we may drift away from them. Heb 2:1
on to us by those who * him speak? Heb 2:3
I speak of, who * God's voice Heb 3:16
But God graciously * and answered Heb 5:7f
And God * his prayers because of Heb 5:7
When he * God's warning about the Heb 11:7
Whoever * of a son who was never Heb 12:7
God his Father; I * that glorious, 2Pe 1:17,18
actually seen and *, so that you 1Jn 1:3
You have * it all before. 1Jn 2:7
You have * about the Antichrist 1Jn 2:18
you have * about who is going to 1Jn 4:3
and everything he * and saw. Rev 1:2
when suddenly I * a loud voice Rev 1:10
And then I * him say, "Write Rev 1:11
Go back to what you * and Rev 3:3
same voice I had * before, that Rev 4:1
Then in my vision I * the singing Rev 5:11
And then I * everyone in heaven Rev 5:13
And I * the second Living Being Rev 6:3
the third seal, I * the third Rev 6:5
seal was broken, I * the fourth Rev 6:7
given this mark? I * the number—it Rev 7:4-8
his trumpet and I * a voice Rev 9:13
—I * an announcement of how many Rev 9:16
Then I * a loud voice shouting Rev 12:10
And I * a sound from heaven like Rev 14:2
And I * a voice in the heavens Rev 14:13
AND I * a mighty voice shouting Rev 16:1
And I * this angel of the waters Rev 16:5
And I * the angel of the altar Rev 16:7
Literally, "I * the altar cry. Rev 16:7f
Then I * another voice calling Rev 18:4
AFTER THIS I * the shouting of a Rev 19:1
Then I * again what sounded like Rev 19:6
I * a loud shout from the throne Rev 21:3
I, John, saw and * all these Rev 22:8

HEARING
left in him after * things like Jos 2:11
silently and, * no sound, thought 1Sa 1:12,13
"I have been * terrible reports 1Sa 2:23,24,25
to assist him in * these cases. 2Sa 15:3
"You have said it in my *, yes, Job 33:8
shouts in the streets for a *. Pro 1:20
good eyesight and good *, thank Pro 20:12
Upon * this, he sent messengers Is 37:8,9
Upon * this, the king was Dan 2:12
* this, the king was very angry Dan 6:14
but of * the words of the Lord. Amo 8:11
Upon * this, the Angel of the Zec 1:12
in their ears to keep from * me. Zec 7:11
unlike what they were used to *! Mk 1:22
And the poor are * the Good News. Lk 7:20,21,22
* this, a man sitting at the Lk 14:15
to believe in him after * him. Jn 4:40,41
"Father, thank you for * me. Jn 11:41
you are seeing and * today. Act 2:33
the Romans.' " * this, all of Act 21:12
I demand my privilege of a * Act 25:10,11
I will keep on * good reports that Php 1:27
because I keep * of your love and Phm 1:5

HEARS
him Ishmael ('God *'), because God Gen 16:9-12
He * the words of God Num 24:15-19
and her father * that she has made Num 30:4
on the first day he * about it; Num 30:5
he * of it, her vow shall stand. Num 30:7
and her husband * of it and does Num 30:11
the first day he * of it, her vow Num 30:12
think, when he * the warnings of Deu 29:19
If Saul * about it, he will kill 1Sa 16:2
he goes he * that the Jews are Neh 6:5,6
I scream for help and no one * Job 19:7
Yes, he * the cries of those Job 34:28
know he does! He * me from highest Ps 20:6
Yes, the Lord * the good man Ps 34:17
For Jehovah * the cries of his Ps 69:33
I LOVE THE Lord because he * my Ps 116:1
and trust him; he * their cries for Ps 145:19
he * the prayers of the righteous. Pro 15:29
When Egypt * the news, there Is 23:5
forefather David * you praying and Is 38:5
then anyone who * the alarm and Eze 33:4
of a person who * the Good News Mt 13:19
heart of a man who * the message Mt 13:20
a man who * the message, but the Mt 13:22
"If the governor * about it," Mt 28:14
will do when he * what happened? Mk 12:9
If anyone * me and doesn't obey Jn 12:47
But not everyone who * the Good Rom 10:16
to church and * you all talking in 1Co 14:23
be pricked by everything he *. 1Co 14:24
heart color all he sees and *. Tit 1:15
If anyone * me calling him and Rev 3:20
Let each one who * them say the Rev 22:17

HEARSAY
false evidence, or *, but will Is 11:3

HEART
It broke his *. Gen 6:6
The * of his empire included Gen 10:10
will bless me with all your *!" Gen 27:19
it and bless you with all my *." Gen 27:25
But Jacob's * was like a stone; Gen 45:26
This touched her *. Ex 2:6
Pharaoh's * was still hard and Ex 7:13
that Pharaoh's * had been unmoved, Ex 7:14
so Pharaoh's * remained hard and Ex 7:22
he hardened his * and refused to Ex 8:15
But Pharaoh's * was hard and Ex 8:19
But Pharaoh hardened his * again Ex 8:31,32
hardened Pharaoh's * and he did not Ex 10:20
So the Lord hardened Pharaoh's * Ex 10:27
Lord hardened his * so that he Ex 11:10
the head, legs, *, and liver. Ex 12:9
* and he will chase after you. Ex 14:4
over his * (it is God's oracle) Ex 28:29
to be carried over Aaron's * when Ex 28:30,31
* when he goes in before the Lord. Ex 28:30,31
of you from the * of the fire, Deu 5:22
his voice from the * of the fire. Deu 5:24
from the * of the fire, and live? Deu 5:26,27
always have such a * for me, Deu 5:29
with all your *, soul, and might. Deu 6:5
given you from the * of the fire on Deu 10:4
love him with all your * and soul. Deu 13:3
shut your * or hand against them; Deu 15:7
wives, lest his * be turned away Deu 17:17
as slaves. Your * will break with Deu 28:32
was pouring out my * to the Lord. 1Sa 1:15,16
battle, for his * trembled for the 1Sa 4:13
I'm with you * and soul, whatever 1Sa 14:7
Literally, "his * died within him 1Sa 25:37,38f
them into the * of Absalom as he 2Sa 18:14
They shall lose * 2Sa 22:46
for you know each *. 1Ki 8:39
they turned his * away from the 1Ki 11:3
was, and his * was not right with 1Ki 15:3
Literally, "nevertheless, the * 1Ki 15:14f
and the arrow pierced his *, and 2Ki 9:24
with all his *, for he continued to 2Ki 10:31
me, because of your own great *. 1Ch 17:19
him with a clean * and a willing 1Ch 28:9
Lord sees every * and understands 1Ch 28:9
Give my son Solomon a good * 1Ch 29:19
my eyes and my * shall always be 2Ch 7:16
the wisdom God had put into his *. 2Ch 9:23
and Benjamin the * of King Asa was 2Ch 15:17
with all his * and soul, and to do 2Ch 34:31
it into his * to be kind to me." Neh 1:11
which God had put into my *. Neh 2:11,12
had put into my *, and of my Neh 2:18
poisoned arrows deep within my *. Job 6:4
majesty strike terror to your *? Job 13:11
and store them in your *. Job 22:22
God has given me a fainting *; Job 23:16,17
a strong wind. My * is broken. Job 30:16
Darkness came. My * is troubled Job 30:27
pathway, or if my * has lusted for Job 31:7,8
pathway, and my * has been Job 31:27
"MY * TREMBLES at this. Job 37:1
soft and fat. His * is hard as Job 41:24
Literally, "the upright in *." Ps 7:10f
you with all my *, and tell Ps 9:1
I be hiding daily anguish in my *? Ps 13:2
or to fall. *, body, and soul are Ps 16:9
what is right, and I am pure of *. Ps 18:24
what sins are lurking in my *? Ps 19:12
out of joint. My * melts like wax; Ps 22:14
me, my * shall know no fear! Ps 27:3
My * has heard you say, "Come Ps 27:8
And my * responds, "Lord, I am Ps 27:8
Joy rises in my * until I burst Ps 28:7
"all who are upright in *." Ps 32:11f
all who are discouraged take *. Ps 34:2
From the bottom of my * praise Ps 35:10
Or, "because of the pains in my * Ps 38:8f
You hear my every sigh. My * Ps 38:10
bring no special joy to your *. Ps 40:6
your law is written upon my *!" Ps 40:8
hidden in my *, but have Ps 40:10
to look up. My * quails within me. Ps 40:12
he knows the secrets of every *. Ps 44:21
MY * IS overflowing with a Ps 45:1
You deserve honesty from the *; Ps 51:6
Create in me a new, clean *, O Ps 51:10
A broken and a contrite *, O God, Ps 51:17
And when my * is right, Ps 51:19
Because of his wicked *, his dark Ps 53:1
me. My * is in anguish within me. Ps 55:4
entrenched in the * of the city. Ps 55:10
oily smooth, but in his * was war. Ps 55:21
O God, my * is quiet and Ps 57:7
When my * is faint and Ps 61:2
like arrows straight at my *. Ps 64:3
and the * of everyone is deep." Ps 64:6f
Their contempt has broken my *; Ps 69:20
this, what turmoil filled my *! Ps 73:21
He is the strength of my *; Ps 73:26
desert years and grieved his *. Ps 78:40
with a true * and skillful hands. Ps 78:71,72
With all my * I will praise you. Ps 86:12
"All my * is in Jerusalem." Ps 87:7
my mind, when my * is in turmoil, Ps 94:19
and * were far away from me. Ps 95:10
My health is broken and my * is Ps 102:3,4
holy name of God with all my *. Ps 103:1
O GOD, MY * is ready to praise Ps 108:1
stored them in my * so that they Ps 119:11
I weep with grief; my * is heavy Ps 119:28
Revive my * toward you. Ps 119:37
With all my * I want your Ps 119:58
I obey your laws with all my *. Ps 119:69
of * and mind and do not stumble. Ps 119:165
* was so filled with turmoil? Ps 132:1
LORD, WITH ALL my * I thank you. Ps 138:1
O LORD, YOU have examined my * and Ps 139:1
Search me, O God, and know my *; Ps 139:23
Write them deep within your *. Pro 3:3
deep within your *, for they will Pro 4:21
Next, his * is full of Pro 6:14
Take to * all of their advice. Pro 6:21
also keep them deep within your *. Pro 7:3
with an arrow through its *. Pro 7:23
Hope deferred makes the * sick; Pro 13:12
Laughter cannot mask a heavy *. Pro 14:13
A happy face means a glad *; Pro 15:13
a sad face means a breaking *. Pro 15:13
a rebel who has no * for truth. Pro 17:16
Literally, "no *." Pro 17:16f
A cheerful * does good like Pro 17:22
*, the wise man will draw it out. Pro 20:5
ever say, "I have cleansed my *; Pro 20:9
that hurts chases evil from the *. Pro 20:30

(HEART Con't)
A youngster's * is filled with Pro 22:15
Yes, my * will thrill to your Pro 23:15,16
Whose * is filled with anguish Pro 23:29,30
a person whose * is heavy is as bad Pro 25:20
Pretty words may hide a wicked *, Pro 26:23
A man with hate in his * may Pro 26:24,25,26
for he is cursing you in his *. Pro 26:24,25,26
Literally, "the woman whose * is Ecc 7:26f
A wise man's * leads him to do Ecc 10:2
a fool's * leads him to do evil. Ecc 10:2
You have ravished my *, my Sol 4:9
my * awakened in a dream. Sol 5:2
door and my * was moved for him. Sol 5:4
but he was gone. My * stopped. Sol 5:6
and how you capture my *. Sol 6:4
The Girl: "Seal me in your * Sol 8:6
My * weeps for Moab! Is 15:5
to the Lord in the * of Egypt in Is 19:19
My mind reels; my * races; Is 21:4
But my * is heavy with grief, for Is 24:15,16
have gladness of *, as when a Is 30:29
BECAUSE I LOVE Zion, because my * Is 62:1
*, who trembles at my word. Is 66:2
When you see Jerusalem, your * Is 66:14
after my own *, who will guide you Jer 3:15
My *, my heart—I writhe in pain; Jer 4:19
My heart, my *—I writhe in pain; Jer 4:19
in pain; my * pounds within me. Jer 4:19
My grief is beyond healing; my * Jer 8:18
own stubborn will and his proud *. Jer 11:8
you know my *—you know how much it Jer 12:3
Then in loneliness my breaking * Jer 13:17
They bring joy to my sorrowing * Jer 15:16
man and turns his * away from God. Jer 17:5
The * is the most deceitful thing Jer 17:9
his word in my * is like fire that Jer 20:9
right into the * of this city, and Jer 21:3,4
My * is broken for the false Jer 23:9
And I will give them one * and Jer 32:39
David, the man after God's own *. Jer 33:15f
your arrogance and your haughty *. Jer 48:29
Yes, I wail for Moab, my * is Jer 48:31
Sad sings my * for Moab and Jer 48:36
See, O Lord, my anguish; my * is Lam 1:20
sighs are many and my * is faint. Lam 1:22
no longer come; my * is broken, my Lam 2:11
sent his arrows deep within my *. Lam 3:13
to my cry! My * is breaking over Lam 3:51
sink deep into your own * first; Eze 3:10
I will give you one * and a new Eze 11:19
What a filthy * you have, says Eze 16:30
receive a new * and a new spirit. Eze 18:31
sigh with grief and broken *. Eze 21:6
When it comes true, the boldest * Eze 21:7
and you are wrecked in the * of Eze 27:26
bitterness of * and deep mourning. Eze 27:31
your island in the * of the seas. Eze 28:8
Your * was filled with pride Eze 28:17
And I will give you a new *—I Eze 36:26
listen and take to * everything I Eze 40:4
who have no * for God—when you Eze 44:7
But when his * and mind were Dan 5:20
My * cries out within me; Hos 11:8
your *, O daughter of Jerusalem. Zep 3:14
adultery with her in his *. Mt 5:28
heaven your * will be there too. Mt 6:21
For a man's * determines his Mt 12:34
shall be in the * of the earth Mt 12:39,40
finds the man's * clean but empty! Mt 12:43,44,45
represents the * of a person who Mt 13:19
away the seeds from his *. Mt 13:19
represents the * of a man who hears Mt 13:20
The good ground represents the * Mt 13:23
come from an evil *, and defile the Mt 15:18
For from the * come evil Mt 15:19
with all your *, soul, and mind.' Mt 22:37
contact with your *, but only Mk 7:19
* and soul and mind and strength.' Mk 12:30
him with all my * and understanding Mk 12:33
* and often thought about them. Lk 2:19
away all these things in her *. Lk 2:51
produces good deeds from a good *. Lk 6:45
Whatever is in the * overflows Lk 6:45
When the Lord saw her, his * Lk 7:13
God with all your *, and with all Lk 10:27
your * and thoughts will also be. Lk 12:34
"LET NOT YOUR * be troubled. Jn 14:1
with a gift—peace of mind and *! Jn 14:27
you will have peace of * and mind. Jn 16:33
will be of one * and mind, just as Jn 17:21
"Lord, you know my *; Jn 21:17
they said, "you know every *; Act 1:24,25
'No wonder my * is filled with Act 2:26
All the believers were of one * Act 4:32
Satan has filled your *. Act 5:3
your * is not right before God. Act 8:21
and sin in your *." Act 8:23
you believe with all your *." Act 8:37
my own *, for he will obey me.' Act 13:22
Lord opened her * and she accepted Act 16:14
You are breaking my *! Act 21:13
No, a real Jew is anyone whose * Rom 2:29
with all your * the teaching to Rom 6:17
the sin in my *—the evil desires Rom 7:7
not have evil desires in your *." Rom 7:7
come to Christ. My * is heavy Rom 9:1
BROTHERS, THE longing of my * Rom 10:1
in your own * that God has raised Rom 10:9
For it is by believing in his * Rom 10:10
you with a happy * by the will of Rom 15:32
and great peace of * and mind. 1Co 1:3
as God sees into my * right now. 1Co 13:12
It almost broke my * and I tell 2Co 2:4
I love you with all my *. 2Co 6:11
you are in my * forever and I live 2Co 7:3
me and let me say what is on my *. 2Co 11:1
So please don't lose * at what Eph 3:13
For though once your * was full Eph 5:8
When I pray for you, my * is Php 1:4
have a very special place in my *. Php 1:7
with one * and mind and purpose. Php 2:2
away from you my * is with you, Col 2:5
Let the peace of * which comes Col 3:15
and peace of * be your rich gifts 1Th 1:1
you great peace of * and mind. 1Ti 1:2
A person who is pure of * sees Tit 1:15
but a person whose own * is evil Tit 1:15
* color all he sees and hears. Tit 1:15
you, and with him comes my own *. Phm 1:12
my weary * will praise the Lord. Phm 1:20
brother is really a murderer at *; 1Jn 3:15
Literally, "If our * condemns 1Jn 3:20f
us, God is greater than our *." 1Jn 3:20f
be, "at the * of the throne." Rev 7:17f

HEART'S
David did. His * desire was always 1Ki 14:8
He built to his * desire in 2Ch 8:6
My hopes have disappeared. My * Job 17:11
May he grant you your * desire Ps 20:4
For you have given him his * Ps 21:2
Then he will give you all your * Ps 37:4

HEARTFELT
his people my * thanks to God for Ps 111:1

HEARTH
be left upon the * of the altar all Lev 6:9
coals from the *, or a little water Is 30:14

HEARTILY
For we all * agreed to this oath Neh 10:29

HEARTLESS
succeed forever in their * wars? Hab 1:17
broke their promises, and were * Rom 1:31

HEARTS
I will harden the * of the Ex 14:17
with generous *, may bring these Ex 35:5-9
Those whose * were stirred by Ex 35:21
When at last their evil * are Lev 26:40,41
fear into the * of the people were Num 14:36,37,38
for him with all your * and souls. Deu 4:29
him with all your * and souls? Deu 10:12,13
Therefore, cleanse your sinful * Deu 10:16
God with all your * and souls, and Deu 11:13
"But beware that your * do not Deu 11:16
give you trembling *, darkness, and Deu 28:65
hasn't given you * that understand Deu 29:4
He will cleanse your * and the Deu 30:6
hearts and the * of your children Deu 30:6
God with all your * and souls, and Deu 30:6
God with all your * and souls. Deu 30:10
at hand —in your * and on your Deu 30:14
But if your * turn away and you Deu 30:17
band of men whose * the Lord had 1Sa 10:26
the * of all the people of Israel. 2Sa 15:6
though they have * of lions, will 2Sa 17:10
for you know the * of all mankind. 2Ch 6:30
you with all their * to forgive 2Ch 6:37,38
it with all their * and wills, and 2Ch 15:15
for people whose * are perfect 2Ch 16:9
in the fear of God, with honest *. 2Ch 19:9
in their *." Job 1:5
* give birth only to wickedness." Job 15:35
those with pure * shall become Job 17:9
And I caused the widows' * to Job 29:13
Their * are filled to the brim Ps 5:9
deep within the * of men and Ps 7:9
He saves those whose * and lives Ps 7:10
comfort their * by helping them. Ps 10:17
"We will lie to our * content. Ps 12:3,4
Their * shall rejoice with Ps 22:26
Only those with pure hands and * Ps 24:4
He has made their * and closely Ps 33:13,14,15
to those whose * are breaking; Ps 34:18
SIN LURKS DEEP in the * of the Ps 36:1
into their own * and all their Ps 37:15
Our * have not deserted you! Ps 44:18
In your enemies' *; Ps 45:5
my face while cursing in their *! Ps 62:3,4
Though sins fill our *, you Ps 65:3
Israel—to those whose * are pure. Ps 73:1
their * could ever wish for! Ps 73:7
refusing to give their * to God. Ps 78:8
followed him, not with their *; Ps 78:36
their * were far away. Ps 78:37
Come before him with thankful *. Ps 95:2
Don't harden your * as Israel did Ps 95:8
whose * are right with the Lord; Ps 125:4
Deceit fills * that are plotting Pro 12:20
joy fills * that are planning for Pro 12:20
Anxious * are very heavy but a Pro 12:25
Wisdom is enshrined in the * of Pro 14:33
How much more the * of all Pro 15:11
by fire, but God purifies *. Pro 17:3
For God, who knows all *, knows Pro 24:11,12
eternity in the * of men, even so, Ecc 3:11
the * of the king and his Is 7:2
the strongest * melt, and are Is 13:7
the idols of Egypt tremble; the * Is 19:1
terror in their *, for the Lord of Is 19:17
*' desire is to glorify your name. Is 26:8
deep terror into many * again. Is 47:12
my laws in your *: don't be afraid Is 51:7
courage to those with repentant *. Is 57:15
everything their evil * desired. Is 57:17
with joy, your * will thrill, for Is 60:5
you hardened our * and made us sin Is 63:17
Plow up the hardness of your *; Jer 4:3
remove the foreskin of your *." Jer 4:4f
your minds and *, not just your Jer 4:4
weep with broken *, for the fierce Jer 4:8
O Jerusalem, cleanse your * while Jer 4:14
striking deep within your *. Jer 4:18
But my people have rebellious *; Jer 5:23,24
Unless you circumcise your * by Jer 9:25,26
See the * and motives of these Jer 11:20
But in their * they give no Jer 12:2
out of their own lying *. Jer 14:14
You follow evil to your *' Jer 16:12
upon their stony * or on the Jer 17:1
He searches all * and examines Jer 17:10
thoughts of * and minds, let me see Jer 20:12
I will give them * that respond Jer 24:7
inscribe my laws upon their *, Jer 31:33
inscribed on their *, so that they Jer 31:33f
I will put a desire into their * Jer 32:40
her strongholds are seized. The * Jer 48:41
Their * are troubled like a wild Jer 49:23
Pour out your * like water to the Lam 2:19
Let us lift our * and hands to Lam 3:41
Harden their * and curse them, Lam 3:65
The joy of our * has ended; Lam 5:15
Woe upon us for our sins. Our * Lam 5:17
their adulterous *—their love of Eze 6:9
I will take from your * of Eze 11:19
give you tender * of love for God, Eze 11:19
idols in their *—should I let them Eze 14:3
the minds and * of those who turn Eze 14:5
stop worshiping them in your *. Eze 14:6,7
* were with their idols! Eze 20:16
see the great change in your *. Eze 20:41
Let their * melt with terror, Eze 21:15
the joy of their * and their glory Eze 24:25
grief will be in many * among the Eze 32:9
terror into the * of everyone are Eze 32:23
struck terror to the * of all; Eze 32:26
* they are loving their money. Eze 33:31
I will take out your stony * of Eze 36:26
of sin and give you new * of love. Eze 36:26
Literally, "* of flesh," in Eze 36:26f
in contrast to "* of stone." Eze 36:26f
Their * blaze like a furnace Hos 7:6
hard * would not accept the truth. Hos 7:13
she erects. The * of her people Hos 10:2
plow the hard ground of your *, Hos 10:12
Give me all your *. Joe 2:12
Let your remorse tear at your * Joe 2:13
They have hardened their * and Amo 2:4
I will make your * miserable for Mic 6:13
empty shambles; * melt in horror; Nah 2:10
attitudes and evil *—and not only Hag 2:14
They hardened their * like Zec 7:12
Their * shall rejoice in the Zec 10:7
do their work for God with pure *. Mal 3:3
Happy are those whose * are Mt 5:8
For their * are fat Mt 13:15
me, but their * are far away. Mt 15:8
And the disciples' * were Mt 17:22,23
your hard and evil *, but it was Mt 19:8
robes of yours are * besmirched Mt 23:28
Sorrow chilled their *, and each Mt 26:22
the hard * of some of those who Mk 4:15
The rocky soil represents the * Mk 4:16
represents the * of people who Mk 4:18
*, so that no crop is produced. Mk 4:19
represents the * of those who truly Mk 4:20
much as was planted in their *." Mk 4:20
Literally, "for their * were Mk 6:52f
For from within, out of men's *, Mk 7:21
Are your * too hard to take it Mk 8:17
He will soften adult * to become Lk 1:17
Literally, "to turn the * of the Lk 1:17f
He has satisfied the hungry * Lk 1:53
of many * shall be revealed." Lk 2:34,35
the hard * of those who hear the Lk 8:12

(HEARTS Con't)
someday everything [in men's * Lk 8:17
realize what your * are like. Lk 9:55f
public, but God knows your evil *. Lk 16:15
to men who have * as trusting as Lk 18:16,17
other how their * had felt Lk 24:32
not find a home within your *. Jn 8:37
and hardened their * so that they Jn 12:40
God, who knows men's *, Act 15:8
for your * are too fat and your Act 28:27
has put this knowledge in their *. Rom 1:19
* they know right from wrong. Rom 2:12-15
those with changed * and minds. Rom 2:29
to fill our * with his love. Rom 5:5
way, [with all of your * and minds Rom 7:6
to us deep in our *, and tells us Rom 8:16
And the Father who knows all * Rom 8:27
as near as our own * and mouths. Rom 10:8
the seed in your *, and Apollos' 1Co 3:6
made the garden grow in your *. 1Co 3:6
really like, deep down in our *. 1Co 4:5
Holy Spirit in our * as guarantee 2Co 1:22
change in your *, everyone can see 2Co 3:2
carved on stone, but in human *. 2Co 3:3
as though Jewish * and minds are 2Co 3:14
writings their * are blind and they 2Co 3:15
God knows our *, that they are 2Co 5:11
but don't have true and honest *. 2Co 5:12
from death. Our * ache, but at the 2Co 6:10
Open your * to us! 2Co 6:13
Please open your * to us again, 2Co 7:2
within us, our * were full of 2Co 7:5
*' desire is obedience to Christ. 2Co 10:5
his Son into our *, so now we can Gal 4:6
and sincere *, especially if they Gal 4:18
I pray that your * will be Eph 1:18
right now in the * of those who are Eph 2:2
(But their *, too, were still Eph 2:11
at home in your *, living within Eph 3:17
Their closed * are full of Eph 4:17,18
music in your * to the Lord. Eph 5:19
the will of God with all your *. Eph 6:6,7
peace in your * and your lives. Php 1:2
Are your * tender and sympathetic Php 2:1
thoughts and your * quiet and at Php 4:7
your * is your only hope of glory. Col 1:26,27
present in your * and lives, for Col 3:15
to the Lord with thankful *. Col 3:16
examines our *' deepest thoughts. 1Th 2:4
while (though our * never left 1Th 2:17
This will result in your * being 1Th 3:13
and peace-filled * and minds. 2Th 1:2
with all their *, and all of them 2Th 2:11
comfort your * with all comfort, 2Th 2:17
comes from pure *, and that their 1Ti 1:5
have rebellious *, curse and swear, 1Ti 1:9
who love the Lord and have pure *. 2Ti 2:22
with cleansed * and real enthusiasm Tit 2:14
refreshed the * of God's people. Phm 1:7
and not let our * become set Heb 3:7,8
them, for their * were always Heb 3:10
Beware then of your own *, dear Heb 3:12
do not harden your * against him, Heb 3:15
not harden your * against him." Heb 4:7
will be in their * so that they Heb 8:10
* of the people who brought them. Heb 9:9
will transform our lives and *. Heb 9:14
my laws in their * so that they Heb 10:16
himself, with true * fully trusting Heb 10:22
*, and with holy fear and awe. Heb 12:28
souls as it takes hold of our *. Jas 1:21
and let your * be filled with God Jas 4:8
fat * are ready for the slaughter. Jas 5:5
at work in your *, cleansing you 1Pe 1:2
other warmly, with all your *. 1Pe 1:22
Be beautiful inside, in your *, 1Pe 3:4
with tender * and humble minds. 1Pe 3:8
him to cleanse our * from sin. 1Pe 3:21
Morning Star will shine in your *. 2Pe 1:19
God's Word in your *, and have won 1Jn 2:14
you, in your *, so that you don't 1Jn 2:27
is someone in your * who is 1Jn 4:4
Spirit into our * as a proof to us 1Jn 4:13
Holy Spirit in our *, the voice 1Jn 5:6,7,8
know in their * that it is true. 1Jn 5:10
might take God's place in your *. 1Jn 5:21
Since the Truth is in our * 2Jn 1:2
deep within men's *, and minds; Rev 2:23

HEARTY
celebrate with a * meal, and to Neh 8:10
said before, give Mark a * welcome Col 4:10
stay warm and eat *," and then Jas 2:16

HEAT
harvest, cold and *, winter and Gen 8:22
the scorching * of the day, and Gen 31:40
that will stand *—such as gold, Num 31:22
But anything that won't stand * Num 31:23
as drought and * consume snow. Job 24:19
DON'T punish me in the * of your Ps 6:1
and nothing can hide from its *. Ps 19:6
and song in the * of battle, and Ps 118:14
* and from rains and storms. Is 4:6
a shadow from the *, a shelter from Is 25:4
I've burned it for * and used it Is 44:19
bothered by the * nor worried by Jer 17:8
Literally, "I went in the * of my Eze 3:14,15f
smelt you with the * of my wrath. Eze 22:18,19,20
silver in fierce *, and you will Eze 22:22
For the * has withered the Joe 1:19
withered in the *, the Lord Jon 4:6
all day in the scorching *.' Mt 20:11,12
*, fastened itself onto his hand! Act 28:3
from the scorching noontime *. Rev 7:16
by this blast of *, and they cursed Rev 16:9

HEATED
the furnace be * up seven times Dan 3:19

HEATHEN
evil example of these * people; Ex 23:24
break down their * altars, smash Ex 34:13
so don't act like *—like the Lev 18:3
for these are the things the * do; Lev 18:24
edges of your beard, as the * do. Lev 19:27
"You must break down the * Deu 7:5
"You must destroy all the * Deu 12:2
as the * sacrifice to their gods. Deu 12:4,5
* do when they worship their idols Deu 14:1
to * gods, must be killed. Deu 18:10
There you will worship * gods Deu 28:64
And you have seen their * idols Deu 29:17
They sacrificed to * gods, Deu 32:17
not mix with the * people still Jos 23:7
I told you to destroy their * Ju 2:2
the worshiping of * gods. Ju 2:11
They prayed to * gods again, Ju 2:19
and worshiped the * gods Baal and Ju 10:6
a wife from these * Philistines? Ju 14:3
fall to the mercy of these *?" Ju 15:18
can't stay in this * city where Ju 19:12,13
"Yes, let's go across to those * 1Sa 14:6
"Who is this * Philistine, 1Sa 17:26
I'll do it to this * Philistine 1Sa 17:36
sent me away to worship * gods. 1Sa 26:19
sword before these * Philistines 1Sa 31:3,4
Lest the * nations laugh in 2Sa 1:20
own land where the * nations won't 2Sa 7:10,11
as depraved as the * nations which 1Ki 14:24
Ahab summoned his four hundred * 1Ki 22:6
following the * customs of the 2Ki 16:3
an unusual altar in a * temple. 2Ki 16:10
they worshiped * idols despite the 2Ki 17:15
or make sacrifices to any * gods. 2Ki 17:35,36
Israel had done. * altars to the 2Ki 21:3,4,5
as a burnt offering on a * altar. 2Ki 21:6
He killed the * priests who had 2Ki 23:5
He executed the priests of the * 2Ki 23:20
* capture and torture me." 1Ch 10:4
have appointed * priests instead. 2Ch 13:9
He demolished the * altars on 2Ch 14:3
knocking down the * altars on the 2Ch 17:6
So King Ahab summoned 400 of his * 2Ch 18:3,4,5
you drive out the * who lived in 2Ch 20:7
just like the * nations that were 2Ch 28:3
made altars to the * gods in every 2Ch 28:24
and destroyed the * altars in 2Ch 30:14
and other * centers of worship. 2Ch 31:1
one of the * gods—a handmade idol! 2Ch 32:19
the idols of the * nations 2Ch 33:2
He rebuilt the * altars his 2Ch 33:3
He even constructed * altars in 2Ch 33:4,5
destroying the * altars and the 2Ch 34:3
the bones of the * priests upon 2Ch 34:5
He broke down the * altars, 2Ch 34:7
and have worshiped * gods, and I am 2Ch 34:25
worshiped the * idols of the 2Ch 36:14
And some of the * people who had Ez 6:21,22
customs of the * people who lived Ez 9:1
girls from these * nations, and had Ez 9:2
were slain by the * kings—we were Ez 9:7
for we have married these * women. Ez 10:2
God to divorce our * wives and to Ez 10:3
for you have married * women; Ez 10:10
from the * people about you and Ez 10:11
Everyone who has a * wife will Ez 10:14
who had married * wives (they vowed Ez 10:16-19
Each of these men had * wives, Ez 10:44
So once again you allowed the * Neh 9:30
from the * people of the land in Neh 10:28
We further agreed that if the * Neh 10:31
"You talk like some * woman. Job 2:10
literally, "Why do the * rage?" Ps 2:1f
how you drove the * nations from Ps 44:1
the * nations surrounding us. Ps 59:5
been conquered by the * nations. Ps 79:1
Why should the * nations be Ps 79:10
* from your land and planted us. Ps 80:8
Where among the * gods is there a Ps 86:8
in among the * and learned their Ps 106:35
That is why he let the * nations Ps 106:41,42
The * worship idols of gold and Ps 135:15
you lest the * say their gods have Is 48:11
I crushed the * nations in my Is 63:6
though we were a * nation that Is 63:19
is only a * rite like theirs, and Jer 9:25,26
And if these * nations quickly Jer 12:16
What * god can give us rain? Jer 14:22
of sorrow (as is their * custom). Jer 16:6
Even among the *, no one has ever Jer 18:13
and Buz, and the other * there; Jer 25:23
yours, and I will scatter these * Jer 49:32
nor be shamed by * conquest. Eze 34:29
and mocked by * nations all around: Eze 36:4
No longer will those * nations Eze 36:15
For the * mock at you because Dan 9:16
My people mingle with the *, Hos 7:8
Instead, they worship * gods, Hos 7:14
it on the altars of her * gods; Hos 10:1
God will break down their * Hos 10:2
don't let the * rule them, for Joe 2:17
the taunts of the * who say, 'Where Joe 2:17
them off to your * temples. Joe 3:5
has been in your * gods—in Amo 5:25,26,27
You yourself will die in a * Amo 7:17
I will abolish the * shrines from Mic 5:14
and all others wearing * clothing. Zep 1:8
those who follow * customs and who Zep 1:9
I am very angry with the * Zec 1:15
as Judah,' the * used to say to Zec 8:13
* women who worship idols. Mal 2:11
Even the * do that. Mt 5:47
and over as the * do, who think Mt 6:7,8
Why be like the *? Mt 6:31,32
said, "Among the *, kings are Mt 20:25
'Why do the * rage against the Act 4:25,26
was in your * gods—Sakkuth, and the Act 7:43
"You stiff-necked *! Act 7:51
He will punish the * when they Rom 2:12-15
you are no better off than the *. Rom 2:25
And if the * obey God's laws, Rom 2:26
In fact, those * will be much Rom 2:27
And the *, of whom it once was Rom 9:26
to the foolish * nations. Rom 10:19
evil that even the * don't do it: 1Co 5:1
to law" and ask a * court to 1Co 6:1
When with the * I agree with 1Co 9:21
idols to whom the * bring 1Co 10:19
along with the *, that has been 1Co 10:20
Never forget that once you were * Eph 2:11
passion as the * do, in their 1Th 4:5
Such a person is worse than the * 1Ti 5:8

HEAVEN
under the whole *, standing Gen 7:19
*, brought him bread and wine. Gen 14:18
* and earth, be upon you, Abram; Gen 14:19,20
God, Creator of * and earth, that Gen 14:22
has reached to * and God has sent Gen 19:13
flaming tar from * upon Sodom and Gen 19:24
shouted to him from *, "Abraham! Gen 22:11
called again to Abraham from *. Gen 22:15
"Swear by Jehovah, the God of * Gen 24:3
For the Lord God of * told me to Gen 24:7
reached from earth to *, and he Gen 28:12
This is the awesome entrance to * Gen 28:16,17
with blessings of * above and of Gen 49:25
He heard their cries from *, and Ex 2:23
has risen to me in *, and I have Ex 3:9
your hand toward * and cause the Ex 9:22
his hands to * to the Lord, and the Ex 9:33
your hands to *, and darkness Ex 10:21
to rain down food from * for them. Ex 16:4
Literally, "of anything in * or Ex 20:4f
the Lord made the *, earth, and Ex 20:11
made known my will to you from *. Ex 20:22
For in six days the Lord made * Ex 31:17
as the stars of *, and I will give Ex 32:13
for what God in all of * or earth Deu 3:23,24,25
of your sin, * and earth are Deu 4:26
you from *, and he let you see his Deu 4:36
in * and down here upon the earth; Deu 4:39
name from under *, and I will make Deu 9:13,14
Earth and highest * belong to Deu 10:14
the name of Amalek from under *. Deu 25:19
your holy home in * and bless your Deu 26:15
blot out his name from under *. Deu 29:20
"I call * and earth to witness Deu 30:19
to them, and call * and earth to Deu 31:28
I raise my hand to * Deu 32:40,41
With the choicest gifts of * Deu 33:13
the gentle rains descend from *. Deu 33:28
of *, not just an ordinary god. Jos 2:11
The very stars of * Ju 5:20
vow: "O Lord of *, if you will 1Sa 1:11
He thunders against them from *. 1Sa 2:10
Ark of the Lord of * who is 1Sa 4:4
of thunder from *, and they were 1Sa 7:10
they stank to high * as far as the 1Sa 13:3,4
of the armies of * and of 1Sa 17:45
the Lord God of * was with him. 2Sa 5:10
of * enthroned above the cherubim. 2Sa 6:1
of the Lord of *, and gave a 2Sa 6:18
from the Lord of *: 'I chose you to 2Sa 7:8
to me, O Lord of *, God of Israel, 2Sa 7:27
The Lord thundered from *; 2Sa 22:14
spread out towards * and said, "O 1Ki 8:22,23

(HEAVEN Con't)

no god like you in * or earth, for	1Ki 8:22,23
yes, hear in * where you live,	1Ki 8:30
him in * and do what is right;	1Ki 8:32
hear them from * and forgive them	1Ki 8:33,34
hear them from * and forgive them	1Ki 8:35,36
hear them from * and forgive and	1Ki 8:39
from * and answer their prayers.	1Ki 8:43
and pleadings from * where you	1Ki 8:49
his hands outstretched toward *.	1Ki 8:54,55
of the armies of *, in whose	1Ki 18:15
flashed down from * and burned up	1Ki 18:38
of the armies of *, but the people	1Ki 19:14
the armies of * stood around him.	1Ki 22:19
come down from * and destroy you	2Ki 1:10
come down from * and destroy you	2Ki 1:12
to *—by means of a whirlwind!	2Ki 2:1
was carried by a whirlwind into *.	2Ki 2:11
Lord opened the windows of *!"	2Ki 7:19
'The Lord of * says to you, I took	1Ch 17:7
They will exclaim, 'The Lord of *	1Ch 17:24
standing between * and earth with	1Ch 21:16
down fire from * to burn up the	1Ch 21:26
Israel like to the stars of *."	1Ch 27:23f
Not even the highest * would be	2Ch 2:6
toward *, and prayed this prayer:	2Ch 6:12,13
like you in all of * and earth.	2Ch 6:14
Why, even the * and the heaven of	2Ch 6:18
Why, even the heaven and the * of	2Ch 6:18
yes, hear us from *, and when you	2Ch 6:20,21
then hear from * and punish him if	2Ch 6:23
to them from * and forgive their	2Ch 6:25
then listen from * and forgive the	2Ch 6:27
Hear from * where you live, and	2Ch 6:30
hear them from * where you live,	2Ch 6:33
from * and give them success.	2Ch 6:35
then hear from * where you live	2Ch 6:39
* and burned up the sacrifices!	2Ch 7:1
hear them from * and forgive their	2Ch 7:14
mercy, and all * is disturbed.	2Ch 28:9
prayers from his holy temple in *.	2Ch 30:27
prayer to God in *, and the Lord	2Ch 32:20
by the Lord God of *, and he has	2Ch 36:22,23
the God of * who gave me my vast	Ez 1:2
of the God of * and earth and we	Ez 5:11
angered the God of *, and he	Ez 5:12
burnt offerings to the God of *;	Ez 6:9
*, and to pray for me and my sons.	Ez 6:10
of the laws of the God of *.	Ez 7:12
of *), up to $200,000 in silver;	Ez 7:21
and whatever else the God of *	Ez 7:23
time in prayer to the God of *.	Neh 1:4
to the God of *, I replied, "If it	Neh 2:4
But I replied, "The God of *	Neh 2:20
and lifted their hands toward *;	Neh 8:6
and all the angels of * worship	Neh 9:6
with them from * and gave them good	Neh 9:13
"You gave them bread from * when	Neh 9:15
from * or water for their thirst.	Neh 9:20
heard them from *, and in great	Neh 9:27
you listened from *, and in your	Neh 9:28
has fallen from * and burned up	Job 1:16
He is as faultless as * is	Job 11:8
to my innocence is there in *;	Job 16:19
there, walking on the vault of *.'	Job 22:14
And the light of * will shine	Job 22:28
He enforces peace in *.	Job 25:2
God stretches out * over empty	Job 26:7
The pillars of * tremble at his	Job 26:11
Or, "the bars of * are afraid of	Job 26:13f
mean that I denied the God of *.	Job 31:28
"But if a messenger from * is	Job 33:23,24
*, clothed in dazzling splendor.	Job 37:22
Who can tilt the water jars of *,	Job 38:37,38
Everything under the * is mine.	Job 41:11
(Ten were in *.	Job 42:13,14f
But God in * merely laughs!	Ps 2:4
look to you in * and lay my	Ps 5:3
he still rules from *.	Ps 11:4
The Lord looks down from * on all	Ps 14:2
And when I awake in *, I will be	Ps 17:15
And he heard me from *;	Ps 18:6
He reached down from * and took	Ps 18:16
He hears me from highest * and	Ps 20:6
Lord, I lift my hands to *	Ps 28:2
mankind from * where he lives.	Ps 33:13,14,15
Where is his equal in all of *	Ps 35:10
The Commander of the armies of *	Ps 46:7
the Commander of the armies of *.	Ps 48:8
his people. To * and earth he	Ps 50:4
all * declares that he is just.	Ps 50:6
God looks down from *, searching	Ps 53:2
I will cry to the God of * who	Ps 57:2
He will send down help from * to	Ps 57:3
O Lord God of the armies of *,	Ps 69:6
Praise him, all * and earth!	Ps 69:34
receive me into the glories of *!	Ps 73:24
Whom have I in * but you?	Ps 73:25
pronounce sentence on them from *;	Ps 76:8
lifting my hands to *, pleading.	Ps 77:2
the windows of *— and rained down	Ps 78:23
He gave them bread from *!	Ps 78:24
wounded by iceballs from *.	Ps 78:48
of the armies of *, and bless us.	Ps 80:14
Look down from * and see our	Ps 80:14
O God of the armies of *.	Ps 80:19
Temple, O Lord of the armies of *.	Ps 84:1
O Lord of the armies of *,	Ps 84:12
righteousness smiles down from *.	Ps 85:11
All * shall praise your miracles,	Ps 89:5
For who in all of * can be	Ps 89:6
be as endless as the days of *.	Ps 89:29
from his temple in *, and heard	Ps 102:19
and gave them manna—bread from *.	Ps 105:40
and fire fell from * to consume	Ps 106:18
Yes, Jehovah who made * and	Ps 115:15
Lord, your Word stands firm in *.	Ps 119:89
O GOD ENTHRONED in *, I lift my	Ps 123:1
the Lord who made * and earth.	Ps 124:8
Lord who made * and earth.	Ps 134:3
throughout all of * and earth, and	Ps 135:6
Oh, give thanks to the God of *,	Ps 136:26
in *. I face your Temple as I	Ps 138:1
If I go up to *, you are there;	Ps 139:8
Reach down from * and rescue me;	Ps 144:7
both earth and *, the seas and	Ps 146:6
his angels, all the armies of *.	Ps 148:2
greater than all of earth and *.	Ps 148:13
the height of *, the size of the	Pro 25:2,3
but God goes back and forth to *?	Pro 30:4
God, for he is in * and you are	Ecc 5:1
Listen, O * and earth, to what	Is 1:2
out to *, I won't look or listen.	Is 1:15
Ask anything you like, in * or on	Is 7:11
be deep as Sheol or high as *."	Is 7:11f
the Lord of the armies of *!	Is 8:13
their fists at * and curse their	Is 8:21
of the armies of *, is chopping	Is 10:33
were when God sent fire from *;	Is 13:19
How you are fallen from *, O	Is 14:12
ascend to * and rule the angels.	Is 14:13
says the Lord of the armies of *.	Is 14:23
of the armies of * has told me	Is 22:15,16
The Commander of the armies of *	Is 23:9
is poured down on us from *.	Is 32:15
is very great, and lives in *.	Is 33:5
and the highlands of * far away.	Is 33:17
You alone made * and earth.	Is 37:16,17
"With what in all of * and earth	Is 46:5
come down from * and stay upon the	Is 55:10
O Lord, look down from * and see	Is 63:15
* IS MY throne and the earth is my	Is 66:1
to offer to "The Queen of *"	Jer 7:18
the "Queen of *" among the gods	Jer 7:18f
Am I not everywhere in all of *	Jer 23:24
his holy temple in *, and against	Jer 25:30
The Lord, the Maker of * and	Jer 33:2
burn incense to the 'Queen of *'	Jer 44:17
"Queen of *";	Jer 44:17f
to the 'Queen of *' and stopped	Jer 44:18
the 'Queen of *' and pouring out	Jer 44:19
to the 'Queen of *,' and you have	Jer 44:25
for God is judging her from *.	Jer 51:9
in the streets. * and earth shall	Jer 51:48
be as powerful as *, though she	Jer 51:53
He has sent fire from * that	Lam 1:13
the heights of * at his command.	Lam 2:1
to him in *, for we have sinned;	Lam 3:41
down from * and respond to my cry!	Lam 3:50
They asked the God of * to show	Dan 2:18
Then Daniel praised the God of *,	Dan 2:19
there is a God in * who reveals	Dan 2:28
for the God of * has given you your	Dan 2:37
kings, the God of * will set up a	Dan 2:44
coming down from *.	Dan 4:13
Let the dews of * drench him and	Dan 4:15
your greatness reaches up to *,	Dan 4:22
coming down from * and saying,	Dan 4:23
Let him be wet with the dew of *.	Dan 4:23
your back wet with dew from *.	Dan 4:25
you have learned that * rules.	Dan 4:26
called down from *, "O King	Dan 4:31
I, Nebuchadnezzar, looked up to *	Dan 4:34
among the hosts of *, as well as	Dan 4:35
honor the King of *, the Judge of	Dan 4:37
with the dew of *, until at last he	Dan 5:21
defied the Lord of *, and brought	Dan 5:23
he does great miracles in * and	Dan 6:27
be—brought there on clouds from *;	Dan 7:13
Then every nation under *, and	Dan 7:27
Literally, "host of *" and "the	Dan 8:10f
Literally, "host of *" and "the	Dan 8:10f
of the army of * by canceling the	Dan 8:11
But the army of * was restrained	Dan 8:12
has been heard in * and was	Dan 10:12
the messenger from *, "Sir, I am	Dan 10:16
you in * against satanic forces	Dan 12:1
hands lifted to *, taking oath by	Dan 12:7
They look everywhere except to *,	Hos 7:16
Israel like the dew from *;	Hos 14:5
it smells to highest *.'	Jon 1:2
I worship Jehovah, the God of *,	Jon 1:9,10
He leaves his throne in * and	Mic 1:3
* and giving you such scant crops.	Hag 1:10
from *, from his holy home."	Zec 2:13
up the windows of * for you and	Mal 3:10
for the Kingdom of * is coming	Mt 3:2
And a voice from * said, "This	Mt 3:17
for the Kingdom of * is near."	Mt 4:17
Good News about the Kingdom of *.	Mt 4:23
the Kingdom of * is given to them.	Mt 5:3
for the Kingdom of * is theirs.	Mt 5:10
reward awaits you up in *.	Mt 5:12
be the least in the Kingdom of *.	Mt 5:19
be great in the Kingdom of *.	Mt 5:19
get into the Kingdom of * at all!	Mt 5:20
as true sons of your Father in *.	Mt 5:45
as your Father in * is perfect.	Mt 5:48
the reward from your Father in *.	Mt 6:1
in *, we honor your holy name.	Mt 6:9
here on earth, just as it is in *.	Mt 6:10
Store them in * where they will	Mt 6:20
If your profits are in * your	Mt 6:21
your Father in * even more	Mt 7:11
"* can be entered only through	Mt 7:13
'Lord,' but still won't get to *.	Mt 7:21
whether they obey my Father in *.	Mt 7:21
* with Abraham, Isaac, and Jacob.	Mt 8:11
that the Kingdom of * is near.	Mt 10:7
my friend before my father in *.	Mt 10:32
deny him before my Father in *.	Mt 10:33
of * will be greater than he is!	Mt 11:11
crowding toward the Kingdom of *,	Mt 11:12
Literally, "the Kingdom of *	Mt 11:12f
Father, Lord of * and earth, thank	Mt 11:25
obeys my Father in * is my brother,	Mt 12:50
Kingdom of *, and others were not.	Mt 13:11
"The Kingdom of * is like a farmer	Mt 13:24
"The Kingdom of * is like a tiny	Mt 13:31,32
"The Kingdom of * can be compared	Mt 13:33
"The Kingdom of * is like a	Mt 13:44
"Again, the Kingdom of * is like	Mt 13:45
"Again, the Kingdom of * can be	Mt 13:47,48
"for my Father in * has personally	Mt 16:17
you the keys of the Kingdom of *;	Mt 16:19
on earth shall be locked in *;	Mt 16:19
on earth shall be open in *!"	Mt 16:19
him. "* forbid, sir," he said.	Mt 16:22
be greatest in the Kingdom of *!	Mt 18:1
never get into the Kingdom of *.	Mt 18:3
the greatest in the Kingdom of *.	Mt 18:4
Better to enter * crippled than	Mt 18:8
Better to enter * with one eye	Mt 18:9
For I tell you that in * their	Mt 18:10
earth is bound in *, and whatever	Mt 18:18
free on earth will be freed in *.	Mt 18:18
my Father in * will do it for you.	Mt 18:19
"The Kingdom of * can be	Mt 18:23
for the sake of the Kingdom of *.	Mt 19:12
For of such is the Kingdom of *	Mt 19:14
* if you keep the commandments."	Mt 19:17
and you will have treasure in *;	Mt 19:21
man to get into the Kingdom of *.	Mt 19:23
illustration of the Kingdom of *.	Mt 20:1
"Praise God in highest *!"	Mt 21:9
what the Kingdom of * is like.	Mt 22:1
everyone is as the angels in *.	Mt 22:30
* should be addressed like that.	Mt 23:9
of *, and won't go in yourselves.	Mt 23:13,14
"the stars shall fall from *."	Mt 24:29f
of *, with power and great glory.	Mt 24:30
farthest ends of the earth and *.	Mt 24:31
from one end of * to the other."	Mt 24:31f
"* and earth will disappear, but	Mt 24:35
"THE KINGDOM OF * can be	Mt 25:1
"Again, the Kingdom of * can be	Mt 25:14
returning on the clouds of *."	Mt 26:64
came down from * and rolled aside	Mt 28:2
all authority in * and earth.	Mt 28:18
* said, "You are my beloved Son;	Mk 1:11
up to *, gave thanks for the food.	Mk 6:41
Then, looking up to *, he sighed	Mk 7:34
what must I do to get to *?"	Mk 10:17
in *—and come, follow me."	Mk 10:21
your Father in * will forgive you	Mk 11:25
is in * forgive your trespasses."	Mk 11:26,f
farthest bounds of earth and *.	Mk 13:27
* and earth shall disappear, but	Mk 13:31
the angels in *, nor I myself,	Mk 13:32
to earth in the clouds of *."	Mk 14:62
was taken up into * and sat down at	Mk 16:19
armies of *—praising God:	Lk 2:13
"Glory to God in the highest *	Lk 2:14
returned again to *, the shepherds	Lk 2:15
and a voice from * said, "You are	Lk 3:22
a great reward awaiting you in *.	Lk 6:23
Then your reward from * will be	Lk 6:35
for his return to *, he moved	Lk 9:51
down from * to burn them up?"	Lk 9:54
Will you be exalted to *?	Lk 10:15
from * as a flash of lightning!	Lk 10:18
are registered as citizens of *."	Lk 10:20
O Father, Lord of * and earth, for	Lk 10:21

(HEAVEN Con't)
need to do to live forever in *?" Lk 10:25
sought of him a sign from *." Lk 11:16f
gets rich on earth but not in *." Lk 12:21
This will fatten your purses in * Lk 12:33
And the purses of * have no rips Lk 12:33
And he replied, "The door to * Lk 13:24,25
"Well, in the same way * will be Lk 15:7
against both * and you, and am no Lk 15:18
sinned against * and you, and am Lk 15:21
into an everlasting home in *? Lk 16:9
befriend you when you get to *." Lk 16:9f
you with the true riches of *? Lk 16:11
and unshakable as * and earth. Lk 16:17
from * and destroyed them all. Lk 17:29
lift his eyes to * as he prayed, Lk 18:13
what shall I do to get to *?" Lk 18:18
you in *—and come, follow me." Lk 18:22
Let all * rejoice! Lk 19:38
message was from *, then we are Lk 20:5
dead get to *, they do not marry. Lk 20:34,35
And though all * and earth shall Lk 21:33
Then an angel from * appeared Lk 22:43
and fills you with power from *." Lk 24:49
his hands to *, he blessed them, Lk 24:50
into the sky, and went on to *. Lk 24:51
from * and resting upon Jesus. Jn 1:32
You will even see * open and the Jn 1:51
Holy Spirit gives new life from *; Jn 3:6
next bestow this life from *." Jn 3:8
I tell you what is going on in *? Jn 3:12
earth and will return to * again. Jn 3:13
the Light from * came into the Jn 3:19
John replied, "God in * appoints Jn 3:27
"He has come from * and is Jn 3:31
shall never see *, but the wrath of Jn 3:36
souls into the granaries of *! Jn 4:36
laws you set your hopes of *. Jn 5:45
'Moses gave them bread from *.' Jn 6:30,31
he offers you true Bread from *. Jn 6:32
sent by God from *, and he gives Jn 6:33
For I have come here from * to Jn 6:38
he claimed to be the Bread from *. Jn 6:41
that he came down from *?" Jn 6:42
But the Bread from * gives Jn 6:48-51
Bread that came down out of *. Jn 6:48-51
I am the true Bread from *; Jn 6:58
they ate bread from *." Jn 6:58
return to * again? Jn 6:62
yet returned to his glory in *. Jn 7:39
Then Jesus looked up to * and Jn 11:41
to his glory in *, then they Jn 12:16
to his glory in *, and that "I Jn 12:23,24
Then a voice spoke from * saying, Jn 12:28
he looked up to * and said, Jn 17:1
how he returned to * after giving Act 1:1
Jesus has gone away to *, and Act 1:11
day he was taken from us into *." Act 1:21,22
highest honor in *, next to God. Act 2:33
For he must remain in * until Act 3:21,22
Under all * there is no other Act 4:12
"O Lord, Creator of * and earth Act 4:24
human hands. 'The * is my throne,' Act 7:48,49
Didn't I make both * and earth?' Act 7:50
upward into * and saw the glory of Act 7:55
from * spotted down upon him! Act 9:3
sheet was pulled up again to *. Act 10:16
it contained disappeared into *. Act 11:10
God who made * and earth and sea Act 14:15
he is Lord of * and earth, he Act 17:24
image fell down to us from *. Act 19:35
light from * shone around me. Act 22:6
sir, a light from * brighter than Act 26:13
disobedient to that vision from *! Act 26:19
bringing all who believe it to *. Rom 1:16
makes us ready for *—makes us right Rom 1:17
But God shows his anger from * Rom 1:18
has shown us a different way to * Rom 3:21,22
But didn't he earn his right to * Rom 4:4,5
God, pleading for us there in *. Rom 8:34
want a sign from * as proof that 1Co 1:22
to bring us into the glories of *. 1Co 2:7
and reward the very angels in *? 1Co 6:3
many gods, both in * and on earth. 1Co 8:5
there is in all of * and earth, but 1Co 13:1
in * have bodies far different 1Co 15:40
but Christ came from * above. 1Co 15:47
kind of body as his—a body from *. 1Co 15:48
in * which we have not yet seen. 2Co 4:18
new bodies in *, homes that will be 2Co 5:1
our eternal home in * with Jesus. 2Co 5:6
from this body and with him in *. 2Co 5:9
was taken up to * 2Co 12:2,3
Literally, "the third *." 2Co 12:2,3f
different "way to *," which Gal 1:6
really doesn't go to * at all. Gal 1:6
yes, if an angel comes from * and Gal 1:8
that the way to * which I preach is Gal 1:11
him fit for * only because he Gal 3:6
to get to * by obeying God's laws? Gal 4:9
in * because we belong to Christ. Eph 1:3
wherever we are—in * or on earth—to Eph 1:10
right hand in *, far, far above Eph 1:20
and foreigners to *, but you are Eph 2:19
To show to all the rulers in * Eph 3:10
of them already in * and some down Eph 3:14,15
triumphantly to * after his Eph 4:8
that it says he returned to *. Eph 4:9
the heights of *, far down to the Eph 4:9
to the heights of * and gave him a Php 2:9
knee shall bow in * and on earth Php 2:10
calling us up to * because of what Php 3:14
But our homeland is in *, where Php 3:20
to the joys of *, and have been Col 1:5
made everything in * and earth, the Col 1:16
him—all things in * and on Col 1:20
and joys of * where he sits beside Col 3:1
power. Let * fill your thoughts; Col 3:2
Your real life is in * with Col 3:3
in * who is closely watching you. Col 4:1
of God's Son from *—Jesus, whom God 1Th 1:10
come down from * with a mighty 1Th 4:16
suddenly from * in flaming fire 2Th 1:7
up again to his glory in *. 1Ti 3:16
be revealed from * by the blessed 1Ti 6:15
for themselves in *—it is the only 1Ti 6:19
will begin living with him in *. 2Ti 2:11
soon now I will be on my way to *. 2Ti 4:6
and rest. In * a crown is waiting 2Ti 4:8
honor beside the great God of *. Heb 1:3
multitudes of God's people to *; Heb 2:10
who are chosen for *—I want you to Heb 3:1
has gone to * itself to help us; Heb 4:14
the good things of * and shared in Heb 6:4
sacred curtains of *, where Christ Heb 6:19
given the place of honor in *. Heb 7:26
Priest, and is in * at the place of Heb 8:1
He ministers in the temple in *, Heb 8:2
model of the real tabernacle in *; Heb 8:5
But Christ, as a Minister in *, Heb 8:6
tabernacle in *, not made by men Heb 9:11
from things in *—all had to be made Heb 9:23
But the real things in *, of Heb 9:23
For Christ has entered into * Heb 9:24
a copy of the real temple in *. Heb 9:24
awaiting you in *, things that Heb 10:34
took him away to * without dying; Heb 11:5
forward to their real home in *. Heb 11:14
They were living for *. Heb 11:16
of all those registered in *; Heb 12:23
in *, already made perfect; Heb 12:23
to God who speaks to us from *! Heb 12:25
to our everlasting home in *. Heb 13:14
and the Kingdom of * is theirs, for Jas 2:5
But the wisdom that comes from * Jas 3:17
by * or earth or anything else; Jas 5:12
it is kept in * for you, pure and 1Pe 1:4
joy that comes from * itself. 1Pe 1:8
even the angels in * would give a 1Pe 1:12
from now on until you get to *. 1Pe 1:17
impossible road to * which your 1Pe 1:18
Since your real home is in * I 1Pe 2:11
And now Christ is in *, sitting 1Pe 3:22
and powers of * bowing before him 1Pe 3:22
wide the gates of * for you to 2Pe 1:11
calling down from *, saying, "This 2Pe 1:17,18
the angels in * who stand in the 2Pe 2:11
I am on my way to *; 1Jn 2:4
with a voice from * when Jesus was 1Jn 5:6,7,8
the voice from * at Christ's 1Jn 5:6,7,8
and then an angel was sent from * Rev 1:1
the secret nourishment from *; Rev 2:17
coming down from * from my God; Rev 3:12
standing open in *, and the same Rev 4:1
in * and saw—oh, the glory of it! Rev 4:2
But no one in all * or earth Rev 5:3
And then I heard everyone in * Rev 5:13
Then the stars of * appeared to Rev 6:13
Literally, "the stars of * fell Rev 6:13f
throughout all * for what seemed Rev 8:1
star fell from * upon a third of Rev 8:10
Literally, "a star fallen from * Rev 9:1f
who was fallen to earth from *, Rev 9:1
coming down from *, surrounded by a Rev 10:1
* called to me, "Don't do it. Rev 10:4
his right hand to *, and swore by Rev 10:5
ever, who created * and everything Rev 10:6
Then the voice from * spoke to me Rev 10:8
will shout from *, "Come up!" Rev 11:12
And they will rise to * in a Rev 11:12
give glory to the God of *. Rev 11:13
shouting down from *, "The kingdom Rev 11:15
Then, in *, the temple of God was Rev 11:19
THEN A GREAT pageant appeared in * Rev 12:1
Then there was war in *; Rev 12:7
the battle and was forced from *. Rev 12:8
thrown down from * onto earth—he Rev 12:10
You citizens of *, rejoice! Rev 12:12
temple and all those living in *. Rev 13:6
And I heard a sound from * like Rev 14:2
Worship him who made the * and Rev 14:7
good deeds follow them to *!" Rev 14:13
*, and he also had a sharp sickle. Rev 14:17
AND I SAW in * another mighty Rev 15:1
temple in * was thrown wide open! Rev 15:5
cursed the God of * for their pains Rev 16:11
in *, saying, "It is finished!" Rev 16:17
an incredible hailstorm from *; Rev 16:21
come down from * with great Rev 18:1
voice calling from *, "Come away Rev 18:4
piled as high as * and God is ready Rev 18:5
But you, O *, rejoice over her Rev 18:20
a vast crowd in *, "Hallelujah! Rev 19:1
Then I saw * opened and a white Rev 19:11
The armies of *, dressed in Rev 19:14
of * were gorged with their flesh. Rev 19:21
come down from * with the key to Rev 20:1
But fire from God in * will flash Rev 20:9
coming down from God out of *. Rev 21:2

HEAVEN-SENT
demonstration of his * power. Jn 2:11
* Holy Spirit who spoke to them; 1Pe 1:12

HEAVEN'S
The Commander of all of * armies! Ps 24:10
(And O Jehovah, God of * armies, Ps 59:5
O Jehovah, God of * armies, how Ps 80:4
GOD STANDS UP to open * court. Ps 82:1
of * armies, my King and my God! Ps 84:3
bless you with * blessings Ps 128:5
the King, the Lord of * armies." Is 6:5
of the Lord of * armies for his Is 8:18
the Lord of * armies has dedicated Is 9:7
turn to him, the Lord of * armies. Is 9:13
the wrath of the Lord of * armies. Is 9:19,20
says the Lord of * armies, and will Is 14:22
from the Lord God of * armies! Is 22:5
Then the Lord of * armies will Is 24:23
very tender, and * dawn is about to Lk 1:78

HEAVENLY
The Commander of the * armies is Ps 46:11
O Jehovah, God of the * armies, Ps 84:8
O Jehovah, Commander of the * Ps 89:8
Praise him who made the * Ps 136:7
officers of the * army, came to Dan 10:13
are the four * spirits who stand Zec 6:5
they will praise your * Father. Mt 5:15,16
Your * Father will forgive you Mt 6:14,15
food—for your * Father feeds them. Mt 6:26
But your * Father already knows Mt 6:31,32
* Father speaking through you! Mt 10:20
So shall my * Father do to you Mt 18:35
realize that your * Father will do Lk 11:13
your * Father knows your needs. Lk 12:30
of the only Son of the * Father! Jn 1:14
They hated the * Light because Jn 3:20
but we do it for a * reward that 1Co 9:25
God gives us spiritual, * bodies. 1Co 15:46
transformed into * bodies that 1Co 15:53
was full of * glory, the glory of 2Co 3:11
when we shall have * bodies which 2Co 5:2
confidence to our * bodies, 2Co 5:6
But our mother-city is the * Gal 4:26
with him in the * realms—all Eph 2:6
will bring me into his * kingdom. 2Ti 4:18
the pattern of the * tabernacle as Heb 8:5
him to that strong * city whose Heb 11:10
for he has made a * city for them. Heb 11:16
living God, the * Jerusalem, and to Heb 12:22
Sometimes it praises our * Jas 3:9
And remember that your * Father 1Pe 1:17
noise and the * bodies will 2Pe 3:10
on fire, and the * bodies will melt 2Pe 3:12
SEE HOW VERY much our * Father 1Jn 3:1
poverty (but you have * riches! Rev 2:9

HEAVENS
the * and the earth, the earth Gen 1:1
NOW AT LAST the * and earth were Gen 2:1
creation of the * and earth which Gen 2:4
* and count the stars if you can. Gen 15:5
stones, as clear as the *. Ex 24:10
and make your * as iron, and your Lev 26:19
one end of the * to the other to Deu 4:32
he will shut the *—there will be no Deu 11:17
of rain in the *, to give you fine Deu 28:12
"The * above you will be as Deu 28:23
are not in the far *, so distant Deu 30:12
"LISTEN, O * and earth! Deu 32:1
He descends from the * Deu 33:26
So the sun stopped in the * and Jos 10:13
of the * and to sacrifice to him. 1Sa 1:3
The foundations of the * quaked 2Sa 22:8
He bent the * down and came to 2Sa 22:10
and the highest * cannot contain 1Ki 8:27
hard for the Lord God of the *; 1Ki 19:10
You created the * and the earth. 2Ki 19:15
the Lord of the * was with him. 1Ch 11:9
But the Lord made the *. 1Ch 16:26
Let the * be glad, the earth 1Ch 16:31
Everything in the * and earth is 1Ch 29:11
who made the * and the earth and 2Ch 2:12
and the heaven of * cannot contain 2Ch 6:18
If I shut up the * so that there 2Ch 7:13
God in all the *, the Ruler of all 2Ch 20:6

(HEAVENS Con't)
guilt is as boundless as the *. Ez 9:6
You have made the skies and the * Neh 9:6
Only he has stretched the * out Job 9:8
again until the * are no more; Job 14:11,12
Even the * can't be absolutely Job 15:15
be proud as the *, and walk with Job 20:6
he has left. The * will reveal his Job 20:27
than the *, higher than the stars. Job 22:12
its pride! The * are made Job 26:13
the whole earth, under all the *. Job 28:23,24
* and knock God from his throne? Job 35:6
It rolls across the * and his Job 37:3
with her satellites across the *? Job 38:32
and how the * influence the earth? Job 38:33
all the earth and overflows the *. Ps 8:1
He bent the * down and came to Ps 18:9
The Lord thundered in the *; Ps 18:13
THE * ARE telling the glory of Ps 19:1
The sun lives in the * where God Ps 19:3,4
The sun crosses the * from end Ps 19:6
He merely spoke, and the * were Ps 33:6
O Lord, is as great as all the *. Ps 36:5
be exalted above the highest *! Ps 57:5
and love are as vast as the *. Ps 57:10
be exalted, O God, above the *. Ps 57:11
earth trembled and the * shook. Ps 68:8
upon the ancient *, whose mighty Ps 68:33
his strength is mighty in the *. Ps 68:34
Lord, reach to the highest *. Ps 71:19
They boast against the very *, Ps 73:9
enduring as the * and the earth. Ps 78:69
truth is as enduring as the *. Ps 89:2
power. The * are yours, the world, Ps 89:11
exalted in the *, while his Ps 92:8
idols, but our God made the *! Ps 96:5
Let the * be glad, the earth Ps 96:11
the earth. The * declare his Ps 97:6
and made the * with your hands! Ps 102:25
height of the * above the earth. Ps 103:11
The Lord has made the * his Ps 103:19
curtain of the *, and hollowed out Ps 104:1
Their ships are tossed to the * Ps 107:26
beyond measure, high as the *. Ps 108:4
glory is far more vast than the *. Ps 108:5
glory is far greater than the *. Ps 113:4
Far below him are the * and the Ps 113:6
For he is in the *, and does as Ps 115:3
bless you! The * belong to the Ps 115:16
And the * too! Ps 121:2
Praise him who made the *, for Ps 136:5
Bend down the *, Lord, and come. Ps 144:5
He covers the * with clouds, Ps 147:8
PRAISE THE LORD, O *! Ps 148:1
the * he made with mighty power. Ps 150:1
he established the * and formed the Pro 8:27,28,29
and sorrow and the * are black. Is 5:30
The * will be black above them. Is 13:10
For I will shake the * in my Is 13:13
I will climb to the highest * Is 14:14
falls from the * upon you; Is 24:18
angels in the *, and the proud Is 24:21
The Lord is coming from the * to Is 26:21
At that time the * above will Is 34:4
its work in the *, then watch, for Is 34:5
measured off the * with his ruler? Is 40:12
stretches out the * like a curtain Is 40:22
Look up into the *! Is 40:26
The Lord God who created the * Is 42:5
Sing, O *, for the Lord has done Is 44:23
I alone stretched out the *. Is 44:24
Open up, O *. Is 45:8
stretched out the * and commanded Is 45:12
For Jehovah created the * and Is 45:18
right hand spread out the * above; Is 48:13
Sing for joy, O *; Is 49:13
For just as the * are higher Is 55:9
For see, I am creating new * and Is 65:17
As surely as my new * and earth Is 66:22
silly idols! The * are shocked at Jer 2:12
And all the * were dark. Jer 4:23
and the birds of the * had fled. Jer 4:25
The earth shall mourn, the * Jer 4:28
have not made the * and earth, Jer 10:11
in space and stretched out the *. Jer 10:12
Not until the * can be measured Jer 31:37
You have made the * and earth by Jer 32:17
He stretched out the * by his Jer 51:15
is thunder in the * and he causes Jer 51:16
earth, beneath the * of the Lord. Lam 3:66
the * were suddenly opened to me Eze 1:1
And all the birds of the * will Eze 32:4
veil the * and darken the stars. Eze 32:7
high into the * for all the world Dan 4:20
before them and the * tremble. Joe 2:10
though they climb into the *, I Amo 9:2
*, the first floor on the earth. Amo 9:6
his glory fills the *, and the Hab 3:3
begin to shake the * and earth—and Hag 2:6
about to shake the * and the earth, Hag 2:21
stretched out the * and laid the Zec 12:1
of the water, the * were opened to Mt 3:16
And even to say, 'By *!' Mt 5:34
God, for the * are God's throne. Mt 5:34
sign in the *, but no further proof Mt 16:4
And when you swear 'By *' you Mt 23:22
to fall from the *, and the Mt 24:29
Literally, "the powers of the * Mt 24:29f
will appear in the * and there Mt 24:30
water, he saw the * open and the Mk 1:10
will fall—the * will convulse. Mk 13:25
and as he was praying, the * Lk 3:21
Glory to God in the highest *!" Lk 19:38
things happening in the *. Lk 21:11
of the very * will be broken up. Lk 21:26
in the * and on the earth—blood and Act 2:19
the * opened and Jesus the Messiah Act 7:56
need to search the * to find Christ Rom 10:6
the * are the work of your hands. Heb 1:10
shake the earth, but the * too." Heb 12:26
he had made the * by the word of 2Pe 3:5,6
the earth and the * be stored away 2Pe 3:7
and then the * will pass away with 2Pe 3:10
God will set the * on fire, and the 2Pe 3:12
promise of new * and a new earth 2Pe 3:13
And the starry * disappeared Rev 6:14
flying through the * crying loudly, Rev 8:13
the *, "It has happened at last! Rev 12:10
Rejoice, O *! Rev 12:12
flying through the *, carrying the Rev 14:6
And I heard a voice in the * Rev 14:13

HEAVIER
burdens but I will give you *!" 2Ch 10:14
For they are * than the sand of Job 6:3
A rebel's frustrations are * than Pro 27:3

HEAVIEST
Therefore God's * sentence awaits Lk 20:47

HEAVILY
book shall lie * upon him, and the Deu 29:20
I will lay my hand * upon you, Eze 25:7
of God lies very * upon the Jews, Rom 3:19

HEAVINESS
Praise instead of *. Is 61:3

HEAVING
finds its way across the * ocean. Pro 30:18,19

HEAVY
But a * stone covered the mouth Gen 29:2
them down under * burdens while Ex 1:11
carry * loads of mortar and brick. Ex 1:13,14
I have seen the * tasks the Ex 3:9
you go except under * pressure. Ex 3:19
Moses, this job is too * a burden Ex 18:18
its feet beneath a * load, you must Ex 23:5
and no * work is permitted. Lev 23:36
The load is far too *! Num 11:14
Ordinary sin receives * 1Sa 2:23,24,25
hand will be as * upon you as it 1Sa 12:15
carry such a * responsibility?" 1Ki 3:9
because they were too * to weigh! 1Ki 7:47
with clouds, and a * wind brought a 1Ki 18:45
to pay * annual taxes to Assyria. 2Ki 17:3
Solomon—because they were so *. 2Ki 25:16
hard pressed with * fighting all 1Ch 10:3
bronze were used, too * to weigh. 2Ch 4:17,18
"My father gave you * burdens but 2Ch 10:14
and because of the * rainfall. Ez 10:9
made my life so * a burden to me? Job 7:20
all night your hand was * on me. Ps 32:4
the wicked; * penalties are meted Ps 34:21
they are a burden too * to bear. Ps 38:3,4
my spirit is * within me. Ps 69:20
your hands from their * tasks." Ps 81:6
Your wrath lies * on me; Ps 88:7
and * here beneath your wrath. Ps 90:9
my heart is * with sorrow; Ps 119:28
Anxious hearts are very * but a Pro 12:25
Laughter cannot mask a * heart. Pro 14:13
whose heart is * is as bad as Pro 25:20
man's trouble lies * upon him; Ecc 8:6,7
When the clouds are *, the rains Ecc 11:3
his hand is * on them still. Is 5:25
His hand is still * upon them, to Is 9:21
But my heart is * with grief, for Is 24:15,16
but I will send * judgment upon Is 29:2
when a woman is in * labor trying Is 37:3
Take * millstones and grind the Is 47:2
the old folks carry * burdens. Is 47:6
Therefore your wrath is * on us. Is 64:5
iron pillar and * gates of brass. Jer 1:18
Day and night his hand is * on Lam 3:3
he has fastened me with * chains. Lam 3:7
stagger beneath their * loads. Lam 5:13
A * rainstorm will undermine it; Eze 13:11
flounders in the * eastern gale, Eze 27:26
carrying * basketfuls of earth); Eze 29:18
saying: 'Our sins are * upon us; Eze 33:10
There will be * crops of fruit to Eze 36:8
I have never put her under a * Hos 10:11
Suddenly the * lead cover on the Zec 5:7
and clamped down the * lid again. Zec 5:8
Jerusalem will be a * stone Zec 12:3
who work so hard beneath a * yoke. Mt 11:28
and *, and their ears Mt 13:15
and they were fighting * seas. Mt 14:23,24
their eyes were *, so he went back Mt 26:43
A * veil hung in front of the room Mk 15:38f
the stone—a very * one—was already Mk 16:4
It was a cave with a * stone Jn 11:37,38
abruptly and a * wind of typhoon Act 27:14,15
My heart is * within me and I Rom 9:1
forever with a * load." Rom 11:10
They must not be * drinkers and 1Ti 3:8
be thoughtful, not * drinkers, not 1Ti 3:11
and must not be * drinkers, but Tit 2:3
all nations with a * hand, and he Rev 12:5
pit and a * chain in his hand. Rev 20:1

HEBER
Beriah's sons were * and Malchiel. Gen 46:16,17
named after their ancestor *. Num 26:44-47
with them. (*, the Kenite—the Ju 4:11
Jael, the wife of * the Kenite, for Ju 4:17
Jabin of Hazor and the clan of *. Ju 4:17
The wife of * the Kenite— Ju 5:24
she was the mother of Jered, *, 1Ch 4:18
*, Malchi-el (the father of 1Ch 7:31
Zebadiah, Meshullam, Hizki, *, 1Ch 8:17,18

HEBER'S
* children were: 1Ch 7:32

HEBERITES
The *, named after their ancestor Num 26:44-47

HEBREW
Many * names are based on puns. Gen 3:20f
In this case for instance, the * Gen 3:20f
* word that means "life-giving." Gen 3:20f
Or, by * usage, "When his son, Gen 5:3,4,5f
Or, by * usage, "After this Gen 5:3,4,5f
Or, by * usage, "there was born Gen 11:12,13f
and told Abram the *, who was Gen 14:13
Which sounds a little like the * Gen 25:25f
The meaning is not of the actual * Gen 30:6f
a * word sounding like the name. Gen 30:6f
The name given is a * pun. Gen 30:6f
The * word is not specific. Gen 39:12f
in this * slave to insult us!" Gen 39:14,15
"That * slave you've had around Gen 39:17
We told the dreams to a young * Gen 41:12
and made the * slavery more bitter Ex 1:13,14
instructed the * midwives (their Ex 1:15,16
Puah) to kill all * boys as soon as Ex 1:15,16
"Sir," they told him, "the * Ex 1:19
* boys into the Nile River. Ex 1:22
THERE WERE AT this time a * fellow Ex 2:1
"He must be one of the * Ex 2:6
find one of the * women to nurse Ex 2:7
* word meaning "to draw out." Ex 2:10f
Egyptian knock a * to the Ex 2:11
ground—one of his own * brothers! Ex 2:11
your own * brother like that?" Ex 2:13
The * word here translated Ex 12:3,4f
a * slave, he shall serve only Ex 21:2
between a * slave-girl and his son, Ex 21:9
seventh month" of the * calendar. Lev 16:29,30f
first month" (of the * calendar). Lev 23:5f
month" (of the * calendar). Lev 23:23,24f
month" (of the * calendar). Lev 23:26,27f
month" (of the * calendar). Lev 23:33,34f
month" (of the * calendar). Lev 25:9f
'Added in the * text is this Num 1:17,18,19f
first month of the * calendar Num 9:2,3f
Joshua is the same name in * as Num 13:16f
month" (of the * calendar). Num 29:1f
month" (of the * calendar). Num 29:7f
month" (of the * calendar). Num 29:12f
first month" (of the * calendar). Num 33:3,4f
fifth month" (of the * calendar). Num 33:38,39f
month" (of the * calendar). Deu 1:1f
"If you buy a * slave, whether a Deu 15:12
"But if your * slave doesn't Deu 15:16
first month of the * calendar. Deu 16:1f
The word Samuel in * sounds like 1Sa 1:19,20f
The *, from which the numbers have 1Sa 13:1f
The meaning of the * wording is 2Sa 23:20f
eighth month" of the * calendar. 1Ki 12:32,33f
The * is unclear. 2Ki 16:18f
Don't use *, for the people 2Ki 18:26
shouted in * to the people on the 2Ki 18:28
Jabez sounds like ozeb, the * 1Ch 4:9f
The word in the * for 1Ch 28:12f
seventh month" of the * calendar. Ez 3:6f
first month" of the * calendar. Ez 6:19f
first month" of the * calendar. Ez 8:31f
ninth month" of the * calendar. Ez 10:9f
day" of the * month. Neh 9:1f
The * text adds here: "Higgaion. Ps 9:16f
The * is obscure. Pro 14:9f
The * of this verse is not clear. Pro 18:19f
the prophets: the * words for Is 5:7f
The controversial * word used here Is 7:14f
begin to speak the * language. Is 19:18
Don't speak in *, for the people Is 36:11
Then he shouted in * to the Jews Is 36:13
The meaning of the * word is Is 52:14,15f
It is not clear from the * whether Is 66:19f

(HEBREW Con't)
(the days of the * patriarchs), Jer 5:15f
This is a * pun. Jer 23:38,39f
his * slaves, both men and women. Jer 34:9
I told them that every * slave Jer 34:14
in the * expression used here. Jer 36:30f
which does not, in * usage, Eze 38:15,16f
April was the first month of the * Eze 45:18f
The * text is obscure. Dan 8:12f
*: "two others," probably Dan 12:5f
The * text is uncertain. Hos 4:18f
Literally, "a *." Jon 1:9,10f
The * text makes no distinction Jon 3:3f
In the *, there is frequent word Mic 1:11f
Shaphir sounds like the * word Mic 1:11f
In the *, there is frequent word Mic 1:11f
Shaphir sounds like the * word Mic 1:11f
In the *, there is frequent word Mic 1:11f
Shaphir sounds like the * word Mic 1:11f
The * text of this verse is very Hab 1:11f
of my returning people to pure * Zep 3:9
possible from the * text, but many Zec 9:10f
it to the potter" is the *. Zec 11:13f
The * is uncertain. Zec 14:6f
Pavement, but in *, Gabbatha." Jn 19:13f
"The Skull," in *, "Golgotha." Jn 19:17
was written in *, Latin, and Greek, Jn 19:20
as the widows who spoke *. Act 6:1
"Tabitha," her name in *. Act 9:40f
custom for the * Christians and Act 21:24
he addressed them in * as follows: Act 21:40
*, the silence was even greater. Act 22:2
speaking to me in *, 'Saul, Saul, Act 26:14
Greek to *, becomes Balaamites; Rev 2:6f
pit whose name in * is Abaddon, and Rev 9:11
a place called, in *, Rev 16:16

HEBREWS
homeland among the *, and now Gen 40:15
for Egyptians despise * and never Gen 43:32
visit his fellow * and saw the Ex 2:11
visiting among the * again, he saw Ex 2:13
the God of the *, has met with us Ex 3:18
"The God of the * has met with Ex 5:3
the God of the *, has sent me back Ex 7:16
the God of the *, demands that you Ex 9:1
the God of the * says, "Let my Ex 9:13
the God of the *, asks, 'How long Ex 10:3
about over in the camp of the *?" 1Sa 4:6
swords and spears for the *. 1Sa 13:19
And now the * who had been 1Sa 14:21
See Exodus 12:22, * 9:18–22. Ps 51:7f
See * 8:9b. Jer 31:32f
as being only "half-breed" *. Lk 17:16f
They brag that they are *; do 2Co 11:22
11:30). And * 6:4–8 speaks of the 1Jn 5:17f

HEBRON
of Mamre, near *, and built an Gen 13:18
died in * in the land of Canaan; Gen 23:1
*), where Abraham too had lived. Gen 35:27
Shechem from his home at * Valley. Gen 37:13,14
The sons of Kohath:Amram, Izhar,* Ex 6:18
grandsons Amram Izhar * Num 3:25-30
the Negeb and arrived at *. Num 13:22
(By the way, * was very ancient, Num 13:22
King Hoham of *, Jos 10:3
*, Jarmuth, Lachish, and Eglon. Jos 10:22,23
Eglon they went to *, and captured Jos 10:36
*, Debir, Anab, Judah, and Israel; Jos 11:21
The king of *; Jos 12:8-24
him and gave him * as a permanent Jos 14:13,14
(Before that time * had been Jos 14:15
Arba (also called *), which had Jos 15:13
Kiriath-arba (or, *), Zior, Maon, Jos 15:48-62
and Kiriath-arba (also known as * Jos 20:7
*, in the Judean hills, as a City Jos 21:9-16
the Canaanites in * (formerly Ju 1:10
The city of * was given to Caleb Ju 1:20
top of the mountain across from *! Ju 16:3
Hormah, Borashan, Athach, *. 1Sa 30:27-31
And the Lord replied, "*." 2Sa 2:1
and their families all moved to *. 2Sa 2:3
was reigning in * as king of the 2Sa 2:10,11
night and reached * at daybreak. 2Sa 2:32
born to David while he was at *. 2Sa 3:2
then he went to * and reported to 2Sa 3:19
When Abner arrived at *, Joab 2Sa 3:27
They buried Abner in * 2Sa 3:32
Abner's death at *, he was 2Sa 4:1
presented the head to David at *. 2Sa 4:8
their bodies beside the pool in *. 2Sa 4:12
buried it in Abner's tomb in *. 2Sa 4:12
came to David at * and gave him 2Sa 5:1
of Israel there at *, and they 2Sa 5:3
After moving from * to Jerusalem, 2Sa 5:13
"Let me go to * to sacrifice to 2Sa 15:7,8
So Absalom went to *. 2Sa 15:9
* was King David's first capital, 2Sa 15:9f
Absalom has been crowned in *." 2Sa 15:10
* and thirty-three in Jerusalem. 1Ki 2:11
Father of *. 1Ch 2:42
The sons of *: Korah, Tappuah, 1Ch 2:43
These six were born to him in *, 1Ch 3:4
Amram, Izhar, *, Uzziel. 1Ch 6:2
were:Amram, Izhar, *, Uzziel. 1Ch 6:18
* and its surrounding 1Ch 6:55,56,57
went to David at * and told him, 1Ch 11:1
of recruits who joined David at *. 1Ch 12:23
in battle array to * with the 1Ch 12:38
80 from the subclan of *; 1Ch 15:4-10
Amram, Izhar, *, and 1Ch 23:12
The sons of * were led by Jeriah. 1Ch 23:19
Jahath. The * group:Jeriah, 1Ch 24:23
after Amram, Izhar, *, and Uzziel. 1Ch 26:23,24
his clansmen from *, all 1Ch 26:30
* and thirty-three in Jerusalem. 1Ch 29:26,27
Zorah, Aijalon, and *. 2Ch 11:5-10

HEBRON'S
The Hebron group:Jeriah, * 1Ch 24:23

HEBRONITES
Libnites, the *,The Mahlites, the Num 26:58,59
of the clan of the *, under the 1Ch 26:31,32

HECALIAH
OF Nehemiah, the son of *: Neh 1:1

HEDGE
more crooked than a * of thorns. Mic 7:4
a vineyard with a * around it, and Mt 21:33

HEDGEHOGS
homes in her. * will burrow there; Zep 2:14

HEDGES
weep and wail, hiding in the *, Jer 49:3
in the * in the cold, but all of Nah 3:17
and out behind the * and urge Lk 14:23

HEED
You must * all of my Lev 19:37
that you carefully * all the Deu 15:4,5
to him and * his messages from me. Deu 18:19
and to * all he tells you to do. Deu 26:17
"How I pray that you will * my 2Ch 6:19
O Lord, please hear my prayer! * Neh 1:11
too busy to * their requests. Ps 102:17
now give me sense to * your laws. Ps 119:73
is right but won't * nor do it; Is 42:20
is the man who does not * it! Jer 11:1
and refuses to * it—well, if he Eze 33:4
they will * my warnings, so that Zep 3:7
also, and they will * my voice; Jn 10:16
* the truth stated in this Book. Rev 22:9

HEEDED
So God * Abraham's plea and kept Gen 19:29
The Lord * their request and Num 21:3
their cries and * their distress; Ps 106:44
For the words may not be *. Pro 29:19
If he had * the warning, he would Eze 33:5

HEEDING
If you insist on * them, I must Jer 27:15

HEEDLESS
* of their babies' cries. Lam 4:3,4

HEEDS
no one *—the wicked know no shame. Zep 3:5

HEEL
while you will strike at his *." Gen 3:15
born with his hand on Esau's *! Gen 25:26
kept beneath the * of earthly Is 49:7

HEELS
*, so that the rider falls off. Gen 49:17
the usual great crowd at his *. Lk 7:11

HEGAI
the royal harem. *, the eunuch in Est 2:3
young girls. *, who was Est 2:9
the advice of *, the eunuch in Est 2:15

HEGLAM
Gera (also called *), the father 1Ch 8:6,7

HEIFER
a three-year-old *, a Gen 15:9
to bring you a red * without Num 19:1
Then someone shall burn the * as Num 19:5
the ashes of the * and place them Num 19:9
the ashes of the * must wash his Num 19:10
through the ashes of the red * Num 19:12
ashes from the red * sin offering Num 19:17
city shall take a * that has never Deu 21:3
hands over the *, and say, 'Our Deu 21:6
"If you hadn't plowed with my *, Ju 14:18
"Take a * with you," the Lord 1Sa 16:2
Egypt is sleek as a *, but a Jer 46:20,21
stubborn as a *, resisting the Hos 4:16

HEIGHT
on end. The * of each frame was Ex 36:21
So he went up to a barren *, Num 23:3,4
or *, for this is not the one. 1Sa 16:7
was at the * of his popularity and 2Ch 12:1
strongly laid. The * will be ninety Ez 6:3
half its original * around the Neh 4:6
* of the heavens above the earth. Ps 103:11
You cannot understand the * of Pro 25:2,3
suddenly, at the * of his power, Dan 8:8
of a cube, for its * was exactly Rev 21:16

HEIGHTS
On the * of the Arnon River. Num 21:27-30
Climb to its *, and look out Deu 32:49
He ascends the *, leading many Ps 68:18
You will be afraid of * and of Ecc 12:5
you down from your * and leave you, Jer 51:25
the * of heaven at his command. Lam 2:1
your ancient * as theirs, and Eze 36:2
come down from the * of heaven, far Eph 4:9
him up to the * of heaven and gave Php 2:9

HEIR
else will be your *, for you will Gen 15:4
child of Pharaoh, * to his throne, Ex 11:5
died and left no *, in which case Lev 18:16f
can give Naomi an * by marrying me Ru 3:10
"For her son would become an * Ru 4:6
He will always have an *; Ps 89:29
"the * of David's royal line." Is 11:10f
* sitting on the throne of Israel. Jer 33:17
been broken, and I have fallen *! Eze 26:2
'Here comes the * to this estate; Mt 21:38
shall be an * in the house of Rom 15:12

HEIRESSES
of Israel who are * must marry Num 36:8

HEIRS
you will be your brother's *." Gen 38:8
to the original owners or their *. Lev 25:10
a multitude of children, many *. Is 53:10

HELAH
*, and 1Ch 4:5
Haahashtari; and * bore him 1Ch 4:7

HELAM
These troops arrived at * under 2Sa 10:15,16
*, where the Syrians attacked him. 2Sa 10:17

HELBAH
Ahlab, Achzib, *, Aphik, or Rehob; Ju 1:31,32

HELBON
She brings wines from *, and Eze 27:18

HELD
So Noah * out his hand and drew Gen 8:9
took a robe and * it over their Gen 9:23
"That is why I * you back from Gen 20:6
He has * back nothing from me Gen 39:9
days later, and he * a party for Gen 40:20
Jordan River, they * a very great Gen 50:10
So Moses * out his hand, and the Ex 9:23
feast to the Lord shall be *. Ex 13:6,7
the manna—* about three quarts; Ex 16:36
And as long as Moses * up the Ex 17:11
owner shall not be *— unless the Ex 21:28
150 feet, and be * up by twenty Ex 27:9,10
The curtains will be * up with Ex 27:9,10
feet of curtains * up by twenty Ex 27:11
feet of curtain, * up by three Ex 27:14,15
The ephod was * together by Ex 39:4,5
The chestpiece was * securely Ex 39:21
pot * above running water. Lev 14:5
"and will be * liable for any Num 18:1
You Levites will not be * guilty Num 18:32
A great mob formed, and they * a Num 20:3
of all the people shall be *. Num 29:7
"This feast will be * at the Deu 16:15
you will not be * responsible for Deu 19:10
flowing as though * back by a dam, Jos 3:13,14
of Lappidoth. She * court at a Ju 4:5
Shechem that year, * in the temple Ju 9:27
when we * our council before the Ju 21:5
religious festival * in the fields Ju 21:19
sons, * court in Beer-sheba; 1Sa 8:2
he is * in high honor by all the 1Sa 9:6
who, with David, * back the 2Sa 23:9
Festival would be * at Bethel on 1Ki 12:32,33
and his mother * him on her lap; 2Ki 4:20
it in water and * it over the 2Ki 8:15
being * as prisoners in Babylon. 2Ki 25:28
run away, but he * his ground in 1Ch 11:14
He is to be * in awe above all 1Ch 16:25
lily. It * 3,000 barrels of water. 2Ch 4:5
A final religious service was * 2Ch 7:9
of Tabernacles to be * that month. Neh 8:14
days of revelry, * in the courtyard Est 1:5
And again the king * out the Est 8:4
you are old, so I * back and did Job 32:6
But the Lord * me steady. Ps 18:18
Many and many a time he * back Ps 78:38
Why were they * back? Ps 114:5
Being kidnapped and * for ransom Pro 13:8
for to be * in loving esteem is Pro 22:1
I found him and * him and would not Sol 3:4
The king is * captive in your Sol 7:5
* the nations in your angry grip. Is 14:6
the night when holy feasts are *; Is 30:29
Who else has * the oceans in his Is 40:12
and the Lord * back the terrible Jer 26:19
the Day of Fasting * in December of Jer 36:9
Each of them * a censer of Eze 8:11
In your proud days you * Sodom Eze 16:56
He was * in captivity so that his Eze 19:9
"the great waters were * back." Eze 31:15f
sworn with hand * high, that those Eze 36:7
Daniel * this appointment as the Dan 1:21
to strike. It * three ribs between Dan 7:5
him to walk, I * him in my arms. Hos 11:3
for the waves will be * back. Zec 10:11
stick and * it up to him to drink. Mt 27:48
mob arrested Jesus and * him fast. Mk 14:46

(HELD Con't)
and * it up to him on a stick. Mk 15:36
Soon Levi * a reception in his Lk 5:29
generation will be * responsible Lk 11:50
has * her for eighteen years?" Lk 13:16
As he spoke, he * out his Lk 24:40
purposes and * perhaps twenty to Jn 2:6
branch and * up to his lips. Jn 19:29
to Jerusalem and * a prayer Act 1:13
—is * in a perishable container, 2Co 4:7
the shore. He * seven stars in his Rev 1:16
* bound at the great River Rev 9:14
And he * open in his hand a Rev 10:2
and pearls, and * in her hand a Rev 17:4
In his mouth he * a sharp sword Rev 19:15
The angel * in his hand a golden Rev 21:15

HELDAI
Division was * from Netophah in the 1Ch 27:15
"*, Tobijah, and Jedaiah will Zec 6:10,11
those who gave it—*, Tobijah, Zec 6:14

HELEB
* (son of Baanah) from Netophah; 2Sa 23:24-39

HELECH
Men from Arvad and from * Eze 27:11

HELED
* (son of Baanah) from Netophah; 1Ch 11:26-47

HELEK
named after their ancestor *. Num 26:28-37
clans of Abiezer, *, Asri-el, Jos 17:2

HELEKITES
The *, named after their ancestor Num 26:28-37

HELEM
Literally, "*." 1Ch 7:35f

HELEPH
began near * and ran past Jos 19:34

HELEZ
* from Palti; 2Sa 23:24-39
Azariah's son was *; 1Ch 2:39
* from Pelon; 1Ch 11:26-47
Division was * from Pelona in 1Ch 27:10

HELEZ'S
Azariah's son was Helez; * son 1Ch 2:39

HELI
Joseph's father was *; Lk 3:23-38

HELI'S
Joseph's father was Heli;* father Lk 3:23-38

HELIODORUS
III, sent * to rob and desecrate Dan 11:20f

HELIOPOLIS
of Potiphera, priest of *. Gen 41:45
priest of the sun god Re of *. Gen 41:50
of Potiphera, priest of *); Gen 46:19-22
One of these will be *, "The Is 19:18
in the city of *, and burn down the Jer 43:13
The young men of * and Bubastis Eze 30:17

HELKAI
*, leader of the Meraioth clan; Neh 12:12-21

HELKATH
*, Hali, Beten, Achshaph, Jos 19:24,25,26
Mishal, Abdon, *, and Rehob. Jos 21:30,31

HELL
By * and death; 2Sa 22:6
that destroys to *, and would root Job 31:12
wicked shall be sent away to *; Ps 9:17
one soul, to keep it out of *. Ps 49:8,9
shall go down to the depths of *. Ps 63:9
have rescued me from deepest *. Ps 86:13
He ransoms me from *. Ps 103:4
lie along the road to death and *. Pro 2:18
She leads you down to death and *. Pro 5:5
the road to *, look for her house. Pro 7:27
guests are now citizens of *. Pro 9:18
The depths of * are open to God's Pro 15:11
leads upward, leaving * behind. Pro 15:24
will keep them out of *. Pro 23:13,14
conscience will drive him into *. Pro 28:17
no, four!*The barren wombA barren Pro 30:15,16
* is licking its chops in Is 5:14
The denizens of * crowd to meet Is 14:9
of *, down to its lowest depths. Is 14:15
Terror and the captivity of * Is 24:17
You have traveled far, even to * Is 57:9
I will send you to the pit of * Eze 26:20
you to the pit of * and you shall Eze 28:8
they will land in *, along with all Eze 31:14
to * with all the others like her. Eze 31:16
to find her there with them in *. Eze 31:16
of * with all these other nations. Eze 31:18
of *, surrounded by their allies. Eze 32:23
and now they lie undone in *; Eze 32:24
Shall I ransom him from *? Hos 13:14
and *, they are never satisfied. Hab 2:5
are in danger of the fires of *. Mt 5:22
Literally, "the * of fire." Mt 5:22f
for all of you to be cast into *. Mt 5:29
that than find yourself in *. Mt 5:30
The highway to * Mt 7:13
destroy both soul and body in *. Mt 10:28
shall go down to *! Mt 11:23
and all the powers of * shall not Mt 16:18
than to be in * with both of your Mt 18:8
one eye than to be in * with two. Mt 18:9
the son of * you are yourselves. Mt 23:15
you escape the judgment of *? Mt 23:33
unquenchable fires of * with two! Mk 9:43,44
have two feet that carry you to *. Mk 9:45,46
see the fires of *, where the worm Mk 9:47
You are trying to escape * Lk 3:7
you shall be brought down to *." Lk 10:15
to kill and then cast into *. Lk 12:5
buried, and his soul went into *. Lk 16:23
of *, as the Scriptures foretold. Jn 17:12
'You will not leave my soul in * Act 2:27
in * and his body would not decay. Act 2:31
all the powers of * itself cannot Rom 8:38
in everlasting *, forever separated 2Th 1:9
rebellion will come—the son of *. 2Th 2:3
of rebellion and * will do when he 2Th 2:7
on their way to * because they have 2Th 2:10
and finally send them to * itself. 1Ti 6:9
is set on fire by * itself, and can Jas 3:6
threw them into *, chained in 2Pe 2:4
all the demons and powers of *. 2Pe 2:12
from * and given eternal life. 1Jn 3:14
a * in which sinners are punished. Jud 1:7
from the very flames of * itself. Jud 1:23
of * and death—don't be afraid! Rev 1:17,18
horse whose rider's name was *. Rev 6:8
And Death and * were thrown into Rev 20:14

HELLENIST
removed by the * Menelaus. Dan 11:22f

HELLO
with this message: "* from Jacob! Gen 32:4
"* there," he said. 1Sa 15:13
to Jesus and said, "*, Master!" Mt 26:49
Tell Priscilla and Aquila "*." Rom 16:3
Say "*" to Ampliatus, whom I Rom 16:8
Say "*" to Tryphaena and Rom 16:12
Gaius says to say "*" to you Rom 16:23
me to say "*" to you for them. 1Co 16:20
Say "*" for me to all the Php 4:21
Please say "*" for me to 2Ti 4:19
Please say "*" to all of the Tit 3:15

HELMET
He wore a bronze *, a 1Sa 17:4-7
bronze * and a coat of mail. 1Sa 17:38,39
the land of Ephraim is the * on Ps 108:8
the * of salvation on his head. Is 59:17
And you will need the * of Eph 6:17
our * the happy hope of salvation. 1Th 5:8

HELMETS
shields, spears, *, coats of mail, 2Ch 26:14
them—don your *, sharpen your Jer 46:4

HELMSMEN
your * are skilled men from Zemer. Eze 27:8

HELON
Zebulun -Eliab (son of * Num 1:2-15
Eliab (son of *) Num 2:3-31
Eliab, the son of *, chief of the Num 7:24-29
led by Eliab, the son of *. Num 10:16

HELP
For, as she said, "With God's *, Gen 4:1
master Abraham and * me to Gen 24:12
God: "If God will * and protect me Gen 28:20
whether I could * it or not. Gen 31:39
you, for I will * you to speak Ex 4:12
him, and I will * both of you to Ex 4:15
cried out to the Lord to * them. Ex 14:10
Moses pleaded with the Lord to * Ex 15:25
"God is my *," for Moses said at Ex 18:4
here all day long to get your *?" Ex 18:14
for my *, I will surely give it. Ex 22:23
he cries to me for *, I will hear Ex 22:27
must not go on by, but must * him. Ex 23:5
you are responsible to * him; Lev 25:35
and will be a great * to us. Num 10:31
They screamed to Moses for *, Num 11:2
that if he would * them conquer the Num 21:2
He begged Balaam to come and * Num 22:5,6
time I told the people, 'I need *! Deu 1:9
as the Lord agreed to * you do. Deu 6:19
He did it to * you realize that Deu 8:3
the Lord punishes you to * you. Deu 8:5
believe that he would * you; Deu 9:23
Go and *! Deu 22:4
didn't scream for *, and the man Deu 22:23,24
you live, try to * the Ammonites or Deu 23:6
one intervenes to * her husband by Deu 25:11
you will not be able to * them. Deu 28:32
And * them! Deu 32:38
"A blessing upon those who * Gad. Deu 33:20
In majestic splendor to * you. Deu 33:26
not abandon you or fail to * you. Jos 1:5
Jordan River to * them conquer Jos 1:14
"Come and * me destroy Gibeon," Jos 10:4
"Come and * your servants!" Jos 10:6
for the Lord will * you to Jos 10:19
his army to try to * defend the Jos 10:33
asked * from the tribe of Simeon. Ju 1:3
we will * you conquer yours." Ju 1:3
they begged the Lord for *. Ju 4:2,3
'Because they did not come to * Ju 5:23
to cry out to the Lord for *. Ju 6:6,7
you are going to * me like that, Ju 6:17
mob, "Does Baal need your *? Ju 6:31
will know you are going to * me!" Ju 6:37
that if God would * Israel conquer Ju 11:30,31
us to * you fight against Ammon? Ju 12:1
"You failed to * us in our time Ju 12:2
There was no one to * the Ju 18:28
when you are thirsty, go and * Ru 2:8,9
and pleaded with him to * Israel. 1Sa 7:9
"the Stone of *"), for he said, 1Sa 7:12
but the Lord will not * you." 1Sa 8:18
to see if we can get some *!" 1Sa 11:3
Other gods can't * you. 1Sa 12:21
even asked for the Lord's *!' 1Sa 13:12
that he will * us defeat them!" 1Sa 14:10
the Lord will * us defeat them!" 1Sa 14:12
Will you * us defeat them?" 1Sa 14:37
to * his father with the sheep. 1Sa 17:14,15
to kill me if I didn't * him." 1Sa 19:17
* you conquer the Philistines." 1Sa 23:4
good it did us to * this fellow. 1Sa 25:21
"Come and * us fight," King 1Sa 28:1
"You will soon see what a * we 1Sa 28:2
when they came to * Hadadezer. 2Sa 8:5
and * me," Joab instructed him. 2Sa 10:11
for you, I will come and * you. 2Sa 10:11
And the Syrians were afraid to * 2Sa 10:19
and cried out, "O king! * me!" 2Sa 14:4
father and now I will * you!" 2Sa 16:19
and send us * if we need it." 2Sa 18:3
They looked in vain for *; 2Sa 22:42
Literally, "He will cause my * 2Sa 23:5f
they agreed to * him become king. 1Ki 1:7
punished them, * them to follow the 1Ki 8:35,36
hear their prayer and * them. 1Ki 8:45
able-bodied man to * demolish Ramah 1Ki 15:22
plains,' I will * you defeat this 1Ki 20:28
for God will * you conquer it." 1Ki 22:6
Will you * me fight him?" 2Ki 3:6,7,8
to him, "*, my lord the king!" 2Ki 6:26-30
"If the Lord doesn't * you, what 2Ki 6:26-30
"Why should I expect any * from 2Ki 6:33
*, and the Lord listened to him; 2Ki 13:4
of Israel—she had no one to * her. 2Ki 14:26
begging him to * him fight the 2Ki 16:7
So of Egypt to * him shake free of 2Ki 17:4
of * before rebelling against me. 2Ki 18:20,21
bless me and * me in my work; 1Ch 4:10
They cried out to God to * them, 1Ch 5:20
have come to * me, we are friends; 1Ch 12:17
and carpenters to * build David's 1Ch 14:1
from Damascus to * King Hadadezer, 1Ch 18:5
and * me," Joab told his brother; 1Ch 19:12
for you, I'll come and * you. 1Ch 19:12
desire is to * your people, and you 2Ch 1:11
and I will send my men to * them. 2Ch 2:8
where you live and * them and 2Ch 6:39
alone may * them in their work. 2Ch 13:10
to God, "no one else can * us! 2Ch 14:11
army. Oh, * us, Lord our God! 2Ch 14:11
beside you and * you give justice 2Ch 19:6
for them and * them to decide 2Ch 19:10
to beg for * from the Lord; 2Ch 20:3
And kill anyone who tries to * 2Ch 23:13,14
for God has power to * or to 2Ch 25:8
Syria, they would * him too if he 2Ch 28:23
and cried out humbly to God for *. 2Ch 33:12
not to * those nations in any way. Ez 9:12
Please * me now as I go in and Neh 1:11
God of heaven will * us, and we, Neh 2:20
leaders were lazy and didn't *. Neh 3:5
all we can to * our Jewish brothers Neh 5:8
been done with the * of our God. Neh 6:16
cried to you for *, once more you Neh 9:28
"THEY CRY FOR * but no one Job 5:1
from me in terror and refuse to *. Job 6:19-21
Have I ever asked your *? Job 6:23
and many will look to you for *. Job 11:19
I, the man who begged God for *, Job 12:4
Does God want your * if you are Job 13:8
you use lies to try to * him out. Job 13:10
me, what have I done wrong? * me! Job 13:23
in such a way that it would * you. Job 16:5
nor does it * if I refuse to Job 16:6
I scream for * and no one hears Job 19:7
the humble, and * even sinners by Job 22:30
the wounded cry for *; Job 24:12
They refuse to * the needy Job 24:21
who had no one to * them. Job 29:12
well that I have no one to * me. Job 30:13
or cries for * in his calamity. Job 30:24
up and cry to the assembly for *. Job 30:28,29
out of my way to * others— (oh, Job 31:34
many say that God will never * me. Ps 3:2
Many say that God will never * Ps 4:6
Lord, will count on you for *. Ps 9:10
when they call to him for *. Ps 9:12
LORD! *! Ps 12:1
I have no other * but yours." Ps 16:2
I AM PLEADING for your *, O Lord; Ps 17:1

(HELP Con't)

seeking your * against their foes.	Ps 17:7
I screamed to the Lord for his *.	Ps 18:6
They shouted for * but no one	Ps 18:41
wrongs; * me to stop doing them.	Ps 19:13
Why do you refuse to * me or even	Ps 22:1
crying for your *, but there is no	Ps 22:2
You heard their cries for * and	Ps 22:5
and no one else can possibly *.	Ps 22:9,10,11
for *, for he alone can rescue me.	Ps 25:15
Be merciful and send the * I	Ps 27:7
You have been my * in all my	Ps 27:9
Yes, wait and he will * you.	Ps 27:14
I PLEAD WITH you to * me, Lord,	Ps 28:1
and implore your *.	Ps 28:2
oh, have pity and * me."	Ps 30:10
Only he can * us;	Ps 33:20
calls to him for *, and saves him	Ps 34:17
Trust him to * you do it and he	Ps 37:5
Come quickly! * me, O my Savior.	Ps 38:22
with God: Lord, * me to realize	Ps 39:4
on earth will be. * me to know that	Ps 39:4
I WAITED PATIENTLY for God to *	Ps 40:1
Come and * me!	Ps 40:13
Day and night I weep for his *,	Ps 42:3
shall again praise him for his *.	Ps 42:4,5
Literally, "for the * of his	Ps 42:4,5f
He is my *!	Ps 42:11
praise him for his wondrous *;	Ps 43:5
Literally, "He is the * of my	Ps 43:5f
Rise up, O Lord, and come and *	Ps 44:26
a tested * in times of trouble.	Ps 46:1
He will not delay his *.	Ps 46:5
You see a thief and * him, and	Ps 50:18
apart—and no one can * you then.	Ps 50:22
Israel for my sins—* your people	Ps 51:18
The very day I call for *, the	Ps 56:9
Lord, and thank you for your *.	Ps 56:12
He will send down * from heaven	Ps 57:3
See what is happening! * me!	Ps 59:4
for me and he will come and * me.	Ps 59:10
God has promised to * us.	Ps 60:6,7
Yes, Lord, * us against our	Ps 60:11
enemies, for man's * is useless.	Ps 60:11
With God's * we shall do mighty	Ps 60:12
earth, I will cry to you for *.	Ps 61:2
longings before him, for he can *!	Ps 62:8
I cried to him for *, with praises	Ps 66:17
for only you can * and save me.	Ps 70:5
There is no one to * him now!"	Ps 71:11
Come quickly! *!	Ps 71:12
keep on expecting you to * me.	Ps 71:14
O GOD, * the king to judge as you	Ps 72:1
* his son to walk in godliness.	Ps 72:1
in godliness. * him to give	Ps 72:2
his good reign. * him to defend	Ps 72:4
trouble and I need his * so badly.	Ps 77:2
with longing for his *.	Ps 77:3
dust. * us, God of our salvation!	Ps 79:9
Help us, God of our salvation! *	Ps 79:9
strikes, and you will * me.	Ps 86:7
face because you * and comfort me.	Ps 86:17
Each day I beg your *;	Ps 88:9
Forgetfulness talk about your *?	Ps 88:12
and refused to * him in battle.	Ps 89:43
* us to spend them as we should.	Ps 90:12
to him for *, he answered them.	Ps 99:6
how I need your *, especially in my	Ps 101:2
* me to refuse the low and vulgar	Ps 101:3
and vulgar things; * me to abhor	Ps 101:3
pity her—the time you promised *.	Ps 102:13
"Lord, *!"	Ps 107:6
they fell and none could * them	Ps 107:12
our army? Oh, * us fight against	Ps 108:12
But with the * of God we shall	Ps 108:13
* me, O Lord my God!	Ps 109:26
Lord is on my side, he will * me.	Ps 118:7
O Lord, please * us.	Ps 118:25
Keep me far from every wrong; *	Ps 119:29,30
If you will only * me to want	Ps 119:32
* me to prefer obedience to	Ps 119:36
* me to love your every wish;	Ps 119:80
but I expect your *, for you have	Ps 119:81
will you comfort me with your *?	Ps 119:82
* me, for you love only truth.	Ps 119:85,86
Your laws are always fair; * me	Ps 119:144
Stand ready to * me because I	Ps 119:173
pled with God to * me and he did!	Ps 120:1
I LOOK to the mountain gods for *?	Ps 121:1
No! My * is from Jehovah who	Ps 121:2
Our * is from the Lord who made	Ps 124:8
That man shall have the * he	Ps 127:5
I cry for your *: "Hear me!	Ps 130:1
Answer! * me!"	Ps 130:2
God to *, for he has promised.	Ps 130:5
But the Lord will surely * those	Ps 140:12
Listen when I cry to you for *!	Ps 141:1
* me, Lord, to keep my mouth shut	Ps 141:3
know that I am trying to * them.	Ps 141:6,7
I look to you for *, O Lord God.	Ps 141:8
No one will * me;	Ps 142:4
rejoice with me for all your *."	Ps 142:7
you to hide me. * me to do your	Ps 143:10
all mankind look up to you for *;	Ps 145:15
he hears their cries for * and	Ps 145:19
Don't look to men for *;	Ps 146:3
I will not answer your cry for *.	Pro 1:28
Rulers rule well with my *.	Pro 8:16
only hate you for trying to * him.	Pro 9:7,8
Your riches won't * you on	Pro 11:4
good men long to * each other.	Pro 12:12
To * the poor is to honor God.	Pro 14:31
God will * the king to judge the	Pro 16:10
is born to * in time of need.	Pro 17:17
When you * the poor you are	Pro 19:17
you can't do much to * him.	Pro 19:19
get all the *	Pro 23:12
for * in your time of need.	Pro 27:10
First, * me never to tell a lie.	Pro 30:8
those who cannot * themselves.	Pro 31:8
She will not hinder him, but *	Pro 31:12
Everyone is eager to * a youth	Ecc 4:15
even to * him usurp the throne.	Ecc 4:15
is not going to * him then.	Ecc 8:8
you yourself may need much *.	Ecc 11:2
We will * you find him."	Sol 6:1
have cut themselves off from my *.	Is 1:4
to be fair and to * the poor, the	Is 1:17
If you will only let me * you,	Is 1:19
"I cannot be of any *!	Is 3:7
I will wait for the Lord to * us,	Is 8:17
will you turn then for your *?	Is 10:3
I will not * you;	Is 10:4
The nations of the world will *	Is 14:2
plead for advice and *.	Is 16:3
their idols for * in that day,	Is 17:8
to the Lord for * against those who	Is 19:20
you never ask for * from God, who	Is 22:9,10,11
shame—he won't * one little bit!	Is 30:5
"We will get our * from Egypt;	Is 30:16
those who wait for him to * them.	Is 30:18
run to Egypt for *, trusting their	Is 31:1
among those they are trying to *.	Is 31:3
that the king of Egypt will * you.	Is 36:4
*, and have rebelled against me!	Is 36:5
who has ever looked to her for *.	Is 36:6
For you'll get no * from Egypt.	Is 36:8,9
grew weary of looking up for *.	Is 38:14
I cried, 'I am in trouble—* me.'	Is 38:14
I will * you;	Is 41:10
I am here to * you.	Is 41:13
for I will * you.	Is 41:14
Look! * is on the way!"	Is 41:27
O my people, you won't ask my *;	Is 43:22
The Lord who made you, who will *	Is 44:2
idol that can * him not one whit!	Is 44:10
can never give him any * at all.	Is 44:20
and I will not forget to * you.	Is 44:21
Call on them to * you strike deep	Is 47:12
You'll get no * from them at all.	Is 47:14
away and disappear, unable to *.	Is 47:15
alive to * or tell her what to do.	Is 51:18
of your idols can * you when you	Is 57:13
from relatives who need your *.	Is 58:7
Feed the hungry! * those in	Is 58:10
No one was there to * me.	Is 63:3
I looked but no one came to *	Is 63:5
Return and * us, for we who	Is 63:17
you still refuse to * us, Lord?	Is 64:12
one ally to another for their *;	Jer 2:36
ever find her * and her salvation.	Jer 3:23
pleading for *, prostrate before	Jer 4:31
you trust for *, and this place I	Jer 7:13,14
* them, for I will not listen.	Jer 7:16
Why doesn't he *?	Jer 8:22
harm nor *, nor do you any good.	Jer 10:5
There is no one left to * me	Jer 10:20
desperate enough to beg me for *.	Jer 11:14
for Jerusalem cannot *;	Jer 13:19
grievously, yet * us for the sake	Jer 14:7
we will wait for you to * us."	Jer 14:22
I wouldn't * them—away with them!	Jer 15:1
hurting me? Your * is as uncertain	Jer 15:17,18
O Lord, * me!	Jer 18:19
me when you promised me your *.	Jer 20:7
"Ask the Lord to * us, for	Jer 21:1
Do what is right! * those in need	Jer 22:3
He saw to it that justice and *	Jer 22:16
Not one is left to * you!	Jer 22:20
I will * them and not hurt them;	Jer 24:6
There is no one to * you or to	Jer 30:13
not pity them when they cry for *.	Jer 33:5
it came here to * you, is about to	Jer 37:7
no good to seek my * and blessing	Jer 44:26
saying, 'O Lord our God, * us!'	Jer 44:26
shall * your exiles as they flee.	Jer 49:5
We would * her if we could, but	Jer 51:9
there is none to * her.	Lam 1:2
far away—he who alone could * me.	Lam 1:16
Jerusalem pleads for * but no one	Lam 1:17
for their *.	Lam 1:19
False hope—they could not * at	Lam 1:19
And there is no one anywhere to *	Lam 1:21
The nation we expected most to *	Lam 4:17
* him—he shall die in his sin.	Eze 3:20
They refuse to even offer *	Eze 13:18
idols and then comes to ask my *.	Eze 14:4
to ask for my * and advice.	Eze 14:6,7
army shall fail to * Israel when	Eze 17:17
How dare you come to ask my *?	Eze 20:3
between us to * you remember that I	Eze 20:20
I listen to you or * you, Israel?	Eze 20:31
to Egypt for * during the reigns of	Eze 23:17f
no longer expect any * from Egypt.	Eze 29:16
I will come and * you as you	Eze 36:9
Everyone in Israel will *, for	Eze 39:13
and be present to * the people.	Eze 44:11
and they are not here to *."	Dan 2:11
For no one else can * me;	Dan 4:18
stand against it or * its victims.	Dan 8:4
We don't ask because we merit *,	Dan 9:18
to * you understand God's plans.	Dan 9:22
army, came to * me, so that I was	Dan 10:13
will be there to * me.	Dan 10:20,21
to strengthen and * Darius the Mede	Dan 11:1
Claiming his * he will have	Dan 11:39
and there will be no one to * him.	Dan 11:45
without any * from her armies or	Hos 1:7
but he can neither * nor cure.	Hos 5:13
and look to me for * again, for as	Hos 5:15
and none cries out to me for *.	Hos 7:7
with anxiety, but won't ask my *.	Hos 7:14
"* us, for you are our God!"	Hos 8:2
off from my * by worshiping the	Hos 8:4
how I long to * you!	Hos 11:8
to get their *, and in return she	Hos 12:1
Why don't you call on him for *?	Hos 13:10
Lord, * us!	Joe 1:19
*, for there is no water for them.	Joe 1:20
No one will * her.	Amo 5:2
that your brothers need your *.	Amo 6:6
* to push you out of your land.	Ob 1:7
lift a finger to * him when	Ob 1:11
to their gods for * and threw the	Jon 1:5
she promised * she cannot give.	Mic 1:14
for his * in times of trouble!	Mic 3:4
Moses, Aaron, and Miriam to * you.	Mic 6:4
me, I look to the Lord for his *;	Mic 7:7
call for * before you will listen?	Hab 1:2
there is no answer. "*!	Hab 1:2
a foolish lie that they could *!	Hab 2:18
* us, as you did in years gone by.	Hab 3:2
reign, and volunteered their *.	Hag 1:14,15
to ask for his blessing and *.	Zec 8:22
arrived to * his flock of Judah.	Zec 10:3
'Friend, let me * you get that	Mt 7:4
Then you can see to * your	Mt 7:5
what to do or where to go for *.	Mt 9:36
for those you * should feed and	Mt 10:10
walking without *, and the cured	Mt 11:5
"I was sent to * the Jews—the lost	Mt 15:24
him and pled again, "Sir, * me!"	Mt 15:25
Or a stranger, and * you?	Mt 25:38
sick or in prison, and not * you?'	Mt 25:44
you refused to * the least of these	Mt 25:45
you were refusing * to me.'	Mt 25:45
that he would *, Jesus said to the	Mk 2:5
seeds grew and grew without his *.	Mk 4:27
them, 'Sorry, I can't * you!	Mk 7:11
I should * my own family—the Jews.	Mk 7:27
faith; oh, * me to have more!"	Mk 9:24
be served, but to * others, and to	Mk 10:45
badly need your *, and you can aid	Mk 14:7
used a miracle to * the widow of	Lk 4:25,26
widows needing * in those days of	Lk 4:25,26
many Jewish lepers needing *."	Lk 4:27
A shout for * brought their	Lk 5:7
'Brother, let me * you get rid of	Lk 6:42
to come with them and * the man.	Lk 7:4
"If anyone deserves your *, it is	Lk 7:4
And so they are never able to *	Lk 8:14
more laborers to * you, for the	Lk 10:2
Tell her to come and * me."	Lk 10:40
I just can't * you this time.'	Lk 11:7
that stones those sent to * her.	Lk 13:34
* them and promised him a reward.	Lk 22:5
"I can't * you now," he said.	Jn 2:4
Do we have the Holy Spirit's *?	Jn 4:21-24
his * to worship as we should.	Jn 4:21-24
I have no one to * me into the pool	Jn 5:7
many a miracle to * the people.	Jn 10:32
You can always * the poor, but I	Jn 12:8
him to * them, but they didn't.	Act 7:25
to Antioch to * the new converts.	Act 11:22
him, "Come over here and * us."	Act 16:9
him, yelling, "Men of Israel! *!	Act 21:28
Help! *!	Act 21:28
that will * your church grow	Rom 1:11,12
Then, too, I need your *, for I	Rom 1:11,12
us—they * us learn to be patient.	Rom 5:3
But I can't * myself, because	Rom 7:17
bring him down to * you," and,	Rom 10:6
you be the one to * them out.	Rom 12:13

(HELP Con't)
policeman is sent by God to * you. Rom 13:4
Jesus Christ to * you live as you Rom 13:14
and encouragement * you to live in Rom 15:5
to his promises and to * the Jews. Rom 15:8
I pray that God will * you Rom 15:13
Christian welcome. * her in every Rom 16:1
who has worked so hard to * us. Rom 16:6
and with our * you believed. 1Co 3:5
sending Timothy—to * you do this. 1Co 4:17
with the * of his Christian wife. 1Co 7:14
the * of her Christian husband. 1Co 7:14
direction and *, and accepting 1Co 7:17
now the Lord is there to * him. 1Co 7:24
I am saying this to * you, not to 1Co 7:35
I want you to do whatever will * 1Co 7:35
should be paid by those they *. 1Co 9:10
our own needs without your *. 1Co 9:12
agree, because I want to * them. 1Co 9:20
and * them too. 1Co 9:21
they are willing to let me * them. 1Co 9:22
Those who can * others, 1Co 12:28
understand, how would that * you? 1Co 14:6
that is what will * you. 1Co 14:6
be of real * to the whole church. 1Co 14:12
you can to * them as well as all 1Co 16:16
the * you aren't here to give me. 1Co 16:17
* and comfort God has given us. 2Co 1:3,4
this, too, to * you: to show you 2Co 1:6,7
powerless we were to * ourselves; 2Co 1:9
And he did * us, and saved us 2Co 1:10
But you must * us too, by 2Co 1:11
his *, and not on our own skills. 2Co 1:12
I can't do much to * your faith, 2Co 1:24
that he will * us to be true to 2Co 3:4
in our lives to * us turn away from 2Co 7:10
and longed for me to come and *. 2Co 7:11
even more than to * the man 2Co 7:12
very rich, yet to * you he became 2Co 8:9
you have plenty and can * them; 2Co 8:14
our eagerness to * each other. 2Co 8:19
him all about your eagerness to *. 2Co 8:22
and praise to God for your *. 2Co 9:11
Those you * will be glad not 2Co 9:13
you—authority to * you, not to hurt 2Co 10:8
Who falls without my longing to * 2Co 11:29
have said this to * you, dear 2Co 12:19
spiritually and not to * myself. 2Co 12:19
always remember to * the poor, and Gal 2:10
But we by the * of the Holy Gal 5:5
gently and humbly * him back onto Gal 6:1
* their teachers by paying them. Gal 6:6
is to * those who believe him. Eph 1:19
and he had promised you no *. Eph 2:12
the Holy Spirit's * because of what Eph 2:18
all your wonderful * in making Php 1:5
be of more * to you by staying! Php 1:24
little longer, to * you grow and Php 1:25
love me enough to want to * me? Php 2:1
You sent him to * me in my need; Php 2:25
Please, please, with the Lord's * Php 4:2
true teammate, to * these women, Php 4:3
me to with the * of Christ who Php 4:13
in Thessalonica you sent * twice. Php 4:16
slave, here to * us in your place. Col 1:7
and asking God to * you understand Col 1:9
God has sent me to * his church Col 1:25
and perfect and to * you know his Col 4:12
they are straining to * you. 1Th 5:13
all comfort, and * you in every 2Th 2:17
how can he * the whole church? 1Ti 3:5
because that will * you not only 1Ti 4:8
bless you and use you to * others. 1Ti 4:16
don't have anyone else to * them. 1Ti 5:3
to God for his * and spending much 1Ti 5:5
when they need *, especially those 1Ti 5:8
and may the Lord * you to 2Ti 2:7
to us and will * us, for he cannot 2Ti 2:13
likely, with God's *, to turn away 2Ti 2:25
around to * you very much longer. 2Ti 4:6
the judge no one was here to * me. 2Ti 4:16
was needed to * strengthen each of Tit 1:5
Do everything you can to * Zenas Tit 3:13
For our people must learn to * Tit 3:14
sent out to * and care for those Heb 1:14
he is wonderfully able to * us. Heb 2:18
has gone to heaven itself to * us; Heb 4:14
to * us in our times of need. Heb 4:16
he promised to * would be perfectly Heb 6:17
to give gifts to * their priests Heb 7:5
For by the * of the eternal Holy Heb 9:14
With Jesus' * we will continually Heb 13:15
must love and * your neighbors just Jas 2:8
lift you up, encourage and * you. Jas 4:10
Instead, pray for God's * for 1Pe 3:9
be sure to use them to * each 1Pe 4:10
Are you called to * others? 1Pe 4:11
* you to stand firmly in his love. 1Pe 5:12
their words * us to understand many 2Pe 1:19
in need, and won't * him—how can 1Jn 3:17
by trusting Christ to * him. 1Jn 5:4
Son, has come to * us understand 1Jn 5:20
Try to * those who argue against Jud 1:22
And as for others, * them to find Jud 1:23

HELPED
The Lord had similarly * the Deu 2:22
So the Lord * us fight against Deu 3:3
has * us because we are so good!' Deu 9:4
fair after the way I have * you." Jos 2:12,13
the Lord * them destroy all their Jos 21:44
And the Lord * them defeat the Ju 1:4,5,6
The Lord * the tribe of Judah Ju 1:19
so he * them as long as that Ju 2:18
* Israel conquer him completely. Ju 3:10
ways, so God * King Eglon of Moab Ju 3:12
But the Lord our God * Israel Ju 11:21,22
Lord * me to conquer the enemy. Ju 12:3
So the Lord * Israel defeat Ju 20:35-39
"The Lord has certainly * us!" 1Sa 7:12
"He has always * you in any way 1Sa 19:4
So she * him get down to the 1Sa 19:12
The Lord has kept us safe and * 1Sa 30:23
why shouldn't I? I * your father 2Sa 16:19
* them in every way they could. 2Sa 19:18
Men from Gebal * Solomon's and 1Ki 5:18
he * him into the royal chariot. 2Ki 10:15
custodial work and * perform the 1Ch 23:28
searched for him, he has * them. 2Ch 15:4
country. God * him not only with 2Ch 26:7
for the Lord * him wonderfully 2Ch 26:15
these gods had * the kings of 2Ch 28:23
the Levites * them until the work 2Ch 29:34
So they did and the prophets * Ez 5:1
"Then you * them conquer great Neh 9:22
* them during the service. Neh 12:9
Their fellow-clansmen * them Neh 12:24
* the Jews for fear of Mordecai; Est 9:3
* the poor in their need, and the Job 29:12
to help them. I * those who were Job 29:13
Lord, how you have * me before! Ps 22:9,10,11
I trusted in him, and he * me. Ps 28:7
and have not * us in our battles. Ps 44:9
how much you have * me—and how I Ps 63:7
birth and have * me constantly—no Ps 71:6
O God, you have * me from my Ps 71:17
died unless the Lord had * me. Ps 94:17
and he * them and delivered them. Ps 107:19
me, O my enemy, but the Lord * me. Ps 118:13
with a touch, and * me to my feet. Dan 8:18
I have * them, and made them Hos 7:15
by the hand and * her to sit up, Mk 1:31
by the hand and * him to his feet Mk 9:27
And how he has * his servant Lk 1:54
He gave her his hand and * her Act 9:41
where they * the believers to grow Act 14:22
can, for she has * many in their Rom 16:1
He has * you speak out for him 1Co 1:5
other people present won't be *. 1Co 14:17
understand and be * by, than ten 1Co 14:19
learn and be encouraged and *. 1Co 14:31
how much the Lord has * you earn. 1Co 16:2
He is the one who has * us tell 2Co 3:6
were wide open. I * you on a day 2Co 6:2
in need are *, and they overflow 2Co 9:12
if that would have * me. Gal 4:15
Has she * those who are sick and 1Ti 5:10
faith is being * by their efforts. 1Ti 6:2
you how much he * me at Ephesus. 2Ti 1:18
hasn't * those who have tried it! Heb 13:9
Jewish laws can never be *. Heb 13:10
but the earth * her by opening Rev 12:16

HELPER
him, a * suited to his needs." Gen 2:18
But still there was no proper * Gen 2:19,20
my fathers was my *, and delivered Ex 18:4
He is your shield and your *! Deu 33:29
and the child became the Lord's * 1Sa 2:11
was the Lord's * and wore a little 1Sa 2:18
you are known as the * of the Ps 10:14
O my God, you are my *. Ps 40:17
But God is my *. Ps 54:4
He is your *. Ps 115:9
He is your *; Ps 115:10
He is your *; Ps 115:11
of Jacob as his *, whose hope is in Ps 146:5
your *, as you have claimed he is. Amo 5:14
Or, "*." Jn 14:26f
is my partner, my * in helping you, 2Co 8:23
and faithful * in the Lord's work, Eph 6:21
"The Lord is my * and I am not Heb 13:6

HELPERS
Or, "the * of Rahab." Job 9:13f
"What wonderful * you all are! Job 26:2
and Apollos and Peter as your *. 1Co 3:22

HELPFUL
The upright speak what is *; Pro 10:32
your sermons are strong and *. Rom 12:8
but it may not be best and *. 1Co 10:23
Say only what is good and * to Eph 4:29
other in being * and kind to each Heb 10:24

HELPING
MEANWHILE LITTLE SAMUEL was * 1Sa 3:1
criticized for * me like this." 2Sa 14:9
purpose of * David become king. 1Ch 12:24-37
of praise and of * the priests in 2Ch 8:14
show his great power in * them. 2Ch 16:9
"Should you be * the wicked, and 2Ch 19:2
for King Ahaz instead of * him. 2Ch 28:20
anyone was interested in * Israel. Neh 2:10
for * another Israelite?" Neh 5:7
You sent widows away without * Job 22:9
comfort their hearts by * them. Ps 10:17
the Lord who enjoys * his child!" Ps 35:27
you have been actively * me Ps 74:12
and no one * them, while on the Ecc 4:1
and comfort them, * them to mourn Is 57:18
He saw no one was * you, and Is 59:16
our husbands knowing it and * us? Jer 44:19
to offer a * hand, only to take Dan 11:34
Anyone who isn't * me is harming Mt 12:30
if he isn't * me, he is hurting Lk 11:23
"He was so good at * others," Lk 23:35
He is * me. Act 2:25
them and * them grow in the Lord. Act 18:23
example to you in * the poor; Act 20:35
us when our sins are * him?" Rom 3:5
be generous in * others with it. Rom 12:8
unless the Holy Spirit is * him. 1Co 12:3
as a means of * the entire church. 1Co 12:7
of God, is * others grow in the 1Co 14:3
their lives * and serving 1Co 16:15
God's power * us in all we do. 2Co 6:7
of * the Christians in Jerusalem. 2Co 8:4
my helper in * you, and you can 2Co 8:23
this to you, about * God's people. 2Co 9:1
up many of them to begin *. 2Co 9:2
of God's two ways of * people. Gal 4:24,25
spend these lives in * others. Eph 2:10
people to Christ, * them to trust Eph 4:11
will keep right on * you grow in Php 1:6
For God is at work within you, * Php 2:13
and then * you do what he wants. Php 2:13
me in * me preach the Good News. Php 2:22
the Lord that you are * me again. Php 4:10
in * me in my present difficulty. Php 4:14
and I am glad, for I am * to Col 1:24
instead of * people accept God's 1Ti 1:3,4
would have been * me through him, Phm 1:13
still do—by * his children? Heb 6:10
you aren't proving it by * others? Jas 2:14

HELPLESS
and we are * to redeem them, for Neh 5:5
Like aged, * lions they shall Job 4:11
They die in * frustration, Job 5:2
For I am utterly *, without any Job 6:13
That would be like injuring a * Job 6:27
are known as the helper of the *. Ps 10:14
Trapped and *, I struggled Ps 18:5
me—I who was * in their hands. Ps 18:17
all were * before me. Ps 18:38
*, overwhelmed, in deep distress; Ps 25:16
Who else protects the weak and * Ps 35:10
He will take care of the * and Ps 72:12
I stand * before your terrors. Ps 88:15
over and hold me * in its meshes. Ps 140:5
You stand there * and abandoned Is 1:8
extorted from the * peasants. Is 3:14
You look at one another, *, as Is 13:8
"We are sick and *," for the Lord Is 33:24
him: My people—the * virgin Is 37:22
They were as * as the grass, as Is 37:27
* as wild goats caught in a net. Is 51:20
who are *, poor and destitute. Is 58:7
this nation! * as a girl, you are Jer 6:2
like a * scarecrow in a garden! Jer 10:5
Lord, drag them off like * sheep Jer 12:3
in this land with * Jer 13:13
Are you * to save us? Jer 14:9
As for me, I am * and in your Jer 26:14
Egypt is as * as a girl before Jer 46:24
glance at their * children, for Jer 47:3
his hands fell * at his sides; Jer 50:43
search for pasture—* game too weak Lam 1:6
my enemies; I am * in their hands. Lam 1:14
I was * in the hand of God, and Eze 3:22
will stand *, weeping in despair. Eze 7:26,27
and exposed you * before the Eze 28:17
when they were *, when I had Eze 35:4,5
Lord, saying, 'His people are *; Eze 35:12
from your hands and leave you *. Eze 39:3
God's people will be * in his Dan 7:25
Now the ram was * and the buck Dan 8:7
How weak and * he must be!' Joe 2:17
and * to prevent the slaughter. Ob 1:9
threshing floor, * before Israel. Mic 4:13
The nations will be like * sheep Mic 5:8
Your troops will be weak and * Nah 3:13
while you stand trembling and *. Hab 2:7
"I will make you as * as a blind Zep 1:17
I will save the weak and * ones, Zep 3:19
When we were utterly * with no Rom 5:6
that we are * to save ourselves. Php 3:3
I am no * widow. Rev 18:7

HELPLESSNESS
boasts are false—her * is great. Jer 48:30
HELPS
God * you in everything you do; Gen 21:22
you forever; it * you to remember Ex 31:12,13
night, so that he * me and all of 1Ki 8:59
strength, and * them in many ways. Job 24:22,23
proudly. He * them hear his Job 36:10
* me do what honors him the most. Ps 23:2,3
But the Lord * him in each and Ps 34:19
Because they trust in him, he * Ps 37:40
He * them out of their troubles. Ps 41:1
are, so he * us by punishing us. Ps 94:12,13
The Lord mocks at mockers, but * Pro 3:34
A man's goodness * him all Pro 13:6
Scolding and spanking a child * Pro 29:15
and the molder * at the anvil. Is 41:7
Because the Lord God * me, I will Is 50:7
It is the Lord who * one and Lam 3:38
he no longer * them, for they Lam 4:16
the needy, and * the poor and does Eze 18:17
"Only those whom God *. Mt 19:11
in us and * us trust God more each Rom 5:4
—the Holy Spirit * us with our Rom 8:26
in tongues" * himself grow 1Co 14:4
messages from God, * the entire 1Co 14:4
own special way * the other parts, Eph 4:15,16
as the Holy Spirit * me, this is Php 1:19
it straightens us out and * us do 2Ti 3:16
Lord, and someone * him understand Jas 5:19
HEM
It is the * of your robe! 1Sa 24:11
HEMAN
(the son of Seir) were Hori and *. Gen 36:22
the Ezrahite and *, Calcol, and 1Ki 4:31
Ethan, *, 1Ch 2:6
of choir leaders: * the Cantor 1Ch 6:33-38
and cymbals. * (son of Joel), 1Ch 15:17
*, Asaph, and Ethan were chosen 1Ch 15:19
David also appointed *, 1Ch 16:41
groups of Asaph, *, and Jeduthun. 1Ch 25:1
Under the direction of *, the 1Ch 25:4,5
Asaph, Jeduthun, and * reported 1Ch 25:6,7
The singers were Asaph, *, 2Ch 5:11,12
King David, Asaph, *, and Jeduthun 2Ch 35:15
HEMAN'S
* assistant 1Ch 6:39-43
* second assistant was Ethan, a 1Ch 6:44-47
HEMANITE
From the * clan, Jehuel and 2Ch 29:12,13,14
HEMDAN
The children of Dishon:*, Gen 36:26
HEMORRHAGE
sick for twelve years with a *. Mk 5:25
HEMS
tassels for the * of their clothes Num 15:37,38
HEN
The marsh *, Lev 11:13-19
together as a * gathers her chicks Mt 23:37
together even as a * protects her Lk 13:34
HENA
Arpad, Sepharvaim, *, and Ivvah? 2Ki 18:34
of Sepharvaim, *, and Ivvah?" 2Ki 19:13
of Sepharvaim, *, and Ivvah." Is 37:13
HENADAD
Jeshua, Kadmi-el, *, and their sons Ez 3:9
by Bavvai (son of *), the mayor of Neh 3:18
Next was Binnui (son of *), who Neh 3:24
(son of *), Kadmi-el, Neh 10:9-13
HENCE
Literally, "* it is said, 'Is 1Sa 19:24f
of the cherubim. * it could not be Eze 10:17f
HEPHER
named after their ancestor *. Num 26:28-37
his son * was their grandfather, Num 27:1
The king of *; Jos 12:8-24
Asri-el, Shechem, Shemida, and *. Jos 17:2
Socoh and all the land of *; 1Ki 4:8-19
Naarah bore him Ahuzzam, *, 1Ch 4:6
* from Mecherath; 1Ch 11:26-47
HEPHER'S
(* son, Zelophehad, had no sons. Num 26:28-37
However, * son Zelophehad Jos 17:3
HEPHERITES
The *, named after their ancestor Num 26:28-37
HEPHZIBAH
Name of his mother: * 2Ki 21:1
HERALD
the monument, a * shouted out, "O Dan 3:4
These * only the early stages of Mk 13:8
HERBS
and * from Gilead to Egypt. Gen 37:25
unleavened bread and bitter *. Ex 12:8
unleavened bread and bitter *. Num 9:11
Wine drugged with bitter * was Mk 15:23
HERD
Then he ran out to the * and Gen 18:7
bull calf from the * for a sin Lev 9:2
the Lord from the * or flock, Lev 22:21
A * of pigs was feeding in the Mt 8:30
send us into that * of pigs." Mt 8:31
and the whole * rushed over a cliff Mt 8:32
there was a huge * of hogs rooting Mk 5:11
and the entire * plunged down the Mk 5:13
A * of pigs was feeding on the Lk 8:32
the whole * rushed down the Lk 8:33
HERDING
out in the fields * cattle, so he Gen 34:5
HERDS
Lot with all their flocks and *. Gen 13:6
of sheep and * of cattle, and a Gen 24:35
* of cattle, and many servants. Gen 26:14
how your flocks and * have grown. Gen 30:29
and * and camels, into two groups; Gen 32:7
flocks and * I met as I came?" Gen 33:8
and the flocks and * have their Gen 33:13
with pens for his flocks and *. Gen 33:17
all the flocks and * and Gen 34:28
and *, and all that you have. Gen 45:10
and * and everything they own.' Gen 46:32
flocks and * and possessions. Gen 47:1
Soon all the horses, flocks, *, Gen 47:17
and * in the land of Goshen. Gen 50:8
donkeys, camels, flocks, and *. Ex 9:3
none of the Israeli * and flocks Ex 9:4
of the Israeli * was even sick. Ex 9:6
flocks and *," Moses replied. Ex 10:9
let your flocks and * stay here; Ex 10:24
our flocks and * for sacrifices and Ex 10:25
Take your flocks and * and be Ex 12:32
and there were flocks and *—a Ex 12:38
Do not let the flocks or * feed Ex 34:3
animals from your * and flocks. Lev 1:2,3
animal of your * and flocks and Lev 27:32
flocks and * it won't be enough! Num 11:22
goats, or from their * of cattle. Num 15:3,4
us, along with our flocks and *. Num 20:4
your flocks and * have become very Deu 8:12,13
animals of your flocks and *. Deu 12:6
of your flocks and *, nor anything Deu 12:17
your flocks and * may be butchered Deu 12:20-23
firstborn of your flocks and *. Deu 14:23
of your crops and * and take the Deu 14:25
males from your flocks and *. Deu 15:19
firstborn of your * to work your Deu 15:19
Large flocks and *; Deu 28:2-6
* and drove them on ahead of them. 1Sa 30:20
flocks of sheep and * of goats; 2Sa 12:1
entire * at wholesale prices. 2Ch 1:16
and captured great * of sheep and 2Ch 14:15
for he had great * of cattle out in 2Ch 26:10
of all our cattle, *, and flocks, Neh 10:36
state of your flocks and your *; Pro 27:23,24
I also bred great * and flocks, Ecc 2:7,8
whole flocks and * will be Is 7:21,22
cities empty. Wild * of donkeys and Is 32:14
* will graze in green pastures. Is 32:20
shall be a place to pasture *. Is 65:10
had—flocks and * and sons and Jer 3:24
of sheep and * of cattle, yes, and Jer 5:17
given him all your flocks and *. Jer 28:14
oil, and the healthy flocks and * Jer 31:12
Egypt, and destroy both men and *. Eze 29:8
flocks and * gave birth to young. Eze 31:6
your flocks and * that graze beside Eze 32:13
and * will also greatly multiply. Eze 36:11
their flocks and * to sacrifice to Hos 5:6
with hunger; the * stand perplexed Joe 1:18
"Let the flocks and * forget Joe 2:22
HERDSMAN
Saul's chief *, was there at that 1Sa 21:7
AMOS WAS A * living in the village Amo 1:1
I am just a * and fruit picker. Amo 7:14
HERDSMEN
out between the * of Abram and Lot, Gen 13:7
and argued over it with Isaac's *. Gen 26:20
sheep and all the *, and I alone Job 1:16
water below. The * fled to the Mt 8:33
The * fled to the nearby towns Mk 5:14
they drowned. The * rushed away to Lk 8:34
HERE
* is a summary of the events in Gen 2:4
* IS A list of some Gen 5:1
Literally, "sons of God" used * Gen 6:1f
to the Lord. * is the story of Gen 6:8
of Japheth. * is a list of Shem's Gen 10:22
sister? *, take her and be gone!" Gen 12:19
stay * in the western section. Gen 13:9
they will return * to this land; Gen 15:16
the Amorite nations living * now Gen 15:16
Stop awhile and rest * in the Gen 18:3,4
stretch out * along the street." Gen 19:2
"What relatives do you have * in Gen 19:12
daughters who are * and get out Gen 19:15
Don't stay down * on the plain or Gen 19:17
"Stay * with the donkey," Gen 22:5
"* I am, a visitor in a foreign Gen 23:4
any charge. * in the presence of my Gen 23:11
See, * I am, standing beside Gen 24:13
why stand * outside the city when Gen 24:31
I have told you why I am *." Gen 24:33
but to come to his relatives * Gen 24:38
a girl from * to marry his son. Gen 24:38
me in this way: * I am, standing Gen 24:43
brought you *, so what can we say? Gen 24:50
"But we want Rebekah * at least Gen 24:55
* is a list, in the order of Gen 25:12-15
Do as I say and stay * in this Gen 26:3
good—and bring it * for me to eat, Gen 27:2,3,4
I've done as you told me to. * is Gen 27:19
Isaac: "Come over *. Gen 27:21
Isaac: "Come * and kiss me, my Gen 27:26
Esau: "* I am, father, with the Gen 27:31
is it who was just * with venison, Gen 27:33
Isaac: "Your brother was * and Gen 27:35
"God lives *!" Gen 28:16,17
shepherds are *," they replied. Gen 29:8
are all because of your being *. Gen 30:27
There's nothing for us *—none of Gen 31:14
But see *—though you feel you Gen 31:30
Now put everything I stole out * Gen 31:36,37
he exclaimed, "God lives *!" Gen 32:1
you folks to live * among us and to Gen 34:9,10
with you and live * and unite with Gen 34:16
"Let's invite them to live * Gen 34:21
consider staying * on one Gen 34:22
they will settle * among us." Gen 34:23
the God who met me * at Bethel" Gen 35:7
* are the names of the twelve sons Gen 35:22
* IS A list of the descendants of Gen 36:1
* are the names of Esau's Gen 36:9
clans, as listed *:The clan of Gen 36:15,16
* are the names of the sub-tribes Gen 36:40-43
told him, "they are no longer *. Gen 37:17
"* comes that master-dreamer," Gen 37:19,20
throw him alive into this well *; Gen 37:21,22
others. "* come some Ishmaelites. Gen 37:26,27
prostitute *," they replied. Gen 38:21
no more authority * than I have! Gen 39:9
you've had around * tried to rape Gen 39:17
one * to tell us what they mean." Gen 40:8
and ask him to let me out of *. Gen 40:14
and now this—* I am in jail when I Gen 40:15
to do * in the land of Egypt. Gen 41:25
this youngest brother comes *. Gen 42:15
I'll keep the rest of you *, Gen 42:16
"my money is * in my sack." Gen 42:28
Leave one of your brothers * with Gen 42:33
had paid for the grain. * it is; Gen 43:21
him * so that I can see him.' Gen 44:21
'Don't come back * unless your Gen 44:23
Please sir, let me stay * as a Gen 44:33
"Come over *," he said. Gen 45:4
He sent me * ahead of you to Gen 45:5
God has sent me * to keep you Gen 45:7
Yes, it was God who sent me *, Gen 45:8
about all my power * in Egypt, and Gen 45:13
and come * to Egypt to live. Gen 45:18
ones, and to bring your father *. Gen 45:19
* are the names of his sons and Gen 46:8-14
that you are *, and that you have Gen 46:31
live * in the land of Goshen." Gen 46:34
"My father and my brothers are * Gen 47:1
We have come to live * in Egypt, Gen 47:4
your land for Pharaoh. * is grain. Gen 47:23
and Manasseh, born * in the land of Gen 48:5
God has given me * in Egypt." Gen 48:9
This one over * is the older. Gen 48:18
God * upon this mountain!" Ex 3:12
appearing to you * in this burning Ex 3:16
And he is coming * to look for Ex 4:14
your God, but do it * in the land. Ex 8:25
we do this right * before their Ex 8:26
let your flocks and herds stay *; Ex 10:24
"Get out of * and don't let me Ex 10:28
The Hebrew word * translated Ex 12:3,4f
you brought us out * to die in the Ex 14:11
"Let's get out of *," the Ex 14:25
Why did you bring us * to die, Ex 17:3
* all day long to get your help?" Ex 18:14
They must not come up * to try to Ex 19:21
up *, or I will destroy them." Ex 19:24
"* ARE OTHER laws you must obey: Ex 21:1
Moses, "Come up * with Aaron, Ex 24:1
He told the elders, "Stay * and Ex 24:14
am showing you * on the mountain. Ex 25:40
us * from Egypt has disappeared; Ex 32:1
side, come over * and join me." Ex 32:26
However, stand * on this rock Ex 33:21
and sprinkle it * and there upon Ex 40:9
"* ARE THE instructions Lev 7:1
"* are the instructions Lev 7:11
"* are the conditions for his Lev 16:3
* is the final tabulation: Num 1:20-46
* are the tribal locations: Num 2:3-31
the Lord who is * among you, and Num 11:19,20
*, you three," he commanded. Num 12:3,4
milk and honey.' * is some fruit we Num 13:27
wailed, "or even * in the Num 14:2
Let's get out of * and return to Num 14:3
will all die * in this wilderness! Num 14:29
shall die * in this wilderness.' Num 14:34,35
"* we are!" Num 14:40

(HERE Con't)
Egypt to kill us * in this terrible Num 16:13
And Moses said to Korah, "Come * Num 16:16
Aaron will be * too. Num 16:16
and Aaron will also be * with Num 16:17
Aaron, "* is another of my laws: Num 19:1
and bring us * to this evil place? Num 20:5
and now we are * at Kadesh, Num 20:16
to die * in the wilderness?" Num 21:5
"There is nothing to eat *, and Num 21:5
"Stay * overnight," Balaam Num 22:8
However, stay * tonight so that Num 22:19
seven altars *, and prepare seven Num 23:1
the king, "Stand * by your burnt Num 23:3,4
the king, "Stand * by your burnt Num 23:15
Get out of *! Num 24:11
* are the results of the census: Num 26:3,4
* are the names of his daughters: Num 26:28-37
"You mean you want to sit * Num 32:6
died. But * you are, a brood of Num 32:14
walled cities * for our families, Num 32:17
We will not settle down * until Num 32:18
stay * in the cities of Gilead. Num 32:26
be * on this side of the Jordan." Num 32:32
near Edre-i. *, then, is Moses' Deu 1:1
'You have stayed * long enough. Deu 1:6
us, bringing us * from Egypt to be Deu 1:27
again and again * in the Deu 1:31
" 'You have stayed * long Deu 2:3
them, 'may live * in the cities the Deu 3:19
may return * to your own land.' Deu 3:20
Lord our God is * among us whenever Deu 4:7
I must die * on this side of the Deu 4:21,22
heaven and down * upon the earth; Deu 4:39
with you who are * alive today. Deu 5:2,3
Then you come back and stand * Deu 5:31
wilderness, until your arrival *. Deu 11:5
"* is an example of the purpose Deu 19:4
she married; yet * is the proof.' Deu 22:17,18
will say, 'Oh, that night were *!' Deu 28:67
say, 'Oh, that morning were *!' Deu 28:67
"When we came *, King Sihon of Deu 29:7
You are standing * to enter into Deu 29:12
while I am still * with you, you Deu 31:27
you a homeland * on the east side Jos 1:12,13
cattle may remain *, but your Jos 1:14
Only then may you settle down * Jos 1:15
"The men were * earlier, but I Jos 2:4
else—are * inside the house. Jos 2:17,18
these stones are * and what they Jos 4:21
actually living right * among us? Jos 9:22
hills are * with their armies." Jos 10:6
on the second day; *, too, the Jos 10:32
* IS THE list of the kings on the Jos 12:1
* is a list of the kings Jos 12:7
to be conquered. * is a list of Jos 13:2-7
of the Amorites * in this land? Jos 24:15
nations living * in the land. Jos 24:18
* IS A list of the nations the Ju 3:1
You will be safe * in our Ju 4:18
me, tell them that no one is *." Ju 4:20
The same name is used * as in Ju 6:16f
But stay * until I go and get a Ju 6:18
"I'll stay * until you return." Ju 6:18
your God, built * on this hill, Ju 6:26
"Well, * they are!" Ju 8:15
Israel has been living * for all Ju 11:26
him, "The same man is * again!" Ju 13:10
"Please stay * until we can get Ju 13:15
"Why have you come *?" Ju 15:10
The Philistines are *!" Ju 16:9
are * to capture you, Samson!" Ju 16:20
"Well, stay * with me," Micah Ju 17:10,11
asked him, "What are you doing *? Ju 18:3
let's stay * tonight." Ju 19:11
for you mustn't stay * in the Ju 19:20
he is my guest. *, take my virgin Ju 19:24
"Stay right * with us to glean; Ru 2:8,9
come * to live among strangers. Ru 2:10,11
Stay * tonight, and in the Ru 3:13
was * at the threshing-floor." Ru 3:14
"Say, come over *," he called to Ru 4:1
"Must you come * drunk?" 1Sa 1:14
"I am the woman who stood * that 1Sa 1:26
up and ran to Eli. "* I am. 1Sa 3:4,5
"Let's bring the Ark * from 1Sa 4:3
of the God of Israel * any longer. 1Sa 5:7
God of Israel * to kill us too!" 1Sa 5:10
can we send the Ark from *?" 1Sa 6:20
There is a prophet who lives * in 1Sa 9:6
Is he * among us?" 1Sa 10:22
Bring them * and we will kill 1Sa 11:12
and now I stand *, an old, 1Sa 12:2
"Now stand * quietly before the 1Sa 12:7
All right, * is the king you 1Sa 12:13
"Come on up * and we'll show you 1Sa 14:12
"Find out who isn't *," Saul 1Sa 14:17
"Roll a great stone over *, and 1Sa 14:33
the oxen and sheep * to kill and 1Sa 14:34
I will stand over *, and all of you 1Sa 14:40
Now be sure that you obey him. * 1Sa 15:2
"What are you doing around *, 1Sa 17:28
"Come over * and I'll give your 1Sa 17:44
hasn't David been * for dinner 1Sa 20:27
me not to tell anybody why I am *. 1Sa 21:2
it, for there is nothing else *." 1Sa 21:9
have enough of them around *! 1Sa 21:14,15
"Listen *, you men of 1Sa 22:7
me and to come * and attack me?" 1Sa 22:13
Stay * with me, and I'll protect 1Sa 22:23
"We're afraid even * in Judah; 1Sa 23:3
and destroy Keilah because I am *. 1Sa 23:10
And now, * is a present I have 1Sa 25:27
for my boldness in coming out *. 1Sa 25:28
of water and then get out of *!" 1Sa 26:11
"* is your spear, sir," David 1Sa 26:22
instead of * in the royal city." 1Sa 27:5
"Now he will have to stay * and 1Sa 27:12
and your sons will be * with me." 1Sa 28:19
are these Israelis doing *?" 1Sa 29:3
elders of Judah. "* is a present 1Sa 30:26
It is quoted * from the book, 2Sa 1:17,18
shouted to him, "Get away from *. 2Sa 2:22
they exclaimed. "* is the head 2Sa 4:8
"You'll never come in *," they 2Sa 5:6
prophet, "Look! * I am living in 2Sa 7:2
you shall live * at the palace!" 2Sa 9:7
but he will live * with me." 2Sa 9:10,11
men aren't * to honor your father! 2Sa 10:3
"Well, stay * tonight," David 2Sa 11:12
"Everyone get out of *," he told 2Sa 13:9
me the food again * in my bedroom 2Sa 13:10
"Get out of *!" 2Sa 13:15
around *, and this is a command. 2Sa 13:28
"Did Joab send you *?" 2Sa 14:19
"but he must never come *. 2Sa 14:24
to him, "What are you doing *? 2Sa 15:19,20
told Zadok, "Look, * is my plan. 2Sa 15:27
"Get out of *, you murderer, you 2Sa 16:7,8
has left them * to keep the house. 2Sa 16:21
that you stay * in the city and 2Sa 18:3
He shouted down, "* comes 2Sa 18:26
"Wait *," the king told him. 2Sa 18:30
will remain * during the night; 2Sa 19:7
That is why I have come * today, 2Sa 19:20
are buried. But * is Chimham. 2Sa 19:37
men of Israel, let's get out of *. 2Sa 20:1
Come over * so I can talk to 2Sa 20:16
told the king. "* are oxen for the 2Sa 24:22
the prophet is * to see you." 1Ki 1:22,23
When you bring him back *, 1Ki 1:35
"No," he said, "I'll die *." 1Ki 2:30
"Build a house * in Jerusalem, and 1Ki 2:36,37
way around. And * I am among your 1Ki 3:8
* IS A list of King Solomon's 1Ki 4:1
* is a list of the items he made: 1Ki 7:41-46
and then, standing * before your 1Ki 8:31
and have put my name * forever. 1Ki 9:2,3
things going on * is all true. 1Ki 10:6
for they stand * day after day 1Ki 10:8
"What do you lack *? 1Ki 11:22
Zeruah, a widow. * is the story 1Ki 11:27,28
hills who come * to burn incense; 1Ki 13:2
water while I'm *, and not to 1Ki 13:9
and have come *, and have eaten and 1Ki 13:21,22
Have you come * to punish my sins 1Ki 17:18
"Now go and tell the king I am * 1Ki 18:8
told 'Elijah isn't *,' King Ahab 1Ki 18:10
'Go and tell him Elijah is *'! 1Ki 18:11
tell the king that Elijah is *'! 1Ki 18:14
to the people, "Come over *." 1Ki 18:30
"What are you doing *, Elijah?" 1Ki 19:9
And a voice said, "Why are you *; 1Ki 19:13
And we're sitting * without doing 1Ki 22:3
there a prophet of the Lord *? 1Ki 22:7
Gilgal, "Stay *, for the Lord has 2Ki 2:1
"Please stay * in Bethel, for the 2Ki 2:4
"Please stay *, for the Lord has 2Ki 2:6,7
"The Lord has brought us * to 2Ki 3:10
"Elisha is *," one of the king 2Ki 3:11
who has called us * to be destroyed 2Ki 3:13
true prophet of God * in Israel." 2Ki 5:8
"Why sit * until we die?" 2Ki 7:3
"We will starve if we stay * 2Ki 7:4
* and die with the rest of us!" 2Ki 7:13
Gehazi exclaimed. "* is the 2Ki 8:5
'I will repay him * on Naboth's 2Ki 9:26
only those who worship Baal are *; 2Ki 10:23
"Get her out of *," shouted 2Ki 11:15
"Don't kill her * in the Temple. 2Ki 11:15
"We colonists * in Israel don't 2Ki 17:26
And do you think we have come * 2Ki 18:25
You can live in peace * in your 2Ki 18:31,32
happen * at the altar at Bethel!" 2Ki 23:17
* is a list of the names of the 1Ch 1:43
* is a list of the men from 1Ch 12:20
army of God. * is the registry of 1Ch 12:23
I'm living * in a cedar-paneled 1Ch 17:1
" 'When your time * on earth is 1Ch 17:11
They are * to spy out the land so 1Ch 19:2,3
THEN DAVID SAID, "Right * at 1Ch 22:1
and Jeduthun. * is a list of their 1Ch 25:1
month each year. * is the list of 1Ch 27:1
"* before the leaders of Israel, 1Ch 28:8
For we are * for but a moment, 1Ch 29:15
his father is from * in Tyre. 2Ch 2:14
and pray to you * in this Temple, 2Ch 6:24
and my heart shall always be *. 2Ch 7:16
got * and saw it with my own eyes. 2Ch 9:6
to stand * and listen to you talk! 2Ch 9:7
else can help us! * we are, 2Ch 14:11
not removed. But * in Judah and 2Ch 15:17
my father. See, * is silver and 2Ch 16:3
of the Lord around * too?" 2Ch 18:6,7
"Look *," the king said 2Ch 18:15
"Get me out of *," he groaned 2Ch 18:33
Your people settled * and built 2Ch 20:8
can stand * before this Temple and 2Ch 20:9
you—for you are * in this 2Ch 20:9
"Don't do it * at the Temple. 2Ch 23:13,14
must not bring the captives *!" 2Ch 28:13
so is referred to * in this unusual 2Ch 28:19f
will be honored * in this Temple, 2Ch 33:7
these laws that are written *." 2Ch 34:21
* IS THE list of the Jewish exiles Ez 2:1
* is a census of those who Ez 2:2
* are the statistics concerning Ez 2:36-39
* are the statistics concerning Ez 2:40,41,42
of Assyria brought us *." Ez 4:2
* is the text of the letter they Ez 4:11
was constructed * many centuries Ez 5:11
* IS THE genealogy of Ezra, who Ez 7:1
* before you in our wickedness?" Ez 9:15
we can't stay out * much longer. Ez 10:13
* is the list of ordinary Ez 10:25
to Jerusalem from their exile *?" Neh 1:2
"* are the statistics concerning Neh 7:39-42
"* are the statistics concerning Neh 7:43,44,45
"So now we are slaves * in the Neh 9:36
* IS A list of the priests who Neh 12:1
out *, camping around the wall? Neh 13:21
the queen right * in the palace, Est 7:8
If they have done that *, I Est 9:12
the Jews who are * at Shushan do Est 9:13
our days * on earth are as Job 8:9
a giant. * I sit in sackcloth; Job 16:15
I seek him *, I seek him there, Job 23:8
" 'It's not *,' the oceans say; Job 28:14
and the seas reply, 'Nor is it * Job 28:14
"All right, * is my reply: In Job 33:12
* shall your proud waves stop!' Job 38:11
The Hebrew text adds *: Ps 9:16f
that happens * on earth. Ps 11:4
were already *, that God would come Ps 14:7
to me * in the land of the living. Ps 27:13
death itself, and * I am alive! Ps 30:3
then you will live safely * in Ps 37:3
Help me to know that I am * for Ps 39:4
Yet I am standing * depressed Ps 42:6
armies of heaven is * among us. Ps 46:7
the heavenly armies is * among us! Ps 46:11
Lord, * in your Temple we Ps 48:9
Listen! * are my charges against Ps 50:7
God who judges justly * on earth. Ps 58:11
"He will never notice them *," Ps 64:5
God will live among us *. Ps 68:18
What awe we feel, kneeling * Ps 68:35
names of those who were born *. Ps 87:6
They have left me * to die, like Ps 88:5
and heavy * beneath your wrath. Ps 90:9
praises to Jehovah * on earth, Ps 115:17
Yes, in his presence—* on earth! Ps 116:9
of thanksgiving. * in the courts Ps 116:18,19
I am but a pilgrim * on earth: Ps 119:19
* come these lawless men to Ps 119:150
I am tired of being * among these Ps 120:5,6
Now we are standing * inside the Ps 122:2,3
and my friends who live *; Ps 122:8
God's permanent home * on earth. Ps 132:7
praise the Lord, for he lives * Ps 135:21
Don't let liars prosper * in our Ps 140:11
* is my description of Ps 144:12-15
And praise him down * on earth, Ps 148:7
Come * and listen to me! Pro 1:23
to look for you and * you are! Pro 7:15
shall be rewarded * on earth; Pro 11:31
* are some additional proverbs: Pro 24:21,22
The wind blows south and north, * Ecc 1:3-7
remember what we have done back *. Ecc 1:8-11
who please him. So *, too, we see Ecc 2:24-26
is what they are * for, and no one Ecc 3:22
and you are only * on earth, so let Ecc 5:1
all that goes on * in the world, Ecc 8:9,10
thing happening * upon the earth: Ecc 8:14
in anything * on earth any more. Ecc 9:6
down * for all your earthly toil. Ecc 9:9
* is another thing that has made Ecc 9:13
down * is futile in comparison. Ecc 11:8
* is my final conclusion: fear Ecc 12:13
you are, lying * upon the grass, Sol 1:16
him—my beloved! * he comes, leaping Sol 2:8
Yes, spring is *. Sol 2:12
KING SOLOMON: "I am * in my Sol 5:1

HERE Con't)
The term used *, "branch of the Is 4:2,3,4f
Zechariah 3:8). * it is used Is 4:2,3,4f
may prefer to see * a reference to Is 4:2,3,4f
* is an example of serious punning Is 5:7f
Hebrew word used * sometimes means Is 7:14f
Its immediate use * refers to Is 7:14f
Some see * a reference to the Is 10:27f
them *, from countries far away. Is 13:4
her time of doom will soon be *. Is 13:22
* IS GOD'S message to Moab: Is 15:1
night I have been * at my post. Is 21:8,9
Now at last—look! * come riders Is 21:8,9
ruthless nations. * on Mount Zion Is 25:6
Now at last he is *." Is 25:9
selecting them * and there from his Is 27:12
"No, this is the way; walk *." Is 30:21
cry, "can live * in the presence Is 33:14
I will tell you who can live * Is 33:15
COME * AND listen, O nations of Is 34:1
only at the altars * in Jerusalem? Is 36:7
think I have come * without the Is 36:10
Don't listen to Hezekiah, for * Is 36:16
Then God said to Hezekiah, "* is Is 37:30
the Lord, and * is my guarantee: Is 38:7
be afraid; I am * to help you. Is 41:13
It's crowded *!' Is 49:20
into exile, leaving me * alone. Is 49:21
Is that why you aren't *? Is 50:1
But see *, you who live in your Is 50:11
*, is the Messiah, our Lord Jesus. Is 52:13f
covenant with David, * remembered. Is 55:3f
But you—come *, you witches' Is 57:3
"Yes, I am *," he will quickly Is 58:9
See, * is my decree all written Is 65:6
There is word play * between Jer 1:12f
First *, then there, you flit Jer 2:36
of Israel—one from * and two from Jer 3:14
for you to be * among my children. Jer 3:19
to it, all of you who worship *. Jer 7:2
of the Lord is *, God will never Jer 7:4
is *, you will never suffer? Jer 7:8
and then come * and stand before Jer 7:10
do the same thing * because of all Jer 7:13,14
"Why should we wait * to die? Jer 8:14
O Lord, you are right * among us, Jer 14:9
not marry and have children *. Jer 16:2
on the throne * in Jerusalem; Jer 17:25
* IS ANOTHER message to Jeremiah Jer 18:1
armies kill you * and leave your Jer 19:7
Stay * in Jerusalem and Jer 21:9
no one can touch us *!' Jer 21:13
the people living * forgot the Lord Jer 22:9
* in my own Temple, says the Lord. Jer 23:11
I will bring them back * again. Jer 24:6
of Jerusalem left * in this land; Jer 24:8
continue to live * in this land Jer 25:5
dishes still * in the Temple, left Jer 27:18
articles left * by Nebuchadnezzar, Jer 27:19,20,21
the people left * in Jerusalem—on Jer 29:16,17
For he has written to us * in Jer 29:28
for we will be * to eat the fruit Jer 29:28
they shall possess it and live * Jer 30:3
O virgin Israel, to your cities *. Jer 31:21
the number of cattle * in Israel. Jer 31:27
again own property * in this Jer 32:15
of Benjamin and * in Jerusalem, in Jer 32:44
about what is going to happen *. Jer 33:3
and is not * in its chronological Jer 35:1f
That's why we are *." Jer 35:11
you live in peace * in the land I Jer 35:15
I am a prisoner *, you read the Jer 36:5
in the Hebrew expression used *. Jer 36:30f
though it came * to help you, is Jer 37:7
"Stay * and serve the king of Jer 40:9
* to oversee my administration. Jer 40:10
"Stay * in this land. Jer 42:10
will let you stay * in your land. Jer 42:12
'We will not stay *,'—and insist on Jer 42:13,14
that we will stay * and be killed Jer 43:2,3
Pharaoh's palace * in Tahpanhes, Jer 43:9
* to Egypt, for he is my servant. Jer 43:10
you who has come * from Judah, not Jer 44:7
made and worshiped * in Egypt, Jer 44:8
insisted on coming * to Egypt and I Jer 44:12
They shall fall * in Egypt, Jer 44:12
of Judah who are * in Egypt! Jer 44:24
*: I will turn Pharaoh Hophra, Jer 44:29
* ARE THE messages given to Jer 46:1
away from all this slaughter *!" Jer 46:16
(* the prophecy concerning Moab Jer 48:47
Jeremiah * sees the long-range Jer 51:26f
for this hour and it is finally *! Lam 2:16
but indicated * by this reaction. Eze 3:14,15f
See the dietary laws Ezekiel * Eze 4:14f
*, to push me from my Temple? Eze 8:6
And begin right * at the Eze 9:6
If Noah, Daniel and Job were * Eze 14:14
three men were *, the Lord God Eze 14:16
and they come * to join you as Eze 14:22
your final day of reckoning is *. Eze 21:25
* in the land of those who live. Eze 26:20
The text * is uncertain. Eze 27:19f
* IS ANOTHER message given to me Eze 28:1
for the terrible day is almost *; Eze 30:2,3
* IS ANOTHER message to me from Eze 38:1
* so I can show you many things; Eze 40:4
and measured it. * too there were Eze 40:21
* at the north entry, just as at Eze 40:23
the walls. And * again, if one Eze 40:27
* and so it shall remain shut. Eze 44:2
They do it * to avoid the Eze 46:19,20
* are the instructions for Eze 47:13
"* IS THE list of the tribes and Eze 48:1
and they are not * to help." Dan 2:11
Come out! Come *!" Dan 3:26
* among the inhabitants of earth. Dan 4:35
* these cups from his Temple; Dan 5:23
"I am *," he said, "to tell Dan 8:19
me, "Daniel, I am * to help you Dan 9:22
was given. I am * to tell you what Dan 9:23
that very day I was sent * to Dan 10:12
Now I am * to tell you what will Dan 10:14
I have come? I am * to tell you Dan 10:20,21
The prophecy takes a turn *. Dan 11:40f
* is the first message: Hos 1:2
You may no longer stay * in this Hos 9:3
the day of recompense is almost * Hos 9:7
from the Almighty is almost *! Joe 1:15
And you will know that I am * Joe 2:27
of the Lord were *, for then God Amo 5:18
"Get out of *, you prophet, you! Amo 7:12
Don't bother us * with your Amo 7:13
your visions, not * in the capital, Amo 7:13
searching, running * and going Amo 8:12
"Who can ever reach us way up * Ob 1:3
and you first told me to come *. Jon 4:2
* contrasted with their shame; Mic 1:11f
"to go forth," * contrasted with Mic 1:11f
* contrasted with their shame; Mic 1:11f
"to go forth," * contrasted with Mic 1:11f
* contrasted with their shame; Mic 1:11f
"to go forth," * contrasted with Mic 1:11f
is well—the Lord is * among us. Mic 3:11
time of punishment is almost *; Mic 7:4
do it! And * I will give peace,' Hag 2:8,9
* seen as one of the Godhead. Zec 2:8f
* is your part: Tell the truth. Zec 8:16
* is another message that came to Zec 8:18
The translation * follows the Zec 11:13f
a yet future disaster foretold *? Zec 13:8f
* IS THE Lord's message to Israel, Mal 1:1
God can change these stones * Mt 3:9
"Get out of *, Satan," Jesus Mt 4:10
May your will be done * on earth, Mt 6:10
Some manuscripts add *, "For Mt 6:13f
"Don't store up treasures * on Mt 6:19
flowers that are * today and gone Mt 6:30
If you will only stand * and say, Mt 8:8,9
Literally, "Have you come * to Mt 8:29f
* are the names of his twelve Mt 10:2,3,4
it would still be * today. Mt 11:23
And truly, one is * who is Mt 12:6
And now a greater than Jonah is * Mt 12:41
*—and you refuse to believe him. Mt 12:42
"Now * is the explanation of the Mt 13:18
* is another illustration Jesus Mt 13:24
in the barn.' " * is another of Mt 13:31,32
And his sisters—they all live *. Mt 13:56
is nothing to eat * in the desert; Mt 14:15
"Bring them *," he said. Mt 14:18
been * with me for three days now, Mt 15:32
we get enough * in the desert for Mt 15:33
And some of you standing right * Mt 16:28
it's wonderful that we can be *! Mt 17:4
Bring him * to me." Mt 17:17
of you agree down * on earth Mt 18:19
wretch! * I forgave you all that Mt 18:32
Omitted * in many manuscripts, but Mt 19:29f
* IS ANOTHER illustration of the Mt 20:1
Untie them and bring them *. Mt 21:2
"God's Man is *! Mt 21:9
"* comes the heir to this estate; Mt 21:38
you are * without a wedding robe?' Mt 22:12
questions? *, show me a coin." Mt 22:19
And don't address anyone * on Mt 23:9
* or there,' don't believe it. Mt 24:23
you know that summer is almost *. Mt 24:32
money in the earth and * it is!' Mt 25:24,25
stay * Mt 26:38
Look! * comes the man who is Mt 26:46
was crucified, but he isn't *! Mt 28:6
* BEGINS THE wonderful story of Mk 1:1
* is a sample of his preaching: Mk 1:7
"* is another story illustrating Mk 4:26
many of us * within this man." Mk 5:9
And his sisters live right * Mk 6:2,3
is nothing to eat * in this Mk 6:35,36
they have been * three days, and Mk 8:1
food for them * in the desert?" Mk 8:4
who are standing * right now will Mk 9:1
"We will make three shelters *, Mk 9:5
Mentioned * so quietly, this Mk 10:1f
"All these will be his * on Mk 10:30
least * shall be greatest there." Mk 10:31
am not * to be served, but to Mk 10:45
and said, "Tell him to come *." Mk 10:49
Untie him and bring him *. Mk 11:2
demanding, "What's going on *? Mk 11:27,28
* ARE SOME of the Mk 12:1
* was their question: Mk 12:18
* are some of the other things he Mk 12:38
"Now, * is a lesson from a fig Mk 13:28
but I won't be * much longer. Mk 14:7
of you who is * eating with me." Mk 14:18
"Sit *, while I go and pray." Mk 14:32
death; stay * and watch with me." Mk 14:34
My betrayer is *!" Mk 14:42
He spoke * in Aramaic. Mk 15:34f
He isn't *! Mk 16:6
that I would be * at the Temple, in Lk 2:49
* is a sample of John's preaching Lk 3:7
you do miracles * in your home town Lk 4:23
every Saturday. *, too, the people Lk 4:32
stand * where everyone can see." Lk 6:8
* are their names: Lk 6:14,15,16
have their only happiness down *. Lk 6:24
* are some of the Lk 6:39
seen and heard * today: how those Lk 7:20,21,22
See this woman kneeling *! Lk 7:44
"For there is nothing to eat * Lk 9:12
who are standing * right now will Lk 9:27
this boy * is my only son, and a Lk 9:38
Bring him *." Lk 9:41
difference the next time I am *.' Lk 10:35
sits * while I do all the work? Lk 10:40
is * [and few pay any attention Lk 11:31
is * [but this nation won't listen Lk 11:32
me * on earth as your Friend. Lk 12:8
those who deny me * among men. Lk 12:9
flowers that are * today and gone Lk 12:28
west, you say, '* comes a shower.' Lk 12:54
You can't come in *, guilty as Lk 13:27
him, "Get out of * if you want to Lk 13:31
say, 'Let this man sit * instead.' Lk 14:9
and * I am, dying of hunger! Lk 15:17
I'm through *, and I haven't the Lk 16:3
'Yes, * is the contract you Lk 16:5,6
was the reply. '*,' the accountant Lk 16:7
Send Lazarus over * if only to Lk 16:24
So now he is * being comforted Lk 16:25
you from * is stopped at its edge; Lk 16:26
lest they come * when they die.' Lk 16:28
say, 'It has begun * in this place Lk 17:21
day, but I won't be *," he said. Lk 17:22
"Bring the blind man over *," Lk 18:40
Jesus said, "and bring him *. Lk 19:30
died also. Now * is our question: Lk 20:33
is for people * on earth, but when Lk 20:34,35
and down * on earth the nations Lk 21:25
But * at this table, sitting Lk 22:21
But not *! Lk 22:27
me a Kingdom, I, * and now, grant Lk 22:29
He isn't *! Lk 24:6,7
"Do you have anything * to eat?" Lk 24:41
Literally, "but wait * in the Lk 24:49f
yet—stay * in the city until the Lk 24:49
became a human being and lived * Jn 1:14
water, but right * in the crowd Jn 1:26
the one, but I am * baptizing with Jn 1:31
Jesus said, "* comes an honest Jn 1:47
them, "Get these things out of *. Jn 2:16
these that happen * among men, how Jn 3:12
there instead of coming * to us." Jn 3:26
the Messiah. I am * to prepare the Jn 3:28
this long trip out * every day." Jn 4:15
claim it is * [at Mount Gerazim Jn 4:20
the Father * or in Jerusalem. Jn 4:21-24
in fact, it is *, when the dead Jn 5:25
"There's a youngster * with five Jn 6:8,9
said, "Sir, how did you get *?" Jn 6:25
For I have come * from heaven to Jn 6:38
to kill? But * he is preaching in Jn 7:26
I am to be * a little longer. Jn 7:33
I am not * on my own, but he sent Jn 8:42
But while I am still * in the Jn 9:5
*, my brother wouldn't have died. Jn 11:21
"He is * and wants to see you." Jn 11:28
if you had been *, my brother would Jn 11:32
people standing *, so that they Jn 11:42
If you love your life down *—you Jn 12:25
If you despise your life down * Jn 12:25
The Greek * is a very free Jn 12:40f
that isn't true of everyone *." Jn 13:10
I love you. And * is how to Jn 15:13
fact, it is *—when you will be Jn 16:32
of heart and mind. * on earth you Jn 16:33
I brought glory to you * on Jn 17:4
During my time * I have kept Jn 17:12
You have some of them *. Jn 18:21
their chief priests brought you *. Jn 18:35
And Pilate said to the Jews, "* Jn 19:14
events and have recorded them *. Jn 21:24

(HERE Con't)
you standing * staring at the sky? Act 1:11
* is the list of those who were Act 1:14
we were born! * we are—Parthians, Act 2:9
and his tomb is still * among us. Act 2:29
said to him, Sit * in honor beside Act 2:34
and then Peter said, "Look *!" Act 3:4
that this man stands * healed! Act 4:10
"That is what is happening * in Act 4:27
Then God brought him * to the Act 7:4
land of Israel and worship me *.' Act 7:7
that he came * to arrest them all Act 9:21
come so soon. Now * we are, waiting Act 10:33
These six brothers * accompanied Act 11:12
"and all others * who reverence Act 13:16
of you Gentiles * who reverence Act 13:26
"And now Barnabas and I are * to Act 13:32,33
believers from * have upset you and Act 15:24
him, "Come over * and help us." Act 16:9
We are all *!" Act 16:28
and now they are * disturbing our Act 17:6
Many people * in this city belong Act 18:10
evident not only * in Ephesus, but Act 19:26
Yet you have brought these men * Act 19:37
Our Jewish Christians * at Act 21:21
We have four men * who are Act 21:23
but educated * in Jerusalem under Act 22:3
Leave Jerusalem, for the people * Act 22:17,18
And I am being tried * today Act 23:6
people about me * in Jerusalem, so Act 23:11
(who ought to be * if they have Act 24:19
Ask these men right * what Act 24:20
when I shouted out, 'I am * Act 24:21
"There is a prisoner *," he Act 25:14
"When they came * for the trial, Act 25:17
you and everyone * in this audience Act 26:29
I asked you to come * today so Act 28:20
But perhaps he is referring *, Act 28:20f
will soon be *. Rom 13:12,13
with my work *, and I am ready to Rom 15:23
All the churches * send you their Rom 16:16
the church meets * in his home. Rom 16:23
that comes from * on earth, and not 1Co 2:6
down * on earth easily enough. 1Co 6:3
Obviously, Paul is not * 1Co 6:12f
* I want to add some suggestions 1Co 7:12
* is the problem: We Christians 1Co 7:26
they are fakes? * is the test: no 1Co 12:3
Now * is what I am trying to say: 1Co 12:27
part of it. * is a list of some of 1Co 12:28
what I gain in this life down *? 1Co 15:32
NOW * ARE the directions about the 1Co 16:1
I will be staying * at Ephesus 1Co 16:8
door for me to preach and teach *. 1Co 16:9
have arrived * for a visit. 1Co 16:17
the help you aren't * to give me. 1Co 16:17
The churches * in Asia send you 1Co 16:19
All the friends * have asked me 1Co 16:20
do, whether we are * in this body 2Co 5:9
himself were * pleading with you, 2Co 5:20
we live close to death, but * we 2Co 6:9
the assemblies * and are splendid 2Co 8:23
but when he gets * he will be 2Co 10:1
When he gets * you will see that 2Co 10:10
they are, so * I go: (You think 2Co 11:18
All the Christians * send you 2Co 13:13
and all the other Christians *. Gal 1:1
self-control; and * there is no Gal 5:23
of Christ, am * in jail because of Eph 3:1
at what they are doing to me *. Eph 3:13
and some down * on earth— that out Eph 3:14,15
I BEG YOU—I, a prisoner * in jail Eph 4:1
even to mention * those pleasures Eph 5:12
him even * in prison, as I should. Eph 6:20
has happened to me * has been a Php 1:12
For everyone around *, including Php 1:13
of the Christians * seem to have Php 1:14
* to use me to defend the Truth. Php 1:16,17
will add to my sorrows * in jail! Php 1:16,17
*, just as I have in the past; Php 1:20
much happier for me than being *! Php 1:23
Yes, I am still needed down * and Php 1:25
what is going to happen to me *. Php 2:23
about is this life * on earth. Php 3:19
And all the other Christians * Php 4:22
slave, * to help us in your place. Col 1:7
time worrying about things down *. Col 3:2
Christ for which I am * in jail. Col 4:3
Aristarchus, who is with me * as Col 4:10
working with me *, and what a Col 4:11
* is my own greeting in my own Col 4:18
Remember me * in jail. Col 4:18
and suffering *, now that we know 1Th 3:7
keeping him from being * already; 2Th 2:6
Now * is a command, dear 2Th 3:6
Now * is my greeting which I am 2Th 3:17
Now, Timothy, my son, * is my 1Ti 1:18
* ARE MY directions: Pray much for 1Ti 2:1
Christian life down * as well. 1Ti 6:19
I am * in jail for Christ's sake. 2Ti 1:8
That is why I am suffering * in 2Ti 1:12
came * from Asia have deserted me; 2Ti 1:15
I am in trouble * and have been put 2Ti 2:9
the judge no one was * to help me. 2Ti 4:16
Do try to be * before winter. 2Ti 4:21
seriously. And * you yourself must Tit 2:7
Everybody * sends greetings. Tit 3:15
an old man now, * in jail for the Phm 1:8,9
to the Lord while * in my chains. Phm 1:10
I really wanted to keep him * Phm 1:13
this by writing it * with my own Phm 1:19
who is also * for preaching Christ Phm 1:23
to his Son, "Sit * beside me in Heb 1:13
time, "See, * am I and the Heb 2:13
Yet while Christ was * on earth Heb 5:7
(But even so, if he were * on Heb 8:4
because down * the priests still Heb 8:4
was a sacred tent down * on earth. Heb 9:1
sacred tent down * on earth, and Heb 9:23
which these down * are copies, were Heb 9:23
high priest down * on earth offers Heb 9:25
system, he then added, "* I am. Heb 10:9
just strangers visiting down *. Heb 11:13
Since we respect our fathers * Heb 12:9
if he comes * soon, I will come Heb 13:23
are * with me send you their love. Heb 13:24,25
Look *, you people who say, Jas 4:13
LOOK *, YOU rich men, now is the Jas 5:1
You have spent your years * on Jas 5:5
He is almost *. Jas 5:9
going is rough for a while down *. 1Pe 1:6
brothers, you are only visitors *. 1Pe 2:11
What I have told you * should 1Pe 5:12
The church * in Rome 1Pe 5:13
sister church * in Babylon salutes 1Pe 5:13f
me that my days * on earth are 2Pe 1:13,14
As long as I am still * I intend 2Pe 1:13,14
of your children *, and to see that 2Jn 1:4
They have told the church * of 3Jn 1:6
Friends * send their love, and 3Jn 1:15
As used * the expression Rev 1:5f
said, "Come up * and I will show Rev 4:1
tribes of Israel, as listed *: Rev 7:4-8
That is why they are * before Rev 7:15
of his Christ are finally *; Rev 12:10
But do not be dismayed, for * is Rev 13:10
of his name. * is a puzzle that Rev 13:18
of life"—used * as a collective Rev 22:2f
to what is written *, God shall add Rev 22:18

HERE'S
"* another opportunity to see 1Sa 18:21
came in, he said, "* your son!" 2Ki 4:36
* what you should do. 1Co 10:25
means Christ. * what I am trying Gal 3:17

HEREAFTER
pleasant * for those who love God. Ps 6:5f

HEREBY
You are * banished from this Gen 4:11
I am * appointing you to be in Gen 41:40
"Cyrus, King of Persia, * Ez 1:2
I and my Council of Seven * Ez 7:14

HERES
spread into Mount *, Aijalon, and Ju 1:35
Gideon returned by way of * Pass. Ju 8:13

HERESH
Bakbakkar, *, Galal, 1Ch 9:15,16

HERETH
So David went to the forest of *. 1Sa 22:5

HERITAGE
That is their wonderful *. Jos 18:7
good men's sons have a special *. Ps 112:2
It is a wonderful * to have an Pro 20:7
This is the * of the servants of Is 54:17
And the wonderful * I reserved Jer 17:4
not own any, for I am their *! Eze 44:28

HERMAS
Hermes, Patrobas, *, and the other Rom 16:14

HERMES
Phlegon, *, Patrobas, Hermas, and Rom 16:14

HERMOGENES
even Phygellus and * are gone. 2Ti 1:15

HERMON
valley of the Arnon to Mount *. Deu 3:8
(The Sidonians called Mount * Deu 3:9
*, as it is sometimes called; Deu 4:48
of Mount *, in the land of Mizpah. Jos 11:1
Lebanon, at the foot of Mount *. Jos 11:17
River to Mount *, including the Jos 12:1
from Mount * in the north to Jos 12:5
beneath Mount * in the south to the Jos 13:2-7
all of Mount *; Jos 13:11
Baal-hermon, Senir, and Mount *. 1Ch 5:23
Mount * and Mount Mizar stand. Ps 42:6
Mount Tabor and Mount * rejoice Ps 89:12
*, on the mountains of Israel. Ps 133:3
mountain, from the top of Mount *, Sol 4:8
from the peak of Senir and *." Sol 4:8f
crags of Mount * never run dry. Jer 18:14

HERMON'S
they are hiding on Mount * Ps 68:22

HERMOPOLIS
found at * in Egypt, mentions Jer 7:18f

HERO
after a great * of the Anakim. Jos 14:15
So he was a great *, but he was a 2Ki 5:1
was Nimrod, who became a great *. 1Ch 1:10
YOU CALL YOURSELF a *, do you? Ps 52:1
for he was a * to the people—they Lk 19:48

HEROD
Judea, during the reign of King *. Mt 2:1
King * was deeply disturbed by Mt 2:3
Then * sent a private message to Mt 2:7
to report to *, for God had warned Mt 2:12
return, for King * is going to try Mt 2:13
* was furious when he learned Mt 2:16
When * died, an angel of the Lord Mt 2:19
* heard about Jesus, he said to Mt 14:1
For * had arrested John and Mt 14:3
But at a birthday party for *, Mt 14:6
after John was arrested by King *, Mk 1:14
King * soon heard about Jesus, Mk 6:14
"No," * said, "it is John, the Mk 6:16
For * had sent soldiers to arrest Mk 6:17,18
powerless. And * respected John, Mk 6:20
his protection. * was disturbed Mk 6:20
of King * and of the Pharisees." Mk 8:15
lived when * was king of Judea. Lk 1:5
at that time; *, over Galilee; Lk 3:1
criticized *, governor of Galilee, Lk 3:19,20
he had done, * put John in prison, Lk 3:19,20
miracles reached *, the governor, Lk 9:7
Literally, "* the Tetrarch." Lk 9:7f
"I beheaded John," * said, "so Lk 9:9
live, for King * is after you!" Lk 13:31
take him to King *, for Galilee was Lk 23:7
jurisdiction; and * happened to be Lk 23:7
at the time. * was delighted at Lk 23:8
Now * and his soldiers began Lk 23:11
That day * and Pilate—enemies Lk 23:12
him innocent. * came to the same Lk 23:15
city today! For * the king, and Act 4:27
ABOUT THAT TIME King * moved Act 12:1
When * saw how much this pleased Act 12:3
and saved me from * and from what Act 12:11
When * sent for him and found Act 12:19
An appointment with * was Act 12:21
of the Lord struck * with a Act 12:23
of King *), and Paul. Act 13:1

HEROD'S
stayed there until King * death. Mt 2:15
This brutal action of * Mt 2:17
the new king was * son, Archelaus. Mt 2:22
* approval she was powerless. Mk 6:19
It was * birthday and he gave a Mk 6:21
(Chuza was King * business manager Lk 8:3
Galilee was under * jurisdiction; Lk 23:7
sixteen soldiers. * intention was Act 12:4
upon trade with * country. Act 12:20
in the prison at King * palace. Act 23:35

HERODIANS
some of their men along with the * Mt 22:16
The * were a Jewish political Mt 22:16f
went away and met with the * Mk 3:6
Literally, "Pharisees and *." Mk 12:13f

HERODIAS
his wife *, his brother Philip's Mt 14:3
party for Herod, *' daughter Mt 14:6
*, his brother Philip's wife. Mk 6:17,18
Philip's wife. * wanted John Mk 6:19
*' chance finally came. Mk 6:21
Then *' daughter came in and Mk 6:22,23
for marrying *, his brother's wife, Lk 3:19,20

HERODION
Remember me to * my relative. Rom 16:11

HEROES
chose five army * from the cities Ju 18:2
Mighty * have fallen. 2Sa 1:19
These mighty * have fallen in the 2Sa 1:25
greatest * among David's men. 1Ch 11:11
my *, and invite them to my home. Ps 101:6
with a thousand *' shields. Sol 4:4
Woe to those who are "*" when Is 5:22
the atheists, will not be *! Is 32:5
"We are *, mighty men of war"? Jer 48:14

HEROIC
You shall do * deeds and be a 1Sa 26:25
here from the book, * Ballads. 2Sa 1:17,18
Top Three—the most * men in David's 2Sa 23:8
a * soldier from Kabzeel. 2Sa 23:20
and his * achievements and his wars 1Ki 22:45
to Saul, their * warriors went out 1Ch 10:12

HERON
The * (all kinds), Lev 11:13-19
The stork, the * (any variety), Deu 14:11-18

HERSELF
she scoffed to *. Gen 18:12
* said, 'Yes, he is my brother.' Gen 20:5
and covered * with a veil to Gen 38:14
a veil to disguise *, and sat Gen 38:14
and a woman must never give * to Lev 18:23
borne, so that she * can eat them: Deu 28:56,57
she *—replied, Ju 5:29
where she found * belonged to Boaz, Ru 2:3

HERSELF Con't)
a girl will let * be seduced." Pro 30:18,19f
Like a wanton wife who gives * to Jer 3:6
left me and given * to Jer 3:8
she * will perish too. Jer 49:9,10
She indulged * in immorality, and Lam 1:9
their idols, defiling *. Eze 23:7
she longed to give * to the men Eze 23:16
she flaunted * before them and gave Eze 23:18
them and gave * to their lust. Eze 23:18
never again will she raise * Eze 29:15
Therefore because she has set * Eze 31:10
to quit giving * to others. Hos 1:2
All this because Nineveh sold * Nah 3:4
a drunkard and hide * in fear. Nah 3:11
that said to *, "In all the world Zep 2:15
Though Tyre has armed * to the Zec 9:3
For she thought to *, "If I can Mk 5:28
and was unable to straighten *. Lk 13:11
Jezebel, who calls * a prophetess, Rev 2:20
and his bride has prepared *. Rev 19:7

HESHBON
the city of *, which had been King Num 21:25,26
Come to *, Num 21:27-30
at *," the Lord assured him. Num 21:34
*, Elealeh, Sebam, Nebo, and Beon. Num 32:3,4
*, Elealeh, Num 32:37,38
been defeated at *, and King Og of Deu 1:1
King Sihon the Amorite, king of *. Deu 2:24
of * with a proposal of peace. Deu 2:26
King Sihon of the Amorites, at *.' Deu 3:1
Sihon's kingdom at *, killing the Deu 3:6
King Sihon, whose capital was *; Deu 4:44,45,46
King Sihon of * and King Og of Deu 29:7
king of *, and Og, king of Bashan. Jos 9:10
of the Amorites, who lived in *. Jos 12:2
the kingdom of Sihon, king of *. Jos 12:5
who reigned in *, and extended as Jos 13:10
It included * and the other Jos 13:17
who had lived in * and was killed Jos 13:21
It also extended from * to Jos 13:26
of the kingdom of King Sihon of *. Jos 13:27,28
Refuge), Mahanaim, *, and Jazer. Jos 21:38,39
who lived in *, and asked Ju 11:19
the land from * to Aroer, and all Ju 11:26
Gilead, Mahanaim, *, and Jazer, 1Ch 6:81
Sihon of * and King Og of Bashan. Neh 9:22
in * by the gate of Bath-rabbim. Sol 7:4
The cries from the cities of * Is 15:4
of * and the vineyards at Sibmah. Is 16:8
My tears shall flow for * and Is 16:9
her life. In *, plans have been Jer 48:2,3,4
over the land—from * clear across Jer 48:34
They flee to *, unable to go Jer 48:45
But a fire comes from *—Sihon's Jer 48:45
Cry out, O *, for Ai is Jer 49:3

HESHMON
Hazar-gaddah, *, Beth-pelet, Jos 15:21-32

HESITATE
Don't * to answer me if you can. Job 33:5
* to take Mary as your wife! Mt 1:20
And don't * to accept Lk 10:7

HESITATED
When Lot still *, the angels Gen 19:16

HETH
and he was also the father of *; Gen 10:15-19
her body, he said to the men of *: Gen 23:3
to the men of *, and replied to Gen 23:12
of the men of * at the city gate. Gen 23:17,18
by the men of * as a burial plot. Gen 23:19,20
purchased from the sons of *." Gen 49:32
Sidon (his firstborn) and *. 1Ch 1:13-16

HETHITE
son of Zohar, the *, where Sarah, Gen 25:9,10
Judith, daughter of Be-eri the *; Gen 26:34
Basemath, daughter of Elon the *. Gen 26:34
Adah (daughter of Elon the *), Gen 36:2,3
Ephron the * for a burial ground. Gen 49:29,30
of Ephron the *, close to Mamre. Gen 50:12,13

HETHLON
toward *, then on through Labweh Eze 47:15
across to *, then to Labweh, and Eze 48:1

HEW
shall * your way with your sword. Gen 27:39,40

HEWED
of acacia wood and * out two stone Deu 10:3

HEWN
three layers of * stone and one 1Ki 6:36
three courses of * stone in its 1Ki 7:12
* out for himself in Jerusalem. 2Ch 16:13,14
walled up my ways with * stone." Lam 3:9f
Petra, the city * from rocks; Ob 1:1f
a new, unused tomb * into the rock Lk 23:53

HEY
"*, who's that girl over there?" Ru 2:4,5
"* there, Messiah!" Mk 15:32

HEZEKIAH
and his son * became the new king. 2Ki 16:20
NEW KING OF Judah: * 2Ki 18:1
even though, as King * 2Ki 18:4
the reign of King * and the ninth 2Ki 18:10
the reign of King *, King 2Ki 18:13
King * sued for peace and sent 2Ki 18:14
To gather this amount, King * 2Ki 18:15
They demanded that King * come 2Ki 18:18
message to King *: "The great King 2Ki 18:19
'Don't let King * fool you. 2Ki 18:29
Don't listen to King *. 2Ki 18:31,32
Don't listen to King * when he 2Ki 18:31,32
went to King * with their clothes 2Ki 18:37
WHEN KING * heard their report he 2Ki 19:1
"King * says, 'This is a day of 2Ki 19:3
sent back this message to King *: 2Ki 19:9
* took the letter from the 2Ki 19:14
this message to *: "The Lord God 2Ki 19:20
* NOW BECAME deathly sick, and 2Ki 20:1
* turned his face to the wall. 2Ki 20:2
"Go back to *, the leader of my 2Ki 20:5
Isaiah then instructed * to boil 2Ki 20:7
Meanwhile, King * had said to 2Ki 20:8
always moves forward," * replied; 2Ki 20:10
and a present to *, for he had 2Ki 20:12
of his sickness. * welcomed them 2Ki 20:13
Then Isaiah went to King * and 2Ki 20:14
"From far away in Babylon," * 2Ki 20:14
And * replied, "Everything. 2Ki 20:15
Then Isaiah said to *, "Listen 2Ki 20:16
"All right," * replied, "if 2Ki 20:19
The rest of the history of * and 2Ki 20:20
which his father * had destroyed. 2Ki 21:3,4,5
Jotham, Ahaz, *, 1Ch 3:10-14
So during the reign of King * of 1Ch 4:40,41
and his son * became the new king. 2Ch 28:27
* WAS TWENTY-FIVE years old when 2Ch 29:1
reported to King *, "We have 2Ch 29:18
Early the next morning, King * 2Ch 29:20
Then * ordered the burnt 2Ch 29:27
Then King * ordered the Levites 2Ch 29:30
ceremony is now ended," * said. 2Ch 29:31
again. And * and all the people 2Ch 29:36
KING * NOW sent letters throughout 2Ch 30:1
Then King * prayed for them and 2Ch 30:17,18,19
God's rules. But * said, "May the 2Ch 30:17,18,19
(King * spoke very 2Ch 30:22
King * gave the people 1,000 2Ch 30:24
* now organized the priests and 2Ch 31:2
October. When * and his officials 2Ch 31:7,8
* asked the priests and Levites. 2Ch 31:9
* decided to prepare storerooms 2Ch 31:11
* and Azariah the High Priest. 2Ch 31:12,13
In this way King * handled the 2Ch 31:20
good work of King *, King 2Ch 32:1
attack Jerusalem, * summoned his 2Ch 32:3
Then * further strengthened his 2Ch 32:5
* and the citizens of Jerusalem: 2Ch 32:9
King * is trying to persuade you 2Ch 32:11
Don't you realize that * is the 2Ch 32:12
Don't let * fool you! 2Ch 32:15
servant *, heaping up insults. 2Ch 32:16
of * will fail, too," he wrote. 2Ch 32:17
Then King * and Isaiah the 2Ch 32:20
That is how the Lord saved * and 2Ch 32:22
From then on King * became 2Ch 32:23
valuable presents for King *, too. 2Ch 32:23
But about that time * became 2Ch 32:24
However, * didn't respond with 2Ch 32:25
But finally * and the residents 2Ch 32:26
So * became very wealthy and was 2Ch 32:27
The rest of the story of * and 2Ch 32:32
When * died he was buried in the 2Ch 32:33
altars his father * had 2Ch 33:3
Ater (the descendants of *), 98; Ez 2:3-35
From the family of * of the Neh 7:8-38
Ater, *, Azzur, Hodiah, Neh 10:14-27
and copied by the aides of King * Pro 25:1
* lived 200 years after Solomon. Pro 25:1f
and King *—all kings of Judah. Is 1:1
* was seeking a defensive alliance Is 30:2f
confer with King * in Jerusalem. Is 36:2
to go and say to *, "The mighty Is 36:4
"Don't let * fool you—nothing he Is 36:14
Don't listen to *, for here is Is 36:16
Don't let * deprive you of all Is 36:18
not a word, for * had told them to Is 36:21
went back to * with clothes ripped Is 36:22
WHEN KING * heard the results of Is 37:1
brought him this message from *: Is 37:3
"Tell King * that the Lord says, Is 37:6
Jerusalem to * with this message: Is 37:8,9
As soon as King * had read this Is 37:14
message to King *: "The Lord God Is 37:21
Then God said to *, "Here is the Is 37:30
IT WAS JUST before all this that * Is 38:1
When * heard this, he turned his Is 38:2
"Go and tell * that the Lord God Is 38:5
When King * was well again, he Is 38:9
Perhaps * was unaware of the Is 38:18f
And then * had asked, "What sign Is 38:22
* a present and his best wishes, Is 39:1
for he had heard that * had been Is 39:1
was well again. * appreciated this Is 39:2
"From far away in Babylon," * Is 39:3
And * replied, "I showed them Is 39:4
"All right," * replied. Is 39:8
Manasseh, son of *, king of Judah, Jer 15:4
in the days of * (Isaiah 36–37). Jer 21:1f
the days of King * of Judah, he Jer 26:18
But did King * and the people Jer 26:19
This occurred when * entertained Eze 23:16f
*; and one of the kings of Israel, Hos 1:1
and King *, all kings of Judah. Mic 1:1
and great-great-grandson of *). Zep 1:1
Ahaz was the father of *; Mt 1:9
* was the father of Manasseh; Mt 1:10

HEZEKIAH'S
And the Lord listened to * 2Ch 30:20
fall upon them during * lifetime. 2Ch 32:26
year of King * reign, Sennacherib, Is 36:1
(For Isaiah had told * servants, Is 38:21
in * activities in the west. Is 39:1f

HEZIR
Seventeenth, the group led by *; 1Ch 24:7-18
Meshullam, *, Meshezabel, Neh 10:14-27

HEZRO
* from Carmel; 2Sa 23:24-39
* from Carmel; 1Ch 11:26-47

HEZRON
Reuben's sons: Hanoch, Pallu, *, Gen 46:8-14
The sons of Perez were * and Gen 46:8-14
oldest son:Hanoch, Pallu,*, Carmi. Ex 6:14
of the family of *, house of Caleb Ex 17:10f
named after their ancestor *. Num 26:5-11
named after their ancestor *. Num 26:19-22
of Zin to * (south of Jos 15:2,3,4
Perez, *, Ram, Amminadab, Nashon, Ru 4:18-22
* and Hamul. 1Ch 2:5
The sons of * were Jerahmeel, 1Ch 2:9
*) had two wives, 1Ch 2:18
* married Machir's daughter at the 1Ch 2:21
Jerahmeel (the oldest son of *): 1Ch 2:25
Perez, *, Carmi, Hur, 1Ch 4:1
Hanoch, Pallu, *, Carmi. 1Ch 5:3
Perez was the father of *; Mt 1:3
Perez was the father of Hezron; * Mt 1:3
Arni's father was *; Lk 3:23-38

HEZRON'S
Soon after his father * death, 1Ch 2:24
Arni's father was Hezron;* father Lk 3:23-38

HEZRONITES
The *, named after their ancestor Num 26:5-11
The *, named after their ancestor Num 26:19-22

HID
and they * themselves among the Gen 3:8
you to see me naked. So I *." Gen 3:10
* him at home for three months. Ex 2:1
and * his body in the sand. Ex 2:12
because she * the spies sent to Jos 6:25
and * in a cave at Makkedah. Jos 10:16
inches long and * it in his Ju 3:16
Jotham, who escaped and *. Ju 9:5
So David * himself in the field. 1Sa 20:24,25
where a man * them inside a well in 2Sa 17:18
prophets, and I * a hundred of them 1Ki 18:13
into the city and * in the inner 1Ki 20:30
Then he * the money in his house. 2Ki 5:24
so we can eat him,' she * him." 2Ki 6:26-30
to be slain, and * him and his 2Ki 11:2,3
and his four sons ran and *. 1Ch 21:19,20
For it is * from the eyes of all Job 28:21
So I did; I * it as the Lord had Jer 13:5
Then the officials * the Jer 36:20
But the Lord * them! Jer 36:26
are obscured and the stars are *. Joe 2:10
and * the money for safekeeping. Mt 25:18
so I * your money in the earth Mt 25:24,25
His parents * him at home for Act 7:20
and they * him for three months, Heb 11:23
she did when she * those messengers Jas 2:25
slave and free, * themselves in the Rev 6:15

HIDDAI
* from the brooks of Gaash; 2Sa 23:24-39

HIDDEN
But she had * them, so she told Jos 2:4
up to the roof and * them beneath Jos 2:6
have * it among their belongings. Jos 7:10,11
them, and they are * in the ground Jos 7:21
the stolen goods * there just as Jos 7:22
he has probably already * in 2Sa 17:9
Literally, "there was nothing * 1Ki 10:3f
Obadiah had * one hundred of them 1Ki 18:3,4
camp and have * in the fields, 2Ki 7:12
Nothing was * from him; 2Ch 9:2
and was * away in a storage room 2Ch 22:11
Joash remained * in the Temple 2Ch 22:12
the light the things that are *." Job 28:11f
the lotus plants, * by the reeds, Job 40:21
Cleanse me from these * faults. Ps 19:12
* in my heart, but have Ps 40:10
I could have * and escaped. Ps 55:12
for lost money or * treasure, then Pro 2:3,4,5
exposing his * motives. Pro 20:27
Open rebuke is better than * Pro 27:5
every * thing, good or bad. Ecc 12:14

(HIDDEN Con't)
And I will give you treasures * Is 45:3
He has * me in the shadow of his Is 49:2
and * you safe within my hand. Is 51:16
idols that are * behind a tree in Is 66:17
out of the hole where I had * it. Jer 13:7
they have * traps along my path. Jer 18:22
oil and honey they had * away. Jer 41:8
upon these stones that I have *. Jer 43:10
and uncovered a door to a * room. Eze 8:8
for no secret is * from you. Eze 28:2,3
He knows all * things, for he is Dan 2:22
I will explain mysteries * since Mt 13:34,35
* to those outside the Kingdom: Mk 4:11,12
"All that is now * will someday Mk 4:22
evil deeds from his * wickedness. Lk 6:45
For you are like * graves in a Lk 11:44
But such hypocrisy cannot be * Lk 12:1
But Jesus was * from them, and Jn 8:59
went away and was * from them. Jn 12:36
no longer keep him *, and had to Act 7:21
desires that are * there—if the law Rom 7:7
This plan was * in former times, 1Co 2:7
If the Good News we preach is * 2Co 4:3
to anyone, it is * from the one who 2Co 4:3
In him lie * all the mighty, Col 2:3
is the * Source of their faith. 1Ti 3:9
nothing can be * from him to whom Heb 4:13
shall eat of the * manna, the Rev 2:17

HIDE
"Should I * my plan from Gen 18:17
a strip of the * around his neck; Gen 27:16
Then, when she could no longer * Ex 2:3
also be given the animal's *. Lev 7:8
bull, with its * and dung, was Lev 8:17
the meat and * outside the camp. Lev 9:11
*, meat, blood, and dung. Num 19:5
to drive out those who * from you! Deu 7:20
She will * from them the Deu 28:56,57
she told them. "* there for three Jos 2:16
bravest troops to * in ambush close Jos 8:3,4
Come by night with an army and * Ju 9:32
wives, "Go and * in the vineyards, Ju 21:20
And may God punish you if you * 1Sa 3:16,17
and tried to * in caves, thickets, 1Sa 13:6
* something like this from me. 1Sa 20:2
but tomorrow I'll * in the field 1Sa 20:5
* it from the cities of Gath and 2Sa 1:20
I will * in God, 2Sa 22:3
He shields all who * behind him. 2Sa 22:31
to the east and * by Cherith Brook 1Ki 17:3
"Let us * in the Temple and bolt Neh 6:10
Oh, that you would * me with the Job 14:13
Shall we all go and *? Job 18:4
I have tried to * my sins, fearing Job 31:33
No darkness is thick enough to * Job 34:22
The wild animals * in the rocks Job 37:8
Will his * be hurt by darts, or Job 41:7
Who can penetrate his *, or who Job 41:13
Why do you * when I need you the Ps 10:1
pupil of your eye; * me in the Ps 17:8
He is a rugged mountain where I * Ps 18:2
and nothing can * from its heat. Ps 19:6
He will * me. Ps 27:5
Oh, do not * yourself when I am Ps 27:9
* your loved ones in the shelter Ps 31:20
you and stopped trying to * them. Ps 32:5
think they can * their evil deeds Ps 36:2
don't * yourself when I cry to Ps 55:1
their plans; they * beside the Ps 56:6
I will * beneath the shadow of Ps 57:1
Don't * from me, Ps 69:17
Will you * yourself from me Ps 89:46
mighty Rock where I can *. Ps 94:21,22
Though the wicked * along the Ps 119:95
If I try to * in the darkness, Ps 139:11
For even darkness cannot * from Ps 139:12
O Lord, I run to you to * me. Ps 143:9
"We'll * and rob and kill," Pro 1:11
Pretty words may * a wicked Pro 26:23
in the rocks and * in terror from Is 2:10
the caverns to * among the jagged Is 2:21
you; * them from our enemies! Is 16:4,5
save you—the Rock who can * you; Is 17:10
O caravans from Dedam, you will * Is 21:13
lock the doors! * for a little Is 26:20
The earth will no longer * the Is 26:21
Woe to those who try to * their Is 29:15
I do not * from shame—they spit Is 50:6
are cold and don't * from relatives Is 58:7
What bride will seek to * her Jer 2:32
The people * in the bushes and Jer 4:29
the world shall * before his Jer 10:10
and * it in a hole in the rocks. Jer 13:4
You cannot hope to * from me. Jer 16:17
Can anyone * from me? Jer 23:24
And you will find no place to *, Jer 25:35
"You and Jeremiah both *," the Jer 36:19
"and don't try to * the truth." Jer 38:14
I will * nothing from you." Jer 42:4
Flee for your lives; * in the Jer 48:6
and there will be no place to *. Jer 49:9,10
If we * in the wilderness, they Lam 4:19
and sandals made of dolphin *. Eze 16:9,10
And I will never * my face from Eze 39:29
ran to *, and I was left alone. Dan 10:7
Though they * among the rocks at Amo 9:3
Though they * at the bottom of Amo 9:3
the ship to * there from the Lord. Jon 1:3
a drunkard and * herself in fear. Nah 3:11
Don't * your light! Mt 5:15,16
For you * the truth from the Lk 11:52
"You can't be famous when you * Jn 7:4
will be no place to *. 1Th 5:3
pleaded, "and * us from the face Rev 6:16
but they found no place to *. Rev 20:11

HIDEAWAY
altar, which was near Joash's *. 2Ki 11:11

HIDEOUS
lizards and * creatures, besides Eze 8:10

HIDEOUT
you, so be at the * where you were 1Sa 20:19

HIDES
the * and internal organs. Lev 16:27
there, too, he * himself. Job 23:9
He is a shield for everyone who * Ps 18:30
where the thunder *. Ps 81:7
She groans and * her face. Lam 1:8
"No one lights a lamp and * it! Lk 11:33

HIDING
called to Adam, "Why are you *?" Gen 3:9
and springs out of * and kills him, Deu 19:11
will abandon them, * my face from Deu 31:17
thousand men already * there. Jos 8:11,12,13f
the cave where they had been *; Jos 10:27
he was * from the Midianites. Ju 6:11
into three groups * in the fields. Ju 9:43
* places and began killing them. Ju 9:43
Some men were * in the next Ju 16:9
The men were * in the next room, Ju 16:12
And the Lord replied, "He is * in 1Sa 10:22
Finally even the men * in the 1Sa 14:22
find a * place out in the fields. 1Sa 19:2
where he had been * near the south 1Sa 20:41
"We know where he is *," they 1Sa 23:19
Discover his * places and then 1Sa 23:23
and his men were * in the cave! 1Sa 24:3
and was * on Hachilah Hill. 1Sa 26:1
where David was *, but David knew 1Sa 26:3,4
From their * places. 2Sa 22:46
yourself * in an inner room." 1Ki 22:25
and gold and clothing and * it. 2Ki 7:8
were discovered * in the city, 2Ki 25:19
went to David while he was * in 1Ch 11:15
while he was * from King Saul. 1Ch 12:1
you are * in an inner room!" 2Ch 18:24
they found him * in the city of 2Ch 22:9
who was still in * at the Temple. 2Ch 23:2,3
How long must I be * daily Ps 13:2
lions * and waiting their chance. Ps 17:12
You are my * place from every Ps 32:7
A Psalm of David when he was * in Ps 63:1
they are * on Mount Hermon's Ps 68:22
Literally, "in the * place of Ps 81:7f
"My dove is * behind some rocks, Sol 2:14
to help us, though he is * now. Is 8:17
man who waits in * to beat up the Is 29:21
like a hunter * in a blind. Jer 5:26
where you are * from my wrath. Jer 16:16
weep and wail, * in the hedges, Jer 49:3
other men of importance found *. Jer 52:24,25
as mourning doves * on the Eze 7:16
thank you for * the truth from Mt 11:25
Or, that he is * at a certain Mt 24:26
and earth, for * these things from Lk 10:21
There are more than forty men * Act 23:21
mountains, * in dens and caves. Heb 11:37,38

HIEL
(It was during his reign that *, 1Ki 16:34

HIERAPOLIS
the Christians in Laodicea and *. Col 4:13

HIGGAION
The Hebrew text adds here: "*. Ps 9:16f

HIGH
long, 75 feet wide, and 45 feet *. Gen 6:15
the boat * above the earth. Gen 7:17
covered all the * mountains under Gen 7:19
for the water was still too *. Gen 8:9
into a family of * nobility, his Gen 41:45f
brought me to this * position I Gen 50:20
long, 2¼ feet wide, and 2¼ feet *. Ex 25:10
long, 1½ feet wide, and 2¼ feet *. Ex 25:23
being fifteen feet * and 2¼ feet Ex 26:15,16
7½ feet wide, and three feet *. Ex 27:1
*, made from fine-twined linen. Ex 27:18
and used by the * Priest to Ex 28:30,31f
Whoever is the next * Priest Ex 29:30
and three feet *, with horns carved Ex 30:2
long, 2¼ feet wide, and 2¼ feet *. Ex 37:1
long, 1½ feet wide and 2¼ feet *. Ex 37:10
A rim four inches * was Ex 37:12
and three feet *, with its Ex 37:25
square at the top, and 4½ feet *. Ex 38:1
by the anointed * Priest, Lev 16:32
"The * Priest—anointed with the Lev 21:10
applied to the * Priest, while the Lev 21:11f
"Every Sabbath day the * Priest Lev 24:5-8
years away, the price will be *; Lev 25:14,15,16
has knowledge from the Most *; Num 24:15-19
until the death of the * Priest. Num 35:25
until the death of the * Priest. Num 35:28
But after the death of the * Num 35:28
before the death of the * Priest. Num 35:32
their cities rise * into the sky! Deu 1:28
with * walls and barred gates. Deu 3:5
They live in * walled cities. Deu 9:1
I lifted the tablets * above my Deu 9:17
you find them—* in the mountains, Deu 12:2
the death of the * Priest who was Jos 20:6
In this delegation were ten * Jos 22:14
of Manasseh to these * officials: Jos 22:21
the priest and the * officials Jos 22:30
he is held in * honor by all the 1Sa 9:6
that they stank to * heaven as far 1Sa 13:3,4
Abiathar) were the * Priests, and 2Sa 8:17
My refuge and * tower. 2Sa 22:3
Azariah (son of Zadok) was the * 1Ki 4:1
feet wide, and forty-five feet *. 1Ki 6:2
These rooms were three stories * 1Ki 6:6
story of the annex was 7½ feet *. 1Ki 6:10
feet wide, and thirty feet *. 1Ki 6:20
olive wood, each fifteen feet *. 1Ki 6:23-28
long, 75 feet wide, and 45 feet *. 1Ki 7:2
twenty-seven feet * and eighteen 1Ki 7:15
each 7½ feet *, and 6 feet wide. 1Ki 7:16-22
* and 15 feet from brim to brim; 1Ki 7:23
each 6 feet square and 4½ feet *. 1Ki 7:27-30
stand was a round piece 1½ feet *. 1Ki 7:31
inches *, and were similar to 1Ki 7:32
* hill and under every green tree. 1Ki 14:23
THE KING OF Syria had * admiration 2Ki 5:1
the wife of Jehoiada the * Priest. 2Ki 11:2,3f
the * Priest instructed him. 2Ki 12:2
secretary and the * Priest counted 2Ki 12:10
Literally, "built them * places 2Ki 17:9f
on your throne * above the angels, 2Ki 19:15
to Hilkiah, the * Priest: 2Ki 22:3,4
One day Hilkiah the * Priest went 2Ki 22:8
Hilkiah the * Priest and the rest 2Ki 23:4
Literally, "the priests of the * 2Ki 23:9f
twenty-seven feet *, with an 2Ki 25:17
Azariah (the * Priest in Solomon's 1Ch 6:4-15
as * or higher than The Thirty); 1Ch 12:3-7
and Abiathar, the * Priests, and 1Ch 15:11
of Israel and the * officers of the 1Ch 15:25
famous men and * officials of the 1Ch 24:5
(He was the son of Jehoiada the * 1Ch 27:5,6
The roof was 180 feet *. 2Ch 3:4
pillars 52½ feet *, topped by a 2Ch 3:15
feet wide, and fifteen feet *. 2Ch 4:1
7½ feet square and 4½ feet *. 2Ch 6:12,13
Literally, "* places." 2Ch 16:1f
Then he appointed Amariah, the * 2Ch 19:11
for Jehoiada, the * Priest, and 2Ch 24:6
of the * Priest counted the money, 2Ch 24:11
Azariah the * Priest went in 2Ch 26:17,18
And Azariah the * Priest from the 2Ch 31:10
Hezekiah and Azariah the * Priest. 2Ch 31:12,13
Hill, where it was built very *. 2Ch 33:14
to Hilkiah the * Priest for 2Ch 34:9
One day when Hilkiah, the * 2Ch 34:14
including the * Priests, worshiped 2Ch 36:14
THEN ELIASHIB THE * Priest and the Neh 3:1
the home of Eliashib the * Priest. Neh 3:20
served under the * Priest Joiakim: Neh 12:12-21
of Eliashib the * Priest) was a Neh 13:28
king was feeling *, half drunk from Est 1:10
* officials of Media-Persia. Est 1:13-15
as heaven is *—but who are you? Job 11:8
my Advocate is there on *. Job 16:19
Look up there into the sky, * Job 35:5
the eagle rises * upon the cliffs Job 39:27
* above them, judging their sins. Ps 7:7,8
Literally, "O Most *." Ps 9:2f
his debtors with * interest rates, Ps 15:5
He will set me on a * rock out Ps 27:5
* above the plains for all to Ps 48:2
in her palaces for a * tower." Ps 48:3f
LISTEN, EVERYONE! * and low, rich Ps 49:1
Show your glory * above the Ps 57:5
JUSTICE? YOU * and mighty Ps 58:1
For you have been my * tower of Ps 59:16
for you are my * tower of safety, Ps 59:17
For you are my refuge, a * tower Ps 61:3
his holy temple * upon Mount Zion. Ps 68:17
Pile their sins * and do not Ps 69:27
hand of the Most * has changed." Ps 77:10f
and "sons of the Most *." Ps 82:6
* ON HIS holy mountain stands Ps 87:1
Your right hand is lifted * in Ps 89:13
in the firs. * in the mountains Ps 104:18
the waves rise *. Ps 107:25
beyond measure, * as the heavens. Ps 108:4

(HIGH Con't)
For he is * above the nations; Ps 113:4
compared with God enthroned on *? Ps 113:5
My troubles pile * among these Ps 120:5,6
O Israel, bless Jehovah! * Ps 135:19
Praise him, vapors * above the Ps 148:4
earth and fields, and * plateaus. Pro 8:26
defense, a * wall of safety. Pro 18:11
low, and all the * mountains and Is 2:14
hills, and every * tower and wall, Is 2:15
be deep as Sheol or * as heaven." Is 7:11f
heavens and be like the Most *." Is 14:14
you down from your * position. Is 22:19
evil works. The * walls of Moab Is 25:12
it is piled * with wood. Is 30:33
Such as these shall dwell on *. Is 33:16
up rivers for them on * plateaus! Is 41:18
Look * in the skies and watch Is 51:6
The * and lofty one who inhabits Is 57:15
I live in that * and holy place Is 57:15
it that you ride *, and get your Is 58:14
I hear voices * upon the Jer 3:21
search * and low and see if you Jer 5:1
army against a * city wall. Jer 15:20
beneath each tree, * in the Jer 17:2,3
throne, eternal, * and glorious. Jer 17:12
The snow never melts * up in the Jer 18:14
They have built * altars to Baal Jer 19:5
When the * officials of Judah Jer 26:10
And they have built * altars to Jer 32:35
For my anger rose * against them Jer 44:2,3
and her * gates shall be burned; Jer 51:58
twenty-seven feet * and eighteen Jer 52:21
He has shut me into a place of * Lam 3:9
For * in the sky above them was Eze 1:26
who cuts down the * trees and Eze 17:24
every * hill and under every tree! Eze 20:27,28
of * rank, riding their steeds. Eze 23:23
its head * up among the clouds. Eze 31:2,3
has set herself so * above the Eze 31:10
pasture on the * hills of Israel. Eze 34:14
with hand held *, that those Eze 36:7
set me down on a * mountain where I Eze 40:2
is 10½ feet * and 10½ feet wide." Eze 40:5
inches * and eighteen inches wide. Eze 40:7-12
the porch to be about 100 feet *. Eze 40:14
2⅝ feet square and 1¾ feet *. Eze 40:42
was 3½ feet square, and 5¼ feet *; Eze 41:22
The base is twenty-one inches *, Eze 43:13
is a stone platform 3½ feet *. Eze 43:14
on all sides, and seven feet *. Eze 43:14
statue ninety feet * and nine feet Dan 3:1
servants of the Most * God! Dan 3:26
that the Most * God did to me. Dan 4:2
that the Most * dominates the Dan 4:17
so tall, reaching * into the Dan 4:20
"Your Majesty, the Most * God Dan 4:24
that the Most * God dominates the Dan 4:25
worshiped the Most * God and Dan 4:34
Your Majesty, the Most * God Dan 5:18
knew that the Most * overrules the Dan 5:21
people of the Most * God shall rule Dan 7:18
He will defy the Most * God, and Dan 7:25
of the saints of the Most *." Dan 7:27f
Menelaus, the * Priest, who Dan 11:32f
to heaven, to the Most * God. Hos 7:16
The threshing floors will pile * Joe 2:24
in those *, inaccessible cliffs. Ob 1:3
Though you soar as * as eagles, Ob 1:4
Literally, "and lifts * its Hab 3:10f
the mighty waters piled *. Hab 3:15
walls 100 feet * and so thick that Zep 2:15f
of Josedech), the * Priest—for it Hag 1:1
of Josedech), the * Priest, and the Hag 1:12
the governor and * Priest and Hag 2:2
vision) Joshua the * Priest Zec 3:1
Listen to me, O Joshua the * Zec 3:8
*, can stand before Zerubbabel! Zec 4:7
flew off with it, * in the sky. Zec 5:9
(son of Josedech) the * Priest. Zec 6:10,11
the peak of a very * mountain and Mt 4:8
was in bed with a * fever. Mt 8:14
around at the * waves, he was Mt 14:30
to the top of a * and lonely hill, Mt 17:1
of Caiaphas the * Priest, to Mt 26:3
the ear of the * Priest's servant. Mt 26:51
of Caiaphas the * Priest, where all Mt 26:57
courtyard of the * Priest's house Mt 26:58
Then the * Priest stood up and Mt 26:62
Then the * Priest said to him, "I Mt 26:63
Then the * Priest tore at his own Mt 26:65,66
sick in bed with a * fever. Mk 1:29,30
God—Abiathar was * Priest then—and Mk 2:25,26
storm arose. * waves began to break Mk 4:37
me, Jesus, Son of the Most * God? Mk 5:7,8
and slashed at the * Priest's Mk 14:47
Jesus was led to the * Priest's Mk 14:53
the gates of the * Priest's Mk 14:54
Then the * Priest stood up before Mk 14:60
Then the * Priest asked him. Mk 14:61
Then the * Priest tore at his Mk 14:63,64
who worked for the * Priest noticed Mk 14:66,67
and Annas and Caiaphas were * Lk 3:1
to Jerusalem to a * roof of the Lk 4:9,10,11
very sick with a * fever. Lk 4:38
with me, Jesus, Son of God Most *? Lk 8:28
until it has risen * and light." Lk 13:20,21
slashed at the * Priest's servant, Lk 22:50
and led him to the * Priest's Lk 22:54
Caiaphas, who was * Priest that Jn 11:49
in his position as * Priest—he Jn 11:51
Malchus, the * Priest's servant. Jn 18:10
Caiaphas, the * Priest that year. Jn 18:13
was acquainted with the * Priest. Jn 18:15
Inside, the * Priest began asking Jn 18:19
"Is that the way to answer the * Jn 18:22
bound, to Caiaphas the * Priest. Jn 18:24
slaves of the * Priest—a relative Jn 18:26
a new * of about 5,000 men! Act 4:4
Annas the * Priest was there, and Act 4:6
of the * Priest's relatives. Act 4:6
The * Priest and his relatives Act 5:17
the * Priest and his courtiers Act 5:21
the * Priest demanded. Act 5:28
THEN THE * Priest asked him, "Are Act 7:1
went to the * Priest in Jerusalem. Act 9:1
to prison. The * Priest or any Act 22:5
Instantly Ananias the * Priest Act 23:2
way to talk to God's * Priest?" Act 23:4
"I didn't realize he was the * Act 23:5
FIVE DAYS LATER Ananias the * Act 24:1
as authorized by the * Priests; Act 26:10
to hold our heads * no matter what Rom 5:5
or where we are—* above the sky, Rom 8:39
profound words and * sounding 1Co 1:17
and how * his love really is; Eph 3:18,19
are in places of * responsibility, 1Ti 2:2
and holds * the truth of God. 1Ti 3:15
and faithful * Priest before God, a Heb 2:17
and the * Priest of our faith. Heb 3:1
who appointed him * Priest, just as Heb 3:2
God is our great * Priest who has Heb 4:14
This * Priest of ours Heb 4:15
THE JEWISH * priest is merely a Heb 5:1
no one can be a * priest just Heb 5:4
to the honor of being * Priest; Heb 5:5
chosen him to be a * Priest with Heb 5:10
Literally, "having become our * Heb 6:20f
our * Priest, with the honor and Heb 6:20
also a priest of the Most * God. Heb 7:1
Christ, the new * Priest who came Heb 7:15
the kind of * Priest we need; Heb 7:26
Under the old system, even the * Heb 7:28
described, is our * Priest, and is Heb 8:1
And since every * priest is Heb 8:3
But only the * priest went into Heb 9:7
He came as * Priest of this Heb 9:11
and again, as the * priest down Heb 9:25
And since this great * Priest of Heb 10:21
of Jewish laws the * priest brought Heb 13:11
long and as * as a horse's bridle. Rev 14:20
For her sins are piled as * as Rev 18:5
Its walls were broad and *, with Rev 21:12

HIGH-RANKING
Each was a * officer of Manasseh's 1Ch 12:20
and rich men, and * military Rev 6:15

HIGHER
As the water rose * and higher Gen 7:18
As the water rose higher and * Gen 7:18
as high or * than The Thirty); 1Ch 12:3-7
our sins are piled * than our heads Ez 9:6
"God is so great—* than the Job 22:12
the heavens, * than the stars. Job 22:12
They are like a flood, * than my Ps 38:3,4
to solve are piled * than my head. Ps 40:12
Your faithfulness is * than the Ps 57:10
his grain for * prices, but they Pro 11:26
under orders from * up, and the Ecc 5:8
higher up, and the * officials look Ecc 5:8
Literally, "and there are yet * Ecc 5:8f
properly used this * meaning, Is 7:14f
For just as the heavens are * Is 55:9
so are my ways * than yours, and my Is 55:9
though it be * than the clouds, for Eze 31:14
of the Temple wall as it rose *. Eze 41:7
a field, growing * and higher into Dan 4:10,11
growing higher and * into the sky Dan 4:10,11
up, with waves * than the boat. Mt 8:24
who has far * authority than mine; Lk 3:16
'If his bill runs * than that,' Lk 10:35
went * into the mountains alone. Jn 6:15
The next day as the seas grew *, Act 27:18

HIGHEST
feet and more above the * peaks. Gen 7:20
of the God of * Heaven, brought him Gen 14:18
Earth and * heaven belong to the Deu 10:14
knock down your * walls—the walls Deu 28:52
Why, even the skies and the * 1Ki 8:27
have conquered the * mountains, 2Ki 19:23
Not even the * heaven would be 2Ch 2:6
That would be your * wisdom. Job 13:5
their mouths. The * officials of Job 29:10
He is my food and drink, my * Ps 16:5
He hears me from * heaven and Ps 20:6
Yes, sing your * praises to our Ps 47:6,7
Lord, be exalted above the * Ps 57:5
* slopes and deep within the sea! Ps 68:22
Lord, reach to the * heavens. Ps 71:19
But someday the * honor will be Ps 87:5
is anything like him? The * of Ps 89:7
my * joy, let me never sing again. Ps 137:5,6
as the * of the mountains." Is 2:2f
I will take the * throne. Is 14:13
I will climb to the * heavens Is 14:14
or three in the * branches, four or Is 17:6
I conquered their * mountains and Is 37:24
things beyond our * expectations, Is 64:3
our fuel is sold to us at the * Lam 5:4
the top of the * cedar, and I, Eze 17:22,23
on the top of Israel's * mountain. Eze 17:22,23
it smells to * heaven.' Jon 1:2
"Praise God in * heaven!" Mt 21:9
"Glory to God in the * heaven," Lk 2:14
Glory to God in the * heavens!" Lk 19:38
the * rank [in the coming Kingdom Lk 22:24
of * honor in heaven, next to God. Act 2:33
but all had the * regard for them. Act 5:13
into this place of * privilege Rom 5:2
at the place of * honor next to Rom 8:34
I have the * confidence in you, 2Co 7:4
went beyond our * hopes, for their 2Co 8:5
beyond our * prayers, desires, Eph 3:20
the very lowest to the very *. Eph 4:10
He is the * Ruler, with authority Col 2:10
can use you for his * purposes. 2Ti 2:21
then sat down in * honor beside the Heb 1:3
in the place of * honor at God's Heb 10:12

HIGHEST-RANKING
"The Thirty" were the * officers 1Ch 11:15f
thirty * officers in David's army. 1Ch 27:5,6

HIGHLAND
the land, even on the * plains; Ps 72:16

HIGHLANDS
whose area was the * of Dor; 1Ki 4:8-19
and the * of heaven far away. Is 33:17
the land, yes, and in the *, too; Hag 1:11
hurried to the * of Judea to the Lk 1:39,40

HIGHLY
was * respected and very popular. Gen 34:18,19
He is * capable as an artistic Ex 31:4
Moses too was * displeased. Num 11:10
evidently was * decorated with Ju 8:27f
bodyguard and a * honored member of 1Sa 22:14
is great, and should be * praised; 1Ch 16:25
all trained and * skilled in the 2Ch 25:5,6
very wealthy and was * honored. 2Ch 32:27
and they were * honored. Neh 11:2
He is * honored everywhere. Ps 47:9
he shall be * exalted. Is 52:13
And Capernaum, though * honored, Mt 11:23
* honored by Christ's being there. Mt 11:23f
The paraphrase is of course * Mt 13:52f
Just at that time the * prized Lk 7:2
and some who are * thought of now Lk 13:30
* regarded by both God and man. Lk 24:19
He was * displeased with the Act 12:20
with him, who is * praised as a 2Co 8:18
to think more * of me than he 2Co 12:6
Think * of them and give them 1Th 5:13
well and should be * appreciated, 1Ti 5:17
is this Son of Man you honor so *? Heb 2:6
itself, speaks * of Demetrius. 3Jn 1:12

HIGHWAY
and they camped along the * 2Ki 18:17
He will make a * from Assyria Is 11:16
will be connected by a *, and the Is 19:23
it will be named "The Holy *." Is 35:8
Prepare a glorious * for my Is 57:14
the narrow gate! The * to hell Mt 7:13

HIGHWAYS
for them; the * shall be raised Is 49:11
from the ancient * of good, and Jer 18:15

HIKE
can't be counted! * in all Gen 13:17

HIKED
their son. She * out into the Gen 21:14

HILAKKU
known from Assyrian records as *. Eze 27:11f

HILEN
Libnah, Jattir, Eshtemoa, *, 1Ch 6:58,59

HILKIAH
Then Eliakim (son of *) the 2Ki 18:37
instruction to *, the High Priest: 2Ki 22:3,4
One day * the High Priest went to 2Ki 22:8
mentioned the scroll found by *. 2Ki 22:9,10
He commanded * the priest, and 2Ki 22:12,13
So * the priest, and Ahikam, and 2Ki 22:14
Then the king instructed * the 2Ki 23:4
in the book that * the priest had 2Ki 23:24
*, the father of 1Ch 6:4-15
Amaziah, *, Amzi, Bani, Shemer, 1Ch 6:44-47
Azariah (the son of *, son of 1Ch 9:10,11
*, the second; 1Ch 26:11

(HILKIAH Con't)
The money was taken to * the High 2Ch 34:9
One day when *, the High Priest, 2Ch 34:14
"Look!" * exclaimed to Shaphan, 2Ch 34:15,16
These are the laws of God!" * 2Ch 34:15,16
and how * had discovered it. 2Ch 34:18
and summoned *, Ahikam (son of 2Ch 34:20
and Levites. *, Zechariah, and 2Ch 35:8
Azariah was the son of *; Ez 7:1
* was the son of Shallum; Ez 7:1
Anaiah, Uriah, *, and Ma-aseiah. Neh 8:1
Seraiah (son of *, son of Neh 11:10-14
*, Jedaiah. Neh 12:1
Hashabiah, leader of the * clan; Neh 12:12-21
the son of *, to replace you. Is 22:20
Then Eliakim (son of *), the Is 36:22
priest (the son of *) who lived in Jer 1:1
Gemariah (son of *) when they went Jer 29:3

HILKIAH'S
Then Eliakim, * son, who was the Is 36:3

HILL
at the top of the *, with the rod Ex 17:9
went to the top of the *. Ex 17:10
northward into the * country of the Num 13:17
while in the * country there are Num 13:29
But they went ahead into the * Num 14:44
Now go and occupy the * country Deu 1:7
on up into the * country to fight. Deu 1:43
all the Mount Seir * country as Deu 2:5
River and the * country cities, the Deu 2:37
named "The * of the Foreskins." Jos 5:2,3
racing down the * to Beth-horon, Jos 10:11
and kings of the * country, the Jos 10:40
All the kings of the northern * Jos 11:1
The kings in the Jebusite * Jos 11:1
entire land—the * country, the Jos 11:16
who lived in the * country in Jos 11:21
The area included the * country, Jos 12:8-24
All the * country from Lebanon to Jos 13:2-7
you give me the * country which the Jos 14:12
shoulder of the * north of Ekron, Jos 15:10,11
cities in the * country with Jos 15:48-62
and the * country to Bethel. Jos 16:1
"If the * country of Ephraim is Jos 17:15
west through the * country and the Jos 18:12
in the * country south of Lower Jos 18:13
He chose Timnath-serah in the * Jos 19:50
in the * country of Naphtali; Jos 20:7
Shechem, in the * country of Jos 20:7
Hebron) in the * country of Judah. Jos 20:7
in the * country of Ephraim, on the Jos 24:30
he was buried in the * country of Jos 24:33
Canaanites in the * country and in Ju 1:9
the people of the * country, though Ju 1:19
them into the * country and Ju 1:34
in the * country of Ephraim, north Ju 2:7-9
When he arrived in the * country Ju 3:27
in the * country of Ephraim; Ju 4:5
*, laying the stones carefully. Ju 6:26
the valley beside the * of Moreh. Ju 7:1
throughout the * country of Ephraim Ju 7:24
in the * country of Ephraim. Ju 10:1
the * country of the Amalekites. Ju 12:15
called "Jawbone *" ever since. Ju 15:16,17
IN THE * country of Ephraim lived Ju 17:1
Arriving in the * country of Ju 18:2
up into the * country of Ephraim. Ju 18:13
far side of the * country of Ju 19:1
(He was originally from the * Ju 19:16
Ephraim * country, near Shiloh. Ju 19:18
They traveled all through the * 1Sa 9:4
As they were climbing a * toward 1Sa 9:9,10,11
in a public sacrifice up on the *. 1Sa 9:12,13
out toward them to go up the *. 1Sa 9:14
"Go on up the * ahead of me and 1Sa 9:19
known as "God's *," where the 1Sa 10:5
coming down the * playing a 1Sa 10:5
arrived at the * of God they saw 1Sa 10:10
he climbed the * to the altar. 1Sa 10:13
caves in the * country of Ziph. 1Sa 23:14,15
Horesh on Hachilah *, down in the 1Sa 23:19
and was hiding on Hachilah *. 1Sa 26:1
arrived at Ammah * near Giah, along 2Sa 2:24
at the top of the *, and Abner 2Sa 2:25
the road at the side of the *. 2Sa 13:34
the top of the * when Ziba, the 2Sa 16:1
Sheba from the * country of 2Sa 20:21
was the * country of Ephraim; 1Ki 4:8-19
in the * country, and thirty-three 1Ki 5:15
of Shechem in the * country of 1Ki 12:25
high * and under every green tree. 1Ki 14:23
Then Omri bought the * now known 1Ki 16:24
found him sitting on top of a *. 2Ki 1:9
But when they arrived at the * 2Ki 5:24
* and under every green tree; 2Ki 17:10
of the Lord on the * of Gibeon 1Ch 16:39
were on the * of Gibeon, but David 1Ch 21:29
He led them up to the * to the 2Ch 1:2,3
returned down the *, and went back 2Ch 1:13
Zemaraim, in the * country of 2Ch 13:4
captured in the * country of 2Ch 15:8
Beer-sheba to the * country of 2Ch 19:4
* where the Temple was situated. 2Ch 27:3
And he built cities in the * 2Ch 27:4
*, where it was built very high. 2Ch 33:14
your tabernacle up on your holy *? Ps 15:1
I am slipping down the * to Ps 109:22,23
and to the * of frankincense. Sol 4:6
a vineyard on a very fertile *. Is 5:1
down each mountain and every *. Is 30:25
On every * and under every tree Jer 2:20
every *, beneath every shady tree. Jer 3:6
God said: 'This * shall be plowed Jer 26:18
of righteousness, O holy *!" Jer 31:23
and from the * of Gareb at the Jer 31:38,39
Judah and in the * country, in the Jer 32:44
altars on every * and mountain and Eze 6:13
every high * and under every tree! Eze 20:27,28
towers and make a * against the Eze 21:22
homes around my * a blessing. Eze 34:26
The entire top of the * where the Eze 43:12
occupy the * country of Edom; Ob 1:19
fire, like water pouring down a *. Mic 1:4
of the * where the city is built. Zep 1:10
light—a city on a *, glowing in the Mt 5:14
and climbed a * and sat there. Mt 15:29
a high and lonely *, and as they Mt 17:1
the bottom of the *, a huge crowd Mt 17:14
that is, "Skull *," where the Mt 27:33
around on the * above the lake. Mk 5:11
to the edge of the * on which the Lk 4:29
descended from the *, a huge crowd Lk 9:37
into the rock [at the side of a * Lk 23:53
climbing the *, looking for him. Jn 6:2-5
him to the forum at Mars *. Act 17:19
them at the Mars * forum, addressed Act 17:22

HILLEL
Next was Abdon (son of *) from Ju 12:13

HILLS
Mesha to the eastern * of Sephar. Gen 10:26-30
bounds of the everlasting *. Gen 49:26
the altars on the * where you Lev 26:30
who lived in the * came down and Num 14:45
I watch them from the *. Num 23:7-10
* where they worship their idols. Num 33:52
among the Amorite * to which the Deu 1:19,20,21
They crossed into the * and came Deu 1:24,25
with its rolling *—and Lebanon. Deu 3:23,24,25
gushing springs, valleys, and *; Deu 8:7
and copper is abundant in the *. Deu 8:9
It is a land of * and valleys Deu 11:11
up in the *, or under the trees. Deu 12:2
And of the everlasting *. Deu 33:15
* are here with their armies." Jos 10:6
and the * and lowlands of Israel. Jos 11:16
Hebron, in the Judean *, as a City Jos 21:9-16
me go up into the * and roam with Ju 11:37
in the * of Ephraim. 1Sa 1:1
men hiding in the * joined the 1Sa 14:22
*, with the valley between them. 1Sa 17:3
and joy lies dead upon the *; 2Sa 1:19
Jonathan is slain upon the *. 2Sa 1:25
on altars in the *, for the Temple 1Ki 3:2
the * and to offer incense there. 1Ki 3:3
He also made shrines on the * 1Ki 12:31
priests for the shrines on the *. 1Ki 12:32,33
* who come here to burn incense; 1Ki 13:2
to idols in the shrines on the *. 1Ki 13:33
However, the shrines on the * 1Ki 15:14
Israeli God is a god of the *; 1Ki 20:23
is a God of the * and not of the 1Ki 20:28
the shrines on the *, so the people 1Ki 22:43
prophets from the * of Ephraim have 2Ki 5:22
the shrines on the *—the people 2Ki 12:3
the shrines on the *, so the people 2Ki 14:4
the shrines on the * where the 2Ki 15:4
the shrines on the * where the 2Ki 15:34,35
the shrines on the * and at the 2Ki 16:4
on the * near their cities. 2Ki 17:29
He removed the shrines on the *, 2Ki 18:4
the shrines on the * throughout 2Ki 23:5
the shrines on the * where they had 2Ki 23:8
the shrines on the * east of 2Ki 23:13
on the * in all of Samaria. 2Ki 23:19
in the *, and 3,600 foremen. 2Ch 2:2
calves which he placed on the *. 2Ch 11:15
altars on the *, and broke down the 2Ch 14:3
from the *, and the incense altars 2Ch 14:5
altars on the *, and destroying the 2Ch 17:6
shrines on the *, nor had the 2Ch 20:33
and towers on the wooded *. 2Ch 27:4
the * and under every green tree. 2Ch 28:4
gods from the * and took his idol 2Ch 33:15
*, but only to the Lord their God. 2Ch 33:17
built idols on the * and set up 2Ch 33:19
and the shame-idols on the *. 2Ch 34:3
to go to the * to get branches from Neh 8:15
Were you born before the * were Job 15:7,8
The cattle on a thousand *! Ps 50:10,11
May the mountains and * flourish Ps 72:3
this land of * he made for them. Ps 78:54
in glee, and the * sing out their Ps 98:8,9
rams, the little * like lambs! Ps 114:4
Why, little *, like lambs? Ps 114:6
Let the mountains and *, the Ps 148:9
before the mountains and the * Pro 8:25
mountains and bounding over the *. Sol 2:8
high mountains and *, and every Is 2:14
to smash them. The * will tremble, Is 5:25
of the *, but it will do no good; Is 16:12
the distant wooded * and mountain Is 17:9
and altars in the * and making Is 36:7
level the *; Is 40:4
weighs the mountains and the *? Is 40:12
and * and blight their greenery. Is 42:15
pastures and on the grassy *. Is 49:8,9
may depart and the * disappear, but Is 54:10
The mountains and *, the trees of Is 55:12
and insulted me upon the *. Is 65:7
idols on the * and of having orgies Jer 3:23
in the fields and on the *. Jer 13:27
* panting like thirsty jackals. Jer 14:6
watchmen on the * of Ephraim will Jer 31:6
of joy upon the * of Zion, and Jer 31:12
Her refugees will climb the * of Jer 48:5
And I will cover the * with your Eze 32:5
the mountains and * and over the Eze 34:6
pasture on the high * of Israel. Eze 34:14
with the dead—your *, your valleys Eze 35:8
He says to the * and mountains, Eze 36:4
and say to the * and mountains, Eze 36:6
they go up into the * to burn Hos 4:13
the mountains and * to fall upon Hos 10:8
and the * shall flow with milk. Joe 3:18
* of Israel will drip sweet wine! Amo 9:13
marches across our *, he will Mic 5:5
Let the mountains and * be called Mic 6:1
and from distant * and mountains. Mic 7:12
mountains quake and * melt; Nah 1:5
mountains and leveling the *. Hab 3:6
he went up into the * to pray. Mt 14:23,24
the * to search for the lost one? Mt 18:12
Judea must flee into the Judean *. Mt 24:16
Afterwards he went up into the * Mk 3:13
and in the wild *, screaming and Mk 5:5
Afterwards he went up into the * Mk 6:46
—flee, if you can, to the Judean * Mk 13:14
spread through the Judean *. Lk 1:65
John with him into the * to pray. Lk 9:28
the people of Judea flee to the *. Lk 21:21
them, and the * to bury them. Lk 23:30
So when Jesus went up into the * Jn 6:2-5
built on seven * where this woman Rev 17:9

HILLSIDE
Like showers on the *. Deu 32:2
the Ark to the * home of Abinadab; 1Sa 7:1
taken from the * home of Abinadab. 2Sa 6:3
them on a nearby *, cursing as he 2Sa 16:13
in the royal * cemetery among the 2Ch 32:33
he went up the * with his disciples Mt 5:1
Jesus as he came down the *. Mt 8:1
steep * into the lake and drowned. Mk 5:13

HILLSIDES
the * and in the fertile valleys. 2Ch 26:10
wilderness; * blossom with joy. Ps 65:11,12
No one will go to the fertile * Is 7:25
All day long he sat on the * Amo 1:1

HILLTOP
The most famous of the * altars 1Ki 3:4
to the Lord on the * altars. 2Ki 17:32
whose * altars you've destroyed. 2Ki 18:22
He rebuilt the * shrines which 2Ki 21:3,4,5
Literally, "bamah"—a * area Eze 20:29f

HILLTOPS
God gave them fertile *, Deu 32:13

HILLY
to the * country between Bethel Gen 12:8

HILT
king's belly. The * of the dagger Ju 3:22,23
herself to the *, and become so Zec 9:3

HIM.OBEY
pleasing to him. * your spiritual Heb 13:17

HIMSHI
Then anoint Jehu (son of *) to 1Ki 19:16

HIND
Literally, "as a loving * and a Pro 5:19f

HINDER
But he pleaded, "Don't * my Gen 24:56
She will not * him, but help him Pro 31:12

HINDRANCE
their armies westward without *. Rev 16:12

HINDS
Or, "makes the * to calve." Ps 29:9f

HINGED
was * to fold back upon itself. 1Ki 6:34

HINGES
firepans, the * of the doors to the 1Ki 7:50
to his bed like a door to its *! Pro 26:14

HINNOM
the Valley of *, along the southern Jos 15:8
the Valley of * and on up to the Jos 15:8
*, north of the valley of Rephaim. Jos 18:16
the valley of *, crossed south of Jos 18:16

(HINNOM Con't)
of the Sons of *, so that no one 2Ki 23:10
to the Valley of *, and it was not 2Ch 28:3
offerings in the Valley of *. 2Ch 33:6
Beer-sheba to the valley of *. Neh 11:25-30
altars to Baal in the Valley of *. Jer 32:35

HINT
And I am not writing this to * 1Co 9:15

HIP
he struck Jacob's *, and knocked it Gen 32:25
he was limping because of his *. Gen 32:31
muscle where it attaches to the *. Gen 32:32

HIPS
to cover themselves around the *. Gen 3:7
bodies, reaching from * to knees. Ex 28:42
on her * and dandled on her knees. Is 66:12

HIRAH
lived there with a man named *. Gen 38:1
and his friend *, the Adullamite, Gen 38:12
Judah asked his friend * the Gen 38:20
her, but * couldn't find her! Gen 38:20

HIRAM
Then King * of Tyre sent cedar 2Sa 5:11
KING * OF Tyre had always been a 1Ki 5:1
pointed out to *, had not been able 1Ki 5:2,3
"But now," Solomon said to *, 1Ki 5:4
* was very pleased with the 1Ki 5:7
So * produced for Solomon as much 1Ki 5:10
had promised. And * and Solomon 1Ki 5:12
for a man named * to come from 1Ki 7:13
in two rows. * set these pillars at 1Ki 7:16-22
Then * cast a round bronze tank, 1Ki 7:23
side of the room. * also made the 1Ki 7:40
of Galilee to King * of Tyre as 1Ki 9:11,12
palace and Temple. * came from Tyre 1Ki 9:11,12
For * had sent gold to Solomon 1Ki 9:14
King * supplied experienced 1Ki 9:27,28
KING * OF Tyre sent masons and 1Ch 14:1
ambassador to King * at Tyre, 2Ch 2:3
lumber such as * had supplied to 2Ch 2:3
the Lord my God," Solomon told *. 2Ch 2:4
King * replied to King Solomon: 2Ch 2:11
cities which King * of Tyre had 2Ch 8:2
fleet presented to him by King *. 2Ch 8:17,18
supplied by King *, to bring back 2Ch 9:21

HIRAM'S
Solomon's and * builders in cutting 1Ki 5:18
(And when King * ships brought 1Ki 10:11
with King *, and once every three 1Ki 10:22
These ships, with King * 2Ch 8:17,18
King * and King Solomon's crews 2Ch 9:10

HIRE
it would cost to * a servant for Lev 25:50
they even tried to * Balaam, the Deu 23:4
which he used to * some worthless Ju 9:4
so that they can * carpenters and 2Ki 22:5,6
He also paid $200,000 to * 2Ch 25:5,6
"Sir, do not * troops from Israel, 2Ch 25:7
free from rot and * a man to carve Is 40:20
with gold? They * a goldsmith to Is 46:6
return to the * of an harlot." Mic 1:7f
* workers for his harvest field. Mt 20:1
He persuaded a local farmer to * Lk 15:15

HIRED
circumcised. A * servant or a Ex 12:45
shall pay your * workers promptly. Lev 19:13
a * servant, may eat this food. Lev 22:10
as a * servant or as a guest; Lev 25:40
treat him as a * servant rather Lev 25:53
than half the price of a * hand! Deu 15:18
"Never oppress a poor * man, Deu 24:14,15
David, so they * twenty thousand 2Sa 10:6
horses, and * fifty footmen to run 2Sa 15:1
So he * chariots and drivers and 1Ki 1:5
"The king of Israel has * the 2Ki 7:6
and Zobah. He * thirty-two 1Ch 19:7
who * masons and carpenters to 2Ch 24:12
Then they * masons and Ez 3:7
and Sanballat had * him to scare me Neh 6:12,13
Instead, they had * Balaam to Neh 13:2
Assyrians you have * to save you Is 7:20
is common. * murderers, loan Eze 22:12
for you have * foreigners to take Eze 44:8
who cheat their * hands, or oppress Mal 3:5
" 'Because no one * us,' they Mt 20:7
When the men * at five o'clock Mt 20:9
So when the men * earlier came Mt 20:10
with the * men and went with him. Mk 1:20
'At home even the * men have food Lk 15:17
Please take me on as a * man." Lk 15:19
"A rich man * an accountant to Lk 16:1
for the sheep. A * man will run Jn 10:12
the flock. The * man runs because Jn 10:13
runs because he is * and has no Jn 10:13

HIRELING
to the year of a *," like 16:14. Is 21:16f

HIRES
friends she has are those she *; Hos 8:9
But though she * "friends" from Hos 8:10

HIRING
"for I am * you with some Gen 30:16

he was passing a * hall and saw Mt 20:3

HISS
deride you. They * and grind their Lam 2:16

HISSED
the serpent *. Gen 3:4
will be cursed and * and mocked, Jer 29:18

HISTORIAN
was the * who kept the records. 2Sa 20:24
* and in charge of the archives; 1Ki 4:1
and Joah, his royal *. 2Ki 18:18
(son of Asaph) the * went to King 2Ki 18:37
(son of Ahilud) was the *; 1Ch 18:15

HISTORIC
of gifts this * day when the Jews Est 9:22
was mutual, due to * reasons. Lk 10:33f

HISTORICAL
He ordered the * records of his Est 6:1
an * figure like Nebuchadnezzar. Eze 38:2,3f

HISTORICALLY
this * rebellious and evil city; Ez 4:12

HISTORIES
is recorded in the * written by 2Ch 12:15

HISTORY
Never in all the * of Egypt had Ex 9:24
Never in the * of Egypt has there Ex 10:6
locust plague in all Egyptian *; Ex 10:14
"You know our sad *, how our Num 20:14
"In all *, going back to the Deu 4:32
in Israel's * that this was done. Jos 5:2,3
The rest of Abijam's * is 1Ki 15:7
The rest of the * of Elah's 1Ki 16:14
The rest of Omri's * is recorded 1Ki 16:27
The rest of Ahab's *—including 1Ki 22:39
The rest of the * of Ahaziah's 2Ki 1:18
The rest of the * of King Joram 2Ki 8:23
The rest of the * of Joash is 2Ki 12:19
The rest of the * of Jehoahaz is 2Ki 13:8
The rest of the * of the reign 2Ki 13:12
The rest of the * of Joash and 2Ki 14:15
The rest of the * of Azariah is 2Ki 15:6
The rest of the * of Zechariah's 2Ki 15:11
The rest of the * of King 2Ki 15:21
The rest of the * of King 2Ki 15:26
The rest of the * of Pekah's 2Ki 15:31
The rest of Jotham's * is 2Ki 15:36
The rest of the * of the reign of 2Ki 16:19
The rest of the * of Hezekiah and 2Ki 20:20
The rest of the * of Manasseh's 2Ki 21:17
The rest of the * of the life of 2Ki 24:5
written in the * of Samuel the 1Ch 29:29
the prophet, the * written by 1Ch 29:29
the * written by the prophet Gad. 1Ch 29:29
is written in the * of Nathan the 2Ch 9:29
in the prophet Iddo's * of Judah. 2Ch 13:22
are written in the * of Jehu the 2Ch 20:34
The remainder of his *, including 2Ch 27:7
of its long * of sedition against Ez 4:15
Our whole * has been one of sin; Ez 9:7
of the * of King Ahasuerus' reign. Est 2:23
Mordecai wrote a * of all these Est 9:20
"Read the * books and see— for Job 8:8
lessons from our *, stories handed Ps 78:2,3
* merely repeats itself. Ecc 1:8-11
What a * was yours! Is 23:7
had a long and illustrious *. Jer 5:15f
Alas, in all * when has there Jer 30:7
From her earliest * Moab has Jer 48:11
of the city's *, and does not Jer 51:26f
wiped out, your memory lost in *. Eze 21:32
future—in the latter years of *. Eze 38:15,16
astronomy and *—plus a strong dose Dan 1:3,4f
pertains to that final event in *. Dan 8:19
Antichrist at the end of human *. Dan 8:23f
for never in all * has there been a Dan 9:12
previous suffering in Jewish *. Dan 12:1
yes, in all your *, have you ever Joe 1:2
*, no longer nations any more. Ob 1:16
its *, and will never see again. Mt 24:21
begin my remarks with a bit of * Act 13:16
An epoch of human * has come to Rev 16:17f
unprecedented in human *. Rev 16:18

HIT
For I have instructed Moses to * Ex 7:17
watched, Aaron * the surface of the Ex 7:20
the man who * him will be Ex 21:19
realizing it will * anyone, and Num 35:22,23
* our tent and knocked it flat!" Ju 7:12,13
Delilah began to * him, but she Ju 16:19
They could * a target within a Ju 20:16
* the Philistine in the forehead. 1Sa 17:48,49
the villages they *, and took for 1Sa 27:9
a mighty windstorm * the mountain; 1Ki 19:11
Lord, don't * me anymore—I am Ps 39:10
they even * the bottom of the den. Dan 6:24
"Who * you that time, you Mk 14:65
They blindfolded him and * him Lk 22:63,64
"Who * you that time, prophet?" Lk 22:63,64
"Should you * a man for telling Jn 18:23
But the ship * a sandbar Act 27:41

HITCH
told Gideon to * his father's best Ju 6:25

Now build a new cart and * to it 1Sa 6:7
He wove my sins into ropes to * Lam 1:14

HITCHED
Two fresh cows were * to the cart 1Sa 6:10

HITLER
Roman wars, six million under *. Zec 13:8f

HITS
"Anyone who * a man so hard that Ex 21:12
fighting, and one * the other with Ex 21:18
"If a man * his slave in the Ex 21:26

HITTING
"What are you doing, * your own Ex 2:13
is as harmful as * him with an axe, Pro 25:18
it is always * him and hardly Lk 9:39

HITTITE
David asked Ahimelech (the *) 1Sa 26:5,6,7
to Joab: "Send me Uriah the *." 2Sa 11:6
and Uriah the * is dead too." 2Sa 11:24
Uriah the *—thirty-seven 2Sa 23:24-39
resold to the * and Syrian kings. 1Ki 10:29
the affair concerning Uriah the *. 1Ki 15:5
Uriah the *; 1Ch 11:26-47
an Amorite and your mother a *! Eze 16:3
a * and your father an Amorite. Eze 16:45

HITTITES
Kenizzites, Kadmonites, * Gen 15:19,20,21
the Canaanites, *, Amorites, Ex 3:8
by the Canaanites, *, Amorites, Ex 3:17
of the Canaanites, *, Amorites, Ex 13:4,5
of the Amorites, *, Perizzites, Ex 23:23
Canaanites, and * from before you. Ex 23:28
Amorites, *, Perizzites, Hivites, Ex 33:2
Canaanites, *, Perizzites, Hivites, Ex 34:11
the *, Jebusites, and Amorites; Num 13:29
The *, the Girgashites, Deu 7:1
Utterly destroy the *, the Deu 20:17
including all the land of the *.' Jos 1:4
the Canaanites, *, Hivites, Jos 3:10
mountains—the *, Amorites, Jos 9:1
The kings of the *; Jos 11:1
there were the *, the Amorites, the Jos 12:8-24
Canaanites, the *, the Girgashites, Jos 24:11
the Canaanites, *, Hivites, Ju 3:5
Amorites, *, Perizzites, Hivites, 1Ki 9:20,21
and from the *— even though the 1Ki 11:1
has hired the * and Egyptians to 2Ki 7:6
to the kings of the * and Syria. 2Ch 1:17
slave laborers the *, Amorites, 2Ch 8:7,8
Canaanites, *, Perizzites, Ez 9:1
of the Canaanites, *, Amorites, Neh 9:8
The Amorites and * were nations Eze 16:3f

HIVITE
of King Hamor the *, saw her, he Gen 34:2
granddaughter of Zibeon the *), Gen 36:2,3
The * kings in the cities on the Jos 11:1

HIVITES
Girgashites,*, Arkites, Gen 10:15-19
Perizzites, *, and Jebusites live. Ex 3:8
Perizzites, *, and Jebusites, a Ex 3:17
Amorites, *, and Jebusites—the land Ex 13:4,5
*, and Jebusites, to live there. Ex 23:23
to drive out the *, Canaanites, and Ex 23:28
Perizzites, *, and Jebusites. Ex 33:2
Perizzites, *, and Jebusites. Ex 34:11
The Perizzites, the *, Deu 7:1
the *, and the Jebusites. Deu 20:17
Hittites, *, Perizzites, Jos 3:10
Perizzites, *, and Jebusites. Jos 9:1
The Israelis replied to these *, Jos 9:7
treaty except the * of Gibeon; Jos 11:19
the *, and the Jebusites): Jos 12:8-24
the *, and the Jebusites. Jos 24:11
The * living in Mount Lebanon, Ju 3:1
Hittites, *, Perizzites, Amorites, Ju 3:5
the cities of the * and Canaanites, 2Sa 24:7
Perizzites, *, and Jebusites. 1Ki 9:20,21
Girgashites, *, Arkites, Sinites, 1Ch 1:13-16
Perizzites, *, and Jebusites—the 2Ch 8:7,8

HIZKI
Zebadiah, Meshullam, *, Heber, 1Ch 8:17,18

HIZKIAH
Eli-o-enai, *, Azrikam. 1Ch 3:23

HOARDED
They will not be * but used for Is 23:18

HOARFROST
as small as * on the ground. Ex 16:14

HOARSE
my throat is dry and *; Ps 69:3

HOARY
Literally, "the * head." Pro 20:29f

HOBAB
his brother-in-law * (son of Reuel, Num 10:29
father-in-law *—had moved away from Ju 4:11

HOBAH
fleeing army to *, north of Gen 14:15

HOBBLING
aged men and women * through her Zec 8:4

HOD
Bezer, *, Shamma, Shilshah, 1Ch 7:36,37

HODAVIAH
*, Eliashib, Pelaiah, Akkub, 1Ch 3:24

(HODAVIAH Con't)
Azri-el, Jeremiah, *, Jahdi-el. 1Ch 5:24
son of *, the son of Hassenuah); 1Ch 9:7,8
Kedmi-el of the subclan of *, 74; Ez 2:40,41,42

HODESH
land of Moab by *, his new wife: 1Ch 8:8,9,10

HODEVAH
of * of the clan of Jeshua, 74; Neh 7:43,44,45

HODIAH
Akkub, Shabbethai, *, Ma-aseiah, Neh 8:7,8
*, Shebaniah, and Pethahiah. Neh 9:5
Shebaniah, *, Kelita, Neh 10:9-13
Shebaniah, *, Neh 10:9-13
Ater, Hezekiah, Azzur, *, Neh 10:14-27

HODIAH'S
* wife was the sister of Naham. 1Ch 4:19

HOE
I won't prune it or * it, but Is 5:6

HOGLAH
Mahlah, Noah, *, Milcah,Tirzah. Num 26:28-37
These girls, Mahlah, Tirzah, *, Num 36:11,12
Noah, *, Milcah, and Tirzah. Jos 17:3

HOGS
was a huge herd of * rooting around Mk 5:11
"Send us into those *," the Mk 5:12
and entered the *, and the entire Mk 5:13

HOHAM
King * of Hebron, Jos 10:3

HOISTED
difficulty we * aboard the lifeboat Act 27:16

HOLD
For the land is large enough to * Gen 34:21
Then the Lord said to Moses, "* Ex 10:12
Use your rod—* it out over the Ex 14:16
They stood as solid walls to * the Ex 15:8
tired to * up the rod any longer; Ex 17:12
and make gold rings to * the bars; Ex 26:29
rings to * the carrying poles. Ex 30:4
to * the carrying poles in place. Ex 37:14
molding, to * the carrying poles. Ex 37:27
There were twenty posts to * Ex 38:10
* up the drapes were solid silver. Ex 38:17
until you can * no more, then Deu 6:10,11,12
to * him back, and tore his robe. 1Sa 15:27
Literally, "took * of him and 2Sa 15:5f
Yes, you * me safe above their 2Sa 22:49
hand was too tired to * his sword; 2Sa 23:10
and caught * of the horns of the 1Ki 1:49,50
* of the horns of the altar. 1Ki 2:28
Then Jehovah will * him 1Ki 2:32
to * the water he will send. 2Ki 3:16
him and caught * of his feet. 2Ki 4:27
But the Lord still did not * back 2Ki 23:26
For I know that you will not * me Job 9:28
Horror takes * upon me and I Job 21:6
"I live in terror now. They * me Job 30:15
"Can you * back the stars? Job 38:31
O God, * them responsible. Ps 5:10
They have no fear of God to * Ps 36:1
O Lord, don't * back your tender Ps 40:11
Why do you delay? Why * back Ps 74:11
gave them all that they could *. Ps 78:25
Oh, do not * us guilty for our Ps 79:8
He will * sway from the Ps 89:25
they would * me back from sin. Ps 119:11
Proud men * me in contempt for Ps 119:51
God failed me. * me safe above the Ps 119:117
and * me helpless in its meshes. Ps 140:5
and kind. * these virtues tightly. Pro 3:3
will exalt you. * her fast and she Pro 4:8,9
they are ropes that catch and * Pro 5:22
Can a man * fire against his Pro 6:27
Let her * you back from visiting Pro 7:5
It is also possible to * on too Pro 11:24,25
at any price, and * on tightly to Pro 23:23
stop the wind or * onto anything Pro 27:16
and reservoirs to * the water to Ecc 2:4,5,6
No one can * back his spirit from Ecc 8:8
and take * of its branches. Sol 7:8
boast about the liquor they can *. Is 5:22
the men of Kir * up the shields. Is 22:6,7
by fraud, who * back their hands Is 33:15
of my name I will * back my anger Is 48:9
He will * you aloft in his hands Is 62:3
cisterns that can't * water! Jer 2:13
you all that you * dear, and I will Jer 15:7
and I can't * it in any longer. Jer 20:9
the door of the Temple to * court. Jer 26:10
Their captors * them and refuse Jer 50:33
They have not tried to * you back Lam 2:14
we could * our own against any Lam 4:20
But I will * you responsible for Eze 3:20
strong enough to * a sword again. Eze 30:21
* you responsible for his death. Eze 33:8
and I will * them responsible for Eze 34:9,10
Now * them together in your Eze 37:17
down into the dark * of the ship to Jon 1:3
was sound asleep down in the *. Jon 1:5
sin, and don't * us responsible for Jon 1:14
us live, and will * back his fierce Jon 3:9
she cannot * them back. Nah 2:8
have come to take * of the four Zec 1:21
ate until they could * no more! Mk 6:42
Jewish leaders got * of him and Act 25:2
we are able to * our heads high no Rom 5:5
perfectly good and * out against Rom 10:5
rather than let it * you back from 1Co 3:18
It does not * grudges and will 1Co 13:5
Who has interfered with you to * Gal 5:7
never * grudges. Col 3:13
Fight on for God. * tightly to 1Ti 6:12
* tightly to the pattern of truth 2Ti 1:13
souls as it takes * of our hearts. Jas 1:21
some among you who * that "only Jas 2:19
run after it to catch and * it! 1Pe 3:11
anything to get * of your money. 2Pe 2:3
of you; only * tightly to what you Rev 2:24,25
believed at first; * to it firmly Rev 3:3
* tightly to the little strength Rev 3:11

HOLDERS
fitting into twenty bronze post *. Ex 27:9,10
Lamp *, with lamps and oil; Ex 35:10-19

HOLDING
slipped off and she was left * it Gen 39:12
I was * Pharaoh's wine cup in my Gen 40:11
* tightly to the "rod of God"! Ex 4:20
meet him there, * in your hand the Ex 7:15
side, * up his hands until sunset. Ex 17:12
down the mountain, * in his hands Ex 32:15
the court and the posts * them up; Ex 39:33-40
stand before her * the jar of Num 5:18
burning mountain, * in my hands the Deu 9:15
right hands, and * the flaming Ju 7:19,20
is ready, and only you are * out. 2Sa 19:11,12
Ten movable stands * ten vats; 1Ki 7:41-46
down the incense burner he was *. 2Ch 26:19
* out the golden scepter to her. Est 5:2
* myself back from doing wrong. Ps 18:23
You are * my right hand! Ps 73:23
There are the judges * court Ps 122:5
drink, while still * steadily to my Ecc 2:3
I am * you by your right hand—I, Is 41:13
that I'm * in my hand, a lie?" Is 44:20
I am weary of * it in. Jer 6:11
why he was * back the rain: Jer 14:1
where the king was * court. Jer 38:8
Then I looked and saw a hand * Eze 2:9,10
creditor, not * on to the items Eze 18:7
Tell these people (* the sticks Eze 37:18,19,20
* in his hand a measuring tape Eze 40:3
I ruined your crops by * back Amo 4:7
That is why I am * back the Hag 1:10
a golden lampstand * seven lamps, Zec 4:2
* his feet and worshiping him. Mt 28:9
anyone you are * a grudge against, Mk 11:25
was * tightly to Peter and John! Act 3:11
is * you responsible as overseers. Act 20:28
to be used for * flowers, and Rom 9:21
* out to them the Word of Life. Php 2:16
* him back steps out of the way. 2Th 2:7
by rejecting him, * him up to Heb 6:6
* a pair of balances in his hand. Rev 6:5
of the earth, * back the four winds Rev 7:1
All were * harps of God, and Rev 15:2

HOLDINGS
*, as were their brother-tribes. Gen 49:7f

HOLDS
"The same law * if the ox gores Ex 21:31
promissory note he * against a Deu 15:2
the king * out his golden scepter; Est 4:11
my enemies; he * me safely out of Ps 18:48
for the Lord * them with his hand. Ps 37:24
for he * our lives in his hands. Ps 66:9
And he * our feet to the path. Ps 66:9
A wise man * his tongue. Pro 10:14
a man with good sense * his Pro 11:12
People curse the man who * his Pro 11:26
a wise man * his temper in and Pro 29:11
Who else * the wind in his fists, Pro 30:4
The Lord * out his hand over the Is 23:11
gone by, or what the future *. Is 41:22
try to tell you what the future *. Is 47:13
I will show you what the future *. Dan 11:2
law no longer * him in its power? Rom 7:1
power that * everything together. Col 1:17
and * high the truth of God. 1Ti 3:15
slows us down or * us back, and Heb 12:1
Christ, God's Son, * him securely 1Jn 5:18
Literally, "from him who * the Rev 2:1f
and * their leaders in his right Rev 2:1
For them the Second Death * no Rev 20:6
what the future *, has sent his Rev 22:6,7

HOLE
and there was a * at the center Ex 39:23
he must dig a * with the spade and Deu 23:13
Jehoiada the priest bored a * in 2Ki 12:9
his troops made a * in the inner 2Ki 25:4,5
and hide it in a * in the rocks. Jer 13:4
I dug it out of the * where I had Jer 13:7
in the city tore a * in the city Jer 52:7
possessions out through the *. Eze 12:5
at night through a * in the wall, Eze 12:12
tear away and make the * worse. Mt 9:16
the $1,000 dug a * in the ground Mt 25:18
leaves the * worse than before. Mk 2:21
and basket from a * in the city 2Co 11:33

HOLES
are crawling out of their *!" 1Sa 14:11
with fear into the * in the rocks Is 2:19
as worms crawling from their *. Mic 7:17
it into pockets filled with *! Hag 1:6
heaven have no rips or * in them. Lk 12:33

HOLIDAY
we have come at a happy time of *. 1Sa 25:8
"This isn't a religious *." 2Ki 4:23
celebration and declared a *. Est 8:17
declare an annual * on the last Est 9:21
annual Jewish * when no bread made Mk 14:1
means be at Jerusalem for the *," Act 18:21
Ephesus until the * of Pentecost, 1Co 16:8
And there will be a worldwide * Rev 11:10

HOLIDAYS
new moon and all the other *. Ps 81:3
joys, her parties, *, and feasts. Hos 1:11
and the religious * to be over, so Amo 8:5
for one of the Jewish religious *. Jn 5:1
the annual Jewish *, and Jesus' Jn 7:2
the climax of the *, Jesus shouted Jn 7:37
observe the Jewish * as special Rom 14:5
celebrating Jewish * and feasts or Col 2:16

HOLIER
For I am * than you!" Is 65:5

HOLIES
the Ark within the Holy of *. Ex 40:3
bars the way to the Holy of *. Lev 4:6
veil that secludes the Holy of *. Lev 24:3,4
Holy of *—and the tasks relating to 1Ch 6:49
Holy of *—thirty feet square. 2Ch 3:8
room, the Holy of *, Solomon placed 2Ch 3:10
in the Holy of *, and " 2Ch 3:16f
to the Holy of * were of gold. 2Ch 4:22
Temple—the Holy of *—and placed it 2Ch 5:7,8
priests came out of the Holy of *! 2Ch 5:11,12
the Holy of * within the Ps 28:2f
and the Holy of * and the entry Eze 41:15,16
the Holy of * was also paneled. Eze 41:17,18
of the Holy of * was what appeared Eze 41:21
Both the nave and the Holy of * Eze 41:23
"The Holy of *," a place reserved Mk 15:38f
was a room called the Holy of *. Heb 9:3
into the Holy of * as long as the Heb 9:8
room, the Holy of *, and sprinkled Heb 9:12
blood in the Holy of * each year. Heb 9:25
the very Holy of * where God is, Heb 10:19
that the Holy of * of the temple in Rev 15:5

HOLIEST
The curtain secluding the * Place Mt 27:51

HOLINESS
Who is glorious in * like him? Ex 15:11
you profane the * of Jehovah, and Lev 19:8
her father's * as well as her own, Lev 21:9
the Lord when clothed with *! 1Ch 16:29
He has vowed it by his *! Ps 60:6,7
cannot be changed. * is forever the Ps 93:5
mighty victory by his power and *. Ps 98:1
Lift your hands in * and bless Ps 134:2
and defiled my Temple and my *. Eze 22:26
You defiled your * with lust for Eze 28:18
and show forth my * upon you then Eze 28:22
of the world my * among my people. Eze 28:25
my land, and my * will be Eze 38:15,16
vindicate my * before the nations. Eze 39:27
is the basic law of the Temple: *! Eze 43:12
The Lord God has sworn by his * Amo 4:2
"No," the priests replied. "* Hag 2:12
your name be honored for its *; Lk 11:2
need for growth in truth and *. Jn 17:19
include * and everlasting life. Rom 6:22
church grow in * and happiness. 1Co 14:4
you will marry in * and honor— not 1Th 4:3,4
good, that we may share his *. Heb 12:10
will continue on in greater *." Rev 22:11

HOLLOW
The altar is to be *, made from Ex 27:8
The altar was *, with plank Ex 38:7
to gush out from a * in the ground Ju 15:19
He cast two * bronze pillars, 1Ki 7:15
This is absurd, a * mockery, and Ecc 6:2
*, with three-inch walls. Jer 52:21

HOLLOWED
It was *With their stavesAnd Num 21:17,18
the heavens, and * out the surface Ps 104:3

HOLON
Anim, Goshen, *, Giloh, Arab, Jos 15:48-62
Libnah, Jattir, Eshtemoa, *, Jos 21:9-16
upon them all—on * and Jahzah and Jer 48:21

HOLY
and declared it *, because it was Gen 2:3
for you are standing on * ground. Ex 3:5
they must make a * pilgrimage out Ex 5:1
for we must all join in the * Ex 10:9
To your * land. Ex 15:13
and rest, a * Sabbath to the Lord Ex 16:23

(HOLY Con't)
of priests to God, a * nation.' Ex 19:6
to observe the Sabbath as a * day. Ex 20:8
"And since you yourselves are * Ex 22:31
The curtain will separate the * Ex 26:33
Holy Place and the Most * Place. Ex 26:33
of the Ark—in the Most * Place. Ex 26:34
south side of the * Place and the Ex 26:35
flame in the outer * room, tending Ex 27:21
when he goes in to the * Place; Ex 28:29
* Place, so that he will not die. Ex 28:35
the altar in the * Place, lest they Ex 28:43
in the Tabernacle and the * Place. Ex 29:30
these things are set apart and *. Ex 29:33
shall not be eaten, for it is *. Ex 29:34
be exceedingly *, so that whatever Ex 29:37
Or, "shall become *," or, "only Ex 29:37f
those who are * may touch it." Ex 29:37f
is the Lord's supremely * altar." Ex 30:10
all this into a * anointing oil. Ex 30:25
Sanctify them, to make them *; Ex 30:29
touches them shall become *. Ex 30:29
"only what is * may touch them." Ex 30:29f
always be my * anointing oil. Ex 30:31
for it is *, and it shall be Ex 30:32
it shall be treated by you as *. Ex 30:32
it shall be a pure and * incense. Ex 30:35
this incense is most *. Ex 30:36
Lord and you must treat it as *. Ex 30:37
the beautifully made, * garments Ex 31:10
incense for the * Place. Ex 31:11
that I am Jehovah who makes you *. Ex 31:12,13
rest on the Sabbath, for it is *. Ex 31:14,15
day of solemn rest, * to the Lord. Ex 31:16
of solemn rest, a * day to be used Ex 35:2
The veil to enclose the * Place; Ex 35:10-19
when ministering in the * Place; Ex 35:10-19
The * garments for Aaron the Ex 35:10-19
equipment, and for the * garments. Ex 35:21
while ministering in the * Place. Ex 39:1
Finally they made the * plate of Ex 39:30
ministering in the * Place, and the Ex 39:41
Place, and the * garments for Aaron Ex 39:41
the Ark within the * of Holies. Ex 40:3
and it shall become *. Ex 40:9
altar shall then become most *. Ex 40:10
and clothe Aaron with the * Ex 40:13
but all of it is counted as a * Lev 2:3
as a * burnt offering to the Lord. Lev 2:10
bars the way to the * of Holies. Lev 4:6
defiling what is *, then he shall Lev 5:15
for the * thing he has spoiled, or Lev 5:16
However, all of it is most *, Lev 6:17
Literally, "(only) whoever is * Lev 6:18f
touches them shall become *." Lev 6:18f
"This sacrifice is most *, and Lev 6:25
it must be washed in a * place. Lev 6:27
but only they, for it is most *. Lev 6:29
to make atonement in the * Place. Lev 6:30
the most * offering for guilt: Lev 7:1
must be eaten in a * place, for Lev 7:6
for this is a most * sacrifice. Lev 7:6
for he has defiled what is *." Lev 7:21
at its front—the * crown—as the Lev 8:9
will show myself * among those who Lev 10:3
between what is * and what is Lev 10:10
The offering is most *; Lev 10:12
it in the sanctuary, in a * place. Lev 10:13
him, may be eaten in any * place. Lev 10:14
since it is most *, and God has Lev 10:17
things, and be *, for I am holy; Lev 11:44
things, and be holy, for I am *; Lev 11:44
You must therefore be *, for I am Lev 11:45
therefore be holy, for I am *." Lev 11:45
It is a most * offering. Lev 14:13
to enter into the * Place behind Lev 16:1
atonement for the * place because Lev 16:16
atonement in the * Place—not until Lev 16:17
of Israel, and making it *. Lev 16:19
atonement for the * Place, the Lev 16:20
was taken into the * Place by Lev 16:27
one to put on the * linen garments, Lev 16:32
atonement for the * sanctuary, the Lev 16:33
"You must be * because I, the Lord Lev 19:1
I, the Lord your God, am *. Lev 19:1
live in, and insulting my * name. Lev 20:3
So sanctify yourselves and be *, Lev 20:7
You shall be * to me, for I the Lev 20:26
for I the Lord am *, and I have set Lev 20:26
They shall be * unto their God, Lev 21:6
woman, for he is a * man of God. Lev 21:7
he is *, for I, the Lord who Lev 21:8
the Lord who sanctifies you, am *. Lev 21:8
the * and most holy offerings. Lev 21:22
the holy and most * offerings. Lev 21:22
not to defile my * name by Lev 22:1
eat the * sacrifices until healed. Lev 22:4
not eat of the * sacrifices until Lev 22:6
and may eat the * food, for it is Lev 22:7
"No one may eat of the * Lev 22:10
"the elevation of the * things." Lev 22:12f
"If someone should eat of the * Lev 22:14
for the * sacrifices brought by Lev 22:15
the Lord, made you * to myself and Lev 22:32,33
These are the * festivals which Lev 23:4
They are * to the Lord, and will Lev 23:20
regular weekly days of * rest. Lev 23:38
that secludes the * of Holies. Lev 24:3,4
law of God, and are most *." Lev 24:9
For the fiftieth year shall be * Lev 25:10
for it is a * Year of Jubilee Lev 25:12
for they are most * to the Lord. Lev 27:28
or fruit, is the Lord's, and is *. Lev 27:30
but they must not touch the * Num 4:15
carry the most * things: Aaron Num 4:17,18,19
Lord, and take * water in a clay Num 5:17
is * and consecrated to the Lord; Num 6:5
all of it is a * portion for the Num 6:20
It will remind you to be * to Num 15:40
his, and who is *, and whom he has Num 16:5
Jehovah chooses to be the * one." Num 16:6,7f
for they are *, dedicated to the Num 16:36,37
these censers are * because they Num 16:38
All these are most * offerings. Num 18:9
a most * place, and only by males. Num 18:10
Literally, "they are *." Num 18:17f
do not treat the * gifts of the Num 18:32
himself to be * before them. Num 20:13
in the * place before the Lord. Num 28:7
of the festival a * assembly of all Num 28:18
shall again be a * and solemn Num 28:25
" 'Keep the Sabbath day *. Deu 5:12
For you are a * people, Deu 7:6
you are * to the Lord your God. Deu 14:21
The camp must be *, for the Lord Deu 23:14
Look down from your * home in Deu 26:15
you must be a * people to the Lord Deu 26:19
He will change you into a * Deu 28:9
Surrounded by ten thousands of * Deu 33:2
Literally, "* ones." Deu 33:2f
His * ones are in his hands. Deu 33:3
him, "for this is * ground." Jos 5:15
Lord God, for he is * and jealous; Jos 24:19
No one is as * as the Lord! 1Sa 2:2
before Jehovah, this * God?" 1Sa 6:20
"but there is the * bread, which I 1Sa 21:4
gave him the * bread—the Bread of 1Sa 21:6
The Urim and Thummim were * 1Sa 28:5,6f
Temple—the Most * Place—was also 1Ki 6:16
Most * Place—was sixty feet long. 1Ki 6:17
the entrance to the Most * Place. 1Ki 6:21,22
front of the Most * Place), the 1Ki 7:49
doors to the Most * Place, and the 1Ki 7:50
Temple—the Most * Place—and placed 1Ki 8:6
from time to time is a * prophet. 2Ki 4:9
It is the * One of Israel! 2Ki 19:22
sanctuary—the * of Holies—and the 1Ch 6:49
Then the * Spirit came upon them, 1Ch 12:18
Glory in his * name; 1Ch 16:10
Then we will thank your * name, 1Ch 16:35
Ark and the other * articles of 1Ch 22:19
set apart for the * service of 1Ch 23:13
chosen you to build his * temple. 1Ch 28:10
For the * Spirit had given David 1Ch 28:12
for your * name comes from you! 1Ch 29:16
* of Holies—thirty feet square. 2Ch 3:8
Within the innermost room, the * 2Ch 3:10
Literally, "chains in the * of 2Ch 3:16f
to the * of Holies were of gold. 2Ch 4:22
of the Temple—the * of Holies—and 2Ch 5:7,8
came out of the * of Holies! 2Ch 5:11,12
was there and it is * ground." 2Ch 8:11
of the Presence upon the * table. 2Ch 13:11
all the debris from the * place. 2Ch 29:4,5
sheep were brought as * gifts. 2Ch 29:32,33
from his * temple in heaven. 2Ch 30:27
and boiled the * offerings in pots, 2Ch 35:13
So the * people of God were being Ez 9:2
For this is a day of * joy, not Neh 8:11
the laws about the * Sabbath; Neh 9:14
* day, we would refuse to buy it. Neh 10:31
the * City, at this time; Neh 11:1
not denied the words of the * God. Job 6:10
him in Jerusalem, my * city." Ps 2:6
Literally, "Upon Zion, my * Ps 2:6f
Literally, "from his * Ps 3:4f
But the Lord is still in his * Ps 11:4
your tabernacle up on your * hill? Ps 15:1
there is no reply— for you are *. Ps 22:3,4
e., the * of Holies within the Ps 28:2f
give thanks to his * name. Ps 30:4
We trust his * name. Ps 33:21
Temple on your * mountain, Zion. Ps 43:3
nations, sitting on his * throne. Ps 47:8
Don't take your * Spirit from me. Ps 51:11
the Temple of the Lord on * days. Ps 55:14
within the * tabernacle courts! Ps 65:4
to the widows, for he is *. Ps 68:5
Literally, "in his * Ps 68:5f
his * temple high upon Mount Zion. Ps 68:17
your promises, O * One of Israel. Ps 71:22
O God, your ways are *. Ps 77:13
and limited the * One of Israel Ps 78:41
and praise your great and * name. Ps 86:9
HIGH ON HIS * mountain stands Ps 87:1
Literally, "the assembly of the * Ps 89:5f
Literally, "the assembly of the * Ps 89:7f
and he, the * One of Israel, has Ps 89:18
I have anointed him with my * Ps 89:20
to David (and a * God can never Ps 89:35,36
Lord with the beauty of * lives. Ps 96:9
Literally, "give glory to his * Ps 97:12f
him, our * God. Ps 97:12
reverence your great and * name. Ps 99:3
Exalt the Lord our * God! Ps 99:5
and worship at his * mountain in Ps 99:9
in Jerusalem, for he is *. Ps 99:9
I BLESS THE * name of God with all Ps 103:1
Literally, "the * one of Ps 106:16f
* name and rejoice and praise you. Ps 106:47
dressed in * altar robes. Ps 110:3
Literally, "in * array." Ps 110:3f
a *, awe-inspiring name that is). Ps 111:9
his * name forever and forever. Ps 145:21
and thus insult God's * name. Pro 30:9
have despised the * One of Israel. Is 1:4
my nostrils. Your * celebrations of Is 1:12,13
They will be God's * people. Is 4:2,3,4
for he alone is *, just and good. Is 5:16
They even mock the * One of Is 5:19
the Word of the * One of Israel. Is 5:24
they sang, "*, holy, holy is the Is 6:3
*, holy is the Lord of Hosts; Is 6:3
holy, * is the Lord of Hosts; Is 6:3
God, the Light and * One of Is 10:17
the Lord, the * One of Israel, Is 10:20
destroy in all my * mountain, for Is 11:9
For great and mighty is the * One Is 12:6
respect for the * One of Israel. Is 17:7
the Lord in his * mountain. Is 27:13
exult in the * One of Israel. Is 29:19
and praise the * One of Israel, and Is 29:23
enough about your '* One of Israel' Is 30:10,11
This is the reply of the * One of Is 30:12
For the Lord God, the * One of Is 30:15
the night when * feasts are held; Is 30:29
of looking to the * One of Israel Is 31:1
it will be named "The * Is 35:8
It was against the * One of Is 37:23
asks the * One. Is 40:25
I am the * One of Israel. Is 41:14
is God who did it, Israel's * One. Is 41:20
your Savior, the * One of Israel. Is 43:3
The Lord, your Redeemer, the * Is 43:14
I am the Lord, your * One, Is 43:15
Jehovah, the * One of Israel, Is 45:11
is his name, the * One of Israel. Is 47:4
of living in the * City and brag Is 48:1
your Redeemer, the * One of Israel, Is 48:17
The Lord, the Redeemer and * One Is 49:7
he, the faithful Lord, the * One Is 49:7
beautiful clothes, O Zion, * City; Is 52:1
The Lord has bared his * arm Is 52:10
You are the * people of the Lord; Is 52:11
he is your Redeemer, the * One of Is 54:5
keep his Sabbaths * and choose the Is 56:4
them also to my * mountain of Is 56:7
land and inherit my * Mountain. Is 57:13
eternity, the * One, says this: I Is 57:15
in that high and * place where Is 57:15
If you keep the Sabbath *, not Is 58:13
as the Lord's * day, and honoring Is 58:13
the Lord: "My * Spirit shall not Is 59:21
For the * One of Israel, known Is 60:9
Mountain of the * One of Israel." Is 60:14
be called "The * People" and Is 62:12
him and grieved his * Spirit. Is 63:10
Where is the God who sent his * Is 63:11
see us from your *, glorious home; Is 63:15
Your * cities are destroyed; Is 64:10
wilderness. Our *, beautiful Is 64:11
all my * Mountain, says the Lord. Is 65:25
and camels, to my * mountain, to Is 66:20
In those days Israel was a * Jer 2:3
Sabbath day but make it a * day. Jer 17:21,22
special and *, then this nation Jer 17:24
keep the Sabbath *, if on the Jer 17:27
for God has decreed * words of Jer 23:9
his own from his * temple in Jer 25:30
of righteousness, O * hill!" Jer 31:23
valley shall be * to the Lord, and Jer 31:40
the Lord, the * One of Israel. Jer 50:29
is filled with sin against the * Jer 51:5
their * feasts and Sabbaths. Lam 2:6
used to do on days of * feasts! Lam 2:7
Such desecration of my * name Eze 20:39
For at Jerusalem in my * Eze 20:40
my Sabbaths, so my * name is Eze 22:26
You had access to the * mountain Eze 28:14
a blight upon my * name because the Eze 36:20
I am doing it to protect my * Eze 36:22
"Thus I will make known my * Eze 39:7
am the Lord, the * One of Israel. Eze 39:7

(HOLY Con't)
told me, "is the Most * Place." Eze 41:4
The nave of the Temple and the * Eze 41:15,16
the * of Holies was also paneled. Eze 41:17,18
in front of the * of Holies was Eze 41:21
Both the nave and the * of Holies Eze 41:23
facing the Temple yard are *; Eze 42:13
eat of the most * offerings and Eze 42:13
offerings, for these rooms are *. Eze 42:13
When the priests leave the * Eze 42:14
be removed, for these robes are *. Eze 42:14
Literally, "between the * and the Eze 42:16-20f
will not defile my * name any Eze 43:7
Because they sullied my * name by Eze 43:8
where the Temple is built is *. Eze 43:12
concerning these * affairs, for you Eze 44:8
they may not touch any of my * Eze 44:13
between what is * and what is Eze 44:23
it to the Lord as his * portion. Eze 45:1
It shall all be * ground. Eze 45:1
All this section shall be * Eze 45:4
Adjacent to the * lands will be Eze 45:6
each side of the * lands and city; Eze 45:7
it is *. Eze 48:14
alongside the * grounds, is garden Eze 48:18
* gods, and I told him the dream. Dan 4:8
the spirit of the * gods is in you Dan 4:9
Literally, "a watcher, a * one." Dan 4:13f
Watchers, demanded by the * Ones. Dan 4:17
spirit of the * gods is in you." Dan 4:18
Literally, "a * watcher." Dan 4:23f
him the spirit of the * gods. Dan 5:11
Then I heard two of the * angels Dan 8:13
your own city, your * mountain. Dan 9:16
for Jerusalem, his * mountain, Dan 9:20
and the Most * Place (in the Dan 9:24
of the * people comes to an end." Dan 12:7f
What then will you do on * days, Hos 9:5
I am the * One living among you, Hos 11:9
God and is faithful to the * One. Hos 11:12
be heard upon my * mountain! Joe 2:1
your God in Zion, my * mountain. Joe 3:17
temple-girl, corrupting my * name. Amo 2:7
punishment upon my * mountain, and Ob 1:16
How shall I ever again see your * Jon 2:4
went to you in your * Temple. Jon 2:7
For the Lord in his * Temple has Mic 1:2
O Lord my God, my * One, you who Hab 1:12
"But the Lord is in his * Hab 2:20
or haughtiness on my * mountain. Zep 3:11
you is carrying a * sacrifice in Hag 2:12
or meat, will it too become *?" Hag 2:12
inheritance in the * Land, for God Zec 2:11,12
from heaven, from his * home." Zec 2:13
charge of my Temple, to keep it *; Zec 3:7
And even now in your * feasts to Zec 7:6
City,' and 'The * Mountain,' and Zec 8:3
Literally, "his * ones." Zec 14:5f
on them, "These Are * Property"; Zec 14:20
Literally, "* to the Lord." Zec 14:20f
have defiled God's * and beloved Mal 2:11
became pregnant by the * Spirit. Mt 1:18
been conceived by the * Spirit. Mt 1:20
Or, "in the * Spirit and in Mt 3:11f
the * Spirit and with fire. Mt 3:11
wilderness by the * Spirit, to be Mt 4:1
in heaven, we honor your * name. Mt 6:9
"Don't give * things to depraved Mt 7:6
against the * Spirit shall never be Mt 12:31,32
the * Spirit, call him 'Lord'?" Mt 22:43
They act * Mt 23:5
And you pretend to be *, with all Mt 23:13,14
the prophet) standing in a * Mt 24:15
the Son and of the * Spirit, and Mt 28:19
God's * Spirit!" Mk 1:8
open and the * Spirit in the form Mk 1:10
Immediately the * Spirit urged Mk 1:12,13
I know who you are—the * Son of Mk 1:24
but blasphemy against the * Mk 3:29
it was by the * Spirit's power Mk 3:30
he was a good and * man, and so he Mk 6:20
of my Father, with the * angels." Mk 8:38
For David himself said—and the * Mk 12:36
speaking, but the * Spirit will. Mk 13:11
called "The * of Holies," a place Mk 15:38f
had opened up access to the * God. Mk 15:38f
be filled with the * Spirit, even Lk 1:15
The angel replied, "The * Spirit Lk 1:35
will be utterly *—the Son of God. Lk 1:35
she was filled with the * Spirit. Lk 1:41
For he, the mighty * One, has Lk 1:49
* Spirit and gave this prophecy: Lk 1:67
through his * prophets long ago— Lk 1:70
and by making us * and acceptable, Lk 1:75
filled with the * Spirit and Lk 2:25
For the * Spirit had revealed to Lk 2:26
King. The * Spirit had impelled Lk 2:27
you with fire—with the * Spirit. Lk 3:16
opened, and the * Spirit in the Lk 3:22
THEN JESUS, FULL of the * Spirit, Lk 4:1
full of the * Spirit's power. Lk 4:14
I know who you are—the * Son of Lk 4:34
the Father and the * angels, I will Lk 9:26
the joy of the * Spirit and said, Lk 10:21
much, and give the * Spirit to Lk 11:13
* Spirit shall never be forgiven. Lk 12:10
defense, for the * Spirit will Lk 12:12
"And now I will send the * Lk 24:49
the city until the * Spirit comes Lk 24:49
Then John told about seeing the * Jn 1:32
'When you see the * Spirit Jn 1:33
the * Spirit.' I saw it happen Jn 1:33
life, but the * Spirit gives new Jn 3:6
Do we have the * Spirit's help? Jn 4:21-24
Only the * Spirit gives eternal Jn 6:63
know you are the * Son of God." Jn 6:69
(He was speaking of the * Jn 7:39
on Saturday, the weekly Jewish * Jn 9:14f
The Passover, a Jewish * day, was Jn 11:55
He is the * Spirit, the Spirit Jn 14:17
I mean the * Spirit—he will teach Jn 14:26
* Spirit, the source of all truth. Jn 15:26
When the * Spirit, who is truth, Jn 16:13
and coming to you. * Father, keep Jn 17:11
Make them pure and * through Jn 17:17
told them, "Receive the * Spirit. Jn 20:22
instructions from the * Spirit. Act 1:1
until the * Spirit came upon them Act 1:4
the * Spirit in just a few Act 1:5
But when the * Spirit has come Act 1:8
long ago by the * Spirit, speaking Act 1:16
filled with the * Spirit and began Act 2:4
for the * Spirit gave them this Act 2:4
will pour out my * Spirit upon all Act 2:17
Yes, the * Spirit shall come Act 2:18
let the body of your * Son decay. Act 2:27
to send the * Spirit—with the Act 2:33
receive this gift, the * Spirit. Act 2:38
You didn't want him freed—this * Act 3:14
Then Peter, filled with the * Act 4:8
long ago by the * Spirit through Act 4:25,26
your anointed Son, your * servant. Act 4:27
name of your * servant Jesus." Act 4:30
filled with the * Spirit and boldly Act 4:31
you were lying to the * Spirit. Act 5:3
and so is the * Spirit, who is Act 5:32
and full of the * Spirit, who are Act 6:3
full of faith and the * Spirit), Act 6:5
of faith and the * Spirit's power, Act 6:8
for you are standing on * ground. Act 7:33
Must you forever resist the * Act 7:51
But Stephen, full of the * Act 7:55
to receive the * Spirit, for as Act 8:15
and they received the * Spirit. Act 8:17
When Simon saw this—that the * Act 8:18
they will receive the * Spirit!" Act 8:19
The * Spirit said to Philip, "Go Act 8:29
be filled with the * Spirit and get Act 9:17
in the comfort of the * Spirit. Act 9:31
the vision, the * Spirit said to Act 10:19
by God with the * Spirit and with Act 10:38
these things, the * Spirit fell Act 10:44
the gift of the * Spirit would be Act 10:45
the * Spirit just as we did?" Act 10:46,47
was staying! The * Spirit told me Act 11:12
my sermon, the * Spirit fell on Act 11:15
the * Spirit.' And since it was Act 11:16
the * Spirit and strong in faith. Act 11:24
and fasting the * Spirit said, Act 13:2
Directed by the * Spirit they Act 13:4
Then Paul, filled with the * Act 13:9
will not let his * One decay.' Act 13:35
with joy and with the * Spirit. Act 13:52
by giving them the * Spirit, just Act 15:8
"For it seemed good to the * Act 15:27,28,29
because the * Spirit had told them Act 16:6
"Did you receive the * Spirit Act 19:2
What is the * Spirit?" Act 19:2
their heads, the * Spirit came on Act 19:6
Paul felt impelled by the * Spirit Act 19:21
irresistibly by the * Spirit, Act 20:22
except that the * Spirit has told Act 20:23
his blood—for the * Spirit is Act 20:28
These disciples warned Paul—the * Act 21:4
it and said, "The * Spirit Act 21:11
their ears: "The * Spirit was Act 28:25
with the * nature of God himself. Rom 1:4
God's very own—yes, his * people. Rom 1:6,7
has given us the * Spirit to fill Rom 5:5
slaves to all that is right and *. Rom 6:19
follow after the * Spirit and no Rom 8:4
follow after the * Spirit find Rom 8:5
Following after the * Spirit Rom 8:6
Or possibly, "but the * Spirit Rom 8:10f
same * Spirit living within you. Rom 8:11
the power of the * Spirit you crush Rom 8:13
For his * Spirit speaks to us Rom 8:16
we have the * Spirit within us as a Rom 8:23
—the * Spirit helps us with our Rom 8:26
but the * Spirit prays for us Rom 8:26
Christ knows and the * Spirit Rom 9:1
are *, the branches will be too. Rom 11:16
Let them be a living sacrifice, * Rom 12:1
peace and joy from the * Spirit. Rom 14:17
the * Spirit's power within you. Rom 15:13
pleasing to him by the * Spirit. Rom 15:15,16
God—all by the * Spirit's power. Rom 15:19
to you by the * Spirit—pray much Rom 15:30
he made us pure and * 1Co 1:30
wisdom, but the * Spirit's power 1Co 2:4
given to us by the * Spirit, not 1Co 2:13
So we use the * Spirit's words to 1Co 2:13
to explain the * Spirit's facts. 1Co 2:13
which the * Spirit teaches us. 1Co 2:14
those who have the * Spirit within 1Co 2:14
what the * Spirit means. 1Co 2:14
For God's home is * and clean, 1Co 3:17
is the home of the * Spirit God 1Co 6:19
abilities the * Spirit gives to 1Co 12:1
the * Spirit is helping him. 1Co 12:3
but it is the same * Spirit who is 1Co 12:4
who are his. The * Spirit displays 1Co 12:7
It is the same and only * Spirit 1Co 12:11
But the * Spirit has fitted us 1Co 12:13
all been given that same * Spirit. 1Co 12:13
abilities the * Spirit gives, and 1Co 14:1
gifts from the * Spirit, ask him 1Co 14:12
ability from the * Spirit should be 1Co 14:37
given us his * Spirit in our hearts 2Co 1:22
life for them from the * Spirit. 2Co 3:6
in the new way, the * Spirit 2Co 3:6
when the * Spirit is giving life? 2Co 3:8
he has given us his * Spirit. 2Co 5:5
and filled with the * Spirit. 2Co 6:6
spirit than the * Spirit you 2Co 11:4
For we have the same * Spirit, 2Co 12:18
May God's love and the * Spirit's 2Co 13:14
you receive the * Spirit by trying Gal 3:2
Of course not, for the * Spirit Gal 3:2
the power of the * Spirit and work Gal 3:5
* Spirit through this faith. Gal 3:14
And so we who are born of the * Gal 4:29
But we by the help of the * Gal 5:5
I advise you to obey only the * Gal 5:16
that the * Spirit tells us to do; Gal 5:17
When you are guided by the * Gal 5:18
But when the * Spirit controls Gal 5:22
If we are living now by the * Gal 5:25
let us follow the * Spirit's Gal 5:25
life which the * Spirit gives him. Gal 6:8
he decided then to make us * in Eph 1:4
to Christ by the * Spirit, who long Eph 1:13
Father with the * Spirit's help Eph 2:18
revealed it by the * Spirit to his Eph 3:5
strengthening of his * Spirit. Eph 3:16
together by the * Spirit, and so be Eph 4:3
and different person, * and good. Eph 4:24
Don't cause the * Spirit sorrow Eph 4:30
be filled instead with the * Eph 5:18
her * and clean, washed by baptism Eph 5:26
* and without a single fault. Eph 5:27
line with the * Spirit's wishes. Eph 6:18
for me, and as the * Spirit helps Php 1:19
which the * Spirit has given you. Col 1:8
upon you, for the * Spirit gave you 1Th 1:5
with joy from the * Spirit in spite 1Th 1:6
sinless and * by God our Father, so 1Th 3:13
For God wants you to be * and 1Th 4:3,4
of lust, but to be * and clean. 1Th 4:7
God who gives his * Spirit to you. 1Th 4:8
Do not smother the * Spirit. 1Th 5:19
by the work of the * Spirit and by 2Th 2:13
to pray with * hands lifted up to 1Ti 2:8
BUT THE * Spirit tells us clearly 1Ti 4:1
Christ and of the * angels to do 1Ti 5:21
For the * Spirit, God's gift, 2Ti 1:7
chose us for his * work, not 2Ti 1:9
the * Spirit who lives within you. 2Ti 1:14
you were taught the * Scriptures; 2Ti 3:15
of the indwelling * Spirit whom he Tit 3:5
the * Spirit to those who believe; Heb 2:4
We who have been made * by Jesus, Heb 2:11
much superior, the * Spirit warns Heb 3:7,8
and shared in the * Spirit, and Heb 6:4
for he is * and blameless, Heb 7:26
special loaves of * bread upon it; Heb 9:1
this part was called the * Place. Heb 9:1
was a room called the * of Holies. Heb 9:3
And the * Spirit uses all this to Heb 9:8
not go into the * of Holies as long Heb 9:8
inner room, the * of Holies, and Heb 9:12
For by the help of the eternal * Heb 9:14
in the * of Holies each year. Heb 9:25
God all those whom he is making *. Heb 10:14
And the * Spirit testifies that Heb 10:15
into the very * of Holies where God Heb 10:19
let us into the * presence of God. Heb 10:20
and outraged the * Spirit who Heb 10:29
live a clean and * life, for one Heb 12:14
is not * will not see the Lord. Heb 12:14
hearts, and with * fear and awe. Heb 12:28
it says that the * Spirit, whom God Jas 4:5
And the * Spirit has been at work 1Pe 1:2

(HOLY Con't)
* Spirit who spoke to them; 1Pe 1:12
But be * now in everything you 1Pe 1:15
as the Lord is *, who invited you 1Pe 1:15
"You must be *, for I am holy." 1Pe 1:16
"You must be holy, for I am *." 1Pe 1:16
What's more, you are his * 1Pe 2:5
the King, you are * and pure, you 1Pe 2:9
I was there on the * mountain when 2Pe 1:17,18
It was the * Spirit within these 2Pe 1:20,21
his back on the * commandments that 2Pe 2:21
learned from the * prophets and 2Pe 3:1
to melt away, what *, godly lives 2Pe 3:11
like that, for the * Spirit has 1Jn 2:20
But you have received the * 1Jn 2:27
true because the * Spirit he has 1Jn 3:24
is from the * Spirit is to ask: 1Jn 4:2
And he has put his own * Spirit 1Jn 4:13
And the * Spirit, forever 1Jn 5:6,7,8
the voice of the * Spirit in our 1Jn 5:6,7,8
Blasphemy against the * Spirit 1Jn 5:17f
*, but turned to a life of sin. Jud 1:6
with millions of his * ones. Jud 1:14
they do not have the * Spirit Jud 1:19
foundation of our * faith, learning Jud 1:20
and strength of the * Spirit. Jud 1:20
aspects of the * Spirit are Rev 1:4f
by the one who is * and true, and Rev 3:7
kept on saying, "*, holy, holy, Rev 4:8
on saying, "Holy, *, holy, Lord Rev 4:8
"Holy, holy, *, Lord God Rev 4:8
Sovereign Lord, * and true, how Rev 6:10
They will trample the * City for Rev 11:2
of the * angels and the Lamb. Rev 14:10
For you alone are *. Rev 15:3,4
Then I looked and saw that the * Rev 15:5
this judgment, O * One, who is and Rev 16:5
Blessed and * are those who Rev 20:6
And I, John, saw the * City, the Rev 21:2
wondrous city, the * Jerusalem, Rev 21:10
those who are * will continue on Rev 22:11
and in the * City just described. Rev 22:19

HOMAM
Lotan's sons: Hori and *. 1Ch 1:38,39

HOME
"Sirs," he said, "come to my * Gen 19:2
at last they went * with him, and Gen 19:3
from my childhood *, I told her, Gen 20:13
of his army, returned * again. Gen 21:32
traveled * again to Beer-sheba. Gen 22:19
who will come so far from *?" Gen 24:5
The girl ran * to tell her folks, Gen 24:28
So the man went * with Laban, and Gen 24:32
Meanwhile, Isaac, whose * was in Gen 24:62
quiet sort who liked to stay at *. Gen 25:27
venison he brought *, and Rebekah's Gen 25:28
arrived * exhausted from the hunt. Gen 25:29
Then Isaac sent them happily * Gen 26:31
"I've stumbled into his *! Gen 28:16,17
him warmly and brought him *. Gen 29:12,13
Jacob was coming * from the fields, Gen 30:16
to Laban, "I want to go back * Gen 30:25
*—why have you stolen my idols?" Gen 31:30
and blessed them, and returned *. Gen 31:55
For when I left * Gen 32:10
from his * at Hebron Valley. Gen 37:13,14
ABOUT THIS TIME, Judah left * and Gen 38:1
to her childhood * and to her Gen 38:11
So Tamar went * to her parents. Gen 38:11
there in the * of his master, so Gen 39:2
her husband came * that night, she Gen 39:16
for the loss of his father's *). Gen 41:51
on * with grain for your families; Gen 42:19
with the grain and started for *. Gen 42:26
families and go on *, but bring Gen 42:33
Take them * and prepare a big Gen 43:16
we were returning *, we stopped for Gen 43:21
When Joseph came * they gave him Gen 43:26
Joseph was still * when Judah Gen 44:14
The rest of you can go on * to Gen 44:17
she hid him at * for three months. Ex 2:1
So the little girl rushed * and Ex 2:8
"Take this child * and nurse him Ex 2:9
So she took him * and nursed Ex 2:9
Invite him * for supper." Ex 2:20
Moses returned * and talked it Ex 4:18
Every * in Egypt will be filled Ex 8:3,4
palace and in every * in Egypt. Ex 8:24
* and on the panel above the door. Ex 12:7
blood of the lamb eaten in that *. Ex 12:7
the door of that * and not permit Ex 12:23f
that * and not permit the Ex 12:23
for each person in his *." Ex 16:16
no lack! Each * had just enough. Ex 16:18
each * according to its need; Ex 16:21
he had sent her *), along with Ex 18:2
"This * of mine shall be a tent Ex 25:9
and has returned * to her father's Lev 22:13
rest in every *, times for Lev 23:3
shall return * to his original Lev 25:13
with you as a guest in your *. Lev 25:35
"If someone donates his * to the Lev 27:14,15
He is completely at * in my Num 12:7,8
Balaam told the men, "Go on *! Num 22:13
I will go back * if you don't Num 22:34
Go back *! Num 24:11
is still a girl at * in her Num 30:3
in her father's *, and her father Num 30:3
in her husband's * when she makes Num 30:10
his daughter who is living at *. Num 30:16
may return to his own land and *. Num 35:28
to return to his * before the death Num 35:32
envy him for his *, land, servants, Deu 5:21
you are at * or out for a walk; Deu 6:7
Do not bring an idol into your * Deu 7:26
you are sitting at *, when you are Deu 11:19
he himself will select as his *. Deu 12:4,5
the place he will choose as his *. Deu 12:11
the offerings may be eaten at *. Deu 12:17
your pleasant * and gets along well Deu 15:16
it for food for your family at *. Deu 15:22
the elders of his * town shall Deu 19:12
shall bring him * and deliver him Deu 19:12
If so, go *! Deu 20:5
If so, go *! Deu 20:6
Well, go * and get married! Deu 20:7
If you are, go * before you Deu 20:8
your wife, take her * with you. Deu 21:12
remain in your * in mourning for Deu 21:13
of her father's * where the men of Deu 22:21
living at * with her parents; Deu 22:21
to be at *, happy with his wife. Deu 24:5
to as 'the * of the man who had his Deu 25:10
Look down from your holy * in Deu 26:15
out of house and * until your Deu 28:51
Are your *." Deu 33:23
to Rahab's *, demanding that she Jos 2:3
to return to his own city and *." Jos 20:6
So go * now to the land given you Jos 22:4
blessed them and sent them *. Jos 22:6
relatives back *—their booty of Jos 22:7,8
they were leaving for their new *, Ju 1:14
he started * again. Ju 3:17,18,19
Why did you sit at * among the Ju 5:16
And he will bring * Ju 5:30
Gideon hurried * and roasted a Ju 6:19
Send * any of your men who are Ju 7:3
"Send all the others *!" Ju 7:7
them, he sent them *, leaving only Ju 7:8,9
and put it in Ophrah, his * town. Ju 8:27
He returned *, and eventually Ju 8:29
He took them to his father's * Ju 9:5
* and lived in the land of Tob. Ju 11:3
when he returned * in peace, the Ju 11:30,31
When Jephthah returned * his Ju 11:34
and when he got * he told his Ju 14:2
wife and went back * to live with Ju 14:19
brought him back * and buried him Ju 16:31
Ephraim, they stayed at Micah's *. Ju 18:2
As they passed the * of Micah, Ju 18:13
to one man in his private *?" Ju 18:19
from Micah's *, Micah and some of Ju 18:22
him to handle, he turned back *. Ju 18:26
who brought * a girl from Bethlehem Ju 19:1
to her father's * in Bethlehem, and Ju 19:2
When he arrived at her *, she let Ju 19:3
way * from his work in the fields. Ju 19:16
"We're on the way * from Ju 19:18
So he took them * with him. Ju 19:21
the donkey's back and took her *. Ju 19:28
of us will return * until we have Ju 20:8,9,10
them * with you to be your wives! Ju 21:21
and returned to her childhood *; Ru 1:14
the Lord has brought me * empty; Ru 1:21
asked her when she arrived *. Ru 3:15-18
mustn't go * without a present. Ru 3:15-18
now come into your *, as fertile as Ru 4:11
Then they returned * to Ramah, 1Sa 1:19,20
So she stayed * until the baby was 1Sa 1:23
So they returned * to Ramah 1Sa 2:11
Before they returned * Eli would 1Sa 2:20
Ark to the hillside * of Abinadab; 1Sa 7:1
to Ramah, for his * was there, and 1Sa 7:17
agreed and sent the men * again. 1Sa 8:22
said to the servant, "Let's go *; 1Sa 9:5
Then Samuel sent the people * 1Sa 10:25
When Saul returned to his * at 1Sa 10:26
to Gibe-ah, Saul's * town, and told 1Sa 11:4
The rest of the army was sent *. 1Sa 13:2
and the Philistines returned *. 1Sa 14:46
Then Samuel went * to Ramah, and 1Sa 15:34
let him return * any more. 1Sa 18:4
* after David had killed Goliath. 1Sa 18:6
was sitting at *, listening to 1Sa 19:9,10
permission to go * to Bethlehem for 1Sa 20:6
Horesh while Jonathan returned *. 1Sa 23:18
So the men of Ziph returned *. 1Sa 23:24,25
and Saul went *, but David and his 1Sa 24:22
told her to return * without fear, 1Sa 25:35
When she arrived * she found 1Sa 25:36
me out of my * so that I can't be 1Sa 26:19
Come back *, my son, and I'll no 1Sa 26:21
went away and Saul returned *. 1Sa 26:25
He was buried in Ramah, his * 1Sa 28:3
He went to the woman's * at 1Sa 28:7,8
his men arrived * at their city of 1Sa 30:1
have gone * tomorrow morning." 2Sa 2:27
with him returned * too, and when 2Sa 2:30
Then Abner told him, "Go on * 2Sa 3:16
* one noon as he was taking a nap. 2Sa 4:5
to bring * the Ark of the Lord of 2Sa 6:1
from the hillside * of Abinadab. 2Sa 6:3
can I ever bring the Ark *?" 2Sa 6:9
it instead to the * of Obed-edom, 2Sa 6:10
So Israel brought * the Ark of 2Sa 6:15
everyone had gone *, David 2Sa 6:19
in a temple. My * has been a tent 2Sa 7:6
"At the * of Machir." 2Sa 9:4
and sent them * half naked. 2Sa 10:4
Then she returned *. 2Sa 11:4
Then he told him to go * and 2Sa 11:8
he sent a present to him at his *. 2Sa 11:8
Why didn't you go * to your wife 2Sa 11:10
and should I go * to wine and dine 2Sa 11:11
but even so he didn't go * that 2Sa 11:13
arrived at the * of the rich man. 2Sa 12:4
Then Nathan returned to his *. 2Sa 12:15
to bring * your own banished son. 2Sa 14:13
was also Absalom's * town, its 2Sa 15:9f
went to his * town, set his affairs 2Sa 17:23
blessed Barzillai, he returned *. 2Sa 19:39
"Go on *," he said. 1Ki 1:53
"Go back to your * in Anathoth. 1Ki 2:26
and each family had its own * and 1Ki 4:25
in Lebanon and two months at *. 1Ki 5:14
built you a lovely * on earth, a 1Ki 8:12,13
sent the people *, happy for all 1Ki 8:66
even so, I'd like to go back *." 1Ki 11:22
Let's go *! 1Ki 12:16,17
Tell them to disband and go *, 1Ki 12:23,24
So the army went * as the Lord 1Ki 12:23,24
and his sons went * and told him 1Ki 13:11
"Come * with me and eat." 1Ki 13:15
* by the same road I came on." 1Ki 13:16,17
I am to take you * with me and 1Ki 13:18
some water at the old man's *. 1Ki 13:19
So his wife went to Ahijah's * at 1Ki 14:4
disaster upon your * and will 1Ki 14:10
wife, "Go on *, and when you step 1Ki 14:12
walked through the door of her *. 1Ki 14:17
half drunk at the * of Arza, the 1Ki 16:9
So the king of Israel went * to 1Ki 20:43
"It's all over—return *! 1Ki 22:36,37
"Carry him * to his mother." 2Ki 4:19
So he took him *, and his mother 2Ki 4:20
that I won't go * without you." 2Ki 4:30
stood at the door of Elisha's *. 2Ki 5:9
at * and get rid of my leprosy." 2Ki 5:12
So Naaman started * again. 2Ki 5:19
and drink and send them * again." 2Ki 6:22
then sent them * to their king. 2Ki 6:23
with your glory and stay *! 2Ki 14:10
was defeated and the army fled *. 2Ki 14:12
he turned around and returned *. 2Ki 15:19,20
from * and will decide to return; 2Ki 19:7
The Babylonians carried * all the 2Ki 24:13
I ever get the Ark of God *?" 1Ch 13:12
to take it to the * of Obed-edom 1Ch 13:13
we transfer the Ark to its new * 1Ch 15:2
for bringing * the Ark of Jehovah, 1Ch 15:14
great joy to the * of Obed-edom to 1Ch 15:25
in a cedar-paneled * while the Ark 1Ch 17:1
tent to tent as my * from the time 1Ch 17:5
And I will give a permanent * to 1Ch 17:9
who can ever build him a worthy *? 2Ch 2:6
Zion, [to its new * in the Temple 2Ch 5:2
he sent the people *, joyful and 2Ch 7:10
sanctified it to be my * forever; 2Ch 7:16
Let's go *!" 2Ch 10:16
your brothers. Go *, for I am 2Ch 11:4
Send them *.' 2Ch 18:16
of Judah returned *, uninjured, 2Ch 19:1
didn't release them to go *. 2Ch 23:8
So Amaziah sent them * again to 2Ch 25:10
that had been sent * raided several 2Ch 25:13
advice is to stay * and don't 2Ch 25:19
was defeated, and its army fled *. 2Ch 25:22
So Sennacherib returned * in deep 2Ch 32:21
He also took * with him all the 2Ch 36:18
the * of Eliashib the High Priest. Neh 3:20
nearby cities went * for a visit, Neh 4:12
section of wall next to his own *. Neh 7:3
now returned * to their own towns Neh 7:73
should rule his *, and should Est 1:22
orders, just as she had in his *. Est 2:20
and went on * and gathered together Est 5:10
hurried * utterly humiliated. Est 6:12
to his * for a celebration. Job 1:4
* and his property from all harm. Job 1:10
A messenger rushed to Job's * Job 1:14,15
oldest brother's *, when suddenly Job 1:18
"You need not worry about your * Job 5:24
their *—never to be seen again. Job 7:10

(HOME Con't)
you, and bless you with a happy *. Job 8:6
If he counts on his * for Job 8:15
every * where there is wickedness. Job 18:6
of Terrors. His * shall disappear Job 18:15
Those living in my *, even my Job 19:15
your *, then you will be restored. Job 22:23
and live in caves for want of a *. Job 24:8
of God was felt in my *; Job 29:4
in another man's *, and someone Job 31:10
for orphans in our *, treating them Job 31:18
Where is the * of the east wind? Job 38:24
her * in her mountain fortress. Job 39:28
with him in his *, consoling him Job 42:11
live with you forever in your *. Ps 23:6
Lord, I love your *, this shrine Ps 26:8
So if you want an eternal *, Ps 37:27
* of the God above all gods. Ps 46:4
sight and hurry * again, afraid of Ps 48:5
pull you from your *, and drag you Ps 52:5
at his * to capture and kill him. Ps 59:1
this * when they were destitute. Ps 68:9,10
The women at * Ps 68:11,12,13
as your * on earth! Ps 74:2
in Israel. His * is in Jerusalem. Ps 76:2
its apportioned place as its *. Ps 78:55
people Israel, invading every *. Ps 79:7
nor ever have an idol in your *. Ps 81:9
generations you have been our *! Ps 90:1
in my own *, where I long to act as Ps 101:2
heroes, and invite them to my *. Ps 101:6
in each Egyptian *, their pride and Ps 105:36
evicted from the ruins of their *. Ps 109:9,10
* of many nations living there. Ps 111:6
became God's new * and kingdom. Ps 114:2
wife shall be contented in your *. Ps 128:3
to build a permanent * for the Ark Ps 132:2-5
God's permanent * here on earth. Ps 132:7
as your *: "This is my Ps 132:13
is my permanent * where I shall Ps 132:14
in each Egyptian *, along with the Ps 135:8
with those outside your *? Pro 5:17
or waits for me outside my *! Pro 8:34
"Come * with me," she urges Pro 9:16
for good, a curse is upon your *. Pro 17:13
with a crabby woman in a lovely *. Pro 21:9
in a beautiful * with a cranky, Pro 25:24
A man who strays from * is like a Pro 27:8
his everlasting * as the mourners Ecc 12:5
*, into my mother's old bedroom. Sol 3:4
would bring you to my childhood *, Sol 8:2
every * and all its public Is 4:5
"Many a beautiful * will lie Is 5:9
the desert will make it their *. Is 13:21
* comes the sound of weeping. Is 15:3
Weep, O ships of Tyre, returning * Is 23:1
for your * port is destroyed! Is 23:14
every * and shop is locked up Is 24:10
Go *, my people, and lock the Is 26:20
quietly at *, but the Assyrians Is 32:18
He will make Jerusalem the * of Is 33:5
of jackals and a * for ostriches. Is 34:13
the Lord, will go * along that road Is 35:10
he is needed at * at once, and he Is 37:7
my people to go *, and create Is 43:19
is silent and empty when I come *? Is 50:2
redeemed will all come * again. Is 51:11
Lord God bring his people * again. Is 52:8
carry * the vessels of the Lord. Is 52:11
spread out your *! Is 54:2
* to you from distant lands. Is 60:4
to bring the sons of Israel * Is 60:9
see us from your holy, glorious *; Is 63:15
* to me again, for I am merciful; Jer 3:12
O sinful children, come *, for I Jer 3:14
but I must bear it. My * is gone; Jer 10:20
one left to help me rebuild my *. Jer 10:20
and will bring you * to your own Jer 12:15
his people * from the countries of Jer 16:14,15
promised, and bring you * again. Jer 29:10
you back * again to your own land. Jer 29:14
Nehelam was Shemaiah's * town, Jer 29:24f
I will bring them * to this land Jer 30:3
for I will bring you * again from Jer 30:10
when I bring you * again from your Jer 30:18
will lead them * with great care. Jer 31:9
They shall come * and sing songs Jer 31:12
them and send them scurrying *. Jer 37:7
to take him back to his *. Jer 39:14
Moabite * and on the streets; Jer 48:38
ancestral *—and devours the land Jer 48:45
Hazor shall be a * for wild Jer 49:33
to Zion and start back * again. Jer 50:5
lead my people * again, for see, Jer 50:8
And I will bring Israel * again Jer 50:19
it shall be a * for the wild Jer 50:39
me; at *, disease and death. Lam 1:20
has destroyed every * in Israel. Lam 2:2
of Judah in my *, the power of the Eze 8:1
leave your *—go somewhere else. Eze 12:3
Then, when I have brought you * Eze 20:42
island * in the midst of the seas. Eze 28:2,3
the Egyptians * again from the Eze 29:13
they were, back * to their own land Eze 34:13
and bring them safely * again. Eze 34:15,16
they will be coming * again soon! Eze 36:8
For I will bring you back * Eze 36:24
I will bring you * again to Israel, Eze 36:33
return * again to your own land. Eze 37:14
and bringing them * from around the Eze 37:21
And I will make my * among them. Eze 37:27
they will be * again, in peace Eze 39:26
I will bring them * from the Eze 39:27
responsible for bringing them *. Eze 39:29
Then he went * and told Hananiah, Dan 2:17
about it, he went * and knelt down Dan 6:10
will then return * with great Dan 11:28
and he will withdraw and return *. Dan 11:30,31
and return to my * until they admit Hos 5:15
There, far from *, you are not Hos 9:4
And I will bring them * again; Hos 11:11
For my * is in Jerusalem Joe 3:21
The upper stories of his * are Amo 9:6
Micah's * town. Mic 1:14f
This is no more your land and *, Mic 2:10
quietly in his own * in peace and Mic 4:4
will be found in his own *. Mic 7:6
and bring you * again, and give you Zep 3:20
And when you bring it *, I blow Hag 1:9
from heaven, from his holy *." Zec 2:13
of you will own a * of your own Zec 3:10
curse into the * of every thief and Zec 5:4
his * and completely destroy it." Zec 5:4
meet them at the * of Josiah (son Zec 6:10,11
I will bring them * again to Zec 8:8
they will come * again to Israel. Zec 10:9
a brawl at the * of a friend!' Zec 13:6
and brought Mary * to be his wife, Mt 1:24
in a dream to go * another way. Mt 2:12
he left Judea and returned * Mt 4:12,13
only angry, even in your own *, Mt 5:22
him to come to his * and heal his Mt 8:5,6
am not worthy to have you in my *; Mt 8:8,9
to the Roman officer, "Go on *. Mt 8:13
have no * of my own—no place to Mt 8:20
the lake to Capernaum, his * town. Mt 9:1
and go on *, for you are healed." Mt 9:5,6
to the rabbi's *, a woman who had Mt 9:19
at the rabbi's * and saw the noisy Mt 9:23
As Jesus was leaving her *, two Mt 9:27
and stay in his * until you leave Mt 10:11
a godly *, give it your blessing; Mt 10:13
Any city or * that doesn't Mt 10:14
will be right in his own *! Mt 10:36
A city or * divided against Mt 12:25
his * town, Nazareth in Galilee, Mt 13:53,54
to get the people started *. Mt 14:22
Then Jesus sent the people * and Mt 15:39
the ninety-nine others safe at *! Mt 18:13
And anyone who gives up his *, Mt 19:29
to the * of Simon the leper. Mt 26:6
from every Jewish *, the disciples Mt 26:17
Then the mob led him to the * of Mt 26:57
Simon and Andrew's *, where they Mk 1:29,30
and go on *, for you are healed!" Mk 2:9,10,11
to try to take him * with them. Mk 3:21
will collapse. A * filled with Mk 3:25
"Go * to your friends," he told Mk 5:19
from Jairus' * with the news that Mk 5:35
* except Peter and James and John. Mk 5:37
disciples to Nazareth, his * town. Mk 6:1
except in his * town and among his Mk 6:4
"Stay at one * in each Mk 6:10
good-bye and get them started *. Mk 6:45
So when they come * from the Mk 7:4
Go on *, for the demon has left Mk 7:29
And when she arrived *, her Mk 7:30
And if I send them * without Mk 8:3
and afterwards he sent them *. Mk 8:8,9
Jesus sent him * to his family. Mk 8:26
given up anything—*, brothers, Mk 10:29
at the * of Simon the leper; Mk 14:3
the High Priest's * where all of Mk 14:53
Temple duties and then returned *. Lk 1:23
and then went back to her own *. Lk 1:56
ancestral * for this registration. Lk 2:3
David's ancient *—journeying there Lk 2:4
returned * to Nazareth in Galilee. Lk 2:39
over they started * to Nazareth, Lk 2:43
his boyhood *, he went as usual to Lk 4:16
here in your * town like those you Lk 4:23
is accepted in his own * town! Lk 4:24
he went to Simon's * where he found Lk 4:38
and go on *, for you are healed!" Lk 5:23,24
his mat and went * praising God! Lk 5:25
a reception in his * with Jesus as Lk 5:29
by coming to my *, for I am not Lk 7:6,7,8
to come to his * for lunch and Lk 7:36
When I entered your *, you didn't Lk 7:44
begged him to come * with him, for Lk 8:41
from the Jairus' * with the news Lk 8:49
and mother. The * was filled with Lk 8:52
Be a guest in only one * at each Lk 9:4
have no earthly * at all." Lk 9:58
me ask permission of those at *." Lk 9:61
"bid them farewell at *." Lk 9:61f
"Whenever you enter a *, give it Lk 10:5
shift around from * to home, but Lk 10:7
from home to *, but stay in one Lk 10:7
Martha welcomed them into her *. Lk 10:38
so is a * filled with argument Lk 11:17
former * is all swept and clean. Lk 11:25
Pharisees asked him * for a meal. Lk 11:37,38
ONE SABBATH AS he was in the * of Lk 14:1
carry it * on your shoulders. Lk 15:5
to himself, 'At * even the hired Lk 15:17
I will go * to my father and Lk 15:18
"So he returned * to his father. Lk 15:20
when he returned *, he heard Lk 15:25
his coming * again unharmed.' Lk 15:27
into an everlasting * in heaven? Lk 16:9
him to my father's *— for I have Lk 16:27
"Those away from * that day must Lk 17:31
the Pharisee, returned * forgiven! Lk 18:14
you have, leaving *, wife, Lk 18:29
to be a guest in your * today!" Lk 19:5
that salvation has come to this * Lk 19:9,10
dead, they went * in deep sorrow. Lk 23:48
Then they went * and prepared Lk 23:56
and then he went back * again, Lk 24:12
So he went * with them. Lk 24:29
Andrew and Peter's * town. Jn 1:44
Then Jesus told him, "Go back *. Jn 4:50
man believed Jesus and started *. Jn 4:50
your sleeping mat and go on *!" Jn 5:8
broke up and everybody went *. Jn 7:53
not find a * within your hearts. Jn 8:37
But Mary stayed at *. Jn 11:20
to his own *, leaving me alone. Jn 16:32
from then on I took her into my *. Jn 19:27
went on *, and by that time Mary Jn 20:10
he says, 'Let his * become desolate Act 1:20
and in their * Bible classes, they Act 5:42
His parents hid him at * for Act 7:20
What kind of * could you build?' Act 7:48,49
and then sent him to his * Act 9:30
As Peter entered his *, Act 10:25
come into a Gentile * like this. Act 10:28
is staying in the * of Simon, a Act 10:32
arrived at the * of the man who had Act 11:12
he went to the * of Mary, mother of Act 12:12
said, "come and stay at my *." Act 16:15
returned to the * of Lydia where Act 16:40
They attacked the * of Jason, Act 17:5
Jason has let them into his *. Act 17:7
went aboard and they returned *. Act 21:6
and stayed at the * of Philip the Act 21:8
were guests at the * of Mnason, Act 21:16
of inviting guests * for dinner or, Rom 12:13
who meet to worship in their *. Rom 16:5
the church meets here in his *. Rom 16:23
God's *, God will destroy him. 1Co 3:17
For God's * is holy and clean, 1Co 3:17
and clean, and you are that *. 1Co 3:17
your body is the * of the Holy 1Co 6:19
and drinking at *, to avoid 1Co 11:22
he should eat at * so that he won't 1Co 11:34
their husbands at *, for it is 1Co 14:35
make him feel at *, for he is doing 1Co 16:10
their * for their church service. 1Co 16:19
eternal * in heaven with Jesus. 2Co 5:6
we will be at * with the Lord. 2Co 5:8
For you are God's temple, the * 2Co 6:16
inherit Abraham's * and lands along Gal 4:30
more and more at * in your hearts, Eph 3:17
Now I am sending him * again, Php 2:26
Jewish * that was a branch of the Php 3:5
and to those who meet in his *. Col 4:15
guests in his *, and must be a good 1Ti 3:2
at *, supporting needy parents. 1Ti 5:4
In a wealthy * there are dishes 2Ti 2:20
living at the * of Onesiphorus. 2Ti 4:19
that meets in your *, and to Apphia Phm 1:1
When Abraham was returning * Heb 7:1
told him to leave * and go far away Heb 11:8
was not their real * but that they Heb 11:13
forward to their real * in heaven. Heb 11:14
For this world is not our *; Heb 13:14
to our everlasting * in heaven. Heb 13:14
Since your real * is in heaven I 1Pe 2:11
he might bring us safely * to God. 1Pe 3:18
Cheerfully share your * with 1Pe 4:9
don't even invite him into your *. 2Jn 1:10
rank and left their proper *." Jud 1:6f
"Look, the * of God is now among Rev 21:3

HOME-BORN
as for the * citizen, for I am Lev 24:22

HOMELAND
Go instead to my *, to my Gen 24:4
For I was kidnapped from my * Gen 40:15
Your own *, Lord— Ex 15:17
land as your *), "the southern Num 34:1
has given you a * here on the east Jos 1:12,13

HOMELAND Con't)
River to their own * of Gilead. Jos 22:9
I have selected a * for my 2Sa 7:10,11
your parents in your * far away. Ps 45:10,11
return to their * and conquer the Ob 1:20
But our * is in heaven, where Php 3:20

HOMELESS
They were wandering * in the Ps 107:4
of the Arnon River like * birds. Is 16:2
They will be wandering Jews, * Hos 9:17
for a long time. * and naked, he Lk 8:27

HOMEOWNER
and that each * who lived near the Neh 7:3

HOMER
bushels, honest gallons. A * Eze 45:11
The * was about 220 litres, or 6½ Eze 45:11f
(one-tenth of a *) for dry measure, Eze 45:11
(one-tenth of a *) for liquid. Eze 45:11

HOMES
quickly to their * in Canaan, and Gen 45:17
in the * will turn to blood." Ex 7:19
and filled the nation's *. Ex 8:13
Egypt. Your * will be filled with Ex 8:21
palace, and the * of your Ex 10:6
be no trace of yeast in your *; Ex 12:19
he passed over the * of the people Ex 12:27
don't even have any in your *. Ex 13:3
no yeast in your *, or anywhere Ex 13:6,7
the fires in your * that day." Ex 35:3
of bread from your * to be waved Lev 23:17
"There is one exception: The * Lev 25:32
eat it in their * or anywhere they Num 18:31
Joys in the * of Jacob. Num 24:3-9
Then Balaam looked over at the * Num 24:20
and Balak returned to their *. Num 24:25
These cities are for their *, Num 35:3
have built fine * to live in, and Deu 8:12,13
shall be in your *, and none of the Deu 16:4
is not to be eaten in your *. Deu 16:5
back to your * the next morning. Deu 16:7
their cities and *, you must set Deu 19:1
us Levites for our *, and Jos 21:2
They left their * in Jericho, Ju 1:16
disbanded and returned to their *. Ju 9:55
and they returned to their *; Ju 21:14
of Israel returned to their *. Ju 21:24
* instead of coming with me? Ru 1:8
to your parents' *, for I am too Ru 1:12
before returning to their *. 1Sa 27:9
army of Israel fled to their *. 2Sa 18:17
cities for * for his cavalry and 1Ki 9:19
Pharaoh had given them * and 1Ki 11:16,17,18
palace and the * of your people, 1Ki 20:5,6
palace and the * of the people.' 1Ki 20:9
send them to their *.' 1Ki 22:17
were living in the * of the chief 2Ki 10:6
returned to their *, and David 1Ch 16:43
abandoned their * and moved to 2Ch 11:13,14
of yours to their *, for now the 2Ch 28:11
returned again to their own *. 2Ch 31:1
from their * in the other towns. Ez 3:1
your families, and your *!" Neh 4:14
and * to these rich men; Neh 5:2,3,4
oliveyards, and * to them this very Neh 5:11
"May God destroy your * and Neh 5:13
* in the various cities of Judah). Neh 11:3
* to comfort and console him. Job 2:11
the poor and foreclosed their *; Job 20:19
Their * are safe from every Job 21:9
filled their * with good things. Job 22:18
rich and build their lovely *. Ps 49:16
is sin in their *, and they are Ps 55:15
Let their * be desolate and Ps 69:25
are sung in the * of the godly. Ps 118:15,16
A father can give his sons * and Pro 19:14
works program: *, vineyards, Ecc 2:4,5,6
to live. Your * are built on great Is 5:8
their * will be sacked, and their Is 13:16
your joyous * and happy cities Is 32:13
into your own * those who are Is 58:7
on the rooftops of their *. Is 65:3
their * are full of evil plots. Jer 5:27
* and take their fields and wives. Jer 6:12
We must leave our land and *!' Jer 9:19
through your windows into your *. Jer 9:21
heard from their * as troops of Jer 18:22
And I will defile all the * in Jer 19:13
* shall lie in silent darkness. Jer 25:10
Build * and plan to stay; Jer 29:5
build permanent * and plan to stay Jer 29:28
and all the larger *, and set the Jer 52:13
we must bear! Our *, our nation, Lam 5:2
to occupy your *, break down your Eze 7:24
their * and sent away into exile. Eze 12:11
They will burn your *, punishing Eze 16:40,41
and daughters and burn their * Eze 23:47
They will destroy your lovely * Eze 26:12
their * and plant their vineyards. Eze 28:26
their * around my hill a blessing. Eze 34:26
again you will be filled with *. Eze 36:11
that the Lord will bless your *. Eze 44:30
for their * and for my Temple. Eze 45:4
and expelling them from their *. Eze 45:9
is for public use—*, pasture and Eze 48:15
"Their beautiful * are full of Amo 3:10
and plunder those beautiful *." Amo 3:11
the beautiful * of the Amo 3:15
your beautiful * and tossed out Amo 4:3
and hate their beautiful *. Amo 6:8
this: That * both great and small Amo 6:11
widows from their *, and stripped Mic 2:9
by cheating? The * of the wicked Mic 6:10
* with captured goods and slaves. Nah 2:12
the walls of your * cry out against Hab 2:11
their masters' * with evil gain of Zep 1:9
enemy, whose * will be ransacked; Zep 1:13
live in the new * they have built. Zep 1:13
animals will have their * in her. Zep 2:14
*, when the Temple lies in ruins? Hag 1:3,4
only concern is your own fine *. Hag 1:9
are evicting widows from their *. Mt 23:13,14
to their * for their clothes. Mt 24:18
and you invited me into your *; Mt 25:35
times over, *, brothers, sisters, Mk 10:30
out of their * and then, to cover Mk 12:40
people in their *, no matter what Lk 4:40
left our * and followed you." Lk 18:28
There are many * up there where Jn 14:2,3
in small groups in * for Communion, Act 2:46
entering private * and dragging out Act 8:3
returning to their * in Turkey, Act 20:4
either publicly or in your *. Act 20:20
around without * of our own. 1Co 4:11
have of being a guest in your *? 1Co 9:4
bodies in heaven, * that will be 2Co 5:1
and take care of their own *; 1Ti 5:14
other people's * and make 2Ti 3:6
* and must love all that is good. Tit 1:8
time in their own *, being kind and Tit 2:5
doorposts of their *, so that God's Heb 11:28
*, as he did among the Egyptians. Heb 11:28

HOMESICK
for he has been * for all of you Php 2:26

HOMESICKNESS
with terrible * and wanted to be Sol 6:12

HOMEWARD
and went on their * way, taking Gen 14:11
But after they had begun their * Ru 1:8
He will turn * again, but will Dan 11:19

HOMONYM
is a * of the word "good." Lev 2:13f

HOMOSEXUAL
The penalty for * acts is death Lev 20:13
a prostitute or a *, for both are Deu 23:17,18
yourselves through * practices and Eze 22:10f

HOMOSEXUALITY
"* is absolutely forbidden, for Lev 18:22
There was * throughout the land, 1Ki 14:24

HOMOSEXUALS
adulterers or *—will have no share 1Co 6:9,10
and impure: *, kidnappers, liars, 1Ti 1:10,11

HONEST
We are all brothers and * men, Gen 42:11
'No, no,' we said, 'we are * Gen 42:31
whether you are spies or * men; Gen 42:34
"Find some capable, godly, * men Ex 18:21
scales and * measurements, so Deu 25:13,14,15
because he was * and true and 1Ki 3:6
all who have made an * confession; 1Ki 8:39
for they were * and faithful men. 2Ki 12:15
expenditures, for they were * men. 2Ki 22:7
in the fear of God, with * hearts. 2Ch 19:9
job was to make an * distribution Neh 13:13
Fair and * men could reason with Job 23:7
"For I, as an * judge, Job 29:12
All I did was just and *, for Job 29:14
I am telling you the * truth, Job 36:4
for I have been * and have done Ps 17:1
accusing * men of evil deeds." Ps 31:18
have preserved me because I was *; Ps 41:12
mind is filled with * thoughts; Pro 12:5
And to punish nobles for being *! Pro 17:26
BETTER BE POOR and * than rich Pro 19:1
heritage to have an * father. Pro 20:7
If a king is kind, * and fair, Pro 20:28
be punished; an * witness is safe. Pro 21:28
but with *, sensible leaders Pro 28:2
Better to be poor and * than rich Pro 28:6
both known as * men, to watch me as Is 8:2
King is coming, with * princes! Is 32:1
here: All who are * and fair, who Is 33:15
to live good, *, clean lives, then Jer 4:2
you can find one fair and * man! Jer 5:1
to get them to be *, for you have Jer 5:3
and stays away from sin, and is * Eze 18:8
Always be fair and *. Eze 45:9
"You must use * scales, honest Eze 45:10
"You must use honest scales, * Eze 45:10
scales, honest bushels, * gallons. Eze 45:10
He was faithful and *, and made Dan 6:4
How long will it be before one * Hos 8:5
How you hate * judges! Amo 5:10
It is as hard to find an * man as Mic 7:1
"Tell them to be * and fair—and Zec 7:8,9
know you are very * and teach the Mt 22:16
"But the good soil represents *, Lk 8:15
For unless you are * in small Lk 16:10
* with greater responsibilities. Lk 16:10
agents pretending to be * men. Lk 20:20
we know what an * teacher you are. Lk 20:21
an * man—a true son of Israel." Jn 1:47
God's warning: Be * in your Rom 12:3
can see you are * clear through. Rom 12:17
but don't have true and * hearts. 2Co 5:12
least, are well intentioned and *. 2Co 5:12
We are *, but they call us liars. 2Co 6:8
God knows we are *, but I want 2Co 8:21
they weren't being * about what Gal 2:14
hands of his for * work so he can Eph 4:28
have been pure and * and faultless 1Th 2:10
obedient and ready for any * work. Tit 3:1
feasts as though they were * men. 2Pe 2:13

HONESTLY
if they * return to you and pray 1Ki 8:48
A little, gained *, is better Pro 16:8
I tell you * that I cried over it. 2Co 2:4

HONESTY
And if you live in * and truth 1Ki 9:4
in your stand for truth and *. 2Ch 19:11
You deserve * from the heart; Ps 51:6
HATES cheating and delights in *. Pro 11:1
A good man is guided by his *; Pro 11:3
upright are directed by their *; Pro 11:5
trouble, but * is its own defense. Pro 12:13
"By your *," he replied. Lk 3:13
up his * in contrast to my lies. Rom 3:7
can say with utter * that in all 2Co 1:12

HONEY
man as gifts—balm, *, spices, Gen 43:11
with milk and *'—the land where the Ex 3:8
land "flowing with milk and *." Ex 3:17
a land 'flowing with milk and *.' Ex 13:4,5
and flat, and tasted like * bread. Ex 16:31
a land 'flowing with milk and *'; Ex 33:3
for no yeast or * is permitted in Lev 2:11
You may offer yeast bread and * Lev 2:12
a land 'flowing with milk and *.' Lev 20:24
land 'flowing with milk and *.' Num 13:27
a land 'flowing with milk and *'! Num 14:8
with milk and *,' even as the God Deu 6:3
pomegranates, olives, and *; Deu 8:8
land 'flowing with milk and *'! Deu 11:9
land "flowing with milk and *!" Deu 26:9
land "flowing with milk and *"!' Deu 26:15
with milk and *'—take out boulders Deu 27:2,3,4
with milk and *'—and when they have Deu 31:20
* from the rock, Deu 32:13
that "flowed with milk and *." Jos 5:6
a swarm of bees in it, and some *! Ju 14:8
He took some of the * with him, Ju 14:9
"What is sweeter than *?" Ju 14:18
eaten the * he felt much better. 1Sa 14:27
I have eaten this little bit of *. 1Sa 14:29
"I tasted a little *," Jonathan 1Sa 14:43
lentils, *, butter, and cheese. 2Sa 17:28,29
bars, and a jar of * and ask him 1Ki 14:3
grain, wine, olive trees, and *. 2Ki 18:31,32
they will not be butter and * to Job 20:17
They are sweeter than * dripping Ps 19:10
He would satisfy you with * for Ps 81:16
Literally, "* out of the rock." Ps 81:16f
your words are sweeter than *. Ps 119:102,103
are as sweet as *, and smooth Pro 5:3
Kind words are like *—enjoyable Pro 16:24
My son, * whets the appetite, and Pro 24:13,14
Do you like *? Pro 25:16
to eat too much *, so also it is Pro 25:27
Even * seems tasteless to a man Pro 27:7
Your lips, my dear, are made of *. Sol 4:11
of honey. Yes, * and cream are Sol 4:11
and eat my honeycomb with my *. Sol 5:1
old enough to) eat curds and *." Is 7:15,16f
will live on curds and wild *. Is 7:21,22
with milk and *," as it is today. Jer 11:5
land that 'flows with milk and *.' Jer 32:22
oil and * they had hidden away. Jer 41:8
I ate it, it tasted sweet as *. Eze 3:3
flour and oil and * I gave you; Eze 16:19
*, the best of all lands anywhere. Eze 20:5,6
full of milk and *, the choicest Eze 20:15
and with *, oil and balm. Eze 27:17
his food was locusts and wild *. Mt 3:4
locusts and wild * were his food. Mk 1:6
"At first it will taste like *, Rev 10:9

HONEYCOMB
though they found * on the ground 1Sa 14:24,25
so he dipped a stick into a *, 1Sa 14:27
than honey dripping from a *. Ps 19:10
spices and eat my * with my honey. Sol 5:1

HONOR
Now he will * me, for I have Gen 30:20
that you will * this, my last Gen 47:29
May these boys be an * to my name Gen 48:16

(HONOR Con't)
head of the list in rank and in *. Gen 49:3
this to gain great * and glory over Ex 14:4
you will see the * I will get in Ex 14:17
"* your father and mother, that Ex 20:12
to give them * and respect. Ex 28:40
"You shall give due * and Lev 19:32
you to great *, but Jehovah has Num 24:11
as angry as I, concerning my *; Num 25:10,11
" '* your father and mother Deu 5:16
to receive praise, *, and renown; Deu 26:19
but to attain this * and renown Deu 26:19
give you great *, so that all Jos 3:7
to the * of your great name?" Jos 7:9
you now that the * of conquering Ju 4:9
Sitting in the seats of *. 1Sa 2:8
I will * only those who honor me, 1Sa 2:30
I will honor only those who * me, 1Sa 2:30
he is held in high * by all the 1Sa 9:6
been set aside for the guest of *. 1Sa 9:23
but oh, at least * me before the 1Sa 15:30
"Isn't he the one the people * at 1Sa 21:11
men aren't here to * your father! 2Sa 10:3
with you is all the * I need! 2Sa 19:36
you didn't ask for—riches and *! 1Ki 3:13
calling it Samaria in * of Shemer. 1Ki 16:24
had selected to * his own name. 2Ki 21:3,4,5
Majesty and * march before him, 1Ch 16:27
dog, yet you have decided to * me! 1Ch 17:18
And may this bring eternal * to 1Ch 17:24
sent these men to * your father! 1Ch 19:2,3
Riches and * come from you 1Ch 29:12
wealth and * than his father. 1Ch 29:25
wealth and *, and you haven't asked 2Ch 1:11
wealth, and * as no other king has 2Ch 1:12
is not going to * you for this!" 2Ch 26:17,18
those of us who delight to * you. Neh 1:11
to * a man who truly pleases me?" Est 6:6
would he want to * more than me?" Est 6:6
And an * guard keeps watch at his Job 21:30-32
establish my * and truth before Ps 7:7,8
and placed a crown of glory and * Ps 8:5
You have given him fame and *. Ps 21:5
Oh, pardon them for the * of your Ps 25:11
and my fortress; * your name by Ps 31:3
he will * you with every blessing, Ps 37:34
she is, led beside her maids of * Ps 45:14
fear him or even * his commands. Ps 55:19
All day long I'll praise and * Ps 71:8
You will give me greater * than Ps 71:21
Or, "you will bring me unto *." Ps 73:24f
Help us for the * of your name. Ps 79:9
But someday the highest * will Ps 87:5
trouble, and rescue him and * him. Ps 91:15
Give a joyous shout in * of the Ps 95:1
* and majesty surround him; Ps 96:6
those who fear and * him is as Ps 103:11
You are robed with * and with Ps 104:1
them—to defend the * of your name Ps 106:8
*, majesty, and eternal goodness. Ps 111:3
He shall have influence and *. Ps 112:9
backed by all the * of your name. Ps 138:2
Let his people rejoice in this *. Ps 149:4,5
* the Lord by giving him the Pro 3:9,10
good lifeRiches*PleasurePeace Pro 3:16,17
The wise are promoted to *, but Pro 3:35
and she will lead you to great *; Pro 4:8,9
and lose your *, and give the Pro 5:9
Unending riches, *, justice and Pro 8:18
* goes to kind and gracious Pro 11:16
To help the poor is to * God. Pro 14:31
humility ends in *. Pro 18:12
It is an * for a man to stay out Pro 20:3
finds life, righteousness and *. Pro 21:21
a man to riches, * and long life. Pro 22:4
It is an * to receive a frank Pro 24:26
It is a badge of * to accept Pro 25:12
* DOESN'T GO with fools any more Pro 26:1
It will be a public * to me. Pro 27:11
a fall, while humility brings *. Pro 29:23
shall bring her * and recognition Pro 31:31
great wealth and *, so that they Ecc 6:2
can outweigh much wisdom and *. Ecc 10:1
your Creator. * him in your youth Ecc 12:1
will be an * to his family name." Is 22:23,24
O LORD, I will * and praise your Is 25:1
For my own * I will defend it, Is 37:35
large enough to * him, nor are all Is 40:16
some day * me before the world. Is 43:21
of glory, pomp and * are ended. Is 47:1
sake and for the * of my name I Is 48:9
greater than the * they would Is 56:5
They were my people, an * to my Jer 13:11
so that they shall want to * me; Jer 31:33
Then this city will be an * to Jer 33:9
to protect the * of my name, lest Eze 20:9,10
to protect the * of my name, lest Eze 20:14
it is the ultimate of *. Eze 27:10
buried in great * with their Eze 32:27
And I will * my name in Israel by Eze 35:11
I will * my great name that you Eze 36:23
and bring * upon my name, and all Eze 38:23
* of one of the tribes of Israel. Eze 48:30,31
so did my * and glory and kingdom. Dan 4:36
with even greater * than before. Dan 4:36
and glorify and * the King of Dan 4:37
robes of royal * with a gold chain Dan 5:7
and majesty and glory and *. Dan 5:18
brought lasting * to your name by Dan 9:15
He will * those who submit to Dan 11:39
for shame is greater than for *. Hos 4:18
For they have betrayed the * of Hos 5:7
* of their shattered gods. Hos 10:5
indignant for the * of his land! Joe 2:18
will come and * you—from Assyria to Mic 7:12
restore their * and power again! Nah 2:2
my servant, and * you like a signet Hag 2:23
of the Lord, to * those who gave Zec 6:14
yet you don't * me, O priests, but Mal 1:6
pure offerings in * of my name. Mal 1:11
in heaven, we * your holy name. Mt 6:9
For instance, God's law is '* Mt 15:4
to * and care for your parents. Mt 15:5,6
people say they * me, but their Mt 15:8
steal, don't lie, * your father Mt 19:19
I invited aren't worthy of the *. Mt 22:8
God: '* your father and mother.' Mk 7:10
at the places of * at banquets— Mk 12:39
that week—the * fell to him by lot Lk 1:8,9
What an * this is, that the Lk 1:43
home with Jesus as the guest of *. Lk 5:29
* or even to come and meet you. Lk 7:6,7,8
For how you love the seats of * Lk 11:43
will publicly * you in the Lk 12:8
For everyone who tries to * Lk 14:11
Your pretense brings you * from Lk 16:15
lie, * your parents, and so on." Lk 18:20
And how they love the seats of * Lk 20:46
that everyone will * the Son, just Jn 5:23
Son, just as they * the Father. Jn 5:23
But if you refuse to * God's Son, Jn 5:23
For you gladly * each other, but Jn 5:44
* that comes from the only God! Jn 5:44
anyone seeking to * the one who Jn 7:18
For I * my Father—and you Jn 8:49
banquet was prepared in Jesus' *. Jn 12:2
follow me, the Father will * them. Jn 12:26
Father, bring glory and * to Jn 12:28
He told me, "It is the one I * Jn 13:26
great * by showing you my glory. Jn 16:14
highest * in heaven, next to God. Act 2:33
him, Sit here in * beside me until Act 2:34
a people to bring * to his name. Act 15:14
I became very anxious to * God in Act 22:3
glory and * and eternal life that Rom 2:7
But there will be glory and * Rom 2:10
place of highest * next to God, Rom 8:34
they have for the * of God, but it Rom 10:2
over you, and give * and respect to Rom 13:7
the Lord, you are trying to * him; Rom 14:6
of * and sincerity and truth. 1Co 5:8
a way that extra * and care are 1Co 12:24
whether others * us or despise us, 2Co 6:8
His good deeds will be an * to 2Co 9:9
in the place of * at God's right Eph 1:20
Yes, his * is far more glorious Eph 1:21
* Christ by submitting to each Eph 5:21
you. * your father and mother. Eph 6:2
that if you * your father and Eph 6:3
and that I will always be an * to Php 1:20
the Lord and * him, so that you Col 1:10
God in the place of * and power. Col 3:1
had a right to some * from you. 1Th 2:6
in holiness and *—not in lustful 1Th 4:3,4
Dear brothers, * the officers of 1Th 5:12
Glory and * to God forever and 1Ti 1:17
Unto him be * and everlasting 1Ti 6:16
* beside the great God of heaven. Heb 1:3
the * that goes with that name." Heb 1:5,6
here beside me in * until I crush Heb 1:13
And who is this Son of Man you * Heb 2:6
have crowned him with glory and *. Heb 2:7
God with glory and * because he Heb 2:9
to the * of being High Priest; Heb 5:5
our High Priest, with the * and Heb 6:20
given the place of * in heaven. Heb 7:26
of greatest * next to God himself. Heb 8:1
place of highest * at God's right Heb 10:12
and now he sits in the place of * Heb 12:2
* your marriage and its vows, and Heb 13:4
All * to God, the God and Father 1Pe 1:3
and * on the day of his return. 1Pe 1:7
and to * those who do right. 1Pe 2:14
Fear God and * the government. 1Pe 2:17
in the place of * next to God the 1Pe 3:22
glory and his * when he returns. 1Pe 5:1
share in his glory and *. 1Pe 5:4
* given him by God his Father; 2Pe 1:17,18
*, both now and forevermore. 2Pe 3:18
gave glory and * and thanks to the Rev 4:9
the glory and the * and the power, Rev 4:11
strength, and the *, and the glory, Rev 5:12
blessing and the * and the glory Rev 5:13
thanksgiving, and *, and power, and Rev 7:12
Salvation is from our God. * and Rev 19:1
Let us be glad and rejoice and * Rev 19:7
And the glory and * of all the Rev 21:26

HONORABLE
to take a chance that you are *: Gen 42:19
be as numerous and * as those of Ru 4:12
Literally, "* women." Ps 45:9f
criminals sneering at * men. Is 3:5
said to them, "* leaders and Act 4:8

HONORED
are an * prince of God among us; Gen 23:5,6
This is a law to be * from Lev 23:21
He doesn't feel * by such gifts! Deu 17:1
used mockingly, "Let Baal be *!" Ju 6:32f
Why have you * your sons more 1Sa 2:29
* member of your own household! 1Sa 22:14
And may you be eternally * when 2Sa 7:26
instead you have * me among all 2Sa 19:28
(For God had * him with fourteen 1Ch 25:4,5
died at an old age, wealthy and *; 1Ch 29:28
very wealthy and was highly *. 2Ch 32:27
and Jerusalem * him at his death. 2Ch 32:33
said that he would be * forever. 2Ch 33:4,5
"I will be * here in this Temple, 2Ch 33:7
have chosen to be * forever above 2Ch 33:7
and they were highly *. Neh 11:2
gladness, and were * everywhere. Est 8:16
never knows it if his sons are *; Job 14:20,21
took my place among the * elders. Job 29:7
"I will cause your name to be * Ps 45:17
I will be * by every nation in Ps 46:10
He is highly * everywhere. Ps 47:9
His name will be * forever; Ps 72:17
His children shall be * Ps 112:2
will make you both wise and *. Pro 15:33
Your great and * men will starve, Is 5:13
to me and *, and I love you. Is 43:4
you have not * me with Is 43:23
of God or the * name of Israel. Is 44:5
this task and * me for doing it! Is 49:5
be known and * among the nations; Is 61:9
Go to Shiloh, the city I first * Jer 7:12
gods * by the Jewish community. Jer 7:18f
make of them a great and * nation. Jer 30:19
All who * her despise her now, Lam 1:8
And when I have * my name by Eze 20:44
I will be * before their eyes by Eze 36:23
Most High God and * him who lives Dan 4:34
be greatly * all around the world. Mic 5:4
"But my name will be * by the Mal 1:11
And Capernaum, though highly *, Mt 11:23
Highly * by Christ's being there. Mt 11:23f
"A prophet is * everywhere except Mt 13:57
has been made the * cornerstone; Mt 21:42
"A prophet is * everywhere except Mk 6:4
the most * stone in the building! Mk 12:10
from Arimathea, an * member of the Mk 15:42,43
your name be * for its holiness; Lk 11:2
and the decision of an * Lk 12:53
now will be greatly * then; Lk 13:30
Thus you will be * in front of Lk 14:10
who humbles himself shall be *." Lk 14:11
but the humble shall be *." Lk 18:14
will be widely known and *. Lk 21:13
"A prophet is * everywhere except Jn 4:43,44
The * guest was thus singled Jn 13:26f
And the Lord * this effort so Act 11:21
our ancestors and * them in Egypt Act 13:17
'Today I have * you as my son.' Act 13:32,33
of the Lord Jesus was greatly *. Act 19:17
part is *, all the parts are glad. 1Co 12:26
you should feel * and encouraged. Eph 3:13
to him, "My Son, today I have * Heb 5:5
the first and most * of all God's Heb 7:4
the most * and important part of 1Pe 2:7

HONORING
head of the table, * them above the 1Sa 9:22
and also he was * his contract with 2Ki 13:23
by * me before the king and his Ez 7:28
He has made his people strong, * Ps 148:14
* a rebel will backfire like a Pro 26:8
holy day, and * the Lord in what Is 58:13
hypocrisy of '*' me with your Amo 5:21
are certainly not * the Father. Jn 5:23
and take delight in * each other. Rom 12:10
It would be far more * to the 1Co 6:7
praising and * him. Eph 5:33
* him as head of the house. 1Pe 3:6
and * them as the weaker sex. 1Pe 3:7

HONORS
He promises you great * plus any Num 22:16,17
I said I would give you great *?" Num 22:37
* those who truly please him!' Est 6:9
the king * those he delights in." Est 6:11
Mordecai and the * given him by the Est 10:2
Fresh * were constantly given Job 29:20
the good men but * them by placing Job 36:7
He helps me do what * him the Ps 23:2,3
he publicly * them and destroys Ps 41:2

HONORS Con't)
Their * will not follow them. Ps 49:17
this really * me. Ps 50:23
This * the Lord, and exhibits Ps 92:15
it will gain you many *. Pro 1:7,8,9
To do right * God; Pro 14:2
about all the * they deserve! Pro 25:27
Therefore I will give him the * Is 53:12
Sabbath days of rest, but * them; Is 56:2
gifts and * if you tell me what the Dan 2:6
"A son * his father, a servant Mal 1:6
father, a servant * his master. Mal 1:6
Literally, "*." Act 28:10f
and * he planned to give the Jews? Rom 2:26
Then we won't need to look for * Gal 5:26

HOOF
Not a * shall be left behind; Ex 10:26

HOOFS
only semi-parted *, or any animal Lev 11:26
she was trampled by the horses' *. 2Ki 9:33
sparks fly from their horses' *, Is 5:28
trampled and mangled by horses' *. Is 14:19
Hear the clattering * and Jer 47:3
your forts. The * of his cavalry Eze 26:10
horns of iron and * of brass and Mic 4:13
rumbling, horses' * pounding, and Nah 3:2

HOOK
am going to put a * in your nose 2Ki 19:28
"CAN YOU CATCH leviathan with a * Job 41:1
—I have put a * in your nose and a Is 37:29

HOOKS
with gold, with four golden *. Ex 26:32
Hang the curtain from the *. Ex 26:33
with gold, with * of gold, and a Ex 26:37
up with silver * attached to silver Ex 27:9,10
sockets, with silver * and rods. Ex 27:11
rods, using silver *, the posts Ex 27:17
to four gold * set into four posts Ex 36:36
connected by five * to five posts. Ex 36:38
basins, meat *, and fire pans. Ex 38:3
bronze and with silver * and rods. Ex 38:10
bases and with silver * and rods. Ex 38:11
bases, and with silver * and rods. Ex 38:12
all the * and rods were silver; Ex 38:17
bases, and with silver * and rods; Ex 38:19
tops, and for the rods and *. Ex 38:28
firepans, *, shovels, basins, and Num 4:14
for the solid gold * used in 1Ch 28:17
seized him with * and bound him 2Ch 33:11
and their spears into pruning *." Is 2:4f
those who fish with * and those Is 19:8
I will put * into your jaws and Eze 29:4
I will put * into your jaws and Eze 38:4
There were *, three or four Eze 40:43
beat your pruning * into spears. Joe 3:10
when he will put * in your noses Amo 4:2
Must we be strung up on their * Hab 1:15

HOOPOE
The *, the bat. Lev 11:13-19
The *, the bat. Deu 14:11-18

HOOTING
* from the gaping windows; Zep 2:14

HOOVES
with cloven * which chews its cud. Lev 11:2,3
cud but does not have cloven *); Lev 11:4-7
cud, it does not have cloven *); Lev 11:4-7
cud, it does not have cloven *); Lev 11:4-7
*, it does not chew the cud). Lev 11:4-7
"Any animal that has cloven * Deu 14:6
the cud but do not have cloven *. Deu 14:7
cloven *, they don't chew the cud. Deu 14:8

HOPE
curse them, in the * that he can Num 22:11
"I * you won't turn me down." 1Ki 2:20
grab this straw of * and hurried to 1Ki 20:33
"I * you will agree with them and 2Ch 18:12
a just God; what * can we have if Ez 9:15
But there is * for Israel in Ez 10:2
integrity of your ways, your *." Job 4:6f
And so at last the poor have *, Job 5:16
utterly helpless, without any *. Job 6:13
those who forget God have no *. Job 8:11-13
courage because you will have *. Job 11:18
their only * is death." Job 11:20
"For there is * for a tree—if Job 14:7
This thought gives me *, so that Job 14:14
So every * of man is worn away. Job 14:18,19
and have laid all * in the dust. Job 16:15
Where then is my *? Job 17:15
No, my * will go down with me to Job 17:16
He has destroyed all *. Job 19:10
What a glorious *! Job 19:27
"But what * has the godless when Job 27:8
God opposes me, what * is there? Job 31:23
shield, my glory, and my only *. Ps 3:3
I have no * except in you. Ps 25:5
And so, Lord, my only * is in Ps 39:7
My only * is in your love and Ps 40:11
Why be discouraged and sad? * in Ps 42:4,5
You are the only * of all mankind Ps 65:5
O Lord, you alone are my *; Ps 71:5
and to set its * anew on God and Ps 78:7
burn till every * is gone? Ps 79:5
looking up to you in constant *. Ps 86:3
and give me renewed * and cheer. Ps 94:19
for they are my only *. Ps 119:43
servant, for they are my only *. Ps 119:49,50
promises are my only source of *. Ps 119:114
O Israel, * in the Lord; Ps 130:7
I am losing all *; Ps 143:4
his helper, whose * is in the Lord Ps 146:5
broken beyond * of healing. Pro 6:15
The * of good men is eternal Pro 10:28
* deferred makes the heart sick; Pro 13:12
when courage dies, what * is left? Pro 18:14
his early years while there is *. Pro 19:18
There is * for you yet! Pro 23:17,18
becoming wise, there is * for you! Pro 24:13,14
flood sweeping away their last *. Pro 28:3
There is more * for a fool than Pro 29:20
be merry, with the * that this Ecc 8:15
for they have no *—there is nothing Ecc 9:2,3
There is * only for the living. Ecc 9:4
My only * is in him. Is 8:17
They cannot be filled with * and Is 38:18
LISTEN TO ME, all who * for Is 51:1
own reputation! O * of Israel, our Jer 14:8
You cannot * to hide from me. Jer 16:17
desert, with no * for the future; Jer 17:6
the Lord his * and confidence. Jer 17:7
O Lord, the * of Israel, all who Jer 17:13
You alone are my *. Jer 17:17
come true! I * the Lord will do Jer 28:6
to give you a future and a *. Jer 29:11
There is * for your future, says Jer 31:17
justice, the * of their fathers." Jer 50:7
False *—they could not help at Lam 1:19
what enjoyment is. All * is gone; Lam 3:18
Yet there is one ray of *: his Lam 3:21
therefore I will * in him. Lam 3:24
It is good both to * and wait Lam 3:26
then at last there is * for him. Lam 3:29
That is our only *! Lam 5:21
is finished. No * remains, for I Eze 7:3
In the * that they would draw Eze 20:26
of dried-out bones—all * is gone.' Eze 37:11
of Troubles into a Door of *. Hos 1:15
not a ray of joy or * will shine. Amo 5:18
against Israel, what * is there? Amo 7:2
If you turn against them, what * Amo 7:5
"When I had lost all *, I turned Jon 2:7
The people of Maroth vainly * Mic 1:12
there is no * of saving her. Mic 1:14
"You * for much but get so Hag 1:9
you prisoners, for there is yet *! Zec 9:12
Peg on which all * hangs, the Bow Zec 10:4
Or quench the smallest *; Mt 12:20
And his name shall be the * Mt 12:21
day to attain this same * I have! Act 26:7
until at last all * was gone. Act 27:20
Literally, "the * of Israel." Act 28:20f
* and faith are strong and steady. Rom 5:4
* and trust that he will get it. Rom 8:24
God who gives you * will keep you Rom 15:13
you overflow with * in him through Rom 15:13
in the * that his soul will be 1Co 5:5
that remain—faith, *, and love—and 1Co 13:13
to you, too. I * you properly 1Co 16:18
me very well (I * someday you 2Co 1:13,14
this matter, and I * that, deep 2Co 5:11
I * I won't need to show you when 2Co 10:2
Instead, we * that your faith 2Co 10:15
I * YOU will be patient with me as 2Co 11:1
aren't at all? I * you can agree 2Co 13:6
at all times, not to * for evil. 2Co 13:8
to you now in the * that I won't 2Co 13:10
were lost, without God, without *. Eph 2:12
expectation and * that I will never Php 1:20
the Good News. I * to send him to Php 2:23
ever had reason to * that he could Php 3:4
my trust and * in Christ alone. Php 3:7
I * all of you who are mature Php 3:15
hearts is your only * of glory. Col 1:26,27
for, that gives us * and joy and is 1Th 2:19
as those are who have no *. 1Th 4:13
helmet the happy * of salvation. 1Th 5:8
comfort and * which we don't 2Th 2:16
Jesus Christ our Lord—our only *. 1Ti 1:1
now, even though I * to be with you 1Ti 3:14
it, for our * is in the living God 1Ti 4:9,10
Everyone had run away. I * that 2Ti 4:16
This certain * of being saved is Heb 6:19
But now we have a far better *, Heb 7:19
that what we * for is waiting for Heb 11:1
Now we live in the * of eternal 1Pe 1:3
Now your faith and * can rest in 1Pe 1:21
brother. I * I have encouraged you 1Pe 5:12
this letter, for I * to come to see 2Jn 1:12
write it, for I * to see you soon 3Jn 1:14

HOPED
"Perhaps," Jacob *, "he will Gen 32:20
But Reuben * to spare Joseph's Gen 37:21,22
Jews' enemies had * to vanquish Est 9:1
He also * that Paul would bribe Act 24:26
and, I *, agree that it was right. Gal 2:2

HOPEFULLY
patiently and * for that future day Rom 8:19

HOPELESS
to give him a * life of uselessness Job 3:23
My life flies by—day after * Job 7:6
my life is ebbing out—a * case. Ps 88:4
Yes, that will be a dark and * Amo 5:20
in God is empty, worthless, *; 1Co 15:14

HOPES
water there, their * are dashed. Job 6:19-21
And so my * in you are dashed—you Job 6:19-21
How little will come of his *! Job 15:33
the past. My * have disappeared. Job 17:11
so let whoever * to master him Job 40:19
forever; the * of the poor shall Ps 9:18
Lord, you know the * of humble Ps 10:17
us, for our * are in you alone. Ps 33:22
and slink away, their * thwarted. Ps 112:10
and so will the good man's *. Pro 10:24
the * of evil men are all in vain. Pro 10:28
When an evil man dies, his * all Pro 11:7
Their * remain unanswered. Is 44:9
But Zedekiah's * were dashed. Jer 21:1f
to you, filling you with futile *. Jer 23:16
saw that all her * for him were Eze 19:5
not only will her * be blighted, Dan 11:6
terror, for their * that Tyre would Zec 9:5
laws you set your * of heaven. Jn 5:45
Her masters' * of wealth were now Act 16:19
they will pin their * on him Rom 15:12
beyond our highest *, for their 2Co 8:5
prayers, desires, thoughts, or *. Eph 3:20

HOPHNI
two sons of Eli—* and Phinehas. 1Sa 1:3
your two sons, * and Phinehas, to 1Sa 2:34
above the angels. * and Phinehas, 1Sa 4:4
and * and Phinehas were killed. 1Sa 4:11
the battlefield. * and Phinehas 1Sa 4:17

HOPHRA
When the army of Pharaoh * of Jer 37:5
you here: I will turn Pharaoh *, Jer 44:30
*, or Apries, ruled Egypt from 588 Jer 44:30f
Pharaoh * was killed by Amasis, Jer 44:30f
Rename Pharaoh * and call him Jer 46:17
When Pharaoh * sent an army to Eze 30:21f

HOPING
you of my coming, * that you will Gen 32:5
(They were, of course, * he Mt 12:10
* to see him perform a miracle. Lk 23:8
the Jews were * to do to me!" Act 12:11
for me, for I am * that God will Phm 1:22
reminders to you, * to impress 2Pe 1:15

HOPPER-LOCUSTS
After them will come the *! Joe 1:4

HOR
journeyed from Kadesh to Mount *. Num 20:21,22
and lead them up onto Mount *. Num 20:25
Mount * as all the people watched. Num 20:27
returned to Mount *, and from there Num 21:4
From Kadesh to Mount * (at the Num 33:15-37
the foot of Mount *, Aaron the Num 33:38,39
from Mount * and camped in Num 33:41
eastward to Mount *, then to Num 34:7,8,9
died in Mount * and joined them. Deu 32:50

HOR-HAGGIDGAD
From Bene-jaakan to *; Num 33:15-37
From * to Jotbathah; Num 33:15-37

HORAM
on Lachish, King * of Gezer arrived Jos 10:33

HORDE
"A vast * of people has arrived Num 22:5,6
"The king says that a vast * of Num 22:11
your name we attack this vast *. 2Ch 14:11

HORDES
I will send vast * of frogs across Ex 8:2
These enemy * arrived on droves Ju 6:5
quickly destroy the Midianite *!" Ju 6:16
nations and their * of chariots and 1Ki 20:1
He spoke, and * of locusts came, Ps 105:34
They will come in vast *, Is 7:19
wives raped by the attacking *. Is 13:16
Call out the demon * you've Is 47:12
Gomer and all his * and the armies Eze 38:6

HOREB
of the desert near *, the mountain Ex 3:1
So Aaron traveled to Mount *, Ex 4:27
and lead the people out to Mt. *. Ex 17:5,6
Or, "Mt. *." Ex 18:5,6f
Israel left Mount *—though it takes Deu 1:1
from Mount * to Kadesh-barnea, Deu 1:1
ago, at Mount *, that Jehovah our Deu 1:6
"Then we left Mount * and Deu 1:19,20,21
the Lord at Mount *, and he told Deu 4:10
the fire at Mount *, so do not Deu 4:15
with you at Mount *—not with your Deu 5:2,3
how angry you made him at Mount *? Deu 9:8
begged of God at Mount *. Deu 18:16
the people of Israel at Mount *. Deu 29:1

(HOREB Con't)
there at Mount * at the time the 1Ki 8:9
nights to Mount *, the mountain of 1Ki 19:8
put there at Mount *, when the Lord 2Ch 5:10
Moses my servant on Mount *. Mal 4:4

HOREM
*, Beth-anath, and Beth-shemesh. Jos 19:35-39

HORESH
One day near * he received the 1Sa 23:14,15
he met him at * and encouraged 1Sa 23:16
and David stayed at * while 1Sa 23:18
"He is in the caves of * on 1Sa 23:19

HORI
son of Seir) were * and Heman. Gen 36:22
Shaphat, son of *, from the tribe Num 13:3-15
Lotan's sons: * and Homam. 1Ch 1:38,39

HORITE
from Seir, the *—one of the native Gen 36:20,21

HORITES
The * in Mount Seir, as far as Gen 14:5,6
In earlier days the * lived in Deu 2:12
he destroyed the * who were living Deu 2:22

HORMAH
them and chased them to *. Num 14:45
* (meaning "Utterly Destroyed"). Num 21:3
and killed them from Seir to *. Deu 1:44
The king of *; Jos 12:8-24
Eltolad, Chesil, *, Ziklag, Jos 15:21-32
Eltolad, Bethul, *, Ziklag, Jos 19:2-7
So now the city is named * Ju 1:17
*, Borashan, Athach, Hebron. 1Sa 30:27-31
Tolad, Bethuel, *, Ziklag, 1Ch 4:30

HORN
a ram's * sounding one long blast; Ex 19:13
loud blast as from a ram's *; Ex 19:16
a trumpet made from a ram's *. Jos 6:3,4
He is like the strong * of a Ps 18:2
Literally, "lift not up the *." Ps 75:4f
another small * appeared among Dan 7:8
this little * had a man's eyes Dan 7:8
and the boasting of its little *. Dan 7:11
and the little * that came up Dan 7:20
of the others—the * with the eyes, Dan 7:20
For I had seen this * warring Dan 7:21
had one very large * between its Dan 8:5
of his power, his * was broken, and Dan 8:8
and its long * represents the first Dan 8:21
When you saw the * break off, Dan 8:22

HORNED
The * owl, the pelican, Deu 14:11-18

HORNETS
and I will send * to drive out Ex 23:28
your God will send * to drive out Deu 7:20
And I sent * ahead of you to Jos 24:12

HORNS
a ram caught by its * in a bush. Gen 22:13
Make * for the four corners of Ex 27:2
Place its blood upon the * of Ex 29:12
feet high, with * carved from the Ex 30:2
Overlay the top, sides, and * of Ex 30:3
upon its * the blood of the sin Ex 30:10
There were four * at the four Ex 38:2
the blood upon the * of the incense Lev 4:7
put blood upon the * of the altar Lev 4:18
finger upon the * of the altar of Lev 4:25
the * of the burnt offering altar. Lev 4:30
smear it upon the * of the burnt Lev 4:34
upon the four * of the altar, and Lev 8:15,16
it upon the * of the altar, and Lev 9:9
the goat on the * of the altar, Lev 16:18
With the strong * of a wild ox Deu 33:17
hold of the * of the sacred altar. 1Ki 1:49,50
caught hold of the * of the altar. 1Ki 2:28
made some iron * and declared, 1Ki 22:11
* until they are destroyed." 1Ki 22:11
the blowing of * and trumpets, the 1Ch 15:28
trumpets blaring and * sounding. 2Ch 15:14
made some iron * for the occasion 2Ch 18:10
and from the * of these wild oxen. Ps 22:21
with stringed instruments and *. Ps 150:4
Moab is ended—her * are cut off; Jer 48:25
altar, with four * projecting Eze 43:15
it on the four * of the altar and Eze 43:20
other animals, and it had ten *. Dan 7:7
As I was looking at the *, Dan 7:8
I asked, too, about the ten * Dan 7:20
His ten * are ten kings that Dan 7:24
long * standing on the river bank; Dan 8:3
and as I watched, one of these * Dan 8:3
the ram and broke off both his *. Dan 8:7
its place grew four good-sized * Dan 8:8
"The two * of the ram you saw Dan 8:20
and four smaller * replace it, this Dan 8:22
at Bethel. The * of the altar will Amo 3:14
I will give you * of iron and Mic 4:13
I looked and saw four animal *! Zec 1:18
hold of the four * that scattered Zec 1:21
He had seven * and seven eyes, Rev 5:6
from the four * of the golden altar Rev 9:13
*, and seven crowns on his heads. Rev 12:3
It had seven heads and ten *, and Rev 13:1
horns, and ten crowns upon its *. Rev 13:1
with two little * like those of a Rev 13:11
that had seven heads and ten *, Rev 17:3
His ten * are ten kings who have Rev 17:12
animal and his ten *—which Rev 17:16

HORONAIM
be heard all along the road to *. Is 15:5
will surge against *, for all Moab Jer 48:2,3,4
from Zoar to * and to Jer 48:34

HORONITE
But when Sanballat (the *) and Neh 2:10
of Sanballat the *, so I chased him Neh 13:28

HOROSCOPES
people who make * and try to read Jer 10:2,3

HORRIBLE
and to do so is * wickedness. Lev 18:17
practice any of these * customs. Lev 18:29,30
for causing her * disease, for she Num 5:31
for it is * to the Lord your God. Deu 7:25
These nations have done * things Deu 12:31
don't conceal his * suggestion. Deu 13:8
that such a * thing is happening Deu 13:12,13,14
corrupted by the * customs of the Deu 18:9
"There hasn't been such a * crime Ju 19:30
destroy Gibe-ah for this * deed." Ju 20:8,9,10
laws of God and done this * deed? 2Sa 12:9
the * god of the Ammonites. 1Ki 11:5
had taken up the * customs of the Ez 9:1
defiled by the * practices of the Ez 9:11
have committed the * sin of not Neh 1:6,7
It is a * thing for a king to do Pro 16:12
A * thing has happened in this Jer 5:30
gods—a deed so * I've never even Jer 7:31
something too * to understand. Jer 18:13
The things they do are *; Jer 23:14
not to do this * thing I hate, but Jer 44:4
The fate of Edom will be *; Jer 49:17
by jackals, a land * to see, Jer 51:37
taken away and the * Thing is set Dan 12:11
Yes, I have seen a * thing in Hos 6:10
leaving * carnage everywhere. Zec 9:15
wicked men to a * death, and lease Mt 21:41
"So, when you see the * thing Mt 24:15
"When you see the * thing Mk 13:14
do many * things to the followers Act 26:9
the earth, and *, malignant sores Rev 16:2

HORRIBLY
am innocent. I am * punished, even Job 34:6
For Jerusalem sinned so *; Lam 1:8
Their kings are * afraid and look Eze 27:35
the child *, and he fell to the Mk 9:20

HORRIFIED
Old and young alike will be * by Job 18:20

HORRIFY
will * the peoples of the world. Jer 15:4

HORROR
foreboding, darkness, and *. Gen 15:12
is an object of * and disgust to Deu 18:12
You will become an object of *, Deu 28:37
their clothes in * and sorrow. 2Sa 13:31
king, and to the * of the Israeli 2Ki 3:27
hear about it will tingle with *. 2Ki 21:12
make it a public * and disgrace. 2Ch 7:20
to be objects of *, amazement, and 2Ch 29:8
Look at me in *, and lay your Job 21:5
when I see myself. * takes hold Job 21:6
and darkness and waves of *. Job 22:10,11
Trembling and * overwhelm me. Ps 55:5
vision: oh, the * of it all! Is 21:2
sharp pangs of * are upon me, Is 21:3
last the unmixed * of the truth of Is 28:19
and shrink back in * and dismay. Jer 2:12
prophets will be stricken with *. Jer 4:9
always it is disaster and * and Jer 20:8
For she is a sign of * and of Jer 48:39
oh, the *; Jer 50:45
hands in * and shake your head Eze 6:11
and * and shame shall cover you; Eze 7:18
would draw back in *, and know that Eze 20:26
you are an example of *; Eze 28:19
hearts melt in *; Nah 2:10
*: "Nineveh lies in utter ruin." Nah 3:7
is crushed with * and sadness to Mt 26:38
For those will be days of such * Mk 13:19
with * and deepest distress. Mk 14:33
But, oh, the * awaiting that man Lk 22:22
take away this cup of * from me. Lk 22:41,42
never forgot the * of it. Rev 1:7f
or "kept through" the coming *. Rev 3:10f
I stared at her in *. Rev 17:6

HORRORS
These * shall befall you and Deu 28:46
of the awesome * surrounding you. Deu 28:67
moral filth by the * and the fire. Is 4:2,3,4
the beginning of the * to come. Mt 24:8
What * await you, you cities of Lk 10:13
"Yes," said Jesus, "the same * Lk 11:46
having to experience these *. Lk 21:36
safely through these coming *." Lk 21:36f
Then God released him from the * Act 2:24

HORSE
He has thrown both * and rider Ex 15:1
The * and rider have been drowned Ex 15:21
wall beyond the * Gate, each one Neh 3:28
and the king's own *, and the royal Est 6:7,8
on the king's own *, shouting Est 6:9
these robes and my *, and do just Est 6:10
the swiftest * with its rider. Job 39:18
"Have you given the * strength, Job 39:19
Don't be like a senseless * or Ps 32:9
A war * is a poor risk for Ps 33:16,17
The speed of a * is nothing to Ps 147:10
Literally, "The * is prepared Pro 21:31f
Guide a * with a whip, a donkey Pro 26:3
When the * is stolen, it is too Ecc 10:11
as a * rushing to the battle! Jer 8:6
from there to the * Gate on the Jer 31:40
destroying the * and his rider, the Jer 51:21
sitting on a red * that was Zec 1:8
Then the rider on the red *—he Zec 1:10
Give Paul a * to ride and get him Act 23:23,24
We can make a large * turn Jas 3:3
in front of me was a white *. Rev 6:2
This time a red * rode out. Rev 6:4
And I saw a black *, with its Rev 6:5
And now I saw a pale *, and Rev 6:8
* whose rider's name was Hell. Rev 6:8
and a white * standing there; Rev 19:11
and the one sitting on the * was Rev 19:11
one sitting on the * and his army. Rev 19:19
riding the white *, and all the Rev 19:21

HORSE-TRADERS
Solomon sent * to Egypt to 2Ch 1:16

HORSE'S
long and as high as a * bridle. Rev 14:20

HORSEHOOFS
Of the * of the enemy! Ju 5:22

HORSEMEN
all his armies, chariots, and *. Ex 14:17
Pharaoh's horses, chariots, and *. Ex 14:23
and their chariots and *." Ex 14:26
the path and the chariots and *. Ex 14:28
The horses of Pharaoh, his *, and Ex 15:19
six thousand *, and so many 1Sa 13:5
chariots of Israel and its *!" 2Ki 13:14f
he sees a troop, * in pairs, riders Is 21:6,7f
behind them. * will occupy every Eze 26:11
of * can't outrun the danger then. Amo 2:15
Your * marched across the sea; Hab 3:15
Literally, "*." Rev 9:16f

HORSES
Soon all the *, flocks, herds, Gen 47:17
that bites the *' heels, so that Gen 49:17
your cattle, *, donkeys, camels, Ex 9:3
Pharaoh's entire cavalry—*, Ex 14:9
*, chariots, and horsemen. Ex 14:23
The * of Pharaoh, his horsemen, Ex 15:19
Egypt and to their * and Deu 11:4
a large stable of * for himself, Deu 17:16
to Egypt to raise * for him there, Deu 17:16
vast numbers of * and chariots, an Deu 20:1
a vast array of * and chariots, Jos 11:4
Hamstring their * and burn their Jos 11:6
the * and burned all the chariots. Jos 11:9
* except for one hundred teams. 2Sa 8:4
and chariot *, and hired fifty 2Sa 15:1
thousand chariot * and employed 1Ki 4:26
for the royal * in the stables. 1Ki 4:28
myrrh, spices, *, and mules. 1Ki 10:25
a great stable of * with a vast 1Ki 10:26
Solomon's * were brought to him 1Ki 10:28
the * were valued at $150 each. 1Ki 10:29
at least some of my * and mules. 1Ki 18:5
of chariots and *, besieged 1Ki 20:1
and a few others escaped on *. 1Ki 20:20
However, the great bulk of the * 1Ki 20:21
give us the same number of *, 1Ki 20:25
and my * are at your service. 1Ki 22:4
of fire, drawn by * of fire, 2Ki 2:11
"My people and * are yours to 2Ki 3:6,7,8
So Naaman arrived with his * and 2Ki 5:9
and * to surround the city. 2Ki 6:14
*, and chariots everywhere. 2Ki 6:15
that he could see * of fire and 2Ki 6:17
loud galloping of * and the sounds 2Ki 7:6
*, donkeys, and everything else. 2Ki 7:7
one was there! The * and donkeys 2Ki 7:10
of the remaining *—if something 2Ki 7:13
against the wall and on the *; 2Ki 9:33
and she was trampled by the *' 2Ki 9:33
For you have chariots and * and a 2Ki 10:2,3
His body was returned on *, and 2Ki 14:20
ride *, we'll furnish the horses! 2Ki 18:23
ride horses, we'll furnish the *! 2Ki 18:23
Even if Egypt supplies you with * 2Ki 18:24
He tore down the statues of * 2Ki 23:11
for $400 each and * for $100, 2Ch 1:17
his chariots and * were kept. 2Ch 8:6
armor, spices, *, and mules. 2Ch 9:24
4,000 stalls of * and chariots, and 2Ch 9:25
common sycamore. * were brought to 2Ch 9:28
And they brought him back on * 2Ch 25:28
They took with them 736 *, 245 Ez 2:66,67

(HORSES Con't)
They took with them 736 *, 245 Neh 7:68,69
great numbers of * and chariots Is 2:7
sparks fly from their *' hoofs, Is 5:28
trampled and mangled by *' hoofs. Is 14:19
they will give us swift * for Is 30:16
Their * are puny flesh, not Is 31:3
you 2,000 * for them to ride on! Is 36:8,9
its chariots and *, to lie beneath Is 43:17
on * and in chariots, and in Is 66:20
of their war * can be heard all the Jer 8:16f
you race against *, against the Jer 12:5
Harness the * and prepare to Jer 46:4
Then come, O * and chariots and Jer 46:9
War shall devour her * and Jer 50:37
bring a multitude of *! Jer 51:27
* to fight against Nebuchadnezzar. Eze 17:15
blue, dashing about on their *. Eze 23:6
will shake as the * gallop through Eze 26:10
come chariot *, steeds and mules. Eze 27:14
table—feast on *, riders and Eze 39:20
They look like tiny *, and they Joe 2:4
lads in war and drove away your *. Amo 4:10
to pieces. Can * run on rocks? Amo 6:12
wheels rumbling, *' hoofs pounding, Nah 3:2
Their * are swifter than Hab 1:8
sin that you rode upon your *? Hab 3:8,9f
Behind him were other *, red and Zec 1:8
"Sir, what are all those * for?" Zec 1:9
was pulled by red *, the second by Zec 6:2
* and the fourth by dappled-greys. Zec 6:3
by the black * will go north, and Zec 6:6
by white * will follow it there, Zec 6:6
* were impatient to be off, to Zec 6:7
will strike the *, mules, camels, Zec 14:15
In that day the bells on the * Zec 14:20
The locusts looked like * armored Rev 9:7
I saw their * spread out before Rev 9:17,18
others yellow. The *' heads looked Rev 9:17,18
wheat, cattle, sheep, *, Rev 18:13
clean, followed him on white *. Rev 19:14
great generals; of * and riders; Rev 19:18

HOSAH
to the Mediterranean Sea at *. Jos 19:29
son of Jeduthun), * and sixty-eight 1Ch 16:38
real leaders. *, one of the Merari 1Ch 26:10
the upper road, to Shuppim and *. 1Ch 26:16

HOSAH'S
* sons and brothers numbered 1Ch 26:11

HOSEA
for it by the prophet * (1:4). 2Ki 10:11f
from the Lord to *, son of Beeri, Hos 1:1
The Lord said to *, "Go and marry Hos 1:2
So * married Gomer, daughter of Hos 1:3
And God said to *, "Name her Hos 1:6
Baal-worship flourished (* 4:15; Hos 9:15f
* 11:1. Mt 2:15f
* 6:6. Mt 9:13f
Remember what the prophecy of * Rom 9:25
* 2:23. Rom 9:26f

HOSEA'S
during * lifetime—Zechariah, Hos 7:7f

HOSHAIAH
Judah, including *, Azariah, Ezra, Neh 12:33
Azariah (son of *) and Johanan Jer 43:2,3

HOSHAMA
Pedaiah, Shenazzar, Jekamiah, *, 1Ch 3:17,18

HOSHEA
* son of a nun from the Num 13:3-15
"*" means "salvation". Num 13:16f
Then * (the son of Elah) plotted 2Ki 15:30
New king of Israel: * 2Ki 15:30
NEW KING OF Israel: * 2Ki 17:1
and defeated King *, so Israel had 2Ki 17:3
Then * conspired against the 2Ki 17:4
at this time: King * (son of Elah), 2Ki 18:1
the reign of King * in Israel) that 2Ki 18:9
of King * of Israel) Samaria fell. 2Ki 18:10
Over Ephraim, * (son of Azaziah); 1Ch 27:16-22
Hanan, Anaiah, *, Neh 10:14-27

HOSHEA'S
Moses changed * name to Joshua. Num 13:16
ninth year of King * reign, Samaria 2Ki 17:6

HOSPITAL
of the large * bill the child was Gen 30:6f

HOSPITALITY
a stranger, and you refused me * Mt 25:43
And don't hesitate to accept *, Lk 10:7
with friends and receive their *. Act 27:3

HOST
and an unnumbered * of 2Ch 12:3
* of men have been her victims. Pro 7:26
destroyed the vast * of the Is 9:4
yourself to a * of foreign gods; Jer 3:20
you a mighty *, all fully armed. Eze 38:4
with your vast * of cavalry and Eze 38:15,16
Literally, "* of heaven" and Dan 8:10f
of heaven" and "the starry *." Dan 8:10f
Literally, "* of heaven" and Dan 8:10f
of heaven" and "the starry *." Dan 8:10f
joined by a vast * of others—the Lk 2:13
When Jesus' *, a Pharisee, saw Lk 7:39
This greatly surprised his *. Lk 11:37,38
fiercely with a * of questions, Lk 11:53,54
you shows up, the * will bring him Lk 14:9
and when your * sees you he will Lk 14:10
Then he turned to his *. Lk 14:12
Usually a * uses the best wine Jn 2:10
battle—a mighty *, numberless as Rev 20:8

HOSTAGE
to Babylon as a political *. Jer 37:1f

HOSTAGES
King Joash took many * and all 2Ki 14:14
and he took *, including 2Ch 25:24

HOSTS
Who is able to number his * of Job 25:3
us again to yourself, O God of *. Ps 80:7
If the Lord of * had not stepped Is 1:9
Therefore the Lord of *, the Is 1:24
On that day the Lord of * will Is 2:12
THE LORD OF * will cut off Is 3:1
the Lord of * will demand of Is 3:15
But the Lord of * has sworn your Is 5:9
but the Lord of * is exalted Is 5:16
holy, holy is the Lord of *; Is 6:3
the Lord of * will send a plague Is 10:16
the Lord God of * to consume them. Is 10:23
Therefore the Lord God of * says, Is 10:24
The Lord of * will send his angel Is 10:26
The Lord of * has brought them Is 13:4
disappear, declares the Lord of *. Is 17:3
to the Lord of * in Jerusalem, Is 18:7
vicious king, says the Lord of *. Is 19:4
* has laid his plans against them. Is 19:17
follow the Lord of * and will begin Is 19:18
sign of loyalty to the Lord of *; Is 19:20
of *, the God of Israel, has said. Is 21:10
The Lord God of * called you to Is 22:12
The Lord of * has revealed to Is 22:14
the Lord of * will spread a Is 25:6
Then at last the Lord of * Is 28:5
the Lord God of * has plainly told Is 28:22
The Lord of * is a wonderful Is 28:29
In an instant, I, the Lord of *, Is 29:6
He, the Lord of *, will hover Is 31:4,5
"O Lord of *, God of Israel Is 37:16,17
the power of the Lord of * will Is 37:32
this message from the Lord of *: Is 39:5
the Lord of *, who says it—I am the Is 44:6
the Lord of * is his name, the Is 47:4
God, the Lord of *, who dried a Is 51:15
The Lord of * is his name; Is 54:5
him, says the Lord, the God of *. Jer 2:19
the Lord God of * says to his Jer 5:14
For the Lord of * has said to Jer 6:6
again, the Lord of * has said; Jer 6:9
The Lord of *, the God of Israel Jer 7:3
The Lord of *, the God of Israel Jer 7:21
scatter them, says the Lord of *. Jer 8:3
Therefore the Lord of * says Jer 9:7
what the Lord of *, the God of Jer 9:15
"The Lord of * says: Send for Jer 9:17,18
The Lord of * is his name. Jer 10:16
that the Lord of * who planted the Jer 11:17
O Lord of *, you are just. Jer 11:20
For the Lord of *, the God of Jer 16:9
The Lord of *, the God of Israel, Jer 19:3
from the Lord of *: As this jar Jer 19:11
The Lord of *, the God of Israel, Jer 19:15
O Lord of *, who knows those who Jer 20:12
Therefore the Lord of * says: I Jer 23:15
to my people, says the Lord of *. Jer 23:16
And now the Lord God of * says, Jer 25:8,9
Tell them, "The Lord of *, the Jer 25:27
Lord of * says you must drink it! Jer 25:28
See, declares the Lord of *, the Jer 25:32
that the Lord of *, the God of Jer 27:4
to the Lord of * that the golden Jer 27:18
"For the Lord of * says, The Jer 27:19,20,21
"The Lord of *, the God of Jer 28:2
The Lord of *, the God of Jer 28:14
The Lord of *, the God of Israel, Jer 29:4
The Lord of *, the God of Israel, Jer 29:8
The Lord of *, the God of Jer 29:21
The Lord of *, the God of Israel, Jer 29:25
says the Lord of *, I will break Jer 30:8
The Lord of *, the God of Israel, Jer 31:23
name is Lord of *—says this: Jer 31:35
"The Lord of *, God of Israel, Jer 32:14
For the Lord of *, God of Jer 32:15
and mighty God, the Lord of *. Jer 32:18
The Lord of *, the God of Israel, Jer 35:13
Therefore the Lord God of *, the Jer 35:17
"The Lord of *, the God of Israel, Jer 35:18,19
Lord, the God of *, the God of Jer 38:17
The Lord of *, the God of Israel, Jer 39:16
Judah: The Lord of *, the God of Jer 42:15
"For the Lord of *, the God of Jer 42:18
this: The Lord of *, the God of Jer 43:10
The Lord of *, the God of Israel, Jer 44:2,3
And now the Lord, the God of *, Jer 44:7
Therefore the Lord of *, the God Jer 44:11
The Lord of *, the God of Jer 44:25
of the Lord God of *, a day of Jer 46:10
the Lord God of * will receive a Jer 46:10
King, the Lord of *, one is coming Jer 46:18
The Lord of *, the God of Israel, Jer 46:25
of the Lord of *, the God of Jer 48:1
says the King, the Lord of *. Jer 48:15
upon you, says the Lord God of *. Jer 49:5
The Lord of * says: Where are all Jer 49:7
in one day, says the Lord of *. Jer 49:26
The Lord of * says: I will Jer 49:35
Therefore the Lord of *, the God Jer 50:18
work of the Lord, the God of *. Jer 50:25
The Lord of * says: The people of Jer 50:33
His name is the Lord of *. Jer 50:34
For the Lord of * has not Jer 51:5
The Lord of * has taken this Jer 51:14
the Lord of * is his name. Jer 51:19
For the Lord of *, the God of Jer 51:33
So says the King, the Lord of *. Jer 51:57
best among the * of heaven, as well Dan 4:35
to him— the Lord, the God of *; Hos 12:5
Lord, the God of *: "On the same Amo 3:13
Lord, the God of *, is his name." Amo 4:13
Then the Lord God of * will truly Amo 5:14
the Lord God of * will have mercy Amo 5:15
Therefore the Lord God of * says Amo 5:16
says the Lord, the God of *. Amo 5:25,26,27
Jehovah, the Lord God of *, has Amo 6:8
says the Lord, the God of *. Amo 6:14
The Lord God of * touches the Amo 9:5
But now the Lord of * has turned Nah 2:13
against you," says the Lord of *; Nah 3:5
says the Lord of *, God of Israel, Zep 2:9
at the people of the Lord of *. Zep 2:10
it over," says the Lord of *. Hag 1:7
am with you,' says the Lord of *. Hag 2:4
"For the Lord of * says, 'In Hag 2:6
my glory,' says the Lord of *. Hag 2:7
chosen you," says the Lord of *. Hag 2:23
The Lord of * was very angry with Zec 1:2
"O Lord of *, for seventy years Zec 1:12
from the Lord of *: Don't you think Zec 1:14
of *, and so will all Jerusalem. Zec 1:16
Say it again: The Lord of * Zec 1:17
it was the Lord of * who sent me. Zec 2:9
the Lord of * who sent me to you. Zec 2:11,12
"The Lord of * declares: 'If you Zec 3:7
And after that,' the Lord of * Zec 3:10
says the Lord of *—you will succeed Zec 4:6
are from God, the Lord of *. Zec 4:9
by my name," says the Lord of *. Zec 5:4
Tell him that the Lord of * Zec 6:12
have been from God, the Lord of *. Zec 6:15
God, the Lord of *, commanded Zec 7:12
"The Lord of * says, I am Zec 8:2
'The Mountain of the Lord of *.' Zec 8:3
The Lord of * declares that Zec 8:4
The Lord of * says, "Get on with Zec 8:9
says the Lord of *. Zec 8:11
came to me from the Lord of *: Zec 8:18
to the Lord of * in Jerusalem to Zec 8:22
For the Lord of * has arrived to Zec 10:3
in the Lord of *, their God.' Zec 12:5
And the Lord of * declares, "In Zec 13:2
and equal," says the Lord of *. Zec 13:7
the Lord of *, to celebrate a time Zec 14:16
the Lord of *, will have no rain. Zec 14:17
shall be sacred to the Lord of *; Zec 14:21
in the Temple of the Lord of *! Zec 14:21
then the Lord of * will say, 'Try Mal 1:4
says the Lord of *, "and I will Mal 1:10
the nations," says the Lord of *. Mal 1:11
says the Lord of *, "and my name Mal 1:14
this warning from the Lord of *: Mal 2:1
father Levi," says the Lord of *. Mal 2:4
of the Lord of *, and men should Mal 2:7
parody," says the Lord of *. Mal 2:8
coming," says the Lord of *. Mal 3:1
not fear me," says the Lord of *. Mal 3:5
to me," says the Lord of *. Mal 3:7
they ripen," says the Lord of *. Mal 3:11
are the promises of the Lord of *. Mal 3:12
says the Lord of *, "in that day Mal 3:17
"WATCH NOW," THE Lord of * Mal 4:1
underfoot," says the Lord of *. Mal 4:3
reached the ears of the Lord of *. Jas 5:4
Dragon and his * of fallen angels. Rev 12:7

HOT
it happened: One * summer afternoon Gen 18:1
him, he set out in * pursuit and Gen 31:23
who discovered a * springs in the Gen 36:24
and when the sun became * upon Ex 16:21
is your anger so * against your own Ex 32:11
and the anger of the Lord grew *; Num 11:10
Then the anger of the Lord grew * Num 12:9
and the anger of the Lord was * Num 25:3
And the Lord's anger was * Num 32:10,11
the Lord would be * against you and Deu 7:4
where it was so * and dry. Deu 8:15
the Lord will be * against you, and Deu 11:17

(HOT Con't)
His anger and jealousy will be * Deu 29:20
of the Lord was * against this Deu 29:27
This bread was * from the ovens Jos 9:12
His anger will rise * against Jos 23:15,16
on * stones, and a jar of water! 1Ki 19:6
beneath the * sun, and like grain 2Ki 19:26
but in * weather, disappears. Job 6:15-18
burns * within me. Ps 69:9
Why is your anger * against Ps 74:1
Can he walk on * coals and not Pro 6:28
in the * summertime. Pro 25:13
Literally, "like * embers to Pro 26:21f
the Lord is * against his people; Is 5:25
As a *, dry land is cooled by Is 25:5
rock within a * and weary land. Is 32:2
his * rebuke with flames of fire. Is 66:15
No matter how * the fire, they Jer 6:29
thrown out to the * sun and frosty Jer 36:30
demanded such a * fire in the Dan 3:22
Then, when the sun was *, God Jon 4:8
soil, but the * sun soon scorched Mt 13:6
wilted beneath the * sun and died Mk 4:5,6
but when the * winds of Lk 8:13
long walk in the * sun and sat Jn 4:5,6
well—you are neither * nor cold; Rev 3:15

HOT-HEAD
THEN A * whose name was Sheba (son 2Sa 20:1

HOT-HEADED
Don't be * and rush to court! Pro 25:8,9,10

HOT-TEMPERED
A * man starts fights and gets Pro 29:22

HOTBED
times past been a * of insurrection Ez 4:19

HOTHAM
Japhlet, Shomer, *, 1Ch 7:32
The sons of his brother * 1Ch 7:35
Shama and Je-iel (sons of *) from 1Ch 11:26-47

HOTHEADED
they will be *, puffed up with 2Ti 3:4

HOTHEADS
by fierce lions—* whose teeth are Ps 57:4
Even the * among them will be Is 32:4

HOTHIR
Mallothi, *, and Mahazi-oth. 1Ch 25:4,5
Twenty-first, * and twelve of his 1Ch 25:9-31

HOTTER
The battle grew * and hotter 2Ch 18:34
The battle grew hotter and * 2Ch 18:34
The more I mused, the * the fires Ps 39:2,3
the refining fire grows *, but it Jer 6:29
up seven times * than usual, and Dan 3:19

HOTTEST
the front of the * part of the 2Sa 11:15
all remains despite the * fire. Eze 24:12

HOUND
that you must * me for sins you Job 10:4-7
synagogues, and * them from city to Mt 23:34

HOUNDED
and * brokenhearted ones to death. Ps 109:16
them that I even * them in distant Act 26:11

HOUNDING
the Christians, * them to death, Act 22:4

HOUR
Let them save you in your * of Ju 10:14
They are like a single *! Ps 90:4
sleeps away his * of opportunity. Pro 10:5
And even until this very * there Jer 44:10
Long have we waited for this * Lam 2:16
against me until this very *. Eze 2:3
a flaming furnace within the *. Dan 3:15
and silent for an *, aghast at the Dan 4:19
That very same * this prophecy Dan 4:33
Yet to this very * my people rise Mic 2:8
the boy was healed that same *! Mt 8:13
worked only one *, and yet you've Mt 20:11,12
But no one knows the date and * Mt 24:36
you even stay awake with me one *? Mt 26:40
knows the day or * when these Mk 13:32
* awaiting him might never come. Mk 14:35
Literally, "that the * might pass Mk 14:35f
you watch with me even one *? Mk 14:37
This was the question of the *, Lk 3:15
knew the exact * of his return—just Lk 12:39
right up to the * of my return. Lk 17:30
Or, "the * I am revealed." Lk 17:30f
forward to this * with deep Lk 22:15
About an * later someone else Lk 22:59
Within the * they were on their Lk 24:33,34
and during every * of it a man can Jn 11:9
That same * he washed their Act 16:33
And that very * I could see him! Act 22:13
To this very * we have gone 1Co 4:11
our lives, facing death * by hour? 1Co 15:30
our lives, facing death hour by *? 1Co 15:30
this world's last * has come. 1Jn 2:18
in the * of testing " Rev 3:10f
for what seemed like half an *. Rev 8:1
month and day and *, and now they Rev 9:15
The same * there will be a Rev 11:13
And now in a single * all is Rev 18:19

HOURS
there for almost twenty-four *! Jos 10:13
Temple and were on duty at all *. 1Ch 9:33,34
for two or three *, and for several Neh 9:3
for several more * they took turns Neh 9:3
their waking * planning treachery. Ps 38:12
They spend long * with all their Ps 64:6
"I, Wisdom, will make the * of Pro 9:11
Reverence for God adds * to each Pro 10:27
It is the one who spends long * Pro 23:29,30
"A couple of * later he was Mt 20:3
*, from noon until three o'clock. Mt 27:45
for three *, until three o'clock. Lk 23:44
"There are twelve * of daylight Jn 11:9
in the early * of the morning. Jn 18:28
About three * later his wife came Act 5:7
kept it up for two *: "Great is Act 19:34

HOUSE
the * and shouted to Lot, "Bring Gen 19:4
Literally, "go into my father's * Gen 24:38f
were there in the *—and instructed Gen 27:15
to the * of your grandfather Gen 28:2
He named the place Bethel ("* Gen 28:19
from Shechem's * and returned to Gen 34:26
Jacob named the spot Bethel ("* Gen 35:15
Then one day as he was in the * Gen 39:11
holding it as he fled from the *. Gen 39:12
or gold from your master's *? Gen 44:8
a * where there was not one dead. Ex 12:30
one *, and not carry it outside; Ex 12:46
* of Caleb (1 Chronicles 2:18,19). Ex 17:10f
your cattle or your * guests. Ex 20:10
of your neighbor's *, or want to Ex 20:17
of breaking into a * and is killed, Ex 22:2
into the * of Jehovah thy God." Ex 23:19f
the Tabernacle to * the Ark, so Ex 38:21
leprosy in some * there, then the Lev 14:33,34
the owner of the * shall come and Lev 14:35
there may be leprosy in my *!' Lev 14:35
"The priest shall order the * to Lev 14:36
everything in the * will not be Lev 14:36
the walls of the * which seem to be Lev 14:37
shall close up the * for seven Lev 14:38
walls of the * scraped thoroughly, Lev 14:41
used, and the * replastered. Lev 14:42
is leprosy, and the * is defiled. Lev 14:44
destruction of the *—all its Lev 14:45
Anyone entering the * while it Lev 14:46
in the * shall wash his clothing. Lev 14:47
will pronounce the * cleansed, and Lev 14:48
shall sprinkle the * seven times. Lev 14:51,52
In this way the * shall be Lev 14:51,52
for the * and cleansing it." Lev 14:53
a garment or in a *, or in any Lev 14:55
born in the same * or elsewhere. Lev 18:9
like an ordinary *, for the Lev 21:12
"If a man sells a * in the city, Lev 25:29
and the * will be his again. Lev 27:14,15
He is completely at home in my *! Num 12:7,8
them on the doorposts of your *! Deu 6:9
a new *, but not yet dedicated it? Deu 20:5
"Every new * must have a Deu 22:8
guilt to both the * and its owner. Deu 22:8
enter his * to get his security. Deu 24:10
refuses to build his brother's *.' Deu 25:9
And ever afterwards his * shall Deu 25:10
someone else will live in the * Deu 28:30
They will eat you out of * and Deu 28:51
Then, since her * was on top of Jos 2:15
anyone else—are here inside the *. Jos 2:17,18
this * will be killed or injured. Jos 2:19
*, for she protected our spies. Jos 6:17
with her in the *, and they still Jos 6:25
driven me out of my father's *? Ju 11:7
coming out of his * to meet him Ju 11:30,31
We are going to burn down your *, Ju 12:1
your father's * with you in it. Ju 14:15
He happened to stop at Micah's * Ju 17:7,8
went over to the * and with all of Ju 18:15,16
around the * and began beating at Ju 19:22
at the door of the * and lay there Ju 19:26
surrounded the *, planning to kill Ju 20:5
tell me where the seer's * is?" 1Sa 9:18
to watch David's * and kill him 1Sa 19:11
man in his own * and on his bed! 2Sa 4:11
you build me a * to dwell in?" 2Sa 7:5f
has left them here to keep the *. 2Sa 16:21
* should be placed in seclusion. 2Sa 20:3
and he was buried beside his * in 1Ki 2:34
him, "Build a * here in Jerusalem, 1Ki 2:36,37
live in the same *, just the two of 1Ki 3:17,18
a single piece of bread in the *. 1Ki 17:12
much food do you have in the *?" 2Ki 4:2
"Go into your * with your sons 2Ki 4:4
and forth in the * a few times; 2Ki 4:35
Then he hid the money in his *. 2Ki 5:24
Elisha was sitting in his * at a 2Ki 6:32
about getting back her * and land. 2Ki 8:3
and went into the *, and the young 2Ki 9:6
so he lived in a * by himself. 2Ki 15:5
years that he was under * arrest: 1Ch 3:17,18
It was taken from the * of 1Ch 13:7
new Tabernacle to * the Ark of God, 1Ch 15:1
width of the *, with the inner 2Ch 3:4
were brought into the Lord's *. 2Ch 31:12,13
pulled from his * and built into a Ez 6:11
and his * shall be reduced to a Ez 6:11
walls, and for a * for myself." Neh 2:8
beside his own *, and next to him Neh 3:10
Literally, "the * of the mighty Neh 3:16f
* to the side of the house. Neh 3:21
house to the side of the *. Neh 3:21
from Azariah's * to the corner. Neh 3:24
immediately opposite his own *. Neh 3:28
next to his own *, and beyond him Neh 3:29
who built next to his own *. Neh 3:30
brother's *, tragedy struck. Job 1:12,13
and engulfed the * so that the roof Job 1:19
Every * built by the wicked is Job 27:18
Literally, "for your *." Ps 69:9f
deceive and lie to stay in my *. Ps 101:7
UNLESS THE LORD builds a *, the Ps 127:1
Don't go near her *, lest you Pro 5:8
in his * to pay it back. Pro 6:31
the window of my * one day, and Pro 7:6
the street to the * of this wayward Pro 7:8,9
the road to hell, look for her *. Pro 7:27
road, and at the door of every *. Pro 8:1
She sits at the door of her * or Pro 9:14
A WISE WOMAN builds her *, while a Pro 14:1
first before building your *. Pro 24:27
Literally, "my mother's *." Sol 8:2f
Then Isaiah said, O * of Is 7:13
them his treasure * full of silver, Is 39:2
Is that why the * is silent and Is 50:2
Enlarge your *; Is 54:2
give them—in my *, within my walls Is 56:5
full of joy within my * of Prayer. Is 56:7
"A * of Prayer for All People"! Is 56:7
a man builds a *, he will keep on Is 65:21;22
suddenly, in a moment, every * is Jer 4:20
dungeon under the * of Jonathan the Jer 37:15,16
*, for you would die there." Jer 38:26
in your *, and I will paralyze Eze 3:24
outside your * during the daylight Eze 12:4
Then leave the * at night, just Eze 12:4
* knocked into a heap of rubble. Dan 3:29
to Daniel's * and found him praying Dan 6:11
even one *, they too will perish. Amo 6:9
his body from the *, he will ask Amo 6:10
* (though it is all he has); Mic 2:2
for you to make, O * of Jacob? Mic 2:7
received in the * of my friends." Zec 13:6f
Entering the * where the baby and Mt 2:11
who builds his * on solid rock. Mt 7:24
beat against his *, it won't Mt 7:25
a man who builds his * on sand. Mt 7:26
beat against his *, it will fall Mt 7:27
When Jesus arrived at Peter's *, Mt 8:14
were eating dinner [at Matthew's * Mt 9:10
They went right into the * where Mt 9:28
"then will he spoil his *." Mt 12:29f
Jesus was speaking in a crowded * Mt 12:46,47
Jesus left the * and went down to Mt 13:1
outside, he went into the *. Mt 13:36
Then he went into the * to talk to Mt 17:25
And now your * is left to you, Mt 23:38
meal with my disciples at your *.' Mt 26:18
the High Priest's * and went in and Mt 26:58
before Pilate's * that morning he Mt 27:17
Soon the * where he was staying Mk 2:2
he went into the * of God—Abiathar Mk 2:25,26
When he returned to the * where Mk 3:20
tied up before his * can be Mk 3:27
at the crowded * where he was Mk 3:31,32
shift around from * to house while Mk 6:10
* while you are there," he said. Mk 6:10
Then he went into a * to get away Mk 7:17
was alone in the * with his Mk 9:28
When they were settled in the * Mk 9:33
disciples in the *, they brought up Mk 10:10
in the street, tied outside a *. Mk 11:4,5
don't even go back into the *. Mk 13:15,16
the master of the * will come." Mk 13:34f
At the * he enters, tell the man Mk 14:14
at the Temple, in my Father's *?" Lk 2:49
a man who builds a * on a strong Lk 6:47,48
break against the *, it stands Lk 6:47,48
builds a * without a foundation. Lk 6:49
down against that *, it crumbles Lk 6:49
but just before arriving at the * Lk 7:6,7,8
returned to his *, they found the Lk 7:10
get into the * where he was Lk 8:19
When they arrived at the * Jesus Lk 8:51
went to a friend's * at midnight, Lk 11:5,6
the head of the * has locked the Lk 13:24,25
And now—now your * is left Lk 13:35
come, so that the * will be full. Lk 14:23
corner of the * and sweep every Lk 15:8
Bring the finest robe in the * Lk 15:22
coming from the *, and he asked Lk 15:25
his * in great excitement and joy. Lk 19:6

HOUSE Con't)
Follow him into the * he enters, Lk 22:10
Don't turn my Father's * into a Jn 2:16
for God's * will be my undoing." Jn 2:17
who were at the * trying to console Jn 11:31
And the * was filled with Jn 12:3
By Jewish law, entering the * of a Jn 18:28f
of the * where they were staying. Act 1:13
the * where they were meeting. Act 2:2
the sky above the *, crowds came Act 2:6
and find the * of a man named Judas Act 9:11
on the flat roof of his * to pray. Act 10:9,10
had found the * and were standing Act 10:17
at the * where I was staying! Act 11:11
his * and set a meal before them. Act 16:34
of his * naked and badly injured. Act 19:16
day large numbers came to his *. Act 28:23
the next two years in his rented * Act 28:30
be an Heir in the * of Jesse, and Rom 15:12
working at the * of Aristobulus. Rom 16:10
slaves over at Narcissus *. Rom 16:11
live at Chloe's * have told me of 1Co 1:11
But if the * he has built burns 1Co 3:15
together are the * of God, and that 1Co 3:16
of God lives among you in his *? 1Co 3:16
Gentiles are a part of God's *. Eph 3:1
around from * to house, getting 1Ti 5:13
from house to *, getting into other 1Ti 5:13
very best in the *—so that Christ 2Ti 2:21
also faithfully served in God's *. Heb 3:2
who builds a fine * gets more Heb 3:3
gets more praise than his * does. Heb 3:3
*, but he was only a servant; Heb 3:5
is in complete charge of God's *. Heb 3:6
And we Christians are God's *—he Heb 3:6
best seat in the * and say to the Jas 2:3
for God's use in building his *. 1Pe 2:5
honoring him as head of the *. 1Pe 3:6

HOUSEHOLD

Literally, "into the * of Gen 12:15f
* on account of her being there. Gen 12:17
and all his * and possessions. Gen 12:20
men born into his *, 318 of them in Gen 14:14
a son, some other member of my * Gen 15:2,3
as to everyone born in your *. Gen 17:12
male—born in his * or bought from Gen 17:23
and boys of the *, whether born Gen 17:24-27
and a godly *—men who are just and Gen 18:19
to death along with all your *." Gen 20:7
other women of the *, so that they Gen 20:17
One day Abraham said to his * Gen 24:2
stole her father's * gods and took Gen 31:21
But as for your * idols, a Gen 31:32
SO JACOB AND his * Gen 32:1
He divided his *, along with the Gen 32:7
Meanwhile Jacob and his * went Gen 33:17
all those in his * to destroy the Gen 35:2
Leaving Bethel, he and his * Gen 35:16
wives, children, * servants, cattle Gen 36:6,7,8
of Potiphar's *, and all of his Gen 39:4
All his * affairs began to run Gen 39:5
with everything in the entire *; Gen 39:8
all of his officials and * staff. Gen 40:20
the manager of his *, "These men Gen 43:16
over to Joseph's * manager, and Gen 43:19
"Don't worry about it," the * Gen 43:23
Joseph ordered his * manager to Gen 44:1
So the * manager did as he was Gen 44:2
Joseph said to his * manager, Gen 44:4
poverty along with all your *." Gen 45:11,12
Also in the total of Jacob's * Gen 46:19-22
* there in Egypt totaled seventy. Gen 46:27
for his *—about three quarts Ex 16:16
your *—your slaves and visitors. Ex 23:12
himself and his * and for all the Lev 16:17
children born in his * may eat it. Lev 22:11
to her father's *, she may eat of Lev 22:13
or by any of your *—your sons, Deu 5:14
God, and to rejoice with your *. Deu 14:26
the Lord with your family and *. Deu 16:11
of his father's *, and for fear of Ju 6:27
cattle, and * goods at the front of Ju 18:21
honored member of your own *! 1Sa 22:14
blessed Obed-edom and all his *. 2Sa 6:11
All the * of Ziba became 2Sa 9:12
your own * to rebel against you. 2Sa 12:11
So the king and his * set out at 2Sa 15:16
*, caught up with him. 2Sa 16:1
the king's * and troops across, and 2Sa 19:18
him and his * across the Jordan. 2Sa 19:41
from the people for the king's *. 1Ki 4:7
You can pay me with food for my * 1Ki 5:9
of wheat for his * and 96 gallons 1Ki 5:11
The man in charge of Ahab's * 1Ki 18:3,4
David returned to bless his own *. 1Ch 16:43
food for all your * after the hay Pro 27:25,26,27
breakfast for her *, and plans the Pro 31:15
of winter for her *, for she has Pro 31:21
her *, and is never lazy. Pro 31:27
and others were born within my *. Ecc 2:7,8
your family and * shall become Jer 20:6
mock and make my name a * joke. Jer 20:8
the Lord, with all their * goods. Jer 49:29
"Those of his own * will bring Dan 11:26
And since I, the master of the *, Mt 10:25
will be going about their * tasks; Mt 24:41
*, to feed my children day by day? Mt 24:45
be working together at * tasks; Lk 17:35,36
and his entire * believed that Jn 4:53
The police and the * servants Jn 18:18
But one of the * slaves of the Jn 18:26
reverent, as was his entire *. Act 10:2
called two of his * servants and a Act 10:7
you and all your * can be saved!' Act 11:14
* and asked us to be her guests. Act 16:15
be saved, and your entire *." Act 16:31
Then they told him and all his * Act 16:32
How he and his * rejoiced because Act 16:34
and all his * believed in the Lord Act 18:8
* with every other Christian. Eph 2:19
rules over God's *, let us go Heb 10:21

HOUSEHOLDS

and to all their *, "I'll go and Gen 46:31
and for your * and little ones." Gen 47:24
them, with their * and tents and Deu 11:6

HOUSEKEEPING

things such as * and the likes and 1Co 7:34

HOUSES

come out into your *, even into Ex 8:3,4
officials, and all the * of Egypt. Ex 10:6
he passed over our * and did not Ex 12:27
But village *—a village is a Lev 25:31
will receive only * in their Lev 25:33
the doors of your * and upon your Deu 11:20
in the inner room of one of the *. 1Ki 20:30
He also closed all the * of male 1Ki 22:46
He also tore down the * of male 2Ki 23:7
and all the other * of any worth. 2Ki 25:9
and * of the descendants of Ham; 1Ch 4:40,41
the sections next to their own *. Neh 3:23
and only a few * were scattered Neh 7:4
the roofs of their *, or in their Neh 8:16
they took over * full of good Neh 9:25
They break into * at night and Job 24:16
Their * lie along the road to Pro 2:18
it their home. The * will be Is 13:21
You check over the * and tear Is 22:9,10,11
silent and empty, * abandoned, Is 27:10
of your * from precious jewels. Is 54:11
heaps of ruined * where only Jer 9:11
* and vineyards and fields." Jer 32:15
down all these * where the roofs Jer 32:29
have torn down the * of this city, Jer 33:4
He also told us not to build * Jer 35:7
We haven't built * or owned Jer 35:9
knock down her walls and * into Jer 50:26
The invaders have burned the * Jer 51:30
They talk about you in their * Eze 33:30
your * made into heaps of rubble! Dan 2:5
they climb up into the *, coming Joe 2:9
and their summer *, too—and Amo 3:15
beautiful stone * you are building, Amo 5:11
in the abandoned * in Ashkelon. Zep 2:7
the city will be taken, the * Zec 14:1
who owned land or * sold them and Act 4:34,35
And many people can build *, but Heb 3:4

HOUSETOPS

the *, burnt yellow by the sun. Is 37:27
in your ears, proclaim from the *! Mt 10:27
from the * for all to hear! Lk 12:3

HOVER

of your wings as you * over me. Ps 17:8
He, the Lord of Hosts, will * Is 31:4,5
Jerusalem as birds * round their Is 31:4,5

HOVERING

with his glory. * about him were Is 6:2

HOWEVER

farm the soil. (*, water welled up Gen 2:6
owned to Isaac; *, he gave gifts Gen 25:6
Pharaoh's wine taster, *, Gen 40:23
to buy grain. *, Jacob wouldn't Gen 42:4
Perez, Zerah (*, Er and Onan died Gen 46:8-14
for making bricks! *, don't reduce Ex 5:7,8
shall be killed. *, you must buy Ex 13:13
get protection. *, if a man Ex 21:14
be punished. *, if the slave does Ex 21:21
on ahead of you; *, when I come to Ex 32:34
see me and live. *, stand here on Ex 33:21
"* it is prepared—whether baked, Lev 2:8
"*, if he chooses to bring a Lev 4:32
made to me. *, all of it is most Lev 6:17
"*, if someone brings a Lev 7:16
is not leprosy. *, if in the Lev 13:42
it is in. *, if it then reappears, Lev 13:57
inside the camp; *, he must stay Lev 14:8
will be rivals. *, if your wife Lev 18:18
brother's wife." * such a marriage Lev 20:21f
physical defect. *, he shall be Lev 21:22
eat this food. *, there is one Lev 22:11
"*, you may purchase slaves from Lev 25:44
to someone else. *, anything Lev 27:28
the Tabernacle. *, only Aaron and Num 3:10
of their animals. *, you may Num 18:16
"*, the firstborn of cows, Num 18:17
the Lord my God. *, stay here Num 22:19
of them to us. *, we stayed away Deu 2:37
your offerings. *, the meat you Deu 12:15
a natural death. *, a foreigner Deu 14:21
at his sanctuary. *, if this Deu 15:21
stoned to death. *, never put a Deu 17:6
After that you may marry her. *, Deu 21:14
or injured. *, if you betray us, Jos 2:20
will guide you. *, stay about a Jos 3:2,3,4
long before. (*, Joshua did not Jos 11:13
driven them out. *, the people of Jos 13:13
*, Hepher's son Zelophehad Jos 17:3
Later on, *, when the Israelis Jos 17:13
to each tribe. *, remember that Jos 18:7
First, *, they sent a delegation Jos 22:13
tribe of Judah, *, asked help from Ju 1:3
*, the Lord's reply through the Ju 6:8
the Lord is your King! *, I have Ju 8:23,24
to battle again. *, someone had Ju 9:42
and captured it. *, there was a Ju 9:51
not eat anything. *, if you wish to Ju 13:16
There were, *, some bums and 1Sa 10:27
Jonathan, *, had not heard his 1Sa 14:27
everyone else. *, Saul and his men 1Sa 15:9
*, this was their song: "Saul 1Sa 18:7
this to Amnon. *, he hated him with 2Sa 13:21-24
"*, if you or your children turn 1Ki 9:6
to someone else. *, for the sake 1Ki 11:12,13
take the kingdom from him now, *; 1Ki 11:34
at Kidron Brook. *, the shrines on 1Ki 15:14
on horses. *, the great bulk of 1Ki 20:21
they turned back! *, someone 1Ki 22:34
*, may the Lord pardon me this 2Ki 5:18
Later on, *, King Ben-hadad of 2Ki 6:24
give you. *, what's the matter?" 2Ki 6:26-30
Baal from Israel. *, he didn't 2Ki 10:29
and faithful men. *, the money 2Ki 12:16
his father Joash. *, he didn't 2Ki 14:4
but they did not conquer it. *, 2Ki 16:6
the city gate. *, these priests 2Ki 23:9
wiped out. *, he didn't make 2Ch 8:9
*, remained loyal to Rehoboam. 2Ch 10:17
*, the priests and Levites from 2Ch 11:13,14
My troops are at your command! *, 2Ch 18:3,4,5
cities of Judah. *, he gave the 2Ch 21:3,4
of doing evil. *, the Lord was 2Ch 21:7
None of his sons, *, except for 2Ch 22:9
his father. *, he didn't kill 2Ch 25:4
*, King Amaziah of Judah lived on 2Ch 25:25
Uzziah—who had, *, sinned by 2Ch 27:2
and scorn! *, some from the tribes 2Ch 30:11
and old alike. *, the priests on 2Ch 31:16
with a miracle. *, Hezekiah didn't 2Ch 32:25
*, when ambassadors arrived from 2Ch 32:31
God of Israel. *, the people still 2Ch 33:17
Addan, and Immer. *, they had lost Ez 2:59
was located. *, the Temple workers Neh 11:21
he was furious. *, he restrained Est 5:10
* long the Lord may let him live. Ecc 5:18
of the land." *, some may prefer Is 4:2,3,4f
the city stood. *, when the news Is 7:2
be destroyed. *, the Gospel of Is 7:14f
ways and live. *, if a righteous Eze 18:24
"*, the sons of Zadok, of the Eze 44:15
tribe of Judah. *, their Dan 1:7
to his own land. *, the sons of Dan 11:10,11
early fig, * much I long for it! Mic 7:1
But no; * much I punish them, Zep 3:7
Therefore no mountain, * high, Zec 4:7
citizens are free! *, we don't want Mt 17:26,27
"*, no one, not even the angels Mk 13:32
There was, *, a young man Mk 14:51,52
eyewitnesses. *, it occurred to me Lk 1:3
Nothing shall injure you! *, the Lk 10:20
*, Peter ran to the tomb to look. Lk 24:12
Implied. *, most commentators Jn 5:32,33f
(actually, *, this tradition of Jn 7:21,22,23
*, even many of the Jewish Jn 12:42
didn't break his. *, one of the Jn 19:34
"*, God promised that eventually Act 7:5
built it. *, God doesn't live in Act 7:48,49
to murder him. *, when the other Act 9:30
but only to Jews. *, some of the Act 11:20
to the synagogue. *, Crispus, the Act 18:8
worthy of death. *, he appealed his Act 25:25
it is no sin. *, marriage will 1Co 7:28
*, some Christians don't realize 1Co 8:7
First, *, let me tell you about 1Co 12:31
to the unsaved. *, prophecy 1Co 14:22
in tongues"; *, be sure that 1Co 14:40
Each, *, in his own turn: Christ 1Co 15:23
every part of us. *, Christ has Eph 4:7

HOWLING

God protected them in the * Deu 32:10
are satisfied, * like dogs and Ps 59:14,15
The houses will be haunted by * Is 13:21
I will wail and lament, * as a Mic 1:8

HOWLS

Their * will fill the night. Is 34:14

HUBS
the axles, spokes, rims, and *. 1Ki 7:33
HUCKSTERS
We are not like those *—and there 2Co 2:17
HUDDLE
Gaza will * in desperation and Zec 9:5
HUDDLING
among the bushes, * together for Job 30:7
HUG
A time to *; Ecc 3:5
A time not to *; Ecc 3:5
HUGE
For God made two * lights, the Gen 1:16
storm, and a * cloud came down upon Ex 19:16
of God, and took a * stone as a Jos 24:26
there was this * loaf of barley Ju 7:12,13
The Philistines in turn sent a * Ju 15:9
ahead of him with a * shield. 1Sa 17:4-7
And have you heard about the * 1Sa 17:25
so that you will have a * force. 2Sa 17:11
whose spearhandle was as * as a 2Sa 21:19
and shaped * blocks of stone—a very 1Ki 5:17
It was *—measuring 150 feet long, 1Ki 7:2
entirely from *, expensive stones, 1Ki 7:9
feet across. The * stones in the 1Ki 7:11
gold, along with a * quantity of 1Ki 10:10
He also made a * ivory throne and 1Ki 10:18
He built up a * force of 1,400 2Ch 1:14
be * and incredibly beautiful. 2Ch 2:9
Then he forged a * round tank 2Ch 4:2
the * tank and five to the left. 2Ch 4:6
with bronze. The * tank was in the 2Ch 4:10
The * tank and the twelve oxen 2Ch 4:12-16
He also made a * ivory throne 2Ch 9:17
and he had a * army stationed at 2Ch 17:13
shoot arrows and * stones from the 2Ch 26:15
came and saw these * piles, how 2Ch 31:7,8
They organized a * work crew to 2Ch 32:4
It is being built with * stones, Ez 5:8
There will be three layers of * Ez 6:4
and we needed a * supply of all Neh 5:18
terrible storms and * hailstones. Is 30:30
palace with * rooms and many Jer 22:14
before it a * cloud glowing with Eze 1:4
famous, * pillars will topple. Eze 26:11
I will give you * harvests from Eze 36:30
"O king, you saw a * and Dan 2:31
Then four * animals came up out Dan 7:3
apart with its * iron teeth, and Dan 7:7
"These four * animals," he Dan 7:17
a * crowd was waiting for them. Mt 17:14
and a * crowd of people from all Mk 1:32,33
followed by a * crowd from all over Mk 3:7,8
Now as it happened there was a * Mk 5:11
for that man if a * millstone were Mk 9:42
the * stone from the entrance. Mk 16:3
from the hill, a * crowd met him, Lk 9:37
the sea with a * rock tied to his Lk 17:2,3
and found that the * stone covering Lk 24:2
And a * crowd, many of them Jn 6:2-5
the city, and a * crowd of Passover Jn 12:12
I saw a vision—a * sheet, let down Act 11:5
and against * numbers of wicked Eph 6:12
SINCE WE HAVE such a * crowd of Heb 12:1
And a tiny rudder makes a * ship Jas 3:4
appeared to be a * burning mountain Rev 8:8,9
though from some * furnace, and the Rev 9:2
the shouting of a * crowd, or like Rev 19:6
HUKKOK
then to *, and coincided with the Jos 19:34
HUKOK
Abdon, Mashal, *, and Rehob, with 1Ch 6:75
HUL
were:Uz, *, Gether, Mash. Gen 10:23
Arpachshad, Lud, Aram, Uz, *, 1Ch 1:17
HULDAH
to find * the prophetess. 2Ki 22:14
So the men went to * the 2Ch 34:22
HULL
with ropes to strengthen the *. Act 27:17
HUMAN
involved with * women, their Gen 6:4
saw the extent of * wickedness, and Gen 6:5
Or if he touches * discharge of Lev 5:3
"Anyone who touches a dead * Num 19:11
works without regard to * means! 1Sa 17:47
is far beyond any * standard! 2Sa 7:19
by scattering * bones over them. 2Ki 23:14
and he burned * bones upon the 2Ki 23:20
pass away, removed by no * hand. Job 34:20
as well as with * joys. Ps 128:5
Why bother at all with the * Ps 144:3
even to call myself a * being! Pro 30:2
as I have watched * affairs: There Ecc 9:13
manner in which a * spirit is Ecc 11:5
your children as * sacrifices down Is 57:5
to him than * sacrifice. Is 66:3
shall it be lived in by * beings; Jer 50:39
their wings I could see * hands. Eze 1:8
* race of which he is the head. Eze 2:1f
dried * dung as fuel, and eat it. Eze 4:12
use cow dung instead of * dung." Eze 4:15
what looked like * hands) and took Eze 10:7,8
like * hands under their wings. Eze 10:21
phrases apply to a * king of Tyre, Eze 28:12f
mountain without * hands—the Rock Dan 2:45
at the end of * history. Dan 8:23f
no * means could overpower him. Dan 8:25
you worship was made by * hands! Hos 8:6
you—this is not from any * source. Mt 16:17
You are thinking merely from a * Mt 16:23
indifference to * need, he said to Mk 3:5
this only from a * point of view Mk 8:33
Temple made with * hands and in Mk 14:58
another, made without * hands!' Mk 14:58
resulting from * passion or Jn 1:13
became a * being and lived here Jn 1:14
him how changeable * nature is! Jn 2:24,25
observed during every * birth. Jn 3:5f
Men can only reproduce * life, Jn 3:6
Vast fields of * souls are Jn 4:35
live in temples made by * hands. Act 7:48,49
men are gods in * bodies!" Act 14:11
We are merely * beings like Act 14:15
temples; and * hands can't Act 17:25
who came as a * baby, born into Rom 1:3
sin entered the entire * race. Rom 5:12
He sent his own Son in a * body Rom 8:3
Jew so far as his * nature is Rom 9:5
will destroy all * plans of 1Co 1:19
find God through * brilliance, and 1Co 1:21
of oratory and * wisdom, but the 1Co 2:4
full well how the * mind reasons, 1Co 3:20
They are just * bodies at death, 1Co 15:44
For just as there are natural, * 1Co 15:44
Adam, was given a natural, * body 1Co 15:45
First, then, we have these * 1Co 15:46
Every * being has a body just 1Co 15:48
not one carved on stone, but in * 2Co 3:3
God himself, and not by * hands. 2Co 5:1
merely as a * being like myself. 2Co 5:16
an ordinary, weak * being, but I 2Co 10:3
but I don't use * plans and methods 2Co 10:3
His weak, * body died on the 2Co 13:4
on some mere * whim or dream. Gal 1:11
than the * mind can understand. Php 4:7
cross of his own * body, and now as Col 1:22
there is all of God in a * body; Col 2:9
Such rules are mere * teachings, Col 2:22
that no * being can approach him. 1Ti 6:16
Since we, God's children, are * Heb 2:14
blood too by being born in * form; Heb 2:14
for only as a * being could he Heb 2:14
angel but as a * being—yes, a Jew. Heb 2:16
Christ's body, being *, was frail Heb 5:7f
And can a * body live long Heb 5:7f
to Abraham in * form, or simply Heb 7:3f
by the Lord and not by * hands. Heb 8:2
the curtain—his * body—to let us Heb 10:20
no * being can tame the tongue. Jas 3:8
Elijah was as completely * as we Jas 5:17
to him with a * voice, scolding and 2Pe 2:16
actually became man with a * body? 1Jn 4:2
a * being with a body like ours. 2Jn 1:7
An epoch of * history has come Rev 16:17f
unprecedented in * history. Rev 16:18
Literally, "144 cubits by * Rev 21:17f
HUMANITY
love, O God! All * takes refuge in Ps 36:7
In all * there is no one Lk 7:28
is my flesh given to redeem *." Jn 6:48-51
and of all *, both great and Rev 19:18
HUMANLY
and said, "* speaking, no one. Mt 19:26
ABRAHAM WAS, * speaking, the Rom 4:1
HUMANS
He doesn't change his mind like * Num 23:18-24
Why then should we, mere * as we Lam 3:39
kinds of flesh. *, animals, fish, 1Co 15:39
HUMBLE
in it you shall * your souls and be Lev 23:32
you would become * and so that your Deu 8:16
to the ground in * worship. Ju 2:19
and * yourselves beneath my shade! Ju 9:15
if my people will * themselves and 2Ch 7:14
And when the Lord saw them * 2Ch 12:7
would * ourselves before our God; Ez 8:21
*, and takes sufferers to safety. Job 5:11
Yes, he will save the *, and Job 22:29
Lord, you know the hopes of * Ps 10:17
of the poor and * when evildoers Ps 14:6
You deliver the * but condemn Ps 18:27
Both proud and * together, all Ps 22:29
But all who * themselves before Ps 37:11
or an ox. The * shall see their Ps 69:32
he respects the *, but proud men Ps 138:6
The Lord supports the *, but Ps 147:6
he will save the *. Ps 149:4,5
mocks at mockers, but helps the *. Pro 3:34
Pride leads to arguments; be *, Pro 13:10
Better poor and * than proud and Pro 16:19
with contrite, * spirits dwell; Is 57:15
and I refresh the * and give new Is 57:15
the man who has a * and a contrite Is 66:2
all this, yet you have not been *. Dan 5:22
are *—all who have tried to obey. Zep 2:3
the poor and the *, and they will Zep 3:12
"* men are very fortunate!" Mt 5:3
for I am gentle and *, and you Mt 11:29,30
and those who * themselves shall Mt 23:12
but the * shall be honored." Lk 18:14
Do not be proud; be * and Rom 11:20
I come God will * me before you and 2Co 12:21
as these. Be * and gentle. Eph 4:2
on others. Be *, thinking of others Php 2:3
*) have a very clever imagination. Col 2:18
who are wrong. Be * when you are 2Ti 2:25
strength to the *, but sets himself Jas 4:6
with tender hearts and * minds. 1Pe 3:8
each other with * spirits, for God 1Pe 5:5
to those who are *, but sets 1Pe 5:5
If you will * yourselves under 1Pe 5:6
HUMBLED
evil hearts are * and they accept Lev 26:40,41
Yes, he * you by letting you go Deu 8:3
AFTER THIS DAVID subdued and * the 2Sa 8:1
how Ahab has * himself before me? 1Ki 21:29
and concerned and * yourself before 2Ki 22:18,19
"Because you have * yourselves, I 2Ch 12:7
When the king * himself, the 2Ch 12:12
of Jerusalem * themselves, so the 2Ch 32:26
are sorry and have * yourself 2Ch 34:27
These young men, having * me, now Job 30:11
the proud shall be *; Is 5:15
great shall be disappointed and *; Mt 23:12
tries to honor himself shall be *; Lk 14:11
For the proud shall be *, but the Lk 18:14
And he * himself even further, Php 2:8
HUMBLES
strength. He * the proud and Is 26:5
Therefore anyone who * himself Mt 18:4
and he who * himself shall be Lk 14:11
HUMBLEST
(Now Moses was the * man on Num 12:3,4
HUMBLING
those forty years, * you and Deu 8:2
HUMBLY
they stood * before him and 2Ki 5:15
and cried out * to God for help. 2Ch 33:12
best to those who * turn to him. Ps 25:9
he rescues those who are * sorry Ps 34:18
and to walk * with your God. Mic 6:8
Walk * and do what is right; Zep 2:3
riding * on a donkey's colt!" Mt 21:5
the Lord's work *—yes, and with Act 20:19
should gently and * help him back Gal 6:1
listen and learn quietly and *. 1Ti 2:11
and outside, and * be glad for the Jas 1:21
So give yourselves * to God. Jas 4:7
HUMILIATE
* the haughty with a glance; Job 40:12
HUMILIATED
as a slave, for you have * her. Deu 21:14
frightened and *, and they realized Neh 6:16
but Haman hurried home utterly *. Est 6:12
be disappointed, * and disgraced, Is 30:3
and thoroughly *, and they shall Jer 20:11
seen her stripped naked and *. Lam 1:8
HUMILIATING
devotion and are * and hard on the Col 2:23
HUMILIATION
the drudgery and * they are Ex 3:17
show my * and sorrow for my sins! Ps 69:11
in his *, justice was denied Act 8:33
HUMILITY
the day in self-examination and *. Lev 16:29,30
shall spend the day in quiet *; Lev 16:31
This will be a day of solemn * Num 29:7
in deep *, bowing low before him. 2Sa 9:5,6
and went about in deep *. 1Ki 21:27
Defending truth, *, and justice. Ps 45:4
* and reverence for the Lord will Pro 15:33
Pride ends in destruction; * ends Pro 18:12
True * and respect for the Lord Pro 22:4
Pride ends in a fall, while * Pro 29:23
as a sign of * and mourning, and Is 37:1
repented long ago in shame and *. Mt 11:21
HUMPED
or hand, or has a * back, or is a Lev 21:20
HUMTAH
Aphekah, *, Kiriath-arba (or, Jos 15:48-62
HUNDRED
and sat down a * yards or so away. Gen 21:16
and three * pieces of silver! Gen 45:22
four * years after Joseph's death. Ex 1:8f
there were six * thousand of Ex 12:37
under him, each in charge of a *; Ex 18:21
Literally, "five * shekels." Ex 30:22,23f
Five of you will chase a *, and Lev 26:8
and a * of you, ten thousand! Lev 26:8
against Moses. Two * and fifty Num 16:2
share is one out of every five *. Num 31:28
and fine him one * dollars Deu 22:19

(HUNDRED Con't)
Literally, "a * shekels of Deu 22:19f
He once killed six * Philistines Ju 3:31
He had nine * iron chariots, and Ju 4:2,3
including the nine * iron chariots, Ju 4:13
Only three * of the men drank from Ju 7:5,6
Midianites with these three *!" Ju 7:7
leaving only three * men with him. Ju 7:8,9
He divided the three * men into Ju 7:16
Gideon and the * men with him crept Ju 7:19,20
Then the other two * of his men Ju 7:19,20
Jordan River with his three * men. Ju 8:4
for one * twenty thousand had Ju 8:10
But now after three * years you Ju 11:26
So he went out and caught three * Ju 15:4
So six * armed troops of the Ju 18:11
to join the seven * local men in Ju 20:14,15
there were seven * men who were Ju 20:16
leaving only six * men who escaped Ju 20:46,47
There were four * of these, and Ju 21:10,11,12
The four * girls were given to Ju 21:14
there were three * thousand of them 1Sa 11:8
there were only about six * left! 1Sa 13:15
and these six * men set up their 1Sa 13:16
Saul and his six * men were 1Sa 14:2
Then Saul and his six * men 1Sa 14:20
There were two * thousand troops 1Sa 15:4
I need is one * dead Philistines! 1Sa 18:25
Literally, "one * foreskins of 1Sa 18:25f
out and killed two * Philistines 1Sa 18:27
the leader of about four * men. 1Sa 22:2
So David and his men—about six * 1Sa 23:13
on his own. Four * of them started 1Sa 25:13
with David and two * remained 1Sa 25:13
Then Abigail hurriedly took two * 1Sa 25:18
roasted grain, one * raisin cakes, 1Sa 25:18
cakes, and two * fig cakes, and 1Sa 25:18
So David took his six * men and 1Sa 27:2,3
So David and his six * men set 1Sa 30:9,10
Besor Brook, two * of the men were 1Sa 30:9,10
but the other four * kept going. 1Sa 30:9,10
No one escaped except four * 1Sa 30:17
Brook and the two * men who had 1Sa 30:21
But three * and sixty of Abner's 2Sa 2:31
the lives of one * Philistines." 2Sa 3:14
David captured seventeen * 2Sa 8:4
horses except for one * teams. 2Sa 8:4
time leaving seven * charioteers 2Sa 10:18
He took two * men from 2Sa 15:11
lead the way—six * Gittites who had 2Sa 15:17,18
captain of the six * Gittites, and 2Sa 15:19,20
Then Ittai and his six * men 2Sa 15:22
loaded with two * loaves of bread, 2Sa 16:1
of bread, one * clusters of 2Sa 16:1
of raisins, one * bunches of 2Sa 16:1
He once killed eight * men in one 2Sa 23:8
Once he took on three * of the 2Sa 23:18,19
there will be a * times as many 2Sa 24:3
and thirty-three * foremen. 1Ki 5:16
four * pomegranates in two rows. 1Ki 7:16-22
Four * pomegranates in two rows on 1Ki 7:41-46
beaten into two * pieces of armor 1Ki 10:16,17
piece) and three * shields ($1,800 1Ki 10:16,17
He had seven * wives and three 1Ki 11:3
wives and three * concubines; 1Ki 11:3
had hidden one * of them in two 1Ki 18:3,4
and I hid a * of them in two caves 1Ki 18:13
So King Ahab summoned his four * 1Ki 22:6
"Feed one * men with only 2Ki 4:43
a distance of about six * feet. 2Ki 14:13
Later, five * of these invaders 1Ch 4:42
the weakest was worth a * normal 1Ch 12:14
a * that he kept for his own use. 1Ch 18:4
his people a * times, would they 1Ch 21:3
Literally, "six * shekels of gold 1Ch 21:25f
Literally, "a * thousand talents 1Ch 22:14f
Twenty-seven * outstanding men 1Ch 26:31,32
also, two * fifty of them were 2Ch 8:10
with twelve * chariots, sixty 2Ch 12:3
to the Lord seven * oxen and seven 2Ch 15:11
Three * thousand Judean troops 2Ch 17:14,15
Then King Joash ordered two * 2Ch 25:23
Twenty-six * brave clan leaders 2Ch 26:12
of the * and the Tower of Hananel; Neh 3:1
to the gate of the Tower of the *; Neh 12:39
a * lashes on the back of a rebel. Pro 17:10
Even if a man has a * sons and as Ecc 6:3
But though a man sins a * times Ecc 8:12
* pieces to those who care for it. Sol 8:12
round about there were a * more. Jer 52:23
Fifteen * feet after that it was Eze 47:5
replied, "Twenty-three * days Dan 8:14
Literally, "Twenty-three * Dan 8:14f
the twenty-three * days to pass Dan 8:26
men to battle, a * will return. Amo 5:3
The city that sends a * only ten Amo 5:3
* times as much as he had planted. Mt 13:8
a * others into the Kingdom." Mt 13:23
or even a * times as much." Mt 13:23f
"If a man has a * sheep, and one Mt 18:12
shall receive a * times as much in Mt 19:29
even sixty or a * times as much! Mk 4:8
sixty, or even a * times as much as Mk 4:20
of fifty or a * each were sitting Mk 6:39,40
be given back, a * times over, Mk 10:30
a crop one * times as large as he Lk 8:8
"If you had a * sheep and one of Lk 15:3,4
came too, bringing a * pounds of Jn 19:39
eating, all two * seventy-six of Act 27:37
at the age of one *, and that Sarah Rom 4:19
by more than five * Christian 1Co 15:6
or changed four * and thirty years Gal 3:17
hailstones weighing a * pounds Rev 16:21
the waves of a * oceans crashing on Rev 19:6

HUNDREDS
*, fifties, and tens. Ex 18:25
of thousands, *, fifties, and tens Deu 1:15
to him and * of millions of people Dan 7:10
men, though dead for * of years, Mk 12:27
I suppose that there are * of 1Co 14:10
out of sight for * of years until Heb 10:4f

HUNG
of its weight, * upon a wall. Ju 8:27f
* its doors, and dedicated it. Neh 3:1
the beams, * the doors, and made Neh 3:3
the Valley Gate, * the doors, and Neh 3:13
and after building it, he * the Neh 3:14
He rebuilt it, roofed it, * its Neh 3:15
we had not yet * all the doors of Neh 6:1
and we had * the doors in the gates Neh 7:1
Shushan, and they * up the bodies Est 9:14
then * me up as his target. Job 16:12
intelligence he * the stars in Jer 10:12
a golden chain was * around his Dan 5:29
and watched him as he * there. Mt 27:36
A heavy veil * in front of the Mk 15:38f
* on every word he said. Lk 19:48
Jesus was * upon a wooden cross Gal 3:13

HUNGER
will be the * during the siege and Deu 28:56,57
I will waste them with *, Deu 32:24
He was also faint with *, for he 1Sa 28:20
"His vigor is depleted by *; Job 18:12
struggle up from their nest in *? Job 38:41
You constantly satisfy the * and Ps 145:16
* is good—if it makes you work to Pro 16:26
They shall neither * nor thirst; Is 49:10
He will die of *, for almost all Jer 38:9
free from war and * and alarms, Jer 42:13,14
they faint with * in the streets. Lam 2:19
The cattle groan with *; Joe 1:18
flocks and herds forget their *; Joe 2:22
"I sent you *," says the Lord, Amo 4:6
never have enough; * pangs and Mic 6:14
years, and * stalked the land; Lk 4:25,26
a time of awful * is before them. Lk 6:25
spare, and here I am, dying of *! Lk 15:17
In fact, I would rather die of * 1Co 9:15
full stomach or *, plenty or want; Php 4:12

HUNGRILY
fig is * snatched and gobbled up! Is 28:4

HUNGRY
"They'll be * if you stop so Gen 29:7
and you will still be * after Lev 26:26
by letting you go * and then Deu 8:3
and you will be *, thirsty, naked, Deu 28:47,48
we were tired and *," he said. Ju 8:15
But * as they were, they chased 1Sa 14:31
be very tired and * and thirsty 2Sa 17:28,29
when they were * and water from the Neh 9:15
or refused food to * orphans— (but Job 31:17
have ever gone *— (actually I have Job 31:31
lions sometimes go *, but those of Ps 34:10
the children of the godly go *. Ps 37:25
If I were *, I would not mention Ps 50:12
desert, * and thirsty and faint. Ps 107:5
and fills the * soul with good. Ps 107:9
He brings the * to settle there Ps 107:36
* to save them from their enemies. Ps 109:31
the dirt, and the * from the Ps 113:7
and oppressed, and food to the *. Ps 146:7
A wise man is * for truth, while Pro 15:14
man sleeps soundly—and goes *! Pro 19:15
If your enemy is *, give him Pro 25:21,22
but if he is *, he'll eat Pro 27:7
captive, stumbling, weary and *. Is 8:21
And because they are * they will Is 8:21
As a * man dreams of eating, but Is 29:8
but is still *, and as a thirsty Is 29:8
* will be plain for all to see. Is 32:6
everyone is so * and thirsty that Is 36:12
He grows *, and thirsty, weak and Is 44:12
for the *, so also is my Word. Is 55:10
your food with the * and bring Is 58:7
Feed the *! Is 58:10
You roar like * bears; Is 59:11
they are food to my * soul. Jer 15:16
gives food to the * and clothes to Eze 18:7
but feeds the * and clothes the Eze 18:16
crowd my sick and * flock until Eze 34:21
never again go * nor be shamed by Eze 34:29
They will eat and still be *. Hos 4:10
he ate nothing and became very *. Mt 4:2
suspect you are *, except your Mt 6:18
worship, and his disciples were *; Mt 12:1
when he and his friends were *? Mt 12:3
I don't want to send them away * Mt 15:32
Jerusalem, he was *, and noticed a Mt 21:18
For I was * and you fed me; Mt 25:35
we ever see you * and feed you? Mt 25:37
For I was * and you wouldn't Mt 25:42
we ever see you * or thirsty or a Mt 25:44
companions were *, and he went into Mk 2:25,26
as they left Bethany, he felt *. Mk 11:12
He has satisfied the * hearts Lk 1:53
give it away to those who are *." Lk 3:11
all that time, and was very *. Lk 4:1
Do wedding guests go * while Lk 5:34
did when he and his men were *? Lk 6:3
you who are now *, for you are Lk 6:21
The boy became so * that even Lk 15:16
coming to me will ever be * again. Jn 6:35
It was noon and he was *, but Act 10:9,10
"I have never been * for money Act 20:33
And if we are *, or penniless, or Rom 8:35
feed your enemy if he is *. Rom 12:20
To this very hour we have gone * 1Co 4:11
enough and goes * while another has 1Co 11:21
if anyone is really * he should 1Co 11:34
and I was getting * I still 2Co 11:8,9
Often I have been * and thirsty 2Co 11:27
They were * and sick and Heb 11:37,38
He prowls around like a *, 1Pe 5:8
they will never be * again, nor Rev 7:16

HUNT
arrived home exhausted from the *. Gen 25:29
for the field to * for the venison, Gen 27:5
troops and went to * him down. 1Sa 26:2
Israel come out to * my life like a 1Sa 26:20
Rescue me from those who * me Ps 31:14,15
Lions will * down the survivors, Is 15:9
We went into the wilderness to * Lam 5:9
Literally, "Will you * the souls Eze 13:18f
you because you * my people's souls Eze 13:20
went on to Tarsus to * for Paul. Act 11:25

HUNTED
and kill him. Saul * him day after 1Sa 23:14,15
when we are * down or destroyed, is Rom 8:35
We are * down, but God never 2Co 4:9
name of Christ. I * down his 1Ti 1:13

HUNTER
He was a mighty *, blessed of Gen 10:9
Or, "a mighty * against the Gen 10:9f
mighty *, blessed of God." Gen 10:9
Or, "a mighty * against the Gen 10:9f
became a skillful *, while Jacob Gen 25:27
from a *, or a bird from the net. Pro 6:5
like a * hiding in a blind. Jer 5:26

HUNTER'S
lives as a bird from a * snare. Ps 124:7

HUNTERS
the poor. Like * they catch their Ps 10:9
I am sending for * to chase you Jer 16:16
called out their * and trapped him Eze 19:4

HUNTING
arrives, coming in from his *. Gen 27:30
you, who goes * and kills an animal Lev 17:13
you have been * for my life? 1Sa 24:11
Saul gives up and quits * for me; 1Sa 27:1
to Gath, so he quit * for him. 1Sa 27:4
While Jehu was * down and killing 2Ch 22:8
game he gets while *, but the Pro 12:27
a * ground overrun by wildlife. Is 7:24
like roaring lions * for their Zep 3:3
mercilessly, * them down and doing Gal 1:13

HUPHAM
named after their ancestor *. Num 26:38-41

HUPHAMITES
The *, named after their ancestor Num 26:38-41

HUPPAH
Thirteenth, the group led by *; 1Ch 24:7-18

HUPPIM
*, and Ard. Gen 46:19-22
The sons of Ir were Shuppim and * 1Ch 7:12
who found wives for * and Shuppim. 1Ch 7:15

HUR
Meanwhile Moses, Aaron, and * Ex 17:10
* was a man of Judah, of the Ex 17:10f
so Aaron and * rolled a stone for Ex 17:12
gone, consult with Aaron and *." Ex 24:14
and grandson of *, of the tribe of Ex 31:1
and grandson of * of the tribe of Ex 35:30,31
and grandson of *, of the tribe of Ex 38:22
Rekem, Zur, *, and Reba. Num 31:8
Rekem, Zur, *, and Reba. Jos 13:21
with a son, * 1Ch 2:19
The sons of * (who was the oldest 1Ch 2:50
Perez, Hezron, Carmi, *, 1Ch 4:1
The son of *, the oldest son of 1Ch 4:3-4
of Uri, son of *) still stood in 2Ch 1:5,6
Rephaiah (son of *), the mayor of Neh 3:9

HUR'S
* son was 1Ch 2:20

HURAI
* from near the brooks of Gaash; 1Ch 11:26-47
HURAM
Ahoah, Gera, Shephuphan, *. 1Ch 8:3,4,5
HURAMABI
a master crafts-man—my famous *! 2Ch 2:13
of the Temple. * also made the 2Ch 4:11
This skillful craftsman, *, made 2Ch 4:12-16
HURI
Gilead, Jaroah, *, Abihail. 1Ch 5:14
HURL
And * my punishments upon my Deu 32:40,41
For God shall * at him Job 27:22
so gorgeously will * you away, Is 22:17
* her fortifications into the sea; Zec 9:4
said, "All right, * the stones at Jn 8:7
HURLED
took out a stone, * it from his 1Sa 17:48,49
spear, suddenly * it at David, 1Sa 18:11,12
in his hand, and * it at David in 1Sa 19:9,10
Then Saul * his spear at 1Sa 20:33
laughs at the javelins * at him. Job 41:29
have * against you all day long. Ps 74:22
of Israel—will be * to the ground Is 28:3
And the people passing by * Mt 27:39
HURLING
and blasphemed, * abuse at Jesus, Act 18:6
gathered around, * many serious Act 25:7
HURLS
bolts. He * each at its target. Job 36:32
and * the hail upon the earth. Ps 147:17
HURRICANE
bring your ship of state into a *! Eze 27:26
HURRIED
was up early and * out to the place Gen 19:27
They left proudly, * along by the Num 33:3,4
you left Egypt in * flight." Deu 16:3f
Meanwhile, the people had * Jos 4:10
Gideon * home and roasted a young Ju 6:19
officer and * out to the ranks to 1Sa 17:22
Then David * on, for he was 1Sa 21:10
a calf, so she * out and killed it 1Sa 28:24
the well and * on to King David. 2Sa 17:21
man from Bahurim, * across with the 2Sa 19:16
straw of hope and * to clinch the 1Ki 20:33
* them out to the people to eat. 2Ch 35:13
and Shimshai, they * to Jerusalem Ez 4:23
Haman * home utterly humiliated. Est 6:12
Then Ari-och * Daniel in to the Dan 2:25
Very early the next morning he * Dan 6:19
So she * back to the king and Mk 6:25
A few days later Mary * to the Lk 1:39,40
That night the Christians * Paul Act 17:10
HURRIEDLY
eat it *. Ex 12:11
The men of Gibeon * sent Jos 10:6
Then Abigail * took two hundred 1Sa 25:18
Zacchaeus * climbed down and took Lk 19:6
HURRIES
The sun rises and sets and * Ecc 1:3-7
the carver * the goldsmith, and Is 41:7
HURRY
a servant to * and butcher it. Gen 18:7
became urgent. "*," they said to Gen 19:15
destroy that little city. But *! Gen 19:22
"*, return to my father and tell Gen 45:9
* and plead with God for me." Ex 8:28
Egypt in such a * that there was no Deu 16:3
If you * you can probably catch Jos 2:5
up on the hill. So *, because he'll 1Sa 9:12,13
of you. *, hurry, don't wait." 1Sa 20:38
Hurry, *, don't wait." 1Sa 20:38
Then Elijah shouted, "* to Ahab 1Ki 18:44
his aides, "Go get Micaiah. *!" 1Ki 22:9
so that I can * to the prophet and 2Ki 4:22
and said to the servant, "*! 2Ki 4:24
talk to anyone along the way. *! 2Ki 4:29
God has told me to *! 2Ch 35:21
"Tell Haman to *!" Est 5:5
the king said to Haman. "* and Est 6:10
O God my Strength, * to my aid. Ps 22:19
They marvel at the sight and * Ps 48:5
Lord, * to my aid! Ps 70:1
"* up and punish us, O Lord," Is 5:19
and the roast is in the oven. *!' Mt 22:4
you can, to the Judean hills. *! Mk 13:15,16
Then Jesus told him, "*—do it Jn 13:27
and Timothy to * and join him. Act 17:15
a vision of God saying to me, '*! Act 22:17,18
Never be in a * about choosing a 1Ti 5:22
to that day and * it along—the day 2Pe 3:12
HURRYING
time, as he was * to get to Act 20:16
HURT
don't * the lad in any way," the Gen 22:12
and in the process * a pregnant Ex 21:22
and it dies, or is *, or gets away, Ex 22:10
and have not * one of them." Num 16:15
tell Jonathan—why should I * him?' 1Sa 20:3
day, for he was * by his father's 1Sa 20:34
to * us more than Absalom did. 2Sa 20:6
were killed who sought to * them. 1Ch 16:21
you and all Judah get badly *." 2Ch 25:19
"If I have * the poor or caused Job 31:16
Your sins may * another man, or Job 35:8
Will his hide be * by darts, or Job 41:7
For all who tried to * me have Ps 71:24
"and do not * my prophets." Ps 105:15
There in prison they * his feet Ps 105:18
scorn her, you * only yourself. Pro 9:12
discipline won't * them! Pro 23:13,14
Nothing will * or destroy in all Is 11:9
Who let Israel be robbed and *? Is 42:24
no one shall be * or destroyed in Is 65:25
idols as you do now to your *. Jer 7:6
Most of all they * themselves, to Jer 7:19
I weep for the * of my people; Jer 8:21
I will help them and not * them; Jer 24:6
"See that he isn't *," he said. Jer 39:11,12
they aren't even * by the flames! Dan 3:25
idols at Beth-aven should be *; Hos 10:5
vengeance on those who * them. Nah 1:2
'You'll * the wheat if you do. Mt 13:29
poisonous, it won't * them; Mk 16:18
God's blessing on those who * you. Lk 6:28
whose consciences * them when they Rom 14:1f
of others who might be * by it. Rom 14:22
lest the answer * your conscience. 1Co 10:25
I didn't want to * you, but I had 2Co 2:4
But it * you only for a little 2Co 7:8
it, not because it * you, but 2Co 7:9
help you, not to * you—but I shall 2Co 10:8
Who is spiritually * without my 2Co 11:29
rising against the one who * him? 2Co 11:29
from Satan to * and bother me, and 2Co 12:7
helped those who are sick and *? 1Ti 5:10
money, things that * them and make 1Ti 6:9
and * for a long time to come. 2Ti 2:17
* themselves, but become strong. Heb 12:13
Usually no one will * you for 1Pe 3:13
not be * by the Second Death. Rev 2:11
Don't do anything yet—* neither Rev 7:3
They were told not to * the Rev 9:4
and their power to *, given to them Rev 9:10
HURTING
has kept me from * you, that if you 1Sa 25:34
my life, and delight in * me. Ps 70:2,3
Am I the one that they are *? Jer 7:19
Will they never stop * me? Jer 15:17,18
left him without * him further. Lk 4:35
if he isn't helping me, he is * Lk 11:23
You are only * yourself.' Act 26:14
Oh, my children, how you are * Gal 4:19
to each other we are * ourselves. Eph 4:25
for those who are * you. 2Th 1:6
* many in their spiritual lives. Heb 12:15
HURTLING
It came * toward the statue and Dan 2:34
there and send it * into the sea! Lk 17:6
stones came * at him, Stephen Act 7:59
HURTS
A bribe * the cause of the person Ex 23:8
"A command like that only * us. 1Sa 14:29
Punishment that * chases evil Pro 20:30
I will punish anyone who * them. Jer 30:20
and * their tender consciences. 1Co 8:7
while it is happening—it *! Heb 12:11
HUSBAND
some to her *, and he ate it too. Gen 3:6
"And with a * as old as mine?" Gen 18:12
Now restore her to her *, and he Gen 20:7
trouble—now my * will love me." Gen 29:32
"Surely now my * will feel Gen 29:34
"Wasn't it enough to steal my *? Gen 30:15
giving my slave-girl to my *." Gen 30:18
has given me good gifts for my *. Gen 30:20
hysterically. "My * had to bring Gen 39:14,15
and when her * came home that Gen 39:16
Well, when her * heard his wife's Gen 39:19
* you've turned out to be!" Ex 4:25,26
amount the woman's * shall demand, Ex 21:22
* lived, but also after his death. Lev 18:14f
responsibility since she has no *. Lev 21:2,3
you except your *, be free from the Num 5:19
against her *, the water will Num 5:27
above. Her * shall not be brought Num 5:31
marries, and her * learns of her Num 30:7
But if her * refuses to accept Num 30:8
the vow, and her * hears of it and Num 30:11
So her * may either confirm or Num 30:13
wives while their * was living. Deu 22:30f
and the second * also divorces Deu 24:3
dies, the former * may not marry Deu 24:4
to help her * by grabbing the Deu 25:11
her beloved *, son, and daughter. Deu 28:56,57
The woman ran and told her *, "A Ju 13:6
ran and found her * and told him, Ju 13:10
answer from your *, or we'll burn Ju 14:15
Then her *, taking along a Ju 19:3
Then the girl's * pushed her out Ju 19:25
When her * opened the door to be Ju 19:27
murdered woman's * and asked him Ju 20:3
left alone, without her * or sons. Ru 1:4,5
a younger brother of her former *. Ru 1:11f
for I am too old to have a *. Ru 1:12
Boaz, this relative of Naomi's *. Ru 2:3
the death of your *, and how you Ru 2:10,11
to us as well as to your dead *!" Ru 2:20
I try to find a * for you, and get Ru 3:1
the family name of her dead *." Ru 4:10
for she told her *, "Wait until 1Sa 1:21,22
came with her * for the sacrifice. 1Sa 2:19
and that her * and father-in-law 1Sa 4:19
* and her father-in-law were dead. 1Sa 4:21,22
But she didn't tell her * what 1Sa 25:19
fear, for he would not kill her *. 1Sa 25:35
took her away from her * Palti. 2Sa 3:15
When Bath-sheba heard that her * 2Sa 11:26
Give your * this message from 1Ki 14:7
She said to her *, "I'm sure 2Ki 4:9
a son, and her * is an old man." 2Ki 4:14
then she sent a message to her * 2Ki 4:22
See if her * is all right and if 2Ki 4:26
Abigail, whose * was Jether from 1Ch 2:17
and someone else become her *. Job 31:10
Your royal * delights in your Ps 45:10,11
and his murder of Uriah, her *. Ps 51:1
of vengeance from the wronged *. Pro 5:9f
for the woman's * will be furious Pro 6:34
for my * is away on a long trip. Pro 7:19
girl who marries her mistress' *. Pro 30:21,22,23
gems! Her * can trust her, and she Pro 31:11
pure linen. Her * is well known, Pro 31:23
so does her *. Pro 31:28
now than she whose * stayed! Is 54:1
your Creator will be your "*." Is 54:5
young wife abandoned by her *. Is 54:6
a faithless wife who leaves her *. Jer 3:20
for them as a * does his wife." Jer 31:32f
other men instead of her own *. Eze 16:32
For your mother loathed her * Eze 16:45
man's wife—I am no longer her *. Hos 1:2
well return to my *, for I was Hos 1:7
"My *" instead of "My Master." Hos 1:16
me as a prostitute leaves her *; Hos 5:3
I am as jealous as a * for his Zec 1:14
(who was the * of Mary, the mother Mt 1:16
Literally, "her *." Mt 1:19f
And if a wife divorces her * and Mk 10:12
"Go and get your *," Jesus told Jn 4:16
could you and your * even think of Act 5:9
who buried your *, and they will Act 5:9
out and buried her beside her *. Act 5:10
to her * as long as he is alive. Rom 7:2
Your "*," your master, used to Rom 7:4
having her own *, because otherwise 1Co 7:2
the same for her *: for a girl who 1Co 7:3
* then has his rights to it, too; 1Co 7:4
and in the same way the * no 1Co 7:4
agreement of both * and wife to 1Co 7:5
God gives some the gift of a * or 1Co 7:7
said: A wife must not leave her *. 1Co 7:10
And the * must not divorce his 1Co 7:11
And if a Christian woman has a * 1Co 7:13
For perhaps the * who isn't a 1Co 7:14
with the help of her Christian *. 1Co 7:14
But if the * or wife who isn't a 1Co 7:15
In such cases the Christian * or 1Co 7:15
the likes and dislikes of her *. 1Co 7:34
The wife is part of her * as long 1Co 7:39
if her * dies, then she may marry 1Co 7:39
responsible to her *, her husband 1Co 11:3
her husband, her * is responsible 1Co 11:3
head dishonors her * [for her 1Co 11:5
for the one who will be her *. 2Co 11:2
For a * is in charge of his wife Eph 5:23
(That the * and wife are one body Eph 5:31
respects her *—obeying, praising Eph 5:33
who already has a *, also said you Jas 2:11
Sarah, for instance, obeyed her * 1Pe 3:6
HUSBAND'S
shall welcome your * affections, Gen 3:16
her * suspicions are justified. Num 5:18
wayward wife—or a * suspicions Num 5:29
and living in her * home when she Num 30:10
instead, her * brother must marry Deu 25:5
say to them, 'My * brother refuses Deu 25:7
* name, and to inherit the land." Ru 4:5
one left, and my * name will be 2Sa 14:7
Elisha to tell him of her * death. 2Ki 4:1
A worthy wife is her * joy and Pro 12:4
wife who loves her * enemies. Jas 4:4
HUSBANDS
faithfulness to your * and to me. Ru 1:8
who could grow up to be your *? Ru 1:11
to disobey their * when they learn Est 1:17
talking to us * the same way, and Est 1:18
great kingdom, * everywhere, Est 1:20
* and flouted the laws of God. Pro 2:16,17
Their * shall die in battle; Is 3:25,26
on * and wives and grandparents. Jer 6:11
one to bury them. *, wives, sons Jer 14:16
our * knowing it and helping us? Jer 44:19

(HUSBANDS Con't)
their * and their children. Eze 16:45
who encourage your * to rob the Amo 4:1
private mourning, * and wives Zec 12:12,13,14
"For you have had five *, and Jn 4:17,18
* will be converted if they stay; 1Co 7:16
and the same may be said to you * 1Co 7:16
let them ask their * at home, for 1Co 14:35
You wives must submit to your *' Eph 5:22
obey your * in everything, just as Eph 5:24
And you *, show the same kind of Eph 5:25
That is how * should treat their Eph 5:28
yourselves to your *, for that is Col 3:18
And you * must be loving and Col 3:19
of women whose * have died, if they 1Ti 5:3
to love their * and their children, Tit 2:4
obedient to their *, so that the Tit 2:5
WIVES, FIT IN with your *' plans; 1Pe 3:1
and fitted in with their *' plans. 1Pe 3:5
not need to fear [offending your * 1Pe 3:6
You * must be careful of your 1Pe 3:7

HUSH
of Jesus tried to * the man, but he Lk 18:39

HUSHAH
Gedor),Ezer (the ancestor of *), 1Ch 4:3-4

HUSHAI
God, David found * the Archite 2Sa 15:32
So David's friend * returned to 2Sa 15:37
When David's friend, * the 2Sa 16:16
Lord and by Israel," * replied. 2Sa 16:18
said, "Ask * the Archite what he 2Sa 17:5
When * arrived, Absalom told him 2Sa 17:6
"Well," * replied, "this time 2Sa 17:7
Then * reported to Zadok and 2Sa 17:15
Baana (son of *), whose areas were 1Ki 4:8-19
counselor and * the Archite was his 1Ch 27:33

HUSHAI'S
of Israel said, "* advice is 2Sa 17:14

HUSHAM
Succeeded by: King *, from the Gen 36:31-39
When Jobab died, * from the 1Ch 1:45
When * died, Hadad the son of 1Ch 1:46

HUSHATH
Mebunnai from *; 2Sa 23:24-39
Sibbecai from *; 1Ch 11:26-47
But Sibbecai, a man from *, 1Ch 20:4

HUSHATHITE
the * killed Saph, another giant. 2Sa 21:18

HUSHED
in fact, all the world stands * Rom 3:19

HUSHIM
Dan and his son: *. Gen 46:23,24,25
* was one of the sons of Aher. 1Ch 7:12
* and Baara, but he had children 1Ch 8:8,9,10
His wife * had borne him Abitub 1Ch 8:11

HUSHITE
Sibbecai of the * subclan from 1Ch 27:11

HUSKS
rubbing off the * in their hands Lk 6:1

HUSTLING
where once your * port was full of Is 23:2,3

HUTS
is called Succoth, meaning "*." Gen 33:17
trees and to make * in which to Neh 8:15
used them to build * on the roofs Neh 8:16
They lived in these * for the Neh 8:17

HYENAS
there to dance. * and jackals will Is 13:22
mingle there with wolves and *. Is 34:14

HYMENAEUS
God like that. * and Alexander are 1Ti 1:20
long time to come. * and Philetus, 2Ti 2:17

HYMN
And when they had sung a *, they Mt 26:30
Then they sang a * and went out Mk 14:26

HYMNS
in * of praise and thanks to God. Neh 12:46
Away with your * of praise—they Amo 5:23
and singing * to the Lord—and the Act 16:25
quoting psalms and * and singing Eph 5:19
out in psalms and * and spiritual Col 3:16

HYPNOTIZED
What magician has * you and cast Gal 3:1

HYPOCRISY
and pretence—your * of 'honoring' Amo 5:21
with every sort of * and sin. Mt 23:28
But such * cannot be hidden Lk 12:1

HYPOCRITE
of the board in your own? *! Mt 7:5
see past the board in yours? *! Lk 6:42
But the Lord replied, "You *! Lk 13:15

HYPOCRITES
vengeance on these *, and make Is 29:14
and * will fool no one at all. Is 32:6
False prophets and *—evil people Eze 14:10
about it as the * do—blowing Mt 6:2
don't be like the * who pretend Mt 6:5
publicly, as the * do, who try to Mt 6:16
and care for your parents. You *! Mt 15:7
"You *!" Mt 22:18
you other religious leaders. *! Mt 23:13,14
widows from their homes. *! Mt 23:13,14
Yes, woe upon you *. Mt 23:15
and you other religious leaders—*! Mt 23:23
and you religious leaders—*! Mt 23:25
and you religious leaders—*! Mt 23:29,30
you off to the judgment of the *; Mt 24:51
Jesus replied, "You bunch of *! Mk 7:6,7
And it is. *! Lk 12:56
Barnabas became * too, following Gal 2:13

HYPOCRITICAL
they are false and *. Ps 26:4

HYSSOP
take a cluster of * branches and Ex 12:22
and strike the * against the lintel Ex 12:22
string, and some * branches, to be Lev 14:4
scarlet thread, and the * branch. Lev 14:6
scarlet thread, and * branches. Lev 14:49
the cedar wood, * branch, and Lev 14:51,52
cedar wood and * branches and Num 19:6
defiled shall take * branches and Num 19:18
down to the tiny * which grows in 1Ki 4:33
Literally, "purge me with *." Ps 51:7f
* branch and held up to his lips. Jn 19:29
using branches of * bushes and Heb 9:19

HYSTERICAL
The king grew more and more *; Dan 5:9

HYSTERICALLY
had happened, she was crying *. Gen 39:14,15

I.E.
Literally, "clean," *. Gen 8:20f
ruin my own inheritance," *. Ru 4:6f
and all Israel went to Baalah (*. 1Ch 13:6
"the king's daughter," *. 2Ch 22:11f
"Your innermost shrine," *. Ps 28:2f
"the cup of salvation," *. Ps 116:13f
*., "Christians"? Is 65:15f
Literally, "dust (*. Is 65:25f
*., from Babylon. Jer 4:6f
*., rather than upon tablets of Jer 31:33f
*., when Ahaz paid "protection Eze 23:12f
*., during the reign of Josiah. Eze 23:19,20f
*., Nebuchadnezzar of Babylonia. Eze 27:26f
*., showing their desire for Zep 1:8f
*., Christ, the Messiah. Hag 2:7f
*., the Messiah, Christ. Zec 3:8f
*., the Messiah. Zec 10:4f
*., if Abraham, Isaac, and Jacob, Mt 22:32f
"even the tax collectors"; *. Lk 7:29f
*., on Saturday, the weekly Jewish Jn 9:14f
that anyone should ask you," *. Jn 16:30f
*., the book of Luke; Act 1:1f
"the breaking of bread," *. Act 2:42f
"as the sand of the sea," *. Rom 9:27f
the center of the throne"; *. Rev 7:17f

I'D
these local girls. * rather die Gen 27:46
Laban replied. "* rather give Gen 29:19
even so, * like to go back home." 1Ki 11:22
here? * like to ask him, too." 1Ki 22:7
was you who said * have a son. 2Ki 4:28
he asked. "* like to ask him 2Ch 18:6,7
But perhaps * sermonize the same Job 16:4
"Please kill me, Lord; * rather Jon 4:3
"* like to hear the man Act 25:22

IBEX
The wild goat, the *, Deu 14:3,4,5

IBHAR
Nathan, Solomon, *, Elishu-a, 2Sa 5:14,15,16
*, Elishama, Eliphelet, Nogah, 1Ch 3:6-8
Nathan, Solomon, *, Elishu-a, 1Ch 14:4-7

IBIS
The cormorant, the *, Lev 11:13-19

IBLE-AM
Asher: Beth-shean, *, Dor, En-dor, Jos 17:11

IBLEAM
Taanach, Dor, *, Megiddo, with Ju 1:27
the road climbs to Gur, near *. 2Ki 9:27
at * and took the crown himself. 2Ki 15:10

IBNEIAH
* (the son of Jeroham); 1Ch 9:7,8

IBNIJAH
the son of Reuel, the son of *). 1Ch 9:7,8

IBRI
brothers Shoham, Zaccur, and *. 1Ch 24:26,27

IBSAM
Uzzi, Rephaiah, Jeri-el, Jahmai, * 1Ch 7:2

IBZAN
The next judge was *, who lived Ju 12:8

ICE
it floods when there is * and Job 6:15-18
Who is the mother of the * and Job 38:29
and turns to *, as hard as rock. Job 38:30
and all the river * is broken. Ps 147:18

ICEBALLS
mortally wounded by * from heaven. Ps 78:48

ICHABOD
"*,' for Israel's glory is gone." 1Sa 4:21,22
(* means "there is no glory." 1Sa 4:21,22

ICHABOD'S
(the son of Ahitub, * brother; 1Sa 14:3

ICONIUM
town and went on to the city of *. Act 13:51
AT *, PAUL and Barnabas went Act 14:1
from Antioch and * and turned the Act 14:19
again to Lystra, * and Antioch, Act 14:21
in Lystra and *, so Paul asked him Act 16:2
in Antioch, * and Lystra, but the 2Ti 3:11

IDALAH
Nahalal, Shimron, *, Bethlehem, and Jos 19:15,16

IDBASH
Ishma, *,Hazzelelponi (his 1Ch 4:3-4

IDDO
Ahinadab (the son of *), whose 1Ki 4:8-19
Libni, Jahath, Zimmah, Joah, *, 1Ch 6:19,20,21
in Gilead, * (son of Zechariah); 1Ch 27:16-22
in the visions of * the seer 2Ch 9:29
the prophet and by * the seer, and 2Ch 12:15
(the son of *)—who brought messages Ez 5:1
Haggai and Zechariah (son of *). Ez 6:14
I sent them to *, the leader of Ez 8:17
Rehum, Meremoth, *, Neh 12:1
Zechariah, leader of the * clan; Neh 12:12-21
and grandson of * the prophet) in Zec 1:1
and grandson of * the prophet), in Zec 1:7

IDDO'S
in the prophet * History of Judah. 2Ch 13:22

IDEA
I have no * who is responsible. Gen 21:26
sure, sell the * to the other men Gen 34:18,19
We have no * how the money got Gen 43:22
The * swept the camp. Num 14:4
"This seemed like a good *, so I Deu 1:23
But you have no * what you ask. Amo 5:18
the means, an unbiblical *. Lk 16:9f
"We haven't any * where you are Jn 14:5
of this *, otherwise obscure. Jn 16:26f
But Paul didn't like that * at Act 15:38
through with that * you come to Rom 3:8
a message or * from the Lord, the 1Co 14:29,30
many of them—whose * in getting out 2Co 2:17
to propose this *, but the first to 2Co 8:10
Let your enthusiastic * at the 2Co 8:11
fables, and their * of being saved 1Ti 1:3,4
missed this whole * and spend their 1Ti 1:6
* what those laws really show us. 1Ti 1:7

IDEAL
sheep country, * for our flocks. Num 32:3,4
fall short of God's glorious *; Rom 3:23
more and more closely to that *. 1Th 4:1
* of hard work we set up for you. 2Th 3:6
Be their *; 1Ti 4:12

IDEALS
and your truth as my *. Ps 26:3

IDEAS
man is always open to new *. Pro 18:15
Anyone presenting his own * is Jn 7:18
telling you my own *, but have Jn 8:28
For these are not my own *, but Jn 12:49
presenting his own *, but will be Jn 16:13
time discussing the latest new *! Act 17:21
to think up silly * of what God was Rom 1:21
having different * from yours about Rom 14:1
and high sounding *, for fear of 1Co 1:17
ignore the best * of men, even the 1Co 1:19
chosen to use * the world considers 1Co 1:27
* to tell you God's message. 1Co 2:1
upon God, not on man's great *. 1Co 2:5
against their own little *. 2Co 10:12
men's thoughts and *, instead of on Col 2:8
the world's * of how to be saved—by Col 2:20
up to God—wild * that stir up 1Ti 1:3,4
of teachers with devil-inspired *. 1Ti 4:1
* and silly myths and legends. 1Ti 4:7
wrong * and believe what is true. 2Ti 2:25
follow their own misguided *. 2Ti 4:4
and controversial theological *; Tit 3:9
be attracted by strange, new *. Heb 13:9

IDENTICAL
with * carvings of blossoms. Ex 37:19
they were * to those brought by Num 7:78-83
The two angels were * in all 1Ki 6:23-28
He made the * assignments of the 2Ch 23:18
Their faces too were * to the Eze 10:22
and exit hall were * to all the Eze 40:29,30
exits and doors—they were * units. Eze 42:11
Verses 44 and 46 (which are * with Mk 9:43,44f
Verses 44 and 46 (which are * with Mk 9:45,46f

IDENTIFICATION
"Your * seal and your walking Gen 38:18
man who owns this * seal and Gen 38:25
it is simply a way of easier * of 1Ch 1:1f
commodities, their * is uncertain. Eze 27:17f

IDENTIFIED
fatal error is not clearly *. Lev 10:1f
can be * as Mushki, Tabal, Eze 38:2,3f
be * by examining their fruit. Mt 7:17
"A tree is * by its fruit. Mt 12:33
A tree is * by the kind of fruit Lk 6:44

IDENTIFY
and to * the day and the night; Gen 1:14,15
father and asked him to * it. Gen 37:32
celebration shall * you as God's Ex 13:16
I will use these rods to * the Num 17:5

(IDENTIFY Con't)
shouted out to * himself, 1Ki 22:32,33
You can * a fool just by the way Ecc 10:3
as you can * a tree by its fruit. Mt 7:16
Yes, the way to * a tree or a Mt 7:20
he was only a witness to * it. Jn 1:8
Yes, these laws are made to * as 1Ti 1:10,11

IDENTIFYING
Then the Lord put an * mark on Gen 4:15
The headings * the speakers are Sol 1:1f

IDENTITY
be respected and maintain her *. Eze 17:14
revealed his * to his brothers, and Act 7:13

IDIOT
If you call your friend an *, you Mt 5:22

IDIOTS
said, "You stupid *— let this one Jn 11:49

IDLE
years you refused to let it lie *; Lev 26:34,35
* hands are the devil's workshop; Pro 16:27
* lips are his mouthpiece. Pro 16:27
You sing * songs to the sound of Amo 6:5
Day for every * word you speak. Mt 12:36

IDLES
only a fool * away his time. Pro 12:11

IDLY
O GOD, DON'T sit * by, silent and Ps 83:1
nor talking *— then the Lord will Is 58:13
* by while they swallow us up? Hab 1:13

IDOL
his *, you are apt to do it. Ex 34:15
a statue of God—an * in any form, Deu 4:16,17
Do not bring an * into your home Deu 7:26
had made an * from molten metal. Deu 9:12
luring you into * worship and into Deu 20:18
and worships an *, even in secret, Deu 27:15
down the wooden * of the goddess Ju 6:25
using the wooden * as wood for the Ju 6:26
knocked apart, the * beside it was Ju 6:28
for cutting down the Asherah *." Ju 6:30
offerings of the * Baal-berith, Ju 9:4
"I'll have an * carved for you Ju 17:3
and the * he made from it was Ju 17:4,5
* Dagon in the city of Ashdod. 1Sa 5:1
had happened—the * had fallen face 1Sa 5:4
Then she took an * 1Sa 19:13
discovered that it was only an *! 1Sa 19:16
she had made an *—which he cut down 1Ki 15:13
a shameful Asherah *, just as Ahab 2Ki 21:3,4,5
He removed the shameful * of 2Ki 23:6
burned the shameful * of Asherah. 2Ki 23:15
and every kind of * worship, both 2Ki 23:24
he cut down the * and crushed and 2Ch 15:16
not destroy the * shrines on the 2Ch 20:33
constructed * shrines in the 2Ch 21:11
incense at the * shrines on the 2Ch 28:4
against * worship was begun. 2Ch 31:1
and tore down the * altars, the 2Ch 31:1
of the heathen gods—a handmade *! 2Ch 32:19
He placed an * in the very Temple 2Ch 33:7
hills and took his * from the 2Ch 33:15
nor ever have an * in your home. Ps 81:9
gods in their * temples, but none Is 16:12
her sins, to rid her of all her * Is 27:9
With an *? Is 40:19
With an idol? An *, made from a Is 40:19
But they rush to make a new *; Is 41:7
* that can help him not one whit! Is 44:10
the axe and uses it to make an *. Is 44:13
Now he has a wonderful * that Is 44:13
* to fall down before and praise! Is 44:15
left he makes his god: a carved *! Is 44:17
this thing, this * that I'm holding Is 44:20
* ever told you they would happen? Is 45:21
Will you compare me with an * Is 46:6
could never say, "My * did it; Is 48:5
same as though they blessed an *. Is 66:3
have an * chiseled out from stone. Jer 2:26,27
tree and carve an *, and decorate Jer 10:2,3
your abominable * worship in the Jer 13:27
be ashamed of her * Chemosh, as Jer 48:13
But the God of Israel is no *! Jer 51:19
and the * altars abandoned. Eze 6:4-7
where the large * was that had made Eze 8:3
in the entrance, stood the *. Eze 8:5
every trace of all this * worship. Eze 11:18
you for making * shrines and to Eze 16:16
your lovers, and * altars on every Eze 16:24
building your * altars, your Eze 16:31
your brothels and * altars, and Eze 16:39
said to them: Get rid of every *; Eze 20:7
their children on * altars. Eze 36:12
washed away, your * worship gone. Eze 36:25
They built their * temples Eze 43:8
burned to Baal her * and for the Hos 1:13
this calf—this * you have made. Hos 8:5
This *—this calf-god thing—will Hos 10:6
laughed at for trusting in this *; Hos 10:6
And the * altars of Aven at Hos 10:8
destroy the * altars at Bethel. Amo 3:14
punishing. The * altars and Amo 7:9
her ornate * temples, built with Mic 1:7
Israel in her sin of * worship. Mic 1:13
cities where your * temples stand. Mic 5:14
every vestige of * worship Zec 13:2
think of God as an * made by men Act 17:29
and thieves and * worshipers. 1Co 5:10
lives, who are * worshipers, 1Co 6:9,10
Well, we all know that an * is 1Co 8:4
around from one * to another, not 1Co 12:2
is really an * worshiper—he loves Eph 5:5
them to go to * feasts. Rev 2:14
Prostitutes and of * Worship Rev 17:5
with demons, and * worshipers and Rev 21:8

IDOL-GODS
angered the Lord by worshiping *. 1Ki 14:15
nations, and have burned their *. 2Ki 19:18
and to their other *! Jer 7:18

IDOL-TEMPLES
Over in Israel the * were not 2Ch 15:17

IDOL-WORSHIP
he continued the * begun by 2Ki 15:24
from the guilt of their sin of *. 2Ch 34:5
and state your proofs that * pays! Is 45:21
carefully avoid * of every kind. 1Co 10:14

IDOLATERS
armies—all of them *—who once Eze 32:26
broken among the *, among those who Eze 32:28
* who have gone down to the pit. Eze 32:29
* who are slain by the sword." Eze 32:32
and murderers and *, and all who Rev 22:15

IDOLATORS
Murderers! *! Eze 33:26

IDOLATRIES
Literally, "lawless *." 1Pe 4:3f

IDOLATROUS
I will put an end to their * Zep 1:4

IDOLATRY
into *, and then you must die." Num 31:1
of Judah into *: I will bring such 2Ki 21:11
In addition to the * which God 2Ki 21:16
but even so he was led into * by Neh 13:26
against me and gone off into *. Jer 5:23,24
whole nation into *, thumbing their Eze 8:17
are guilty both of murder and *. Eze 22:4
Thus will I make lewdness and * Eze 23:48
a lesson against * for all to see. Eze 23:48
from her, for she is wedded to *. Hos 4:17
from my land because of their *. Hos 9:15
Then I will cure you of * and Hos 14:4
What sins? The * and oppression Mic 1:5
center of world * and wickedness. Zec 5:11f
I will yank her * out of her Zec 9:7
lustful pleasure, *, spiritism Gal 5:20
things of life, for that is *. Col 3:5

IDOLS
home—why have you stolen my *?" Gen 31:30
But as for your household *, a Gen 31:32
was the one who had stolen the *; Gen 31:34
to destroy the * they had brought Gen 35:2
So they gave Jacob all their * Gen 35:4
yourselves any *: any images Ex 20:4
make or worship * made of silver or Ex 20:23
and break down their shameful *. Ex 23:24
and cut down their shameful *. Ex 34:13
must have nothing to do with *. Ex 34:17
Do not make or worship *, for I Lev 19:3,4
"YOU MUST HAVE no *; Lev 26:1
you worship your *, and I will cut Lev 26:30
dead bodies to rot among your *; Lev 26:30
bowing down and worshiping the *. Num 25:2
Israel to worship * on Mount Peor, Num 31:16
destroy all their *—their carved Num 33:52
hills where they worship their *. Num 33:52
many people for worshiping *. Deu 4:3
it if you make any *, for the Lord Deu 4:23
by making *, and the Lord your God Deu 4:25
you will worship * made from wood Deu 4:28
wood and stone, * that neither see Deu 4:28
" 'Never make *; Deu 5:8
shameful images and burn the *. Deu 7:5
"Burn their * and do not touch Deu 7:25
cut down the metal *, and leave Deu 12:3
do when they worship their * Deu 14:1
seen their heathen * made of wood, Deu 29:17
made me very jealous of their *, Deu 32:21
Put away forever the * which your Jos 24:14
destroy all the * you now own, and Jos 24:23
the * of the neighboring nations. Ju 2:12-14
Baal and the Ashtaroth *. Ju 2:12-14
worshiped Baal and the Asheroth *. Ju 3:7
the * Baal and Baal-berith. Ju 8:33
worshiped *," they confessed. Ju 10:10
Micah had many * in his Ju 17:4,5
some teraphim, and many plated *. Ju 18:14
*, the ephod, and the teraphim. Ju 18:17
ephod, the teraphim, and the *. Ju 18:20
Then, with Micah's * and the Ju 18:27
Then they set up the * and Ju 18:30
So Micah's * were worshiped by Ju 18:31
foreign gods and your Ashtaroth *. 1Sa 7:3
So they destroyed their * of Baal 1Sa 7:4
the Baal and Ashtaroth *. 1Sa 12:10
is as bad as worshiping *. 1Sa 15:23
death to their * and to the people 1Sa 31:9
confiscated many * which had been 2Sa 5:21
nations where * were worshiped 1Ki 11:1
to * in the shrines on the hills. 1Ki 13:33
and obelisks and * on every high 1Ki 14:23
all the * his father had made. 1Ki 15:12
* and led all of Israel into sin. 1Ki 15:26
into the sin of worshiping *. 1Ki 15:34
into worshiping * and the Lord was 1Ki 16:13
he had worshiped * and had led 1Ki 16:19
he worshiped * as Jeroboam had, 1Ki 16:26
Then he made other * and did 1Ki 16:33
he worshiped * just as the Amorites 1Ki 21:26
into the sin of worshiping *. 1Ki 22:52,53
of Israel into the worship of *. 2Ki 3:3
worship * and led them into sin. 2Ki 13:11
into the sin of worshiping *. 2Ki 14:24
Israel in the sin of worshiping *. 2Ki 15:9
He worshiped *, as King Jeroboam 2Ki 15:18
into the sin of worshiping *. 2Ki 15:28
They had placed obelisks and * 2Ki 17:10
Yes, they worshiped *, despite 2Ki 17:12
worshiped heathen * despite the 2Ki 17:15
They made detestable, shameful * 2Ki 17:16
Those from Babylon worshiped * 2Ki 17:30
they also worshiped their *. 2Ki 17:41
down the shameful * of Asherah, and 2Ki 18:4
worshiped the same *, and turned 2Ki 21:21
down the shameful * of Asherah; 2Ki 23:14
instead they worshiped the * of 1Ch 5:25
because the people worshiped *. 1Ch 9:1
the wonderful news before their *. 1Ch 10:9
picked up many * left by the 1Ch 14:12
you, and worship *, then I will 2Ch 7:19
people to worship * instead of God, 2Ch 11:15
destroyed all the * in the land of 2Ch 15:8
years, and did not worship *. 2Ch 17:3
and destroying the Asherim *. 2Ch 17:6
of Jerusalem in worshiping *; 2Ch 21:11
and Judah worship * just as in the 2Ch 21:13
knocked down the *, and killed 2Ch 23:15,16,17
brought with him * taken from the 2Ch 25:14
worshiped these *, and have not 2Ch 25:16
and worshiped the * of Baal. 2Ch 28:2
incense to the *, for he even 2Ch 28:3
destroyed all the *, and commanded 2Ch 32:12
to worship the * of the heathen 2Ch 33:2
where he built * on the hills and 2Ch 33:19
for Amon sacrificed to all the * 2Ch 33:22
So Josiah removed all * from the 2Ch 34:33
the heathen * of the surrounding 2Ch 36:14
these silly *, when every claim Ps 4:2
worship *, those imitation gods. Ps 31:5,6
who are proud, or who trust in *. Ps 40:4
*, would God not know it? Ps 44:20
their * to flaunt their victory. Ps 74:4
* and altars to other gods. Ps 78:58
*, but our God made the heavens! Ps 96:5
Let those who worship * be Ps 97:7
Or, "to lifeless *." Ps 106:28f
*, and were led away from God. Ps 106:36
to the demons—the * of Ps 106:37,38
for their love of * was adultery in Ps 106:39
just as foolish as their * are. Ps 115:8
The heathen worship * of gold and Ps 135:15
made by men— * with speechless Ps 135:16
the gods," or "before the *." Ps 138:1f
you sacrificed to * in your groves Is 1:29
and *—the land is full of them! Is 2:8
And all * will be utterly Is 2:18
gold and silver * to the moles and Is 2:20
a kingdom whose * were far greater Is 10:10
Samaria and her * we will destroy Is 10:11
anguish to their * at the tops of Is 16:12
They will no longer ask their * Is 17:8
cloud; the * of Egypt tremble; Is 19:1
they plead with their * for Is 19:3
and all the * of Babylon lie Is 21:8,9
of all her idol altars and her *. Is 27:9
all your silver * and golden images Is 30:22
away his golden * and silver Is 31:7
at all, but merely *, carved by men Is 37:19
Can your * make such claims as Is 41:21
Not one of your * told you Is 41:28
* are all as empty as the wind. Is 41:29
not share my praise with carved *. Is 42:8
But those who trust in * and Is 42:17
Which of all their * ever has Is 43:9
your *, I have shown you my power. Is 43:12
who manufacture * for their gods. Is 44:9
for their * neither see nor know. Is 44:9
All who worship * shall be Is 45:16
around the wooden * and pray to Is 45:20
THE * OF Babylon, Bel and Nebo, Is 46:1
Among all your *, which one has Is 48:14
You worship your * with great Is 57:5
you worship * there, deserting me. Is 57:7,8
doors you set your * up and worship Is 57:7,8
* your love, instead of loving me. Is 57:7,8

(IDOLS Con't)
collection of your * can help you Is 57:13
face by worshiping * in many Is 65:3
Those who worship * that are Is 66:17
* they themselves have made! Jer 1:16
them into fools who worship *? Jer 2:4,5
up their glorious God for silly *! Jer 2:10,11
tree you've bowed low before *. Jer 2:20
so, that you haven't worshiped *? Jer 2:23
worship * made of wood and stone. Jer 3:9
by worshiping * under every tree; Jer 3:13
We are weary of worshiping * on Jer 3:23
on priests and *. Jer 3:24
discard your *, and if you will Jer 4:1
ashamed when they worshiped *? Jer 6:15
And stop worshiping * as you do Jer 7:6
They have set up their * right in Jer 7:30
ashamed because they worship *? Jer 8:12
carved * and strange evil rites?" Jer 8:19
and worshiped the * of Baal, as Jer 9:14
The wisest of men who worship * Jer 10:8
goldsmiths who make their *; Jer 10:9
of God bow before their *. Jer 10:14
Jacob is not like these foolish *. Jer 10:16
to listen to me and worshiping *. Jer 11:10
Then they will pray to their * Jer 11:12
own evil desires and worships *; Jer 13:10
and worship your * all you like—and Jer 16:13
your detestable *, and filled it up Jer 16:18
they have worshiped worthless *! Jer 16:19
to sin, worshiping * beneath each Jer 17:2,3
me and turned to foolish *. Jer 18:15
The people burn incense to * Jer 19:4
incense to idols—* that neither Jer 19:4
with them, for they worshiped *." Jer 22:9
who turned away to the * of Baal. Jer 23:27
Don't anger me by worshiping *; Jer 25:6
and made me furious with your *. Jer 25:7
their abominable * there. Jer 32:34
Egypt and burn the * and carry off Jer 43:12
my anger with the * you have made Jer 44:8
burned incense to * (it was a great Jer 44:15
burning incense to * in the cities Jer 44:21
gods and burning incense to *. Jer 48:35
are madly in love with their *. Jer 50:38
in them at all! * are nothing! Jer 51:18
this great city and all her *; Jer 51:47
destruction of the * of Babylon. Jer 51:52
my Temple with * and evil Eze 5:11
war upon you to destroy your *. Eze 6:3
love of *—and I will blind their Eze 6:9
among your * and altars on every Eze 6:13
on you for your worshiping of *. Eze 7:3
and you used it instead to make *! Eze 7:20
all the various * worshiped by the Eze 8:10
who long for *, I will repay them Eze 11:21
these men worship * in their Eze 14:3
* and then comes to ask my help. Eze 14:4
of those who turn from me to *. Eze 14:5
and destroy your *, and stop Eze 14:6,7
who rejects me for *, and then Eze 14:6,7
worship *," says the Lord God. Eze 15:8
I gave you—to cover your *! Eze 16:18
worshiping of *—and the slaying of Eze 16:36
She insolently worshiped many * Eze 16:50
You have worshiped * far more Eze 16:51
feast before the * of Israel and Eze 18:6
God, but worships * on the Eze 18:11
pledge, and loves * and worships Eze 18:12
feast before the * and worship Eze 18:15
They didn't get rid of their *, Eze 20:8
hearts were with their *! Eze 20:16
*, for I am the Lord your God. Eze 20:18
and longed for their fathers' *. Eze 20:23,24
did, and keep on worshiping *? Eze 20:30
on worshiping your *, go right Eze 20:39
they will sacrifice to * and Eze 21:21
and damned—City of *, filthy and Eze 22:3
mountain top is filled with *; Eze 22:9
their *, defiling herself. Eze 23:7
yourself with all their *. Eze 23:30
they have worshiped * and Eze 23:37
in front of their *, then even that Eze 23:39
harlotry, your worshiping of *. Eze 23:49
lewdness, of worshiping your *. Eze 24:13
And I will smash the * of Egypt Eze 30:13
you worship *, and murder. Eze 33:25
the worshiping of *, so I poured Eze 36:18
themselves with * and their other Eze 37:23
between, and worshiped their *. Eze 43:8
Now let them put away their * Eze 43:9
away from God to * must be punished Eze 44:10
when Israel abandoned me for *. Eze 44:15
from them to their * made of gold Dan 5:2,3,4
carry back their * with him, along Dan 11:8
worshiping * inside the Temple. Dan 11:30,31
because applied to *, so it will no Hos 1:16f
you to forget your *, and their Hos 1:17
altar, temple, priests, or even *! Hos 3:4
of God for the disgrace of *. Hos 4:7
Longing after * has made them Hos 4:12
They sacrifice to * on the tops Hos 4:13
because they sacrifice to *. Hos 4:19
the people with * at Mizpah and Hos 5:1
she is determined to follow *. Hos 5:11
by worshiping the * that they made Hos 8:4
the statues and * she erects. Hos 10:1
heathen altars and smash their *. Hos 10:2
* at Beth-aven should be hurt; Hos 10:5
to Baal and burning incense to *. Hos 11:2
used for sacrifices to your *. Hos 12:11
who worship *. Hos 12:11
to mold into *, formed with skill Hos 13:2
never again will we call the * we Hos 14:3
Stay away from *! Hos 14:8
Go ahead and sacrifice to * at Amo 4:4
Don't seek the * of Bethel, Amo 5:5
of the * in Bethel can put it out. Amo 5:6
And those who worship the * of Amo 8:14
the nations around us worship *! Mic 4:5
consult— and destroy all your *. Mic 5:13
in worshiping all your man-made *? Hab 2:18
lifeless wooden * to arise and save Hab 2:19
Mankind and all the * that he Zep 1:3
How foolish to ask the * for Zec 10:2
names of the * will be forgotten. Zec 13:2
heathen women who worship *. Mal 2:11
They told Aaron, 'Make * for us, Act 7:40
meat sacrificed to *, from all Act 15:20
food offered to * and from unbled Act 15:27,28,29
by all the * he saw everywhere Act 17:16
put away * and worship only him. Act 17:30
food offered to *, not to eat Act 21:25
and stone and made * for Rom 1:23
You say, "Don't pray to *," and Rom 2:22
me and have not bowed down to *!" Rom 11:4
meat that has been offered to *. Rom 14:2
meat that has been offered to *; Rom 14:6
meat that has been offered to *. Rom 14:14
*, or is a drunkard, or abusive. 1Co 5:11
that has been sacrificed to *. 1Co 8:1
that has been sacrificed to *? 1Co 8:4
to thinking of * as alive, and have 1Co 8:7
offered to the * is really being 1Co 8:7
So if eating meat offered to * 1Co 8:13
did, nor worship * as they did. 1Co 10:7
Am I saying that the * to whom 1Co 10:19
food to these * are united together 1Co 10:20
that has been offered to these *. 1Co 10:20
food offered to * if you want to; 1Co 10:23
it was offered to *, lest the 1Co 10:25
as a sacrifice to *, and you won't 1Co 10:27
been offered to *, then don't eat 1Co 10:28
be between God's temple and *? 2Co 6:16
away from your * to God so that now 1Th 1:9
of *, and other terrible sins. 1Pe 4:3
that has been sacrificed to *. Rev 2:20
nor their * made of gold and Rev 9:20

IDUMEA
Judea, Jerusalem, *, from beyond Mk 3:7,8

IGAL
*, son of Joseph, from the tribe Num 13:3-15
* (son of Nathan) from Zobah; 2Sa 23:24-39
including Hattush, *, Bariah, 1Ch 3:21,22

IGDALIAH
Hanan the prophet (the son of *). Jer 35:4

IGNOMINIOUS
the Jews be brought to * defeat. Ps 129:5

IGNOMINY
they lie in * with all the other Eze 32:30

IGNORANCE
"Why are you using your * to Job 38:2
Where there is * of God, the Pro 29:18
Such stupidity and *! Is 44:18
through error or *, and so the Eze 45:20
is caused by your * of the Mt 22:29
you did to Jesus was done in *; Act 3:17
God tolerated man's past * about Act 17:30
answers, he is just showing his *. 1Co 8:2
we will leave him in his *. 1Co 14:38
in their * of God and his ways. 1Th 4:5

IGNORANT
I saw myself so stupid and so *; Ps 73:22
But you are so foolish and so *! Ps 82:5
Are you so *? Is 40:21
can we expect from the poor and *? Jer 5:4
are foolish and *, for he, too, is Heb 5:1

IGNORE
O Lord God, do not * me—do not 2Ch 6:42
his charioteers: "* everyone but 2Ch 18:30
Do not * their sin. Neh 4:5
He does not * the good men but Job 36:7
He does not * the prayers of men Ps 9:12
Why do you * our sorrows and Ps 44:24
heart, O God, you will not *. Ps 51:17
They * the fact that it was I, Jer 2:6
instructions and * them are Mt 7:26
"For they * our ritual of Mt 15:2
shall be rooted up, so * them. Mt 15:13,14
your garden, but * the important Mt 23:23
For you * God's specific orders Mk 7:8
seem to be, and * the best ideas of 1Co 1:19
Or, "If he disagrees, * his 1Co 14:38f
Don't let anyone despise or * 1Co 16:11
remember that you can't * God and Gal 6:7

IGNORED
them roughly. He * the old men's 1Ki 12:13,14
Warnings from the Lord were * by 2Ch 33:10
the needy shall not be * forever; Ps 9:18
when half grown, * by the reaper, Ps 129:6,7
will be * in his own time of need. Pro 21:13
the Lord, and their judges * me; Jer 2:8
at my laws, * my wishes, and Eze 20:16
and mothers are contemptuously *; Eze 22:7
my Sabbaths are *. Eze 22:8
my Temple and * my Sabbaths, for Eze 23:38
But Jesus * their comments and Mk 5:36
The judge * her for a while, but Lk 18:4,5

IGNORES
destroy them. She * her young as Job 39:16
The world * us, but we are known 2Co 6:9

II
and Jeroboam * became the new 2Ki 13:13
Israel, Jeroboam * had become king 2Ki 14:23
Jeroboam * recovered the lost 2Ki 14:25
used King Jeroboam * to save her. 2Ki 14:27
When Jeroboam * died he was 2Ki 14:29
Zuph, Elkanah *, Mahath, Amasai, 1Ch 6:33-38
Nabopolasser and Nebuchadnezzar * Jer 4:6f
* (2 Kings 16:7, 8). Eze 23:12f
"the southern king"—Ptolemy *. Dan 11:5f
Ptolemy * of Egypt gave his Dan 11:6f
to Antiochus * of Syria to conclude Dan 11:6f
Seleucus *. Dan 11:9f

II'S
by Antiochus * former wife Laodice, Dan 11:7f

III
Tilgath-pilneser *) to invade the 1Ch 5:26
Joel, Samuel, Elkanah *, Jeroham, 1Ch 6:33-38
sister of Ptolemy *, who now Dan 11:7f
Possibly Antiochus * the Great, Dan 11:13f
of Antiochus *, sent Heliodorus to Dan 11:20f

IIM
Baalah, *, Ezem, Eltolad, Chesil, Jos 15:21-32

IJON
and he destroyed *, Dan, 1Ki 15:20
He captured the cities of *, 2Ki 15:29
They destroyed the cities of *, 2Ch 16:4

IKKESH
Ira (son of *) from Tekoa; 2Sa 23:24-39
Ira (son of *) from Tekoa; 1Ch 11:26-47
was Ira, the son of * from Tekoa; 1Ch 27:9

ILAI
* from Ahoh; 1Ch 11:26-47

ILL
who didn't die were deathly *; 1Sa 5:12
his love for her that he became *. 2Sa 13:2
When they were *, I mourned Ps 35:13
Others, the fools, were * because Ps 107:17
with these men of * repute, they Mk 2:16
God and curing those who were *. Lk 9:11
long he had been *, he asked him, Jn 5:6
About this time she became * and Act 9:37
was * with fever and dysentery. Act 28:8
because you heard that he was *. Php 2:26

ILL-GOTTEN
* gain brings no lasting Pro 10:2
they buy with such * gain will turn Pro 20:17

ILL-MANNERED
churlish, stubborn, and *. 1Sa 25:3

ILL-TREATED
They were hungry and sick and * Heb 11:37,38

ILL-TREATMENT
but chose to share * with God's Heb 11:24,25

ILLEGAL
"It is * to take a millstone as Deu 24:6
Under Mosaic law, it was * to keep Amo 2:8f
some Pharisees said, "That's *! Lk 6:2
Lord, and ate it—* as this was—and Lk 6:4
* to carry that sleeping mat!" Jn 5:10

ILLEGITIMATE
"You * bastard, Jn 9:34

ILLNESS
When Elisha was in his last *, 2Ki 13:14
you will not recover from this * Is 38:1
And whatever their * and pain, or Mt 4:24
healed people of every sort of *. Mt 9:35
purpose of his * is not death, but Jn 11:4

ILLUMINATE
glory of God and of the Lamb * it. Rev 21:23

ILLUSTRATE
This will * the way my people Hos 1:2
This will * the way my people Zec 11:5
What story shall I use to * it? Mk 4:30
"How can I * it? Lk 13:18
To further * the point, he told Lk 15:10
a story to * their need for Lk 18:1
Let me *: when a woman marries, Rom 7:2
as examples to * what I have been 1Co 4:6
and his work was mostly to * and Heb 3:5

ILLUSTRATED
of Heaven can be * by a Mt 13:47,48
said, "it can be * by the story of Mt 22:1

(ILLUSTRATED Con't)
"THE KINGDOM OF Heaven can be * Mt 25:1
of Heaven can be * by the story of Mt 25:14

ILLUSTRATES
Then the Lord said: This * the Jer 13:8,9
The Lord God says, "This * what Eze 5:5,6,7
This * the fact that Israel will Hos 3:4
And he said to me, "This * how I Zec 11:16
This * the fact that someday Lk 8:17

ILLUSTRATING
"Here is another story * what Mk 4:26

ILLUSTRATION
A rebel will misapply an * so Pro 26:9
Here is another * Jesus used: Mt 13:24
to them without at least one *. Mt 13:34,35
* of the thistles and the wheat. Mt 13:36
HERE IS ANOTHER * of the Kingdom Mt 20:1
this simple *, what will you do Mk 4:13
for using this *, for they knew he Mk 12:12
Then Jesus used this *: "No one Lk 5:36
One day he gave this * to a large Lk 8:4
(As he was giving this * he Lk 8:8
Jesus replied with an *: "A Jew Lk 10:30
he used this *: "Suppose you Lk 11:5,6
Then he gave an *: "A rich man Lk 12:16
Then he used this *: "A man Lk 13:6
Jesus replied with this *: "A Lk 14:16
So Jesus used this *: "If you Lk 15:3,4
"Or take another *: A woman has Lk 15:8
Pharisees, to whom he gave this *. Lk 16:31f
were the wicked tenants in his *. Lk 20:19
Then he gave them this *: Lk 21:29
Those who heard Jesus use this * Jn 10:6
I speak this way, using the * of Rom 6:19
Now this true story is an * of Gal 4:24,25
Arabs—and in my * Abraham's Gal 4:24,25
but it is an * of the way we are Eph 5:32

ILLUSTRATIONS
I will give you many * of the Job 36:3
are * of the good things to come. Zec 3:8
He used many * such as this one Mt 13:2,3
hard-to-understand *? Mt 13:10
That is why I use these *, so Mt 13:12,13
spiritual truth understood the *. Mt 13:12,13f
Here is another of his *: Mt 13:31,32
Jesus constantly used these * Mt 13:34,35
giving these *, he returned to his Mt 13:53,54
He used many such * to teach the Mk 4:33
In fact, he taught only by * in Mk 4:34
Think over these three *, and 2Ti 2:7

ILLUSTRIOUS
had a long and * history. Jer 5:15f

ILLYRICUM
from Jerusalem clear over into *. Rom 15:19

IMAGE
man in our *, in our likeness." Gen 1:26f
Seth was born, the very * of his Gen 5:3,4,5
his own likeness, after his *." Gen 5:3,4,5f
You must never bow to an * or Ex 20:5
my carved * commanded it to Is 48:5
for her with her * on them, without Jer 44:19
up the bronze * of a serpent on a Jn 3:14
* fell down to us from heaven. Act 19:35
God's glory is man made in his *, 1Co 11:7
Literally, "who is the * of 2Co 4:4f

IMAGES
any idols: any * resembling Ex 20:4
Then make * of angels, Ex 25:18
you must never worship carved *, Lev 26:1
stones, molten *, and the open-air Num 33:52
don't worship *, whether of Deu 5:8
You shall not bow down to any * Deu 5:9,10
the shameful * and burn the idols. Deu 7:5
burn the shameful *, cut down the Deu 12:3
to erect shameful * beside the Deu 16:21
the altars and * and killing 2Ki 11:18
and graven * (this of course was 2Ch 33:19
* of Ashtaroth and the sun-idols. Is 17:8
idols and golden * and cast them Is 30:22
idols and silver *—which in your Is 31:7
land is full of *, and the people Jer 50:38
is dulled by the * he makes, for in Jer 51:17
of Egypt and the * at Memphis, and Eze 30:13
and in all the * of them you Amo 5:25,26,27
All her carved * will be smashed Mic 1:7
what to do. Can * speak for God? Hab 2:19
Kaiway, and in all the * you made. Act 7:43

IMAGINABLE
themselves in every evil way *. Jud 1:18

IMAGINATION
so humble) have a very clever *. Col 2:18

IMAGINE
We cannot * the power of the Job 37:23
and cannot * suggesting. Jer 32:35
You set before them—* it—the Eze 16:19
"Don't * that I came to bring Mt 10:34
and we can't even * what it is 1Jn 3:2

IMAGINED
greater than I could ever have *. 2Ch 9:6
your * grievances against others. Job 36:17
heard or even * what wonderful 1Co 2:9

IMBEDDED
by three posts * in three sockets. Ex 27:14,15
posts * in their four sockets. Ex 27:16
being * in solid bronze bases. Ex 27:17
spear * in the timber of the wall. 1Sa 19:9,10
tied to silver rings * in marble Est 1:6

IMITATES
a much loved child * his father. Eph 5:1

IMITATION
who worship idols, those * gods. Ps 31:5,6

IMLAH
His name is Micaiah, the son of * 1Ki 22:8
His name is Micaiah (son of *)." 2Ch 18:6,7
Go and get Micaiah (son of *)," 2Ch 18:8

IMMANUEL
and bore a son, *, the Christ. Is 7:14f
And she shall call him * Is 7:14
land of Judah, O *, submerging it Is 8:7,8
Or, "*." Is 8:9,10f

IMMEASURABLY
*, she shall die, says the Lord. Jer 51:53

IMMEDIATE
an * bond of love between them. 1Sa 18:1
and he put the plan into * effect. Est 2:4
Its * use here refers to Is 7:14f
Your command would bring * Lk 17:6

IMMEDIATELY
and must wash his clothes *. Lev 11:25
and he shall * give that estimated Lev 27:23
But the Lord heard them. * he Num 12:3,4
land of Bashan. He * mobilized his Deu 3:1
river bottom and * pile them into a Deu 27:2,3,4
The king * dismissed all those who Ju 3:17,18,19
his people, so he * permitted the Ju 10:7,8
will mean that you must leave *. 1Sa 20:22
King Saul * summoned Ahimelech 1Sa 22:11,12
arrived, he went * to see Absalom. 2Sa 16:16
Asa of Judah. He * killed all of 1Ki 15:29
He * killed the entire royal 1Ki 16:11
this, they returned * to the king. 2Ki 1:4,5
* Elisha warned the king of 2Ki 6:9
The people responded * and 2Ch 31:5,6
and it was used * to sacrifice Ez 3:3
shall be punished * by death, Ez 7:26
section * opposite his own house. Neh 3:28
were * expelled from the assembly. Neh 13:3
to their farms. I * confronted the Neh 13:11
* the king's secretaries were Est 8:9,10
and its * surrounding yards. Eze 41:13
his dream! He * called in all his Dan 2:1
to obey will * be thrown into a Dan 3:6
So he returned * to Israel with Mt 2:21
and children.) * after this, Jesus Mt 14:22
But Jesus * spoke to them, Mt 14:27
Or, "*." Mt 21:19f
"* after the persecution of Mt 24:29
the $5,000 began * to buy and sell Mt 25:16
And * the cock crowed. Mt 26:74
* the Holy Spirit urged Jesus Mk 1:12,13
He called them too, and * they Mk 1:20
Be healed!" * the leprosy was Mk 1:42
examined * by the Jewish priest. Mk 1:43,44
* after this Jesus instructed his Mk 6:45
* after this he got into a boat Mk 8:10
And *, while he was still Mk 14:43
And * the rooster crowed the Mk 14:72
rebuking it, and * her temperature Lk 4:39
And *, as everyone watched, the Lk 5:25
into the pigs, and * the whole herd Lk 8:33
him arrested *, for they realized Lk 20:19
end won't follow *— for nation Lk 21:9
to let him in, and * the boat was Jn 6:21
* so that they could arrest him. Jn 11:57
Again Peter denied it. And * a Jn 18:27
daybreak, and * began preaching! Act 5:21
could see, and was * baptized. Act 9:18
of the Temple, and * the gates were Act 21:30
his trumpet and * a third of the Rev 8:12

IMMENSE
to help them. An * amount of 2Ch 2:9
where an * crowd soon gathered. Mt 13:2,3
ONCE AGAIN AN * crowd gathered Mk 4:1

IMMENSELY
with David and how * popular he was 1Sa 18:28
Hezekiah became * respected among 2Ch 32:23
This pleased Haman * and he Est 5:14
daughters, and was * wealthy, Job 1:2,3
than the man who is * rich! Pro 3:13,14,15

IMMER
son of Meshillemith, son of *). 1Ch 9:12
Sixteenth, the group led by *; 1Ch 24:7-18
From the subclan of *, 1,052; Ez 2:36-39
Tel-harsha, Cherub, Addan, and *. Ez 2:59
The sons of *: Ez 10:20
Zadok (son of *) also rebuilt the Neh 3:29
From the subclan of *, 1,052; Neh 7:39-42
Tel-harsha, Cherub, Addon, and *. Neh 7:61
son of Meshillemoth, son of *); Neh 11:10-14
NOW WHEN PASHHUR (son of *), the Jer 20:1

IMMERSED
you and your people will be * in Ex 8:3,4

IMMIGRANTS
Benjamin, and the * from Israel 2Ch 15:9
They murder widows, *, and Ps 94:6,7
He protects the *, and cares for Ps 146:9
aliens and *, orphans and widows; Jer 22:3
ignored; * and visitors are forced Eze 22:7
All these * are to be given land Eze 47:23
of a great wave of * to the Zep 2:5f

IMMINENT
him from seemingly * and premature Heb 5:7f

IMMORAL
turned from their * customs and Ez 6:21,22
your time with evil and * men. Ps 50:18
Those who live * lives, who are 1Co 6:9,10
all who are * and impure: 1Ti 1:10,11
who are * or commit adultery. Heb 13:4
living their evil, * lives, Jud 1:8
along with all her * followers, Rev 2:22
the world have had * relations with Rev 17:2
took part in her * acts and enjoyed Rev 18:9
murderers, and the *, and those Rev 21:8
in it—no one * or dishonest—but Rev 21:27
sorcerers and the * and murderers Rev 22:15

IMMORALITY
wild party, followed by sexual *. Ex 32:6
She indulged herself in *, and Lam 1:9
your lust and *, and the taking of 2Co 12:21
and will think nothing of *. 2Ti 3:3
she urges them to practice * and Rev 2:20
and witchcraft, their * and theft. Rev 9:21
made drunk by the wine of her *." Rev 17:2
the fatal wine of her intense *. Rev 18:3

IMMOVABLE
BLESS THE LORD who is my * Rock. Ps 144:1

IMNA
Zophah, *, Shelesh, Amal. 1Ch 7:35

IMNAH
Asher and his sons: *, Ishvah, Gen 46:16,17
named after their ancestor *. Num 26:44-47
*, Ishvah, Ishvi, 1Ch 7:30
Kore (son of *, the Levite), who 2Ch 31:14,15

IMNITES
The *, named after their ancestor Num 26:44-47

IMPACT
The double dream gives double *, Gen 41:32

IMPALE
off your head and * your body on a Gen 40:18,19

IMPALED
*, just as Joseph had predicted. Gen 40:22
was executed, and * on a pole." Gen 41:13
The men of Gibeon * them in the 2Sa 21:9
Philistines had * them after they 2Sa 21:12,13,14
Literally, "*." Ez 6:11f
two men found guilty, and * alive. Est 2:23

IMPART
so that I can * to you the faith Rom 1:11,12

IMPARTIAL
"You must be * in judgment. Lev 19:35,36

IMPATIENT
Don't be *. Ps 27:14
Don't be * for the Lord to act! Ps 37:34
horses were * to be off, to Zec 6:7
But I became * with these Zec 11:8
They must not be proud or *; Tit 1:7

IMPEDIMENT
to me, for I have a speech *." Ex 4:10
A deaf man with a speech * was Mk 7:32

IMPELLED
The Holy Spirit had * him to go Lk 2:27
Afterwards, Paul felt * by the Act 19:21

IMPENDING
didn't realize the * disaster. Ju 20:34
concerning the * doom of Nineveh: Nah 1:1

IMPENETRABLE
me, thick, * darkness everywhere. Job 23:16,17
he causes deep, * darkness to fall Jer 13:16

IMPENITENCE
sin in such a way? * at the 1Jn 5:17f

IMPERFECT
skin, or has * testicles— although Lev 21:20

IMPERIAL
Julius, a member of the * guard. Act 27:1

IMPERIL
* them by deserting to King Saul. 1Ch 12:19

IMPERVIOUS
For see, today I have made you * Jer 1:18

IMPLACABLE
as though I were an * foe; Jer 30:14

IMPLEMENTS
weapons of war into * of peace. Is 2:4
knives and other * were laid. Eze 40:42

IMPLIES
therefore * "to die no more." Rev 1:5f
Verse 12 * death from Rev 14:13f

IMPLORE
and * your help. Ps 28:2
HOW I PLEAD with God, how I * his Ps 142:1
who curse you; * God's blessing on Lk 6:28

IMPLY
But this would * the end Lk 16:9f

IMPLYING
* jealousy, as in Mark 6:2–6. Mk 6:52f

(IMPLYING Con't)
as a collective noun, * plurality. Rev 22:2f

IMPORT
pay your taxes and * duties gladly, Rom 13:7

IMPORTANCE
But no doubt you gave men of * Job 22:8
me teach you the * of trusting and Ps 34:11
you will soon learn the * of Pro 2:3,4,5
it will bring you before men of * Pro 18:16
Evil men don't understand the * Pro 28:5
the men of *, and speak to them, Jer 5:5
sixty other men of * found hiding. Jer 52:24,25
and *—these are not from God. 1Jn 2:16

IMPORTANT
* month of the Jewish calendar. Ex 12:2
Anything that is too * or Ex 18:22
* than ours at the beginning!" Ju 8:2,3
is the least * of all the families 1Sa 9:21
But she said, "It's *. 2Ki 4:23
well as all of his * officials, 2Ki 10:11
that these persons were more *; 1Ch 1:1f
Because of their * positions 1Ch 9:27
All the * people of the nation, 2Ch 36:14
"Your sons shall become * men; Job 5:25
For I have * information for you. Pro 8:6,7
They nail down * truths. Ecc 12:11
he exiled all the * people of Judah Jer 27:19,20,21
the Ethiopian, an * palace Jer 38:7
are no more * than any daily task. Eze 22:26
my altar is not *, and encouraging Mal 1:12
the things that are most * to me. Mal 2:1
more * than what to eat and wear. Mt 6:25
* command in the laws of Moses?" Mt 22:36
The second most * is similar: Mt 22:38,39
but ignore the * things—justice and Mt 23:23
leave the more * things undone. Mt 23:23
But many people who seem to be * Mk 10:31
now will be the least * then; Mk 10:31
which is the most *?" Mk 12:28
And I know it is far more * to Mk 12:33
life are much more * than bread!' Lk 4:4
However, the * thing is not that Lk 10:20
of now will be least * then." Lk 13:30
Nor is the messenger more * than Jn 13:16
and also many * women of the city. Act 17:4
He has something * to tell him." Act 23:17
Remember that you are * only Rom 11:18
the good graces of * people, but Rom 12:16
For, after all, the * thing for Rom 14:17
isn't very *, but God is important 1Co 3:7
but God is * because he is the one 1Co 3:7
Now the most * thing about a 1Co 4:2
Don't think of eating as *, 1Co 6:13
That is the * thing. 1Co 7:19
The * thing to remember is that 1Co 7:29
makes us feel *, what is really 1Co 8:1
it is the * thing, not yours. 1Co 10:29
* are really the most necessary. 1Co 12:22
that might otherwise seem less *. 1Co 12:24
to have the more * of these gifts. 1Co 12:31
I or they; the * thing is that we 1Co 15:11
isn't * how much you have to give. 2Co 8:12
* and is a tonic for all you do. 1Ti 4:8
missed the most * thing in 1Ti 6:21
think that what you say is not *. Tit 2:15
with a far more * work than those Heb 8:6
This has an * lesson for us Heb 9:9
well, I say that good works are * Jas 2:18
and * part of the building." 1Pe 2:7
Most * of all, continue to show 1Pe 4:8

IMPORTED
For I saw a beautiful robe * Jos 7:21
of finest linen * from Egypt, Pro 7:16,17
She buys * foods, brought by Pro 31:14

IMPOSES
The sentence he * is to be fully Deu 17:11

IMPOSSIBLE
Let me out of this * situation!" Num 11:15
territory proved * to conquer, so Jos 19:47,48
and it seemed * to Amnon to do 2Sa 13:2f
It was * to estimate the weight 2Ki 25:16
This is an * thing the king Dan 2:11
Nothing would be *. Mt 17:20
"It is almost * for a rich man to Mt 19:23
They load you with * demands Mt 23:4
"It's almost * for the rich to get Mk 10:23
"Without God, it is utterly *. Mk 10:27
to the angel, "But this is *! Lk 1:18
For you crush men beneath * Lk 11:46
and riches! How * it is for us to Rom 11:33
the doom of that * system by taking Gal 3:13
for it is * for God to tell a lie. Heb 6:18
save you from the * road to heaven 1Pe 1:18

IMPREGNABLE
* defense, a high wall of safety. Pro 18:11
and Medes sacked * Nineveh. Nah 2:1f

IMPRESS
to you, hoping to * them so 2Pe 1:15

IMPRESSED
was very much * with her, and did Est 2:9
For he is not * by the world's Job 37:24
They weren't * by the wonder of Ps 106:7
and it is silly to be * by it. Ecc 7:6
"Why aren't you *? Is 58:3
and none of them * him as much as Dan 1:18,19
The crowds were profoundly * by Mt 22:33

IMPRESSION
make a deep * on all who see it. Ps 112:6
has made a deep * on me as I have Ecc 9:13
them: You're getting the wrong *. Jer 13:13
to correct the * that the Kingdom Lk 19:11
don't live to make a good * on Php 2:3
Don't worry about making a good * Col 3:12

IMPRISON
At his pleasure he could * the Ps 105:22
you to Babylon and * you there for Jer 32:5
He talked to me and said: "Go, * Eze 3:24
to arrest and * John because he Mk 6:17,18

IMPRISONED
and Jehoiachin was * in Babylon 2Ki 24:12
like prisoners and * in a dungeon Is 24:22
for they are robbed, enslaved, *, Is 42:22
At this time Jeremiah was * in Jer 32:2
(Jeremiah had not been * yet, so Jer 37:4
I was locked out of life and * in Jon 2:6
celebration and * him, placing him Act 12:4
know that I * and beat those in Act 22:19
of Jesus of Nazareth. I * many Act 26:10
imprisons you, he will be *! Rev 13:10f

IMPRISONMENT
confiscation of goods, or *." Ez 7:26
broached the subject of his *. Jer 37:18
37th year of the * in Babylon of Jer 52:31
tenth year (of the * of King Eze 29:1
nothing worthy of * or death. Act 23:29
anything worthy of death or *." Act 26:31
And because of my * many of the Php 1:14

IMPRISONS
Or, "If anyone * you, he will be Rev 13:10f

IMPROBABLE
"Nothing then seemed more * than Zep 2:15f

IMPROPER
at home, for it is * for women to 1Co 14:35

IMPROPERLY
*—you were not carrying it." 1Ch 15:13

IMPROPRIETY
for any * in your priestly work. Num 18:1

IMPROVEMENT
may notice your * and progress. 1Ti 4:15
constant * in all these things. Rev 2:19

IMPUDENT
of them are hard, * and stubborn. Eze 3:7

IMPULSIVELY
I * cried out in desperation? Job 6:25,26

IMPURE
what is pure and what is *; Lev 10:10
is ceremonially * at the time. Num 18:11
so that David was ceremonially *. 1Sa 20:26
were ceremonially * because they 2Ch 30:17,18,19
you demand purity in one born *? Job 14:4
We are all infected and * with Is 64:6
I must label them "*, Rejected Jer 6:30
ceremonially *, and then brushes Hag 2:13
Perhaps the reference is to * Lk 14:34f
about the wicked, * things you have 2Co 12:21
evil results: * thoughts, eagerness Gal 5:19
given themselves over to * ways. Eph 4:19
to anyone who is * or greedy, for a Eph 5:5
are immoral and *: homosexuals, 1Ti 1:10,11

IMPURITY
her ceremonial *, she must not Lev 12:4
ceremonial * shall last two weeks, Lev 12:5
this is *; Lev 20:21
Let there be no sex sin, * or Eph 5:3
sin, *, lust and shameful desires; Col 3:5
wine of her intense * and sin." Rev 14:8

IMRAH
Suah, Harnepher, Shual, Beri, *, 1Ch 7:36,37

IMRI
of Omri, son of *, son of Bani) of 1Ch 9:4
crew led by Zaccur (son of *). Neh 3:2

IN-GATHERING
And, finally, the Pilgrimage of * Ex 23:16

IN-LAW
NOW NAOMI HAD an * there in Ru 2:1

INACCESSIBLE
or mountain goats on * crags. Jer 16:16
you live in those high, * cliffs. Ob 1:3

INACTIVE
by, silent and * when we pray. Ps 83:1

INADEQUATE
the need for these * special gifts 1Co 13:10

INAUGURATE
realm agreed to * this tradition Est 9:27

INAUGURATED
Damascus, * it with an offering. 2Ki 16:11,12

INAUGURATING
* his annual Feast of Purim. Est 9:29-31
fulfillment by * a great public Ecc 2:4,5,6

INAUGURATION
REHOBOAM'S * WAS at Shechem, and 1Ki 12:1

INCALCULABLE
there would be * damage to the king Est 7:4

INCANTATION
Lord Jesus. The * they decided on Act 19:13
and brought their * books and Act 19:18,19

INCANTATIONISTS
all his magicians, *, sorcerers, Dan 2:1

INCENSE
for the fragrant *, onyx stones, Ex 25:1
MAKE A small altar for burning *. Ex 30:1
he shall burn the * before the Ex 30:8
Offer no unauthorized *, burnt Ex 30:9
its utensils, the * altar, the Ex 30:26,27
Anyone who compounds any * like Ex 30:33
concerning the *: "Use sweet Ex 30:34
it shall be a pure and holy *. Ex 30:35
Tabernacle; this * is most holy. Ex 30:36
the altar of *; Ex 31:8
and the sweet-spice * for the Ex 31:11
the anointing oil and for the *; Ex 35:5-9
The * altar and its carrying Ex 35:10-19
The anointing oil and sweet *; Ex 35:10-19
the anointing oil and the sweet *. Ex 35:28
The * altar was made of acacia Ex 37:25
and the pure *, using the Ex 37:29
The sweet *; Ex 39:33-40
for the * in front of the Ark. Ex 40:5
burned upon it the * made from Ex 40:27
to pour olive oil and * upon it. Lev 2:1
Put olive oil and * on the Lev 2:15
oil and all of the * as a Lev 2:16
the horns of the * altar before the Lev 4:7
oil or put any * on it, because it Lev 5:11
olive oil and the * mixed into it, Lev 6:15
censers, laid * on the fire, and Lev 10:1
and offered the * before the Lord Lev 10:1
hands with sweet * beaten into fine Lev 16:12
he shall put the * upon the coals, Lev 16:13
so that a cloud of * will cover the Lev 16:13
will cut down your * altars, Lev 26:30
not respond to your * offerings. Lev 26:31
light, the sweet *, the daily grain Num 4:16
gold box of * which weighed only Num 7:14
them, and put * upon them before Num 16:6,7
bring your censers with * on them; Num 16:17
and placed the * on them, and stood Num 16:18
the 250 men who were offering *. Num 16:35
the burning * from the cen-sers of Num 16:36,37
the Lord to burn *, lest the same Num 16:40
the altar; lay * on it, and carry Num 16:46
and he put on the * and made Num 16:47
And shall work before you at the * Deu 33:10
*, and to wear a priestly robe 1Sa 2:28
in the hills and to offer * there. 1Ki 3:3
And he also burned * upon it. 1Ki 9:25
* and sacrificing to their gods. 1Ki 11:8
at Bethel, and burned * to them. 1Ki 12:32,33
the altar to burn * to the golden 1Ki 13:1
the hills who come here to burn *; 1Ki 13:2
sacrificed and burned * there. 1Ki 22:43
sacrificed and burned * there. 2Ki 12:3
sacrificed and burned * there. 2Ki 14:4
people sacrificed and burned *. 2Ki 15:4
people sacrificed and burned *. 2Ki 15:34,35
He also sacrificed and burned * 2Ki 16:4
and they had burned * to the 2Ki 17:11
to worship it by burning * to it; 2Ki 18:4
they had burned * in the shrines on 2Ki 23:5
They had also offered * to Baal 2Ki 23:5
they had burned *, even those as 2Ki 23:8
offerings and *, handling all the 1Ch 6:49
fine flour, wine, *, and spices. 1Ch 9:29
priests prepared the spices and *. 1Ch 9:30
for the altar of * and for the gold 1Ch 28:18
where I can burn * and sweet spices 2Ch 2:4
Literally, "a place to burn * 2Ch 2:6f
offerings and sweet *; 2Ch 13:11
the hills, and the * altars from 2Ch 14:5
of * for him at his funeral. 2Ch 16:13,14
and bowls used for *, and for 2Ch 24:14
before them, and burned * to them! 2Ch 25:14
burning * upon the altar. 2Ch 26:16
to burn *," they declared. 2Ch 26:17,18
down the * burner he was holding. 2Ch 26:19
not just to burn * to the idols, 2Ch 28:3
Yes, he sacrificed and burned * 2Ch 28:4
put out, and the * and burnt 2Ch 29:7
minister to him and to burn *." 2Ch 29:11
down all the * altars, and threw 2Ch 30:14
and to burn * upon it alone? 2Ch 32:12
and as * wafting up to you. Ps 141:2
from every other * tree, as well as Sol 4:13,14
for your sins? The * you bring me Is 1:12,13
and * have been very few! Is 43:23
no sweet-smelling * nor pleased me Is 43:24
You have taken pleasant * and Is 57:9
and * to add to the praise of God. Is 60:6
* on the rooftops of their homes. Is 65:3
they also burned * on the mountains Is 65:7
When they burn * to him, he Is 66:3
sweet * from Sheba before me! Jer 6:20
idols and burn * before them, but Jer 11:12
altars to burn * to Baal) are along Jer 11:13

(INCENSE Con't)
Judah in offering * to Baal that — Jer 11:17
offerings and *, bringing their — Jer 17:26
The people burn * to idols—idols — Jer 19:4
of Judah—wherever * has been burned — Jer 19:13
been used to offer * to Baal, and — Jer 32:29
and they will burn * in your — Jer 34:5
and were bringing offerings and *. — Jer 41:5
in Egypt, burning * to them, and — Jer 44:8
wives had burned * to idols (it was — Jer 44:15
We will burn * to the 'Queen of — Jer 44:17
But ever since we quit burning * — Jer 44:18
were burning * to idols in the — Jer 44:21
you have burned * and sinned — Jer 44:23
false gods and burning * to idols. — Jer 48:35
where they offered * to their — Eze 6:13
censer of burning *, so there was a — Eze 8:11
And used my oil and * to worship — Eze 16:18
sacrifices and * on every high hill — Eze 20:27,28
their perfumes and * and poured out — Eze 20:27,28
of perfumed * when I bring you back — Eze 20:41
bed and put my * and my oil upon a — Eze 23:41
and burn sweet * before him. — Dan 2:46
For all the * that she burned to — Hos 1:13
the hills to burn * in the pleasant — Hos 4:13
to Baal and burning * to idols. — Hos 11:2
their nets and burn * before them! — Hab 1:16
will offer sweet * and pure — Mal 1:11
and burn * before the Lord. — Lk 1:8,9
when the * was being burned. — Lk 1:10
to the right of the altar of *! — Lk 1:11,12
*—the prayers of God's people! — Rev 5:8
and a great quantity of * was — Rev 8:3
And the perfume of the * mixed — Rev 8:4
and spices and perfumes and *, — Rev 18:13

INCENSE-ALTAR
were a golden * and the golden — Heb 9:4

INCENSED
They were * with Jeremiah and — Jer 37:15,16

INCENSEMAKER
the *, and seasoning it with salt; — Ex 30:35

INCH
every * of the entire land!" — 1Sa 23:23
of ornaments an * or two apart, — 1Ki 7:24
and don't budge an * in the face of — Lk 20:21

INCHES
ship, eighteen * below the roof; — Gen 6:16
Put a molding four * wide around — Ex 25:25
It is to be eighteen * square — Ex 30:2
A rim four * high was — Ex 37:12
It was eighteen * square and — Ex 37:25
It was a piece nine * square, — Ex 39:9
dagger eighteen * long and hid it — Ju 3:16
javelin several * thick, tipped — 1Sa 17:4-7
of the tank were four * thick; — 1Ki 7:26
The wheels were twenty-seven * — 1Ki 7:32
the tank were five * thick, flaring — 2Ch 4:5
* high and eighteen inches wide. — Eze 40:7-12
inches high and eighteen * wide. — Eze 40:7-12
three or four * long, fastened — Eze 40:43
The base is twenty-one * high, — Eze 43:13
* beyond the altar on all sides. — Eze 43:13
This platform is twenty-one * — Eze 43:14
twenty-one * narrower on all sides, — Eze 43:14
twenty-one * up from the corners. — Eze 43:15
the top twenty-one * on all sides. — Eze 43:17

INCIDENT
Implied. This * occurred about — Ex 1:8f
He was referring to the * at — Num 27:14
This * took place at Bethany, a — Jn 1:28

INCIDENTALLY
"*, King Og of Bashan was the — Deu 3:11
(*, Doeg the Edomite, Saul's — 1Sa 21:7
by Elisha! And *, there are 7,000 — 1Ki 19:18

INCITE
to * a rebellion against Moses. — Num 16:2
to * rebellion against the king. — 2Sa 15:10
of a plot to * a mob of Gentiles, — Act 14:5,6

INCITED
Then the ten spies who had * the — Num 14:36,37,38
of the city and * a mob against — Act 13:50
were jealous and * some worthless — Act 17:5
that I have never * a riot in any — Act 24:12

INCITING
who is constantly * the Jews — Act 24:5

INCLINATIONS
your own wrong * your lives will — Gal 5:19

INCLUDE
be used for food * any animal with — Lev 11:2,3
This total does not * the — Num 1:47,48,49
not * their number in the census. — Num 1:47,48,49
And don't forget to * the local — Deu 16:11
And don't forget to * the — Deu 16:14
south to * the northern half of — Jos 12:5
of Israel, so * all this territory — Jos 13:2-7
(This list does not * the sons of — 1Ch 3:9
But he didn't * the tribes of — 1Ch 21:6
census he didn't * the — 1Ch 27:23
All * this in Matthew 6:15. — Mk 11:26,f
* holiness and everlasting life. — Rom 6:22

INCLUDED
The heart of his empire * Babel, — Gen 10:10
Shem's line of descendants * — Gen 11:10,11
With Joseph's two sons *, this — Gen 46:27
Aaron and Moses, * in that list, — Ex 6:26
was * in the original rental fee. — Ex 22:15
shall be * with the sacrifice, — Lev 7:12
them, lest you be * in their sins — Num 16:26
This census also * the sub-clans — Num 26:19-22
of Ephraim * the following clans, — Num 26:28-37
But the Levites were not * in the — Num 26:62
(Cities in the area * Suph, — Deu 1:1
The area * the hill country, the — Jos 12:8-24
the Arnon River, * the city in the — Jos 13:9
it also * all the cities of King — Jos 13:10
borders of Ammon. It * Gilead; — Jos 13:11
near Medeba. It * Heshbon and the — Jos 13:17
The land of Reuben also * the — Jos 13:21
This territory * Jazer, all the — Jos 13:25
from Mahanaim, * all of Bashan, the — Jos 13:30
of Judah also * all the towns and — Jos 15:45
Mediterranean, and * the cities — Jos 15:46
cities were * in the land given — Jos 18:21-28
Their inheritance * these — Jos 19:2-7
* Kattath, Nahalal, Shimron, — Jos 19:15,16
Its boundaries * the following — Jos 19:17-23
The boundaries * these cities: — Jos 19:24,25,26
The territory also * Mahalab, — Jos 19:29
The fortified cities * in this — Jos 19:35-39
So altogether the territory * — Jos 19:35-39
The cities within its area *: — Jos 19:41-46
His territory * Gilead, Ashuri, — 2Sa 2:9
solid gold. This * the altar, the — 1Ki 7:48
These * Ishmael, the son of — 2Ki 25:23
also * — 1Ch 1:38,39
Shobal's sons * — 1Ch 2:52
they also * the families of the — 1Ch 2:55
The sons of Elah * Kenaz. — 1Ch 4:15
Mishma's sons * Hammu-el (the — 1Ch 4:26
were * in the official genealogy: — 1Ch 5:7,8
All were * in the official — 1Ch 5:17
The booty * 50,000 camels, — 1Ch 5:21
Amram's descendants *: — 1Ch 6:3
Their duties * sacrificing burnt — 1Ch 6:49
all * in the official genealogy. — 1Ch 7:5
their descendants * 17,200 warriors — 1Ch 7:11
Elpaal's sons also *: — 1Ch 8:14
The sons of Elpaal also *: — 1Ch 8:17,18
Saul's sons *: — 1Ch 8:33
Other Levites who returned *: — 1Ch 9:15,16
This group * Obed-edom (the son — 1Ch 16:38
Eliezer were * with the tribe of — 1Ch 23:14,15
by his son Beno, * his brothers — 1Ch 24:26,27
Their music ministry * the — 1Ch 25:6,7
clan of Gershom * Zetham and — 1Ch 26:20,21,22
These men * Ben-hail, Obadiah, — 2Ch 17:7,8,9
were not * in this distribution. — 2Ch 31:16
The items Cyrus donated *: — Ez 1:9,10
Those who made the trip also * — Ez 2:55,56,57
This group * the subclans of — Ez 2:60
had * this provision in his grant. — Ez 3:7
the literature would have * — Dan 1:3,4f
manuscripts, but * in Luke 18:29. — Mt 19:29f
This clause is not * in some of — Lk 8:43,44f
The word "yet" is * in the — Jn 7:8f
and you are * in God's promise to — Act 3:25
too, are * in his kindness. — Eph 3:2,3

INCLUDES
not be eaten. This * all reptiles — Lev 11:41,42
Ammonites. This * half of the — Jos 12:2
This account * a report of — 2Ch 25:27
"Your army * men from far-off — Eze 27:10
plan * our working there with you. — 2Co 10:13
This * you who were once so far — Col 1:21

INCLUDING
* the women and other captives. — Gen 14:16
man there, * Hamor and Shechem. — Gen 34:26
and Leah, not * their daughter — Gen 46:15
but roasted, * the head, legs, — Ex 12:9
of the Tabernacle, * all the pins — Ex 27:19
Then take the body, * the skin — Ex 29:14
"Then take the fat of the ram, * — Ex 29:22
These frames, * those at the — Ex 36:29
altar all its fat, * the tail, the — Lev 7:3
piece by piece, * the head, and he — Lev 9:13
* the hides and internal organs. — Lev 16:27
603,550 (not * the Levites, who — Num 2:32,33
Kohath division, * all of the men — Num 4:35
of the Tabernacle, * the altar and — Num 7:1
The lampstand, * the floral — Num 8:4
shall be forgiven, * the foreigners — Num 15:26
(* Aaron) brought him a rod. — Num 17:6
sacred service, * the altar and all — Num 18:7
shall be yours, * the firstborn — Num 18:14,15
shall be yours, * the breast and — Num 18:18
and lived in them, * the city of — Num 21:25,26
of Judah—but not * Er and Onan — Num 26:19-22
booty, * the people and animals; — Num 31:26
* the women and babies. — Deu 2:33,34
* all the cities in the valley. — Deu 2:35,36
of Mount Gilead, * its cities. — Deu 3:12
* all the land of the Hittites.' — Jos 1:4
Then all the people of Israel—* — Jos 8:33
entire assembly, * the women and — Jos 8:35
to Mount Hermon, * the cities of — Jos 12:1
all the land of the Canaanites, * — Jos 13:2-7
* all the land of the Sidonians. — Jos 13:2-7
assignment of land—* part of the — Jos 19:1
'Your ancestors, * Terah the father — Jos 24:2
* the worshiping of heathen gods. — Ju 2:11
his entire army, * the nine hundred — Ju 4:13
at $25,000, not * the crescents and — Ju 8:26
Aroer to Minnith, * twenty cities, — Ju 11:33
cavalrymen, * General Shobach. — 2Sa 10:18
all of his sons attend, * Amnon. — 2Sa 13:27
were with him, * Ziba, the servant — 2Sa 19:17
area was Arubboth, * Socoh and all — 1Ki 4:8-19
was Ramoth-gilead, * the villages — 1Ki 4:8-19
Argob in Bashan, * sixty walled — 1Ki 4:8-19
area was Gilead, * the territories — 1Ki 4:8-19
men of the East, * those in Egypt. — 1Ki 4:30
paneled it all, * the beams and — 1Ki 6:9
* the cedar altar—with pure gold; — 1Ki 6:21,22
molten bronze, * the axles, spokes, — 1Ki 7:33
stole everything, * all the gold — 1Ki 14:26
The rest of Ahab's history—* the — 1Ki 22:39
reign of Joash, * his wars against — 2Ki 13:12
people, * their drink offerings. — 2Ki 16:15
his great deeds—* the pool and — 2Ki 20:20
from Jerusalem, * all the princes — 2Ki 24:14
Shemaiah had six sons, * Hattush, — 1Ch 3:21,22
pastures—* Geba, Alemeth, and — 1Ch 6:60
family to return, * Asaiah — 1Ch 9:5
the sons of Zerah, * Jeuel and his — 1Ch 9:6
sons, *: — 1Ch 9:35,36,37
land of Israel, * the priests and — 1Ch 13:2
24,000 troops, * officers and — 1Ch 27:1
accompanied her, * camel-loads of — 2Ch 9:1
for this purpose, * Shemaiah, — 2Ch 17:7,8,9
palace, * his sons and his wives; — 2Ch 21:17
and he took hostages, * — 2Ch 25:24
The remainder of his history, * — 2Ch 27:7
sins and errors, * a list of the — 2Ch 33:19
And all Judah and Jerusalem, * — 2Ch 35:24,25
of the nation, * the High Priests, — 2Ch 36:14
Jew in my realm, * the priests and — Ez 7:13
* the laws about the holy Sabbath; — Neh 9:14
leaders of Judah, * Hoshaiah, — Neh 12:33
him from his many enemies, * Saul. — Ps 18:1
seen everything, * the fact that — Ecc 7:15-17
* every hidden thing, good or bad. — Ecc 12:14
off his clothing, * his shoes, and — Is 20:2
in Jerusalem, * the palace of the — Jer 19:13
And the entire city * the — Jer 31:40
burned Jerusalem, * the palace, and — Jer 39:8
All of them, * all those who had — Jer 43:5
Then Jeremiah said to them all, * — Jer 44:24
with eyes, * the rims and spokes. — Eze 10:9-13
men of the city, * two officers, — Eze 11:1
of the Temple, * its two walls. — Eze 41:15,16
"The entire area—* sacred lands — Eze 48:20
him, * a leader of the priests. — Dan 11:22
lands on the way, * Israel, the — Dan 11:41
A nation southeast of Israel, * — Ob 1:1f
of the earth, * my people in — Zec 9:10
Jewish leaders, * some Pharisees, — Mt 12:38
message to his disciples * Peter: — Mk 16:7
Court assembled, * the chief — Lk 22:66
Meanwhile, Jesus' friends, * the — Lk 23:49
Several women, * Jesus' mother, — Act 1:14
became converts—* a large number of — Act 17:4
of them believed, * several — Act 17:12
congregation * wives and children — Act 21:5
as his children, * the new bodies — Rom 8:23
helped many in their needs, * me. — Rom 16:1
enemies, * the last enemy—death. — 1Co 15:26
fall on anyone, * myself, who — Gal 1:8
For everyone around here, * all — Php 1:13
But everyone, * Truth itself, — 3Jn 1:12
kind * lust of men for other men. — Jud 1:7
the temple of God, * the inner — Rev 11:1
and The Books were opened, * the — Rev 20:12

INCOME
will not be a division of the *; — Ex 21:36
*, for I am all that you need. — Num 18:20
"Don't forget to share your * — Deu 14:27
no other source of * because their — 2Ch 31:17,18
part of all your *, and he will — Pro 3:9,10
is no * from an empty stable. — Pro 14:4
* from exploiting the poor will — Pro 28:8
the limits of your *, so what is — Ecc 5:11
you warm. Your * disappears, as — Hag 1:6
part of your *, you completely — Lk 11:42
this business is our *. — Act 19:25
and our loss of *, but also of the — Act 19:27

INCOMPARABLE
* quality, and many, many jewels. — 2Ch 9:9
in his * perfections and glory. — Ps 27:4

INCONSISTENCIES
you can always justify your *." — Lk 7:35

INCONSISTENCY
you can justify your every *!" — Mt 11:19

INCONVENIENCE
say, "Sir, don't * yourself by — Lk 7:6,7,8

INCREASE
he said, "Let your numbers *. Gen 1:21,22
And may his tribe *!" Deu 33:6
had said he would * Israel like to 1Ch 27:23f
Crime was on the * everywhere. 2Ch 15:5
"and * the power of good men in Ps 75:10
more my grief; to * knowledge only Ecc 1:16-18
kingdom will not * its boundaries. Is 7:8
and King Pekah's power will not *. Is 7:9
and they shall be fruitful and *. Jer 23:3
I will greatly * the population and Jer 31:27
heaven, though she * her strength Jer 51:53
I will greatly * your population Eze 36:10
will * in power, but this king's Dan 11:5

INCREASED
and your wealth has * enormously; Gen 30:30
As a result, Jacob's flocks * Gen 30:43
has * enough to fill the land. Ex 23:30
and education shall be vastly *!" Dan 12:4
disciples * vastly in Jerusalem; Act 6:7

INCREASES
to increase knowledge only * Ecc 1:16-18

INCREASING
fertile, * rapidly in numbers; Ex 1:7
a great earthquake, * the terror. 1Sa 14:15
and grant you * freedom from all 1Pe 1:2

INCREDIBLE
bless you with * blessings and Gen 22:17
the * things I am doing in Egypt! Ex 10:2
stand quietly and see the * 2Ch 20:17
"He does * miracles, too many to Job 9:10
himself be led away into * folly. Pro 5:23
You have done * things in the Jer 32:20
What an * evil, causing Judah to Jer 32:35
land desolate, an * ruin, cursed, Jer 44:22
to see, *, without a living soul. Jer 51:37
It was *—a mighty miracle! Dan 4:3
*, and he does not easily forgive. Nah 1:3
"He was a Prophet who did * Lk 24:19
Does it seem * to you that God Act 26:8
it is no longer *, in view of a Rev 9:16f
was an * hailstorm from heaven; Rev 16:21

INCREDIBLY
will be huge and * beautiful. 2Ch 2:9
dreadful to describe and * strong. Dan 7:7
to understand how * great his power Eph 1:19

INCREDULOUS
Saul's men were *! 1Sa 19:24
famous, all who pass by will be *. 2Ch 7:21
You are amazed, *? Is 29:9
along the coastlands watch, *. Eze 27:35
The disciples were *! Mk 10:26

INCURABLE
him down with the * bowel disease. 2Ch 21:18
be a pile of grief and * pain. Is 17:11
My sickness is *, but I must bear Jer 10:19
For your sin is an * bruise, a Jer 30:12

INDECENT
* lest he turn away from you. Deu 23:14

INDEED
women will think me blessed *!" Gen 30:13
For it was little * you had Gen 30:30
"Shall I *, and your mother and Gen 37:10
No, don't be afraid. *, I myself Gen 50:21
they were * in a bad situation. Ex 5:19
find out that I am * God when I Ex 7:5
If the spot has * turned Lev 13:16,17
to see, and it is * a magnificent Num 13:27
the plague had * already begun; Num 16:47
us that it was * a good land the Deu 1:24,25
that it had * been the Angel of the Ju 6:22
For you are * God, and your 2Sa 7:28
shall know that I am * the Lord." 1Ki 20:28
the child was * dead, lying there 2Ki 4:32
of heaven is * the God of Israel!' 1Ch 17:24
records and have * found that Ez 4:19
by Queen Esther; *, the Jews Est 9:29-31
And if * I was wrong, you have Job 19:4
love and follow me are * wealthy. Pro 8:21
This pleasure was, *, my only Ecc 2:10
in life—that is * a gift from God. Ecc 5:19,20
prove that I will * crush your Is 7:11
every step? Who, *, but the Lord? Is 41:2
"Yes," they said, "we did *, Dan 3:24
you with curses. *, I have cursed Mal 2:1
"You shall * drink from it," he Mt 20:23
For the spirit * is willing, but Mt 26:41
And Jesus said, "You shall * Mk 10:39
will be counted fortunate *. Lk 23:29
that he was * the Messiah. Jn 2:23
He is * the Savior of the Jn 4:42
Don't be so surprised! * the Jn 5:28
you free, you will * be free— Jn 8:36
synagogues, and * the time is Jn 16:2
Jesus—that he is * the Son of God! Act 9:20
that Jesus was * the Christ. Act 9:22
that Jesus is * the Messiah. Act 18:28
love one another. *, your love is 1Th 4:10
Yes *, it is good when you truly Jas 2:8
to faith is blind *, or at least 2Pe 1:9
they are blest *, for now they Rev 14:13

INDENTURED
of them. He * 70,000 as common 2Ch 2:18

INDEPENDENCE
Moab declared its * and refused to 2Ki 1:1
So Edom has maintained its * to 2Ki 8:22
declaring his * of Judah. 2Ch 21:8
declaration of *, stating that they Lk 19:14

INDEPENDENT
to Israel as an * kingdom, breaking Hos 1:4,5
now and restore us as an * Act 1:6

INDESTRUCTIBLE
but it shall stand forever, *. Dan 2:44

INDETERMINATE
It is * from the text as to Num 12:1f

INDIA
stretching from * to Ethiopia. Est 1:1
from * to Ethiopia, 127 in all; Est 8:9,10

INDICATE
heads of grain) * that there will Gen 41:27
for Aaron, to * his separation to Ex 28:2
Lord would * what to do with him. Lev 24:12
Isaiah 57:1,2 may * that Old Ps 6:5f
* Christ's universal rule. Zec 9:10f
He said this to * how he was Jn 12:33

INDICATED
following tribes at the places *: Gen 14:5,6
rules apply as * above, so that Lev 15:25
to its size, as * by the amount of Lev 27:16
locations * by the Lord to Moses. Num 2:34
population, as * by the census— Num 26:52,53
and the tribe of Judah was *. Jos 7:16
and the family of Zabdi was *. Jos 7:17
where sub-totals are *. Jos 19:2-7f
the tribes, with the boundaries *; Jos 19:49
is * in the original text. Jos 21:9-16f
The first toss * Joseph of the 1Ch 25:9-31
the following year was the date *. Est 3:7
but * here by this reaction. Eze 3:14,15f
of this prophecy * for the future; Dan 8:9f
what is * in the paraphrase above. Act 27:4f

INDICATES
Deuteronomy 2:19 * that God had Num 21:24f
the original text * sub-totals of Jos 15:48-62f
original manuscript * sub-totals. Jos 18:21-28f
20:19, which * his death by Jn 18:32f
This * how deeply the whole Act 19:20

INDICATING
skin or leather, * whether to Lev 13:59
to war, * their tribe and family. Num 1:2-15
register, each man * his tribe and Num 1:17,18,19
of Levi, * each person's clan; Num 3:14,15

INDICATION
thus a good * of the water level. Gen 8:7f

INDICT
"Son of dust, * Jerusalem as the Eze 22:2

INDICTMENT
as an * of Israel's unbelief. Is 30:8

INDICTMENTS
let him approve the * made Job 31:35

INDIFFERENCE
disturbed by their * to human need, Mk 3:5
you turn from your * and become Rev 3:19

INDIFFERENT
his business, * to the loss of the Gen 25:34
in their sins, * to God, thinking Zep 1:12
the world will be [as * to the Lk 17:26
escape if we are * to this great Heb 2:3
dull and *, but you will be anxious Heb 6:12

INDIGNANT
I am * and angry because of the Ps 119:139
be * for the honor of his land! Joe 2:18
The Pharisees were *. Mt 9:11
The other ten disciples were * Mt 20:24
were disturbed and * and asked him, Mt 21:15
The disciples were *. Mt 26:8,9
John had asked, they were very *. Mk 10:41
Some of those at the table were * Mk 14:4,5

INDIGNATION
enemies with angry * and with Is 30:30
I burst with * at their sins. Jer 15:17,18
with a storm of * and with a great Eze 13:13
In the day of my * you shall be Eze 22:24
moved with * and deeply troubled. Jn 11:33

INDIGNITIES
Or, "and great * were perpetrated Dan 8:12f

INDISCREET
Watch yourself, lest you be * Pro 5:2

INDISPUTABLE
Since this is an * fact, you Act 19:36

INDIVIDUAL
offering for an *, only this time Lev 4:21
made by a single *, then he shall Num 15:27
This same law applies to * Num 15:29
and twenty * loaves of barley 2Ki 4:42

INDIVIDUAL'S
listen to every * prayer 2Ch 6:29

INDUCE
to * you to ask God to bless us?" 2Sa 21:3
See, here is silver and gold to * 2Ch 16:3
to discuss how to * the Roman Mt 27:1
the Lord enough to * him to act? Rom 11:35

INDUCED
to King Joash and * him to abandon 2Ch 24:17,18
followers of the man who * the Rev 2:6f

INDUCTED
are anointed and * into the Lev 6:19,20
they shall be * into office by Lev 6:22,23

INDULGED
She * herself in immorality, and Lam 1:9
and * in sex sin with each other. Rom 1:26

INDULGENCES
magic veils and selling them *. Eze 13:18

INDULGES
Christian but * in sexual sins, or 1Co 5:11

INDUSTRIOUS
Solomon saw how * he was, he put 1Ki 11:27,28

INDUSTRY
No * of any kind will ever again Rev 18:22

INDWELLING
the new joy of the * Holy Spirit Tit 3:5

INEDIBLE
fruit never produces an * kind. Mt 7:18
And a tree producing an * kind Mt 7:18
So the trees having the * fruit Mt 7:19

INEFFECTIVE
Slingstones are as * as straw. Job 41:27,28

INEVITABLE
Temptation to do wrong is *, but Mt 18:7

INEVITABLY
is right, I * do what is wrong. Rom 7:21

INEXPERIENCED
is still young and *, and the work 1Ch 29:1

INEXPRESSIBLE
are happy with the * joy that comes 1Pe 1:8

INEXPRESSIBLY
it was * beautiful. Eze 1:22
Gate, they were * surprised! Act 3:10

INFAMOUS
name shall be * through the ages. Jer 23:40
will mock you, a city of * rebels. Eze 22:5

INFANCY
brought me through the years of *. Ps 22:9,10,11
I trained him from *, I taught Hos 11:3

INFANT
* at a mother's generous breasts. Is 66:11
will rise and your * mortality rate Eze 36:14

INFANTRY
cavalry and twenty thousand *; 2Sa 8:4
ten chariots, and ten thousand *; 2Ki 13:7
These "soldiers" charge like * Joe 2:7

INFANTRYMEN
100,000 Syrian * that first day. 1Ki 20:29
unnumbered host of *—Egyptians, 2Ch 12:3

INFECT
For I know that they will * you Ex 23:33
among you to * all the others. Gal 5:9

INFECTED
article is * through and through. Lev 13:55
* wounds, unanointed and unbound. Is 1:5,6
We are all * and impure with Is 64:6

INFECTION
if the * seems to be below the Lev 13:29,30
and if the * does not seem to be Lev 13:32
* that has broken out in the skin. Lev 13:39

INFECTIONS
fever, *, plague, and war. Deu 28:22

INFERENCE
The * is not clear in the Greek Rev 3:10f

INFERIOR
This empire will be * to yours. Dan 2:39
should never think of anyone as *. Act 10:28

INFESTED
and suddenly lice * the entire Ex 8:17

INFINITE
call on them for * assistance, as Nah 3:9

INFINITELY
or even dream of—* beyond our Eph 3:20

INFLAMED
And while they lie * with all Jer 51:39

INFLAMMATION
My loins burn with * Ps 38:7

INFLUENCE
and how the heavens * the earth? Job 38:33
He shall have * and honor. Ps 112:9
For they * everything else in Pro 4:23
The good * of godly citizens Pro 11:11
sadness has a refining * on us. Ecc 7:3
You are to * them, not let them Jer 15:19
them, not let them * you! Jer 15:19
but she will lose her * over him Dan 11:6
will lose its *, and that Act 19:27
don't let this bad example * you. 3Jn 1:11

INFLUENCED
You aren't * by the opinions and Mk 12:14

INFLUENTIAL
KISH WAS A rich, * man from the 1Sa 9:1
was a powerful and * tribe in 1Ch 5:2
They are * men, these who plot to Ps 69:4
one of the most * Jews in the Roman Lk 19:1
he was a very *, proud man Act 8:9,10,11

INFORM
I have sent these messengers to * Gen 32:5

(INFORM Con't)
Lord to Moses: "* the people of Num 5:1
Turn northward. * the people Deu 2:4
she sent a message to * him. 2Sa 11:5
"We wish to * you that we went Ez 5:8
had come to * David of God's Ps 51:1
"I write to * you of a message Rev 2:1
INFORMATION
have decided to send you this *. Ez 4:14
and passed on the * to Queen Est 2:22
crediting Mordecai with the *. Est 2:22
and betray some vital *. Pro 5:2
For I have important * for you. Pro 8:6,7
they could obtain * from the gods. Eze 21:21f
And in all matters requiring * Dan 1:20
secret plots will become public *. Mt 10:26
they want to get some more *. Act 23:20
tell some special * God has given 1Co 14:26
INFORMED
So the taskmasters and officers * Ex 5:10,11
the people were * of Aaron's death, Num 20:29
but someone * the king of Jericho Jos 2:2
Please be * that the Jews sent Ez 4:12
when the king was * of the number Est 9:11
fields, are well *, alert and Dan 1:3,4
ABOUT THIS TIME he was * that Lk 13:1
But when I was * of a plot to Act 23:30
INFORMING
Who has been * the king of Israel 2Ki 6:11
INFURIATE
Day in and day out they * me. Is 65:5
INFURIATED
Evil-minded men will be * when Ps 112:10
they have * me with all their Jer 32:30
INFUSED
a human spirit is * into the little Ecc 11:5
INGRATIATED
was assassinated, * himself with Dan 11:21f
INHABITANT
cities will lie in ruin without *. Jer 4:7
without an *, as it is today. Jer 44:22
INHABITANTS
"the land vomits out her *." Lev 18:25f
They have told this to the * of Num 14:14
safe from attack by the local *. Num 32:17
its *, and even all of the cattle. Deu 13:15
so Caleb drove out the * of the Ju 1:20
There was no one to help the *, Ju 18:28
ancestor of the * of Craftsman 1Ch 4:14
they killed the * of the land and 1Ch 4:40,41
they chased out the * of Gath. 1Ch 8:13
original * of the land—lived. 1Ch 11:4
Literally, "* of the coastland." Is 20:5,6f
well as here among the * of earth. Dan 4:35
fear of its * to venture outside; Mic 1:11f
fear of its * to venture outside; Mic 1:11f
fear of its * to venture outside; Mic 1:11f
be desolate because of its *." Mic 7:13f
the sea and its *, that there Rev 10:6
INHABITED
(This area was * by Canaanites at Gen 12:6
"(That area, too, used to be * Deu 2:20
become * by ostriches and jackals; Jer 50:39
Never again will you be * or be Eze 26:20
And Jerusalem shall be *, safe Zec 14:11
INHABITING
of the people * these areas: Gen 10:13,14
INHABITS
The high and lofty one who * Is 57:15
INHERIT
will * all my wealth." Gen 15:2,3
a son to * everything you own." Gen 15:4
own, and they will * from me just Gen 48:5
own, and shall * Ephraim's and Gen 48:6
and they shall * it forever.' Ex 32:13
shall * what you have despised. Num 14:31
name, and to * the land." Ru 4:5
his children shall * the earth. Ps 25:13
by the Lord shall * the earth, but Ps 37:22
Their children shall * the land; Ps 69:36
the land and * my Holy Mountain. Is 57:13
those I select will * it and Is 65:9
Didn't they * them from me? Jer 49:1
fathers, and you shall * it now. Eze 47:14
Who will * your possessions left Hos 9:6
This fellow will * all the land Lk 20:14
son could not * Abraham's home and Gal 4:30
will not * the kingdom of God. Gal 5:21
Everyone who conquers will * all Rev 21:7
INHERITANCE
on the name and * of the deceased. Lev 18:16f
these are their *, and so they Num 18:24
no sons, then his * shall be passed Num 27:8
brought them safely to their *. Num 32:17
of Israel have received their *. Num 32:18
Levites as their * certain cities Num 35:2
"and to give the * of our brother Num 36:1
tribe, for the * of every tribe is Num 36:7
In this way no * shall move from Num 36:9
so their * remained in their Num 36:11,12
as his personal * some of the land Deu 1:36
be his special people, his own *; Deu 4:20
land he has given you as your *. Deu 4:21,22
land as an *, as it is today. Deu 4:38
They are your * saved from Egypt Deu 9:26
people and your * which you brought Deu 9:29
told them, he himself is their *. Deu 10:9
who have no * among you, or to Deu 14:29
not give a larger * to his younger Deu 21:16
half-tribe of Manasseh as their *. Deu 29:8
of Israel as their *, dividing the Jos 11:23
received their * on the east side Jos 13:8
to them, the Lord God was their *. Jos 13:33
as a permanent * because he had Jos 14:13,14
were given an * along with their Jos 17:5,6
and the total * came to ten Jos 17:5,6
Their * included these seventeen Jos 19:2-7
So the Simeon tribe's * came Jos 19:9
Or, "that would ruin my own *," Ru 4:6f
for they are your people—your * 1Ki 8:51
As your *.' 1Ch 16:18
to our children as an *. Ez 9:12
their family * was located. Neh 11:20
The Lord himself is my *, my Ps 16:5
What a wonderful *! Ps 16:6
the land of Canaan as your *." Ps 105:10,11
leaves an * to his grandchildren; Pro 13:22
blessed be Israel, my *!" Is 19:25
them and they, not I, are your *. Is 57:6
turned my * into an evil thing. Jer 2:7
their fathers as an * forever. Jer 3:18
I have abandoned my people, my *; Jer 12:7
own land again, each man to his *. Jer 12:15
My soul claims the Lord as my *; Lam 3:24
Distribute the land as an * for Eze 47:22
for scattering my * among the Joe 3:2
And Judah shall be the Lord's * Zec 2:11,12
mountains and *, to give it to the Mal 1:2,3
the * and have some security. Lk 9:59f
gave Israel their land as an *. Act 13:19,20
give you all the * of those who are Act 20:32
sins and God's * along with all Act 26:18
INHERITED
animals, or * fields—shall not be Lev 27:28
The tribe of Judah also * Jos 15:37-44
in all the riches * by God's sons; Eph 3:6
INHERITS
* all my efforts, free of charge. Ecc 2:20-23
INIQUITIES
Literally, "their iniquity (*) Eze 32:27f
INIQUITY
Literally, "forgiving * and Ex 34:7f
but pardon our * and our sins, and Ex 34:9
to take away the * and guilt of the Lev 10:17
off; his * shall be upon him." Num 15:31f
and to refuse to forgive my *. Job 10:13,14
sins and leave all * behind you. Job 11:13,14
let him be destroyed for his *. Job 21:20
* is atoned for by mercy and Pro 16:6
Literally, "their * (iniquities) Eze 32:27f
INITIALS
as * are engraved upon a ring. Ex 39:6,7
INITIATION
Jewish * ceremony of circumcision. Rom 2:28
Jewish * ceremony of circumcision. Rom 4:10
For I went through the Jewish * Php 3:5
INJURE
"If her eye is injured, * his; Ex 21:24
If you * them he will punish you. Pro 22:22,23
he doesn't punish those who * you. Is 59:9
Nothing shall * you! Lk 10:19
power to * earth and sea, "Wait! Rev 7:2
INJURED
He has been severely * by those Gen 49:23
then the man who * her shall be Ex 21:22
"If her eye is *, injure his; Ex 21:24
and it is * or killed, and the Ex 22:14
An animal that has * Lev 22:24
anyone is to be * in exactly the Lev 24:19
this house will be killed or *. Jos 2:19
at Samaria and was seriously *. 2Ki 1:2
But the one who misses me has * Pro 8:36
or that I found * or dead; Eze 4:14
for his head was seriously *. Mk 12:4
of his house naked and badly *. Act 19:16
been patient with those who * us. 1Co 4:12
We have been * but kept from 2Co 6:9
INJURES
with his fist and * him so that he Ex 21:18
"If a man's ox * another, and it Ex 21:35
punished me in a way that * you." Ru 1:13
is "Their speech * others." Rom 3:13f
INJURIES
loss of cargo, *, and death." Act 27:10
INJURING
The penalty for * anyone is to Lev 24:19
That would be like * a helpless Job 6:27
have the power of * each other. Ecc 8:9,10
INJURY
have avoided all this * and loss! Act 27:21
INJUSTICE
They are men of violence and *. Gen 49:5
For there must be no * among 2Ch 19:7
but * robs him of its riches. Pro 13:23
you are building * into its walls Jer 22:13
full of murder and *, for they say, Eze 9:9
It is never glad about *, but 1Co 13:6
INK
them down in * upon the scroll. Jer 36:18
with pen and *, but by the Spirit 2Co 3:3
INLAID
It was made of gold * with gems 1Ch 20:2
Beautiful jewels were * into the 2Ch 3:6
In your * palaces of ivory, Ps 45:8
and the back is * with these Sol 3:10
For the * Lam 4:1
of foundation stones * with gems: Rev 21:18,19,20
INLAND
can take them * to Jerusalem." 2Ch 2:16
INMOST
flow from the * being of anyone who Jn 7:38
their * thoughts and motives; Rom 2:16
INN
They arrived at an * operated by Jos 2:1
at a shepherd's * along the way. 2Ki 10:12
As he left the *, he met 2Ki 10:15
no room for them in the village *. Lk 2:7
they came to an *, where he nursed Lk 10:34
INNER
Literally, "* parts." Ex 12:9f
that covers the * parts, also the Ex 29:13
The blue, purple, and scarlet * Ex 36:35
the fat upon the * organs, the gall Lev 8:25
fat covering the * organs—and the Lev 9:19
the items from the * sanctuary. Num 10:21
Put these rods in the * room of Num 17:4
the Lord in the * room of the Num 17:7
The thirty-foot * room at the 1Ki 6:16
The * room was where the Ark of 1Ki 6:19
This * sanctuary was thirty feet 1Ki 6:20
Within the * sanctuary Solomon 1Ki 6:23-28
wall, while their * wings touched 1Ki 6:23-28
The doorway to the * sanctuary 1Ki 6:31
The wall of the * court had three 1Ki 6:36
just like the * court of the Temple 1Ki 7:12
the Ark into the * sanctuary of the 1Ki 8:6
returning from the * sanctuary, a 1Ki 8:10
the * room of one of the houses. 1Ki 20:30
yourself hiding in an * room." 1Ki 22:25
he was wearing an * robe made of 2Ki 6:26-30
Then Jehu's men went into the * 2Ki 10:25
made a hole in the * wall and fled 2Ki 25:4,5
relating to the * sanctuary—the 1Ch 6:49
house, with the * walls and ceiling 2Ch 3:4
main door, and the * doors to the 2Ch 4:22
the Ark into the * room of the 2Ch 5:7,8
Solomon consecrated the * court 2Ch 7:7
you are hiding in an * room!" 2Ch 18:24
The priests cleaned up the * 2Ch 29:16
into the king's * court without his Est 4:11
and entered the * court just beyond Est 5:1
there in the * court, he welcomed Est 5:2
You made all the delicate, * Ps 139:13
Take them into one of the * rooms Jer 35:2
Then he brought me into the * Eze 8:16
cloud of glory filled the * court. Eze 10:3
Beyond this hall, at the * end of Eze 40:7-12
it, he came to an * wall and a Eze 40:23
through it to an * court. Eze 40:23
it, he came to the * wall and a Eze 40:27
through it to the * court. Eze 40:27
Then he took me over to the * Eze 40:28
of the * wall, and measured it. Eze 40:32
north gate of the * wall, and the Eze 40:35
In the * court, there were two Eze 40:44
beside the * northern gate is for Eze 40:45
The building beside the * Eze 40:46
Then he measured the * court [in Eze 40:47
Ten steps led up to it from the * Eze 40:48,49
Then he went into the * room at Eze 41:3
behind it. The * room was Eze 41:4
row of rooms down in the * court. Eze 41:10
feet square. The * court at the Eze 41:14
windows. The * walls of the Temple Eze 41:15,16
And so it was, all around the * Eze 41:19,20
back into the * court to the rooms Eze 42:1
were the * wall of the court. Eze 42:3
strip of * court on the other. Eze 42:3
as long as the * wing that faced Eze 42:7,8
south side of the * court, between Eze 42:9,10
and brought me into the * court; Eze 43:5
passageway to the * court, for they Eze 44:17
in the * court or in the Temple. Eze 44:17
wine before coming to the * court. Eze 44:21
and enters the * court and the Eze 44:27
walls at the entry of the * court. Eze 45:19
"THE LORD GOD says, the * wall's Eze 46:1
and proceed to the * wall at the Eze 46:2
to the Lord, the * eastern gate Eze 46:12
to enter the * sanctuary and burn Lk 1:8,9
be the * circle of his disciples. Lk 6:13
whispered in the * rooms shall be Lk 12:3
put them into the * dungeon and Act 16:24

(INNER Con't)
Or, "by an * compulsion." Act 20:22f
are dying, our * strength in the 2Co 4:16
you the mighty * strengthening of Eph 3:16
If you will stir up this * 2Ti 1:8
went into the * room, and then only Heb 9:7
blood into that * room, the Holy of Heb 9:12
God, including the * court where Rev 11:1

INNERMOST
Within the * room, the Holy of 2Ch 3:10
Literally, "Your * shrine," i.e. Ps 28:2f
and deep into our * thoughts and Heb 4:12

INNKEEPER
The next day he handed the * two Lk 10:35

INNOCENCE
How can we prove our *? Gen 44:16
to swear to his * before this 2Ch 6:22
to my * is there in heaven; Job 16:19
Will no one anywhere confirm my *? Job 17:3,4
until I die I will vow my *. Job 27:5
he kept insisting on his *. Job 32:1
I wash my hands to prove my * Ps 26:6
Your * will be clear to Ps 37:6

INNOCENT
"Lord, will you slay an * man? Gen 20:4
whether in * fun or otherwise is Gen 21:9f
the man who hit him will be * Ex 21:19
never let an * person be put to Ex 23:7
swear that she is *, and then he Num 5:19
catch and kill the * slayer, even Deu 19:6,7
avoid the death of * people, and Deu 19:10
them with murdering an * man. Deu 21:8
The girl is as * as a murder Deu 22:25,26,27
a bribe to kill an * person.' Deu 27:25
When the * killer reaches any of Jos 20:4
in revenge, the * slayer must not Jos 20:5
and the people were declared *. 1Sa 14:41
Why should you now murder an * 1Sa 19:5
for who can remain * after 1Sa 26:9
are * of this crime against Abner. 2Sa 3:28
great numbers of * people. 2Ki 21:16
enemies when I am *, then may the 1Ch 12:17
is lying, or else declare him *. 2Ch 6:23
*," was his final word to them. 2Ch 19:11
and * person who was punished? Job 4:7,8
And even if I am utterly *, I Job 9:21
I despise what I am. * or evil, Job 9:22
laugh when calamity crushes the *. Job 9:23
me *, O God, but will condemn me. Job 9:28
"Yet I am *, and my prayer is Job 16:17
"Yet, finally, the * shall come Job 17:8
* shall laugh the wicked to scorn. Job 22:19
*—as pure as solid gold! Job 23:10
tailor, but the * shall wear that Job 27:17
knows that I am *— or if I have Job 31:6
and again— 'I am pure, I am *; Job 33:9
For Job has said, 'I am *, but Job 34:5
called a liar, even though I am *. Job 34:6
against the * despite the bribes Ps 15:5
guilt and * of some great crime. Ps 19:13
But all who harm the * shall be Ps 25:3
against the * and demands bribes. Ps 26:9,10
of plots against * men who are Ps 35:20
They shoot from ambush at the *. Ps 64:4
who plot to kill me though I am *. Ps 69:4
those who condemn the * to death? Ps 94:21,22
of Canaan—shedding * blood and Ps 106:37,38
the wicked and condemn the *. Pro 18:5
wicked, "You are *," shall be Pro 24:24
spitefully against an * neighbor. Pro 24:28,29
with the blood of your * victims. Is 1:15
go free and putting * men in jail. Is 5:23
the blood of the * and the poor. Jer 2:34
with the blood of * children. Jer 19:4
stop murdering the *! Jer 22:3
You murder the *, oppress the Jer 22:17
will be killing an * man and the Jer 26:15
The Lord says to Edom: If the * Jer 49:12
the city by shedding * blood. Lam 4:13
with you, your sisters seem *! Eze 16:52
for I am * before God, nor, sir, Dan 6:22
killed * people in those nations. Joe 3:19
men who trick the *, against Mal 3:5
"for I have betrayed an * man." Mt 27:4
* of the blood of this good man. Mt 27:24
on this point and find him *. Lk 23:14
said, "Surely this man was *." Lk 23:47
own heads—I am *—from now on I will Act 18:6
But if I am *, neither you nor Act 25:10,11
one in all the world is *." Rom 3:10
go free, and say that they are *? Rom 3:26
right, and to stay * of any wrong. Rom 16:19
these things. Be * babies when it 1Co 14:20
You are to live clean, * lives as Php 2:15
he himself was * of any sin at any 1Pe 3:18

INQUIRE
I took the opportunity to * about Neh 1:2

INQUIRED
*, "Why are you doing that?" Gen 21:28,29
"Well, what do you want?" he *. Gen 38:18
the king eagerly *. Num 23:17
they *. Ju 1:1
the king *. Est 6:4
who never before * about me are Is 65:1

INQUIRING
he would be * whether Jesus was Jn 18:34f
at the gate, * whether this was Act 10:18

INQUIRY
This * was perhaps ostensibly to 1Ki 21:9f
Jesus' chest," to whisper his *. Jn 13:25f

INQUISITOR
Must you be his * every morning, Job 7:18

INSANE
to him, so he pretended to be *! 1Sa 21:13
by demons, or were *, or Mt 4:24
Festus shouted, "Paul, you are *. Act 26:24
But Paul replied, "I am not *, Act 26:25
Are we * [to say such things 2Co 5:13,14

INSCRIBE
will * my laws upon their hearts, Jer 31:33

INSCRIBED
rod with his name * upon it. Num 17:1
tablets with the laws * upon them. Deu 9:9
tablets * with the laws of God. Deu 9:15
In Jeremiah 17:1 their sin was * Jer 31:33f
and he will have my new Name * Rev 3:12

INSCRIPTION
engrave this * on it seven times: Zec 3:9
and I will engrave its *." Zec 3:9f
this * on it—'To the Unknown God.' Act 17:23

INSECT
of some forbidden *—is guilty, even Lev 5:2

INSECTS
"Flying * with four legs must Lev 11:20
winged * are a defilement to you Deu 14:19,20
flies and other * swarmed in vast Ps 105:31
guard them from * and plagues. Mal 3:11

INSERT
them continually. * into the Ex 28:30,31
grating, to * the carrying poles. Ex 38:5
Then they shall * the carrying Num 4:8
leather, and * the carrying poles Num 4:11

INSERTED
The carrying poles were * into Ex 38:7
not * into the walls themselves. 1Ki 6:6
Hanani, which is * in The Annals of 2Ch 20:34

INSIDE
trees with seeds * the fruit, so Gen 1:11,12
and make three decks * the boat—a Gen 6:16
the Lord, but * he was laughing in Gen 17:17
were fighting each other * her! Gen 25:22
hands on, both * the city and Gen 34:28
Now reach your hand * your robe, Ex 4:6
Overlay it * and outside with Ex 25:11
is finished, place * it the tablets Ex 25:16
"[* the Tabernacle Ex 26:31
lower, * edges of the chestpiece; Ex 28:26
pillar of cloud. * the tent the Ex 33:11
It was plated with pure gold * Ex 37:2
* the Ark he placed the stones Ex 40:20
* its pouch; Lev 8:8
was not taken * the sanctuary, you Lev 10:18
and return to live * the camp; Lev 14:8
Then he shall order the * walls Lev 14:41
powder, and bring it * the veil. Lev 16:12
Not another soul shall be * the Lev 16:17
should have stayed * the City until Num 35:28
*, the plague Deu 32:25
anyone else—are here * the house. Jos 2:17,18
but we swear that no one * this Jos 2:19
in ambush were * the city, so they Jos 8:20,21
Then the Israelis who were * the Jos 8:22
and finished off everyone left *. Jos 8:24
placed there to keep the kings *. Jos 10:18
just as a man * had wakened from a Ju 7:12,13
So all the people * died, about a Ju 9:49
However, there was a fort * the Ju 9:51
He lives just * the city gates. 1Sa 9:12,13
though you were safe * his purse! 1Sa 25:29
were sleeping * a ring formed by 1Sa 26:5,6,7
The Ark was placed * the tent 2Sa 6:17
hid them * a well in his backyard. 2Sa 17:18
The entire *, from floor to 1Ki 6:15
rooms, the * rooms, and the 1Ch 28:11
I mused, the hotter the fires *. Ps 39:2,3
Now we are standing here * the Ps 122:2,3
and those trapped * begin to eat Jer 19:9
Then, when they were all * the Jer 41:7
fire * that flashed continually; Eze 1:4
with a second wheel crosswise *. Eze 1:16
If you stay *, famine and disease Eze 7:15
will lick the * to get every drop. Eze 23:34
the passageway to the court *. Eze 40:17
A stone pavement ran around the * Eze 40:17
the doorway to the entry hall *. Eze 40:22
eight tables, four * and four Eze 40:41
the prince—may sit * the passageway Eze 44:3
He shall worship * the passageway Eze 46:2
Around the * of these walls Eze 46:23
and worshiping idols * the Temple. Dan 11:30,31
alive *, "Are any others left?" Amo 6:10
And Jonah was * the fish three Jon 1:17
the Lord his God from * the fish: Jon 2:1
but there is no breath at all *! Hab 2:19
see a woman sitting * the basket! Zec 5:7
speak because a demon was * him. Mt 9:32
boxes with Scripture verses *, Mt 23:5
the cup, but the * is foul with Mt 23:25
First cleanse the * of the cup, Mt 23:26
must not even go * to pack before Mt 24:17
He went * and spoke to the Mk 5:39
and then slipped * the gates of the Mk 14:54
*, the chief priests and the Mk 14:55
the outside, but * you are still Lk 11:39
Didn't God make the * as well as Lk 11:40
holidays. * the city, near the Jn 5:2
*, the High Priest began asking Jn 18:19
Simon Peter arrived and went on *. Jn 20:6
When the people * saw him walking Act 3:9
from the sky. * the sheet were all Act 11:6
that she ran back * to tell Act 12:14
colony just * the Macedonian Act 16:12
*, the people were all shouting, Act 19:32
As Paul was about to be taken *, Act 21:37,38
So the commander brought him * Act 22:24
It is sin * me that is stronger Rom 7:17
that is still * me loves to sin. Rom 7:23,24,25
he becomes a brand new person *. 2Co 5:17
here on earth. * this place of Heb 9:1
with pure gold. * the ark were the Heb 9:4
in your life, both * and outside, Jas 1:21
Be beautiful *, in your hearts, 1Pe 3:4
writing on the * and on the back, Rev 5:1
of his covenant could be seen *. Rev 11:19

INSIDES
that covers the *, also the gall Ex 29:22
which covers the *, the two Lev 3:14
that covers the *, the two kidneys Lev 7:3
He then washed the * and the Lev 8:21
Then he washed the * and the Lev 9:14

INSIDIOUS
But not before Balaam gave * Num 24:25f

INSIGHT
orators, and the * of the elders. Job 12:20
they are wise and filled with *. Ps 49:3
Literally, "but without *." Ps 49:20f
Yes, if you want better * and Pro 2:3,4,5
considerable * and understanding. Act 13:6,7
But the spiritual man has * into 1Co 2:15
knowledge and *, for I want you Php 1:9

INSIGNIFICANT
on such an * person as I am? 2Sa 7:18

INSINCERELY
with those who * worship me at Hos 4:15

INSIPID
drink, and we hate this * manna." Num 21:5

INSIST
"If you * on having a king, he 1Sa 8:11
"But they * that King Cyrus of Ez 5:13
Don't * that I be cautious lest Job 32:21,22
Only fools * on quarreling. Pro 20:3
"Why do you * on dying—you and Jer 27:13
If you * on heeding them, I must Jer 27:15
stay here,'—and * on going to Egypt Jer 42:13,14
says: If you * on going to Egypt, Jer 42:15
in Egypt, where you * on going." Jer 42:22
to go back—who * on living in Jer 44:28
God says: If you * on worshiping Eze 20:39
the Jewish leaders * Elijah must Mt 17:10
If you * on saving your life, Mk 8:35
it that you Jews * that Jerusalem Jn 4:20
that we should not * that the Act 15:19
or wife should not * that the other 1Co 7:15
* we are all its prisoners. Gal 3:21,22
you are all true. * on them so that Tit 3:8

INSISTED
So Jacob *, and finally Esau Gen 33:11
"No," Jacob *, "we'll get along Gen 33:15
"Yes, you are," he *. Gen 42:12
that you will do it," Jacob *. Gen 47:31
* on their having breakfast first. Ju 19:5
but Ruth * on staying with Naomi. Ru 1:14
I have obeyed the Lord," Saul *. 1Sa 15:20
But Achish *, "As far as I'm 1Sa 29:9
"Take $4,000," Naaman *. 2Ki 5:23
of Judah that * on coming here to Jer 44:12
Peter *. Mt 26:35
but Jesus * that they not tell Lk 8:56
When she * they decided, "It Act 12:15
legalists, who * that circumcision Gal 2:12

INSISTENT
they are all very * that Jewish Act 21:20

INSISTING
he kept * on his innocence. Job 32:1

INSISTS
who * on going to live in Egypt. Jer 42:17
it, but whoever * on keeping his Lk 9:24
who died, but Paul * is alive! Act 25:19

INSOLENCE
Hear their *! Ps 94:4
His arrogance and * are all gone Is 16:6
I know her *, the Lord has said, Jer 48:30
of the enemy for their * to me. Hos 7:16

INSOLENT
the wicked to lower their * gaze, Ps 75:4
O God, proud and * men defy me; Ps 86:14
They are * as brass, hard and Jer 6:28
haters of God, *, proud braggarts, Rom 1:30
INSOLENTLY
But one of the Israeli men * Num 25:6
her door. She * worshiped many Eze 16:50
INSOMNIA
the rich must worry and suffer *. Ecc 5:12
INSPECT
arrived together to * the city. Ps 48:4
treated fairly. Go, * the city! Ps 48:12
She goes out to * a field, and Pro 31:16
your weapons! You * the walls of Is 22:9,10,11
sacrifice to idols and * the liver Eze 21:21
to * it, and asked to be excused. Lk 14:18
INSPECTED
And Moses * all their work and Ex 39:43
INSPECTING
the brook, * the wall, and entered Neh 2:14,15
INSPECTION
They also brought for his * the Ex 39:41
INSPIRATION
speaking under the * of the Holy Mt 22:43
was given to us by * from God and 2Ti 3:16
INSPIRED
"The * men are mad." Hos 9:7
and wise men, and * writers, and Mt 23:34
by himself, but was * to say it. Jn 11:51
they are really * by God or whether 1Co 12:3
unspiritual, * by the devil. Jas 3:15
INSTALL
the gold lid. * the lid upon the Ex 25:21
"Now * the mercy place—the Ex 26:34
Commandments; and * the veil to Ex 40:3
into Jerusalem and * the son of Is 7:6
INSTALLED
to the Ark and * the golden lid, Ex 40:20
* one of his sons as the priest. Ju 17:4,5
of Abinadab; and * his son Eleazar 1Sa 7:1
Or, "and they * him as 1Ch 29:22f
doors, and * the bolts and bars. Neh 3:6
doors, and * the bolts and bars; Neh 3:13
doors and * the bolts and bars. Neh 3:14
doors, and * its locks and bars. Neh 3:15
INSTALLING
their walls and * barred gates. 2Ch 8:5
INSTALLMENT
and as the first * of all that he 2Co 1:22
INSTANCE
In this case for *, the Hebrew Gen 3:20f
to God. For *, if a man is blind Lev 21:18
no one visiting the priest, for * Lev 22:10
you to decide—for *, whether Deu 17:8
of thread: for *, wool and linen. Deu 22:11
defiled (for *, while I was in Deu 26:14
He knew, for *, that his sons 1Sa 2:22
*) counted together as one tribe. 1Ki 12:20f
"For *, you must have refused to Job 22:6
in this *, fifth removed. Dan 5:11f
of God? For *, God's law is 'Honor Mt 15:4
"For *," he said, "it can be Mt 22:1
For *, Moses gave you this law Mk 7:10
Moses, for *, said long ago, 'The Act 3:21,22
For *, there was Joseph (the one Act 4:36
Philip, for *, went to the city Act 8:5
predicted. For *, listen to this Act 15:15
For *, don't argue with him Rom 14:2
For *, take the matter of eating. 1Co 6:13
For *, a man who already has gone 1Co 7:18
flute, for *, or the harp—are 1Co 14:7
the truth. For *, in Damascus the 2Co 11:32
For *, there was God's promise to Heb 6:13
Sarah, for *, obeyed her husband 1Pe 3:6
he promised; for *, the promise to 2Pe 1:4
INSTANCES
"LOOK, I HAVE seen many * such as Job 13:1
INSTANT
God knows very well that the * Gen 3:5
can doom me in an *, as though you Gen 44:18
From the * he saw David, Saul 1Sa 16:21
was David's * response to his 2Sa 15:14
by * punishment of the tyrants. Job 35:12
destruction: an * end to all their Ps 73:19
In an *, I, the Lord of Hosts, Is 29:6
the throat and demanded * payment. Mt 18:28
greeted me, the * I heard your Lk 1:44
But the * she touched the edge of Lk 8:43,44
INSTANTLY
Joseph recognized them *, but Gen 42:7
so that I may * destroy them." Num 16:21
so that I can * destroy them." Num 16:45
and shook his fist at him. * 1Ki 13:4
the king roared. * the death Est 7:8
be rejected * from his presence. Job 13:16
he does not * respond in anger? Job 35:14,15
who have never seen me submit *. Ps 18:43,44,45
not punish sinners *, people feel Ecc 8:11
And * the leprosy disappears. Mt 8:3
demon, and * the man could talk. Mt 9:33
* Jesus reached out his hand and Mt 14:31
their eyes. And * they could see, Mt 20:34
us, and he would send them *? Mt 26:53
He did, and * his hand was Mk 3:5
"Open!" * the man could hear Mk 7:35
The father * replied, "I do have Mk 9:24
And * the blind man could see, and Mk 10:52
name is John!" * Zacharias could Lk 1:64
And the leprosy left him *! Lk 5:13
He touched her, and * she Lk 13:13
And * the man could see, and Lk 18:43
*, the man was healed! Jn 5:9
* she fell to the floor, dead, Act 5:10
* (it was as though scales fell Act 9:18
And he was healed *. Act 9:34
*, an angel of the Lord struck Act 12:23
* mist and darkness fell upon him, Act 13:11
her," he said. And * it left her. Act 16:18
* Ananias the High Priest Act 23:2
And * I was, in spirit, there in Rev 4:2
INSTEAD
but they stopped * at the city of Gen 11:31
village over there * of into the Gen 19:18,19,20
Please, please, let me go there * Gen 19:18,19,20
and sacrificed it, * of his son, as Gen 22:13
Canaanites. Go * to my homeland, Gen 24:4
to Gerar Valley and lived there *. Gen 26:17
you before his death, * of Esau!" Gen 27:8,9,10
and curse me * of blessing me!" Gen 27:11,12
Canaanite girls. *, go at once to Gen 28:2
here as a slave * of the lad, and Gen 44:33
to place it on Manasseh's head *. Gen 48:17
of Shekem to you * of to your Gen 48:22
return to Egypt. *, God led them Ex 13:17,18
as usual, six quarts * of three; Ex 16:22
may accept a fine *, if they wish. Ex 21:30
into a great nation * of them." Ex 32:10
Or, "then kill me * of them." Ex 32:32f
their evil ways. *, you must break Ex 34:13
be accepted by God * of the death Lev 1:4
and enjoy— * of the people's Lev 17:7
and wizards * of me and I will cut Lev 20:6
these payments *: A man from the Lev 27:1
shall be told how much to pay *. Lev 27:11,12
courts to die may pay a fine *; Lev 27:29
me the Levites * of the eldest sons Num 3:45
of the Levites * of the firstborn Num 3:45
Well, * I will bring them safely Num 14:31
to obey his laws * of following Num 15:39
permit for food. *, there must be a Num 18:16
But King Sihon refused. * he Num 21:23
as he had earlier. *, he went at Num 24:1
my enemies and * you have blessed Num 24:10
as our portion * of the land on the Num 32:5
Promised Land! *, your assistant, Deu 1:38
wouldn't listen. *, they rebelled Deu 1:43
worship other gods *, and follow Deu 8:19
but remember * your promises to Deu 9:27
with the meat. *, pour the blood Deu 12:24,25
sheep and goats. *, you and your Deu 15:20
not sacrifice it. *, use it for Deu 15:22
"*, he will raise up for you a Deu 18:15
listen to Balaam; *, he turned the Deu 23:5
the family; *, her husband's Deu 25:5
Israelis * of asking for peace; Jos 11:20
the tribe of Levi: *, they were Jos 13:14
as we thought; *, you have saved us Jos 22:31
*, just as he has promised you. Jos 23:4,5
from your land. *, they will be a Jos 23:13
But I wouldn't listen to him. * Jos 24:10
them out of Egypt. *, they were Ju 2:12-14
by worshiping other gods *. Ju 2:17
when he died. *, I will use these Ju 2:22
Jebusites. But * of destroying Ju 3:6
will go to a woman * of to you!" Ju 4:9
had been built *, with the remains Ju 6:28
"Sibboleth" * of "Shibboleth," Ju 12:6
So his wife was married * to the Ju 14:20
Marry her *." Ju 15:2
tribe in Israel * of just to one Ju 18:19
wouldn't listen. *, twenty-six Ju 20:14,15
homes * of coming with me? Ru 1:8
and have said, 'We want a king *!' 1Sa 10:18,19
had left Saul, and *, the Lord had 1Sa 16:14
to Adriel, a man from Meholath, *. 1Sa 18:19
* of here in the royal city." 1Sa 27:5
clothing * of his royal robes. 1Sa 28:7,8
but carried it * to the home of 2Sa 6:10
the rich man. But * of killing a 2Sa 12:4
credit for the victory * of me." 2Sa 12:28
sending my brother Amnon *?" 2Sa 13:26
let him, but shook his hand *! 2Sa 15:5
what he himself had suggested *. 2Sa 17:15
we made our king *, chased him out 2Sa 19:8,9,10
from you, but * you have honored me 2Sa 19:28
But he refused to drink it! *, he 2Sa 23:16
your throne. But *, Adonijah is 1Ki 1:18
everything went to my brother *; 1Ki 2:15
and Zadok as priest * of Abiathar. 1Ki 2:35
made me the king * of my father 1Ki 3:7
they worshiped other gods *. 1Ki 9:9
worship their gods * of trusting 1Ki 11:4
and ask him to be their king *." 1Ki 12:27
his evil ways; *, he made more 1Ki 13:33
the palace guards used these *. 1Ki 14:27
Lord, and have worshiped Baal *. 1Ki 18:18
people shall perish * of his.' 1Ki 20:42
And Hazael became king *. 2Ki 8:15
king * of one of Ahab's sons." 2Ki 10:5
former practices * of truly 2Ki 17:34
wanted them to do. *, they had 2Ki 18:12
speak to them, but * he sent a 2Ki 18:18
All of this * of death! 2Ki 18:31,32
of their fathers; * they worshiped 1Ch 5:25
But he refused to drink it! * he 1Ch 11:18,19
David become king * of Saul, just 1Ch 12:23
the Gittite * of bringing it to the 1Ch 13:13
it for myself. *, I will make it a 2Ch 7:20
and disgrace. * of its being 2Ch 7:21
and they worshiped other gods *. 2Ch 7:22
He had appointed other priests * 2Ch 11:15
to worship idols * of God, and to 2Ch 11:15
have appointed heathen priests *. 2Ch 13:9
them to build Geba and Mizpah *. 2Ch 16:6
the king of Syria * of in the Lord 2Ch 16:7
and to worship shame-idols *! 2Ch 24:17,18
for King Ahaz * of helping him. 2Ch 28:20
to them. But *, they were his ruin, 2Ch 28:23
did; * he sinned more and more. 2Ch 33:23
to turn back. * he led his army 2Ch 35:22
us to slavery; * you caused the Ez 9:9
you did for them; *, they rebelled Neh 9:17
people of Israel. *, they had hired Neh 13:2
shall be the queen * of Vashti." Est 2:4
declared her queen * of Vashti. Est 2:17
But now, *, you give me so few Job 14:16
Evil came *. Job 30:26
grow on that land * of wheat, and Job 31:40
of wheat, and weeds * of barley." Job 31:40
absurd or evil? *, glorify him for Job 36:24
Look at me * through eyes of Ps 25:6,7
to the Lord * of lying in silence Ps 30:12
hold them back. *, in their Ps 36:2
their evil plots, * of planning how Ps 36:4
Trust in the Lord *. Ps 37:3
godly go hungry. *, the godly are Ps 37:26
I eat ashes * of bread. Ps 102:9,10
to the other. * of rain he sent Ps 105:32
kindness to them. * they rebelled Ps 106:7
to care for them. *, they pouted Ps 106:25
Follow the steps of the godly *, Pro 2:20
your own wisdom. *, trust and Pro 3:7,8
So I worked hard to be wise * Ecc 1:16-18
Dreaming * of doing is Ecc 5:6,7
fear God *. Ecc 5:6,7
to be good, but * choose their own Ecc 9:2,3
and join you there * of wandering Sol 1:7
and veils. * of smelling of sweet Is 3:24
they'll wear sacks * of robes. Is 3:24
give me wild grapes * of sweet? Is 5:4
of justice, but found bloodshed *. Is 5:7
* of fearing the Assyrians. Is 10:20
But *, you will be brought Is 14:15
your remorse. But *, you sing and Is 22:13
tell you and trust * in frauds and Is 30:12
and chariots * of looking to the Is 31:1
* you will see Jerusalem at Is 33:20
idols your love, * of loving me. Is 57:7,8
for ashes;Joy * of mourning; Is 61:3
Praise * of heaviness. Is 61:3
in their riches. * of shame and Is 61:7
would not hear. *, they did wrong Is 66:4
They went backward * of forward. Jer 7:24
obeyed my laws. * they have done Jer 9:14
me as their God * of Baal (whom Jer 12:16
evil against you now * of good; Jer 18:11
Don't weep for the dead! * weep Jer 22:10
were to care for. * of leading my Jer 23:2
are doing evil, * of turning them Jer 23:14
Isaac and Jacob. * I will restore Jer 33:25,26
* he chose Zedekiah (son of Jer 37:1
the palace prison *, and that he be Jer 37:21
shouting of joy. * the awful cries Jer 48:34
Let us examine ourselves *, and Lam 3:40
use cow dung * of human dung." Eze 4:15
and you used it * to make idols! Eze 7:20
Give them this one *: 'The time Eze 12:23
in the Lord? * you have lied when Eze 13:6
me—you trusted in your beauty *; Eze 16:15
other men * of her own husband. Eze 16:32
out toward him *, even though it Eze 17:7
to other gods * of me, and gave her Eze 23:4,5
on you for aid [* of trusting me Eze 29:6
feed themselves * of their flocks. Eze 34:2
away and are lost. * you have ruled Eze 34:4
steps leading up to it * of seven. Eze 40:31
were eight steps * of seven going Eze 40:34
permission to eat other things *. Dan 1:8
the mind of an animal * of a man. Dan 4:16
This totals 483 years, * of the Dan 9:25f
than them all. * of these he will Dan 11:38
Then, * of saying to them, 'You Hos 1:10

NSTEAD Con't)
"My Husband" * of "My Master." Hos 1:16
won't ask my help. *, they worship Hos 7:14
blessing * of his terrible curse. Joe 2:14
Beor, but I made him bless you *? Mic 6:5
that cannot walk; *, he will eat Zec 11:16
upon you, and * of giving you Mal 2:1
Galilee *, and lived in Nazareth. Mt 2:22
bread, will he be given a stone *? Mt 7:9
about it, but * they spread his Mt 9:31
*.' And so, by your man-made Mt 15:5,6
laws * of those from God.' Mt 15:9
haven't enough. Go * to the shops Mt 25:9
by Satan's power [* of Mk 3:30
release of Barabbas * of Jesus. Mk 15:11
knew the truth, * of merely quoting Lk 4:32
were feasting * of fasting. Lk 5:33
lamp and hides it! *, he puts it on Lk 11:33
say, 'Let this man sit here *.' Lk 14:9
"Do this *—start at the foot; Lk 14:10
the invitation. *, invite the Lk 14:13
now, * of waiting until you die!' Lk 15:12
there * of coming here to us." Jn 3:26
good example. But * you are trying Jn 8:40
* of me Jn 14:26
* you are only filled with Jn 16:6
righteous one. * you demanded the Act 3:14
God wants us to obey you * of him! Act 4:19
"And * you have filled all Act 5:28
* of giving the glory to God. Act 12:23
things and to pray * to the living Act 14:15
Jesus said no. So * they went on Act 16:8
took them before the Council *. Act 17:6
king, Jesus, * of Caesar." Act 17:7
the light of God * of in Satan's Act 26:18
God, they became utter fools *. Rom 1:22
And then, * of worshiping the Rom 1:23
other's bodies. * of believing Rom 1:25
And the men, * of having a Rom 1:27
and then make money your god *. Rom 2:22
* of doing all these evil things; Rom 3:19
sins and gives glorious life *. Rom 5:16
kindness rules *, giving us right Rom 5:21
to sin, and * be alive to God, Rom 6:11
of life resulted * in my being Rom 7:10
servant but * I find myself still Rom 7:23,24,25
good * of by depending on faith. Rom 9:32
right with God. * they are trying Rom 10:3
gifts God was merciful to you *. Rom 11:30
*, feed your enemy if he is Rom 12:20
any more. Try * to live in such a Rom 14:13
power or wealth. *, God has 1Co 1:27
Let us feast * upon the pure 1Co 5:8
decide the matter * of taking it to 1Co 6:1
But, *, one Christian sues 1Co 6:6
But, *, you yourselves are the 1Co 6:8
done among you. *, we hope that 2Co 10:15
you anything? * I "robbed" other 2Co 11:8,9
of Christ's power, * of showing off 2Co 12:9
afterward to do something else *. Gal 3:15
But if * of showing love among Gal 5:15
like the truth. *, we will Eph 4:15,16
in your lives. *, be kind to each Eph 4:32
are not for you. *, remind each Eph 5:4
but *, rebuke and expose them. Eph 5:11
be filled * with the Holy Spirit, Eph 5:18
Don't worry about anything; *, Php 4:6
* of on what Christ has said. Col 2:8
and arguments * of helping people 1Ti 1:3,4
things and work * at what is right 1Ti 6:11
somewhere else * of up to me, and Heb 3:10
others, but * you have dropped back Heb 5:12,13
Let us go on * to other things Heb 6:1
of Melchizedek, * of sending Heb 7:11
guilt * of relieving their minds. Heb 10:3
with God's people * of enjoying the Heb 11:24,25
forgives * of crying out for Heb 12:24
Let there be sadness * of Jas 4:9
of laughter, and gloom * of joy. Jas 4:9
things about you. *, pray for God's 1Pe 3:9
to happen to you. *, be really 1Pe 4:13
of something else *, urging you to Jud 1:3

INSTINCT
"Who gives intuition and *? Job 38:36
Doesn't even * itself teach us 1Co 11:14,15

INSTINCTIVELY
truth about God is known to them * Rom 1:19

INSTITUTED
employees first * by King David. Ez 8:20
of God, was * (1 Samuel 11:15). Hos 9:15f

INSTRUCT
Then the Lord said to Moses, "* Ex 8:5
"* the people of Israel to bring Ex 27:20
to his work. * those to whom I Ex 28:3
THE LORD TOLD Moses, "* Aaron and Lev 22:1
at this time, "* the people of Num 15:17,18
"* the people of Israel to give Num 35:2
me and I will * them, so that they Deu 4:10
I was with Moses. * the priests Jos 3:8
Lord told Gad to * David to build 1Ch 21:18
of Seven hereby * you to take a Ez 7:14
You sent your good Spirit to * Neh 9:20
royal crown, and * one of the Est 6:9
I will * you (says the Lord) and Ps 32:8
I when there is no one to * me?" Act 8:31

INSTRUCTED
Lord had * him, and Lot went too; Gen 12:4
house—and * Jacob to put them on. Gen 27:15
He * his servants to drive them Gen 32:16
So Jacob * all those in his Gen 35:2
he tells you to," he * them. Gen 41:55
along the lines he had been *. Gen 44:6
died, your father * us to tell you Gen 50:16,17
the king of Egypt, * the Hebrew Ex 1:15,16
me," the princess * the baby's Ex 2:9
of Israel," God * him, "and tell Ex 3:16
met with us and * us to go three Ex 3:18
as Jehovah had * them—Aaron threw Ex 7:10
For I have * Moses to hit the Ex 7:17
Then the Lord * Moses: "Tell Ex 7:19
THE LORD * Moses, "Dedicate to me Ex 13:1
JEHOVAH NOW * Moses, "Tell the Ex 14:1
as the Lord had * Moses, and Ex 16:34
Moses * Joshua to issue a call Ex 17:9
Then the Lord * Moses, "Write Ex 17:14
THE LORD NOW * Moses, "Come up Ex 24:1
The Lord * skilled Ex 30:25
* you to make: the Tabernacle; Ex 31:6
days, just as I * you, at the dates Ex 34:18
blue cord, just as the Lord had *. Ex 39:31
it was all as the Lord had * him. Ex 39:43
just as the Lord had * him. Lev 8:29
just as I * you to do. Lev 8:31
of Israel," Moses *, "to select a Lev 9:3
Now the Lord * Aaron, "Never Lev 10:8,9
The Lord also * Moses, "The Num 8:23,24
for so the Lord had * them. Num 9:19
JEHOVAH NOW * Moses, "Send spies Num 13:1
So Moses did as *. Num 20:9
the Lord *, "and let the smaller Num 26:55,56
and are offered as I have * you. Num 28:1
movements as the Lord had * him. Num 33:2
"The Lord * you to divide the land Num 36:1
in every way. I * them to be Deu 1:16
Red Sea, for so the Lord had * me. Deu 2:1
Then Moses * the people of Israel Deu 4:41
new commander, as the Lord has *. Deu 31:3
the Lord *, "—men, women, Deu 31:12
in this book, he * the Levites who Deu 31:25
armed as Moses had *, and forty Jos 4:12,13
The Lord * them to manufacture Jos 5:2,3
So our elders and our people * Jos 9:11
told that Jehovah * his disciple Jos 9:24
Joshua now * his men to remove Jos 10:22,23
going down, Joshua * that their Jos 10:27
as the Lord had *, for they Jos 11:9
land just as the Lord had * Moses; Jos 11:23
The Lord * Joshua to assign some Jos 15:13
Cities of Refuge, as I * Moses. Jos 20:2
The Lord also * that three Jos 20:8
"The Lord * Moses to give cities Jos 21:2
oldest son, he * him to kill them. Ju 8:20
Samuel then * the chef to bring 1Sa 9:23
Then Saul * his men to say 1Sa 18:22
Saul then * his aides to try to 1Sa 28:7,8
So David did as the Lord had * 2Sa 5:25
out and help me," Joab * him. 2Sa 10:11
The letter * Joab to put Uriah 2Sa 11:15
you are in mourning," Joab * her. 2Sa 14:2,3
the king * that his ten wives he 2Sa 20:3
Then the king * Amasa to mobilize 2Sa 20:4
he * my father that I should do. 1Ki 5:5
Lord had clearly * his people not 1Ki 11:2
Meanwhile, the Lord * one of the 1Ki 20:35
friends and neighbors!" he *. 2Ki 4:3
to the other. He * the head of the 2Ki 10:22
Jehoiada the High Priest * him. 2Ki 12:2
that eastern window," he *. 2Ki 13:16,17
the new altar. He * Uriah the 2Ki 16:15
the priest did as King Ahaz * him. 2Ki 16:16
king had * them to say nothing. 2Ki 18:36
Isaiah then * Hezekiah to boil 2Ki 20:7
Then the king * Hilkiah the High 2Ki 23:4
just as the Lord had * Moses. 1Ch 15:15
Temple," David *, "six thousand 1Ch 23:4,5
the larger cities, and * them: 2Ch 19:6
So now the king * that a chest 2Ch 24:7,8
He * the priests, the sons of 2Ch 29:21
They stood at their posts as * 2Ch 30:16
as the king had *, then the 2Ch 35:10
of the Lord, as Josiah had *. 2Ch 35:16
heaven, and he has * me to build 2Ch 36:22,23
his own gods. He * Mithredath, the Ez 1:8
upon it, as * in the laws of Moses, Ez 3:1
The king * him to return the Ez 5:15
of God as * in the laws of Moses. Ez 6:18
For the king had * his officers Est 1:8
Literally, "Thou hast * many." Job 4:3,4f
The wise man is glad to be *, but Pro 10:8
was growing, he * his disciples to Mt 8:18
He * his disciples to bring Mk 3:9
Jesus * them very earnestly not Mk 5:43
Immediately after this Jesus * Mk 6:45
Gethsemane, and he * his disciples, Mk 14:32
Then Jesus * him to go at once Lk 5:14
stick," he * them, "nor a Lk 9:3
this Council, and * to state Lk 22:67,68
how an angel had * him to send for Act 10:22
He ordered Paul to prison but * Act 24:23
Then he * me, "Do not seal up Rev 22:10

INSTRUCTING
wrong, and * them in God's ways. Ex 18:15,16
He let you hear his voice * you Deu 4:36
of our God, I am * you to search 1Ch 28:8
Euphrates River * them to let me Neh 2:7
the king's forest, * him to give me Neh 2:8

INSTRUCTION
them this further * from the Lord: Ex 16:32
(Stress this *, that if it is Lev 6:17
This is a permanent * to be Num 10:8
* to Hilkiah, the High Priest: 2Ki 22:3,4
them wisdom and *, causing them to Job 33:16
He helps them hear his * to turn Job 36:10
is only open! My * is far more Pro 8:10
Did he need * as to what is right Is 40:14
of * for us come and give it!" Act 13:15
you don't need further * about Heb 6:2

INSTRUCTIONS
to follow Abraham's *. Gen 24:9
So Jacob followed his mother's *, Gen 27:14
Jacob gave the same * to each Gen 32:19
also gave secret * to put each Gen 42:25
of Jehovah's * to Moses and Aaron. Ex 12:50
they will follow my * or not. Ex 16:4
"Give these * to the people of Ex 19:2,3
"Be sure to obey all of these *; Ex 23:13
him and obey all of his *; Ex 23:21
following all my *, then I will be Ex 23:22
These are * to Aaron and his Ex 30:21
gave these further * to Moses: Ex 31:12,13
people whatever * God had given Ex 34:34
with the Lord's * to Moses. Ex 39:1
with the Lord's * to Moses. Ex 39:6,7
all of the Lord's * to Moses. Ex 39:32
all the Lord's * to Moses. Ex 39:42
following all the *, and placed Ex 40:25
give the following * to the people Lev 1:2,3
THEN THE LORD gave these further * Lev 4:1
the * concerning the sin offering: Lev 6:25
"HERE ARE THE * concerning the Lev 7:1
"The same * apply to both the Lev 7:7
"Here are the * concerning the Lev 7:11
These were the * concerning the Lev 7:37
these * were given to Moses by Lev 7:38
*, his glory will appear to you." Lev 9:6
with the * God had given. Lev 9:16
these * to the people of Israel: Lev 12:1
(the following * are applicable Lev 12:6
people of Israel these further *: Lev 15:1
The same * apply to anyone Lev 15:7
And Aaron followed all these * Lev 16:35
these additional * for Aaron and Lev 17:1
* for the people of Israel: Lev 20:1
while the contrary * in verse 1 Lev 21:11f
So Moses gave these * to Aaron Lev 21:24
to follow these * carefully, lest Lev 22:9
these * for the people of Israel: Lev 25:1
ordinances, and * that Jehovah gave Lev 26:46
issued the following * to Moses. Num 1:1
So all these * of the Lord to Num 1:54
THE LORD GAVE these further * to Num 2:1
They will follow his * and Num 3:7,8,9
carry out the Lord's * to Moses. Num 4:37
response to the Lord's * to Moses. Num 4:49
THESE ARE FURTHER * from the Num 5:1
These * were put into effect. Num 5:4
these further * for the people of Num 6:1
following Jehovah's * to Moses. Num 8:20
JEHOVAH GAVE THESE * to Moses Num 9:1
Be sure to follow all of my * Num 9:2,3
regular * concerning the Passover. Num 9:12
he shall follow all these same *. Num 9:14
the Lord's travel * to Moses. Num 10:13
Moses sent them out with these *: Num 13:17
to give these * to the people of Num 15:1
"These are the * for what is to Num 15:11,12
These * apply both to Num 15:13,14
So Moses gave the * to the Num 17:6
If you follow these * the wrath Num 18:5
The Lord gave these further * to Num 18:8
* concerning the water at Meribah. Num 20:24
Balak followed his *, and a young Num 23:2
census * to the leaders of Israel. Num 26:3,4
my * in the wilderness of Zin. Num 27:14
before them by following my * to Num 27:14
these * to Joshua and the people. Num 27:21
THE LORD GAVE Moses these * to Num 28:1
So Moses gave all of these * to Num 29:40
"We will follow your * Num 32:25
giving them these * from the Lord: Num 36:5
And I gave them other * at that Deu 1:18
all of his * as long as you live; Deu 6:2
These * apply only to distant Deu 20:15

(INSTRUCTIONS Con't)
"Be very careful to follow the * Deu 24:8
people these further * to obey: Deu 27:1
where I can give him his *." Deu 31:14
He obeyed your * Deu 33:9
Then Joshua issued * to the Jos 1:10,11
camp giving these *: "When you see Jos 3:2,3,4
until all these * of the Lord, Jos 4:10
gave them their *: the armed men Jos 6:6-9
You now have your *." Jos 8:8
the * given long before by Moses. Jos 8:33
all of the Lord's * to Moses. Jos 11:15
to follow all the * written in the Jos 23:6
went to the Lord to receive his *. Ju 1:1
When Gideon had followed these *, Ju 6:20
and give us more * about the child Ju 13:8
us any special * about how we Ju 13:12
wife follows the * I gave her. Ju 13:13,14
followed her mother-in-law's *. Ru 3:6,7
So these * were carried out. 1Sa 6:10
I will give you further * when I 1Sa 10:8
"Yes, I have disobeyed your * 1Sa 15:24
obey the Lord's * when he was so 1Sa 28:18
Then, following David's *, Zadok 2Sa 15:25,26
"Now listen to my * 1Ki 2:5
to the king for further *. 1Ki 2:30
his father David's * except that he 1Ki 3:3
commandments and *, I will do what 1Ki 6:11,12
and * he has given our ancestors. 1Ki 8:58
he has not kept my laws and * as 1Ki 11:33
I have given her my *." 1Ki 17:8,9
fathers followed the queen's *. 1Ki 21:11
* to destroy the dynasty of Ahab. 2Ki 10:30
Then he gave them their *: "A 2Ki 11:5
officers followed Jehoiada's *. 2Ki 11:9
only follow the * I gave them 2Ki 21:8
He refused to listen to God's *. 2Ki 21:22
been following the * of this book: 2Ki 22:12,13
and issued these *: [When we 1Ch 15:2
commandments and * as he has until 1Ch 28:7
on to Solomon the * concerning the 1Ch 28:13
Carefully following God's *, he 2Ch 4:7
with the * Moses had given; 2Ch 8:13
way from David's * concerning these 2Ch 8:15
follow the * of the Lord our God; 2Ch 13:11
had issued these * to his 2Ch 18:30
These were his * to them: "You 2Ch 19:9
and Levites and gave them these *: 2Ch 24:5
received their * from the Lord. 2Ch 29:25,26
the laws and * given to you by 2Ch 33:8
Follow all of the * of the Lord 2Ch 35:6
I issued * to them not to open Neh 7:3
The * concerning these girls were Est 2:12,13,14
dressing according to his *. Est 2:15
Listen to his * and store them Job 22:22
of cloud and they followed his *. Ps 99:7
followed his * and he sent thick Ps 105:28
let me wander off from your *. Ps 119:10
I long for your * more than I Ps 119:20
Now give me your *. Ps 119:26
to me and obeys my * will be given Pro 2:1
life, closely follow my *. Pro 3:1
Carry out my *; Pro 4:13
Tie their * around your finger Pro 6:21
* guide you into the new day. Pro 6:22
and gave them his * not to spread Pro 8:27,28,29
how happy are all who follow my *. Pro 8:32
Israel came to ask * from the Lord, Eze 20:1
Here are the * for dividing the Eze 47:13
"All who listen to my * and Mt 7:24
"But those who hear my * and Mt 7:26
Jesus sent them out with these *: Mt 10:5
giving these * to his twelve Mt 11:1
These were his * to them: "Plead Lk 10:2
ahead, with * to go to the next Lk 19:30
And I know his * lead to eternal Jn 12:50
further * from the Holy Spirit. Act 1:1
the city and await my further *." Act 9:6
but they had no such * from us. Act 15:24
in Damascus, with * to let me bring Act 22:5
Please follow their * and do 1Co 16:16
to obey only the Holy Spirit's *. Gal 5:16
always so careful to follow my *. Php 2:12
who would follow the * I gave you. Tit 1:5

INSTRUCTOR
eyes on Jesus, our leader and *. Heb 12:2

INSTRUCTS
or as a king * his army, and as one Job 29:25

INSTRUMENT
sort of musical * before the 2Sa 6:5
threshing * to tear all enemies Is 41:15
voice or plays well on an *. Eze 33:32
and every other sort of *." Dan 3:5f
and every other sort of *." Dan 3:7f
and every other sort of *." Dan 3:10f
For Paul is my chosen * to take Act 9:15

INSTRUMENTS
forging * of bronze and iron. Gen 4:22
table and all its *, the lampstand Ex 30:26,27
altar with all its *, and the Ex 30:28
the table and its *; Ex 31:8
pure gold lampstand with its *; Ex 31:8
burnt offering altar with its *; Ex 31:9
The Urim and Thummim were holy * 1Sa 28:5,6f
use the threshing * and ox yokes 2Sa 24:22
bronze * used for the sacrifices. 2Ki 25:14,15
pillars, and the * used in offering 1Ch 18:8
use the threshing * for wood for 1Ch 21:23
with the musical * I have made." 1Ch 23:4,5
and its * from place to place." 1Ch 23:26
of other musical *—all praising and 2Ch 5:13,14
using the musical * that King David 2Ch 7:6
* in all the land of Judah. 2Ch 9:11
and for making the * used in the 2Ch 24:14
began, the * of music began to play 2Ch 29:27
(They used the original musical * Neh 12:35,36
Praise him with stringed * and Ps 150:4
to be accompanied by stringed *. Hab 3:19
Even musical *—the flute, for 1Co 14:7
whatever * were used for worship. Heb 9:21

INSUFFICIENT
when there is * evidence, or Deu 17:8

INSULT
to overlook the *, for it was an Gen 34:6,7
in this Hebrew slave to * us!" Gen 39:14,15
You must not * the Lord your God Deu 12:31
What an * to a god! Ju 6:31
a day of trouble, *, and dishonor. 2Ki 19:3
be cautious lest I * someone, and Job 32:21,22
* me even as they insult you. Ps 69:9
insult me even as they * you. Ps 69:9
steal, and thus * God's holy name. Pro 30:9
All day long they * me to my Is 65:3
exclude you and * you and smear Lk 6:22

INSULTED
"He has * the entire army of 1Sa 17:25
but he * them and railed at them. 1Sa 25:14
have * me by taking Uriah's wife. 2Sa 12:10
know that you have * him beyond the 2Sa 16:21
So King Hanun * King David's 1Ch 19:4
which made them very angry and *. 2Ch 25:10
He flew into a rage, and * and Neh 4:1
people be constantly *. Ps 74:21
a wise man stays cool when *. Pro 12:16
Isn't he the one your king *, Is 36:7
mountains and * me upon the hills. Is 65:7
there, "you have * my profession, Lk 11:45
he was beaten up and * and sent Lk 20:11
unhallowed, and * and outraged the Heb 10:29
lie, never answered back when *; 1Pe 2:23
Be happy if you are cursed and * 1Pe 4:14

INSULTING
unfit for me to live in, and * my Lev 20:3
His sons and daughters were * him. Deu 32:19
"He must die for * the altar of Ju 6:30
ones who should die for * Baal! Ju 6:31
When the * message from the 2Sa 5:8
he will slap them in the face, * Ps 3:7
the poor is * God who made them. Pro 14:31
and what * language he is using. 3Jn 1:10
names, each one defying and * God. Rev 13:1

INSULTS
and ending his * to Israel?" 1Sa 17:26
that I get for my trouble is *. 1Sa 25:21
servant Hezekiah, heaping up *. 2Ch 32:16
I hear them shouting * and Ps 59:7
Remember the * these rebels have Ps 74:22
quarrels, but love overlooks *. Pro 10:12
and the rich man answers with *. Pro 18:23
his anger and overlooks *. Pro 19:11
away forever all * and mockery Is 25:8
accept their awful *, for the Lord Lam 3:30
threw all sorts of other * at him. Lk 22:65
under the * of those who were Rom 15:3
thorn," and about * and hardships, 2Co 12:10

INSURGENTS
against Egypt. * among your own Dan 11:14

INSURRECTION
a hotbed of * against many kings; Ez 4:19
others for murder during an *. Mk 15:7
for starting an * in Jerusalem Lk 23:19
* and murder, at their request. Lk 23:25

INSURRECTIONS
And when you hear of wars and * Lk 21:9

INTACT
the trunk of his body was left *. 1Sa 5:4

INTEGRITY
Literally, "the * of your ways, Job 4:6f
Assign me Godliness and * as my Ps 25:21
with all his *: "I will never Is 62:8
are men of *, sent by God, speaking 2Co 2:17

INTELLECTUALS
things from the * and worldly wise Lk 10:21

INTELLIGENCE
you a reputation for wisdom and *. Deu 4:6
wisdom, and by his * he hung the Jer 10:12
wisdom, and scholars their *. Dan 2:21
power with great shrewdness and *. Dan 8:23
above average in *, as judged by 1Co 3:18
but be men of * in understanding 1Co 14:20

INTELLIGENT
very * woman, was named Abigail. 1Sa 25:3
David such a wise, *, and 2Ch 2:12
of the Almighty which makes him *. Job 32:8,9
The * man is always open to new Pro 18:15
Whoever is *, let him listen. Hos 14:9
You are * people. 1Co 10:15

INTELLIGENTLY
soberly and * to more of God's 1Pe 1:13

INTEND
(But he didn't really * for Gen 38:11
to make a vow you don't * to keep. Deu 5:11
Geshur if he didn't * to see me. 2Sa 14:32
They make promises they don't * Hos 10:4
your teaching and * to bring the Act 5:28
As long as I am still here I * to 2Pe 1:13,14

INTENDED
destroying all Israel as I had *. Num 25:10,11
instead, he turned the * curse Deu 23:5
he * to make him the next king. 2Ch 11:22
has no effect. Its * victim will be Pro 26:2
was not what God had originally *. Mt 19:8
are living as God *, marrying or 1Co 7:17
laws are good when used as God *. 1Ti 1:8

INTENDING
attacks another, * to kill him, Ex 21:14
to his wife, * to sleep with her; Ju 15:1
David, * to pin him to the wall. 1Sa 18:11,12
spear at Jonathan, * to kill him; 1Sa 20:33
Sennacherib was * to attack 2Ch 32:2

INTENSE
children in * pain and suffering; Gen 3:16
The battle became more and more * 1Ki 22:35
butchered because his anger was *. Ps 78:62
"I was blinded by the * light, Act 22:11
upon a sickbed of * affliction, Rev 2:22
wine of her * impurity and sin." Rev 14:8
fatal wine of her * immorality. Rev 18:3

INTENSELY
go, and long so * for your Gen 31:30
enemies, for they hated Israel *. 1Ki 11:25

INTENT
"Don't join mobs * on evil. Ex 23:2,3
who are so * upon destroying me. Ps 57:3
the law but often violated its *. Mt 3:7f

INTENTION
I hadn't the slightest * of Gen 20:5
* that you be slaves no longer; Lev 26:13
We have no * whatever of doing Jer 18:12
"I have no * whatever of doing Jer 37:14
But they have no * of doing what Eze 33:31
Herod's * was to deliver Peter to Act 12:4

INTENTIONAL
act of God—and not *, then I will Ex 21:13

INTENTIONED
at least, are well * and honest. 2Co 5:12

INTENTIONS
fled without telling Laban his *. Gen 31:17-20
look at a man's thoughts and *." 1Sa 16:7
but they knew nothing of his *. 2Sa 15:11
their * were friendly or not. 2Ki 9:19
or try to flatter you from your *? Job 41:3
forever. His * are the same for Ps 33:11
he signals his true * to his Pro 6:12,13
afflicted them far beyond my *. Zec 1:15

INTENTLY
For the eyes of the Lord are * Ps 34:15
Jesus looked at them * and said, Mt 19:26
as the man stared *, his sight was Mk 8:25
Jesus looked at them *, then Mk 10:27
in the synagogue gazed at him *. Lk 4:20
John looked at him * and then Jn 1:36
Jesus looked * at Peter for a Jn 1:42
They looked at him *, and then Act 3:4
Crowds listened * to what he had Act 8:6
GAZING * AT the Council, Paul Act 23:1

INTER-REGNUM
A three-month * by his son Jer 36:30f

INTERCEDE
for Joab to ask him to * for him; 2Sa 14:29
heaven is there to * for him as a Job 33:23,24
stay at Mizpah and * for you with Jer 40:10

INTERCEDED
But Aaron * with Moses. Lev 10:19

INTERCEPT
thousand were to * the forces Jos 8:11,12,13f

INTERCESSION
in penitence and * before God. 2Ch 20:3

INTERCESSORS
O Jerusalem, I have set * Is 62:6,7

INTERCOURSE
THEN ADAM HAD sexual * with Eve Gen 4:1
and had sexual * with her father; Gen 19:33
have sexual * with your wives." Ex 19:15
After sexual *, the woman as Lev 15:18
A man having sexual * with her Lev 15:24
and for anyone who has sexual * Lev 15:33
that is, "have sexual * with." Lev 18:6f
A man shall have no sexual * Lev 18:23
And if a man has sexual * with Lev 20:12
If a man has sexual * with a Lev 20:14
"If a man has sexual * with an Lev 20:15
If a woman has sexual * with an Lev 20:16

INTERCOURSE Con't)
"If a man has sexual * with his Lev 20:17
If a man has sexual * with a Lev 20:18
"Sexual * is outlawed between a Lev 20:19
If a man has * with his uncle's Lev 20:20
the women who have had sexual *. Num 31:17
had premarital * with another man, Deu 22:13,14
" 'Cursed is he who has sexual * Deu 27:21
" 'Cursed is he who has sexual * Deu 27:22
" 'Cursed is he who has sexual * Deu 27:23
Then I had sexual * with my wife Is 8:3

NTEREST
in an ordinary way, with *. Ex 22:25
and don't charge him * on the Lev 25:36
Remember—no *; Lev 25:37
"Don't demand * on loans you Deu 23:19
You may take * from a foreigner, Deu 23:20
For if you take * from a brother, Deu 23:20
because of the Lord's *. 2Sa 12:25
and expressed * in his problem. 2Sa 15:2
naturalist, with * in animals, 1Ki 4:33
to our fellow-Jews without any *. Neh 5:10
in the king's * to let them live. Est 3:8
debtors with high * rates, and Ps 15:5
will listen with * and respect. Ps 119:44,45,46
own best * and will be a success. Pro 19:8
he pays wonderful * on your loan! Pro 19:17
after their own *, each trying to Is 56:11
No one had the slightest * in Eze 16:5
need, and grants loans without *, Eze 18:8
and loans out his money at * Eze 18:13
Or, "at usurious *." Eze 18:13f
poor and does not loan money at *, Eze 18:17
Or, "at usurious *." Eze 18:17f
always your real * has been in Amo 5:25,26,27
the bank so I could have some *. Mt 25:27
they listened to him with great *. Mk 12:37
of persecution blow, they lose *. Lk 8:13
could at least get some * on it?' Lk 19:23
No, your real * was in your Act 7:43
Because of that cross my * in all Gal 6:14
world's * in me is also long dead. Gal 6:14
for having a real * in you; Php 2:20
no, you listened with great *. 1Th 1:5

INTERESTED
He is much more * in your 1Sa 15:22
was no longer * in the Lord God of 1Ki 11:9,10
just as * in your God as you are; Ez 4:2
anyone was * in helping Israel. Neh 2:10
You aren't * in offerings burned Ps 51:16
he was especially * in Hezekiah's Is 39:1f
and none of you seems * in the Jn 16:5
I'm not * and I'm not touching Act 18:15
you might be less * in our message 1Co 9:12
are not * in fooling anyone. 2Co 4:2
He is especially *, as he looks 2Co 8:22
affairs, but be * in others, too, Php 2:4

INTERESTING
to pass these * comments on to King Neh 6:7
but taught them in an * manner. Ecc 12:10

INTERESTS
and a mind with broad *. 1Ki 4:29
harm yourself and your own best *. Pro 15:31,32
rewarded who protects another's *. Pro 27:18
* closely. Pro 27:23,24
his wife. His * are divided. 1Co 7:34
is, outside the * of this world, Heb 13:13

INTERFERE
and Sidon, don't you try to *! Joe 3:4
will not try to * with the Lord in Amo 5:13
do as they like, and no one can *. Hab 1:7

INTERFERED
name in Greek), * and urged the Act 13:8
Who has * with you to hold you Gal 5:7

INTERFERENCE
'Because of your *, your wife will Amo 7:17

INTERFERING
more foolish than * in an argument Pro 26:17

INTERIOR
Then he overlaid the * of the 1Ki 6:21,22

INTERMARRIAGE
other through * of their rulers; Dan 2:43

INTERMARRIED
the people of Israel * with them. Ju 3:6
again and * with people who do Ez 9:14

INTERMARRY
then we will * with you and live Gen 34:16
hold them, and we can * with them. Gen 34:21
Do not * with them, nor let your Deu 7:3
if you begin to * with the nations Jos 23:12
their children * with non-Jews. Neh 13:25
of Ekron will * with the Jews, just Zec 9:7

INTERMEDIARY
I stood as an * between you and Deu 5:5

INTERNAL
the wood. The * organs and the Lev 1:9
But the * organs and the legs Lev 1:13
fat covering the * organs, the two Lev 3:9,10,11
meat, head, legs, * organs, and Lev 4:11,12
including the hides and * organs. Lev 16:27
I have no foreign enemies or * 1Ki 5:4
There were external wars, and * 2Ch 15:6
real problem is *—wickedness and Ps 55:10
you with * turmoil and you sinned. Eze 28:16
twelve years with * bleeding came Mt 9:20

INTERNATIONAL
The Lord will settle * disputes; Is 2:4
Aramaic was the language used in * Is 36:11f

INTERPRET
But I have heard that you can * Gen 41:15
able to analyze them and * them. Ecc 8:1
the dream, they couldn't * it. Dan 4:7
He can * dreams, explain riddles, Dan 5:12
Hypocrites! You * the sky well Lk 12:56
Some commentators would * this Lk 16:9f
Narratives from that period * Act 27:4f
ready to * what they are saying. 1Co 14:27
*, they must not speak out loud. 1Co 14:28
Let those who are able, * this Rev 13:18

INTERPRETATION
the dream and the *, all he could Ju 7:15
This was the * of this passage by Is 52:13f
expect me to believe your *!" Dan 2:8,9
future, and this * of your dream is Dan 2:45
Either * is possible from the Zec 9:10f
some unusual *—they have twisted 2Pe 3:15,16

INTERPRETATIONS
Both * are possible. 1Co 6:4f
Other * of this verse are equally 1Jn 5:6,7,8f

INTERPRETED
could also be * "descendant." 1Ch 1:24-27f
"spirit" can be * either way. 1Ch 28:12f

INTERPRETER
speaking to them through an *. Gen 42:23

INTERPRETING
"* dreams is God's business," Gen 40:8
Or, "* spiritual truth in 1Co 2:13f

INTERPRETS
This alternate paraphrase * Jn 3:5f

INTERRUPTED
Then the other woman *, "It 1Ki 3:22
Agrippa * him. Act 26:28

INTERSECTIONS
She calls from the busiest * in Pro 9:3

INTERSPERSED
their selections were * with 2Ch 5:13,14

INTERTWINED
is * with everything he does. Ps 145:9

INTERVAL
29:10. This * had now almost Dan 9:2f

INTERVENED
you, and wondered that no one *. Is 59:16

INTERVENES
the wife of one * to help her Deu 25:11

INTERVENING
On each of the * days you shall Lev 23:8

INTERVENTION
He was driven off by special * of Hos 1:7f

INTERVIEW
so that he could have a private *. Ju 3:17,18,19
Let me have an * with the king; 2Sa 14:32
many lands came to * him and listen 1Ki 10:24
After this * the astrologers Mt 2:9
arrived from Jerusalem to * Jesus. Mt 15:1
Some Pharisees came to * him, Mt 19:3
came for an * with Jesus. Jn 3:1
who came secretly to * Jesus. Jn 7:50

INTERVIEWED
cent of the men I * could be said Ecc 7:27,28

INTESTINAL
You will be stricken with an * 2Ch 21:15

INTESTINES
organs, and *—shall be carried to a Lev 4:11,12
of two years, his * came out and he 2Ch 21:19

INTOLERABLE
This is *. Amo 7:10

INTRICATE
feet high, with an * bronze network 2Ki 25:17

INTRIGUE
the kingdom by flattery and *. Dan 11:21
blaze like a furnace with *. Hos 7:6

INTRIGUES
might read, "skilled in *." Dan 8:23f

INTRODUCED
she let him in and * him to her Ju 19:3
But John * the Good News that the Lk 16:16
and they were * to Pharaoh. Act 7:13

INTRODUCTION
"I will send a letter of * for 2Ki 5:5

INTRUSION
The penalty for * is death. Lev 16:1
guards to protect it from *. Mt 27:66

INTUITION
"Who gives * and instinct? Job 38:36

INVADE
*, and they will flee before you; Ex 23:27
subdued and didn't * Israel again 1Sa 7:13
to get an excuse to * us again." 2Ki 5:7
used to * the land each spring. 2Ki 13:20,21
III) to * the land and deport the 1Ch 5:26
You wouldn't let our ancestors * 2Ch 20:10
"They say, 'We will * Judah and Is 7:6
of Assyria will * both Damascus and Is 8:4
the nations—will * her land and cut Eze 31:12
will * Egypt briefly, but will Dan 11:9
He will * various lands on the Dan 11:41
Assyrians when they * our land. Mic 5:6
to come upon the people who * us. Hab 3:16

INVADED
the army of Midian when it * Gen 36:31-39
people of Caphtor * and destroyed Deu 2:23
*, and they made unleavened bread. Jos 5:11,12
Bands of Syrians had * the land 2Ki 5:2
Then King Pul of Assyria * the 2Ki 15:19,20
these princes * the land and struck 1Ch 4:40,41
Meanwhile, the Philistines had * 2Ch 28:17,18
of Assyria * Judah and laid siege 2Ch 32:1
Our enemies have * our land and Ps 44:10
Then frogs * in enormous Ps 105:30
and though Israel is * again and Is 6:13
* Judah and besieged Jerusalem. Hos 1:7f
Moab, who * Gilead around 740 B.C. Hos 10:14f

INVADER
I will send against them an * who Jer 50:44

INVADERS
Later, five hundred of these * 1Ch 4:42
and day against *, their real Ps 55:10
they have become as women. The * Jer 51:30
At least to these * you will be Eze 28:9
to help him when * carried off his Ob 1:11
glad news: "The * have been wiped Nah 1:15

INVADES
is he who * and sacks your city." Ps 137:9f
And when the Assyrian * our land Mic 5:5

INVADING
of Adullam and the * Philistines 2Sa 23:13
however, sinned by * the Temple—but 2Ch 27:2
For Edom was * Judah and 2Ch 28:16
your people Israel, * every home. Ps 79:7
two * kings would be destroyed. Is 7:14f
For your sakes I will send an * Is 43:14
by * armies as in the past. Is 65:21,22
raped and destroyed by the * army. Jer 13:22
and I will let * armies kill you Jer 19:7
flees; the * army marches in. Jer 46:22,23
be killed by the * army, her babies Hos 13:16
my people and * their land. Zep 2:8
* armies from entering Israel. Zec 9:8

INVALID
will automatically become *. Num 30:5

INVASION
at the time of the * and conquest 1Ki 9:20,21
in fact, even after Shishak's *, 2Ch 12:12
"When I send an * of dangerous Eze 14:15
The Assyrian * came about twenty Hos 4:19f

INVASIONS
there undisturbed from all *. Jer 48:11

INVENT
privilege to discover and *. Pro 25:2,3
dreams that they *, for they Jer 29:8

INVENTED
in Jerusalem, * by brilliant men to 2Ch 26:15

INVENTING
of deceit, * everything they say. Jer 23:26
You are twisting my words and * Jer 23:36
of Israel who are * their own Eze 13:2,3

INVENTOR
Jubal, the first musician—the * Gen 4:21
is an engraver besides, and an *! 2Ch 2:14
Does a machine call its * dumb? Is 29:16

INVEST
to * for him while he was gone. Mt 25:14
$2,000 to * while he was gone. Lk 19:13

INVESTIGATE
burn up, he went over to *. Ex 3:3,4
set out at once to *, and reached Jos 9:17
from Jerusalem to * him, and Mk 7:1

INVESTIGATED
have * the matter more thoroughly. Ez 4:21

INVESTIGATION
information. An * was made, the Est 2:23
* to pass this summary on to you, Lk 1:3

INVESTMENT
is the only safe * for eternity! 1Ti 6:19

INVESTMENTS
are put into risky * that turn Ecc 5:13,14

INVINCIBLE
The Lord, strong and mighty, * in Ps 24:8

INVISIBLE
up as though against an * wall!" Jos 3:13,14
He passes by, *; Job 9:11

INVITATION
to accept Reuel's * to live with Ex 2:21
no good is going to come of his *. Pro 23:1
It is better to wait for an * Pro 25:6,7
lunch and Jesus accepted the *. Lk 7:36
For they will return the *. Lk 14:12
accept the * if you want to. 1Co 10:27

INVITATIONS
a great feast and sent out many *. Lk 14:16

INVITE
Moreover, we * you folks to live Gen 34:9,10
"Let's * them to live here among Gen 34:21

(INVITE Con't)
"Did you just leave him there? * Ex 2:20
to help him; * him to live with you Lev 25:35
and remember to * the Levites to Deu 12:12
and orphans. * them to accompany Deu 16:11
why didn't you * the rest of us? 2Sa 19:43
But he didn't * Nathan the 1Ki 1:10
But he didn't * Solomon. 1Ki 1:19
my heroes, and * them to my home. Ps 101:6
And I will * him to be a priest Jer 30:21
live and * them to the Temple. Jer 35:2
to Chaldea to * them to come to Eze 23:16
where you can * your neighbors.' Zec 3:10
corners and * everyone you see.' Mt 22:9
My purpose is to * sinners to Lk 5:32
he said, "don't * friends, Lk 14:12
Instead, * the poor, the Lk 14:13
of the city and to * the beggars, Lk 14:21
don't even * him into your home. 2Jn 1:10

INVITED
So Laban * all the men of the Gen 29:22
the mountain, and * his companions Gen 31:54
These girls also * them to Num 25:2
Were we * to this party just to Ju 14:15
But as no one * them in, they Ju 19:15
even before I * these others!" 1Sa 9:24
and his sons, and * them too. 1Sa 16:5
David * him to dinner and got 2Sa 11:13
Ephraim, Absalom * his father and 2Sa 13:21-24
many sheep and has * all your sons 1Ki 1:19
sheep, and has * your sons to 1Ki 1:25
He also * General Joab and 1Ki 1:25
and Solomon and I weren't *. 1Ki 1:26
Then he * all of his officials to 1Ki 3:15
And when Ben-hadad arrived, he * 1Ki 20:33
A prominent woman of the city * 2Ki 4:8
and those he had * assembled 2Ch 1:5,6
which the emperor * all his Est 1:1
Esther the queen * only me and the Est 5:12
and tomorrow we are * again! Est 5:12
had a birthday, he * his brothers Job 1:4
* to meet with the Lord in Zion. Ps 84:7
lovers, yet I have * you to come to Jer 3:1
who would dare to come unless *. Jer 30:21
before them and * them to have a Jer 35:5
Gedaliah * them to dinner. Jer 41:1
BELSHAZZAR THE KING * a thousand Dan 5:1
Many guests were *, and when the Mt 22:3
"But the guests he had * merely Mt 22:5
I * aren't worthy of the honor. Mt 22:8
I was a stranger and you * me Mt 25:35
That night Levi * his fellow tax Mk 2:15
Another time, when he * a man to Lk 9:59
"If you are * to a wedding feast, Lk 14:8
For none of those I * first will Lk 14:24
"So he * each one who owed money Lk 16:5,6
and his disciples were * too. Jn 2:2
So Peter * them in and lodged Act 10:23
The governor * Barnabas and Paul Act 13:6,7
News that you are * to turn from Act 14:15
But they * him to the forum at Act 17:19
you, too, are * by Jesus Christ Rom 1:6,7
* to come to God in this same way. Rom 1:16
To: The Christians in Corinth, * 1Co 1:2
he is the one who * you into this 1Co 1:9
love and mercy, * you to share the Gal 1:6
both are * to belong to his Eph 3:6
joy to him who * you into his 1Th 2:12
that all who are * may come and Heb 9:15
holy, who * you to be his child. 1Pe 1:15
are those who are * to the wedding Rev 19:9

INVITES
and one of them * you to go with Ex 34:15

INVITING
* them to come and join us. 1Ch 13:2
and Manasseh, * everyone to come to 2Ch 30:1
Dan to Beer-sheba, * everyone. 2Ch 30:5
out her maidens * all to come. Pro 9:3
* them to come and join him there; Mk 3:13
for * those who can't repay you." Lk 14:14
And get into the habit of * Rom 12:13

INVOCATION
Now King Solomon prayed this *: 1Ki 8:12,13

INVOKE
Or, "This man was the first to * Gen 4:26f
when all who * a blessing or take Is 65:16

INVOKED
And I * the curse of God upon Neh 5:13

INVOKING
out demons by * the powers of Mt 12:27

INVOLVED
were sexually * with human women, Gen 6:4
The man * shall bring his guilt Lev 19:21
* in such error and forgiveness. Num 15:26
members of the Assembly, were *. Num 16:2
(The area * stretched all the way Jos 12:1
of us * in this sinful affair. Ez 10:13
the expenses * in this purge." Est 3:9
Only the person * can know his Pro 14:10
Don't get me *!" Is 3:7
The men * were about twelve in Act 19:7
Again I say, don't get * in 2Ti 2:23
Don't get * in arguing over Tit 3:9
Watch out that no one becomes * Heb 12:16

INVOLVING
* violation of sacred affairs; 2Ch 19:11
in this respect, * so many of the 2Ch 35:18
this were a case * some crime, I Act 18:14
of Israel by * them in sexual sin Rev 2:14

INWARD
that covers the * parts, the two Lev 3:3,4,5
Or, "Who has put wisdom in the * Job 38:36f
Literally, "And the * thought and Ps 64:6f
that narrowed * through the walls Eze 40:16
Your eyes light up your * being. Lk 11:34

INWARDLY
but an evil man * curses his luck. Pro 10:6
wrong, and to be * clean, no one Php 1:10

IOB
his sons: Tola, Puvah, *, Shimron. Gen 46:8-14

IOTA
is not an * of truth in him. Jn 8:44

IPHDEIAH
Elam, Anthothijah, *, Penuel. 1Ch 8:22-25

IPHTAH
Ether, Ashan, *, Ashnah, Nezib, Jos 15:37-44

IPHTAHEL
and ended at the Valley of *. Jos 19:14
in the Valley of *, running north Jos 19:27

IR
The sons of * were Shuppim and 1Ch 7:12

IR-SHEMESH
Zorah, Eshta-ol, *, Sha-alabbin, Jos 19:41-46

IRA
chief priests. * the Jairite was 2Sa 20:26
* (son of Ikkesh) from Tekoa; 2Sa 23:24-39
* from Ithra; 2Sa 23:24-39
* (son of Ikkesh) from Tekoa; 1Ch 11:26-47
* from Ithra; 1Ch 11:26-47
*, the son of Ikkesh from Tekoa; 1Ch 27:9

IRAD
of *; Gen 4:18
* was the father Gen 4:18

IRAM
clan of Magdiel,The clan of *. Gen 36:40-43
Mibzar, Chief Magdi-el, Chief *. 1Ch 1:51-54

IRAQ
to *, to Nahor's village. Gen 24:10
Babylon, in *, still lies in utter Is 13:20f
In that day Egypt and * Is 19:23
and * because of their friendship Is 19:25
blessed be *, the land I have Is 19:25
to our ancestor Abraham in * Act 7:2

IRAQI
Egyptians and the * will move Is 19:23

IRI
Ezbon, Uzzi, Uzziel, Jerimoth, *. 1Ch 7:7

IRIJAH
The guard making the arrest was * Jer 37:13
But * wouldn't listen; Jer 37:14

IRNAHASH
Tehinnah was the father of *. 1Ch 4:11,12

IRON
metal workers in bronze and *." Gen 4:22f
instruments of bronze and *. Gen 4:22
as *, and your earth as bronze. Lev 26:19
silver, bronze, *, tin, or lead— Num 31:22
by a piece of *, it must be Num 35:16
giant Rephaim. His * bedstead is Deu 3:11
it is a land where * is as common Deu 8:9
the earth beneath will be as *. Deu 28:23
A yoke of * shall be placed Deu 28:47,48
Of * and bronze, Deu 33:25
of bronze and * will be dedicated Jos 6:19
and the bronze and * utensils were Jos 6:24
of Jezreel have * chariots and are Jos 17:16,17,18
are strong and have * chariots." Jos 17:16,17,18
gold, bronze, *, and clothing. Jos 22:7,8
of the valley, who had * chariots. Ju 1:19
He had nine hundred * chariots, Ju 4:2,3
the nine hundred * chariots, and Ju 4:13
twenty-five-pound * spearhead, and 1Sa 17:4-7
Or, "killed them with saws and * 2Sa 12:31f
made some * horns and declared, 1Ki 22:11
work with saws, * picks, and axes, 1Ch 20:3
They also manufactured * into 1Ch 22:3
and so much * and bronze that I 1Ch 22:14
smiths and bronze and * workers. 1Ch 22:16
silver, bronze, *, wood, and great 1Ch 29:2
and 4,600 tons of *. 1Ch 29:6,7
silversmiths, brass and * workers; 2Ch 2:7
with brass and *, and knows all 2Ch 2:14
made some * horns for the occasion 2Ch 18:10
who made articles of * and brass. 2Ch 24:12
with an * pen in the rock forever. Job 19:23,24
gold, to dig * from the earth and Job 28:2
His ribs are like * bars. Job 40:18
pointed shaft. * is nothing but Job 41:27,28
Rule them with an * rod; Ps 2:9
and gives me strength to draw an * Ps 18:34
his neck in an * collar, until Ps 105:18
brass and cut apart their * bars. Ps 107:16
and leaders with * chains, and Ps 149:8
His anger shuts you out like * Pro 18:19
that fly when * strikes iron. Pro 27:17
that fly when iron strikes *. Pro 27:17
city gates of brass and * bars. Is 45:2
Your necks are as unbending as *; Is 48:4
for gold, your * for silver, your Is 60:17
wood for brass, your stones for *. Is 60:17
* pillar and heavy gates of brass. Jer 1:18
as brass, hard and cruel as *. Jer 6:28
bars of northern * or bronze? Jer 15:12,13
chiseled with an * pen or diamond Jer 17:1
have yokes of * on their necks. Jer 28:13
have put a yoke of * on the necks Jer 28:14
And put an * plate between you Eze 4:3
and the city, like a wall of *. Eze 4:3
for our city is an * shield and Eze 11:3
think this city is an * shield? Eze 11:7
No, this city will not be an * Eze 11:11
I will rule you with an * fist Eze 20:33
the tin, the * and the lead. Eze 22:18,19,20
markets—silver, *, tin and lead. Eze 27:12
wrought *, cassia and calamus, Eze 27:19
its legs of *, its feet part iron Dan 2:33
its feet part * and part clay. Dan 2:33
* and clay, smashing them to bits. Dan 2:34
*, clay, brass, silver, and gold; Dan 2:35
will be strong as *—smashing, Dan 2:40
The feet and toes you saw—part * Dan 2:41,42
as *, and some as weak as clay. Dan 2:41,42
This mixture of * with clay also Dan 2:43
but this will not succeed, for * Dan 2:43
to powder all the * and brass, the Dan 2:45
with a chain of * and brass, Dan 4:15
with a chain of * and brass. Dan 4:23
brass and *, wood and stone. Dan 5:2,3,4
gold, brass, *, wood, and Dan 5:23
with its huge * teeth, and others Dan 7:7
shocking, with its * teeth and Dan 7:19
as grain is threshed with * rods. Amo 1:3
I will give you horns of * and Mic 4:13
towards Jerusalem with an * will. Lk 9:51
and came to the * gate to the Act 12:10
them with a rod of * just as my Rev 2:27
seemed to be of *, and their wings Rev 9:9
and brass and * and marble; Rev 18:12
he ruled them with an * grip; Rev 19:15

IRONICALLY
Literally, and probably *, "Make Lk 16:9f

IRPEEL
Mozah, Rekem, *, Taralah, Zela, Jos 18:21-28

IRRATIONAL
hate life because it is all so *; Ecc 2:17

IRREGULAR
time, or at some * time during the Lev 15:25

IRRELIGIOUS
religious or *, profane or godly. Ecc 9:2,3

IRREPARABLY
misses me has injured himself *. Pro 8:36

IRRESISTIBLE
And no temptation is *. 1Co 10:13

IRRESISTIBLY
drawn there * by the Holy Spirit, Act 20:22

IRREVERENTLY
the name of Jehovah your God *, Ex 20:7

IRREVOCABLE
and blessed him with * blessing?" Gen 27:33
should make a law, * under any Dan 6:7

IRRIGATE
the water to * my plantations. Ecc 2:4,5,6

IRRIGATION
come from, where * is necessary. Deu 11:10
JUST AS WATER is turned into * Pro 21:1
a vine beside an * ditch, with Eze 19:10

IRRITABLE
It is not * or touchy. 1Co 13:5

IRU
Caleb (the son of Jephunneh):*, 1Ch 4:15

ISAAC
and you are to name him * Gen 17:19
But my contract is with *, who Gen 17:21
and Abraham named him * (meaning Gen 21:3
*, she turned upon Abraham and Gen 21:9
do as Sarah says, for * is the Gen 21:12
your only son—yes, * whom you love Gen 22:2
with him his son * and two young Gen 22:3
"Father," * asked, "we have Gen 22:7
and then tied * and laid him on the Gen 22:9
"Then shall I take * there, to Gen 24:5
* marry one of the local girls, Gen 24:37
Meanwhile, *, whose home was in Gen 24:62
Then the servant told * the Gen 24:66
And * brought Rebekah into his Gen 24:67
deeded everything he owned to *; Gen 25:5
off into the east, away from *. Gen 25:6
175, and his sons * and Ishmael Gen 25:9,10
poured out rich blessings upon *. Gen 25:11
upon Isaac. (* had now moved south Gen 25:11
Isaac's children: * was forty Gen 25:20
sister of Laban. * pleaded with Gen 25:21
"Grabber"). * was sixty years old Gen 25:26

(ISAAC Con't)
time, and so * moved to the city of Gen 26:1
So * stayed in Gerar. Gen 26:6
and saw * petting with Rebekah. Gen 26:8
Abimelech called for * and Gen 26:9
I would be murdered," * replied. Gen 26:9
And King Abimelech asked * to Gen 26:16
So * moved to Gerar Valley and Gen 26:17
instead. And * redug the wells of Gen 26:18
Then * built an altar and Gen 26:25
One day * had visitors from Gen 26:26
"Why have you come?" * asked Gen 26:27
So * prepared a great feast for Gen 26:30
* sent them happily home again. Gen 26:31
the Hethite. But * and Rebekah Gen 26:35
*: "My son?" Gen 27:1
*: "I am an old man now, and Gen 27:2,3,4
*: "Yes? Gen 27:18
*: "How were you able to find it Gen 27:20
*: "Come over here. Gen 27:21
*: (to himself) "The voice is Gen 27:22
(The ruse convinces * and he Gen 27:23
*: "Are you really Esau?" Gen 27:24
*: "Then bring me the venison, Gen 27:25
(Jacob takes it over to him and * Gen 27:25
*: "Come here and kiss me, my Gen 27:26
him on the cheek. * sniffs his Gen 27:26
*: "The smell of my son is the Gen 27:27,28,29
(As soon as * has blessed Jacob, Gen 27:30
*: "Who is it?" Gen 27:32
(* begins to tremble noticeably. Gen 27:33
*: "Then who is it who was just Gen 27:33
*: "Your brother was here and Gen 27:35
*: "I have made him your master, Gen 27:37
(* says nothing Gen 27:38
*: "Yours will be no life of Gen 27:39,40
Then Rebekah said to *, "I'm Gen 27:46
SO * CALLED for Jacob and blessed Gen 28:1
So * sent Jacob away, and he went Gen 28:5
of Abraham, and of your father *. Gen 28:13
father * in the land of Canaan. Gen 31:17-20
glorious God of *, my father—you Gen 31:42
*, to respect the boundary line. Gen 31:53
and of my father *—O Jehovah who Gen 32:9
the land I gave to Abraham and *. Gen 35:12
So Jacob came at last to * his Gen 35:27
too had lived. * died soon Gen 35:28,29
there to the God of his father *. Gen 46:1
Abraham and *, the God who has Gen 48:15
names of my fathers Abraham and *; Gen 48:16
there they buried * and Rebekah Gen 49:31
of Abraham, * and Jacob." Gen 50:24
to Abraham, *, and Jacob [to bring Ex 2:24
God of Abraham, *, and Jacob." Ex 3:6
*, and Jacob, has sent me to you.' Ex 3:15
ancestors Abraham, *, and Jacob, Ex 4:5
to Abraham, *, and Jacob—though I Ex 6:2,3
to give to Abraham, *, and Jacob. Ex 6:8,9
Abraham, *, and Israel. Ex 32:13
I promised Abraham, *, and Jacob; Ex 33:1
to Abraham, *, and Jacob, and I Lev 26:42
promised Abraham, *, and Jacob, Num 32:10,11
ancestors Abraham, *, and Jacob, Deu 1:8
Abraham, *, and Jacob, and when Deu 6:10,11,12
*, and Jacob, that he will do it. Deu 9:5
servants Abraham, *, and Jacob. Deu 9:27
ancestors, Abraham, *, and Jacob. Deu 29:13
Abraham, *, and Jacob." Deu 30:20
"I promised Abraham, *, and Deu 34:4
descendants through * his son. Jos 24:3
God of Abraham, *, and Israel, 1Ki 18:36
with Abraham, *, and Jacob. 2Ki 13:23
* and 1Ch 1:28-31
Abraham's son * had two sons, 1Ch 1:34
And his oath to *, 1Ch 16:16
fathers: Abraham, *, and Israel! 1Ch 29:18
God of Abraham, *, and Israel," 2Ch 30:6
and *, and confirmed with Jacob. Ps 105:8,9
of Abraham, * and Jacob. Jer 33:25,26
Abraham was the father of *; Mt 1:2
Abraham was the father of Isaac; * Mt 1:2
Heaven with Abraham, *, and Jacob. Mt 8:11
the God of Abraham, *, and Jacob'? Mt 22:32
if Abraham, *, and Jacob, long Mt 22:32f
of *, and I am the God of Jacob.' Mk 12:26
Jacob's father was *; Lk 3:23-38
and see Abraham, *, Jacob, and all Lk 13:28
God of *, and the God of Jacob.' Lk 20:37,38
For it is the God of Abraham, *, Act 3:13
And so *, Abraham's son, was Act 7:8
eight days old. * became the father Act 7:8
Abraham, * and Jacob.' Act 7:32
to Abraham's son * and Isaac's Rom 9:7
when this son, *, was grown up and Rom 9:10-13
promises to Abraham, *, and Jacob. Rom 11:28
that God promised, just as * was. Gal 4:28
laws, just as * the child of Gal 4:29
a son, *, just as he had promised. Heb 6:15
visitor, as did * and Jacob, to Heb 11:9
offered up his son *, and was ready Heb 11:17
yes, to slay even *, through Heb 11:18
He believed that if * died God Heb 11:19
was concerned, * was doomed to Heb 11:19
It was by faith that * knew God Heb 11:20
his son * to die on the altar? Jas 2:21

ISAAC'S
offering upon * shoulders, while he Gen 22:6
one you have appointed as * wife. Gen 24:14
This is the story of * children: Gen 25:19
to stay at home. * favorite was Gen 25:28
That year * crops were Gen 26:12
argued over it with * herdsmen. Gen 26:20
* men then dug another well, but Gen 26:21
That very same day * servants Gen 26:32
ONE DAY, IN * old age when he was Gen 27:1
Isaac his son. * children, whom I Jos 24:4
Jacob's father was Isaac;* father Lk 3:23-38
son Isaac and * descendants, though Rom 9:7

ISAIAH
and to go to * (son of Amoz), the 2Ki 19:2
* replied, "The Lord says, 'Tell 2Ki 19:5,6
Then * sent this message to 2Ki 19:20
* the prophet went to visit him. 2Ki 20:1
and prepare to die," * told him. 2Ki 20:1
So before * had left the 2Ki 20:4
* then instructed Hezekiah to 2Ki 20:7
had said to *, "Do a miracle to 2Ki 20:8
give you a proof," * told him. 2Ki 20:9
So * asked the Lord to do this, 2Ki 20:11
Then * went to King Hezekiah and 2Ki 20:14
seen in your palace?" * asked. 2Ki 20:15
Then * said to Hezekiah, "Listen 2Ki 20:16
by the prophet * (son of Amoz). 2Ch 26:22
Then King Hezekiah and * the 2Ch 32:20
in The Book of * (the prophet, the 2Ch 32:32
give you thanks?" * 57:1,2 may Ps 6:5f
that came to *, son of Amoz, in the Is 1:1
THIS IS ANOTHER message to * from Is 2:1
Then the Lord said to *, "Go out Is 7:3
Then * said, O House of Is 7:13
and her newborn son (* 8:1-4). Is 7:14f
for his people: * means "Jehovah Is 8:18
See 2 Kings 19:35 and * 37:36. Is 10:17f
THIS IS THE vision God showed * Is 13:1
it, the Lord told *, the son of Is 20:2
And * did as he was told. Is 20:2
Then the Lord said, My servant *, Is 20:3
"Who does * think he is," the Is 28:9
* the prophet, son of Amoz. Is 37:2
Oh, *, pray for us who are left!" Is 37:4
they took the king's message to *. Is 37:5
Then * replied, "Tell King Is 37:6
Then *, the son of Amoz, sent Is 37:21
deathly sick and * the prophet Is 38:1
Lord sent another message to *: Is 38:4
those who trust in God (* 57:1,2). Is 38:18f
(For * had told Hezekiah's Is 38:21
Then * the prophet came to the Is 39:3
asked *. Is 39:4
Then * said to him, "Listen to Is 39:5
the Great of Persia. See * 44:28. Is 41:2f
in the days of Hezekiah (* 36–37). Jer 21:1f
See also, * 44:28; Jer 51:20f
from Babylon (* 38–39), also during Eze 23:16f
of God's angel (* 36–37). Hos 1:7f
See * 19:18. Zep 3:9f
* the prophet had told about Mt 3:3
Implied. * 40:3. Mt 3:3f
* 9:1, 2. Mt 4:15,16f
This fulfilled the prophecy of * Mt 8:17
* 53:4. Mt 8:17f
This fulfilled the prophecy of * Mt 12:17
* 42:1–4. Mt 12:21f
"This fulfills the prophecy of * Mt 13:14
Well did * prophesy of you, Mt 15:7
* 29:13. Mt 15:9f
by the prophet *, God announced Mk 1:2
out in the barren wilderness," * Mk 1:3
book of *, appears in Malachi 3:1. Mk 1:3f
of hypocrites! * the prophet Mk 7:6,7
How right * was! Mk 7:6,7
The quotation is from * 53:12. Mk 15:28f
In the words of * the prophet, Lk 3:4
The book of * the prophet was Lk 4:17
shouting as * prophesied, 'Get Jn 1:23
This is exactly what * the Jn 12:38
the Lord been revealed?" * 53:1. Jn 12:38f
for as * also said: "God Jn 12:39
or paraphrase, of * 6:10. Jn 12:40f
to heal them." * was referring to Jn 12:41
from the book of the prophet *. Act 8:28
The eunuch asked Philip, "Was * Act 8:34
he said through * the prophet, Act 28:25
* 6:9, 10. Act 28:27f
* the prophet cried out Rom 9:27
* 10:22; 28:22. Rom 9:28f
And * says in another place that Rom 9:29
* 1:9. Rom 9:29f
* 28:16. Rom 9:33f
* 52:7. Rom 10:15f
welcomed it, for * the prophet Rom 10:16
* 53:1. Rom 10:16f
And later on * said boldly that Rom 10:20
* 65:1. Rom 10:20f
And the prophet * said, "There Rom 15:12
Scriptures where * says that those Rom 15:21
That is what * meant when he Gal 4:27
But see * 11:2, where various Rev 1:4f

ISAIAH'S
use here refers to * young wife and Is 7:14f
This fulfilled * prophecy: Mt 4:14

ISCAH
and she had a brother named *. Gen 11:29

ISCARIOT
Judas * (the one who betrayed Mt 10:2,3,4
Then Judas *, one of the twelve Mt 26:14
Judas * (who later betrayed him). Mk 3:16-19
Then Judas *, one of his Mk 14:10
Judas * (who later betrayed him). Lk 6:14,15,16
Then Satan entered into Judas *, Lk 22:3
son of Simon *, one of the Twelve, Jn 6:71
But Judas *, one of his Jn 12:4
suggested to Judas *, Simon's son, Jn 13:1
gave it to Judas, son of Simon *. Jn 13:26
Judas (not Judas *, but his other Jn 14:22

ISH-BOSHETH
to crown Saul's son * as king. 2Sa 2:8
* was forty years old at the time. 2Sa 2:10,11
But when * accused Abner of this, 2Sa 3:7
* made no reply, for he was 2Sa 3:11
this message to *: "Give me back 2Sa 3:14
So * took her away from her 2Sa 3:15
WHEN KING * heard about Abner's 2Sa 4:1
"Here is the head of *, the son 2Sa 4:8

ISH-BOSHETH'S
Abner led some of * troops to 2Sa 2:12
captains of King * raiding bands. 2Sa 4:2,3
arrived at King * home one noon as 2Sa 4:5
And they took * head and buried 2Sa 4:12

ISHBAH
Shammai, and *—an ancestor of 1Ch 4:17

ISHBAK
Jokshan, Medan,Midian, *, Shuah. Gen 25:1
Midian, *, and Shuah. 1Ch 1:32

ISHBI-BENOB
and exhausted. *, a giant whose 2Sa 21:16

ISHHOD
bore *, Abiezer, and Mahlah. 1Ch 7:18

ISHI
*; Ishi's son was 1Ch 2:31
The sons of *:Zoheth, Ben-zoheth. 1Ch 4:20
and Uzziel—all sons of *. 1Ch 4:42
Epher, *, Eliel, Azri-el, 1Ch 5:24

ISHI'S
Ishi; * son was 1Ch 2:31

ISHMA
of Etam:Jezreel, *, 1Ch 4:3-4

ISHMAEL
are to name him * ('God hears'), Gen 16:9-12
a son, and Abram named him *. Gen 16:15
said to God, "Yes, do bless *!" Gen 17:18
As for *, all right, I will Gen 17:20
day, Abraham took * his son and Gen 17:23
at that time, and * was thirteen. Gen 17:24-27
But when Sarah noticed *—the son Gen 21:9
for after all, * too was his son. Gen 21:11
his sons Isaac and * buried him in Gen 25:9,10
the descendants of *, who was the Gen 25:12-15
bore their names. * finally died Gen 25:17
These descendants of * were Gen 25:18
and daughter of *, Abraham's son. Gen 28:9
Literally, "the daughter of *." Gen 36:2,3f
—she was a daughter of *—the Gen 36:2,3
These included *, the son of 2Ki 25:23
But seven months later, *, who 2Ki 25:25
sons were Isaac and *. 1Ch 1:28-31
The sons of *: 1Ch 1:28-31
land of *, had a son named Amasa. 1Ch 2:17
Azrikam, Bocheru, *, She-ariah, 1Ch 8:38
Azrikam, Bocheru, *, 1Ch 9:44
Obil, from the territory of *, 1Ch 27:30
and Zebadiah (son of *), a ruler 2Ch 19:11
(son of Jeroham), * (son of 2Ch 23:1
Eli-o-enai, Ma-aseiah, *, Ez 10:22
leaders who came: * (son of Jer 40:8
had sent * (son of Nethaniah) to Jer 40:13,14
Johanan volunteered to kill * Jer 40:15
for you are lying about *." Jer 40:16
BUT IN OCTOBER, * (son of Jer 41:1
While they were eating, * and Jer 41:2
and incense. * went out from the Jer 41:6
inside the city, * and his men Jer 41:7
The ten had talked * into Jer 41:8
The cistern where * dumped the Jer 41:9
* made captives of the king's Jer 41:10
leaders heard what * had done, Jer 41:11
The people with * shouted for Jer 41:13,14
Meanwhile * escaped with eight of Jer 41:15
reached them that * had killed Jer 41:18
by * the slave-wife's son. Gal 4:29

ISHMAEL'S
So Esau went to his Uncle * Gen 28:9

ISHMAELITE
distance, probably * traders who Gen 37:25

(ISHMAELITE Con't)
a captive of the * traders, he was Gen 39:1
his father was Ithra, an *, and 2Sa 17:25

ISHMAELITES
"Here come some *. Gen 37:26,27
being *, all wore golden earrings. Ju 8:23,24
God— these * and Edomites and Ps 83:6

ISHMAIAH
Jehu from Anathoth; * from Gibeon 1Ch 12:3-7
Over Zebulun, * (son of Obadiah); 1Ch 27:16-22

ISHMERAI
Hizki, Heber, *, Izliah, Jobab. 1Ch 8:17,18

ISHPAH
Zebadiah, Arad, Eder, Michael, *, 1Ch 8:15,16

ISHPAN
*, Eber, Eliel, Abdon, Zichri, 1Ch 8:22-25

ISHTAR
A name by which *, the Jer 7:18f

ISHVAH
Asher and his sons: Imnah, *, Gen 46:16,17
Imnah, *, Ishvi, 1Ch 7:30

ISHVI
and his sons: Imnah, Ishvah, *, Gen 46:16,17
named after their ancestor *. Num 26:44-47
Saul had three sons, Jonathan, *, 1Sa 14:49
Imnah, Ishvah, *, 1Ch 7:30

ISHVITES
The *, named after their ancestor Num 26:44-47

ISLAND
Send to the west to the * of Jer 2:10,11
a bare rock! Her * shall become Eze 26:5
I will make your * a bare rock, Eze 26:14
happened to the * settlement later Eze 26:14f
dirge: 'O mighty * city, with your Eze 26:17
* warehouse is filled to the brim! Eze 27:25
* home in the midst of the seas. Eze 28:2,3
your * in the heart of the seas. Eze 28:8
of Levi, from the * of Cyprus). Act 4:36
across the entire * until finally Act 13:6,7
We sighted the * of Cyprus, Act 21:3
between the * and the mainland, Act 27:4
behind a small * named Clauda, Act 27:16
we will be shipwrecked on an *." Act 27:26
that we were on the * of Malta. Act 28:1
The people of the * were very Act 28:1
The people of the * saw it Act 28:4
to Publius, the governor of the *. Act 28:7
in the * came and were cured. Act 28:9
a ship that had wintered at the *. Act 28:11
I left you there on the * of Tit 1:5
I was on the * of Patmos, exiled Rev 1:9
and every mountain and * shook Rev 6:14

ISLANDS
but even on the * of the sea. Est 10:1
Tarshish and the *—and those from Ps 72:10
Tell the farthest * to be glad. Ps 97:1
He picks up the * as though they Is 40:15
How the * tremble at your fall! Eze 26:18
of his wrath. And * vanished, and Rev 16:20

ISMACHIAH
Eliel, *, Mahath, Benaiah. 2Ch 31:12,13

ISOLATED
then * for seven more days. Lev 13:54

ISOLATION
death and lived in *, cut off from 2Ch 26:21

ISRAEL
"It is *—one who has power with Gen 32:28
(That is why the people of * Gen 32:32
"The Altar to the God of *." Gen 33:20
* ('One who prevails with God'). Gen 35:10
Then * journeyed on and camped Gen 35:21
and someone told * about it. Gen 35:22
(before * had her first king): Gen 36:31-39
Now as it happened, * loved Gen 37:3
A few days later * called for Gen 37:13,14
Then * tore his garments and put Gen 37:34
had another brother?" * moaned. Gen 43:6
So their father * finally said to Gen 43:11
SO * SET out with all his Gen 46:1
Canaan, before * went to Egypt). Gen 46:8-14
Then * said to Joseph, "Now let Gen 46:30
So * lived in the land of Goshen Gen 47:27
soon the people of * began to Gen 47:27
Then * looked over at the two Gen 48:8
And * said, "Bring them over to Gen 48:9
* was half blind with age, so Gen 48:10
And * said to Joseph, "I never Gen 48:11
at his right. But * crossed his Gen 48:14
the people of * bless each other by Gen 48:20
Then * said to Joseph, "I am Gen 48:21
listen to * your father. Gen 49:2
their descendants throughout *. Gen 49:7
people like any other tribe in *. Gen 49:16
the Shepherd, the Rock of *. Gen 49:24
the blessings that * their father Gen 49:28
So his sons did as * commanded Gen 50:12,13
So the people of * continued to Ex 1:20
Yes, the wail of the people of * Ex 3:9
to the people of * and tell them Ex 3:13
all the elders of *," God Ex 3:16
of * will accept your message. Ex 3:18
'Jehovah says, "* is my eldest Ex 4:22
people of * to a council meeting. Ex 4:29
from Jehovah, the God of *. Ex 5:1
listen to him, and let * go? Ex 5:2
Jehovah and I will not let * go." Ex 5:2
over the people of *: "Don't give Ex 5:6
of the people of *, in slavery now Ex 6:5
the descendants of * that I will Ex 6:6
he must let the people of * go." Ex 6:11
to the people of * and to Pharaoh, Ex 6:13
clans of the various tribes of *: Ex 6:14
all the people of * out of the land Ex 6:26
of * be allowed to leave Egypt. Ex 7:2
where the people of * lived. Ex 9:26
people of * had light as usual. Ex 10:23
Tell all the men and women of * Ex 11:2
to the people of *, and Moses was a Ex 11:3
of the people of *, nor shall any Ex 11:7
of *) each family shall get a lamb Ex 12:3,4
shall be excommunicated from *. Ex 12:15
from the congregation of *. Ex 12:19
all the elders of * and said to Ex 12:21
*, though he killed the Egyptians; Ex 12:27
So the people of * did as Moses Ex 12:28
upon the people of *, to get them Ex 12:33
And the people of * did as Moses Ex 12:35
That night the people of * left Ex 12:37
All the congregation of * shall Ex 12:47
to those born in * and to Ex 12:49
So the people of * followed all Ex 12:50
out the people of * from the land Ex 12:51
of *, and every firstborn male Ex 13:1
made the sons of * vow before God Ex 13:19
He pursued the people of *, for Ex 14:8
the people of * as they were camped Ex 14:9
the people of * saw them far in the Ex 14:10
all the people of * shall walk Ex 14:16
the people of *, moved the cloud Ex 14:19
the people of * and the Egyptians. Ex 14:20
but light to the people of *! Ex 14:20
So the people of * walked Ex 14:22
that chased after * through the Ex 14:28
The people of * had walked Ex 14:29
Thus Jehovah saved * that day Ex 14:30
and the people of * saw the Ex 14:30
When the people of * saw the Ex 14:31
THEN MOSES AND the people of * Ex 15:1
While the people of * walked Ex 15:19
Then Moses led the people of * on Ex 15:22
all the people of * and told them, Ex 16:6
When the people of * saw it they Ex 16:15
So the people of * went out and Ex 16:17
So the people of * ate the manna Ex 16:35
the people of * left the Sihn Ex 17:1
the elders of * with you and lead Ex 17:5,6
that the people of * argued against Ex 17:7
The people of * at Rephidim. Ex 17:8
rod in his hands, * was winning; Ex 17:11
order to deliver *, and all the Ex 18:8
Lord had done for *, and about his Ex 18:9
from Pharaoh, and has rescued *. Ex 18:10
and the leaders of * came to meet Ex 18:12
men from all over * and made them Ex 18:25
instructions to the people of *. Ex 19:2,3
his spokesman to the people of *. Ex 20:22
year, every man in * shall appear Ex 23:17
and seventy of the elders of *. Ex 24:1
there were twelve tribes of *. Ex 24:4
of * went up into the mountain. Ex 24:9
And they saw the God of *; Ex 24:10
the people of * that everyone who Ex 25:1
For I want the people of * to Ex 25:8
commandments for the people of *. Ex 25:22
"Instruct the people of * to Ex 27:20
rule for the people of *. Ex 27:21
them the names of the tribes of *. Ex 28:9
for the people of *: Aaron will Ex 28:12
of the tribes of * and the name of Ex 28:21
of the tribes of * on the Ex 28:29
the offerings of the people of *. Ex 28:37,38
The people of * must always Ex 29:28
with the people of * there, and the Ex 29:43
the people of * and be their God, Ex 29:45
of the people of *, each man who is Ex 30:11,12
you, the people of *, to the Lord's Ex 30:16
And say to the people of *, Ex 30:31
the people of * to rest on my Ex 31:12,13
obligation for the people of *. Ex 31:16
between me and the people of *. Ex 31:17
The people exclaimed, "O *, this Ex 32:4
*, that brought you out of Egypt.' Ex 32:8
servants—to Abraham, Isaac, and *. Ex 32:13
the God of * says, 'Get your swords Ex 32:27
all the people of * shall see the Ex 34:10
of * shall appear before the Lord. Ex 34:23
my covenant with you and with *." Ex 34:27
of * were afraid to come near him. Ex 34:30
So the people of *—every man and Ex 35:29
of the tribes of *, just as Ex 39:6,7
concerning the people of *; Ex 39:6,7
memorial for the children of *." Ex 39:6,7f
names of the twelve tribes of *. Ex 39:1
So the people of * followed all Ex 39:4
* journeyed onward, following it. Ex 40:3
all the people of * could see it. Ex 40:3
to the people of *: "When you Lev 1:2,
"Tell the people of * that these Lev 4:
"If the entire nation of * sins Lev 4:1
the people of * never to eat fat, Lev 7:2
the people of * that anyone Lev 7:2
people of * to the sons of Aaron. Lev 7:34
of * give these portions to them; Lev 7:36
to the people of * so that they Lev 7:38
and summon all * to a meeting Lev 8:1
and the elders of *, and told Lev 9:1
"And tell the people of *," Lev 9:3
come upon all the people of *. Lev 10:6
But the rest of the people of * Lev 10:6
sacrifices of the people of *. Lev 10:14
"Tell the people of * that the Lev 11:2,3
instructions to the people of *: Lev 12:1
of * these further instructions: Lev 15:1
the people of * from their Lev 15:31
The people of * shall then bring Lev 16:5
of the people of *, and for the Lev 16:16
and for all the people of *. Lev 16:17
of *, and making it holy. Lev 16:19
all the sins of the people of *. Lev 16:21
living among the people of *; Lev 16:29,30
for the people of * once each year, Lev 16:34
and for all the people of *: Lev 17:1
stop the people of * from Lev 17:5
to the people of *, that neither Lev 17:12
told the people of * never to eat Lev 17:14
Moses to tell the people of *, Lev 18:1
in the nation of * and to Lev 18:26
tell the people of *, "You must be Lev 19:1
instructions for the people of *: Lev 20:1
be cut off from the people of *. Lev 20:17
sons and to all the people of *. Lev 21:24
by the people of * must not be Lev 22:15
all the people of * that if an Lev 22:17,18
to the people of * that they are to Lev 23:1
* will assemble and worship me. Lev 23:1
This is a law of * from Lev 23:30,31
the people of *, generation after Lev 23:43
of the Lord to the people of *. Lev 23:44
the people of * to bring you pure Lev 24:1
covenant with the people of *. Lev 24:5-8
a fight with one of the men of *. Lev 24:10
And tell the people of * that Lev 24:15,16
instructions for the people of *: Lev 25:1
of *, shall not be treated so. Lev 25:46
For the people of * are my Lev 25:55
*, through Moses, on Mount Sinai. Lev 26:46
the people of * that when a person Lev 27:1
the people of * on Mount Sinai. Lev 27:34
at the camp of * on the Sinai Num 1:1
all the men of * who were twenty Num 1:17,18,19
Each tribe of * shall have a Num 1:52
the people of * and God's wrath—to Num 1:53
up the rear whenever * traveled. Num 2:3-31
In summary, the armies of * Num 2:32,33
So the people of * set up their Num 2:34
on behalf of all the people of *. Num 3:7,8,9
of all the people of *. Num 3:7,8,9
oldest sons of the people of *. Num 3:11,12
in * of both men and animals! Num 3:13
on behalf of the people of *. Num 3:38
the eldest sons in * who are a Num 3:40
for the eldest sons of *; Num 3:41
of the people of *, as the Lord had Num 3:42
eldest sons of the people of *; Num 3:45
cattle of the people of *; Num 3:45
273 eldest sons of * who were in Num 3:49
and the leaders of * found that Num 4:46,47,48
the people of * that they must Num 5:1
the people of * that when anyone, Num 5:5,6
When the people of * bring a Num 5:9,10
the people of * that if a man's Num 5:11,12
for the people of *: "When either Num 6:1
to the people of *: 'May the Lord Num 6:22,23
my name upon the people of *." Num 6:27f
upon the people of *; Num 6:27
Then the leaders of *—the chiefs Num 7:2
the chiefs of the tribes of *. Num 7:84,85,86
from the other people of *. Num 8:5,6
gift from the entire nation of *. Num 8:11
*, and the Levites shall be mine. Num 8:14
all the people of *, and I have Num 8:16
* are mine, both men and animals; Num 8:17
place of all the eldest sons of *. Num 8:18
of the people of * in the Num 8:19
all the people of * dedicated the Num 8:20
"The people of * must celebrate Num 9:2,3
"If any of the people of *, now Num 9:10
from the people of * for refusing Num 9:13
the people of * moved on to Num 9:17
how long the people of * stayed; Num 9:22
the tribes of * shall come to you. Num 10:4
given wonderful promises to *!" Num 10:29
O Lord, to the millions of *." Num 10:36

(ISRAEL Con't)
of the people of * and they wept, Num 11:4,5
me seventy of the leaders of *; Num 11:16
to the camp with the elders of *. Num 11:30
Canaan—the land I am giving to *; Num 13:2
all the people of * in the Num 13:26
the ground before the people of *; Num 14:5
that you are with * and that you Num 14:14
But now, since the people of * Num 14:25
to the people of *: "When your Num 15:1
the people of * that when they Num 15:17,18
of * and they shall be forgiven; Num 15:25
One day while the people of * Num 15:32
the people of * to make tassels for Num 15:37,38
everyone in * has been chosen of Num 16:3
that the God of * has chosen you Num 16:8,9
all the people of * to be near to Num 16:8,9
All of the people of * fled at Num 16:34
a reminder to the people of *." Num 16:38
to the people of * that no Num 16:40
the people of * that each of their Num 17:1
But the people of * only grumbled Num 17:12,13
of * for violating this law. Num 18:5
of the people of *, and the Num 18:14,15
by the people of * to the Lord; Num 18:19
tithes from the entire land of *. Num 18:21
own no property in *, for the Num 18:23
of the people of * as though they Num 18:32
"Tell the people of * to bring Num 19:1
for the people of * as a source of Num 19:9
of the people of * and any Num 19:10
shall be excommunicated from *. Num 19:13
THE PEOPLE OF * arrived in the Num 20:1
of the people of *, you shall not Num 20:12
the people of * fought against Num 20:13
the people of * were descended from Num 20:14f
whose name was later changed to *. Num 20:14f
*," he declared. Num 20:14
Because Edom refused to allow * Num 20:21,22
their country, * turned back and Num 20:21,22
the people of *, for the two of you Num 20:24
army and attacked *, taking some of Num 21:1
Then the people of * vowed to Num 21:2
Then the people of * returned to Num 21:4
* journeyed next to Oboth and Num 21:10
Then * traveled to Beer (meaning Num 21:16
in the distance. * now sent Num 21:21
army and attacked * in the Num 21:23
at Jahaz. But * slaughtered them Num 21:24
So * captured all the cities of Num 21:25,26
While * was there in the Amorite Num 21:31,32
And sure enough, * was Num 21:35
remained; and * occupied the land. Num 21:35
THE PEOPLE OF * now traveled to Num 22:1
people of * spread out before him. Num 22:41
Let your anger rise on *.' Num 23:7-10
only a portion of the nation of *. Num 23:13
He will not trouble *! Num 23:18-24
* has the strength of a wild ox. Num 23:18-24
For now it shall be said of *, Num 23:18-24
planned to bless *, so he didn't Num 24:1
toward the camp of * which Num 24:1
Oh, the joys awaiting *, Num 24:3-9
* has the strength of a wild ox, Num 24:3-9
* sleeps as a lion or a lioness— Num 24:3-9
is everyone who blesses you, O *, Num 24:3-9
I see in the future of *, Num 24:15-19
This ruler of * Num 24:15-19
* shall possess all Edom and Seir. Num 24:15-19
WHILE * WAS camped at Acacia, Num 25:1
Before long all * was joining Num 25:3
all the tribal leaders of *. Num 25:4
all * as I had intended. Num 25:10,11
for the people of * by what he Num 25:12,13
of all the men of * who are twenty Num 26:2
instructions to the leaders of *. Num 26:3,4
men throughout * was 601,730. Num 26:51
of the people of *, for the Levites Num 26:62
I have given to the people of *. Num 27:12
When the people of * rebelled, Num 27:14
all the people of * will obey him. Num 27:20
to the people of *: "The offerings Num 28:1
instructions to the people of *. Num 29:40
many thousands of *, 12,000 armed Num 31:4,5
of the people of * who were camped Num 31:12
the people of * to worship idols on Num 31:16
is to be given to the people of *. Num 31:27
that are given to the people of *. Num 31:30
to the people of *—Moses had Num 31:42-46
as a memorial of the people of *. Num 31:54
WHEN * ARRIVED in the land of Num 32:1
Lord has used * to destroy the Num 32:3,4
* will be even fiercer this time. Num 32:14
of the people of *, until we have Num 32:17
* have received their inheritance. Num 32:18
to the rest of the people of *. Num 32:22
tribal leaders of *, "If all the Num 32:28
of the nation of * from the time Num 33:1
the people of * had left Egypt. Num 33:38,39
of * were approaching his land. Num 33:40
tell the people of *, "When you Num 33:50,51
tell the people of *, "When they Num 34:1
WHILE * WAS camped beside the Num 35:1
"Instruct the people of * to Num 35:2
* from generation to generation. Num 35:29
and the leaders of * with a Num 36:1
the people of *," they reminded Num 36:1
the tribes of * who are heiresses Num 36:8
to the people of * through Moses, Num 36:13
to the people of * when they were Deu 1:1
forty years after the people of * Deu 1:1
Moses' address to *, stating all Deu 1:1
of Esau, just as * would displace Deu 2:12
been assigned to * by the Lord. Deu 2:12
" 'Today * shall cross the Deu 2:18
hands of *, as has now been done. Deu 2:30
it, it shall belong to * forever.' Deu 2:31
"AND NOW, O *, listen carefully Deu 4:1
is as wise and prudent as *!' Deu 4:6
the people of * to set apart three Deu 4:41
to the people of * when they left Deu 4:44,45,46
and the Israelis. * conquered his Deu 4:47
of the Jordan. * also conquered Deu 4:48
to the people of * and said, Deu 5:1
Therefore, O *, listen closely Deu 6:3
"O *, listen: Jehovah is our Deu 6:4
"O *, LISTEN! Deu 9:1
"The people of * then journeyed Deu 10:6
"And now, *, what does the Lord Deu 10:12,13
belongings, as all * watched! Deu 11:6
Then all * will hear about his Deu 13:11
of the cities of * that some Deu 13:12,13,14
"Every man in * shall appear Deu 16:16
sinners must be purged from *. Deu 17:12
in the land of *, has the right to Deu 18:6,7
Purge all murderers from *! Deu 19:13
'Listen to me, all you men of *! Deu 20:3
O Lord, forgive your people * Deu 21:8
the young men of * will hear about Deu 21:21
has falsely accused a virgin of *. Deu 22:19
She has defiled * by flagrant Deu 22:21
way evil will be cleansed from *. Deu 22:22
in *, either men or women; Deu 23:17,18
THEN MOSES AND the elders of * Deu 27:1
* as follows: "O Israel, listen! Deu 27:9
Israel as follows: "O *, listen! Deu 27:9
them shall shout to all *, Deu 27:14
the people of * at Mount Horeb. Deu 29:1
He summoned all * before him and Deu 29:2,3
future generations of * as well. Deu 29:14,15
family or tribe of *—begins to turn Deu 29:18
all the tribes of *, to pour out Deu 29:21
and * shall come alive again! Deu 30:6
to the people of *, he told them, Deu 31:1
as all * watched, "Be strong! Deu 31:7
of the laws to the elders of *. Deu 31:9
when all * would assemble before Deu 31:10,11
people of * as my warning to them. Deu 31:19
the people of * into the land the Deu 31:23
solemn warning to the people of *. Deu 31:26
song to the whole assembly of *: Deu 31:30
But * has become corrupt, Deu 32:5
But he appointed none for *; Deu 32:9
For * was God's own personal Deu 32:9
But * Deu 32:15
* began to follow foreign gods, Deu 32:16
"* is destroyed by our own might; Deu 32:27
* is a stupid nation; Deu 32:28
But * Deu 32:34
I am giving to the people of *. Deu 32:49
the people of * at the springs of Deu 32:51
of *, but you will not enter it." Deu 32:52
the people of * before his death: Deu 33:1
And unite him with *; Deu 33:7
shall teach God's laws to * Deu 33:10
out God's penalties for *." Deu 33:21
So * dwells safely, Deu 33:28
What blessings are yours, O *! Deu 33:29
The people of * mourned for him Deu 34:8
so the people of * obeyed him, Deu 34:9
the people of * in the wilderness. Deu 34:11,12
dead, [you are the new leader of * Jos 1:2
of the land of *— all the way from Jos 1:3
to the leaders of * to tell the Jos 1:10,11
if the word * is even mentioned. Jos 2:9
all the people of * left Acacia, Jos 3:1
honor, so that all * will know that Jos 3:7
of * of this amazing miracle." Jos 4:7
all the people of *, and they Jos 4:14
the nation of * crossed the Jordan Jos 4:22
so the people of * could cross, Jos 5:1
the entire male population of *. Jos 5:2,3
that although when * left Egypt all Jos 5:4,5
For the nation of * had traveled Jos 5:6
he had promised to *—a land that Jos 5:6
fall upon the entire nation of *. Jos 6:18
and the people of * poured into the Jos 6:20
to live outside the camp of *. Jos 6:23
nation of * because of this. Jos 7:1
Joshua and the elders of * tore Jos 7:6
that * has fled from her enemies! Jos 7:8
up off your face! * has sinned and Jos 7:10,11
That is why the people of * are Jos 7:12
Lord your God of * says that Jos 7:13
brought calamity upon all of *.' Jos 7:15
the tribes of * before the Lord, Jos 7:16
God of * and make your confession. Jos 7:19
against the Lord, the God of *. Jos 7:20
And the men of * stoned them to Jos 7:25
by the elders of *, and stopped at Jos 8:10
When the army of * had finished Jos 8:24
of * kept these for themselves. Jos 8:27
to the Lord God of * at Mount Ebal, Jos 8:30
And as the people of * watched, Jos 8:32
Then all the people of * Jos 8:33
at the camp of * at Gilgal, they Jos 9:6
and the men of *, "We have come Jos 9:6
go to the people of * and declare Jos 9:11
And the leaders of * ratified the Jos 9:14,15
of * had made before the Lord God. Jos 9:18
The people of * were angry with Jos 9:18
the Lord God of * that we will not Jos 9:19
the people of * to kill them, but Jos 9:26
for the people of * and for the Jos 9:27
made peace with * and were now Jos 10:1
with Joshua and the people of *." Jos 10:4
that the army of * slaughtered Jos 10:10
As the men of * were pursuing and Jos 10:12
But the Lord was fighting for *. Jos 10:14
that no one dared to attack *. Jos 10:21
as the Lord God of * had commanded, Jos 10:40
of * was fighting for his people. Jos 10:42
armies, and uniting to crush *. Jos 11:4
and the hills and lowlands of *. Jos 11:16
Hebron, Debir, Anab, Judah, and *; Jos 11:21
in all the land of *, though some Jos 11:22
and he gave it to the people of * Jos 11:23
Moses and the people of * had Jos 12:6
* on the west side of the Jordan. Jos 12:7
Joshua to the other tribes of *. Jos 12:7
the nation of *, so include all Jos 13:2-7
However, the people of * had not Jos 13:13
The people of * also killed Jos 13:22
nine and a half tribes of *. Jos 14:1
he had followed the Lord God of *. Jos 14:13,14
of the tribes of * had not yet Jos 18:1
had given them—all * gathered at Jos 18:1
and the nation of * gave a Jos 19:49
of the tribes of * supervised the Jos 19:51
"Tell the people of * to Jos 20:2
living in * as well as for the Jos 20:9
So in this way the Lord gave to * Jos 21:43
left the army of * at Shiloh in Jos 22:9
But when the rest of * heard Jos 22:11
high officials of *, one from each Jos 22:14
against the God of * by turning Jos 22:16
He knows (and let all * know it Jos 22:22,23
have to worship the Lord God of *? Jos 22:24,25
to the people of * and told them Jos 22:32
happened, and all * rejoiced and Jos 22:33
to the people of * against their Jos 23:1
for the leaders of *—the elders, Jos 23:2
all the people of * to him at Jos 24:1
"The Lord God of * says, 'Your Jos 24:2
Then * cried out to me and I put Jos 24:7
You saw what I did. Then * lived Jos 24:7
a war against *, and he asked Jos 24:9
and so I delivered * from him. Jos 24:10
before the eyes of *, as we Jos 24:17
you must obey the Lord God of *." Jos 24:23
* obeyed the Lord throughout the Jos 24:31
which the Lord had done for *. Jos 24:31
the people of * had brought with Jos 24:32
AFTER JOSHUA DIED, the nation of * Ju 1:1
to the people of *, "I brought you Ju 2:1
the armies of *, the tribes moved Ju 2:6
miracles the Lord had done for *. Ju 2:7-9
mighty miracles he had done for *. Ju 2:10
the Lord flamed out against all *. Ju 2:12-14
So now when the nation of * went Ju 2:15
Yet even then * would not listen Ju 2:17
the people of * from their enemies Ju 2:18
would flame out against * again. Ju 2:20
them out, nor let * destroy them. Ju 2:23
new generation of * who had not Ju 3:1
the youth of * to exercise faith Ju 3:1
the people of * . Ju 3:1f
new generation of *, to see whether Ju 3:4
So * lived among the Canaanites, Ju 3:5
of * intermarried with them. Ju 3:6
The young men of * took their Ju 3:6
And soon * was worshiping their Ju 3:6
So the people of * were very Ju 3:7
flamed out against *, and he let Ju 3:8
But when * cried out to the Ju 3:9
and purged * so that when he led Ju 3:10
led the forces of * against the Ju 3:10
helped * conquer him completely. Ju 3:10
the people of * turned once again Ju 3:12
to conquer part of * at that time. Ju 3:12
the people of * were required to Ju 3:14
So Moab was conquered by * that Ju 3:30
thereby saving * from disaster. Ju 3:31

(ISRAEL Con't)
EHUD'S DEATH the people of * Ju 4:1
"The Lord God of * has commanded Ju 4:6
So that day the Lord used * to Ju 4:23
And from that time on * became Ju 4:24
The God of *. Ju 5:3
At the presence of the God of *! Ju 5:5
Until Deborah became a mother to * Ju 5:7
When * chose new gods, Ju 5:8
Among forty thousand men of *, Ju 5:8
In the leaders of * Ju 5:9
Let all *, rich and poor, Ju 5:10
Of how the Lord saved * Ju 5:11
THEN THE PEOPLE of * began once Ju 6:1
devastated. So * was reduced to Ju 6:6,7
Then at last the people of * Ju 6:6,7
"The Lord God of * brought you out Ju 6:8
Go and save * from the Ju 6:14
replied, "Sir, how can I save *? Ju 6:15
Moses and rescued * from Egypt Ju 6:16f
it again, rescuing * from Midian. Ju 6:16f
in one vast alliance against *. Ju 6:33
to use me to save * as you Ju 6:36
then the people of * will boast to Ju 7:2
Now the men of * said to Gideon, Ju 8:22
But all * soon began worshiping Ju 8:27
of how Midian was subdued by *. Ju 8:28
Abimelech was acclaimed king of *. Ju 9:6
the next judge of * was Tola (son Ju 10:1
who judged * for twenty-two years. Ju 10:3
Then the people of * turned away Ju 10:6
began their war against *. Ju 11:4
to know why * was being attacked. Ju 11:12
Jephthah replied, "* did not Ju 11:14,15
When the people of * arrived at Ju 11:16
the people of * stayed in Kadesh. Ju 11:17
Then * sent messengers to King Ju 11:19
But King Sihon didn't trust *, Ju 11:20
But the Lord our God helped * Ju 11:21,22
your people, so * took over all of Ju 11:21,22
the Lord God of * who took away the Ju 11:23
the Amorites and gave it to *. Ju 11:23
his land after * defeated him? Ju 11:25
an issue of this! * has been living Ju 11:26
which of us is right—* or Ammon." Ju 11:27
if God would help * conquer the Ju 11:30,31
were subdued by the people of *. Ju 11:33
became a custom in *, that the Ju 11:39
He judged * for seven years Ju 12:9,10
He judged * for ten years and was Ju 12:11,12
ONCE AGAIN * sinned by worshiping Ju 13:1
and he will begin to rescue * Ju 13:5
the people of * you could marry?" Ju 14:3
at that time were the rulers of *. Ju 14:4
"You have given * such a wonderful Ju 15:18
He had judged * for twenty years. Ju 16:31
(For in those days * had no Ju 17:6
was no king in * at that time. Ju 18:1
a whole tribe in * instead of just Ju 18:19
AT THIS TIME before * had a king, Ju 19:1
sent one piece to each tribe of *. Ju 19:29
* left Egypt," everyone said. Ju 19:30
THEN THE ENTIRE nation of * sent Ju 20:1
The chiefs of * now called for Ju 20:3
the land of *, for these men have Ju 20:6
Now then, sons of *, express Ju 20:7
them and purge * of her evil." Ju 20:13
defense against the rest of *. Ju 20:14,15
The army of *, not counting the Ju 20:17
So the men of * took courage Ju 20:22,23,24
The men of * asked the Lord, Ju 20:27,28
the town as they chased after *. Ju 20:31
to kill the men of * along the Ju 20:31
But the armies of * had agreed Ju 20:32
But when the main army of * Ju 20:33
So the Lord helped * defeat Ju 20:35-39
The army of * retreated from the Ju 20:35-39
THE LEADERS OF * had vowed at Ju 21:1
"O Lord God of *," they cried Ju 21:3
"Was any tribe of * not Ju 21:5
throughout all * for the loss of Ju 21:6
* has been cut off, and is gone. Ju 21:6
Then * sent a peace delegation to Ju 21:13
(What a sad time it was in * in Ju 21:15
made a breach in the tribes of *. Ju 21:15
the leaders of * asked. Ju 21:16
of * will not be lost forever. Ju 21:17
So the people of * returned to Ju 21:24
(There was no king in * in those Ju 21:25
LONG AGO WHEN judges ruled in *, a Ru 1:1
She decided to return to * with Ru 1:6,7
May the Lord God of *, under Ru 2:12
was the custom in * for a man Ru 4:7
all the nation of * descended! Ru 4:11
may he be famous in *. Ru 4:14
May the Lord of * grant you your 1Sa 1:17
people of * were slaves in Egypt? 1Sa 2:27
"Therefore, I, the Lord God of * 1Sa 2:30
going to do a shocking thing in *. 1Sa 3:11
And all * from Dan to Beer-sheba 1Sa 3:20
passed them on to the people of *. 1Sa 3:21,4:1
AT THAT TIME * was at war with the 1Sa 4:1
And the Philistines defeated *, 1Sa 4:2
over, the army of * returned to 1Sa 4:3
us from these mighty gods of *? 1Sa 4:8
when * was in the wilderness. 1Sa 4:8
and * was defeated again. 1Sa 4:10
Thirty thousand men of * died 1Sa 4:10
told Eli, "and * has been 1Sa 4:17
He had judged * for forty years. 1Sa 4:18
of the God of * here any longer. 1Sa 5:7
God of * here to kill us too!" 1Sa 5:10
praise the God of *, perhaps he 1Sa 6:4,5
They wouldn't let * go until God 1Sa 6:6
that time all * was in sorrow 1Sa 7:2
and pleaded with him to help *. 1Sa 7:9
and didn't invade * again at that 1Sa 7:13
now returned to *, for the Israeli 1Sa 7:14
And there was peace between * and 1Sa 7:14
Finally the leaders of * met in 1Sa 8:4
was the most handsome man in *. 1Sa 9:2
you own all the wealth of * now!" 1Sa 9:20
the smallest in *, and my family is 1Sa 9:21
to be the king of his people, *! 1Sa 10:1
convocation of all * at Mizpah, 1Sa 10:17
There isn't his equal in all of * 1Sa 10:24
of you as a disgrace upon all *!" 1Sa 11:2
to carry them throughout all *. 1Sa 11:7
for today the Lord has rescued * 1Sa 11:13
Saul and all * were very happy. 1Sa 11:15
and two years over *." 1Sa 13:1f
the call to arms throughout *. 1Sa 13:3,4
When the men of * saw the vast 1Sa 13:6
kings of * forever, but now your 1Sa 13:13
all in the land of * in those days, 1Sa 13:19
entire "army" of * that day, 1Sa 13:22
the people of * at that time. 1Sa 14:18
So the Lord saved * that day, 1Sa 14:23
the God who saved * that though the 1Sa 14:39
Then Saul said, "O Lord God of * 1Sa 14:41
who saved * today, shall die? 1Sa 14:45
saddle as king of *, Saul sent the 1Sa 14:47
and saved * from all those who had 1Sa 14:48
king of * because God told me to. 1Sa 15:1
territory when * came from Egypt. 1Sa 15:2
to the people of * when they came 1Sa 15:6
yourself, God made you king of *. 1Sa 15:17
you from being the king of *." 1Sa 15:26
the kingdom of * from you today and 1Sa 15:28
And he who is the glory of * is 1Sa 15:29
he had ever made Saul king of *. 1Sa 15:35
I have rejected him as king of *. 1Sa 16:1
ranks to face the forces of *. 1Sa 17:4-7
I defy the armies of *! 1Sa 17:10
strutted before the armies of *. 1Sa 17:16
his challenge to the army of *. 1Sa 17:23
has insulted the entire army of *. 1Sa 17:25
and ending his insults to *?" 1Sa 17:26
of heaven and of *—the very God 1Sa 17:45
know that there is a God in *! 1Sa 17:46
in Israel! And * will learn that 1Sa 17:47
but all * and Judah loved him, 1Sa 18:15,16
a great victory to * as a result? 1Sa 19:5
by the Lord God of * that about 1Sa 20:12
"Isn't he the top leader of *?" 1Sa 21:11
"O Lord God of *," David said, 1Sa 23:10
O Lord God of *, please tell 1Sa 23:11
You are going to be the king of * 1Sa 23:17
were raiding * again, so Saul quit 1Sa 23:27
And who is the king of * trying 1Sa 24:14
and * shall be yours to rule. 1Sa 24:20
died and all * gathered for his 1Sa 25:1
made you king of *, you won't want 1Sa 25:30,31
the Lord God of * who has sent you 1Sa 25:32
Lord, the God of * who has kept me 1Sa 25:34
"Where in all * is there anyone 1Sa 26:15
Why should the king of * come out 1Sa 26:20
* must hate him bitterly by now. 1Sa 27:12
armies for another war with *. 1Sa 28:1
and all * had mourned for him. 1Sa 28:3
and wizards from the land of *. 1Sa 28:3
the armies of * were at Gilboa. 1Sa 28:4
runaway servant of King Saul of *. 1Sa 29:3
man the women of * sang about in 1Sa 29:5
of *, and it is still followed. 1Sa 30:25
the battle against *, and the 1Sa 31:1
men of * who had died that day. 2Sa 1:12
that it be sung throughout *. 2Sa 1:17,18
O *, your pride and joy lies dead 2Sa 1:19
But now, O women of *, weep for 2Sa 1:24
Benjamin, and all the rest of *. 2Sa 2:9
men of * had been defeated by Joab 2Sa 2:17
stopped chasing the troops of *. 2Sa 2:28
the kingdom of * to him in exchange 2Sa 3:12
combined armies of * and Judah. 2Sa 3:12
the leaders of * and reminded them 2Sa 3:17
with the people of * and Benjamin. 2Sa 3:19
all the people of *, and they will 2Sa 3:21
both Judah and *, understood from 2Sa 3:37
a great man has fallen today in *; 2Sa 3:38
all the tribes of * came to David 2Sa 5:1
the leaders of * there at Hebron, 2Sa 5:3
and they crowned him king of *. 2Sa 5:3
as king of both * and Judah; 2Sa 5:4,5
kindness on *, his chosen people. 2Sa 5:12
of *, they tried to capture him; 2Sa 5:17
other leaders of *, who were 2Sa 6:5
So * brought home the Ark of the 2Sa 6:15
the king of * looked today! 2Sa 6:20
of *, the people of the Lord! 2Sa 6:21
upon the land, and * was no longer 2Sa 7:1
the time I brought * out of Egypt. 2Sa 7:6
of my people * when you were a mere 2Sa 7:8
such blessings as *, your people? 2Sa 7:23
You chose * to be your people 2Sa 7:24
have established * as your people 2Sa 7:26
of heaven, God of *, that I am the 2Sa 7:27
to pay tribute to *—another example 2Sa 8:14
David reigned with justice over * 2Sa 8:15
that they were no match for *. 2Sa 10:15,16
The Lord God of * says, 'I made 2Sa 12:7
made you king of * and saved you 2Sa 12:7
and the kingdoms of * and Judah; 2Sa 12:8
openly, in the sight of all *.' 2Sa 12:12
what a serious crime it is in *. 2Sa 13:12
such thing ought to be done in *; 2Sa 13:12f
one of the greatest fools in *. 2Sa 13:13
who would end our existence in *. 2Sa 14:15,16
Now no one in * was such a 2Sa 14:25
the hearts of all the people of *. 2Sa 15:6
to every part of * to incite 2Sa 15:10
King David, "All * has joined 2Sa 15:13
guest in *, a foreigner in exile. 2Sa 15:19,20
Lord and by *," Hushai replied. 2Sa 16:18
Then all * will know that you 2Sa 16:21
Absalom and all the elders of * 2Sa 17:4
for all * knows what a mighty man 2Sa 17:10
the entire army of *, bringing them 2Sa 17:11
the entire army of * there at your 2Sa 17:13
Then Absalom and all the men of * 2Sa 17:14
the entire army of * and was 2Sa 17:24
from chasing the army of *. 2Sa 18:16
And the army of * fled to their 2Sa 18:17
For all * is ready, and only you 2Sa 19:11,12
I am once more king of *!" 2Sa 19:22
And most of Judah and half of * 2Sa 19:40
But the men of * complained to 2Sa 19:41
"But there are ten tribes in * 2Sa 19:43
Come on, you men of *, let's get 2Sa 20:1
traveled across * to mobilize his 2Sa 20:14
peace-loving city, loyal to *. 2Sa 20:19
They were not part of *, but were 2Sa 21:2
* had sworn not to kill them; 2Sa 21:2
were at war with *, and David and 2Sa 21:15
snuffing out the light of *?" 2Sa 21:17
each foot defied *, and David's 2Sa 21:20,21
David, sweet psalmist of *: 2Sa 23:1
The Rock of * said to me: 2Sa 23:3
flared against *, and David was 2Sa 24:1
went out to count the people of *. 2Sa 24:4
age in *, and 500,000 in Judah. 2Sa 24:9
So the Lord sent a plague upon * 2Sa 24:15
And now, my lord the king, all * 1Ki 1:20
you before by the Lord God of *." 1Ki 1:30
to anoint him there as king of *. 1Ki 1:34
him king of * and Judah." 1Ki 1:35
be the Lord God of * who has 1Ki 1:48
of *—my dynasty will never end. 1Ki 2:4
He had reigned over * for forty 1Ki 2:11
of the army of *, and General 1Ki 2:32
At that time the people of * 1Ki 3:2
* and Judah were a wealthy, 1Ki 4:20
and * lived in peace and safety; 1Ki 4:25
the new king of *, he sent 1Ki 5:1
has given * peace on every side; 1Ki 5:4
for as you know, no one in * can 1Ki 5:6
the great nation of *," he said. 1Ki 5:7
from all over *, and rotated them 1Ki 5:13
of * left their slavery in Egypt. 1Ki 6:1
of * and never forsake them." 1Ki 6:13
all the leaders of *—the heads of 1Ki 8:1
people of * after they left Egypt. 1Ki 8:9
"Blessed be the Lord God of *," 1Ki 8:15
*, but the Lord told him not to. 1Ki 8:17
father as king of *, and now this 1Ki 8:20
been built for the Lord God of *. 1Ki 8:20
"O Lord God of *, there is no god 1Ki 8:22,23
and now, O Lord God of *, 1Ki 8:25
always sit upon the throne of *. 1Ki 8:25
Yes, O God of *, fulfill this 1Ki 8:26
of the people of * whenever they 1Ki 8:30
name just as your own people * do; 1Ki 8:43
you had chosen * from among all the 1Ki 8:53
upon all the people of *: 1Ki 8:54,55
and given rest to his people *; 1Ki 8:56
me and all of * in accordance with 1Ki 8:59
servant David and to his people *. 1Ki 8:66
to be the kings of * forever, just 1Ki 9:5
always be upon the throne of *.' 1Ki 9:5
away the people of * from this land 1Ki 9:7
of my sight; and * will become a 1Ki 9:7
be, 'The people of * abandoned the 1Ki 9:9
For the people of * had not been 1Ki 9:20,21

ISRAEL Con't)
and conquest of *, and they 1Ki 9:20,21
And there were 550 men of * who 1Ki 9:23
and set you on the throne of *. 1Ki 10:9
How the Lord must love *—for he 1Ki 10:9
in the Lord God of * who had 1Ki 11:9,10
for they hated * intensely. 1Ki 11:25
the Lord God of * says, 'I will 1Ki 11:31
above all the other cities of *. 1Ki 11:32
of *, and give you absolute power. 1Ki 11:37
and your descendants shall rule * 1Ki 11:38
Shechem, and all * came for the 1Ki 12:1
joined the rest of * at Shechem, 1Ki 12:2,3,4
to Jerusalem. And * has been in 1Ki 12:19
When the people of * learned of 1Ki 12:20
and there he was made king of *. 1Ki 12:20
force the rest of * to acknowledge 1Ki 12:21
their brothers, the people of *. 1Ki 12:23,24
the Lord God of *: 'I promoted you 1Ki 14:7
people and made you king of *. 1Ki 14:7
All of * will mourn for him and 1Ki 14:13
the Lord God of * sees in the 1Ki 14:13
up a king over * who will destroy 1Ki 14:14
Then the Lord will shake * like 1Ki 14:15
he will uproot the people of * 1Ki 14:15
He will abandon * because 1Ki 14:16
all of * sin along with him." 1Ki 14:16
in The Annals of the Kings of *. 1Ki 14:19
*, the Lord had chosen to live in. 1Ki 14:21
like those in *, did wrong and 1Ki 14:22
year of Jeroboam's reign in *. 1Ki 15:1
constant war between * and Judah. 1Ki 15:6
*, and reigned forty-one years. 1Ki 15:9
Asa of Judah and King Baasha of *. 1Ki 15:16
King Baasha of * so that he will 1Ki 15:19
against some of the cities of *; 1Ki 15:20
Meanwhile, over in *, Nadab the 1Ki 15:25
idols and led all of * into sin. 1Ki 15:26
as the king of * in Tirzah, during 1Ki 15:28
the Lord God of * by sinning and 1Ki 15:30
leading the rest of * into sin. 1Ki 15:30
in The Annals of the Kings of *. 1Ki 15:31
Asa of Judah and King Baasha of *. 1Ki 15:32,33
led the people of * into the sin of 1Ki 15:34
"to make you king of my people *; 1Ki 16:2
in The Annals of the Kings of *. 1Ki 16:4-7
himself to be the new king of *. 1Ki 16:10
for they had led * into 1Ki 16:13
in The Annals of the Kings of *. 1Ki 16:14
for when the army of *, which was 1Ki 16:15,16
the people of * to sin with him. 1Ki 16:19
in The Annals of the Kings of *. 1Ki 16:20
But now the kingdom of * was 1Ki 16:21
his reign over *, which lasted 1Ki 16:23
had, and led * into this same sin. 1Ki 16:26
in The Annals of the Kings of *. 1Ki 16:27
when Ahab became the king of *; 1Ki 16:29
worse than any other king of *! 1Ki 16:30
the Lord God of * than any of the 1Ki 16:33
the other kings of * before him. 1Ki 16:33
as the Lord God of * lives—the God 1Ki 17:1
For the Lord God of * says that 1Ki 17:14
brought this disaster upon *!" 1Ki 18:17
Now bring all the people of * to 1Ki 18:19
represent each of the tribes of *, 1Ki 18:31
had said, '* shall be your name.' 1Ki 18:31f
Isaac, and *, prove today that you 1Ki 18:36
of * and that I am your servant; 1Ki 18:36
but the people of * have broken 1Ki 19:10
to be king of *, and anoint Elisha 1Ki 19:16
are 7,000 men in * who have never 1Ki 19:18
to King Ahab of *: "Your silver 1Ki 20:2,3
The king of * retorted, "Don't 1Ki 20:11
* again, this time at Aphek. 1Ki 20:26
time at Aphek. * then mustered its 1Ki 20:27
to the king of * with this message 1Ki 20:28
the kings of * are very merciful. 1Ki 20:31
So they went to the king of * and 1Ki 20:32
the king of * asked. 1Ki 20:32
"Go and get him," the king of * 1Ki 20:33
So the king of * went home to 1Ki 20:43
"Are you the king of * or not?" 1Ki 21:7
and have led all of * into sin. 1Ki 21:22
to make room for the people of *. 1Ki 21:26
was no war between Syria and *. 1Ki 22:1
King Ahab of *, Ahab said to his 1Ki 22:2
him, "I saw all * scattered upon 1Ki 22:17
So King Ahab of * and King 1Ki 22:29
in The Annals of the Kings of *. 1Ki 22:39
his son became the new king of *. 1Ki 22:40
of the reign of King Ahab of *. 1Ki 22:41
peace with Ahab, the king of *. 1Ki 22:44
began to reign over * in Samaria; 1Ki 22:51
who had led * into the sin of 1Ki 22:52,53
So Ahaziah made the Lord God of * 1Ki 22:52,53
to pay tribute to * any longer. 2Ki 1:1
it true that there is no God in *? 2Ki 1:3
it because there is no God in *? 2Ki 1:6
there is no God in * to ask? 2Ki 1:16
in The Annals of the Kings of *. 2Ki 1:18
The Chariot of * and the 2Ki 2:12
his reign over * during the 2Ki 3:1
of * into the worship of idols. 2Ki 3:3
They paid * an annual tribute of 2Ki 3:4
king of Moab rebelled against *. 2Ki 3:5
the king of * cried out. 2Ki 3:10
So the kings of *, Judah, and 2Ki 3:12
snarled at King Jehoram of *. 2Ki 3:13
camp, the army of * rushed out and 2Ki 3:24
Then the men of * moved forward 2Ki 3:24
So the army of * turned back in 2Ki 3:27
the land of * and among their 2Ki 5:2
you to carry to the king of *." 2Ki 5:5
The letter to the king of * 2Ki 5:6
When the king of * read it, he 2Ki 5:7
a true prophet of God here in *." 2Ki 5:8
all the rivers of * put together? 2Ki 5:12
God in all the world except in *; 2Ki 5:15
was at war with *, he said to his 2Ki 6:8
warned the king of *, "Don't go 2Ki 6:9
the king of * about my plans?" 2Ki 6:11
tells the king of * even the words 2Ki 6:12
in Samaria, the capital city of *! 2Ki 6:20
When the king of * saw them, he 2Ki 6:21
stayed away from the land of *. 2Ki 6:23
One day as the king of * was 2Ki 6:26-30
with the elders of * when the king 2Ki 6:32
"The king of * has hired the 2Ki 7:6
down a famine on * that will last 2Ki 8:1
to the land of * and went to see 2Ki 8:3
to the people of *: you will burn 2Ki 8:12
King Joram of *, the son of Ahab. 2Ki 8:16
as Ahab and the other kings of *; 2Ki 8:18
King Joram of *, the son of Ahab. 2Ki 8:24,25
granddaughter of King Omri of *. 2Ki 8:26
He joined King Joram of * (son of 2Ki 8:28
anointed him to be the king of *; 2Ki 9:3
"The Lord God of * says, 'I anoint 2Ki 9:6
you king of the Lord's people, *. 2Ki 9:6
he had been anointed king of *! 2Ki 9:12
defending * against the forces of 2Ki 9:14
of the reign of King Joram of *. 2Ki 9:29
throughout all * summoning those 2Ki 10:20,21
every trace of Baal from *. 2Ki 10:28
for it resulted in all * sinning. 2Ki 10:29
to be the kings of *." 2Ki 10:30
the Lord God of * with all his 2Ki 10:31
the cause of such great sin in *. 2Ki 10:31
to whittle down the size of *. 2Ki 10:32,33
in The Annals of the Kings of *. 2Ki 10:34
reigned as king of *, in Samaria, 2Ki 10:36
* that Joash became king of Judah. 2Ki 12:1
reign over * during the 2Ki 13:1
Jeroboam, who had caused * to sin. 2Ki 13:2
very angry with *, and he 2Ki 13:3
king of Syria was oppressing *. 2Ki 13:4
and then * lived in safety again 2Ki 13:5
in The Annals of the Kings of *. 2Ki 13:8
in The Annals of the Kings of *. 2Ki 13:12
Samaria with the other kings of *; 2Ki 13:13
You are the strength of *!" 2Ki 13:14
Literally, "The chariots of * and 2Ki 13:14f
had oppressed * during the entire 2Ki 13:22
to the people of *, and they were 2Ki 13:23
King Joash of * 2Ki 13:25
of King Joash of *, King Amaziah 2Ki 14:1
to King Joash of * (the son of 2Ki 14:8
King Joash of * mustered his army. 2Ki 14:11
and the army of * marched on 2Ki 14:13
in The Annals of the Kings of *. 2Ki 14:15
Samaria with the other kings of *. 2Ki 14:16
Meanwhile, over in *, Jeroboam II 2Ki 14:23
who had led * into the sin of 2Ki 14:24
territories of * between Hamath and 2Ki 14:25
as the Lord God of * had predicted 2Ki 14:25
of *—she had no one to help her. 2Ki 14:26
out the name of *, so he used King 2Ki 14:27
in The Annals of the Kings of *. 2Ki 14:28
the other kings of *, and his son 2Ki 14:29
became the new king of *. 2Ki 14:29
Reigning in * at this time: King 2Ki 15:1
New king of *: Zechariah 2Ki 15:8
* in the sin of worshiping idols. 2Ki 15:9
in The Annals of the Kings of *. 2Ki 15:11
great-grandson would be kings of * 2Ki 15:12
New king of *: Shallum 2Ki 15:13
in The Annals of the Kings of *. 2Ki 15:15
Name of new king of *: Menahem 2Ki 15:17
the people of * into grievous sin. 2Ki 15:18
in The Annals of the Kings of *. 2Ki 15:21
Name of new king of *: Pekahiah 2Ki 15:23
who led * down that evil trail. 2Ki 15:24
in The Annals of the Kings of *. 2Ki 15:26
New king of *: Pekah 2Ki 15:27
who led all of * into the sin of 2Ki 15:28
led an attack against *. 2Ki 15:29
New king of *: Hoshea 2Ki 15:30
in The Annals of the Kings of *. 2Ki 15:31
Reigning in * at this time: Pekah 2Ki 15:32,33
King Pekah of * to attack Judah. 2Ki 15:37
Reigning in * at this time: King 2Ki 16:1
was as wicked as the kings of *. 2Ki 16:3
the people of * entered the land. 2Ki 16:3
of Remaliah) of * declared war on 2Ki 16:5
attacking armies of Syria and *. 2Ki 16:7
new king of * 2Ki 17:1
as some of the other kings of * 2Ki 17:1
King Hoshea, so * had to pay heavy 2Ki 17:3
Now the land of * was filled with 2Ki 17:5
Samaria, the capital city of *. 2Ki 17:5
of * were exiled to Assyria. 2Ki 17:6
upon the nation of * because the 2Ki 17:7
The people of * had also 2Ki 17:9
out of the land when * came in. 2Ki 17:11
So the people of * had done many 2Ki 17:11
to warn both * and Judah to turn 2Ki 17:13
prophets, but * wouldn't listen. 2Ki 17:14
in the same evil paths as * had. 2Ki 17:19
Literally, "descendants of *." 2Ki 17:20f
destroyed. For * split off from 2Ki 17:21
Then Jeroboam drew * away from 2Ki 17:21
and the people of * never quit 2Ki 17:22
would happen. So * was carried off 2Ki 17:23
replacing the people of *. 2Ki 17:24
Samaria and the other cities of *. 2Ki 17:24
colonists here in * don't know the 2Ki 17:26
should return to * and teach the 2Ki 17:27,28
name was later changed to *). 2Ki 17:34
But * didn't listen, and the 2Ki 17:40
Reigning in * at this time: King 2Ki 18:1
the people of * had begun to 2Ki 18:4
strongly in the Lord God of *. 2Ki 18:5
of King Hoshea in *) that King 2Ki 18:9
Assyria attacked * and began a 2Ki 18:9
of King Hoshea of *) Samaria fell. 2Ki 18:10
"O Lord God of *, sitting on your 2Ki 19:15
God of * says, 'I have heard you! 2Ki 19:20
It is the Holy One of *! 2Ki 19:22
to make room for the people of * 2Ki 21:1
as Ahab the king of * had done. 2Ki 21:3,4,5
all the cities of the tribes of *. 2Ki 21:7
If the people of * will only 2Ki 21:8
the people of * entered the land. 2Ki 21:9
I will cause the kings of * to 2Ki 21:13
message from the Lord God of *: 2Ki 22:15,16
I had made when he led * into sin. 2Ki 23:15
various kings of * and had made the 2Ki 23:19
of the judges of *, and there was 2Ki 23:22
years of the kings of * and Judah. 2Ki 23:22
Judah just as I have destroyed *; 2Ki 23:27
King Solomon of * had placed in the 2Ki 24:13
Esau and *. 1Ch 1:34
before the kingdom of * began: 1Ch 1:43
THE SONS OF * were: 1Ch 2:1
father of Nahshon, a leader of *. 1Ch 2:10
to the God of *, "Oh, that you 1Ch 4:10
THE OLDEST SON of * was Reuben, 1Ch 5:1
*, and from Judah came a Prince. 1Ch 5:2
of Judah and King Jeroboam of *. 1Ch 5:17
Korah, Izhar, Kohath, Levi, *. 1Ch 6:33-38
the annual Day of Atonement for *. 1Ch 6:49
Joseph the son of *, controlled the 1Ch 7:29
of every person in * was carefully 1Ch 9:1
in The Annals of the Kings of *. 1Ch 9:1
from the tribes of *, and also the 1Ch 9:2
THEN THE LEADERS of * went to 1Ch 11:1
be the shepherd of my people *. 1Ch 11:2
him as king of *, just as the Lord 1Ch 11:3
the leaders of * to make David 1Ch 11:10
the best course for * to take. 1Ch 12:24-37
of making David the king of *. 1Ch 12:38
In fact, all of * was ready for 1Ch 12:38
the assembled men of * as follows: 1Ch 13:2
the land of *, including the 1Ch 13:2
of * from all across the nation 1Ch 13:5
Then David and all * went to 1Ch 13:6
Then David summoned all * to 1Ch 15:3
the God of *, to the place I have 1Ch 15:12
the Ark of Jehovah, the God of *. 1Ch 15:14
Then David and the elders of * 1Ch 15:25
So the leaders of * took the Ark 1Ch 15:28
and the leaders of * sacrificed 1Ch 16:1
to the Lord God of * and by asking 1Ch 16:4
He promised * 1Ch 16:17
When * was few in number—oh, so 1Ch 16:19
Blessed be Jehovah, God of *, 1Ch 16:36
just as the Lord had commanded *. 1Ch 16:40
the time I brought * out of Egypt. 1Ch 17:5
of the leaders of *—the shepherds I 1Ch 17:6
home to my people *, and will plant 1Ch 17:9
to be kings of * just as you are. 1Ch 17:10
the kingdom of * forever—and his 1Ch 17:14
nation in all the earth is like *? 1Ch 17:21
that your people * belong to you 1Ch 17:22
of heaven is indeed the God of *!' 1Ch 17:24
of Israel!' And * shall always be 1Ch 17:24
David reigned over all of * and 1Ch 18:14
and the mightiest warriors of *. 1Ch 19:8
he mobilized all *, crossed the 1Ch 19:17,18
a giant) defied and taunted *; 1Ch 20:6,7
SATAN BROUGHT disaster upon * 1Ch 21:1
Why must you cause * to sin?" 1Ch 21:3
he traveled all through * and 1Ch 21:4

(ISRAEL Con't)

age in * and 470,000 in Judah. 1Ch 21:5
the census and punished * for it. 1Ch 21:7
by the enemies of *, or three days 1Ch 21:12
So the Lord sent a plague upon * 1Ch 21:14
and the elders of * clothed 1Ch 21:16
resident aliens in * to prepare 1Ch 22:2
a temple for the Lord God of *. 1Ch 22:6
quietness to * during his reign. 1Ch 22:9
reign over every generation of *.' 1Ch 22:10
laws when he makes you king of *. 1Ch 22:12
* through Moses, you will prosper. 1Ch 22:13
all the leaders of * to assist his 1Ch 22:17
son Solomon as the new king of *. 1Ch 23:1
of * for the coronation ceremony. 1Ch 23:2
"The Lord God of * has given us 1Ch 23:25
of * west of the Jordan River; 1Ch 26:30
the tribes of * were as follows: 1Ch 27:16-22
* like to the stars of heaven." 1Ch 27:23f
the anger of God broke out upon *; 1Ch 27:24
villages, and fortresses of *. 1Ch 27:25
"Nevertheless, the Lord God of * 1Ch 28:4
dynasty that will rule * forever; 1Ch 28:4
and has made me king over all *. 1Ch 28:4
on the throne of his Kingdom of *. 1Ch 28:5
"Here before the leaders of *, 1Ch 28:8
the next king of *, is still young 1Ch 29:1
God of our father *, praise your 1Ch 29:10
fathers: Abraham, Isaac, and *! 1Ch 29:18
sacrifices on behalf of all *. 1Ch 29:21
greatly, and all * obeyed him. 1Ch 29:23
all the people of *, and he amassed 1Ch 29:25
David was king of the land of * 1Ch 29:26,27
to him and to * and to the kings of 1Ch 29:30
ruler of *, for the Lord his God 2Ch 1:1
and religious leaders of *. 2Ch 1:2,3
went back to Jerusalem to rule *. 2Ch 1:13
For God wants * always to 2Ch 2:4
Blessed be the Lord God of * who 2Ch 2:12
of a Jewish woman from Dan in *; 2Ch 2:14
of the leaders of *—the heads of 2Ch 5:2
As the leaders of * watched, the 2Ch 5:4,5
of * as they were leaving Egypt. 2Ch 5:10
"Blessed be the Lord God of *," 2Ch 6:4
a city anywhere in * as the 2Ch 6:5,6
I chosen a king for my people *. 2Ch 6:5,6
of *, and placed the Ark there. 2Ch 6:10
the Lord and his people *." 2Ch 6:11
"O Lord God of *, there is no 2Ch 6:14
And now, O God of *, carry out 2Ch 6:16
always reign over * if they will 2Ch 6:16
Yes, Lord God of *, please 2Ch 6:17
of your people * when they pray 2Ch 6:20,21
"If your people * are destroyed 2Ch 6:24
you, just as your people * do; 2Ch 6:33
crowds coming in from all over *; 2Ch 7:8
and Solomon and to his people *. 2Ch 7:10
will always be the kings of *; 2Ch 7:18
some of the people of * into them. 2Ch 8:2
How he must love * to give them a 2Ch 9:8
over all of * for forty years. 2Ch 9:30
ALL THE LEADERS of * came to 2Ch 10:1
*, the people stoned him to death. 2Ch 10:18
to Jerusalem. And * has refused to 2Ch 10:19
the rest of * in an attempt to 2Ch 11:1
Laymen, too, from all over * 2Ch 11:16
and the leaders of * confessed 2Ch 12:6
all the other cities of *. 2Ch 12:13
the reign of King Jeroboam of *. 2Ch 13:1
war broke out between Judah and *. 2Ch 13:1
the Lord God of * swore that 2Ch 13:5
would always be the kings of *? 2Ch 13:5
O people of *, do not fight 2Ch 13:12
and the army of *, and they 2Ch 13:15,16
elite troops of * that day. 2Ch 13:17
fathers, defeated *, and chased 2Ch 13:18,19
King Jeroboam of * never 2Ch 13:20
For a long time now, over in *, 2Ch 15:3
to the Lord God of * in their 2Ch 15:4
immigrants from * (for many had 2Ch 15:9
and Simeon, in *, when they saw 2Ch 15:9
Over in * the idol-temples were 2Ch 15:17
King Baasha of * declared war on 2Ch 16:1
King Baasha of *, so that he will 2Ch 16:3
mobilized his armies to attack *. 2Ch 16:4
As soon as King Baasha of * 2Ch 16:5
of the Kings of * and Judah. 2Ch 16:11
and mobilized for war against *. 2Ch 17:1
the border in the land of *. 2Ch 17:4
King Ahab of *. 2Ch 18:1
So the king of * called one of 2Ch 18:8
vision I saw all * scattered upon 2Ch 18:16
the king of * exclaimed to 2Ch 18:17
Joash," the king of * ordered. 2Ch 18:25
So the king of * and the king of 2Ch 18:28
The king of * said to 2Ch 18:29
everyone but the king of *!" 2Ch 18:30
of *, they stopped chasing him. 2Ch 18:32
struck the king of * at the opening 2Ch 18:33
no more trips to * after that, but 2Ch 19:4
those nations when * left Egypt, so 2Ch 20:10

the Lord God of * with songs of 2Ch 20:19
*, the fear of God fell upon them. 2Ch 20:29
in The Annals of the Kings of *. 2Ch 20:34
of *, who was a very wicked man. 2Ch 20:35
and many other leaders of *. 2Ch 21:3,4
as the kings who were over in *. 2Ch 21:6
the kings over in *, and have made 2Ch 21:13
King Jehoram of * (the son of 2Ch 22:5
King Jehoram of * was wounded, 2Ch 22:5
of God had assessed upon *. 2Ch 24:9
*, for God, and for the Temple. 2Ch 24:16
experienced mercenaries from *. 2Ch 25:5,6
*, for the Lord is not with them. 2Ch 25:7
Meanwhile, the army of * that had 2Ch 25:13
on King Joash of * (son of 2Ch 25:17
King Joash of * captured the 2Ch 25:23
the death of King Joash of *. 2Ch 25:25
of the Kings of Judah and *. 2Ch 25:26
of the Kings of * and Judah. 2Ch 27:7
* and worshiped the idols of Baal. 2Ch 28:2
by the Lord to make room for *. 2Ch 28:3
The armies from * also 2Ch 28:5
The armies from * also captured 2Ch 28:8
the evil deeds of King Ahaz of *, 2Ch 28:19
King Ahaz ruled two tribes of * 2Ch 28:19f
this unusual way as a king of *. 2Ch 28:19f
of the Kings of Judah and *. 2Ch 28:26
the Lord God of * so that his 2Ch 29:10
atonement for all * as the king had 2Ch 29:24
throughout all of *, Judah, 2Ch 30:1
throughout *, from Dan to 2Ch 30:5
tribe of * for a long time; 2Ch 30:5f
Isaac, and *," the king's letter 2Ch 30:6
So the people of * celebrated the 2Ch 30:21
from *, were filled with deep joy. 2Ch 30:25
scorning the Lord God of *. 2Ch 32:17
of the Kings of Judah and *. 2Ch 32:32
the people of * entered the land. 2Ch 33:2
above all the other cities of *. 2Ch 33:7
ever again exile * from this land 2Ch 33:8
destroyed when * entered the land. 2Ch 33:9
Judah worship the Lord God of *. 2Ch 33:16
in The Annals of the Kings of *. 2Ch 33:18
* before returning to Jerusalem. 2Ch 34:7
of the remnant of *, as well as 2Ch 34:9
"Pray for all the remnant of * 2Ch 34:21
* says, Tell the man who sent you, 2Ch 34:23
the Lord God of * says, 'Because 2Ch 34:26
the religious teachers in *: 2Ch 35:3
David of * and by his son Solomon. 2Ch 35:4,5
of the kings of * could vie with 2Ch 35:18
of Judah, and from over in *. 2Ch 35:18
of the Kings of * and Judah. 2Ch 35:27
the Lord God of * was concerned, 2Ch 36:13
people, return to * for this task, 2Ch 36:22,23
is the God of * and of Jerusalem. Ez 1:3
rebuilt the altar of the God of *; Ez 3:1
toward * will last forever." Ez 3:11
The Temple of the God of * must Ez 4:3
from the God of * to Zerubbabel Ez 5:1
ago by a great king of *. Ez 5:11
for the twelve tribes of *. Ez 6:17
to be generous to * and to assist Ez 6:21,22
had given to the people of *. Ez 7:6
those laws to the people of *. Ez 7:10
as an offering to the God of *. Ez 7:15
* to return with me to Jerusalem. Ez 7:28
the son of Levi and grandson of *. Ez 8:18
and people of * had presented to Ez 8:25
and the elders of * at Jerusalem, Ez 8:29
to the God of *—twelve oxen for the Ez 8:35
oxen for the nation of *; Ez 8:35
The men of * had married girls Ez 9:2
feared the God of * because of this Ez 9:4
O Lord God of *, you are a just Ez 9:15
But there is hope for * in spite Ez 10:2
all the people of * swear that they Ez 10:5
and excommunicated from *. Ez 10:7,8
night and day for your people *. Neh 1:6,7
was interested in helping *. Neh 2:10
assistance from the people of *. Neh 5:14
that the people of * should live in Neh 8:14
Temple and for the atonement of *. Neh 10:33
been friendly to the people of *. Neh 13:2
upon the people of * by permitting Neh 13:18
and made him the king over all *; Neh 13:26
throughout * to this day have an Est 9:19
when the Lord has rescued *! Ps 14:7
Let all * sing his praises, for Ps 22:23
to ransom * from all her troubles. Ps 25:22
Bless the Lord, the God of *, who Ps 41:13
to us, spreading * from one end of Ps 44:1
And Lord, don't punish * for my Ps 51:18
come from Zion now and save *! Ps 53:6
armies, God of *, arise and punish Ps 59:5
that God rules in * and will reign Ps 59:12,13
quailed before you—the God of *. Ps 68:8
Now all the women of * are Ps 68:11,12,13
Let all the people of * praise Ps 68:26
His majesty shines down on *; Ps 68:34
The God of * gives strength and Ps 68:35

O God of *, don't let me cause Ps 69:6
your promises, O Holy One of *. Ps 71:22
*, who only does wonderful things! Ps 72:18
HOW GOOD GOD is to *—to those Ps 73:1
IS very great in Judah and in *. Ps 76:1
For he gave his laws to *, and Ps 78:5
burned against *, because they Ps 78:21
* from giving them his blessings. Ps 78:41
gave each tribe of * its Ps 78:55
people *, invading every home. Ps 79:7
O SHEPHERD OF * who leads Israel Ps 80:1
O SHEPHERD OF Israel who leads * Ps 80:1
are scheduled in the laws of *. Ps 81:4
O *, if you will only listen! Ps 81:8
listen. * doesn't want me around. Ps 81:11
Oh, that * would follow me, Ps 81:13
let us wipe out * as a nation—we Ps 83:4
Listen, God of *. Ps 84:8
of *, and forgiven the sins of Ps 85:1
One of *, has given us our king. Ps 89:18
Don't harden your hearts as * did Ps 95:8
his promise to be kind to *. Ps 98:2,3
He gives justice throughout *. Ps 99:4
to Moses and the people of *. Ps 103:7
with the people of *: "I will give Ps 105:10,11
Then Jacob (*) arrived in Egypt Ps 105:23
the people of * multiplied Ps 105:24
At Meribah, too, * angered God, Ps 106:32
Nor did * destroy the nations in Ps 106:34
Blessed be the Lord, the God of * Ps 106:48
them the land of *, though it was Ps 111:6
of Judah and of * became God's new Ps 114:2
O *, trust the Lord! Ps 115:9
He will bless the people of * and Ps 115:12
Let the congregation of * praise Ps 118:2
crowded city. All *—Jehovah's Ps 122:4
our side (let all * admit it), if Ps 124:1
And let * have quietness and Ps 125:5
And may God bless *! Ps 128:6
MY earliest youth (* is speaking), Ps 129:1
O *, hope in the Lord; Ps 130:7
He himself shall ransom * from Ps 130:8
O *, you too should quietly trust Ps 131:3
a Temple for the mighty one of *. Ps 132:2-5
Hermon, on the mountains of *. Ps 133:3
For the Lord has chosen * as his Ps 135:4
an eternal gift to his people *. Ps 135:12
O *, bless Jehovah! Ps 135:19
Egypt, for his lovingkindness to * Ps 136:10
for his lovingkindness to * Ps 136:11,12
sea, for his lovingkindness to * Ps 136:15
for his lovingkindness to * Ps 136:18
God's lovingkindness to * Ps 136:19
Bashan—for his lovingkindness to * Ps 136:20
of these kings to * as a gift Ps 136:21
for his lovingkindness to * Ps 136:21
to his servant *, for his Ps 136:22
of worship to *— something he has Ps 147:19
of *, the people closest to him. Ps 148:14
O *, rejoice in your Maker. Ps 149:2
of King Solomon of *, David's son: Pro 1:1
I, the Preacher, was king of *, Ecc 1:12-15
for them, but not my people *. Is 1:3
have despised the Holy One of *. Is 1:4
Listen, you leaders of *, you men Is 1:10
the Mighty One of *, says: I will Is 1:24
to the Temple of the God of *; Is 2:3
will end. O *, come, let us walk Is 2:5
* has vast treasures of silver Is 2:7
I spoke about. * and Judah are his Is 5:7
They even mock the Holy One of * Is 5:19
the Word of the Holy One of *. Is 5:24
Over all * lies a pall of Is 5:30
all the land of * lies deserted! Is 6:12
and though * is invaded again and Is 6:13
and destroyed, yet * will be like a Is 6:13
Pekah of * (the son of Remaliah). Is 7:1
is allied with * against us!" Is 7:2
Yes, the kings of Syria and * Is 7:5
so much—the kings of * and Syria Is 7:15,16
empire into * and Judah—the mighty Is 7:17
Do your worst, O Syria and *, Is 8:9,10
Judah to surrender to Syria and *. Is 8:11
of Syria and * attacking you. Is 8:12
He will be your safety; but * Is 8:14,15
of death. For * will again be Is 9:3
that braggart * who says that Is 9:8,9,10
bared fangs they will devour *. Is 9:11,12
of * and the lying prophets. Is 9:14,15
God, the Light and Holy One of * Is 10:17
who destroyed the land of *. Is 10:17
Then at last, those left in * and Is 10:20
the Holy One of *, instead of Is 10:20
But though * be now as many as Is 10:22
to the land of * from Assyria, Is 11:11
between * and Judah will end; Is 11:13
he did for all of * long ago when Is 11:16
One of *, who lives among you. Is 12:6
Shout to them, O *, and wave them Is 13:2
once again in the land of *. Is 14:1
Those enslaving * will be Is 14:2

(ISRAEL Con't)
enslaved—* shall rule her enemies! Is 14:2
when they are in * and to crush Is 14:25
The strength of * and the power Is 17:3
Yes, the glory of * will be very Is 17:4
stalks the land. * will be as Is 17:5
be in Damascus and *—stripped bare Is 17:6
respect for the Holy One of *. Is 17:7
In the evening * waits in Is 17:14
now advance against the land of *. Is 18:4
Just to speak the name of * will Is 19:17
God. And * will be their ally; Is 19:24
the three will be together, and * Is 19:24
with *. He will say, "Blessed be Is 19:25
blessed be *, my inheritance!" Is 19:25
of Hosts, the God of *, has said. Is 21:10
The Lord, the God of *, has Is 21:17
* -is my vineyard Is 27:3
My anger against * Is 27:4,5
The time will come when * will Is 27:6
Has God punished * as much as he Is 27:7,8
while he has punished * but a Is 27:7,8
and delight of the drunkards of *! Is 28:1
the drunkards of *—will be hurled Is 28:3
shall exult in the Holy One of *. Is 29:19
One of *, and stand in awe of him. Is 29:23
'Holy One of *' and all he says." Is 30:10,11
is the reply of the Holy One of *: Is 30:12
the Holy One of *, says: Only in Is 30:15
of the Lord, the Rock of *. Is 30:29
Holy One of * and consulting him. Is 31:1
battle flags of *, says the Lord. Is 31:9
He will shelter * from the storm Is 32:2
Then at last the eyes of * will Is 32:3
All the land of * is in trouble; Is 33:9
The people of * will no longer Is 33:24
for what Edom has done to *. Is 34:8
prime minister of *, and Shebna, Is 36:3
of Hosts, God of * enthroned above Is 37:16,17
"The Lord God of * says, This is Is 37:21
It was against the Holy One of *! Is 37:23
O Jacob, O *, how can you say Is 40:27
But as for you, O *, you are Is 41:8
though you are, fear not, O *; Is 41:14
I am the Holy One of *. Is 41:14
you shall glory in the God of *. Is 41:16
says God, the King of *. Is 41:21
He will bring blind * along a Is 42:16
Who let * be robbed and hurt? Is 42:24
who created you, O *, says, Don't Is 43:1
your Savior, the Holy One of *. Is 43:3
daughters back to * from the Is 43:6
But I have witnesses, O *, says Is 43:10
Redeemer, the Holy One of *, says: Is 43:14
I have made * for myself, and Is 43:21
destroyed *, leaving her to shame. Is 43:28
LISTEN TO ME, O my servant *, O my Is 44:1
of God or the honored name of *. Is 44:5
The Lord, the King of *, Is 44:6
Pay attention, *, for you are my Is 44:21
Jacob and is glorified in *! Is 44:23
Lord, the God of *, the one who Is 45:3
of Jacob, my servant—*, my chosen. Is 45:4
Jehovah, the Holy One of *, Is 45:11
Truly, O God of *, Savior, you Is 45:15
and ashamed. But * shall be saved Is 45:17
And I didn't tell * to ask me for Is 45:19
* shall be justified, triumphant. Is 45:25
"Listen to me, all * who are Is 46:3
Jerusalem, and *, who is my glory. Is 46:13
* from Babylon's mighty power; Is 47:4
is his name, the Holy One of *. Is 47:4
with my people * and began to Is 47:6
about depending on the God of *. Is 48:1
the Holy One of *, says, I am the Is 48:17
Or, "*." Is 49:3f
to him his people *, who has given Is 49:5
do more than restore * to me. Is 49:6
and Holy One of *, says to the one Is 49:7
the Holy One of *, chooses you." Is 49:7
and pledge to *, proof that I will Is 49:8,9
the land of * and reassign it to Is 49:8,9
Redeemer, the Mighty One of *." Is 49:26
And the Lord will bless * again, Is 51:3
listen, O *, for I will see that Is 51:4
I am the one who says to *, "You Is 51:16
the news that the God of * reigns. Is 52:7
*, will protect you from behind. Is 52:12
of *, the God of all the earth. Is 54:5
the outcasts of * says, I will Is 56:8
others too besides my people *. Is 56:8
to *, like doves to their nests? Is 60:8
to bring the sons of * home again Is 60:9
For the Holy One of *, known Is 60:9
Mountain of the Holy One of *." Is 60:14
and Redeemer, the Mighty One of *. Is 60:16
To all who mourn in * he will Is 61:3
boulders, raise the flag of *." Is 62:10
great goodness to *, which he has Is 63:7
one who brought * through the sea, Is 63:11
so I will not destroy all *, Is 65:8
people to possess the land of *; Is 65:9
a nation, *, shall be born, even Is 66:7,8
or survivors of the Jews in *. Is 66:19f
In those days * was a holy Jer 2:3
O *, says the Lord, why did your Jer 2:4,5
Why has * become a nation of Jer 2:14
that * knows is getting caught. Jer 2:26,27
of God: Have I been unjust to *? Jer 2:31
Have you seen what * does? Jer 3:6
every chance, so * has worshiped Jer 3:6
saw the continued rebellion of *. Jer 3:7
saw that I divorced faithless *. Jer 3:8
In fact, faithless * is less Jer 3:11
Therefore go and say to *, O Jer 3:12
say to Israel, O *, my sinful Jer 3:12
to the land of *—one from here and Jer 3:14
of Judah and of * will return Jer 3:18
It is the sons of * who have Jer 3:21
Only in the Lord our God can * Jer 3:23
O *, IF you will truly return to Jer 4:1
For the people of * and Judah are Jer 5:11
against you, O *, says the Lord—a Jer 5:15
announcement to Judah and to *: Jer 5:20
Even the few who remain in * Jer 6:9
The Lord of Hosts, the God of * Jer 7:3
all the wickedness of my people *. Jer 7:12
The Lord of Hosts, the God of * Jer 7:21
Hosts, the God of *, says: Lo, I Jer 9:15
HEAR THE WORD of the Lord, O *: Jer 10:1
He is the Creator of all, and * Jer 10:16
have destroyed * and made a Jer 10:25
And now, *, obey me, says the Jer 11:5
the wickedness of * and Judah in Jer 11:17
gave his people *: See, I will Jer 12:14
* to cling to me, says the Lord. Jer 13:11
Tell them this: The Lord God of * Jer 13:12
O Hope of *, our Savior in times Jer 14:8
Hosts, the God of *, says: In your Jer 16:9
O Lord, the Hope of *, all who Jer 17:13
O *, can't I do to you as this Jer 18:6
The Lord of Hosts, the God of *, Jer 19:3
will prickle. For * has forsaken Jer 19:4
Hosts, the God of *, says: I will Jer 19:15
the Lord God of * says, I will make Jer 21:3,4
be saved and * will live in peace. Jer 23:5,6
the people of * from the land of Jer 23:7
their own land of * from the Jer 23:8
Baal and led my people * into sin; Jer 23:13
from the land of *, which I gave to Jer 24:10
that befalls you. * and her Jer 25:11
Hosts, the God of *, says, Drink Jer 25:27
God of *, sends you this message: Jer 27:4
"The Lord of Hosts, the God of * Jer 28:2
The Lord of Hosts, the God of *, Jer 28:14
The Lord of Hosts, the God of *, Jer 29:4
The Lord of Hosts, the God of *, Jer 29:8
The Lord of Hosts, the God of *, Jer 29:21
The Lord of Hosts, the God of *, Jer 29:25
The Lord God of * says, Write Jer 30:2
of my people, * and Judah, and I Jer 30:3
And write this also concerning * Jer 30:4
don't be dismayed, O *; Jer 30:10
* shall recognize me as the Lord; Jer 31:1
when * sought for rest. Jer 31:2
Lord had said to *: I have loved Jer 31:3
your nation, O virgin of *. Jer 31:4
*, the greatest of the nations! Jer 31:7
his people, the remnant of *." Jer 31:7
For I am a Father to *, and Jer 31:9
He will save * from those who Jer 31:11
up road signs pointing back to *. Jer 31:21
O virgin *, to your cities here. Jer 31:21
to happen—* shall seek him! Jer 31:22
The Lord of Hosts, the God of *, Jer 31:23
the number of cattle here in *. Jer 31:27
with the people of * and Judah. Jer 31:31
reject my people * as I am to do Jer 31:36
"The Lord of Hosts, God of *, Jer 32:14
For the Lord of Hosts, God of *, Jer 32:15
in * and all around the world. Jer 32:20
"You brought * out of Egypt with Jer 32:21
You gave * this land that you Jer 32:22
fury to rise! For * and Judah have Jer 32:30
The sins of * and Judah—the sins Jer 32:32
Now therefore the Lord God of * Jer 32:36
and * and restore their fortunes. Jer 33:7
when I will do for * and Judah all Jer 33:14
heir sitting on the throne of *. Jer 33:17
—that the Lord chose Judah and * Jer 33:24
and saying that * isn't worthy to Jer 33:24
The Lord, the God of *, says: Jer 34:13
The Lord of Hosts, the God of *, Jer 35:13
Hosts, the God of *, says: Because Jer 35:17
Hosts, the God of *, says that Jer 35:18,19
*, Judah and the other nations. Jer 36:2
"The Lord, the God of *, says: Jer 37:7
Hosts, the God of *, says: If you Jer 38:17
Hosts, the God of *, says: I will Jer 39:16
himself against Baasha, king of *. Jer 41:9
Lord, the God of *, with your Jer 42:9
Hosts, the God of *, says: If you Jer 42:15
Hosts, the God of *, says: Just as Jer 42:18
Hosts, the God of *, says: I will Jer 43:10
The Lord of Hosts, the God of *, Jer 44:2,3
Hosts, the God of *, asks you: Why Jer 44:7
Hosts, the God of *, says: There is Jer 44:11
The Lord of Hosts, the God of *, Jer 44:25
O Baruch, the Lord God of * says Jer 45:2
The Lord of Hosts, the God of *, Jer 46:25
distant land. Yes, * shall return Jer 46:27
Hosts, the God of *, against Moab: Jer 48:1
* was of her calf-idol at Bethel. Jer 48:13
For you scorned * and robbed Jer 48:27
be burned. Then * shall come and Jer 49:2
Then the people of * and Judah Jer 50:4
Hosts, the God of *, says: Now I Jer 50:18
And I will bring * home again to Jer 50:19
shall be found in * or in Judah, Jer 50:20
the Lord, the Holy One of *. Jer 50:29
of * and Judah have been wronged. Jer 50:33
to live again in quietness in *. Jer 50:34
has not forsaken * and Judah. Jer 51:5
sin against the Holy One of *. Jer 51:5
But the God of * is no idol! Jer 51:19
there is, and * is his nation; Jer 51:19
Hosts, the God of *, says: Babylon Jer 51:33
of *, so must she be killed. Jer 51:49
and the people of * were ejected Jer 52:3
the fairest city of * lies in the Lam 2:1
has destroyed every home in *. Lam 2:2
All the strength of * vanishes Lam 2:3
God burns across the land of * Lam 2:3
Yes, the Lord has vanquished * Lam 2:5
in the Temple as * used to do on Lam 2:7
their young, but not my people, *. Lam 4:3,4
to the nation of *, to a nation Eze 2:3
its message to the people of *." Eze 3:1
the people of * with my messages. Eze 3:4
to the people of *, and they won't Eze 3:7
appointed you as a watchman for *; Eze 3:17
is a warning to the people of *. Eze 4:3
days, to show that * will be Eze 4:4,5
a year of punishment ahead for *. Eze 4:4,5
For the Lord declares, * shall Eze 4:13
this remnant and destroy all *." Eze 5:4
And all * will know that what I Eze 5:13
of * and prophesy against them. Eze 6:2
Say to them, O mountains of *, Eze 6:3
destroy those in the land of *; Eze 6:12
"Tell *, Wherever you look—east, Eze 7:2
your final doom is waiting. O *, Eze 7:7
against all the people of *; Eze 7:13
has come for the cutting off of *. Eze 7:25
of the God of * was there, just as Eze 8:4
sins the people of * are doing Eze 8:6
worshiped by the people of *. Eze 8:10
Seventy elders of * were Eze 8:11
of * are doing in their minds? Eze 8:12
And the glory of the God of * Eze 9:3
wipe out everyone left in *?" Eze 9:8
of the people of * and Judah are Eze 9:9
And the glory of the God of * was Eze 10:19
God of * beside the Chebar Canal. Eze 10:20
of *: Is that what you are saying? Eze 11:5
to the borders of *, and you will Eze 11:10
to the borders of *, and you will Eze 11:11
going to kill everyone in all *?" Eze 11:13
and give you the land of * again. Eze 11:17
of the God of * stood above them. Eze 11:22
to the people of * of the evil that Eze 12:6
*, have asked what all this means. Eze 12:9
and to all the people of *. Eze 12:10
that the people of * and Jerusalem Eze 12:19
they quote in *—'The days as they Eze 12:22
be no more delays, O rebels of *! Eze 12:25
"Son of dust, the people of * Eze 12:27
false prophets of * who are Eze 13:2,3
"O *, these 'prophets' of yours Eze 13:4
the walls of * against her Eze 13:5
strengthening * in the Lord? Eze 13:5
off from among the leaders of *; Eze 13:9
THEN SOME OF the elders of * Eze 14:1
with anyone in * who worships idols Eze 14:4
whether people of * or the Eze 14:6,7
him from among my people *. Eze 14:9
that the people of * will learn not Eze 14:11
remainder of *, says the Lord God. Eze 14:14
things are being done to *." Eze 14:23
this riddle to the people of *: Eze 17:2
"Ask these rebels of *: Don't Eze 17:12,13
so that * would not be strong Eze 17:14
But by keeping her promises, * Eze 17:14
But will * prosper after breaking Eze 17:15
the Lord, the king of * shall die. Eze 17:16
shall fail to help * when the king Eze 17:17
For the king of * broke his Eze 17:18
And all the best soldiers of * Eze 17:21
about the land of *: The children Eze 18:2
any more in *, for all souls are Eze 18:3
the idols of * and worship them, Eze 18:6
Listen to me, O people of *. Eze 18:25
"And yet the people of * keep Eze 18:29

(ISRAEL Con't)
O people of *, it is you who are Eze 18:29
I will judge each of you, O *, Eze 18:30
For why will you die, O *? Eze 18:31
for the leaders of *: What a woman Eze 19:1
"When *, the mother lion, saw Eze 19:5
be heard upon the mountains of *. Eze 19:9
of the elders of * came to ask Eze 20:1
to the elders of *: The Lord God Eze 20:3
says: When I chose * and revealed Eze 20:5,6
"But * rebelled against me. Eze 20:13
I listen to you or help you, *? Eze 20:31
in returning to * from Babylon. Eze 20:35,36f
They shall not enter *, but I Eze 20:38
"O *, the Lord God says: If you Eze 20:39
the Lord, all * shall worship me. Eze 20:40
*, you will know I am the Lord." Eze 20:44
against * and against my Temple! Eze 21:2
Lord says: I am against you, *. Eze 21:3
evil prince of *, your final day Eze 21:25
"Every leader in * who lives Eze 22:6
"Son of dust, the people of * Eze 22:18,19,20
to the people of *: In the day of Eze 22:24
this parable to these rebels, *; Eze 24:3
to the people of *: I will destroy Eze 24:20,21
and mocked * in her anguish, and Eze 25:3
By the hand of my people, *, Eze 25:14
the kingdom of * send merchants Eze 27:17
prick and tear at * like thorns and Eze 28:24
"The people of * will once more Eze 28:25
They will live safely in *, and Eze 28:26
collapsed when * called on you for Eze 29:6
I am the Lord. * leaned on you Eze 29:7
"* will no longer expect any Eze 29:16
* will know that I alone am God." Eze 29:16
ancient glory of * to revive, and Eze 29:21
as a watchman for the people of *; Eze 33:7
"O people of *, you are saying: Eze 33:10
for why will you die, O *? Eze 33:11
And the mountain villages of * Eze 33:28
the leaders of *, and say to them: Eze 34:2
their own land of *, and I will Eze 34:13
the mountains of * and by the Eze 34:13
pasture on the high hills of *. Eze 34:14
in * so that my people will Eze 34:29
the people of *, are my people, Eze 34:30
Because you hate my people *, I Eze 35:4,5
"For you said, 'Both * and Judah Eze 35:10
And I will honor my name in * by Eze 35:11
Therefore, O mountains of *, Eze 36:4
and valleys of *: The Lord God Eze 36:6
but for *, good times will return. Eze 36:8
throughout all *, and the ruined Eze 36:10
O mountains of *, again you will Eze 36:11
you, saying, '* is a land that Eze 36:13
when the people of * were living in Eze 36:17
to the people of *: The Lord God Eze 36:22
back home again to the land of *. Eze 36:24
"And you shall live in *, the Eze 36:28
O my people *, be utterly ashamed Eze 36:32
again to *, and rebuild the ruins. Eze 36:33
"represent all the people of *. Eze 37:11
again and return to the land of *. Eze 37:12
all the other tribes of *.' Eze 37:16
take the tribes of * and join them Eze 37:18,19,20
the people of * from among the Eze 37:21
They shall live in the land of * Eze 37:25
* apart for special blessings." Eze 37:28
onto the land of *, that will be Eze 38:8
You will have said, '* is an Eze 38:11
the prophets of *, saying that Eze 38:17
the land of *, my fury will rise! Eze 38:18
in the land of * on that day. Eze 38:19
the mountains of *, bringing you Eze 39:2
my holy name among my people *; Eze 39:7
I am the Lord, the Holy One of *. Eze 39:7
"The people of the cities of * Eze 39:9
people of * to bury the bodies. Eze 39:12
Everyone in * will help, for it Eze 39:13
victory for * on that day when I Eze 39:13
and near to the mountains of *. Eze 39:17
the people of * will know I am the Eze 39:22
And the nations will know why * Eze 39:23
me to the land of * and set me down Eze 40:2
to the people of * to tell them all Eze 40:4
God of * appeared from the east. Eze 43:2
among the people of * forever. Eze 43:7
have shown you to the people of *. Eze 43:10
for the Lord, the God of *, Eze 44:2
the people of *, The Lord God says: Eze 44:6
Lord God says: O *, you have sinned Eze 44:6
abandoned me when * strayed away Eze 44:10
gods, causing * to fall into deep Eze 44:12
when * abandoned me for idols. Eze 44:15
the tribes of *, you shall first Eze 45:1
for a city open to everyone in *. Eze 45:6
flocks in *, give him one sheep. Eze 45:15
All the people of * shall bring Eze 45:16
for the people of *. Eze 45:17
himself and all the people of *. Eze 45:22
twelve tribes of *: The tribe of Eze 47:13
River separating * from Gilead, Eze 47:18
boundaries among the tribes of *. Eze 47:21
when the people of * and the rest Eze 48:11
matter where he comes from in *. Eze 48:19
of *, shall belong to the prince. Eze 48:21,22
entire country of *, from its Eze 48:23
honor of one of the tribes of *. Eze 48:30,31
from * as a Jewish captive? Dan 5:13
and warred against the land of *. Dan 8:9
glorious land." * was attacked by Dan 8:9f
Jerusalem, and all *, scattered Dan 9:7
prophets. All * has disobeyed; Dan 9:11
angel who guards your people *, Dan 10:20,21
* into Egypt, to a fortress there. Dan 11:10,11
Land' of *, and pillage it. Dan 11:16
tax collector into *, but after a Dan 11:20
through * and destroying it. Dan 11:28
the way, including *, the Pleasant Dan 11:41
and one of the kings of *, Hos 1:1
in fact, I will put an end to * Hos 1:4,5
of * twenty-five years later. Hos 1:4,5f
upon *, to forgive her again. Hos 1:6
Soon after defeating *, the Hos 1:7f
'Not mine'), for * is not mine and Hos 1:9
"Yet the time will come when * Hos 1:10
Then the people of Judah and * Hos 1:11
O *, I will cause you to forget Hos 1:17
For the Lord still loves * though Hos 3:1
This illustrates the fact that * Hos 3:4
WORD of the Lord, O people of *. Hos 4:1
and I will destroy your mother, * Hos 4:5
But though * is a prostitute, may Hos 4:15
Don't be like *, stubborn as a Hos 4:16
The men of * finish up their Hos 4:18
I have seen your evil deeds: *, Hos 5:3
The very arrogance of * testifies Hos 5:5
Hear this announcement, *: When Hos 5:9
horrible thing in *—Ephraim chasing Hos 6:10
other gods, * utterly defiled. Hos 6:10
I WANTED TO forgive *, but her Hos 7:1
Now * pleads with me and says, Hos 8:2
But it is too late! * has Hos 8:3
* is destroyed; Hos 8:8
* has built great palaces; Hos 8:14
O *, REJOICE no more as others do, Hos 9:1
soon * will know it all too well. Hos 9:7
O *, how well I remember those Hos 9:10
The glory of * flies away like a Hos 9:11
I have seen the sons of * doomed. Hos 9:13
The roots of * are dried up; Hos 9:16
the people of * because they will Hos 9:17
HOW PROSPEROUS * is—a luxuriant Hos 10:1
this idol; * will be put to shame. Hos 10:6
where * sinned will crumble. Hos 10:8
O *, ever since that awful night Hos 10:9
too, you people of *, because of Hos 10:15
In one morning the king of * Hos 10:15
WHEN * WAS a child I loved him as Hos 11:1
so I led * with my ropes of love. Hos 11:4
* surrounds me with lies and Hos 11:12
* IS CHASING the wind, yes, Hos 12:1
IT USED TO be when * spoke, the Hos 13:1
O *, if I destroy you, who can Hos 13:9
to the kings of * assassinated Hos 13:11f
O *, RETURN to the Lord, your God, Hos 14:1
I will refresh * like the dew Hos 14:5
Listen, you aged men of *! Joe 1:2
among my people *, and that I alone Joe 2:27
But to his people *, the Lord Joe 3:16
"But * will prosper forever, and Joe 3:20
going to happen to his nation, *. Amo 1:2
*—two years before the earthquake. Amo 1:2
treaty with their brother, *; Amo 1:9
For he chased his brother, *, Amo 1:11
The Lord says, "The people of * Amo 2:6
and prophets—can you deny this, * Amo 2:11
Lord against both * and Amo 3:1
it throughout all *," says the Amo 3:13
day that I punish * for her sins, I Amo 3:14
to meet your God in judgment, *. Amo 4:12
this song of grief for you, O *: Amo 5:1
"Beautiful * lies broken and Amo 5:2
The Lord says to the people of *, Amo 5:4
like fire through * and consume Amo 5:6
in the desert, *—but always your Amo 5:25,26,27
and popular among the people of *. Amo 6:1
*, and hate their beautiful homes. Amo 6:8
"O *, I will bring against you a Amo 6:14
If you turn against *, what hope Amo 7:2
is there? For * is so small!" Amo 7:2
is there? For * is so small!" Amo 7:5
The idol altars and temples of * Amo 7:9
be killed, and * will be sent far Amo 7:11
'Go and prophesy to my people *.' Amo 7:15
say, 'Don't prophesy against *.' Amo 7:16
and the people of * will certainly Amo 7:17
my people *—ripe for punishment. Amo 8:2
Lord, the Pride of *, has sworn: Amo 8:7
"O people of *, are you any more Amo 9:7
God are watching *, that sinful Amo 9:8
For I have commanded that * be Amo 9:9
former glory, and * will possess Amo 9:12
hills of * will drip sweet wine! Amo 9:13
of my people *, and they shall Amo 9:14
A nation southeast of *, including Ob 1:1f
of what you did to your brother *. Ob 1:10
For you deserted * in his time Ob 1:11
into the land of * in the day of Ob 1:13
As you have done to *, so will it Ob 1:15
escape. * will reoccupy the land. Ob 1:17
Israel will reoccupy the land. * Ob 1:18
Because of the sins of * and Mic 1:5
* in her sin of idol worship. Mic 1:13
the kings of *, for she promised Mic 1:14
to Adúllum, the "Pride of *." Mic 1:15
The time will come, O *, when I Mic 2:12
LISTEN, YOU LEADERS of *—you are Mic 3:1
punishment on * for her sins. Mic 3:8
Listen to me, you leaders of * Mic 3:9
see the Temple of the God of *; Mic 4:2
floor, helpless before *. Mic 4:13
strike the Judge of * on the face. Mic 5:1
exile remnants of * will rejoin Mic 5:3
Then the nation of * will refresh Mic 5:7
and * will be as strong as a lion. Mic 5:8
has a case against his people *! Mic 6:2
comes terrible destruction to * Mic 7:13
thinking * would be an easy prey. Hab 3:14
of Hosts, God of *, "Moab and Zep 2:9
shout, O *; Zep 3:14
King of *, will live among you! Zep 3:15
that the cities of * will again Zec 1:17
Judah, *, and Jerusalem." Zec 1:19
as much as do the tribes of *." Zec 9:1f
as well as *. Zec 9:1
be adopted into * as a new clan: Zec 9:7
invading armies from entering *. Zec 9:8
my people in *, and he shall bring Zec 9:10
Judah and * have been led astray Zec 10:2
strengthen Judah, yes, and * too; Zec 10:6
they will come home again to *. Zec 10:9
them in *—in Gilead and Lebanon; Zec 10:10
the people of * were miraculously Zec 10:11f
between Judah and * was broken. Zec 11:14
THIS IS THE fate of *, as Zec 12:1
All of * will weep in profound Zec 12:12,13,14
to the people of * and Jerusalem, a Zec 13:1
of * will be cut off and die, Zec 13:8
HERE IS THE Lord's message to *, Mal 1:1
O *, lift your eyes to see what Mal 1:5
In Judah, in *, and in Mal 2:11
For the Lord, the God of *, says Mal 2:16
laws I gave all * through Moses my Mal 4:4
from you to rule my people *.' Mt 2:6
his mother back to *, for those who Mt 2:20
So he returned immediately to * Mt 2:21
like this in all the land of *! Mt 8:10
the people of *—God's lost sheep. Mt 10:6
sheep of *—not the Gentiles." Mt 15:24
and praised the God of *. Mt 15:31
judging the twelve tribes of *. Mt 19:28
by the people of *— and purchased Mt 27:9
So you are the King of *, are Mt 27:41,42,43
"The one that says, 'Hear, O *! Mk 12:29
"You 'King of *'! Mk 15:32
And he shall reign over * Lk 1:33
how he has helped his servant *! Lk 1:54
"Praise the Lord, the God of *, Lk 1:68
he began his public ministry to *. Lk 1:80
Literally, "the Consolation of * Lk 2:25f
be the glory of your people *!" Lk 2:32
in *, and this to their undoing. Lk 2:34,35
all the Jews in * have I met a man Lk 7:9
judging the twelve tribes of *. Lk 22:30
and that he had come to rescue *. Lk 24:21
him out to the nation of *." Jn 1:31
an honest man—a true son of *." Jn 1:47
the Son of God—the King of *!" Jn 1:49
would not be for * only, but for Jn 11:52
God bless the King of *! Jn 12:13
King, people of *, for he will come Jn 12:15
are you going to free * [from Rome Act 1:6
"O men of *, listen! Act 2:22
to everyone in * that God has made Act 2:36
"Men of *," he said, "what is Act 3:12
all to you men of *, to bless you Act 3:26
all the people of * that it was Act 4:10
as the people of *—are united Act 4:27
that the people of * would have an Act 5:31
"Men of *, take care what you are Act 5:35
to the land of *, but gave him no Act 7:4
land of * and worship me here.' Act 7:7
his brothers, the people of *. Act 7:23
Egyptian mistreating a man of *. Act 7:24
and saw two men of * fighting. Act 7:26
told the people of *, 'God will Act 7:37
the people of * and the Angel who Act 7:38
forty years in the desert, *? Act 7:42
as well as to the people of *. Act 9:15
for the people of *—that there is Act 10:36,37
he did throughout * and in Act 10:39
was coming upon the land of *. Act 11:28

(ISRAEL Con't)

"Men of *," he said, "and all	Act 13:16
"The God of this nation * chose	Act 13:17
* their land as an inheritance.	Act 13:19,20
who is God's promised Savior of *!	Act 13:23
in * to turn from sin to God.	Act 13:24
grabbed him, yelling, "Men of *!	Act 21:28
The twelve tribes of * strive	Act 26:7
Literally, "the hope of *."	Act 28:20f
OH, *, MY people!	Rom 9:1
And then all * will be saved.	Rom 11:26
him, as the people of * did.	Heb 3:7,8
as the people of * did when they	Heb 3:15
of * that Joshua led them into.	Heb 4:8
of * did, thus failing to get in.	Heb 4:11
of * and the people of Judah.	Heb 8:8
with the people of *, says the	Heb 8:10
with the people of *, though they	Heb 10:16
the people of * out of Egypt;	Heb 11:22
The people of * trusted God and	Heb 11:29
the people of * had walked around	Heb 11:30
For if the people of * did not	Heb 12:25
ruin the people of * by involving	Rev 2:14
tribes of *, as listed here:	Rev 7:4-8
of * were written on the gates.	Rev 21:12

ISRAEL'S

So it was that * sons arrived in	Gen 42:5
knees—Ephraim at * left hand and	Gen 48:12,13
The sons of Reuben, * oldest	Ex 6:14
of the second year of * leaving	Num 10:11
(Reuben was * eldest son.	Num 26:5-11
(It was the second time in *	Jos 5:2,3
chosen to carry * annual tax money	Ju 3:15
* leader at that time, the one	Ju 4:4
* leaders bravely led;	Ju 5:2
* population dwindled,	Ju 5:7
He was * judge for twenty-three	Ju 10:2
to attack * army at Mizpah.	Ju 10:17
Jephthah was * judge for six	Ju 12:7
He was * judge for eight years.	Ju 12:14
Samson was * judge for the next	Ju 15:20
their ancestor, * son, but it had	Ju 18:29
'Ichabod,' for * glory is gone."	1Sa 4:21,22
Mizpah that Samuel became * judge.	1Sa 7:6
Samuel continued as * judge for	1Sa 7:15
once complained to * leaders, the	2Sa 7:7
or if * enemies besiege one of her	1Ki 8:37
to besiege Tirzah, * capital.	1Ki 16:17
* new king, Ahaziah, had fallen	2Ki 1:2
of the king of * officers replied.	2Ki 3:11
about the king of * plight, he sent	2Ki 5:8
could worship Jehovah on * soil.	2Ki 5:17f
The sons of Reuben, * son, were:	1Ch 5:3
that David was * new king, they	1Ch 14:8
the altar for * burnt offering!"	1Ch 22:1
the Lord, who is * fountain.	Ps 68:26
killed the finest of * young men.	Ps 78:31
Sing to * God!	Ps 81:1
and politicians. * kings will be	Is 3:4
* civil government will be in	Is 3:8
For as * glory departed, so	Is 17:3
In that day [of * freedom	Is 27:2
as an indictment of * unbelief.	Is 30:8
* God, will not ever forsake them.	Is 41:17
it is God who did it, * Holy One.	Is 41:20
I am the Lord, your Holy One, *	Is 43:15
says—yes, it is * Redeemer, the	Is 44:6
One of Israel, * Creator, says:	Is 45:11
In a moment, just as * anguish	Is 66:7,8
utterly destroy * glory and power.	Jer 2:16
The reference is to Egypt and *	Lam 1:2f
of the Lord. * exile for her sins	Lam 4:22
"The trumpets shout to * army,	Eze 7:14
the top men of * government, so	Eze 17:12,13
on the top of * highest mountain.	Eze 17:22,23
Egyptians laugh at * God who	Eze 20:9,10
No longer shall you and * other	Eze 28:24
You rejoiced at * fearful fate.	Eze 35:15
"SON OF DUST, prophesy to *	Eze 36:1
I am ready to hear * prayers for	Eze 36:37,38
you priests and all of * leaders;	Hos 5:1
The time of * punishment has	Hos 9:7
spectacle of all * crimes.	Amo 3:9
the time of * spiritual rebirth;	Mic 5:3
Listen to the wailing of *	Zec 11:3

ISRAELI

Then they whipped the *	Ex 5:14
none of the * herds and flocks	Ex 9:4
one of the * herds was even sick.	Ex 9:6
that none of the * cattle were	Ex 9:7
he is a native * or a foreigner, is	Num 15:30
closely by the 250 * leaders.	Num 16:25
"But, sir," protested the *	Num 20:19
But one of the * men insolently	Num 25:6
Then the * army took as captives	Num 31:9,10,11
For example, any * who presents	Deu 18:10
No * may practice black magic, or	Deu 18:10
like me, an *, a man to whom you	Deu 18:15
them a Prophet, an * like you.	Deu 18:18
stand before the * army and say,	Deu 20:2
a foreigner, but not from an *.	Deu 23:20
from a brother, an *, the Lord your	Deu 23:20
two spies from the * camp at Acacia	Jos 2:1
"They have been sent by the *	Jos 2:3
the quarries. The * army was	Jos 7:5
Joshua and the * army fled	Jos 8:15
neighbors. The * army set out at	Jos 9:17
So Joshua and the * army left	Jos 10:7
move until the * army had finished	Jos 10:13
(Afterwards Joshua and the *	Jos 10:15
So Joshua and the * army	Jos 10:20
The * army then captured Eglon on	Jos 10:34,35
of Israel. The * territory now	Jos 11:17
the * leaders and reminded them,	Jos 17:4
escaped, but the * army soon	Ju 1:4,5,6
and the * girls married their men.	Ju 3:6
Gideon, the son of Joash, the *,	Ju 7:14
of the * forces at Mizpah soon	Ju 20:3
Before the battle the * army went	Ju 20:18
Then the * army wept before the	Ju 20:22,23,24
So the * army set an ambush all	Ju 20:29
to attack, the * forces retreated	Ju 20:31
Benjamin, and the * army killed	Ju 20:35-39
the signal for the * army to turn	Ju 20:35-39
Then the * army returned and	Ju 20:48
And now the * leaders met at	Ju 21:2
Philistines. The * army was camped	1Sa 4:1
thousands of the * troops are dead	1Sa 4:17
lifetime. The * cities between	1Sa 7:14
to Israel, for the * army rescued	1Sa 7:14
the * city of Jabesh-gilead.	1Sa 11:1
So the entire * army mobilized	1Sa 13:3,4
Saul sent the * army out in every	1Sa 14:47
and the * army heard this, they	1Sa 17:11
(Saul and the * army were camped	1Sa 17:19
camp just as the * army was leaving	1Sa 17:20
Soon the * and Philistine forces	1Sa 17:21
As soon as they saw him the *	1Sa 17:24
Then the * army returned and	1Sa 17:53
the victorious * army was returning	1Sa 18:6
What's more, the entire * army	1Sa 28:19
arrived from the * army with his	2Sa 1:1
"From the * army," he replied.	2Sa 1:3
The command of the * troops then	2Sa 4:2,3
the entire * army to attack them.	2Sa 10:7,8
personally led the * army to Helam,	2Sa 10:17
* army to destroy the Ammonites.	2Sa 11:1
with several other * soldiers.	2Sa 11:17
Meanwhile Joab and the * army	2Sa 12:26,27
Absalom and the * army now	2Sa 17:26
Ephraim, and the * troops were	2Sa 18:7
when the rest of the * army fled.	2Sa 23:9
officers of the * army—went down at	2Sa 23:13
burned, killing the * population;	1Ki 9:16
peacocks arrived at the * ports.	1Ki 10:22
the burial of some * soldiers who	1Ki 11:15
in battle, the * army had killed	1Ki 11:15
he was with the * army laying siege	1Ki 15:27
besieged Samaria, the * capital.	1Ki 20:1
"The * God is a god of the hills;	1Ki 20:23
but the * army looked like two	1Ki 20:27
So King Jehoram mustered the *	2Ki 3:6,7,8
But when they arrived at the *	2Ki 3:24
the horror of the * army, killed	2Ki 3:27
When the * guerrilla forces	2Ki 25:23
and defeated the * troops, who	1Ch 10:1
at Pas-dammim. The * army was in a	1Ch 11:13
deserted the * army and joined	1Ch 12:19
Joab led the * army in successful	1Ch 20:1
THE * ARMY was divided into twelve	1Ch 27:1
commander-in-chief of the * army.	1Ch 27:34
of any of the * citizens, but used	2Ch 8:9
twice as many * troops—strong,	2Ch 13:3
to King Jeroboam and the * army:	2Ch 13:4
haphazardly at the * troops, and it	2Ch 18:33
THE * OFFICIALS were living in	Neh 11:1
The * exiles shall return and	Ob 1:20

ISRAELIS

He told his people, "These * are	Ex 1:9
the more the * seemed to multiply!	Ex 1:12
of Egypt died. The * were groaning	Ex 2:23
land of Goshen where the * live.	Ex 8:22
between Egyptians and *.'	Ex 11:7
The * took with them their bread	Ex 12:34
And the Lord gave the * favor	Ex 12:36
of Egypt that the * were not	Ex 14:5
the Egyptians couldn't find the *!	Ex 14:20
THE * ARRIVED in the Sinai	Ex 19:1
of the second year after the *	Num 1:1
in line whenever the * traveled.	Num 2:3-31
the rest of the * were on the Sinai	Num 9:1
(The * were camped in the	Num 13:3-15
and figs. The * named the valley	Num 13:24
to native-born * and to foreigners	Num 15:13,14
heard that the * were approaching	Num 21:1
and the * completely destroyed	Num 21:3
After dealing with him, the *	Num 33:41
were destroyed by Moses and the *.	Deu 4:44,45,46
Jericho that two * who were	Jos 2:2
the people were afraid of the *;	Jos 6:1
Then the * burned the city and	Jos 6:24
BUT THERE WAS sin among the *.	Jos 7:1
About thirty-six of the * were	Jos 7:5
for they will say, 'The * are	Jos 8:6
The King of Ai, seeing the *	Jos 8:14
Then the * who were inside the	Jos 8:22
foreigners who lived among the *.	Jos 8:35
lives against Joshua and the *.	Jos 9:1
The * replied to these Hivites,	Jos 9:7
So they became servants of the *,	Jos 9:21
hail than by the swords of the *.	Jos 10:11
Then the * returned to their	Jos 10:21
Then the * went to Libnah.	Jos 10:29
vast army to the *, who chased them	Jos 11:8
were taken by the * for themselves,	Jos 11:14
the * instead of asking for peace;	Jos 11:20
destroyed by the *: (The area	Jos 12:1
as the * resettled the land.	Jos 14:15
Later on, however, when the *	Jos 17:13
as well as for the * themselves, so	Jos 20:9
there today, mingled with the *.	Ju 1:21
In later years when the * were	Ju 1:28
so the * still live among the	Ju 1:31,32
These forces defeated the * and	Ju 3:13
for the * for twenty years.	Ju 4:2,3
so cruel that the * took to the	Ju 6:2
and the * took the heads of Oreb	Ju 7:25
was dead, the * began to worship	Ju 8:33
the Jordan to attack the *.	Ju 10:9
Finally the * turned to Jehovah	Ju 10:10
said, when the * came from Egypt;	Ju 11:13
twenty-two thousand * that day.	Ju 20:21
thirty of the *, they were	Ju 20:35-39
but the * chased after them, and	Ju 20:42
When the * saw the Ark coming,	1Sa 4:5
and advanced. The * were badly	1Sa 7:7
confusion, and the * routed them,	1Sa 7:10
"Look! The * are crawling out of	1Sa 14:11
revolted and joined with the *.	1Sa 14:21
The * fought constantly with the	1Sa 14:52
So the Philistines and * faced	1Sa 17:3
across to the *, "Do you need a	1Sa 17:8
Then the * gave a great shout of	1Sa 17:52
at Aphek, and the * camped at the	1Sa 29:1
"What are these * doing here?"	1Sa 29:3
Israel, and the * fled from them	1Sa 31:1
When the * on the other side of	1Sa 31:7
fled from the *, this time leaving	2Sa 10:18
and the * were fighting at Gath, a	2Sa 21:20,21
Solomon didn't conscript any *	1Ki 9:22
and fled. The * chased them, but	1Ki 20:20
And the * killed 100,000 Syrian	1Ki 20:29
leaders among the * to rescue them	2Ki 13:5
transported the * to Assyria and	2Ki 18:11
When the * in the valley below	1Ch 10:7
After the battle the * picked up	1Ch 14:12
* had not completely wiped out.	2Ch 8:7,8
be built by the *, just as King	Ez 4:3
the * in worshiping the Lord God.	Ez 6:21,22
And the * separated themselves	Neh 9:1
among the * and brought them into	Neh 9:23
the Egyptians against the *;	Ps 105:25
LONG AGO WHEN the * escaped from	Ps 114:1
THE LORD will have mercy on the *;	Is 14:1
face so that the * could not see	2Co 3:13

ISRAELITE

"Any * who sacrifices	Lev 17:3,4
I repeat: Anyone, whether an *	Lev 17:8,9
anyone, whether an * or a foreigner	Lev 17:10
Anyone, whether an * or a	Lev 17:13
"Anyone—whether an * or a	Lev 20:1
Israel that if an * or other person	Lev 22:17,18
mother was an * and whose father	Lev 24:10
Literally, "the * woman's son."	Lev 24:11f
as well as to the * who blasphemes	Lev 24:15,16
"If a fellow * becomes poor and	Lev 25:39
rich, and an * becomes poor and	Lev 25:47
only I could die as happy as an *!	Num 23:7-10
against a fellow *, for the Lord	Deu 15:2
He must be an *, not a foreigner.	Deu 17:15
make to a brother *, whether it is	Deu 23:19
If anyone kidnaps a brother *,	Deu 24:7
whether a fellow * or a foreigner	Deu 24:14,15
Literally, "to each *."	1Ch 16:3f
condition for helping another *?"	Neh 5:7
Three * kings were assassinated	Hos 7:7f
And many an *—those for whom the	Mt 8:12

ISRAELITES

For Pharaoh will think, 'Those *	Ex 14:3
When all the * were on the other	Ex 14:26
*, to fight the army of Amalek.	Ex 17:9
* are to live in these shelters.	Lev 23:42
the * traveled to a new campsite.	Num 2:3-31
children of the *: I have taken the	Num 8:16
plague among the *—as there would	Num 8:19
so the * left the Sinai	Num 10:12
"From now on, * other than the	Num 18:22
tell you what the * are going to do	Num 24:14
* in Egypt, leaving them unharmed	Num 28:16
(The * later changed the names of	Num 32:37,38
the protection of *, but also for	Num 35:15
the song and taught it to the *.	Deu 31:22
live among the * because she hid	Jos 6:25

(ISRAELITES Con't)
Then Joshua and all the * took Jos 7:24
there among the * to this day. Jos 13:13
and the * came to her to decide Ju 4:5
where there are no *—we will go on Ju 19:12,13
They treated all of the * in this 1Sa 2:13,14
"When the * were in Egypt and 1Sa 12:8
So whenever the * needed to 1Sa 13:20
the tallest of the *, and was 1Sa 17:11f
to see * executed in revenge." 2Sa 21:4
not prove that they were really *. Ez 2:59
he will gather the scattered * Is 11:12
when the * approached (so long ago Is 17:9
to * rather than to the nations. Is 65:1f
to * rather than to the nations. Is 65:1f
The * are like sheep the lions Jer 50:17
* and raise them for myself ! Hos 1:23
like saying to the * that they must Amo 1:5f
So it will be when the * in Amo 3:12
And they say that they are *, 2Co 11:22
storm, as the * did at Mount Sinai Heb 12:18
who induced the * to fall by lust. Rev 2:6f

ISSACHAR
She named him * (meaning Gen 30:18
Simeon, Levi, Judah, *, Zebulun. Gen 35:23
* and his sons: Tola, Puvah, Iob, Gen 46:8-14
"* is a strong beast of burden Gen 49:14
Levi,Judah, *, Zebulun,Benjamin, Ex 1:1
* -Nethanel (son of Zuar Num 1:2-15
* 54,400 Num 1:20-46
Tribe: * Nethanel (son of Num 2:3-31
Next to * Num 2:3-31
of the tribe of *, brought his Num 7:18-23
Next came the tribe of *, led by Num 10:15
of Joseph, from the tribe of *; Num 13:3-15
The tribe of *: 64,300. Num 26:23-25
clans named after the sons of *: Num 26:23-25
* Paltiel (son of Azzan) Num 34:16-28
Levi, Judah, *, Joseph, and Deu 27:12
And *, you lovers of your tents; Deu 33:18
boundary was the territory of *. Jos 17:10
areas assigned to * and Asher: Jos 17:11
The Land Given to the Tribe of *: Jos 19:17-23
to be assigned its land was *. Jos 19:17-23
The boundary of * ended at the Jos 19:17-23
by the tribes of *, Asher, Jos 21:6
The tribe of * gave four cities: Jos 21:28,29
Went the princes of * Ju 5:15
He was from the tribe of *, but Ju 10:1
(son of Paruah), whose area was *; 1Ki 4:8-19
from the tribe of *) plotted 1Ki 15:27
Reuben, Simeon, Levi, Judah, *, 1Ch 2:1
*, Asher, Naphtali, and Manasseh. 1Ch 6:62
The tribe of * gave them Kedesh, 1Ch 6:72
THE SONS OF *: 1Ch 7:1
of the tribe of * numbered 87,000 1Ch 7:5
From the tribe of * there were 200 1Ch 12:24-37
as far away as *, Zebulun, and 1Ch 12:40
* (the seventh), 1Ch 26:4,5
Over *, Omri (son of Michael); 1Ch 27:16-22
Ephraim, Manasseh, *, and 2Ch 30:17,18,19
Next is *, with the same Eze 48:25
gates of Simeon, * and Zebulun; Eze 48:33
* 12,000 Rev 7:4-8

ISSHIAH
and *, all chiefs of subclans. 1Ch 7:3
Elkanah, *, Azarel, Jo-ezer, 1Ch 12:3-7
and * was the second in command. 1Ch 23:20
group, led by his oldest son *; 1Ch 24:21
*, and by Isshiah's son Zechariah. 1Ch 24:24,25

ISSHIAH'S
Isshiah, and by * son Zechariah. 1Ch 24:24,25

ISSHIJAH
Eliezer, *, Malchijah, Shemaiah, Ez 10:31,32

ISSUE
Moses instructed Joshua to * a Ex 17:9
Literally, "an * out of his Lev 15:1f
Literally, "has an *." Lev 15:32f
commanded me to * the laws you must Deu 4:14
years you make an * of this! Ju 11:26
of the priests to * food and other 2Ch 31:19
agreement, you * a royal edict, a Est 1:19
If it please the king, * a Est 3:9
and to those who * unfair laws, Is 10:1
He will * his laws and announce Mic 4:2

ISSUED
THEN GOD * this edict: Ex 20:1
that the Lord * the following Num 1:1
He * the following command to Num 25:4
So Moses and Eleazar * census Num 26:3,4
Listed below are the laws Moses * Deu 4:44,45,46
Then Joshua * instructions to the Jos 1:10,11
Lord's command, * the orders to the Jos 4:15,16
So Joshua * the order. Jos 4:17
been found, he * a command that a Jos 10:18
The king then * orders for his 2Ki 23:21
Ark of God, and * these 1Ch 15:2
Now the king of Syria had * these 2Ch 18:30
Then Jehoiada * spears and 2Ch 23:9
Uzziah * to them shields, 2Ch 26:14
Temple again. He * this order to 2Ch 35:3
directions * centuries earlier by 2Ch 35:15
year of his reign, * a decree that Ez 5:13
SO KING DARIUS * orders that a Ez 6:1
I, Darius, have * this decree; Ez 6:12
most people do. I * instructions Neh 7:3
laws as * by his servant Moses. Neh 10:29
The same decree was also * at Est 8:14
the king, he * a decree causing Est 9:24,25
For you have * the order to save Ps 71:3
For he * his command, and they Ps 148:5
Then the king * a command to Dan 6:24
guests, he * the necessary orders. Mt 14:9
And Pilate * an order to release Mt 27:58
Lightning and thunder * from the Rev 4:5

ISSUES
discussing various * with the local Ju 9:35

ISSUING
no longer be the * of battle gear; Is 9:5

ITALIAN
a captain of an * regiment. Act 10:1

ITALIC
The use of bold type or * type 1Ch 1:1f
* means that the name has 1Ch 1:5-9f

ITALY
from * with his wife, Priscilla. Act 18:2,3
They had been expelled from * as Act 18:2,3
bound for *, and put us aboard. Act 27:6
The Christians from * who are Heb 13:24,25

ITCH
which has sores or * or any other Lev 22:22
scurvy, and *, for none of which Deu 28:27

ITEM
on each * in it, sanctifying them. Lev 8:10
for each * in the Temple which was 1Ch 28:13
A receipt was given for each *, Ez 8:34
he came across the * telling how Est 6:1

ITEMS
They alone shall eat those * Ex 29:33
repairs needed on any of these *. Num 3:31-35
touch the holy *, lest they die. Num 4:15
for the transportation of these *. Num 4:26
the * from the inner sanctuary. Num 10:21
Here is a list of the * he made: 1Ki 7:41-46
All these * were made of burnished 1Ki 7:41-46
the furniture, the * in the 1Ch 9:29
the care of the * dedicated to the 1Ch 26:28
make these various *, as well as 1Ch 28:14
above-mentioned * for King Solomon, 2Ch 4:12-16
bowls and other * from the Temple, 2Ch 36:7
with him all the *, great and 2Ch 36:18
and other valuable * which King Ez 1:7
The * Cyrus donated included: Ez 1:9,10
1,000 miscellaneous *. Ez 1:9,10
gold and silver * turned over to Ez 1:11
They say these * were delivered Ez 5:14
bowls and other * we are giving you Ez 7:19
and the other * which the king and Ez 8:25
purchase the other * necessary for Neh 10:33
the other * used in the Temple. Jer 52:18
holding on to the * given to him in Eze 18:7
Next on my list of * to write you 1Co 11:17

ITHAI
* (son of Ribai) a Benjaminite 1Ch 11:26-47

ITHAMAR
were:Nadab, Abihu,Eleazar, *. Ex 6:23
Eleazer, and *, to be priests, to Ex 28:1
by *, son of Aaron the priest. Ex 38:21
sons Eleazar and *, "Do not Lev 10:6
left, Eleazar and *, "Take the Lev 10:12
*, the remaining sons of Aaron. Lev 10:16
(his oldest), Abihu, Eleazar, *. Num 3:2
* to assist their father Aaron. Num 3:4
responsible to Aaron's son *. Num 4:28
also report to Aaron's son *." Num 4:33
the leadership of *, Aaron's son. Num 7:8
born Nadab, Abihu, Eleazar, and *. Num 26:60
Nadab, Abihu, Eleazar, *. 1Ch 6:3
Eleazar and * 1Ch 24:1
so only Eleazar and * were left 1Ch 24:1
who represented the * clan; 1Ch 24:3
of * were assigned to each task. 1Ch 24:6
From the clan of *—Daniel; Ez 8:2-14

ITHAMAR'S
sixteen groups and * into eight 1Ch 24:4

ITHI-EL
son of *, son of Jeshaiah). Neh 11:7,8,9

ITHIEL
Massa, addressed to * and Ucal: Pro 30:1

ITHLAH
Aijalon, *, Elon, Timnah, Ekron, Jos 19:41-46

ITHMAH
* from Moab; 1Ch 11:26-47

ITHNAN
Kedesh, Hazor, *, Ziph, Telem, Jos 15:21-32

ITHRA
his father was *, an Ishmaelite, 2Sa 17:25
Ira from *; 2Sa 23:24-39
Gareb from *; 2Sa 23:24-39
Ira from *; 1Ch 11:26-47
Gareb from *; 1Ch 11:26-47

ITHRAN
Dishon:Hemdan, Eshban,*, Cheran. Gen 36:26
Hamran, Eshban, *, and Cheran. 1Ch 1:41
*, Be-era. 1Ch 7:36,37
The sons of * 1Ch 7:38

ITHREAM
Abital, and * was born to Eglah. 2Sa 3:5
The sixth was *, the son of his 1Ch 3:3

ITHRITES
were the *, the Puthites, the 1Ch 2:53

ITINERANT
A team of * Jews who were Act 19:13

ITINERARY
THIS IS THE * of the nation of Num 33:1

ITSELF
science feeds upon * and grows. Gen 11:6f
of animals by *, separated by a Gen 32:16
The central shaft * will be Ex 25:34,35
the Tabernacle * and on each item Lev 8:10
and upon the altar *, to sanctify Lev 8:15,16
not on the spot *) and the priest Lev 13:33
that dies of *, or is torn by wild Lev 17:15
that dies of * or is torn by wild Lev 22:8
the Tabernacle * with its Num 4:25
sacred duties in the Tabernacle *. Num 18:2,3
in the Promised Land * Deu 20:15
was hinged to fold back upon *. 1Ki 6:34
Temple *, for they are sanctified. 2Ch 23:5,6
from death *, and here I am alive! Ps 30:3
are better to me than life *. Ps 63:3
History merely repeats *. Ecc 1:8-11
Can a cane walk by *?" Is 10:15
hell *, to find new gods to love. Is 57:9
The land * is mourning—the Jer 23:10
The nave * was seventy feet long Eze 41:2
the Mediterranean * will be your Eze 47:20
The city * is to be 1½ miles Eze 48:16
the seaweed wrapped * around my Jon 2:5
A city or home divided against * Mt 12:25
more evil than *, and all enter the Mt 12:43,44,45
altar * that sanctifies the gift? Mt 23:19
A kingdom divided against * will Mk 3:24
strife and division destroys *. Mk 3:25
*, and they all enter the man. Lk 11:26
heat, fastened * onto his hand! Act 28:3
But still, you see, the law * Rom 7:12
* cannot keep God's love away. Rom 8:38
Doesn't even instinct * teach us 1Co 11:14,15
and finally send them to hell *. 1Ti 6:9
has gone to heaven * to help us; Heb 4:14
into heaven *, to appear now before Heb 9:24
Faith that doesn't show * by good Jas 2:17
on fire by hell *, and can turn our Jas 3:6
joy that comes from heaven *. 1Pe 1:8
They are from this evil world *. 1Jn 2:16
But everyone, including Truth *, 3Jn 1:12
as from the very flames of hell *. Jud 1:23
The city * was pure, transparent Rev 21:18,19,20

ITTAI
But suddenly the king turned to * 2Sa 15:19,20
But * replied, "I vow by God and 2Sa 15:21
Then * and his six hundred men 2Sa 15:22
and a third under *, the Gittite. 2Sa 18:2
Joab, Abishai, and *, "For my 2Sa 18:5
and Abishai and *, 'For my sake, 2Sa 18:12
* (son of Ribai) from Gibe-ah, of 2Sa 23:24-39

ITUREA
his brother Philip, over * and Lk 3:1

IV
by Antiochus * Epiphanes, with a Dan 8:9f
Ptolemy *. Dan 11:10,11f
Seleucus *, successor of Antiochus Dan 11:20f
This may refer to Antiochus * Dan 11:21f
Probably Antiochus * and Ptolemy Dan 11:27f
Antiochus IV and Ptolemy *. Dan 11:27f
Antiochus * fades from view and Dan 11:40f

IVORY
He also made a huge * throne and 1Ki 10:18
of gold, silver, *, apes, and 1Ki 10:22
the story of the * palace and the 1Ki 22:39
He also made a huge * throne 2Ch 9:17
silver, *, apes, and peacocks. 2Ch 9:21
In your inlaid palaces of *, Ps 45:8
his body is bright * encrusted Sol 5:14
Your neck is stately as an * Sol 7:4
giving payment in ebony and *. Eze 27:15
demolish their * palaces." Amo 3:15
You lie on * beds surrounded with Amo 6:4
perfumed wood, and * goods and most Rev 18:12

IVVAH
Arpad, Sepharvaim, Hena, and *? 2Ki 18:34
of Sepharvaim, Hena, and *?" 2Ki 19:13
of Sepharvaim, Hena, and *." Is 37:13

IYE-ABARIM
Then they went on to *, in the Num 21:11

IYEABARIM
then * (at the border of Moab). Num 33:44

IZHAR
The sons of Kohath:Amram,* Ex 6:18
The sons of *:Korah, Nepheg, Ex 6:21
(clan names) Amram * Num 3:25-30
ONE DAY KORAH (son of *, Num 16:1
and Helah bore him Zereth, *, 1Ch 4:7

(ZHAR Con't)
Amram, *, Hebron, Uzziel. 1Ch 6:2
The sons of Kohath were:Amram, *, 1Ch 6:18
Korah, *, Kohath, Levi, Israel. 1Ch 6:33-38
Amram, *, Hebron, and 1Ch 23:12
The sons of * were led by 1Ch 23:18
son Isshiah; the * group, 1Ch 24:22
Amram, *, Hebron, and Uzziel. 1Ch 26:23,24
the subclan of *) were appointed 1Ch 26:29

ZLIAH
Hizki, Heber, Ishmerai, *, Jobab. 1Ch 8:17,18

ZRAH
was Shamuth from *, with 24,000 men 1Ch 27:8

ZRAHIAH
Uzzi's son was * among whose five 1Ch 7:3

ZRI
The fourth, * and twelve of his 1Ch 25:9-31

ZZIAH
Ramiah, *, Malchijah, Mijamin, Ez 10:25

A-AKOBAH
Jehu, Eli-o-enai, *, Jeshohaiah, 1Ch 4:34-39

A-ASIEL
Obed; * from Mezoba. 1Ch 11:26-47
Over Benjamin, * (son of Abner); 1Ch 27:16-22

JA-AZANIAH
Netophathite; and *, son of 2Ki 25:23
So I went over to see * (son of Jer 35:3
there along with * (son of Shaphan) Eze 8:11
two officers, * (son of Azzur) and Eze 11:1

JA-AZIAH'S
Mushi. (* group, led by his son 1Ch 24:26,27

JA-AZIEL
Zechariah, *, Shemiramoth, Jehiel, 1Ch 15:18

JAAKAN
of Ezer: Bilhan, Zaavan, and *. 1Ch 1:42

JAALA
*, Darkon, Giddel, Neh 7:57,58,59

JAALAH
Sotai, Hassophereth, Peruda, *, Ez 2:55,56,57

JAAR
in the distant countryside of *. Ps 132:6

JAARESHIAH
Shamsherai, Shehariah, Athaliah, * 1Ch 8:26,27

JAASU
Mattenai, *, Bani, Binnui, Shime-i, Ez 10:34-42

JABAL
To Adah was born a baby named *. Gen 4:20

JABBERING
with a strange, * language you Is 33:19

JABBOK
River at the * ford, then returned Gen 32:22,23,24
Arnon River to the * River, as far Num 21:24
Ammon and from the * River and the Deu 2:37
extending from the * River in Deu 3:16
Arnon River to the * River, which Jos 12:2
which lies north of the * River. Jos 12:2
Arnon River to the * and the Jordan Ju 11:13
Arnon River to the *, and from the Ju 11:21,22

JABESH
But the citizens of * asked for 1Sa 11:1
replied the elders of *. 1Sa 11:3
told him about the message from *. 1Sa 11:5
The men of * then told their 1Sa 11:10
to *, where they cremated them. 1Sa 31:12
at * and fasted for seven days. 1Sa 31:13
Then Shallum (the son of *) 2Ki 15:10
Father's name: * 2Ki 15:13
the oak tree at * and mourned and 1Ch 10:12

JABESH-GILEAD
that no one had attended from *. Ju 21:8,9
to destroy the people of *. Ju 21:10,11,12
when we destroyed *, and you Ju 21:22
against the Israeli city of *. 1Sa 11:1
messengers back to * to say, "We 1Sa 11:9
But when the people of * heard 1Sa 31:11
When David heard that the men of * 2Sa 2:4
to the men of *, asking them to 2Sa 21:12,13,14
But when the people of * heard 1Ch 10:11

JABEZ
writers living at *—the Tirathites, 1Ch 2:55
* was more distinguished than any 1Ch 4:9
His mother named him * because 1Ch 4:9
a hard time at his birth (* means 1Ch 4:9
A play on words. * sounds like 1Ch 4:9f

JABIN
WHEN KING * of Hazor heard what Jos 11:1
by King * of Hazor, in Canaan. Ju 4:2,3
* of Hazor and the clan of Heber. Ju 4:17
Israel to subdue King * of Canaan. Ju 4:23
against King *, until he and all Ju 4:24
did to Sisera and * at the river Ps 83:9

JABIN'S
to fight King * mighty army with Ju 4:7

JABNEEL
north, it passed * and ended at the Jos 15:10,11
to Adami-nekeb, *, and Lakkum, Jos 19:33

JABNEH
walls, also those of * and Ashdod. 2Ch 26:6

JACAN
Sheba, Jorai, *, Zia, and Eber. 1Ch 5:13

JACHIN
Jamin, Ohad, *, Zohar, and Shaul Gen 46:8-14
*, Zohar, Ex 6:15
named after their ancestor *. Num 26:12-14
was named the * Pillar, and the one 1Ki 7:16-22
* means "to establish," and Boaz 1Ki 7:16-22f
Jedaiah, Jehoiarib, *, 1Ch 9:10,11
Twenty-first, the group led by *; 1Ch 24:7-18
And he gave them names: * (the 2Ch 3:17
*; Seraiah (son of Neh 11:10-14

JACHINITES
The *, named after their ancestor Num 26:12-14

JACINTH
In the third row were a *, an Ex 39:12
The eleventh with *; Rev 21:18,19,20

JACK
your lust?) Any * wanting you need Jer 2:24

JACKAL
howling as a *, mournful as an Mic 1:8

JACKAL'S
Gate toward the * Well and over to Neh 2:13

JACKALS
to * and a companion to ostriches. Job 30:28,29
sword, to become the food of *. Ps 63:10
Hyenas and * will den within the Is 13:22
of * and a home for ostriches. Is 34:13
Where desert * lived, there will Is 35:7
will thank me, the * and ostriches Is 43:20
where only * have their dens. Jer 9:11
of Judah shall become dens of *. Jer 10:22
bare hills panting like thirsty *. Jer 14:6
inhabited by ostriches and *; Jer 50:39
ruins, haunted by *, a land Jer 51:37
Even the * feed their young, but Lam 4:3,4
to give it to the * of the desert. Mal 1:2,3

JACKET
himself away, but as he did, his * Gen 39:12
When she saw that she had his *, Gen 39:13
ran, and forgot to take his *." Gen 39:14,15
She kept the *, and when her Gen 39:16
He fled, leaving his * behind!" Gen 39:18
as stealing his * in cold weather, Pro 25:20

JACOB
So they called him * (meaning Gen 25:26
hunter, while * was a quiet sort Gen 25:27
and Rebekah's favorite was *. Gen 25:28
One day * was cooking stew when Gen 25:29
*: "All right, trade me your Gen 25:31
*: "Well then, vow to God that Gen 25:33
Then * gave Esau bread, peas, Gen 25:34
she called her son * and told him Gen 27:6,7
*: "But mother! Gen 27:11,12
So * followed his mother's Gen 27:14
instructed * to put them on. Gen 27:15
bread. * carried the platter of Gen 27:18
*: "Father?" Gen 27:18
Who is it, my son—Esau or *?" Gen 27:18
*: "It's Esau, your oldest son. Gen 27:19
*: "Because Jehovah your God put Gen 27:20
(* goes over to his father. Gen 27:22
and he gives * his blessings): Gen 27:23
*: "Yes, of course." Gen 27:24
(* takes it over to him and Isaac Gen 27:25
he also drinks the wine * brings Gen 27:25
(* goes over and kisses him on the Gen 27:26
(As soon as Isaac has blessed *, Gen 27:30
and almost before * leaves the Gen 27:30
"*" means "Cheater." Gen 27:36f
So Esau hated * because of what Gen 27:41
be gone, and then I will kill *." Gen 27:41
She sent for * and told him that Gen 27:42
I'd rather die than see * marry Gen 27:46
SO ISAAC CALLED for * and blessed Gen 28:1
So Isaac sent * away, and he went Gen 28:5
mother had sent * to Paddan-aram, Gen 28:6,7,8
girl, and that * had agreed and had Gen 28:6,7,8
So * left Beer-sheba and Gen 28:10
Then * woke up. Gen 28:16,17
And * vowed this vow to God: "If Gen 28:20
* TRAVELED ON, finally arriving in Gen 29:1
the well again.) * went over to Gen 29:4
get back to grazing?" * asked. Gen 29:7
were his uncle's, * went over to Gen 29:10
Then * kissed Rachel and started Gen 29:11
home. Then * told him his story. Gen 29:12,13
After * had been there about a Gen 29:14
Well, * was in love with Rachel. Gen 29:18
So * spent the next seven years Gen 29:20
my contract," * said to Laban. Gen 29:21
celebrate with * at a big party. Gen 29:22
Leah to *, and he slept with her. Gen 29:23
"What sort of trick is this?" * Gen 29:25
So * agreed to work seven more Gen 29:28
be her maid. So * slept with Gen 29:30
But because * was slighting Leah, Gen 29:31
or I'll die," she exclaimed to *. Gen 30:1
* flew into a rage. Gen 30:2
again and gave * a second son. Gen 30:7
Zilpah to *, to be his wife, and Gen 30:9
That evening as * was coming home Gen 30:16
Joseph to Rachel, * said to Laban, Gen 30:25
* replied, "You know how Gen 30:29
* replied, "If you will do one Gen 30:31,32
formed a flock for * of all the Gen 30:35,36
distance, and * stayed and cared Gen 30:35,36
Then * took fresh shoots from Gen 30:37
and * added them to his flock. Gen 30:39,40
BUT * LEARNED that Laban's sons Gen 31:1
Soon * noticed a considerable Gen 31:2
Jehovah now spoke to * and told Gen 31:3
So one day * sent for Rachel and Gen 31:4
shearing sheep, * set his wives and Gen 31:17-20
"Watch out what you say to *," Gen 31:24
Laban finally caught up with * Gen 31:25
careful not to be too hard on *!' Gen 31:29
I was afraid," * answered. Gen 31:31
For * didn't know that Rachel Gen 31:32
Now * got mad at Laban. Gen 31:36,37
So * took a stone and set it up Gen 31:45
make a heap, and * and Laban ate Gen 31:46
So * took oath before the mighty Gen 31:53
Then * presented a sacrifice to Gen 31:54
SO * AND his household Gen 32:1
* now sent messengers to his Gen 32:3
with this message: "Hello from *! Gen 32:4
to meet *—with an army of 400 men! Gen 32:6
400 men! * was frantic with fear. Gen 32:7
Then * prayed, "O God of Abraham Gen 32:9
* stayed where he was for the Gen 32:13,14,15
"These belong to your servant *. Gen 32:18
* gave the same instructions to Gen 32:19
"Perhaps," * hoped, "he will Gen 32:20
* spent that night in the camp. Gen 32:21
But * panted, "I will not let you Gen 32:26
"*," was the reply. Gen 32:27
"What is your name?" * asked Gen 32:29
* named the place "Peniel" Gen 32:30
THEN, FAR IN the distance, * saw Gen 33:1
with his 400 men. * now arranged Gen 33:2
Then * went on ahead. Gen 33:3
"My children," * replied. Gen 33:5
And * replied, "They are my Gen 33:8
"No, but please accept them," * Gen 33:10
have enough." So * insisted, and Gen 33:11
But * replied, "As you can see, Gen 33:13
"No," * insisted, "we'll get Gen 33:15
Meanwhile * and his household Gen 33:17
Word soon reached * of what had Gen 34:5
went to talk with *, arriving just Gen 34:6,7
Hamor told *, "My son Shechem is Gen 34:8
Then * said to Levi and Simeon, Gen 34:30
God said to *, "and build an altar Gen 35:1
So * instructed all those in his Gen 35:2
So they gave * all their idols Gen 35:4
in Canaan. And * erected an altar Gen 35:7
longer be called * ('Grabber'), but Gen 35:10
Afterwards * built a stone pillar Gen 35:13,14
with olive oil. * named the spot Gen 35:15
Bethlehem). And * set up a Gen 35:20
the names of the twelve sons of *: Gen 35:22
So * came at last to Isaac his Gen 35:27
And his sons Esau and * buried Gen 35:28,29
from his brother * to Mount Seir. Gen 36:6,7,8
SO * SETTLED again in the land of Gen 37:1
So one day * gave him a special Gen 37:3
WHEN * HEARD that there was grain Gen 42:1
However, * wouldn't let Joseph's Gen 42:4
So they came to their father * Gen 42:29
Then * exclaimed, "You have Gen 42:36
But * replied, "My son shall not Gen 42:38
land of Canaan, to * their father. Gen 45:25
* -Jacob: he called Gen 46:2
"Jacob! *!" Gen 46:2
"Yes?" * answered. Gen 46:2
So * left Beer-sheba, and his Gen 46:5
and came to Egypt—* and all his Gen 46:6
So these descendants of * and Gen 46:15
Dinah, born to * in Paddan-aram, Gen 46:15
were the sons of * and Zilpah, the Gen 46:18
and descendants of * and Rachel: Gen 46:19-22
and descendants of * and Bilhah, Gen 46:23,24,25
* sent Judah on ahead to tell Gen 46:28
Then Joseph brought his father * Gen 47:7
to Pharaoh. And * blessed Pharaoh. Gen 47:7
* replied, "I have lived 130 Gen 47:9
Then * blessed Pharaoh again Gen 47:10
among them. * lived seventeen Gen 47:28
"Swear that you will do it," * Gen 47:31
Soon afterwards * took to his Gen 47:31
When * heard that Joseph had Gen 48:2
So * blessed the boys that day Gen 48:20
THEN * CALLED together all his Gen 49:1
Listen to me, O sons of *; Gen 49:2
the Mighty One of *, the Shepherd, Gen 49:24
Then, when * had finished his Gen 49:33
of Abraham, Isaac and *." Gen 50:24
THIS IS THE list of the sons of * Ex 1:1
Isaac, and * [to bring their Ex 2:24
God of Abraham, Isaac, and *." Ex 3:6
Isaac, and *, has sent me to you.' Ex 3:15
and *, has really appeared to you. Ex 4:5
Isaac, and *—though I did not Ex 6:2,3
to give to Abraham, Isaac, and *. Ex 6:8,9
The sons of * and their Ex 12:40,41

(JACOB Con't)
I promised Abraham, Isaac, and *; Ex 33:1
Isaac, and *, and I will remember Lev 26:42
(the oldest son of *) Num 1:20-46
from his brother *, whose name was Num 20:14f
'Come,' he told me, 'curse * for Num 23:7-10
He has not seen sin in *. Num 23:18-24
No curse can be placed on *, Num 23:18-24
Joys in the homes of *; Num 24:3-9
there shall come a star from *! Num 24:15-19
* shall arise in power Num 24:15-19
Isaac, and *, for they had refused Num 32:10,11
*, and all of their descendants.' Deu 1:8
Isaac, and *, and when he has given Deu 6:10,11,12
Isaac, and *, that he will do it. Deu 9:5
servants Abraham, Isaac, and *. Deu 9:27
ancestors, Abraham, Isaac, and *. Deu 29:13
Abraham, Isaac, and *." Deu 30:20
Isaac, and * that I would give it Deu 34:4
whom I gave him, were * and Esau. Jos 24:4
Mount Seir while * and his children Jos 24:4
of ground which * had bought for Jos 24:32
the anointed of the God of *; 2Sa 23:1
of the sons of * to whom the Lord 1Ki 18:31f
with Abraham, Isaac, and *. 2Ki 13:23
rejected all the descendants of *. 2Ki 17:20
the descendants of * (whose name 2Ki 17:34
The descendants of * were to 2Ki 17:37
O chosen sons of *, 1Ch 16:12,13
And his confirmation to *. 1Ch 16:17
May the God of * keep you from Ps 20:1
Literally, "all you sons of *." Ps 22:23f
the Lord and worship the God of *. Ps 24:6
He, the God of *, has come to Ps 46:7
He, the God of *, has come to Ps 46:11
Literally, "the pride of *." Ps 47:4f
the praises of the God of *. Ps 75:9
When you rebuked them, God of *, Ps 76:6
of * and of Joseph by your might. Ps 77:15
Literally, "the God of *." Ps 94:6,7f
God's servant Abraham, and of *. Ps 105:5,6
and Isaac, and confirmed with *. Ps 105:10,11
Then * (Israel) arrived in Egypt Ps 105:23
of the Lord, the God of *. Ps 114:7
who has the God of * as his helper, Ps 146:5
O *, O Israel, how can you say Is 40:27
for the Lord redeemed * and is Is 44:23
For the sake of *, my Is 45:4
I promised to *, your father. Is 58:14
Even if Abraham and * would Is 63:16
But the God of * is not like Jer 10:16
for my people—for *—such as they Jer 30:7
So don't be afraid, O * my Jer 30:10
of Abraham, Isaac and *. Jer 33:25,26
Fear not, O *, my servant, says Jer 46:28
the land I gave their father *. Eze 28:25
the land I gave my servant *. Eze 37:25
Literally, "*." Hos 12:2f
who worship idols. * fled to Hos 12:12
for you to make, O House of *? Mic 2:7
us as you promised * long ago. Mic 7:20
for you by loving your father, *. Mal 1:2,3
Isaac was the father of *; Mt 1:2
Isaac was the father of Jacob; * Mt 1:2
Matthan was the father of *; Mt 1:15
* was the father of Joseph (who Mt 1:16
Heaven with Abraham, Isaac, and *. Mt 8:11
the God of Abraham, Isaac, and *'? Mt 22:32
if Abraham, Isaac, and *, long Mt 22:32f
of Isaac, and I am the God of *.' Mk 12:26
Judah's father was *; Lk 3:23-38
Abraham, Isaac, *, and all the Lk 13:28
God of Isaac, and the God of *.' Lk 20:37,38
ground * gave to his son Joseph. Jn 4:5,6
you greater than our ancestor *? Jn 4:12
of Abraham, Isaac, * and of all our Act 3:13
Isaac became the father of *, and Act 7:8
of Jacob, and * was the father of Act 7:8
When their food was gone, * Act 7:12
for his father * and all his Act 7:14
in all. So * came to Egypt, where Act 7:15
Abraham, Isaac and *.' Act 7:32
permanent Temple for the God of *. Act 7:46
a servant to *, his twin brother. Rom 9:10-13
chose to bless *, but not Esau." Rom 9:10-13
promises to Abraham, Isaac, and *. Rom 11:28
as did Isaac and *, to whom God Heb 11:9
to his two sons, * and Esau. Heb 11:20
By faith *, when he was old and Heb 11:21

JACOB'S
is *, but the hands are Esau's!" Gen 27:22
as he heard of * arrival, he rushed Gen 29:12,13
He gave them to * sons to take Gen 30:35,36
them mate only with * black rams. Gen 30:39,40
and the stronger ones were *! Gen 30:42
As a result, * flocks increased Gen 30:43
He drove the flocks before him—* Gen 31:17-20
Laban went first into * tent to Gen 31:33
language, and "Galeed" in *. Gen 31:47,48
the same message. * strategy was Gen 32:20
match, he struck * hip, and knocked Gen 32:25
arriving just as * sons came in Gen 34:6,7
Then all of * sons went over and Gen 34:27
Upon * arrival at Bethel, en Gen 35:9
Reuben, * oldest child, Simeon, Gen 35:23
* son Joseph was now seventeen Gen 37:2
But * heart was like a stone; Gen 45:26
Also in the total of * household Gen 46:19-22
wives of * sons, was sixty-six. Gen 46:26
this total of * household there in Gen 46:27
of Naphtali (descendants of * wife 1Ch 7:13
Judah's father was Jacob;* father Lk 3:23-38
Sychar, he came to * Well, located Jn 4:5,6

JADA
Shammai and *. 1Ch 2:28
Shammai's brother * had two sons, 1Ch 2:32

JADDAI
Zabad, Zebina, *, Joel, Benaiah. Ez 10:43

JADDU-A
Zadok, *, Pelatiah, Neh 10:14-27
Jonathan was the father of *. Neh 12:10,11
and *—all of whom were Levites. Neh 12:22

JADON
from Gibeon; * from Meronoth; Neh 3:7

JAEL
to the tent of *, the wife of Heber Ju 4:17
* went out to meet Sisera and Ju 4:18
Then * took a sharp tent peg and Ju 4:21
for Sisera, * went out to meet him Ju 4:22
In the days of Shamgar and of *, Ju 5:6
Blessed be *, Ju 5:24

JAGGED
to hide among the * rocks at the Is 2:21

JAGUR
Kabzeel, Eder, *, Kinah, Dimonah, Jos 15:21-32

JAHATH
was the father of *, the ancestor 1Ch 4:2
Libni, *, Zimmah, Joah, Iddo, 1Ch 6:19,20,21
Zimmah, Shime-i, *, Gershom, Levi. 1Ch 6:39-43
four sons: * was greatest, Zizah 1Ch 23:10,11
of Shelamoth and his descendant *. 1Ch 24:22
the leadership of * and Obadiah, 2Ch 34:12

JAHAZ
wilderness, battling them at *. Num 21:23
us and mobilized his forces at *. Deu 2:32
Beth-baal-meon, *, Kedemoth, Jos 13:18
Bezer, *, Kedemoth, and Mepha-ath. Jos 21:36,37
an army at * and attacked them. Ju 11:20
are heard far away, even in *. Is 15:4
clear across to Elealeh and to *; Jer 48:34

JAHAZIEL
Jeremiah; *; 1Ch 12:3-7
The priests Benaiah and * played 1Ch 16:6
Amariah was second in command, * 1Ch 23:19
Amariah, his second son;*, his 1Ch 24:23
men standing there—* (son of 2Ch 20:14
son of *, and 300 other men; Ez 8:2-14

JAHDAI
The sons of *: 1Ch 2:47

JAHDI-EL
Azri-el, Jeremiah, Hodaviah, *. 1Ch 5:24

JAHDO
*, Jeshishai, Michael, Gilead, 1Ch 5:14

JAHLEEL
and his sons: Sered, Elon, *. Gen 46:8-14
named after their ancestor *. Num 26:26,27

JAHLEELITES
The *, named after their ancestor Num 26:26,27

JAHMAI
Uzzi, Rephaiah, Jeri-el, *, Ibsam, 1Ch 7:2

JAHZAH
(a desert town), *, Kedemoth and 1Ch 6:78,79
all—on Holon and * and Mepha-ath, Jer 48:21

JAHZEEL
Naphtali and his sons: *, Guni, Gen 46:23,24,25
named after their ancestor *. Num 26:48-50

JAHZEELITES
The *, named after their ancestor Num 26:48-50

JAHZEIAH
Only Jonathan (son of Asahel), * Ez 10:15

JAHZERAH
of Adi-el, son of *, son of 1Ch 9:12

JAHZI-EL
*, Guni, Jezer, Shallum. 1Ch 7:13

JAIL
this—here I am in * when I did Gen 40:15
the chief baker in * in the castle Gen 41:10
So he threw them all into * for Gen 42:17
in chains in *, and the rest of you Gen 42:19
He was put in * until the Lord Lev 24:12
put this fellow in * and feed him 1Ki 22:27
this that he threw him into *. 2Ch 16:10
from *, singing with joy! Ps 68:6
and putting innocent men in *. Is 5:23
WHILE JEREMIAH WAS still in *, the Jer 33:1
criminal in * named Barabbas, and Mt 27:16
judge, lest he sentence you to *; Lk 12:58
am ready to go to * with you, and Lk 22:33
and put them in the public *. Act 5:18
of the * and brought them out. Act 5:19
arrived at the *, the men weren't Act 5:22
reported, "The * doors were Act 5:23
the Lord had brought him out of *. Act 12:17
At dawn, the * was in great Act 12:18
So they came to the * and begged Act 16:39
that * and suffering lie ahead. Act 20:23
So I ordered him back to * until Act 25:21
We have been beaten, put in *, 2Co 6:5
been put in * oftener, been whipped 2Co 11:23
Christ, am here in * because of Eph 3:1
I BEG YOU—I, a prisoner here in * Eph 4:1
will add to my sorrows here in *! Php 1:16,17
Christ for which I am here in *. Col 4:3
Remember me here in *. Col 4:18
I am here in * for Christ's sake. 2Ti 1:8
suffering here in * and I am 2Ti 1:12
never ashamed of my being in *. 2Ti 1:16
been put in * like a criminal. 2Ti 2:9
FROM: PAUL, IN * for preaching the Phm 1:1
in * for the sake of Jesus Christ. Phm 1:8,9
those thrown into *, and you were Heb 10:34
Don't forget about those in *. Heb 13:3
Brother Timothy is now out of *; Heb 13:23

JAILED
wine taster, so he * them both in Gen 40:1
They * him until they could find Num 15:34
Pharaoh-Neco * him at Riblah in 2Ki 23:33
and sword, or being * and robbed. Dan 11:33
He had the man arrested and * Mt 18:30
already evening, * them overnight. Act 4:3
the men they had * were out in the Act 5:25
* us—and we are Roman citizens! Act 16:37
For I am ready not only to be * Act 21:13

JAILER
him favor with the chief *. Gen 39:21
In fact, the * soon handed over Gen 39:22
The chief * had no more worries Gen 39:23
with no brutal * to curse them. Job 3:18
into prison. The * was threatened Act 16:23
The * wakened to see the Act 16:27
Trembling with fear, the * called Act 16:29
tell the *, "Let those men go!" Act 16:35
So the * told Paul they were Act 16:36

JAILING
men and women alike and * them. Act 8:3

JAIR
The men of *, another clan of Num 32:41
The clan of *, of the tribe of Deu 3:14
the sixty cities of * in Bashan. Jos 13:30
was succeeded by *, a man from Ju 10:3
still called "The Cities of *." Ju 10:4
When * died he was buried in Ju 10:5
* (the son of Manasseh) in Gilead; 1Ki 4:8-19
Segub was the father of *, who 1Ch 2:22
(the son of *) killed Lahmi, the 1Ch 20:5
Mordecai (son of *, son of Shime-i, Est 2:5

JAIR'S
(meaning '* Villages') as it is Deu 3:14

JAIRITE
Ira the * was David's personal 2Sa 20:26

JAIRUS
whose name was *, came and fell Mk 5:22
arrived from *' home with the news Mk 5:35
and said to *, "Don't be afraid. Mk 5:36
go on with him to *' home except Mk 5:37
And now a man named *, a leader Lk 8:41
arrived from the *' home with the Lk 8:49

JAKEH
of Agur, son of *, from Massa, Pro 30:1

JAKIM
*, Zichri, Zabdi, Eli-enai, 1Ch 8:19,20,21
Twelfth, the group led by *; 1Ch 24:7-18

JALAM
sons named Jeush, *, and Korah. Gen 36:5
clan of *,The clan of Korah. Gen 36:18,19
Eliphaz, Reuel, Jeush, *, and 1Ch 1:35

JALON
Mered, Epher, *. 1Ch 4:17

JAMBRES
Jannes and * fought against Moses. 2Ti 3:8
as was the sin of Jannes and *. 2Ti 3:9

JAMES
other brothers, * and John, sitting Mt 4:21
* (Zebedee's son), Mt 10:2,3,4
John (*' brother), Mt 10:2,3,4
* (Alphaeus' son), Mt 10:2,3,4
* Joseph, Simon, and Judas. Mt 13:55
SIX DAYS LATER Jesus took Peter, * Mt 17:1
Then the mother of * and John, Mt 20:20
Then he turned to * and John Mt 20:22
what * and John had asked for. Mt 20:24
Zebedee's two sons * and John, and Mt 26:37
Mary the mother of * and Joseph, Mt 27:56
* and John (the sons of Zebedee). Mt 27:56
Zebedee's sons, * and John, in a Mk 1:19
* and John (the sons of Zebedee, Mk 3:16-19
* (the son of Alphaeus), Mk 3:16-19
home except Peter and * and John. Mk 5:37
of * and Joseph, Judas and Simon. Mk 6:2,3
Jesus took Peter, * and John to the Mk 9:2
Then * and John, the sons of Mk 10:35
discovered what * and John had Mk 10:41
Jerusalem, Peter, *, John, and Mk 13:3,4

JAMES Con't)
He took Peter, * and John with Mk 14:33
(the mother of * the Younger and of Mk 15:40
Mary the mother of * went out and Mk 16:1
* and John, the sons of Zebedee. Lk 5:10
*, John Lk 6:14,15,16
* (the son of Alphaeus), Lk 6:14,15,16
Judas (son of *), Lk 6:14,15,16
room except Peter, *, John, and the Lk 8:51
Eight days later he took Peter, * Lk 9:28
what had happened, * and John said Lk 9:54
mother of *, and several others. Lk 24:10
in Galilee, my brother * and I Jn 21:2
John, *, Act 1:14
* (son of Alphaeus), Act 1:14
Judas (son of *), Act 1:14
* (John's brother). Act 12:2
"Tell * and the others what Act 12:17
When they had finished, * took Act 15:13
him to meet with * and the elders Act 21:18
Then * saw him and later all the 1Co 15:7
time was *, our Lord's brother. Gal 1:19
In fact, when Peter, *, and Gal 2:7,8,9
Jewish friends of * came, he Gal 2:12
FROM: *, A servant of God and of Jas 1:1
Sincerely,* Jas 5:20
Jesus Christ, and a brother of *. Jud 1:1

JAMIESON
* Fausset and Brown Commentary Zep 2:15f

JAMIN
Simeon and his sons: Jemuel, *, Gen 46:8-14
Jemuel, *, Ohad, Ex 6:15
named after their ancestor *. Num 26:12-14
Maaz, *, and Eker. 1Ch 2:27
Nemu-el, *, Jarib, 1Ch 4:24
Bani, Sherebiah, *, Akkub, Neh 8:7,8

JAMINITES
The *, named after their ancestor Num 26:12-14

JAMLECH
Meshobab, *, Joshah, Joel, Jehu, 1Ch 4:34-39

JAMMED
dust, with closets * full of Job 27:16

JANAI
by Shapham, also * and Shaphat. 1Ch 5:12

JANIM
Dumah, Eshan, *, Beth-tappu-ah, Jos 15:48-62

JANITORS
and officials—* and cabinet Est 1:5

JANNAI
Melchi's father was *; Lk 3:23-38

JANNAI'S
Melchi's father was Jannai;* Lk 3:23-38

JANNES
truth just as * and Jambres fought 2Ti 3:8
as was the sin of * and Jambres. 2Ti 3:9

JANOAH
on past Taanath-shiloh and *. Jos 16:5,6
From * it turned southward to Jos 16:7
Abel-beth-maacah, *, Kedesh, Hazor, 2Ki 15:29

JANUARY
of the king in * of the seventh Est 2:16
IT WAS IN * of the ninth year of Jer 39:1
in July, August, October, and * Zec 8:19

JAPHETH
had three sons, Shem, Ham, and *. Gen 5:32
had three sons—Shem, Ham, and *. Gen 6:9,10
Shem, Ham, and *, and their wives. Gen 7:13
three sons were Shem, Ham, and *. Gen 9:18
Then Shem and * took a robe and Gen 9:23
To the descendants of Shem and* Gen 9:24,25
God bless * Gen 9:26,27
of Shem, Ham, and *, who were the Gen 10:1
of * were:Gomer, Magog, Gen 10:2
Shem, the oldest brother of *. Gen 10:21
Shem, Ham, and * 1Ch 1:1
The sons of * 1Ch 1:5-9

JAPHIA
King * of Lachish, Jos 10:3
and from there to Daberath and *; Jos 19:12
*, Elishama, Eliada, Eliphelet. 2Sa 5:14,15,16
Nogah, Nepheg, *, Elishama, Eliada, 1Ch 3:6-8
*, Elishama, Beeliada, Eliphelet. 1Ch 14:4-7

JAPHLET
*, Shomer, Hotham, 1Ch 7:32

JAPHLET'S
* sons were: 1Ch 7:33

JAPHLETITES
and west to the border of the * Jos 16:1

JAR
water in a clay * and mix into it Num 5:17
her holding the * of bitter water Num 5:18
and a clay * with a torch in it. Ju 7:16
fig bars, and a * of honey and ask 1Ki 14:3
oil in the bottom of the *. 1Ki 17:12
on hot stones, and a * of water! 1Ki 19:6
"Nothing at all, except a * of 2Ki 4:2
Then pour olive oil from your * 2Ki 4:4
"Bring me another *," she said 2Ki 4:6
But the * that he was forming Jer 18:4
THE LORD SAID, Buy a clay * and Jer 19:1
watch, smash the * you brought with Jer 19:10
of Hosts: As this * lies shattered, Jer 19:11
and as this * cannot be mended, Jer 19:11
into a pottery * to preserve them Jer 32:14
spill her out from * to jar and Jer 48:12
to * and then shatter the jars! Jer 48:12
kinds of flour together in a *. Eze 4:9
Then Mary took a * of costly Jn 12:3
thirsty." A * of sour wine was Jn 19:29
When a man makes a * out of Rom 9:21
clay to make one * beautiful, to be Rom 9:21
them, and a golden * with some Heb 9:4

JARAH
Ahaz was the father of *; 1Ch 9:42
* was the father of Alemeth, 1Ch 9:42

JARED
years old when his son * was born. Gen 5:15,16,17
*: Jared was 162 years old when Gen 5:18,19,20
Jared: * was 162 years old when Gen 5:18,19,20
Kenan, Mahalalel, *, Enoch, 1Ch 1:1
Enoch's father was *; Lk 3:23-38

JARED'S
Enoch's father was Jared;* father Lk 3:23-38

JARHA
wife of *, his Egyptian servant. 1Ch 2:34,35

JARIB
Nemu-el, Jamin, *, 1Ch 4:24
Elnathan, *, Elnathan, Nathan, Ez 8:16
*, Gedaliah. Ez 10:16-19

JARMUTH
King Piram of *, Jos 10:3
Hebron, *, Lachish, and Eglon. Jos 10:22,23
The king of *; Jos 12:8-24
Tappu-ah, Enam, *, Adullam, Socoh, Jos 15:33-36
Kishion, Daberath, *, and Jos 21:28,29
En-rimmon, Zorah, *, Neh 11:25-30

JAROAH
Michael, Gilead, *, Huri, Abihail. 1Ch 5:14

JARS
all the clay * and trumpets they Ju 7:8,9
broke their clay * so that their Ju 7:19,20
Who can tilt the water * of Job 38:37,38
greater than you, the * he makes? Is 29:16
clay pots and * are made and I will Jer 18:2
jar to jar and then shatter the *! Jer 48:12

JASHAR
greater detail in The Book of *. Jos 10:13

JASHEN
The sons of *; 2Sa 23:24-39

JASHOBE-AM
Azarel, Jo-ezer, *—all Korahites; 1Ch 12:3-7

JASHOBEAM
* (the son of a man from Hachmon) 1Ch 11:11
of the First Division was *. 1Ch 27:2,3

JASHUB
named after their ancestor *. Num 26:23-25
Tola, Puah, *, Shimron. 1Ch 7:1
Meshullam, Malluch, Adaiah, *, Ez 10:29

JASHUBITES
The *, named after their ancestor Num 26:23-25

JASON
Probably *, treacherously removed Dan 11:22f
They attacked the home of *, Act 17:5
they dragged out * and some of the Act 17:6
* has let them into his home. Act 17:7
and Lucius and * and Sosipater, my Rom 16:21

JASPER
and a *—all set in gold settings. Ex 28:20
and a *—all set in gold filigree. Ex 39:13
chrysolite, onyx, *, sapphire, Eze 28:13
gem, crystal clear like *. Rev 21:11
The wall was made of *, and was Rev 21:18,19,20
with *; Rev 21:18,19,20

JATHNI-EL
* (the fourth), 1Ch 26:2,3

JATTIR
Shamir, *, Socoh, Dannah, Jos 15:48-62
Libnah, *, Eshtemoa, Holon, Debir, Jos 21:9-16
Bethel, South Ramoth, *, Aroer, 1Sa 30:27-31
Libnah, *, Eshtemoa, Hilen, Debir, 1Ch 6:58,59

JAVAN
Madai,*, Tubal,Meshech, Tiras. Gen 10:2
The sons of *:Elishah, Gen 10:4
*, Tubal, Meshech, and Tiras. 1Ch 1:5-9
The sons of *: 1Ch 1:5-9
Rosh, Tubal, *, and to the lands Is 66:19
Merchants from *, Tubal and Eze 27:13
Vedan and * bring Arabian yarn, Eze 27:19

JAVELIN
carried a bronze * several inches 1Sa 17:4-7
him, or the flashing spear and *. Job 39:21-23

JAVELINS
he laughs at the * hurled at him. Job 41:29
bows and arrows, * and spears, to Eze 39:9

JAW
All with a donkey's *! Ju 15:16,17
All with a donkey's *!" Ju 15:16,17
it by the * and club it to death. 1Sa 17:35
or pierce his * with a spike? Job 41:2

JAWBONE
Then he picked up a donkey's * Ju 15:15
Tossing away the *, he remarked, Ju 15:16,17
(The place has been called "* Ju 15:16,17

JAWS
ripped the lion's * apart, and did Ju 14:6
These 'comforters' have gaping * Job 16:10
dares come within reach of his *? Job 41:13
Lord, snatch me back from the * Ps 9:13
They come at me with open *, Ps 22:13
Save me from these lions' * and Ps 22:21
I will put hooks into your * Eze 29:4
I will put hooks into your * and Eze 38:4
me from the yawning * of death! Jon 2:6

JAZAR
in the land of * and Gilead, the Num 32:1

JAZER
spies to look over the * area; Num 21:31,32
Dibon, *, Nimrah, Heshbon, Elealeh, Num 32:3,4
Atroth-shophan, *, Num 32:34,35,36
This territory included *, all Jos 13:25
Refuge), Mahanaim, Heshbon, and *. Jos 21:38,39
of the valley of Gad, near *; 2Sa 24:5
Heshbon, and *, each with their 1Ch 6:81
and ability at * in Gilead in the 1Ch 26:31,32
out as far as * in the deserts, and Is 16:8
So I wail and lament for * and Is 16:9
weep for you even more than for *. Jer 48:32

JAZIZ
under the care of * the Hagrite. 1Ch 27:31

JE-IEL
*, Zechariah, 1Ch 5:7,8
*, the father of Gibeon, lived at 1Ch 8:29
Shama and * (sons of Hotham) 1Ch 11:26-47
Obed-edom and *, the door keepers. 1Ch 15:18
*, and Azaziah were the harpists. 1Ch 15:21
His associates were Zechariah, *, 1Ch 16:5
Eliab, Benaiah, Obed-edom, and *; 1Ch 16:5
of Benaiah, son of *, son of 2Ch 20:14
quotas set by *, the secretary of 2Ch 26:11
Hashabiah, *, and Jozabad—gave 2Ch 35:9
*, Mattithiah, Zabad, Zebina, Ez 10:43

JEALOUS
And the Philistines became * of Gen 26:14
and he is * and suspicious, the Num 5:14
But Moses replied, "Are you * Num 11:29
He is a devouring fire, a * God. Deu 4:24
I am a * God, and I will bring Deu 5:9,10
among you is a * God, and his anger Deu 6:15
He was * of his people. Deu 32:16
They have made me very * of their Deu 32:21
Now I, in turn, will make them * Deu 32:21
Lord God, for he is holy and *; Jos 24:19
King Saul kept a * watch on David. 1Sa 18:9
afraid of him and * because the 1Sa 18:11,12
Crooks are * of each other's Pro 12:12
and governors very *, and they Dan 6:4
God is * over those he loves; Nah 1:2
I am as * as a husband for his Zec 1:14
These men were very * of Joseph Act 7:9
saw the crowds, they were *, and Act 13:45
But the Jewish leaders were * and Act 17:5
make his people * and try to wake Rom 10:19
the Jews would be * and begin to Rom 11:11
When you are * of one another and 1Co 3:3
and kind, never * or envious, never 1Co 13:4
are * of the way God has used me. Php 1:15
And some preach to make me *, Php 1:16,17
you are bitter and * and selfish; Jas 3:14

JEALOUSY
His anger and * will be hot Deu 29:20
Will your * burn till every hope Ps 79:5
be furious in his *, and he will Pro 6:34
a man's life; * rots it away. Pro 14:30
* is more dangerous and cruel Pro 27:4
the driving force of envy and *! Ecc 4:4
death and * is as cruel as Sheol. Sol 8:6
Then, at last, the * between Is 11:13
will die away; my * against you Eze 16:42
And I will send my * against you Eze 23:25
For in my * and blazing wrath, I Eze 38:19
be devoured by the fire of his *. Zep 1:18
be devoured with the fire of my *. Zep 3:8
implying *, as in Mark 6:2-6. Mk 6:52f
with violent * and arrested the Act 5:17
for I can see that there is * Act 8:23
and lust, or fighting, or *. Rom 13:12,13
and fighting, * and anger, constant Gal 5:20
which lead to * and hard feelings. Gal 5:26
ending in * and anger, which only 1Ti 6:4
sort of lie. For * and selfishness Jas 3:15
For wherever there is * or Jas 3:16
us, watches over us with tender *? Jas 4:5
Be done with dishonesty and * and 1Pe 2:1

JEARIM
*, and went down to Beth-shemesh. Jos 15:10,11

JEATHERAI
Zimmah, Joah, Iddo, Zerah, *. 1Ch 6:19,20,21

JEBERECHIAH
the son of *, both known as honest Is 8:2

JEBUS
shoulder of * (where the city of Jos 15:8
Zela, Ha-eleph, * (or, Jerusalem), Jos 18:21-28
(also called *) before dark. Ju 19:10

(JEBUS Con't)
to Jerusalem (or *, as it used to 1Ch 11:4
But the people of * refused to 1Ch 11:5,6

JEBUSITE
The kings in the * hill country; Jos 11:1
of Araunah the * at the time. 2Sa 24:16
floor of Araunah the *." 2Sa 24:18
man to kill a * shall be made 1Ch 11:5,6
threshing-floor of Ornan the *. 1Ch 21:15
threshing-floor of Ornan the *. 1Ch 21:18
of Ornan the * had been. 2Ch 3:1

JEBUSITES
these nations:*, Amorites, Gen 10:15-19
Canaanites, Girgashites, *." Gen 15:19,20,21
Perizzites, Hivites, and * live. Ex 3:8
Hivites, and *, a land "flowing Ex 3:17
Hivites, and *—the land he promised Ex 13:4,5
Hivites, and *, to live there. Ex 23:23
Perizzites, Hivites, and *. Ex 33:2
Perizzites, Hivites, and *. Ex 34:11
are the Hittites, *, and Amorites; Num 13:29
The *. Deu 7:1
the Hivites, and the *. Deu 20:17
Amorites, and *—all the people who Jos 3:10
Perizzites, Hivites, and *. Jos 9:1
the Hivites, and the *): Jos 12:8-24
not drive out the * who lived in Jos 15:63
Jerusalem, so the * live there Jos 15:63
where the * lived, and continued Jos 18:16
the Hivites, and the *. Jos 24:11
to exterminate the * living in Ju 1:21
Perizzites, Amorites, and *. Ju 3:5
against the * who lived there. 2Sa 5:6
those 'lame' and 'blind' *. 2Sa 5:8
Perizzites, Hivites, and *. 1Ki 9:20,21
ancestor of the *, Amorites, 1Ch 1:13-16
called) where the *—the original 1Ch 11:4
Hivites, and *—the descendants of 2Ch 8:7,8
Perizzites, *, Ammonites, Moabites, Ez 9:1
Perizzites, *, and Girgashites; Neh 9:8
just as the * did so long ago. Zec 9:7

JECHONIAH
Josiah was the father of * and Mt 1:11
* was the father of Shealtiel; Mt 1:12

JECOLIAH
Name of his mother: * of Jerusalem 2Ki 15:1
His mother's name was *, from 2Ch 26:3

JECONIAH
*, Zedekiah. 1Ch 3:16
were born to King * during the 1Ch 3:17,18
King * of Judah and many others. Est 2:6
* and Jehoiachin, his other names. Jer 22:24,25f
and enslaved * (son of Jehoiakim), Jer 24:1
along with * (son of Jehoiakim), Jer 27:19,20,21
and I will bring back King *, Jer 28:4
AFTER * THE king, and the Jer 29:1
called Coniah and *) evidently did Jer 36:30f
years after King * was captured, Eze 20:1

JECONIAH'S
the seventh year of * captivity." Eze 20:1f

JEDAIAH
of Allon, son of *, son of Shimri, 1Ch 4:34-39
*, Jehoiarib, Jachin, 1Ch 9:10,11
Second, the group led by *; 1Ch 24:7-18
From the families of * of the Ez 2:36-39
wall from them. * (son of Neh 3:10
Jeshua of the subclan of *, 973; Neh 7:39-42
* (son of Joiarib); Neh 11:10-14
Joiarib, *, Sallu, Amok, Neh 12:1
Hilkiah, *. Neh 12:1
Uzzi, leader of the * clan; Neh 12:12-21
Nethanel, leader of the * clan. Neh 12:12-21
"Heldai, Tobijah, and * will Zec 6:10,11
Tobijah, *, and also Josiah. Zec 6:14

JEDIA-EL
Bela, Becher, *. 1Ch 7:6
The son of * was 1Ch 7:10
of the subclans of *, and their 1Ch 7:11
* (son of Shimri); 1Ch 11:26-47
Adnah, Jozabad, *, Michael, 1Ch 12:20
* (the second), 1Ch 26:2,3

JEDIDAH
Name of his mother: * (daughter of 2Ki 22:1

JEDIDIAH
David nicknamed the baby * 2Sa 12:25

JEDUTHUN
Shemaiah, son of Galal, son of *). 1Ch 9:15,16
(the son of *), Hosah and 1Ch 16:38
David also appointed Heman, *, 1Ch 16:41
the groups of Asaph, Heman, and *. 1Ch 25:1
Under *, who led in giving thanks 1Ch 25:3
Asaph, *, and Heman reported 1Ch 25:6,7
The singers were Asaph, Heman, * 2Ch 5:11,12
From the * clan, Shemaiah and 2Ch 29:12,13,14
Heman, and * the king's prophet. 2Ch 35:15
son of *) were his assistants. Neh 11:15,16,17

JEDUTHUN'S
* sons were appointed as guards. 1Ch 16:42

JEER
chains, you will * at the king of Is 14:4
even Satan, or * at him, but simply Jud 1:9

JEERED
they *. Mk 14:65
The people * at him as they Mk 15:29,30

JEGAR-SAHADUTHA
Witness Pile"—"*," in Laban's Gen 31:47,48

JEHALLELEL
of Abdi) and Azariah (son of *); 2Ch 29:12,13,14

JEHALLELEL'S
* sons were:Ziph, Ziphah, Tiri-a, 1Ch 4:16

JEHDEIAH
and Shuba-el's descendant *; 1Ch 24:20
of the camels, and * from Meronoth 1Ch 27:30

JEHEZKEL
Twentieth, the group led by *; 1Ch 24:7-18

JEHIAH
And Obed-edom and * guarded the 1Ch 15:24

JEHIEL
Shemiramoth, *, Unni, Eliab, 1Ch 15:18
Shemiramoth, *, Unni, Eliab, 1Ch 15:20
Shemiramoth, *, Mattithiah, Eliab, 1Ch 16:5
Ladan: * the leader, Zetham, Joel; 1Ch 23:8,9
* (the son of Hachmoni) was their 1Ch 27:32
with * (a descendant of Gershom). 1Ch 29:8
Azariah, *, Zechariah, Azariah, 2Ch 21:2
*, Azaziah, Nahath, Asahel, 2Ch 31:12,13
Hilkiah, Zechariah, and *, the 2Ch 35:8
(son of *), and 218 other men; Ez 8:2-14
Then Shecaniah (the son of * of Ez 10:2
*, Uzziah. Ez 10:21
Mattaniah, Zechariah, *, Ez 10:26

JEHIELI
Zetham and Joel, the sons of *. 1Ch 26:20,21,22

JEHIZKIAH
of Meshillemoth, * the son of 2Ch 28:12

JEHO-ADDAN
His mother's name was *, a native 2Ch 25:1

JEHO-ADDIN
(His mother was *, a native of 2Ki 14:2

JEHO-HANAN
* (the sixth), 1Ch 26:2,3
Next in command was * with an 2Ch 17:14,15
Then I went into the room of * Ez 10:6
*, Hananiah, Ez 10:28

JEHOADDAH
Ahaz was the father of *, 1Ch 8:36
* was the father of: 1Ch 8:36

JEHOAHAZ
and his son * became the new 2Ki 10:35
* (THE SON of Jehu) began a 2Ki 13:1
conquer them. But * prayed for the 2Ki 13:4
The rest of the history of * is 2Ki 13:8
* died and was buried in Samaria, 2Ki 13:9,10
during the entire reign of King *. 2Ki 13:22
(the son of *) was successful on 2Ki 13:25
Israel (the son of * and the 2Ki 14:8
And his son * was chosen by the 2Ki 23:30
New king of Judah: * 2Ki 23:31,32
Then he took King * to Egypt, 2Ki 23:34
Or, "*" (see 2 Kings 23:30 f.). 1Ch 3:15f
only his youngest son, *, 2Ch 21:17
Also called "*." 2Ch 22:1f
(son of *, grandson of Jehu). 2Ch 25:17
JOSIAH'S SON * was selected as the 2Ch 36:1
of *, as the new king of Judah. 2Ch 36:4
to Jehoiakim.) * was taken to Egypt 2Ch 36:4
For the Lord says this about * Jer 22:11
*, or Shallum, reigned for three Jer 22:11f
to replace *, whom they took back Jer 22:13f
One of her cubs [King * Eze 19:3

JEHOAHAZ'S
Finally the Lord reduced * army 2Ki 13:7

JEHOHANAN
Ishmael (son of *), Azariah (son of 2Ch 23:1
because his son * was married to Neh 6:18
*, leader of the Amariah clan; Neh 12:12-21
Uzzi, *, Malchijah, Neh 12:42

JEHOIACHIN
When he died, his son * became 2Ki 24:6
New king of Judah, * 2Ki 24:8,9
siege, and King *, all of his 2Ki 24:12
The surrender was accepted, and * 2Ki 24:12
Nebuchadnezzar took King *, his 2Ki 24:15
King * was released from prison 2Ki 25:27
He treated * kindly and gave him 2Ki 25:28
in Babylon. * was given civilian 2Ki 25:29
Also known as * or Coniah. 1Ch 3:16f
and his son * became the new 2Ch 36:8
* was eight years old when he 2Ch 36:9
King * and his mother Nehashta. Jer 13:18f
Jeconiah and *, his other names. Jer 22:24,25f
Or, "*," as he is also called. Jer 28:4f
by his son * (also called Coniah Jer 36:30f
in Babylon of *, king of Judah, Jer 52:31
was kind to King * and brought him Jer 52:31
took another of her cubs [King * Eze 19:5
* was taken away to captivity). Eze 26:1
of King *), this message came to me Eze 29:1

JEHOIACHIN'S
appointed King * great-uncle, 2Ki 24:17
appointed * brother Zedekiah as the 2Ch 36:10
sixth year of King * captivity, Eze 8:1
year (of King * captivity), another Eze 24:1
year of King * captivity, Eze 29:17
year of King * captivity, this Eze 30:20
eleventh year of King * captivity, Eze 31:1
year of King * captivity, this Eze 32:1

JEHOIADA
Benaiah (son of *) was captain 2Sa 8:18
There was also Benaiah (son of * 2Sa 23:20
Benaiah (son of *) was 1Ki 4:1
was the wife of * the High Priest. 2Ki 11:2,3f
Athaliah's reign, * the priest 2Ki 11:4
They brought to * the men who 2Ki 11:9
Then * brought out the young 2Ki 11:12
* to the officers of the guard. 2Ki 11:15
* made a treaty between the Lord, 2Ki 11:17
of the altar. And * set guards at 2Ki 11:18
* the High Priest instructed him. 2Ki 12:2
One day King Joash said to *, 2Ki 12:4,5
So Joash called for * and the 2Ki 12:7
personal needs. * the priest bored 2Ki 12:9
man of unusual courage, and *. 1Ch 12:24-37
Benaiah (son of *) was in charge 1Ch 18:17
(He was the son of * the High 1Ch 27:5,6
Ahithophel was assisted by * 1Ch 27:34
and the wife of * the priest. 2Ch 22:11
of Queen Athaliah, * the priest got 2Ch 23:1
son to reign!" * exclaimed. 2Ch 23:2,3
going off duty—for * the chief 2Ch 23:8
Then * issued spears and shields 2Ch 23:9
as * and his sons anointed him. 2Ch 23:11
"Take her out and kill her," * 2Ch 23:13,14
Then * made a solemn contract 2Ch 23:15,16,17
before his altar. * now appointed 2Ch 23:18
the lifetime of * the priest. 2Ch 24:2
the priest. * arranged two 2Ch 24:3
So the king called for *, the 2Ch 24:6
The king and * gave the money to 2Ch 24:12
to the king and *, and it was 2Ch 24:14
the lifetime of * the priest. 2Ch 24:14
That was how King Joash repaid * 2Ch 24:22
murdering the son of * the priest. 2Ch 24:25
One of the sons of * (the son of Neh 13:28
replace * as priest in Jerusalem. Jer 29:26

JEHOIADA'S
So the officers followed * 2Ki 11:9
of God came upon Zechariah, * son. 2Ch 24:20

JEHOIAKIM
and he changed his name to *. 2Ki 23:34
where he died. * taxed the people 2Ki 23:35
New king of Judah: * 2Ki 23:36,37
DURING THE REIGN of King *, King 2Ki 24:1
Jerusalem. * surrendered and paid 2Ki 24:1
of the life of * is recorded in The 2Ki 24:5
of his reign: evil, like that of * 2Ki 24:18,19
*, Zedekiah, Shallum. 1Ch 3:15
The sons of *: 1Ch 3:16
(Eliakim's name was changed to *. 2Ch 36:4
as a prisoner. * was twenty-five 2Ch 36:5
The rest of the deeds of *, and 2Ch 36:8
of Josiah's son *, king of Judah, Jer 1:3
And woe to you, King *, Jer 22:13
against King *, who succeeded his Jer 22:18
son of * king of Judah—even if Jer 22:24,25
Jeconiah (son of *), king of Judah, Jer 24:1
King * of Judah (son of Josiah). Jer 25:1
* (son of Josiah), king of Judah: Jer 26:1
But when King * and the army Jer 26:21
Then King * sent Elnathan (son Jer 26:22
him back to King *, who butchered Jer 26:23
at the beginning of the reign of * Jer 27:1
Jeconiah (son of *), king of Judah, Jer 27:19,20,21
son of *, king of Judah, and all Jer 28:4
gave Jeremiah when * (son of Jer 35:1
of the reign of King * of Judah Jer 36:1
reign of King * (son of Josiah). Jer 36:9
concerning you, *, king of Judah: Jer 36:30
assassinated King * appointed his Jer 37:1f
the reign of King * (son of Jer 45:1
* (son of Josiah), king of Judah: Jer 46:2
a wicked king, just as * had been. Jer 52:2
two Judean kings, * and Zedekiah. Eze 23:17f
THREE YEARS AFTER King * began Dan 1:1
the Lord gave him victory over *. Dan 1:1

JEHOIAKIM'S
Coniah (King * son) to be the new Jer 37:1

JEHOIARIB
Jedaiah, *, Jachin, 1Ch 9:10,11
First, the group led by *; 1Ch 24:7-18

JEHONADAB
As he left the inn, he met *, the 2Ki 10:15
"Yes," * replied. 2Ki 10:15
Lord." So * rode along with him. 2Ki 10:16
Then Jehu and * (son of Rechab) 2Ki 10:23

JEHONATHAN
Shemiramoth, *, Adonijah, Tobijah, 2Ch 17:7,8,9
*, leader of the Shemaiah clan; Neh 12:12-21

JEHORAM
and his son * took the throne. 1Ki 22:50
and his brother * became the new 2Ki 1:17
* (son of Jehoshaphat) of Judah. 2Ki 1:17
AHAB'S SON * began his reign over 2Ki 3:1

JEHORAM Con't)
Chapter 1, verse 17, says King * 2Ki 3:1f
So King * mustered the Israeli 2Ki 3:6,7,8
wilderness of Edom," * replied. 2Ki 3:6,7,8
snarled at King * of Israel. 2Ki 3:13
But King * replied, "No! 2Ki 3:13
King *, the son of King 2Ki 8:16
the son of Ahab. * was thirty-two 2Ki 8:17
King * 2Ki 8:21
(son of *) came to visit him. 2Ki 8:29
of King *, Ahaziah's father). 2Ki 11:2,3
*, and Ahaziah, the kings of 2Ki 12:18
Or, "*." 1Ch 3:10-14f
also the priests, Elishama and *. 2Ch 17:7,8,9
* became the new ruler of Judah. 2Ch 21:1
to * because he was the oldest. 2Ch 21:3,4
But when * had become solidly 2Ch 21:3,4
Yes, as wicked as Ahab, for * had 2Ch 21:6
of Judah. * attacked him with his 2Ch 21:9
Literally, "* .I.I. 2Ch 21:9f
Libnah revolted too, because * 2Ch 21:10
What's more, * constructed idol 2Ch 21:11
to the Ethiopians to attack *. 2Ch 21:16
alliance with King * of Israel (the 2Ch 22:5
the battle. King * of Israel was 2Ch 22:5
Ahaziah for his alliance with *. 2Ch 22:7
went out with * to challenge Jehu 2Ch 22:7
She was a daughter of King *, and 2Ch 22:11

JEHORAM'S
During * reign, the people in 2Ki 8:20
King * daughter, verse 11. 2Ch 22:11f

JEHOSHABEATH
Joash was rescued by his Aunt *, 2Ch 22:11

JEHOSHAPHAT
of state was * (son of Ahilud). 2Sa 8:16
battalions, and * was the historian 2Sa 20:24
* (son of Ahilud) was the official 1Ki 4:1
* (son of Paruah), whose area was 1Ki 4:8-19
Then his son * became the new 1Ki 15:24
year, while King * of Judah was 1Ki 22:2
Then he turned to * and asked 1Ki 22:4
And King * of Judah replied, "Of 1Ki 22:4
But * asked, "Isn't there a 1Ki 22:7
"Oh, come now!" * replied. 1Ki 22:8
Turning to *, Ahab complained, 1Ki 22:18
So King Ahab of Israel and King * 1Ki 22:29
Ahab said to *, "You wear your 1Ki 22:30
When they saw King * in his 1Ki 22:32,33
But when * shouted out to 1Ki 22:32,33
Meanwhile, over in Judah, * the 1Ki 22:41
Ahab of Israel. * was thirty-five 1Ki 22:42
The rest of the deeds of * and 1Ki 22:45
King * built great freighters to 1Ki 22:48
had proposed to * that his men go 1Ki 22:49
too, but * had refused the offer. 1Ki 22:49
When King * died he was buried 1Ki 22:50
the reign of King * of Judah that 1Ki 22:51
King Jehoram (son of *) of Judah. 2Ki 1:17
year of the reign of King * 2Ki 3:1
this message to King * of Judah: 2Ki 3:6,7,8
"Of course I will," * replied. 2Ki 3:6,7,8
But *, the king of Judah, asked, 2Ki 3:11
"Fine," * said. 2Ki 3:12
King * of Judah," Elisha replied. 2Ki 3:14
King Jehoram, the son of King * 2Ki 8:16
(the son of *, the son of Nimshi). 2Ki 9:2
That is how Jehu (son of *, son 2Ki 9:14
that his ancestors—*, Jehoram, and 2Ki 12:18
Rehoboam, Abijah, Asa, *, Joram, 1Ch 3:10-14
of the army; * (son of Ahilud) was 1Ch 18:15
THEN HIS SON * became the king and 2Ch 17:1
The Lord was with * because he 2Ch 17:3
of them declared war on King *. 2Ch 17:10
male goats. So * became very 2Ch 17:12
BUT RICH, POPULAR King * of Judah 2Ch 18:1
Then he asked King * to join 2Ch 18:2
King * replied. 2Ch 18:3,4,5
But * wasn't satisfied. 2Ch 18:6,7
talk like that!" * exclaimed. 2Ch 18:6,7
the king of Israel exclaimed to *. 2Ch 18:17
The king of Israel said to *, 2Ch 18:29
saw King * of Judah in his royal 2Ch 18:31
were after. But * cried out to the 2Ch 18:31
AS KING * of Judah returned home, 2Ch 19:1
So * made no more trips to Israel 2Ch 19:4
* set up courts in Jerusalem, 2Ch 19:8
war on * and the people of Judah. 2Ch 20:1
Word reached * that "a vast 2Ch 20:2
called Engedi). * was badly shaken 2Ch 20:3
with him. * stood among them as 2Ch 20:5
Jerusalem, and you, O king *!" 2Ch 20:15
Then King * fell to the ground 2Ch 20:18
On the way * stopped and called 2Ch 20:20
King * and his people went out 2Ch 20:25
to Jerusalem, with * leading them, 2Ch 20:27
A thumbnail sketch of King *: He 2Ch 20:31
But at the close of his life, *, 2Ch 20:35
prophesied against *, telling him, 2Ch 20:37
WHEN * DIED, he was buried in the 2Ch 21:1
His brothers—other sons of * 2Ch 21:2
of your father *, nor the good ways 2Ch 21:12
grandson of King *—a man who 2Ch 22:9
Or, "Valley of *." Joe 3:2f
bring them to the Valley of *, Joe 3:12
Asa was the father of *; Mt 1:8
* was the father of Joram; Mt 1:8

JEHOSHAPHAT'S
upon them. So * kingdom was quiet, 2Ch 20:30
The details of * reign from first 2Ch 20:34

JEHOSHAZ
an alternate form of the name *. 2Ki 8:24,25f

JEHOSHEBA
Joash was rescued by his Aunt *, 2Ki 11:2,3
practical because * was the wife of 2Ki 11:2,3f

JEHOVAH
first to invoke the name of *." Gen 4:26f
Then * said, "My Spirit must Gen 6:3
Literally, "*." Gen 7:16f
for that purpose. And * was Gen 8:21
Literally, "and * smelled the Gen 8:21f
Or, "Blessed be *, the God of Gen 9:26,27f
it was there that * confused them Gen 11:9
Then * appeared to Abram and Gen 12:7
* destroyed Sodom and Gomorrah); Gen 13:10
Literally, "the Garden of *." Gen 13:10f
and sinned greatly against *. Gen 13:13
and built an altar to * there. Gen 13:18
solemnly promised *, the supreme Gen 14:22
AFTERWARDS * SPOKE to Abram in a Gen 15:1
But Abram replied, "O Lord *, Gen 15:2,3
Then * told him, "No, no one Gen 15:4
And he told him, "I am * who Gen 15:7
But Abram replied, "O Lord *, Gen 15:8
Then * told him to take a Gen 15:9
Then * told Abram, "Your Gen 15:13
So that day * made this covenant Gen 15:18
Hagar spoke of *—for it was he Gen 16:13
Abraham named the place "* Gen 22:14
"Swear by *, the God of heaven Gen 24:3
"O *, the God of my master," he Gen 24:12
with head bowed, worshiping *. Gen 24:26
Literally, "blessed of *." Gen 24:31f
"And * has overwhelmed my Gen 24:35
this prayer: 'O *, the God of my Gen 24:42
and blessed *, the God of my master Gen 24:48
master's son, as * has directed." Gen 24:51
fell to his knees before *. Gen 24:52
Isaac pleaded with * to give Gen 25:21
* appeared to him there and told Gen 26:2
grain he sowed. For * blessed him. Gen 26:12
When he went to Beer-sheba, * Gen 26:24
built an altar and worshiped *; Gen 26:25
see that * is blessing you. Gen 26:28
Jacob: "Because * your God put it Gen 27:20
and fields that * has blessed. Gen 27:27,28,29
"I am *," he said, "the God of Gen 28:13
then I will choose * as my God! Gen 28:21
slighting Leah, * let her have a Gen 29:31
for she said, "* has noticed my Gen 29:32
Simeon (meaning "* heard"), for Gen 29:33
for she said, "* heard that I was Gen 29:33
she said, "Now I will praise *!" Gen 29:35
for she said, "May * give me Gen 30:23,24
enormously; * has blessed you from Gen 30:30
* now spoke to Jacob and told Gen 31:3
my father Isaac—O * who told me to Gen 32:9
the Angel of * appeared to him as a Ex 3:2
Yes, tell them, '*, Ex 3:15
either "*" or "Lord." Ex 3:15f
tell them about * appearing to you Ex 3:16
and tell him, '*, the God of the Ex 3:18
They'll say, '* never appeared to Ex 4:1
"Then they will realize that *, Ex 4:5
"Now put it in again," * said. Ex 4:7
"Who makes mouths?" * asked Ex 4:11
Before Moses left Midian, * said Ex 4:19
* told him, "When you arrive Ex 4:21
Then you are to tell him, '* Ex 4:22
for the night, * appeared to Moses Ex 4:24
Now * said to Aaron, "Go into Ex 4:27
Aaron told them what * had said Ex 4:30
they heard that * had visited them Ex 4:31
message from *, the God of Israel. Ex 5:1
"And who is *, that I should Ex 5:2
I don't know * and I will not let Ex 5:2
and sacrifice there to * our God; Ex 5:3
'Let us go and sacrifice to *.' Ex 5:17
I am *, the Almighty God who Ex 6:2,3
not reveal my name, *, to them. Ex 6:2,3
And they shall know that I am * Ex 6:7
and Moses to whom * said, "Lead Ex 6:26
to whom the Lord said, "I am *. Ex 6:28,29
the miracle, as * had instructed Ex 7:10
Say to him, '*, the God of the Ex 7:16
and tell him, '* says, "Let my Ex 8:1
and say to him, '* says, "Let my Ex 8:20
And * did as he had said, so that Ex 8:24
* our God, as he commanded us." Ex 8:27
"and tell him, '*, the God of the Ex 9:1
Then * said to Moses and Aaron, Ex 9:8
them too. But * hardened Pharaoh Ex 9:12
and tell him, '* the God of the Ex 9:13
of * left them out in the storm. Ex 9:21
Then * said to Moses, "Point Ex 9:22
he confessed. "* is right, and I Ex 9:27
that the earth is controlled by *. Ex 9:29
how I proved to you that I am *." Ex 10:2
and told him: "*, the God of the Ex 10:3
Let the men go and serve * their Ex 10:7
"All right, go and serve * your Ex 10:8
You that are men, go and serve *, Ex 10:11
So Moses lifted his rod and * Ex 10:13
* your God and against you. Ex 10:16
this once, and beg * your God to Ex 10:17
Then * said to Moses, "Lift your Ex 10:21
"Go and worship *—but let your Ex 10:24
and burnt offerings to * our God. Ex 10:25
"* says, 'About midnight I will Ex 11:4
Then you will know that * makes a Ex 11:7
all the gods of Egypt—for I am *. Ex 12:12
"For * will pass through the Ex 12:23
And that night, at midnight, * Ex 12:29
go and serve * as you said. Ex 12:31
Then * said to Moses and Aaron, Ex 12:43
each year, when * brings you into Ex 13:4,5
mighty miracles * brought us out of Ex 13:14
Pharaoh wouldn't let us go, so * Ex 13:15
* NOW INSTRUCTED Moses, "Tell Ex 14:1
Egypt shall know that I am *." Ex 14:18
But in the early morning * Ex 14:24
yelled. "* is fighting for them Ex 14:25
Thus * saved Israel that day Ex 14:30
Yes, * is his name. Ex 15:3
* shall reign forever and Ex 15:18
Come now before *, and hear his Ex 16:7,8,9
appeared the awesome glory of *. Ex 16:10
And * said to Moses, "I have Ex 16:11,12
shall know that I am * your God.' Ex 16:11,12
the food * has given you to eat. Ex 16:15
given you to eat. * has said for Ex 16:16
is the Sabbath to * and there will Ex 16:25
Then Moses pleaded with *. Ex 17:4
Then * said to Moses, "Take the Ex 17:5,6
"tempting * to slay us"), and Ex 17:7
them by saying, "Is * going to Ex 17:7
(meaning "* is my flag"). Ex 17:15,16
with smoke because * descended upon Ex 19:18
priests who come near to *." Ex 19:22f
must sanctify themselves, lest * Ex 19:22
But * said, "Go on down, and Ex 19:24
"I am * your God who liberated Ex 20:2
"You shall not use the name of * Ex 20:7
god than * shall be executed. Ex 22:20
into the house of * thy God." Ex 23:19f
* SAID TO Moses, "Tell the people Ex 25:1
Holy Place; thus * will be reminded Ex 28:29
heart when he goes in before *. Ex 28:30,31
upon a seal, 'Consecrated to *.' Ex 28:36
live among them. I am * their God. Ex 29:46
And * said to Moses, "Whenever Ex 30:11,12
a shekel for an offering to *." Ex 30:13f
that I am * who makes you holy. Ex 31:12,13
there will be a feast to *!" Ex 32:5
He told them, "* the God of Ex 32:27
to consult with * went out there. Ex 33:7
His name, *, means "I will be Ex 33:19f
*, the Lord. Ex 33:19
"proclaimed the name of *." Ex 34:5,6f
"I am *, the merciful and Ex 34:5,6
and truth. I, *, show this Ex 34:7
gods, but only *, for he is a God Ex 34:14
are the laws of * you must obey. Ex 35:1
holy day to be used to worship *; Ex 35:2
may bring these offerings to *: Ex 35:5-9
And Moses told them, "* has Ex 35:30,31
These stones were reminders to * Ex 39:6,7
just as * had commanded Moses. Ex 39:28,29
the words, "Consecrated to *." Ex 39:30
head and kill it there before *. Lev 4:4
something that * has said not to Lev 4:13
other sacrifice made to * by fire; Lev 4:35
other offering to * made by fire; Lev 5:12
And * said to Moses, "On the day Lev 6:19,20
Literally, "it pertains unto *." Lev 7:20f
to do has been commanded by *." Lev 8:5
to the Lord; and * was pleased by Lev 8:28
For today," Moses said, "* will Lev 9:4
anointing oil of * is upon you." Lev 10:7
and to teach them all the laws * Lev 10:11
the offerings to * made by fire; Lev 10:13
"I am * your God, so don't act Lev 18:1
the name of your God, for I am *. Lev 18:21
For I am * your God." Lev 18:29,30
idols, for I am * your God. Lev 19:3,4
the holiness of *, and you shall be Lev 19:8
through, for I am * your God. Lev 19:10
the name of your God, for I am *. Lev 19:12
Fear your God; I am *! Lev 19:14
for I am *. Lev 19:16
neighbor as yourself, for I am *. Lev 19:18
"I am * your God! Lev 19:26
and wizards, for I am * your God. Lev 19:31
in the fear of God. I am *. Lev 19:32

(JEHOVAH Con't)
land of Egypt. I am * your God. Lev 19:34
measure, for I am * your God who Lev 19:35,36
obeying them, for I am *." Lev 19:37
of his God is upon him; I am *. Lev 21:12
for it is * who sanctifies it." Lev 21:23
for I am *. Lev 22:1
gifts dedicated to *, he shall be Lev 22:3
For I am *! Lev 22:3
for this will defile him. I am *. Lev 22:8
for I am * who sanctifies the Lev 22:16
to be my own people! I am *!" Lev 22:32,33
offerings, very acceptable to *. Lev 23:18
of their own; I am * your God! Lev 23:22
in shelters. I am * your God." Lev 23:43
who blasphemes the name of *. Lev 24:15,16
citizen, for I am * your God." Lev 24:22
he died, as * had commanded Moses. Lev 24:23
For I am *. Lev 25:17,18
with them, for I am * their God. Lev 26:44
watched in wonder. I am *." Lev 26:45
instructions that * gave to the Lev 26:46
They are mine; I am *." Num 3:13
be mine (I am *) as substitutes for Num 3:41
the Levites shall be mine; I am *. Num 3:45
adultery, then * shall make you a Num 5:21,22
*, and carry it to the altar. Num 5:25
* GAVE THESE instructions to Moses Num 9:1
sacrifice to * at the proper time; Num 9:13
For I am *, your God." Num 10:10
Literally, "the mount of *." Num 10:33f
* NOW INSTRUCTED Moses, "Send Num 13:1
"Joshua" means "* is Num 13:16f
ahead of us. * will kill us there, Num 14:3
to reject me. I, *, have spoken. Num 14:34,35
rebellion against * by striking Num 14:36,37,38
shall the foreigner be before *." Num 15:15,16f
is blaspheming *, and shall be cut Num 15:30
For I am * your God who brought Num 15:41
Literally, "whom * chooses to be Num 16:6,7f
the Tabernacle of *, and to stand Num 16:8,9
why you are revolting against *. Num 16:11,12
Then the glory of * appeared to Num 16:19
the people, and * said to Moses Num 16:20
shall know that * has sent me to do Num 16:28
disease, then * has not sent me. Num 16:29
Then fire came forth from * and Num 16:35
and the glory of * appeared to Num 20:6
fought against *, and where he Num 20:13
spoken against * and against you. Num 21:7
of the Wars of *, where it is Num 21:14
except what * tells me to?" Num 23:12
"What has * said?" Num 23:17
* their God is with them. Num 23:18-24
must say whatever * tells me to?" Num 23:26
BALAAM REALIZED BY now that * Num 24:1
but * has kept you from it!" Num 24:11
the words of *, and could not say a Num 24:13
that I would say only what * says! Num 24:13
AFTER THE PLAGUE had ended, * Num 26:1
to the Lord, "O *, the God of the Num 27:16
So Moses did as * commanded, and Num 27:22
and then * will forgive her Num 30:5
it void, and * will forgive her. Num 30:8
is void and * will forgive her. Num 30:12
is the commandment * has given Num 31:21
for I, *, will be living there." Num 35:34
Mount Horeb, that * our God told Deu 1:6
as the Anakim; but * destroyed them Deu 2:21
refused because * your God made him Deu 2:30
cities, the places * our God had Deu 2:37
destroyed. * will scatter you Deu 4:27
search again for * your God, and Deu 4:29
would realize that * is God, and Deu 4:35
for the day: * is God both in Deu 4:39
between you and *, for you were Deu 5:5
" 'I am * your God who rescued Deu 5:6
"O Israel, listen: * is our God, Deu 6:4
Jehovah is our God, * alone. Deu 6:4
nations, for * your God who lives Deu 6:15
I say it yet again: * your God Deu 9:6
the contract which * had made with Deu 9:9
It was there that * set apart Deu 10:8
Commandments of *, and to stand Deu 10:8
"* your God is God of gods and Deu 10:17
in the land which *, the God of Deu 12:1
must never worship any God but *; Deu 13:4
as a burnt offering to * your God. Deu 13:16
and then * your God will bless Deu 14:29
for that was when * your God Deu 16:1
fearful name of * your God, then Deu 28:58,59
your God, then * will send Deu 28:58,59
a contract with * your God, a Deu 29:12
made with them by *, the God of Deu 29:25
Is this the way you treat *? Deu 32:6
And * was very angry; Deu 32:16
will realize that * is the mighty Jos 4:24
to the Lord, "O *, why have you Jos 7:7
the wrath of * will be upon us." Jos 9:20
we were told that * instructed his Jos 9:24
"We swear by *, the God of gods, Jos 22:22,23
patterned after the altar of *. Jos 22:28
and them that * is our God, too." Jos 22:34
"So revere * and serve him in Jos 24:14
did not worship * as their God, and Ju 2:10
They abandoned *, the God loved Ju 2:12-14
had departed from * and were Ju 2:12-14
broke faith with * by worshiping Ju 2:17
turned against * their God and Ju 3:7
But the Angel of * Ju 5:23
the Lord said to him, "But I, *, Ju 6:16
Prove that it is really * who is Ju 6:17
it "The Altar of Peace with *." Ju 6:24
they no longer worshiped * at all. Ju 10:6
This made * very angry with his Ju 10:7,8
Finally the Israelis turned to * Ju 10:10
keep whatever * our God gives us! Ju 11:24
against me; but * the Judge will Ju 11:27
and said, "O Lord *, remember me Ju 16:28
won't, then I will, I swear by *; Ru 3:13
never had a message from * before. 1Sa 3:7
Literally, "did not yet know *." 1Sa 3:7f
to the ground before the Ark of *! 1Sa 5:3
"Who is able to stand before *, 1Sa 6:20
the word of *, he has rejected you 1Sa 15:23
and the Spirit of * came upon him 1Sa 16:13
soil, far from the presence of *? 1Sa 26:20
Literally, "* sent word by Nathan 2Sa 12:25f
"Beloved of *") because of the 2Sa 12:25
Today * has rescued you from all 2Sa 18:31
for I swear by * that if you don't, 2Sa 19:7
"* is my rock, 2Sa 22:2
the decree of * at Shiloh 1Ki 2:27
Then * will hold him personally 1Ki 2:32
the altar of * and cried out this 1Ki 8:54,55
* was very angry with Solomon 1Ki 11:9,10
perfect toward * all his days." 1Ki 15:14f
the ground shouting, "* is God! 1Ki 18:39
"Jehovah is God! * is God!" 1Ki 18:39
"I swear by * my God that I will 2Ki 5:16
could worship * on Israel's soil. 2Ki 5:17f
done, even though * had destroyed 2Ki 21:9
bring the Ark of *, the God of 1Ch 15:12
the Ark of *, the God of Israel. 1Ch 15:14
Blessed be *, God of Israel, 1Ch 16:36
the drawn sword of the angel of *. 1Ch 21:30
It was after this that * struck 2Ch 21:18
of them to worship * their God. 2Ch 34:33
*, the God of their ancestors. 2Ch 34:33
in Jerusalem. * the God of their 2Ch 36:15
announces that *, the God of heaven Ez 1:2
this Temple of *, who is the God of Ez 1:3
they noted that * had told Moses Neh 8:14
in the sea. O *, our Lord, the Ps 8:9
(And O *, God of heaven's Ps 59:5
* is his name—oh, rejoice in his Ps 68:4
threatens me. O *, answer my Ps 69:16
live in joy. For * hears the cries Ps 69:33
Blessed be * God, the God of Ps 72:18
scoff at you. O *, an arrogant Ps 74:18
that you have made to * your God. Ps 76:11
glorious deeds of * to your Ps 78:4
they grumbled. * heard them Ps 78:21
O *, how long will you be angry Ps 79:5
only then shall we be saved. O * Ps 80:4
For it was I, * your God, who Ps 81:10
that you alone, *, are the God Ps 83:18
O *, God of the heavenly armies, Ps 84:8
of wickedness. For * God is our Ps 84:11
O *, GOD of my salvation, I have Ps 88:1
day by day. O *, why have you Ps 88:14
him? O *, Commander of the Ps 89:8
O *, how long will this go on? Ps 89:46
O *, come and bless us! Ps 90:13
not share it. For * is my refuge! Ps 91:9
* IS KING! Ps 93:1
* our God will cut them off. Ps 94:23
Tell the nations that * reigns! Ps 96:10
* IS KING! Ps 97:1
* IS KING! Ps 99:1
* sits in majesty in Zion, Ps 99:2
his instructions. O * our God! Ps 99:8
For * will rebuild Jerusalem! Ps 102:16
Literally, "the holy one of *." Ps 106:16f
* SAID TO my Lord the Messiah, Ps 110:1
* has established your throne Ps 110:2
like morning dew. * has taken Ps 110:4
free to come to * (what a holy, Ps 111:9
mind that * will take care of him. Ps 112:7
O SERVANTS of *, praise his name. Ps 113:1
* is constantly thinking about us Ps 115:12
Yes, * who made heaven and earth Ps 115:15
The dead cannot sing praises to * Ps 115:17
But now what can I offer * for Ps 116:12
* God is our light. Ps 118:27,28
* is mine! Ps 119:57
My help is from * who made the Ps 121:2
* himself is caring for you! Ps 121:5
We look to * our God for his Ps 123:2
Blessed be * who has not let them Ps 124:6
WHEN * BROUGHT back his exiles to Ps 126:1
O *, your name endures forever; Ps 135:13
generation. For * will vindicate Ps 135:14
O Israel, bless *! Ps 135:19
Levite priests, bless the Lord *! Ps 135:20
O *, do not forget what these Ps 137:7
O *, my Lord and Savior, my God Ps 140:6,7,8
Then I prayed to *. Ps 142:5
a truly happy land where * is Ps 144:12-15
happy are those whose God is *. Ps 144:12-15
Great is *! Ps 145:3
* is kind and merciful, slow to Ps 145:8
For * enjoys his people; Ps 149:4,5
flashes fire, the very flame of *. Sol 8:6
Isaiah means "* will save (his Is 8:18
* is your everlasting strength. Is 26:4
I am *; Is 45:5
I am * and there is no one else. Is 45:6
I send good times and bad. I, *, Is 45:7
the earth. I, *, created them. Is 45:8
*, the Holy One of Israel, Is 45:11
* says: The Egyptians, Ethiopians Is 45:14
But Israel shall be saved by * Is 45:17
all eternity. For * created the Is 45:18
*, he says, and there is no other! Is 45:18
No, for I, *, speak only truth Is 45:19
"In * is all my righteousness Is 45:24
be ashamed. In * all the Is 45:25
and claim that you yourself are *. Is 47:10
will come to an evil end, says *. Is 66:17
and earth—* is his name—says this: Jer 33:2
the God of Hosts; * is his name. Hos 12:5
into the "Valley Where * Judges" Joe 3:2
his feet: *, the Lord, the God of Amo 4:13
The Lord, *, is his name. Amo 5:8
*, the Lord God of Hosts, has Amo 6:8
ground. *, the Lord, is his name. Amo 9:6
I worship *, the God of heaven, Jon 1:9,10
out a prayer to *, Jonah's God. Jon 1:14
Jonah's God. "O *," they pleaded, Jon 1:14
in awe before *, and sacrificed to Jon 1:16

JEHOVAH-NISSI
and called it "*" (meaning Ex 17:15,16

JEHOVAH-SHAMMAH
Literally, "*," "The Lord is Eze 48:35f

JEHOVAH'S
there to commemorate * visit. Gen 12:7
the celebration of * passing over Ex 12:27
all of * people left the land. Ex 12:40,41
* instructions to Moses and Aaron. Ex 12:50
All the fat is *. Lev 3:15,16
very much, for * directions to Lev 8:21
be excommunicated from * people. Lev 19:8
by * commandment to Moses). Num 2:32,33
following * instructions to Moses. Num 8:20
reported * words to the people; Num 11:24
arms to wage * war against Midian. Num 31:3
Only there are more of you, so * Num 32:14
arm yourselves for * war, and keep Num 32:20
was well versed in * laws which Ez 7:6
another. In * hand there is a cup Ps 75:8
That is why * anger burned Ps 106:40
All Israel—* people—have come to Ps 122:4
saying, "* blessings be upon you; Ps 129:8
we bless you in * name." Ps 129:8
Yes, they shall sing about * Ps 138:5
THIS IS * message to Cyrus, God's Is 45:1
a flood-tide driven by * breath. Is 59:19
you sticks his finger in * eye! Zec 2:8

JEHOZABAD
of Shimeath, and *, the son of 2Ki 12:21
* (the second), 1Ch 26:4,5
His second in command was *, 2Ch 17:18
from Ammon; and *, whose mother was 2Ch 24:26

JEHOZADAK
* (who went into exile when the 1Ch 6:4-15

JEHU
at this time by the prophet *: 1Ki 16:1
predicted through the prophet *. 1Ki 16:12
Then anoint * (son of Himshi) to 1Ki 19:16
shall be killed by *, and those who 1Ki 19:17
* shall be killed by Elisha! 1Ki 19:17
you, and find * (the son of 2Ki 9:2
he found * sitting around with the 2Ki 9:5
"For which one of us?" * asked. 2Ki 9:5
So * left the others and went 2Ki 9:6
* went back to his friends and 2Ki 9:11
and what he wanted," * replied. 2Ki 9:11
trumpet, shouting, "* is king!" 2Ki 9:13
That is how * (son of 2Ki 9:14
me to be king," * told the men who 2Ki 9:15
Then * jumped into a chariot and 2Ki 9:16
of Jezreel saw * and his company 2Ki 9:17
So a soldier rode out to meet *. 2Ki 9:18
* replied, "What do you know 2Ki 9:18
* answered, "What do you know 2Ki 9:19
"It must be *, for he is driving 2Ki 9:20
of Judah rode out to meet *. 2Ki 9:21
"Do you come as a friend, *?" 2Ki 9:22
* replied, "How can there be 2Ki 9:22
Then * drew his bow with his full 2Ki 9:24
* said to Bidkar, his assistant, 2Ki 9:25
to Beth-haggan. * rode after him, 2Ki 9:27

JEHU Con't)
When Jezebel heard that * had 2Ki 9:30
When * entered the gate of the 2Ki 9:31
Then * went into the palace for 2Ki 9:34
THEN * WROTE a letter to the city 2Ki 10:1
"*, we are your servants and will 2Ki 10:5
* responded with this message: 2Ki 10:6
and presented to * at Jezreel. 2Ki 10:7
When a messenger told * that the 2Ki 10:8
* then killed all the rest of the 2Ki 10:11
Apparently * in his zeal exceeded 2Ki 10:11f
"Grab them!" * shouted to his 2Ki 10:14
each other, * said to him, "Are 2Ki 10:15
"Then give me your hand," * 2Ki 10:15
"Now come along with me," * 2Ki 10:16
Then * called a meeting of all the 2Ki 10:17
Then * and Jehonadab (son of 2Ki 10:23
burnt offerings, * surrounded the 2Ki 10:24
burnt offering, * went out and told 2Ki 10:25
Thus * destroyed every trace of 2Ki 10:28
Afterwards the Lord said to *, 2Ki 10:30
But * didn't follow the Lord God 2Ki 10:31
When * died, he was buried in 2Ki 10:35
In all, * reigned as king of 2Ki 10:36
IT WAS SEVEN years after * had 2Ki 12:1
JEHOAHAZ (THE SON of *) began a 2Ki 13:1
the grandson of *), daring him to 2Ki 14:8
(So the Lord's statement to * 2Ki 15:12
Obed's son was *; 1Ch 2:38
Meshobab, Jamlech, Joshah, Joel, * 1Ch 4:34-39
Beracah; * from Anathoth; 1Ch 12:3-7
the prophet * (son of Hanani) went 2Ch 19:2
in the history of * the son of 2Ch 20:34
to challenge * (son of Nimshi), 2Ch 22:7
While * was hunting down and 2Ch 22:8
brought him to *, who killed him. 2Ch 22:9
(son of Jehoahaz, grandson of *). 2Ch 25:17

JEHU'S
But * plan was to exterminate 2Ki 10:18,19
outside. Then * men went into the 2Ki 10:25
The rest of * activities are 2Ki 10:34
came true, that * son, grandson, 2Ki 15:12
Obed's son was Jehu; * son was 1Ch 2:38
* dynasty to avenge the murders Hos 1:4,5

JEHUBBAH
Rohgah, *, Aram. 1Ch 7:34

JEHUCAL
King Zedekiah sent * (son of Jer 37:3

JEHUD
Baalath, *, Bene-berak, Jos 19:41-46

JEHUDI
the officials sent * (son of Jer 36:14,15
The king sent * to get the Jer 36:21
to get the scroll. * brought it Jer 36:21
And whenever * finished reading Jer 36:23

JEHUEL
From the Hemanite clan, * and 2Ch 29:12,13,14

JEIEL
* (whose wife was Maacah) lived 1Ch 9:35,36,37

JEKABZEEL
Kiriath-arba, Dibon, * (and their Neh 11:25-30

JEKAMEAM
was third, and * was fourth. 1Ch 23:19
Jahaziel, his third son;*, his 1Ch 24:23

JEKAMIAH
Shallum's son was *; 1Ch 2:41
Pedaiah, Shenazzar, *, Hoshama, 1Ch 3:17,18

JEKAMIAH'S
Shallum's son was Jekamiah; * 1Ch 2:41

JEKUTHIEL
Jered, Heber, and *, who were, 1Ch 4:18

JEMIMA
*, Kezia, Keren. Job 42:13,14

JEMUEL
Simeon and his sons: *, Jamin, Gen 46:8-14
*, Jamin, Ohad, Ex 6:15

JEOKNE-AM
it reached the brook east of *. Jos 19:11

JEOPARDY
For God has placed my life in *. Job 30:11

JEPHTHAH
NOW * WAS a great warrior from the Ju 11:1
they chased * out of the country. Ju 11:1
So * fled from his father's home Ju 11:3
The leaders of Gilead sent for * Ju 11:5
But * said to them, "Why do you Ju 11:7
"Sure!" * exclaimed. Ju 11:9
So * accepted the commission and Ju 11:11
Then * sent messengers to the Ju 11:12
* replied, "Israel did not steal Ju 11:14,15
the Lord came upon * and he led his Ju 11:29
Meanwhile * had vowed to the Ju 11:30,31
So * led his army against the Ju 11:32
When * returned home his Ju 11:34
this message to *: "Why didn't you Ju 12:1
you refused to come!" * retorted. Ju 12:2
Then *, furious at the taunt of Ju 12:4
* was Israel's judge for six Ju 12:7
Gideon, Barak, *, and Samuel to 1Sa 12:11
and Samson and * and David and Heb 11:32

JEPHTHAH'S
paid no attention to * message. Ju 11:28
to lament the fate of * daughter. Ju 11:40

JEPHUNNEH
Caleb, son of *, from the tribe of Num 13:3-15
Caleb (the son of *), ripped their Num 14:6
Only Caleb (son of *) and Joshua Num 14:30
of *) and Joshua (son of Nun). Num 26:64,65
were Caleb (son of * the Kenizzite) Num 32:12
Caleb (son of *) Num 34:16-28
Caleb (the son of *), who, because Deu 1:36
to Caleb (son of *), so he was Jos 15:13
were given to Caleb, the son of *; Jos 21:9-16
The sons of Caleb (the son of * 1Ch 4:15
Caleb the son of *), and the 1Ch 6:55,56,57
*, Pispa, Ara. 1Ch 7:38

JERAH
Almodad, Sheleph, Hazarmaveth, *, Gen 10:26-30
Almodad, Sheleph, Hazarmaveth, *, 1Ch 1:20-23

JERAHMEEL
the people of * and the Kenites." 1Sa 27:10
The sons of Hezron were *, Ram, 1Ch 2:9
* (the oldest son of Hezron): 1Ch 2:25
and Kish, among whose sons was *. 1Ch 24:29
Then the king commanded * (a Jer 36:26

JERAHMEEL'S
* second wife Atarah was the 1Ch 2:26
Caleb (* brother) was Mesha; 1Ch 2:42

JERAHMEELITES
the cities of the *, the cities of 1Sa 30:27-31

JERED
she was the mother of *, Heber, 1Ch 4:18

JEREMAI
Matattah, Zabad, Eliphelet, *, Ez 10:33

JEREMIAH
(the daughter of * of Libnah) 2Ki 23:31,32
Hamutal (daughter of * of Libnah) 2Ki 24:18,19
Epher, Ishi, Eliel, Azri-el, *, 1Ch 5:24
or higher than The Thirty); *; 1Ch 12:3-7
* was fifth in command; 1Ch 12:8-13
* was tenth in command; 1Ch 12:8-13
including even * the prophet, 2Ch 35:24,25
the counsel of * the prophet, who 2Ch 36:12
spoken through * came true, that 2Ch 36:21
the prediction of * the prophet. 2Ch 36:22,23
* had predicted (in Jeremiah 25:12 Ez 1:1f
Jeremiah had predicted (in * 25:12 Ez 1:1f
*, Pashhur, Amariah, Neh 10:1
Seraiah, *, Ezra, Amariah, Neh 12:1
Hananiah, leader of the * clan; Neh 12:12-21
Judah, Benjamin, Shemaiah, and *. Neh 12:34
Messiah (* 23:5, Zechariah 3:8). Is 4:2,3,4f
THESE ARE GOD'S messages to * the Jer 1:1
the Lord said to me, "Look, *! Jer 1:11
*, I have made you an assayer of Jer 6:27
THEN THE LORD said to *: Jer 7:1
Pray no more for these people, *. Jer 7:16
THEN THE LORD spoke to * once Jer 11:1
Therefore, *, pray no longer for Jer 11:14
THIS MESSAGE CAME to * from the Jer 14:1
Then * said, "What sadness is Jer 15:10
Then * replied, "Lord, you know Jer 15:15
HERE IS ANOTHER message to * from Jer 18:1
said, "Come, let's get rid of *. Jer 18:18
And now, *, as these men watch, Jer 19:10
As * returned from Topheth where Jer 19:14
Lord, heard what * was saying, he Jer 20:1
he arrested * and had him whipped Jer 20:2
released him, * said, "Pashhur, Jer 20:3
of Ma-aseiah) to *, and begged, Jer 21:1
* replied, "Go back to King Jer 21:3,4
asks you, "Well, *, what is the Jer 23:33
You may respectfully ask *, Jer 23:37
to me, "What do you see, *?" Jer 24:3
from the Lord to * during the Jer 25:1
years, * said, from the thirteenth Jer 25:2,3
by * against the nations. Jer 25:13
THIS MESSAGE CAME to * from the Jer 26:1
When * had finished his message, Jer 26:7,8
Then * spoke in his defense. Jer 26:12
If we kill * for giving us the Jer 26:19
nation at the same time as * was. Jer 26:20
stood with * and persuaded the Jer 26:24
THIS MESSAGE CAME to * from the Jer 27:1
* repeated all these prophecies Jer 27:12
Then * said to Hananiah, in front Jer 28:5
At that point * walked out. Jer 28:11
the Lord gave this message to *: Jer 28:12
Then * said to Hananiah, the Jer 28:15
by Nebuchadnezzar, * wrote them a Jer 29:1
this false prophet * of Anathoth? Jer 29:27
over to * and read it to him! Jer 29:29
the Lord gave this message to *: Jer 29:30
of the Lord's messages to *: Jer 30:1
(Then * wakened. Jer 31:26
In * 17:1 their sin was inscribed Jer 31:33f
FOLLOWING MESSAGE came to * Jer 32:1
At this time * was imprisoned in Jer 32:2
Surrender now!" * had told him Jer 32:5
the Lord came to *: Your cousin Jer 32:6,7
Then this message came to *: Jer 32:26
WHILE * WAS still in jail, the Jer 33:1
Then this message came to * from Jer 33:19
The Lord spoke to * again and Jer 33:23
THIS IS THE message that came to * Jer 34:1
So * delivered the message to Jer 34:6
that came to * from the Lord after Jer 34:8
lifted (* 37:6–11) they became bold Jer 34:11f
the Lord gave * when Jehoiakim (son Jer 35:1
early message to *, and is not here Jer 35:1f
Ja-azaniah (son of *, who was the Jer 35:3
the Lord gave this message to *: Jer 35:12
Then * turned to the Rechabites Jer 35:18,19
the Lord gave this message to *: Jer 36:1
So * sent for Baruch (son of Jer 36:4
of Neriah), and as * dictated, Jer 36:4
When all was finished, * said to Jer 36:5
Baruch did as * told him to, and Jer 36:8
* himself dictate them to you?" Jer 36:17
So Baruch explained that * had Jer 36:18
"You and * both hide," the Jer 36:19
of Abdeel) to arrest Baruch and *. Jer 36:26
the scroll, the Lord said to *: Jer 36:27
Then * took another scroll and Jer 36:32
to what the Lord said through *. Jer 37:2
to ask * to pray for them. Jer 37:3
pray for them. (* had not been Jer 37:4
the Lord sent this message to *: Jer 37:6
army in battle, * started to leave Jer 37:12
"That's not true," * said. Jer 37:14
he took * before the city Jer 37:14
They were incensed with * and Jer 37:15,16
into a prison. * was kept there for Jer 37:15,16
"Yes," said *, "there is! Jer 37:17
Then * broached the subject of Jer 37:18
commanded that * not be returned to Jer 37:21
* was kept in the palace prison. Jer 37:21
heard what * had been telling the Jer 38:1
They took * from his cell and Jer 38:6
bottom, and * sank down into it. Jer 38:6
heard that * was in the cistern, Jer 38:7
in putting * into the cistern. Jer 38:9
him and pull * out before he died. Jer 38:10
and lowered to * on a rope. Jer 38:11
Ebed-melech called down to *, Jer 38:12
Then, when * was ready, they Jer 38:12
One day King Zedekiah sent for * Jer 38:14
* said, "If I tell you the Jer 38:15
he would not kill * or give him to Jer 38:16
Then * said to Zedekiah, "The Jer 38:17
* replied, "You won't get into Jer 38:20
Then Zedekiah said to *, "On Jer 38:24
officials came to * and asked him Jer 38:27
by anyone. And * remained confined Jer 38:28
had told Nebuzaradan to find *. Jer 39:11,12
They sent soldiers to bring * Jer 39:14
to his home. And * lived there Jer 39:14
message to * before the Babylonians Jer 39:15
OF the guard, took * to Ramah along Jer 40:1
The captain called for * and Jer 40:2,3
Then Nebuzaradan gave * some food Jer 40:5
let him go. So * returned to Jer 40:6
and small, came to * and said, Jer 42:1
"All right," * replied. Jer 42:4
Then they said to *, "May the Jer 42:5
the Lord gave his reply to *. Jer 42:7
* concluded: "Never forget the Jer 42:19
WHEN * HAD finished giving this Jer 43:1
proud men, said to *, "You lie! Jer 43:2,3
They even forced * and Baruch to Jer 43:6
Lord spoke to * again and said: Jer 43:8
THIS IS THE message God gave to * Jer 44:1
in southern Egypt) answered *: Jer 44:15
Then * said to all of them, men Jer 44:20
Then * said to them all, Jer 44:24
* gave to Baruch in the fourth Jer 45:1
as * was dictating them to him: Jer 45:1
HERE ARE THE messages given to * Jer 46:1
Then God gave * this message Jer 46:13
THIS IS GOD'S message to * Jer 47:1
city at the time of * and Ezekiel. Jer 49:8f
Elam came to * in the beginning of Jer 49:34
spoken by * the prophet: Jer 50:1
Persian kings. * here sees the Jer 51:26f
message came to * to give to Jer 51:59
Zedekiah's army.) * wrote on a Jer 51:60
Hamutal (daughter of * of Libnah). Jer 52:1
he was taken to Babylon, * 52:11. Eze 12:12f
he was taken to Babylon, * 52:11. Eze 12:13f
from the book of * the prophet, Dan 9:2
* 25:11–12; Dan 9:2f
The prophet * was active during Zep 1:1f
fulfilled the prophecy of *, Mt 2:17
* 31:15. Mt 2:17f
some, * or one of the other Mt 16:14
This fulfilled the prophecy of * Mt 27:9

JEREMIAH'S
the Lord fulfilled * prophecy Ez 1:1
revived in * time (around 626 B.C. Jer 5:15f
the yoke off * neck and broke it. Jer 28:10
(This ends * messages. Jer 51:64

JEREMOTH
Eli-o-enai, Omri, *, Abijah, 1Ch 7:8
Shashak, *. 1Ch 8:14

(JEREMOTH Con't)
sons were Mahli, Eder, and *. 1Ch 23:23
Fifteenth, * and twelve of his 1Ch 25:9-31
Over Naphtali, * (son of Azriel); 1Ch 27:16-22
Abdi, *, Elijah. Ez 10:26
Eli-o-enai, Eliashib, Mattaniah, * Ez 10:27
Malluch, Adaiah, Jashub, Sheal, *. Ez 10:29

JERI-EL
Uzzi, Rephaiah, *, Jahmai, Ibsam, 1Ch 7:2

JERIAH
The sons of Hebron were led by *. 1Ch 23:19
The Hebron group:*, Hebron's 1Ch 24:23

JERIBAI
* and Joshaviah (sons of Elna-am); 1Ch 11:26-47

JERICHO
west of the Jordan River, near *. Gen 50:10f
of the Jordan River opposite *. Num 22:1
the Jordan River, opposite *. Num 26:3,4
from * Num 26:64,65
the Jordan River, across from *. Num 31:12
the river Jordan, opposite *. Num 33:48
side of the Jordan, opposite *." Num 34:14,15
*, the Lord said to Moses, Num 35:1
the Jordan River, across from *. Num 36:13
in the land of Moab across from *. Deu 32:49
Peak in Mount Nebo, across from *. Deu 34:1
and the Jordan Valley; and *, the Deu 34:3
the other side, especially at *. Jos 2:1
the king of * that two Israelis who Jos 2:2
your God that when * is conquered Jos 2:12,13
to the city of *, and the priests Jos 3:15,16
army across to the plains of *. Jos 4:12,13
the eastern edge of the city of *; Jos 4:19
on the plains of *, they celebrated Jos 5:10
up the city of *, a man appeared Jos 5:13
THE GATES OF * were kept tightly Jos 6:1
But the Lord said to Joshua, "* Jos 6:2
And suddenly the walls of * Jos 6:20
hid the spies sent to * by Joshua. Jos 6:25
who might rebuild *, warning that Jos 6:26
them as you did to * and her king; Jos 8:2
army remained in the camp at *. Jos 8:9
had happened to *, they quickly Jos 9:1
had happened to * and Ai, they Jos 9:3,4,5
as he had done at *, and how the Jos 10:1
was slaughtered, just as at *. Jos 10:30
The king of *; Jos 12:8-24
camped at that time across from *. Jos 13:32
Jordan River at * through the Jos 16:1
*, and ended at the Jordan River. Jos 16:7
went north of *, then west through Jos 18:12
*, Beth-hoglah, Emek-keziz, Jos 18:21-28
the Jordan River, across from *. Jos 20:8
the Jordan River and came to *. Jos 24:11
The men of * fought against you, Jos 24:11
They left their homes in *, "The Ju 1:16
took possession of *, often called Ju 3:13
at * until their beards grew out; 2Sa 10:5
a man from Bethel, rebuilt *. 1Ki 16:34
this was the Lord's curse upon * 1Ki 16:34
for the Lord has sent me to *." 2Ki 2:4
So they went on together to *. 2Ki 2:4
Then the students at * Seminary 2Ki 2:5
When the young prophets of * saw 2Ki 2:15
Elisha was still at * when they 2Ki 2:18
officials of * visited Elisha. 2Ki 2:19
From * he went to Bethel. 2Ki 2:23
of *, and all his men scattered. 2Ki 25:4,5
River, opposite *, the tribe of 1Ch 6:78,79
them to stay at * until their 1Ch 19:5
in *, the City of Palm Trees. 2Ch 28:15
From the subclan of *, 345; Ez 2:3-35
Men from the city of * worked Neh 3:2
From the subclan of *, 345; Neh 7:8-38
on the plains of * and brought him Jer 39:5
some fields near *—for all his army Jer 52:8
left the city of *, a vast crowd Mt 20:29
And so they reached *. Mk 10:46
to * was attacked by bandits. Lk 10:30
As they approached *, a blind man Lk 18:35
AS JESUS WAS passing through *, a Lk 19:1
the walls of * tumbling down after Heb 11:30

JERICHO'S
Soon after * defeat, Joshua sent Jos 7:2

JERIJAH
the supervision of *, were 1Ch 26:31,32

JERIMOTH
Ezbon, Uzzi, Uzziel, *, Iri. 1Ch 7:7
Eluzai; *; 1Ch 12:3-7
of Mushi were Mahli, Eder, and *. 1Ch 24:30
Uzziel, Shebuel, *, Hananiah, 1Ch 25:4,5
of David's son * and of Abihail, 2Ch 11:18
Jehiel, Azaziah, Nahath, Asahel, * 2Ch 31:12,13

JERIOTH
Azubah and *. 1Ch 2:18

JEROBOAM
Another rebel leader was * (the 1Ki 11:26
father had built. * was very able, 1Ki 11:27,28
One day as * was leaving 1Ki 11:29
and said to *, "Take ten of these 1Ki 11:31
Solomon tried to kill *, but he 1Ki 11:40
ceremony. *, who was still in 1Ki 12:2,3,4
So when * and the people returned 1Ki 12:12
his promise to *, made through 1Ki 12:15
* now built the city of Shechem 1Ki 12:25
Later he built Penuel. * 1Ki 12:26
of Levi. * also announced that the 1Ki 12:32,33
AS * APPROACHED the altar to burn 1Ki 13:1
Despite the prophet's warning, * 1Ki 13:33
became very sick. * told his wife, 1Ki 14:2
called out, "Come in, wife of *! 1Ki 14:6
sees in the entire family of *. 1Ki 14:13
who will destroy the family of *. 1Ki 14:14
He will abandon Israel because * 1Ki 14:16
Kings of Israel. * reigned 1Ki 14:20
war between Rehoboam and *. 1Ki 14:30
"between Rehoboam and *." 1Ki 15:6f
of the reign of * over Israel, and 1Ki 15:9
the son of * had become king. 1Ki 15:25
of King *, so that not one of the 1Ki 15:29
This was done because * had 1Ki 15:30
He followed the evil paths of *, 1Ki 15:34
walked in the evil paths of *. 1Ki 16:2
as I did the descendants of *. 1Ki 16:3
He was as evil as * despite the 1Ki 16:4-7
For he, too, had sinned like *; 1Ki 16:19
he worshiped idols as * had, and 1Ki 16:26
the family of King * and the family 1Ki 21:22
and mother and of *, who had led 1Ki 22:52,53
the great sin of * (the son of 2Ki 3:3
the families of * (son of Nebat) 2Ki 9:9
the great sin of * (son of Nebat), 2Ki 10:29
*, who had caused Israel to sin. 2Ki 13:2
sin, following the evil ways of *; 2Ki 13:6
man, for, like *, he encouraged the 2Ki 13:11
and * II became the new king. 2Ki 13:13
And his son * became the new 2Ki 14:16
Meanwhile, over in Israel, * II 2Ki 14:23
But he was as evil as * I (the 2Ki 14:24
worshiping idols. * II recovered 2Ki 14:25
so he used King * II to save her. 2Ki 14:27
When * II died he was buried 2Ki 14:29
at this time: King *, who had been 2Ki 15:1
Name of his father: * 2Ki 15:8
ancestors. Like * I (the son of 2Ki 15:9
He worshiped idols, as King * I 2Ki 15:18
begun by * I (son of Nebat) who led 2Ki 15:24
in the example of * I (son of 2Ki 15:28
of David and chose * I (the son of 2Ki 17:21
as its king. Then * drew Israel 2Ki 17:21
evil things that * led them into, 2Ki 17:22
at Bethel which * I had made when 2Ki 23:15
of Judah and King * of Israel. 1Ch 5:17
concerning * the son of Nebat. 2Ch 9:29
Meanwhile, friends of * (son of 2Ch 10:2,3
So when * and the people returned 2Ch 10:12
spoken to * by Ahijah, the 2Ch 10:15
and refused to fight against *. 2Ch 11:4
for King * had fired them, telling 2Ch 11:13,14
wars between Rehoboam and *. 2Ch 12:15
of the reign of King * of Israel. 2Ch 13:1
courageous men led by King *. 2Ch 13:3
to King * and the Israeli army: 2Ch 13:4
Your King * is a mere servant of 2Ch 13:6
with you, that * made for you—he 2Ch 13:8
Meanwhile, * had secretly sent 2Ch 13:13,14
against King * and the army of 2Ch 13:15,16
King * of Israel never regained 2Ch 13:20
and one of the kings of Israel, * Hos 1:1
Judah, and while * (son of Joash) Amo 1:2
dynasty of King * by the sword." Amo 7:9
a message to *, the king: "Amos is Amo 7:10

JEROBOAM'S
Israel learned of * return from 1Ki 12:20
the destruction of * kingdom and 1Ki 13:34
* SON ABIJAH now became very sick. 1Ki 14:1
Then Ahijah said to * wife, "Go 1Ki 14:12
So * wife returned to Tirzah; 1Ki 14:17
The rest of * activities—his wars 1Ki 14:19
year of * reign in Israel. 1Ki 15:1
of * descendants for their sins. 1Ki 16:4-7
to worship * gold calves that had 2Ki 10:31
* reign lasted forty-one years. 2Ki 14:23
The rest of * biography—all that 2Ki 14:28
declared would happen to * altar. 2Ki 23:16
and chased King * troops, and 2Ch 13:18,19

JEROHAM
His father's name was *, 1Sa 1:1
*, Elkanah. 1Ch 6:25,26,27
Joel, Samuel, Elkanah III, *, 1Ch 6:33-38
The sons of * were: 1Ch 8:26,27
Ibneiah (the son of *); 1Ch 9:7,8
was Adaiah (son of *, son of 1Ch 9:12
Jo-elah and Zebadiah (sons of * 1Ch 12:3-7
Over Dan, Azarel (son of *). 1Ch 27:16-22
Azariah (son of *), Ishmael (son of 2Ch 23:1
of Adaiah (son of *, son of Neh 11:10-14

JEROME
Some expositors (Origen, *, Rev 1:20f

JERUBBAAL
was called "*," a nickname Ju 6:32
* (THAT IS, Gideon—his other name) Ju 7:1

JERUEL
opens into the wilderness of *. 2Ch 20:16

JERUSALEM
the king of Salem (*), who was a Gen 14:18
The Lord became king in *, Deu 33:5
There is none like the God of *— Deu 33:26
WHEN ADONI-ZEDEK, THE king of *, Jos 10:1
So King Adoni-zedek of * sent Jos 10:3
the five kings—of *, Hebron, Jos 10:22,23
The king of *; Jos 12:8-24
(where the city of * is located), Jos 15:8
in the city of *, so the Jebusites Jos 15:63
crossed south of the old city of * Jos 18:16
*), Gibe-ah, and Kiriath-jearim. Jos 18:21-28
He was taken to *, and died Ju 1:7
(Judah had conquered *, and Ju 1:8
living in *, so they still live Ju 1:21
* (also called Jebus) before dark. Ju 19:10
Goliath's head to *, but stored his 1Sa 17:54
King Saul now kept David at * and 1Sa 18:4
years in * as king of both Israel 2Sa 5:4,5
David now led his troops to * to 2Sa 5:6
After moving from Hebron to *, 2Sa 5:13
his children who were born at *: 2Sa 5:14,15,16
gold shields to * which King 2Sa 8:7
He also carried back to * a very 2Sa 8:8
moved to * to live at the palace. 2Sa 9:13
Afterwards Joab returned to *. 2Sa 10:14
But David stayed in *. 2Sa 11:1
So the messenger arrived at *, 2Sa 11:22
carried back to *, and David took 2Sa 12:29,30
David and the army returned to *. 2Sa 12:31
As they were on the way back to * 2Sa 13:29,30
Now the watchman on the * wall 2Sa 13:34
and brought Absalom back to *. 2Sa 14:23
After Absalom had been in * for 2Sa 14:28
to *, I would sacrifice to him." 2Sa 15:7,8
He took two hundred men from * 2Sa 15:11
A messenger soon arrived in * to 2Sa 15:13
and the city of * will be saved." 2Sa 15:14
Go on back with your men to *, to 2Sa 15:19,20
Let me know what happens in * 2Sa 15:28
return to * and tell Absalom, 'I 2Sa 15:33,34
"He stayed at *," Ziba replied. 2Sa 16:3
at *, accompanied by Ahithophel. 2Sa 16:15
without success and returned to *. 2Sa 17:20
So the king started back to *. 2Sa 19:15
thing I did when you left *; 2Sa 19:19
arrived from * to meet the king. 2Sa 19:24,25
since the day the king left *. 2Sa 19:24,25
*," the king said to Barzillai. 2Sa 19:33
him from the Jordan to *. 2Sa 20:2
at his palace in *, the king 2Sa 20:3
they returned to the king at *. 2Sa 20:22
to destroy *, the Lord was sorry 2Sa 24:16
with him to *, making a joyous and 1Ki 1:40
David died and was buried in *. 1Ki 2:10
in Hebron and thirty-three in *. 1Ki 2:11
a house here in *, and don't step 1Ki 2:36,37
So he lived in * for a long 1Ki 2:38
slaves, he took them back to *. 1Ki 2:40
Shime-i had left * and had gone to 1Ki 2:41
name of God to stay in * or die? 1Ki 2:42
He brought her to * to live in 1Ki 3:1
He returned to * and went into 1Ki 3:15
a convocation at * of all the 1Ki 8:1
chosen city of * and toward this 1Ki 8:44
this city of * which you have 1Ki 8:48
Millo, the wall of *, and the 1Ki 9:15
resort cities near * and in the 1Ki 9:19
old sector of *—to the new quarters 1Ki 9:24
She arrived in * with a long 1Ki 10:2
cities and with the king at *. 1Ki 10:26
as stones in * in those days, and 1Ki 10:27
delivered to * cost $400, and the 1Ki 10:29
the valley from *, for Chemosh, the 1Ki 11:7
the sake of *, my chosen city." 1Ki 11:12,13
One day as Jeroboam was leaving * 1Ki 11:29
for the sake of *, which I have 1Ki 11:32
to reign in *, the city I have 1Ki 11:36
He ruled in * for forty years, 1Ki 11:42
escaped by chariot and fled to *. 1Ki 12:18
When King Rehoboam arrived in *, 1Ki 12:21
When they go to * to offer 1Ki 12:27
trouble to go to * to worship; 1Ki 12:28
in *, which God had ordained. 1Ki 12:32,33f
to the annual festival at *; 1Ki 12:32,33
seventeen years in *, the city 1Ki 14:21
of Egypt attacked and conquered *. 1Ki 14:25
his ancestors in *, and his son 1Ki 14:31
king of Judah in * during the 1Ki 15:1
When he died he was buried in *, 1Ki 15:8
Asa became king of Judah, in *, 1Ki 15:9
to cut off all trade with *. 1Ki 15:17
buried in the royal cemetery in *. 1Ki 15:24
in * for twenty-five years. 1Ki 22:42
his ancestors in *, the city of his 1Ki 22:50
he reigned in * for eight years. 2Ki 8:17
of David—the old section of *. 2Ki 8:24,25
he reigned only one year, in *. 2Ki 8:26

(JERUSALEM Con't)

him by chariot to * where they	2Ki 9:28
He reigned in * for forty years.	2Ki 12:1
then he moved on toward * to	2Ki 12:17
royal cemetery in *, and his son	2Ki 12:21
in * for twenty-nine years.	2Ki 14:2
was Jeho-addin, a native of *.	2Ki 14:2
Israel marched on * and broke down	2Ki 14:13
life in *, and he fled to Lachish;	2Ki 14:19
in the City of David section of *.	2Ki 14:20
Name of his mother: Jecoliah of *	2Ki 15:1
of his reign: 52 years, in *	2Ki 15:1
of his reign: 16 years, in *	2Ki 15:32,33
in the City of David section of *.	2Ki 15:38
Duration of reign: 16 years, in *	2Ki 16:1
war on Ahaz and besieged *;	2Ki 16:5
of David sector of *, and his son	2Ki 16:20
of his reign: 29 years, in *	2Ki 18:1
to worship at the altar in *!'	2Ki 18:22
you think the Lord can save *?'	2Ki 18:35
he says that I won't conquer *.	2Ki 19:10
The daughter of * scorns and	2Ki 19:21
people shall become strong in *.	2Ki 19:31
of his reign: 55 years, in *	2Ki 21:1
Temple, and in *—the city I have	2Ki 21:7
such evil upon * and Judah that the	2Ki 21:12
Israel to conquer *, and I will	2Ki 21:13
and I will wipe * as a man wipes a	2Ki 21:13
people. And * was filled from one	2Ki 21:16
Length of his reign: 2 years, in *	2Ki 21:19,20
of his reign: 31 years in *	2Ki 22:1
* to find Huldah the prophetess.	2Ki 22:14
* to go to the Temple with him.	2Ki 23:1
and great, of * and Judah gathered	2Ki 23:1
Valley outside *, and he carried	2Ki 23:4
throughout Judah and even in *.	2Ki 23:5
took it outside * to Kidron Brook;	2Ki 23:6
He brought back to * the priests	2Ki 23:8
former mayor of *, located on the	2Ki 23:8
of the Lord in *, even though they	2Ki 23:9
the hills east of * and south of	2Ki 23:13
Finally he returned to *.	2Ki 23:20
and it was celebrated in *.	2Ki 23:23
both in * and throughout the land.	2Ki 23:24
my chosen city of * and the Temple	2Ki 23:27
from Megiddo to * and buried him in	2Ki 23:30
of his reign: 3 months, in *	2Ki 23:31,32
his reigning in *, and he levied a	2Ki 23:33
of Josiah's sons, to reign in *;	2Ki 23:34
of his reign: 11 years, in *	2Ki 23:36,37
of Babylon attacked *.	2Ki 24:1
for he had filled * with blood, and	2Ki 24:3,4
of his reign: 3 months, in *	2Ki 24:8,9
of Elnathan, a citizen of *)	2Ki 24:8,9
of Babylon besieged the city of *.	2Ki 24:10
captives from *, including all the	2Ki 24:14
of his reign: 11 years, in *	2Ki 24:18,19
the people of * and Judah.	2Ki 24:20
and laid siege to *, arriving on	2Ki 25:1
arrived at * from Babylon on July	2Ki 25:8
in tearing down the walls of *.	2Ki 25:10
Then he moved the capital to *,	1Ch 3:4
While he was in *, his wife	1Ch 3:5
Temple at *), the father of	1Ch 6:4-15
of Judah and * into captivity under	1Ch 6:4-15
the Temple at *, the choirs carried	1Ch 6:32
of the subclans living at *.	1Ch 8:28
families lived together near *.	1Ch 8:30,31,32
and Manasseh arrived in *:	1Ch 9:3
They lived in * at the Temple and	1Ch 9:33,34
Shime-am in * near his relatives.	1Ch 9:38
leaders went to * (or Jebus, as it	1Ch 11:4
of * is called the City of David.	1Ch 11:7
while Joab rebuilt the rest of *.	1Ch 11:8
After David moved to *, he	1Ch 14:3
of the sons born to him in *:	1Ch 14:4-7
for himself in *, and he also built	1Ch 15:1
all Israel to * to celebrate the	1Ch 15:3
of Obed-edom to take the Ark to *.	1Ch 15:25
took the Ark to * with shouts of	1Ch 15:28
(But as the Ark arrived in *,	1Ch 15:29
officers to *, as well as a great	1Ch 18:7
Then Joab returned to *.	1Ch 19:15
Meanwhile, David had stayed in *.	1Ch 20:1
and all his army returned to *.	1Ch 20:3
through Israel and returned to *.	1Ch 21:4
God sent an angel to destroy *;	1Ch 21:15
pointing toward *, he and the	1Ch 21:16
and he will always live in *.	1Ch 23:25
his officials to *—the political	1Ch 28:1
in Hebron and thirty-three in *.	1Ch 29:26,27
Tabernacle in *, built by King	2Ch 1:4
and went back to * to rule Israel.	2Ch 1:13
were stationed at * near the king.	2Ch 1:14
in * as rocks on the road!	2Ch 1:15
horses for $100, delivered at *.	2Ch 1:17
of Judah and * who were selected by	2Ch 2:7
you can take them inland to *."	2Ch 2:16
Its location was in * at the top	2Ch 3:1
Solomon now summoned to * all of	2Ch 5:2
But now I have chosen * as that	2Ch 6:5,6
this city of * which you have	2Ch 6:34
heart's desire in * and Lebanon and	2Ch 8:6
of David sector of * to the new	2Ch 8:11
* to test him with hard questions.	2Ch 9:1
well as in * to protect the king.	2Ch 9:25
in * as stones in the road!	2Ch 9:27
So Solomon reigned in * over all	2Ch 9:30
Then he died and was buried in *	2Ch 9:31
into his chariot and fled to *.	2Ch 10:18
UPON ARRIVAL AT *, Rehoboam	2Ch 11:1
Rehoboam stayed in * and	2Ch 11:5-10
moved to Judah and *, for King	2Ch 11:13,14
began moving to * where they could	2Ch 11:16
of Egypt attacked * in the fifth	2Ch 12:2
cities and soon arrived at *.	2Ch 12:4
(they had fled to * for safety),	2Ch 12:5
to pour out my anger upon *.	2Ch 12:7
of Egypt conquered * and took away	2Ch 12:9
seventeen years in *, the city God	2Ch 12:13
he was buried in *, and his son	2Ch 12:16
king of Judah, in *, in the	2Ch 13:1
KING ABIJAH WAS buried in *.	2Ch 14:1
before finally returning to *.	2Ch 14:15
They all came to * in June of	2Ch 15:10
he had hewn out for himself in *.	2Ch 16:13,14
army stationed at *, his capital.	2Ch 17:13
These were the troops in * in	2Ch 17:19
that, but remained quietly at *.	2Ch 19:4
Jehoshaphat set up courts in *,	2Ch 19:8
to * to plead unitedly with him.	2Ch 20:4
*, and you, O king Jehoshaphat!"	2Ch 20:15
for you, O people of Judah and *!	2Ch 20:17
and the people of * did the same,	2Ch 20:18
people of Judah and *," he said.	2Ch 20:20
Then they returned to *, with	2Ch 20:27
They marched into * accompanied	2Ch 20:28
reigned twenty-five years, in *.	2Ch 20:31
of the kings in *, and his son	2Ch 21:1
and he reigned eight years, in *.	2Ch 21:5
people of * in worshiping idols;	2Ch 21:11
made the people of * and Judah	2Ch 21:13
* eight years, and died unmourned.	2Ch 21:20
He was buried in *, but not in	2Ch 21:20
THEN THE PEOPLE of * chose	2Ch 22:1
and he reigned one year, in *.	2Ch 22:2
his plans and to summon them to *.	2Ch 23:2,3
and he reigned forty years, in *.	2Ch 24:1
the cities of Judah, and from *?	2Ch 24:6
and throughout * telling the people	2Ch 24:9
came down upon Judah and * again.	2Ch 24:17,18
Judah and *, killing all the	2Ch 24:23
reigned twenty-nine years, in *.	2Ch 25:1
was Jeho-addan, a native of *.	2Ch 25:1
and took him as a prisoner to *.	2Ch 25:23
of the walls of * dismantled, from	2Ch 25:23
against him in *, and how he fled	2Ch 25:27
back on horses to * and buried him	2Ch 25:28
he reigned fifty-two years, in *.	2Ch 26:3
name was Jecoliah, from *.	2Ch 26:3
He built fortified towers in * at	2Ch 26:9
manufactured in *, invented by	2Ch 26:15
he reigned sixteen years, in *.	2Ch 27:1
he reigned sixteen years, in *.	2Ch 27:8
When he died, he was buried in *	2Ch 27:9
he reigned sixteen years, in *.	2Ch 28:1
of these people from Judah and *?	2Ch 28:10
heathen gods in every corner of *.	2Ch 28:24
he was buried in * but not in the	2Ch 28:27
reigned twenty-nine years, in *.	2Ch 29:1
Lord has been upon Judah and *.	2Ch 29:8
to the Temple at * for the annual	2Ch 30:1
the assembly of * had voted to	2Ch 30:2,3
turned to God and came to *.	2Ch 30:11
crowd assembled at * in the month	2Ch 30:13
heathen altars in *, and knocked	2Ch 30:14
* for seven days with great joy.	2Ch 30:21
deep joy. For * hadn't seen a	2Ch 30:26
Those who were at * for the	2Ch 31:1
the people in * to bring their	2Ch 31:4
to attack *, Hezekiah summoned his	2Ch 32:2
Hezekiah and the citizens of *:	2Ch 32:9
you can survive my siege of *?	2Ch 32:10
Judah and * to use only the one	2Ch 32:12
about the God of * just as though	2Ch 32:19
Hezekiah and the people of *.	2Ch 32:22
Lord arrived at *, with valuable	2Ch 32:23
was upon him and upon Judah and *.	2Ch 32:25
the residents of * humbled	2Ch 32:26
of the City of David sector in *.	2Ch 32:30
and * honored him at his death.	2Ch 32:33
he reigned fifty-five years, in *.	2Ch 33:1
Temple, and in *—the city I have	2Ch 33:7
of Judah and * to do even more evil	2Ch 33:9
him to * and to his kingdom!	2Ch 33:13
that were in *, and dumped them	2Ch 33:15
began to reign in *, but he lasted	2Ch 33:20,21
He reigned thirty-one years, in *	2Ch 34:1
clean up Judah and *, destroying	2Ch 34:3
of Judah and * from the guilt of	2Ch 34:5
of Israel before returning to *.	2Ch 34:7
governor of *, and Joah (son of	2Ch 34:8
as well as from the people of *.	2Ch 34:9
of Judah and *, and the priests	2Ch 34:29
And he required everyone in *	2Ch 34:32
on the first day of April, in *.	2Ch 35:1
Everyone present in * took part	2Ch 35:17
and people from * and from all	2Ch 35:18
him back to * where he died.	2Ch 35:24,25
And all Judah and *, including	2Ch 35:24,25
and he reigned eleven years, in *;	2Ch 36:5
Babylon conquered *, and took away	2Ch 36:6
as the new king of Judah and *.	2Ch 36:10
and he reigned eleven years, in *.	2Ch 36:11
the Temple of the Lord in *.	2Ch 36:14
down the walls of * and burned all	2Ch 36:19
Temple in *, in the land of Judah.	2Ch 36:22,23
Temple in *, in the land of Judah.	Ez 1:2
may now return to * to rebuild this	Ez 1:3
who is the God of Israel and of *.	Ez 1:3
* at once to rebuild the Temple.	Ez 1:5
from the Temple at * and had placed	Ez 1:7
to Shesh-bazzar to take back to *.	Ez 1:11
now returned to * and to the other	Ez 2:1
Another group returned to * at	Ez 2:59
family name)—also returned to *.	Ez 2:61
in * and its nearby villages;	Ez 2:70
to Judah came to * from their homes	Ez 3:1
second year of their arrival at *.	Ez 3:8
of Judah and *, and did the same	Ez 4:6
and relocated in *, Samaria, and	Ez 4:10
the Jews sent to * from Babylon are	Ez 4:12
indeed found that * has in times	Ez 4:19
great kings in * who have ruled the	Ez 4:20
they hurried to * and forced the	Ez 4:23
BUT THERE WERE prophets in * and	Ez 5:1
soon arrived in * and demanded,	Ez 5:3
from the Temple in * and had placed	Ez 5:14
the bowls to * and to let the	Ez 5:15
foundations of the Temple at *;	Ez 5:16
* where the Jews offer sacrifices.	Ez 6:3
be taken back to * and put into the	Ez 6:5
Give the priests in * young	Ez 6:9
chosen the city of * will destroy	Ez 6:12
who traveled from Babylon to *	Ez 7:1
to return to *, and the king	Ez 7:6
at * in the month of August;	Ez 7:7,8,9
Levites, may return to * with you.	Ez 7:13
laws to Judah and * and to send	Ez 7:14
take with you to * the silver and	Ez 7:15
your Temple when you arrive in *.	Ez 7:17
for the Temple of your God at *.	Ez 7:19
the Temple of the Lord in *!	Ez 7:27
of Israel to return with me to *.	Ez 7:28
for the Temple of God at *.	Ez 8:17
of Israel at *, where they are to	Ez 8:29
of taking it to God's Temple in *.	Ez 8:30
and started off to *;	Ez 8:31
So at last we arrived safely at *.	Ez 8:32
us to return to * from our exile.	Ez 9:8
us * as a walled city in Judah.	Ez 9:9
Judah and * that everyone should	Ez 10:7,8
should appear at * within three	Ez 10:7,8
about how things were going in *	Neh 1:2
"—the Jews who returned to *	Neh 1:2
the wall of * is still torn down,	Neh 1:3
I will bring you back to *.	Neh 1:9
to Jerusalem. For * is the place in	Neh 1:9
Three days after my arrival at *	Neh 2:11,12
* which God had put into my heart.	Neh 2:11,12
Let us rebuild the wall of * and	Neh 2:17
mayor of half of *, was next down	Neh 3:9
the mayor of the other half of *.	Neh 3:12
the City of David section of *.	Neh 3:15
an army against * to bring about	Neh 4:8
talk them out of returning to *.	Neh 4:12
walls to move into * so that their	Neh 4:22
for you at * by saying, 'Look!	Neh 6:7
of governing * to my brother Hanani	Neh 7:2
not to open the * gates until well	Neh 7:3
be residents of *, and that they	Neh 7:3
Another group returned to * at	Neh 7:61
of September, they came back to *.	Neh 7:73
especially in *, telling the people	Neh 8:15
in *, the Holy City, at this time;	Neh 11:1
Some who moved to * at this time	Neh 11:2
who came to * (though most of the	Neh 11:3
of Perez who lived in *.	Neh 11:4,5,6
all, there were 284 Levites in *.	Neh 11:18
of the Levites in * and of those	Neh 11:22,23
of the new * wall, all the Levites	Neh 12:27
the land came to * to assist in the	Neh 12:27
The choir members also came to *	Neh 12:28
own villages as suburbs of *.	Neh 12:29
people of * was heard far away!	Neh 12:43
I was not in * at the time, for I	Neh 13:6
permission to go back again to *).	Neh 13:6
When I arrived back in * and	Neh 13:7
which they took that day into *.	Neh 13:15
on the Sabbath to the people of *.	Neh 13:16
camped outside * once or twice,	Neh 13:20
He had been captured when * was	Est 2:6
him in *, my holy city."	Ps 2:6

(JERUSALEM Con't)

he heard me from his Temple in *. Ps 3:4
praises to the God who lives in *. Ps 9:11
He lives upon Mount Zion in *. Ps 48:1
God himself is the defender of *. Ps 48:3
God has established * forever. Ps 48:8
throughout the world. O *, Ps 48:11
your people and protect *. Ps 51:18
build the walls of *." Ps 51:18f
their gifts to your temple in *. Ps 68:29
For God will save *; Ps 69:35
You chose * Ps 74:2
His home is in *. Ps 76:2
Your Temple is defiled and * is a Ps 79:1
the entire population of *; Ps 79:3
HIGH ON HIS holy mountain stands * Ps 87:1
honor will be to be a native of *! Ps 87:5
sing, "All my heart is in *." Ps 87:7
must bow to him! * and all the Ps 97:8,9
mountain in *, for he is holy. Ps 99:9
and have mercy on *—and now is the Ps 102:13
For Jehovah will rebuild *! Ps 102:16
to the Temple in * to praise him, Ps 102:21,22
in * Ps 110:2
of the Temple in *, before all the Ps 116:18,19
to *, to the Temple of the Lord. Ps 122:1
Pray for the peace of *. Ps 122:6
city prosper. O *, may there be Ps 122:7
and protect *, so the Lord Ps 125:2
exiles to *, it was like a dream! Ps 126:1
Literally, "of *." Ps 128:5f
O Lord, you have chosen * Ps 132:13
this eternal blessing on *, Ps 133:3
All people of *, Ps 135:21
the Lord, for he lives here in *. Ps 135:21
rivers of Babylon thinking of *. Ps 137:1
If I forget you, O *, let my Ps 137:5,6
the armies of Babylon captured *. Ps 137:7
The Lord will reign forever. O *, Ps 146:10
He is rebuilding * and bringing Ps 147:2
Praise him, O *! Ps 147:12
O people of *, exult in your Ps 149:2
descendant) of David, King of *." Ecc 1:1f
of *, King David's son, "The Ecc 1:1
was king of Israel, living in *. Ecc 1:12-15
any of the kings before me in *. Ecc 1:16-18
of the kings in * before me, and Ecc 2:9
O girls of *, tanned as the dark Sol 1:5
O girls of *, I adjure you by Sol 2:7
I adjure you, O women of *, by Sol 3:5
The Young Women of *: "Who is Sol 3:5
'With love from the girls of *!' Sol 3:10
The Young Women of *: "Oh, lover Sol 5:1
I adjure you, O women of *, if Sol 5:8
The Young Women of *: "O woman Sol 5:8
Such, O women of *, is my Sol 5:16
THE YOUNG WOMEN of *: "O rarest Sol 6:1
*, and how you capture my heart. Sol 6:4
The women of * were delighted Sol 6:9
The Young Women of *: "Return, Sol 6:12
I adjure you, O women of *, not Sol 8:4
The Young Women of *: "Who is Sol 8:4
to Judah and * in the days ahead. Is 1:1
*, once my faithful wife! Is 1:21
the Lord concerning Judah and *: Is 2:1
In the last days * and the Temple Is 2:2
the world will be ruled from *. Is 2:3
the destruction of * will be washed Is 4:2,3,4
of the Messiah in * at that time. Is 4:2,3,4f
shade on all *—over every home and Is 4:5
Now, men of * and Judah, you have Is 5:3
of this delicious morsel, *. Is 5:14
they will come racing toward *. Is 5:26
of Uzziah), * was attacked by King Is 7:1
Then we'll fight our way into * Is 7:6
"Since the people of * are Is 8:6
than those in * and Samaria, so Is 10:10
we will destroy * with hers." Is 10:11
"O my people in *, don't be afraid Is 10:24
He shakes his fist at * on Mount Is 10:32
Let all the people of * shout Is 12:6
Lord has founded * and is Is 14:32
who accompany the gift to * Is 16:3
from his Temple in *—serene as on a Is 18:4
*, where he has placed his name. Is 18:7
THIS IS GOD'S message concerning * Is 22:1
The walls of * are breached and Is 22:5
You inspect the walls of * to Is 22:9,10,11
to the people of * and all Judah. Is 22:21
rule gloriously in *, in the sight Is 24:23
Here on Mount Zion in *, the Is 25:6
will rest upon *, and Moab will be Is 25:10
brought back to * to worship the Is 27:13
But * is now led by drunks! Is 28:7
Lord, you scoffing rulers in *: Is 28:14
WOE TO *, Is 29:1
and sorrow. For * shall become as Is 29:2
I will surround * and lay siege Is 29:3
And all the nations fighting * Is 29:7
O my people in *, you shall weep Is 30:19
a pilgrim band to * to the Mountain Is 30:29
will hover over * as birds hover Is 31:4,5
flame of God burns brightly in *. Is 31:9
and vines, so * will strip the Is 33:4
He will make * the home of Is 33:5
Instead you will see * at peace, Is 33:20
to confer with King Hezekiah in *. Is 36:2
only at the altars here in *? Is 36:7
in * to hear this, not just you. Is 36:12
of yours can deliver * from me? Is 36:20
Now the Assyrian envoy left * and Is 37:8,9
* to Hezekiah with this message: Is 37:8,9
by promising that * will not be Is 37:10
out from * to repopulate the land; Is 37:32
shall not enter *, nor shoot their Is 37:33
Speak tenderly to * and tell her Is 40:2
O Crier of Good News, shout to * Is 40:9
I was the first to tell *, Is 41:27
don't be afraid. O *, my chosen Is 44:2
when they say * will be delivered Is 44:26
do as I say; and * will be rebuilt Is 44:28
*, and Israel, who is my glory. Is 46:13
They shall come with singing to * Is 51:11
Wake up, wake up, *! Is 51:17
WAKE UP, WAKE up, *, and clothe Is 52:1
Rise from the dust, *; Is 52:2
Let the ruins of * break into Is 52:9
he has redeemed *. Is 52:9
out into loud and joyful song, *, Is 54:1
holy mountain of *, and make them Is 56:7
They will call * "The City of Is 60:14
heart yearns for *, I will not Is 62:1
care for you, O *, with joy like Is 62:5
O *, I have set intercessors Is 62:6,7
he establishes * and makes her Is 62:6,7
The Lord has sworn to * with all Is 62:8
Redeemed," and * shall be called Is 62:12
How briefly we possessed *! Is 63:18
Your holy cities are destroyed; * Is 64:10
I will recreate * as a place of Is 65:18
And I will rejoice in *, and in Is 65:19
Rejoice with *; Is 66:10
Delight in *; Is 66:11
Prosperity shall overflow * like Is 66:12
When you see *, your heart will Is 66:14
*, where they shall see my glory. Is 66:18
mountain, to *, says the Lord. Is 66:20
of Judah, when * was captured and Jer 1:3
north to come to * and set their Jer 1:15
I see great armies marching on * Jer 2:15
the whole city of * will be known Jer 3:17
men of Judah and *, Plow up the Jer 4:3
Shout to * and to all Judea, Jer 4:5
Send a signal from *: "Flee Jer 4:6
you promised great blessings on *. Jer 4:10
O *, cleanse your hearts while Jer 4:14
against * and the cities of Judah. Jer 4:16
They surround * like shepherds Jer 4:17
through every street in all *; Jer 5:1
Flee from *! Jer 6:1
smash down the walls of *. Jer 6:6
This is your last warning, O *. Jer 6:8
I will pour it out over *, even Jer 6:11
listen to it, O my people in *; Jer 6:18,19
O *, pride of my people, put on Jer 6:26
God will never let * be destroyed. Jer 7:4
of Judah and in the streets of *? Jer 7:17
After the fall of * the refugees Jer 7:18f
O *, shave your head in shame and Jer 7:29
in the streets of * and in the Jer 7:34
"And I will turn * into heaps of Jer 9:11
Hear * weeping in despair. Jer 9:19
all the people of * that I made a Jer 11:1
me among the men of Judah and *. Jer 11:9
Baal) are along every street in *. Jer 11:13
will rot the pride of Judah and *. Jer 13:8,9
to the south of * have closed their Jer 13:19
themselves, for * cannot help; Jer 13:19
Where is your flock, *, Jer 13:20
Woe upon you, O *! Jer 13:27
and a great cry rises from *. Jer 14:2
of *, victims of famine and war; Jer 14:16
Do you abhor *? Jer 14:19
of Judah, did in *, I will punish Jer 15:4
Who will feel sorry for you, *? Jer 15:5
in the gates of *, first at the Jer 17:19
nation, and all you citizens of *. Jer 17:20
sitting on the throne here in *; Jer 17:25
And from all around * and from Jer 17:26
these gates of *, just as on other Jer 17:27
warn all Judah and *, saying: Hear Jer 18:11
kings of Judah and citizens of *! Jer 19:3
plans of Judah and * and I will let Jer 19:7
And I will wipe * off the earth, Jer 19:8
so I will shatter the people of *; Jer 19:11
this valley, so it will be in *. Jer 19:12
For I will fill * with dead Jer 19:12
all the homes in *, including the Jer 19:13
I will let your enemies loot *. Jer 20:5
deliverance of * from Sennacherib, Jer 21:1f
Stay here in * and Jer 21:9
of *, which boasts, 'We are safe; Jer 21:13
out of * and thrown on the garbage Jer 22:19
but the prophets of * are even Jer 23:14
Later, when * has fallen, Jer 23:20
in front of the Temple in *. Jer 24:2
of * left here in this land; Jer 24:8
I went to * and to the cities of Jer 25:18
and I will make * a curse word in Jer 26:6
"What do you mean—* destroyed Jer 26:9
and this city of * razed into heaps Jer 26:18
ambassadors in *, saying, Tell Jer 27:3
in the palaces in * will not be Jer 27:18
of Judah and * to Babylon, along Jer 27:19,20,21
bring them all back to * again." Jer 27:22
them a letter from *, addressing it Jer 29:1
he has exiled to Babylon from *: Jer 29:4
left here in *—on your relatives Jer 29:16,17
priests and to everyone in *. Jer 29:25
replace Jehoiada as priest in *. Jer 29:26
and "*, the Place Nobody Wants." Jer 30:17
* will be rebuilt upon her ruins; Jer 30:18
the Lord, when all * shall be Jer 31:38,39
Babylonian army was besieging *. Jer 32:2
and here in *, in the cities of Jer 32:44
* and in all the cities of Judah. Jer 33:13
of Judah and * shall live in safety Jer 33:16
against * and the cities of Judah: Jer 34:1
army was besieging *, Lachish and Jer 34:7
all the slaves in *— (for King Jer 34:8
gave the following message to *. Jer 34:12
afraid and decided to move to *. Jer 35:11
say to Judah and *, Won't you learn Jer 35:13
upon Judah and * all the evil I Jer 35:17
of Judah and *, for they wouldn't Jer 36:31
The people of * who had Jer 37:1f
besieged city of *, the Babylonian Jer 37:5
from * to fight the Egyptians. Jer 37:5
army set out from * to engage Jer 37:11
remaining in * would die by sword, Jer 38:2
that the city of * would surely be Jer 38:3
* was retaken by the Babylonians. Jer 38:28
against * again and besieged it. Jer 39:1
Meanwhile the army burned *, Jer 39:8
exiled people of * and Judah who Jer 40:1
upon the people of *, so it will be Jer 42:18
* and to all the cities of Judah. Jer 44:2,3
the streets of *, and there is Jer 44:6
sins of your wives in Judah and *? Jer 44:9
*, by sword, famine and disease. Jer 44:13
of Judah and in the streets of *; Jer 44:17
of Judah and in the streets of *? Jer 44:21
Come, let us declare in * all the Jer 51:10
Remember the Lord and return to * Jer 51:50
and he reigned eleven years in *. Jer 52:1
Lord's presence in * and Judah, and Jer 52:3
his army against * and built forts Jer 52:4
guard, arrived in *, and burned Jer 52:12
punished * for all her many sins; Lam 1:5
For * sinned so horribly; Lam 1:8
* pleads for help but no one Lam 1:17
from the Lord has overcast *; Lam 2:1
and tears are his portion for *. Lam 2:5
The Lord determined to destroy *. Lam 2:8
The elders of * sit upon the Lam 2:10
The virgins of * hang their heads Lam 2:10
such sorrow? O *, what can I Lam 2:13
He has destroyed * without mercy Lam 2:17
O walls of *, let tears fall down Lam 2:18
happening to the young girls of *. Lam 3:51
He started a fire in * that Lam 4:11
They rape the women of * and the Lam 5:11
our eyes grow dim. * and the Lam 5:18
draw a map of the city of * on it. Eze 4:1
how an enemy army will capture *! Eze 4:3
demonstration of the siege of *; Eze 4:7
will be tightly rationed in *. Eze 4:16
it at the center of your map of *. Eze 5:2
will happen to *, for she has Eze 5:5,6,7
of bloody crimes. * is filled with Eze 7:23
by bringing to * the worst of the Eze 7:24
to transport me to *, to the Eze 8:3
the streets of * and put a mark on Eze 9:4
Will your fury against * wipe out Eze 9:8
is time to rebuild *, for our city Eze 11:3
will take you from * and hand you Eze 11:9
remnant left in * are saying about Eze 11:15
But as for those now in *, Eze 11:21
ended the vision of my visit to *. Eze 11:24
the evil that will come upon *." Eze 12:6
Literally, "to the prince in *." Eze 12:10f
in * and to all the people of Eze 12:10
of Israel and * shall ration their Eze 12:19
of safety and security for *. Eze 12:24
prophets, claiming * will have Eze 13:16
punishments await * to destroy all Eze 14:21
it was right for me to destroy *. Eze 14:22
The people of * are like the vines Eze 15:5,6
to * about her loathsome sins. Eze 16:2
came to * and took away her Eze 17:12,13
* again and slaughters many lives. Eze 17:17
For at * in my holy mountain, Eze 20:40
"Son of dust, look toward * and Eze 20:46

JERUSALEM Con't)

"Son of dust, face toward * and	Eze 21:2
smite * and satisfy my fury."	Eze 21:17
to follow—one to * and the other to	Eze 21:19,20
whether to attack * or Rabbah.	Eze 21:21
They will decide to turn toward *!	Eze 21:22
* won't understand this treachery;	Eze 21:23
ally and has sworn to defend *!	Eze 21:23
"Son of dust, indict * as the	Eze 22:2
to my crucible in *, to smelt you	Eze 22:18,19,20
(I am speaking of Samaria and *!	Eze 23:4,5
"But when Oholibah (*) saw what	Eze 23:11
you, O Oholibah (*), those very	Eze 23:22
"Son of dust, you must accuse *	Eze 23:36
Samaria and *, these shameless	Eze 23:44
king of Babylon has attacked *.	Eze 24:2
"For the Lord God says: Woe to *	Eze 24:6
"Woe to *, City of Murderers.	Eze 24:9
from them in * the joy of their	Eze 24:25
day a refugee from * will start on	Eze 24:26
over the fall of *, saying, 'Ha!	Eze 26:2
the year * fell to	Eze 30:20f
an army to relieve * in 588,	Eze 30:21f
the year * fell.	Eze 31:1f
who escaped from * arrived to tell	Eze 33:21
year after * was captured—the hand	Eze 40:1
Chebar Canal, and then later at *	Eze 43:3
attacked * with his armies, and the	Dan 1:1
from the Temple in * during	Dan 5:2,3,4
open toward *, and prayed three	Dan 6:10
the prophet, that * must lie	Dan 9:2
the people of *, and all Israel,	Dan 9:7
at * to us and our rulers.	Dan 9:12
furious anger from *, your own	Dan 9:16
Lord my God for *, his holy	Dan 9:20
of further punishment upon * and	Dan 9:24
Or, consider the destruction of *	Dan 9:25f
*, until the Anointed One comes!	Dan 9:25
rob and desecrate the Temple in *.	Dan 11:20f
* and pollute the sanctuary,	Dan 11:30,31
He will halt between * and the	Dan 11:45
invaded Judah and besieged *.	Hos 1:7f
SOUND THE ALARM in *!	Joe 2:1
"Rejoice, O people of *, rejoice	Joe 2:23
even in * some will escape, just	Joe 2:32
of Judah and *," says the Lord,	Joe 3:1
of Judah and * to the Greeks, who	Joe 3:6
from his Temple in * and the earth	Joe 3:16
mountain. * shall be mine forever;	Joe 3:17
* will thrive as generations pass.	Joe 3:20
For my home is in *	Joe 3:21
in luxury at * and Samaria, so	Amo 6:1
and divided * among them by lot;	Ob 1:11
But * will become a refuge, a way	Ob 1:17
For deliverers will come to *	Ob 1:21
the capital cities, Samaria and *!	Mic 1:5
the Lord stands poised against *.	Mic 1:12
and fill * with murder and sin of	Mic 3:10
It is because of you that *	Mic 3:12
will be ruled by the Lord from *!	Mic 4:2
Zion forever. O *—the Watchtower	Mic 4:8
THE ENEMY lays siege to *!	Mic 5:1
calls out to all *—listen to the	Mic 6:9
I will crush Judah and * with my	Zep 1:4
farthest gate of *, coming closer	Zep 1:10
"Wail in sorrow, you people of *	Zep 1:11
WOE TO FILTHY, sinful *, city of	Zep 3:1
all your heart, O daughter of *.	Zep 3:14
On that day the announcement to *	Zep 3:16
from Babylon to rebuild *.	Hag 1:1f
against * and the cities of Judah.	Zec 1:12
what has happened to Judah and *?	Zec 1:14
returned to * filled with mercy;	Zec 1:16
Lord of Hosts, and so will all *	Zec 1:16
* and bless her and live in her."	Zec 1:17
scattered Judah, Israel, and *."	Zec 1:19
"To measure *," he said.	Zec 2:2
angel, "that * will some day be so	Zec 2:4
of fire protecting them and all *;	Zec 2:5
Sing, *, and rejoice!	Zec 2:10
once more choose to bless *.'	Zec 2:11,12
even the Lord, who has chosen *,	Zec 3:2f
to be merciful to *—I rebuke you.	Zec 3:2
Lord's Temple at *, to seek his	Zec 7:2
Long years ago, when * was	Zec 7:7
will live within *, and Jerusalem	Zec 8:3
Jerusalem, and * shall be called	Zec 8:3
The Lord of Hosts declares that *	Zec 8:4
to live safely in *, and they will	Zec 8:8
and pour into * from many foreign	Zec 8:20,21
say, 'Let's go to * to ask the Lord	Zec 8:20,21
Lord of Hosts in * to ask for his	Zec 8:22
"I will make * and Judah like a	Zec 12:2
send their armies to surround *.	Zec 12:2
Jerusalem. * will be a heavy stone	Zec 12:3
'The people of * have found	Zec 12:5
and left, while * stands unmoved.	Zec 12:6
first, before *, so that the people	Zec 12:7
that the people of * and the royal	Zec 12:7
Lord will defend the people of *;	Zec 12:8
the nations that come against *.	Zec 12:9
all the people of *, and they will	Zec 12:10
The sorrow and mourning in * at	Zec 12:11
of Israel and *, a Fountain to	Zec 13:1
together the nations to fight *;	Zec 14:1
to the east of *, and the Mount of	Zec 14:4
on the eastern outskirts of *.	Zec 14:5f
will flow out from *, half toward	Zec 14:8
vast plain, but * will be on an	Zec 14:10
wine presses. And * shall be	Zec 14:11
on all the people who fought *.	Zec 14:12
Or, "against *."	Zec 14:14f
*. The wealth of all the	Zec 14:14
will go up to * each year to	Zec 14:16
refuses to come to * to worship the	Zec 14:17
In fact, every container in *	Zec 14:21
In Judah, in Israel, and in *,	Mal 2:11
of Judah and *, as he did before.	Mal 3:4
lands arrived in *, asking,	Mt 2:1
and all * was filled with rumors.	Mt 2:3
Literally, "and all * with him."	Mt 2:3f
didn't go through * to report to	Mt 2:12
People from * and from all over	Mt 3:5
Then Satan took him to * to the	Mt 4:5
Ten Cities, and *, and from all	Mt 4:25
And don't swear 'By *!'	Mt 5:35
Jerusalem!' for * is the capital of	Mt 5:35
arrived from * to interview Jesus.	Mt 15:1
about going to *, and what would	Mt 16:21
As Jesus was on the way to *, he	Mt 20:17
approached *, and were near the	Mt 21:1
prophecy, "Tell * her King is	Mt 21:5
The entire city of * was stirred	Mt 21:10
was returning to *, he was hungry,	Mt 21:18
"O *, Jerusalem, the city that	Mt 23:37
"O Jerusalem, *, the city that	Mt 23:37
for foreigners who died in *.	Mt 27:7
and went into *, and appeared to	Mt 27:53
People from * and from all over	Mk 1:5
Galilee, Judea, *, Idumea, from	Mk 3:7,8
had arrived from * said, "His	Mk 3:22
arrived from * to investigate him,	Mk 7:1
Now they were on the way to *,	Mk 10:32
to him when they arrived at *.	Mk 10:32
the outskirts of * and came to the	Mk 11:1
And so he entered * and went into	Mk 11:11
When they arrived back to * he	Mk 11:15
had arrived in * again, and as he	Mk 11:27,28
the valley from *, Peter, James,	Mk 13:3,4
He sent two of them into * to	Mk 14:13
and had come with him to *.	Mk 15:41
were walking from * into the	Mk 16:12
rushed back to * to tell the	Mk 16:13
to * to present him to the Lord;	Lk 2:22
That day a man named Simeon, a *	Lk 2:25
everyone in * who had been awaiting	Lk 2:38
for the redemption of *."	Lk 2:38f
his parents to * for the annual	Lk 2:41,42
but Jesus stayed behind in *.	Lk 2:43
back to * to search for him there.	Lk 2:45
Then Satan took him to * to a	Lk 4:9,10,11
and Judea, as well as from *.	Lk 5:17
Judea and from * and from as far	Lk 6:17,18
of his death at *, to be carried	Lk 9:31
towards * with an iron will.	Lk 9:51
because they were headed for *.	Lk 9:53
on a trip from * to Jericho was	Lk 10:30
continued on their way to *	Lk 10:38
sacrificing at the Temple in *.	Lk 13:1
Were they the worst sinners in *?	Lk 13:4
always pressing onward toward *.	Lk 13:22
of God to be killed except in *!	Lk 13:33
"O *, Jerusalem!	Lk 13:34
"O Jerusalem, *!	Lk 13:34
As they continued onward toward *	Lk 17:11
"As you know, we are going to *.	Lk 18:31
And because Jesus was nearing *,	Lk 19:11
went on towards *, walking along	Lk 19:28
But as they came closer to * and	Lk 19:41
"But when you see * surrounded	Lk 21:20
Let those in * try to escape, and	Lk 21:21
of the world; and * shall be	Lk 21:24
replied, "As soon as you enter *,	Lk 22:10
over Judea, from Galilee to *!"	Lk 23:5
and Herod happened to be in * at	Lk 23:7
an insurrection in * against the	Lk 23:19
just coming into * from the	Lk 23:26
"Daughters of *, don't weep for	Lk 23:28
remembered, and rushed back to *	Lk 24:9
of Emmaus, seven miles out of *.	Lk 24:13
the only person in * who hasn't	Lk 24:18
their way back to *, where the	Lk 24:33,34
be taken from * to all the nations:	Lk 24:47
and returned to * filled with	Lk 24:52
priests from * to ask John whether	Jn 1:19
celebration, and Jesus went to *.	Jn 2:13
miracles he did in * at the	Jn 2:23
his disciples left * and stayed for	Jn 3:22
Jews insist that * is the only	Jn 4:20
worship the Father here or in *.	Jn 4:21-24
they had been in * at the Passover	Jn 4:45
JESUS RETURNED to * for	Jn 5:1
on their way to * for the annual	Jn 6:2-5
who lived there in * said among	Jn 7:25
and Jesus was in * at the time of	Jn 10:22,23
down the road from *, and many of	Jn 11:18
his public ministry and left *;	Jn 11:54
people arrived in * several days	Jn 11:55
When the ordinary people of *	Jn 12:9
was on the way to * swept through	Jn 12:12
Some Greeks who had come to * to	Jn 12:20
them not to leave * until the Holy	Act 1:4
to the people in *, throughout	Act 1:8
half mile back to * and held a	Act 1:12
all the people of *, and they named	Act 1:19
Many godly Jews were in * that	Act 2:5
visitors and residents of * alike!	Act 2:14
was in session in *— Annas the	Act 4:5
and everybody in * knows about it.	Act 4:16
And crowds came in from the *	Act 5:16
have filled all * with your	Act 5:28
disciples increased vastly in *;	Act 6:7
over the church in *, and everyone	Act 8:1
who had fled * went everywhere	Act 8:4
When the apostles back in * heard	Act 8:14
John returned to *, stopping at	Act 8:25
that runs from * through the Gaza	Act 8:26
He had gone to * to worship at	Act 8:27
went to the High Priest in *.	Act 9:1
could bring them in chains to *.	Act 9:2
has done to the believers in *!	Act 9:13
followers so bitterly in *?"	Act 9:21
Upon arrival in * he tried to	Act 9:26
Israel and in *, where he was	Act 10:39
But when Peter arrived back in *	Act 11:2
who fled from * during the	Act 11:19
When the church at * heard what	Act 11:22
came down from * to Antioch, and	Act 11:27
to the elders of the church in *.	Act 11:30
Barnabas and Paul now visited *	Act 12:25
them and returned to *.	Act 13:13
The Jews in * and their leaders	Act 13:27
accompanied him to * from	Act 13:31
sent them to *, accompanied by some	Act 15:2
went on to *, stopping along the	Act 15:3
Arriving in *, they met with the	Act 15:4
elders and brothers at *.	Act 15:23
Silas returned to * taking	Act 15:33
by the apostles and elders in *.	Act 16:4
a sacrifice in * in thanksgiving	Act 18:18f
Possibly in order to arrive in *	Act 18:20f
"I must by all means be at * for	Act 18:21
where he visited the church [at *	Act 18:22
a sacrifice in * in thanksgiving	Act 18:22f
to Greece before returning to *.	Act 19:21
hurrying to get to *, if possible,	Act 20:16
"And now I am going to *, drawn	Act 20:22
through them—not to go on to *.	Act 21:4
* and turned over to the Romans.'	Act 21:11
Paul not to go on to *.	Act 21:12
to be jailed at *, but also to die	Act 21:13
packed our things and left for *.	Act 21:15
and all the believers at *	Act 21:17
and the elders of the * church.	Act 21:18
Our Jewish Christians here at *	Act 21:21
that all * was in an uproar.	Act 21:31
educated here in * under Gamaliel,	Act 22:3
to * in chains to be punished.	Act 22:5
"One day after my return to *,	Act 22:17,18
Leave *, for the people here	Act 22:17,18
"But God said to me, 'Leave *,	Act 22:21
in *, so you must also in Rome."	Act 23:11
that I arrived in * to worship at	Act 24:11
I returned to * with money to aid	Act 24:17
he left for *, where the chief	Act 25:1
him to bring Paul to * at once.	Act 25:3
the Jews from * gathered around,	Act 25:7
to * and stand trial before me?"	Act 25:9
When I was in *, the chief	Act 25:15
stand trial on these charges in *.	Act 25:20
the local Jews and by those in *!	Act 25:24
and later at *, and I lived	Act 26:4
of the saints in *, as authorized	Act 26:10
Damascus, then in * and through	Act 26:20
by the Jews in * and handed over to	Act 28:17
from those arriving from *.	Act 28:21
from * clear over into Illyricum.	Rom 15:19
I must go down to * to take a gift	Rom 15:25
for those in * who are going	Rom 15:26
a real debt to the * Christians.	Rom 15:27
Gentiles from the church in *.	Rom 15:27
be protected in * from those who	Rom 15:31
to send to the Christians in *;	1Co 16:1
with a letter to *, to be taken	1Co 16:3
of helping the Christians in *.	2Co 8:4
with me to take the gift to *.	2Co 8:19
I didn't go up to * to consult	Gal 1:17
I finally went to * for a visit	Gal 1:18
* again, this time with Barnabas;	Gal 2:1
Hagar represents *, the mother-city	Gal 4:24,25
is the heavenly *, and she is not a	Gal 4:26
God, the heavenly *, and to the	Heb 12:22
driven out of * and scattered	1Pe 1:1

(JERUSALEM Con't)
of my God—the New *, coming down Rev 3:12
in the streets of * (the city Rev 11:8,9
on Mount Zion in *, and with him Rev 14:1
people and the beloved city of * Rev 20:9
Holy City, the new *, coming down Rev 21:2
city, the holy *, descending out of Rev 21:10

JERUSALEM'S
before all the people at * Ps 9:14
THE LORD OF Hosts will cut off * Is 3:1
is a picture of * walls in ruins. Is 49:16
Go and shout this in * streets: Jer 2:2
this message in * streets—go from Jer 11:6
when I will heal * damage and give Jer 33:6
* STREETS, ONCE thronged with Lam 1:1
And now in the midst of all * Lam 1:7
* gates are useless. Lam 2:9
enemy could enter through * gates! Lam 4:12
* streets at time of sacrifice. Eze 36:37,38
One comes! * streets and walls will Dan 9:25
down all * palaces and forts." Amo 2:5
The Lord stands ready at * gates Mic 1:9
with lanterns in * darkest corners Zep 1:12
that * enemies have done to her. Zec 8:2

JERUSHA
Mother's name: * (daughter of 2Ki 15:32,33

JERUSHAH
His mother was *, daughter of 2Ch 27:1

JESHA-IAH
*, Joram, Zichri, and Shelomoth. 1Ch 26:25

JESHAIAH
sons were Pelatiah and *; 1Ch 3:21,22
Gedaliah, Zeri, *, Shime-i, 1Ch 25:3
Eighth, * and twelve of his sons 1Ch 25:9-31
From the clan of Elam—* (son of Ez 8:2-14
God also sent Hashabiah; and * Ez 8:19
son of Ithi-el, son of *). Neh 11:7,8,9

JESHAIAH'S
* son was Rephaiah; 1Ch 3:21,22

JESHANAH
between Mizpah and * and named it 1Sa 7:12
*, Ephron, and their suburbs. 2Ch 13:18,19

JESHARELAH
Seventh, * and twelve of his sons 1Ch 25:9-31

JESHEBE-AB
Fourteenth, the group led by *; 1Ch 24:7-18

JESHER
*, Shobab, and Ardon. 1Ch 2:18

JESHISHAI
Jahdo, *, Michael, Gilead, Jaroah, 1Ch 5:14

JESHOHAIAH
Ja-akobah, *, Asaiah, Adi-el, 1Ch 4:34-39

JESHUA
Ninth, the group led by *; 1Ch 24:7-18
Eden, Miniamin, *, Shemaiah, 2Ch 31:14,15
Zerubbabel, *, Nehemiah, Seraiah, Ez 2:2
descendants of * and Joab), 2,812; Ez 2:3-35
Jedaiah of the subclan of *, 973; Ez 2:36-39
From the families of * and Ez 2:40,41,42
other towns. Then * (son of Ez 3:1
of She-alti-el), * (son of Ez 3:8
was given to *, Kadmi-el, Henadad, Ez 3:9
But Zerubbabel and * and the Ez 4:3
She-alti-el) and * (son of Ez 5:1
Jozabad (son of *), and Noadiah Ez 8:33
by Ezer (son of *), the mayor of Neh 3:19
were: Zerubbabel, *, Nehemiah; Neh 7:7
From the families of * and Joab of Neh 7:8-38
From the family of * of the Neh 7:39-42
of Hodevah of the clan of *, 74; Neh 7:43,44,45
As Ezra read from the scroll, *, Neh 8:7,8
These men were *, Kadmi-el, Bani, Neh 9:4
the service were *, Kadmi-el, Bani, Neh 9:5
* (son of Azaniah), Binnui Neh 10:9-13
*, Moladah, Beth-pelet, Neh 11:25-30
(son of She-altiel) and *: Neh 12:1
*, Binnui, Kadmi-el, Sherebiah, Neh 12:8
* was the father of Joiakim; Neh 12:10,11
Hashabiah, Sherebiah, and * (son Neh 12:24
of Joiakim (son of *, son of Neh 12:26

JESHURUN
Literally, "*." Deu 32:15f

JESIMI-EL
Asaiah, Adi-el, *, Benaiah, Ziza 1Ch 4:34-39

JESSE
He was the father of * and Ru 4:16,17
Salmon, Boaz, Obed, *, David. Ru 4:18-22
find a man named *, for I have 1Sa 16:1
Then call * to the sacrifice and 1Sa 16:3
rite on * and his sons, and invited 1Sa 16:5
Then * told his son Abinadab to 1Sa 16:8
Next * summoned Shammah, but the 1Sa 16:9
any of them," Samuel told *. 1Sa 16:10,11
"Well, there is the youngest," * 1Sa 16:10,11
So * sent for him. 1Sa 16:12
son of a man named *, who was not 1Sa 16:18
So Saul sent messengers to *, 1Sa 16:19
the shepherd. * responded by 1Sa 16:20
Then Saul wrote to *, "Please 1Sa 16:22
David (the son of aging *, a 1Sa 17:12
One day * said to David, "Take 1Sa 17:17
And David replied, "His name is * 1Sa 17:58
Literally, "son of *." 1Sa 20:30f
"Who does this son of * think he 1Sa 25:10
"David, the son of *, speaks. 2Sa 23:1
and Obed was the father of *. 1Ch 2:12
kingdom to David, the son of *. 1Ch 10:14
We are on your side, son of *. 1Ch 12:18
the psalms of David, son of *. Ps 72:20
Literally, "*." Is 11:1f
Literally, "the Root of *." Is 11:10f
Obed was the father of *; Mt 1:5
* was the father of King David. Mt 1:6
David's father was *; Lk 3:23-38
'David (son of *) is a man after my Act 13:22
in the house of *, and he will be Rom 15:12

JESSE'S
* first son was Eliab, his second 1Ch 2:13
David's father was Jesse;* father Lk 3:23-38

JESUS
in Hebrew as the Greek name "*." Num 13:16f
Solomon's son to * the Messiah. Ps 72:6f
In Matthew 22:41-45, * applies Ps 110:1f
here, is the Messiah, our Lord *. Is 52:13f
THESE ARE THE ancestors of * Mt 1:1
mother of * Christ the Messiah). Mt 1:16
the birth of * Christ: His mother, Mt 1:18
you shall name him * (meaning Mt 1:21
and Joseph named him "*." Mt 1:25
* WAS BORN in the town of Mt 2:1
to Israel with * and his mother. Mt 2:21
Then * went from Galilee to the Mt 3:13
But * said, "Please do it, for I Mt 3:15
After his baptism, as soon as * Mt 3:16
THEN * WAS led out into the Mt 4:1
But * told him, "No! Mt 4:4
* retorted, "It also says not to Mt 4:7
"Get out of here, Satan," * Mt 4:10
and angels came and cared for *. Mt 4:11
When * heard that John had been Mt 4:12,13
From then on, * began to preach, Mt 4:17
* called out, "Come along with Mt 4:19
* traveled all through Galilee Mt 4:23
The crowds were amazed at *' Mt 7:28
LARGE CROWDS FOLLOWED * as he Mt 8:1
* touches the man. Mt 8:3
Then * says to him, "Don't stop Mt 8:4
When * arrived in Capernaum, a Mt 8:5,6
"Yes," * said, "I will come Mt 8:7
* stood there amazed! Mt 8:10
Then * said to the Roman officer, Mt 8:13
When * arrived at Peter's house, Mt 8:14
But when * touched her hand, the Mt 8:15
people were brought to *; Mt 8:16
When * noticed how large the Mt 8:18
But * said, "Foxes have dens and Mt 8:20
But * told him, "Follow me now! Mt 8:22
than the boat. But * was asleep. Mt 8:24
But * answered, "O you men of Mt 8:26
"All right," * told them. Mt 8:32
rushing out to see *, and begged Mt 8:34
SO * CLIMBED into a boat and went Mt 9:1
boy on a mat. When * saw their Mt 9:2
* knew what they were thinking Mt 9:4
As * was going on down the road, Mt 9:9
"Come and be my disciple," * Mt 9:9
Later, as * and his disciples Mt 9:10
was *' reply. Mt 9:12
Baptist came to * and asked him, Mt 9:14
while he is with them?" * asked. Mt 9:15
As * and the disciples were going Mt 9:19
* turned around and spoke to her. Mt 9:22
When * arrived at the rabbi's Mt 9:23
finally outside, * went in where Mt 9:25
As * was leaving her home, two Mt 9:27
was staying, and * asked them, "Do Mt 9:28
And suddenly they could see! * Mt 9:30
Leaving that place, * met a man Mt 9:32
inside him. So * cast out the Mt 9:33
* traveled around through all the Mt 9:35
* CALLED HIS twelve disciples to Mt 10:1
* sent them out with these Mt 10:5
WHEN * HAD finished giving these Mt 11:1
disciples to ask *, "Are you Mt 11:2
* told them, "Go back to John Mt 11:4
When John's disciples had gone, * Mt 11:7
And * prayed this prayer: "O Mt 11:25
ABOUT THAT TIME, * was walking Mt 12:1
But * said to them, "Haven't you Mt 12:3
asked *, "Is it legal to work by Mt 12:10
to plot *' arrest and death. Mt 12:14
brought to *, and Jesus healed him Mt 12:22
to Jesus, and * healed him so that Mt 12:22
"Maybe * is the Messiah!" Mt 12:23
* knew their thoughts and Mt 12:25
Pharisees, came to * asking him to Mt 12:38
But * replied, "Only an evil, Mt 12:39,40
As * was speaking in a crowded Mt 12:46,47
LATER THAT SAME day, * left the Mt 13:1
Here is another illustration * Mt 13:24
* constantly used these Mt 13:34,35
When * had finished giving these Mt 13:53,54
Then * told them, "A prophet is Mt 13:57
HEROD heard about *, he said to Mt 14:1
came to tell * what had happened. Mt 14:12
As soon as * heard the news, he Mt 14:13
So when * came out of the Mt 14:14
But * replied, "That isn't Mt 14:16
Immediately after this, * told Mt 14:22
in the morning * came to them, Mt 14:25
But * immediately spoke to them, Mt 14:27
and walked on the water toward *. Mt 14:29
Instantly * reached out his hand Mt 14:31
"O man of little faith," * Mt 14:31
from Jerusalem to interview *. Mt 15:1
Then * called to the crowds and Mt 15:10
* replied, "Every plant not Mt 15:13,14
Then Peter asked * to explain Mt 15:15
"Don't you understand?" * asked Mt 15:16
* then left that part of the Mt 15:21
But * gave her no reply—not even Mt 15:23
"Woman," * told her, "your Mt 15:28
* now returned to the Sea of Mt 15:29
before *, and he healed them all. Mt 15:30
Then * called his disciples to Mt 15:32
* asked them, "How much food do Mt 15:34
Then * told all of the people to Mt 15:35
Then * sent the people home and Mt 15:39
came to test *' claim of being Mt 16:1
Then * walked out on them. Mt 16:4
"Watch out!" * warned them; Mt 16:6
* knew what they were thinking Mt 16:8
When * came to Caesarea Philippi, Mt 16:13
son of Jonah," * said, "for my Mt 16:17
From then on * began to speak Mt 16:21
* turned on Peter and said, "Get Mt 16:23
Then * said to the disciples, Mt 16:24
SIX DAYS LATER * took Peter, Mt 17:1
* came over and touched them. Mt 17:7
And when they looked, only * was Mt 17:8
down the mountain, * commanded them Mt 17:9
* replied, "They are right. Mt 17:11
A man came and knelt before * and Mt 17:14
* replied, "Oh, you stubborn, Mt 17:17
Then * rebuked the demon in Mt 17:18
Afterwards the disciples asked * Mt 17:19
your little faith," * told them. Mt 17:20
still in Galilee, * told them, "I Mt 17:22,23
house to talk to * about it, but Mt 17:25
a chance to speak, * asked him, Mt 17:25
"Well, then," * said, "the Mt 17:26,27
disciples came to * to ask which of Mt 18:1
* called a small child over to Mt 18:2
"No!" * replied, "seventy Mt 18:22
AFTER * HAD finished this address, Mt 19:1
* replied, "Moses did that in Mt 19:8
*' disciples then said to him, Mt 19:10
accept this statement," * said. Mt 19:11
were brought for * to lay his hands Mt 19:13
But * said, "Let the little Mt 19:14
Someone came to * with this Mt 19:16
calling me God," * replied, "for Mt 19:17
And * replied, "Don't kill, don't Mt 19:18
* told him, "If you want to be Mt 19:21
Then * said to his disciples, Mt 19:23
* looked at them intently and Mt 19:26
And * replied, "When I, the Mt 19:28
As * was on the way to Jerusalem, Mt 20:17
* and respectfully asked a favor. Mt 20:20
But * told her, "You don't know Mt 20:22
But * called them together and Mt 20:25
As * and the disciples left the Mt 20:29
they heard that * was coming that Mt 20:30
When * came to the place where Mt 20:32,33
* was moved with pity for them Mt 20:34
AS * AND the disciples approached Mt 21:1
Mount of Olives, * sent two of them Mt 21:1
The two disciples did as * said, Mt 21:6
And the crowds replied, "It's *, Mt 21:11
* went into the Temple, drove out Mt 21:12
"Yes," * replied. Mt 21:16
Then * told them, "Truly, if you Mt 21:21
one question first," * replied. Mt 21:24
And * said, "Then I won't answer Mt 21:27
Then * explained his meaning: Mt 21:31
Then * asked them, "Didn't you Mt 21:42
realized that * was talking about Mt 21:45
for they accepted * as a prophet. Mt 21:46
* TOLD SEVERAL other stories to Mt 22:1
some way to trap * into saying Mt 22:15
But * saw what they were after. Mt 22:18
But * said, "Your error is Mt 22:29
* replied, " 'Love the Lord your Mt 22:37
call him 'Lord'?" * asked. Mt 22:43
THEN * SAID to the crowds, and to Mt 23:1
AS * WAS leaving the Temple Mt 24:1
* told them, "Don't let anyone Mt 24:4
WHEN * HAD finished this talk with Mt 26:1
* quietly, and killing him. Mt 26:4
* now proceeded to Bethany, to Mt 26:6
* knew what they were thinking, Mt 26:10
pay me to get * into your hands?" Mt 26:15
opportunity to betray * to them. Mt 26:16

JESUS Con't)

disciples came to * and asked,	Mt 26:17
And * had told him, "Yes."	Mt 26:25
As they were eating, * took a	Mt 26:26
Then * said to them, "Tonight	Mt 26:31
* told him, "The truth is that	Mt 26:34
Then * brought them to a garden	Mt 26:36
So now Judas came straight to *	Mt 26:49
* said, "My friend, go ahead and	Mt 26:50
One of the men with * pulled out	Mt 26:51
"Put away your sword," * told	Mt 26:52
Then * spoke to the crowd.	Mt 26:55
what was going to be done to *.	Mt 26:58
would lie about *, in order to	Mt 26:59
said to *, "Well, what about it?	Mt 26:62
But * remained silent.	Mt 26:63
"Yes," * said, "I am.	Mt 26:64
"You were with *, for both of you	Mt 26:69
Literally, "with * the	Mt 26:69f
man was with *—from Nazareth."	Mt 26:71
Then Peter remembered what * had	Mt 26:75
government to sentence * to death.	Mt 27:1
against * to put him to death."	Mt 27:1f
when he saw that * had been	Mt 27:3
Now * was standing before Pilate,	Mt 27:11
"Yes," * replied.	Mt 27:11
against him, * remained silent.	Mt 27:12
But * said nothing, much to the	Mt 27:14
you—Barabbas, or * your Messiah?"	Mt 27:17
Literally, "* who is called	Mt 27:17f
had arrested * out of envy because	Mt 27:18
release, and for *' death.	Mt 27:20
"Then what shall I do with *,	Mt 27:22
And after he had whipped *, he	Mt 27:26
forced him to carry *' cross.	Mt 27:32
is *, the King of the Jews."	Mt 27:37
About three o'clock, * shouted,	Mt 27:46
Then * shouted out again,	Mt 27:50
After *' resurrection, they left	Mt 27:53
from Galilee with * to care for him	Mt 27:55
Joseph, one of *' followers, went	Mt 27:57
to Pilate and asked for *' body.	Mt 27:58
"I know you are looking for *,	Mt 28:5
* was there in front of them!	Mt 28:9
Then * said to them, "Don't be	Mt 28:10
been asleep when *' disciples came	Mt 28:12,13
* had said they would find him.	Mt 28:16
them weren't sure it really was *!	Mt 28:17
of * the Messiah, the Son of God.	Mk 1:1
Then one day * came from Nazareth	Mk 1:9
The moment * came up out of the	Mk 1:10
Spirit urged * into the desert.	Mk 1:12,13
* went to Galilee to preach God's	Mk 1:14
One day as * was walking along	Mk 1:16
* called out to them, "Come,	Mk 1:17
* and his companions now arrived	Mk 1:21
you bothering us, * of	Mk 1:24
* curtly commanded the demon to	Mk 1:25
They told * about her right away.	Mk 1:29,30
door to watch. So * healed great	Mk 1:34
And *, moved with pity, touched	Mk 1:41
* then told him sternly, "Go and	Mk 1:43,44
soon surrounded * that he couldn't	Mk 1:45
They couldn't get to * through	Mk 2:4
right down in front of *.	Mk 2:4
When * saw how strongly they	Mk 2:5
he would help, * said to the sick	Mk 2:5
* could read their minds and said	Mk 2:8
Then * went out to the seashore	Mk 2:13
"Come with me," * told him.	Mk 2:14
could meet * and his disciples.	Mk 2:15
When * heard what they were	Mk 2:17
One day some people came to * and	Mk 2:18
* replied, "Do friends of the	Mk 2:19
a Sabbath day as * and his	Mk 2:23
*, "They shouldn't be doing that!	Mk 2:24
But * replied, "Didn't you ever	Mk 2:25,26
WHILE IN CAPERNAUM * went over	Mk 3:1
Since it was the Sabbath, *'	Mk 3:2
* asked the man to come and stand	Mk 3:3
to discuss plans for killing *.	Mk 3:6
Meanwhile, * and his disciples	Mk 3:7,8
of Zebedee, but * called them	Mk 3:16-19
* summoned these men and asked	Mk 3:23
* asked, "How can I describe the	Mk 4:30
As evening fell, * said to his	Mk 4:35
about to sink. * was asleep at the	Mk 4:38
as * was climbing from the boat.	Mk 5:1
When * was still far out on the	Mk 5:6
Then * spoke to the demon within	Mk 5:7,8
me, *, Son of the Most High God?	Mk 5:7,8
"What is your name?" * asked,	Mk 5:9
And * gave them permission.	Mk 5:13
crowd soon gathered where * was;	Mk 5:15
* to go away and leave them alone!	Mk 5:17
begged * to let him go along.	Mk 5:18
let him go along. But * said no.	Mk 5:19
great things * had done for him;	Mk 5:20
When * had gone across by boat to	Mk 5:21
* went with him, and the crowd	Mk 5:24
wonderful miracles * did, and that	Mk 5:27
* realized at once that healing	Mk 5:30
was no point in *' coming now.	Mk 5:35
coming now. But * ignored their	Mk 5:36
Then * halted the crowd and	Mk 5:37
When they arrived, * saw that	Mk 5:38
get over it. * instructed them	Mk 5:43
Then * told them, "A prophet is	Mk 6:4
King Herod soon heard about *,	Mk 6:14
The king thought * was John the	Mk 6:14
Others thought * was Elijah	Mk 6:15
The apostles now returned to *	Mk 6:30
Then * suggested, "Let's get	Mk 6:31
But * said, "You feed them."	Mk 6:37
Then * told the crowd to sit	Mk 6:39,40
Immediately after this *	Mk 6:45
* replied, "You bunch of	Mk 7:6,7
Then * called to the crowd to	Mk 7:14
She had heard about * and now she	Mk 7:25
* told her, "First I should help	Mk 7:27
everyone begged * to lay his hands	Mk 7:32
* led him away from the crowd and	Mk 7:33
* told the crowd not to spread	Mk 7:36
out of food again. * called his	Mk 8:1
found, too, so * also blessed these	Mk 8:7
As they were crossing, * said to	Mk 8:15
* realized what they were	Mk 8:17
and heal him. * took the blind man	Mk 8:23
"Can you see anything now?" *	Mk 8:23
Then * placed his hands over the	Mk 8:25
* sent him home to his family.	Mk 8:26
* and his disciples now left	Mk 8:27
But * warned them not to tell	Mk 8:30
say things like that," he told *.	Mk 8:32
* turned and looked at his	Mk 8:33
* WENT ON to say to his disciples,	Mk 9:1
Six days later * took Peter,	Mk 9:2
appeared and began talking with *!	Mk 9:4
gone, and only * was with them.	Mk 9:8
* agreed that Elijah must come	Mk 9:12,13
predicted. Then * asked them what	Mk 9:12,13
The crowd watched * in awe as he	Mk 9:15
* said [to his disciples	Mk 9:19
but when he saw * the demon	Mk 9:20
this way?" * asked the father.	Mk 9:21
"If I can?" * asked.	Mk 9:23
When * saw the crowd was growing	Mk 9:25
But * took him by the hand and	Mk 9:27
Afterwards, when * was alone in	Mk 9:28
* replied, "Cases like this	Mk 9:29
"Don't forbid him!" * said.	Mk 9:39
say about divorce?" * asked them.	Mk 10:3
"And why did he say that?" *	Mk 10:5
were bringing their children to *	Mk 10:13
But when * saw what was happening	Mk 10:14
"Why do you call me good?" *	Mk 10:18
* felt genuine love for this man	Mk 10:21
* watched him go, then turned	Mk 10:23
This amazed them. So * said it	Mk 10:24
* looked at them intently, then	Mk 10:27
And * replied, "Let me assure	Mk 10:29
and * was walking along ahead;	Mk 10:32
Taking them aside, * once more	Mk 10:32
But * answered, "You don't know	Mk 10:38
And * said, "You shall indeed	Mk 10:39
indignant. So * called them to him	Mk 10:42
beside the road as * was going by.	Mk 10:46
When Bartimaeus heard that * from	Mk 10:47
to shout out, "*, Son of David,	Mk 10:47
When * heard him he stopped there	Mk 10:49
it aside, jumped up and came to *.	Mk 10:50
want me to do for you?" * asked.	Mk 10:51
And * said to him, "All right,	Mk 10:52
see, and followed * down the road!	Mk 10:52
Mount of Olives, * sent two of his	Mk 11:1
So they said what * had told them	Mk 11:6
So the colt was brought to * and	Mk 11:7
Then * said to the tree, "You	Mk 11:14
so enthusiastic about *' teaching.	Mk 11:18
Then Peter remembered what * had	Mk 11:21
In reply * said to the disciples,	Mk 11:22,23
* replied, "I'll tell you if you	Mk 11:29
To which * replied, "Then I won't	Mk 11:33
* gave to the people at that time:	Mk 12:1
* saw their trick and said,	Mk 12:15
* replied, "Your trouble is that	Mk 12:24
realized that * had answered well.	Mk 12:28
* replied, "The one that says,	Mk 12:29
understanding, * said to him, "You	Mk 12:34
Later, as * was teaching the	Mk 12:35
* replied, "Yes, look!	Mk 13:2
So * launched into an extended	Mk 13:5
* secretly and put him to death.	Mk 14:1
Meanwhile * was in Bethany, at	Mk 14:3
But * said, "Let her alone;	Mk 14:6
to arrange to betray * to them.	Mk 14:10
right time and place to betray *.	Mk 14:11
everything as * had said, and	Mk 14:16
In the evening * arrived with the	Mk 14:17
the table eating, * said, "I	Mk 14:18
As they were eating, * took bread	Mk 14:22
"All of you will desert me," *	Mk 14:27
"Peter," * said, "before the	Mk 14:30
as they arrived he walked up to *.	Mk 14:45
Then the mob arrested * and held	Mk 14:46
* asked them, "Am I some	Mk 14:48
* was led to the High Priest's	Mk 14:53
something against * that would be	Mk 14:55
Court and asked *, "Do you refuse	Mk 14:60
To this * made no reply.	Mk 14:61
* said, "I am, and you will see	Mk 14:62
"You were with *, the Nazarene."	Mk 14:66,67
There's that disciple of *!"	Mk 14:69
Suddenly *' words flashed through	Mk 14:72
Their decision was to send *	Mk 15:1
"Yes," * replied, "it is as you	Mk 15:2
But * said no more, much to	Mk 15:5
because they envied *' popularity.	Mk 15:10
release of Barabbas instead of *.	Mk 15:11
And he ordered * flogged with a	Mk 15:15
into service to carry *' cross.	Mk 15:21
And they brought * to a place	Mk 15:22
standing around joking about *.	Mk 15:31
Then * called out with a loud	Mk 15:34
Then * uttered another loud cry,	Mk 15:37
to Pilate and asked for *' body.	Mk 15:42,43
Pilate couldn't believe that *	Mk 15:44
cloth and, taking *' body down from	Mk 15:46
were watching as * was laid away.	Mk 15:47
Aren't you looking for *, the	Mk 16:6
" * is going ahead of you to	Mk 16:7
morning when * came back to life,	Mk 16:9
she had seen *, and he was alive!	Mk 16:10,11
When the Lord * had finished	Mk 16:19
boy, and you are to name him '*.'	Lk 1:31
he was named *, the name given him	Lk 2:21
At that time *' parents also	Lk 2:24
present the baby * to the Lord in	Lk 2:27
at what was being said about *.	Lk 2:33
When *' parents had fulfilled all	Lk 2:39
When * was twelve years old he	Lk 2:41,42
but * stayed behind in Jerusalem.	Lk 2:43
in her heart. So * grew both tall	Lk 2:52
baptized, * himself was baptized;	Lk 3:21
* was about thirty years old when	Lk 3:23-38
* was known as the son of	Lk 3:23-38
THEN *, FULL of the Holy Spirit,	Lk 4:1
But * replied, "It is written in	Lk 4:4
* replied, "We must worship God,	Lk 4:8
* replied, "The Scriptures also	Lk 4:12
left * for a while and went away.	Lk 4:13
Then * returned to Galilee, full	Lk 4:14
began shouting at *, "Go away!	Lk 4:33
We want nothing to do with you, *	Lk 4:34
* cut him short.	Lk 4:35
diseases were, brought them to *;	Lk 4:40
one of the boats, * asked Simon,	Lk 5:3
his knees before * and said, "Oh,	Lk 5:8
* replied, "Don't be afraid!	Lk 5:10
When he saw * he fell to the	Lk 5:12
* reached out and touched the man	Lk 5:13
Then * instructed him to go at	Lk 5:14
crowd to * but couldn't reach him.	Lk 5:18,19
sleeping mat, right in front of *.	Lk 5:18,19
Seeing their faith, * said to the	Lk 5:20
* knew what they were thinking,	Lk 5:22
Later on as * left the town he	Lk 5:27
The man's name was Levi. * said	Lk 5:27
home with * as the guest of honor.	Lk 5:29
bitterly to *' disciples about his	Lk 5:30
* answered them, "It is the sick	Lk 5:31
Their next complaint was that *'	Lk 5:33
* asked, "Do happy men fast?	Lk 5:34
Then * used this illustration:	Lk 5:36
ONE SABBATH AS * and his disciples	Lk 6:1
* replied, "Don't you read the	Lk 6:3
And * added, "I	Lk 6:5
Then * said to the Pharisees and	Lk 6:9
At this, the enemies of * were	Lk 6:11
they stood with * on a large, level	Lk 6:17,18
* used in his sermons: "What good	Lk 6:39
WHEN * HAD finished his sermon he	Lk 7:1
When the captain heard about *,	Lk 7:3
earnestly with * to come with them	Lk 7:4
* went with them;	Lk 7:6,7,8
* was amazed.	Lk 7:9
Not long afterwards * went with	Lk 7:11
And * gave him back to his mother.	Lk 7:15
heard of all that * was doing.	Lk 7:18
his disciples to * to ask him,	Lk 7:19
The two disciples found * while	Lk 7:20,21,22
After they left, * talked to the	Lk 7:24
I say about such men?" * asked.	Lk 7:31
and you say, 'What a glutton * is!	Lk 7:34
One of the Pharisees asked * to	Lk 7:36
and * accepted the invitation.	Lk 7:36
When *' host, a Pharisee, saw	Lk 7:39
"This proves that * is no prophet,	Lk 7:39
Then * spoke up and answered his	Lk 7:40
Then * told him this story: "A	Lk 7:41
"Correct," * agreed.	Lk 7:43
And * said to the woman, "Your	Lk 7:50
among them were Mary Magdalene (*	Lk 8:2

(JESUS Con't)

support of * and his disciples. Lk 8:3
When * heard they were standing Lk 8:20
As soon as he saw * he shrieked Lk 8:28
with me, *, Son of God Most High? Lk 8:28
For * was already commanding the Lk 8:29
"What is your name?" * asked Lk 8:30
the pigs. And * said they could. Lk 8:32
at *' feet, clothed and sane! Lk 8:35
And everyone begged * to go away Lk 8:37
begged to go too, but * said no. Lk 8:38
everyone about *' mighty miracle. Lk 8:39
and fell down at *' feet and begged Lk 8:41
twelve years old. * went with him, Lk 8:42
"Who touched me?" * asked. Lk 8:45
But * told him, "No, it was Lk 8:46
When the woman realized that * Lk 8:47
But when * heard what had Lk 8:50
When they arrived at the house * Lk 8:51
happiness, but * insisted that they Lk 8:56
ONE DAY * called together his Lk 9:1
When reports of *' miracles Lk 9:7
After the apostles returned to * Lk 9:10
But * replied, "You feed them!" Lk 9:13
of about fifty each," * replied. Lk 9:14
* took the five loaves and two Lk 9:16
Now they woke up and saw * Lk 9:32
Then, as the voice died away, * Lk 9:36
people," * said [to his disciples Lk 9:41
convulsion. But * ordered the demon Lk 9:42
he was doing, * said to his Lk 9:43
But * knew their thoughts, so Lk 9:47
But * said, "You shouldn't have Lk 9:50
and John said to *, "Master, shall Lk 9:54
But * turned and rebuked them, Lk 9:55
55 and 56, "And * said, You don't Lk 9:55f
someone said to *, "I will always Lk 9:57
But * replied, "Remember, I Lk 9:58
* replied, "Let those without Lk 9:60
But * told him, "Anyone who lets Lk 9:62
laws came to test *' orthodoxy by Lk 10:25
* replied, "What does Moses' law Lk 10:26
"Right!" * told him. Lk 10:28
* replied with an illustration: Lk 10:30
Then * said, "Yes, now go and do Lk 10:37
As * and the disciples continued Lk 10:38
listening to * as he talked. Lk 10:39
She came to * and said, "Sir, Lk 10:40
ONCE WHEN * had been out praying, Lk 11:1
Once, when * cast out a demon Lk 11:14
for a meal. When * arrived, he sat Lk 11:37,38
Then * said to him, "You Lk 11:39
"Yes," said *, "the same Lk 11:46
But * replied, "Man, who made me Lk 12:14
Calling her over to him * said, Lk 13:12
about it because * had healed her Lk 13:14
* replied, "Go tell that fox Lk 13:32
* said to the Pharisees and legal Lk 14:3
refused to answer, * took the sick Lk 14:4
at the table with * exclaimed, Lk 14:15
* replied with this illustration: Lk 14:16
came to listen to *' sermons; Lk 15:1
with them! So * used this Lk 15:3,4
* NOW TOLD this story to his Lk 16:1
rich man," * said, "who was Lk 16:19
to sin," * said one day to his Lk 17:1
a mustard seed," * answered, "it Lk 17:6
out, "*, sir, have mercy on us!" Lk 17:13
One of them came back to *, Lk 17:15
ground in front of *, face downward Lk 17:16
* asked, "Didn't I heal ten men? Lk 17:17
And * said to the man, "Stand up Lk 17:19
One day the Pharisees asked *, Lk 17:20
of God begin?" * replied, "The Lk 17:20
* replied, "Where the body is, Lk 17:37
ONE DAY * told his disciples a Lk 18:1
Then * called the children over Lk 18:16,17
you call me 'good'?" * asked him. Lk 18:19
one thing you lack," * said. Lk 18:22
* watched him go and then said to Lk 18:24
"Yes," * replied, "and Lk 18:29
He was told that * from Nazareth Lk 18:37
began shouting, "*, Son of David, Lk 18:38
The crowds ahead of * tried to Lk 18:39
When * arrived at the spot, he Lk 18:40
Then * asked the man, "What do Lk 18:41
And * said, "All right, begin Lk 18:42
see, and followed *, praising God. Lk 18:43
AS * WAS passing through Jericho, Lk 19:1
to get a look at *, but he was too Lk 19:3
When * came by he looked up at Lk 19:5
down and took * to his house in Lk 19:6
* told him, "This shows Lk 19:9,10
And because * was nearing Lk 19:11
After telling this story, * went Lk 19:28
"Untie him," * said, "and bring Lk 19:30
They found the colt as * said, Lk 19:32
So they brought the colt to * Lk 19:35
across its back for * to sit on. Lk 19:35
the wonderful miracles * had done. Lk 19:36,37
And * responded, "Then I won't Lk 20:8
* looked at them and said, "Then Lk 20:17
They said to *, "Sir, we know Lk 20:21
came to * with this: Lk 20:28
* replied, "Marriage is for Lk 20:34,35
But * said, "The time is coming Lk 21:6
Every day * went to the Temple to Lk 21:37,38
actively plotting *' murder, trying Lk 22:2
the best way to betray * to them. Lk 22:4
for them to arrest * quietly when Lk 22:6
unleavened bread. * sent Peter and Lk 22:8
everything just as * had said, and Lk 22:13
Then * and the others arrived, Lk 22:14
* told them, "In this world the Lk 22:25
But * said, "Peter, let me tell Lk 22:34
Then * asked them, "When I sent Lk 22:35
Judas walked over to * and kissed Lk 22:47
Literally, "approached * to kiss Lk 22:47f
But * said, "Judas, how can you Lk 22:48
But * said, "Don't resist any Lk 22:51
Then * addressed the chief Lk 22:52
spoke: "This man was with *!" Lk 22:56
fellow is one of *' disciples, for Lk 22:59
At that moment * turned and Lk 22:61
Now the guards in charge of * Lk 22:63,64
of the nation. * was led before Lk 22:66
THEN THE ENTIRE Council took * Lk 23:1
"Yes," * replied, "it is as you Lk 23:3
opportunity to see *, for he had Lk 23:8
He asked * question after Lk 23:9
began mocking and ridiculing *; Lk 23:11
them, for he wanted to release *. Lk 23:20
and louder for *' death, and their Lk 23:23
So Pilate sentenced * to die as Lk 23:24
But he delivered * over to them Lk 23:25
As the crowd led * away to his Lk 23:26
to follow, carrying *' cross. Lk 23:26
But * turned and said to them, Lk 23:28
were crucified—* on the center Lk 23:32,33
these people," * said, "for they Lk 23:34
Then he said, "*, remember me Lk 23:42
And * replied, "Today you will Lk 23:43
Then * shouted, "Father, I Lk 23:46
saw that * was dead, they went home Lk 23:48
Meanwhile, *' friends, including Lk 23:49
and asked for the body of *. Lk 23:50,51,52
So he took down *' body and Lk 23:53
So they went in—but the Lord *' Lk 24:3
That same day, Sunday, two of *' Lk 24:13
were talking of *' death, when Lk 24:14
when suddenly * himself came along Lk 24:15
"What things?" * asked. Lk 24:19
"The things that happened to *, Lk 24:19
there who told them * is alive! Lk 24:22,23
and sure enough, *' body was gone, Lk 24:24
Then * said to them, "You are Lk 24:25
Then * quoted them passage after Lk 24:27
of their journey. * would have gone Lk 24:28
other followers of * greeted them Lk 24:33,34
their story of how * had appeared Lk 24:35
telling about it, * himself was Lk 24:36
Then * led them out along the Lk 24:50
that * Christ is the true Light. Jn 1:6,7
justice, while * Christ brought us Jn 1:17
The next day John saw * coming Jn 1:29
from heaven and resting upon *. Jn 1:32
of his disciples, * walked by. Jn 1:36
disciples turned and followed *. Jn 1:37
* looked around and saw them Jn 1:38
And he brought Peter to meet * Jn 1:42
* looked intently at Peter for a Jn 1:42
The next day * decided to go to Jn 1:43
His name is *, the son of Joseph Jn 1:45
As they approached, * said, Jn 1:47
And * replied, "I could see you Jn 1:48
* asked him, "Do you believe all Jn 1:50
TWO DAYS LATER *' mother was a Jn 2:1
in Galilee, and * and his Jn 2:2
festivities, and *' mother came to Jn 2:3
Then * told the servants to fill Jn 2:7,8
in Galilee was *' first public Jn 2:11
and * went to Jerusalem. Jn 2:13
their counters. * made a whip from Jn 2:15
"All right," * replied, "this Jn 2:19
the Messiah. But * didn't trust Jn 2:24,25
came for an interview with *. Jn 3:1
* replied, "With all the Jn 3:3
* replied, "What I am telling Jn 3:5
* replied, "You, a respected Jn 3:10,11
Afterwards * and his disciples Jn 3:22
them that *' baptism was best. Jn 3:25
disciples—(though * himself didn't Jn 4:1
to his son Joseph. * was tired from Jn 4:5,6
and * asked her for a drink. Jn 4:7
—and she remarked about this to *. Jn 4:9
* replied that people soon became Jn 4:13
"Go and get your husband," * Jn 4:16
"All too true!" * said. Jn 4:17,18
* replied, "The time is coming, Jn 4:21-24
Then * told her, "I am the Jn 4:26
disciples were urging * to eat. Jn 4:31
Then * explained: "My Jn 4:34
on into Galilee. * used to say, "A Jn 4:43,4
sick, heard that * had come from Jn 4:46,4
to Cana, found *, and begged him to Jn 4:46,4
* asked, "Won't any of you Jn 4:48
Then * told him, "Go back home. Jn 4:50
And the man believed * and Jn 4:50
same moment that * had told him, Jn 4:53
believed that * was the Messiah. Jn 4:53
This was *' second miracle in Jn 4:54
AFTERWARDS * RETURNED to Jn 5:1
When * saw him and knew how long Jn 5:6
* told him, "Stand up, roll up Jn 5:8
The man didn't know, and * had Jn 5:13
But afterwards * found him in Jn 5:14
them it was * who had healed him. Jn 5:15
So they began harassing * as a Jn 5:16
breaker. But * replied, "My Jn 5:17
* replied, "The Son can do Jn 5:19
AFTER THIS, * crossed over the Sea Jn 6:1
So when * went up into the hills Jn 6:2-5
"Tell everyone to sit down," * Jn 6:10
Then * took the loaves and gave Jn 6:11
"Now gather the scraps," * told Jn 6:12
* saw that they were ready to Jn 6:15
But as darkness fell and * still Jn 6:17
saw * walking toward the boat! Jn 6:18,19
on the shore [waiting to see * Jn 6:22,23
people saw that * wasn't there, nor Jn 6:24
you get here?" * replied, "The Jn 6:26
* told them, "This is the will Jn 6:29
* said, "Moses didn't give it to Jn 6:32
* replied, "I am the Bread of Jn 6:35
"Why, he is merely * the son of Jn 6:42
But * replied, "Don't murmur Jn 6:43
So * said it again, "With all Jn 6:53
* knew within himself that his Jn 6:61
(For * knew from the beginning Jn 6:64
Then * turned to the Twelve and Jn 6:67
Then * said, "I chose the twelve Jn 6:70
AFTER THIS, * went to Galilee, Jn 7:1
holidays, and *' brothers urged Jn 7:3
* replied, "It is not the right Jn 7:6
the festival, * went up to the Jn 7:14
So * told them, "I'm not Jn 7:16
* replied, "I worked on the Jn 7:21,22,23
So *, in a sermon in the Temple, Jn 7:28
priests sent officers to arrest *. Jn 7:32
But * told them, "[Not yet! Jn 7:33
of the holidays, * shouted to the Jn 7:37
given, because * had not yet Jn 7:39
who came secretly to interview *. Jn 7:50
* RETURNED TO the Mount of Olives, Jn 8:1
"Teacher," they said to *, Jn 8:4
against him, but * stooped down and Jn 8:6
eldest, until only * was left in Jn 8:9
Then * stood up again and said to Jn 8:10
And * said, "Neither do I. Jn 8:11
Later, in one of his talks, * Jn 8:12
* told them, "These claims are Jn 8:14
* answered, "You don't know who I Jn 8:19
* made these statements while in Jn 8:20
So * said, "When you have killed Jn 8:28
* said to them, "You are truly my Jn 8:30,31
* replied, "You are slaves of Jn 8:34
"No!" * replied, "for if he Jn 8:39
* told them, "If that were so, Jn 8:42
"No," * said, "I have no demon Jn 8:49
Then * told them this: "If I Jn 8:54
*: "The absolute truth is that I Jn 8:58
to kill him. But * was hidden from Jn 8:59
"Neither," * answered. Jn 9:3
"A man they call * made mud and Jn 9:11
So he told them how * had Jn 9:15
"Then this fellow * is not from Jn 9:16
that anyone saying * was the Jn 9:22,23
to God, not to *, for we know Jesus Jn 9:24
for we know * is an evil person." Jn 9:24
When * heard what had happened, Jn 9:35
"You have seen him," * said, Jn 9:37
And he worshiped *. Jn 9:38
Then * told him, "I have come Jn 9:39
wouldn't be guilty," * replied. Jn 9:41
Those who heard * use this Jn 10:6
and * was in Jerusalem at the Jn 10:22,23
and you don't believe me," * Jn 10:25
* said, "At God's direction I Jn 10:32
costly perfume on *' feet and wiped Jn 11:1
sent a message to * telling him, Jn 11:3
But when * heard about it he Jn 11:4
Although * was very fond of Jn 11:5
* replied, "There are twelve Jn 11:9
The disciples, thinking * meant Jn 11:12,13
But * meant Lazarus had died. Jn 11:12,13
When Martha got word that * was Jn 11:20
Martha said to *, "Sir, if you Jn 11:21
* told her, "Your brother will Jn 11:23
* told her, "I am the one who Jn 11:25
Now * had stayed outside the Jn 11:30
When Mary arrived where * was, Jn 11:32
When * saw her weeping and the Jn 11:33
Tears came to *' eyes. Jn 11:35

(JESUS Con't)
And again * was moved with deep Jn 11:37,38
"Roll the stone aside," * told Jn 11:39
God if you believe?" * asked her. Jn 11:40
stone aside. Then * looked up to Jn 11:41
in a head swath. * told them, Jn 11:44
This prophecy that * should die Jn 11:51
It was a prediction that *' Jn 11:52
leaders began plotting *' death. Jn 11:53
* now stopped his public ministry Jn 11:54
They wanted to see *, and as Jn 11:56
that anyone seeing * must report Jn 11:57
ceremonies began, * arrived in Jn 12:1
A banquet was prepared in *' Jn 12:2
nard, and anointed *' feet with it Jn 12:3
* replied, "Let her alone. Jn 12:7
believed in * as their Messiah. Jn 12:11
The next day, the news that * was Jn 12:12
* rode along on a young donkey, Jn 12:14
but after * returned to his glory Jn 12:16
crowd who had seen * call Lazarus Jn 12:17
said, "Sir, we want to meet *." Jn 12:21
and they went together to ask *. Jn 12:22
* replied that the time had come Jn 12:23,24
Then * told them, "The voice was Jn 12:30
* replied, "My light will shine Jn 12:35
After saying these things, * went Jn 12:36
Isaiah was referring to * when Jn 12:41
* shouted to the crowds, "If you Jn 12:44
* KNEW ON the evening of Passover Jn 13:1
to carry out his plan to betray *. Jn 13:1
to betray Jesus. * knew that the Jn 13:1
* replied, "You don't understand Jn 13:7
can't be my partner," * replied. Jn 13:8
* replied, "One who has bathed Jn 13:10
For * knew who would betray Jn 13:11
Now * was in great anguish of Jn 13:21
Literally, "reclining on *' Jn 13:23f
John, next to *, was at his side. Jn 13:23f
to * at the table, being his Jn 13:23
back against *' chest," to whisper Jn 13:25f
* told him, "Hurry—do it now." Jn 13:27
at the table knew what * meant. Jn 13:28
their treasurer, * was telling him Jn 13:29
As soon as Judas left the room, * Jn 13:31
And * replied, "You can't go with Jn 13:36
* answered, "Die for me? Jn 13:38
* told him, "I am the Way—yes, Jn 14:6
* replied, "Don't you even yet Jn 14:9
* replied, "Because I will only Jn 14:23
* realized they wanted to ask him Jn 16:19
finally believe this?" * asked. Jn 16:31
WHEN * HAD finished saying all Jn 17:1
only true God, and * Christ, the Jn 17:3
AFTER SAYING THESE things * Jn 18:1
this place, for * had gone there Jn 18:2
* fully realized all that was Jn 18:4,5
"* of Nazareth," they replied. Jn 18:4,5
"I am he," * said. Jn 18:4,5
And again they replied, "* of Jn 18:7
"I told you I am he," * said; Jn 18:8
But * said to Peter, "Put your Jn 18:11
arrested * and tied him. Jn 18:12
along with *, while Peter stood Jn 18:15
you one of *' disciples?" Jn 18:17
began asking * about his followers Jn 18:19
* replied, "What I teach is Jn 18:20
there struck * with his fist. Jn 18:22
"If I lied, prove it," * Jn 18:23
Then Annas sent *, bound, to Jn 18:24
there in the olive grove with *?" Jn 18:26
*' trial before Caiaphas ended in Jn 18:28
This fulfilled *' prediction Jn 18:32
called for * to be brought to him. Jn 18:33
or as the Jews use it?" * asked. Jn 18:34
inquiring whether * was setting up Jn 18:34f
Then * answered, "I am not an Jn 18:36
"Yes," * said. Jn 18:37
THEN PILATE LAID open *' back with Jn 19:1
Then * came out wearing the crown Jn 19:5
He took * back into the palace Jn 19:9
but * gave no answer. Jn 19:9
Then * said, "You would have no Jn 19:11
At these words Pilate brought * Jn 19:13
Then Pilate gave * to them to be Jn 19:16
either side, with * between them. Jn 19:18
him reading, "* of Nazareth, the Jn 19:19
The place where * was Jn 19:20
When the soldiers had crucified * Jn 19:23,24
Standing near the cross were *' Jn 19:25
When * saw his mother standing Jn 19:26
* knew that everything was now Jn 19:28
When * had tasted Jn 19:30
of the two men crucified with *; Jn 19:32
secret disciple of * for fear of Jn 19:38
permission to take *' body down; Jn 19:38
man who had come to * at night, Jn 19:39
Together they wrapped *' body in Jn 19:40
other disciple whom * loved." Jn 20:2f
that had covered *' head was rolled Jn 20:7
the body of * had been lying. Jn 20:12
It was *, but she didn't Jn 20:14
"Mary!" * said. Jn 20:16
* was standing there among them! Jn 20:19
but suddenly, as before, * was Jn 20:26
Then * told him, "You believe Jn 20:29
*' disciples saw him do many Jn 20:30,31
LATER * APPEARED again to the Jn 21:1
disciple therefore whom * loved." Jn 21:7f
fish you've just caught," * said. Jn 21:10
and have some breakfast!" * said; Jn 21:12
Then * went around serving us Jn 21:13
This was the third time * had Jn 21:14
After breakfast * said to Simon Jn 21:15
"Then feed my lambs," * told Jn 21:15
* repeated the question: "Simon, Jn 21:16
"Then take care of my sheep," * Jn 21:16
Peter was grieved at the way * Jn 21:17
* said, "Then feed my little Jn 21:17
want to go." * said this to let Jn 21:19
Then * told him, "Follow me." Jn 21:19
saw the disciple * loved following, Jn 21:20
that time to ask *, "Master, which Jn 21:20
Peter asked *, "What about Jn 21:21
* replied, "If I want him to Jn 21:22
But that isn't what * said at Jn 21:23
other events in *' life were Jn 21:25
I told you about *' life and Act 1:1
at the sky? * has gone away to Act 1:11
And the brothers of *. Act 1:14
Several women, including *' Act 1:14
who betrayed * by guiding the mob Act 1:16
as witnesses of *' resurrection. Act 1:21,22
SEVEN WEEKS HAD gone by since *' Act 2:1
God publicly endorsed * of Act 2:22
"King David quoted * as Act 2:25
He was speaking of *, and we all Act 2:32
that * rose from the dead. Act 2:32
God has made this * you crucified Act 2:36
in the name of * Christ for the Act 2:38
telling about * and strongly urging Act 2:40
I command you in the name of * Act 3:6
to his servant * by doing this. Act 3:13
I refer to the * whom you Act 3:13
"*' name has healed this man—and Act 3:16
Faith in *' name—faith given us Act 3:16
did to * was done in ignorance; Act 3:17
* your Messiah back to you again. Act 3:20
that * had risen from the dead. Act 4:2
name and power of * from Nazareth, Act 4:10
here healed! For * the Messiah is Act 4:11
being with * had done for them! Act 4:13
them never again to speak about *. Act 4:18
we saw * do and heard him say." Act 4:20
united against *, your anointed Act 4:27
the name of your holy servant *." Act 4:30
*, and there was warm fellowship Act 4:33
again to preach about this *?" Act 5:28
ancestors brought * back to life Act 5:30
of *, and finally let them go. Act 5:40
and preach that * is the Messiah. Act 5:42
that this fellow * of Nazareth will Act 6:14
* standing at God's right hand. Act 7:55
heavens opened and * the Messiah Act 7:56
"Lord *, receive my spirit." Act 7:59
preaching the Good News about *! Act 8:4
message that * was the Messiah, and Act 8:12
in the name of the Lord *. Act 8:16
many others to tell him about *. Act 8:35
that * Christ is the Son of God." Act 8:37
And the voice replied, "I am *, Act 9:5
Paul, the Lord *, who appeared to Act 9:17
Good News about *—that he is indeed Act 9:20
man who persecuted *' followers so Act 9:21
that * was indeed the Christ. Act 9:22
preaching in the name of *. Act 9:27
Peter said to him, "Aeneas! * Act 9:34
with God through *, the Messiah, Act 10:36,37
And you no doubt know that * of Act 10:38
to testify that * is ordained of Act 10:42
in the name of *, the Messiah. Act 10:48
* Christ, who was I to argue?" Act 11:17
about the Lord * to some Greeks. Act 11:20
descendants, *, who is God's Act 13:23
fulfilled prophecy by killing *; Act 13:27
God brought * back to life again. Act 13:32,33
it says concerning *, 'Today I have Act 13:32,33
In this man *, there is Act 13:38
by the free gift of the Lord *?" Act 15:11
sake of our Lord * Christ—will Act 15:26
but again the Spirit of * said no. Act 16:7
"I command you in the name of * Act 16:18
on the Lord * and you will be Act 16:31
and proving that * is the Messiah. Act 17:3
king, *, instead of Caesar." Act 17:7
he told them about * and his Act 17:18
to the Jews that * is the Messiah. Act 18:5
hurling abuse at *, Paul shook off Act 18:6
about *, but that is all he knew. Act 18:25,26
had happened to * since the time of Act 18:25,26
that * is indeed the Messiah. Act 18:28
on to believe in *, the one John Act 19:4
the name of the Lord *. Act 19:5
persuading many to believe in *. Act 19:8
by using the name of the Lord *. Act 19:13
"I adjure you by *, whom Paul Act 19:13
replied, "I know * and I know Act 19:15
of the Lord * was greatly honored. Act 19:17
faith in our Lord * Christ. Act 20:21
me by the Lord *—the work of Act 20:24
words of the Lord *, 'It is more Act 20:35
die for the sake of the Lord *." Act 21:13
And he replied, 'I am * of Act 22:8
told them about faith in Christ *. Act 24:24
someone called * who died, but Paul Act 25:19
of * of Nazareth. Act 26:9
"And the Lord replied, 'I am *, Act 26:15
taught them about * from the Act 28:23
God and about the Lord * Christ; Act 28:31
is from Paul, * Christ's slave, Rom 1:1
about his Son, * Christ our Lord, Rom 1:3
you, too, are invited by * Christ Rom 1:6,7
Father and from * Christ our Lord. Rom 1:6,7
How I thank God through * Christ Rom 1:8
at God's command * Christ will Rom 2:16
* Christ to take away our sins. Rom 3:21,22
him if we trust in * Christ, who in Rom 3:24
For God sent Christ * to take the Rom 3:25
because * took away their sins. Rom 3:26
in * who took away their sins. Rom 3:26
In fact, only when we trust * can Rom 3:31
back * our Lord from the dead. Rom 4:24
* Christ our Lord has done for us. Rom 5:1
of what our Lord * Christ has done Rom 5:11
But this one man, * Christ, Rom 5:15
because of this one man, * Rom 5:17
life through * Christ our Lord. Rom 5:21
to become a part of * Christ; Rom 6:2,3
to him, through * Christ our Lord. Rom 6:11
life through * Christ our Lord. Rom 6:23
God through * Christ our Lord." Rom 7:23,24,25f
by * Christ our Lord. Rom 7:23,24,25
those who belong to Christ *. Rom 8:1
through Christ *—has freed me from Rom 8:2
God, who raised up * from the dead, Rom 8:11
to his Son * is now ours too. Rom 8:17
Lord * Christ when he died for us. Rom 8:39
many will stumble over him (*). Rom 9:33
own mouth that * Christ is your Rom 10:9
But ask the Lord * Christ to Rom 13:14
of the Lord * that there is nothing Rom 14:14
the Father of our Lord * Christ. Rom 15:6
Remember that * Christ came to Rom 15:8
messenger from * Christ to you Rom 15:15,16
all Christ * has done through me. Rom 15:17
For the Lord * Christ's sake, and Rom 15:30
in the affairs of Christ *. Rom 16:3
for our Lord *, but only want gain Rom 16:18
The blessings from our Lord * Rom 16:20
May the grace of our Lord * Rom 16:24
forever through * Christ our Lord. Rom 16:25,26,27
PAUL, CHOSEN by God to be * 1Co 1:1
Or, "chosen by Christ *." 1Co 1:2f
"sanctified in Christ *." 1Co 1:2f
to him by Christ *. 1Co 1:2
of * Christ, our Lord and theirs. 1Co 1:2
May God our Father and the Lord * 1Co 1:3
the return of our Lord * Christ. 1Co 1:7
name of the Lord * Christ to stop 1Co 1:10
lost, when they hear that * died 1Co 1:18
have your life through Christ *. 1Co 1:30
speak only of * Christ and his 1Co 2:2
that one we already have—* Christ. 1Co 3:11
name of the Lord * Christ I have 1Co 5:3,4
power of the Lord * will be with 1Co 5:3,4
when our Lord * Christ returns. 1Co 5:5
of what the Lord * Christ and the 1Co 6:11
as he raised up the Lord * Christ. 1Co 6:14
and one Lord * Christ, who made 1Co 8:6
I am one who has actually seen * 1Co 9:1
him, the Lord * took bread, and 1Co 11:23
of God can curse *, and no one can 1Co 12:3
no one can say, "* is Lord," and 1Co 12:3
The name given to *' twelve 1Co 15:5f
through * Christ our Lord! 1Co 15:57
person is cursed. Lord *, come! 1Co 16:22
the Lord * Christ rest upon you. 1Co 16:23
for we all belong to Christ *. 1Co 16:24
by God to be * Christ's messenger; 2Co 1:1
and the Lord * Christ mightily 2Co 1:2
Father of our Lord * Christ, the 2Co 1:3,4
when our Lord * comes back again. 2Co 1:13,14
you about * Christ the Son of God. 2Co 1:19
but about Christ * as Lord. 2Co 4:5
because of what * has done for us. 2Co 4:5
is seen in the face of * Christ. 2Co 4:6
facing death just as * did; 2Co 4:10
* Christ within our dying bodies. 2Co 4:11
brought the Lord * back from death 2Co 4:14
to life again with *, and present 2Co 4:14
our eternal home in heaven with *. 2Co 5:6
himself through what Christ * did. 2Co 5:18
kindness our Lord * was: though he 2Co 8:9

(JESUS Con't)
about another * than the one we 2Co 11:4
God, the Father of our Lord * 2Co 11:31
May the grace of our Lord * 2Co 13:14
My call is from * Christ himself, Gal 1:1
Father and from the Lord * Christ. Gal 1:3
less a person than * Christ Gal 1:12
show them the Good News about *. Gal 1:16
enjoyed in Christ *, as to whether Gal 2:4
in * Christ to take away our sins. Gal 2:16
And so we, too, have trusted * Gal 2:16
see the meaning of * Christ's death Gal 3:1
[as * was hung upon a wooden cross Gal 3:13
out is through faith in * Christ; Gal 3:21,22
through faith in * Christ, and we Gal 3:26
we are one in Christ *. Gal 3:28
God, or even * Christ himself. Gal 4:14
the cross of our Lord * Christ. Gal 6:14
and wounds from *' enemies that Gal 6:17
our Lord * Christ be with you all. Gal 6:18
by God to be * Christ's messenger. Eph 1:1
our Father and * Christ our Lord. Eph 1:2
Father of our Lord * Christ, who Eph 1:3
by sending * Christ to die for us. Eph 1:5
faith in the Lord * and of the love Eph 1:15
Father of our Lord * Christ, to Eph 1:16,17
because of what Christ * did. Eph 2:6
has done for us through * Christ. Eph 2:7
given us new lives from Christ *; Eph 2:10
But now you belong to Christ *, Eph 2:13
because of what * Christ has done Eph 2:13
the building is * Christ himself! Eph 2:20
it through * Christ our Lord. Eph 3:11
for the church through * Christ. Eph 3:21
in the name of our Lord * Christ. Eph 5:20
the Father and the Lord * Christ. Eph 6:23
sincerely love our Lord * Christ. Eph 6:24
AND Timothy, slaves of * Christ. Php 1:1
and the Lord * Christ will give Php 1:2
on that day when * Christ returns. Php 1:6
the tenderness of * Christ. Php 1:8
to glorify Christ * for keeping me Php 1:26
was shown us by * Christ, who, Php 2:5
at the name of * every knee shall Php 2:10
shall confess that * Christ is Php 2:11
plans and not those of * Christ. Php 2:21
in what Christ * has done for us Php 3:3
gain of knowing Christ * my Lord. Php 3:8
of what Christ * did for us. Php 3:14
our Savior the Lord * Christ is; Php 3:20
at rest as you trust in Christ *. Php 4:7
of what Christ * has done for us. Php 4:19
The blessings of our Lord * Php 4:23
PAUL, CHOSEN by God to be * Col 1:1
Father of our Lord * Christ, for Col 1:3
He is * Christ's faithful slave, Col 1:7
the Good News that * died for you, Col 1:23
of the Lord *, and come with him Col 3:17
if he comes your way. * Justus Col 4:11
of Christ *, sends you his love. Col 4:12
and the Lord * Christ: May blessing 1Th 1:1
and from * Christ our Lord. 1Th 1:1
the return of our Lord * Christ. 1Th 1:3
Son from heaven—*, whom God brought 1Th 1:10
they even executed the Lord *; 1Th 2:15
* Christ when he comes back again. 1Th 2:19
Lord * send us back to you again. 1Th 3:11
day when our Lord * Christ returns 1Th 3:13
gave you from the Lord * himself. 1Th 4:1
name of the Lord *—that you live 1Th 4:1
For since we believe that * died 1Th 4:14
believe that when * returns, God 1Th 4:14
save us through our Lord * Christ; 1Th 5:9
for you who belong to Christ *. 1Th 5:18
Lord * Christ comes back again. 1Th 5:23
* Christ be with you, every one. 1Th 5:28
Father and in the Lord * Christ. 2Th 1:1
May God the Father and the Lord * 2Th 1:2
us when the Lord * appears suddenly 2Th 1:7
them through our Lord * Christ. 2Th 1:8
name of the Lord * Christ because 2Th 1:12
and of the Lord * Christ has made 2Th 1:12
again of our Lord * Christ, and our 2Th 2:1
whom the Lord * will burn up with 2Th 2:8
in the glory of our Lord * Christ. 2Th 2:14
May our Lord * Christ himself and 2Th 2:16
name of our Lord * Christ by his 2Th 3:6
In the name of the Lord * Christ 2Th 3:12
May the blessing of our Lord * 2Th 3:18
FROM: PAUL, A missionary of * 1Ti 1:1
* Christ our Lord—our only hope. 1Ti 1:1
May God our Father and * Christ 1Ti 1:2
How thankful I am to Christ * our 1Ti 1:12
full of the love of Christ *. 1Ti 1:14
it, that Christ * came into the 1Ti 1:15
me so that Christ * could use me as 1Ti 1:16
side, and Christ *, himself man, is 1Ti 2:5
God and the Lord * Christ and of 1Ti 5:21
of the Lord * Christ and are the 1Ti 6:3
and before Christ * who gave a 1Ti 6:13
until our Lord * Christ returns. 1Ti 6:14
FROM: PAUL, * Christ's missionary, 2Ti 1:1
them through faith in * Christ. 2Ti 1:1
May God the Father and Christ * 2Ti 1:2
of our Savior * Christ, who broke 2Ti 1:10
and love Christ * offers you. 2Ti 1:13
"and love that is in Christ *." 2Ti 1:13f
the strength Christ * gives you. 2Ti 2:1
a good soldier of * Christ, just as 2Ti 2:3
fact that * Christ was a Man, born 2Ti 2:8
Christ * to those God has chosen. 2Ti 2:10
to please Christ * by living godly 2Ti 3:12
salvation by trusting in Christ *. 2Ti 3:15
and before Christ *—who will some 2Ti 4:1
May the Lord * Christ be with 2Ti 4:22
God and the messenger of * Christ. Tit 1:1
May God the Father and Christ * Tit 1:4
our great God and Savior * Christ. Tit 2:13
because of what * Christ our Savior Tit 3:6
Good News about * Christ, and from Phm 1:1
May God our Father and the Lord * Phm 1:3
in the Lord * and in his people. Phm 1:5
in you that come from Christ *. Phm 1:6
in jail for the sake of * Christ. Phm 1:8,9
Christ *, sends you his greetings. Phm 1:23
The blessings of our Lord * Phm 1:25
But God said it about *. Heb 1:5,6
by the Lord * himself, and passed Heb 2:3
but we do see *—who for awhile was Heb 2:9
great kindness, * tasted death for Heb 2:9
should allow * to suffer, for in Heb 2:10
for his suffering made * a Heb 2:10
We who have been made holy by *, Heb 2:11
That is why * is not ashamed to Heb 2:11
And it was necessary for * to be Heb 2:17
now about this * who is God's Heb 3:1
For * was faithful to God who Heb 3:2
God's house. But * has far more Heb 3:3
But * the Son of God is our great Heb 4:14
And even though * was God's Son, Heb 5:8
experience that * became the Giver Heb 5:9
But * lives forever and continues Heb 7:24
* Christ came to die on the cross. Heb 10:4f
God is, because of the blood of *. Heb 10:19
Keep your eyes on *, our leader Heb 12:2
and to * himself, who has Heb 12:24
* Christ is the same yesterday, Heb 13:8
That is why * suffered and died Heb 13:12
With *' help we will continually Heb 13:15
the dead our Lord *, equip you with Heb 13:20,21
of God and of the Lord * Christ. Jas 1:1
belong to the Lord * Christ, the Jas 2:1
ones who laugh at * Christ, whose Jas 2:7
FROM: PETER, * Christ's 1Pe 1:1
with the blood of * Christ and 1Pe 1:2
and Father of our Lord * Christ; 1Pe 1:3
to you when * Christ returns. 1Pe 1:13
to him because of * Christ 1Pe 2:5
glorified through * Christ—to him 1Pe 4:11
and missionary of * Christ. 2Pe 1:1
is the kind that * Christ our God 2Pe 1:1
and useful to our Lord * Christ. 2Pe 1:8
of our Lord and Savior * Christ. 2Pe 1:11
But the Lord * Christ has showed 2Pe 1:13,14
* Christ and his coming again. 2Pe 1:16
Lord and Savior * Christ, and then 2Pe 2:20
* promised to come back, did he? 2Pe 3:4
with our Lord and Savior * Christ. 2Pe 3:18
Father and with * Christ his Son. 1Jn 1:3
and the blood of * his Son cleanses 1Jn 1:7
His name is * Christ, the one who 1Jn 2:1
in the name of * our Savior. 1Jn 2:12
The one who says that * is not 1Jn 2:22
* Christ, and love one another. 1Jn 3:23
really agree that * Christ, God's 1Jn 4:2
and says that * is the Son of God 1Jn 4:15
IF YOU BELIEVE that * is the 1Jn 5:1
that * is truly the Son of God? 1Jn 5:5
from heaven when * was baptized, 1Jn 5:6,7,8
that * Christ is the Son of God. 1Jn 5:6,7,8
And God declares that * is his 1Jn 5:9
because we are in * Christ his Son, 1Jn 5:20
God the Father and * Christ his Son 2Jn 1:3
don't believe that * Christ came to 2Jn 1:7
FROM: JUDE, A servant of * Christ, Jud 1:1
only Master and Lord, * Christ. Jud 1:4
of our Lord * Christ told you, Jud 1:17
life that our Lord * Christ in his Jud 1:21
us through * Christ our Lord; Jud 1:24,25
to occur in the life of * Christ. Rev 1:1
(concerning, or, from) * Christ." Rev 1:1f
words of God and * Christ and Rev 1:2
and from * Christ who faithfully Rev 1:5
piercing of *—and never forgot the Rev 1:7f
the patience * gives, and we shall Rev 1:9
what I knew about * Christ. Rev 1:9
who looked like * who called Rev 1:13
fellow servants of *, had been Rev 6:11
confessing that they belong to *. Rev 12:17
to his commands and trust in *." Rev 14:12
who die in the faith of *." Rev 14:13f
it who looked like *, who was Rev 14:14
the martyrs of * she had killed. Rev 17:6
who testify of their faith in *. Rev 19:10
shown you is to tell about *." Rev 19:10
Literally, "The testimony of * is Rev 19:10f
testimony about *, for proclaiming Rev 20:4
I, too, am a servant of * as you Rev 22:9
and do so. I, *, have sent my Rev 22:16

JETHER
Then, turning to *, his oldest Ju 8:20
Abigail, whose husband was * from 1Ch 2:17
* and 1Ch 2:32
Jonathan. * died without children, 1Ch 2:32
Ezrah's sons were:*, 1Ch 4:17
Literally, "*." 1Ch 7:38f

JETHETH
Alvah,The clan of *,The clan of Gen 36:40-43
Chief Timna, Chief Aliah, Chief *, 1Ch 1:51-54

JETHRO
the flock of his father-in-law *, Ex 3:1
in these chapters, * and Reuel. Ex 3:1f
it over with *, his father-in-law. Ex 4:18
"Go with my blessing," * Ex 4:18
WORD SOON REACHED *, Moses' Ex 18:1
Then * took Moses' wife, Ex 18:2
"*, your father-in-law, has come Ex 18:5,6
from all of them. * was very happy Ex 18:9
"Bless the Lord," * said, "for Ex 18:10
* offered sacrifices Ex 18:12
came to meet *, and they all ate Ex 18:12

JETUR
Hadad, Tema,*, Naphish, Kedemah. Gen 25:12-15
Tema, *, Naphish, and Kedemah. 1Ch 1:28-31

JETURITES
the Hagrites, the *, the 1Ch 5:19

JEUEL
* and his relatives: 690 in all. 1Ch 9:6
the Elizaphan clan, Shimri and *; 2Ch 29:12,13,14
*, Shemaiah, and 60 other men (they Ez 8:2-14

JEUSH
sons named *, Jalam, and Korah. Gen 36:5
Anah):The clan of *,The clan of Gen 36:18,19
Eliphaz, Reuel, *, Jalam, and 1Ch 1:35
*, Benjamin, Ehud, Chenaanah, 1Ch 7:10
*, the second, 1Ch 8:39
was next, and * and Beriah were 1Ch 23:10,11
marriage—*, Shemariah, and Zaham. 2Ch 11:19

JEUZ
*, Sachia, Mirmah. 1Ch 8:8,9,10

JEW
"I decree that any * in my Ez 7:13
Now there was a certain * at the Est 2:5
of his being a *, which was the Est 3:3,4
I see Mordecai the * just sitting Est 5:13
*, who works at the Chancellery. Est 6:10
"If Mordecai is a *, you will Est 6:13
and Mordecai the *, "I have given Est 8:7
by Mordecai the *) had written a Est 9:29-31
the * and by Queen Esther; Est 9:29-31
Mordecai the * was the Prime Est 10:3
You have made the word "*" a Ps 44:14
say, or, "I am a *," and tattoo Is 44:5
He had said that no * should be Jer 34:9
another * for all were brothers. Jer 34:9
And he said, "I am a *; Jon 1:9,10
sleeves of one * and say, 'Please Zec 8:23
And he will persuade many a * to Lk 1:16
illustration: "A * going on a trip Lk 10:30
The woman was surprised that a * Jn 4:9
name was Greek, though he was a *. Jn 12:21f
"Am I a *?" Jn 18:35
acquainted with a * named Aquila, Act 18:2,3
As it happened, a * named Act 18:24
realized he was a *, they started Act 19:34
"No," Paul replied, "I am a * Act 21:39
"I am a *," he said, "born Act 22:3
Being a * is worth something if Rom 2:25
No, a real * is anyone whose Rom 2:29
THEN WHAT'S THE use of being a *? Rom 3:1
Yes, being a * has many Rom 3:2
It was before he became a* Rom 4:10
was one of you, a * so far as his Rom 9:5
into a Jewish family is truly a *! Rom 9:6
be disappointed. * and Gentile are Rom 10:12
Remember that I myself am a *, a Rom 11:1
"Though you are a * by birth, you Gal 2:14
a woman, born as a *, to buy Gal 4:4
So I was a real * if there ever Php 3:5
but as a human being—yes, a *. Heb 2:16

JEWEL
He took them into his * rooms, Is 39:2
and supple, a * among jewels. Eze 16:6,7

JEWELED
sparkles like a * necklace, and Ps 73:6
as the tower of David, * with a Sol 4:4
Take off your * crown, the Lord Eze 21:26
And a * ring for his finger; Lk 15:22

JEWELER
He is skilled, too, as a * and Ex 31:5
a *, and can do beautiful carving; Ex 35:33

JEWELERS
unusual skills as *, carpenters, Ex 35:35

EWELRY

for costly gold and silver *." Ex 11:2
and gold *, and for clothing. Ex 12:35
of their * and ornaments. Ex 33:4
Remove your * and ornaments until Ex 33:5
So, after that, they wore no * Ex 33:6
offerings of gold, *—earrings, Ex 35:22
The total booty (besides the *, Num 31:32-35
our booty—gold *, bracelets, Num 31:50
great amounts of *, which were 1Ch 29:8
of clothing or * she wished, to Est 2:12,13,14
* of finest gold from Ophir. Ps 45:9
clothing and * and brighten your Jer 4:30
linen, and * of coral and agate. Eze 27:16
that depends on *, or beautiful 1Pe 3:3
and beautiful * made of gold and Rev 17:4

JEWELS

Then he brought out * set in Gen 24:53
Every woman will ask for *, Ex 3:22
Sealed as * within my treasury. Deu 32:34
carrying spices, gold, and *; 1Ki 10:2
stones, costly *, and marble. 1Ch 29:2
Beautiful * were inlaid into the 2Ch 3:6
of spices, gold, and *. 2Ch 9:1
quality, and many, many *. 2Ch 9:9
from Ophir, also sandalwood and *. 2Ch 9:10
garments, and * stripped from the 2Ch 20:25
gifts of money and *, also the 2Ch 21:3,4
It cannot be bought for * mounted Job 28:17
See them sparkle with * of silver Ps 68:11,12,13
far more valuable than precious *. Pro 3:13,14,15
valuable than gold or precious *. Pro 20:15
neck with that long string of *. Sol 1:10
is bright ivory encrusted with *. Sol 5:14
Your rounded thighs are like *, Sol 7:1
their rings and *, and party Is 3:21
They will be as * to display, as Is 49:18
of your houses from precious *. Is 54:11
suit or a bride with her *. Is 61:10
Can a girl forget her *? Jer 2:32
with the precious * and gold and Jer 20:5
and supple, a jewel among *. Eze 16:6,7
You took the very * and gold and Eze 16:17
* and leave you naked and ashamed. Eze 16:39
of your beautiful clothes and *. Eze 23:26
and put on your finest * for them. Eze 23:40
all kinds of spices, * and gold. Eze 27:22
her earrings and * and went out Hos 1:13
land as glittering * in a crown. Zec 9:16,17
"in that day when I make up my *. Mal 3:17
Some use gold and silver and *; 1Co 3:12
of their * or fancy clothes. 1Ti 2:9,10

JEWESS

Eshtemoa's wife was a *; 1Ch 4:18
a *, for Mordecai had said not to. Est 2:10
anyone she was a *, for she was Est 2:20
* but his father a Greek. Act 16:1
wife, a *. Act 24:24

JEWISH

important month of the * calendar. Ex 12:2
month" (of the * calendar). Num 1:1f
month" (of the * calendar). Num 1:17,18,19f
first month" (of the * calendar). Jos 4:19f
"Why don't you marry a * girl?" Ju 14:3
He was half *, being the son of 1Ki 7:14
the city and the * deserters who 2Ki 25:11
of a * woman from Dan in Israel; 2Ch 2:14
threats in the * language to the 2Ch 32:18
And all the * exiles Ez 1:6
HERE IS THE list of the * exiles Ez 2:1
and the other * leaders replied, Ez 4:3
So the * leaders continued in Ez 6:14
As a * religious leader, Ezra was Ez 7:6
BUT THEN THE * leaders came to Ez 9:1
that many of the * people and even Ez 9:1
we can to help our * brothers who Neh 5:8
regularly fed 150 * officials at my Neh 5:17
could not prove their * ancestry; Neh 7:61
never perish from the * race. Est 9:28
blessings for his * people Ps 47:4
Next, he will judge the haughty * Is 3:16
gods honored by the * community. Jer 7:18f
it to the * elders and priests and Jer 29:1
* captives over there in Babylon. Jer 29:20
Now when the leaders of the * Jer 40:7
all the * officials and Babylonian Jer 41:3
of the * army (who was in charge of Jer 52:24,25
who lived with the * exiles beside Eze 1:1
* exiles beside the Chebar River. Eze 3:14,15
He may marry only a * maiden, or Eze 44:22
to select some of the * youths Dan 1:3,4
found one of the * captives who Dan 2:25
from Israel as a * captive? Dan 5:13
Daniel, one of the * captives, is Dan 6:13
previous suffering in * history. Dan 12:1
He called a meeting of the * Mt 2:4
* religious leaders who strictly Mt 3:7f
* political leaders. Mt 3:7f
teaching in the * synagogues, Mt 4:23
and other * leaders, you can't get Mt 5:20
and not as their * leaders. Mt 7:29
one of the * religious teachers Mt 8:19
teaching in the * synagogues and Mt 9:35
It was on the Sabbath, the * day Mt 12:1
One day some of the * leaders, Mt 12:38
"Those experts in * law who are Mt 13:52
SOME PHARISEES AND other * Mt 15:1
the ancient * traditions?" Mt 15:2
* politico-religious leaders of Mt 16:1f
at the hands of the * leaders, Mt 16:21
"Why do the * leaders insist Mt 17:10
priests and other * leaders, and Mt 20:18
priests and other * leaders saw Mt 21:15
priests and other * leaders came up Mt 21:23
The * leaders replied, "He will Mt 21:41
priests and other * leaders Mt 21:45
The Herodians were a * political Mt 22:16f
would think these * leaders and Mt 23:2
priests and other * officials were Mt 26:3
purged from every * home, the Mt 26:17
and clubs, sent by the * leaders. Mt 26:47
all the * leaders were gathering. Mt 26:57
fact, the entire * Supreme Court Mt 26:59
chief priests and * leaders met Mt 27:1
chief priests and other * leaders. Mt 27:3
priests and other * leaders made Mt 27:12
was to release one * prisoner each Mt 27:15
For he knew very well that the * Mt 27:18
Meanwhile the chief priests and * Mt 27:20
And the chief priests and * Mt 27:41,42,43
A meeting of all the * leaders Mt 28:12,13
went into the * place of Mk 1:21
immediately by the * priest. Mk 1:43,44
But some of the * religious Mk 2:6
But when some of the * Mk 2:16
John's disciples and the * Mk 2:18
Some of the * religious leaders Mk 2:24
But the * teachers of religion Mk 3:22
ONE DAY SOME * religious leaders Mk 7:1
the usual * rituals before eating. Mk 7:2
When the local * leaders learned Mk 8:11
and the other * leaders—and be Mk 8:31
something the * religious leaders Mk 9:11
some * leaders argued with them. Mk 9:14
priests and the * leaders, who will Mk 10:33
priests and other * leaders heard Mk 11:18
chief priests and other * leaders Mk 11:27,28
The * leaders wanted to arrest Mk 12:12
later—an annual * holiday when no Mk 14:1
The chief priests and other * Mk 14:1
chief priests and other * leaders. Mk 14:43
and other * leaders soon gathered. Mk 14:53
and the whole * Supreme Court were Mk 14:55
to release one * prisoner each year Mk 15:6
member of the * Supreme Court (who Mk 15:42,43
My story begins with a * priest, Lk 1:5
of Phanuel, of the * tribe of Lk 2:36,37
There were many * widows needing Lk 4:25,26
the many * lepers needing help." Lk 4:27
and be examined by the * priest. Lk 5:14
teaching, some * religious leaders Lk 5:17
* law to work on the Sabbath." Lk 6:2
some respected * elders to ask him Lk 7:3
a leader of a * synagogue, came and Lk 8:41
be rejected by the * leaders—the Lk 9:22
"By chance a * priest came Lk 10:31
him by. A * Temple-assistant Lk 10:32
washing required by * custom. Lk 11:37,38
trial before these * rulers and Lk 12:11
But the local * leader in charge Lk 13:14
day, to free this * woman from the Lk 13:16
of a member of the * Council, the Lk 14:1
from the * religious leaders and Lk 15:2
and the experts on * law because he Lk 15:2
said, "Go to the * priest and show Lk 17:14
Once a * religious leader asked Lk 18:18
the * law who were standing there. Lk 20:39
drawing near—the * festival when Lk 22:1
at daybreak the * Supreme Court Lk 22:66
priests and other * leaders, along Lk 23:13
And the * leaders laughed and Lk 23:35
a member of the * Supreme Court, Lk 23:50,51,52
actions of the other * leaders. Lk 23:50,51,52
that day as required by the * law. Lk 23:56
The * leaders Jn 1:19
they were used for * ceremonial Jn 2:6
Then it was time for the annual * Jn 2:13
the * leaders Jn 2:18
AFTER DARK ONE night a * religious Jn 3:1
"You, a respected * teacher, and Jn 3:10,11
one of the * religious holidays. Jn 5:1
So the * leaders objected. Jn 5:10
Then the man went to find the * Jn 5:15
Then the * leaders were all the Jn 5:18
* leaders were plotting his death. Jn 7:1
one of the annual * holidays, and Jn 7:2
public eye. The * leaders tried to Jn 7:11
of reprisals from the * leaders. Jn 7:13
openly. The * leaders were Jn 7:15
Then the * leaders sought to Jn 7:30
The * leaders were puzzled by Jn 7:35
"Is there a single one of us * Jn 7:48
He was the * leader who came Jn 7:50
As he was speaking, the * Jn 8:3
And the * leaders slipped away Jn 8:9
Then many of the * leaders who Jn 8:30,31
the * leaders snarled. Jn 8:48
The * leaders: "You aren't even Jn 8:57
At that point the * leaders Jn 8:59
on Saturday, the weekly * holy Jn 9:14f
The * leaders wouldn't believe he Jn 9:18
They said this in fear of the * Jn 9:22,23
When he said these things, the * Jn 10:19
Hall. The * leaders surrounded him Jn 10:24
Then again the * leaders picked Jn 10:31
a few days ago the * leaders in Jn 11:8
and many of the * leaders had come Jn 11:19
When the * leaders who were at Jn 11:31
weeping and the * leaders wailing Jn 11:33
friends," the * leaders said. Jn 11:36
And so at last many of the * Jn 11:45
and take over the * government." Jn 11:48
So from that time on the * Jn 11:53
The Passover, a * holy day, was Jn 11:55
that many of the * leaders had Jn 12:11
However, even many of the * Jn 12:42
me—just as I told the * leaders. Jn 13:33
So the * police, with the Jn 18:12
who told the other * leaders, Jn 18:14
I have been heard by all the * Jn 18:20
By * law, entering the house of a Jn 18:28f
I was arrested by the * leaders. Jn 18:36
chief priests and * officials began Jn 19:6
him, but the * leaders told him, Jn 19:12
The * leaders didn't want the Jn 19:31
for fear of the * leaders, boldly Jn 19:38
as is the * custom of burial. Jn 19:40
in fear of the * leaders, when Jn 20:19
Rome—both Jews and * converts— Act 2:10
world through the * race—that is Act 3:25
The Sadducees were members of a * Act 4:1f
Council of all the * leaders was in Act 4:5
and, convening the * Council and Act 5:21
convert to the * faith, who had Act 6:5
and many of the * priests were Act 6:7
the men from the * cult of "The Act 6:9
against Stephen, and the * leaders Act 6:12
twelve patriarchs of the * nation. Act 7:8
from slavery, the * people greatly Act 7:17,18
The * leaders were stung to fury Act 7:54
After a while the * leaders Act 9:23
are forbidden by our * laws." Act 10:14
it is against the * laws for me to Act 10:28
the * believers argued with him. Act 11:2
anything forbidden by our * laws!' Act 11:8
this pleased the * leaders, he Act 12:3
to the * synagogue and preached. Act 13:5
where they met a * sorcerer, a fake Act 13:6,7
the * law could never do. Act 13:39
But when the * leaders Act 13:45
Then the * leaders stirred up Act 13:50
Some agreed with the * leaders, Act 14:4
Jews, and * leaders to attack and Act 14:5,6
to the ancient * custom of Act 15:1
all the * customs and ceremonies. Act 15:5
God must obey our * laws, except Act 15:19
against in * synagogues in every Act 15:21
greater burden of * laws on you Act 15:27,28,29
where there was a * synagogue. Act 17:1
But the * leaders were jealous Act 17:5
silly * laws, you take care of it. Act 18:15
* custom, for he had taken a vow. Act 18:18
refuted all the * arguments in Act 18:28
Seven sons of Sceva, a * Act 19:14
of the week," by * reckoning, from Act 20:7f
insistent that * believers must Act 21:20
the * traditions and customs. Act 21:20
Our * Christians here at Act 21:21
Moses, against our * customs, and Act 21:21
yourself obey the * laws and are in Act 21:24
to follow these * customs at Act 21:25
everybody to disobey the * laws. Act 21:28
* laws and customs very carefully. Act 22:3
for letters to the * leaders in Act 22:5
into session with the * Council. Act 22:30
Some of the * leaders Act 23:9
about their * beliefs, certainly Act 23:29
arrived with some of the * leaders Act 24:1
been a judge of * affairs for many Act 24:10
I firmly believe in the * law and Act 24:14
priests and other * leaders got Act 25:2
"I have not opposed the * laws Act 25:8
priests and other * leaders gave me Act 25:15
an expert on * laws and customs. Act 26:3
given a thorough * training from my Act 26:4
obedience to * laws and customs. Act 26:5
together the local * leaders and Act 28:17
demanded by the * leaders. Act 28:18
you were born of * parents or Rom 2:28
gone through the * initiation Rom 2:28
Is there any value in the * Rom 3:1
the founder of our * nation. Rom 4:1
but also keep the * laws, or is the Rom 4:9

(JEWISH Con't)
* rules, but only trust in Christ? Rom 4:9
Or because he also kept the * Rom 4:9
went through the * initiation Rom 4:10
are saved without obeying * laws. Rom 4:11
or not we follow * customs if we Rom 4:16
YOU UNDERSTAND yet, dear * Rom 7:1
your master, used to be the * law; Rom 7:4
worry about the * laws and customs Rom 7:6
Oh, my * brothers! Rom 9:1
And not everyone born into a * Rom 9:6
are not from his * family) and will Rom 9:25
that the * people might be saved Rom 10:1
by keeping the * laws and customs, Rom 10:3
has rejected his * people forever? Rom 11:11
should observe the * holidays as Rom 14:5
a gift to the * Christians there. Rom 15:25
gone through the * ceremony of 1Co 7:18
who follow * customs and ceremonies 1Co 9:20
And the * people, all who eat 1Co 10:18
it seems as though * hearts and 2Co 3:14
I followed the * religion—how I Gal 1:13
we obeyed the * laws or not. Gal 2:4
circumcised and by obeying * laws. Gal 2:5
and the many other * laws Gal 2:12
But afterwards when some * Gal 2:12
of what these * legalists, who Gal 2:12
and then all the other * Gal 2:13
long since discarded the * laws; Gal 2:14
and yet we * Christians know very Gal 2:16
God by obeying our * laws, but only Gal 2:16
because we have obeyed the * laws. Gal 2:16
and obeying all the other * laws? Gal 2:17
saved by keeping * laws, for it Gal 2:18
saved by keeping * laws, then there Gal 2:21
by trying to keep the * laws? Gal 3:2
For if trying to obey the * laws Gal 3:3
of your trying to obey the * laws? Gal 3:5
who depend on the * laws to save Gal 3:10
trying to keep the * laws, because Gal 3:11
Let me put it another way. The * Gal 3:24
We were slaves to * laws and Gal 4:3
have to obey the * laws to be Gal 4:21
and she is not a slave to * laws. Gal 4:26
us to keep the * laws, just as Gal 4:29
obligated to the * laws, but Gal 4:31
slavery to * laws and ceremonies. Gal 5:1
and keeping the * laws to make you Gal 5:2
obey every other * law or perish. Gal 5:3
obeying the * ceremonies or not; Gal 5:6
circumcision and * laws are Gal 5:11
force yourself to obey * laws. Gal 5:18
there is no conflict with * laws. Gal 5:23
try to keep the other * laws; Gal 6:13
us, caused by the * laws which Eph 2:15
annul that whole system of * laws. Eph 2:15
For I went through the * Php 3:5
a pure-blooded * home that was a Php 3:5
to every * law and custom. Php 3:5
and I tried to obey every * rule Php 3:6
not celebrating * holidays and Col 2:16
These are the only * Christians Col 4:11
Christians must obey the * laws. Tit 1:10
from listening to * folk tales and Tit 1:14
about obedience to * laws, for this Tit 3:9
THE * HIGH priest is merely a man Heb 5:1
had been a * priest, for later on Heb 7:5
(c) The * priests, though mortal, Heb 7:8
ancestor of all * priests, of all Heb 7:9
(e) If the * priests and their Heb 7:11
the old * system of sacrifices. Heb 8:4
THE OLD SYSTEM of * laws gave only Heb 10:1
* laws can never be helped. Heb 13:10
Under the system of * laws the Heb 13:11
To: * Christians scattered Jas 1:1
To: The * Christians driven out of 1Pe 1:1

JEWS

he drove out the * and sent 2Ki 16:6
the * and the Babylonians. 2Ki 25:25
occupied by the *, and required all 2Ch 34:33
29:10) that the * would remain in Ez 1:1f
of Judah. All * throughout the Ez 1:3
Those * Ez 1:4
Please be informed that the * Ez 4:12
for the * will then refuse to pay Ez 4:13
and forced the * to stop building. Ez 4:23
where the * offer sacrifices. Ez 6:3
and gold from the * and their Ez 7:16
the leader of the * at Casiphia, to Ez 8:17
one of my fellow * named Hanani Neh 1:2
"—the * who returned to Neh 1:2
feeble * think they are doing?" Neh 4:1
* who were profiteering on them. Neh 5:1
he hears that the * are planning to Neh 6:5,6
the names of the * who returned to Neh 7:6
cancel the debts of our brother *. Neh 10:31
that some of the * had married Neh 13:23
people, the *, and destroy all of Est 3:5,6
decreeing that the *—young and old, Est 3:13
mourning among the *, fasting, Est 4:3
for the destruction of the *. Est 4:7
decree dooming all *, and told him Est 4:8
when all other * are killed? Est 4:13
will deliver the * from some other Est 4:14
the * of Shushan and fast for me; Est 4:16
the *' enemy, to Queen Esther. Est 8:1
stop Haman's plot against the *. Est 8:3
* throughout the king's provinces. Est 8:5
a message to the *, telling them Est 8:8
decree to the * and to the Est 8:9,10
This decree gave the * Est 8:11
for the extermination of the *. Est 8:12f
people so that the * would be ready Est 8:13
And the * had joy and gladness, Est 8:16
arrived, the * were filled with joy Est 8:17
pretended to be *, for they feared Est 8:17
what the * might do to them. Est 8:17
effect—the day the *' enemies had Est 9:1
the contrary—the * gathered in Est 9:1
the * for fear of Mordecai; Est 9:3
But the * went ahead on that Est 9:5
(son of Hammedatha), the *' enemy— Est 9:7-10
"The * have killed 500 men in Est 9:12
Majesty, let the * who are here at Est 9:13
Then the * at Shushan gathered Est 9:15
Meanwhile, the other * throughout Est 9:16
But the * at Shushan went on Est 9:18
And so it is that the * in the Est 9:19
letters to the * near and far, Est 9:20
day when the * were saved from Est 9:22
So the * adopted Mordecai's Est 9:23
enemy of all the *, had plotted to Est 9:24,25
All the * throughout the realm Est 9:27
and to all who became *; Est 9:27
sent to all the * throughout the Est 9:29-31
indeed, the * themselves had Est 9:29-31
great among the *, and respected by Est 10:3
May all who hate the * be brought Ps 129:5
ruin because the * have spoken out Is 3:8
in Hebrew to the * listening on the Is 36:13
has redeemed his servants, the *. Is 48:20
or survivors of the * in Israel. Is 66:19f
who brought the * back to their own Jer 23:8
I will never abandon the *, or Jer 33:25,26
me over to the * who have defected Jer 38:19
When the * in Moab and among the Jer 40:11
"What will happen then to the * Jer 40:15
concerning all the * who were Jer 44:1
crowd of all the * in southern Jer 44:15
the Lord, all you * who are living Jer 44:26
(Then the remnant of the * will Jer 46:16
you living in the cities of the *? Jer 49:1
Aren't the * enough to fill them Jer 49:1
The * in Babylon say, Jer 51:34,35
Babylon, to the * in exile there. Eze 11:24
of the * of refusing to worship! Dan 3:8
But there are some * out Dan 3:12
of 1,000,000 * during the following Dan 9:25f
and stop the * from all their Dan 9:27
your people, the *, at the end Dan 10:14
own people, the *, will join them, Dan 11:14
He will leave godless * in power Dan 11:30,31
* who were loyal to God's laws. Dan 11:32f
of anguish for the * greater than Dan 12:1
They will be wandering *, Hos 9:17
against the *, for they killed Joe 3:19
gold from the * exiled in Babylon. Zec 6:10,11
The * of the city of Bethel had Zec 7:2
with the *, just as the Jebusites Zec 9:7
twice: Two million * perished in Zec 13:8f
is the newborn King of the *? Mt 2:2
we are *—descendants of Abraham.' Mt 3:9
change these stones here into *! Mt 3:9
sent to help the *—the lost sheep Mt 15:24
"Are you the *' Messiah?" Mt 27:11
Literally, " 'King' of the *." Mt 27:11f
"Hail, King of the *," they Mt 27:29
is Jesus, the King of the *." Mt 27:37
widely among the *, and is still Mt 28:15
were a religious sect of the *. Mk 3:6f
(For the *, especially the Mk 7:3
I should help my own family—the *. Mk 7:27
"Are you the King of the *?" Mk 15:2
giving you the 'King of *'?" Mk 15:9
King of the *!" Mk 15:18
It read, "The King of the *." Mk 15:26
of the *, a descendant of Aaron. Lk 1:5
"for he loves the * and even paid Lk 7:5
among all the * in Israel have I Lk 7:9
John 4:9). The * called the Lk 9:53f
Samaritans naturally hated the *. Lk 9:53f
were despised by *, and the feeling Lk 10:33f
had butchered some * from Galilee Lk 13:1
Samaritans were despised by * as Lk 17:16f
most influential * in the Roman Lk 19:1
"Are you the King of the *?" Lk 23:3f
King of the *, save yourself ! Lk 23:37
"This is the King of the *." Lk 23:38
the *, he was not accepted. Jn 1:11,12
Literally, "the *." Jn 1:19f
Literally, "the *." Jn 2:18f
why is it that you * insist that Jn 4:20
blindly, while we * know all about Jn 4:21-24
to the world through the *." Jn 4:21-24
the feast of the *, was at hand." Jn 6:2-5f
Then the * began to murmur Jn 6:41
Then the * began arguing with Jn 6:52
among the * in other lands, or Jn 7:35
The * asked, "Is he planning Jn 8:22
The leaders of the * said, "Now Jn 8:52
"Are you the King of the *?" Jn 18:33
use the word or as the * use it?" Jn 18:34
But the * were using the word Jn 18:34f
I'll release the 'King of the *.' Jn 18:39
"Hail, 'King of the *!' Jn 19:3
and said to the *, "I am going to Jn 19:4
And Pilate said to the *, "Here Jn 19:14
of Nazareth, the King of the *." Jn 19:19
'The King of the *' to 'He said, I Jn 19:21
to 'He said, I am King of the *.' Jn 19:21
Many godly * were in Jerusalem Act 2:5
from Rome—both * and Jewish Act 2:10
soon joined by * from Cyrene, Act 6:9
(But some godly * Act 8:2
they were godly and sympathetic *. Act 8:2f
and the Damascus * couldn't Act 9:22
But then some Greek-speaking * Act 9:29
birds [forbidden to the * for food Act 10:12
thought of by the *, and how an Act 10:22
* are not God's only favorites! Act 10:34
listening! The * who came with Act 10:45
the Good News, but only to *. Act 11:19
Peter to the * for execution after Act 12:4
the * were hoping to do to me!" Act 12:11
all of us! The * in Jerusalem and Act 13:27
And many * and godly Gentiles Act 13:43
Literally, "the *." Act 13:45f
should be given first to you *. Act 13:46
many—both * and Gentiles—believed. Act 14:1
But the * who spurned God's Act 14:2
a mob of Gentiles, *, and Jewish Act 14:5,6
Yet only a few days later, some * Act 14:19
In deference to the * of the Act 16:3
"These * are corrupting our Act 16:20,21
But when the * in Thessalonica Act 17:13
with the * and the devout Gentiles, Act 17:17
order to deport all * from Rome. Act 18:2,3
convince the * and Greeks alike. Act 18:4
the * that Jesus is the Messiah. Act 18:5
But when the * opposed him and Act 18:6
of Achaia, the * rose in concerted Act 18:12
"Listen, you *, if this were a Act 18:14
for a discussion with the *. Act 18:19
of Ausia—both * and Greeks—heard Act 19:10
A team of itinerant * who were Act 19:13
Ephesus, to * and Greeks alike; Act 19:17
some of the * and dragged forward. Act 19:33
a plot by the * against his life, Act 20:3
plots of the * against my life. Act 20:19
I have had one message for * and Act 20:21
be bound by the * in Jerusalem and Act 21:11
many thousands of * have also Act 21:20
ended when some * from Turkey saw Act 21:26,27
of by all the * ot Damascus, came Act 22:12
or more of the * got together and Act 23:12,13
he told him, "the * are going to Act 23:20
"This man was seized by the * Act 23:27
and peace to us * and have greatly Act 24:2
inciting the * throughout the Act 24:5
Then all the other * chimed in, Act 24:9
money to aid the *, and to offer a Act 24:17
But some * from Turkey were there Act 24:18
told the * to wait for the Act 24:22
the *, he left Paul in chains. Act 24:27
On Paul's arrival in court the * Act 25:7
to please the *, asked him, "Are Act 25:9
local * and by those in Jerusalem! Act 25:24
"As the * are well aware, I was Act 26:4
good deeds. The * arrested me in Act 26:21
light to * and Gentiles alike." Act 26:23
arrested by the * in Jerusalem and Act 28:17
But when the * protested the Act 28:19
" 'Say to the *, "You will hear Act 28:26
these words, the * departed, having Act 28:28,29f
first to the * alone, but now Rom 1:16
and suffering for * and Gentiles Rom 2:9
whether they are * or Gentiles. Rom 2:10
And God will punish the * for Rom 2:12-15
You * think all is well between Rom 2:17
honors he planned to give the *? Rom 2:26
than you * who know so much about Rom 2:27
For you are not real * just Rom 2:28
Well, then, are we * better than Rom 3:9
sinners, whether * or Gentiles. Rom 3:9
heavily upon the *, for they are Rom 3:19
And does God save only the * in Rom 3:29
all, whether * or Gentiles, are Rom 3:30
those * who have been circumcised. Rom 4:12
to fulfill his promises to the *? Rom 9:6
are only to those who are truly *. Rom 9:6
whether we are * or Gentiles, and Rom 9:23,24
out concerning the * that though Rom 9:27
mercy all the * would be Rom 9:29

EWS Con't)
But the *, who tried so hard to Rom 9:31
in the path of the *, and many will Rom 9:33
But what about the *? Rom 10:18
to the *, but they keep arguing Rom 10:21
and deserted his people the *? Rom 11:1
to God about the *, telling God how Rom 11:2,3
Not all the * have turned away Rom 11:5
Most of the * have not found the Rom 11:7
and then the * would be jealous and Rom 11:11
when the * stumbled over it and Rom 11:12
when the *, too, come to Christ. Rom 11:12
and remind the * about it as often Rom 11:13
when the * come to Christ. Rom 11:15
of the *, have been broken off. Rom 11:17
branches, the *, were broken off Rom 11:20
On the other hand, if the * Rom 11:23
ready to put the * back again, who Rom 11:24
that some of the * have set Rom 11:25
turn the * from all ungodliness. Rom 11:26
Now many of the * are enemies of Rom 11:28
Yet the * are still beloved of Rom 11:28
God, but when the * refused his Rom 11:30
And now the * are the rebels, Rom 11:31
to his promises and to help the *. Rom 15:8
along with his people the *." Rom 15:10
It seems foolish to the * 1Co 1:22
to save them, the * are offended 1Co 1:23
to salvation, both * and Gentiles, 1Co 1:24
When I am with the * I seem as 1Co 9:20
are * or Gentiles or Christians. 1Co 10:32
Some of us are *, some are 1Co 12:13
Five different times the * gave 2Co 11:24
my own people, the *, as well as 2Co 11:26
the most religious * of my own age Gal 1:14
preaching to the *—for the same God Gal 2:7,8,9
continued their work with the *. Gal 2:7,8,9
You and I are * by birth, not Gal 2:15
his sons—all the *—were being Gal 3:16
We are no longer * or Greeks or Gal 3:28
mother-city of the *, the center of Gal 4:24,25
and the *, who try to follow that Gal 4:24,25
godless and "unclean" by the *. Eph 2:11
He has made peace between us * Eph 2:14
which favored the * and excluded Eph 2:15
him, and to us * who were near. Eph 2:17
Now all of us, whether * or Eph 2:18
share with the * in all the riches Eph 3:6
all of his family—* and Gentiles Eph 3:10
from their own people the *. 1Th 2:14
say that they are *—the children of Rev 2:9
Literally, "say they are * but Rev 3:9f

JEZANIAH
Netophathite), * (son of a Jer 40:8

JEZEBEL
enough, he married *, the daughter 1Ki 16:31
Once when Queen * had tried to 1Ki 18:3,4
time when Queen * was trying to 1Ki 18:13
Asherah who are supported by *." 1Ki 18:19
WHEN AHAB TOLD Queen * what 1Ki 19:1
his wife, *, asked him. 1Ki 21:5
of Israel or not?" * demanded. 1Ki 21:7
word to * that Naboth was dead. 1Ki 21:14
When * heard the news, she said 1Ki 21:15
apart the body of your wife, *. 1Ki 21:23
Ahab, for his wife * encouraged him 1Ki 21:25
other people who were killed by *. 2Ki 9:7
Dogs shall eat Ahab's wife * at 2Ki 9:10
your mother * are all around us?" 2Ki 9:22
When * heard that Jehu had come 2Ki 9:30
Ahab and of the Queen Mother, *." 2Ki 10:13
that woman *, who calls herself a Rev 2:20

JEZER
Jahzeel, Guni, *, and Shillem. Gen 46:23,24,25
named after their ancestor *. Num 26:28-37
named after their ancestor *. Num 26:48-50
Jahzi-el, Guni, *, Shallum. 1Ch 7:13

JEZERITES
The *, named after their ancestor Num 26:28-37
The *, named after their ancestor Num 26:48-50

JEZI-EL
His brother Joash; * and Pelet, 1Ch 12:3-7

JEZRAHIAH
direction of * the choirmaster. Neh 12:42

JEZREEL
Ziph, Juttah, *, Jokde-am, Zanoah, Jos 15:48-62
and the Valley of * have iron Jos 17:16,17,18
*, Chesulloth, Shunem, Hapharaim, Jos 19:17-23
and camped in the valley of *. Ju 6:33
also married Ahino-am from *. 1Sa 25:43
him—Ahino-am of * and Abigail of 1Sa 27:2,3
camped at the springs in *. 1Sa 29:1
the Philistine army went on to *. 1Sa 29:11
from * and Abigail the widow of 2Sa 2:2
Gilead, Ashuri, *, Ephraim, the 2Sa 2:9
were killed at the battle of *. 2Sa 4:4
Zarethan below *, and all the 1Ki 4:8-19
Ahab left hastily for *, and the 1Ki 18:45
NABOTH, A MAN from *, had a 1Ki 21:1
leaders of *, where Naboth lived. 1Ki 21:8
that the dogs of * shall tear apart 1Ki 21:23
so he went to * to rest and 2Ki 8:29
at *, and no one will bury her.' 2Ki 9:10
But he had returned to * to 2Ki 9:15
* to report what we have done." 2Ki 9:15
and rode to * himself to find King 2Ki 9:16
The watchman on the Tower of * 2Ki 9:17
Jehu had come to *, she painted her 2Ki 9:30
* at about this time tomorrow." 2Ki 10:6
and presented to Jehu at *. 2Ki 10:7
Ahab who were in *, as well as all 2Ki 10:11
born to his wife, Ahino-am of *. 1Ch 3:1
The descendants of Etam:*, Ishma, 1Ch 4:3-4
and returned to * to recover. 2Ch 22:6
"Name the child *, for in the Hos 1:4,5
in the Valley of * I am about to Hos 1:4,5
the nation in the Valley of *." Hos 1:4,5
Literally, "the day of * ('God Hos 1:11f
O *, Hos 1:11
"*" is implied in the preceding Hos 1:11f
Literally, "*." Hos 1:21,22f

JIDLAPH
*,Bethuel (father of Rebekah). Gen 22:20-23

JITTERY
But Martha was the * type, and Lk 10:40

JO-ELAH
Korahites; * and Zebadiah (sons of 1Ch 12:3-7

JO-EZER
Elkanah, Isshiah, Azarel, *, 1Ch 12:3-7

JOAB
and General * (the son of Zeruiah) 2Sa 2:13
Then Abner suggested to *, 2Sa 2:14
* agreed, so twelve men were 2Sa 2:14
of Israel had been defeated by * 2Sa 2:17
I could never face your brother * 2Sa 2:22
Now * and Abishai set out after 2Sa 2:24
shouted down to *, "Must our 2Sa 2:26
* shouted back, "I swear by God 2Sa 2:27
at Mahanaim. * and the men who 2Sa 2:30
were dead. * and his men took 2Sa 2:32
But just after Abner left, * and 2Sa 3:22
When * was told that Abner had 2Sa 3:23
Then * sent messengers to catch 2Sa 3:26
When Abner arrived at Hebron, * 2Sa 3:27
against Abner. * and his family 2Sa 3:29
So * and his brother Abishai 2Sa 3:30
Then David said to * and to all 2Sa 3:31
The general of his army was * 2Sa 8:16
this, he sent * and the entire 2Sa 10:7,8
When * realized that he would 2Sa 10:9
and help me," * instructed him. 2Sa 10:11
And when * and his troops 2Sa 10:13
Afterwards * returned to 2Sa 10:14
begin, David sent * and the Israeli 2Sa 11:1
So David dispatched a memo to *: 2Sa 11:6
asked him how * and the army were 2Sa 11:7
* and gave it to Uriah to deliver. 2Sa 11:14
The letter instructed * to put 2Sa 11:15
there to die! So * assigned Uriah 2Sa 11:16
When * sent a report to David of 2Sa 11:18
"Well, tell * not to be 2Sa 11:25
Meanwhile * and the Israeli army 2Sa 12:26,27
capital of Ammon. * sent messengers 2Sa 12:26,27
WHEN GENERAL * realized how much 2Sa 14:1
"Pretend you are in mourning," * 2Sa 14:2,3
"Did * send you here?" 2Sa 14:19
* sent me and told me what to say. 2Sa 14:19
So the king sent for * and told 2Sa 14:21
* fell to the ground before the 2Sa 14:22
Then * went to Geshur and brought 2Sa 14:23
* to ask him to intercede for him; 2Sa 14:29
for him; but * wouldn't come. 2Sa 14:29
Then * came to Absalom and 2Sa 14:31
So * told the king what Absalom 2Sa 14:33
general of the army, replacing *. 2Sa 17:25
And the king commanded *, 2Sa 18:5
of David's men saw him and told *. 2Sa 18:10
and didn't kill him?" * demanded. 2Sa 18:11
"Enough of this nonsense," * 2Sa 18:14
Then * blew the trumpet, and his 2Sa 18:16
"No," * told him, "it wouldn't 2Sa 18:20
Then * said to a man from Cush, 2Sa 18:21
But Ahima-az pleaded with *, 2Sa 18:22
need you now, my boy." * replied. 2Sa 18:22
And * finally said, "All right, 2Sa 18:23
"When * told me to come, there 2Sa 18:29
WORD SOON REACHED * that the 2Sa 19:1
Then * went to the king's room 2Sa 19:5
of my army in place of *." 2Sa 19:13
So Abishai and * set out after 2Sa 20:7
face with Amasa. * was wearing his 2Sa 20:8,9,10
you, my brother," * said, and took 2Sa 20:8,9,10
his left hand, and * stabbed him in 2Sa 20:8,9,10
and he died there. * and his 2Sa 20:8,9,10
for David, come and follow *." 2Sa 20:11
went on with * to capture Sheba. 2Sa 20:13
out to *, "Listen to me, Joab. 2Sa 20:16
out to Joab, "Listen to me, *. 2Sa 20:16
the woman asked, "Are you *?" 2Sa 20:17
And * replied, "That isn't it at 2Sa 20:20
head and threw it out to *. 2Sa 20:22
* was commander-in-chief of the 2Sa 20:23
the brother of * (son of Zeruiah), 2Sa 23:18,19
Asahel, the brother of *, was 2Sa 23:24-39
bearer of * (son of Zeruiah); 2Sa 23:24-39
*, Abishai, Asahel, and Benaiah. 2Sa 23:24-39f
The king said to *, 2Sa 24:2
But * replied, "God grant that 2Sa 24:3
remonstrance; so * and the other 2Sa 24:4
twenty days. And * reported the 2Sa 24:9
He took General * and Abiathar 1Ki 1:7
Abiathar the priest and General *. 1Ki 1:19
He also invited General * and 1Ki 1:25
"What's going on?" * demanded. 1Ki 1:41
You know that * murdered my two 1Ki 2:5
and General * would take over!" 1Ki 2:22
When * heard about Adonijah's 1Ki 2:28
Adonijah's death (* had joined 1Ki 2:28
*, "The king says to come out!" 1Ki 2:30
of Judah. May * and his 1Ki 2:33
to the Tabernacle and killed *; 1Ki 2:34
been in Edom with * to arrange for 1Ki 11:15
that David and * were both dead, he 1Ki 11:21
Zeruiah's sons were Abishai, *, 1Ch 2:16
Seraiah was the father of *, the 1Ch 4:14
*, the son of Zeruiah, was 1Ch 11:5,6
* rebuilt the rest of Jerusalem. 1Ch 11:8
* (son of Zeruiah) was 1Ch 18:15
of this, he sent * and the 1Ch 19:8
When * realized that the enemy 1Ch 19:10
and help me," * told his brother; 1Ch 19:12
So * and his troops attacked the 1Ch 19:14
Then * returned to Jerusalem. 1Ch 19:15
usually began) * led the Israeli 1Ch 20:1
he told * and the other leaders. 1Ch 21:2
But * objected. 1Ch 21:3
and * did as he was told; 1Ch 21:4
the son of Ner, * the son of 1Ch 26:28
(the brother of *), who was later 1Ch 27:7
* began the census, but he never 1Ch 27:24
and by Abiathar. * was 1Ch 27:34
of Jeshua and *), 2,812; Ez 2:3-35
From the clan of *—Obadiah (son of Ez 8:2-14
From the families of Jeshua and * Neh 7:8-38
this was when *, captain of his Ps 60:1

JOAB'S
(* brother and the son of Zeruiah). 1Sa 26:5,6,7
and the forces of David. * 2Sa 2:18
of * next to mine," and they did. 2Sa 14:30
(Amasa was * second cousin; 2Sa 17:25
the sister of * mother Zeruiah. 2Sa 17:25
A third were placed under * 2Sa 18:2
Ten of * young armor bearers 2Sa 18:15
elite guard from * army and the 2Sa 20:7
One of * young officers shouted 2Sa 20:11
the road, and when * young officers 2Sa 20:12
When * forces arrived, they 2Sa 20:15
But the king's command overcame * 2Sa 24:4
Abishai, * brother, was commander 1Ch 11:20
Asahel (* brother); 1Ch 11:26-47
was General * armor bearer; 1Ch 11:26-47

JOAH
Shebnah, his secretary; and *, 2Ki 18:18
Then Eliakim, Shebnah, and * said 2Ki 18:26
secretary, and * (son of Asaph) the 2Ki 18:37
Libni, Jahath, Zimmah, *, Iddo, 1Ch 6:19,20,21
* (the third), 1Ch 26:4,5
From the Gershon clan, * (son of 2Ch 29:12,13,14
of Zimmah) and Eden (son of *). 2Ch 29:12,13,14
of Jerusalem, and * (son of 2Ch 34:8
king's scribe, and * (Asaph's son), Is 36:3
Then Eliakim and Shebna and * Is 36:11
royal scribe, and * (son of Asaph), Is 36:22

JOAHAZ
and Joah (son of *), the city 2Ch 34:8

JOANAN
Joda's father was *; Lk 3:23-38

JOANAN'S
Joda's father was Joanan;* father Lk 3:23-38

JOANNA
demons from her), *, Chuza's wife Lk 8:3
Mary Magdalene and * and Mary the Lk 24:10

JOASH
on the farm of * the Abiezrite. Ju 6:11
that it was Gideon, the son of *. Ju 6:29
out your son," they shouted to *. Ju 6:30
But * retorted to the whole mob, Ju 6:31
Gideon, the son of *, the Ju 7:14
of his father * in Ophrah, in the Ju 8:32
of the city, and to my son *. 1Ki 22:26
son *. Joash was rescued by his 2Ki 11:2,3
son Joash. * was rescued by his 2Ki 11:2,3
Athaliah's death. * was seven 2Ki 11:21
that * became king of Judah. 2Ki 12:1
All his life * did what was 2Ki 12:2
One day King * said to Jehoiada, 2Ki 12:4,5
in disrepair. So * called for 2Ki 12:7
King * took all the sacred 2Ki 12:18
The rest of the history of * is 2Ki 12:19
of the reign of King * of Judah. 2Ki 13:1
and his son * reigned in Samaria 2Ki 13:9,10
of the reign of King * of Judah. 2Ki 13:9,10
of the reign of *, including his 2Ki 13:12

(JOASH Con't)
Kings of Israel. * died and was 2Ki 13:13
* visited him and wept over him. 2Ki 13:14
King * of Israel 2Ki 13:25
the reign of King * of Israel, King 2Ki 14:1
as good a king as his father *. 2Ki 14:3
a message to King * of Israel (the 2Ki 14:8
But King * replied, "The thistle 2Ki 14:9
* of Israel mustered his army. 2Ki 14:11
King * took many hostages and 2Ki 14:14
The rest of the history of * and 2Ki 14:15
When * died, he was buried in 2Ki 14:16
years longer than *, and the rest 2Ki 14:17
Ahaziah, *, Amaziah, Azariah, 1Ch 3:10-14
* , Saraph 1Ch 4:21-22
Zemirah, *, Eliezer, Eli-o-enai, 1Ch 7:8
His brother *; 1Ch 12:3-7
territory, while * had charge of 1Ch 27:28
*," the king of Israel ordered. 2Ch 18:25
except for *, lived to succeed him 2Ch 22:9
* was rescued by his Aunt 2Ch 22:11
the priest. * remained hidden in 2Ch 22:12
* WAS SEVEN years old when he 2Ch 24:1
from Beer-sheba. * tried hard to 2Ch 24:2
Later on, * decided to repair and 2Ch 24:4
Judah came to King * and induced 2Ch 24:17,18
and finally King * himself ordered 2Ch 24:21
That was how King * repaid 2Ch 24:22
way God executed judgment upon *. 2Ch 24:24
When the Syrians left—leaving * 2Ch 24:25
about the sons of *, and the curses 2Ch 24:27
curses laid upon *, and about the 2Ch 24:27
When * died, his son Amaziah 2Ch 24:27
war on King * of Israel (son of 2Ch 25:17
King * replied with this parable: 2Ch 25:18
King * of Israel captured the 2Ch 25:23
Then King * ordered two hundred 2Ch 25:23
the death of King * of Israel. 2Ch 25:25
of Israel, Jeroboam, son of *. Hos 1:1
Jeroboam (son of *) was king of Amo 1:2

JOASH'S
the Abiezrite. * son, Gideon, had Ju 6:11
altar, which was near * hideaway. 2Ki 11:11

JOB
to see if she would finish the *, Gen 24:21
years old. His *, along with his Gen 37:2
back your * as his wine taster. Gen 40:13
appointed for the *, Pharaoh said, Gen 41:38
"But I'm not the person for a * Ex 3:11
Moses, this * is too heavy a Ex 18:18
on hand now to complete the *!" Ex 36:4-7
have given me the * of nursing them Num 11:12
do a complete * of it—don't make Deu 7:2
for this *," they promised. Ju 16:5
say, 'give me a * among the priests 1Sa 2:36
and finish the *, so that you will 2Sa 12:28
very expensive *—for the foundation 1Ki 5:17
And when they had finished that * 2Ch 20:23
* was completed in sixteen days. 2Ch 29:17
to the Levites—a * classification Ez 8:20
and their * was to make an honest Neh 13:13
returned to his *, but Haman Est 6:12
land of Uz a man named *—a good Job 1:1
several days—* would summon his Job 1:5
each of them. For * said, "Perhaps Job 1:5
"Have you noticed my servant *? Job 1:8
Then * stood up and tore his robe Job 1:20
In all of this, * did not sin or Job 1:22
have you noticed my servant *?" Job 2:3
Lord and struck * with a terrible Job 2:7
Then * took a broken piece of Job 2:8
So in all this * said nothing Job 2:10
the Naamathite. * was so changed Job 2:12
AT LAST * spoke, and cursed the Job 3:1
A REPLY TO * from Eliphaz the Job 4:1
BILDAD THE SHUHITE replies to *: Job 8:1
*, blowing words around like wind? Job 8:2
THE NAAMATHITE replies to * Job 11:1
THE REPLY OF *: Job 19:1
THE REPLY OF *: Job 23:1
* CONTINUED: Job 29:1
reply further to * because he kept Job 32:1
angry because * refused to admit he Job 32:2
them has convinced * that he is a Job 32:11,12
of his sin.' If * had been arguing Job 32:14
"PLEASE LISTEN, *, to what I have Job 33:1
Mark this well, O *. Job 33:31
what is good. For * has said, 'I Job 34:5
"Who else is as arrogant as *? Job 34:7,8
you, *, are speaking like a fool. Job 34:34,35
*, you have spoken like a fool." Job 35:16
"Listen, O *, stop and consider Job 37:14
THEN THE LORD answered * from the Job 38:1
Then * replied to God: Job 40:2
Then the Lord spoke to * again Job 40:6
THEN * REPLIED TO GOD: Job 42:1
speaking with *, he said to Eliphaz Job 42:7
about me, as my servant * was. Job 42:7
go to my servant * and offer a Job 42:8
and my servant * will pray for Job 42:8
rightly concerning my servant *." Job 42:8
Then, when * prayed for his Job 42:10
So the Lord blessed * at the end Job 42:12
as lovely as the daughters of *; Job 42:15
* lived 140 years after that, Job 42:16
his food and drink, and his *. Ecc 2:24-26
work whatever his * may be, for Ecc 5:18
If Noah, Daniel and * were here Eze 14:14
Noah, Daniel and * were living Eze 14:20
out the grain—an easy * she loves. Hos 10:11
"Get on with the * and finish it! Zec 8:9
"Go and take a * as shepherd of a Zec 11:4
again and get a * as a shepherd; Zec 11:15
he has done a good *, there will be Lk 12:42,43,44
for a special * I have for them." Act 13:2
If you are a teacher, do a good * Rom 12:7
As it says in the book of *, God 1Co 3:19
It isn't our * to judge 1Co 5:12
But it certainly is our * to 1Co 5:12
Well, Moses did a fine * working Heb 3:5
But your * is not to decide Jas 4:11
greatly for it. * is an example of Jas 5:11
And no one could get a * or even Rev 13:17

JOB'S
Every year when each of * sons Job 1:4
This was * regular practice. Job 1:5
not long afterwards when * sons Job 1:12,13
A messenger rushed to * home with Job 1:14,15
When three of * friends heard of Job 2:11
* REPLY: Job 6:1
* REPLY: Job 9:1
* REPLY: Job 12:1
* REPLY: Job 16:1
* REPLY: Job 21:1
* REPLY: Job 26:1
* FINAL DEFENSE: Job 27:1
* words are ended. Job 31:40
But he was also angry with * Job 32:3
unable to answer * arguments and Job 32:3
accepted * prayer on their behalf. Job 42:9
Eliphaz, the wisest of * three Ob 1:8f

JOBAB
Sheba, Ophir, Havi-lah, *. Gen 10:26-30
by: King * (son of Zerah), from Gen 36:31-39
King * of Madon; Jos 11:1
Sheba, Ophir, Havilah, and *. 1Ch 1:20-23
When Bela died, * the son of 1Ch 1:44
When * died, Husham from the 1Ch 1:45
*, Zibia, Mesha, Malcam, 1Ch 8:8,9,10
Hizki, Heber, Ishmerai, Izliah, *. 1Ch 8:17,18

JOBS
Get back to your *!" Ex 5:4,5
were no *, no wages, no security; Zec 8:10
around waiting for *, so he sent Mt 20:3
be given other * in the church as a 1Ti 3:10

JOCHEBED
married *, his father's sister; Ex 6:20
Egypt, a daughter, *, was born to Num 26:58,59

JODA
Josech's father was *; Lk 3:23-38

JODA'S
Josech's father was Joda;* father Lk 3:23-38

JOED
Sallu (son of Meshullam, son of *, Neh 11:7,8,9

JOEL
in his place. * and Abijah, his 1Sa 8:2
Meshobab, Jamlech, Joshah, *, 1Ch 4:34-39
great grandson of *). 1Ch 5:7,8
* was a cattle man, and he 1Ch 5:9
* was the greatest and was 1Ch 5:12
by Samuel's sons:*, the oldest; 1Ch 6:28
*, Samuel, Elkanah III, Jeroham, 1Ch 6:33-38
Amasai, Elkanah I, *, Azariah, 1Ch 6:33-38
Michael, Obadiah, *, and Isshiah, 1Ch 7:3
* (brother of Nathan); 1Ch 11:26-47
Gershom; with * as their leader; 1Ch 15:4-10
*, Shemaiah, Eliel, and Amminadab. 1Ch 15:11
Heman (son of *), Asaph (son of 1Ch 15:17
Jehiel the leader, Zetham, *; 1Ch 23:8,9
Zetham and *, the sons of Jehieli. 1Ch 26:20,21,22
Over the half-tribe of Manasseh, * 1Ch 27:16-22
of Amasai) and * (son of 2Ch 29:12,13,14
Zabad, Zebina, Jaddai, *, Benaiah. Ez 10:43
Their chief was *, son of Zichri, Neh 11:7,8,9
the Lord to *, son of Pethuel: Joe 1:1
ago by the prophet *— 'In the Act 2:16

JOEL'S
* descendants were his son 1Ch 5:4

JOGBEHAH
*, Beth-nimrah, Num 32:34,35,36
east of Nobah and *, striking at Ju 8:11

JOGLI
Dan Bukki (son of *) Num 34:16-28

JOHA
Arad, Eder, Michael, Ishpah, *. 1Ch 8:15,16
* (his brother) from Tiza; 1Ch 11:26-47

JOHANAN
Nethaniah; *, the son of Kareah; 2Ki 25:23
Josiah and *. 1Ch 3:15
Pelaiah, Akkub, *, Delaiah, Anani. 1Ch 3:24
*, the father of 1Ch 6:4-15
Jahaziel; *; 1Ch 12:3-7
* was eighth in command; 1Ch 12:8-13
Azariah the son of *, Berechiah the 2Ch 28:12
From the clan of Azgad—* (son of Ez 8:2-14
Eliashib, Joiada, *, and Neh 12:22
days of *, the son of Eliashib. Neh 12:23
of Nethaniah), * and Jonathan (sons Jer 40:8
But soon afterwards * (son of Jer 40:13,14
Then * had a private conference Jer 40:15
with Gedaliah. * volunteered to Jer 40:15
come and murder you?" * asked. Jer 40:15
But when * (son of Kareah) and Jer 41:11
joy when they saw * and his men, Jer 41:13,14
Then * and his men went to the Jer 41:16,17
THEN * AND the army captains and Jer 42:1
So he called for * and the Jer 42:8
of Hoshaiah) and * (son of Kareah) Jer 43:2,3
So * and all the guerrilla Jer 43:4
off for Egypt with * and the other Jer 43:5

JOHN
applying to himself. See * 4:34. Ps 40:7f
* the Baptist began preaching out Mt 3:1
River to be baptized there by *. Mt 3:13
by John. * didn't want to do it. Mt 3:14
So then * baptized him. Mt 3:15
When Jesus heard that * had been Mt 4:12,13
James and *, sitting in a boat with Mt 4:21
One day the disciples of * the Mt 9:14
* (James' brother), Mt 10:2,3,4
* the Baptist, who was now in Mt 11:2
Jesus told them, "Go back to * Mt 11:4
wilderness to see *, what did you Mt 11:7
a prophet. For * is the man Mt 11:10
more brightly than * the Baptist. Mt 11:11
And from the time * the Baptist Mt 11:12
Then * appeared, and if you Mt 11:13
For * the Baptist doesn't even Mt 11:18
"This must be * the Baptist, come Mt 14:2
For Herod had arrested * and Mt 14:3
ex-wife, because * had told him it Mt 14:4
He would have killed * but was Mt 14:5
people believed * was a prophet. Mt 14:5
* the Baptist's head on a tray. Mt 14:8
So * was beheaded in the prison, Mt 14:10
replied, "some say * the Baptist; Mt 16:14
and his brother * to the top of a Mt 17:1
he was speaking of * the Baptist. Mt 17:13
Then the mother of James and *, Mt 20:20
Then he turned to James and * Mt 20:22
what James and * had asked for. Mt 20:24
"Was * the Baptist sent from Mt 21:25
why we didn't believe what * said. Mt 21:25
you do. For * the Baptist told you Mt 21:32
two sons James and *, and began to Mt 26:37
James and * (the sons of Zebedee). Mt 27:56
This messenger was * the Baptist. Mk 1:4
to see and hear *, and when they Mk 1:5
by * there in the Jordan River. Mk 1:9
Later on, after * was arrested by Mk 1:14
*, in a boat mending their nets. Mk 1:19
James and * (the sons of Zebedee, Mk 3:16-19
home except Peter and James and *. Mk 5:37
The king thought Jesus was * the Mk 6:14
"No," Herod said, "it is *, Mk 6:16
and imprison * because he kept Mk 6:17,18
Herodias wanted * killed in Mk 6:19
And Herod respected *, knowing Mk 6:20
he talked with *, but even so he Mk 6:20
"Ask for * the Baptist's head!" Mk 6:24
want the head of * the Mk 6:25
The soldier killed * in the Mk 6:27
"Some of them think you are * Mk 8:28
and * to the top of a mountain. Mk 9:2
One of his disciples, *, told him Mk 9:38
Then James and *, the sons of Mk 10:35
what James and * had asked, they Mk 10:41
What about * the Baptist? Mk 11:30
strongly that * was a prophet. Mk 11:32
Peter, James, *, and Andrew got Mk 13:3,4
He took Peter, James and * with Mk 14:33
It was Peter. * 18:10. Mk 14:47f
And you are to name him *. Lk 1:13
He must be named *!" Lk 1:60
surprise wrote, "His name is *!" Lk 1:63
came from God to * (the son of Lk 3:1
Then * went from place to place Lk 3:3
the prophet, * was "a voice Lk 3:4
* replied, "Don't extort money by Lk 3:14
to know whether or not * was he. Lk 3:15
* answered the question by Lk 3:16
(But after * had publicly Lk 3:19,20
done, Herod put * in prison, thus Lk 3:19,20
and *, the sons of Zebedee. Lk 5:10
of fasting. "* the Baptist's Lk 5:33
*, Philip Lk 6:14,15,16
The disciples of * the Baptist Lk 7:18
When they told * about it, he Lk 7:18
"Go back to * and tell him all you Lk 7:20,21,22
Jesus talked to the crowd about *. Lk 7:24
there is no one greater than *. Lk 7:28
And all who heard * preach—even Lk 7:29
For * the Baptist used to go Lk 7:33

JOHN Con't)
Peter, James, *, and the little Lk 8:51
saying, "This is * the Baptist Lk 9:7
"I beheaded *," Herod said, Lk 9:9
"* the Baptist," they told him, Lk 9:19
* with him into the hills to pray. Lk 9:28
His disciple * came to him and Lk 9:49
of discrimination (cf. * 4:9). Lk 9:53f
James and * said to Jesus, Lk 9:54
just as * taught one to his Lk 11:1
Until * the Baptist began to Lk 16:16
your guides. But * introduced the Lk 16:16
"Was * sent by God, or was he Lk 20:4
But if we say * was not sent Lk 20:6
Jesus sent Peter and * ahead to Lk 22:8
God sent * the Baptist as a Jn 1:6,7
* himself was not the Light; Jn 1:8
* pointed him out to the people, Jn 1:15
Jerusalem to ask * whether he Jn 1:19
* told them, "I merely baptize Jn 1:26
River where * was baptizing. Jn 1:28
The next day * saw Jesus coming Jn 1:29
Then * told about seeing the Holy Jn 1:32
he was the one," * said again, Jn 1:33
The following day as * was Jn 1:35
Jesus walked by. * looked at him Jn 1:36
At this time * the Baptist was Jn 3:23,24
So they came to * and said, Jn 3:26
* replied, "God in heaven Jn 3:27
to him than to * to be baptized and Jn 4:1
See * 2:23. Jn 4:45f
someone else, yes, * the Baptist, Jn 5:32,33
me and be saved. * shone brightly Jn 5:35
I have a greater witness than *. Jn 5:36
See * 1:13. Literally, "the flesh Jn 6:63f
Most ancient manuscripts omit * Jn 7:53f
place where * was first baptizing. Jn 10:40
"* didn't do miracles," they Jn 10:41
See * 12:3. Jn 11:1f
to be *, the writer of this book. Jn 13:23f
*, next to Jesus, was at his side. Jn 13:23f
been asked before (* 13:36, 14:5), Jn 16:5f
"Simon, son of *, do you love me Jn 21:15
son of *, do you really love me?" Jn 21:16
of *, are you even my friend?" Jn 21:17
"* baptized you with Act 1:5
*, James, Act 1:14
he was baptized by * until the day Act 1:21,22
PETER AND * went to the Temple one Act 3:1
As Peter and * were passing by, Act 3:3
holding tightly to Peter and *! Act 3:11
to life again. And * and I are Act 3:15
that Peter and * were claiming that Act 4:2
and Caiaphas, *, Alexander, and Act 4:6
of Peter and *, and could see that Act 4:13
But Peter and * replied, "You Act 4:19
freed, Peter and * found the other Act 4:23
they sent down Peter and *. Act 8:14
Then Peter and * laid their Act 8:17
Samaria, Peter and * returned to Act 8:25
with * the Baptist in Galilee. Act 10:36,37
he said, 'Yes, * baptized with Act 11:16
of Mary, mother of * Mark, where Act 12:12
taking * Mark with them. Act 12:25
and preached. (* Mark went with Act 13:5
There * deserted Act 13:13
"But before he came, * the Act 13:24
sin to God. As * was finishing his Act 13:25
and wanted to take along * Mark. Act 15:37
* had deserted them in Pamphylia. Act 15:38
had told him about * the Baptist Act 18:25,26
Baptist and what * had said about Act 18:25,26
time of *, and all that it meant! Act 18:25,26
And they replied, "What * the Act 19:3
the one * said would come later. Act 19:4
Peter, James, and *, who were known Gal 2:7,8,9
Luke 9:31, 35; * 12:27, 28, 32, 1Jn 5:6,7,8f
Sincerely,* 1Jn 5:21
FROM: *, THE old Elder of the 2Jn 1:1
Sincerely,* 2Jn 1:13
FROM: *, THE Elder. 3Jn 1:1
Sincerely,* 3Jn 1:15
to his servant * in a vision; Rev 1:1
vision's meaning. * wrote it all Rev 1:2
From: * Rev 1:4
* saw this happen with his own Rev 1:7f
It is I, your brother *, a fellow Rev 1:9
a Son of Man"; * recognizes him Rev 1:13f
Literally, "The Logos," as in * Rev 19:13f
And I, *, saw the Holy City, the Rev 21:2
that * could understand. Rev 21:17f
I, *, saw and heard all these Rev 22:8

JOHN'S
about * ministry centuries before! Mt 3:3
* clothing was woven from camel's Mt 3:4
When * disciples had gone, Jesus Mt 11:7
Then * disciples came for his Mt 14:12
* disciples and the Jewish Mk 2:18
off * head and bring it to him. Mk 6:27
When * disciples heard what had Mk 6:29
Here is a sample of * preaching Lk 3:7
When they asked him * question, Lk 7:20,21,22
for them and refused * baptism. Lk 7:30
Then * two disciples turned and Jn 1:37
"You are Simon, * son—but you Jn 1:42
an argument with * disciples, Jn 3:25
reminded you about * witness so Jn 5:34
James (* brother). Act 12:2
out to them that * baptism was to Act 19:4

JOIADA
The Old Gate was repaired by * Neh 3:6
Eliashib was the father of *; Neh 12:10,11
* was the father of Jonathan; Neh 12:10,11
days of Eliashib, *, Johanan, and Neh 12:22

JOIAKIM
Jeshua was the father of *; Neh 12:10,11
* was the father of Eliashib; Neh 12:10,11
served under the High Priest *: Neh 12:12-21
in the time of * (son of Jeshua, Neh 12:26

JOIARIB
I also sent for * and Elnathan, Ez 8:16
of Adaiah, son of *, son of Neh 11:4,5,6
Jedaiah (son of *); Neh 11:10-14
*, Jedaiah, Sallu, Amok, Neh 12:1
Mattenai, leader of the * clan; Neh 12:12-21

JOIN
from the land of Canaan to * me. Gen 46:31
out, they will * our enemies and Ex 1:10
for we must all * in the holy Ex 10:9
"Don't * mobs intent on evil. Ex 23:2,3
on them. * five sheets end to end Ex 26:3
Use loops at the edges to * Ex 26:4,5
wide pieces, to * them together Ex 26:10,11
side, come over here and * me." Ex 32:26
then all the people shall * in. Deu 17:7
shall die and * your ancestors. Deu 31:16
you must die and * your ancestors, Deu 32:50
thousand men to * the troops in Jos 8:11,12,13
is defiled, then * us on our side Jos 22:19
tribe of Simeon. "* us in clearing Ju 1:3
* in his praises— Ju 5:10
in Gibe-ah to * the seven hundred Ju 20:14,15
"Please let David * my staff, for 1Sa 16:22
So David let them * him, and he 1Ch 12:18
inviting them to come and * us. 1Ch 13:2
Jehoshaphat to * forces with him 2Ch 18:2
Ahaziah led his army there to * 2Ch 22:5
Let all others * me, who trust Ps 119:79
and * us"—turn your back on them! Pro 1:10
For I will come and * you there Sol 1:7
will come and * them there and be Is 14:1
Carefully they * the parts Is 41:7
beyond the sea! * in the chorus, Is 42:11
the outsiders who * the people of Is 56:6
don't you * them any more in Jer 16:8
and Judah shall * together, weeping Jer 50:4
they come here to * you as exiles Eze 14:22
of Israel and * them to Judah and Eze 37:18,19,20
Peras, Cush and Put shall * you Eze 38:5
* him in a crusade against Egypt. Dan 11:14
* them, thus fulfilling prophecy, Dan 11:14
O Judah, do not * with those who Hos 4:15
" 'Then go on out and * the Mt 20:7
them to come and * him there; Mk 3:13
where he would * them later. Mk 6:45
place and to * us as witnesses of Act 1:21,22
didn't dare * them, though, but all Act 5:13
him to * them on their journey. Act 16:3
and Timothy to hurry and * him. Act 17:15
who wants to * you, even though his Rom 14:1
Christ and * him to a prostitute? 1Co 6:15
How can they * you in giving 1Co 14:16
you don't eagerly * them any more 1Pe 4:4
side while they * your love feasts 2Pe 2:13
When these men * you at the love Jud 1:12

JOINED
and mother and is * to his wife in Gen 2:24
age of 137, and * his ancestors. Gen 25:17
and back, * at the shoulders. Ex 28:7
* its beautifully woven sash. Ex 39:20
died in Mount Hor and * them. Deu 32:50
Afterwards the army of Judah * Ju 1:17
and * the slaughter from the rear. Ju 20:42
mobilized again and * at Gilgal. 1Sa 13:3,4
revolted and * with the Israelis. 1Sa 14:21
in the hills * the chase when they 1Sa 14:22
and other relatives soon * him. 1Sa 22:1
they were * by additional Syrian 2Sa 10:15,16
"All Israel has * Absalom in a 2Sa 15:13
death (Joab had * Adonijah's 1Ki 2:28
where others * them and 1Ki 11:16,17,18
They urged him to attend, so he * 1Ki 12:2,3,4
By now Ahab's entire army had * 1Ki 20:19
So their two armies, now * also 2Ki 3:9
He * King Joram of Israel (son of 2Ki 8:28
and their men * him at Mizpah. 2Ki 25:23
warriors who * David at Ziklag 1Ch 12:1
Israeli army and * David just as he 1Ch 12:19
More men * David almost every day 1Ch 12:22
of recruits who * David at Hebron. 1Ch 12:23
where they were * by the troops 1Ch 19:7
worthless rebels * him, defying 2Ch 13:7
customs and * the Israelis in Ez 6:21,22
Those with me were * by the Neh 12:40,41
world have * with us in praising Ps 47:9
Assyria has * them too, and is Ps 83:8
Then our fathers * the Ps 106:28
I have not * the people in their Jer 15:17,18
The four living beings were * Eze 1:9
divorce what God has * together." Mt 19:5,6
and woman to be * together Mk 10:6,7
what God has * together." Mk 10:9
Suddenly, the angel was * by a Lk 2:13
warmth, and Peter * them there. Lk 22:55
came along and * them and began Lk 24:15
They * with the other believers Act 2:42
About 400 others * him, but he Act 5:36
and they were soon * by Jews from Act 6:9
of this book, now * Paul and Act 16:10f
a few * him and became believers. Act 17:34
ahead by ship. He * us there and Act 20:14
Others * us at The Three Taverns Act 28:15
are * together as one person. 1Co 6:17
We who believe are carefully * Eph 2:21
And you also are * with him and Eph 2:22
seen to be * together in his Eph 3:10
can be perfectly * to his wife, and Eph 5:31
all of us who are his body are *; Col 2:19
for we are * together by his Col 2:19
martyred on the earth and * them. Rev 6:11

JOINING
Each frame had two clasps * it Ex 36:22
Before long all Israel was * Num 25:3

JOINS
know that if a man * himself to a 1Co 6:16

JOINT
knocked it out of * at the socket. Gen 32:25
and all my bones are out of *. Ps 22:14
shoulder out of * and made her Eze 29:7

JOINTS
Ahab between the * of his armor. 1Ki 22:34

JOKDE-AM
Juttah, Jezreel, *, Zanoah, Kain, Jos 15:48-62

JOKE
and Israel will become a * to the 1Ki 9:7
I am a * among them! Job 30:9
Your enemies * about me, the one Ps 89:51
and make my name a household *. Jer 20:8
and people who * about "today's Jer 23:34

JOKES
coarse *—these are not for you. Eph 5:4

JOKIM
*, the clans of Cozeba 1Ch 4:21-22

JOKING
standing around * about Jesus. Mk 15:31

JOKME-AM
Gezer; *; 1Ch 6:66-69

JOKMEAM
to Abel-meholah and over to *; 1Ki 4:8-19

JOKNE-AM
The king of *, in Carmel; Jos 12:8-24
*, Kartah, Dimnah, and Nahalal. Jos 21:34,35

JOKSHAN
*, Medan,Midian, Ishbak, Shuah. Gen 25:1
*, Medan, 1Ch 1:32

JOKSHAN'S
* two sons were Sheba and Dedan. Gen 25:3
* sons were Sheba and Dedan. 1Ch 1:32

JOKTAN
and * (Peleg's brother). Gen 10:25
* was the father Gen 10:26-30
These descendants of * lived all Gen 10:26-30
different language groups), and *. 1Ch 1:19
The sons of *: 1Ch 1:20-23

JOKTHE-EL
Dilean, Mizpeh, *, Lachish, Jos 15:37-44
to *, as it is called to this day. 2Ki 14:7

JONADAB
friend—his cousin * (the son of 2Sa 13:3
One day * said to Amnon, "What's 2Sa 13:4
"Well," * said, "I'll tell you 2Sa 13:5
But just then * (the son of 2Sa 13:32,33
"See!" * told the king. 2Sa 13:35
"We don't drink, for * our Jer 35:6
that * our father commanded us. Jer 35:10

JONAH
predicted through * (son of 2Ki 14:25
The Lord sent this message to *, Jon 1:1
But * was afraid to go and ran Jon 1:3
And all this time * was sound Jon 1:5
storm; and * drew the short one. Jon 1:7
Then they picked up * and threw Jon 1:15
for a great fish to swallow *. Jon 1:17
swallow Jonah. And * was inside the Jon 1:17
THEN * PRAYED to the Lord his God Jon 2:1
up * on the beach, and it did. Jon 2:10
THEN THE LORD spoke to * again: Jon 3:1
So * obeyed, and went to Nineveh. Jon 3:3
But the very first day when * Jon 3:4,5
people repented. * shouted to the Jon 3:4,5
Nineveh heard what * was saying, he Jon 3:6
THIS CHANGE OF plans made * very Jon 4:1
So * went out and sat sulking Jon 4:5

(JONAH Con't)
wind to blow on *, and the sun beat Jon 4:8
And God said to *, "Is it right Jon 4:9
"Yes," * said, "it is; Jon 4:9
what happened to * the prophet! Mt 12:39,40
For as * was in the great fish Mt 12:39,40
For when * preached to them, they Mt 12:41
And now a greater than * is Mt 12:41
the miracle that happened to *." Mt 16:4
you, Simon, son of *," Jesus said, Mt 16:17
like that of *, whose experiences Lk 11:29,30
repented at the preaching of *; Lk 11:32
and someone far greater than * is Lk 11:32

JONAH'S
out a prayer to Jehovah, * God. Jon 1:14
leaves over * head to shade him. Jon 4:6

JONAM
Joseph's father was *; Lk 3:23-38

JONAM'S
Joseph's father was Jonam;* father Lk 3:23-38

JONATHAN
a man named * (son of Gershom and Ju 18:30
remained with *, Saul's son, in 1Sa 13:2
Then * attacked and destroyed 1Sa 13:3,4
Saul and * and these six hundred 1Sa 13:16
A DAY OR so later, Prince * said 1Sa 14:1
No one realized that * had gone. 1Sa 14:3
garrison, * had to go over a narrow 1Sa 14:4
* had said to his bodyguard. 1Sa 14:6
is what we'll do," * told him. 1Sa 14:8
Then they shouted to *, "Come 1Sa 14:12
right behind me," * exclaimed to 1Sa 14:12
fell back as * and the lad killed 1Sa 14:13
* and his bodyguard were gone. 1Sa 14:17
Saul's curse. *, however, had not 1Sa 14:27
"That's ridiculous!" * 1Sa 14:29
own son *, he shall surely die!" 1Sa 14:39
Then Saul proposed, "* and I 1Sa 14:40
What is wrong? Are * and I 1Sa 14:41
And * and Saul were chosen by 1Sa 14:41
draw lots between me and *." 1Sa 14:42
And * was chosen as the guilty 1Sa 14:42
you've done," Saul demanded of *. 1Sa 14:43
"I tasted a little honey," * 1Sa 14:43
"Yes, *," Saul said, "you must 1Sa 14:44
But the troops retorted, "*, who 1Sa 14:45
So the people rescued *. 1Sa 14:45
Saul had three sons, *, Ishvi, 1Sa 14:49
David, David met *, the king's son, 1Sa 18:1
love between them. * swore to be 1Sa 18:1
his son * to assassinate David. 1Sa 19:1
David. But *, because of his close 1Sa 19:1
as * and his father were talking 1Sa 19:4
anything to harm you," * pleaded. 1Sa 19:4
Afterwards * called David and 1Sa 19:7
from Naioth in Ramah, and found *. 1Sa 20:1
"That's not true!" * protested. 1Sa 20:2
not tell *—why should I hurt him?' 1Sa 20:3
"Tell me what I can do," * 1Sa 20:4
"Of course not!" * exclaimed. 1Sa 20:9
to the field with me," * replied. 1Sa 20:11
Then * told David, "I promise by 1Sa 20:12
So * made a covenant with the 1Sa 20:16
his promise. But * made David 1Sa 20:17
Then * said, "Yes, they will 1Sa 20:18
against the wall. * sat opposite 1Sa 20:24,25
day, Saul asked *, "Why hasn't 1Sa 20:27
a family celebration," * replied. 1Sa 20:28,29
"But what has he done?" * 1Sa 20:32
Then Saul hurled his spear at *, 1Sa 20:33
so at last * realized that his 1Sa 20:33
David must die. * left the table 1Sa 20:34
The next morning, as agreed, * 1Sa 20:35
So the boy ran and * shot an 1Sa 20:36
reached the arrow, * shouted, "The 1Sa 20:37
didn't understand what * meant; 1Sa 20:39
meant; only * and David knew. 1Sa 20:39
Then * gave his bow and arrows 1Sa 20:40
At last * said to David, "Cheer 1Sa 20:42
away and * returning to the city. 1Sa 20:42
(Prince * now went to find David; 1Sa 23:16
"Don't be afraid," * reassured 1Sa 23:17
at Horesh while * returned home. 1Sa 23:18
sons *, Abinidab, and Malchishua. 1Sa 31:2
and his son * have been killed." 2Sa 1:4
Saul and his son *, and for the 2Sa 1:12
dirge for Saul and * and afterward 2Sa 1:17,18
Both Saul and * slew their 2Sa 1:22
Both Saul and *! 2Sa 1:23
* is slain upon the hills. 2Sa 1:25
How I weep for you, my brother *; 2Sa 1:26
who was the son of Prince *. 2Sa 4:4
the time Saul and * were killed at 2Sa 4:4
them, as he had promised Prince *. 2Sa 9:1
of my vow to your father *. 2Sa 9:7
son Ahima-az and Abiathar's son *. 2Sa 15:27
sons Ahima-az and * to find me and 2Sa 15:35,36
* and Ahima-az had been staying 2Sa 17:17
seen Ahima-az and *, she said they 2Sa 17:20
of the oath between himself and *. 2Sa 21:7
bring him the bones of Saul and *. 2Sa 21:12,13,14
and David's nephew *—the son of 2Sa 21:20,21
* -from harar 2Sa 23:24-39
still speaking, *, the son of 1Ki 1:42
Solomon as king!" * shouted. 1Ki 1:43
*. Jether died without children, 1Ch 2:32
children, but * had two sons named 1Ch 2:33
*, Malchishua, Abinadab, Eshbaal. 1Ch 8:33
The son of * was Mephibosheth; 1Ch 8:34
Saul was the father of *, 1Ch 9:39
* was the father of Mephibosheth; 1Ch 9:40
his three sons, *, Abinadab, and 1Ch 10:2
* (son of Shagee) from Harar; 1Ch 11:26-47
by David's nephew *, the son of 1Ch 20:6,7
treasuries, and * (son of Uzziah) 1Ch 27:25
king's sons was *, David's uncle, a 1Ch 27:32
(son of *), and 50 other men; Ez 8:2-14
Only * (son of Asahel), Jahzeiah Ez 10:15
Joiada was the father of *; Neh 12:10,11
* was the father of Jaddu-a. Neh 12:10,11
*, leader of the Malluchi clan; Neh 12:12-21
Zechariah (son of *, son of Neh 12:35,36
under the house of * the scribe, Jer 37:15,16
Johanan and * (sons of Kareah), Jer 40:8

JONATHAN'S
that day, except for Saul's and *. 1Sa 13:22
"Yes," Ziba replied, "* lame 2Sa 9:3
* son and Saul's grandson. 2Sa 9:5,6
He spared * son Mephibosheth, who 2Sa 21:7
to the dungeon in * house, for you Jer 38:26

JOPPA
Rakkon, also the territory near *. Jos 19:41-46
across the sea to *, and from there 2Ch 2:16
Sea to *, for King Cyrus had Ez 3:7
to the port of *, where he found a Jon 1:3
In the city of * there was a Act 9:36
beg him to return with them to *. Act 9:38
*, living with Simon, the tanner. Act 9:43
Now send some men to * to find a Act 10:5,6
happened and sent them off to *. Act 10:8
by some other believers from *. Act 10:23
Now send some men to * and Act 10:32
"One day in *," he said, Act 11:5
to * to find Simon Peter! Act 11:13

JORAH
From the subclan of *, 112; Ez 2:3-35

JORAI
Sheba, *, Jacan, Zia, and Eber. 1Ch 5:13

JORAM
he sent his son * to congratulate 2Sa 8:10
King * of Israel, the son of Ahab. 2Ki 8:16
Literally, "*." 2Ki 8:21f
The rest of the history of King * 2Ki 8:23
King * of Israel, the son of Ahab. 2Ki 8:24,25
He joined King * of Israel (son 2Ki 8:28
King * was wounded in the battle, 2Ki 8:28
Nimshi) rebelled against King *. 2Ki 9:14
(King * had been with the army at 2Ki 9:14
*, who was lying there wounded. 2Ki 9:16
or foe," King * shouted back. 2Ki 9:17
King * commanded. 2Ki 9:21
Naboth, and King * demanded, "Do 2Ki 9:22
Then King * reined the 2Ki 9:23
and shot * between the shoulders; 2Ki 9:24
year of the reign of King * of 2Ki 9:29
Abijah, Asa, Jehoshaphat, *, 1Ch 3:10-14
*, Zichri, and Shelomoth. 1Ch 26:25
Jehoshaphat was the father of *; Mt 1:8
Joram; * was the father of Uzziah; Mt 1:8

JORDAN
plains of the * River, well watered Gen 13:10
So that is what Lot chose—the * Gen 13:11
Literally, "passed over this *." Gen 32:10f
them across the * River at the Gen 32:22,23,24
Located just west of the * River, Gen 50:10f
beyond the * River, they held a Gen 50:10
Sea and in the * River valley are Num 13:29
of the * River opposite Jericho. Num 22:1
the * River, opposite Jericho. Num 26:3,4
the * River, across from Jericho. Num 26:63
the * River, across from Jericho. Num 31:12
the other side of the * River." Num 32:5
land on the other side of the *; Num 32:19
troops across the * until the Lord Num 32:21
go with you over *, then, when the Num 32:29
be here on this side of the *." Num 32:32
the river *, opposite Jericho. Num 33:48
places along the * River, from Num 33:49
pass across the * River into the Num 33:50,51
* River, ending at the Dead Sea." Num 34:12
side of the *, opposite Jericho." Num 34:14,15
camped beside the * on the plains Num 35:1
on the east side of the * River. Num 35:13,14
the * River, across from Jericho. Num 36:13
of Moab, east of the * River. Deu 1:1
We are on our way across the * Deu 2:29
east of the * River—all the land Deu 3:8
bounded by the * River on the west, Deu 3:17
tribes across the * to the land the Deu 3:18
them across the * River, then you Deu 3:20
on the other side of the *. Deu 3:21
land beyond the * River with its Deu 3:23,24,25
But you shall not cross the * Deu 3:27
not go over the * River into the Deu 4:21,22
Soon, now, you will cross the * Deu 4:26
cities east of the * River, where Deu 4:41
camped east of the * River near the Deu 4:44,45,46
two Amorite kings east of the *. Deu 4:47
and all the Arabah east of the * Deu 4:49
Today you are to cross the * Deu 9:1
west of the * River, where the Deu 11:30
For you are to cross the * and Deu 11:31
But when you cross the * River Deu 12:10
"When you cross the * River and Deu 27:2,3,4
I shall not cross the * River. Deu 31:2
to possess across the * River." Deu 32:47
and the * Valley; Deu 34:3
Lead my people across the * River Jos 1:2
to get ready to cross the * River. Jos 1:10,11
east side of the * River," Moses Jos 1:12,13
tribes across the * River to help Jos 1:14
here on the east side of the *." Jos 1:15
to the * River looking for them; Jos 2:7
kings east of the *, and how you Jos 2:10
the banks of the * River, where Jos 3:1
* was overflowing all its banks; Jos 3:13,14
the middle of the * and waited as Jos 3:17
the middle of the *, and to carry Jos 4:2,3
middle of the * where the Ark is. Jos 4:5
remind us that the * River stopped Jos 4:7
the middle of the * river—one for Jos 4:8
nation crossed the * River and Jos 4:19
the * were piled up as a monument. Jos 4:20
crossed the * River on dry ground! Jos 4:22
WHEN THE NATIONS west of the * Jos 5:1
had dried up the * River so the Jos 5:1
us over the * River if you are Jos 7:7
west of the * River, along the Jos 9:1
east side of the * River whose Jos 12:1
Sihon also controlled the * Jos 12:3
Israel on the west side of the *. Jos 12:7
east side of the *, for Moses had Jos 13:8
son of Beor. The * River was the Jos 13:23
of Heshbon. The * River was the Jos 13:27,28
turned east from the * River. Jos 13:27,28
land east of the * River where the Jos 13:32
on the east side of the * River. Jos 14:3,4
Sea to the mouth of the * River. Jos 15:5
the bay where the * River empties Jos 15:5
This boundary extended from the * Jos 16:1
Jericho, and ended at the * River. Jos 16:7
[on the east side of the * River Jos 17:1
land on the west side of the * Jos 17:2
and Bashan across the * River). Jos 17:5,6
east side of the * where Moses Jos 18:7
began at the * River, went north of Jos 18:12
the southern end of the * River. Jos 18:19
The eastern border was the * Jos 18:20
of Issachar ended at the * River. Jos 19:17-23
and Lakkum, ending at the * River. Jos 19:33
and with the * River at the east. Jos 19:34
the * River, across from Jericho. Jos 20:8
on the other side of the * River. Jos 22:4
d on the west side of the *. Jos 22:7,8
and crossed the * River to their Jos 22:9
The Lord has placed the * River Jos 22:24,25
All the land from the * River to Jos 23:4,5
on the other side of the *; Jos 24:8
"Then you crossed the * River Jos 24:11
the fords of the * River near Moab, Ju 3:28
did Gilead remain across the *, Ju 5:17
They crossed the * and camped in Ju 6:33
the fords of the * River at Ju 7:24
and Zeeb across the * to Gideon. Ju 7:25
Gideon now crossed the * River Ju 8:4
place east of the * River in the Ju 10:7,8
For the Ammonites crossed the * Ju 10:9
and the * was his, he claimed. Ju 11:13
the wilderness to the * River. Ju 11:21,22
He captured the fords of the * Ju 12:5
the * in the land of Gilead. Ju 20:1
Some of them crossed the * River 1Sa 13:7
and beyond the * heard that their 1Sa 31:7
across the * Valley, crossed the 2Sa 2:29
I will stop at the ford of the * 2Sa 15:28
the ford of the * River tonight. 2Sa 17:16
they told him, "cross the * 2Sa 17:21
the men across the * River. 2Sa 17:24
And when he arrived at the * 2Sa 19:15
they rushed down to the * to 2Sa 19:17
So all the people crossed the * 2Sa 19:39
and his household across the *. 2Sa 19:41
him from the * to Jerusalem. 2Sa 20:2
First they crossed the * and 2Sa 24:5
to meet me at the * River I 1Ki 2:8
the plains of the * River between 1Ki 7:41-46
of where it enters the * River. 1Ki 17:3
Lord has sent me to the * River." 2Ki 2:6,7
stood beside the * River as fifty 2Ki 2:6,7
to the bank of the * River, and 2Ki 2:13,14
go and wash in the * River seven 2Ki 5:10
So Naaman went down to the * 2Ki 5:14
down beside the * River, where 2Ki 6:1

(JORDAN Con't)

When they arrived at the *, they	2Ki 6:4
all the way to the * River—thrown	2Ki 7:15
he crossed the * River and attacked	2Ki 8:21
east of the * River, as well as all	2Ki 10:32,33
And across the * River, opposite	1Ch 6:78,79
They crossed the * River during	1Ch 12:15
From the other side of the *	1Ch 12:24-37
crossed the * River, and engaged	1Ch 19:17,18
of Israel west of the * River;	1Ch 26:30
claybanks of the * valley between	2Ch 4:17,18
swelling * rushes down upon him.	Job 40:23
land where the * River flows and	Ps 42:6
them across the ever-flowing *.	Ps 74:15
before them. The * River opened up	Ps 114:3
What happened, * River, to your	Ps 114:5
them at the fording points of *.	Jer 22:20
the fields toward the * valley.	Jer 39:4
* stalking the sheep in the fold.	Jer 49:19
the jungles of * that leaps upon	Jer 50:44
along the course of the * River	Eze 26:2
the desert and the * Valley to the	Eze 47:8
westward to the * at the southern	Eze 47:18
and down along the * River	Eze 47:18
glorious * valley lies in ruins.	Zec 11:3
from all over the * Valley, and, in	Mt 3:5
he baptized them in the * River.	Mt 3:6
Galilee to the * River to be	Mt 3:13
beyond the * River, and Upper	Mt 4:15,16
and even from across the * River.	Mt 4:25
to Judea from across the * River.	Mt 19:1
he baptized them in the * River.	Mk 1:5
by John there in the * River.	Mk 1:9
from beyond the * River, and even	Mk 3:7,8
into the area east of the * River.	Mk 10:1
both sides of the * River,	Lk 3:3
Holy Spirit, left the * River,	Lk 4:1
* River where John was baptizing.	Jn 1:28
other side of the * River—the one	Jn 3:26
went beyond the * River to stay	Jn 10:40

JORDAN'S

what will you do in * jungles?	Jer 12:5

JORIM

Eliezer's father was *;	Lk 3:23-38

JORIM'S

Eliezer's father was Jorim;*	Lk 3:23-38

JORKE-AM

of Raham, who was the father of *.	1Ch 2:44

JOSECH

Semein's father was *;	Lk 3:23-38

JOSECH'S

Semein's father was Josech;*	Lk 3:23-38

JOSEDECH

and to Joshua (son of *), the	Hag 1:1
and Joshua (son of *), the High	Hag 1:12
Joshua (son of *) the High Priest.	Zec 6:10,11

JOSEPH

And she named him * (meaning	Gen 30:23,24
Soon after the birth of * to	Gen 30:25
next, and Rachel and * last.	Gen 33:2
and * came and made their bows.	Gen 33:7
The sons of Rachel:*, Benjamin.	Gen 35:24
Jacob's son * was now seventeen	Gen 37:2
flocks. But * reported to his	Gen 37:2
Israel loved * more than any of his	Gen 37:3
* was born to him in his old age.	Gen 37:3
and consequently hated *;	Gen 37:4
One night * had a dream and	Gen 37:5
Israel called for *, and told him,	Gen 37:13,14
"Very good," * replied.	Gen 37:13,14
and their flocks," * replied.	Gen 37:16
to Dothan." So * followed them to	Gen 37:17
So when * got there, they	Gen 37:23
Let's sell * to them!	Gen 37:26,27
came by, his brothers pulled *	Gen 37:28
returned to get * out of the	Gen 37:29
of the well. When * wasn't there,	Gen 37:29
A wild animal has eaten him. * is	Gen 37:33
the traders sold * to Potiphar, an	Gen 37:36
WHEN * ARRIVED in Egypt as a	Gen 39:1
The Lord greatly blessed * there	Gen 39:2
was with * in a very special way.	Gen 39:3
special way. So * naturally became	Gen 39:4
So Potiphar gave * the complete	Gen 39:6
in the world with * there, except	Gen 39:6
he wanted to eat! *, by the way,	Gen 39:6
making eyes at *, and suggested	Gen 39:7
* refused.	Gen 39:8
He threw * into prison, where	Gen 39:20
But the Lord was with * there,	Gen 39:21
administration to *, so that all	Gen 39:22
after that, for * took care of	Gen 39:23
the prison where * was, in the	Gen 40:1
assigned * to wait on them.	Gen 40:4
The next morning * noticed that	Gen 40:6
is God's business," * replied.	Gen 40:8
what the dream means," * said.	Gen 40:12
he told his dream to *, too.	Gen 40:16
mean three days," * told him.	Gen 40:18,19
impaled, just as * had predicted.	Gen 40:22
*, never giving him a thought.	Gen 40:23
Pharaoh sent at once for *.	Gen 41:14
"I can't do it by myself," *	Gen 41:16
the same thing," * told Pharaoh.	Gen 41:25
"Who could do it better than *?	Gen 41:38
Turning to *, Pharaoh said to	Gen 41:39
Pharaoh also gave * the chariot	Gen 41:43
And Pharaoh declared to *,	Gen 41:44
* thus married into a family of	Gen 41:45f
So * became famous throughout the	Gen 41:45
of the king. * went out from the	Gen 41:46
During those years, *	Gen 41:48
sons were born to * by Asenath, the	Gen 41:50
Re of Heliopolis. * named his	Gen 41:51
began, just as * had predicted.	Gen 41:54
for food, and he sent them to *.	Gen 41:55
over the world, * opened up the	Gen 41:56,57
came to Egypt to buy grain from *.	Gen 41:56,57
to him [as it had to his brother *	Gen 42:4
Since * was governor of all	Gen 42:6
to the earth. * recognized them	Gen 42:7
Then * remembered the dreams of	Gen 42:8,9
"So?" * asked.	Gen 42:14
The third day * said to them, "I	Gen 42:18
of what we did to * long ago.	Gen 42:21
Of course they didn't know that *	Gen 42:23
their eyes. * then ordered his	Gen 42:25
me of my children—* didn't come	Gen 42:36
for his brother * is dead and he	Gen 42:38
went to Egypt, and stood before *.	Gen 43:15
When * saw that Benjamin was	Gen 43:16
When * came home they gave him	Gen 43:26
Then * made a hasty exit, for	Gen 43:30
* ate by himself, his brothers	Gen 43:32
* ordered his household manager	Gen 44:1
out of the city, * said to his	Gen 44:4
to the city. * was still home when	Gen 44:14
"What were you trying to do?" *	Gen 44:15
"No," * said.	Gen 44:17
* COULD STAND it no longer.	Gen 45:1
"I am *!"	Gen 45:3
And he said again, "I am *, your	Gen 45:4
him, 'Your son * says, "God has	Gen 45:9
Then Pharaoh said to *, "Tell	Gen 45:17
So * gave them wagons, as Pharaoh	Gen 45:21
"* is alive," they shouted to	Gen 45:26
with food that * had sent him, his	Gen 45:27
And he said, "It must be true! *	Gen 45:28
but you shall die in Egypt with *	Gen 46:3,4
* and Benjamin;	Gen 46:19-22
on ahead to tell * that they were	Gen 46:28
they did. * jumped into his	Gen 46:29
Then Israel said to *, "Now let	Gen 46:30
And * said to his brothers and to	Gen 46:31
UPON THEIR ARRIVAL, * went in to	Gen 47:1
And Pharaoh said to *, "Choose	Gen 47:5,6
Then * brought his father Jacob	Gen 47:7
So * assigned the best land of	Gen 47:11
commanded. And * furnished food to	Gen 47:12
were starving. * collected all the	Gen 47:14
came to * crying again for food.	Gen 47:15
"Well then," * replied, "give	Gen 47:16
So they brought their cattle to *	Gen 47:17
So * bought all the land of Egypt	Gen 47:20
Then * said to the people, "See,	Gen 47:23
So * made it a law throughout the	Gen 47:26
called for his son * and said to	Gen 47:29
And * promised.	Gen 47:30
it," Jacob insisted. And * did.	Gen 47:31
this, word came to * that his	Gen 48:1
When Jacob heard that * had	Gen 48:2
"Yes," * told him, "these are	Gen 48:9
hardly see. So * brought the boys	Gen 48:10
And Israel said to *, "I never	Gen 48:11
* took the boys by the hand,	Gen 48:12,13
Then he blessed * with this	Gen 48:15
But * was upset and displeased	Gen 48:17
Then Israel said to *, "I am	Gen 48:21
"* is a fruitful tree beside a	Gen 49:22
upon the head of * who was exiled	Gen 49:26
* THREW HIMSELF upon his father's	Gen 50:1
mourning was over, * approached	Gen 50:4
father made * swear to take his	Gen 50:5
So * went, and a great number of	Gen 50:7
cavalry, and people accompanied *.	Gen 50:9
Then * returned to Egypt with his	Gen 50:14
"Now * will pay us back for all	Gen 50:15
When * read the message, he	Gen 50:16,17
But * told them, "Don't be	Gen 50:19
So * and his brothers and their	Gen 50:22
* was 110 years old when he died.	Gen 50:22
"Soon I will die," * told his	Gen 50:24
Then * made his brothers	Gen 50:25
to Canaan. So * died at the age of	Gen 50:26
seventy (for * was already there).	Ex 1:5
In due season * and each of his	Ex 1:6
Literally, "who did not know *."	Ex 1:8f
to the descendants of *.	Ex 1:8
Moses took the bones of * with	Ex 13:19
with them, for * had made the sons	Ex 13:19
Ephraim (son of *)	Num 1:2-15
Manassh (son of *)	Num 1:2-15
*: Manasseh (son of	Num 1:20-46
son of *)	Num 1:20-46
*: Ephraim (son of Joseph	Num 1:20-46
* -40,500	Num 1:20-46
Igal, son of *, from the tribe of	Num 13:3-15
from the tribe of * (actually, the	Num 13:3-15
The tribe of *: 32,500 in the	Num 26:28-37
of Manasseh (a son of *).	Num 27:1
half-tribe of Manasseh (son of *).	Num 32:33
one of the sons of *) came to Moses	Num 36:1
of * have a proper complaint.	Num 36:5
own tribe of Manasseh (son of *);	Num 36:11,12
Judah, Issachar, *, and Benjamin	Deu 27:12
Concerning the tribe of *, he	Deu 33:13
all these blessings come upon *,	Deu 33:16
The tribe of * had become two	Jos 14:3,4
of the Tribes of * (Ephraim and the	Jos 16:1
Then the two tribes of * came to	Jos 17:14
"Fine," said the tribes of *,	Jos 17:16,17,18
to the tribes of Judah and *.	Jos 18:11
The bones of *, which the people	Jos 24:32
assigned to the tribes of *.	Jos 24:32
As for the tribe of *, they	Ju 1:22,23
the tribe of * conquered them and	Ju 1:35
all the tribe of * to greet you."	2Sa 19:20
battalions from the tribe of *.	1Ki 11:27,28
*, Benjamin, Naphtali, Gad, Asher.	1Ch 2:1
was given to his half brother, *.	1Ch 5:1
Although * received the	1Ch 5:2
descendants of * the son of Israel,	1Ch 7:29
*, Nethaniah, and Asharelah.	1Ch 25:2
The first toss indicated * of the	1Ch 25:9-31
Amariah, *.	Ez 10:34-42
*, leader of the Shebaniah clan;	Neh 12:12-21
of Jacob and of * by your might.	Ps 77:15
Then he sent * as a slave to	Ps 105:17
tribe of * (Ephraim and Manesseh	Eze 47:13
be named for *, Benjamin and Dan.	Eze 48:32
Jacob was the father of * (who	Mt 1:16
was engaged to be married to *.	Mt 1:18
Then *, her fiancé,	Mt 1:19
beside him. "*, son of David,"	Mt 1:20
When * awoke, he did as the angel	Mt 1:24
born; and * named him "Jesus."	Mt 1:25
the Lord appeared to * in a dream.	Mt 2:13
in a dream to * in Egypt, and told	Mt 2:19
*, Simon, and Judas.	Mt 13:55
of James and *, and the mother of	Mt 27:56
Arimathea named *, one of Jesus'	Mt 27:57
it to him. * took the body and	Mt 27:59
of James and *, Judas and Simon.	Mk 6:2,3
Late that afternoon * from	Mk 15:42,43
told * he could have the body.	Mk 15:45
* bought a long sheet of linen	Mk 15:46
*, a descendant of King David.	Lk 1:27
And because * was a member of	Lk 2:4
and found their way to Mary and *.	Lk 2:16
and so, when Mary and * arrived	Lk 2:27
* and Mary just stood there,	Lk 2:33
with Mary and *, and she also began	Lk 2:38
*.Joseph's father was Heli;	Lk 3:23-38
Jannai's father was *;	Lk 3:23-38
Judah's father was *;	Lk 3:23-38
Then a man named *, a member of	Lk 23:50,51,52
His name is Jesus, the son of *	Jn 1:45
of ground Jacob gave to his son *.	Jn 4:5,6
Jesus the son of *, whose father	Jn 6:42
Afterwards * of Arimathea, who	Jn 19:38
The assembly nominated two men: *	Act 1:23
For instance, there was * (the	Act 4:36
These men were very jealous of *	Act 7:9
God also gave * unusual wisdom,	Act 7:10
The second time they went, *	Act 7:13
Then * sent for his father Jacob	Act 7:14
And it was by faith that *, as he	Heb 11:22
* 12,000	Rev 7:4-8

JOSEPH'S

One day * brothers took their	Gen 37:12
But Reuben hoped to spare * life.	Gen 37:21,22
its blood on * coat, and took the	Gen 37:31
"Is it * coat or not?"	Gen 37:32
blessing Potiphar for * sake.	Gen 39:5
* suggestions were well received	Gen 41:37
own signet ring on * finger as a	Gen 41:41,42
So * ten older	Gen 42:3
However, Jacob wouldn't let *	Gen 42:4
told and took them to * palace.	Gen 43:17
they went over to * household	Gen 43:19
presents ready for * arrival at	Gen 43:25
He was also told to put * own	Gen 44:2
Pharaoh—"* brothers have come";	Gen 45:16
But when they had given him *	Gen 45:27
* sons, born in the land of Egypt,	Gen 46:19-22
With * two sons included, this	Gen 46:27
them, "that * father made Joseph	Gen 50:5
as well as all of * people—his	Gen 50:8
of lamentation for * father.	Gen 50:10
dead, * brothers were frightened.	Gen 50:15
four hundred years after * death.	Ex 1:8f
of Manasseh (* oldest son):	Jos 17:1
But he rejected * family, the	Ps 78:67

(JOSEPH'S Con't)
Joseph.* father was Heli; Lk 3:23-38
Jannai's father was Joseph;* Lk 3:23-38
Judah's father was Joseph;* father Lk 3:23-38
"Isn't this * son?" Lk 4:22
who had no respect for * memory. Act 7:17,18
blessed each of * two sons as he Heb 11:21

JOSEPHUS
According to *, Chimham was 2Sa 19:37f

JOSES
and of *), Salome, and others. Mk 15:40
Mary the mother of * were watching Mk 15:47

JOSHAH
Meshobab, Jamlech, *, Joel, Jehu, 1Ch 4:34-39

JOSHAPHAT
* from Mithna; 1Ch 11:26-47
Shebaniah, *, Nethanel, Amasai, 1Ch 15:24

JOSHAVIAH
Jeribai and * (sons of Elna-am); 1Ch 11:26-47

JOSHBEKASHA
Seventeenth, * and twelve of his 1Ch 25:9-31

JOSHBEKASHAH
Romamti-ezer, *, Mallothi, Hothir, 1Ch 25:4,5

JOSHEB-BASSHEBETH
the first was * from Tah-chemon, 2Sa 23:8

JOSHUA
Moses instructed * to issue a Ex 17:9
So * and his men went out to Ex 17:10
As a result, * and his troops Ex 17:13
and announce to * that I will Ex 17:14
So Moses and *, his assistant, Ex 24:13
When * heard the noise below Ex 32:17
who assisted him, * (son of Nun), Ex 33:11
happening, and * (the son of Nun), Num 11:28
Or, "*." See verse 16. Num 13:3-15f
Moses changed Hoshea's name to *. Num 13:16
"salvation"; "*" means Num 13:16f
is salvation." * is the same name Num 13:16f
two of the spies, * (the son of Num 14:6
of Jephunneh) and * (son of Nun) Num 14:30
Of all the spies, only * and Num 14:36,37,38
of Jephunneh) and * (son of Nun). Num 26:64,65
The Lord replied, "Go and get * Num 27:18
instructions to * and the people. Num 27:21
and took * to Eleazar the priest. Num 27:22
the Kenizzite) and * (son of Num 32:12
saying to Eleazar, *, and the Num 32:28
the priest, * (son of Nun), and one Num 34:16-28
Instead, your assistant, * (the Deu 1:38
"Then I said to *, 'You have Deu 3:21
Commission * to replace you, and Deu 3:28
overcome them. * is your new Deu 31:3
Then Moses called for * and said Deu 31:7
Summon * and come into the Deu 31:14
So Moses and * came and stood Deu 31:14
Then he charged * (son of Nun) Deu 31:23
When Moses and * had recited all Deu 32:44,45
* (son of Nun) was full of the Deu 34:9
whose name was * (the son of Nun), Jos 1:1
Then * issued instructions to the Jos 1:10,11
* as their commander-in-chief. Jos 1:16
THEN * SENT two spies from the Jos 2:1
* all that had happened to them. Jos 2:23
EARLY THE NEXT morning * and all Jos 3:1
Then * told the people to perform Jos 3:5
In the morning * ordered the Jos 3:6
"Today," the Lord told *, "I Jos 3:7
Then * summoned all the people Jos 3:9
safely across, the Lord said to *, Jos 4:1
So * summoned the twelve men, Jos 4:4
So the men did as * told them. Jos 4:8
just as the Lord had commanded *. Jos 4:8
a monument there. * also built Jos 4:9
* by Moses, had been carried out. Jos 4:10
It was a tremendous day for *! Jos 4:14
For it was * who, at the Lord's Jos 4:15,16
So * issued the order. Jos 4:17
Then * explained again the Jos 4:21
The Lord then told * to set aside Jos 5:2,3
So now * circumcised their Jos 5:7
And the Lord said to *, "Today I Jos 5:8,9
As * was sizing up the city of Jos 5:13
a drawn sword. * strode over to him Jos 5:13
* fell to the ground before him Jos 5:14
And * did. Jos 5:15
But the Lord said to *, "Jericho Jos 6:2
So * summoned the priests and Jos 6:6-9
for the trumpets," * commanded. Jos 6:10
* yelled to the people, "Shout! Jos 6:16
Then * said to the two spies, Jos 6:22
Thus * saved Rahab the Jos 6:25
the spies sent to Jericho by *. Jos 6:25
Then * declared a terrible curse Jos 6:26
So the Lord was with *, and his Jos 6:27
Soon after Jericho's defeat, * Jos 7:2
Upon their return they told * Jos 7:3
turn of events. * and the elders Jos 7:6
* cried out to the Lord, "O Jos 7:7
But the Lord said to *, "Get up Jos 7:10,11
So, early the next morning, * Jos 7:16
* said to Achan, "My son, give Jos 7:19
So * sent some men to search for Jos 7:22
They brought it all to * and Jos 7:23
Then * and all the Israelites Jos 7:24
Then * said to Achan, "Why have Jos 7:25
THEN THE LORD said to *, "Don't Jos 8:1
army left for Ai, * sent thirty Jos 8:3,4
side of Ai; but * and the rest of Jos 8:9
Early the next morning * roused Jos 8:10
That night * sent another five Jos 8:11,12,13
behind the city. * and the Israeli Jos 8:15
Then the Lord said to *, "Point Jos 8:18
I will give you the city." * did. Jos 8:18
to go. When * and the troops who Jos 8:20,21
who was captured and brought to *. Jos 8:23
out that day. For * kept his spear Jos 8:26
(The Lord had told * they could. Jos 8:27
* hanged the king of Ai on a tree Jos 8:29
Then * built an altar to the Lord Jos 8:30
of Israel watched, * carved upon Jos 8:32
before by Moses.) * then read to Jos 8:34
lives against * and the Israelis. Jos 9:1
They sent ambassadors to * Jos 9:3,4,5
Gilgal, they told * and the men of Jos 9:6
"But who are you?" * demanded. Jos 9:8
* and the other leaders finally Jos 9:14,15
* summoned their leaders and Jos 9:22
So * would not allow the people Jos 9:26
heard how * had captured and Jos 10:1
with * and the people of Israel." Jos 10:4
sent messengers to * at Gilgal. Jos 10:6
So * and the Israeli army left Jos 10:7
the Lord said to *, "for they are Jos 10:8
* traveled all night from Gilgal Jos 10:9
harassing the foe, * prayed aloud, Jos 10:12
(Afterwards * and the Israeli Jos 10:15
When the news was brought to * Jos 10:17
Then * commanded the rest of the Jos 10:19
So * and the Israeli army Jos 10:20
* now instructed his men to Jos 10:22,23
and Eglon. * told the captains of Jos 10:24
discouraged," * said to his men. Jos 10:25
With that, * plunged his sword Jos 10:26
As the sun was going down, * Jos 10:27
On that same day * destroyed the Jos 10:28
So * and his army conquered the Jos 10:40
Then * and his army returned to Jos 10:43
But the Lord said to *, "Don't Jos 11:6
their chariots." * and his troops Jos 11:7
Then * and his men did as the Jos 11:9
On the way back, * captured Hazor Jos 11:10
(However, * did not burn any of Jos 11:13
commandment on to *, who did as he Jos 11:15
So * conquered the entire Jos 11:16
Mount Hermon. And * killed all the Jos 11:17
During this period * routed all Jos 11:21
So * took the entire land just as Jos 11:23
kings destroyed by * and the armies Jos 12:7
* to the other tribes of Israel. Jos 12:7
* WAS NOW an old man. Jos 13:1
Eleazar the priest, *, and the Jos 14:1
led by Caleb, came to * in Gilgal. Jos 14:6
Caleb asked *. Jos 14:6
So * blessed him and gave him Jos 14:13,14
The Lord instructed * to assign Jos 15:13
the priest and to * and the Israeli Jos 17:4
of Joseph came to * and asked, Jos 17:14
enough for you," * replied, "and Jos 17:15
forests," * replied, "and since Jos 17:16,17,18
Then * asked them, "How long are Jos 18:3
to bring back their report to *. Jos 18:8
Then they returned to * and the Jos 18:9
the Lord showed * by the sacred Jos 18:10
piece of land to *, for the Lord Jos 19:49
Eleazar the priest, *, and the Jos 19:51
THE LORD SAID to *, Jos 20:1
priest and with * and the leaders Jos 21:1
* NOW CALLED together the troops Jos 22:1
So * blessed them and sent them Jos 22:6
of the Jordan.) As * sent away Jos 22:7,8
enemies and when * was very old, Jos 23:1
THEN * SUMMONED all the people of Jos 24:1
Then * addressed them as follows: Jos 24:2
But * replied to the people, Jos 24:19
say it," * said—"you have chosen Jos 24:22
The people replied to *, "Yes, Jos 24:24
So * made a covenant with them Jos 24:25
and God. * recorded the people's Jos 24:26
Then * said to all the people, Jos 24:27
Then * sent the people away to Jos 24:28
the lifetimes of * and the other Jos 24:31
AFTER * DIED, the nation of Israel Ju 1:1
When * finally disbanded the Ju 2:6
of the land. *, the man of God, Ju 2:7-9
unconquered by * when he died. Ju 2:21
* and stopped beside a large rock. 1Sa 6:14
still be seen in the field of *. 1Sa 6:18
See * 6:26. 1Ki 16:34f
as declared by *, the son of Nun. 1Ki 16:34
of the palace of *, the former 2Ki 23:8
*. 1Ch 7:25,26,27
carried out since the days of *. Neh 8:17
Not the Hazor mentioned in * and Jer 49:30
Compare * 5:13-15. Dan 8:11
and to * (son of Josedech), the Hag 1:1
of Judah, and * (son of Josedech), Hag 1:12
and * and all the people; Hag 2:4
me (in my vision) * the High Priest Zec 3:1
hand, accusing * of many things. Zec 3:1
I have decreed mercy to * and his Zec 3:2
And turning to * he said, Zec 3:4
very solemnly to * and said, "The Zec 3:5,6
Listen to me, O * the High Zec 3:8
Don't you see?—* represents my Zec 3:8
of the Temple that * is standing Zec 3:9
I have set before *, and I will Zec 3:9f
on the head of * (son of Josedech) Zec 6:10,11
Er's father was *; Lk 3:23-38
Years later, when * led the Act 7:45
of Israel that * led them into. Heb 4:8

JOSHUA'S
the city, but * men killed him and Jos 10:33
Lord throughout * lifetime, and as Ju 2:7-9
* clothing was filthy as he stood Zec 3:3
Er's father was Joshua; * father Lk 3:23-38

JOSIAH
that a child named * shall be born 1Ki 13:2
Amon's son * upon the throne. 2Ki 21:24
and his son * became the new king. 2Ki 21:26
NEW KING OF Judah: * 2Ki 22:1
of his reign, King * sent his 2Ki 22:3,4
As * was looking around, he 2Ki 23:16
So King * replied, "Leave it 2Ki 23:18
* demolished the shrines on the 2Ki 23:19
the reign of King *, and it was 2Ki 23:23
* also exterminated the mediums 2Ki 23:24
the land. For * wanted to follow 2Ki 23:24
and no king since the time of * 2Ki 23:25
The rest of the biography of * is 2Ki 23:28
and King * went to assist him; 2Ki 23:29
but King Neco killed * at Megiddo 2Ki 23:29
Manasseh, Amon, *. 1Ch 3:10-14
The sons of * were: 1Ch 3:15
his son * to be the new king. 2Ch 33:25
* WAS ONLY eight years old when he 2Ch 34:1
So * removed all idols from the 2Ch 34:33
THEN * ANNOUNCED that the 2Ch 35:1
of the Lord, as * had instructed. 2Ch 35:16
vie with King * in this respect, 2Ch 35:18
eighteenth year of the reign of *. 2Ch 35:19
River, and * declared war on him. 2Ch 35:20
ambassadors to * with this message: 2Ch 35:21
But * refused to turn back. 2Ch 35:22
recognize him.) * refused to 2Ch 35:22
The enemy archers struck King * 2Ch 35:23
The other activities of *, and 2Ch 35:26
of Amon's son *, king of Judah. Jer 1:1
to me during the reign of King *: Jer 3:6
his father King *, and was taken Jer 22:11
Why did your father * reign so Jer 22:15
his father * on the throne: His Jer 22:18
Jehoiakim of Judah (son of *). Jer 25:1
of the reign of * (son of Amon) Jer 25:2,3
(son of *), king of Judah: Jer 26:1
(son of *), king of Judah: Jer 27:1
(son of *) was the king of Judah: Jer 35:1
of Judah (son of *) the Lord gave Jer 36:1
in the days of *, and write down Jer 36:2
of King Jehoiakim (son of *). Jer 36:9
he chose Zedekiah (son of *). Jer 37:1
Jehoiakim (son of *), after Baruch Jer 45:1
(son of *), king of Judah: Jer 46:2
the year King * died. Jer 47:1f
during the reign of *. Eze 23:19,20f
When: During the reign of * (son Zep 1:1
Revival under King * followed about Zep 1:1f
at the home of * (son of Zec 6:10,11
Tobijah, Jedaiah, and also *. Zec 6:14
mourning for the godly King *, Zec 12:11
Amos was the father of *; Mt 1:10
* was the father of Jechoniah and Mt 1:11

JOSIAH'S
of * sons, to reign in Jerusalem; 2Ki 23:34
* SON JEHOAHAZ was selected as the 2Ch 36:1
the reign of * son Jehoiakim, king Jer 1:3
of the reign of * son Zedekiah, Jer 1:3

JOSIPHIAH
(son of *), and 160 other men; Ez 8:2-14

JOTBAH
(daughter of Haruz, of *) 2Ki 21:19,20

JOTBATHAH
From Hor-haggidgad to *; Num 33:15-37
From * to Abronah; Num 33:15-37
to *, a land of brooks and water. Deu 10:7

JOTHAM
youngest, *, who escaped and hid. Ju 9:5
When * heard about this, he stood Ju 9:7
Then * escaped and lived in Beer Ju 9:21
So the curse of *, Gideon's son, Ju 9:56,57
And his son * was the acting 2Ki 15:5
David, and his son * became king. 2Ki 15:7
Concurrent with: * (son of Uzziah) 2Ki 15:30
New king of Judah: * 2Ki 15:32,33

(JOTHAM Con't)
Generally speaking, * was a good 2Ki 15:34,35
When * died he was buried with 2Ki 15:38
Father's name: * 2Ki 16:1
Regem, *, Geshan, Pelet, Ephah, 1Ch 2:47
*, Ahaz, Hezekiah, 1Ch 3:10-14
the time of King * of Judah and 1Ch 5:17
His son * became vice-regent, in 2Ch 26:21
and his son * became the new king. 2Ch 26:23
* WAS TWENTY-FIVE years old at the 2Ch 27:1
King * became powerful because 2Ch 27:6
King Uzziah, King *, King Ahaz and Is 1:1
Ahaz (the son of * and grandson of Is 7:1
Uzziah, *, Ahaz, and Hos 1:1
the reigns of King *, King Ahaz, Mic 1:1
Uzziah was the father of *; Mt 1:9
Jotham; * was the father of Ahaz; Mt 1:9

JOTHAM'S
It was during King * reign that 2Ki 15:34,35
The rest of * history is written 2Ki 15:36

JOTTED
He * down its dimensions and made 2Ki 16:10

JOURNEY
awhile before continuing your *." Gen 18:5
food for the *, and strapped a Gen 21:14
On the third day of the * Gen 22:4
to accomplish the purpose of my *. Gen 24:12
protect me on this * and give me Gen 28:20
and was with me on my *." Gen 35:3
gave them provisions for their *. Gen 42:25
provisions for the *, and he gave Gen 45:21
of other food, to eat on his *. Gen 45:23
to go three days' * into the desert Ex 3:18
for a long *, wearing your walking Ex 12:11
if they are on a * and cannot be Num 9:10
This was their first * after Num 10:13
Egypt in ships, a * I promised you Deu 28:68
though from a long *, with patched Jos 9:3,4,5
us, 'Prepare for a long *; Jos 9:11
sent us on that *, and I can still Jos 14:11
Before he went on this * he made Ju 3:16
Kadesh, on their * from Egypt after Ju 11:16
their homeward *, she changed her Ru 1:8
there is a long * ahead of you." 1Ki 19:7
supplies for the *, and a freewill Ez 1:4
give us a good * and protect us, Ez 8:21
will start on a * to come to you in Eze 24:26
make their weary * for a drink of Amo 4:8
on a long, hard * to listen to the Lk 11:31
Emmaus and the end of their *. Lk 24:28
In the course of his * through Jn 4:46,47
where their * had begun, and where Act 14:26
asked him to join them on their *. Act 16:3
Paul and accompanied him on his *. Act 16:10f

JOURNEYED
and * to Iraq, to Nahor's village. Gen 24:10
So Jacob left Beer-sheba and * Gen 28:10
the cities they * through, so that Gen 35:5
Then Israel * on and camped Gen 35:21
his chariot and * to Goshen to meet Gen 46:29
NOW THEY LEFT Elim and * on into Ex 16:1
of Israel * onward, following it. Ex 40:36
In this way they * at the Num 9:18
And from that place they * to Num 11:35
and * from Kadesh to Mount Hor. Num 20:21,22
Israel * next to Oboth and camped Num 21:10
him, the Israelis * from Mount Hor Num 33:41
"The people of Israel then * Deu 10:6
"Then they * to Gudgodah, and Deu 10:7
and his families * to the 1Sa 1:3
they * through the wilderness! Jn 6:30,31

JOURNEYING
ancient home—* there from the Lk 2:4

JOURNEYS
continued throughout all their *. Ex 40:38

JOY
It can be bright with * if you Gen 4:7
for she said, "What * is mine! Gen 30:13
Then, weeping with *, he embraced Gen 45:14
radiate with * because of you; Num 6:24,25,26
it shall be a time of great *. Deu 16:15
great * before the Lord your God. Deu 27:7
on a tambourine and dancing for *. Ju 11:34
their shout of * was so loud that 1Sa 4:5
saw the Ark they went wild with *! 1Sa 6:13
What * there was throughout the 1Sa 11:9
* with tambourines and cymbals. 1Sa 18:6
and dancing with * because of the 1Sa 30:16
O Israel, your pride and * lies 2Sa 1:19
in order to show my * in the Lord. 2Sa 6:21
for his son, the * of that day's 2Sa 19:2
* had spread throughout the land. 1Ch 12:40
reason—to give * to God's people! 1Ch 14:2
went with great * to the home of 1Ch 15:25
with shouts of *, the blowing of 1Ch 15:28
woods sing for * before the Lord, 1Ch 16:33
King David was moved with deep *. 1Ch 29:9
before the Lord with great *. 1Ch 29:22
them, full of * that the Lord had 2Ch 20:27
They sang with * as they worked. 2Ch 23:18
for seven days with great *. 2Ch 30:21
Israel, were filled with deep *. 2Ch 30:25
while others were shouting for *! Ez 3:12
with great * by the priests, the Ez 6:16
There was great * throughout the Ez 6:21,22
You have given us a moment of * Ez 9:8
* of the Lord is your strength. Neh 8:10
For this is a day of holy *, not Neh 8:11
and everyone was filled with *! Neh 8:17
the Lord God with songs of *. Neh 9:4
had given us cause for great *. Neh 12:43
too, and the * of the people of Neh 12:43
And the Jews had * and gladness, Est 8:16
were filled with * and had a great Est 8:17
and your lips with shouts of *. Job 8:21
and to send * and prosperity to Job 10:3
* of the godless but for a moment? Job 20:5
wealth will give him no *. Job 20:18
the widows' hearts to sing for *. Job 29:13
The voice of * and gladness has Job 30:31
*, and return him to his duties. Job 33:26
and all the angels shouted for *? Job 38:6,7
Keep them shouting for * because Ps 5:11
yes, filled with * because of you. Ps 9:2
in mercy and * upon the good." Ps 11:7f
my food and drink, my highest *! Ps 16:5
body, and soul are filled with *. Ps 16:9
us wise, and give us * and light. Ps 19:7,8
May there be shouts of * when we Ps 20:5
unquenchable * of your presence. Ps 21:6
shall rejoice with everlasting *. Ps 22:26
and sing his praises with much *. Ps 27:6
and he helped me. * rises in my Ps 28:7
but in the morning there is *. Ps 30:5
Then he turned my sorrow into *! Ps 30:11
I am radiant with * because of Ps 31:7
and shout for *, all those who Ps 32:11
But give great * to all who wish Ps 35:27
Burnt animals bring no special * Ps 40:6
But may the * of the Lord be Ps 40:16
singing with *, praising the Lord? Ps 42:4,5
*, and praise him with my harp. Ps 43:4
There is a river of * flowing Ps 46:4
COME, EVERYONE, AND clap for *! Ps 47:1
to see—Mount Zion, * of all the Ps 48:2
me, give me back my * again. Ps 51:8
Restore to me again the * of Ps 51:12
I will praise you with great *. Ps 63:5
The dawn and sunset shout for *! Ps 65:8
hillsides blossom with *. Ps 65:11,12
All the world shouts with *, and Ps 65:13
What excitement and * there was Ps 66:6
let your face beam with * as you Ps 67:1
for * because you are their King Ps 67:4
from jail, singing with *! Ps 68:6
who seek for God shall live in *. Ps 69:32
fill the followers of God with *. Ps 70:4
There can be no * for me until he Ps 77:2
beginning of its strength and *. Ps 78:51
Look down on us in * and love; Ps 80:3
Look down on us in * and love; Ps 80:7
face aglow with * and love—only Ps 80:19
God has given us these times of *; Ps 81:4
* to the end of our lives. Ps 90:14
I sing for *. Ps 92:4
for the godly and * for the good. Ps 97:11
to God, and sings for utter *! Ps 98:4
out their songs of * before the Ps 98:8,9
SHOUT WITH * before the Lord, O Ps 100:1
come before him, singing with *. Ps 100:2
for he is the source of all my *. Ps 104:34
their pride and *— and brought his Ps 105:36
Songs of * at the news of our Ps 118:15,16
been my source of * and singing Ps 119:54
them to restore my * and health. Ps 119:93
How we laughed and sang for *. Ps 126:2
What wonder! What *! Ps 126:3
Those who sow tears shall reap *. Ps 126:5
May our nation shout for *. Ps 132:9
her saints shall shout for *. Ps 132:16
*, let me never sing again. Ps 137:5,6
But his * is in those who Ps 147:11
Let them sing for * as they lie Ps 149:4,5
being, filling your life with *. Pro 2:10
A worthy wife is her husband's * Pro 12:4
plotting for evil; * fills hearts Pro 12:20
true at last, there is life and *. Pro 13:12
*—no one else can really share it. Pro 14:10
A wise teacher makes learning a * Pro 15:2
for *—what pleasure a wise son is! Pro 23:24,25
So give your parents *! Pro 23:24,25
good men stay away and sing for *. Pro 29:5,6
not restrain myself from any *. Ecc 2:10
him wisdom, knowledge, and *; Ecc 2:24-26
on his past, for God gives him *. Ecc 5:19,20
great, filled with * like that of Is 9:3
That is why the Lord has no * in Is 9:17
Oh, the * of drinking deeply Is 12:3
Jerusalem shout his praise with *. Is 12:6
gladness, gone the * of harvest. Is 16:10
* has reached its lowest ebb; Is 24:11
left will shout and sing for *; Is 24:14
dust shall awake and sing for *! Is 26:19
Samaria—yes, the * and delight of Is 28:3
filled with fresh * from the Lord, Is 29:19
a song of solemn *, like songs in Is 30:29
of flowers and singing and *! Is 35:2
the songs of everlasting *. Is 35:10
only * and gladness will be there. Is 35:10
cannot be filled with hope and *. Is 38:18
And the * of the Lord shall fill Is 41:16
Sing for *, O heavens; Is 49:13
Garden of Eden. * and gladness will Is 51:3
with * and everlasting gladness; Is 51:11
you and gives you all this *. Is 51:12
and sing with *, for right before Is 52:8
You will live in * and peace. Is 55:12
of * within my House of Prayer. Is 56:7
Your eyes will shine with *, Is 60:5
forever, a * for all the Is 60:15
for ashes;* instead of mourning; Is 61:3
of prosperity and everlasting *. Is 61:7
O Jerusalem, with * like that of a Is 62:5
despair, while they sing for *. Is 65:14
and her people shall be a *! Is 65:18
and give you life and * again? Jer 11:15
They bring * to my sorrowing Jer 15:16
shall return to me with great *. Jer 24:7
I will take away your *, your Jer 25:10
The cities will be filled with * Jer 30:19
For the Lord says, Sing with * Jer 31:7
Shout out with praise and *: Jer 31:7
Tears of * shall stream down Jer 31:9
and sing songs of * upon the hills Jer 31:12
The young girls will dance for * Jer 31:13
mourning into * and I will comfort Jer 31:13
weary and * to all the sorrowing. Jer 31:25
them in this land, with great *. Jer 32:41
it will give me * and be a source Jer 33:9
shouted for * when they saw Johanan Jer 41:13,14
He has plucked you bare! * and Jer 48:33
the grapes with shouts of *. Jer 48:33
yes, but not the shouting of *. Jer 48:33
O famous city, city of *, how Jer 49:25
and "* of All the Earth'?" Lam 2:15
The * of our hearts has ended; Lam 5:15
of anguish, not shouts of *! Eze 7:7
in Jerusalem the * of their hearts Eze 24:25
himself with * and ordered that Dan 6:23
with peace and * upon your desolate Dan 9:17
singing with * as in days long ago Hos 1:15
all * has withered with them. Joe 1:12
our eyes; all * and gladness will Joe 1:16
not a ray of * or hope will Amo 5:18
and your songs of * will be turned Amo 8:10
their hands for *, for where can Nah 3:19
Shout with *! Zec 9:9
promises, to bring you great *. Mal 3:1
* like calves let out to pasture. Mal 4:2
Their * knew no bounds! Mt 2:10
it with real *, but he doesn't Mt 13:20
also filled with *, and rushed to Mt 28:8
the message with *, but, like Mk 4:16
You will both have great * and Lk 1:14
voice, my baby moved in me for *! Lk 1:44
But he will be the greatest * of Lk 2:34,35
come when you shall laugh with *! Lk 6:21
Yes, leap for *! Lk 6:23
Then he was filled with the * of Lk 10:21
There will be great * for those Lk 12:37
* for his servants who are ready! Lk 12:38
In the same way there is * in Lk 15:10
house in great excitement and *. Lk 19:6
filled with * and doubt. Lk 24:41
filled with mighty *, and were Lk 24:52
I am filled with * at his success. Jn 3:29
that you will be filled with my *. Jn 15:11
Yes, your cup of * will overflow! Jn 15:11
wonderful * [when you see me again Jn 16:20
It will be the same * as that of Jn 16:21
* and the pain is forgotten. Jn 16:21
and no one can rob you of that *. Jn 16:22
and your cup of * will overflow. Jn 16:24
they would be filled with my *. Jn 17:13
And how wonderful was their * as Jn 20:20
is filled with * and my tongue Act 2:26
me wonderful * in your presence.' Act 2:28
* and thankfulness, praising God. Act 2:46
so there was much * in that city! Act 8:8
excitement and *, and encouraged Act 11:23
were filled with * and with the Act 13:52
to everyone's *—that the Gentiles, Act 15:3
And there was great * throughout Act 15:31
What a wave of awesome * swept Act 20:10,11,12
Yes, what * there is for anyone Rom 4:8
peace and * from the Holy Spirit. Rom 14:17
It is the special * I get from 1Co 9:18
about your *: I want to make you 2Co 1:24
who ought to give me greatest *. 2Co 2:3
either, unless I came with *. 2Co 2:3
time we have the * of the Lord. 2Co 6:10
Not only was his presence a *, 2Co 7:7
for me, well, I overflowed with *! 2Co 7:7

(JOY Con't)
still by Titus' * when you gave him 2Co 7:13
their wonderful * with their deep 2Co 8:2
could share in the * of helping the 2Co 8:4
you can shout with * though you Gal 4:27
fruit in us: love, *, peace, Gal 5:22
for this special * of telling the Eph 3:8
heart is full of *, because of all Php 1:4
will share my * with each of you. Php 2:17
Lord with great *, and show your Php 2:29
my * and my reward for my work. Php 4:1
Always be full of * in the Lord; Php 4:4
full of the * of the Lord, and Col 1:11
And I, Paul, have the * of Col 1:23
Let your lives overflow with * Col 2:7
your faith and * with their Col 2:8
our message with * from the Holy 1Th 1:6
God, but bring * to him who invited 1Th 2:12
gives us hope and * and is our 1Th 2:19
Yes, you will bring us much * as 1Th 2:19
For you are our trophy and *. 1Th 2:20
our visit with * and want to see us 1Th 3:6
you and for the * and delight you 1Th 3:9
giving us the new * of the Tit 3:5
I myself have gained much * and Phm 1:7
Yes, dear brother, give me * Phm 1:20
our * and our trust in the Lord. Heb 3:6
* he knew would be his afterwards; Heb 12:2
laughter, and gloom instead of *. Jas 4:9
There is wonderful * ahead, even 1Pe 1:6
* that comes from heaven itself. 1Pe 1:8
have the wonderful * of sharing his 1Pe 4:13
will be full of *, and so will we. 1Jn 1:4
fellowship and * with each other, 1Jn 1:7
confidence and *, because he loves 1Jn 4:17
I could have no greater * than 3Jn 1:4
mighty shouts of everlasting *. Jud 1:24,25

JOYFUL
the people home, * and happy 2Ch 7:10
it was a time of great and * Neh 8:12
What a *, glad procession as Ps 45:15
Blessed are those who hear the * Ps 89:14,15
Make a * symphony before the Ps 98:6
Break out into loud and * song, Is 54:1
"I bring you the most * news Lk 2:10
Always be *. 1Th 5:16
you were actually * when all you Heb 10:34

JOYFULLY
to go on, David greeted them *. 1Sa 30:21
skillfully on the harp; sing *. Ps 33:3
returned, they * reported to him, Lk 10:17
And then you would * carry it Lk 15:5
we confidently and * look forward Rom 5:2
left over to give * to others. 2Co 9:8
Give them reason to report * Heb 13:17

JOYLESS
Let that night be bleak and *. Job 3:7

JOYOUS
It is a * celebration, and no Lev 23:36
On the following day, a great, * Num 28:17
making a * and noisy celebration 1Ki 1:40
take part in the * occasion with Neh 12:27
offered on that * day, for God had Neh 12:43
or as * as an athlete looking Ps 19:5
Play * melodies of praise upon Ps 33:2
nights were filled with * songs. Ps 77:6
Come to the * celebrations at Ps 81:3
Give a * shout in honor of the Ps 95:1
Your laws are my * treasure Ps 119:111
* song: "Your power is broken; Is 14:8
that's left of your once * land. Is 23:7
and briars; your * homes and happy Is 32:13
break into * song, for the Lord has Is 52:9
of Judah, and the * voices of the Jer 7:34
of brides, and the * song of those Jer 33:10,11
longer filled with * throngs who Lam 1:4
Is that a * choir I hear? Zep 3:17,18
They will be changed to * Zec 8:19
Begin the * tasks I have assigned Mt 25:21
things together and have a * time. 2Jn 1:12
No more * wedding bells and happy Rev 18:23

JOYOUSLY
Israel, who were * waving branches 2Sa 6:5
played loudly and * upon psaltries, 1Ch 15:16
offer their gifts willingly and *. 1Ch 29:17

JOYS
Oh, the * awaiting Israel, Num 24:3-9
* in the homes of Jacob. Num 24:3-9
OH, THE * of those who do not Ps 1:1
But oh, the * of those who put Ps 2:12
What * he gives to all his people. Ps 3:8
greater than their * at harvest Ps 4:7
You have let me experience the * Ps 16:11
What * when sins are covered over! Ps 32:1
LET ALL THE * of the godly well up Ps 33:1
courts! What * await us among all Ps 65:4
Let their * Ps 69:22
do not give them the * of life Ps 69:28
in all their *, and receive the Ps 106:5
as well as with human *. Ps 128:5
I have ended all their harvest *. Is 16:10

All the * of life will go: the Is 24:7
No more are the * of wine and Is 24:9
She thinks of all the precious * Lam 1:7
Give us back the * we used to Lam 5:21
their glory and *—their wives and Eze 24:25
I will put an end to all her *, Hos 1:11
"I'll preach to you the * of Mic 2:11
of heaven! What * await the sower Jn 4:36
forward to the * in heaven which we 2Co 4:18
the * to come will last forever. 2Co 4:18
forward to the * of heaven, and Col 1:5
rich treasures and * of heaven Col 3:1
fellowship and the * we have with 1Jn 1:3

JOZABAD
Johanan; * from Gederah; 1Ch 12:3-7
Adnah, *, Jedia-el, Michael, 1Ch 12:20
Michael, *, Elihu, Zillethai. 1Ch 12:20
Asahel, Jerimoth, *, Eliel, 2Ch 31:12,13
Je-iel, and *—gave 5,000 sheep and 2Ch 35:9
(son of Phinehas), * (son of Ez 8:33
Ishmael, Nethanel, *, Elasah. Ez 10:22
*, Shime-i, Ez 10:23
Kelita, Azariah, *, Hanan, Pelaiah, Neh 8:7,8
Shabbethai and *, who were in Neh 11:15,16,17

JOZACHAR
The assassins were *, the son of 2Ki 12:21

JOZADAK
Then Jeshua (son of *) with his Ez 3:1
Jeshua (son of *), and their fellow Ez 3:8
and Jeshua (son of *), encouraging Ez 5:1
of Jeshua, son of *), and when I Neh 12:26

JUBAL
His brother's name was *, the Gen 4:21

JUBILEE
for it is a holy Year of * for Lev 25:12
Yes, during the Year of * Lev 25:13
the number of years until the *. Lev 25:14,15,16
If the * is many years away, the Lev 25:14,15,16
harvests until the *, and the owner Lev 25:27
the new owner until the Year of *; Lev 25:28
but at the * year it must be Lev 25:28
original owner in the Year of *. Lev 25:30
original owner in the Year of *. Lev 25:31
original owners in the Year of *; Lev 25:33
you only until the Year of *. Lev 25:40
before the Year of *—whatever it Lev 25:50
years until the *, he shall pay Lev 25:51
remain until the *, then he will Lev 25:52
time the Year of * arrives, then he Lev 25:54
in the Year of *, then the whole Lev 27:17
but if it is after the Year of * Lev 27:18
until the next Year of *. Lev 27:18
his rights to it at the Year of * Lev 27:20
in the Year of *, it shall belong Lev 27:21
until the Year of *, and he shall Lev 27:23
and in the Year of * the field Lev 27:24
be returned at the Year of *." Num 36:4

JUCAL
of Pashhur) and * (son of Jer 38:1

JUDAH
at the southern border of *. Gen 15:18f
son and named him * (meaning Gen 29:35
Levi, *, Issachar, Zebulun. Gen 35:23
"Look there," * said to the Gen 37:26,27
ABOUT THIS TIME, * left home and Gen 38:1
When his oldest son Er grew up, * Gen 38:6
Then * said to Er's brother, Gen 38:8
Then * told Tamar, his Gen 38:11
mourning was over, * and his friend Gen 38:12
way to Timnah. * noticed her as he Gen 38:15
as usual. * asked his friend Hirah Gen 38:20
So he returned to * and told him Gen 38:22
"Then let her keep them!" * Gen 38:23
later word reached * that Tamar, Gen 38:24
"Bring her out and burn her," * Gen 38:24
* admitted that they were his and Gen 38:26
But * told him, "The man wasn't Gen 43:3,4,5
* said to his father, "Send the Gen 43:8
Joseph was still home when * and Gen 44:14
And * said, "Oh, what shall we Gen 44:16
Then * stepped forward and said, Gen 44:18
* and his sons: Er, Onan, Shelah, Gen 46:8-14
Jacob sent * on ahead to tell Gen 46:28
"*, your brothers shall praise Gen 49:8
bow before you. * is a young lion Gen 49:9
not depart from * until Shiloh Gen 49:10
Simeon, Levi,*, Issachar, Ex 1:1
Hur was a man of *, of the family Ex 17:10f
of the tribe of *), and have Ex 31:1
of the tribe of *) as general Ex 35:30,31
of the tribe of *) was the master Ex 38:22
* -Nahshon (son of) Num 1:2-15
* -74,600 Num 1:20-46
Tribe: * Issachar Num 2:3-31
Next to * Num 2:3-31
*, brought his gift the first day. Num 7:12
was the tribe of * grouped behind Num 10:14
of Jephunneh, from the tribe of *; Num 13:3-15
The tribe of *: 76,500. Num 26:19-22
after the sons of *—but not Num 26:19-22
* Caleb (son of Jephunneh Num 34:16-28

of Simeon, Levi, *, Issachar, Deu 27:1
And Moses said of *: Deu 33:
"O Lord, hear the cry of * Deu 33:
and across there, *, extending to Deu 34:
of the tribe of *) took some loot Jos 7:
and the tribe of * was indicated. Jos 7:1
Then he brought the clans of *, Jos 7:1
Debir, Anab, *, and Israel; Jos 11:2
A delegation from the tribe of *, Jos 14:6
THE LAND GIVEN to the Tribe of * Jos 15:
of land to the tribe of *: Jos 15:20
The cities of * which were Jos 15:21-32
the lowlands were also given to *: Jos 15:33-36
The tribe of * also inherited Jos 15:37-44
The territory of the tribe of * Jos 15:45
* also received these fortyfour Jos 15:48-62
number of cities assigned to *. Jos 15:48-62
But the tribe of * could not Jos 15:63
among the people of * to this day. Jos 15:63
to the tribes of * and Joseph. Jos 18:11
of the cities of the tribe of *. Jos 18:14
the land previously assigned to *. Jos 19:1
been given to *, for Judah's Jos 19:9
Its boundary began at *, at the Jos 19:33
Hebron) in the hill country of *. Jos 20:7
tribes of *, Simeon, and Benjamin. Jos 21:4
The tribes of * and Simeon gave Jos 21:9-16
God's answer came, "*. Ju 1:2
The leaders of the tribe of *, Ju 1:3
of Simeon went with the army of *. Ju 1:3
(* had conquered Jerusalem, and Ju 1:8
Afterward the army of * fought Ju 1:9
Then * marched against the Ju 1:10
When the tribe of * moved into Ju 1:16
Afterwards the army of * joined Ju 1:17
The army of * also conquered the Ju 1:18
The Lord helped the tribe of * Ju 1:19
also in *, Benjamin, and Ephraim. Ju 10:9
huge posse into * and raided Lehi. Ju 15:9
the men of * asked. Ju 15:10
So three thousand men of * went Ju 15:11
the men of * told him. Ju 15:12,13
from the town of Bethlehem, in *, Ju 17:7,8
from Bethlehem, in *, and I am Ju 17:9
Kiriath-jearim in * (which is still Ju 18:12
in * to be his concubine. Ju 19:1
in *," the man replied. Ju 19:18
And the Lord replied, "* shall go Ju 20:18
Ephrathites from Bethlehem in *." Ru 1:1f
Perez, the son of Tamar and *." Ru 4:12
to thirty thousand from *. 1Sa 11:8
to ten thousand men from *. 1Sa 15:4
in * and Azekah in Ephes-dammim. 1Sa 17:1
of the tribe of * who lived in 1Sa 17:12
but all Israel and * loved him, 1Sa 18:15,16
cave and return to the land of *. 1Sa 22:5
The news of his arrival in * 1Sa 22:6
"We're afraid even here in *; 1Sa 23:3
to the kings of * to this day), 1Sa 27:6
the south of * and the people of 1Sa 27:10
the south of * and the land of 1Sa 30:14
Philistines and from the men of *. 1Sa 30:16
of the loot to the elders of *. 1Sa 30:26
Lord, "Shall I move back to *?" 2Sa 2:1
Then the leaders of * came to 2Sa 2:4
Be like the tribe of * who have 2Sa 2:7
combined armies of Israel and *. 2Sa 3:12
Thus the whole nation, both * 2Sa 3:37
been the king of * for seven years, 2Sa 5:4,5
as king of both Israel and *. 2Sa 5:4,5
and the kingdoms of Israel and *; 2Sa 12:8
to the elders of *, "Why are you 2Sa 19:11,12
*, and they responded as one man. 2Sa 19:14
as if everyone in * had come to 2Sa 19:15
men of * to welcome King David. 2Sa 19:16
And most of * and half of Israel 2Sa 19:40
only men from * had ferried him and 2Sa 19:41
the men of * replied. 2Sa 19:42
and the men of * were very rough in 2Sa 19:43
So all except * and Benjamin 2Sa 20:2
But the men of * stayed with 2Sa 20:2
the army of * within three days and 2Sa 20:4
south to * as far as Beer-sheba. 2Sa 24:7
age in Israel, and 500,000 in *. 2Sa 24:9
royal officials of *, requesting 1Ki 1:9
him king of Israel and *." 1Ki 1:35
of the army of *. 1Ki 2:32
Israel and * were a wealthy, 1Ki 4:20
of Solomon, all of * and Israel 1Ki 4:25
Of the twelve tribes, * and 1Ki 11:32f
for the tribe of *, who remained 1Ki 12:16,17
Only the tribe of * 1Ki 12:20
* and Benjamin were sometimes (as 1Ki 12:20f
able-bodied men of * and Benjamin: 1Ki 12:21
Solomon, king of *, and all the 1Ki 12:23,24
all the people of * and Benjamin 1Ki 12:23,24
the Lord from * walked up to him. 1Ki 13:1
to * by the road I came on." 1Ki 13:9
the prophet from * had done and 1Ki 13:11
you the prophet who came from *?" 1Ki 13:14
the prophet from *, "The Lord says 1Ki 13:21,22

(JUDAH Con't)

the son of Solomon was king in *.	1Ki 14:21
the people of *, like those in	1Ki 14:22
and the people of * became as	1Ki 14:24
in The Annals of the Kings of *.	1Ki 14:29
reign as king of * in Jerusalem	1Ki 15:1
constant war between Israel and *.	1Ki 15:6
in The Annals of the Kings of *.	1Ki 15:7
Asa became king of *, in	1Ki 15:9
of * and King Baasha of Israel.	1Ki 15:16
to all *, asking every able-bodied	1Ki 15:22
in The Annals of the Kings of *.	1Ki 15:23
became the new king of *.	1Ki 15:24
of the reign of King Asa of *.	1Ki 15:25
of the reign of King Asa of *.	1Ki 15:28
of * and King Baasha of Israel.	1Ki 15:32,33
*, but he reigned only two years.	1Ki 16:8
of the reign of King Asa of *.	1Ki 16:10
King Asa of * had been on the	1Ki 16:23
King Asa of * had been on the	1Ki 16:29
of *, and left his servant there.	1Ki 19:3
Jehoshaphat of * was visiting King	1Ki 22:2
And King Jehoshaphat of * replied,	1Ki 22:4
Jehoshaphat of * led their armies	1Ki 22:29
Meanwhile, over in *, Jehoshaphat	1Ki 22:41
in The Annals of the Kings of *.	1Ki 22:45
Jehoshaphat of * that Ahaziah,	1Ki 22:51
Jehoram (son of Jehoshaphat) of *.	2Ki 1:17
was the king of * at this time.	2Ki 3:1f
of *; and he reigned twelve	2Ki 3:1
message to King Jehoshaphat of *:	2Ki 3:6,7,8
But Jehoshaphat, the king of *,	2Ki 3:11
So the kings of Israel, *, and	2Ki 3:12
of *," Elisha replied.	2Ki 3:14
Jehoshaphat of *, began his reign	2Ki 8:16
descendants, he did not destroy *.	2Ki 8:19
* and appointed their own king.	2Ki 8:20
in The Annals of the Kings of *.	2Ki 8:23
King Ahaziah of * (son of Jehoram)	2Ki 8:29
(King Ahaziah of * was there too,	2Ki 9:16
Then he and King Ahaziah of * rode	2Ki 9:21
Meanwhile, King Ahaziah of * had	2Ki 9:27
(Ahaziah's reign over * had	2Ki 9:29
the brothers of King Ahaziah of *.	2Ki 10:13
of King Ahaziah of *, learned that	2Ki 11:1
that Joash became king of *.	2Ki 12:1
the kings of *—had dedicated, along	2Ki 12:18
in The Annals of the Kings of *.	2Ki 12:19
of the reign of King Joash of *.	2Ki 13:1
of the reign of King Joash of *.	2Ki 13:9,10
King Amaziah of *, are written in	2Ki 13:12
Amaziah began his reign over *.	2Ki 14:1
for both yourself and *?"	2Ki 14:10
of the cities of *, and Judah was	2Ki 14:11
of Judah, and * was defeated and	2Ki 14:12
King Amaziah of * are recorded in	2Ki 14:15
in The Annals of the Kings of *.	2Ki 14:18
built Elath and restored it to *.	2Ki 14:22
of the reign of King Amaziah of *.	2Ki 14:23
been captured by *)—is recorded in	2Ki 14:28
NEW KING OF *: Azariah	2Ki 15:1
in The Annals of the Kings of *.	2Ki 15:6
Reigning in * at that time: King	2Ki 15:8
Reigning in * at that time: King	2Ki 15:13
Concurrent with: King Azariah of *	2Ki 15:17
Concurrent with: King Azariah of *	2Ki 15:23
Concurrent with: King Azariah of *	2Ki 15:27
of Uzziah) king of *, who had been	2Ki 15:30
New king of *: Jotham	2Ki 15:32,33
in The Annals of the Kings of *.	2Ki 15:36
King Pekah of Israel to attack *.	2Ki 15:37
the other kings of * in the royal	2Ki 15:38
new king of *	2Ki 16:1
the nations around *—nations which	2Ki 16:3
in The Annals of the Kings of *.	2Ki 16:19
Reigning in * at this time: King	2Ki 17:1
* to turn from their evil ways;	2Ki 17:13
tribe of * remained in the land.	2Ki 17:18
But even * refused to obey the	2Ki 17:19
new King of *	2Ki 18:1
all the fortified cities of *.	2Ki 18:13
"O my people *, those of you	2Ki 19:30
in The Annals of the Kings of *.	2Ki 20:20
new king of *	2Ki 21:1
led the people of * into idolatry:	2Ki 21:11
upon Jerusalem and * that the ears	2Ki 21:12
led the people of *, he murdered	2Ki 21:16
in The Annals of the Kings of *.	2Ki 21:17
Name of the new king of *: Amon	2Ki 21:19,20
in The Annals of the Kings of *.	2Ki 21:25
new king of *	2Ki 22:1
For the people of * have thrown	2Ki 22:17
other leaders of * and Jerusalem to	2Ki 23:1
of Jerusalem and * gathered there	2Ki 23:1
previous kings of *, for they had	2Ki 23:5
* and even in Jerusalem.	2Ki 23:5
in other cities of *, and tore down	2Ki 23:8
former kings of * to the sun god.	2Ki 23:11
which the kings of * had built on	2Ki 23:12
who came from * and proclaimed that	2Ki 23:17
of the kings of Israel and *.	2Ki 23:22
anger against *, caused by the	2Ki 23:26
* just as I have destroyed Israel;	2Ki 23:27
in The Annals of the Kings of *.	2Ki 23:28
New king of *: Jehoahaz	2Ki 23:31,32
a tax against * totaling $230,000.	2Ki 23:33
New king of *: Jehoiakim	2Ki 23:36,37
Ammonites against * in order to	2Ki 24:2
disasters befell * at the direct	2Ki 24:3,4
He had decided to wipe * out of	2Ki 24:3,4
in The Annals of the Kings of *.	2Ki 24:5
by Egypt—all of * from the Brook of	2Ki 24:7
New king of *, Jehoiachin	2Ki 24:8,9
New king of *: Zedekiah	2Ki 24:18,19
the people of Jerusalem and *.	2Ki 24:20
the reign of King Zedekiah of *.	2Ki 25:1
A commander of the army of *,	2Ki 25:19
So * was exiled from its land.	2Ki 25:21
over the people left in *.	2Ki 25:22
Then all the men of * and the	2Ki 25:26
Reuben, Simeon, Levi, *, Issachar,	1Ch 2:1
* had three sons by Bath-shua, a	1Ch 2:3
her father-in-law, *, became the	1Ch 2:4
Zerah. So * had five sons.	1Ch 2:4
THESE ARE THE sons of *:	1Ch 4:1
The sons of Shelah (the son of *	1Ch 4:21-22
children than was normal in *.	1Ch 4:27
King Hezekiah of * these princes	1Ch 4:40,41
birthright, yet * was a powerful	1Ch 5:2
Israel, and from * came a Prince.	1Ch 5:2
of * and King Jeroboam of Israel.	1Ch 5:17
sent the people of * and Jerusalem	1Ch 6:4-15
pasturelands in * (although the	1Ch 6:55,56,57
tribes of *, Simeon, and Benjamin.	1Ch 6:64,65
* was exiled to Babylon because	1Ch 9:1
from the tribes of *, Benjamin,	1Ch 9:3
of the clan of Perez (son of *).	1Ch 9:4
came to David from Benjamin and *.	1Ch 12:16
From *, 6,800 troops armed with	1Ch 12:24-37
Kiriath-jearim) in * to bring	1Ch 13:6
age in Israel and 470,000 in *.	1Ch 21:5
Over *, Elihu (a brother of King	1Ch 27:16-22
he has chosen the tribe of *, and	1Ch 28:4
families of *, my father's family;	1Ch 28:4
the craftsmen of * and Jerusalem	2Ch 2:7
instruments in all the land of *.	2Ch 9:11
Rehoboam rule his own tribe of *!	2Ch 10:16
The people of the tribe of *,	2Ch 10:17
the armies of * and Benjamin,	2Ch 11:1
King Rehoboam of *, Solomon's son,	2Ch 11:3
the people of * and of Benjamin:	2Ch 11:3
these cities of * with walls and	2Ch 11:5-10
For only * and Benjamin remained	2Ch 11:12
homes and moved to * and Jerusalem,	2Ch 11:13,14
the kingdom of *, so King Rehoboam	2Ch 11:17
the land of * and Benjamin, and	2Ch 11:23
the economy of * remained strong.	2Ch 12:12
ABIJAH BECAME THE new king of *,	2Ch 13:1
broke out between * and Israel.	2Ch 13:1
Judah and Israel. *, led by King	2Ch 13:3
When the army of * arrived at	2Ch 13:4
the men of * to ambush them;	2Ch 13:13,14
to ambush them; so * was	2Ch 13:13,14
The men of * began to shout.	2Ch 13:15,16
and the men of * to turn the tide	2Ch 13:15,16
So *, depending upon the Lord God	2Ch 13:18,19
Meanwhile, King Abijah of *	2Ch 13:21
the prophet Iddo's History of *.	2Ch 13:22
the new king of *, and there was	2Ch 14:1
build walled cities throughout *.	2Ch 14:6
and the army of * triumphed as the	2Ch 14:12
Then the army of * carried off	2Ch 14:13
Listen, armies of * and	2Ch 15:2
But you men of *, keep up the	2Ch 15:7
in the land of * and Benjamin, and	2Ch 15:8
all the people of * and Benjamin,	2Ch 15:9
But here in * and Benjamin the	2Ch 15:17
in order to control the road to *.	2Ch 16:1
and gave up his plan to attack *.	2Ch 16:5
and the people of * went out to	2Ch 16:6
of the Kings of Israel and *.	2Ch 16:11
cities of *, in various other	2Ch 17:2
his position as king of *.	2Ch 17:5
All the people of * cooperated by	2Ch 17:5
teachers in all the cities of *.	2Ch 17:7,8,9
all the cities of *, to teach the	2Ch 17:7,8,9
and supply cities throughout *.	2Ch 17:12
Jehoshaphat of * made a marriage	2Ch 18:1
and the king of * led their armies	2Ch 18:28
Jehoshaphat of * in his royal	2Ch 18:31
AS KING JEHOSHAPHAT of *	2Ch 19:1
a ruler in *, as the court of final	2Ch 19:11
Jehoshaphat and the people of *.	2Ch 20:1
all the people of * should go	2Ch 20:3
from every part of * stood before	2Ch 20:13
all you people of * and Jerusalem,	2Ch 20:15
you, O people of * and Jerusalem!	2Ch 20:17
all the people of * and the people	2Ch 20:18
the army of * went out into the	2Ch 20:20
"Listen to me, O people of * and	2Ch 20:20
So, when the army of * arrived	2Ch 20:24
He became king of * when he was	2Ch 20:31
king of *, went into partnership	2Ch 20:35
Jehoram became the new ruler of *.	2Ch 21:1
some of the fortified cities of *.	2Ch 21:3,4
declaring his independence of *.	2Ch 21:8
in throwing off the yoke of *.	2Ch 21:10
the mountains of *, and led the	2Ch 21:11
of Jerusalem and * worship idols	2Ch 21:13
They marched against *, broke	2Ch 21:17
the princes of *, and killed them.	2Ch 22:8
"Go to all the cities of * and	2Ch 24:5
cities of *, and from Jerusalem?	2Ch 24:6
all the cities of * and throughout	2Ch 24:9
the leaders of * came to King Joash	2Ch 24:17,18
down upon * and Jerusalem again.	2Ch 24:17,18
and conquered * and Jerusalem,	2Ch 24:23
the great army of * be conquered by	2Ch 24:24
to each clan from * and Benjamin.	2Ch 25:5,6
of the cities of * in the vicinity	2Ch 25:13
King Amaziah of * now took the	2Ch 25:17
you and all * get badly hurt."	2Ch 25:19
Beth-shemesh in *, and Judah was	2Ch 25:21
in Judah, and * was defeated, and	2Ch 25:22
King Amaziah of * and took him as a	2Ch 25:23
However, King Amaziah of * lived	2Ch 25:25
of the Kings of * and Israel.	2Ch 25:26
THE PEOPLE OF * now crowned	2Ch 26:1
of Eloth and restored it to *.	2Ch 26:2
hill country of *, and erected	2Ch 27:4
of the Kings of Israel and *.	2Ch 27:7
was angry with * and let you	2Ch 28:9
these people from * and Jerusalem?	2Ch 28:10
About that time King Ahaz of *	2Ch 28:16
For Edom was invading * and	2Ch 28:16
For the Lord brought * very low	2Ch 28:19
tribes of Israel—* and Benjamin—and	2Ch 28:19f
spiritual fiber of * and had been	2Ch 28:19
in every city of *, thus angering	2Ch 28:25
of the Kings of * and Israel.	2Ch 28:26
became the king of *, and he	2Ch 29:1
has been upon * and Jerusalem.	2Ch 29:8
all of Israel, *, Ephraim, and	2Ch 30:1
But in * the entire nation felt	2Ch 30:12
Then the people of *, together	2Ch 30:25
to the cities of *, Benjamin,	2Ch 31:1
The people who had moved to *	2Ch 31:5,6
and the people of * living in the	2Ch 31:5,6
throughout all *, doing what was	2Ch 31:20
of Assyria invaded * and laid siege	2Ch 32:1
and commanded * and Jerusalem to	2Ch 32:12
upon him and upon * and Jerusalem.	2Ch 32:25
of the Kings of * and Israel.	2Ch 32:32
kings, and all * and Jerusalem	2Ch 32:33
the people of * and Jerusalem to do	2Ch 33:9
all of the fortified cities of *.	2Ch 33:14
* worship the Lord God of Israel.	2Ch 33:16
began to clean up * and Jerusalem,	2Ch 34:3
the people of * and Jerusalem from	2Ch 34:5
earlier kings of * had torn down.	2Ch 34:10,11
all the remnant of Israel and *!	2Ch 34:21
to the king of * who sent you to	2Ch 34:26
all the elders of * and Jerusalem,	2Ch 34:29
of *, and from over in Israel.	2Ch 35:18
a fight with you, O king of *!	2Ch 35:21
And all * and Jerusalem,	2Ch 35:24,25
of the Kings of Israel and *.	2Ch 35:27
annual tribute from * of $250,000.	2Ch 36:3
of Jehoahaz, as the new king of *.	2Ch 36:4
in The Annals of the Kings of *;	2Ch 36:8
the new king of * and Jerusalem.	2Ch 36:10
in Jerusalem, in the land of *,	2Ch 36:22,23
in Jerusalem, in the land of *.	Ez 1:2
of the tribes of * and Benjamin,	Ez 1:5
of the exiles returning to *.	Ez 1:8
of *, from which their parents	Ez 2:1
of 42,360 persons returned to *;	Ez 2:64,65
of * from which they had come.	Ez 2:70
had returned to * came to Jerusalem	Ez 3:1
WHEN THE ENEMIES of * and	Ez 4:1
the people of * and Jerusalem, and	Ez 4:6
in Jerusalem and * at that	Ez 5:1
the Temple of the great God of *.	Ez 5:8
Cyrus appointed as governor of *.	Ez 5:14
the governor of * and the other	Ez 6:7
been relocated in * turned from	Ez 6:21,22
of God's laws to * and Jerusalem	Ez 7:14
Jerusalem as a walled city in *.	Ez 9:9
made throughout * and Jerusalem	Ez 10:7,8
all the men of * and Benjamin had	Ez 10:9
Petha-haiah, *, Eliezer.	Ez 10:23
some men who had arrived from *.	Neh 1:2
favor, send me to * to rebuild the	Neh 2:4
their countries on my way to *;	Neh 2:7
I was governor of *—from the	Neh 5:14
and the wealthy politicians of *.	Neh 6:17
For many in * had sworn	Neh 6:18
had returned to * before, and this	Neh 7:5
who returned to * after being	Neh 7:6
officials who returned to *:	Neh 7:57,58,59
who returned to * at that time;	Neh 7:66
towns and villages throughout *.	Neh 7:73
and towns of * and Benjamin were	Neh 11:1

(JUDAH Con't)
homes in the various cities of *). Neh 11:3
Leaders from the tribe of *: Neh 11:4,5,6
assisted by *, son of Hassenu-ah. Neh 11:7,8,9
of Zerah, a son of *) assisted in Neh 11:24
where the people of * lived were: Neh 11:25-30
who lived in * were sent to live Neh 11:36
Sherebiah, *, Mattaniah—who was the Neh 12:8
of the leaders of *, including Neh 12:31,32
Ezra, Meshullam, *, Benjamin, Neh 12:34
*, and Hanani. Neh 12:35,36
for the people of * appreciated the Neh 12:44
all the people of * began bringing Neh 13:12
Then I asked the leaders of *, Neh 13:17
speak the language of * at all. Neh 13:24
Jeconiah of * and many others. Est 2:6
O people of *, rejoice! Ps 48:11
he says. "* shall continue to Ps 60:6,7
The princes and elders of *, and Ps 68:27
he rebuilds the cities of *. Ps 69:35
IS very great in * and in Israel. Ps 76:1
*—and Mount Zion which he loved. Ps 78:68
all the cities of * have heard of Ps 97:8,9
on my head. * is my scepter. Ps 108:8
then the lands of * and of Israel Ps 114:2
of *: Pro 25:1
and King Hezekiah—all kings of *. Is 1:1
* and Jerusalem in the days ahead. Is 1:1
Lord concerning * and Jerusalem: Is 2:1
Now, men of Jerusalem and *, you Is 5:3
Israel and * are his pleasant Is 5:7
"They say, 'We will invade * and Is 7:6
into Israel and *—the mighty king Is 7:17
into your land of *, O Immanuel, Is 8:7,8
with the plans of * to surrender to Is 8:11
but Israel and * have refused his Is 8:14,15
Manasseh—and both against *. Is 9:21
in Israel and in * will trust the Is 10:20
between Israel and * will end; Is 11:13
of alliance with the king of *. Is 16:1
the people of Jerusalem and all *. Is 22:21
the land of * and making it a vast Is 24:1
In that day the whole land of * Is 26:1
is stored up for * in a safe place, Is 33:6
cities of * and conquered them. Is 36:1
making everyone in * worship only Is 36:7
And you who are left in * will Is 37:31
of *, "Your God is coming!" Is 40:9
and the cities of * lived in once Is 44:26
of Amon's son Josiah, king of *. Jer 1:1
Jehoiakim, king of *, and at Jer 1:3
Zedekiah, king of *, when Jerusalem Jer 1:3
southward, spilling over *." Jer 1:13
and in all the other cities of *. Jer 1:15
All the kings of * and its Jer 1:18
gods as there are cities in *. Jer 2:28
And her faithless sister * saw Jer 3:7
But now * too has left me and Jer 3:8
is less guilty than treacherous *! Jer 3:11
At that time the people of * and Jer 3:18
to the men of * and Jerusalem, Plow Jer 4:3
Jerusalem and the cities of *. Jer 4:16
For the people of Israel and * Jer 5:11
Make this announcement to * and Jer 5:20
to the people: O *, listen to this Jer 7:2
* and in the streets of Jerusalem? Jer 7:17
For the people of * have sinned Jer 7:30
in the cities of *, and the joyous Jer 7:34
of the kings of * and of the Jer 8:1
The cities of * shall be ghost Jer 9:11
and yes, even you people of *. Jer 9:25,26
The cities of * shall become dens Jer 10:22
Remind the men of * and all the Jer 11:1
among the men of * and Jerusalem. Jer 11:9
of Israel and * in offering incense Jer 11:17
as * will be forced from hers; Jer 12:14
rot the pride of * and Jerusalem. Jer 13:8,9
loins, so I made * and Israel to Jer 13:11
and all * shall be taken away as Jer 13:19
* mourns; business has ground to Jer 14:2
"have you completely rejected *? Jer 14:19
Hezekiah, king of *, did in Jer 15:4
the Lord, kings of * and all the Jer 17:20
from the cities of * and Benjamin, Jer 17:26
lowlands west of *, the people Jer 17:26
Therefore go and warn all * and Jer 18:11
of * and citizens of Jerusalem! Jer 19:3
nor the kings of * have worshiped Jer 19:4
battle plans of * and Jerusalem and Jer 19:7
of the kings of *—wherever incense Jer 19:13
I will hand over * to the king of Jer 20:4
"And to the king of *, the Lord Jer 21:11
to the king of * and say, Listen Jer 22:1
of *, sitting on David's throne; Jer 22:2
son of Jehoiakim king of *—even Jer 22:24,25
the throne of David or rule in *. Jer 22:30
At that time * will be saved and Jer 23:5,6
king of *, and exiled him to Jer 24:1
the princes of * and the skilled Jer 24:1
Zedekiah, king of *, his officials Jer 24:8
all the people of * came from the Jer 25:1
Jehoiakim of * (son of Josiah). Jer 25:1
of Amon) king of *, until now, God Jer 25:2,3
to the cities of *, and their kings Jer 25:18
(son of Josiah), king of *: Jer 26:1
to worship from many parts of *. Jer 26:2
When the high officials of * Jer 26:10
King Hezekiah of *, he told the Jer 26:18
(son of Josiah), king of *: Jer 27:1
prophecies to Zedekiah, king of *. Jer 27:12
of the king of * and in the palaces Jer 27:18
people of * and Jerusalem to Jer 27:19,20,21
king of *, will all yet be carried Jer 27:19,20,21
Zedekiah, king of *—Hananiah (son Jer 28:1
son of Jehoiakim, king of *, and Jer 28:4
people, Israel and *, and I will Jer 30:3
this also concerning Israel and *: Jer 30:4
they shall say in * and her cities, Jer 31:23
with the people of Israel and *. Jer 31:31
Zedekiah, king of * (which was the Jer 32:1
For Israel and * have done Jer 32:30
The sins of Israel and *—the sins Jer 32:32
evil, causing * to sin so greatly! Jer 32:35
in the cities of * and in the hill Jer 32:44
the cities of both * and Israel and Jer 33:7
and in all the cities of *. Jer 33:13
* all the good I promised them. Jer 33:14
In that day the people of * and Jer 33:16
—that the Lord chose * and Israel Jer 33:24
Jerusalem and the cities of *: Jer 34:1
Go tell Zedekiah, king of *, that Jer 34:2
Zedekiah, king of *: God says you Jer 34:4
walled cities of * still standing. Jer 34:7
King Zedekiah of * had freed all Jer 34:8
Zedekiah, king of *, and his Jer 34:21
that the cities of * are completely Jer 34:22
(son of Josiah) was the king of *: Jer 35:1
Go and say to * and Jerusalem, Jer 35:13
I will send upon * and Jerusalem Jer 35:17
King Jehoiakim of * (son of Josiah) Jer 36:1
Israel, * and the other nations. Jer 36:2
Perhaps when the people of * see Jer 36:3
will be there from all over *. Jer 36:6
People came from all over * to Jer 36:9
of *: He shall have no one to sit Jer 36:30
all the people of * and Jerusalem, Jer 36:31
son) to be the new king of *. Jer 37:1
southern border of * to relieve the Jer 37:5
Tell the king of *, who sent you to Jer 37:7
King Zedekiah of *, that King Jer 39:1
children and all the nobles of *. Jer 39:6
But throughout the land of * he Jer 39:10
of Jerusalem and * who were being Jer 40:1
as governor of * by the king of Jer 40:5
and lived in * with the people left Jer 40:6
were still left in *, and that the Jer 40:11
began to return to * from the many Jer 40:12
O remnant of *: The Lord of Hosts, Jer 42:15
of *, do not go to Egypt!" Jer 42:19
to obey the Lord and stay in *. Jer 43:4
"Call together the men of * and, Jer 43:9
tell the men of * this: The Lord of Jer 43:10
and to all the cities of *. Jer 44:2,3
upon the cities of * and into the Jer 44:6
*, not even the babies in arms. Jer 44:7
and queens of *, and your own sins, Jer 44:9
of your wives in * and Jerusalem? Jer 44:9
I will take this remnant of * Jer 44:12
* and in the streets of Jerusalem; Jer 44:17
* and in the streets of Jerusalem? Jer 44:21
of * who are here in Egypt! Jer 44:24
"Only those who return to * (it Jer 44:28
Zedekiah, king of *, over to Jer 44:30
(son of Josiah), king of *: Jer 46:2
us return again to * where we were Jer 46:16
the reign of Zedekiah, king of *: Jer 49:34
Then the people of Israel and * Jer 50:4
in Israel or in *, for I will Jer 50:20
of Israel and * have been wronged. Jer 50:33
has not forsaken Israel and *. Jer 51:5
along with Zedekiah, king of *. Jer 51:59
in Jerusalem and *, and were taken Jer 52:3
all the princes of * were killed Jer 52:10
king of *, Evil-merodach, who Jer 52:31
Why is * led away, a slave? Lam 1:3
with the elders of * in my home, Eze 8:1
to the people of * that they commit Eze 8:17
of Israel and * are very great and Eze 9:9
Samaria again, and those of * too. Eze 16:53
* too will prosper in that day. Eze 16:55
The anti-Babylonian party in * Eze 23:17f
and laughed at * when she was Eze 25:3
have said that * is no better off Eze 25:8
upon the people of *, I will smash Eze 25:12
have acted against * out of revenge Eze 25:15
coral and agate. * and the cities Eze 27:17
remnants of * living among the Eze 33:24
'Both Israel and * shall be mine. Eze 35:10
* and her allied tribes.' Eze 37:16
and join them to * and make Eze 37:18,19,20
Reuben and then *, all with the Eze 48:5,6,7
"South of * is the land set Eze 48:8
alloted to * and Benjamin, is 8 Eze 48:21,22
one for * and one for Levi. Eze 48:30,31
began to rule in *, Babylon's King Dan 1:1
and nobility of *—and to teach them Dan 1:3,4
chosen, all from the tribe of *. Dan 1:6
yes, all of us—the men of *, the Dan 9:7
reigns of these four kings of *: Hos 1:1
will have mercy on the tribe of *. Hos 1:7
invaded * and besieged Jerusalem. Hos 1:7f
Then the people of * and Israel Hos 1:11
may * stay far from such a life. Hos 4:15
such a life. O *, do not join with Hos 4:15
of guilt, and *, too, shall fall. Hos 5:5
The leaders of * have become the Hos 5:10
I will sap away the strength of * Hos 5:12
When Ephraim and * see how sick Hos 5:13
I will tear Ephraim and * as a Hos 5:14
O Ephraim and *, what shall I do Hos 6:4
O *, for you also there is a Hos 6:11
Israel has built great palaces; * Hos 8:14
and deceit, but * still trusts in Hos 11:12
is bringing a lawsuit against *, Hos 12:2
too. * also will be justly Hos 12:2
the prosperity of * and Joe 3:1
You have sold the people of * Joe 3:6
to the people of * and they will Joe 3:8
dry stream beds of *, and a Joe 3:18
Uzziah was king of *, and while Amo 1:2
The Lord says, "The people of * Amo 2:4
So I will destroy * with fire, Amo 2:5
both Israel and *—against the Amo 3:1
Flee to the land of * and do your Amo 7:12
and King Hezekiah, all kings of *. Mic 1:1
both Samaria and *, and came to Mic 1:1
of the sins of Israel and *. Mic 1:5
of the cities of * to follow Israel Mic 1:13
we are safe!" O *, proclaim a day Nah 1:15
of Josiah (son of Amon) king of *. Zep 1:1
I will crush * and Jerusalem Zep 1:4
and princes of *, and all others Zep 1:8
riddance of all the people of *. Zep 1:18
the tribe of * will be pastured. Zep 2:7
of She-alti-el), governor of *; Hag 1:1
the governor of *, and Joshua (son Hag 1:12
the governor of *, "I am about to Hag 2:21
Jerusalem and the cities of *, Zec 1:12
has happened to * and Jerusalem? Zec 1:14
*, Israel, and Jerusalem." Zec 1:19
that scattered * so terribly, and Zec 1:21
me to you. And * shall be the Zec 2:11,12
Governor of *, who was given the Zec 4:6f
'May you be as poor as *,' the Zec 8:13
For now '*' is a word of Zec 8:13
and happy as * is,' they'll say. Zec 8:13
of your woes! *, you are my bow! Zec 9:13
don't come true? * and Israel have Zec 10:2
arrived to help his flock of *. Zec 10:3
"I will strengthen *, yes, and Zec 10:6
between * and Israel was broken. Zec 11:14
"I will make Jerusalem and * Zec 12:2
of *, but blind all her enemies. Zec 12:4
"And the clans of * shall say to Zec 12:5
make the clans of * like a little Zec 12:6
to the rest of * first, before Zec 12:7
of Uzziah, king of *, and the Lord Zec 14:5
northern border of *) to Rimmon Zec 14:10
combat. All * will be fighting at Zec 14:14
in Jerusalem and * shall be sacred Zec 14:21
our fathers! In *, in Israel, and Mal 2:11
for the men of * have defiled God's Mal 2:11
* and Jerusalem, as he did before. Mal 3:4
Jacob was the father of * and his Mt 1:2
* was the father of Perez and Mt 1:3
Simeon's father was *; Lk 3:23-38
Perez' father was *; Lk 3:23-38
from the tribe of *, which had not Heb 7:12,13,14
of Israel and the people of *. Heb 8:8
The Lion of the tribe of *, the Rev 5:5
* 12,000 Rev 7:4-8

JUDAH'S
In the process of time * wife Gen 38:12
So the total of all those on * Num 2:3-31
* southern boundary began at the Jos 15:1
to assign some of * territory to Jos 15:13
to Judah, for * section had been Jos 19:9
He quickly conquered * fortified 2Ch 12:4
altars from every one of * cities. 2Ch 14:5
Jerusalem's and * food and water Is 3:1
He was * last ruler before the Jer 21:1f
So it was that * exile was Jer 52:27
and the girls in * cities. Lam 5:11
signify the years of * punishment. Eze 4:6
For Babylon is * ally and has Eze 21:23
Simeon's father was Judah;* father Lk 3:23-38
Perez' father was Judah;* father Lk 3:23-38

JUDAS
* Iscariot (the one who betrayed Mt 10:2,3,4
Joseph, Simon, and *. Mt 13:55
Then * Iscariot, one of the Mt 26:14
From that time on, * watched for Mt 26:16
*, too, had asked him, "Rabbi, Mt 26:25

(JUDAS Con't)
still speaking, *, one of the Mt 26:47
Jewish leaders. * had told them to Mt 26:48
So now * came straight to Jesus Mt 26:49
About that time *, who betrayed Mt 27:3
* Iscariot (who later betrayed Mk 3:16-19
of James and Joseph, * and Simon. Mk 6:2,3
Then * Iscariot, one of his Mk 14:10
still speaking, * (one of his Mk 14:43
* had told them, "You will know Mk 14:44
* (son of James), Lk 6:14,15,16
* Iscariot (who later betrayed Lk 6:14,15,16
Then Satan entered into * Lk 22:3
by *, one of his twelve disciples. Lk 22:47
twelve disciples. * walked over to Lk 22:47
But Jesus said, "*, how can you Lk 22:48
He was speaking of *, son of Jn 6:71
But * Iscariot, one of his Jn 12:4
suggested to * Iscariot, Simon's Jn 13:1
it to *, son of Simon Iscariot. Jn 13:26
As soon as * had eaten it, Satan Jn 13:27
Some thought that since * was Jn 13:29
to the poor. * left at once, going Jn 13:30
As soon as * left the room, Jesus Jn 13:31
* (not Judas Iscariot, but his Jn 14:22
Judas (not * Iscariot, but his Jn 14:22
of olive trees. *, the betrayer, Jn 18:2
had given * a squad of soldiers and Jn 18:3
* (son of James), Act 1:14
true concerning *, who betrayed Act 1:16
King David. * was one of us, Act 1:17
else to take *' place and to join Act 1:21,22
apostle to replace * the traitor, Act 1:24,25
taxation, there was * of Galilee. Act 5:37
of a man named * and ask there for Act 9:11
the church leaders—* (also called Act 15:22
These men—* and Silas, who have Act 15:26
Then * and Silas, both being Act 15:32
and then * and Silas returned to Act 15:33
on the night when * betrayed him, 1Co 11:23
after * was gone from among them. 1Co 15:5f

JUDE
FROM: *, A servant of Jesus Jud 1:1
shouts of everlasting joy. Amen.* Jud 1:24,25

JUDEA
was hiding in the wilderness of *. Ps 63:1
Shout to Jerusalem and to all *, Jer 4:5
And your sons and daughters in * Eze 24:20,21
*, during the reign of King Herod. Mt 2:1
not to go to *, so they went to Mt 2:22
every section of * went out to the Mt 3:5
he left * and returned home Mt 4:12,13
and from all over *, and even from Mt 4:25
to * from across the Jordan River. Mt 19:1
then those in * must flee into Mt 24:16
and from all over * traveled out Mk 1:5
all over Galilee, *, Jerusalem, Mk 3:7,8
lived when Herod was king of *. Lk 1:5
the highlands of * to the town Lk 1:39,40
go to Bethlehem in *, King David's Lk 2:4
(Pilate was governor over * at Lk 3:1
wastelands of *, where Satan Lk 4:1
in synagogues throughout *. Lk 4:44
and *, as well as from Jerusalem. Lk 5:17
For people from all over * and Lk 6:17,18
* and even out across the borders. Lk 7:17
Then let the people of * flee to Lk 21:21
*, from Galilee to Jerusalem!" Lk 23:5
of Arimathea in *, went to Pilate Lk 23:50,51,52
a while in * and baptized there. Jn 3:22
did)— he left * and returned to Jn 4:3
* and was traveling in Galilee. Jn 4:46,47
in Galilee after coming from *. Jn 4:54
to stay out of * where the Jewish Jn 7:1
to go to * for the celebration. Jn 7:3
his disciples, "Let's go to *." Jn 11:7
in * were trying to kill you. Jn 11:8
throughout *, in Samaria, and to Act 1:8
*, Cappadocia, Pontus, Ausia, Act 2:9
apostles fled into * and Samaria. Act 8:1
peace throughout *, Galilee and Act 9:31
spread all through *, beginning Act 10:36,37
other brothers in * that Gentiles Act 11:1
the Christians in *, each giving as Act 11:29
some men from * arrived and began Act 15:1
arrived from * and visited us. Act 21:10
and through *, and also to the Act 26:20
We have had no letters from * or Act 28:21
you could send me on my way to *. 2Co 1:15,16
And still the Christians in * Gal 1:22
the churches in * did, persecution 1Th 2:14

JUDEAN
the * Desert, and the Negeb. Jos 12:8-24
Hebron, in the * hills, as a City Jos 21:9-16
him king of the * confederacy. 2Sa 2:4
as king of the * confederacy for 2Sa 2:10,11
"Am I a * dog to be kicked around 2Sa 3:8
Rehoboam and the * leaders from 2Ch 12:5
King Asa's * army was 300,000 2Ch 14:8
Three hundred thousand * troops 2Ch 17:14,15
captured 200,000 * women and 2Ch 28:8
I led the * leaders to the top of Neh 12:31,32
* kings, Jehoiakim and Zedekiah. Eze 23:17f
those living in * lowlands shall Ob 1:19
are but a small * village, yet you Mic 5:2
an unimportant * village, for a Mt 2:6
preaching out in the * wilderness. Mt 3:1
Judea must flee into the * hills. Mt 24:16
out into the * wastelands to see Mk 1:5
and went southward to the * Mk 10:1
—flee, if you can, to the * hills. Mk 13:14
spread through the * hills. Lk 1:65
into the * wilderness to see?" Lk 7:24

JUDGE
May the Lord * you for doing this Gen 16:5
Literally, "Let the Lord * Gen 16:5f
Should not the * of all the earth Gen 18:25
Am I God, to * and punish you? Gen 50:19
think you are our prince and *! Ex 2:14
"May God * you for making us Ex 5:21
"I am their *, deciding who is Ex 18:15,16
one * for each 1000 people; Ex 18:21
the people shall * whether or not Num 35:24
and the chief * on duty at the time Deu 17:9
of the priest or * appointed by God Deu 17:12
is a beating, the * shall command Deu 25:1
Each * rescued the people of Ju 2:18
them as long as that * lived. Ju 2:18
But when the * died, the people Ju 2:19
The next * after Ehud was Shamgar Ju 3:31
DEATH, the next * of Israel was Ju 10:1
He was Israel's * for Ju 10:2
but Jehovah the * will soon show Ju 11:27
Jephthah was Israel's * for six Ju 12:7
The next * was Ibzan, who lived Ju 12:8
The next * was Elon from Zebulun. Ju 12:11,12
He was Israel's * for eight Ju 12:14
Samson was Israel's * for the Ju 15:20
And he will * your deeds. 1Sa 2:3
that Samuel became Israel's *. 1Sa 7:6
Samuel continued as Israel's * 1Sa 7:15
to Samuel, "Don't * by a man's 1Sa 16:7
way you do! Men * by outward 1Sa 16:7
May the Lord * as to which of us 1Sa 24:15
I surely wish I were the *; 2Sa 15:4
right; * whether or not he did it. 1Ki 8:32
of our fathers see and * you." 1Ch 12:17
For he comes to * the earth. 1Ch 16:33
Are you qualified to * the Job 11:7
who can rebuke God, the supreme *? Job 21:22
How can he * through the thick Job 22:13
him, and be acquitted by my *. Job 23:7
"For I, as an honest *, Job 29:12
going to condemn the Almighty *? Job 34:17
God is a * who is perfectly fair, Ps 7:11
he sits upon his throne to * Ps 9:7,8
O Lord, arise and * and punish Ps 9:19
Literally, "* me according to Ps 35:24f
they are brought before the *. Ps 37:33
He has come to * his people. Ps 50:4
God will * them with complete Ps 50:6
O GOD, HELP the king to * as you Ps 72:1
Stand up, O God, and * the earth. Ps 82:8
Arise and * the earth; Ps 94:1
He will * all nations fairly. Ps 96:10
For the Lord is coming to * the Ps 96:13
he will * the nations fairly and Ps 96:13
* the world with perfect justice. Ps 98:8,9
him to court before an unfair *. Ps 109:6
God will help the king to * the Pro 16:10
It is wrong for a * to favor the Pro 18:5
A king sitting as * weighs all Pro 20:8
Don't fawn on the *, but ask the Pro 29:26
season God will * everything man Ecc 3:17
For God will * us for everything Ecc 12:14
Next, he will * the haughty Is 3:16
He will not * by appearance, Is 11:3
to beat up the * who sentenced him, Is 29:21
For the Lord is our *, our Is 33:22
to the slaughter. * them, O God! Jer 12:3
I am ready to * you because of all Jer 21:12
Give justice to these you *! Jer 21:12
of rebels, a land that I will *! Jer 50:21
be my *, to prove me right. Lam 3:59
souls are mine to *—fathers and Eze 18:4
I will * each of you, O Israel, Eze 18:30
you nothing. * them, son of dust; Eze 20:4
I will * you there, and get rid Eze 20:35,36
everywhere will * them for what Eze 23:45
But I will * each of you in Eze 33:20
I will surely * between these fat Eze 34:20
of Heaven, the * of all, whose Dan 4:37
Almighty God—sat down to *. Dan 7:9
the * of Israel on the face. Mic 5:1
The governor and * alike demand Mic 7:3
And he will * the nations. Mt 12:18
of my Father and * each person Mt 16:27
who made me a * over you to decide Lk 12:14
*, lest he sentence you to jail; Lk 12:58
"There was a city *," he said, Lk 18:2
harmed her. The * ignored her for Lk 18:4,5
"If even an evil * can be worn Lk 18:6
himself, and to * the sins of all Jn 5:27
the Father. I * as I am told. Jn 5:30
me, I am not his *—for I have come Jn 12:47
to save the world and not to * it. Jn 12:47
"Then take him away and * him Jn 18:31
'Who made you a ruler and * over Act 7:27
made you a ruler and * over us?' Act 7:35
be the * of all—living and dead. Act 10:42
What kind of * are you to break Act 23:3
you have been a * of Jewish affairs Act 24:10
Do you think that God will * and Rom 2:3
be the just * of all the world. Rom 2:5
Jesus Christ will * the secret Rom 2:16
For he could not * and condemn Rom 3:7
not in those days * them guilty of Rom 5:13
I dare not * how effectively he Rom 15:18
It isn't our job to * outsiders. 1Co 5:12
But it certainly is our job to * 1Co 5:12
God alone is the * of those on 1Co 5:13
going to * and govern the world? 1Co 6:2
we Christians will * and reward the 1Co 6:3
our sins, will no longer be our *. 1Co 15:55,56
will some day * the living and the 2Ti 4:1
the righteous *, will give me on 2Ti 4:8
the * no one was here to help me. 2Ti 4:16
and to God who is * of all; Heb 12:23
* them on how well they do this. Heb 13:17
the law can rightly * among us. Jas 4:12
So what right do you have to * or Jas 4:12
The great * is coming. Jas 5:9
He will * you with perfect 1Pe 1:17
the * of all, living and dead; 1Pe 4:5
it be before you * the people of Rev 6:10
It is time to * the dead, and Rev 11:18
has come when he will sit as *. Rev 14:7
is ready to * her for her crimes. Rev 18:5
who had been given the right to *. Rev 20:4

JUDGED
* the smaller matters themselves. Ex 18:26
lest they be * guilty and die. Num 18:22
Whenever anyone is * guilty of Num 35:31
* by the amount of your harvest. Deu 16:10
who * Israel for twenty-two years. Ju 10:3
marry his sons. He * Israel for Ju 12:9,10
from Zebulun. He * Israel for ten Ju 12:11,12
He had * Israel for twenty years. Ju 16:31
He had * Israel for forty years. 1Sa 4:18
stood before him, waiting to be *. Dan 7:10
been * and sentenced to death." Zec 5:3
my message will be * at the Day of Jn 12:48
of this world has already been *. Jn 16:11
intelligence, as * by this world's 1Co 3:18
not need to be * and punished. 1Co 11:31
Yet, when we are * and punished 1Co 11:32
Christ to be * and have our lives 2Co 5:10
will be justly * for believing 2Th 2:12
You will be * on whether or not Jas 2:12
Christians must be *, what terrible 1Pe 4:17
And the dead were * according to Rev 20:12
Each was * according to his Rev 20:13

JUDGES
*, one judge for each 1000 people; Ex 18:21
he in turn will have ten * under Ex 18:21
them will be two *, each Ex 18:21
will have five * beneath him, each Ex 18:21
and made them * over the Ex 18:25
him before the * and shall publicly Ex 21:6
demand, and as the * approve. Ex 21:22
The * will determine the amount. Ex 21:30
officials—your * and your rulers. Ex 22:28
"* must always be just in their Lev 19:15
Moses and Aaron and the other *. Num 15:33
So Moses ordered the * to execute Num 25:5
"Appoint * and administrative Deu 16:18
the priests and * on duty before Deu 19:17
the elders and * shall measure Deu 21:2
of her virginity to the city *. Deu 22:15
spread the garment before the *. Deu 22:17,18
the judges. The * shall sentence Deu 22:17,18
not a virgin, the * shall take the Deu 22:21
the people, your *, and your Deu 29:10
elders, officers, *, and the Jos 8:33
been tried by the *, and must live Jos 20:6
Israel—the elders, *, and Jos 23:2
elders, officers, and *. Jos 24:1
* to save them from their enemies. Ju 2:16
not listen to the *, but broke Ju 2:17
was from Shechem (* 8:30–31), so Ju 9:2f
LONG AGO WHEN * ruled in Israel, a Ru 1:1
He * throughout the earth. 1Sa 2:10
his sons as * in his place. 1Sa 8:1
did when the * ruled my people. 2Sa 7:10,11
the days of the * of Israel, and 2Ki 23:22
before, when the * ruled them. 1Ch 17:10
to be bailiffs and *, four thousand 1Ch 23:4,5
public administrators and *. 1Ch 26:29
the army officers and * to Gibeon 2Ch 1:2,3
He appointed * throughout the 2Ch 19:5
among God's *, no partiality, no 2Ch 19:7
priests and clan leaders and *. 2Ch 19:8
to you by the * out in the 2Ch 19:10

(JUDGES Con't)
scribe), several * and other local Ez 4:8,9
select and appoint * and other Ez 7:25
with the elders and * of his city; Ez 10:14
and I were designated as *; Ez 10:16-19
God blinds the eyes of the * and Job 9:24
makes fools of counselors and *. Job 12:17
too, must be punished by the *. Job 31:28
a God who * justly here on earth. Ps 58:11
He pronounces judgment on the *. Ps 82:1
Literally, "He * among the Ps 82:1f
How long will you * refuse to Ps 82:2
* 7:25. Ps 83:11f
* 7:25. Ps 83:11f
* 8:21. Ps 83:11f
* 8:21. Ps 83:11f
There are the * holding court Ps 122:5
rulers and their *, young men and Ps 148:11
Street, and to the * in their Pro 1:21
I show the * who is right and who Pro 8:14,15
will give you good * and wise Is 1:26
he will destroy her armies, *, Is 3:2
You be the *! Is 5:3
WOE TO UNJUST * and to those who Is 10:1
justice to your * and great courage Is 28:6
the Lord, and their * ignored me; Jer 2:8
in Joshua and *—a great city north Jer 49:30f
"They will serve as * to resolve Eze 44:24
captains, *, treasurers, Dan 3:2
See * 19:14ff. Hos 9:9f
*, chapters 19 and 20. Hos 10:9f
the "Valley Where Jehovah *" Joe 3:2
How you hate honest *! Amo 5:10
they can get. Her * are like Zep 3:3
for me and * [those who reject me Jn 8:50
"There is one who seeks and *." Jn 8:50f
as an inheritance. * ruled for Act 13:19,20
before the * at the marketplace. Act 16:19
and Silas, and the * ordered them Act 16:22
The next morning the * sent Act 16:35
reported to the *, who feared for Act 16:38
as well as the *, were concerned at Act 17:8,9
the * can take the case at once. Act 19:38
Why then go to outside * who are 1Co 6:4
pray has no favorites when he *. 1Pe 1:17
hands of God who always * fairly. 1Pe 2:23
for mighty is the Lord who * Rev 18:8

JUDGING
for you are * in the place of God. Deu 1:17
the * of the people of the land. 2Ch 26:21
sit high above them, * their Ps 7:7,8
on the throne, * righteously." Ps 9:4f
for God is * her from heaven. Jer 51:9
and fair when * others, and obeys Eze 18:8
* the twelve tribes of Israel. Mt 19:28
and you will sit on thrones * the Lk 22:30
I am not * you now; Jn 8:15
a day for justly * the world by the Act 17:31
the floor"—well, * a man by his Jas 2:4

JUDGMENT
Egypt, and execute * upon all the Ex 12:12
"You must be impartial in *. Lev 19:35,36
and was brought to Moses for *. Lev 24:11
defy the court's * a second time. Deu 17:13
and strong, and had good, solid *. 1Sa 16:18
the Throne Room or * Hall, where 1Ki 7:7
give you the good * to follow all 1Ch 22:12
In that way God executed * upon 2Ch 24:24
and the king trusted their *. Est 1:13-15
Rather that than face the * sent Job 31:23
a man is called before God in *. Job 34:23
They are not safe on * Day; Ps 1:5
be forgiven. * will not touch him Ps 32:6
he knows their * day is coming. Ps 37:12,13
David of God's * against him Ps 51:1
It is his *, poured out upon the Ps 75:8
He pronounces * on the judges. Ps 82:1
Give fair * to the poor man, the Ps 82:3
are his prize. * will again be Ps 94:15
When his case is called for *, Ps 109:7
Now teach me good * as well as Ps 119:66
for good * and common sense, then Pro 3:4,5
and has good * and common sense Pro 3:13,14,15
develop good * and common sense! Pro 4:5
develop common sense and good *. Pro 4:7
Wisdom and good * live together, Pro 8:12
you simple ones without good *; Pro 9:4
Your riches won't help you on * Pro 11:4
It is poor * to countersign Pro 17:18
God's contempt and *, yet in the Is 9:1
The watchman replies, "Your * Is 21:12
for only when you come in * on Is 26:9
I will send heavy * upon you and Is 29:2
This * on Edom will never end. Is 34:10
God will make my words of * Is 49:2
unaided, I meted out *. Is 63:5
Lord and the * that follows sin. Jer 5:5
say, "God won't bring * on us. Jer 12:4
Wherever you run to escape my *, Jer 16:16
And now I will pour out * upon Jer 23:2
holy words of * against them. Jer 23:9
That cry of * will reach the Jer 25:31
where he pronounced * upon him. Jer 39:5
too, for God's * has been poured Jer 48:21
for the time of your * has come. Jer 48:44
You must drink this cup of *! Jer 49:12
and there * was passed upon him. Jer 52:9
died before the hand of * fell. Lam 5:7
The day of * has come; Eze 7:10,11
I withdrew my * against them to Eze 20:22
bring you into my desert * hall. Eze 20:35,36
from the land. My * will be a Eze 23:48
Thus I will bring down my * upon Eze 25:11
She will be drawn down to *. Eze 32:20
That day of * will come; Eze 39:8
and balanced *, the king found Dan 1:20
But in God's time and plan, his * Dan 9:27
Suddenly, without warning, my * Hos 6:5
day of the Lord's * approaches. Joe 2:1
The day of the * of the Lord is Joe 2:11
sit to pronounce * on them all. Joe 3:12
Lord is near, in the Valley of *. Joe 3:14
Prepare to meet your God in *, Amo 4:12
deeds you bring the Day of * near. Amo 6:3
But your * day is coming swiftly Mic 7:4
Drink down God's * on yourselves. Hab 2:16
For the awesome Day of his * has Zep 1:7
"On that Day of * I will punish Zep 1:8
is time—before * begins, and your Zep 2:2
for the * is against you, too. Zep 2:5
remove his hand of *, and disperse Zep 3:15
my * and quieted my anger there." Zec 6:8
OPEN YOUR DOORS, O Lebanon, to *. Zec 11:1
"the day of * is coming, burning Mal 4:1
"And even now the axe of God's * Mt 3:10
you are in danger of *! Mt 5:22
At the * Mt 7:22
be better off at * Day than they. Mt 10:15
better off on the * Day than you! Mt 11:22
off at the * Day than you." Mt 11:24
give account on * Day for every Mt 12:36
nation at the * and condemn you. Mt 12:41
nation in the *, and condemn it; Mt 12:42
How shall you escape the * of Mt 23:33
Yes, all the accumulated * of Mt 23:36
off to the * of the hypocrites; Mt 24:51
The axe of his * is poised over Lk 3:9
off than such a city on the * Day. Lk 10:12
Cities destroyed by God in * for Lk 10:13f
punishment on the * Day than you. Lk 10:14
"And at the * Day the Queen of Lk 11:31
Yes, awesome * is awaiting you. Lk 11:44
For those will be days of God's *, Lk 21:22
And the Father leaves all * of Jn 5:22
who have continued in evil, to *. Jn 5:29
"But I pass no * without Jn 5:30
And my * is absolutely fair and Jn 5:30
You pass * on me without knowing Jn 8:15
absolutely correct * in every Jn 8:16
The time of * for the world has Jn 12:31
of * by the truths I have spoken. Jn 12:48
and of deliverance from *. Jn 16:8
of sin and righteousness and *." Jn 16:8f
there is deliverance from * Jn 16:11
sat down at the * bench on the Jn 19:13
Literally, "the * seat in a place Jn 19:13f
"And so my * is that we should Act 15:19
him before the governor for *. Act 18:12
* to come, Felix was terrified. Act 24:25
they stand before God at * Day Rom 1:20
So the * of God lies very heavily Rom 3:19
before the * Seat of God. Rom 14:10
at Christ's * Day to see what kind 1Co 3:13
I don't even trust my own * on 1Co 4:3
and drinking God's * upon himself; 1Co 11:29
he is preparing * and punishment 2Th 1:6
angels, bringing * on those who do 2Th 1:8
But in other cases only the * day 1Ti 5:24
He died under God's * against Tit 2:14
of the dead and eternal *. Heb 6:2
after that comes *, so also Christ Heb 9:27
win out over his * against you. Jas 2:13
receive on that coming day of *. Jas 5:3
For the time has come for *, and 1Pe 4:17
and darkness until the * day. 2Pe 2:4
until the day of final * comes. 2Pe 2:9
bonfire at the * day, when all 2Pe 3:7
at the day of *, but can face him 1Jn 4:17
darkness, waiting for the * day. Jud 1:6
before him in *, to receive just Jud 1:15
for they are fully ripe for *." Rev 14:18
in sending this *, O Holy One, who Rev 16:5
coming * Day of God Almighty. Rev 16:14
In one moment her * fell." Rev 18:10
For at last God has given * Rev 18:20

JUDGMENTS
Literally, "His *." Ps 105:7f
experienced) your righteous *." Ps 119:7f
will carry out my * against you. Eze 11:9
the way; my * will be fulfilled!" Eze 21:7
for his * are just and true. Rev 19:2

JUDITH
*, daughter of Be-eri the Hethite; Gen 26:34

JUG
with a water * on her shoulder and Gen 24:15,1
lowered the * for him to drink. Gen 24:1
So she emptied the * into the Gen 24:2
her water * upon her shoulder; Gen 24:4
and drew water and filled the *. Gen 24:4
She quickly lifted the * down Gen 24:4
his spear and his * of water and 1Sa 26:1
So David took the spear and * of 1Sa 26:12
spear and the * of water that was 1Sa 26:16

JUGS
All your * will be full of wine. Jer 13:12
I set cups and * of wine before Jer 35:5

JUICE
and squeezed the * into it, and Gen 40:11
wine, grape *, grapes, or raisins! Num 6:3,4
* as they suffer from thirst. Job 24:11
will not produce a gallon of *! Is 5:10
who tread the * from the grapes. Jer 25:30
but get no * to make your wine. Mic 6:15
*, and built a watchman's tower. Mk 12:1

JULIA
Give my love to Philologus, *, Rom 16:15

JULIUS
*, a member of the imperial guard. Act 27:1
docked at Sidon, * was very kind to Act 27:3
swim ashore and escape. But * Act 27:43

JULY
The date of his death was * 15, Num 33:38,39
city was eaten on * 24, and that 2Ki 25:3
from Babylon on * 22 of the 2Ki 25:8
of the month of *—and they wrote as Est 8:9,10
other times until * of the eleventh Jer 1:3
in the month of *, they breached Jer 39:2
Late in *, 587 B.C. Jer 52:12f
LATE IN *, six Eze 20:1
in *, August, October, and January Zec 8:19

JUMP
the exception of those that *; Lev 11:21,22
Then you will * up from your Jos 8:7
of the Temple. "* off," he said, Mt 4:6
you are the Son of God, * off! Lk 4:9,10,11
road ready to * him and kill him. Act 23:21
who could swim to * overboard and Act 27:43
So be careful not to * to 1Co 4:5

JUMPED
Joseph * into his chariot and Gen 46:29
saw this, he * up, grabbed a spear, Num 25:7
his signal, they * up and poured Jos 8:19
he and his men * up from their Ju 9:43
west of Geba * up from where they Ju 20:33
"What is it?" He * up and ran 1Sa 3:4,5
And again Samuel * up and ran 1Sa 3:6
more Samuel * up and ran to Eli. 1Sa 3:8
But David * aside and escaped. 1Sa 18:11,12
Then the other sons of the king * 2Sa 13:29,30
The king * up, ripped off his 2Sa 13:31
Then Adonijah and his guests * up 1Ki 1:49,50
When Naaman saw him coming, he * 2Ki 5:21
Then Jehu * into a chariot and 2Ki 9:16
man revived and * to his feet! 2Ki 13:20,21
King Rehoboam he * into his chariot 2Ch 10:18
The king * to his feet and went Est 7:7
moved for him. I * up to open it Sol 5:5
with him suddenly * up, pulled out Jer 41:2
Nebuchadnezzar * up in amazement Dan 3:24
And the boy * up and left! Mt 9:7
* up and went along with him. Mt 9:9
she * up and was all right again! Mt 9:25
"All the girls * up and trimmed Mt 25:7,8
The man * up, took the stretcher, Mk 2:12
And Levi * to his feet and went Mk 2:14
And she * up and walked around! Mk 5:41,42
it aside, * up and came to Jesus. Mk 10:50
watched, the man * to his feet, Lk 5:25
her life returned and she * up! Lk 8:55
* into the water [and swam ashore Jn 21:7
* up to argue that Paul was all Act 23:9

JUMPING
the crippled were walking and * Mt 15:31
them to fury; and * up, they Lk 4:29

JUMPS
But whenever she * up to run, Job 39:18
a person falls, he * up again; Jer 8:4,5

JUNE
They all came to Jerusalem in * 2Ch 15:10
tithes arrived in *, and the piles 2Ch 31:7,8
Temple began in * of the second Ez 3:8
One day late in *, when I was Eze 1:1

JUNGLE
dens, or lie in wait in the *? Job 38:39,40
her—and let them grow into a *; Hos 1:12

JUNGLES
what will you do in Jordan's *? Jer 12:5
a lion from the * of Jordan that Jer 50:44

JUNIAS
Then there are Andronicus and *, Rom 16:7

JUNIPER
waving branches of * trees and 2Sa 6:5

JUPITER
was the Greek god *, and that Paul, Act 14:12

JUPITER Con't)	
of the Temple of *, located on the	Act 14:13
JURISDICTION	
for Galilee was under Herod's *;	Lk 23:7
JUSHAB-HESED	
*, Shelomith (a daughter).	1Ch 3:19,20
JUST	
female, * as God commanded Noah.	Gen 7:8,9
female, * as God had commanded.	Gen 7:16
when they have * begun to exploit	Gen 11:6
political unity, * think of what	Gen 11:6
The king of Sodom told him, "*	Gen 14:21
also, * as you have asked me to.	Gen 17:20
* as God had told him to.	Gen 17:23
Next year, * as I told you, I	Gen 18:14
who are * and good—so that I can do	Gen 18:19
they said, "we'll * stretch out	Gen 19:2
close by and it is * a small one.	Gen 19:18,19,20
had led me along * the right path	Gen 24:48
your descendants, * as I promised	Gen 26:3
will not harm us, * as we have not	Gen 26:29
and prepare it * the way I like	Gen 27:2,3,4
dear son. * do what I tell you.	Gen 27:13
Isaac: "Then who is it who was *	Gen 27:33
"* think, my very own flesh and	Gen 29:14
to him one day, "* because we are	Gen 29:15
and again * as you promised me.	Gen 32:10
"we'll get along * fine.	Gen 33:15
Jacob, arriving * as Jacob's sons	Gen 34:6,7
too, * as he had his two brothers.	Gen 38:11
* as Joseph had predicted.	Gen 40:22
And everything happened * as he	Gen 41:13
began, * as Joseph had predicted.	Gen 41:54
let me say * this one word to you.	Gen 44:18
* as Pharaoh had commanded.	Gen 47:11
me * as Reuben and Simeon will.	Gen 48:5
as we were * a short distance from	Gen 48:7
a man, and maimed oxen * for fun.	Gen 49:6
Located * west of the Jordan	Gen 50:10f
"Did you * leave him there?	Ex 2:20
was the reply. "* say, 'I Am has	Ex 3:14
again, it was normal, * as before!	Ex 4:7
Lord, I'm * not a good speaker.	Ex 4:10
but you must produce * as many	Ex 5:10,11
"Fulfill your daily quota * as	Ex 5:13
* as the Lord had predicted.	Ex 7:13
Moses and Aaron, * as the Lord had	Ex 7:22
go, * as the Lord had predicted.	Ex 8:15
them, * as the Lord had predicted.	Ex 8:19
refused to listen, * as the Lord	Ex 9:12
the people leave, * as the Lord had	Ex 9:35
"But * who is it you want to	Ex 10:8
"I will send * one more disaster	Ex 11:1
living among you * as much as to	Ex 12:19
will give you, * as he promised,	Ex 12:25
they shall be * as though they had	Ex 12:48
own unique people, * as though he	Ex 13:9
as God's people, * as much as if	Ex 13:16
"Don't be afraid. * stand where	Ex 14:13
measure, there was * enough for	Ex 16:18
Each home had * enough.	Ex 16:18
Aaron did this, * as the Lord	Ex 16:34
to report * what happened to it,	Ex 22:10
of a man * because he is poor.	Ex 23:2,3
* as I commanded you before.	Ex 23:15
made from planks, * as was shown	Ex 27:8
this opening, * as on the neck of a	Ex 28:32
and engrave on it, * as you would	Ex 28:36
Place the altar * outside the	Ex 30:6
for seven days, * as I instructed	Ex 34:18
and 7½ feet wide, * the same as the	Ex 38:18
* as God had directed Moses.	Ex 39:4,5
tribes of Israel, * as initials are	Ex 39:6,7
piece of work, * like the ephod,	Ex 39:8
hole at the center * as in a coat	Ex 39:23
* as the Lord had commanded Moses.	Ex 39:25,26
* as Jehovah had commanded Moses.	Ex 39:28,29
* as the Lord had instructed.	Ex 39:31
* as the Lord had commanded him.	Ex 40:19
it, * as the Lord had commanded.	Ex 40:21
Lord, * as the Lord had commanded.	Ex 40:23
* as the Lord had commanded.	Ex 40:27
* as the Lord had commanded him.	Ex 40:29
* as the Lord had commanded Moses.	Ex 40:32
of burnt offering, * as in the case	Lev 4:10
and burn it there, * as though it	Lev 4:21
upon the altar, * as if it were the	Lev 4:26
be taken off, * as in the procedure	Lev 4:31
The fat shall be used * as in	Lev 4:35
it on the altar * as any other	Lev 5:12
to the priest, * as was the case	Lev 5:13
it is most holy, * as is the entire	Lev 6:17
* as the Lord had instructed him.	Lev 8:29
* as I instructed you to do.	Lev 8:31
and offered it in * the same way as	Lev 9:15
to him, * as Moses had commanded.	Lev 9:21
—contrary to what the Lord had *	Lev 10:1
of his right foot—* as he did with	Lev 14:17
of his right foot, * as he did with	Lev 14:28
time is defiled, * as it would be	Lev 15:26
mercy are, * whenever he chooses.	Lev 16:1
in front of it, * as he did with	Lev 16:15
of the land, * as I will throw out	Lev 18:28
"Judges must always be * in	Lev 19:15
its own flag, * as each was	Num 2:3-31
and his sons, * as any other gift	Num 8:13
everything was done * as the Lord	Num 8:22
* as the Lord had commanded.	Num 9:4,5
of the men had * attended a	Num 9:6,7
You shall eat it, not for * a	Num 11:19,20
steadfast love, * as you have	Num 14:19
But I vow by my own name that *	Num 14:20,21
It shall be credited to you * as	Num 18:30
* seen by the death of Cozbi."	Num 25:18
disappear * because he had no son?	Num 27:3,4
the Lord, * as you have said."	Num 32:27
* as you saw him do in Egypt.	Deu 1:30
in the wilderness, * as a father	Deu 1:31
of Esau, * as Israel would displace	Deu 2:12
kingdom of Bashan * as we had	Deu 3:6
from these; * obey them, for they	Deu 4:2
It was * because he loves you,	Deu 7:8
But don't be afraid of them! *	Deu 7:18
certainly perish, * as the Lord	Deu 8:20
day, * as the Lord commanded me.	Deu 10:5
his name, * as is done today.	Deu 10:8
the second time, * as I had the	Deu 10:10
you go, * as he has promised.	Deu 11:25
to your God * anywhere, as the	Deu 12:4,5
your burnt offerings * anywhere;	Deu 12:13
anywhere, * as you do now with	Deu 12:15
on your own farms, * as you do	Deu 12:20-23
* as he promised your ancestors.	Deu 13:17
time, may eat it, * as anyone may	Deu 15:22
evening * as the sun goes down.	Deu 16:6
name of the Lord, * like his	Deu 18:6,7
his right, not * if he is in need.	Deu 18:8
'Has anyone * built a new house,	Deu 20:5
Has anyone * planted a vineyard	Deu 20:6
Has anyone * become engaged?	Deu 20:7
Eat all the fruit you wish; *	Deu 20:19
the widows, * as you commanded me;	Deu 26:13
very own people, * as he promised,	Deu 26:18
in the land, * as he promised: many	Deu 28:11
bright sunlight * as the blind man	Deu 28:29
"* as the Lord has rejoiced over	Deu 28:63
he is your God, * as he promised	Deu 29:13
of vegetation—* like Sodom and	Deu 29:23
in the land, * as he destroyed	Deu 31:4
Everything he does is * and fair.	Deu 32:4
your ancestors, * as Aaron your	Deu 32:50
be with you * as I was with Moses;	Jos 1:5
"We will obey you * as we obeyed	Jos 1:17,18
of heaven, not * an ordinary god.	Jos 2:11
am with you * as I was with Moses.	Jos 3:7
for each tribe, * as the Lord had	Jos 4:8
goods hidden there * as Achan had	Jos 7:22
away again * as they did before!'	Jos 8:6
was slaughtered, * as at Jericho.	Jos 10:30
was slaughtered, * as at Libnah.	Jos 10:32
And they killed everyone * as	Jos 10:39
in the land, * as the Lord God of	Jos 10:40
were slaughtered, * as Moses had	Jos 11:12
So Joshua took the entire land *	Jos 11:23
of Canaan you were * in shall	Jos 14:9
And the Lord gave them peace, *	Jos 21:44
instead, * as he has promised you.	Jos 23:4,5
But follow the Lord your God *	Jos 23:8
for you, * as he has promised.	Jos 23:10
he promised, * as certainly he will	Jos 23:15,16
And it happened * that way!	Ju 6:38
in the valley * below, the Lord	Ju 7:8,9
one of the tents * as a man inside	Ju 7:12,13
was * stand there worshiping God!	Ju 7:15
he told them, "do * as I do.	Ju 7:17
It was * after midnight and the	Ju 7:19,20
Then they * stood and watched as	Ju 7:21
* like you—like sons of kings!"	Ju 8:18
God and man, * to wave to and fro	Ju 9:9
and fruit * to lift my head above	Ju 9:11
both God and man, * to be mightier	Ju 9:13
* because he is your relative.	Ju 9:18
* punishment for these murders.	Ju 9:24
"You're * seeing shadows that	Ju 9:36
And besides, * who do you think	Ju 11:25
found her to be * what he wanted,	Ju 14:7
Were we invited to this party *	Ju 14:15
So while he slept, she did * that	Ju 16:14
"Come * this once more," she	Ju 16:18
I'll * shake myself free."	Ju 16:20
armed men standing * outside the	Ju 18:15,16
Israel instead of * to one man in	Ju 18:19
pleaded, "Stay * today and leave	Ju 19:8
getting late. Stay * tonight, and	Ju 19:9
The sun was setting * as they	Ju 19:14
village square. * then an old man	Ju 19:16
supper together. * as they were	Ju 19:22
Finally, * at dawn, they let her	Ju 19:25
and asked him * what had happened.	Ju 20:3
* as on the previous days.	Ju 20:35-39
Then Naomi said to her, "* be	Ru 3:15-18
Please don't think that I am *	1Sa 1:15,16
linen robe * like the priest's.	1Sa 2:18
slaves * as they have been ours."	1Sa 4:9
"I have * come from the battle—I	1Sa 4:16
suddenly began. * before she died,	1Sa 4:20
two cows that have * had	1Sa 6:7
And the Lord responded. * as	1Sa 7:10
But the servant said, "I've *	1Sa 9:6
He lives * inside the city gates.	1Sa 9:12,13
He has * arrived back from a trip	1Sa 9:12,13
* then Saul approached Samuel and	1Sa 9:18
himself—* because he wanted to!	1Sa 12:22
himself. But * as he was	1Sa 13:10
then we will do * that;	1Sa 14:10
the raiders. And * then there was a	1Sa 14:15
of the camp * as the Israeli army	1Sa 17:20
you * want to see the battle!"	1Sa 17:28
this from me. It * isn't so."	1Sa 20:2
It had * been replaced that day	1Sa 21:6
"* the thing!"	1Sa 21:9
was no use. But * then a message	1Sa 23:27
He is a fool—* like his name	1Sa 25:25
the Lord your God, * as though you	1Sa 25:29
He has done * as he said he	1Sa 28:17
The sun was * going down as they	2Sa 2:24
David, * as the Lord predicted."	2Sa 3:9,10
But * after Abner left, Joab and	2Sa 3:22
that Abner had * been there	2Sa 3:23
This pleased his people, * as	2Sa 3:35,36
You are doing all these things *	2Sa 7:21
(She had * completed the	2Sa 11:4
Please, * speak to the king about	2Sa 13:13
But * then Jonadab (the son of	2Sa 13:32,33
Your sons are coming, * as I	2Sa 13:35
there * as Absalom arrived.	2Sa 15:37
DAVID WAS * past the top of the	2Sa 16:1
told him to, * as David had;	2Sa 16:23
"I am content * to have you back	2Sa 19:30
my lord the king. * to go across	2Sa 19:36
David asked. "* tell me and I	2Sa 21:4
upon my throne, * as I swore to you	1Ki 1:30
and shouting * as they were	1Ki 1:41
They have * returned, and the	1Ki 1:44,45
But now I have * a small favor	1Ki 2:16
in the same house, * the two of us,	1Ki 3:17,18
the Lord my God, * as he instructed	1Ki 5:5
to Solomon * as he had promised.	1Ki 5:12
with cedar beams, * like the inner	1Ki 7:12
* as your own people Israel do;	1Ki 8:43
* as you are doing today."	1Ki 8:61
of Israel forever, * as I promised	1Ki 9:5
And you give your people a *,	1Ki 10:9
ashes poured out, * as the prophet	1Ki 13:5
am a prophet too, * as you are;	1Ki 13:18
and the child died * as she	1Ki 14:17
the land, * as the Lord had	1Ki 14:18
"Let us be allies * as our	1Ki 15:19
family was left, * as the Lord had	1Ki 15:29
and your family, * as I did the	1Ki 16:3
I was * gathering a few sticks to	1Ki 17:12
in the containers, * as the Lord	1Ki 17:16
and gold, * as he demanded."	1Ki 20:7
outside the city * as they licked	1Ki 21:19
he worshiped idols * as the	1Ki 21:26
evening, he died. * as the sun was	1Ki 22:36,37
the king's blood * as the Lord had	1Ki 22:38
"Sir," they said, "* say the	2Ki 2:16
The water was purified, * as	2Ki 2:22
"He's * the man we want."	2Ki 3:12
year, * as Elisha had predicted.	2Ki 4:17
And sure enough, there was, * as	2Ki 4:44
of Ephraim have * arrived, and he	2Ki 5:22
dollar, * as the Lord had said!	2Ki 7:16
house and land. * as she came in,	2Ki 8:4
He was an evil king, * as all of	2Ki 8:27
field, * as the Lord said."	2Ki 9:26
* what the Lord said would happen.	2Ki 9:36
and relatives, * as Elijah,	2Ki 10:17
for my son.' But * then a wild	2Ki 14:9
and the Dead Sea, * as the Lord God	2Ki 14:25
Lord * as his father Amaziah had.	2Ki 15:3
opinion, * like his ancestors.	2Ki 15:9
Uriah built one * like it by	2Ki 16:11,12
swept them away, * as all his	2Ki 17:23
to rescue us"—* remember that he	2Ki 18:22
to another land * like this	2Ki 18:31,32
of Egypt * by walking by!"	2Ki 19:24
Asherah idol, * as Ahab the king of	2Ki 21:3,4,5
and its people, * as I stated in	2Ki 22:15,16
to defile it, * as the Lord's	2Ki 23:16
that what you have * done would	2Ki 23:17
dust, * as he had done at Bethel.	2Ki 23:19
* as I have destroyed Israel;	2Ki 23:27
the nation, * as the Lord had	2Ki 24:2
of the sanctuary, * as their	1Ch 9:19
* as the Lord had told Samuel.	1Ch 11:3
and joined David * as he was going	1Ch 12:19
instead of Saul, * as the Lord had	1Ch 12:23
carrying poles, * as the Lord had	1Ch 15:15
for that purpose, * as the Lord had	1Ch 16:40
be kings of Israel * as you are.	1Ch 17:10
wonderful promises * because you	1Ch 17:19

(JUST Con't)

This is * another example of how 1Ch 18:13
all of Israel and was a * ruler. 1Ch 18:14
will build is not * another 1Ch 29:1
in the country (* as his father 2Ch 2:17
you, * as your people Israel do; 2Ch 6:33
to give them a * king like you! 2Ch 9:8
* wait and see what I'll be like!' 2Ch 10:10
BUT * WHEN Rehoboam was at the 2Ch 12:1
priests instead. * like the people 2Ch 13:9
he has determined * the opposite of 2Ch 18:22
the Syrians, but * as the sun sank 2Ch 18:34
He was a good king, * as his 2Ch 20:32
worship idols * as in the times of 2Ch 21:13
to my son.' * then a wild animal 2Ch 25:18
and it was not * to burn incense to 2Ch 28:3
in the fire, * like the heathen 2Ch 28:3
Lord's opinion, * as his ancestor 2Ch 29:2
doing what was * and fair in the 2Ch 31:20
Name * one time when anyone, 2Ch 32:14
God of Jerusalem * as though he 2Ch 32:19
all the idols * as his father had. 2Ch 33:22
you, for we are * as interested in Ez 4:2
* as King Cyrus has commanded." Ez 4:3
and disgraced, * as we are today. Ez 9:7
God of Israel, you are a * God; Ez 9:15
our children are * like theirs," Neh 5:5
Nehemiah is * the man we need!' Neh 6:7
You're * trying to scare us into Neh 6:9
—* fifty-two days after we had Neh 6:15
and flocks, * as the law requires; Neh 10:36
and thanksgiving, * as commanded by Neh 12:24
orders, * as she had in his home. Est 2:20
and found Mordecai * outside the Est 4:6
for * such a time as this?" Est 4:14
the inner court * beyond the royal Est 5:1
Mordecai the Jew * sitting there in Est 5:13
Now, as it happened, Haman had * Est 6:4
my horse, and do * as you have Est 6:10
was reclining, * as the king Est 7:8
"Sir, Haman has * ordered a Est 7:9
you! But * take away his wealth, Job 1:11
" 'Is mere man more * than God? Job 4:17
Are you going to condemn me * Job 6:25,26
Why not * pardon my sin and take Job 7:21
He alone is strong and *. Job 9:19
I will say to God, 'Don't * Job 10:2
my iniquity. * the slightest Job 10:15
of all mankind. * as my mouth can Job 12:11
stupid and dumb? * because you Job 18:4
destroy him. * as he is about to Job 20:23
all their time * getting barely Job 24:5
All I did was * and honest, for Job 29:14
fall to be broken, * as one who Job 30:24
God had * cause for punishing him. Job 32:2
fight against him * because he does Job 33:13
an entire nation * as easily. Job 34:29,30
and yet he is so * and merciful Job 37:23
I made him, too, * as I made you! Job 40:15
His heart is hard as rock, * Job 41:24
Literally, "the *." Ps 7:9f
God's laws are pure, eternal, *. Ps 19:9
save me * because you are so Ps 31:16
He loves whatever is * and good; Ps 33:5
me "not guilty," for you are *. Ps 35:24
because he is * and fair and knows Ps 37:30,31
said, "See, I have come, * as Ps 40:7
eternal life for * one soul, to Ps 49:8,9
all heaven declares that he is *. Ps 50:6
and your sentence against me is *. Ps 51:4
me from my enemies, for you are *! Ps 71:2
that you alone are * and good. Ps 71:16
Judgment will again be * and all Ps 94:15
others and are always * and good. Ps 106:3
All he does is * and good, and Ps 111:7
* as foolish as their idols are. Ps 115:8
* tell me what to do and I will Ps 119:33,34
Be merciful * as you promised. Ps 119:58
your blessings, * as you promised. Ps 119:65
comfort me, * as you promised. Ps 119:75,76,77
oh, give me back my life again, * Ps 119:107
O Lord, you are * and your Ps 119:137
Your demands are * and right. Ps 119:138
life again * as you have promised. Ps 119:154
wonder, for each of them is *. Ps 119:172
mercy and kindness * as a servant Ps 123:2
* as the mountains surround and Ps 125:2
before the Lord, * as a child who Ps 131:2
(There's one—* over there to the Ps 142:4
* and fair in everything they did. Pro 1:3
proof of his love. * as a father Pro 3:11,12
Sure, * a little more! Pro 6:10
I was * coming to look for you Pro 7:15
Literally, "a * balance and Pro 16:11f
* AS WATER is turned into Pro 21:1
God is more pleased when we are * Pro 21:3
* as the rich rule the poor, so Pro 22:7
his reign will be * and fair. Pro 25:4,5
* as surely a retort causes Pro 25:23
* as it is harmful to eat too Pro 25:27
and says, "I was * fooling," is Pro 26:18,19
a wicked heart, * as a pretty glaze Pro 26:23
A * king gives stability to his Pro 29:4
Give me * enough to satisfy my Pro 30:8
than foolishness, * as light is Ecc 2:13,14
* as the fool will die, so will I. Ecc 2:15
your words be few. * as being too Ecc 5:1
You can identify a fool * by the Ecc 10:3
* because my complexion is so Sol 1:6
are * and good, shall be redeemed. Is 1:27
You too shall get your * deserts. Is 3:11
for he alone is holy, * and good. Is 5:16
scourges them, * as he did when he Is 9:4
"We will destroy Calno * as we Is 10:9
and we will destroy Samaria * as Is 10:9
* as the Egyptians did long ago. Is 10:24
the remnant there, * as he did for Is 11:16
place a * and righteous King." Is 16:4,5
will be left, * as a few stray Is 17:6
This is the * reward of those who Is 17:14
fist of God. * to speak the name Is 19:17
accomplished them, * as you said! Is 25:1
God will push them down * as a Is 25:11
He knows * what to do, for God Is 28:26
you to bless you, * as he said. Is 30:18
In a short time—in * a little more Is 32:10
the nations flee. * as locusts Is 33:4
away and disappear * like a Is 34:4
Jerusalem to hear this, not * you. Is 36:12
people from my power? Name * one! Is 36:20
king of Assyria! * remember what Is 37:11
all those nations, * as the letter Is 37:18
IT WAS * before all this that Is 38:1
"Why, it's * a block of wood! Is 44:19
Woe to the baby * being born who Is 45:10
* God and a Savior—no, not one! Is 45:21
when suddenly I did * what I said. Is 48:3
your Redeemer. * as in the time of Is 54:9
a government that is * and fair. Is 54:14
as yours! For * as the heavens are Is 55:9
BE * AND fair to all, the Lord God Is 56:1
reading of my laws—* as though they Is 58:2
would obey them—* as though they Is 58:2
what it means to be * and good; Is 59:8
says the Lord; for * as good grapes Is 65:8
In a moment, * as Israel's Is 66:7,8
Surely you will * forget it?" Jer 3:4,5
your minds and hearts, not * your Jer 4:4
* one, I'll not destroy the city! Jer 5:1
you into exile, * as I did your Jer 7:15
O Lord of Hosts, you are *. Jer 11:20
you from your land * as Judah will Jer 12:14
of Jerusalem, * as on other days, Jer 17:27
Because he was * and fair in all Jer 22:15
been that way—you * won't listen! Jer 22:21
* as they enslaved my people; Jer 25:14
and cursed, * as they are today. Jer 25:18
Everything has happened * as you Jer 32:24
with great joy. * as I have sent Jer 32:42
* as they did for your fathers. Jer 34:5
will cut you apart * as you cut Jer 34:18,19
(This room was * off the upper Jer 36:10
everything again * as you did Jer 36:28
we discussed, * say that you Jer 38:26
this land, * as he said he would. Jer 40:2,3
of Israel, says: * as my anger and Jer 42:18
for you and said, '* tell us what Jer 42:20
I will punish them in Egypt * as Jer 44:13
and sacrifice to her * as much as Jer 44:17
as much as we like—* as we and our Jer 44:17
who seek his life, * as I turned Jer 44:30
destroy Babylon * as he destroyed Jer 50:40
floor; in * a little while the Jer 51:33
says the Lord. * as Babylon killed Jer 51:49
the Lord God gives * punishment and Jer 51:56
But he was a wicked king, * as Jer 52:2
But it is the Lord who did it, * Lam 2:17
there, * as in my first vision! Eze 3:23
Keep * a bit of the hair and tie Eze 5:3
and give them all their * deserts. Eze 7:26,27
Israel was there, * as I had seen Eze 8:4
* then the man in linen clothing, Eze 9:11
ahead, * as the others did. Eze 10:22
Then leave the house at night, * Eze 12:4
"But if a man is * and does what Eze 18:5
laws—that man is *, says the Lord, Eze 18:9
and do what is * and right, he Eze 18:21
pollute yourselves * as your Eze 20:30
rid of the rebels, * as I did in Eze 20:35,36
my * attacks, but I found not one. Eze 22:30
"And I despised her * as I Eze 23:18
* as your sister Samaria did. Eze 23:33
prostitutes. But * persons Eze 23:45
her, * as they will upon Ammon. Eze 25:9,10
from the siege * long enough to Eze 30:21f
what's fair and * that shall live. Eze 33:19
from God, * as he told me to; Eze 37:7
have done * what I promised you." Eze 37:14
everything will happen * as I Eze 39:8
* the same as on the east side. Eze 40:22
Here at the north entry, * as at Eze 40:23
were * the same as in the others. Eze 40:24
on the pillars, * as the others. Eze 40:31
there were * like the others: The Eze 40:35
and palm trees, * as on the walls. Eze 41:25
It was * as I had seen it in the Eze 43:3
sacrifices * as on the Sabbaths. Eze 46:12
* as they do the Mediterranean! Eze 47:10
three times a day, * as he always Dan 6:10
is literal, and means * that. Dan 8:26
with sin, * as you see us now; Dan 9:7
us up. In * a couple of days, Hos 6:2
it is polluted, * as food of Hos 9:4
* as at Beth-arbel, which Shalman Hos 10:14
of Gilgal flourish * the same. Hos 12:11
some will escape, * as the Lord has Joe 2:32
and right. And * as stupid is your Amo 6:13
am * a herdsman and fruit picker. Amo 7:14
back to you again, * as before. Mic 4:8
is: to be fair and * and merciful, Mic 6:8
How could God be * while saying Mic 6:11
surely come to pass. * be patient! Hab 2:3
Now you will get your * deserts Hab 2:6
His power is * the same as Hab 3:6
of Hosts says, 'In * a little while Hag 2:6
"He has done * what he warned us Zec 1:5,6
will be their God, * and true and Zec 8:8
with the Jews, * as the Jebusites Zec 9:7
Literally, "a * man." Mt 1:19f
you are not * an unimportant Judean Mt 2:6
who long to be * and good, for they Mt 5:6
or black. Say * a simple 'Yes, I Mt 5:37
on the * and on the unjust too. Mt 5:45
on earth, * as it is in heaven. Mt 6:10
us our sins, * as we have forgiven Mt 6:12
the way they act, * as you can Mt 7:16
* then Mt 8:19
The disciples * sat there, awed! Mt 8:27
"My little daughter has * Mt 9:18
Yes, and he is more than * a Mt 11:9
"If you had * one sheep, and it Mt 12:11
normal, * like the other one! Mt 12:13
"* as in this story the thistles Mt 13:40
"He's * a carpenter's son, and Mt 13:55
The crowds * marveled, and Mt 15:31
safe at home! * so, it is not my Mt 18:14
tremendous debt, * because you Mt 18:32
others, * as I had mercy on you?' Mt 18:33
you've paid them * as much as those Mt 20:11,12
"* as you enter," he said, Mt 21:2
you are doing, * say, 'The Master Mt 21:3
is almost here. * so, when you see Mt 24:33
and weddings—* as it was in Noah's Mt 24:37,38
"* as a man can prevent trouble Mt 24:43
* as was prophesied, but woe to Mt 26:24
* then, as he was presiding over Mt 27:19
life again, * as he said he would. Mt 28:6
* as a strong man must be tied Mk 3:27
So they took him * as he was Mk 4:36
from a graveyard, * as Jesus was Mk 5:1
"If I can * touch his clothing, I Mk 5:28
"Don't be afraid. * trust me." Mk 5:36
Her parents * couldn't get over Mk 5:41,42
was * a local man like themselves. Mk 6:2,3
"He's * a carpenter, Mary's boy, Mk 6:2,3
They * sat there, unable to take Mk 6:51
by the statement he had * made. Mk 7:17
He said this * to be talking, for Mk 9:6
* as the prophets had predicted. Mk 9:12,13
told them, "and * as you enter you Mk 11:2
you are doing, * say, 'Our Master Mk 11:3
and asked him, "* when is all this Mk 13:3,4
* say what God tells you to. Mk 13:11
* then, a rooster crowed. Mk 14:68
from the country * then, was Mk 15:21
Early the following morning, * at Mk 16:1
You will see him there, * as he Mk 16:7
to the wisdom of the *." Lk 1:17f
servant David, * as he promised Lk 1:70
* as the angel had told them. Lk 2:20
Joseph and Mary * stood there, Lk 2:33
She came along * as Simeon was Lk 2:38
* at that time the highly prized Lk 7:2
Jesus went with them; but * Lk 7:6,7,8
come and meet you. * speak a word Lk 7:6,7,8
he does it. So * say, 'Be healed!' Lk 7:6,7,8
do not understand, * as the ancient Lk 8:10
"Don't be afraid! * trust me, and Lk 8:50
"* tell them to sit down on the Lk 9:14
And you must love your neighbor * Lk 10:27
you that my sister * sits here Lk 10:40
* as John taught one to his Lk 11:1
friend of mine has * arrived for a Lk 11:5,6
I * can't help you this time.' Lk 11:7
* because of your persistence. Lk 11:8
too, in what you * said." Lk 11:45
hour of his return—* as they would Lk 12:39
talking * to us or to everyone?" Lk 12:41
And is it wrong for me, * Lk 13:16
One said he had * bought a field Lk 14:18
Another said he had * bought Lk 14:19
Another had * been married and Lk 14:20
I know * the thing! Lk 16:4

(JUST Con't)
sheep, he doesn't * sit down and Lk 17:7,8,9
supposed to do. * so, if you Lk 17:10
married—everything * as usual right Lk 17:27
* say, 'The Lord needs him.' Lk 19:31
you can be * as sure that the Lk 21:31
found everything * as Jesus had Lk 22:13
of Cyrene, who was * coming into Lk 23:26
gone, * as the women had said." Lk 24:24
the bread. And * as they were Lk 24:36
upon you, * as my Father Lk 24:49
"* come and see for yourself," Jn 1:46
believe all this * because I told Jn 1:50
be born again! * as you can hear Jn 3:8
* then his disciples arrived. Jn 4:27
not * because of what you told us. Jn 4:42
he wants to, * as the Father does. Jn 5:21
Son, * as they honor the Father. Jn 5:23
fair and *, for it is according to Jn 5:30
when Christ comes, he will * Jn 7:27
will come * before the Messiah." Jn 7:40
you * naturally don't believe it! Jn 8:45
and they know me, * as my Father Jn 10:15
for you * a little while longer. Jn 12:35
and head as well—not * my feet!" Jn 13:9
me—* as I told the Jewish leaders. Jn 13:33
other * as much as I love you. Jn 13:34
work through me. * believe it—that Jn 14:11
come to you. In * a little while I Jn 14:19
living in my love, * as I obey my Jn 15:10
you my glory. In * a little while Jn 16:16
me no more; but * a little while Jn 16:16
* as we are, with none missing. Jn 17:11
fit in with it, * as I don't. Jn 17:14
heart and mind, * as you and I are, Jn 17:21
I are, Father—that * as you are in Jn 17:21
prophecy he had * made, "I have Jn 18:9
"Bring some of the fish you've * Jn 21:10
the Holy Spirit in * a few Act 1:5
* as he went, he will return!" Act 1:11
to be an apostle * as we were. Act 1:17
next to God. And * as promised, the Act 2:33
* outside that door are the young Act 5:9
* then the men sent by Cornelius Act 10:17
the Holy Spirit * as we did?" Act 10:46,47
into heaven. * then three men who Act 11:11
the Good News, but * as I was Act 11:15
fell on them, * as he fell on us at Act 11:15
They found no * cause to execute Act 13:28
Spirit, * as he gave him to us. Act 15:8
through faith, * as he did ours. Act 15:9
colony * inside the Macedonian Act 16:12
they were tentmakers * as he was. Act 18:2,3
But * as Paul started to make Act 18:14
and preacher, had * arrived in Act 18:24
* as you have tried to do today. Act 22:3
worry, Paul; * as you have told the Act 23:11
and I believe, * as these men Act 24:15
* then a light wind began blowing Act 27:13
It will be * as he said! Act 27:25
see good results, * as I have among Rom 1:13
You are * as bad. Rom 2:1
be the * Judge of all the world. Rom 2:5
For you are not real Jews * Rom 2:28
unfaithful, but * because they Rom 3:3
of those who say such things is *. Rom 3:8
obey God's laws? * the opposite! Rom 3:31
and declared him * and good in his Rom 4:11
a promise * couldn't come to pass! Rom 4:18
* for Abraham's benefit. Rom 4:23
Christ came at * the right time and Rom 5:6
to understand: * as you used to be Rom 6:19
is truly a Jew! * the fact that Rom 9:7
are not given * because someone Rom 9:16
is kind to some * because he wants Rom 9:18
of them—* as everyone in the cities Rom 9:29
these things? * this, that God has Rom 9:30
you are * a branch, not a root. Rom 11:18
their sins, * as I promised." Rom 11:27
has given you. * as there are many Rom 12:4,5
Don't * pretend that you love Rom 12:9
Be at peace with everyone, * as Rom 12:18
* because you know you should. Rom 13:5
still we cannot * go ahead and do Rom 15:1
into the church, * as Christ has Rom 15:7
in the Lord, * as the Gospel says, Rom 16:25,26,27
says, and * as I have told you. Rom 16:25,26,27
for he always does * what he says, 1Co 1:9
Others * can't take it in. 1Co 2:14
you were still * babies in the 1Co 3:1
Why, we're * God's servants, each 1Co 3:5
* what his master tells him to. 1Co 4:2
proud men are * big talkers or 1Co 4:19
The Kingdom of God is not * 1Co 4:20
to do, * as though I were there. 1Co 5:3,4
Why not * accept mistreatment and 1Co 6:7
some of you were * like that but 1Co 6:11
sins such as have * been expressly 1Co 6:12f
dead by his power * as he raised up 1Co 6:14
along without marrying, * as I do. 1Co 7:7
unmarried if you can, * as I am. 1Co 7:8
a command, not * a suggestion. 1Co 7:10
he is * showing his ignorance. 1Co 8:2
consciences. * remember that God 1Co 8:8
on these trips * as the other 1Co 9:5
charge. For * preaching the Gospel 1Co 9:16
* because he pays my salary; 1Co 9:19
all this trouble * to win a blue 1Co 9:25
I'm not * shadow-boxing or 1Co 9:26
* because he thinks I am wrong? 1Co 10:30
example, * as I follow Christ's. 1Co 11:1
you, and I can * about believe it. 1Co 11:18
has many parts, not * one part. 1Co 12:14
Or if your whole body were * one 1Co 12:17
put each part * where he wants it. 1Co 12:18
never learned? Can * anyone 1Co 12:30
clearly, * as clearly as God sees 1Co 13:12
died for our sins * as the 1Co 15:3
grave * as the prophets foretold. 1Co 15:4
* the kind he wants it to have; 1Co 15:38
kind of seed. And * as there are 1Co 15:39
They are * human bodies at 1Co 15:44
bodies. For * as there are natural, 1Co 15:44
Every human being has a body * 1Co 15:48
body from heaven. * as each of us 1Co 15:49
This time I don't want to make * 1Co 16:7
doing the Lord's work * as I am. 1Co 16:10
to some extent; * as I shall be of 2Co 1:13,14
facing death * as Jesus did; 2Co 4:10
* as the Psalm writer did when 2Co 4:13
* see how much good this grief 2Co 7:11
to completion * as gladly, giving 2Co 8:11
But I am sending these men * to 2Co 9:3
A farmer who plants * a few seeds 2Co 9:6
not think I am * blustering when I 2Co 10:9
is going to be * as rough on you as 2Co 10:11
for Christ alone, * as a pure 2Co 11:2
to our Lord, * as Eve was deceived 2Co 11:3
work in * the same way we are. 2Co 11:12
or * my spirit, for I don't know; 2Co 12:2,3
and all others, * as I did then, 2Co 13:2
Or are you * pretending to be 2Co 13:5
He died for our sins * as God Gal 1:4
all understand * what I had been Gal 2:2
the Gentiles, * as Peter had been Gal 2:7,8,9
Now are you going to * throw it Gal 3:4
doing it * when I am with you! Gal 4:18
that God promised, * as Isaac was. Gal 4:28
the Jewish laws, * as Isaac the Gal 4:29
things that are * the opposite from Gal 5:17
way with us are * the opposite of Gal 5:17
reap * the kind of crop he sows! Gal 6:7
are doing it for * one reason: so Gal 6:12
happen * as he decided long ago. Eph 1:11
This is * one more reason for us Eph 1:14
the crowd and were * like all the Eph 2:2
All of us used to be * as they Eph 2:3
God's anger * like everyone else. Eph 2:3
* think! Eph 3:8
the Gentiles too, * as he who made Eph 3:9
in his church, in * the way he had Eph 3:11
one another, * as God has forgiven Eph 4:32
everything you do * as a much loved Eph 5:1
* as the church obeys Christ. Eph 5:24
cares for it, * as Christ cares for Eph 5:29,30
your slaves right, * as I have told Eph 6:9
I am sending him to you for * Eph 6:22
here, * as I have in the past; Php 1:20
Don't * think about your own Php 2:4
He has been * like a son to me in Php 2:22
I hope to send him to you * as Php 2:23
lives everywhere, * as it changed Col 1:6
And now * as you trusted Christ Col 2:6
at all you do, * as though you were Col 3:23
YOU SLAVE OWNERS must be * and Col 4:1
this special trip * to see how you Col 4:8
not * meaningless chatter to you; 1Th 1:5
at Philippi * before we came to 1Th 2:2
knows we were not * pretending to 1Th 2:5
we spoke as being * our own, but 1Th 2:13
own countrymen, * as they suffered 1Th 2:14
And now Timothy has * returned 1Th 3:6
* as much as we want to see you. 1Th 3:6
* as our love does toward you. 1Th 3:12
own work, * as we told you before. 1Th 4:11
up, * as you are already doing. 1Th 5:11
this for you, * as he promised. 1Th 5:24
of the fair, * way God does things, 2Th 1:5
Lord's battles, * as the Lord told 1Ti 1:18
him respectfully * as though he 1Ti 5:1
to them the Good News is * a 1Ti 6:5
trust the Lord, * as your mother 2Ti 1:5
of Jesus Christ, * as I do, and as 2Ti 2:3
doing his work, * as an athlete 2Ti 2:5
for him is hard, * remember that 2Ti 2:12
And these teachers fight truth * 2Ti 3:8
them * what they want to hear. 2Ti 4:3
And not * to me, but to all those 2Ti 4:8
you and prefer * to ask you—I, Phm 1:8,9
its commands are always * and Heb 1:8
him High Priest, * as Moses also Heb 3:2
glory than Moses, * as a man who Heb 3:3
end, trusting God * as we did when Heb 3:14
been given to us * as it was to Heb 4:2
He is resting from his work, * as Heb 4:10
priest * because he wants to be. Heb 5:4
He had said * a few moments Heb 5:7f
son, Isaac, * as he had promised. Heb 6:15
priesthood we have * described, is Heb 8:1
bodies from sin, * think how much Heb 9:14
And * as it is destined that men Heb 9:27
But * the opposite happened: Heb 10:3
lay down my life, * as the Heb 10:7
* strangers visiting down here. Heb 11:13
and that is * about what Heb 11:19
to obey, not * to listen to. Jas 1:22
For if a person * listens and Jas 1:23
sharp tongue is * fooling himself, Jas 1:26
your neighbors * as much as you Jas 2:8
little slip, is * as guilty as the Jas 2:10
So you see, it isn't enough * to Jas 2:17
And so it happened * as the Jas 2:23
a different road. * as the body is Jas 2:26
or anything else; * say a simple Jas 5:12
everything you do, * as the Lord is 1Pe 1:15
Don't * pretend to be good! 1Pe 2:1
and scorn. But * remember that 1Pe 4:5
How precious it is, and how * and 2Pe 1:1
in those days, * as there will be 2Pe 2:1
* escaped from such wicked living. 2Pe 2:18
what he meant, * as they do the 2Pe 3:15,16
of God's presence, * as Christ 1Jn 1:7
Literally, "he is *." 1Jn 1:9f
for you * as it did for Christ; 1Jn 2:8
and so, * as he has said, you 1Jn 2:27
Little children, let us stop * 1Jn 3:18
you hear * because someone says it 1Jn 4:1
we can do * as we like without fear Jud 1:4
to receive * punishment, and to Jud 1:15
Write down what you have * seen, Rev 1:19
* as I do. Rev 2:6
with a rod of iron * as my Father Rev 2:27
me on my throne, * as I took my Rev 3:21
and ate it! And * as he had said, Rev 10:10
For * then the seventh angel blew Rev 11:15
* then the angel who has power to Rev 14:18
* and true Rev 15:3,4
"You are * in sending this Rev 16:5
it is their * reward." Rev 16:6
your punishments are * and true." Rev 16:7
for his judgments are * and Rev 19:2
For I am a servant of God * as Rev 19:10

JUST-RIPENED
In one basket there were fresh, * Jer 24:2

JUSTICE
matter. Now * has been done." Gen 20:16
"*"), for she said, "God has Gen 30:6
"God has given me *, and heard my Gen 30:6
the people with * at all times. Ex 18:22
available to administer *. Ex 18:26
excuse for twisting * against him. Ex 23:6
He gives * to the fatherless and Deu 10:18
They will administer * in every Deu 16:18
Never twist * to benefit a rich Deu 16:19
their decisions. * must prevail. Deu 16:20
"* must be given to migrants and Deu 24:17
in the administration of *. 1Sa 8:3
David reigned with * over Israel 2Sa 8:15
to me, and I would give him *!" 2Sa 15:4
and help you give * in each case 2Ch 19:6
if you give us * as we stand here Ez 9:15
as Persian law and *, and the king Est 1:13-15
Does God twist *? Job 8:3
I shriek, but get no *. Job 19:7
and dispenses * for the world. Job 34:13
Could God govern if he hated *? Job 34:17
"Must God tailor his * to your Job 34:33
He does bring about * at last, if Job 35:14,15
Are you going to discredit my * Job 40:8
Demand * for me, Lord! Ps 7:6
ear to those who cry to him for *. Ps 9:12
Your * is as solid as God's Ps 36:6
blazing light of * shining down as Ps 37:6
For the Lord loves * and Ps 37:28
Defending truth, humility, and *. Ps 45:4
* is your royal scepter. Ps 45:6
*? Ps 58:1
give "*" in exchange for bribes. Ps 58:1
and will give true * to their Ps 67:4
he gives * to the widows, for he Ps 68:5
about your * and your goodness. Ps 71:24
Help him to give * to your Ps 72:2
truth have met together. Grim * Ps 85:10
bountiful crops. * goes before him Ps 85:13
is * and the other Righteousness. Ps 89:14,15
Righteousness and * are the Ps 97:2
have heard of your *, Lord, and are Ps 97:8,9
to judge the world with perfect *. Ps 98:8,9
King is determined to give *. Ps 99:4
He gives * throughout Israel. Ps 99:4
lovingkindness and your *, Lord. Ps 101:1
He gives * to all who are Ps 103:6
Your * is eternal for your laws Ps 119:142

(JUSTICE Con't)
and gives * to the poor and Ps 146:7
Unending riches, honor, * and Pro 8:18
My paths are those of * and Pro 8:20
to accept a bribe to twist *. Pro 17:23
A good man loves *, but it is a Pro 21:15
the importance of *, but those who Pro 28:5
Do you want *? Pro 29:26
give * to those who are oppressed. Pro 31:5
and needy and see that they get *. Pro 31:9
the earth * is giving way to crime Ecc 3:16
miscarriage of * anywhere Ecc 5:8
of *," and "The Faithful Town." Is 1:26
of *, but found bloodshed instead. Is 5:7
Hebrew words for "*" and Is 5:7f
They take bribes to pervert *, Is 5:23
fairness and * from the throne of Is 9:7
He will bring true * and peace to Is 9:7
that there is no * for the poor, Is 10:2
He will give a longing for * to Is 28:6
and plummet of * to check the Is 28:17
Then * will rule through all the Is 32:16
the land, and out of *, peace. Is 32:17
* and goodness and righteousness. Is 33:5
he will reveal * to the nations Is 42:1
He will see full * given to all Is 42:3
He who gives me * is near. Is 50:8
My mercy and * are coming soon; Is 51:5
but my * and mercy shall last Is 51:8
* against every courtroom lie. Is 54:17
in the streets, and * is outlawed. Is 59:14
through his mighty power and *. Is 59:16
For I, the Lord, love *; Is 61:8
the nations of the world his *; Is 61:11
They refuse * to orphans and the Jer 5:28
I am the Lord of * and of Jer 9:24
I look to you for *. Jer 11:20
O LORD, YOU always give me * when Jer 12:1
Quick! Give * to these you judge! Jer 21:12
Help those in need of *! Jer 22:3
He saw to it that * and help Jer 22:16
with wisdom and * and cause Jer 23:5,6
of *, the hope of their fathers." Jer 50:7
rights, and refused them *. Lam 3:34,35,36
and open his court of * and take Dan 7:26
and * and love and mercy. Hos 1:19
of love and *, and always be Hos 12:6
For they have perverted * by Amo 2:6
O evil men, you make "*" a Amo 5:7
you refuse * to the poor. Amo 5:12
your courts into true halls of *. Amo 5:15
of *—a torrent of doing good. Amo 5:24
make a mockery of *, and corrupt Amo 6:12
of Israel who hate * and love Mic 3:9
ruin. * is twisted between them. Mic 7:3
and there is no * given in the Hab 1:4
At last * has caught up with you! Hab 2:6
Day by day his * is more evident, Zep 3:5
things—* and mercy and faith. Mt 23:23
about * and the love of God. Lk 11:42
to appeal for * against a man who Lk 18:3
I'm going to see that she gets *, Lk 18:4,5
will surely give * to his people Lk 18:7
and merciless *, while Jesus Christ Jn 1:17
in his humiliation, * was denied Act 8:33
Though he escaped the sea, * will Act 28:4
And we know that God, in *, will Rom 2:2
Melchizedek's name means "*," so Heb 7:2
so he is the King of *; Heb 7:2
For we know him who said, "* Heb 10:30
He will judge you with perfect * 1Pe 1:17

JUSTIFICATION
Literally, "raised for our *." Rom 4:25f

JUSTIFIED
her husband's suspicions are *. Num 5:18
of Israel shall be *, triumphant. Is 45:25
Literally, "wisdom is * by her Mt 11:19f
either you will be * by them or you Mt 12:37
Literally, "but wisdom is * of Lk 7:35f
Literally, "*." Rom 3:28f
rules are * by God through faith. Rom 4:11

JUSTIFIES
But this would imply the end * Lk 16:9f

JUSTIFY
it, for I am anxious to * you. Job 33:32
their sins. But * me publicly; Ps 7:7,8
We can * our every deed but God Pro 21:2
But brilliant men like you can * Mt 11:19
But I am sure you can always * Lk 7:35
The man wanted to * (his lack of Lk 10:29
Literally, "wanting to * Lk 10:29f

JUSTLY
them to decide *, lest the wrath of 2Ch 19:10
judge * the nations of the world. Ps 9:7,8
a God who judges * here on earth. Ps 58:11
of David, and he shall rule *. Jer 33:15
Judah also will be * punished for Hos 12:2
For he has set a day for * Act 17:31
given him what he * deserves, but Act 24:6
dealings, * cutting them short." Rom 9:28
upon their heads to * crush them. Rom 11:9
of them will be * judged for 2Th 2:12
one who * punishes and makes war. Rev 19:11

JUSTUS
two men: Joseph * (also called Act 1:23
After that he stayed with Titus * Act 18:7
Jesus * also sends his love. Col 4:11

JUTTAH
Carmel, Ziph, *, Jezreel, Jokde-am, Jos 15:48-62
Debir, Ain, *, and Beth-shemesh. Jos 21:9-16

KABUL
It then passed to the east of *, Jos 19:27

KABZEEL
*, Eder, Jagur, Kinah, Dimonah, Jos 15:21-32
a heroic soldier from *. 2Sa 23:20
*, killed the two famous giants 1Ch 11:22

KADESH
(later called *) and destroyed the Gen 14:7
It lies between * and Bered. Gen 16:14
and settled between * and Shur. Gen 20:1
of Paran at *, and they showed the Num 13:26
and camped at *, where Miriam Num 20:1
While Moses was at * he sent Num 20:14
now we are here at *, encamped on Num 20:16
and journeyed from * to Mount Num 20:21,22
in *, in the wilderness of Zin. Num 27:14
From Ezion-geber to * (in the Num 33:15-37
From * to Mount Hor (at the edge Num 33:15-37
So they stayed there at * for a Deu 1:46
get across Zered Brook from *! Deu 2:14,15
Israel arrived at *, on their Ju 11:16
the people of Israel stayed in *. Ju 11:17
and shakes the wilderness of *. Ps 29:8

KADESH-BARNE-A
Hezron (south of *), and then up Jos 15:2,3,4

KADESH-BARNEA
I sent them from * to spy out the Num 32:8
Its southernmost point will be *, Num 34:4
by foot from Mount Horeb to *, Deu 1:1
* was at the southern edge of the Deu 1:1f
We were then at * [on the border Deu 1:19,20,21
At *, when the Lord told you to Deu 9:23
them from * to Gaza, and from Jos 10:41
you and me when we were at *?" Jos 14:6
* to spy out the land of Canaan. Jos 14:7

KADMI-EL
given to Jeshua, *, Henadad, and Ez 3:9
From the family of * of the Neh 7:43,44,45
These men were Jeshua, *, Bani, Neh 9:4
were Jeshua, *, Bani, Hashabneiah, Neh 9:5
(son of Henadad), *, Neh 10:9-13
Jeshua, Binnui, *, Sherebiah, Neh 12:8
Sherebiah, and Jeshua (son of *). Neh 12:24

KADMONITES
Kenites, Kenizzites, *, Hittites, Gen 15:19,20,21

KAIN
Jokde-am, Zanoah, *, Gibe-ah, Jos 15:48-62

KAIWAN
your king, and in *, your god of Amo 5:25,26,27

KAIWAY
*, and in all the images you made. Act 7:43

KALLAI
*, leader of the Sallai clan; Neh 12:12-21

KAMON
When Jair died he was buried in *. Ju 10:5

KANAH
* Brook to the Mediterranean Sea. Jos 16:8
of * to the Mediterranean Sea. Jos 17:9
Hammon, *, and Greater Sidon. Jos 19:28

KAREAH
Johanan, the son of *; 2Ki 25:23
Jonathan (sons of *), Seraiah (son Jer 40:8
Johanan (son of *) and the other Jer 40:13,14
But when Johanan (son of *) and Jer 41:11
Johanan (son of *) and all the Jer 43:2,3

KARKA
then up through * and Azmon, until Jos 15:2,3,4

KARKOR
fifteen thousand troops were in *. Ju 8:10

KARTAH
Jokne-am, *, Dimnah, and Nahalal. Jos 21:34,35

KARTAN
of Refuge), Hammoth-dor, and *. Jos 21:32

KATTATH
included *, Nahalal, Shimron, Jos 19:15,16

KEDAR
girl:Nebaioth, *, Abdeel,Mibsam, Gen 25:12-15
Nabaioth (the oldest), *, Adbeel, 1Ch 1:28-31
Lord, these men of Meshech and *. Ps 120:5,6
tanned as the dark tents of *." Sol 1:5
the mighty tribe of *, will end. Is 21:16
you desert cities—* and Sela! Is 42:11
The flocks of * shall be given Is 60:7
to the east to the deserts of *. Jer 2:10,11
palaces of Benhadad.* and Hazor Jer 49:27
Hazor This prophecy is about * Jer 49:28

KEDAR'S
"The Arabians, and * wealthy Eze 27:21

KEDEMAH
Hadad, Tema,Jetur, Naphish, *. Gen 25:12-15
Tema, Jetur, Naphish, and *. 1Ch 1:28-31

KEDEMOTH
"Then from the wilderness of * I Deu 2:26
Jahaz, *, Mepha-ath, Kiriathaim, Jos 13:18
Bezer, Jahaz, *, and Mepha-ath. Jos 21:36,37
town), Jahzah, * and Mepha-ath, 1Ch 6:78,79

KEDESH
The king of *; Jos 12:8-24
Dimonah, Adadah, *, Hazor, Ithnan, Jos 15:21-32
Ramah, Hazor, *, Edre-i, Enhazor, Jos 19:35-39
of Refuge were * of Galilee in the Jos 20:7
*, in Galilee (a City of Refuge), Jos 21:32
who lived in *, in the land of Ju 4:6
So she went with him to *. Ju 4:9
*, ten thousand men volunteered. Ju 4:10
as the Oak of Za-anannim, near *. Ju 4:11
Janoah, *, Hazor, Gilead, Galilee, 2Ki 15:29
The tribe of Issachar gave them * 1Ch 6:72
The tribe of Naphtali gave them * 1Ch 6:76

KEDMI-EL
From the families of Jeshua and * Ez 2:40,41,42

KEENLY
I am * aware of your apostasy, Jer 13:27

KEEP
"Am I supposed to * track of him Gen 4:9
But I promise to * you safe in Gen 6:18
to * them alive through the flood. Gen 6:19,20
they said, "and * us from Gen 11:3,4
who were captured; * for yourself Gen 14:21
see to it that we * this bargain Gen 31:49
Esau laughed. "* what you have." Gen 33:9
"Then let her * them!" Gen 38:23
I refused to * my promise to give Gen 38:26
your brother! I'll * the rest of Gen 42:16
God has sent me here to * you Gen 45:7
to Pharaoh. * four parts for Gen 47:24
three days, but to * on going, Ex 14:5
and * what is left overnight." Ex 16:23
manna in it and to * it in a sacred Ex 16:33
Now if you will obey me and * Ex 19:5
goods to anyone to * for him, and Ex 22:7
"If a man asks his neighbor to * Ex 22:10
"* far away from falsely Ex 23:7
and always * the special Bread Ex 25:30
afterwards, * it for yourself. Ex 29:26
"I am the Lord your God. * Lev 11:44
them, don't even * it overnight. Lev 19:13
"* my Sabbath laws and reverence Lev 19:30
"You must * all of my Lev 22:31
you may * them for yourselves. Num 31:18
our families, to * them safe from Num 32:17
war, and * your troops across the Num 32:21
who love me and * my commandments. Deu 5:9,10
make a vow you don't intend to *. Deu 5:11
" '* the Sabbath day holy. Deu 5:12
Why should you * the Sabbath? Deu 5:15
Lord your God will * his part of Deu 7:12
a wooden Ark to * them in, and to Deu 10:1
has given you. So * these Deu 11:18
be rebuilt. * none of the booty! Deu 13:17
each district; and * the roads to Deu 19:2,3
but you may * for yourselves all Deu 20:14
to your farm and * it there until Deu 22:2
else you find. * it for its owner. Deu 22:3
to obey and * his laws and Deu 26:17
Literally, "* all the Deu 27:1f
his paths and to * his laws, so Deu 30:16
the two spies, "* your promise. Jos 6:22
but this time you may * the loot Jos 8:2
there to * the kings inside. Jos 10:18
So be very careful to * on Jos 23:11
the city gate to * the men of Ju 9:44
it to you? You * whatever your god Ju 11:24
you, and we will * whatever Jehovah Ju 11:24
"We can't * the Ark of the God of 1Sa 5:7
it that I let them * the best of 1Sa 15:21
And may the Lord make us * our 1Sa 20:23
"Even the blind and lame could * 2Sa 5:6
wives to * the palace in order. 2Sa 15:16
has left them here to * the house. 2Sa 16:21
he had left to * house should be 2Sa 20:3
To * them from slipping. 2Sa 22:37
She will lie in your arms and * 1Ki 1:2
all his ways; * each of his 1Ki 2:3
and kind and you * your promises to 1Ki 8:22,23
cities in which to * his chariots, 1Ki 9:19
a prisoner and said, '* this man; 1Ki 20:39
only enough to * him alive 1Ki 22:27
shut the door and * him out, for 2Ki 6:32
not required to * account of their 2Ki 22:7
* me from all evil and disaster!" 1Ch 4:10
that no one tried to * count! 2Ch 5:6
But you men of Judah, * up the 2Ch 15:7
to * this promise," I declared. Neh 5:13
O my God, please * in mind all Neh 5:19
God, you who * your promises of Neh 9:32
telling him, "* the money, but Est 3:11
If you * quiet at a time like Est 4:14
For who could * from speaking Job 4:2
"He will * you from death in Job 5:20
answer—then I will * quiet. Job 6:24
or grass without water to * it Job 8:11-13
God won't let him * it down. Job 20:15
to * soul and body together. Job 24:5

KEEP Con't)
from my sheep to * him warm, or if Job 31:19,20
But if not, then listen to me. * Job 33:33
alone, O Lord, you will * me safe. Ps 4:8
his trust in you. * them shouting Ps 5:11
nor man can ever * them Ps 10:6
I did my best to * them all, Ps 18:23
Day and night they * on telling Ps 19:2
And * me from deliberate wrongs; Ps 19:13
May the God of Jacob * you from Ps 20:1
Day and night I * on weeping, Ps 22:2
I have tried to * your laws and Ps 26:1
O Lord my God, I will * on Ps 30:12
you even * me from getting into Ps 32:7
bit in its mouth to * it in line! Ps 32:9
He will * them from death even in Ps 33:18,19
Then watch your tongue! * your Ps 34:13
planning how to * away from wrong. Ps 36:4
the Lord to act! * traveling Ps 37:34
complaining! I'll * quiet, Ps 39:1
one soul, to * it out of hell. Ps 49:8,9
Literally, "comes, and does not * Ps 50:3f
Don't * looking at my sins—erase Ps 51:9
They * a sharp lookout for Ps 64:6
But I * right on praying to you, Ps 69:13
Don't let them * on mocking me! Ps 70:2,3
I will * on expecting you to Ps 71:14
You will * on guiding me all my Ps 73:24
I * thinking of the good old days Ps 77:5
They did not * their promises. Ps 78:37
and will * on pleading day by day. Ps 88:13
their hands to * you from stumbling Ps 91:12
his strength, and * on searching! Ps 105:4
words. * me far from every wrong; Ps 119:29,30
Therefore I will * on obeying Ps 119:44,45,46
I obey them even at night and * Ps 119:55
* my mind upon your promises. Ps 119:95
of me, and * me from stumbling. Ps 119:105
Lord, if you * in mind our sins Ps 130:3,4
proud men must * their distance. Ps 138:6
snakes. * me out of their power. Ps 140:4
Help me, Lord, to * my mouth shut Ps 141:3
Don't let them slay me. * me out Ps 141:9
Only you can * me safe. Ps 142:5
They * you safe from defeat and Pro 3:23
Listen carefully. * these Pro 4:21
Their counsel will * you far Pro 6:24
always * it in mind and stick to Pro 7:1
and also * them deep within your Pro 7:3
Don't talk so much. You * putting Pro 10:19
God delights in those who * their Pro 12:22
its waters * a man from death. Pro 14:27
It pays him to * his mouth shut. Pro 17:27,28
* the commandments and keep your Pro 19:16
Keep the commandments and * your Pro 19:16
* your mouth closed and you'll Pro 21:23
* away from angry, short-tempered Pro 22:24,25
Punishment will * them out of Pro 23:13,14
while wise men try to * peace. Pro 29:8
a nation to know and * his laws! Pro 29:18
he works hard to * gaining more Ecc 4:8
AS YOU ENTER the Temple, * your Ecc 5:1
in fools. * your promise to him. Ecc 5:4
mother's womb. * on sowing your Ecc 11:6
But if you * on turning your Is 1:20
make promises to God and * them. Is 19:21
locked up tight to * out looters. Is 24:10
He will * in perfect peace all Is 26:3
them good; they * on doing wrong Is 26:10
I'll watch to * all enemies away. Is 27:3
so he doesn't * on pounding it. Is 28:28
God, who try to * him in the dark Is 29:15
his meat and to * him warm and fed Is 44:16
I will * you from premature Is 49:8,9
to the eunuchs who * his Sabbaths Is 56:4
fasting, and you * right on Is 58:3
you * on fighting and quarreling? Is 58:4
things, and * you healthy too; Is 58:11
If you * the Sabbath holy, not Is 58:13
You look for God to * you, but he Is 59:11
For your sins * piling up before Is 59:12
you shall * it, praising God. Is 62:9
a house, he will * on living in Is 65:21,22
to me, and will * on pleading; Jer 2:9
So you talk, and * right on Jer 3:4,5
me! * your expensive perfumes! Jer 6:20
gave to your fathers to * forever. Jer 7:7
But these people * on along their Jer 8:4,5
You have let them * right on with Jer 15:17,18
they did not * my laws, and you Jer 16:11
of the Lord you * talking about? Jer 17:15
Sabbath day and * it separate, Jer 17:24
if you refuse to * the Sabbath Jer 17:27
They * saying to these rebels Jer 23:17
false prophets who * telling you Jer 27:14
your life and * you safe." Jer 39:18
For rumors will * coming year by Jer 51:46
to * on running from their foes. Lam 1:6
But if you warn them and they * Eze 3:19
with the sword. * just a bit of Eze 5:3
to me, yet I will * the pledge I Eze 16:59,60
for you did not * my covenant. Eze 16:61
"And yet the people of Israel * Eze 18:29
couldn't * them back from harm. Eze 20:9,10
Follow my laws; * my ordinances; Eze 20:19
did, and * on worshiping idols? Eze 20:30
the ruined cities * saying, Eze 33:24
that you not only * the best of the Eze 34:18
and the rules for them to *. Eze 43:11
the servant may * it only until the Eze 46:17
He told me to * in mind what I Eze 47:6
Daniel answered, "* your gifts, Dan 5:17
who love you and * your laws. Dan 9:4
"But Daniel, * this prophecy a Dan 12:4
promises they don't intend to *. Hos 10:4
it was illegal to * pledged Amo 2:8f
Bethel and Gilgal. * Amo 4:4
The only commands you * are those Mic 6:16
full force, and * a sharp watch for Nah 2:1
she shouts, but they * on running. Nah 2:8
not enough clothes to * you warm. Hag 1:6
charge of my Temple, to * it holy; Zec 3:7
their ears to * from hearing me. Zec 7:11
like a guard to * invading armies Zec 9:8
movements and I will * them away; Zec 9:8
you promised to care for and *. Mal 2:14
Therefore guard your passions! * Mal 2:15
angels to * you from harm,'. Mt 4:6
if not, * the blessing. Mt 10:13
for, or shall we * on looking?" Mt 11:3
if you * the commandments." Mt 19:17
if you obey them. * only these and Mt 22:40
way they * making up so many laws! Mt 23:2
themselves don't even try to *. Mt 23:4
me one hour? * alert and pray. Mt 26:41
and tried to * it a secret that Mk 7:24
"* a sharp lookout! Mk 13:35,36,37
guard you and to * you from Lk 4:9,10,11
Or shall we * on looking for Lk 7:19
both, letting them * the money! Lk 7:42
it up to * it from shining? Lk 8:16
him every day and * close to me! Lk 9:23
a friend, if you * knocking long Lk 11:8
And so it is with prayer—* on Lk 11:9
asking and you will * on getting; Lk 11:9
keep on getting; * on looking and Lk 11:9
keep on looking and you will * on Lk 11:9
evil people. They * asking for some Lk 11:29,30
would never think of trying to *. Lk 11:46
fox that I will * on casting out Lk 13:32
* praying until the answer comes. Lk 18:1
He replied, "If they * quiet, Lk 19:40
of the world. * a constant watch. Lk 21:36
you will * a man from dying! Jn 8:52
are you going to * us in suspense? Jn 10:24
he * Lazarus from dying?" Jn 11:37,38
Holy Father, * them in your own Jn 17:11
to * them safe from Satan's power. Jn 17:15
to them, and will * on revealing Jn 17:26
not * this man within its grip. Act 2:24
could no longer * him hidden, and Act 7:21
to * him from trusting the Lord. Act 13:8
it difficult to * the ship on Act 27:4
And one of the things I * on Rom 1:10
Gentiles alike who * on sinning. Rom 2:9
are responsible to * God's laws Rom 3:19
and trying to * his laws, but by a Rom 3:21,22
in Christ but also * the Jewish Rom 4:9
those who do not * the Jewish Rom 4:9
those who do not * these rules are Rom 4:11
he trusted God to * his promise. Rom 4:13
for we always fail to * them. Rom 4:15
The only way we can * from Rom 4:15
WELL THEN, SHALL we * on sinning Rom 6:1
so that God can * on showing us Rom 6:1
Should we * on sinning when we Rom 6:2,3
we can't and don't * them, but God Rom 8:3
For if you * on following it you Rom 8:13
But if we must * trusting God Rom 8:25
Who then can ever * Christ's love Rom 8:35
itself cannot * God's love away. Rom 8:38
to the Jews, but they * arguing Rom 10:21
want to be afraid, * the laws and Rom 13:3
reasons: first, to * from being Rom 13:5
so that they can * on doing God's Rom 13:6
of view, but * it to yourself; Rom 14:22
you hope will * you happy and full Rom 15:13
even enough clothes to * us warm. 1Co 4:11
you are not to * company with 1Co 5:11
Usually a person should * on with 1Co 7:20
* anyone from doing God's work. 1Co 7:30
not to try to * you from marrying. 1Co 7:35
And must Barnabas and I alone * 1Co 9:6
muzzle on an ox to * it from eating 1Co 9:9
to me—I couldn't * from preaching 1Co 9:16
would * you from doing your best. 1Co 9:25
You can trust God to * the 1Co 10:13
very foolish to * on trusting God 1Co 15:17
* your eyes open for spiritual 1Co 16:13
* from being outsmarted by Satan; 2Co 2:11
but we get up again and * going. 2Co 4:9
built to * men from finding him. 2Co 10:5
me as I * on talking like a fool. 2Co 11:1
Yet those other men * telling 2Co 11:18
enough clothing to * me warm. 2Co 11:27
encouraged us to * right on with Gal 2:7,8,9
by trying to * the Jewish laws? Gal 3:2
favor by trying to * the Jewish Gal 3:11
who want us to * the Jewish laws, Gal 4:29
try to * the other Jewish laws; Gal 6:13
Don't * on scolding and nagging Eph 6:4
Don't * threatening them; Eph 6:9
of your needs, and * praying Eph 6:18
But pray that I will * on Eph 6:20
within you will * right on helping Php 1:6
at the same time * on growing in Php 1:9
I am going to * on being glad, Php 1:19
or not, I will * on hearing good Php 1:27
even yet, but I * working toward Php 3:12
His peace will * your thoughts Php 4:7
be glad about. * putting into Php 4:9
so that you can * going no matter Col 1:11
—why do you * right on following Col 2:20
Don't be weary in prayer; * at Col 4:2
it, for they * telling us about 1Th 1:9
man, trying to * us from preaching 1Th 2:16
you, and to * you from becoming 1Th 3:2,3
and pure, and to * clear of all 1Th 4:3,4
live in the light * sober, 1Th 5:8
Always * on praying. 1Th 5:17
* away from every kind of evil. 1Th 5:22
And so we * on praying for you 2Th 1:11
stand firm and * a strong grip on 2Th 2:15
Christ and always * your conscience 1Ti 1:19
and progress. * a close watch on 1Ti 4:16
of making money. * away from them. 1Ti 6:5
entrusted to you. * out of foolish 1Ti 6:20
But you must * on believing the 2Ti 3:14
theological ideas; * out of Tit 3:9
because I * hearing of your love Phm 1:5
I really wanted to * him here Phm 1:13
Please * a guest room ready for Phm 1:22
—if we * up our courage firm to Heb 3:6
And we are anxious that you * Heb 6:11
men who could not * from doing Heb 7:28
they did not * their part in that Heb 8:9
The people had to * these rules Heb 9:10
You need to * on patiently doing Heb 10:36
* your eyes on Jesus, our leader Heb 12:2
If you want to * from becoming Heb 12:3
and we want to * it that way. Heb 13:18
He should * on praying about it. Jas 5:13
I beg you to * away from the evil 1Pe 2:11
If you want a happy, good life, * 1Pe 3:10
to God's will, * on doing what is 1Pe 4:19
I plan to * on reminding you of 2Pe 1:12
here I intend to * sending these 2Pe 1:13,14
So * on believing what you have 1Jn 2:24
But those who * on sinning are 1Jn 3:4
but as for those who * on 1Jn 3:6
But if you * on sinning, it 1Jn 3:8
so he can't * on sinning, for 1Jn 3:9
Dear children, * away from 1Jn 5:21
to his people to * without change Jud 1:3
And he is able to * you from Jud 1:24,25
Or, "I will * you from failing in Rev 3:10f
awaiting me, who * their robes in Rev 16:15

KEEPERS
Obed-edom and Je-iel, the door *. 1Ch 15:18

KEEPING
came out, * himself under control. Gen 43:31
Bless you for * me from murdering 1Sa 25:33
their minds, and * them from pride, Job 33:17,18
of sin, and * them from falling Job 33:17,18
I publicly praise the Lord for * Ps 26:12
by * abreast of the facts. Pro 24:3,4
A time for *; Ecc 3:6
But by * her promises, Israel Eze 17:14
laws so they could live by * them. Eze 20:11
Through the * of them they could Eze 20:25
the sheep, * them from straying. Amo 1:1
respect and awe for me, by * them. Mal 2:5
from thieves by * watch for them, Mt 24:43
on * his life will lose it; Lk 9:24
there agreeing—* the coats they Act 22:20
and salvation by * his laws we Rom 4:15
does not depend on * the law, but Rom 6:15
by * his laws, never succeeded. Rom 9:31
to be saved by * the law and being Rom 9:32
God's favor by * the Jewish laws Rom 10:3
are trying to get by * his laws. Rom 10:4
God and * God's commandments. 1Co 7:19
to be saved by * the Ten 2Co 3:6
to be saved by * the laws of God 2Co 3:17
to be saved by * Jewish laws, for Gal 2:18
For if we could be saved by * Gal 2:21
circumcision and * the Jewish laws Gal 5:2
your debt to God by * those laws; Gal 5:4
Christ Jesus for * me safe, when I Php 1:26
And you know what is * him from 2Th 2:6
the exercise of * spiritually fit. 1Ti 4:7
who were * God's commandments and Rev 12:17

KEEPS
generations * his promises and Deu 7:9

(KEEPS Con't)
gives you rest and * you safe from Deu 12:10
You are the God who * his kind 2Ch 6:14
"O great and awesome God who * Neh 1:5
And an honor guard * watch at his Job 21:30-32
of the Lord, * a promise even if it Ps 15:4
You have rescued me, O God who * Ps 31:5,6
He protects them and * them Ps 41:2
day and night. He * you from all Ps 121:7
your life. He * his eye upon you Ps 121:8
just as a servant * his eyes upon Ps 123:2
He is the God who * every Ps 146:6
happy is the man who * on eating Pro 3:18
everywhere and * his eye on both Pro 15:3
Someone from among you * calling, Is 21:11
* my laws, he shall surely live. Eze 18:19
If anyone * them, he shall live. Eze 20:11
if a person * them, he shall live. Eze 20:21
For anyone who * his life for Mt 16:25
Literally, "Blessed is he who * Lk 7:23f
* seizing him, making him scream; Lk 9:39
In the meantime, he * on Rom 10:21
whether or not it * its value, and 1Co 3:13
Everyone * telling me about the 1Co 11:18
Christ within [who * us safe 2Co 4:10
But if it * on having crops of Heb 6:8
But if anyone * looking steadily Jas 1:25
And the person who * every law of Jas 2:10
who * you safe from all attacks. 1Pe 2:25
it, but whoever * doing the will of 1Jn 2:17
love God," but * on hating his 1Jn 4:20
to the very end * on doing things Rev 2:26

KEHELATHAH
From Rissah to *; Num 33:15-37
From * to Mount Shepher; Num 33:15-37

KEILAH
Nezib, *, Achzib, and Mareshah. Jos 15:37-44
at * robbing the threshing floors. 1Sa 23:1
"Yes, go and save *," the Lord 1Sa 23:2
want to go to * to fight the whole 1Sa 23:3
"Go down to *, for I will help you 1Sa 23:4
They went to * and slaughtered 1Sa 23:5
and so the people of * were saved. 1Sa 23:5
(Abiathar the priest went to * 1Sa 23:6
soon learned that David was at *. 1Sa 23:7
* and besiege David and his men. 1Sa 23:8
and destroy * because I am here. 1Sa 23:10
Will the men of * surrender me 1Sa 23:11
"And will these men of * betray 1Sa 23:12
of them now—left * and began 1Sa 23:13
was the father of * the Garmite, 1Ch 4:19
mayor of half the * district, who Neh 3:17
the other half of the * district. Neh 3:18

KELAIAH
* (also called Kelita), Ez 10:23

KELITA
Kelaiah (also called *), Ez 10:23
Hodiah, Ma-aseiah, *, Azariah, Neh 8:7,8
Shebaniah, Hodiah, *, Neh 10:9-13

KEMUEL
the next oldest,* (father of Gen 22:20-23
* (son of Shiptan) Num 34:16-28
Over Levi, Hashabiah (son of *); 1Ch 27:16-22

KENAN
years old when his son * was born. Gen 5:9,10,11
*: Kenan was seventy years old Gen 5:12,13,14
Kenan: * was seventy years old Gen 5:12,13,14
Adam, Seth, Enosh, *, Mahalalel, 1Ch 1:1

KENATH
to * and its surrounding Num 32:42
him and also took * and its sixty 1Ch 2:23

KENAZ
Teman, Omar, Zepho, Gatam, *, Gen 36:10,11,12
Zepho,The clan of *,The clan of Gen 36:15,16
Pinon,The clan of *,The clan of Gen 36:40-43
Othni-el (son of *), Caleb's Jos 15:17
*, volunteered to lead the attack; Ju 1:13
Othni-el (son of *, Caleb's younger Ju 3:9
Teman, Omar, Zephi, Gatam, *, 1Ch 1:36
Chief Pinon, Chief *, Chief Teman, 1Ch 1:51-54
The sons of * were 1Ch 4:13
The sons of Elah included *. 1Ch 4:15

KENITE
of the * tribe—accompanied them. Ju 1:16
(Heber, the *—the Kenites were Ju 4:11
wife of Heber the *, for there was Ju 4:17
The wife of Heber the *— Ju 5:24

KENITES
*, Kenizzites, Kadmonites, Gen 15:19,20,21
Then he looked over at the *: Num 24:21,22
But the * shall be destroyed, Num 24:21,22
(Heber, the Kenite—the * were Ju 4:11
Saul sent a message to the *, 1Sa 15:6
So the * packed up and left. 1Sa 15:6
people of Jerahmeel and the *." 1Sa 27:10
the cities of the *, Hormah, 1Sa 30:27-31
All these are * who descended 1Ch 2:55

KENIZZITE
of Jephunneh the *) and Joshua (son Num 32:12

KENIZZITES
Kenites, *, Kadmonites, Hittites, Gen 15:19,20,21

KEPT
Abraham's plea and * Lot safe, Gen 19:29
spring again and * carrying water Gen 24:20
But she * on with her suggestions Gen 39:10
to listen, and * out of her way as Gen 39:10
She * the jacket, and when her Gen 39:16
king's prisoners were * in chains. Gen 39:20
that no one * track of the amount. Gen 41:49
He is the Angel who has * me Gen 48:16
as before," they * demanding. Ex 5:13
quarts of it to be * as a museum Ex 16:32
* in the Ark in the Tabernacle. Ex 16:34
the ox was not * under control; Ex 21:29
its owner has not * it under Ex 21:36
lamb may be * over until the Ex 34:25
with the altar fire * burning. Lev 6:9
be * burning—it must not go out. Lev 6:12
The fire must be * burning upon Lev 6:13
The other goat shall be * alive Lev 16:10
they shall be * for the people of Num 19:9
where it was * before the Lord; Num 20:9
but Jehovah has * you from it!" Num 24:11
donkeys, and flocks * by the army. Num 31:28
which the soldiers * for Num 31:32-35
(The soldiers had also * Num 31:53
the Tabernacle and * there before Num 31:54
But we * the cattle and loot for Deu 3:7
His iron bedstead is * in a Deu 3:11
* his promise to your ancestors. Deu 7:8
how the Lord has * them powerless Deu 11:4
the book * by the Levite-priests. Deu 17:18
meanwhile, the city gates were * Jos 2:7
* it dry until we were all across! Jos 4:23
THE GATES OF Jericho were * Jos 6:1
were * for the Lord's treasury. Jos 6:24
For Joshua * his spear pointed Jos 8:26
of Israel * these for themselves. Jos 8:27
now the Lord has * me alive and Jos 14:10
Philistines, who * them in Ju 13:1
was with him and * it up for the Ju 14:17
So the men of Dan * going. Ju 18:26
his father-in-law * urging him Ju 19:7
"Gone," they * saying to Ju 21:6
Parents * a widowed Ru 1:11f
However, Saul and his men * the 1Sa 15:9
King Saul now * David at Jerusalem 1Sa 18:4
So from that time on King Saul * 1Sa 18:9
Sir, since the Lord has * you 1Sa 25:26
of Israel who has * me from hurting 1Sa 25:34
God has paid back Nabal and * me 1Sa 25:39
BUT DAVID * thinking to himself, 1Sa 27:1
the other four hundred * going. 1Sa 30:9,10
The Lord has * us safe and helped 1Sa 30:23
for anything, but * on, 2Sa 2:19
But Asahel refused and * on 2Sa 2:21
young men were * strictly apart. 2Sa 13:2
Absalom * on urging the matter 2Sa 13:27
on, and Shime-i * pace with them on 2Sa 16:13
* on weeping, "O my son Absalom! 2Sa 19:4
the historian who * the records. 2Sa 20:24
And * myself from sin. 2Sa 22:24
Then why have you not * your 1Ki 2:43
And he * them in his palace in 1Ki 10:16,17
you have not * our agreement and 1Ki 11:11
he has not * my laws and 1Ki 11:33
But they * urging until he was 2Ki 2:17
hundred that he * for his own use. 1Ch 18:4
And you have * your promise to 2Ch 6:15
his chariots and horses were *. 2Ch 8:6
The guards at the Temple gates * 2Ch 23:19
They had not * it in great 2Ch 30:5
And he has * his faith in me Job 2:3
But you, O God, have * them back Job 17:3,4
he * insisting on his innocence. Job 32:1
I * close watch on all his laws; Ps 18:22
Literally, "when I * silence." Ps 32:3f
They will be * safe forever; Ps 37:28
I have not * this Good News Ps 40:10
Yet they * on with their Ps 78:17
Yet even so the people * on Ps 78:32
wilderness. He * them safe, so Ps 78:53
by mankind, and * beneath the heel Is 49:7
But they wouldn't listen; they * Jer 7:24
until now, I have * on sending them Jer 7:25
of Egypt—and have * on saying it Jer 11:7
Jeremiah was * there for several Jer 37:15,16
So Jeremiah was * in the palace Jer 37:21
where used clothing was *. Jer 38:11
they have * right on with their Jer 44:5
* us from complete destruction. Lam 3:22
They and their fathers have * on Eze 2:3
You have not * the laws I gave Eze 44:8
the Sabbath is * a sacred day. Eze 44:24
mourning you have * in July, Zec 8:19
But they * shouting, "Crucify! Mt 27:23
But he * on looking around to see Mk 5:32
John because he * saying it was Mk 6:17,18
so he * him under his protection. Mk 6:20
So they * it to themselves, but Mk 9:10
They * begging him not to order Lk 8:31
'I've * it safe,' he said, Lk 19:20
him, for God * them from it. Lk 24:1
But you have * the best for the Jn 2:1
* asking if anyone had seen him. Jn 7:1
They * demanding an answer, so Jn 8:7
During my time here I have * Jn 17:12
Literally, "* in your name those Jn 17:12
When they * telling him, "We Jn 20:25
In it they * the stone tablets Act 7:44
shouting again and * it up for two Act 19:34
and ordered him * in the prison at Act 23:35
No one anywhere has * on doing Rom 3:12
Or because he also * the Jewish Rom 4:9
for you Gentiles, * secret from Rom 16:25,26,27
be offended or * back from finding 2Co 6:3
We have been injured but * from 2Co 6:9
under King Aretas * guards at the 2Co 11:32
by the law, * in protective Gal 3:23
about you we have * on praying and Col 1:9
He has * this secret for Col 1:26,27
soul and body be * strong and 1Th 5:23
To: The church of Thessalonica—* 2Th 1:1
it all I have * true to him. 2Ti 4:7
sorely; he * right on doing his Heb 3:9
Remember how you * right on with Heb 10:32
Moses * right on going; Heb 11:27
they were * from harm in a den of Heb 11:33
it is * in heaven for you, pure 1Pe 1:4
began to sin has * steadily at it. 1Jn 3:8
Literally, "you have * my word." Rev 3:8f
this means "* from" or "kept Rev 3:10f
"* through" the coming horror. Rev 3:10f
after night they * on saying, Rev 4:8
And the four Living Beings * Rev 5:14
They had been * in readiness Rev 9:15

KEREN
Jemima, Kezia, *. Job 42:13,14

KEREN-HAPPUCH
Literally, "*." Job 42:13,14f

KERI-OTH
Beth-meon, and * and Bozrah—and Jer 48:24

KERI-OTH-HEZRON
Hazor-hadattah, * (or, Hazor), Jos 15:21-32

KERIOTH
will destroy all the palaces in *. Amo 2:2

KERNEL
every * well formed and plump. Gen 41:5
yet not one true * will be lost. Amo 9:9
and die like a * of wheat that Jn 12:23,24

KERNELS
remove the * from a fresh ear, Lev 2:14
* nor bread nor parched grain. Lev 23:14
many new wheat *—a plentiful Jn 12:23,24

KEROS
Ziha, Hasupha, Tabbaoth, *, Siaha, Ez 2:43-54
Ziha, Hasupha, Tabbaoth, *, Neh 7:46-56

KETTLE
or if a bronze * is used, it must Lev 6:28
be added to spring water in a *. Num 19:17
put them into a * without realizing 2Ki 4:39
He threw it into the * and said, 2Ki 4:41

KETTLES
offerings in pots, *, and pans, and 2Ch 35:13
bronze pots and *, and ash shovels Jer 52:18

KETURAH
NOW ABRAHAM MARRIED again. * Gen 25:1
these were the children of *." Gen 25:4f
also had sons by his concubine *: 1Ch 1:32
of Abraham by his concubine *. 1Ch 1:33

KEY
they became concerned and got a *. Ju 3:25
true, and has the * of David to Rev 3:7
given the * to the bottomless pit. Rev 9:1
heaven with the * to the bottomless Rev 20:1

KEYNOTE
Holiness is forever the * of your Ps 93:5

KEYS
And I will give you the * of the Mt 16:19
who has the * of hell and Rev 1:17,18

KEZIA
Jemima, *, Keren. Job 42:13,14

KIBROTH-HATTAAVAH
Literally, "*." Num 11:34f
the wilderness of Sinai to *; Num 33:15-37
From * to Hazeroth; Num 33:15-37
the Lord, and yet again at *. Deu 9:22

KIBZA-IM
Refuge), Gezer, *, and Beth-horon. Jos 21:20,21,22

KICK
in the dust and * aside the meek. Amo 2:7
for you to * against the oxgoad!" Act 26:14f

KICKED
* me out in a most uncivil way." Gen 26:27
"Am I a Judean dog to be * around 2Sa 3:8
The needy are * aside; Job 24:4
I * myself for my stupidity. Jer 31:19
We have been * around without 1Co 4:11

KID
can also mean "*"—a baby goat. Ex 12:3,4f
"How can a * like you fight with 1Sa 17:33

KIDNAP
so no one can * them from me. Jn 10:29

KIDNAPPED
For I was * from my homeland Gen 40:15
they were told and * the girls who Ju 21:23
Being * and held for ransom never Pro 13:8

KIDNAPPER
"A * must be killed, whether he Ex 21:16
or sells him, the * must die, in Deu 24:7

KIDNAPPERS
homosexuals, *, liars, and all 1Ti 1:10,11

KIDNAPS
If anyone * a brother Israelite, Deu 24:7

KIDNEYS
bladder and two *, and the fat on Ex 29:13
and the two * and the fat Ex 29:22
parts, the two * and the loin-fat Lev 3:3,4,5
organs, the two * with the loin-fat Lev 3:9,10,11
insides, the two * and the Lev 3:15,16
entrails, the two * and the Lev 4:9
insides, the two * and the Lev 7:4
liver, and the two * and their fat, Lev 8:15,16
bladder, the two * with their fat, Lev 8:25
the altar the fat, *, and gall Lev 9:10
the * and gall bladders. Lev 9:19

KIDRON
passed by, crossed * Brook, and 2Sa 15:23
The moment you go beyond * Brook, 1Ki 2:36,37
he cut down and burned at * Brook. 1Ki 15:13
the fields of the * Valley outside 2Ki 23:4
it outside Jerusalem to * Brook; 2Ki 23:6
scattered the pieces in * Valley. 2Ki 23:12
crushed and burned it at * Brook. 2Ch 15:16
then carted it out to the brook *. 2Ch 29:16
and threw them into * Brook. 2Ch 30:14
of Gihon in the * Valley, and then 2Ch 33:14
to the brook of *, and from there Jer 31:40
Jesus crossed the * ravine with his Jn 18:1

KIDS
the dressed *, which she prepared Gen 27:14
Lambs and calves and * will Is 5:17
from * and rams from billy goats! Eze 34:17

KILL
who sees me will try to * me." Gen 4:14
The Lord replied, "They won't * Gen 4:15
on Cain as a warning not to * him. Gen 4:15
for to * a man is to kill one Gen 9:5,6
for to kill a man is to * one Gen 9:5,6
Let's * him and then we can have Gen 12:11,12,13
"Will you * good and bad alike? Gen 18:22,23
to * the godly with the wicked! Gen. 18:25
will * me to get her,' I thought. Gen 20:11,12
he was afraid they would * him to Gen 26:7
"I thought someone would * me to Gen 26:9
gone, and then I will * Jacob." Gen 27:41
he is coming to * me and these Gen 32:11
distance, they decided to * him! Gen 37:18
"Come on, let's * him and toss Gen 37:19,20
"Let's not * him," he said; Gen 37:21,22
Let's sell Joseph to them! Why * Gen 37:26,27
for fear God would * him, too, just Gen 38:11
taking her out to * her she sent Gen 38:25
to his father, "* my two sons if I Gen 42:37
and Puah) to * all Hebrew boys as Ex 1:15,16
And do you plan to * me as you Ex 2:14
who wanted to * you are dead." Ex 4:19
to Moses and threatened to * him. Ex 4:24
giving them an excuse to * us." Ex 5:21
before their eyes, they will * us. Ex 8:26
Egypt tonight and * all the oldest Ex 12:12
the families, and * the lamb so Ex 12:21
the land and * the Egyptians; Ex 12:23
to enter and * your firstborn. Ex 12:23
to * us with starvation." Ex 16:3
directly to us, or it will * us." Ex 20:19
intending to * him, drag him even Ex 21:14
him even from my altar, and * him. Ex 21:14
you, and I will * you with enemy Ex 22:24
and you shall * it before the Ex 29:11
to the other and * even your Ex 32:27
Or, "then * me instead of them." Ex 32:32f
The man shall then * the animal Lev 1:5
The man who brings it will * it Lev 1:11
upon its head and * it at the door Lev 3:2
upon its head and * it at the Lev 3:7,8
upon its head and * it at the Lev 3:13
and * it there before Jehovah. Lev 4:4
head and * it before the Lord. Lev 4:15
upon its head and * it at the Lev 4:24
head of the sin offering and * it. Lev 4:29
and * it there as a sin offering. Lev 4:33
Then he shall * the lamb at the Lev 14:13
and afterwards the priest shall * Lev 14:19
Then he shall * the lamb for the Lev 14:25
He shall * one of the birds over Lev 14:50
with an animal, * the woman and the Lev 20:16
I will send wild animals to * Lev 26:22
like this, please * me right now; Num 11:15
Jehovah will * us there, and our Num 14:3
Now if you * all your people, Num 14:15
The Lord had to * them because he Num 14:16
of lovely Egypt to * us here in Num 16:13
someone shall * her as he watches. Num 19:1
to stand in the road to * him. Num 22:22,23
with me, for I would * you." Num 22:29
destroyed us. Now * all the boys Num 31:17
* the murderer when he meets him. Num 35:19
might catch and * the innocent Deu 19:6,7
the dead man's avenger, to * him. Deu 19:12
to you, * every male in the city; Deu 20:13
a bribe to * an innocent person.' Deu 27:25
I * and make live. Deu 32:39
(He had told them previously, "* Jos 6:17
going to let the Amorites * us? Jos 7:7
of Israel to * them, but they Jos 9:26
who may try to * him in revenge. Jos 20:3
dead man comes to * him in revenge, Jos 20:5
killed them I wouldn't * you." Ju 8:19
son, he instructed him to * them. Ju 8:20
"* me!" Ju 9:54
Lord were going to * us he wouldn't Ju 13:23
that you won't * me yourselves." Ju 15:12,13
light, we'll find him and * him." Ju 16:2
angry and * every one of you." Ju 18:25
house, planning to * me, and they Ju 20:5
Benjamin began to * the men of Ju 20:31
of their oath to * anyone who Ju 21:8,9
was already planning to * them. 1Sa 2:23,24,25
God of Israel here to * us too!" 1Sa 5:10
Bring them here and we will * 1Sa 11:12
where you are or we'll * you!' 1Sa 14:9
and sheep here to * and drain them, 1Sa 14:34
If Saul hears about it, he will * 1Sa 16:2
If your man is able to * me, 1Sa 17:9
But if I * him, then you must be 1Sa 17:9
will * you and cut off your head; 1Sa 17:46
and let them * him rather than 1Sa 18:17
risked his life to * Goliath, and 1Sa 19:5
at David in an attempt to * him. 1Sa 19:9,10
David's house and * him when he 1Sa 19:11
bed, then, so that he could * him. 1Sa 19:15
"He threatened to * me if I 1Sa 19:17
father so determined to * me?" 1Sa 20:1
know that he is planning to * me. 1Sa 20:7
Or else * me yourself if I have 1Sa 20:8
my father was planning to * you?" 1Sa 20:9
then may the Lord * me if I don't 1Sa 20:13
Now go and get him so I can * 1Sa 20:31
at Jonathan, intending to * him; 1Sa 20:33
David to come and * me!" 1Sa 22:8
He ordered his bodyguards, "* 1Sa 22:17
Ziph to search for him and * him. 1Sa 23:14,15
persuaded his men not to * Saul. 1Sa 24:7,8
me to * you, but I spared you. 1Sa 24:9,10
I cut it off, but I didn't * you! 1Sa 24:11
Perhaps he will * you for what 1Sa 24:12
into your hand, you didn't * me. 1Sa 24:18
you will not * my family and 1Sa 24:21
for he would not * her husband. 1Sa 25:35
"Don't * him, for who can remain 1Sa 26:9
But God forbid that I should * 1Sa 26:11
king when someone came to * him? 1Sa 26:15
and I refused to * you even when 1Sa 26:23
that you will not * me or give me 1Sa 30:15
armor bearer, "* me with your 1Sa 31:3,4
"Why did you * God's chosen 2Sa 1:14
one of his young men, "* him!" 2Sa 1:15
brother Joab if I have to * you!" 2Sa 2:22
continue to * each other forever? 2Sa 2:26
enemy Saul who tried to * you. 2Sa 4:8
to wicked men who * a good man in 2Sa 4:11
young men to * them, and they did. 2Sa 4:12
drunk, then, at my signal, * him! 2Sa 13:28
My own son is trying to * me, 2Sa 16:11
and I will * only the king, and 2Sa 17:2,3
You saw him there and didn't * 2Sa 18:11
Israel had sworn not to * them; 2Sa 21:2
on David and was about to * him. 2Sa 21:16
River I promised I wouldn't * him. 1Ki 2:8
king replied. "* him there beside 1Ki 2:31
Give her the child—don't * him!" 1Ki 3:26
Solomon tried to * Jeroboam, but 1Ki 11:40
then they will * me and ask him 1Ki 12:27
by causing the lion to * him." 1Ki 13:26
had tried to * all of the Lord's 1Ki 18:3,4
and can't find you, he will * me; 1Ki 18:12
was trying to * the Lord's 1Ki 18:13
that I am going to * you by this 1Ki 19:2
and now they are trying to * me, 1Ki 19:10
and now they are trying to * me, 1Ki 19:14
* you as soon as you leave me." 1Ki 20:36
Am I God, that I can * and give 2Ki 5:7
Elisha, "Oh, sir, shall I * them? 2Ki 6:21
Shall I * them?" 2Ki 6:21
"Do we * prisoners of war? 2Ki 6:22
day when I said, '* your son so we 2Ki 6:26-30
"May God * me if I don't execute 2Ki 6:31
murderer has sent a man to * me. 2Ki 6:32
but if they * us, we would have 2Ki 7:4
burn their forts, * the young men, 2Ki 8:12
him, but I didn't * his sons! 2Ki 10:9,10
in and * the whole bunch of them. 2Ki 10:25
in hand, and * anyone who tries to 2Ki 11:6,7,8
"Don't * her here in the Temple. 2Ki 11:15
in the Temple. But * anyone who 2Ki 11:15
but he didn't * their children, 2Ki 14:6
among them to * some of them. 2Ki 17:25
"Quick, * me with your sword 1Ch 10:4
"The first man to * a Jebusite 1Ch 11:5,6
from him and used it to * him. 1Ch 11:23
in hand, and * any unauthorized 2Ch 23:7
"Take her out and * her," 2Ch 23:13,14
* anyone who tries to help her." 2Ch 23:13,14
Then the leaders plotted to * 2Ch 24:21
decided to * him for murdering the 2Ch 24:25
However, he didn't * their 2Ch 25:4
to the Temple. * the Passover 2Ch 35:6
us and * us, thus ending our work. Neh 4:11
were plotting to * me, so I Neh 6:2
are coming tonight to * you." Neh 6:10
God may * me for saying this—in Job 13:15
dawn to * the poor and needy; Job 24:14,15
those who are trying to * me. Ps 35:4
my enemies are trying to * me. Ps 38:12
me with terror and plot to * me. Ps 55:3
for my steps, waiting to * me. Ps 56:6
at his home to capture and * him. Ps 59:1
Yet they prepare to * me. Ps 59:4
Don't * them—for my people soon Ps 59:11
plot to * me though I am innocent. Ps 69:4
and tempted God to * them, and Ps 78:41
godless men are trying to * me. Ps 86:14
that he would * them in the Ps 106:26
You did your best to * me, O my Ps 118:13
along the way to * me, I will Ps 119:95
"We'll hide and rob and *," Pro 1:11
your own complacency will * you. Pro 1:32
pray for those who long to * them. Pro 29:10
easy to catch and *, yet are found Pro 30:24-28
A time to *; Ecc 3:3
water supplies and * her leaders; Is 3:2
you, like bees to sting and to *. Is 7:18
will turn to fire and * you. Is 33:11
allies despise you and will * you. Jer 4:30
enemy is everywhere, ready to *; Jer 6:25
while planning to * them. Jer 9:8
that they were planning to * me! Jer 11:19
"Let's * him so that his name Jer 11:19
be punished for planning to * you. Jer 11:21,22
Lord—the sword to *, the dogs to Jer 15:3
Don't let them * me! Jer 15:15
They have set a trap to * me, yet Jer 18:20
invading armies * you here and Jer 19:7
as slaves to Babylon and * them. Jer 20:4
he did not * me at my birth! Jer 20:17
those who seek to * you, of whom Jer 22:24,25
mobbed him, shouting, "* him! Jer 26:7,8
him, shouting, "Kill him! * him! Jer 26:7,8
thing sure, if you * me, you will Jer 26:15
the people * him for saying this? Jer 26:19
If we * Jeremiah for giving us Jer 26:19
saying, the king sent to * him. Jer 26:21
turn him over to the mob to * him. Jer 26:24
your enemies and they shall * you. Jer 34:20
tell you the truth, you will * me. Jer 38:15
that he would not * Jeremiah or Jer 38:16
Johanan volunteered to * Ishmael Jer 40:15
that he will not * you or make Jer 42:12
to them, too! * them all! Jer 50:27
them to * their finest youth. Lam 2:4
you and * you and your families; Eze 5:17
there stands the enemy to * you. Eze 7:15
the city and * everyone whose Eze 9:5
Spare not nor pity them— * them Eze 9:6
with the bodies of those you *! Eze 9:7
to * everyone in all Israel?" Eze 11:13
the gates, shouting for the *; Eze 21:22
stone them and * them with swords; Eze 23:47
came to * them, Daniel handled the Dan 2:14
Babylon, and said, "Don't * them. Dan 2:24
You swear and lie and * and Hos 4:2
They * their kings one after Hos 7:7
of Damascus, and * her people as Amo 1:5
I will * the people of Ashdod, Amo 1:8
command the sword to * them there. Amo 9:4
"Please * me, Lord; Jon 4:3
and who rob and * to fill their Zep 1:9
and companions will * each other. Hag 2:22
is going to try to * the child." Mt 2:13
he ordered them to * every baby boy Mt 2:16
trying to * the child are dead." Mt 2:20
was, 'If you *, you must die.' Mt 5:21
of those who can * only your Mt 10:28
of those who will * me, and on the Mt 17:22,23
And Jesus replied, "Don't *, Mt 19:18
come on, let's * him and get it Mt 21:38
and you will * some by crucifixion, Mt 23:34
the fire or into water to * him. Mk 9:22
don't *, don't commit adultery, Mk 10:19
flog me with their whips and * me; Mk 10:34
Come on, let's * him—and then the Mk 12:7
He will come and * them all, and Mk 12:9
prophets, 'I will * the Shepherd, Mk 14:27
you, and you will * some of them Lk 11:49
They can only * the body; Lk 12:4

(KILL Con't)
to * and then cast into hell. Lk 12:5
and shoes! And * the calf we Lk 15:23
Let's * him, and then it will be Lk 20:14
I'll tell you—he will come and * Lk 20:16
to find a way to * him without Lk 22:2
they shouted, "* him, and release Lk 23:18
the more eager to * him because in Jn 5:18
them? Why * me for this?" Jn 7:19
Who's trying to * you?" Jn 7:20
this the man they are trying to *? Jn 7:25
Moses' law says to * her. Jn 8:5
you are trying to * me because my Jn 8:37
But instead you are trying to * Jn 8:40
leaders picked up stones to * him. Jn 8:59
is to steal, * and destroy. Jn 10:10
No one can * me without my Jn 10:18
leaders picked up stones to * him. Jn 10:31
in Judea were trying to * you. Jn 11:8
army will come and * us and take Jn 11:48
priests decided to * Lazarus too. Jn 12:10
when those who * you will think Jn 16:2
the people would * them if they Act 5:26,27
furious, and decided to * them. Act 5:33
'Are you going to * me as you Act 7:28
leaders determined to * him. Act 9:23
Then a voice said to him, "Go * Act 10:13
And I heard a voice say, '* and Act 11:7
he drew his sword to * himself. Act 16:27
"Away with such a fellow! * him! Act 22:22
We will * him on the way." Act 23:15
road ready to jump him and * him. Act 23:21
of a plot to * him, I decided to Act 23:30
(Their plan was to waylay and * Act 25:3
turn me over to these men to * me. Act 25:10,11
this, and tried to * me, but God Act 26:21
to let them * the prisoners lest Act 27:42
They are quick to *, hating Rom 3:15
now they were trying to * him too. Rom 11:2,3
him, or * him or steal from him. Rom 13:9
commanded them to * a lamb as God Heb 11:28
don't have, so you * to get it. Jas 4:2
Why did he * him? 1Jn 3:12
of the earth, to * with war and Rev 6:8
They were not to * them, but to Rev 9:5
In those days men will try to * Rev 9:6
loose to * a third of all mankind. Rev 9:15
them and conquer and * them; Rev 11:7

KILLED
Cain attacked and * his brother. Gen 4:8
I have * a youth who attacked and Gen 4:23
another son for the one Cain *." Gen 4:25
any man who murders shall be *; Gen 9:5,6
If any were attacked and * by Gen 31:39
crush us, and we will all be *." Gen 34:30
Then the brothers * a goat and Gen 37:31
wicked man, and so the Lord * him. Gen 38:7
so he * him, too. Gen 38:10
was watching, then * the Egyptian Ex 2:12
I could have * you all by now, Ex 9:15
animals alike, was *, and the trees Ex 9:25
lambs shall be *, and their blood Ex 12:6
Israel, though he * the Egyptians; Ex 12:27
midnight, Jehovah * all the Ex 12:29
to trade, the donkey shall be *. Ex 13:13
us go, so Jehovah * all the Ex 13:15
that the Lord had * us there! Ex 16:3
"A kidnapper must be *, whether Ex 21:16
and the owner also shall be *. Ex 21:29
a house and is *, the one who Ex 22:2
the one who * him is not guilty. Ex 22:2
it is injured or *, and the owner Ex 22:14
attacked and * by a wild animal. Ex 22:31
of one of the rams as it is *. Ex 29:15,16
hands upon its head as it is *. Ex 29:19,20
any work on that day shall be *. Ex 31:14,15
are *, and present it to the Lord. Lev 4:24
offerings are *, and there lay his Lev 4:29
offerings are *, and lay his hand Lev 4:33
holy, and shall be * before the Lev 6:25
where the burnt offerings are *. Lev 6:25
animal shall be * at the place Lev 7:2
or is attacked and * by wild Lev 7:24
upon its head as Moses * it. Lev 8:15,16
head, and Moses * it and sprinkled Lev 8:19
Moses * it and took some of its Lev 8:23
to the altar and * the calf as a Lev 9:8
Next he * the burnt offering Lev 9:12
offering; he * the goat and offered Lev 9:15
Next he * the ox and ram—the Lev 9:18
one of the birds * in an Lev 14:5
are *, there at the Tabernacle; Lev 14:13
the bird that was * over the fresh Lev 14:51,52
be executed and the animal *. Lev 20:15
From the day I * all the oldest Num 3:13
I * all the firstborn Egyptians. Num 8:17
So the people caught and * quail Num 11:32
the people and he * large numbers Num 11:33
* him as the Lord had commanded. Num 15:36
"You have * the Lord's people." Num 16:41
who has been * in battle, or who Num 19:16
who has been * or is otherwise Num 19:18
our dear brothers the Lord *!" Num 20:3
was victorious and * King Og, his Num 21:35
* you by now, and spared her." Num 22:33
The name of the man who was * Num 25:14
And every man of Midian was * in Num 31:7
Among those * were all five of Num 31:8
the son of Beor, was also *. Num 31:8
* anyone or touched a dead body. Num 31:19
* by the Lord the night before. Num 33:3,4
has accidentally * someone can run Num 35:6
if he has * someone accidentally. Num 35:11
for the slayer must not be * Num 35:12
"But if someone is struck and * Num 35:16
The same is true if he is * with Num 35:18
and * them from Seir to Hormah. Deu 1:44
and his people, and we * them all. Deu 3:3
* someone could flee for safety. Deu 4:42
to heathen gods, must be *. Deu 18:10
since he had not * deliberately. Deu 19:6,7
For you might be * in the battle, Deu 20:5
the other man's wife must be *; Deu 22:22
this house will be * or injured. Jos 2:19
the Israelis were * during the Jos 7:5
Ai and had * its king, the same as Jos 10:1
and * its king and everyone in it. Jos 10:28
but Joshua's men * him and Jos 10:33
they * everyone in the city. Jos 10:34,35
And they * everyone just as they Jos 10:39
captured Hazor and * its king. Jos 11:10
Every person there was * and Jos 11:11
but they * all the people. Jos 11:14
And Joshua * all the kings of Jos 11:17
so they were mercilessly *, as Jos 11:20
and Israel; he * them all and Jos 11:21
in Heshbon and was * by Moses along Jos 13:21
The people of Israel also * Jos 13:22
who accidentally * another man Jos 20:9
a trial, and not be * in revenge. Jos 20:9
the Moabites and * about ten Ju 3:29
He once * six hundred Philistines Ju 3:31
Oreb was * at the rock now known Ju 7:25
thousand had already been *. Ju 8:10
and * the entire male population. Ju 8:17
* at Tabor—what were they like?" Ju 8:18
"I swear that if you hadn't * Ju 8:19
we'd rather be * by a man!" Ju 8:21
So Gideon * them and took the Ju 8:21
* his seventy sons upon one stone. Ju 9:18
captured the city, * its people, Ju 9:45
said that a woman * Abimelech!" Ju 9:54
It is not clear whether he * her Ju 11:39f
he was dragged away and *. Ju 12:6
city of Ashkelon, * thirty men, Ju 14:19
great fury and * many of them. Ju 15:8
* a thousand Philistines with it. Ju 15:15
I've * a thousand men, Ju 15:16,17
"The scourge of our nation who * Ju 16:23,24
So those he * at the moment of Ju 16:30
had * during his entire lifetime. Ju 16:30
stormed out and * twenty-two Ju 20:21
the Israeli army * 25,100 men of Ju 20:35-39
When the men of Benjamin had * Ju 20:35-39
Gibe-ah, and * most of them there. Ju 20:43
five thousand were * along the way, Ju 20:45
and Hophni and Phinehas were *. 1Sa 4:11
Hophni and Phinehas were * too, 1Sa 4:17
for a fire and * the cows and 1Sa 6:14
But the Lord * seventy of the 1Sa 6:19
many people whom the Lord had *. 1Sa 6:19
and the lad * them right and left, 1Sa 14:13
they chased and * the Philistines 1Sa 14:31
Amalekites, but * everyone else. 1Sa 15:8
and I brought King Agag but * 1Sa 15:20
your sword has * the sons of many 1Sa 15:33
its sheath and * him with it, and 1Sa 17:50,51
After David had * Goliath, Abner 1Sa 17:57
home after David had * Goliath. 1Sa 18:6
to see him * by the Philistines!" 1Sa 18:21
David would be * in the fight. 1Sa 18:25
men went out and * two hundred 1Sa 18:27
Lord lives, he shall not be *." 1Sa 19:6
If he is angry and wants you *, 1Sa 20:13
you * in the valley of Elah. 1Sa 21:9
So Doeg turned on them and * them, 1Sa 22:18
the priests, and * the priests' 1Sa 22:19
then died, for the Lord * him. 1Sa 25:37,38
"Are you trying to get me *?" 1Sa 28:9
hurried out and * it and kneaded 1Sa 28:24
in on Saul, and * his sons 1Sa 31:2
his son Jonathan have been *." 2Sa 1:4
"So I * him, for I knew he 2Sa 1:10
that you * God's appointed king." 2Sa 1:16
out a dagger and * him in revenge 2Sa 3:27
or be * by the sword!" 2Sa 3:29
So Joab and his brother Abishai * 2Sa 3:30
were * at the battle of Jezreel. 2Sa 4:4
bringing me good news, I * him; 2Sa 4:10
Uzzah and he * him for doing this, 2Sa 6:7
and Uriah was * along with 2Sa 11:17
Wasn't Abimelech * at Thebez by 2Sa 11:19,20,21
—then tell him, 'Uriah was *, 2Sa 11:19,20,21
and some of our men were *, and 2Sa 11:24
Or, "* them with saws and iron 2Sa 12:31f
"Absalom has * all of your sons, 2Sa 13:29,30
said, "No, not all have been *! 2Sa 13:32,33
to part them, one of them was *. 2Sa 14:5,6
advised that he be captured and *. 2Sa 17:21
in the forest than were *. 2Sa 18:8
his rescue and * the Philistine. 2Sa 21:17
Hushathite * Saph, another giant. 2Sa 21:18
place, Elhanan * the brother of 2Sa 21:19
of David's brother Shime-i—* him. 2Sa 21:20,21
and were * by David's troops. 2Sa 21:22
He once * eight hundred men in 2Sa 23:8
army fled. He * the Philistines 2Sa 23:10
enemy singlehanded and * them all. 2Sa 23:18,19
Benaiah * two giants, 2Sa 23:20
that was caught there and * it. 2Sa 23:20
with a staff, he * an Egyptian 2Sa 23:21
Egyptian's hand and * him with it. 2Sa 23:21
him, and he * him with a sword. 1Ki 2:25
You should be *, too, but I won't 1Ki 2:26
to the Tabernacle and * Joab; 1Ki 2:34
took Shime-i outside and * him. 1Ki 2:46
Israeli army had * nearly every 1Ki 11:15
but they finally * all except 1Ki 11:16,17,18
along, a lion came out and * him. 1Ki 13:24,25
He immediately * all of the 1Ki 15:29
in and struck him down and * him. 1Ki 16:10
He immediately * the entire royal 1Ki 16:11
General Omri won and Tibni was *; 1Ki 16:22
God, why have you * the son of this 1Ki 17:20
to Kishon Brook and * them there. 1Ki 18:40
to Elijah: "You * my prophets, and 1Ki 19:2
your altars and * your prophets, 1Ki 19:10
they have * every one of your 1Ki 19:14
Hazael shall be * by Jehu, and 1Ki 19:17
escape Jehu shall be * by Elisha! 1Ki 19:17
to his oxen, * them, and used wood 1Ki 19:21
Each one * a Syrian soldier, and 1Ki 20:20
army was * in a great slaughter. 1Ki 20:21
And the Israelis * 100,000 Syrian 1Ki 20:29
fell on them and * another 27,000. 1Ki 20:30
to go a lion attacked and * him. 1Ki 20:36
struck them and * them all! 2Ki 1:10
the woods and * forty-two of them. 2Ki 2:24
have attacked and * each other! 2Ki 3:23
the Israeli army, * him and 2Ki 3:27
and * as the people rushed out. 2Ki 7:17
people who were * by Jezebel. 2Ki 9:7
* him, but I didn't kill his sons! 2Ki 10:9,10
Jehu then * all the rest of the 2Ki 10:11
and * all forty-two of them. 2Ki 10:14
son was dead, she * all of his 2Ki 11:1
palace stables and * her there. 2Ki 11:16
on the kingdom, he * the men who 2Ki 14:5
shall not be * for their children, 2Ki 14:6
Once Amaziah * ten thousand 2Ki 14:7
sent assassins and * him there. 2Ki 14:19
as their king; he * the entire 2Ki 15:16
He even * his own son by offering 2Ki 16:3
and King Rezin of Syria was *. 2Ki 16:9
he is * when he arrives there." 2Ki 19:7
angel of the Lord * 185,000 2Ki 19:35
Adrammelech and Sharezer * him. 2Ki 19:37
him and * him in the palace. 2Ki 21:23
Then a posse of civilians * all 2Ki 21:24
to Bethel. He * the heathen 2Ki 23:5
but King Neco * Josiah at Megiddo 2Ki 23:29
his sons were * before his eyes; 2Ki 25:7
with ten men and * Gedaliah and his 2Ki 25:25
was so wicked that the Lord * him. 1Ch 2:3
of Ham; they * the inhabitants of 1Ch 4:40,41
they were * by the local farmers. 1Ch 7:20,21
and Malchishua, and * them all. 1Ch 10:2
dead, * himself in the same way. 1Ch 10:5
bodies of the men * in action and 1Ch 10:8
So the Lord * him and gave the 1Ch 10:14
He once * 300 men with his spear. 1Ch 11:11
Kabzeel, * the two famous giants 1Ch 11:22
He also * a lion in a slippery 1Ch 11:22
Once he * an Egyptian who was 1Ch 11:23
against Uzza, and * him because he 1Ch 13:10
Even kings were * who sought to 1Ch 16:21
* twenty-two thousand of them; 1Ch 18:5
from David, and he * seven thousand 1Ch 19:17,18
He also * Shophach, the 1Ch 19:17,18
man from Hushath, * one of the sons 1Ch 20:4
(the son of Jair) * Lahmi, the 1Ch 20:5
but he was * by David's nephew 1Ch 20:6,7
were * by David and his soldiers. 1Ch 20:8
'You have * too many men in great 1Ch 22:8
said, 'Their master has been *. 2Ch 18:16
Ramoth-gilead and be * there?' 2Ch 18:19,20
Seir and * every one of them. 2Ch 20:23
as king, he * all of his brothers 2Ch 21:3,4
because you have * your brothers 2Ch 21:13
of Arabs had * his older sons). 2Ch 22:1
the princes of Judah, and * them. 2Ch 22:8
brought him to Jehu, who * him. 2Ch 22:9
Athaliah * them when she heard the 2Ch 22:10

(KILLED Con't)
they * her at the palace stables. 2Ch 23:15,16,17
the idols, and * Mattan the priest 2Ch 23:15,16,17
and there * 10,000 men from Seir. 2Ch 25:11
quiet now, before I have you *." 2Ch 25:16
went after him and * him there. 2Ch 25:27
son of Remaliah, * 120,000 of his 2Ch 28:6
from Ephraim, * the king's son 2Ch 28:7
Our fathers have been * in war, 2Ch 29:9
So they * the young bulls, and 2Ch 29:22
altar, and they * the rams and 2Ch 29:22
Then the priests * the animals 2Ch 29:24
the people * their Passover lambs. 2Ch 30:15
rites, the Levites * their Passover 2Ch 30:17,18,19
some of his own sons * him there. 2Ch 32:21
citizens * all of those who 2Ch 33:25
then the Levites * the Passover 2Ch 35:11
against them and * their young men, 2Ch 36:17
They threw away your law, * the Neh 9:26
all be * on the 28th day of Est 3:13
given to those who * them. Est 3:13
palace, when all other Jews are *? Est 4:13
They even * 500 men in Shushan. Est 9:6
They also * the ten sons of Est 9:7-10
"The Jews have * 500 men in Est 9:12
next day also and * 300 more men, Est 9:15
and * all the farmhands except me. Job 1:14,15
your camels and * your servants, Job 1:17
against them and * the finest of Ps 78:31
Their sheep were * by lightning. Ps 78:48
Then he * the eldest son Ps 78:51
Their young men were * by fire Ps 78:63
Then he * the oldest child in Ps 105:36
forever, and * famous kings who Ps 136:18
* with an arrow through its heart. Pro 7:23
a lion in the street and be *!" Pro 22:13
me, you will be * by your enemies; Is 1:20
their owners * or gone." Is 5:9
evil will be *— the violent man Is 29:20
land, where I will have him *." Is 37:7
Assyrians and * 185,000 soldiers; Is 37:36
Sharezer * him with their swords; Is 37:38
For most of my children were * Is 49:21
And you yourselves have * my Jer 2:30
He has * off the flower of your Jer 9:21
bodies of those the sword has *; Jer 14:18
for all her children have been *. Jer 15:9
by your enemies, * by starvation Jer 21:9
C. and * Belshazzar, the last Jer 25:12f
says you won't be * in war and Jer 34:4
watch as they * his children and Jer 39:6
You shall not be * by those you Jer 39:17
out their swords and * Gedaliah. Jer 41:2
and his men * all but ten of them Jer 41:7
that Ishmael had * Gedaliah the Jer 41:18
stay here and be * by the Jer 43:2,3
all those I want *, and capturing Jer 43:11
They shall fall here in Egypt, * Jer 44:12
Pharaoh Hophra was * by Amasis, Jer 44:30f
who want them *—into the hands of Jer 46:26
her warriors will all be *. Jer 50:30
Just as Babylon * the people of Jer 51:49
of Israel, so must she be *. Jer 51:49
of Judah were * before his eyes, Jer 52:10
where the king * them all. Jer 52:27
girls, * by the enemies' swords. Lam 2:21
You have * them, Lord, in your Lam 2:21
you have * them without mercy. Lam 2:21
Those * by the sword are far Lam 4:9
myths, he had been *, and fertility Eze 8:14f
of Israel will be * by the sword, Eze 17:21
They stripped her and * her and Eze 23:10
your survivors will be *; Eze 23:25
you despise, * by the sword. Eze 31:18
filled with those the sword has *. Eze 35:8
up with the others to be *. Dan 2:13
leaped out and * the soldiers as Dan 3:22
him in fear. He * any who offended Dan 5:19
king, was *, and Darius the Mede Dan 5:30
fourth animal was * and its body Dan 7:11
One will be *, his kingdom still Dan 9:26
of his enemies, * but his success Dan 11:12
army will desert, and many be *. Dan 11:26
Her people will be * by the Hos 13:16
the Jews, for they * innocent Joe 3:19
Egypt long ago. I * your lads in Amo 4:10
He says you will be *, and Amo 7:11
be * and your land divided up. Amo 7:17
they all will be *. Amo 9:1
and * those trying to escape; Ob 1:14
we but fish, to be caught and *? Hab 1:14
her king *, and Ashkelon will be Zec 9:5
if you are *, I don't care. Zec 11:9
who was * in the valley of Zec 12:11
He would have * John but was Mt 14:5
that he would be *, and that Mt 16:21
one, * one and stoned another. Mt 21:35
him out of the vineyard and * him. Mt 21:39
to the prophets * by your fathers Mt 23:29,30
"Then you will be tortured and * Mt 24:9
"Those using swords will get *. Mt 26:52
Herodias wanted John * in Mk 6:19
The soldier * John in the prison, Mk 6:27
leaders—and be *, and that he would Mk 8:31
am going to be betrayed and * and Mk 9:30,31
me over to the Romans to be *. Mk 10:33
The next man he sent was *; Mk 12:5
either beaten or *, until there Mk 12:5
will betray their parents to be *. Mk 13:12
when the bridegroom will be *; Lk 5:35
and teachers of the Law—and be *; Lk 9:22
who * the prophets long ago. Lk 11:47
God to be * except in Jerusalem! Lk 13:33
your father has * the calf we were Lk 15:27
and spat upon, and lashed and *. Lk 18:33
him out of the vineyard and * him. Lk 20:15
and some of you will be *. Lk 21:16
They will be brutally * by enemy Lk 21:24
Passover lamb was * and eaten with Lk 22:7
So Jesus said, "When you have * Jn 8:28
And you * the Author of Life; Act 3:15
after you * him we saw him alive! Act 3:15
* him by hanging him on a cross. Act 5:30
him, but he was *, and his Act 5:36
So Moses * the Egyptian. Act 7:24
as you * that Egyptian yesterday?' Act 7:28
They even * the ones who Act 7:52
the believers, and * the apostle Act 12:2
[They must have * him. Act 12:15
asked Pilate to have him * anyway. Act 13:28
Stephen was *, I was standing there Act 22:20
nor drink until they had * Paul! Act 23:12,13
story and asked me to have him *. Act 25:15
God how they had * the prophets and Rom 11:2,3
soon to be *, put on display at the 1Co 4:9
of the world was * long ago, and Gal 6:14
After they had * their own 1Th 2:15
given by Moses was * without mercy Heb 10:28
faith, then were * with the sword. Heb 11:37,38
* by the scorching summer sun. Jas 1:10,11
You have condemned and * good Jas 5:6
those who were dead—* by the flood 1Pe 4:6
born only to be caught and *, 2Pe 2:12
to Satan and * his brother. 1Jn 3:12
of Egypt, and then * every one of Jud 1:5
example of Cain who * his brother; Jud 1:11
and a third of the fish were *. Rev 8:8,9
harm them will be * by bursts of Rev 11:5
destined for death will be *. Rev 13:10
If anyone kills you, he will be * Rev 13:10f
of the martyrs of Jesus she had *. Rev 17:6
And their entire army was * with Rev 19:21
As they were * him, word reached Act 21:31
Jews and they were * him when I Act 23:27
war and * broke out everywhere. Rev 6:4
* one-third of all mankind. Rev 9:17,18

KILLER
or not to hand the * over to the Num 35:24
shall save the * from the avenger; Num 35:25
the avenger; the * shall be Num 35:25
When the innocent * reaches any Jos 20:4

KILLING
against me for * that youth should Gen 4:24
* your own sons and brothers; Ex 32:29
at Heshbon, * the entire Deu 3:6
their pursuers and began * them. Jos 8:20,21
Makkedah, * them along the way. Jos 10:10
each of the five kings, * them. Jos 10:26
If a man is guilty of * someone Jos 20:3
begin fighting and * each other Ju 7:22
hiding places and began * them. Ju 9:43
Israel, * four thousand of them. 1Sa 4:2
* them all along the way. 1Sa 7:11
the Philistines * each other, and 1Sa 14:20
"What will a man get for * this 1Sa 17:26
murder an innocent man by * him? 1Sa 19:5
his men began talking of * him. 1Sa 30:6
would reward him for * his rival. 2Sa 1:10f
But instead of * a lamb from his 2Sa 12:4
the king by * his son (and the king 2Sa 18:13
burned, * the Israeli population; 1Ki 9:16
to punish my sins by * my son?" 1Ki 17:18
me: 'Isn't * Naboth bad enough? 1Ki 21:19
rushed out and began * them; 2Ki 3:24
and images and * Mattan, the priest 2Ki 11:18
The Thirty by * 300 men at one time 1Ch 11:20
While Jehu was hunting down and * 2Ch 22:8
his love and loyalty—by * his son. 2Ch 24:22
and Jerusalem, * all the leaders of 2Ch 24:23
toward Samaria, * 3,000 people and 2Ch 25:13
* even young girls and old men. 2Ch 36:17
* 75,000 of those who hated them; Est 9:16
at Shushan went on * their enemies Est 9:18
cities after * off its citizens. Job 15:27,28
will you gain, O Lord, from * me? Ps 30:9
me, you will be * an innocent man Jer 26:15
the land of Egypt, * all those I Jer 43:11
And so they began by * the Eze 9:6
of Mount Seir, * off all those who Eze 35:7
shamefully, even * some of them. Mt 22:6
to discuss plans for * Jesus. Mt 26:4
Jesus quietly, and * him. Mk 3:6
you celebrate by * the finest calf Lk 15:30
For which one are you * me?" Jn 10:32
agreement with the * of Stephen. Act 8:1
fulfilled prophecy by * Jesus; Act 13:27

KILLS
If anyone who * Cain will be Gen 4:24
in that case, if it * someone, Ex 21:29
or sheep and then * or sells it, he Ex 22:1
and the man who * him is guilty. Ex 22:3
goes hunting and * an animal or Lev 17:13
Anyone who * an animal [that Lev 24:18
"To repeat, whoever * an animal Lev 24:21
it, and whoever * a man must die. Lev 24:21
So, if anyone * another out of Num 35:20
him outside and * him, it is not Num 35:27
* someone may flee to safety. Deu 19:2,3
off the handle and * the man's Deu 19:5
out of hiding and * him, and then Deu 19:11
The Lord *, 1Sa 2:6
has offered to anyone who * him? 1Sa 17:25
"The sword * one as well as 2Sa 11:25
even a young one, * a sheep, he Is 31:4,5
my prophets as a lion * its prey. Jer 2:30
and the plague * man and beast Eze 14:19
the city that * the prophets, and Mt 23:37
If anyone * you, he will be Rev 13:10f

KILN
Aaron, "Take ashes from the *. Ex 9:8
So they took ashes from the * and Ex 9:10

KILNS
and axes and work in the brick *; 2Sa 12:31
iron harrows, and in brick *." 2Sa 12:31f

KIN
live near the rest of his *." Gen 16:9-12
his father—for they are near of *; Lev 20:19

KINAH
Kabzeel, Eder, Jagur, *, Dimonah, Jos 15:21-32

KIND
be filled with birds of every *." Gen 1:20
sort of fish and every * of bird. Gen 1:21,22
bring forth every * of Gen 1:24
and wildlife of every *." Gen 1:24
the soil every * of animal and Gen 2:19,20
Bring in a pair of each * of bird Gen 6:19,20
of every * of bird. Gen 7:3
Thus there will be every * of Gen 7:3
pairs of every * of animal—domestic Gen 7:14,15
you've been so * to me and saved Gen 19:18,19,20
the matter, be so * as to ask Gen 23:8
"thank you for being so * and Gen 24:27
Will you or won't you be * to my Gen 24:49
"Please be * to me and let me Gen 34:11
children, and wealth of every *. Gen 34:29
they couldn't say a * word to Gen 37:4
too, and was * to him by granting Gen 39:21
benefactor has been so * to them? Gen 44:4
"What * of people do you think Gen 44:7
"Simeon and Levi are two of a *. Gen 49:5
"Be so * as to tell me when you Ex 8:9
and no work of any * may be done on Ex 12:16
do no work of any *, nor shall your Ex 20:10
treaty of any * with the people Ex 34:15
gold objects of every *. Ex 35:22
discharge of any *, he becomes Lev 5:3
this *, and he shall be forgiven. Lev 5:13
Apparently a * of sacred lot used Lev 8:8f
living birds of a * permitted for Lev 14:4
or bird of a * permitted for food, Lev 17:13
defiled with this * of activity; Lev 18:25
your cattle with a different *; Lev 19:19
who does any * of work that day. Lev 23:30,31
the Lord is not a * that is Lev 27:11,12
If the animal is a * that may be Lev 27:13
* of man—he has obeyed me fully. Num 14:24
and no work of any * may be done. Num 29:7
This is the same * of thing your Num 32:8
(it was a * of bread unknown Deu 8:16
"You have been * enough to give me Ju 1:15
some * man to glean the free grain Ru 2:2
"How can you be so * to me?" Ru 2:10,11
for whoever was so * to you." Ru 2:19
He has been so * to us, and is a Ru 3:2
"For you were * to the people of 1Sa 15:6
who were in any * of trouble, such 1Sa 22:2
Yes, you have been wonderfully * 1Sa 24:18
And I too will be * to you 2Sa 2:6
he wanted to be * to them, as he 2Sa 9:1
a sacred vow by being * to him." 2Sa 9:3
so that I can be * to you because 2Sa 9:7
was always so loyal and * to me." 2Sa 10:2
But be * to the sons of 1Ki 2:7
were wonderfully * to my father 1Ki 3:6
you are loving and * and you keep 1Ki 8:22,23
But there was no reply of any * 1Ki 18:26
wizards, and every * of idol 2Ki 23:24
equipped with every * of weapon. 1Ch 12:24-37
you want to be * to me, because of 1Ch 17:19
* things his father did for me." 1Ch 19:2,3
and craftsmen of every *. 1Ch 22:15
Others with skills of every * 1Ch 28:21
you have been so * and good to my 2Ch 1:8

(KIND Con't)
You are the God who keeps his * 2Ch 6:14
saints rejoice in your * deeds. 2Ch 6:41
"He is always so loving and *." 2Ch 7:3
required to pay taxes of any *.' Ez 7:24
* to those who love and obey him! Neh 1:5
it into his heart to be * to me." Neh 1:11
"One should be * to a fainting Job 6:14
You gave me life and were so * Job 10:12
not answer with that * of logic! Job 32:14
You have been loving and * to me Ps 18:50
save me just because you are so * Ps 31:16
to the test and see how * he is! Ps 34:8
Trust in the Lord instead. Be * Ps 37:3
GOD BLESSES THOSE who are * to Ps 41:1
"O Lord," I prayed, "be * and Ps 41:4
O LOVING AND * God, have mercy. Ps 51:1
He is loving and * and rewards Ps 62:12
so plentiful, so tender and so *. Ps 69:16
Has he forgotten to be * to one Ps 77:9
O Lord, you are so good and *, Ps 86:5
You are constantly so *! Ps 86:13
forever, and be * to him always; Ps 89:28
things, the * you used to do, and Ps 90:16
and he was * and saved me. Ps 94:18
his promise to be * to Israel. Ps 98:2,3
He is always loving and *, and Ps 100:5
every *, to have no part in them. Ps 101:3
of every *, both great and small. Ps 104:25
for always being so loving and *. Ps 107:1
Let no one be * to him; Ps 109:12,13
Because you are so *, O Lord, Ps 109:21
me because you are loving and *. Ps 109:26
He is * and merciful— and all Ps 112:4
How * he is! Ps 116:5
Because you are so loving and *, Ps 119:149
and health because you are so *. Ps 119:159
for he is loving and *, and comes Ps 130:7
And because you are loving and * Ps 143:12
He is always * and loving to me; Ps 144:2
to the brim with crops of every *. Ps 144:12-15
Jehovah is * and merciful, slow Ps 145:8
who expect him to be loving and *. Ps 147:11
Never forget to be truthful and *. Pro 3:3
If you live that * of life, Pro 4:12
lies and every * of deception. Pro 8:6,7
corruption and deceit of every *. Pro 8:13
in every other * of understanding. Pro 9:10
Honor goes to * and gracious Pro 11:16
soul is nourished when you are *; Pro 11:17
the other * corrodes his strength Pro 12:4
Literally, "but * words are Pro 15:26f
in * words. Pro 15:26
* words are like honey—enjoyable Pro 16:24
The Lord despises every * of Pro 20:10
If a king is *, honest and fair, Pro 20:28
good, loving and * finds life, Pro 21:21
Though he pretends to be so *, Pro 26:24,25,26
by the * of friends he chooses. Pro 27:19
obey him, if they were * and good. Is 28:12
quarreling? This * of fasting will Is 58:4
No, the * of fast I want is that Is 58:6
You are loving and * to Jer 32:18
must die. That * of talk will Jer 38:4
you by making him * so that he will Jer 42:12
a different * of feast for them, Jer 51:39
that year, was * to King Jehoiachin Jer 52:31
done, I will be * to you again; Eze 16:63
its branches will shelter every * Eze 17:22,23
against that * of life, and Eze 18:14
I will summon every * of terror Eze 38:21
defects or unhealthiness of any *. Eze 43:25
Fish of every * will fill the Eze 47:10
and practice every * of sin. Hos 6:9
is the * of drunken, lying prophet Mic 2:11
*— you leaders who take bribes; Mic 3:10
to be merciful and * to everyone. Zec 7:8,9
But when you bring that * of Mal 1:9
and refuse this * of sacrifice. Mal 1:10
And he healed every * of sickness Mt 4:23
Happy are the * and merciful, Mt 5:7
never produces an inedible *. Mt 7:18
* can't produce what is good. Mt 7:18
is by the * of fruit produced. Mt 7:20
every * of sickness and disease. Mt 10:1
every *, valuable and worthless. Mt 13:47,48
But this * of demon won't leave Mt 17:21
you be angry because I am *? Mt 20:15
to do * deeds on Sabbath days? Mk 3:4
that every * of food is kosher. Mk 7:19
to cover up the * of men they Mk 12:40
the day I drink a different * Mk 14:25
"How * the Lord is," she Lk 1:25
relatives of how * the Lord had Lk 1:58
to their own * for full return! Lk 6:34
of God: for he is * to the Lk 6:35
A tree is identified by the * of Lk 6:44
what * of woman this one is!" Lk 7:39
doesn't have their * of faith will Lk 18:16,17
The Father wants this * of Jn 4:21-24
let him know what * of death he Jn 21:19
What * of home could you build?' Act 7:48,49
was always doing * things for Act 9:36
his reminders—the * things he did Act 14:17
What * of judge are you to break Act 23:3
a case of this * and asked him Act 25:20
Julius was very * to Paul and let Act 27:3
island were very * to us, building Act 28:1
full of every * of wickedness and Rom 1:29
Whoever has that * of change in Rom 2:29
Then what * of God would he be, Rom 3:6
I want to be * to someone, I will. Rom 9:15
So you see, God is * to some Rom 9:18
and to be * to us so that everyone Rom 9:23,24
Notice how God is both * and Rom 11:22
holy—the * he can accept. Rom 12:1
rather than eat that * of meat. Rom 14:2
On questions of this * everyone Rom 14:5
but not the * that comes from here 1Co 2:6
earth, and not the * that appeals 1Co 2:6
Day to see what * of material each 1Co 3:13
payment of any * for fear that, if 1Co 9:12
avoid idol-worship of every *. 1Co 10:14
Love is very patient and *, never 1Co 13:4
understanding matters of this *. 1Co 14:20
put down all enemies of every *. 1Co 15:24
What * of bodies will they have?" 1Co 15:35
the * he wants it to have; 1Co 15:38
a different * of plant grows from 1Co 15:38
plant grows from each * of seed. 1Co 15:38
The sun has one * of glory while 1Co 15:41
the moon and stars have another *. 1Co 15:41
will have the same * of body as 1Co 15:48
not the right * to live forever. 1Co 15:50
hardship and trouble of every *. 2Co 6:4
We have been * and truly loving 2Co 6:6
It was a good * of sorrow you 2Co 7:9
you felt, the * of sorrow God wants 2Co 7:9
will produce this * of fruit in us: Gal 5:22
reap just the * of crop he sows! Gal 6:7
should always be * to everyone, and Gal 6:10
Instead, be * to each other, Eph 4:32
And you husbands, show the same * Eph 5:25
doing those good, * things which Php 1:11
Your attitude should be the * Php 2:5
be doing good, * things for others, Col 1:10
for rules of this * require strong Col 2:23
You are living a brand new * of Col 3:10
given you this new * of life, and Col 3:12
must be loving and * to your wives Col 3:19
Keep away from every * of evil. 1Th 5:22
will make you the * of children he 2Th 1:11
from satanic attacks of every *. 2Th 3:3
Oh, how * our Lord was, for he 1Ti 1:14
noticed for being * and good, not 1Ti 2:9,10
*, and not be one who loves money. 1Ti 3:3
you will know what * of men you 1Ti 3:15
Has she been * to strangers as 1Ti 5:10
They are the * who craftily sneak 2Ti 3:6
Women of that * are forever 2Ti 3:7
me that I am not that * of person. 2Ti 3:10
God's truth—the * of truth that Tit 1:1
own homes, being * and obedient to Tit 2:5
to them of good deeds of every *. Tit 2:7
for doing * things for others. Tit 2:14
this * of thing isn't worthwhile; Tit 3:9
I didn't want you to be * because Phm 1:14
And when God sends a new * of Heb 7:12,13,14
He is, therefore, exactly the * Heb 7:26
* to each other and in doing good. Heb 10:24
Don't forget to be * to Heb 13:2
Will that * of faith save anyone? Jas 2:14
the * that results in good deeds. Jas 2:26
can train, every * of animal or Jas 3:7
lives and every * of reptile and Jas 3:7
are not God's * of wisdom. Jas 3:15
and every other * of evil. Jas 3:16
Now that you realize how * the 1Pe 2:2,3
only if they are * and reasonable, 1Pe 2:18
That * of deep beauty was seen 1Pe 3:5
for we are to be * to others, and 1Pe 3:9
To: All of you who have our * of 2Pe 1:1
The faith I speak of is the * 2Pe 1:1
who are loving and * show that they 1Jn 4:7
isn't loving and *, it shows that 1Jn 4:8
of lust of every * including lust Jud 1:7
the Lord by being * to them, but be Jud 1:23
and to send every * of plague upon Rev 11:6
devils and every * of evil spirit. Rev 18:2
and every * of perfumed wood, and Rev 18:12
No industry of any * will ever Rev 18:22

KINDER

"For you are being even * to Ru 3:10
been * to you than seven sons!" Ru 4:15

KINDLE

Yes, his breath would * Job 41:21

KINDLED

For my anger has * a fire Deu 32:22
Literally, "coals were * by it." 2Sa 22:9f
Literally, "coals were * by it." Ps 18:8f
For you have * a fire of my anger Jer 17:4
that a fire was * and fish were Jn 21:9

KINDLING

burn up these people like * wood. Jer 5:1

KINDLY

And he spoke very * to them, Gen 50:2
He treated Jehoiachin * and gave 2Ki 25:2
him back, so he * forgave them Lk 7:4
Barnabas was a * person, full of Act 11:2
But lest I bore you, * give me Act 24:

KINDNESS

her, 'Have the * to mention, Gen 20:1
he prayed, "show * to my master Gen 24:1
I show * and mercy to anyone I Ex 33:1
it will be a *! Num 11:1
but I will show * to a thousand Deu 5:9,1
Nor did they show any * to the Ju 8:3
all the love and * you have shown Ru 2:10,1
God has continued his * to us as Ru 2:2
the love and * of the Lord not only 1Sa 20:1
for the * you have shown me today. 1Sa 24:1
* on Israel, his chosen people. 2Sa 5:1
but my love and * shall not leave 2Sa 7:1
"Should the king show * to a 2Sa 9:
And you have continued your * to 1Ki 3:6
that we appreciate her * to us. 2Ki 4:13
His love and his * go on forever. 1Ch 16:34
for David and your * to him." 2Ch 6:42
reply and treat them with *." 2Ch 10:7
God is full of * and mercy and will 2Ch 30:9
of love and *—do not let all the Neh 9:32
Remember me, my God, with your *. Neh 13:31
In your * save me. Ps 6:4
Your goodness and unfailing * Ps 23:6
eyes of everlasting love and *. Ps 25:6,7
I will boast of all his * to me. Ps 34:2
meditate upon your * to this lovely Ps 42:6
upon your * and your love. Ps 48:9
Your * and love are as vast as Ps 57:10
for your love and * are better to Ps 63:3
didn't refuse me his * and love. Ps 66:20
a plentiful supply of love and *. Ps 69:13
Pour out your love and * on us, Ps 85:7
about the tender * of the Lord! Ps 89:1
Your love and * are forever; Ps 89:2
Where is your * that you promised Ps 89:49
you for your *," and every evening Ps 92:2
get angry and full of * and love. Ps 103:8
your many acts of * to them. Ps 106:7
For he refused all * to others, Ps 109:16
Now spare me by your * and your Ps 119:40,41,42
In your *, spare my life; Ps 119:88
for his mercy and * just as a Ps 123:2
It will be a *! Ps 141:5
Let me see your * to me in the Ps 143:8
everything he does, and full of *. Ps 145:17
the * of godless men is cruel. Pro 12:10
* makes a man attractive. Pro 19:22
Their * is a trick; Pro 23:6,7,8
of appreciation for their "*." Pro 23:6,7,8
are wise, and * is the rule for Pro 31:26
God will reward you for your * to Is 16:4,5
Your * to the wicked doesn't make Is 26:10
but my * shall not leave you. Is 54:10
let me speak a word of * to them; Jer 20:8
faithfulness, no *, no knowledge of Hos 4:1
our feet again, to live in his *! Hos 6:2
he is full of *, and anxious not Joe 2:13
slow to get angry, and full of *; Jon 4:2
That is the * I showed you again Mic 6:5
his people in * and restore their Zep 2:7
But when you do a * to someone, Mt 6:3
about God's mighty * and love. Act 20:24
Christ, all the * of God has been Rom 1:5
from your sin? His * is meant to Rom 2:4
his * freely takes away our sins. Rom 3:24
but now God's * rules instead, Rom 5:21
more and more * and forgiveness? Rom 6:1
of God's * in choosing them. Rom 11:5
And if it is by God's *, then it Rom 11:6
God, in his *, has taught me how 1Co 3:10
But the Lord in his * has given 1Co 7:25
poured out such * and grace upon 1Co 15:10
you do, do it with * and love. 1Co 16:14
him for his great *, and the more 2Co 4:15
message of God's great * 2Co 6:1
You know how full of love and * 2Co 8:9
and called me—what * and grace— to Gal 1:15
peace, patience, *, goodness, Gal 5:22
for his wonderful * to us and his Eph 1:6
So overflowing is his * towards Eph 1:7
very rich his * is, as shown in all Eph 2:7
Because of his * you have been Eph 2:8
too, are included in his *. Eph 3:2,3
you will have because of your *. Php 4:17
about God's great * to sinners. Col 1:6
mercy and * to others. Col 3:12
Lord show you his * and mercy and 1Ti 1:2
for * should begin at home, 1Ti 5:4
Is she always ready to show *? 1Ti 5:10
you with his *, mercy and peace. 2Ti 1:2
love and * to us through Christ. 2Ti 1:9
But when the time came for the * Tit 3:4

(KINDNESS Con't)
but because of his * and pity—by Tit 3:5
eyes—all because of his great *; Tit 3:7
because your * has so often Phm 1:7
My plea is that you show * to my Phm 1:10
Yes, because of God's great *, Heb 2:9
to more of God's * to you when 1Pe 1:13
goodness and *, cry for more, as a 1Pe 2:2,3f
you knew very little of God's *; 1Pe 2:10
who is full of * through Christ, 1Pe 5:10
and more of God's * and peace? 2Pe 1:2
more of God's *, peace, and love. Jud 1:2
good deeds—your * to the poor, your Rev 2:19

KINDNESSES
of all your loving * shown me again Gen 32:10

KINDS
will produce the * of plants and Gen 1:11,12
each, except those * I have chosen Gen 7:2
With him were all the various * Gen 7:8,9
In the top basket were all * of Gen 40:17
with grain and all * of other food, Gen 45:23
(The various * of bread shall be Ex 29:2
The falcon (all *), the kite, Lev 11:13-19
The raven (all *), the ostrich, Lev 11:13-19
The hawk (all *), the owl, Lev 11:13-19
The heron (all *), Lev 11:13-19
don't sow your field with two * Lev 19:19
have planted all * of fruit trees, Lev 19:23
all other * are ceremonially Deu 14:10
woven from two * of thread: for Deu 22:11
of all * of wines every ten days. Neh 5:18
to him, for he destroys both *. Job 9:22
And the loot we'll get! All * of Pro 1:13
and gets into all * of trouble. Pro 29:22
all the various * of work God has Ecc 3:10
plant his many * of grain, each in Is 28:25
I will appoint over them four * Jer 15:3
Mix the various * of flour Eze 4:9
* of animals our law forbids." Eze 4:14
pictures of all * of snakes, Eze 8:10
"From Tarshish come all * of Eze 27:12
all * of spices, jewels and gold. Eze 27:22
they will still be salty. All * Eze 47:12
you can solve all * of mysteries. Dan 5:16
Different * of fruit trees can Mt 7:17
than to offer all * of sacrifices Mk 12:33
of love for some * of people), Lk 10:29
be slaves to all * of sin, so now Rom 6:19
* of forbidden desires within me! Rom 7:8
But there are various * of 1Co 3:12
Now God gives us many * of 1Co 12:4
There are different * of service 1Co 12:5
are different * of seeds and 1Co 15:39
there are different * of flesh. 1Co 15:39
begin to do all * of wrong things 1Ti 6:9
first step toward all * of sin. 1Ti 6:10
others God's many * of blessings. 1Pe 4:10

KINFOLK
return to my own land and *." Num 10:30

KING
her to their *, the Pharaoh, and Gen 12:15
Amraphel, * of Shinar, Gen 14:1
Arioch, * of Ellasar, Gen 14:1
Ched-or-laomer, * of Elam, and Gen 14:1
Tidal, * of Goiim Gen 14:1
Bera, * of Sodom, Gen 14:2
Birsha, * of Gomorrah, Gen 14:2
Shinab, * of Admah, Gen 14:2
Shemeber, * of Zeboiim, and Gen 14:2
The * of Bela (later called Zoar). Gen 14:2
been subject to * Ched-or-laomer, Gen 14:4
Valley), the * of Sodom came out to Gen 14:17
Melchizedek, the * of Salem Gen 14:18
The * of Sodom told him, "Just Gen 14:21
his sister! Then * Abimelech sent Gen 20:2
The * was up early the next Gen 20:8
Then the * called for Abraham. Gen 20:9,10
Then * Abimelech took sheep and Gen 20:14
want to live," the * told him. Gen 20:15
God to cure the * and queen and the Gen 20:17
About this time * Abimelech, and Gen 21:22
complained to the * about a well Gen 21:25
heard of it," the * exclaimed, Gen 21:26
and oxen to the *, as sacrifices to Gen 21:27
by themselves, the * inquired, Gen 21:28,29
Then * Abimelech, and Phicol, Gen 21:32
* of the Philistines, lived. Gen 26:1
But sometime later, * Abimelech, Gen 26:8
King Abimelech, * of the Gen 26:8
And * Abimelech asked Isaac to Gen 26:16
from Gerar. * Abimelech arrived Gen 26:26
Shechem, son of * Hamor the Hivite, Gen 34:2
Meanwhile * Hamor, Shechem's Gen 34:6,7
(before Israel had her first *): Gen 36:31-39
* Bela (son of Beor), from Gen 36:31-39
by: * Jobab (son of Zerah), from Gen 36:31-39
Succeeded by: * Husham, from the Gen 36:31-39
Succeeded by: * Hadad (son of Gen 36:31-39
Succeeded by: * Samlah, from Gen 36:31-39
Succeeded by: * Shaul, from Gen 36:31-39
Succeeded by: * Baal-hanan (son of Gen 36:31-39
Succeeded by: * Hadad, from the Gen 36:31-39
* Hadad's wife was Mehetabel, Gen 36:31-39
"So you want to be our *, do Gen 37:8
of the Pharaoh—the * of Egypt. Gen 37:36
staff of Pharaoh, the * of Egypt. Gen 39:1
happened that the * of Egypt became Gen 40:1
Joseph, "I, the * of Egypt, swear Gen 41:44
he entered the service of the *. Gen 41:46
a new * came to the throne of Ex 1:8
Then Pharaoh, the * of Egypt, Ex 1:15,16
the *—they let the boys live too. Ex 1:17
The * summoned them before him Ex 1:18
Several years later the * of Ex 2:23
They must go with you to the * of Ex 3:18
"But I know that the * of Egypt Ex 3:19
and to Pharaoh, * of Egypt, Ex 6:13
When word reached the * of Egypt Ex 14:5
you want to make yourself our *? Num 16:13
messengers to the * of Edom: "We Num 20:14
But the * of Edom said, "Stay Num 20:18
But the * of Edom was adamant. Num 20:20
WHEN THE * of Arad heard that the Num 21:1
them conquer the * of Arad and his Num 21:2
Israel now sent ambassadors to * Num 21:21
But * Sihon refused. Num 21:23
which had been * Sihon's capital. Num 21:25,26
referred to * Sihon in this poem: Num 21:27-30
* Sihon's capital, Num 21:27-30
By * Sihon of the Amorites. Num 21:27-30
of Bashan, but * Og of Bashan met Num 21:33
"The same thing will happen to * Num 21:34
Og as happened to * Sihon at Num 21:34
and killed * Og, his sons, and his Num 21:35
When * Balak of Moab (the son of Num 22:2,3
So * Balak sent messengers to Num 22:4
"They have come from * Balak of Num 22:10
"The * says that a vast horde Num 22:11
So * Balak's ambassadors returned Num 22:14
"* Balak pleads with you to come. Num 22:16,17
When * Balak heard that Balaam Num 22:36
Balaam accompanied the * to Num 22:39
where * Balak sacrificed oxen and Num 22:40
BALAAM SAID TO the *, "Build Num 23:1
Then Balaam said to the *, Num 23:3,4
gave Balaam a message for * Balak. Num 23:5
When Balaam returned, the * was Num 23:6
"* Balak, king of Moab, has Num 23:7-10
"King Balak, * of Moab, has Num 23:7-10
demanded * Balak. Num 23:11
So * Balak took Balaam into the Num 23:14
Then Balaam said to the *, Num 23:15
So he returned to where the * Num 23:17
the * eagerly inquired. Num 23:17
He is their *! Num 23:18-24
the * exclaimed to Balaam. Num 23:25
Then the * said to Balaam, "I Num 23:27
So * Balak took Balaam to the Num 23:28
Balaam again told the * to build Num 23:29
sacrifice. The * did as Balaam Num 23:30
Their * will be greater than Agag; Num 24:3-9
* Balak was livid with rage by Num 24:10
And the mighty army of the * of Num 24:21,22
the territory of * Sihon of the Num 32:33
Amorites, and of * Og of Bashan—all Num 32:33
It was then that the Canaanite * Num 33:40
At the time of this address, * Deu 1:1
at Heshbon, and * Og of Bashan had Deu 1:1
into the land of * Sihon the Deu 2:24
Sihon the Amorite, * of Heshbon. Deu 2:24
ambassadors to * Sihon of Heshbon Deu 2:26
"But * Sihon refused because Deu 2:30
to give you the land of * Sihon; Deu 2:31
"* Sihon then declared war on us Deu 2:32
"NEXT WE TURNED toward * Og's Deu 3:1
him as you did to * Sihon of the Deu 3:1
us fight against * Og and his Deu 3:3
we had destroyed * Sihon's kingdom Deu 3:6
"Incidentally, * Og of Bashan Deu 3:11
kingdom of * Og, the Argob region. Deu 3:13
the Amorites under * Sihon, whose Deu 4:44,45,46
land and that of * Og of Deu 4:47
ought to have a * like the other Deu 17:14
that you select as * the man the Deu 17:15
upon his throne as *, then he must Deu 17:18
"He will exile you and the * you Deu 28:36
"When we came here, * Sihon of Deu 29:7
of Heshbon and * Og of Bashan came Deu 29:7
The Lord became * in Jerusalem, Deu 33:5
informed the * of Jericho that two Jos 2:2
"Jericho and its * and all its Jos 6:2
I have given the * of Ai and all Jos 8:1
as you did to Jericho and her *; Jos 8:2
The * of Ai, seeing the Israelis Jos 8:14
except for the * of Ai, who was Jos 8:23
Joshua hanged the * of Ai on a Jos 8:29
Amorites—Sihon, * of Heshbon, and Jos 9:10
of Heshbon, and Og, * of Bashan. Jos 9:10
WHEN ADONI-ZEDEK, THE * of Jos 10:1
and had killed its *, the same as Jos 10:1
hard fighters. So * Adoni-zedek of Jos 10:3
* Hoham of Hebron, Jos 10:3
* Piram of Jarmuth, Jos 10:3
* Japhia of Lachish, Jos 10:3
* Debir of Eglon. Jos 10:3
killed its * and everyone in it. Jos 10:28
Lord gave them the city and its *. Jos 10:30
During the attack on Lachish, * Jos 10:33
WHEN * JABIN of Hazor heard what Jos 11:1
* Jobab of Madon; Jos 11:1
The * of Shimron; Jos 11:1
The * of Achshaph; Jos 11:1
captured Hazor and killed its *. Jos 11:10
* Sihon of the Amorites, who Jos 12:2
* Og of Bashan, the last of the Jos 12:4
kingdom of Sihon, * of Heshbon. Jos 12:5
The * of Jericho; Jos 12:8-24
The * of Ai, near Bethel; Jos 12:8-24
The * of Jerusalem; Jos 12:8-24
The * of Hebron; Jos 12:8-24
The * of Jarmuth; Jos 12:8-24
The * of Lachish; Jos 12:8-24
The * of Eglon; Jos 12:8-24
The * of Gezer; Jos 12:8-24
The * of Debir; Jos 12:8-24
The * of Geder; Jos 12:8-24
The * of Hormah; Jos 12:8-24
The * of Arad; Jos 12:8-24
The * of Libnah; Jos 12:8-24
The * of Adullam; Jos 12:8-24
The * of Makkedah; Jos 12:8-24
The * of Bethel; Jos 12:8-24
The * of Tappu-ah; Jos 12:8-24
The * of Hepher; Jos 12:8-24
The * of Aphek; Jos 12:8-24
The * of Lasharon; Jos 12:8-24
The * of Madon; Jos 12:8-24
The * of Hazor; Jos 12:8-24
The * of Shimron-meron; Jos 12:8-24
The * of Achshaph; Jos 12:8-24
The * of Taanach; Jos 12:8-24
The * of Megiddo; Jos 12:8-24
The * of Kedesh; Jos 12:8-24
The * of Jokne-am, in Carmel; Jos 12:8-24
The * of Dor in the city of Jos 12:8-24
The * of Goiim in Gilgal; Jos 12:8-24
The * of Tirzah. Jos 12:8-24
all the cities of * Sihon of the Jos 13:10
and all the territory of * Og of Jos 13:12
Sihon was the * who had lived in Jos 13:21
the kingdom of * Sihon of Heshbon. Jos 13:27,28
former kingdom of * Og, and the Jos 13:30
Half of Gilead and * Og's royal Jos 13:31
Then * Balak of Moab started a Jos 24:9
slain at Bezek. * Adoni-bezek Ju 1:4,5,6
my table!" * Adoni-bezek said. Ju 1:7
Israel, and he let * Ju 3:8
the army of * Cushan-rishathaim, Ju 3:10
so God helped * Eglon of Moab to Ju 3:12
to pay crushing taxes to * Eglon. Ju 3:14
After delivering the money to * Ju 3:17,18,19
on and returned alone to the *. Ju 3:17,18,19
The * immediately dismissed all Ju 3:17,18,19
* Eglon stood up at once to Ju 3:20
by * Jabin of Hazor, in Canaan. Ju 4:2,3
Tabor, to fight * Jabin's mighty Ju 4:7
agreement between * Jabin of Hazor Ju 4:17
to subdue * Jabin of Canaan. Ju 4:23
stronger against * Jabin, until he Ju 4:24
By this time * Zebah and King Ju 8:10
By this time King Zebah and * Ju 8:10
would never catch * Zebah and King Ju 8:15
King Zebah and * Zalmunna, and you Ju 8:15
Then Gideon asked * Zebah and Ju 8:18
King Zebah and * Zalmunna, "The Ju 8:18
Israel said to Gideon, "Be our *! Ju 8:22
not be your *, nor shall my son; Ju 8:23,24
the Lord is your *! Ju 8:23,24
was acclaimed * of Israel. Ju 9:6
the trees decided to elect a *. Ju 9:8
to the fig tree, 'You be our *!' Ju 9:10
'You be our *!' Ju 9:14
Abimelech your *, that you have Ju 9:16
to be your * just because he is Ju 9:18
up trouble between * Abimelech and Ju 9:22,23
"and why should he be our *? Ju 9:28
Make me your * and you'll soon Ju 9:29
and why should he be our *?' Ju 9:38
volunteers shall be our *!" Ju 10:18
will make you the * of Gilead." Ju 11:8
was made commander-in-chief and *. Ju 11:11
messengers to the * of Ammon, Ju 11:12
attacked. The * of Ammon replied Ju 11:13
a message to the * of Edom asking Ju 11:17
Then they asked the * of Moab for Ju 11:17
Then Israel sent messengers to * Ju 11:19
destination. But * Sihon didn't Ju 11:20
Israel defeat * Sihon and all your Ju 11:21,22
Are you better than * Balak, the Ju 11:25
than King Balak, the * of Moab? Ju 11:25
But the * of Ammon paid no Ju 11:28
days Israel had no *, so everyone Ju 17:6
was no * in Israel at that time. Ju 18:1

(KING Con't)

AT THIS TIME before Israel had a * Ju 19:1
(There was no * in Israel in Ju 21:25
Jesse and grandfather of * David. Ru 4:16,17
He gives mighty strength to his *, 1Sa 2:10
"Give us a * like all the other 1Sa 8:5
want me to be their * any longer. 1Sa 8:7
it will be like to have a *!" 1Sa 8:9
"If you insist on having a *, he 1Sa 8:11
because of this * you are 1Sa 8:18
"Even so, we still want a *," 1Sa 8:19
as they say and give them a *." 1Sa 8:22
to be the * of his people, Israel! 1Sa 10:1
that he had been anointed as *! 1Sa 10:16
have said, 'We want a * instead!' 1Sa 10:18,19
man the Lord has chosen as your *. 1Sa 10:24
shouted, "Long live the *!" 1Sa 10:24
the rights and duties of a * were; 1Sa 10:25
said that Saul shouldn't be our *? 1Sa 11:12
and reconfirm Saul as our *." 1Sa 11:14
the Lord they crowned him *. 1Sa 11:15
I have given you a *. 1Sa 12:1
his anointed *—whose ox or donkey 1Sa 12:3
"The Lord and his anointed * are 1Sa 12:5
the general of * Hazor's army, and 1Sa 12:9
the Philistines and the * of Moab. 1Sa 12:9
of Nahash, the * of Ammon, you came 1Sa 12:12
you wanted a * to reign over you. 1Sa 12:12
was already your *, for he has 1Sa 12:12
for he has always been your *. 1Sa 12:12
All right, here is the * you 1Sa 12:13
both you and your * follow the Lord 1Sa 12:14
wickedness in asking for a *!" 1Sa 12:17
other sins by asking for a *." 1Sa 12:19
and your * will be destroyed." 1Sa 12:25
him as * over his people; 1Sa 13:14
in the saddle as * of Israel, Saul 1Sa 14:47
"I crowned you * of Israel because 1Sa 15:1
He captured Agag, the * of the 1Sa 15:8
I ever made Saul *, for he has 1Sa 15:11
God made you * of Israel. 1Sa 15:17
and I brought * Agag but killed 1Sa 15:20
has rejected you from being *." 1Sa 15:23
you from being the * of Israel." 1Sa 15:26
Then Samuel said, "Bring * Agag 1Sa 15:32
he had ever made Saul * of Israel. 1Sa 15:35
have rejected him as * of Israel. 1Sa 16:1
one of his sons to be the new *." 1Sa 16:1
Probably * Saul was especially 1Sa 17:11f
huge reward the * has offered to 1Sa 17:25
And the * will give him one of 1Sa 17:25
* Saul, and the king sent for him. 1Sa 17:31
King Saul, and the * sent for him. 1Sa 17:31
the * told him. 1Sa 17:56
AFTER * SAUL had finished his 1Sa 18:1
* Saul now kept David at Jerusalem 1Sa 18:4
and to cheer for * Saul, and were 1Sa 18:6
they'll be making him their *!" 1Sa 18:8
So from that time on * Saul kept 1Sa 18:9
When * Saul saw this, he became 1Sa 18:15,16
to David that the * really liked 1Sa 18:22
to marry the daughter of a *?" 1Sa 18:23
their foreskins to * Saul. 1Sa 18:27
When the * realized how much the 1Sa 18:28
began, the * sat down to eat at his 1Sa 20:24,25
to be * in your place, shaming 1Sa 20:30
is alive, you'll never be *. 1Sa 20:31
"The * has sent me on a private 1Sa 21:2
and went to * Achish of Gath. 1Sa 21:10
was afraid of what * Achish might 1Sa 21:12
finally * Achish said to his men, 1Sa 21:14,15
permission of the * for his father 1Sa 22:3
* Saul immediately summoned 1Sa 22:11,12
the * shouted. 1Sa 22:16
Then the * said to Doeg, "You do 1Sa 22:18
You are going to be the * of 1Sa 23:17
God's chosen * in any way." 1Sa 24:6
after him, "My lord the *!" 1Sa 24:7,8
him—he is the Lord's chosen *.' 1Sa 24:9,10
And who is the * of Israel 1Sa 24:14
surely going to be *, and Israel 1Sa 24:20
and has made you * of Israel, you 1Sa 25:30,31
from Jezreel. * Saul, meanwhile, 1Sa 25:44
to look around. * Saul and General 1Sa 26:5,6,7
attacking the Lord's chosen *? 1Sa 26:9
the man he has chosen to be *! 1Sa 26:11
* when someone came to kill him? 1Sa 26:15
Why should the * of Israel come 1Sa 26:20
under the protection of * Achish. 1Sa 27:2,3
the * thought. 1Sa 27:12
"Come and help us fight," * 1Sa 28:1
his home town. * Saul had banned 1Sa 28:3
the * told her. 1Sa 28:13
She brought the meal to the * 1Sa 28:25
marched at the rear with * Achish. 1Sa 29:2
And * Achish told them, "This is 1Sa 29:3
servant of * Saul of Israel. 1Sa 29:3
"Why did you kill God's chosen * 2Sa 1:14
you killed God's appointed *." 2Sa 1:16
He is God's appointed * no more. 2Sa 1:21
him * of the Judean confederacy. 2Sa 2:4

* and giving him a decent burial. 2Sa 2:5
appointed me as their new *." 2Sa 2:7
crown Saul's son Ish-bosheth as *. 2Sa 2:8
in Hebron as * of the Judean 2Sa 2:10,11
daughter of * Talmai of Geshur. 2Sa 3:3
they had wanted David as their *. 2Sa 3:17
*, as you've so long desired." 2Sa 3:21
there visiting the * and had been 2Sa 3:23
he rushed to the *, demanding, 2Sa 3:24,25
And * David accompanied the 2Sa 3:31
And the * and all the people wept 2Sa 3:32
the * lamented. 2Sa 3:33,34
I am God's chosen *, I can do 2Sa 3:39
WHEN * ISH-BOSHETH heard about 2Sa 4:1
of * Ish-bosheth's raiding bands. 2Sa 4:2,3
lame grandson of * Saul's named 2Sa 4:4
Rechab and Baanah arrived at * 2Sa 4:5
"And even when Saul was our * 2Sa 5:2
and they crowned him * of Israel. 2Sa 5:3
(He had already been the * of 2Sa 5:4,5
as * of both Israel and Judah; 2Sa 5:4,5
Then * Hiram of Tyre sent cedar 2Sa 5:11
had made him the * and blessed his 2Sa 5:12
had been crowned * of Israel, they 2Sa 5:17
a window and saw * David leaping 2Sa 6:16
the * of Israel looked today! 2Sa 6:20
He also destroyed the forces of * 2Sa 8:3
* Hadadezer's officers had used. 2Sa 8:7
When * Toi of Hamath heard about 2Sa 8:9
Amalek, and * Hadadezer. 2Sa 8:11,12
the * asked. 2Sa 9:2
The * then asked him, "Is anyone 2Sa 9:3
the * asked. 2Sa 9:4
So * David sent for 2Sa 9:5,6
and greeted the * in deep humility, 2Sa 9:5,6
fell to the ground before the *. 2Sa 9:8
"Should the * show kindness to a 2Sa 9:8
Then the * summoned Saul's 2Sa 9:9
ate regularly with * David, as 2Sa 9:10,11
this the Ammonite * died and his 2Sa 10:1
thousand from the * of Maacah, and 2Sa 10:6
with the other servants of the *. 2Sa 11:9
"If the * is angry and asks, 'Why 2Sa 11:19,20,21
says, 'I made you * of Israel and 2Sa 12:7
and David took the * of Rabbah's 2Sa 12:29,30
Why should the son of a * look so 2Sa 13:4
And when the * came to see him, 2Sa 13:6
Please, just speak to the * about 2Sa 13:13
for virgin daughters of the *. 2Sa 13:17,18
When * David heard what had 2Sa 13:21-24
The * replied, "No, my boy; 2Sa 13:25
the * asked. 2Sa 13:26
until finally the * agreed, and let 2Sa 13:27
Then the other sons of the * 2Sa 13:29,30
The * jumped up, ripped off his 2Sa 13:31
Jonadab told the *. 2Sa 13:35
sobbing, and the * and his 2Sa 13:36
Absalom fled to * Talmai of 2Sa 13:37,38,39
* Talmai was his grandfather—his 2Sa 13:37,38,39f
how much the * was longing to see 2Sa 14:1
ask for an appointment with the *. 2Sa 14:2,3
When the woman approached the *, 2Sa 14:4
of him, and cried out, "O *! 2Sa 14:4
"Leave it with me," the * told 2Sa 14:8
the * replied. 2Sa 14:10
'Perhaps the * will listen to me 2Sa 14:15,16
Yes, the * will give us peace 2Sa 14:17
know one thing," the * replied. 2Sa 14:18
So the * sent for Joab and told 2Sa 14:21
ground before the * and blessed him 2Sa 14:22
quarters," the * ordered, "but he 2Sa 14:24
not yet seen the *, he sent for 2Sa 14:28
you to ask the * why he brought me 2Sa 14:32
me have an interview with the *; 2Sa 14:32
So Joab told the * what Absalom 2Sa 14:33
the *, and David kissed him. 2Sa 14:33
a case to the * for trial, Absalom 2Sa 15:2
it's unfortunate that the * 2Sa 15:3
said to the *, "Let me go to 2Sa 15:7,8
"All right," the * told him, 2Sa 15:9
Hebron was * David's first 2Sa 15:9f
to incite rebellion against the *. 2Sa 15:10
Jerusalem to tell * David, "All 2Sa 15:13
So the * and his household set 2Sa 15:16
But suddenly the * turned to 2Sa 15:19,20
Jerusalem, to your *, for you are a 2Sa 15:19,20
the city as the * and his retinue 2Sa 15:23
Then the * told Zadok, "Look, 2Sa 15:27
the * asked Ziba. 2Sa 16:2
the * asked him. 2Sa 16:3
"He said, 'Now I'll get to be *! 2Sa 16:3
"In that case," the * told 2Sa 16:4
He threw stones at the * and the 2Sa 16:6
murdering * Saul and his family; 2Sa 16:7,8
dead dog curse my lord the *?" 2Sa 16:9
the * said. 2Sa 16:10
into the air. The * and all those 2Sa 16:14
"Long live the *!" 2Sa 16:16
"Long live the *!" 2Sa 16:16
and I will kill only the *, and 2Sa 17:2,3
they were to take to * David. 2Sa 17:17

well and hurried on to * David. 2Sa 17:21
the Gittite. The * planned to lead 2Sa 18:2
best," the * finally replied. 2Sa 18:4
And the * commanded Joab, 2Sa 18:5
And all the troops heard the * 2Sa 18:5
"We all heard the * say to you 2Sa 18:12
And if I had betrayed the * by 2Sa 18:13
his son (and the * would certainly 2Sa 18:13
"Let me run to * David with the 2Sa 18:19
to the * that his son is dead. 2Sa 18:20
tell the * what you have seen." 2Sa 18:21
to David, and the * replied, "If 2Sa 18:25
And the * replied, "He will have 2Sa 18:26
with good news," the * replied. 2Sa 18:27
Then Ahima-az cried out to the *, 2Sa 18:28
the * demanded. 2Sa 18:29
the * what actually had happened. 2Sa 18:29f
"Wait here," the * told him. 2Sa 18:30
have good news for my lord the *. 2Sa 18:31
the * demanded. 2Sa 18:32
Then the * broke into tears, and 2Sa 18:33
SOON REACHED Joab that the * 2Sa 19:1
The * covered his face with his 2Sa 19:4
So the * went out and sat at the 2Sa 19:8,9,10
about bringing the * back?" 2Sa 19:8,9,10
and Absalom, whom we made our * 2Sa 19:8,9,10
to return and be our * again." 2Sa 19:8,9,10
the last ones to reinstate the *? 2Sa 19:11,12
They sent word to the *, "Return 2Sa 19:14
So the * started back to 2Sa 19:15
men of Judah to welcome * David. 2Sa 19:16
Jordan to arrive ahead of the *. 2Sa 19:17
As the * was crossing, Shime-i 2Sa 19:18
"My lord the *, please forgive me 2Sa 19:19
he cursed the Lord's chosen *!" 2Sa 19:21
I am once more * of Israel!" 2Sa 19:22
from Jerusalem to meet the *. 2Sa 19:24,25
the day the * left Jerusalem. 2Sa 19:24,25
the * asked him. 2Sa 19:24,25
And he replied, "My lord, O *, 2Sa 19:26
so that I can go with the *.' 2Sa 19:26
Barzillai, who had fed the * and 2Sa 19:31,32
to conduct the * across the river. 2Sa 19:31,32
the * said to Barzillai. 2Sa 19:33
only be a burden to my lord the *. 2Sa 19:35
"Good," the * agreed. 2Sa 19:38
crossed the Jordan with the *; 2Sa 19:39
home. The * then went on to 2Sa 19:40
complained to the * because only 2Sa 19:41
"The * is one of our own tribe. 2Sa 19:42
as much right in the * as you do; 2Sa 19:43
him back to be our * again." 2Sa 19:43
He's not our *!" 2Sa 20:1
stayed with their *, accompanying 2Sa 20:2
in Jerusalem, the * instructed that 2Sa 20:3
Then the * instructed Amasa to 2Sa 20:4
who has revolted against * David. 2Sa 20:21
returned to the * at Jerusalem. 2Sa 20:22
So * David summoned the 2Sa 21:2
in Gibeon, the city of * Saul." 2Sa 21:5,6
"All right," the * said, "I 2Sa 21:5,6
wonderful deliverance to his *, 2Sa 22:51
The * said to Joab, 2Sa 24:2
the * delight in this thing?" 2Sa 24:3f
the people to the *—800,000 men of 2Sa 24:9
When Araunah saw the * and his 2Sa 24:20
you like," Araunah told the *. 2Sa 24:22
But the * said to Araunah, "No, 2Sa 24:24
IN HIS OLD age * David was 1Ki 1:1
They brought her to the * and she 1Ki 1:3,4
* in place of his aged father. 1Ki 1:5
Now his father, * David, had 1Ki 1:6
they agreed to help him become *. 1Ki 1:7
remained loyal to * David and 1Ki 1:8
other sons of * David—and all the 1Ki 1:9
is now the * and that our lord 1Ki 1:11
Go at once to * David and ask 1Ki 1:13
* and would sit upon your throne? 1Ki 1:13
* and would sit upon your throne. 1Ki 1:17
is the new *, and you don't even 1Ki 1:18
And now, my lord the *, all 1Ki 1:20
low before the *, and asked, "My 1Ki 1:22,23
Adonijah to be the next *? 1Ki 1:24
shouting, 'Long live * Adonijah!' 1Ki 1:25
have chosen to be the next *." 1Ki 1:27
back in and stood before the *. 1Ki 1:28
And the * vowed, "As the Lord 1Ki 1:29
shall be the next * and shall sit 1Ki 1:30
"did reverence to the *." 1Ki 1:31f
May my lord the * live forever!" 1Ki 1:31
"Call Zadok the priest," the * 1Ki 1:32
anoint him there as * of Israel. 1Ki 1:34
and shout, 'Long live * Solomon!' 1Ki 1:34
him upon my throne as the new *; 1Ki 1:35
for I have appointed him * of 1Ki 1:35
riding on * David's own mule. 1Ki 1:38
shouted, "Long live * Solomon!" 1Ki 1:39
"Our lord * David has declared 1Ki 1:43
David has declared Solomon as *!" 1Ki 1:43
"The * sent him to Gihon with 1Ki 1:44,45
have anointed him as the new *! 1Ki 1:44,45

(KING Con't)
are congratulating * David, saying, 1Ki 1:46,47
And the * is lying in bed, 1Ki 1:46,47
So * Solomon summoned him, and 1Ki 1:53
He came to bow low before the *; 1Ki 1:53
AS THE TIME of * David's death 1Ki 2:1
always be the * of Israel—my 1Ki 2:4
guests of the *, for they took care 1Ki 2:7
And Solomon became the new *, 1Ki 2:12
expected me to be the next *. 1Ki 2:15
He replied, "Speak to * Solomon 1Ki 2:17
So she went to ask the favor of * 1Ki 2:19
King Solomon. The * stood up from 1Ki 2:19
Then * Solomon swore with a 1Ki 2:23,24
So * Solomon sent Benaiah to 1Ki 2:25
Then the * said to Abiathar the 1Ki 2:26
When news of this reached * 1Ki 2:29
Joab, "The * says to come out!" 1Ki 2:30
So Benaiah returned to the * for 1Ki 2:30
"Do as he says," the * replied. 1Ki 2:31
Then the * appointed Benaiah as 1Ki 2:35
The * now sent for Shime-i and 1Ki 2:36,37
escaped to * Achish of Gath. 1Ki 2:39
and went to Gath to visit the *. 1Ki 2:40
you did to my father, * David? 1Ki 2:44
with Pharaoh, the * of Egypt, and 1Ki 3:1
Gibeon and now the * went there and 1Ki 3:4
have made me the * instead of my 1Ki 3:7
the * to have an argument settled. 1Ki 3:16
back and forth before the *. 1Ki 3:22
Then the * said, "Let's get the 1Ki 3:23
So a sword was brought to the * 1Ki 3:24
Then the * said, "Give the baby 1Ki 3:27
HERE IS A list of * Solomon's 1Ki 4:1
the territories of * Sihon of the 1Ki 4:8-19
the Amorites and * Og of Bashan. 1Ki 4:8-19
at this time. * Solomon ruled the 1Ki 4:21
food for * Solomon and his court; 1Ki 4:27
* HIRAM OF Tyre had always been a 1Ki 5:1
was the new * of Israel, he sent 1Ki 5:1
a wise son to be * of the great 1Ki 5:7
* Solomon then asked for a man 1Ki 7:13
So he came to work for * Solomon. 1Ki 7:14
been assigned to him by * Solomon. 1Ki 7:40
the Tabernacle. * Solomon and all 1Ki 8:5
Now * Solomon prayed this 1Ki 8:12,13
Then the * turned around and 1Ki 8:14
my father as * of Israel, and now 1Ki 8:20
Then the * and all the people 1Ki 8:62,63
As a temporary measure the * 1Ki 8:64
And they blessed the *. 1Ki 8:66
land of Galilee to * Hiram of Tyre 1Ki 9:11,12
Gezer was the city the * of 1Ki 9:16
* Solomon moved Pharaoh's 1Ki 9:24
* Solomon had a shipyard in 1Ki 9:26
* Hiram supplied experienced 1Ki 9:27,28
bringing gold to * Solomon, the 1Ki 9:27,28
hidden from the * which he could 1Ki 10:3f
he gave you to them as their *! 1Ki 10:9
Then she gave the * a gift of 1Ki 10:10
* Solomon had ever received. 1Ki 10:10
(And when * Hiram's ships brought 1Ki 10:11
queen of Sheba, * Solomon gave her 1Ki 10:13
All of * Solomon's cups were of 1Ki 10:21
* Solomon's merchant fleet was in 1Ki 10:22
partnership with * Hiram's, and 1Ki 10:22
So * Solomon was richer and wiser 1Ki 10:23
and with the * at Jerusalem. 1Ki 10:26
* SOLOMON MARRIED many other 1Ki 11:1
And even so I will let him be * 1Ki 11:12,13
the officials of * Hadad-ezer of 1Ki 11:23
*) when David destroyed Zobah. 1Ki 11:24
but he fled to * Shishak of Egypt 1Ki 11:40
he had fled from * Solomon, heard 1Ki 12:2,3,4
"We don't want you as our * 1Ki 12:2,3,4
you can be their * forever." 1Ki 12:7
the new * answered them roughly. 1Ki 12:13,14
so the * refused the people's 1Ki 12:15
caused the new * to do this in 1Ki 12:15
realized that the * meant what he 1Ki 12:16,17
Let Rehoboam be * of his own 1Ki 12:16,17
and accepted Rehoboam as their *. 1Ki 12:16,17
When * Rehoboam sent Adoram (who 1Ki 12:18
him to death. But * Rehoboam 1Ki 12:18
and there he was made * of 1Ki 12:20
When * Rehoboam arrived in 1Ki 12:21
to acknowledge him as their *. 1Ki 12:21
son of Solomon, * of Judah, and all 1Ki 12:23,24
a descendant of David as their *. 1Ki 12:26
become friendly with * Rehoboam; 1Ki 12:27
ask him to be their * instead." 1Ki 12:27
counselors, the * had two gold 1Ki 12:28
The * was very angry with the 1Ki 13:4
"Oh, please, please," the * 1Ki 13:6
Then the * said to the prophet, 1Ki 13:7
But the prophet said to the *, 1Ki 13:8
and what he had said to the *. 1Ki 13:11
who told me that I would become *. 1Ki 14:2
people and made you * of Israel. 1Ki 14:7
And the Lord will raise up a * 1Ki 14:14
the son of Solomon was * in Judah. 1Ki 14:21
Rehoboam's reign, * Shishak of 1Ki 14:25
Whenever the * went to the 1Ki 14:28
reign as * of Judah in Jerusalem 1Ki 15:1
right with God, as * David's was. 1Ki 15:3
Asa became * of Judah, in 1Ki 15:9
Lord like his ancestor * David. 1Ki 15:11
There was lifelong war between * 1Ki 15:16
of Judah and * Baasha of Israel. 1Ki 15:16
Baasha of Israel. * Baasha built 1Ki 15:17
to Damascus, to * Ben-hadad of 1Ki 15:18
Now break your alliance with * 1Ki 15:19
Then * Asa made a proclamation 1Ki 15:22
and timbers. And * Asa used these 1Ki 15:22
became the new * of Judah. 1Ki 15:24
the son of Jeroboam had become *. 1Ki 15:25
of the reign of * Asa of Judah. 1Ki 15:25
But he was not a good *; 1Ki 15:26
Nadab as the * of Israel in Tirzah, 1Ki 15:28
of the reign of * Asa of Judah. 1Ki 15:28
the descendants of * Jeroboam, so 1Ki 15:29
warfare between * Asa of Judah and 1Ki 15:32,33
of Judah and * Baasha of Israel. 1Ki 15:32,33
was delivered to * Baasha at this 1Ki 16:1
make you * of my people Israel; 1Ki 16:2
of the reign of * Asa of Judah, but 1Ki 16:8
One day * Elah was half drunk at 1Ki 16:9
of the reign of * Asa of Judah. 1Ki 16:10
himself to be the new * of Israel. 1Ki 16:10
assassinated the *, they decided on 1Ki 16:15,16
* Asa of Judah had been on the 1Ki 16:23
son Ahab became * in his place. 1Ki 16:28
* Asa of Judah had been on the 1Ki 16:29
when Ahab became the * of Israel; 1Ki 16:29
he was worse than any other * of 1Ki 16:30
the daughter of * Ethbaal of the 1Ki 16:31
from Tishbe in Gilead, told * 1Ki 17:1
"Go and tell * Ahab that I will 1Ki 18:1
was on the way to see * Ahab, 1Ki 18:5
the * said to Obadiah, "We must 1Ki 18:5
"Now go and tell the * I am 1Ki 18:8
For I swear by God that the * 1Ki 18:10
isn't here,' * Ahab forced the king 1Ki 18:10
Ahab forced the * of that nation to 1Ki 18:10
And now you say, 'Go tell the * 1Ki 18:14
anoint Hazael to be * of Syria. 1Ki 19:15
of Himshi) to be * of Israel, and 1Ki 19:16
* BEN-HADAD OF Syria now mobilized 1Ki 20:1
into the city to * Ahab of Israel: 1Ki 20:2,3
"Tell my lord the *, 'I will give 1Ki 20:9
Then the Syrian * sent this 1Ki 20:10
The * of Israel retorted, "Don't 1Ki 20:11
Then a prophet came to see * Ahab 1Ki 20:13
The Israelis chased them, but * 1Ki 20:20
Then the prophet approached * 1Ki 20:22
attack by the * of Syria." 1Ki 20:22
* Ben-hadad did as they suggested. 1Ki 20:25
Then a prophet went to the * of 1Ki 20:28
and go out to * Ahab to see if he 1Ki 20:31
So they went to the * of Israel 1Ki 20:32
the * of Israel asked. 1Ki 20:32
"Go and get him," the * of 1Ki 20:33
The prophet waited for the * 1Ki 20:38
As the * passed by, the prophet 1Ki 20:39
your own fault," the * replied. 1Ki 20:40
his eyes, and the * recognized him 1Ki 20:41
So the * of Israel went home to 1Ki 20:43
of the city near * Ahab's palace. 1Ki 21:1
One day the * talked to him 1Ki 21:2
"I want it for a garden," the * 1Ki 21:2
"Are you the * of Israel or 1Ki 21:7
him of cursing God and the *. 1Ki 21:10
him of cursing God and the *; 1Ki 21:13
"Go to Samaria to meet * Ahab. 1Ki 21:18
did the family of * Jeroboam and 1Ki 21:22
and the family of * Baasha, for you 1Ki 21:22
third year, while * Jehoshaphat of 1Ki 22:2
Judah was visiting * Ahab of 1Ki 22:2
And * Jehoshaphat of Judah 1Ki 22:4
So * Ahab summoned his four 1Ki 22:6
"Well, there's one," * Ahab 1Ki 22:8
So * Ahab called to one of his 1Ki 22:9
When he arrived, the * asked him, 1Ki 22:15
the * demanded. 1Ki 22:16
And the Lord said, 'Their * is 1Ki 22:17
Then * Ahab ordered Micaiah's 1Ki 22:26
Tell them, 'The * says to put 1Ki 22:27
So * Ahab of Israel and King 1Ki 22:29
So King Ahab of Israel and * 1Ki 22:29
For the * of Syria had commanded 1Ki 22:31
no one except * Ahab himself. 1Ki 22:31
When they saw * Jehoshaphat in 1Ki 22:32,33
and it struck * Ahab between the 1Ki 22:34
day wore on, and * Ahab went back 1Ki 22:35
over—return home! The * is dead!" 1Ki 22:36,37
son became the new * of Israel. 1Ki 22:40
of Asa had become * during the 1Ki 22:41
of the reign of * Ahab of Israel. 1Ki 22:41
peace with Ahab, the * of Israel. 1Ki 22:44
(There was no * in Edom at that 1Ki 22:47
* Jehoshaphat built great 1Ki 22:48
Ahaziah, * Ahab's son and 1Ki 22:49
When * Jehoshaphat died he was 1Ki 22:50
of the reign of * Jehoshaphat of 1Ki 22:51
But he was not a good *, for he 1Ki 22:52,53
AFTER * AHAB'S death the nation of 2Ki 1:1
Israel's new *, Ahaziah, had 2Ki 1:2
ask whether the * will get well? 2Ki 1:3
Because * Ahaziah has done this, 2Ki 1:4,5
returned immediately to the *. 2Ki 1:4,5
to go back to the * and tell him, 2Ki 1:6
the * demanded. 2Ki 1:7
the * exclaimed. 2Ki 1:8
man of God, the * has commanded you 2Ki 1:9
So the * sent another captain 2Ki 1:11
man of God, the * says that you 2Ki 1:11
Once more the * sent fifty men, 2Ki 1:13
So Elijah went to the *. 2Ki 1:15
became the new *—for Ahaziah did 2Ki 1:17
of the reign of * Jehoram (son of 2Ki 1:17
year of the reign of * Jehoshaphat 2Ki 3:1
Chapter 1, verse 17, says * 2Ki 3:1f
was the * of Judah at this time. 2Ki 3:1f
* Mesha of Moab and his people 2Ki 3:4
but after Ahab's death, the * of 2Ki 3:5
Israel. So * Jehoram mustered the 2Ki 3:6,7,8
message to * Jehoshaphat of Judah: 2Ki 3:6,7,8
"The * of Moab has rebelled 2Ki 3:6,7,8
the * of Israel cried out. 2Ki 3:10
to let the * of Moab defeat us." 2Ki 3:10
But Jehoshaphat, the * of Judah, 2Ki 3:11
"Elisha is here," one of the * 2Ki 3:11
snarled at * Jehoram of Israel. 2Ki 3:13
But * Jehoram replied, "No! 2Ki 3:13
be destroyed by the * of Moab!" 2Ki 3:13
the presence of * Jehoshaphat of 2Ki 3:14
When the * of Moab saw that the 2Ki 3:26
to break through to the * of Edom; 2Ki 3:26
have been the next *, and to the 2Ki 3:27
* or to the general of the army?" 2Ki 4:13
THE * OF Syria had high admiration 2Ki 5:1
Naaman told the * what the little 2Ki 5:4
the prophet," the * told him. 2Ki 5:5
you to carry to the * of Israel." 2Ki 5:5
The letter to the * of Israel 2Ki 5:6
When the * of Israel read it, he 2Ki 5:7
heard about the * of Israel's 2Ki 5:8
my master the * goes into the 2Ki 5:18
Once when the * of Syria was at 2Ki 6:8
Immediately Elisha warned the * 2Ki 6:9
The * sent a scout to see if 2Ki 6:10
The * of Syria was puzzled. 2Ki 6:11
Who has been informing the * of 2Ki 6:11
prophet, tells the * of Israel even 2Ki 6:12
to seize him," the * exclaimed. 2Ki 6:13
So one night the * of Syria sent 2Ki 6:14
When the * of Israel saw them, he 2Ki 6:21
So the * made a great feast for 2Ki 6:23
then sent them home to their *. 2Ki 6:23
Later on, however, * Ben-hadad of 2Ki 6:24
One day as the * of Israel was 2Ki 6:26-30
to him, "Help, my lord the *!" 2Ki 6:26-30
When the * heard this he tore his 2Ki 6:26-30
this very day," the * vowed. 2Ki 6:31
* sent a messenger to summon him. 2Ki 6:32
arrived [followed by the * 2Ki 6:33
caused this mess," the * stormed. 2Ki 6:33
The officer assisting the * said, 2Ki 7:2
"The * of Israel has hired the 2Ki 7:6
The * got out of bed and told his 2Ki 7:12
were found and the * sent out two 2Ki 7:14
and told the *, and the people of 2Ki 7:15
The * appointed his special 2Ki 7:17
day when the * had come to arrest 2Ki 7:17
had told the * that flour and 2Ki 7:18
went to see the * about getting 2Ki 8:3
Just as she came in, the * was 2Ki 8:4
And Gehazi was telling the * 2Ki 8:5
the * asked her. 2Ki 8:6
where * Ben-hadad lay sick. 2Ki 8:7
Someone told the * that the 2Ki 8:7
When the * heard the news, he 2Ki 8:8,9
son Ben-hadad, the * of Syria, has 2Ki 8:8,9
are going to be the * of Syria." 2Ki 8:13
When Hazael went back, the * 2Ki 8:14
And Hazael became * instead. 2Ki 8:15
* Jehoram, the son of King 2Ki 8:16
King Jehoram, the son of * 2Ki 8:16
of the reign of * Joram of Israel, 2Ki 8:16
old when he became *, and he 2Ki 8:17
Judah and appointed their own *. 2Ki 8:20
their own king. * Jehoram 2Ki 8:21
The rest of the history of * 2Ki 8:23
became the new * during the 2Ki 8:24,25
of the reign of * Joram of Israel, 2Ki 8:24,25
granddaughter of * Omri of Israel. 2Ki 8:26
He was an evil *, just as all of 2Ki 8:27
just as all of * Ahab's descendants 2Ki 8:27
He joined * Joram of Israel (son 2Ki 8:28
the * of Syria, at Ramoth-gilead. 2Ki 8:28
at Ramoth-gilead. * Joram was 2Ki 8:28
While he was there, * Ahaziah of 2Ki 8:29
him to be the * of Israel; 2Ki 9:3

(KING Con't)
* of the Lord's people, Israel. 2Ki 9:6
he had been anointed * of Israel! 2Ki 9:12
trumpet, shouting, "Jehu is *!" 2Ki 9:13
Nimshi) rebelled against * Joram. 2Ki 9:14
King Joram. (* Joram had been with 2Ki 9:14
the forces of * Hazael of Syria. 2Ki 9:14
"Since you want me to be *," 2Ki 9:15
himself to find * Joram, who was 2Ki 9:16
there wounded. (* Ahaziah of Judah 2Ki 9:16
or foe," * Joram shouted back. 2Ki 9:17
"The * wants to know whether you 2Ki 9:18
The watchman called out to the * 2Ki 9:18
So the * sent out a second 2Ki 9:19
in the name of the * to know 2Ki 9:19
Get my chariot ready!" * Joram 2Ki 9:21
Then he and * Ahaziah of Judah 2Ki 9:21
of Naboth, and * Joram demanded, 2Ki 9:22
Then * Joram reined the 2Ki 9:23
fled, shouting to * Ahaziah, 2Ki 9:23
Meanwhile, * Ahaziah of Judah had 2Ki 9:27
year of the reign of * Joram of 2Ki 9:29
for she is the daughter of a *." 2Ki 9:34
sons to be your *, and prepare to 2Ki 10:2,3
* instead of one of Ahab's sons." 2Ki 10:5
(These seventy sons of * Ahab were 2Ki 10:6
brothers of * Ahaziah of Judah. 2Ki 10:13
of * Ahaziah. 2Ki 10:13
visit the sons of * Ahab and of the 2Ki 10:13
size of Israel. * Hazael conquered 2Ki 10:32,33
his son Jehoahaz became the new *. 2Ki 10:35
In all, Jehu reigned as * of 2Ki 10:36
WHEN ATHALIAH, THE mother of * 2Ki 11:1
was a sister of * Ahaziah (for she 2Ki 11:2,3
of * Jehoram, Ahaziah's father). 2Ki 11:2,3
surround the *, weapons in hand, 2Ki 11:6,7,8
Stay with the * at all times." 2Ki 11:6,7,8
that had belonged to * David. 2Ki 11:10
and anointed him as *. 2Ki 11:12
and shouted, "Long live the *!" 2Ki 11:12
and saw the new * standing beside 2Ki 11:13,14
the Lord, the *, and the people, 2Ki 11:17
between the * and the people. 2Ki 11:17
the people led the * from the 2Ki 11:19
seven years old when he became *. 2Ki 11:21
had become the * of Israel that 2Ki 12:1
that Joash became * of Judah. 2Ki 12:1
One day * Joash said to Jehoiada, 2Ki 12:4,5
About this time, * Hazael of 2Ki 12:17
to attack it. * Joash took all the 2Ki 12:18
his son Amaziah became the new *. 2Ki 12:21
of the reign of * Joash of Judah. 2Ki 13:1
But he was an evil *, and he 2Ki 13:2
allowed * Hazael of Syria and his 2Ki 13:3
* of Syria was oppressing Israel. 2Ki 13:4
for the * of Syria had destroyed 2Ki 13:7
of the reign of * Joash of Judah. 2Ki 13:9,10
his wars against * Amaziah of 2Ki 13:12
and Jeroboam II became the new *. 2Ki 13:13
his last illness, * Joash visited 2Ki 13:14
Then he told the * to put his hand 2Ki 13:16,17
So the * picked them up and struck 2Ki 13:18
* Hazael of Syria had oppressed 2Ki 13:22
the entire reign of * Jehoahaz. 2Ki 13:22
Then * Hazael of Syria died, and 2Ki 13:24
in his place. * Joash of Israel 2Ki 13:25
of the reign of * Joash of Israel, 2Ki 14:1
Joash of Israel, * Amaziah began 2Ki 14:1
He was a good * in the Lord's 2Ki 14:3
but he was as good a * as his 2Ki 14:3
One day he sent a message to * 2Ki 14:8
But * Joash replied, "The 2Ki 14:9
to listen, so * Joash of Israel 2Ki 14:11
army fled home. * Amaziah was 2Ki 14:13
six hundred feet. * Joash took 2Ki 14:14
and his war with * Amaziah of Judah 2Ki 14:15
his son Jeroboam became the new *. 2Ki 14:16
became the new * at the age of 2Ki 14:21
II had become * during the 2Ki 14:23
the reign of * Amaziah of Judah. 2Ki 14:23
he used * Jeroboam II to save her. 2Ki 14:27
became the new * of Israel. 2Ki 14:29
NEW * OF Judah: Azariah 2Ki 15:1
his father: Amaziah, the former * 2Ki 15:1
Reigning in Israel at this time: * 2Ki 15:1
had been the * there for 27 years. 2Ki 15:1
Azariah was a good *, and he 2Ki 15:3
his son Jotham was the acting *. 2Ki 15:5
and his son Jotham became *. 2Ki 15:7
New * of Israel: Zechariah 2Ki 15:8
Reigning in Judah at that time: * 2Ki 15:8
had been the * there for 38 years 2Ki 15:8
But Zechariah was an evil * in 2Ki 15:9
New * of Israel: Shallum * 2Ki 15:13
Reigning in Judah at that time: * 2Ki 15:13
had been the * there for 39 years 2Ki 15:13
One month after Shallum became *, 2Ki 15:14
Additional details about * 2Ki 15:15
refused to accept him as their *; 2Ki 15:16
Name of new * of Israel: Menahem 2Ki 15:17
Concurrent with: * Azariah of 2Ki 15:17
had been the * there for 39 years 2Ki 15:17
But Menahem was an evil *. 2Ki 15:18
He worshiped idols, as * Jeroboam 2Ki 15:18
Then * Pul of Assyria invaded 2Ki 15:19,20
the land; but * Menahem bought him 2Ki 15:19,20
The rest of the history of * 2Ki 15:21
his son Pekahiah became the new *. 2Ki 15:22
Name of new * of Israel: Pekahiah 2Ki 15:23
Father's name: * Menahem 2Ki 15:23
Concurrent with: * Azariah of 2Ki 15:23
had been the * there for 50 years 2Ki 15:23
But Pekahiah was an evil *, and 2Ki 15:24
So Pekah became the new *. 2Ki 15:25
The rest of the history of * 2Ki 15:26
New * of Israel: Pekah 2Ki 15:27
Concurrent with: * Azariah of 2Ki 15:27
had been the * there for 52 years 2Ki 15:27
Pekah, too, was an evil *, and he 2Ki 15:28
It was during his reign that * 2Ki 15:29
New * of Israel: Hoshea 2Ki 15:30
(son of Uzziah) * of Judah, who had 2Ki 15:30
had been the * there for 20 years 2Ki 15:30
New * of Judah: Jotham 2Ki 15:32,33
Father's name: * Uzziah 2Ki 15:32,33
His age when he became *: 25 years 2Ki 15:32,33
had been the * there for 2 years 2Ki 15:32,33
speaking, Jotham was a good *. 2Ki 15:34,35
It was during * Jotham's reign 2Ki 15:34,35
In those days the Lord caused * 2Ki 15:37
* Pekah of Israel to attack Judah. 2Ki 15:37
his son Ahaz became the new *. 2Ki 15:38
new * of Judah 2Ki 16:1
Reigning in Israel at this time: * 2Ki 16:1
had been the * there for 17 years 2Ki 16:1
Then * Rezin of Syria and King 2Ki 16:5
Then King Rezin of Syria and * 2Ki 16:5
However, at that time * Rezin of 2Ki 16:6
do to this day. * Ahaz sent a 2Ki 16:7
King Ahaz sent a messenger to * 2Ki 16:7
it as a payment to the Assyrian *. 2Ki 16:8
and * Rezin of Syria was killed. 2Ki 16:9
* Ahaz now went to Damascus to 2Ki 16:10
to meet with * Tiglath-pileser, and 2Ki 16:10
it ready for the *, who, upon his 2Ki 16:11,12
an offering. The * presented a 2Ki 16:13
Uriah the priest did as * Ahaz 2Ki 16:16
Then the * dismantled the 2Ki 16:17
In deference to the * of Assyria 2Ki 16:18
of the reign of * Ahaz is recorded 2Ki 16:19
his son Hezekiah became the new *. 2Ki 16:20
new * of Israel 2Ki 17:1
Reigning in Judah at this time: * 2Ki 17:1
had been the * there for 12 years 2Ki 17:1
* Shalmaneser of Assyria attacked 2Ki 17:3
and defeated * Hoshea, so Israel 2Ki 17:3
against the * of Assyria by asking 2Ki 17:4
Assyria by asking * So of Egypt to 2Ki 17:4
So the * of Assyria put him in 2Ki 17:4
Finally, in the ninth year of * 2Ki 17:6
I (the son of Nebat) as its *. 2Ki 17:21
And the * of Assyria transported 2Ki 17:24
Then they sent a message to the * 2Ki 17:26
The * of Assyria then decreed 2Ki 17:27,28
new * of Judah 2Ki 18:1
Reigning in Israel at this time: * 2Ki 18:1
had been the * there for 3 years 2Ki 18:1
even though, as * Hezekiah 2Ki 18:4
Then he rebelled against the * of 2Ki 18:7
of the reign of * Hoshea in Israel) 2Ki 18:9
in Israel) that * Shalmaneser of 2Ki 18:9
of the reign of * Hezekiah and the 2Ki 18:10
* Hoshea of Israel) Samaria fell. 2Ki 18:10
It was at that time that the * 2Ki 18:11
of the reign of * Hezekiah, King 2Ki 18:13
of King Hezekiah, * Sennacherib of 2Ki 18:13
cities of Judah. * Hezekiah sued 2Ki 18:14
message to the * of Assyria at 2Ki 18:14
The * of Assyria then demanded 2Ki 18:14
To gather this amount, * 2Ki 18:15
and gave it all to the Assyrian *. 2Ki 18:16
Nevertheless the * of Assyria 2Ki 18:17
They demanded that * Hezekiah 2Ki 18:18
this message to * Hezekiah: "The 2Ki 18:19
"The great * of Assyria says, 'No 2Ki 18:19
with my master, the * of Assyria! 2Ki 18:23
to the great * of Assyria! 2Ki 18:28
'Don't let * Hezekiah fool you. 2Ki 18:29
Don't listen to * Hezekiah. 2Ki 18:31,32
Don't listen to * Hezekiah when 2Ki 18:31,32
people from the * of Assyria? 2Ki 18:33
silent, for the * had instructed 2Ki 18:36
historian went to * Hezekiah with 2Ki 18:37
WHEN * HEZEKIAH heard their report 2Ki 19:1
"* Hezekiah says, 'This is a day 2Ki 19:3
For the * of Assyria will 2Ki 19:7
returned to his * at Libnah (for he 2Ki 19:8
news reached the * that King 2Ki 19:9
the king that * Tirhakah of 2Ki 19:9
back this message to * Hezekiah: 2Ki 19:9
What happened to the * of Hamoth 2Ki 19:13
king of Hamoth and the * of Arpad? 2Ki 19:13
And this is my reply to * 2Ki 19:21
concerning the * of Assyria is that 2Ki 19:32
Then * Sennacherib returned to 2Ki 19:36
son Esarhaddon became the new *. 2Ki 19:37
this city from the * of Assyria. 2Ki 20:6
Meanwhile, * Hezekiah had said to 2Ki 20:8
(the son of * Baladan of Babylon) 2Ki 20:12
Then Isaiah went to * Hezekiah 2Ki 20:14
the palace of the * of Babylon." 2Ki 20:18
his son Manasseh became the new *. 2Ki 20:21
new * of Judah 2Ki 21:1
as Ahab the * of Israel had done. 2Ki 21:3,4,5
"Because * Manasseh has done 2Ki 21:11
and his son Amon became the new *. 2Ki 21:18
Name of the new * of Judah: Amon 2Ki 21:19,20
his son Josiah became the new *. 2Ki 21:26
new * of Judah 2Ki 22:1
of his ancestor * David, obeying 2Ki 22:1
year of his reign, * Josiah sent 2Ki 22:3,4
When Shaphan reported to the * 2Ki 22:9,10
Then Shaphan read it to the *. 2Ki 22:9,10
When the * heard what was 2Ki 22:11
So they took the message to the *. 2Ki 22:20
THEN THE * sent for the elders and 2Ki 23:1
Temple so that the * could read to 2Ki 23:1
Then the * instructed Hilkiah the 2Ki 23:4
and stars. The * had it all burned 2Ki 23:4
Then the * destroyed the altar of 2Ki 23:10
So * Josiah replied, "Leave it 2Ki 23:18
The * then issued orders for his 2Ki 23:21
of the reign of * Josiah, and it 2Ki 23:23
There was no other * who so 2Ki 23:25
and no * since the time of Josiah 2Ki 23:25
caused by the evils of * Manasseh. 2Ki 23:26
In those days * Neco of Egypt 2Ki 23:29
Egypt attacked the * of Assyria at 2Ki 23:29
and * Josiah went to assist him; 2Ki 23:29
to assist him; but * Neco killed 2Ki 23:29
chosen by the nation as its new *. 2Ki 23:30
New * of Judah: Jehoahaz 2Ki 23:31,32
His age when he became *: 23 years 2Ki 23:31,32
The Egyptian * then chose 2Ki 23:34
Then he took * Jehoahaz to Egypt, 2Ki 23:34
New * of Judah: Jehoiakim 2Ki 23:36,37
His age when he became *: 25 years 2Ki 23:36,37
DURING THE REIGN of * Jehoiakim, 2Ki 24:1
of King Jehoiakim, * Nebuchadnezzar 2Ki 24:1
son Jehoiachin became the new *. 2Ki 24:6
that, for the * of Babylon occupied 2Ki 24:7
New * of Judah, Jehoiachin 2Ki 24:8,9
During his reign the armies of * 2Ki 24:10
the siege, and * Jehoiachin, all 2Ki 24:12
gold bowls which * Solomon of 2Ki 24:13
directions. * Nebuchadnezzar took 2Ki 24:14
Nebuchadnezzar took * 2Ki 24:15
Then the * of Babylon appointed 2Ki 24:17
* Jehoiachin's great-uncle, 2Ki 24:17
Mattaniah, to be the next *; 2Ki 24:17
New * of Judah: Zedekiah 2Ki 24:18,19
His age when he became *: 21 years 2Ki 24:18,19
But now * Zedekiah rebelled 2Ki 24:20
rebelled against the * of Babylon. 2Ki 24:20
THEN * NEBUCHADNEZZAR of 2Ki 25:1
the reign of * Zedekiah of Judah. 2Ki 25:1
and that night the * and his troops 2Ki 25:4,5
sentenced before the * of Babylon. 2Ki 25:6
of the reign of * Nebuchadnezzar. 2Ki 25:8
allegiance to the * of Babylon were 2Ki 25:11
for the Temple by * Solomon—because 2Ki 25:16
Nebuzaradan to the * of Babylon at 2Ki 25:20
Then * Nebuchadnezzar appointed 2Ki 25:22
learned that the * of Babylon had 2Ki 25:23
* Jehoiachin was released from 2Ki 25:27
of * Evil-merodach of Babylon. 2Ki 25:27
king's table. The * also gave him 2Ki 25:30
from Bozrah became the new *. 1Ch 1:44
of the Temanites became the *. 1Ch 1:45
of Moab—became * and ruled from the 1Ch 1:46
town of Rehoboth became the new *. 1Ch 1:48
the son of Achbor became *. 1Ch 1:49
died, Hadad became * and ruled from 1Ch 1:50
* DAVID'S OLDEST son was Amnon, 1Ch 3:1
daughter of * Talmai of Geshur. 1Ch 3:2
These are the descendants of * 1Ch 3:10-14
who were born to * Jeconiah during 1Ch 3:17,18
they all worked for the *: 1Ch 4:23
So during the reign of * Hezekiah 1Ch 4:40,41
by * Tilgath-pilneser of Assyria. 1Ch 5:6
During the reign of * Saul, the 1Ch 5:10
at the time of * Jotham of Judah 1Ch 5:17
of Judah and * Jeroboam of Israel. 1Ch 5:17
So God caused * Pul of Assyria 1Ch 5:26
* David appointed songleaders and 1Ch 6:31
At the time of * David, the total 1Ch 7:2
* David, numbered 36,000 troops; 1Ch 7:4
warriors at the time of * David. 1Ch 7:11
and even when Saul was *, you 1Ch 11:2
You shall be their *.' 1Ch 11:2
anointed him as * of Israel, just 1Ch 11:3
make David their *, as the Lord had 1Ch 11:10
while he was hiding from * Saul. 1Ch 12:1

KING Con't)
their right! Like * Saul, they were 1Ch 12:2
the Philistines against * Saul. 1Ch 12:19
them by deserting to * Saul. 1Ch 12:19
see David become * instead of Saul, 1Ch 12:23
purpose of helping David become *. 1Ch 12:24-37
of making David the * of Israel. 1Ch 12:38
I should be your *, and since the 1Ch 13:2
it ever since Saul became *." 1Ch 13:3
* HIRAM OF Tyre sent masons and 1Ch 14:1
Lord had made him * and why he had 1Ch 14:2
was Israel's new *, they mobilized 1Ch 14:8
* David also ordered the Levite 1Ch 15:16
the daughter of * Saul, felt a deep 1Ch 15:29
and made you the * of my people. 1Ch 17:7
So Nathan told * David everything 1Ch 17:15
Then * David went in and sat 1Ch 17:16
He conquered the dominion of * 1Ch 18:3
Damascus to help * Hadadezer, David 1Ch 18:5
He brought the gold shields of * 1Ch 18:7
Tibhath and Cun. (* Solomon later 1Ch 18:8
When * Tou of Hamath learned that 1Ch 18:9
learned that * David had destroyed 1Ch 18:9
and congratulate * David on his 1Ch 18:10
between them. * David dedicated 1Ch 18:11
WHEN * NAHASH of Ammon died, his 1Ch 19:1
his son Hanun became the new *. 1Ch 19:1
arrived, * Hanun's counselors 1Ch 19:2,3
So * Hanun insulted King David's 1Ch 19:4
So King Hanun insulted * David's 1Ch 19:4
When * Hanun realized his 1Ch 19:6
* of Maacah and his entire army. 1Ch 19:7
by the troops * Hanun had recruited 1Ch 19:7
* Hadadezer's commander-in-chief. 1Ch 19:16
Then * Hadadezer's troops 1Ch 19:19
* David and became his subjects. 1Ch 19:19
crown from the head of * Milcom 1Ch 20:2
But the * won the argument, and 1Ch 21:4
at what the * had made him do. 1Ch 21:6
Then Ornan saw the * 1Ch 21:21
to the ground before * David. 1Ch 21:21
"No," the * replied, "I will 1Ch 21:24
when he makes you * of Israel. 1Ch 22:12
Solomon as the new * of Israel. 1Ch 23:1
presence of the * and of these 1Ch 24:6
It was done in the presence of * 1Ch 24:31
Heman reported directly to the *. 1Ch 25:6,7
to the Lord by * David and the 1Ch 26:26
fortieth year of * David's reign. 1Ch 26:31,32
Over Judah, Elihu (a brother of * 1Ch 27:16-22
put into the annals of * David. 1Ch 27:24
These men were * David's 1Ch 27:31
and has made me * over all Israel. 1Ch 28:4
The * also passed on to Solomon 1Ch 28:13
THEN * DAVID turned to the entire 1Ch 29:1
to be the next * of Israel, is 1Ch 29:1
* pledged $145,000,000 in gold; 1Ch 29:6,7
* David was moved with deep joy. 1Ch 29:9
low before the Lord and the *. 1Ch 29:20
him as co-regent" (with * David). 1Ch 29:22f
they crowned * David's son 1Ch 29:22
David's son Solomon as their *. 1Ch 29:22
their allegiance to * Solomon. 1Ch 29:24
David was * of the land of Israel 1Ch 29:26,27
Detailed biographies of * David 1Ch 29:29
* DAVID'S SON Solomon was now the 2Ch 1:1
before the reign of * Solomon. 2Ch 1:2,3f
built by * David for the Ark of God 2Ch 1:4
and have made me * over a nation as 2Ch 1:9
other * has ever had before you! 2Ch 1:12
so great a * in all the world!" 2Ch 1:12
stationed at Jerusalem near the *. 2Ch 1:14
Solomon sent an ambassador to * 2Ch 2:3
* Hiram replied to King Solomon: 2Ch 2:11
King Hiram replied to * Solomon: 2Ch 2:11
that he has made you their *! 2Ch 2:11
Solomon's father, * David, and 2Ch 3:1
fourth year of * Solomon's reign. 2Ch 3:2
work assigned to him by * Solomon: 2Ch 4:11
* Solomon, using polished bronze. 2Ch 4:12-16
bronze. The * did the casting at 2Ch 4:17,18
the Lord by his father, * David. 2Ch 5:1
sacred vessels. * Solomon and the 2Ch 5:6
Then the * turned around to the 2Ch 6:3
I chosen a * for my people Israel. 2Ch 6:5,6
that city, and David as that *.' 2Ch 6:5,6
for I have become * in my father's 2Ch 6:10
Then the * and all the people 2Ch 7:4,5
to the Lord. * Solomon's 2Ch 7:4,5
instruments that * David himself 2Ch 7:6
Solomon had become *, and the great 2Ch 8:1
the cities which * Hiram of Tyre 2Ch 8:2
must not live in * David's palace, 2Ch 8:11
fleet presented to him by * Hiram. 2Ch 8:17,18
These ships, with * Hiram's 2Ch 8:17,18
Finally she exclaimed to the *, 2Ch 9:5
to give them a just * like you! 2Ch 9:8
She gave the * a gift of over a 2Ch 9:9
* Hiram's and King Solomon's 2Ch 9:10
King Hiram's and * Solomon's 2Ch 9:10
and jewels. The * used the 2Ch 9:11
* Solomon gave the Queen of Sheba 2Ch 9:12
$140,000. The * placed these in the 2Ch 9:16
All of * Solomon's cups were 2Ch 9:20
Every three years the * sent his 2Ch 9:21
supplied by * Hiram, to bring back 2Ch 9:21
So * Solomon was richer and wiser 2Ch 9:22
than any other * in all the earth. 2Ch 9:22
as in Jerusalem to protect the *. 2Ch 9:25
his son Rehoboam became the new *. 2Ch 9:31
had gone to escape from * Solomon. 2Ch 10:2,3
and we will let you be our *!" 2Ch 10:4
"If you want to be their *," 2Ch 10:7
three days to hear * Rehoboam's 2Ch 10:12
So the * turned down the people's 2Ch 10:15
realized what the * was saying they 2Ch 10:16
get someone else to be our *. 2Ch 10:16
Afterwards, when * Rehoboam sent 2Ch 10:18
When this news reached * Rehoboam 2Ch 10:18
"Go and say to * Rehoboam of 2Ch 11:3
and Jerusalem, for * Jeroboam had 2Ch 11:13,14
of Judah, so * Rehoboam survived 2Ch 11:17
* David and King Solomon had done. 2Ch 11:17
King David and * Solomon had done. 2Ch 11:17
intended to make him the next *. 2Ch 11:22
As a result, * Shishak of Egypt 2Ch 12:2
the fifth year of * Rehoboam's 2Ch 12:2
Then the * and the leaders of 2Ch 12:6
So * Shishak of Egypt conquered 2Ch 12:9
gold shields. * Rehoboam replaced 2Ch 12:10
Whenever the * went to the 2Ch 12:11
When the * humbled himself, the 2Ch 12:12
* Rehoboam reigned seventeen 2Ch 12:13
He had become * at the age of 2Ch 12:13
But he was an evil *, for he 2Ch 12:14
his son Abijah became the new *. 2Ch 12:16
ABIJAH BECAME THE new * of Judah, 2Ch 13:1
the reign of * Jeroboam of Israel. 2Ch 13:1
Judah, led by * Abijah, fielded 2Ch 13:3
courageous men led by * Jeroboam. 2Ch 13:3
of Ephraim, * Abijah shouted to 2Ch 13:4
* Jeroboam and the Israeli army: 2Ch 13:4
Your * Jeroboam is a mere 2Ch 13:6
And as they shouted, God used * 2Ch 13:15,16
of battle against * Jeroboam and 2Ch 13:15,16
Israel, and chased * Jeroboam's 2Ch 13:18,19
their suburbs. * Jeroboam of 2Ch 13:20
Meanwhile, * Abijah of Judah 2Ch 13:21
* ABIJAH WAS buried in Jerusalem. 2Ch 14:1
Then his son Asa became the new * 2Ch 14:1
* Asa's Judean army was 300,000 2Ch 14:8
of Zephathah, and * Asa sent his 2Ch 14:9,10
went out to meet * Asa as he was 2Ch 15:2
When * Asa heard this message 2Ch 15:8
that the Lord God was with * Asa). 2Ch 15:9
fifteenth year of * Asa's reign, 2Ch 15:10
* Asa even removed his mother 2Ch 15:16
the heart of * Asa was perfect 2Ch 15:17
year of * Asa's reign. 2Ch 15:19
IN THE THIRTY-SIXTH year of * 2Ch 16:1
King Asa's reign, * Baasha of 2Ch 16:1
and to send it to * Ben-hadad of 2Ch 16:2
your alliance with * Baasha of 2Ch 16:3
Ben-hadad agreed to * Asa's 2Ch 16:4
As soon as * Baasha of Israel 2Ch 16:5
Then * Asa and the people of 2Ch 16:6
Hanani came to * Asa and told him, 2Ch 16:7
your trust in the * of Syria 2Ch 16:7
* of Syria has escaped from you. 2Ch 16:7
became the * and mobilized for war 2Ch 17:1
his position as * of Judah. 2Ch 17:5
declared war on * Jehoshaphat. 2Ch 17:10
placed by the * in the fortified 2Ch 17:19
BUT RICH, POPULAR * Jehoshaphat of 2Ch 18:1
* Ahab of Israel. 2Ch 18:1
Samaria to visit * Ahab, and King 2Ch 18:2
King Ahab, and * Ahab gave a great 2Ch 18:2
Then he asked * Jehoshaphat to 2Ch 18:2
"Why, of course!" * Jehoshaphat 2Ch 18:3,4,5
So * Ahab summoned 400 of his 2Ch 18:3,4,5
So the * of Israel called one of 2Ch 18:8
would end in triumph for the *. 2Ch 18:12
them and give the * a favorable 2Ch 18:12
When he arrived before the *, the 2Ch 18:14
the king, the * asked him, 2Ch 18:14
"Look here," the * said 2Ch 18:15
the * of Israel exclaimed to 2Ch 18:17
said, 'Who can get * Ahab to go to 2Ch 18:19,20
Joash," the * of Israel ordered. 2Ch 18:25
"Tell them, 'The * says to put 2Ch 18:26
So the * of Israel and the king 2Ch 18:28
So the king of Israel and the * 2Ch 18:28
The * of Israel said to 2Ch 18:29
Now the * of Syria had issued 2Ch 18:30
everyone but the * of Israel!" 2Ch 18:30
charioteers saw * Jehoshaphat of 2Ch 18:31
he was not the * of Israel, they 2Ch 18:32
and it struck the * of Israel at 2Ch 18:33
all that day, and * Ahab went back 2Ch 18:34
AS * JEHOSHAPHAT of Judah returned 2Ch 19:1
and you, O * Jehoshaphat!" 2Ch 20:15
Then * Jehoshaphat fell to the 2Ch 20:18
had escaped. * Jehoshaphat and his 2Ch 20:25
A thumbnail sketch of * 2Ch 20:31
He became * of Judah when he was 2Ch 20:31
He was a good *, just as his 2Ch 20:32
life, Jehoshaphat, * of Judah, went 2Ch 20:35
with Ahaziah, * of Israel, who was 2Ch 20:35
yourself with * Ahaziah, the Lord 2Ch 20:37
established as *, he killed all of 2Ch 21:3,4
At that time the * of Edom 2Ch 21:8
the good ways of * Asa, but you 2Ch 21:12
as in the times of * Ahab, and 2Ch 21:13
his youngest son, as their new * 2Ch 22:1
an alliance with * Jehoram of 2Ch 22:5
was at war with * Hazael of Syria 2Ch 22:5
join the battle. * Jehoram of 2Ch 22:5
of Ahab, he met * Ahaziah's 2Ch 22:8
the grandson of * Jehoshaphat—a man 2Ch 22:9
to succeed him as *, for their 2Ch 22:9
who was * Ahaziah's sister 2Ch 22:11
* Jehoram's daughter, verse 11. 2Ch 22:11f
She was a daughter of * Jehoram, 2Ch 22:11
to the young *, who was still in 2Ch 23:2,3
a descendant of * David shall be 2Ch 23:2,3
shall be our *—will be true again. 2Ch 23:2,3
bodyguard for the *, weapons in 2Ch 23:7
Stay right beside the *." 2Ch 23:7
These had once belonged to * 2Ch 23:9
law of God, and proclaimed him *. 2Ch 23:11
went up, "Long live the *!" 2Ch 23:11
of praise to the *, she rushed over 2Ch 23:12
there stood the * by his pillar at 2Ch 23:12
that he and the * and the people 2Ch 23:15,16,17
the Levite clans that * David had. 2Ch 23:18
escorted the * from the Temple, 2Ch 23:20
and seated the * upon his throne. 2Ch 23:20
old when he became *, and he 2Ch 24:1
So the * called for Jehoiada, the 2Ch 24:6
So now the * instructed that a 2Ch 24:7,8
to pour in. The * and Jehoiada 2Ch 24:12
was brought to the * and Jehoiada, 2Ch 24:14
of Judah came to * Joash and 2Ch 24:17,18
and finally * Joash himself ordered 2Ch 24:21
That was how * Joash repaid 2Ch 24:22
of booty to the * of Damascus. 2Ch 24:23
his son Amaziah became the new *. 2Ch 24:27
old when he became *, and he 2Ch 25:1
as the new *, he executed the men 2Ch 25:3
When * Amaziah returned from this 2Ch 25:14
the * retorted. 2Ch 25:16
* Amaziah of Judah now took the 2Ch 25:17
declared war on * Joash of Israel 2Ch 25:17
* Joash replied with this 2Ch 25:18
army fled home. * Joash of Israel 2Ch 25:23
the defeated * Amaziah of Judah and 2Ch 25:23
to Jerusalem. Then * Joash ordered 2Ch 25:23
However, * Amaziah of Judah lived 2Ch 25:25
the death of * Joash of Israel. 2Ch 25:25
The complete biography of * 2Ch 25:26
Uzziah as their new *. 2Ch 26:1
in general, a good * so far as the 2Ch 26:4
And as long as the * followed the 2Ch 26:5
So * Uzziah was a leper until the 2Ch 26:21
his son Jotham became the new *. 2Ch 26:23
the time he became *, and he 2Ch 27:1
sacks of barley. * Jotham became 2Ch 27:6
and his son Ahaz became the new *. 2Ch 27:9
old when he became * and he reigned 2Ch 28:1
But he was an evil *, unlike his 2Ch 28:1
king, unlike his ancestor * David. 2Ch 28:1
God allowed the * of Syria to 2Ch 28:5
About that time * Ahaz of Judah 2Ch 28:16
of Judah asked the * of Assyria to 2Ch 28:16
evil deeds of * Ahaz of Israel, 2Ch 28:19
* Ahaz ruled two tribes of 2Ch 28:19f
this unusual way as a * of Israel. 2Ch 28:19f
But when Tilgath-pilneser, * of 2Ch 28:20
for * Ahaz instead of helping him. 2Ch 28:20
In this time of deep trial, * 2Ch 28:22
his people. The * took the gold 2Ch 28:24
When * Ahaz died, he was buried 2Ch 28:27
his son Hezekiah became the new *. 2Ch 28:27
when he became the * of Judah, and 2Ch 29:1
the Temple, as the * (who was 2Ch 29:15
and reported to * Hezekiah, "We 2Ch 29:18
* Ahaz when he closed the Temple. 2Ch 29:19
Early the next morning, * 2Ch 29:20
brought before the * and his 2Ch 29:23
all Israel as the * had 2Ch 29:24
commanded—for the * had specified 2Ch 29:24
Afterwards the * and his aides 2Ch 29:29
Then * Hezekiah ordered the 2Ch 29:30
* HEZEKIAH NOW sent letters 2Ch 30:1
celebration. The *, his aides, and 2Ch 30:2,3
notices out. The * and his 2Ch 30:4
by the * and his officers. 2Ch 30:12
them. Then * Hezekiah prayed for 2Ch 30:17,18,19
day after day. (* Hezekiah spoke 2Ch 30:22
seven days. * Hezekiah gave the 2Ch 30:24
the days of * David's son Solomon. 2Ch 30:26
These appointments were made by * 2Ch 31:12,13
In this way * Hezekiah handled 2Ch 31:20

(KING Con't)
this good work of * Hezekiah, King 2Ch 32:1
of King Hezekiah, * Sennacherib of 2Ch 32:1
"Why should the * of Assyria come 2Ch 32:4
be afraid of the * of Assyria or 2Ch 32:7
Then * Sennacherib of Assyria, 2Ch 32:9
this message to * Hezekiah and the 2Ch 32:9
"* Sennacherib of Assyria asks, 2Ch 32:10
of Jerusalem? * Hezekiah is trying 2Ch 32:11
us from the * of Assyria"! 2Ch 32:11
* Sennacherib also sent letters 2Ch 32:17
Then * Hezekiah and Isaiah the 2Ch 32:20
From then on * Hezekiah became 2Ch 32:23
presents for * Hezekiah, too. 2Ch 32:23
his son Manasseh became the new *. 2Ch 32:33
old when he became *, and he 2Ch 33:1
and his son Amon became the new *. 2Ch 33:20,21
his son Josiah to be the new *. 2Ch 33:25
eight years old when he became *. 2Ch 34:1
example of his ancestor * David. 2Ch 34:2
took it to the *, along with his 2Ch 34:15,16
and workmen," he said to the *. 2Ch 34:17
So he read it to the *. 2Ch 34:18
When the * heard what these laws 2Ch 34:19
the * told them. 2Ch 34:21
says this to the * of Judah who 2Ch 34:26
So they brought back to the * 2Ch 34:28
Then the * summoned all the 2Ch 34:29
There the * read the scroll to 2Ch 34:30
As the * stood before them, he 2Ch 34:31
first organized by * David of 2Ch 35:4,5
Then the * contributed 30,000 2Ch 35:7
corps as the * had instructed, 2Ch 35:10
earlier by * David, Asaph, Heman, 2Ch 35:15
could vie with * Josiah in this 2Ch 35:18
Afterwards * Neco of Egypt led 2Ch 35:20
But * Neco sent ambassadors to 2Ch 35:21
a fight with you, O * of Judah! 2Ch 35:21
I have come only to fight the * 2Ch 35:21
The enemy archers struck * 2Ch 35:23
was selected as the new *. 2Ch 36:1
Then he was deposed by the * of 2Ch 36:3
The * of Egypt now appointed 2Ch 36:4
Jehoahaz, as the new * of Judah. 2Ch 36:4
old when he became *, and he 2Ch 36:5
Finally Nebuchadnezzar * of 2Ch 36:6
away the * in chains to Babylon. 2Ch 36:6
son Jehoiachin became the new *. 2Ch 36:8
to Babylon by * Nebuchadnezzar. 2Ch 36:10
at that time, and * Nebuchadnezzar 2Ch 36:10
the new * of Judah and Jerusalem. 2Ch 36:10
old when he became * and he reigned 2Ch 36:11
He rebelled against * 2Ch 36:13
Then the Lord brought the * of 2Ch 36:17
The Lord used the * of Babylon to 2Ch 36:17
as slaves to the * and his sons 2Ch 36:20
But in the first year of * Cyrus 2Ch 36:22,23
of the reign of * Cyrus of Persia, Ez 1:1
by giving * Cyrus the desire to Ez 1:1
"Cyrus, * of Persia, hereby Ez 1:2
* Cyrus himself donated the gold Ez 1:7
items which * Nebuchadnezzar had Ez 1:7
had been deported to Babylon by * Ez 2:1
of * Solomon's officials: Ez 2:55,56,57
Sea to Joppa, for * Cyrus had Ez 3:7
in the manner ordained by * David. Ez 3:10
to him ever since * Esar-haddon of Ez 4:2
just as * Cyrus has commanded." Ez 4:3
tell lies about them to * Cyrus. Ez 4:4,5
until * Darius took the throne. Ez 4:4,5
And afterwards, when * Ahasu-erus Ez 4:6
they sent to * Ar-ta-xerxes: Ez 4:11
Then the * made this reply to Ez 4:17
When this letter from * Ez 4:23
the reign of * Darius of Persia. Ez 4:24
us continue while * Darius looked Ez 5:5
other officials sent to * Darius: Ez 5:6
"To * Darius: Ez 5:7
ago by a great * of Israel. Ez 5:11
them and let * Nebuchadnezzar Ez 5:12
"But they insist that * Cyrus of Ez 5:13
and they say * Cyrus returned the Ez 5:14
Shesh-bazzar, whom * Cyrus Ez 5:14
of Judah. The * instructed him to Ez 5:15
* Cyrus ever made such a decree; Ez 5:17
SO * DARIUS issued orders that a Ez 6:1
of the reign of * Cyrus, a decree Ez 6:3
expenses will be paid by the *. Ez 6:4
So * Darius sent this message Ez 6:6
will destroy any * and any nation Ez 6:12
once with the command of * Darius. Ez 6:13
year of the reign of * Darius. Ez 6:15
had caused the * of Assyria to be Ez 6:21,22
during the reign of * Ez 7:1
and the * granted his request; Ez 7:6
* Ar-ta-xerxes presented this Ez 7:11
"From: Ar-ta-xerxes, the * of Ez 7:12
"I, Ar-ta-xerxes the *, send Ez 7:21
wrath against the * and his sons? Ez 7:23
and the law of the * shall be Ez 7:26
who made the * want to beautify the Ez 7:27
by honoring me before the * and Ez 7:28
the reign of * Ar-ta-xerxes: Ez 8:1
first instituted by * David. Ez 8:20
For I was ashamed to ask the * Ez 8:22
After all, we had told the * that Ez 8:22
items which the * and his council Ez 8:25
reign of * Ar-ta-xerxes of Persia, Neh 1:1
go in and ask the * for a great Neh 1:11
I was serving the * his wine he Neh 2:1
Literally, "Let the * live Neh 2:3f
the * asked. Neh 2:4
The * replied, with the queen Neh 2:5,6
"If it please the *, give me Neh 2:7
And the * granted these requests, Neh 2:8
there. (The *, I should add, had Neh 2:9
with the *, and the plan to which Neh 2:18
against the * like this?" Neh 2:19
of the reign of * Ar-ta-xerxes—my Neh 5:14
He claims you plan to be their * Neh 6:5,6
comments on to * Ar-ta-xerxes! Neh 6:7
by * Nebuchadnezzar of Babylon. Neh 7:6
over the land of * Sihon of Heshbon Neh 9:22
of Heshbon and * Og of Bashan. Neh 9:22
He was appointed by * David, Neh 11:22,23
from the * concerning them." Neh 11:22,23f
the reign of * Darius of Persia, in Neh 12:22
musical instruments of * David. Neh 12:35,36
of the reign of * Ar-ta-xerxes Neh 13:6
"Wasn't this exactly * Solomon's Neh 13:26
"There was no * who could Neh 13:26
made him the * over all Israel; Neh 13:26
of the reign of * Ahasuerus, Est 1:1
When it was all over, the * gave Est 1:5
the * was feeling very generous. Est 1:7
For the * had instructed his Est 1:8
On the final day, when the * was Est 1:10
to come. The * was furious, but Est 1:12
and the * trusted their judgment. Est 1:13-15
not only the * but every official Est 1:16
The * and all his aides thought Est 1:21
BUT AFTER * Ahasuerus' anger had Est 2:1
them to the * for his pleasure. Est 2:2
pleased the * very much, and he put Est 2:4
was destroyed by * Nebuchadnezzar, Est 2:6
Babylon along with * Jeconiah of Est 2:6
the night with * Ahasuerus, she was Est 2:12,13,14
never seeing the * again unless he Est 2:12,13,14
turn to go to the *, she accepted Est 2:15
the palace of the * in January of Est 2:16
Well, the * loved Esther more Est 2:17
Later, the * demanded a second Est 2:19
* and plotted to assassinate him. Est 2:21
who told the *, crediting Mordecai Est 2:22
the history of * Ahasuerus' reign. Est 2:23
SOON AFTERWARDS * Ahasuerus Est 3:1
the empire next to the * himself. Est 3:1
by, for so the * had commanded. Est 3:2
Haman now approached the * about Est 3:8
If it please the *, issue a Est 3:9
The * agreed, confirming his Est 3:10
in the name of * Ahasuerus and Est 3:12
Then the * and Haman sat down for Est 3:15
to the * to plead for her people. Est 4:8
* holds out his golden scepter; Est 4:11
and the * has not called for me Est 4:11
I will go in to see the *; Est 4:16
palace, where the * was sitting Est 5:1
Then the * asked her, "What do Est 5:3
The * turned to his aides. Est 5:5
So the * and Haman came to Est 5:5
During the wine course the * said Est 5:6
and promotions the * had given him, Est 5:11
the kingdom next to the * himself. Est 5:11
only me and the * himself to the Est 5:12
* to let you hang Mordecai on it; Est 5:14
way with the * to the banquet." Est 5:14
THAT NIGHT THE * had trouble Est 6:1
the * asked. Est 6:3
the * inquired. Est 6:4
palace to ask the * to hang Est 6:4
So the courtiers replied to the * Est 6:5
"Bring him in," the * ordered. Est 6:5
So Haman came in and the * said Est 6:6
royal robes the * himself has worn, Est 6:7,8
is the way the * honors those who Est 6:9
the * said to Haman. Est 6:10
* honors those he delights in." Est 6:11
SO THE * and Haman came to Est 7:1
wine course, the * asked her, Est 7:2
won your favor, O *, and if it Est 7:3
damage to the * that no amount of Est 7:4
"What are you talking about?" * Est 7:5
fright before the * and queen. Est 7:6
and queen. The * jumped to his Est 7:7
* returned from the palace garden. Est 7:8
the * roared. Est 7:8
saved the * from assassination! Est 7:9
"Hang Haman on it," the * Est 7:9
ON THAT SAME day * Ahasuerus gave Est 8:1
brought before the *, for Esther Est 8:1
had told the * that he was her Est 8:1
The * took off his ring—which he Est 8:2
came before the *, falling down at Est 8:3
And again the * held out the Est 8:4
Then * Ahasuerus said to Queen Est 8:7
not be reversed, even by the *. Est 8:8f
Now the * is giving permission Est 8:8f
Mordecai wrote in the name of * Est 8:9,10
the provinces of * Ahasuerus was Est 8:12
presence of the * through the city Est 8:15
two decrees of the * were to be put Est 9:1
Late that evening, when the * was Est 9:11
So the * agreed, and the decree Est 9:14
came before the *, he issued a Est 9:24,25
* AHASUERUS NOT only laid tribute Est 10:1
given him by the *, are written in Est 10:2
to that of * Ahasuerus himself. Est 10:3
His enemies conquer him as a * Job 15:23,24
brought down to the * of Terrors. Job 18:14
chief, or as a * instructs his Job 29:25
and his Messiah, Christ the *. Ps 2:2
"This is the * of my choice, and Ps 2:6
listen to my plea, O God my *, Ps 5:1
The Lord is * forever and Ps 10:16
rescued me, the * you appointed. Ps 18:50
"God save the *"—I know he Ps 20:6
Give victory to our *, O Lord; Ps 20:9
HOW THE * rejoices in your Ps 21:1
And because the * trusts in the Ps 21:7
For the Lord is * and rules the Ps 22:28
gates, and let the * of Glory in. Ps 24:7
Who is this * of Glory? Ps 24:8
gates and let the * of Glory in. Ps 24:9
Who is this * of Glory? Ps 24:10
gives victory to his anointed *. Ps 28:8
army cannot save a *—for great Ps 33:16,17
You are my * and my God. Ps 44:4
lovely poem to the *, for I am as Ps 45:1
her maids of honor to the *! Ps 45:14
he is the great * of all the Ps 47:2
your praises to our God, our *. Ps 47:6,7
our *, the King of all the earth. Ps 47:6,7
our King, the * of all the earth. Ps 47:6,7
the residence of the great *. Ps 48:2
Written by David at the time * Ps 59:1
Literally, "to the days of the * Ps 61:6f
Literally, "the *." Ps 63:11f
for joy because you are their * Ps 67:4
The procession of God my * moves Ps 68:24
O GOD, HELP the * to judge as you Ps 72:1
God is my * from ages past; Ps 74:12
heaven's armies, my * and my God! Ps 84:3
one you have anointed as your *. Ps 84:9
One of Israel, has given us our *. Ps 89:18
who was sent to anoint David as *. Ps 89:19f
be the *— he is my servant David! Ps 89:19
the mightiest * in all the earth. Ps 89:27
angry with the one you chose as *? Ps 89:38
the one you anointed as their *. Ps 89:51
JEHOVAH IS *! Ps 93:1
is a great God, the great * of Ps 95:3
JEHOVAH IS *! Ps 97:1
symphony before the Lord, the *! Ps 98:6
JEHOVAH IS *! Ps 99:1
This mighty * is determined to Ps 99:4
you, Lord, are a famous * forever. Ps 102:12
He destroyed many a * who tried! Ps 105:14
Then the * sent for him and set Ps 105:20
in him than in the mightiest *! Ps 118:9
* you chose for your people. Ps 132:10
but he shall be a glorious *." Ps 132:18
kings— Sihon, * of Amorites; Ps 135:11
and Og, the * of Bashan; Ps 135:11
continues forever: Sihon, * of Ps 136:19
continues forever— and Og, * of Ps 136:20
Every * in all the earth shall Ps 138:4
I WILL PRAISE you, my God and *, Ps 145:1
your God is * in every Ps 146:10
of Jerusalem, exult in your *. Ps 149:2
THESE ARE THE proverbs of * Pro 1:1
For though they have no * to Pro 6:7
A * rejoices in servants who know Pro 14:35
God will help the * to judge the Pro 16:10
It is a horrible thing for a * to Pro 16:12
The * rejoices when his people Pro 16:13
The anger of the * is a messenger Pro 16:14
on those who please the *. Pro 16:15
lies from a * are both unexpected. Pro 17:7
A * sitting as judge weighs all Pro 20:8
A wise * stamps out crime by Pro 20:26
If a * is kind, honest and fair, Pro 20:28
the Lord and the *, and don't Pro 24:21,22
copied by the aides of * Hezekiah Pro 25:1
audience with the * as though you Pro 25:6,7
his people, but a * will have a Pro 28:16
A just * gives stability to his Pro 29:4
A * who is fair to the poor shall Pro 29:14
A slave who becomes a *. Pro 30:21,22,23
The lion, * of the animals. Pro 30:29,30,31
A * as he leads his army. Pro 30:29,30,31
These are the wise sayings of * Pro 31:1
Or, "of * Lemuel the oracle." Pro 31:1f

KING Con't)
of David, * of Jerusalem." Ecc 1:1f
of Jerusalem, * David's son, Ecc 1:1
I, the Preacher, was * of Israel, Ecc 1:12-15
man do who comes after the *?" Ecc 2:12f
foolish * who refuses all advice. Ecc 4:13
He might even become *, though Ecc 4:14
And over them all is the *. Ecc 5:9
Oh, for a * who is devoted to his Ecc 5:9
Obey the * as you have vowed to Ecc 8:2,3
For the * punishes those who Ecc 8:2,3
in it, and a great * came with his Ecc 9:14
than the shout of a * of fools. Ecc 9:17
Woe to the land whose * is a Ecc 10:16,17
Happy the land whose * is a Ecc 10:16,17
Never curse the *, not even in Ecc 10:20
composed by * Solomon:The Girl: Sol 1:1
The Girl: "The * has brought me Sol 1:4
* Solomon: "But lovely as the Sol 1:5
* Solomon: "If you don't know, O Sol 1:7
The Girl: "The * lies on his Sol 1:12
* Solomon: "My beloved is a Sol 1:13
* Solomon: "Yes, a lily among Sol 2:1
to defend his * against any Sol 3:8
in the night. For * Solomon made Sol 3:9
The Girl: "Go out and see * Sol 3:11
* SOLOMON: "How beautiful you Sol 4:1
* SOLOMON: "I am here in my Sol 5:1
* Solomon: "O my beloved, you Sol 6:3
* Solomon: "Because you dance so Sol 6:13
* SOLOMON: "How beautiful your Sol 7:1
is your crown. The * is held Sol 7:5
* Solomon: "Under the apple tree Sol 8:5
* Solomon: "If she has no Sol 8:8
the reigns of * Uzziah, King Is 1:1
of King Uzziah, * Jotham, King Ahaz Is 1:1
King Jotham, * Ahaz and King Is 1:1
and * Hezekiah—all kings of Judah. Is 1:1
* and take care of this mess." Is 3:6
as little children playing *. Is 3:12
THE YEAR * Uzziah died I saw the Is 6:1
and I have looked upon the *, the Is 6:5
was attacked by * Rezin of Syria Is 7:1
Rezin of Syria and * Pekah of Is 7:1
the hearts of the * and his Is 7:2
"Go out to meet * Ahaz, you and Is 7:3
the son of Tabeel as their *.' Is 7:6
Syria alone, and * Rezin's kingdom Is 7:8
* Pekah's power will not increase. Is 7:9
this further message to * Ahaz: Is 7:10
But the * refused. Is 7:12
Judah—the mighty * of Assyria will Is 7:17
or 'Mommy,' the * of Assyria will Is 8:4
about asking * Rezin and King Pekah Is 8:6
King Rezin and * Pekah to come and Is 8:6
mighty flood; the * of Assyria and Is 8:7,8
and curse their * and their God. Is 8:21
But the * of Assyria will not Is 10:7
be a *, ruling a conquered land. Is 10:8
After the Lord has used the * of Is 10:12
evil boasting, O * of Assyria, the Is 10:16
will jeer at the * of Babylon and Is 14:4
son will not succeed you as the *. Is 14:20
came to me the year * Ahaz died: Is 14:28
that the * who smote you is dead. Is 14:29
of alliance with the * of Judah. Is 16:1
place a just and righteous *." Is 16:4,5
vicious *, says the Lord of Hosts. Is 19:4
Their best counsel to the * of Is 19:11
IN THE YEAR when Sargon, * of Is 20:1
For the * of Assyria will take Is 20:4
Then, in the days of another *, Is 23:15,16
LOOK, A RIGHTEOUS * is coming, Is 32:1
Your eyes will see the * in his Is 33:17
our Judge, our Lawgiver and our *; Is 33:22
SO IN THE fourteenth year of * Is 36:1
Sennacherib, * of Assyria, came to Is 36:1
with * Hezekiah in Jerusalem. Is 36:2
"The mighty * of Assyria says you Is 36:4
that the * of Egypt will help you. Is 36:4
Isn't he the one your * insulted, Is 36:7
My master, the * of Assyria, Is 36:8,9
the great *, the king of Assyria: Is 36:13
the great king, the * of Assyria: Is 36:13
be conquered by the * of Assyria. Is 36:15
for here is the * of Assyria's Is 36:16
the armies of the * of Assyria? Is 36:18
WHEN * HEZEKIAH heard the results Is 37:1
blasphemy of the * of Assyria's Is 37:4
Then Isaiah replied, "Tell * Is 37:6
* of Assyria, and his blasphemy. Is 37:6
will reach the * that he is needed Is 37:7
to consult his *, who had left Is 37:8,9
But at this point the Assyrian * Is 37:8,9
be captured by the * of Assyria! Is 37:10
happened to the * of Hamath, to the Is 37:13
of Hamath, to the * of Arpad, and Is 37:13
As soon as * Hezekiah had read Is 37:14
Look at this letter from * Is 37:16,17
this message to * Hezekiah: "The Is 37:21
against Sennacherib, Assyria's *. Is 37:21
from the * of Assyria: This year Is 37:30
"As for the * of Assyria, his Is 37:33
Then Sennacherib, * of Assyria, Is 37:37
and Esar-haddon his son became *. Is 37:38
this city from the * of Assyria. Is 38:6
When * Hezekiah was well again, Is 38:9
SOON AFTERWARDS, THE * of Is 39:1
* and said, "What did they say? Is 39:3
the palace of the * of Babylon." Is 39:7
says God, the * of Israel. Is 41:21
Holy One, Israel's Creator and *. Is 43:15
The Lord, the * of Israel, Is 44:6
and love that I had for * David. Is 55:3
splendid crown for the * of kings. Is 62:3
of Amon's son Josiah, * of Judah. Jer 1:1
son Jehoiakim, * of Judah, and at Jer 1:3
son Zedekiah, * of Judah, when Jer 1:3
me during the reign of * Josiah: Jer 3:6
says the Lord, the * and the Jer 4:9
Who would not fear you, O * of Jer 10:7
the living God, the everlasting *. Jer 10:10
against the *, his court and all Jer 12:5
the * sitting on David's throne, Jer 13:13
Say to the * and queen-mother, Jer 13:18
* Jehoiachin and his mother Jer 13:18f
son of Hezekiah, * of Judah, did in Jer 15:4
the gate where the * goes out, and Jer 17:19
I will hand over Judah to the * Jer 20:4
THEN * ZEDEKIAH sent Pashhur (son Jer 21:1
Nebuchadnezzar, * of Babylon, has Jer 21:1
* Zedekiah doubtless had in mind Jer 21:1f
from Sennacherib, * of Assyria, in Jer 21:1f
Jeremiah replied, "Go back to * Jer 21:3,4
against the * of Babylon and the Jer 21:3,4
And finally I will deliver * Jer 21:7
into the hands of * Nebuchadnezzar Jer 21:7
It shall be captured by the * of Jer 21:10
"And to the * of Judah, the Lord Jer 21:11
directly to the * of Judah and say, Jer 22:1
from God, O * of Judah, sitting on Jer 22:2
his father * Josiah, and was Jer 22:11
And woe to you, * Jehoiakim, Jer 22:13
palace does not make a great *! Jer 22:15
punishment against * Jehoiakim, who Jer 22:18
son of Jehoiakim * of Judah—even Jer 22:24,25
* of Babylon, and his mighty army. Jer 22:24,25
was briefly governor, but not *. Jer 22:30f
Branch upon * David's throne. Jer 23:5,6
He shall be a * who shall rule Jer 23:5,6
AFTER NEBUCHADNEZZAR, * of Jer 24:1
of Jehoiakim), * of Judah, and Jer 24:1
Zedekiah, * of Judah, his officials Jer 24:8
of the reign of * Jehoiakim of Jer 25:1
* of Babylon, began his reign. Jer 25:1
(son of Amon) * of Judah, until Jer 25:2,3
Nebuchadnezzar, * of Babylon (I Jer 25:8,9
* of Babylon for seventy years. Jer 25:11
I will punish the * of Babylon Jer 25:12
And finally, the * of Babylon Jer 25:26
(son of Josiah), * of Judah: Jer 26:1
in the days of * Hezekiah of Judah, Jer 26:18
But did * Hezekiah and the Jer 26:19
But when * Jehoiakim and the Jer 26:21
saying, the * sent to kill him. Jer 26:21
Then * Jehoiakim sent Elnathan Jer 26:22
him back to * Jehoiakim, who Jer 26:23
(son of Josiah), * of Judah: Jer 27:1
your countries to * Nebuchadnezzar Jer 27:6
* of Babylon will not enslave you. Jer 27:9
to submit to the * of Babylon, I Jer 27:10
submitting to the * of Babylon will Jer 27:11
to Zedekiah, * of Judah. Jer 27:12
to the * of Babylon," he said. Jer 27:12
will not submit to Babylon's *? Jer 27:13
telling you the * of Babylon will Jer 27:14
Surrender to the * of Babylon and Jer 27:17
the palace of the * of Judah and in Jer 27:18
by Nebuchadnezzar, * of Babylon, Jer 27:19,20,21
of Jehoiakim), * of Judah, will Jer 27:19,20,21
reign of Zedekiah, * of Jer 28:1
the * of Babylon from your necks. Jer 28:2
and I will bring back * Jeconiah, Jer 28:4
son of Jehoiakim, * of Judah, and Jer 28:4
your necks by the * of Babylon." Jer 28:4
to * Nebuchadnezzar of Babylon." Jer 28:11
to Nebuchadnezzar, * of Babylon. Jer 28:14
AFTER JECONIAH THE *, and the Jer 29:1
went to Babylon as * Zedekiah's Jer 29:3
and on the * who sits on David's Jer 29:16,17
the * of Babylon burned alive!" Jer 29:22
Lord their God, and David their *, Jer 30:9
reign of Zedekiah, * of Judah Jer 32:1
Jerusalem. * Zedekiah had put him Jer 32:3
conquered by the * of Babylon, and Jer 32:3
Babylon, and that * Zedekiah would Jer 32:4
before the * of Babylon for trial Jer 32:4
to Nebuchadnezzar, * of Babylon; Jer 32:28
will fall to the * of Babylon Jer 32:36
Nebuchadnezzar, * of Babylon, and Jer 34:1
Go tell Zedekiah, * of Judah, Jer 34:2
* of Babylon and he shall burn it. Jer 34:2
taken before the * of Babylon and Jer 34:3
this, O Zedekiah, * of Judah: God Jer 34:4
and say, "Alas, our * is dead!" Jer 34:5
the message to * Zedekiah. Jer 34:6
the Lord after * Zedekiah of Judah Jer 34:8
Jerusalem— (for * Zedekiah had Jer 34:9
And I will surrender Zedekiah, * Jer 34:21
to the army of the * of Babylon, Jer 34:21
of Josiah) was the * of Judah: Jer 35:1
But when Nebuchadnezzar, * of Jer 35:11
of the reign of * Jehoiakim of Jer 36:1
of * Jehoiakim (son of Josiah). Jer 36:9
"We must tell the *," they Jer 36:16
the scribe and went to tell the *. Jer 36:20
The * sent Jehudi to get the Jer 36:21
* as all his officials stood by. Jer 36:21
stood by. The * was in a Jer 36:22
four columns, the * would take his Jer 36:23
They pled with the * not to burn Jer 36:24,25
Then the * commanded Jerahmeel (a Jer 36:26
"a son of the *." Jer 36:26f
After the * had burned the Jer 36:27
say this to the *: "The Lord says, Jer 36:29
it said the * of Babylon would Jer 36:29
you, Jehoiakim, * of Judah: He Jer 36:30
NEBUCHADNEZZAR, * OF Babylon, Jer 37:1
appoint Coniah (* Jehoiakim's son) Jer 37:1
son) to be the new * of Judah. Jer 37:1
had assassinated * Jehoiakim Jer 37:1f
But neither * Zedekiah nor his Jer 37:2
Nevertheless, * Zedekiah sent Jer 37:3
says: Tell the * of Judah, who sent Jer 37:7
but eventually * Zedekiah sent for Jer 37:17
secretly. The * asked him if there Jer 37:17
You shall be defeated by the * of Jer 37:17
he asked the *. Jer 37:18
the * of Babylon would not come? Jer 37:19
Listen, O my lord the *: I beg Jer 37:20
Then * Zedekiah commanded that Jer 37:21
be captured by the * of Babylon— Jer 38:3
they went to the * and said: Jer 38:4
So * Zedekiah agreed. Jer 38:5
where the * was holding court. Jer 38:8
"My lord the *," he said, Jer 38:9
Then the * commanded Ebedmelech Jer 38:10
One day * Zedekiah sent for Jer 38:14
something," the * said, "and Jer 38:14
So * Zedekiah swore before Jer 38:16
surrender," the * said, "for the Jer 38:19
You will be seized by the * of Jer 38:23
him why the * had called for him. Jer 38:27
So he said what the * had told Jer 38:27
of the reign of * Zedekiah of Jer 39:1
of Judah, that * Nebuchadnezzar and Jer 39:1
When * Zedekiah and his soldiers Jer 39:4
But the Babylonians chased the * Jer 39:5
to Nebuchadnezzar, * of Babylon who Jer 39:5
upon him. The * of Babylon made Jer 39:6
Meanwhile * Nebuchadnezzar had Jer 39:11,12
to do as the * had commanded. Jer 39:13
of Judah by the * of Babylon, and Jer 40:5
heard that the * of Babylon had Jer 40:7
"Stay here and serve the * of Jer 40:9
and that the * of Babylon had not Jer 40:11
that Baalis, * of the Ammonites, Jer 40:13,14
one constructed by * Asa when he Jer 41:9
against Baasha, * of Israel. Jer 41:9
Don't fear the * of Babylon any Jer 42:11
Nebuchadnezzar, * of Babylon, here Jer 43:10
* of Egypt, over to those. Jer 44:30
I turned Zedekiah, * of Judah, over Jer 44:30
to Nebuchadnezzar, * of Babylon." Jer 44:30
of the reign of * Jehoiakim (son of Jer 45:1
Pharaoh Necho, * of Egypt, and his Jer 46:2
by Nebuchadnezzar, * of Babylon, in Jer 46:2
(son of Josiah), * of Judah: Jer 46:2
* of Babylon, to attack Egypt: Jer 46:13
As I live, says the *, the Lord Jer 46:18
* of Babylon, and his army. Jer 46:26
the year * Josiah died. Jer 47:1f
says the *, the Lord of Hosts. Jer 48:15
by Nebuchadnezzar, * of Babylon, Jer 49:28
for Nebuchadnezzar, * of Jer 49:30
"Go," said the Lord to * Jer 49:31
the reign of Zedekiah, * of Judah: Jer 49:34
I will destroy her * and princes. Jer 49:38
First the * of Assyria ate them Jer 50:17
then Nebuchadnezzar, the * of Jer 50:17
I will punish the * of Babylon and Jer 50:18
as I punished the * of Assyria. Jer 50:18
When the * of Babylon received Jer 50:43
to the * to tell him all is lost! Jer 51:31
"Nebuchadnezzar, * of Babylon, has Jer 51:34,35
So says the *, the Lord of Hosts. Jer 51:57
along with Zedekiah, * of Judah. Jer 51:59
old when he became *, and he Jer 52:1
But he was a wicked *, just as Jer 52:2
against the * of Babylon until he Jer 52:3
Nebuchadnezzar, * of Babylon, came Jer 52:4
them and caught * Zedekiah in some Jer 52:8
They brought him to the * of Jer 52:9

(KING Con't)

of the reign of Nebuchadnezzar, *	Jer 52:12
made in the days of * Solomon.	Jer 52:20
He took them to the * of Babylon	Jer 52:26
where the * killed them all.	Jer 52:27
of Jehoiachin, * of Judah,	Jer 52:31
who became * of Babylon that year,	Jer 52:31
year, was kind to * Jehoiachin and	Jer 52:31
Not a * in all the earth—no one	Lam 4:12
for us there. Our *—the life of	Lam 4:20
Yes, even our mighty *, about	Lam 4:20
year of * Jehoiachin's captivity,	Eze 8:1
says it is a message to * Zedekiah	Eze 12:10
"Even * Zedekiah shall go out at	Eze 12:12
Nebuchadnezzar, * of Babylon [the	Eze 17:12,13
and took away her * and princes	Eze 17:12,13
Lord, the * of Israel shall die.	Eze 17:16
shall die in Babylon, where the *	Eze 17:16
Israel when the * of Babylon lays	Eze 17:17
For the * of Israel broke his	Eze 17:18
One of her cubs [* Jehoahaz	Eze 19:3
another of her cubs [* Jehoiachin	Eze 19:5
and taught him to be '* of the	Eze 19:5
him before the * of Babylon.	Eze 19:9
years after * Jeconiah was	Eze 20:1
two routes for the * of Babylon to	Eze 21:19,20
For the * of Babylon stands at a	Eze 21:21
But (the * of Babylon) will think	Eze 21:23
has come. O * Zedekiah,	Eze 21:25
save you from the * of Babylon.	Eze 21:29
the ninth year (of * Jehoiachin's	Eze 24:1
for today the * of Babylon has	Eze 24:2
year (after * Jehoiachin was taken	Eze 26:1
Nebuchadnezzar, * of Babylon—the	Eze 26:7
of Babylon—the * of kings from the	Eze 26:7
"Son of dust, weep for the * of	Eze 28:12
apply to a human * of Tyre, and	Eze 28:12f
imprisonment of * Jehoiachin), this	Eze 29:1
Pharaoh her * and all her people.	Eze 29:2
enemy, Pharaoh, * of Egypt—mighty	Eze 29:3
In the twenty-seventh year of *	Eze 29:17
"Son of dust, the army of *	Eze 29:18
to Nebuchadnezzar, * of Babylon,	Eze 29:19
Nebuchadnezzar, * of Babylon, will	Eze 30:10
and there will be no * in Egypt;	Eze 30:13
eleventh year of * Jehoiachin's	Eze 30:20
of Pharaoh, * of Egypt, and it	Eze 30:21
against Pharaoh, * of Egypt, and I	Eze 30:22
the arms of the * of Babylon and	Eze 30:24
arms of Pharaoh, * of Egypt, and he	Eze 30:24
groan before the * of Babylon as	Eze 30:24
the hands of the * of Babylon,	Eze 30:25
the hand of the * of Babylon, and	Eze 30:25
year of * Jehoiachin's captivity,	Eze 31:1
"Son of dust, tell Pharaoh, * of	Eze 31:2,3
twelfth year of * Jehoiachin's	Eze 32:1
mourn for Pharaoh, * of Egypt, and	Eze 32:2
* of Babylon shall come upon you.	Eze 32:11
One * shall be king of them all;	Eze 37:22
One king shall be * of them all;	Eze 37:22
be their *, their only Shepherd;	Eze 37:24
* of Meshech and Tubal.	Eze 38:2,3
THREE YEARS AFTER * Jehoiakim	Dan 1:1
Judah, Babylon's * Nebuchadnezzar	Dan 1:1
The * assigned them the best of	Dan 1:5
and wine given to them by the *.	Dan 1:8
"and then the * will behead me for	Dan 1:10
eating the food supplied by the *!	Dan 1:15
young men to the * for oral exams,	Dan 1:18,19
ordered to do. * Nebuchadnezzar had	Dan 1:18,19
judgment, the * found these young	Dan 1:20
year of the reign of * Cyrus.	Dan 1:21
said to the *, "Sir, tell us the	Dan 2:4
But the * replied, "I tell you,	Dan 2:5
The * retorted, "I can see your	Dan 2:8,9
The Chaldeans replied to the *,	Dan 2:10
And there isn't a * in all the	Dan 2:10
impossible thing the * requires.	Dan 2:11
Upon hearing this, the * was	Dan 2:12
asking, "Why is the * so angry?	Dan 2:15
So Daniel went in to see the *.	Dan 2:16
Daniel what the * had dreamed.	Dan 2:19
Take me to the * and I will tell	Dan 2:24
Daniel in to the * and said, "I've	Dan 2:25
The * said to Daniel, "Is this	Dan 2:26
can tell the * such things, but	Dan 2:27
"O *, you saw a huge and	Dan 2:31
"Your Majesty, you are a * over	Dan 2:37
"Truly, O Daniel," the * said,	Dan 2:47
Then the * made Daniel very	Dan 2:48
Then, at Daniel's request, the *	Dan 2:49
* NEBUCHADNEZZAR MADE a	Dan 3:1
* Nebuchadnezzar's golden statue;	Dan 3:5
But some officials went to the *	Dan 3:8
And because the *, in his anger,	Dan 3:22
Then the * gave promotions to	Dan 3:30
Nebuchadnezzar the *, which he sent	Dan 4:1
Finally the * said to him:	Dan 4:19
"O * Nebuchadnezzar, listen to	Dan 4:27
from heaven, "O * Nebuchadnezzar,	Dan 4:31
and honor the * of Heaven, the	Dan 4:37
BELSHAZZAR THE * invited a	Dan 5:1
the lampstand. The * himself saw	Dan 5:5
The * grew more and more	Dan 5:9
And in the reign of *	Dan 5:11
Literally, "* Nebuchadnezzar your	Dan 5:11f
as the * called him—for his mind is	Dan 5:12
Daniel was rushed in to see the *.	Dan 5:13
see the king. The * asked him,	Dan 5:13
the Daniel that * Nebuchadnezzar	Dan 5:13
the Chaldean *, was killed, and	Dan 5:30
them) so that the * could	Dan 6:2
ability, and the * began to think	Dan 6:3
could complain to the * about him.	Dan 6:4
They decided to go to the * and	Dan 6:6
and say, "* Darius, live forever!	Dan 6:6
So * Darius signed the law.	Dan 6:9
They rushed back to the * and	Dan 6:12
"Yes," the * replied, "it is 'a	Dan 6:12
Then they told the *, "That	Dan 6:13
Hearing this, the * was very	Dan 6:14
came again to the * and said,	Dan 6:15
So at last the * gave the order	Dan 6:16
den of lions. The * said to him,	Dan 6:16
and the * sealed it with his own	Dan 6:17
Then the * returned to his palace	Dan 6:18
The * was beside himself with joy	Dan 6:23
Then the * issued a command to	Dan 6:24
Afterward * Darius wrote this	Dan 6:25,26
then another *	Dan 7:24
from this vicious *, to consume and	Dan 7:26
of the reign of * Belshazzar, I had	Dan 8:1
the first great * of that country.	Dan 8:21
rotten, an angry * shall rise to	Dan 8:23
my duties for the *, but I was	Dan 8:27
of * Darius, the son of Ahasuerus.	Dan 9:1
(Darius was a Mede but became *	Dan 9:1
and a * will arise whose armies	Dan 9:26
This * will make a seven-year	Dan 9:27
reign of Cyrus, * of Persia, Daniel	Dan 10:1
"Then a mighty * will rise in	Dan 11:3
rise in Greece, a * who will rule a	Dan 11:3
One of them, the * of Egypt,	Dan 11:5
Literally, "the southern *	Dan 11:5f
be formed between the * of Syria	Dan 11:6
Literally, "the * of the north,"	Dan 11:6f
and the * of Egypt.	Dan 11:6
The daughter of the * of Egypt	Dan 11:6
* of Syria as a gesture of peace,	Dan 11:6
of her father, the * of Egypt, and	Dan 11:6
takes over as * of Egypt, he will	Dan 11:7
army against the * of Syria, and	Dan 11:7
he will leave the Syrian * alone.	Dan 11:8
"Meanwhile the * of Syria	Dan 11:9
of this Syrian * will assemble a	Dan 11:10,11
Then the * of Egypt,	Dan 11:10,11
"A few years later the Syrian *	Dan 11:13
Then the Syrian * and his allies	Dan 11:15
"The Syrian * will march onward	Dan 11:16
with the Egyptian *, giving him a	Dan 11:17
will be remembered as the * who	Dan 11:20
"The Syrian * will then return	Dan 11:28
the Syrian * will again pillage	Dan 11:30,31
"The * will do exactly as he	Dan 11:36
the * of the south will attack	Dan 11:40
and the northern * will react with	Dan 11:40
am about to punish * Jehu's dynasty	Hos 1:4,5
time without a * or prince, and	Hos 3:4
God, and to the Messiah, their *,	Hos 3:5
Literally, "to David, their *."	Hos 3:5f
to the great * there, but he can	Hos 5:13
I see them all. The * is glad	Hos 7:3
of the burden of her wonderful *!	Hos 8:10
the Lord and he took away our *.	Hos 10:3
a present to the great * there.	Hos 10:6
As for Samaria, her * shall	Hos 10:7
Shalman: probably Salaman, * of	Hos 10:14f
In one morning the * of Israel	Hos 10:15
Where is your *?	Hos 13:10
time Uzziah was * of Judah, and	Amo 1:2
(son of Joash) was * of Israel—two	Amo 1:2
So I will set fire to * Hazael's	Amo 1:4
Ekron and the * of Ashkelon;	Amo 1:8
And their * and his princes will	Amo 1:15
And I will destroy their * and	Amo 2:3
Sakkuth your *, and in Kaiwan,	Amo 5:25,26,27
as great musicians as * David was.	Amo 6:5
which went as taxes to the *.	Amo 7:1
of * Jeroboam by the sword."	Amo 7:9
to Jeroboam, the *: "Amos is a	Amo 7:10
And the Lord shall be *!	Ob 1:21
from the * on down, everyone put	Jon 3:4,5
For when the * of Nineveh heard	Jon 3:6
And the * and his nobles sent	Jon 3:7
the reigns of * Jotham, King Ahaz,	Mic 1:1
of King Jotham, * Ahaz, and King	Mic 1:1
* Hezekiah, all kings of Judah.	Mic 1:1
own land. Your * will go before	Mic 2:13
their * from Mount Zion forever.	Mic 4:7
Where is your * to lead you?	Mic 4:9
birthplace of my * who is alive	Mic 5:2
people, how Balak, * of Moab, tried	Mic 6:5
Who is this *	Nah 1:11
of slavery to this Assyrian *."	Nah 1:13
And to the * he says, "I have	Nah 1:14
The * shouts for his officers;	Nah 2:5
O Assyrian *, your princes lie	Nah 3:18
Josiah (son of Amon) * of Judah.	Zep 1:1
Note: The Great Revival under *	Zep 1:1f
And the Lord himself, the * of	Zep 3:15
year of the reign of * Darius I.	Hag 1:1
the second year of * Darius' reign,	Hag 1:14,15
of the reign of * Darius, this	Hag 2:10
year of the reign of * Darius.	Zec 1:1
of the reign of * Darius, another	Zec 1:7
He will rule both as * and as	Zec 6:13
year of the reign of * Darius.	Zec 7:1
officer of the *, and Regem-melech,	Zec 7:2
Gaza will be conquered, her *	Zec 9:5
For look—your * is coming!	Zec 9:9
them will be as mighty as * David!	Zec 12:8
mourning for the godly * Josiah,	Zec 12:11
* prophet, priest, and people.	Zec 12:12,13,14
days of Uzziah, * of Judah, and the	Zec 14:5
And the Lord shall be * over all	Zec 14:9
to worship the *, the Lord of	Zec 14:16
to worship the *, the Lord of	Zec 14:17
For I am a Great *," says the	Mal 1:14
of * David and of Abraham:	Mt 1:1
Jesse was the father of * David.	Mt 1:6
from Abraham to * David;	Mt 1:17
and fourteen from * David's time	Mt 1:17
during the reign of * Herod.	Mt 2:1
is the newborn * of the Jews?	Mt 2:2
* Herod was deeply disturbed by	Mt 2:3
you to return, for * Herod is going	Mt 2:13
there until * Herod's death.	Mt 2:15
new * was Herod's son, Archelaus.	Mt 2:22
is the capital of the great *.	Mt 5:35
about theirs. Yet * Solomon in all	Mt 6:29
of * David, have mercy on us."	Mt 9:27
by Satan, the demon *!"	Mt 9:34
you ever read what * David did when	Mt 12:3
* of devils."	Mt 12:24
WHEN *	Mt 14:1
The * was grieved, but because of	Mt 14:9
on me, O Lord, * David's Son!	Mt 15:22
be compared to a * who decided to	Mt 18:23
He couldn't pay, so the *	Mt 18:25
down before the *, his face in the	Mt 18:26
"Then the * was filled with pity	Mt 18:27
"But when the man left the *, he	Mt 18:28
* and told him what had happened.	Mt 18:31
And the * called before him the	Mt 18:32
"Then the angry * sent the man	Mt 18:34
* David's Son, have mercy on us!"	Mt 20:30
Jerusalem her * is coming to her,	Mt 21:5
"God bless * David's Son!"	Mt 21:9
by the story of a * who prepared a	Mt 22:1
"Then the angry * sent out his	Mt 22:7
But when the * came in to meet	Mt 22:11
"Then the * said to his aides,	Mt 22:13
"Then I, the *, shall say to	Mt 25:34
"And I, the *, will tell them,	Mt 25:40
Literally, " '*' of the Jews."	Mt 27:11f
"Hail, * of the Jews," they	Mt 27:29
is Jesus, the * of the Jews."	Mt 27:37
So you are the * of Israel, are	Mt 27:41,42,43
John was arrested by * Herod,	Mk 1:14
about the time * David and his	Mk 2:25,26
possessed by Satan, * of demons.	Mk 3:22
* Herod soon heard about Jesus,	Mk 6:14
everywhere. The * thought Jesus was	Mk 6:14
was wrong for the * to marry	Mk 6:17,18
you like," the * vowed, "even	Mk 6:22,23
So she hurried back to the * and	Mk 6:25
Then the * was sorry, but he was	Mk 6:26
of * Herod and of the Pharisees."	Mk 8:15
them shouting, "Hail to the *!"	Mk 11:9
"Hail to the * of the	Mk 11:10
must be a descendant of * David?	Mk 12:35
Pilate asked him, "Are you the *	Mk 15:2
"How about giving you the '* of	Mk 15:9
with this man you call your *?"	Mk 15:12
yelling, "Yea! * of the Jews!"	Mk 15:18
It read, "The * of the Jews."	Mk 15:26
"You '* of Israel'!	Mk 15:32
lived when Herod was * of Judea.	Lk 1:5
Joseph, a descendant of * David.	Lk 1:27
in Judea, * David's ancient	Lk 2:4
he had seen him—God's anointed *.	Lk 2:26
Haven't you ever read what *	Lk 6:3
wife (Chuza was * Herod's business	Lk 8:3
Many a prophet and * of old has	Lk 10:24
the * of demons!"	Lk 11:15
live, for * Herod is after you!"	Lk 13:31
"Or what * would ever dream of	Lk 14:31
to be crowned * of his province.	Lk 19:12
not acknowledge him as their *.	Lk 19:14
" 'Fine!' the * exclaimed.	Lk 19:17
and wicked slave,' the * roared.	Lk 19:22
" 'Yes,' the * replied, 'but it	Lk 19:26
"God has given us a *!"	Lk 19:38

(KING Con't)
"Long live the *! Lk 19:38
to be a descendant of * David? Lk 20:41
claiming he is our Messiah—a *." Lk 23:2
"Are you their Messiah—their *?" Lk 23:3
Literally, "Are you the * of the Lk 23:3f
to take him to * Herod, for Galilee Lk 23:7
* of the Jews, save yourself! Lk 23:37
"This is the * of the Jews." Lk 23:38
the Son of God—the * of Israel!" Jn 1:49
and make him their *, so he went Jn 6:15
God bless the * of Israel! Jn 12:13
be afraid of your *, people of Jn 12:15
"Are you the * of the Jews?" Jn 18:33
" '*' as you use the word or as Jn 18:34
mean their *, or their Messiah?" Jn 18:34f
using the word "*" to mean their Jn 18:34f
answered, "I am not an earthly *. Jn 18:36
Pilate replied, "But you are a * Jn 18:37
I'll release the '* of the Jews.' Jn 18:39
"Hail, '* of the Jews!' Jn 19:3
Anyone who declares himself a * Jn 19:12
to the Jews, "Here is your *!" Jn 19:14
Crucify your *?" Jn 19:15
"We have no * but Caesar," the Jn 19:15
of Nazareth, the * of the Jews." Jn 19:19
it from 'The * of the Jews' to 'He Jn 19:21
to 'He said, I am * of the Jews.' Jn 19:21
Spirit, speaking through * David. Act 1:16
Field of Blood.' * David's Act 1:20
"* David quoted Jesus as Act 2:25
our ancestor * David, your servant, Act 4:25,26
For Herod the *, and Pontius Act 4:27
favor before Pharaoh, * of Egypt. Act 7:10
but then a * was crowned who had Act 7:17,18
This * plotted against our race, Act 7:19
used until the time of * David. Act 7:45
ABOUT THAT TIME * Herod moved Act 12:1
of * Herod), and Paul. Act 13:1
"Then the people begged for a *, Act 13:21
him with David as *, a man about Act 13:22
And it is one of * David's Act 13:23
*, Jesus, instead of Caesar." Act 17:7
in the prison at * Herod's palace. Act 23:35
A few days later * Agrippa Act 25:13
discussed Paul's case with the *. Act 25:14
So the next day, after the * and Act 25:23
the audience: "* Agrippa and all Act 25:24
especially you, * Agrippa, to Act 25:26
"I am fortunate, * Agrippa," he Act 26:2
Yet, O *, for me it is a crime, Act 26:7
"And so, O * Agrippa, I was not Act 26:19
sober truth. And * Agrippa knows Act 26:26
done in a corner! * Agrippa, do Act 26:27
Then the *, the governor, Act 26:30
into * David's royal family line; Rom 1:3
* David spoke of this, describing Rom 4:6
caused death to be * over all, but Rom 5:17
Pharaoh, * of Egypt, was an Rom 9:17
* David spoke of this same thing Rom 11:9
he will be * over the Gentiles; Rom 15:12
For Christ will be * until he 1Co 15:25
the governor under * Aretas kept 2Co 11:32
* or ruler or dictator or leader. Eph 1:21
He is the * of the ages, the 1Ti 1:17
Almighty God, the * of kings and 1Ti 6:15
a Man, born into * David's family; 2Ti 2:8
He announced this through * David Heb 4:7
THIS MELCHIZEDEK WAS * of the Heb 7:1
so he is the * of Justice; Heb 7:2
and he is also the * of Peace Heb 7:2
from the death the * commanded, and Heb 11:23
grandson of the *, but chose to Heb 11:24,25
are priests of the *, you are holy 1Pe 2:9
those of the * as head of the 1Pe 2:13
He is far greater than any * in Rev 1:5
Their * is the Prince of the Rev 9:11
O * of Ages. Rev 15:3,4
Some manuscripts read, "* of the Rev 15:3,4f
died is the eighth *, having Rev 17:11
all lords, and * of kings, and his Rev 17:14
"* of Kings and Lord of Lords." Rev 19:16

KING'S
(later called * Valley), the king Gen 14:17
about a well the * servants had Gen 21:25
the captain of the * bodyguard and Gen 39:1
* prisoners were kept in chains. Gen 39:20
Then the * wine taster spoke up. Gen 41:9
"The * chief assistant spoke Gen 42:30
plunged it deep into the * belly. Ju 3:21
When the * servants returned and Ju 3:24
met Jonathan, the * son, and there 1Sa 18:1
"Who am I that I should be the * 1Sa 18:18
should accept the * proposition and 1Sa 18:22
"The * business required such 1Sa 21:8
Where is the * spear and the jug 1Sa 26:16
was the * private secretary. 2Sa 8:17
the king and the * officers and all 2Sa 16:6
to himself in the * Valley, for he 2Sa 18:18
As the people heard of the * 2Sa 19:2
Then Joab went to the * room and 2Sa 19:5
hard ferrying the * household and 2Sa 19:18
army and the * own bodyguard. 2Sa 20:7
was in charge of the * bodyguard. 2Sa 20:23
But the * command overcame Joab's 2Sa 24:4
So Bath-sheba went into the * 1Ki 1:15
While she was speaking, the * 1Ki 1:22,23
protected by the * own bodyguard; 1Ki 1:44,45
and he rode on the * own mule. 1Ki 1:44,45
Then, at the * command, Benaiah 1Ki 2:46
Word of the * decision spread 1Ki 3:28
Zabud (son of Nathan) was the * 1Ki 4:1
the people for the * household. 1Ki 4:7
Instantly the * arm became 1Ki 13:4
and the * arm became normal again. 1Ki 13:6
and licked the * blood just as the 1Ki 22:38
The * officer had replied, "That 2Ki 7:19
held it over the * face until he 2Ki 8:15
the heads of the * sons had 2Ki 10:8
the rest of the * children who were 2Ki 11:2,3
and showed them the * son. 2Ki 11:4
And he sat upon the * throne. 2Ki 11:19
became full, the * financial 2Ki 12:10
his own hands upon the * hands. 2Ki 13:16,17
offering, the * burnt offering and 2Ki 16:15
and Shebnah the * secretary, and 2Ki 18:37
and Asaiah, the * assistant, and 2Ki 22:12,13
double walls near the * garden. 2Ki 25:4,5
five of the * counselors, and sixty 2Ki 25:19
he ate regularly at the * table. 2Ki 25:29
Shavsha was the * special 1Ch 18:16
in charge of the * bodyguard—the 1Ch 18:17
of Asaph, the * private prophet, 1Ch 25:2
of Heman, the * private chaplain, 1Ch 25:4,5
of the laborers on the * estates. 1Ch 27:26
the oversight of the * vineyards; 1Ch 27:27
for the * olive yards and sycamore 1Ch 27:28
The attendant to the * sons was 1Ch 27:32
Ahithophel was the * official 1Ch 27:33
mouth of all of the * prophets!' 2Ch 18:21
of value in the * palace, including 2Ch 21:17
Literally, "the * daughter," 2Ch 22:11f
has come for the * son to reign!" 2Ch 23:2,3
the chest to the * accounting 2Ch 24:11
in charge of the * affairs and of 2Ch 26:21
killed the * son Ma-aseiah, and the 2Ch 28:7
Ma-aseiah, the * administrator 2Ch 28:7
the * second-in-command Elkanah. 2Ch 28:7
and Israel," the * letter said, 2Ch 30:6
to Shaphan, the * secretary. 2Ch 34:15,16
and Asaiah, the * personal aide. 2Ch 34:20
(Shallum was the * tailor, living 2Ch 34:22
When they told her of the * 2Ch 34:22
young bulls. The * officials made 2Ch 35:8
Heman, and Jeduthun the * prophet. 2Ch 35:15
sin offering. The * decrees were Ez 8:36
(I was the * cupbearer. Neh 1:11
the manager of the * forest, Neh 2:8
* letters to the governors there. Neh 2:9
Gate and to the * Pool, but my Neh 2:14,15
of Siloam to the * garden and the Neh 3:15
* castle beside the prison yard. Neh 3:25
to obey the * orders, properly sent Est 1:13-15
So now, as a result of the * Est 2:8
was brought to the * harem at Est 2:8
being taken to the * bed, each Est 2:12,13,14
She was taken to the * apartment Est 2:12,13,14
harem where the * wives lived. Est 2:12,13,14
another of the * eunuchs, and lived Est 2:12,13,14
palace, two of the * eunuchs, Est 2:21
Now all the * officials bowed Est 3:2
"Why are you disobeying the * Est 3:3,4
they refuse to obey the * laws; Est 3:8
therefore, it is not in the * Est 3:8
Haman called in the * secretaries Est 3:12
The edict went out by the * Est 3:15
and despair at the * decree; Est 4:3
one of the * eunuchs who had been Est 4:5
to pay into the * treasury for the Est 4:7
a copy of the * decree dooming all Est 4:8
who goes into the * inner court Est 4:11
* gate, refusing to bow to me." Est 5:13
Teresh, two of the * eunuchs, Est 6:1
has worn, and the * own horse, and Est 6:7,8
one of the * most noble princes to Est 6:9
the streets on the * own horse, Est 6:9
mounted him on the * own steed, and Est 6:11
it with him, the * messengers Est 6:14
Then Harbona, one of the * aides, Est 7:9
So they did, and the * wrath was Est 7:10
Jews throughout the * provinces. Est 8:5
you want to in the * name, and seal Est 8:8
seal it with the * ring, so that it Est 8:8
sealed with the * ring and could Est 8:8f
Immediately the * secretaries Est 8:9,10
message with the * ring and sent Est 8:9,10
dromedaries used in the * service. Est 8:9,10
carried by the * couriers and Est 8:14
and speeded by the * commandment. Est 8:14
province, as the * decree arrived, Est 8:17
throughout all the * provinces to Est 9:1
mighty name in the * palace and his Est 9:4
throughout the * provinces had Est 9:16
throughout all the * provinces, Est 9:20
Literally, "The * daughter." Ps 45:13f
charge of all the * possessions. Ps 105:21
could imprison the * aides and Ps 105:22
aides and teach the * advisors. Ps 105:22
they were found even in the * Ps 105:30
A growing population is a * Pro 14:28
The * anger is as dangerous as a Pro 19:12
The * fury is like that of a Pro 20:2
the Lord directs the * thoughts. Pro 21:1
grace and truth is the * friend. Pro 22:11
things, and the * privilege to Pro 25:2,3
or all that goes on in the * mind! Pro 25:2,3
men from the * court, his reign Pro 25:4,5
And the * crown doesn't stay in Pro 27:23,24
yet are found even in * palaces! Pro 30:24-28
who disobey. The * command is Ecc 8:4
and Shebna, the * scribe, and Joah Is 36:3
So they took the * message to Is 37:5
this city, and the * palace too, Jer 33:4
had obeyed the * command and freed Jer 34:10
Not another of the * officials Jer 36:24,25
the * chief assistant, and many Jer 39:3
the * advisor, and all the Jer 39:13
and one of the * top officials, Jer 41:1
Ishmael made captives of the * Jer 41:10
and children, the * daughters and Jer 43:6
two walls near the * gardens (for Jer 52:7
army, seven of the * special Jer 52:24,25
the * kitchen as long as he lived. Jer 52:33
who ate the * rich food, and decide Dan 1:13
appointment as the * counselor Dan 1:21
this vision of the * dream, and the Dan 2:23
chief magistrate in the * court. Dan 2:49
languages, this is the * command: Dan 3:4
they defied the * commandment, and Dan 3:28
in power, but this * own officials Dan 11:5
On the * birthday, the princes Hos 7:5
capital, where the * chapel is!" Amo 7:13
of Hananel to the * wine presses. Zec 14:10
and wasn't afraid of the * anger. Heb 11:27
and those of the * officers, for 1Pe 2:14

KINGDOM
and my * guilty of this great sin? Gen 20:9,10
"Look my * over, and choose the Gen 20:15
And you shall be a * of priests Ex 19:6
Their * is exalted. Num 24:3-9
We utterly destroyed the * of Deu 3:6
King Sihon's * at Heshbon, killing Deu 3:6
* of King Og, the Argob region. Deu 3:13
in Heshbon. His * extended from Jos 12:2
and Ma-acah. His * also stretched Jos 12:5
the * of Sihon, king of Heshbon. Jos 12:5
the tableland and the * of Sihon. Jos 13:21
of the * of King Sihon of Heshbon. Jos 13:27,28
Bashan, the former * of King Og, Jos 13:30
The Lord has torn the * of Israel 1Sa 15:28
and has taken the * from you and 1Sa 28:17
away the entire * from you, all the 2Sa 3:9,10
surrender the * of Israel to him in 2Sa 3:12
and blessed his * so greatly—it was 2Sa 5:12
and I will make his * strong. 2Sa 7:12
And I will continue his * into 2Sa 7:13
Your family shall rule my * 2Sa 7:16
Today I will get back the * of my 2Sa 16:3
people in your * as there are now! 2Sa 24:3
and his * prospered. 1Ki 2:12
he said, "and the * was mine: 1Ki 2:15
I would be giving him the * too! 1Ki 2:22
David and this * he promised me." 1Ki 2:23,24
So Solomon's grip upon the * 1Ki 2:46
I will tear the * away from you and 1Ki 11:11
I will take the * away from your 1Ki 11:12,13
'I will tear the * from the hand of 1Ki 11:31
I will not take the * from him 1Ki 11:34
" 'But I will take away the * 1Ki 11:35
of Jeroboam's * and the death of 1Ki 13:34
I ripped the * away from the 1Ki 14:8
But now the * of Israel was split 1Ki 16:21
every nation and * on earth from 1Ki 18:10
a firm grip on the *, he killed the 2Ki 14:5
For Israel split off from the * 2Ki 17:21
before the * of Israel began: 1Ch 1:43
the * to David, the son of Jesse. 1Ch 10:14
why he had made his * so great; 1Ch 14:2
From one * to another— 1Ch 16:20
and I will make his * strong. 1Ch 17:11
and over the * of Israel 1Ch 17:14
other men of authority in his *. 1Ch 28:1
on the throne of his * of Israel. 1Ch 28:5
I will make his * last forever.' 1Ch 28:7
yours, O Lord, and this is your *. 1Ch 29:11
me the *— this is all I want! 2Ch 1:8
in an attempt to reunite the *. 2Ch 11:1
This strengthened the * of 2Ch 11:17
you can defeat the * of the Lord 2Ch 13:8
That is why God gave his * peace. 2Ch 14:5
So Jehoshaphat's * was quiet, 2Ch 20:30
him to Jerusalem and to his *! 2Ch 33:13
the * of Persia conquered Babylon. 2Ch 36:20

(KINGDOM Con't)
his *, putting it into writing: 2Ch 36:22,23
All Jews throughout the * may Ez 1:3
your great *, husbands everywhere, Est 1:20
the whole * of Ahasuerus. Est 3:5,6
provinces of your *," he began, Est 3:8
you, even if it is half the *!" Est 5:3
even if it is half of the *!" Est 5:6
in the * next to the king himself. Est 5:11
records of his * from the library, Est 6:1
you, even if it is half of my *!" Est 7:2
of all the people of the *. Est 8:9,10
provinces of the * of Ahasuerus Est 9:29-31
He will be driven out from the * Job 18:18
were driven from one * to another; Ps 105:13
became God's new home and *. Ps 114:2
the glory of your * and mention Ps 145:11
For your * never ends. Ps 145:13
and fair, his * stands secure. Pro 20:28
and King Rezin's * will not Is 7:8
this oracle—ending the Northern *. Is 7:8f
off many a * whose idols were far Is 10:10
never end, Queen * of the world. Is 47:7
O pleasure-mad *, living at ease, Is 47:8
The * of Babylonia, being revived Jer 5:15f
certain nation or * is to be taken Jer 18:7
of Riblah in the * of Hamath, and Jer 52:9
He has brought the * to dust, Lam 2:2
overturn the *, so that even the Eze 21:27
what was once the * of Israel send Eze 27:17
will be an unimportant, minor *. Eze 29:14
your *, power, strength and glory. Dan 2:37
"But after your * has come to an Dan 2:39
And after that * has fallen, yet Dan 2:39
Following it, the fourth * Dan 2:40
later on, this * will be divided. Dan 2:41,42
a * that will never be destroyed; Dan 2:44
sure that his * is everlasting; Dan 4:3
all the wisest men of my * have Dan 4:18
you will get your * back again, Dan 4:26
You are no longer ruler of this *. Dan 4:31
is everlasting, his * evermore. Dan 4:34
so did my honor and glory and *. Dan 4:36
as head of my *, with even greater Dan 4:36
in the *!" Dan 5:7
For there is a man in your * who Dan 5:11
you the third ruler in the *." Dan 5:16
* and majesty and glory and honor. Dan 5:18
"Parsin means 'divided'—your * Dan 5:28
proclaimed third ruler in the *. Dan 5:29
DARIUS DIVIDED THE * into 120 Dan 6:1
administer the * efficiently. Dan 6:2
of Daniel in every part of my *. Dan 6:25,26
God whose * shall never be Dan 6:25,26
then the * of everlasting Dan 9:24
his * still unrealized. Dan 9:26
who overrules the * of Persia Dan 10:13
will rule a vast * and accomplish Dan 11:3
of his power, his * will break Dan 11:4
* and make it still more powerful. Dan 11:5
the * by flattery and intrigue. Dan 11:21
as an independent *, breaking the Hos 1:4,5
for the * of Heaven is coming Mt 3:2
for the * of heaven is near." Mt 4:17
Good News about the * of Heaven. Mt 4:23
he told them, "for the * of Mt 5:3
for the * of Heaven is theirs. Mt 5:10
be the least in the * of Heaven. Mt 5:19
shall be great in the * of Heaven. Mt 5:19
get into the * of Heaven at all! Mt 5:20
We ask that your * will come Mt 6:10
"For yours is the * and the power Mt 6:13f
sit down in the * of Heaven with Mt 8:11
for whom the * was prepared—shall Mt 8:12
the Good News about the *. Mt 9:35
them that the * of Heaven is near. Mt 10:7
lights in the * of Heaven will be Mt 11:11
crowding toward the * of Heaven, Mt 11:12
Literally, "the * of Heaven Mt 11:12f
come [at the time the * begins Mt 11:14
"A divided * ends in ruin. Mt 12:25
himself, and destroying his own *. Mt 12:26
* of God has arrived among you. Mt 12:28
One cannot rob Satan's * without Mt 12:29
* of Heaven, and others were not. Mt 13:11
the * and doesn't understand it; Mt 13:19
a hundred others into the *." Mt 13:23
Jesus used: "The * of Heaven is Mt 13:24
"The * of Heaven is like a tiny Mt 13:31,32
"The * of Heaven can be compared Mt 13:33
represents the people of the *; Mt 13:38
out of the * every temptation and Mt 13:41
as the sun in their Father's *. Mt 13:43
"The * of Heaven is like a Mt 13:44
"Again, the * of Heaven is like Mt 13:45
"Again, the * of Heaven can be Mt 13:47,48
you the keys of the * of Heaven; Mt 16:19
live to see me coming in my *." Mt 16:28
be greatest in the * of Heaven! Mt 18:1
never get into the * of Heaven. Mt 18:3
the greatest in the * of Heaven. Mt 18:4
"The * of Heaven can be compared Mt 18:23
for the sake of the * of Heaven. Mt 19:12
For of such is the * of Heaven." Mt 19:14
man to get into the * of Heaven. Mt 19:23
rich man to enter the * of God!" Mt 19:24
upon my glorious throne in the *, Mt 19:28
illustration of the * of Heaven. Mt 20:1
She replied, "In your *, will Mt 20:21
will get into the * before you do. Mt 21:31
"What I mean is that the * of Mt 21:43
show what the * of Heaven is like. Mt 22:1
others enter the * of Heaven, and Mt 23:13,14
"And the Good News about the * Mt 24:14
"THE * OF Heaven can be Mt 25:1
"Again, the * of Heaven can be Mt 25:14
Father, into the * prepared for you Mt 25:34
new with you in my Father's *." Mt 26:29
"God's * is near! Mk 1:15
cast out Satan? A * divided Mk 3:24
truths about the * of God that are Mk 4:11,12
are hidden to those outside the *: Mk 4:11,12
what the * of God is like: Mk 4:26
"How can I describe the * of God? Mk 4:30
my *, and I will give it to you!" Mk 6:22,23
* of God arrive in great power!" Mk 9:1
Better enter the * of God half Mk 9:47
* of God belongs to such as they. Mk 10:14
never be allowed into his *." Mk 10:15
rich to get into the * of God!" Mk 10:23
to enter the * of God. Mk 10:24
rich man to enter the * of God." Mk 10:25
to yours in your *," they said, Mk 10:37
of our father David's * " Mk 11:10
are not far from the * of God." Mk 12:34
in the * of God." Mk 14:25
arrival of God's *), gathered his Mk 15:42,43
forever; his * shall never end!" Lk 1:33
Good News of the * of God in other Lk 4:43
poor, for the * of God is yours! Lk 6:20
the * of God is greater than he." Lk 7:28
to announce the coming of the * Lk 8:1
a great deal about the * of God. Lk 8:10
the * of God and to heal the sick. Lk 9:2
again about the * of God and curing Lk 9:11
you have seen the * of God." Lk 9:27
would be greatest [in the coming * Lk 9:46
the * of God to all the world." Lk 9:60
him is not fit for the * of God." Lk 9:62
and as you heal them, say, 'The * Lk 10:8,9
close you were to the * of God!' Lk 10:11
send your * soon. Lk 11:2
* filled with civil war is doomed; Lk 11:17
his demons, how can his * survive? Lk 11:18
that the * of God has arrived. Lk 11:20
the * of God your primary concern. Lk 12:31
great happiness to give you the *. Lk 12:32
again about the * of God: "What is Lk 13:18
of God: "What is the * like?" Lk 13:18
within the * of God— for people Lk 13:28
be to get into the * of God!" Lk 14:15
that the * of God would come soon. Lk 16:16
"When will the * of God begin?" Lk 17:20
Jesus replied, "The * of God Lk 17:20
For the * of God is within Lk 17:21
For the * of God belongs to men Lk 18:16,17
the rich to enter the * of God! Lk 18:24
rich man to enter the * of God." Lk 18:25
the sake of the * of God, will be Lk 18:29
* of God would begin right away. Lk 19:11
against nation and * against Lk 21:10
kingdom against *, and there will Lk 21:10
as sure that the * of God is near. Lk 21:31
has occurred in the * of God." Lk 22:16
until the * of God has come." Lk 22:18
the highest rank [in the coming * Lk 22:24
has granted me a *, I, here and Lk 22:29
and drink at my table in that *; Lk 22:30
me when you come into your *." Lk 23:42
can never get into the * of God." Jn 3:3
he cannot enter the * of God. Jn 3:5
But my * is not of the world." Jn 18:36
talked to them about the * of God. Act 1:3
his words concerning the * of God; Act 8:12
enter into the * of God through Act 14:22
Literally, "concerning the * of Act 19:8f
the * will ever see me again. Act 20:25
He told them about the * of God Act 28:23
boldness about the * of God and Act 28:31
had given him the * of Egypt for Rom 9:17
The * of God is not just talking; 1Co 4:20
have no share in the * of God? 1Co 6:9,10
have no share in his *. 1Co 6:9,10
he will turn the * over to God the 1Co 15:24
and blood cannot get into God's *. 1Co 15:50
will not inherit the * of God. Gal 5:21
You can be sure of this: The * of Eph 5:5
those who live in the * of light. Col 1:12
gloom of Satan's * and brought us Col 1:13
us into the * of his dear Son, who Col 1:13
you into his * to share his glory. 1Th 2:12
you ready for his *, while at the 2Th 1:5
to set up his *— to preach the 2Ti 4:1
will bring me into his heavenly *. 2Ti 4:18
but of his Son he says, "Your * Heb 1:8
Since we have a * nothing can Heb 12:28
in faith, and the * of Heaven is Jas 2:5
into the eternal * of our Lord and 2Pe 1:11
He has gathered us into his * Rev 1:6
gives, and we shall share his *! Rev 1:9
them into a * and made them priests Rev 5:10
from heaven, "The * of this world Rev 11:15
and his * was plunged into Rev 16:10

KINGDOM'S

never get within the * gates." Lk 18:16,17

KINGDOMS

You will do the same to all the * Deu 3:21
of the federation of all those *. Jos 11:10
of the * of Geshur and Ma-acah. Jos 12:5
and the * of Israel and Judah; 2Sa 12:8
over all the * west of the 1Ki 4:24
the God of all the * of the earth. 2Ki 19:15
then all the * of the earth will 2Ki 19:19
He ruled over all kings and * 2Ch 9:26
the surrounding * so that none of 2Ch 17:10
Ruler of all the * of the earth—you 2Ch 20:6
the surrounding * heard that the 2Ch 20:29
"All the * of the earth have been 2Ch 36:22,23
them conquer great * and many Neh 9:22
submission and * totter into ruin. Ps 46:6
Sing to the Lord, O * of the Ps 68:32
And on * that refuse to pray, Ps 79:6
and gathered up * as a farmer Is 10:14
most glorious of *, the flower of Is 13:19
the earth and the * of the world? Is 14:16
he shakes the * of the earth; Is 23:11
are God of all the * of the earth. Is 37:16,17
us so that all the * of the earth Is 37:20
you be called "The Queen of *." Is 47:5
nations and the * of the world. Jer 1:10
I am calling the armies of the * Jer 1:15
and earlier * had ruled on Jer 5:15f
and in all the * of the world there Jer 10:7
and all the * of the world. Jer 25:26
from all the * he ruled, came and Jer 34:1
and the * of Hazor, which are Jer 49:28
in pieces and to destroy many *. Jer 51:20
shows that these * will try to Dan 2:43
It will shatter all these * into Dan 2:44
High dominates the * of the world, Dan 4:17
God dominates the * of men, and Dan 4:25
parcels out the * of men and gives Dan 4:32
High overrules the * of men, and Dan 5:21
animals, their * were taken from Dan 7:12
"Toward the end of their *, when Dan 8:23
together the * of the earth, and Zep 3:8
strength of the * of the nations. Hag 2:22
The nations and * of the earth Mt 24:7
"For nations and * will proclaim Mk 13:8
to him all the * of the world in a Lk 4:5
all these splendid * and their Lk 4:6,7
and *, its rulers and authorities; Col 1:16
battles, overthrew *, ruled their Heb 11:33
they will be appointed to their * Rev 17:12

KINGLY

them upon eternal, * thrones. Job 36:7
You set a * crown of purest gold Ps 21:3
Who is this in * robes, marching Is 63:1
then they clothe these gods in * Jer 10:9
and putting a * robe on him, they Lk 23:11

KINGS

who became the first of the *. Gen 10:8
These * (of Sodom, Gomorrah, Gen 14:3
army, that of the * of Sodom, Gen 14:8,9
Sea Valley (four * against five). Gen 14:8,9
And as the army of the * of Sodom Gen 14:10
and the other * at the Valley of Gen 14:17
* shall be among your descendants! Gen 17:6
* shall be among your posterity." Gen 17:16
* shall be among your descendants. Gen 35:11
These are the names of the * of Gen 36:31-39
produce rich foods, fit for *! Gen 49:20
*—Evi, Rekem, Zur, Hur, and Reba. Num 31:8
land of the two * of the Amorites Deu 3:8
your God has done to those two *. Deu 3:21
two Amorite * east of the Jordan. Deu 4:47
He will deliver their * into Deu 7:24
and Og, the * of the Amorites. Deu 31:4
the two Amorite * east of the Jos 2:10
See 1 * 16:34 for the fulfillment Jos 6:26f
WHEN THE * of the surrounding area Jos 9:1
These were the * of the nations Jos 9:1
you did to the two * of the Jos 9:10
messengers to several other *: Jos 10:3
So these five Amorite * combined Jos 10:5
For all the * of the Amorites who Jos 10:6
During the battle the five * Jos 10:16
placed there to keep the * inside. Jos 10:18
bring out the five *—of Jerusalem, Jos 10:22,23
to put their feet on the *' necks. Jos 10:24
each of the five *, killing them. Jos 10:26
nations and * of the hill country, Jos 10:40
messages to the following *: Jos 11:1

KINGS Con't)
All the * of the northern hill Jos 11:1
The * in the Arabah, south of Jos 11:1
The * in the mountain areas of Jos 11:1
The * of Canaan, both east and Jos 11:1
The * of the Amorites; Jos 11:1
The * of the Hittites; Jos 11:1
The * of the Perizzites; Jos 11:1
The * in the Jebusite hill Jos 11:1
The Hivite * in the cities on the Jos 11:1
All these * responded by Jos 11:4
all the other cities of those *. Jos 11:12
And Joshua killed all the * of Jos 11:17
For the Lord made the enemy * Jos 11:20
HERE IS THE list of the * on the Jos 12:1
Here is a list of the * destroyed Jos 12:7
So in all, thirty-one * and their Jos 12:8-24
drive out the two * of the Amorites Jos 24:12
"I have treated seventy * in Ju 1:7
Listen, O you * and princes, Ju 5:3
The * of Canaan fought in Taanach Ju 5:19
the * of Midian," he said. Ju 8:5
The two * fled, but Gideon Ju 8:12
just like you—like sons of *!" Ju 8:18
clothing of the *, or the chains Ju 8:26
ruled by seventy *—Gideon's seventy Ju 9:2
shall be priests to my * forever. 1Sa 2:35
your descendants * of Israel 1Sa 13:13
* of Zobah, and the Philistines. 1Sa 14:47
belongs to the * of Judah to this 1Sa 27:6
in the wall. And * from many lands 1Ki 4:34
to be the * of Israel forever, just 1Ki 9:5
trade with the * of Arabia and the 1Ki 10:15
wiser than all the * of the earth. 1Ki 10:23
to the Hittite and Syrian *. 1Ki 10:29
than all the other * before you; 1Ki 14:9
in The Annals of the * of Israel. 1Ki 14:19
in The Annals of the * of Judah. 1Ki 14:29
in The Annals of the * of Judah. 1Ki 15:7
See 1 * 14:27. 1Ki 15:15f
in The Annals of the * of Judah. 1Ki 15:23
in The Annals of the * of Israel. 1Ki 15:31
in The Annals of the * of Israel. 1Ki 16:4-7
in The Annals of the * of Israel. 1Ki 16:14
in The Annals of the * of Israel. 1Ki 16:20
than any of the * before him; 1Ki 16:25
in The Annals of the * of Israel. 1Ki 16:27
the other * of Israel before him. 1Ki 16:33
and the other * as they were 1Ki 20:12
thirty-two allied * were still 1Ki 20:16
Only this time replace the * 1Ki 20:24
the * of Israel are very merciful. 1Ki 20:31
See 1 * 18:19 and 40. 1Ki 22:6f
before the two *, who were dressed 1Ki 22:10
in The Annals of the * of Israel. 1Ki 22:39
in The Annals of the * of Judah. 1Ki 22:45
in The Annals of the * of Israel. 2Ki 1:18
So the * of Israel, Judah, and 2Ki 3:12
as Ahab and the other * of Israel; 2Ki 8:18
in The Annals of the * of Judah. 2Ki 8:23
Implied in 2 * 8:25. 2Ki 9:29f
"Two * couldn't stand against 2Ki 10:4
to be the * of Israel." 2Ki 10:30
in The Annals of the * of Israel. 2Ki 10:34
and Ahaziah, the * of Judah—had 2Ki 12:18
in The Annals of the * of Judah. 2Ki 12:19
in The Annals of the * of Israel. 2Ki 13:8
in The Annals of the * of Israel. 2Ki 13:12
with the other * of Israel; 2Ki 13:13
in The Annals of the * of Israel. 2Ki 14:15
with the other * of Israel. 2Ki 14:16
in The Annals of the * of Judah. 2Ki 14:18
in The Annals of the * of Israel. 2Ki 14:28
with the other * of Israel, and his 2Ki 14:29
in The Annals of the * of Judah. 2Ki 15:6
in The Annals of the * of Israel. 2Ki 15:11
would be * of Israel 2Ki 15:12
See 2 * 10:30. 2Ki 15:12f
in The Annals of the * of Israel. 2Ki 15:15
in The Annals of the * of Israel. 2Ki 15:21
in The Annals of the * of Israel. 2Ki 15:26
in The Annals of the * of Israel. 2Ki 15:31
in The Annals of the * of Judah. 2Ki 15:36
with the other * of Judah in the 2Ki 15:38
he was as wicked as the * of 2Ki 16:3
in The Annals of the * of Judah. 2Ki 16:19
as some of the other * of Israel 2Ki 17:1
In fact, none of the * before or 2Ki 18:5
well what the * of Assyria have 2Ki 19:11
The former * of Assyria destroyed 2Ki 19:12
What happened to the * of 2Ki 19:13
Lord, it is true that the * of 2Ki 19:17
in The Annals of the * of Judah. 2Ki 20:20
I will cause the * of Israel to 2Ki 21:13
in The Annals of the * of Judah. 2Ki 21:17
in The Annals of the * of Judah. 2Ki 21:25
by the previous * of Judah, for 2Ki 23:5
former * of Judah to the sun god. 2Ki 23:11
altars which the * of Judah had 2Ki 23:12
See 1 * 13:2. 2Ki 23:16f
See 1 * 13:31, 32. 2Ki 23:18f
by the various * of Israel and had 2Ki 23:19
of the * of Israel and Judah. 2Ki 23:22
in The Annals of the * of Judah. 2Ki 23:28
the other * who had preceded him 2Ki 23:31,32
like the other * preceding him 2Ki 23:36,37
in The Annals of the * of Judah. 2Ki 24:5
over all the other * who were being 2Ki 25:28
the names of the * of Edom who 1Ch 1:43
Hadad's death, the * of Edom were: 1Ch 1:51-54
Or, "Jehoahaz" (see 2 * 23:30 1Ch 3:15f
in The Annals of the * of Israel. 1Ch 9:1
Even * were killed who sought to 1Ch 16:21
to be * of Israel just as you are. 1Ch 17:10
his descendants will always be *.' 1Ch 17:14
of my children being * too! 1Ch 17:17
see 1 * 11:5. 1Ch 20:2f
to the * of the nearby nations. 1Ch 29:30
the * of the Hittites and Syria. 2Ch 1:17
will always be the * of Israel; 2Ch 7:18
each year from the * of Arabia and 2Ch 9:13,14
in all the earth. * from every 2Ch 9:23
He ruled over all * and kingdoms 2Ch 9:26
See 1 * 11:30, 31. 2Ch 10:15f
would always be the * of Israel? 2Ch 13:5
of the * of Israel and Judah. 2Ch 16:11
The two * were sitting on thrones 2Ch 18:9
LATER ON, THE armies of the * of 2Ch 20:1
in The Annals of the * of Israel. 2Ch 20:34
cemetery of the * in Jerusalem, and 2Ch 21:1
But he was as wicked as the * 2Ch 21:6
as evil as the * over in Israel, 2Ch 21:13
but see 2 * 8:26. 2Ch 22:2f
of David among the *, because he 2Ch 24:16
but not in the cemetery of the *. 2Ch 24:25
Temple, see The Annals of the *. 2Ch 24:27
of the * of Judah and Israel. 2Ch 25:26
of the * of Israel and Judah. 2Ch 27:7
the example of the * over in Israel 2Ch 28:2
had helped the * of Syria, they 2Ch 28:23
of the * of Judah and Israel. 2Ch 28:26
the power of the * of Assyria. 2Ch 30:6
I and the other * of Assyria before 2Ch 32:13
of the * of Judah and Israel. 2Ch 32:32
among the other *, and all Judah 2Ch 32:33
in The Annals of the * of Israel. 2Ch 33:18
He now rebuilt what earlier * of 2Ch 34:10,11
one of the * of Israel could vie 2Ch 35:18
See 2 * 23:29. 2Ch 35:20f
of the * of Israel and Judah. 2Ch 35:27
of The Annals of the * of Judah; 2Ch 36:8
against the * and countries who Ez 4:15
of insurrection against many *; Ez 4:19
some very great * in Jerusalem who Ez 4:20
and Ar-ta-xerxes, the * of Persia. Ez 6:14
Ar-ta-xerxes, the king of *. Ez 7:12
that is why we and our * and our Ez 9:7
by the heathen *—we were captured, Ez 9:7
instead you caused the * of Ez 9:9
them—even the * and the princes of Neh 9:24
us and upon our * and princes and Neh 9:32
the days when the * of Assyria Neh 9:32
we deserved. Our *, princes, Neh 9:34
the hands of the * whom you have Neh 9:37
of the * of Media and Persia. Est 10:2
ministers and * with all their Job 3:14,15
He reduces * to slaves and frees Job 12:18
of presidents and *, and leaves Job 12:24,25
God who says to * and nobles, 'You Job 34:18
O * and rulers of the earth, Ps 2:10
your enjoyment. *' daughters are Ps 45:9
"Your sons will some day be * Ps 45:16
The * of the earth have arrived Ps 48:4
though rich as *, can ransom his Ps 49:7
*, and Ephraim great warriors. Ps 60:6,7
The * of the earth are bringing Ps 68:29
in the dust. * along the Ps 72:10
coast—the * of Tarshish and the Ps 72:10
Yes, * from everywhere! Ps 72:11
things to the * of the earth. Ps 76:12
his descendants as * forever on his Ps 89:3,4
He will strike down many * in the Ps 110:5
I will speak to * about their Ps 119:44,45,46
*— Sihon, king of Amorites; Ps 135:10
and the * of Canaan— and gave Ps 135:11
power of mighty *, for his Ps 136:17
and killed famous * who were their Ps 136:18
God gave the land of these * to Ps 136:21
For you grant victory to *! Ps 144:10
and birds, the * and all the Ps 148:11
Bind their * and leaders with Ps 149:8
Because of my strength, * reign Pro 8:14,15
be successful and stand before *! Pro 22:29
1 * 4:32. Pro 25:1f
And it is not for *, O Lemuel, to Pro 31:4
of the * before me in Jerusalem. Ecc 1:16-18
more than any of the * before me. Ecc 2:7,8
taxes from many * and provinces. Ecc 2:7,8
than any of the * in Jerusalem Ecc 2:9
concerning * and rulers: For I Ecc 10:5
and King Hezekiah—all * of Judah. Is 1:1
Israel's * will be like babies, Is 3:4
Yes, the * of Syria and Israel Is 7:5
two invading * would be destroyed. Is 7:14f
wrong, the two * you fear so Is 7:15,16
so much—the * of Israel and Syria Is 7:15,16
will be deserted (of their *)." Is 7:15,16f
2 * 16:7-8. Is 7:20f
See 2 * 19:35 and Isaiah 37:36. Is 10:17f
earth's mightiest *, long dead, are Is 14:9
The * of the nations lie in Is 14:18
2 * 19:35. Is 33:4f
2 * 18:14-17. Is 33:8f
wherever the * of Assyria have Is 37:11
No, the Assyrian * completely Is 37:12
Arpad, and to the * of the cities Is 37:13
It is true, O Lord, that the * Is 37:18
him to trample * underfoot and to Is 41:2
him victory over * and princes. Is 41:25
crush the strength of mighty *. Is 45:1
earthly rulers: "* shall stand at Is 49:7
* and queens shall serve you; Is 49:23
foreign nations and their *; Is 52:14,15
mighty * will come to see the Is 60:3
Presidents and * will send you Is 60:10
* of the world will cater to you. Is 60:11
Powerful * and mighty nations Is 60:16
* shall be blinded by your glory; Is 62:2
splendid crown for the King of *. Is 62:3
All the * of Judah and its Jer 1:18
is getting caught. *, princes, Jer 2:26,27
the graves of the * of Judah and of Jer 8:1
word of the Lord, * of Judah and Jer 17:20
there shall always be * and Jer 17:25
word of the Lord, * of Judah and Jer 19:3
nor the * of Judah have worshiped Jer 19:4
the palace of the * of Jer 19:13
and silver of your *, shall be Jer 20:5
and once more give * to sit on Jer 22:4
For many nations and great * Jer 25:14
Judah, and their * and princes Jer 25:18
So did all the * of the land of Jer 25:19,20
land of Uz and the * of the Jer 25:19,20
and all the * of Tyre and Sidon, Jer 25:22
* of the regions across the sea; Jer 25:22
and all the * of Arabia and of Jer 25:24
and all the * of Zimri, Elam and Jer 25:25
and all the * of the northern Jer 25:26
See 2 * 22:12. Jer 26:24f
Then send messages to the * of Jer 27:3
nations and great * shall conquer Jer 27:7
priests as well as *) as well as to Jer 30:21f
people, of their *, officers, Jer 32:32
See 1 * 15:22. Fifty-three Jer 41:9f
the sins of the * and queens of Jer 44:9
before us, and our * and princes Jer 44:17
fathers and your * and princes and Jer 44:21
It is accompanied by many * Jer 50:41
the spirit of the * of the Medes to Jer 51:11
accomplished by later Persian *. Jer 51:26f
the armies of the * of the Medes Jer 51:28
over all the other * in Babylon, Jer 52:32
and Sabbaths. * and priests Lam 2:6
crushed them. Her * and princes are Lam 2:9
and elders and the * and princes Eze 7:26,27
Tiglath-pileser II (2 * 16:7, 8). Eze 23:12f
Judean *, Jehoiakim and Zedekiah. Eze 23:17f
king of * from the north—against Eze 26:7
of many nations. * at the ends of Eze 27:33
Their * are horribly afraid and Eze 27:35
before the curious gaze of *. Eze 28:17
lands, and their * shall be Eze 32:10
"Great * of Elam lie there with Eze 32:24
"Edom is there with her * and Eze 32:29
They and their * will not defile Eze 43:7
totem poles erected by their *. Eze 43:7
erected by their *, and I will Eze 43:9
See 2 * 20:17, 18. Dan 1:3,4f
He removes * and sets others on Dan 2:21
a king over many *, for the God of Dan 2:37
"During the reigns of those *, Dan 2:44
of gods, Ruler of *, the Revealer Dan 2:47
* who will someday rule the earth. Dan 7:17
His ten horns are ten * that Dan 7:24
saw are the * of Media and Persia; Dan 8:20
sections with four *, none of them Dan 8:22
messages to our * and princes and Dan 9:6
O Lord, we and our * and princes Dan 9:8
Three more Persian * will reign, Dan 11:2
"Both these * Dan 11:27
reigns of these four * of Judah: Hos 1:1
and one of the * of Israel, Hos 1:1
See 1 * 21:21 and 2 Kings 10:11. Hos 1:4,5f
See 1 Kings 21:21 and 2 * 10:11. Hos 1:4,5f
They kill their * one after Hos 7:7
Three Israelite * were Hos 7:7f
She has appointed * and princes, Hos 8:4
I gave you * in my anger, and I Hos 13:11
Probably an allusion to the * of Hos 13:11f
the tombs of the * of Edom, with no Amo 2:1
and King Hezekiah, all * of Judah. Mic 1:1
has deceived the * of Israel, for Mic 1:14
"They scoff at * and princes, Hab 1:10

(KINGS Con't)
See 1 * 18:28. Zec 13:6f
governors and * for my sake. Mt 10:18
was one of four "*" over the Mt 14:1f
think, Peter? Do * levy assessments Mt 17:25
the heathen, * are tyrants and each Mt 20:25
"As you know, the * and great men Mk 10:42
and * of being my followers. Mk 13:9
See 1 *, chapter 10. Lk 11:31f
prisons and before * and governors Lk 21:12
this world the * and great men Lk 22:25
Literally, "they (the * and great Lk 22:25f
Almighty God? The * of the earth Act 4:25,26
nations and before *, as well as to Act 9:15
and acquittal are * of life Rom 5:17
1 * 19:18. Rom 11:4f
contented, rich * on your thrones, 1Co 4:8
the spirit world with its * and Col 1:16
Pray in this way for * and all 1Ti 2:2
God, the King of * and Lord of 1Ti 6:15
against many *, Melchizedek met him Heb 7:1
from the * he had been fighting. Heb 7:4
and shifted. The * of the earth, Rev 6:15
peoples, nations, tribes, and *." Rev 10:11
up so that the * from the east Rev 16:12
of the world. The * of the world Rev 17:2
They also represent seven *. Rev 17:10
His ten horns are ten * who have Rev 17:12
lords, and King of *, and his Rev 17:14
represent ten * who will reign with Rev 17:16
rules over the * of the earth." Rev 17:18
"King of * and Lord of Lords." Rev 19:16
Come and eat the flesh of *, and Rev 19:18

KINGSHIP
continued under the * of the 1Ki 12:20
However, he gave the * to Jehoram 2Ch 21:3,4

KINSHIP
so Abimelech felt close * there. Ju 9:2f

KINSMAN
Literally, "brother," or "*." 1Ch 6:39-43f

KINSMEN
Your *, the tribe of Levi, are Num 18:2,3
I say it again—your * the Num 18:6
Literally, "*." 2Ki 10:13f

KIR
resettling them in *, and King 2Ki 16:9
of Ar and * will be destroyed. Is 15:1
the men of * hold up the shields. Is 22:6,7
people of Syria shall return to * Amo 1:5
should go back to * as slaves was Amo 1:5f
exodus from * and now were free. Amo 1:5f
Caphtor and the Syrians out of *. Amo 9:7

KIR-HARESETH
finally, only Fort * was left, 2Ki 3:25
mourn for stricken *, and for the Is 16:7

KIR-HARESH
and my sorrow for * will be very Is 16:11

KIR-HERES
heart is broken for the men of *. Jer 48:31
heart for Moab and *, for all their Jer 48:36

KIRIATH-ARBA
father at Mamre in * (now called Gen 35:27
had been called *, after a great Jos 14:15
Aphekah, Humtah, * (or, Hebron), Jos 15:48-62
of Ephraim; and * (also known as Jos 20:7
was also called * (Arba was the Jos 21:9-16
(formerly called *), destroying the Ju 1:10
*, Dibon, Jekabzeel (and their Neh 11:25-30

KIRIATH-BAAL
Eltekon, * (also known as Jos 15:48-62
at the village of * (sometimes Jos 18:14
from the edge of *, over Mount Jos 18:15

KIRIATH-JEARIM
Chephirah, Be-eroth, and *. Jos 9:17
(which is another name for *). Jos 15:9
(also known as *), Rabbah, Jos 15:48-62
(sometimes called *), one of the Jos 18:14
(or, Jerusalem), Gibe-ah, and *. Jos 18:21-28
at a place west of * in Judah Ju 18:12
to the people at * and told them 1Sa 6:21
SO THE MEN of * came and took the 1Sa 7:1
Shobal (the father of *), 1Ch 2:50
* and Haroeh, the ancestor of half 1Ch 2:52
The families of * were the 1Ch 2:53
the Ark of God was brought from *. 1Ch 13:5
to Baalah (i.e., *) in Judah to 1Ch 13:6
of God when he removed it from *. 2Ch 1:4
From the subclans of *, Chephirah, Neh 7:8-38
of Shemaiah) from *, was also Jer 26:20

KIRIATH-SANNAH
Shamir, Jattir, Socoh, Dannah, * Jos 15:48-62

KIRIATH-SEPHER
city of Debir (formerly called *). Jos 15:15
anyone who would go and capture *. Jos 15:16
city of Debir (formerly called *). Ju 1:11

KIRIATHAIM
The Emim in the plain of *; Gen 14:5,6
*, Nebo, Num 32:37,38
Mepha-ath, *, Sibmah, Jos 13:19
Hammon, and * with pasturelands. 1Ch 6:76
The city of * and its forts are Jer 48:1
and * and Beth-gamul and Jer 48:23
Baal-meon and *. Eze 25:9,10

KIRIATHARIM
From the subclans of *, Chephirah, Ez 2:3-35

KIRIATHHUZOTH
the king to *, where King Balak Num 22:39

KISH
* WAS A rich, influential man from 1Sa 9:1
lot selected Saul, the son of *. 1Sa 10:21
Saul's father, *, were brothers; 1Sa 14:50,51
in the grave of Saul's father, *. 2Sa 21:12,13,14
Zur, *, Baal, Nadab, Gedor, Ahio, 1Ch 8:30,31,32
Ner was the father of *, and Kish 1Ch 8:33
Ner was the father of Kish, and * 1Ch 8:33
Gibeon, Abdon (the oldest), Zur, * 1Ch 9:35,36,37
Ner was the father of *, 1Ch 9:39
* was the father of Saul, 1Ch 9:39
Literally, "the son of *." 1Ch 12:1f
Eleazar and *. 1Ch 23:21
to their cousins, the sons of *. 1Ch 23:22
*, among whose sons was Jerahmeel. 1Ch 24:29
Saul the son of *, Abner the son of 1Ch 26:28
From the Merari clan, * (son of 2Ch 29:12,13,14
Shime-i, son of *, a Benjaminite). Est 2:5
them Saul (son of *), a man of the Act 13:21

KISH'S
One day * donkeys strayed away, 1Sa 9:3

KISHI
*, Abdi, Malluch, Hashabiah, 1Ch 6:44-47

KISHION
Rabbith, *, Ebez, Remeth, Jos 19:17-23
*, Daberath, Jarmuth, and Jos 21:28,29

KISHON
draw them to the * River, and you Ju 4:7
Harosheth-ha-goiim to the * River. Ju 4:13
The rushing * River Ju 5:21
to * Brook and killed them there. 1Ki 18:40
Jabin at the river *, and as you Ps 83:9

KISLEV
"The 24th day of *." Hag 2:18,19f

KISS
Isaac: "Come here and * me, my Gen 27:26
Why didn't you let me * my Gen 31:28
his right hand as though to * him. 2Sa 20:8,9,10
Fall down before his Son and * Ps 2:12
Spurn the careless * of a Pro 4:24
"* me again and again, for your Sol 1:2
then I could * you no matter who Sol 8:1
They will * your feet! Is 60:14
Literally, "*"—the usual Mk 14:44f
You refused me the customary * Lk 7:45
Literally, "approached Jesus to * Lk 22:47f
the Messiah with a *?" Lk 22:48

KISSED
Then Jacob * Rachel and started Gen 29:11
next morning and * his daughters Gen 31:55
him affectionately and * him; Gen 33:4
to him and he * and embraced them. Gen 48:10
body and wept over him and * him. Gen 50:1
Then she * them and they all Ru 1:9
and Orpah * her mother-in-law Ru 1:14
and * him on the cheek and said, 1Sa 10:1
times and they * each other and 1Sa 20:41f
before the king, and David * him. 2Sa 14:33
"took hold of him and * him." 2Sa 15:5f
and after David had * and blessed 2Sa 19:39
never bowed to Baal nor * him!" 1Ki 19:18
and peace have *! Ps 85:10
She put her arms around him and * Pro 7:13
Literally, "*," the greeting Mt 26:49f
with her hair and * them and poured Lk 7:38
but she has * my feet again and Lk 7:45
ran and embraced him and * him. Lk 15:20
Judas walked over to Jesus and * Lk 22:47

KISSES
(Jacob goes over and * him on the Gen 27:26
are better than * from an enemy! Pro 27:6
apples, and your * as exciting as Sol 7:9

KISSING
worshiped them by * my hand to Job 31:27
they say—men * calves! Hos 13:2

KITCHEN
They walked into the * as though 2Sa 4:6,7
the king's * as long as he lived. Jer 52:33
wine from his own * during their Dan 1:5
in the * or to put garbage in. 2Ti 2:20

KITE
The falcon (all kinds), the *, Lev 11:13-19
not one * will be there without a Is 34:16

KITES
her wings, and the * will come, Is 34:15

KITRON
the people of * or Nahalol, but Ju 1:30

KITTIM
Tarshish,*, Dodanim. Gen 10:4
Elishah, Tarshish, *, and Rodanim. 1Ch 1:5-9

KNAPSACK
sticks—no food, no *, no money, not Mk 6:8,9

KNEAD
and the women * dough and make Jer 7:18

KNEADED
and killed it and * dough and baked 1Sa 28:24
he wished, so he * it into a lump Jer 18:
It is like yeast * into dough, Lk 13:20,2

KNEADING
fill your ovens and your * bowls; Ex 8:3,
and bound their * troughs into Ex 12:34

KNEADS
while he * the dough and waits for Hos 7:4

KNEE
taught to him at his mother's *: Pro 31:
is true—that every * in all the Is 45:23
the Lord, "every * shall bow to me Rom 14:11
of Jesus every * shall bow in Php 2:10

KNEEL
There he made the camels * down Gen 24:11
went the shout arose, "* down!" Gen 41:43
In Group 2 will be those who *, Ju 7:5,6
Come, * before the Lord our Ps 95:6
you will only * and worship me." Mt 4:9

KNEELING
Solomon had been * with his hands 1Ki 8:54,55
What awe we feel, * here before Ps 68:35
See this woman * here! Lk 7:44
felt deep pity. * beside him the Lk 10:34

KNEELS
A leper is approaching. He * Mt 8:2

KNEES
fell to his * before Jehovah. Gen 24:52
grandfather's *—Ephraim at Israel's Gen 48:12,13
from the shoulders to below the *. Ex 28:4f
bodies, reaching from hips to *. Ex 28:42
on their hands and *, and the 1Sa 14:13
got down on his *, with his face 1Ki 18:42
face between his *, and said to 1Ki 18:42
fell to his * before Elijah and 2Ki 1:13
then I fell to my * and lifted my Ez 9:5
power and bring them to their *. Ps 59:11
from his arm. My * are weak from Ps 109:24
fall down on their * before you and Is 45:14
on her hips and dandled on her *. Is 66:12
those they bounced upon their *? Lam 2:20
and all * as weak as water. Eze 7:17
strong * will tremble and become Eze 21:7
time the water was up to my *. Eze 47:4
him that his * knocked together and Dan 5:6
trembling, to my hands and *. Dan 10:10
hearts melt in horror; * quake; Nah 2:10
on their * to "worship" him. Mk 15:19
down on your * and worship me." Lk 4:6,7
he fell to his * before Jesus and Lk 5:8
and fell to her * before him and Lk 8:47
And he fell to his *, Act 7:60
fall down on his * and worship God, 1Co 14:25
I fall down on my * and pray to the Eph 3:14,15

KNELT
people watched, he * down, reached 2Ch 6:12,13
he went home and * down as usual in Dan 6:10
A man came and * before Jesus and Mt 17:14
and * before him in mockery. Mt 27:29
Once a leper came and * in front Mk 1:40
running to him and * down and Mk 10:17
Going in, she * behind him at Lk 7:38
stone's throw, and * down and Lk 22:41,42
then he * and prayed. Act 9:40
speaking, he * and prayed with Act 20:36

KNEW
So Noah * that the water was Gen 8:11
Looking down upon them, he * Ex 2:25
Literally, "* their condition." Ex 2:25f
Lord from the first day I * you. Deu 9:24
the smoke, they * that their men Jos 8:20,21
for he * what would happen if Ju 6:27
on around him. He *, for instance, 1Sa 2:22
Dan to Beer-sheba * that Samuel was 1Sa 3:20
* whether the seer was in town. 1Sa 9:9,10,11
One of them said he * a young 1Sa 16:18
"Look, wouldn't I say so if I * 1Sa 20:9
only Jonathan and David *. 1Sa 20:39
until David * what God was going to 1Sa 22:3
matter, for we * nothing of any 1Sa 22:15
with David; they * he was running 1Sa 22:17
done, David exclaimed, "I * it! 1Sa 22:22
When I saw Doeg there, I * he 1Sa 22:22
hiding, but David * of Saul's 1Sa 26:3,4
"So I killed him, for I * he 2Sa 1:10
but David * nothing about it. 2Sa 3:26
city where he * that the enemies' 2Sa 11:16
they * nothing of his intentions. 2Sa 15:11
I * his laws, 2Sa 22:23
of the times and * the best course 1Ch 12:24-37
Our enemies learned that we * of Neh 4:15
people, for you * how brutally the Neh 9:10
certain that each * his work. Neh 13:30
They were men of wisdom who * the Est 1:13-15
for he * that he was doomed. Est 7:7
Those who * him will wonder where Job 20:7
Oh, that I * where to find Job 23:3
I was talking about things I * Job 42:3
sea—a pathway no one * was there! Ps 77:19
knows yours, and he knows you *! Pro 24:11,12
very poor, and he * what to do to Ecc 9:15
on teaching the people all he *; Ecc 12:9

(KNEW Con't)
he not only taught what he * to Ecc 12:10
* how hard and obstinate you are. Is 48:4
Then you can't say, "We * that Is 48:7
and chose what they * I despised. Is 66:4
The Lord said to me, "I * you Jer 1:5
of things they * nothing about. Jer 14:18
I * the prophets of Samaria were Jer 23:13
Then I * for sure that the Jer 32:8
the outside world * what had Jer 41:4
all the men who * that their wives Jer 44:15
Chebar Canal. I * they were the Eze 10:20
until at last he * that the Most Dan 5:21
O Belshazzar—you * all this, yet Dan 5:22
But though Daniel * about it, he Dan 6:10
—a god his fathers never *—and Dan 11:38
For I * you were a gracious God, Jon 4:2
of kindness; I * how easily you Jon 4:2
Their joy * no bounds! Mt 2:10
Literally, "I never * you." Mt 7:23f
Jesus * what they were thinking Mt 9:4
But he * what they were Mt 12:15
Jesus * their thoughts and Mt 12:25
Jesus * what they were thinking Mt 16:8
Literally, "* not." Mt 24:39f
and said, 'Sir, I * you were a hard Mt 25:24,25
Since you * I would demand your Mt 25:26
Jesus * what they were thinking, Mt 26:10
For he * very well that the Mt 27:18
speak, because they * who he was. Mk 1:34
stopped and she * she was well! Mk 5:29
for they * he was pointing at Mk 12:12
For he spoke as one who * the Lk 4:32
But because they * he was the Lk 4:41
Jesus * what they were thinking, Lk 5:22
How well he * their thoughts! Lk 6:8
that Jesus *, she began to tremble Lk 8:47
for they all * she was dead. Lk 8:53
But Jesus * their thoughts, so Lk 9:47
He * the thoughts of each of Lk 11:17
for him if they * the exact hour of Lk 12:39
if they * when he was coming. Lk 12:39
he * his duty he refused to do it. Lk 12:47
If you * so much about me and how Lk 19:22
for he * mankind to the core. Jn 2:24,25
WHEN THE LORD * that the Pharisees Jn 4:1
He replied, "If you only * what Jn 4:10
When Jesus saw him and * how Jn 5:6
already * what he was going to do. Jn 6:6
For they * that he and his Jn 6:22,23
Jesus * within himself that his Jn 6:61
(For Jesus * from the beginning Jn 6:64
* the one who would betray him. Jn 6:64
If you * me, then you would know Jn 8:19
He * I was coming and was glad." Jn 8:56
His neighbors and others who * Jn 9:8
JESUS * ON the evening of Passover Jn 13:1
Jesus * that the Father had given Jn 13:1
For Jesus * who would betray Jn 13:11
None of the others at the table * Jn 13:28
Judas, the betrayer, * this Jn 18:2
Jesus * that everything was now Jn 19:28
But he was a prophet, and * God Act 2:30
door, their surprise * no bounds. Act 12:16
left, for everyone * that his Act 16:3
about Jesus, but that is all he *. Act 18:25,26
Felix, who * Christians didn't go Act 24:22
At this rate they * they would Act 27:29
Yes, they * about him all right, Rom 1:21
Instead of believing what they * Rom 1:25
all along he * who would—should Rom 8:29
of prophecy and * all about what is 1Co 13:2
in the future, * everything about 1Co 13:2
Literally, "Him who * no sin, he 2Co 5:21f
All they * was what people were Gal 1:23
though they certainly * better. Gal 2:13
Before you Gentiles * God you Gal 4:8
done what they * was wrong. 1Ti 1:19
It was by faith that Isaac * God Heb 11:20
joy he * would be his afterwards; Heb 12:2
for us that they * how, but God's Heb 12:10
* you would become his children. 1Pe 1:2
evil because you * no better. 1Pe 1:14
Once you * very little of God's 1Pe 2:10
doing wrong and he * very well that 1Jn 3:12
after Adam, * about these men and Jud 1:14
what I * about Jesus Christ. Rev 1:9
and only he * its meaning. Rev 19:12

KNIFE
carried the * and the flint for Gen 22:6
And Abraham took the * and Gen 22:10
"Lay down the *; Gen 22:12
wife took a flint * and cut off the Ex 4:25,26
When he got there he took a * Ju 19:29
would take his *, and slit off the Jer 36:23
your map and slash at it with a *. Eze 5:2

KNIT
You gave me skin and flesh and * Job 10:11
his thighs are tightly * together. Job 40:17
of my body, and * them together in Ps 139:13
be encouraged and * together by Col 2:2

KNIVES
flint * for this purpose. Jos 5:2,3
themselves with * and swords until 1Ki 18:28
the poor with teeth as sharp as *! Pro 30:13,14
* and other implements were laid. Eze 40:42

KNOCK
he saw an Egyptian * a Hebrew to Ex 2:11
if her tooth is knocked out, * Ex 21:24
to your cities and * down your Deu 28:52
heavens and * God from his throne? Job 35:6
where they stand. * them into the Job 40:13
a storm of hail will * it down! Is 28:17
break open her granaries; * down Jer 50:26
and mighty winds will * it down. Eze 13:11
and they will * down your brothels Eze 16:39
I will * your weapons from your Eze 39:3
If a tooth gets knocked out, * Mt 5:38
Seek, and you will find. *, and Mt 7:7
If only you will *, the door will Mt 7:8
* and the door will be opened. Lk 11:9
to * down the devil's strongholds. 2Co 10:4

KNOCKED
* it out of joint at the socket. Gen 32:25
All the flax and barley were * Ex 9:31
if her tooth is * out, knock out Ex 21:24
altar of Baal was * apart, the idol Ju 6:28
It hit our tent and * it flat!" Ju 7:12,13
He also went to Penuel and * Ju 8:17
gate, but he was * down and 2Ki 7:17
down the obelisks, * down the 2Ki 18:4
temple of Baal and * it down, and 2Ch 23:15,16,17
up the altars and * down the 2Ch 23:15,16,17
in Jerusalem, and * down all the 2Ch 30:14
of Baal were * apart, the obelisks 2Ch 34:4
a few of them and * them around and Neh 13:25
If you are attacked and * down, Job 22:29
a fair trial. I * out the fangs of Job 29:17
They have * me to the ground. Ps 143:3
Because the Lord * him down Jer 46:15
But the Rock that * the statue Dan 2:35
his house * into a heap of rubble. Dan 3:29
him that his knees * together and Dan 5:6
and the buck goat * him down and Dan 8:7
If a tooth gets * out, knock out Mt 5:38
the merchants, and * over the Mt 21:12
buildings will be * down, with not Mt 24:2
customers, and * over the tables of Mk 11:15
As the boy was coming the demon * Lk 9:42
admiring will be * down, and not Lk 21:6
He * at the door in the gate, and Act 12:13
We get * down, but we get up 2Co 4:9

KNOCKING
paths of God—even * down the 2Ch 17:6
he was * at my bedroom door. Sol 5:2
if you keep * long enough he will Lk 11:8
Then if you stand outside *, and Lk 13:24,25
Meanwhile Peter continued *. Act 12:16
at the door and I am constantly *. Rev 3:20

KNOCKS
And if a master * out his Ex 21:27
door is opened to everyone who *. Lk 11:10
in the moment he arrives and *. Lk 12:36

KNOTTY
riddles, and solve * problems. Dan 5:12

KNOW
"How should I *?" Gen 4:9
Then I will *." Gen 18:21
he didn't * that anyone was there. Gen 19:35
"Yes, I *," the Lord replied. Gen 20:6
said, "for I * that God is first Gen 22:12
That is how I will *." Gen 24:14
so that he would * whether she Gen 24:21
When you tell me, then I'll * Gen 24:49
"Do you * a fellow there named Gen 29:5
be gone, for you * how fully I have Gen 30:26
Jacob replied, "You * how Gen 30:29
my flock, you will * that I have Gen 30:33
spoken to me. You * how hard I've Gen 31:6
For Jacob didn't * that Rachel Gen 31:32
I won't *, but God will see it. Gen 31:50
"I * what the dream means," Gen 40:12
then I'll * you are spies." Gen 42:16
In this way I will * whether you Gen 42:20
Of course they didn't * that Gen 42:23
Then I shall * whether you are Gen 42:34
"He wanted to * whether our Gen 43:7
How could we * that he was going Gen 43:7
"Didn't you * such a man as I Gen 44:15
a man as I would * who stole it?" Gen 44:15
a moment, for I * you can doom me Gen 44:18
said to us, 'You * that my wife had Gen 44:27
you again and * you are alive." Gen 46:30
But his father refused. "I * Gen 48:19
Literally, "who did not * Ex 1:8f
"But I * that the king of Egypt Ex 3:19
I don't even * whether they are Ex 4:18
I don't * Jehovah and I will not Ex 5:2
And they shall * that I am Ex 6:7
then you will * that there is no Ex 8:10
thus you will * that I am the Ex 8:22
your officials, I * that even yet Ex 9:30
Don't you * even yet that all Ex 10:7
God, and we do not * what he will Ex 10:26
Then you will * that Jehovah Ex 11:7
shall * that I am the Lord." Ex 14:4
And all Egypt shall * that I am Ex 14:18
* that I am Jehovah your God.' Ex 16:11,12
rescued Israel. I * now that the Ex 18:11
stand something you * is false. Ex 23:1
foreigners; you * what it's like to Ex 23:9
For I * that they will infect you Ex 23:33
* that I am the Lord their God. Ex 29:46
"You * these people and what a Ex 32:22
Literally, "You have said you * Ex 33:12f
us, who will ever * that I and my Ex 33:16
Literally, "I * you by name." Ex 33:17f
so that they would * how to offer Lev 7:38
In this way you will * whether Lev 14:57
they do not * what the man has Lev 20:4
that you won't * what to do with Lev 26:10
the people will * that they are to Num 10:3
pleaded, "for you * the ways of Num 10:31
Literally, "you * how we are to Num 10:31f
"They * full well the power you Num 14:13
above us, and they * that you lead Num 14:14
this you shall * that Jehovah has Num 16:28
then you will * that these men have Num 16:30
"You * our sad history, how our Num 20:14
for I * what fantastic blessings Num 22:5,6
bless, and I also * that those whom Num 22:5,6
And you * how he has cared for Deu 1:31
Now we * that a man may speak to Deu 5:24
If you wonder, 'How shall we * Deu 18:21
this is the way to *: If the Deu 18:22
If you don't * who the owner is, Deu 22:2
to generation.) I * now, even Deu 31:21
"For I * how rebellious and Deu 31:27
against them. I * that after my Deu 31:29
Oh, that they would * what they Deu 32:29
but I didn't * they were spies. Jos 2:4
and I don't * where they went. Jos 2:5
"I * perfectly well that your Jos 2:9
And we * what you did to Sihon Jos 2:10
all Israel will * that I am with Jos 3:7
Today you are going to * for Jos 3:10
do we * you don't live nearby? Jos 9:7
Lord demands to * why you are Jos 22:16
For you * that if you rebel today Jos 22:17,18
He knows (and let all Israel * it Jos 22:22,23
them, "Today we * that the Lord is Jos 22:31
around you, then * for a certainty Jos 23:13
"You * very well that God's Jos 23:14
might * war." Ju 3:1f
will * you are going to help me!" Ju 6:37
* why Israel was being attacked. Ju 11:12
so that they would * how to Ju 16:5
"I * the Lord will really bless Ju 17:13
asking, "Did you * about the Ju 20:12
"You must * I am only a Ru 2:10,11
"Yes, I *," Boaz replied, "and Ru 2:10,11
"and I also * about all the love Ru 2:10,11
I happen to * that he will be Ru 3:2
relative, "You * Naomi, who came Ru 4:3
let me * right away, for if you Ru 4:4
Literally, "did not yet * 1Sa 3:7f
Then, if it doesn't, you will * 1Sa 6:3
then you will * that it was God who 1Sa 6:9
then we will * that the plague 1Sa 6:9
to * and send you on your way. 1Sa 9:19
miracles. You * that it does not 1Sa 12:17
of? I * what a cocky brat you are; 1Sa 17:28
* that there is a God in Israel! 1Sa 17:46
wanted to * more about his family! 1Sa 17:55f
"I really don't *," Abner said. 1Sa 17:55
things, and I * he wouldn't hide 1Sa 20:2
"Of course you don't * about 1Sa 20:3
then I'll * that all is well. 1Sa 20:7
But if he is angry, then I'll * 1Sa 20:7
Then David asked, "How will I * 1Sa 20:10
* at once how he feels about you. 1Sa 20:12
then you will * that all is well 1Sa 20:21
"Do you think I don't * that you 1Sa 20:30
"We * where he is hiding," they 1Sa 23:19
for I * that he is very crafty. 1Sa 23:22
"You * that Saul has had all of 1Sa 28:9
"How do you * they are dead?" 2Sa 1:5
him get away? You * perfectly well 2Sa 3:24,25
For you * what I am like! 2Sa 7:20
Didn't they * there would be 2Sa 11:19,20,21
Don't do this to me! You * what a 2Sa 13:12
us peace again.' I * that you are 2Sa 14:17
"I want to * one thing," the 2Sa 14:18
you * everything that happens!" 2Sa 14:20
"At last I * that you like me! 2Sa 14:22
read, "you will * that Absalom has 2Sa 15:10
Let me * what happens in 2Sa 15:28
Then all Israel will * that you 2Sa 16:21
You * your father and his men; 2Sa 17:8
but I didn't * what was 2Sa 18:29
for I * very well how much I 2Sa 19:20
For as you * I am lame. 2Sa 19:26
But I * that you are as an angel 2Sa 19:27

(KNOW Con't)

* how many of them there are."	2Sa 24:2
Think this over and let me * what	2Sa 24:13
David doesn't even * about it?	1Ki 1:11
and you don't even * about it.	1Ki 1:18
instructions. You * that Joab	1Ki 2:5
You are a wise man and will *	1Ki 2:6
man, and you will * how to arrange	1Ki 2:9
my behalf (for I * he will do	1Ki 2:17
"You * I won't refuse you."	1Ki 2:20
who doesn't * his way around.	1Ki 3:7
people well and * the difference	1Ki 3:9
for as you *, no one in Israel	1Ki 5:6
for you * each heart.	1Ki 8:39
of the earth will * and fear your	1Ki 8:43
and all the earth will * that	1Ki 8:43
May people all over the earth *	1Ki 8:60
"Now I * for sure that you are a	1Ki 17:24
Answer me so these people will *	1Ki 18:37
Then at last you will * that I am	1Ki 20:13
* that I am indeed the Lord."	1Ki 20:28
to Ahab, "You * the vineyard	1Ki 21:15
'The Lord wants to * why you are	2Ki 1:6
Elisha, "Did you * that the Lord	2Ki 2:3
"Of course I * it."	2Ki 2:3
him, "Do you * that the Lord is	2Ki 2:5
"Of course I * it!"	2Ki 2:5
Naaman said, "I * at last that	2Ki 5:15
officers, "I * what has happened.	2Ki 7:12
The Syrians * we are starving, so	2Ki 7:12
Elisha replied, "I * the terrible	2Ki 8:12
"You * very well who he was and	2Ki 9:11
"The king wants to * whether you	2Ki 9:18
Jehu replied, "What do you *	2Ki 9:18
of the king to * whether their	2Ki 9:19
Jehu answered, "What do you *	2Ki 9:19
in Israel don't * the laws of the	2Ki 17:26
Jerusalem. You * perfectly well	2Ki 19:11
will * that you alone are God."	2Ki 19:19
grown. I * everything about you.	2Ki 19:27
I know everything about you. I *	2Ki 19:27
and I also * the evil things you	2Ki 19:27
What else can I say? You * that	1Ch 17:18
Think it over and let me * what	1Ch 21:12
Solomon, my son, get to * the	1Ch 28:9
It all belongs to you! I *, my	1Ch 29:17
you * the hearts of all mankind.	2Ch 6:30
and they too will * that this	2Ch 6:33
We don't * what to do, but we are	2Ch 20:12
"God wants to * why you are	2Ch 24:20
warning: "I * that God has	2Ch 25:16
But we wish you to * that if	Ez 4:13
and then let us * your pleasure	Ez 5:17
The city officials did not * I	Neh 2:16
But now I told them, "You * full	Neh 2:17
My reply was, "You * you are	Neh 6:8
curse the sea, who * how to rouse	Job 3:8f
Don't I * the difference between	Job 6:30
but yesterday and * so little;	Job 8:9
"Sure, I * all that.	Job 9:2
For I * that you will not hold me	Job 9:28
* full well I've not committed?	Job 10:4-7
Is it because you * no one can	Job 10:4-7
"Do you * the mind and purposes	Job 11:7
can you * in comparison?	Job 11:8
"Yes, I realize you *	Job 12:2
Well, I * a few things	Job 12:3
And who doesn't * these things	Job 12:3
"Who doesn't * that the Lord	Job 12:7,8,9
saying. I * as much as you do.	Job 13:2
You are doctors who don't * what	Job 13:4
"This is my case: I * that I am	Job 13:18
What do you * more than we do?	Job 15:9
"But as for me, I * that my	Job 19:25
And I * that after this body has	Job 19:26
"I * what you are going to say—	Job 21:27
down, you will * that there is	Job 22:29
their faces so no one will * them.	Job 24:14,15
* as much about him as I do;	Job 27:12
"MEN * HOW to mine silver and	Job 28:1
from stone. Men * how to put light	Job 28:3,4
"Men * how to obtain food from	Job 28:5
"They * how to find sapphires	Job 28:6
paw there. Men * how to tear apart	Job 28:9
things, they don't * where to find	Job 28:12
They not only don't * how to get	Job 28:13
And I * that your purpose for me	Job 30:23
upon a girl. I * full well that	Job 31:2,3
Or, 'We * not what evil we have	Job 34:32
that we cannot begin to * him.	Job 36:26
Do you * how God controls all	Job 37:15
Do you * why you become warm	Job 37:16,17
"You who think you * so much,	Job 37:19,20
For we are too dull to *!	Job 37:19,20
Tell me, if you * so much.	Job 38:4
Do you * how its dimensions were	Job 38:5
Tell me about it if you *!	Job 38:17,18
But of course you * all this!	Job 38:21
Do you * the laws of the	Job 38:33
"DO YOU * how mountain goats give	Job 39:1
Do you * how many months of	Job 39:2,3
"Do you * how a hawk soars and	Job 39:26
"I * that you can do anything	Job 42:2
I * you get no pleasure from	Ps 5:4
All those who * your mercy,	Ps 9:10
last they * they are but puny men.	Ps 9:20
"he'll never *!"	Ps 10:11
each evil act. You * what trouble	Ps 10:14
Lord, you * the hopes of humble	Ps 10:17
O Lord, we * that you will	Ps 12:7
Don't they really * any better?	Ps 14:4
and * that I have told the truth.	Ps 17:3
Because I * you will answer me, O	Ps 17:6
Even those I didn't * before come	Ps 18:43,44,45
But how can I ever * what sins	Ps 19:12
"God save the king"—I * he	Ps 20:6
me, my heart shall * no fear!	Ps 27:3
* some of those who were there.	Ps 35:15
Lord, you * all about it.	Ps 35:22
unfailing love on those who * you!	Ps 36:10
Lord, you * how I long for my	Ps 38:9
Help me to * that I am here for	Ps 39:4
about it, as you well *, O Lord.	Ps 40:9
pay them back! I * you are pleased	Ps 41:11
For I * that I shall again have	Ps 42:11
idols, would God not * it?	Ps 44:21
"Stand silent! * that I am God!	Ps 46:10
This one thing I *: God is for	Ps 56:9
even * the meaning of the word!	Ps 58:1
Then at last everyone will *	Ps 58:11
O God, you * so well how stupid I	Ps 69:5
I am, and you * all my sins.	Ps 69:5
brothers pretend they don't * me!	Ps 69:8
my enemies. You * how they talk	Ps 69:19
You see them all and * what each	Ps 69:19
he also * what you are doing?	Ps 94:10
I * that you will come and have	Ps 102:13
* how delightful they really are.	Ps 119:35
I *, O Lord, that your decisions	Ps 119:75,76,77
for them. You * this because	Ps 119:168
I don't pretend to "* it all."	Ps 131:1
I * the greatness of the	Ps 135:5
heart and * everything about me.	Ps 139:1
me. You * when I sit or stand.	Ps 139:2
When far away you * my every	Ps 139:2
Every moment, you * where I am.	Ps 139:3
where I am. You * what I am going	Ps 139:4
is marvelous—and how well I * it.	Ps 139:14
Search me, O God, and * my heart;	Ps 139:23
* that I am trying to help them.	Ps 141:6,7
and you alone * which way I ought	Ps 142:3
LISTEN TO ME, my son! I * what I	Pro 5:1
For she does not * the path to	Pro 5:6
someone you hardly *, guaranteeing	Pro 6:1
Be sure you * a person well	Pro 11:15
Only the person involved can *	Pro 14:10
A king rejoices in servants who *	Pro 14:35
contradicts what you * is right.	Pro 19:27
Do you * a hard-working man?	Pro 22:29
* it when they beat me up .	Pro 23:35
by saying you didn't * about it.	Pro 24:11,12
Don't you * that this good man,	Pro 24:15,16
interests closely. * the state of	Pro 27:23,24
a nation to * and keep his laws!	Pro 29:18
his son's name—if you * it?	Pro 30:4
How do you * it didn't exist long	Ecc 1:8-11
And I * this, that whatever God	Ecc 3:14
Who can * what will prove best	Ecc 6:12
for you don't * whether they were	Ecc 7:10
For you * how often you yourself	Ecc 7:21,22
he doesn't * is going to happen?	Ecc 8:6,7
and still lives, I * very well that	Ecc 8:12
For the living at least * that	Ecc 9:5
But the dead * nothing	Ecc 9:5
But who can really * what is	Ecc 10:14
for you never * which will	Ecc 11:6
King Solomon: "If you don't *, O	Sol 1:8
donkey and the ox—* their owner and	Is 1:3
you neither * nor care that I have	Is 5:13
still you won't * what they mean.'	Is 6:9
this child shall * (is old enough)	Is 7:15,16f
not * that it is I who sent him.	Is 10:7
their wits' ends to * what to do;	Is 19:3
Yes, they will * the Lord and	Is 19:21
"He doesn't * what is going	Is 29:15
return to God. I * the glorious	Is 31:7
He wants them to * that if you	Is 36:12
of the earth will * that you are	Is 37:20
But do you not yet * that it was	Is 37:26
But I * you well—your comings	Is 37:28
Don't you * by now that the	Is 40:28
chosen to * and to believe me and	Is 43:10
None that I * about!	Is 44:8
for their idols neither see nor *.	Is 44:9
and you will * that I am doing	Is 45:3
you by name when you didn't * me.	Is 45:4
though you don't * me, and all the	Is 45:5
west will * there is no other God.	Is 45:6
so that no one can * what I mean.	Is 45:19
you won't * where it comes from.	Is 47:11
new, for I * so well what traitors	Is 48:8
then you shall * I am the Lord.	Is 49:23
All the world shall * that I, the	Is 49:26
so that I may * what I should say	Is 50:4
will, and I * that I will triumph.	Is 50:7
Listen to me, you who * the right	Is 51:7
shall * the power in that name.	Is 52:6
* it was a person standing there.	Is 52:14,15
You don't * what true peace is,	Is 59:8
Yes, we * what sinners we are.	Is 59:12
we are. We * our disobedience;	Is 59:13
Lord our God. We * what rebels we	Is 59:13
need, and you will * at last and	Is 60:16
to do what you * I despise.	Is 65:12
they are doing; I * what they are	Is 66:18
They don't * the ways of God.	Jer 5:4
to them, for they * the ways of the	Jer 5:5
It will let you * when trouble	Jer 6:17
they don't even * how to blush!	Jer 8:12
That they truly * me, and	Jer 9:24
O Lord, I * it is not within the	Jer 10:23
I didn't * that they were	Jer 11:19
But as for me—Lord, you * my	Jer 12:3
* how much it longs for you.	Jer 12:3
Lord, you * how I have pled with	Jer 15:11
"Lord, you * it is for your sake	Jer 15:15
behold, I will cause them to *."	Jer 16:21f
No one can really * how bad it	Jer 17:9
Lord, you * all their murderous	Jer 18:23
For I * the plans I have for	Jer 29:11
lied in my name. I *, for I have	Jer 29:23
one another to * the Lord.	Jer 31:34
shall really * me then, says the	Jer 31:34
God, for as you * so well, we are	Jer 42:2
Therefore * for a certainty that	Jer 42:22
"Do you think the Lord didn't *	Jer 44:21
is very great. We * your loftiness,	Jer 48:29
haughty heart. I * her insolence,	Jer 48:30
they will at least * they have had	Eze 2:5
And all Israel will * that what I	Eze 5:13
Then at last you will * I am the	Eze 6:4-7
Then you will * I am the Lord."	Eze 6:14
and you shall * I am the Lord."	Eze 7:4
* that I, the Lord, am doing it.	Eze 7:8,9
Yes, I * it is, for I know	Eze 11:5
Yes, I know it is, for I *	Eze 11:5
and you will * I am the Lord.	Eze 11:10
and you will * I am the Lord—you	Eze 11:12
rebels who could * the truth if	Eze 12:2
then they shall * I am the Lord.	Eze 12:15
and they shall * I am the Lord."	Eze 12:16
and you shall * I am the Lord."	Eze 12:20
And you shall * I am the Lord.	Eze 13:9
and you shall * I am the Lord.	Eze 13:14
and you shall * I am the Lord.	Eze 13:21
and you shall * I am the Lord."	Eze 13:23
and you shall * I am the Lord.	Eze 14:8
are, and you will * it was right	Eze 14:22
and then you shall * I am the	Eze 15:7
You will * you don't deserve this	Eze 16:61
you, and you will * I am the Lord.	Eze 16:62
Then you will * that I, the Lord,	Eze 17:21
And everyone shall * that it is	Eze 17:24
in horror, and * that I alone am	Eze 20:26
"The Lord God wants to * whether	Eze 20:30
And when that happens, you will *	Eze 20:38
fathers, you will * I am the Lord.	Eze 20:42
you will * I am the Lord."	Eze 20:44
All the world shall * that it is	Eze 21:5
and you shall * I am the Lord."	Eze 22:16
heat, and you will * that I, the	Eze 22:22
you will * that I alone am God."	Eze 23:49
then you will * I am the Lord."	Eze 24:24
and they shall * I am the Lord."	Eze 24:27
Then you will * I am the Lord.	Eze 25:5
then you shall * I am the Lord.	Eze 25:7
and they shall * I am the Lord.	Eze 25:11
then they shall * I am the Lord."	Eze 25:17
Then they shall * I am the Lord.	Eze 26:6
All who * you are appalled at	Eze 28:19
all who see shall * I am the Lord.	Eze 28:22
Then you will * I am the Lord.	Eze 28:23
shall * I am the Lord their God."	Eze 28:26
all of you shall * I am the	Eze 29:6
* that I, the Lord, have done it.	Eze 29:9
Then Israel will * that I alone	Eze 29:16
and Egypt shall * I am the Lord."	Eze 29:21
And they will * I am the Lord	Eze 30:8
and they shall * I am the Lord."	Eze 30:19
Egypt shall * I am the Lord.	Eze 30:25
then they shall * I am the	Eze 30:26
* that I, the Lord, have done it.	Eze 32:15
then they shall * I am the Lord.	Eze 33:29
* a prophet has been among them."	Eze 33:33
they shall * I am the Lord.	Eze 34:27
In this way they will * that I,	Eze 34:30
then you shall * I am the Lord.	Eze 35:4,5
Then you shall * I am the Lord.	Eze 35:9
And you shall * that I have	Eze 35:12
And then you will * I am the	Eze 35:15
Then you shall * I am the Lord.	Eze 36:11
the world shall * I am the Lord.	Eze 36:23
still left—will * that I, the Lord,	Eze 36:36

KNOW Con't)
everyone will * I am the Lord." Eze 36:37,38
I replied, "Lord, you alone * the Eze 37:3
shall live and * I am the Lord." Eze 37:6
people, you will * I am the Lord. Eze 37:13
Then you will * that I, the Lord, Eze 37:14
the nations shall * that I, the Eze 37:28
the nations will * that I am God. Eze 38:15,16
I have done, and * that I am God! Eze 38:23
and they shall * I am the Lord. Eze 39:6
And the nations too shall * I am Eze 39:7
of Gog and * that I have done it. Eze 39:21
will * I am the Lord their God. Eze 39:22
And the nations will * why Eze 39:23
Then my people will * I am the Eze 39:28
tell him what he wants to *." Dan 2:24
person that I * this secret of your Dan 2:30
I want you all to * about the Dan 4:2
And now I * for sure that his Dan 4:3
I said, "I * that the spirit of Dan 4:9
do what you * is right; Dan 4:27
nor hear, nor * anything at all. Dan 5:23
He replied, "Do you * why I have Dan 10:20,21
But the people who * their God Dan 11:32
to learn will * what it means. Dan 12:10
you will really * me then as you Hos 1:20
because they don't * me, and it is Hos 4:6
for you yourselves refuse to * me; Hos 4:6
you, and you cannot * the Lord. Hos 5:4
Oh, that we might * the Lord! Hos 6:3
Let us press on to * him, and he Hos 6:3
your offerings—I want you to * me. Hos 6:6
strength, but they don't * it. Hos 7:9
Israel will * it all too well. Hos 9:7
But he doesn't * or even care Hos 11:3
and my love will * no bounds, for Hos 14:4
And you will * that I am here Joe 2:27
"Then you shall * at last that Joe 3:17
your sins. I * them all so well. Amo 5:12
For I * this terrible storm has Jon 1:12
children who don't * their right Jon 4:11f
are supposed to * right from wrong, Mic 3:1
But they do not * my thoughts Mic 4:12
one heeds—the wicked * no shame. Zep 3:5
Then you will * it was the Lord Zec 2:9
Then you will * it was the Lord Zec 2:11,12
"Don't you really *?" Zec 4:5
(Then you will * these messages Zec 4:9
"Don't you *?" Zec 4:13
And when this happens you will * Zec 6:15
for I * that God is with you.' Zec 8:23
Then at last you will * it was I Mal 2:4
sinful men * how to give good gifts Mt 7:11
will get well! I *, because I am Mt 8:8,9
And I * you have authority to Mt 8:8,9
and they didn't * what to do or Mt 9:36
son, and we * Mary his mother and Mt 13:55
But Jesus told her, "You don't * Mt 20:22
and demanded to * by whose Mt 21:23
finally replied, "We don't *!" Mt 21:27
"Sir, we * you are very honest and Mt 22:16
the reader: You * what is meant! Mt 24:15
you * that summer is almost here. Mt 24:32
to happen, you can * that my Mt 24:33
"So be prepared, for you don't * Mt 24:42
Literally, "I * you not!" Mt 25:12f
* the date or moment of my return. Mt 25:13
"As you *, the Passover Mt 26:2
"I don't even * what you are Mt 26:70
"I don't even * the man," he Mt 26:72
him and said, "We * you are one of Mt 26:73
"I don't even * the man," he Mt 26:74
he said. "I * you are looking Mt 28:5
us demons? I * who you are—the holy Mk 1:24
than before. You * better than to Mk 2:22
are permitted to * some truths Mk 4:11,12
them many things they needed to *. Mk 6:34
* what it means to really live. Mk 8:35
for he didn't * what else to say Mk 9:6
I tell you as seriously as I * Mk 10:15
But as for your question—you * Mk 10:19
But Jesus answered, "You don't * Mk 10:38
and said, "As you *, the kings and Mk 10:42
We don't *." Mk 11:33
spies said, "we * you tell the Mk 12:14
"What we want to * is this: Mk 12:23
is that you don't * the Scriptures, Mk 12:24
and don't * the power of God. Mk 12:24
And I * it is far more important Mk 12:33
you * that spring has come. Mk 13:28
And since you don't * when it Mk 13:33
Literally, "You do not * when the Mk 13:34f
For you do not * when I Mk 13:35,36,37
And they didn't * what to say. Mk 14:40
Judas had told them, "You will * Mk 14:44
"I don't * what you're talking Mk 14:68
"I don't even * this fellow you Mk 14:71
His parents didn't * what to Lk 2:48
don't accuse anyone of what you * Lk 3:14
to * whether or not John was he. Lk 3:15
You have come to destroy us. I * Lk 4:34
How can a student * more than Lk 6:40
will be healed! I *, because I am Lk 7:6,7,8
sent him, he would * what kind of Lk 7:39
has granted you to * the meaning of Lk 8:10
and grow. They * the message is Lk 8:13
But the disciples didn't * Lk 9:45
exclaimed, 'I *—I'll tear down my Lk 12:18
he will reply, 'I do not * you.' Lk 13:24,25
reply, 'I tell you, I don't * you. Lk 13:27
proud to beg. I * just the thing! Lk 16:4
For when I return, you will * it Lk 17:24
"But as to your question, you * Lk 18:20
you *, we are going to Jerusalem. Lk 18:31
They demanded to * by what Lk 20:2
they replied, "We don't *!" Lk 20:7
the owner asked himself. 'I *! Lk 20:13
They said to Jesus, "Sir, we * Lk 20:21
* of a family of seven brothers. Lk 20:29
then you will * that the time of Lk 21:20
When the leaves come out, you * Lk 21:30
delighted to * that he was ready to Lk 22:5
that you don't even * me." Lk 22:34
said, "I don't even * the man!" Lk 22:57
flatly stated, "I * this fellow is Lk 22:59
But Peter said, "Man, I don't * Lk 22:60
don't * what they are doing." Lk 23:34
I didn't * he was the one, but Jn 1:31
"I didn't * he was the one," Jn 1:33
"How do you * what I am like?" Jn 1:48
"Sir," he said, "we all * that Jn 3:1
We do not * on whom he will next Jn 3:8
I am telling you what I * and Jn 3:10,11
You yourselves * how plainly I Jn 3:28
But you Samaritans * so little Jn 4:21-24
while we Jews * all about him, for Jn 4:21-24
"Well, at least I * that the Jn 4:25
some food you don't * about." Jn 4:32
The man didn't *, and Jesus had Jn 5:13
to me, for as I * so well, you Jn 5:41,42
within you. I *, because I have Jn 5:43
whose father and mother we *. Jn 6:42
* you are the holy Son of God." Jn 6:69
"How can he * so much when he's Jn 7:15
you will certainly * whether my Jn 7:17
For we * where this man was born; Jn 7:27
one will * where he comes from." Jn 7:27
out, "Yes, you * me and where I Jn 7:28
one you don't *, and he is Truth. Jn 7:28
he is Truth. I * him because I was Jn 7:29
but what do they * about it? Jn 7:49
For I * where I came from and Jn 8:14
but you don't * this about me. Jn 8:14
Jesus answered, "You don't * who Jn 8:19
so you don't * who my Father is. Jn 8:19
If you knew me, then you would * Jn 8:19
to, and you will * the truth, and Jn 8:32
we * you are possessed by a demon. Jn 8:52
But you do not even * him. Jn 8:55
But it is true—I * him and fully Jn 8:55
"I don't *," he replied. Jn 9:12
His parents replied, "We * this Jn 9:20
but we don't * what happened to Jn 9:21
we * Jesus is an evil person." Jn 9:24
"I don't * whether he is good or Jn 9:25
replied, "but I * this: I was Jn 9:25
of Moses. We * God has spoken to Jn 9:29
we don't * anything about him." Jn 9:29
you don't * anything about him! Jn 9:30
you claim to * what you are doing. Jn 9:41
"I am the Good Shepherd and * my Jn 10:14
sheep, and they * me, just as my Jn 10:14
knows me and I * the Father; Jn 10:15
and I * them, and they follow me. Jn 10:27
too late, for I * that God will Jn 11:22
And I * his instructions lead to Jn 12:50
You * these things—now do them! Jn 13:17
* so well each one of you I chose. Jn 13:18
you will deny that you even * me! Jn 13:38
And you * where I am going and Jn 14:4
going, so how can we * the way?" Jn 14:5
From now on you * him—and have Jn 14:7
you even yet * who I am, Philip, Jn 14:9
again, you will * that I am in my Jn 14:20
will * that I love the Father. Jn 14:31
for they don't * God who sent me. Jn 15:21
We don't * what he means." Jn 16:17,18
Now we understand that you * Jn 16:30
Now they * that everything I Jn 17:7
and they accepted them and * of a Jn 17:8
the world will * you sent me and Jn 17:23
the world doesn't * you, but I do; Jn 17:25
and these disciples * you sent Jn 17:25
them here. They * what I said." Jn 18:21
don't * where they have put him!" Jn 20:2
don't * where they have put him." Jn 20:13
"Yes," Peter replied, "You * I Jn 21:15
"Yes, Lord," Peter said, "you * Jn 21:16
"Lord, you * my heart; Jn 21:17
you * I am," he said. Jn 21:17
Jesus said this to let him * Jn 21:19
And we all * that my account of Jn 21:24
"and they are not for you to *. Act 1:7
"O Lord," they said, "you * Act 1:24,25
in languages they didn't *, Act 2:4
through him, as you well *. Act 2:22
* the Lord is always with me. Act 2:25
For I * all will be well with me Act 2:26
you * how lame he was before. Act 3:16
they didn't * how to punish them Act 4:21
ability to * what is going on? Act 5:9
in the area we now * as Syria. Act 7:2f
for we don't * what has become of Act 7:40
Peter told them, "You * it is Act 10:28
And you no doubt * that Jesus of Act 10:38
you all * that God chose me from Act 15:7
"No," they replied, "we don't * Act 19:2
demon replied, "I * Jesus and I Act 19:15
and I * Paul, but who are you?" Act 19:15
As you * so well from what Act 19:26
didn't even * why they were there. Act 19:32
I won't * what to say." Act 19:40
them, "You men * that from the day Act 20:18
"And now I * that none of you Act 20:25
as overseers. I * full well that Act 20:29
clothing— you * that these hands Act 20:34
then said, "You *, dear brother, Act 21:20
"Then everyone will * that you Act 21:24
"Do you * Greek?" Act 21:37,38
* his will and to see the Messiah Act 22:14
'they certainly * that I imprisoned Act 22:19
"Don't let a soul * you told me Act 23:22
Paul began: "I *, sir, that you Act 24:10
You * very well I am not guilty. Act 25:10,11
before you, for I * you are an Act 26:3
If they would admit it, they * Act 26:5
But I * you do—" Act 26:27
the only thing we * about these Act 28:22
I want you to *, dear brothers, Rom 1:13
And we * that God, in justice, Rom 2:2
hearts they * right from wrong. Rom 2:12-15
* what is right but don't do it. Rom 2:12-15
* what to do, unless they do it. Rom 2:12-15
Yes, you * what he wants; Rom 2:18
what he wants; you * right from Rom 2:18
for you really * his laws, which Rom 2:20
than you Jews who * so much about Rom 2:27
that they could * and do his will Rom 3:2
For the more we * of God's laws, Rom 3:20
and trials for we * that they are Rom 5:3
what happens and * that all is Rom 5:5
is well, for we * how dearly God Rom 5:5
for all sinned. [We * that it Rom 5:13
with Christ, we * that you will Rom 6:8
Literally, "men who * (the) Rom 7:1f
to—what I hate. I * perfectly well Rom 7:16
I * I am rotten through and Rom 7:18
For we * that even the things of Rom 8:22
For we don't even * what we Rom 8:26
And we * that all that happens Rom 8:28
would * what he wanted you to do. Rom 9:4
might be saved. I * what Rom 10:2
As you *, God has appointed me as Rom 11:13
I want you to * about this truth Rom 11:25
For who among us can * the mind Rom 11:34
And don't think you * it all! Rom 12:16
just because you * you should. Rom 13:5
is this: you * how late it is; Rom 13:11
you * that what you do is right. Rom 14:16
You may * that there is nothing Rom 14:22
I * that you are wise and good, Rom 15:14
and that you * these things so well Rom 15:14
used others, but I * this: he has Rom 15:18
I * very well how foolish it 1Co 1:18
But we * about these things 1Co 2:10
No one can really * what anyone 1Co 2:11
And no one can * God's thoughts 1Co 2:11
never been one to * the Lord's 1Co 2:16
Then everyone will * why we have 1Co 4:5
I * that some of you will have 1Co 4:18
Don't you * that some day we 1Co 6:2
Don't you * that those doing such 1Co 6:9,10
And don't you * that if a man 1Co 6:16
might never come to * the Lord; 1Co 7:14
Well, we all * that an idol is 1Co 8:4
But we * that there is only one 1Co 8:6
for you * there is no harm in it. 1Co 8:10
So because you "* it is all 1Co 8:11
act as though I * it all and don't 1Co 9:22
Then you won't * whether or not 1Co 10:27
How can you * whether they are 1Co 12:3
else the power to * whether evil 1Co 12:10
and others, who do not * the 1Co 12:10
Now we * so little, even with 1Co 13:9
Now all that I * is hazy and 1Co 13:12
you the things I *, and what is 1Co 14:6
will the soldiers * that they are 1Co 14:8
how will he * what you mean? 1Co 14:9
but I don't * what I am saying. 1Co 14:14
they don't * what you are saying? 1Co 14:16
Or, "there are some who * nothing 1Co 15:34f
work, for you * that nothing you do 1Co 15:58
I think you ought to *, dear 2Co 1:8

(KNOW Con't)
And even though you don't * me 2Co 1:13,14
for we * what he is trying to do. 2Co 2:11
while to those who * Christ we are 2Co 2:16
Since we * that this new glory 2Co 3:12
truth, as all who * us will agree. 2Co 4:2
because we don't * why things 2Co 4:8
We * that the same God who 2Co 4:14
FOR WE * that when this tent we 2Co 5:1
with Jesus. We * these things are 2Co 5:7
deep within, you really * it too. 2Co 5:11
You * how full of love and 2Co 8:9
I want everyone else to * it too. 2Co 8:21
brother, whom we * from experience 2Co 8:22
For I * how eager you are to do 2Co 9:2
at least I * what I am talking 2Co 11:6
or just my spirit, for I don't *; 2Co 12:2,3
Since I * it is all for Christ's 2Co 12:10
You * what I was like when I Gal 1:13
didn't even * what I looked like. Gal 1:22
Jewish Christians * very well that Gal 2:16
For in those days I * you would Gal 4:15
I frankly don't * what to do. Gal 4:20
No doubt you already * that God Eph 3:2,3
to you how I * about these things. Eph 3:4
of it or fully * or understand it. Eph 3:18,19
I * this is hard to Eph 5:32
to let you * how we are and be Eph 6:22
And I want you to * this, dear Php 1:12
love me, for they * that the Lord Php 1:16,17
being glad, for I * that as you Php 1:19
* which is better, to live or die! Php 1:22
struggle now, as you * so well. Php 1:30
But you * Timothy. Php 2:22
you again, for I * how thankful you Php 2:28
only way to really * Christ and to Php 3:10
me again. I * you have always been Php 4:10
much or little. I * how to live on Php 4:12
As you well *, when I first Php 4:15
to * God better and better. Col 1:10
teaching them as well as we * how. Col 1:28
I WISH YOU could * how much I have Col 2:1
they say, and * you should. Col 2:18
* his will in everything you do. Col 4:12
We * that God has chosen you, 1Th 1:4
And you * how our very lives were 1Th 1:5
YOU YOURSELVES *, dear brothers, 1Th 2:1
visit was. You * how badly we had 1Th 2:2
as you very well *, and God knows 1Th 2:5
(But of course you * that such 1Th 3:2,3
here, now that we * you are 1Th 3:7
* that you remain strong in him. 1Th 3:8
You already * how to please God in 1Th 4:1
living, for you * the commands we 1Th 4:1
I want you to * what happens to a 1Th 4:13
brothers, for you * perfectly well 1Th 5:2
who do not wish to * God, and who 2Th 1:8
And you * what is keeping him 2Th 2:6
For you well * that you ought to 2Th 3:7
because I didn't * what I was 1Ti 1:13
I didn't * Christ at that time. 1Ti 1:13
everyone should * it, that Christ 1Ti 1:15
clear, doing what you * is right. 1Ti 1:19
awhile you will * what kind of men 1Ti 3:15
will * and do what is right. 1Ti 5:7
sin—don't * how to tell the truth; 1Ti 6:5
thing in life—they don't * God. 1Ti 6:21
I * how much you trust the Lord, 2Ti 1:5
or to let them * that I am your 2Ti 1:8
of it, for I * the one in whom I 2Ti 1:12
As you *, all the Christians who 2Ti 1:15
And you * better than I can tell 2Ti 1:18
* what his Word says and means. 2Ti 2:15
YOU MAY AS well * this too, 2Ti 3:1
But you * from watching me that I 2Ti 3:10
of person. You * what I believe and 2Ti 3:10
what I want. You * my faith in 2Ti 3:10
have suffered. You * my love for 2Ti 3:10
my patience. You * how many 2Ti 3:11
the Good News. You * about all that 2Ti 3:11
been taught. You * they are true 2Ti 3:14
You know they are true for you * 2Ti 3:14
taught you. You * how, when you 2Ti 3:15
to teach them to * God's truth—the Tit 1:1
Such persons claim they * God, Tit 1:16
against by those who * them. Tit 2:5
We all * he did not come as an Heb 2:16
We * he is ready and waiting Heb 4:4
life, and doesn't * much about the Heb 5:12,13
Holy Spirit, and * how good the Heb 6:5
now they can * without doubt that Heb 6:18
As we all *, Christ did not Heb 7:12,13,14
so that they will * what I want Heb 8:10
'You, too, should * the Lord,' Heb 8:11
and small, will * me already. Heb 8:11
they will always * my will, and I Heb 10:16
For we * him who said, "Justice Heb 10:30
By faith—by believing God—we * Heb 11:3
you * what they are going through. Heb 13:3
I want you to * that Brother Heb 13:23
If you want to * what God wants Jas 1:5
who should * better, do wrong, our Jas 3:1
How do you * what is going to Jas 4:14
prophets. We * how happy they are Jas 5:11
a great deal to * more about it. 1Pe 1:12
or silver, as you very well *. 1Pe 1:18
Then learn to * him better and 2Pe 1:2
For as you * him better, he will 2Pe 1:3
For then you must learn to * God 2Pe 1:5
though you already * them and are 2Pe 1:12
which they * so little about; 2Pe 2:12
facts you already *: facts you 2Pe 3:1
That is the way to * whether or 1Jn 2:5
and doesn't * where he is going, 1Jn 2:11
because you really * Christ, the 1Jn 2:13
have learned to * God our Father. 1Jn 2:13
And so I say to you fathers who * 1Jn 2:14
upon you, and you * the truth. 1Jn 2:20
those who need to * the truth, but 1Jn 2:21
Since we * that God is always 1Jn 2:29
But since most people don't * 1Jn 3:1
But we do * this, that when he 1Jn 3:2
And you * that he became a man 1Jn 3:5
and you * that no one wanting to 1Jn 3:15
life within. We * what real love 1Jn 3:16
Then we will * for sure, by our 1Jn 3:19
he with them. We * this is true 1Jn 3:24
That is another way to * whether 1Jn 4:6
they are getting to * him better. 1Jn 4:7
he doesn't * God—for God is love. 1Jn 4:8
We * how much God loves us 1Jn 4:16
And we * he is, because God said 1Jn 5:6,7,8
All who believe this * in their 1Jn 5:10
you may * you have eternal life. 1Jn 5:13
And if we really * he is 1Jn 5:15
hands on him. We * that we are 1Jn 5:19
And we * that Christ, God's Son, 1Jn 5:20
is as healthy as I * your soul is. 3Jn 1:2
him, and you * I speak the truth. 3Jn 1:12
fact—which you * already—that the Jud 1:5
"He says to you: I * how many Rev 2:2
your patience; I * you don't Rev 2:2
"I * how much you suffer for the Rev 2:9
the Lord, and I * all about your Rev 2:9
riches!). I * the slander of those Rev 2:9
also I * your love and faith and Rev 2:19
And all the churches shall * that Rev 2:23
"I * your reputation as a live Rev 3:1
"I * you well; Rev 3:8
"I * you well—you are neither Rev 3:15
asked me, "Do you * who these are, Rev 7:13

KNOW-IT-ALL
But although being a "*" makes 1Co 8:1

KNOWING
become as we are, * good from bad, Gen 3:22
There is no way of * the value 2Sa 18:11f
speak of * something about it! Job 28:22
my calamity, * full well that I Job 30:13
you and * all is well between us. Ps 17:15
Have two goals: wisdom—that is, * Pro 3:21
not * the fate awaiting it there. Pro 7:23
to all wisdom. * God results in Pro 9:10
—to decide before * the facts! Pro 18:13
the sun or even * its existence, Ecc 6:5
planning, or *, or understanding. Ecc 9:10
our husbands * it and helping us? Jer 44:19
ground without your Father * it. Mt 10:29
And Herod respected John, * that Mk 6:20
and not even * what he was saying, Lk 9:33
was now wine, not * where it had Jn 2:9
on me without * the facts. Jn 8:15
eternal life—by * you, the only Jn 17:3
came in, not * what had happened. Act 5:7
him without * who he is, and now I Act 17:23
not * what awaits me, except Act 20:22
You are so proud of * God's laws, Rom 2:23
sin's grasp by * the commandments Rom 8:3
of these points, * that all you Rom 15:15,16
for the gift of * what he has said, 1Co 14:13
gain of * Christ Jesus my Lord. Php 3:8
rich experience of * Christ with Col 2:2
they must be sensible, * and Tit 2:2
Then, * what lies ahead for you, Heb 6:12
the Savior after * the truth of Heb 10:26
taken from you, * that better Heb 10:34
Away he went, not even * where he Heb 11:8
Remember, too, that * what is Jas 4:17
the Gospel without * what it can do 1Pe 2:15
* that he has little time." Rev 12:12

KNOWLEDGE
giving * of Good and Bad. Gen 2:9
of an explosion of *, nipped in the Gen 11:6f
and wrong use of the * gained. Gen 11:6f
And has * from the Most High; Num 24:15-19
Has this been done with your *? 1Ki 1:27
Now give me wisdom and * to rule 2Ch 1:10
but for wisdom and * to properly 2Ch 1:11
the wisdom and * you asked for! 2Ch 1:12
for I am a man of well-rounded *. Job 36:4
me good judgment as well as *. Ps 119:66
given you, and * of God himself; Pro 2:3,4,5
His every word is a treasure of * Pro 2:6
*, and the skies poured down rain. Pro 3:20
to discover * and understanding. Pro 8:12
A wise man doesn't display his *, Pro 12:23
the wise man is crowned with *. Pro 14:18
of hell are open to God's *. Pro 15:11
Literally, "*." Pro 23:12f
I have greater wisdom and *." Ecc 1:16-18
to increase * only increases Ecc 1:16-18
for wisdom, *, and skill, I must Ecc 2:20-23
who please him wisdom, *, and joy; Ecc 2:24-26
* of God's truth on these points! Ecc 9:5f
* of God's truth on these points! Ecc 9:5f
* of God's truth on these points! Ecc 9:10f
the Spirit of * and of the fear Is 11:2
be full of the * of the Lord. Is 11:9
and * and reverence for God. Is 33:6
Your "wisdom" and "*" have Is 47:10
But foolish men without * of God Jer 10:14
their backs to all * of God. Eze 16:3f
with divine * and understanding. Dan 5:12
no * of God in your land. Hos 4:1
flow with the * of God so the Mal 2:7
Men go by you with no * of the Lk 11:44
"having more accurate *." Act 24:22f
God has put this * in their Rom 1:19
which are full of all * and truth. Rom 2:20
How great are his wisdom and * Rom 11:33
is the one who is open to God's *. 1Co 8:3
*—these gifts will disappear. 1Co 13:8
And do you think that the * of 1Co 14:36
in spiritual * and insight, for I Php 1:9
treasures of wisdom and *. Col 2:3
boast of their "*" and thus prove 1Ti 6:20
in the eternal plan and * of God. Rev 13:8f

KNOWN
his deed was *, he was frightened. Ex 2:14
The exact measure is not *. Ex 16:16f
And the food became * as Ex 16:31
made * my will to you from heaven. Ex 20:22
unless the ox was * to gore people Ex 21:29
But if the ox was * from past Ex 21:36
The exact weight is not *. Ex 25:39f
to all who are * as experts, so Ex 31:6
Ever after, the area was * as Num 11:3
Babylon were also * as Cush, so it Num 12:1f
Then they came to what is now * Num 13:23
Villages') as it is still * today. Deu 3:14
*, gods made of wood and stone! Deu 28:64
who have not * these laws will hear Deu 31:13
its men were * as hard fighters. Jos 10:2
Kiriath-baal (also * as Jos 15:48-62
Baalath-beer (also * as Jos 19:8
and Kiriath-arba (also * as Jos 20:7
Bethel, formerly * as Luz, and the Ju 1:22,23
Luz, too, as it is still * today. Ju 1:26
Oreb was killed at the rock now * Ju 7:25
"Don't let it be * that a woman Ru 3:14
also * as "God's Hill," where the 1Sa 10:5
The place has been * ever since 2Sa 2:16
as it is still * today. 2Sa 18:18
* also as Adino, the Eznite. 2Sa 23:8
pieces was not * because they were 1Ki 7:47
(And they are still * as "The 1Ki 9:13
Then Omri bought the hill now * 1Ki 16:24
Also * as "Uzziah." 2Ki 14:21f
was Abram (later * as Abraham). 1Ch 1:24-27
Also * as Jehoiachin or Coniah. 1Ch 3:16f
These were * as the Zorathite 1Ch 4:2
of Assyria (also * as 1Ch 5:26
the place has been * as 1Ch 14:11
City of David, also * as Zion, 2Ch 5:2
province, and made * to all your Est 3:14
Literally, "had made * how they Est 8:1f
and his fame was * throughout all Est 9:4
Have you ever * a truly good and Job 4:7,8
Will long searching make them * Job 11:7
who have never * anything good. Job 21:25
meanings of these words are not *. Ps 9:16f
you are * as the helper of the Ps 10:14
Turn from all * sin and spend Ps 34:14
has made himself * in her palaces Ps 48:3f
Your name is * throughout the Ps 48:10
I have * from earliest days that Ps 119:152
everything I do is * to you. Ps 119:168
your fame is * to every Ps 135:13
He has made * his laws and Ps 147:19
they have not * his commands. Ps 147:20
A good man is * by his Pro 12:17
The wise man is * by his common Pro 16:21
a child can be * by the way he Pro 20:11
A man is * by his actions. Pro 21:8
Her husband is well *, for he Pro 31:23
it was * long ago what each man Ecc 6:10
as has not been * since the Is 7:17
Jeberechiah, both * as honest men, Is 8:2
* his praise around the world. Is 12:5
make himself * to the Egyptians. Is 19:21
One generation makes * your Is 38:19
and you will be * as "The People Is 58:12
For the Holy One of Israel, * Is 60:9

(KNOWN Con't)
Their descendants shall be * and Is 61:9
Jerusalem will be * as the throne Jer 3:17
we are * as your people. Jer 14:9
be * that he really is from God." Jer 28:9
as they have never * before. Jer 30:7
any of your fathers have ever *. Jer 44:2,3
Her name was * to every woman in Eze 23:10
A region in ancient Cilicia * from Eze 27:11f
"Thus I will make * my holy name Eze 39:7
and the Father is * only by the Son Mt 11:27
But if you had * the meaning of Mt 12:7
Then they went out to an area * Mt 27:33
warned them not to make him *. Mk 3:12
more they made it *, for they were Mk 7:36
must first be made * in every Mk 13:10
was * for wisdom beyond his years; Lk 2:40
Jesus was * as the son of Lk 3:23-38
Soon he became well * throughout Lk 4:14
will be widely * and honored. Lk 21:13
also * as the Sea of Tiberias. Jn 6:1
of the Temple * as the Treasury. Jn 8:20
the section * as Solomon's Hall. Jn 10:22,23
If you had * who I am, then you Jn 14:7
you would have * who my Father is. Jn 14:7
have never * the Father or me. Jn 16:3
I teach is widely *, for I have Jn 18:20
cross to the place * as "The Jn 19:17
Temple in the area * as Solomon's Act 5:12
Paul is also * as Saul. Act 7:58f
to city, making * the decision Act 16:4
He is a ringleader of the sect * Act 24:5
is becoming * around the world. Rom 1:8
For the truth about God is * to Rom 1:19
God made, and have * of his Rom 1:20
they have never * what it is to Rom 3:17
I would never have * the sin in Rom 7:7
will become * and recognized! 1Co 11:19
all and have never really * God. 1Co 15:34
ignores us, but we are * to God; 2Co 6:9
and John, who were * as the pillars Gal 2:7,8,9
help in making * the Good News Php 1:5
who have never * me personally. Col 2:1
at last made *, is Christ himself. Col 2:2
aren't * until long afterward. 1Ti 5:25
will be well * to everyone, as was 2Ti 3:9
if he had never * about Christ at 2Pe 2:21
never really * him or become his. 1Jn 3:6
Her businessmen were * around the Rev 18:23

KNOWS
"You'll not die! God * very Gen 3:5
what he * about a crime is guilty. Lev 5:1
but no one * the exact place. Deu 34:6
the Lord. He * (and let all Israel Jos 22:22,23
* what a wonderful person you are. Ru 3:11
The Lord * what you have done, 1Sa 2:3
"Your father * perfectly well 1Sa 20:3
men who come from God * where." 1Sa 25:11f
to wander with us, who * where? 2Sa 15:19,20
for all Israel * what a mighty 2Sa 17:10
you away, who * where, and when 1Ki 18:12
understands and * every thought. 1Ch 28:9
and iron, and * all about 2Ch 2:14
"All the world * that anyone, Est 4:11
for he * everything you've done. Job 11:6
For he * perfectly all the Job 11:11
Ask the dumbest beast—he * that Job 12:7,8,9
He alone * what we should do; Job 12:13
He never * it if his sons are Job 14:20,21
face disaster, but he * it not. Job 14:20,21
But he * every detail of what is Job 23:10
And God surely * where it is to Job 28:23,24
the lightning. He * where wisdom Job 28:27
deceived— but God * that I am Job 31:6
Surely everyone * that God Job 34:10
This he *, for he watches my Ps 18:24
he * their judgment day is coming. Ps 37:12,13
Literally, "* the days of the Ps 37:18f
and fair and * right from wrong. Ps 37:30,31
Yes, he * the secrets of every Ps 44:21
* what a merciful God you are. Ps 52:9
punish you? He * everything—doesn't Ps 94:10
For he * we are but dust, and Ps 103:14
The man who * right from wrong Pro 3:13,14,15
for wisdom * where to discover Pro 8:12
a fool blurts out everything he *; Pro 10:14
everyone * his reputation." Pro 11:9f
He * that anger causes mistakes. Pro 14:29
For God, who * all hearts, knows Pro 24:11,12
For God, who knows all hearts, * Pro 24:11,12
knows yours, and he * you knew! Pro 24:11,12
and who * where it all will end? Pro 24:21,22
The good man * the poor man's Pro 29:7
For he * the consequence but does Pro 29:24
For who * the future? Ecc 6:12
who says he * everything, doesn't! Ecc 8:16,17
no one * whether he will favor Ecc 9:1
A man never * when he is going Ecc 9:12
A fool * all about the future Ecc 10:14
and * right from wrong, the two Is 7:15,16
of his land? He * just what to do, Is 28:26
Who else * the weight of all the Is 40:12
that Israel * is getting caught. Jer 2:26,27
The stork * the time of her Jer 8:7
Only the Lord *! Jer 17:10
O Lord of Hosts, who * those who Jer 20:12
who * what God will do to us!" Jer 26:19
who * what they will do to me?" Jer 38:19
understanding. He * all hidden Dan 2:22
everyone * that it is yours. Dan 9:18
Who *? Joe 2:14
winds, and * your every thought; Amo 4:13
And he * everyone who trusts in Nah 1:7
Only the Lord * how! Zec 14:7
And your Father who * all Mt 6:4
* your secrets, will reward you. Mt 6:6
Remember, your Father * exactly Mt 6:7,8
your Father who * every secret. Mt 6:18
Father already * perfectly well Mt 6:31,32
Only the Father * the Son, and Mt 11:27
But no one * the date and hour Mt 24:36
Only the Father *. Mt 24:36
* the day or hour when these Mk 13:32
only the Father *. Mk 13:32
and no one really * the Son Lk 10:22
and no one really * the Father Lk 10:22
And he * the number of hairs on Lk 12:7
your heavenly Father * your needs. Lk 12:30
but God * your evil hearts. Lk 16:15
Father * me and I know the Father; Jn 10:15
and he * what he says is true, Jn 19:35f
everybody in Jerusalem * about it. Act 4:16
God, who * men's hearts, Act 15:8
* that Ephesus is the center Act 19:35
And King Agrippa * about these Act 26:26
God * how often I pray for you. Rom 1:9
And the Father who * all hearts Rom 8:27
knows all hearts *, of course, what Rom 8:27
Christ * and the Holy Spirit Rom 9:1
the Holy Spirit * that it is no Rom 9:1
of the Lord? Who * enough to be his Rom 11:34
sin by doing what he * is right. Rom 14:22
But everyone * that you stand Rom 16:19
told that the Lord * full well how 1Co 3:20
If anyone thinks he * all the 1Co 8:2
to win others. God * our hearts, 2Co 5:11
large gift. God * we are honest, 2Co 8:21
Because I don't love you? God * I 2Co 11:11
and ever, * I tell the truth. 2Co 11:31
understands us and * what is best Eph 1:8
Only God * how deep is my love Php 1:8
at the barracks, * that I am in Php 1:13
well know, and God * we were not 1Th 2:5
know perfectly well that no one *. 1Th 5:2
sinful lives and everyone * it. 1Ti 5:24
In the same way, everyone * how 1Ti 5:25
on it: "The Lord * those who are 2Ti 2:19
way they act, one * they don't. Tit 1:16
He is sinning, and he * it. Tit 3:11
and temptation, he * what it is Heb 2:18
He * about everyone, everywhere. Heb 4:13
and as everyone *, a person who Heb 7:7
for he * everything we do. 1Jn 3:20
* except the one receiving it. Rev 2:17

KOA
from Pekod and Shoa and *; Eze 23:23

KOHATH
Levi and his sons: Gershon, *, Gen 46:8-14
Gershon, *, Merari. Ex 6:16
The sons of *:Amram, Ex 6:18
(* lived 133 years. Ex 6:18
Levi's son * Num 3:25-30
* division of the Levite tribe. Num 4:1
the clan of * shall come and carry Num 4:15
the sacred work of the sons of *. Num 4:15
families of * destroy themselves! Num 4:17,18,19
a census of the * division, Num 4:34
was given to the * division, for Num 7:9
Izhar, grandson of *, and a Num 16:1
named after their ancestor *. Num 26:57
the wife of Amram, son of *. Num 26:58,59
the priests of the * division (of Jos 21:4
The other families of the Jos 21:5
of the * division of the Levites. Jos 21:9-16
The other families of the * Jos 21:20,21,22
of the * division was ten. Jos 21:26
Gershom, *, Merari. 1Ch 6:1
Gershom, *, Merari. 1Ch 6:16
The sons of * were:Amram, Izhar, 1Ch 6:18
In the * clan: 1Ch 6:22,23,24
the Cantor was from the clan of *; 1Ch 6:33-38
Korah, Izhar, *, Levi, Israel. 1Ch 6:33-38
whom were members of the * clan: 1Ch 6:54
descendants of *, and they received 1Ch 6:61
pasturelands to the subclans of *: 1Ch 6:66-69
Some members of the * clan were 1Ch 9:32
120 from the clan of *; 1Ch 15:4-10
* division and the 1Ch 23:6
The division of * was subdivided 1Ch 23:12
Then the Levites of the * clan 2Ch 20:19
From the * clan, Mahath (son of 2Ch 29:12,13,14
of the subclan of *, were the 2Ch 34:12

KOHATH'S
* sons were: 1Ch 6:2

KOHATHITES
Next came the * carrying the Num 10:21
The *, named after their ancestor Num 26:57
* by the half-tribe of Manasseh: 1Ch 6:70

KOLAIAH
of Pedaiah, son of *, son of Neh 11:7,8,9
Ahab (son of *) and Zedekiah (son Jer 29:21

KORAH
sons named Jeush, Jalam, and *. Gen 36:5
Kenaz,The clan of *,The clan of Gen 36:15,16
clan of Jalam,The clan of *. Gen 36:18,19
The sons of Izhar:*, Nepheg, Ex 6:21
The sons of *:Assir, Elkanah, Ex 6:24
the families within the clan of *. Ex 6:24
ONE DAY * (son of Izhar, grandson Num 16:1
Then he said to * and to those Num 16:5
Do this: You, *, and all those Num 16:6,7
Then Moses spoke again to *: Num 16:8,9
And Moses said to *, "Come here Num 16:16
Meanwhile, * had stirred up the Num 16:19
tents of *, Dathan, and Abiram." Num 16:23,24
tents of *, Dathan, and Abiram. Num 16:27
happened to * and his associates. Num 16:40
had died the previous day with *). Num 16:49
who conspired with * against Moses Num 26:5-11
Reuel, Jeush, Jalam, and *. 1Ch 1:35
The sons of Hebron: *, Tappuah, 1Ch 2:43
Amminadab, *, Assir, 1Ch 6:22,23,24
*, Izhar, Kohath, Levi, Israel. 1Ch 6:33-38
through Kore and Ebiasaph to *. 1Ch 9:19
the Asaph division of the * clan. 1Ch 26:1
from the clans of * and Merari. 1Ch 26:19
clan and the * clan stood to praise 2Ch 20:19
and like *, they have disobeyed Jud 1:11

KORAH'S
who perished in * revolt against Num 27:3,4

KORAHITE
son of Shallum the *) was entrusted 1Ch 9:31

KORAHITES
Mahlites, the Mushites,The *. Num 26:58,59
He and his close relatives the * 1Ch 9:19
Azarel, Jo-ezer, Jashobe-am—all *; 1Ch 12:3-7

KORE
through * and Ebiasaph to Korah. 1Ch 9:19
was Meshelemiah, the son of *. 1Ch 26:1
* (son of Imnah, the Levite), who 2Ch 31:14,15

KOSHER
don't eat any food that isn't *. Ju 13:4
food that isn't *, for the baby is Ju 13:7
or eat anything that isn't *." Ju 13:13,14
that every kind of food is *. Mk 7:19
If he says something is *, then Act 10:15

KOZ
* was the father of Anub and 1Ch 4:8

KUSHAIAH
and Ethan (son of *) from the clan 1Ch 15:17

LAADAH
* (the father of Mareshah), 1Ch 4:21-22

LABAN
and when her brother * saw the Gen 24:29,30
So the man went home with *, and Gen 24:32
with Laban, and * gave him straw to Gen 24:32
"All right," * said, "tell us Gen 24:33
Then * and Bethuel replied, "The Gen 24:50
from Paddam-aram, sister of *. Gen 25:20
"Flee to your Uncle * in Haran. Gen 27:43
to visit his Uncle *, his mother's Gen 28:5
there named *, the son of Nahor?" Gen 29:5
told her father, *, and as soon as Gen 29:12,13
flesh and blood," * exclaimed. Gen 29:14
about a month, * said to him one Gen 29:15
Now * had two daughters, Leah, Gen 29:16
"Agreed!" * replied. Gen 29:19
my contract," Jacob said to *. Gen 29:21
So * invited all the men of the Gen 29:22
when it was dark, * took Leah to Gen 29:23
(And * gave to Leah a servant Gen 29:24
Jacob raged at *. Gen 29:25
her sister," * replied smoothly. Gen 29:26
Then * gave him Rachel, too. Gen 29:28
Rachel, too. And * gave to Rachel Gen 29:29
to *, "I want to go back home. Gen 30:25
"Please don't leave me," * Gen 30:27
"What wages do you want?" * Gen 30:31,32
"All right!" * replied. Gen 30:34
So that very day * went out and Gen 30:35,36
'For I have seen all that * has Gen 31:12
So one day while * was out Gen 31:17-20
without telling * his intentions. Gen 31:17-20
of Gilead. * didn't learn of their Gen 31:22
That night God appeared to * in Gen 31:24
curse him." * finally caught up Gen 31:25
top of a ridge; *, meanwhile, Gen 31:25
off like this?" * demanded. Gen 31:26
* went first into Jacob's tent to Gen 31:33
So although * searched the tents Gen 31:34
Now Jacob got mad at *. Gen 31:36,37
* replied, "These women are my Gen 31:43
and Jacob and * ate together beside Gen 31:46

(LABAN Con't)
* said. So it was also Gen 31:47,48
(Mizpah). For * said, "May the Gen 31:49
This heap," * continued, Gen 31:51,52
on the mountain. * was up early Gen 31:55
I have been living with Uncle * Gen 32:4
given to Leah by her father, *. Gen 46:18
given to Rachel by her father, *: Gen 46:23,24,25
Tophel, *, Hazeroth, and Dizahab. Deu 1:1

LABAN'S
* daughters. Gen 28:2
stayed and cared for * flock. Gen 30:35,36
out the ewes from * flock and Gen 30:39,40
Thus he built his flocks from *. Gen 30:39,40
So the less healthy lambs were * Gen 30:42
BUT JACOB LEARNED that * sons Gen 31:1
cooling in * attitude towards him. Gen 31:2
in * language, and "Galeed" in Gen 31:47,48

LABEL
I must * them "Impure, Rejected Jer 6:30

LABOR
dead, her * pains suddenly began. 1Sa 4:19
city and made them * with saws, 2Sa 12:31
of the forced * battalions, and 2Sa 20:24
superintendent of this * camp. 1Ki 5:14
Solomon had conscripted forced * 1Ki 9:15
Solomon conscripted his * forces 1Ki 9:20,21
were overseers of the * forces. 1Ki 9:23
in charge of his * battalions from 1Ki 11:27,28
that he made them * with saws or 1Ch 20:3f
to draft forced * from the other 2Ch 10:18
hard * shall repay his debts. Job 20:10
is why he broke them with hard *; Ps 107:12
work, yet they * hard all summer, Pro 6:8
pangs, like those of a woman in *. Is 13:8
woman is in heavy * trying to give Is 37:3
your great palace with forced *. Jer 22:13
as of a woman in *. Jer 22:23
their sides like women in *?" Jer 30:6
disappear like that of women in *. Jer 49:22
gripped her as they do women in *. Jer 49:24
like the pangs of a woman in *. Jer 50:43
has gripped you like a woman in *. Mic 4:9
I rewarded all your * with rust Hag 2:16,17
the payment for a day's *; Mt 20:2f
that of a woman in * when her child Jn 16:21
of her *, awaiting her delivery. Rev 12:2

LABORERS
while others will be slave *; 1Sa 8:12
thirty thousand * from all over 1Ki 5:13
additional *, eighty thousand 1Ki 5:15
of the * on the king's estates. 1Ch 27:26
a force of 70,000 *, 80,000 2Ch 2:2
He indentured 70,000 as common * 2Ch 2:18
as slave * the Hittites, Amorites, 2Ch 8:7,8
the unskilled * who carried in the 2Ch 34:13
And the masons and * worked with Neh 4:17
to send out more * to help you, for Lk 10:2

LABORS
all. His * shall not be rewarded; Job 20:18
an evil plot, * with its dark Ps 7:14
my only reward for all my *. Ecc 2:10
*, for these are gifts from God. Ecc 3:13

LABWEH
toward Hethlon, then on through * Eze 47:15
Hethlon, then to *, and then on to Eze 48:1

LACHISH
King Japhia of *, Jos 10:3
Hebron, Jarmuth, *, and Eglon. Jos 10:22,23
From Libnah they went to * and Jos 10:31
During the attack on *, King Jos 10:33
day and, as at *, they killed Jos 10:34,35
The king of *; Jos 12:8-24
Mizpeh, Jokthe-el, *, Bozkath, Jos 15:37-44
in Jerusalem, and he fled to *; 2Ki 14:19
Assyria at *: "I have done wrong. 2Ki 18:14
of staff from * with a great army; 2Ki 18:17
received word that he had left *). 2Ki 19:8
Adoraim, *, Azekah, 2Ch 11:5-10
and how he fled to *—but they went 2Ch 25:27
the city of *, sent ambassadors 2Ch 32:9
surrounding villages), * Neh 11:25-30
a great army from * to confer with Is 36:2
left * and was besieging Libnah. Is 37:8,9
Jerusalem, * and Azekah—the only Jer 34:7
flee, O people of *, for you were Mic 1:13

LACK
Will you destroy the city for * Gen 18:28
who gathered little had no *! Ex 16:18
as dry as dust for * of rain, and Deu 28:24
"What do you * here? 1Ki 11:22
because of their * of good sense. Job 36:12
Lord will never * any good thing. Ps 34:10
is destroyed by * of common sense. Pro 10:21
Fire goes out for * of fuel, and Pro 26:20
The fishermen will weep for * of Is 19:8
parched and cracked for * of rain; Jer 14:4
I will cause the people to * Eze 4:17
"You * only one thing," he told Mk 10:21
and died for * of moisture. Lk 8:6
The man wanted to justify (his * Lk 10:29
"There is still one thing you * Lk 18:22
of their * of self-control. 1Co 7:5
not because of any * of love on my 2Co 6:12
and thus prove their * of it. 1Ti 6:20

LACKED
and you have * nothing in all Deu 2:7
they * nothing in all that time. Neh 9:21

LACKING
superfluous or * in its body parts, Lev 22:23
is plentiful, and nothing is *; Deu 8:9
lad, a young man * common sense, Pro 7:7
A beautiful woman * discretion Pro 11:22

LAD
canteen and gave the * a drink. Gen 21:19
men, "and the * and I will travel Gen 22:5
don't hurt the * in any way," Gen 22:12
father, "Send the * with me and we Gen 43:8
But we said to you, 'Sir, the * Gen 44:22
my father and the * is not with Gen 44:30
that I would take care of the *. Gen 44:32
instead of the *, and let the lad Gen 44:33
the * return with his brothers. Gen 44:33
my father if the * is not with me? Gen 44:34
But the boy was only a * and was Ju 8:20
service from the time he was a *. 1Sa 12:2
Jonathan and the * killed them 1Sa 14:13
Then I'll send a * to bring the 1Sa 20:21
a simple-minded *, a young man Pro 7:7
a shame to see a * who sleeps away Pro 10:5
happy, but a * who hangs around Pro 29:3
Such a * could come from prison Ecc 4:14
they traded a young * for a Joe 3:3
a strong, robust *, and was known Lk 2:40
He asked them when the * had Jn 4:52
is it you want to tell me, *?" Act 23:19

LAD'S
Then God answered the * cries, Gen 21:17
For God has heard the * cries as Gen 21:17
is bound up in the * life— when he Gen 44:30

LADAN
*, the father of 1Ch 7:25,26,27
* and 1Ch 23:7
after the sons of *: Jehiel the 1Ch 23:8,9
These men of the * subclan from 1Ch 26:20,21,22

LADDER
Literally, "*." Gen 28:12f

LADDERS
Use them for the siege [to make * Deu 20:20

LADDIE
bearers stopped. "*," he said, Lk 7:14

LADEN
of fruit trees * with fruit, and Lev 23:40
and camels * down with treasure to Is 30:6

LADIES-IN-WAITING
But her *—and she Ju 5:29

LADS
good-looking *," he said; Dan 1:3,4
I killed your * in war and drove Amo 4:10

LADY
"Congratulations, favored *! Lk 1:28

LAEL
Elisaph (son of *) Num 3:16-24

LAGGING
and weary and * behind, with no Deu 25:18

LAHAD
the ancestor of Ahumai and *. 1Ch 4:2

LAHMAM
Eglon, Cabbon, *, Chitlish, Jos 15:37-44

LAHMI
of Jair) killed *, the brother of 1Ch 20:5

LAID
* him on the altar over the wood. Gen 22:9
fully grown, she * aside her Gen 38:14
his father had * his right hand on Gen 48:17
baby in it, and * it among the Ex 2:3
that the Lord * before them the Ex 15:25
if a ransom is * upon him, then he Ex 21:30f
his life whatever is * upon him." Ex 21:30f
Aaron and his sons * their hands Lev 8:14
Aaron and his sons * their hands Lev 8:18
Aaron and his sons * their hands Lev 8:22
in their censers, * incense on the Lev 10:1
As the people watched, Moses * Num 27:23
whole way he has * out for you; Deu 5:32
Moses had * his hands upon him; Deu 34:9
the foundation was *, the builder's Jos 6:26
all to Joshua and * it on the Jos 7:23
and * it on her back. Ru 3:15-18
the cart and * them on the rock. 1Sa 6:15
his father had * a curse upon 1Sa 14:28
men * down their lives that day. 2Sa 18:7
I was asleep, and * her dead child 1Ki 3:20
the cedar paneling * over the stone 1Ki 6:18
of the Temple was * in the month of 1Ki 6:37
So the prophet * the body upon 1Ki 13:29
He * the body in his own grave, 1Ki 13:30
When he * the foundations, his 1Ki 16:34
he lived, and * the body on his 1Ki 17:19
and * the pieces on the wood. 1Ki 18:33
Gehazi went on ahead and * the 2Ki 4:31
bow, and Elisha * his own hands 2Ki 13:16,17
entire army and * siege to 2Ki 25:
After destroying them, he * siege 1Ch 20:
He was * on a bed perfumed with 2Ch 16:13,1
and the curses * upon Joash, and 2Ch 24:2
who * their hands upon them. 2Ch 29:2
Everything was * out in great 2Ch 31:5,6
invaded Judah and * siege to the 2Ch 32:
of Megiddo. (He * aside his royal 2Ch 35:2
of the Temple had been *. Ez 3:1
is being * in the city walls. Ez 5:8
So Shesh-bazzar came and * the Ez 5:16
foundations are to be strongly *. Ez 6:3
Besodeiah). They * the beams, set Neh 3:6
KING AHASUERUS NOT only * tribute Est 10:1
and have * all hope in the dust. Job 16:15
* their hands upon their mouths. Job 29:9
"Where were you when I * the Job 38:4
and who * its cornerstone, as the Job 38:6,7
of rain? Who * out the path for the Job 38:25-27
breath the depths were * bare. Ps 18:15
have * me in the dust of death. Ps 22:15
no wrong, yet they * a trap for me Ps 35:7
and * great burdens on our backs. Ps 66:11
protecting him and * in ruins every Ps 89:40
In ages past you * the Ps 102:25
has * his plans against them. Is 19:17
destroyed and their cities * low. Is 32:19
It was my hand that * the Is 48:13
Yet God * on him the guilt and Is 53:6
their land has been * waste by Jer 25:38
* siege to the city for two years. Jer 52:5
Jerusalem. He * out an unalterable Lam 2:8
plots my foes have * against me. Lam 3:60
Because she has been * waste, I Eze 26:2
you will be * beside the people Eze 32:19
and other implements were *. Eze 40:42
flesh of the offering was to be *. Eze 40:43
his throne and * aside his royal Jon 3:6
* bare his bones from head to toe. Hab 3:13
"Zerubbabel * the foundation of Zec 4:9
the heavens and * the foundation of Zec 12:1
many others, and * them before Mt 15:30
on the farms—they * the sick in the Mk 6:56
eyes, and * his hands over them. Mk 8:23
country. He * out his employees' Mk 13:34
in the cloth and * it in a Mk 15:46
were watching as Jesus was * away. Mk 15:47
and * him in a manger, because Lk 2:7
* upon the underlying rock. Lk 6:47,48
beggar, was * at his door. Lk 16:20
linen cloth and * it in a new, Lk 23:53
but no hand was * on him, for Jn 7:30
THEN PILATE * open Jesus' back Jn 19:1
close at hand, they * him there. Jn 19:42
the street and * beside the Temple Act 3:2
* their hands on them in blessing. Act 6:6
their coats and * them at the feet Act 7:58
Then Peter and John * their Act 8:17
and found Paul and * his hands on Act 9:17
and * her in an upstairs room. Act 9:37
prayer, the men * their hands on Act 13:3
And now God has * his hand of Act 13:11
Then, when Paul * his hands upon Act 19:6
man's blood can be * at my door. Act 20:26
they * aside as they stoned him.' Act 22:20
called forward, he * charges Act 24:2
I have * the foundation and 1Co 3:10
thoughts will be * bare and he will 1Co 14:25
have our lives * bare—before him. 2Co 5:10
as God, but * aside his mighty Php 2:7
* their hands upon your head. 1Ti 4:14
into you when I * my hands upon 2Ti 1:6
enemies to be * under his feet. Heb 10:13
but he * his right hand on me and Rev 1:17,18
lives but * them down for him. Rev 12:11

LAIN
have * there many generations. Is 61:4

LAIR
of nations—stalks from his *; Jer 4:7
He has left his * like a lion Jer 25:38
*—from his Temple on Mount Zion. Amo 1:2

LAISH
on to the town of *, and noticed Ju 18:7
of Dan arrived at the city of *. Ju 18:27
it had originally been called *. Ju 18:29
Gallim named Palti (the son of *). 1Sa 25:44
Shout out a warning to *, for the Is 10:30

LAKE
shores of the * of Galilee; Jos 12:3
as far as the * of Galilee; Jos 13:27,28
As water evaporates from a *, as Job 14:11,12
beside the * of Galilee, close to Mt 4:12,13
beside the *, and the countryside Mt 4:15,16
beach beside the * of Galilee, he Mt 4:18
cross to the other side of the *. Mt 8:18
across the * with his disciples. Mt 8:23
other side of the *, in the country Mt 8:28
the * to Capernaum, his home town. Mt 9:1
other side of the * while he stayed Mt 14:22
Night fell, and out on the * the Mt 14:23,24
Arriving across the *, the Mt 16:5

LAKE Con't)
to the other side of the *." Mk 4:35
other side of the * a Mk 5:1
around on the hill above the *. Mk 5:11
hillside into the * and drowned. Mk 5:13
other side of the *, a vast crowd Mk 5:21
out across the * to Bethsaida, Mk 6:45
the middle of the *, and he was Mk 6:47
other side of the * they moored the Mk 6:53
to the other side of the *. Mk 8:13
on the shore of * Gennesaret, great Lk 5:1
cross to the other side of the *. Lk 8:22
country across the * from Galilee. Lk 8:26
the * below, where they drowned. Lk 8:33
back to the other side of the *. Lk 8:37
On the other side of the * the Lk 8:40
out across the * toward Capernaum. Jn 6:17
back across the *, crowds began Jn 6:22,23
disciples beside the * of Galilee. Jn 21:1
* of Fire that burns with sulphur. Rev 19:20
be thrown into the * of Fire Rev 20:10
were thrown into the * of Fire. Rev 20:14
This is the Second Death—the * of Rev 20:14
he was thrown into the * of Fire. Rev 20:15
doom is in the * that burns with Rev 21:8

LAKES
"The oceans, * and rivers that Rev 17:15

LAKKUM
and *, ending at the Jordan River. Jos 19:33

LAMA
"Eli, Eli, * sabachthani," which Mt 27:46
"Eli, Eli, * sabachthani?" Mk 15:34

LAMB
is the * for the sacrifice?" Gen 22:7
Israel) each family shall get a * Ex 12:3,4
here translated "*" can also mean Ex 12:3,4f
let it share the * with another Ex 12:3,4
Use the blood of the * eaten in Ex 12:7
Everyone shall eat roast * that Ex 12:8
your flocks, a * for one or more Ex 12:21
and kill the * so that God will Ex 12:21
No foreigners shall eat the *, Ex 12:43
you who eat each *, eat it together Ex 12:46
person shall ever eat the *. Ex 12:48
in exchange for a * or baby goat; Ex 13:13
Offer the other * in the Ex 29:41
by giving a * in its place. Ex 34:20
of the Passover * may be kept over Ex 34:25
"If it is a *, the man who Lev 3:7,8
chooses to bring a * as his sin Lev 4:32
*—the priest shall burn the fat Lev 4:35
the Lord, a female * or goat, and Lev 5:6
"If he is too poor to bring a * Lev 5:7
and a yearling *, all without Lev 9:3
bring a yearling * as a burnt Lev 12:6
poor to bring a *, then she must Lev 12:8
Then he shall kill the * at the Lev 14:13
only one, a male * for the guilt Lev 14:21
The priest shall take the * for Lev 14:24
Then he shall kill the * for the Lev 14:25
an ox, *, or goat anywhere except Lev 17:3,4
If the young bull or * presented Lev 22:23
a male yearling * without defect as Lev 23:12
along with a * for atonement. Num 5:8
* a year old for a guilt offering. Num 6:12
Lord, a year-old * without defect. Num 6:14
a yearling ewe * without defect; Num 6:14
shoulder of the *, one of the Num 6:19
yearling * as burnt offerings; Num 7:15
eat the Passover * that night. Num 9:6,7
They are to eat the * at that Num 9:11
offering. If a * is being Num 15:3,4
bull, ram, *, or young goat. Num 15:11,12
offering. One * shall be Num 28:4
wine with each *, poured out in the Num 28:7
Offer the second * in the Num 28:8
and for each *, three quarts of Num 28:13
a ram, and three pints for a *. Num 28:14
shall be either a * or an ox, Deu 16:2
of the Passover * shall be left Deu 16:4
Roast the * and eat it, then Deu 16:7
So Samuel took a suckling * and 1Sa 7:9
comes and grabs a * from the flock, 1Sa 17:34
and take the * from its mouth. 1Sa 17:35
could sacrifice an ox and a fat *. 2Sa 6:13
a little * he had managed to buy. 2Sa 12:3
But instead of killing a * from 2Sa 12:4
* and roasted it and served it." 2Sa 12:4
In that day the wolf and the * Is 11:6
He was brought as a * to the Is 53:7
The wolf and * shall feed Is 65:25
If they sacrifice a *, or bring Is 66:3
a * or ox on the way to slaughter. Jer 11:19
is willing for, to go with each *. Eze 46:5
With the *, he is to bring Eze 46:7
is willing to give with each *; Eze 46:11
"Each morning a yearling * must Eze 46:13
ordinance—the *, the grain offering Eze 46:14,15
when the Passover * was killed and Lk 22:7
There is the * of God who takes Jn 1:29
There is the * of God!" Jn 1:36
be allowed to eat the Passover *. Jn 18:28
and as a * is silent before the Act 8:32
Christ, God's *, has been slain 1Co 5:7
them to kill a * as God had told Heb 11:28
the sinless, spotless * of God. 1Pe 1:19
I looked and saw a * standing Rev 5:6
Beings, and on the * were wounds Rev 5:6
down before the *, each with a harp Rev 5:8
* is worthy" (loudly they sang Rev 5:12
"—the * who was slain. Rev 5:12
and to the * forever and ever." Rev 5:13
AS I WATCHED, the * broke the Rev 6:1
the anger of the *, because the Rev 6:16
and before the *, clothed in white, Rev 7:9
upon the throne, and from the *." Rev 7:10
them by the blood of the *. Rev 7:14
For the * standing in front of Rev 7:17
WHEN THE * had broken the seventh Rev 8:1
of the *, and by their testimony; Rev 12:11
of Life of the * slain before the Rev 13:8f
like those of a * but a fearsome Rev 13:11
THEN I SAW a * standing on Mount Rev 14:1
following the * wherever he goes. Rev 14:4
offering to God and the *. Rev 14:4
of the holy angels and the *. Rev 14:10
of God, and the song of the *: Rev 15:3,4
*, and the Lamb will conquer them; Rev 17:14
Lamb, and the * will conquer them; Rev 17:14
banquet of the *, and his bride has Rev 19:7
to the wedding feast of the *." Rev 19:9
of the twelve apostles of the *. Rev 21:14
* are worshiped in it everywhere. Rev 21:22
of God and of the * illuminate it. Rev 21:23
of God and the *, coursing down Rev 22:1
of God and of the * will be there, Rev 22:3

LAMB'S
Drain the * blood into a basin, Ex 12:22
dip them into the * blood, and Ex 12:22
then there will be * wool enough Pro 27:25,26,27
* Book of Life—worshiped the evil Rev 13:8
show you the bride, the * wife." Rev 21:9
are written in the * Book of Life. Rev 21:27

LAMBS
*, and presented them to the Lord. Gen 4:4
But when he took seven ewe * and Gen 21:28,29
So the less healthy * were Gen 30:42
then all the * were streaked! Gen 31:8
month, all these * shall be killed, Ex 12:6
them, "Go and get * from your Ex 12:21
"Each day offer two yearling * Ex 29:38
take two male * without physical Lev 14:10
take one of the * and the pint of Lev 14:12
cannot afford two *, then he shall Lev 14:21
seven yearling * without defects, Lev 23:18
yearling * for a peace offering. Lev 23:19
goats, and five male yearling *. Num 7:17
60 male * a year old. Num 7:88
male *—each without defect. Num 28:3
two yearling male *—both without Num 28:9,10
yearling *—all without defect. Num 28:11
male *—all without defect. Num 28:19
and with each of the seven * Num 28:20,21
ram, and seven yearling male *. Num 28:27
quarts with each of the seven *. Num 28:28,29
male *—all without defect. Num 29:2
quarts with each of the seven *. Num 29:3,4
yearling male *—each without Num 29:8
three with each of the seven *. Num 29:9,10
male yearling * —each without Num 29:13
quarts for each of the fourteen *. Num 29:15
male yearling *—each without Num 29:17
male yearling *—each without Num 29:20
male yearling *—each without Num 29:23
male yearling *—each without Num 29:26,27
male yearling *—each without Num 29:29
male yearling *—each without Num 29:32
male yearling *—each without Num 29:36
calves, and * will all disappear. Deu 28:51
the fattest of the *—everything, in 1Sa 15:9
he shall repay four * to the 2Sa 12:6
* and the wool of 100,000 rams; 2Ki 3:4
seven bulls and seven *. 1Ch 15:26
* as burnt offerings to the Lord; 1Ch 29:21
seven rams, seven *, and seven male 2Ch 29:21
and did the same with the *. 2Ch 29:22
offerings, 100 rams, and 200 *. 2Ch 29:32,33
people killed their Passover *. 2Ch 30:15
* for them, to sanctify them. 2Ch 30:17,18,19
The Passover * were slain that 2Ch 35:1
Kill the Passover * and sanctify 2Ch 35:6
contributed 30,000 * and young 2Ch 35:7
the Passover * and presented the 2Ch 35:11
the Passover * and boiled the holy 2Ch 35:13
bulls, rams, and * for burnt Ez 6:9
rams, and 400 * were sacrificed; Ez 6:17
of oxen, rams, *, grain offerings, Ez 7:17
seventy-seven *; Ez 8:35
from following the ewes with *; Ps 78:71,72
rams, the little hills like *! Ps 114:4
Why, little hills, like *? Ps 114:6
there feed your sheep and their *. Sol 1:8
among the ruins. * and calves and Is 5:17
MOAB'S REFUGEES AT Sela send * as Is 16:1
slaying * and goats for sacrifice. Is 34:6
he will carry the * in his arms Is 40:11
You have not brought me the * Is 43:23
see shepherds leading sheep and *. Jer 33:12
I will bring them like * to the Jer 51:40
bring you * and rams and goats. Eze 27:21
I will distinguish * from kids and Eze 34:17
are the rams, the *, the goats and Eze 39:18
six * and a ram, all unblemished. Eze 46:4
condition; six * and one ram, all Eze 46:6
* and the choicest calves. Amo 6:4
and comfort and care for the *. Zec 13:7
the day the * were sacrificed, his Mk 14:12
sending you out as * among wolves. Lk 10:3
"Then feed my *," Jesus told Jn 21:15

LAME
a man is blind or *, or has a Lev 21:18
such as being * or blind, or if Deu 15:21
(There was a little * grandson of 2Sa 4:4
she was running, and he became *. 2Sa 4:4
"Even the blind and * could keep 2Sa 5:6
those '*' and 'blind' Jebusites. 2Sa 5:8
and the * could conquer you!" 2Sa 5:8
* son is still alive." 2Sa 9:3
(who was * in both feet) moved to 2Sa 9:13
For as you know I am *. 2Sa 19:26
for the blind and feet for the *. Job 29:15
even the * will win their share. Is 33:23
of the deaf. The * man will leap Is 35:6
their blind and *, young mothers Jer 31:8
people—sick and * and dispossessed— Mic 4:6
nor carry the * that cannot walk; Zec 11:16
You tell the people, "* animals Mal 1:8
Stolen animals, * and sick—as Mal 1:13
healed, and the * people now Mt 11:5
brought him their *, blind, maimed, Mt 15:30
Better be * and live forever than Mk 9:45,46
the * and the blind and casting out Lk 7:20,21,22
The * are walking without a limp. Lk 7:20,21,22
crippled, the *, and the blind. Lk 14:13
beggars, crippled, *, and blind. Lk 14:21
Crowds of sick folks—*, blind, Jn 5:3
they saw a man * from birth carried Act 3:2
The * man looked at them eagerly, Act 3:5
Then Peter took the * man by the Act 3:7,8
he was the * beggar they had seen Act 3:10
you know how * he was before. Act 3:16
who had been * for forty years. Act 4:22
were paralyzed or * were healed, Act 8:7
though weak and *, will not fall Heb 12:13

LAMECH
of *; Gen 4:18
* married two wives—Adah and Gen 4:19
One day * said to Adah and Gen 4:23
years old when his son * was born; Gen 5:25,26,27
*: Lamech was 182 years old when Gen 5:28-31
Lamech: * was 182 years old when Gen 5:28-31
son Noah was born. * named him Gen 5:28-31
Afterwards * lived 595 years, Gen 5:28-31
Enoch, Methuselah, *, Noah, 1Ch 1:1
Noah's father was *; Lk 3:23-38

LAMECH'S
of the harp and flute. To * Gen 4:22
Noah's father was Lamech;* father Lk 3:23-38

LAMED
then he * all of the chariot 2Sa 8:4

LAMENT
of Israel may * the death of Nadab Lev 10:6
* the fate of Jephthah's daughter. Ju 11:40
they could even begin their *. Ps 78:64
So I wail and * for Jazer and Is 16:9
Anakim, how you will * and mourn! Jer 47:5
mourners to wail and *. Amo 5:16
I will wail and *, howling as a Mic 1:8

LAMENTATION
period of * for Joseph's father. Gen 50:10

LAMENTATIONS
recorded among the official *. 2Ch 35:24,25

LAMENTED
the king *. 2Sa 3:33,34

LAMP
* holders, with lamps and oil; Ex 35:10-19
a chair, and a *, and he will have 2Ki 4:10
tongs, * snuffers, basins, spoons, 2Ch 4:22
someone lights a *, does he put a Mk 4:21
be seen or used. A * is placed on a Mk 4:21
someone lighting a * and then Lk 8:16
"No one lights a * and hides it! Lk 11:33
Won't she light a * and look in Lk 15:8
not even a * in a window will Rev 18:23

LAMP-HOLDERS
Its base, shaft, *, and Ex 37:17

LAMPS
olive oil for the *, spices for the Ex 25:1
base, shaft, *, and blossoms. Ex 25:31
Then make seven * for the Ex 25:37
oil to use in the * of the Ex 27:20
Aaron trims the *, he shall burn Ex 30:7
when he lights the * he shall burn Ex 30:8

(LAMPS Con't)
Olive oil for the *; Ex 35:5-9
Lamp holders, with * and oil; Ex 35:10-19
Then he made the seven * at the Ex 37:23,24
lampstand with its *, utensils, Ex 39:33-40
in the lampstand and light the *. Ex 40:4
Then he lighted the * before the Ex 40:25
the lampstand, the *, snuffers, Num 4:9
lights the seven * in the Num 8:2
the flowers, *, tongs, cups, 1Ki 7:49
needed for the lampstands and *. 1Ch 28:15
and *, each according to its use. 1Ch 28:15
also the * and lampstands, the 2Ch 4:20
holding seven *, and at the top Zec 4:2
oil that feeds the *, flowing into Zec 4:2
For these seven * represent the Zec 4:10
who took their * and went to meet Mt 25:1
to fill their * with oil, while the Mt 25:2,3,4
jumped up and trimmed their *. Mt 25:7,8
them, for their * were going out. Mt 25:7,8
from shining? No, * are mounted in Lk 8:16
lighted with many flickering *; Act 20:8
were seven lighted * representing Rev 4:5
* are equated with the one Spirit. Rev 4:5f
the seven * and the one Spirit. Rev 5:6f
there—no need for * or sun—for the Rev 22:5

LAMPSTAND
"Make a * of pure, beaten gold. Ex 25:31
The entire * and its decorations Ex 25:31
Then make seven lamps for the *, Ex 25:37
pounds of pure gold for the * and Ex 25:39
Place the table and * across the Ex 26:35
of the veil. The * will be on the Ex 26:35
instruments, the * and all its Ex 30:26,27
the pure gold * with its Ex 31:8
Then he made the *, again using Ex 37:17
of one piece. The * had six Ex 37:18
The main stem of the * was Ex 37:20,21
The entire * weighed 107 pounds, Ex 37:23,24
* with its lamps, utensils, and Ex 39:33-40
in the * and light the lamps. Ex 40:4
And he placed the * next to the Ex 40:24
flame in the * of pure gold which Lev 24:3,4
the table, the *, the altars, the Num 3:31-35
a blue cloth the *, the lamps, Num 4:9
seven lamps in the *, he is to set Num 8:2
So Aaron did this. The *, Num 8:4
The golden * is lighted every 2Ch 13:11
of the wall opposite the *. Dan 5:5
I answered, "I see a golden * Zec 4:2
carved upon the *, one on each side Zec 4:3
each side of the *, and about the Zec 4:11
Instead, he puts it on a * to Lk 11:33

LAMPSTANDS
displayed, the * (five on the 1Ki 7:49
gold needed for the * and lamps. 1Ch 28:15
then cast ten gold * and placed 2Ch 4:7
also the lamps and *, the 2Ch 4:20

LAND
so that the dry * will emerge." Gen 1:9,10
Then God named the dry * Gen 1:9,10
places and flowed across the *. Gen 2:6
A river from the * of Eden Gen 2:10
entire length of the * of Havilah, Gen 2:11,12
entire length of the * of Cush. Gen 2:13
in the * of Nod, east of Eden. Gen 4:16
breathed and lived upon dry * Gen 7:22
and Calneh in the * of Shinar. Gen 10:10
discovered in the * of Babylon, Gen 11:2
Literally, "the * of Shinar," Gen 11:2f
But Haran died young, in the * Gen 11:28
to go to the * of Canaan; Gen 11:31
go to the * I will guide you to. Gen 12:1
give this * to your descendants." Gen 12:7
famine in the *: and so Abram went Gen 12:10
But the * could not support both Gen 13:6
and Perizzites present in the *. Gen 13:7
* you want, and we will separate. Gen 13:9
For Abram stayed in the * of Gen 13:12
NOW WAR FILLED the *— Gen 14:1
to give you this * forever." Gen 15:7
in a foreign * for 400 years. Gen 15:13
they will return here to this *; Gen 15:16
have given this * to your Gen 15:18
first arrived in the * of Canaan. Gen 16:2,3
And I will give all this * of Gen 17:7,8
much—and go to the * of Moriah and Gen 22:2
died in Hebron in the * of Canaan; Gen 23:1
*, with no place to bury my wife. Gen 23:4
"Well, the * is worth 400 pieces Gen 23:14,15
This is the * he bought: Gen 23:17,18
me to leave that * and my people, Gen 24:7
to give me and my children this *. Gen 24:7
man among the people of his *. Gen 24:35
this far-off *, to his brother's Gen 24:38
overshadowed the *, as had happened Gen 26:1
as I say and stay here in this *. Gen 26:3
will give all this * to you and to Gen 26:3
"This is our * and our well," Gen 26:20
May you own this * where we now Gen 28:4
They will cover the * from east Gen 28:14
bring you back safely to this *; Gen 28:15
arriving in the * of the East. Gen 29:1
"Return to the * of your fathers, Gen 31:3
return to the * of your birth.' Gen 31:13
father Isaac in the * of Canaan. Gen 31:17-20
in Edom, in the * of Seir, with Gen 32:3
to return to the * of my relatives, Gen 32:9
(He bought the * he camped on Gen 33:19
For the * is large enough to hold Gen 34:21
ours and the * will be enriched. Gen 34:23
the people of this *—all the Gen 34:30
And I will pass on to you the * Gen 35:12
born to Esau in the * of Canaan. Gen 36:5
had gained in the * of Canaan—and Gen 36:6,7,8
(For there was not * enough to Gen 36:6,7,8
families of the * of Seir:The tribe Gen 36:20,21
from the * of the Temanites. Gen 36:31-39
SO JACOB SETTLED again in the * of Gen 37:1
specimens in all the * of Egypt. Gen 41:19
to do here in the * of Egypt. Gen 41:25
throughout all the * of Egypt; Gen 41:29
famine will consume the *. Gen 41:30
throughout all the * of Egypt. Gen 41:40
in charge of all the * of Egypt." Gen 41:41,42
charge over all the * of Egypt." Gen 41:44
famous throughout the * of Egypt. Gen 41:45
began traveling all across the *. Gen 41:46
this * of my slavery," he said). Gen 41:52
"From the * of Canaan," they Gen 42:7
the famine has made our *." Gen 42:8,9
our father is in the * of Canaan. Gen 42:13
Jacob in the * of Canaan and told Gen 42:29
our father in the * of Canaan.' Gen 42:32
terrible famine throughout the *. Gen 43:1
with the best products of the *. Gen 43:11
ruler of all the * of Egypt. Gen 45:8
me chief of all the * of Egypt. Gen 45:9
You shall live in the * of Gen 45:10
best territory in the * of Egypt. Gen 45:18
shall live off the fat of the *!' Gen 45:18
of all the * of Egypt is yours." Gen 45:20
returned to the * of Canaan, to Gen 45:25
"And he is ruler over all the * Gen 45:26
accumulated in the * of Canaan, and Gen 46:6
Joseph's sons, born in the * of Gen 46:19-22
from the * of Canaan to join me. Gen 46:31
live here in the * of Goshen." Gen 46:34
They wish to settle in the * of Gen 47:1
to live in the * of Goshen." Gen 47:4
Give them the best * of Egypt. Gen 47:5,6
The * of Goshen will be fine. Gen 47:5,6
So Joseph assigned the best * of Gen 47:11
land of Egypt—the * of Rameses—to Gen 47:11
so that all the * of Egypt and Gen 47:13
nothing left but our bodies and *. Gen 47:18
Buy us and our * and we will be Gen 47:19
and the * won't be abandoned." Gen 47:19
So Joseph bought all the * of Gen 47:20
And the * became Pharaoh's. Gen 47:20
The only * he didn't buy was Gen 47:22
bought you and your * for Pharaoh. Gen 47:23
Go and sow the *. Gen 47:23
law throughout the * of Egypt—and Gen 47:26
on the * owned by the temples. Gen 47:26
So Israel lived in the * of Gen 47:27
me at Luz in the * of Canaan and Gen 48:3
I will give this * of Canaan to you Gen 48:4
born here in the * of Egypt before Gen 48:5
to Canaan, the * of your fathers. Gen 48:21
And I have given the choice * of Gen 48:22
portion of that * which I took from Gen 48:22
were not given * holdings, as were Gen 49:7f
how pleasant the *, he willingly Gen 49:15
my fathers in the * of Canaan, in Gen 49:29,30
* of Canaan, to bury him there. Gen 50:5
officers of the *, as well as all Gen 50:7
and herds in the * of Goshen. Gen 50:8
his body into the * of Canaan and Gen 50:12,13
you out of this * of Egypt and take Gen 50:24
you back to the * he promised to Gen 50:24
and they filled the * of Goshen. Ex 1:7
But Moses ran away into the * of Ex 2:15
am a stranger in a foreign *." Ex 2:22
back into the * of Canaan Ex 2:24
Egypt into a good *, a large land, Ex 3:8
good land, a large *, a land Ex 3:8
a large land, a * 'flowing with Ex 3:8
and honey'—the * where the Ex 3:8
take them to the * now occupied by Ex 3:17
* "flowing with milk and honey." Ex 3:17
*, and it will turn to blood." Ex 4:9
returned to the * of Egypt, holding Ex 4:20
but will drive them out of his *! Ex 6:1
descendants the * of Canaan where Ex 6:4
I will bring them into the * I Ex 6:8,9
Israel out of the * of Egypt," Ex 6:26
people from the *, and to whom the Ex 6:27
my miracles in the * of Egypt. Ex 7:3
blood throughout the * of Egypt. Ex 7:21
* from one border to the other. Ex 8:2
frogs in every corner of the *." Ex 8:5
frogs to come up upon the *. Ex 8:7
terrible stench throughout the *. Ex 8:14
throughout all the * of Egypt." Ex 8:16
different in the * of Goshen where Ex 8:22
your God, but do it here in the *. Ex 8:25
dust over all the * of Egypt and Ex 9:9
animals alike, throughout the *." Ex 9:9
that day was the * of Goshen where Ex 9:26
your hand over the * of Egypt to Ex 10:12
will cover the * and eat everything Ex 10:12
And the locusts covered the * of Ex 10:14
sun so that the * was darkened; Ex 10:15
throughout all the * of Egypt. Ex 10:15
one locust in all the * of Egypt! Ex 10:19
descend upon the * of Egypt." Ex 10:21
over all the * for three days. Ex 10:22
on Pharaoh and his *, and after Ex 11:1
great man in the * of Egypt and was Ex 11:3
throughout the entire * of Egypt; Ex 11:6
let the people leave the *. Ex 11:10
For I will pass through the * of Ex 12:12
animals in all the * of Egypt, and Ex 12:12
when I smite the * of Egypt. Ex 12:13
brought you out of the * of Egypt; Ex 12:17
as much as to those born in the *. Ex 12:19
the * and kill the Egyptians; Ex 12:23
And when you come into the * Ex 12:25
sons in the * of Egypt, from Ex 12:29
throughout all the * of Egypt, for Ex 12:30
of the * as quickly as possible. Ex 12:33
of Jehovah's people left the *. Ex 12:40,41
people out from the * of Egypt; Ex 12:42
of Israel from the * of Egypt, wave Ex 12:51
from the * of Egypt, all of the Ex 12:51f
you into the * of the Canaanites, Ex 13:4,5
and Jebusites—the * he promised Ex 13:4,5
a * 'flowing with milk and honey.' Ex 13:4,5
within the borders of your *! Ex 13:6,7
you into the * he promised to your Ex 13:11
throughout the * of Egypt, both of Ex 13:15
them through the * of the Ex 13:17,18
from Egypt to the Promised *. Ex 13:17,18
through on dry *, and the waters Ex 14:29
To your holy *. Ex 15:13
of Israel walked through on dry *. Ex 15:19
brought you out of the * of Egypt. Ex 16:6
arrived in the * of Canaan, where Ex 16:35
in a foreign *") and Eliezer Ex 18:3
father-in-law return to his own *. Ex 18:27
* the Lord your God will give you. Ex 20:12
were foreigners in the * of Egypt. Ex 22:21
own experience in the * of Egypt. Ex 23:9
but let the * rest and lie fallow Ex 23:11
to the * I have prepared for you. Ex 23:20
bring you into the * of the Ex 23:23
throughout your *, and you will Ex 23:26
the people whose * you invade, and Ex 23:27
one year, for the * would become a Ex 23:29
increased enough to fill the *. Ex 23:30
now living in the *, and you will Ex 23:31
brought from the * of Egypt with Ex 32:11
them all of this * I have promised Ex 32:13
from Egypt to the * I promised Ex 33:1
for I said, 'I will give this * Ex 33:1
It is a * 'flowing with milk and Ex 33:3
to the Promised *,' but you haven't Ex 33:12
go with us to the Promised *; Ex 34:9
there in the * where you are going, Ex 34:12
living in the *, for they are Ex 34:15
and conquer your * when you go up Ex 34:24
throughout your *, that you shall Lev 3:17
of the * of Egypt to be your God. Lev 11:45
you arrive in the * of Canaan which Lev 14:33,34
into a * where no one lives, Lev 16:22
Literally, "a solitary *." Lev 16:22f
are born in the * or are a Lev 16:29,30
the * into which you are going. Lev 18:24
and will throw them out of the *. Lev 18:25
Literally, "the * vomits out her Lev 18:25f
the people of the * where I am Lev 18:27
taking you, and the * is defiled. Lev 18:27
of the *, just as I will throw out Lev 18:28
Literally, "that the * vomit not Lev 18:28f
in the * where you are going. Lev 18:29,30
"When you enter the * and have Lev 19:23
lest the * become full of enormous Lev 19:29
advantage of foreigners in your *; Lev 19:33
were foreigners in the * of Egypt. Lev 19:34
brought you from the * of Egypt. Lev 19:35,36
And if the people of the * Lev 20:4
not throw you out of your new *. Lev 20:22
Literally, "that the * I give you Lev 20:22f
I have promised you their *; Lev 20:24
It is a * 'flowing with milk and Lev 20:24
though the * teem with them. Lev 20:25
you arrive in the * I will give you Lev 23:9,10,11
you who have no * of their own; Lev 23:22
"When you come into the * I am Lev 25:1
you must let the * rest before the Lev 25:1
seventh year the * is to lie fallow Lev 25:4
it is a year of rest for the *. Lev 25:5

LAND Con't)
loud and long throughout the *. Lev 25:9
throughout the * to all enslaved Lev 25:10
Because of this, if the * is Lev 25:14,15,16
* before it is returned to you. Lev 25:14,15,16
you want to live safely in the *. Lev 25:17,18
When you obey, the * will yield Lev 25:19
And remember, the * is mine, so Lev 25:23
that the * can be redeemed at any Lev 25:24
sells some of his *, then his Lev 25:25
the money and return the * to him. Lev 25:27
fields of common * surrounding Lev 25:34
you out of the * of Egypt to give Lev 25:38
* of Canaan, and to be your God. Lev 25:38
For I brought you from the * of Lev 25:42
they have been born in your *. Lev 25:45
I brought them from the * of Lev 25:55
rains, and the * will yield bumper Lev 26:4,5
live safely in the *, for I will Lev 26:4,5
you out of the * of Egypt, with the Lev 26:13
for your * shall not yield its Lev 26:20
Yes, I will desolate your *; Lev 26:32
as you go. Your * shall be desolate Lev 26:33
Then at last the * will rest and Lev 26:34,35
Yes, then the * will rest and Lev 26:34,35
them into the * of their enemies. Lev 26:40,41
the * (and its desolation). Lev 26:42
For the * shall enjoy its Lev 26:43
A section of * that requires ten Lev 27:16
"A tenth of the produce of the * Lev 27:30
in the Promised * and go to war Num 10:9
are on our way to the Promised *. Num 10:29
return to my own * and kinfolk." Num 10:30
* you promised their ancestors? Num 11:12
for the * of Midian from which Num 12:1f
spies into the * of Canaan—the land Num 13:2
* I am giving to Israel; Num 13:2
and see what the * is like; Num 13:18
and whether the * is fertile or Num 13:19
whether the * is rich or poor, Num 13:20
So they spied out the * all the Num 13:21
arrived in the * you sent us to Num 13:27
* 'flowing with milk and honey.' Num 13:27
negative: "The * is full of Num 13:32
into the * and give it to us. Num 14:8
It is very fertile, a * 'flowing Num 14:8
do not fear the people of the *. Num 14:9
of this *, who are well aware that Num 14:14
* he swore he would give them.' Num 14:16
shall even see the * I promised to Num 14:23
I will bring him into the * he Num 14:24
me, shall enter the Promised *. Num 14:30
slaves of the people of the *. Num 14:31
safely into the * and they shall Num 14:31
" 'Since the spies were in the * Num 14:34,35
started towards the Promised *. Num 14:40
the * the Lord has promised us." Num 14:40
live in the * I am going to give Num 15:1
they arrive in the * that I am Num 15:17,18
brought you out of the * of Egypt; Num 15:41
from the entire * of Israel. Num 18:21
Where is the fertile * of Num 20:5
into the * I have promised them!" Num 20:12
encamped on the borders of your *. Num 20:16
If you attempt to enter my * Num 20:18
the border of the * of Edom, "The Num 20:23
not enter the * I have given the Num 20:24
order to go around the * of Edom. Num 21:4
"Let us travel through your *," Num 21:22
and occupied their * from the Arnon Num 21:24
had promised the * of the Ammonites Num 21:24f
and Israel occupied the *. Num 21:35
in his native * of Pethor, near the Num 22:5,6
that I can drive them out of my *; Num 22:5,6
River, at the border of his *. Num 22:36
From the * of Aram, Num 23:7-10
shall deport you from this *!" Num 24:21,22
Onan who died in the * of Canaan: Num 26:19-22
to divide the * among the tribes in Num 26:52,53
*, the smaller tribes less land. Num 26:54
land, the smaller tribes less *. Num 26:54
were given no * when it was divided Num 26:62
Give them * along with their Num 27:6,7
the river to the * I have given to Num 27:12
WHEN ISRAEL ARRIVED in the * of Num 32:1
Please let us have this * as our Num 32:5
instead of the * on the other side Num 32:5
* that the Lord has given them? Num 32:7
to spy out the *, but when they Num 32:8
from going on into the Promised *. Num 32:9
would ever see the * he promised Num 32:10,11
to go on into the Promised *. Num 32:12
We don't want * on the other Num 32:19
then, when the * is finally Num 32:22
And the * on the eastern side Num 32:22
then, when the * is conquered, you Num 32:29
must give them the * of Gilead; Num 32:29
they must accept * among the rest Num 32:30
rest of you in the * of Canaan." Num 32:30
but our own * shall be here on this Num 32:32
of Bashan—all the * and cities—to Num 32:33
(at the edge of the * of Edom). Num 33:15-37
the Negeb, in the * of Canaan, Num 33:40
of Israel were approaching his *. Num 33:40
River into the * of Canaan, you Num 33:50,51
I have given the * to you; Num 33:53
You will be given * in Num 33:54
The larger sections of * will be Num 33:54
they come into the * of Canaan (I Num 34:1
you the entire * as your homeland), Num 34:1
been assigned * on the east side of Num 34:14,15
dividing up of the *: Eleazar the Num 34:16-28
of the * among the tribes." Num 34:29
they arrive in the *, Cities of Num 35:9,10
be located in the * of Canaan, and Num 35:13,14
may return to his own * and home. Num 35:28
In this way the * will not be Num 35:33
pollutes the *, and no atonement Num 35:33
You shall not defile the * where Num 35:34
you to divide the * by lot among Num 36:1
tribe, their * will go with them to Num 36:3
In this way none of the * of the Num 36:7
their * won't leave the tribe. Num 36:8
southern edge of the Promised *. Deu 1:1f
Negeb, and all the * of Canaan and Deu 1:7
it, for it is the * the Lord Deu 1:8
[on the border of the Promised * Deu 1:19,20,21
'The Lord God has given us this *. Deu 1:19,20,21
* the Lord our God had given us. Deu 1:24,25
Our brothers who spied out the * Deu 1:28
They say that the people of the * Deu 1:28
to see the good * he had promised Deu 1:34,35
some of the * he had walked over. Deu 1:36
shall not enter the Promised *! Deu 1:37
I will give the * to the Deu 1:39
We will go into the * and fight Deu 1:41
you even a tiny piece of their *. Deu 2:5
will not give you any of their *; Deu 2:9
of Canaan, whose * had been Deu 2:12
Ar, into the * of the Ammonites. Deu 2:19
will not give you any of their *. Deu 2:19
River into the * of King Sihon the Deu 2:24
begin to take possession of his *. Deu 2:24
'Let us pass through your *,' we Deu 2:27
* the Lord our God has given us.' Deu 2:29
to give you the * of King Sihon; Deu 2:31
toward King Og's * of Bashan. Deu 3:1
'All his people and his * are Deu 3:1
"We now possessed all the * of Deu 3:8
River—all the * from the valley of Deu 3:8
gave the conquered * to the tribes Deu 3:12
called 'The * of the Rephaim.' Deu 3:13
had given them the *, they could Deu 3:18
to the * the Lord was giving them. Deu 3:18
When they conquer the * the Lord Deu 3:20
may return here to your own *.' Deu 3:20
into the Promised *—the good land Deu 3:23,24,25
Land—the good * beyond the Deu 3:23,24,25
will see the * in the distance. Deu 3:27
to conquer the * you will see from Deu 3:28
and possess the * given you by the Deu 4:1
in the * where you will live. Deu 4:5
when you arrive in the Promised *. Deu 4:14
into the good * he has given you as Deu 4:21,22
have been in the * a long time, and Deu 4:25
be quickly destroyed from the *. Deu 4:26
Jordan River and conquer that *. Deu 4:26
and gave you their * as an Deu 4:38
forever in the * the Lord your God Deu 4:40
(This was the * formerly occupied Deu 4:44,45,46
Israel conquered his * and that Deu 4:47
life in the * he is giving you. Deu 5:16
him for his home, *, servants, Deu 5:21
and they will obey them in the * Deu 5:31
* you are to enter and possess. Deu 5:33
are to obey in the * you will soon Deu 6:1
in a glorious * 'flowing with milk Deu 6:3
you into the * he promised your Deu 6:10,11,12
* of Egypt, the land of slavery. Deu 6:10,11,12
land of Egypt, the * of slavery. Deu 6:10,11,12
possess the good * which the Lord Deu 6:18
living in your *, as the Lord Deu 6:19
could give us this * he had Deu 6:23
into the Promised *, as he soon Deu 7:1
you arrive in the * he promised Deu 7:13
Pharaoh and to all the * of Egypt. Deu 7:18
and take over the * promised to Deu 8:1
you into a good * of brooks, pools, Deu 8:7
it is a * of wheat and barley, Deu 8:8
it is a * where food is Deu 8:9
it is a * where iron is as common Deu 8:9
for the good * he has given you. Deu 8:10
of your slavery in the * of Egypt. Deu 8:14
you this good * because you are Deu 9:6
you to enter the * he had given Deu 9:23
bring them to the * he promised Deu 9:28
a * of brooks and water. Deu 10:7
have a portion of * reserved for it Deu 10:9
*, as their brother tribes do; Deu 10:9
to the * I promised their fathers. Deu 10:11
were foreigners in the * of Egypt. Deu 10:19
against Pharaoh and all his *. Deu 11:3
the * you are about to enter. Deu 11:8
good life in the * the Lord Deu 11:9
* 'flowing with milk and honey'! Deu 11:9
For the * you are about to enter Deu 11:10
is not like the * of Egypt where Deu 11:10
It is a * of hills and valleys Deu 11:11
plenty of rain— a * that the Lord Deu 11:12
the good * the Lord has given you. Deu 11:17
the * the Lord has promised you. Deu 11:21
nations in your *, no matter how Deu 11:23
Wherever you go, the * is yours. Deu 11:24
you into the * to possess it, a Deu 11:29
in the * the Lord is giving you. Deu 11:31
you arrive in the * which Jehovah, Deu 12:1
in the Promised *, and the Lord Deu 12:10
for they have no * of their own. Deu 12:12
the nations in the * where you will Deu 12:29
out of slavery in the * of Egypt. Deu 13:5
* of Egypt, the place of slavery. Deu 13:10
bless you in the * he is giving you Deu 15:4,5
you arrive in the * the Lord will Deu 15:7
were slaves in the * of Egypt and Deu 15:15
justice in every part of the *. Deu 16:18
successful in the * which the Lord Deu 16:20
throughout your * violates your Deu 17:2,3
"When you arrive in the * the Deu 17:14
he lives in the * of Israel, has Deu 18:6,7
in the Promised * you must be very Deu 18:9
gives you all the * he promised Deu 19:8
"When you arrive in the * the Deu 19:14
* by moving the boundary marker. Deu 19:14
not to those in the Promised * Deu 20:15
Promised * you are to save no one; Deu 20:16
the people of the * from luring you Deu 20:18
in the Promised *, a murder victim Deu 21:1
Don't defile the * the Lord your Deu 21:23
when you arrive in the Promised *. Deu 23:20
this would bring guilt upon the * Deu 24:4
were slaves in the * of Egypt—that Deu 24:22
* the Lord your God is giving Deu 25:13,14,15
in the Promised *, you are utterly Deu 25:19
"WHEN YOU ARRIVE in the * and Deu 26:1
the * he promised our ancestors.' Deu 26:2,3
* "flowing with milk and honey!" Deu 26:9
people and the * you have given us, Deu 26:15
make it a * "flowing with milk Deu 26:15
into the Promised *—a land 'flowing Deu 27:2,3,4
Promised Land—a * 'flowing with Deu 27:2,3,4
into the Promised *, the tribes of Deu 27:12
between his * and his neighbor's.' Deu 27:17
* the Lord your God is giving you. Deu 28:8
good things in the *, just as he Deu 28:11
the face of the * which you are Deu 28:21
be as iron. The * will become as Deu 28:24
much, and they shall plague the *. Deu 28:60
you shall disappear from the *. Deu 28:63
and his people in the * of Egypt. Deu 29:2,3
and took their * and gave it to Deu 29:8
we lived in the * of Egypt, and how Deu 29:16
devastation of the * and the Deu 29:22
They will see that the whole * Deu 29:23
has the Lord done this to his *?' Deu 29:24
the people of the * broke the Deu 29:25
them out of the * of Egypt. Deu 29:25
hot against this *, so that all his Deu 29:27
them out of their * and threw them Deu 29:28
*, where they still live today!' Deu 29:28
again to the * of your ancestors. Deu 30:5
You shall possess the * again, Deu 30:5
the * you are about to possess. Deu 30:16
the * you are going in to possess. Deu 30:18
live safely in the * the Lord Deu 30:20
living in the *, just as he Deu 31:4
people into the * promised by the Deu 31:7
as you live in the Promised *." Deu 31:13
foreign gods in the Promised *. Deu 31:16
them into the * I promised their Deu 31:20
their ancestors—a * 'flowing with Deu 31:20
*, what these people are like." Deu 31:21
into the * the Lord promised them; Deu 31:23
Purifying his * Deu 32:40,41
lives in the * you are going to Deu 32:47
the * of Moab across from Jericho. Deu 32:49
out across the * of Canaan, the Deu 32:49
of Canaan, the * I am giving to the Deu 32:49
After you see the * you must die Deu 32:50
out before you the * I am giving Deu 32:52
"May his * be blessed by God Deu 33:13
He chose the best of the * for Deu 33:21
Prospering in a * of corn and Deu 33:28
him the Promised *, as they gazed Deu 34:1
"It is the Promised *," the Deu 34:4
* of Moab as the Lord had said. Deu 34:5
Jordan River into the Promised *. Jos 1:2
be part of the * of Israel— all Jos 1:3
all the * of the Hittites.' Jos 1:4
and they shall conquer all the * Jos 1:6
in the * which God has given us!" Jos 1:10,11
you ruined their * and completely Jos 2:10
give us the entire *," they said, Jos 2:24
in the * you will soon occupy. Jos 3:10

(LAND Con't)

let them enter the * he had	Jos 5:6
to Israel—a * that "flowed with	Jos 5:6
from a distant * to ask for a peace	Jos 9:6
lived in a distant *, when you were	Jos 9:22
this entire * and destroy all the	Jos 9:24
They destroyed everyone in the *,	Jos 10:40
Mount Hermon, in the * of Mizpah.	Jos 11:1
So Joshua conquered the entire*	Jos 11:16
the Negeb, the * of Goshen, the	Jos 11:16
None was left in all the * of	Jos 11:22
So Joshua took the entire * just	Jos 11:23
dividing the * among the tribes.	Jos 11:23
So the * finally rested from its	Jos 11:23
and Moses gave the * to the tribes	Jos 12:6
(This * which lay between	Jos 12:7
All the * of the Philistines;	Jos 13:2-7
The * of the Geshurites;	Jos 13:2-7
The * of the Avvim in the south;	Jos 13:2-7
all the * of the Canaanites,	Jos 13:2-7
The * of the Gebalites on the	Jos 13:2-7
all the * of the Sidonians.	Jos 13:2-7
you divide the * among the nine	Jos 13:2-7
assigned this * to them.	Jos 13:8
The * Given to the Tribe of Levi:	Jos 13:14
Moses hadn't assigned any * to the	Jos 13:14
The * Given to the Tribe of	Jos 13:15
of Reuben: Their * extended from	Jos 13:16
The * of Reuben also included the	Jos 13:21
The * Given to the Tribe of Gad:	Jos 13:24
Moses also assigned * to the tribe	Jos 13:24
and half of the * of Ammon as far	Jos 13:25
The * Given to the Half-Tribe of	Jos 13:29
That was how Moses divided the *	Jos 13:32
But Moses had given no * to the	Jos 13:33
(Moses had already given * to the	Jos 14:3,4
were given no * at all, except	Jos 14:3,4
So the distribution of the * was	Jos 14:5
The * Given to Caleb:	Jos 14:6
to spy out the * of Canaan.	Jos 14:7
them from entering the Promised *.	Jos 14:8
I shall drive them out of the *."	Jos 14:12
as the Israelis resettled the *.	Jos 14:15
THE * GIVEN to the Tribe of Judah	Jos 15:1
The * Given to Caleb:	Jos 15:13
For the * you gave me is a	Jos 15:18,19
So this was the assignment of *	Jos 15:20
The * Given to the Tribe of	Jos 16:5,6
THE * GIVEN to the Half-tribe of	Jos 17:1
been given the * of Gilead and	Jos 17:1
So now, * on the west side of	Jos 17:2
to ten sections of * (in addition	Jos 17:5,6
addition to the * of Gilead and	Jos 17:5,6
(The * of Tappu-ah belonged to	Jos 17:8
of Manasseh's *, belonged to the	Jos 17:8
The * south of the brook and as	Jos 17:10
Ephraim, and the * north of the	Jos 17:10
one portion of * when the Lord has	Jos 17:14
out the forest * where the	Jos 17:15
and conquered the * God had given	Jos 18:1
living in the * which the Lord your	Jos 18:3
the Levites won't receive any *;	Jos 18:7
they already have * on the east	Jos 18:7
the sections of * to the tribes by	Jos 18:8
The * Given to the Tribe of	Jos 18:11
The section of * assigned to the	Jos 18:11
This was the * assigned to the	Jos 18:20
cities were included in the *	Jos 18:21-28
THE * GIVEN to the Tribe of	Jos 19:1
next assignment of *—including part	Jos 19:1
* previously assigned to Judah.	Jos 19:1
The * Given to the Tribe of	Jos 19:10
its assignment of * was Zebulun.	Jos 19:10
The * Given to the Tribe of	Jos 19:17-23
to be assigned its * was Issachar.	Jos 19:17-23
The * Given to the Tribe of	Jos 19:24,25,26
to be assigned its * was Asher.	Jos 19:24,25,26
The * Given to the Tribe of	Jos 19:32
The * Given to the Tribe of Dan:	Jos 19:40
to be assigned its * was Dan.	Jos 19:40
So all the * was divided among	Jos 19:49
a special piece of * to Joshua,	Jos 19:49
to divide the * among the tribes.	Jos 19:51
of the * of the tribe of Reuben;	Jos 20:8
and Golan of Bashan, in the * of	Jos 20:8
to Israel all the * he had promised	Jos 21:43
So go home now to the * given you	Jos 22:4
(Moses had assigned the * of	Jos 22:7,8
* on the west side of the Jordan.	Jos 22:7,8
When they arrived in the * of	Jos 22:15
altar because your * is defiled,	Jos 22:19
and we will share our * with you.	Jos 22:19
enemies and has given you their *.	Jos 23:3
And I have divided to you the *	Jos 23:4,5
as well as the * of those you have	Jos 23:4,5
All the * from the Jordan River	Jos 23:4,5
people still remaining in the *;	Jos 23:7
chase those nations from your *.	Jos 23:13
from this good * which the Lord	Jos 23:13
* which the Lord has given you.	Jos 23:15,16
Abraham from that * across the	Jos 24:3
led him into the * of Canaan and	Jos 24:3
you into the * of the Amorites on	Jos 24:8
them and gave you their *.	Jos 24:8
I gave you * you had not worked	Jos 24:13
of the Amorites here in this *?	Jos 24:15
their slavery in the * of Egypt.	Jos 24:17
when we passed through their *.	Jos 24:17
nations living here in the *.	Jos 24:18
of Hamor. (The * was located in the	Jos 24:32
piece of *.	Ju 1:14
enough to give me * in the Negeb,	Ju 1:15
moved into its new * in the Negeb	Ju 1:16
the original people of that *.	Ju 1:31,32
of Egypt into this * which I	Ju 2:1
with the people living in this *;	Ju 2:2
the nations living in your *;	Ju 2:3
and took possession of the *.	Ju 2:6
nations in the * and did not drive	Ju 2:23
Lord left in the * to test the new	Ju 3:1
there was peace in the *.	Ju 3:11
that day, and the * was at peace	Ju 3:30
in Kedesh, in the * of Naphtali,	Ju 4:6
peace in the * for forty years.	Ju 5:31
stayed until the * was completely	Ju 6:5
before you, and gave you their *.	Ju 6:9
Ophrah in the * of the Abiezrites.	Ju 6:24
Midian never recovered, and the *	Ju 8:28
in the * of the Abiezrites.	Ju 8:32
cities in the * of Gilead which are	Ju 10:4
River in the * of the Amorites	Ju 10:7,8
warrior from the * of Gilead, but	Ju 11:1
home and lived in the * of Tob.	Ju 11:3
living off the * as bandits.	Ju 11:3
* belonged to the people of Ammon;	Ju 11:13
"Give us back our * peaceably,"	Ju 11:13
"Israel did not steal the *.	Ju 11:14,15
permission to pass through his *.	Ju 11:17
his * to get to their destination.	Ju 11:19
over all of your * from the Arnon	Ju 11:21,22
who took away the * from the	Ju 11:23
Did he try to recover his * after	Ju 11:25
spread across the * from Heshbon to	Ju 11:26
army across the * of Gilead and	Ju 11:29
still controlled the *.	Ju 15:20
living in the * assigned to them.	Ju 18:1
* they were supposed to settle in.	Ju 18:2
We have seen the * and it is ours	Ju 18:9,10
the Jordan in the * of Gilead.	Ju 20:1
soon reached the * of Benjamin.	Ju 20:3
throughout the * of Israel, for	Ju 20:6
city and village in the entire *.	Ju 20:48
carried them off to their own *.	Ju 21:23
famine and moved to the * of Moab.	Ru 1:1
that girl from the * of Moab who	Ru 2:6
mother in your own * and have come	Ru 2:10,11
purchase of the * from Naomi	Ru 4:5
name, and to inherit the *."	Ru 4:5
when we return it to its own *?"	1Sa 6:2
ravaged the whole *—the capital	1Sa 6:4,5
the border of our * and go into	1Sa 6:9
taller than anyone else in the *!	1Sa 9:2
of Ephraim, the * of Shalisha, the	1Sa 9:4
and the entire * of Benjamin, but	1Sa 9:4
searching in the * of Zuph, Saul	1Sa 9:5
you a man from the * of Benjamin.	1Sa 9:16
at Zelzah, in the * of Benjamin;	1Sa 10:2
ancestors out of the * of Egypt.	1Sa 12:6
Aaron to bring them into this *.	1Sa 12:8
in Gibe-ah in the * of Benjamin.	1Sa 13:2
throughout the * of the	1Sa 13:3,4
to the * of Gad and Gilead.	1Sa 13:7
to Gibe-ah in the * of Benjamin.	1Sa 13:15
camp in Geba in the * of Benjamin;	1Sa 13:16
one went toward Ophrah in the *	1Sa 13:17
at all in the * of Israel in those	1Sa 13:19
over about half an acre of *.	1Sa 14:14
of the * of Egypt," he explained.	1Sa 15:6
very famous throughout the *.	1Sa 18:30
cave and return to the * of Judah.	1Sa 22:5
every inch of the entire *!"	1Sa 23:23
and wizards from the * of Israel.	1Sa 28:3
So David headed back into the *	1Sa 29:11
of Judah and the * of Caleb, and	1Sa 30:14
to the people throughout their *.	1Sa 31:9
peace upon the *, and Israel was no	2Sa 7:1
It will be their own * where the	2Sa 7:10,11
this * for generations to come!	2Sa 7:10,11
He also devastated the * of	2Sa 8:2
I will restore to you all the *	2Sa 9:7
are to farm the * for him, to	2Sa 9:10,11
ten thousand from the * of Tob.	2Sa 10:6
now camped in the * of Gilead.	2Sa 17:26
the * equally between you."	2Sa 19:29
to Gilead in the * of Tahtim-hodshi	2Sa 24:6
Having gone through the entire *	2Sa 24:8
famine across the *, or to flee for	2Sa 24:13
most beautiful girl in all the *.	1Ki 1:3,4
Socoh and all the * of Hepher;	1Ki 4:8-19
River to the * of the Philistines,	1Ki 4:21
there was peace throughout the *.	1Ki 4:24
them out of the * of Egypt."	1Ki 8:21
Bring them back again to this *	1Ki 8:33,34
send rain upon the * which you have	1Ki 8:35,36
"If there is a famine in the *	1Ki 8:37
to live in this * which you have	1Ki 8:40
to some foreign *, whether far or	1Ki 8:46
pray toward this * which you have	1Ki 8:48
fathers out of the * of Egypt, you	1Ki 8:53
one end of the * to the other.	1Ki 8:65
this * which I have given them.	1Ki 9:7
things to this * and this Temple?'	1Ki 9:8
them out of the * of Egypt;	1Ki 9:9
cities in the * of Galilee to King	1Ki 9:11,12
and elsewhere throughout the *.	1Ki 9:19
the Red Sea in the * of Edom, where	1Ki 9:26
servants returned to their own *.	1Ki 10:13
from this good * of their fathers	1Ki 14:15
him throughout the *, just as the	1Ki 14:18
throughout the *, and the people of	1Ki 14:24
the cities in the * of Naphtali.	1Ki 15:20
was no rainfall anywhere in the *.	1Ki 17:7
and we will search the entire *."	1Ki 18:5
to him about selling him this *.	1Ki 21:2
a piece of better * in trade.	1Ki 21:2
on your life! That * has been in my	1Ki 21:3
chased out of the * to make room	1Ki 21:26
Literally, "the * is	2Ki 2:19f
ruin all the good * with stones."	2Ki 3:19
forward into the * of Moab,	2Ki 3:24
good piece of *, stopped up the	2Ki 3:25
back in disgust to their own *.	2Ki 3:27
but there was a famine in the *.	2Ki 4:38
had invaded the * of Israel and	2Ki 5:2
Thus even in a foreign * he could	2Ki 5:17f
stayed away from the * of Israel.	2Ki 6:23
and lived in the * of the	2Ki 8:2
returned to the * of Israel and	2Ki 8:3
getting back her house and *.	2Ki 8:3
produce of the * as presents for	2Ki 8:8,9
used to invade the * each spring.	2Ki 13:20,21
King Pul of Assyria invaded the *;	2Ki 15:19,20
and all the * of Naphtali;	2Ki 15:29
people of Israel entered the *.	2Ki 16:3
Now the * of Israel was filled	2Ki 17:5
to other gods throughout the *.	2Ki 17:9
out of the * when Israel came in.	2Ki 17:11
tribe of Judah remained in the *.	2Ki 17:18
carried off to the * of Assyria	2Ki 17:23
of the god of the *, and he has	2Ki 17:26
the laws of the god of the *.	2Ki 17:27,28
them out of the * of Egypt with	2Ki 17:35,36
here in your own * until I take you	2Ki 18:31,32
you to another * just like this	2Ki 18:31,32
and Eden in the * of Telassar?	2Ki 19:12
eastern Turkey—the * of Ararat—and	2Ki 19:37
thrown out of the * to make room	2Ki 21:1
from this * of their fathers."	2Ki 21:8
people of Israel entered the *.	2Ki 21:9
who were in this * long ago, and	2Ki 21:11
warnings that this * would be	2Ki 22:18,19
in Jerusalem and throughout the *.	2Ki 23:24
skilled people were left in the *.	2Ki 24:14
people were left to farm the *.	2Ki 25:12
So Judah was exiled from its *.	2Ki 25:21
in the * and would not be exiled.	2Ki 25:24
Jether from the * of Ishmael, had a	1Ch 2:17
twenty-three cities in the * of	1Ch 2:22
but the * belonged to the	1Ch 4:40,41
invaded the * and struck down the	1Ch 4:40,41
inhabitants of the * and took	1Ch 4:40,41
many cattle in the * of Gilead.	1Ch 5:9
Across from them, in the * of	1Ch 5:11
Gilead (in the * of Bashan) and	1Ch 5:16
spread through the * from Bashan to	1Ch 5:23
III) to invade the * and deport the	1Ch 5:26
of the cities and * assigned by lot	1Ch 6:54
Lots were then drawn to assign *	1Ch 6:61
* of Moab by Hodesh, his new wife:	1Ch 8:8,9,10
inhabitants of the *—lived.	1Ch 11:4
joy had spread throughout the *.	1Ch 12:40
throughout the * of Israel,	1Ch 13:2
'I will give you the * of Canaan	1Ch 16:18
strangers in the Promised *;	1Ch 16:19
and will plant them in their *.	1Ch 17:9
They are here to spy out the * so	1Ch 19:2,3
a complete census throughout the *	1Ch 21:2
Lord brings destruction to the *.	1Ch 21:12
to rule this good * and leave it to	1Ch 28:8
* as our fathers were before us;	1Ch 29:15
David was king of the * of Israel	1Ch 29:26,27
my people from the * of Egypt,	2Ch 6:5,6
this * you gave to their fathers.	2Ch 6:25
and send rain upon this * which	2Ch 6:27
"If there is a famine in the *,	2Ch 6:28
enemies are in the * besieging our	2Ch 6:28
* which you gave to our fathers."	2Ch 6:31f
and if in that * of exile they	2Ch 6:37,38
face toward this * you gave their	2Ch 6:37,38
their sins and heal their *.	2Ch 7:14
people from this * of mine which I	2Ch 7:20
to this * and to this Temple?'	2Ch 7:21
them out of the * of Egypt, and	2Ch 7:22

LAND Con't)
instruments in all the * of Judah. 2Ch 9:11
retinue returned to their own *. 2Ch 9:12
River to the * of the Philistines 2Ch 9:26
throughout the * of Judah and 2Ch 11:23
was peace in the * for the first 2Ch 14:1
the idols in the * of Judah and 2Ch 15:8
the border in the * of Israel. 2Ch 17:4
throughout the *, and you have 2Ch 19:3
this * when your people arrived? 2Ch 20:7
And didn't you give this * 2Ch 20:7
of your * which you have given us. 2Ch 20:11
from all over the * rejoicing and 2Ch 23:12
So all the people of the * 2Ch 23:21
judging of the people of the *. 2Ch 26:21
thrown out of the * by the Lord to 2Ch 28:3
will be able to return to this *. 2Ch 30:9
home in deep shame to his own *. 2Ch 32:21
people of Israel entered the *. 2Ch 33:2
* which I gave your ancestors." 2Ch 33:8
when Israel entered the *. 2Ch 33:9
the whole * of Israel before 2Ch 34:7
he had purged the * and cleaned up 2Ch 34:8
true, that the * must rest for 2Ch 36:21
in Jerusalem, in the * of Judah. 2Ch 36:22,23
in Jerusalem, in the * of Judah. Ez 1:2
ruled the entire * beyond the Ez 4:20
joy throughout the * because the Ez 6:21,22
who lived in the *—the Canaanites, Ez 9:1
warned us that the * we would Ez 9:11
become captives in a foreign *! Neh 4:4
and refused to speculate in *; Neh 5:16
the cities of the *, especially in Neh 8:15
descendants the * of the Neh 9:8
so they could go through on dry *! Neh 9:11
the * you had sworn to give them; Neh 9:15
people in every corner of the *; Neh 9:22
they completely took over the * Neh 9:22
them into the * you had promised to Neh 9:23
fortified cities and fertile *; Neh 9:25
You gave them a large, fat *, but Neh 9:35
slaves here in the * of plenty Neh 9:36
The lush yield of this * passes Neh 9:37
of the * in order to serve God. Neh 10:28
people in the * should bring any Neh 10:31
of everything our * produced, for Neh 10:37
throughout the * came to Jerusalem Neh 12:27
And many of the people of the * Est 8:17
THERE LIVED IN the * of Uz a man Job 1:1
I leave for the * of darkness and Job 10:20,21
to return— a * as dark as Job 10:22
as midnight, a * of the shadow of Job 10:22
to whom alone the * was given—and Job 15:17-19
"Or if my * accuses me because I Job 31:38,39
to get their * for myself, then Job 31:38,39
grow on that * instead of wheat, Job 31:40
And in all the * there were no Job 42:15
gods shall be swept from his *. Ps 10:16
is praised throughout the *. Ps 12:8
the godly men and women in the *; Ps 16:3
oceans back to let dry * appear. Ps 24:2
to me here in the * of the living. Ps 27:13
* and prosper, feeding in safety. Ps 37:3
in the *, and live there forever. Ps 37:29
Literally, "to possess the *." Ps 37:34f
to this lovely * where the Jordan Ps 42:6
nations from this * and gave it all Ps 44:1
Our enemies have invaded our * Ps 44:10
you away from the * of the living. Ps 52:5
the Lord in the * of the living. Ps 56:13
you publicly throughout the *. Ps 57:9
violence of your hands in the *." Ps 58:1f
weary * where there is no water. Ps 63:1
seeds to sprout across the *. Ps 65:10
rain upon your *, O God, to refresh Ps 68:9,10
children shall inherit the *; Ps 69:36
*, even on the highland plains; Ps 72:16
me everywhere throughout the *. Ps 74:12
For the * is full of darkness and Ps 74:20
flies to fill the *, and how the Ps 78:45
the border of his * of blessing, to Ps 78:54
this * of hills he made for them. Ps 78:54
occupying the *, and gave each Ps 78:55
the Promised * and disobeyed as Ps 78:57
O GOD, YOUR * has been conquered Ps 79:1
from your * and planted us. Ps 80:8
and we took root and filled the *. Ps 80:9
covering the entire * from the Ps 80:11
brought you out of the * of Egypt. Ps 81:10
out amazing blessings on this *! Ps 85:1
* will be filled with his glory. Ps 85:9
blessings on the * and it yields Ps 85:12
Can anyone in the * of Ps 88:12
He made the sea and formed the * Ps 95:5
enter the Promised *, the place of Ps 95:11
I will make the godly of the * Ps 101:6
seen everywhere throughout the *. Ps 105:7
* of Canaan as your inheritance." Ps 105:10,11
He called for a famine on the * Ps 105:16
of terror upon the * of Egypt. Ps 105:27
through the *, and turned the Ps 105:28
through the dry and barren *; Ps 105:41
ones singing into the Promised *. Ps 105:43
enter the Promised *, for they Ps 106:24
the nations in the * as God had Ps 106:34
and polluting the * with murder. Ps 106:37,38
and turns the good * of the wicked Ps 107:34
to give us all the * of Shechem, Ps 108:7
as well; the * of Ephraim is the Ps 108:8
by giving them the * of Israel, Ps 111:6
Egypt, from that * of foreign Ps 114:1
and gave their * as an eternal Ps 135:12
God gave the * of these kings to Ps 136:21
let liars prosper here in our *; Ps 140:11
I thirst for you as parched * Ps 143:6
a truly happy * where Jehovah is Ps 144:12-15
in all the *: "You simpletons!" Pro 1:21
Literally, "shall dwell in the *" Pro 2:21f
"shall be cut off from the *." Pro 2:22f
Don't steal the * of defenseless Pro 23:10,11
the *, don't be surprised! Ecc 5:8
Woe to the * whose king is a Ecc 10:16,17
Happy the * whose king is a Ecc 10:16,17
turtledove is heard in our *." Sol 2:12f
as the lovely * of Tirzah, yes, Sol 6:4
and idols—the * is full of them! Is 2:8
And the * will produce for them Is 4:2,3,4
phrase, "fruit of the *." Is 4:2,3,4f
the Glorious *, protecting it from Is 4:5
all the * of Israel lies deserted! Is 6:12
across the whole *, even into the Is 7:19
your *, your crops, your people. Is 7:20
All the * will be one vast Is 7:24
sweep into your * of Judah, O Is 8:7,8
Though soon the * of Zebulun and Is 9:1
in the * of the shadow of death. Is 9:2
that though our * lies in ruins Is 9:8,9,10
burning. The * is blackened by Is 9:19,20
upon you from a distant *? Is 10:3
be a king, ruling a conquered *. Is 10:8
who destroyed the * of Israel. Is 10:17
to him, for the * where he lives Is 11:10
them to the * of Israel from Is 11:11
possessing their * on the east and Is 11:14
and will destroy your whole *. Is 13:5
fierce anger. The * shall be Is 13:9
back to their own * like deer Is 13:14
* will never again be lived in. Is 13:20
once again in the * of Israel. Is 14:1
live in their * will serve them. Is 14:2
and conquer the * nor rebuild the Is 14:21
into a desolate * of porcupines, Is 14:23
I will sweep the * with the broom Is 14:23
The whole * of Moab is a land of Is 15:8
The whole land of Moab is a * of Is 15:8
dim when poverty stalks the *. Is 17:4
armies thundering toward God's *. Is 17:12
AH, * BEYOND the upper reaches of Is 18:1
Literally, "* beyond the rivers Is 18:1f
along the river! * that sends Is 18:2
nation whose * the upper Nile Is 18:2
Literally, "whose * the rivers Is 18:2f
advance against the * of Israel. Is 18:4
nation whose * the rivers divide, Is 18:7
blessed be Iraq, the * I have Is 19:25
you away into a distant, barren *; Is 22:18
that's left of your once joyous *. Is 23:7
THE LORD is overturning the * of Is 24:1
be spared. The * will be Is 24:3
The Lord has spoken. The * Is 24:4,5
rain. The * is defiled by crime; Is 24:4,5
has been banished from the *. Is 24:11
Throughout the * Is 24:13
As a hot, dry * is cooled by Is 25:5
mockery against his * and people. Is 25:8
In that day the whole * of Judah Is 26:1
widened the boundaries of our *! Is 26:15
far from her own * as though blown Is 27:7,8
rest in their own * if they would Is 28:12
each in its own section of his *? Is 28:25
rock within a hot and weary *. Is 32:2
the *, and out of justice, peace. Is 32:16
All the * of Israel is in Is 33:9
will fill the *, and the mountains Is 34:3
veterans too. The * will be soaked Is 34:7
up forever. The * will lie deserted Is 34:10
For God will observe that * and Is 34:11
It will be called "The * of Is 34:12
and subdivided the * and deeded it Is 34:17
springs of water in the thirsty *. Is 35:7
go through that once-deserted *. Is 35:8
Lord's telling me to take this *? Is 36:10
grain and grapes, a * of plenty. Is 36:17
*, where I will have him killed." Is 37:7
many a conquered *, and Egypt with Is 37:25
own * by the same road you came." Is 37:29
Jerusalem to repopulate the *; Is 37:32
then they escaped into the * of Is 37:38
the Lord in the * of the living. Is 38:11
cypress, fir and pine—on barren *. Is 41:19
reestablish the * of Israel and Is 49:8,9
of your abandoned * shall soon be Is 49:19
* and inherit my Holy Mountain. Is 57:13
out of your *—all war will end. Is 60:18
They will possess their * Is 60:21
"The God-forsaken *" or the Is 62:4
or the "* that God Forgot." Is 62:4
Your new name will be "The * Is 62:4
to every * and said, "Tell my Is 62:11
be called "The * of Desire" and Is 62:12
people to possess the * of Israel; Is 65:9
of Anathoth in the * of Benjamin. Jer 1:1
out upon all the people of this *. Jer 1:14
wilderness, a * of deserts and Jer 2:6
into a fruitful *, to eat of its Jer 2:7
made it into a * of sin and Jer 2:7
and look in any valley in the *! Jer 2:23
Have I been to them a * of Jer 2:31
spot in all the * where you haven't Jer 3:2
You have polluted the * with your Jer 3:2
And so the * was greatly polluted Jer 3:9
you again to the * of Israel—one Jer 3:14
Then, when your * is once more Jer 3:16
the north, to the * I gave their Jer 3:18
*, the finest in the world. Jer 3:19
sound the alarm throughout the *. Jer 4:5
and he is headed for your *. Jer 4:7
from a distant * and they shout Jer 4:16
*, until it lies in utter ruin; Jer 4:20
I looked down upon their * and as Jer 4:23
of desolation covers all the *. Jer 4:27
to other gods while in your *; Jer 5:19
happened in this *— the priests Jer 5:30
don't listen, I will empty the *. Jer 6:8
of this *, the Lord has said. Jer 6:12
I will let you stay in your own *. Jer 7:3
you stay in this * that I gave to Jer 7:7
For the * shall lie in Jer 7:34
The whole * trembles at the Jer 8:16
is devouring the * and everything Jer 8:16
of my people all across the *. Jer 8:19
Why is the * a wilderness so that Jer 9:12
We must leave our * and homes!' Jer 9:19
* and pour great troubles down; Jer 10:18
I want to give you a * that Jer 11:5
throughout the * and say, Remember Jer 11:6
How long must this * of yours put Jer 12:4
away, leaving the * deserted. Jer 12:4
The whole * is desolate and no Jer 12:11
Destroying armies plunder the *; Jer 12:12
surrounding the * God gave his Jer 12:14
you from your * just as Judah will Jer 12:14
home to your own * again, each man Jer 12:15
living in this * with helpless Jer 13:13
through the * who is merely Jer 14:8
you as slaves to a * where you have Jer 15:14
shall die in this *, unburied and Jer 16:6
laughter in this *—the happy songs, Jer 16:9
you out of this * and chase you Jer 16:13
you into a foreign * where neither Jer 16:13
this same * I gave your fathers. Jer 16:14,15
have defiled my * with your Jer 16:18
Therefore their * shall become Jer 18:16
to see their native * again. Jer 22:10
He shall die in a distant * Jer 22:12
and you shall die in a foreign *. Jer 22:26
return to the * of your desire. Jer 22:27
Or, "throughout the *." Jer 23:5,6f
of Israel from the * of Egypt," Jer 23:7
back to their own * of Israel from Jer 23:8
For the * is full of adultery Jer 23:10
God is on it. The * itself is Jer 23:10
them that wickedness fills this *. Jer 23:15
of Jerusalem left here in this *; Jer 24:8
destroyed from the * of Israel, Jer 24:10
live here in this * which the Lord Jer 25:5
all against this * and its people Jer 25:8,9
This entire * shall become a Jer 25:11
I will make the * of Chaldea an Jer 25:12
population living in his *. Jer 25:19,20
So did all the kings of the * of Jer 25:19,20
their * has been laid waste by Jer 25:38
* and send you far away to perish. Jer 27:10
country and farm the * as usual." Jer 27:11
you from this * to die—you and all Jer 27:15
you back home again to your own *. Jer 29:14
* that I gave to their fathers; Jer 30:3
quiet in their own *, and no one Jer 30:10
from the distant * of the enemy. Jer 31:16
will come again to their own *. Jer 31:17
them out of the * of Egypt—a Jer 31:32
Anathoth, in the * of Benjamin," Jer 32:8
things in the * of Egypt—things Jer 32:20
You gave Israel this * that you Jer 32:22
ago—a wonderful * that 'flows with Jer 32:22
them in this *, with great joy. Jer 32:41
and sold in this *, now ravaged by Jer 32:43
be heard again in this doomed *. Jer 33:10,11
For I will make this * happier Jer 33:10,11
This *—though every man and Jer 33:12
the Negeb, in the * of Benjamin, in Jer 33:13
long, good lives in our own *. Jer 35:7
* I gave to you and your fathers. Jer 35:15

(LAND Con't)
were left in the * listened to what Jer 37:2
city to go to the * of Benjamin, to Jer 37:12
at Riblah, in the * of Hamath, Jer 39:5
But throughout the * of Judah he Jer 39:10
his people who were left in the *. Jer 39:14
this *, just as he said he would. Jer 40:2,3
with the people left in the *. Jer 40:6
the poor of the * who were left Jer 40:7
city you wish and live off the *. Jer 40:10
men into the * of the Ammonites. Jer 41:15
"Stay here in this *. Jer 42:10
will let you stay here in your *. Jer 42:12
will never again see your own *. Jer 42:18
shall destroy the * of Egypt, Jer 43:11
And he shall plunder the * of Jer 43:12
by returning again to their own *. Jer 44:14
that he made your * desolate, an Jer 44:22
are living in the * of Egypt: I Jer 44:26
flood time, overflowing all the *? Jer 46:7
But afterwards the * shall Jer 46:26
to your own *, don't be dismayed; Jer 46:27
your children from a distant *. Jer 46:27
overflow the * of the Philistines; Jer 47:2
in terror and all the * will weep. Jer 47:2
of the * of Moab, far and near. Jer 48:24
from all over the *—from Heshbon Jer 48:34
the * of Moab, says the Lord. Jer 48:40
devours the * from end to end with Jer 48:45
take back her * from you again. Jer 49:2
you from your * and none shall help Jer 49:5
strip bare the * of Esau, and there Jer 49:9,10
But now, flee from Babylon, the * Jer 50:8
wilderness, a dry and desert *. Jer 50:12
of Babylon and his * as I punished Jer 50:18
again to her own *, to feed in the Jer 50:19
against the * of Merathaim Jer 50:21
Yes, march against Babylon, the * Jer 50:21
of rebels, a * that I will judge! Jer 50:21
*, a shout of great destruction. Jer 50:22
has come. * of pride, you will Jer 50:32
Because the whole * is full of Jer 50:38
Babylon, the * of the Chaldeans. Jer 50:45
against that whole * of the Jer 51:1
down slain in the * of the Jer 51:4
He is still their God, but the * Jer 51:5
return to your own *, for God is Jer 51:9
by jackals, a * horrible to see, Jer 51:37
All through the * will be heard Jer 51:52
Babylon, the * the Chaldeans rule! Jer 51:54
we are a conquered *. Lam 1:16
God burns across the * of Israel Lam 2:3
O people of Edom, in the * of Uz? Lam 4:21
far-off foreign * where you can't Eze 3:5
past the ruins of your *. Eze 5:14
disease and war will stalk your * Eze 5:17
war will destroy those in the * Eze 6:12
north or south—your * is finished. Eze 7:2
for the wrath of God is on the *. Eze 7:12
the * is full of bloody crimes. Eze 7:23
great and all the * is full of Eze 9:9
Now the Lord has given us their * Eze 11:15
give you the * of Israel again. Eze 11:17
may not see the * with his eyes." Eze 12:12f
Babylon, the * of the Chaldeans; Eze 12:13
may not see the * with his eyes." Eze 12:13f
the people of this * sin against Eze 14:13
animals into the * to devastate the Eze 14:15
to devastate the *, even if these Eze 14:15
but the * would be devastated. Eze 14:16
war against that * and tell the Eze 14:17
men were in the *, the Lord God Eze 14:18
disease into the *, and the plague Eze 14:19
And I will make the * desolate Eze 15:8
great merchant * of Babylon—and you Eze 16:29
"planted the seed of the *." Eze 17:5f
proverb about the * of Israel: The Eze 18:2
everyone in the * shook with Eze 19:7
out of Egypt to a * I had Eze 20:5,6
for them—a good *, flowing as it Eze 20:5,6
them into the * I had given them, a Eze 20:15
had given them, a * full of milk Eze 20:15
them into the * I promised them, Eze 20:27,28
you home to the * I promised your Eze 20:42
throughout the * from the Negeb to Eze 21:4
they multiply the widows in the * Eze 22:25
that guards the *, who could stand Eze 22:30
every woman in the * as a sinner Eze 23:10
brought from the * of Egypt; Eze 23:27
and idolatry to cease from the * Eze 23:48
"Son of dust, look toward the * Eze 25:2
to the east of you overrun your *. Eze 25:4
* where flocks of sheep can graze. Eze 25:5
my fist over the * of the Eze 25:16
here in the * of those who live. Eze 26:20
Ships come from every * with all Eze 27:9
out at sea come to * and watch upon Eze 27:29
live in their own *, the land I Eze 28:25
the * I gave their father Jacob. Eze 28:25
you out onto the * with fish Eze 29:4
and herds. The * of Egypt shall Eze 29:9
destroy the * of Egypt, from Migdol Eze 29:10
people back to the * of Pathros in Eze 29:14
I will give the * of Egypt to Eze 29:19
Yes, I have given him the * of Eze 29:20
The * of Cush has been ravished. Eze 30:4
sent to demolish the *. Eze 30:11
sell the whole * to wicked men. Eze 30:12
swings it over the * of Egypt, Eze 30:25
invade her * and cut her down and Eze 31:12
and valleys and rivers of the *. Eze 31:12
and they will * in hell, along with Eze 31:14
you stranded on the * to die. Eze 32:4
across your *—even the bright stars Eze 32:8
is drawn against the * of Egypt. Eze 32:20
the people of that * choose a Eze 33:2
suppose I'll let you have the *? Eze 33:25
Should you possess the *? Eze 33:26
I will desolate the * and her Eze 33:28
When I have ruined the * because Eze 33:29
home to their own * of Israel, and Eze 34:13
where the * is fertile and good. Eze 34:13
animals from the * so that my Eze 34:25
for grabbing my * with relish, in Eze 36:5
is a * that devours her people!' Eze 36:13
They polluted the * with murder Eze 36:18
home again to the * of Israel. Eze 36:24
in Israel, the * which I gave your Eze 36:28
scoff at your * for its famines. Eze 36:30
see the extent of ruin in your *. Eze 36:34
* has become like Eden's garden! Eze 36:35
and return to the * of Israel. Eze 37:12
return home again to your own *. Eze 37:14
*, to unify them into one nation. Eze 37:21
They shall live in the * of Eze 37:25
the * I gave my servant Jacob. Eze 37:25
toward the * of Magog, and Eze 38:2,3
down onto the * of Israel, that Eze 38:8
and cover the * like a cloud. Eze 38:9
* of unwalled villages! Eze 38:11
*, then you will rouse yourself. Eze 38:14
and cover the * like a cloud. Eze 38:15,16
I will bring you against my *, Eze 38:15,16
* of Israel, my fury will rise! Eze 38:18
in the * of Israel on that day. Eze 38:19
men to search the * systematically Eze 39:14
so that the * will be cleansed. Eze 39:14
And so the * will finally be Eze 39:15,16
in their own *, with no one Eze 39:26
he took me to the * of Israel and Eze 40:2
"WHEN YOU DIVIDE the * among the Eze 45:1
"A section of this *, 875 feet Eze 45:2
All this section shall be holy * Eze 45:4
"Two special sections of * shall Eze 45:7
remainder of the * to the people, Eze 45:8
out of their *, and expelling them Eze 45:9
gives a gift of * to one of his Eze 46:16
But if he gives a gift of * to Eze 46:17
then the * returns to the prince. Eze 46:17
be from his own *, for I don't want Eze 46:18
for dividing the * to the twelve Eze 47:13
truth to give the * to your Eze 47:14
"Divide the * within these Eze 47:21
Distribute the * as an Eze 47:22
All children born in the * Eze 47:22
are to be given * according to the Eze 47:23
and western limits of the *. Eze 48:1
Naphtali's * lies south of Eze 48:3
"South of Judah is the * set Eze 48:8
"A strip of * measuring 8 Eze 48:10
portion when the * is distributed, Eze 48:12
the most sacred * of all. Eze 48:12
None of this special * shall Eze 48:14
"The strip of * 8 Eze 48:15
Open * for pastures shall Eze 48:17
"The * on both sides of this Eze 48:21,22
the prince. This *, lying between Eze 48:21,22
of his god in the * of Shinar. Dan 1:1
warred against the * of Israel. Dan 8:9
Literally, "the glorious *." Dan 8:9f
and send us back to our own * Dan 9:3
soon return again to his own *. Dan 11:9
*' of Israel, and pillage it. Dan 11:16
areas of the * without warning and Dan 11:24
the * to them as their reward. Dan 11:39
the Pleasant *, and overthrow the Dan 11:41
soil of their own * again." Hos 1:11
* riddled with famine and drought. Hos 1:3
no knowledge of God in your *. Hos 4:1
That is why your * is not Hos 4:3
tremble, * of Benjamin! Hos 5:8
longer stay here in this * of God; Hos 9:3
I will drive them from my * Hos 9:15
in that dry and thirsty *. Hos 13:5
are all the leaders of the *? Hos 13:10
hard upon him and dry up his *. Hos 13:15
covers the *. Joe 1:6
Ahead of them the * lies fair as Joe 2:3
indignant for the honor of his *! Joe 2:18
stench will rise upon the *. Joe 2:20
the nations and dividing up my *. Joe 3:2
took them far from their own *. Joe 3:6
I cleared the * of the Amorites Amo 2:
to possess the * of the Amorites. Amo 2:1
am sending disaster into your *. Amo 3:
pours it out as rain upon the *. Amo 5:
to Gath in the Philistines' *. Amo 6:
and was devouring the entire *. Amo 7:
to rebellion all across the *. Amo 7:1
Flee to the * of Judah and do Amo 7:1
be killed and your * divided up. Amo 7:1
die in a heathen *, and the people Amo 7:1
in exile, far from their *.' Amo 7:1
your deeds! The * will tremble as Amo 8:8
a famine on the *—not a famine of Amo 8:1
Hosts touches the * and it melts, Amo 9:5
upon the * that I have given them; Amo 9:1
the future of the * of Edom. Ob 1:1
help to push you out of your *. Ob 1:7
You yourselves went into the * Ob 1:13
Israel will reoccupy the *. Ob 1:17
and imprisoned in the * of death. Jon 2:6
You want a certain piece of *, Mic 2:2
God has confiscated our * and Mic 2:4
This is no more your * and home, Mic 2:10
of captivity, back to your own *. Mic 2:13
again in their own *, a mighty Mic 4:7
their brethren in their own *. Mic 5:3
invades our * and marches across Mic 5:5
the gates of the * of Nimrod. Mic 5:6
Assyrians when they invade our *. Mic 5:6
Literally, "But the * will be Mic 7:13f
For the * of the people of God Nah 2:2
Ethiopia and the whole * of Nah 3:9
The gates of your * will be Nah 3:13
proudly forward from a distant *; Hab 1:8
You marched across the * in Hab 3:12
in all your *," says the Lord. Zep 1:2
For the whole * will be devoured Zep 1:18
living on the coast and in the * Zep 2:5
my people and invading their *. Zep 2:8
in his own * throughout the world. Zep 2:11
*, yes, and in the highlands, too; Hag 1:11
remaining in the * obeyed Haggai's Hag 1:12
Priest and everyone left in the *: Hag 2:2
too, and the dry *— I will shake Hag 2:6
" 'Come, flee from the * of the Zec 2:6,7
in the Holy *, for God shall once Zec 2:11,12
I will remove the sins of this * Zec 3:9
curse going out over the entire *. Zec 5:3
everywhere throughout the *." Zec 5:6
Their * became desolate; Zec 7:14
the Pleasant * lay bare and Zec 7:14
Now I am going to return to my * Zec 8:3
given to the people left in the *. Zec 8:12
will again overrun my people's *. Zec 9:8
Or, "to the ends of the *" of Zec 9:10f
They shall shine in his * as Zec 9:16,17
They shall turn the * into a Zec 11:6
throughout the *, so that even the Zec 13:2
but a third will be left in the * Zec 13:8
All the * from Geba (the Zec 14:10
is named 'The * of Wickedness' and Mal 1:4
be a * sparkling with happiness. Mal 3:12
to their own *, they didn't go Mt 2:12
"The * of Zebulun and the land Mt 4:15,16
"The land of Zebulun and the * Mt 4:15,16
they sat in the * of death, and Mt 4:15,16
like this in all the * of Israel! Mt 8:10
Literally, "in all that *." Mt 9:31f
for she came from a distant * to Mt 12:42
followed by * from many villages. Mt 14:13
Or, "*." Mt 27:45f
to send them to some distant *. Mk 5:10
he was alone on *, he saw that Mk 6:47
children, and *—with persecutions! Mk 10:30
darkness fell across the entire *, Mk 15:33
foreigner from the * of Sidon. Lk 4:25,26
years, and hunger stalked the *; Lk 4:25,26
were circulating all over the *. Lk 9:8
trip to a distant *, and there Lk 15:13
the *, and he began to starve. Lk 15:14
* to live for several years. Lk 20:9
all the * when his father dies. Lk 20:14
Literally, "upon the *," or, Lk 21:23f
darkness fell across the whole * Lk 23:44
Even in his own * and among his Jn 1:11,12
the boat was at the *." Jn 6:21f
all who owned * or houses sold them Act 4:34,35
* for such and such a price?" Act 5:8
leave his native *, to say good-bye Act 7:3
So he left the * of the Act 7:4
him here to the * of Israel, but Act 7:4
own, not one little tract of *. Act 7:5
would leave the * and live in a Act 7:6
* of Israel and worship me here.' Act 7:7
and lived in the * of Midian, where Act 7:29
was coming upon the * of Israel. Act 11:28
Israel their * as an inheritance. Act 13:19,20
Paul was going by * to Assos, and Act 20:13
the sailors suspected * was near. Act 27:27
and make for *, and the rest to Act 27:43
left in all the * who still loved Rom 11:2,3

(LAND Con't)
the * he had promised his people? Heb 3:18
does not mean the * of Israel that Heb 4:8
When a farmer's * has had many Heb 6:7
come up, that * has experienced Heb 6:7
and thorns, the * is considered no Heb 6:8
lead them out of the * of Egypt; Heb 8:9
away to another * which he promised Heb 11:8
God's promised *, he lived in tents Heb 11:9
that he left the * of Egypt and Heb 11:27
people out of the * of Egypt, and Jud 1:5
blowing over dry * without giving Jud 1:12
on the sea and * lifted his right Rev 10:5
there upon the sea and *." Rev 10:8
the laws of the * are refusing to Rom 13:2

LANDED
a millstone. It * on Abimelech's Ju 9:53
how their staffs * on the ground Hos 4:12f
They * at Gennesaret. Mt 14:34
the shore and met them as they *. Mk 6:33
And as soon as they *, they left Lk 5:11
Other seed * in thistle patches, Lk 8:7
But when we * at Miletus, he Act 20:17
it on our left and * at the harbor Act 21:3
Near the shore where we * was an Act 28:7

LANDING
* at the port town of Perga. Act 13:13
and Pamphylia, * at Myra, in the Act 27:5

LANDMARKS
has engulfed us—* are moved, flocks Job 24:2

LANDOWNER
story: A certain * planted a Mt 21:33

LANDS
*, each with a separate language. Gen 10:5
abroad in many * and nations, with Gen 10:20
I will give them all of these *; Gen 26:4
those from other * who came to Gen 41:56,57
others from many * to buy food, for Gen 42:5
that you are captives in enemy *. Lev 26:34,35
* as prisoners of war, and slaves. Lev 26:36
pine away in enemy * because of Lev 26:39
cities and surrounding pasture *. Num 35:2
the surrounding * for their cattle, Num 35:3
by from distant * shall see the Deu 29:22
to scatter them to distant *, Deu 32:26
THE CONQUERED * of Canaan were Jos 14:1
from the * of Rehob and Zobah, one 2Sa 10:6
The conquered peoples of those * 1Ki 4:21
And kings from many * sent their 1Ki 4:34
come from distant * to worship you 1Ki 8:41,42
Great men from many * came to 1Ki 10:24
his enemies in the surrounding *. 1Ch 22:9
come from distant * to worship your 2Ch 6:32
* that paid annual tribute to him. 2Ch 9:13,14
Just like the people of other *, 2Ch 13:9
to do a thing to save their *! 2Ch 32:13
from their own * by the great and Ez 4:10
* west of the Euphrates River. Ez 4:10
governor of the * west of the Ez 5:3
slaves in distant *, but you are Neh 5:8
* and sell them their children. Neh 5:12
as though your * could be forever Ps 49:11
O rebel *, he will deflate your Ps 66:7
And peoples from remotest * will Ps 67:6,7
people from the * of Gebal, Ps 83:7
He gave them the * of the Ps 105:44
away to distant * as exiles. Ps 106:27
tongue, then the * of Judah and of Ps 114:2
and people from many * will flow Is 2:2
Or, "the * will be deserted (of Is 7:15,16f
future these very *, Galilee and Is 9:1
and all the distant coastal *. Is 11:11
between their *, and they shall Is 19:23
returning home from distant *! Is 23:1
colonists you sent to distant *! Is 23:7
Beautiful palaces in distant * Is 25:2
For your * will thrive with Is 32:13
Of all the gods of these *, Is 36:20
LISTEN IN SILENCE before me, O * Is 41:1
The * beyond the sea watch in Is 41:5
Remote * tremble and mobilize for Is 41:5
until even distant * beyond the Is 42:4
live in distant * beyond the sea! Is 42:10
he has chosen to conquer many *. Is 45:1
in many eastern * today) only Is 47:2f
of you in far-off *: The Lord Is 49:1
the nations that took their *. Is 54:3
for his foes in distant *. Is 59:18
coming home to you from distant *. Is 60:4
bringing you the wealth of many *. Is 60:5
ships of many *, the very best, Is 60:9
to receive the wealth of many *. Is 60:11
Javan, and to the * beyond the sea Is 66:19
slaves to foreigners in their *." Jer 5:19
people: (Listen to it, distant *; Jer 6:18,19
to be strangers in distant *; Jer 9:16
to your enemies in distant *. Jer 17:4
will be exiled to distant *. Jer 22:28
Israel and her neighboring * Jer 25:11
again from distant *, and your Jer 30:10
shall be taken away to distant *! Jer 48:7
Let them rush back to their own * Jer 50:16
come against her from distant *; Jer 50:26
* shall become as weak as women. Jer 50:37
kings called by God from many *. Jer 50:41
the builders from many * have Jer 51:58
far away as slaves to distant *. Lam 1:18
in far-off *, without a temple, Lam 2:9
They flee to distant * and Lam 4:15
Gentile * to which I exile them!" Eze 4:13
their long march to distant *. Eze 12:4
honey, the best of all * anywhere. Eze 20:5,6
you out from the * where you are Eze 20:34
it and the forest * of the Negeb. Eze 20:46
"You even sent away to distant * Eze 23:40
again from distant * where I have Eze 28:25
exile the Egyptians to other *. Eze 29:12
banish the Egyptians to many *. Eze 30:23
strike in many *, and their kings Eze 32:10
sent you away as slaves to many *. Eze 36:3
And I exiled them to many *; Eze 36:19
return of its people from many *. Eze 38:8
them home from the * of their Eze 39:27
Adjacent to the holy * will be a Eze 45:6
each side of the holy * and city; Eze 45:7
sacred * and city lands—is 8 Eze 48:20
sacred lands and city *—is 8 Eze 48:20
side of the sacred and city *. Eze 48:21,22
of peace between their two *. Dan 11:6f
He will invade various * on the Dan 11:41
and many other * will be occupied. Dan 11:42
*, I will send her off to exile. Hos 8:10
took him far away to foreign *; Ob 1:12
have gone as slaves to distant *. Mic 1:16
Citizens of many * will come and Mic 7:12
your neighboring * reel and stagger Hab 2:15
and so will the * of the north; Zep 2:13
come from distant * to rebuild the Zec 6:15
God's curse on the * of Hadrach and Zec 9:1
from eastern * arrived in Mt 2:1
*, and have come to worship him." Mt 2:2
still used among men in Eastern *. Mt 26:49f
in many *, and famines. Mk 13:8
famines in many *, and epidemics, Lk 21:11
greeting among men in eastern *. Lk 22:47f
*, or maybe even to the Gentiles! Jn 7:35
of the * where we were born! Act 2:8
and even to those in distant *!" Act 2:39
in distant cities in foreign *. Act 26:11
men from other * to speak in 1Co 14:21
* along with the free woman's son. Gal 4:30

LANDSCAPE
covered the * around the Springs of Jos 11:4
all across the * in the morning. 2Ki 19:35
whole * lighted up with his glory. Eze 43:2
them, and the * shone bright with Lk 2:9

LANES
into the country * and out behind Lk 14:23

LANGUAGE
lands, each with a separate *. Gen 10:5
TIME all mankind spoke a single *. Gen 11:1
* is the basis on which science Gen 11:6f
*, and "Galeed" in Jacob's. Gen 31:47,48
a nation whose * you don't Deu 28:49
different * groups), and Joktan. 1Ch 1:19
in the Jewish * to the people 2Ch 32:18
*, and it was translated to him. Ez 4:7
spoke in the * of Ashdod and Neh 13:24
speak the * of Judah at all. Neh 13:24
You curse and lie, and vile * Ps 50:19
will begin to speak the Hebrew *. Is 19:18
Literally, "the * of Canaan." Is 19:18f
the only * they can understand is Is 28:11
strange, jabbering * you can't Is 33:19
Aramaic was the * used in Is 36:11f
nation whose * you don't Jer 5:15
understand the *— no, not to Eze 3:5
the Chaldean * and literature. Dan 1:3,4
The * was Aramaic; Dan 1:3,4f
his nation, *, or religion Dan 3:7
of any nation, *, or religion Dan 3:29
* in every nation of the world: Dan 4:1
people of every * must obey him. Dan 7:14
Egypt, the Cyrene * areas of Libya, Act 2:10
spiritual truth in spiritual *." 1Co 2:13f
and others, who do not know the * 1Co 12:10
speak in every * there is in all of 1Co 13:1
talking in some * you don't 1Co 14:6
The local *, whatever it is. 1Co 14:7f
a person in some * he doesn't 1Co 14:9
For if I pray in a * I don't 1Co 14:14
* that everyone understands. 1Co 14:15
also in ordinary *, so that I can 1Co 14:15
in another *, how can those who 1Co 14:16
in tongues" in an unknown *. 1Co 14:19
in an unknown *, or tell what 1Co 14:26
in the unknown *, but everything 1Co 14:26
in an unknown *, and they must 1Co 14:27
in the unknown * but not publicly. 1Co 14:28
Don't use bad *. Eph 4:29
hatred, cursing, and dirty *. Col 3:8
and what insulting * he is using. 3Jn 1:10
and * groups throughout the world. Rev 13:7
every nation, tribe, * and people. Rev 14:6

LANGUAGES
lands and nations, with many *. Gen 10:20
*, and geographical locations. Gen 10:31
them different *, so that they Gen 11:7
giving them many *, thus widely Gen 11:9
In many of the * of the ancient Lev 2:13f
in all the local *, stressing that Est 1:22
in its own * and dialects; Est 3:12
into the * and dialects of all the Est 8:9,10
and *, this is the king's command: Dan 3:4
and they shall speak new *. Mk 16:17
speaking in * they didn't know, Act 2:4
* being spoken by the disciples. Act 2:6
* of the lands where we were born! Act 2:8
telling in our own * about the Act 2:11
spoke in other * and prophesied. Act 19:6
to speak in * he never learned; 1Co 12:10
Those who speak in * they have 1Co 12:28
to speak in * we've never learned? 1Co 12:30
to speak in other * without 1Co 13:1
in unknown *, and special 1Co 13:8
is, to speak in * you haven't 1Co 14:2
speak in unknown *—unless, of 1Co 14:5
rather than in unknown *. 1Co 14:7
of different * in the world, and 1Co 14:10
me in one of these * will be a 1Co 14:11
speak in foreign * to his people, 1Co 14:21
talking in other *, he is likely to 1Co 14:23
and provinces and *, standing in Rev 7:9

LANGUISHES
The earth *, the crops wither, Is 24:4,5

LANTERNS
"I will search with * in Zep 1:12
Now with blazing torches, *, and Jn 18:3

LAODICE
II's former wife *, was the sister Dan 11:7f

LAODICEA
for the church at *, and for my Col 2:1
Christians in * and Hierapolis. Col 4:13
friends at *, and to Nymphas, and Col 4:15
you pass it on to the church at *? Col 4:16
Sardis, Philadelphia, and *." Rev 1:11
of the church in *: Rev 3:14

LAP
their mouths and * it like dogs. Ju 7:5,6
his head in her *, and they brought Ju 16:19
and his mother held him on her *; 2Ki 4:20
shook out the * of my gown." Neh 5:13f
Literally, "cast dice into the * Pro 16:33f
the people; they * it up and lick Hos 4:8

LAPIS
bdellium and even * lazuli. Gen 2:11,12
Literally, "* lazuli." Eze 10:1f

LAPPIDOTH
a prophetess, the wife of *. Ju 4:4

LARGE
He had * flocks of sheep and Gen 26:14
"Because of the * hospital bill Gen 30:6f
For the land is * enough to hold Gen 34:21
they soon became a * nation, and Ex 1:7
a good land, a * land, a land Ex 3:8
one oven will be * enough to bake Lev 26:26
* numbers of them with a plague. Num 11:33
of grapes so * that it took two of Num 13:23
cities are fortified and very *; Num 13:28
and Gad (who had * flocks of sheep) Num 32:1
From there it will make a * Num 34:10,11
struck down with a * stone, it is Num 35:17
that area, a very * tribe, tall as Deu 2:10
They were a * and powerful Deu 2:21
that you will have * crops of Deu 7:13
have become very *, and your silver Deu 8:12,13
Give him a * farewell present Deu 15:14
doesn't build up a * stable of Deu 17:16
* flocks and herds; Deu 28:2-6
has given us such * populations?" Jos 17:14
of Ephraim is not * enough for Jos 17:15
you are such a *, strong tribe you Jos 17:16,17,18
section had been too * for them. Jos 19:9
they built a * monument for Jos 22:10
and stopped beside a * rock. 1Sa 6:14
(By the way, that * rock at 1Sa 6:18
Jerusalem a very * amount of bronze 2Sa 8:8
One * tank and twelve oxen 1Ki 7:41-46
in the lid of a * chest and set it 2Ki 12:9
cities both * and small. 2Ki 18:8
his brothers had * families—they 1Ch 4:27
him a * sum of money every year. 1Ch 18:2
him * amounts of money every year. 1Ch 18:6
* sums of money annually to David. 1Ch 18:13
Festival, with * crowds coming in 2Ch 7:8
gold to make 200 * shields, each 2Ch 9:15
and gave them * allowances and 2Ch 11:23
Your army is twice as * as mine, 2Ch 13:8
armed with * shields and bows. 2Ch 14:8
him and deport * numbers of his 2Ch 28:5
And so it was that a very * 2Ch 30:13
And at this time another * group 2Ch 30:24

(LARGE Con't)
* numbers of weapons and shields. 2Ch 32:5
this confession, a * crowd of men, Ez 10:1
and a * number of domestic fowls; Neh 5:18
For the city was *, but the Neh 7:4
You gave them a *, fat land, but Neh 9:35
He had a * family of seven sons Job 1:2,3
"Make a * signboard and write on Is 8:1
Not a piece will be left * enough Is 30:14
a sacrifice * enough to honor him, Is 40:16
More literally, "a * brazier in Jer 36:22f
murdered was the * one constructed Jer 41:9
watch you, bury * rocks between the Jer 43:9
dismantled the two * bronze pillars Jer 52:17
"AND NOW, SON of dust, take a * Eze 4:1
gate, where the * idol was that had Eze 8:3
which she drank was full and *. Eze 23:32
into the nave, the * main room of Eze 41:1
A * building stood on the west, Eze 41:12
This goat, which had one very * Dan 8:5
Now Nineveh was a very * city, Jon 3:3
suburbs—so * that it would take Jon 3:3
* and clear, so that anyone can Hab 2:2
Your crops will be *, for I will Mal 3:11
* CROWDS FOLLOWED Jesus as he Mt 8:1
When Jesus noticed how * the Mt 8:18
*, and your request is granted." Mt 15:28
And a * crowd soon gathered Mk 5:15
seven very * basketfuls left over! Mk 8:8,9
Some who were rich put in * Mk 12:41
upstairs to a * room all set up. Mk 14:15
with Jesus on a *, level area, Lk 6:17,18
you use to give—* or small—will be Lk 6:38
illustration to a * crowd that was Lk 8:4
times as * as he had planted." Lk 8:8
matters, you won't be in * ones. Lk 16:10
"it would be * enough to uproot Lk 17:6
to a * room all ready for us. Lk 22:12
The world at * cannot receive Jn 14:17
and not to the world at *?" Jn 14:22
shall produce a * crop of fruit. Jn 15:5
By his count there were 153 * Jn 21:11
effort so that * numbers of these Act 11:21
As a result * numbers of people Act 11:24
a * number of godly Greek men, and Act 17:4
day * numbers came to his house. Act 28:23
way we are handling this * gift. 2Co 8:20
See how * I have to make the Gal 6:11
paid well if he raises a * crop. 2Ti 2:6
We can make a * horse turn Jas 3:3

LARGER
upon the earth—the * one, the sun, Gen 1:16
spot grows no * and does not Lev 13:23
This time he sent a * number of Num 22:15
the census— the * tribes to be Num 26:54
of the * tribes have a lottery, Num 26:55,56
drawing for the * sections," the Num 26:55,56
your tribes. The * sections of land Num 33:54
by lot among the * tribes, and the Num 33:54
of the nation; the * tribes with Num 35:8
because you were a * nation than Deu 7:7
he may not give a * inheritance to Deu 21:16
cities and much * than Ai—and its Jos 10:2
* cities, and instructed them: 2Ch 19:5
palace and all the * homes, and Jer 52:13
* and more prosperous than before. Mic 7:11
"Then he sent a * group of his Mt 21:36
that bear fruit for even * crops. Jn 15:2

LARGEST
He gave the * serving to Gen 43:34
by conquering Gath, their * city. 2Sa 8:1
in fact, it was the * single gift 1Ki 10:10
before the * crowd I can find. Ps 35:18
Their * cities will be as Is 17:9
but becomes the * of plants, and Mt 13:31,32
become one of the * of plants, with Mk 4:31,32

LASEA
Fair Havens, near the city of *. Act 27:7,8

LASH
burn, wound for wound, * for lash. Ex 21:25
burn, wound for wound, lash for *. Ex 21:25
As they tied Paul down to * him, Act 22:25
The soldiers standing ready to * Act 22:29

LASHA
Admah, and Zeboiim, near *. Gen 10:15-19

LASHARON
The king of *; Jos 12:8-24

LASHED
he was *—and we were healed! Is 53:5
and spat upon, and * and killed. Lk 18:33
and ordered him * with whips to Act 22:24

LASHES
hundred * on the back of a rebel. Pro 17:10
me their terrible thirty-nine *. 2Co 11:24

LAST
NOW AT * the heavens and earth Gen 2:1
Then at * the earth was dry. Gen 8:14
urgent, until at * they went home Gen 19:3
"I slept with my father * night. Gen 19:34
Then at *, when the camels had Gen 24:22
Then at * she became pregnant. Gen 25:21
Well of Room Enough for Us at *!" Gen 26:22
"For now at *," he said, "the Gen 26:22
appeared to me * night and told me, Gen 31:29
why he appeared to you * night." Gen 31:42
next, and Rachel and Joseph *. Gen 33:2
And with Rachel's * breath Gen 35:18
So Jacob came at * to Isaac his Gen 35:27
both had dreams * night, but there Gen 40:8
"I had a dream * night," Gen 41:15
So at * the seven years of plenty Gen 41:53
honor this, my * request: do not Gen 47:29
the bed, breathed his *, and died. Gen 49:33
Then, when at * the mourning was Gen 50:4
and then at * he will let you go. Ex 3:20
The celebration shall * seven Ex 12:15
and it was on the * day of the Ex 12:40,41
So at * Pharaoh let the people Ex 13:17,18
Then at * the people were Ex 36:4-7
And so at * the Tabernacle was Ex 39:32
So at * Moses finished the work. Ex 40:33
impurity shall * two weeks, during Lev 12:5
strip every * piece of fruit from Lev 19:10
later, on the * day of September, Lev 23:33,34
"This * day of September, at the Lev 23:39
Remember that the first and * Lev 23:39
year that will * you until the Lev 25:21,22
Then at * the land will rest and Lev 26:34,35
"But at * they shall confess Lev 26:40,41
When at * their evil hearts are Lev 26:40,41
But then at * they shall accept Lev 26:43
son of Gideoni. * of all were the Num 10:25
Midianite), "At * we are on our Num 10:29
* of you lies dead in the desert. Num 14:33
Then at * this murmuring and Num 17:5
Then at * the Lord said, Deu 2:2
Then at * the Lord said to me, Deu 2:16,17
was the * of the giant Rephaim. Deu 3:11
you do, until at * you are Deu 28:20
Ai until the * person was dead. Jos 8:26
Every * person was slaughtered, Jos 10:30
King Og of Bashan, the * of the Jos 12:4
(He was the * of the Rephaim, for Jos 13:12
The * tribe to be assigned its Jos 19:40
Then at * the people of Israel Ju 6:6,7
More literally, "Are not the * Ju 8:2,3f
border until at * they arrived Ju 11:18
was the * they ever saw of him. Ju 13:21
celebration. At *, on the seventh Ju 14:17
at * Naomi has a son again!" Ru 4:16,17
and destroy every * one of them." 1Sa 14:36
Listen to what the Lord told me * 1Sa 15:16
so at * Jonathan realized that 1Sa 20:33
At * Jonathan said to David, 1Sa 20:42
Saul said. "At * someone has 1Sa 23:21
home to your wife * night after 2Sa 11:10
"At * I know that you like me! 2Sa 14:22
Then at * David summoned Absalom, 2Sa 14:33
son Absalom! At * you will taste 2Sa 16:7,8
the * ones to reinstate the king? 2Sa 19:11,12
Then at * God answered prayer 2Sa 21:12,13,14
THESE ARE THE * words of David: 2Sa 23:1
At * the Temple was finished. 1Ki 6:14
and basins and at * completed the 1Ki 7:40
to cook this * meal, and then my 1Ki 17:12
Go ahead and cook that '* meal,' 1Ki 17:13
end of the line with the * team. 1Ki 19:19
Then at * you will know that I am 1Ki 20:13
his swordsmen in a * desperate 2Ki 3:26
said, "I know at * that there is 2Ki 5:15
that will * for seven years." 2Ki 8:1
When Elisha was in his * illness, 2Ki 13:14
The * food in the city was eaten 2Ki 25:3
day of the * month of the 2Ki 25:27
At * the celebration ended and 1Ch 16:43
was one of the * things David did 1Ch 23:27
will make his kingdom * forever.' 1Ch 28:7
So at * he completed the work 2Ch 4:11
from first to * are written in the 2Ch 20:34
"At * the time has come for the 2Ch 23:2,3
Zechariah's * words as he died 2Ch 24:22
from first to * are recorded by the 2Ch 26:22
And now there was peace at * 2Ch 32:22
Then at * he came to his senses 2Ch 33:12
more and more. At * his own 2Ch 33:24
toward Israel will * forever." Ez 3:11
So at * we arrived safely at Ez 8:32
At * the wall was completed to Neh 4:6
And that was the * time they Neh 13:21
And at * Queen Esther replied, Est 7:3
holiday on the * days of the month, Est 9:21
AT * JOB spoke, and cursed the day Job 3:1
is free at * from his master. Job 3:19
What blessed relief when at * Job 3:22
And so at * the poor have hope, Job 5:16
his home for security, it won't *. Job 8:15
lies down for the * time, and does Job 14:11,12
he will stand upon the earth at *. Job 19:25
'See,' they will say, 'the * of Job 22:20
him and you will have peace at *! Job 22:21
He does bring about justice at *, Job 35:14,15
Then at * he died, an old, old Job 42:17
* they know they are but puny men. Ps 9:20
Go after them until the * of them Ps 10:15
lips quieted at *—the lips of these Ps 31:18
and, "At * we have him!" Ps 35:25
Then at * I spoke, and pled with Ps 39:2,3
This is the * chance for all of Ps 50:22
Then at * everyone will know Ps 58:11
At * I shall be fully satisfied; Ps 63:5
of God; at * they will realize what Ps 64:9
Then at *, when he had ruined Ps 78:34
their desolation would * forever. Ps 81:15
I will praise God to my * breath! Ps 104:33
Then at * his people believed Ps 106:12
but when dreams come true at *, Pro 13:12
Dishonest gain will never *, so Pro 21:6
flood sweeping away their * hope. Pro 28:3
and beauty doesn't *, but a woman Pro 31:30
In the * days Jerusalem and the Is 2:2
Then at the * all wars will stop Is 2:4
Then at * they will abandon Is 2:20
bouts that * till late at night—woe Is 5:11
Then at *, those left in Israel Is 10:20
It will not * very long; Is 10:25
Then, at *, the jealousy between Is 11:13
* you have what was coming to you! Is 14:4
But at * the whole earth is at Is 14:7
no one will bother us now; at * Is 14:8
Then at * they will think of God Is 17:7
barefoot for the * three years, is Is 20:3
the wall, and at * he shouted, Is 21:8,9
Now at *—look! Is 21:8,9
Now at * he is here." Is 25:9
Then at * the Lord of Hosts Is 28:5
to the * before your gates. Is 28:6
you off, until at * the unmixed Is 28:19
Then at * the eyes of Israel Is 32:3
are, until at * the Spirit is Is 32:15
is I, the Lord, the First and *; Is 41:4
who says it—I am the First and *; Is 44:6
I am the *. Is 48:12
but my justice and mercy shall * Is 51:8
and squeezed out the * drops. Is 51:17
it is gone at *. Is 51:22
Then at * they will recognize Is 52:6
Then at * they will reverence Is 59:19
you will know at * and really Is 60:16
Why then do my people say, "At * Jer 2:31
This is your * warning, O Jer 6:8
at * you shall feel my wrath. Jer 10:18
We thought, Now at * he will heal Jer 14:19
at * that I alone am God. Jer 16:21
He was Judah's * ruler before the Jer 21:1f
Surely at * you will see your Jer 22:22
had from God * night," they say. Jer 23:25
and killed Belshazzar, the * Jer 25:12f
Then at * Moab shall be ashamed Jer 48:13
Things became so bad at * that Jer 52:3
serious, with the * of the food Jer 52:6
say, "We have destroyed her at *! Lam 2:16
then at * there is hope for him. Lam 3:29
But now at * the anger of the Lam 4:11
will end at *, but Edom's never. Lam 4:22
Scatter the * third to the wind, Eze 5:2
Then at * my anger will be Eze 5:13
Then at * you will know I am the Eze 6:4-7
Then at * they will loathe Eze 6:9
So at * I will expend my fury on Eze 6:12
it were your *, and say to the Eze 12:18
Then at * my wrath against the Eze 13:15
"Then at * my fury against you Eze 16:42
So then I said: Now at * I will Eze 20:21
the reigns of the * two Judean Eze 23:17f
and then at * her words will be Eze 29:21
And, then at *, O my people, you Eze 37:13
fuel—enough to * them seven years. Eze 39:9
interpret it. At * Daniel came Dan 4:8
heaven, until at * he knew that the Dan 5:21
So at * the king gave the order Dan 6:16
to happen in the * days of the Dan 8:19
Then at * they will learn to stay Dan 9:24
will * for only a short while. Dan 11:24
Antichrist of the * days becomes Dan 11:40f
your full share of those * days." Dan 12:13
Then at *, they will come with Hos 5:6
This is the * time I will destroy Hos 11:9
during her * tempestuous years: Hos 13:11f
"Then you shall know at * that Joe 3:17
they will drag the * of you away Amo 4:2
Then at * you will cover your Mic 3:7
BUT IN THE * days Mount Zion will Mic 4:1
then at * the exile remnants of Mic 5:3
* justice has caught up with you! Hab 2:6
live among you! At * your troubles Zep 3:15
blow it away—it doesn't * at all. Hag 1:9
Then at * they repented. Zec 1:5,6
inhabited, safe at *, never again Zec 14:11
Then at * you will know it was I Mal 2:4
his covenant every * man, whether Mal 2:12
until you have paid the * penny. Mt 5:26
Then at * they understood that by Mt 16:12
he had paid every * penny due. Mt 18:34

(LAST Con't)
who are first now will be * then; Mt 19:30
and some who are * now will be Mt 19:30
beginning with the * men first. Mt 20:8
And so it is that the * shall Mt 20:16
be first, and the first, *." Mt 20:16
For you tithe down to the * mint Mt 23:23
"And then at * the signal of my Mt 24:30
Then at * this age will come to Mt 24:34
and $1,000 to the *—dividing it in Mt 25:15
concerning him * night." Mt 27:19
"At * the time has come!" Mk 1:15
and * of all, the woman died too. Mk 12:20,21,22
while she gave up her * penny." Mk 12:43,44
from first to * and after thorough Lk 1:3
* night and didn't catch a thing. Lk 5:5
the * penny is paid in full." Lk 12:59
more earnestly. At * he stood up Lk 22:45
that happened there * week." Lk 24:18
at * these many Scriptures! Lk 24:45
have kept the best for the *!" Jn 2:10
them to eternal life at the * Day. Jn 6:39
I should raise him at the * Day." Jn 6:40
to me, and at the * Day I will Jn 6:44
and I will raise him at the * Day. Jn 6:54
On the * day, the climax of the Jn 7:37
And so at * many of the Jewish Jn 11:45
it would be his * night on earth Jn 13:1
"At * you are speaking Jn 16:29
So they had him at *, and he was Jn 19:17
Joel— 'In the * days,' God said, Act 2:17
and when at * they could no longer Act 7:21
At * the mayor was able to quiet Act 19:35
until at * all hope was gone. Act 27:20
"For * night an angel of the God Act 27:23
to come at * to see you and, if Rom 1:10
now, but this will * only until all Rom 11:25
But now at * I am through with my Rom 15:23
you asked in your * letter: my 1Co 7:1
* days as the world nears its end. 1Co 10:11
all the apostles. * of all I saw 1Co 15:8
including the * enemy—death. 1Co 15:26
Literally, "the * Adam." 1Co 15:45f
eye, when the * trumpet is blown. 1Co 15:52
When this happens, then at * this 1Co 15:54
as I did in my * letter, so that 2Co 2:3
quite small and won't * very long. 2Co 4:17
the joys to come will * forever. 2Co 4:18
been sinning when I was there *; 2Co 13:2
I close my letter with these * 2Co 13:11
But this system of law was to * Gal 3:19
person, and at * there was peace. Eph 2:15
And so the feud ended at * at the Eph 2:16
And so at * you will be filled up Eph 3:18,19
* of all I want to remind you Eph 6:10
right down to the very * point. Php 3:6
past, but now at * it has pleased Col 1:26,27
For God's secret plan, now at * Col 2:2
God has caught up with them at *. 1Th 2:16
that in the * times some in the 1Ti 4:1
that in the * days it is going to 2Ti 3:1
O God, will * forever and ever; Heb 1:8
It will be yours in that coming * 1Pe 1:5
And now at * this Good News has 1Pe 1:12
* days, as a blessing to you. 1Pe 1:20
This new one will * forever, for 1Pe 1:23
but the Word of the Lord will * 1Pe 1:25
you that in the * days there will 2Pe 3:3
Dear children, this world's * 1Jn 2:18
you, that in the * times there Jud 1:18
these are the first and * letters Rev 1:8f
"I am A and Z, the First and *!" Rev 1:11
Though I am the First and *, the Rev 1:17,18
is the First and *, who was dead Rev 2:8
heavens, "It has happened at *! Rev 12:10
this down: At * the time has come Rev 14:13
to earth the seven * plagues—and Rev 15:1
at * God's anger will be finished. Rev 15:1
punished to the * drop of anger in Rev 16:19
For at * God has given judgment Rev 18:20
the seven * plagues, came and said Rev 21:9
and the End, the First and *. Rev 22:13

LASTED
has * for such a long time. Jos 22:2,3
David's reign that * year after 2Sa 21:1
The harvest * six months, from 2Sa 21:10f
morning, and it * for three days; 2Sa 24:15
The celebration * for fourteen 1Ki 8:65
But Zimri * only seven days; 1Ki 16:15,16
over Israel, which * twelve years, 1Ki 16:23
Jeroboam's reign * forty-one 2Ki 14:23
* until the day of his death; 2Ki 15:5
of Israel. He * three years. 2Ch 13:1
but he * for only two years. 2Ch 33:20,21
to reign, but * only three months. 2Ch 36:2
But he * only three months and 2Ch 36:9
entire reign and * until King Ez 4:4,5
The celebration * six months, a Est 1:4
sometimes they * several days—Job Job 1:5
The old Babylonian Empire * from Jer 5:15f

LASTING
Ill-gotten gain brings no * Pro 10:2
O Lord our God, you brought * Dan 9:15
* until three o'clock that Mk 15:33
anything of * value by ourselves. 2Co 3:5
hearts, with the * charm of a 1Pe 3:4

LASTS
As long as the disease *, he is Lev 13:46
His lovingkindness * forever!" 2Ch 5:13,14
His anger * a moment; Ps 30:5
his favor * for life! Ps 30:5
the good man's reward * forever. Pro 11:18
But my salvation * forever; Is 51:6
as long as life *, so that you will Heb 6:11

LATE
the event annually in * March. Ex 13:10
But Moses said, "It's too *. Num 14:41
both the early and * rains that Deu 11:14
said, "Look, it's getting *. Ju 19:9
"It's getting too * to travel; Ju 19:11
at once or it will be too *!" 2Sa 15:14
We worked early and *, from Neh 4:20,21
* that evening, when the king was Est 9:11
Soon it will be too *! Ps 88:10
morning until * at night, fearing Ps 127:2
It will be too * though you Pro 1:28
it is too * to lock the barn. Ecc 10:11
It will be too * then to try to Ecc 12:2
that last till * at night—woe to Is 5:11
Although it is too * now to plant Is 37:30
before it is too *, before he Jer 13:16
before it is too *, even though Jer 36:7
* in July, 587 B.C. Jer 52:12f
One day * in June, when I was Eze 1:1
THEN, * IN August of the sixth Eze 8:1
* IN JULY, six Eze 20:1
ONE DAY * in December of the ninth Eze 24:1
* IN DECEMBER of the tenth year Eze 29:1
year of our exile, * in December, Eze 33:21
be too *—they will not find him. Hos 5:6
But it is too *! Hos 8:3
from a lion, but it was too *; Amo 3:12
But too *! Nah 2:6
When: In * August of the second Hag 1:1
from the Lord in * November of the Zec 7:1
before it is too * and he drags you Mt 5:25
It is too *!' Mt 25:12
that it was too *—his daughter was Mk 5:35
* in the afternoon his disciples Mk 6:35,36
spot, and it is getting *." Mk 6:35,36
now it was * in the afternoon—and Mk 11:11
early dawn or * daybreak. Mk 13:35,36,37
the Sabbath. * that afternoon Mk 15:42,43
* in the afternoon all twelve of Lk 9:12
locked the door, it will be too *. Lk 13:24,25
he wept, "and now it is too *. Lk 19:42
This was done * on Friday Lk 23:54
with them, as it was getting *. Lk 24:29
And even now it's not too *, for Jn 11:22
be too * for you to find your way. Jn 12:35
because it was * in the year, Act 27:9
is this: you know how * it is; Rom 13:11
been born almost too * for this. 1Co 15:8
again, it was too *, even though he Heb 12:17

LATER
* on Eve gave birth to another Gen 4:25
One week *, when Noah was 600 Gen 7:10,11,12
Three months *, Gen 8:5
Seven days * Noah released the Gen 8:10
A week * he released the dove Gen 8:12
just think of what they will do *! Gen 11:6
The king of Bela (* called Zoar). Gen 14:2
One year *, Ched-or-laomer and Gen 14:5,6
to Enmishpat (* called Kadesh) and Gen 14:7
Valley of Shaveh (* called King's Gen 14:17
* that well was named "The Well Gen 16:14
* ON, GOD tested Abraham's [faith Gen 22:1
But sometime *, King Abimelech, Gen 26:8
seven days *, at Mount Gilead. Gen 31:23
which, under the * Mosaic law, Gen 31:35f
But three days *, when their Gen 34:25
A few days * Israel called for Gen 37:13,14
* and return him to his father. Gen 37:21,22
Some time *, Reuben (who was Gen 37:29
About three months * word Gen 38:24
SOME TIME * it so happened that Gen 40:1
came three days *, and he held a Gen 40:20
ONE NIGHT TWO years *, Pharaoh Gen 41:1
"A little * I had another dream. Gen 41:22
*, when he was older, she brought Ex 2:10
One day, many years * Ex 2:11
Several years * the king of Egypt Ex 2:23
and when the dew disappeared * Ex 16:14
forever, so that * generations Ex 16:32
doesn't die, if * he is able to Ex 21:19
and even * generations." Ex 34:7
But if the raw flesh * changes Lev 13:16,17
But if, * on, this spot begins Lev 13:35
This ceremony, in * generations, Lev 16:32
Fifty days * you shall bring to the Lev 23:15,16
of the new grain of your * crops. Lev 23:15,16
first sampling of your * crops. Lev 23:17
first sampling of your * crops. Lev 23:20
of Atonement follows nine days *: Lev 23:26,27
*, on the last day of September, Lev 23:33,34
* he shall shave his defiled head; Num 6:9
but one month *, on the Num 9:10
Forty days * they returned from Num 13:25
name was * changed to Israel. Num 20:14f
"Ten days * Num 29:7
"Five days * Num 29:12
pledge, and * marries, and her Num 30:6
(The Israelites * changed the Num 32:37,38
Three days * the facts came Jos 9:16
remained. * on, however, when the Jos 17:13
and Talmai. * they attacked the Ju 1:11
and his family. * the man moved to Ju 1:26
stayed there. In * years when the Ju 1:28
but when the Amorites * spread Ju 1:35
entire force. *, Gideon returned Ju 8:13
Three years * God stirred up Ju 9:22,23
Three days * they were still Ju 14:14
* ON, DURING the wheat harvest, Ju 15:1
* on he fell in love with a girl Ju 16:4
entire lifetime. *, his brothers Ju 16:31
and Ruth. But *, both men died, so Ru 1:4,5
A DAY OR so *, Prince Jonathan 1Sa 14:1
(* David took Goliath's head to 1Sa 17:54
told my men where to meet me *. 1Sa 21:2
(* David went to Mizpeh in Moab 1Sa 22:3
THREE DAYS *, when David and his 1Sa 30:1
Three days * a man arrived from 2Sa 1:1
Then, two years *, when Absalom's 2Sa 13:21-24
*, during a war with the 2Sa 21:18
But three years * two of 1Ki 2:39
population; * he had given the city 1Ki 9:16
Damascus (where he * became king) 1Ki 11:24
three days *, the new king 1Ki 12:12
his capital. * he built Penuel. 1Ki 12:25
This was a month * than the 1Ki 12:32,33f
IT WAS THREE years * that the Lord 1Ki 18:1
* on, however, King Ben-hadad of 2Ki 6:24
name was * changed to Israel). 2Ki 17:34
Three years * (during the sixth 2Ki 18:10
*, during the fourteenth year of 2Ki 18:13
But seven months *, Ishmael, who 2Ki 25:25
The son of Terah was Abram (* 1Ch 1:24-27
*, five hundred of these invaders 1Ch 4:42
fortress of Zion, * called the City 1Ch 11:5,6
* the Philistines raided the 1Ch 14:13
(King Solomon * melted the bronze 1Ch 18:8
* replaced by his son Zebadiah. 1Ch 27:7
(There was a * Tabernacle in 2Ch 1:4
* he married Maacah, the daughter 2Ch 11:20
A few years * he went down to 2Ch 18:2
at Jerusalem. * he went out again 2Ch 19:4
* ON, THE armies of the kings of 2Ch 20:1
* on, Joash decided to repair and 2Ch 24:4
A few months * the Syrian army 2Ch 24:23
SOME TIME *, after this good work 2Ch 32:1
and four years * he began to 2Ch 34:3
men (they arrived at a * time); Ez 8:2-14
ONE DAY IN April four months *, as Neh 2:1
A few days * I went to visit Neh 6:10
(though I * received his permission Neh 13:6
*, the king demanded a second Est 2:19
Two or three weeks *, Est 3:12
THREE DAYS * Esther put on her Est 5:1
of Abihail and * adopted by Est 9:29-31
(1 Samuel 22), who * slaughtered Ps 52:1
in Canaan. * they were dispersed Ps 105:13
Better refuse than suffer *. Pro 11:15
your gifts will return to you *. Ecc 11:1
But * on, Is 7:17
Sooner or * he will lose his Jer 17:11
*, when Jerusalem has fallen, Jer 23:20
And sure enough, two months * Jer 28:17
destruction he has planned. * on Jer 30:24
Two years *, in the month of Jer 39:2
Ten days * the Lord gave his Jer 42:7
accomplished by * Persian kings. Jer 51:26f
Then, eleven years *, he took Jer 52:29
"*, when I passed by and saw you Eze 16:8
island settlement * as a result of Eze 26:14f
A year *, Eze 30:20
Two weeks *, Eze 32:17
Canal, and then * at Jerusalem Eze 43:3
clay—show that * on, this kingdom Dan 2:41,42
to me (Daniel said *) I had been in Dan 10:2
"Several years * an alliance Dan 11:6
many years * in the Seleucid wars Dan 11:6f
"A few years * the Syrian king Dan 11:13
the Great, who was * defeated by Dan 11:13f
of Israel twenty-five years *. Hos 1:4,5f
* and the nation disappeared. Hos 4:19f
and twenty-five years * had Hab 1:6f
*, the deportation and exile. Zep 1:1f
*, came often to this Temple. Hag 2:8,9f
*, as Jesus and his disciples Mt 9:10
* THAT SAME day, Jesus left the Mt 13:1
that three days * he would be Mt 16:21
SIX DAYS * Jesus took Peter, Mt 17:1
"A couple of hours * he was Mt 20:3
'I won't,' he answered, but * Mt 21:29

(LATER Con't)
the disciples asked him *, as Mt 24:3
"*, when the other five Mt 25:11
*, out by the gate, another girl Mt 26:71
* on, after John was arrested by Mk 1:14
*, Simon and the others went out Mk 1:36,37
SEVERAL DAYS * he returned to Mk 2:1
Judas Iscariot (who * betrayed Mk 3:16-19
through, and * the wheat-heads Mk 4:28
where he would join them *. Mk 6:45
Six days * Jesus took Peter, Mk 9:2
* I will return to life again." Mk 9:30,31
*, when he was alone with his Mk 10:10
And so they reached Jericho. *, Mk 10:46
was killed; and *, others were Mk 12:5
*, as Jesus was teaching the Mk 12:35
began two days *—an annual Jewish Mk 14:1
A little * others standing around Mk 14:70
* that day Mk 16:12
Still * he appeared to the eleven Mk 16:14
A few days * Mary hurried to the Lk 1:39,40
Eight days *, at the baby's Lk 2:21
Three days * they finally Lk 2:46,47
* on as Jesus left the town he Lk 5:27
Judas Iscariot (who * betrayed Lk 6:14,15,16
and three days * I will come back Lk 9:22
Eight days * he took Peter, Lk 9:28
* manuscripts add to verses 55 and Lk 9:55f
villages he planned to visit *. Lk 10:1
A few minutes * some Pharisees Lk 13:31
"A few days * this younger son Lk 15:13
* he talked again about this with Lk 17:22
About an hour * someone else Lk 22:59
to identify it. * on, the one who Jn 1:9
TWO DAYS * Jesus' mother was a Jn 2:1
You go on, and I'll come * Jn 7:8
*, in one of his talks, Jesus Jn 8:12
* he said to them again, "I am Jn 8:21
but you will follow me *." Jn 13:36
Eight days * the disciples were Jn 20:26
* JESUS APPEARED again to the Jn 21:1
About three hours * his wife came Act 5:7
began preaching! * that morning Act 5:21
"Forty years *, in the desert Act 7:30
Years *, when Joshua led the Act 7:45
again three days * and showed him Act 10:40,41
Yet only a few days *, some Jews Act 14:19
Several days * Paul suggested to Act 15:36
want to hear more about this *." Act 17:32
to Ephesus * if God permitted; Act 18:21
the one John said would come *. Act 19:4
and five days * arrived in Troas, Act 20:6
and a day * we arrived at Act 20:15
days * with the others. Act 21:26,27
FIVE DAYS * Ananias the High Act 24:1
A few days * Felix came with Act 24:24
Eight or ten days * he returned Act 25:6
A few days * King Agrippa arrived Act 25:13
and * at Jerusalem, and I lived Act 26:4
A little * they sounded again, Act 27:28
a day * a south wind began Act 28:13
It wasn't until * on, after God Rom 4:11
to the glory he will give us *. Rom 8:18
And years *, when this son, Rom 9:10-13
nations. And * on Isaiah said Rom 10:20
will share in * on when the Jews, Rom 11:12
He was seen by Peter and * by 1Co 15:5
Then James saw him and * all the 1Co 15:7
human bodies and * on God gives us 1Co 15:46
he will be seeing you * on when 1Co 16:12
to plant, and * on, good crops to 2Co 9:10
It was not until three years * Gal 1:18
THEN FOURTEEN YEARS * I went Gal 2:1
and thirty years * when God gave Gal 3:17
things that would happen * on. Heb 3:5
him if he * refuses to do it; Heb 6:16
Jewish priest, for * on God's Heb 7:5
doing wrong, but * God appointed by Heb 7:28
but long years *, during yours. 1Pe 1:12
the vast flood. *, he turned the 2Pe 2:6
what it is going to be like * on. 1Jn 3:2

LATEST
"Listen to my * dream," he Gen 37:9
it, or the next day at the *; Lev 19:6
next day at the *, I will talk to 1Sa 20:12
time discussing the * new ideas! Act 17:21
will give you all the * news. Col 4:9

LATIN
spoke Greek and *, misunderstood Mk 15:34f
written in Hebrew, *, and Greek, so Jn 19:20

LATTER
upon you in the * times, you will Deu 4:30
Literally, "in the * days." Jer 23:20f
Literally, "in the * days." Jer 30:24f
But in the * days, says the Jer 48:47
But in the * days I will bring Jer 49:39
future—in the * years of history. Eze 38:15,16
Literally, "in the * days," an Eze 38:15,16f

LATTICES
chain-designed * and four hundred 1Ki 7:16-22

LATTICEWORK
* covering the bases of the 1Ki 7:41-46
in two rows on the *, to cover the 1Ki 7:41-46

LAUDED
Babylon, * by all the earth! Jer 51:41

LAUGH
to Abraham, "Why did Sarah *? Gen 18:13
"I didn't *," she lied, for she Gen 18:15
Lest the heathen nations * in 2Sa 1:20
"You shall * at war and famine; Job 5:22
He will * when calamity crushes Job 9:23
the innocent shall * the wicked Job 22:19
they *. Ps 22:8
And when they leave, they * and Ps 41:6
The neighboring nations * and Ps 44:13
Then they will * and say, "See Ps 52:6
Lord, * at them! Ps 59:8
nations. They * among themselves. Ps 80:6
you'll be in trouble, and I'll *! Pro 1:26
A time to *; Ecc 3:4
and no one would * at me. Sol 8:1
My own people * at me; Lam 3:14
See how they * and sing with Lam 3:63
lest the Egyptians * at Israel's Eze 20:9,10
Now will you *? Eze 21:9,10,11
the princes * about their lies. Hos 7:3
And all Egypt will * at them. Hos 7:16
come when you shall * with joy! Lk 6:21
And then how everyone would *! Lk 14:29
are the ones who * at Jesus Christ, Jas 2:7
* at you in contempt and scorn. 1Pe 4:4
and killed, they * at the 2Pe 2:12
can think of, and * at the truth. 2Pe 3:3

LAUGHED
So Sarah * silently. Gen 18:12
I have plenty," Esau *. Gen 33:9
and mocked us and * at us, and so Neh 4:1
How we * and sang for joy. Ps 126:2
because they * at my laws, ignored Eze 20:16
her anguish, and * at Judah when Eze 25:3
Ephraim will be * at for trusting Hos 10:6
had invited merely * and went on Mt 22:5
They * at him in bitter derision, Mk 5:40
And the Jewish leaders * and Lk 23:35
been dead, some *, but others said, Act 17:32
thought of, while we are * at. 1Co 4:10
teaching be * at because of this. 1Ti 6:1
Sometimes you were * at and Heb 10:33
Some were * at and their backs Heb 11:36

LAUGHING
inside he was * in disbelief! Gen 17:17
scoffing and * at her as they went 1Sa 1:7
The Lord is * at those who plot Ps 37:12,13
I was his constant delight, * and Pro 8:30
For it is silly to be * all the Ecc 2:1
their bodies and * at those in Jud 1:8
smears among you, * and carrying Jud 1:12

LAUGHINGSTOCK
We'd be the * of the town to go Gen 38:23
have become a * to my neighbors. Job 12:4
the * of the city, mocked by all. Jer 20:7
You will become a * to the world Eze 5:15
I will make you a * and a Eze 22:4
No longer will I make you a * Joe 2:19
I will make you the * of the Mic 6:16

LAUGHS
Clubs do no good, and he * at Job 41:29
But God in heaven merely *! Ps 2:4
daughter of Zion—* at you and Is 37:22

LAUGHTER
and you are to name him Isaac ("* Gen 17:19
named him Isaac (meaning "*!" Gen 21:3
declared, "God has brought me *! Gen 21:6
were received with * and scorn! 2Ch 30:10
your mouth with * and your lips Job 8:21
* cannot mask a heavy heart. Pro 14:13
When the * ends, the grief Pro 14:13
Sorrow is better than *, for Ecc 7:3
A party gives *, and wine gives Ecc 10:19
happy singing and * in the streets Jer 7:34
I will end all * in this land—the Jer 16:9
Their careless * now means sorrow Lk 6:25
This brought scoffing and *, Lk 8:53
Let there be sadness instead of * Jas 4:9

LAUNCH
Eloth, in Edom, to * a fleet 2Ch 8:17,18

LAUNCHED
detachments, and * a surprise 1Sa 11:11
Perhaps Xerxes (486-465) who * an Dan 11:2f
So Jesus * into an extended Mk 13:5

LAVER
the * and its pedestal; Ex 31:9
and the bronze * and bronze bulls Jer 52:17
* and twelve bulls was tremendous. Jer 52:20

LAVISH
but I * my love upon thousands Ex 20:6
knew—and * on him costly gifts! Dan 11:38

LAVISHLY
made * with silver and with gold? Is 46:6

LAW
the later Mosaic *, caused Gen 31:35f
Tamar, as our * requires of a dead Gen 38:8
So Joseph made it a * throughout Gen 47:26
it is still the *—that Pharaoh Gen 47:26
is a permanent *) to remind you of Ex 12:14
so it is a * that you must Ex 12:17
* for you and your posterity. Ex 12:24
The same * applies to those born Ex 12:49
"The same * holds if the ox Ex 21:31
to the Lord. This * is a perpetual Ex 31:16
This is a permanent * throughout Lev 3:17
"Anyone who disobeys some * of Lev 5:17,18
This is a perpetual *. Lev 6:22,23
This, then, is the * for the man Lev 15:32
"This is a permanent *: You must Lev 16:29,30
this is a permanent *. Lev 16:31
This shall be an everlasting * Lev 16:34
The purpose of this * is to stop Lev 17:5
This shall be a permanent * for Lev 17:7
*, for I am the Lord your God. Lev 19:1
Anyone who violates this * is Lev 22:16
This is a permanent * throughout Lev 23:14
This is a * to be honored from Lev 23:21
This is a * of Israel from Lev 23:30,31
a * from generation to generation. Lev 23:41
* of God, and are most holy." Lev 24:9
stone him; this * applies to the Lev 24:15,16
You shall have the same * for Lev 24:22
"This, then, is the * concerning Num 5:29
There is one * for all." Num 9:14
For there is the same * for all, Num 15:15,16
Yes, one * for all!" Num 15:15,16
This same * applies to Num 15:29
deliberately failed to obey his *; Num 15:31
of Israel for violating this *. Num 18:5
you and your sons, by permanent *. Num 18:8
This is a permanent * among you, Num 18:23
this is a permanent * for the Num 19:10
This is a permanent *. Num 19:21
Moreover, this is a general * Num 27:8
living among you must obey this *. Deu 5:14
The general * against adultery Deu 22:30f
The reason for this * is that Deu 23:4
no special * would be needed to Deu 27:23f
this book of the *, and if you turn Deu 30:10
this book of the * beside the Ark, Deu 31:26
the letter every * Moses gave you, Jos 1:7
Literally, "the * of Moses." Jos 8:32f
according to God's *, for you are Ru 3:9
be burned," [as the * requires 1Sa 2:16
who took the * into his own hands! 1Sa 25:30,31
From then on David made this a * 1Sa 30:25
written in the * of Moses so that 1Ki 2;3
through the * of Moses that fathers 2Ki 14:6
of The Book of the * of the Lord to 2Ch 17:7,8,9
* of God, and proclaimed him king. 2Ch 23:11
as prescribed in the * of Moses. 2Ch 23:18
The tax * enacted by Moses the 2Ch 24:6
written in the * of Moses, that the 2Ch 25:4
by the * of Moses the man of God; 2Ch 30:16
as required in the * of God. 2Ch 31:3
as required in the * of God. 2Ch 31:4
as required by * to be given to the 2Ch 31:5,6
the Temple, the *, and godly 2Ch 31:21
it is written in the * of Moses. 2Ch 35:12
Anyone refusing to obey the * of Ez 7:26
your God and the * of the king Ez 7:26
read to them the * of God which he Neh 8:1
they heard the commands of the *. Neh 8:9
go over the * in greater detail. Neh 8:13
They threw away your *, killed Neh 9:26
the Temple as required in the *. Neh 10:34
flocks, just as the * requires; Neh 10:36
were required by * to bring these Neh 10:39,40
as well as Persian * and justice, Est 1:13-15
"What penalty does the * provide Est 1:13-15
a royal edict, a * of the Medes and Est 1:19
be proclaimed as * in every Est 3:14
This was part of the famed "* of Est 8:8f
everywhere as *, must be broadcast Est 8:13
dates and it was recorded as *. Est 9:32
"* and order have collapsed," Ps 11:3
your * is written upon my heart!" Ps 40:8
For your * is my delight. Ps 119:75,76,77
my choice is clear—I love your *. Ps 119:113
Every * of God is right, Ps 119:128
and your * is my delight. Ps 119:174
to worship as the * requires, to Ps 122:4
To complain about the * is to Pro 28:4
To obey the * is to fight evil. Pro 28:4
Young men who are wise obey the * Pro 28:7
prayers of men who flout the *. Pro 28:9
The Lord has magnified his * and Is 42:21
all the world the glory of his *; Is 42:22
your forebears transgressed my *. Is 43:27
THERE IS A * Jer 3:1
They reject my *. Jer 6:18,19
Anathoth, for by * you have a Jer 32:6,7
he said, "for the * gives you the Jer 32:8
without a divine * to govern them, Lam 2:9
kinds of animals our * forbids." Eze 4:14
and obeys the *, and does right, he Eze 18:27
them the sentences the * demands. Eze 23:45
And this is the basic * of the Eze 43:12

(LAW Con't)
Yes, this is the primary * Eze 43:12
him, "you made a * that everyone Dan 3:10
you should make a *, irrevocable Dan 6:7
request your signature on this *; Dan 6:8
it will be a '* of the Medes and Dan 6:8
So King Darius signed the *. Dan 6:9
king and reminded him about his *. Dan 6:12
"it is 'a * of the Medes and Dan 6:12
no attention to you or your *. Dan 6:13
*, and determined to save Daniel. Dan 6:14
You signed the * and it cannot be Dan 6:15
"change the times and the *." Dan 7:25f
in the * of Moses your servant. Dan 9:11
in the * of Moses has come true; Dan 9:13
Under Mosaic *, it was illegal to Amo 2:8f
and to fight. The * is not Hab 1:4
question about the *: "If one of Hag 2:11
break the * without rebuke." Mal 2:9
* but often violated its intent. Mt 3:7f
have I say: Every * in the Book Mt 5:18
"The * of Moses says, 'If anyone Mt 5:31
"Again, the * of Moses says, Mt 5:33
"The * of Moses says, 'If a man Mt 5:38
Literally, "this is the * and the Mt 7:12f
required by Moses' * for lepers who Mt 8:4
disciples are breaking the *. Mt 12:2
That was breaking the * too. Mt 12:4
ever read in the * of Moses how the Mt 12:5
experts in Jewish * who are now my Mt 13:52
For instance, God's * is 'Honor Mt 15:4
is it against the * to give away Mt 20:15
That was against the * too. Mk 2:25,26
gave you this * from God: 'Honor Mk 7:10
And so you break the * of God Mk 7:12,13
"Teacher, Moses gave us a * that Mk 12:19
obedience to the *, Simeon was Lk 2:27
of the * of God they returned home Lk 2:39
the teachers of *, discussing deep Lk 2:46,47
"Offer the sacrifice Moses' * Lk 5:14
and teachers of the * were Lk 5:17
the * exclaimed among themselves. Lk 5:21
teachers of the * complained Lk 5:30
Jewish * to work on the Sabbath." Lk 6:2
The teachers of the * and the Lk 6:7
*, "I have a question for you. Lk 6:9
and teachers of Moses' *. Lk 7:30
teachers of the *—and be killed; Lk 9:22
does Moses' * say about it?" Lk 10:26
in religious * who was standing Lk 11:45
is it within the * to heal a man on Lk 14:3
experts on Jewish * because he was Lk 15:2
But that doesn't mean that the * Lk 16:17
Jewish * who were standing there. Lk 20:39
day as required by the Jewish *. Lk 23:56
For Moses gave us only the * Jn 1:17
you obey Moses' * of circumcision Jn 7:21,22,23
is older than the Mosaic *); Jn 7:21,22,23
Moses' * says to kill her. Jn 8:5
"In your own * it says that men Jn 10:34,35,36
By Jewish *, entering the house of Jn 18:28f
a practice under Roman *. Jn 18:32f
Literally, "men without the *." Act 2:23f
on religious * and very popular Act 5:34
who gave them the * of God—the Act 7:38
Literally, "the * as it was Act 7:53f
the Jewish * could never do. Act 13:39
that are contrary to Roman *." Act 18:13
are all zealous for the *." Act 21:20f
for obeying the *, and well thought Act 22:12
you to break the * yourself by Act 23:3
that he be tried by Roman *. Act 24:8
I firmly believe in the Jewish * Act 24:14
to them that Roman * does not Act 25:16
Or, "you rely upon the * for your Rom 2:17f
by doing what the * commands. Rom 3:20
God's special * against eating the Rom 5:14
longer tied to the * where sin Rom 6:14
*, but on receiving God's grace! Rom 6:15
Literally, "men who know (the) * Rom 7:1f
a person dies the * no longer holds Rom 7:1
woman marries, the * binds her to Rom 7:2
master, used to be the Jewish *; Rom 7:4
"married to the *," and it has no Rom 7:4
we are delivered from the *." Rom 7:6f
No, the * is not sinful but it Rom 7:7
was the * that showed me my sin. Rom 7:7
there—if the * had not said, "You Rom 7:7
But sin used this * against Rom 7:8
what the * really demanded. Rom 7:9
* and was a sinner, doomed to die. Rom 7:9
the good * which was supposed to Rom 7:10
But still, you see, the * itself Rom 7:12
Didn't the * cause my doom? Rom 7:13
purposes. The * is good, then, and Rom 7:14
by keeping the * and being good Rom 9:32
[Don't take the * into your own Rom 12:19
It is the only * you need. Rom 13:10
you "go to *" and ask a heathen 1Co 6:1
I'm telling you what God's * 1Co 9:8
For in the * God gave to Moses 1Co 9:9
and the *, which reveals our 1Co 15:55,56
must obey every * of God or die; 2Co 3:6
Yet that old system of * that led 2Co 3:7
For as he gave them God's * to 2Co 3:7
Literally, "For I through the * Gal 2:19f
*, that I might live unto God." Gal 2:19f
written in God's Book of the *." Gal 3:10
is the way of * which says that a Gal 3:12
every * of God, without one slip. Gal 3:12
But this system of * was to last Gal 3:19
guarded by the *, kept in Gal 3:23
were slaves to the * so that he Gal 4:5
every other Jewish * or perish. Gal 5:3
For the whole * can be summed up Gal 5:14
to every Jewish * and custom. Php 3:5
were required by * to give gifts to Heb 7:5
* must be changed to permit it. Heb 7:12,13,14
into God's * for free men, he will Jas 1:25
But you are breaking this * of Jas 2:9
And the person who keeps every * Jas 2:10
who has broken every * there is. Jas 2:10
against God's * of loving one Jas 4:11
whether this * is right or wrong, Jas 4:11
Only he who made the * can Jas 4:12
sake, obey every * of your 1Pe 2:13
You are free from the *, but 1Pe 2:16
"freedom" from * are themselves 2Pe 2:19

LAWFUL
and does what is * and right, and Eze 18:5
Literally, "It is not * for us to Jn 18:31f
Literally, "All things are * for 1Co 6:12f

LAWGIVER
For the Lord is our Judge, our * Is 33:22

LAWLESS
Here come these * men to attack Ps 119:150
a son who is a member of a * gang Pro 28:7
remember their sins and * deeds." Heb 10:17
Literally, "* idolatries." 1Pe 4:3f

LAWLESSNESS
with * and all the cities too. Hab 2:8
Literally, "the mystery of * is 2Th 2:7f

LAWS
obeyed my commandments and *." Gen 26:5
I apply the * of God to their Ex 18:15,16
them God's *, and showing them the Ex 18:19,20
"HERE ARE OTHER * you must obey: Ex 21:1
the people all the * and Ex 24:3
Moses wrote down the *; Ex 24:4
God's directions and *. Ex 24:7
with you in giving you these *." Ex 24:8
I give you the * and commandments I Ex 24:12
and the Ark will contain the * of Ex 25:22
tablets engraved with God's *. Ex 26:33
have quickly abandoned all my *. Ex 32:8
That is, the preceding * in verses Ex 34:27f
* that I have given you, for they Ex 34:27
the * of Jehovah you must obey. Ex 35:1
that these are the * concerning Lev 4:2
one of God's *, as soon as it is Lev 4:22
and to teach them all the * Lev 10:11
These are the * concerning Lev 11:46
These, then, are the * concerning Lev 14:32
These, then, are the * concerning Lev 14:54
That is why these * are given. Lev 14:57
You must obey only my *, and you Lev 18:4,5
obey all of my * and ordinances, Lev 18:26
these * apply both to you who are Lev 18:26
So be very sure to obey my *, and Lev 18:29,30
"Obey my *: Do not mate your Lev 19:19
"Keep my Sabbath * and reverence Lev 19:30
"You must obey all of my * and Lev 20:22
Obey my * if you want to live Lev 25:17,18
You must obey my Sabbath * of Lev 26:2
me, but reject my *, this is what Lev 26:15
my * and for despising my rule. Lev 26:43
These were the *, ordinances, and Lev 26:46
are to obey his * instead of Num 15:39
Aaron, "Here is another of my *: Num 19:1
These are permanent * for all Num 35:29
stating all the * God had commanded Deu 1:1
carefully to these * I teach you, Deu 4:1
Do not add other * or subtract Deu 4:2
"These are the * for you to obey Deu 4:5
nations hear these * they will Deu 4:6
how great, has * as fair as these I Deu 4:8
can teach my * to their children.' Deu 4:10
He proclaimed the * you must Deu 4:13
me to issue the * you must obey Deu 4:14
You must obey these * that I Deu 4:40
Listed below are the * Moses Deu 4:44,45,46
to all these * God has given you; Deu 5:1
me and I passed on his * to you. Deu 5:5
"The Lord has given these * to Deu 5:22
The purpose of these * is to Deu 6:2
purpose of these * which the Lord Deu 6:20
obey all of these * and to Deu 6:24
all the * of the Lord our God.' Deu 6:25
"Obey the * of the Lord your Deu 8:6
with the * inscribed upon them. Deu 9:9
away from the * of God, and had Deu 9:12
inscribed with the * of God. Deu 9:15
But you must obey all the * I am Deu 11:32
"THESE ARE THE * you must obey Deu 12:1
(for these * don't go into Deu 12:9
he must copy these * from the book Deu 17:18
That copy of the * shall be his Deu 17:19
This regular reading of God's * Deu 17:20
away from God's * in the slightest Deu 17:20
obey and keep his * and ordinances, Deu 26:17
that you must obey all of his *. Deu 26:18
and then write the * of God in Deu 27:2,3,4
Write all of these * plainly Deu 27:8
anyone who does not obey these *.' Deu 27:26
Lord your God, the * I am declaring Deu 28:1
way from the * I have given you; Deu 28:14
won't obey these * I am giving you Deu 28:15-19
"If you refuse to obey all the * Deu 28:58,59
for these * are not in the far Deu 30:12
and to keep his *, so that you will Deu 30:16
Then Moses wrote out the * he had Deu 31:9
Moses also gave copies of the * Deu 31:9
The Lord commanded that these * Deu 31:10,11
you—to hear the * of God and to Deu 31:12
the Lord your God and obey his *. Deu 31:12
not known these * will hear them Deu 31:13
down all the * that are recorded in Deu 31:24
"Meditate upon all the * I have Deu 32:46
These * are not mere words—they Deu 32:47
The * I have given Deu 33:4
The Levites shall teach God's * Deu 33:10
people about these *, and you Jos 1:8
in the book of his *: "Make me Jos 8:31
written in the book of God's *. Jos 8:34
in the book of the * of Moses; Jos 23:6
in the book of the * of God, and Jos 24:26
you despised the * of God and done 2Sa 12:9
I knew his *, 2Sa 22:23
Obey the * of God and follow all 1Ki 2:3
my * as your father David did." 1Ki 3:14
may you always obey his * and 1Ki 8:61
and do not obey my *, then I will 1Ki 9:6
have not obeyed my *, I will tear 1Ki 11:11
he has not kept my * and 1Ki 11:33
They rejected his * and the 2Ki 17:15
don't know the * of the god of the 2Ki 17:26
the * of the god of the land. 2Ki 17:27,28
or obeying the * he gave to the 2Ki 17:34
* and never worship other gods. 2Ki 17:37
disobeyed all the * given to them 2Ki 18:12
with God's * written on it!" 2Ki 22:8
book of God's * which had been 2Ki 23:1
to follow all the * which were 2Ki 23:24
and followed all the * of Moses; 2Ki 23:25
to follow all his * when he makes 1Ch 22:12
they will obey my * as you have.' 2Ch 6:16
if you refuse the * I have given 2Ch 7:19
They have lived without God's *. 2Ch 15:3
violations of the * and ordinances 2Ch 19:10
Temple, as required by God's *. 2Ch 23:5,6
commands—all the * and instructions 2Ch 33:8
be the * of God as given to Moses! 2Ch 34:14
These are the * of God!" 2Ch 34:15,16
When the king heard what these * 2Ch 34:19
these * that are written here." 2Ch 34:21
Then, as directed by the * of 2Ch 35:13
he followed the * of the Lord, all 2Ch 35:26
in the * of Moses, the man of God. Ez 3:1
prescribed in the * of Moses, Ez 3:4
as instructed in the * of Moses. Ez 6:18
in Jehovah's * which Moses had Ez 7:6
study and obey the * of the Lord Ez 7:10
those * to the people of Israel. Ez 7:10
of the * of the God of heaven. Ez 7:12
a copy of God's * to Judah and Ez 7:14
and teacher of the * of the God of Ez 7:21
familiar with the * of your God, Ez 7:25
abandoned you and broken your *! Ez 9:10
We will obey the * of God. Ez 10:3
to me and obey my *, even though Neh 1:9
to them the scroll of Moses' *. Neh 8:1
as required by the * of Moses. Neh 8:18
foreigners. The * of God were read Neh 9:3
and gave them good * and true Neh 9:13
the * about the holy Sabbath; Neh 9:14
order to turn them toward your *; Neh 9:29
your * or listen to your warnings. Neh 9:34
* as issued by his servant Moses. Neh 10:29
as decreed by the * of Moses. Neh 12:44
* of David and his son Solomon. Neh 12:45
ON THAT SAME day, as the * of Neh 13:1
began, "and their * are different Est 3:8
they refuse to obey the king's *; Est 3:8
He makes the * of the rain and a Job 28:26
Do you know the * of the Job 38:33
meditating on his * and thinking Ps 1:2
I kept close watch on all his *; Ps 18:22
God's * are perfect. Ps 19:7,8
God's * are pure, eternal, just. Ps 19:9
tried to keep your * and have Ps 26:1
men: Recite my * no longer, and Ps 50:16
my discipline, disregarding my *. Ps 50:17
For he gave his * to Israel, and Ps 78:5

(LAWS Con't)
Thus his * pass down from Ps 78:6
able to obey his * and to set its Ps 78:7
because they didn't obey his *. Ps 78:10
they are scheduled in the * of Ps 81:4
for I try to follow all your *. Ps 86:2
If his children forsake my * and Ps 89:30,31,32
They refused to accept my *. Ps 95:10
faithful and obedient to his *. Ps 105:45
good, and all his * are right, for Ps 111:7
wisdom comes from obeying his *. Ps 111:10
who perfectly follow the * of God. Ps 119:1
You have given us your * to Ps 119:4
I have recited your *, and Ps 119:13
Your * are both my light and my Ps 119:24
*, for I have chosen to do right. Ps 119:29,30
follow your * even more closely. Ps 119:32
for your * are right and good. Ps 119:39
free within the limits of your *. Ps 119:44,45,46
How I love your *! Ps 119:47
For these * of yours have been Ps 119:54
I am firmly anchored to your *. Ps 119:61
my thanks to you for your good *. Ps 119:62
For your * are my guide. Ps 119:66
I obey your * with all my heart. Ps 119:69
me to pay attention to your *. Ps 119:71,72
now give me sense to heed your *. Ps 119:73
my thoughts upon your *. Ps 119:78
you, and we will discuss your *. Ps 119:79
But still I cling to your * and Ps 119:83
your truth and * have dug deep pits Ps 119:85,86
to yield and disobey your *. Ps 119:87
* had been my deepest delight. Ps 119:92
I will never lay aside your *, Ps 119:93
obey these wonderful * of yours. Ps 119:106
not give up obedience to your *. Ps 119:109
Your * are my joyous treasure Ps 119:111
I can continue to obey your *. Ps 119:117
rejected all who reject your *. Ps 119:118
no wonder I love to obey your *! Ps 119:119
have violated your *, while I love Ps 119:126
Your * are wonderful; Ps 119:129
Guide me with your * so that I Ps 119:133
upon me and teach me all your *. Ps 119:135
I weep because your * are Ps 119:136
enemies have disregarded your *. Ps 119:139
but I don't despise your *. Ps 119:141
for your * are perfectly fair. Ps 119:142
Your * are always fair; Ps 119:144
O Lord, and I will obey your *. Ps 119:145
for they do not care for your *. Ps 119:155
they care nothing for your *. Ps 119:158
is utter truth in all your *; Ps 119:160
I rejoice in your * like one who Ps 119:162
falsehood but how I love your *. Ps 119:163
a day because of your wonderful *. Ps 119:164
Those who love your * have great Ps 119:165
Lord, and so I have obeyed your *. Ps 119:166
you for letting me learn your *. Ps 119:171
let your * assist me. Ps 119:175
He has made known his * and Ps 147:19
husbands and flouted the * of God. Pro 2:16,17
a nation to know and keep his *! Pro 29:18
there he will teach us his *, and Is 2:3
Lord, and be obedient to his *! Is 2:5
thrown away the * of God and Is 5:24
who issue unfair *, says the Lord, Is 10:1
the people have twisted the * of Is 24:4,5
he sent them nor listen to his *. Is 42:24
Oh, that you had listened to my * Is 48:18
and cherish my * in your hearts: Is 51:7
to grips with his *: I will give Is 56:4
the reading of my *—just as though Is 58:2
They don't accept the * of God. Jer 8:7
understand his *," when your Jer 8:8
commandments and not obeyed my *. Jer 9:13
they did not keep my *, and you Jer 16:11
their evil were * chiseled with an Jer 17:1
to me and obey the * I have given Jer 26:4
inscribe my * upon their hearts, Jer 31:33
to do away with these * of nature! Jer 31:36
to obey you or to follow your *; Jer 32:23
I would change my * of night and Jer 33:25,26
me, or follow the * I gave you and Jer 44:10
See the dietary * Ezekiel here Eze 4:14f
away from my * and has been even Eze 5:5,6,7
you can obey my * and be my people, Eze 11:20
and obeys my *—that man is just, Eze 18:9
to obey the * of God, but worships Eze 18:11
and obeys my *—he shall not die Eze 18:17
keeps my *, he shall surely live. Eze 18:19
begins to obey my * and do what is Eze 18:21
There I gave them my * so they Eze 20:11
the wilderness they refused my *. Eze 20:13
they laughed at my *, ignored my Eze 20:16
Follow my *; Eze 20:19
They refused my *—the laws that, Eze 20:21
They refused my laws—the * that, Eze 20:21
did not obey my * but scorned them Eze 20:23,24
customs and * which were Eze 20:25
Your priests have violated my * Eze 22:26
my * and do whatever I command. Eze 36:27
and they shall obey my * and all Eze 37:24
tell you about the * and rules of Eze 44:5
You have not kept the * I gave Eze 44:8
decisions must be based upon my *. Eze 44:24
change all *, morals, and customs. Dan 7:25
who love you and who keep your *. Dan 9:4
we have flouted all the * you Dan 9:10
Jews who were loyal to God's *. Dan 11:32f
Since you have forgotten my *, I Hos 4:6
treaty and revolted against my *. Hos 8:1
her ten thousand *, she'd say they Hos 8:12
For they have rejected the * of Amo 2:4
He will issue his * and announce Mic 4:2
by their disobedience to God's *. Zep 3:4
commanded them—the * he had Zec 7:12
to return to the * I gave your Mal 2:4
"The purpose of these * was to Mal 2:5
so the people will learn God's *. Mal 2:7
"Though you have scorned my * Mal 3:7
it do to obey his *, and to sorrow Mal 3:14,15
"Remember to obey the * I gave Mal 4:4
to cancel the * of Moses and the Mt 5:17
But those who teach God's * and Mt 5:19
"Under the * of Moses the rule Mt 5:21
"The * of Moses said, 'You shall Mt 5:27
This is the teaching of the * of Mt 7:12
for all the * and prophets Mt 11:13
* instead of those from God.' Mt 15:9
command in the * of Moses?" Mt 22:36
from these two * and are fulfilled Mt 22:40
way they keep making up so many *! Mt 23:2
it's against our * to accept money Mt 27:6
It's against our * to work by Mk 2:24
many examples of * and regulations Mk 7:4
You are simply rejecting God's * Mk 7:9
broken a single one of those *." Mk 10:20
* in spirit as well as in letter. Lk 1:6
as required by the * of Moses after Lk 2:22
for in these * God had said, Lk 2:23
One day an expert on Moses' * Lk 10:25
to preach, the * of Moses and the Lk 16:16
* since I was a small child." Lk 18:21
"The * of Moses state that if a Lk 20:28
their Sabbath *, he had spoken of Jn 5:18
Moses, on whose * you set your Jn 5:45
None of you obeys the * of Jn 7:19
Your * say that if two men agree Jn 8:17
by your own *," Pilate told them. Jn 18:31
They replied, "By our * he ought Jn 19:7
Temple and against the * of Moses. Act 6:13
and throw out all of Moses' *." Act 6:14
destroyed God's *, though you Act 7:53
are forbidden by our Jewish *." Act 10:14
against the Jewish * for me to come Act 10:28
forbidden by our Jewish *!' Act 11:8
obey our Jewish *, except that we Act 15:19
burden of Jewish * on you than to Act 15:27,28,29
that are against the Roman *." Act 16:20,21
Jewish *, you take care of it. Act 18:15
are against the * of Moses, against Act 21:21
obey the Jewish * and are in line Act 21:24
everybody to disobey the Jewish *. Act 21:28
* and customs very carefully. Act 22:3
I had shaved my head as their * Act 24:18
"I have not opposed the Jewish * Act 25:8
an expert on Jewish * and customs. Act 26:3
obedience to Jewish * and customs. Act 26:5
had God's written *, for down in Rom 2:12-15
God's * are written within them; Rom 2:12-15
his written * but don't obey them. Rom 2:12-15
God because he gave his * to you; Rom 2:17
taught his * from earliest youth. Rom 2:18
really know his *, which are full Rom 2:20
of knowing God's *, but you Rom 2:23
something if you obey God's *; Rom 2:25
And if the heathen obey God's *, Rom 2:26
his promises but don't obey his *. Rom 2:27
them with his * [so that they could Rom 3:2
to keep God's * instead of doing Rom 3:19
For the more we know of God's *, Rom 3:20
obeying them; his * serve only to Rom 3:20
trying to keep his *, but by a new Rom 3:21,22
we no longer need obey God's *? Rom 3:31
keep the Jewish *, or is the Rom 4:9
saved without obeying Jewish *. Rom 4:11
obeyed God's * but because he Rom 4:13
by keeping his * we always end up Rom 4:15
* is not to have any to break! Rom 4:15
for breaking his *—because he had Rom 5:13
not yet given his * to them, nor Rom 5:13
of their failure to obey God's *. Rom 5:20
bound to him; the * of marriage no Rom 7:2
about the Jewish * and customs Rom 7:6
that these * of God are evil? Rom 7:7
Only if there were no * to break Rom 7:8
by taking the good * of God and Rom 7:11
For it uses God's good * for its Rom 7:13
agree with these * I am breaking. Rom 7:16
So now we can obey God's * if we Rom 8:4
It never did obey God's * and it Rom 8:7
by keeping his *, never succeeded. Rom 9:31
keeping the Jewish * and customs, Rom 10:3
trying to get by keeping his *. Rom 10:4
refuse to obey the * of the land Rom 13:2
the * and you will get along well. Rom 13:3
Obey the *, then, for two Rom 13:5
all of God's *, fulfilling all his Rom 13:8
it's not against God's * to eat 1Co 10:23
be saved by keeping the * of God 2Co 3:17
we obeyed the Jewish * or not. Gal 2:4
and by obeying Jewish *. Gal 2:5
and the many other Jewish * Gal 2:12
long since discarded the Jewish *; Gal 2:14
obeying our Jewish *, but only by Gal 2:16
we have obeyed the Jewish *. Gal 2:16
obeying all the other Jewish *? Gal 2:17
by keeping Jewish *, for it was Gal 2:18
trying—and failing—to obey the *. Gal 2:19
by keeping Jewish *, then there was Gal 2:21
by trying to keep the Jewish *? Gal 3:2
to obey the Jewish * never gave you Gal 3:3
your trying to obey the Jewish *? Gal 3:5
on the Jewish * to save them are Gal 3:10
one of these * that are written in Gal 3:10
to keep the Jewish *, because God Gal 3:11
If obeying those * could save Gal 3:18
Well then, why were the * given? Gal 3:19
they are of breaking God's *. Gal 3:19
God gave his * to angels to give Gal 3:19
Well then, are God's * and God's Gal 3:21,22
If we could be saved by his *, Gal 3:21,22
The Jewish * were our teacher and Gal 3:24
don't need those * any longer to Gal 3:25
We were slaves to Jewish * and Gal 4:3
get to heaven by obeying God's *? Gal 4:9
to obey the Jewish * to be saved: Gal 4:21
find out what those * really mean? Gal 4:21
One way was by giving them his * Gal 4:24,25
she is not a slave to Jewish *. Gal 4:26
to keep the Jewish *, just as Isaac Gal 4:29
to the Jewish *, but children of Gal 4:31
to Jewish * and ceremonies. Gal 5:1
keeping the Jewish * to make you Gal 5:2
debt to God by keeping those *; Gal 5:4
and Jewish * are necessary to the Gal 5:11
force yourself to obey Jewish *. Gal 5:18
is no conflict with Jewish *. Gal 5:23
try to keep the other Jewish *; Gal 6:13
by the Jewish * which favored the Eph 2:15
that whole system of Jewish *. Eph 2:15
by obeying God's *, but by trusting Php 3:9
as teachers of the * of Moses when 1Ti 1:7
idea what those * really show us. 1Ti 1:7
Those * are good when used as 1Ti 1:8
Yes, these * are made to 1Ti 1:10,11
Christians must obey the Jewish *. Tit 1:10
to Jewish *, for this kind of thing Tit 3:9
priests and their * had been able Heb 7:11
under the old *, because the new Heb 8:6
I will write my * in their minds so Heb 8:10
them, and these * will be in their Heb 8:10
all of God's *, he took the blood Heb 9:19
the book of God's * and over all Heb 9:19
THE OLD SYSTEM of Jewish * gave Heb 10:1
I will write my * into their minds Heb 10:16
and I will put my * in their hearts Heb 10:16
A man who refused to obey the * Heb 10:28
Sinai when God gave them his *. Heb 12:18
Jewish * can never be helped. Heb 13:10
Under the system of Jewish * the Heb 13:11
the marriage * by committing Jas 2:11
broken God's * and stand utterly Jas 2:11

LAWSUIT
then anyone with a * could come 2Sa 15:4
The Lord has filed a * against Hos 4:1
But the Lord is bringing a * Hos 12:2

LAWSUITS
and decide * and punishments), and Deu 21:5
true. Your * are based on lies; Is 59:4
To have such * at all is a real 1Co 6:7

LAWYER
Be these people's *—their Ex 18:19,20
He is my * and defender, and he 1Sa 24:15
Lord replies: I will be your *; Jer 51:36
O Lord, you are my *! Lam 3:58
One of them, a *, spoke up: Mt 22:34,35
and the * Act 24:1
the * and Apollos with their trip; Tit 3:13

LAWYERS
consulted his *, for he did nothing Est 1:13-15
*, magicians and politicians. Is 3:3

LAY
One day as he was drunk and * Gen 9:20,21
girl went in and * with him, and, Gen 19:35
"* down the knife; Gen 22:12
for a headrest and * down to sleep, Gen 28:11
they could * their hands on, both Gen 34:28
them out to * his hands upon the Gen 48:14
to his sons, he * back in the bed, Gen 49:33
All Egypt * in ruins. Ex 9:25
shall * their hands upon its head; Ex 29:10

(LAY Con't)
and his sons shall * their hands Ex 29:15,16
and his sons shall * their hands Ex 29:19,20
ground and they * broken at the Ex 32:19
The person bringing it is to * Lev 1:4
the priests will * the pieces, with Lev 1:12
the animal shall * his hand upon Lev 3:2
brings it shall * his hand upon its Lev 3:7,8
Lord, he shall * his hand upon its Lev 3:13
and shall * his hand upon its head Lev 4:4
of the nation shall * their hands Lev 4:15
He shall * his hand upon its Lev 4:24
killed, and there * his hand upon Lev 4:29
are killed, and * his hand upon its Lev 4:33
each morning, and * the daily burnt Lev 6:12
He shall * all their sins upon Lev 16:21
to * their hands upon his head; Lev 24:13,14
of the tribes shall * their hands Num 8:10
shall * their hands upon the Num 8:12
it from the altar; * incense on it, Num 16:46
So she * down in the road! Num 22:27
days and nights I * before the Deu 9:18
That nation will * siege to your Deu 28:52
their clothing and * prostrate Jos 7:6
So they left that night and * in Jos 8:9
(This land which * between Jos 12:7
tribe of Benjamin * between the Jos 18:11
And he * at her feet, Ju 5:27
men of the city * in wait all night Ju 16:2
and * there until it was light. Ju 19:26
a good meal, he * down very Ru 3:6,7
covering off his feet and * there. Ru 3:6,7
So she * at his feet until the Ru 3:14
He tore off his clothes and * 1Sa 19:24
he had a stroke and * paralyzed 1Sa 25:37,38
they came to the place where he *. 2Sa 2:23
without food and * all night before 2Sa 12:16
But Amasa * in his blood in the 2Sa 20:12
the king and she * in his arms to 1Ki 1:3,4
His body * there on the road, 1Ki 13:24,25
* my bones beside his bones. 1Ki 13:31
it into pieces and * it on the wood 1Ki 18:23
young bull and * it on the wood on 1Ki 18:23
Then he * down and slept beneath 1Ki 19:5
So he ate and drank and * down 1Ki 19:6
Hurry! * the staff upon the 2Ki 4:29
Then he * upon the child's body, 2Ki 4:34
where King Ben-hadad * sick. 2Ki 8:7
a gate that * between the double 2Ki 25:4,5
They assassinated him as he * in 2Ch 24:25
AS I * on the ground in front of Ez 10:1
but decided not to * hands on Est 3:5,6
and many * in sackcloth and Est 4:3
Look at me in horror, and * your Job 21:5
rocks and * bare precious stones. Job 28:10
the dew * all night upon my Job 29:19
This rabble trip me and * traps Job 30:12
the answers? I * my hand upon my Job 40:4
"If you * your hands upon him, Job 41:8
Then I * down and slept in peace Ps 3:5
you in heaven and * my requests Ps 5:3
all the trees * broken on the Ps 105:33
I will never * aside your laws, Ps 119:93
they trap themselves! They * a Pro 1:18
But one calamity is enough to * Pro 24:15,16
They will * siege to it, raze its Is 23:13
I will surround Jerusalem and * Is 29:3
make her nest and * her eggs and Is 34:15
all these * dead before them. Is 37:36
that your enemies * siege to the Jer 19:9
survivors and they * wounded in Jer 37:10
Literally, "* bands upon you." Eze 3:25f
a large brick and * it before you Eze 4:1
Literally, "I will * bands upon Eze 4:8f
therefore I will * my hand heavily Eze 25:7
their thrones and * aside their Eze 26:16
* empty as a barren wilderness; Eze 36:34
Then as I * there dreaming, I Dan 4:13
will come and * siege to a Dan 11:15
the Pleasant Land * bare and Zec 7:14
As he * awake Mt 1:20
of my own—no place to * my head." Mt 8:20
to * his hands on them and pray. Mt 19:13
your fathers and * flowers on the Mt 23:29,30
was delayed, they * down to rest Mt 25:5,6
begged Jesus to * his hands on the Mk 7:32
and the boy * there limp and Mk 9:26
came and ate it as it * exposed. Lk 8:5
On the way across he * down for Lk 8:23
even own a place to * my head. Lk 9:58
As he * there longing for scraps Lk 16:21
paralyzed limbs—* on the platforms Jn 5:3
and I * down my life for the Jn 10:15
"The Father loves me because I * Jn 10:17
* down my life voluntarily. Jn 10:18
right and power to * it down when I Jn 10:18
"so that when I * my hands on Act 8:19
took him upstairs where Dorcas * Act 9:39
and to us to * no greater burden Act 15:27,28,29
else they could * their hands on. Act 27:19
of sticks to * on the fire, a Act 28:3
to you Gentiles. I * great stress Rom 11:13
And no one can ever * any other 1Co 3:11
* as a sacrifice upon your altar. Heb 10:5
do your will, to * down my life, Heb 10:7
And so we also ought to * down 1Jn 3:16
am saying: I will * her upon a Rev 2:22

LAYER
with a thick * of locusts so that Ex 10:4,5
is placed a * of rams' skins, dyed Ex 26:14
over them a top * of goatskins. Ex 26:14
Above the ceiling was a second * Ex 36:14,15
The top * of the roof was made of Ex 36:19
stone and one * of cedar beams. 1Ki 6:36
topped with a * of new timber. Ez 6:4
there was a thick * of mire at the Jer 38:6
The first * Rev 21:18,19,20
The sixth * with sardus; Rev 21:18,19,20

LAYERS
bases; * of covering for the roof Ex 39:33-40
and put on the top *, just as the Ex 40:19
court had three * of hewn stone and 1Ki 6:36
There will be three * of huge Ez 6:4
built on twelve * of foundation Rev 21:18,19,20

LAYING
live goat and, * both hands upon Lev 16:21
her clothing, * aside that which Deu 21:13
this hill, * the stones carefully. Ju 6:26
They began by * siege to the city 2Sa 11:1
the Israeli army * siege to the 1Ki 15:27
your people, * plans to slay your Ps 83:3
"I have cut off many nations, * Zep 3:6
For since you began * the Zec 8:9
coming in and * his hands on him so Act 9:12
* his hands on him, healed him! Act 28:8
Literally, "the * on of hands." Heb 6:2f

LAYMAN
or *, who has done this thing! Mal 2:12

LAYMEN
on the hills. *, too, from all 2Ch 11:16

LAYS
love. She * her eggs on top of the Job 39:14
king of Babylon * siege to Eze 17:17
THE ENEMY * siege to Jerusalem! Mic 5:1
The Good Shepherd * down his life Jn 10:11
* down his life for his friends; Jn 15:13

LAZARUS
One day *, a diseased beggar, Lk 16:20
There, in torment, he saw * in Lk 16:23
some pity! Send * over here if only Lk 16:24
you wanted, and * had nothing. Lk 16:25
Well, her brother *, who lived in Jn 11:1
Martha, Mary, and *, he stayed Jn 11:5
Then he said, "Our friend * Jn 11:11
Jesus meant * was having a good Jn 11:12,13
But Jesus meant * had died. Jn 11:12,13
Then he told them plainly, "* is Jn 11:14
were told that * had already been Jn 11:17
she was going to *' tomb to weep; Jn 11:31
couldn't he keep * from dying?" Jn 11:37,38
Then he shouted, "*, come Jn 11:43
And * came—bound up in the Jn 11:44
in Bethany where * was—the man he Jn 12:1
Martha served, and * sat at the Jn 12:2
and also to see *—the man who had Jn 12:9
decided to kill * too, for it was Jn 12:10
seen Jesus call * back to life were Jn 12:17
Others (*, etc. Rev 1:5f

LAZINESS
the tasks ahead! * lets the roof Ecc 10:18
were pride and * and too much food, Eze 16:49
spends his days in * and does not 2Th 3:6
you are living in *, refusing to 2Th 3:11

LAZULI
bdellium and even lapis *. Gen 2:11,12
Literally, "lapis *." Eze 10:1f

LAZY
leaders were * and didn't help. Neh 3:5
I was not fat and *, yet trouble Job 3:26
from the ants, you * fellow. Pro 6:6
* men are soon poor; Pro 10:4
A * fellow is a pain to his Pro 10:26
a leader; be * and never succeed. Pro 12:24
A * man won't even dress the game Pro 12:27
* people want much but get Pro 13:4
A * fellow has trouble all Pro 15:19
A * man is brother to the Pro 18:9
A * man sleeps soundly—and goes Pro 19:15
Some men are so * they won't even Pro 19:24
The * man longs for many things Pro 21:25,26
The * man is full of excuses. Pro 22:13
field of a certain * fellow and saw Pro 24:30,31
The * man won't go out and work. Pro 26:13
her household, and is never *. Pro 31:27
it is better to be * and barely get Ecc 4:5,6
women who loll around in * ease; Is 32:9
replied, 'Wicked man! * slave! Mt 25:26
Never be * in your work but Rom 12:11
brothers, warn those who are *; 1Th 5:14
Besides, they are likely to be * 1Ti 5:13
they are like * animals, living Tit 1:12

LEAD
stay with you and * the way." Gen 33:12
you * my people out of Egypt." Ex 3:10
Jehovah said, "* all the people of Ex 6:26
ask permission to * the people from Ex 6:27
disaster and then * my people out. Ex 7:4
God did not * them through the Ex 13:17,18
They sank as * in the mighty Ex 15:10
you and * the people out to Mt. Ex 17:5,6
before you to * you safely to the Ex 23:20
"make us a god to * us, for this Ex 32:1
'Make us a god to * us, for Ex 32:23
And now go, * the people to the Ex 32:34
THE LORD SAID to Moses, "* these Ex 33:1
* and protect us day and night. Num 14:14
and * them up onto Mount Hor. Num 20:25
a man who will * them into battle Num 27:17
iron, tin, or *— shall be passed Num 31:22
son of Nun), shall * the people. Deu 1:38
him, for he shall * the people Deu 3:28
"But he said to me, 'Arise and * Deu 10:11
"The prophet who tries to * you Deu 13:5
been yoked, and * it to a valley Deu 21:4
I am no longer able to * you, Deu 31:2
But the Lord himself will * you, Deu 31:3
For you shall * these people into Deu 31:7
* my people across the Jordan Jos 1:2
fully armed, must * the other Jos 1:14
* on with courage and strength!" Jos 1:17,18
Ark and * us across the river!" Jos 3:6
will * you across the river! Jos 3:11
armed men would * the procession Jos 6:6-9
"Who will * the attack against Ju 1:12
volunteered to * the attack; Ju 1:13
and Zebulun. * them to Mount Tabor, Ju 4:6
O son of Abino-am, * away your Ju 5:12
"Who will * our forces against Ju 10:18
him to come and * their army Ju 11:6
"Which tribe shall * us against Ju 20:18
some will be made to * his 1Sa 8:12
He will govern us and * us to 1Sa 8:20
move past him to * the way—six 2Sa 15:17,18
should personally * the troops. 2Sa 17:11
The king planned to * the army 2Sa 18:2
let their enemies * them away as 1Ki 8:46
Literally, "were to * with 1Ch 15:21f
will * us into battle against you. 2Ch 13:12
They plotted to * an army Neh 4:8
choir directors to * the choirs in Neh 12:46
the man and to * him through the Est 6:9
Don't let your anger at others * Job 36:18
a ring in his nose and * him away. Job 40:24
paths of the godless * to doom. Ps 1:6
Lord, * me as you promised me you Ps 5:8
right road for me to walk. * me; Ps 25:5
your chosen ones. * them like a Ps 28:9
and your truth—let them * me. Ps 43:3
Let them * me to your Temple on Ps 43:3
and overwhelmed, * me to the Ps 61:2
Who else can * me into Edom? Ps 108:10
make me follow your *. Ps 119:68
but * evil men to execution. Ps 125:5
makes you sad, and * me along the Ps 139:24
you are my God. * me in good paths, Ps 143:10
Hold her fast and she will * you Pro 4:8,9
they will * you to real living. Pro 4:13
will * you and save you from harm; Pro 6:22
for the Lord * a man to riches, Pro 22:4
A curse on those who * astray the Pro 28:10
a little child shall * them all. Is 11:6
them and * them off to their doom. Is 30:28
and gently * the ewes with young. Is 40:11
For the Lord in his mercy will * Is 49:10
I will * them and comfort them, Is 57:18
your godliness will * you Is 58:8
to * you and show you the way! Jer 2:17
lies that * my people into sin. Jer 23:32
will * them home with great care. Jer 31:9
of the Chaldeans; * my people home Jer 50:8
the tin, the iron and the *. Eze 22:18,19,20
markets—silver, iron, tin and *. Eze 27:12
to * her in green pastures. Hos 4:16
The fathers are forced to * their Hos 9:13
As a man would * his favorite ox, Hos 11:4
in your noses and * you away like Amo 4:2
It will * to rebellion all across Amo 7:10
will * you out of exile and bring Mic 2:13
You who * his people astray! Mic 3:5
Where is your king to * you? Mic 4:9
over us, eight princes to * us. Mic 5:5
rule your people; * your flock; Mic 7:14
Suddenly the heavy * cover on the Zec 5:7
surely * to ruin, as it has.' Zec 7:7
The Lord shall * his people as Zec 9:14
my contract to * and protect them. Zec 11:10
Messiah, and will * many astray. Mt 24:5
will appear and * many astray. Mt 24:11
Messiah, and will * many astray. Mk 13:6
it for one blind man to * another? Lk 6:39
Sabbath and * them out for water? Lk 13:15
And I know his instructions * to Jn 12:50
we will have gods to * us back; Act 7:40
to take his hand and * him. Act 13:11

(LEAD Con't)
the Gentiles, to * them from the Act 13:47
His kindness is meant to * you to Rom 2:4
we no right to * about a wife that 1Co 9:5f
we no right to * about a wife that 1Co 9:5f
to guard us and * us to him. Gal 3:25
* to jealousy and hard feelings. Gal 5:26
our evil thoughts might * us into. Eph 2:3
without freedom to * his flock. 1Ti 3:7
men, even pastors, * sinful lives 1Ti 5:24
anger, which only * to 1Ti 6:4
discussions which * people into the 2Ti 2:16
* them out of the land of Egypt; Heb 8:9
These evil thoughts * to evil Jas 1:15
Don't be tyrants, but * them by 1Pe 5:3
to blindfold you and * you astray. 1Jn 2:26
their Shepherd and * them to the Rev 7:17

LEADED
flogged with a * whip, and handed Mk 15:15
with * thongs, and release him." Lk 23:16
Jesus' back with a * whip, and the Jn 19:1

LEADER
of Bedad), the * of the forces that Gen 36:31-39
atonement for the * concerning his Lev 4:26
For the priest is a * among his Lev 21:4
* Num 1:2-15
*: Nahshon (son of Num 2:3-31
* Num 3:16-24
* Num 3:25-30
* Num 3:31-35
send one * from each tribe. Num 13:2
"Let's elect a * to take us back Num 14:4
Salu, a * of the tribe of Simeon. Num 25:14
please appoint a new * for the Num 27:16
of Nun), and one * from each tribe, Num 34:16-28
* Num 34:16-28
The Lord God is your *, and he Deu 1:30
Because it is reserved for a *. Deu 33:21
dead, [you are the new * of Israel Jos 1:2
be a successful * of my people; Jos 1:6
the ten tribes, and each a clan *. Jos 22:14
Israel's * at that time, the one Ju 4:4
You are to anoint him as the * of 1Sa 9:16
"Isn't he the top * of Israel?" 1Sa 21:11
the * of about four hundred men. 1Sa 22:2
* among the followers of Saul. 2Sa 3:6
people, "A great * and a great man 2Sa 3:38
was our king you were our real *. 2Sa 5:2
shepherd and * of his people." 2Sa 5:2
appointed me as * of Israel, the 2Sa 6:21
you to be the * of my people Israel 2Sa 7:8
of the army—and was their *. 2Sa 23:18,19
a man to be my people's *.' 1Ki 8:16
He had become the * of a gang of 1Ki 11:24
Another rebel * was Jeroboam (the 1Ki 11:26
"Go back to Hezekiah, the * of 2Ki 20:5
father of Nahshon, a * of Israel. 1Ch 2:10
of Guni, was the * of the clan. 1Ch 5:15
reputation as a warrior and *. 1Ch 5:24
Hachmon) was the * of The Top 1Ch 11:11
a * of The Thirty, replied, 1Ch 12:18
with Uriel as their *; 1Ch 15:4-10
with Asaiah as their *; 1Ch 15:4-10
with Joel as their *; 1Ch 15:4-10
with Shemaiah as their *; 1Ch 15:4-10
with Eliel as their *; 1Ch 15:4-10
with Amminadab as their *. 1Ch 15:4-10
The song * was Chenaniah, the 1Ch 15:22
* were all dressed in linen robes. 1Ch 15:27
Asaph, the * of this detail, 1Ch 16:5
Ladan: Jehiel the *, Zetham, Joel; 1Ch 23:8,9
Rehabiah, was the * of his clan, 1Ch 23:17
Shimri as the * among his sons, 1Ch 26:10
the Lord as their *, and they 1Ch 29:22
he is our *. 2Ch 13:12
Shesh-bazzar, the * of the exiles Ez 1:8
As a Jewish religious *, Ezra was Ez 7:6
I sent them to Iddo, the * of Ez 8:17
their religious *, to read to them Neh 8:1
and appointed a * to take them back Neh 9:17
Meraiah, * of the Seraiah clan; Neh 12:12-21
Hananiah, * of the Jeremiah clan; Neh 12:12-21
Meshullam, * of the Ezra clan; Neh 12:12-21
Jehohanan, * of the Amariah clan; Neh 12:12-21
Jonathan, * of the Malluchi clan; Neh 12:12-21
Joseph, * of the Shebaniah clan; Neh 12:12-21
Adna, * of the Harim clan; Neh 12:12-21
Helkai, * of the Meraioth clan; Neh 12:12-21
Zechariah, * of the Iddo clan; Neh 12:12-21
Meshullam, * of the Ginnethon Neh 12:12-21
Zichri, * of the Abijah clan; Neh 12:12-21
Piltai, * of the Moadiah and Neh 12:12-21
Shammu-a, * of the Bilgah clan; Neh 12:12-21
Jehonathan, * of the Shemaiah Neh 12:12-21
Mattenai, * of the Joiarib clan; Neh 12:12-21
Uzzi, * of the Jedaiah clan; Neh 12:12-21
Kallai, * of the Sallai clan; Neh 12:12-21
Eber, * of the Amok clan; Neh 12:12-21
Hashabiah, * of the Hilkiah clan; Neh 12:12-21
Nethanel, * of the Jedaiah clan. Neh 12:12-21
Work hard and become a *; Pro 12:24
The locusts: though they have no * Pro 30:24-28
He can become the * of millions Ecc 4:16
Appoint a *; Jer 51:27
He became a * among the lions Eze 19:6
"Every * in Israel who lives Eze 22:6
be, the * of one of these nations. Eze 38:2,3f
You are their *, Gog! Eze 38:7
I stand against you, Gog, * of Eze 39:1
him, including a * of the priests. Dan 11:22
Israel will unite and have one *; Hos 1:11
* to defend them from their foes? Hab 1:14
Anyone wanting to be a * among Mt 20:26
The * of the local synagogue, Mk 5:22
And now a man named Jairus, a * Lk 8:41
But the local Jewish * in charge Lk 13:14
Once a Jewish religious * asked Lk 18:18
serves you best will be your *. Lk 22:26
a Jewish religious * named Jn 3:1
He was the Jewish * who came Jn 7:50
However, Crispus, the * of the Act 18:8
grabbed Sosthenes, the new * of Act 18:17
commitment to him as their *. 1Co 10:2
king or ruler or dictator or *. Eph 1:21
and he is the * of all those who Col 1:18
More literally, "church *" or 1Ti 3:1f
Jesus a perfect *, one fit to bring Heb 2:10
out of Egypt with Moses their *. Heb 3:16
Keep your eyes on Jesus, our * Heb 12:2
forward as the * of the Christians 3Jn 1:9
"Write a letter to the * Rev 2:1
"To the * Rev 2:8
"Write this letter to the * Rev 2:12
"Write this letter to the * Rev 2:18
"To the * Rev 3:1
"Write this letter to the * Rev 3:7
"Write this letter to the * Rev 3:14

LEADERS
The * of Edom are appalled, Ex 15:15
then the * of the people came and Ex 16:22
Aaron and the * of Israel came to Ex 18:12
together the * of the people and Ex 19:7
and Aaron and the * of the Ex 34:31
into cloth. The * brought onyx Ex 35:27
it to the Tabernacle where the * Lev 4:15
"If one of the * sins without Lev 4:22
assisted by * from each tribe:" Num 1:2-15
These were the tribal * elected Num 1:16
the above-named * summoned all Num 1:17,18,19
over the * of the Levites, with Num 3:31-35
and the other * took a census of Num 4:34
Thus Moses and Aaron and the * Num 4:46,47,48
Then the * of Israel—the chiefs Num 7:2
two * and an ox for each one; Num 7:3
The * also presented dedication Num 7:10
There the * Num 8:10
"Next, the Levite * Num 8:12
me seventy of the * of Israel; Num 11:16
and sent these twelve tribal *: Num 13:3-15
Two hundred and fifty popular *, Num 16:2
closely by the 250 Israeli *. Num 16:25
This is a wellThe * dug. Num 21:17,18
consulted with the * of Midian. Num 22:4
of the top * of Moab and Midian. Num 22:7
"Execute all the tribal * of Num 25:4
instructions to the * of Israel. Num 26:3,4
were the two * who conspired with Num 26:5-11
*, and others who were there. Num 27:1
NOW MOSES SUMMONED the * of Num 30:1
priest and all the * of the people Num 31:13
the army officers and battalion *. Num 31:14
the priest and the * of the tribes Num 31:26
Then the officers and battalion * Num 31:48,49
and battalion * and company Num 31:51,52
the other tribal * and said, "The Num 32:2
and the tribal * of Israel, "If Num 32:28
to Moses and the * of Israel with a Num 36:1
I will appoint them as your *.' Deu 1:13
all your tribal * came to me and Deu 5:23
the names of the battalion *. Deu 20:9
All of you—your *, the people, Deu 29:10
Elected by a convocation of the * Deu 33:5
to the * of Israel to tell the Jos 1:10,11
Then he summoned the * of the Jos 1:12,13
by the Israeli * to discover the Jos 2:3
Joshua and the other * finally Jos 9:14,15
And the * of Israel ratified the Jos 9:14,15
the vow which the * of Israel had Jos 9:18
* because of the peace treaty. Jos 9:18
But the * replied, "We have Jos 9:19
Joshua summoned their * and Jos 9:22
tribal * supervised the lottery. Jos 14:1
the Israeli * and reminded them, Jos 17:4
Joshua, and the * of the tribes of Jos 19:51
THEN THE * of the tribe of Levi Jos 21:1
and the * of the various tribes. Jos 21:1
he called for the * of Israel—the Jos 23:2
along with their *—the elders, Jos 24:1
The * of the tribe of Judah, Ju 1:3
Israel's * bravely led; Ju 5:2
In the * of Israel Ju 5:9
BUT THE TRIBAL * of Ephraim were Ju 8:1
But the * of Succoth replied, Ju 8:6
and religious * of the city. Ju 8:14
Then he took the * of the city Ju 8:16
"Go and talk to the * of Ju 9:2
So his uncles went to the * of Ju 9:3
with the local *, Abimelech and his Ju 9:35
the * of Gilead asked each Ju 10:18
Israel. The * of Gilead sent for Ju 11:5
sent for the five Philistine *. Ju 16:18
The Philistine * declared a great Ju 16:23,24
The five Philistine * were there Ju 16:27
Philistine * and all the people. Ju 16:30
Israel sent their * and 450,000 Ju 20:1
THE * OF Israel had vowed at Ju 21:1
And now the Israeli * met at Ju 21:2
the * of Israel asked. Ju 21:16
camp and their * discussed why the 1Sa 4:3
When the Philistine * heard about 1Sa 7:7
Finally the * of Israel met in 1Sa 8:4
So Samuel called the tribal * 1Sa 10:20
Then Saul said to the *, 1Sa 14:38
me before the * and before my 1Sa 15:30
But the Philistine * were angry. 1Sa 29:4
Then the * of Judah came to 2Sa 2:4
consulted with the * of Israel and 2Sa 3:17
Abner also talked to the * of the 2Sa 3:19
the Lord with the * of Israel there 2Sa 5:3
and the other * of Israel, who were 2Sa 6:5
*, the shepherds of my people. 2Sa 7:7
bare earth. The * of the nation 2Sa 12:17
Then Amasa convinced all the * 2Sa 19:14
of all the * of Israel—the heads of 1Ki 8:1
* of Jezreel, where Naboth lived. 1Ki 21:8
So the Lord raised up * among 2Ki 13:5
elders and other * of Judah and 2Ki 23:1
these underground * and their men 2Ki 25:23
and the guerrilla * fled in panic 2Ki 25:26
(Their * were Pelatiah, Ne-ariah, 1Ch 4:42
of choir *: Heman the Cantor was 1Ch 6:33-38
and were the * of 22,034 troops 1Ch 7:7
THEN THE * of Israel went to David 1Ch 11:1
Then David and the * went to 1Ch 11:4
encouraged the * of Israel to make 1Ch 11:10
* of the tribe of Reuben; 1Ch 11:26-47
there were 200 * of the tribe with 1Ch 12:24-37
and for the Levite *: Uriel, 1Ch 15:11
"You are the * of the clans of 1Ch 15:12
ordered the Levite * to organize 1Ch 15:16
So the * of Israel took the Ark 1Ch 15:28
for it, and the * of Israel 1Ch 16:1
to any of the * of Israel—the 1Ch 17:6
he told Joab and the other *. 1Ch 21:2
Then David ordered all the * of 1Ch 22:17
and religious * of Israel for the 1Ch 23:2
king and of these *: Zadok the 1Ch 24:6
* of the priests and the Levites. 1Ch 24:31
and brothers, too, were real *. 1Ch 26:9
guards were named after the *. 1Ch 26:12
and the other * of the nation such 1Ch 26:26
political *, the commanders of the 1Ch 28:1
"Here before the * of Israel, the 1Ch 28:8
Then the clan *, the heads of the 1Ch 29:6,7
The national *, the army 1Ch 29:24
and religious * of Israel. 2Ch 1:2,3
all of the * of Israel—the heads of 2Ch 5:2
As the * of Israel watched, the 2Ch 5:4,5
ALL THE * of Israel came to 2Ch 10:1
and the Judean * from every part of 2Ch 12:5
Then the king and the * of Israel 2Ch 12:6
and priests and clan * and judges. 2Ch 19:8
After consultation with the * of 2Ch 20:21
and many other * of Israel. 2Ch 21:3,4
Levites and clan * about his plans 2Ch 23:2,3
Each of the three * led a third 2Ch 23:8
And all the * and the people 2Ch 24:10
But after his death the * of 2Ch 24:17,18
Then the * plotted to kill 2Ch 24:21
killing all the * of the nation and 2Ch 24:23
army, assigning * to each clan from 2Ch 25:5,6
Twenty-six hundred brave clan * 2Ch 26:12
Some of the top * of Ephraim also 2Ch 28:12
political * to decide what to do. 2Ch 28:14
The Levite *—Conaniah, Shemaiah, 2Ch 35:9
desire to the * of the tribes of Ez 1:5
The * were: Ez 2:2
so the * refused to allow them to Ez 2:62,63
Some of the * were able to give Ez 2:68
Levites and other *—the old men who Ez 3:12
and the other * and suggested, Ez 4:2
the other Jewish * replied, "No, Ez 4:3
and other local *, the Persians, Ez 4:8,9
We asked the *, 'Who has given Ez 5:9
and the other * in their work. Ez 6:7
So the Jewish * continued in Ez 6:14
and I persuaded some of the * of Ez 7:28
genealogies of the * who Ez 8:1
and Meshullam, the Levite *; Ez 8:16
I appointed twelve * of the Ez 8:24
council and the * and people of Ez 8:25
and the Levite * and the elders of Ez 8:29
BUT THEN THE Jewish * came to tell Ez 9:1

LEADERS Con't)
and the political * were some of Ez 9:2
demanded that the * of the priests Ez 10:5
days and that the * and elders had Ez 10:7,8
Let our * arrange trials for us. Ez 10:14
* and I were designated as judges; Ez 10:16-19
or religious *, or even to those Neh 2:16
their * were lazy and didn't help. Neh 3:5
Then some of the * began Neh 4:10
together the * and the people and Neh 4:14
together all the * of the city, Neh 7:5
"Their * were: Neh 7:7
Some of their * gave gifts for Neh 7:70
The other * gave a total of Neh 7:71
The next day the clan * and the Neh 8:13
Then the Levite * called out to Neh 9:5
The * in this part of the service Neh 9:5
The political * who signed: Neh 10:14-27
Levites, and * should supply the Neh 10:34
most of the *, the priests, the Neh 11:3
* from the tribe of Judah: Neh 11:4,5,6
* from the tribe of Benjamin: Neh 11:7,8,9
* from among the priests: Neh 11:10-14
Levite *: Neh 11:15,16,17
workers (whose * were Ziha and Neh 11:21
The following were the clan * of Neh 12:12-21
I led the Judean * to the top of Neh 12:31,32
of half of the * of Judah, Neh 12:31,32
I immediately confronted the * Neh 13:11
Then I asked the * of Judah, Neh 13:17
and before the * of the nation. Ps 107:32
When their * are condemned, and Ps 141:6,7
their greatest * fail; Ps 146:3
Bind their kings and * with iron Ps 149:8
wiser and become * by exploring the Pro 1:5,6
but with honest, sensible * there Pro 28:2
chamber with the other civic *. Pro 31:23
from even the * of the nations. Pro 31:31
a child and whose * are already Ecc 10:16,17
and whose * work hard before they Ecc 10:16,17
Listen, you * of Israel, you men Is 1:10
Your * are rebels, companions of Is 1:23
water supplies and kill her *; Is 3:2
children playing king. True *? Is 3:12
will destroy the * of Israel and Is 9:14,15
For the * of his people have led Is 9:16
World * and earth's mightiest Is 14:9
All your * flee; Is 22:3
For the * of my people—the Is 56:10
And I will give you * after my Jer 3:15
I will go now to their *, the men Jer 5:5
I will send disaster upon the * of Jer 23:1
let the * of mankind beat their Jer 25:34
and to the * shouting in despair, Jer 25:36
Now when the * of the Jewish Jer 40:7
These are the names of the * who Jer 40:8
other guerrilla * came to Mizpah to Jer 40:13,14
of the guerrilla * heard what Jer 41:11
all the guerrilla * and all the Jer 43:4
off from among the * of Israel; Eze 13:9
"SING THIS DEATH dirge for the * Eze 19:1
slay my people and all their *. Eze 21:12
Your * are like wolves, who tear Eze 22:27
the shepherds, the * of Israel, and Eze 34:2
and defeated some of their *. Dan 8:10
you priests and all of Israel's *; Hos 5:1
The * of Judah have become the Hos 5:10
their * will perish by the sword Hos 7:16
more, for all their * are rebels. Hos 9:15
Where are all the * of the land? Hos 13:10
and slay all the * under him." Amo 2:3
and Egyptian *, saying, "Take your Amo 3:9
LISTEN, YOU * of Israel—you are Mic 3:1
Listen to me, you * of Israel who Mic 3:9
kind— you * who take bribes; Mic 3:11
All her * were bound in chains. Nah 3:10
I will punish the * and princes of Zep 1:8
Her * are like roaring lions Zep 3:3
'shepherds'—your *—and I will Zec 10:3
of Israel's *—all these evil Zec 11:3
by wicked *, who go unpunished. Zec 11:5
wicked *, and they will slay them. Zec 11:6
And I said to their *, "If you Zec 11:12
meeting of the Jewish religious *. Mt 2:4
Jewish religious * who strictly Mt 3:7f
Jewish political *. Mt 3:7f
and other Jewish *, you can't get Mt 5:20
and not as their Jewish *. Mt 7:29
These * only quoted others, and Mt 7:29f
of the religious * to themselves. Mt 9:3
One day some of the Jewish *, Mt 12:38
PHARISEES AND other Jewish * Mt 15:1
Jewish politico-religious * of two Mt 16:1f
at the hands of the Jewish *, Mt 16:21
do the Jewish * insist Elijah must Mt 17:10
and other Jewish *, and they will Mt 20:18
and other Jewish * saw these Mt 21:15
and other Jewish * came up to him Mt 21:23
The Jewish * replied, "He will Mt 21:41
and other Jewish * realized that Mt 21:45
think these Jewish * and these Mt 23:2
and you other religious *. Mt 23:13,14
you other religious *—hypocrites! Mt 23:23
and you religious *—hypocrites! Mt 23:25
Pharisees, and you religious *! Mt 23:27
and you religious *—hypocrites! Mt 23:29,30
and clubs, sent by the Jewish *. Mt 26:47
all the Jewish * were gathering. Mt 26:57
priests and Jewish * met again to Mt 27:1
chief priests and other Jewish *. Mt 27:3
and other Jewish * made their many Mt 27:12
that the Jewish * had arrested Mt 27:18
and Jewish * also mocked him. Mt 27:41,42,43
A meeting of all the Jewish * Mt 28:12,13
But some of the Jewish religious * Mk 2:6
some of the Jewish religious * Mk 2:16
John's disciples and the Jewish * Mk 2:18
Some of the Jewish religious * Mk 2:24
ONE DAY SOME Jewish religious * Mk 7:1
So the religious * asked him, Mk 7:5
When the local Jewish * learned Mk 8:11
the other Jewish *—and be killed, Mk 8:31
Jewish religious * often spoke of, Mk 9:11
as some Jewish * argued with them. Mk 9:14
and the Jewish *, who will sentence Mk 10:33
and other Jewish * heard what he Mk 11:18
chief priests and other Jewish * Mk 11:27,28
The Jewish * wanted to arrest him Mk 12:12
other religious and political * Mk 12:13
and other Jewish * were still Mk 14:1
chief priests and other Jewish *. Mk 14:43
and other Jewish * soon gathered. Mk 14:53
The chief priests and religious * Mk 15:31
teaching, some Jewish religious * Lk 5:17
by the Jewish *—the elders, chief Lk 9:22
Jewish religious * and the experts Lk 15:2
* and the business community Lk 19:47
other religious * and councilmen. Lk 20:1
and religious * heard about this Lk 20:19
other religious * were actively Lk 22:2
religious * who headed the mob. Lk 22:52
other religious * stood there Lk 23:10
and other Jewish *, along with the Lk 23:13
And the Jewish * laughed and Lk 23:35
and actions of the other Jewish *. Lk 23:50,51,52
and our religious * arrested him Lk 24:20
The Jewish * Jn 1:19
the Jewish * Jn 2:18
So the Jewish * objected. Jn 5:10
to find the Jewish * and told them Jn 5:15
Then the Jewish * were all the Jn 5:18
Jewish * were plotting his death. Jn 7:1
The Jewish * tried to find him Jn 7:11
of reprisals from the Jewish *. Jn 7:13
The Jewish * were surprised when Jn 7:15
Can it be that our * have Jn 7:26
Then the Jewish * sought to Jn 7:30
The Jewish * were puzzled by this Jn 7:35
As he was speaking, the Jewish * Jn 8:3
And the Jewish * slipped away Jn 8:9
Then many of the Jewish * who Jn 8:30,31
the Jewish * snarled. Jn 8:48
The * of the Jews said, "Now we Jn 8:52
The Jewish *: "You aren't even Jn 8:57
At that point the Jewish * picked Jn 8:59
The Jewish * wouldn't believe he Jn 9:18
fear of the Jewish * who had Jn 9:22,23
things, the Jewish * were again Jn 10:19
The Jewish * surrounded him and Jn 10:24
Then again the Jewish * picked up Jn 10:31
ago the Jewish * in Judea were Jn 11:8
many of the Jewish * had come to Jn 11:19
When the Jewish * who were at Jn 11:31
and the Jewish * wailing with her, Jn 11:33
friends," the Jewish * said. Jn 11:36
many of the Jewish * who were with Jn 11:45
* began plotting Jesus' death. Jn 11:53
many of the Jewish * had deserted Jn 12:11
many of the Jewish * believed him Jn 12:42
to me—just as I told the Jewish *. Jn 13:33
the other Jewish *, "Better that Jn 18:14
by all the Jewish * and teach Jn 18:20
I was arrested by the Jewish *. Jn 18:36
but the Jewish * told him, "If you Jn 19:12
The Jewish * didn't want the Jn 19:31
fear of the Jewish *, boldly asked Jn 19:38
fear of the Jewish *, when suddenly Jn 20:19
the same can be said of your *. Act 3:17
of all the Jewish * was in session Act 4:5
them, "Honorable * and elders of Act 4:8
against Stephen, and the Jewish * Act 6:12
The Jewish * were stung to fury Act 7:54
After a while the Jewish * Act 9:23
pleased the Jewish *, he arrested Act 12:3
and their * fulfilled prophecy by Act 13:27
But when the Jewish * Act 13:45
Then the Jewish * stirred up both Act 13:50
and the civic * of the city and Act 13:50
Some agreed with the Jewish *, Act 14:4
Jews, and Jewish * to attack and Act 14:5,6
with the church *—all the apostles Act 15:4
two of the church *—Judas (also Act 15:22
But the Jewish * were jealous and Act 17:5
to the Jewish * in Damascus, with Act 22:5
Some of the Jewish * Act 23:9
arrived with some of the Jewish * Act 24:1
and other Jewish * got hold of him Act 25:2
and other Jewish * gave me their Act 25:15
* and spoke to them as follows: Act 28:17
sentence demanded by the Jewish *. Act 28:18
You people there are * in so 2Co 8:7
Now I want you to be * also in 2Co 8:7
I talked privately to the * of Gal 2:2
And the great * of the church who Gal 2:6
(By the way, their being great * Gal 2:6
Remember your * who have taught Heb 13:7
Obey your spiritual * and be Heb 13:17
Give my greetings to all your * Heb 13:24,25
Watch out for the false *—and 2Jn 1:7
The seven stars are the * Rev 1:20
and holds their * in his right Rev 2:1
earth, and world * and rich men, Rev 6:15
And the world *, who took part in Rev 18:9

LEADERSHIP
the * of Ithamar, Aaron's son. Num 7:8
of Dan under the * of Ahiezer, the Num 10:25
as he prepares to take over the *. Deu 1:38
there was more * ability among the 1Ch 24:4
Under the * of Asaph, the king's 1Ch 25:2
under the * of General Zerah. 2Ch 14:9,10
under the * of Jahath and Obadiah, 2Ch 34:12
Temple under the * of these men. Neh 11:10-14
priests under the * of Adaiah (son Neh 11:10-14
men under the * of Amashsai (son Neh 11:10-14
Without wise *, a nation is in Pro 11:14
to your husbands' * in the same way Eph 5:22
You younger men, follow the * of 1Pe 5:5

LEADING
to him, and for * me straight to Gen 24:27
Then the Angel of God, who was * Ex 14:19
the son of Shedeur * his people. Num 10:18
Baal, and they are * you astray, as Num 25:18
responsibility of * the people. Num 27:19
the Midianites for * you into Num 31:1
When the Lord alone was * them, Deu 32:12
he became one of the * citizens. Ju 9:26
Samson said to the boy who was * Ju 16:25,26
captains were * out their troops by 1Sa 29:2
He was * two donkeys loaded with 2Sa 16:1
* the men across the Jordan River. 2Sa 17:24
and * the rest of Israel into sin. 1Ki 15:30
should be a choir * the march, 2Ch 20:21
with Jehoshaphat * them, full of 2Ch 20:27
by an orchestra * the people in a 2Ch 23:12
honor your name by * me out of Ps 31:3
He ascends the heights, * many Ps 68:18
where are you * your flock today? Sol 1:7
No, misleaders! * you down the Is 3:12
of Ethiopia, was * an army against Is 37:8,9
Instead of * my flock to safety, Jer 23:2
see shepherds * sheep and lambs. Jer 33:12
terrible sins, * the whole nation Eze 8:17
And there were seven steps * up Eze 40:22
of seven steps * up to it, and Eze 40:26
steps * up to it instead of seven. Eze 40:31
eight steps * up to the entrance. Eze 40:37
The space above the door * into Eze 41:17,18
The doors * into the nave were Eze 41:25
the outer wall * to the east. Eze 43:1
They are blind guides * the Mt 15:13,14
and the * citizens of Galilee. Mk 6:21
Literally, "the * men among the Lk 19:47f
fellow has been * our people to Lk 23:2
accusing him of * a revolt against Lk 23:14
* them out of their slavery. Act 13:17
of the wives of the * men." Act 17:4f
by the hand, and * him aside asked, Act 23:19
* in every part of our lives. Gal 5:25
does his sheep, * and teaching them Eph 4:11
chain of angels * up to God—wild 1Ti 1:3,4
* you away from the living God. Heb 3:12

LEADS
The Lord * on! Ju 4:14
Anyone who * a blameless life and Ps 15:2
upon the crags. He * me safely Ps 18:33
and * me beside the quiet streams. Ps 23:2,3
Don't fret and worry—it only * to Ps 37:8
The little tribe of Benjamin * Ps 68:27
O SHEPHERD OF Israel who * Israel Ps 80:1
She * you down to death and hell. Pro 5:5
doesn't even realize where it *. Pro 5:6
Winking at sin * to sorrow; Pro 10:10
bold reproof * to peace. Pro 10:10
that only * to sorrow and Pro 10:14
The path of the godly * to life. Pro 12:28
Pride * to arguments; Pro 13:10
The road of the godly * upward, Pro 15:24
The path of the godly * away from Pro 16:17
Wickedness loves company—and * Pro 16:29
neighbor and * him into loss." Pro 16:29f
hard liquor * to brawls; Pro 20:1
quick is evil and * to poverty. Pro 28:22
trusting God * to prosperity. Pro 28:25

(LEADS Con't)
A king as he * his army. Pro 30:29,30,31
A wise man's heart * him to do Ecc 10:2
a fool's heart * him to do evil. Ecc 10:2
the aqueduct which * from Gihon Is 7:3
* down to the bleaching field. Is 7:3
as when a flutist * a pilgrim band Is 30:29
is good and * to life and health. Is 38:16
* his sheep, calling each by its Is 40:26
your own good and * you along the Is 48:17
The Lord * them with a shout. Joe 2:11
will go before you—the Lord * on. Mic 2:13
Literally, "the way that * to Mt 7:13f
own sheep by name and * them out. Jn 10:3
the Spirit who * into all truth. Jn 14:17
the Holy Spirit * to life and Rom 8:6
the old nature * to death, because Rom 8:6
If the plan that * to doom was 2Co 3:9

LEAF
him with an olive * in her beak. Gen 8:11
The sound of a * driven in the Lev 26:36
Would you blame a * that is Job 13:25
to the last mint * in your garden, Mt 23:23
a fig tree in full *, so he went Mk 11:13
so that not a * rustled in the Rev 7:1

LEAF-BLADE
First a * pushed through, and Mk 4:28

LEAFY
A * plant eaten by peasant women Gen 30:14f
and the boughs of * trees—such as Lev 23:40
as full of cracks as a * booth! Job 27:18
and he made a * shelter to shade Jon 4:5
down * branches from the fields. Mk 11:8

LEAGUE
and the ten men in * with him Jer 41:2

LEAGUED
all the countries * with them shall Eze 30:5

LEAH
Now Laban had two daughters, * Gen 29:16
sister, Rachel. * had lovely eyes, Gen 29:17
* to Jacob, and he slept with her. Gen 29:23
(And Laban gave to * a servant Gen 29:24
But in the morning—it was *! Gen 29:25
her more than *, and stayed and Gen 29:30
But because Jacob was slighting * Gen 29:31
was barren. So * became pregnant Gen 29:32
Meanwhile, when * realized that Gen 30:9
him with a son. * named him Gad Gen 30:11
a second son, and * named him Gen 30:13
and brought them to his mother *. Gen 30:14
Rachel begged * to give some of Gen 30:14
But * angrily replied, "Wasn't Gen 30:15
fields, * went out to meet him. Gen 30:16
for Rachel and * to come out to the Gen 31:4
Rachel and * replied, "That's Gen 31:14
at the head, * and her children Gen 33:2
Next came * with her children, Gen 33:7
The sons of *: Gen 35:23
of Jacob and *, not including their Gen 46:15
given to * by her father, Laban. Gen 46:18
and there I buried *. Gen 49:31
as Rachel and *, from whom all the Ru 4:11

LEAH'S
there, then into *, and then Gen 31:33
ONE DAY DINAH, * daughter, went Gen 34:1
The sons of Zilpah, * Gen 35:26

LEAK
Laziness lets the roof *, and Ecc 10:18

LEAKING
Nineveh is like a * water tank! Nah 2:8

LEAN
If you * on Egypt, you will find 2Ki 18:20,21
pierce your hand if you * on it. Is 36:6
Our princes were * and tanned, Lam 4:7

LEANED
Israel * on you but, like a Eze 29:7
the one who had * around at supper Jn 21:20

LEANING
and saw Saul * against his spear 2Sa 1:6
the desert, * on her beloved?" Sol 8:5
the table, * on the left elbow. Jn 13:23f
Literally, "* back against Jesus' Jn 13:25f
prayed, * on the top of his cane. Heb 11:21

LEANNESS
but sent them * in their souls. Ps 106:15

LEANS
worship there and * on my arm, may 2Ki 5:18
in a dark room who * against a Amo 5:19

LEAP
By your strength I * over a wall. 2Sa 22:30
the ground, you * upon me like a Job 10:16
Have you made him able to * Job 39:20
coals—flames * from his mouth. Job 41:21
Mount Sirion. They * and skip Ps 29:5,6
The lame man will * up like a Is 35:6
happens, rejoice! Yes, * for joy! Lk 6:23
he came up with a *, stood there a Act 3:7,8
disguised as frogs * from the mouth Rev 16:13

LEAPED
and Sisera * from his chariot and Ju 4:15
Fire * from his mouth 2Sa 22:9
Fierce flames * from his mouth, Ps 18:8
the flames * out and killed the Dan 3:22
and the lions * upon them and tore Dan 6:24
Elizabeth's child * within her and Lk 1:41
and the man * to his feet and Act 14:10
And he * on two of them and Act 19:16

LEAPING
* out from Bashan." Deu 33:22
the altar were * up toward the sky, Ju 13:20
* and dancing before the Lord; 2Sa 6:16
Here he comes, * upon the Sol 2:8
Look at them * along the tops of Joe 2:5
And you will go free, * with joy Mal 4:2
Then, walking, *, and praising Act 3:7,8

LEAPS
Fire * from his mouth. Job 41:19
that * upon the grazing sheep. Jer 50:44
And so the wolf * on them and Jn 10:12

LEARN
Laban didn't * of their flight Gen 31:22
so that they will * always to Deu 4:10
* them, and be sure to obey them! Deu 5:1
so that he will * to respect the Deu 17:19
laws of God and to * his will, so Deu 31:12
will hear them and * how to revere Deu 31:13
And Israel will * that the Lord 1Sa 17:47
In this way they will always * 1Ki 8:40
Send Naaman to me, and he will * 2Ki 5:8
they * what Queen Vashti has done. Est 1:17
until they * that you alone, Ps 83:18
Literally, "when I * (have Ps 119:7f
I praise you for letting me * Ps 119:171
What you * from them will stand Pro 1:7,8,9
you will soon * the importance of Pro 2:3,4,5
and happy life. * to be wise," he Pro 4:5
I would have you * this great Pro 4:11
* from their ways and be wise! Pro 6:6
begin to live; * how to be wise." Pro 9:6
teach a good man, and he will * Pro 9:9
TO *, YOU must want to be taught. Pro 12:1
Punish a mocker and others will * Pro 19:25
the simpleton can * only by Pro 21:11
The godly * by watching ruin Pro 21:12
men, lest you * to be like them and Pro 22:24,25
spanking a child helps him to *. Pro 29:15
Or, "I sought to * about Ecc 1:16-18f
quit your evil ways. * to do Is 1:17
must * to believe what I say." Is 7:9
then your enemies would * the Is 64:2
harlot could * a lot from you! Jer 2:33
nations quickly * my people's ways Jer 12:16
Won't you * a lesson from the Jer 35:13
They shall * that I am the Eze 7:26,27
of Israel will * not to desert me Eze 14:11
great ability to * and they soon Dan 1:17
life, until you * that the Most Dan 4:25
Then at last they will * to stay Dan 9:24
Only those who are willing to * Dan 12:10
so the people will * God's laws. Mal 2:7
was frightened to * that the new Mt 2:22
"Now go away and * the meaning of Mt 9:13
"Now * a lesson from the fig Mt 24:32
But if he works hard, he may * as Lk 6:40
speaks to, who * the truth from Jn 6:45
us—they help us * to be patient. Rom 5:3
Then you will * from your own Rom 12:2
about them and * from them in these 1Co 10:11
* and be encouraged and helped. 1Co 14:31
* as you go along what pleases Eph 5:10
until they could * not to bring 1Ti 1:20
Women should listen and * 1Ti 2:11
For our people must * to help Tit 3:14
Son, he had to * from experience Heb 5:8
Christians and * right from wrong Heb 5:14
dead, we can still * lessons from Heb 11:4
When will you ever * that Jas 2:20
* to know him better and better. 2Pe 1:2
For then you must * to know God 2Pe 1:5
Next, * to put aside your own 2Pe 1:6
at all than to * of him and then 2Pe 2:21
will * to love God more and more. 1Jn 2:5

LEARNED
stupor, and * what had happened and Gen 9:24,25
When Abram * that Lot had been Gen 14:14
Literally, "I have * by Gen 30:27f
BUT JACOB * that Laban's sons were Gen 31:1
were, and when he * what they had Num 22:2,3
Finally they * that it was Ju 6:29
When Abimelech * of this, he led Ju 9:47,48
when they * that the Philistines 1Sa 7:7
Saul soon * that David was at 1Sa 23:7
But David * of Saul's plan and 1Sa 23:9
his casualties, he * that only 2Sa 2:30
When David * what she had done, 2Sa 21:11
When Shime-i * where they were, 1Ki 2:39
David, so when he * that David's 1Ki 5:1
When the people of Israel * of 1Ki 12:20
Ahaziah of Judah, * that her son 2Ki 11:1
for he had * of his sickness. 2Ki 20:12
guerrilla forces * that the king of 2Ki 25:23
But David * that they were on the 1Ch 14:8
When King Tou of Hamath * that 1Ch 18:
When David * of this, he sent 1Ch 19.
WAS VERY angry when he * Neh 4:
Our enemies * that we knew of Neh 4:1
in Jerusalem and * of this evil Neh 13:
I also * that the Levites had not Neh 13:1
WHEN MORDECAI * what had been Est 4:
the heathen and * their evil ways, Ps 106:3
Then, as I looked, I * this Pro 24:32,3
Literally, "I have not * Pro 30:3
to mere words * by rote, therefore Is 29:1
young lion, and * to catch prey and Eze 19:
the lions and * to catch prey, and Eze 19:
when you have * that heaven rules. Dan 4:2
reign, I, Daniel, * from the book Dan 9:
they *, that God's Word endures! Zec 1:5,
Herod was furious when he * that Mt 2:1
When the local Jewish leaders * Mk 8:1
Can it be that our leaders have * Jn 7:2
The believers * how to walk in Act 9:3
But when they * that Peter was Act 9:38
When Paul and Barnabas * of a Act 14:5,
in Thessalonica * that Paul was Act 17:1
at whose feet I * to follow our Act 22:3
I * that he was a Roman citizen. Act 23:27
WE SOON * that we were on the Act 28:1
But when I * the truth, I Rom 7:9
Haven't you yet * that your body 1Co 6:19
to speak in languages he never *; 1Co 12:10
in languages they have never *. 1Co 12:28
speak in languages we've never *? 1Co 12:30
you haven't *, you will be talking 1Co 14:2
his voice and * from him the truths Eph 4:21
I haven't * all I should even Php 3:12
practice all you * from me and saw Php 4:9
need, for I have * how to get along Php 4:11
I have * the secret of Php 4:12
when you first * about Christ. Heb 10:32
know: facts you * from the holy 2Pe 3:1
have * to know God our Father. 1Jn 2:13

LEARNING
A wise teacher makes * a joy; Pro 15:2
languages without * them, and could 1Co 13:1
preachers, so much *, so much 2Co 8:7
* to know God better and better. Col 1:10
is continually * more and more of Col 3:10
is right and good, * to trust him 1Ti 6:11
of the world by * about our Lord 2Pe 2:20
of our holy faith, * to pray in the Jud 1:20

LEARNS
and her husband * of her vow and Num 30:7
The wise man * by listening; Pro 21:11
make sure everyone * them well. 1Ti 4:11

LEASE
You have no greater * on life Ps 49:10
death, and * the vineyard to others Mt 21:41
all, and * the vineyard to others. Mk 12:9

LEASED
the watchman, then * the vineyard Mt 21:33
Then he * the farm to tenant Mk 12:1

LEAST
is my sister—or at * a half-sister Gen 20:11,12
"But we want Rebekah here at * Gen 24:55
not worthy of the * of all your Gen 32:10
"Well," Esau said, "at * let Gen 33:15
be avoided, then at * do this. Gen 43:11
* anyone gathered was 100 bushels! Num 11:32
Curse at * that many!" Num 23:13
them, at * don't bless them!" Num 23:25
there must be at * two or three. Deu 17:6
There must be at * two, and three Deu 19:15
do not deviate from them the * Jos 23:6
and I am the * thought of in the Ju 6:15
the loss of at * one of my eyes." Ju 16:28
We can at * offer it to him and 1Sa 9:8
my family is the * important of all 1Sa 9:21
but oh, at * honor me before the 1Sa 15:30
at * some of my horses and mules. 1Ki 18:5
been, for he at * tore down the 2Ki 3:2
"I thought at * he would come out 2Ki 5:11
you are no threat to even the * 2Ki 18:24
thinking, "At * there will be 2Ki 20:19
So only the poorest and * skilled 2Ki 24:14
This is at * a beginning, 1Ch 22:14
This, at *, gives me comfort Job 6:10
This at * will be in my favor, Job 13:16
" 'Well,' you say, 'at * God Job 21:19
Well, one thing, at *, is good: Ecc 5:18
For the living at * know that Ecc 9:5
says is good. At * there will be Is 39:8
the * of them right to the top! Jer 6:13
No, not in the *; Jer 8:12
all shall die, from the * to the Jer 44:12
shall become the * of the nations—a Jer 50:12
they will at * know they have had a Eze 2:5
boast as a god? At * to these Eze 28:9
front of me—or at * he looked like Dan 8:15
a half years as at * a partial Dan 9:25f
Then for a while at * she will be Hos 8:10
at * the gleanings would be left! Ob 1:5
And so if anyone breaks the * Mt 5:19

(LEAST Con't)
be the * in the Kingdom of Heaven. Mt 5:19
without at * one illustration. Mt 13:34,35
you should at * have put my money Mt 25:27
to help the * of these my brothers, Mt 25:45
him to let them at * touch the Mk 6:56
be the *—the servant of all!" Mk 9:35
now will be the * important then; Mk 10:31
and many who are considered * Mk 10:31
And yet the * citizen of the Lk 7:28
Father will do at * as much, and Lk 11:13
will come when * expected." Lk 12:40
of now will be * important then." Lk 13:30
at * get some interest on it?" Lk 19:23
The woman said, "Well, at * I Jn 4:25
mats so that at * Peter's shadow Act 5:15
they feel that the * they can do in Rom 15:27
Or, "Even the * capable people in 1Co 6:4f
seem weakest and * important are 1Co 12:22
For I am the * worthy of all the 1Co 15:9
us that we, at *, are well 2Co 5:12
If I am a poor speaker, at * I 2Co 11:6
should be at * sixty years old 1Ti 5:9
indeed, or at * very shortsighted, 2Pe 1:9

LEATHER
or in a piece of * or leather-work, Lev 13:47,48
covering, or * article, for it is Lev 13:52
or * goods or whatever it is in. Lev 13:56
made of skin or *, indicating Lev 13:59
veil with goatskin *, cover the Num 4:6
* on top of the scarlet cloth. Num 4:8
with goatskin *, and the bundle Num 4:10
of goatskin *, and insert the Num 4:11
with goatskin *, and placed on the Num 4:12
* will be spread over them. Num 4:14
the goatskin * roof, and the Num 4:25
made of *, goat's hair, or wood." Num 31:20
replied, "with a wide * belt." 2Ki 1:8
on your neck with * thongs as you Jer 27:2
camel's hair and he wore a * belt; Mt 3:4
These were * bags for storing Mt 9:17f
camel's hair and he wore a * belt; Mk 1:6

LEATHER-WORK
of leather or *, and there is a Lev 13:47,48

LEAVE
God told him, "* your own country Gen 12:1
as you wish. But * these men alone, Gen 19:8
heaven told me to * that land and Gen 24:7
asked Isaac to * the country. Gen 26:16
"Please don't * me," Laban Gen 30:27
to serve me. Now * this country and Gen 31:13
"at least let me * you some of my Gen 33:15
are not going to * Egypt until this Gen 42:15
you claim to be. * one of your Gen 42:33
HIS BROTHERS were ready to *, Gen 44:1
the lad cannot * his father, for Gen 44:22
"Did you just * him there? Ex 2:20
gifts when you *, so that you will Ex 3:21
that the people be permitted to *. Ex 6:13
of Israel be allowed to * Egypt. Ex 7:2
to let the people *, just as the Ex 9:35
begging, 'Please * at once, and Ex 11:8
let the people * the land. Ex 11:10
during the night and said, "* us; Ex 12:31
Why did you make us * Egypt? Ex 14:11
we were slaves, to * us alone? Ex 14:12
And Moses told them, "Don't * it Ex 16:19
may * freely without any payment. Ex 21:11
* its carcass for the dogs to eat. Ex 22:31
that may come up; * the rest for Ex 23:11
Next he told them not to * the Lev 8:33
"If you *," he told them, "you Lev 8:35
But you are not to * the Lev 10:7
* them there in the Tabernacle. Lev 16:23
to the ground. * them for the poor Lev 19:10
He shall not * the sanctuary Lev 21:12
day it is slain. * none of it for Lev 22:29,30
the fallen grain; * it for the poor Lev 23:22
At that time he can * with his Lev 25:41
They must not * any of it until Num 9:12
of the Tabernacle shall * first; Num 10:5,6,7
Why did you ever make us * Egypt Num 20:5
main road and not * it until we Num 20:17
"We will not * the road until we Num 21:22
that their land won't * the tribe. Num 36:8
metal idols, and * nothing even to Deu 12:3
doesn't want to *—if he says he Deu 15:16
the night must * the camp, and Deu 23:9,10
go back after it. * it for the Deu 24:19
the boughs twice; * anything Deu 24:20
* what's left for those in need. Deu 24:21
did force them to * the country. Ju 1:28
to capture him if he tried to *. Ju 16:2
my strength would * me, and I would Ju 16:16,17
up early, ready to *, but the Ju 19:5
and * sometime this evening." Ju 19:8
were preparing to *, his Ju 19:9
"Don't make me * you, for I want Ru 1:16
the Tabernacle and * him there." 1Sa 1:21,22
When you * me, you will see two 1Sa 10:2
asked for peace. "* us alone and 1Sa 11:1
mean that you must * immediately. 1Sa 20:22
Gad told David to * the cave and 1Sa 22:5
They didn't * one person alive 1Sa 27:9
and * as soon as it is light." 1Sa 29:10
kindness shall not * him as I took 2Sa 7:15
pull back and * him there to die!" 2Sa 11:15
"* it with me," the king told 2Sa 14:8
me, we will * the city in peace." 2Sa 20:21
But I will * him one tribe 1Ki 11:32
so that he will * me alone." 1Ki 15:19
But as soon as I * you, the 1Ki 18:12
kill you as soon as you * me." 1Ki 20:36
the Lord * me and speak to you?" 1Ki 22:24
never * the bed he is lying on; 2Ki 1:4,5
not * the bed you are lying on; 2Ki 1:6
this, you shall not * this bed; 2Ki 1:16
swear to God that I won't * you!" 2Ki 2:1
swear to God that I won't * you." 2Ki 2:4
swear to God that I won't * you." 2Ki 2:6,7
city gate, and to * them there 2Ki 10:8
So King Josiah replied, "* it 2Ki 23:18
this good land and * it to your 1Ch 28:8
so that he will * me alone." 2Ch 16:3
of the Lord * me and enter you?" 2Ch 18:23
see their mistake and * him. 2Ch 18:31
and didn't need to * their posts of 2Ch 35:15
* me alone! 2Ch 35:21
nation and forever * that Ez 9:12
wild animals will * you alone. Job 5:22
comfort before I * for the land of Job 10:20,21
and * all iniquity behind you. Job 11:13,14
* no property for their children. Job 24:18
open field, then * their parents Job 39:4
Go, * me now, you men of evil Ps 6:8
For you will not * me among the Ps 16:10
pain to those who * your paths. Ps 18:26
Don't * me now, for trouble is Ps 22:9,10,11
don't * me now. Ps 27:9
So if you want an eternal home, * Ps 37:27
Don't * me, Lord; Ps 38:21
And when they *, they laugh and Ps 41:6
You must * your wealth to others. Ps 49:10
to * their guilty, stubborn ways. Ps 68:21
Don't * me to the mercy of my Ps 119:121
up and * me dangling in the air; Ps 140:5
I have mixed. * behind your Pro 9:6
O evil man, * the upright man Pro 24:15,16
this, that I must * the fruits of Ecc 2:18
and skill, I must * all of it to Ecc 2:20-23
and to whom will he * it all? Ecc 4:8
And if you * God's paths and go Is 30:21
but half done and I must * it all. Is 38:10
* Babylon, singing as you go; Is 48:20
Yet I * it all with God for my Is 49:4
Go now, * your bonds and slavery. Is 52:11
You shall not * in haste, Is 52:12
but my kindness shall not * you. Is 54:10
you go you * behind a trail of Is 59:7
Spirit shall not * them, and they Is 59:21
to destroy her and * her cities Jer 2:15
"Until my people * their Jer 4:22
But * a scattered few to live. Jer 5:10
We must * our land and homes!' Jer 9:19
Get ready now to *; Jer 10:17
up and * you broken and charred. Jer 11:16
kill you here and * your dead Jer 19:7
but I will destroy you and * you Jer 22:6
don't * out one word of all I Jer 26:2
me, and they shall never * me. Jer 32:40
started to * the city to go to the Jer 37:12
to prepare to * for Egypt. Jer 41:16,17
And he himself shall * unharmed. Jer 43:12
get ready to * for exile, you Jer 46:19
Those who gather grapes * a few Jer 49:9,10
and * you, a burnt-out mountain. Jer 51:25
you so you can't *; Eze 3:25
and * the Temple in ruins. Eze 7:22
and * your home—go somewhere else. Eze 12:3
can watch. Then * the house at Eze 12:4
and * you naked and ashamed. Eze 16:39
Egypt, she did not * her spirit of Eze 23:8
And I will * you and all the Eze 29:5
and * her fallen on the ground. Eze 31:12
go away and * her lying there. Eze 31:12
I will haul you out, and * you Eze 32:4
Literally, "* one-sixth of you." Eze 39:2f
your hands and * you helpless. Eze 39:3
I will * none of them remaining Eze 39:28
When the priests * the Holy Eze 42:14
The prince shall enter and * Eze 46:10
its branches, but * its stump and Dan 4:15
destroy it, but * the stump and the Dan 4:23
Then, when I *, I will go again Dan 10:20,21
he will * the Syrian king alone. Dan 11:8
He will * godless Jews in power Dan 11:30,31
when I turn away and * you alone. Hos 9:12
I will not * her unpunished any Amo 1:3
I will not * her unpunished any Amo 1:6
I will not * them unpunished any Amo 1:9
I will not * him unpunished any Amo 1:11
I will not * them unpunished any Amo 1:13
I will not * them unpunished any Amo 2:1
I will not * them unpunished any Amo 2:4
I will not * them unpunished any Amo 2:6
Zion, for you must * this city and Mic 4:10
against you, * your sacrifice Mt 5:24
him to go away and * them alone. Mt 8:34
until you * for the next town. Mt 10:11
place from your feet as you *. Mt 10:14
But this kind of demon won't * Mt 17:21
Won't he * the ninety-nine others Mt 18:12
that a man should * his father and Mt 19:5,6
but you shouldn't * the more Mt 23:23
message: "* that good man alone; Mt 27:19
But the rest said, "* him Mt 27:49
Go tell my brothers to * at once Mt 28:10
Jesus to go away and * them alone! Mk 5:17
told them all to *, and taking the Mk 5:40
the dust from your feet as you *; Mk 6:11
therefore a man is to * his Mk 10:6,7
* them, but to stay at Capernaum. Lk 4:42
"Oh, sir, please * us—I'm too much Lk 5:8
commanding the demon to * him. Lk 8:29
to go away and * them alone (for a Lk 8:37
turn around and *, demonstrating Lk 9:5
were starting to *, Peter, all Lk 9:33
not * these other things undone. Lk 11:42
* your evil ways and turn to God? Lk 13:3
answered. '* it another year, and Lk 13:8
wouldn't you * the ninety-nine Lk 15:3,4
to take care of me when I *!' Lk 16:4
your enemies will not * one stone Lk 19:44
coming and will * the sheep, for Jn 10:12
Mary saw her * so hastily, they Jn 11:31
before I must go away and * you! Jn 13:33
and he will never * you. Jn 14:15,16
No, I will not abandon you or * Jn 14:18
the world and will * the world and Jn 16:28
told them not to * Jerusalem until Act 1:4
'You will not * my soul in hell Act 2:27
"And so my advice is, * these Act 5:38
and told him to * his native Act 7:3
of his would * the land and live in Act 7:6
But Peter asked them all to * Act 9:40
told Paul they were free to *. Act 16:36
So now they want us to * Act 16:37
and pled with them to * the city. Act 16:39
I know full well that after I * Act 20:29
to me, 'Hurry! * Jerusalem, for the Act 22:17,18
"But God said to me, '* Act 22:21
soldiers ready to * for Caesarea at Act 23:23,24
Wherever they go they * misery Rom 3:16
On the other hand, if the Jews * Rom 11:23
avenge yourselves. * that to God, Rom 12:19
mistreatment and * it at that? 1Co 6:7
A wife must not * her husband. 1Co 7:10
he must not * her or divorce her. 1Co 7:12
stay with him, she must not * him. 1Co 7:13
is eager to *, it is permitted. 1Co 7:15
we will * him in his ignorance. 1Co 14:38
we die and * these bodies—we will 2Co 5:1
why the Lord has said, "* them; 2Co 6:17
off from you and * you alone! Gal 5:12
says, "A man must * his father and Eph 5:31
accusations, and * him without 1Ti 3:7
not * this to the church to do. 1Ti 5:16
Bring others to Christ. * nothing 2Ti 4:5
God told him to * home and go far Heb 11:8
They will soon die and * behind Jas 1:10,11
of Christ, you will * God behind; 2Jn 1:9
All they * behind them is shame Jud 1:13
* her naked and ravaged by fire. Rev 17:16

LEAVEN
sure there is no * in it, and eat Lev 10:12

LEAVENED
shall be offered with * bread; Ex 23:18
"You must not use * bread with Ex 34:25
with loaves of * bread. Lev 7:13
but no * bread shall be served. Num 28:17

LEAVES
This explains why a man * his Gen 2:24
So they strung fig * together to Gen 3:7
before Jacob * the room, Esau Gen 27:30
heals, but which * a white Lev 13:19
"If the slayer * the City, and Num 35:26
and kings, and * them wandering, Job 12:24,25
They eat roots and *, having Job 30:4
He churns the depths. He * a Job 41:31,32
Their * shall never wither, and Ps 1:3
When a good man dies, he * an Pro 13:22
be very old, but * so little money Ecc 6:3
The * are coming out Sol 2:13
*, as ripe fruit from the trees. Is 34:4
Like autumn * we fade, wither and Is 64:6
faithless wife who * her husband. Jer 3:20
of drought. Its * stay green and it Jer 17:8
of * and branches in a garden! Lam 2:6
strong branches and luxuriant *. Eze 17:6
vine, producing * and fruit. Eze 17:8
and let its * wither and die. Eze 17:9
river banks. The * will never turn Eze 47:12
for food and the * for medicine. Eze 47:12

(LEAVES Con't)
the world. Its * were fresh and Dan 4:12
shake off its *, and scatter its Dan 4:14
its fresh green *, loaded with Dan 4:21
in power when he *—men who have Dan 11:30,31
comes to them through tea *! Hos 4:12
me as a prostitute * her husband; Hos 5:3
And when the * of the shelter Jon 4:6
* over Jonah's head to shade him. Jon 4:6
He is coming! He * his throne in Mic 1:3
For if the demon *, it goes into Mt 12:43,44,45
any figs, but there were only *. Mt 21:19
is tender and the * begin to Mt 24:32
The patch pulls away and * the Mk 2:21
But no, there were only *, for it Mk 11:13
tender and its * begin to sprout, Mk 13:28
him and hardly ever * him alone. Lk 9:39
When the * come out, you know Lk 21:30
And the Father * all judgment of Jn 5:22
a father dies and * great wealth Gal 4:1
Now, if someone dies and * a Heb 9:16
each month; the * were used for Rev 22:2

LEAVING
God destroyed them all, * only Gen 7:23
* Bethel, he and his household Gen 35:16
He fled, * his jacket behind!" Gen 39:18
was his parting shot! And *, Gen 45:25
day of * Egypt and your slavery; Ex 13:3
* Succoth, they camped in Etham Ex 13:20
of the second month after * Egypt. Ex 16:1
eighth day, after * it with its Ex 22:30
incense altars, * your dead bodies Lev 26:30
of the second year after * Egypt: Num 9:1
of the second year of Israel's * Num 10:11
three days after * Mount Sinai, Num 10:33
in Egypt, * them unharmed Num 28:16
After * Rameses, they stayed in Num 33:5,6
* Marah, they came to Elim, Num 33:9
* Elim, they camped beside the Num 33:10
After * Eglon they went to Jos 10:36
As she was * with him, she urged Jos 15:18,19
As they were * for their new Ju 1:14
oozed out. * the dagger there, Ehud Ju 3:22,23
far away as Gaza, * nothing to eat, Ju 6:3,4
* only three hundred men with him. Ju 7:8,9
see that his strength was * him. Ju 16:19
Benjamin that day, * but a tiny Ju 20:35-39
warriors that day, * only six Ju 20:46,47
be * about the time you get there; 1Sa 9:12,13
tell his father that he was *. 1Sa 14:1
Israeli army was * for the 1Sa 17:20
into the night, * the spear 1Sa 19:9,10
this time * seven hundred 2Sa 10:18
be seen entering and * the city. 2Sa 17:17
But a boy saw them * En-rogel to 2Sa 17:18
His mule went on, * him dangling 2Sa 18:9
One day as Jeroboam was * 1Ki 11:29
family—* not a single male child. 1Ki 16:11
Before * to meet the attack, he 2Ki 19:9
of Israel as they were * Egypt. 2Ch 5:10
When the Syrians left—* Joash 2Ch 24:25
walls, * us without protection. Ps 80:12
godly leads upward, * hell behind. Pro 15:24
destroyed Israel, * her to shame. Is 43:28
away into exile, * me here alone. Is 49:21
moved away, * the land deserted. Jer 12:4
you own, * you naked and bare. Eze 23:29
boldly murders, * blood upon the Eze 24:7
my flock, * them to be attacked and Eze 34:8
was 8¾ feet thick, * a free space Eze 41:9
ministering to me, * them in the Eze 44:19
in verse 24, * seven years Dan 9:25f
the fig trees, * trunks and Joe 1:7
he found a ship * for Tarshish. Jon 1:3
in earnest about * your sins Zec 7:5
They will slaughter their foes, * Zec 9:15
their work and, * their father Mt 4:22
As Jesus was * her home, two Mt 9:27
* that place, Jesus met a man who Mt 9:32
Then, * the crowds outside, he Mt 13:36
AS JESUS WAS * the Temple grounds, Mt 24:1
Then, * the synagogue, he and his Mk 1:29,30
and started out, * the crowds Mk 4:36
But many people saw them * and Mk 6:33
* that region they traveled Mk 9:30,31
AS HE WAS * the Temple that day, Mk 13:1
After * the synagogue that day, Lk 4:38
drains out, * a tasteless residue. Lk 14:34f
done as you have, * home, wife, Lk 18:29
her and died, * no children. Lk 20:31
off in their boat, * him behind. Jn 6:22,23
"Maybe he is thinking of * the Jn 7:35
"I am * you with a gift—peace of Jn 14:27
to his own home, * me alone. Jn 16:32
Now I am * the world, and Jn 17:11
* them behind, and coming to you. Jn 17:11
a cloud, * them staring after him. Act 1:9
to them once more before * town. Act 16:40
And since he was * the next day, Act 20:7
The next stop after * Tyre was Act 21:7
the next morning, * him with the Act 23:32
Cutting off the anchors and * Act 27:40
on your thrones, * us far behind! 1Co 4:8
Christian life, * entirely behind 1Co 5:8
went on my way, * Macedonia, only Php 4:15
a tenth of the city, * 7,000 dead. Rev 11:13

LEBANA
Sia, Padon, *, Hagaba, Neh 7:46-56

LEBANAH
Siaha, Padon, *, Hagabah, Akkub, Ez 2:43-54

LEBANON
land of Canaan and *—the entire Deu 1:7
with its rolling hills—and *. Deu 3:23,24,25
southern Negeb to *, and from the Deu 11:24
the south to the * mountains in the Jos 1:4
far north as the * mountains—the Jos 9:1
of *, at the foot of Mount Hermon. Jos 11:17
in the Valley of * and Mount Halak, Jos 12:7
and all of the * mountain area Jos 13:2-7
All the hill country from * to Jos 13:2-7
The Hivites living in Mount *, Ju 3:1
burn down the great cedars of *!' Ju 9:15
great cedars of * down to the tiny 1Ki 4:33
the mountains of * to cut cedar 1Ki 5:6
the logs from the * mountains to 1Ki 5:9
rotated them to *, ten thousand a 1Ki 5:14
month in * and two months at home. 1Ki 5:14
the Hall of the Forest of *. 1Ki 7:2
and in the * mountains and 1Ki 9:19
in the Hall of the Forest of *. 1Ki 10:16,17
of the Forest of * his entire 1Ki 10:21
"The thistle of * demanded of the 2Ki 14:9
mountains, yes, the peaks of *. 2Ki 19:23
the Forests of *, for your men are 2Ch 2:8
wood from the * mountains, as much 2Ch 2:16
* and throughout the entire realm. 2Ch 8:6
Forest of * Room in his palace. 2Ch 9:16
in the Forest of * Room. 2Ch 9:20
"Out in the * mountains a thistle 2Ch 25:18
down from the * mountains and Ez 3:7
It splits the giant trees of *. Ps 29:5,6
It shakes Mount * and Mount Ps 29:5,6
like a cedar of *, but when I Ps 37:35,36
may there be fruit like that of * Ps 72:16
and grow tall as the cedars of *. Ps 92:12
The Lord planted the cedars of * Ps 104:16
a chariot from the wood of *. Sol 3:9
"Come with me from *, my bride. Sol 4:8
of the mountains and cedars of *. Sol 4:11
streams from the * mountains." Sol 4:15
of finest gold, like cedars of *; Sol 5:15
like the tower of * overlooking Sol 7:4
All the tall cedars of * and all Is 2:13
cuts down the forest trees in *. Is 10:34
and cedars of *—sing out this Is 14:8
wilderness of * will be a fruitful Is 29:17
in trouble; * has been destroyed; Is 33:9
as green as the * mountains, as Is 35:2
The glory of * will be yours—the Is 60:13
melts high up in the * mountains. Jer 18:14
Gilead and the green forests of *; Jer 22:6
Search for them in *; Jer 22:20
the cedars of *, but soon you will Jer 22:23
feathers came to * and plucked off Eze 17:3,4
They took a cedar from * to make Eze 27:5
a cedar of *, full of thick Eze 31:2,3
I clothed * in black and caused Eze 31:15
and caused the trees of * to weep. Eze 31:15
and the best of *, the ones whose Eze 31:16
in the soil like cedars in *. Hos 14:5
fragrant as the forests of *. Hos 14:6
be as fragrant as the wines of *. Hos 14:7
the green forests of * wilt. Nah 1:4
You cut down the forests of * Hab 2:17
them in Israel—in Gilead and *; Zec 10:10
OPEN YOUR DOORS, O *, to Zec 11:1

LEBANON'S
All of * forests do not contain Is 40:16

LEBAOTH
*, Shilhim, Ain, and Rimmon. Jos 15:21-32

LEBO-HAMATH
Mount Hor, then to *, and on Num 34:7,8,9
It was originally called *. Eze 47:15f

LEBONAH
of Shiloh, between * and Bethel, Ju 21:19

LECAH
Er (the father of *), 1Ch 4:21-22

LECHEROUS
* eyes that long for other gods. Eze 6:9

LECTURE
meeting at the * hall of Tyrannus Act 19:9

LECTURING
He began * in the morning and Act 28:23

LED
because he had * me along just the Gen 24:48
deeply to him, and * the boys to Gen 48:12,13
you: When you have * the people out Ex 3:12
Instead, God * them along a route Ex 13:17,18
with them when God * them out of Ex 13:19
So Pharaoh * the chase in his Ex 14:6
You have * the people you Ex 15:13
timbrel and * the women in dances. Ex 15:20
Then Moses * the people of Israel Ex 15:22
Moses * them out from the camp Ex 19:17
Moses who * us out of Egypt.' Ex 32:23
* by a man appointed for the task. Lev 16:21
These three tribes * the way Num 2:3-31
its flag, and * by Nahshon, the son Num 10:14
tribe of Issachar, * by Nethanel, Num 10:15
* by Eliab, the son of Helon. Num 10:16
and the tribe of Gad * by Num 10:20
* by Elishama, the son of Ammihud; Num 10:22
and the tribe of Manasseh * by Num 10:23
and the tribe of Benjamin, * by Num 10:24
the tribe of Asher, * by Pagiel, Num 10:26
and the tribe of Naphtali, * by Num 10:27
the priest) * them into battle, Num 31:6
Meanwhile, a man named Nobah * Num 32:42
and Aaron * them out of Egypt. Num 33:1
our God who had * them all the Deu 1:33
their armed men * the other tribes Deu 3:18
Do you remember how the Lord * Deu 8:2
forget the God who * you through Deu 8:15
the people I had * out of Egypt had Deu 9:12
rabble have * their fellow citizens Deu 13:12,13,14
For forty years God has * you Deu 29:5
He * the people Deu 33:21
thousand strong—* the other tribes Jos 4:12,13
tribe of Judah, * by Caleb, came to Jos 14:6
sent a delegation * by Phinehas, Jos 22:13
the river and * him into the land Jos 24:3
so that when he * the forces of Ju 3:10
So Barak * his ten thousand men Ju 4:14
Israel's leaders bravely *; Ju 5:2
When you * us out from Seir, Ju 5:4
So Gaal * the men of Shechem into Ju 9:39
of this, he * his forces to Mount Ju 9:47,48
Jephthah and he * his army across Ju 11:29
So Jephthah * his army against Ju 11:32
with two new ropes and * him away. Ju 15:12,13
AT THIS TIME Nahash * the army of 1Sa 11:1
that and David * his troops against 1Sa 19:8
So he * them to the Amalekite 1Sa 30:16
One day General Abner * some of 2Sa 2:12
* David's troops out to meet them. 2Sa 2:13
David now * his troops to 2Sa 5:6
special troops and * them to 2Sa 6:1
he personally * the Israeli army to 2Sa 10:17
So David * his army to Rabbah and 2Sa 12:29,30
David walked up the road that * 2Sa 15:30
another flight of stairs * from 1Ki 6:8
and * all of Israel into sin. 1Ki 15:26
Jeroboam, for he * the people of 1Ki 15:34
for they had * Israel into 1Ki 16:13
So Omri * the army of Gibbethon 1Ki 16:17
he had worshiped idols and had * 1Ki 16:19
and * Israel into this same sin. 1Ki 16:26
and have * all of Israel into sin. 1Ki 21:22
* their armies to Ramoth-gilead. 1Ki 22:29
Jeroboam, who had * Israel into the 1Ki 22:52,53
of Nebat), who had * the people of 2Ki 3:3
had been lost, he * 700 of his 2Ki 3:26
army, for he had * his troops to 2Ki 5:1
And he * them to Samaria! 2Ki 6:19
and all the people * the king from 2Ki 11:19
worship idols and * them into sin. 2Ki 13:11
of Nebat), who had * Israel into 2Ki 14:24
before, and he * the people of 2Ki 15:18
who * Israel down that evil trail. 2Ki 15:24
of Nebat), who * all of Israel into 2Ki 15:28
* an attack against Israel. 2Ki 15:29
that Jeroboam * them into, until 2Ki 17:22
and because he has * the people of 2Ki 21:11
which Manasseh * the people of 2Ki 21:16
made when he * Israel into sin. 2Ki 23:15
and they were * by their clan 1Ch 7:9
were the one who * our armies to 1Ch 11:2
Euphrates River, * personally by 1Ch 19:16
began) Joab * the Israeli army in 1Ch 20:1
Gershom's sons were * by 1Ch 23:16
The sons of Izhar were * by 1Ch 23:18
The sons of Hebron were * by 1Ch 23:19
The sons of Uzziel were * by 1Ch 23:20
First, the group * by Jehoiarib; 1Ch 24:7-18
Second, the group * by Jedaiah; 1Ch 24:7-18
Third, the group * by Harim; 1Ch 24:7-18
Fourth, the group * by Se-orim; 1Ch 24:7-18
Fifth, the group * by Malchijah; 1Ch 24:7-18
Sixth, the group * by Mijamin; 1Ch 24:7-18
Seventh, the group * by Hakkoz; 1Ch 24:7-18
Eighth, the group * by Ahijah; 1Ch 24:7-18
Ninth, the group * by Jeshua; 1Ch 24:7-18
Tenth, the group * by Shecaniah; 1Ch 24:7-18
Eleventh, the group * by Eliashib; 1Ch 24:7-18
Twelfth, the group * by Jakim; 1Ch 24:7-18
Thirteenth, the group * by Huppah; 1Ch 24:7-18
Fourteenth, the group * by 1Ch 24:7-18
Fifteenth, the group * by Bilgah; 1Ch 24:7-18
Sixteenth, the group * by Immer; 1Ch 24:7-18
Seventeenth, the group * by Hezir; 1Ch 24:7-18
Eighteenth, the group * by 1Ch 24:7-18
Nineteenth, the group * by 1Ch 24:7-18
Twentieth, the group * by 1Ch 24:7-18

LED Con't)

Twenty-first, the group * by 1Ch 24:7-18
Twenty-second, the group * by 1Ch 24:7-18
Twenty-third, the group * by 1Ch 24:7-18
Twenty-fourth, the group * by 1Ch 24:7-18
the Rehabiah group, * by his 1Ch 24:21
The Uzziel group was * by his son 1Ch 24:24,25
The Merari group was * by his 1Ch 24:26,27
(Ja-aziah's group, * by his son 1Ch 24:26,27
Under Jeduthun, who * in giving 1Ch 25:3
Other Levites, * by Ahijah, were 1Ch 26:20,21,22
* them up to the hill to the old 2Ch 1:2,3
coronation, and * the people's 2Ch 10:2,3
Judah, * by King Abijah, fielded 2Ch 13:3
courageous men * by King Jeroboam. 2Ch 13:3
is * by a descendant of David? 2Ch 13:8
* their armies to Ramoth-gilead. 2Ch 18:28
of Judah, and * the people of 2Ch 21:11
death, and they * him on to ruin. 2Ch 22:4
Ahaziah * his army there to join 2Ch 22:5
Each of the three leaders * a 2Ch 23:8
Then Amaziah took courage and * 2Ch 25:11
Afterwards King Neco of Egypt * 2Ch 35:20
Instead he * his army into the 2Ch 35:22
crew * by Zaccur (son of Imri). Neh 3:2
The people from Zanoah, * by Neh 3:13
his clan brothers * by Bavvai (son Neh 3:18
Next to them the workers were * Neh 3:19
waters. You * our ancestors by a Neh 9:12
The pillar of cloud * them Neh 9:19
172 gatekeepers, * by Akkub, Neh 11:19
I * the Judean leaders to the top Neh 12:31,32
Ezra the priest * this Neh 12:35,36
but even so he was * into Neh 13:26
own steed, and * him through the Est 6:11
Priests are * away as slaves. Job 12:19
me steady. He * me to a place of Ps 18:19
when you * a great procession to Ps 42:4,5
she is, * beside her maids of Ps 45:14
O God, when you * your people Ps 68:7
Your road * by a pathway through Ps 77:19
was there! You * your people along Ps 77:20
before them and * them through! Ps 78:13
In the daytime he * them by a Ps 78:14
And he * forth the east wind and Ps 78:26
But he * forth his own people Ps 78:52
idols, and were * away from God. Ps 106:36
they cried, and he did! He * Ps 107:7
rescued them! He * them from the Ps 107:14
forever, and * them safely Ps 136:14
Praise him who * his people Ps 136:16
he has let himself be * away into Pro 5:23
My people will be * away Is 8:21
* them down the paths of ruin. Is 9:16
But Jerusalem is now * by Is 28:7
in your mouth and * you back to Is 37:29
They were not thirsty when he * Is 48:21
From prison and trial they * him Is 53:8
God's servant, * his people out of Is 63:11
forever? Who * them through the Is 63:13
out of Egypt and * them through the Jer 2:6
Why is she captured and * far Jer 2:14
when I * them out of Egypt. Jer 7:22
Instead weep for the captives * Jer 22:10
and * my people Israel into sin; Jer 23:13
children will be * out to the Jer 38:23
Their shepherds * them astray and Jer 50:6
Why is Judah * away, a slave? Lam 1:3
You have * those to death who Eze 13:19
and * them into the wilderness. Eze 20:9,10
the ground. He * me around among Eze 37:1
But a door * from its entry hall Eze 40:38
Ten steps * up to it from the Eze 40:48,49
Temple * up from floor to floor. Eze 41:7
THEN HE * me out of the Temple, Eze 42:1
measurements, he * me out through Eze 42:15
passageway, he * me through the Eze 46:19,20
court again and * me to each of the Eze 46:21,22
then * me back along the bank. Eze 47:6
I * you through the wilderness! Hos 9:10
so I * Israel with my ropes of Hos 11:4
Then the Lord * his people out Hos 12:13
and * him into slavery to Edom. Amo 1:9
out from Egypt and * you through Amo 2:10
* away as slaves—stripped, naked Mic 1:11
the streets, and * away, a slave, Nah 2:7
her people were * off as slaves; Nah 3:10
Judah and Israel have been * Zec 10:2
THEN JESUS WAS * out into the Mt 4:1
Then the mob * him to the home of Mt 26:57
Jesus * him away from the crowd Mk 7:33
by the hand and * him out of the Mk 8:23
Jesus was * to the High Priest's Mk 14:53
fists on him as they * him away. Mk 14:65
and * him away to be crucified. Mk 15:20
a mob approached, * by Judas, one Lk 22:47
So they seized him and * him to Lk 22:54
Jesus was * before this Council, Lk 22:66
As the crowd * Jesus away to his Lk 23:26
Two others, criminals, were * out Lk 23:32,33
Then Jesus * them out along the Lk 24:50
"So you also have been * Jn 7:47
miracles he * them out of Egypt and Act 7:36
Years later, when Joshua * the Act 7:45
was this:"He was * as a sheep to Act 8:32
He had to be * into Damascus and Act 9:8,9
"Aren't you that Egyptian who * Act 21:37,38
* into Damascus by my companions. Act 22:11
For all who are * by the Spirit Rom 8:14
chosen people and * you along with Rom 9:4
Yet that old system of law that * 2Co 3:7
Not one of you was * astray. 2Co 7:2
way you will be * away from your 2Co 11:3
Try always to be * along Eph 4:3
church and been * astray by Satan. 1Ti 5:15
of Israel that Joshua * them into. Heb 4:8
They * an army of 200,000,000 Rev 9:16

LEDGE

resting it upon the * built there. Ex 27:5
that rested upon a * about halfway Ex 38:4

LEE

sailed under the * of Cyprus." Act 27:4f

LEECH

satisfied, like a * forever craving Pro 30:15,16

LEEKS

and melons, *, onions, and garlic! Num 11:4,5

LEFT

* the ark in pairs and groups. Gen 8:18,19
Sarai, and * Ur of the Chaldeans to Gen 11:31
Afterwards Abram * that place Gen 12:8
SO THEY * Egypt and traveled north Gen 13:1
ended the conversation and God *. Gen 17:22
Afterwards Lot * Zoar, fearful of Gen 19:30
When the water was gone she * Gen 21:15
residents finally * him alone. Gen 26:22
So when Esau * for the field to Gen 27:5
wine—what is there * to give?" Gen 27:37
Esau: "Not one blessing * for Gen 27:38
agreed and had * for Paddan-aram. Gen 28:6,7,8
So Jacob * Beer-sheba and Gen 28:10
For when I * home Gen 32:10
ABOUT THIS TIME, Judah * home and Gen 38:1
father-in-law had * for the Gen 38:13
slipped off and she was * holding Gen 39:12
Now he * the room and found a Gen 42:24
is * of his mother's children. Gen 42:38
and he alone is * of his mother's Gen 44:20
he was * alone with his brothers. Gen 45:1
So Jacob * Beer-sheba, and his Gen 46:5
blessed Pharaoh again before he *. Gen 47:10
nothing * but our bodies and land. Gen 47:18
* hand and Manasseh at his right. Gen 48:12,13
boy, and his * hand was upon the Gen 48:14
But they * their little children Gen 50:8
Before Moses * Midian, Jehovah Ex 4:19
man and animal * out in the fields Ex 9:19
Jehovah * them out in the storm. Ex 9:21
Everything * in the fields, men Ex 9:25
soon as I have * the city I will Ex 9:29
So Moses * Pharaoh and went out Ex 9:33
eat everything the hail has *." Ex 10:12
bit of vegetation the hail had *; Ex 10:15
Not a hoof shall be * behind; Ex 10:26
eaten that night, burn what is *. Ex 12:10
That night the people of Israel * Ex 12:37
of Jehovah's people * the land. Ex 12:40,41
Lord did for you when you * Egypt. Ex 13:8
though they had * Egypt armed; Ex 13:17,18
NOW THEY * Elim and journeyed on Ex 16:1
in the morning it * tiny flakes of Ex 16:14
a lot had nothing * over and those Ex 16:18
listen, and * it until morning; Ex 16:20
and keep what is * overnight." Ex 16:23
people of Israel * the Sihn desert, Ex 17:1
in March, the month you * Egypt; Ex 23:15
no sacrificial fat shall be * Ex 23:18
but are to be * there permanently. Ex 25:15
that was the month you * Egypt. Ex 34:18
But finally the workmen all * Ex 36:4-7
The silver * over was used for Ex 38:28
"The burnt offering shall be * Lev 6:9
none * to be eaten the next day. Lev 7:15
But anything * over until the Lev 7:17,18
Anything * of the meat and bread Lev 8:32
his sons who were *, Eleazar and Lev 10:12
the palm of his * hand, and dip Lev 14:15
remaining in his * hand shall then Lev 14:17
palm of his own * hand, and with Lev 14:26
Except when the brother died and * Lev 18:16f
case his wife was * to a brother to Lev 18:16f
born, it shall be * with its mother Lev 22:26,27
number of years * before the Year Lev 25:50
"And for those who are * alive, Lev 26:36
Those * shall pine away in enemy Lev 26:39
after the Israelis * Egypt that the Num 1:1
no children, this * only Eleazar Num 3:4
so the Israelites * the Sinai Num 10:12
It was daytime when they *, with Num 10:34
about all you * behind in Egypt, Num 11:18
So Moses * the Tabernacle and Num 11:24
Afterwards they * Hazeroth and Num 12:16
from when we * Egypt until now." Num 14:19
the Ark nor Moses * the camp. Num 14:44
Then they * the desert and Num 21:17,18
was on the way, he * the capital Num 22:36
They * the city of Rameses, Num 33:3,4
the Passover. They * proudly, Num 33:3,4
the people of Israel had * Egypt. Num 33:38,39
people of Israel * Mount Deu 1:1
"Then we * Mount Horeb and Deu 1:19,20,21
and babies. We * nothing alive Deu 2:33,34
Israel when they * Egypt, and as Deu 4:44,45,46
the day you * Egypt until now? Deu 9:7
This is to remind you that you * Deu 16:3
Literally, "For you * Egypt in Deu 16:3f
shall be * until the next morning. Deu 16:4
leave what's * for those in need. Deu 24:21
There will be few of you *, Deu 28:62
and how as we *, we came safely Deu 29:16
They * the city at dusk as the Jos 2:5
Red Sea for you when you * Egypt! Jos 2:10
No one has any fight * in him Jos 2:11
But before they *, the men had Jos 2:17,18
And she * the scarlet rope Jos 2:21
people of Israel * Acacia, and Jos 3:1
when Israel * Egypt all of the men Jos 5:4,5
arms when they * Egypt were dead; Jos 5:6
Before the main army * for Ai, Jos 8:3,4
us until they have all * the city; Jos 8:6
So they * that night and lay in Jos 8:9
so the city was * defenseless; Jos 8:16
there was not a soldier * in Ai Jos 8:17
the city gates were * wide open. Jos 8:17
finished off everyone * inside. Jos 8:24
the ovens when we *, but now as you Jos 9:12
So Joshua and the Israeli army * Jos 10:7
in the entire city was * alive. Jos 10:28
Not one person was * alive. Jos 10:37
None was * in all the land of Jos 11:22
it bent to the *, passing south of Jos 15:10,11
of Manasseh * the army of Israel at Jos 22:9
them when they * Egypt, were buried Jos 24:32
them. They * their homes in Ju 1:16
all Israel. He * them to the mercy Ju 2:12-14
out the nations * unconquered by Ju 2:21
So the Lord * those nations in Ju 2:23
nations the Lord * in the land to Ju 3:1
with his strong * hand, pulled out Ju 3:21
not one man was * alive. Ju 4:16
So twenty-two thousand of them *, Ju 7:3
torches in their * hands, all Ju 7:19,20
That was all that was * of the Ju 8:10
of Shechem were * wounded all the Ju 9:40
realize that the Lord had * him. Ju 16:20
my priest, and I have nothing *!" Ju 18:24
adamant, so they *, getting as far Ju 19:10
Israel * Egypt," everyone said. Ju 19:30
So the entire army * early the Ju 20:19,20
* the country because of a famine Ru 1:1
and Naomi was * with her two sons. Ru 1:3
so that Naomi was * alone, without Ru 1:4,5
and how you * your father and Ru 2:10,11
with what was * of her lunch. Ru 2:18
So she * him there at the 1Sa 1:28
Those who are * alive will live 1Sa 2:33
only the trunk of his body was * 1Sa 5:4
no two of them were * together. 1Sa 11:11
Samuel then * Gilgal and went to 1Sa 13:15
were only about six hundred *! 1Sa 13:15
* the camp of the Philistines; 1Sa 13:17
them right and *, about twenty men 1Sa 14:13
So the Kenites packed up and *. 1Sa 15:6
But the Spirit of the Lord had * 1Sa 16:14
So David * the sheep with another 1Sa 17:20
David * his luggage with a 1Sa 17:22
had * him and was now with David. 1Sa 18:11,12
Jonathan * the table in fierce 1Sa 20:34
such haste, and I * in such a rush 1Sa 21:8
SO DAVID * Gath and escaped to the 1Sa 22:1
of them now—* Keilah and began 1Sa 23:13
After Saul had * the cave and gone 1Sa 24:7,8
No one was * alive to come to 1Sa 27:11
us, and God has * me and won't 1Sa 28:15
* you and has become your enemy? 1Sa 28:16
"My master * me behind three 1Sa 30:13
As Abner *, he promised David, 2Sa 3:21
But just after Abner *, Joab and 2Sa 3:22
"Is anyone * from Saul's family? 2Sa 9:3
in the fields. He * the rest of 2Sa 10:10
so they all * the apartment. 2Sa 13:9
sons, and not one is * alive!" 2Sa 13:29,30
I will have no one *, and my 2Sa 14:7
out at once. He * no one behind 2Sa 15:16
has * them here to keep the house. 2Sa 16:21
that not one of them is * alive. 2Sa 17:12
thing I did when you * Jerusalem; 2Sa 19:19
the day the king * Jerusalem. 2Sa 19:24,25
ten wives he had * to keep house 2Sa 20:3
the dagger in his * hand, and Joab 2Sa 20:8,9,10
Joab and his brother Abishai * 2Sa 20:8,9,10
* of the nation of the Amorites. 2Sa 21:2
that Shime-i had * Jerusalem and 1Ki 2:41
Israel * their slavery in Egypt. 1Ki 6:1

(LEFT Con't)

arranged on the * and five on the 1Ki 7:39
and five on the *, in front of the 1Ki 7:49
of Israel after they * Egypt. 1Ki 8:9
Benjamin were * to Solomon's son. 1Ki 11:32f
So the people *. 1Ki 12:5
silver and gold * in the Temple 1Ki 15:18
royal family was *, just as the 1Ki 15:29
a handful of flour * and a little 1Ki 17:12
of flour and oil * in your 1Ki 17:14
was always plenty * in the 1Ki 17:16
of the Lord who is *," he told 1Ki 18:22
rainstorm. Ahab * hastily for 1Ki 18:45
of Judah, and * his servant there. 1Ki 19:3
your prophets, and only I am *; 1Ki 19:10
Elisha * the oxen standing there 1Ki 19:20
Asherah priests * alive by Elijah 1Ki 22:6f
Elijah said to Elisha as they * 2Ki 2:1
of the Lord has * him on some 2Ki 2:16
Kir-hareseth was *, but even that 2Ki 3:25
be enough money * for you and your 2Ki 4:7
and some will even be * over!" 2Ki 4:43
so they have * their camp and have 2Ki 7:12
So Jehu * the others and went 2Ki 9:6
Finally, no one was * who had 2Ki 10:11
As he * the inn, he met 2Ki 10:15
If you have two thousand men * 2Ki 18:23
pray for the few of us who are *.' 2Ki 19:4
word that he had * Lachish). 2Ki 19:8
So before Isaiah had * the 2Ki 20:4
will be taken—nothing shall be *. 2Ki 20:17
my people who are *, and I will 2Ki 21:14
located on the * side as one enters 2Ki 23:8
skilled people were * in the land. 2Ki 24:14
people were * to farm the land. 2Ki 25:12
over the people * in Judah. 2Ki 25:22
of Merari, who stood on his *. 1Ch 6:44-47
* hands as readily as their right! 1Ch 12:2
up many idols * by the Philistines, 1Ch 14:12
David * Zadok the priest and his 1Ch 16:39
So he * the threshing-floor and 1Ch 21:21
and Ithamar were * to carry on. 1Ch 24:1
Solomon then * the Tabernacle, 2Ch 1:13
the right and the other on the *. 2Ch 3:17
and Boaz (the one on the *). 2Ch 3:17
the huge tank and five to the *. 2Ch 4:6
each wall on the right and *. 2Ch 4:8
when Israel * Egypt, so we went 2Ch 20:10
When the Syrians *—leaving Joash 2Ch 24:25
The prophet * with this parting 2Ch 25:16
but all this is * over, for the 2Ch 31:10
being healed, God * him to himself 2Ch 32:31
with him. They * Babylon in the Ez 7:7,8,9
The money that is * over may be Ez 7:18
To his * were Pedaiah, Misha-el, Neh 8:1
man was Haman as he * the banquet! Est 5:9
I am the only one *." Job 1:14,15
a breath, and nothing good is *. Job 7:7
you see how little time I have *? Job 10:20,21
*, nor any other relatives. Job 18:19
his goods, consuming all he has *. Job 20:26
There is no sincerity *. Ps 12:2
We have not * your path by a Ps 44:18
Which of you has any *? Ps 58:1
There is nothing * to show that Ps 74:9,10
No one is * even to bury them. Ps 79:3
They have * me here to die, like Ps 88:5
is * to you, sharp as a Pro 5:4
of food on hand, * from her Pro 7:14f
finally have nothing worthwhile *. Pro 11:29
when courage dies, what hope is *? Pro 18:14
the poor man has none *. Pro 19:4
him to learn. * to himself, he Pro 29:15
nothing * to pass on to one's son. Ecc 5:13,14
silver lining * among your clouds. Ecc 12:2
lovesick. His * hand is under my Sol 2:6
wine. His * hand would be under my Sol 8:3
all that will be * to them is Is 3:24
AT THAT TIME so few men will be * Is 4:1
a person *—and the whole country is Is 6:11
to have a cow and two sheep *. Is 7:21,22
milk, and everyone * will live on Is 7:21,22
all that mighty army will be *; Is 10:19
Then at last, those * in Israel Is 10:20
will be * to return at that time; Is 10:22
The women of Moab are * at the Is 16:2
of all its people will be * alive. Is 16:13,14
her people will be *, just as a few Is 17:6
stray olives are * on the trees Is 17:6
Your mighty army will be * dead Is 18:6
How much time is *?" Is 21:11
This silent ruin is all that's * Is 23:7
they are * desolate, destroyed by Is 24:6
Few will be * alive. Is 24:6
The city is * in ruins; Is 24:12
is the same—only a remnant is *. Is 24:13
But all who are * will shout and Is 24:14
beneath his feet and * to rot. Is 25:10
of beauty to his people who are *. Is 28:5
Not a piece will be * large Is 30:14
not two of you are * together. Is 30:17

Their dead will be * unburied, Is 34:3
—that you don't have 2,000 men * Is 36:8,9
Oh, Isaiah, pray for us who are * Is 37:4
Now the Assyrian envoy * Is 37:8,9
his king, who had * Lachish and was Is 37:8,9
And you who are * in Judah will Is 37:31
Nothing will be *. Is 39:6
* he makes his god: a carved idol! Is 44:17
to me, all Israel who are *; Is 46:3
Not one of her sons is * alive Is 51:18
And who is * to sympathize? Is 51:19
Who is * to comfort you? Is 51:19
We, who * God's paths to follow Is 53:6
possess the cities * behind during Is 54:3
You will be * in despair, and Jer 2:37
But though you have * me and Jer 3:1
But now Judah too has * me and Jer 3:8
a little remnant of my people *. Jer 4:27
day your fathers * Egypt until now, Jer 7:25
one shall be * to scare them away. Jer 7:33
who are still * alive shall long to Jer 8:3
There is no one * to help me Jer 10:20
animals to finish up what's *. Jer 15:3
Temple. He * him there all night. Jer 20:3
all the remnant * in the city into Jer 21:7
Not one is * to help you! Jer 22:20
of Jerusalem * here in this land; Jer 24:8
He has * his lair like a lion Jer 25:38
in the Temple, * from before, and Jer 27:18
articles * here by Nebuchadnezzar, Jer 27:19,20,21
upon the people * here in Jer 29:16,17
All your lovers have * you and Jer 30:14
* desolate without a living soul. Jer 34:22
people who were * in the land Jer 37:2
as there was any * in the city. Jer 37:21
have *, and of all the people too. Jer 38:4
that all the women * in your palace Jer 38:21,22
They have betrayed you and * you Jer 38:21,22
him to, and they * without finding Jer 38:27
land of Judah he * a few people, Jer 39:10
his people who were * in the land. Jer 39:14
with the people * in the land. Jer 40:6
the land who were * behind, and had Jer 40:7
people were still * in Judah, and Jer 40:11
who had been * under Gedaliah's Jer 41:10
of the guard, had * with Gedaliah. Jer 43:6
and * without a soul alive. Jer 46:19
shall be * without a living soul. Jer 48:9
Is there not one * in all of Jer 49:7
let nothing be *. Jer 50:26
Babylon will be * desolate Jer 51:29
and the tradesmen who were *. Jer 52:15
But he * some of the poorest Jer 52:16
with no one * to lift her out. Lam 1:9
He has * me sick and desolate the Lam 1:13
and * me bleeding and desolate. Lam 3:11
to water, for the Lord has * me. Lam 3:18
there is not a drop of water *. Lam 4:3,4
there is no one * to save us. Lam 5:8
and the face of an ox on his * Eze 1:10
"Now lie on your * side for 390 Eze 4:4,5
one will be * to bewail your fate. Eze 7:10,11
wipe out everyone * in Israel?" Eze 9:8
"Son of dust, the remnant * in Eze 11:15
a field and * to die, unwanted. Eze 16:5
and slash to the *, wherever you Eze 21:16
slag * when silver is smelted. Eze 22:18,19,20
For when she * Egypt, she did Eze 23:8
and everything * will be burned. Eze 23:25
And I have * it there, Eze 24:8
There was little * to pay the Eze 29:18f
There was little * to pay the Eze 29:20f
All that's * for my flock is Eze 34:19
those still *—will know that I, the Eze 36:36
for any skeletons * and bury them, Eze 39:14
As I followed, he * the eastern Eze 40:20
strip all around is to be * empty. Eze 45:2
the roots were * in the ground! Dan 4:26
fly, and it was * standing on the Dan 7:4
ran to hide, and I was * alone. Dan 10:8
vision my strength * me, and I grew Dan 10:8
Israel, you have * me as a Hos 5:3
from them and they are * alone. Hos 5:6
inherit your possessions * behind? Hos 9:6
will take what's *! Joe 1:4
all Philistines * will perish." Amo 1:8
they will have * is half a chair Amo 3:12
those * are like half-burned Amo 4:11
She is * alone to die." Amo 5:2
few as ten of them *, and even one Amo 6:9
be the only one * to bury him, and Amo 6:10
inside, "Are any others *?" Amo 6:10
possess what is * of Edom, and of Amo 9:12
at least the gleanings would be *! Ob 1:5
will be * in all of Edom! Ob 1:8
their right hands from their *." Jon 4:11f
you—all that are *—and bring you Mic 2:12
not one fair-minded man is *. Mic 7:1
is neither blossom * nor fruit, and Hab 3:17
be rooted out and * in desolation. Zep 2:4
you until not one of you is *. Zep 2:5

those of my people who are * will Zep 2.
have * no trace of their prey. Zep 3:
I have * their streets in silent Zep 3
Those who are * will be the poor Zep 3:1
Priest and everyone * in the land: Hag 2:
'For I promised when you * Egypt Hag 2:
Then the angel * me for awhile, Zec 5:
So they * at once. Zec 6:
if you * the city, there was no Zec 8:1
given to the people * in the land. Zec 8:1
Everyone * will worship God and Zec 9:
From the few that are *, their Zec 10:
*, while Jerusalem stands unmoved. Zec 12:
but a third will be * in the Zec 13:
be * in what remains of the city. Zec 14:
For you have * God's paths. Mal 2:
night he * for Egypt with Mary Mt 2:1
he * Judea and returned home Mt 4:12,1
And they * their nets at once Mt 4:2
tell your * hand what your right Mt 6:
touched her hand, the fever * her; Mt 8:1
And the boy jumped up and *! Mt 9:
were planning, and * the synagogue, Mt 12:1
LATER THAT SAME day, Jesus * the Mt 13:1
were twelve basketfuls * over! Mt 14:2
Jesus then * that part of the Mt 15:2
now, and have nothing * to eat; Mt 15:3
were seven basketfuls * over! Mt 15:37,38
loaves, and the basketfuls * over? Mt 16:9
4,000 I fed, and all that was *? Mt 16:10
in the boy and it * him, and from Mt 17:18
"But when the man * the king, he Mt 18:28
this address, he * Galilee and Mt 19:1
and blessed them before he *. Mt 19:15
Then Peter said to him, "We * Mt 19:27
As Jesus and the disciples * the Mt 20:29
And now your house is * to you, Mt 23:38
one stone * on top of another!" Mt 24:2
one will be taken, the other *. Mt 24:40
one will be taken, the other *. Mt 24:41
abilities—and then * on his trip. Mt 25:15
right hand, and the goats at my *. Mt 25:33
to those on my * and say, 'Away Mt 25:41
Again he * them and prayed, "My Mt 26:42
resurrection, they * the cemetery Mt 27:53
stone across the entrance as he *. Mt 27:60
Then the eleven disciples * for Mt 28:16
At once they * their nets and Mk 1:18
immediately they * their father Mk 1:20
the man violently and * him. Mk 1:26
the fever suddenly *, and she got Mk 1:31
SOON AFTERWARDS HE * that Mk 6:1
So they * by boat for a quieter Mk 6:32
Then he * Galilee and went to the Mk 7:24
Go on home, for the demon has * Mk 7:29
days, and have nothing * to eat. Mk 8:1
very large basketfuls * over! Mk 8:8,9
into the boat and * them, and Mk 8:13
food before they *, and had only Mk 8:14
seven loaves, how much was *?" Mk 8:20
Jesus and his disciples now * Mk 8:27
convulsed the boy again and * him; Mk 9:26
THEN HE * Capernaum Mk 10:1
the other disciples had * behind. Mk 10:28
right and the other at your *!" Mk 10:37
Later, as they * town, a great Mk 10:46
and then *—for now it was late in Mk 11:11
The next morning as they * Mk 11:12
That evening as usual they * the Mk 11:19
there was only one *—his only son. Mk 12:6
So they * him and went away. Mk 12:12
and died, and * no children. Mk 12:20,21,22
he died too, and * no children. Mk 12:20,21,22
For not one stone will be * upon Mk 13:2
She never * the Temple but stayed Lk 2:36,37
Holy Spirit, * the Jordan River, Lk 4:1
* Jesus for a while and went away. Lk 4:13
away through the crowd and * them. Lk 4:30
* him without hurting him further. Lk 4:35
* everything and went with him. Lk 5:11
And the leprosy * him Lk 5:13
Later on as Jesus * the town he Lk 5:27
So Levi * everything, sprang Lk 5:28
After they *, Jesus talked to the Lk 7:24
So they * the man and went into Lk 8:33
So he returned to the boat and *, Lk 8:37
beat him up and * him lying half Lk 10:30
to the person it *, and finds that Lk 11:24
And now—now your house is * Lk 13:35
is * at the foot of the table! Lk 14:9
until the morning Lot * Sodom. Lk 17:29
will be taken away, the other *. Lk 17:34
one will be taken, the other *; Lk 17:35,36
their bodies * to the vultures. Lk 17:37f
And Peter said, "We have * our Lk 18:28
Before he * he called together Lk 19:13
stone will be * on top of another; Lk 21:6
the disciples, he * the upstairs Lk 22:39
After the wedding he * for Jn 2:12
and his disciples * Jerusalem and Jn 3:22
did)— he * Judea and returned to Jn 4:3

(LEFT Con't)
Then the woman * her waterpot Jn 4:28,29
But after his brothers had * for Jn 7:10
only Jesus was * in front of the Jn 8:9
walked past them and * the Temple. Jn 8:59
is little time * before the night Jn 9:4
But he walked away and * them, Jn 10:39
Then she * him and returned to Jn 11:28
public ministry and * Jerusalem; Jn 11:54
the table, leaning on the * elbow. Jn 13:23f
Judas * at once, going out into Jn 13:30
As soon as Judas * the room, Jn 13:31
soul would not be * in hell and his Act 2:31
They * the Council chamber Act 5:41
So he * the land of the Act 7:4
screaming as they * their victims, Act 8:7
So Peter * the cell, following Act 12:9
a block, and then the angel * him. Act 12:10
he said—and * for safer quarters. Act 12:17
Afterwards he * to live in Act 12:19
Now Paul and those with him * Act 13:13
As the people * the synagogue Act 13:42
never * himself without a witness; Act 14:17
The next day he * with Barnabas Act 14:20
of the believers, * for Syria and Act 15:40,41
before they *, for everyone knew Act 16:3
And instantly it * her. Act 16:18
THEN PAUL * Athens and went to Act 18:1
of Ephesus, he * us aboard ship Act 18:19
time there, he * for Turkey again, Act 18:23
Christ, so he *, refusing to preach Act 19:9
said good-bye and * for Greece, Act 20:1
was dawn when he finally * them! Act 20:10,11,12
passed it on our * and landed at Act 21:3
our things and * for Jerusalem. Act 21:15
commander warned the boy as he *. Act 23:22
the Jews, he * Paul in chains. Act 24:27
he * for Jerusalem, where the Act 25:1
case was * for me by Felix. Act 25:14
and all the others stood and *. Act 26:30
imperial guard. We * on a boat Act 27:2
place and not * Fair Havens—you Act 27:21
themselves, they * with this final Act 28:25
was the only one * in all the land Rom 11:2,3
"No, you are not the only one *. Rom 11:4
him before he * me of my pride in 2Co 7:14
much had nothing * over, and he 2Co 8:15
* over to give joyfully to others. 2Co 9:8
him with nothing * against Col 1:22
you—nothing * that he could even Col 1:22
Dear brothers, after we * you and 1Th 2:17
our hearts never * you), we tried 1Th 2:17
As I said when I * for Macedonia, 1Ti 1:3,4
your tears as we * each other. 2Ti 1:4
to have any faith *, he remains 2Ti 2:13
They have * the path of truth, 2Ti 2:18
as you can, for Demas has * me. 2Ti 4:10
bring the coat I * at Troas with 2Ti 4:13
and I * Trophimus sick at Miletus. 2Ti 4:20
I * you there on the island of Tit 1:5
Nothing is * out." Heb 2:8
his bones with them when they *! Heb 11:22
God that he * the land of Egypt and Heb 11:27
only unshakable things will be *. Heb 12:27
to get even; he * his case in the 1Pe 2:23
When they * us it proved that 1Jn 2:19
rank and * their proper home." Jud 1:6f
the dirty foam * along the beach by Jud 1:13
is * is at the point of death. Rev 3:2
But the men * alive after these Rev 9:20
on the sea and his * foot on the Rev 10:2
Then everyone * will, in their Rev 11:13
So the first angel * the temple Rev 16:2
is no one * to buy their goods. Rev 18:11

LEFT-HANDED
Gera, a Benjaminite), who was *. Ju 3:15
men who were * sharpshooters. Ju 20:16

LEFTOVERS
baskets were filled with the *! Jn 6:13

LEG
as useless as a paralyzed *. Pro 26:7

LEGAL
* affairs were usually transacted. Ru 4:1f
Solomon sat to hear * matters; 1Ki 7:7
asked Jesus, "Is it * to work by Mt 12:10
pigeons" was the * requirement. Lk 2:24
The Pharisees and * experts were Lk 11:53,54
Jesus said to the Pharisees and * Lk 14:3
"Is it * to convict a man Jn 7:51
Let them go through * channels. Act 19:38
there, "Is it * for you to whip a Act 22:25
Felix came with Drusilla, his * Act 24:24
It may be perfectly *, but it may 1Co 10:23

LEGALISTS
what these Jewish *, who insisted Gal 2:12

LEGALLY
our father were * ours and our Gen 31:16
you to * declare my marriage vow. Eze 16:8
children will * belong to the dead Lk 20:28

LEGENDS
of whom so many * are told. Gen 6:4

ideas and silly myths and *. 1Ti 4:7

LEGGINGS
of mail, bronze *, and carried a 1Sa 17:4-7

LEGION
demon replied, "*, for there are Mk 5:9
Jesus asked the demon. "*," Lk 8:30
Implied; a * consisted of 6,000 Lk 8:30f

LEGITIMATE
other sons by his * wife, and when Ju 11:1

LEGS
the head, *, heart, and liver. Ex 12:9
of the four *, close to the top; Ex 25:26,27
wash off the entrails and the *; Ex 29:17
the four table *, close to the Ex 37:13
The internal organs and the * Lev 1:9
organs and the * shall first be Lev 1:13
skin, meat, head, *, internal Lev 4:11,12
insides and the * with water, and Lev 8:21
insides and the *, and offered Lev 9:14
"Flying insects with four * must Lev 11:20
as well as those that have *. Lev 11:41,42
and your strong * will become weak, Ecc 12:3
with jewels. His * are as pillars Sol 5:15
Their * were like those of men, Eze 1:7
of brass, its * of iron, its feet Dan 2:33
and his * gave way beneath him. Dan 5:6
mouth two * and a piece of ear. Amo 3:12
my lips quiver with fear. My * Hab 3:16
missing arms and * had new ones; Mt 15:31
to order the * of the men broken to Jn 19:31
came and broke the * of the two men Jn 19:32
firm on your shaky *, and mark out Heb 12:12

LEHABIM
Ludim, Anamim, *, Naphtuhim, Gen 10:13,14
the Ludim, the Anamim, the *, the 1Ch 1:11,12

LEHEM
in Moab before he returned to *). 1Ch 4:21-22

LEHI
posse into Judah and raided *. Ju 15:9
captors arrived at *, the Ju 15:14

LEMUEL
wise sayings of King * of Massa, Pro 31:1
Or, "of King * the oracle." Pro 31:1f
And it is not for kings, O *, to Pro 31:4

LEND
"If you * money to a needy Ex 22:25
that will * dignity to his work. Ex 28:2
interest on the money you * him. Lev 25:36
You shall * money to many nations Deu 15:6
you must * them as much as they Deu 15:8
You must * him what he needs, Deu 15:10
You must * to them liberally. Deu 15:11
"If you * anything to another Deu 24:10
and you shall * to many nations, Deu 28:12
They shall * to you, not you to Deu 28:44
And if you * money only to those Lk 6:34
Even the most wicked will * to Lk 6:34
Do good to them! * to them! Lk 6:35

LENDER
the borrower is servant to the *. Pro 22:7

LENDERS
and sellers, * and borrowers, Is 24:2

LENDING
The rest of us are * money and Neh 5:10
When you help the poor you are * Pro 19:17

LENGTH
it winds across the entire * of Gen 2:11,12
the entire * of the land of Cush. Gen 2:13
There will be a 1½-foot * of Ex 26:12
and a 1½-foot * at the front. Ex 26:13
your life and the * of your days. Deu 30:20
And may your strength match the * Deu 33:25
Saul now fell full * upon the 1Sa 28:20
along the full * of both sides of 1Ki 6:5
* of his reign: 52 years, in 2Ki 15:1
* of reign: 6 months 2Ki 15:8
* of reign: 1 month 2Ki 15:13
* of reign: 10 years, in Samaria 2Ki 15:17
* of reign: 3 years, in Samaria 2Ki 15:23
* of reign: 20 years, in Samaria 2Ki 15:27
* of his reign: 9 years, in 2Ki 17:1
* of his reign: 29 years, in 2Ki 18:1
* of his reign: 55 years, in 2Ki 21:1
* of his reign: 2 years, in 2Ki 21:19,20
* of his reign: 3 months, in 2Ki 23:31,32
* of his reign: 11 years, in 2Ki 23:36,37
* of his reign: 3 months, in 2Ki 24:8,9
* of his reign: 11 years, in 2Ki 24:18,19
The full * of the entrance Eze 40:15
the others, with a * of 87½ feet Eze 40:36
the entire *, with the doors of the Eze 42:4
the court—the same * and width and Eze 42:11
it is contiguous with them in *, Eze 45:7
The south wall, also the same *, Eze 48:33
this with them at *, and finally Act 15:2
For the * of your lives is as Jas 4:14
A cubit was the average * of a Rev 21:17f

LENGTHENING
and by * the memorial fringes of Mt 23:5

LENGTHENS
A relaxed attitude * a man's Pro 14:30

LENGTHS
Use accurate measurements—*, Lev 19:35,36
For you go to all * to make one Mt 23:15

LENGTHY
This was Stephen's * reply: "The Act 7:2

LENTILS
*, honey, butter, and cheese. 2Sa 17:28,29
* and beat back the Philistines; 2Sa 23:11,12
barley, beans, *, and spelt. Eze 4:9

LEOPARD
the * and goats will be at peace. Is 11:6
upon them, and a "*" shall lurk Jer 5:6
skin? or a * take away his spots? Jer 13:23
looked like a *, but on its back it Dan 7:6
or a * lurking along the road. Hos 13:7
This Creature looked like a * Rev 13:2

LEOPARDS
Their horses are swifter than *. Hab 1:8

LEPER
the priest must declare him a *. Lev 13:3
the priest must pronounce him a *. Lev 13:8
the man shall be declared a *. Lev 13:14,15
to white, the * will return to the Lev 13:16,17
the priest must declare him a *. Lev 13:22
the priest must pronounce him a *. Lev 13:25
the priest must pronounce him a *. Lev 13:27
the priest must pronounce him a *. Lev 13:29,30
hair develops, declare him a *. Lev 13:36
and is not a *, and the priest Lev 13:37
him a * even though he is bald! Lev 13:40
then he is a *, and the priest Lev 13:44
goes, "I am a *, I am a leper." Lev 13:45
goes, "I am a leper, I am a *." Lev 13:45
"No priest who is a * or who has Lev 22:4
was a great hero, but he was a *. 2Ki 5:1
"This man sends me a * to heal! 2Ki 5:7
a *, his skin as white as snow. 2Ki 5:27
So King Uzziah was a * until the 2Ch 26:21
though he was a *, and his son 2Ch 26:23
Look! A * is approaching. Mt 8:2
"Sir," the * pleads, "if you Mt 8:2
to the home of Simon the *. Mt 26:6
Once a * came and knelt in front Mk 1:40
by Moses for a * who is healed, so Mk 1:43,44
at the home of Simon the *; Mk 14:3

LEPERS
must expel all * from the camp, and Num 5:1
of cancer, or be *, or be sterile, 2Sa 3:29
Now there were four * sitting 2Ki 7:3
When the * arrived at the edge of 2Ki 7:8
by Moses' law for * who are Mt 8:4
cure the *, and cast out demons. Mt 10:8
and the cured *, and the deaf who Mt 11:5
the many Jewish * needing help." Lk 4:27
for * who are healed," he said. Lk 5:14
limp. The * are completely healed. Lk 7:20,21,22
village there, ten * stood at a Lk 17:12

LEPROSY
it out again, it was white with *! Ex 4:6
skin, * is to be suspected. Lev 13:1
skin-deep, it is *, and the priest Lev 13:3
of having * is brought to the Lev 13:9,10
case of *, and the priest must Lev 13:11
sees that the * has erupted and Lev 13:12
of *, for it has all turned white; Lev 13:13
* has broken out from the boil. Lev 13:20
skin-deep, it is * that has broken Lev 13:25
declare that he does not have *. Lev 13:28
this is not *, but an ordinary Lev 13:39
bald forehead, but this is not *. Lev 13:41
spot, it may be * breaking out. Lev 13:42
that looks like *, then he is a Lev 13:43
discovered to have * must tear his Lev 13:45
"If * is suspected in a woolen Lev 13:47,48
it, it is probably *, and must be Lev 13:49
it is a contagious *, and he must Lev 13:51
not spread, it is * and shall be Lev 13:55
it is * and he must burn it. Lev 13:57
concerning * in a garment or Lev 13:59
a person whose * disappears: Lev 14:1
If the priest sees that the * is Lev 14:3
man cured of his *, and the priest Lev 14:7
be declared fully cured of his *. Lev 14:9
person being cleansed from his *; Lev 14:19
are cleansed of * but are not able Lev 14:32
you, and I place * in some house Lev 14:33,34
that there may be * in my house!' Lev 14:35
he decides that there is * there. Lev 14:36
it is *, and the house is defiled. Lev 14:44
cleansed, and declare the * gone. Lev 14:48
places where * may appear: in a Lev 14:54
whether or not it is actually *. Lev 14:57
suddenly became white with *. Num 12:10
priest in cases of *, for I have Deu 24:8
He would heal him of his *!" 2Ki 5:3
I want you to heal him of his * 2Ki 5:6
be healed of every trace of his *! 2Ki 5:10
his hand over the * and call upon 2Ki 5:11
at home and get rid of my *." 2Ki 5:12
this, Naaman's * shall be upon you 2Ki 5:27
the Lord struck him with *, which 2Ki 15:5

(LEPROSY Con't)
Suddenly—* appeared in his 2Ch 26:19
And instantly the * disappears. Mt 8:3
Immediately the * was gone—the Mk 1:42
a man with an advanced case of *. Lk 5:12
And the * left him instantly! Lk 5:13
And as they were going, their * Lk 17:14

LEPROUS
whether to pronounce it * or not. Lev 13:59

LESHEM
the city of *, slaughtered its Jos 19:47,48

LESS
So the * healthy lambs were Gen 30:42
shall not give *, for it is an Ex 30:15
land, the smaller tribes * land. Num 26:54
he has cost you * than half the Deu 15:18
* swear by them or worship them. Jos 23:7
"A quick death is * painful." Ju 8:21f
much * this Temple I have built! 1Ki 8:27
* this Temple which I have built! 2Ch 6:18
how much * your God!' 2Ch 32:15
been punished far * than we Ez 9:13
how much * men made of dust, who Job 4:18,19
and even my clothing would be * Job 9:31
you far * than you deserve! Job 11:6
How much * someone like you, who Job 15:16
* than nothing as compared to him. Job 25:5
How much * is man, who is but a Job 25:6
whose fathers are * than my dogs. Job 30:1
They weigh * than air on scales. Ps 62:9
The more words you speak, the * Ecc 6:11
in his eyes they are * than Is 40:17
You are * than nothing, and can Is 41:24
In fact, faithless Israel is * Jer 3:11
exchanged for twenty gerahs, no *; Eze 45:12
be valued at five shekels, no *; Eze 45:12
are, when you are * than nothing! Amo 6:13
and he does * and less for God. Mt 13:22
and he does less and * for God. Mt 13:22
Sidon will receive * punishment on Lk 10:14
brings out the * expensive brands. Jn 2:10
and I must become * and less. Jn 3:30
and I must become less and *. Jn 3:30
But Gallio couldn't have cared *. Act 18:17
did, you might be * interested in 1Co 9:12
make it any * a part of the body. 1Co 12:15
Would that make it any * a part 1Co 12:16
might otherwise seem * important. 1Co 12:24
I am strong—the * I have, the more 2Co 12:10
I love you, the * you love me. 2Co 12:15
For my message comes from no * a Gal 1:12
counting it worth * than nothing, Php 3:8
Once you were * than nothing; 1Pe 2:10

LESSER
And yet, even the * lights in the Mt 11:11

LESSON
Take a * from the ants, you lazy Pro 6:6
as I looked, I learned this *: Pro 24:32,33
a * from the families of Rechab? Jer 35:13
My judgment will be a * against Eze 23:48
but remember the * they learned, Zec 1:5,6
"Now learn a * from the fig Mt 24:32
"Now, here is a * from a fig Mk 13:28
From this * we are warned that we 1Co 10:6
Another * for us is what happened 1Co 10:8
This has an important * for us Heb 9:9

LESSONS
soon forget such *—but stagger them Ps 59:11
For I will show you * from our Ps 78:2,3
of you apply these * from the past Is 42:23
examples—as object * to us—to warn 1Co 10:11
those first * about Christ. Heb 6:1
* from him about trusting God. Heb 11:4

LEST
thread from you, * you say, 'Abram Gen 14:23
must sanctify themselves, * Ex 19:22
Place, * they be guilty and die. Ex 28:43
go into the Tabernacle, * you die; Lev 10:8,9
their defilement, * they die Lev 15:31
her a prostitute, * the land become Lev 19:29
carefully, * they be declared Lev 22:9
touch the holy items, * they die. Num 4:15
for even a moment, * they look at Num 4:20
belongs to them, * you be included Num 16:26
to burn incense, * the same thing Num 16:40
* I destroy both them and you. Num 18:2,3
* they be judged guilty and die. Num 18:22
they were common, * you die." Num 18:32
Beware * you break the contract Deu 4:23
more, then beware * you forget the Deu 6:10,11,12
too many wives, * his heart be Deu 17:17
be very careful * you be corrupted Deu 18:9
fire on the mountain, * you die. Deu 18:16
Literally, "* the fulness of the Deu 22:9f
indecent * he turn away from you. Deu 23:14
may be given * the punishment seem Deu 25:1
country, * the entire city die. 1Sa 5:11
"Pray for us * we die!" 1Sa 12:19
Don't tell the Philistines, * 2Sa 1:20
* the heathen nations laugh in 2Sa 1:20
their hands, * it be diverted to 2Ki 12:8
to decide justly, * the wrath of 2Ch 19:10
meddle with me, * you and all Judah 2Ch 25:19
the darkness, * he be murdered. Job 15:22
sipping it slowly, * it disappear. Job 20:13
that I be cautious * I insult Job 32:21,22
Let me be frank, * God should Job 32:21,22
give me light in my darkness * I Ps 13:3
* the godly be forced to do wrong. Ps 125:3
Watch yourself, * you be Pro 5:2
Don't go near her house, * you Pro 5:9
* strangers obtain your wealth, Pro 5:10
of foreigners. * afterwards you Pro 5:11
stay away from where she walks, * Pro 7:25
men, * you learn to be like them Pro 22:24,25
Don't tell anyone else, * he Pro 25:8,9,10
Do not add to his words, * he Pro 30:6
* he curse you for your sin. Pro 30:10
So scoff no more, * your Is 28:22
not destroy you * the heathen say Is 48:11
honor of my name, * the Egyptians Eze 20:9,10
honor of my name, * the nations who Eze 20:14
on other clothes * they consecrate Eze 44:19
The people of Samaria tremble * Hos 10:5
Watch with me and pray * the Mk 14:38
judge, * he sentence you to jail; Lk 12:58
* they come here when they die.' Lk 16:28
able to stop them, * you find Act 5:39
to you. But * I bore you, kindly Act 24:4
Literally, "fearing * they should Act 27:17f
kill the prisoners * any of them Act 27:42
freedom to eat it, * you cause some 1Co 8:9
* the answer hurt your conscience. 1Co 10:25
dear brothers, * you find that Heb 3:12
these wicked men, * you yourselves 2Pe 3:17

LET'S
"* go out into the fields." Gen 4:8
'This is his wife. * kill him and Gen 12:11,12,13
Come, * fill him with wine and Gen 19:32
father last night. * fill him with Gen 19:34
"Well, * be going," Esau said. Gen 33:12
they said. "* invite them to live Gen 34:21
Come on, * agree to this so that Gen 34:23
"Come on, * kill him and toss Gen 37:19,20
life. "* not kill him," he said; Gen 37:21,22
"we'll shed no blood—* throw him Gen 37:21,22
"Here come some Ishmaelites. * Gen 37:26,27
guilty conscience? * not be Gen 37:26,27
under control. "* eat," he said. Gen 43:31
so many of them. * figure out a Ex 1:10
the dry ground. "* get out of Ex 14:25
become slaves. * get out of here Num 14:3
The idea swept the camp. "* Num 14:4
"But they replied, 'First * send Deu 1:22
"All right," they agreed, "* Ju 14:13
And the men replied, "* attack! Ju 18:9,10
Come on, * go! Ju 18:9,10
to travel; * stay here tonight." Ju 19:11
"Well, come on," he said. "* Ju 19:28
"* bring the Ark here from 1Sa 4:3
said to the servant, "* go home; 1Sa 9:5
says comes true; * go and find him 1Sa 9:6
"All right," Saul agreed, "* 1Sa 9:9,10,11
called seers. "* go and ask the 1Sa 9:9,10,11
rather than, "* go and ask the 1Sa 9:9,10,11
"Come on, * cross the valley to 1Sa 14:1
"Yes, * go across to those 1Sa 14:6
Afterwards Saul said, "* chase 1Sa 14:36
But the priest said, "* ask God 1Sa 14:36
to Joab, "* watch some sword play 2Sa 2:14
Absalom is dead. * ask David to 2Sa 19:8,9,10
Come on, you men of Israel, * get 2Sa 20:1
Then the king said, "* get the 1Ki 3:23
and all his relatives! * go home! 1Ki 12:16,17
* go and collect the loot!" 2Ki 3:23
a holy prophet. * make a little 2Ki 4:10
come on, * go back and tell the 2Ki 7:9
own tribe of Judah! * go home!" 2Ch 10:16
However, * check with the Lord 2Ch 18:3,4,5
Jehoshaphat exclaimed. "* hear 2Ch 18:6,7
They replied at once, "Good! * Neh 2:18
Lord. "* wipe out every trace of Ps 74:8
Come on, * take our fill of love Pro 7:18
* go and have another Pro 23:35
come, * run!" Sol 1:4
Come, * talk this over! Is 1:18
and have a party; * all get drunk. Is 56:12
will save you. * see if the whole Is 57:13
to kill me! "* destroy this man Jer 11:19
they said. "* kill him so that his Jer 11:19
Then the people said, "Come, * Jer 18:18
need his advice. * silence him that Jer 18:18
saying, 'Come on, * have some fun! Eze 33:30
have some fun! * go hear him tell Eze 33:30
cities and say, '* go to Jerusalem Zec 8:20,21
Please come with me. * go now!' Zec 8:20,21
come on, * kill him and get it Mt 21:38
of evil men! Up! * be going! Mt 26:46
"Leave him alone. * see whether Mt 27:49
his disciples, "* cross to the Mk 4:35
Then Jesus suggested, "* get Mk 6:31
Come on, * kill him—and then the Mk 12:7
"* see if Elijah will come and Mk 15:3
"Come on! * go to Bethlehem! Lk 2:1
Let's go to Bethlehem! * see this Lk 2:1
Come on. * kill him, and then it Lk 20:1
they said, "* see him save himself Lk 23:3
his disciples, "* go to Judea." Jn 11:
Come, * go to him." Jn 11:1
"* go too—and die with him." Jn 11:1
Come, * be going. Jn 14:3
But they said, "* not tear up Jn 19:23,2
'* throw dice to see who gets it." Jn 19:23,2
things are wrong. * please the Rom 15:
Well, my brothers, * add up what 1Co 14:2

LETS
"If someone deliberately * his Ex 22:
Lord, who * you do these things? 2Ki 19:2
the judges and * them be unfair. Job 9:2
He * me rest in the meadow grass Ps 23:2,
Literally, "as when one * out Pro 17:14
Laziness * the roof leak, and Ecc 10:18
God, who * this come upon you. Is 22:9,10,1
him, "Anyone who * himself be Lk 9:62
A pure eye * sunshine into your Lk 11:34

LETTER
and is to be followed to the *. Deu 17:10
he may write a * stating that he Deu 24:1
give her the *, and send her away. Deu 24:1
must obey to the *: Remember what Deu 24:8
and to obey to the * every law Jos 1:7
and bring us back a * 1Sa 17:18
David wrote a * to Joab and gave it 2Sa 11:14
to deliver. The * instructed Joab 2Sa 11:15
In her * she commanded: "Call 1Ki 21:9
"I will send a * of introduction 2Ki 5:5
of clothing. The * to the king of 2Ki 5:6
this * is my servant Naaman; 2Ki 5:6
THEN JEHU WROTE a * to the city 2Ki 10:1
"Upon receipt of this *, select 2Ki 10:2,3
When the * arrived, all seventy 2Ki 10:7
Hezekiah took the * from the 2Ki 19:14
wrote him this *: "The Lord God of 2Ch 21:12
the king's * said, "so that he 2Ch 30:6
they wrote him a * of accusation Ez 4:6
associates wrote a * to him in the Ez 4:7
Here is the text of the * they Ez 4:11
"Gentlemen: Greetings! The * you Ez 4:18
When this * from King Ez 4:23
Following is the * which governor Ez 5:6
presented this * to Ezra the Ez 7:11
also a * to Asaph, the manager Neh 2:8
came with an open * in his hand and Neh 6:5,6
"A copy of this edict," the * Est 3:14
Jew) had written a * throwing her Est 9:29-31
behind Mordecai's * inaugurating Est 9:29-31
had read this *, he went over to Is 37:14
Look at this * from King Is 37:16,17
just as the * says, and thrown Is 37:18
wrote them a * from Jerusalem, Jer 29:1
He sent the * with Elasah (son Jer 29:3
And this is what the * said: Jer 29:3
You have written a * to Zephaniah Jer 29:25
And in this * you have said to Jer 29:26
Zephaniah took the * over to Jer 29:29
Send an open * to all the exiles Jer 29:31
followed the * of the law but often Mt 3:7f
by giving her a * of dismissal.' Mt 5:31
writing her a * of dismissal?" Mt 19:7
write his wife a * of dismissal." Mk 10:4
laws in spirit as well as in *. Lk 1:6
In my first * Act 1:1
He requested a * addressed to Act 9:2
This is the * they took along Act 15:23
Christians and gave them the *. Act 15:30
Then he wrote this * to the Act 23:25
Paul and the * to the governor. Act 23:33
DEAR FRIENDS IN Rome: This * is Rom 1:1
thing to say before I end this *. Rom 16:17
is writing this * for Paul, send my Rom 16:22
asked in your last *: my answer is 1Co 7:1
loving gift with a * to Jerusalem, 1Co 16:3
words of this * with my own hand: 1Co 16:21
This * is from me, Paul, appointed 2Co 1:1
I did in my last *, so that you 2Co 2:3
Oh, how I hated to write that *! 2Co 2:4
* to tell you about us, do you? 2Co 3:1
The only * I need is you 2Co 3:2
They can see that you are a * 2Co 3:3
It is not a * written with pen 2Co 3:3
that I sent that * to you, though I 2Co 7:8
I close my * with these last 2Co 13:11
as I close this * let me say this Php 4:8
you have read this * will you pass Col 4:16
And read the * I wrote to them. Col 4:16
read this * to all the Christians. 1Th 5:27
this * I ask you to pray for us. 2Th 3:1
we say in this *, notice who he is 2Th 3:14
I've written you this * because I Phm 1:21
in this *, for it is a short one. Heb 13:22
you by this * for I have given you 1Pe 5:12
THIS IS MY second * to you, dear 2Pe 3:1
And if you do as I say in this * 1Jn 1:4

LETTER Con't)
to say it in this *, for I hope to 2Jn 1:12
I sent a brief * to the church 3Jn 1:9
who is writing this * to you. Rev 1:9
* to the seven churches in Turkey: Rev 1:11
"Write a * to the leader Rev 2:1
the church in Smyrna write this *: Rev 2:8
"Write this * to the leader Rev 2:12
"Write this * to the leader Rev 2:18
the church in Sardis write this *: Rev 3:1
"Write this * to the leader Rev 3:7
"Write this * to the leader Rev 3:14

LETTERS
So she wrote * in Ahab's name, 1Ki 21:8
KING HEZEKIAH NOW sent * 2Ch 30:1
King Sennacherib also sent * 2Ch 32:17
The messengers who brought the * 2Ch 32:18
the king, give me * to the Neh 2:7
king's * to the governors there. Neh 2:9
days many * went back and forth Neh 6:17
many threatening * to frighten me. Neh 6:19
counsel, and sent * to all of his Est 1:22
and dictated * to the governors and Est 3:12
these * were signed in the name Est 3:12
ring and sent the * by swift Est 8:9,10
events, and sent * to the Jews near Est 9:20
In addition, * were sent to all Est 9:29-31
Use capital *! Is 8:1
For I asked them for * to the Act 22:5
We have had no * from Judea or Act 28:21
toward you. My * have been 2Co 1:13,14
* of recommendation with them? 2Co 3:1
saying, "Paul's * are bold enough 2Co 10:1
when I scold you in my *. 2Co 10:9
"Don't bother about his *," 2Co 10:10
just as rough on you as my * are! 2Co 10:11
how large I have to make the *! Gal 6:11
mentioned before in one of my *. Eph 3:2,3
God about this, or * that are 2Th 2:1
taught you in our * and during the 2Th 2:15
the end of all my *, for proof that 2Th 3:17
same things in many of his *. 2Pe 3:15,16
have twisted his * around to mean 2Pe 3:15,16
these are the first and last * of Rev 1:8f
of the * in his name add to 666! Rev 13:18

LETTING
"What is this we have done, * Ex 14:5
Yes, he humbled you by * you go Deu 8:3
fighting men, * not one escape. Ju 3:29
What do you mean by * him get 2Sa 3:24,25
mother's womb, for * me be born to Job 3:10
His archers surround me, * fly Job 16:13
of his wickedness, * it melt in his Job 20:12
O Lord, by * the light of your Ps 4:6
So I am * them go their blind Ps 81:12
I praise you for * me learn your Ps 119:171
while * the wicked fall into it. Pro 11:8
And then I realized that God is * Ecc 3:18
pervert justice, * the wicked go Is 5:23
them a little by * them fall into Is 47:6
Ishmael into * them go by promising Jer 41:8
greatly, by * the uncircumcised Eze 44:7
them both, * them keep the money! Lk 7:42
brother stumble by * him see you Rom 14:13
* God have his way with you. 2Pe 1:6

LETUSHIM
Dedan's sons were Asshurim, *, Gen 25:3

LEUMMIM
were Asshurim, Letushim, and *. Gen 25:3

LEVEL
a good indication of the water *. Gen 8:7f
Fill the valleys; * the hills; Is 40:4
He will * the mountains and Is 42:15
you, Cyrus, and * the mountains and Is 45:2
mountains into * paths for them; Is 49:11
are on the same *, as brothers. Mt 23:8
Widen the pathway before him! * Lk 3:5
Jesus on a large, * area, Lk 6:17,18
They must be clean minded and * Tit 1:8

LEVEL-HEADED
HAPPY IS THE man with a * son; Pro 10:1

LEVELED
people, and * it to the ground. Ju 9:45
Babylon shall be * to the ground Jer 51:58

LEVELING
mountains and * the hills. Hab 3:6

LEVELS
valleys sank to the * you decreed. Ps 104:7,8
the strong man and * his defenses. Pro 21:22
earthquake that * a tenth of the Rev 11:13

LEVI
son, and named him * (meaning Gen 29:34
Simeon and *, took their swords, Gen 34:25
Then Jacob said to * and Simeon, Gen 34:30
*, Judah, Issachar, Zebulun. Gen 35:23
* and his sons: Gershon, Kohath, Gen 46:8-14
"Simeon and * are two of a kind. Gen 49:5
of Simeon and * were not given land Gen 49:7f
Simeon, *,Judah, Issachar, Ex 1:1
of the tribe of * who married and Ex 2:1
of *, in the order of their ages: Ex 6:16
(* lived 137 years. Ex 6:16
entire tribe of * from the draft, Num 1:47,48,49
the tribe of * and present them to Num 3:6
*, indicating each person's clan; Num 3:14,15
of the tribe of *, all of the men Num 4:21,22,23
of the tribe of * were next in the Num 10:17
a descendant of *) conspired with Num 16:1
ones, you sons of *." Num 16:6,7
be on the rod of the tribe of *. Num 17:1
the tribe of *, had budded and was Num 17:8
Your kinsmen, the tribe of *, Num 18:2,3
of * shall assist you in any way. Num 18:4
As for the tribe of *, your Num 18:21
of the tribe of *:The Libnites, the Num 26:58,59
While * was in Egypt, a daughter, Num 26:58,59
apart the tribe of * to carry the Deu 10:8
(That is why the tribe of * does Deu 10:9
the tribe of *, of all the tribes, Deu 18:5
tribes of Simeon, *, Judah, Deu 27:12
the sons of *, who carried the Ark Deu 31:9
said concerning the tribe of *: Deu 33:8
"Give to godly * Deu 33:8
You tested * at Massah and at Deu 33:8
The Land Given to the Tribe of *: Jos 13:14
to the tribe of *: instead, they Jos 13:14
to the tribe of * for, as he had Jos 13:33
THEN THE LEADERS of the tribe of * Jos 21:1
tribe of *, descendants of Aaron). Jos 21:4
of the tribe of * living on the far Ju 19:1
Didn't I choose your ancestor * 1Sa 2:28
of the tribe of * could always be 1Sa 2:30
Several men of the tribe of * 1Sa 6:15
not from the priest-tribe of *. 1Ki 12:31
Reuben, Simeon, *, Judah, 1Ch 2:1
THE names of the sons of *: 1Ch 6:1
the sons of * were: 1Ch 6:16
Korah, Izhar, Kohath, *, Israel. 1Ch 6:33-38
Shime-i, Jahath, Gershom, *. 1Ch 6:39-43
Shemer, Mahli, Mushi, Merari, *. 1Ch 6:44-47
the tribes of * and Benjamin in his 1Ch 21:6
* who were thirty years or older. 1Ch 23:3
named after the sons of *—the 1Ch 23:6
were included with the tribe of *. 1Ch 23:14,15
In the census, all the men of * 1Ch 23:24
(This census of the tribe of * 1Ch 23:27
the other descendants of *: Amram; 1Ch 24:20
These were the descendants of * in 1Ch 24:30
Over *, Hashabiah (son of Kemuel); 1Ch 27:16-22
son of * and grandson of Israel. Ez 8:18
And the men of the tribe of * Eze 44:10
of the tribe of *, continued as my Eze 44:15
the rest of their tribe of * did. Eze 48:11
one for Judah and one for *. Eze 48:30,31
*," says the Lord of Hosts. Mal 2:4
the covenant of *, and made it into Mal 2:8
the beach he saw *, the son of Mk 2:14
And * jumped to his feet and went Mk 2:14
That night * invited his fellow Mk 2:15
Matthat's father was *; Lk 3:23-38
Matthat's father was *; Lk 3:23-38
The man's name was *. Lk 5:27
So * left everything, sprang Lk 5:28
Soon * held a reception in his Lk 5:29
He was of the tribe of *, from Act 4:36
(d) One might even say that * Heb 7:9
For although * wasn't born yet, Heb 7:10
priest-tribe of *, but came from Heb 7:12,13,14
to the tribe of *, but on the basis Heb 7:16
* 12,000 Rev 7:4-8

LEVI'S
* son Gershon Num 3:16-24
* grandsons (clan names) Num 3:16-24
* son Kohath Num 3:25-30
* grandsons (clan names) Num 3:25-30
* son Merari Num 3:31-35
* grandsons (clan names) Num 3:31-35
Matthat's father was Levi;* father Lk 3:23-38
Matthat's father was Levi;* father Lk 3:23-38
Many of * fellow tax collectors Lk 5:29

LEVIATHAN
"CAN YOU CATCH * with a hook and Job 41:1
sword and punish *, the swiftly Is 27:1

LEVIED
Jerusalem, and he * a tax against 2Ki 23:33

LEVITE
Literally, "your brother the *." Ex 4:14f
(Anyone who was not a priest or * Num 3:38
Kohath division of the * tribe. Num 4:1
division of the * tribe, all of the Num 4:29
"Next, the * leaders Num 8:12
members of the * tribe will not be Deu 18:1
"Any *, no matter where he lives Deu 18:6,7
Literally, "a *." Ju 17:7,8f
Literally, "a *." Ju 17:9f
Literally, "a * as a priest." Ju 17:13f
And Mattithiah (a * and the 1Ch 9:31
and for the * leaders: Uriel, 1Ch 15:11
King David also ordered the * 1Ch 15:16
Shemaiah, a * and the son of 1Ch 24:6
of Mattaniah the *, who was one of 2Ch 20:14
Jehoiada now appointed the * 2Ch 23:18
the * clans that King David had. 2Ch 23:18
Conaniah, the *, was put in 2Ch 31:12,13
Kore (son of Imnah, the *), who 2Ch 31:14,15
offerings. The * leaders—Conaniah, 2Ch 35:9
to them by their * brothers. 2Ch 35:15
I also decree that no priest, *, Ez 7:24
and I found that not one * had Ez 8:15
and Meshullam, the * leaders; Ez 8:16
priests and the * leaders and the Ez 8:29
* opposed this course of action. Ez 10:15
Then the * leaders called out to Neh 9:5
* leaders: Neh 11:15,16,17
the Chronicles the * names were Neh 12:23
and Pedaiah the * in charge of the Neh 13:13
* priests, bless the Lord Jehovah! Ps 135:20
and my covenant with the * Jer 33:20,21
family of the * tribe, who are my Eze 43:19
Literally, "*." Lk 10:32f

LEVITE-PRIESTS
laws from the book kept by the *. Deu 17:18
Then Moses and the * addressed Deu 27:9

LEVITE'S
Noticing the young * accent, Ju 18:3

LEVITES
*, listed according to their ages. Ex 6:19
the clans of the *, and the Ex 6:25
And all the * came. Ex 32:26
Then Moses told the *, "Today Ex 32:29
* could carry on their ministry. Ex 38:21
The homes of the *, even though in Lev 25:32
for the * will not be given Lev 25:33
The * are not permitted to sell Lev 25:34
This total does not include the * Num 1:47,48,49
For the * are assigned for the Num 1:50
is moved, the * are to take it down Num 1:51
its own flag. The *' tents shall Num 1:53
was the Tabernacle, with the *. Num 2:3-31
(not including the *, who were Num 2:32,33
have accepted the * in substitution Num 3:11,12
of Israel. The * are mine in Num 3:11,12
these two clans of * was the care Num 3:25-30
four clans of * was the care of the Num 3:31-35
the leaders of the *, with special Num 3:31-35
So all the *, as numbered by Num 3:39
each name. The * shall be mine (I Num 3:41
and the *' cattle are mine as Num 3:41
"Give me the * instead of the Num 3:45
and give me the cattle of the * Num 3:45
yes, the * shall be mine; Num 3:45
the number of *, pay five dollars Num 3:46
were in excess of the number of *. Num 3:49
because the * had been given to the Num 3:49
total of all the * who were thirty Num 4:46,47,48
Give them to the * for whatever Num 7:4,5
the wagons and the oxen to the *. Num 7:6
* from the other people of Israel. Num 8:5,6
Then bring the * to the door of Num 8:9
of Israel. The * will represent all Num 8:11
to make atonement for the *. Num 8:12
Then the * are to be presented Num 8:13
will dedicate the * from among the Num 8:14
Israel, and the * shall be mine. Num 8:14
taken the * as their substitutes. Num 8:16
Yes, I have accepted the * in Num 8:18
And I will give the * as a gift Num 8:19
and his sons. The * will carry out Num 8:19
dedicated the *, carefully Num 8:20
to Moses. The * purified Num 8:21
Moses, "The * are to begin serving Num 8:23,24
has given this task to only you *? Num 16:10
itself. The * must be careful not Num 18:2,3
kinsmen the * are your assistants Num 18:6
the priests and * shall not enter Num 18:22
Only the * shall do the work Num 18:23
you, that the * shall own no Num 18:23
the altar, shall belong to the *; Num 18:24
Moses, "Tell the * to give to the Num 18:25,26
Tabernacle. You * will not be held Num 18:32
These are the clans of the * Num 26:57
The total number of * in the Num 26:62
But the * were not included in Num 26:62
of Israel, for the * were given no Num 26:62
Present this to the * in charge Num 31:30
girls (of whom 32 went to the *). Num 31:36-40
two percent of these to the *. Num 31:47
to give to the * as their Num 35:2
"You shall give the * the six Num 35:6
pastureland given to the *. Num 35:7
several to the *, while the smaller Num 35:8
and remember to invite the * to Deu 12:12
children, and the * shall eat them Deu 12:18
careful not to forget about the *. Deu 12:19
income with the * in your Deu 14:27
Give it to the * who have no Deu 14:29
include the local *, foreigners, Deu 16:11
And don't forget to include the * Deu 16:14
to the priests and *, and the chief Deu 17:9
So the priests and * are to be Deu 18:1
* who work there regularly. Deu 18:6,7
* or migrants living among you. Deu 26:11
your tithes to the *, migrants, Deu 26:12

(LEVITES Con't)
my tithes to the *, the migrants, Deu 26:13
Then the * standing between Deu 27:14
he instructed the * who carried Deu 31:25
The * shall teach God's laws to Deu 33:10
O Lord, prosper the * Deu 33:11
Ephraim, and the * were given no Jos 14:3,4
However, remember that the * Jos 18:7
give cities to us * for our homes, Jos 21:2
of the Kohath division of the *. Jos 21:9-16
division of the *, received two Jos 21:27
The remainder of the *—the Merari Jos 21:34,35
So the Merari division of the * Jos 21:40
to the * came to forty-eight. Jos 21:41,42
Abiathar and Zadok and the * 2Sa 15:24
The subclans of the * were: 1Ch 6:19,20,21
Their relatives—all the other * 1Ch 6:48
by lot to the * (and then renamed) 1Ch 6:64,65
the *, and the Temple assistants. 1Ch 9:2
Among the * who returned was 1Ch 9:14
Other * who returned included: 1Ch 9:15,16
Akkub, Talmon, and Ahiman—all *. 1Ch 9:17,18
The four head gatekeepers, all *, 1Ch 9:26
The cantors were all prominent *. 1Ch 9:33,34
From the *, 4,600. 1Ch 12:24-37
the priests and *, inviting them to 1Ch 13:2
no one except the * may carry 1Ch 15:2
These were the priests and * 1Ch 15:4-10
clans of the *," he told them. 1Ch 15:12
So the priests and the * 1Ch 15:14
Then the * carried the Ark on 1Ch 15:15
*, who was selected for his skill. 1Ch 15:22
didn't destroy the * who were 1Ch 15:26
David, the * carrying the Ark, 1Ch 15:27
He appointed certain of the * to 1Ch 16:4
and his fellow * to minister 1Ch 16:37
Now the * will no longer need to 1Ch 23:26
The work of the * was to assist 1Ch 23:28
There were always as many * 1Ch 23:31
the heads of the priests and *. 1Ch 24:6
leaders of the priests and the *. 1Ch 24:31
Like the other *, they were 1Ch 26:12
Other *, led by Ahijah, were 1Ch 26:20,21,22
various groups of priests and *; 1Ch 28:13
and * will serve in the Temple. 1Ch 28:21
watched, the * lifted the Ark and 2Ch 5:4,5
And how the * were praising the 2Ch 5:11,12
of duty, and the * were playing 2Ch 7:6
he also assigned the * to their 2Ch 8:14
However, the priests and * from 2Ch 11:13,14
the Lord and the *, and have 2Ch 13:9
priests, and the * alone may help 2Ch 13:10
He also used the * for this 2Ch 17:7,8,9
too, with the * and priests and 2Ch 19:8
with the * as their assistants. 2Ch 19:11
Then the * of the Kohath clan 2Ch 20:19
to tell the * and clan leaders 2Ch 23:2,3
of you priests and * who come off 2Ch 23:4
For only the priests and * on 2Ch 23:5,6
sanctified. You *, form a 2Ch 23:7
He summoned the priests and * 2Ch 24:5
But the * took their time. 2Ch 24:5
demanded that the * go out and 2Ch 24:6
Then the * carried the chest to 2Ch 24:11
He summoned the priests and * to 2Ch 29:4,5
"Listen to me, you *. 2Ch 29:4,5
Then the * went into action: 2Ch 29:12,13,14
their fellow * and sanctified 2Ch 29:15
found there. The * then carted it 2Ch 29:16
He organized * at the Temple into 2Ch 29:25,26
Then King Hezekiah ordered the * 2Ch 29:30
their brothers the * helped them 2Ch 29:34
to work—for the * were much more 2Ch 29:34
Then the priests and * became 2Ch 30:15
the blood received from the *. 2Ch 30:16
rites, the * killed their Passover 2Ch 30:17,18,19
Meanwhile the * and priests 2Ch 30:21
to the * of their excellent music. 2Ch 30:22
the priests, the *, the foreign 2Ch 30:25
Then the priests and * stood and 2Ch 30:27
the priests and * into service 2Ch 31:2
to the priests and *, so that they 2Ch 31:4
Hezekiah asked the priests and *. 2Ch 31:9
by clans, and the * twenty years 2Ch 31:17,18
the area, and to all registered *. 2Ch 31:19
by the * on guard duty there. 2Ch 34:9
then used by the * to pay the 2Ch 34:10,11
* of the subclan of Merari. 2Ch 34:12
The * who were skilled musicians 2Ch 34:12
Other * superintended the 2Ch 34:13
the priests and * and all the 2Ch 34:30
to the sanctified *, the religious 2Ch 35:3
to the priests and *. 2Ch 35:8
* for their Passover offerings. 2Ch 35:9
places, and the * were formed into 2Ch 35:10
then the * killed the Passover 2Ch 35:11
altar as the * removed the skins. 2Ch 35:11
Afterwards the * prepared a meal 2Ch 35:14
of the priests, *, and people from 2Ch 35:18
to the priests and *, to return to Ez 1:5
concerning the * who returned: Ez 2:40,41,42
So the priests and * and some of Ez 2:70
their fellow priests and the *. Ez 3:8
the Levites. The * who were twenty Ez 3:8
and relatives, all of whom were *. Ez 3:9
But many of the priests and * and Ez 3:12
the *, and all the people. Ez 6:16
Then the priests and * were Ez 6:18
and * had consecrated themselves. Ez 6:20
well as priests, *, singers, Ez 7:7,8,9
the priests and *, may return to Ez 7:13
assistants to the *—a job Ez 8:20
So the priests and the * accepted Ez 8:30
of Binnui)—all of whom were *. Ez 8:33
of the priests and * had taken up Ez 9:1
priests and the * and all the Ez 10:5
The * who were guilty: Ez 10:23
Next was a group of * working Neh 3:17
singers, and *, I gave the Neh 7:1
the statistics concerning the *: Neh 7:43,44,45
The priests, the *, the Neh 7:73
and the * went among the people Neh 8:7,8
governor, and the * who were Neh 8:9
And the *, too, quieted the Neh 8:11
the priests and * met with Ezra to Neh 8:13
Some of the * were on the Neh 9:4
And we and our princes and * and Neh 9:38
These were the * who signed: Neh 10:9-13
the priests; the *; Neh 10:28
of the priests, *, and leaders Neh 10:34
And we promised to bring to the * Neh 10:37
produced, for the * were Neh 10:37
be with the * as they received Neh 10:38
The people and the * were Neh 10:39,40
the priests, the *, the Temple Neh 11:3
In all, there were 284 * in Neh 11:18
The other priests, *, and people Neh 11:20
The supervisor of the * in Neh 11:22,23
Some of the * who lived in Judah Neh 11:36
The * who went with them were: Neh 12:8
of the priests and * was compiled Neh 12:22
and Jaddu-a—all of whom were *. Neh 12:22
These were the chiefs of the * at Neh 12:24
wall, all the * throughout the land Neh 12:27
The priests and * first Neh 12:30
to the priests and *, for the Neh 12:44
priests and * and their ministry. Neh 12:44
choir, the gatekeepers, and the *. Neh 12:47
the Levites. The *, in turn, gave a Neh 12:47
belonged to the *, the members of Neh 13:5
I also learned that the * had not Neh 13:10
Then I called all the * back Neh 13:11
Then I commanded the * to purify Neh 13:22
and vows of the priests and *. Neh 13:29
to the priests and *, making Neh 13:30
my priests and *, says the Lord. Is 66:21
And there shall always be * to Jer 33:18
the line of the * who minister to Jer 33:22
alone of all the * may come near to Eze 40:46
for the * who work at the Temple. Eze 45:5
assistants—the *—boil the Eze 46:24
area where the other * will live. Eze 48:12
He will purify the *, the Mal 3:3

LEVITICUS
all that was sat upon. See * 15. Gen 31:35f
See * 11:20-23. Deu 14:19,20f
See * 19:9 and Deuteronomy 24:19. Ru 2:2f
Ezekiel here refers to, in * 11. Eze 4:14f
pork or other foods outlawed in *. Dan 1:8f
Christ was crucified. See * 23:16. Act 2:1f
Implied; see * 11 for the Act 10:12f

LEVY
Also * a two percent tribute of Num 31:30
Yet I refused to make a special * Neh 5.18
Do kings * assessments against Mt 17:25

LEWD
but was still as * as in her youth, Eze 23:8
many men carousing—* men and Eze 23:42

LEWDNESS
with idols; * is everywhere. Eze 22:9
put a stop to your * and Eze 23:27
Thus will I make * and idolatry Eze 23:48
*, of worshiping your idols. Eze 24:13
deceit, *, envy, slander, pride, Mk 7:22

LIABLE
"and will be held * for any Num 18:1

LIAR
"You *!" 2Ch 18:23
Who can prove me a * and claim Job 24:25
I am called a *, even though I Job 34:6
first, he is a constant *; Pro 6:12,13
To hate is to be a *; Pro 10:18
punished and a * shall be caught. Pro 19:9
rebuke you, and you be found a *. Pro 30:6
being a *, thief, and bandit! Hos 7:1
him, "Sir, that * once said, Mt 27:63
I would be as great a * as you! Jn 8:55
in the world is a *, God is not. Rom 3:4
a *, for he says we have sinned. 1Jn 1:10
Christ tells him to, he is a *. 1Jn 2:4
And who is the greatest *? 1Jn 2:22
and he is the Truth, and no *; 1Jn 2:27
on hating his brother, he is a *; 1Jn 4:20
calling God a *, because he doesn't 1Jn 5:10

LIAR'S
but the * counsel is shunned. Pro 10:31

LIARS
he will destroy those proud * who Ps 12:3,4
Murderers and * will not live out Ps 55:23
He will rescue me from these * Ps 57:3
They are proud, cursing *. Ps 59:12,13
exult, while * shall be silenced. Ps 63:11
said in my alarm, all men are *." Ps 116:10,11f
Deliver me, O Lord, from *. Ps 120:2
Don't let * prosper here in our Ps 140:11
these *, these treacherous men. Ps 144:11
who are wicked; * enjoy liars. Pro 17:4
liars enjoy *. Pro 17:4
Track down *. Pro 19:5
are all filthy-mouthed, wicked *. Is 9:17
I am the one who shows what * all Is 44:25
You children of sinners and *! Is 57:4
They are swindlers and *, from Jer 6:13
For they are all *, and if you Jer 27:10
not conquer you, for they are *. Jer 27:14
pass make * out of every prophet.' Eze 12:22
Her "prophets" are * seeking Zep 3:4
adulterers, and *, against all Mal 3:5
for he is the father of *. Jn 8:44
and we apostles are all * 1Co 15:15
We are honest, but they call us * 2Co 6:8
kidnappers, *, and all others who 1Ti 1:10,11
they will be constant * and 2Ti 3:3
"These men of Crete are all *; Tit 1:12
worshipers and all *—their doom is Rev 21:8

LIBATION
also 2½ pints of wine, as a *. Ex 29:40
flour and the wine * as in the Ex 29:41

LIBATIONS
and * poured out to them. Jer 19:13
and to pour out * to other gods, Jer 32:29
pouring out our * to her and making Jer 44:19

LIBERAL
Yes, the * man shall be rich! Pro 11:24,25

LIBERALLY
You must lend to them *. Deu 15:11

LIBERATED
"I am Jehovah your God who * you Ex 20:2

LIBERTY
a time to proclaim * throughout the Lev 25:10
to announce * to captives and to Is 61:1

LIBNAH
From Rimmon-parez to *; Num 33:15-37
From * to Rissah; Num 33:15-37
Then the Israelis went to *. Jos 10:29
From * they went to Lachish and Jos 10:31
was slaughtered, just as at *. Jos 10:32
everyone just as they had at *. Jos 10:39
The king of *; Jos 12:8-24
Naamah, Makkedah, *, Ether, Ashan, Jos 15:37-44
*, Jattir, Eshtemoa, Holon, Debir, Jos 21:9-16
day. * also rebelled at that time. 2Ki 8:22
to his king at * (for he received 2Ki 19:8
(the daughter of Jeremiah of *) 2Ki 23:31,32
(daughter of Jeremiah of *) 2Ki 24:18,19
*, Jattir, Eshtemoa, Hilen, Debir, 1Ch 6:58,59
the yoke of Judah. * revolted too, 2Ch 21:10
left Lachish and was besieging *. Is 37:8,9
(daughter of Jeremiah of *). Jer 52:1

LIBNI
The sons of Gershon were:*, Ex 6:17
grandsons * Shime-i Num 3:16-24
The sons of Gershom were:*, 1Ch 6:17
*, Jahath, Zimmah, Joah, Iddo, 1Ch 6:19,20,21
Mahli, *, Shime-i, Uzzah, Shime-a, 1Ch 6:29,30

LIBNITES
tribe of Levi:The *, the Num 26:58,59

LIBRARY
in the royal * of Babylon to Ez 5:17
kingdom from the *, and in them he Est 6:1

LIBYA
Lud, Arabia and * and all the Eze 30:5
assistance, as well as Put and *. Nah 3:9
language areas of *, visitors from Act 2:10

LIBYANS
*, Sukkiim, and Ethiopians. 2Ch 12:3
the Ethiopians and * and their vast 2Ch 16:8
of Egypt, and the * and Ethiopians Dan 11:43

LICE
and it will become *, throughout Ex 8:16
and suddenly * infested the entire Ex 8:17

LICENTIOUS
the deeds of the * Nicolaitans, Rev 2:6

LICK
this, dogs shall * your blood 1Ki 21:19
and * the dust from off your feet; Is 49:23
* the inside to get every drop. Eze 23:34
they lap it up and * their lips Hos 4:8
would come and * his open sores. Lk 16:21

LICKED
as they * the blood of Naboth!' 1Ki 21:19
dogs came and * the king's blood 1Ki 22:38

LICKING
Hell is * its chops in Is 5:14

D

"And make a * of pure gold, 3¾ Ex 25:17
the two ends of the * of the Ark. Ex 25:18
wings spread out above the gold *. Ex 25:20
Install the * upon the Ark, and Ex 25:21
place—the golden * of the Ark—in Ex 26:34
Then, from pure gold, he made a * Ex 37:6
at the two ends of the golden *. Ex 37:7
the golden *—it was all one piece. Ex 37:8
the golden *, the place of mercy. Ex 40:20
without a * over it is defiled. Num 19:15
a hole in the * of a large chest 2Ki 12:9
clamped down the heavy * again. Zec 5:8

IE

"That's a *!" Gen 3:4
and you go in and * with him, so Gen 19:34
must never again * to us by Ex 8:29
"You must not *. Ex 20:16
the land rest and * fallow during Ex 23:11
"You must not steal nor * nor Lev 19:11
the land is to * fallow before the Lev 25:4
you refused to let it * idle; Lev 26:34,35
for it will * desolate all the Lev 26:34,35
city of Waheb, * between the Num 21:15
God is not a man, that he should * Num 23:18-24
They shall not * down Num 23:18-24
command him to * down and be beaten Deu 25:1
days of siege that * ahead. Deu 28:53
in this book shall * heavily upon Deu 29:20
You told me a *! Ju 16:10
off his feet and * down there, and Ru 3:4
* down until the morning." Ru 3:13
So he said to Samuel, "Go and * 1Sa 3:9
them * down side by side in rows. 2Sa 8:2
tent to * with his father's wives. 2Sa 16:22
She will * in your arms and keep 1Ki 1:2
"don't * to me like that!" 2Ki 4:15,16
And I begged you not to * to 2Ki 4:28
or falling, or * crushed upon the Job 4:3,4
Would I * to your face? Job 6:28
For all so soon I'll * down in Job 7:21
You will * down unafraid and Job 11:19
his bones shall * in the dust. Job 20:11
All night they * naked in the Job 24:7
on men as they * on their beds. Job 33:15
appetites as they * in their dens, Job 38:39,40
dens, or * in wait in the jungle? Job 38:39,40
His vertebrae * straight as a Job 40:18
and do not sin against him. * Ps 4:4
I will * down in peace and Ps 4:8
will * to our hearts' content. Ps 12:3,4
let them * silently in their Ps 31:17
These evil men swear to a *. Ps 35:11
They * awake at night to hatch Ps 36:4
We * face downward in the dust. Ps 44:25
You curse and *, and vile Ps 50:19
I * awake at night thinking of Ps 63:6
* before us in the sleep of death; Ps 76:5
The bodies of your people * Ps 79:2
you speak, and they * still. Ps 89:9
holy God can never *), that his Ps 89:35,36
deceive and * to stay in my house. Ps 101:7
in the desert. I * awake, lonely Ps 102:7
I am completely discouraged—I * Ps 119:25
Let them sing for joy as they * Ps 149:4,5
Their houses * along the road to Pro 2:18
wicked men * Pro 13:5
neighbor. Why * about him? Pro 24:28,29
First, help me never to tell a *. Pro 30:8
the pride of men will * in the Is 2:17
home will * deserted, their owners Is 5:9
salvation and * fallen and crushed Is 8:14,15
as prisoners or * among the slain. Is 10:4
and the lamb will * down together, Is 11:6
cubs and calves will * down Is 11:7
Your arms * paralyzed with fear; Is 13:7
The kings of the nations * in Is 14:18
The needy shall * down in peace. Is 14:30
gone; I * awake, trembling. Is 21:4
and all the idols of Babylon * Is 21:8,9
made is far too short to * on; Is 28:20
from the earth where you * buried. Is 29:4
Your roads * in ruins; Is 33:8
The land will * deserted from Is 34:10
See, all your angry enemies * Is 41:11
and horses, to * beneath the waves, Is 43:17
I'm holding in my hand, a *?" Is 44:20
For your sons have fainted and * Is 51:20
justice against every courtroom *. Is 54:17
They love to * there, love to Is 56:10
* and grumble and oppose the good. Is 59:3
and idols. We * in shame and in Jer 3:25
Your cities will * in ruin Jer 4:7
Even under oath, they *. Jer 5:2
Therefore they shall * among the Jer 6:15
by those who * to you and say that Jer 7:4
commit adultery, *, and worship Jer 7:9
She continues to live a *. Jer 7:28
For the land shall * in Jer 7:34
it that they * among the fallen. Jer 8:12
"They pile evil upon evil, * Jer 9:6
evil, lie upon *, and utterly Jer 9:6
* mortally wounded on the ground. Jer 14:17
the fields, there * the bodies of Jer 14:18
the streets, there * those dead Jer 14:18
their bodies shall * on the ground Jer 16:4
And then they proceed to * in my Jer 23:25
homes shall * in silent darkness. Jer 25:10
will * upon you and upon this city Jer 26:15
It is all a *. Jer 27:16
men, said to Jeremiah, "You *! Jer 43:2,3
wickedness they * in heaps and Jer 44:2,3
to the ground and * in ruins. Jer 47:5
of Nebo, for it shall * in ruins. Jer 48:1
All the cities of the tableland * Jer 48:21
Your young men * dead in the Jer 49:26
it shall * desolate forever. Jer 50:39
And while they * inflamed with Jer 51:39
Her cities * in ruins—she is a Jer 51:43
her dead shall * in the streets. Jer 51:47
All my little children * dead Lam 2:22
to * face downward in the dust; Lam 3:29
"Now * on your left side for 390 Eze 4:4,5
Each day you * there represents a Eze 4:4,5
Afterwards, turn over and * on Eze 4:6
of Jerusalem; * there with your arm Eze 4:7
will * scattered among the altars. Eze 6:4-7
When your slain * scattered Eze 6:13
Your slain will * within it, but Eze 11:7
But you will * no more; Eze 13:23
him a message anyway, it is a *. Eze 14:9
adultery, nor * with any woman Eze 18:6
with their fathers' wives and * Eze 22:10
to * there with those of long ago. Eze 26:20
Your city will * in ruins, dead, Eze 26:20
Now you * broken beneath the Eze 27:34
* as wastelands for forty years. Eze 29:12
and Zoan and Thebes shall * in Eze 30:14
animals will * among her branches; Eze 31:13
her friends, to * there beside the Eze 32:21
"The princes of Assyria * there Eze 32:22
"Great kings of Elam * there Eze 32:24
and now they * undone in hell; Eze 32:24
but now they * in shame in the pit, Eze 32:25
now they * dead. Eze 32:26
Now you will * crushed and Eze 32:28
mighty as they were, they too * Eze 32:29
Once a terror, now they * in Eze 32:30
lie in shame; they * in ignominy Eze 32:30
And Pharaoh and his army shall * Eze 32:32
There they will * down in peace Eze 34:14
and cause them to * down in peace, Eze 34:15,16
must * desolate for seventy years. Dan 9:2
But a further fulfillment may * Dan 11:32f
those whose bodies * dead and Dan 12:2
Then you will * down in peace and Hos 1:18
You swear and * and kill and Hos 4:2
They * there sleepless with Hos 7:14
of trusting in a *—believing that Hos 10:13
O ministers of my God, * all Joe 1:13
You * on ivory beds surrounded Amo 6:4
WOE TO YOU who * awake at night, Mic 2:1
Your finest youth * dead. Nah 2:13
O Assyrian king, your princes * Nah 3:18
What a foolish * that they could Hab 2:18
all fail, and the fields * barren; Hab 3:17
* there rotting on the ground." Zep 1:17
They will * down to rest in the Zep 2:7
All her cedar paneling will * Zep 2:14
in peace, and * down in safety, and Zep 3:13
It says that all who steal and * Zec 5:3
He did not * or cheat; Mal 2:6
don't steal, don't *, honor your Mt 19:18
who would * about Jesus, in order Mt 26:59
don't steal, don't *, don't cheat, Mk 10:19
Finally some men stood up to * Mk 14:57
don't steal, don't *, honor your Lk 18:20
So they brought in some men to * Act 6:11
that jail and suffering * ahead. Act 20:23
made the * sound like the truth. Eph 4:14
other and when we * to each other Eph 4:25
for many evils * along that path; Eph 5:18
In him * hidden all the mighty, Col 2:3
preaching the * that the 2Ti 2:18
the world began—and he cannot *. Tit 1:1
is impossible for God to tell a *. Heb 6:18
that is the worst sort of *. Jas 3:14
never told a *, never answered 1Pe 2:22
You have found out how they *. Rev 2:2
and all who love to *, and do so. Rev 22:15

LIED

"I didn't laugh," she *, for Gen 18:15
Her brothers then * to Shechem Gen 34:13
it, they have * about it and Jos 7:10,11
"Why have you * to us by saying Jos 9:22
me on a private matter," David *. 1Sa 21:2
"If I have * and deceived— but Job 31:5
They have * and said, "He won't Jer 5:12
those to whom you * when you Jer 20:6
wives and have * in my name. Jer 29:23
They * and said that all was well. Lam 2:14
Instead you have * when you Eze 13:6
and persecuted and * about because Mt 5:11
"If I *, prove it," Jesus Jn 18:23
or has cleverly * to us and made Eph 4:14

LIES

It * between Kadesh and Bered. Gen 16:14
listen to Moses' and Aaron's *!" Ex 5:9
yet that all Egypt * in ruins? Ex 10:7
Anyone who * down or eats in the Lev 14:47
Any bed he * on and anything he Lev 15:4
Anything she * on or sits on Lev 15:20
bed he * upon shall be defiled. Lev 15:24
that anything she * upon during Lev 15:26
its Sabbaths as it * desolate. Lev 26:43
last of you * dead in the desert. Num 14:33
" 'You must not tell *. Deu 5:20
to tell * on the witness stand. Deu 19:20
And of the earth that * below. Deu 33:13
which * north of the Jabbok River. Jos 12:2
me again, and told me more *!" Ju 16:13
Notice where he * down to sleep; Ru 3:4
O Israel, your pride and joy * 2Sa 1:19
of the city that * in the middle of 2Sa 24:5
tell * about them to King Cyrus. Ez 4:4,5
of our city; it * in ruins and its Neh 2:17
you use * to try to help him out. Job 13:10
drought, so a man * down for the Job 14:11,12
evil, my tongue shall speak no *. Job 27:4
he preys. He * down under the Job 40:21
You will destroy them for their *; Ps 5:6
to birth his treachery and *; Ps 7:14
full of profanity and * and fraud. Ps 10:7
deceives and flatters and *. Ps 12:2
I heard the * about me, the Ps 31:13
they plot my death and use * and Ps 62:3,4
Everything * in shambles like a Ps 74:5,6
Your wrath * heavy on me; Ps 88:7
There before me * the mighty Ps 104:25
slander me and tell their *. Ps 109:2
Let * be told about him, and Ps 109:6
enemies who tell * about me and Ps 109:20
Proud men have made up * about Ps 119:69
have cut me down with all their *. Ps 119:78
Their * have brought me into deep Ps 119:85,86
Their mouths are filled with *; Ps 144:8
* and every kind of deception. Pro 8:6,7
evil man's mind is crammed with *. Pro 12:5
* will get any man into trouble, Pro 12:13
a false man by deceit and *. Pro 12:17
Truth stands the test of time; * Pro 12:19
A good man hates *; Pro 13:5
A truthful witness never *; Pro 14:5
a false witness always *. Pro 14:5
Before every man there * a wide Pro 14:12
Before every man there * a wide Pro 16:25
Truth from a rebel or * from a Pro 17:7
Though good advice * deep within Pro 20:5
A bright future * ahead! Pro 24:13,14
Telling * about someone is as Pro 25:18
man's trouble * heavy upon him; Ecc 8:6,7
the die is cast, for there it *. Ecc 11:3
The Girl: "The king * on his Sol 1:12
Your country * in ruins; Is 1:7
Over all Israel * a pall of Is 5:30
all the land of Israel * deserted! Is 6:12
Transjordan, where * the road to Is 9:1
though our land * in ruins now, we Is 9:8,9,10
Babylon, in Iraq, still * in utter Is 13:20f
broken branch; it * in an open Is 14:19
in battle. It * as a carcass in the Is 14:19
The city * in chaos; Is 24:10
tell us *. Is 30:10,11
in frauds and * and won't repent, Is 30:12
Their * about God and their Is 32:6
as will all the * they use to Is 32:7
Your lawsuits are based on *; Is 59:4
are, for we carefully plan our *. Is 59:13
land, until it * in utter ruin; Jer 4:20
and spread their slanderous *. Jer 9:4
For their tongues aim * like Jer 9:8
theirs, for it is all a pack of *. Jer 10:2,3
prophets are telling * in my name. Jer 14:14
Hosts: As this jar * shattered, so Jer 19:11
* that lead my people into sin. Jer 23:32
they are telling you * in my name. Jer 27:15
the people are believing your *. Jer 28:15
for they prophesy * in my name. Jer 29:9
who are declaring * to you in my Jer 29:21
into believing his *, I will Jer 29:31
And they reply, "Moab * in Jer 48:20
the earth, * broken and shattered. Jer 50:23
he makes, for in making them he *; Jer 51:17
They are *! Jer 51:18
Now she * in the gutter with no Lam 1:9
the fairest city of Israel * in Lam 2:1
you for these 'visions' and *. Eze 13:8
Your * have discouraged the Eze 13:22
have told you * of safety and Eze 21:29
Asher's territory * south of Eze 48:2
Naphtali's land * south of Eze 48:3
Next to it * the area where the Eze 48:12
South of Benjamin's area * that Eze 48:24

(LIES Con't)
your city * in ruins for our sins. Dan 9:16
how your city * in ruins—for Dan 9:18
the princes laugh about their *. Hos 7:3
Israel is destroyed; she * among Hos 8:8
Israel surrounds me with * and Hos 11:12
Ahead of them the land * fair as Joe 2:3
"Beautiful Israel * broken and Amo 5:2
the people of God * empty and Nah 2:2
full of *, crammed with plunder. Nah 3:1
"Nineveh * in utter ruin." Nah 3:7
be sinners, full of * and deceit. Zep 3:13
homes, when the Temple * in ruins? Hag 1:3,4
Because my Temple * in ruins and Hag 1:9
are all a bunch of silly *; Zec 10:2
glorious Jordan valley * in ruins. Zec 11:3
* in the name of the Lord.' Zec 13:3
When he *, it is perfectly Jn 8:44
save me from what * ahead'? Jn 12:27
be staggered [by all that * ahead. Jn 16:1
deliberately chose to believe *. Rom 1:25
his honesty in contrast to my *. Rom 3:7
Their tongues are loaded with *. Rom 3:13
So the judgment of God * very Rom 3:19
forward to what * ahead, I strain Php 3:13
Don't tell * to each other; Col 3:9
them to believe * with all their 2Th 2:11
But the answer * in Christ, who 1Ti 3:16
These teachers will tell * with 1Ti 4:2
Then, knowing what * ahead for Heb 6:12
guard your lips from telling *. 1Pe 3:10
They will cleverly tell their * 2Pe 2:1

LIEUTENANT
to even the least * in charge of 2Ki 18:24
*, arrested Jesus and tied him. Jn 18:12

LIEUTENANTS
delivered to his * and the Ez 8:36

LIFE
fish and other *, and let the skies Gen 1:20
to be the master of all * upon Gen 1:26
breathed into it the breath of *. Gen 2:7
placed the Tree of *, and also the Gen 2:9
All your * you will struggle to Gen 3:17
All your * you will sweat to Gen 3:19
the Tree of * and lives forever?" Gen 3:22
the entrance to the Tree of *. Gen 3:24
in which there is the breath of *. Gen 6:17
be every kind of * reproducing Gen 7:3
the floods come and destroy all *. Gen 9:15
because of you, and spare my *!" Gen 12:11,12,13
Literally, "when * would be Gen 18:10f
to me and saved my *, and you've Gen 19:18,19,20
And my * will be saved." Gen 19:18,19,20
eliminating all *—people, plants, Gen 19:25
is first in your *—you have not Gen 22:12
For he feared for his * if he Gen 26:7
Isaac: "Yours will be no * of Gen 27:39,40
* was being threatened by Esau. Gen 27:42
to face, and yet my * is spared." Gen 32:30
Reuben hoped to spare Joseph's *. Gen 37:21,22
god-like power of * and death!" Gen 41:45
I swear by the * of Pharaoh that Gen 42:15
that our father's * is bound up in Gen 44:30
up in the lad's *— when he sees Gen 44:30
*, wonderfully bless these boys. Gen 48:15
have a long, good * in the land the Ex 20:12
his * whatever is laid upon him." Ex 21:30f
full quota of the days of your *. Ex 23:26
among all animal * upon the earth. Lev 11:47
For the * of the flesh is in the Lev 17:11
atonement, because it is the *. Lev 17:11
dust, for the blood is the *. Lev 17:14
for the * of every bird and animal Lev 17:14
food, for it is his source of *. Lev 22:7
Literally, "shall make it good, * Lev 24:18f
make it good, life for *." Lev 24:18f
and your * shall ebb away; Lev 26:16
like this before in my entire *?" Num 22:30
* in the land he is giving you. Deu 5:16
and that real * comes by obeying Deu 8:3
a long and good * in the land the Deu 11:9
enjoy the good * awaiting you in Deu 11:21
the blood is the *, and you shall Deu 12:20-23
shall not eat the * with the meat. Deu 12:20-23
every day of his * so that he will Deu 17:19
a false witness. * for life, eye Deu 19:21
Life for *, eye for eye, tooth Deu 19:21
have a long, good * in the land Deu 25:13,14,15
set before you * and death, Deu 30:15
you will not have a long, good * Deu 30:18
you * or death, blessing or curse. Deu 30:19
Oh, that you would choose *; Deu 30:19
* and the length of your days. Deu 30:20
not mere words—they are your *! Deu 32:47
him deeply all the rest of his *. Jos 4:14
They offered to spare his * and Ju 1:24
chariots, and made * unbearable for Ju 4:2,3
you and risked his * and delivered Ju 9:17
have a long and happy * together. Ju 9:19
so I risked my * and went to Ju 12:3
Their manner of * was Phoenician, Ju 18:7
The Lord gives *. 1Sa 2:6
judge for the remainder of his *. 1Sa 7:15
We vow by the * of God that not 1Sa 14:45
time he risked his * to kill 1Sa 19:5
I'll protect you with my own *. 1Sa 22:23
you have been hunting for my *? 1Sa 24:11
I pray by the * of God, and by your 1Sa 25:26
and by your own * too, that all 1Sa 25:26
do wrong throughout your entire *. 1Sa 25:28
who seek your *, you are safe in 1Sa 25:29
out to hunt my * like a partridge 1Sa 26:20
for you saved my * today. 1Sa 26:21
Now may the Lord save my *, even 1Sa 26:24
for *," Achish told him. 1Sa 28:2
your command at the risk of my *. 1Sa 28:21
terrible pain but * lingers on.' 2Sa 1:9
They were together in * and in 2Sa 1:23
was childless throughout her *. 2Sa 6:23
you with a longer * if you will 2Sa 14:14
Or, "God does not sweep * away, 2Sa 14:14f
my son because my * and my son's 2Sa 14:15,16
life and my son's * have been 2Sa 14:15,16
and by your own * that wherever you 2Sa 15:21
it means * or death." 2Sa 15:21
"We saved your * today and the 2Sa 19:5
have ever been in your entire *." 2Sa 19:7
he vowed, "Your * is spared." 2Sa 19:23
and * has lost its excitement. 2Sa 19:35
If you want to save your own * 1Ki 1:12
own life and the * of your son 1Ki 1:12
asked for a long * or riches for 1Ki 3:11
as you for the rest of your *! 1Ki 3:13
And I will give you a long * if 1Ki 3:14
reign for the rest of his *. 1Ki 11:34
during his entire * except for the 1Ki 15:5
true servant of the Lord all my *. 1Ki 18:12
So Elijah fled for his *; 1Ki 19:3
"Take away my *. 1Ki 19:4
Naboth replied, "Not on your *! 1Ki 21:3
please spare my * and the lives of 2Ki 1:13
There was no sign of *. 2Ki 4:31
I God, that I can kill and give *? 2Ki 5:7
brought back to *, "Take your 2Ki 8:1
brought a little boy back to *. 2Ki 8:5
one Elisha brought back to *!" 2Ki 8:5
then run for your *!" 2Ki 9:3
pay for it with your own *." 2Ki 10:24
All his * Joash did what was 2Ki 12:2
There was a plot against his * 2Ki 14:19
years to his * and save him and 2Ki 20:6
the remainder of my own *!" 2Ki 20:19
The rest of the history of the * 2Ki 24:5
allowance for the rest of his *. 2Ki 25:30
asked for a long *, but for wisdom 2Ch 1:11
But at the close of his *, 2Ch 20:35
and his whole * was one constant 2Ch 21:6
The other details of his * and 2Ch 28:26
of joy and new * in our slavery. Ez 9:8
a priest, I would forfeit my *. Neh 6:11
the rest of her *, never seeing the Est 2:12,13,14
my * and the lives of my people. Est 7:3
to plead for his * to Queen Esther, Est 7:7
will give anything to save his *. Job 2:4,5
"only spare his *." Job 2:6
"Oh, why should light and * be Job 3:20,21
* of uselessness and frustration? Job 3:23
Their candle of * is snuffed Job 4:21
You shall live a long, good *; Job 5:26
A man's * is long and hard, like Job 7:1
* flies by—day after hopeless day. Job 7:6
hopeless day. My * is but a Job 7:7
I hate my *. Job 7:16
made my * so heavy a burden to me? Job 7:20
"My * passes swiftly away, Job 9:25
Is your * so short that you must Job 10:4-7
You gave me * and were so kind Job 10:12
And your * will be cloudless; Job 11:17
Yes, I will take my * in my hand Job 13:14
of *—months is all you give him! Job 14:5
upon the stage of *, and notice Job 14:16
in trouble throughout his *. Job 15:20
to snuff out any sign of *. Job 16:9
to * when anyone else would die. Job 24:22,23
cuts him off and takes away his *? Job 27:8
in my nest after a long, good *.' Job 29:18
For God has placed my * in Job 30:11
breath of the Almighty gives me *. Job 33:4
his Spirit, all * would disappear Job 34:15
getting into a * of evil that God Job 36:21
let you make him your slave for *? Job 41:4
his * more than at the beginning. Job 42:12
and trample my * in the dust. Ps 7:5
fish, and all the * in the sea. Ps 8:8
whose only goal in * is money. Ps 10:3
Anyone who leads a blameless * Ps 15:2
the joys of * and the exquisite Ps 16:11
He asked for a long, good *, and Ps 21:4
the days of his * stretch on and Ps 21:4
spare my precious * from all Ps 22:20
with me all of my *, and afterwards Ps 23:6
Deliver my * from their power! Ps 25:20
every day of my *, delighting in Ps 27:
his favor lasts for *! Ps 30:
they were plotting against my *. Ps 31:1
place from every storm of *; Ps 32:
along the best pathway for your *; Ps 32:
Do you want a long, good *? Ps 34:1
for I have but one * and these Ps 35:1
For you are the Fountain of *; Ps 36:
My * is no longer than my hand! Ps 39:5,
and pray to God who gives me *. Ps 42:
to buy eternal * for just one soul, Ps 49:8,
You have no greater lease on * Ps 49:1
all through his *—and the world Ps 49:1
deeds. His * is corroded with sin. Ps 53:
nothing for God are seeking my * Ps 54:
They lurk in ambush for my *. Ps 59:
added years of *, as rich and Ps 61:6
are better to me than * itself. Ps 63:
Oh, preserve my * from the Ps 64:1
be blotted out of the book of *." Ps 69:28
do not give them the joys of * Ps 69:28
They are after my *, and delight Ps 70:2,3
But you will bring me back to * Ps 71:20
Yes, all through * their road is Ps 73:4
a finger—theirs is a * of ease; Ps 73:12
Their present * is only a dream! Ps 73:20
my * with your wisdom and counsel; Ps 73:24
oh, listen to my cry, for my * Ps 88:3
They say my * is ebbing out—a Ps 88:4
O Lord, I plead for my * and will Ps 88:13
why have you thrown my * away? Ps 88:14
Is it an empty, futile * you give Ps 89:47
Who can rescue his * from the Ps 89:48
I will satisfy him with a full * Ps 91:16
Literally, "with long *." Ps 91:16f
thrown me out. My * is passing Ps 102:11
He has cut me down in middle *, Ps 102:23
He fills my * with good things! Ps 103:5
teeming with * of every kind, both Ps 104:25
your Spirit, and new * is born Ps 104:30
I am shaken off from * as easily Ps 109:22,23
Bless me with * Ps 119:17
Therefore in fairness renew my *, Ps 119:40,41,42
them and will let them fill my *. Ps 119:48
In your kindness, spare my *; Ps 119:88
oh, give me back my * again, just Ps 119:107
your desires. My * hangs in the Ps 119:109
* again just as you have promised. Ps 119:154
oh, give me back my * again. Ps 119:156
Now give me back my * and health Ps 119:159
all evil, and preserves your *. Ps 121:7
even * forevermore. Ps 133:3
his plans for my *—for your Ps 138:8
of my * before I began to breathe. Ps 139:16
along the path of everlasting *. Ps 139:24
His breathing stops, * ends, and Ps 146:4
*, and murder is their specialty. Pro 1:16
being, filling your * with joy. Pro 2:10
"never return to the ways of *." Pro 2:19f
only good men enjoy * to the full; Pro 2:21
*, closely follow my instructions. Pro 3:1
Wisdom gives:A long, good * Pro 3:16,17
Wisdom is a tree of * to those Pro 3:18
will have a long and happy *. Pro 4:4
and you will have a long, good *. Pro 4:10
great fact: that a * of doing right Pro 4:11
right is the wisest * there is. Pro 4:11
If you live that kind of *, Pro 4:12
* for you, and radiant health. Pro 4:22
everything else in your *. Pro 4:23
she does not know the path to *. Pro 5:6
your * to the cruel and merciless; Pro 5:9
danger and to give you a good *. Pro 6:23
may cost him his very *. Pro 6:26
For whoever finds me finds * and Pro 8:35
years of your * more fruitful." Pro 9:11
corrected is on the pathway to *. Pro 10:17
the wicked expect a long, good *? Pro 10:27
are based upon this earthly *. Pro 11:7
The good man finds *; Pro 11:19
The path of the godly leads to *. Pro 12:28
him all through *, while evil men Pro 13:6
The good man's * is full of Pro 13:9
true at last, there is * and joy. Pro 13:12
Literally, "it is a tree of *." Pro 13:12f
the godly man's * is exciting. Pro 14:14
for the Lord is a fountain of *; Pro 14:27
attitude lengthens a man's *; Pro 14:30
Gentle words cause * and health; Pro 15:4
fellow has trouble all through *; Pro 15:19
Wisdom is a fountain of * to Pro 16:22
the commandments and keep your *; Pro 19:16
If you don't you will ruin his *. Pro 19:18
and be wise the rest of your *. Pro 19:20
Reverence for God gives *, Pro 19:23
rouse his anger is to risk your *. Pro 20:2
An evil man lives an evil *; Pro 21:8
a good man lives a godly *. Pro 21:8
finds *, righteousness and honor. Pro 21:21
a man to riches, honor and long *. Pro 22:4
him, but help him all her *. Pro 31:12

(LIFE Con't)
So now I hate * because it is Ecc 2:17
For though I spend my * searching Ecc 2:20-23
hasn't done a day's work in his *; Ecc 2:20-23
bring them back to * to enjoy what Ecc 3:22
All the rest of his * he is Ecc 5:17
his position in *, and enjoy his Ecc 5:18
*—that is indeed a gift from God. Ecc 5:19,20
who is wise lives a far better *. Ecc 6:7,8
that nothing is certain in this *. Ecc 7:14
In this silly * I have seen Ecc 7:15-17
fleeting days of *, for the wife Ecc 9:9
in every day of *, but let him also Ecc 11:8
with a whole * before it, can make Ecc 11:10
the silver cord of * snaps, and the Ecc 12:6
city will come back to * again; Is 23:15,16
All the joys of * will go: the Is 24:7
For God's light of * will fall Is 26:19
"My * is but half done and I Is 38:10
in this world. My * is blown away Is 38:12
In one short day my * hangs by a Is 38:12
is good and leads to * and health. Is 38:16
of the future * for those who trust Is 38:18f
Every day of my * from now on I Is 38:20
in it, and gives * and breath and Is 42:5
and destroy its *, so now I swear Is 54:9
Listen, for the * of your soul Is 55:3
tries a better * is soon attacked. Is 59:15
gods without * or power in them. Jer 10:14
of man to map his * and plan his Jer 10:23
doom and give you * and joy again? Jer 11:15
of his * become a poor old fool. Jer 17:11
For my * has been but trouble and Jer 20:18
Take your choice of * or death! Jer 21:8
His * will amount to nothing. Jer 22:30
This very year your * will end Jer 28:16
Their * shall be like a watered Jer 31:12
according to his * and deeds. Jer 32:19
to the men who were after his *. Jer 38:16
the Lord; your * will be spared and Jer 38:20
your * and keep you safe." Jer 39:18
who seek his *, just as I turned Jer 44:30
for there is a plot against her *. Jer 48:2,3,4
the thread of your * is cut. Jer 51:13
not a breath of * in them at all! Jer 51:17
in prison for the rest of his *. Jer 52:11
For you have redeemed my *. Lam 3:58
Our king—the * of our life, the Lam 4:20
Our king—the life of our *, the Lam 4:20
and save your *—they will die in Eze 3:18
you have saved your own * too." Eze 3:21
been defiled before in all my *. Eze 4:14
And you have promised * to those Eze 13:19
by promising *, though they Eze 13:22
to destroy all *: war, famine, Eze 14:21
that kind of *, and doesn't go up Eze 18:14
from his sins and live a good *. Eze 18:28
even though obeying them means *. Eze 20:13
of them they could not attain *. Eze 20:25
by which they could not have *." Eze 20:25f
he would have saved his *. Eze 33:5
this will be your *, until you Dan 4:25
of * and controls your destiny! Dan 5:23
to everlasting * and some to shame Dan 12:2
the end of your * and your rest; Dan 12:13
may Judah stay far from such a *. Hos 4:15
I was locked out of * and Jon 2:6
was to give him * and peace, to be Mal 2:5
good and righteous *, and turned Mal 2:6
For you already have * and a Mt 6:25
add a single moment to your *? Mt 6:27
* and live as he wants you to. Mt 6:33
But the Gateway to * is small, Mt 7:14
bring her back to * again if you Mt 9:18
"If you cling to your *, you Mt 10:39
hear, and the dead raised to *; Mt 11:5
much depth in his *, and the seeds Mt 13:21
the cares of this * and his longing Mt 13:22
the Baptist, come back to * again. Mt 14:2
he would be raised to * again. Mt 16:21
For anyone who keeps his * for Mt 16:25
and anyone who loses his * for me Mt 16:25
whole world—and lose eternal *? Mt 16:26
with the value of eternal *? Mt 16:26
will be brought back to * again." Mt 17:22,23
must I do to have eternal *?" Mt 19:16
return, and shall have eternal *. Mt 19:29
day I will rise to * again." Mt 20:19
give my * as a ransom for many." Mt 20:28
righteous into everlasting *." Mt 25:46
brought back to * again I will go Mt 26:32
who had died came back to * again. Mt 27:52
days I will come back to * again.' Mt 27:63
everyone he came back to *! Mt 27:64
For he has come back to * again, Mt 28:6
straighten out his * to be ready Mk 1:3
the Baptist come back to * again. Mk 6:14
prophet, now returned to * again; Mk 6:15
prophet come back to * again." Mk 8:28
If you insist on saving your *, Mk 8:35
later I will return to * again." Mk 9:30,31

to come he shall have eternal *. Mk 10:30
I will come back to * again." Mk 10:34
give my * as a ransom for many." Mk 10:45
But after I am raised to * Mk 14:28
He has come back to *! Mk 16:6
Jesus came back to *, and the first Mk 16:9
'Other things in * are much more Lk 4:4
To save *, or to destroy it?" Lk 6:9
he said, "come back to * again." Lk 7:14
The dead come back to *. Lk 7:20,21,22
of liquor all his *, and you said, Lk 7:33
and pleasures of *. Lk 8:14
And at that moment her * Lk 8:55
Baptist come back to * again"; Lk 9:7
I will come back to * again!" Lk 9:22
Whoever loses his * for my sake Lk 9:24
on keeping his * will lose it; Lk 9:24
without eternal * concern Lk 9:60
For real * and real living are Lk 12:15
to wear. For * consists of far Lk 12:23
it add a single day to your *? Lk 12:25
more than his own *—otherwise he Lk 14:26
was dead and has returned to *. Lk 15:24
was dead and has come back to *! Lk 15:32
Whoever clings to his * shall Lk 17:33
whoever loses his * shall save it. Lk 17:33
eternal * in the world to come." Lk 18:30
raised up in new * from the dead. Lk 20:36
*, like all the rest of the world. Lk 21:34,35
He has come back to * again! Lk 24:6,7
Eternal * is in him, and this Jn 1:4
this * gives light to all mankind. Jn 1:4
all mankind. His * is the light Jn 1:5
After he came back to * again, Jn 2:22
Men can only reproduce human *, Jn 3:6
Spirit gives new * from heaven; Jn 3:6
next bestow this * from heaven." Jn 3:8
in me will have eternal *. Jn 3:15
not perish but have eternal *. Jn 3:16
Son—to save them have eternal *; Jn 3:36
them forever with eternal *." Jn 4:14
me has eternal *, and will never be Jn 5:24
passed out of death into *. Jn 5:24
The Father has * in himself, and Jn 5:26
his Son to have * in himself, and Jn 5:26
who have done good, to eternal *; Jn 5:29
believe they give you eternal *. Jn 5:39
I can give you this * eternal! Jn 5:40
the eternal * that I, the Messiah, Jn 6:27
and he gives * to the world." Jn 6:33
replied, "I am the Bread of *. Jn 6:35
them to eternal * at the Last Day. Jn 6:39
have eternal *—that I should raise Jn 6:40
in me already has eternal *! Jn 6:47
Yes, I am the Bread of *! Jn 6:48-51
eternal * to everyone who eats it. Jn 6:48-51
cannot have eternal * within you. Jn 6:53
blood has eternal *, and I will Jn 6:54
the Holy Spirit gives eternal *. Jn 6:63
how to get this true spiritual *. Jn 6:63
that give eternal *, and we Jn 6:68
My purpose is to give * in all Jn 10:10
The Good Shepherd lays down his * Jn 10:11
and I lay down my * for the Jn 10:15
* that I may have it back again. Jn 10:17
lay down my * voluntarily. Jn 10:18
I give them eternal * and they Jn 10:28
my brother back to * again, if you Jn 11:22
will come back to * again." Jn 11:23
the dead and gives them * again. Jn 11:25
He is given eternal * for Jn 11:26
man he had brought back to *. Jn 12:1
man who had come back to * again. Jn 12:9
to * were telling all about it. Jn 12:17
If you love your * down here—you Jn 12:25
If you despise your * down Jn 12:25
instructions lead to eternal *; Jn 12:50
Way—yes, and the Truth and the *. Jn 14:6
When I come back to * again, you Jn 14:20
lays down his * for his friends; Jn 15:13
He gives eternal * to each one Jn 17:2
to have eternal *—by knowing you, Jn 17:3
said he would come to * again! Jn 20:9
believing in him you will have *. Jn 20:30,31
events in Jesus' * were written, Jn 21:25
I told you about Jesus' * and Act 1:1
him back to * again, for death Act 2:24
'You will give me back my *, and Act 2:28
And you killed the Author of *; Act 3:15
but God brought him back to * Act 3:15
his servant to * again, he sent him Act 3:26
God raised back to * again. Act 4:10
Temple and preach about this *!" Act 5:20
Jesus back to * again after you had Act 5:30
For his * is taken from the Act 8:33
never in all my * eaten such Act 10:14
But God brought him back to * Act 10:40,41
to him and receiving eternal *!" Act 11:18
"But God brought him back to * Act 13:30
God brought Jesus back to * again. Act 13:32,33
back to * again, no more to die. Act 13:34

—someone God brought back to *, Act 13:37
of eternal *—well, we will offer it Act 13:46
eternal *, believed. Act 13:48
his coming back to *, and proving Act 17:3
He himself gives * and breath to Act 17:25
by bringing him back to * again." Act 17:31
him not to risk his * by entering. Act 19:31
Jews against his *, so he decided Act 20:3
plots of the Jews against my *. Act 20:19
lie ahead. But * is worth nothing Act 20:24
God can bring men back to * again? Act 26:8
man who finds * will find it Rom 1:17
He will give eternal * to those Rom 2:7
glory and honor and eternal * Rom 2:7
of change in his * will get his Rom 2:29
sins and gives glorious * instead. Rom 5:16
and acquittal are kings of * Rom 5:17
Literally, "reign in *." Rom 5:17f
* through Jesus Christ our Lord. Rom 5:21
him back to * again, you were given Rom 6:4
his wonderful new * to enjoy. Rom 6:4
and now you share his new *, and Rom 6:5
that you will share his new *. Rom 6:8
holiness and everlasting *. Rom 6:22
* through Jesus Christ our Lord. Rom 6:23
Then you came back to * again Rom 7:4
show me the way of * resulted Rom 7:10
It seems to be a fact of * that Rom 7:21
So you see how it is: my new * Rom 7:23,24,25
Spirit leads to * and peace, but Rom 8:6
you will give you *, for he has Rom 8:10f
is * because of righteousness." Rom 8:10f
and came back to * again for us and Rom 8:34
Death can't, and * can't. Rom 8:38
He gave you his rules for daily * Rom 9:4
temptation all his * and never sin Rom 10:5
to bring Christ back to * again." Rom 10:7
like dead people coming back to *. Rom 11:15
he has enriched your whole *. 1Co 1:5
have your * through Christ Jesus. 1Co 1:30
in the Christian *, who are not 1Co 3:1
world to use, and * and even death 1Co 3:22
in the Christian *, leaving 1Co 5:8
the cancerous old * with all its 1Co 5:8
made everything and gives us *. 1Co 8:6
come into your * aren't anything 1Co 10:13
will never come back to * again? 1Co 15:12
dead do not come back to * again. 1Co 15:15
only now in this *, we are the most 1Co 15:19
who will come back to * again 1Co 15:20
not come back to * again, then what 1Co 15:29
what I gain in this * down here? 1Co 15:32
dead be brought back to * again? 1Co 15:35
* again, for they will never die. 1Co 15:42
when we come back to * again. 1Co 15:43
* they will be superhuman bodies. 1Co 15:44
but we tell them there is * for 2Co 3:6
way, the Holy Spirit gives them *. 2Co 3:6
when the Holy Spirit is giving *? 2Co 3:8
who gives them *, and where he is 2Co 3:17
has resulted in eternal * for you. 2Co 4:12
bring us back to * again with 2Co 4:14
be swallowed up by everlasting *. 2Co 5:4
died to the old * we used to live. 2Co 5:13,14
received eternal * from him—might 2Co 5:15
A new * has begun! 2Co 5:17
away from sin and seek eternal *. 2Co 7:10
see in my * and my message. 2Co 12:6
eternal * he gives through Christ; Gal 1:6
And the real * I now have within Gal 2:20
gave you spiritual * in the first Gal 3:3
man who finds * will find it Gal 3:11
even in everyday * a promise made Gal 3:15
has given eternal * don't need to Gal 5:6
that sort of * will not inherit the Gal 5:21
* which the Holy Spirit gives him. Gal 6:8
they are far away from the * of Eph 4:17,18
things of this * more than God. Eph 5:5
(He gave his very * to take care Eph 5:23
be a long *, full of blessing. Eph 6:3
has given you eternal * with him. Php 1:28
holding out to them the Word of *. Php 2:16
for he risked his * for the work Php 2:30
him back to * again, and to find Php 3:10
fresh newness of * of those who are Php 3:11
about is this * here on earth. Php 3:19
are written in the Book of *. Php 4:3
him into a new * because you Col 2:12
share in the very * of Christ, for Col 2:13
Your real * is in heaven with Col 3:3
who is our real * comes back again, Col 3:4
things of *, for that is idolatry. Col 3:5
You used to do them when your * Col 3:7
it was your old * with all its Col 3:9
brand new kind of * that is Col 3:10
who created this new * within you. Col 3:10
In this new * one's nationality Col 3:11
this new kind of *, and because of Col 3:12
love guide your *, for then the Col 3:14
brought back to *—and he is our 1Th 1:10
to live a quiet *, minding your own 1Th 4:11

(LIFE Con't)
then came back to * again, we can 1Th 4:14
they, too, can have everlasting *. 1Ti 1:16
by giving his * for all mankind. 1Ti 2:6
whose * cannot be spoken against. 1Ti 3:2
a godly * is not an easy matter. 1Ti 3:16
this *, but in the next life too. 1Ti 4:8
this life, but in the next * too. 1Ti 4:8
are the foundation for a godly *. 1Ti 6:3
Hold tightly to the eternal * 1Ti 6:12
God who gives * to all, and before 1Ti 6:13
Christian * down here as well. 1Ti 6:19
thing in *—they don't know God. 1Ti 6:21
about the eternal * he has promised 2Ti 1:1
purpose in * is to please him. 2Ti 1:3
* through trusting him. 2Ti 1:10
this * and went to Thessalonica. 2Ti 4:10
can have eternal *, which God Tit 1:1
carefully, taking * seriously. Tit 2:6
of the eternal * he gives us, and Tit 3:7
in the Christian *, and doesn't Heb 5:12,13
others as long as * lasts, so that Heb 6:11
never died but his * is like that Heb 7:3
flowing from a * that cannot end. Heb 7:16
to lay down my *, just as the Heb 10:7
I have come to give my *." Heb 10:9
would bring him back to * again; Heb 11:19
the end of his *, confidently spoke Heb 11:22
rise to a better * afterwards. Heb 11:35
a clean and holy *, for one who is Heb 12:14
Dear brothers, is your * full of Jas 1:2
the crown of * that God has Jas 1:12
is wrong in your *, both inside and Jas 1:21
If you are wise, live a * of Jas 3:13
hope of eternal * because Christ 1Pe 1:3
the priceless gift of eternal *; 1Pe 1:4
For you have a new *. 1Pe 1:23
* they gave you will fade away. 1Pe 1:23
sin and live a good * from now on. 1Pe 2:24
If you want a happy, good *, keep 1Pe 3:10
the rest of your * chasing after 1Pe 4:2
a truly good *: he even shares his 2Pe 1:3
him from the old * of sin so that 2Pe 1:9
a strong, good * for the Lord. 2Pe 1:9
He is God's message of *. 1Jn 1:1
This one who is * from God has 1Jn 1:2
of Christ, who is eternal *. 1Jn 1:2
light of * in Christ shines in. 1Jn 2:8
has promised us this: eternal *. 1Jn 2:25
because now God's * is in him; 1Jn 3:9
for this new * has been born into 1Jn 3:9
Whoever is living a * of sin and 1Jn 3:10
brother's * was better than his. 1Jn 3:12
from hell and given eternal *. 1Jn 3:14
to murder has eternal * within. 1Jn 3:15
to us eternal * through his death. 1Jn 4:9
That he has given us eternal *, 1Jn 5:11
and that this * is in his Son. 1Jn 5:11
So whoever has God's Son has *; 1Jn 5:12
not have his Son, does not have *. 1Jn 5:12
you may know you have eternal *. 1Jn 5:13
God will give him *, unless he has 1Jn 5:16
and he is eternal *. 1Jn 5:20
me that your * stays clean and 3Jn 1:3
holy, but turned to a * of sin. Jud 1:6
whole purpose in * is to enjoy Jud 1:18
Wait patiently for the eternal * Jud 1:21
to occur in the * of Jesus Christ. Rev 1:1
Tree of * in the Paradise of God. Rev 2:7
was dead and then came back to *. Rev 2:8
of *—an unending, glorious future. Rev 2:10
from the Book of *, but I will Rev 3:5
to the springs of the Water of *. Rev 7:17
the spirit of * from God will enter Rev 11:11
in the Book of * of the Lamb slain Rev 13:8f
Lamb's Book of *—worshiped the Rev 13:8
wounded and then came back to *. Rev 13:14
in the Book of * before the world Rev 17:8
They had come to * again and now Rev 20:4
not come back to * until the Rev 20:5
opened, including the Book of *. Rev 20:12
in the Book of *, he was thrown Rev 20:15
of the Water of *—as a gift! Rev 21:6
written in the Lamb's Book of *. Rev 21:27
of pure Water of *, clear as Rev 22:1
Literally, "the tree of *"—used Rev 22:2f
of *, bearing twelve crops of Rev 22:2
eat the fruit from the Tree of *. Rev 22:14
the Water of * without charge. Rev 22:17
in the Tree of *, and in the Holy Rev 22:19

LIFE-BLOOD
their * has been drained off. Gen 9:4

LIFE-GIVING
to a Hebrew word that means "*." Gen 3:20f
"The * one"), for he said, Gen 3:20
a tree that bears * fruit, and all Pro 11:30
me, the Fountain of * Water; Jer 2:13
still be light. * waters will flow Zec 14:8
For the power of the * Rom 8:2
than that, for he was * Spirit. 1Co 15:45
know Christ we are a * perfume. 2Co 2:16

This is the fresh, new, * way Heb 10:20

LIFE'S
answer to one of * most perplexing Ps 49:4

LIFEBLOOD
And if my * is, so to speak, to Php 2:17
with the precious * of Christ, the 1Pe 1:19
sins by pouring out his * for us. Rev 1:5

LIFEBOAT
hoisted aboard the * that was being Act 27:16

LIFELESS
* mound and may never be rebuilt. Deu 13:16
Or, "to * idols." Ps 106:28f
Woe to those who command their * Hab 2:19

LIFELONG
There was * war between King Asa 1Ki 15:16
the offer of my * service. Ps 40:6

LIFESPAN
how short you have made man's *. Ps 89:47

LIFETIME
It was during his * that men Gen 4:26
for during his * the people of the Gen 10:25
God has done for you during my *. Jos 23:3
Joshua's *, and as long afterward Ju 2:7-9
throughout his *, for the Lord was Ju 2:18
forty years—all during Gideon's *. Ju 8:28
he had killed during his entire *. Ju 16:30
for his entire *, and his hair 1Sa 1:11
the remainder of Samuel's *. 1Sa 7:13
Philistines throughout Saul's *. 1Sa 14:52
me during my own *, but also to my 1Sa 20:14
to serve him throughout his *. 1Ki 4:21
Throughout the * of Solomon, all 1Ki 4:25
During Solomon's entire *, Rezon 1Ki 11:25
do what I promised during his *; 1Ki 21:29
it was during his * that the people 1Ch 1:19
during Abijah's *, and eventually 2Ch 13:20
before God throughout his *. 2Ch 15:17
the * of Jehoiada the priest. 2Ch 24:2
the * of Jehoiada the priest. 2Ch 24:14
upon them during Hezekiah's *. 2Ch 32:26
remainder of his * they continued 2Ch 34:33
My whole * is but a moment to Ps 39:5,6
there will be peace during my *!" Is 39:8
through all your *, yes, even when Is 46:4
says: In your own *, before your Jer 16:9
You will be in Babylon for a *. Jer 29:10
I will do it in your own *!" Eze 12:25
during Hosea's *—Zechariah, Hos 7:7f
In all your *, yes, in all your Joe 1:2
in your own * that you will have to Hab 1:5
that during your * you had Lk 16:25
occur during their *, but long 1Pe 1:12

LIFETIMES
throughout the * of Joshua and the Jos 24:31
In these few days of our empty *, Ecc 6:12
Whatever they did in their * Ecc 9:6

LIFT
Then Jehovah said to Moses, "* Ex 10:21
you won't need to * a finger!" Ex 14:14
and fruit just to * my head above Ju 9:11
then go and * the cover off his Ru 3:4
I blush to * up my face to you, Ez 9:6
someone who will * you up again. Job 22:29
You alone can * my head, now Ps 3:3
Lord, I * my hands to heaven Ps 28:2
in front. * your spear in my Ps 35:3
they never have to * a Ps 73:12
Literally, "* not up the horn." Ps 75:4f
not one can * a hand against us. Ps 76:5
O GOD ENTHRONED in heaven, I * Ps 123:1
every night. * your hands in Ps 134:2
He is too tired even to * his Pro 26:15
* up your eyes and see! Is 60:4
Sharpen the arrows! * up the Jer 51:11
and they shall * to the skies their Jer 51:14
I will * my hand against you and Jer 51:25
with no one left to * her out. Lam 1:9
the Lord; * up your hands to him; Lam 2:19
Let us * our hearts and hands to Lam 3:41
As they watch, * your pack to Eze 12:6
You stood aloof, refusing to * a Ob 1:11
O Israel, * your eyes to see what Mal 1:5
and dared not even * his eyes to Lk 18:13
* you up, encourage and help you. Jas 4:10
in his good time he will * you up. 1Pe 5:6

LIFTED
And Abraham took the knife and * Gen 22:10
She quickly * the jug down from Gen 24:46
so he * it to place it on Gen 48:17
of the city and * his hands to Ex 9:33
So Moses * his rod and Jehovah Ex 10:13
Whenever the cloud * and moved, Ex 40:36
When the Cloud *, the people of Num 9:17
The Cloud * from the Tabernacle Num 10:11
Then Moses * the rod and struck Num 20:11
away from him! I * the tablets Deu 9:17
the city gates and * them, with the Ju 16:3
Then Ruth came quietly and * the Ru 3:6,7
the tribe of Levi * the Ark and the 1Sa 6:15
"I * you out of the dust," the 1Ki 16:2
the Levites * the Ark and carried 2Ch 5:4,5

So they * him out of his chariot 2Ch 35:24,25
then I fell to my knees and * my Ez 9:5
and * their hands toward heaven; Neh 8:6
heard my cry. He * me out of the Ps 40:2
Your right hand is * high in Ps 89:13
redeemed them and * them up and Is 63:9
them when Moses * up his hand, and Is 63:12
When the siege was temporarily * Jer 34:11f
Then the Spirit * me up and the Eze 3:12
The Spirit * me up and took me Eze 3:14,15
And the Spirit * me up into the Eze 8:3
THEN THE SPIRIT * me and brought Eze 11:1
Then the cherubim * their wings Eze 11:22
that Daniel be * from the den. Dan 6:23
But a hand touched me and * me, Dan 10:10
He replied, with both hands * to Dan 12:7
on the basket was * off, and I Zec 5:7
And as Moses in the wilderness * Jn 3:14
even so I must be * up upon a pole, Jn 3:14
Literally, "when you have * up Jn 8:28f
And when I am * up [on the cross Jn 12:32
that the soldiers * Paul to their Act 21:35
been saved— and * us up from the Eph 2:6
with holy hands * up to God, free 1Ti 2:8
the sea and land * his right hand Rev 10:5

LIFTING
* the boat high above the earth. Gen 7:17
* up my hands to you in prayer. Ps 63:4
All night long I pray, * my hands Ps 77:2
to Bethany, and * his hands to Lk 24:50

LIFTS
And * another up. 1Sa 2:7
He * the poor from the dust— 1Sa 2:8
he stoops to look, and * the Ps 113:7
The Lord * the fallen and those Ps 145:14
of the blind; he * the burdens from Ps 146:8
Literally, "and * high its Hab 3:10f

LIGHT
God said, "Let there be *." Gen 1:3
And * appeared. Gen 1:3
divided the * from the darkness. Gen 1:4,5
He called the * "daytime," and Gen 1:4,5
in the sky to give * to the earth Gen 1:14,15
And God set them in the sky to * Gen 1:17
to divide the * from the darkness. Gen 1:18
found no place to *, and returned Gen 8:9
without a ray of * will descend Ex 10:21
people of Israel had * as usual. Ex 10:23
but * to the people of Israel! Ex 14:20
to normal beneath the morning *. Ex 14:27
that they reflect their * forward. Ex 25:37
Don't even * the fires in your Ex 35:3
and spices, and oil—for the *, Ex 35:28
in the lampstand and * the lamps. Ex 40:4
the oil for the *, the sweet Num 4:16
they will throw their * forward." Num 8:2
with various * duties in the Num 8:25,26
tomorrow and * them, and put Num 16:6,7
that you will see the morning *. Deu 28:66
*, we'll find him and kill him." Ju 16:2
and lay there until it was *. Ju 19:26
and leave as soon as it is *." 1Sa 29:10
before you in a different *. 2Sa 14:20
snuffing out the * of Israel?" 2Sa 21:17
O Lord, you are my *! 2Sa 22:29
He shall be as the * of the 2Sa 23:4
But when it became * outside, I 1Ki 3:21
to * the wood is the true God!" 1Ki 18:24
with * shields and spears. 2Ch 14:8
Let it long for *, but never see Job 3:9
see it, never see the morning *. Job 3:9
have never breathed or seen the *. Job 3:16
"Oh, why should * and life be Job 3:20,21
brightest * is dark as midnight.' Job 10:22
He floods the darkness with *, Job 12:22
and groping, without a guiding *. Job 12:24,25
the kingdom of * into darkness, and Job 18:18
path and turned my * to darkness. Job 19:8
And the * of heaven will shine Job 22:28
"The wicked rebel against the * Job 24:13
are not acquainted with the *. Job 24:16
And his * shines down on all the Job 25:3
Men know how to put * into Job 28:3,4
* the things that are hidden." Job 28:11f
I waited for the *. Job 30:26
go on living in the realm of *.' Job 33:28
may live in the * of the living. Job 33:30
Where does the * come from, and Job 38:19
to the distribution point of *? Job 38:24
O Lord, by letting the * of your Ps 4:6
give me * in my darkness lest I Ps 13:3
You have turned on my *! Ps 18:28
has made my darkness turn to *. Ps 18:28
us wise, and give us joy and *. Ps 19:7,8
THE LORD IS my * and my salvation; Ps 27:1
of life; our * is from your Light. Ps 36:9
our light is from your *. Ps 36:9
with the blazing * of justice Ps 37:6
Oh, send out your * and your Ps 43:3
For Jehovah God is our * and our Ps 84:11
walk in the * of your presence. Ps 89:14,15

(LIGHT Con't)
from the wicked. * is sown for the Ps 97:11
with honor and with majesty and *! Ps 104:1
of flame at night to give them *. Ps 105:39
When darkness overtakes him, * Ps 112:4
Jehovah God is our *. Ps 118:27,28
Your laws are both my * and my Ps 119:24
Your words are a flashlight to Ps 119:105
the night becomes * around me. Ps 139:11
Darkness and * are both alike to Ps 139:12
ever-brightening * of God's favor; Pro 4:18
For their advice is a beam of * Pro 6:23
The good man's life is full of *. Pro 13:9
God puts out the * of the man who Pro 20:20
future; his * will be snuffed out. Pro 24:19,20
finally come to * for all to see. Pro 26:24,25,26
this: each depends on God for *. Pro 29:13
just as * is better than darkness; Ecc 2:13,14
when the sun and * and moon and Ecc 12:2
let us walk in the * of the Lord, Is 2:5
for they have no * or truth in Is 8:20
shall see a great *—a Light that Is 9:2
a great Light—a * that will shine Is 9:2
God, the * and Holy One of Is 10:17
above them. No * will shine from Is 13:10
For God's * of life will fall Is 26:19
You shall also be a * to guide Is 42:6
I form the * and make the dark. Is 45:7
I will make you a * to the Is 49:6
without one ray of *, let them Is 50:10
live in your own *, and warm Is 50:11
shed his own glorious * upon you. Is 58:8
Then your * will shine out from Is 58:10
in darkness when you expected *. Is 59:9
Let your * shine for all the Is 60:1
All nations will come to your *; Is 60:3
moon to give you *, for the Lord Is 60:19
*, and he will be your glory. Is 60:19
Lord will be your everlasting *; Is 60:20
then, when you look for *, you Jer 13:16
I will * a fire in the forests Jer 21:14
moon and stars to * the night, and Jer 31:35
for the Lord will * a fire in the Jer 50:32
darkness, shutting out all *. Lam 3:2
the heavens will * upon you and the Eze 32:4
the moon shall not give you her *. Eze 32:7
things, for he is *, and darkness Dan 2:22
and the stars withdraw their *. Joe 3:15
For that day will not be * and Amo 5:18
the Lord himself will be my *. Mic 7:8
*, and I will see his goodness. Mic 7:9
hands flash rays of brilliant *. Hab 3:4
evening time it will still be *. Zec 14:7
in darkness have seen a great *; Mt 4:15,16
the * broke through upon them." Mt 4:15,16
You are the world's *—a city on Mt 5:14
Don't hide your *! Mt 5:15,16
for I give you only * burdens." Mt 11:29,30
give *, and the stars will seem Mt 24:29
a box over it to shut out the *? Mk 4:21
Of course not! The * couldn't be Mk 4:21
now hidden will someday come to *. Mk 4:22
upon us, to give * to those who Lk 1:79
He is the * that will shine upon Lk 2:32
shall be brought to * and made Lk 8:17
dazzling white and blazed with *. Lk 9:29
give * to all who enter the room. Lk 11:33
Your eyes * up your inward Lk 11:34
A lustful eye shuts out the * and Lk 11:34
If you are filled with * within, Lk 11:36
be heard in the *, and what you Lk 12:3
until it has risen high and *." Lk 13:20,21
Won't she * a lamp and look in Lk 15:8
Literally, "sons of the *." Lk 16:8f
o'clock. The * from the sun was Lk 23:45
this life gives * to all mankind. Jn 1:4
His life is the * that shines Jn 1:5
that Jesus Christ is the true *. Jn 1:6,7
John himself was not the *; Jn 1:8
who is the true * arrived to shine Jn 1:9
fact: that the * from heaven came Jn 3:19
the *, for their deeds were evil. Jn 3:19
They hated the heavenly * Jn 3:20
They stayed away from that * for Jn 3:20
come gladly to the * to let Jn 3:21
people, "I am the * of the world. Jn 8:12
living * will flood your path." Jn 8:12
in the world, I give it my *." Jn 9:5
Jesus replied, "My * will shine Jn 12:35
Make use of the * while there is Jn 12:36
then you will become * bearers." Jn 12:36
Literally, "sons of *." Jn 12:36f
I have come as a * to shine in Jn 12:46
a brilliant * from heaven spotted Act 9:3
there was a * in the cell and an Act 12:7
'I have made you a * to the Act 13:47
* from heaven shone around me. Act 22:6
The men with me saw the * but Act 22:9
"I was blinded by the intense *, Act 22:11
about noon, sir, a * from heaven Act 26:13
and live in the * of God instead of Act 26:18
* to Jews and Gentiles alike." Act 26:23
Just then a * wind began blowing Act 27:13
*, Paul begged everyone to eat. Act 27:33
will turn on the * so that everyone 1Co 4:5
see the glorious * of the Gospel 2Co 4:4
"Let there be * in the darkness," 2Co 4:6
But this precious treasure—this * 2Co 4:7
How can * live with darkness? 2Co 6:14
into an angel of *, so is it no 2Co 11:14
be flooded with * so that you can Eph 1:18
now it is full of * from the Lord, Eph 5:8
Because of this * within you, Eph 5:9
But when you expose them, the * Eph 5:13
may even become children of *! Eph 5:13
and Christ shall give you *." Eph 5:14
who live in the kingdom of *. Col 1:12
children of the * and of the day, 1Th 5:5
But let us who live in the * 1Th 5:8
die, who lives in * so terrible 1Ti 6:16
the Creator of all *, and he shines Jas 1:17
the darkness into his wonderful *. 1Pe 2:9
words, then the * will dawn in your 2Pe 1:19
you: that God is * and in him is no 1Jn 1:5
But if we are living in the * of 1Jn 1:7
new * of life in Christ shines in. 1Jn 2:8
is walking in the * of Christ but 1Jn 2:9
"walking in the *" and can see 1Jn 2:10
Great bursts of * flashed forth Rev 4:3
of sun or moon to * it, for the Rev 21:23
it. Its * will light the nations Rev 21:24
Its light will * the nations of Rev 21:24
the Lord God will be their *; Rev 22:5

LIGHTED
Then he * the lamps before the Ex 40:25
The golden lampstand is * every 2Ch 13:11
of me, when he * the way before me Job 29:3
the lightning * up the world! Ps 77:18
landscape * up with his glory. Eze 43:2
was * with many flickering lamps; Act 20:8
throne were seven * lamps Rev 4:5

LIGHTEN
the cargo overboard to * the ship. Jon 1:5
make me happy and * all my cares. Php 2:28

LIGHTENED
them, and * their spirits. Job 29:24
After eating, the crew * the Act 27:38

LIGHTER
Don't be surprised then by the * Eze 16:52

LIGHTING
Apparently * from time to time Gen 8:7f
"Who ever heard of someone * a Lk 8:16

LIGHTLY
and he does not * let them die. Ps 116:15
She treated it all so *—to her Jer 3:9
promises. You * broke your solemn Eze 16:59,60
wrong will be punished only *. Lk 12:48

LIGHTNING
Lord sent thunder and hail and *. Ex 9:23
thunder and * storm, and a huge Ex 19:16
All the people saw the * and the Ex 20:18
That I will whet the * of my Deu 32:40,41
He shot forth his arrows of * 2Sa 22:15
Then * struck them and killed 2Ki 1:10
of the rain and a path for the *. Job 28:26
See how he spreads the * around Job 36:30
He fills his hands with * bolts. Job 36:32
* flashes out in every direction. Job 37:3
and they send forth his *. Job 37:11
lightning. The * bolts are Job 37:12
* to flash forth from the clouds? Job 37:15
Who laid out the path for the *, Job 38:25-27
Can you make * appear and cause Job 38:35
like * across the vapor droplets. Job 41:18
broke through the clouds with * Ps 18:12
of * and routed all my enemies. Ps 18:14
the Lord thunders through the *. Ps 29:7
in the sky. Your * flashed. Ps 77:17
the * lighted up the world! Ps 77:18
Their sheep were killed by *. Ps 78:48
* flashes out across the world. Ps 97:4
* flashes overwhelmed the nation. Ps 105:32
the * to bring down the rain; Ps 135:7
Let loose your * bolts, your Ps 144:6
he sends the * and brings the Jer 10:13
he brings the * with the rain and Jer 51:16
it was from these the * flashed. Eze 1:13
darted to and fro, swift as *. Eze 1:14
it flashes like *; Eze 21:15
and polished and flashes like *. Eze 21:28
flashes like *, and his eyes were Dan 10:5,6
like *, gleaming like torches. Nah 2:4
His arrows shall fly like *; Zec 9:14
he will answer with * and showers. Zec 10:1
For as the * flashes across the Mt 24:27
His face shone like * and his Mt 28:3
from heaven as a flash of *! Lk 10:18
It will be as evident as the * Lk 17:24
upon their heads. * and thunder Rev 4:5
and rumbled, * flashed, and there Rev 8:5
be seen inside. * flashed and Rev 11:19
crashed and rolled, and * flashed; Rev 16:18

LIGHTS
there be bright * in the sky to Gen 1:14,15
For God made two huge *, the sun Gen 1:16
evening when he * the lamps he Ex 30:8
Aaron that when he * the seven Num 8:2
made the heavenly *, for his Ps 136:7
Wisdom * up a man's face, Ecc 8:1
And yet, even the lesser * in the Mt 11:11
"When someone * a lamp, does he Mk 4:21
"No one * a lamp and hides it! Lk 11:33
jailer called for * and ran to the Act 16:29
as beacon *, directing men who are Rom 2:19
them like beacon *, holding out to Php 2:15
written, for, like * shining into 2Pe 1:19

LIKE
—someone * ourselves, Gen 1:26
So God made man * his Maker. Gen 1:27
* God did God make man; Gen 1:27
it you will become * him, for your Gen 3:5
of Adam—the man who was * Gen 5:1
a man is to kill one made * God. Gen 9:5,6
someone as being "* Nimrod—a Gen 10:9
the whole section was * the Gen 13:10
or * the beautiful countryside Gen 13:10
* dust, they can't be counted! Gen 13:16
Your descendants will be * Gen 15:5
an old woman * me have a baby?' Gen 18:13
you can get up as early as you * Gen 19:2
deserves treatment * this, to make Gen 20:9,10
you would do a thing * this to me? Gen 20:9,10
and millions, * the stars above you Gen 22:17
* the sands along the seashore. Gen 22:17
Which sounds a little * the Hebrew Gen 25:25f
it just the way I * it—savory and Gen 27:2,3,4
a Hebrew word sounding * the name. Gen 30:6f
you mean by sneaking off * this?" Gen 31:26
you have rushed them away * this? Gen 31:26
"Should he treat our sister * a Gen 34:31
often as you * to purchase grain.' Gen 42:34
"Why did you have to treat me * Gen 43:6
they are acting * this when their Gen 44:4
But Jacob's heart was * a Gen 45:26
are shepherds * our ancestors. Gen 47:3
anywhere you * for them to live. Gen 47:5,6
"Dan shall govern his people * Gen 49:16
They are not slow * the Egyptian Ex 1:19
The name Moses sounds * another Ex 2:10f
your own Hebrew brother * that?" Ex 2:13
not the person for a job * that!" Ex 3:11
"Don't treat us * this," they Ex 5:15
mistreat your own people * this? Ex 5:22
is no one * the Lord our God. Ex 8:10
It will spread * fine dust over Ex 9:9
had there been a storm * that. Ex 9:24
been a plague * this will be!' Ex 10:6
will never again be another * it. Ex 10:14
They went down into the depths * a Ex 15:5
Who else is * the Lord among the Ex 15:11
Who is glorious in holiness * him? Ex 15:11
it was white, * coriander seed, Ex 16:31
flat, and tasted * honey bread. Ex 16:31
you know what it's * to be a Ex 23:9
top looked * a raging fire. Ex 24:17
are not told what they looked *. Ex 25:18f
will be engraved upon it * a seal. Ex 28:21
What these looked * has been lost Ex 28:30,31f
any incense * it or puts any of it Ex 30:33
two stone tablets * the first ones Ex 34:1
tablets of stone * the first ones, Ex 34:4
he can cut and set stones * a Ex 35:33
of work, just * the ephod, made Ex 39:8
The stones were engraved * a Ex 39:14
lump that looks * leprosy, then he Lev 13:43
God, so don't act * heathen—like Lev 18:3
act like heathen—* the people of Lev 18:3
They must be treated * any other Lev 19:34
nor treat my Tabernacle * an Lev 21:12
around it—are * farmland, Lev 25:31
be given farmland * the other Lev 25:33
seed, and looked * droplets of gum Num 11:7
* pancakes fried in vegetable oil. Num 11:8
me the burden of a people * this? Num 11:11
nursing them along * babies until Num 11:12
If you are going to treat me * Num 11:15
and see what the land is *; Num 13:18
see also what the people are * Num 13:18
We felt * grasshoppers before Num 13:33
You must wander in the desert * Num 14:33
"This mob will eat us * an ox Num 22:4
"Because you have made me look * Num 22:29
"Have I ever done anything * Num 22:30
He doesn't change his mind * Num 23:18-24
If you turn away from God * Num 32:15
to anyone they *, so long as it is Num 36:6
Lord has multiplied you * stars! Deu 1:10
"This seemed * a good idea, so I Deu 1:23
and chased them * bees and killed Deu 1:44
can find anything * this: An Deu 4:32
that there is no one else * him. Deu 4:35
more stone tablets * the first Deu 10:1
two stone tablets * the first two, Deu 10:3

(LIKE Con't)

and possess is not * the land of	Deu 11:10
it out on the ground, * water.	Deu 12:16
insult the Lord your God * that!	Deu 12:31
pour it out upon the ground *	Deu 15:23
to have a king * the other nations	Deu 17:14
given property * the other tribes.	Deu 18:1
of the Lord, just * his brother	Deu 18:6,7
for you a Prophet * me, an Israeli,	Deu 18:15
them a Prophet, an Israeli * you.	Deu 18:18
decide you don't * her, you must	Deu 21:14
"IF A MAN doesn't * something	Deu 24:1
swooping down upon you * an eagle;	Deu 28:49
of vegetation—just * Sodom and	Deu 29:23
land, what these people are *."	Deu 31:21
* the gentle rain and dew,	Deu 32:2
* rain upon the tender grass,	Deu 32:2
* showers on the hillside.	Deu 32:2
Is not * our Rock;	Deu 32:31
They act * men of Sodom and	Deu 32:32
He crouches * a lion,	Deu 33:20
"Dan is * a lion's cub	Deu 33:22
There is none * the God of	Deu 33:26
another prophet * Moses, for the	Deu 34:10
hearing things * that, for your God	Jos 2:11
going to help me * that, then do	Ju 6:17
to their mouths and lap it * dogs.	Ju 7:5,6
Purah if you *— and listen to what	Ju 7:10
across the valley * locusts—yes,	Ju 7:12,13
like locusts—yes, * the sand upon	Ju 7:12,13
at Tabor—what were they *?"	Ju 8:18
just * you—like sons of kings!"	Ju 8:18
just like you—* sons of kings!"	Ju 8:18
Doesn't it look * people coming	Ju 9:36
seeing shadows that look * men!"	Ju 9:36
if they would * to hear a riddle,	Ju 14:12
* thread and fell from his wrists!	Ju 15:14
Then he snapped the bowstrings *	Ju 16:9
Literally, "* a string of tow	Ju 16:9f
ropes from his arms * spiderwebs!	Ju 16:12
want, chasing after us * this?"	Ju 18:23
do whatever you * to them—but don't	Ju 19:24
"Praise the Lord for a man *	Ru 2:20
"Thank God for a girl * you!"	Ru 3:10
sounds * the word "to ask."	1Sa 1:19,20f
Nor any Rock * our God.	1Sa 2:2
linen robe just * the priest's.	1Sa 2:18
to face anything * this before!	1Sa 4:7
but they were not * their	1Sa 8:3
"Give us a king * all the other	1Sa 8:5
it will be * to have a king!"	1Sa 8:9
to be * the nations around us.	1Sa 8:20
feel and act * a different person.	1Sa 10:6
added, "With a father * his?"	1Sa 10:12
"A command * that only hurts us.	1Sa 14:29
talking * that, he was angry.	1Sa 17:28
"How can a kid * you fight with	1Sa 17:33
like you fight with a man * him?	1Sa 17:33
to see what it was *, for he had	1Sa 17:38,39
and he began to rave * a madman.	1Sa 18:10
can a poor man * me from an unknown	1Sa 18:23
hide something * this from me.	1Sa 20:2
night they were * a wall of	1Sa 25:15,16
He is a fool—just * his name	1Sa 25:25
disappear * stones from a sling!	1Sa 25:29
* a partridge on the mountains?"	1Sa 26:20
"What does he look *?"	1Sa 28:14
to you when you talk * this?	1Sa 30:24
Saul is dead. Be * the tribe of	2Sa 2:7
Asahel could run * a deer, and	2Sa 2:18
dog to be kicked around * this?"	2Sa 3:8
"Should Abner have died * a	2Sa 3:33,34
"He burst through my enemies * a	2Sa 5:20
When you hear a sound * marching	2Sa 5:24
the street * a common pervert!"	2Sa 6:20
So I am willing to act * a fool	2Sa 6:21
For you know what I am *!	2Sa 7:20
heard of any other god * you.	2Sa 7:22
kindness to a dead dog * me?"	2Sa 9:8
We must really act * men today if	2Sa 10:12
be guilty of acting * that."	2Sa 11:11
he cuddled it in his arms * a	2Sa 12:3
* that should be put to death;	2Sa 12:5
for helping me * this."	2Sa 14:9
our lives are * water that is	2Sa 14:14
I know that you are * the angel	2Sa 14:17
"At last I know that you * me!	2Sa 14:22
"The first man looks * Ahima-az,	2Sa 18:27
and yet you act * this, making us	2Sa 19:5
"Don't talk to me * that!"	2Sa 19:22
* mountain goats upon the rocks.	2Sa 22:34
* dust along the streets.	2Sa 22:43
"Use anything you *," Araunah	2Sa 24:22
can cut timber * you Sidonians!"	1Ki 5:6
cedar beams, just * the inner court	1Ki 7:12
its brim was shaped * a goblet,	1Ki 7:26
there is no god * you in heaven or	1Ki 8:22,23
even so, I'd * to go back home."	1Ki 11:22
will shake Israel * a reed whipped	1Ki 14:15
people of Judah, * those in Israel,	1Ki 14:22
He pleased the Lord * his	1Ki 15:11
But he was not a good king; *	1Ki 15:26
For he, too, had sinned *	1Ki 16:19
will take away whatever they *!"	1Ki 20:5,6
Recruit another army * the one	1Ki 20:25
but the Israeli army looked * two	1Ki 20:27
here? I'd * to ask him, too."	1Ki 22:7
"Don't talk * that!"	1Ki 22:8
"What did he look *?"	2Ki 1:7
"don't lie to me * that!"	2Ki 4:15,16
and he would * $2,000 in silver and	2Ki 5:22
would be scattered * manure upon	2Ki 9:36
But he was an evil man, for, *	2Ki 13:11
not quite * his ancestor David;	2Ki 14:3
Amaziah had. But * his	2Ki 15:4
opinion, just * his ancestors.	2Ki 15:9
his ancestors. * Jeroboam I (the	2Ki 15:9
a good king. * his father Uzziah,	2Ki 15:34,35
Uriah built one just * it by	2Ki 16:11,12
another land just * this one—with	2Ki 18:31,32
They were * grass shriveling	2Ki 19:26
the hot sun, and * grain blighted	2Ki 19:26
celebration * that since the days	2Ki 23:22
was never another * it in all the	2Ki 23:22
Character of his reign: evil, *	2Ki 23:31,32
Character of his reign: evil, *	2Ki 23:36,37
Character of his reign: evil, *	2Ki 24:18,19
Jabez sounds * ozeb, the Hebrew	1Ch 4:9f
as their right! * King Saul, they	1Ch 12:2
* water bursting through a dam!"	1Ch 14:11
When you hear a sound * marching	1Ch 14:15
and saw him dancing * a madman.	1Ch 15:29
O Lord, there is no one *	1Ch 17:20
even heard of another god * you!	1Ch 17:20
in all the earth is * Israel?	1Ch 17:21
Be courageous and let us act *	1Ch 19:13
the handle of his spear was * a	1Ch 20:5
various clans. * the descendants	1Ch 24:31
after the leaders. * the other	1Ch 26:12
Israel * to the stars of heaven."	1Ch 27:23f
our days on earth are * a shadow,	1Ch 29:15
lumber was used * common sycamore!	2Ch 1:15
flaring out * the cup of a lily.	2Ch 4:5
* you in all of heaven and earth.	2Ch 6:14
to give them a just king * you!	2Ch 9:8
just wait and see what I'll be *!'	2Ch 10:10
instead. Just * the people of other	2Ch 13:9
"I'd * to ask him the same	2Ch 18:6,7
"Oh, come now, don't talk *	2Ch 18:6,7
that in a time * this—whenever we	2Ch 20:9
in the fire, just * the heathen	2Ch 28:3
Do not be * your fathers and	2Ch 30:7
seen a celebration * this one since	2Ch 30:26
and to see what he was really *.	2Ch 32:31
It was an evil reign * the early	2Ch 33:22
You look * a man with deep	Neh 2:1
against the king * this?"	Neh 2:19
* theirs," the people protested.	Neh 5:5
I would * to mention that for the	Neh 5:14
they sank * stones beneath the	Neh 9:11
and do as you * with these	Est 3:11
was, and why he was acting * that.	Est 4:5
If you keep quiet at a time *	Est 4:14
do anything you * with his wealth,	Job 1:12,13
But he replied, "You talk * some	Job 2:10
my groans pour out * water.	Job 3:24
and destroyed. * aged, helpless	Job 4:11
They grope * blind men in the	Job 5:14
a long, good life; * standing	Job 5:26
Am I unfeeling, * stone?	Job 6:12
That would be * injuring a	Job 6:27
A man's life is long and hard, *	Job 7:1
than go on and on * this.	Job 7:15
"How long will you go on * this,	Job 8:2
Job, blowing words around * wind?	Job 8:2
They are * rushes without any	Job 8:11-13
and virile, * a green plant;	Job 8:16
My years disappear * swift	Job 9:26
like swift ships, * the eagle that	Job 9:26
* men?	Job 10:4-7
bottle to bottle * milk, and	Job 10:10
milk, and curdled me * cheese.	Job 10:10
you leap upon me * a lion and	Job 10:16
that the Lord does things * that?	Job 12:7,8,9
And as you say, older men * me	Job 12:12
every side. I am * a fallen, rotten	Job 13:27,28
rotten tree, * a moth-eaten coat.	Job 13:27,28
He blossoms for a moment * a	Job 14:2
touch of water, * a new seedling.	Job 14:8,9
How much less someone * you, who	Job 15:16
to the ground * a withered grape.	Job 15:33
me, running upon me * a giant.	Job 16:14
Have we become * animals to you,	Job 18:3
I am * a foreigner to them.	Job 19:15
forever, cast away * his own dung.	Job 20:7
He will fade * a dream.	Job 20:8
It is * poison and death to him.	Job 20:16
even to deal with people * that.	Job 21:16
driven before the wind * straw?	Job 21:18
that I should say a thing * that.	Job 22:18
they must get out of the way. *	Job 24:5
For wicked men are broken * a	Job 24:20
they shall be gone * all others,	Job 24:24
others, cut off * heads of grain.	Job 24:24
accumulate money * dust, with	Job 27:16
They sound * animals among the	Job 30:7
to all)— or if, * Adam, I have	Job 31:33
I would treasure it * a crown.	Job 31:36
I am * a wine cask without a	Job 32:19
He opens their ears in times *	Job 33:16
you, Job, are speaking * a fool.	Job 34:34,35
Job, you have spoken * a fool."	Job 35:16
Who is a teacher * him?	Job 36:22
Can you stalk prey * a lioness,	Job 38:39,40
able to leap forward * a locust?	Job 39:20
"Stand up * a man and brace	Job 40:7
He eats grass * an ox.	Job 40:15
His ribs are * iron bars.	Job 40:18
Can you make a pet of him * a	Job 41:5
sunlight sparkles * lightning	Job 41:18
His eyes glow * sparks.	Job 41:18
Smoke flows from his nostrils, *	Job 41:20
hard as rock, just * a millstone.	Job 41:24
he drags across the ground * a	Job 41:30
They are * trees along a river	Ps 1:3
They blow away * chaff before the	Ps 1:4
smash them * clay pots!"	Ps 2:9
murder passersby. * lions they	Ps 10:9
upon the poor. * hunters they catch	Ps 10:9
gently with people who act * that;	Ps 12:3,4
all he says is purest truth, *	Ps 12:6
Anyone who talks * that is	Ps 14:1
They eat my people * bread and	Ps 14:4
Why am I praying * this?	Ps 17:6
They are * lions eager to tear	Ps 17:12
to tear me apart, * young lions	Ps 17:12
He is * the strong horn of a	Ps 18:2
I threw them away * sweepings	Ps 18:42
Literally, "is * a bridegroom."	Ps 19:5f
me with open jaws, * roaring lions	Ps 22:13
My strength has drained away *	Ps 22:14
My heart melts * wax;	Ps 22:14
my strength has dried up *	Ps 22:15
men, circles me * a pack of dogs;	Ps 22:16
No, I am not * that, O Lord;	Ps 26:11
dismantle them * old buildings,	Ps 28:5
Lead them * a shepherd and carry	Ps 28:9
They leap and skip before him *	Ps 29:5,6
I am forgotten * a dead man,	Ps 31:12
man, * a broken and discarded pot.	Ps 31:12
protects me * the walls of a fort!	Ps 31:21
My strength evaporated * water on	Ps 32:4
Don't be * a senseless horse or	Ps 32:9
he protects us * a shield.	Ps 33:20
Blow them away * chaff in the	Ps 35:5
Soon they fade away * grass and	Ps 37:2
* grass, and disappear like smoke.	Ps 37:20
like grass, and disappear * smoke.	Ps 37:20
evil man, towering * a cedar of	Ps 37:35,36
They are * a flood, higher than	Ps 38:3,4
upon me * a thundering cataract.	Ps 42:7
Their taunts pierce me * a	Ps 42:10
You have treated us * sheep in a	Ps 44:11
We are * sheep awaiting	Ps 44:22
some day be kings * their father.	Ps 45:16
they are filled with panic * a	Ps 48:6
You must die * all the rest!	Ps 49:10
his pomp must die * any animal.	Ps 49:12
in the end he dies * everyone else,	Ps 49:19
must die * any animal.	Ps 49:20
and they—guilty * me—will repent	Ps 51:13
But I am * a sheltered olive tree	Ps 52:8
For they devour my people * bread	Ps 53:4
Oh, for wings * a dove, to fly	Ps 55:6
But it was you, a man * myself,	Ps 55:13
Their tongues are * swords.	Ps 57:4
Let them disappear * water into	Ps 58:7
trodden down and wither * grass."	Ps 58:7f
around * dogs that prowl the city.	Ps 59:6
* dogs and searching for food.	Ps 59:14,15
they aim their bitter words *	Ps 64:3
O Lord, * silver in a crucible.	Ps 66:10
Drive them off * smoke before	Ps 68:2
melt them * wax in fire!	Ps 68:2
God scattered their enemies *	Ps 68:14
Where is there another God * you?	Ps 71:19
* showers that water the earth!	Ps 72:6
may there be fruit * that of	Ps 72:16
with problems * everyone else, so	Ps 73:5
pride sparkles * a jeweled	Ps 73:6
I must seem * an animal to you, O	Ps 73:22
Everything lies in shambles * a	Ps 74:5,6
along that road * a flock of sheep,	Ps 77:20
from the rock, flowing * a river!	Ps 78:16
of them * sands along the shore!	Ps 78:27
in a moment * a breath of wind.	Ps 78:39
But he led forth his own people *	Ps 78:52
their fathers had. * a crooked	Ps 78:57
from sleep, and * a mighty man	Ps 78:65
blood has flowed * water.	Ps 79:3
Israel who leads Israel * a flock;	Ps 80:1
we were * the mighty cedar trees,	Ps 80:10
let all their princes die * Zebah	Ps 83:11

LIKE Con't)
O my God, blow them away * dust; Ps 83:13
away like dust; * chaff before the Ps 83:13
heathen gods is there a god * you? Ps 86:8
They have left me here to die, * Ps 88:5
is anything * him? Ps 89:6
there any other Mighty One * you? Ps 89:8
How long will your wrath burn * Ps 89:46
They are * a single hour! Ps 90:4
We are * grass that is green in Ps 90:5,6
wicked flourish * weeds, there is Ps 92:7
But the godly shall flourish * Ps 92:12
The mountains melt * wax before Ps 97:5
for my days disappear * smoke. Ps 102:3,4
it is trampled * grass and is Ps 102:3,4
I am * a vulture in a far-off Ps 102:6
or * an owl alone in the desert. Ps 102:6
I am withering * grass, while Ps 102:11
They will grow old, * worn-out Ps 102:26
will change them * a man putting on Ps 102:26
My youth is renewed * the Ps 103:5
He is * a father to us, tender Ps 103:13
are few and brief, * grass, like Ps 103:15
brief, like grass, * flowers, Ps 103:15
They reel and stagger * Ps 107:27
to him * his clothing or his belt. Ps 109:19
Then let them curse me if they * Ps 109:28
renewed day by day * morning dew. Ps 110:3
that you are a priest forever * Ps 110:4
The mountains skipped * rams, Ps 114:4
rams, the little hills * lambs! Ps 114:4
Why, mountains, did you skip * Ps 114:6
Why, little hills, * lambs? Ps 114:6
They swarm around me * bees; Ps 118:12
they blaze against me * a roaring Ps 118:12
I am shriveled * a wineskin in Ps 119:83
* the earth you created; Ps 119:90,91
I rejoice in your laws * one who Ps 119:162
I have wandered away * a lost Ps 119:176
to Jerusalem, it was * a dream! Ps 126:1
are * sharp arrows to defend him. Ps 127:4
Those who make them become * Ps 135:18
Their words sting * poisonous Ps 140:3
the darkness * those in the grave. Ps 143:3
his days are * a passing shadow. Ps 144:4
Daughters of graceful beauty * the Ps 144:12-15
Stay far from men * that, for Pro 1:15
saved yourself * a deer that Pro 6:5
you * a robber and destroys you; Pro 6:11
Love wisdom * a sweetheart; Pro 7:4
I was always at his side * a Pro 8:30
Or, "* a master workman." Pro 8:30f
Disaster strikes * a cyclone and Pro 10:25
to his employers—* smoke in their Pro 10:26
and modesty is * a fine gold ring Pro 11:22
Some people * to make cutting Pro 12:18
* water from a mountain spring. Pro 13:14
Kind words are * honey—enjoyable Pro 16:24
A bribe works * magic. Pro 17:8
A cheerful heart does good * Pro 17:22
His anger shuts you out * iron Pro 18:19
advice satisfies * a good meal! Pro 18:20
wife annoys * constant dripping. Pro 19:13
The king's fury is * that of a Pro 20:2
be * them and endanger your soul. Pro 22:24,25
and narrow grave. * a robber, she Pro 23:26,27,28
For in the end it bites * a Pro 23:32
it stings * an adder. Pro 23:32
You will stagger * a sailor Pro 23:34
upon you suddenly * a robber, and Pro 24:34
robber, and violently * a bandit. Pro 24:34
he promised is * a cloud blowing Pro 25:14
Do you * honey? Pro 25:16
unreliable man is * chewing with a Pro 25:19
Literally, "* vinegar upon Pro 25:20f
Good news from far away is * cold Pro 25:25
the wicked, it is * polluting a Pro 25:26
Honoring a rebel will backfire * Pro 26:8
He sticks to his bed * a door to Pro 26:14
just fooling," is * a madman Pro 26:18,19
Literally, "* hot embers to coals Pro 26:21f
A man who strays from home is * a Pro 27:8
what he is really * is shown by the Pro 27:19
even poorer, he is * an unexpected Pro 28:3
never satisfied, * a leech forever Pro 30:15,16
even this was * chasing the wind. Ecc 1:16-18
to help a youth * that, even to Ecc 4:15
He is * a fish caught in a net, Ecc 9:12
while princes walk * servants! Ecc 10:7
The wise man's words are * goads Ecc 12:11
of wandering * a vagabond among the Sol 1:7
My beloved is * a gazelle or Sol 2:9
my beloved, and be * a gazelle or a Sol 2:17
from the deserts * a cloud of smoke Sol 3:6
across your face * flocks of goats Sol 4:1
Your lips are * a thread of Sol 4:3
Literally, "* halves of a Sol 4:3f
Your breasts are * twin fawns of Sol 4:5
your garments is * the scent of the Sol 4:11
"My darling bride is * a private Sol 4:12
You are * a lovely orchard Sol 4:13,14

His eyes are * doves beside the Sol 5:12
His cheeks are * sweetly scented Sol 5:13
lilies, his breath * myrrh. Sol 5:13
finest gold, * cedars of Lebanon; Sol 5:15
your face, is * a flock of goats Sol 6:5
Literally, "* the halves of a Sol 6:7f
Your rounded thighs are * jewels, Sol 7:1
is * a heap of wheat set about Sol 7:2
Your two breasts are * two Sol 7:3
* the tower of Lebanon Sol 7:4
You are tall and slim * a palm Sol 7:7
are * its clusters of dates. Sol 7:7
Now may your breasts be * grape Sol 7:8
of your breath * apples, and your Sol 7:8
my beloved, and be * a gazelle or Sol 8:14
and abandoned * a watchman's shanty Is 1:8
Once * sterling silver; Is 1:22
Once so pure, but now diluted * Is 1:22
* those you used to have. Is 1:26
You will perish * a withered Is 1:30
will disappear * burning straw; Is 1:31
Israel's kings will be * babies, Is 3:4
my people in the dust * that?" Is 3:15
their sins behind them * a bullock Is 5:18
They will disappear * straw on Is 5:24
of their chariots spin * the wind. Is 5:28
They roar * lions and pounce Is 5:29
They growl over their victims * Is 5:30
yet Israel will be * a tree cut Is 6:13
Ask anything you *, in heaven or Is 7:11
the Lord with anything * that." Is 7:12
down upon you * flies and destroy Is 7:18
you, * bees to sting and to kill. Is 7:18
filled with joy * that of reapers Is 9:3
time has come, and * that of men Is 9:3
them * dirt beneath his feet. Is 10:5,6
Assyria's vast army is * a Is 10:18
a mighty slaughter * the time when Is 10:26
will be cut off, chopped down * a Is 11:1
lions will eat grass * the cows. Is 11:7
* those of a woman in labor. Is 13:8
to their own land * deer chased by Is 13:14
by dogs, wandering * sheep deserted Is 13:14
heavens and be * the Most High." Is 14:14
is thrown out * a broken branch; Is 14:19
the Arnon River * homeless birds. Is 16:2
tops and become * the abandoned Is 17:9
But though they roar * breakers Is 17:13
They will flee, scattered * chaff Is 17:13
* whirling dust before a storm. Is 17:13
plans are ripening * grapes, he Is 18:5
they make Egypt stagger * a sick Is 19:14
terrible desert, * a whirlwind Is 21:1
are upon me, * the pangs of a woman Is 21:3
the year of a hireling," * 16:14. Is 21:16f
up in his hands * a ball and toss Is 22:18
The world staggers * a drunkard; Is 24:20
it shakes * a tent in a storm. Is 24:20
They will be rounded up * Is 24:22
men who are * a driving rain that Is 25:4
of life will fall * dew upon them! Is 26:19
My people are * the dead branches Is 27:11
one by one * handpicked grain, Is 27:12
against you; * a mighty hailstorm Is 28:2
say, "to speak to us * this! Is 28:9
The enemy will come * a flood and Is 28:17
Your voice will whisper * a Is 29:4
away * chaff before the wind. Is 29:5
Jerusalem will vanish * a dream! Is 29:7
God will smash you * a broken Is 30:14
You will be * lonely trees on the Is 30:17
* filthy things you hate to touch. Is 30:22
his words consume * fire. Is 30:27
His wrath pours out * floods Is 30:28
of solemn joy, * songs in the night Is 30:29
The breath of the Lord, * fire Is 30:33
be burned to lime, * thorns cut Is 33:12
and disappear just * a rolled-up Is 34:4
The lame man will leap up * a Is 35:6
My life is blown away * a Is 38:12
it was * being torn apart by Is 38:13
Delirious, I chattered * a Is 38:14
a swallow and mourned * a dove; Is 38:14
"Shout that man is * the grass Is 40:6
his beauty fades * dying flowers. Is 40:6
He will feed his flock * a Is 40:11
buy expensive gods * that will find Is 40:20
must seem to him * grasshoppers! Is 40:22
out the heavens * a curtain and Is 40:22
the wind carries them off * straw. Is 40:24
They shall mount up with wings * Is 40:31
he will groan and cry * a woman Is 42:14
lives snuffed out * candlewicks. Is 43:17
They shall thrive * watered Is 44:4
grass, * willows on a river bank. Is 44:4
they are gone * morning mist at Is 44:22
there is no other * me who can Is 46:9
had peace flowing * a gentle river, Is 48:18
am * a sharp arrow in his quiver. Is 49:2
therefore, I have set my face * Is 50:7
* old clothes eaten up by moths! Is 50:9

shall disappear * smoke, the earth Is 51:6
shall wear out * a garment, and the Is 51:6
of the earth shall die * flies. Is 51:6
shall destroy them * garments; Is 51:8
the worm shall eat them * wool; Is 51:8
wither * the grass and disappear? Is 51:12
he was * a tender green shoot, Is 53:2
the ones who strayed away * sheep! Is 53:6
He was buried * a criminal in a Is 53:9
are * the restless sea, which is Is 57:20
penance and bowing * reeds in the Is 58:5
and you will be * a well-watered Is 58:11
garden, * an ever-flowing spring. Is 58:11
No wonder you grope * blind men Is 59:10
No wonder you are * corpses when Is 59:10
You roar * hungry bears; Is 59:11
you moan with mournful cries * Is 59:11
For he will come * a flood-tide Is 59:19
And who are these who fly * a Is 60:8
to Israel, * doves to their nests? Is 60:8
For God has planted them * strong Is 61:3
I am * a bridegroom in his wedding Is 61:10
His righteousness shall be * a Is 61:11
a budding tree, or * a garden in Is 61:11
with joy * that of a young man who Is 62:5
have trodden my enemies * grapes. Is 63:3
bottom of the sea? * fine stallions Is 63:13
never stumbled. * cattle grazing Is 63:14
* autumn leaves we fade, wither Is 64:6
And our sins, * the wind, sweep Is 64:6
overflow Jerusalem * a river, says Is 66:12
It will be * offerings flowing Is 66:20
You are strong * a fortified city Jer 1:18
be captured, * an iron pillar and Jer 1:18
How can you say a thing * that? Jer 2:23
* a thief, the only shame that Jer 2:26,27
How can you disown your God * Jer 2:32
You sit * a prostitute beside the Jer 3:2
You sit alone * a Bedouin in the Jer 3:2
Have you seen what Israel does? * Jer 3:6
you have been * a faithless wife Jer 3:20
roll down upon us * a storm wind; Jer 4:13
his chariots are * a whirlwind; Jer 4:13
They surround Jerusalem * Jer 4:17
I have heard great crying * that Jer 4:31
Because of talk * this I'll take Jer 5:14
up these people * kindling wood. Jer 5:14
* a hunter hiding in a blind. Jer 5:26
They set their traps for men. * Jer 5:27
prophets, and my people * it so! Jer 5:31
She spouts evil * a fountain! Jer 6:7
The noise of their army is * a Jer 6:23
Fright and pain have gripped us * Jer 6:24
scattered * dung upon the ground. Jer 8:2
troops among you * poisonous snakes Jer 8:17
"They bend their tongues * bows Jer 9:3
refine them and test them * metal. Jer 9:7
For their tongues aim lies * Jer 9:8
across the fields * manure, like Jer 9:22
like manure, * sheaves after the Jer 9:22
rite * theirs, and nothing more. Jer 9:25,26
Don't act * the people who make Jer 10:2,3
stands their god * a helpless Jer 10:5
O Lord, there is no other god * Jer 10:6
world there isn't anyone * you. Jer 10:7
But the God of Jacob is not * Jer 10:16
Lord, drag them off * helpless Jer 12:3
My people have roared at me * a Jer 12:8
You will writhe in pain * a woman Jer 13:21
hills panting * thirsty jackals. Jer 14:6
* fire, and it shall consume you. Jer 15:14
They will fight against you * a Jer 15:20
*—and I will grant you no favors! Jer 16:13
to chase you down * deer in the Jer 16:16
He is * a stunted shrub in the Jer 17:6
He is * a tree planted along a Jer 17:8
* a bird that fills her nest with Jer 17:11
in my heart is * fire that burns in Jer 20:9
But the Lord stands beside me * a Jer 20:11
be destroyed * the cities of old Jer 20:16
you * a fire no man can quench. Jer 21:12
He shall be buried * a dead Jer 22:19
This man Coniah is * a Jer 22:28
And the priests are * the Jer 23:11
Does not my word burn * fire? Jer 23:29
Is it not * a mighty hammer that Jer 23:29
you not to mock * that, then I, the Jer 23:38,39
I will treat them * spoiled figs, Jer 24:8
they shall fall * fragile women. Jer 25:34
He has left his lair * a lion Jer 25:38
this Temple * the one at Shiloh?" Jer 26:9
shall be plowed * an open field and Jer 26:18
* rotting figs, too bad to eat. Jer 29:16,17
Lord make you * Zedekiah and Ahab Jer 29:22
their sides * women in labor?" Jer 30:6
they shall act * my people. Jer 31:1
Their life shall be * a watered Jer 31:12
It won't be * the one I made Jer 31:32
very much *, if not the same as, Jer 31:33f
"Do as you *—I can't stop you." Jer 38:5
is before you—go where you *. Jer 40:4

(LIKE Con't)
go where you *." Jer 40:5
Whether we * it or not, we will Jer 42:6
just as much as we *—just as we and Jer 44:17
army, rising * the Nile at flood Jer 46:7
* a flood, destroying every foe. Jer 46:8
have become * frightened calves. Jer 46:20,21
down your people * woodsmen who Jer 46:22,23
She is * wine that has not been Jer 48:11
Let her stagger and fall * a Jer 48:26
live in the caves * doves that nest Jer 48:28
Moab * an old, unwanted bottle. Jer 48:38
fail with fear * women in the pains Jer 48:41
one who will come * a lion from the Jer 49:19
For who is * me and who can call Jer 49:19
* that of women in labor. Jer 49:22
Their hearts are troubled * a Jer 49:23
and neigh * stallions, yet your Jer 50:11
The Israelites are * sheep the Jer 50:17
their battle cry roars * the surf Jer 50:42
pangs of terror gripped him * the Jer 50:43
them suddenly, * a lion from the Jer 50:44
For who is * me? Jer 50:44
with enemies, * fields filled with Jer 51:14
says: Babylon is * the wheat upon a Jer 51:33
he has swallowed us * a great Jer 51:34,35
the men of Babylon roar * lions. Jer 51:38
I will bring them * lambs to the Jer 51:40
the slaughter, * rams and goats. Jer 51:40
are silent now. * a widow broken Lam 1:1
her princes are * starving deer Lam 1:6
therefore she is tossed away * Lam 1:8
is any sorrow * my sorrow, because Lam 1:12
Let her be thrown out * filthy Lam 1:17
land of Israel * a raging fire. Lam 2:3
His fury is poured out * fire Lam 2:4
has vanquished Israel * an enemy. Lam 2:5
Their lives ebb away * those Lam 2:12
fall down upon you * a river; Lam 2:18
Pour out your hearts * water to Lam 2:19
He buried me in dark places, * Lam 3:6
He lurks * a bear, like a lion, Lam 3:10
He lurks like a bear, * a lion, Lam 3:10
They are * cruel desert Lam 4:3,4
rubies, polished * sapphires." Lam 4:7f
that shone * polished brass. Eze 1:4
that looked * men, except that Eze 1:5
Their legs were * those of men, Eze 1:7
feet were cloven * calves' feet, Eze 1:7
feet, and shone * burnished brass. Eze 1:7
forms that glowed * bright coals of Eze 1:13
their wings roared * waves against Eze 1:24
the shore, or * the voice of God, Eze 1:24
* the shouting of a mighty army. Eze 1:24
was what looked * a throne made of Eze 1:26
glowing bronze, dazzling * fire; Eze 1:27,28
halo * a rainbow all around him. Eze 1:27,28
and barbed and sting * scorpions. Eze 2:6
and the city, * a wall of iron. Eze 4:3
Toss it out * worthless rubbish, Eze 7:19
will I stop them. * robbers, they Eze 7:22
wings, what looked * human hands) Eze 10:7,8
within, sparkled * chrysolite, Eze 10:9-13
* human hands under their wings. Eze 10:21
them what being exiled will be *. Eze 12:3
my people free * birds from cages. Eze 13:20
of Jerusalem are * the vines of the Eze 15:5,6
Thrive * a plant in the field!' Eze 16:6,7
You looked * a queen, and so you Eze 16:13
There has never been anything * Eze 16:16
" '* mother, like daughter'—that Eze 16:44
" 'Like mother, * daughter'—that Eze 16:44
And you are exactly * your Eze 16:45
breaking all her promises * that? Eze 17:15
"Do you think I * to see the Eze 18:23
sinning and acts * any other Eze 18:24
woman your mother was—* a lioness! Eze 19:2
Her children were * lion's cubs! Eze 19:2
"Your mother was * a vine beside Eze 19:10
not be done—to be * the nations all Eze 20:32
it flashes * lightning; Eze 21:15
polished and flashes * lightning. Eze 21:28
and you will melt * silver in Eze 22:22
you shall be * an uncleared Eze 22:24
against you * lions stalking prey. Eze 22:25
Your leaders are * wolves, who Eze 22:27
You will reel * a drunkard Eze 23:33
nations against you * ocean waves. Eze 26:3
in ruins, dead, * the bodies of Eze 26:20
You are * a ship built of finest Eze 27:5
you boast yourself to be * God. Eze 28:2,3
You will die * an outcast at the Eze 28:10
mountain of God * a common sinner. Eze 28:16
and tear at Israel * thorns and Eze 28:24
Israel leaned on you but, * a Eze 29:7
and mighty nation—* a cedar of Eze 31:2,3
to hell with all the others * her. Eze 31:16
to them, * someone who sings lovely Eze 33:32
I will be * a shepherd looking Eze 34:12
land has become * Eden's garden! Eze 36:35
will multiply them * the flocks Eze 36:37,38
figure * Nebuchadnezzar. Eze 38:2,3f
down upon them * a storm and cover Eze 38:9
and cover the land * a cloud. Eze 38:9
and cover the land * a cloud. Eze 38:15,16
whose face shone * bronze, standing Eze 40:3
an entry hall. And * the others, it Eze 40:25
and entry. And, * the others, it Eze 40:29,30
there were just * the others: The Eze 40:35
The sound of his coming was * the Eze 43:2
And the fourth looks * a god!" Dan 3:25
Literally, "looks * a son of the Dan 3:25f
live in the fields * an animal, Dan 4:25
eating grass * a cow, your back wet Dan 4:25
and to eat grass * the cows for Dan 4:32
and ate grass * the cows, and his Dan 4:33
and his nails were * birds' claws. Dan 4:33
he ate grass * the cows and his Dan 5:21
The first was * a lion, but it Dan 7:4
the ground, on two feet, * a man; Dan 7:4
The second animal looked * a Dan 7:5
animals looked * a leopard, but on Dan 7:6
back it had wings * those of birds, Dan 7:6
as snow, his hair * whitest wool. Dan 7:9
at least he looked * a man— and I Dan 8:15
been a disaster * what happened at Dan 9:12
blinding flashes * lightning, and Dan 10:5,6
his arms and feet shone * Dan 10:5,6
and his voice was * the roaring of Dan 10:5,6
Then someone—he looked * a Dan 10:16
will glitter * stars forever. Dan 12:3
to count—* sand along a seashore! Hos 1:10
And thus it is: "* priests, Hos 4:9
"Like priests, * people"—because Hos 4:9
Don't be * Israel, stubborn as a Hos 4:16
down upon them * a waterfall, and Hos 5:10
the strength of Judah * dry rot. Hos 5:12
For your love vanishes * morning Hos 6:4
clouds, and disappears * dew. Hos 6:4
But * Adam, you broke my Hos 6:7
Their hearts blaze * a furnace Hos 7:6
it flames forth * raging fire. Hos 7:6
her down * a bird from the sky; Hos 7:12
They are * a crooked bow that Hos 7:16
They are coming! * a vulture, the Hos 8:1
How satisfying, * the early figs Hos 9:10
The glory of Israel flies away * Hos 9:11
up among them * poisonous weeds in Hos 10:4
shall disappear * a chip of wood Hos 10:7
How can I forsake you * Admah and Hos 11:8
from the west. * a flock of birds, Hos 11:11
Egypt—* doves flying from Assyria. Hos 11:11
But no, my people are * crafty Hos 12:7
Row on row of altars—* furrows in Hos 12:11
They shall disappear * morning Hos 13:3
like morning mist, * dew that Hos 13:3
dries away, * chaff blown by the Hos 13:3
by the wind, * a cloud of smoke. Hos 13:3
So I will come upon you * a Hos 13:7
I will rip you to pieces * a Hos 13:8
and * a lion I will devour you. Hos 13:8
him, but he is * a child resisting Hos 13:13
I will refresh Israel * the dew Hos 14:5
in the soil * cedars in Lebanon. Hos 14:5
garden and blossom * grapes and be Hos 14:7
care for you. I am * an evergreen Hos 14:8
It covers the mountains * night! Joe 2:2
They look * tiny horses, and Joe 2:4
Listen to the noise they make, * Joe 2:5
a field, and * a mighty army moving Joe 2:5
These "soldiers" charge * Joe 2:7
they scale the walls * picked and Joe 2:7
* thieves through the windows. Joe 2:9
again be dealt a blow * this. Joe 2:27
The Lord roared—* a ferocious lion Amo 1:2
Kir as slaves was * saying to the Amo 1:5f
* a whirlwind in a mighty storm. Amo 1:14
you away * the cattle you are; Amo 4:2
"I sent you plagues * those of Amo 4:10
those left are * half-burned Amo 4:11
else he will sweep * fire through Amo 5:6
It will rise up * the river Nile Amo 8:8
It rises * the river Nile in Amo 9:5
"sleeping at a time * this? Jon 1:6
for a great city * Nineveh with its Jon 4:11
into the valleys * wax in fire, Mic 1:4
fire, * water pouring down a hill. Mic 1:4
Shaphir sounds * the Hebrew word Mic 1:11f
Zaanan sounds * a verb meaning Mic 1:11f
Beth-ezel sounds * a word for Mic 1:11f
Shaphir sounds * the Hebrew word Mic 1:11f
Zaanan sounds * a verb meaning Mic 1:11f
Beth-ezel sounds * a word for Mic 1:11f
Shaphir sounds * the Hebrew word Mic 1:11f
Zaanan sounds * a verb meaning Mic 1:11f
Beth-ezel sounds * a word for Mic 1:11f
"Don't harp on things * that. Mic 2:6
drunken, lying prophet that you *! Mic 2:11
you together again * sheep in a Mic 2:12
sheep in a fold, * a flock in a Mic 2:12
and chop them up * meat for the Mic 3:3
will be plowed * a field, and Mic 3:12
Pain has gripped you * a woman in Mic 4:
of his people * sheaves upon the Mic 4:1
refresh the world * a gentle dew or Mic 5
The nations will be * helpless Mic 5
trampled down * mud in the street. Mic 7:1
miracles for you, * those when I Mic 7:1
Where is another God * you, who Mic 7:1
His fury is * fire; Nah 1:
fire * a tangled mass of thorns. Nah 1:1
They burst into flames * straw. Nah 1:1
squares, darting * lightning, Nah 2:
lightning, gleaming * torches. Nah 2:
listen to them mourn * doves, and Nah 2:
Nineveh is * a leaking water Nah 2:
Nineveh, too, will stagger * a Nah 3:1
They will be devoured * Nah 3:1
the enemy will consume you * Nah 3:1
you multiply * grasshoppers. Nah 3:1
swarm * locusts and carry it away. Nah 3:1
crowd together * grasshoppers in Nah 3:1
and disappear, * locusts when the Nah 3:1
They do as they *, and no one can Hab 1:
a distant land; * eagles they come Hab 1:
They collect captives * sand. Hab 1:
They sweep past * wind and are Hab 1:1
many nations, but * death and hell, Hab 2:
reel and stagger * drunkards Hab 2:1
those who came out * a whirlwind, Hab 3:14
opportunity is blown away * chaff; Zep 2:2
will be destroyed * Sodom and Zep 2:9
desolate wasteland * a wilderness. Zep 2:13
Her leaders are * roaring lions Zep 3:3
Her judges are * ravenous wolves Zep 3:3
* a signet ring upon my finger; Hag 2:23
Don't be * your fathers were! Zec 1:4
they are * a burning stick pulled Zec 3:2
us, with wings * those of a stork. Zec 5:9
* two mountains made of brass. Zec 6:1
They hardened their hearts * Zec 7:12
that silver is * dirt to her, and Zec 9:3
her, and fine gold * dust in the Zec 9:3
And I will surround my Temple * Zec 9:8
Both of you will be my sword, * Zec 9:13
His arrows shall fly * lightning; Zec 9:14
his enemies * a whirlwind off the Zec 9:14
ask the idols for anything * that! Zec 10:2
astray and wander * lost sheep; Zec 10:2
* a proud steed in battle. Zec 10:3
They shall be * mighty warriors. Zec 10:7
Though I have scattered them * Zec 10:9
leaders, "If you *, give me my Zec 11:12
and Judah * a cup of poison to all Zec 12:2
the clans of Judah * a little fire Zec 12:6
the forest aflame—* a burning match Zec 12:6
will be as God, * the Angel of the Zec 12:8
Literally, "* the mourning of Zec 12:11f
They will become * walking Zec 14:12
'Try to if you *, but I will Mal 1:4
When have we ever done a thing * Mal 1:7
* that—and see how pleased he is! Mal 1:8
as I would * to, I will turn on you Mal 2:1
me, and throw you out * dung. Mal 2:3
For he is * a blazing fire Mal 3:2
garments! * a refiner of silver he Mal 3:3
God, refining them * gold or Mal 3:3
is coming, burning * a furnace. Mal 4:1
wicked will be burned up * straw; Mal 4:1
up like straw; * a tree, they will Mal 4:1
joy * calves let out to pasture. Mal 4:2
I will send you another prophet * Mal 4:5
When you pray, don't be * the Mt 6:5
Why be * the heathen? Mt 6:31,32
them are wise, * a man who builds Mt 7:24
them are foolish, * a man who Mt 7:26
* this in all the land of Israel! Mt 8:10
Gentiles [* this Roman officer Mt 8:11
associate with men * that?" Mt 9:11
anything * this," they exclaimed. Mt 9:33
They were * sheep without a Mt 9:36
will be given a reward * theirs. Mt 10:41
what did you expect him to be *? Mt 11:7
These people are * children Mt 11:16
But brilliant men * you can Mt 11:19
normal, just * the other one! Mt 12:13
How could evil men * you speak Mt 12:34
"This evil nation is * a man Mt 12:43,44,45
of Heaven is * a farmer sowing good Mt 13:24
of Heaven is * a tiny mustard seed Mt 13:31,32
"The Kingdom of Heaven is * a Mt 13:44
of Heaven is * a pearl merchant on Mt 13:45
his face shone * the sun and his Mt 17:2
a little child * this because you Mt 18:5
the top, you must serve * a slave. Mt 20:27
must be * my own, for I, the Mt 20:28
do things * this and much more. Mt 21:21
what the Kingdom of Heaven is *. Mt 22:1
heaven should be addressed * that. Mt 23:9
You are * beautiful Mt 23:27
You try to look * saintly men, Mt 23:28
His face shone * lightning and Mt 28:3
"We've never seen anything * Mk 2:12

(LIKE Con't)
It is * patching an old garment Mk 2:21
One of them went * this: Mk 4:2
with joy, but, * young plants in Mk 4:17
what the Kingdom of God is *: Mk 4:26
It is * a tiny mustard seed! Mk 4:31,32
was just a local man * themselves. Mk 6:2,3
* the great ones of the past. Mk 6:15
"Ask me for anything you *," the Mk 6:22,23
because they were * sheep without a Mk 6:34
they look * tree trunks walking Mk 8:24
"You shouldn't say things * Mk 8:32
Jesus replied, "Cases * this Mk 9:29
a little child * this in my name is Mk 9:37
married—they will be * the angels. Mk 12:25
that you come * this, armed to the Mk 14:48
(His wife Elizabeth was, * Lk 1:5
spirit and power * Elijah, the Lk 1:17
hearts to become * little Lk 1:17
* those you did in Capernaum?' Lk 4:23
he had done spread * wildfire Lk 4:37
and obey me are * a man who builds Lk 6:47,48
and don't obey are * a man who Lk 6:49
I met a man with faith * this." Lk 7:9
They are * a group of children Lk 7:32
'You don't * it if we play Lk 7:32
* it if we play "funeral" '! Lk 7:32
child * this is caring for me! Lk 9:48
realize what your hearts are *. Lk 9:55f
themselves with things * that. Lk 9:60
"And if even sinful persons * Lk 11:13
them is a miracle * that of Jonah, Lk 11:29,30
For you are * hidden graves in a Lk 11:44
For you are exactly * your Lk 11:47
of God: "What is the Kingdom *?" Lk 13:18
It is * a tiny mustard seed Lk 13:19
It is * yeast kneaded into Lk 13:20,21
were watching him * hawks to see if Lk 14:1
can be worn down * that, don't you Lk 18:6
I am not a sinner * everyone else, Lk 18:11
* that tax collector over there! Lk 18:11
for saying things * that!" Lk 19:39
* that," his listeners protested. Lk 20:16
in these respects they are * Lk 20:36
life, * all the rest of the world. Lk 21:34,35
slaves have no choice but to * it! Lk 22:25
you, to sift you * wheat, but I Lk 22:31
But the story sounded * a fairy Lk 24:11
"How do you know what I am *?" Jn 1:48
him, "Would you * to get well?" Jn 5:6
about perishable things * food. Jn 6:27
Give us free bread every day, * Jn 6:30,31
be famous when you hide * this! Jn 7:4
"We've never heard anything * Jn 7:46
Abraham wouldn't do a thing * Jn 8:40
"but he surely looks * him!" Jn 9:9
Why listen to a man * that?" Jn 10:20
us * a man possessed by a demon! Jn 10:21
* anyone else, shall live again. Jn 11:25
must fall and die * a kernel of Jn 12:23,24
be washing our feet * this!" Jn 13:6
* the peace the world gives. Jn 14:27
he is thrown away * a useless Jn 15:6
you *, and it will be granted! Jn 15:7
there was a sound * the roaring of Act 2:2
Then, what looked * flames or Act 2:3
Literally, "* unto me." Act 3:21,22f
How could you do a thing * this? Act 5:4
of doing a thing * this—conspiring Act 5:9
and shouldn't be fighting * this! Act 7:26
will raise up a Prophet much * me Act 7:37
Literally, "* unto me." Act 7:37f
Paul was * a wild man, going Act 8:3
come into a Gentile home * this. Act 10:28
We are merely human beings * Act 14:15
But Paul didn't * that idea at Act 15:38
false teachers, * vicious wolves, Act 20:29
by ordering me struck * that?" Act 23:3
"I'd * to hear the man myself," Act 25:22
"With trivial proofs * these, Act 26:28
* a perfect day for the trip; Act 27:13
* and what he wanted them to do. Rom 1:21
them to look * mere birds and Rom 1:23
Their talk is foul and filthy * Rom 3:13
who we are or what we have been *. Rom 3:21,22
if we have faith * Abraham's, for Rom 4:16
in a human body * ours—except that Rom 8:3
But you are not * that. Rom 8:9
And so we should not be * Rom 8:15
we should behave * God's very own Rom 8:15
things of nature, * animals and Rom 8:22
Literally, "in * manner." Rom 8:26f
become * his Son, so that his Son Rom 8:29
are * sheep awaiting slaughter; Rom 8:36
"Why have you made me * this?" Rom 9:20
It will be * dead people coming Rom 11:15
*, except that person himself. 1Co 2:11
In fact, you are acting * people 1Co 3:3
He himself will be saved, but * a 1Co 3:15
really *, deep down in our hearts. 1Co 4:5
end of the line, * prisoners soon 1Co 4:9
* dirt under foot, like garbage. 1Co 4:13
like dirt under foot, * garbage. 1Co 4:13
without being with people * that. 1Co 5:10
of you were just * that but now 1Co 6:11
In times * these I think it is 1Co 7:26
in times * these, it is no sin. 1Co 7:28
hint that I would * to start now. 1Co 9:15
Yes, whatever a person is *, I 1Co 9:22
playing around. * an athlete I 1Co 9:27
would never behave * that"—let 1Co 10:12
not doing what I * or what is best 1Co 10:33
It's * this: when I was a child I 1Co 13:11
them you will start acting * them. 1Co 15:33
has a body just * Adam's, made of 1Co 15:48
us now has a body * Adam's, so we 1Co 15:49
some day have a body * Christ's. 1Co 15:49
stand true to the Lord; act * 1Co 16:13
well as all others * them who work 1Co 16:16
Or am I * a man of the world who 2Co 1:17
the Gospel * a sweet perfume. 2Co 2:14
Only those who, * ourselves, are 2Co 2:17
We are not * those hucksters—and 2Co 2:17
ARE WE BEGINNING to be * those 2Co 3:1
us, we become more and more * him. 2Co 3:18
we shall put on * new clothes. 2Co 5:2
but we wouldn't * to think of dying 2Co 5:4
they seem to be * on the outside. 2Co 5:16
merely as a human being * myself. 2Co 5:16
me as I keep on talking * a fool. 2Co 11:1
too, and seem * godly ministers. 2Co 11:15
have lost my wits to talk * this; 2Co 11:16
I am acting * a brainless fool. 2Co 11:17
I'm not strong and daring * that! 2Co 11:21
about—I'm talking * a fool again—I 2Co 11:21
(Have I gone mad to boast * this? 2Co 11:23
You have made me act * a 2Co 12:11
a fool—boasting * this—for you 2Co 12:11
visit you I won't * what I find, 2Co 12:20
* the way I will have to act. 2Co 12:20
You know what I was * when I Gal 1:13
didn't even know what I looked *. Gal 1:22
their rules, * slaves in chains. Gal 2:4
to reason with you * this, for at Gal 4:20
and were just * all the others, Eph 2:2
God's anger just * everyone else. Eph 2:3
Then we will no longer be * Eph 4:14
made the lie sound * the truth. Eph 4:14
more in every way * Christ who is Eph 4:15,16
you was * sweet perfume to him. Eph 5:2
of a slave and becoming * men. Php 2:7
Shine out among them * beacon Php 2:15
There is no one * Timothy for Php 2:20
He has been just * a son to me in Php 2:22
glorious bodies * his own, using Php 3:21
be more and more * Christ who Col 3:10
way that you won't *—for he has no Col 3:25
* a thief in the night. 1Th 5:2
guard, not asleep * the others. 1Th 5:6
Timothy, you are * a son to me in 1Ti 1:2
Christ after defying God * that. 1Ti 1:19
His visits revived me * a breath 2Ti 1:16
Work hard, * a farmer who gets 2Ti 2:6
been put in jail * a criminal. 2Ti 2:9
love of argument, are men * that. 2Ti 2:17
But God's truth stands firm * a 2Ti 2:19
sin you will be * one of these 2Ti 2:21
Don't be taken in by people * 2Ti 3:5
they are * lazy animals, living Tit 1:12
to Archippus who * myself is a Phm 1:1
They will become worn out * old Heb 1:11
for Jesus to be * us, his brothers, Heb 2:17
knows what it is * when we suffer Heb 2:18
is merely a man * anyone else, but Heb 5:1
was frail and weak * ours (except Heb 5:7f
what it was * to obey, when obeying Heb 5:8
There is much more I would * to Heb 5:11
You are * babies who can drink Heb 5:12,13
I am talking * this I really don't Heb 6:9
but his life is * that of the Son Heb 7:3
This new agreement will not be * Heb 8:9
he lived in tents * a mere visitor, Heb 11:9
of people that, * the stars of the Heb 11:12
when they talked * that, they were Heb 11:14
will soon be gone, * a flower that Jas 1:10,11
obey, he is * a man looking at his Jas 1:23
or remember what he looks *. Jas 1:24
over there if you *, or else sit on Jas 2:3
against men who are made * God. Jas 3:9
You are * an unfaithful wife who Jas 4:4
you, and eat your flesh * fire. Jas 5:3
be patient, * a farmer who waits Jas 5:7
All our greatness is * a flower 1Pe 1:24
But you are not * that, for you 1Pe 2:9
have healed ours! * sheep you 1Pe 2:25
in her steps * good daughters and 1Pe 3:6
you: You should be * one big happy 1Pe 3:8
He prowls around * a hungry, 1Pe 5:8
people and to * them, and finally 2Pe 1:7
have written, for, * lights shining 2Pe 1:19
They do whatever they feel *; 2Pe 2:12
and become lost * Balaam, the son 2Pe 2:15
Do what you *, be free." 2Pe 2:19
now is * tomorrow to the Lord. 2Pe 3:8
But you are not * that, for the 1Jn 2:20
what it is going to be * later on. 1Jn 3:2
comes we will be * him, as a result 1Jn 3:2
We are not to be * Cain, who 1Jn 3:12
is against Christ, * the 1Jn 4:3
a human being with a body * ours. 2Jn 1:7
Beware of being * them, and 2Jn 1:8
Well, I would * to say much more, 2Jn 1:12
can do just as we * without fear of Jud 1:4
understand, and, * animals, they do Jud 1:10
*, thereby ruining their souls. Jud 1:10
his brother; and, * Balaam, they Jud 1:11
for money; and * Korah, they have Jud 1:11
They are * clouds blowing over Jud 1:12
They are * fruit trees without Jud 1:12
shame and disgrace * the dirty foam Jud 1:13
doing whatever evil they feel *; Jud 1:16
voice that sounded * a trumpet Rev 1:10
was one who looked * Jesus who Rev 1:13
Literally, "* unto a Son of Rev 1:13f
head—the hair—was white * wool." Rev 1:14f
eyes penetrated * flames of fire. Rev 1:14
His feet gleamed * burnished Rev 1:15
* the waves against the shore. Rev 1:15
and his face shone * the power of Rev 1:16
eyes penetrate * flames of fire, Rev 2:18
whose feet are * glowing brass. Rev 2:18
they will be shattered * a pot of Rev 2:27
that sounded * a mighty trumpet Rev 4:1
* an emerald encircled his throne. Rev 4:3
the second looked * an ox; Rev 4:7
sounded * thunder, said, "Come!" Rev 6:1
and the sun became dark * black Rev 6:12
—* green fruit from fig trees Rev 6:13
as though rolled up * a scroll Rev 6:14
for what seemed * half an hour. Rev 8:1
given power to sting * scorpions. Rev 9:3
* the pain of scorpion stings. Rev 9:5
The locusts looked * horses Rev 9:7
They had what looked * golden Rev 9:7
and their faces looked * men's. Rev 9:7
Their hair was long * women's, Rev 9:8
their wings roared * an army of Rev 9:9
They had stinging tails * Rev 9:10
The horses' heads looked much * Rev 9:17,18
his face shone * the sun and his Rev 10:1
great shout—it was * the roar of a Rev 10:3
"At first it will taste * honey, Rev 10:9
But she was given two wings * Rev 12:14
This Creature looked * a leopard Rev 13:2
two little horns * those of a lamb Rev 13:11
a fearsome voice * the Dragon's. Rev 13:11
sound from heaven * the roaring of Rev 14:2
on it who looked * Jesus, who was Rev 14:14
Literally, "one * a Son of Man." Rev 14:14f
* the watery blood of a dead man; Rev 16:3
city, so beautiful—* a woman Rev 18:16
a boulder shaped * a millstone and Rev 18:21
Then I heard again what sounded * Rev 19:6
a huge crowd, or * the waves of a Rev 19:6
on the shore, or * the mighty Rev 19:6
His eyes were * flames, and on Rev 19:12
flashed and glowed * a precious Rev 21:11
gem, crystal clear * jasper. Rev 21:11
pure, transparent gold * glass! Rev 21:18,19,20
pure, transparent gold, * glass. Rev 21:21
"No, don't do anything * that. Rev 22:9

LIKED
quiet sort who * to stay at home. Gen 25:27
the king really * him a lot, and 1Sa 18:22
offended him, and spared any he *. Dan 5:19
but even so he * to listen to him. Mk 6:20
* and go wherever you wanted to; Jn 21:18

LIKELY
"Mere man is as * to be wise as Job 11:12
colt is * to be born a man! Job 11:12
I am as * to reject my people Jer 31:36
he is * to think you are crazy. 1Co 14:23
awhile they are * to disregard 1Ti 5:11
Besides, they are * to be lazy 1Ti 5:13
them they are more *, with God's 2Ti 2:25

LIKENESS
make man in our image, in our *." Gen 1:26f
Literally, "In the * of God." Gen 5:1f
Literally, "In his own *, after Gen 5:3,4,5f
with him in the * of his death." Rom 6:5f
Literally, "was made in the * of Php 2:7f
Christ is the exact * of the Col 1:15

LIKES
are! The * of them have not been Joe 2:2
Lord * to talk to you so roughly? Mic 2:7
worse we are, the better God * it! Rom 3:8
the * and dislikes of her husband. 1Co 7:34
God is not one who * things to 1Co 14:33
and upset. He * harmony, and he 1Co 14:33
them whenever he *, and then they 2Ti 2:26

LIKETHEIRS
Oh, that my end might be *!" Num 23:7-10

LIKEWISE
who is at Babylon is * chosen"; 1Pe 5:13f

LIKHI
were Ahian, Shechem, *, and Aniam. 1Ch 7:19
LILIES
He is feeding among the *! Sol 2:16
of a gazelle, feeding among the *. Sol 4:5
His lips are perfumed *, his Sol 5:13
his flock and to gather the *. Sol 6:2
He pastures his flock among the * Sol 6:3
a heap of wheat set about with *. Sol 7:2
Look at the field *! Mt 6:28
"Look at the *! Lk 12:27
LILY
flaring out like the cup of a *. 2Ch 4:5
of Sharon, the * of the valley." Sol 2:1
King Solomon: "Yes, a * among Sol 2:2
she will blossom as the * and Hos 14:5
LILY-SHAPED
he made two * capitals of molten 1Ki 7:16-22
LIMB
I'll have you torn * from limb and Dan 2:5
you torn limb from * and your Dan 2:5
shall be torn * from limb and his Dan 3:29
be torn limb from * and his house Dan 3:29
LIMBS
strength in his *, and throughout Job 41:12
a time when your * will tremble Ecc 12:3
or five out on the tips of the *. Is 17:6
their broken * and heal the sick. Eze 34:15,16
or with paralyzed *—lay on the Jn 5:3
LIME
the stones with a coating of * Deu 27:2,3,4
write the laws of God in the *. Deu 27:2,3,4
Your armies will be burned to *, Is 33:12
LIMIT
So, before the time * expired, 1Sa 18:26
to the * to pay their taxes. Neh 5:2,3,4
is no * to their wicked deeds. Jer 5:28
You have reached the * of your Eze 22:4
chosen ones he will * those days. Mk 13:20
is upon him without measure or *. Jn 3:33,34
LIMITED
to kill them, and * the Holy One of Ps 78:41
The Lord is fully aware of how * Ps 94:11
is * to the things of earth. Jn 3:31
of marriage for a * time, so that 1Co 7:5
and * by what someone else thinks? 1Co 10:29
LIMITING
and barred them by * their shores, Job 38:10
LIMITS
to declare it off * because it is Ex 19:23
free within the * of your laws. Ps 119:44,45,46
I was there when he set the * of Pro 8:27,28,29
right up to the * of your income, Ecc 5:11
eastern and western * of the land. Eze 48:1
goes beyond the * of this book's Jn 18:34f
still within the * set for us, our 2Co 10:15
LIMP
able to walk again, even with a *, Ex 21:19
not * or stumble as you run. Pro 4:12
and the boy lay there * and Mk 9:26
The lame are walking without a *. Lk 7:20,21,22
LIMPID
your eyes as * pools in Heshbon by Sol 7:4
LIMPING
and he was * because of his hip. Gen 32:31
LINE
to the "godly *" of Seth, and Gen 6:1f
men" to the men of the * of Cain. Gen 6:1f
Shem's * of descendants included Gen 11:10,11
that our family * will continue." Gen 19:34
of us trespasses across this * Gen 31:47,48
not cross this * to attack you and Gen 31:51,52
Isaac, to respect the boundary *. Gen 31:53
on down the * to the youngest. Gen 44:12
These three tribes were next in * Num 2:3-31
Next in the * of march was the Num 2:3-31
they were next in the * of march. Num 2:3-31
were next in the * of march, Num 10:17
Next in * was the tribe of Num 10:22
is the boundary * between the Num 21:13
the boundary * proceeded past the Jos 15:10,11
the boundary * went east to the Jos 19:12
by lot as a supply * to bring us Ju 20:8,9,10
and destroy my * of descendants!" 1Sa 24:21
into the family * of David, and he 1Ki 13:2
and did not end the * of David's 1Ki 15:4
of Baasha was in * with what the 1Ki 16:12
he was at the end of the * with 1Ki 19:19
of the royal *, went to Mizpah with 2Ki 25:25
This is Ephraim's * of descent: 1Ch 7:25,26,27
his royal * of descent forever. 1Ch 17:12
The * of descendants from Eliezer 1Ch 26:25
armed, formed a * from one side to 2Ch 23:10
Next down the * were his clan Neh 3:18
his final punch *: "Yes, and Est 5:12
And don't give me that * about Job 32:13
CATCH leviathan with a hook and *? Job 41:1
bit in its mouth to keep it in *! Ps 32:9
a good neighbor is out of his *. Pro 21:10
end of the *, publicly disgraced! Pro 25:6,7
God does things and fall into *. Ecc 7:13
THE ROYAL * of David Is 11:1
"the Heir of David's royal *." Is 11:10f
* of wise men they have come from? Is 19:11
and over again, a * at a time and Is 28:10
I will take the * and plummet Is 28:17
my servant and the * of the Levites Jer 33:22
He laid out an unalterable * of Lam 2:8
walls there ran a * of brick Eze 46:23
in * for royal succession. Dan 11:21
and the royal * of David won't be Zec 12:7
And the royal * will be as God, Zec 12:8
and throw in a *, and open the Mt 17:26,27
from the royal * of his servant Lk 1:69
of the royal *, he had to go to Lk 2:4
born of the royal * of David, in Jn 7:41,42
laws and are in * with our thinking Act 21:24
into King David's royal family *; Rom 1:3
very end of the *, like prisoners 1Co 4:9
Ask God for anything in * with Eph 6:18
This will be their * of 2Pe 3:4
for anything in * with his will. 1Jn 5:14
LINEN
cloth, fine-twined *, goat's hair, Ex 25:1
of fine-twined *, forty-two feet Ex 26:1
the fine-twined *, with cherubim Ex 26:31
purple, and scarlet fine-twined *. Ex 26:36
curtains made from fine-twined *. Ex 27:9,10
fine-twined *, and attached to four Ex 27:16
high, made from fine-twined *. Ex 27:18
scarlet threads of fine-twined *. Ex 28:5,6
purple, and scarlet fine-twined *. Ex 28:8
* as you did in the ephod. Ex 28:15
*, using a checkerboard pattern; Ex 28:39
make the turban, too, of this *; Ex 28:39
Also make * undershorts for Ex 28:42
fine-twined * or of goat's hair; Ex 35:5-9
the fine-twined * or goats' hair; Ex 35:23
*, and brought them in. Ex 35:25
and scarlet on * backgrounds, and Ex 35:35
and scarlet *, with cherubim Ex 36:8,9
veil was made from woven *, with Ex 36:35
it was woven from finespun *, Ex 36:37
woven from fine-twined * thread. Ex 38:9
court were woven of fine-twined *. Ex 38:16
of fine-twined *, beautifully Ex 38:18
scarlet threads into fine * cloth. Ex 38:23
woven from fine-twined * thread. Ex 39:2
the blue, purple, and scarlet *; Ex 39:3
from fine-twined * thread, just as Ex 39:4,5
gold, blue, purple, and scarlet *. Ex 39:8
these were made of * cloth, Ex 39:24
sons from fine-twined * thread. Ex 39:27
all made of this *, and the linen Ex 39:28,29
linen, and the * belt was Ex 39:28,29
shall put on his * undergarments Lev 6:10
and his * outer garments and clean Lev 6:10
in a woolen or * garment or fabric, Lev 13:47,48
clothing, fabric, * or woolen Lev 13:52
* coat, shorts, belt, and turban. Lev 16:4
and take off the * garments he wore Lev 16:23
to put on the holy * garments, and Lev 16:32
made of half wool and half *. Lev 19:19
thread: for instance, wool and *. Deu 22:11
An ephod was usually a * pouch Ju 8:27f
* robe just like the priest's. 1Sa 2:18
Literally, "wore a * ephod." 1Sa 2:18f
was girded with a * ephod." 2Sa 6:14f
The families of the * workers who 1Ch 4:21-22
were all dressed in * robes. 1Ch 15:27
David also wore a * ephod. 1Ch 15:27
and blue * and crimson cloth. 2Ch 2:14
*, decorated with angels. 2Ch 3:14
in finespun * robes and standing at 2Ch 5:11,12
of fine * and purple thread." Est 1:6f
cloak of fine * and purple, and Est 8:15
sheets of finest * imported from Pro 7:16,17
made—a purple gown of pure *. Pro 31:22
She makes belted * garments to Pro 31:24
me, Go and buy a * loincloth and Jer 13:1
One of them wore * clothing and Eze 9:2
Just then the man in * clothing, Eze 9:11
to the man in * clothing and said: Eze 10:2
When the Lord told the man in * Eze 10:6
of the man in * clothes, who took Eze 10:7,8
and * and beautifully embroidered. Eze 16:13
*, and jewelry of coral and agate. Eze 27:16
"They must wear only * clothing Eze 44:17
They must wear * turbans and Eze 44:18
wear linen turbans and * trousers; Eze 44:18
a person robed in * garments, with Dan 10:5,6
asked the man in * robes who was Dan 12:6
it in a clean * cloth, and placed Mt 27:59
clothed only in a * nightshirt. Mk 14:51,52
Literally, "wearing only a * Mk 14:51,52f
Joseph bought a long sheet of * Mk 15:46
it in a long * cloth and laid it in Lk 23:53
in and saw the empty * wrappings; Lk 24:12
body in a long * cloth saturated Jn 19:40
in and saw the * cloth lying there, Jn 20:5
spotlessly white *, with golden Rev 15:6
(Fine * represents the good Rev 19:8
dressed in finest *, white and Rev 19:14
LINENS
clothes of * and silk, embroidered, Eze 16:9,10
are made of Egypt's finest *; Eze 27:7
*, purple silks, and scarlet; Rev 18:12
purple and scarlet *, decked out Rev 18:16
and whitest and finest of *." Rev 19:8
LINES
the * he had been instructed. Gen 44:6
Set boundary * the people may Ex 19:12
*, and moved into the battle; 1Ki 20:27
them into two long * to walk in Neh 12:31,32
Literally, "The boundary * are Ps 16:6f
* on the east and the west. Eze 48:3
eastern and western boundary *. Eze 48:4
"Pray along these *: 'Our Father Mt 6:9
nothing is written between the *! 2Co 1:13,14
to say along these *, but you don't Heb 5:11
based on family * was canceled Heb 7:18
LINGERIE
their mirrors, lovely *, Is 3:23
LINGERS
in terrible pain but life * on.' 2Sa 1:9
LINGUISTIC
to exploit their * and political Gen 11:6
LINGUISTS
Some * believe the meaning is, Pro 30:18,19f
LINING
silver * left among your clouds. Ecc 12:2
LINKED
the corners, were * to each other Ex 36:29
LINTEL
hyssop against the * above the door Ex 12:22
LINUS
*, Claudia, and all the others. 2Ti 4:21
LION
Judah is a young * that has Gen 49:9
He has settled down as a *—who Gen 49:9
These people rise up as a *; Num 23:18-24
Israel sleeps as a * or a lioness— Num 24:3-9
He crouches like a *, Deu 33:20
to Timnah, a young * attacked Ju 14:5
to look at the carcass of the *. Ju 14:8
"and what is stronger than a *?" Ju 14:18
he said, "and a * or a bear comes 1Sa 17:34
and teeth of the * and the bear 1Sa 17:37
ground, took on a * that was caught 2Sa 23:20
and a * standing on each side. 1Ki 10:19
a * came out and killed him. 1Ki 13:24,25
and the * standing beside it. 1Ki 13:24,25
the road and the * standing quietly 1Ki 13:24,25
by causing the * to kill him." 1Ki 13:26
and the donkey and * were still 1Ki 13:28
beside it, for the * had not eaten 1Ki 13:28
of the Lord, a * shall kill you as 1Ki 20:36
to go a * attacked and killed him. 1Ki 20:36
He also killed a * in a slippery 1Ch 11:22
each flanked by a gold *. 2Ch 9:18
a * and quickly finish me off. Job 10:16
no * has set his paw there. Job 28:8
upon me as a * would and maul me Ps 7:2
You can safely meet a * or step Ps 91:13
fury is like that of a roaring *; Pro 20:2
a * in the street and be killed!" Pro 22:13
"There might be a * outside!" Pro 26:13
as a * or bear attacking them. Pro 28:15
The *, king of the animals. Pro 30:29,30,31
to be a live dog than a dead *!" Ecc 9:4
me this: When a *, even a young Is 31:4,5
miss the way. No * will lurk along Is 35:9
feed together, the * shall eat Is 65:25
my prophets as a * kills its prey. Jer 2:30
A *—a destroyer of Jer 4:7
fury of the "* from the forest"; Jer 5:6
at me like a * of the forest, so I Jer 12:8
He has left his lair like a * Jer 25:38
will come like a * from the wilds Jer 49:19
suddenly, like a * from the jungles Jer 50:44
He lurks like a bear, like a *, Lam 3:10
grew into a strong young *, and Eze 19:3
"When Israel, the mother *, saw Eze 19:5
as a strong young * among the Eze 32:2
of a young *—looked toward the Eze 41:19,20
The first was like a *, but it Dan 7:4
Judah as a * rips apart its prey; Hos 5:14
I shall roar as a * [at their Hos 11:10
So I will come upon you like a * Hos 13:7
and like a * I will devour you. Hos 13:8
a ferocious * from his lair—from Amo 1:2
"Would I be roaring as a * Amo 3:4
Even a young *, when it growls, Amo 3:4
The * has roared—tremble in fear. Amo 3:8
from a *, but it was too late; Amo 3:12
who is chased by a *—and met by a Amo 5:19
Israel will be as strong as a *. Mic 5:8
great Nineveh, * of the nations, Nah 2:11
O Nineveh, once mighty *! Nah 2:12
out of the mouth of the *." 2Ti 4:17f
a hungry, roaring *, looking for 1Pe 5:8
Beings was in the form of a *; Rev 4:7
for look! The * of the tribe of Rev 5:5

.ION Con't)
like the roar of a *—and the seven Rev 10:3

.ION-FACED
spear and were "* men, swift as 1Ch 12:8-13

.ION'S
"Dan is like a * cub Deu 33:22
he ripped the * jaws apart, and did Ju 14:6
anger is as dangerous as a *. Pro 19:12
with a * face on the right side Eze 1:10
the third, a *; Eze 10:14
Her children were like * cubs! Eze 19:2
he snatched from the * mouth two Amo 3:12
but had bear's feet and a * mouth! Rev 13:2

.IONESS
Israel sleeps as a lion or a *— Num 24:3-9
Can you stalk prey like a *, to Job 38:39,40
a woman your mother was—like a *! Eze 19:2

.IONS
I have done this to both * and 1Sa 17:36
than eagles, stronger than *. 2Sa 1:23
of *, will be paralyzed with fear; 2Sa 17:10
with carved *, oxen, and angels. 1Ki 7:27-30
Above and below the * and oxen 1Ki 7:27-30
Cherubim, *, and palm trees 1Ki 7:36
And there were two * on each 1Ki 10:20
* among them to kill some of them. 2Ki 17:25
and he has sent * among us to 2Ki 17:26
Gold * also stood at each side 2Ch 9:19
fierce as young *, they shall all Job 4:10
Like aged, helpless * they shall Job 4:11
satisfy the young *' appetites as Job 38:39,40
Like * they crouch silently, Ps 10:9
They are like * eager to tear me Ps 17:12
* hiding and waiting their chance. Ps 17:12
roaring * attacking their prey. Ps 22:13
Save me from these *' jaws and Ps 22:21
Even strong young * sometimes go Ps 34:10
these young * are out to get it. Ps 35:17
I am surrounded by fierce * Ps 57:4
the teeth of these young *, Lord. Ps 58:6
Then the young * roar for their Ps 104:21
But the godly are bold as *! Pro 28:1
where the * have their dens, and Sol 4:8
They roar like * and pounce upon Is 5:29
will be safe among *, and a little Is 11:6
* will eat grass like the cows. Is 11:7
with Dibon yet! * will hunt down Is 15:9
they go, where * and swift venomous Is 30:6
it was like being torn apart by * Is 38:13
Literally, "The * have roared Jer 2:15f
are like sheep the * chase. Jer 50:17
the men of Babylon roar like *. Jer 51:38
He became a leader among the * Eze 19:6
against you like * stalking prey. Eze 22:25
Majesty—shall be thrown to the *. Dan 6:7
will be thrown to the *?" Dan 6:12
and he was taken to the den of *. Dan 6:16
could rescue Daniel from the *. Dan 6:17
hurried out to the *' den, and Dan 6:19
able to deliver you from the *?" Dan 6:20
"to shut the *' mouths so that Dan 6:22
and wives, and the * leaped upon Dan 6:24
Daniel from the power of the *." Dan 6:27
with teeth as sharp as those of *! Joe 1:6
Her leaders are like roaring * Zep 3:3
Hear the young * roaring—the Zec 11:3
me from being thrown to the *. 2Ti 4:17
den of *, and in a fiery furnace. Heb 11:33
and their teeth were those of *. Rev 9:8
looked much like *', and smoke and Rev 9:17,18

LIP
cover his upper * and call out as Lev 13:45

LIPS
your *—so that you can obey them. Deu 30:14
and your * with shouts of joy. Job 8:21
from God, my * shall speak no Job 27:4
content. Our * are our own; Ps 12:3,4
their lying * quieted at last—the Ps 31:18
at last—the * of these arrogant men Ps 31:18
Keep your * from lying. Ps 34:13
for my * will be unsealed—oh, how Ps 51:14,15
my mouth shut and my * sealed. Ps 141:3
For the * of a prostitute are as Pro 5:3
idle * are his mouthpiece. Pro 16:27
and in his * there is a scorching Pro 16:27f
space with pursed *, deep in Pro 16:30
Then let your * be tightly Ecc 12:4
Your * are like a thread of Sol 4:3
Your *, my dear, are made of Sol 4:11
of spices. His * are perfumed Sol 5:13
causing the * of those who are Sol 7:9
He touched my * with it and Is 6:7
this coal has touched your *. Is 6:7
smoke. His * are filled with fury; Is 30:27
a man—touched my * and I could talk Dan 10:16
they lap it up and lick their * Hos 4:8
all this; my * quiver with fear. Hab 3:16
"Priests' * should flow with the Mal 2:7
words that fell from his *. Lk 4:22
branch and held up to his *. Jn 19:29
guard your * from telling lies. 1Pe 3:10

LIQUID
for both * and dry measure. Eze 45:11
bath (one-tenth of a homer) for *. Eze 45:11

LIQUOR
WINE GIVES FALSE courage; hard * Pro 20:1
Hard * is for sick men at the Pro 31:6,7
boast about the * they can hold. Is 5:22
touch wine or hard *—and he will be Lk 1:15
took a drop of * all his life, and Lk 7:33

LIST
HERE IS A * of some Gen 5:1
Here is a * of Shem's other Gen 10:22
Here is a *, in the order of Gen 25:12-15
HERE IS A * of the descendants of Gen 36:1
You are the head of the * in rank Gen 49:3
THIS IS THE * of the sons of Jacob Ex 1:1
included in that *, are the same Ex 6:26
bring me an offering from this *: Ex 25:1
it is not on the * of those Lev 27:27
are to make a * of all the booty, Num 31:26
HERE IS THE * of the kings on the Jos 12:1
Here is a * of the kings Jos 12:7
Here is a * of the areas still Jos 13:2-7
HERE IS A * of the nations the Ju 3:1
HERE IS A * of King Solomon's 1Ki 4:1
Here is a * of the items he made: 1Ki 7:41-46
Here is a * of the names of the 1Ch 1:43
(This * does not include the sons 1Ch 3:9
Here is a * of the men from 1Ch 12:20
Here is a * of their names and 1Ch 25:1
Here is the * of the units and 1Ch 27:1
including a * of the locations 2Ch 33:19
HERE IS THE * of the Jewish exiles Ez 2:1
They also asked for a * of the Ez 5:4
Following is the * of priests who Ez 10:16-19
Here is the * of ordinary Ez 10:25
"The following is a * of the Neh 7:6
"Following is a * of the Neh 7:57,58,59
Following is a * of the names of Neh 11:3
HERE IS A * of the priests who Neh 12:1
has come, and I * all the above Ps 50:21
these men be blotted from the * Ps 69:28
Who can ever * the glorious Ps 106:2
"HERE IS THE * of the tribes and Eze 48:1
Here is the * of those who were Act 1:14
Leviticus 11 for the forbidden *. Act 10:12f
Next on my * of items to write 1Co 11:17
Here is a * of some of the parts 1Co 12:28
against you, the * of his Col 2:14
He took this * of sins and Col 2:14
leaves a will—a * of things to be Heb 9:16

LISTED
All of the men * above descended Gen 10:32
of the names * in verse 5. Gen 36:13,14f
became the heads of clans, as * Gen 36:15,16
the names * in verses 20, 21. Gen 36:28,29,30f
* according to their ages. Ex 6:19
from each tribe, as * below: Num 34:16-28
* below are the laws Moses issued Deu 4:44,45,46
the curses I have *—you will Deu 30:1
cities * below, with their Jos 21:9-16
The priests were * in the 2Ch 31:17,18
old and older were * under the 2Ch 31:17,18
who returned (* by subclans): Ez 2:2
These 220 men were all * by Ez 8:20
(All those * Neh 10:1
tribes of Israel, as * here: Rev 7:4-8

LISTEN
and Zillah, "* to me, my wives. Gen 4:23
said to Abraham, "please * to me. Gen 23:11
"* to this," he proudly Gen 37:6
to his brothers. "* to my latest Gen 37:9
he refused to *, and kept out of Gen 39:10
pleadings, but we wouldn't *." Gen 42:21
"But you wouldn't *. Gen 42:22
come. * to me, O sons of Jacob. Gen 49:2
Listen to me, O sons of Jacob; * Gen 49:2
* to him, and let Israel go? Ex 5:2
that will teach them to * to Ex 5:9
but they wouldn't * any more Ex 6:8,9
won't even * to me any more; Ex 6:12
should Pharaoh * to me?" Ex 6:30
Yet even then Pharaoh won't * to Ex 7:4
*, just as the Lord had predicted. Ex 7:13
You wouldn't * before, and now Ex 7:16
and he wouldn't * to Moses and Ex 7:22
and he wouldn't * to them, just as Ex 8:19
that he refused to *, just as the Ex 9:12
"Pharaoh won't *, and this will Ex 11:9
"If you will * to the voice of Ex 15:26
*, and left it until morning; Ex 16:20
by yourself. Now *, and let me Ex 18:19,20
"But if you will not * to me or Lev 26:14
not obey me and * to me, I will Lev 26:21
"And if you still won't * to me Lev 26:27
and he said to them, "*, you Num 20:10
* to me, you son of Zippor. Num 23:18-24
told them, but they wouldn't *. Deu 1:43
the Lord, but he wouldn't *. Deu 1:45
"AND NOW, O Israel, * carefully Deu 4:1
God and * to what he tells you. Deu 4:30
Israel and said, "* carefully now Deu 5:1
You go and * to all that God Deu 5:26,27
tell us, and we will * and obey.' Deu 5:26,27
Therefore, O Israel, * closely Deu 6:3
"O Israel, *: Jehovah is our Deu 6:4
"O ISRAEL, *! Deu 9:1
of you except to * carefully to all Deu 10:12,13
every one of his commands. *! Deu 11:2
other nations,' don't * to him. Deu 13:3
do not consent nor *, and have no Deu 13:8
you must * and whom you must obey. Deu 18:15
might not have to * to the Deu 18:16
who will not * to him and heed his Deu 18:19
" "* to me, all you men of Deu 20:3
But the Lord wouldn't * to Deu 23:5
Israel as follows: "O Israel, *! Deu 27:9
If you will only * and obey the Deu 28:13
"If you won't * to the Lord your Deu 28:15-19
refuse to * to the Lord your God. Deu 28:45
All this if you do not * to the Deu 28:62
away and you won't *—if you are Deu 30:17
"*, O HEAVENS and earth! Deu 32:1
* to what I say! Deu 32:1
them, "Come and * to what the Lord Jos 3:9
But I wouldn't * to him. Jos 24:10
Yet even then Israel would not * Ju 2:17
Or, "to * to her speak to them Ju 4:5f
*, O you kings and princes, Ju 5:3
if you like— and * to what they Ju 7:11
you want God's blessing, * to me! Ju 9:7
But they wouldn't * to him. Ju 19:25
the people of Benjamin wouldn't *. Ju 20:13
"*, my child," he said to her. Ru 2:8,9
But they wouldn't * to their 1Sa 2:23,24,25
But the people refused to * to 1Sa 8:19
the Lord and * to his commandments 1Sa 12:14
and refuse to * to him, then his 1Sa 12:15
to Saul, "Stop! * to what the Lord 1Sa 15:16
"* here, you men of Benjamin!" 1Sa 22:7
"* to me, you son of Ahitub!" 1Sa 22:11,12
Saul, "Why do you * to the people 1Sa 24:9,10
"Please * to what I want to say. 1Sa 25:24
Do you think that anyone will * 1Sa 30:24
But he wouldn't * to her; 2Sa 13:14
But he wouldn't * to her. 2Sa 13:16
the king will * to me and rescue us 2Sa 14:15,16
out to Joab, "* to me, Joab. 2Sa 20:16
"Now * to my instructions. 1Ki 2:5
* to me and answer my requests. 1Ki 8:29
my requests. * to every plea of 1Ki 8:30
him and * to his God-given wisdom. 1Ki 10:24
If you * to what I tell you and 1Ki 11:38
was refusing to * to them, they 1Ki 12:16,17
Then Micaiah said, "* to this 1Ki 22:19
But Amaziah refused to *, so King 2Ki 14:11
prophets, but Israel wouldn't *. 2Ki 17:14
But Israel didn't *, and the 2Ki 17:40
For they had refused to * to the 2Ki 18:12
"* to the great king of Assyria! 2Ki 18:28
Don't * to King Hezekiah. 2Ki 18:31,32
Don't * to King Hezekiah when he 2Ki 18:31,32
Bend low, O Lord, and *. 2Ki 19:16
O Lord, and see. * to this man's 2Ki 19:16
Then Isaiah said to Hezekiah, "* 2Ki 20:16
But the people did not * to the 2Ki 21:9
He refused to * to God's 2Ki 21:22
contrition, I will * to your plea. 2Ki 22:18,19
O Lord my God! * to my prayer that 2Ch 6:19
toward this place. * to my prayers 2Ch 6:20,21
this Temple, then * to them from 2Ch 6:25
punished us, then * from heaven 2Ch 6:27
the trouble is— * to every 2Ch 6:29
I will *, wide awake, to every 2Ch 7:15
to stand here and * to you talk! 2Ch 9:7
"*! 2Ch 13:5
"* to me, Asa! 2Ch 15:2
"Listen to me, Asa! *, armies of 2Ch 15:2
"* to what else the Lord has 2Ch 18:18
"* to me, all you people of 2Ch 20:15
to attention. "* to me, O people 2Ch 20:20
Lord, but the people wouldn't *. 2Ch 24:19
But Amaziah wouldn't *, for God 2Ch 25:20
Lord your God? * to me and return 2Ch 28:11
"* to me, you Levites. 2Ch 29:4,5
Hear my prayer! * carefully to Neh 1:6,7
refused to * to your commandments. Neh 9:16
they were proud and wouldn't *, Neh 9:29
sins, but still they wouldn't *. Neh 9:30
your laws or * to your warnings. Neh 9:34
For your own good, * to my Job 5:27
knows everything you've done. *! Job 11:6
"* to me now, to my reasons for Job 13:6
his presence. * closely to what I Job 13:17
"*, and I will answer you from Job 15:17-19
that he will * as a man would Job 16:21
as a man would * to his neighbor. Job 16:21
"* to me; let me speak, and Job 21:2,3
you were wrong. * to his Job 22:22
this argument, and * to his reply, Job 23:4,5
No, he would * with sympathy. Job 23:6
open the court and * to my case? Job 24:1

(LISTEN Con't)
Will God * to his cry when Job 27:9
and declares it to all who will *. Job 28:27
someone who would * to me and try Job 31:35
intelligent. So * to me awhile and Job 32:10
"PLEASE *, JOB, to what I have to Job 33:1
Mark this well, O Job. * to me, Job 33:31
But if not, then * to me. Job 33:33
"* to me, you wise men. Job 34:2
choose the sounds we want to * to; Job 34:3
"* to me, you with Job 34:10
"* now and try to understand. Job 34:16
"If they * and obey him, then Job 36:11
If they won't * to him, they Job 36:12
This makes them * to him! Job 36:15
"MY HEART TREMBLES at this. *, Job 37:2
Listen, * to the thunder of his Job 37:2
"*, O Job, stop and consider the Job 37:14
'* and I will speak! Job 42:4
the earth, * while there is time. Ps 2:10
Therefore he will * to me and Ps 4:3
O LORD, HEAR me praying; * to my Ps 5:1
others, does not * to gossip, never Ps 15:3
and you must * to my earnest cry! Ps 17:1
me, O God! Yes, * as I pray. Ps 17:6
and arrogant. * to their boasting. Ps 17:10
help me or even to * to my groans? Ps 22:1
much joy. * to my pleading, Lord! Ps 27:7
and implore your help. Oh, * to Ps 28:2
Sons and daughters, come and * Ps 34:11
earnestness, but God did not *. Ps 35:13
Hear my prayer, O Lord; * to my Ps 39:12
*, EVERYONE! Ps 49:1
around the world—* to my words, Ps 49:1
O my people, *! Ps 50:7
For I am your God. *! Ps 50:7
Defend me with your might! Oh, * Ps 54:2
* TO MY prayer, O God; Ps 55:1
Hear me, Lord! * to me! Ps 55:2
O GOD, * to me! Ps 61:1
LORD, * TO my complaint: Oh, Ps 64:1
Bend down your ear and * to my Ps 71:2
Oh, that he would *. Ps 77:1
O MY PEOPLE, * to my teaching. Ps 78:1
of your people! * to the sighing Ps 79:11
down your ear and * as I plead. Ps 80:1
was no water. * to me, O my Ps 81:8
O Israel, if you will only *! Ps 81:8
But no, my people won't *. Ps 81:11
But oh, that my people would * to Ps 81:13
refuse to * to the evidence? Ps 82:2
hear my prayer! *, God of Israel. Ps 84:8
* closely to my prayer, O God. Ps 86:6
Now hear my prayers; oh, * to my Ps 88:2
LORD, HEAR MY prayer! * to my Ps 102:1
He will * to the prayers of the Ps 102:17
*, if you are wise, to what I am Ps 107:43
will * with interest and respect. Ps 119:44,45,46
* to me and make me well again. Ps 119:149
O Lord, * to my prayers; Ps 119:169
* when I cry to you for help! Ps 141:1
then these men will finally * to Ps 141:6,7
Only fools refuse to be taught. * Pro 1:7,8,9
Come here and * to me! Pro 1:23
But all who * to me shall live Pro 1:33
YOUNG MEN, * to me as you would to Pro 4:1
to your father. *, and grow wise, Pro 4:1
My son, * to me and do as I say, Pro 4:10
*, son of mine, to what I say. Pro 4:20
mine, to what I say. * carefully. Pro 4:20
* TO ME, my son! Pro 5:1
I know what I am saying; *! Pro 5:1
Young men, * to me, and never Pro 5:7
he will not * to the truth; Pro 5:23
* to me, young men, and not only Pro 7:24
men, and not only * but obey; Pro 7:24
of every house. * to what she says: Pro 8:1
Listen to what she says: "*, Pro 8:4,5
show you common sense! * to me! Pro 8:6,7
And so, young men, * to me, for Pro 8:32
"* to my counsel—oh, don't Pro 8:33
* to this wise advice; Pro 22:17,18,19
a man with rags. * to your Pro 23:22
God doesn't * to the prayers of Pro 28:9
It is pleasant to * to wise Ecc 10:12,13
companions may * to your voice; Sol 8:13
*, O heaven and earth, to what Is 1:2
*, you leaders of Israel, you men Is 1:10
as I call you now. * to the Lord. Is 1:10
out to heaven, I won't look or *. Is 1:15
and refusing to * to me, you will Is 1:20
be before they are ready to *?" Is 6:11
will be shattered. * to me, all you Is 8:9,10
Don't * to their whisperings and Is 8:19
mountains! * as the armies march! Is 13:4
When I blow the trumpet, *! Is 18:3
* to their plea and heal them. Is 19:22
* TO THEM singing! Is 26:1
They do not * when you threaten; Is 26:11
But they won't *; Is 28:11
Only then will they * to him! Is 28:11
that, but they wouldn't * to him. Is 28:12
* to me, listen as I plead: Does Is 28:23,24
Listen to me, * as I plead: Does Is 28:23,24
his people will * to his voice. Is 32:3
*, you women who loll around in Is 32:9
in lazy ease; * to me and I will Is 32:9
* to what I have done, O nations Is 33:13
who refuse to * to those who plot Is 33:15
COME HERE AND *, O nations of the Is 34:1
Don't * to Hezekiah, for here is Is 36:16
heaven and earth. * as I plead; Is 37:16,17
Then Isaiah said to him, "* to Is 39:5
* -I hear the voice of Is 40:3
* IN SILENCE before me, O lands Is 41:1
Why won't you *? Is 42:18
you hear but you won't *. Is 42:20
he sent them nor * to his laws. Is 42:24
* TO ME, O my servant Israel, O my Is 44:1
"* to me, all Israel who are Is 46:3
* to me, you stubborn, evil men! Is 46:12
in the world—* to the sentence of Is 47:8
* to me, my people, my chosen Is 48:12
Come, all of you, and *. Is 48:14
Come closer and *. Is 48:16
* TO ME, all of you in far-off Is 49:1
* TO ME, all who hope for Is 51:1
* to me, my people; Is 51:4
Listen to me, my people; *, O Is 51:4
* to me, you who know the right Is 51:7
upon them. But * now to this, Is 51:21
Who will *? Is 53:1
do you any good? * and I'll tell Is 55:2
ears wide open. *, for the life of Is 55:3
* NOW! Is 59:1
from you and will not * anymore. Is 59:2
when I spoke, you wouldn't *. Is 65:12
O my people, * to the words of Jer 2:31
for they refuse to * to me; Jer 4:22
*, O foolish, senseless Jer 5:21
ears that do not *— have you no Jer 5:21
If you don't *, I will empty the Jer 6:8
But who will * when I warn them? Jer 6:10
"* for the sound of the trumpet! Jer 6:17
people: (* to it, distant lands; Jer 6:18,19
* to it, O my people in Jerusalem; Jer 6:18,19
Jerusalem; * to it, all the earth! Jer 6:18,19
because they will not * to me. Jer 6:18,19
their value. * to what they are Jer 6:27
Judah, * to this message from God. Jer 7:2
message from God. * to it, all of Jer 7:2
help them, for I will not *. Jer 7:16
But they wouldn't *; Jer 7:24
But they wouldn't * to them or Jer 7:26
them, but don't expect them to *. Jer 7:27
I warn them. I * to their Jer 8:6
my heart is broken. * to the Jer 8:19
and homes!' " * to the words of Jer 9:20
their flocks are scattered. *! Jer 10:22
They wouldn't even *. Jer 11:8
to * to me and worshiping idols. Jer 11:10
I will not * to their pleas. Jer 11:11
for I will not * to them when Jer 11:14
This evil nation refuses to * to Jer 13:10
Then you would * to the Lord, for Jer 13:15
Do you still refuse to *? Jer 13:17
content and refuse to * to me. Jer 16:12
but they didn't * or obey. Jer 17:23
But if you will not * to me, if Jer 17:27
to them and said: * to the word of Jer 19:3
refused to * to the Lord. Jer 19:15
of Judah and say, * to this Jer 22:2
servants and your people * too. Jer 22:2
been that way—you just won't *! Jer 22:21
Don't * to these false prophets Jer 23:16
one of them cared enough to *? Jer 23:18
"* to the dream I had from God Jer 23:25
But you won't *; Jer 25:7
* to the frantic cries of the Jer 25:36
For perhaps they will * and turn Jer 26:3
If you will not * to me and obey Jer 26:4
if you will not * to my servants, Jer 26:5
but you would not * to them— then Jer 26:5
"Do not * to your false Jer 27:9
Don't * to the false prophets Jer 27:14
Lord says, Don't * to your prophets Jer 27:16
Don't * to them. Jer 27:17
loved ones. But * now to the Jer 28:7
false prophet, "*, Hananiah, the Jer 28:15
Don't * to the dreams that they Jer 29:8
days when you pray, I will *. Jer 29:12
for they refuse to * to me though I Jer 29:19
Therefore * to the word of God, Jer 29:20
* to this message from the Lord, Jer 31:10
but they would not * or obey. Jer 32:33
to Babylon. But * to this, O Jer 34:4
you will not * to me and release Jer 34:17
and again and you won't * or obey. Jer 35:14
But you wouldn't * or obey. Jer 35:15
but you have refused to * to me. Jer 35:16
you refuse to * or answer when I Jer 35:17
scroll, but he wouldn't * to them. Jer 36:24,25
they wouldn't * to my warnings." Jer 36:
But Irijah wouldn't *; Jer 37:
would not come? *, O my lord the Jer 37:
And you won't * to me anyway." Jer 38:
but they wouldn't * and wouldn't Jer 44
"We will not * to your false Jer 44:
the women: "* to the word of the Jer 44:2
vows to her! But * to the word of Jer 44:2
Who can call me to account? * to Jer 50:4
*! Hear the cry of great Jer 51:5
And whether they * or not (for Eze 2:
they * or not (but they won't, Eze 2
for they are utter rebels). *, Eze 2:
(If I did, they would *! Eze 3
and they won't * to you any more Eze 3:
* to them carefully for yourself. Eze 3:1
or not they will *, tell them: This Eze 3:1
says, Let anyone * who wants to, Eze 3:2
scream for mercy, I will not *." Eze 8:1
me if they would *, but they won't, Eze 12:
* to me, O people of Israel. Eze 18:2
against me and would not *. Eze 20:
I * to you or help you, Israel? Eze 20:3
Tell them: * to what the Lord Eze 25:
heard the warning and wouldn't *; Eze 33:
therefore * to what I say and Eze 33:
Tell them: * to this message from Eze 36:
"O dry bones, * to the words of Eze 37:
of dust, watch and * and take to Eze 40:
use your eyes and ears. * to all Eze 44:
"O King Nebuchadnezzar, * to Dan 4:27
We have refused to * to your Dan 9:6
servant's prayer! * as I plead! Dan 9:17
down your ear and * to my plea. Dan 9:18
O Lord, * to me and act! Dan 9:19
you very much. *, and try to Dan 9:23
prophets have declared. Now *! Dan 9:25
"stand up and * carefully to what Dan 10:11
* TO THIS, you priests and all of Hos 5:1
Israel's leaders; *, all you men of Hos 5:1
because they will not * or obey. Hos 9:17
Whoever is intelligent, let him * Hos 14:9
*, you aged men of Israel! Joe 1:2
Everyone, *! Joe 1:2
of the mountain! * to the noise Joe 2:5
*! THIS IS your doom! Amo 3:1
The alarm has sounded—* and Amo 3:6
"* to this announcement, and Amo 3:13
* TO ME, you "fat cows" of Amo 4:1
I will not * to your music, no Amo 5:23
"Now therefore * to this message Amo 7:16
*, you merchants who rob the Amo 8:4
all the peoples of the world *. Mic 1:2
*, YOU LEADERS of Israel—you are Mic 3:1
Do you really expect him to *? Mic 3:4
* to me, you leaders of Israel Mic 3:9
* TO WHAT the Lord is saying to Mic 6:1
And now, O mountains, * to the Mic 6:2
* to the Lord if you are wise! Mic 6:9
weeping after her; * to them mourn Nah 2:7
of lies, crammed with plunder. *! Nah 3:2
I call for help before you will *? Hab 1:2
In her pride she won't * even to Zep 3:2
I thought, 'Surely they will * Zep 3:7
But no, they wouldn't *; Zec 1:4
these angels. * to me, O Joshua Zec 3:8
Your fathers would not * to this Zec 7:11
I called but they refused to *, Zec 7:13
forests felled. * to the wailing Zec 11:3
*, YOU PRIESTS, to this warning Mal 2:1
"*: I WILL send my messenger Mal 3:1
"*; you have said, 'It is Mal 3:14,15
*! The virgin shall Mt 1:23
"All who * to my instructions Mt 7:24
If ever you were willing to *, Mt 11:15
you were willing to listen, * now! Mt 11:15
If you have ears, *!" Mt 13:9
Let those with ears, *! Mt 13:43
crowds and said, "* to what I say Mt 15:10
If he still refuses to *, then Mt 18:17
"Now * to this story: A certain Mt 21:33
"*! Mk 4:3
If you have ears, *!" Mk 4:9
of people who * to the Good News Mk 4:18
If you have ears, *! Mk 4:23
accept you or * to you, shake off Mk 6:11
but even so he liked to * to him. Mk 6:20
"All of you *," he said, "and Mk 7:14
don't you open your ears and *?' Mk 8:18
and the crowds to come over and *. Mk 8:34
is my beloved Son. * to him." Mk 9:7
and have no doubt! * to me! Mk 11:24
in on him to * to the Word of God. Lk 5:1
"*, all of you. Lk 6:27
But all those who come and * and Lk 6:47,48
"But those who * and don't obey Lk 6:49
those who * and believe God's words Lk 8:14
people. They * to God's words and Lk 8:15
So be careful how you *; Lk 8:18
"If the people of a town won't * Lk 9:5
my Son, my Chosen One; * to him." Lk 9:35

STEN Con't)
* to me and remember what I say. Lk 9:44
o * to the wisdom of Solomon; Lk 11:31
s here [but this nation won't * Lk 11:32
e thrown out. * well, if you would Lk 14:35
ften came to * to Jesus' sermons; Lk 15:1
If they won't * to Moses and the Lk 16:31
hey won't * even though someone Lk 16:31
f God—and those who * shall live. Jn 5:25
You have gone out to * to his Jn 5:32,33
didn't you *? Jn 9:27
Well, God doesn't * to evil men, Jn 9:31
But the true sheep did not * to Jn 10:8
crazy. Why * to a man like that?" Jn 10:20
to me, they would * to you! Jn 15:20
to the crowd, "*, all of you, Act 2:14
"O men of Israel, *! Act 2:22
* carefully to everything he Act 3:21,22
Anyone who will not * to him Act 3:23
"Brothers! *! Act 13:38
"Brothers," he said, "* to me. Act 15:13
For instance, * to this passage Act 15:15
and said, "*, you Jews, if this Act 18:14
be obliged to * to you, but since Act 18:14
"BROTHERS AND FATHERS, * to me Act 22:1
Now please * patiently! Act 26:3
your ears don't * and you have Act 28:27
But no, you won't *; Rom 2:5
but still you will not * to him. Rom 9:4
be, and he makes some refuse to *. Rom 9:18
so that they will * to the Gospel 1Co 9:20
but even then they would not *. 1Co 14:21
the gift, while all the others *. 1Co 14:29,30
If you * to them you will start 1Co 15:33
but even if you do, * to me 2Co 11:16
you * gladly to those fools; 2Co 11:19,20
Lord's brother. (* to what I am Gal 1:20
But we did not * to them for a Gal 2:5
* to me, you friends who think Gal 4:21
and ceremonies. * to me, for this Gal 5:2
to all who will *, warning them and Col 1:28
Women should * and learn quietly 1Ti 2:11
Don't * to complaints against the 1Ti 5:19
when people won't * to the truth, 2Ti 4:3
They won't * to what the Bible 2Ti 4:4
SO WE MUST * very carefully to the Heb 2:1
Spirit warns us to * to him, to be Heb 3:7,8
you don't seem to *, so it's hard Heb 5:11
they refused to * to Moses, the Heb 12:25
if we refuse to * to God who speaks Heb 12:25
Brethren, please * patiently to Heb 13:22
that it is best to * much, speak Jas 1:19
message to obey, not just to * to. Jas 1:22
* to me, dear brothers: God has Jas 2:5
coming day of judgment. For *! Jas 5:4
they will not * to God's Word, nor 1Pe 2:8
for then if they refuse to * when 1Pe 3:1
had refused to * to God, though he 1Pe 3:20
and talked with God will * to us. 1Jn 4:6
for if it is, the world won't * 1Jn 4:6
this, that he will * to us whenever 1Jn 5:14
over him and refuses to * to me. 3Jn 1:9
Those who * to it being read and Rev 1:3
Let everyone who can hear, * to Rev 2:11
"Let everyone who can hear, * to Rev 2:17
"Let all who can hear, * to what Rev 2:29
"Let all who can hear, * to what Rev 3:6
"Let all who can hear, * to what Rev 3:13
Let those who can hear, * to Rev 3:22
Anyone who can hear, * carefully: Rev 13:9

LISTENED
"Because you * to your wife and Gen 3:17
as the others *, speaking publicly Gen 23:10
*: "No, let me buy it from you. Gen 23:13
Moses * to his father-in-law's Ex 18:24
'I have * to the word of God, Num 24:3-9
But that time, too, he * to me. Deu 9:19
But you have not * to him." Ju 6:10
people * carefully to his advice. 1Sa 3:19
But he hadn't *, so now the Lord 1Ki 11:9,10
help, and the Lord * to him; 2Ki 13:4
And the Lord * to Hezekiah's 2Ch 30:20
And the Lord *, and answered his 2Ch 33:13
once more you * from heaven, and in Neh 9:28
Everyone * to me and valued my Job 29:21
Oh, praise the Lord, for he has * Ps 28:6
for you have * to my troubles and Ps 31:7
you * to my plea and answered me. Ps 31:22
then he * and heard my cry. Ps 40:1
He would not have * if I had not Ps 66:18
But he *! Ps 66:19
Yet, even so, he * to their Ps 106:44
you say, "Oh, if only I had *! Pro 5:12
Oh, that you had * to my laws! Is 48:18
God has spoken to me and I have *; Is 50:5
them on to you, but you haven't *. Jer 25:2,3
you have not * to me, I will gather Jer 25:8,9
all the priests and people *. Jer 28:1
And I said to him as they all *: Jer 32:13
left in the land * to what the Lord Jer 37:2
heard me! You * to my pleading; Lam 3:56
to you any more than they * to me! Eze 3:7
you and haven't * to your voice. Dan 9:11
while the people * on the beach. Mt 13:2,3
they * to him with great interest. Mk 12:37
And if they had * to me, they Jn 15:20
Crowds * intently to what he had Act 8:6
and everyone now * as Barnabas and Act 15:12
of God and, as she * to us, the Act 16:14
Some who * were persuaded and Act 17:4
and gladly * to the message. Act 17:11
The crowd * until Paul came to Act 22:22
Sending for Paul, they * as he Act 24:24
of the prisoners * more to the Act 27:11
you should have * to me in the Act 27:21
the way you * to him so willingly 2Co 7:15
no, you * with great interest. 1Th 1:5
my own eyes and * to him speak. 1Jn 1:1

LISTENERS
like that," his * protested. Lk 20:16
urging all his * to save themselves Act 2:40

LISTENING
(Sarah was * from the tent door Gen 18:10
again, say, 'Yes, Lord, I'm *.' 1Sa 3:9
And Samuel replied, "Yes, I'm * 1Sa 3:10
interested in your * to him than in 1Sa 15:22
sitting at home, * to David playing 1Sa 19:9,10
and your ears * to their pleas. 1Ki 8:52
day after day * to your wisdom! 1Ki 10:8
"I have waited all this time, * Job 32:11,12
they hide beside the trail, * for Ps 56:6
I am * carefully to all the Lord Ps 85:8
* for each of his commands. Ps 103:20
from * to her flattery. Pro 7:5
he is worth * to, but the words of Pro 10:20
Stop * to teaching that Pro 19:27
The wise man learns by *; Pro 21:11
Hebrew to the Jews * on the wall, Is 36:13
are sincere and sit before you *. Eze 33:31
You have been * long enough! Zec 8:9
was standing there * to the Mk 12:28
anyone has * ears, use them now!" Lk 8:8
those who enjoy * to sermons, but Lk 8:13
floor, * to Jesus as he talked. Lk 10:39
Then, with the crowds *, he Lk 20:45
But you are not * to him, for Jn 5:38
Holy Spirit fell upon all those *! Act 10:44
He was * as Paul preached, and Act 14:9
When the * crowd saw what Paul Act 14:11
prisoners were *— suddenly there Act 16:25
why does God blame them for not *? Rom 9:19
Yet faith comes from * to this Rom 10:17
I tell you, with God * as I say 2Co 12:19
to stop them from * to Jewish folk Tit 1:14
his children, * to their prayers; 1Pe 3:12
And if we really know he is * 1Jn 5:15

LISTENS
"THEY CRY FOR help but no one *; Job 5:1
my defense as one he * to). Job 31:37
Because he bends down and *, I Ps 116:2
EVERY YOUNG MAN who * to me Pro 2:1
but a wise man * to others. Pro 12:15
but no one *, for my wrath is on Eze 7:14
heart of a man who * to the message Mt 13:23
If he * and confesses it, you Mt 18:15
that anyone who * to my message and Jn 5:24
Anyone whose Father is God * Jn 8:47
As he *, his secret thoughts 1Co 14:25
For if a person just * and Jas 1:23
ears of anyone who * to what the Rev 2:7

LISTIA
*. Ex 15:14

LISTING
* the cities in each section. Jos 18:9
against you * the following Hos 4:1

LISTS
The original text repeats the * of Num 7:18-23f
The original text repeats the * of Num 7:24-29f
The original text repeats the * of Num 7:30-35f
The original text repeats the * of Num 7:36-41f
The original text repeats the * of Num 7:42-47f
The original text repeats the * of Num 7:48-53f
The original text repeats the * of Num 7:54-59f
The original text repeats the * of Num 7:60-65f
The original text repeats the * of Num 7:66-71f
The original text repeats the * of Num 7:72-77f
The original text repeats the * of Num 7:78-83f
I went over the * of the people and Ez 8:15

LIT
their censers and * them and placed Num 16:18
Then he * the torches and let Ju 15:5
The soldiers * a fire in the Lk 22:55

LITERAL
This number is *, and means just Dan 8:26
If this is a * figure, it is no Rev 9:16f

LITERATURE
them the Chaldean language and *. Dan 1:3,4
The language was Aramaic; the * Dan 1:3,4f
mastered all the * and science of Dan 1:17

LITRES
The homer was about 220 *, or 6½ Eze 45:11f

LITTER
Literally, "*." Sol 3:7f

LITTERS
chariots, and in *, and on mules Is 66:20

LITTLE
me flee to that * village over Gen 19:18,19,20
and won't destroy that * city. Gen 19:21
named Zoar, meaning "* City." Gen 19:22
Shur (which is a * way to the Gen 25:18
Which sounds a * like the Hebrew Gen 25:25f
For it was * indeed you had Gen 30:30
"A * later I had another dream. Gen 41:22
"Go again and buy us a * food." Gen 43:2
we, but you and all our * ones. Gen 43:8
a child of his old age, a * one. Gen 44:20
again and buy us a * food,' we Gen 44:25
their wives and * ones, and to Gen 45:19
along with their * ones and their Gen 46:5
for your households and * ones." Gen 47:24
But they left their * children Gen 50:8
him, she made a * boat from papyrus Ex 2:3
she spied the * boat among the Ex 2:5
So the * girl rushed home and Ex 2:8
not let you take your * ones!" Ex 10:10
those who gathered * had no lack! Ex 16:18
shall be my own * flock from among Ex 19:5
But I will drive them out a * at Ex 23:30
and * ones will become slaves. Num 14:3
their wives and sons and * ones. Num 16:27
The * children Num 21:27-30
Only the * girls may live; Num 31:18
and cities for our * ones, but we Num 32:16
He will cast them out a * at a Deu 7:22
"You will sow much but reap *, Deu 28:38
along with your * ones and your Deu 29:11
Do this so that your * children Deu 31:13
us—so * that you must rebel again? Jos 22:17,18
deviate from them the least * bit. Jos 23:6
in Sidon, and had * or no contact Ju 18:7
delegation to the * remnant of the Ju 21:13
who has given you this * grandson; Ru 4:14
helper and wore a * linen robe just 1Sa 2:18
Each year his mother made a * 1Sa 2:19
* Samuel was growing in two 1Sa 2:26
MEANWHILE * SAMUEL was helping 1Sa 3:1
I have eaten this * bit of honey. 1Sa 14:29
"I tasted a * honey," Jonathan 1Sa 14:43
"It was only a * bit on the end 1Sa 14:43
women, babies, * children, oxen, 1Sa 15:3
at this nice * red-cheeked boy! 1Sa 17:41,42
going to do, even * things, and I 1Sa 20:2
men to ask for a * contribution 1Sa 25:8
(There was a * lame grandson of 2Sa 4:4
a * lamb he had managed to buy. 2Sa 12:3
cook a * something for him to eat. 2Sa 13:6
but I am as a * child who doesn't 1Ki 3:7
flour left and a * cooking oil in 1Ki 17:12
bake me a * loaf of bread first; 1Ki 17:13
him, "I saw a * cloud about the 1Ki 18:44
looked like two * flocks of baby 1Ki 20:27
Let's make a * room for him on 2Ki 4:10
This time the * boy sneezed seven 2Ki 4:35
captives was a * girl who had been 2Ki 5:2
One day the * girl said to her 2Ki 5:3
Naaman told the king what the * 2Ki 5:4
as a * child's, and he was healed! 2Ki 5:14
for so * on the following day. 2Ki 7:18
brought a * boy back to life. 2Ki 8:5
Tell them, 'My * finger is 2Ch 10:10
Lord with their * ones, wives, and 2Ch 20:13
Then they brought out the * 2Ch 23:11
not even this * remnant escapes. Ez 9:14
And though you started with *, Job 8:7
born but yesterday and know so *; Job 8:9
Can't you see how * time I have Job 10:20,21
that I may have a * moment of Job 10:20,21
So give him a * rest, won't you? Job 14:6
Is God's comfort too * for you? Job 15:11
How * will come of his hopes! Job 15:33
Poor widows must surrender the * Job 24:3
and makes us a * wiser than the Job 35:11
him to your * girls to play with? Job 41:5
You have taught the * children Ps 8:2
only a * lower than the angels, Ps 8:5
Or, "only a * lower than God!" Ps 8:5f
Only a * while and the wicked Ps 37:10
It is better to have * and be Ps 37:16
* tribe of Benjamin leads the way. Ps 68:27
They even sacrificed their * Ps 106:37,38
like rams, the * hills like lambs! Ps 114:4
rams? Why, * hills, like lambs? Ps 114:6
"Let me sleep a * longer!" Pro 6:10
Sure, just a * more! Pro 6:10
always at his side like a * child. Pro 8:30
Lazy people want much but get *, Pro 13:4
Better a * with reverence for Pro 15:16
A *, gained honestly, is better Pro 16:8
"A * extra sleep, Pro 24:32,33
A * more slumber, Pro 24:32,33
A * folding of the hands to rest" Pro 24:32,33
Cliff badgers: delicate * animals Pro 30:24-28
whether he eats * or much, but the Ecc 5:12
old, but leaves so * money at his Ecc 6:3

(LITTLE Con't)
A fool is so upset by a * work Ecc 10:15
for a * bird will tell them what Ecc 10:20
infused into the * body of a baby Ecc 11:5
"The * foxes are ruining the Sol 2:15
It was only a * while Sol 3:4
The Girl: "We have a * sister Sol 8:8
Foolish as * children playing Is 3:12
the Midianites by Gideon's * band. Is 9:4
very long; in a * while my anger Is 10:25
and a * child shall lead them all. Is 11:6
snakes, and a * child who puts his Is 11:8
Their * children will be dashed Is 13:16
Hide for a * while until the Is 26:20
Israel but a *, exiling her far Is 27:7,8
Are we * children, barely old Is 28:9
shame—he won't help one * bit! Is 30:5
or a * water from the well. Is 30:14
time—in just a * more than a Is 32:10
wants to make a * bet with you! Is 36:8,9
That's why their people had so * Is 37:27
to punish them a * by letting them Is 47:6
Can a mother forget her * child Is 49:15
shall carry your * sons back to you Is 49:22
anger I turned my face a * while; Is 54:8
I will comfort you there as a * Is 66:13
be angry about such a * thing! Jer 3:4,5
upon them—not in * gusts but in a Jer 4:11,12
be a * remnant of my people left. Jer 4:27
to death their * sons and daughters Jer 7:31
* ones, those ready to give birth. Jer 31:8
from the city for a * while. Jer 34:21
of Teman—even * children will be Jer 49:20
For even * children shall be Jer 50:45
in just a * while the flailing Jer 51:33
for food to give a * strength. Lam 1:11
to my people; * children and tiny Lam 2:11
Shall mothers eat their * Lam 2:20
All my * children lie dead upon Lam 2:22
grain and the * children stagger Lam 5:13
girls, women and * children; Eze 9:6
them and give your * sons to be Eze 20:31
There was * left to pay the Eze 29:18f
There was * left to pay the Eze 29:20f
"Give me a * time," he said, Dan 2:16
give it room; this * horn had a Dan 7:8
and the boasting of its * horn. Dan 7:11
ten horns and the * horn that came Dan 7:20
prostitute, and a * girl for wine Joe 3:3
Weep, weep for your * ones. Mic 1:16
the end, and what * you succeed in Mic 6:14
There the * remnant of the tribe Zep 2:7
You plant much but harvest *. Hag 1:6
"You hope for much but get so *. Hag 1:9
says, 'In just a * while I will Hag 2:6
for I was only a * displeased with Zec 1:15
So they counted out thirty * Zec 11:12
of Judah like a * fire that sets Zec 12:6
'O * town of Bethlehem, you are Mt 2:6
A * farther up the beach he saw Mt 4:21
care for you, O men of * faith? Mt 6:30
answered, "O you men of * faith! Mt 8:26
him. "My * daughter has just Mt 9:18
out, for the * girl isn't dead; Mt 9:24
went in where the * girl was lying Mt 9:25
of cold water to a * child, you Mt 10:42
who say to their * friends, 'We Mt 11:16
for revealing it to * children. Mt 11:25
where there was * depth of earth; Mt 13:5
and died, for they had so * root. Mt 13:6
the * he has will be taken away. Mt 13:12,13
"O man of * faith," Jesus said. Mt 14:31
and told them, "O men of * faith! Mt 16:8
"Because of your * faith," Mt 17:20
to him and set the * fellow down Mt 18:2
sins and become as * children, you Mt 18:3
himself as this * child, is the Mt 18:4
And any of you who welcomes a * Mt 18:5
one of these * ones who trusts in Mt 18:6
a single one of these * children. Mt 18:10
one of these * ones should perish. Mt 18:14
begged him to give him a * time. Mt 18:29
* children were brought for Jesus Mt 19:13
But Jesus said, "Let the * Mt 19:14
and heard even the * children in Mt 21:15
For they say, 'Even * babies Mt 21:16
by wearing on their arms * prayer Mt 23:5
even what * responsibility he has Mt 25:29
He went forward a *, and fell Mt 26:39
A * farther up the beach, he saw Mk 1:19
with him to heal his * daughter. Mk 5:23
and taking the * girl's father and Mk 5:40
said to her, "Get up, * girl!" Mk 5:41,42
* girl was possessed by a demon. Mk 7:25
that I have healed your * girl. Mk 7:29
And when she arrived home, her * Mk 7:30
Then he placed a * child among Mk 9:36
who welcomes a * child like this in Mk 9:37
one of these * ones who believe in Mk 9:42
come to God as a * child will never Mk 10:15
he felt hungry. A * way off he Mk 11:13
For they gave a * of their extra Mk 12:43,44
He went on a * further and fell Mk 14:35
A * later others standing around Mk 14:70
to become like * children's, and Lk 1:17
"And you, my * son, shall be Lk 1:76
The * boy greatly loved God Lk 1:80
to push out a * into the water, so Lk 5:3
in someone else's eye—his * fault Lk 6:41
but one who is forgiven *, shows Lk 7:47
forgiven little, shows * love." Lk 7:47
dying, a * girl twelve years old. Lk 8:42
the news that the * girl was dead. Lk 8:49
the * girl's father and mother. Lk 8:51
and called, "Get up, * girl!" Lk 8:54
so he stood a * child beside him Lk 9:47
takes care of a * child like this Lk 9:48
who are as trusting as * children. Lk 10:21
can't even do such * things as Lk 12:26
"So don't be afraid, * flock. Lk 12:32
If you cheat even a *, you won't Lk 16:10
who harm these * children's souls. Lk 17:2,3
"Let the * children come to me! Lk 18:16,17
as trusting as these * children's. Lk 18:16,17
You have been faithful with the * Lk 19:17
who have *, soon lose even that. Lk 19:26
For they have given a * of what Lk 21:4
But you Samaritans know so * Jn 4:21-24
I am to be here a * longer. Jn 7:33
me, for there is * time left before Jn 9:4
out for you just a * while longer. Jn 12:35
In just a * while I will be gone Jn 14:19
In just a * while I will be Jn 16:16
but just a * while after that, Jn 16:16
Jesus said, "Then feed my * Jn 21:17
* plots against Almighty God? Act 4:25,26
his own, not one * tract of land. Act 7:5
After a * thought he went to Act 12:12
On the Sabbath, we went a * way Act 16:13
Literally, "with * Act 26:28f
below them. A * later they sounded Act 27:28
So it is right for me to be a * Rom 15:17
together for a * while, you can Rom 15:24
foolish and of * worth in order to 1Co 1:27
Doesn't this show how * you have 1Co 3:4
these * things among yourselves? 1Co 6:2
Now we know so *, even with our 1Co 13:9
understand only a * about God now, 1Co 13:12
ground is a dry * seed of wheat, or 1Co 15:37
staying there only for a * while. 1Co 16:5
But it hurt you only for a * 2Co 7:8
he that gathered * had enough." 2Co 8:15
But remember this—if you give *, 2Co 9:6
you give little, you will get *. 2Co 9:6
against their own * ideas. 2Co 10:12
I also boast a * as they do. 2Co 11:16
my children, and * children don't 2Co 12:14
wealth for his * son, that child is Gal 4:1
those in your own * group—and there Gal 5:20
staying on earth a * longer, to Php 1:25
happily whether I have much or *. Php 4:11
You should have as * desire for Col 3:3
you but a very * while (though our 1Th 2:17
to fill up any * cracks there may 1Th 3:10
can't make his own * family behave, 1Ti 3:5
Don't let anyone think * of you 1Ti 4:12
You ought to take a * sometimes 1Ti 5:23
from you for a * while so that now Phm 1:15
telling them * by little about Heb 1:1
telling them little by * about Heb 1:1
the angels for a * while, now you Heb 2:7
for awhile was a * lower than the Heb 2:9
speak *, and not become angry; Jas 1:19
God, but makes one * slip, is just Jas 2:10
him and pour a * oil upon him, Jas 5:14
Once you knew very * of God's 1Pe 2:10
After you have suffered a * 1Pe 5:10
which they know so * about; 2Pe 2:12
MY * CHILDREN, I am telling you 1Jn 2:1
to all of you, my * children, 1Jn 2:12
And now, my * children, stay in 1Jn 2:28
be within him? * children, let us 1Jn 3:18
Strengthen what * remains—for Rev 3:2
Hold tightly to the * strength Rev 3:11
told to rest a * longer until their Rev 6:11
knowing that he has * time." Rev 12:12
earth, with two * horns like those Rev 13:11
be released again for a * while. Rev 20:3

LIVE
*, crawling along on your belly. Gen 3:14
Abram went on down to Egypt to *. Gen 12:10
But he will * near the rest of Gen 16:9-12
obey me and * as you should. Gen 17:1
there, and went to * in a cave in Gen 19:30
he is a prophet) and you shall *. Gen 20:7
want to *," the king told him. Gen 20:15
to * among your relatives?" Gen 24:5
and I, and will * by its terms." Gen 31:44
you folks to * here among us and to Gen 34:9,10
And you shall * among us wherever Gen 34:9,10
with you and * here and unite with Gen 34:16
"Let's invite them to * here Gen 34:21
the prostitute * who was soliciting Gen 38:
You shall * in the land of Gen 45:
and come here to Egypt to *. Gen 45:
You shall * off the fat of the Gen 45:
* here in the land of Goshen." Gen 46:
We have come to * here in Egypt, Gen 47
We request permission to * in the Gen 47
anywhere you like for them to *. Gen 47:5
food, then we will *, and the land Gen 47:1
families continued to * in Egypt. Gen 50:2
were born, but to let the girls *. Ex 1:15,1
the king—they let the boys * too. Ex 1:1
command and let the baby boys *?" Ex 1:1
But the girls, he said, could *. Ex 1:2
invitation to * with them, and Ex 2:2
Hivites, and Jebusites *. Ex 3:
of Goshen where the Israelis *. Ex 8:2
you made for them to * in. Ex 15:1
shall sell the * ox and divide the Ex 21:3
act of stealing a * ox or donkey or Ex 22:
and Jebusites, to * there. Ex 23:2
land, and you will * out the full Ex 23:2
Don't let them * among you! Ex 23:3
Temple where I can * among them. Ex 25:
And I will * among the people of Ex 29:4
so that I could * among them. Ex 29:4
for man may not see me and *. Ex 33:2
and must * outside the camp. Lev 13:4
and return to * inside the camp; Lev 14:
Then he shall let the * bird fly Lev 14:5
a censer full of * coals from the Lev 16:1
he shall bring the * goat and, Lev 16:2
If you obey them you shall *. Lev 18:4,
Literally, "shall * in Lev 18:4,5
in them" or "shall * by them." Lev 18:4,5
the nations that * there now. Lev 18:2
unfit for me to * in, and Lev 20:
are to * in these shelters. Lev 23:42
and caused you to * in shelters. Lev 23:4
Obey my laws if you want to * Lev 25:17,1
invite him to * with you as a Lev 25:35
and let your brother * with you; Lev 25:36
You shall eat your fill, and * Lev 26:4,5
And I will * among you, and not Lev 26:11
your enemies shall * in it, Lev 26:32
There they will * in constant Lev 26:36
They are to * near the Num 1:50
the camp where I * among you." Num 5:3
are like who * there, whether they Num 13:18
The Amalekites * in the south, Num 13:29
children finally * in the land I am Num 15:1
anyone who is bitten shall * if Num 21:8
They * alone, Num 23:7-10
And they shall * in many places. Num 24:3-9
"Alas, who can * when God does Num 24:23,24
have you let all the women *?" Num 31:15
Only the little girls may *; Num 31:18
take it and * there. Num 33:53
and he must * there until the Num 35:25
you are going to *, for I, Jehovah, Num 35:34
generation would * to see the good Deu 1:34,35
descendants of Esau who * in Seir; Deu 2:4
"(The Emim used to * in that Deu 2:10
I told them, 'may * here in the Deu 3:19
if you want to * and enter into and Deu 4:1
in the land where you will *. Deu 4:5
so that you will * forever in the Deu 4:40
from the heart of the fire, and *? Deu 5:26,27
only then will you * long and Deu 5:33
be entering, where you will *. Deu 6:1
his instructions as long as you *; Deu 6:2
If you do, you will not only *, Deu 8:1
fine homes to * in, and when your Deu 8:12,13
are! They * in high walled cities. Deu 9:1
the Canaanites *, in the wasteland Deu 11:30
the Jordan and * in the land the Deu 11:31
Jordan River and * in the Promised Deu 12:10
where you will *, don't follow Deu 12:29
You must never, as long as you * Deu 23:6
let him * among you in whatever Deu 23:15,16
someone else will * in the house Deu 28:30
You will * night and day in fear, Deu 28:66
land, where they still * today!' Deu 29:28
so that you will * and become a Deu 30:16
you and your children might *! Deu 30:19
You will then be able to * safely Deu 30:20
as you * in the Promised Land." Deu 31:13
(For this song will * from Deu 31:21
I kill and make *. Deu 32:39
Through obeying them you will * Deu 32:47
Let Reuben * forever Deu 33:6
you as long as you *, for I will be Jos 1:5
and conquer and * in the land which Jos 1:10,11
you will let me *, along with my Jos 2:12,13
the people who now * in the land Jos 3:10
to * outside the camp of Israel. Jos 6:23
and they still * among the Jos 6:25
do we know you don't * nearby? Jos 9:7
We must let them *, for if we Jos 9:20
the Amorites who * in the hills are Jos 10:6
who still * there among the Jos 13:13

LIVE Con't)
cities in which to * and the Jos 14:3,4
so the Jebusites * there among the Jos 15:63
out, so they still * as slaves Jos 16:10
the Perizzites and Rephaim *." Jos 17:15
able to clear it all and * there. Jos 17:16,17,18
give him a place to * among them. Jos 20:4
judges, and must * there until the Jos 20:6
now, and you will * there instead, Jos 23:4,5
so they still * there today, Ju 1:21
they still * among the tribe of Ju 1:29
so the Israelis still * among the Ju 1:31,32
to * among them as servants. Ju 1:33
Above all women who * in tents. Ju 5:24
who * around you on every side. Ju 6:10
have come to * in Shechem, and now Ju 9:31
let them * there any longer. Ju 9:41
to * with his father and mother. Ju 14:19
Then he went to * in a cave in Ju 15:8
looking for a good place to *. Ju 17:7,8
I am looking for a place to *." Ju 17:9
man replied. "I * on the far edge Ju 19:18
go, and to * wherever you live; Ru 1:16
go, and to live wherever you *; Ru 1:16
come here to * among strangers. Ru 2:10,11
None shall * to be old. 1Sa 2:31
Not one of them will * out his 1Sa 2:32
Those who are left alive will * 1Sa 2:33
shouted, "Long * the king!" 1Sa 10:24
is Jesse and we * in Bethlehem." 1Sa 17:58
David with him to * at Naioth. 1Sa 19:18
tell you, so you can escape and *. 1Sa 20:13
and mother to * there under royal 1Sa 22:3
David then went to * in the 1Sa 23:29
their families to * at Gath under 1Sa 27:2,3
we would rather * in one of the 1Sa 27:5
him, for I knew he couldn't *. 2Sa 1:10
where they now *. 2Sa 4:2,3
you shall * here at the palace!" 2Sa 9:7
but he will * here with me." 2Sa 9:10,11
to Jerusalem to * at the palace. 2Sa 9:13
to me and let the child *.' 2Sa 12:22
"Long * the king!" 2Sa 16:16
"Long * the king!" 2Sa 16:16
him *, and restore them to you." 2Sa 17:2,3
"Come across with me and * in 2Sa 19:33
that you will * to see the day when 2Sa 24:3
shouting, 'Long * King Adonijah!' 1Ki 1:25
May my lord the king * forever!" 1Ki 1:31
and shout, 'Long * King Solomon!' 1Ki 1:34
shouted, "Long * King Solomon!" 1Ki 1:39
He brought her to Jerusalem to * 1Ki 3:1
them began, "we * in the same 1Ki 3:17,18
him to *, for she is the mother!" 1Ki 3:27
would do: I will * among the 1Ki 6:13
he would * in the thick darkness; 1Ki 8:12,13
a place for you to * forever." 1Ki 8:12,13
that God would really * on earth? 1Ki 8:27
have promised to * in—and as I face 1Ki 8:29
yes, hear in heaven where you *, 1Ki 8:30
they continue to * in this land 1Ki 8:40
*, and come to their assistance. 1Ki 8:49
O my people, may you * good and 1Ki 8:61
And if you * in honesty and 1Ki 9:4
the Lord had chosen to * in. 1Ki 14:21
to him, "Go and * in the village 1Ki 17:8,9
to see if he will let you *." 1Ki 20:31
Ben-hadad pleads, 'Let me *!' 1Ki 20:32
for you and your sons to * on!" 2Ki 4:7
If they let us *, so much the 2Ki 7:4
and shouted, "Long * the king!" 2Ki 11:12
* there, as they do to this day. 2Ki 16:6
You can * in peace here in your 2Ki 18:31,32
be allowed to * in the land and 2Ki 25:24
The first to return and * again 1Ch 9:2
and he will always * in Jerusalem. 1Ch 23:25
rest—a place for our God to * in. 1Ch 28:2
he would * in the thick darkness, 2Ch 6:1
you, O Lord, to * in forever!" 2Ch 6:1
But will God really * upon the 2Ch 6:18
Hear from heaven where you *, 2Ch 6:30
heaven where you *, and do what 2Ch 6:33
heaven where you * and help them 2Ch 6:39
For he said, "She must not * in 2Ch 8:11
A great shout went up, "Long * 2Ch 23:11
in which I have chosen to *.' Neh 1:9
Literally, "Let the king * Neh 2:3f
slavery to get enough money to *. Neh 5:5
of Israel should * in tents during Neh 8:14
* for the duration of the feast. Neh 8:15
of which a man shall *." Neh 9:29f
selected by lot to * there too. Neh 11:1
continued to * in their own homes Neh 11:3
to * with the tribe of Benjamin. Neh 11:36
the king's interest to let them *. Est 3:8
Why did the midwife let me *? Job 3:12
You shall * a long, good life; Job 5:26
* in terror of his punishment. Job 9:34
Not one bit longer may he *. Job 14:5
"If a man dies, shall he * Job 14:14
"The truth is that the wicked * Job 21:7

They * to see their children Job 21:8
the wealthy * wherever they chose. Job 22:8
and * in caves for want of a home. Job 24:8
that as long as I *, while I have Job 27:3
is clear for as long as I *. Job 27:6
So now they * in frightening Job 30:6
"I * in terror now. Job 30:15
may * in the light of the living. Job 33:30
given them salt plains to * in. Job 39:6
* with you forever in your home. Ps 23:6
He shall * within God's circle of Ps 25:13
Try to * in peace with everyone; Ps 34:14
watching all who * good lives, and Ps 34:15
then you will * safely here in Ps 37:3
low-down ways and * good lives. Ps 37:27
in the land, and * there forever. Ps 37:29
and you could * on them eternally. Ps 49:11
Murderers and liars will not * Ps 55:23
I shall * forever in your Ps 61:4
And I shall * before the Lord Ps 61:7
I will bless you as long as I *, Ps 63:4
chosen to come and * with you Ps 65:4
where God has chosen to * forever. Ps 68:15,16
God will * among us here. Ps 68:18
All who seek for God shall * in Ps 69:32
His people shall * in them and Ps 69:35
all who love his name shall * Ps 69:36
And he shall *; Ps 72:15
and all its people * in turmoil, Ps 75:3
How happy are those who can * in Ps 84:4
Temple of my God than * in palaces Ps 84:10
No man can * forever. Ps 89:48
And some may even * to eighty. Ps 90:10
WE * WITHIN the shadow of the Ps 91:1
God, you * forever and forever! Ps 102:24
sing to the Lord as long as I *. Ps 104:33
to safety and a place to *. Ps 107:7
He does not fear bad news, nor * Ps 112:7
I shall *! Ps 116:9
I shall not die, but * to tell Ps 118:17
"deal bountifully that I may *." Ps 119:17f
As long as I * I'll Ps 119:33,34
your tender mercies, that I may *. Ps 119:75,76,77
For I have tried to * according Ps 119:94
Lord, you promised to let me *! Ps 119:116
to understand them and I shall *. Ps 119:144
If you will let me *, I will Ps 119:175
and my friends who * here; Ps 122:8
May you * to enjoy your Ps 128:6
home where I shall *," you said, Ps 132:14
when brothers * in harmony! Ps 133:1
for they shall * in your presence. Ps 140:13
They force me to * in the Ps 143:3
I will praise him as long as I * Ps 146:2
his people how to *—how to act in Pro 1:2
Such is the fate of all who * by Pro 1:19
But all who listen to me shall * Pro 1:33
If you * that kind of life, Pro 4:12
Obey me and *! Pro 7:2
Wisdom and good judgment * Pro 8:12
your foolishness and begin to *; Pro 9:6
The good man eats to *, while the Pro 13:25
Literally, "you will *." Pro 15:27f
The wicked * for rebellion; Pro 17:11
It is better to * in the corner Pro 21:9
Better to * in the desert than Pro 21:19
It is better to * in a corner of Pro 25:24
but good men will * to see the Pro 29:16
long the Lord may let him *. Ecc 5:18
some of the wicked * on and on. Ecc 7:15-17
who will not * long, good Ecc 8:13
"It is better to be a * dog than Ecc 9:4
dash of cologne! * happily with Ecc 9:9
so others have no place to *. Is 5:8
will * on curds and wild honey. Is 7:21,22
on all those who * in the land of Is 9:2
Few will * when I have finished Is 13:12
Ostriches will * there, and the Is 13:21
* in their land will serve them. Is 14:2
who belong to God shall * again. Is 26:19
venomous snakes *—and Egypt will Is 30:6
My people will * in safety, Is 32:18
they cry, "can * here in the Is 33:14
I will tell you who can * Is 33:15
no one will * there anymore. Is 34:10
will *, and owls and ravens. Is 34:11
will let you * fifteen more years. Is 38:5
Oh, heal me and make me *! Is 38:16
sing his praises, all you who * Is 42:10
Sing, all you who * in distant Is 42:10
Others died that you might *; Is 43:4
But see here, you who * in your Is 50:11
you will * among sorrows. Is 50:11
He shall * again Is 53:10
you will no longer * in shame. Is 54:4
You will * under a government Is 54:14
you will * in peace. Is 54:14
You will * in joy and peace. Is 55:12
One, says this: I * in that high Is 57:15
For my people will * as long as Is 65:21,22
God, and begin to * good, honest, Jer 4:2

But leave a scattered few to *. Jer 5:10
Their enemies shall * in their Jer 6:12
She continues to * a lie. Jer 7:28
die, rather than * where I will Jer 8:3
forget them and * in some wayside Jer 9:2
The Lord says: Take warning and *; Jer 17:21,22
We will continue to * as we want Jer 18:12
to the Chaldean army and *. Jer 21:9
It's very nice to * graciously Jer 22:23
saved and Israel will * in peace. Jer 23:5,6
and to those who * the way they Jer 23:17
those too who * in Egypt. Jer 24:8
Only then can you continue to * Jer 25:5
"If you want to *, submit to the Jer 27:12
of Babylon and *, for otherwise Jer 27:17
they shall possess it and * here Jer 30:3
* together in peace and happiness. Jer 31:24
make them * in peace and safety. Jer 32:37
Jerusalem shall * in safety and Jer 33:16
* and invite them to the Temple. Jer 35:2
farms, but always to * in tents; Jer 35:7
and that if we obeyed we would * Jer 35:7
I would let you * in peace here in Jer 35:15
Babylonians would *, and that the Jer 38:2
* and the city will not be burned. Jer 38:17
Settle in any city you wish and * Jer 40:10
insists on going to * in Egypt. Jer 42:17
For not one of you shall *—not a Jer 44:7
As I *, says the King, the Lord Jer 46:18
your cities and * in the caves like Jer 48:28
But though you * among the peaks Jer 49:16
No one will * there anymore. Jer 49:18
No one shall ever * there again. Jer 49:33
that no one shall * in her again; Jer 50:3
to * again in quietness in Israel. Jer 50:34
no one will * again in Babylon. Jer 50:40
always my soul will * in utter Lam 3:20
repents, he shall * and you have Eze 3:21
and wicked men of pride shall *. Eze 7:10,11
and took some * coals from the Eze 10:7,8
"Son of dust," he said, "you * Eze 12:2
who should not *, by lying to my Eze 13:19
your own blood, and I said, '*! Eze 16:6,7
"As I *, the Lord God says, Eze 16:48
For as I *, says the Lord, the Eze 17:16
"The Lord God says: As I *, Eze 17:19
As I *, says the Lord God, you Eze 18:3
the Lord, and he shall surely *. Eze 18:9
—shall that man *? Eze 18:13
he shall surely *. Eze 18:17
keeps my laws, he shall surely *. Eze 18:19
he shall surely * and not die. Eze 18:21
shall * because of his goodness. Eze 18:22
turn from his wicked ways and *. Eze 18:23
sinner, should he be allowed to *? Eze 18:24
from his sins and * a good life. Eze 18:28
He shall surely *—he shall not Eze 18:28
Turn, turn and *! Eze 18:32
so they could * by keeping them. Eze 20:11
If anyone keeps them, he shall *. Eze 20:11
a person keeps them, he shall *. Eze 20:21
you, Israel? As I *, the Lord God Eze 20:31
here in the land of those who *. Eze 26:20
All who * along the coastlands Eze 27:35
will once more * in their own land, Eze 28:25
They will * safely in Israel, Eze 28:26
All those who * beneath her shade Eze 31:12
How can we *?' Eze 33:10
Tell them: As I *, says the Eze 33:11
turn from his evil ways and *. Eze 33:11
"I have said the good man will * Eze 33:13
not doing evil—he shall surely *. Eze 33:15
to the good and shall surely *. Eze 33:16
what's fair and just, he shall *. Eze 33:19
God says: As I *, surely those Eze 33:27
"As I *, says the Lord God, you Eze 34:8
and everyone will * in safety. Eze 34:27
They shall * in safety and no one Eze 34:28
As I *, the Lord God says, since Eze 35:6
Therefore as I *, the Lord God Eze 35:11
Mount Seir and all who * in Edom! Eze 35:15
"And you shall * in Israel, the Eze 36:28
I am going to make you * and Eze 37:5
shall * and know I am the Lord." Eze 37:6
bodies, that they may * again." Eze 37:9
you, and you shall * and return Eze 37:14
They shall * in the land of Eze 37:25
after them shall * there, and their Eze 37:25
your allies who * safely on the Eze 39:6
and I will * among them forever. Eze 43:9
the water of this river shall *. Eze 47:9
water flows, everything will *. Eze 47:9
* among you with their families. Eze 47:22
to the tribe where they now *. Eze 47:23
where the other Levites will *. Eze 48:12
and you will * in the fields like Dan 4:25
of the palace to * with the animals Dan 4:32
and say, "King Darius, * forever! Dan 6:6
"Your Majesty, * forever!" Dan 6:21
allowed to * a short time longer. Dan 7:12
"You must * alone for many days; Hos 3:3

(LIVE Con't)
feet again, to * in his kindness! Hos 6:2
one can even * in Samaria without Hos 7:1
and * there on scraps of food. Hos 9:3
Oh, come back to God. * by the Hos 12:6
people of Israel, "Seek me—and *. Amo 5:4
Seek the Lord and *, or else he Amo 5:6
therefore you will never * in the Amo 5:11
Be good, flee evil—and *! Amo 5:14
ruined cities, and * in them again, Amo 9:14
You are proud because you * in Ob 1:3
Then my people who * in the Negeb Ob 1:19
decide to let us *, and will hold Jon 3:9
"The People of the Lord" will * Mic 2:5
Everyone will * quietly in his Mic 4:4
this city and * in the fields; Mic 4:10
make them * in peace and Mic 7:14
Or, "shall * by his Hab 2:4f
to * beyond the reach of danger. Hab 2:9
have a chance to * in the new homes Zep 1:13
Therefore as I *," says the Zep 2:9
the vultures and the owls will * Zep 2:14
ruins, a place for animals to *! Zep 2:15
Those who * far beyond the Zep 3:10
They will * quietly, in peace, Zep 3:13
King of Israel, will * among you! Zep 3:15
God has arrived to * among you. Zep 3:17,18
time for you to * in luxurious Hag 1:3,4
and bless her and * in her." Zec 1:17
Many will * outside the city Zec 2:4
For I have come to * among you,' Zec 2:10
I will * among them all. Zec 2:11,12
'you will all * in peace and Zec 3:10
I, myself, will * within Jerusalem, Zec 8:3
them home again to * safely in Zec 8:8
Be fair. * at peace with Zec 8:16
"But who can * when he appears? Mal 3:2
so many foreigners *—there the Mt 4:15,16
life and * as he wants you to. Mt 6:33
tomorrow too. * one day at a time. Mt 6:34
all enter the man and * in him. Mt 12:43,44,45
And his sisters—they all * here. Mt 13:56
now will certainly * to see me Mt 16:28
went away to * in another country. Mt 21:33
"This messenger will * out in Mk 1:3
hands on her and make her *." Mk 5:23
And his sisters * right here Mk 6:2,3
know what it means to really *. Mk 8:35
right now will * to see the Kingdom Mk 9:1
Better * forever with one hand Mk 9:43,44
Better be lame and * forever than Mk 9:45,46
So don't lose your flavor! * in Mk 9:50
* that you really have repented. Lk 3:8
Literally, "Man shall not * by Lk 4:4f
Men who * in luxury are found in Lk 7:25
Foxes have dens to * in, and Lk 9:58
to do to * forever in heaven?" Lk 10:25
"Do this and you shall *!" Lk 10:28
the birds * among its branches. Lk 13:19
*, for King Herod is after you!" Lk 13:31
"Long * the King! Lk 19:38
land to * for several years. Lk 20:9
they replied, "where do you *?" Jn 1:38
God—and those who listen shall *. Jn 5:25
Anyone eating this Bread shall * Jn 6:48-51
and I in him. I * by the power of Jn 6:57
of me shall * because of me! Jn 6:57
this Bread shall * forever, and not Jn 6:58
disciples if you * as I tell you Jn 8:30,31
like anyone else, shall * again. Jn 11:25
would * forever and never die. Jn 12:34
For I will * again—and you will Jn 14:19
will come to them and * with them. Jn 14:23
Take care to * in me, and let me Jn 15:4
live in me, and let me * in you. Jn 15:4
has loved me. * within my love. Jn 15:9
obey my Father and * in his love. Jn 15:10
replied, "If I want him to * Jn 21:22
He only said, "If I want him to * Jn 21:23
leave the land and * in a foreign Act 7:6
However, God doesn't * in Act 7:48,49
Afterwards he left to * in Act 12:19
he doesn't * in man-made temples; Act 17:24
For in him we * and move and Act 17:28
He isn't fit to *!" Act 22:22
may repent and * in the light of Act 26:18
will not permit him to *!" Act 28:4
was permitted to * wherever he Act 28:16
who makes the dead * again and Rom 4:17
with God, so that they can *. Rom 5:18
lower natures * only to please Rom 8:5
but your spirit will *, for Rom 8:10
your dying bodies * again after you Rom 8:11
and its evil deeds, you shall *. Rom 8:13
we who * in the daylight should! Rom 13:12,13
Christ to help you * as you should, Rom 13:14
We are not our own bosses to * Rom 14:7
both while we * and when we die. Rom 14:9
For it is written, "As I *," Rom 14:11
Try instead to * in such a way Rom 14:13
help you to * in complete harmony Rom 15:5
For some of those who * at 1Co 1:11
unbelievers who * in sexual sin, or 1Co 5:10
For you can't * in this world 1Co 5:10
Those who * immoral lives, who 1Co 6:9,10
to * in peace and harmony. 1Co 7:15
of it as long as I *, because I 1Co 8:13
If we will never * again after we 1Co 15:32
now, but when we * again they will 1Co 15:43
not the right kind to * forever. 1Co 15:50
cannot perish but will * forever. 1Co 15:53
we would never * through it. 2Co 1:8
Yes, we * under constant danger 2Co 4:11
when this tent we * in now is taken 2Co 5:1
died to the old life we used to *. 2Co 5:13,14
so that all who *—having received 2Co 5:15
from him—might * no longer for 2Co 5:15
We try to * in such a way that no 2Co 6:3
known to God; we * close to death, 2Co 6:9
How can light * with darkness? 2Co 6:14
of you, "I will * in them and walk 2Co 6:16
forever and I * and die with you. 2Co 7:3
he was, but now we * and are 2Co 13:4
I pray that you will * good 2Co 13:7
* in harmony and peace. 2Co 13:11
this evil world in which we *. Gal 1:4
law, that I might * unto God." Gal 2:19f
longer *, but Christ lives in me. Gal 2:20
all of you who * by this principle Gal 6:16
the Lord—to * and act in a way Eph 4:1
for the Lord: * no longer as the Eph 4:17,18
Spirit sorrow by the way you *. Eph 4:30
For I * in eager expectation and Php 1:20
whether I * or whether I must die. Php 1:20
know which is better, to * or die! Php 1:22
Sometimes I want to * and at Php 1:23
remember always to * as Christians Php 1:27
don't * to make a good impression Php 2:3
You are to * clean, innocent Php 2:15
I know how to * on almost Php 4:12
and asking that the way you * Col 1:10
who * in the kingdom of light. Col 1:12
who love him and * for him, and the Col 1:26,27
* in vital union with him. Col 2:6
to earn enough to * on so that our 1Th 2:9
For what is it we * for, that 1Th 2:19
Jesus—that you * more and more 1Th 4:1
If anyone refuses to * by these 1Th 4:8
your ambition: to * a quiet life, 1Th 4:11
But let us who * in the light 1Th 5:8
he died for us so that we can * 1Th 5:10
money we needed to * on, in order 2Th 3:8
so that we can * in peace and 1Ti 2:2
that the way to * a godly life is 1Ti 3:16
follow the way you teach and *; 1Ti 4:12
and the way I * and what I want. 2Ti 3:10
younger women to * quietly, to love Tit 2:4
pleasures and to * good, Tit 2:12
Christ's longing was to * until Heb 5:7f
And can a human body * long Heb 5:7f
so that he could * to accomplish Heb 5:7f
Since he will * forever, he will Heb 7:25
God's sight must * by faith, Heb 10:38
so that we can begin really to *? Heb 12:9
and seek to * a clean and holy Heb 12:14
If you are wise, * a life of Jas 3:13
we shall * and do this or that." Jas 4:15
Now we * in the hope of eternal 1Pe 1:3
free to do wrong. * as those who 1Pe 2:16
sin and * a good life from now on. 1Pe 2:24
Try to * in peace even if you 1Pe 3:11
* in their spirits as God lives. 1Pe 4:6
so that now he can * a strong, good 2Pe 1:9
For they * in evil pleasures day 2Pe 2:13
try hard to * without sinning; 2Pe 3:14
Christian should * as Christ did. 1Jn 2:6
the will of God will * forever. 1Jn 2:17
has said, you must * in Christ, 1Jn 2:27
money enough to * well, and sees a 1Jn 3:17
And as we * with Christ, our 1Jn 4:17
I am fully aware that you * in Rev 2:13
"I know your reputation as a * Rev 3:1
men, and he will * with them and Rev 21:3

LIVED

Adam * another 800 years, Gen 5:3,4,5
Afterwards he * another 807 Gen 5:6,7,8
Afterwards he * another 815 Gen 5:9,10,11
Afterwards he * another 840 Gen 5:12,13,14
Afterwards he * 830 years, Gen 5:15,16,17
Afterwards he * another 800 Gen 5:18,19,20
Afterwards he * another 300 years Gen 5:21-24
afterwards he * another 782 Gen 5:25,26,27
Afterwards Lamech * 595 years, Gen 5:28-31
that breathed and * upon dry land. Gen 7:22
Noah * another 350 years after Gen 9:28
These descendants of Joktan * all Gen 10:26-30
The people who * there began to Gen 11:3,4
after that he * another 500 Gen 11:10,11
and after that he * another 403 Gen 11:12,13
Peleg was born. He * another 430 Gen 11:16,17
Reu was born. He * another 209 Gen 11:18,19
Serug was born. He * 207 years Gen 11:20,21
Nahor was born. He * 200 years Gen 11:22,23
his son Terah. He * 119 years Gen 11:24,25
Canaan, while Lot * among the Gen 13:12
who * in Sodom—and all he owned. Gen 14:12
"I saw God and * to tell it." Gen 16:13
And Abraham * in the Philistine Gen 21:34
king of the Philistines, *. Gen 26:1
Gerar Valley and * there instead. Gen 26:17
and asked them where they *. Gen 29:4
Hebron), where Abraham too had *. Gen 35:27
while they * in Canaan:The clan of Gen 36:17
of Canaan, where his father had *. Gen 37:1
* there with a man named Hirah. Gen 38:1
They * at Chezib and had three Gen 38:3,4,5
Jacob replied, "I have * 130 Gen 47:9
So Israel * in the land of Goshen Gen 47:27
Jacob * seventeen years after Gen 47:28
when he died. He * to see the Gen 50:23
(Levi * 137 years. Ex 6:16
(Kohath * 133 years. Ex 6:18
Amram * to the age of 137. Ex 6:20
where the people of Israel *. Ex 9:26
descendants had * in Egypt 430 Ex 12:40,41
of Egypt where you * so long, or Lev 18:3
*, but also after his death. Lev 18:14f
seventh year when you * upon it. Lev 26:34,35
the Canaanites who * in the hills Num 14:45
the Amorites and * in them, Num 21:25,26
given to their father if he had *. Num 27:6,7
the Machirites, and they * there. Num 32:40
king of Arad, who * in the Negeb, Num 33:40
But the Amorites who * there Deu 1:44
where our brothers *, crossing the Deu 2:8
In earlier days the Horites * in Deu 2:12
Ammonites * there in their place. Deu 2:21
it from fire, as you did, and *! Deu 4:33
and you * among the Egyptians. Deu 23:7
"Surely you remember how we * in Deu 29:16
And they * without foreign gods, Deu 32:12
and Canaanites who * along the Jos 5:1
So from that time on they * on Jos 5:11,12
who * among the Israelis. Jos 8:35
by saying that you * in a distant Jos 9:22
of Anak who * in the hill country Jos 11:21
King Sihon of the Amorites, who * Jos 12:2
the Rephaim, who * at Ashtaroth and Jos 12:4
The people who * there were the Jos 12:8-24
Sihon was the king who had * in Jos 13:21
the Jebusites who * in the city of Jos 15:63
out the people who * in those Jos 17:12
where the Jebusites *, and Jos 18:16
its people, and * there; Jos 19:47,48
he rebuilt it and * there. Jos 19:50
in and conquered it and * there. Jos 21:43
* east of the Euphrates River; Jos 24:2
Then Israel * in the wilderness Jos 24:7
when they * beyond the Euphrates Jos 24:14
two tribes * together after that. Ju 1:16
them as long as that judge *. Ju 2:18
So Israel * among the Canaanites, Ju 3:5
who * in Harosheth-ha-goiim. Ju 4:2,3
of Abinoam), who * in Kedesh, in Ju 4:6
Then Jotham escaped and * in Beer Ju 9:21
of Issachar, but * in the city of Ju 10:1
home and * in the land of Tob. Ju 11:3
the Amorites, who * in Heshbon, and Ju 11:19
The next judge was Ibzan, who * Ju 12:8
Dan, who * in the city of Zorah. Ju 13:2,3
IN THE HILL country of Ephraim * a Ju 17:1
were wealthy. They * quietly, and Ju 18:7
to try it. They * a great distance Ju 18:7
Dan rebuilt the city and * there. Ju 18:28
where they * for four months. Ju 20:46,47
their cities and * in them. Ju 21:23
of Ephraim who * in 1Sa 1:1
into the city where the prophet *. 1Sa 9:9,10,11
to save you, and you * in safety. 1Sa 12:11
of Judah who * in 1Sa 17:12
David now * in the wilderness 1Sa 23:14,15
While your shepherds have * among 1Sa 25:7
day), and they * there among the 1Sa 27:7
who had * near Shur along the road 1Sa 27:8
and the Philistines * in them. 1Sa 31:7
against the Jebusites who * there. 2Sa 5:6
For I have never * in a temple. 2Sa 7:6
So Tamar * as a desolate woman in 2Sa 13:20
David's counselors who * in Giloh. 2Sa 15:12
if Absalom had * and all of us 2Sa 19:6
So he * in Jerusalem for a long 1Ki 2:38
and Israel * in peace and safety; 1Ki 4:25
cavalrymen who * in the chariot 1Ki 10:26
in Bethel where the old prophet *. 1Ki 13:24,25
room where he *, and laid the body 1Ki 17:19
of God, where he * in a cave. 1Ki 19:9
of Jezreel, where Naboth *. 1Ki 21:8
at the hill where Elisha *, 2Ki 5:24
her family and * in the land of the 2Ki 8:2
They * there for six years while 2Ki 11:2,3
and then Israel * in safety again 2Ki 13:5
Amaziah * fifteen years longer 2Ki 14:17
so he * in a house by himself. 2Ki 15:5

LIVED Con't)
for as long as he *, he ate 2Ki 25:29
Bela (the son of Beor), who * in 1Ch 1:43
because many craftsmen * there). 1Ch 4:14
They * at Beer-sheba, Moladah, 1Ch 4:28
Their descendants also * in or 1Ch 4:32,33
And they have * there ever since. 1Ch 4:43
* in Aroer and as far distant as 1Ch 5:7,8
land of Bashan, * the descendants 1Ch 5:11
The clan * in and around Gilead 1Ch 5:16
So the Reubenites * in the 1Ch 5:22
They * in an area bounded on one 1Ch 7:28
Je-iel, the father of Gibeon, * 1Ch 8:29
All of these families * together 1Ch 8:30,31,32
of El-kanah, who * in the area of 1Ch 9:15,16
positions they * near the 1Ch 9:27
Levites. They * in Jerusalem at the 1Ch 9:33,34
Jeiel (whose wife was Maacah) * 1Ch 9:35,36,37
Mikloth * with his son Shime-am 1Ch 9:38
And the Philistines came and * in 1Ch 10:7
inhabitants of the land—*. 1Ch 11:4
David * in the fortress and that 1Ch 11:7
of Manasseh *—there were 120,000 1Ch 12:24-37
They have * without God's laws. 2Ch 15:3
the heathen who * in this land when 2Ch 20:7
except for Joash, * to succeed him 2Ch 22:9
the priest. He * to a very old 2Ch 24:15
However, King Amaziah of Judah * 2Ch 25:25
of his death and * in isolation, 2Ch 26:21
heathen people who * in the Ez 9:1
And whenever the workers who * Neh 4:12
each homeowner who * near the wall Neh 7:3
They * in these huts for the Neh 8:17
of Perez who * in Jerusalem. Neh 11:4,5,6
and people * wherever their family Neh 11:20
Ziha and Gishpa) all * in Ophel. Neh 11:21
where the people of Judah * were: Neh 11:25-30
of the tribe of Benjamin * at: Neh 11:31-35
Some of the Levites who * in Neh 11:36
harem where the king's wives *. Est 2:12,13,14
eunuchs, and * there the rest of Est 2:12,13,14
THERE * IN the land of Uz a man Job 1:1
and rich, and has * in conquered Job 15:27,28
Job * 140 years after that, Job 42:16
There your people *, for you gave Ps 68:9,10
where he had * among mankind, and Ps 78:60
Egypt and * there with his sons. Ps 105:23
earth began. I * before the oceans Pro 8:24
Hezekiah * 200 years after Pro 25:1f
the land will never again be * in. Is 13:20
Where desert jackals *, there Is 35:7
* in once again—it shall be done! Is 44:26
be * in, not to be an empty chaos. Is 45:18
of Hilkiah) who * in the town of Jer 1:1
to his deeds—how he has *. Jer 17:10
conquered it and * in it, but they Jer 32:23
We have * in tents and have Jer 35:10
And Jeremiah * there among his Jer 39:14
to Gedaliah and * in Judah with the Jer 40:6
history Moab has * there Jer 48:11
Never again shall it be * in by Jer 50:39
No one has * in them since, and Jer 50:40
king's kitchen as long as he *. Jer 52:33
son of Buzi) who * with the Jewish Eze 1:1
of the world * beneath its shadow. Eze 31:6
that had * beneath her shade. Eze 31:17
nations while they *, and now they Eze 32:24
nations while they *, but now they Eze 32:25
were a terror to all while they *. Eze 32:27
them for the evil way they *. Eze 36:19
*, and stood up—a very great army. Eze 37:10
their fathers *, the land I gave my Eze 37:25
peoples who * in the mountainous Eze 38:2,3f
and he * among the wild donkeys; Dan 5:21
Lord to Micah, who * in the town of Mic 1:1
gave to Nahum, who * in Elkosh, Nah 1:1
the young and tender, * unafraid? Nah 2:11
city that * in such security, that Zep 2:15
instead, and * in Nazareth. Mt 2:23
them met him. They * in a cemetery Mt 8:28
the Baptist. He * in the wilderness Mk 1:4
This man * among the gravestones, Mk 5:3,4
* when Herod was king of Judea. Lk 1:5
Zacharias *, to visit Elizabeth. Lk 1:39,40
and when he grew up he * out in Lk 1:80
Homeless and naked, he * in a Lk 8:27
* each day in mirth and luxury. Lk 16:19
became a human being and * here Jn 1:14
Some of the people who * there in Jn 7:25
Well, her brother Lazarus, who * Jn 11:1
the Chaldeans and * in Haran, in Act 7:4
the country, and * in the land of Act 7:29
IN CAESAREA THERE * a Roman Act 10:1
was the place where Simon Peter *! Act 10:18
from Rome. Paul * and worked with Act 18:2,3
who worshiped God and * next door Act 18:7
"Brothers, I have always * before Act 23:1
and later at Jerusalem, and I * Act 26:4
Paul * for the next two years in Act 28:30
good way I have * before them, and Rom 15:19
I have * with weariness and pain 2Co 11:27

those who * in the time of Moses. Heb 4:2
those who * under their rules. Heb 10:1
promised land, he * in tents like a Heb 11:9
died, his spirit * on, and it was 1Pe 3:18
punished for the way they have *. 1Pe 4:5
of the people who * in ancient 2Pe 2:5
Enoch, who * seven generations Jud 1:14
John recognizes him from having * Rev 1:13f
She has * in luxury and Rev 18:7

LIVELIHOOD
by which its owner gains his *. Deu 24:6
"May God destroy your homes and * Neh 5:13
The soil has been my * from my Zec 13:5

LIVER
the head, legs, heart, and *. Ex 12:9
mass above the *, and the two Lev 8:15,16
to idols and inspect the * Eze 21:21

LIVES
the Tree of Life and * forever?" Gen 3:22
direction of men's * were only Gen 6:5
"Flee for your *," the angels Gen 19:17
"God * here!" Gen 28:16,17
them he exclaimed, "God * here!" Gen 32:1
ahead of you to preserve your *. Gen 45:5
"You have saved our *," they Gen 47:25
I could save the * of many people. Gen 50:20
but she *, then the man who injured Ex 21:22
people into a land where no one *, Lev 16:22
sinned at the cost of their *. Num 16:38
and permanent effect upon your *! Deu 4:9
and prosperous * in the land you Deu 5:33
your God who * among you is a Deu 6:15
always to put God first in your *. Deu 14:23
that day all the rest of your *! Deu 16:3
no matter where he * in the land of Deu 18:6,7
Your * will hang in doubt. Deu 28:66
long, plentiful * in the land you Deu 32:47
And * in safety beside him. Deu 33:12
"We'll defend you with our *." Jos 2:15
* against Joshua and the Israelis. Jos 9:1
So we feared for our * because of Jos 9:24
and follow his plan for your *. Jos 22:5
where the Lord * among us in his Jos 22:19
to the Lord for as long as he *." 1Sa 1:28
There is a prophet who * here in 1Sa 9:6
He * just inside the city gates. 1Sa 9:12,13
Lord *, he shall not be killed." 1Sa 19:6
But the * of your enemies shall 1Sa 25:29
* of one hundred Philistines." 2Sa 3:14
Shall I not demand your *?" 2Sa 4:11
eventually; our * are like water 2Sa 14:14
men laid down their * that day. 2Sa 18:7
life today and the * of your sons, 2Sa 19:5
The Lord *. 2Sa 22:47
men who have risked their *." 2Sa 23:17
"As the Lord * who has rescued me 1Ki 1:29
for they were fearful for their * 1Ki 1:49,50
perfect * before the Lord our God; 1Ki 8:61
Lord God of Israel *—the God whom I 1Ki 17:1
* of these, your fifty servants. 2Ki 1:13
who risked their * to get it." 1Ch 11:18,19
* from everlasting to everlasting. Neh 9:5
my life and the * of my people. Est 7:3
defense of their * and their Est 8:11
stood for their * and destroyed all Est 9:16
* in fear, distress, and anguish. Job 15:23,24
that my Redeemer *, and that he Job 19:25
of their * washed out forever? Job 22:15,16
prosperity throughout their *. Job 36:11
They die young after * of Job 36:14
her nest? She * upon the cliffs, Job 39:28
He saves those whose hearts and * Ps 7:10
But the Lord * on forever; Ps 9:7,8
to the God who * in Jerusalem. Ps 9:11
The sun * in the heavens where Ps 19:3,4
of the Lord and enter where he *? Ps 24:3
* by God himself, their Savior. Ps 24:5
splendor of your presence *. Ps 26:8
mankind from heaven where he *. Ps 33:13,14,15
all who live good *, and he gives Ps 34:15
low-down ways and live good *. Ps 37:27
He * upon Mount Zion in Jerusalem. Ps 48:1
for he holds our * in his hands. Ps 66:9
for their * are precious to him. Ps 72:14
His home is in Jerusalem. He * Ps 76:2
So he cut their * short and gave Ps 78:33
the Egyptians' *, but handed them Ps 78:50
constant joy to the end of our *. Ps 90:14
Lord with the beauty of holy *. Ps 96:9
he protects the * of his people, Ps 97:10
We have escaped with our * as a Ps 124:7
praise the Lord, for he * here in Ps 135:21
lay a booby trap for their own *. Pro 1:18
live, while the evil man * to eat. Pro 13:25
An evil man * an evil life; Pro 21:8
a good man * a godly life. Pro 21:8
most men have throughout their *. Ecc 2:3
many daughters and * to be very Ecc 6:3
Though a man * a thousand years Ecc 6:6
alike spend their * scratching for Ecc 6:7,8
who is wise * a far better life. Ecc 6:7,8

times and still *, I know very well Ecc 8:12
live long, good *—their days shall Ecc 8:13
If a person * to be very old, Ecc 11:8
stump still * to grow again." Is 6:13
of Saul—are running for their *. Is 10:28,29
he * will be a glorious place. Is 11:10
One of Israel, who * among you. Is 12:6
The Lord is very great, and * in Is 33:5
I traded their * for yours Is 43:4
* snuffed out like candlewicks. Is 43:17
in haste, running for your *; Is 52:12
sinners and have been all our *. Is 64:5
where no one * or even travels. Jer 2:6
honest, clean *, then you will be a Jer 4:2
"Run for your *! Jer 4:5
OF Benjamin, run for your *! Jer 6:1
for the future; he * on the Jer 17:6
you 'The Man Who * in Terror.' Jer 20:3
This is how a man * close to God. Jer 22:16
"As the Lord * who rescued the Jer 23:7
say, "As the Lord * who brought Jer 23:8
these prophets who * close enough Jer 23:18
live long, good * in our own land. Jer 35:7
it will be at the cost of your *. Jer 42:20
Flee for your *; Jer 48:6
Flee for your *, says the Jer 49:30
one * nor even travelers pass by. Jer 51:43
Their * ebb away like those Lam 2:12
streets without danger to our *. Lam 4:18
And even if a merchant *, his Eze 7:13
Not one of those whose * are Eze 7:13
wife who * with other men instead Eze 16:32
where the king * who gave him his Eze 17:16
again and slaughters many *. Eze 17:17
"Every leader in Israel who * Eze 22:6
They devour many *; Eze 22:25
and they destroy * for profit. Eze 22:27
their * on the day of your fall. Eze 32:10
honored him who * forever, whose Dan 4:34
oath by him who * for-ever and Dan 12:7
and run for their * that day." Amo 2:16
Fearing for their *, the Jon 1:5
righteous man trusts in me, and *! Hab 2:4
your name and forfeited your *. Hab 2:10
turned many from their * of sin. Mal 2:6
"Never in all our * have we seen Mt 9:33
by it, and by God who * in it. Mt 23:21
Is it a day to save * or to Mk 3:4
to plant good seed within their *. Mk 4:14
Only those who throw away their * Mk 8:35
men's *, but to save them." Lk 9:55f
say to the man who * there, 'Our Lk 22:11
that bread every day of our *!" Jn 6:34
plentiful harvest of new *. Jn 12:23,24
where my Father *, and I am going Jn 14:2,3
are from my Father who * in me. Jn 14:10
But you do, for he * with you now Jn 14:17
Whoever * in me and I in him Jn 15:5
fled for their *, going to the Act 14:5,6
he cleansed their * through faith, Act 15:9
have risked their * for the sake of Act 15:26
feared for their * when they heard Act 16:38
Not one of us will lose our *, Act 27:22
* of all those sailing with you.' Act 27:24
Their * became full of every Rom 1:29
judge the secret * of everyone, Rom 2:16
power, but now he * forever in Rom 6:10
Yet, even though Christ * Rom 8:10
Holy Spirit who * in you will give Rom 8:10f
from the dead, * in you, he will Rom 8:11
Everything * by his power, and Rom 11:36
In fact, they risked their * for Rom 16:4
of God * among you in his house? 1Co 3:16
Those who live immoral *, who are 1Co 6:9,10
you, and that he * within you? 1Co 6:19
great dangers to our * at present. 1Co 7:26
of her husband as long as he *; 1Co 7:39
All their * they have been used 1Co 8:7
And your changed * are the result 1Co 9:1
God works in our *, but it is the 1Co 12:6
our *, facing death hour by hour? 1Co 15:30
are spending their * helping and 1Co 16:15
wholesome fragrance in our *. 2Co 2:15
danger to our * because we serve 2Co 4:11
have our * laid bare—before him. 2Co 5:10
but to spend their * pleasing 2Co 5:15
by our wholesome * and by our 2Co 6:6
uses sorrow in our * to help us 2Co 7:10
he * by the mighty power of God. 2Co 13:4
I pray that you will live good *, 2Co 13:7
longer live, but Christ * in me. Gal 2:20
inclinations your * will produce Gal 5:19
controls our * he will produce this Gal 5:22
leading in every part of our *. Gal 5:25
as they are, our * expressing the Eph 2:3
sins, he gave us back our * again Eph 2:5
given us new * from Christ Jesus; Eph 2:10
spend these * in helping others. Eph 2:10
should have no place in your *. Eph 4:31
Or, "your * should be an Eph 5:10f
peace in your hearts and your *. Php 1:2

(LIVES Con't)
You are to live clean, innocent * Php 2:15
I will be one who * in the fresh Php 3:11
Dear brothers, pattern your * Php 3:17
who else * up to my example. Php 3:17
world and changing * everywhere, Col 1:6
Let your * overflow with joy and Col 2:7
in your hearts and *, for this is Col 3:15
enrich your * and make you wise; Col 3:16
And you know how our very * were 1Th 1:5
God's message, but our own * too. 1Th 2:8
that your daily * should not 1Th 2:12
your * when you believed it. 1Th 2:13
living quiet, good, and loving *. 1Ti 2:15
sinful * and everyone knows it. 1Ti 5:24
can never die, who * in light so 1Ti 6:16
the Holy Spirit who * within you. 2Ti 1:14
by living godly * will suffer at 2Ti 3:12
us realize what is wrong in our *; 2Ti 3:16
to all those whose * show that they 2Ti 4:8
truth that changes *—so that they Tit 1:1
well thought of for their good *; Tit 1:6
must be men of blameless * Tit 1:7
good, God-fearing * day after day, Tit 2:12
desires. Our * were full of Tit 3:3
that their * will be fruitful. Tit 3:14
it will grip their * too, as they Phm 1:6
* as slaves to constant dread. Heb 2:15
are God's house—he * in us! Heb 3:6
we are told that Melchizedek * on. Heb 7:8
But Jesus * forever and continues Heb 7:24
will transform our * and hearts. Heb 9:14
hurting many in their spiritual *. Heb 12:15
come from their *, and try to trust Heb 13:7
when he gave us our new *, Jas 1:18
can turn our whole * into a blazing Jas 3:6
or bird that * and every kind of Jas 3:7
For the length of your * is as Jas 4:14
Yes, our natural * will fade as 1Pe 1:24
now your very * have been changed 1Pe 2:10
It is God's will that your good * 1Pe 2:15
Your godly * will speak to them 1Pe 3:1
live in their spirits as God *. 1Pe 4:6
holy, godly * we should be living! 2Pe 3:11
darkness in our * disappears and 1Jn 2:8
Holy Spirit and he * within you, in 1Jn 2:27
our * for our Christian brothers. 1Jn 3:16
each other God * in us and his love 1Jn 4:12
God is love, and anyone who * in 1Jn 4:16
evil, immoral *, degrading their Jud 1:8
must build up your * ever more Jud 1:20
on the throne, who * forever and Rev 4:9
swore by him who * forever and Rev 10:6
for they did not love their * but Rev 12:11
God who * forever and forever. Rev 15:7

LIVESTOCK
very rich in *, silver, and gold. Gen 13:1
They brought their * too, and Gen 46:6
Joseph replied, "give me your *. Gen 47:16
their cattle, flocks, and other *. Num 35:3
his property and * and all the 1Ch 28:1

LIVID
King Balak was * with rage by Num 24:10

LIVING
And man became a * person. Gen 2:7
struggle to extract a * from it. Gen 3:17
cattlemen and those * in tents. Gen 4:20
man * on the earth at that time. Gen 6:9,10
and destroy every * Gen 6:17
And all * things upon the earth Gen 7:21
destroying all * things, even Gen 8:21
to every * being on the earth." Gen 9:16,17
many generations, * in the various Gen 10:32
son Eber was born, * 403 years Gen 11:14,15
the Amorites * in Hazazan-tamar. Gen 14:7
of the Amorite nations * here now Gen 15:16
Well of the * One Who Sees Me." Gen 16:14
was * in the oak grove at Mamre. Gen 18:1
I have been * with Uncle Laban Gen 32:4
of Esau, * in the localities named Gen 36:40-43
"God (or Pharaoh) says 'He is *.' Gen 41:45f
father was still * and he asked us Gen 43:7
Or, "the * God." Ex 3:14f
land of Canaan where they were *. Ex 6:4
foreigners who are * among you just Ex 12:19
"As to foreigners, if they are * Ex 12:48
and to foreigners * among you." Ex 12:49
Canaanites are now *, all Ex 13:11
them the principles of godly *. Ex 18:19,20
but the owner of the * ox shall Ex 21:36
the people now * in the land, and Ex 23:31
with the people * in the land, for Ex 34:15
shall require two * birds of a kind Lev 14:4
The other bird, still *, shall Lev 14:6
* bird fly into the open field. Lev 14:7
as well as the * bird, into the Lev 14:51,52
* among the people of Israel; Lev 16:29,30
or a foreigner * among you who Lev 17:8,9
or a foreigner * among you, who Lev 17:10
* among them, may eat blood. Lev 17:12
or a foreigner * among you, who Lev 17:13
the people * there, and will throw Lev 18:25
and to foreigners * among you. Lev 18:26
* in the land where you are going. Lev 18:29,30
or a foreigner * among you—who Lev 20:1
or other person * among you offers Lev 22:17,18
and for foreigners * among you who Lev 23:22
and any foreigners * among you. Lev 25:6,7
foreign nations * around you, and Lev 25:44
of the foreigners * among you, even Lev 25:45
"If a foreigner * among you Lev 25:47
And if a foreigner is * among Num 9:14
But the people * there are Num 13:28
and the Canaanites * in the Num 14:25
and to foreigners * among you who Num 15:13,14
the foreigners * among them, for Num 15:26
foreigners who are * among you. Num 15:29
And he stood between the * and Num 16:48
and any foreigners * among them. Num 19:10
of Beor) who was * in his native Num 22:5,6
"If she is married and * in her Num 30:10
and his daughter who is * at home. Num 30:16
out the Amorites who were * there. Num 32:39
out all the people * there and Num 33:52
out the people * there, those who Num 33:55
for I, Jehovah, will be * there." Num 35:34
who were * there before them. Deu 2:22
the tribe of Avvim * in villages Deu 2:23
even foreigners * among you must Deu 5:14
the voice of the * God speaking Deu 5:26,27
all the enemies * in your land, as Deu 6:19
of the nations now * there. Deu 18:9
and when you are * in their cities Deu 19:1
destroy every * thing. Deu 20:16
while * at home with her parents; Deu 22:21
wives while their husband was *. Deu 22:30f
or a foreigner * in your town. Deu 24:14,15
it and are * there, you must Deu 26:1
Levites or migrants * among you. Deu 26:11
Foreigners * among you shall Deu 28:43
them as you are * among the nations Deu 30:1
the nations * there, and you shall Deu 31:3
the nations * in the land, just as Deu 31:4
to you the people * there, and you Deu 31:5
and foreigners * among you—to hear Deu 31:12
for sure that the * God is among Jos 3:10
and the foreigners * among Jos 8:33
actually * right here among us? Jos 9:22
destroy all the people * in it. Jos 9:24
found the Anakim * there in great, Jos 14:12
against the people * in the city of Jos 15:15
The Canaanites * in Gezer were Jos 16:10
out the people * in the land which Jos 18:3
for foreigners * in Israel as well Jos 20:9
out all the people * there now, and Jos 23:4,5
cities where you are now *. Jos 24:13
other nations * here in the land. Jos 24:18
out the people * in the territory Ju 1:3
the Jebusites * in Jerusalem, so Ju 1:21
out the people * in Beth-shean, Ju 1:27
true of the Canaanites * in Gezer; Ju 1:29
with the people * in this land; Ju 2:2
the nations * in your land; Ju 2:3
were still *—those who had seen the Ju 2:7-9
The Hivites * in Mount Lebanon, Ju 3:1
clan, and had been * in various Ju 4:11
mountains, * in caves and dens. Ju 6:2
Abimelech was * at Arumah at Ju 9:41
* off the land as bandits. Ju 11:3
Israel has been * here for all Ju 11:26
* in the land assigned to them. Ju 18:1
the tribe of Levi * on the far side Ju 19:1
Ephraim, but was * now in Gibe-ah, Ju 19:16
to defy the armies of the * God?" 1Sa 17:26
defied the armies of the * God! 1Sa 17:36
when David was * in the cave. 1Sa 22:4
he was * among the Philistines. 1Sa 27:11
Here I am * in this beautiful 2Sa 7:2
family was still *, for he wanted 2Sa 9:1
"I swear by the * God," he 2Sa 12:5
"While the baby was still *, you 2Sa 12:21
One time when David was * in the 2Sa 23:13
I swear it by the * God who has 1Ki 2:23,24
son, and the * child is mine." 1Ki 3:22
is yours and the * one is mine." 1Ki 3:22
of you claim the * child, and each 1Ki 3:23
Then he said, "Divide the * 1Ki 3:25
His cedar-paneled * quarters 1Ki 7:8
(He designed similar * quarters, 1Ki 7:8
was an old prophet * in Bethel, and 1Ki 13:11
sons—all of whom were * there. 2Ki 10:1
of King Ahab were * in the homes of 2Ki 10:6
the * God, and will rebuke him. 2Ki 19:4
this man's defiance of the * God. 2Ki 19:16
the Lord, who were * in other 2Ki 23:8
of the writers * at Jabez—the 1Ch 2:55
of the subclans * at Geba, were 1Ch 8:6,7
chiefs of subclans * in Aijalon; 1Ch 8:13
of the subclans * at Jerusalem. 1Ch 8:28
AFTER DAVID HAD been * in his new 1Ch 17:1
"Look! I'm * here in a 1Ch 17:1
Or, "as long as they are * in 2Ch 6:31f
and the Arabs * next to the 2Ch 21:
villages, and were * there. 2Ch 28:17,
people of Judah * in the provinces 2Ch 31:5
godly *, and was very successful. 2Ch 31:2
(Shallum was the king's tailor, * 2Ch 34:2
their companions * in Samaria and Ez 4:
practices of the people * there. Ez 9:1
The Temple attendants * in Ophel Neh 3:2
I told everyone * outside the Neh 4:2
THE ISRAELI OFFICIALS were * in Neh 11:
"I AM WEARY of *. Job 10:
For the soul of every * thing is Job 12:1
"I was * quietly until he broke Job 16:1
Those * in my home, even my Job 19:1
"I vow by the * God, who has Job 27:
it is not to be found among the *. Job 28:1
I will go on * in the realm of Job 33:2
he may live in the light of the *. Job 33:3
Job lived 140 years after that, * Job 42:1
man, after * a long, good life. Job 42:1
in his Temple, * in his presence Ps 27:
to me here in the land of the *. Ps 27:1
I thirst for God, the * God. Ps 42:
God himself is * in that City; Ps 46:
you away from the land of the *. Ps 52:
the Lord in the land of the *. Ps 56:1
of the *; Ps 69:28
* according to their own desires. Ps 81:1
and come near to the * God. Ps 84:
Let the earth and all those * on Ps 98:
to replenish all the * of the Ps 104:30
the home of many nations * there. Ps 111:6
me I will thank you by * as I Ps 119:7
He gives food to every * thing, Ps 136:25
he does. All * things shall thank Ps 145:10
and thirst of every * thing. Ps 145:16
they fill you with * energy, and Pro 3:22
for they will lead you to real *. Pro 4:13
right * does. Pro 10:2
There is * truth in what a good Pro 10:11
themselves by * among the rocks. Pro 30:24-28
king of Israel, * in Jerusalem. Ecc 1:12-15
dead were better off than the *. Ecc 4:2
There is hope only for the *. Ecc 9:4
For the * at least know that Ecc 9:5
only a few people * in it, and a Ecc 9:14
you'll no longer enjoy *. Ecc 12:1
a well of * water, refreshing as Sol 4:15
"O my beloved, * in the gardens, Sol 8:13
Can the * find out the future Is 8:19
as he scoffed at the * God. Is 37:4
for he has mocked the * God. Is 37:16,17
you will be * in luxury again. Is 37:30
when the * wakened the next Is 37:36
see the Lord in the land of the *. Is 38:11
hope and joy. The *, only the Is 38:19
The living, only the *, can Is 38:19
O pleasure-mad kingdom, * at Is 47:8
when you boast of * in the Holy Is 48:1
This is really *; Is 56:12
Because you are * in evil Is 58:3
he will keep on * in it—it will not Is 65:21,22
by me alone, the * God, and begin Jer 4:2
are desolate, without a * soul. Jer 9:10
towns, with no one * in them." Jer 9:11
the * God, the everlasting King. Jer 10:10
I will fill everyone * in this Jer 13:13
Lord, the Fountain of * waters. Jer 17:13
the people * here forgot the Lord Jer 22:9
foreign population * in his land. Jer 25:19,20
against all those * on the earth. Jer 25:30
People now * undisturbed will be Jer 25:37
and upon every person * in it; Jer 26:15
left desolate without a * soul. Jer 34:22
the Jews who were * in the north of Jer 44:1
heaps and ashes, without a * soul. Jer 44:2,3
you Jews who are * in the land of Jer 44:26
back—who insist on * in Egypt—shall Jer 44:28
* along the sea must be destroyed. Jer 47:7
shall be left without a * soul. Jer 48:9
Why are you * in the cities of Jer 49:1
and your pride, * there in the Jer 49:16
An Arab tribe * in the desert east Jer 49:28f
Bedouin tribes * alone in the Jer 49:31
be left desolate without a * soul. Jer 51:29
see, incredible, without a * soul. Jer 51:37
so that not a * creature will Jer 51:61,62
The four * beings were joined Eze 1:9
the wings of the * beings on each Eze 1:11
flashed. The * beings darted to Eze 1:14
When the four * beings flew Eze 1:19,20,21
When the * beings stopped, the Eze 1:19,20,21
For the spirit of the four * Eze 1:19,20,21
and the * beings went there too. Eze 1:19,20,21
the wings of the * beings as they Eze 3:13
That is, the wheel was a * part of Eze 10:17f
These were the * beings I had Eze 10:20
or the foreigners * among you, who Eze 14:6,7
and Job were * there, the Lord God Eze 14:20
breaking wedlock * with other men. Eze 16:38
"Your older sister is Samaria, * Eze 16:46

(LIVING Con't)
my terror to fall upon all the *. Eze 32:32
remnants of Judah * among the Eze 33:24
live, surely those * in the ruins Eze 33:27
Those * in the open fields shall Eze 33:27
of Israel were * in their own Eze 36:17
these people * in such confidence! Eze 38:11
When my people are * in peace in Eze 38:14
on that day. All * things shall Eze 38:20
I shall remain, * among the people Eze 43:7
am wiser than any * person that I Dan 2:30
I, Nebuchadnezzar, was * in peace Dan 4:4
the wild animals * in its shade, Dan 4:21
servant of the * God, was your God, Dan 6:20
For his God is the *, unchanging Dan 6:25,26
my sons, children of the * God.' Hos 1:10
all * things grow sick and die; Hos 4:3
I am the Holy One * among you, Hos 11:9
consign you to * in tents again, as Hos 12:9
Stay away from idols! I am * and Hos 14:8
AMOS WAS A herdsman * in the Amo 1:1
cows" of Bashan * in Samaria—you Amo 4:1
those * in Judean lowlands shall Ob 1:19
Chaldeans: a tribe of Semites * Hab 1:6f
* on the coast and in the land of Zep 2:5
your sacrifices by * with selfish Hag 2:14
he walked with me, * a good and Mal 2:6
WHILE THEY WERE * in Nazareth, Mt 3:1
A woman from Canaan who was * Mt 15:22
Messiah, the Son of the * God." Mt 16:16
God of the dead, but of the *." Mt 22:32
in the name of the * God that you Mt 26:63
as he was * out in the deserts. Lk 3:1
For real life and real * are not Lk 12:15
"A nobleman * in a certain Lk 19:12
point of view, all men are *." Lk 20:37,38
don't let me find you * in Lk 21:34,35
done to me, the * Tree, what will Lk 23:31
would ask me for some * water!" Jn 4:10
Where would you get this * water? Jn 4:11
to the man you're * with now." Jn 4:17,18
I am that * Bread that came down Jn 6:48-51
I live by the power of the * Jn 6:57
that rivers of * water shall flow Jn 7:38
* light will flood your path." Jn 8:12
When you obey me you are * in my Jn 15:10
desolate with no one * in it.' Act 1:20
of God—the * Word—on Mount Sinai. Act 7:38
Joppa, * with Simon, the tanner. Act 9:43
to be the Judge of all—* and dead. Act 10:42
instead to the * God who made Act 14:15
friends, and he is * within us! Rom 5:10
have the Spirit of God * in you. Rom 8:9
Spirit of Christ * in him, he is Rom 8:9
same Holy Spirit * within you. Rom 8:11
be called "sons of the * God." Rom 9:26
Let them be a * sacrifice, Rom 12:1
Another reason for right * is Rom 13:11
the armor of right *, as we who Rom 13:12,13
* or dying we follow the Lord. Rom 14:8
with our hands to earn our *. 1Co 4:12
it is * by God's power. 1Co 4:20
* in sin with his father's wife. 1Co 5:1
that you are * as God intended, 1Co 7:17
*, while you supply these others? 1Co 9:6
Literally, "was made a * soul." 1Co 15:45f
is to make a good * out of it. 2Co 2:17
but by the Spirit of the * God; 2Co 3:3
* Christ within [who keeps us safe 2Co 4:10
the home of the * God, and God has 2Co 6:16
purify ourselves, * in the 2Co 7:1
I am glad to be a * demonstration 2Co 12:9
that anyone * that sort of life Gal 5:21
If we are * now by the Holy Gal 5:25
were * utterly apart from Christ; Eph 2:12
* within you as you trust in him. Eph 3:17
and * through every part of us. Eph 4:6
truly, dealing truly, * truly Eph 4:15,16
For to me, * means opportunities Php 1:21
But if * will give me more Php 1:22
You are * a brand new kind of Col 3:10
so that now the * and true God only 1Th 1:9
God in your daily *, for you know 1Th 4:1
we who are still * when the Lord 1Th 4:15
how you should work for your *. 2Th 3:9
some of you are * in laziness, 2Th 3:11
get to work, and earn their own *. 2Th 3:12
our time in godly * and thinking 1Ti 2:2
* quiet, good, and loving lives. 1Ti 2:15
the church of the * God, which 1Ti 3:15
our hope is in the * God who died 1Ti 4:9,10
especially those * in his own 1Ti 5:8
should be in the * God who always 1Ti 6:17
And they will be * a fruitful 1Ti 6:19
will begin * with him in heaven. 2Ti 2:11
Christ Jesus by * godly lives will 2Ti 3:12
some day judge the * and the dead 2Ti 4:1
* at the home of Onesiphorus. 2Ti 4:19
they are like lazy animals, * Tit 1:12
up for the right * that goes along Tit 2:1
turn from godless * and sinful Tit 2:12
of death have been * all their Heb 2:15
leading you away from the * God. Heb 3:12
to us is full of * power: it is Heb 4:12
the all-seeing eyes of our * God; Heb 4:13
And when a person is still * on Heb 5:12,13
makes us want to serve the * God. Heb 9:14
fall into the hands of the * God. Heb 10:31
They were * for heaven. Heb 11:16
to the city of the * God, the Heb 12:22
Come to Christ, who is the * 1Pe 2:4
And now you have become * 1Pe 2:5
face the Judge of all, * and dead; 1Pe 4:5
you need for * a truly good life: 2Pe 1:3
deceiving you by * in foul sin on 2Pe 2:13
just escaped from such wicked *. 2Pe 2:18
holy, godly lives we should be *! 2Pe 3:11
friends, but go on * in spiritual 1Jn 1:6
But if we are * in the light of 1Jn 1:7
Whoever is * a life of sin and 1Jn 3:10
are * with God and he with them. 1Jn 3:24
we are * with him and he with us. 1Jn 4:13
Son of God has God * in him, and he 1Jn 4:15
in him, and he is * with God. 1Jn 4:15
lives in love is * with God and God 1Jn 4:16
with God and God is * in him. 1Jn 4:16
see that they are * as they should, 2Jn 1:4
* by the standards of the Gospel. 3Jn 1:3
go right on * their evil, immoral Jud 1:8
have the Holy Spirit * in them. Jud 1:19
and Last, the * One who died, who Rev 1:17,18
crystal sea. Four * Beings, dotted Rev 4:6
The first of these * Beings was Rev 4:7
Each of these * Beings had six Rev 4:8
And when the * Beings gave glory Rev 4:9
him, the Eternal * One, and cast Rev 4:10
the throne and the * Beings, and on Rev 5:6
the throne and the * Beings and the Rev 5:11
And the four * Beings kept Rev 5:14
Then one of the four * Beings, Rev 6:1
And I heard the second * Being Rev 6:3
the third * Being say, "Come!" Rev 6:5
among the four * Beings said, "A Rev 6:6
the fourth * Being say, "Come!" Rev 6:7
against those * on the earth?" Rev 6:10
the Great Seal of the * God. Rev 7:2
and the four * Beings, and falling Rev 7:11
temple and all those * in heaven. Rev 13:6
before the four * Beings and the Rev 14:3
And one of the four * Beings Rev 15:7
wrath of the * God who lives Rev 15:7
rich from all her luxurious *." Rev 18:3
Elders and four * Beings fell down Rev 19:4

LIZARD
The great *, the gecko, Lev 11:29,30
The mouse, the *, Lev 11:29,30

LIZARDS
The *: they are easy to catch and Pro 30:24-28
kinds of snakes, * and hideous Eze 8:10

LO
*, they taste the riches of the Deu 33:19
Literally, "*, we heard of it in Ps 132:6f
of Israel, says: *, I will feed Jer 9:15

LO-AMMI
And God said, "Call him * Hos 1:9

LO-DEBAR
Betonim, and from Mahanaim to *. Jos 13:26
"In *," Ziba told him. 2Sa 9:4

LO-RUHAMAH
Hosea, "Name her * (meaning 'No Hos 1:6
After Gomer had weaned *, she Hos 1:8

LOAD
at least do this. * your donkeys Gen 43:11
your brothers to * their pack Gen 45:17
that the Egyptians * you down with Ex 3:21
to their God. * them with work and Ex 5:9
beneath a heavy *, you must not go Ex 23:5
by myself! The * is far too heavy! Num 11:14
when it has slipped beneath its *, Deu 22:4
carrying a * of food and wine. 1Sa 16:20
too much of a * to carry around! 2Sa 14:26
years a great * of gold, silver, 1Ki 10:22
fall beneath their * of sins. Pro 11:5
beneath their * of guilt. Is 1:4
They * the tables with food; Is 21:5
they will * him with Is 22:23,24
She will stumble under her * of Hos 5:5
They * you with impossible Mt 23:4
forever with a heavy *." Rom 11:10
He personally carried the * of 1Pe 2:24

LOADED
Abraham's camels * with samples of Gen 24:10
So they * up their donkeys with Gen 42:26
on their way with their * donkeys. Gen 44:3
in despair, * the donkeys again, Gen 44:13
and ten donkeys * with grain and Gen 45:23
the trees will be * with fruit long Lev 26:4,5
He was leading two donkeys * with 2Sa 16:1
and came away * with money, 2Ch 20:25
Egypt, * with silver and gold; Ps 105:37
Oxen * down with produce. Ps 144:12-15
green leaves, * with fruit for all Dan 4:21
groans that is * with sheaves. Amo 2:13
and pulled the * net to the beach, Jn 21:8
Their tongues are * with lies. Rom 3:13
on the earth and * the grapes into Rev 14:19

LOADING
in sheaves, and * their donkeys Neh 13:15

LOADS
carry heavy * of mortar and brick. Ex 1:13,14
freeze. He * the clouds with Job 37:11
and those bent beneath their *. Ps 145:14
those bent down beneath their *. Ps 146:8
you bring in * of merchandise Jer 17:27
stagger beneath their heavy *. Lam 5:13
from bringing in * of merchandise. Mk 11:16

LOAF
his sons— and one * of bread, one Ex 29:23
crops by making a *, using coarse Num 15:19,20,21
each year. This * must be waved Num 15:19,20,21
was this huge * of barley bread Ju 7:12,13
women alike—of a * of bread, some 2Sa 6:19
bake me a little * of bread first; 1Ki 17:13
(men and women alike) a * of 1Ch 16:3
be given a small * of fresh bread Jer 37:21
his father for a * of bread, will Mt 7:9
Jesus took a small * of bread and Mt 26:26
only one * of bread in the boat. Mk 8:14
stone to become a * of bread." Lk 4:3
Then he took a * of bread; Lk 22:19
then took a small * of bread and Lk 24:30
the bread from the * to eat there 1Co 10:16
eat from the same *, showing that 1Co 10:17
Beings said, "A * of bread for Rev 6:6

LOAFERS
some worthless * who agreed to do Ju 9:4
some bums and * who exclaimed, 1Sa 10:27

LOAFING
our example: you never saw us *; 2Th 3:7

LOAN
Don't refuse a * because the year Deu 15:9
If you refuse to make the * and Deu 15:9
have refused to * money to needy Job 22:6
they have as a pledge to get a *. Job 24:3
will * him any money or grain. Job 24:9
pays wonderful interest on your *! Pro 19:17
and does not * money at interest, Eze 18:17
Hired murderers, * racketeers Eze 22:12
all your * sharks—all will die. Zep 1:11

LOANED
his servants and * them money to Mt 25:14
story: "A man * money to two Lk 7:41

LOANS
"Don't demand interest on * you Deu 23:19
their gifts and * to others, and Ps 37:26
It is risky to make * to Pro 20:16
and grants * without interest, Eze 18:8
and * out his money at interest Eze 18:13

LOATHE
seen you, and I * myself and Job 42:6
You have made my friends to * Ps 88:8
Then at last they will * Eze 6:9
all your sins and * yourselves Eze 20:43
to your enemies, to those you *. Eze 23:28
your past sins and * yourselves for Eze 36:31

LOATHED
from your will. I * these traitors Ps 119:158
They shall be despised and *, Jer 44:12
For your mother * her husband Eze 16:45

LOATHES
The Lord * all cheating and Pro 20:23
God * the gifts of evil men, Pro 21:27

LOATHSOME
in their * customs, thus sinning Deu 20:18
of grain, it is as * to God as Is 66:3
to Jerusalem about her * sins. Eze 16:2

LOAVES
Literally, "unleavened * mingled Lev 7:12f
with olive oil and * from a batter Lev 7:12
with * of leavened bread. Lev 7:13
This shall consist of two * of Lev 23:17
along with the * representing the Lev 23:20
shall place twelve * of bread in Lev 24:5-8
These * shall be baked from Lev 24:5-8
will have three * of bread, and the 1Sa 10:3
of the *, which you are to accept. 1Sa 10:4
ten * of bread to your brothers. 1Sa 17:17
Give me five * of bread, or 1Sa 21:3
took two hundred * of bread, two 1Sa 25:18
with two hundred * of bread, one 2Sa 16:1
Take him a gift of ten * of 1Ki 14:3
and twenty individual * of barley 2Ki 4:42
changing stones into * of bread. Mt 4:3
"We have exactly five small * of Mt 14:17
and he took the five * and two Mt 14:19
then broke the * apart and gave Mt 14:19
And they replied, "Seven * of Mt 15:34
he took the seven * and the fish, Mt 15:36
*, and the basketfuls left over? Mt 16:9
were five * of bread and two fish. Mk 6:38
He took the five * and two fish Mk 6:41
Breaking the * into pieces, he Mk 6:41
"How many * of bread do you Mk 8:5

(LOAVES Con't)
Then he took the seven *, thanked Mk 8:6
men I fed with five * of bread? Mk 8:19
with seven *, how much was left?" Mk 8:20
"Why, we have only five * of Lk 9:13
Jesus took the five * and two Lk 9:16
to borrow three * of bread. Lk 11:5,6
barley * and a couple of fish! Jn 6:8,9
Then Jesus took the * and gave Jn 6:11
special * of holy bread upon it; Heb 9:1

LOBE
it upon the * of Aaron's right ear Lev 8:23

LOBES
sons—upon the * of their right Lev 8:24

LOCAL
these * girls, these Canaanites. Gen 24:3
Isaac marry one of the * girls, Gen 24:37
Then the * shepherds came and Gen 26:20
dug again, and the * residents Gen 26:22
sick and tired of these * girls. Gen 27:46
despised the * girls, and that his Gen 28:6,7,8
Esau married three * girls from Gen 36:2,3
father. The * residents, the Gen 50:11
parties with the * Moabite girls. Num 25:1
from attack by the * inhabitants. Num 32:17
with samples of the * fruit. Deu 1:24,25
entire tithe for * welfare Deu 14:28
And don't forget to include the * Deu 16:11
from the * populations as the Jos 14:15
the temple of the * god, the wine Ju 9:27
issues with the * leaders, Ju 9:35
and they had no * allies, for they Ju 18:28
the seven hundred * men in their Ju 20:14,15
But when the * citizens went to 1Sa 5:3
they were killed by the * farmers. 1Ch 7:20,21
Then the * residents tried to Ez 4:4,5
judges and other * leaders, the Ez 4:8,9
in all the * languages, stressing Est 1:22
the rabbi of the * synagogue came Mt 9:18
The leader of the * synagogue, Mk 5:22
was just a * man like themselves. Mk 6:2,3
When the * Jewish leaders Mk 8:11
But the * Jewish leader in charge Lk 13:14
He persuaded a * farmer to hire Lk 15:15
shouted (in their * dialect, of Act 14:11
was Mercury! The * priest of the Act 14:13
by some * men, to talk to the Act 15:2
We went ashore, found the * Act 21:4
all of us—the * believers and his Act 21:12
* Jews and by those in Jerusalem! Act 25:24
together the * Jewish leaders and Act 28:17
The * language, whatever it is. 1Co 14:7f
by God to oversee each * church. Rev 1:20f

LOCALITIES
living in the * named after Gen 36:40-43

LOCATED
* along the border of Babylonia. Gen 2:11,12f
Resen (which is * between Nineveh Gen 10:11,12
land of Shinar," * at the mouth of Gen 11:2f
* just west of the Jordan River, Gen 50:10f
the Tabernacle, * right among them Lev 16:16
Refuge are to be * in the land of Num 35:13,14
you where this altar must be *. Deu 12:18
which will be * at the place the Deu 16:15
of Jerusalem is *), then west to Jos 15:8
were * in Manasseh's territory. Jos 17:9
(The land was * in the territory Jos 24:32
the tribe of Dan, * between the Ju 13:25
"This city is * in beautiful 2Ki 2:19
of Jerusalem, * on the left side as 2Ki 23:8
and chariots * near the entrance of 2Ki 23:11
their family inheritance was *. Neh 11:20
This room was * next to the one Jer 35:4
to Jacob's Well, * on the parcel of Jn 4:5,6
Temple of Jupiter, * on the Act 14:13

LOCATION
*: East side of the Num 2:3-31
Camp * Num 3:16-24
Camp * Num 3:25-30
Camp * Num 3:31-35
new * by the time they arrived. Num 10:21
Temple began. Its * was in 2Ch 3:1
in Israel as the * of my Temple 2Ch 6:5,6
Has the * of the gates of Death Job 38:17,18

LOCATIONS
languages, and geographical *. Gen 10:31
Here are the tribal *: Num 2:3-31
* indicated by the Lord to Moses. Num 2:34
a list of the * where he built 2Ch 33:19

LOCK
out and * the door behind her." 2Sa 13:17,18
and to close and * them while the Neh 7:3
it is too late to * the barn. Ecc 10:11
Go home, my people, and * the Is 26:20
whatever doors you * on earth Mt 16:19

LOCKED
Leaving the dagger there, Ehud * Ju 3:22,23
the doors were *, they waited, Ju 3:24
every home and shop is * up tight Is 24:10
I will snap the bars that * the Amo 1:5
I was * out of life and Jon 2:6
on earth shall be * in heaven; Mt 16:19
feast, and the door was *. Mt 25:10
The door is * for the night and Lk 11:7
* the door, it will be too late. Lk 13:24,25
meeting behind * doors, in fear of Jn 20:19
The doors were *; Jn 20:26
jail doors were *, and the guards Act 5:23
he then shut and *, so that he Rev 20:3

LOCKS
and installed its * and bars. Neh 3:15
behind your *. Sol 4:3
All their * and bars are broken, Lam 2:9

LOCUST
it was the worst * plague in all Ex 10:14
one * in all the land of Egypt! Ex 10:19
if I command the * swarms to eat up 2Ch 7:13
him able to leap forward like a *? Job 39:20

LOCUSTS
a thick layer of * so that you Ex 10:4,5
of Egypt to bring *—they will cover Ex 10:12
the east wind had brought the *. Ex 10:13
And the * covered the land of Ex 10:14
For the * covered the face of Ex 10:15
wind that blew the * out into the Ex 10:19
those that jump; * of all Lev 11:21,22
varieties—ordinary *, bald locusts, Lev 11:21,22
locusts, bald *, crickets, and Lev 11:21,22
for the * will eat your crops. Deu 28:38
as slaves. The * shall destroy Deu 28:42
the valley like *—yes, like the Ju 7:12,13
plant disease or * or caterpillers, 1Ki 8:37
or attacks of * or caterpillars, or 2Ch 6:28
Their harvest was consumed by *. Ps 78:46
He spoke, and hordes of * came, Ps 105:34
The *: though they have no leader, Pro 30:24-28
Just as * strip the fields and Is 33:4
fields filled with * in a plague, Jer 51:14
A vast army of * Joe 1:6
give you back the crops the * ate! Joe 2:25
* ate your figs and olive trees. Amo 4:9
a vast swarm of * to destroy all Amo 7:1
you like young * that eat up Nah 3:15
swarm like * and carry it away. Nah 3:16
disappear, like * when the sun Nah 3:17
his food was * and wild honey. Mt 3:4
* and wild honey were his food. Mk 1:6
Then * came from the smoke and Rev 9:3
The * looked like horses armored Rev 9:7

LOD
Shemed (who built Ono and * and 1Ch 8:12
From the subclans of *, Hadid, and Ez 2:3-35
From the subclans of *, Hadid, and Neh 7:8-38
Zeboim, Neballat, *, Ono (the Neh 11:31-35

LODEBAR
(son of Ammiel of *) and Barzillai 2Sa 17:27

LODGED
So Peter invited them in and * Act 10:23

LODGING
to find food and * for the night. Lk 9:12
or, if they need *, for the night. Rom 12:13

LOFTINESS
We know your *, your arrogance Jer 48:29

LOFTY
He was sitting on a * throne, and Is 6:1
The high and * one who inhabits Is 57:15
The * sun and moon began to Hab 3:11
you I didn't use * words and 1Co 2:1

LOG
bring it to you in * floats across 2Ch 2:16

LOGGERS
80,000 as * and 3,600 as foremen. 2Ch 2:18

LOGIC
not answer with that kind of *! Job 32:14
words and such * that none of your Lk 21:15

LOGICAL
be so sensible and * that anyone Tit 2:8

LOGOS
Literally, "The *," as in John Rev 19:13f

LOGS
My men will bring the * from the 1Ki 5:9
where there are plenty of *." 2Ki 6:1
great rafts of cedar * to David. 1Ch 22:4
and bought cedar * from the people Ez 3:7
and olive oil. The * were brought Ez 3:7

LOIN-FAT
* on them, and the gall bladder. Lev 3:3,4,5
kidneys with the * on them, and the Lev 3:9,10,11
* on them, and the gall bladder. Lev 3:15,16
kidneys and the * on them, and the Lev 4:9
kidneys and the *, and the gall Lev 7:4

LOINCLOTH
Go and buy a linen * and wear it, Jer 13:1
So I bought the * and put it on. Jer 13:2
This time he said, Take the * Jer 13:4
to the river again and get the *. Jer 13:6
become as this *—good for nothing. Jer 13:10
Even as a * clings to a man's Jer 13:11

LOINS
is thicker than my father's *! 2Ch 10:10
See his powerful * and the Job 40:16
My * burn with inflammation Ps 38:7
clings to a man's *, so I made Jer 13:11
wrapped a towel around his *, Jn 13:

LOIS
Eunice and your grandmother * do; 2Ti 1:5

LOLL
Listen, you women who * around in Is 32:9

LONE
saw a * man running towards them. 2Sa 18:24

LONELINESS
Then in * my breaking heart shall Jer 13:17

LONELY
He gives families to the *, and Ps 68:6
I lie awake, * as a solitary Ps 102:7
You will be like * trees on the Is 30:17
Any who escape will be * as Eze 7:16
She is a *, wandering wild ass. Hos 8:9
top of a high and * hill, and as Mt 17:1
lived out in the * wilderness until Lk 1:80

LONG
You shall grovel in the dust as * Gen 3:14
Make it 450 feet *, 75 feet Gen 6:15
wicked things. As * as the earth Gen 8:22
Lot took a * look at the fertile Gen 13:10
old, and Sarah was * since past the Gen 18:11
Philistine country for a * time. Gen 21:34
you must go, and * so intensely for Gen 31:30
they were still a * way away. Gen 35:16
remembered the dreams of * ago! Gen 42:8,9
of what we did to Joseph * ago. Gen 42:21
other's arms and wept a * while. Gen 46:29
"I have lived 130 *, hard years, Gen 47:9
ONE DAY NOT * after this, word Gen 48:1
them to toil * and hard in the Ex 1:13,14
* will you refuse to submit to me? Ex 10:3
on, prepared for a * journey, Ex 12:11
to your ancestors * ago, where the Ex 13:11
"How * will these people refuse Ex 16:28,29
And as * as Moses held up the Ex 17:11
here all day * to get your help?" Ex 18:14
a ram's horn sounding one * blast; Ex 19:13
and there was a *, loud blast as Ex 19:16
you may have a *, good life in the Ex 20:12
the *, frightening trumpet blast; Ex 20:18
*, 2¼ feet wide, and 2¼ feet high. Ex 25:10
gold, 3¾ feet * and 2¼ feet wide. Ex 25:17
*, 1½ feet wide, and 2¼ feet high. Ex 25:23
forty-two feet * and six feet wide, Ex 26:1
two * pieces, one for each side. Ex 26:3
* pieces together side by side. Ex 26:4,5
will be 150 feet *, and 75 feet Ex 27:18
forming two * roof-sheets. Ex 36:10
edges of these two * sheets, each Ex 36:11,12
its mate on the other * sheet. Ex 36:11,12
thus tying the two * sheets Ex 36:13
feet * and six feet wide). Ex 36:14,15
to make one * piece, and six others Ex 36:16
others to make another * piece. Ex 36:16
*, 2¼ feet wide, and 2¼ feet high. Ex 37:1
it was 3¾ feet * and 2¼ feet Ex 37:6
*, 1½ feet wide and 2¼ feet high. Ex 37:10
The south wall was 150 feet *; Ex 38:9
was also 150 feet *, with twenty Ex 38:11
It was thirty feet * and 7½ feet Ex 38:18
As * as the disease lasts, he is Lev 13:46
where you lived so *, or the people Lev 18:3
let the trumpets blow loud and * Lev 25:9
fruit * after the normal time! Lev 26:4,5
shall shave his * hair—the sign of Num 6:18
there as * as the Cloud stayed. Num 9:18
If it stayed a * time, then they Num 9:19
time, then they stayed a * time. Num 9:19
how * the people of Israel stayed; Num 9:22
to * for the good things of Egypt. Num 11:4,5
* will these people despise me? Num 14:10,11
to Aaron, "How * will these wicked Num 14:26,27
stayed there so *, and became Num 20:15
"Why did you delay so *?" Num 22:37
Before * all Israel was joining Num 25:3
they stayed there for quite a * Num 33:9
* as it is within their own tribe. Num 36:6
'You have stayed here * enough. Deu 1:6
there at Kadesh for a * time. Deu 1:46
" 'You have stayed here * Deu 2:3
a half feet * by six feet wide. Deu 3:11
been in the land a * time, and you Deu 4:25
if you do so, you shall have a *, Deu 5:16
only then will you live * and Deu 5:33
his instructions as * as you live; Deu 6:2
if you do, you will have *, Deu 6:2
you will have a * and good life in Deu 11:9
gates, so that as * as there is Deu 11:21
ensure his having a *, good reign. Deu 17:20
You must never, as * as you Deu 23:6
you will have a *, good life in the Deu 25:13,14,15
you will not have a *, good life Deu 30:18
Lord your God as * as you live in Deu 31:13
Remember the days of * ago! Deu 32:7
them you will live *, plentiful Deu 32:47
to oppose you as * as you live, for Jos 1:5
Then, when they give one *, loud Jos 6:5
the priests blew a *, loud trumpet Jos 6:16

(LONG Con't)
given * before by Moses. Jos 8:33
as though from a * journey, with Jos 9:3,4,5
us, 'Prepare for a * journey; Jos 9:11
worn out from our *, hard trip." Jos 9:13
as Moses had commanded * before. Jos 11:12
Literally, "a * time." Jos 11:18f
Then Joshua asked them, "How * Jos 18:3
has lasted for such a * time. Jos 22:2,3
* AFTER THIS, when the Lord had Jos 23:1
care of you for such a * time." Jos 24:20
lifetime, and as * afterward as the Ju 2:7-9
so he helped them as * as that Ju 2:18
eighteen inches * and hid it in his Ju 3:16
But when, after a * time, he Ju 3:25
'Why is his chariot so * in Ju 5:28
have a * and happy life together. Ju 9:19
been barren so *, you will soon Ju 13:2,3
But before * his hair began to Ju 16:22
tribe of Dan as * as the Tabernacle Ju 18:31
* AGO WHEN judges ruled in Israel, Ru 1:1
the Lord for as * as he lives." 1Sa 1:28
And all the people shouted, "* 1Sa 10:24
"You have mourned * enough for 1Sa 16:1
your mother? As * as that fellow 1Sa 20:31
other forever? How * will it be 2Sa 2:26
THAT WAS THE beginning of a * war 2Sa 3:1
them that for a * time they had 2Sa 3:17
king, as you've so * desired." 2Sa 3:21
night after being away for so *?" 2Sa 11:10
She was wearing a * robe with 2Sa 13:17,18
in deep sorrow for a * time." 2Sa 14:2,3
"* live the king!" 2Sa 16:16
he exclaimed. "* live the 2Sa 16:16
* march through the wilderness." 2Sa 17:28,29
shouting, '* live King Adonijah!' 1Ki 1:25
and shout, '* live King Solomon!' 1Ki 1:34
shouted, "* live King Solomon!" 1Ki 1:39
lived in Jerusalem for a * time. 1Ki 2:38
asked for a * life or riches for 1Ki 3:11
And I will give you a * life if 1Ki 3:14
The Temple was ninety feet *, 1Ki 6:2
feet * and fifteen feet deep. 1Ki 6:3
Most Holy Place—was sixty feet *. 1Ki 6:17
was thirty feet *, thirty feet 1Ki 6:20
each wing was 7½ feet *, so each 1Ki 6:23-28
It was huge—measuring 150 feet *, 1Ki 7:2
It was seventy-five feet * and 1Ki 7:6
The poles were so * that they 1Ki 8:8
Jerusalem with a * train of camels 1Ki 10:2
and oil as * as it was needed. 1Ki 17:15
"How * are you going to waver 1Ki 18:21
is a * journey ahead of you." 1Ki 19:7
city, and after a * while even a 2Ki 6:25
be friendship as * as the evils of 2Ki 9:22
and shouted, "* live the king!" 2Ki 11:12
I had done so * before, and he led 2Ki 15:18
" 'Why haven't you realized * 2Ki 19:25
were in this land * ago, and 2Ki 21:11
garb, and for as * as he lived, he 2Ki 25:29
mourned for them a * time, and his 1Ch 7:22
asked for a * life, but for wisdom 2Ch 1:11
The foundation was ninety feet * 2Ch 3:3
wing of a cherub, five cubits *." 2Ch 3:11,12,13f
altar thirty feet *, thirty feet 2Ch 4:1
These carrying poles were so * 2Ch 5:9
Or, "as * as they are living in 2Ch 6:31f
you as * as you stay with him! 2Ch 15:2
For a * time now, over in 2Ch 15:3
A great shout went up, "* live 2Ch 23:11
And as * as the king followed the 2Ch 26:5
tribe of Israel for a * time; 2Ch 30:5f
because of its * history of Ez 4:15
him, "How * will you be gone? Neh 2:5,6
them into two * lines to walk in Neh 12:31,32
not * afterwards when Job's sons Job 1:12,13
Let it * for light, but never see Job 3:9
* for death, and it won't come; Job 3:20,21
You shall live a *, good life; Job 5:26
grant the thing I * for most—to die Job 6:8,9
A man's life is * and hard, like Job 7:1
these * and weary nights. Job 7:3
You see me now, but not for *. Job 7:8
me alone—even * enough to spit? Job 7:19
"How * will you go on like this, Job 8:2
of God? Will * searching make them Job 11:7
Oh, how I * to speak directly to Job 13:3
"How * are you going to trouble Job 19:2
my soul, that as * as I live, Job 27:3
My conscience is clear for as * Job 27:6
in my nest after a *, good life.' Job 29:18
those in droughttime * for rain. Job 29:23
All night * I toss and turn, and Job 30:18
him, you will * remember the Job 41:8
man, after living a *, good life. Job 42:17
HOW * WILL you forget me, Lord? Ps 13:1
Forever? How * will you look the Ps 13:1
I am in need? How * must I be Ps 13:2
in my heart? How * shall my enemy Ps 13:2
He asked for a *, good life, and Ps 21:4
Do you want a *, good life? Ps 34:12
Lord, how * will you stand there, Ps 35:17
I will praise you all day *. Ps 35:28
to those who * to do your will. Ps 36:10
Lord, you know how I * for my Ps 38:9
for water, so I * for you, O God. Ps 42:1
you did in the days of * ago. Ps 44:1
all day * the enemy troops press Ps 56:1
how they * to conquer me. Ps 56:1
How I * to find you! Ps 63:1
I will bless you as * as I live, Ps 63:4
They spend * hours with all their Ps 64:6
All day * I'll praise and honor Ps 71:8
I will talk to others all day * Ps 71:24
you constantly, as * as sun and Ps 72:5
will bless him all day *. Ps 72:15
and woe—every day and all day *! Ps 73:14
all will end? How *, O God, will Ps 74:9,10
have hurled against you all day *. Ps 74:22
All night * I pray, lifting my Ps 77:2
days of the past, * since ended. Ps 77:5
miracles he did for me so * ago. Ps 77:11
O Jehovah, how * will you be Ps 79:5
armies, how * will you be angry and Ps 80:4
How * will you judges refuse to Ps 82:2
the evidence? How * will you shower Ps 82:2
I *, yes, faint with longing to Ps 84:2
They flow around me all day *. Ps 88:17
They rejoice all day * in your Ps 89:16
O Jehovah, how * will this go on? Ps 89:46
* will your wrath burn like fire? Ps 89:46
No wonder the years are * and Ps 90:9
bless us! How * will you delay? Ps 90:13
Literally, "with * life." Ps 91:16f
Lord, how * shall the wicked be Ps 94:3
where I * to act as I should. Ps 101:2
I will sing to the Lord as * as I Ps 104:33
* AGO WHEN the Israelis escaped Ps 114:1
I will pray as * as I breathe! Ps 116:2
and guide. I * for your Ps 119:20
do it, Lord. As * as I live I'll Ps 119:33,34
right and good. I * to obey them! Ps 119:40,41,42
obey them. How * must I wait Ps 119:84
I think about them all day *. Ps 119:97
do not stumble. I * for your Ps 119:166
has promised. I * for him more Ps 130:6
than sentinels * for the dawn. Ps 130:6
and stir up trouble all day *. Ps 140:2
miracles you did in days of * ago. Ps 143:5
I will praise him as * as I Ps 146:2
"How * will you go on being Pro 1:22
being fools? How * will you scoff Pro 1:22
If you want a * and satisfying Pro 3:1
Wisdom gives:A *, good Pro 3:16,17
will have a * and happy life. Pro 4:4
and you will have a *, good life. Pro 4:10
Every day and all night * their Pro 6:22
my husband is away on a * trip. Pro 7:19
so how can the wicked expect a *, Pro 10:27
good men * to help each other. Pro 12:12
a man to riches, honor and * life. Pro 22:4
don't * for their favors and Pro 23:6,7,8
It is the one who spends * hours Pro 23:29,30
a king will have a * reign if he Pro 28:16
The godly pray for those who * to Pro 29:10
to the poor shall have a * reign. Pro 29:14
How do you know it didn't exist * Ecc 1:8-11
to come both will be * forgotten. Ecc 2:16
to enjoy himself as * as he can; Ecc 3:12
Whatever is, has been * ago; Ecc 3:15
in the * run, it is all so futile. Ecc 4:5,6
* the Lord may let him live. Ecc 5:18
it was known * ago what each man Ecc 6:10
Don't * for "the good old Ecc 7:10
who will not live *, good Ecc 8:13
hating, envying—is * gone, and they Ecc 9:6
How stately your neck with that * Sol 1:10
and cared for so * and tenderly Is 1:2
morning to go on * drinking bouts Is 5:11
Then I said, "Lord, how * will Is 6:11
Not * after this, the Lord sent Is 7:10
just as the Egyptians did * ago. Is 10:24
It will not last very *; Is 10:25
for all of Israel * ago when they Is 11:16
* dead, are there to see you. Is 14:9
Israelites approached (so * ago Is 17:9
Pharaoh about the * line of wise Is 19:11
"But a * year from now," Is 21:16
He is the one who planned it * Is 22:9,10,11
harlot sings who, * absent from her Is 23:15,16
You planned them * ago, and now Is 25:1
All night * I search for you; Is 26:9
them, and they are * forgotten. Is 26:14
Soon—and it will not be very Is 29:17
The funeral pyre has * been Is 30:33
was I who decided all this * ago? Is 37:26
prevail. * has he been silent; Is 42:14
they shall wait for me and * for Is 51:5
and fear their anger all day *? Is 51:13
repairing cities * ago destroyed, Is 61:4
them all day *—have rebelled; Is 65:2
All day * they insult me to my Is 65:3
For my people will live as * as Is 65:21,22
will * enjoy their hard-won gains. Is 65:21,22
as a young bride * ago and how you Jer 2:2
the God of Hosts. * ago you shook Jer 2:20
good old days of * ago" when you Jer 3:16
crushed. How * must this go on? Jer 4:21
How long must this go on? How * Jer 4:21
had a * and illustrious history. Jer 5:15f
to walk in, in the days of * ago. Jer 6:16
left alive shall * to die, rather Jer 8:3
How * must this land of yours put Jer 12:4
Then, a * time afterwards, the Jer 13:6
Woe upon you, O Jerusalem! How * Jer 13:27
worried by * months of drought. Jer 17:8
Terrify him all day * with battle Jer 20:16
did your father Josiah reign so *? Jer 22:15
name. How * will this continue? Jer 23:26
captivity will be *, and that we Jer 29:28
from them for a * time to come." Jer 29:28
for rest. For * ago the Lord had Jer 31:3
still love him. I * for him and Jer 31:20
cities here. How * will you Jer 31:22
jar to preserve them for a * time. Jer 32:14
their fathers * ago—a wonderful Jer 32:22
with your fathers * ago when I Jer 34:13
*, good lives in our own land. Jer 35:7
bread every day as * as there was Jer 37:21
And sure enough, it wasn't * Jer 38:27
king's kitchen as * as he lived. Jer 52:33
her at last! * have we waited for Lam 2:16
promises of doom he made so * ago. Lam 2:17
in dark places, like those * dead. Lam 3:6
all day * they sing their ribald Lam 3:14
prosperity have * since gone, for Lam 3:17
Why do you forsake us for so *? Lam 5:20
eyes that * for other gods. Eze 6:9
You will * for a prophet to guide Eze 7:26,27
who * for idols, I will repay Eze 11:21
their * march to distant lands. Eze 12:4
come true for a *, long time.' Eze 12:27
come true for a long, * time.' Eze 12:27
of those days * ago when you were Eze 16:22
you will no more * for Egypt and Eze 23:27
to lie there with those of * ago. Eze 26:20
who entered * ago the nether world Eze 26:20
the siege just * enough to defeat Eze 30:21f
It prospered and grew * thick Eze 31:5
which I gave your fathers * ago. Eze 36:28
"A * time from now you will be Eze 38:8
the one I spoke of * ago through Eze 38:17
stick, which was 10½ feet *. Eze 40:5
22¾ feet wide and 17½ feet *. Eze 40:7-12
feet * and 43¾ feet from side to Eze 40:21
was 87½ feet * and 43¾ feet wide. Eze 40:25
37½ feet * and 8¾ feet broad." Eze 40:29,30f
was 87½ feet * by 43¾ feet wide. Eze 40:29,30
and it was 87½ feet * by 43¾ feet Eze 40:33
or four inches *, fastened along Eze 40:43
was 35 feet wide and 19¼ feet *. Eze 40:48,49
feet * by thirty-five feet. Eze 41:2
122½ feet wide by 157½ feet *. Eze 41:12
was 175 feet * by 87½ feet wide. Eze 42:2
were 87½ feet *—only half as long Eze 42:7,8
long—only half as * as the inner Eze 42:7,8
court, which was 175 feet *. Eze 42:7,8
a square, 875 feet * on each side, Eze 42:16-20
hair grow too *, nor shave it off. Eze 44:20
miles * and 6 Eze 45:1
miles * and 3 Eze 45:3
miles * and 3 Eze 45:5
was a room 70 feet * by 52½ feet Eze 46:21,22
miles * and 6 Eze 48:9
miles * by 3 Eze 48:10
miles * by 1 Eze 48:15
King Nebuchadnezzar had * talks Dan 1:18,19
his hair grew as * as eagles' Dan 4:33
silver cups taken * before from the Dan 5:2,3,4
who * ago preceded you, a kingdom Dan 5:18
saw a ram with two * horns standing Dan 8:3
One of them said, "How * will it Dan 8:13
again? How * until the destruction Dan 8:13
of Greece, and its * horn Dan 8:21
will happen for a * time, so don't Dan 8:26
the river, "How * will it be until Dan 12:6
joy as in days * ago in her youth, Hos 1:15
Israel will be a * time without a Hos 3:4
My fury burns against you. How * Hos 8:5
* ago. The Lord does not forget. Hos 9:9
how I * to help you! Hos 11:8
All day * he sat on the hillsides Amo 1:1
plagues like those of Egypt * ago. Amo 4:10
you who * for the Sabbath to end Amo 8:5
fig, however much I * for it! Mic 7:1
and Gilead as they did * ago. Mic 7:14
us as you promised Jacob * ago. Mic 7:20
he pursues them all night *. Nah 1:8
O Lord, how * must I call for Hab 1:2
prophets are now * dead, but Zec 1:5,6
of Judah. How * will it be until Zec 1:12
feet * and fifteen feet wide!" Zec 5:2
year, as they had been doing so *. Zec 7:3

(LONG Con't)
and fun. * years ago, when Zec 7:7
and prosperity so * that there will Zec 8:4
You have been listening * enough! Zec 8:9
as the Jebusites did so * ago. Zec 9:7
as your people did * centuries ago Zec 14:5
"Happy are those who * to be Mt 5:6
* ago in shame and humility. Mt 11:21
How * shall I bear with you? Mt 17:17
if Abraham, Isaac, and Jacob, * Mt 22:32f
with all your *, public prayers in Mt 23:13,14
"After a * time their master Mt 25:19
made a crown from * thorns and put Mt 27:29
The next morning he was up * Mk 1:35
of plants, with * branches where Mk 4:31,32
All day * and through the night Mk 5:5
For some of them have come a * Mk 8:3
"How * has he been this way?" Mk 9:21
by praying * prayers in public. Mk 12:40
as the prophets declared * ago; Mk 14:21
made a crown of *, sharp thorns and Mk 15:16,17
Joseph bought a * sheet of linen Mk 15:46
wondered why he was taking so *. Lk 1:21
about it thought * thoughts and Lk 1:66
his holy prophets * ago— someone Lk 1:70
Not * afterwards Jesus went with Lk 7:11
NOT * AFTERWARDS he began a tour Lk 8:1
been demon-possessed for a * time. Lk 8:27
they had seen until * afterwards. Lk 9:36
"how * should I put up with Lk 9:41
in deep repentance * ago, clothed Lk 10:13
you keep knocking * enough he will Lk 11:8
for she went on a *, hard journey Lk 11:31
who killed the prophets * ago. Lk 11:47
be back for a * time,' and begins Lk 12:45
And while he was still a * Lk 15:20
is coming when you will * for me Lk 17:22
Or, "* for the Son of Man." Lk 17:22f
they exulted. "* live the Lk 19:38
they are praying * prayers with Lk 20:47
wrapped it in a * linen cloth and Lk 23:53
it was written * ago that the Lk 24:46
am—for he existed * before I did!' Jn 1:15
coming, who existed * before me!' Jn 1:30
Jesus was tired from the * walk Jn 4:5,6
this * trip out here every day." Jn 4:15
and he did, for two days, * Jn 4:40,41
him and knew how * he had been ill, Jn 5:6
and asked, "How * are you going to Jn 10:24
the one we have so * awaited." Jn 11:27
but I won't be with you very *." Jn 12:8
Jesus' body in a * linen cloth Jn 19:40
It was not * afterwards that he Act 1:9
this was predicted * ago by the Act 1:16
Then Peter preached a * sermon, Act 2:40
Moses, for instance, said * ago, Act 3:21,22
them— you spoke * ago by the Holy Act 4:25,26
And Peter stayed a * time in Act 9:43
stayed there a * time, preaching Act 14:3
at Antioch for a * while. Act 14:28
At the meeting, after * Act 15:7
me from among you * ago to preach Act 15:7
preached * sermons to the Act 15:32
then Paul preached another * Act 20:10,11,12
* studying has broken your mind!" Act 26:24
dangerous for * voyages by then, Act 27:9
No one had eaten for a * time, Act 27:21
but when they had waited a * time Act 28:6
This Good News was promised * Rom 1:2
For I * to visit you so that I Rom 1:11,12
Scriptures told about it * ago). Rom 3:21,22
her husband as * as he is alive. Rom 7:2
That is why I felt fine so * as I Rom 7:9
How I * for you to come to Rom 9:1
the Scriptures so * ago are to Rom 15:4
been so * in coming to visit you. Rom 15:22
all these * years of waiting. Rom 15:23
of her husband as * as he lives; 1Co 7:39
eat any of it as * as I live, 1Co 8:13
people in the wilderness * ago. 1Co 10:1
For women are proud of their * 1Co 11:14,15
with * hair tends to be ashamed. 1Co 11:14,15
So, my fellow believers, * to be 1Co 14:39
Last of all I saw him too, * 1Co 15:8
and bring * letters of 2Co 3:1
quite small and won't last very *. 2Co 4:17
* since discarded the Jewish laws; Gal 2:14
God told Abraham about this * ago Gal 3:8,9
world was killed * ago, and the Gal 6:14
interest in me is also * dead. Gal 6:14
* ago, even before he made the Eph 1:4
plan he decided on in mercy * ago; Eph 1:9
happen just as he decided * ago. Eph 1:11
Holy Spirit, who * ago had been Eph 1:13
Christ Jesus; and * ages ago he Eph 2:10
should, how *, how wide, how deep, Eph 3:18,19
be a * life, full of blessing. Eph 6:3
for I * to go and be with Christ. Php 1:23
I love you and * to see you, for Php 4:1
We can bear anything as * as we 1Th 3:8
How true it is, and how I * that 1Ti 1:15
aren't known until * afterward. 1Ti 5:25
But people who * to be rich soon 1Ti 6:9
times during the * nights I beg my 2Ti 1:3
How I * to see you again. 2Ti 1:4
that was his plan * before the 2Ti 1:9
and hurt for a * time to come. 2Ti 2:17
I have fought * and hard for my 2Ti 4:7
* AGO GOD spoke in many different Heb 1:1
through King David * years after Heb 4:7
not have spoken * afterwards about Heb 4:8
And can a human body live * Heb 5:7f
You have been Christians a * time Heb 5:12,13
loving others as * as life lasts, Heb 6:11
Holy of Holies as * as the outer Heb 9:8
and though Abel is * dead, we can Heb 11:4
It would take too * to recount Heb 11:32
to get it. You * for what others Jas 4:2
Father chose you * ago and knew you 1Pe 1:2
but * years later, during yours. 1Pe 1:12
God chose him for this purpose * 1Pe 1:20
envy, and fraud. * to grow up into 1Pe 2:2,3
of those who, * before in the days 1Pe 3:20
am soon to die. As * as I am still 2Pe 1:13,14
remember them * after I have gone. 2Pe 1:15
But God condemned them * ago and 2Pe 2:3
a mighty flood, * after he had made 2Pe 3:5,6
people was written * ago, for they Jud 1:4
wearing a * robe circled with a Rev 1:13
Its rider was given a * sword and Rev 6:4
holy and true, how * will it be Rev 6:10
They will * to die—but death will Rev 9:6
Their hair was * like women's, Rev 9:8
* and as high as a horse's bridle. Rev 14:20
crews will stand a * way off, Rev 18:17
was a square as wide as it was *; Rev 21:16
they stay open all day *—and Rev 21:25

LONG-DESERTED
Your sons will rebuild the * Is 58:12
farms and the * cities, destroyed Eze 36:4

LONG-RANGE
Jeremiah here sees the * picture Jer 51:26f

LONG-SLEEVED
tunic," or "* tunic." Gen 37:3f

LONG-STANDING
out of revenge and * hatred, I Eze 25:15

LONGED
to Amnon's death, * day after day 2Sa 13:37,38,39
They * for me to speak as those Job 29:23
"Or if I have * for another Job 31:9
I will rescue them as they have * Ps 12:5
O Lord, I have * for your Ps 119:174
and * for their fathers' idols. Eze 20:23,24
paintings she * to give herself to Eze 23:16
and godly man has * to see what you Mt 13:17
king of old has * for these days, Lk 10:24
and * for me to come and help. 2Co 7:11

LONGER
blood. No * will it yield crops Gen 4:12
no * godly in character (verse 3). Gen 6:1f
It is no * 'Abram' ('Exalted Gen 17:5
name is no * 'Sarai' but 'Sarah' Gen 17:15
"You shall no * be called Jacob Gen 35:10
told him, "they are no * here. Gen 37:17
JOSEPH COULD STAND it no *. Gen 45:1
sea, and you shall be first no *. Gen 49:4
Then, when she could no * hide Ex 2:3
tired to hold up the rod any *; Ex 17:12
* wanting her after marrying her. Ex 21:8
then he may no * treat her as a Ex 21:9
she is no * ceremonially defiled. Lev 15:28
intention that you be slaves no *; Lev 26:13
before his defilement no * count. Num 6:12
people stay even * in the Num 32:15
"You will no * go your own way Deu 12:8
I am no * able to lead you, Deu 31:2
Literally, "I am no * able to go Deu 31:2f
will say, 'God is no * among us!' Deu 31:17
They are no * his; Deu 32:5
will no * bind us in any way." Jos 2:20
I will not stay with you any * Jos 7:12
your God will no * chase those Jos 23:13
contract, it is no * in effect, and Ju 2:3
effect, and I no * promise to Ju 2:3
I will no * drive out the nations Ju 2:21
They no * considered the Lord as Ju 8:34
let them live there any *. Ju 9:41
Not only this, but they no * Ju 10:6
* and finally told her his secret. Ju 16:16,17
it will no * serve as priests. 1Sa 2:31
of the God of Israel here any *. 1Sa 5:7
want me to be their king any *. 1Sa 8:7
and I'll no * try to harm you; 1Sa 26:21
and Israel was no * at war with the 2Sa 7:1
But God will bless you with a * 2Sa 14:14
Food and wine are no * tasty, and 2Sa 19:35
no * sleep with them as his wives. 2Sa 20:3
but it took him * than the three 2Sa 20:5
now Solomon was no * interested in 1Ki 11:9,10
old man now, and could no * see. 1Ki 14:4
to pay tribute to Israel any *. 2Ki 1:1
They shall no * cause death or 2Ki 2:21
Amaziah lived fifteen years * 2Ki 14:1
and refused to pay tribute any *. 2Ki 18
Now the Levites will no * need 1Ch 23:2
your duties any *, for the Lord has 2Ch 29:1
the Lord could no * be restrained, 2Ch 36:1
and there was no * any remedy. 2Ch 36:1
we can't stay out here much *. Ez 10:1
so that I need no * live in terror Job 9:3
Not one bit * may he live. Job 14:
"Let him no * trust in foolish Job 15:3
let him no * deceive himself, for Job 15:3
and carry their burden no *? Job 39:2,
man will terrify them no *. Ps 10:1
they are no * wise and good. Ps 36:
My life is no * than my hand! Ps 39:5,
Recite my laws no *, and stop Ps 50:1
"Let me sleep a little *!" Pro 6:1
eternity is far *, and that Ecc 11:
you'll no * enjoy living. Ecc 12:
Let me no * see you doing all Is 1:1
all to see. No * shall they tinkle Is 3:1
* be the issuing of battle gear; Is 9:
my people shall no * be their Is 14:2
It is no * a city—it has become a Is 17:
They will no * ask their idols Is 17:
They will no * have respect for Is 17:
The earth will no * hide the Is 26:2
* pale with fear, or be ashamed. Is 29:2
The people of Israel will no * Is 33:2
Have I no * power to deliver? Is 50:
God—will no * enter your gates. Is 52:
you will no * live in shame. Is 54:
No * will you need the sun or Is 60:1
No * will babies die when only a Is 65:2
a few days old; no * will men be Is 65:2
Lord, you will no * wish for "the Jer 3:16
him there and no * stubbornly Jer 3:17
Why continue the process *? Jer 6:29
Children no * play in the Jer 9:21
they no * follow God nor ask his Jer 10:21
Therefore, Jeremiah, pray no * Jer 11:14
They are no * yours. Jer 13:18
Now I will no * accept you as my Jer 14:10
You will look back no * to the Jer 16:14,15
valley shall no * be called Jer 19:6
and I can't hold it in any *. Jer 20:9
In that day people will no * say Jer 23:7
shall no * be their masters! Jer 30:8
*, for I have heard your prayers Jer 31:16
The people shall no * quote this Jer 31:29
At that time it will no * be Jer 31:34
It was because he could no * Jer 44:22
Moab shall no * be a nation, for Jer 48:42
Her mightiest soldiers no * Jer 51:30
The nations shall no * come and Jer 51:44
The roads to Zion mourn, no * Lam 1:4
in a garden! No * can the people Lam 2:6
I have cried until the tears no * Lam 2:11
he no * helps them, for they Lam 4:16
The old men sit no * in the city Lam 5:14
the young no * dance and sing. Lam 5:14
they will no * be your victims, Eze 13:21
But you will lie no more; no * Eze 13:23
to be polluted any * with sin, but Eze 14:11
And Moab will no * be counted Eze 25:9,10
I am the Lord. No * shall you and Eze 28:24
"Israel will no * expect any Eze 29:16
and you will no * be a place for Eze 36:12
says the Lord. No * will those Eze 36:15
for you will no * be a nation of Eze 36:15
of them all; no * shall they be Eze 37:22
wing, parallel to the * wing. Eze 42:7,8
my holy name any * through the Eze 43:7
My princes shall no * oppress and Eze 45:8
are no * ruler of this kingdom. Dan 4:31
that it could no * fly, and it was Dan 7:4
allowed to live a short time *. Dan 7:12
so that it was * than the other. Dan 8:3
man's wife—I am no * her husband. Hos 1:2
will no * give her rich harvests of Hos 1:9
so it will no * be used in Hos 1:16f
You may no * stay here in this Hos 9:3
your need. No * will I make you a Joe 2:19
ones can no * save themselves. Amo 2:14
I will no * turn away from Amo 7:8
history, no * nations any more. Ob 1:16
nations shall no * fight each Mic 4:3
Lord, but now no * do, and those Zep 1:6
And then you will no * need to Zep 3:11
will no * be rebels against me. Zep 3:11
But no *! Zec 8:13
"I won't be your shepherd any *. Zec 11:9
moon and stars will no * shine, Zec 14:6
The two shall become one—no * Mt 19:5,6
how much * must I stay with you Mk 9:19
How much * must I be patient with Mk 9:19
that they are no * two, but one. Mk 10:8
but I won't be here much *. Mk 14:7
'Why bother with it any *? Lk 13:7
* worthy of being called your son. Lk 15:19
when we will no * be concerned Jn 4:21-24

LONGER Con't)
I am to be here a little *. Jn 7:33
out for you just a little while *. Jn 12:35
will no * wander in the darkness. Jn 12:46
I no * call you slaves, for a Jn 15:15
to be with you for a while *. Jn 16:4
Don't be faithless any *. Jn 20:27
last they could no * keep him Act 7:21
he stayed awhile * in Turkey. Act 19:22
that we no * need obey God's laws? Rom 3:31
whose sins are no * counted against Rom 4:8
body is no * under sin's control, Rom 6:6
no * needs to be a slave to sin; Rom 6:6
Death no * has any power over Rom 6:9
sin control your puny body any *; Rom 6:12
for now you are no * tied to the Rom 6:14
law no * holds him in its power? Rom 7:1
But if he dies, she is no * bound Rom 7:2
the laws of marriage no * apply Rom 7:2
you are no * "married to the Rom 7:4
But now you need no * worry Rom 7:6
myself, because I'm no * doing it. Rom 7:17
Holy Spirit and no * obey the old Rom 8:4
free gift would no * be free—it Rom 11:6
who marries no * has full right to 1Co 7:4
way the husband no * has full right 1Co 7:4
our sins, will no * be our judge. 1Co 15:55,56
It could be that I will stay * 1Co 16:6
him—might live no * for themselves, 2Co 5:15
to himself, no * counting men's 2Co 5:19
I am no * sorry that I sent that 2Co 7:8
You no * shrugged your shoulders, 2Co 7:11
no * live, but Christ lives in me. Gal 2:20
* to guard us and lead us to him. Gal 3:25
We are no * Jews or Greeks or Gal 3:28
Now we are no * slaves, but Gal 4:7
Spirit you need no * force yourself Gal 5:18
Now you are no * strangers to God Eph 2:19
Then we will no * be like Eph 4:14
the Lord: Live no * as the unsaved Eph 4:17,18
on earth a little *, to help you Php 1:25
one with him, no * counting on Php 3:9
could stand it no *, I decided to 1Th 3:1
the suspense no * I sent Timothy to 1Th 3:5
be around to help you very much *. 2Ti 4:6
yours forever, no * only a slave, Phm 1:16
There is no * any room for doubt, Heb 10:23
coming will not be delayed much *. Heb 10:37
from God and no * trusts the Lord, Jas 5:19
to rest a little * until their Rev 6:11
figure, it is no * incredible, in Rev 9:16f
Literally, "There was no * any Rev 20:11f

LONGING
Sin is waiting to attack you, * Gen 4:7
Your heart will break with * for Deu 28:32
much the king was * to see Absalom, 2Sa 14:1
overwhelmed with * for his help. Ps 77:3
I long, yes, faint with * to be Ps 84:2
My eyes grow dim with * for you Ps 119:123
He will give a * for justice to Is 28:6
* after idols has made them Hos 4:12
this life and his * for money choke Mt 13:22
As he lay there * for scraps Lk 16:21
hour with deep *, anxious to eat Lk 22:15
DEAR BROTHERS, THE * of my Rom 10:1
Who falls without my * to help 2Co 11:29
child to be born—* for the time Gal 4:19
is my love and * for you—with the Php 1:8
Christ's * was to live until he Heb 5:7f

LONGINGS
Pour out your * before him, for Ps 62:8
to stand against all such evil *. Jas 4:6

LONGS
and * for her to be his wife. Gen 34:8
How he * for the day to end. Job 7:2
He * to flee from God. Job 27:22
The lazy man * for many things Pro 21:25,26
know how much it * for you. Jer 12:3
Savior, for he * for all to be 1Ti 2:4

LOOK
birds and all the animals. And *! Gen 1:29
* I am going to cover the Gen 6:17
Noah opened the door to *, and Gen 8:13
mankind was making, he said, "*! Gen 11:6
Lot took a long * at the fertile Gen 13:10
said to Abram, "* as far as you Gen 13:14
and told him, "* up into the Gen 15:5
a wicked thing. *—I have two Gen 19:8
"And don't * back. Gen 19:17
"* my kingdom over, and choose Gen 20:15
Then he turned to Sarah. "*," Gen 20:16
"He's well and prosperous. *, Gen 29:6
"* there," Judah said to the Gen 37:26,27
Joseph refused. "*," he told Gen 39:8
"*," he exclaimed to his Gen 42:28
for he was afraid to * at God. Ex 3:6
And he is coming here to * for Ex 4:14
"But *," Moses objected, "my Ex 6:12
Then the Lord said to Moses, "*, Ex 16:4
or someone might * up beneath the Ex 20:26
went to Aaron. "*," they said, Ex 32:1
the priest shall * again, and if Lev 13:8
the priest is to * to see if there Lev 13:9,10
* at it again on the seventh day. Lev 13:51
the seventh day to * at it again. Lev 14:39
come again and *, and if he sees Lev 14:44
comes again to *, the spots have Lev 14:48
I will * after you, and multiply Lev 26:9
moment, lest they * at the sacred Num 4:20
spies to * over the Jazer area; Num 21:31,32
"Because you have made me * like Num 22:29
Look! I have received Num 23:18-24
Mount Abarim and * across the river Num 27:12
local fruit. One * was enough to Deu 1:24,25
where you can * out in every Deu 3:27
And do not * up into the sky to Deu 4:19
don't * the other way. Deu 22:4
But don't * down on the Edomites Deu 23:7
you commanded me. * down from your Deu 26:15
"*, today I have set before you Deu 30:15
Climb to its heights, and * out Deu 32:49
can reply, '* at the altar of the Jos 22:28
Zebul, "* over at that mountain! Ju 9:36
Doesn't it * like people coming Ju 9:36
seeing shadows that * like men!" Ju 9:36
"No, * over there," Gaal said. Ju 9:37
people coming towards us. And *! Ju 9:37
was almost too glorious to * at. Ju 13:6
to * at the carcass of the lion. Ju 14:8
your best man. But *, her sister is Ju 15:2
said, "*, it's getting late. Ju 19:9
if you will * down upon my sorrow 1Sa 1:11
Saul and a servant to * for them. 1Sa 9:3
And Saul replied, "We went to * 1Sa 10:14
"*," he said, "I have done as 1Sa 12:1
king you have chosen. * him over. 1Sa 12:13
saw them coming they shouted, "*! 1Sa 14:11
Samuel took one * at Eliab and 1Sa 16:6
appearance, but I * at a man's 1Sa 16:7
Jonathan exclaimed. "*, 1Sa 20:9
Saul's camp one night to * around. 1Sa 26:5,6,7
was beside his head? * and see!" 1Sa 26:16
"What does he * like?" 1Sa 28:14
* -they exclaimed 2Sa 4:8
Yes, and I am willing to * even 2Sa 6:22
said to Nathan the prophet, "*! 2Sa 7:2
Why should the son of a king * so 2Sa 13:4
Then the king told Zadok, "*, 2Sa 15:27
He will constantly * after 2Sa 23:5
"*, I am the one who has sinned! 2Sa 24:17
* as the priest are 1Ki 8:10
"Go and * out toward the sea." 1Ki 18:43
his advisors. "* what this man is 1Ki 20:7
"What did he * like?" 2Ki 1:7
morning sacrifice was offered—*! 2Ki 3:20
said to Gehazi, "*, that woman 2Ki 4:25
"*," he said, "I thought at 2Ki 5:11
said to Nathan the prophet, "*! 1Ch 17:1
detail, and will * forward eagerly 1Ch 29:19
to you now! * down with favor day 2Ch 6:20,21
Whenever you * for him, you will 2Ch 15:2
"* here," the king said 2Ch 18:15
far as they could * there were dead 2Ch 20:24
burner he was holding. But *! 2Ch 26:19
Look! he exclaimed. 2Ch 28:9
"*!" 2Ch 34:15,16
to what I say! * down and see me Neh 1:6,7
You aren't sick, are you? You * Neh 2:1
Majesty and if you * upon me with Neh 2:4
sacrifices? And * at those charred Neh 4:1
you at Jerusalem by saying, "*! Neh 6:7
he does—* how rich he is! Job 1:10
appetite is gone when I * at it; Job 6:5,6,7
or selling a friend. * at me! Job 6:28
Soon you'll * upon me dead. Job 7:8
you * for me, I shall be gone." Job 7:21
That is all he can * forward to! Job 8:19
"But *! Job 8:20
and many will * to you for help. Job 11:19
"*, I HAVE seen many instances Job 13:1
is so troubled. * at me in horror, Job 21:5
"*, everything the wicked touch Job 21:16
in the Lord, and * up to God. Job 22:26
to all mankind: '*, to fear the Job 28:28
you and you don't bother to *. Job 30:20
not to * with lust upon a girl. Job 31:1
of this argument. *, I will sign my Job 31:35
"*, I am the one you were Job 33:6
your friends too. * up there into Job 35:5
"*, God is all-powerful. Job 36:22
For as we cannot * at the sun Job 37:21
"Take a * at the behemoth! Job 40:15
Each morning I will * to you in Ps 5:3
for you, the righteous God, * Ps 7:9
When I * up into the night skies Ps 8:3
How long will you * the other way Ps 13:1
sins, O Lord! * at me instead Ps 25:6,7
They dread meeting me and * the Ps 31:11
Theirs was no downcast * of Ps 34:5
wicked hands push me around. *! Ps 36:12
You will * for them in vain. Ps 37:10
with me and I am ashamed to * up. Ps 40:12
Why do you * the other way? Ps 44:24
in the markets and wherever you *. Ps 55:11
dug a pitfall in my path. But *! Ps 57:6
beam with joy as you * down at us. Ps 67:1
Well may you * with envy at Mount Ps 68:15,16
and does not * the other way. Ps 69:33
The reference seems to * beyond Ps 72:6f
they ask. "* at these men of Ps 73:12
God. * down on us in joy and love; Ps 80:3
* down on us in joy and love; Ps 80:7
and bless us. * down from heaven Ps 80:14
armies of heaven. * down on us, Ps 80:19
and of truth; so * down in pity Ps 86:16
both great and small. And *! Ps 104:26
he stoops to *, and lifts the Ps 113:6
then I can obey you. * down in Ps 119:135
never changes. * down upon my Ps 119:153
SHALL I * to the mountain gods for Ps 121:1
to thank and praise the Lord. *! Ps 122:5
We * to Jehovah our God for his Ps 123:2
home. And * at all those children! Ps 128:3
I * to you for help, O Lord God. Ps 141:8
The eyes of all mankind * up to Ps 145:15
Don't * to men for help; Ps 146:3
Stay far from her. * straight Pro 4:25
don't even turn your head to *. Pro 4:25
and with a saucy * she said, Pro 7:13
I was just coming to * for you Pro 7:15
the road to hell, * for her house. Pro 7:27
The good man can * forward to Pro 11:23
I said to myself, "*, I am Ecc 1:16-18
officials * up to their superiors. Ecc 5:8
will not need to * back with sorrow Ecc 5:19,20
The Girl: "Don't * down on me, Sol 1:6
or young deer. *, there he is Sol 2:9
I got up to * for him but Sol 3:1
be bought? *, it is the chariot Sol 3:7
We will * down from the summit of Sol 4:8
* the other way, for your eyes Sol 6:5
to heaven, I won't * or listen. Is 1:15
The very * on their faces gives Is 3:9
Wherever they * there will be Is 8:22
*, the mighty armies of Assyria Is 10:28,29
Then, *, look! Is 10:33
Then, look, *! Is 10:33
in labor. You * at one another, Is 13:8
*, Damascus is gone! Is 17:1
*, see the armies thundering Is 17:12
*, the Lord is coming against Is 19:1
*! They are preparing Is 21:5
Now at last—*! Is 21:8,9
the streets to * for them again and Is 23:15,16
*! The Lord is Is 24:1
they will not * to see your Is 26:11
your enemies has passed. *! Is 26:21
*, A RIGHTEOUS King is coming, Is 32:1
see me as I pray. * at this Is 37:16,17
* up into the heavens! Is 40:26
You will * for them in vain—they Is 41:12
the first to tell Jerusalem, "*! Is 41:27
to tell Jerusalem, "Look! *! Is 41:27
Let all the world * to me for Is 45:22
hauled away on ox carts! But *! Is 46:1
destroying you. * and see, for the Is 49:18
for me to come. * high in the Is 51:6
shepherds who only * after their Is 56:11
your workers. *, what good is Is 58:4
like doves. You * for God to keep Is 59:11
O Lord, * down from heaven and Is 63:15
our sins. Oh, * and see that we are Is 64:9
rejoice forever in my creation. * Is 65:18
Yet I will * with pity on the man Is 66:2
And they shall go out and * at Is 66:24
Then the Lord said to me, "*, Jer 1:11
* around you and see if you can Jer 2:10,11
Go and * in any valley in the Jer 2:23
planned! I * to you for justice. Jer 11:20
then, when you * for light, you Jer 13:16
You will * back no longer to the Jer 16:14,15
me, if you * for me in earnest. Jer 29:13
to you in my name: *, I am turning Jer 29:21
hurt," he said. "* after him well Jer 39:11,12
spears, put on your armor. But *! Jer 46:5
against her from every side. *! Jer 50:15
little strength. "*, O Lord," she Lam 1:11
you who pass by? * and see if there Lam 1:12
* also on their sins, O Lord, and Lam 1:22
Oh, that the Lord might * down Lam 3:50
We * for our allies Lam 4:17
to come and save us, but we * in Lam 4:17
and water, and to * at one another Eze 4:17
"Son of dust, * over toward the Eze 6:2
"Tell Israel, Wherever you Eze 7:2
I will not * when they defile Eze 7:22
He said to me, "Son of dust, * Eze 8:5
Then you will * back at all your Eze 20:43
"Son of dust, * toward Jerusalem Eze 20:46
"Son of dust, * toward the land Eze 25:2
and * on with twisted faces. Eze 27:35
"Son of dust, * toward the city Eze 28:21
to * good around the palace." Dan 1:3,4

(LOOK Con't)
superintendent to * after Daniel, Dan 1:11
"Well, *!" Dan 3:25
the blame to him! *, priest, I am Hos 4:4
their guilt and * to me for help Hos 5:15
They * everywhere except to Hos 7:16
I am living and strong! I * after Hos 14:8
They * like tiny horses, and Joe 2:4
they run as fast. * at them Joe 2:5
I will not * at your offerings of Amo 5:22
than you, but * at them now. Amo 6:2
*! He is coming! Mic 1:3
He will * the other way! Mic 3:4
As for me, I * to the Lord for Mic 7:7
Wherever I * there is oppression Hab 1:3
The Lord replied: "*, and be Hab 1:5
lies in ruins? * at the result: Hag 1:5
but he returned and said, "* up! Zec 5:5
Shout with joy! For *—your King Zec 9:9
dying ones, nor * after the young, Zec 11:16
and they will * on him they Zec 12:10
started out again. And *! Mt 2:9
do, who try to * wan and disheveled Mt 6:16
to eat and wear. * at the birds! Mt 6:26
clothes? * at the field lilies! Mt 6:28
*! A leper is approaching Mt 8:2
"* at my Servant. Mt 12:18
pointed to his disciples. "*!" Mt 12:49
they *, but don't see! Mt 13:14
"Beware that you don't * down Mt 18:10
You try to * like saintly men, Mt 23:28
desert, don't bother to go and *. Mt 24:26
Let's be going! *! Mt 26:46
his spirit, and died. And *! Mt 27:51
are to see with—why don't you *? Mk 8:18
very clearly; they * like tree Mk 8:24
day, and exclaimed, "*, Teacher! Mk 11:21
these are! * at the decorated Mk 13:1
Jesus replied, "Yes, *! Mk 13:2
The time for sleep has ended! *! Mk 14:41
We must go! *! Mk 14:42
"Ha! * at you now!" Mk 15:29,30
He has come back to life! *, Mk 16:6
they started to * for him among Lk 2:44
Then—*! Lk 5:18,19
* worse with a new patch on it! Lk 5:36
refer when they say, "*! Lk 7:27
the woman and said to Simon, "*! Lk 7:44
food and clothes. * at the Lk 12:24
"* at the lilies! Lk 12:27
Won't she light a lamp and * in Lk 15:8
" '*, dear son,' his father said Lk 15:31
don't believe it or go out to * Lk 17:23
tried to get a * at Jesus, but he Lk 19:3
they were to * for a donkey tied Lk 19:30
happen, stand straight and * up! Lk 21:28
So he began to * for an Lk 22:6
Peter ran to the tomb to *. Lk 24:12
it is really I? * at my hands! Lk 24:39
Look at my hands! * at my feet! Lk 24:39
coming toward him and said, "*! Jn 1:29
Philip now went off to * for Jn 1:45
months from now? * around you! Jn 4:35
across to Capernaum to * for him. Jn 6:24
* -the man exclaimed Jn 9:27
"We've lost. *—the whole world has Jn 12:19
* on him whom they pierced." Jn 19:36,37
and then Peter said, "* here!" Act 3:4
And why * at us as though we by Act 3:12
they said "Now * around among Act 6:3
shook with terror and dared not *. Act 7:32
And he told them, "*, I see the Act 7:56
water, and the eunuch said, "*! Act 8:36
For they said, '* and perish, Act 13:41
anything against me) — but *! Act 24:20
carving them to * like mere birds Rom 1:23
and joyfully * forward to actually Rom 5:2
with God. So * upon your old sin Rom 6:11
not * down on those who won't. Rom 14:3
your brother or * down on him. Rom 14:10
so that we will * forward Rom 15:4
God has made them all * foolish, 1Co 1:20
You are intelligent people. * now 1Co 10:15
not bear to * at Moses' face. 2Co 3:7
So we do not * at what we can 2Co 4:18
around us, but we * forward to the 2Co 4:18
That is why we * forward eagerly 2Co 5:2
Now we * forward with confidence 2Co 5:6
how well they * and preach, but 2Co 5:12
real gift and not * as if it were 2Co 9:5
you is that you * at me and I seem 2Co 10:7
you don't * beneath the surface. 2Co 10:7
and make you * down on me because I 2Co 11:7
Then we won't need to * for Gal 5:26
will * as if you approve of them. 1Ti 5:22
Now we can * forward to the Heb 10:23
There will be nothing to * Heb 10:27
those who sincerely * for him. Heb 11:6
not see the Lord. * after each Heb 12:15
people and * down on poor people? Jas 2:1
* here, you people who say, Jas 4:13
* HERE, YOU rich men, now is the Jas 5:1
* at the Lord's prophets. Jas 5:10
So now you can * forward soberly 1Pe 1:13
future to * back upon and fear. 2Pe 2:6
You should * forward to that day 2Pe 3:12
alive. *, I am coming soon! Rev 3:11
"*! Rev 3:20
said to me, "Stop crying, for *! Rev 5:5
throne saying, "*, the home of God Rev 21:3

LOOKED
And God * at them with pleasure, Gen 1:21,22
Then God * over all that he Gen 1:31
* upon the beautiful earth women Gen 6:1
nakedness as they * the other way. Gen 9:23
"the God who * upon me," for she Gen 16:13
But the young men * at him as Gen 19:14
But Lot's wife * back as she was Gen 19:26
the Lord. He * out across the Gen 19:28
he * up and saw the camels coming. Gen 24:63
the Philistines, * out of a window Gen 26:8
Then Esau * at the women and Gen 33:5
that they * dejected and sad. Gen 40:6
Then Israel * over at the two Gen 48:8
Moses * this way and that to be Ex 2:12
morning Jehovah * down from the Ex 14:24
and when they *, it was full of Ex 16:20
mountain top * like a raging fire. Ex 24:17
We are not told what they * Ex 25:18f
What these * like has been lost in Ex 28:30,31f
seed, and * like droplets of gum Num 11:7
suddenly, as they * toward the Num 16:42
had been bitten * at the bronze Num 21:9
Instead, he went at once and * Num 24:1
Then Balaam * over at the homes Num 24:20
Then he * over at the Kenites: Num 24:21,22
When the men of Ai * behind Jos 8:20,21
Benjamin, who now * behind them Ju 20:40,41
because they * into the Ark. 1Sa 6:19
for I have * down on them in mercy 1Sa 9:16
But when they * for him, he had 1Sa 10:21
And when Saul * around, David 1Sa 24:7,8
As David and his men * at the 1Sa 30:3
When Abner * behind and saw him 2Sa 2:20
the king of Israel * today! 2Sa 6:20
As he * out over the city, he 2Sa 11:2
were gone. They * for them without 2Sa 17:20
They * in vain for help; 2Sa 22:42
up and eat! He * around and saw 1Ki 19:6
but the Israeli army * like two 1Ki 20:27
morning the sun * red as it shone 2Ki 3:22
He * up and saw her at the window 2Ki 9:32
And two or three eunuchs * out 2Ki 9:32
while King Darius * into the matter Ez 5:5
Then as I * over the situation, I Neh 4:14
I therefore * for good to come. Job 30:26
or if I have * at the sun shining Job 31:26
Everywhere I * I was afraid, for Ps 31:13
but when I * again, he was gone! Ps 37:35,36
Tell them that God * down from Ps 102:19
I have * for your commandments Ps 119:167
Then, as I *, I learned this Pro 24:32,33
But as I * at everything I had Ecc 2:11
Again I * throughout the earth Ecc 9:11
and I have * upon the King, the Is 6:5
who has ever * to her for help. Is 36:6
We turned our backs on him and * Is 53:3
I * but no one came to help them; Is 63:5
in the world. I * forward to your Jer 3:19
I * down upon their land and as Jer 4:23
were dark. I * at the mountains Jer 4:24
and shook. I *, and mankind was Jer 4:25
no peace came; we * for health but Jer 8:15
appeared that * like men, except Eze 1:5
The wheels * as if they were Eze 1:16
out above them * as though it were Eze 1:22
them was what * like a throne made Eze 1:26
Then I * and saw a hand holding Eze 2:9,10
So I * and, sure enough, north Eze 8:5
his wings, what * like human hands) Eze 10:7,8
of the four ways their faces *. Eze 10:9-13
wings, with what * like human hands Eze 10:21
my shoulder while the people * on. Eze 12:7
* like a queen, and so you were! Eze 16:13
"I * in vain for anyone who Eze 22:30
party in Judah * to Egypt for help Eze 23:17f
One face—that of a man—* toward Eze 41:19,20
of a young lion—* toward the palm Eze 41:19,20
of the Temple. I * and saw that the Eze 44:4
could see how they * in comparison Dan 1:13
his three friends * healthier and Dan 1:15
I, Nebuchadnezzar, * up to Dan 4:34
The second animal * like a bear Dan 7:5
strange animals * like a leopard, Dan 7:6
me—or at least he * like a man— Dan 8:15
Tigris River, I * up and suddenly Dan 10:5,6
Then someone—he * like a Dan 10:16
Then I, Daniel, * and saw two men Dan 12:5
Then I * and saw four animal Zec 1:18
WHEN I * around me again, I saw a Zec 2:1
I * UP again and saw a scroll Zec 5:1
THEN I * up again and saw four Zec 6:1
from between what * like two Zec 6:
for all the laws and prophets * Mt 11:1
and two fish, * up into the sky and Mt 14:
But when he * around at the high Mt 14:3
And when they *, only Jesus was Mt 17:
Jesus * at them intently and Mt 19:2
there and * for witnesses who would Mt 26:5
The man * around. Mk 8:2
Jesus turned and * at his Mk 8:3
Then suddenly they * around and Mk 9:
love for this man as he * at him. Mk 10:2
Jesus * at them intently, then Mk 10:2
the Temple. He * around carefully Mk 11:1
She * at him closely and then Mk 14:66,6
But when they arrived they * up Mk 16:
He * around at them one by one Lk 6:1
* up into the sky and gave thanks; Lk 9:1
walked over and * at him lying Lk 10:3
feeding the swine * good to him. Lk 15:1
He * at them and said, "Go to Lk 17:1
When Jesus came by he * up at Lk 19:
Jesus * at them and said, "Then Lk 20:1
and he said, "I have * forward Lk 22:1
After a while someone else * at Lk 22:58
At that moment Jesus turned and * Lk 22:6
walked by. John * at him intently Jn 1:36
Jesus * around and saw them Jn 1:38
Jesus * intently at Peter for a Jn 1:42
Then Jesus * up to heaven and Jn 11:4
The disciples * at each other, Jn 13:22
these things he * up to heaven and Jn 17:1
and stooped and * in and saw the Jn 20:5
she stooped and * in and saw two Jn 20:11
Then, what * like flames or Act 2:3
They * at him intently, and then Act 3:4
The lame man * at them eagerly, Act 3:5
* like a perfect day for the trip; Act 27:13
SO APOLLOS AND I should be * upon 1Co 4:1
didn't even know what I * like. Gal 1:22
What's more, the Scriptures * Gal 3:8,9
them was one who * like Jesus who Rev 1:13
THEN AS I *, I saw a door standing Rev 4:1
the second * like an ox; Rev 4:7
I * and saw a Lamb standing there Rev 5:6
I *, and there in front of me was Rev 6:2
The locusts * like horses armored Rev 9:7
They had what * like golden Rev 9:7
and their faces * like men's. Rev 9:7
The horses' heads * much like Rev 9:17,18
This Creature * like a leopard Rev 13:2
sitting on it who * like Jesus, who Rev 14:14
Then I * and saw that the Holy of Rev 15:5

LOOKING
How lovely and fresh * it was! Gen 3:6
"Who are you * for?" Gen 37:15
standing around * at one another? Gen 42:1
* at his brother Gen 43:29
* down upon them, he knew that Ex 2:25
The Egyptians you are * at—you Ex 14:13
facing each other, * down upon the Ex 25:20
place of mercy, * down upon it. Ex 37:9
* for it, and then give it to him. Deu 22:2
to the Jordan River * for them; Jos 2:7
anyone comes by, * for me, tell Ju 4:20
When Barak came by * for Sisera, Ju 4:22
show you the man you are * for." Ju 4:22
* for a good place to live. Ju 17:7,8
and I am * for a place to live." Ju 17:9
He was a fine * boy, ruddy-faced, 1Sa 16:12
them—they will be * only for you. 2Sa 18:3
they pray to you, * toward your 1Ki 8:44
you to the man you're * for." 2Ki 6:19
As Josiah was * around, he 2Ki 23:16
the whole earth, * for people whose 2Ch 16:9
what to do, but we are * to you." 2Ch 20:12
They wouldn't think of * for him! Ps 10:4
or as joyous as an athlete * Ps 19:5
My eyes are ever * to the Lord Ps 25:15
Don't keep * at my sins—erase Ps 51:9
Be merciful, O Lord, for I am * Ps 86:3
face from me, and * the other way? Ps 88:14
*," they say, "and besides, he Ps 94:6,7
I was * out the window of my Pro 7:6
he claims he is * for, yet it comes Pro 14:6
If you are * for advice, stay Pro 14:7
boasting is * for trouble. Pro 17:19
the wall, now * in at the windows. Sol 2:9
What are they * at? Is 22:1
instead of * to the Holy One of Is 31:1
my eyes grew weary of * up for Is 38:14
They strain their eyes * for Jer 14:6
bones nor gone * for those who have Eze 34:4
I will be like a shepherd * for Eze 34:12
As I was * at the horns, suddenly Dan 7:8
As I was * around, I saw a ram Dan 8:3
All this time I was * down, Dan 10:15
and went out * for her lovers, and Hos 1:13
you are * for will come suddenly Mal 3:1
for, or shall we keep on *?" Mt 11:3
"I know you are * for Jesus, who Mt 28:5
answer him. * around at them Mk 3:5

(LOOKING Con't)
Who are my brothers?" * at Mk 3:34
But he kept on * around to see Mk 5:32
and two fish and * up to heaven, Mk 6:41
Then, * up to heaven, he sighed Mk 7:34
You are * at this only from a Mk 8:33
leaders were still * for an Mk 14:1
So he began * for the right time Mk 14:11
Aren't you * for Jesus, the Mk 16:6
Literally, "* for the redemption Lk 2:38f
Or shall we keep on * for him?" Lk 7:19
keep on * and you will keep on Lk 11:9
"Why are you * in a tomb for Lk 24:5
is the one you are * for. Jn 1:33
climbing the hill, * for him. Jn 6:2-5
his own ideas is * for praise for Jn 7:18
What does he mean about our * Jn 7:36
him, for it isn't * for him and Jn 14:17
he asked, "Whom are you * for?" Jn 18:4,5
"Whom are you * for?" Jn 20:15
David was * far into the future Act 2:31
"I'm the man you're * for," he Act 10:21
is because I am * forward to the Act 26:6
For God is not * for those who Rom 2:29
but he is * for those with changed Rom 2:29
For he was * forward to the time Rom 3:25
And trusting means * forward to Rom 8:24
people who weren't even * for him. Rom 10:20
the favor of God they are * for. Rom 11:7
among you; I am * forward to seeing 1Co 16:11
you yourselves! By * at the good 2Co 3:2
how much you were * forward to my 2Co 7:7
and then shirk when he isn't *; Eph 6:6,7
the past and * forward to what lies Php 3:13
and we are * forward to his Php 3:20
And you are * forward to the Col 1:5
faith and steady * forward to the 1Th 1:3
And they speak of how you are * 1Th 1:10
world, if they are * to God for his 1Ti 5:5
but will go around * for teachers 2Ti 4:3
they are eagerly * forward to his 2Ti 4:8
day after day, * forward to that Tit 2:13
eagerly * forward to receiving it. Tit 3:7
hearts were always * somewhere else Heb 3:10
that, they were * forward to their Heb 11:14
Egypt, for he was * forward to the Heb 11:26
we are * forward to our Heb 13:14
a man * at his face in a mirror; Jas 1:23
But if anyone keeps * steadily Jas 1:25
* for some victim to tear apart. 1Pe 5:8
But we are * forward to God's 2Pe 3:13
belong to him? By * within 1Jn 2:3
They wander around * as bright as Jud 1:13

LOOKOUT
They keep a sharp * for Ps 64:6
on the * for choice pearls. Mt 13:45
"Keep a sharp *! Mk 13:35,36,37

LOOKOUTS
Saul's * in Gibe-ah saw a strange 1Sa 14:16

LOOKS
and if the spot * to be more than Lev 13:3
foot wherever he *, then the Lev 13:12
white lump that * like leprosy, Lev 13:43
shall live if he simply * at it!" Num 21:8
"The first man * like Ahima-az, 2Sa 18:27
watchtower that * out over the 2Ch 20:24
be found, for he * throughout the Job 28:23,24
The Lord * down from heaven on Ps 14:2
God * down from heaven, searching Ps 53:2
The wise man * ahead. Pro 14:8
In fact, he * for them. Pro 18:15
deed but God * at our motives. Pro 21:2
The simpleton never *, and Pro 27:12
your proud * will be brought low; Is 2:11
wall you built; it * so fine, but Is 28:17
sullen, angry *, even though they Eze 3:9
And the fourth * like a god!" Dan 3:25
Literally, "* like a son of the Dan 3:25f
But I say: Anyone who even * at Mt 5:28
"but he surely * like him!" Jn 9:9
interested, as he * forward to this 2Co 8:22
or remember what he * like. Jas 1:24

LOOM
his hair away, breaking the *. Ju 16:14
weaver stops his working at the *. Is 38:12
you weave my hair into your *!" Ju 16:13

LOOP
long sheets, each * being opposite Ex 36:11,12

LOOPED
Fifty blue ribbons were * along Ex 36:11,12

LOOPS
each side. Use * at the edges to Ex 26:4,5
There are to be fifty * on each Ex 26:4,5
to fasten the * together, so that Ex 26:6
Use fifty * along the edges of Ex 26:10,11
to connect the *, thus tying the Ex 36:13
Then he made fifty * along the Ex 36:17
to couple the * so that the Ex 36:18

LOOSE
shake * from him and be free." Gen 27:39,40
"Naphtali is a deer let *, Gen 49:21
lets his animal * and it gets into Ex 22:5
from coming * from the ephod. Ex 28:28
let your hair hang * as a sign of Lev 10:6
and the man shall let it * in the Lev 16:22
let his hair hang * in mourning, Lev 21:10
then I will let * my great anger Lev 26:28
rocks were torn *, but the Lord was 1Ki 19:11
your touch. Let * your lightning Ps 144:6
The enemies' sails hang * on Is 33:23
turned them * in the mountains. Jer 50:6
No hope remains, for I will * my Eze 7:3
* to kill a third of all mankind. Rev 9:15

LOOSED
by lightning. He * on them the Ps 78:49

LOOSEN
then I will * your tongue and let Eze 3:27

LOOSENED
I * his muzzle so he could eat. Hos 11:4

LOOSING
Literally, "of * (the sandal Lk 3:16f

LOOT
everything—the * that had been Gen 14:16
But we kept the cattle and * for Deu 3:7
Don't take any *, for everything Jos 6:18
Judah) took some * for himself, and Jos 7:1
and has taken * when I said it was Jos 7:10,11
sent some men to search for the *. Jos 7:22
but this time you may keep the * Jos 8:2
Only the cattle and the * were Jos 8:27
All the * and cattle of the Jos 11:14
'There is much * to be divided, Ju 5:30
Why did you rush for the * and do 1Sa 15:19
and * to sacrifice to the Lord." 1Sa 15:21
the vast amount of * they had taken 1Sa 30:16
so they can't have any of the *. 1Sa 30:22
of the * to the elders of Judah. 1Sa 30:26
a raid, bringing much * with them. 2Sa 3:22
Tremendous amounts of * were 2Sa 12:29,30
it was time to collect the *! 2Sa 23:10
Let's go and collect the *!" 2Ki 3:23
their war * to support the 1Ch 26:27
And the * we'll get! Pro 1:13
of each other's *, while good men Pro 12:12
And I will let your enemies * Jer 20:5
is sated with *, says the Lord. Jer 50:10
Like robbers, they will * the Eze 7:22
* from their thefts and banditry. Amo 3:10
* the silver! Nah 2:9
Loot the silver! * the gold! Nah 2:9
the * divided, the women raped; Zec 14:1

LOOTED
will be completely emptied and *. Is 24:3
the day of his calamity and * him. Ob 1:13

LOOTERS
is locked up tight to keep out *. Is 24:10

LOP
down the tree; * off its branches; Dan 4:14

LOPPED
all his branches will be * off. Job 18:16
But I * off their fruit and cut Amo 2:9

LOPS
the Gardener. He * off every Jn 15:2

LORD
and earth which the * God made. Gen 2:4
the * God hadn't sent any rain; Gen 2:5
The time came when the * God Gen 2:7
Then the * God planted a garden Gen 2:8
had formed. The * God planted all Gen 2:9
The * God placed the man in the Gen 2:15
But the * God gave the man this Gen 2:16,17
And the * God said, "It isn't Gen 2:18
So the * God formed from the Gen 2:19,20
Then the * God caused the man to Gen 2:21
the creatures the * God had made. Gen 3:1
the * God walking in the garden; Gen 3:8
the trees. The * God called to Gen 3:9
the * God asked. Gen 3:11
Then the * God asked the woman, Gen 3:13
So the * God said to the serpent, Gen 3:14
and the * God clothed Adam and Gen 3:21
Then the * said, "Now that the Gen 3:22
So the * God banished him Gen 3:23
Cain brought the * a gift of his Gen 4:3
and presented them to the *. Gen 4:4
And the * accepted Abel's Gen 4:4
the * asked him. Gen 4:6
But afterwards the * asked Cain, Gen 4:9
But the * said, "Your brother's Gen 4:10
Cain replied to the *, "My Gen 4:13
The * replied, "They won't kill Gen 4:15
Then the * put an identifying Gen 4:15
presence of the * and settled in Gen 4:16
When the * God saw the extent of Gen 6:5
But Noah was a pleasure to the *. Gen 6:8
FINALLY THE DAY came when the * Gen 7:1
So Noah did everything the * Gen 7:5
Then the * God Gen 7:16
"a mighty hunter against the *." Gen 10:9f
"a mighty hunter against the *." Gen 10:9f
So Abram departed as the * had Gen 12:4
altar to the * and prayed to him. Gen 12:8
But the * sent a terrible plague Gen 12:17
there he again worshiped the *. Gen 13:3,4
After Lot was gone, the * said to Gen 13:14
But Abram replied, "O * Jehovah, Gen 15:2,3
But Abram replied, "O * Jehovah, Gen 15:8
"Since the * has given me no Gen 16:2,3
May the * judge you for doing Gen 16:5
Literally, "Let the * judge Gen 16:5f
The Angel of the * found her Gen 16:7
worship before the *, but inside he Gen 17:17
THE * APPEARED again to Abraham Gen 18:1
Then the * said, "Next year Gen 18:10
So the * told Abraham, "I have Gen 18:20
* remained with Abraham a while. Gen 18:22,23
*, though I am but dust and ashes. Gen 18:27
"Oh, let not the * be angry; Gen 18:32
And the * went on his way when he Gen 18:33
the * is going to destroy it." Gen 19:14
the city, for the * was merciful. Gen 19:16
Then the * rained down fire and Gen 19:24
where he had stood before the *. Gen 19:27
will you slay an innocent man? Gen 20:4
"Yes, I know," the * replied. Gen 20:6
there to the *, calling upon the Gen 21:33
"Yes, *?" Gen 22:1
"Yes, *!" Gen 22:11
"I, the *, have sworn by myself Gen 22:16
For the * God of heaven told me Gen 24:7
As he was still speaking to the * Gen 24:15,16
"Thank you, * God of my master Gen 24:27
'She will,' he told me—'for my * Gen 24:40
replied, "The * has obviously Gen 24:50
my return; the * has made my Gen 24:56
So she asked the * about it. Gen 25:22
he said, "the * has made room for Gen 26:22
we bless you in the name of the * Gen 26:29
the top of the stairs stood the *. Gen 28:13
For Laban said, "May the * see Gen 31:49
And now I am two armies! O *, Gen 32:11
I am God Almighty," the * said Gen 35:11
man, and so the * killed him. Gen 38:7
So far as the * was concerned, Gen 38:10
executioner. The * greatly blessed Gen 39:2
realized that the * was with Joseph Gen 39:3
At once the * began blessing Gen 39:5
But the * was with Joseph there, Gen 39:21
and the * was with him so that Gen 39:23
"Oh, what shall we say to my *? Gen 44:16
I trust in your salvation, *. Gen 49:18
and weeping bitterly before the *. Ex 2:23
Then the * told him, "I have Ex 3:7
either "Jehovah" or "*." Ex 3:15f
the * asked him. Ex 4:2
on the ground," the * told him. Ex 4:3
Then the * told him, "Grab it by Ex 4:4
the * told him. Ex 4:5
the second," the * said, "and if Ex 4:8
But Moses pleaded, "O *, I'm Ex 4:10
"Isn't it I, the *? Ex 4:11
But Moses said, "*, please! Ex 4:13
Then the * became angry. Ex 4:14
Then Moses went back to the *. Ex 5:22
to the Lord. "*," he protested, Ex 5:22
do to Pharaoh," the * told Moses. Ex 6:1
Now the * spoke to Moses again Ex 6:10
Then the * ordered Moses and Ex 6:13
whom the * said, "I am Jehovah. Ex 6:28,29
with the *, "I can't do it; Ex 6:30
THEN THE * said to Moses, "See, I Ex 7:1
So Moses and Aaron did as the * Ex 7:6
Then the * said to Moses and Ex 7:8
just as the * had predicted. Ex 7:13
predicted. The * pointed this out Ex 7:14
"Nevertheless," the * said, Ex 7:15
and now the * says this: "You are Ex 7:17
Then the * instructed Moses: Ex 7:19
So Moses and Aaron did as the * Ex 7:20
Aaron, just as the * had predicted, Ex 7:22
THE * SAID to Moses, "Go in again Ex 8:1
Then the * said to Moses, Ex 8:5
is no one like the * our God. Ex 8:10
pleaded with the * concerning the Ex 8:12
And the * did as Moses Ex 8:13
go, just as the * had predicted. Ex 8:15
Then the * said to Moses, "Tell Ex 8:16
them, just as the * had predicted. Ex 8:19
Next the * told Moses, "Get up Ex 8:20
know that I am the * God of all the Ex 8:22
the * to get rid of the flies. Ex 8:30
And the * did as Moses asked and Ex 8:31,32
"GO BACK TO Pharaoh," the * Ex 9:1
The * announced that the plague Ex 9:5
as the * had predicted to Moses. Ex 9:12
Then the * said to Moses, "Get Ex 9:13
his hand, and the * sent thunder Ex 9:23
my hands to the *, and the thunder Ex 9:29
to heaven to the *, and the thunder Ex 9:33
as the * had predicted to Moses. Ex 9:35
THEN THE * said to Moses, "Go Ex 10:1
Then the * said to Moses, "Hold Ex 10:12
and entreated the *, and he sent a Ex 10:18

(LORD Con't)

But the * hardened Pharaoh's	Ex 10:20
sacrifices for the * our God, and	Ex 10:26
So the * hardened Pharaoh's heart	Ex 10:27
THEN THE * said to Moses, "I will	Ex 11:1
The * had told Moses, "Pharaoh	Ex 11:9
eyes, the * hardened his heart so	Ex 11:10
THEN THE * said to Moses and	Ex 12:1
the land that the * will give you,	Ex 12:25
And the * gave the Israelis	Ex 12:36
This night was selected by the *	Ex 12:42
That very day the * brought out	Ex 12:51
THE * INSTRUCTED Moses, "Dedicate	Ex 13:1
for the * has brought you out	Ex 13:3
feast to the * shall be held.	Ex 13:6,7
* did for you when you left Egypt.	Ex 13:8
And remember, when the * brings	Ex 13:11
*, and you shall give them to him.	Ex 13:12
back from the * in exchange for a	Ex 13:13
males to the *—except that all the	Ex 13:15
It is a reminder that the *	Ex 13:16
wilderness. The * guided them by a	Ex 13:21
shall know that I am the *."	Ex 14:4
cried out to the * to help them.	Ex 14:10
way the * will rescue you today.	Ex 14:13
them again. The * will fight for	Ex 14:14
Then the * said to Moses, "Quit	Ex 14:15
the sea, and the * opened up a path	Ex 14:21
the * said to Moses, "Stretch	Ex 14:26
but the * drowned them in the sea.	Ex 14:27
mighty miracle the * had done for	Ex 14:31
and revered the *, and believed in	Ex 14:31
of Israel sang this song to the *:	Ex 15:1
I will sing to the *, for he has	Ex 15:1
The * is my strength, my song,	Ex 15:2
The * is a warrior—	Ex 15:3
Your right hand, O *, is glorious	Ex 15:6
Who else is like the * among the	Ex 15:11
O *, because of your great power	Ex 15:16
Your own homeland, *—	Ex 15:17
But the * let down the walls of	Ex 15:19
Sing to the *, for he has	Ex 15:21
Moses pleaded with the * to help	Ex 15:25
help them, and the * showed him a	Ex 15:25
It was there at Marah that the *	Ex 15:25
the voice of the * your God, and	Ex 15:26
for I am the * who heals you."	Ex 15:26
that the * had killed us there!	Ex 16:3
Then the * said to Moses, "Look,	Ex 16:4
that it was the * who brought you	Ex 16:6
The * will give you meat to eat	Ex 16:7,8,9
And he told them, "Because the *	Ex 16:23
Sabbath to the * when we must	Ex 16:23
the * asked Moses.	Ex 16:28,29
For the * has given you the	Ex 16:28,29
from the *: they were to take three	Ex 16:32
see the bread the * had fed them	Ex 16:32
Aaron did this, just as the *	Ex 16:34
Then the * instructed Moses,	Ex 17:14
"Raise the banner of the *!"	Ex 17:15,16
"For the * will be at war with	Ex 17:15,16
* had brought them out of Egypt.	Ex 18:1
and what the * had done to Pharaoh	Ex 18:8
way, and how the * had delivered	Ex 18:8
everything the * had done for	Ex 18:9
"Bless the *," Jethro said,	Ex 18:10
I know now that the * is greater	Ex 18:11
meal together before the *.	Ex 18:12
advice, and if the * agrees, you	Ex 18:23
and told them what the * had said.	Ex 19:7
the words of the people to the *.	Ex 19:8
So the * came down upon the top	Ex 19:20
But the * told Moses, "Go back	Ex 19:21
for I, the * your God, am very	Ex 20:5
Or, "use the name of the * your	Ex 20:7f
rest before the * your God.	Ex 20:10
For in six days the * made the	Ex 20:11
land the * your God will give you.	Ex 20:12
And the * told Moses to be his	Ex 20:22
shall appear before the * God.	Ex 23:17
to the * your God.	Ex 23:19
"You shall serve the * your God	Ex 23:25
"The terror of the * shall fall	Ex 23:27
THE * NOW instructed Moses, "Come	Ex 24:1
alone shall come near to the *;	Ex 24:2
and peace offerings to the *.	Ex 24:5
the covenant that the * has made with	Ex 24:8
had a meal together before the *.	Ex 24:11
And the * said to Moses, "Come	Ex 24:12
And the glory of the * rested	Ex 24:16
the glory of the * on the mountain	Ex 24:17
the *, so that it never goes out.	Ex 27:21
the * as a constant reminder.	Ex 28:12
when he goes in before the *.	Ex 28:30,31
he goes in to minister to the *;	Ex 28:35
presence of the * in the Holy	Ex 28:35
presence of the *, so that the	Ex 28:37,38
kill it before the *, at the	Ex 29:11
it is a burnt offering to the *,	Ex 29:18
shall be sanctified to the *.	Ex 29:21
placed before the *: Place these	Ex 29:23
in a gesture of offering to the *.	Ex 29:24
the * in a gesture of offering;	Ex 29:26
their contribution to the *.	Ex 29:28
fragrant burnt offering to the *.	Ex 29:41
before the *, where I will meet	Ex 29:42
know that I am the * their God.	Ex 29:46
incense before the *, and this	Ex 30:8
a ransom to the * for his soul, so	Ex 30:11,12
an offering to the * to make	Ex 30:15
And the * said to Moses, "Make a	Ex 30:17,18
appear before the *, or when they	Ex 30:20
altar to burn offerings to the *.	Ex 30:20
Then the * told Moses to collect	Ex 30:22,23
of olive oil. The * instructed	Ex 30:25
* and you must treat it as holy.	Ex 30:37
THE * ALSO said to Moses, "See, I	Ex 31:1
The * then gave these further	Ex 31:12,13
day of solemn rest, holy to the *.	Ex 31:16
For in six days the * made heaven	Ex 31:17
Then the * told Moses, "Quick!	Ex 32:7
Then the * said, "I have seen	Ex 32:9
not to do it. "*," he pleaded,	Ex 32:11
So the * changed his mind and	Ex 32:14
the service of the *, for you	Ex 32:29
will return to the * on the	Ex 32:30
So Moses returned to the * and	Ex 32:31
And the * replied to Moses,	Ex 32:33
And the * sent a great plague	Ex 32:35
THE * SAID to Moses, "Lead these	Ex 33:1
For the * had told Moses to tell	Ex 33:5
door while the * spoke with Moses.	Ex 33:9
Inside the tent the * spoke to	Ex 33:11
Moses talked there with the * and	Ex 33:12
And the * replied, "I myself	Ex 33:14
And the * had replied to Moses,	Ex 33:17
The * replied, "I will make my	Ex 33:19
Jehovah, the *.	Ex 33:19
THE * TOLD Moses, "Prepare two	Ex 34:1
Sinai, as the * had told him to,	Ex 34:4
Then the * descended in the form	Ex 34:5,6
Moses fell down before the * and	Ex 34:8
in your sight, O *, then please go	Ex 34:9
The * replied, "All right, this	Ex 34:10
the power of the *—the terrible	Ex 34:10
Israel shall appear before the *.	Ex 34:23
appear before the * your God those	Ex 34:24
the Tabernacle of the * your God.	Ex 34:26
And the * said to Moses, "Write	Ex 34:27
mountain with the * for forty days	Ex 34:28
* had given him upon the mountain.	Ex 34:32
to speak with the *, he removed the	Ex 34:34
"This is what the * has commanded:	Ex 35:4
They brought to the * their	Ex 35:22
bronze as their offering to the *;	Ex 35:24
was commanded to Moses by the *.	Ex 39:21
ministered to the *, just as the	Ex 39:25,26
just as the * had commanded Moses.	Ex 39:25,26
just as the * had instructed.	Ex 39:31
all as the * had instructed him.	Ex 39:43
THE * NOW said to Moses, "Put	Ex 40:1
do all as the * had commanded him.	Ex 40:16
just as the * had commanded him.	Ex 40:19
it, just as the * had commanded.	Ex 40:21
*, just as the Lord had commanded.	Ex 40:23
Lord, just as the * had commanded.	Ex 40:23
lamps before the *, following all	Ex 40:25
just as the * had commanded.	Ex 40:27
just as the * had commanded him.	Ex 40:29
just as the * had commanded Moses.	Ex 40:32
and the glory of the * filled it.	Ex 40:34
of the * filled the Tabernacle.	Ex 40:35
THE * NOW spoke to Moses from the	Lev 1:1
sacrifice to the *, use animals	Lev 1:2,3
will accept your gift for the *.	Lev 1:2,3
there before the *, and Aaron's	Lev 1:5
blood before the *, sprinkling it	Lev 1:5
with which the * is pleased.	Lev 1:9
be a sweet savor unto the *."	Lev 1:9f
kill it before the * on the north	Lev 1:11
the altar as an offering to the *;	Lev 1:13
give much pleasure to the *.	Lev 1:13
the altar, and the * will have	Lev 1:15,16,17
be a sweet savor unto the *."	Lev 1:15,16,17f
offering to the * is to bring fine	Lev 2:1
and the * will be fully pleased.	Lev 2:2
as a holy burnt offering to the *.	Lev 2:3
an offering to the *, it must be	Lev 2:4
the altar to present it to the *.	Lev 2:8
be fully appreciated by the *.	Lev 2:9
as a holy burnt offering to the *.	Lev 2:10
in burnt offerings to the *.	Lev 2:11
them, then offer them to the *.	Lev 2:14
portion before the *.	Lev 2:16
to the *, he may use either a bull	Lev 3:1
if it is to be offered to the *!	Lev 3:1
burn before the * the fat that	Lev 3:3,4,5
And it will give the * much	Lev 3:3,4,5
to the *, it must have no defect	Lev 3:6
as a burnt offering to the *.	Lev 3:9,10,11
offering to the *, he shall lay	Lev 3:12
offering to the *, the fat which	Lev 3:14
is very pleasing to the *.	Lev 3:15,16
THEN THE * gave these further	Lev 4:1
defect as a sin offering to the *.	Lev 4:3
times before the * in front of the	Lev 4:6
before the * in the Tabernacle;	Lev 4:7
head and kill it before the *.	Lev 4:15
the *, in front of the veil.	Lev 4:17
before the *, and all the remainder	Lev 4:18
killed, and present it to the *.	Lev 4:24
and the * will appreciate it.	Lev 4:31
offering to the *, a female lamb or	Lev 5:6
a lamb to the *, then he shall	Lev 5:7
And the * said to Moses, "If	Lev 5:14
as his guilt offering to the *.	Lev 5:15
certainly guilty before the *."	Lev 5:19
AND THE * said to Moses, "If	Lev 6:1
the *, and he shall be forgiven."	Lev 6:7
Then the * said to Moses, "Give	Lev 6:8
altar to offer it before the *.	Lev 6:14
representative portion for the *;	Lev 6:15
received with pleasure by the *.	Lev 6:15
offerings made by fire to the *."	Lev 6:18
shall bring to the * a regular	Lev 6:19,20
brought to the * as an offering	Lev 6:21
entirely burned up before the *;	Lev 6:22,23
Then the * said to Moses, "Tell	Lev 6:24
killed before the * at the place	Lev 6:25
burned with fire before the *.	Lev 6:30
as a guilt offering to the *.	Lev 7:5
offerings to the * shall be given	Lev 7:9
the * as special peace offerings:	Lev 7:11
presented to the * by a gesture of	Lev 7:14
presented to the * as a peace	Lev 7:15
offering to the *, any portion of	Lev 7:16
day, the * will not accept it;	Lev 7:17,18
detestable to the *, and the person	Lev 7:17,18
Then the * said to Moses, "Tell	Lev 7:22
by fire to the * shall be outlawed	Lev 7:25
And the * said to Moses, "Tell	Lev 7:28
offering to the * must bring it	Lev 7:29
* by waving it before the altar.	Lev 7:30
to minister to the * as priests—to	Lev 7:35
For on the day the * anointed	Lev 7:36
to Moses by the * on Mount Sinai,	Lev 7:38
THE * SAID to Moses, "Now bring	Lev 8:1
the * had commanded Moses.	Lev 8:9
caps, as the * had commanded him.	Lev 8:13
as the * had commanded Moses.	Lev 8:17
Then he presented to the * the	Lev 8:18
ram was consumed before the *;	Lev 8:21
that pleased the * very much, for	Lev 8:21
been placed there before the *.	Lev 8:26
to present to the * by a gesture of	Lev 8:27
to the *;	Lev 8:28
* by waving it before the altar;	Lev 8:29
just as the * had instructed him.	Lev 8:29
commanded by the * in order to make	Lev 8:34
die—this is what the * has said."	Lev 8:35
that the * had commanded Moses.	Lev 8:36
and to offer them before the *.	Lev 9:2
to bring to the * a peace offering	Lev 9:4
came and stood there before the *.	Lev 9:5
people, as the * had commanded.	Lev 9:7
offering, as the * had commanded	Lev 9:10
offering to the *, in accordance	Lev 9:16
slowly before the * as a gesture of	Lev 9:21
and the glory of the * appeared	Lev 9:23
Then fire came from the * and	Lev 9:24
flat upon the ground before the *.	Lev 9:24
offered the incense before the *	Lev 10:1
—contrary to what the * had just	Lev 10:1
of the * and destroyed them.	Lev 10:2
"This is what the * meant when he	Lev 10:3
the terrible fire the * has sent.	Lev 10:6
Now the * instructed Aaron,	Lev 10:8,9
offered to the * by burning it on	Lev 10:12
offered to the * by the gesture of	Lev 10:14
* by the gesture of waving them.	Lev 10:15
for the * has commanded this."	Lev 10:15
atonement for them before the *?"	Lev 10:17
before the *," he said, "but if I	Lev 10:19
would it have pleased the *?"	Lev 10:19
THEN THE * said to Moses and	Lev 11:1
"I am the * your God.	Lev 11:44
For I am the * who brought you	Lev 11:45
THE * TOLD Moses to give these	Lev 12:1
the * and make atonement for her;	Lev 12:7
THE * SAID to Moses and Aaron,	Lev 13:1
AND THE * gave Moses these	Lev 14:1
before the * at the entrance of the	Lev 14:11
offer them to the * as a guilt	Lev 14:12
finger seven times before the *.	Lev 14:16
atonement for him before the *.	Lev 14:18
presented to the * in the rite of	Lev 14:21
of cleansing before the *.	Lev 14:23
as a gesture of offering to the *.	Lev 14:24
of it seven times before the *.	Lev 14:27
atonement for him before the *.	Lev 14:29
for the man before the *."	Lev 14:31
Then the * said to Moses and	Lev 14:33,34
THE * TOLD Moses and Aaron to give	Lev 15:1

(LORD Con't)

come before the * at the entrance Lev 15:14
before the * for the man because of Lev 15:15
*, for her menstrual defilement. Lev 15:30
died before the *, the Lord said to Lev 16:1
the Lord, the * said to Moses, Lev 16:1
First he shall present to the * Lev 16:6
goats before the * at the entrance Lev 16:7
The goat allotted to the * shall Lev 16:9
alive and placed before the *. Lev 16:10
the altar of the *, and fill his Lev 16:12
There before the * he shall put Lev 16:13
the * and make atonement for it. Lev 16:18
that the * gave to Moses. Lev 16:35
THE * GAVE to Moses these Lev 17:1
fat as a savor the * will Lev 17:5
the altar of the * at the entrance Lev 17:6
fat as a savor the * will Lev 17:6
to the *, shall be excommunicated. Lev 17:8,9
THE * THEN told Moses to tell the Lev 18:1
detail, for I am the * your God. Lev 18:4,5
I am the *. Lev 18:4,5
a near relative, for I am the *. Lev 18:6
THE * ALSO told Moses to tell the Lev 19:1
I, the * your God, am holy. Lev 19:1
law, for I am the * your God. Lev 19:1
offering to the *, offer it Lev 19:5
offering to the * at the entrance Lev 19:21
be devoted to the *, and shall be Lev 19:24
given to the * in praise to him. Lev 19:24
I am the *. Lev 19:28
my Tabernacle, for I am the *. Lev 19:30
THE * GAVE Moses these further Lev 20:1
be holy, for I am the * your God. Lev 20:7
for I am the * who sanctifies you. Lev 20:8
I am the * your God who has made Lev 20:24
to me, for I the * am holy, and I Lev 20:26
THE * SAID to Moses: "Tell the Lev 21:1
by fire to the * their God. Lev 21:6
he is holy, for I, the * who Lev 21:8
And the * said to Moses, "Tell Lev 21:16,17
* because of his physical defect. Lev 21:21
THE * TOLD Moses, "Instruct Aaron Lev 22:1
I am the * who sanctifies them. Lev 22:9
have been offered to the *. Lev 22:15
And the * said to Moses, "Tell Lev 22:17,18
sacrifice to the *—whether it is to Lev 22:17,18
acceptable to the * if it is a male Lev 22:19
offering to the * from the herd or Lev 22:21
must not be offered to the *; Lev 22:22
offering for the altar of the *. Lev 22:22
presented to the * has anything Lev 22:23
be offered to the * at any time. Lev 22:24
And the * said to Moses, "When a Lev 22:26,27
as a sacrifice by fire to the *. Lev 22:26,27
When you offer the * a sacrifice Lev 22:29,30
I am the *. Lev 22:29,30
my commandments, for I am the *. Lev 22:31
me, for I, the *, made you holy to Lev 22:32,33
THE * SAID to Moses, "Announce to Lev 23:1
festivals of the *—times when all Lev 23:1
"The Passover of the *: This is Lev 23:5
make an offering by fire to the *. Lev 23:8
He shall wave it before the * in Lev 23:9,10,11
be accepted by the * as your gift. Lev 23:9,10,11
sacrifice to the * a male yearling Lev 23:12
to be offered by fire to the *; Lev 23:13
shall bring to the * an offering of Lev 23:15,16
the * in a gesture of offering. Lev 23:17
It is an offering to the * of the Lev 23:17
"as first fruits to the *." Lev 23:17f
offerings to the * seven yearling Lev 23:18
"of a sweet odor to the *." Lev 23:18f
before the * along with the loaves Lev 23:20
They are holy to the *, and will Lev 23:20
a sacrifice by fire to the *. Lev 23:25
the *, saddened by their sin; Lev 23:26,27
offer sacrifices by fire to the *. Lev 23:26,27
atonement before the * your God. Lev 23:28
to be celebrated before the * for Lev 23:33,34
an offering by fire to the *. Lev 23:36
be an offering by fire to the *. Lev 23:36
to the * are to be made by fire. Lev 23:37
seven-day festival before the *. Lev 23:39
rejoicing before the * your God Lev 23:40
of the * to the people of Israel. Lev 23:44
THE * SAID to Moses, "Tell the Lev 24:1
* from generation to generation. Lev 24:3,4
table that stands before the *. Lev 24:5-8
by fire to the *, in memory of his Lev 24:5-8
by fire to the * under a permanent Lev 24:9
He was put in jail until the * Lev 24:12
And the * said to Moses, "Take Lev 24:13,14
Mount Sinai, the * gave him these Lev 25:1
before the * every seventh year. Lev 25:1
fallow before the *, uncultivated. Lev 25:4
For I, the * your God, brought Lev 25:38
I am the * your God. Lev 25:55
stones, for I am the * your God. Lev 26:1
my Tabernacle, for I am the *. Lev 26:2
For I am the * your God who Lev 26:13

THE * SAID to Moses, "Tell the Lev 27:1
himself to the *, he shall give Lev 27:1
to be given to the * as a Lev 27:9
giving it to the *, nor substitute Lev 27:10
the second shall belong to the *! Lev 27:10
But if the animal given to the * Lev 27:11,12
his home to the * and then wishes Lev 27:14,15
his field to the *, value it in Lev 27:16
has given to the * his rights to it Lev 27:20
belong to the * as a field devoted Lev 27:21
"If a man dedicates to the * a Lev 27:22
value to the *, and in the Year of Lev 27:23
"You may not dedicate to the * Lev 27:26
acceptable to the *, then the owner Lev 27:27
devoted to the *—people, animals, Lev 27:28
for they are most holy to the *. Lev 27:28
And the * owns every tenth Lev 27:32
The tenth given to the * shall Lev 27:33
*, and may not be bought back!" Lev 27:33
These are the commandments the * Lev 27:34
Egypt that the * issued the Num 1:1
as the * had commanded Moses. Num 1:17,18,19
Levites, for the * had said to Num 1:47,48,49
* to Moses were put into effect. Num 1:54
THE * GAVE these further Num 2:1
indicated by the * to Moses. Num 2:34
AT THE TIME when the * spoke to Num 3:1
died before the * in the wilderness Num 3:4
Then the * said to Moses, Num 3:5
And the * said to Moses, "I have Num 3:11,12
The * now spoke again to Moses at Num 3:14,15
the command of the *, were 22,000 Num 3:39
Then the * said to Moses, "Now Num 3:40
of Israel, as the * had commanded, Num 3:42
Now the * said to Moses, "Give Num 3:44
given to the * in their place. Num 3:49
his sons as the * had commanded. Num 3:51
THEN THE * said to Moses and Num 4:1
Then the * said to Moses and Num 4:17,18,19
And the * said to Moses, "Take a Num 4:21,22,23
from the * to Moses: "Inform the Num 5:1
Then the * said to Moses, "Tell Num 5:5,6
* by betraying a trust, it is sin. Num 5:5,6
* it shall go to the priests." Num 5:9,10
And the * said to Moses, "Tell Num 5:11,12
her before the *, and take holy Num 5:16
He shall bring her before the * Num 5:30
THE * GAVE Moses these further Num 6:1
himself to the * in a special way, Num 6:1
to the *, taste strong drink or Num 6:3,4
is holy and consecrated to the *; Num 6:5
* throughout the entire period. Num 6:8
separation to the *, he must go to Num 6:13
*, a year-old lamb without defect. Num 6:14
before the *: first the sin Num 6:16
the * in a gesture of offering; Num 6:20
that were waved before the *. Num 6:20
Now the * said to Moses, "Tell Num 6:22,23
'May the * bless and protect you; Num 6:24,25,26
and they presented them to the * Num 7:3
"Accept their gifts," the * Num 7:4,5
the altar. The * said to Moses, Num 7:11
THE * SAID to Moses, "Tell Aaron Num 8:1
design the * had shown Moses. Num 8:4
Then the * said to Moses, "Now Num 8:5,6
them to the * as a gift from the Num 8:11
all the people in serving the *. Num 8:11
bulls and offer them before the *; Num 8:12
to the * is given to the priests! Num 8:13
to the * in a gesture of offering. Num 8:21
everything was done just as the * Num 8:22
The * also instructed Moses, Num 8:23,24
just as the * had commanded. Num 9:4,5
* at the time he had appointed. Num 9:6,7
Moses said he would ask the * Num 9:8
Passover to the *, he shall follow Num 9:14
the command of the * and stopped Num 9:18
for so the * had instructed them. Num 9:19
at the commandment of the *; Num 9:23
and whatever the * told Moses Num 9:23
NOW THE * said to Moses, "Make Num 10:1
for the * has given wonderful Num 10:29
good things the * does for us." Num 10:32
O *, and scatter your enemies; Num 10:35
O *, to the millions of Israel." Num 10:36
misfortunes, and the * heard them. Num 11:1
so the fire of the * began Num 11:1
because the fire from the * Num 11:3
and the anger of the * grew hot; Num 11:10
Moses said to the *, "Why pick Num 11:11
Then the * said to Moses, Num 11:16
Tell them, 'The * has heard your Num 11:18
for you have rejected the * who Num 11:19,20
Then the * said to Moses, "When Num 11:23
And the * came down in the Cloud Num 11:25
Moses, and the * took of the Spirit Num 11:25
and that the * would put his Spirit Num 11:29
The * sent a wind that brought Num 11:31
the anger of the * rose against the Num 11:33
the * spoken only through Moses? Num 12:2
But the * heard them. Num 12:2

So they stood before the *. Num 12:3,4
Then the * descended in the Cloud Num 12:5
And the * said to them, "Even Num 12:6
Then the anger of the * grew hot Num 12:9
And Moses cried out to the *, Num 12:13
And the * said to Moses, "If her Num 12:14
Moses did as the * had commanded Num 13:3-15
ahead, and the * loves us. Num 14:8
Oh, do not rebel against the *, Num 14:9
for us to eat! The * is with us and Num 14:9
Then the glory of the * appeared, Num 14:10,11
appeared, and the * said to Moses, Num 14:10,11
Moses pleaded with the *. Num 14:13
will say, 'The * had to kill them Num 14:16
Then the * said, "All right, I Num 14:20,21
the glory of the *, so it is true Num 14:20,21
Then the * added to Moses and to Num 14:26,27
Tell them, 'The * vows to do to Num 14:28
were struck dead before the *. Num 14:36,37,38
the land the * has promised us." Num 14:40
for the * is not with you. Num 14:42
You have deserted the *, and now Num 14:43
THE * TOLD Moses to give these Num 15:1
want to please the * with a burnt Num 15:3,4
is a pleasing fragrance to the *. Num 15:7
as a pleasing fragrance to the *. Num 15:10
* with sacrifices offered by fire; Num 15:13,14
all are equal before the *. Num 15:15,16
The * also said to Moses at this Num 15:17,18
present to the * a sample of each Num 15:19,20,21
in a gesture of offering to the *. Num 15:19,20,21
which the * has given you over the Num 15:22
odor before the *, and must be Num 15:23,24
the *, and by their sin offering. Num 15:25
the *, and he shall be forgiven. Num 15:28
commandment of the * and Num 15:31
Then the * said to Moses, "The Num 15:35
killed him as the * had commanded. Num 15:36
The * said to Moses, "Tell the Num 15:37,38
of the *, and that you are to obey Num 15:39
yes, I am the *, your God." Num 15:41
the *, and he is with all of us. Num 16:3
among all these people of the *?" Num 16:3
the morning the * will show you who Num 16:5
them before the *, and we will find Num 16:6,7
find out whom the * has chosen. Num 16:6,7
and said to the *, "Do not accept Num 16:15
the * with all your friends; Num 16:16
to the ground before the *. Num 16:22
And the * said to Moses, "Then Num 16:23,24
But if the * does a miracle and Num 16:30
these men have despised the *." Num 16:30
And the * said to Moses, "Tell Num 16:36,37
they are holy, dedicated to the *. Num 16:36,37
they were used before the *; Num 16:38
come before the * to burn incense, Num 16:40
awesome glory of the * was seen. Num 16:42
and the * said to Moses, Num 16:43,44
to the earth before the *. Num 16:45
THEN THE * said to Moses, "Tell Num 17:1
He put them before the * in the Num 17:7
his rod. The * told Moses to place Num 17:10
So Moses did as the * commanded Num 17:11
THE * NOW spoke to Aaron: "You Num 18:1
They are a gift to you from the * Num 18:6
The * gave these further Num 18:8
brought to the * by the people; Num 18:8
presented to the * by the gesture Num 18:8
the * by burning upon the altar. Num 18:9
offerings to the *—the best of the Num 18:12
dedicated to the * shall be yours, Num 18:14,15
they must be sacrificed to the *. Num 18:17
it is very pleasant to the *. Num 18:17
presented to the * by the gesture Num 18:18
by the people of Israel to the *; Num 18:19
between the * and you and your Num 18:19
offered to the * by the gesture of Num 18:24
The * also said to Moses, "Tell Num 18:25,26
to give to the * a tenth of the Num 18:25,26
presented to the * by the gesture Num 18:25,26
the altar. The * will consider Num 18:27
THE * SAID to Moses and Aaron, Num 19:1
Tabernacle of the *, and shall be Num 19:13
sanctuary of the *, and the water Num 19:20
our dear brothers the * killed!" Num 20:3
fell face downward before the *; Num 20:6
where it was kept before the *; Num 20:9
But the * said to Moses and Num 20:12
The * had said to speak to the Num 20:12f
But when we cried to the * he Num 20:16
Then the * said to Moses and Num 20:23
So Moses did as the * commanded Num 20:27
vowed to the * that if he would Num 21:2
of that area. The * heeded their Num 21:3
So the * sent poisonous snakes Num 21:6
Then the * told him, "Make a Num 21:8
This is the place where the * Num 21:16
at Edre-i. The * told Moses not to Num 21:34
at Heshbon," the * assured him. Num 21:34
the * directs me to say." Num 22:8
home! The * won't let me do it." Num 22:13

(LORD Con't)
to the command of the * my God. Num 22:18
out whether the * will add anything Num 22:19
the angel of the * standing in the Num 22:22,23
Now the angel of the * stood at Num 22:24
Then the angel of the * moved Num 22:26
Then the * caused the donkey to Num 22:28
Then the * opened Balaam's eyes Num 22:31
I will see if the * will meet me; Num 23:3,4
Balaam told the *, "I have Num 23:3,4
Then the * gave Balaam a Num 23:5
while I go to meet the *." Num 23:15
And the * met Balaam and told Num 23:16
to meet the * as he had earlier. Num 24:1
As aloes planted by the * himself; Num 24:3-9
and the anger of the * was hot Num 25:3
Hang them up before the * in Num 25:4
Then the * said to Moses, Num 25:10,11
Then the * said to Moses, Num 25:16,17
by fire from the * that day, as a Num 26:5-11
Then the * told Moses to divide Num 26:52,53
sections," the * instructed, "and Num 26:55,56
offered unholy fire before the *. Num 26:61
had died, as the * had decreed Num 26:64,65
revolt against the * —it was a Num 27:3,4
brought their case before the *. Num 27:5
And the * replied to Moses, "The Num 27:6,7
One day the * said to Moses, "Go Num 27:12
Then Moses said to the *, "O Num 27:15
the people of the * will not be as Num 27:17
The * replied, "Go and get Num 27:18
to get directions from the *. Num 27:21
from the Lord. The * will speak to Num 27:21
In this way the * will continue Num 27:21
as the * had commanded. Num 27:23
THE * GAVE Moses these Num 28:1
an offering made by fire to the *. Num 28:6
in the holy place before the *. Num 28:7
the *, an offering made by fire. Num 28:8
offering to the * of two young Num 28:11
and will please the * very much. Num 28:13
goat for a sin offering to the *. Num 28:15
sacrifices to the * two young Num 28:19
will be very pleasant to the *. Num 28:24
as a grain offering to the *; Num 28:26
the *, shall be offered that day. Num 28:27
These are sacrifices which the * Num 29:2
before the *, and no work of any Num 29:7
sacrifice to the *—it will be very Num 29:8
a seven-day festival before the *. Num 29:12
pleasure to the *, shall be Num 29:13
pleasant to the *—of one young Num 29:36
told them, "The * has commanded Num 30:1
a promise to the *, either to do Num 30:1
"If a woman promises the * to do Num 30:3
commandments the * gave Moses Num 30:16
THEN THE * said to Moses, "Take Num 31:1
And the * said to Moses, "You Num 31:25
But first, the * gets a share of Num 31:28
presented to the * by the gesture Num 31:29
the priest did as the * commanded. Num 31:31
which 675 were given to the *); Num 31:36-40
(of which 72 were given to the *); Num 31:36-40
(of which 61 were given to the *); Num 31:36-40
as the * had directed Moses. Num 31:41
to the * from our booty—gold Num 31:50
for our souls before the *." Num 31:50
there before the * as a memorial of Num 31:54
and said, "The * has used Israel Num 32:3,4
land that the * has given them? Num 32:7
followed the * and urged the people Num 32:12
"The * made us wander back and Num 32:13
Jordan until the * has driven out Num 32:21
before the *, you may return. Num 32:22
your duty to the * and to the rest Num 32:22
be your possession from the *. Num 32:22
sinned against the *, and you may Num 32:23
the *, just as you have said." Num 32:27
again, "As the * has commanded, so Num 32:31
we will follow the * fully armed Num 32:32
as the * had instructed him. Num 33:2
killed by the * the night before. Num 33:3,4
night before. The * had certainly Num 33:3,4
directed by the * to go up into the Num 33:38,39
there that the * told Moses to tell Num 33:50,51
THE * TOLD Moses to tell the Num 34:1
And the * said to Moses, "These Num 34:16-28
Jericho, the * said to Moses, Num 35:1
And the * said to Moses, "Tell Num 35:9,10
a petition: "The * instructed you Num 36:1
from the *: "The men of the tribe Num 36:5
This is what the * has further Num 36:6
did as the * commanded Moses. Num 36:10
which the * gave to the people of Num 36:13
it is the land the * promised to Deu 1:8
* has multiplied you like stars! Deu 1:10
the * our God had directed us. Deu 1:19,20,21
and I said to the people, 'The * Deu 1:19,20,21
land the * our God had given us. Deu 1:24,25
and said, 'The * must hate us, Deu 1:27
be afraid! The * God is your Deu 1:30
"They refused to believe the * Deu 1:32
"Well, the * heard their Deu 1:34,35
followed the *, would receive as Deu 1:36
"And the * was even angry with Deu 1:37
as the * our God has told us to.' Deu 1:41
"But the * said to me, 'Tell Deu 1:42
the *, but he wouldn't listen. Deu 1:45
for so the * had instructed me. Deu 2:1
Then at last the * said, Deu 2:2
you use. The * your God has Deu 2:7
"Then the * warned us, 'Don't Deu 2:9
been assigned to Israel by the *. Deu 2:12
" 'Now cross Zered Brook,' the * Deu 2:13
For the * had decreed that this Deu 2:14,15
Yes, the hand of the * was Deu 2:14,15
Then at last the * said to me, Deu 2:16,17
their place. The * had similarly Deu 2:22
"Then the * said, 'Cross the Deu 2:24
land the * our God has given us.' Deu 2:29
"Then the * said to me, 'I have Deu 2:31
But the * our God crushed him, Deu 2:33,34
* our God gave all of them to us. Deu 2:35,36
But the * told me not to be Deu 3:1
land are yours,' the * told me. Deu 3:1
So the * helped us fight Deu 3:3
that although the * had given them Deu 3:18
to the land the * was giving them. Deu 3:18
in the cities the * has given you, Deu 3:19
return after the * has given Deu 3:20
When they conquer the land the * Deu 3:20
have seen what the * your God has Deu 3:21
* your God will fight for you.' Deu 3:22
plea to God: 'O * God, please let Deu 3:23,24,25
"But the * was angry with me Deu 3:26
by the * God of your ancestors. Deu 4:1
for they are from the * your God. Deu 4:2
You have seen what the * did to Deu 4:3
* your God are still alive today. Deu 4:4
They are from the * our God. Deu 4:5
among them, as the * our God is Deu 4:7
stood before the * at Mount Horeb, Deu 4:10
And the * spoke to you from the Deu 4:12
that time that the * commanded me Deu 4:14
or stars. The * may permit other Deu 4:19
but not you. The * has rescued you Deu 4:20
the * your God has made with you! Deu 4:23
any idols, for the * your God has Deu 4:23
idols, and the * your God is very Deu 4:25
return to the * your God and listen Deu 4:30
For the * your God is Deu 4:31
Yet that is what the * your God Deu 4:34
the * your God is giving you." Deu 4:40
"The * our God made a contract Deu 5:2,3
any way, for I am the * your God. Deu 5:9,10
of the * your God to misuse it." Deu 5:11f
is the Sabbath of the * your God; Deu 5:14
in Egypt, and the * your God Deu 5:15
a commandment of the * your God); Deu 5:16
"The * has given these laws to Deu 5:22
'Today the * our God has shown us Deu 5:24
"And the * agreed to your Deu 5:28
of the * your God, following his Deu 5:32
"THE * YOUR God told me to give Deu 6:1
to reverence the * your God by Deu 6:2
"When the * your God has brought Deu 6:10,11,12
you forget the * who brought you Deu 6:10,11,12
the * promised your ancestors. Deu 6:18
as the * agreed to help you do. Deu 6:19
which the * our God has given us?' Deu 6:20
in Egypt, and the * brought us out Deu 6:21
all the laws of the * our God.' Deu 6:25
"WHEN THE * brings you into the Deu 7:1
When the * your God delivers Deu 7:2
Then the anger of the * would be Deu 7:4
dedicated to the * your God. Deu 7:6
that the * your God is the faithful Deu 7:9
Because of your obedience, the * Deu 7:12
And the * will take away all Deu 7:15
nations which the * your God Deu 7:16
Just remember what the * your God Deu 7:18
the terrors the * sent upon Deu 7:19
Well, the * your God will use Deu 7:19
Moreover, the * your God will Deu 7:20
nations, for the * your God is Deu 7:21
it is horrible to the * your God. Deu 7:25
promised to your fathers by the *. Deu 8:1
Do you remember how the * led Deu 8:2
the * punishes you to help you. Deu 8:5
"Obey the laws of the * your Deu 8:6
For the * your God is bringing Deu 8:7
fill, bless the * your God for the Deu 8:10
you don't forget the * your God Deu 8:11
and forget the * your God who Deu 8:14
Always remember that it is the * Deu 8:18
"But if you forget about the * Deu 8:19
just as the * has caused other Deu 8:20
if you don't obey the * your God. Deu 8:20
But the * your God will go Deu 9:3
"Then, when the * has done this Deu 9:4
yourselves, 'The * has helped us Deu 9:4
people that the * will drive them Deu 9:5
angry you made the * your God out Deu 9
and nights the * gave me the Deu 9:10,1
people!' the * told me, 'and I will Deu 9:13,1
sin against the * your God. Deu 9:1
I lay before the *, neither eating Deu 9:1
had done what the * hated most, Deu 9:1
How I feared for you—for the * Deu 9:1
the * was so angry with him; Deu 9:2
but I prayed, and the * spared Deu 9:2
you angered the *, and yet again at Deu 9:2
At Kadesh-barnea, when the * Deu 9:2
* from the first day I knew you. Deu 9:2
the * was ready to destroy you. Deu 9:2
"I prayed to him, 'O * God, Deu 9:2
is because the * wasn't able to Deu 9:2
"AT THAT TIME the * told me to Deu 10:
day, just as the * commanded me. Deu 10:
stand before the * and to do his Deu 10:
for as the * told them, he Deu 10:
before the * for forty days and Deu 10:1
the first, and the * again yielded Deu 10:1
what does the * your God require of Deu 10:12,1
heaven belong to the * your God. Deu 10:1
God is God of gods and * of lords. Deu 10:1
You must fear the * your God Deu 10:2
them, but now the * your God has Deu 10:2
"YOU MUST LOVE the * your God and Deu 11:1
you, and how the * has kept them Deu 11:4
They didn't see how the * cared Deu 11:5
in the land the * promised to your Deu 11:9
* your God personally cares for! Deu 11:12
you will love the * your God with Deu 11:13
the anger of the * will be hot Deu 11:17
the good land the * has given you. Deu 11:17
the land the * has promised you. Deu 11:21
you, loving the * your God, walking Deu 11:22
to him, then the * will drive out Deu 11:23
you, for the * your God will send Deu 11:25
of the * your God which I am giving Deu 11:27
When the * your God brings you Deu 11:29
in the land the * is giving you. Deu 11:31
There you shall bring to the * Deu 12:6
feast before the * your God, and Deu 12:7
of rest the * will give to you). Deu 12:9
Land, and the * gives you rest and Deu 12:10
there before the * with your sons Deu 12:12
so in the place the * will choose. Deu 12:14
because the * has prospered you. Deu 12:15
vowed to give the *, nor your Deu 12:17
* by waving them before his altar. Deu 12:17
eat them before the * your God. Deu 12:18
Rejoice before the * your God in Deu 12:18
"If, when the * enlarges your Deu 12:20-23
Only your gifts to the *, and Deu 12:26,27
upon the altar of the * your God. Deu 12:26,27
in the eyes of the * your God, all Deu 12:28
You must not insult the * your Deu 12:31
For the * is testing you to find Deu 13:3
against the * your God who brought Deu 13:5
you away from the * your God who Deu 13:10
of the cities the * has given you, Deu 13:12,13,14
Then the * will turn from his Deu 13:17
Of course, the * your God will Deu 13:18
is right in the eyes of the *. Deu 13:18
You belong exclusively to the * Deu 14:2
you are holy to the * your God. Deu 14:21
to eat before the * your God at the Deu 14:23
If the place the * chooses for Deu 14:24
there before the * your God, and to Deu 14:26
Israelite, for the * has released Deu 15:2
of this, for the * will greatly Deu 15:4,5
commands of the * your God that I Deu 15:4,5
in the land the * will give you, Deu 15:7
cries out to the *, it will be Deu 15:9
For the * will prosper you in Deu 15:10
as the * your God has blessed you. Deu 15:14
and the * your God rescued you! Deu 15:15
And the * your God will prosper Deu 15:18
animals before the * your God each Deu 15:20
the * your God at his sanctuary. Deu 16:2
* shall choose as his sanctuary. Deu 16:6
each city before the * your God. Deu 16:8
before the * your God called the Deu 16:10
* with your family and household. Deu 16:11
at the place the * will designate. Deu 16:15
to the * for blessing you with a Deu 16:15
appear before the * your God three Deu 16:16
occasions bring a gift to the *. Deu 16:16
as the * has blessed you. Deu 16:17
the * your God is giving you. Deu 16:18
the * your God is giving you. Deu 16:20
the altar of the * your God. Deu 16:21
an obelisk, for the * hates them! Deu 16:22
ox or sheep to the * your God. Deu 17:1
sanctuary of the * your God, to Deu 17:8
in the land the * your God will Deu 17:14
man the * your God shall choose. Deu 17:15
him there, for the * has told you, Deu 17:16
away from the *, neither shall he Deu 17:17
to respect the * his God by obeying Deu 17:19
the altar of the * and by the other Deu 18:1

LORD Con't)

for the * is their property!	Deu 18:2
to the *—the first of the grain,	Deu 18:4
For the * your God has chosen	Deu 18:5
* from generation to generation.	Deu 18:5
in the name of the *, just like his	Deu 18:6,7
and disgust to the *, and it is	Deu 18:12
the * your God will displace them.	Deu 18:12
blamelessly before the * your God.	Deu 18:13
things, but the * your God will not	Deu 18:14
" 'All right,' the * said to me,	Deu 18:17
prophecy is from the * or not?'	Deu 18:21
* who has given him the message;	Deu 18:22
"WHEN THE * your God has	Deu 19:1
"If the * enlarges your	Deu 19:8
today—loving the * your God and	Deu 19:9
in the land the * your God is	Deu 19:14
on duty before the * at the time.	Deu 19:17
be frightened! The * your God is	Deu 20:1
For the * your God is going with	Deu 20:4
When the * your God has given it	Deu 20:13
This is the commandment of the *	Deu 20:17
deeply against the * your God.	Deu 20:18
come (for the * your God has chosen	Deu 21:5
eyes seen it. O *, forgive your	Deu 21:8
"When you go to war and the *	Deu 21:10
Don't defile the land the * your	Deu 21:23
This is abhorrent to the * your	Deu 22:5
The * will bless you for it.	Deu 22:7
But the * wouldn't listen to	Deu 23:5
for you, because the * loves you.	Deu 23:5
may enter the sanctuary of the *.	Deu 23:8
The camp must be holy, for the *	Deu 23:14
and the * does not want to see	Deu 23:14
you must not bring to the * any	Deu 23:17,18
are detestable to the * your God.	Deu 23:17,18
an Israeli, the * your God won't	Deu 23:20
"When you make a vow to the *,	Deu 23:21
him, for the * demands that you	Deu 23:21
you have vowed to the * your God.	Deu 23:23
land the * your God is giving you.	Deu 24:4
Remember what the * your God did	Deu 24:9
and the * your God will count it	Deu 24:12,13
otherwise he may cry out to the *	Deu 24:14,15
that the * your God rescued you;	Deu 24:18
then the * your God will bless	Deu 24:19
land the * your God is giving you.	Deu 25:13,14,15
are detestable to the * your God.	Deu 25:16
Therefore, when the * your God	Deu 25:19
present to the * at his sanctuary	Deu 26:2,3
that the * my God has brought me to	Deu 26:2,3
You shall then say before the *	Deu 26:5
us and we cried to the * God.	Deu 26:6,7
And now, O *, see, I have	Deu 26:10
the * your God, and worship him.	Deu 26:10
declare before the * your God, 'I	Deu 26:13
I have obeyed the * my God and	Deu 26:14
* your God is giving you today.	Deu 26:16
And the * has declared today	Deu 26:18
the * your God, as he requires."	Deu 26:19
an altar there to the * your God.	Deu 27:5,6
burnt offerings to the * your God.	Deu 27:5,6
great joy before the * your God.	Deu 27:7
the people of the * your God, so	Deu 27:9
handmade gods are hated by the *.'	Deu 27:15
of the * your God, the laws I am	Deu 28:1
"The * will defeat your enemies	Deu 28:7
directions! The * will bless you	Deu 28:8
land the * your God is giving you.	Deu 28:8
the *, and they will stand in awe.	Deu 28:10
"The * will give you an	Deu 28:11
of the * your God that I am giving	Deu 28:13
"If you won't listen to the *	Deu 28:15-19
"For the * himself will send his	Deu 28:20
"The * will cause you to be	Deu 28:25
around you. The * will cover you	Deu 28:35
for the * will thrust you away.	Deu 28:37
to listen to the * your God.	Deu 28:45
has given you. The * will send your	Deu 28:47,48
"The * will bring a distant	Deu 28:49
And that is not all! The * will	Deu 28:61
do not listen to the * your God.	Deu 28:62
"Just as the * has rejoiced over	Deu 28:63
you, so the * at that time will	Deu 28:63
For the * will scatter you among	Deu 28:64
no rest, but the * will give you	Deu 28:65
Then the * will send you back to	Deu 28:68
covenant which the * had made with	Deu 29:1
miracles that the * brought upon	Deu 29:2,3
But even yet the * hasn't given	Deu 29:4
that it is the * your God who has	Deu 29:6
today before the * your God, along	Deu 29:10
turn away from the * our God and	Deu 29:18
For the * will not pardon!	Deu 29:20
upon him, and the * will blot out	Deu 29:20
under heaven. The * will separate	Deu 29:21
the * will have sent upon it.	Deu 29:22
destroyed by the * in his anger.	Deu 29:23
" 'Why has the * done this to	Deu 29:24
That is why the anger of the *	Deu 29:27
In great anger the * rooted them	Deu 29:28
"There are secrets the * your	Deu 29:29
* your God will have driven you.	Deu 30:1
to return to the * your God, and	Deu 30:2
today, then the * your God will	Deu 30:3
you will love the * your God with	Deu 30:6
"If you return to the * and obey	Deu 30:7,8
you today, the * your God will take	Deu 30:7,8
you. The * your God will prosper	Deu 30:9
for the * will again rejoice over	Deu 30:9
if you turn to the * your God with	Deu 30:10
today to love the * your God and to	Deu 30:16
and so that the * your God will	Deu 30:16
Choose to love the * your God	Deu 30:20
in the land the * promised your	Deu 30:20
for the * has told me that I	Deu 31:2
But the * himself will lead you,	Deu 31:3
as the * has instructed.	Deu 31:3
instructed. The * will destroy the	Deu 31:4
the Amorites. The * will deliver	Deu 31:5
For the * your God will be with	Deu 31:6
by the * to their ancestors;	Deu 31:7
Don't be afraid, for the * will	Deu 31:8
the Ten Commandments of the *.	Deu 31:9
of Israel. The * commanded that	Deu 31:10,11
before the * at the sanctuary.	Deu 31:10,11
"Call them all together," the *	Deu 31:12
the * your God and obey his laws.	Deu 31:12
how to revere the * your God as	Deu 31:13
Then the * said to Moses, "The	Deu 31:14
came and stood before the *.	Deu 31:14
into the land the * promised them;	Deu 31:23
for the * says, 'I will be with	Deu 31:23
rebels against the *, how much more	Deu 31:27
will do what the * says is evil,	Deu 31:29
proclaim the greatness of the *.	Deu 32:3
As does the * his people!	Deu 32:11
When the * alone was leading	Deu 32:12
It was not the *	Deu 32:27
Unless the * had destroyed them?	Deu 32:30
The * will see his people	Deu 32:36
That same day, the * said to	Deu 32:48
"The * came to us at Mount	Deu 33:2
They followed in your steps, O *.	Deu 33:3
The * became king in Jerusalem,	Deu 33:5
"O *, hear the cry of Judah	Deu 33:7
O *, prosper the Levites	Deu 33:11
With all the blessings of the *;	Deu 33:23
Who else has been saved by the *?	Deu 33:29
And the * pointed out to him the	Deu 34:1
and Zoar," the * told him.	Deu 34:3
Promised Land," the * told Moses.	Deu 34:4
So Moses, the disciple of the *,	Deu 34:5
land of Moab as the * had said.	Deu 34:5
had said. The * buried him in a	Deu 34:6
that the * had given to Moses.	Deu 34:9
the * talked to him face to face.	Deu 34:10
For remember, the * your God is	Jos 1:9
with Moses: "The * your God has	Jos 1:12,13
him, "and may the * your God be	Jos 1:17,18
For we have heard how the * made	Jos 2:10
"The * will certainly give us	Jos 2:24
Ark of the covenant of the *."	Jos 3:2,3,4f
"the * will do a great miracle."	Jos 3:5
"Today," the * told Joshua, "I	Jos 3:7
to what the * your God has said.	Jos 3:9
The Ark of God, who is * of the	Jos 3:11
across, the * said to Joshua,	Jos 4:1
as the * had commanded Joshua.	Jos 4:8
of the *, which had been given to	Jos 4:10
for Joshua! The * made him great in	Jos 4:14
* now told him to command them.	Jos 4:15,16
Tell them how the * our God	Jos 4:23
It is the same thing the * did	Jos 4:23
that the * had dried up the Jordan	Jos 5:1
The * then told Joshua to set	Jos 5:2,3
was done.) The * instructed them to	Jos 5:2,3
they had not obeyed the *, and he	Jos 5:6
And the * said to Joshua, "Today	Jos 5:8,9
But the * said to Joshua,	Jos 6:2
The * has given us the city!"	Jos 6:16
dedicated to the *, and must be	Jos 6:19
So the * was with Joshua, and his	Jos 6:27
himself, and the * was very angry	Jos 7:1
the Ark of the * until evening,	Jos 7:6
Joshua cried out to the *, "O	Jos 7:7
the other side? O *, what am I to	Jos 7:8
But the * said to Joshua, "Get	Jos 7:10,11
tomorrow, for the * your God of	Jos 7:13
by tribes, and the * will point out	Jos 7:14
* will point out the guilty clan;	Jos 7:14
belongs to the * shall be burned	Jos 7:15
covenant of the * and has brought	Jos 7:15
Israel before the *, and the tribe	Jos 7:16
brought before the * and the family	Jos 7:17
against the *, the God of Israel.	Jos 7:20
upon us? The * will now bring	Jos 7:25
fierce anger of the * was ended.	Jos 7:26
THEN THE * said to Joshua, "Don't	Jos 8:1
for the * will give it to you.	Jos 8:7
Set the city on fire, as the *	Jos 8:8
Then the * said to Joshua,	Jos 8:18
(The * had told Joshua they could.	Jos 8:27
an altar to the * God of Israel at	Jos 8:30
* had said concerning Mount Ebal.	Jos 8:31
offerings to the * on the altar.	Jos 8:31
the might of the * your God and of	Jos 9:9
They did not bother to ask the *,	Jos 9:14,15
Israel had made before the * God.	Jos 9:18
sworn before the * God of Israel	Jos 9:19
the altar of the *—wherever it	Jos 9:27
be built (for the * hadn't yet told	Jos 9:27
of them," the * said to Joshua,	Jos 10:8
Then the * threw them into a	Jos 10:10
to Beth-horon, the * destroyed them	Jos 10:11
since, when the * stopped the sun	Jos 10:14
But the * was fighting for	Jos 10:14
cities, for the * will help you to	Jos 10:19
for the * is going to do this to	Jos 10:25
There, too, the * gave them the	Jos 10:30
And the * gave it to them on the	Jos 10:32
land, just as the * God of Israel	Jos 10:40
campaign, for the * God of Israel	Jos 10:42
But the * said to Joshua, "Don't	Jos 11:6
And the * gave all that vast	Jos 11:8
his men did as the * had	Jos 11:9
For so the * had commanded his	Jos 11:15
For the * made the enemy kings	Jos 11:20
as the * had commanded Moses.	Jos 11:20
as the * had instructed Moses;	Jos 11:23
"You are growing old," the *	Jos 13:1
the offerings brought to the *.	Jos 13:14
the * God was their inheritance.	Jos 13:33
dice before the *, and he caused	Jos 14:1
"Remember what the * said to	Jos 14:6
But since I had followed the * my	Jos 14:8
time until now the * has kept me	Jos 14:10
country which the * promised me.	Jos 14:12
cities, but if the * is with me I	Jos 14:12
had followed the * God of Israel.	Jos 14:13,14
The * instructed Joshua to assign	Jos 15:13
"The * told Moses that we were to	Jos 17:4
So, as the * had commanded	Jos 17:5,6
of land when the * has given us	Jos 17:14
the * your God has given to you?	Jos 18:3
they are priests of the *.	Jos 18:7
Then the * could assign the	Jos 18:8
at Shiloh the * showed Joshua by	Jos 18:10
Joshua, for the * had said that he	Jos 19:50
THE * SAID to Joshua,	Jos 20:1
of Judah. The * also instructed	Jos 20:8
"The * instructed Moses to give	Jos 21:2
So in this way the * gave to	Jos 21:43
And the * gave them peace, just	Jos 21:44
against them; the * helped them	Jos 21:44
Every good thing the * had	Jos 21:45
you—every order of the * your God.	Jos 22:2,3
And now the * our God has given	Jos 22:4
Love the * and follow his plan	Jos 22:5
"The whole congregation of the *	Jos 22:16
altar of rebellion against the *.	Jos 22:16
rebel today the * will be angry	Jos 22:17,18
river where the * lives among us in	Jos 22:19
But do not rebel against the * by	Jos 22:19
sinned against the *, the entire	Jos 22:20
altar in rebellion against the *.	Jos 22:22,23
we love the * and because we fear	Jos 22:24,25
to worship the * God of Israel?	Jos 22:24,25
God of Israel? The * has placed the	Jos 22:24,25
You have no part in the *.'	Jos 22:24,25
may worship the * with our burnt	Jos 22:26,27
have no part in the * our God.'	Jos 22:26,27
the altar of the * which our	Jos 22:28
turn away from the * or to rebel	Jos 22:29
we know that the * is among us	Jos 22:31
against the * as we thought;	Jos 22:31
LONG AFTER THIS, when the * had	Jos 23:1
seen all that the * your God has	Jos 23:3
be yours, for the * your God will	Jos 23:4,5
But follow the * your God just	Jos 23:8
the enemy, for the * your God	Jos 23:10
certainty that the * your God will	Jos 23:13
the * your God has given you.	Jos 23:13
But as certainly as the * has	Jos 23:15,16
land which the * has given you.	Jos 23:15,16
as follows: "The * God of Israel	Jos 24:2
Worship the * alone.	Jos 24:14
to obey the *, then decide today	Jos 24:15
my family, we will serve the *."	Jos 24:15
the * and worship other gods!	Jos 24:16
For the * our God is the one who	Jos 24:17
It was the * who drove out the	Jos 24:18
Yes, we choose the *, for he	Jos 24:18
* God, for he is holy and jealous;	Jos 24:19
answered, "We choose the *!"	Jos 24:21
have chosen to obey the *."	Jos 24:22
must obey the * God of Israel."	Jos 24:23
worship and obey the * alone."	Jos 24:24
everything the * said, so it will	Jos 24:27
Israel obeyed the * throughout	Jos 24:31
which the * had done for Israel.	Jos 24:31
the * to receive his instructions.	Ju 1:1
And the * helped them defeat the	Ju 1:4,5,6

(LORD Con't)

villages. The * helped the tribe	Ju 1:19
to Caleb as the * had promised;	Ju 1:20
as Luz, and the * was with them.	Ju 1:22,23
ONE DAY THE Angel of the * arrived	Ju 2:1
they offered sacrifices to the *.	Ju 2:5
true to the * throughout Joshua's	Ju 2:7-9
the * had done for Israel.	Ju 2:7-9
They did many things which the *	Ju 2:11
So the anger of the * flamed out	Ju 2:12-14
enemies, the * blocked their path.	Ju 2:15
plight, the * raised up judges to	Ju 2:16
lifetime, for the * was moved to	Ju 2:18
Then the anger of the * would	Ju 2:20
the * as their ancestors did."	Ju 2:22
So the * left those nations in	Ju 2:23
of the nations the * left in the	Ju 3:1
* had given to them through Moses.	Ju 3:4
Then the anger of the * flamed	Ju 3:8
cried out to the *, he gave them	Ju 3:9
The Spirit of the * took control	Ju 3:10
the * helped Israel conquer him	Ju 3:10
But when they cried to the *, he	Ju 3:15
them, "for the * has put your	Ju 3:28
sinned against the *, so the Lord	Ju 4:1
the Lord, so the * let them be	Ju 4:2,3
But finally they begged the * for	Ju 4:2,3
said to him, "The * God of Israel	Ju 4:6
command. The * says, 'I will draw	Ju 4:7
time for action! The * leads on!	Ju 4:14
Then the * threw the enemy into	Ju 4:15
So that day the * used Israel to	Ju 4:23
"Praise the *!	Ju 5:2
Yes, bless the *!	Ju 5:2
For I shall sing about the *,	Ju 5:3
Praise the *!	Ju 5:9
To sing of the triumphs of the *.	Ju 5:11
Of how the * saved Israel	Ju 5:11
The people of the *	Ju 5:11
The people of the *	Ju 5:13,14
they did not come to help the *	Ju 5:23
O *, may all your enemies	Ju 5:31
But may those who love the *	Ju 5:31
* let their enemies harass them.	Ju 6:1
to cry out to the * for help.	Ju 6:6,7
was this: "The * God of Israel	Ju 6:8
He told you that he is the *	Ju 6:10
But one day the Angel of the *	Ju 6:11
The Angel of the * appeared to	Ju 6:12
soldier, the * is with you!"	Ju 6:12
replied, "if the * is with us, why	Ju 6:13
Now the * has thrown us away and	Ju 6:13
Then the * turned to him and	Ju 6:14
Whereupon the * said to him,	Ju 6:16
the Angel of the *, he cried out,	Ju 6:22
out, "Alas, O * God, for I have	Ju 6:22
the Angel of the * face to face!"	Ju 6:22
"It's all right," the *	Ju 6:23
That night the * told Gideon to	Ju 6:25
an altar for the * your God, built	Ju 6:26
offering to the *, using the wooden	Ju 6:26
and did as the * had commanded.	Ju 6:27
Then the Spirit of the * came	Ju 6:34
Then Gideon said to the *,	Ju 6:39
So the * did as he asked;	Ju 6:40
The * then said to Gideon,	Ju 7:2
But the * told Gideon, "There	Ju 7:4
There the * told him, "Divide	Ju 7:5,6
the * told Gideon.	Ju 7:7
the * said to Gideon, "Get up!	Ju 7:8,9
For the * is going to use you to	Ju 7:15
"For the * and for Gideon!"	Ju 7:19,20
For in the confusion the *	Ju 7:22
them, "When the * has delivered	Ju 8:7
shall my son; the * is your King!	Ju 8:23,24
They no longer considered the *	Ju 8:34
away from the * again, and	Ju 10:6
But the * replied, "Didn't I	Ju 10:11
gods and worshiped only the *;	Ju 10:16
before the * in Mizpah at a general	Ju 11:11
But the * our God helped Israel	Ju 11:21,22
"So you see, it was the * God of	Ju 11:23
At that time the Spirit of the *	Ju 11:29
had vowed to the * that if God	Ju 11:30,31
as a burnt offering to the *!	Ju 11:30,31
and the * gave him the victory.	Ju 11:32
For I have made a vow to the *	Ju 11:35
you promised the *, for he has	Ju 11:36
* helped me to conquer the enemy.	Ju 12:3
other gods, so the * let them be	Ju 13:1
Then one day the Angel of the *	Ju 13:2,3
the Angel of the *, for he was	Ju 13:6
Then Manoah prayed, "O *, please	Ju 13:8
The * answered his prayer, and	Ju 13:9
offering to sacrifice to the *."	Ju 13:16
that he was the Angel of the *.	Ju 13:16
it as a sacrifice to the *;	Ju 13:19
it had been the Angel of the *.	Ju 13:21
But his wife said, "If the *	Ju 13:23
the * blessed him as he grew up.	Ju 13:24
And the Spirit of the * began to	Ju 13:25
realize that the * was behind the	Ju 14:4
the Spirit of the * came mightily	Ju 14:6
Then the Spirit of the * came	Ju 14:19
but then the strength of the *	Ju 15:14
he prayed to the * and said, "You	Ju 15:18
So the * caused water to gush	Ju 15:19
realize that the * had left him.	Ju 16:20
Then Samson prayed to the * and	Ju 16:28
Lord and said, "O * Jehovah,	Ju 16:28
"I am going to give it to the *	Ju 17:3
"I know the * will really bless	Ju 17:13
The * is taking care of you."	Ju 18:6
one mind before the * at Mizpah.	Ju 20:1
And the * replied, "Judah shall	Ju 20:18
wept before the * until evening and	Ju 20:22,23,24
And the * said, "Yes."	Ju 20:22,23,24
wept before the * and fasted until	Ju 20:26
The men of Israel asked the *,	Ju 20:27,28
And the * said, "Go, for tomorrow	Ju 20:27,28
So the * helped Israel defeat	Ju 20:35-39
"O * God of Israel," they cried	Ju 21:3
council before the * at Mizpah?"	Ju 21:5
have sworn by the * that we will	Ju 21:7
days, because the * had made a	Ju 21:15
had heard that the * had blessed	Ru 1:6,7
And may the * reward you for your	Ru 1:8
for you that the * has punished me	Ru 1:13
May the * do terrible things to	Ru 1:17
I went out full and the * has	Ru 1:21
me Naomi when the * has turned his	Ru 1:21
May the * God of Israel, under	Ru 2:12
Praise the * for whoever was so	Ru 2:19
"Praise the * for a man like	Ru 2:20
May the * make this woman, who	Ru 4:11
descendants the * will give you	Ru 4:12
with her, the * gave her a son.	Ru 4:13
Naomi, "Bless the * who has given	Ru 4:14
to worship the * of the heavens and	1Sa 1:3
for the * had sealed her womb;	1Sa 1:5
bitterly as she prayed to the *.	1Sa 1:10
And she made this vow: "O * of	1Sa 1:11
was pouring out my heart to the *.	1Sa 1:15,16
May the * of Israel grant you	1Sa 1:17
to worship the * once more.	1Sa 1:19,20
the * remembered her petition;	1Sa 1:19,20
said, "I asked the * for him."	1Sa 1:19,20
here that time praying to the *!	1Sa 1:26
and now I am giving him to the *	1Sa 1:28
the Tabernacle for the * to use.	1Sa 1:28
"How I rejoice in the *!	1Sa 2:1
For the * has solved my problem.	1Sa 2:1
No one is as holy as the *!	1Sa 2:2
The * knows what you have done,	1Sa 2:3
The * kills,	1Sa 2:6
The * gives life.	1Sa 2:6
Those who fight against the *	1Sa 2:10
evil men who didn't love the *.	1Sa 2:12
very great in the eyes of the *;	1Sa 2:17
offerings to the * with contempt.	1Sa 2:17
this one they had given to the *.	1Sa 2:20
And the * gave Hannah three sons	1Sa 2:21
grew up in the service of the *.	1Sa 2:21
been committed against the *?"	1Sa 2:23,24,25
father, for the * was already	1Sa 2:23,24,25
message from the *: "Didn't I	1Sa 2:27
"Therefore, I, the * God of	1Sa 2:30
helping the * by assisting Eli.	1Sa 3:1
Messages from the * were very	1Sa 3:1
Ark, the * called out, "Samuel!	1Sa 3:4,5
Then the * called again,	1Sa 3:6
So now the * called the third	1Sa 3:8
Then Eli realized it was the * who	1Sa 3:8
say, 'Yes, *, I'm listening.'	1Sa 3:9
And the * came and called as	1Sa 3:10
Then the * said to Samuel, "I am	1Sa 3:11
Eli what the * had said to him.	1Sa 3:15
said, "what did the * say to you?	1Sa 3:16,17
So Samuel told him what the * had	1Sa 3:18
As Samuel grew, the * was with	1Sa 3:19
going to be a prophet of the *.	1Sa 3:20
Then the * began to give messages	1Sa 3:21,4:1
the * had let them be defeated.	1Sa 4:3
with us, the * will be among us and	1Sa 4:3
So they sent for the Ark of the *	1Sa 4:4
the * had arrived, they panicked.	1Sa 4:6
before the Ark of the * again.	1Sa 5:4
Then the * began to destroy the	1Sa 5:6
at Gath, the * began destroying its	1Sa 5:9
Then the Ark of the * and the	1Sa 6:11
them to the * as a burnt offering.	1Sa 6:14
offered to the * that day by the	1Sa 6:15
offering to the * were gifts from	1Sa 6:17
But the * killed seventy of the	1Sa 6:19
many people whom the * had killed.	1Sa 6:19
had brought back the Ark of the *.	1Sa 6:21
* had seemingly abandoned them.	1Sa 7:2
to return to the *, get rid of your	1Sa 7:3
Determine to obey only the *;	1Sa 7:3
and worshiped only the *.	1Sa 7:4
I will pray to the * for you."	1Sa 7:5
and poured it out before the *.	1Sa 7:6
offered it to the * as a whole	1Sa 7:
And the * responded.	1Sa 7:
battle, but the * spoke with a	1Sa 7:1
"The * has certainly helped us!"	1Sa 7:1
time, because the * was against	1Sa 7:1
And he built an altar to the * at	1Sa 7:1
and went to the * for advice.	1Sa 8:
"Do as they say," the *	1Sa 8:
the people what the * had said:	1Sa 8:1
but the * will not help you."	1Sa 8:1
So Samuel told the * what the	1Sa 8:2
had said, and the * replied again,	1Sa 8:2
up the hill. The * had told Samuel	1Sa 9:1
When Samuel saw Saul the * said,	1Sa 9:1
message for you from the *."	1Sa 9:26,2
"I am doing this because the *	1Sa 10:
the Spirit of the * will come	1Sa 10:
for the * will guide you.	1Sa 10:
message from the * God: "I brought	1Sa 10:18,1
the * by tribes and clans."	1Sa 10:18,1
before the *, and the tribe of	1Sa 10:2
before the *, and the family of the	1Sa 10:21
So they asked the *, "Where is	1Sa 10:22
And the * replied, "He is hiding	1Sa 10:22
man the * has chosen as your king.	1Sa 10:24
in a special place before the *.	1Sa 10:25
whose hearts the * had touched	1Sa 10:26
for today the * has rescued	1Sa 11:13
the * they crowned him king.	1Sa 11:15
offerings to the *, and Saul and	1Sa 11:15
I stand before the * and before his	1Sa 12:3
"The * and his anointed king are	1Sa 12:5
"It was the * who appointed	1Sa 12:6
quietly before the * as I remind	1Sa 12:7
cried out to the *, he sent Moses	1Sa 12:8
But they soon forgot about the *	1Sa 12:9
"Then they cried to the * again	1Sa 12:10
Then the * sent Gideon, Barak,	1Sa 12:11
But the * your God was already	1Sa 12:12
You have asked for him, and the *	1Sa 12:13
and worship the * and listen to his	1Sa 12:14
rebel against the *, and if both	1Sa 12:14
* your God, then all will be well.	1Sa 12:14
"Now watch as the * does great	1Sa 12:16
I will pray for the * to send	1Sa 12:17
So Samuel called to the *, and	1Sa 12:18
and the * sent thunder and rain;	1Sa 12:18
afraid of the * and of Samuel.	1Sa 12:18
you worship the * with true	1Sa 12:20
help you. The * will not abandon	1Sa 12:22
* by ending my prayers for you;	1Sa 12:23
"Trust the * and sincerely	1Sa 12:24
the commandment of the * your God.	1Sa 13:13
for the * wants a man who will	1Sa 13:14
the priest of the * in Shiloh).	1Sa 14:3
"Perhaps the * will do a miracle	1Sa 14:6
the * will help us defeat them!"	1Sa 14:12
So the * saved Israel that day,	1Sa 14:23
against the * by eating blood.	1Sa 14:33
the * by eating the blood."	1Sa 14:34
And Saul built an altar to the	1Sa 14:35
But the * made no reply all	1Sa 14:37
Then Saul said, "O * God of	1Sa 14:41
O * God, show us who is guilty."	1Sa 14:41
Then the * said to Samuel,	1Sa 15:10
that he cried to the * all night.	1Sa 15:11
sacrifice them to the * your God;	1Sa 15:15
Listen to what the * told me last	1Sa 15:16
Then why didn't you obey the *?	1Sa 15:19
"But I have obeyed the *," Saul	1Sa 15:20
and loot to sacrifice to the *."	1Sa 15:21
Samuel replied, "Has the * as	1Sa 15:22
the command of the *, for I was	1Sa 15:24
and go with me to worship the *."	1Sa 15:25
commandment of the *, he has	1Sa 15:26
to him, "See? The * has torn the	1Sa 15:28
me to worship the * your God."	1Sa 15:30
in pieces before the * at Gilgal.	1Sa 15:33
and the * was sorry that he had	1Sa 15:35
FINALLY THE * said to Samuel,	1Sa 16:1
"Take a heifer with you," the *	1Sa 16:2
come to make a sacrifice to the *.	1Sa 16:2
So Samuel did as the * had told	1Sa 16:4
I have come to sacrifice to the *	1Sa 16:5
is the man the * has chosen!"	1Sa 16:6
But the * said to Samuel, "Don't	1Sa 16:7
But the * said, "This is not the	1Sa 16:8
Shammah, but the * said, "No, this	1Sa 16:9
"The * has not chosen any of	1Sa 16:10,11
And the * said, "This is the	1Sa 16:12
But the Spirit of the * had left	1Sa 16:14
and instead, the * had sent a	1Sa 16:14
he added, "the * is with him."	1Sa 16:18
living God! The * who saved me	1Sa 17:37
"and may the * be with you!"	1Sa 17:37
in the name of the * of the armies	1Sa 17:45
Today the * will conquer you and	1Sa 17:46
And Israel will learn that the *	1Sa 17:47
because the * had left him and was	1Sa 18:11,12
undertook, for the * was with him.	1Sa 18:14
how much the * was with David and	1Sa 18:28

LORD Con't)
and how the * brought a great 1Sa 19:5
* lives, he shall not be killed." 1Sa 19:6
spirit from the * attacked him. 1Sa 19:9,10
I swear it by the * and by your 1Sa 20:3
"I promise by the * God of Israel 1Sa 20:12
then may the * kill me if I don't 1Sa 20:13
May the * be with you as he used 1Sa 20:13
kindness of the * not only to me 1Sa 20:14
children after the * has destroyed 1Sa 20:15
And may the * make us keep our 1Sa 20:23
Literally, "The * is our mediator 1Sa 20:23f
before the * in the Tabernacle. 1Sa 21:6
Literally, "detained before the * 1Sa 21:7f
Ahimelech consulted the * to find 1Sa 22:9,10
David asked the *, "Shall I go 1Sa 23:2
"Yes, go and save Keilah," the * 1Sa 23:2
David asked the * again, and the 1Sa 23:4
again, and the * again replied, 1Sa 23:4
get answers for David from the *. 1Sa 23:6
to ask the * what he should do. 1Sa 23:9
"O * God of Israel," David 1Sa 23:10
* God of Israel, please tell me." 1Sa 23:11
And the * said, "He will come." 1Sa 23:11
And the * replied, "Yes, they 1Sa 23:12
but the * didn't let him find him. 1Sa 23:14,15
"Well, praise the *!" 1Sa 23:21
"Today is the day the * was 1Sa 24:4
after him, "My * the king!" 1Sa 24:7,8
it isn't true. The * placed you at 1Sa 24:9,10
"The * will decide between us. 1Sa 24:12
May the * judge as to which of 1Sa 24:15
for when the * delivered me into 1Sa 24:18
May the * reward you well for the 1Sa 24:19
Oh, swear to me by the * that 1Sa 24:21
in this matter, my *," she said. 1Sa 25:24
Sir, since the * has kept you 1Sa 25:26
out here. The * will surely reward 1Sa 25:28
in the care of the * your God, just 1Sa 25:29
When the * has done all the good 1Sa 25:30,31
And when the * has done these 1Sa 25:30,31
"Bless the * God of Israel who has 1Sa 25:32
For I swear by the *, the God 1Sa 25:34
then died, for the * killed him. 1Sa 25:37,38
was dead, he said, "Praise the *! 1Sa 25:39
the * had put them sound asleep. 1Sa 26:12
I swear by the * that you ought 1Sa 26:16
If the * has stirred you up 1Sa 26:19
and get it. The * gives his own 1Sa 26:23
when the * placed you in my power. 1Sa 26:23
Now may the * save my life, even 1Sa 26:24
to Achish, "My *, if it is all 1Sa 27:5
and asked the * what he should do. 1Sa 28:5,6
But the * refused to answer him, 1Sa 28:5,6
ask me if the * has left you and 1Sa 28:16
"I swear by the *," he told 1Sa 29:6
David took strength from the *. 1Sa 30:6
David asked the *, "Shall I 1Sa 30:8
And the * told him, "Yes, go 1Sa 30:8
my brothers! The * has kept us safe 1Sa 30:23
bracelets to bring to you, my *." 2Sa 1:10
DAVID THEN ASKED the *, "Shall I 2Sa 2:1
And the * replied, "Yes." 2Sa 2:1
And the * replied, "Hebron." 2Sa 2:1
message: "May the * bless you for 2Sa 2:5
May the * be loyal to you in 2Sa 2:6
David, just as the * predicted." 2Sa 3:9,10
"For the * has said, 'It is 2Sa 3:18
"I vow by the * that I and my 2Sa 3:28
May the * repay wicked men for 2Sa 3:39
Today the * has given you revenge 2Sa 4:8
"I swear by the * who saved me 2Sa 4:9
real leader. The * has said that 2Sa 5:2
before the * with the leaders of 2Sa 5:3
the * God of heaven was with him. 2Sa 5:10
David now realized why the * had 2Sa 5:12
Then David asked the *, "Shall I 2Sa 5:19
And the * replied, "Yes, go 2Sa 5:19
"The * did it!" 2Sa 5:20
When David asked the * what to 2Sa 5:23
For it will signify that the * 2Sa 5:24
So David did as the * had 2Sa 5:25
the Ark of the * of heaven 2Sa 6:1
before the *—lyres, harps, 2Sa 6:5
Then the anger of the * flared 2Sa 6:7
David was angry at what the * 2Sa 6:8
David was now afraid of the * and 2Sa 6:9
months, and the * blessed Obed-edom 2Sa 6:11
And David danced before the * 2Sa 6:14
the Ark of the * with much shouting 2Sa 6:15
leaping and dancing before the *; 2Sa 6:16
and peace offerings to the *. 2Sa 6:17
in the name of the * of heaven, 2Sa 6:18
dancing before the * who chose me 2Sa 6:21
of Israel, the people of the *! 2Sa 6:21
in order to show my joy in the *. 2Sa 6:21
WHEN THE * finally sent peace upon 2Sa 7:1
"for the * is with you." 2Sa 7:3
But that night the * said to 2Sa 7:4
to David from the * of heaven: 'I 2Sa 7:8
him everything the * had said. 2Sa 7:17
and sat before the * and prayed, 2Sa 7:18
and prayed, "O * God, why have you 2Sa 7:18
any human standard! Oh, * God! 2Sa 7:19
How great you are, * God! 2Sa 7:22
"And now, * God, do as you have 2Sa 7:25
For you have revealed to me, O * 2Sa 7:27
for you, * God, have promised it. 2Sa 7:29
So the * gave him victories 2Sa 8:6
of these to the *, along with the 2Sa 8:11,12
of the way the * made him 2Sa 8:14
But the * was very displeased 2Sa 11:27
SO THE * sent the prophet Nathan 2Sa 12:1
that rich man! The * God of Israel 2Sa 12:7
"I have sinned against the *," 2Sa 12:13
"Yes, but the * has forgiven you, 2Sa 12:13
the enemies of the * to despise and 2Sa 12:14
And the * made Bath-sheba's baby 2Sa 12:15
before the * on the bare earth. 2Sa 12:16
Tabernacle and worshiped the *. 2Sa 12:20
said, 'Perhaps the * will be 2Sa 12:22
And the * loved the baby, and 2Sa 12:24
Literally, "because of the *." 2Sa 12:25f
"Oh, thank you, my *," she 2Sa 14:9
"Yes, my *?" 2Sa 14:18
sacrifice to the * in fulfillment 2Sa 15:7,8
may the * be merciful to you." 2Sa 15:19,20
"If the * sees fit," David 2Sa 15:25,26
David prayed, "O *, please make 2Sa 15:31
"The * is paying you back for 2Sa 16:7,8
throne and now the * has given it 2Sa 16:7,8
dead dog curse my * the king?" 2Sa 16:9
"If the * has told him to curse 2Sa 16:10
Let him alone, for no doubt the * 2Sa 16:11
And perhaps the * will see that 2Sa 16:12
* and by Israel," Hushai replied. 2Sa 16:18
For the * had arranged to 2Sa 17:14
good news that the * has saved him 2Sa 18:19
"Blesssed be the * your God who 2Sa 18:28
have good news for my * the king. 2Sa 18:31
and pleaded, "My * the king, 2Sa 19:19
And he replied, "My *, O king, 2Sa 19:26
I would only be a burden to my * 2Sa 19:35
Then the * said, "The famine is 2Sa 21:1
We will hang them before the * in 2Sa 21:5,6
them in the mountain before the *. 2Sa 21:9
DAVID SANG THIS song to the * 2Sa 22:1
I will call upon the *, 2Sa 22:4
But I called upon the * in my 2Sa 22:7
The * thundered from heaven; 2Sa 22:14
But the * was my salvation. 2Sa 22:19
The * rewarded me for my 2Sa 22:21
That is why the * has done so 2Sa 22:25
O *, you are my light! 2Sa 22:29
The word of the * is true. 2Sa 22:31
Our * alone is God; 2Sa 22:32
The * lives. 2Sa 22:47
to you, O *, among the nations, 2Sa 22:50
The Spirit of the * spoke by me, 2Sa 23:2
and the * gave him a great 2Sa 23:10
he poured it out before the *. 2Sa 23:16
ONCE AGAIN THE anger of the * 2Sa 24:1
Literally, "But why does my * the 2Sa 24:3f
*, "What I did was very wrong. 2Sa 24:10
the word of the * came to the 2Sa 24:11
The * said to Gad, "Tell David 2Sa 24:11
the hand of the * (for his mercy is 2Sa 24:14
So the * sent a plague upon 2Sa 24:15
Jerusalem, the * was sorry for what 2Sa 24:16
he said to the *, "Look, I am the 2Sa 24:17
an altar to the * on the threshing 2Sa 24:18
So David went to do what the * 2Sa 24:19
*, and he will stop the plague." 2Sa 24:21
the * God accept your sacrifice." 2Sa 24:23
to offer to the * my God burnt 2Sa 24:24
altar there to the * and offered 2Sa 24:25
And the * answered his prayer, 2Sa 24:25
king and that our * David doesn't 1Ki 1:11
and ask him, 'My *, didn't you 1Ki 1:13
She replied, "My *, you vowed to 1Ki 1:17
vowed to me by the * your God that 1Ki 1:17
And now, my * the king, all 1Ki 1:20
and asked, "My *, have you 1Ki 1:24
And the king vowed, "As the * 1Ki 1:29
before by the * God of Israel." 1Ki 1:30
May my * the king live forever!" 1Ki 1:31
added, "May the * be with Solomon 1Ki 1:37
"Our * King David has declared 1Ki 1:43
He is saying, 'Blessed be the * 1Ki 1:48
If you do this, then the * will 1Ki 2:4
for that is the way the * wanted 1Ki 2:15
For you carried the Ark of the * 1Ki 2:26
the priest of the *, thereby 1Ki 2:27
and may the * declare David and his 1Ki 2:33
May the * take revenge on you, 1Ki 2:44
of the * hadn't yet been built. 1Ki 3:2
(Solomon loved the * and followed 1Ki 3:3
offerings! The * appeared to him 1Ki 3:5
to succeed him. O * my God, now 1Ki 3:7
The * was pleased with his reply 1Ki 3:10
Covenant of the *, he sacrificed 1Ki 3:15
of the * he wanted to build. 1Ki 5:2,3
for the * to give him peace. 1Ki 5:2,3
to Hiram, "the * my God has given 1Ki 5:4
a Temple for the * my God, just as 1Ki 5:5
For the * told him, 'Your son, 1Ki 5:5
So the * gave great wisdom to 1Ki 5:12
Then the * sent this message to 1Ki 6:11,12
the Covenant of the * was placed. 1Ki 6:19
the Temple of the * which had been 1Ki 7:40
Covenant of the * from the 1Ki 8:1
at the time the * made his covenant 1Ki 8:9
* is filling the entire building! 1Ki 8:11
"The * has said that he would 1Ki 8:12,13
But, O *, I have built you a 1Ki 8:12,13
"Blessed be the * God of 1Ki 8:15
a Temple for the * God of Israel, 1Ki 8:17
but the * told him not to. 1Ki 8:18
And now the * has done what he 1Ki 8:20
built for the * God of Israel. 1Ki 8:20
made by the * with our fathers, at 1Ki 8:21
the altar of the * with his hands 1Ki 8:22,23
and said, "O * God of Israel, 1Ki 8:22,23
and now, O * God of Israel, 1Ki 8:25
And yet, O * my God, you have 1Ki 8:28
to their pleas. O *, hear and 1Ki 8:52
"Blessed be the * who has 1Ki 8:56
May the * our God be with us as 1Ki 8:57
know that the * is God, and that 1Ki 8:60
lives before the * our God; 1Ki 8:61
offerings to the *—a total of 1Ki 8:62,63
goodness that the * had shown to 1Ki 8:66
wanted, the * appeared to him the 1Ki 9:2,3
'Why has the * done such things to 1Ki 9:8
abandoned the * their God who 1Ki 9:9
That is why the * has brought 1Ki 9:9
* had blessed Solomon with wisdom, 1Ki 10:1
concerning the name of the *." 1Ki 10:1f
for him, for the * gave him the 1Ki 10:3
by fire to the *—well, there was no 1Ki 10:5
Blessed be the * your God who 1Ki 10:9
How the * must love Israel—for he 1Ki 10:9
even though the * had clearly 1Ki 11:2
the *, especially in his old age. 1Ki 11:3
* as his father David had done. 1Ki 11:4
the * as his father David did. 1Ki 11:6
interested in the * God of Israel 1Ki 11:9,10
so now the * said to him, "Since 1Ki 11:11
So the * caused Hadad the Edomite 1Ki 11:14
pieces, for the * God of Israel 1Ki 11:31
So the army went home as the * 1Ki 12:23,24
the * from Judah walked up to him. 1Ki 13:1
"O altar, the * says that a child 1Ki 13:2
was from the *: 'This altar will 1Ki 13:3
prophet, "beg the * your God to 1Ki 13:6
So he prayed to the *, and the 1Ki 13:6
For the * has given me strict 1Ki 13:9
* strictly warned me against it; 1Ki 13:16,17
gave me a message from the *. 1Ki 13:18
a message from the * came to the 1Ki 13:20
from Judah, "The * says that 1Ki 13:21,22
command; the * fulfilled his 1Ki 13:26
For the * told him to shout 1Ki 13:32
But the * told him that the 1Ki 14:5
And the * told him what to tell 1Ki 14:5
message from the * God of Israel: 1Ki 14:7
thing which the * God of Israel 1Ki 14:13
And the * will raise up a king 1Ki 14:14
Then the * will shake Israel 1Ki 14:15
the * by worshiping idol-gods. 1Ki 14:15
* had predicted through Ahijah. 1Ki 14:18
the * had chosen to live in. 1Ki 14:21
and angered the * with their sin, 1Ki 14:22
nations which the * drove out to 1Ki 14:24
But despite Abijam's sin, the * 1Ki 15:4
He pleased the * like his 1Ki 15:11
left, just as the * had said would 1Ki 15:29
had angered the * God of Israel by 1Ki 15:30
he continually disobeyed the *. 1Ki 15:34
from the * was delivered to King 1Ki 16:1
the * by all his evil deeds. 1Ki 16:4-7
the fact that the * had destroyed 1Ki 16:4-7
line with what the * had predicted 1Ki 16:12
and the * was very angry about it. 1Ki 16:13
more to anger the * God of Israel 1Ki 16:33
"As surely as the * God of Israel 1Ki 17:1
Then the * said to Elijah, "Go 1Ki 17:2
So he did as the * had told him 1Ki 17:5
Then the * said to him, "Go and 1Ki 17:8,9
But she said, "I swear by the * 1Ki 17:12
For the * God of Israel says 1Ki 17:14
the time when the * sends rain, and 1Ki 17:14
the * had promised through Elijah! 1Ki 17:16
cried out to the *, "O Lord my 1Ki 17:20
to the Lord, "O * my God, why have 1Ki 17:20
cried out to the *, "O Lord my 1Ki 17:21
to the Lord, "O * my God, please 1Ki 17:21
And the * heard Elijah's prayer; 1Ki 17:22
whatever you say is from the *!" 1Ki 17:24
later that the * said to Elijah, 1Ki 18:1
was a devoted follower of the *. 1Ki 18:3,4
"Is it really you, my * Elijah?" 1Ki 18:7
the Spirit of the * will carry you 1Ki 18:12

(LORD Con't)
true servant of the * all my life. 1Ki 18:12
"I swear by the * God of the 1Ki 18:15
to obey the *, and have worshiped 1Ki 18:18
"If the * is God, follow him! 1Ki 18:21
"I am the only prophet of the * 1Ki 18:22
god, and I will pray to the *; 1Ki 18:24
of the * which had been torn down. 1Ki 18:30
Jacob to whom the * had said, 1Ki 18:31f
and prayed, "O * God of Abraham, 1Ki 18:36
at your command. O *, answer me! 1Ki 18:37
Jezreel, and the * gave special 1Ki 18:46
"I've had enough," he told the * 1Ki 19:4
Then the angel of the * came 1Ki 19:7
But the * said to him, "What are 1Ki 19:9
hard for the * God of the heavens; 1Ki 19:10
on the mountain," the * told him. 1Ki 19:11
And as Elijah stood there the * 1Ki 19:11
but the * was not in the wind. 1Ki 19:11
the * was not in the earthquake. 1Ki 19:11
but the * was not in the fire. 1Ki 19:12
very hard for the * God of the 1Ki 19:14
Then the * told him, "Go back by 1Ki 19:15
"All right, my *," Ahab 1Ki 20:4
"Tell my * the king, 'I will give 1Ki 20:9
message from the *: "Do you see 1Ki 20:13
you will know that I am the *." 1Ki 20:13
And the prophet replied, "The * 1Ki 20:14
message from the *: "Because the 1Ki 20:28
declared, 'The * is a God of the 1Ki 20:28
know that I am indeed the *." 1Ki 20:28
Meanwhile, the * instructed one 1Ki 20:35
the voice of the *, a lion shall 1Ki 20:36
told him, "The * says, 'Because 1Ki 20:42
But the * said to Elijah, "Go 1Ki 21:17
is evil in the sight of the *." 1Ki 21:20f
The * is going to bring great 1Ki 21:21
into sin. The * has also told me 1Ki 21:23
people whom the * had chased out of 1Ki 21:26
should ask the * first, to be sure 1Ki 22:5
there a prophet of the * here? 1Ki 22:7
declared, "The * promises that you 1Ki 22:11
the * will cause you to triumph!" 1Ki 22:12
say only what the * tells me to!" 1Ki 22:14
the * will cause you to conquer!" 1Ki 22:15
only what the * tells you to?" 1Ki 22:16
And the * said, 'Their king is 1Ki 22:17
to this further word from the *. 1Ki 22:19
I saw the * sitting on his 1Ki 22:19
"Then the * said, 'Who will 1Ki 22:20
the * and said, 'I'll do it!' 1Ki 22:21
" 'How?' the * asked. 1Ki 22:22
"And the * said, 'That will do 1Ki 22:22
"Don't you see? The * has put a 1Ki 22:23
* has decreed disaster upon you." 1Ki 22:23
"When did the Spirit of the * 1Ki 22:24
the * has not spoken through me." 1Ki 22:28
as the * had said would happen. 1Ki 22:38
done, obeying the * in all but one 1Ki 22:43
So Ahaziah made the * God of 1Ki 22:52,53
But an angel of the * told Elijah 2Ki 1:3
has done this, the * says that he 2Ki 1:4,5
and tell him, 'The * wants to know 2Ki 1:6
Then the angel of the * said to 2Ki 1:15
So Ahaziah died as the * had 2Ki 1:17
NOW THE TIME came for the * to 2Ki 2:1
* has told me to go to Bethel." 2Ki 2:1
you know that the * is going to 2Ki 2:3
the * has sent me to Jericho." 2Ki 2:4
you know that the * is going to 2Ki 2:5
stay here, for the * has sent me to 2Ki 2:6,7
"Where is the * God of Elijah?" 2Ki 2:13,14
perhaps the Spirit of the * has 2Ki 2:16
"The * has healed these waters. 2Ki 2:21
cursed them in the name of the *; 2Ki 2:24
"The * has brought us here to 2Ki 3:10
there a prophet of the * with us? 2Ki 3:11
Literally, "the word of the * is 2Ki 3:12f
For it is the * who has called us 2Ki 3:13
"I swear by the * God that I 2Ki 3:14
message of the * came to Elisha: 2Ki 3:15
"The * says to fill this dry 2Ki 3:16
beginning, for the * will make you 2Ki 3:18
the * hasn't told me what it is." 2Ki 4:27
behind him and prayed to the *. 2Ki 4:33
ahead, for the * says there will be 2Ki 4:43
there was, just as the * had said! 2Ki 4:44
of the * his God, and heal me! 2Ki 5:11
to any other God except the *. 2Ki 5:17
However, may the * pardon me 2Ki 5:18
the * pardon me when I bow too." 2Ki 5:18
Then Elisha prayed, "*, open his 2Ki 6:17
And the * opened the young 2Ki 6:17
"*, please make them blind." 2Ki 6:18
Elisha prayed, "*, now open their 2Ki 6:20
And the * did, and they 2Ki 6:20
to him, "Help, my * the king!" 2Ki 6:26-30
"If the * doesn't help you, what 2Ki 6:26-30
"The * has caused this mess," 2Ki 6:33
ELISHA REPLIED, "THE * says that 2Ki 7:1
the * made windows in the sky!" 2Ki 7:2
(For the * had made the whole 2Ki 7:6
dollar, just as the * had said! 2Ki 7:16
* opened the windows of heaven!" 2Ki 7:19
country, for the * has called down 2Ki 8:1
* whether I will get well again." 2Ki 8:8,9
But the * has shown me that he 2Ki 8:10
But Elisha replied, "The * has 2Ki 8:13
Tell him that the * has anointed 2Ki 9:3
and said, "The * God of Israel 2Ki 9:6
father Ahab, the * revealed this 2Ki 9:25
field, just as the * said." 2Ki 9:26
just what the * said would happen. 2Ki 9:36
kill his sons! The * has done that, 2Ki 10:9,10
how much I have done for the *." 2Ki 10:16
speaking for the *, had predicted. 2Ki 10:17
anyone in who worships the *!" 2Ki 10:23
Afterwards the * said to Jehu, 2Ki 10:30
But Jehu didn't follow the * God 2Ki 10:31
At about that time the * began to 2Ki 10:32,33
treaty between the *, the king, and 2Ki 11:17
set guards at the Temple of the *. 2Ki 11:18
to the *, whether it is a regular 2Ki 12:4,5
to repair the Temple of the *. 2Ki 12:11,12
So the * was very angry with 2Ki 13:3
help, and the * listened to him; 2Ki 13:4
for the * saw how terribly the 2Ki 13:4
So the * raised up leaders among 2Ki 13:5
Finally the * reduced Jehoahaz's 2Ki 13:7
But the * was gracious to the 2Ki 13:23
children, for the * had commanded 2Ki 14:6
Sea, just as the * God of Israel 2Ki 14:25
For the * saw the bitter plight 2Ki 14:26
* just as his father Amaziah had. 2Ki 15:3
the * struck him with leprosy, 2Ki 15:5
he followed the *. 2Ki 15:34,35
of the Temple of the * was built. 2Ki 15:34,35
In those days the * caused King 2Ki 15:37
But he did not follow the * as 2Ki 16:2
which the * destroyed when the 2Ki 16:3
against the * their God who had 2Ki 17:7
* had cast out from before them. 2Ki 17:8
nations which the * had cleared out 2Ki 17:11
things, and the * was very angry. 2Ki 17:11
Again and again the * had sent 2Ki 17:13
to believe in the * their God. 2Ki 17:14
of the * their God and made two 2Ki 17:16
So the * was very angry. 2Ki 17:17
commandments of the * their God; 2Ki 17:19
So the * rejected all the 2Ki 17:20
Israel away from following the *. 2Ki 17:21
into, until the * finally swept 2Ki 17:23
not worship the * when they first 2Ki 17:25
first arrived, the * sent lions 2Ki 17:25
from Babylon how to worship the *. 2Ki 17:27,28
They also worshiped the *, and 2Ki 17:32
to the * on the hilltop altars. 2Ki 17:32
worshiping the * or obeying the 2Ki 17:34
For the * had made a contract 2Ki 17:35,36
They were to worship only the * 2Ki 17:35,36
You must worship only the *; 2Ki 17:39
worshiped the *, yes—but they also 2Ki 17:41
strongly in the * God of Israel. 2Ki 18:5
For he followed the * in 2Ki 18:6
So the * was with him and 2Ki 18:7
to listen to the * their God or to 2Ki 18:12
by Moses the servant of the *. 2Ki 18:12
trusting the * to rescue us"—just 2Ki 18:22
No! The * sent us and told us, 2Ki 18:25
trusting in the * to rescue you. 2Ki 18:30
you that the * will deliver you. 2Ki 18:31,32
So what makes you think the * can 2Ki 18:35
Yet perhaps the * your God has 2Ki 19:4
Isaiah replied, "The * says, 2Ki 19:5,6
and the * will see to it that he 2Ki 19:7
and spread it out before the *. 2Ki 19:14
"O * God of Israel, sitting on 2Ki 19:15
Bend low, O *, and listen. 2Ki 19:16
Open your eyes, O *, and see. 2Ki 19:16
the living God. *, it is true that 2Ki 19:17
wood and stone. O * our God, we 2Ki 19:19
to Hezekiah: "The * God of Israel 2Ki 19:20
*, who lets you do these things? 2Ki 19:25
in Jerusalem. The * is eager to 2Ki 19:31
the angel of the * killed 185,000 2Ki 19:35
"The * says you won't recover." 2Ki 20:1
"O *," he pleaded, "remember 2Ki 20:3
the * spoke to him again. 2Ki 20:4
tell him that the * God of his 2Ki 20:5
to me that the * will heal me and 2Ki 20:8
"All right, the * will give you 2Ki 20:9
So Isaiah asked the * to do this, 2Ki 20:11
to the word of the *: The time 2Ki 20:16
is what the * wants, it is good." 2Ki 20:19
the Temple of the *—in the very 2Ki 21:3,4,5
building which the * had selected 2Ki 21:3,4,5
So the * was very angry, for 2Ki 21:6
place which the * had spoken to 2Ki 21:7
not listen to the *, and Manasseh 2Ki 21:9
Then the * declared through the 2Ki 21:10
on the * God of his ancestors. 2Ki 21:22
David, obeying the * completely 2Ki 22:1
to ask the *, "What shall we do? 2Ki 22:12,1
message from the * God of Israel: 2Ki 22:15,1
before the * when you read the book 2Ki 22:18,1
promise to the * to obey him at all 2Ki 23:
the priests of the *, who were 2Ki 23:8
the altar of the * in Jerusalem, 2Ki 23:9
and had made the * very angry. 2Ki 23:19
as recorded by the * their God in 2Ki 23:2
turned to the * and followed all 2Ki 23:25
But the * still did not hold back 2Ki 23:26
For the * had said, "I will 2Ki 23:27
And the * sent bands of 2Ki 24:2
just as the * had warned through 2Ki 24:2
at the direct command of the *. 2Ki 24:3,4
and the * would not pardon it. 2Ki 24:3,4
So the * finally, in his anger, 2Ki 24:20
so wicked that the * killed him. 1Ch 2:3
exile when the * sent the people of 1Ch 6:4-15
And the * was with him. 1Ch 9:20
to the * and because he had 1Ch 10:13
and did not ask the * for 1Ch 10:14
So the * killed him and gave the 1Ch 10:14
And the * your God has told you, 1Ch 11:2
them before the *, and they 1Ch 11:3
just as the * had told Samuel. 1Ch 11:3
the * of the heavens was with him. 1Ch 11:9
as the * had said would happen): 1Ch 11:10
and the * saved them with a great 1Ch 11:14
an offering to the * and said, 1Ch 11:18,19
as the * had said would happen. 1Ch 12:23
and since the * our God has given 1Ch 13:2
* God enthroned above the angels. 1Ch 13:6
danced before the * with great 1Ch 13:8
Then the anger of the * blazed 1Ch 13:10
David was angry at the * for 1Ch 13:11
the * blessed him and his family. 1Ch 13:14
David now realized why the * had 1Ch 14:2
David asked the *, "If I go out 1Ch 14:10
And the * replied, "Yes, I 1Ch 14:10
The * replied, "Go around by the 1Ch 14:14
So David did as the * commanded 1Ch 14:16
and the * caused all the nations to 1Ch 14:17
for it. The * destroyed us before 1Ch 15:13
as the * had instructed Moses. 1Ch 15:15
the people in the name of the *; 1Ch 16:2
and thanks to the * God of Israel 1Ch 16:4
to sing thanksgiving to the *. 1Ch 16:7
"Oh, give thanks to the * and 1Ch 16:8
Let all rejoice who seek the *. 1Ch 16:10
Seek the *; 1Ch 16:11
He is the * our God! 1Ch 16:14
Sing to the *, O earth, 1Ch 16:23
For the * is great, and should be 1Ch 16:25
But the * made the heavens. 1Ch 16:26
Yes, ascribe to the * 1Ch 16:29
Worship the * when clothed with 1Ch 16:29
say, 'It is the * who reigns.' 1Ch 16:31
woods sing for joy before the *, 1Ch 16:33
Oh, give thanks to the *, for he 1Ch 16:34
and praised the *. 1Ch 16:36
Ark of the Covenant of the *." 1Ch 16:37f
Tabernacle of the * on the hill of 1Ch 16:39
to minister to the * there. 1Ch 16:39
offerings to the * each morning and 1Ch 16:40
as the * had commanded Israel. 1Ch 16:40
* for his constant love and mercy. 1Ch 16:41
for it is the will of the *." 1Ch 17:2
"Tell my servant David, 'The * 1Ch 17:7
David everything the * had said. 1Ch 17:15
and sat before the * and said, 1Ch 17:16
"Who am I, O * God, and what is my 1Ch 17:16
For now, O * God, you are 1Ch 17:17
to honor me! O *, you have given 1Ch 17:19
great heart. O *, there is no one 1Ch 17:20
your promise, *, that I and my 1Ch 17:23
They will exclaim, 'The * of 1Ch 17:24
*, it is an eternal blessing!" 1Ch 17:27
And the * gave David victory 1Ch 18:6
these gifts to the *, as he did the 1Ch 18:11
example of how the * gave David 1Ch 18:13
And may the * do what is best." 1Ch 19:13
"If the * were to multiply his 1Ch 21:3
Then the * said to Gad, David's 1Ch 21:9
* has offered you three choices. 1Ch 21:10,11
* brings destruction to the land. 1Ch 21:12
the hands of the * rather than into 1Ch 21:13
So the * sent a plague upon 1Ch 21:14
(The angel of the * was 1Ch 21:15
the angel of the * standing between 1Ch 21:16
fell to the ground before the *. 1Ch 21:16
sheep done? O * my God, destroy me 1Ch 21:17
Then the angel of the * told Gad 1Ch 21:18
an altar to the * at the 1Ch 21:18
the * and the plague will stop." 1Ch 21:22
"Take it, my *, and use it as 1Ch 21:23
is yours and give it to the *. 1Ch 21:24
and built an altar to the * 1Ch 21:26
and he called out to the *, who 1Ch 21:26
Then the * commanded the angel 1Ch 21:27
and when David saw that the * 1Ch 21:28
plead before the *, for he was 1Ch 21:30

LORD Con't)
the Temple of the * and construct 1Ch 22:1
the Temple of the * must be a 1Ch 22:5
a temple for the * God of Israel. 1Ch 22:6
"but the * said not to do it. 1Ch 22:8
"So now, my son, may the * be 1Ch 22:11
do and build the Temple of the *. 1Ch 22:11
And may the * give you the good 1Ch 22:12
So get to work, and may the * be 1Ch 22:16
"The * your God is with you," 1Ch 22:18
name of the * and for his people. 1Ch 22:18
being to obey the * your God, and 1Ch 22:19
into the Temple of the *!" 1Ch 22:19
will praise the * with the musical 1Ch 23:4,5
the people's offerings to the *. 1Ch 23:13
He served the * constantly and 1Ch 23:13
For David said, "The * God of 1Ch 23:25
stood before the * to sing thanks 1Ch 23:30
and praising the * (while 1Ch 25:3
in singing praises to the *; 1Ch 25:6,7
brought to the * and placed in the 1Ch 26:20,21,22
gifts given to the * by King David 1Ch 26:26
dedicated to the * by Samuel the 1Ch 26:28
who brought gifts to the *. 1Ch 26:28
younger, for the * had promised a 1Ch 27:23
Literally, "the * had said he 1Ch 27:23f
Covenant of the * could rest—a 1Ch 28:2
"Nevertheless, the * God of 1Ch 28:4
and from among his sons, the * 1Ch 28:4
And from among my sons—the * has 1Ch 28:5
commandment of the * so that you 1Ch 28:8
mind, for the * sees every heart 1Ch 28:9
So be very careful, for the * 1Ch 28:10
the Ark of the Covenant of the *. 1Ch 28:18
writing from the hand of the *." 1Ch 28:19
for the * my God is with you; 1Ch 28:20
is for the * God himself! 1Ch 29:1
and all that he has to the *?" 1Ch 29:4,5
his praises to the *: "O Lord God 1Ch 29:10
to the Lord: "O * God of our 1Ch 29:10
O *, and this is your kingdom. 1Ch 29:11
a trace. O * our God, all of this 1Ch 29:16
"O * God of our fathers: 1Ch 29:18
"Give praise to the * your God!" 1Ch 29:20
low before the * and the king. 1Ch 29:20
lambs as burnt offerings to the *; 1Ch 29:21
drank before the * with great joy. 1Ch 29:22
They anointed him before the * as 1Ch 29:22
And the * gave him great 1Ch 29:25
of Israel, for the * his God had 2Ch 1:1
it 1,000 burnt offerings to the *. 2Ch 1:5,6
the * and a palace for himself. 2Ch 2:1
* my God," Solomon told Hiram. 2Ch 2:4
festivals of the * our God. 2Ch 2:4
is because the * loves his people 2Ch 2:11
Blessed be the * God of Israel 2Ch 2:12
by my * David, your father. 2Ch 2:14
Moriah, where the * had appeared to 2Ch 3:1
the * by his father, King David. 2Ch 5:1
Horeb, when the * made a covenant 2Ch 5:10
were praising the * as the priests 2Ch 5:11,12
as one to praise and thank the *; 2Ch 5:13,14
praising and thanking the *. 2Ch 5:13,14
the glory of the *, coming as a 2Ch 5:13,14
"The * has said that he would 2Ch 6:1
you, O *, to live in forever!" 2Ch 6:1
"Blessed be the * God of 2Ch 6:4
Temple, but the * said not to. 2Ch 6:8
the desire, the * told him, but he 2Ch 6:8
And now the * has done what he 2Ch 6:10
the Name of the * God of Israel, 2Ch 6:10
the * and his people Israel." 2Ch 6:11
in front of the altar of the *. 2Ch 6:12,13
"O * God of Israel, there is no 2Ch 6:14
Yes, * God of Israel, please 2Ch 6:17
will heed my prayers, O * my God! 2Ch 6:19
And now, O * God, arise and 2Ch 6:41
Let your priests, O * God, be 2Ch 6:41
kind deeds. O * God, do not ignore 2Ch 6:42
And the glory of the * filled the 2Ch 7:1
and worshiped and thanked the *. 2Ch 7:3
burnt offerings to the *. 2Ch 7:4,5
made and had used to praise the *. 2Ch 7:6
happy because the * had been so 2Ch 7:10
One night the * appeared to 2Ch 7:12
" 'Why has the * done such a 2Ch 7:21
abandoned the * God of their 2Ch 7:22
for the Ark of the * was there and 2Ch 8:11
offerings to the * on the altar he 2Ch 8:12
Blessed be the * your God! 2Ch 9:8
But the * told Shemaiah the 2Ch 11:2
" 'The * says, Do not fight 2Ch 11:4
So they obeyed the * and 2Ch 11:4
to stop being priests of the *. 2Ch 11:13,14
freely worship the * God of their 2Ch 11:16
effort to obey the * as King David 2Ch 11:17
he abandoned the *, and the people 2Ch 12:1
told them, "The * says, 'You have 2Ch 12:5
* is right in doing this to us!" 2Ch 12:6
And when the * saw them humble 2Ch 12:7
did decide really to please the *. 2Ch 12:14
Don't you realize that the * God 2Ch 13:5
the kingdom of the * that is led by 2Ch 13:8
the priests of the * and the 2Ch 13:9
"But as for us, the * is our God 2Ch 13:10
They burn sacrifices to the * 2Ch 13:11
the instructions of the * our God; 2Ch 13:11
fight against the * God of your 2Ch 13:12
Then they cried out to the * for 2Ch 13:13,14
So Judah, depending upon the * 2Ch 13:18,19
the * struck him and he died. 2Ch 13:20
was careful to obey the * his God. 2Ch 14:2
of the * God of their ancestors. 2Ch 14:4
do it, while the * is blessing us 2Ch 14:7
"O *," he cried out to God, 2Ch 14:11
Oh, help us, * our God! 2Ch 14:11
Then the * defeated the 2Ch 14:12
for the * and his army destroyed 2Ch 14:13
the * came upon the residents. 2Ch 14:14
"The * will stay with you as 2Ch 15:2
again to the * God of Israel in 2Ch 15:4
of the * in front of the Temple. 2Ch 15:8
that the * God was with King Asa). 2Ch 15:9
sacrificed to the * seven hundred 2Ch 15:11
worship only the * God of their 2Ch 15:12
his father had dedicated to the *. 2Ch 15:18
instead of in the * your God, the 2Ch 16:7
But you relied then on the *, and 2Ch 16:8
For the eyes of the * search 2Ch 16:9
didn't go to the * with the 2Ch 16:12
The * was with Jehoshaphat 2Ch 17:3
So the * strengthened his 2Ch 17:5
of the Law of the * to all the 2Ch 17:7,8,9
Then the fear of the * fell upon 2Ch 17:10
However, let's check with the * 2Ch 18:3,4,5
of the * around here too?" 2Ch 18:6,7
proclaimed, "The * says you will 2Ch 18:10
the * will cause you to conquer." 2Ch 18:11
except what the * tells you to?" 2Ch 18:15
And the * said, 'Their master has 2Ch 18:16
"Listen to what else the * has 2Ch 18:18
"And the * said, 'Who can get 2Ch 18:19,20
the * and said, 'I can do it!' 2Ch 18:19,20
" 'How?' the * asked him. 2Ch 18:19,20
" 'It will work,' the * said; 2Ch 18:21
"So you see, the * has put a 2Ch 18:22
"When did the Spirit of the * 2Ch 18:23
the * has not spoken through me." 2Ch 18:27
cried out to the * to save him, and 2Ch 18:31
save him, and the * made the 2Ch 18:31
and loving those who hate the *?" 2Ch 19:2
to beg for help from the *; 2Ch 20:3
"O * God of our fathers—the only 2Ch 20:6
stood before the * with their 2Ch 20:13
the Spirit of the * came upon one 2Ch 20:14
"The * says, 'Don't be afraid! 2Ch 20:15
Go out there tomorrow, for the * 2Ch 20:17
did the same, worshiping the *. 2Ch 20:18
to praise the * God of Israel with 2Ch 20:19
"Believe in the * your God, and 2Ch 20:20
along praising and thanking the *! 2Ch 20:21
and to praise, the * caused the 2Ch 20:22
today, and how they praised the *! 2Ch 20:26
of joy that the * had given them 2Ch 20:27
heard that the * himself had fought 2Ch 20:29
to follow the *, with the 2Ch 20:32
the * has destroyed your work." 2Ch 20:37
However, the * was unwilling to 2Ch 21:7
from the * God of his fathers. 2Ch 21:10
this letter: "The * God of your 2Ch 21:12
than you, now the * will destroy 2Ch 21:14
Then the * stirred up the 2Ch 21:16
Nimshi), whom the * had appointed 2Ch 22:7
who enthusiastically served the *. 2Ch 22:9
offering to the * as prescribed in 2Ch 23:18
Joash tried hard to please the * 2Ch 24:2
the servant of the * must be 2Ch 24:6
to bring to the * the tax that 2Ch 24:9
*, but the people wouldn't listen. 2Ch 24:19
You have forsaken the *, and now 2Ch 24:20
as he died were "*, see what they 2Ch 24:22
army, but the * let the great army 2Ch 24:24
the * God of their ancestors. 2Ch 24:24
the command of the * written in the 2Ch 25:4
message from the *: "Sir, do not 2Ch 25:7
for the * is not with them. 2Ch 25:7
And the prophet replied, "The * 2Ch 25:9
This made the * very angry and 2Ch 25:15
famous, for the * helped him 2Ch 26:15
He sinned against the * his God 2Ch 26:16
and the * is not going to honor you 2Ch 26:17,18
out, because the * had struck him. 2Ch 26:20
follow the path of the * his God. 2Ch 27:6
by the * to make room for Israel. 2Ch 28:3
That is why the * God allowed the 2Ch 28:5
from the * God of their fathers. 2Ch 28:6
But Oded, a prophet of the *, was 2Ch 28:9
"The * God of your fathers was 2Ch 28:9
own sins against the * your God? 2Ch 28:10
anger of the * is upon you." 2Ch 28:11
"If you do, the * will be angry, 2Ch 28:13
For the * brought Judah very low 2Ch 28:19
and had been faithless to the *. 2Ch 28:19
angering the * God of his fathers. 2Ch 28:25
the Temple of the * God of your 2Ch 29:4,5
a deep sin before the * our God; 2Ch 29:6
they abandoned the * and his 2Ch 29:6
Therefore the wrath of the * has 2Ch 29:8
covenant with the * God of Israel 2Ch 29:10
longer, for the * has chosen you to 2Ch 29:11
for the *) had commanded them. 2Ch 29:15
are beside the altar of the *." 2Ch 29:19
them on the altar of the *. 2Ch 29:21
their instructions from the *. 2Ch 29:25,26
*, accompanied by the trumpets. 2Ch 29:27
worshiped the * as the singers sang 2Ch 29:28
bowed low before the * in worship. 2Ch 29:29
to sing before the * some of the 2Ch 29:30
"Come back to the * God of 2Ch 30:6
sinned against the * God of their 2Ch 30:7
yourselves to the * and come to 2Ch 30:8
and worship the * your God so that 2Ch 30:8
For if you turn to the * again, 2Ch 30:9
For the * your God is full of 2Ch 30:9
"May the good * pardon everyone 2Ch 30:17,18,19
to follow the * God of his fathers, 2Ch 30:17,18,19
And the * listened to 2Ch 30:20
praised the * with music and 2Ch 30:21
to the * God of their fathers. 2Ch 30:22
people, and the * heard their 2Ch 30:27
give thanks and praise to the *. 2Ch 31:2
to be given to the * their God. 2Ch 31:5,6
to give to the * and piled them up 2Ch 31:5,6
the * and praised his people! 2Ch 31:7,8
the * has blessed his people." 2Ch 31:10
in the sight of the * his God. 2Ch 31:20
while we have the * our God to 2Ch 32:8
that "the * our God will deliver 2Ch 32:11
mocked the * God and God's servant 2Ch 32:16
scorning the * God of Israel. 2Ch 32:17
heaven, and the * sent an angel 2Ch 32:21
That is how the * saved Hezekiah 2Ch 32:22
many gifts for the * arrived at 2Ch 32:23
he prayed to the *, and the Lord 2Ch 32:24
and the * replied with a miracle. 2Ch 32:24
the wrath of the * did not fall 2Ch 32:26
destroyed by the * when the people 2Ch 33:2
the Temple of the *, for worshiping 2Ch 33:4,5
place where the * had said that he 2Ch 33:4,5
of evil, making the * very angry. 2Ch 33:6
the nations the * destroyed when 2Ch 33:9
Warnings from the * were ignored 2Ch 33:10
And the * listened, and answered 2Ch 33:13
that the * was really God! 2Ch 33:13
the altar of the * and offered 2Ch 33:16
Judah worship the * God of Israel. 2Ch 33:16
but only to the * their God. 2Ch 33:17
and plead with the * for me!" 2Ch 34:21
she replied, "The * God of Israel 2Ch 34:23
" 'Yes, the * will destroy this 2Ch 34:24
"But the * also says this to the 2Ch 34:26
Tell him, the * God of Israel says, 2Ch 34:26
you, says the *, and I will not 2Ch 34:27
to the king this word from the *. 2Ch 34:28
a pledge to the * to follow his 2Ch 34:31
to the * and to his people. 2Ch 35:3
of the * through Moses." 2Ch 35:6
sacrifices to the *, as it is 2Ch 35:12
the *, as Josiah had instructed. 2Ch 35:16
the laws of the *, all are written 2Ch 35:26
as far as the * was concerned. 2Ch 36:9
evil so far as the * was concerned, 2Ch 36:12
who gave him messages from the *. 2Ch 36:12
far as obeying the * God of Israel 2Ch 36:13
the Temple of the * in Jerusalem. 2Ch 36:14
the anger of the * could no longer 2Ch 36:16
Then the * brought the king of 2Ch 36:17
and old men. The * used the king of 2Ch 36:17
Thus the word of the * spoken 2Ch 36:21
of Persia, the * stirred up the 2Ch 36:22,23
given to me by the * God of heaven, 2Ch 36:22,23
task, and the * be with you." 2Ch 36:22,23
* fulfilled Jeremiah's prophecy Ez 1:1
evening burnt offerings to the *; Ez 3:3
regular annual feasts of the *. Ez 3:5
the burnt offerings to the *. Ez 3:6
to praise the * in the manner Ez 3:10
But because the * was overseeing Ez 5:5
Israelis in worshiping the * God. Ez 6:21,22
land because the * had caused the Ez 6:21,22
for the * his God was blessing Ez 7:6
for the * gave them a good trip. Ez 7:7,8,9
the laws of the * and to become a Ez 7:10
Well, praise the * God of our Ez 7:27
the Temple of the * in Jerusalem! Ez 7:27
because the * my God was with me; Ez 7:28
I consecrated these men to the * Ez 8:28
to the * God of our fathers. Ez 8:28
Finally I stood before the * in Ez 9:5
my hands to the *, and cried out, Ez 9:5
escapes. O * God of Israel, you Ez 9:15
Confess your sin to the * God of Ez 10:11
"O * God," I cried out; Neh 1:5

(LORD Con't)

O *, please hear my prayer!	Neh 1:11
Then I prayed, "Hear us, O *	Neh 4:4
Remember the * who is great and	Neh 4:14
"Amen," and praised the *.	Neh 5:13
(O * God, please strengthen me!	Neh 6:9
Then the * told me to call	Neh 7:5
Then Ezra blessed the *, the	Neh 8:6
and worshiped the * with their	Neh 8:6
day before the * your God— it is a	Neh 8:9
the joy of the * is your strength.	Neh 8:10
And everyone worshiped the *	Neh 9:3
the * God with songs of joy.	Neh 9:4
up and praise the * your God, for	Neh 9:5
"You are the * God who chose	Neh 9:7
we again promise to serve the *!	Neh 9:38
before the *, Satan, the Accuser,	Job 1:6
the * asked Satan.	Job 1:7
Then the * asked Satan, "Have	Job 1:8
And the * replied to Satan, "You	Job 1:12,13
when I die. The * gave me	Job 1:21
Blessed be the name of the *."	Job 1:21
before the *, and Satan with them.	Job 2:1
the * asked Satan.	Job 2:2
the * asked.	Job 2:3
as you please," the * replied;	Job 2:6
presence of the * and struck Job	Job 2:7
chastening of the * when you sin.	Job 5:17
For the * has struck me down	Job 6:4
"Who doesn't know that the *	Job 12:7,8,9
in the *, and look up to God.	Job 22:26
to fear the * is true wisdom;	Job 28:28
THEN THE * answered Job from the	Job 38:1
THE * WENT ON:	Job 40:1
Then the * spoke to Job again	Job 40:6
After the * had finished speaking	Job 42:7
did as the * commanded them, and	Job 42:9
them, and the * accepted Job's	Job 42:9
his friends, the * restored his	Job 42:10
In fact, the * gave him twice as	Job 42:10
trials the * had brought upon him.	Job 42:11
So the * blessed Job at the end	Job 42:12
For the * watches over all the	Ps 1:6
nations are to rage against the *!	Ps 2:1
plot against the * and his Messiah,	Ps 2:2
For the * declares,	Ps 2:6
* has said to me, 'You are my Son.	Ps 2:7
Serve the * with reverent fear;	Ps 2:11
O *, SO many are against me.	Ps 3:1
help me. But *, you are my shield,	Ps 3:3
I cried out to the *, and he	Ps 3:4
for the * was watching over me.	Ps 3:5
I will cry to him, "Arise, O *!	Ps 3:7
The * God asks, "Sons of men,	Ps 4:2
Mark this well: The * has set	Ps 4:3
Stand before the * in awe,	Ps 4:4
Put your trust in the *, and	Ps 4:5
O *, by letting the light of your	Ps 4:6
alone, O *, you will keep me safe.	Ps 4:8
O *, HEAR me praying;	Ps 5:1
*, lead me as you promised me you	Ps 5:8
For you bless the godly man, O *	Ps 5:12
NO, *!	Ps 6:1
Pity me, O *, for I am weak.	Ps 6:2
Come, O *, and make me well.	Ps 6:4
deeds, for the * has heard my	Ps 6:8
I AM DEPENDING on you, O * my	Ps 7:1
It would be different, *, if I	Ps 7:3
But *!	Ps 7:6
Demand justice for me, *!	Ps 7:6
End all wickedness, O *, and	Ps 7:9
am to the * because he is so good.	Ps 7:17
of the * who is above all lords.	Ps 7:17
O * OUR God, the majesty and glory	Ps 8:1
O Jehovah, our *, the majesty	Ps 8:9
O *, I will praise you with all my	Ps 9:1
I will sing your praises, O * God	Ps 9:2
The * will destroy your cities;	Ps 9:6
But the * lives on forever;	Ps 9:7,8
All those who know your mercy, *	Ps 9:10
And now, O *, have mercy on me;	Ps 9:13
those who hate me. *, snatch me	Ps 9:13
on them. The * is famous for the	Ps 9:16
all the nations forgetting the *.	Ps 9:17
O *, arise and judge and punish	Ps 9:19
*, WHY ARE you standing aloof and	Ps 10:1
those the * abhors, whose only goal	Ps 10:3
O *, arise!	Ps 10:12
*, you see what they are doing.	Ps 10:14
Now punish them. O *, the poor	Ps 10:14
The * is King forever and	Ps 10:16
*, you know the hopes of humble	Ps 10:17
when I am trusting in the *?	Ps 11:1
But the * is still in his holy	Ps 11:4
*! HELP!	Ps 12:1
But the * will not deal gently	Ps 12:3,4
The * replies, "I will arise	Ps 12:5
times refined. O *, we know that	Ps 12:7
HOW LONG WILL you forget me, *?	Ps 13:1
Answer me, O * my God;	Ps 13:3
I will sing to the * because he	Ps 13:6
The * looks down from heaven on	Ps 14:2
What gladness when the * has	Ps 14:7
*, WHO MAY go and find refuge and	Ps 15:1
followers of the *, keeps a promise	Ps 15:4
I said to him, "You are my *;	Ps 16:2
The * himself is my inheritance,	Ps 16:5
I will bless the * who counsels	Ps 16:7
I am always thinking of the *;	Ps 16:8
I AM PLEADING for your help, O *;	Ps 17:1
Publicly acquit me, *, for you	Ps 17:2
*, arise and stand against them.	Ps 17:13,14
at a time when the * had delivered	Ps 18:1
*, HOW I love you!	Ps 18:1
The * is my fort where I can	Ps 18:2
him—oh, praise the *—and I am saved	Ps 18:3
I screamed to the * for his help.	Ps 18:6
The * thundered in the heavens;	Ps 18:13
Then at your command, O *, the	Ps 18:15
But the * held me steady.	Ps 18:18
in me. The * rewarded me for doing	Ps 18:20
And so the * has paid me with	Ps 18:24
*, how merciful you are to those	Ps 18:25
on my light! The * my God has made	Ps 18:28
For who is God except our *?	Ps 18:31
Your right hand, O *, supports	Ps 18:35
they cried to the *, but he	Ps 18:41
For this, O *, I will praise you	Ps 18:49
the worship of the * are pure and	Ps 19:9f
you, O * my Rock and my Redeemer.	Ps 19:14
IN YOUR DAY of trouble, may the *	Ps 20:1
but our boast is in the * our God.	Ps 20:7
Give victory to our king, O *;	Ps 20:9
rejoices in your strength, O *!	Ps 21:1
king trusts in the *, he will never	Ps 21:7
Your hand, O *, will find your	Ps 21:8
your presence. The * will destroy	Ps 21:9,10
plot against you, *, but they	Ps 21:11
Accept our praise, O *, for all	Ps 21:13
who rolled his burden on the *?"	Ps 22:8
who claims the * delights in him?	Ps 22:8
*, how you have helped me before!	Ps 22:9,10,11
O *, don't stay away.	Ps 22:19
"Praise the *, each one of you	Ps 22:23
all who seek the * shall find him	Ps 22:26
shall see it and return to the *;	Ps 22:27
For the * is King and rules the	Ps 22:28
us about the wonders of the *;	Ps 22:30
BECAUSE THE * is my Shepherd, I	Ps 23:1
of the * and enter where he lives?	Ps 24:3
Who may stand before the *?	Ps 24:3
* and worship the God of Jacob.	Ps 24:6
Who is this King of Glory? The *	Ps 24:8
TO YOU, O *, I pray.	Ps 25:1
Don't fail me, *, for I am	Ps 25:2
the path where I should go, O *;	Ps 25:4
Overlook my youthful sins, O *!	Ps 25:6,7
The * is good and glad to teach	Ps 25:8
But *, my sins!	Ps 25:11
Where is the man who fears the *?	Ps 25:12
My eyes are ever looking to the *	Ps 25:15
Come, *, and show me your mercy,	Ps 25:16
against me, *, for I have tried to	Ps 26:1
Cross-examine me, O *, and see	Ps 26:2
*, I love your home, this shrine	Ps 26:8
No, I am not like that, O *;	Ps 26:11
I publicly praise the * for	Ps 26:12
THE * IS my light and my	Ps 27:1
Listen to my pleading, *!	Ps 27:7
And my heart responds, "*, I	Ps 27:8
Tell me what to do, O *, and make	Ps 27:11
Don't let them get me, *!	Ps 27:12
I am expecting the * to rescue	Ps 27:13
Wait for the *, and he will come	Ps 27:14
I PLEAD WITH you to help me, *,	Ps 28:1
die. *, I lift my hands to heaven	Ps 28:2
Oh, praise the *, for he has	Ps 28:6
to him. The * protects his people	Ps 28:8
Defend your people, *;	Ps 28:9
PRAISE THE *, you angels of his;	Ps 29:1
The voice of the * echoes from	Ps 29:3
The voice of the * thunders	Ps 29:7
The voice of the * spins and	Ps 29:9
"Glory, glory to the *."	Ps 29:9
At the Flood, the * showed his	Ps 29:10
I WILL PRAISE you, *, for you have	Ps 30:1
over me. O * my God, I pleaded	Ps 30:2
nothing can stop me now! The *	Ps 30:6,7
Then, *, you turned your face	Ps 30:6,7
I cried to you, O *;	Ps 30:8
you gain, O *, from killing me?	Ps 30:9
Hear me, *;	Ps 30:10
praises to the * instead of lying	Ps 30:12
in the grave. O * my God, I will	Ps 30:12
*, I TRUST in you alone.	Ps 31:1
O *, have mercy on me in my	Ps 31:9,10
But I was trusting you, O *.	Ps 31:14,15
Don't disgrace me, *, by not	Ps 31:17
Blessed is the *, for he has	Ps 31:21
when I said, "The * has deserted	Ps 31:22
Oh, love the *, all of you who	Ps 31:23
for the * protects those who are	Ps 31:23
if you are depending on the *.	Ps 31:2
"I will confess them to the *."	Ps 32:
I will instruct you (says the *)	Ps 32:8
those who trust in the *.	Ps 32:10
*, for it is right to praise him.	Ps 33:1
the * and stand in awe of him.	Ps 33:8
whose God is the *, whose people he	Ps 33:12
as his own. The * gazes down upon	Ps 33:13,14,15
But the eyes of the * are	Ps 33:18,19
We depend upon the * alone to	Ps 33:20
No wonder we are happy in the *!	Ps 33:21
Yes, *, let your constant love	Ps 33:22
I WILL PRAISE the * no matter what	Ps 34:1
Let us praise the * together,	Ps 34:3
This poor man cried to the *—and	Ps 34:6
the Lord—and the * heard him and	Ps 34:6
For the Angel of the * guards	Ps 34:7
If you belong to the *,	Ps 34:9
* will never lack any good thing.	Ps 34:10
of trusting and fearing the *.	Ps 34:11
For the eyes of the * are	Ps 34:15
But the * has made up his mind	Ps 34:16
Yes, the * hears the good man	Ps 34:17
The * is close to those whose	Ps 34:18
But the * helps him in each and	Ps 34:19
But as for those who serve the *	Ps 34:22
O *, FIGHT those fighting me;	Ps 35:1
sent by the Angel of the *.	Ps 35:5
the Angel of the * pursuing them.	Ps 35:6
But I will rejoice in the *.	Ps 35:9
mourned before the * in sackcloth,	Ps 35:13
*, how long will you stand there,	Ps 35:17
it." *, you know all about it.	Ps 35:22
Rise up, O * my God;	Ps 35:23
* who enjoys helping his child!"	Ps 35:27
Your steadfast love, O *, is as	Ps 36:5
Trust in the * instead.	Ps 37:3
Be delighted with the *.	Ps 37:4
Commit everything you do to the *.	Ps 37:5
Rest in the *;	Ps 37:7
* shall be given every blessing.	Ps 37:9
before the * shall be given every	Ps 37:11
The * is laughing at those who	Ps 37:12,13
be broken, but the * takes care of	Ps 37:17
Day by day the * observes the	Ps 37:18
Those blessed by the * shall	Ps 37:22
of good men are directed by the *.	Ps 37:23
the * holds them with his hand.	Ps 37:24
the * forsake a man who loves him;	Ps 37:25
For the * loves justice and	Ps 37:28
But the * will not let these	Ps 37:33
Don't be impatient for the * to	Ps 37:34
The * saves the godly!	Ps 37:39
O *, DON'T punish me while you are	Ps 38:1
*, you know how I long for my	Ps 38:9
For I am waiting for you, O * my	Ps 38:15
Don't leave me, *;	Ps 38:21
pled with God: *, help me to	Ps 39:4
And so, *, my only hope is in	Ps 39:7
*, I am speechless before you.	Ps 39:9
*, don't hit me anymore—I am	Ps 39:10
Hear my prayer, O *;	Ps 39:12
Spare me, *!	Ps 39:13
the *, and put their trust in him.	Ps 40:3
who trust the *, and have no	Ps 40:4
O * my God, many and many a time	Ps 40:5
about it, as you well know, O *.	Ps 40:9
O *, don't hold back your tender	Ps 40:11
Please, *, rescue me!	Ps 40:13
But may the joy of the * be given	Ps 40:16
I am poor and needy, yet the * is	Ps 40:17
"O *," I prayed, "be kind and	Ps 41:4
how often we ate together. *,	Ps 41:10
Be gracious, *, and make me well	Ps 41:10
Bless the *, the God of Israel,	Ps 41:13
singing with joy, praising the *?	Ps 42:4,5
Yet day by day the * also pours	Ps 42:8
And yet for a time, O *, you	Ps 44:9
And all this has happened, *,	Ps 44:17
Don't sleep, O *!	Ps 44:23
Rise up, O *, and come and help	Ps 44:26
Reverence him, for he is your *.	Ps 45:10,11
Shout triumphant praises to the *	Ps 47:1
For the *, the God above all	Ps 47:2
HOW GREAT IS the *!	Ps 48:1
*, here in your Temple we	Ps 48:9
THE MIGHTY GOD, the *, has	Ps 50:1
will receive salvation from the *.	Ps 50:23
And *, don't punish Israel for my	Ps 51:18
tree protected by the * himself.	Ps 52:8
and ever. O *, I will praise you	Ps 52:9
Only when the * himself restores	Ps 53:6
Literally, "The * is of them that	Ps 54:4f
I will praise your name, O *, for	Ps 54:6
Hear me, *!	Ps 55:2
O *, make these enemies begin to	Ps 55:9
the Temple of the * on holy days.	Ps 55:14
But I will call upon the * to	Ps 55:16
Give your burdens to the *.	Ps 55:22
*, HAVE MERCY on me;	Ps 56:1
Don't let them, *.	Ps 56:7

LORD Con't)

*, and thank you for your help. Ps 56:12
the * in the land of the living. Ps 56:13
Their tongues are like swords. * Ps 57:5
the teeth of these young lions, *. Ps 58:6
And not, O *, because I've done Ps 59:3
Yet they prepare to kill me. *, Ps 59:4
they think. *, laugh at them! Ps 59:8
Bring them to the dust, O * our Ps 59:11
*, restore us again to your favor. Ps 60:1
you have torn it apart. *, heal Ps 60:2
Yes, *, help us against our Ps 60:11
And I shall live before the * Ps 61:7
I STAND SILENTLY before the *, Ps 62:1
*, waiting for him to rescue me. Ps 62:5
*, LISTEN TO my complaint: Oh, Ps 64:1
the *, and trust and praise him. Ps 64:10
SING TO THE *, all the earth! Ps 66:1
O *, like silver in a crucible. Ps 66:10
who reverence the *, and I will Ps 66:16
the earth will praise the *! Ps 67:3
Sing praises to the *! Ps 68:4
The * speaks. The enemy flees. Ps 68:11,12,13
chariots, the * moves on from Mount Ps 68:17
What a glorious *! Ps 68:19
ways. The * says, "Come," to all Ps 68:22
the *, who is Israel's fountain. Ps 68:26
Rebuke our enemies, O *. Ps 68:30
Sing to the *, O kingdoms of the Ps 68:32
praises to the *, to him who rides Ps 68:32
all my sins. O * God of the armies Ps 69:6
I mourn and fast before the *! Ps 69:10
I keep right on praying to you, *. Ps 69:13
Come, *, and rescue me. Ps 69:18
RESCUE ME, O God! *, hurry to my Ps 70:1
and save me. O *, don't delay. Ps 70:5
*, YOU ARE my refuge! Ps 71:1
men. O *, you alone are my hope; Ps 71:5
I walk in the strength of the * Ps 71:16
Your power and goodness, *, Ps 71:19
of those who hate the *. Ps 73:16
to the ground—your sanctuary, *. Ps 74:7
the winter too. *, see how these Ps 74:18
O *, save me! Ps 74:19
and cruel men. O *, don't let your Ps 74:21
HOW WE THANK you, *! Ps 75:1
"Yes," the * replies, "and Ps 75:2
of evil men," says the *, Ps 75:10
I CRY TO the *; Ps 77:1
Has the * rejected me forever? Ps 77:7
the anger of the * rose against Ps 78:31
Then the * rose up as though Ps 78:65
by saving them. O *, take Ps 79:12
THE * MAKES us strong! Ps 81:1
Those who hate the * would Ps 81:15
these proud men who hate the *? Ps 83:2
your power and name, O *. Ps 83:16
HOW LOVELY IS your Temple, O * of Ps 84:1
their young, O * of heaven's Ps 84:3
are strong in the *, who want above Ps 84:5
to meet with the * in Zion. Ps 84:7
O * of the armies of heaven, Ps 84:12
*, YOU HAVE poured out amazing Ps 85:1
O *, so that your anger will Ps 85:4
*, and grant us your salvation. Ps 85:7
to all the * is saying—for he Ps 85:8
Yes, the * pours down his Ps 85:12
DOWN AND hear my prayer, O *, Ps 86:1
Be merciful, O *, for I am Ps 86:3
Give me happiness, O *, for I Ps 86:4
only you. O *, you are so good and Ps 86:5
bow before you, *, and praise your Ps 86:9
and gentle, *, slow in getting Ps 86:15
Each day I beg your help; O *, I Ps 88:9
O *, I plead for my life and will Ps 88:13
the tender kindness of the *! Ps 89:1
The * God says, Ps 89:3,4
shall praise your miracles, O *; Ps 89:5
is from the * himself and he, the Ps 89:18
*, where is the love you used to Ps 89:49
faithful pledge? *, see how all Ps 89:50
And yet—blessed be the * forever! Ps 89:52
*, THROUGH ALL the generations you Ps 90:1
do, and let the * our God favor us Ps 90:17
For the * says, "Because he Ps 91:14
you" to the *, to sing praises to Ps 92:1
You have done so much for me, O *. Ps 92:4
O *, what miracles you do! Ps 92:5
But the * continues forever, Ps 92:8
This honors the *, and exhibits Ps 92:15
O *, you have reigned from Ps 93:1
* GOD, TO whom vengeance belongs, Ps 94:1
they deserve. *, how long shall Ps 94:3
O *, afflicting those you love. Ps 94:5
orphans, for "The * isn't Ps 94:6,7
The * is fully aware of how Ps 94:11
them. The * will not forsake his Ps 94:14
I would have died unless the * Ps 94:17
I screamed, "I'm slipping, *!" Ps 94:18
*, when doubts fill my mind, when Ps 94:19
No! The * my God is my Ps 94:21,22
OH, COME, LET us sing to the *! Ps 95:1
For the * is a great God, the Ps 95:3
Come, kneel before the * our Ps 95:6
them in disgust," the * God says. Ps 95:10
SING A NEW song to the *! Ps 96:1
For the * is great beyond Ps 96:4
Worship the * with the beauty of Ps 96:9
For the * is coming to judge the Ps 96:13
wax before the * of all the earth. Ps 97:5
of your justice, *, and are glad Ps 97:8,9
The * loves those who hate evil; Ps 97:10
godly be happy in the * and crown Ps 97:12
SING A NEW song to the * telling Ps 98:1
symphony before the *, the King! Ps 98:6
on it shout, "Glory to the *." Ps 98:7
of joy before the *, for he is Ps 98:8,9
Exalt the * our holy God! Ps 99:5
Exalt the * our God, and worship Ps 99:9
SHOUT WITH JOY before the *, O Ps 100:1
what this means—the * is God! Ps 100:3
For the * is always good. Ps 100:5
and your justice, *. Ps 101:1
*, HEAR MY prayer! Ps 102:1
you, *, are a famous King forever. Ps 102:12
before the *, before his glory. Ps 102:15
the * for all that he has done. Ps 102:18
be created shall praise the *. Ps 102:18
Yes, I will bless the * and not Ps 103:2
But the lovingkindness of the * Ps 103:17,18
The * has made the heavens his Ps 103:19
Bless the *, you mighty angels Ps 103:20
Yes, bless the *, you armies of Ps 103:21
everything everywhere bless the *. Ps 103:22
I BLESS THE *: O Lord my God, how Ps 104:1
I BLESS THE Lord: O * my God, how Ps 104:1
* planted the cedars of Lebanon. Ps 104:16
but they are dependent on the *. Ps 104:21
O *, what a variety you have made! Ps 104:24
I will sing to the * as long as I Ps 104:33
THANK THE * for all the glorious Ps 105:1
Glory in the *; Ps 105:3
He is the * our God. Ps 105:7
THANK YOU, *! Ps 106:1
Remember me too, O *, while you Ps 106:4
So the * declared he would Ps 106:23
O * God, save us! Ps 106:47
Blessed be the *, the God of Ps 106:48
SAY "THANK YOU" to the * for Ps 107:1
Has the * redeemed you? Ps 107:2
thirsty and faint. "*, help!" Ps 107:6
would praise the * for his Ps 107:8
They rebelled against the *, Ps 107:11
Then they cried to the * in Ps 107:13
would praise the * for his Ps 107:15
Then they cried to the * in Ps 107:19
would praise the * for his Ps 107:21
Then they cry to the * in their Ps 107:28
would praise the * for his Ps 107:31
about the lovingkindness of the *! Ps 107:43
*, have you thrown us away? Ps 108:11
But as for me, O *, deal with me Ps 109:21
Because you are so kind, O *, Ps 109:21
Help me, O * my God! Ps 109:26
the *, praising him to everyone. Ps 109:30
JEHOVAH SAID TO my * the Messiah, Ps 110:1
Literally, "The * will send forth Ps 110:2f
PRAISE THE *! Ps 112:1
Praise the *. Ps 113:9
of the *, the God of Jacob. Ps 114:7
YOUR NAME, not ours, O *! Ps 115:1
O Israel, trust the *! Ps 115:9
O priests of Aaron, trust the *! Ps 115:10
May the * richly bless both you Ps 115:14
The heavens belong to the *, but Ps 115:16
Praise the *! Ps 115:18
I LOVE THE * because he hears my Ps 116:1
Then I cried, "*, save me!" Ps 116:4
God of ours! The * protects the Ps 116:6
For the * has done this wonderful Ps 116:7
* is the death of his saints." Ps 116:15f
O *, you have freed me from my Ps 116:16
pay everything I vowed to the *. Ps 116:18,19
Praise the *. Ps 116:18,19
PRAISE THE *, all nations Ps 117:1
Praise the *. Ps 117:2
OH, THANK THE *, for he's so good! Ps 118:1
In my distress I prayed to the * Ps 118:5
* is on my side, he will help me. Ps 118:7
It is better to trust the * than Ps 118:8
O my enemy, but the * helped me. Ps 118:13
The strong arm of the * has done Ps 118:15,16
his deeds. The * has punished me, Ps 118:18
the *, and the godly enter there. Ps 118:20
enter there. O *, thank you so Ps 118:21
This is the day the * has made. Ps 118:24
glad in it. O *, please help us. Ps 118:25
Literally, "in the name of the Ps 118:26f
by the *. Ps 118:26
Oh, give thanks to the *, for he Ps 118:29
Blessed *, teach me your rules. Ps 119:12
closely as I can. *, don't let me Ps 119:31
me what to do and I will do it, *. Ps 119:33,34
your promise—yes, *, to save me! Ps 119:40,41,42
and keep my thoughts, O *, on you. Ps 119:55
and trusts the * and obeys him. Ps 119:63
and obeys him. O *, the earth is Ps 119:64
*, I am overflowing with your Ps 119:65
You made my body, *; Ps 119:73
I know, O *, that your decisions Ps 119:75,76,77
Forever, O *, your Word stands Ps 119:89
*, you promised to let me live! Ps 119:116
to rescue me. *, deal with me in Ps 119:124
*, it is time for you to act. Ps 119:126
O *, you are just and your Ps 119:137
answer me, O *, and I will obey Ps 119:145
but you are near, O *; Ps 119:151
laws. *, how great is your mercy; Ps 119:156
for your laws. *, see how much I Ps 119:159
I long for your salvation, *, Ps 119:166
O *, listen to my prayers; Ps 119:169
your will. O *, I have longed for Ps 119:174
Deliver me, O *, from liars. Ps 120:2
*, these men of Meshech and Kedar. Ps 120:5,6
Jerusalem, to the Temple of the *. Ps 122:1
to thank and praise the *. Ps 122:4
protection to the Temple of the *. Ps 122:9
Have mercy on us, *, have mercy. Ps 123:3,4
IF THE * had not been on our side Ps 124:1
admit it), if the * had not been on Ps 124:1
Our help is from the * who made Ps 124:8
THOSE WHO TRUST in the * are Ps 125:1
Jerusalem, so the * surrounds and Ps 125:2
to do wrong. O *, do good to those Ps 125:4
whose hearts are right with the *; Ps 125:4
things the * has done for them." Ps 126:2
"Restore our fortunes, *." Ps 126:4f
UNLESS THE * builds a house, the Ps 127:1
Unless the * protects a city, Ps 127:1
trust the *—on all who obey him! Ps 128:1
May the * continually bless you Ps 128:5
with their whips, the * is good. Ps 129:3,4
O *, FROM the depths of despair I Ps 130:1
*, if you keep in mind our sins Ps 130:3,4
O Israel, hope in the *; Ps 130:7
*, I AM not proud and haughty. Ps 131:1
I am quiet now before the *, Ps 131:2
trust in the *—now, and always. Ps 131:3
*, DO YOU remember that time when Ps 132:1
of the *, a Temple for the mighty Ps 132:2-5
I made a solemn promise to the *. Ps 132:2-5
Arise, O *, and enter your Ps 132:8
O *, you have chosen Jerusalem Ps 132:13
OH, BLESS THE *, you who serve him Ps 134:1
hands in holiness and bless the *. Ps 134:2
The * bless you from Zion—the Ps 134:3
* who made heaven and earth. Ps 134:3
Praise the * because he is so Ps 135:3
For the * has chosen Israel as Ps 135:4
I know the greatness of the Ps 135:5
O Levite priests, bless the * Ps 135:20
Literally, "the * be blessed from Ps 135:21f
praise the *, for he lives here Ps 135:21
OH, GIVE THANKS to the *, for he Ps 136:1
Give thanks to the * of lords, Ps 136:3
Praise the * who opened the Red Ps 136:13
*, WITH ALL my heart I thank you. Ps 138:1
give you thanks, O *, for all of Ps 138:4
Your power will save me. The * Ps 138:8
*, continues forever. Ps 138:8
O*, YOU have examined my heart Ps 139:1
How precious it is, *, to realize Ps 139:17,18
you will slay the wicked, *! Ps 139:19
can they be? O *, shouldn't I hate Ps 139:21
O *, DELIVER me from evil men. Ps 140:1
O Jehovah, my * and Savior, my Ps 140:6,7,8
But the * will surely help those Ps 140:12
QUICK, *, ANSWER me—for I have Ps 141:1
Help me, *, to keep my mouth shut Ps 141:3
I look to you for help, O * God. Ps 141:8
Then I prayed to Jehovah. "*," Ps 142:5
HEAR MY PRAYER, O *; Ps 143:1
Come quickly, *, and answer me, Ps 143:7
Save me from my enemies, O *, I Ps 143:9
*, saving me will bring glory to Ps 143:11
BLESS THE * who is my immovable Ps 144:1
O *, what is man that you even Ps 144:3
Bend down the heavens, *, and Ps 144:5
your arrows, *, upon your enemies, Ps 144:6
*, and your people will bless you. Ps 145:10
The * lifts the fallen and those Ps 145:14
The * is fair in everything he Ps 145:17
I will praise the * and call on Ps 145:21
PRAISE THE *! Ps 146:1
hope is in the * his God— the God Ps 146:5
For the * loves good men. Ps 146:8
The * will reign forever. Ps 146:10
Praise the *! Ps 146:10
YES, PRAISE the *! Ps 147:1
is unlimited. The * supports the Ps 147:6
Yes, praise the *! Ps 147:20
PRAISE THE *, O heavens! Ps 148:1
all praise the * together. Ps 148:13

(LORD Con't)

Yes, praise the *!	Ps 148:14
YES, PRAISE the *!	Ps 149:1
YES, PRAISE the *!	Ps 150:1
alive give praises to the *!	Ps 150:6
is to trust and reverence the *!	Pro 1:7,8,9
and trust the *, and you turned	Pro 1:29
for the * and of trusting him.	Pro 2:3,4,5
For the * grants wisdom!	Pro 2:6
Only wisdom from the * can save a	Pro 2:16,17
then trust the * completely;	Pro 3:4,5
the *, and turn your back on evil;	Pro 3:7,8
Honor the * by giving him the	Pro 3:9,10
him better, so the * corrects you.	Pro 3:11,12
wicked men, for the * is with you;	Pro 3:24,25,26
abomination to the *, but he gives	Pro 3:32
the upright. The * mocks at	Pro 3:34
For there are six things the *	Pro 6:16-19
I fill their treasuries. The *	Pro 8:22
life and wins approval from the *.	Pro 8:35
The * will not let a good man	Pro 10:3
THE * HATES cheating and delights	Pro 11:1
The * hates the stubborn but	Pro 11:20
The * blesses good men and	Pro 12:2
Reverence for the * is a fountain	Pro 14:27
The * is watching everywhere and	Pro 15:3
The * hates the gifts of the	Pro 15:8
The * despises the deeds of the	Pro 15:9,10
If they stop trying, the * will	Pro 15:9,10
The * destroys the possessions of	Pro 15:25
The * hates the thoughts of the	Pro 15:26
The * is far from the wicked, but	Pro 15:29
Humility and reverence for the *	Pro 15:33
are right, but is the * convinced?	Pro 16:2
Commit your work to the *, then	Pro 16:3
The * has made everything for his	Pro 16:4
Pride disgusts the *.	Pro 16:5
The * demands fairness in every	Pro 16:11
man who puts his trust in the *.	Pro 16:20
but it is the * who controls its	Pro 16:33
The * despises those who say that	Pro 17:15
The *	Pro 18:10
Literally, "The name of the *."	Pro 18:10f
is a blessing to him from the *.	Pro 18:22
and then blame it on the *!	Pro 19:3
but only the * can give them	Pro 19:14
are lending to the *—and he pays	Pro 19:17
The * despises every kind of	Pro 20:10
Wait for the * to handle the	Pro 20:22
The * loathes all cheating and	Pro 20:23
Since the * is directing our	Pro 20:24
to the * before counting the cost.	Pro 20:25
the * directs the king's thoughts.	Pro 21:1
he is, can stand against the *.	Pro 21:30
before the * who made them all.	Pro 22:2
respect for the * lead a man to	Pro 22:4
The * preserves the upright but	Pro 22:12
it on to others: Trust in the *.	Pro 22:17,18,19
For the * is their defender.	Pro 22:22,23
to reverence the * all the time,	Pro 23:17,18
he falls— for the * may be	Pro 24:18
step before the * and the king, and	Pro 24:21,22
the * are much concerned about it.	Pro 28:5
the judge, but ask the * for it!	Pro 29:26
dedicated to the *, do not spend	Pro 31:2
long the * may let him live.	Ecc 5:18
wealth from the *, and the good	Ecc 5:19,20
earth, to what the * is saying:	Is 1:2
backs upon the *, and have despised	Is 1:4
If the * of Hosts had not stepped	Is 1:9
Listen to the *.	Is 1:10
says the *;	Is 1:18
I, the *, have spoken.	Is 1:20
Therefore the * of Hosts, the	Is 1:24
Those who return to the *, who	Is 1:27
* concerning Judah and Jerusalem:	Is 2:1
the Temple of the * will become the	Is 2:2
will flow there to worship the *.	Is 2:2
mountain of the *, to the Temple of	Is 2:3
Jerusalem. The * will settle	Is 2:4
*, and be obedient to his laws!	Is 2:5
The * has rejected you because	Is 2:6
low; the * alone will be exalted.	Is 2:11
On that day the * of Hosts will	Is 2:12
be crushed before the * that day.	Is 2:16
and the * alone will be exalted.	Is 2:17
When the * stands up from his	Is 2:19
the terror of the * and the glory	Is 2:21
THE * OF Hosts will cut off	Is 3:1
their * and will not worship him;	Is 3:8
The * stands up!	Is 3:13
the * of Hosts will demand of	Is 3:15
of the men. The * will send a	Is 3:17
For the * will strip away their	Is 3:18
"branch of the *," sometimes	Is 4:2,3,4f
Then the * will provide shade on	Is 4:5
But the * of Hosts has sworn	Is 5:9
But for the * you have no thought	Is 5:12
but the * of Hosts is exalted	Is 5:16
and dare the * to punish them.	Is 5:19
"Hurry up and punish us, O *,"	Is 5:19

That is why the anger of the *	Is 5:25
YEAR KING Uzziah died I saw the *!	Is 6:1
holy, holy is the * of Hosts;	Is 6:3
King, the * of heaven's armies."	Is 6:5
Then I heard the * asking, "Whom	Is 6:8
And I said, "*, I'll go!	Is 6:8
Then I said, "*, how long will	Is 6:11
Then the * said to Isaiah, "Go	Is 7:3
to quit worrying," the * said.	Is 7:4
"But the * God says, This plan	Is 7:7
Not long after this, the * sent	Is 7:10
the * with anything like that."	Is 7:12
All right then, the * himself	Is 7:14
the * will bring a terrible curse	Is 7:17
At that time the * will whistle	Is 7:18
In that day the * will take this	Is 7:20
AGAIN THE * sent me a message:	Is 8:1
me a son, and the * said, "Call	Is 8:3
Then the * spoke to me again and	Is 8:5
The * has said in strongest	Is 8:11
Don't fear anything except the *	Is 8:13
*, and seal it up for the future.	Is 8:16
I will wait for the * to help us,	Is 8:17
the plans of the * of heaven's	Is 8:18
happen because the * of heaven's	Is 9:7
The * has spoken out against that	Is 9:8,9,10
to him, the * of heaven's armies.	Is 9:13
Therefore the *, in one day,	Is 9:14,15
That is why the * has no joy in	Is 9:17
wrath of the * of heaven's armies.	Is 9:19,20
laws, says the *, so that there is	Is 10:1
After the * has used the king of	Is 10:12
But the * says, "Shall the axe	Is 10:15
of Assyria, the * of Hosts will	Is 10:16
be destroyed. The * will destroy	Is 10:18
will trust the *, the Holy One of	Is 10:20
* God of Hosts to consume them.	Is 10:23
Therefore the * God of Hosts	Is 10:24
The * of Hosts will send his	Is 10:26
Then, look, look! The *, the Lord	Is 10:33
The Lord, the * of the armies of	Is 10:33
And the Spirit of the * shall	Is 11:2
and of the fear of the *.	Is 11:2
will be obedience to the *.	Is 11:3
be full of the knowledge of the *.	Is 11:9
At that time the * will bring	Is 11:11
The * will dry a path through the	Is 11:15
DAY you will say, "Praise the *!	Is 12:1
for the * is my strength and song;	Is 12:2
day you will say, "Thank the *!	Is 12:4
Sing to the *, for he has done	Is 12:5
I, the *, have set apart these	Is 13:3
many nations. The * of Hosts has	Is 13:4
For see, the day of the * is	Is 13:9
BUT THE * will have mercy on the	Is 14:1
In that wonderful day when the *	Is 14:3
For the * has crushed your	Is 14:5
him, says the * of heaven's armies,	Is 14:22
the * of the armies of heaven.	Is 14:23
the world. The *, the God of	Is 14:27
Tell them that the * has founded	Is 14:32
but now the * says that within	Is 16:13,14
declares the * of Hosts.	Is 17:3
For the * has told me this: Let	Is 18:4
bring gifts to the * of Hosts in	Is 18:7
Look, the * is coming against	Is 19:1
vicious king, says the * of Hosts.	Is 19:4
the * is going to do to Egypt.	Is 19:12
counsel. The * has sent a spirit	Is 19:14
hearts, for the * of Hosts has laid	Is 19:17
will follow the * of Hosts and will	Is 19:18
be an altar to the * in the heart	Is 19:19
a monument to the * at its border.	Is 19:19
sign of loyalty to the * of Hosts;	Is 19:20
then when they cry to the * for	Is 19:20
In that day the * will make	Is 19:21
Yes, they will know the * and	Is 19:21
keep them. The * will smite Egypt	Is 19:22
will turn to the * and he will	Is 19:22
For the * will bless Egypt and	Is 19:25
captured it, the * told Isaiah,	Is 20:2
Then the * said, My servant	Is 20:3
the * had told me, "Put a	Is 21:6,7
you all that the * of Hosts, the	Is 21:10
says the *, "the great power of	Is 21:16
The *, the God of Israel, has	Is 21:17
from the * God of heaven's armies!	Is 22:5
it long ago. The * God of Hosts	Is 22:12
The * of Hosts has revealed to	Is 22:14
Furthermore, the same * God of	Is 22:15,16
For the * who allowed you to be	Is 22:17
office," says the *, "and pull	Is 22:19
But the * will pull out that	Is 22:25
with it, for the * has spoken.	Is 22:25
is gone. The * holds out his hand	Is 23:11
Yes, after seventy years, the *	Is 23:17
will give their profits to the *!	Is 23:18
clothes for the priests of the *!	Is 23:18
LOOK! THE * is overturning the	Is 24:1
and looted. The * has spoken.	Is 24:3
Hear them singing to the * from	Is 24:15,16

On that day the * will punish the	Is 24:2
Then the * of heaven's armies	Is 24:2
O *, I will honor and praise your	Is 25:
But to the poor, O *, you are a	Is 25:
in Jerusalem, the * of Hosts will	Is 25:
death forever. The * God will wipe	Is 25:
* has spoken—he will surely do it!	Is 25:
all may enter in who love the *.	Is 26:
thoughts turn often to the *!	Is 26:
Trust in the * God always, for	Is 26:
always, for in the * Jehovah is	Is 26:
O *, we love to do your will!	Is 26:
*, grant us peace;	Is 26:1
come from you. O * our God, once	Is 26:1
O praise the *!	Is 26:1
*, in their distress they sought	Is 26:1
How we missed your presence, *!	Is 26:1
Look! The * is coming from the	Is 26:2
IN THAT DAY the * will take his	Is 27:
I, the *, will tend the fruitful	Is 27:
will come when the * will gather	Is 27:1
the * in his holy mountain.	Is 27:1
For the * will send a mighty	Is 28:
Then at last the * of Hosts	Is 28:
So the * will spell it out for	Is 28:1
Therefore hear the word of the *,	Is 28:14
But the * God says, See, I am	Is 28:16
to cover you. The * will come	Is 28:21
greater, for the * God of Hosts has	Is 28:22
pounding it. The * of Hosts is a	Is 28:29
In an instant, I, the * of	Is 29:6
For the * has poured out upon	Is 29:10
And so the * says, "Since these	Is 29:13
fresh joy from the *, and the poor	Is 29:19
That is why the * who redeemed	Is 29:22
rebellious children, says the *;	Is 30:1
For the * God, the Holy One of	Is 30:15
Yet the * still waits for you to	Is 30:18
For the * is faithful to his	Is 30:18
So it will be when the * begins	Is 30:26
See, the * comes from afar,	Is 30:27
of the *, the Rock of Israel.	Is 30:29
And the * shall cause his	Is 30:30
The voice of the * shall punish	Is 30:31
And when the * smites them, his	Is 30:32
The breath of the *, like fire	Is 30:33
When the * clenches his fist	Is 31:3
But the * has told me this: When	Is 31:4,5
In such manner the * will come	Is 31:4,5
He, the * of Hosts, will hover	Is 31:4,5
flags of Israel, says the *.	Is 31:9
But to us, O *, be merciful, for	Is 33:2
The * is very great, and lives in	Is 33:5
But the * says, I will stand up	Is 33:10
The glorious * will be to us as	Is 33:21
For the * is our Judge, our	Is 33:22
for the * will forgive them their	Is 33:24
For the * is enraged against the	Is 34:2
The sword of the * is sated with	Is 34:6
For the * will slay a great	Is 34:6
Search the Book of the * and see	Is 34:16
a mate, for the * has said it, and	Is 34:16
for the * will display his glory	Is 35:2
These, the ransomed of the *,	Is 35:10
are trusting in the * our God!'	Is 36:7
* said to me, 'Go and destroy it!'	Is 36:10
trusting in the * by telling you	Is 36:15
by telling you the * won't let you	Is 36:15
* will deliver you from my armies.	Is 36:18
But perhaps the * your God heard	Is 37:4
Hezekiah that the * says, Don't be	Is 37:6
it out before the *, and prayed,	Is 37:14
saying, "O * of Hosts, God of	Is 37:16,17
It is true, O *, that the kings	Is 37:18
destroy them. O * our God, save us	Is 37:20
Hezekiah: "The * God of Israel	Is 37:21
"The * says to him: My	Is 37:22
your messengers to mock the *.	Is 37:24
against the *—and I heard it all!	Is 37:29
the power of the * of Hosts will	Is 37:32
not enter this city, says the *.	Is 37:34
That night the Angel of the *	Is 37:36
gave him this message from the *:	Is 38:1
"O *, don't you remember how	Is 38:3
So the * sent another message to	Is 38:4
"Go and tell Hezekiah that the *	Is 38:5
I will defend you, says the *,	Is 38:6
Never again will I see the * in	Is 38:11
bitterness. O *, your discipline	Is 38:16
Think of it! The * healed me!	Is 38:20
sign will the * give me to prove	Is 38:22
this message from the * of Hosts:	Is 39:5
"Whatever the * says is good.	Is 39:8
Her sins are pardoned, and the *	Is 40:2
for the * through the wilderness;	Is 40:3
The glory of the * will be seen	Is 40:5
The * has spoken—it shall be.	Is 40:5
Yes, the * God is coming with	Is 40:10
the Spirit of the * or be his	Is 40:13
you say that the * doesn't see your	Is 40:27
But they that wait upon the *	Is 40:31

(LORD Con't)
Who, indeed, but the *? Is 41:2
It is I, the *, the First and Is 41:4
right hand—I, the * your God—and I Is 41:13
I am the *, your Redeemer; Is 41:14
And the joy of the * shall fill Is 41:16
The * God who created the heavens Is 42:5
"I the * have called you to Is 42:6
I am the *! Is 42:8
Sing a new song to the *; Is 42:10
the * and sing his mighty power. Is 42:12
The * will be a mighty warrior, Is 42:13
one," the "Servant of the *"? Is 42:19
The * has magnified his law and Is 42:21
Did not the *? Is 42:24
It is the * they sinned against, Is 42:24
BUT NOW THE * who created you, O Is 43:1
For I am the * your God, your Is 43:3
witnesses, O Israel, says the *! Is 43:10
I am the *, and there is no Is 43:11
The *, your Redeemer, the Holy Is 43:14
I am the *, your Holy One, Is 43:15
I am the *, who opens a way Is 43:16
The * who made you, who will help Is 44:2
The *, the King of Israel, Is 44:6
Redeemer, the * of Hosts, who says Is 44:6
stand before the * in shame, along Is 44:11
Sing, O heavens, for the * has Is 44:23
for the * redeemed Jacob and is Is 44:23
in Israel! The *, your Redeemer Is 44:24
doing this—I, the *, the God of Is 45:3
mighty power; the * of Hosts is his Is 47:4
allegiance to the * without meaning Is 48:1
you this: "The * loves Cyrus. Is 48:14
And now the * God and his Spirit Is 48:16
message): The *, your Redeemer, Is 48:17
says, I am the * your God, who Is 48:17
the earth that the * has redeemed Is 48:20
peace, says the *, for the wicked. Is 48:22
The * called me before my birth. Is 49:1
"And now," said the *—the Lord Is 49:5
"And now," said the Lord—the * Is 49:5
The *, the Redeemer and Holy One Is 49:7
low because the * has chosen you; Is 49:7
he, the faithful *, the Holy One Is 49:7
The * says, "Your request has Is 49:8,9
For the * in his mercy will lead Is 49:10
mountains, for the * has comforted Is 49:13
Yet they say, "My * deserted us; Is 49:14
Look and see, for the * has Is 49:18
The * God says, "See, I will Is 49:22
then you shall know I am the *. Is 49:23
But the * says, "Even the Is 49:25
know that I, the *, am your Savior Is 49:26
THE * ASKS, Did I sell you to my Is 50:1
The * God has given me his words Is 50:4
to his will. The * God has spoken Is 50:5
Because the * God helps me, I Is 50:7
See, the * God is for me! Is 50:9
Who among you fears the * and Is 50:10
*, let them rely upon their God. Is 50:10
for deliverance, who seek the *! Is 51:1
And the * will bless Israel Is 51:3
Awake, O *! Is 51:9
For I am the * your God, the Is 51:15
Lord your God, the * of Hosts, who Is 51:15
from the cup of the fury of the *. Is 51:17
in a net. The * has poured out his Is 51:20
this is what the * says, the Lord Is 51:22
the Lord says, the * your God who Is 51:22
For the * says, When I sold you Is 52:3
asks the *. Is 52:5
* God bring his people home again. Is 52:8
the * has comforted his people; Is 52:9
he has redeemed Jerusalem. The * Is 52:10
You are the holy people of the *; Is 52:11
carry home the vessels of the *. Is 52:11
for the * will go ahead of you, Is 52:12
The Servant of the *, as the term Is 52:13f
here, is the Messiah, our * Jesus. Is 52:13f
The * of Hosts is his name; Is 54:5
For the * has called you back Is 54:6
on you, says the *, your Redeemer. Is 54:8
says the * who has mercy upon you. Is 54:10
heritage of the servants of the *. Is 54:17
I have given you, says the *. Is 54:17
* your God, have glorified you. Is 55:5
Seek the * while you can find Is 55:6
Let them turn to the * that he Is 55:7
BE JUST AND fair to all, the * God Is 56:1
too, when they accept the *; Is 56:3
the people of the * and serve him Is 56:6
For the * God who brings back Is 56:8
* will protect you from behind. Is 58:8
Then, when you call, the * will Is 58:9
And the * will guide you Is 58:11
and honoring the * in what you do, Is 58:13
idly— then the * will be your Is 58:14
your father. The * has spoken. Is 58:14
LISTEN NOW! THE * isn't too weak Is 59:1
we have denied the * our God. Is 59:13
soon attacked. The * saw all the Is 59:15
them," says the *: "My Holy Is 59:21
For the glory of the * is Is 60:1
of the * will shine from you. Is 60:2
see the glory of the * upon you. Is 60:3
"The City of the *" and "The Is 60:14
that I, the *, am your Savior and Is 60:16
you light, for the * your God will Is 60:19
* will be your everlasting light; Is 60:20
I, the *, will bring it all to Is 60:22
THE SPIRIT OF the * God is upon Is 61:1
me, because the * has anointed me Is 61:1
of the *, ministers of our God. Is 61:6
For I, the *, love justice; Is 61:8
her jewels. The * will show the Is 61:11
Bride," for the * delights in you Is 62:4
the earth. The * has sworn to Is 62:8
See, the * has sent his Is 62:11
my people, I, the * your God, am Is 62:11
"It is I, the *, announcing your Is 63:1
I, the *, the one who is mighty Is 63:1
Spirit of the * gave them rest. Is 63:14
O *, look down from heaven and Is 63:15
from ages past. O *, why have you Is 63:17
that never called you "*"? Is 63:19
And yet, O *, you are our Father. Is 64:8
Oh, be not so angry with us, *, Is 64:9
you still refuse to help us, *? Is 64:12
THE * SAYS, People Is 65:1
too, says the *, for they also Is 65:7
not destroy them all, says the *; Is 65:8
have forsaken the * and his Temple Is 65:11
Therefore the * God says, You Is 65:13
my people, for the * God will slay Is 65:15
of those the * has blessed; Is 65:23
all my Holy Mountain, says the *. Is 65:25
"Be happy in the *!" Is 66:5
It is the voice of the * taking Is 66:6
asks the * your God. Is 66:9
says the *, for I will send it; Is 66:12
For see, the * will come with Is 66:15
For the * will punish the world Is 66:16
the slain of the * shall be many! Is 66:16
to the *, transporting them gently Is 66:20
to Jerusalem, says the *. Is 66:20
the Temple of the * at harvest Is 66:20
in vessels consecrated to the *. Is 66:20
priests and Levites, says the *. Is 66:21
The * said to me, "I knew you Jer 1:4
"O * God," I said, "I can't do Jer 1:6
people, for I, the *, will be with Jer 1:8
Then the * said to me, "Look, Jer 1:11
And the * replied, "That's Jer 1:12
Then the * asked me, "What do Jer 1:13
For I am with you," says the *. Jer 1:19
AGAIN THE * spoke to me and said: Jer 2:1
streets: The * says, I remember how Jer 2:2
O Israel, says the *, why did Jer 2:4,5
that it was I, the *, who brought Jer 2:6
*, and their judges ignored me; Jer 2:8
against the * your God when he Jer 2:17
rebel against the * your God, Jer 2:19
him, says the *, the God of Hosts. Jer 2:19
I see it always before me, the * Jer 2:22
me—you are all rebels, says the *. Jer 2:29
hands, for the * has rejected the Jer 2:37
to come to me again, the * says. Jer 3:1
This message from the * came to Jer 3:6
was only faked, the * God says. Jer 3:10
against the * your God and Jer 3:13
people, says the *, you will no Jer 3:16
for the * himself will be among Jer 3:17
the throne of the *, and all Jer 3:17
come, for you are the * our God. Jer 3:22
Only in the * our God can Israel Jer 3:23
childhood against the * our God; Jer 3:25
The * is saying to the men of Jer 4:3
For I the * am bringing vast Jer 4:6
of the * has not stopped yet. Jer 4:8
In that day, says the *, the Jer 4:9
(Then I said, "But *, the people Jer 4:10
rebelled against me, says the *. Jer 4:17
presence of the *, and crushed by Jer 4:26
Even under oath, they lie. O *, Jer 5:3
the ways of the * and the judgment Jer 5:5
treachery against me, says the *. Jer 5:11
Therefore this is what the * God Jer 5:14
the *—a mighty nation, an ancient Jer 5:15
So says the *. Jer 5:18
that the * is doing this to us?" Jer 5:19
at all for me? the * God asks. Jer 5:22
is going on? the * God asks. Jer 5:29
For the * of Hosts has said to Jer 6:6
again, the * of Hosts has said; Jer 6:9
of this land, the * has said. Jer 6:12
Yet the * pleads with you still: Jer 6:16
together. The * God says, See the Jer 6:22
full of evil talk against the *? Jer 6:28
THEN THE * said to Jeremiah: Jer 7:1
the Temple of the * and give this Jer 7:2
worship here. The * of Hosts, the Jer 7:3
the Temple of the * is here, God Jer 7:4
And now, says the *, I will do Jer 7:13,14
asks the *. Jer 7:19
So the * God says, I will pour Jer 7:20
The * of Hosts, the God of Israel Jer 7:21
to obey the * its God, and refuses Jer 7:28
for the * has rejected and Jer 7:29
before my very eyes, says the *. Jer 7:30
The time is coming, says the *, Jer 7:32
THEN, SAYS THE *, the enemy shall Jer 8:1
scatter them, says the * of Hosts. Jer 8:3
message from the *: When a person Jer 8:4,5
have rejected the word of the *. Jer 8:9
For the * our God has decreed our Jer 8:14
"Where is the *?" Jer 8:19
the * replies. Jer 8:19
care nothing for me," says the *. Jer 9:3
to come to me," says the *. Jer 9:6
Therefore the * of Hosts says Jer 9:7
asks the *. Jer 9:9
"Because," the * replies, "my Jer 9:13
Therefore this is what the * of Jer 9:15
"The * of Hosts says: Send for Jer 9:17,18
Tell them this, says the *: Jer 9:22
The * says: Let not the wise man Jer 9:23
that I am the * of justice and of Jer 9:24
A time is coming, says the *, Jer 9:25,26
HEAR THE WORD of the *, O Israel: Jer 10:1
O *, there is no other god like Jer 10:6
But the * is the only true God, Jer 10:10
The * of Hosts is his name. Jer 10:16
O *, I know it is not within the Jer 10:23
his course— so you correct me, *; Jer 10:24
who don't obey the *, for they have Jer 10:25
THEN THE * spoke to Jeremiah once Jer 11:1
obey me, says the *, so that I can Jer 11:5
Then I replied, "So be it, *!" Jer 11:5
Then the * said: Broadcast this Jer 11:6
Again the * spoke to me and said: Jer 11:9
Therefore, the * says, I am Jer 11:11
joy again? The * used to call you Jer 11:16
to Baal that the * of Hosts who Jer 11:17
Then the * told me all about Jer 11:18
O * of Hosts, you are just. Jer 11:20
And the * replied, The men of the Jer 11:21,22
O *, YOU always give me justice Jer 12:1
But as for me—*, you know my Jer 12:3
O *! Jer 12:3
O Lord!) *, drag them off like Jer 12:3
The * replied to me: If racing Jer 12:5
Then the * said: I have abandoned Jer 12:7
the sword of the * devours from Jer 12:12
anger of the * is upon them. Jer 12:13
And now the * says this to the Jer 12:14
again and finished, says the *. Jer 12:17
THE * SAID to me, Go and buy a Jer 13:1
I hid it as the * had told me to. Jer 13:5
afterwards, the * said: Go out to Jer 13:6
Then the * said: This illustrates Jer 13:8,9
Israel to cling to me, says the *. Jer 13:11
Tell them this: The * God of Jer 13:12
against each other, says the *. Jer 13:14
Then you would listen to the *, Jer 13:15
Give glory to the * your God Jer 13:16
Jeremiah from the *, explaining why Jer 14:1
O *, we have sinned against you Jer 14:7
Are you helpless to save us? O *, Jer 14:9
we are known as your people. O *, Jer 14:9
But the * replies: You have loved Jer 14:10
The * told me again: Don't ask me Jer 14:11
Then I said, O * God, their Jer 14:13
Then the * said: The prophets are Jer 14:14
Therefore, the * says, I will Jer 14:15
"O *," the people will cry, Jer 14:19
everywhere. O *, we confess our Jer 14:20
Do not hate us, *, for the sake Jer 14:21
Who but you alone, O * our God, Jer 14:22
THEN THE * said to me, Even if Jer 15:1
tell them the * says: Those who Jer 15:2
says the *—the sword to kill, the Jer 15:3
Well, let them curse! *, you Jer 15:11
Then Jeremiah replied, "*, you Jer 15:15
proud I am to bear your name, O *. Jer 15:16
The * replied: "Stop this Jer 15:19
and deliver you, says the *. Jer 15:20
For the * of Hosts, the God of Jer 16:9
ask, "Why has the * decreed such Jer 16:10
What is our sin against the * our Jer 16:10
day, says the *, when the whole Jer 16:14,15
again, says the *, to this same Jer 16:14,15
O *, my Strength and Fortress, my Jer 16:19
The * says: Cursed is the man who Jer 17:5
who trusts in the * and has made Jer 17:7
the * his hope and confidence. Jer 17:7
Only the * knows! Jer 17:10
and glorious. O *, the Hope of Jer 17:13
*, the Fountain of living waters. Jer 17:13
of living waters. *, you alone can Jer 17:14
of the * you keep talking about? Jer 17:15
*, I don't want the people Jer 17:16
I don't want them doomed! *, Jer 17:17

(LORD Con't)
Then the * said to me, Go and Jer 17:19
the word of the *, kings of Judah Jer 17:20
The * says: Take warning and live; Jer 17:21,22
But if you obey me, says the *, Jer 17:24
to praise the * in his Temple. Jer 17:26
message to Jeremiah from the *: Jer 18:1
Then the * said: Jer 18:5
saying: Hear the word of the *. Jer 18:11
Then the * said: Even among the Jer 18:13
O *, help me! Jer 18:19
Now, *, let their children Jer 18:21
along my path. *, you know all Jer 18:23
THE * SAID, Buy a clay jar and Jer 19:1
Then the * spoke to them and Jer 19:3
to the word of the *, kings of Jer 19:3
of Jerusalem! The * of Hosts, the Jer 19:3
The day is coming, says the *, Jer 19:6
to you from the * of Hosts: As this Jer 19:11
the Temple of the * and said to all Jer 19:14
the people, The * of Hosts, the Jer 19:15
refused to listen to the *. Jer 19:15
the Temple of the *, heard what Jer 20:1
the * has changed your name. Jer 20:3
For the * will send terror on Jer 20:4
Babylon, says the *, and he shall Jer 20:4
Then I said, O *, you deceived me Jer 20:7
again mention the *—never more Jer 20:9
But the * stands beside me like a Jer 20:11
them forever. O * of Hosts, who Jer 20:12
will sing out in thanks to the *! Jer 20:13
begged, "Ask the * to help us, for Jer 21:1
Perhaps the * will be gracious to Jer 21:1
and tell him the * God of Israel Jer 21:3,4
"Tell these people, the * says: Jer 21:8
and not its friend, says the *. Jer 21:10
"And to the king of Judah, the * Jer 21:11
for your sinfulness, says the *. Jer 21:14
THEN THE * said to me: Go over and Jer 22:1
The * says: Be fair-minded. Jer 22:3
own name, says the *, that this Jer 22:5
another, "Why did the * do it? Jer 22:8
here forgot the * their God and Jer 22:9
For the * says this about Jer 22:11
His name means, "The * will Jer 22:24,25f
Hear the word of the *! Jer 22:29
Hear the word of the Lord! The * Jer 22:30
THE * DECLARES: Jer 23:1
coming, says the *, when I will Jer 23:5,6
And this is his name: The * Our Jer 23:5,6
an oath, "As the * lives who Jer 23:7
will say, "As the * lives who Jer 23:8
here in my own Temple, says the *. Jer 23:11
Therefore the * of Hosts says: I Jer 23:15
to my people, says the * of Hosts. Jer 23:16
* has said you shall have peace!" Jer 23:17
See, the * is sending a furious Jer 23:19
The terrible anger of the * will Jer 23:20
asks the *. Jer 23:29
at all for my people, says the *. Jer 23:32
the sad news from the * today?" Jer 23:33
You are the sad news, for the * Jer 23:33
that, then I, the * God, will Jer 23:38,39
burden of the *," or, "the Jer 23:38,39f
or, "the message of the *." Jer 23:38,39f
* gave me this vision. Jer 24:1
Then the * said to me, "What do Jer 24:3
Then the * said: "The good figs Jer 24:4,5
came from the * to Jeremiah during Jer 25:1
land which the * gave to you and to Jer 25:5
And now the * God of Hosts says, Jer 25:8,9
For the * God said to me: "Take Jer 25:15
of fury from the * and made all the Jer 25:17
Tell them, "The * of Hosts, the Jer 25:27
* of Hosts says you must drink it! Jer 25:28
Tell them the * will shout Jer 25:30
the earth, for the * has a case Jer 25:31
See, declares the * of Hosts, Jer 25:32
On that day those the * has Jer 25:33
the * has spoiled their pastures. Jer 25:36
fierceness of the anger of the *. Jer 25:37
of the fierce anger of the *. Jer 25:38
Jeremiah from the * during the Jer 26:1
the Temple of the * and make an Jer 26:2
Tell them the * says: If you Jer 26:4
everything the * had told him to, Jer 26:7,8
have to say the * will destroy this Jer 26:9
"The * sent me," he said, "to Jer 26:12
begin obeying the * your God, he Jer 26:13
true that the * sent me to speak Jer 26:15
us in the name of the * our God." Jer 26:16
and worshiped the * and begged the Jer 26:19
the * to have mercy upon them; Jer 26:19
and the * held back the terrible Jer 26:19
Another true prophet of the *, Jer 26:20
Jeremiah from the * at the Jer 27:1
masters that the * of Hosts, the Jer 27:4
disease, which the * has promised Jer 27:13
I have not sent them, says the * Jer 27:15
told them: "The * says, Don't Jer 27:16
them pray to the * of Hosts that Jer 27:18
"For the * of Hosts says, The Jer 27:19,20,21
"The * of Hosts, the God of Jer 28:2
exiled to Babylon, says the *. Jer 28:4
I hope the * will do everything Jer 28:6
gathered, "The * has promised that Jer 28:11
Soon afterwards, the * gave this Jer 28:12
Go and tell Hananiah that the * Jer 28:13
their necks. The * of Hosts, the Jer 28:14
Hananiah, the * has not sent you, Jer 28:15
Therefore the * says you must Jer 28:16
you have rebelled against the *." Jer 28:16
The * of Hosts, the God of Jer 29:4
The * of Hosts, the God of Jer 29:8
I have not sent them, says the *. Jer 29:9
plans I have for you, says the *. Jer 29:11
Yes, says the *, I will be found Jer 29:14
you and say the * has sent them, I Jer 29:15
in Babylon. The * of Hosts, the Jer 29:21
he will say, "The * make you like Jer 29:22
everything they do, says the *. Jer 29:23
The * of Hosts, the God of Jer 29:25
Zephaniah, "The * has appointed Jer 29:26
Then the * gave this message to Jer 29:30
them this: The * says that because Jer 29:31
taught you to rebel against the *. Jer 29:32
The * God of Israel says, Write Jer 30:2
For on that day, says the * of Jer 30:8
For they shall serve the * their Jer 30:9
raise up for them, says the *. Jer 30:9
and I will save you, says the *. Jer 30:11
But, says the *, when I bring you Jer 30:18
of the * roars with fury; Jer 30:23
the wicked. The * will not call Jer 30:24
AT THAT TIME, says the *, all the Jer 31:1
shall recognize me as the *; Jer 31:1
For long ago the * had said to Jer 31:3
go up to Zion to the * our God." Jer 31:6
For the * says, Sing with joy Jer 31:7
and joy: "The * has saved his Jer 31:7
Listen to this message from the * Jer 31:10
it abroad: The * who scattered his Jer 31:10
goodness of the *—the good crops, Jer 31:12
people with my bounty, says the *. Jer 31:14
The * spoke to me again, saying: Jer 31:15
But the * says: Don't cry any Jer 31:16
future, says the *, and your Jer 31:17
for you alone are the *, my God. Jer 31:18
And the * replies: Ephraim is Jer 31:20
For the * will cause something Jer 31:22
The * of Hosts, the God of Jer 31:23
her cities, "The * bless you, O Jer 31:23
The * says: The time will come Jer 31:27
The day will come, says the *, Jer 31:31
says the *. Jer 31:32
one another to know the *. Jer 31:34
me then, says the *, and I will Jer 31:34
The * who gives us sunlight in Jer 31:35
name is * of Hosts—says this: Jer 31:35
coming, says the *, when all Jer 31:38,39
be rebuilt for the *, from the Jer 31:38,39
be holy to the *, and so shall all Jer 31:40
Jeremiah from the * in the tenth Jer 32:1
Then this message from the * came Jer 32:6,7
So Hanamel came, as the * had Jer 32:8
I had heard was really from the *. Jer 32:8
"The * of Hosts, God of Israel, Jer 32:14
For the * of Hosts, God of Jer 32:15
"O * God! Jer 32:17
and mighty God, the * of Hosts. Jer 32:18
I am the *, the God of all Jer 32:27
Now therefore the * God of Israel Jer 32:36
* sent him this second message: Jer 33:1
The *, the Maker of heaven and Jer 33:2
The * declares that the happy Jer 33:10,11
offerings to the * will be heard Jer 33:10,11
people will sing: "Praise the *! Jer 33:10,11
come, says the *, when I will do Jer 33:14
"The * is our righteousness!" Jer 33:16
For the * declares that from Jer 33:17
offerings and sacrifices to the *. Jer 33:18
came to Jeremiah from the *: Jer 33:19
The * spoke to Jeremiah again and Jer 33:23
—that the * chose Judah and Israel Jer 33:24
Jeremiah from the * when Jer 34:1
of Judah, that the * says this: I Jer 34:2
This I have decreed, says the * Jer 34:5
Jeremiah from the * after King Jer 34:8
That is why the * gave the Jer 34:12
The *, the God of Israel, says: Jer 34:13
Therefore, says the *, because Jer 34:17
THIS IS THE message the * gave Jer 35:1
Then the * gave this message to Jer 35:12
The * of Hosts, the God of Jer 35:13
Therefore the * God of Hosts, Jer 35:17
and said: "The * of Hosts, the God Jer 35:18,19
* gave this message to Jeremiah: Jer 36:1
ways and ask the * to forgive them Jer 36:7
But the * hid them! Jer 36:26
scroll, the * said to Jeremiah: Jer 36:27
to the king: "The * says, You Jer 36:29
And now the * adds this Jer 36:30
this time the * added a lot more! Jer 36:3
what the * said through Jeremiah. Jer 37
Then the * sent this message to Jer 37
"The *, the God of Israel, says: Jer 37
was any recent message from the *. Jer 37:1
Listen, O my * the king: I beg Jer 37:2
"My * the king," he said, Jer 38
to Zedekiah, "The *, the God of Jer 38:1
hands if only you will obey the *; Jer 38:2
to surrender, the * has said that Jer 38:21,2
The * gave the following message Jer 39:1
the Ethiopian: The * of Hosts, the Jer 39:1
and said, "The * your God has Jer 40:2,
people have sinned against the *. Jer 40:2,
to worship at the Temple of the *. Jer 41:
pray for us to the * your God, for Jer 42:
Beg the * your God to show us Jer 42:
we will obey the * our God, to whom Jer 42:
Ten days later the * gave his Jer 42:
sent me to the *, the God of Jer 42:
"But if you refuse to obey the * Jer 42:13,1
this is what the * replies, O Jer 42:1
of Judah: The * of Hosts, the God Jer 42:1
"For the * of Hosts, the God of Jer 42:1
For the * has said: O remnant of Jer 42:1
"You lie! The * our God hasn't Jer 43:2,
to obey the * and stay in Judah. Jer 43:
for they would not obey the *. Jer 43:
Then at Tahpanhes, the * spoke to Jer 43:
of Judah this: The * of Hosts, the Jer 43:1
The * of Hosts, the God of Jer 44:2,
And now the *, the God of Hosts, Jer 44:
Therefore the * of Hosts, the God Jer 44:1
"Do you think the * didn't know Jer 44:2
the * and refused to obey him." Jer 44:2
to the word of the *, all you Jer 44:2
in Egypt! The * of Hosts, the God Jer 44:2
But listen to the word of the *, Jer 44:2
name, says the *, that it will do Jer 44:2
saying, 'O * our God, help us!' Jer 44:2
O Baruch, the * God of Israel Jer 45:2
And now the * has added more! Jer 45:3
But tell Baruch this, The * Jer 45:4
them on every side, says the *. Jer 46:5
For this is the day of the * God Jer 46:1
blood, for the * God of Hosts will Jer 46:10
Because the * knocked him down Jer 46:15
As I live, says the King, the * Jer 46:18
The * of Hosts, the God of Jer 46:25
says the *, for I am with you. Jer 46:28
The * says: A flood is coming Jer 47:2
For the * is destroying the Jer 47:4
O sword of the *, when will you Jer 47:6
the * has sent it on an errand? Jer 47:7
THIS IS THE message of the * of Jer 48:1
destroyed, for the * has said it. Jer 48:8
The time is coming soon, the * Jer 48:12
says the King, the * of Hosts. Jer 48:15
she has rebelled against the *. Jer 48:26
I know her insolence, the * has Jer 48:30
For the * says: I have put a stop Jer 48:35
the land of Moab, says the *. Jer 48:40
for she has boasted against the *. Jer 48:42
be your lot, O Moab, says the *. Jer 48:43
the *, I will reestablish Moab. Jer 48:47
you for this, the * declares, by Jer 49:2
who dispossessed her, says the *. Jer 49:2
upon you, says the * God of Hosts. Jer 49:5
of the Ammonites, says the *. Jer 49:6
The * of Hosts says: Where are Jer 49:7
The * says to Edom: If the Jer 49:12
own name, says the *, that Bozrah Jer 49:13
heard this message from the *: Jer 49:14
and despised by all, says the *. Jer 49:15
I will bring you down, says the *. Jer 49:16
neighboring towns, says the *. Jer 49:18
Take note: The * will certainly Jer 49:20
in one day, says the * of Hosts. Jer 49:26
* will send him to destroy them. Jer 49:28
*, with all their household goods. Jer 49:29
Flee for your lives, says the *. Jer 49:30
"Go," said the * to King Jer 49:31
The * of Hosts says: I will Jer 49:35
Elam, says the *, and I will cause Jer 49:37
set my throne in Elam, says the *. Jer 49:38
bring the people back, says the *. Jer 49:39
THIS IS THE message from the * Jer 50:1
and seeking the * their God. Jer 50:4
be united to the * with an eternal Jer 50:5
sinned against the *, the God of Jer 50:7
is sated with loot, says the *. Jer 50:10
Because of the anger of the *, Jer 50:13
for she has sinned against the *. Jer 50:14
Her walls have fallen. The * has Jer 50:15
Therefore the * of Hosts, the Jer 50:18
In those days, says the *, no Jer 50:20
for you have fought against the *. Jer 50:24
The * has opened his armory and Jer 50:25
work of the *, the God of Hosts. Jer 50:25
to tell how the * their God has Jer 50:28
the *, the Holy One of Israel. Jer 50:29

LORD Con't)

you up, for the * will light a fire	Jer 50:32
The * of Hosts says: The people	Jer 50:33
His name is the * of Hosts.	Jer 50:34
smite the Chaldeans, says the *.	Jer 50:35
forever. The * declares that he	Jer 50:40
Listen to the plan of the *	Jer 50:45
THE * SAYS: I will stir up a	Jer 51:1
For the * of Hosts has not	Jer 51:5
heaven. The * has vindicated us.	Jer 51:10
all the * our God has done.	Jer 51:10
For the * has stirred up the	Jer 51:11
send out an ambush, for the *	Jer 51:12
life is cut. The * of Hosts has	Jer 51:14
the * of Hosts is his name.	Jer 51:19
I will use you, says the *, to	Jer 51:20
done to my people, says the *.	Jer 51:24
for all that the * has planned	Jer 51:29
For the * of Hosts, the God of	Jer 51:33
And the * replies: I will be your	Jer 51:36
never to waken again, says the *.	Jer 51:39
from the fierce anger of the *.	Jer 51:45
against Babylon, says the *.	Jer 51:48
Remember the * and return to	Jer 51:50
the Temple of the * has been	Jer 51:51
Yes, says the *.	Jer 51:52
she shall die, says the *.	Jer 51:53
For the * is destroying Babylon;	Jer 51:55
her hands, for the * God gives just	Jer 51:56
So says the King, the * of Hosts.	Jer 51:57
written and say, '*, you have said	Jer 51:61,62
at last that the *, in his anger,	Jer 52:3
Her enemies prosper, for the *	Lam 1:5
*," she cries, "see my plight.	Lam 1:9
"Look, O *," she prays, "and	Lam 1:11
because of all the * has done to me	Lam 1:12
The * has trampled all my mighty	Lam 1:15
noblest youth. The * has trampled	Lam 1:15
For the * has spoken: "Let her	Lam 1:17
And the * is right, for we	Lam 1:18
See, O *, my anguish;	Lam 1:20
And yet, O *, the time will	Lam 1:21
Look also on their sins, O *, and	Lam 1:22
A CLOUD OF anger from the * has	Lam 2:1
The * without mercy has destroyed	Lam 2:2
Yes, the * has vanquished Israel	Lam 2:5
The * has rejected his own altar,	Lam 2:7
The * determined to destroy	Lam 2:8
But it is the * who did it, just	Lam 2:17
Then the people wept before the *	Lam 2:18
your hearts like water to the *;	Lam 2:19
O *, think!	Lam 2:20
die within the Temple of the *?	Lam 2:20
You have killed them, *, in your	Lam 2:21
ashes and dirt. O *, all peace and	Lam 3:17
to water, for the * has left me.	Lam 3:18
My soul claims the * as my	Lam 3:24
hope in him. The * is wonderfully	Lam 3:25
for the salvation of the *.	Lam 3:26
* will not abandon him forever.	Lam 3:31
No wonder the * has had to deal	Lam 3:34,35,36
It is the * who helps one and	Lam 3:38
repent and turn again to the *.	Lam 3:40
we have rebelled against the *,	Lam 3:42
*, and slain us without mercy.	Lam 3:43
Oh, that the * might look down	Lam 3:50
But I called upon your name, O *	Lam 3:55
O *, you are my lawyer!	Lam 3:58
O *, repay them well for all the	Lam 3:64
their hearts and curse them, *.	Lam 3:65
beneath the heavens of the *.	Lam 3:66
the anger of the * is satisfied;	Lam 4:11
The * himself has dealt with them;	Lam 4:16
feel the awful anger of the *.	Lam 4:21
O *, REMEMBER all that has	Lam 5:1
the Temple of the * are desolate,	Lam 5:18
O *, forever you remain the same!	Lam 5:19
the glory of the * appeared to me.	Eze 1:27,28
messages of the * God.	Eze 2:4
This is what the * God says!"	Eze 3:11
the glory of the * began to move	Eze 3:12
but the hand of the * was strong	Eze 3:14,15
the seven days, the * said to me:	Eze 3:16
and the * destroys him, his	Eze 3:20
the glory of the * there, just as	Eze 3:23
say to them: The * God says, Let	Eze 3:27
For the * declares, Israel shall	Eze 4:13
Then I said, "O * God, must I be	Eze 4:14
Then the * said, "All right, you	Eze 4:15
The * God says, "This	Eze 5:5,6,7
Therefore the * God says, I,	Eze 5:8
happens when the * turns against an	Eze 5:15
I, the *, have spoken it!	Eze 5:15
I, the *, have spoken it!"	Eze 5:17
AGAIN A MESSAGE came from the *:	Eze 6:1
the message of the * God against	Eze 6:3
I, even I the *, will bring war	Eze 6:3
at last you will know I am the *.	Eze 6:4-7
"The * God says: Raise your	Eze 6:11
Then you will know I am the *."	Eze 6:14
and you shall know I am the *."	Eze 7:4
The * God says: "With one blow	Eze 7:5,6
know that I, the *, am doing it.	Eze 7:8,9
They shall learn that I am the *	Eze 7:26,27
power of the * God fell upon me.	Eze 8:1
was that had made the * so angry.	Eze 8:3
Then the * said to me: "Son of	Eze 8:12
For they say, 'The * doesn't see	Eze 8:12
the Temple of the *, facing east,	Eze 8:16
And the * called to the man with	Eze 9:3
Then I heard the * tell the other	Eze 9:5
my face and cried out: "O * God!	Eze 9:8
they say, 'The * doesn't see it!	Eze 9:9
Then the * spoke to the man in	Eze 10:2
Then the glory of the * rose	Eze 10:4
brightness of the glory of the *.	Eze 10:4
When the * told the man in linen	Eze 10:6
Then the glory of the * moved	Eze 10:18
Then the Spirit of the * came	Eze 11:5
me to say: "The * says to the	Eze 11:5
"Therefore the * God says: You	Eze 11:7
feared, says the * God, and I will	Eze 11:8
and you will know I am the *.	Eze 11:10
will know I am the *—you who have	Eze 11:12
and cried out: "O * God, are you	Eze 11:13
Again a message came from the *:	Eze 11:14
that the * has deported them.	Eze 11:15
Now the * has given us their	Eze 11:15
"But tell the exiles that the *	Eze 11:16
for their sins," the * God says.	Eze 11:21
Then the glory of the * rose	Eze 11:23
everything the * had shown me.	Eze 11:25
A MESSAGE came to me from the *:	Eze 12:1
message came to me from the *:	Eze 12:8
Tell them the * God says it is a	Eze 12:10
then they shall know I am the *.	Eze 12:15
and they shall know I am the *."	Eze 12:16
message came to me from the *:	Eze 12:17
to the people, the * God says that	Eze 12:19
and you shall know I am the *."	Eze 12:20
a message came to me from the *:	Eze 12:21
The * God says, I will put an	Eze 12:23
For I am the *!	Eze 12:25
says the * God.	Eze 12:25
Therefore say to them: 'The *	Eze 12:28
strengthening Israel in the *?	Eze 13:5
"Therefore the * God says: I	Eze 13:8
And you shall know I am the *.	Eze 13:9
Yes, it will surely fall. The *	Eze 13:13
and you shall know I am the *.	Eze 13:14
there is no peace, says the * God.	Eze 13:16
the * has given them his messages.	Eze 13:17
Tell them the * God says: Woe to	Eze 13:18
"And so the * says: I will crush	Eze 13:20
and you shall know I am the *.	Eze 13:21
and you shall know I am the *."	Eze 13:23
a message from the *, and this is	Eze 14:1
Tell them, the * God says: I the	Eze 14:4
God says: I the * will personally	Eze 14:4
"Therefore warn them that the *	Eze 14:6,7
I the * will personally punish	Eze 14:6,7
and you shall know I am the *.	Eze 14:8
So says the *."	Eze 14:11
Then this message of the * came	Eze 14:12
of Israel, says the * God.	Eze 14:14
men were here, the * God swears	Eze 14:16
in the land, the * God declares	Eze 14:18
living there, the * God says that	Eze 14:20
"And the * says: Four great	Eze 14:21
MESSAGE came to me from the *:	Eze 15:1
"This is what I mean, the * God	Eze 15:5,6
then you shall know I am the *.	Eze 15:7
worship idols," says the * God.	Eze 15:8
A message came to me from the *.	Eze 16:1
Tell her, the * God says: You	Eze 16:3
gifts I gave you, says the * God.	Eze 16:14
upon you, says the * God— you	Eze 16:23
* God, to do such things as these;	Eze 16:30
hear the word of the *:	Eze 16:35
"The * God says: Because I see	Eze 16:36
for all of your sins, says the *.	Eze 16:43
"As I live, the * God says,	Eze 16:48
for all your sins, says the *.	Eze 16:58
"For the * God says: I will	Eze 16:59,60
you, and you will know I am the *.	Eze 16:62
you have done, says the * God."	Eze 16:63
MESSAGE came to me from the *:	Eze 17:1
"The * God asks: Shall I let	Eze 17:9
message came to me from the *:	Eze 17:11
For as I live, says the *, the	Eze 17:16
"The * God says: As I live,	Eze 17:19
Then you will know that I, the *,	Eze 17:21
"The * God says: I, myself, will	Eze 17:22,23
that it is I, the *, who cuts down	Eze 17:24
I, the *, have said that I would	Eze 17:24
As I live, says the * God, you	Eze 18:3
the *, and he shall surely live.	Eze 18:9
asks the *.	Eze 18:23
"Yet you say: 'The * isn't being	Eze 18:25
keep saying: 'The * is unfair!'	Eze 18:29
seeing you die, the * God says.	Eze 18:32
from the *, and sat before me	Eze 20:1
Then the * gave me this message:	Eze 20:2
of Israel: The * God says: How dare	Eze 20:3
Tell them the * God says: When I	Eze 20:5,6
gods, for I am the * your God.	Eze 20:7
that it is I, the *, who sanctifies	Eze 20:12
idols, for I am the * your God.	Eze 20:19
remember that I am the * your God.	Eze 20:20
tell them that the * God says: Your	Eze 20:27,28
"The * God wants to know whether	Eze 20:30
As I live, the * God says, I will	Eze 20:31
happens, you will know I am the *.	Eze 20:38
"O Israel, the * God says: If	Eze 20:39
*, all Israel shall worship me.	Eze 20:40
fathers, you will know I am the *.	Eze 20:42
you will know I am the *."	Eze 20:44
message came to me from the *:	Eze 20:45
and say: Hear the word of the *.	Eze 20:47
that I, the *, have set the fire.	Eze 20:48
Then I said, "O * God, they say	Eze 20:49
MESSAGE came to me from the *:	Eze 21:1
For the * says: I am against	Eze 21:3
shall know that it is I, the *.	Eze 21:5
And the * God says: Your doom is	Eze 21:7
do they have? the * God asks.	Eze 21:13
hands that I, the *, will smite	Eze 21:17
message came to me. The * said:	Eze 21:18
"The * God says: Again and again	Eze 21:24
jeweled crown, the * God says.	Eze 21:26
For I, the *, have spoken it."	Eze 21:32
MESSAGE came from the *.	Eze 22:1
and my commands, the * God says.	Eze 22:12
For I, the *, have spoken, and I	Eze 22:14
and you shall know I am the *."	Eze 22:16
Then the * said this:	Eze 22:17
Therefore the * God says:	Eze 22:18,19,20
know that I, the *, have poured my	Eze 22:22
Again the message of the * came	Eze 22:23
And so the * God says: I will	Eze 22:31
"And now the * God says that he	Eze 23:22
For the * God says: I will	Eze 23:28
For I have spoken, says the *.	Eze 23:34
"The * God says: Bring an army	Eze 23:46
message came to me from the *.	Eze 24:1
tell them the * God says: Put a	Eze 24:3
"For the * God says: Woe to	Eze 24:6
I, the *, have spoken it;	Eze 24:14
came to me from the *, saying:	Eze 24:15
The next morning I did all the *	Eze 24:18
And I answered, "The * told me	Eze 24:20,21
an example to you, the * God says.	Eze 24:24
then you will know I am the *."	Eze 24:24
and they shall know I am the *."	Eze 24:27
Tell them: Listen to what the *	Eze 25:3
Then you will know I am the *.	Eze 25:5
"For the * God says: Because you	Eze 25:6
then you shall know I am the *.	Eze 25:7
"And the * God says: Because the	Eze 25:8
and they shall know I am the *.	Eze 25:11
"And the * God says: Because the	Eze 25:12
"And the * God says: Because the	Eze 25:15
then they shall know I am the *."	Eze 25:17
to me from the * on the first day	Eze 26:1
"Therefore the * God says: I	Eze 26:3
I have spoken it, says the * God.	Eze 26:5
Then they shall know I am the *.	Eze 26:6
"For the * God says: I will	Eze 26:7
for I, the *, have spoken it.	Eze 26:14
So says the *.	Eze 26:14
"For the * God says: I will	Eze 26:19
enough to find you, says the *."	Eze 26:21
MESSAGE came to me from the *.	Eze 27:1
of the world, the * God speaks.	Eze 27:3
message given to me from the *:	Eze 28:1
of Tyre: The * God says: You are so	Eze 28:2,3
"Therefore the * God says:	Eze 28:6
For I have spoken it, the * God	Eze 28:10
message came to me from the *:	Eze 28:11
Tell him, the * God says: You	Eze 28:12
message came to me from the *:	Eze 28:20
"The * God says: I am your	Eze 28:22
all who see shall know I am the *.	Eze 28:22
Then you will know I am the *.	Eze 28:23
shall know I am the * their God."	Eze 28:26
message came to me from the *:	Eze 29:1
Tell them that the * God says: I	Eze 29:3
all of you shall know I am the *.	Eze 29:6
Therefore the * God says: I will	Eze 29:8
know that I, the *, have done it.	Eze 29:9
"But the * God says that at the	Eze 29:13
message came to me from the *:	Eze 29:17
so the * was giving Egypt to him to	Eze 29:18f
Therefore, the * God says, I	Eze 29:19
so the * was giving Egypt to him to	Eze 29:20f
says the *.	Eze 29:20
and Egypt shall know I am the *."	Eze 29:21
ANOTHER MESSAGE FROM the *!	Eze 30:1
and say: The * God says, Weep, for	Eze 30:2,3
the day of the *;	Eze 30:2,3
"For the * says: All Egypt's	Eze 30:6
And they will know I am the *	Eze 30:8
"For the * God says:	Eze 30:10

(LORD Con't)
I, the *, have spoken it. Eze 30:12
and they shall know I am the *." Eze 30:19
For, the * God says, I am Eze 30:22
Egypt shall know I am the *. Eze 30:25
then they shall know I am the * Eze 30:26
message came to me from the *: Eze 31:1
and arrogant, the * God says. Eze 31:10
"The * God says: When she fell I Eze 31:15
his teeming masses, says the *." Eze 31:18
message came to me from the *: Eze 32:1
"The * God says: I will send a Eze 32:3
"For the * God says: The sword Eze 32:11
as olive oil, the * God says. Eze 32:14
know that I, the *, have done it. Eze 32:15
and for her people, says the *." Eze 32:16
message came to me from the *. Eze 32:17
his army slain, says the * God. Eze 32:31
A message came to me from the *. Eze 33:1
I live, says the * God, I have no Eze 33:11
are saying the * isn't fair. Eze 33:17
Yet you are saying the * isn't Eze 33:20
Now the hand of the * had been Eze 33:22
But the * God says: You are Eze 33:25
"Tell them: The * God says: As I Eze 33:27
then they shall know I am the *. Eze 33:29
him tell us what the * is saying!' Eze 33:30
word is that comes from the *!" Eze 33:30f
about loving the *, but with their Eze 33:31
MESSAGE came to me from the *: Eze 34:1
say to them: The * God says to you: Eze 34:2
shepherds, hear the word of the *: Eze 34:7
"As I live, says the * God, you Eze 34:8
"For the * God says: I will Eze 34:11
lie down in peace, the * God says. Eze 34:15,16
people—the * God says, I will Eze 34:17
"Therefore the * God says: I Eze 34:20
"And I, the *, will be their Eze 34:24
I, the *, have spoken it. Eze 34:24
they shall know I am the *. Eze 34:27
know that I, the * their God, am Eze 34:30
are my people, says the * God. Eze 34:30
I am your God, so says the *." Eze 34:31
AGAIN A MESSAGE came from the *. Eze 35:1
"The * God says: I am against Eze 35:3
then you shall know I am the *. Eze 35:4,5
As I live, the * God says, since Eze 35:6
Then you shall know I am the *. Eze 35:9
Therefore as I live, the * God Eze 35:11
spoke against the *, saying, 'His Eze 35:12
boasted great words against the *. Eze 35:13
And then you will know I am the * Eze 35:15
Listen to this message from the *. Eze 36:1
hear the word of the * God. Eze 36:4
of Israel: The * God says, I am Eze 36:6
Then you shall know I am the *. Eze 36:11
"The * God says: Now the other Eze 36:13
will drop off sharply, says the *. Eze 36:14
of sinners, the * God says." Eze 36:15
word came to me from the *: Eze 36:16
of Israel: The * God says, I am Eze 36:22
the world shall know I am the *. Eze 36:23
"The * God says: When I cleanse Eze 36:33
know that I, the *, rebuilt the Eze 36:36
For I, the *, have promised it, Eze 36:36
"The * God says: I am ready to Eze 36:37,38
everyone will know I am the *." Eze 36:37,38
THE POWER OF the * was upon me Eze 37:1
the Spirit of the * to a valley Eze 37:1
I replied, "*, you alone know the Eze 37:3
of God, for the * God says, See! Eze 37:5
shall live and know I am the *." Eze 37:6
and say: "The * God says: Come Eze 37:9
But tell them, the * God says: Eze 37:12
people, you will know I am the *. Eze 37:13
Then you will know that I, the *, Eze 37:14
Again a message from the * came Eze 37:15
are doing), the * God says: I will Eze 37:18,19,20
"For the * God says: I am Eze 37:21
know that I, the *, have set Israel Eze 37:28
ANOTHER message to me from the *: Eze 38:1
Tell him that the * God says: I Eze 38:2,3
"The * God says to Gog: When my Eze 38:14
"The * God says: You are the one Eze 38:17
you, says the * God, and you will Eze 38:21
for I have spoken, the * God Eze 39:5
and they shall know I am the *. Eze 39:6
am the *, the Holy One of Israel. Eze 39:7
demonstrate my glory, says the *. Eze 39:13
valiant warriors, says the * God. Eze 39:20
will know I am the * their God. Eze 39:22
"But now, the * God says, I will Eze 39:25
will know I am the * their Eze 39:28
upon them, says the * God." Eze 39:29
hand of the * was upon me, and in Eze 40:1
to the * to minister to him." Eze 40:46
me, "is the Table of the *." Eze 41:22
table which is before the *." Eze 41:22f
sacrifices to the * shall eat of Eze 42:13
And the glory of the * came into Eze 43:4
and the glory of the * filled the Eze 43:5
And I heard the * speaking to me Eze 43:6
And the * said to me: Eze 43:7
"Son of dust, the * God says: Eze 43:18
Present them before the *, and Eze 43:24
will accept you, says the * God." Eze 43:27
THEN THE * brought me back to the Eze 44:1
for the *, the God of Israel, Eze 44:2
to feast there before the *. Eze 44:3
the glory of the * filled the Eze 44:4
the Temple of the *, and I fell to Eze 44:4
And the * said to me: Eze 44:5
and rules of the Temple of the *. Eze 44:5
of Israel, The * God says: O Eze 44:6
"The * God says: No foreigner of Eze 44:9
and does not love the *. Eze 44:9
* God, that they must be punished. Eze 44:12
of the sacrifices, says the * God. Eze 44:15
for himself, the * God says. Eze 44:27
Whatever anyone gives to the * Eze 44:29
for the * shall go to the priests. Eze 44:30
that the * will bless your homes. Eze 44:30
it to the * as his holy portion. Eze 45:1
For the * God says to the Eze 45:9
who bring them, says the * God. Eze 45:15
"The * God says: On each New Eze 45:18
prepare a burnt offering to the *. Eze 45:23
"THE * GOD says, the inner wall's Eze 46:1
The people shall worship the * Eze 46:3
sacrifices to the * on the Sabbath Eze 46:4
sacrificed to the *, the inner Eze 46:12
as a burnt offering to the *. Eze 46:13
"The * God says: If the prince Eze 46:16
"The * God says: Eze 47:13
others, for it belongs to the *; Eze 48:14
to each tribe, says the * God. Eze 48:29
"The * is there." Eze 48:35f
* gave him victory over Jehoiakim. Dan 1:1
enemies, my *, and not to you! Dan 4:19
For you have defied the * of Dan 5:23
pleaded with the * God [to end our Dan 9:3
"O *," I prayed, "you are a Dan 9:4
"O *, you are righteous; Dan 9:7
to you. O *, we and our kings and Dan 9:8
"But the * our God is merciful, Dan 9:9
"O * our God, we have disobeyed Dan 9:10
to satisfy the * our God by turning Dan 9:13
"And so the * deliberately Dan 9:14
would not obey. O * our God, you Dan 9:15
display of power. *, do it again! Dan 9:15
faithful mercies, *, please turn Dan 9:16
sanctuary—for your own glory, *. Dan 9:17
"O *, hear; O Lord, forgive. Dan 9:19
"O Lord, hear; O *, forgive. Dan 9:19
O Lord, forgive. O *, listen to Dan 9:19
pleading with the * my God for Dan 9:20
"The * has commanded 490 years Dan 9:24
the * and pray for understanding; Dan 10:12
THESE ARE THE messages from the * Hos 1:1
The * said to Hosea, "Go and Hos 1:2
And the * said, "Name the child Hos 1:4,5
I will punish her, says the *. Hos 1:13
In that coming day, says the *, Hos 1:16
meaning "my *," but this was a Hos 1:16f
In that day, says the *, I will Hos 1:21,22
THEN THE * said to me, "Go, and Hos 3:1
For the * still loves Israel Hos 3:1
will return to the * their God, and Hos 3:5
submissive to the * and to his Hos 3:5
HEAR THE WORD of the *, O people Hos 4:1
of Israel. The * has filed a Hos 4:1
you, and you cannot know the *. Hos 5:4
the honor of the *, bearing Hos 5:7
"COME, LET US return to the *; Hos 6:1
Oh, that we might know the *! Hos 6:3
of feasting to the *, when you are Hos 9:5
even in the Temple of the *. Hos 9:8
long ago. The * does not forget. Hos 9:9
to slaughter. O *, what shall I Hos 9:14
the * and he took away our king. Hos 10:3
time to seek the *, that he may Hos 10:12
the people shall walk after the *. Hos 11:10
it is a promise from the *. Hos 11:11
But the * is bringing a lawsuit Hos 12:2
God spoke to him— the *, the God Hos 12:5
I am the same *, the same God, Hos 12:9
Then the * led his people out of Hos 12:13
has bitterly provoked the *. Hos 12:14
the Lord. The * will sentence him Hos 12:14
I alone am God, your *, and have Hos 13:4
wind—a wind of the * from the Hos 13:15
O ISRAEL, RETURN to the *, your Hos 14:1
Come to the * and say, "O Lord, Hos 14:2
Come to the Lord and say, "O *, Hos 14:2
for in you alone, O *, the Hos 14:3
For the paths of the * are true Hos 14:9
THIS MESSAGE CAME from the * to Joe 1:1
to bring to the Temple of the *; Joe 1:9
the Temple of the * your God, and Joe 1:14
Or, "the Day of the *." Joe 1:15f
*, help us! Joe 1:19
The * leads them with a shout. Joe 2:11
The day of the judgment of the * Joe 2:1
That is why the * says, "Turn to Joe 2:1
Return to the * your God, for Joe 2:1
grain and wine to the * as before! Joe 2:1
Then the * will pity his people Joe 2:1
upon the land. The * has done a Joe 2:2
rejoice in the * your God! Joe 2:2
"Praise the *, who does these Joe 2:2
that I alone am the *, your God. Joe 2:2
terrible Day of the * shall come. Joe 2:3
the name of the * will be saved; Joe 2:3
just as the * has promised, for he Joe 2:3
says the *, "I will gather the Joe 3:
This is a promise from the *." Joe 3:
And now, O *, bring down your Joe 3:1
For the Day of the * is near, in Joe 3:1
their light. The * shouts from his Joe 3:1
But to his people Israel, the * Joe 3:1
last that I am the * your God in Joe 3:1
of the * to water Acacia Valley. Joe 3:1
saw and heard: The * roared—like a Amo 1:
The * says, "The people of Amo 1:
The * has spoken. Amo 1:
The * says, "Gaza has sinned Amo 1:
The * has spoken. Amo 1:
The * says, "The people of Tyre Amo 1:
The * says, "Edom has sinned Amo 1:11
The * says, "The people of Ammon Amo 1:13
The * has spoken. Amo 1:15
THE * SAYS, "The people of Moab Amo 2:1
The * has spoken. Amo 2:3
The * says, "The people of Judah Amo 2:4
The * says, "The people of Amo 2:6
asks the *. Amo 2:11
The * God has spoken. Amo 2:16
It is spoken by the * against Amo 3:1
For I, the *, am sending disaster Amo 3:6
in fear. The * God has sounded your Amo 3:8
means to do right," says the *. Amo 3:10
Therefore," the * God says, Amo 3:11
The * says, "A shepherd tried to Amo 3:12
Israel," says the *, the God of Amo 3:13
to drink! The * God has sworn by Amo 4:2
in the wall. The * has said it. Amo 4:3
"I sent you hunger," says the * Amo 4:6
return to me," says the *. Amo 4:8
return to me," says the *. Amo 4:9
won't return to me," says the *. Amo 4:11
feet: Jehovah, the *, the God of Amo 4:13
For the * God says, "The city Amo 5:3
The * says to the people of Amo 5:4
Seek the * and live, or else he Amo 5:6
land. The *, Jehovah, is his name. Amo 5:8
interfere with the * in the dread Amo 5:13
Then the * God of Hosts will Amo 5:14
Perhaps even yet the * God of Amo 5:15
Therefore the * God of Hosts says Amo 5:16
the Day of the * were here, for Amo 5:18
says the *, the God of Hosts. Amo 5:25,26,27
Jehovah, the * God of Hosts, has Amo 6:8
don't mention the name of the * Amo 6:10
For the * commanded this: That Amo 6:11
says the *, the God of Hosts. Amo 6:14
THIS IS WHAT the * God showed me Amo 7:1
Then I said, "O * God, please Amo 7:2
So the * relented, and did not Amo 7:3
Then the * God showed me a great Amo 7:4
Then I said, "O * God, please Amo 7:5
Then the * turned from this plan Amo 7:6
Then he showed me this: The * was Amo 7:7
And the * said to me, "Amos, Amo 7:8
But the * took me from caring Amo 7:15
to this message to you from the *. Amo 7:16
THEN THE * God showed me, in a Amo 8:1
Then the * said, "This fruit Amo 8:2
The * has spoken. Amo 8:3
moldy wheat— the *, the Pride of Amo 8:7
coming," says the * God, "when I Amo 8:11
but of hearing the words of the *. Amo 8:11
the Word of the *, searching, Amo 8:12
I SAW THE * standing beside the Amo 9:1
The * God of Hosts touches the Amo 9:5
Jehovah, the *, is his name. Amo 9:6
"The eyes of the * God are Amo 9:8
For so the *, who plans it all, Amo 9:12
up again," says the * your God. Amo 9:15
In a vision the * God showed Ob 1:1
"A report has come from the *," Ob 1:1
you plummeting down, says the *. Ob 1:4
says the *. Ob 1:8
survivors, for the * has spoken. Ob 1:18
And the * shall be King! Ob 1:21
The * sent this message to Jonah, Jon 1:1
from the *: 'I am going to destroy Jon 1:2
to go and ran away from the *. Jon 1:3
the ship to hide there from the *. Jon 1:3
suddenly the * flung a terrific Jon 1:4
he was running away from the *. Jon 1:9,10
Now the * had arranged for a Jon 1:17
THEN JONAH PRAYED to the * his Jon 2:1
cried to the * and he answered me; Jon 2:2

LORD Con't)
I called, and *, you heard me! Jon 2:2
Then I said, 'O *, you have Jon 2:4
But, O * my God, you have Jon 2:6
my thoughts once more to the *. Jon 2:7
waiting for them from the *! Jon 2:8
comes from the * alone." Jon 2:9
And the * ordered the fish to Jon 2:10
THEN THE * spoke to Jonah again: Jon 3:1
He complained to the * about it: Jon 4:2
thought you'd do, *, when I was Jon 4:2
"Please kill me, *; Jon 4:3
Then the * said, "Is it right to Jon 4:4
in the heat, the * arranged for a Jon 4:6
Then the * said, "You feel sorry Jon 4:10
These are messages from the * to Mic 1:1
For the * in his holy Temple has Mic 1:2
grapes! The * will tear down her Mic 1:6
deep to heal. The * stands ready at Mic 1:9
* stands poised against Jerusalem. Mic 1:12
But the * God says, I will reward Mic 2:3
"The People of the *" will live Mic 2:5
Do you think the Spirit of the * Mic 2:7
will go before you—the * leads on. Mic 2:13
you plead with the * for his help Mic 3:4
the Spirit of the *, fearlessly Mic 3:8
(And yet you fawn upon the * and Mic 3:11
is well—the * is here among us. Mic 3:11
mountain of the *, and see the Mic 4:2
be ruled by the * from Jerusalem! Mic 4:2
The * himself has promised this. Mic 4:4
(Therefore we will follow the * Mic 4:5
In that coming day, the * says Mic 4:6
nation, and the * himself shall be Mic 4:7
will come when the * will gather Mic 4:12
the *, the Lord of all the earth. Mic 4:13
the Lord, the * of all the earth. Mic 4:13
strength of the *, in the majesty Mic 5:4
of the name of the * his God, and Mic 5:4
At that same time, says the *, I Mic 5:10
LISTEN TO WHAT the * is saying to Mic 6:1
"Shall we bow before the * with Mic 6:6
to the * if you are wise! Mic 6:9
are coming; the * is sending them. Mic 6:9
As for me, I look to the * for Mic 7:7
When I sit in darkness, the * Mic 7:8
I will be patient while the * Mic 7:9
O *, come and rule your people; Mic 7:14
"Yes," replies the *, "I will Mic 7:15
fortresses to meet the * our God. Mic 7:17
The * is good. Nah 1:7
of, Nineveh, to defy the *? Nah 1:9
who dares to plot against the *? Nah 1:11
But the * is not afraid of him! Nah 1:12
the * declares, "it will vanish. Nah 1:12
only the *, as you have vowed. Nah 1:15
attacks but the * will restore Nah 2:2
But now the * of Hosts has turned Nah 2:13
you," says the * of Hosts; Nah 3:5
O *, how long must I call for Hab 1:2
The * replied: "Look, and be Hab 1:5
O * my God, my Holy One, you who Hab 1:12
And the * said to me, "Write my Hab 2:2
Has not the * decreed that Hab 2:13
awareness of the glory of the *. Hab 2:14
"But the * is in his holy Hab 2:20
that Habakkuk sang before the *: Hab 3:1
O *, now I have heard your Hab 3:2
Literally, "Was the * displeased Hab 3:8,9f
Was it in anger, *, you smote the Hab 3:8,9
announcing its surrender to the *. Hab 3:10
yet I will rejoice in the *; Hab 3:18
my salvation. The * God is my Hab 3:19
SUBJECT: A MESSAGE from the *. Zep 1:1
in all your land," says the *. Zep 1:2
They 'follow the *,' but worship Zep 1:5
worshiped the *, but now no longer Zep 1:6
silence in the presence of the *. Zep 1:7
and their contempt for the *. Zep 1:8f
you have sinned against the *; Zep 1:17
before the fierce anger of the * Zep 2:2
perhaps even yet the * will Zep 2:3
you, too. The * will destroy you Zep 2:5
For the * God will visit his Zep 2:7
I live," says the * of Hosts, God Zep 2:9
at the people of the * of Hosts. Zep 2:10
* will do terrible things to them. Zep 2:11
She does not trust the *, nor Zep 3:2
But the * is there within the Zep 3:5
But the * says, "Be patient; Zep 3:8
so that all can worship the * Zep 3:9
will trust in the name of the *. Zep 3:12
For the * will remove his hand Zep 3:15
And the * himself, the King of Zep 3:15
For the * your God has arrived Zep 3:17,18
No, it is the * himself exulting Zep 3:17,18
your very eyes," says the *. Zep 3:20
SUBJECT: A MESSAGE from the *. Hag 1:1
asks the *. Hag 1:2
"Think it over," says the * of Hag 1:7
there in my glory," says the *. Hag 1:8
message from the * their God; Hag 1:12
Then the * told them (again Hag 1:13
And the * gave them a desire Hag 1:14,15
the same year, the * sent them this Hag 2:1
am with you," says the * of Hosts. Hag 2:4
"For the * of Hosts says, 'In Hag 2:6
my glory,' says the * of Hosts. Hag 2:7
says the *." Hag 2:8,9
the * through Haggai the prophet: Hag 2:10
(speaking for the *), "were Hag 2:14
to return to me," says the *. Hag 2:16,17
Haggai from the * that same day: Hag 2:20
chosen you," says the * of Hosts. Hag 2:23
SUBJECT: MESSAGES FROM the *. Zec 1:1
These messages from the * were Zec 1:1
The * of Hosts was very angry Zec 1:2
"Come, return to me," the * God Zec 1:4
message from the * came to Zec 1:7
the Angel of the *—answered me, Zec 1:10
me, "The * has sent them to patrol Zec 1:10
the Angel of the *, "We have Zec 1:11
the Angel of the * prayed this Zec 1:12
this prayer: "O * of Hosts, for Zec 1:12
And the * answered the angel who Zec 1:13
message from the * of Hosts: Don't Zec 1:14
Therefore the * declares: I have Zec 1:16
rebuilt, says the * of Hosts, and Zec 1:16
Say it again: The * of Hosts Zec 1:17
and the * will again comfort Zec 1:17
Then the * showed me four Zec 1:20
For the * himself will be a wall Zec 2:5
the * to all his exiles there; Zec 2:6,7
says the *. Zec 2:6,7
"The * of Glory has sent me Zec 2:8
Then you will know it was the * Zec 2:9
to live among you,' says the *. Zec 2:10
converted to the *, and they too Zec 2:11,12
Then you will know it was the * Zec 2:11,12
before the *, for he has come to Zec 2:13
before the Angel of the *; Zec 3:1
And the * said to Satan, "I Zec 3:2
Literally, "The * rebuke you, O Zec 3:2f
even the *, who has chosen Zec 3:2f
yes, I, the *, for I have decided Zec 3:2
stood before the Angel of the *. Zec 3:3
Then the Angel of the * spoke very Zec 3:5,6
and said, "The * of Hosts Zec 3:7
And after that,' the * of Hosts Zec 3:10
Spirit, says the * of Hosts—you Zec 4:6
or, "The * bless it!" Zec 4:7f
that I received from the * said: Zec 4:8
are from God, the * of Hosts. Zec 4:9
the eyes of the * rejoice to see Zec 4:10
the eyes of the * that see Zec 4:10
assist the * of all the earth." Zec 4:14
by my name," says the * of Hosts. Zec 5:4
before the * of all the earth; Zec 6:5
the earth, so the * said, "Go. Zec 6:7
Then the * summoned me and said, Zec 6:8
In another message the * said: Zec 6:9
Tell him that the * of Hosts Zec 6:12
will build the Temple of the *. Zec 6:12
the Temple of the *, to honor those Zec 6:14
to rebuild the Temple of the *. Zec 6:15
been from God, the * of Hosts. Zec 6:15
commandments of the * your God." Zec 6:15
to me from the * in late November Zec 7:1
Then this message from the * came Zec 7:8,9
that God, the * of Hosts, commanded Zec 7:12
"The * of Hosts says, I am Zec 8:2
'The Mountain of the * of Hosts.' Zec 8:3
The * of Hosts declares that Zec 8:4
The * says, "This seems Zec 8:6
The * of Hosts says, "Get on Zec 8:9
says the * of Hosts. Zec 8:11
says the *. Zec 8:17
came to me from the * of Hosts: Zec 8:18
to ask the * to bless us, and be Zec 8:20,21
will come to the * of Hosts in Zec 8:22
* is closely watching all mankind, Zec 9:1
belong to the *, as much as do the Zec 9:1f
streets, yet the * will dispossess Zec 9:4
The * shall lead his people as Zec 9:14
lightning; the * God shall sound Zec 9:14
everywhere. The * their God will Zec 9:16,17
ASK THE * for rain in the Zec 10:1
For the * of Hosts has arrived to Zec 10:3
The * is with them as they fight; Zec 10:5
away, for I, the * their God, will Zec 10:6
the mercies of the * and be glad. Zec 10:7
hearts shall rejoice in the *. Zec 10:7
The * says, "I will make my Zec 10:12
Then said the * my God to me, Zec 11:4
either," says the *, "for I will Zec 11:6
And the * told me, 'Toss it into Zec 11:13
Then the * told me to go again Zec 11:15
pronounced by the *, who stretched Zec 12:1
"In that day," says the *, "I Zec 12:4
in the * of Hosts, their God.' Zec 12:5
unmoved. The * will give victory Zec 12:7
The * will defend the people of Zec 12:8
of the * who goes before them! Zec 12:8
And the * of Hosts declares, "In Zec 13:2
lies in the name of the *.' Zec 13:3
and equal," says the * of Hosts. Zec 13:7
they will say, 'The * is our God.' Zec 13:9
WATCH, FOR THE day of the * is Zec 14:1
On that day the * will gather Zec 14:1
Then the * will go out fully Zec 14:3
of Judah, and the * my God shall Zec 14:5
Only the * knows how! Zec 14:7
And the * shall be King over all Zec 14:9
In that day there shall be one * Zec 14:9
And the * will send a plague on Zec 14:12
from the *, and will fight against Zec 14:13
* of Hosts, to celebrate a time Zec 14:16
the * of Hosts, will have no rain. Zec 14:17
Literally, "Holy to the *." Zec 14:20f
the Temple of the * will be as Zec 14:20
shall be sacred to the * of Hosts; Zec 14:21
in the Temple of the * of Hosts! Zec 14:21
you very deeply," says the *. Mal 1:2,3
And the * replies, "I showed my Mal 1:2,3
ruins,' then the * of Hosts will Mal 1:4
the altar of the *—yes, even the Mal 1:8
in you," says the * of Hosts, Mal 1:10
nations," says the * of Hosts. Mal 1:11
serve the * and do what he asks.' Mal 1:13
asks the *. Mal 1:13
King," says the * of Hosts, "and Mal 1:14
this warning from the * of Hosts: Mal 2:1
Levi," says the * of Hosts. Mal 2:4
messengers of the * of Hosts, and Mal 2:7
parody," says the * of Hosts. Mal 2:8
May the * cut off from his Mal 2:12
tears because the * doesn't pay Mal 2:13
it is because the * has seen your Mal 2:14
were united to your wife by the *. Mal 2:15
For the *, the God of Israel, Mal 2:16
You have wearied the * with your Mal 2:17
is good, that it pleases the *! Mal 2:17
Literally, "the *." Mal 3:1f
coming," says the * of Hosts. Mal 3:1
Then once more the * will enjoy Mal 3:4
fear me," says the * of Hosts. Mal 3:5
"For I am the *—I do not Mal 3:6
to me," says the * of Hosts. Mal 3:7
they ripen," says the * of Hosts. Mal 3:11
These are the promises of the * Mal 3:12
proud and arrogant," says the *. Mal 3:13
and loved the * spoke often of him Mal 3:16
mine," says the * of Hosts, "in Mal 3:17
"WATCH NOW," THE * of Hosts Mal 4:1
underfoot," says the * of Hosts. Mal 4:3
* appeared to Joseph in a dream. Mt 2:13
an angel of the * appeared in a Mt 2:19
a road for the *—straighten out the Mt 3:3
* your God to a foolish test!" Mt 4:7
say, 'Worship only the * God. Mt 4:10
They may refer to me as '*,' but Mt 7:21
many will tell me, '*, Lord, we Mt 7:22
many will tell me, 'Lord, *, we Mt 7:22
him, shouting, "*, save us! Mt 8:25
"Yes, *," they told him, "we Mt 9:28
Luke 10:1 remarks, "The * Mt 11:1f
"O Father, * of heaven and earth, Mt 11:25
"All right," the * said, "come Mt 14:29
"Save me, *!" Mt 14:30
on me, O *, King David's Son! Mt 15:22
who comes in the name of the *." Mt 21:9f
Bless him, *!" Mt 21:9
what an amazing thing the * has Mt 21:42
Jesus replied, " 'Love the * Mt 22:37
the Holy Spirit, call him '*'?" Mt 22:43
'God said to my *, Sit at my Mt 22:44
Since David called him '*,' how Mt 22:45
Literally, "in the name of the * Mt 23:39f
know what day your * is coming. Mt 24:42
and faithful servant of the *? Mt 24:45
to yourself, 'My * won't be coming Mt 24:48
drunk, your * will arrive Mt 24:50
"Then they will reply, '*, when Mt 25:44
potters as the * directed me." Mt 27:10
for an angel of the * came down Mt 28:2
"make ready the way of the *; Mk 1:3f
prettily about the * but they have Mk 7:6,7
of the earth * it over the people; Mk 10:42
who comes in the name of the *!" Mk 11:9
* our God is the one and only God. Mk 12:29
it—'God said to my *, sit at my Mk 12:36
Since David called him his *, Mk 12:37
And unless the * shortens that Mk 13:20
When the * Jesus had finished Mk 16:19
preaching, and the * was with them Mk 16:20
and burn incense before the *. Lk 1:8,9
a Jew to turn to the * his God. Lk 1:16
"How kind the * is," she Lk 1:25
favored lady! The * is with you!" Lk 1:28
And the * God shall give him the Lk 1:32
mother of my * should visit me! Lk 1:43
"Oh, how I praise the *. Lk 1:46
of how kind the * had been to her, Lk 1:58

(LORD Con't)
For the hand of the * is surely Lk 1:66
"Praise the *, the God of Lk 1:68
bright with the glory of the *. Lk 2:9
the Messiah, the *—has been born Lk 2:11
which the * has told us about." Lk 2:15
Jerusalem to present him to the *; Lk 2:22
he shall be dedicated to the *." Lk 2:23
baby Jesus to the * in obedience to Lk 2:27
"*," he said, "now I can die Lk 2:29,30,31
a road for the * to travel on! Lk 3:4
the * your God to a foolish test.' Lk 4:12
"The Spirit of the * is upon me; Lk 4:18,19
the acceptable year of the *." Lk 4:18,19f
placed before the *, and ate Lk 6:4
"So why do you call me '*' when Lk 6:46
When the * saw her, his heart Lk 7:13
Literally, "But he said, '*, Lk 9:59f
Another said, "Yes, *, I will Lk 9:61
THE * NOW chose seventy other Lk 10:1
"Plead with the * of the harvest Lk 10:2
you, O Father, * of heaven and Lk 10:21
you must love the * your God with Lk 10:27
But the * said to her, "Martha, Lk 10:41
"*, teach us a prayer to recite Lk 11:1
Peter asked, "*, are you talking Lk 12:41
And the * replied, "I'm talking Lk 12:42,43,44
to think, 'My * won't be back for a Lk 12:45
But the * replied, "You Lk 13:15
and pleading, '*, open the door for Lk 13:24,25
who comes in the name of the *.' Lk 13:35
to the *, "We need more faith; Lk 17:5
"*, where will they be taken?" Lk 17:37
Then the * said, "If even an Lk 18:6
"*," he pleaded, "I want to Lk 18:41
stood before the * and said, "Sir, Lk 19:8
just say, 'The * needs him.' Lk 19:31
replied, "The * needs him!" Lk 19:34
To say that the * is Lk 20:37,38
'God said to my *, the Messiah, Lk 20:42,43
Simon said, "*, I am ready to go Lk 22:33
So they went in—but the * Jesus' Lk 24:3
words, "The * has really risen! Lk 24:33,34
ready for the coming of the *!' Jn 1:23
WHEN THE * knew that the Pharisees Jn 4:1
an angel of the * came from time to Jn 5:4
"Yes, *," the man said, "I Jn 9:38
"*, who will believe us? Jn 12:38
the arm of the * been revealed?" Jn 12:38f
You call me 'Master' and '*,' Jn 13:13
And since I, the * and Teacher, Jn 13:14
and asked him, "*, who is it?" Jn 13:25
have taken away my *," she Jn 20:13
told them, "I have seen the *!" Jn 20:18
was their joy as they saw their *! Jn 20:20
"We have seen the *," he replied, Jn 20:25
"My * and my God!" Jn 20:28
said to Peter, "It is the *!" Jn 21:7
*, for we were quite sure of it. Jn 21:12
"Yes, *," Peter said, "you know Jn 21:16
time. "*, you know my heart; Jn 21:17
asked Jesus, "What about him, *? Jn 21:21
they asked him, "*, are you going Act 1:6
with the *—from the time he was Act 1:21,22
to be chosen. "O *," they said, Act 1:24,25
that awesome Day of the * arrives. Act 2:20
for mercy from the * shall have it Act 2:21
know the * is always with me. Act 2:25
'God spoke to my *, the Messiah, Act 2:34
to be the *, the Messiah!" Act 2:36
been called by the * our God, and Act 2:39
presence of the * and send Jesus Act 3:19
long ago, 'The * God will raise up Act 3:21,22
"O *, Creator of heaven and earth Act 4:24
rage against the *, and the foolish Act 4:25,26
And now, O *, hear their Act 4:29
of the * Jesus, and there was warm Act 4:33
"to try the Spirit of the *." Act 5:9f
*, crowds both of men and women. Act 5:14
But an angel of the * came at Act 5:19
the voice of the * called out to Act 7:31
"And the * said to him, 'Take Act 7:33
prophecies the * God asks, 'Was it Act 7:42
throne,' says the * through his Act 7:48,49
asks the *. Act 7:48,49
"* Jesus, receive my spirit." Act 7:59
knees, shouting, "*, don't charge Act 7:60
in the name of the * Jesus. Act 8:16
an angel of the * said to him, "Go Act 8:26
the Spirit of the * caught away Act 8:39
named Ananias. The * spoke to him Act 9:10
"Yes, *!" Act 9:10
And the * said, "Go over to Act 9:11
"But *," exclaimed Ananias, "I Act 9:13
But the * said, "Go and do what Act 9:15
Paul, the * Jesus, who appeared to Act 9:17
Paul had seen the * on the way to Act 9:27
Damascus, what the * had said to Act 9:27
boldly in the name of the *. Act 9:29
in the fear of the * and in the Act 9:31
turned to the * when they saw Act 9:35
town, and many believed in the *. Act 9:42
"Never, *," Peter declared, "I Act 10:14
waiting before the *, anxious to Act 10:33
Messiah, who is * of all creation. Act 10:36,37
" 'Never, *,' I replied. Act 11:8
we believed on the * Jesus Christ, Act 11:17
about the * Jesus to some Greeks. Act 11:20
And the * honored this effort so Act 11:21
close to the *, whatever the cost. Act 11:23
of people were added to the *. Act 11:24
angel of the * stood beside Peter! Act 12:7
"The * has sent his angel and Act 12:11
the * had brought him out of jail. Act 12:17
Instantly, an angel of the * Act 12:23
to keep him from trusting the *. Act 13:8
end your opposition to the *? Act 13:10
For this is as the * commanded Act 13:47
boldly, and the * proved their Act 14:3
of the * in whom they trusted. Act 14:23
by the free gift of the * Jesus?" Act 15:11
'Afterwards' [says the * Act 15:16
*—all those marked with my name.' Act 15:17
That is what the * says, who Act 15:18
the sake of our * Jesus Christ—will Act 15:26
we proclaimed the word of the *." Act 15:36f
to us, the * opened her heart and Act 16:14
am faithful to the *," she said, Act 16:15
hymns to the *—and the other Act 16:25
They replied, "Believe on the * Act 16:31
the Good News from the *. Act 16:32
and since he is * of heaven and Act 17:24
believed in the * and were Act 18:8
One night the * spoke to Paul in Act 18:9
and helping them grow in the *. Act 18:23
the name of the * Jesus. Act 19:5
by using the name of the * Jesus. Act 19:13
the * Jesus was greatly honored. Act 19:17
faith in our * Jesus Christ. Act 20:21
assigned me by the * Jesus—the work Act 20:24
the words of the * Jesus, 'It is Act 20:35
die for the sake of the * Jesus." Act 21:13
"The will of the * be done." Act 21:14
"And I said, 'What shall I do, * Act 22:10
"And the * told me, 'Get up and Act 22:10
calling on the name of the *.' Act 22:16
" 'But *,' I argued, 'they Act 22:19
That night the * stood beside Act 23:11
"And the * replied, 'I am Jesus, Act 26:15
God and about the * Jesus Christ; Act 28:31
Jesus Christ our *, who came as a Rom 1:3
and from Jesus Christ our *. Rom 1:6,7
your church grow strong in the *. Rom 1:11,12
counted against him by the *." Rom 4:8
back Jesus our * from the dead. Rom 4:24
Christ our * has done for us. Rom 5:1
of what our * Jesus Christ has done Rom 5:11
life through Jesus Christ our *. Rom 5:21
him, through Jesus Christ our *. Rom 6:11
life through Jesus Christ our *. Rom 6:23
God through Jesus Christ our *." Rom 7:23,24,25f
by Jesus Christ our *. Rom 7:23,24,25
by our * Jesus Christ when he died Rom 8:39
"For the * will execute his Rom 9:28
Christ is your *, and believe in Rom 10:9
all have the same * who generously Rom 10:12
the name of the * will be saved. Rom 10:13
prophet said, "*, who has believed Rom 10:16
us can know the mind of the *? Rom 11:34
the * enough to induce him to act? Rom 11:35
but serve the * enthusiastically. Rom 12:11
Wake up, for the coming of the * Rom 13:11
But ask the * Jesus Christ to Rom 13:14
*, you are trying to honor him; Rom 14:6
he is thankful to the * for it; Rom 14:6
to please the *, and is thankful. Rom 14:6
Living or dying we follow the *. Rom 14:8
that he can be our * both while we Rom 14:9
I live," says the *, "every knee Rom 14:11
authority of the * Jesus that there Rom 14:14
If you let Christ be * in these Rom 14:18
difference to the * whether we do Rom 15:1
and thus build him up in the *. Rom 15:1
of those who were against the *." Rom 15:3
us can praise the * together with Rom 15:6
the Father of our * Jesus Christ. Rom 15:6
And yet again, "Praise the *, O Rom 15:11
when I come the * will give me a Rom 15:29
For the * Jesus Christ's sake, Rom 15:30
your sister in the *, giving her a Rom 16:1
a good man whom the * approves; Rom 16:10
who has worked so hard for the *. Rom 16:12
Greet Rufus for me, whom the * Rom 16:13
working for our * Jesus, but only Rom 16:18
The blessings from our * Jesus Rom 16:20
May the grace of our * Jesus Rom 16:24
and steady in the *, just as the Rom 16:25,26,27
through Jesus Christ our *. Rom 16:25,26,27
of Jesus Christ, our * and theirs. 1Co 1:2
May God our Father and the * 1Co 1:3
the return of our * Jesus Christ. 1Co 1:7
with his Son, even Christ our *. 1Co 1:9
in the name of the * Jesus Christ 1Co 1:1
only of what the * has done." 1Co 1:3
have crucified the * of Glory. 1Co 2:
ready for those who love the *. 1Co 2:
the *, but your own desires; 1Co 3:
who don't belong to the * at all. 1Co 3:
little you have grown in the *? 1Co 3:
are told that the * knows full well 1Co 3:2
It is the * himself who must 1Co 4:
before the * returns as to whether 1Co 4:
When the * comes, he will turn on 1Co 4:
and trustworthy child in the *. 1Co 4:1
and soon, if the * will let me, and 1Co 4:1
in the name of the * Jesus Christ I 1Co 5:3,
the power of the * Jesus will be 1Co 5:3,
when our * Jesus Christ returns. 1Co 5:
* to let yourselves be cheated. 1Co 6:
of what the * Jesus Christ and the 1Co 6:1
that, but for the *, and the Lord 1Co 6:1
the Lord, and the * wants to fill 1Co 6:1
he raised up the * Jesus Christ. 1Co 6:14
yourself to the *, you and Christ 1Co 6:17
this is what the * himself has 1Co 7:10
commands from the *, but they seem 1Co 7:12
might never come to know the *; 1Co 7:14
If the * calls you, and you are 1Co 7:22
now the * is there to help him. 1Co 7:24
command for them from the *. 1Co 7:25
But the * in his kindness has 1Co 7:25
as free as possible for the *; 1Co 7:29
the * in all she is and does. 1Co 7:34
help you serve the * best, with as 1Co 7:35
and one * Jesus Christ, who made 1Co 8:6
seen Jesus our * with my own eyes. 1Co 9:1
by those offering it to the *. 1Co 9:13
In the same way the * has given 1Co 9:14
* would give me a special reward; 1Co 9:17
Are you tempting the * to be 1Co 10:22
to the * and is yours to enjoy. 1Co 10:26
For this is what the * himself 1Co 11:23
betrayed him, the * Jesus took 1Co 11:23
this cup of the * in an unworthy 1Co 11:27
the body and the blood of the *. 1Co 11:27
punished by the *, it is so that we 1Co 11:32
say, "Jesus is *," and really 1Co 12:3
it is the same * we are serving. 1Co 12:5
others grow in the *, encouraging 1Co 14:3
all, and build them up in the *. 1Co 14:26
or idea from the *, the one who is 1Co 14:29,30
a commandment from the * himself. 1Co 14:37
my pride in your growth in the *. 1Co 15:31
through Jesus Christ our *! 1Co 15:57
you do for the * is ever wasted as 1Co 15:58
much the * has helped you earn. 1Co 16:2
stay awhile, if the * will let me. 1Co 16:7
stand true to the *; 1Co 16:13
love the *, that person is cursed. 1Co 16:22
person is cursed. * Jesus, come! 1Co 16:22
May the love and favor of the * 1Co 16:23
May God our Father and the * 2Co 1:2
the Father of our * Jesus Christ, 2Co 1:3,4
depending upon the * for his help, 2Co 1:12
when our * Jesus comes back again. 2Co 1:13,14
city of Troas, the * gave me 2Co 2:12
others about the * and to spread 2Co 2:14
turns to the * from his sins, then 2Co 3:16
taken away. The * is the Spirit 2Co 3:17
reflect the glory of the *. 2Co 3:18
And as the Spirit of the * works 2Co 3:18
but about Christ Jesus as *. 2Co 4:5
we serve the *, but this gives us 2Co 4:11
who brought the * Jesus back from 2Co 4:14
and the more the * is glorified. 2Co 4:15
in the * is growing every day. 2Co 4:16
we will be at home with the *. 2Co 5:8
solemn fear of the *, which is ever 2Co 5:11
from finding the * by the way we 2Co 6:3
with us and blame it on the *. 2Co 6:3
We stand true to the * whether 2Co 6:8
time we have the joy of the *. 2Co 6:10
do not love the *, for what do the 2Co 6:14
That is why the * has said, 2Co 6:17
this grief from the * did for you! 2Co 7:11
I wrote as I did so the * could 2Co 7:12
themselves to the * and to us, for 2Co 8:5
and kindness our * Jesus was: 2Co 8:9
This will glorify the * and show 2Co 8:19
of those who belong to the *. 2Co 8:23
about what the * has done and not 2Co 10:17
But when the * commends him, 2Co 10:18
devotion to our *, just as Eve was 2Co 11:3
something the * commanded me to do, 2Co 11:17
God, the Father of our * Jesus 2Co 11:31
had, and revelations from the *. 2Co 12:1
test and truly belong to the *. 2Co 13:6
Greet each other warmly in the *. 2Co 13:12
May the grace of our * Jesus 2Co 13:14
and from the * Jesus Christ. Gal 1:3
to think such things about our *. Gal 2:17
I am trusting the * to bring you Gal 5:10
the cross of our * Jesus Christ. Gal 6:14

(LORD Con't)
* Jesus Christ be with you all. Gal 6:18
ever loyal to the *: This is Paul Eph 1:1
our Father and Jesus Christ our *. Eph 1:2
the Father of our * Jesus Christ, Eph 1:3
faith in the * Jesus and of the Eph 1:15
Father of our * Jesus Christ, to Eph 1:16,17
of those who are against the *. Eph 2:2
it through Jesus Christ our *. Eph 3:11
for serving the *—to live and act Eph 4:1
For us there is only one *, one Eph 4:5
full-grown in the *—yes, to the Eph 4:13
speaking for the *: Live no longer Eph 4:17,18
of light from the *, and your Eph 5:8
you go along what pleases the *. Eph 5:10
do whatever the * wants you to. Eph 5:17
much about the *, quoting psalms Eph 5:19
music in your hearts to the *. Eph 5:19
in the name of our * Jesus Christ. Eph 5:20
the same way you submit to the *. Eph 5:22
discipline the * himself approves, Eph 6:4
Remember, the * will pay you for Eph 6:8
others about the *, and as I Eph 6:19
the Father and the * Jesus Christ. Eph 6:23
sincerely love our * Jesus Christ. Eph 6:24
our Father and the * Jesus Christ Php 1:2
you from now until our * returns. Php 1:10
much praise and glory to the *. Php 1:11
they know that the * has brought me Php 1:16,17
in the *, sharing the same Spirit? Php 2:1
*, to the glory of God the Father. Php 2:11
If the * is willing, I will send Php 2:19
And I am trusting the * that Php 2:24
Welcome him in the * with great Php 2:29
DEAR friends, be glad in the *. Php 3:1
gain of knowing Christ Jesus my *. Php 3:8
our Savior the * Jesus Christ is; Php 3:20
friends, stay true to the *. Php 4:1
Always be full of joy in the *; Php 4:4
Remember that the * is coming Php 4:5
* that you are helping me again. Php 4:10
The blessings of our * Jesus Php 4:23
the Father of our * Jesus Christ, Col 1:3
much you trust the *, and how much Col 1:4
always please the * and honor him, Col 1:10
of the joy of the *, and always Col 1:11
strong in the *, convinced of the Col 1:23
on growing in the *, and become Col 2:7
Remember, the * forgave you, so Col 3:13
to the * with thankful hearts. Col 3:16
of the * Jesus, and come with him Col 3:17
is what the * has planned for you. Col 3:18
mothers, for that pleases the *. Col 3:20
your love for the * and because you Col 3:22
working for the * and not merely Col 3:23
that it is the * Christ who is Col 3:24
worker and serves the * with me. Col 4:7
do all the * has told you to." Col 4:17
the Father and the * Jesus Christ: 1Th 1:1
and from Jesus Christ our *. 1Th 1:1
the return of our * Jesus Christ. 1Th 1:3
And now the Word of the * has 1Th 1:8
they even executed the * Jesus; 1Th 2:15
before our * Jesus Christ when he 1Th 2:19
you are standing true to the *. 1Th 3:7
* Jesus send us back to you again. 1Th 3:11
And may the * make your love to 1Th 3:12
that day when our * Jesus Christ 1Th 3:13
gave you from the * Jesus himself. 1Th 4:1
in the name of the * Jesus—that you 1Th 4:1
wife, because the * will punish you 1Th 4:6
directly from the *: that we who 1Th 4:15
living when the * returns will not 1Th 4:15
For the * himself will come down 1Th 4:16
the first to rise to meet the *. 1Th 4:16
clouds to meet the * in the air and 1Th 4:17
That day of the * will come 1Th 5:2
when that day of the * comes. 1Th 5:4
us through our * Jesus Christ; 1Th 5:9
* Jesus Christ comes back again. 1Th 5:23
in the name of the * to read this 1Th 5:27
blessings from our * Jesus Christ 1Th 5:28
Father and in the * Jesus Christ. 2Th 1:1
May God the Father and the * 2Th 1:2
with us when the * Jesus appears 2Th 1:7
them through our * Jesus Christ. 2Th 1:8
separated from the *, never to see 2Th 1:9
the name of the * Jesus Christ 2Th 1:12
our God and of the * Jesus Christ 2Th 1:12
again of our * Jesus Christ, and 2Th 2:1
day of the * has already begun. 2Th 2:1
appear, whom the * Jesus will burn 2Th 2:8
loved by the *, because God chose 2Th 2:13
the glory of our * Jesus Christ. 2Th 2:14
May our * Jesus Christ himself 2Th 2:16
men, for not everyone loves the *. 2Th 3:2
But the * is faithful; 2Th 3:3
And we trust the * that you are 2Th 3:4
May the * bring you into an ever 2Th 3:5
in the name of our * Jesus Christ 2Th 3:6
In the name of the * Jesus 2Th 3:12
May the * of peace himself give 2Th 3:16
happens. The * be with you all. 2Th 3:16
May the blessing of our * Jesus 2Th 3:18
Jesus Christ our *—our only hope. 1Ti 1:1
son to me in the things of the *. 1Ti 1:2
Jesus Christ our * show you his 1Ti 1:2
Christ Jesus our * for choosing me 1Ti 1:12
Oh, how kind our * was, for he 1Ti 1:14
just as the * told us through his 1Ti 1:18
and thinking much about the *. 1Ti 2:2
I never let women teach men or * 1Ti 2:12
and bold trust in the *. 1Ti 3:13
of God and the * Jesus Christ and 1Ti 5:21
teachings of the * Jesus Christ and 1Ti 6:3
until our * Jesus Christ returns. 1Ti 6:14
King of kings and * of lords, who 1Ti 6:15
Christ Jesus our * shower you with 2Ti 1:2
I know how much you trust the *, 2Ti 1:5
others about our *, or to let them 2Ti 1:8
with me for the *, for he will give 2Ti 1:8
May the * bless Onesiphorus and 2Ti 1:16
May the * give him a special 2Ti 1:18
and may the * help you to 2Ti 2:7
in the name of the * not to argue 2Ti 2:14
on it: "The * knows those who are 2Ti 2:19
love the * and have pure hearts. 2Ti 2:22
Lystra, but the * delivered me. 2Ti 3:11
be afraid of suffering for the *. 2Ti 4:5
and hard for my *, and through it 2Ti 4:7
for me which the *, the righteous 2Ti 4:8
me much harm. The * will punish 2Ti 4:14
But the * stood with me and gave 2Ti 4:17
Yes, and the * will always 2Ti 4:18
May the * Jesus Christ be with 2Ti 4:22
my son in the affairs of the *. Tit 1:4
must love the * and not have a Tit 1:6
May God our Father and the * Phm 1:3
in the * Jesus and in his people. Phm 1:5
to the * while here in my chains. Phm 1:10
my weary heart will praise the *. Phm 1:20
The blessings of our * Jesus Phm 1:25
God also called him "*" when he Heb 1:10
when he said, "*, in the beginning Heb 1:10
announced by the * Jesus himself, Heb 2:3
our joy and our trust in the *. Heb 3:6
The * willing, we will go on now Heb 6:3
you back to the * again if you have Heb 6:4
Only to Christ he said, "The * Heb 7:21
by the * and not by human hands. Heb 8:2
Israel, says the *: I will write my Heb 8:10
should know the *,' because Heb 8:11
who also said, "The * himself Heb 10:30
right on with the * even though it Heb 10:32
happy trust in the * die away, no Heb 10:35
be angry when the * punishes you. Heb 12:5
is not holy will not see the *. Heb 12:14
or fear, "The * is my Helper and I Heb 13:6
and try to trust the * as they do. Heb 13:7
about you to the * and not with Heb 13:17
from the dead our * Jesus, equip Heb 13:20,21
of God and of the * Jesus Christ. Jas 1:1
* to give you any solid answer. Jas 1:7,8
nothing to the *, for he will soon Jas 1:10,11
true to the *—not soiled and Jas 1:27
you belong to the * Jesus Christ, Jas 2:1
Jesus Christ, the * of glory, if Jas 2:1
God, and the * declared him good in Jas 2:23
before the *, he will lift you up, Jas 4:10
say is, "If the * wants us to, we Jas 4:15
the ears of the * of Hosts. Jas 5:4
for the coming of the * is near. Jas 5:8
to trust the * in sorrow; Jas 5:11
be singing praises to the *. Jas 5:13
him, calling on the * to heal him. Jas 5:14
him, for the * will make him well; Jas 5:15
some sin, the * will forgive him. Jas 5:15
longer trusts the *, and someone Jas 5:19
and Father of our * Jesus Christ; 1Pe 1:3
do, just as the * is holy, who 1Pe 1:15
but the Word of the * will last 1Pe 1:25
strong in the * and be saved." 1Pe 2:2,3f
how kind the * has been to you, put 1Pe 2:2,3
Praise the * if you are punished 1Pe 2:19
to them about the *, they will be 1Pe 3:1
For the * is watching his 1Pe 3:12
to Christ your * and if anybody 1Pe 3:15
who have never believed in the *? 1Pe 4:17
you are eager to serve the *. 1Pe 5:2
Trust the *; 1Pe 5:9
—she is your sister in the *—sends 1Pe 5:13
and useful to our * Jesus Christ. 2Pe 1:8
a strong, good life for the *. 2Pe 1:9
of our * and Savior Jesus Christ. 2Pe 1:11
But the * Jesus Christ has 2Pe 1:13,14
the power of our * Jesus Christ and 2Pe 1:16
But at the same time the * 2Pe 2:7,8
So also the * can rescue you and 2Pe 2:9
presence of the *, and are far 2Pe 2:11
learning about our * and Savior 2Pe 2:20
you the words of our * and Savior. 2Pe 3:1
now is like tomorrow to the *. 2Pe 3:8
The day of the * is surely 2Pe 3:10
our * and Savior Jesus Christ. 2Pe 3:18
with the * so that when he comes 1Jn 2:28
even when we stand before the *. 1Jn 3:19
* will surely feel it even more, 1Jn 3:20
Or, perhaps, "the * will be 1Jn 3:20f
we can come to the * with perfect 1Jn 3:21
and sisters in the *—by how much 1Jn 5:2
win your full reward from the *. 2Jn 1:8
For they are traveling for the * 3Jn 1:7
only Master and *, Jesus Christ. Jud 1:4
already—that the * saved a whole Jud 1:5
simply said, "The * rebuke you." Jud 1:9
them: "See, the * is coming with Jud 1:14
apostles of our * Jesus Christ told Jud 1:17
life that our * Jesus Christ in his Jud 1:21
them to find the * by being kind to Jud 1:23
us through Jesus Christ our *; Jud 1:24,25
a special blessing from the *. Rev 1:3
God, who is the *, the All Powerful Rev 1:8
you suffer for the *, and I know Rev 2:9
holy, holy, * God Almighty—the one Rev 4:8
singing, "O *, you are worthy to Rev 4:11
They called loudly to the * and Rev 6:10
"O Sovereign *, holy and true, how Rev 6:10
place where their * was crucified. Rev 11:8,9
to our *, and to his Christ; Rev 11:15
Or, "The * and his Anointed shall Rev 11:15f
"We give thanks, * God Almighty, Rev 11:17
great blasphemies against the *; Rev 13:5
* God Almighty. Rev 15:3,4
O *, Rev 15:3,4
say, "Yes, * God Almighty, your Rev 16:7
battle against the * on that great Rev 16:14
for he is * over all lords, and Rev 17:14
for mighty is the * who judges Rev 18:8
Praise the *! Rev 19:1
their voices rang, "Praise the *! Rev 19:3
Praise the *!" Rev 19:4
of great thunder, "Praise the *. Rev 19:6
For the * our God, the Almighty, Rev 19:6
"King of Kings and * of Lords." Rev 19:16
the city, for the * God Almighty Rev 21:22
the * God will be their light; Rev 22:5

LORD'S
call themselves "the * people." Gen 4:26
by stealing my * personal silver Gen 44:5
shall be called the * Passover. Ex 12:11
is the * supremely holy altar." Ex 30:10
of Israel, to the * attention, and Ex 30:16
These were the * directions to Ex 30:34
you who are on the * side, come Ex 32:26
to them by the * command to Ex 35:29
with the * instructions to Moses. Ex 39:1
with the * instructions to Moses. Ex 39:6,7
of the * instructions to Moses. Ex 39:32
all the * instructions to Moses. Ex 39:42
to determine the * will by simple Lev 8:8f
to the * use Aaron and his sons and Lev 8:30
have followed the * instructions, Lev 9:6
* and which is to be sent away. Lev 16:8
the * eyes from all of your sins. Lev 16:29,30
or fruit, is the *, and is holy. Lev 27:30
out the * instructions to Moses. Num 4:37
to the * instructions to Moses. Num 4:49
may the * face radiate with joy Num 6:24,25,26
* travel instructions to Moses. Num 10:13
I only wish that all of the * Num 11:29
Now you are disobeying the * Num 14:41
out the * mind concerning him. Num 15:34
Thus the * directions to Moses Num 16:40
"You have killed the * people." Num 16:41
you receive as the * portion, and Num 18:28,29
for accepting the * tithes if you Num 18:32
for it is the * portion." Num 31:30
Literally, "were the * portion." Num 31:36-40f
All of the * portion was given to Num 31:41
In accordance with the * Num 31:47
And the * anger was hot against Num 32:10,11
for the * battles go with you over Num 32:29
rebelled against the * command. Deu 1:26
again against the * commandment and Deu 1:43
is right and good in the * eyes. Deu 6:18
experienced the * punishments or Deu 11:2
take the money to the * sanctuary. Deu 14:25
you by following the * directions. Deu 21:9
AFTER THE DEATH of Moses, the * Jos 1:1
tribes of the * army across to the Jos 4:12,13
For it was Joshua who, at the * Jos 4:15,16
of the * army," he replied. Jos 5:14
were kept for the * treasury. Jos 6:24
for the * treasury was disobeyed. Jos 7:1
of the * instructions to Moses. Jos 11:15
with the * directions to Moses. Jos 14:5
This was done in the * presence Jos 19:51
So the * command to Moses was Jos 21:8
"You have done as the * disciple Jos 22:2,3
given you by the * servant Moses, Jos 22:4
However, the * reply through the Ju 6:8
"May the * will be done." 1Sa 1:23
For all the earth is the * 1Sa 2:8

(LORD'S Con't)
and the child became the * 1Sa 2:11
a child, was the * helper and wore 1Sa 2:18
reports from the * people about 1Sa 2:23,24,25
thing to make the * people sin. 1Sa 2:23,24,25
he was a favorite of the *, too! 1Sa 2:26
"It is the * will," Eli replied; 1Sa 3:18
But if you rebel against the * 1Sa 12:15
even asked for the * help!' 1Sa 13:12
for you have not obeyed the * 1Sa 13:14
"Well, I have carried out the * 1Sa 15:13
by fighting the * battles." 1Sa 18:17
harm him—he is the * chosen king.' 1Sa 24:9,10
after attacking the * chosen king? 1Sa 26:9
can't be with the * people, and you 1Sa 26:19
did not obey the * instructions 1Sa 28:18
the * enemies," he wrote them. 1Sa 30:26
and for the * people, and for the 2Sa 1:12
May the * will be done." 2Sa 10:12
because of the * interest. 2Sa 12:25
for he cursed the * chosen king!" 2Sa 19:21
Should you destroy what is the * 2Sa 20:19
(But the * hand was in it—he 1Ki 12:15
Then, at the * command, the 1Ki 13:2
who disobeyed the * command; 1Ki 13:26
For this was the * curse upon 1Ki 16:34
to kill all of the * prophets, 1Ki 18:3,4
trying to kill the * prophets, and 1Ki 18:13
* altar, with no fire under it. 1Ki 18:30
the stones to rebuild the * altar. 1Ki 18:32
you king of the * people, Israel. 2Ki 9:6
zeal exceeded the * command in this 2Ki 10:11f
that they would be the * people. 2Ki 11:17
But Jehoahaz prayed for the * 2Ki 13:4
"This is the * arrow, full of 2Ki 13:16,17
He was a good king in the * 2Ki 14:3
evil king in the * opinion, just 2Ki 15:9
(So the * statement to Jehu came 2Ki 15:12
* specific and repeated warnings. 2Ki 17:12
despite the * stern warnings. 2Ki 17:15
it, just as the * prophet had 2Ki 23:16
in the Temple at the * directions. 2Ki 24:13
in charge of the * Tabernacle. 1Ch 9:23
by Moses, the * assistant, while he 2Ch 1:2,3
projects of the * Temple and his 2Ch 8:1
himself, the * anger was turned 2Ch 12:12
"The * promise—that a descendant 2Ch 23:2,3
and the people would be the *. 2Ch 23:15,16,17
* opinion of him was concerned. 2Ch 26:4
a good one in the * opinion, just 2Ch 29:2
desire to obey the * direction as 2Ch 30:12
were brought into the * house. 2Ch 31:12,13
the reason the * great anger has 2Ch 34:21
All among you who are the * 2Ch 36:22,23
The * promise is sure. Ps 12:6
A song to sing on the * Day Ps 92:1
into the * own garden, and are Ps 92:13
This is the * punishment upon my Ps 109:20
This is the * doing, and it is Ps 118:23
The * wisdom founded the earth; Pro 3:19
The * blessing is our greatest Pro 10:22
just balance and scales are the *; Pro 16:11f
is the * searchlight exposing his Pro 20:27
you exhaust the * as well! Is 7:13
with cedars! The * reply to your Is 9:11,12
And even then the * anger against Is 9:11,12
Scream in terror, for the * time Is 13:6
For the * good hand will rest Is 25:10
while until the * wrath against Is 26:20
* telling me to take this land? Is 36:10
"I am the *," they'll proudly Is 44:5
Yet it was the * good plan to Is 53:10
This miracle will make the * name Is 55:13
of my people—the * watchmen, his Is 56:10
delight as the * holy day, and Is 58:13
People" and "The * Redeemed," Is 62:12
fierce anger. The * decree of Jer 4:27
each vine, for they are not the *. Jer 5:10
Where is the * messenger to Jer 9:12
Then the * message came to me Jer 13:3
tears because the * flock shall be Jer 13:17
tell them the * reply is this: Jer 16:11
For this is the * message Jer 22:6
Jeremiah, "What is the * message? Jer 23:37
THIS IS ANOTHER of the * messages Jer 30:1
But this is the * reply: I would Jer 33:25,26
golden cup in the * hands, a cup Jer 51:7
ejected from the * presence in Jer 52:3
It is only the * mercies that Lam 3:22
beneath the * demands, to lie face Lam 3:28
you without the * permission? Lam 3:37
of our life, the * anointed—was Lam 4:20
THEN THE * message came to me Eze 18:1
THE * MESSAGE came to me again, Eze 23:1
THEN THE * message came to me Eze 25:1
resisting the * attempts to lead Hos 4:16
day of the * judgment approaches. Joe 2:1
"The * reply is this: 'Because Amo 7:17
The * vengeance will soon fall Ob 1:15
listen to the * complaint! Mic 6:2
your God. The * voice calls out to Mic 6:9
to you in that day of the * wrath. Zep 1:18
as the foundation of the * Temple Hag 2:18,19
And Judah shall be the * Zec 2:11,12
to the * Temple at Jerusalem, to Zec 7:2
This was the * reply: Zec 7:4
AGAIN THE * message came to me: Zec 8:1
HERE IS THE * message to Israel, Mal 1:1
then you will say, "Truly, the * Mal 1:5
to be ready for the * arrival." Mk 1:3
This is the * doing and it is an Mk 12:11
For he will be one of the * Lk 1:15
Mary said, "I am the * servant, Lk 1:38
And the * healing power was upon Lk 5:17
portions of the * Prayer as Lk 11:5,6f
* return from the wedding feast. Lk 12:36
and said, "They have taken the * Jn 20:2
"the * Supper." Act 2:42f
Then I thought of the * words Act 11:16
and Greeks—heard the * message. Act 19:10
and ate the * Supper together; Act 20:10,11,12
I have done the * work humbly—yes, Act 20:19
and Tryphosa, the * workers, and to Rom 16:12
one to know the * thoughts, or to 1Co 2:16
why we have been doing the * work. 1Co 4:5
opportunities for doing the * work 1Co 7:29
his time doing the * work and 1Co 7:32
* brothers do, and as Peter does? 1Co 9:5
And don't try the * 1Co 10:9
When we ask the * blessing upon 1Co 10:16
cup of wine at the * Table, this 1Co 10:16
* Table and at Satan's table, too. 1Co 10:21
the * Table and at Satan's table. 1Co 10:21
eat, it isn't the * Supper you are 1Co 11:20
* death, that he has died for you. 1Co 11:26
you gather for the * Supper—the 1Co 11:33
abounding in the * work, for you 1Co 15:58
On every * Day each of you 1Co 16:2
is doing the * work just as I am. 1Co 16:10
for I want to use the * authority 2Co 13:10
time was James, our * brother. Gal 1:19
and so obey our * command. Gal 6:2
the * mighty power within you. Eph 6:10
helper in the * work, will tell you Eph 6:21
Please, please, with the * help, Php 4:2
became our followers and the *; 1Th 1:6
Pray first that the * message 2Th 3:1
Fight well in the * battles, just 1Ti 1:18
Follow the * rules for doing his 2Ti 2:5
for he is great in the * sight. Jas 1:9
you truly obey our * command, "You Jas 2:8
this law of our * when you favor Jas 2:9
waiting for the * return, be Jas 5:7
suffering, look at the * prophets. Jas 5:10
we can see how the * plan finally Jas 5:11
have tasted the * goodness and 1Pe 2:2,3f
For the * sake, obey every law 1Pe 2:13
but the * face is hard against 1Pe 3:12
partners with them in the * work. 3Jn 1:8
sufferer for the * sake, who is Rev 1:9
It was the * Day and I was Rev 1:10

LORDS
God is God of gods and Lord of *. Deu 10:17
of the Lord who is above all *. Ps 7:17
Give thanks to the Lord of *, Ps 136:3
not as the fallen * who are buried Eze 32:27
* it over those beneath him. Mt 20:25
kings and Lord of *, who alone can 1Ti 6:15
for he is Lord over all *, and Rev 17:14
"King of Kings and Lord of *." Rev 19:16

LOSE
They shall * heart 2Sa 22:46
see it they will * face because you Ps 86:17
evil men * the good things they Pro 2:22
her temptation and * your honor, Pro 5:9
The good shall never * God's Pro 10:30
but the wicked shall * everything. Pro 10:30
on too tightly and * everything. Pro 11:24,25
The wicked will finally *; Pro 21:18
A time to *; Ecc 3:6
I'll never * my children." Is 47:8
Sooner or later he will * his Jer 17:11
but she will * her influence over Dan 11:6
her to make her * her way, so that Hos 1:6
If you * your flavor, what will Mt 5:13
for then you will * the reward from Mt 6:1
they will never * their value, and Mt 6:20
cling to your life, you will * it; Mt 10:39
his life for himself shall * it; Mt 16:25
whole world—and * eternal life? Mt 16:26
who trusts in me to * his faith, Mt 18:6
saving your life, you will * it. Mk 8:35
solemnly—he won't * his reward. Mk 9:41
believe in me to * faith—it would Mk 9:42
So don't * your flavor! Mk 9:50
who does not * his faith in me.' Lk 7:23
persecution blow, they * interest. Lk 8:13
on keeping his life will * it; Lk 9:24
to his life shall * it, and whoever Lk 17:33
who have little, soon * even that. Lk 19:26
that I should not * even one of all Jn 6:39
your life down here—you will * it. Jn 12:25

he felt that he had no time to *. Act 18:2
goddess Diana will * its influence, Act 19:2
Not one of us will * our lives, Act 27:2
die of hunger then * the 1Co 9:1
So please don't * heart at what Eph 3:1

LOSES
so that a man * all taste and Job 33:2
account * its significance. Is 7:14
and anyone who * his life for me Mt 16:2
and * his soul in the process? Mk 8:3
"Good salt is worthless if it * Mk 9:5
Whoever * his life for my sake Lk 9:2
valuable silver coins and * one. Lk 15:
whoever * his life shall save it. Lk 17:3
body suffers, sin * its power, and 1Pe 4:

LOSING
I am * all hope; Ps 143:
want my people * their property and Eze 46:1
Beware of being like them, and * 2Jn 1:

LOSS
to him after the * of his mother. Gen 24:67
indifferent to the * of the rights Gen 25:34
No, I took the *. Gen 31:39
for the * of his father's home). Gen 41:51
must pay for the * of his time Ex 21:19
by paying for the *, plus a Lev 5:16
* of at least one of my eyes." Ju 16:28
all Israel for the * of their Ju 21:6
be any greater * than if they stay 2Ki 7:13
them in and out to avoid *. 1Ch 9:28
brooding over the * of Vashti, Est 2:1
neighbor and leads him into *." Pro 16:29
widowhood and the * of your Is 47:9
Martha and Mary on their *. Jn 11:19
situation and our * of income, but Act 19:27
* of cargo, injuries, and death." Act 27:10
avoided all this injury and *! Act 27:21
burns up, he will have a great *. 1Co 3:15
Their future is eternal *, for Php 3:19

LOST
him as though he had * his senses. Gen 19:14
gladly agreed, and * no time in Gen 34:18,19
anything else is *, and the owner Ex 22:9
What these looked like has been * Ex 28:30,31f
or by finding a * article and Lev 6:3
without having * a single man! Jos 10:21
And that day they * another Ju 20:25
So the tribe of Benjamin * Ju 20:46,47
of Israel will not be * forever. Ju 21:17
donkeys that were * three days ago, 1Sa 9:20
enemy troops, they * their nerve 1Sa 13:6
not one thing was * or stolen, but 1Sa 25:21
and life has * its excitement. 2Sa 19:35
another army like the one you *; 1Ki 20:25
battle had been *, he led 700 of 2Ki 3:26
his father had * to Ben-hadad. 2Ki 13:25
Jeroboam II recovered the * 2Ki 14:25
However, they had * their Ez 2:59
But they too had * their Ez 2:62,63
for it will be * to you." Ez 4:16
"present them without a penny * Ez 8:29
But they had * their genealogies Neh 7:61
whose genealogies had been *. Neh 7:64,65
Let it be * even to God, shrouded Job 3:4
them wandering, * and groping, Job 12:24,25
"His treasures will be * in Job 20:26
and I have * my appetite. Ps 102:3,4
away from them, then all is *. Ps 104:29
I have wandered away like a * Ps 119:176
I can never be * to your Spirit! Ps 139:7
as you would for * money or hidden Pro 2:3,4,5
Anyone refusing has * his chance. Pro 10:17
wander away and be *, but those who Pro 14:22
And so the matter is * in red Ecc 5:8
everything is *, abandoned and Is 24:19
see that none are * or strayed, so Is 40:26
of my people have * their senses; Jer 10:21
that the city was *, they fled Jer 39:4
this remnant be scattered and *?" Jer 40:15
My people have been * sheep. Jer 50:6
mountains. They * their way and Jer 50:6
to the king to tell him all is *! Jer 51:31
HOW THE FINEST gold has * its Lam 4:1
out, your memory * in history. Eze 21:32
Everything is *. Eze 27:27
who have wandered away and are *. Eze 34:4
I will seek my * ones, those who Eze 34:15,16
than the one he *, and other Dan 11:13
yet not one true kernel will be *. Amo 9:9
"When I had * all hope, I turned Jon 2:7
astray and wander like * sheep; Zec 10:2
people of Israel—God's * sheep. Mt 10:6
help the Jews—the * sheep of Mt 15:24
came to save the *. Mt 18:11
away and is *, what will he do? Mt 18:12
the hills to search for the * one? Mt 18:12
"What good is salt that has * Lk 14:34
away and was * in the wilderness, Lk 15:3,4
for the * one until you found it? Lk 15:3,4
because your * sheep was found. Lk 15:6
happier over one * sinner who Lk 15:7

OST Con't)
He was * and is found.' Lk 15:24
He was * and is found!' Lk 15:32
that the Law has * its force in Lk 16:17
This man was one of the * sons of Lk 19:9,10
said to each other, "We've *. Jn 12:19
made, "I have not * a single one Jn 18:9
men who are * in darkness to God. Rom 2:19
it you are * and will perish, but Rom 8:13
*, when they hear that Jesus died 1Co 1:18
Christians who have died are *! 1Co 15:18
have * my wits to talk like this; 2Co 11:16
you are * from God's grace. Gal 5:4
You were *, without God, without Eph 2:12
to have * their fear of chains! Php 1:14
Don't let anyone declare you * Col 2:18
that soon they * their faith in 1Ti 1:19
a flower that has * its beauty and Jas 1:10,11
road and become * like Balaam, the 2Pe 2:15
And the Dragon * the battle and Rev 12:8

OT
And Haran had a son named *. Gen 11:27
his grandson * (his son Haran's Gen 11:31
instructed him, and * went too; Gen 12:4
Sarai, his nephew *, and all his Gen 12:5
with his wife, and *, and all that Gen 13:1
* too was very wealthy, with Gen 13:5
* with all their flocks and herds. Gen 13:6
of Abram and *, despite the danger Gen 13:7
Then Abram talked it over with * Gen 13:8
* took a long look at the fertile Gen 13:10
So that is what * chose—the Gen 13:11
of Canaan, while * lived among the Gen 13:12
After * was gone, the Lord said Gen 13:14
taking with them *—Abram's nephew Gen 14:12
When Abram learned that * had Gen 14:14
his relative *, and all of Lot's Gen 14:16
city of Sodom, and * was sitting Gen 19:1
and shouted to *, "Bring out Gen 19:5
* stepped outside to talk to Gen 19:6
And they lunged at * and began Gen 19:9
out and pulled * in and bolted the Gen 19:10
So * rushed out to tell his Gen 19:14
"Hurry," they said to *, "take Gen 19:15
When * still hesitated, the Gen 19:16
"Oh no, sirs, please," * Gen 19:18,19,20
The sun was rising as * reached Gen 19:23
plea and kept * safe, removing him Gen 19:29
Afterwards * left Zoar, fearful Gen 19:30
those who gathered a * had Ex 16:18
rebellious * these people are. Ex 32:9
Apparently a kind of sacred * used Lev 8:8f
Ammonites to the descendants of *. Num 21:24f
and a * of miscellaneous booty. Num 31:9,10,11
will be divided by * among the Num 33:54
yourselves by *," Moses said. Num 34:13
divide the land by * among the Num 36:1
given it to the descendants of *.' Deu 2:9
given it to the descendants of *.' Deu 2:19
Literally, "by *." Jos 14:1f
Judah (as assigned by sacred *): Jos 15:1
by sacred * in the area of Bashan. Jos 21:6
be selected by * as a supply line Ju 20:8,9,10
Benjamin was chosen by sacred *. 1Sa 10:20
And finally, the sacred * 1Sa 10:21
chosen by sacred * as the guilty 1Sa 14:41
really liked him a *, and that they 1Sa 18:22
to himself, "A * of good it did us 1Sa 25:21
come, there was a * of shouting; 2Sa 18:29
land assigned by * to the 1Ch 6:54
clan received by * thirteen cities 1Ch 6:62
Merari received by * twelve cities 1Ch 6:63
also assigned by * to the Levites 1Ch 6:64,65
Literally, "by *." 1Ch 24:5f
proud and stubborn *, and they Neh 9:16
selected by * to live there too. Neh 11:1
allied with the descendants of *. Ps 83:8
Come on, throw in your * with Pro 1:14
disgrace are his *, for the Pro 6:33
can cause a * of trouble. Pro 13:17
Literally, "the *." Pro 18:18f
I discovered that the * of man, Ecc 1:12-15
So, after a * of thinking, I Ecc 2:3
and to accept your * in life—that Ecc 5:19,20
still your *, O men of the world. Is 24:17
*: desolation and destruction. Is 51:19
harlot could learn a * from you! Jer 2:33
this time the Lord added a * more! Jer 36:32
be your *, O Moab, says the Lord. Jer 48:43
unending work is now our *. Lam 5:5
For the whole * of them are hard, Eze 3:7
or a * of equipment to do that. Eze 17:9
Literally, "no * has fallen upon Eze 24:6f
divided Jerusalem among them by *; Ob 1:11
week—the honor fell to him by * Lk 1:8,9
and you will catch a * of fish!" Lk 5:4
the * of us," they protested; Lk 9:13
was in the days of *: people went Lk 17:28
until the morning * left Sodom. Lk 17:29
for he had heard a * about him and Lk 23:8
There was a * of discussion Jn 7:12
plain, not with a * of oratory and 1Co 2:4
been thinking a * about this, and 1Co 5:3,4
But it makes a * of difference 1Co 7:19
and you make a * of fuss over the Jas 2:3
the Lord rescued * out of Sodom 2Pe 2:7,8

LOT'S
Lot, and all of * possessions, Gen 14:16
alike. But * wife looked back as Gen 19:26
were among * descendants. Ps 83:8f
remember what happened to * wife! Lk 17:32

LOTAN
Seir:The tribe of *,The tribe of Gen 36:20,21
The children of * (the son of Gen 36:22
and Heman. (* had a sister, Timna. Gen 36:22
*, Shobal, Zibeon, Anah, Dishon, 1Ch 1:38,39

LOTAN'S
* sons: Hori and Homam. 1Ch 1:38,39

LOTION
and olive oil as * for his skin, Ps 104:15

LOTS
and cast * to determine which is Lev 16:8
Then Saul said, "Now draw * 1Sa 14:42
There are * of servants these 1Sa 25:10
* in determining the will of God. 1Sa 28:5,6f
of Benjamin. * were then drawn to 1Ch 6:61
Literally, "cast *," a form of Neh 10:34f
they will cast * by shaking Eze 21:21
them, and cast * for my robe." Jn 19:23,24
Literally, "cast *," or, "threw Act 1:26f

LOTTERY
tribes have a *, drawing for the Num 26:55,56
tribal leaders supervised the *. Jos 14:1
by the sacred * which tribe should Jos 18:10
the sacred * to divide the land Jos 19:51

LOTUS
He lies down under the * plants, Job 40:21

LOUD
* blast as from a ram's horn; Ex 19:16
by * blowing of trumpets. Lev 23:23,24
let the trumpets blow * and long Lev 25:9
But when you heard the * voice Deu 5:23
Then, when they give one long, * Jos 6:5
blew a long, * trumpet blast, Jos 6:16
they shouted as * as they could. Jos 6:20
of joy was so * that it almost made 1Sa 4:5
chariots and a * galloping of 2Ki 7:6
of cymbals, and * playing on the 1Ch 15:28
the singers with * praises to God. 1Ch 16:42
cymbals, and the * playing of other 2Ch 5:13,14
together in a * commotion that Ez 3:13
crying with a * and bitter wail. Est 4:1
cymbals, yes, * clanging cymbals. Ps 150:5
A prostitute is * and brash, and Pro 9:13
Break out into * and joyful song, Is 54:1
the eyes, and the *, bragging Dan 7:20
Then Jesus called out with a * Mk 15:34
Then Jesus uttered another * cry, Mk 15:37
they must not speak out *. 1Co 14:28
suddenly I heard a * voice behind Rev 1:10
A mighty angel with a * voice Rev 5:2
Then a * voice will shout from Rev 11:12
and there were * voices shouting Rev 11:15
Then I heard a * voice shouting Rev 12:10
I heard a * shout from the throne Rev 21:3

LOUD-MOUTHED
they are * "show-offs," and Jud 1:16

LOUDER
As the trumpet blast grew * and Ex 19:19
grew louder and *, Moses spoke and Ex 19:19
the Philistines grew * and louder. 1Sa 14:19
the Philistines grew louder and *. 1Sa 14:19
"You'll have to shout * than 1Ki 18:27
So they shouted * and, as was 1Ki 18:28
it grows * and louder. Ps 74:23
it grows louder and *. Ps 74:23
Shout *—don't be afraid—tell the Is 40:9
quiet, but they only yelled the *. Mt 20:31
But he only shouted the *, again Mk 10:48
They only roared the *, Mk 15:14
he only yelled the *, "Son of Lk 18:39
But they shouted * and louder Lk 23:23
But they shouted louder and * Lk 23:23
The shouting grew * and louder, Act 23:10
The shouting grew louder and *, Act 23:10

LOUDLY
and they played * and joyously upon 1Ch 15:16
They sang * and clearly under the Neh 12:42
Wailing * in despair, they tore Job 2:12
that if you shout * enough against Job 36:19
God, and can you shout as * as he? Job 40:9
life—and the world * applauds Ps 49:18
shout * before fools will hear it. Pro 14:33
against them * and clearly." Eze 11:4
But Peter denied it *. Mt 26:70
Lamb is worthy" (* they sang Rev 5:12
They called * to the Lord and Rev 6:10
the heavens crying *, "Woe, woe, Rev 8:13
shouting * to the birds, "Come! Rev 19:17

LOUNGE
At their religious feasts they * Amo 2:8

LOUNGING
WOE TO THOSE * in luxury at Amo 6:1

LOUT
such a stubborn * that no one can 1Sa 25:17

LOVABLE
His mouth is altogether sweet, * Sol 5:16

LOVE
Isaac whom you * so much—and go to Gen 22:2
Well, Jacob was in * with Gen 29:18
a few days, he was so much in *. Gen 29:20
my husband will * me." Gen 29:32
He fell deeply in * with her, Gen 34:3
is truly in * with your daughter, Gen 34:8
was very much in * with Dinah, and Gen 34:18,19
was overcome with * for his brother Gen 43:30
but I lavish my * upon thousands Ex 20:6
who * me and obey my commandments. Ex 20:6
and rich in steadfast * and truth. Ex 34:5,6
this steadfast * to many thousands Ex 34:7
Don't bear a grudge; but * your Lev 19:18
any other citizen; * them as Lev 19:34
and showing us your steadfast *. Num 14:17,18
steadfast *, just as you have Num 14:19
who * me and keep my Deu 5:9,10
You must * him with all your Deu 6:5
and pour out his * upon you because Deu 7:7
* him and who obey his commands. Deu 7:9
*, he made with your fathers. Deu 7:12
And he will * you and bless you Deu 7:13
you today, and to * him, and to Deu 10:12,13
(You too must * foreigners, for Deu 10:19
"YOU MUST * the Lord your God and Deu 11:1
and if you will * the Lord your God Deu 11:13
or not you really * him with all Deu 13:3
wife he doesn't *, he may not give Deu 21:15
of the wife his father doesn't *. Deu 21:17
so that you will * the Lord your Deu 30:6
I have commanded you today to * Deu 30:16
Choose to * the Lord your God Deu 30:20
Moses gave you. * the Lord and Jos 22:5
We have done it because we * the Jos 22:24,25
But may those who * the Lord Ju 5:31
and said, "You don't * me at all; Ju 14:16
Later on he fell in * with a girl Ju 16:4
"How can you say you * me when Ju 16:15
know about all the * and kindness Ru 2:10,11
evil men who didn't * the Lord. 1Sa 2:12
immediate bond of * between them. 1Sa 18:1
had fallen in * with David, and 1Sa 18:20
demonstrate the * and kindness of 1Sa 20:14
this time by his * for him, for he 1Sa 20:17
And your * for me was deeper 2Sa 1:26
Than the * of women! 2Sa 1:26
with many demonstrations of his *! 2Sa 2:6
him, but my * and kindness shall 2Sa 7:15
fell desperately in * with her. 2Sa 13:1
his * for her that he became ill. 2Sa 13:2
So Amnon told him, "I am in * 2Sa 13:4
Then suddenly his * turned to 2Sa 13:15
You seem to * those who hate 2Sa 19:6
you, and hate those who * you. 2Sa 19:6
How the Lord must * Israel—for he 1Ki 10:9
sin, the Lord remembered David's * 1Ki 15:4
His * and his kindness go on 1Ch 16:34
Lord for his constant * and mercy. 1Ch 16:41
and * from him as I did from Saul. 1Ch 17:13
their * for you never changes. 1Ch 29:18
Oh, remember your * for David and 2Ch 6:42
How he must * Israel to give them 2Ch 9:8
* and loyalty—by killing his son. 2Ch 24:22
is good, and his * and mercy toward Ez 3:11
but in your * and mercy you did not Ez 9:9
kind to those who * and obey him! Neh 1:5
angry, and full of * and mercy; Neh 9:17
your promises of * and kindness—do Neh 9:32
and if you * me, send out a decree Est 8:5
but has no true motherly *. Job 39:13
by your mercy and your *; Ps 5:7
Fill all who * you with your Ps 5:11
protect him with your shield of *. Ps 5:12
hereafter for those who * God. Ps 6:5f
for God is with those who * him. Ps 14:5
Show me your strong * in Ps 17:7
LORD, HOW I * you! Ps 18:1
upon the steadfast * of the God who Ps 21:7
of everlasting * and kindness. Ps 25:6,7
Lord, I * your home, this shrine Ps 26:8
his never-failing * protects me Ps 31:21
Oh, * the Lord, all of you who Ps 31:23
but abiding * surrounds those who Ps 32:10
earth is filled with his tender *. Ps 33:5
him, who rely upon his steady *. Ps 33:18,19
Yes, Lord, let your constant * Ps 33:22
Your steadfast *, O Lord, is as Ps 36:5
How precious is your constant *, Ps 36:7
Pour out your unfailing * on Ps 36:10
but all who * wickedness shall Ps 37:28
My only hope is in your * and Ps 40:11
out his steadfast * upon me, and Ps 42:8
Save us by your constant *. Ps 44:26
You * what is good Ps 45:7
upon your kindness and your *. Ps 48:9
How you * wickedness—far more Ps 52:3

(LOVE Con't)
And lying more than truth! You * Ps 52:4
You love to slander—you * to say Ps 52:4
of his * and his faithfulness. Ps 57:3
Your kindness and * are as vast Ps 57:10
My God is changeless in his * Ps 59:10
all who * truth Ps 60:4,5
glory, for your * and kindness are Ps 63:3
refuse me his kindness and *. Ps 66:20
supply of * and kindness. Ps 69:13
all who * his name shall live Ps 69:36
Let those who * your salvation Ps 70:4
But even so, you * me! Ps 73:23
the door in anger on his *? Ps 77:9
They forgot his power and *, and Ps 78:42
Look down on us in joy and *; Ps 80:3
Look down on us in joy and *; Ps 80:7
Strengthen the man you *, Ps 80:17
and *—only then shall we be saved. Ps 80:19
Pour out your * and kindness on Ps 85:7
forever, for you * me so much! Ps 86:13
Your * and kindness are forever; Ps 89:2
and surround him with my *; Ps 89:24
I will * him forever, and be Ps 89:28
Lord, where is the * you used to Ps 89:49
O Lord, afflicting those you *. Ps 94:5
For your people * every stone in Ps 102:14
angry and full of kindness and *. Ps 103:8
How good you are! Your * for us Ps 106:1
them, for their * of idols was Ps 106:39
of his great *, and caused even Ps 106:45
yet they do! I * them, but even Ps 109:4
evil for good, and hatred for *. Ps 109:5
I * THE Lord because he hears my Ps 116:1
me by your kindness and your *. Ps 119:40,41,42
How I * your laws! Ps 119:47
to them, for I * them and will let Ps 119:48
Help me to * your every wish; Ps 119:80
Help me, for you * only truth. Ps 119:85,86
Oh, how I * them. Ps 119:97
but my choice is clear—I * your Ps 119:113
no wonder I * to obey your laws! Ps 119:119
laws, while I * your commandments Ps 119:127
is your way with those who * you. Ps 119:132
Look down in * upon me and teach Ps 119:135
and that is why I * them so much. Ps 119:140
Lord, see how much I really * Ps 119:159
falsehood but how I * your laws. Ps 119:163
Those who * your laws have great Ps 119:165
and I * them very much; Ps 119:167
May all who * this city prosper. Ps 122:6
If I fail to * her more than my Ps 137:5,6
slow to get angry, full of *. Ps 145:8
He protects all those who * him, Ps 145:20
his punishment is proof of his *. Pro 3:11,12
you. * her—she will guard you. Pro 4:6
Let her * alone fill you with Pro 5:19
* wisdom like a sweetheart; Pro 7:4
take our fill of * until morning, Pro 7:18
my help. I * all who love me. Pro 8:17
I love all who * me. Pro 8:17
Those who * and follow me are Pro 8:21
me show that they * death." Pro 8:36
rebuked, will * you all the more. Pro 9:7,8
Hatred stirs old quarrels, but * Pro 10:12
son, it proves you don't * him; Pro 13:24
for if you * him you will be Pro 13:24
with someone you * than steak with Pro 15:17
* forgets mistakes; Pro 17:9
Sinners * to fight; Pro 17:19
Those who * to talk will suffer Pro 18:21
If you * sleep, you will end in Pro 20:13
to get, while the godly * to give! Pro 21:25,26
rebuke is better than hidden *! Pro 27:5
The growth of * between a man and Pro 30:18,19
with the woman you * through the Ecc 9:9
for your * is sweeter than wine. Sol 1:2
No wonder all the young girls * Sol 1:3
How happy we will be! Your * is Sol 1:4
No wonder all the young girls * Sol 1:4
The Girl: "Tell me, O one I *, Sol 1:7
you are, my *! Sol 1:9
How beautiful you are, my *, how Sol 1:15
Oh, feed me with your *—your Sol 2:5
up nor awaken * until it please." Sol 2:7f
my *, my fair one, and come away. Sol 2:10
Arise, my *, my fair one, and Sol 2:13
anywhere, this one I * so much?' Sol 3:3
* from the girls of Jerusalem!' Sol 3:10
you are, my *, how beautiful! Sol 4:1
You are so beautiful, my *, in Sol 4:7
How sweet is your *, my darling, Sol 4:10
The perfume of your * is more Sol 4:10
tell him that I am sick with *." Sol 5:8
how pleasant, O *, for utter Sol 7:6
And there I will give you my *. Sol 7:12
there I awakened your *." Sol 8:5
betrothal, for * is strong as death Sol 8:6
the flame of *, neither can the Sol 8:7
about his vineyard to the one I *. Is 5:1
the world about his wondrous *. Is 12:4
all may enter in who * the Lord. Is 26:2
O Lord, we * to do your will! Is 26:8
Show them how much you * your Is 26:11
to him, so he can show you his *; Is 30:18
to me and honored, and I * you. Is 43:4
and not have * for her own son? Is 49:15
but with everlasting * I will Is 54:8
and * that I had for King David. Is 55:3
sign [of God's power and * Is 55:13
and serve him and * his name, and Is 56:6
danger comes. They * to lie there, Is 56:10
They love to lie there, * to Is 56:10
your *, instead of loving me. Is 57:7,8
itself, to find new gods to *. Is 57:9
oh, how they * the Temple Is 58:2
For I, the Lord, * justice; Is 61:8
BECAUSE I * Zion, because my heart Is 62:1
accordance with his mercy and *. Is 63:7
In his * and pity he redeemed Is 63:9
where is the * for us you used to Is 63:15
be glad with her, all you who * Is 66:10
I've fallen in * with these Jer 2:25
goddess of * and war, was called. Jer 7:18f
whose * is steadfast; Jer 9:24
and that I * to be this way. Jer 9:24
they commit adultery and * Jer 23:14
my people, with an everlasting *; Jer 31:3
to punish him, but I still * him. Jer 31:20
are madly in * with their idols. Jer 50:38
hearts—their * of idols—and I will Eze 6:9
feed you, for your * of money is Eze 7:19
tender hearts of * for God, so Eze 11:19
to my people—and how they * it! Eze 13:19
have not even charged for your *! Eze 16:31
to your allies for their * Eze 16:40,41
me, and gave her * to the Eze 23:4,5
for she fell in * with pictures she Eze 23:14,15
her in the bed of *, but afterward Eze 23:17
sin and give you new hearts of *. Eze 36:26
and does not * the Lord. Eze 44:9
who * you and who keep your laws. Dan 9:4
and justice and * and mercy. Hos 1:19
faithfulness and *, and you will Hos 1:20
back to you and * her, even though Hos 3:1
Their * for shame is greater than Hos 4:18
For your * vanishes like morning Hos 6:4
your sacrifices—I want your *; Hos 6:6
you refused my *. Hos 6:7
Her people * the ritual of their Hos 8:13
only hatred for those who * God. Hos 9:7
How refreshing was your *! Hos 9:10
I will * them no more, for all Hos 9:15
and you will reap a crop of my *; Hos 10:12
I led Israel with my ropes of *. Hos 11:4
Live by the principles of * and Hos 12:6
dishonest scales—they * to cheat. Hos 12:7
and my * will know no bounds, for Hos 14:4
Hate evil and * the good; Amo 5:15
ones who hate good and * evil; Mic 3:2
hate justice and * unfairness, and Mic 3:9
people, for you * to be merciful. Mic 7:18
You will set your * upon us, as Mic 7:20
men who * to argue and to fight. Hab 1:3
he will * you and not accuse Zep 3:17,18
if you * truth and peace! Zec 8:19
them because I * them. Zec 10:6
"I showed my * for you by loving Mal 1:2,3
"There is a saying, '* your Mt 5:43
But I say: * your enemies! Mt 5:44
If you * only those who love Mt 5:46
If you love only those who * Mt 5:46
For you will hate one and * the Mt 6:24
If you * your father and mother Mt 10:37
more than you * me, you are not Mt 10:37
or if you * your son or daughter Mt 10:37
and * your neighbor as yourself!" Mt 19:19
Jesus replied, " '* the Lord Mt 22:37
is similar: '* your neighbor as Mt 22:38,39
as much as you * yourself.' Mt 22:38,39
And how they * to sit at the Mt 23:6
and will cool the * of many. Mt 24:12
but they have no * for him at all. Mk 7:6,7
Jesus felt genuine * for this man Mk 10:21
or property—for * of me and to tell Mk 10:29
And you must * him with all your Mk 12:30
"The second is: 'You must * Mk 12:31
more important to * him with all my Mk 12:33
strength, and to * others as Mk 12:33
For they * to wear the robes of Mk 12:38
They * to sit in the best seats Mk 12:39
"Listen, all of you. * your Lk 6:27
for merely loving those who * you? Lk 6:32
"* your enemies! Lk 6:35
forgiven little, shows little *." Lk 7:47
"that you must * the Lord your God Lk 10:27
And you must * your neighbor just Lk 10:27
just as much as you * yourself." Lk 10:27
of * for some kinds of people), Lk 10:29
about justice and the * of God. Lk 11:42
For how you * the seats of honor Lk 11:43
follower must * me far more than Lk 14:26
religion, for they * to parade in Lk 20:4
And how they * the seats of honor Lk 20:4
you don't have God's * within you. Jn 5:41,4
so, then you would * me, for I have Jn 8:4
* to do the evil things he does. Jn 8:4
If you * your life down here—you Jn 12:2
to you now—* each other just as Jn 13:3
other just as much as I * you. Jn 13:3
Your strong * for each other Jn 13:3
"If you * me, obey me; Jn 14:15,1
he loves me, my Father will * him; Jn 14:2
to those who * me and obey me. Jn 14:2
The Father will * them too, and Jn 14:2
who doesn't obey me doesn't * me. Jn 14:2
If you really * me, you will be Jn 14:28
will know that I * the Father. Jn 14:31
Live within my *. Jn 15:
are living in my *, just as I obey Jn 15:10
obey my Father and live in his *. Jn 15:10
I demand that you * each other Jn 15:12
each other as much as I * you. Jn 15:12
it—the greatest * is shown when a Jn 15:13
I demand that you * each other, Jn 15:17
The world would * you if you Jn 15:19
dearly because you * me and believe Jn 16:27
you * them as much as you love me. Jn 17:23
you love them as much as you * me. Jn 17:23
so that the mighty * you have for Jn 17:26
All who * the truth are my Jn 18:37
you * me more than these others?" Jn 21:15
son of John, do you really * me?" Jn 21:16
grow in * for God and each other. Act 14:22
about God's mighty kindness and *. Act 20:24
we feel this warm * everywhere Rom 5:5
to fill our hearts with his *. Rom 5:5
But God showed his great * for Rom 5:8
what is wrong. I * to do God's Rom 7:22
for our good if we * God and are Rom 8:28
Who then can ever keep Christ's * Rom 8:35
because he doesn't * us anymore? Rom 8:35
can ever separate us from his *. Rom 8:38
itself cannot keep God's * away. Rom 8:38
us from the * of God demonstrated Rom 8:39
family) and will * them, though no Rom 9:25
you who still * me and have not Rom 11:4
you continue to * and trust him. Rom 11:22
Don't just pretend that you * Rom 12:9
you love others: really * them. Rom 12:9
Stand on the side of the good. * Rom 12:10
except the debt of * for Rom 13:8
For if you * them, you will be Rom 13:8
If you * your neighbor as much Rom 13:9
as much as you * yourself you will Rom 13:9
up in this one, to * your neighbor Rom 13:9
your neighbor as you * yourself. Rom 13:9
* does no wrong to anyone. Rom 13:10
in * if you go ahead and eat it. Rom 14:15
because of your * for me—given to Rom 15:30
Ampliatus, whom I * as one of God's Rom 16:8
Give my * to Philologus, Julia, Rom 16:15
ready for those who * the Lord. 1Co 2:9
come with quiet * and gentleness? 1Co 4:21
needed to build the church is *. 1Co 8:1
earth, but didn't * others, I would 1Co 13:1
* others, what good would it do? 1Co 13:2
be worth nothing at all without *. 1Co 13:2
Gospel but didn't * others, it 1Co 13:3
* is very patient and kind, never 1Co 13:4
* does not demand its own way. 1Co 13:5
If you * someone you will be 1Co 13:7
to an end, but * goes on forever. 1Co 13:8
hope, and *—and the greatest of 1Co 13:13
the greatest of these is *. 1Co 13:13
LET * BE your greatest aim; 1Co 14:1
you do, do it with kindness and *. 1Co 16:14
send you their * and so do all the 1Co 16:19
* the Lord, that person is cursed. 1Co 16:22
May the * and favor of the Lord 1Co 16:23
rest upon you. My * to all of you, 1Co 16:24
that you still do * him very much. 2Co 2:8
Christ's * controls us now. 2Co 5:13,14
you, receive the * he offers you—be 2Co 5:20
I * you with all my heart. 2Co 6:11
of any lack of * on my part, but 2Co 6:12
but because your * is too small and 2Co 6:12
Return our *! 2Co 6:13
those who do not * the Lord, for 2Co 6:14
loyalty and warm * for me, well, I 2Co 7:7
gave us by your *, we were made 2Co 7:13
much enthusiasm, so much * for us. 2Co 8:7
to prove that your * is real, that 2Co 8:8
You know how full of * and 2Co 8:9
Please show your * for me to 2Co 8:24
that your * should be for Christ 2Co 11:2
maiden saves her * for one man 2Co 11:2
Because I don't * you? 2Co 11:11
I * you, the less you love me. 2Co 12:15
I love you, the less you * me. 2Co 12:15
And may the God of * and peace be 2Co 13:11
May God's * and the Holy Spirit's 2Co 13:14
God who, in his * and mercy, Gal 1:6

(LOVE Con't)
need is faith working through *. Gal 5:6
freedom to * and serve each other. Gal 5:13
"* others as you love yourself." Gal 5:14
"Love others as you * yourself." Gal 5:14
But if instead of showing * Gal 5:15
For we naturally * to do evil Gal 5:17
of fruit in us: *, joy, peace, Gal 5:22
before him covered with his *. Eph 1:4
Jesus and of the * you have for Eph 1:15
the soil of God's marvelous *; Eph 3:17
and how high his * really is; Eph 3:18,19
and to experience this * for Eph 3:18,19
other's faults because of your *. Eph 4:2
healthy and growing and full of *. Eph 4:15,16
Be full of * for others, Eph 5:2
for Christ's * for you was like Eph 5:2
the same kind of * to your wives as Eph 5:25
So again I say, a man must * his Eph 5:33
brothers, and *, with faith from Eph 6:23
sincerely * our Lord Jesus Christ. Eph 6:24
Only God knows how deep is my * Php 1:8
more and more with * for others, Php 1:9
because they * me, for they know Php 1:16,17
Do you * me enough to want to Php 2:1
DEAR BROTHER CHRISTIANS, I * Php 4:1
and how much you * his people. Col 1:4
us about the great * for others Col 1:8
it to those who * him and live for Col 1:26,27
by strong ties of *, and that you Col 2:2
of his deep * and concern for you, Col 3:12
Most of all, let * guide your Col 3:14
because of your * for the Lord and Col 3:22
sends you his *, and so does Mark, Col 4:10
Jesus Justus also sends his *. Col 4:11
of Christ Jesus, sends you his *. Col 4:12
Dear doctor Luke sends his *, and Col 4:14
your faith and * are as strong as 1Th 3:6
And may the Lord make your * to 1Th 3:12
just as our * does toward you. 1Th 3:12
the pure brotherly * that there 1Th 4:9
is teaching you to * one another. 1Th 4:9
Indeed, your * is already strong 1Th 4:10
beg you to * them more and more. 1Th 4:10
armor of faith and *, and wearing 1Th 5:8
your wholehearted * because they 1Th 5:13
of your growing * for each other. 2Th 1:3
to believe it and * it, and let it 2Th 2:10
of the * of God and of the patience 2Th 3:5
be filled with * that comes from 1Ti 1:5
full of the * of Christ Jesus. 1Ti 1:14
be a pattern for them in your *, 1Ti 4:12
For the * of money is the first 1Ti 6:10
because of their * for it, and as a 1Ti 6:10
to trust him and * others, and to 1Ti 6:11
* them and enjoy being with them. 2Ti 1:7
began—to show his * and kindness to 2Ti 1:9
and * Christ Jesus offers you. 2Ti 1:13
Literally, "and * that is in 2Ti 1:13f
* of argument, are men like that. 2Ti 2:17
Have faith and *, and enjoy the 2Ti 2:22
* the Lord and have pure hearts. 2Ti 2:22
For people will * only 2Ti 3:2
You know my * for you, and my 2Ti 3:10
children must * the Lord and not Tit 1:6
homes and must * all that is good. Tit 1:8
everything with * and patience. Tit 2:2
live quietly, to * their husbands Tit 2:4
do reflect your * of the truth and Tit 2:7
the kindness and * of God our Tit 3:4
hearing of your * and trust in the Phm 1:5
comfort from your *, my brother, Phm 1:7
you to do, but I * you and prefer Phm 1:8,9
You * right and hate wrong; Heb 1:9
against his * and complained Heb 3:7,8
used to show your * for him—and Heb 6:10
CONTINUE TO * each other with true Heb 13:1
each other with true brotherly *. Heb 13:1
Stay away from the * of money; Heb 13:5
are here with me send you their *. Heb 13:24,25
God has promised those who * him. Jas 1:12
promised to all those who * him. Jas 2:5
"You must * and help your Jas 2:8
you * and take care of yourself." Jas 2:8
You * him even though you have 1Pe 1:8
Now you can have real * for 1Pe 1:22
so see to it that you really do * 1Pe 1:22
Show respect for everyone. * 1Pe 2:17
to show deep * for each other, for 1Pe 4:8
each other, for * makes up for many 1Pe 4:8
Or, "* overlooks each other's 1Pe 4:8f
help you to stand firmly in his *. 1Pe 5:12
the handshake of Christian *. 1Pe 5:14
you will grow to * them deeply. 2Pe 1:7
they join your * feasts as though 2Pe 2:13
Beor, who fell in * with the money 2Pe 2:15
will learn to * God more and more. 1Jn 2:5
commandment, to * one another, the 1Jn 2:8
you, for when you * these things 1Jn 2:15
show that you do not really * God; 1Jn 2:15
who would dearly * to blindfold you 1Jn 2:26
of sin and doesn't * his brother 1Jn 3:10
been that we should * one another. 1Jn 3:11
If we * other Christians it 1Jn 3:14
But a person who doesn't have * 1Jn 3:14
We know what real * is from 1Jn 3:16
him—how can God's * be within him? 1Jn 3:17
us stop just saying we * people; 1Jn 3:18
let us really * them, and show it 1Jn 3:18
Jesus Christ, and * one another. 1Jn 3:23
each other, for * comes from God 1Jn 4:7
he doesn't know God—for God is *. 1Jn 4:8
In this act we see what real * 1Jn 4:10
is: it is not our * for God, but 1Jn 4:10
for God, but his * for us when he 1Jn 4:10
surely ought to * each other too. 1Jn 4:11
seen God, when we * each other God 1Jn 4:12
* within us grows ever stronger. 1Jn 4:12
we have felt his * and because we 1Jn 4:16
God is *, and anyone who lives in 1Jn 4:16
who lives in * is living with God 1Jn 4:16
* grows more perfect and complete; 1Jn 4:17
he loves us and we * him too. 1Jn 4:17
his perfect * for us eliminates 1Jn 4:18
So you see, our * for him comes 1Jn 4:19
If anyone says "I * God," but 1Jn 4:20
for if he doesn't * his brother 1Jn 4:20
he * God whom he has never seen? 1Jn 4:20
said that one must * not only God, 1Jn 4:21
And all who * the Father love his 1Jn 5:1
And all who love the Father * his 1Jn 5:1
out how much you * God's 1Jn 5:2
how much you * and obey God. 1Jn 5:2
children whom I * so much, as does 2Jn 1:1
much peace, and with truth and *. 2Jn 1:3
Christians should * one another. 2Jn 1:5
If we * God, we will do whatever 2Jn 1:6
the very first to * each other. 2Jn 1:6
To: Dear Gaius, whom I truly *. 3Jn 1:1
Friends here send their *, and 3Jn 1:15
of God's kindness, peace, and *. Jud 1:2
When these men join you at the * Jud 1:12
They stir up arguments; they * Jud 1:19
God's * can reach and bless you. Jud 1:21
you don't * me as at first! Rev 2:4
your first * (how different now! Rev 2:5
also I know your * and faith and Rev 2:19
that you are the ones I *. Rev 3:9
and punish everyone I *; Rev 3:19
for they did not * their lives Rev 12:11
and all who * to lie, and do so. Rev 22:15

LOVED
his wife. He * her very much, and Gen 24:67
too, and he * her more than Leah, Gen 29:30
Now as it happened, Israel * Gen 37:3
and granddaughters—all his * ones. Gen 46:7
"It was because he * your Deu 4:37
your fathers and * them so much Deu 10:15
Jehovah, the God * and worshiped by Ju 2:12-14
but although he * Hannah very 1Sa 1:5
saw David, Saul admired and * him; 1Sa 16:21
but all Israel and Judah * him, 1Sa 18:15,16
and that they all * him and thought 1Sa 18:22
* him as much as he loved himself. 1Sa 20:17
loved him as much as he * himself. 1Sa 20:17
How much they were *, how 2Sa 1:23
How much I * you! 2Sa 1:26
And the Lord * the baby, and 2Sa 12:24
hated her more than he had * her. 2Sa 13:15
(Solomon * the Lord and followed 1Ki 3:3
the child, and who * him very much, 1Ki 3:26
He was a man who had * God, she 2Ki 4:1
and Shelomith. He * Maacah more 2Ch 11:21
He was a man who * the soil and 2Ch 26:10
with him, and God * him and made Neh 13:26
Well, the king * Esther more Est 2:17
Those I * have turned against me. Job 19:19
Hide your * ones in the shelter Ps 31:20
going blind. My * ones and friends Ps 38:11
Judah—and Mount Zion which he *. Ps 78:68
to death. He * to curse others; Ps 109:17
I would. His * ones are very Ps 116:15
for God wants his * ones to get Ps 127:2
a son, tenderly * by my mother as Pro 4:3
is it about your * one that is Sol 5:9
women, where has your * one gone? Sol 6:1
ago and how you * me and followed Jer 2:2
—whom they have * and worshiped. Jer 8:2
But the Lord replies: You have * Jer 14:10
this Temple, with all our * ones. Jer 28:6
to Israel: I have * you, O my Jer 31:3
both those you * and those you Eze 16:37
whose gods she * so much. Eze 23:9
WHEN ISRAEL WAS a child I * him as Hos 11:1
never * him and never wanted to." Zep 1:6
"I have * you very deeply," Mal 1:2,3
Then those who feared and * the Mal 3:16
him and * to think about him. Mal 3:16
The little boy greatly * God Lk 1:80
wise, and was * by God and man. Lk 2:52
my much * Son, yes, my delight." Lk 3:22
Which do you suppose * him most Lk 7:42
forgiven, for she * me much; Lk 7:47
The Pharisees, who dearly * their Lk 16:14
For God * the world so much that Jn 3:16
world, but they * the darkness more Jn 3:19
"See how much he * him." Jn 11:36
for they * the praise of men Jn 12:43
And how he * his disciples! Jn 13:1
"I have * you even as the Father Jn 15:9
you even as the Father has * me. Jn 15:9
you * me before the world began! Jn 17:24
by the disciple whom he *." Jn 19:26f
other disciple whom Jesus *." Jn 20:2f
disciple therefore whom Jesus *." Jn 21:7f
the disciple Jesus * following, the Jn 21:20
who * us enough to die for us. Rom 8:37
no one had ever * them before. Rom 9:25
the land who still * God, and now Rom 11:2,3
how very much I * you and cared 2Co 2:4
who * me and gave himself for me. Gal 2:20
we belong to his dearly * Son. Eph 1:6
But God is so rich in mercy; he * Eph 2:4
much * child imitates his father. Eph 5:1
of Christ who * you and gave Eph 5:2
Tychicus, who is a much * brother Eph 6:21
Tychicus, our much * brother, Col 4:7
* brother, one of your own people. Col 4:9
own children. We * you dearly—so 1Th 2:8
you, our brothers * by the Lord, 2Th 2:13
Father, who has * us and given us 2Th 2:16
as you would to much * brothers. 1Ti 5:1
has left me. He * the good things 2Ti 4:10
To: Philemon, our much * fellow Phm 1:1
* ones back again from death. Heb 11:35
But, dearly * friends, if our 1Jn 3:21
DEARLY * FRIENDS, don't always 1Jn 4:1
God showed how much he * us by 1Jn 4:9
Dear friends, since God * us as 1Jn 4:11
Dearly * friends, I had been Jud 1:3
"All the fancy things you * so Rev 18:14

LOVELIES
young * for the royal harem. Est 2:3

LOVELINESS
Your cheeks are matched * Sol 4:3
Your cheeks are matched * Sol 6:7

LOVELY
The woman was convinced. How * Gen 3:6
for Rebekah, and * clothing; Gen 24:53
Leah had * eyes, but Rachel was Gen 29:17
deer let loose, producing * fawns. Gen 49:21
"that you brought us out of * Num 16:13
But, O Lord, I have built you a * 1Ki 8:12,13
This man had a beautiful and * Est 2:7
as * as the daughters of Job; Job 42:15
kindness to this * land where the Ps 42:6
I will write a * poem to the Ps 45:1
palaces of ivory, * music is being Ps 45:8
clothing woven with gold. * Ps 45:14
grow rich and build their * homes. Ps 49:16
HOW * IS your Temple, O Lord of Ps 84:1
He sends the snow in all its * Ps 147:16
My bed is spread with *, colored Pro 7:16,17
with a crabby woman in a * home. Pro 21:9
Timely advice is as * as golden Pro 25:11
King Solomon: "But * as the Sol 1:5
What a * filly Sol 1:9
you are, my love! How * your Sol 1:10
What a *, pleasant thing you Sol 1:16
shade and his fruit is * to eat. Sol 2:3
Call to me and let me hear your * Sol 2:14
You have ravished my heart, my * Sol 4:9
You are like a * orchard bearing Sol 4:13,14
aloes, and every other * spice. Sol 4:13,14
waft its * perfume to my beloved. Sol 4:16
my lover, my * dove,' he said, 'for Sol 5:2
* myrrh as I pulled back the bolt. Sol 5:5
beautiful as the * land of Tirzah, Sol 6:4
Your navel is * as a goblet Sol 7:2
are like two fawns, yes, * twins. Sol 7:3
their mirrors, * lingerie, Is 3:23
You furnish * music at your Is 5:12
summer day or a * autumn morning Is 18:4
mountains, as * as Mount Carmel's Is 35:2
* princess, tender and delicate. Is 47:1
there, thanksgiving and * songs. Is 51:3
cedar and painted a * red." Jer 22:14
I gave you * ornaments, Eze 16:11
ears, and a * tiara for your head. Eze 16:12
You used the * things I gave you Eze 16:16
you used it as a * sacrifice to Eze 16:19
am going to take away your * wife. Eze 24:16
I will destroy my *, beautiful Eze 24:20,21
They will destroy your * homes Eze 26:12
someone who sings * songs with a Eze 33:32
your music, no matter how * it is. Amo 5:23
to go and produce * fruit always, Jn 15:16
that are pure and *, and dwell on Php 4:8

LOVER
me all day long. *, friend, Ps 88:18
The Girl: "My * is an apple Sol 2:3
park, that you do not awaken my *. Sol 2:7
THE GIRL: "One night my * was Sol 3:1

(LOVER Con't)
of the park, not to awake my *. Sol 3:5
* and beloved, eat and drink! Sol 5:1
'Open to me, my darling, my *, my Sol 5:2

LOVER'S
and I have found favor in my * Sol 8:10

LOVERS
And Issachar, you * of your tents; Deu 33:18
every corner for men to be her *. Pro 7:11,12
absent from her *, walks the Is 23:15,16
you plot and scheme to win your *. Jer 2:33
and married many *, yet I have Jer 3:1
All your * have left you and Jer 30:14
Among all her *, Lam 1:2
Literally, "*." Lam 1:19f
brothel for your *, and idol altars Eze 16:24
adultery with your *—your Eze 16:36
your allies—these * of yours you Eze 16:37
I will give you to your *—these Eze 16:39
* she will not catch up with them. Hos 1:7
public for all her * to see, and no Hos 1:10
she claims her * gave her—and let Hos 1:12
looking for her *, and deserted me: Hos 1:13

LOVES
and his father * him very much.' Gen 44:20
country ahead, and the Lord * us. Num 14:8
It was just because he * you, Deu 7:8
and constantly * those who love him Deu 7:9
and widows. He * foreigners and Deu 10:18
he says he * you and enjoys your Deu 15:16
"If a man has two wives but * Deu 21:15
son, the son of the wife he *. Deu 21:16
for you, because the Lord * you. Deu 23:5
How he * his people— Deu 33:3
who * you so much, and who has been Ru 4:15
because the Lord * his people that 2Ch 2:11
if Your Majesty * me, and wants to Est 5:7,8
For God is good, and he * Ps 11:7
He * whatever is just and good; Ps 33:5
the Lord forsake a man who * him; Ps 37:25
For the Lord * justice and Ps 37:28
who * him and his salvation. Ps 40:16
—the very best for those he *. Ps 47:4
the city of God, the city he * Ps 87:1
For the Lord says, "Because he * Ps 91:14
The Lord * those who hate evil; Ps 97:10
For he * us very dearly, and his Ps 117:2
For the Lord * good men. Ps 146:8
but * those who try to be good. Pro 15:9,10
Wickedness * company—and leads Pro 16:29
He who * wisdom loves his own Pro 19:8
He who loves wisdom * his own Pro 19:8
An evil man * to harm others; Pro 21:10
A good man * justice, but it is a Pro 21:15
A man who * pleasure becomes Pro 21:17
He who * money shall never have Ecc 5:10
everyone can see how much he * me. Sol 2:4
told you this: "The Lord * Cyrus. Is 48:14
him in pledge, and * idols and Eze 18:12
it was, for God * you very much. Dan 9:23
"God * you very much," he Dan 10:19
her, even though she * adultery. Hos 3:1
For the Lord still * Israel Hos 3:1
out the grain—an easy job she *. Hos 10:11
God is jealous over those he *; Nah 1:2
DEAR FRIEND WHO * God: Lk 1:1
The name means "one who * Lk 1:1f
said, "for he * the Jews and even Lk 7:5
The Father * this man because he Jn 3:35
For the Father * the Son, and Jn 5:20
"The Father * me because I lay Jn 10:17
who obeys me is the one who * me; Jn 14:21
and because he * me, my Father Jn 14:21
the Father himself * you dearly Jn 16:27
DEAR FRIEND WHO * God: Act 1:1
Rome, are among those he dearly *; Rom 1:6,7
how dearly God * us, and we feel Rom 5:5
that part of you that * to sin Rom 6:6
that is still inside me * to sin. Rom 7:23,24,25
But the person who truly * God 1Co 8:3
proved true! He * you more than 2Co 7:15
idol worshiper—he * and worships Eph 5:5
loving himself when he * his wife! Eph 5:28
men, for not everyone * the Lord. 2Th 3:2
kind, and not be one who * money. 1Ti 3:3
you, it proves that he * you. Heb 12:6
wife who * her husband's enemies. Jas 4:4
But whoever * his fellow man is 1Jn 2:10
heavenly Father * us, for he allows 1Jn 3:1
We know how much God * us because 1Jn 4:16
he tells us that he * us dearly. 1Jn 4:16
he * us and we love him too. 1Jn 4:17
of someone who * us perfectly; 1Jn 4:18
convinced that he really * us. 1Jn 4:18
Diotrephes, who * to push himself 3Jn 1:9
All praise to him who always * us Rev 1:5

LOVESICK
your 'apples'—for I am utterly *. Sol 2:5

LOVING
least of all your * kindnesses Gen 32:10
I give you, * the Lord your God, Deu 11:22
giving you today—* the Lord your Deu 19:9
God surrounds him with his * care, Deu 33:12
So be very careful to keep on * Jos 23:11
earth, for you are * and kind and 1Ki 8:22,23
"He is always so * and kind." 2Ch 7:3
and * those who hate the Lord?" 2Ch 19:2
promises and is so * and kind to Neh 1:5
were so kind and * to me, and I was Job 10:12
he hates those * violence. Ps 11:5
You have been * and kind to me Ps 18:50
O * AND kind God, have mercy. Ps 51:1
He is * and kind and rewards Ps 62:12
Now bring us back to * you, Ps 85:4
He is always * and kind, and his Ps 100:5
for always being so * and kind. Ps 107:1
Save me because you are * and Ps 109:26
Because you are so * and kind, Ps 119:149
for he is * and kind, and comes Ps 130:7
And because you are * and kind Ps 143:12
He is always kind and * to me; Ps 144:2
who expect him to be * and kind. Ps 147:11
Literally, "as a * hind and a Pro 5:19f
The man who tries to be good, * Pro 21:21
for to be held in * esteem is Pro 22:1
A time for *; Ecc 3:8
in their lifetimes—*, hating, Ecc 9:6
idols your love, instead of * me. Is 57:7,8
and I can't stop * them now!" Jer 2:25
your hearts by * me, your Jer 9:25,26
You are * and kind to thousands, Jer 32:18
they talk very sweetly about * Eze 33:31
hearts they are * their money. Eze 33:31
for you by * your father, Jacob. Mal 1:2,3
for merely * those who love you? Lk 6:32
was filled with * pity and ran and Lk 15:20
us and was full of * forgiveness Jn 1:14
brought us * forgiveness as well. Jn 1:17
When I come I will send your * 1Co 16:3
Asia send you their * greetings. 1Co 16:19
And give each other a * handshake 1Co 16:20
We have been kind and truly * and 2Co 6:6
* them as parts of themselves. Eph 5:28
* himself when he loves his wife! Eph 5:28
Rather, bring them up with the * Eph 6:4
Then make me truly happy by * Php 2:2
And you husbands must be * and Col 3:19
We never forget your * deeds as 1Th 1:3
living quiet, good, and * lives. 1Ti 2:15
The church should take * care of 1Ti 5:3
me joy with this * act and my weary Phm 1:20
you keep right on * others as long Heb 6:11
* father does for his children. Heb 12:7
God's law of * one another, Jas 4:11
toward each other, * one another 1Pe 3:8
Satan: Stop * this evil world and 1Jn 2:15
Dear friends, let us practice * 1Jn 4:7
and those who are * and kind show 1Jn 4:7
But if a person isn't * and 1Jn 4:8
as a result of his * us first. 1Jn 4:19
and obey God. * God means doing 1Jn 5:3
your friendship and your * deeds. 3Jn 1:6

LOVINGKINDNESS
But in your * Ex 15:13
is so good! His * lasts forever!" 2Ch 5:13,14
song, "His * Is Forever," using 2Ch 7:6
the song "His * Is Forever" as 2Ch 20:21
God for demonstrating such * to me Ez 7:28
as punishment, or, in his *, to Job 37:13
fragrant with his * and his truth. Ps 25:10
For I have taken your * and your Ps 26:3
proclaimed your * and truth to all Ps 40:10
Literally, "the * of God Ps 52:1f
Oh, send your * and truth to Ps 61:7
prayers, for your * is wonderful; Ps 69:16
Is his * gone forever? Ps 77:8
full of constant * and of truth; Ps 86:15
those in the grave declare your *? Ps 88:11
take away my * from them, nor let Ps 89:33
with your *, giving us constant Ps 90:14
I WILL SING about your * and your Ps 101:1
He surrounds me with * and tender Ps 103:4
But the * of the Lord is from Ps 103:17,18
the Lord for his *, and for all of Ps 107:8
the Lord for his * and for all of Ps 107:15
the Lord for his * and for all of Ps 107:21
the Lord for his * and for all of Ps 107:31
Think about the * of the Lord! Ps 107:43
For your * is great beyond Ps 108:4
Cause everyone to praise your * Ps 115:1
he's so good! His * is forever. Ps 118:1
same words: "His * is forever." Ps 118:2
Aaron chant, "His * is forever." Ps 118:3
chant, "His * is forever." Ps 118:4
For his * is forever. Ps 118:29
Lord, the earth is full of your *! Ps 119:64
Now let your * comfort me, just Ps 119:75,76,77
Lord, deal with me in *, and Ps 119:124
is good; his * continues forever. Ps 136:1
gods, for his * continues forever. Ps 136:2
for his * continues forever. Ps 136:3
for his * continues forever. Ps 136:4
for his * continues forever. Ps 136:
for his * continues forever. Ps 136
lights, for his * continues Ps 136:
day, for his * continues forever; Ps 136:
for his * conti..ues forever. Ps 136:
of Egypt, for his * to Israel Ps 136:1
their enemies, for his * to Israel Ps 136:11,1
them, for his * continues forever, Ps 136:1
through, for his * continues Ps 136:1
in the sea, for his * to Israel Ps 136:1
for his * continues forever. Ps 136:1
kings, for his * continues forever, Ps 136:1
their enemies, for his * to Israel Ps 136:1
of Amorites—for God's * to Israel Ps 136:1
king of Bashan—for his * to Israel Ps 136:2
gift forever, for his * to Israel Ps 136:2
for his * continues forever. Ps 136:2
for his * continues forever. Ps 136:2
foes, for his * continues forever. Ps 136:24
for his * continues forever. Ps 136:25
for his * continues forever. Ps 136:26
you for all your * and your Ps 138:2
your *, Lord, continues forever. Ps 138:8
away my * and my mercies. Jer 16:5
with * I have drawn you to me. Jer 31:3
Great is his faithfulness; his * Lam 3:23
to the greatness of his *. Lam 3:32

LOVINGKINDNESSES
I will tell of the * of God. Is 63:7

LOVINGLY
have * delivered me from death; Is 38:17
Instead, we will * follow the Eph 4:15,16
No one hates his own body but * Eph 5:29,30

LOW
Then Abraham bowed * before them Gen 23:7
May all your relatives bow * Gen 27:27,28,29
he bowed * seven times before him. Gen 33:3
children, and bowed * before him. Gen 33:6
around it and bowed * before it!" Gen 37:7
eleven stars bowed * before me!" Gen 37:9
came, and bowed * before him, with Gen 42:6
presents, bowing * before him. Gen 43:26
to me, bowing * and begging, Ex 11:8
bowing * to the pillar of cloud. Ex 33:10
rings were placed * on the shoulder Ex 39:20
if few years, the price will be * Lev 25:14,15,16
Your enemies shall bow * before Deu 33:29
and bowing * before the idols of Ju 2:12-14
around, David bowed * before him. 1Sa 24:7,8
dismounted and bowed * before him. 1Sa 25:23
was Samuel and bowed * before him. 1Sa 28:14
humility, bowing * before him. 2Sa 9:5,6
he came and bowed * before the 2Sa 14:33
He bowed * with his face to the 2Sa 18:28
Bath-sheba bowed * before him. 1Ki 1:16
Nathan came in and bowed * before 1Ki 1:22,23
Then Bath-sheba bowed * before 1Ki 1:31
He came to bow * before the king; 1Ki 1:53
as she entered and bowed * to her. 1Ki 2:19
Bend *, O Lord, and listen. 2Ki 19:16
And they did, bowing * before 1Ch 29:20
brought Judah very * on account of 2Ch 28:19
* before the Lord in worship. 2Ch 29:29
oxen do not * when they have Job 6:5,6,7
you; bend * and hear my whispered Ps 31:2
HIGH and *, rich and poor, all Ps 49:1
for we are brought * to the dust. Ps 79:8
holy God! Bow * before his feet. Ps 99:5
Help me to refuse the * and Ps 101:3
and make them bow * before you." Ps 110:1
"Hear my cry, for I am very *. Ps 142:6
calamity is enough to lay you *. Pro 24:15,16
proud looks will be brought *; Is 2:11
Bashan shall bend *, and all the Is 2:13
the glory of mankind will bow *; Is 2:17
destroyed and their cities laid *. Is 32:19
princes shall bow * because the Is 49:7
tree you've bowed * before idols. Jer 2:20
search high and * and see if you Jer 5:1
grew and became a * but spreading Eze 17:6
and exalts the *, that I make the Eze 17:24
and the rich brought very *. Eze 21:26
In front of these rooms was a * Eze 40:7-12
and spoke to him in a * voice. Mk 10:35
terrified and bowed * before them. Lk 24:5

LOW-DOWN
evil, * ways and live good lives. Ps 37:27

LOWER
* corners, two rings on each side. Ex 25:12
*, inside edges of the chestpiece; Ex 28:26
also set at the * edge of the Ex 39:19
gave her the upper and * springs. Jos 15:18,19
as far as * Beth-horon, then to Jos 16:1
country south of * Beth-horon. Jos 18:13
So Caleb gave her the upper and * Ju 1:15
stories high, the * floor being 7½ 1Ki 6:6
Gezer along with * Beth-horon, 1Ki 9:17,18
She built * and Upper Beth-horon 1Ch 7:24
Beth-horon and * Beth-horon, both 2Ch 8:5
* armor and the breastplate meet. 2Ch 18:33
and a third will be at the * Gate. 2Ch 23:5,6

LOWER Con't)
only a little * than the angels, Ps 8:5
Or, "only a little * than God!" Ps 8:5f
I told the wicked to * their Ps 75:4
Assyria, Upper and * Egypt, Is 11:11
for water from the * pool! Is 22:9,10,11
This was called "the * Eze 40:18
not as wide as the * one, because Eze 42:5
within me, in my * nature, that is Rom 7:23,24,25
slavery to this deadly * nature? Rom 7:23,24,25
by their * natures live only to Rom 8:5
For though you made him * than Heb 2:7
was a little * than the Heb 2:9

LOWERED
* the jug for him to drink. Gen 24:18
from his cell and * him by ropes Jer 38:6
and * to Jeremiah on a rope. Jer 38:11
above his head and * the sick man Mk 2:4
off some tiles and * the sick man Lk 5:18,19
so they * the topsails and were Act 27:17
the ship, and * the emergency boat Act 27:30
in the sea, they * the rudders, Act 27:40

LOWEST
"May they be the * of slaves Gen 9:24,25
The greatest of men, or the * Ps 62:9
pit of hell, down to its * depths. Is 14:15
joy has reached its * ebb; Is 24:11
have become the * sort of thieves. Hos 5:10
And has the * sort of friends!' Lk 7:34
down to the * parts of the earth. Eph 4:9
the very * to the very highest. Eph 4:10

LOWING
Beth-shemesh, * as they went; 1Sa 6:12
of sheep and * of oxen I heard?" 1Sa 15:14
Gone is the * of cattle, gone the Jer 9:10

LOWLAND
Those in the *; Jos 11:1
had invaded the * cities and the 2Ch 28:17,18

LOWLANDS
the *, and the mountain slopes. Jos 10:40
of Goshen, the *, the Arabah, and Jos 11:16
and the hills and * of Israel. Jos 11:16
hill country, the *, the Arabah, Jos 12:8-24
in the * were also given to Judah: Jos 15:33-36
Canaanites in the * around Jos 17:16,17,18
* on both the east and west banks. 1Ch 12:15
trees in the * bordering Philistine 1Ch 27:28
Negeb and from the * west of Judah, Jer 17:26
those living in Judean * shall Ob 1:19

LOWLIEST
the oldest child of his * slave; Ex 11:5
She will be the * of all the Eze 29:15
he wants to, even the * of men!' Dan 4:17
As the * of slaves would dress. Jn 13:4f

LOWLY
Moab shall become my * servant, Ps 60:8
your feet the * of the world, and Lam 3:34,35,36
snakes they are, * as worms Mic 7:17
Yet he is *, riding on a donkey's Zec 9:9
The meek and * are fortunate! Mt 5:5
"The more * your service to Mt 23:11
For he took notice of his * Lk 1:48
their thrones and exalted the *. Lk 1:52

LOYAL
good and for being *, and I refused 1Sa 26:23
you for being so * to your king and 2Sa 2:5
May the Lord be * to you in 2Sa 2:6
* subjects, now that Saul is dead. 2Sa 2:7
was always so * and kind to me." 2Sa 10:2
peace-loving city, * to Israel. 2Sa 20:19
But among those who remained * 1Ki 1:8
Benaiah, the * army officers, or 1Ki 1:10
who remained * and accepted 1Ki 12:16,17
half the people were * to General 1Ki 16:21
you as * to me as I am to you?" 2Ki 10:15
armed and totally * to David. 1Ch 12:24-37
however, remained * to Rehoboam. 2Ch 10:17
and Benjamin remained * to him. 2Ch 11:12
"Sir: Greetings from your * Ez 4:11
those who are * to him, but harshly Ps 31:23
A true friend is always *, and a Pro 17:17
Most people will tell you what * Pro 20:6
them there and be their * allies. Is 14:1
you out for being * to my name. Is 66:5
the Jews who were * to God's laws. Dan 11:32f
knows that you stand * and true. Rom 16:19
* to him no matter what the cost. 1Co 13:7
at Ephesus, ever * to the Lord: Eph 1:1
while if you are * to Christ's 2Jn 1:9
and yet you have remained * to Rev 2:13

LOYALTY
absolute * and exclusive devotion. Ex 34:14
and gave him their pledge of *. 2Sa 5:1
They shouted out their oath of * 2Ch 15:14
his love and *—by killing his son. 2Ch 24:22
though he had taken an oath of *. 2Ch 36:13
Lord, despite our * to you. Ps 44:17
This will be for a sign of * to Is 19:20
and made him take an oath of *. Eze 17:12,13
You will hate one and show * to Lk 16:13
and about your * and warm love for 2Co 7:7

LUCIFER
heaven, O *, son of the morning! Is 14:12

LUCIUS
Black Man"), * (from Cyrene), Act 13:1
Timothy my fellow-worker, and * Rom 16:21

LUCK
Gad (meaning "My * has turned!" Gen 30:11
I'll try my * among the 1Sa 27:1
an evil man inwardly curses his *. Pro 10:6
he is going to run into bad *. Ecc 9:12

LUCKY
"You * fellow," Mk 10:49

LUCRATIVE
She who controlled the * Eze 26:2

LUD
Asshur,Arpachshad, *, Aram. Gen 10:22
Arpachshad, *, Aram, Uz, Hul, 1Ch 1:17
Put and * were in North Africa; Is 66:19f
Tarshish, Put, *, Meshech, Rosh, Is 66:19
Cush and Put and * who handle the Jer 46:9
men from far-off Paras, * and Put. Eze 27:10
For Cush and Put and *, Arabia Eze 30:5

LUDIM
*, Anamim, Lehabim, Naphtuhim, Gen 10:13,14
the *, the Anamim, the Lehabim, 1Ch 1:11,12

LUGGAGE
David left his * with a baggage 1Sa 17:22

LUGS
tip of each stand, banded with *. 1Ki 7:35

LUHITH
the upward road to *, and their Is 15:5
climb the hills of *, weeping Jer 48:5

LUKE
in their cities." * 10:1 remarks, Mt 11:1f
Implied from * 18:19. Mt 19:17f
but included in * 18:29. Mt 19:29f
the book of *; Act 1:1f
*, the writer of this book, now Act 16:10f
Dear doctor * sends his love, and Col 4:14
Only * is with me. 2Ti 4:11
Demas and *, my fellow workers. Phm 1:24
See Matthew 3:16, 17; * 9:31, 1Jn 5:6,7,8f

LUKEWARM
But since you are merely *, I Rev 3:16

LULLED
with them. She * him to sleep with Ju 16:19

LUMBER
of Tyre sent cedar *, carpenters, 2Sa 5:11
cedar and cypress * and gold he had 1Ki 9:11,12
Temple, and to buy * and stone." 2Ki 22:5,6
he supplied him with much cedar *. 1Ch 14:1
And expensive cedar * was used 2Ch 1:15
shipments of cedar * such as Hiram 2Ch 2:3
An immense amount of * will be 2Ch 2:9
blocks, timber, *, and beams. 2Ch 34:10,11

LUMBERMEN
without equal as *, and I will send 2Ch 2:8

LUMP
Or, "from a * of soil," or, Gen 2:7f
is a reddish white * that looks Lev 13:43
it into a * and started again. Jer 18:4
to use the same * of clay to make Rom 9:21

LUNCH
At * time Boaz called to her, Ru 2:14
with what was left of her *. Ru 2:18
Jehu went into the palace for *. 2Ki 9:34
to his home for * and Jesus Lk 7:36
hungry, but while * was being Act 10:9,10
Don't even eat * with such a 1Co 5:11

LUNGED
And they * at Lot and began Gen 19:9

LURE
"How he wanted to * you away Job 36:16
for success and * of nice things Mk 4:19
their bait, they * back into sin 2Pe 2:18

LURED
that we will be * out of the city. 2Ki 7:12

LURING
of the land from * you into idol Deu 20:18
They make a game of * unstable 2Pe 2:14

LURK
They * in dark alleys of the Ps 10:8
They * in ambush for my life. Ps 59:3
No lion will * along its course, Is 35:9
"leopard" shall * around their Jer 5:6
are wicked men who * for victims Jer 5:26

LURKING
know what sins are * in my heart? Ps 19:12
but wild animals * in the ruins. Lam 5:18
or a leopard * along the road. Hos 13:7
deaden the evil desires * within Col 3:5

LURKS
SIN * DEEP in the hearts of the Ps 36:1
He * like a bear, like a lion, Lam 3:10

LUSCIOUS
* fruit each season without fail. Ps 1:3
on producing all its * fruit. Jer 17:8
and feed in * mountain pastures. Eze 34:14

LUSH
He will give you * pastureland Deu 11:15
abundance! The * yield of this Neh 9:37
* pastures in the wilderness; Ps 65:11,12
At that time the * vineyards Is 7:23
again, a * and fertile forest. Is 29:17
cows that feed in * pastures, and Jer 50:11
ditch, with *, green foliage Eze 19:10
planted * crops in the wilderness. Eze 36:36
And suddenly the * pastures of Amo 1:2
the * vineyards you are planting. Amo 5:11
dry sand; the * pastures of Bashan Nah 1:4
Every field will become a * Zec 10:1

LUSHEST
* bounty and its richest fruit. Is 4:2,3,4

LUST
Place of the Graves Caused by *," Num 11:34
If you give up your * for money, Job 22:24
not to look with * upon a girl. Job 31:1
her husband. For * is a shameful Job 31:11
upon those who * after the tribute Ps 68:30f
Take away my * for evil things; Ps 141:4
Don't * for their beauty. Pro 6:25
never has enough of * and shame. Pro 9:13
Pride, *, and evil actions Pro 21:4
Possibly the reference is to *. Pro 27:20f
(Who can restrain your *? Jer 2:24
them and gave herself to their *. Eze 23:18
You defiled your holiness with * Eze 28:18
people constantly aflame with *. Hos 7:4
at a woman with * in his eye has Mt 5:28
—causes you to *, gouge it out and Mt 5:29
evil thoughts of *, theft, murder, Mk 7:21
women, burned with * for each Rom 1:27
and *, or fighting, or jealousy. Rom 13:12,13
to marry than to burn with *. 1Co 7:9
have done: your * and immorality, 2Co 12:21
and through, full of * and sham. Eph 4:22
impurity, * and shameful desires; Col 3:5
of *, but to be holy and clean. 1Th 4:7
enjoy—sex sin, *, getting drunk, 1Pe 4:3
save us from the * and rottenness 2Pe 1:4
and, using * as their bait, they 2Pe 2:18
towns, all full of * of every kind Jud 1:7
including * of men for other men. Jud 1:7
the Israelites to fall by *. Rev 2:6f

LUSTED
who had * for meat and for Egypt. Num 11:34
or if my heart has * for what my Job 31:7,8
Literally, "* exceedingly." Ps 106:14f

LUSTER
HOW THE FINEST gold has lost its * Lam 4:1

LUSTFUL
And you added * Egypt to your Eze 16:26
sinning with the * men she Eze 23:19,20
of * men who visit prostitutes. Eze 23:44
into your soul. A * eye shuts out Lk 11:34
in the church of * Corinth who were 1Co 6:12f
eagerness for * pleasure, Gal 5:19
and honor— not in * passion as the 1Th 4:5
their own evil, * thoughts, and 2Pe 2:10

LUSTROUS
his waist, and glowing, * skin! Dan 10:5,6

LUSTS
men brag of all their evil *; Ps 10:3
poured out their * upon her and Eze 23:8
their evil minds and reckless *. Eph 4:19

LUSTY
They are well-fed, * stallions, Jer 5:8

LUTE
bring me someone to play the *." 2Ki 3:15
And as the * was played, the 2Ki 3:15
from the harp and * and lyre. Ps 92:3
the trumpet and with * and harp. Ps 150:3

LUXURIANT
strong branches and * leaves. Eze 17:6
HOW PROSPEROUS ISRAEL is—a * Hos 10:1

LUXURIANTLY
It grew * and gave streamlets of Eze 31:4

LUXURIES
"The dainty * and splendor that Rev 18:14

LUXURIOUS
the most * apartment in the harem. Est 2:9
for you to live in * homes, when Hag 1:3,4
rich from all her * living." Rev 18:3

LUXURY
life of ease and *, but you shall Gen 27:39,40
wine and * are not the way to Pro 21:17
you will be living in * again. Is 37:30
WOE TO THOSE lounging in * at Amo 6:1
surrounded with *, eating the meat Amo 6:4
Men who live in * are found in Lk 7:25
and lived each day in mirth and *. Lk 16:19
She has lived in * and Rev 18:7

LUZ
was *. Gen 28:19
Finally they arrived at * (also Gen 35:6
"God Almighty appeared to me at * Gen 48:3
It then went from Bethel to *, Jos 16:1
went south to * (also called Jos 18:13
as *, and the Lord was with them. Ju 1:22,23
there, naming it *, too, as it is Ju 1:26

LYCAONIA
to the cities of *, Lystra, Derbe, Act 14:5,6

LYCIA
at Myra, in the province of *. Act 27:5
LYDDA
to the believers in the town of *. Act 9:32
Then the whole population of * Act 9:35
was nearby at *, they sent two men Act 9:38
LYDIA
One of them was *, a saleswoman Act 16:14
to the home of * where they met Act 16:40
LYE
my hands with * to make them Job 9:30
No amount of soap or * can make Jer 2:22
LYING
but he was unaware of her * down Gen 19:33
the lad's cries as he is * there. Gen 21:17
the room where his father was *. Gen 27:18
The ground you are * on is yours! Gen 28:13
flocks of sheep * beside a well in Gen 29:2
a lost article and * about it, Lev 6:3
if the witness is *, his penalty Deu 19:18
victim is found * in a field and no Deu 21:1
"If a bird's nest is * on the Deu 22:6
and found Sisera * there dead, with Ju 4:22
jawbone that was * on the ground Ju 15:15
There was a woman * at his feet! Ru 3:8
cut off and were * in the doorway; 1Sa 5:4
of Israel is not *, nor will he 1Sa 15:29
He was evidently *. 2Sa 1:10f
* there and continued after Sheba. 2Sa 20:8,9,10
And the king is * in bed, 1Ki 1:46,47
But the old man was * to him. 1Ki 13:18
and saw the body * in the road and 1Ki 13:24,25
He found the prophet's body * in 1Ki 13:28
'I will go as a * spirit in the 1Ki 22:22
The Lord has put a * spirit in 1Ki 22:23
never leave the bed he is * on; 2Ki 1:4,5
not leave the bed you are * on; 2Ki 1:6
* there upon the prophet's bed. 2Ki 4:32
Joram, who was * there wounded. 2Ki 9:16
*, or else declare him innocent. 2Ch 6:23
"He replied, 'I will be a * 2Ch 18:21
the Lord has put a * spirit in the 2Ch 18:22
were dead bodies * on the 2Ch 20:24
reply was, "You know you are *. Neh 6:8
do not practice dishonesty and *. Ps 24:4
of * in silence in the grave. Ps 30:12
graves, their * lips quieted at Ps 31:18
Keep your lips from *. Ps 34:13
I am * there upon my bed of pain. Ps 41:6
than good! And * more than truth! Ps 52:3
do harm, O man with the * tongue. Ps 52:4
These men are born sinners, * Ps 58:3
* when they say I will recover." Ps 116:10,11
* tongue, what shall be your fate? Ps 120:3
seven:Haughtiness*MurderingPlotting Pro 6:16-19
A man who is caught * to his Pro 26:18,19
of myrrh * between my breasts." Sol 1:13
thing you are, * here upon the Sol 1:16
of Israel and the * prophets. Is 9:14,15
Sheep pasture there, * quiet and Is 17:2
Bodies! * everywhere, slain by Is 22:2
of men * drunk in the streets! Is 28:1
out of their own * hearts. Jer 14:14
will punish these * prophets who Jer 14:15
For what is sad is you and your *. Jer 23:36
for you are * about Ishmael." Jer 40:16
See them * in the streets—old and Lam 2:21
For they were * prophets, Eze 13:16
not live, by * to my people—and how Eze 13:19
and through * with women in their Eze 22:10f
* in the middle of your rivers. Eze 29:3
go away and leave her * there. Eze 31:12
that will be * in peace after the Eze 38:8
This land, * between the sections Eze 48:21,22
Then I fainted, * face downward Dan 8:18
* in ambush for their victims; Hos 6:9
which is now * in ruins, and return Amo 9:11
drunken, * prophet that you like! Mic 2:11
of ungodly treasures and * scales. Mic 6:10
your citizens are so used to * Mic 6:12
The dead are * in the Nah 3:3
This is a false prophet who is * Zec 13:6f
little girl was * and took her by Mt 9:25
fornication, theft, * and slander. Mt 15:19
see where his body was * Mt 28:6
into the room where she was *. Mk 5:40
little girl was * quietly in bed, Mk 7:30
Look, that's where his body was * Mk 16:6
* in a manger!" Lk 2:12
And there was the baby, * in the Lk 2:16
him * half dead beside the road. Lk 10:30
and when he saw the man * there, Lk 10:31
walked over and looked at him * Lk 10:32
One of the men * there had been Jn 5:5
"You are boasting—and *!" Jn 8:13
cloth * there, but I didn't go in. Jn 20:5
He also noticed the cloth * Jn 20:6
in a bundle and was * at the side. Jn 20:7
the body of Jesus had been *. Jn 20:12
you were * to the Holy Spirit. Act 5:3
You weren't * to us, but to Act 5:4
the Council. The * witnesses Act 6:13
*, bitterness, and gossip. Rom 1:29
what happened—I am not * to you. Gal 1:20
Stop * to each other; Eph 4:25
darkness and sin, we are *. 1Jn 1:6
not sinned, we are * and calling 1Jn 1:10
(but they aren't—they are *) to Rev 3:9
LYNCH
to call for a mob to * you. Jer 12:6
LYRE
praise upon the * and on the harp. Ps 33:2
Arise, O harp and *! Ps 57:8
pluck the sweet * and harp. Ps 81:2
from the harp and lute and *. Ps 92:3
Wake up, O harp and *! Ps 108:2
accompanied by drums and *. Ps 149:3
LYRES
before the Lord—*, harps, 2Sa 6:5
played the cymbals, *, and harps. 2Ch 5:11,12
harps and * for the choir. 2Ch 9:11
a band of harps, *, and trumpets 2Ch 20:28
We have put away our *, hanging Ps 137:2
LYSANIAS
and Trachonitis; *, over Abilene; Lk 3:1
LYSIAS
"From: Claudius * Act 23:26
deserves, but *, the commander of Act 24:7
for the arrival of *, the garrison Act 24:22
LYSTRA
of Lycaonia, *, Derbe, and the Act 14:5,6
While they were at *, they came Act 14:8
returned again to *, Iconium and Act 14:21
and then on to * where they met Act 16:1
by the brothers in * and Iconium, Act 16:2
and *, but the Lord delivered me. 2Ti 3:11
MA-ACAH
of the kingdoms of Geshur and *. Jos 12:5
MA-ACATHITE
(son of a *), and their men. Jer 40:8
MA-ACATHITES
of the Geshurites and the *; Jos 13:11
Geshurites or the *, who still live Jos 13:13
MA-ACTHITES
borders of the Geshurites and *. Deu 3:14
MA-ADAI
*, Amram, Uel, Banaiah, Bedeiah, Ez 10:34-42
MA-ADIAH
*, Bilgah, Shemaiah, Neh 12:1
MA-ASEIAH
Unni, Eliab, *, and Benaiah 1Ch 15:20
of the army, and his assistant, *. 2Ch 26:11
the king's son *, and the king's 2Ch 28:7
of Azaliah) and *, governor of 2Ch 34:8
*, Eliezer, Ez 10:16-19
*, Elijah, Shemaiah, Ez 10:21
Eli-o-enai, *, Ishmael, Nethanel, Ez 10:22
Adna, Chelal, Benaiah, *, Ez 10:30
Azariah (son of *, son of Ananiah) Neh 3:23
Anaiah, Uriah, Hilkiah, and *. Neh 8:1
Hodiah, *, Kelita, Azariah, Neh 8:7,8
Hashabnah, *, Ahiah, Neh 10:14-27
* (son of Baruch, son of Neh 11:4,5,6
of Kolaiah, son of *, son of Neh 11:7,8,9
Eliakim, *, Miniamin, Neh 12:40,41
*, Shemaiah, Eleazar, Neh 12:42
the priest (son of *) to Jeremiah, Jer 21:1
Zephaniah (son of *) the priest, Jer 29:25
above the room of * (son of Jer 35:4
the priest (son of *) to ask Jer 37:3
MA-ASSEIAH
Eliab, Benaiah, *, Mattithiah, 1Ch 15:18
MA-AZIAH
Mija-min, *, Bilgai, Neh 10:1
MA'AM
time is coming, *, when we will no Jn 4:21-24
MAACAH
Reumah:Tebah, Gaham,Tahash, *. Gen 22:24
The third was Absalom, born to *, 2Sa 3:3
from the king of *, and ten 2Sa 10:6
Tob, and * fought in the fields. 2Sa 10:7,8
Eliphelet (son of Ahasbai) from *; 2Sa 23:24-39
(Abijam's mother was *, the 1Ki 15:1
(His grandmother was *, the 1Ki 15:10
He deposed his grandmother * as 1Ki 15:13
Another of Caleb's concubines, *, 1Ch 2:48,49
son of his wife *, who was the 1Ch 3:2
Machir's sister was *. 1Ch 7:15
Machir's wife, also named *, bore 1Ch 7:16
and his wife's name was *. 1Ch 8:29
Jeiel (whose wife was *) lived in 1Ch 9:35,36,37
Hanan (son of *); 1Ch 11:26-47
the king of * and his entire army. 1Ch 19:7
Over Simeon, Shephatiah (son of * 1Ch 27:16-22
Later he married *, the daughter 2Ch 11:20
He loved * more than any of his 2Ch 11:21
removed his mother * from being the 2Ch 15:16
MAACAH'S
sixty daughters). * son Abijah was 2Ch 11:22
MAACATHITE
was the father of Eshtemoa the *. 1Ch 4:19
MAACHATHITE
and Ja-azaniah, son of *, and 2Ki 25:23
MAAI
Gilalai, *, Nethanel, Neh 12:35,
MAARATH
Beth-zur, Gedor, *, Beth-anoth, Jos 15:48-6
MAASAI
Another priest was * (son of 1Ch 9:1
MAASEIAH
(son of Obed), * (son of Adaiah), 2Ch 23:
Zedekiah (son of *), who are Jer 29:2
MAATH
Naggai's father was *; Lk 3:23-3
MAATH'S
Naggai's father was Maath;* father Lk 3:23-3
MAAZ
*, Jamin, and Eker. 1Ch 2:2
MAAZIAH
Twenty-fourth, the group led by *. 1Ch 24:7-1
MACCABEAN
(the rulers of the * period were Jer 30:21
MACCABEES
Perhaps the valiant * and their Dan 11:32
MACEDONIA
and Antipater of * and Greece. Dan 8:8
saw a man over in *, Greece, Act 16:
would go to *, for we could only Act 16:1
and Timothy from *, Paul spent his Act 18:
he decided to go north to * first. Act 20:
For you see, the Christians in * Rom 15:26
I have been to * first, but I will 1Co 16:
you on my way to *, as well as 2Co 1:15,16
right on to * to try to find him. 2Co 2:1
When we arrived in * there was no 2Co 7:5
has done for the churches in *. 2Co 8:1
to the friends in * that you were 2Co 9:2
from * brought me another gift. 2Co 11:8,9
on my way, leaving *, only you Php 4:15
As I said when I left for *, 1Ti 1:3,4
MACEDONIAN
colony just inside the * border, Act 16:12
some of these * people come with 2Co 9:4
MACH-PELAH
*, down at the end of his field. Gen 23:9
Ephron's field at *, near Mamre, Gen 23:17,18
him in the cave of * near Mamre, in Gen 25:9,10
in the field of *, facing Mamre—the Gen 49:29,30
in the cave of *—the cave Abraham Gen 50:12,13
MACHBANNAI
* was eleventh in command. 1Ch 12:8-13
MACHBENAH
(the father of * and of Gibe-a). 1Ch 2:48,49
MACHI
Geuel, son of *, from the tribe of Num 13:3-15
MACHINE
Does a * call its inventor dumb? Is 29:16
MACHIR
the children of *, Manasseh's son, Gen 50:23
named after their ancestor *. Num 26:28-37
Their ancestor was *, son of Num 27:1
Then the clan of * of the tribe Num 32:39
(of the clan of *, of the tribe of Num 36:1
I gave Gilead to the clan of *. Deu 3:15
clan *, who was Manasseh's son. Jos 13:31
The clan of * (Manasseh's oldest Jos 17:1
great-grandson of *, and Jos 17:3
From * and from Zebulun. Ju 5:13,14
"At the home of *." 2Sa 9:4
an Ammonite) and * (son of Ammiel 2Sa 17:27
Segub. (* was also the father of 1Ch 2:21
* (who became the father of 1Ch 7:14
It was * who found wives for 1Ch 7:15
the grandsons of *, and the 1Ch 7:17
MACHIR'S
Hezron married * daughter at the 1Ch 2:21
* sister was Maacah. 1Ch 7:15
* wife, also named Maacah, bore 1Ch 7:16
Hammolecheth, * sister, bore 1Ch 7:18
MACHIRITES
following clan of *, named after Num 26:28-37
The sub-clan of the * was the Num 26:28-37
So Moses gave Gilead to the *, Num 32:40
MACHNADEBAI
Nathan, Adaiah, *, Shashai, Sharai, Ez 10:34-42
MAD
Now Jacob got * at Laban. Gen 31:36,37
You will go * because of all the Deu 28:34
choose their own * course, for they Ecc 9:2,3
the whole earth drink and go *. Jer 51:7
"The inspired men are *." Hos 9:7
(Have I gone * to boast like 2Co 11:23
stopped from his * course when his 2Pe 2:16
MADAI
of Japheth were:Gomer, Magog, * Gen 10:2
Gomer, Magog, *, 1Ch 1:5-9
MADE
So God * the sky, dividing the Gen 1:7,8
For God * two huge lights, the Gen 1:16
he also * the stars. Gen 1:16
And so it was. God * all sorts Gen 1:25
So God * man like his Maker. Gen 1:27
all that he had *, and it was Gen 1:31
and earth which the Lord God *. Gen 2:4

MADE Con't)
removed it, and * the rib into a Gen 2:22
the creatures the Lord God had *. Gen 3:1
For you were * from the ground, Gen 3:19
garments * from skins of animals. Gen 3:21
not Cain's. This * Cain both Gen 4:5
and * me a fugitive and a tramp; Gen 4:14
evil, he was sorry he had * them. Gen 6:6
For I am sorry I * them." Gen 6:7
and reptiles I have * will die." Gen 7:4
a man is to kill one * like God. Gen 9:5,6
planted a vineyard, and he * wine. Gen 9:20,21
So they * great piles of Gen 11:3,4
There he * camp, and made an Gen 12:8
There he made camp, and * an Gen 12:8
So that day Jehovah * this Gen 15:18
Whatever * you think of this vile Gen 20:9,10
place where they * their covenant. Gen 21:31
There he * the camels kneel down Gen 24:11
And my master * me promise not Gen 24:37
the Lord has * my mission Gen 24:56
Then Abimelech * a public Gen 26:11
"the Lord has * room for us and we Gen 26:22
And she * him a pair of gloves Gen 27:16
Isaac: "I have * him your Gen 27:37
In this way God has * me wealthy Gen 31:9
pillar and * a vow to serve me. Gen 31:13
No, I took the loss. You * me pay Gen 31:39
and Joseph came and * their bows. Gen 33:7
to every move they *, two of Gen 34:25
Simeon, "You have * me stink among Gen 34:30
(meaning "* to Forget"—what he Gen 41:51
was that God had * up to him for Gen 41:51
God has * me fruitful in this land Gen 41:52
the famine has * our land." Gen 42:8,9
Then Joseph * a hasty exit, Gen 43:30
And he has * me a counselor to Gen 45:8
says, "God has * me chief of all Gen 45:9
So Joseph * it a law throughout Gen 47:26
Joseph's father * Joseph swear to Gen 50:5
Then Joseph * his brothers Gen 50:15
So the Egyptians * slaves of them Ex 1:11
alarmed, and * the Hebrew slavery Ex 1:13,14
hide him, she * a little boat from Ex 2:3
Tell them what fools I * of the Ex 10:2
to eat only bread * without yeast. Ex 12:15
not eat anything * with yeast; Ex 12:20
for Joseph had * the sons of Israel Ex 13:19
The sanctuary you * for them to Ex 15:17
over Israel and * them judges over Ex 18:25
For in six days the Lord * the Ex 20:11
fact that I have * known my will to Ex 20:22
or worship idols * of silver or Ex 20:23
no restitution shall be * for it. Ex 22:11
the Lord has * with you in giving Ex 24:8
trays are to be * of pure gold. Ex 25:38
"The roof of the Tabernacle is * Ex 26:7,8
tent shall be * from acacia wood, Ex 26:15,16
pans are all to be * of bronze. Ex 27:3
The altar is to be hollow, * Ex 27:8
curtains * from fine-twined linen. Ex 27:9,10
curtain, * of beautifully Ex 27:16
high, * from fine-twined linen. Ex 27:18
on the walls, will be * of bronze. Ex 27:19
"The ephod shall be * by the Ex 28:5,6
And the sash shall be * of the Ex 28:8
gold shall be * and attached to Ex 28:13,14
"The ephod shall be * of blue Ex 28:30,31
and bread * without yeast, and Ex 29:2
* with finely ground wheat flour. Ex 29:2
It shall be * from acacia wood. Ex 30:1
The poles are to be * of acacia Ex 30:5
* of gold, silver, and bronze. Ex 31:4
the beautifully *, holy garments Ex 31:10
For in six days the Lord * heaven Ex 31:17
water and * the people drink it. Ex 32:20
have * themselves gods of gold. Ex 32:31
Blue, purple, and scarlet cloth, * Ex 35:5-9
and scarlet cloth * from the Ex 35:23
And God has * him and Oholiab Ex 35:34
The skilled weavers first * ten Ex 36:8,9
Then fifty clasps of gold were * Ex 36:13
eleven draperies * of goats' hair Ex 36:14,15
Then he * fifty loops along the Ex 36:17
The top layer of the roof was * Ex 36:19
was its rear, was * from six Ex 36:27
Then he * five sets of bars from Ex 36:31,32
veil was * from woven linen, with Ex 36:35
Then he * a drapery for the Ex 36:37
NEXT BEZALEL * the Ark. Ex 37:1
Then he * poles from acacia Ex 37:4
Then, from pure gold, he * a lid Ex 37:6
2¼ feet wide. He * two cherubim of Ex 37:7
Then he * a table, using acacia Ex 37:10
Next, using pure gold, he * the Ex 37:15,16
Then he * the lampstand, again Ex 37:17
Then he * the seven lamps at the Ex 37:23,24
The incense altar was * of acacia Ex 37:25
its corner-horns * as part of the Ex 37:25
Then, from sweet spices, he * the Ex 37:29
Then he * bronze utensils to be Ex 38:3
Next he * a bronze grating that Ex 38:4
themselves were * of acacia wood, Ex 38:6
the walls were * from drapes Ex 38:12
to the court was * of fine-twined Ex 38:18
the people * beautiful garments of Ex 39:1
The ephod was * from this cloth Ex 39:2
woven sash * of the same gold, Ex 39:4,5
like the ephod, * from the finest Ex 39:8
these were * of linen cloth, Ex 39:24
Robes were now * for Aaron and Ex 39:27
were all * of this linen, and the Ex 39:28,29
Finally they * the holy plate of Ex 39:30
it the incense * from sweet spices, Ex 40:27
altar, an offering * by fire." Lev 2:2f
Lord, it must be * from finely Lev 2:4
Wafers * without yeast and spread Lev 2:4
it shall be * of finely ground Lev 2:5
it too shall be * of fine flour Lev 2:7
sacrifice * to Jehovah by fire; Lev 4:35
offering to Jehovah * by fire; Lev 5:12
of the burnt offerings * to me. Lev 6:17
offerings * by fire to the Lord." Lev 6:18
basket of bread * without yeast; Lev 8:1
offerings to Jehovah * by fire; Lev 10:13
or anything * of skin or leather, Lev 13:59
out again and has * atonement for Lev 16:17
don't wear clothes * of half wool Lev 19:19
I am the Lord your God who has * Lev 20:24
to the sacrifices * by foreigners Lev 22:25
as well as those * by yourselves, Lev 22:25
for I, the Lord, * you holy to Lev 22:32,33
to the Lord are to be * by fire. Lev 23:37
The sacrifices * during the Lev 23:38
memorial offering * by fire to the Lev 24:5-8
For these are offerings * by fire Lev 24:9
Literally, "and * you go Lev 26:13f
for if there is any change *, Lev 27:33
the payment can be *, it must be Num 5:8
a basket of bread * without Num 6:15
pancakes * of fine flour mixed Num 6:15
basket of bread * without yeast; Num 6:17
of the pancakes (* without yeast), Num 6:19
the wafers (also * without yeast), Num 6:19
was * entirely of beaten gold. Num 8:4
it, and then * pancakes from Num 11:8
They * their report to Moses, Num 13:26
their sacrifice * by fire before Num 15:25
"If the error is * by a single Num 15:27
and he put on the incense and * Num 16:47
* for each firstborn child. Num 18:16
So Moses * the replica, and Num 21:9
"Because you have * me look like Num 22:29
and because he has * atonement for Num 25:12,13
an offering * by fire to the Lord. Num 28:6
the Lord, an offering * by fire. Num 28:8
hears that she has * a vow with Num 30:4
and everything * of leather, goat's Num 31:20
order to be * ceremonially pure; Num 31:23
"The Lord * us wander back and Num 32:13
atonement can be * for murder Num 35:33
Jehovah your God * him obstinate, Deu 2:30
"At that time I * this plea to Deu 3:23,24,25
the Lord your God has * with you! Deu 4:23
will worship idols * from wood and Deu 4:28
he has * to your ancestors. Deu 4:31
"The Lord our God * a contract Deu 5:2,3
love, he * with your fathers. Deu 7:12
the silver or gold they are * of. Deu 7:25
and might that * you wealthy. Deu 8:17
how continually angry you * the Deu 9:7
angry you * him at Mount Horeb? Deu 9:8
which Jehovah had * with you—the Deu 9:9
had * an idol from molten metal. Deu 9:12
the calf you had * in your terrible Deu 9:16
calf you had *—and burned it and Deu 9:21
So I * an Ark of acacia wood and Deu 10:3
in the Ark I had *, where they are Deu 10:5
Lord your God has * you as many as Deu 10:22
shall eat no bread * with yeast. Deu 16:8
he has * it up himself. Deu 18:22
carved of wood or * from molten Deu 27:15
known, gods * of wood and stone! Deu 28:64
which the Lord had * with the Deu 29:1
heathen idols * of wood, stone, Deu 29:17
broke the contract * with them by Deu 29:25
the contract I have * with them. Deu 31:16
Has he not established you and * Deu 32:6
They spurned the Rock who had * Deu 32:18
They have * me very jealous of Deu 32:21
people, Moses * these comments: Deu 32:46
For we have heard how the Lord * Jos 2:10
The Lord * him great in the eyes Jos 4:14
and they * unleavened bread. Jos 5:11,12
a trumpet * from a ram's horn. Jos 6:3,4
Arrangements were * for them to Jos 6:23
Israel had * before the Lord God. Jos 9:18
of Gibeon had * peace with Israel Jos 10:1
"for they have * peace with Joshua Jos 10:4
For the Lord * the enemy kings Jos 11:20
which our fathers *, patterned Jos 22:28
Instead I * him bless you; Jos 24:10
So Joshua * a covenant with them Jos 24:25
Nahalol, but * them their slaves; Ju 1:30
them and * them their slaves. Ju 1:35
the treaty I * with their Ju 2:20
on this journey he * himself a Ju 3:16
iron chariots, and * life Ju 4:2,3
Gideon * an ephod Ju 8:27
This * Jehovah very angry with Ju 10:7,8
was * commander-in-chief and king. Ju 11:11
Why have you * no effort to Ju 11:26
For I have * a vow to the Lord Ju 11:35
so the arrangements were *. Ju 14:7
from Samson what * him so strong, Ju 16:5
"You've * fun of me three times Ju 16:15
* to grind grain in the prison. Ju 16:21
The people * sacrifices to their Ju 16:23,24
the prison and * to stand at the Ju 16:25,26
and the idol he * from it was Ju 17:4,5
the Lord had * a breach in the Ju 21:15
saw that Ruth had * up her mind and Ru 1:18
Peninnah * matters worse by 1Sa 1:6
And she * this vow: "O Lord of 1Sa 1:11
Each year his mother * a little 1Sa 2:19
that it almost * the ground shake! 1Sa 4:5
some will be * to lead his 1Sa 8:12
his great name. He * you a special 1Sa 12:22
But the Lord * no reply all 1Sa 14:37
"I am sorry that I ever * Saul 1Sa 15:11
God * you king of Israel. 1Sa 15:17
he had ever * Saul king of Israel. 1Sa 15:35
So Saul * him commander of his 1Sa 18:5
So Jonathan * a covenant with the 1Sa 20:16
But Jonathan * David swear to it 1Sa 20:17
you and has * you king of Israel, 1Sa 25:30,31
From then on David * this a law 1Sa 30:25
Ish-bosheth * no reply, for he 2Sa 3:11
So David * a contract before the 2Sa 5:3
So David * the stronghold of Zion 2Sa 5:9
why the Lord had * him the king and 2Sa 5:12
He gave David presents * from 2Sa 8:10
* him victorious wherever he went. 2Sa 8:14
The Lord God of Israel says, 'I * 2Sa 12:7
And the Lord * Bath-sheba's baby 2Sa 12:15
$50,000 treasure * from solid gold 2Sa 12:29,30
his own head. He * slaves of the 2Sa 12:31
of the city and * them labor with 2Sa 12:31
life away, but has * provision to 2Sa 14:14f
of a vow I * to him while I was at 2Sa 15:7,8
that are being * to capture me, and 2Sa 15:35,36
think Ahithophel has * a mistake. 2Sa 17:7
Arrangements had been * for a 2Sa 17:17
* you a commissioned officer." 2Sa 18:11
and Absalom, whom we * our king 2Sa 19:8,9,10
He has * me safe. 2Sa 22:33
Your gentleness has * me great. 2Sa 22:36
You have * wide steps for my 2Sa 22:37
You have * my enemies 2Sa 22:41
Yes, God has * 2Sa 23:5
And David * him chief of his 2Sa 23:23
SOLOMON * AN alliance with 1Ki 3:1
O Lord my God, now you have * me 1Ki 3:7
And Hiram and Solomon * a formal 1Ki 5:12
floors were * of cypress boards. 1Ki 6:15
gold, and Solomon * a cedar-wood 1Ki 6:20
and he * gold chains to protect 1Ki 6:21,22
Literally, "he * two cherubim." 1Ki 6:23-28f
* from olive wood, each fifteen 1Ki 6:23-28
Then he * square doorposts of 1Ki 6:33
At the tops of the pillars he * 1Ki 7:16-22
Then he * ten four-wheeled 1Ki 7:27-30
supporting posts * of bronze and 1Ki 7:27-30
same size and were * alike, for 1Ki 7:37
Then he * ten brass vats, and 1Ki 7:38
Hiram also * the necessary pots, 1Ki 7:40
Here is a list of the items he *: 1Ki 7:41-46
All these items were * of 1Ki 7:41-46
the Temple were * of solid gold. 1Ki 7:48
Each of these was * of solid 1Ki 7:50
the time the Lord * his covenant 1Ki 8:9
the covenant * by the Lord with our 1Ki 8:21
who have * an honest confession; 1Ki 8:39
He also * a huge ivory throne and 1Ki 10:18
service was * of solid gold. 1Ki 10:21
(I once * this same promise to 1Ki 11:38
to Jeroboam, * through Ahijah, the 1Ki 12:15
and there he was * king of 1Ki 12:20
gold calf-idols * and told the 1Ki 12:28
He also * shrines on the hills 1Ki 12:31
instead, he * more priests than 1Ki 13:33
people and * you king of Israel. 1Ki 14:7
you have * other gods and have 1Ki 14:9
gods and have * me furious with 1Ki 14:9
sinned and * all of Israel sin 1Ki 14:16
the gold shields Solomon had *. 1Ki 14:26
Afterwards Rehoboam * bronze 1Ki 14:27
all the idols his father had *. 1Ki 15:12
because she had * an idol—which he 1Ki 15:13
He * permanent exhibits in the 1Ki 15:15
Then King Asa * a proclamation 1Ki 15:22
You have * my people sin, and I 1Ki 16:2
Then he * other idols and did 1Ki 16:33

(MADE Con't)
What has * you so upset and 1Ki 21:5
for you have * him very angry and 1Ki 21:22
of Chenaanah), * some iron horns 1Ki 22:11
"Various suggestions were *, 1Ki 22:20
He also * peace with Ahab, the 1Ki 22:44
So Ahaziah * the Lord God of 1Ki 22:52,53
to Baal that his father had *. 2Ki 3:2
of barley bread * from the first 2Ki 4:42
So the king * a great feast for 2Ki 6:23
* of sackcloth next to his flesh. 2Ki 6:26-30
the Lord * windows in the sky!" 2Ki 7:2
(For the Lord had * the whole 2Ki 7:6
Jehoiada * a treaty between the 2Ki 11:17
He also * a contract between the 2Ki 11:17
its dimensions and * a sketch and 2Ki 16:10
covenant he had * with their 2Ki 17:15
and * two calves from molten gold. 2Ki 17:16
molten gold. They * detestable, 2Ki 17:16
the Lord. He * them sin a great 2Ki 17:21
For the Lord had * a contract 2Ki 17:35,36
forget the covenant I * with you; 2Ki 17:38
that Moses had *, because the 2Ki 18:4
Assyrians have * against me.' 2Ki 19:5,6
that men had * of wood and stone. 2Ki 19:18
this period were * in the form of 2Ki 20:11f
be taken away and * into eunuchs 2Ki 20:18
and conduit he * and how he brought 2Ki 20:20
He built altars for Baal and * a 2Ki 21:3,4,5
gods and have * me very angry; 2Ki 22:17
and he and they * a solemn promise 2Ki 23:3
had * when he led Israel into sin. 2Ki 23:15
and had * the Lord very angry. 2Ki 23:19
and his troops * a hole in the 2Ki 25:4,5
and its bases—all * for the Temple 2Ki 25:16
So David * a contract with them 1Ch 11:3
be * commander-in-chief!" 1Ch 11:5,6
David * him captain of his 1Ch 11:24,25
he * them captains of his army. 1Ch 12:18
had been * for their arrival. 1Ch 12:39
why the Lord had * him king and why 1Ch 14:2
why he had * his kingdom so great; 1Ch 14:2
But the Lord * the heavens. 1Ch 16:26
and * you the king of my people. 1Ch 17:7
You have * a unique nation and 1Ch 17:21
And you * a great name for 1Ch 17:21
It was * of gold inlaid with gems 1Ch 20:2
Whether this means that he * 1Ch 20:3f
* David decide to take a census. 1Ch 21:1
at what the king had * him do. 1Ch 21:6
The Tabernacle and altar * by 1Ch 21:29
musical instruments I have *." 1Ch 23:4,5
and the wafers * without yeast 1Ch 23:29
and has * me king over all Israel. 1Ch 28:4
for the articles * of gold and 1Ch 29:4,5
are * great and given strength. 1Ch 29:12
* all of these preparations." 1Ch 29:19
God had * him a powerful monarch. 2Ch 1:1
The bronze altar * by Bezalel 2Ch 1:5,6
my father and have * me king over a 2Ch 1:9
that he has * you their king! 2Ch 2:11
God of Israel who * the heavens and 2Ch 2:12
out to the roof. He * chains 2Ch 3:16
HE ALSO * a bronze altar thirty 2Ch 4:1
Huramabi also * the necessary 2Ch 4:11
Huramabi, * all of the 2Ch 4:12-16
of the Presence must be * of gold; 2Ch 4:19
firepans—all were * of pure gold. 2Ch 4:22
when the Lord * a covenant with the 2Ch 5:10
But I have * a Temple for you, O 2Ch 6:1
fulfilled the promise he * to him. 2Ch 6:4
The platform was * of bronze, 7½ 2Ch 6:12,13
prayers * to you in this place. 2Ch 6:40
* and had used to praise the Lord. 2Ch 7:6
to every prayer * in this place. 2Ch 7:15
He also * a huge ivory throne 2Ch 9:17
of Egypt. He * silver become as 2Ch 9:27
* for you—he calls them your gods! 2Ch 13:8
This * it possible for him to 2Ch 14:6
because she * an Asherah-idol; 2Ch 15:16
and his people * a very great 2Ch 16:13,14
* a marriage alliance [for his son 2Ch 18:1
of Chenaanah), * some iron horns 2Ch 18:10
him, and the Lord * the charioteers 2Ch 18:31
So Jehoshaphat * no more trips to 2Ch 19:4
They * ships in Ezion-geber to 2Ch 20:36
David, for he had * a covenant with 2Ch 21:7
Israel, and have * the people of 2Ch 21:13
advice, Ahaziah * an alliance with 2Ch 22:5
So all the arrangements were *. 2Ch 23:8
Then Jehoiada * a solemn 2Ch 23:15,16,17
law of Moses. He * the identical 2Ch 23:18
* and set outside the Temple gate. 2Ch 24:7,8
and to foundrymen who * articles 2Ch 24:12
* them very angry and insulted. 2Ch 25:10
This * the Lord very angry and 2Ch 25:15
in the Negeb, and * many water 2Ch 26:10
worship there, and * altars to the 2Ch 28:24
the animals and * a sin offering 2Ch 29:24
He also * a personal 2Ch 31:3
These appointments were * by King 2Ch 31:12,13
progress being * in the 2Ch 34:15,16
before them, he * a pledge to the 2Ch 34:31
The king's officials * willing 2Ch 35:8
Those who * the trip also Ez 2:55,56,57
The work force was * up of all Ez 3:8
Then the king * this reply to Ez 4:17
I have ordered a search * of the Ez 4:19
King Cyrus ever * such a decree; Ez 5:17
that a search be * in the Ez 6:1
religious progress being * there. Ez 7:14
our ancestors, who * the king want Ez 7:27
Then a proclamation was * Ez 10:7,8
doors, and * the bolts and bars. Neh 3:3
Then I summoned the priests and * Neh 5:12
He stood on a wooden stand * Neh 8:1
should be * throughout the cities Neh 8:15
You have * the skies and the Neh 9:6
to you, you * a contract with him Neh 9:8
even though they * a calf-idol and Neh 9:18
* him the king over all Israel; Neh 13:26
aides thought this * good sense, so Est 1:21
An investigation was *, the two Est 2:23
province, and * known to all your Est 3:14
Literally, "had * known how they Est 8:1f
how much less men * of dust, who Job 4:18,19
Is my flesh * of brass? Job 6:12
Why have you * me your target, Job 7:20
* my life so heavy a burden to me? Job 7:20
the seas. He * the Bear, Orion and Job 9:9
and despise me, a man you have *; Job 10:3
" 'You have * me, and yet you Job 10:8
Oh, please remember that I'm * Job 10:9
you have * have about as much value Job 13:12
you born before the hills were *? Job 15:7,8
"He has * me a mockery among the Job 17:6
The heavens are * beautiful by Job 26:13
he may order them * by his tailor, Job 27:17
and * them drop their victims. Job 29:17
"I * A covenant with my eyes not Job 31:1
For God * me, and made my Job 31:15
For God made me, and * my Job 31:15
let him approve the indictments * Job 31:35
For the Spirit of God has * me, Job 33:4
I, too, am * of common clay. Job 33:7
than to the poor. He * them all. Job 34:19
seen where hail is * and stored? Job 38:22,23
Have you * him able to leap Job 39:20
I * him, too, just as I made you! Job 40:15
I made him, too, just as I * you! Job 40:15
One would think the sea was * of Job 41:31,32
that's * for them is false?" Ps 4:2
arrows * from shafts of fire. Ps 7:13
the stars you have *— I cannot Ps 8:3
And yet you have * him only a Ps 8:5
him in charge of everything you *; Ps 8:6
The Lord my God has * my darkness Ps 18:28
your gentleness has * me great. Ps 18:35
You have * wide steps beneath my Ps 18:36
my feet. You * them turn and run; Ps 18:40
what he has done or what he has *; Ps 28:5
He has * me steady as a Ps 30:6,7
But my dishonesty * me miserable Ps 32:3
of stars. He * the oceans, pouring Ps 33:7
He has * their hearts and closely Ps 33:13,14,15
But the Lord has * up his mind Ps 34:16
You have * the word "Jew" a Ps 44:14
Literally, "God has * himself Ps 48:3f
Literally, "who * a covenant with Ps 50:5f
and * us reel beneath your blows. Ps 60:3
to his people! He * a dry road Ps 66:6
from slavery and * the choicest of Ps 74:2
you * the starlight and the sun. Ps 74:16
you have * to Jehovah your God. Ps 76:11
this land of hills he * for them. Ps 78:54
They * him angry by erecting Ps 78:58
tears, and have * us the scorn of Ps 80:6
Literally, "the son of man you * Ps 80:17f
All the nations—and you * each Ps 86:9
You have * my friends to loathe Ps 88:8
"I have * a solemn agreement Ps 89:3,4
against him and * them rejoice. Ps 89:42
You have * him old before his Ps 89:45
short you have * man's lifespan. Ps 89:47
But you have * me as strong as a Ps 92:10
God has * the sins of evil men Ps 94:23
all are his. He * the sea and Ps 95:5
idols, but our God * the heavens! Ps 96:5
Lord is God! He * us—we are his Ps 100:3
and * the heavens with your hands! Ps 102:25
The Lord has * the heavens his Ps 103:19
O Lord, what a variety you have *! Ps 104:24
And in wisdom you have * them Ps 104:24
And over there, the whale you * Ps 104:26
What's wrong, Red Sea, that * Ps 114:5
Yes, Jehovah who * heaven and Ps 115:15
This is the day the Lord has *. Ps 118:24
Proud men have * up lies about Ps 119:69
You * my body, Lord; Ps 119:73
My help is from Jehovah who * the Ps 121:2
Our help is from the Lord who * Ps 124:8
I * a solemn promise to the Lord. Ps 132:2-5
Lord who * heaven and earth. Ps 134:
gold and silver, * by men— idols Ps 135:1
Praise him who * the heavens, Ps 136:
Praise him who * the heavenly Ps 136:
Don't abandon me—for you * me. Ps 138:
You * all the delicate, inner Ps 139:1
God— the God who * both earth and Ps 146:
He has * known his laws and Ps 147:1
Let everything he has * give Ps 148:
He has * his people strong, Ps 148:1
heavens he * with mighty power. Ps 150:
mountains and the hills were *. Pro 8:2
Yes, I was born before God * the Pro 8:2
I was there when he * the Pro 8:27,28,2
poor is insulting God who * them. Pro 14:3
The Lord has * everything for his Pro 16:
is mocking the God who * them. Pro 17:
A fortune can be * from cheating, Pro 20:2
before the Lord who * them all. Pro 22:
* warm clothes for all of them. Pro 31:2
her own clothing is beautifully * Pro 31:2
And I found that though God has * Ecc 7:29
Here is another thing that has * Ecc 9:13
For King Solomon * himself a Sol 3:9
Your lips, my dear, are * of Sol 4:11
the world and * it into a shambles Is 14:17
worship what their hands have *! Is 17:8
be Iraq, the land I have *; Is 19:25
to wear clothes * of sackcloth to Is 22:12
He has * our nation very great. Is 26:15
Therefore, he who * them will not Is 27:11
The bed you have * is far too Is 28:20
your punishment be * even greater, Is 28:22
God has * him see and understand. Is 28:26
in your sinfulness you have *. Is 31:7
the promises they * in the presence Is 33:8
and the soil * rich with fat. Is 34:7
You alone * heaven and earth. Is 37:16,17
An idol, * from a mold, overlaid Is 40:19
his law and * it truly glorious. Is 42:21
for I have * them for my glory; Is 43:7
I have * Israel for myself, and Is 43:21
The Lord who * you, who will help Is 44:2
claim that they have * a god. Is 44:11
are my servant; I * you, and I will Is 44:21
The Lord, your Redeemer who * Is 44:24
says, All things were * by me; Is 44:24
By myself I * the earth and Is 44:24
I have * the earth and created Is 45:12
in place, and he * the world to be Is 45:18
I * you and I will care for you. Is 46:4
me with an idol * lavishly with Is 46:6
You have * even the old folks Is 47:6
the skies and * the earth. Is 51:13
But when his soul has been * an Is 53:10
very souls that I have *. Is 57:16
tell you how happy God has * me! Is 61:10
in my anger and * them stagger and Is 63:6
and * us sin and turn against you? Is 63:17
My hand has * both earth and Is 66:2
And I replied, "I see a whip * Jer 1:11
idols they themselves have *! Jer 1:16
For see, today I have * you Jer 1:18
goodness, but they * it into a land Jer 2:7
you call on these gods you have *? Jer 2:28
worship idols * of wood and stone. Jer 3:9
people, but I have * up my mind and Jer 4:28
Jeremiah, I have * you an assayer Jer 6:27
fork where he * the wrong turn. Jer 8:4,5
gods, who have not * the heavens Jer 10:11
Israel and * a wasteland of this Jer 10:25
Jerusalem that I * a contract with Jer 11:1
that your fathers * with God, and Jer 11:6
The agreement I * with their Jer 11:10
They have * it desolate; Jer 12:11
man's loins, so I * Judah and Jer 13:11
priests alike have * it their Jer 14:18
The gods they * are not real gods Jer 16:20
the Lord and has * the Lord his Jer 17:7
* and I will talk to you there. Jer 18:2
you have gone ahead and * me Jer 25:7
from the Lord and * all the nations Jer 25:17
"By my great power I have * the Jer 27:5
It won't be like the one I * Jer 31:32
You have * the heavens and earth Jer 32:17
You have * your name very great, Jer 32:20
They changed their minds and * Jer 34:11
I * a covenant with your fathers Jer 34:13
oath and have * them slaves again. Jer 34:16
The king of Babylon * Zedekiah Jer 39:6
Ishmael * captives of the king's Jer 41:10
the idols you have * and worshiped Jer 44:8
were doing that he * your land Jer 44:22
cup from which he * the whole earth Jer 51:7
God * the earth by his power and Jer 51:15
For he * everything there is, and Jer 51:19
Chaldeans), and * a dash for it Jer 52:7
upon him. He * Zedekiah watch Jer 52:10
(They had been * in the days of Jer 52:20
promises of doom he * so long ago. Lam 2:17
He has * me old and has broken Lam 3:4

(MADE Con't)
He has * me eat gravel and Lam 3:16
You have * us as refuse and Lam 3:45
as if they were * of polished amber Eze 1:16
as though it were * of crystal; Eze 1:22
like a throne * of beautiful blue Eze 1:26
But see, I have * you hard and Eze 3:8
I have * your forehead as hard Eze 3:9
390 days eat bread * of flour mixed Eze 4:9
from his waist down, he was * of Eze 8:2
was that had * the Lord so angry. Eze 8:3
I * out an opening in the wall. Eze 8:7
and sandals * of dolphin hide. Eze 16:9,10
And so you were * beautiful with Eze 16:13
I gave to you and * statues of men Eze 16:17
I * to you when you were young. Eze 16:59,60
Nebuchadnezzar * a covenant with Eze 17:12,13
and * him take an oath of Eze 17:12,13
the solemn oath he * in my name. Eze 17:19
sacrifices were * to the gods. Eze 20:29f
your architects have * you Eze 27:4
They * your oars from oaks of Eze 27:6
Your sails are * of Egypt's Eze 27:7
bound with cords and * secure. Eze 27:24
Yes, your wisdom has * you very Eze 28:5
I have * it for myself!' Eze 29:3
and * her stagger with the pain. Eze 29:7
said: 'The Nile is mine! I * it!' Eze 29:10
When she fell I * the oceans mourn Eze 31:15
to weep. I * the nations shake Eze 31:16
be an altar, but it was * of wood. Eze 41:21
of the altar to be * in the future, Eze 43:18
These are the allotments to be * Eze 48:29
But Daniel * up his mind not to Dan 1:8
houses * into heaps of rubble! Dan 2:5
The head of the statue was * of Dan 2:32
Then the king * Daniel very Dan 2:48
KING NEBUCHADNEZZAR * a golden Dan 3:1
to him, "you * a law that Dan 3:10
to their idols * of gold and Dan 5:2,3,4
he was * chief of all the Dan 5:11
This * the other presidents and Dan 6:4
He was faithful and honest, and * Dan 6:4
Longing after idols has * them Hos 4:12
I have helped them, and * them Hos 7:15
they * from their silver and gold. Hos 8:4
this calf—this idol you have *. Hos 8:5
you worship was * by human hands! Hos 8:6
You have * no progress whatever. Hos 10:9
the idols we have * 'our gods'; Hos 14:3
the Syrians had * their exodus from Amo 1:5f
the mountains and * the winds, and Amo 4:13
in all the images of them you *. Amo 5:25,26,27
* yourselves rich at his expense. Ob 1:13
heaven, who * the earth and sea." Jon 1:9,10
THIS CHANGE OF plans * Jonah very Jon 4:1
the city, and he * a leafy shelter Jon 4:5
to shade him. This * him Jon 4:6
has * accusations against you! Mic 1:2
what you have *, and I will Mic 5:13
but I * him bless you instead? Mic 6:5
trust what you yourselves had *. Hab 2:18
Haggai then * his meaning clear. Hag 2:14
like two mountains * of brass. Zec 6:1
I * with you, sealed with blood. Zec 9:11
of Levi, and * it into a grotesque Mal 2:8
"Therefore I have * you Mal 2:9
You aren't * unholy by eating Mt 15:11
been * the honored cornerstone; Mt 21:42
when bread * with yeast was purged Mt 26:17
Jewish leaders * their many Mt 27:12
robe on him, and * a crown from Mt 27:29
But the Sabbath was * to benefit Mk 2:27
For the soil * the seeds grow. Mk 4:28
your faith has * you well; Mk 5:34
by the statement he had just *. Mk 7:17
the more they * it known, for they Mk 7:36
For from the very first he * man Mk 10:6,7
have already been *." Mk 10:40
You have * a serious error." Mk 12:27
News must first be * known in every Mk 13:10
no bread * with yeast was eaten. Mk 14:1
this Temple * with human hands and Mk 14:58
another, * without human hands!' Mk 14:58
To this Jesus * no reply. Mk 14:61
a purple robe, and * a crown of Mk 15:16,17
shall be brought to light and * Lk 8:17
But Jesus replied, "Man, who * Lk 12:14
your faith has * you well." Lk 17:19
builders was * the cornerstone'?" Lk 20:17
bread * without yeast was used. Lk 22:1
But although he * the world, the Jn 1:10
Jesus * a whip from some ropes Jn 2:15
Jesus * these statements while in Jn 8:20
Then he spat on the ground and * Jn 9:6
they call Jesus * mud and smoothed Jn 9:11
days and * no move to go to them. Jn 11:6
of costly perfume * from essence of Jn 12:3
to Jesus when he * this prediction, Jn 12:41
he had just *, "I have not lost a Jn 18:9
fire they had *, for it was cold. Jn 18:18
and the soldiers * a crown of Jn 19:2
ointment * from myrrh and aloes. Jn 19:39
that God has * this Jesus you Act 2:36
and godliness had * this man walk? Act 3:12
* you a ruler and judge over us?' Act 7:27
* you a ruler and judge over us?' Act 7:35
So they * a calf-idol and Act 7:41
rejoiced in this thing they had *. Act 7:41
and in all the images you *. Act 7:43
live in temples * by human hands. Act 7:48,49
garments Dorcas had * for them. Act 9:39
but the delegates * friends with Act 12:20
his throne and * a speech to them. Act 12:21
he said, 'I have * you a light to Act 13:47
the living God who * heaven and Act 14:15
him to us. He * no distinction Act 15:9
his plans * from the beginning. Act 15:18
"He * the world and everything Act 17:24
of God as an idol * by men from Act 17:29
But the accusations * against Act 25:18
God's promise * to our ancestors. Act 26:6
ARRANGEMENTS WERE FINALLY * Act 27:1
headwinds that * it difficult to Act 27:4
sky and all God *, and have known Rom 1:20
wood and stone and * idols for Rom 1:23
to the things God *, but wouldn't Rom 1:25
blessed God who * these things. Rom 1:25
No one can ever be * right in Rom 3:20
they say that God * Abraham the Rom 4:17
SO NOW, SINCE we have been * right Rom 5:1
caused many to be * acceptable to Rom 5:19
salvation which he * to Abraham. Rom 9:8
Haven't they done what he * them Rom 9:19
Should the thing * say to the one Rom 9:20
say to the one who * it, "Why have Rom 9:20
"Why have you * me like this?" Rom 9:20
who have been * for pouring the Rom 9:23,24
Literally, "Confession is * unto Rom 10:10f
for you have been * pure and Rom 15:15,16
to be his people and * acceptable 1Co 1:2
God has * them all look foolish, 1Co 1:20
he was the one who * us 1Co 1:30
to God; he * us pure and holy 1Co 1:30
though it was * for our benefit 1Co 2:7
* the garden grow in your hearts. 1Co 3:6
Religion has * us foolish, you 1Co 4:10
bodies were not * for that, but for 1Co 6:13
won't, he has * a wise decision. 1Co 7:37
and * us to be his own; 1Co 8:6
and one Lord Jesus Christ, who * 1Co 8:6
God's glory is man * in his image, 1Co 11:7
first man, was not * for Eve's 1Co 11:9
benefit, but Eve was * for Adam. 1Co 11:9
But that isn't the way God has * 1Co 12:18
He has * many parts for our 1Co 12:18
So he has * many parts, but 1Co 12:20
But when we have been * perfect 1Co 13:10
Literally, "was * a living 1Co 15:45f
Adam was * from the dust of the 1Co 15:47
just like Adam's, * of dust, but 1Co 15:48
an earthly body * of flesh and 1Co 15:50
Hadn't I really * up my mind yet? 2Co 1:17
It is this God who has * you and 2Co 1:21
I will not be * sad by the very 2Co 2:3
evil world, has * him blind, unable 2Co 4:4
darkness," has * us understand 2Co 4:6
ours forevermore, * for us by God 2Co 5:1
knew no sin, he * sin on our 2Co 5:21f
you have * me so happy in spite 2Co 7:4
your love, we were * happier still 2Co 7:13
That is why we have * this 2Co 8:21
weapons, not those * by men, to 2Co 10:4
You have * me act like a 2Co 12:11
have * money from us some way." 2Co 12:16
great leaders * no difference to Gal 2:6
life a promise * by one man to Gal 3:15
Child to whom God's promise was *. Gal 3:19
SO CHRIST HAS * us free. Gal 5:1
Long ago, even before he * the Eph 1:4
that God has been * rich because we Eph 1:18
under his feet and * him the Eph 1:22
Literally, "he * us alive." Eph 2:5f
It is God himself who has * us Eph 2:10
He has * peace between us Jews Eph 2:14
other and * them parts of himself; Eph 2:15
just as he who * all things had Eph 3:9
* the lie sound like the truth. Eph 4:14
against people * of flesh and Eph 6:12
Literally, "was * in the likeness Php 2:7f
the Father who has * us fit to Col 1:12
He existed before God * anything Col 1:15
is the Creator who * everything in Col 1:16
all were * by Christ for his own Col 1:16
He is the Head of the body * up Col 1:18
on the cross has * peace with God Col 1:20
last * known, is Christ himself. Col 2:2
was * to be eaten and used up. Col 2:22
your hearts being * strong, sinless 1Th 3:13
has * all this possible for you. 2Th 1:12
But they were not * for us, whom 1Ti 1:9
Yes, these laws are * to 1Ti 1:10,11
Because God * Adam first, and 1Ti 2:13
first, and afterwards he * Eve. 1Ti 2:13
For everything God * is good, 1Ti 4:4
it, for it is * good by the Word of 1Ti 4:5
And now he has * all of this 2Ti 1:10
there are dishes * of gold and 2Ti 2:20
well as some * from wood and clay. 2Ti 2:20
of these dishes * of purest 2Ti 2:21
through whom he * the world and Heb 1:2
and as servants * of flaming fire; Heb 1:7
the beginning you * the earth, and Heb 1:10
For though you * him lower than Heb 2:7
that God, who * everything for his Heb 2:10
for his suffering * Jesus a Heb 2:10
We who have been * holy by Jesus, Heb 2:11
are human beings—* of flesh and Heb 2:14
houses, but only God * everything. Heb 3:4
And who was it who * God angry Heb 3:17
There is a strong case to be * Heb 5:7f
It never * anyone really right Heb 7:19
in heaven, not * by men nor part of Heb 9:11
* sure of our eternal salvation. Heb 9:12
had to be * pure by Moses in this Heb 9:23
are copies, were * pure with far Heb 9:23
you, so you have * ready this body Heb 10:5
been forgiven and * clean by Heb 10:10
For by that one offering he * Heb 10:14
And those whose faith has * them Heb 10:38
things—were * at God's command; Heb 11:3
and that they were all * from Heb 11:3
he has * a heavenly city for them. Heb 11:16
sure of it that he * them promise Heb 11:22
Some were * strong again after Heb 11:34
* whole armies turn and run away. Heb 11:34
in heaven, already * perfect; Heb 12:23
his faith was * complete by what Jas 2:22
against men who are * like God. Jas 3:9
Only he who * the law can Jas 4:12
* you, for he will never fail you. 1Pe 4:19
whom reference is * in Matthew 1Pe 5:13f
long after he had * the heavens by 2Pe 3:5,6
the darkness had * him blind so 1Jn 2:11
traveling by have * me very happy 3Jn 1:3
* us priests of God his Father. Rev 1:6
and * them priests of our God; Rev 5:10
nor their idols * of gold and Rev 9:20
Worship him who * the heaven and Rev 14:7
of the world and * them share the Rev 14:8
earth have been * drunk by the wine Rev 17:2
beautiful jewelry * of gold and Rev 17:4
great city! She * us all rich from Rev 18:19
The wall was * of jasper, and was Rev 21:18,19,20
The twelve gates were * of pearls Rev 21:21

MADE-UP
Their * dreams are flippant Jer 23:32

MADLY
are * in love with their idols. Jer 50:38

MADMAN
and he began to rave like a *. 1Sa 18:10
"Must you bring me a *? 1Sa 21:14,15
and saw him dancing like a *. 1Ch 15:29
is like a * throwing around Pro 26:18,19
to arrest any * who claims to be a Jer 29:26

MADMANNAH
Hormah, Ziklag, *, Sansannah, Jos 15:21-32
(the father of *), and Sheva (the 1Ch 2:48,49

MADMEN
a nation." In * all is silent. Jer 48:2,3,4

MADMENAH
There go the people of *, all Is 10:31

MADNESS
He will send *, blindness, fear, Deu 28:28
to learn about composure and *." Ecc 1:16-18f
folly, and that foolishness is *. Ecc 7:25
his conclusion is sheer *. Ecc 10:12,13

MADON
King Jobab of *; Jos 11:1
The king of *; Jos 12:8-24

MAELSTROM
him from the * of death that Gen 19:29

MAGADAN
into the boat and crossed to *. Mt 15:39

MAGBISH
From the subclan of *, 156; Ez 2:3-35

MAGDALENE
Among them were Mary * and Mary Mt 27:56
Both Mary * and the other Mary Mt 27:61
was dawning, Mary * and the other Mt 28:1
a distance—Mary *, Mary (the mother Mk 15:40
(Mary * and Mary the mother of Mk 15:47
ended, Mary * and Salome and Mary Mk 16:1
saw him was Mary *—the woman from Mk 16:9
among them were Mary * (Jesus had Lk 8:2
the tomb were Mary * and Joanna and Lk 24:10
the wife of Cleopas, and Mary *. Jn 19:25
still dark, Mary * came to the tomb Jn 20:1
Mary * found the disciples and Jn 20:18

MAGDI-EL
Chief Mibzar, Chief *, Chief Iram. 1Ch 1:51-54

MAGDIEL
clan of *,The clan of Iram. Gen 36:40-43

MAGGOTS
full of * and had a terrible odor; Ex 16:20
and good, without * or odor. Ex 16:24
has ceased; now * are your sheet, Is 14:11
he was filled with * and Act 12:23
MAGIC
And no * shall be done against Num 23:18-24
No Israeli may practice black *, Deu 18:10
* and sold themselves to evil. 2Ki 17:17
He practiced black * and used 2Ki 21:6
A bribe works like *. Pro 17:8
East who practice * and communicate Is 2:6
despite all your witchcraft and *. Is 47:9
alike, by tying * charms on their Eze 13:18
them with * veils and selling them Eze 13:18
souls with all your * charms. Eze 13:20
I will tear off the * veils and Eze 13:21
nor practice your *, for I will Eze 13:23
a strong dose of alchemy and *! Dan 1:3,4f
practicing black * confessed their Act 19:18,19
MAGICAL
the same thing with their * arts! Ex 7:11
MAGICIAN
Balaam the *, the son of Beor. Jos 13:22
man, astrologer, *, or wizard can Dan 2:27
"O Belteshazzar, master *," I Dan 4:9
OH, FOOLISH GALATIANS! What * Gal 3:1
MAGICIANS
he called for all the * and sages Gen 41:8
I told all this to my *, but not Gen 41:24
his sorcerers—the * of Egypt—and Ex 7:11
But then the * of Egypt used Ex 7:22
But the * did the same with Ex 8:7
Then the * tried to do the same Ex 8:18
And the * couldn't stand before Ex 9:11
lawyers, * and politicians. Is 3:3
mediums and * who say the king of Jer 27:9
He will call his * to use Eze 21:21
Your * and false prophets have Eze 21:29
of all the skilled * and wise Dan 1:20
called in all his *, Dan 2:1
when they came—the *, astrologers, Dan 4:7
"Bring the * and astrologers!" Dan 5:7
he was made chief of all the *, Dan 5:11
MAGISTRATE
Daniel served as chief * in the Dan 2:49
MAGNESIA
later defeated by the Romans at *. Dan 11:13f
MAGNIFICENCE
Because of the * that I gave it, Eze 31:9
MAGNIFICENT
and it is indeed a * country—a land Num 13:27
because of your *, steadfast love, Num 14:19
ABSALOM THEN BOUGHT a * chariot 2Sa 15:1
with his * garments of crimson? Is 63:1
Thus he gave himself a * Is 63:14
You say, "I will build a * Jer 22:14
—this * sum they value you at!" Zec 11:13
that Diana—this * goddess worshiped Act 19:27
MAGNIFIED
The Lord has * his law and made Is 42:21
MAGNITUDE
* unprecedented in human history. Rev 16:18
MAGOG
of Japheth were:Gomer, *, Gen 10:2
Gomer, *, Madai, 1Ch 1:5-9
toward the land of *, and Eze 38:2,3
And I will rain down fire on * Eze 39:6
with Gog and *, for battle—a mighty Rev 20:8
MAGPIASH
Anathoth, Nebai, *, Neh 10:14-27
MAHALAB
The territory also included *, Jos 19:29
MAHALALEEL
Jared's father was *; Lk 3:23-38
MAHALALEEL'S
Jared's father was Mahalaleel;* Lk 3:23-38
MAHALALEL
years old when his son * was born. Gen 5:12,13,14
*: Mahalalel was sixty-five years Gen 5:15,16,17
Mahalalel: * was sixty-five years Gen 5:15,16,17
Adam, Seth, Enosh, Kenan, *, 1Ch 1:1
MAHALATH
One of these new wives was *, the Gen 28:9
*. She was the daughter of 2Ch 11:18
MAHALELEL
son of *, a descendant of Perez); Neh 11:4,5,6
MAHANAIM
Betonim, and from * to Lo-debar. Jos 13:26
north from *, included all of Jos 13:30
Ramoth (a City of Refuge), *, Jos 21:38,39
had gone to * to crown Saul's son 2Sa 2:8
He reigned in * for two years; 2Sa 2:10,11
to Gibeon from *, and General Joab 2Sa 2:12
morning until they arrived at *. 2Sa 2:29
David soon arrived at *. 2Sa 17:24
When David arrived at *, he was 2Sa 17:27
their exile in *, arrived from 2Sa 19:31,32
curse as I was going to *; 1Ki 2:8
son of Iddo), whose area was *; 1Ki 4:8-19
Ramoth in Gilead, *, Heshbon, and 1Ch 6:80
MAHARAI
* from Netophah; 2Sa 23:24-39
* from Netophah; 1Ch 11:26-47
Tenth Division was * from Netophah 1Ch 27:13
MAHATH
Zuph, Elkanah II, *, Amasai, 1Ch 6:33-38
From the Kohath clan, * (son of 2Ch 29:12,13,14
Eliel, Ismachiah, *, Benaiah. 2Ch 31:12,13
MAHAVI
Eliel from *; 1Ch 11:26-47
MAHAZI-OTH
Mallothi, Hothir, and *. 1Ch 25:4,5
Twenty-third, * and twelve of his 1Ch 25:9-31
MAHER-SHALAL-HASH-BAZ
His name will be *, which means Is 8:1
and the Lord said, "Call him *. Is 8:3
return," and * means "Your Is 8:18
MAHIR
whose son was *, the father of 1Ch 4:11,12
MAHLAH
*, Noah, Hoglah, Milcah,Tirzah. Num 26:28-37
These girls, *, Tirzah, Hoglah, Num 36:11,12
whose names were *, Noah, Hoglah, Jos 17:3
bore Ishhod, Abiezer, and *. 1Ch 7:18
MAHLI
The sons of Merari:*, Mushi. Ex 6:19
(clan names) * Mushi Num 3:31-35
The sons of Merari were:*, Mushi. 1Ch 6:19,20,21
*, Libni, Shime-i, Uzzah, Shime-a, 1Ch 6:29,30
Shemer, *, Mushi, Merari, Levi. 1Ch 6:44-47
* and 1Ch 23:21
The sons of * were 1Ch 23:21
Mushi's sons were *, Eder, and 1Ch 23:23
* and 1Ch 24:26,27
The sons of Mushi were *, Eder, 1Ch 24:30
a descendant of *, the son of Levi Ez 8:18
MAHLI'S
and Ibri.) * descendants were 1Ch 24:28
MAHLITES
*, the Mushites,The Korahites. Num 26:58,59
MAHLON
and his two sons, * and Chilion. Ru 1:1
These young men, * and Chilion, Ru 1:4,5
Chilion, and *, from Naomi, and Ru 4:9
the widow of *, to be my wife, so Ru 4:10
MAHOL
Calcol, and Darda, the sons of *; 1Ki 4:31
MAHSEIAH
of Neriah, who was the son of *). Jer 32:12
*), concerning Seraiah's capture Jer 51:59
MAID
Man and * did he make them. Gen 1:27
So Sarai took her *, an Egyptian Gen 16:1
The Angel: "Hagar, Sarai's *, Gen 16:8
servant girl, Zilpah, to be her *. Gen 29:24
servant girl, Bilhah, to be her *. Gen 29:29
given to Naaman's wife as a *. 2Ki 5:2
"the way of a man with a *." Pro 30:18,19f
return to us, O * of Shulam. Sol 6:13
The * saw him standing there and Mk 14:69
MAIDEN
a man and his * aunt—whether the Lev 20:19
your tripping feet, O queenly *. Sol 7:1
He may marry only a Jewish *, or Eze 44:22
just as a pure * saves her love for 2Co 11:2
MAIDENHOOD
And when you reached the age of * Eze 16:6,7
MAIDENS
young men and *, old men and Ps 148:12
out her * inviting all to come. Pro 9:3
young men and *, shepherds and Jer 51:22
with all her * weeping after her; Nah 2:7
MAIDS
and as she and her * were walking Ex 2:5
one of the * to bring it to her. Ex 2:5
the palace as her *, and gave her Est 2:9
When Esther's * and eunuchs came Est 4:4
and I and my * will do the same; Est 4:16
she is, led beside her * of honor Ps 45:14
we won't be mocked as old *." Is 4:1
One of the * who worked for the Mk 14:66,67
MAIL
of *, so that it will not fray. Ex 28:32
as in a coat of *, for the head to Ex 39:23
coat of *, bronze leggings, and 1Sa 17:4-7
bronze helmet and a coat of *. 1Sa 17:38,39
coats of *, bows, and slingstones. 2Ch 26:14
So the * went out swiftly, Est 8:14
her warriors in their coats of *. Jer 51:3
MAIMED
a man, and * oxen just for fun. Gen 49:6
their lame, blind, *, and those who Mt 15:30
MAIN
Calah), the * city of the empire. Gen 10:11,12
of blossoms. The * stem of the Ex 37:20,21
The * part of the ephod was Ex 39:22
will stay on the * road and not Num 20:17
will stay on the * road and will Num 20:19
'We will stay on the * road and Deu 2:27
Before the * army left for Ai, Jos 8:3,4
"When our * army attacks, the Jos 8:5
The * roads were deserted. Ju 5:
But when the * army of Israel Ju 20:3
* entrance doors of the Temple. 1Ki 7:5
them into three * divisions named 1Ch 23:
The * part of the Temple was 2Ch 3:
of the Temple, the * door, and the 2Ch 4:2
the crowds along * Street, and to Pro 1:2
Wisdom is the * pursuit of Pro 17:2
And a * road will go through that Is 35:
nave, the large * room of the Eze 41:
at the side of the * passageway, he Eze 46:19,2
to destroy all the * crop that Amo 7:
naturally go to the * attraction Jn 3:2
That was the * reason why so Jn 12:1
And the * street was pure, Rev 21:2
down the center of the * street. Rev 22:
MAINLAND
tribute upon the *, but even on the Est 10:
* city shall perish by the sword. Eze 26:
then he will attack your * city Eze 26:8
terrorized the *, how you have Eze 26:17
and watch upon the * shore, Eze 27:29
between the island and the *, Act 27:4
MAINTAIN
can * the Temple in good repair. 2Ch 24:5
he will * the rights of the poor. Ps 140:12
be respected and * her identity. Eze 17:14
strength to always * a clear Act 24:16
MAINTAINED
So Edom has * its independence 2Ki 8:22
MAINTENANCE
and * of the Tabernacle. Num 3:7,8,9
the priests who supervise the *. Eze 40:45
caretakers, to do * work and to Eze 44:14
MAJESTIC
In * splendor to help you. Deu 33:26
* snorting is something to hear! Job 39:20
Praise him for his * glory, the Ps 29:2
So glorious, so *! Ps 45:3
And the Lord shall cause his * Is 30:30
I heard that glorious, * voice 2Pe 1:17,18
MAJESTY
"Tell his *," he requested Gen 50:5
Ask his * to permit me to go and Gen 50:5
In the greatness of your * Ex 15:7
ways," or, "show me your *." Ex 33:13f
* and honor march before him, 1Ch 16:27
power and glory and victory and *. 1Ch 29:11
it please Your * and if you look Neh 2:4
it please Your *, I want you and Est 5:4
is that if Your * loves me, and Est 5:7,8
if it please Your *, save my life Est 7:3
it please Your *, and if you love Est 8:5
it please Your *, let the Jews who Est 9:13
Doesn't his * strike terror to Job 13:11
For if the * of God opposes me, Job 31:23
tremendous voice of his *. Job 37:4
at the terrible * of God breaking Job 37:22
of state, your * and splendor. Job 40:10
O LORD OUR God, the * and glory of Ps 8:1
O Jehovah, our Lord, the * and Ps 8:9
clothed him with splendor and *. Ps 21:5
so full of *. Ps 29:4
And in your * Ps 45:4
Power belongs to God! His * Ps 68:34
He is robed in * and strength. Ps 93:1
Honor and * surround him; Ps 96:6
that you reign in * over the entire Ps 97:8,9
Jehovah sits in * in Zion, Ps 99:2
with honor and with * and light! Ps 104:1
honor, *, and eternal goodness. Ps 111:3
glory, splendor, * and miracles. Ps 145:5
the * and glory of your reign. Ps 145:12
from his glorious *, for the day Is 2:10
because of the glory of his *. Is 2:19
the glory of his * when he rises to Is 2:21
will praise the * of God, and Is 24:14
and take no notice of your *. Is 26:10
All her beauty and her * are Lam 1:6
"Your *, you are a king over Dan 2:37
"Your *," they said to him, Dan 3:9
us out of your hand, Your *. Dan 3:17
said, "we did indeed, Your *." Dan 3:24
birds— that tree, Your *, is you. Dan 4:22
"Your *, the Most High God has Dan 4:24
yourself, Your *, don't be so pale Dan 5:10
Your *, the Most High God gave Dan 5:18
kingdom and * and glory and honor. Dan 5:18
He gave him such * that all the Dan 5:19
*—shall be thrown to the lions. Dan 6:7
Your *, we request your Dan 6:8
*, there is nothing you can do. Dan 6:15
"Your *, live forever!" Dan 6:21
the Lord, in the * of the name of Mic 5:4
yes, splendor and *, all power Jud 1:24,25
MAJOR
a * priest-politician of the time. Gen 41:45f
Egypt with a final * disaster and Ex 7:4
MAJORITY
by the mood of the * present, and Ex 23:2,3
So the * report of the spies was Num 13:32

MAKAZ
Ben-deker, whose area was *, 1Ki 4:8-19
MAKE
Then God said, "Let us * a man Gen 1:26
Literally, "Let us * man in our Gen 1:26f
Like God did God * man; Gen 1:27
Man and maid did he * them. Gen 1:27
open your eyes to * you aware of Gen 2:16,17
I will * a companion for him, a Gen 2:18
And it would * her so wise! Gen 3:6
from the earth. * a boat from Gen 6:14
the ship. * it 450 feet long, 75 Gen 6:15
the roof; and * three decks inside Gen 6:16
I will bless you and * your name Gen 12:2
Or, "I will * your name so famous Gen 12:2f
I will * you into a great nation. Gen 16:9-12
to * you into a mighty nation. Gen 17:2,3,4
and * her the mother of nations! Gen 17:16
Use your best flour, and * enough Gen 18:6
like this, to * me and my kingdom Gen 20:9,10
And I will * a nation of the Gen 21:13
him, for I will * a great nation Gen 21:18
and the flint to * the fire, but Gen 22:7
you and * your mission successful. Gen 24:40
are planning to * my mission a Gen 24:42
gather stones and * a heap, and Gen 31:46
to me, 'I will * you a great nation Gen 48:4
by saying, 'God * you as prosperous Gen 48:20
you, but I will * him stubborn so Ex 4:21
go, for they must * a holy Ex 5:1
Load them with work and * them Ex 5:9
straw and told to * as many bricks Ex 5:16
from slavery, and * them free. Ex 6:6
earth, for I will * a distinction Ex 8:23
and * your demand upon Pharaoh; Ex 10:1
Why did you * us leave Egypt? Ex 14:11
then I will not * you suffer the Ex 15:26
"You shall not * yourselves any Ex 20:4
Remember, you must not * or Ex 20:23
"The altars you * for me must be Ex 20:24
would * them unfit for my altar. Ex 20:25
And don't * steps for the altar, Ex 20:26
he must * full restitution; Ex 22:3
the fire shall * full restitution. Ex 22:6
not be required to * restitution. Ex 22:13
religious pilgrimages you must *. Ex 23:14
"You must * no covenant with Ex 23:32
of Israel to * me a sacred Temple Ex 25:8
"Using acacia wood, * an Ark 3¾ Ex 25:10
on each side. * poles from acacia Ex 25:13,14
"And * a lid of pure gold, 3¾ Ex 25:17
Then * images of angels, Ex 25:18
"Then * a table of acacia wood Ex 25:23
all around. * four golden rings Ex 25:26,27
carry the table. * the poles from Ex 25:28
with gold. And * golden dishes, Ex 25:29
"* a lampstand of pure, beaten Ex 25:31
Then * seven lamps for the Ex 25:37
"Be sure that everything you * Ex 25:40
"* THE TABERNACLE-TENT from ten Ex 26:1
Then * fifty golden clasps to Ex 26:6
"* bars of acacia wood to run Ex 26:26,27
and * gold rings to hold the bars; Ex 26:29
* a veil from blue, purple, and Ex 26:31
the sacred tent, * another curtain Ex 26:36
"USING ACACIA WOOD, * a square Ex 27:1
three feet high. * horns for the Ex 27:2
made of bronze. * a bronze Ex 27:4
For moving the altar, * poles Ex 27:6
"Then * a courtyard for the Ex 27:9,10
minister to me. * special clothes Ex 28:2
as tailors to * the garments that Ex 28:3
shall *: a chestpiece, an ephod, Ex 28:4
They shall also * special Ex 28:4
workmanship, * a chestpiece to be Ex 28:15
Then * two more golden rings and Ex 28:26
also * two other golden rings Ex 28:27
"Next, * a plate of pure gold Ex 28:36
* the turban, too, of this linen; Ex 28:39
and * him an embroidered sash. Ex 28:39
"Then, for Aaron's sons, * Ex 28:40
Also * linen undershorts for Ex 28:42
to sanctify it. * atonement for Ex 29:37
"THEN * A small altar for burning Ex 30:1
Literally, "shall * an atonement Ex 30:10f
to * atonement for yourselves. Ex 30:15
and to * atonement for you." Ex 30:16
And the Lord said to Moses, "* a Ex 30:17,18
Sanctify them, to * them holy; Ex 30:29
you shall never * any of it Ex 30:32
Never * it for yourselves, for Ex 30:37
so that they can * all the things I Ex 31:6
you to *: the Tabernacle; Ex 31:6
"Look," they said, "* us a god Ex 32:1
and I will * you, Moses, into a Ex 32:10
he demanded, "to * you bring such Ex 32:21
They said to me, '* us a god to Ex 32:23
The Lord replied, "I will * my Ex 33:19
contract I am going to * with you. Ex 34:10
"No, do not * a peace treaty of Ex 34:15
together to * one long piece, and Ex 36:16
others to * another long piece. Ex 36:16
Then * the courtyard around the Ex 40:8
Literally, "to * atonement for Lev 1:4f
in this way the priest shall * Lev 4:20
thus the priest shall * atonement Lev 4:26
Thus the priest shall * atonement Lev 4:31
and the priest shall * atonement Lev 4:35
the priest shall * atonement for Lev 5:6
so the priest shall * atonement Lev 5:10
In this way the priest shall * Lev 5:13
And he shall * restitution for Lev 5:16
the priest shall * atonement for Lev 5:16
with it the priest shall * Lev 5:17,18
the priest shall * atonement for Lev 6:7
to * atonement in the Holy Place. Lev 6:30
in order to * atonement for them. Lev 8:34
it on the altar—* sure there is no Lev 10:12
of the people, to * atonement for Lev 10:17
the Lord and * atonement for her; Lev 12:7
The priest will * atonement for Lev 12:8
this does not * him a leper even Lev 13:40
Thus the priest shall * atonement Lev 14:18
being cleansed, to * atonement for Lev 14:29
and the priest shall * atonement Lev 14:31
thus the priest shall * atonement Lev 15:15
offering, and * atonement for her Lev 15:30
Thus he shall * atonement for Lev 16:16
Aaron enters to * atonement in the Lev 16:17
the Lord and * atonement for it. Lev 16:18
Place by Aaron, to * atonement) Lev 16:27
garments, and * atonement for the Lev 16:33
law for you, to * atonement for the Lev 16:34
Do not * or worship idols, for I Lev 19:3,4
The priest shall * atonement Lev 19:22
"You shall therefore * a Lev 20:25
yourselves and * yourselves hateful Lev 20:25
otherwise they will be unfit to * Lev 21:6
* an offering by fire to the Lord. Lev 23:8
Literally, "shall * it good, life Lev 24:18f
cost: don't try to * a profit! Lev 25:37
and will * you walk with dignity. Lev 26:13
proud power and * your heavens as Lev 26:19
I will * your cities desolate, Lev 26:31
land will rest and * up for the Lev 26:34,35
It will * up for the rest you Lev 26:34,35
He must confess his sin and * Num 5:7
then Jehovah shall * you a curse Num 5:21,22
for he will * your thigh rot away Num 5:21,22
* atonement for his defilement. Num 6:11
to * atonement for the Levites. Num 8:12
NOW THE LORD said to Moses, "* Num 10:1
protested, "Sir, * them stop!" Num 11:28
plague, and I will * you into a Num 14:12
And the priest shall * atonement Num 15:25
the priest shall * atonement for Num 15:28
of Israel to * tassels for the hems Num 15:37,38
you want to * yourself our king? Num 16:13
people and * atonement for them; Num 16:46
Why did you ever * us leave Num 20:5
Then the Lord told him, "* a Num 21:8
Literally, "* a fiery serpent." Num 21:8f
"When you * offerings by fire, Num 28:3
to * atonement for yourselves. Num 28:22
Also offer one male goat to * Num 28:30
drink offerings. * sure that the Num 28:31
offering, to * atonement for you. Num 29:5
refuses to let her * the vow, or Num 30:5
the tribes are to * a list of all Num 31:26
This is to * atonement for our Num 31:50
like this, he will * the people Num 32:15
From there it will * a large Num 34:10,11
Beginning today I will * people Deu 2:25
by trying to * a statue of God—an Deu 4:16,17
You will break it if you * any Deu 4:23
" 'Never * idols; Deu 5:8
* a vow you don't intend to keep. Deu 5:11
* any treaties or show them mercy; Deu 7:2
you and * you into a great nation. Deu 7:13
He will * you fertile and give Deu 7:13
heaven, and I will * a mighty Deu 9:13,14
first ones, and to * a wooden Ark Deu 10:1
"You must not * sacrifices to Deu 12:4,5
upon you, and * you a great nation Deu 13:17
If you refuse to * the loan and Deu 15:9
at the time will * the decision. Deu 17:9
But if it refuses and won't * Deu 20:12
Use them for the siege [to * Deu 20:20
on loans you * to a brother Deu 23:19
"When you * a vow to the Lord, Deu 23:21
Once you * the vow, you must be Deu 23:23
our ancestors; * it a land Deu 26:15
If you do, he will * you greater Deu 26:19
you today, he will * you the head Deu 28:13
you would never need to * again; Deu 28:68
Now I, in turn, will * them Deu 32:21
I kill and * live. Deu 32:39
of Israel and * your confession. Jos 7:19
in the book of his laws: "* me Jos 8:31
For if you do, we cannot * a Jos 9:7
And your children may * our Jos 22:24,25
your part, would * no peace Ju 2:2
were pressed to * wine—for he was Ju 6:11
and said, "I will * you strong! Ju 6:14
me, but let me * one more test: Ju 6:39
"Now * sure that you have done Ju 9:16
Down with Abimelech! * me your Ju 9:29
will * you the king of Gilead." Ju 11:8
years you * an issue of this! Ju 11:26
to this party just to * us poor?" Ju 14:15
But Ruth replied, "Don't * me Ru 1:16
glean, and not to * any remarks. Ru 2:16
she replied. "* me your wife Ru 3:9
May the Lord * this woman, who Ru 4:11
"Why aren't you eating? Why * 1Sa 1:8
"It is an awful thing to * the 1Sa 2:23,24,25
* them run before his chariots; 1Sa 8:11
without pay; and * his weapons and 1Sa 8:12
and bake and * perfumes for him. 1Sa 8:13
Tell me and I will * right 1Sa 12:3
done wrong, but * sure now that you 1Sa 12:20
He was planning to * you and your 1Sa 13:13
come to * a sacrifice to the Lord. 1Sa 16:2
I don't * decisions the way you 1Sa 16:7
And may the Lord * us keep our 1Sa 20:23
"Where did you * your raid 1Sa 27:10
"Don't * a frontal attack. 2Sa 5:23
And I will * your name greater 2Sa 7:9
and I will * his kingdom strong. 2Sa 7:12
"O Lord, please * Ahithophel give 2Sa 15:31
of us die, it will * no difference 2Sa 18:3
Why should this * you angry? 2Sa 19:42
You * my darkness bright. 2Sa 22:29
you, and may God * Solomon's reign 1Ki 1:37
May God * Solomon's reign even 1Ki 1:46,47
the Gileadite. * them permanent 1Ki 2:7
"Have you come to * trouble?" 1Ki 2:13
"I have one small request to * 1Ki 2:20
* their captors merciful to them; 1Ki 8:50
Solomon used the algum wood to * 1Ki 10:12
* certain demands upon Rehoboam. 1Ki 12:2,3,4
out to * room for his people. 1Ki 14:24
* you king of my people Israel; 1Ki 16:2
* room for the people of Israel. 1Ki 21:26
for the Lord will * you victorious 2Ki 3:18
Let's * a little room for him on 2Ki 4:10
said to Gehazi, "* some stew for 2Ki 4:38
"Lord, please * them blind." 2Ki 6:18
Then they will attack us and * 2Ki 7:12
* sacrifices to any heathen gods. 2Ki 17:35,36
I'll tell you what: * a bet 2Ki 18:23
dried figs and to * a paste of them 2Ki 20:7
replied; "* it go backward." 2Ki 20:10
to * room for the people of Israel 2Ki 21:1
of Israel to * David their king, as 1Ch 11:10
and I will * your name as great as 1Ch 17:8
and I will * his kingdom strong. 1Ch 17:11
decision to *," David replied, 1Ch 21:13
will * his kingdom last forever.' 1Ch 28:7
gold and silver to * these various 1Ch 28:14
Isaac, and Israel! * your people 1Ch 29:18
and send me weavers to * purple, 2Ch 2:7
Instead, I will * it a public 2Ch 7:20
However, he didn't * slaves of 2Ch 8:9
the sandalwood to * terraced steps 2Ch 9:11
He used some of the gold to * 2Ch 9:15
intended to * him the next king. 2Ch 11:22
by the Lord to * room for Israel. 2Ch 28:3
And now are you going to * 2Ch 28:10
"But now I want to * a covenant 2Ch 29:10
upon the altar, to * atonement for 2Ch 29:24
seventy years to * up for the years 2Ch 36:21
spirit of Cyrus to * this 2Ch 36:22,23
Yet I refused to * a special levy Neh 5:18
* me sin by fleeing to the Temple; Neh 6:12,13
fig trees and to * huts in which to Neh 8:15
their job was to * an honest Neh 13:13
and did his best to * her happy; Est 2:9
(for even angels * mistakes), how Job 4:18,19
hands with lye to * them utterly Job 9:30
shouldn't someone * you ashamed? Job 11:3
Oh, that he would * you truly Job 11:6
Will long searching * them known Job 11:7
and notice every mistake I *. Job 14:16
off the scene. You * him old and Job 14:20,21
You have tried to * me feel Job 20:3
and don't * me flatter anyone. Job 32:21,22
to * you nervous and afraid. Job 33:7
say, 'and watches every move I *.' Job 33:11
Do not * him die, for I have Job 33:23,24
shout to the clouds and * it rain? Job 38:34
Can you * lightning appear and Job 38:35
upon the cliffs to * her nest? Job 39:27
Will he agree to let you * him Job 41:4
Can you * a pet of him like a Job 41:5
Arrows cannot * him flee. Job 41:27,28
But * everyone rejoice who puts Ps 5:11
Come, O Lord, and * me well. Ps 6:4
don't let them conquer you! * Ps 9:20
They protect us, * us wise, and Ps 19:7,8
Tell me what to do, O Lord, and * Ps 27:11
of the Lord. * their path dark and Ps 35:6
asking him to * them well; Ps 35:13

(MAKE Con't)
Literally, "You * all his bed in Ps 41:3f
Be gracious, Lord, and * me well Ps 41:10
he will * me smile again, Ps 43:5
and * me willing to obey you. Ps 51:12
O Lord, * these enemies begin to Ps 55:9
thirsty ground. * their weapons Ps 58:7
He waters the earth to * it Ps 65:9
* the summer and the winter too. Ps 74:17
the soil. * their mighty nobles Ps 83:11
and name, O Lord. * them failures Ps 83:17
Justice goes before him to * a Ps 85:13
I will steady him and * him Ps 89:21
firstborn son, and * him the Ps 89:27
I will * him great because he Ps 91:14
trumpets shout! * a joyful symphony Ps 98:6
I will * the godly of the land Ps 101:6
and wine to * him glad, and olive Ps 104:15
There the birds * their nests, Ps 104:17
This was done to * them faithful Ps 105:45
* them fail in everything they Ps 109:29
and * them bow low before you." Ps 110:1
God's constant care of him will * Ps 112:6
And those who * and worship them Ps 115:8
Now give me your instructions. * Ps 119:27
Lord, don't let me * a mess of Ps 119:31
obey. * me walk along the right Ps 119:35
You are good and do only good; * Ps 119:68
They * me wiser than my enemies, Ps 119:98
They * me even wiser than the Ps 119:100
listen to me and * me well again. Ps 119:149
They try to * me disobey, but I Ps 119:157
I will * this city prosperous Ps 132:15
Those who * them become like Ps 135:18
the Red Sea to * a path before Ps 136:13
"I want to * the simple-minded Pro 1:4
wisdom upon you, and * you wise. Pro 1:23
he delights in to * him better, so Pro 3:11,12
have no king to * them work, yet Pro 6:7
Love wisdom like a sweetheart; * Pro 7:4
"I, Wisdom, will * the hours of Pro 9:11
Some people like to * cutting Pro 12:18
Or, "Fools * a mock at sin." Pro 14:9f
will * you both wise and honored. Pro 15:33
WE CAN * our plans, but the final Pro 16:1
We should * plans—counting on God Pro 16:9
It is risky to * loans to Pro 20:16
It is foolish and rash to * a Pro 20:25
much of it, or it will * you sick! Pro 25:16
This will * him feel ashamed of Pro 25:21,22
There are three things that * the Pro 30:21,22,23
it is sinful to * rash promises to Ecc 5:1
it was all a mistake [to * the vow Ecc 5:6,7
That would * God very angry; Ecc 5:6,7
before it, can * serious mistakes. Ecc 11:10
We shall * you golden earrings Sol 1:11
Even though you * many prayers, I Is 1:15
take it out and * you as clean as Is 1:18
I can * you white as wool! Is 1:18
only obey, then I will * you rich! Is 1:19
"* a large signboard and write on Is 8:1
He will * a highway from Assyria Is 11:16
wonderful things. * known his Is 12:5
the desert will * it their home. Is 13:21
I will * Babylon into a desolate Is 14:23
are wrong; they * Egypt stagger Is 19:14
In that day the Lord will * Is 19:21
they will * promises to God and Is 19:21
I will * of him a strong and Is 22:23,24
palaces and * it a heap of ruins. Is 23:13
to the wicked doesn't * them good; Is 26:10
Year after year you * your many Is 29:1
hypocrites, and * their wisest Is 29:14
say to him, "He didn't * us"? Is 29:16
He will * Jerusalem the home of Is 33:5
and * a mighty slaughter there. Is 34:6
There the owl will * her nest Is 34:15
Spirit will * it all come true. Is 34:16
wants to * a little bet with you! Is 36:8,9
Oh, heal me and * me live! Is 38:16
servants, "* an ointment of figs Is 38:21
shouting, "* a road for the Lord Is 40:3
the wilderness; * him a straight, Is 40:3
But they rush to * a new idol; Is 41:7
Can your idols * such claims as Is 41:21
He will * the darkness bright Is 42:16
I will * a road through the Is 43:19
Who but a fool would * his own Is 44:10
at his forge to * an axe, pounding Is 44:12
the axe and uses it to * an idol. Is 44:13
of the wood to * a fire to warm Is 44:15
things they say. I * wise men give Is 44:25
should, and * them into fools. Is 44:25
I form the light and * the dark. Is 45:7
your wealth and * a god from it! Is 46:6
fire to sit beside to * you warm! Is 47:14
God will * my words of judgment Is 49:2
I will * you a Light to the Is 49:6
And I will * my mountains into Is 49:11
For I can rebuke the sea and * it Is 50:2
again, and * her deserts blossom; Is 51:3
at all, nothing to * us want him. Is 53:2
Servant shall * many to be counted Is 53:11
of sapphires and * the walls of Is 54:11
I will * your towers of Is 54:12
I am ready to * an everlasting Is 55:3
This miracle will * the Lord's Is 55:13
will * them second-class citizens. Is 56:3
of Jerusalem, and * them full of Is 56:7
Does all this * me happy? Is 57:6
of the world, for I will * you so. Is 60:15
suffering and * an everlasting Is 61:8
and * them strong and great." Jer 1:10
* a fool of you in front of them. Jer 1:17
No amount of soap or lye can * Jer 2:22
* this announcement to Judah and Jer 5:20
I will * an obstacle course of Jer 6:21
knead dough and * cakes to offer to Jer 7:18
Don't act like the people who * Jer 10:2,3
goldsmiths who * their idols; Jer 10:9
robes that expert tailors *. Jer 10:9
in, for what they * are frauds, Jer 10:14
Can men * God? Jer 16:20
my power and might and * them Jer 16:21
work on the Sabbath day but * it Jer 17:21,22
And if I announce that I will * Jer 18:9
and * my name a household joke. Jer 20:8
says, I will * all your weapons Jer 21:3,4
palace does not * a great king! Jer 22:15
I will * them repulsive to every Jer 24:9
destroy you and * you a byword of Jer 25:8,9
I will * the land of Chaldea an Jer 25:12
with my fury, and * all the nations Jer 25:15
of the Lord and * an announcement Jer 26:2
Shiloh, and I will * Jerusalem a Jer 26:6
* a yoke and fasten it on your Jer 27:2
Babylon and * him their slave. Jer 27:7
David's throne—and * them like Jer 29:16,17
say, "The Lord * you like Zedekiah Jer 29:22
and no one shall * them afraid. Jer 30:10
my people and * of them a great and Jer 30:19
comfort them and * them rejoice, Jer 31:13
Lord, when I will * a new contract Jer 31:31
contract I will * with them: I will Jer 31:33
stirs the sea to * the roaring Jer 31:35
* them live in peace and safety. Jer 32:37
And I will * an everlasting Jer 32:40
For I will * this land happier Jer 33:10,11
not kill you or * slaves of you but Jer 42:12
completely and to * you a curse and Jer 44:8
and nothing shall * her afraid. Jer 46:27
I will * her weak among the Jer 49:15
for them, and * them drink until Jer 51:39
I will * drunk her princes, wise Jer 51:57
and I will * your tongue stick Eze 3:26
"So I will * a public example of Eze 5:14
I will crush you and * your Eze 6:14
you used it instead to * idols! Eze 7:20
* liars out of every prophet.' Eze 12:22
I will turn upon him and * a Eze 14:8
And I will * the land desolate Eze 15:8
hated—and I will * you naked before Eze 16:37
and Sodom, and * them your Eze 16:61
the low, that I * the green tree Eze 17:24
I will * a clean sweep throughout Eze 21:4
"Son of dust, * a map and on it Eze 21:19,20
siege towers and * a hill against Eze 21:22
how could the diviners * this Eze 21:23
I will * you a laughingstock and Eze 22:4
Thus will I * lewdness and Eze 23:48
I will scrape away her soil and * Eze 26:4
I will * your island a bare Eze 26:14
from Lebanon to * a mast for you. Eze 27:5
the rich variety of goods you *. Eze 27:18
I will * Egypt desolate, Eze 29:12
Egypt to him to * up for what he Eze 29:18f
Egypt to him to * up for what he Eze 29:20f
put into a cast to * it strong Eze 30:21
* his sword clatter to the ground. Eze 30:22
I will * a peace pact with them, Eze 34:25
I will * my people and their Eze 34:26
and no one shall * them afraid. Eze 34:28
your cities and * you desolate, and Eze 35:4,5
rejoice when I * you desolate. Eze 35:14
I am going to * you live and Eze 37:5
and * them one stick in my hand. Eze 37:18,19,20
And I will * a covenant of peace Eze 37:26
And I will * my home among them. Eze 37:27
cavalry, and * you a mighty host, Eze 38:4
their goods and * them poor?' Eze 38:13
"Thus I will * known my holy Eze 39:7
"And I will * a vast graveyard Eze 39:11
This will cleanse and * atonement Eze 43:20
to cleanse and * atonement for the Eze 43:26
thank offerings to * atonement for Eze 45:15
thank offerings—to * reconciliation Eze 45:17
waters and * them fresh and pure. Eze 47:8
planning to * them his counselors Dan 1:5
And to * matters worse, he Dan 2:1
Therefore, I * this decree, that Dan 3:29
your neck, and * you the third Dan 5:16
that you should * a law, Dan 6:7
This king will * a seven-year Dan 9:
and * it still more powerful. Dan 1
But it will * no difference, for Dan 11:
cleanse them and * them pure until Dan 11:
road before her to * her lose her Hos 1
At that time I will * a treaty Hos 1:
They * promises they don't intend Hos 10
great armies can * a nation safe! Hos 10:
But riches can't * up for sin. Hos 12
Listen to the noise they *, like Joe 2
No longer will I * you a Joe 2:
"Therefore I will * you groan as Amo 2:
three cities would * their weary Amo 4
O evil men, you * "justice" a Amo 5
you do when you * a mockery of Amo 6:
you who * slaves of the poor, Amo 8
At that time I will * the sun go Amo 8
boat ashore, but couldn't * it. Jon 1:
pleaded, "don't * us die for this Jon 1:
for you to *, O House of Jacob? Mic 2
world will * pilgrimages there. Mic 4
dispossessed— and * them strong Mic 4
"How can we * up to you for what Mic 6
child, would that * him glad? Mic 6
I will * your hearts miserable Mic 6:1
but get no juice to * your wine. Mic 6:1
Therefore I will * an awesome Mic 6:1
I will * you the laughingstock of Mic 6:1
lead your flock; * them live in Mic 7:1
"These are the gods who * us Hab 1:1
"I will * you as helpless as a Zep 1:1
He will * a speedy riddance of Zep 1:1
he will destroy Assyria and * its Zep 2:1
and no one will * them afraid." Zep 3:1
Accept their gifts and * from Zec 6:10,1
and wine will * the young men and Zec 9:16,1
I will * them strong and glorious Zec 10:
The Lord says, "I will * my Zec 10:1
"I will * Jerusalem and Judah Zec 12:
against her, and * fools of them, Zec 12:
"In that day I will * the clans Zec 12:
the fire and * them pure, as gold Zec 13:
that day when I * up my jewels. Mal 3:1
seasoning, to * it tolerable. Mt 5:1
them, and to * them all come true. Mt 5:1
But I say: Don't * any vows! Mt 5:3
tear away and * the hole worse. Mt 9:1
you believe I can * you see?" Mt 9:2
If you want me to, I'll * three Mt 17:4
For you go to all lengths to * Mt 23:1
by potters, and to * it into a Mt 27:
Therefore go and * disciples in Mt 28:19
Literally, "* ready the way of Mk 1:3
the Lord; * his paths straight." Mk 1:3
And I will * you fishermen for Mk 1:17
"If you want to, you can * me Mk 1:40
warned them not to * him known. Mk 3:12
Satan comes at once to try to * Mk 4:15
hands on her and * her live." Mk 5:23
they are what pollute you and * Mk 7:23
"* something happen in the sky. Mk 8:11
earthly process could ever * it! Mk 9:3
"We will * three shelters here, Mk 9:5
I * your enemies your footstool.' Mk 12:36
Jerusalem to * the arrangements. Mk 14:13
he replied. "* sure you collect no Lk 3:13
to * a patch for an old one. Lk 5:36
* room for more, and running over. Lk 6:38
Didn't God * the inside as well Lk 11:40
to day if you will * the Kingdom of Lk 12:31
ironically, "* to yourselves Lk 16:9f
Touch me and * sure that I am not Lk 24:39
exists that he didn't *. Jn 1:3
and won't have to * this long trip Jn 4:15
"When I * claims about myself Jn 5:31
him by force and * him their king, Jn 6:15
and it will * no difference, for Jn 7:6
though I * them concerning myself. Jn 8:14
And though I have no wish to * Jn 8:50
to * him see, or who did it. Jn 9:21
to find your way. * use of the Jn 12:36
more than I am. * them pure and Jn 17:17
They told Aaron, '* idols for Act 7:40
Didn't I * both heaven and Act 7:50
Get up and * your bed." Act 9:34
But just as Paul started to * Act 18:14
whips to * him confess his crime. Act 22:24
Tertullus, to * their accusations Act 24:1
me confidence as I * my defense. Act 24:10
to * his stay more comfortable. Act 24:23
I used torture to try to * Act 26:11
which was scheduled to * several Act 27:2
jump overboard and * for land, and Act 27:43
and then * money your god instead. Rom 2:22
his laws serve only to * us see Rom 3:20
and rose again to * us right with Rom 4:25
them to * me guilty of death. Rom 7:11
I turn I can't * myself do right. Rom 7:18
in you, he will * your dying bodies Rom 8:11
* them truly Abraham's children. Rom 9:7
lump of clay to * one jar Rom 9:21

(MAKE Con't)
has died to * them right with God. Rom 10:3
Instead they are trying to * Rom 10:3
said that he would * his people Rom 10:19
His purpose was to * his Rom 11:11
if possible I can * them want what Rom 11:14
were broken off to * room for me so Rom 11:19
every one of us to * it complete, Rom 12:4,5
and don't * plans to enjoy evil. Rom 13:14
And God is able to * them do as Rom 14:4
you will never * your brother Rom 14:13
who is able to * you strong and Rom 16:25,26,27
these things to * you ashamed, but 1Co 4:14
I am trying to * you ashamed. 1Co 6:5
For it doesn't * any difference 1Co 7:19
offers should * good use of their 1Co 7:31
idols is going to * my brother sin, 1Co 8:13
but the many parts * up only one 1Co 12:12
* it any less a part of the body. 1Co 12:15
Would that * it any less a part 1Co 12:16
to a mountain and * it move, I 1Co 13:2
This time I don't want to * just 1Co 16:7
If Timothy comes * him feel at 1Co 16:10
I want to * you happy, not sad. 2Co 1:24
I'll not * them unhappy with 2Co 2:1
For if I * you sad, who is 2Co 2:2
sad, who is going to * me happy? 2Co 2:2
is to * a good living out of it. 2Co 2:17
These earthly bodies * us groan 2Co 5:4
you could to * it right. 2Co 7:11
by being poor he could * you rich. 2Co 8:9
Every one must * up his own mind 2Co 9:7
God is able to * it up to you by 2Co 9:8
to plant and will * it grow so that 2Co 9:10
I shall * good every claim. 2Co 10:8
cheapen myself and * you look down 2Co 11:7
you don't mind at all when they * 2Co 11:19,20
I begged God to * me well again. 2Co 12:8
with him, did they * any profit? 2Co 12:18
to punish you but to * you strong. 2Co 13:10
to * these Gentiles obey them? Gal 2:14
will * you stronger Christians? Gal 3:3
SO CHRIST HAS made us free. Now * Gal 5:1
the Jewish laws to * you right with Gal 5:2
our sins and * us right with God. Gal 5:5
See how large I have to * the Gal 6:11
It doesn't * any difference now Gal 6:15
he decided then to * us holy in Eph 1:4
be wise: * the most of every Eph 5:15,16
died for her, to * her holy and Eph 5:26
And some preach to * me jealous, Php 1:16,17
my staying will * you glad and Php 1:26
Then * me truly happy by loving Php 2:2
don't live to * a good impression Php 2:3
him, and that will * me happy and Php 2:28
that God will * it plain to you— Php 3:15
asking him to * you wise about Col 1:9
They only * him proud. Col 2:23
enrich your lives and * you wise; Col 3:16
and fully, and * it plain, as, of Col 4:4
* the most of your chances to Col 4:5
you, asking God to * you strong and Col 4:12
And may the Lord * your love to 1Th 3:12
May the God of peace himself * 1Th 5:23
your sufferings to * you ready for 2Th 1:5
that our God will * you the kind of 2Th 1:11
wants to have—will * you as good as 2Th 1:11
he will * you strong and guard 2Th 3:3
For if a man can't * his own 1Ti 3:5
Teach these things and * sure 1Ti 4:11
that hurt them and * them 1Ti 6:9
upset people and * them angry. 2Ti 2:23
people's homes and * friendships 2Ti 3:6
and it is these that * you wise 2Ti 3:15
is true and to * us realize what is 2Ti 3:16
as necessary to * them strong in Tit 1:13
In this way they will * people Tit 2:10
into sin and * us his very own Tit 2:14
all that he had planned to *. Heb 4:4
so it's hard to * you understand. Heb 5:11
give him a son and * him the father Heb 6:14
Christ must * an offering too. Heb 8:3
come when I will * a new agreement Heb 8:8
agreement I will * with the people Heb 8:10
God commanded me to * with you." Heb 9:20
agreement I will * with the people Heb 10:16
Christ's blood to * us clean, and Heb 10:22
and every decision you then * Jas 1:7,8
for anger doesn't * us good, as Jas 1:20
clothes, and you * a lot of fuss Jas 2:3
for we all * many mistakes; Jas 3:1
We can * a large horse turn Jas 3:3
to * them pure and true to him. Jas 4:8
him, for the Lord will * him well; Jas 5:15
mighty power, will * sure that you 1Pe 1:5
the Rock that will * them fall." 1Pe 2:8
these trials will * you partners 1Pe 4:13
and * you stronger than ever. 1Pe 5:10
This will * possible the next 2Pe 1:7
* a game of luring unstable women. 2Pe 2:14
money he could * by doing wrong; 2Pe 2:15
family does not * a practice of 1Jn 3:9
we talk to him and * our requests, 1Jn 5:15
conquers, I will * him a pillar in Rev 3:12
it, it will * your stomach sour!" Rev 10:9
of the world to * a great statue of Rev 13:14
this statue and even * it speak! Rev 13:15

MAKER
So God made man like his *. Gen 1:27
'Where is God my * who gives songs Job 35:9,10
of the righteousness of my *. Job 36:3
be signed by your name as their *! Ps 89:12
Lord our *, for he is our God. Ps 95:6
O Israel, rejoice in your *. Ps 149:2
Does the pot argue with its *? Is 45:9
fear of God, your *—you have Is 51:13
The Lord, the * of heaven and Jer 33:2
but they have forgotten their *. Hos 8:14

MAKERS
they will be crushed when their * Jer 10:15

MAKES
"Who * mouths?" Ex 4:11
"Isn't it I, the Lord? Who * a Ex 4:11
Then you will know that Jehovah * Ex 11:7
"Take no bribes, for a bribe * Ex 23:8
that I am Jehovah who * you holy. Ex 31:12,13
"If anyone * a rash vow, whether Lev 5:4
it is the blood that * atonement, Lev 17:11
that when a person * a special vow Lev 27:1
"But anyone who deliberately * Num 15:30
that when anyone * a promise to the Num 30:1
"If she takes a vow or * a Num 30:6
his disagreement * it void, and Num 30:8
home when she * the vow, and her Num 30:10
be upon anyone who * and worships Deu 27:15
With the best of what the sun * Deu 33:14
told me what * you so strong!" Ju 16:15
For it * no difference to him how 1Sa 14:6
So what * you think the Lord can 2Ki 18:35
laws when he * you king of Israel. 1Ch 22:12
successfully. What * you think your 2Ch 32:14
If he rushes in and * an arrest, Job 11:10
Go ahead and provoke God—it * no Job 12:6
"He * fools of counselors and Job 12:17
destroys it. He * it great, and Job 12:23
What have I said that * you speak Job 16:3
the heavens. He * the winds blow Job 28:25
of the oceans. He * the laws of Job 28:26
but it is not mere age that * Job 32:8,9
Almighty which * him intelligent. Job 32:8,9
in the night, and * us a little Job 35:11
He delivers by distress! This * Job 36:15
"Who * the wild donkeys wild? Job 39:5
"He * the water boil with his Job 41:31,32
Or, "* the hinds to calve." Ps 29:9f
THE LORD * us strong! Ps 81:1
Is God deaf and blind—he who * Ps 94:9
punishing us. This * us follow his Ps 94:12,13
deepest seas. He * mists rise Ps 135:7
find in me that * you sad, and lead Ps 139:24
the showers and * the green grass Ps 147:8
A wise youth * hay while the sun Pro 10:5
* good use of everything he finds. Pro 12:27
Hope deferred * the heart sick; Pro 13:12
A wise teacher * learning a joy; Pro 15:2
to please God, God * even his worst Pro 16:7
Hunger is good—if it * you work Pro 16:26
but a broken spirit * one sick. Pro 17:22
Kindness * a man attractive. Pro 19:22
A wise son * his father happy, Pro 29:3
leaders. She * belted linen Pro 31:24
Generations come and go but it * Ecc 1:3-7
being a fool * you a blabbermouth. Ecc 5:1
for it * no difference to God! Ecc 9:7
greater than you, the jars he *? Is 29:16
One generation * known your Is 38:19
curtain and * his tent from them. Is 40:22
Or do some mighty miracle that * Is 41:23
the rest of it and * himself a Is 44:15
left he * his god: a carved idol! Is 44:17
and * the weapons of destruction. Is 54:16
Jerusalem and * her respected and Is 62:6,7
he *, for in making them he lies; Jer 51:17
most to help us * no move at all. Lam 4:17
get him drunk; he * a fool of Hos 7:5
The Hebrew text * no distinction Jon 3:3f
done that * you turn away from me? Mic 6:3
that * you unclean." Mt 15:11
to the ground and * him foam at the Mk 9:18
the demon often * him fall into the Mk 9:22
tells us that God * us ready for Rom 1:17
ready for heaven—* us right in Rom 1:17
God himself, who * the dead live Rom 4:17
righteousness * men right with Rom 5:18
am that * me do these evil things. Rom 7:17
wins the fight and * me a slave to Rom 7:23,24,25
and he * some refuse to listen. Rom 9:18
When a man * a jar out of Rom 9:21
to eat it if it * another stumble. Rom 14:20
offends your brother or * him sin. Rom 14:21
EVEN IF WE believe that it * no Rom 15:1
and true. This * me very happy. Rom 16:19
he is the one who * things grow. 1Co 3:7
But it * a lot of difference 1Co 7:19
a "know-it-all" * us feel 1Co 8:1
This * for happiness among the 1Co 12:25
to bless me. It * no difference 1Co 15:11
It is he who * us victorious 1Co 15:57
plan that * men right with God. 2Co 3:9
How happy this * me, now that I 2Co 7:16
along: Who * a mistake and I do 2Co 11:29
bodies that * us children of God; Php 3:3
your gifts, what * me happiest is Php 4:17
that * you want to do right. 2Ti 2:22
them, what * us think that we can Heb 2:3
hope, for Christ * us acceptable to Heb 7:19
* us want to serve the living God. Heb 9:14
law of God, but * one little slip, Jas 2:10
And a tiny rudder * a huge ship Jas 3:4
this world—* you an enemy of God? Jas 4:4
love * up for many of your faults. 1Pe 4:8
appeared. This * us all the more 1Jn 2:18
of God's family * a practice of 1Jn 5:18
one who justly punishes and * war. Rev 19:11

MAKHELOTH
From Haradah to *; Num 33:15-37
From * to Tahath; Num 33:15-37

MAKING
mankind was *, he said, "Look! Gen 11:5
He'll think I'm * a fool of him, Gen 27:11,12
wife began * eyes at Joseph, and Gen 39:7
any more straw for * bricks! Ex 5:7,8
for * such unreasonable demands." Ex 5:16
"May God judge you for * us Ex 5:21
into great heaps, * a terrible Ex 8:14
or "place of * propitiation." Ex 25:17f
the same technique as in * a seal; Ex 28:11
purge the altar by * atonement Ex 29:36
Anyone * it for himself shall be Ex 30:38
All the drapes * up the walls of Ex 38:16
for "goodness" in * covenants. Lev 2:13f
thus he sanctified the altar, * Lev 8:15,16
burnt offering, * atonement for Lev 9:7
upon the altar, * atonement for the Lev 14:20
This is the method for * Lev 14:53
for himself, * atonement for Lev 16:6
of Israel, and * it holy. Lev 16:19
for the people, * atonement for Lev 16:24
sanctity by * her a prostitute, Lev 19:29
to Molech, thus * my Tabernacle Lev 20:3
a special day for * atonement Lev 23:28
sacrifices, * atonement for them. Num 8:19
new crops by * a loaf, using Num 15:19,20,21
broken: the person * the vow must Num 30:1
yourselves by * idols, and the Lord Deu 4:25
a contract he is * with you today. Deu 29:12
says is evil, * him very angry." Deu 31:29
the right thing in * Abimelech your Ju 9:16
As his father was * final Ju 14:10,11
to him, "You are * fun of me! Ju 16:10
who were watching Samson and * Ju 16:27
went to Shiloh, * her cry so much 1Sa 1:7
for fear of their * swords and 1Sa 13:19
Next they'll be * him their 1Sa 18:8
He divided his victims by * them 2Sa 8:2
yourself in * this decision, 2Sa 14:13
and yet you act like this, * us 2Sa 19:5
him to Jerusalem, * a joyous and 1Ki 1:40
the timber and * the boards, and in 1Ki 5:18
began mocking and * fun of him 2Ki 2:23
was entrusted with * the flat cakes 1Ch 9:31
of * David the king of Israel. 1Ch 12:38
to use it for * the gold and silver 2Ch 24:14
incense, and for * the instruments 2Ch 24:14
of evil, * the Lord very angry. 2Ch 33:6
and praying and * this confession, Ez 10:1
* certain that each knew his work. Neh 13:30
to everyone and * grants to the Est 2:18
real motive in * me was to destroy Job 10:13,14
Without * a federal case of it, Job 34:24
She lives upon the cliffs, * her Job 39:28
are his pride, * a tight seal, so Job 41:15-17
* a total of twenty children, Job 42:13,14f
Help me to prefer obedience to * Ps 119:36
Thank you for * me so Ps 139:14
it master them, * them reel Pro 20:1
In that case, your mouth is * Ecc 5:6,7
as prisoners, * them walk naked and Is 20:4
land of Judah and * it a vast Is 24:1
* stupid errors and mistakes. Is 28:7
fair, who reject * profit by fraud, Is 33:15
in the hills and * everyone in Is 36:7
cloth used for * sacks, as a sign Is 37:1
apart, * chaff of mountains. Is 41:15
Who else predicted this, * you Is 41:26
* a path right through the sea. Is 43:16
dried up the sea, * a path right Is 51:10
Who is it you mock, * faces and Is 57:4
weak, and to stop * false Is 58:9
They are * up everything they Jer 23:16
The guard * the arrest was Irijah Jer 37:13
merciful to you by * him kind so Jer 42:12
to her and * cakes for her with her Jer 44:19

(MAKING Con't)
he makes, for in * them he lies; Jer 51:17
did to others, * them her slaves. Lam 1:3
* pegs to hang up pots and pans! Eze 15:3
I gave you for * idol shrines and Eze 16:16
Assyrians too [by * them your Eze 16:28
along the banks of the Nile, * Eze 32:2
bothering them or * them afraid. Eze 39:26
When he had finished * these Eze 42:15
Edom, * you small and despised. Ob 1:2
"Woe to you for * your Hab 2:15
will split apart, * a very wide Zec 14:4
be compared to a woman * bread. Mt 13:33
way they keep * up so many laws! Mt 23:2
enemies, and by * us holy and Lk 1:75
keeps seizing him, * him scream; Lk 9:39
But they all began * excuses. Lk 14:18
thereby * himself equal with God. Jn 5:18
is * these claims for me too. Jn 5:32,33
I be condemned for * a man Jn 7:21,22,23
And remember, I am not * up this Jn 14:24
News there and * many disciples, Act 14:21
from city to city, * known the Act 16:4
for our sins—* us friends of God. Rom 5:11
work within you, * you want to do Rom 7:5
others, I would only be * noise. 1Co 13:1
They have been * up for the help 1Co 16:17
and not * me write about myself. 2Co 12:11
Gentiles by * us all one family, Eph 2:14
Literally, "by * us one." Eph 2:14f
Be patient with each other, * Eph 4:2
sacred songs, * music in your Eph 5:19
* them angry and resentful. Eph 6:4
wonderful help in * known the Good Php 1:5
for God's way of * us right with Php 3:9
Don't worry about * a good Col 3:12
News is just a means of * money. 1Ti 6:5
It is God's way of * us well 2Ti 3:17
God all those whom he is * holy. Heb 10:14
Don't you realize that * friends Jas 4:4
Christ and * you to please him. 1Pe 1:2
or stealing or * trouble or being a 1Pe 4:15
face of the earth, * them an 2Pe 2:6
miracles such as * fire flame down Rev 13:13
"See, I am * all things new!" Rev 21:5

MAKKEDAH
and *, killing them along the way. Jos 10:10
escaped and hid in a cave at *. Jos 10:16
to their camp at * without having Jos 10:21
the city of * and killed its king Jos 10:28
The king of *; Jos 12:8-24
Naamah, *, Libnah, Ether, Ashan, Jos 15:37-44

MALACHI
given through the prophet *: Mal 1:1
book of Isaiah, appears in * 3:1. Mk 1:3f

MALCAM
Jobab, Zibia, Mesha, *, 1Ch 8:8,9,10

MALCHI-EL
named after their ancestor *. Num 26:44-47
Heber, * (the father of Birzaith). 1Ch 7:31

MALCHI-ELITES
The *, named after their ancestor Num 26:44-47

MALCHIAH
Pashhur (son of *) and Zephaniah Jer 21:1
Pashhur (son of *) heard what Jer 38:1
(It belonged to *, a member of Jer 38:6

MALCHIEL
Beriah's sons were Heber and *. Gen 46:16,17

MALCHIJAH
Ba-aseiah, *, Ethni, Zerah, Adaiah, 1Ch 6:39-43
son of Pashhur, son of *). 1Ch 9:12
Fifth, the group led by *; 1Ch 24:7-18
Ramiah, Izziah, *, Mijamin, Ez 10:25
Eliezer, Isshijah, *, Shemaiah, Ez 10:31,32
Then came * (son of Harim) and Neh 3:11
The Dung Gate was repaired by * Neh 3:14
to his own house. *, one of the Neh 3:31
Pedaiah, Misha-el, *, Hashum, Neh 8:1
*, Hattush, Shebaniah, Neh 10:1
son of Pashhur, son of *). Neh 11:10-14
Uzzi, Jehohanan, *, Neh 12:42

MALCHIRAM
She-altiel, *, 1Ch 3:17,18

MALCHISHUA
sons, Jonathan, Ishvi, and *; 1Sa 14:49
sons Jonathan, Abinidab, and *. 1Sa 31:2
Jonathan, *, Abinadab, Eshbaal. 1Ch 8:33
Saul was the father of Jonathan, * 1Ch 9:39
and *, and killed them all. 1Ch 10:2

MALCHUS
of *, the High Priest's servant. Jn 18:10

MALCONTENTS
Soon he had quite a band of * as Ju 11:3

MALE
Bring a pair of every animal—a * Gen 6:19,20
Literally, "the * and female." Gen 7:3f
the boat in pairs, * and female, Gen 7:8,9
Two by two they came, * and Gen 7:16
* among you shall be circumcised; Gen 17:9,10
Every * shall be circumcised on Gen 17:12
and every other *—born in his Gen 17:23
Jacob of all the * goats that were Gen 30:35,36
female donkeys,10 * donkeys. Gen 32:13,14,15
be a year-old *, either a sheep or Ex 12:5
sons and firstborn * animals in all Ex 12:12
of Israel, and every firstborn * Ex 13:1
sons and firstborn * animals belong Ex 13:12
the slave is * or female—that man Ex 21:20
a slave, whether * or female, the Ex 21:32
These were carved statues of * Ex 34:13f
"Every firstborn * Ex 34:19
be a *, and without any blemishes. Lev 1:10
may be either a * or female—ram or Lev 3:6
It may be eaten by any * Lev 6:18
Every * among the priests may Lev 6:29
"to select a * goat for their sin Lev 9:3
he shall take two * lambs without Lev 14:10
bring only one, a * lamb for the Lev 14:21
then bring him two * goats for Lev 16:5
to a * animal, to mate with it; Lev 18:23
it is a * animal without defect; Lev 22:19
to the Lord a * yearling lamb Lev 23:12
And you shall offer one * goat Lev 23:19
offering, and two * yearling lambs Lev 23:19
count every * down to one month Num 3:14,15
and must bring a * lamb a year old Num 6:12
bull, a ram, and a * yearling lamb Num 7:15
a * goat for a sin offering; Num 7:16
five rams, five * goats, and five Num 7:17
goats, and five * yearling lambs. Num 7:17
12 yearling * goats (with the Num 7:87
12 * goats. Num 7:87
60 rams, 60 * goats, Num 7:88
60 * lambs a year old. Num 7:88
and one * goat for a sin offering. Num 15:23,24
* lambs—each without defect. Num 28:3
two yearling * lambs—both without Num 28:9,10
one ram, and seven * yearling Num 28:11
shall offer one * goat for a sin Num 28:15
* lambs—all without defect. Num 28:19
You must also offer a * goat as Num 28:22
ram, and seven yearling * lambs. Num 28:27
Also offer one * goat to make Num 28:30
* lambs—all without defect. Num 29:2
In addition, there shall be a * Num 29:5
seven yearling * lambs—each without Num 29:8
You are also to sacrifice one * Num 29:11
rams, and fourteen * yearling lambs Num 29:13
There must also be a * goat Num 29:16
rams, and fourteen * yearling Num 29:17
are to sacrifice a * goat with its Num 29:19
two rams, fourteen * yearling Num 29:20
sacrifice a * goat for a sin Num 29:22
rams, and fourteen * yearling Num 29:23
also a * goat as a sin offering Num 29:25
rams, and fourteen * yearling Num 29:26,27
also sacrifice a * goat with the Num 29:28
rams, and fourteen * yearling Num 29:29
sacrifice a * goat and the usual Num 29:31
rams, and fourteen * yearling Num 29:32
offering of one * goat, with the Num 29:34
one ram, seven * yearling Num 29:36
Sacrifice also one * goat with Num 29:38
not one of you, whether * or Deu 7:14
to you, kill every * in the city; Deu 20:13
the entire * population of Israel. Jos 5:2,3
killed the entire * population. Ju 8:17
every * in the entire country. 1Ki 11:15
Literally, "every *, both bond 1Ki 14:10f
He executed the * prostitutes 1Ki 15:12
not a single * child. 1Ki 16:11
one of your * descendants survive! 1Ki 21:21
all the houses of * prostitution 1Ki 22:46
wiped out—every *, no matter who. 2Ki 9:8
down the houses of * prostitution 2Ki 23:7
7,700 rams and 7,700 * goats. 2Ch 17:11
lambs, and seven * goats for a sin 2Ch 29:21
the lambs. The * goats for the sin 2Ch 29:23
and twelve * goats were presented Ez 6:17
female camel, seeking for a *! Jer 2:23
sacrifice a young * goat without Eze 43:22
"Every day for seven days a * Eze 43:25

MALES
all the mating * are speckled, Gen 31:12f
you, let all the * be circumcised, Ex 12:48
all the firstborn * throughout the Ex 13:15
all the firstborn * to the Ex 13:15
Only * among the priests may Lev 7:6
22,000 * a month old and older. Num 3:39
This census will be of all * Num 4:3
a most holy place, and only by *. Num 18:10
all the * a month old and upward. Num 26:62
* from your flocks and herds. Deu 15:19
Literally, "* from three years 2Ch 31:16f

MALICE
necessary, with no * against them, Act 28:19

MALIGNANT
and horrible, * sores broke out on Rev 16:2

MALLOTHI
*, Hothir, and Mahazi-oth. 1Ch 25:4,5
Nineteenth, * and twelve of his 1Ch 25:9-31

MALLUCH
Kishi, Abdi, *, Hashabiah, 1Ch 6:44-47
Meshullam, *, Adaiah, Jashub, Ez 10:2[...]
Shime-on, Benjamin, *, Shemariah. Ez 10:31,3[...]
*, Harim, Meremoth, Neh 10:[...]
Hanan, Anan, *, Neh 10:14-2[...]
*, Hattush, Shecaniah, Neh 12:[...]

MALLUCHI
Jonathan, leader of the * clan; Neh 12:12-2[...]

MALTA
that we were on the island of *. Act 28:[...]

MAMMA
"*, Mamma, we want food," they Lam 2:1[...]
"Mamma, *, we want food," they Lam 2:1[...]

MAMMON
means of the * of unrighteousness; Lk 16:9

MAMRE
to the oaks of *, near Hebron, and Gen 13:1[...]
oaks belonging to * the Amorite Gen 14:1[...]
Aner, Eshcol, and *, my allies." Gen 14:24
was living in the oak grove at *. Gen 18:1
Mach-pelah, near *, and the cave at Gen 23:17,18
of Mach-pelah near *, in the field Gen 25:9,10
his father at * in Kiriath-arba Gen 35:27
Mach-pelah, facing *—the field Gen 49:29,30
of Ephron the Hethite, close to *. Gen 50:12,13

MAN
Then God said, "Let us make a * Gen 1:26
Literally, "Let us make * in our Gen 1:26f
So God made * like his Maker. Gen 1:27
Like God did God make *; Gen 1:27
* and maid did he make them. Gen 1:27
And * became a living person. Gen 2:7
in the garden the * he had formed. Gen 2:8
The Lord God placed the * in the Gen 2:15
But the Lord God gave the * this Gen 2:16,17
"It isn't good for * to be alone; Gen 2:18
* to see what he would call them; Gen 2:19,20
was no proper helper for the *. Gen 2:19,20
Then the Lord God caused the * Gen 2:21
a woman, and brought her to the *. Gen 2:22
she was taken out of a *." Gen 2:23
This explains why a * leaves Gen 2:24
Now although the * and his wife Gen 2:25
The * named his wife Eve (meaning Gen 3:20
"Now that the * has become as we Gen 3:22
God's help, I have created a *!" Gen 4:1
Or, "This * was the first to Gen 4:26f
of the descendants of Adam—the * Gen 5:1
God created * and woman and Gen 5:2
and called them * from the start. Gen 5:2
in *, wholly evil as he is. Gen 6:3
truly righteous * living on the Gen 6:9,10
is filled with crime because of *. Gen 6:12,13
was blotted out—* and animals Gen 7:23
any * who murders shall be killed; Gen 9:5,6
for to kill a * is to kill one Gen 9:5,6
"There isn't a * anywhere in this Gen 19:31
"You are a dead *, for that woman Gen 20:3
will you slay an innocent *? Gen 20:4
ABRAHAM WAS NOW a very old *, Gen 24:1
The * stood there a moment with Gen 24:26
spring where the * was still Gen 24:29,30
So the * went home with Laban, Gen 24:32
But the old * said, "I don't Gen 24:33
* among the people of his land. Gen 24:35
you willing to go with this *?" Gen 24:58
"Who is that * walking through Gen 24:65
Esau: "When a * is dying of Gen 25:32
this * or his wife shall die." Gen 26:11
He was soon a * of great wealth, Gen 26:13
Isaac: "I am an old * now, and Gen 27:2,3,4
and a * wrestled with him until Gen 32:22,23,24
And when the * saw that he Gen 32:25
Then the * said, "Let me go, for Gen 32:26
the * asked. Gen 32:27
the * told him. Gen 32:28
"No, you mustn't ask," the * Gen 32:29
for her to marry such a *. Gen 34:14
we'll do—if every * of you will be Gen 34:15
slaughtered every * there, Gen 34:25
Hebron Valley. A * noticed him Gen 37:15
"Yes," the * told him, "they Gen 37:17
lived there with a * named Hirah. Gen 38:1
But Er was a wicked *, and so Gen 38:7
"The * who owns this Gen 38:25
Now this * Potiphar was the Gen 39:1
way, was a very handsome young *. Gen 39:6
find the wisest * in Egypt and put Gen 41:33
For he is a * who is obviously Gen 41:38
are the wisest * in the country! Gen 41:39
am a God-fearing * and I'm going to Gen 42:18
Then the * told us, 'This is Gen 42:33
But Judah told him, "The * Gen 43:3,4,5
"But the * specifically asked us Gen 43:7
Take them to the * as gifts—balm, Gen 43:11
mercy before the *, so that he will Gen 43:14
So the * did as he was told Gen 43:17
father—the old * you spoke about? Gen 43:27
"Fair enough," the * replied, Gen 44:10
"Didn't you know such a * as I Gen 44:15
"Only the * who stole the cup, Gen 44:17
a father, an old *, and a child of Gen 44:20

(MAN Con't)
a *, and maimed oxen just for fun. Gen 49:6
up and become a *, he went out to Ex 2:11
the * demanded. Ex 2:14
Who makes a * so that he can Ex 4:11
fields, for every * and animal left Ex 9:19
was a very great * in the land of Ex 11:3
Hur was a * of Judah, of the Ex 17:10f
with arrows, whether * or animal.' Ex 19:13
"But if the * shall plainly Ex 21:5
"If a * sells his daughter as a Ex 21:7
If she does not please the * who Ex 21:8
"Anyone who hits a * so hard Ex 21:12
However, if a * deliberately Ex 21:14
the * who hit him will be Ex 21:19
"If a * beats his slave to Ex 21:20
* shall surely be punished. Ex 21:20
of days, then the * shall not be Ex 21:21
lives, then the * who injured her Ex 21:22
"If a * hits his slave in the Ex 21:26
the eye, whether * or woman, and Ex 21:26
"If an ox gores a * or woman to Ex 21:28
"If a * digs a well and doesn't Ex 21:33
"IF A * steals an ox or sheep and Ex 22:1
and the * who kills him is guilty. Ex 22:3
is found, then the * to whom the Ex 22:8
"If a * asks his neighbor to Ex 22:10
"If a * borrows an animal (or Ex 22:14
* who borrowed it must pay for it. Ex 22:14
"If a * seduces a girl Ex 22:16
Do not cooperate with an evil * Ex 23:1
of a * just because he is poor. Ex 23:2,3
each year, every * in Israel shall Ex 23:17
of Israel, each * who is numbered Ex 30:11,12
face, as a * speaks to his friend. Ex 33:11
but the young * who assisted him, Ex 33:11
for * may not see me and live. Ex 33:20
So the people of Israel—every * Ex 35:29
the death of the * who brings it, Lev 1:4
The * shall then kill the animal Lev 1:5
blemishes. The * who brings it Lev 1:11
Then the * will quarter it, and Lev 1:12
to the Lord! The * who brings the Lev 3:2
"If it is a lamb, the * who Lev 3:7,8
that *, and he shall be forgiven. Lev 4:31
*, and his sin shall be forgiven. Lev 4:35
uncleanness from * or beast, and Lev 7:21
it was only a scab, and the * Lev 13:6
him defiled. The * is not to be Lev 13:11
the * shall be declared a leper. Lev 13:14,15
"In the case of a * who has a Lev 13:18
reddish white, the * must go to the Lev 13:19
"If a * is burned in some way, Lev 13:24
"If a * or woman has a sore on Lev 13:29,30
"If a * or a woman has white, Lev 13:38
times upon the * cured of his Lev 14:7
"Then the * who is cured shall Lev 14:8
shall place the * and his offerings Lev 14:11
right ear of the * being cleansed, Lev 14:14
atonement for the *, who shall then Lev 14:20
right ear—the * on whose behalf the Lev 14:25
the head of the * being cleansed, Lev 14:29
for the * before the Lord." Lev 14:31
"Any * who has a genital Lev 15:1
Anyone sitting on a seat the * Lev 15:6
If the defiled * touches anyone Lev 15:11
by the defiled * must be broken, Lev 15:12
the * because of his discharge. Lev 15:15
as well as the * must bathe, and Lev 15:18
until evening. A * having sexual Lev 15:24
This, then, is the law for the * Lev 15:32
led by a * appointed for the task. Lev 16:21
and the * shall let it loose in Lev 16:22
"(The * who took the goat out Lev 16:26
enormous sin. A * shall have no Lev 18:23
nor trip up a blind * as he walks. Lev 19:14
"If a * seduces a slave Lev 19:20
is not free. The * involved shall Lev 19:21
for the sin the * has committed, Lev 19:22
turn against that * and cut him off Lev 20:3
not know what the * has done, and Lev 20:4
face against that * and his family Lev 20:5
"If a * commits adultery with Lev 20:10
* and woman shall be put to death. Lev 20:10
If a * sleeps with his father's Lev 20:11
both the * and the woman must Lev 20:11
And if a * has sexual Lev 20:12
If a * has sexual intercourse Lev 20:14
"If a * has sexual intercourse Lev 20:15
"If a * has sexual intercourse Lev 20:17
If a * has sexual intercourse Lev 20:18
outlawed between a * and his maiden Lev 20:19
If a * has intercourse with his Lev 20:20
If a * marries his brother's Lev 20:21
"A medium or a wizard—whether * Lev 20:27
woman, for he is a holy * of God. Lev 21:7
For instance, if a * is blind or Lev 21:18
one day, a young * whose mother was Lev 24:10
and whoever kills a * must die. Lev 24:21
"If a * sells a house in the Lev 25:29
though chased by a * with a sword; Lev 26:36
instead: A * from the age of Lev 27:3
a half dollars. A * over sixty Lev 27:7
but the * wants to redeem it, Lev 27:13
its value and the * shall pay that Lev 27:14,15
"If a * dedicates any part of Lev 27:16
If a * dedicates his field in Lev 27:17
If the * decides to redeem the Lev 27:19
"If a * dedicates to the Lord a Lev 27:22
and register, each * indicating his Num 1:17,18,19
"Assign duties to each * by name. Num 4:32
that when anyone, * or woman, Num 5:5,6
suspicious, the * shall bring his Num 5:15
say to her, 'If no * has slept with Num 5:19
"When either a * or a woman takes Num 6:1
(Now Moses was the humblest * on Num 12:3,4
kind of *—he has obeyed me fully. Num 14:24
to Moses, "The * must die—all the Num 15:35
a censer for each *, 250 in all; Num 16:17
all the people when one * sins?" Num 16:22
to identify the * I have chosen: Num 17:5
Then each * except Aaron claimed Num 17:9
"When a * dies in a tent, these Num 19:14
This is a permanent law. The * Num 19:21
God is not a *, that he should Num 23:18-24
The * whose eyes are open says, Num 24:3-9
"Balaam the son of Beor is the * Num 24:15-19
rushed after the * into his tent, Num 25:8
The name of the * who was killed Num 25:14
you, that if a * dies and has no Num 27:8
for the people, a * who will lead Num 27:17
between a * and his wife and Num 30:16
And every * of Midian was killed Num 31:7
Meanwhile, a * named Nobah led Num 32:42
Or if the slain * was struck Num 35:17
an enemy—yet the * dies, then the Num 35:22,23
over to the avenger of the dead *. Num 35:24
murder, for the * should have Num 35:28
High Priest, the * may return to Num 35:28
one witness; no * shall die with Num 35:30
but what can one * do to settle Deu 1:12
favor a * because he is rich; Deu 1:17
form, whether of a *, woman, Deu 4:16,17
when God created * upon the earth, Deu 4:32
Now we know that a * may speak to Deu 5:24
What * can hear, as we have, the Deu 5:26,27
realize that, as a * punishes his Deu 8:5
loan and the needy * cries out to Deu 15:9
slave, whether a * or woman, you Deu 15:12
"Every * in Israel shall appear Deu 16:16
a rich *, and never accept bribes. Deu 16:19
"If anyone, whether * or woman, Deu 17:2,3
true, then that * or woman shall Deu 17:5
However, never put a * to death Deu 17:6
happened to the * who refused God's Deu 17:13
* the Lord your God shall choose. Deu 17:15
me, an Israeli, a * to whom you Deu 18:15
cities: If a * goes into the Deu 19:5
he thought the other * would get. Deu 19:19
them with murdering an innocent *. Deu 21:8
"If a * has two wives but loves Deu 21:15
"If a * has a stubborn, Deu 21:18
"If a * has committed a crime Deu 21:22
* must not wear women's clothing. Deu 22:5
"If a * marries a girl, then Deu 22:13,14
with another *, saying, 'She was Deu 22:13,14
daughter to this * to be his wife, Deu 22:16
The judges shall sentence the * Deu 22:17,18
"If a * is discovered committing Deu 22:22
both she and the * who seduced her Deu 22:23,24
for help, and the * because he has Deu 22:23,24
the country, only the * shall die. Deu 22:25,26,27
If a * rapes a girl who is not Deu 22:28,29
he may never divorce her. A * Deu 22:30
from all evil. Any * who becomes Deu 23:9,10
Each * must have a spade as part Deu 23:13
"IF A * doesn't like something Deu 24:1
"A newly married * is not to be Deu 24:5
to another *, you must not enter Deu 24:10
If the * is poor and gives you Deu 24:12,13
"Never oppress a poor hired *, Deu 24:14,15
every * worthy of death shall be Deu 24:16
"IF A * is guilty of a crime, and Deu 25:1
what happens to a * who refuses to Deu 25:9
* who had his sandal pulled off!' Deu 25:10
of the other *, her hand shall be Deu 25:11
who takes advantage of a blind *.' Deu 27:18
as the blind * gropes in darkness. Deu 28:29
The most tenderhearted * among Deu 28:54
The day that any of you—* or Deu 29:18
will be hot against that *. Deu 29:20
The Lord will separate that * Deu 29:21
that Moses, the * of God, gave to Deu 33:1
and he was as strong as a young *. Deu 34:7
city of Jericho, a * appeared Jos 5:13
to which the guilty * belongs. Jos 7:14
Zabdi's family was brought * by Jos 7:18
was brought man by *, and his Jos 7:18
not one * survived or escaped, Jos 8:22
because of the prayer of one *. Jos 10:14
without having lost a single *! Jos 10:21
JOSHUA WAS NOW an old *. Jos 13:1
If a * is guilty of killing Jos 20:3
of the dead *, who may try to kill Jos 20:3
If a relative of the dead * Jos 20:5
accidental. The * who caused the Jos 20:6
killed another * could run to that Jos 20:9
to the one * who had sinned?" Jos 22:20
"I am an old * now, and you have Jos 23:2
a * coming out of the city. Ju 1:24
except for this * and his family. Ju 1:25
Later the * moved to Syria and Ju 1:26
Joshua, the * of God, died at Ju 2:7-9
Ehud was the * chosen to carry Ju 3:15
not one * was left alive. Ju 4:16
you the * you are looking for." Ju 4:22
Each * receives a girl or two; Ju 5:30
tents just as a * inside had Ju 7:12,13
and gave each * a trumpet and a Ju 7:16
we'd rather be killed by a *!" Ju 8:21
Literally, "For as the * is, so Ju 8:21f
died, an old, old *, and was buried Ju 8:32
sons—or by one *—meaning me, your Ju 9:2
blesses God and *, just to wave to Ju 9:9
both God and *, just to be mightier Ju 9:13
So the young * pierced him with Ju 9:54
by Jair, a * from Gilead, who Ju 10:3
If the * replied that he was not, Ju 12:5
her husband, "A * from God Ju 13:6
please let the * from God come back Ju 13:8
him, "The same * is here again!" Ju 13:10
"Are you the * who talked to my Ju 13:11
been best * at Samson's wedding. Ju 14:20
"so I married her to your best *. Ju 15:2
father gave her to another *." Ju 15:6
Spring of the * Who Prayed," and Ju 15:19
of Ephraim lived a * named Micah. Ju 17:1
The young * agreed to this, and Ju 17:10,11
to one * in his private home?" Ju 18:19
and appointed a * named Jonathan Ju 18:30
king, there was a * of the tribe of Ju 19:1
At first the * refused, but his Ju 19:7
But this time the * was adamant, Ju 19:10
Just then an old * came by on Ju 19:16
in Judah," the * replied. Ju 19:18
"Don't worry," the old * said, Ju 19:20
yelling at the old * to bring out Ju 19:22
to bring out the * who was staying Ju 19:22
The old * stepped outside to Ju 19:23
don't do such a thing to this *." Ju 19:24
And as one * they replied, "Not Ju 20:8,9,10
a * from the tribe of Benjamin. Ju 21:1
days, and every * did whatever he Ju 21:25
* named Elimelech, from Bethlehem, Ru 1:1
who was a very wealthy *. Ru 2:1
kind * to glean the free grain Ru 2:2
"Praise the Lord for a * like Ru 2:20
"Why, that * is one of our Ru 2:20
The * I'm thinking of is Boaz! Ru 3:2
a younger *, even though poor. Ru 3:10
The * replied, "All right, I'll Ru 4:4
"Then I can't do it," the * Ru 4:6
in Israel for a * transferring a Ru 4:7
So, as the * said to Boaz, "You Ru 4:8
and successful * in Bethlehem, and Ru 4:11
THIS IS THE story of Elkanah, a * 1Sa 1:1
If the * offering the sacrifice 1Sa 2:16
Literally, "* of God." 1Sa 2:27f
A * from the tribe of Benjamin 1Sa 4:12
the field of a * named Joshua and 1Sa 6:14
KISH WAS A rich, influential * 1Sa 9:1
was the most handsome * in Israel. 1Sa 9:2
you a * from the land of Benjamin. 1Sa 9:16
"That's the * I told you about! 1Sa 9:17
You must have the wrong *!" 1Sa 9:21
"This is the * the Lord has chosen 1Sa 10:24
"How can this * save us?" 1Sa 10:27
and they came to him as one *. 1Sa 11:7
old, grey-haired * who has been in 1Sa 12:2
for the Lord wants a * who will 1Sa 13:14
And he has discovered the * he 1Sa 13:14
strong young *, he conscripted him 1Sa 14:52
his mind, for he is not a *!" 1Sa 15:29
and find a * named Jesse, for I 1Sa 16:1
is the * the Lord has chosen!" 1Sa 16:6
is not the right * either." 1Sa 16:8
the son of a * named Jesse, who was 1Sa 16:18
He was a giant of a *, measuring 1Sa 17:4-7
If your * is able to kill me, 1Sa 17:9
Send me a * who will fight with 1Sa 17:10
"What will a * get for killing 1Sa 17:26
like you fight with a * like him? 1Sa 17:33
The stone sank in, and the * fell 1Sa 17:48,49
a * from Meholath, instead. 1Sa 18:19
"How can a poor * like me from an 1Sa 18:23
an innocent * by killing him? 1Sa 19:5
"You are a better * than I am, for 1Sa 24:17
A wealthy * from Maon owned a 1Sa 25:2
But the *, who was a descendant 1Sa 25:3
from murdering the * and carrying 1Sa 25:33
to marry a * from Gallim named 1Sa 25:44
the * he has chosen to be king! 1Sa 26:11
a *, then may he be cursed by God. 1Sa 26:19

(MAN Con't)
"I've got to talk to a dead *," 1Sa 28:7,8
"He is an old * wrapped in a 1Sa 28:14
This is the same * the women of 1Sa 29:5
The young * replied, "If you 1Sa 30:15
Three days later a * arrived from 2Sa 1:1
And the * replied, "Our entire 2Sa 1:4
Then David said to the young * 2Sa 1:13
* has fallen today in Israel; 2Sa 3:38
* in his own house and on his bed! 2Sa 4:11
He heard about a * named Ziba 2Sa 9:2
arrived at the home of the rich *. 2Sa 12:4
he vowed, "any * who would do a 2Sa 12:5
lambs to the poor * for the one he 2Sa 12:6
to David, "You are that rich *! 2Sa 12:7
wives to another *, and he will go 2Sa 12:11
passed Bahurim, a * came out of the 2Sa 16:5
"Because I work for the * who is 2Sa 16:18
what a mighty * your father is and 2Sa 17:10
to Bahurim where a * hid them 2Sa 17:18
I wouldn't do it," the * replied. 2Sa 18:12
Then Joab said to a * from Cush, 2Sa 18:21
The * bowed and ran off. 2Sa 18:21
there ahead of the * from Cush. 2Sa 18:23
saw a lone * running towards them. 2Sa 18:24
another * running towards them. 2Sa 18:26
"The first * looks like 2Sa 18:27
"He is a good * and comes with 2Sa 18:27
Then the * from Cush arrived and 2Sa 18:31
And the * replied, "May all of 2Sa 18:32
enemies be as that young * is!" 2Sa 18:32
and they responded as one *. 2Sa 19:14
Benjaminite), the * from Bahurim, 2Sa 19:16
All I want is a * named Sheba 2Sa 20:21
* who did his best to destroy us. 2Sa 21:5,6
David, the * to whom God gave such 2Sa 23:1
He was a very handsome *, and was 1Ki 1:6
He was an old, old * now, and 1Ki 1:15
to him, "for you are a good *; 1Ki 1:42
"I am going where every * on 1Ki 2:2
You are a wise * and will know 1Ki 2:6
You are a wise *, and you will 1Ki 2:9
court—one * from each 1Ki 4:7
so that each * was a month in 1Ki 5:14
King Solomon then asked for a * 1Ki 7:13
a * to be my people's leader.' 1Ki 8:16
This * was my father, David. 1Ki 8:17
"If a * is accused of doing 1Ki 8:31
to his guards, "Arrest that *!" 1Ki 13:4
the donkey," the old * said. 1Ki 13:13
Then the old * said to the 1Ki 13:15
But the old * said, "I am a 1Ki 13:18
But the old * was lying to him. 1Ki 13:18
came to the old *, and he shouted 1Ki 13:20
the meal, the old * saddled the 1Ki 13:23
at Shiloh—the * who told me that I 1Ki 14:2
He was an old * now, and could no 1Ki 14:4
every able-bodied * to help 1Ki 15:22
a * from Bethel, rebuilt Jericho. 1Ki 16:34
"O * of God," she cried, "what 1Ki 17:18
The * in charge of Ahab's 1Ki 18:3,4
"So it's you, is it?—the * who 1Ki 18:17
"Look what this * is doing," he 1Ki 20:7
*, "Strike me with your sword!" 1Ki 20:35
But the * refused. 1Ki 20:35
turned to another * and said, 1Ki 20:37
the battle, and a * brought me a 1Ki 20:39
a prisoner and said, 'Keep this *; 1Ki 20:39
have spared the * I said must die, 1Ki 20:42
NABOTH, A * from Jezreel, had a 1Ki 21:1
"That's the * we're after." 1Ki 22:32,33
"A * came up to us," they said, 2Ki 1:6
"He was a hairy *," they 2Ki 1:8
The captain said to him, "O * of 2Ki 1:9
But Elijah replied, "If I am a * 2Ki 1:10
men to demand, "O * of God, the 2Ki 1:11
Elijah replied, "If I am a * of 2Ki 1:12
with him, "O * of God, please 2Ki 1:13
He was a very evil *, but not as 2Ki 3:2
"He's just the * we want." 2Ki 3:12
mobilized every * who could fight, 2Ki 3:21
He was a * who had loved God, she 2Ki 4:1
"I'm sure this * who stops in from 2Ki 4:9
and her husband is an old *." 2Ki 4:14
"O * of God," she exclaimed, 2Ki 4:15,16
One day a * from Baal-shalishah 2Ki 4:42
Israel said: "The * bringing this 2Ki 5:6
"This * sends me a leper to heal! 2Ki 5:7
you to the * you're looking for." 2Ki 6:19
murderer has sent a * to kill me. 2Ki 6:32
a present to the * of God and tell 2Ki 8:8,9
and the young * poured the oil over 2Ki 9:6
So he told them what the * had 2Ki 9:12
couldn't stand against this *! 2Ki 10:4
But he was an evil *, for, like 2Ki 13:11
* revived and jumped to his feet! 2Ki 13:20,21
was an evil *, in God's opinion. 2Ki 21:6
Jerusalem as a * wipes a dish and 2Ki 21:13
"Tell the * who sent you to me, 2Ki 22:15,16
of Carmi, was the * who robbed God 1Ch 2:7
Joel was a cattle *, and he 1Ch 5:9
But the * was afraid to do it, so 1Ch 10:4
men, "The first * to kill a 1Ch 11:5,6
Jashobeam (the son of a * from 1Ch 11:11
of Zadok, a young * of unusual 1Ch 12:24-37
But Sibbecai, a * from Hushath, 1Ch 20:4
me, 'who will be a * of peace, for 1Ch 22:9
was an old, old *, so he stepped 1Ch 23:1
As for Moses, the * of God, his 1Ch 23:14,15
Zechariah, a * of unusual wisdom; 1Ch 26:14,15
wise counselor and an educated *. 1Ch 27:32
He is a brilliant *, the son of 2Ch 2:13
out so that not one * remained; 2Ch 14:13
old or young, * or woman. 2Ch 15:13
(son of Zichri), a * of unusual 2Ch 17:16
The * who went to get Micaiah 2Ch 18:12
reading," the * ventured. 2Ch 18:12
"Arrest this * and take him back 2Ch 18:25
that he was the * they were after. 2Ch 18:31
Israel, who was a very wicked *. 2Ch 20:35
King Jehoshaphat—a * who 2Ch 22:9
Zechariah was a * who had special 2Ch 26:5
He was a * who loved the soil and 2Ch 26:10
by the law of Moses the * of God; 2Ch 30:16
says, Tell the * who sent you, 2Ch 34:23
hard and stubborn * so far as 2Ch 36:13
the laws of Moses, the * of God. Ez 3:1
safekeeping of a * named Ez 5:14
He sent us an outstanding * named Ez 8:18
he was a very astute * and a Ez 8:18
You look like a * with deep Neh 2:1
Nehemiah is just the * we need!' Neh 6:7
what a wonderful * Tobiah was, and Neh 6:19
very faithful * who revered God Neh 7:2
of which a * shall live." Neh 9:29f
commanded by David, the * of God. Neh 12:24
that every * should rule his home, Est 1:22
This * had a beautiful and Est 2:7
anyone, whether * or woman, who Est 4:11
What a happy * was Haman as he Est 5:9
the greatest * in the kingdom next Est 5:11
honor a * who truly pleases me?" Est 6:6
to robe the * and to lead him Est 6:9
hang Mordecai, the * who saved the Est 7:9
THERE LIVED IN the land of Uz a * Job 1:1
* who feared God and stayed away Job 1:1
He is the finest * in all the Job 1:8
* who fears God and will have Job 1:8
Before this * finished, still Job 1:17
"He is the finest * in all the Job 2:3
the earth—a good * who fears God Job 2:3
Satan replied. "A * will give Job 2:4,5
Why is a * allowed to be born if Job 3:23
" 'Is mere * more just than God? Job 4:17
"How enviable the * whom God Job 5:17
they have food; a * complains when Job 6:5,6,7
What is mere * that you should Job 7:17
it is cut. A * without God is Job 8:14
God will not cast away a good *, Job 8:20
But how can a * be truly good in Job 9:2
with him, can a * answer even one Job 9:3
he sends death to snatch a * away, Job 9:12
The pride of * Job 9:13
for you are no mere * as I am. Job 9:32,33
us, no middle *, no mediator to Job 9:32,33
and despise me, a * you have made; Job 10:3
a * proved right by all this talk? Job 11:2
"Mere * is as likely to be wise Job 11:12
colt is likely to be born a *! Job 11:12
I, the * who begged God for Job 12:4
Yes, I, a righteous *, am now the Job 12:4
man, am now the * they scoff at. Job 12:4
When he closes in on a *, there Job 12:14
"HOW FRAIL IS *, how few his Job 14:1
But when a * dies and is buried, Job 14:10
in drought, so a * lies down for Job 14:11,12
"If a * dies, shall he live Job 14:14
So every hope of * is worn away. Job 14:18,19
"You are supposed to be a wise * Job 15:2
"Are you the wisest * alive? Job 15:7,8
What * in all the earth can be Job 15:14
"A wicked * is always in trouble Job 15:20
"This wicked * is fat and rich, Job 15:27,28
a * would listen to his neighbor. Job 16:21
for I do not find a wise * among Job 17:10
of the wicked * will be shortened; Job 18:7
that ever since * was first placed Job 20:4
Though still a young *, his Job 20:11
This is what awaits the wicked * Job 20:29
not *; no wonder my spirit is so Job 21:4
the * who sins, not his children! Job 21:19
that the evil * is usually spared Job 21:30-32
"Is mere * of any worth to God? Job 22:2
How can mere * stand before God Job 25:4
How much less is *, who is but a Job 25:6
"The evil * may accumulate money Job 27:16
Rather, it is the spirit in a *, Job 32:8,9
For God is greater than *. Job 33:12
broken, so that a * loses all Job 33:20
these things for *— brings back Job 33:29
care how great a * may be, and Job 34:19
crime before a * is called before Job 34:23
Again, he may prevent a vile * Job 34:29,
Your sins may hurt another *, or Job 3
am a * of well-rounded knowledge. Job 36
Well, does a * wish to be Job 37:19,
"Stand up like a * and brace Job 4
*, after living a long, good life. Job 42:
For you bless the godly *, O Ps 5:
The wicked * conceives an evil Ps 7:
*, to pay any attention to him! Ps 8
neither God nor * can ever keep Ps 10
O Lord, the poor * trusts himself Ps 10:
* will terrify them no longer. Ps 10:
THAT * IS a fool who says to Ps 14
a * shall stand firm forever. Ps 15
But I am a worm, not a *, scorned Ps 22
Where is the * who fears the Ps 25:1
I am forgotten like a dead *, Ps 31:1
This poor * cried to the Ps 34
Yes, the Lord hears the good * Ps 34:1
The good * does not escape all Ps 34:1
But the good * returns what he Ps 37:2
Lord forsake a * who loves him; Ps 37:2
The godly * is a good counselor Ps 37:30,3
a proud and evil *, towering like a Ps 37:35,3
But the good *—what a different Ps 37:3
For the good *—the blameless, the Ps 37:3
the upright, the * of peace—he has Ps 37:3
I am silent before them as a * Ps 38:13,1
Proud *! Ps 39:5,
When you punish a * for his Ps 39:1
cloth; yes, * is frail as breath. Ps 39:1
me—a * I completely trusted; Ps 41:
Rich *! Ps 49:1
Proud *! Ps 49:1
Proud man! Wise *! Ps 49:1
eternally. But * with all his pomp Ps 49:1
Though a * calls himself happy Ps 49:1
For * with all his pomp Ps 49:2
harm, O * with the lying tongue. Ps 52:
But it was you, a * like myself, Ps 55:1
him, what can mere * do to me? Ps 56:3,
of anything mere * can do to me! Ps 56:10,1
But may the godly * exult. Ps 68:
and like a mighty * aroused by Ps 78:6
Strengthen the * you love, Ps 80:17
Literally, "the * of your right Ps 80:17
Literally, "the son of * you made Ps 80:17
Give fair judgment to the poor * Ps 82:3
a splendid young * from the common Ps 89:19
of men? No * can live forever. Ps 89:48
A prayer of Moses, the * of God. Ps 90:1
You speak, and * turns back to Ps 90:3
change them like a * putting on a Ps 102:26
and grain for * to cultivate, and Ps 104:14
Literally, "He suffered no * to Ps 105:14f
yes, and Aaron, too, the * Ps 106:16
off his name from the memory of *. Ps 109:15
as easily as a * brushes a Ps 109:22,23
Yes, happy is the * who delights Ps 112:1
for the generous * who conducts his Ps 112:5
Such a * will not be overthrown Ps 112:6
What can mere * do to me? Ps 118:6
How can a young * stay pure? Ps 119:9
Children born to a young * are Ps 127:4
Happy is the * who has his Ps 127:5
full of them. That * shall have the Ps 127:5
Blessed is the * who destroys you Ps 137:8
Blessed is the * who takes your Ps 137:9
O Lord, what is * that you even Ps 144:3
Literally, "or the son of * that Ps 144:3f
For * is but a breath; Ps 144:4
for every * must die. Ps 146:4
But happy is the * who has the Ps 146:5
his sight is the strength of a *. Ps 147:10
How does a * become wise? Pro 1:7,8,9
EVERY YOUNG * who listens to me Pro 2:1
Lord can save a * from the flattery Pro 2:16,17
with both God and *, and a Pro 3:4,5
Young *, do not resent it when Pro 3:11,12
The * who knows right from wrong Pro 3:13,14,15
Literally, "the * that finds Pro 3:13,14,15f
than the * who is immensely rich! Pro 3:13,14,15
happy is the * who keeps on Pro 3:18
But the good * walks along in the Pro 4:18
* gropes and stumbles in the dark. Pro 4:19
The wicked * is doomed by his own Pro 5:22
you a worthless and a wicked *; Pro 6:12,13
Young *, obey your father and Pro 6:20
For a prostitute will bring a * Pro 6:26
Can a * hold fire against his Pro 6:27
So it is with the * who commits Pro 6:29
But the * who commits adultery is Pro 6:32
lad, a young * lacking common Pro 7:7
Happy is the * who is so anxious Pro 8:34
But a wise *, when rebuked, will Pro 9:7,8
Teach a wise *, and he will be Pro 9:9
teach a good *, and he will learn Pro 9:9
HAPPY IS THE * with a level-headed Pro 10:1
The Lord will not let a good * Pro 10:3
The good * is covered with Pro 10:6
evil * inwardly curses his luck. Pro 10:6

MAN Con't)
The wise * is glad to be Pro 10:8
A good * has firm footing, but a Pro 10:9
in what a good * says, but the Pro 10:11
the evil * is filled with curses. Pro 10:11
A wise * holds his tongue. Pro 10:14
The evil * squanders his on sin. Pro 10:16
When a good * speaks, he is worth Pro 10:20
A godly * gives good advice, but Pro 10:21
But the good * has a strong Pro 10:25
The good * gives wise advice, but Pro 10:31
A good * is guided by his Pro 11:3
the evil * is destroyed by his Pro 11:3
When an evil * dies, his hopes Pro 11:7
Or, "When a godless * slanders Pro 11:9f
is foolish; a * with good sense Pro 11:12
trustworthy * tries to quiet them. Pro 11:13
The evil * gets rich for the Pro 11:18
The good * finds life; Pro 11:19
the evil *, death. Pro 11:19
* will not go unpunished forever. Pro 11:21
The good * can look forward to Pro 11:23
Yes, the liberal * shall be rich! Pro 11:24,25
People curse the * who holds his Pro 11:26
but they bless the * who sells it Pro 11:26
shall be the servant of a wiser *. Pro 11:29
Everyone admires a * with good Pro 12:8
* with a warped mind is despised. Pro 12:8
A good * is concerned for the Pro 12:10
Lies will get any * into trouble, Pro 12:13
Telling the truth gives a * great Pro 12:14
but a wise * listens to others. Pro 12:15
a wise * stays cool when Pro 12:16
A good * is known by his Pro 12:17
a false * by deceit and lies. Pro 12:17
A wise * doesn't display his Pro 12:23
The good * asks advice from Pro 12:26
A lazy * won't even dress the Pro 12:27
but the diligent * makes good use Pro 12:27
The good * wins his case by Pro 13:2
A good * hates lies; Pro 13:5
ransom never worries the poor *! Pro 13:8
The advice of a wise * refreshes Pro 13:14
A * with good sense is Pro 13:15
A treacherous * must walk a rocky Pro 13:15
A wise * thinks ahead; Pro 13:16
When a good * dies, he leaves an Pro 13:22
The good * eats to live, while Pro 13:25
while the evil * lives to eat. Pro 13:25
easily to the * with common sense. Pro 14:6
The wise * looks ahead. Pro 14:8
Before every * there lies a wide Pro 14:12
A prudent * checks to see where Pro 14:15
A wise * is cautious and avoids Pro 14:16
A short-tempered * is a fool. Pro 14:17
He hates the * who is patient. Pro 14:17
the wise * is crowned with Pro 14:18
despise the poor *, while the rich Pro 14:20
Reverence for God gives a * deep Pro 14:26
its waters keep a * from death. Pro 14:27
A wise * controls his temper. Pro 14:29
A wise * is hungry for truth, Pro 15:14
When a * is gloomy, everything Pro 15:15
A quick-tempered * starts fights; Pro 15:18
a cool-tempered * tries to stop Pro 15:18
If a * enjoys folly, something is Pro 15:21
A good * thinks before he speaks; Pro 15:28
the evil * pours out his evil Pro 15:28
When a * is trying to please God, Pro 16:7
and a wise * will appease it. Pro 16:14
happy the * who puts his trust in Pro 16:20
The wise * is known by his common Pro 16:21
Before every * there lies a wide Pro 16:25
Literally, "A worthless * devises Pro 16:27f
An evil * sows strife; Pro 16:28
Or, "An evil * deceives his Pro 16:29f
The wicked * stares into space Pro 16:30
A rebuke to a * of common sense Pro 17:10
An evil * is suspicious of Pro 17:20
The * of few words and settled Pro 17:27,28
THE SELFISH * quarrels against Pro 18:1
A lazy * is brother to the Pro 18:9
The rich * thinks of his wealth Pro 18:11
The intelligent * is always open Pro 18:15
The * who finds a wife finds a Pro 18:22
The poor * pleads and the rich Pro 18:23
the rich * answers with insults. Pro 18:23
A * may ruin his chances by his Pro 19:3
A wealthy * has many "friends"; Pro 19:4
the poor * has none left. Pro 19:4
Many beg favors from a * who is Pro 19:6
A wise * restrains his anger and Pro 19:11
A lazy * sleeps soundly—and goes Pro 19:15
A short-tempered * must bear his Pro 19:19
* proposes, but God disposes. Pro 19:21
Kindness makes a * attractive. Pro 19:22
Reprove a wise * and he will be Pro 19:25
It is an honor for a * to stay Pro 20:3
the wise * will draw it out. Pro 20:5
God puts out the light of the * Pro 20:20
A * is known by his actions. Pro 21:8
An evil * lives an evil life; Pro 21:8
a good * lives a godly life. Pro 21:8
An evil * loves to harm others; Pro 21:10
The wise * learns by listening; Pro 21:11
An angry * is silenced by giving Pro 21:14
A good * loves justice, but it is Pro 21:15
The * who strays away from common Pro 21:16
A * who loves pleasure becomes Pro 21:17
The wise * saves for the future, Pro 21:20
but the foolish * spends whatever Pro 21:20
The * who tries to be good, Pro 21:21
The wise * conquers the strong Pro 21:22
strong * and levels his defenses. Pro 21:22
The lazy * longs for many things Pro 21:25,26
An evil * is stubborn, but a Pro 21:29
but a godly * will reconsider. Pro 21:29
Or, "The wicked * is brazen; Pro 21:29f
the godly * is thoughtful." Pro 21:29f
A prudent * foresees the Pro 22:3
* to riches, honor and long life. Pro 22:4
road; the * who values his soul Pro 22:5
Happy is the generous *, the one Pro 22:9
The lazy * is full of excuses. Pro 22:13
Do you know a hard-working *? Pro 22:29
WHEN DINING WITH a rich *, Pro 23:1
if you become a * of common sense. Pro 23:15,16
much sleep clothes a * with rags. Pro 23:19,20,21
The father of a godly * has Pro 23:24,25
Who is the * with bloodshot eyes Pro 23:29,30
A wise * is mightier than a Pro 24:5
man is mightier than a strong *. Pro 24:5
O evil *, leave the upright man Pro 24:15,16
O evil man, leave the upright * Pro 24:15,16
Don't you know that this good *, Pro 24:15,16
For the evil * has no future; Pro 24:19,20
in an unreliable * is like chewing Pro 25:19
If a godly * compromises with the Pro 25:26
A * without self-control is as Pro 25:28
and that is a * who is conceited. Pro 26:12
The lazy * won't go out and work. Pro 26:13
A * who is caught lying to his Pro 26:18,19
A quarrelsome * starts fights as Pro 26:21
A * with hate in his heart may Pro 26:24,25,26
The * who sets a trap for others Pro 26:27
Even honey seems tasteless to a * Pro 27:7
A * who strays from home is like Pro 27:8
A sensible * watches for problems Pro 27:12
credit risk is the * who agrees to Pro 27:13
a crucible, but a * is tested by Pro 27:21
When a poor * oppresses those Pro 28:3
A * who refuses to admit his Pro 28:13
Blessed is the * who reveres God, Pro 28:14
God, but the * who doesn't care is Pro 28:14
The * who wants to do right will Pro 28:20
But the * who wants to get rich Pro 28:20
A * who robs his parents and Pro 28:24
A * is a fool to trust Pro 28:26
THE * WHO is often reproved but Pro 29:1
The good * knows the poor man's Pro 29:7
a wise * holds his temper in and Pro 29:11
fool than for a * of quick temper. Pro 29:20
A hot-tempered * starts fights Pro 29:22
A * who assists a thief must Pro 29:24
Fear of * is a dangerous trap, Pro 29:25
I cannot understand *, Pro 30:3
Never falsely accuse a * to his Pro 30:10
A * who mocks his father and Pro 30:17
The growth of love between a * and Pro 30:18,19
Literally "the way of a * with a Pro 30:18,19f
For what does a * get for all Ecc 1:3-7
I discovered that the lot of *, Ecc 1:12-15
Literally, "for what can the * do Ecc 2:12f
for the wise * sees, while the Ecc 2:13,14
my son will be a wise * or a fool? Ecc 2:19
So what does a * get for all his Ecc 2:20-23
better for a * to do than to enjoy Ecc 2:24-26
of men, even so, * cannot see the Ecc 3:11
better for a * than to be happy and Ecc 3:12
God's purpose in this is that * Ecc 3:14
* does, both good and bad." Ecc 3:17
that the spirit of * goes upward Ecc 3:21
This is the case of a * who is Ecc 4:8
but if a * falls when he is Ecc 4:10
If you see some poor * being Ecc 5:8
your fingers! The * who works hard Ecc 5:12
to one's son. The * who speculates Ecc 5:15
good: it is for a * to eat well, Ecc 5:18
is very good if a * has received Ecc 5:19,20
Even if a * has a hundred sons Ecc 6:3
than to be an old, unhappy *. Ecc 6:5
Though a * lives a thousand Ecc 6:6
yet the poor * who is wise lives a Ecc 6:7,8
it was known long ago what each * Ecc 6:10
Yes, a wise * thinks much of Ecc 7:4
* than to be praised by a fool! Ecc 7:5
The wise * is turned into a fool Ecc 7:7
A wise * is stronger than the Ecc 7:19
And there is not a single * in Ecc 7:20
The wise * will find a time and a Ecc 8:5
But though a * sins a hundred Ecc 8:12
earth than that a * should eat, Ecc 8:15
even the wisest * who says he knows Ecc 8:16,17
nor the strongest * the battle, and Ecc 9:11
the right time. A * never knows Ecc 9:12
There was in the city a wise *, Ecc 9:15
if the wise * is poor, he will be Ecc 9:16
words of a wise * are better than Ecc 9:17
nor the rich *, either; Ecc 10:20
Young *, it's wonderful to be Ecc 11:9
withered old *, dragging himself Ecc 12:5
only a wise *, but a good teacher; Ecc 12:10
for this is the entire duty of *. Ecc 12:13
drown it. If a * tried to buy it Sol 8:7
Puny *! Is 2:22
In those days a * will say to his Is 3:6
But all is well for the godly *. Is 3:10
Entrust it to some godly * to Is 8:16
power than the * who uses it? Is 10:15
Is the saw greater than the * who Is 10:15
as when a sick * wastes away. Is 10:18
* and the haughtiness of the rich. Is 13:11
you into captivity, O strong *! Is 22:17
As a hungry * dreams of eating, Is 29:8
and as a thirsty * dreams of Is 29:8
the violent * who fights at the Is 29:21
drop of a hat, the * who waits in Is 29:21
recognize an evil * when he sees Is 32:6
The lame * will leap up like a Is 35:6
"Shout that * is like the grass Is 40:6
And so it is with fragile *. Is 40:7
its neck? The * too poor to buy Is 40:20
rot and hire a * to carve a face on Is 40:20
Each * encourages his neighbor Is 41:6
wood and carves the figure of a *. Is 44:13
The * never stops to think or Is 44:19
Woe to the * who fights with his Is 45:9
the earth and created * upon it. Is 45:12
east—that * Cyrus from far away. Is 46:11
prey from the hands of a mighty *? Is 49:24
and rejected him—a * of sorrows, Is 53:3
Blessed is the * who refuses to Is 56:2
and blessed is the * who checks Is 56:2
Our courts oppose the righteous *; Is 59:14
of a young * who marries a virgin; Is 62:5
In those days, when a * builds a Is 65:21,22
with pity on the * who has a humble Is 66:2
that if a * divorces a woman who Jer 3:1
can find one fair and honest *! Jer 5:1
The Lord says: Let not the wise * Jer 9:23
nor the mighty * in his might, nor Jer 9:23
nor the rich * in his riches. Jer 9:23
the power of * to map his life and Jer 10:23
is the * who does not heed it! Jer 11:1
"Let's destroy this * and all Jer 11:19
again, each * to his inheritance. Jer 12:15
Can a * break bars of northern Jer 15:12,13
The Lord says: Cursed is the * Jer 17:5
trust in mortal * and turns his Jer 17:5
But blessed is the * who trusts Jer 17:7
away, so is the * who gets his Jer 17:11
you 'The * Who Lives in Terror.' Jer 20:3
Cursed be the * who brought my Jer 20:15
you like a fire no * can quench. Jer 21:12
This is how a * lives close to Jer 22:16
This * Coniah is like a Jer 22:28
Record this * Coniah as childless, Jer 22:30
This * Coniah's grandson, Jer 22:30f
"This * should die!" Jer 26:11
an innocent * and the Jer 26:15
prophets, "This * does not deserve Jer 26:16
"a woman shall encompass a *." Jer 31:22f
This land—though every * and Jer 33:12
the * after God's own heart. Jer 33:15f
people too. This * is a traitor." Jer 38:4
shall live—not a *, woman or child Jer 44:7
and call him "The * with No Power Jer 46:17
I AM THE * who has seen the Lam 3:1
It is good for a young * to be Lam 3:27
in a moment without the hand of *. Lam 4:6
Each had the face of a * [in Eze 1:10
someone who appeared to be a *. Eze 1:26
Or, "son of *" . Eze 2:1f
The connotation is "mortal *." Eze 2:1f
And if a good * becomes bad, and Eze 3:20
I saw what appeared to be a *; Eze 8:2
And the Lord called to the * with Eze 9:3
Just then the * in linen Eze 9:11
Then the Lord spoke to the * in Eze 10:2
of the Temple when the * went in. Eze 10:3
When the Lord told the * in linen Eze 10:6
the wheels, the * went in and stood Eze 10:6
the hands of the * in linen Eze 10:7,8
to destroy both * and beast. Eze 14:13
the plague kills * and beast alike, Eze 14:19
to every * who came along. Eze 16:15
beauty to every * who came by, in Eze 16:25
"But if a * is just and does Eze 18:5
obeys my laws—that * is just, says Eze 18:9
"But if that * has a son who is Eze 18:10
—shall that * live? Eze 18:13
"But if this sinful * has, in Eze 18:14
When a good * turns away from Eze 18:26

(MAN Con't)

* appears who has a right to it.	Eze 21:27
But you are only a *, and not a	Eze 28:2,3
you will be no god, but merely *!	Eze 28:9
and neither * nor animal will	Eze 32:13
'O wicked *, you will die!'	Eze 33:8
of a righteous * will not save him	Eze 33:12
and the sins of an evil * will	Eze 33:12
"I have said the good * will	Eze 33:13
For again I say, when the good *	Eze 33:18
again by the time the * arrived.	Eze 33:22
was only one * and yet he got	Eze 33:24
Going nearer, I saw a * whose	Eze 40:3
The * began to measure the wall	Eze 40:5
One face—that of a *—looked	Eze 41:19,20
the Temple (the * who had been	Eze 43:6
it shall never be opened. No *	Eze 44:2
"There isn't a * alive who can	Dan 2:10
Daniel replied, "No wise *,	Dan 2:27
statue of a *, shining brilliantly,	Dan 2:31
At last Daniel came in—the * I	Dan 4:8
after my god—the * in whom is the	Dan 4:8
mind of an animal instead of a *.	Dan 4:16
For there is a * in your kingdom	Dan 5:11
In the days of your father this *	Dan 5:11
Call for this *, Daniel—or	Dan 5:12
a favor of God or *—except from	Dan 6:7
or *—except you—for thirty days?	Dan 6:12
the ground, on two feet, like a *;	Dan 7:4
Next I saw the arrival of a *—or	Dan 7:13
vision, suddenly a * was standing	Dan 8:15
he looked like a *— and I heard a	Dan 8:15
"Son of *," he said, "you must	Dan 8:17
Then someone—he looked like a *	Dan 10:16
Then the one who seemed to be a *	Dan 10:18
will be an evil * not directly in	Dan 11:21
And one of them asked the * in	Dan 12:6
one honest * is found among you?	Hos 8:5
As a * would lead his favorite	Hos 11:4
For I am God and not *;	Hos 11:9
when he became a *, he even	Hos 12:3
"And a * and his father defile	Amo 2:7
In that day you will be as a *	Amo 5:19
by a bear, or a * in a dark room	Amo 5:19
In that day not one wise *	Ob 1:8
It is as hard to find an honest *	Mic 7:1
not one fair-minded * is left.	Mic 7:1
The rich * pays them off and	Mic 7:3
Sound the alarm! * the ramparts!	Nah 2:1
but the righteous * trusts in me,	Hab 2:4
as a blind * searching for a path,	Zep 1:17
night: I saw a * sitting on a red	Zec 1:8
me again, I saw a * carrying a	Zec 2:1
"Go tell this young *," said	Zec 2:4
'You represent the * who will come,	Zec 6:12
formed the spirit of * within him:	Zec 12:1
my Shepherd, the * who is my	Zec 13:7
"Cursed is that * who promises	Mal 1:14
every last *, whether priest or	Mal 2:12
"Will a * rob God?	Mal 3:8
And I will spare them as a *	Mal 3:17
being a * of stern principle,	Mt 1:19
Literally, "a just *."	Mt 1:19f
But I say that a * who divorces	Mt 5:32
"The law of Moses says, 'If a *	Mt 5:38
are wise, like a * who builds his	Mt 7:24
a * who builds his house on sand.	Mt 7:26
Jesus touches the *.	Mt 8:3
Literally, "See you tell no *."	Mt 8:4f
Literally, "the Son of *."	Mt 8:20f
"Blasphemy! This * is saying he	Mt 9:3
Literally, "the Son of *."	Mt 9:5,6f
it to you by healing this *."	Mt 9:5,6
to the paralyzed *, he commanded,	Mt 9:5,6
for giving such authority to a *!	Mt 9:8
Leaving that place, Jesus met a *	Mt 9:32
and instantly the * could talk.	Mt 9:33
search for a godly * and stay in	Mt 10:11
Literally, "the Son of *."	Mt 10:23f
I have come to set a * against	Mt 10:35
because he is a * of God, you will	Mt 10:41
Or were you expecting to see a *	Mt 11:8
For John is the * mentioned in	Mt 11:10
Literally, "the Son of *."	Mt 11:19f
and a drinking *, and hang around	Mt 11:19
Literally, "the Son of *."	Mt 12:8f
there a * with a deformed hand.	Mt 12:10
Then he said to the *,	Mt 12:13
Then a demon-possessed *—he was	Mt 12:22
Literally, "the Son of *."	Mt 12:31,32f
An evil-hearted * is filled with	Mt 12:35
Literally, "the Son of *."	Mt 12:39,40f
"This evil nation is like a *	Mt 12:43,44,45
will return to the * I came from.'	Mt 12:43,44,45
all enter the * and live in him.	Mt 12:43,44,45
Many a prophet and godly * has	Mt 13:17
the heart of a * who hears the	Mt 13:20
represents a * who hears the	Mt 13:22
the heart of a * who listens to the	Mt 13:23
Literally, "the Son of *."	Mt 13:37f
Literally, "the Son of *."	Mt 13:41f
a * discovered in a field.	Mt 13:44
* of little faith," Jesus said.	Mt 14:31
comes out of a * defiles a man."	Mt 15:11f
comes out of a man defiles a *."	Mt 15:11f
and defile the * who says them.	Mt 15:18
Literally, "the Son of *."	Mt 16:13f
Literally, "the Son of *."	Mt 17:12f
for them. A * came and knelt before	Mt 17:14
to the * who does the tempting.	Mt 18:7
Literally, "the Son of *."	Mt 18:11f
"If a * has a hundred sheep, and	Mt 18:12
"But the * fell down before the	Mt 18:26
"But when the * left the king,	Mt 18:28
he went to a * who owed him $2,000	Mt 18:28
"The * fell down before him and	Mt 18:29
He had the * arrested and jailed	Mt 18:30
before him the * he had forgiven	Mt 18:32
"Then the angry king sent the *	Mt 18:34
God created * and woman, and that	Mt 19:4
woman, and that a * should leave	Mt 19:5,6
And no * may divorce what God has	Mt 19:5,6
"did Moses say a * may divorce his	Mt 19:7
"And the * who marries a divorced	Mt 19:9f
the * asked.	Mt 19:18
But when the young * heard	Mt 19:22
for a rich * to get into the	Mt 19:23
* to enter the Kingdom of God!"	Mt 19:24
Literally, "the Son of *."	Mt 19:28f
Literally, "the Son of *."	Mt 20:18f
Literally, "the Son of *."	Mt 20:28f
"God's * is here!	Mt 21:9
about this? A * with two sons told	Mt 21:28
he noticed a * who wasn't wearing	Mt 22:11
And the * had no reply.	Mt 22:12
said that if a * died without	Mt 22:24
Literally, "the Son of *."	Mt 24:27f
"of the coming of the Son of *."	Mt 24:30f
"Just as a * can prevent trouble	Mt 24:43
by the story of a * going into	Mt 25:14
on his trip. The * who received	Mt 25:16
$5,000. The * with $2,000 went	Mt 25:17
"But the * who received the	Mt 25:18
his money. The * to whom he had	Mt 25:20
"Next came the * who had	Mt 25:22
"Then the * with the $1,000 came	Mt 25:24,25
you were a hard *, and I was afraid	Mt 25:24,25
his master replied, 'Wicked *!	Mt 25:26
Take the money from this * and	Mt 25:28
give it to the * with the $10,000.	Mt 25:28
For the * who uses well what he	Mt 25:29
But from the * who is unfaithful,	Mt 25:29
Literally, "the Son of *."	Mt 25:31f
Literally, "the Son of *."	Mt 26:2f
Literally, "the Son of * goes."	Mt 26:24f
to the * by whom I am betrayed.	Mt 26:24
Literally, "the Son of *."	Mt 26:45f
Here comes the * who is betraying	Mt 26:46
them to arrest the * he greeted,	Mt 26:48
declared, "This * said, 'I am able	Mt 26:60,61
Literally, "the Son of *."	Mt 26:64f
* was with Jesus—from Nazareth."	Mt 26:71
"I don't even know the *," he	Mt 26:72
"I don't even know the *," he	Mt 26:74
I have betrayed an innocent *."	Mt 27:4
"Leave that good * alone;	Mt 27:19
of the blood of this good *.	Mt 27:24
they came across a * from Cyrene,	Mt 27:32
Or, "a godly *."	Mt 27:54f
When evening came, a rich * from	Mt 27:57
A * possessed by a demon was	Mk 1:23
no more and to come out of the *.	Mk 1:25
the * violently and left him.	Mk 1:26
leprosy was gone—the * was healed!	Mk 1:42
But as the * went on his way he	Mk 1:45
a paralyzed * on a stretcher.	Mk 2:3
lowered the sick * on his	Mk 2:4
said to the sick *, "Son, your	Mk 2:5
Literally, "Son of *."	Mk 2:9,10,11f
it to you by healing this *."	Mk 2:9,10,11
to the paralyzed *, he commanded,	Mk 2:9,10,11
The * jumped up, took the	Mk 2:12
made to benefit *, and not man to	Mk 2:27
and not * to benefit the Sabbath.	Mk 2:27
Literally, "the Son of *."	Mk 2:28f
a * there with a deformed hand.	Mk 3:1
Jesus asked the * to come and	Mk 3:3
to the *, "Reach out your hand."	Mk 3:5
just as a strong * must be tied	Mk 3:27
that any sin of * can be forgiven,	Mk 3:28
"Who is this *, that even the	Mk 4:41
a demon-possessed * ran out from a	Mk 5:1
This * lived among the	Mk 5:3,4
on the water, the * had seen him	Mk 5:6
demon within the * and said, "Come	Mk 5:7,8
many of us here within this *."	Mk 5:9
came out of the * and entered the	Mk 5:13
but as they saw the * sitting	Mk 5:15
into the boat. The * who had been	Mk 5:18
So the * started off to visit the	Mk 5:20
just a local * like themselves.	Mk 6:2,3
"it is John, the * I beheaded.	Mk 6:16
a good and holy *, and so he kept	Mk 6:
all right for a * to disregard his	Mk 7:
"If any * has ears to hear, let	Mk 7:15,1
out of the * defiles the man."	Mk 7:15,1
out of the man defiles the *."	Mk 7:15,1
A deaf * with a speech	Mk 7:
his hands on the * and heal him.	Mk 7:
Instantly the * could hear	Mk 7:
brought a blind * to him and begged	Mk 8:2
Jesus took the blind * by the	Mk 8:2
The * looked around.	Mk 8:2
again and as the * stared intently,	Mk 8:2
Literally, "the Son of *."	Mk 8:3
"And how does a * benefit if he	Mk 8:3
Literally, "the Son of *."	Mk 8:3
Literally, "the Son of *."	Mk 9:
Literally, "the Son of *."	Mk 9:12,1
Literally, "the Son of *."	Mk 9:30,3
we saw a * using your name to cast	Mk 9:3
be better for that * if a huge	Mk 9:4
"He said that all a * has to do	Mk 10:
For from the very first he made *	Mk 10:6,
therefore a * is to leave his	Mk 10:6,
And no * may separate what God	Mk 10:
He told them, "When a * divorces	Mk 10:1
out on a trip, a * came running to	Mk 10:1
"Teacher," the * replied,	Mk 10:2
for this * as he looked at him.	Mk 10:2
* to enter the Kingdom of God."	Mk 10:2
can be saved, if not a rich *?"	Mk 10:2
Literally, "the Son of *."	Mk 10:33
Literally, "the Son of *."	Mk 10:45
So they called the blind *.	Mk 10:4
"O Teacher," the blind * said,	Mk 10:5
And instantly the blind * could	Mk 10:5
"A * planted a vineyard and built	Mk 12:
But the farmers beat up the *	Mk 12:
The next * he sent was killed;	Mk 12:
a law that when a * dies without	Mk 12:1
Literally, "the Son of *."	Mk 13:26
can be compared with that of a *	Mk 13:34
"you will see a * coming towards	Mk 14:13
enters, tell the * in charge, 'Our	Mk 14:14
Literally, "the Son of *."	Mk 14:21f
misery ahead for the * by whom I	Mk 14:21
Literally, "the Son of *."	Mk 14:21f
new agreement between God and *.	Mk 14:24
Literally, "the Son of *."	Mk 14:41f
There was, however, a young *	Mk 14:51,52
Literally, "the Son of *."	Mk 14:62f
with this * you call your king?"	Mk 15:12
So one * ran and got a sponge	Mk 15:36
sat a young * clothed in white.	Mk 16:5
He will be a * of rugged	Lk 1:17
I'm an old * now, and my wife is	Lk 1:18
to be married to a * named Joseph,	Lk 1:27
That day a * named Simeon, a	Lk 2:25
He was a good *, very devout,	Lk 2:25
wise, and was loved by God and *.	Lk 2:52
Literally, "* shall not live by	Lk 4:4f
the synagogue, a * possessed by a	Lk 4:33
The demon threw the * to the	Lk 4:35
there was a * with an advanced case	Lk 5:12
* and said, "Of course I will.	Lk 5:13
a paralyzed * on a sleeping mat.	Lk 5:18,19
lowered the sick * down into the	Lk 5:18,19
Jesus said to the *, "My friend,	Lk 5:20
Literally, "the Son of *."	Lk 5:23,24f
it to you by healing this *."	Lk 5:23,24
to the paralyzed *, he commanded,	Lk 5:23,24
watched, the * jumped to his feet,	Lk 5:25
Literally, "the Son of *."	Lk 6:5f
teaching, and a * was present whose	Lk 6:6
he would heal the * that day, since	Lk 6:7
But he said to the * with the	Lk 6:8
to the *, "Reach out your hand."	Lk 6:10
"on account of the Son of *."	Lk 6:22f
for one blind * to lead another?	Lk 6:39
A good * produces good deeds	Lk 6:45
And an evil * produces evil deeds	Lk 6:45
obey me are like a * who builds a	Lk 6:47,48
obey are like a * who builds a	Lk 6:49
to come with them and help the *.	Lk 7:4
I met a * with faith like this."	Lk 7:9
"Who is this * you went out into	Lk 7:24
this story: "A * loaned money to	Lk 7:41
"Who does this * think he is,	Lk 7:49
"Who is this *, that even the	Lk 8:25
out of the boat a * from the city	Lk 8:27
to meet him, a * who had been	Lk 8:27
control of the * so that even when	Lk 8:29
the * was filled with thousands	Lk 8:30
So they left the * and went into	Lk 8:33
and saw the * who had been	Lk 8:35
demon-possessed * had been healed.	Lk 8:36
The * who had been	Lk 8:38
And now a * named Jairus, a	Lk 8:41
"so who is this * about whom I	Lk 9:9
Literally, "the Son of *."	Lk 9:22f
Literally, "the Son of *."	Lk 9:26f
met him, and a * in the crowd	Lk 9:38

MAN Con't)
Literally, "the Son of *." Lk 9:44f
For the Son of * has not come to Lk 9:55f
Literally, "the Son of *." Lk 9:58f
Another time, when he invited a * Lk 9:59
his disciple, the * agreed—but Lk 9:59
meaning that the * could, when his Lk 9:59f
what does a * need to do to live Lk 10:25
The * wanted to justify (his lack Lk 10:29
and when he saw the * lying Lk 10:31
Then he put the * on his donkey Lk 10:34
told him to take care of the *. Lk 10:35
The * replied, "The one who Lk 10:37
out a demon from a * who couldn't Lk 11:14
"When a demon is cast out of a * Lk 11:24
itself, and they all enter the *. Lk 11:26
Literally, "the Son of *." Lk 12:8f
Literally, "the Son of *." Lk 12:10f
But Jesus replied, "*, who made Lk 12:14
"A rich * had a fertile farm that Lk 12:16
"Yes, every * is a fool who gets Lk 12:21
Literally, "the Son of *." Lk 12:40f
faithful, sensible * whose master Lk 12:42,43,44
"But if the * begins to think, Lk 12:45
illustration: "A * planted a fig Lk 13:6
if he would heal a * who was Lk 14:1
a * on the Sabbath day, or not?" Lk 14:3
took the sick * by the hand and Lk 14:4
'Let this * sit here instead.' Lk 14:9
Hearing this, a * sitting at the Lk 14:15
illustration: "A * prepared a Lk 14:16
this story: "A * had two sons. Lk 15:11
Please take me on as a hired *." Lk 15:19
"A rich * hired an accountant to Lk 16:1
of olive oil,' the * replied. Lk 16:5,6
he asked the next *. Lk 16:7
"The rich * had to admire the Lk 16:8
Or, "Do you think the rich * Lk 16:8f
"There was a certain rich *," Lk 16:19
The rich * also died and was Lk 16:22
"Then the rich * said, 'O Father Lk 16:27
"The rich * replied, 'No, Father Lk 16:30
to the * who does the tempting. Lk 17:1
he had done. This * was a despised Lk 17:16
And Jesus said to the *, "Stand Lk 17:19
Or, "long for the Son of *." Lk 17:22f
"a very godless * who had great Lk 18:2
against a * who had harmed her. Lk 18:3
" 'I fear neither God nor *,' he Lk 18:4,5
Literally, "the Son of *." Lk 18:8f
The * replied, "I've obeyed Lk 18:21
But when the * heard this he went Lk 18:23
* to enter the Kingdom of God." Lk 18:25
Jericho, a blind * was sitting Lk 18:35
tried to hush the *, but he only Lk 18:39
"Bring the blind * over here," Lk 18:40
Then Jesus asked the *, "What Lk 18:41
And instantly the * could see, Lk 18:43
through Jericho, a * named Lk 19:1
a very rich *), tried to get a Lk 19:1
home today. This * was one of the Lk 19:9,10
Literally, "the Son of *." Lk 19:9,10f
"The first * reported a Lk 19:16
'You are a good *. Lk 19:17
"The next * also reported a Lk 19:18
"But the third * brought back Lk 19:20
for you are a hard * to deal Lk 19:21
it to the * who earned the most.' Lk 19:24
this story: "A * planted a Lk 20:9
A third * was sent and the same Lk 20:12
state that if a * dies without Lk 20:28
the dead *, to carry on his name. Lk 20:28
Literally, "the Son of *." Lk 21:27f
you will see a * walking along Lk 22:10
and say to the * who lives there, Lk 22:11
is the * who will betray me. Lk 22:21
Literally, "the Son of *." Lk 22:22f
awaiting that * who betrays me." Lk 22:22
Finally she spoke: "This * was Lk 22:56
said, "I don't even know the *!" Lk 22:57
But Peter said, "*, I don't know Lk 22:60
Literally, "the Son of *." Lk 22:69f
"You brought this * to me, Lk 23:14
to us—nothing this * has done calls Lk 23:15
And he released Barabbas, the * Lk 23:25
* hasn't done one thing wrong." Lk 23:40,41
"Surely this * was innocent." Lk 23:47
Then a * named Joseph, a member Lk 23:50,51,52
He was a godly * who had been Lk 23:50,51,52
Literally, "the Son of *." Lk 24:6,7f
the * from Nazareth," they said. Lk 24:19
highly regarded by both God and *. Lk 24:19
I said, 'Soon a * far greater than Jn 1:30
I saw it happen to this *, and Jn 1:34
honest *—a true son of Israel." Jn 1:47
Literally, "the Son of *." Jn 1:51f
How can an old * go back into his Jn 3:4
Literally, "the Son of *." Jn 3:13f
"Master, the * you met on the Jn 3:26
* so that everyone will go to him. Jn 3:28
The Father loves this * because Jn 3:35
to the * you're living with now." Jn 4:17,18
"Come and meet a * who told me Jn 4:28,29
While he was there, a * in the Jn 4:46,47
in Galilee. This * went over to Jn 4:46,47
And the * believed Jesus and Jn 4:50
"I can't," the sick * said, Jn 5:7
Instantly, the * was healed! Jn 5:9
They said to the * who was cured, Jn 5:10
"The * who healed me told me Jn 5:11
The * didn't know, and Jesus had Jn 5:13
Then the * went to find the Jn 5:15
because he is the Son of *. Jn 5:27
have is not from a *, though I have Jn 5:34
Literally, "the Son of *." Jn 6:27f
"How can this * give us his Jn 6:52
Literally, "Son of *." Jn 6:53f
Literally, "the Son of *." Jn 6:62f
Some said, "He's a wonderful * Jn 7:12
a *, and you were surprised. Jn 7:21,22,23
* completely well on the Sabbath? Jn 7:21,22,23
the * they are trying to kill? Jn 7:25
For we know where this * was Jn 7:27
to do that this * hasn't done?" Jn 7:31
declared, "This * surely is the Jn 7:40
"Is it legal to convict a * Jn 7:51
you have lifted up the Son of *." Jn 8:28f
been slaves to any * on earth! Jn 8:33
you will keep a * from dying! Jn 8:52
he saw a * blind from birth. Jn 9:1
him, "why was this * born blind? Jn 9:2
So the * went where he was sent Jn 9:7
"It can't be the same *," they Jn 9:9
beggar said, "I am the same *!" Jn 9:9
And he told them, "A * they call Jn 9:11
Then they took the * to the Jn 9:13
turned on the * who had been blind Jn 9:17
demanded, "This * who opened your Jn 9:17
sent from God," the * replied. Jn 9:17
they called in the * who had been Jn 9:24
good or bad," the * replied, "but Jn 9:25
the * exclaimed. Jn 9:27
the * replied. Jn 9:30
If this * were not from God, he Jn 9:33
he found the * and said, "Do you Jn 9:35
Literally, "the Son of *." Jn 9:35f
The * answered, "Who is he, sir, Jn 9:36
"Yes, Lord," the * said, "I Jn 9:38
A hired * will run when he sees Jn 10:12
The hired * runs because he is Jn 10:13
Why listen to a * like that?" Jn 10:20
us like a * possessed by a demon! Jn 10:21
you, a mere *, have declared Jn 10:33
this * have come true." Jn 10:41
* can walk safely and not stumble. Jn 11:9
healed a blind *—why couldn't he Jn 11:37,38
"For this * certainly does Jn 11:47
let this one * die for the Jn 11:50
* he had brought back to life. Jn 12:1
* who had come back to life again. Jn 12:9
Literally, "if any *." Jn 12:26f
* and woman in all the earth. Jn 17:2
"Should you hit a * for telling Jn 18:23
relative of the * whose ear Peter Jn 18:26
is your charge against this *? Jn 18:29
for us to put any * to death." Jn 18:31f
Not this *, but Barabbas!" Jn 18:40
And Pilate said, "Behold the * Jn 19:5
*, you are no friend of Caesar's. Jn 19:12
Nicodemus, the * who had come to Jn 19:39
At dawn we saw a * standing on Jn 21:4
Literally, "and this *, what?" Jn 21:21f
for the right * to be chosen. Act 1:24,25
not keep this * within its grip. Act 2:24
Temple, they saw a * lame from Act 3:2
The lame * looked at them Act 3:5
Then Peter took the lame * by the Act 3:7,8
godliness had made this * walk? Act 3:12
"Jesus' name has healed this * Act 3:16
the Messiah, the * you Act 4:10
that this * stands here healed! Act 4:10
healing when the * they had healed Act 4:14
the healing of a * who had been Act 4:22
BUT THERE WAS a * named Ananias Act 5:1
Stephen (a * unusually full of Act 6:5
Stephen, the * so full of faith Act 6:8
mistreating a * of Israel. Act 7:24
"But the * in the wrong told Act 7:27
And so God sent back the same * Act 7:35
Literally, "the Son of *." Act 7:56f
the feet of a young * named Paul. Act 7:58
Paul was like a wild *, going Act 8:3
A * named Simon had formerly been Act 8:9,10,11
influential, proud * because of the Act 8:9,10,11
Literally, "this * is that Power Act 8:9,10,11f
the * replied. Act 8:31
the house of a * named Judas and Act 9:11
him a vision of a * named Ananias Act 9:12
things this * has done to the Act 9:13
"Isn't this the same * who Act 9:21
There he met a * named Aeneas, Act 9:33
He was a godly *, deeply Act 10:2
to charity and was a * of prayer. Act 10:2
to Joppa to find a * named Simon Act 10:5,6
"I'm the * you're looking for," Act 10:21
a good and godly *, well thought of Act 10:22
when suddenly a * was standing Act 10:30
the * who had sent the messengers. Act 11:12
voice of a god and not of a *!" Act 12:22
called "The Black *"), Lucius Act 13:1
Sergius Paulus, a * of considerable Act 13:6,7
(son of Kish), a * of the tribe of Act 13:21
David as king, a * about whom God Act 13:22
of Jesse) is a * after my own Act 13:22
In this * Jesus, there is Act 13:38
they came upon a * with crippled Act 14:8
and the * leaped to his feet Act 14:10
In his dream he saw a * over in Act 16:9
of the world from one *, Adam, Act 17:26
the world by the * he has Act 17:31
But when they tried it on a * Act 19:15
and heard, this * Paul has Act 19:26
on and on, a young * named Act 20:9
of several days, a * named Agabus, Act 21:10
This is the * who preaches Act 21:28
There a * named Ananias, as Act 22:12
as godly a * as you could find for Act 22:12
This * is a Roman citizen!" Act 22:26
* to you to tell you something." Act 23:18
"This * was seized by the Jews Act 23:27
outline our case against this *. Act 24:4
a troublemaker, a * who is Act 24:5
clear conscience before God and *. Act 24:16
convict a * before he is tried. Act 25:16
"I'd like to hear the * Act 25:22
"this is the * whose death is Act 25:24
agreed, "This * hasn't done Act 26:31
As the Scripture says it, "The * Rom 1:17
could point it out to a blind *. Rom 2:19
For this one *, Adam, brought Rom 5:15
But this one *, Jesus Christ, Rom 5:15
The sin of this one *, Adam, Rom 5:17
because of this one *, Jesus Rom 5:17
yet have—for a * who already has Rom 8:24
When a * makes a jar out of Rom 9:21
that a * becomes right with God; Rom 10:10
In this situation, happy is the * Rom 14:22
Then there is Apelles, a good * Rom 16:10
plan of the wisest *, and God in 1Co 1:25
cross—is far stronger than any *. 1Co 1:25
say that no mere * has ever seen, 1Co 2:9
But the * who isn't a Christian 1Co 2:14
But the spiritual * has insight 1Co 2:15
and baffles the * of the world, who 1Co 2:15
saved, but like a * escaping 1Co 3:15
do it: you have a * in your church 1Co 5:1
* is removed from your membership? 1Co 5:2
and cast out this * from the 1Co 5:5
* and put him out of your church. 1Co 5:13
And don't you know that if a * 1Co 6:16
be married, each * having his own 1Co 7:2
The * should give his wife all 1Co 7:3
For instance, a * who already has 1Co 7:18
An unmarried * can spend his time 1Co 7:32
But a married * can't do that so 1Co 7:33
But if a * has the willpower not 1Co 7:37
responsible to no mere *. 1Co 9:1
the sake of the * who told you, and 1Co 10:28
That is why, if a * refuses to 1Co 11:4
But a * should not wear anything 1Co 11:7
God's glory is * made in his 1Co 11:7
The first * didn't come from 1Co 11:8
but the first woman came out of *. 1Co 11:8
And Adam, the first *, was not 1Co 11:9
woman came out of *, all men have 1Co 11:12
long hair, while a * with long hair 1Co 11:14,15
That is why a * should examine 1Co 11:28
But when I became a * my thoughts 1Co 13:11
of what one * (Adam) did, and it is 1Co 15:21
of what this other * (Christ) has 1Co 15:21
us that the first *, Adam, was 1Co 15:45
Or am I like a * of the world who 2Co 1:17
Remember that the * I wrote 2Co 2:5,6
But the sorrow of the * who is 2Co 7:10
it up [punishing the * who sinned 2Co 7:11
even more than to help the * 2Co 7:12
In fact, this * was elected by 2Co 8:19
* gives generously to the poor. 2Co 9:9
are merely those of an ordinary *. 2Co 10:2
her love for one * only, for the 2Co 11:2
anyway—a witless *, a fool—while I 2Co 11:16
Literally, "A * in Christ." 2Co 12:2,3f
says it, "The * who finds life Gal 3:11
which says that a * is saved by Gal 3:12
made by one * to another, if it is Gal 3:15
away with it: a * will always reap Gal 6:7
For since a * and his wife are Eph 5:28
are now one, a * is really doing Eph 5:28
which says, "A * must leave his Eph 5:31
So again I say, a * must love his Eph 5:33
They are against both God and *, 1Th 2:15
God, and then the * of rebellion 2Th 2:3
As for the work this * of 2Th 2:7

(MAN Con't)
This * of sin will come as 2Th 2:9
Jesus, himself *, is between them 1Ti 2:5
IT IS A true saying that if a * 1Ti 3:1
For a pastor must be a good * 1Ti 3:2
For if a * can't make his own 1Ti 3:5
came to earth as a *, was proved 1Ti 3:16
SPEAK SHARPLY to an older *, 1Ti 5:1
Oh, Timothy, you are God's *. 1Ti 6:11
No mere * has ever seen him, nor 1Ti 6:16
*, born into King David's family; 2Ti 2:8
Paul, an old * now, here in jail Phm 1:8,9
"What is mere * that you are so Heb 2:6
And who is this Son of * you Heb 2:6
Moses, just as a * who builds a Heb 3:3
priest is merely a * like anyone Heb 5:1
And because he is a * he can deal Heb 5:1
When a * takes an oath, he is Heb 6:16
his enemies. A * who refused to Heb 10:28
that mere * can do to me." Heb 13:6
But a rich * should be glad that Jas 1:10,11
Happy is the * who doesn't give Jas 1:12
* looking at his face in a mirror; Jas 1:23
If a * comes into your church Jas 2:2
moment another * comes in who is Jas 2:2
fuss over the rich * and give him Jas 2:3
say to the poor *, "You can stand Jas 2:3
judging a * by his wealth shows Jas 2:4
you have despised the poor *. Jas 2:6
So you see, a * is saved by Jas 2:24
Job is an example of a * who Jas 5:11
of a righteous * has great power Jas 5:16
Noah, the one * who spoke up for 2Pe 2:5
he was a good *, sick of the 2Pe 2:7,8
For a * is a slave to whatever 2Pe 2:19
fellow *, is still in darkness. 1Jn 2:9
But whoever loves his fellow * 1Jn 2:10
And you know that he became a * 1Jn 3:5
became * with a human body? 1Jn 4:2
who called himself the Son of *, Rev 1:13
Literally, "like unto a Son of * Rev 1:13f
followers of the * who induced Rev 2:6f
the third had the face of a *; Rev 4:7
who was called "The Son of *," Rev 14:14
Literally, "one like a Son of * Rev 14:14f
like the watery blood of a dead *; Rev 16:3
of God's revealing himself to *. Rev 19:13f

MAN-EATER
to catch prey and became a *. Eze 19:3
catch prey, and he too became a *. Eze 19:6

MAN-KILLING
And murder is forbidden. * Gen 9:5,6

MAN-MADE
Their gods are merely * things Ps 115:4
They are *, and yet you worship Is 2:8
in worshiping all your * idols? Hab 2:18
And so, by your * rule, you Mt 15:5,6
* laws instead of those from God.' Mt 15:9
order to protect your * tradition. Mk 7:12,13
he doesn't live in * temples; Act 17:24

MAN'S
* body from the dust of the ground Gen 2:7
even though * bent is always toward Gen 8:21
law requires of a dead * brother; Gen 38:8
each * sack the money he had paid! Gen 44:1
But the dead * relatives may Ex 21:30
"If a * ox injures another, and Ex 21:35
it gets into another * vineyard; Ex 22:5
or if he turns it into another * Ex 22:5
"A * poverty is no excuse for Ex 23:6
"If a * hair is gone, this does Lev 13:40
the tip of the * right ear and the Lev 14:17
be used to anoint the * head. Lev 14:18
the tip of the * right ear—the man Lev 14:25
the tip of the * right ear, and Lev 14:28
so anyone touching the * bed is Lev 15:5
"Whenever a * semen goes out Lev 15:16
with another * wife, both the man Lev 20:10
During the fight the Egyptian * Lev 24:11
Israel that if a * wife commits Num 5:11,12
After the * head has been Num 6:19
and put them all into the * hands. Num 6:19
the * body and into her stomach. Num 25:8
from the dead * relatives who want Num 35:12
desire for another * wife, nor envy Deu 5:21
and kills the * neighbor, he may Deu 19:5
the dead * avenger, to kill him. Deu 19:12
must never steal a * land by moving Deu 19:14
Forgive us the guilt of this * Deu 21:8
But if the * accusations are Deu 22:20
the other * wife must be killed; Deu 22:22
virginity of another * fiancée. Deu 22:23,24
"IF A * testicles are crushed or Deu 23:1
from another * vineyard, but do not Deu 23:24
"If a * brother dies without a Deu 25:5
But if the dead * brother Deu 25:7
virgin daughter and this * wife. Ju 19:24
"Don't judge by a * face or 1Sa 16:7
at a * thoughts and intentions." 1Sa 16:7
he took the poor * lamb and roasted 2Sa 12:4
his backyard. The * wife put a 2Sa 17:19
some water at the old * home. 1Ki 13:19
of a * hand rising from the sea." 1Ki 18:44
And the Lord opened the young * 2Ki 6:17
Listen to this * defiance of the 2Ki 19:16
"HOW MANKIND MUST struggle. A * Job 7:1
and take a poor * baby as a pledge Job 24:9
longed for another * wife, then Job 31:9
wife be in another * home, and Job 31:10
Or, "because of * base pride." Job 35:12f
upon the earth. * work stops at Job 37:7
than to own an evil * wealth; Ps 37:16
enemies, for * help is useless. Ps 60:11
of the earth. * futile wrath will Ps 76:10
short you have made * lifespan. Ps 89:47
wicked * riches continue forever. Pro 10:3
The rich * wealth is his only Pro 10:15
The poor * poverty is his only Pro 10:15
The good * earnings advance the Pro 10:16
a wise * fun is being wise! Pro 10:23
The wicked * fears will all come Pro 10:24
and so will the good * hopes. Pro 10:24
The good * goodness delivers him; Pro 11:6
the evil * treachery is his Pro 11:6
celebrates a good * success—and Pro 11:10
also the godless * death. Pro 11:10
the good * reward lasts forever. Pro 11:18
A good * mind is filled with Pro 12:5
an evil * mind is crammed with Pro 12:5
A * goodness helps him all Pro 13:6
The good * life is full of light. Pro 13:9
A poor * farm may have good soil, Pro 13:23
But the wise * speech is Pro 14:3
the godly * life is exciting. Pro 14:14
A relaxed attitude lengthens a * Pro 14:30
the good * path is easy! Pro 15:19
An old * grandchildren are his Pro 17:6
A wise * words express deep Pro 18:4
A * courage Pro 18:14
A poor * own brothers turn away Pro 19:7
A * conscience Pro 20:27
A mirror reflects a * face, but Pro 27:19
Literally, "a * eyes." Pro 27:20f
The good man knows the poor * Pro 29:7
Wisdom lights up a * face, Ecc 8:1
* trouble lies heavy upon him; Ecc 8:6,7
Certainly a * wickedness is not Ecc 8:8
all the dead * evil deeds, these Ecc 8:9,10
A wise * heart leads him to do Ecc 10:2
The wise * words are like goads Ecc 12:11
like a criminal in a rich * grave; Is 53:9
clings to a * loins, so I made Jer 13:11
the second, a *; Eze 10:14
for a * own sins that he will die. Eze 18:4
mysteries beyond * understanding. Dan 2:22
the fingers of a * hand writing on Dan 5:5
and a * mind was given to it. Dan 7:4
this little horn had a * eyes and Dan 7:8
and I heard a * voice calling from Dan 8:16
* wife—I am no longer her husband. Hos 1:2
will perish. A * uncle will be the Amo 6:10
us die for this * sin, and don't Jon 1:14
Yes, a * enemies will be found in Mic 7:6
mother-in-law— a * worst enemies Mt 10:36
For a * heart determines his Mt 12:34
A good * speech reveals the rich Mt 12:35
So it returns and finds the * Mt 12:43,44,45
"Then the * friends went to the Mt 18:31
would get all the dead * property. Mt 22:24
Would he heal the * hand? Mk 3:2
fingers into the * ears, then spat Mk 7:33
the * tongue with the spittle. Mk 7:33
his hands over the * eyes again and Mk 8:25
Then the * face fell, and he went Mk 10:22
children, the * brother should Mk 12:19
Realizing this * understanding, Mk 12:34
death, for * sin, had opened up Mk 15:38f
"What is in this * words that even Lk 4:36
booth. The * name was Levi. Lk 5:27
from the rich * table, the dogs Lk 16:21
children, the * brother shall marry Lk 20:28
* ear had been and restored it. Lk 22:51
in heaven appoints each * work. Jn 3:27
miracles than this * healing. Jn 5:20
mud over the blind * eyes, and Jn 9:6
But Martha, the dead * sister, Jn 11:39
And as he did, the * feet and Act 3:7,8
blame for this * death on us!" Act 5:28
God tolerated * past ignorance Act 17:30
Let me say plainly that no * Act 20:26
And what a difference between * Rom 5:15
upon God, not on * great ideas. 1Co 2:5
uses * own brilliance to trap him; 1Co 3:19
image, and * glory is the woman. 1Co 11:7
that she is under * authority, 1Co 11:10
All of the godly * 2Co 6:7
they are beyond a * power to 2Co 12:4
by taking another * wife, because 1Th 4:6
long years after * first failure to Heb 4:7
Temptation is the pull of * own Jas 1:14
length of a * arm—not an angel's! Rev 21:17f

MANAEN
(from Cyrene), * (the Act 13:1

MANAGED
* to reach their fortified cities. Jos 10:2
but a little lamb he had * to buy. 2Sa 12
* to subdue him. 2Ch 21

MANAGER
he said to the * of his household, Gen 43:1
Joseph's household *, and said to Gen 43:1
it," the household * told them; Gen 43:2
Joseph ordered his household * to Gen 44:
So the household * did as he was Gen 44:
to his household *, "Chase after Gen 44:
to Pharaoh, and * of this entire Gen 45:
when Ziba, the * of Mephibosheth's 2Sa 16:
Ahishar was * of palace affairs; 1Ki 4:
A general * supervised these 1Ki 4:8-1
So the * of palace affairs and 2Ki 10:
and the city *, together with the 2Ki 10:
men: Eliakam, his business *; 2Ki 18:1
the business *, and Shebnah the 2Ki 18:3
Ezri (son of Chelub) was * of the 1Ch 27:2
also a letter to Asaph, the * of Neh 2:
Herod's business * and was in Lk 8:

MANAGERS
his guardians and * tell him to, Gal 4:

MANAGING
Have I given you the task of * my Mt 24:4

MANAHATH
The children of Shobal:Alvan, *, Gen 36:2
The sons of Shobal: Alian, *, 1Ch 1:4
captured in war and exiled to *. 1Ch 8:6,

MANAHATHITES
half the *, and the Zorites; 1Ch 2:54

MANASSEH
Joseph named his oldest son * Gen 41:5
of Egypt, were * and Ephraim (their Gen 46:19-22
him his two sons, * and Ephraim, he Gen 48:
yours, Ephraim and *, born here in Gen 48:5
left hand and * at his right. Gen 48:12,13
was upon the head of *, the older. Gen 48:14
son," he said. "* too shall Gen 48:19
as prosperous as Ephraim and *.' Gen 48:20
that he put Ephraim before *. Gen 48:20
*: (son of Joseph) Num 1:20-46
Tribe: Ephraim * Num 2:3-31
Next to * Num 2:3-31
of the tribe of *, came the eighth Num 7:54-59
and the tribe of * led by Num 10:23
(actually, the half-tribe of *); Num 13:3-15
and 52,750 in the half-tribe of * Num 26:28-37
In the half-tribe of * was the Num 26:28-37
half-tribe of * (a son of Joseph). Num 27:1
ancestor was Machir, son of *. Num 27:1
half-tribe of * (son of Joseph). Num 32:33
of the tribe of * went to Gilead Num 32:39
of the tribe of *, occupied many of Num 32:41
the half-tribe of * have already Num 34:14,15
* Hanniel (son of Ephod) Num 34:16-28
of the tribe of *, one of the sons Num 36:1
own tribe of * (son of Joseph); Num 36:11,12
Gad, and the half-tribe of *. Deu 3:12
The half-tribe of * received the Deu 3:13
of the tribe of *, took over the Deu 3:14
the half-tribe of *, that although Deu 3:18
in Bashan, for the tribe of *. Deu 4:43
of * as their inheritance. Deu 29:8
And the thousands of *." Deu 33:17
and there is Ephraim and *; Deu 34:2
the half-tribe of * and reminded Jos 1:12,13
the half-tribe of *—fully armed as Jos 4:12,13
of Reuben and the half-tribe of *. Jos 12:6
of * as I have commanded you." Jos 13:2-7
The other half of the tribe of *, Jos 13:8
Land Given to the Half-Tribe of *: Jos 13:29
of * in proportion to its needs: Jos 13:29
separate tribes, * and Ephraim, and Jos 14:3,4
(Ephraim and the half-tribe of *): Jos 16:1
territory of the half-tribe of *. Jos 16:9
of * (Joseph's oldest son): Jos 17:1
of *) had no sons. Jos 17:3
of the tribe of * extended Jos 17:7
belonged to *, but the city of Jos 17:8
the border of * followed the north Jos 17:9
and east of the sea went to *. Jos 17:10
The half-tribe of * was also Jos 17:11
But since the descendants of * Jos 17:12
the half-tribe of * won't receive Jos 18:7
in the land of the tribe of *. Jos 20:8
Dan, and the half-tribe of *. Jos 21:5
Naphtali, and the half-tribe of *. Jos 21:6
The half-tribe of * gave the Jos 21:25
from the half-tribe of *: Jos 21:27
*, and addressed them as follows: Jos 22:1
the half-tribe of *, although the Jos 22:7,8
the half-tribe of * left the army Jos 22:9
the tribes of Reuben, Gad, and *. Jos 22:13
Gad, and the half-tribe of *, Jos 22:15
of * to these high officials: Jos 22:21
Gad, and *, they were very happy. Jos 22:30
The tribe of * failed to drive Ju 1:27
the whole tribe of *, and I am the Ju 6:15
throughout *, Asher, Zebulun, and Ju 6:35

(MANASSEH Con't)
Asher, and * and told them to come Ju 7:23
land of Gilead and *, past Mizpah Ju 11:29
of Jair (the son of *) in Gilead; 1Ki 4:8-19
he also conquered parts of * from 2Ki 10:32,33
When he died, his son * became 2Ki 20:21
NEW KING OF Judah: * 2Ki 21:1
So the Lord was very angry, for * 2Ki 21:6
in God's opinion. * even set up a 2Ki 21:7
to the Lord, and * enticed them to 2Ki 21:9
"Because King * has done these 2Ki 21:11
and into which * led the people of 2Ki 21:16
the altars which * had built in the 2Ki 23:12
caused by the evils of King *. 2Ki 23:26
the many sins of *, for he had 2Ki 24:3,4
*, Amon, 1Ch 3:10-14
Gad, and the half-tribe of *. 1Ch 5:18
The half-tribe of * spread 1Ch 5:23
Gad, and the half-tribe of *. 1Ch 5:26
territory of the half-tribe of *. 1Ch 6:61
Issachar, Asher, Naphtali, and *. 1Ch 6:62
Kohathites by the half-tribe of *: 1Ch 6:70
by the half-tribe of * were: 1Ch 6:71
The sons of *, born to his 1Ch 7:14
and the great-grandsons of *. 1Ch 7:17
The tribe of *, descendants of 1Ch 7:29
and * arrived in Jerusalem: 1Ch 9:3
Some men from * deserted the 1Ch 12:19
Here is a list of the men from * 1Ch 12:20
From the half-tribe of *, 18,000 1Ch 12:24-37
the half-tribe of * lived—there 1Ch 12:24-37
Gad, and the half-tribe of *. 1Ch 26:31,32
Over the half-tribe of *, Joel 1Ch 27:16-22
Over the other half of *, in 1Ch 27:16-22
of Ephraim, *, and Simeon, in 2Ch 15:9
Ephraim, and *, inviting everyone 2Ch 30:1
and * and as far as Zebulun. 2Ch 30:10
tribes of Asher, *, and Zebulun 2Ch 30:11
from Ephraim, *, Issachar, and 2Ch 30:17,18,19
Ephraim, and * and tore down the 2Ch 31:1
Then his son * became the new 2Ch 32:33
* WAS ONLY twelve years old when 2Ch 33:1
forever. And * sacrificed his own 2Ch 33:6
But * encouraged the people of 2Ch 33:9
ignored by both * and his people. 2Ch 33:10
At that point * finally realized 2Ch 33:13
When * died he was buried beneath 2Ch 33:20,21
the early years of his father *; 2Ch 33:22
Then he went to the cities of *, 2Ch 34:6
people coming from *, Ephraim, and 2Ch 34:9
Mattaniah, Bezalel, Binnui, *. Ez 10:30
*, Shime-i. Ez 10:33
"Shechem, Succoth, Gilead, * Ps 60:6,7
Let Ephraim, Benjamin and * see Ps 80:2
you," he says, "and * as well; Ps 108:8
own children! * against Ephraim Is 9:21
against *—and both against Judah. Is 9:21
wicked things that *, son of Jer 15:4
also during the reign of *. Eze 23:16f
Then comes *, south of Naphtali, Eze 48:4
Hezekiah was the father of *; Mt 1:10
* was the father of Amos; Mt 1:10
* 12,000 Rev 7:4-8

MANASSEH'S
Ephraim's and * portion from you. Gen 48:6
so he lifted it to place it on * Gen 48:17
* son, who played at his feet. Gen 50:23
son of Manasseh. * son Gilead was Num 27:1
of the clan Machir, who was * son. Jos 13:31
The clan of Machir (* oldest son Jos 17:1
on the border of * land, belonged Jos 17:8
they were located in * territory. Jos 17:9
went to Manasseh. * northern Jos 17:10
The rest of the history of * 2Ki 21:17
high-ranking officer of * troops. 1Ch 12:20
The rest of * deeds, and his 2Ch 33:18

MANASSH
* (son of Joseph) Num 1:2-15

MANDRAKES
wheat harvest, Reuben found some * Gen 30:14
And now will you steal my son's * Gen 30:15
you tonight because of the *." Gen 30:15
"for I am hiring you with some * Gen 30:16
There the * give forth their Sol 7:13

MANE
his neck with a quivering *? Job 39:19

MANEH
shekels shall always equal one *. Eze 45:12

MANESSEH
The tribe of Joseph (Ephraim and * Eze 47:13

MANEUVER
me open ground in which to *. Ps 31:8

MANEUVERING
give the ambush more room for *. Ju 20:35-39

MANGER
and laid him in a *, because Lk 2:7
lying in a *!" Lk 2:12
was the baby, lying in the *. Lk 2:16

MANGLED
trampled and * by horses' hoofs. Is 14:19

MANHOOD
specimen of * as Absalom, and no 2Sa 14:25
Let your * be a blessing; Pro 5:18

MANIFEST
Literally, "is * in them." Rom 1:19f

MANIFESTED
righteousness of God has been *." Rom 3:21,22f

MANKIND
become the mother of all *"; Gen 3:20
of the earth all * that I created. Gen 6:7
and saw that all * was vicious and Gen 6:12,13
"I have decided to destroy all *; Gen 6:12,13
Yes, I will destroy * from the Gen 6:12,13
reptiles and all *— everything Gen 7:21
AT THAT TIME all * spoke a single Gen 11:1
* was making, he said, "Look! Gen 11:5
"O God, the God of all *," they Num 16:22
of all *, [before I am taken away Num 27:16
ARE THE earliest generations of *: 1Ch 1:1
and you are the Ruler of all *; 1Ch 29:12
for you know the hearts of all *. 2Ch 6:30
seeds of sin. * heads for sin and Job 5:7
"HOW * MUST struggle. Job 7:1
harmed you, O God, Watcher of *? Job 7:20
all the faults and sins of *; Job 11:11
of God, and the breath of all *. Job 12:10
You have set * so brief a span Job 14:5
it is hid from the eyes of all *; Job 28:21
he says to all *: 'Look, to fear Job 28:28
and * would turn again to dust. Job 34:15
watches the goings on of all *; Job 34:21
from heaven on all * to see if Ps 14:2
by my own people and by all *. Ps 22:6
The Lord gazes down upon * from Ps 33:13,14,15
Death is the shepherd of all *. Ps 49:14
summoned all * from east to west! Ps 50:1
among all * to see if there is a Ps 53:2
answer prayer, all * will come to Ps 65:1
You are the only hope of all * Ps 65:5
and your eternal plan for all * Ps 67:2
he had lived among *, and allowed Ps 78:60
the thoughts of * are, so he helps Ps 94:11
I am a symbol of failure to all *; Ps 109:25
he has given the earth to all *. Ps 115:16
The eyes of all * look up to you Ps 145:15
world and all his family of *! Pro 8:31
How much more the hearts of all * Pro 15:11
mocker is the scourge of all *. Pro 24:9
kinds of work God has given to *. Ecc 3:10
that he can test *, and so that men Ecc 3:18
and both die. So * has no real Ecc 3:19
which God gives to * everywhere. Ecc 8:15
All the glory of * will bow low; Is 2:17
for all the greatness of *. Is 23:9
will be seen by all * together." Is 40:5
generations of * as they march by? Is 41:4
rejected by *, and kept beneath the Is 49:7
if I did, all * would perish—the Is 57:16
disappear. All * shall come to Is 66:23
be a disgusting sight to all *. Is 66:24
I looked, and * was gone and the Jer 4:25
against all the nations—all *. Jer 25:31
let the leaders of * beat their Jer 25:34
earth and all * and every animal; Jer 27:5
I am the Lord, the God of all *; Jer 32:27
power was given to it over all *. Dan 7:6
and animals alike. * and all the Zep 1:3
"Be silent, all *, before the Zec 2:13
Lord is closely watching all *, Zec 9:1
For I, the Son of *, shall come Mt 16:27
are shortened, all * will perish. Mt 24:22
"Then all * will see me, the Mk 13:26
veil separated him from sinful *. Mk 15:38f
And then all * shall see the Lk 3:6
it for you. All * scratches for Lk 12:30
fortunate indeed. * will beg the Lk 23:30
this life gives light to all *. Jn 1:4
them, for he knew * to the core. Jn 2:24,25
* because he is the Son of Man. Jn 5:27
Spirit upon all *, and your sons Act 2:17
by giving his life for all *. 1Ti 2:6
could die on the cross for all *. Heb 5:7f
loose to kill a third of all *. Rev 9:15
killing one-third of all *. Rev 9:17,18
And all *—whose names were not Rev 13:8

MANNA
And the food became known as * Ex 16:31
three quarts of * in it and to keep Ex 16:33
So the people of Israel ate the * Ex 16:35
the *—held about three quarts; Ex 16:36
day we have to face this *!" Num 11:6
The * was about the size of Num 11:7
The * fell with the dew during Num 11:9
and we hate this insipid *." Num 21:5
feeding you with *, a food Deu 8:3
He fed you with * in the Deu 8:16
The following day no * fell, and Jos 5:11,12
and rained down * for their food. Ps 78:24
and gave them *—bread from heaven. Ps 105:40
jar with some * in it, and Aaron's Heb 9:4
eat of the hidden *, the secret Rev 2:17

MANNED
the forts, and * them with 2Ch 11:11
your towers are * by men from Eze 27:11

MANNER
Literally, "The * of women is Gen 31:35f
* I showed you in the mountain. Ex 26:30
himself in the * specified, has Num 19:13
the men in this *: 'Has anyone just Deu 20:5
kings in this same * and have fed Ju 1:7
Their * of life was Phoenician, Ju 18:7
in such a * that their wings spread 1Ki 8:7
in the * ordained by King David. Ez 3:10
Literally, "after the * of." Ps 110:4f
wind, and as the * in which a human Ecc 11:5
taught them in an interesting *. Ecc 12:10
In such * the Lord will come and Is 31:4,5
and in this * Matthias was chosen Act 1:26
may come to him in this same *. Rom 3:29
Literally, "in like *." Rom 8:26f
in an unworthy *, he is guilty of 1Co 11:27
and sensible in * and clothing. 1Ti 2:9,10

MANOAH
to the wife of *, of the tribe of Ju 13:2,3
Then * prayed, "O Lord, please Ju 13:8
But again she was alone—* was not Ju 13:9
* ran back with his wife and Ju 13:11
So * asked him, "Can you give us Ju 13:12
Then * said to the Angel, Ju 13:15
to the Lord." (* didn't yet Ju 13:16
Then * asked him for his name. Ju 13:17
Then * took a young goat and a Ju 13:19
the sky, and as * and his wife Ju 13:20
in the fire! * and his wife fell Ju 13:20
It was then that * finally Ju 13:21
"We will die," * cried out to Ju 13:22
where his father, *, was buried. Ju 16:31

MANSIONS
Palaces and * will all be Is 32:14
winter * and their summer houses, Amo 3:15

MANUFACTURE
The Lord instructed them to * Jos 5:2,3
What fools they are who * idols Is 44:9
many craftsmen to * silver shrines Act 19:24

MANUFACTURED
They also * iron into the great 1Ch 22:3
And he produced engines of war * 2Ch 26:15
City of David, and * large numbers 2Ch 32:5

MANUFACTURER
Beyond him was Hananiah, a * of Neh 3:8

MANURE
as a stable hand shovels out *. 1Ki 14:10
be scattered like * upon the field, 2Ki 9:36
the fields like *, like sheaves Jer 9:22
on your faces the * of these Mal 2:3

MANUSCRIPT
original * indicates sub-totals. Jos 18:21-28f
*, where sub-totals are indicated. Jos 19:2-7f
The Dead Sea * reads, "within Is 21:16f

MANUSCRIPTS
is uncertain in the original *. 2Sa 1:21f
Some * read, "In the twelfth Eze 33:21f
Some * add: "And the arches Eze 40:28f
of the ancient *, reads, "There Eze 40:29,30f
Some * add here, "For yours is Mt 6:13f
omitted in many of the ancient *. Mt 17:21f
This verse is omitted in many *, Mt 18:11f
is added in some ancient *. Mt 19:9f
Omitted here in many *, but Mt 19:29f
Many ancient * omit this Mt 24:36f
Some ancient * read, "the Mk 1:3f
omitted in many of the ancient *. Mk 7:15,16f
"And fasting" is added in some * Mk 9:29f
omitted in some of the ancient *. Mk 9:43,44f
omitted in some of the ancient *. Mk 9:45,46f
Some of the ancient * do not Mk 10:24f
Some ancient * read, "new Mk 14:24f
is found in only some of the *. Mk 14:68f
omitted in some of the ancient *. Mk 15:28f
the most ancient *, but may be Mk 16:9f
Some ancient * omit "new." Mk 16:17f
42 which appears in all the *. Lk 1:28f
included in some of the ancient *. Lk 8:43,44f
Later * add to verses 55 and 56, Lk 9:55f
Some ancient * add at this point Lk 11:5,6f
Many of the ancient * omit the Jn 5:4f
in the text of many ancient *. Jn 7:8f
Most ancient * omit John Jn 7:53f
Many ancient * omit verse 37 Act 8:37f
Some * read, "many of the wives Act 17:4f
omitted in many of the ancient *. Act 18:21f
Some of the ancient * add, "And Act 28:28,29f
Some ancient * read, "broken." 1Co 11:24f
Some * read "616." Rev 13:18f
Some * read, "King of the Rev 15:3,4f
Some * add, "and be their God." Rev 21:3f

MANY
* Hebrew names are based on puns. Gen 3:20f
of whom so * legends are told. Gen 6:4
told them to have * children and to Gen 9:1
Yes, have * children and Gen 9:7
spread abroad in * lands and Gen 10:20
and nations, with * languages. Gen 10:20
from Noah, through * generations, Gen 10:32

(MANY Con't)
by giving them * languages, thus Gen 11:9
and had * sons and daughters. Gen 11:10,11
and had * sons and daughters. Gen 11:12,13
and had * sons and daughters. Gen 11:14,15
and had * sons and daughters. Gen 11:16,17
and had * sons and daughters. Gen 11:18,19
that, with * sons and daughters. Gen 11:20,21
with * sons and daughters. Gen 11:22,23
will be a blessing to * others. Gen 12:2
Then Pharaoh gave Abram * gifts Gen 12:16
sheep and cattle and * servants. Gen 13:5
Literally, "* tents." Gen 13:5f
There were too * animals for the Gen 13:6
And I am going to give you so * Gen 13:16
be like that—too * to count!" Gen 15:5
who will form * nations! Gen 17:6
mother of nations! * kings shall be Gen 17:16
* slaves and camels and donkeys. Gen 24:35
and he gave * valuable presents Gen 24:53
becomeThe mother of * millions! Gen 24:60
for even after * years of marriage Gen 25:21
herds of cattle, and * servants. Gen 26:14
will give you so * descendants that Gen 26:24
May * nations be your slaves. Gen 27:27,28,29
bless you and give you * children; Gen 28:2
become a great nation of * tribes! Gen 28:2
have descendants as * as dust! Gen 28:14
told me that the * blessings I've Gen 30:27
you through these * years, and how Gen 30:29
* servants, camels, and donkeys. Gen 30:43
* servants, both men and women. Gen 32:5
along the shores—too * to count." Gen 32:12
a great nation, yes, * nations; Gen 35:11
yes, many nations; * kings shall be Gen 35:11
in deepest mourning for * weeks. Gen 37:34
Egypt along with * others from many Gen 42:5
many others from * lands to buy Gen 42:5
have been for * generations.' Gen 46:34
as old as * of my ancestors." Gen 47:9
could save the lives of * people. Gen 50:20
us because there are so * of them. Ex 1:9
One day, * years later Ex 2:11
is spelled in * modern versions. Ex 3:15f
but you must produce just as * Ex 5:10,11
told to make as * bricks as before, Ex 5:16
would become too * to control. Ex 23:29
steadfast love to * thousands by Ex 34:7
In * of the languages of the Lev 2:13f
No crawling thing with * feet may Lev 11:41,42
If the Jubilee is * years away, Lev 25:14,15,16
If there are still * years until Lev 25:51
make up for the * years you refused Lev 26:34,35
they are strong or weak, * or few; Num 13:18
and whether there are * trees. Num 13:20
* of them were bitten and died. Num 21:6
realized how * of them there were, Num 22:2,3
Curse at least that *!" Num 23:13
And they shall live in * places. Num 24:3-9
And shall shoot them with * Num 24:3-9
And shall destroy * cities." Num 24:15-19
to find out how * of each tribe and Num 26:2
and out of the * thousands of Num 31:4,5
Manasseh, occupied * of the towns Num 32:41
the larger tribes with * cities Num 35:8
instructed me. For * years we Deu 2:1
caring for your * cattle until you Deu 3:19
* people for worshiping idols. Deu 4:3
so that you will have * children. Deu 6:3
you as * as the stars in the sky! Deu 10:22
You shall lend money to * nations Deu 15:6
You shall rule * nations, but Deu 15:6
harvest and in so * other ways; Deu 16:15
He must not have too * wives, Deu 17:17
* children, Deu 28:2-6
as he promised: * children, many Deu 28:11
* cattle, and abundant crops. Deu 28:11
and you shall lend to * nations, Deu 28:12
do and give you * children and much Deu 30:9
[and destroyed * sinners Deu 33:9
the attack, and * others died while Jos 7:5
still * nations to be conquered. Jos 13:1
and gave him * descendants through Jos 24:3
in the wilderness for * years. Jos 24:7
you, and so did * others—the Jos 24:11
They did * things which the Lord Ju 2:11
* gifts for me.' Ju 5:30
Gideon, "There are too * of you! Ju 7:2
Gideon, "There are still too *! Ju 7:4
were too * camels even to count! Ju 7:12,13
sons, for he married * wives. Ju 8:30
was defeated, and * of the men of Ju 9:40
great fury and killed * of them. Ju 15:8
were alerted and * men of the city Ju 16:2
so * of us is now in our power!" Ju 16:23,24
Micah had * idols in his Ju 17:4,5
some teraphim, and * plated idols. Ju 18:14
there were too * of them for him to Ju 18:26
She with * children has no more! 1Sa 2:5
on the rock. And * burnt offerings 1Sa 6:15
* people whom the Lord had killed. 1Sa 6:19

horsemen, and so * soldiers that 1Sa 13:5
how * enemy troops there are!" 1Sa 14:6
enemies, think how * more we could 1Sa 14:30
killed the sons of * mothers, now 1Sa 15:33
and slaughtered * of them, and put 1Sa 19:8
with * demonstrations of his love! 2Sa 2:6
and had * sons and daughters. 2Sa 5:13
troops confiscated * idols which 2Sa 5:21
very rich, owning * flocks of sheep 2Sa 12:1
know how * of them there are." 2Sa 24:2
a hundred times as * people in your 2Sa 24:3
but no matter how * blankets were 1Ki 1:1
fat goats, and * sheep and has 1Ki 1:19
and fat goats and * sheep, and has 1Ki 1:25
are almost too * people to count! 1Ki 3:8
And kings from * lands sent 1Ki 4:34
and the * offerings he sacrificed 1Ki 10:5
Great men from * lands came to 1Ki 10:24
at $150 each. * of these were then 1Ki 10:29
KING SOLOMON MARRIED * other 1Ki 11:1
Egyptian princess. * of them came 1Ki 11:1
like his father, he worshiped * 1Ki 15:26
he said, "for there are * of you; 1Ki 18:25
"How * times must I tell you to 1Ki 22:16
"Then borrow * pots and pans 2Ki 4:3
troops to * glorious victories. 2Ki 5:1
a great army with * chariots and 2Ki 6:14
by her bodyguard and * trumpeters; 2Ki 11:13,14
King Joash took * hostages and 2Ki 14:14
also secretly done * things that 2Ki 17:9
of Israel had done * evil things, 2Ki 17:11
I have been refreshed at * 2Ki 19:24
because of the * sins of Manasseh, 2Ki 24:3,4
because * craftsmen lived there). 1Ch 4:14
* cattle in the land of Gilead. 1Ch 5:9
them had several wives and * sons. 1Ch 7:4
He had * 1Ch 9:35,36,37
father of * sons and daughters. 1Ch 14:3
Israelis picked up * idols left by 1Ch 14:12
present him with * gifts of gold, 1Ch 18:10
had been * wars between them. 1Ch 18:10
'You have killed too * men in 1Ch 22:8
And you have * skilled 1Ch 22:15
because neither had * sons. 1Ch 23:10,11
his clan, for he had * children. 1Ch 23:17
There were always as * Levites 1Ch 23:31
descendants into * groups to serve 1Ch 24:3
for there were * famous men and 1Ch 24:4
Lord has given me * children—he has 1Ch 28:5
offerings and * other sacrifices on 1Ch 29:21
at Jerusalem. * of these were then 2Ch 1:17
for there were too * sacrifices for 2Ch 7:7
tables, and how * servants and 2Ch 9:4
quality, and *, many jewels. 2Ch 9:9
quality, and many, * jewels. 2Ch 9:9
of Arabia and * other lands that 2Ch 9:13,14
against twice as * Israeli 2Ch 13:3
from Israel (for * had come from 2Ch 15:9
sharply, "how * times must I tell 2Ch 18:15
"There were * suggestions, but 2Ch 18:19,20
and * other leaders of Israel. 2Ch 21:3,4
Negeb, and made * water reservoirs, 2Ch 26:10
the soil and had * farms and 2Ch 26:10
sin will be added to our * others. 2Ch 28:13
and capturing * people as slaves. 2Ch 28:16
with each, and * peace offerings. 2Ch 29:35
Since * of the people arriving 2Ch 30:17,18,19
stores of food for * weeks, but all 2Ch 31:10
nations, and * gifts for the Lord 2Ch 32:23
He also built * storehouses for 2Ch 32:28,29
olive oil, with * stalls for his 2Ch 32:28,29
and he acquired * towns, for God 2Ch 32:28,29
involving so * of the priests, 2Ch 35:18
Nebuchadnezzar. * treasures from 2Ch 36:10
But * of the priests and Levites Ez 3:12
of insurrection against * kings; Ez 4:19
constructed here * centuries ago by Ez 5:11
For by that time * of the Ez 6:20
was blessing him. * ordinary Ez 7:7,8,9
to tell me that * of the Jewish Ez 9:1
Then * who feared the God of Ez 9:4
two, for there are * of us involved Ez 10:13
and * had children by these wives. Ez 10:44
During those fifty-two days * Neh 6:17
of Judah. For * in Judah had sworn Neh 6:18
and Tobiah sent * threatening Neh 6:19
They sinned in so * ways, but Neh 9:18
great kingdoms and * nations, and Neh 9:22
and *, many fruit trees; Neh 9:25
and many, * fruit trees; Neh 9:25
they did * other terrible things. Neh 9:26
You were patient with them for * Neh 9:30
* sacrifices were offered on that Neh 12:43
Moab, and that * of their children Neh 13:24
golden goblets of * designs, and Est 1:7
Jeconiah of Judah and * others. Est 2:6
along with * other young girls. Est 2:8
and * lay in sackcloth and ashes. Est 4:3
wealth, and his * children, and Est 5:11
a holiday. And * of the people of Est 8:17
donkeys, and employed * servants. Job 1:2,3

you have told * a troubled soul Job 4:3,
"Thou hast instructed *." Job 4:3,
of * others, not themselves! Job 5:
miracles, too * to count. Job 9:1
You will lie down unafraid and * Job 11:1
"LOOK, I HAVE seen * instances Job 13:
they have * happy children, they Job 21:1
Literally, "and * such things are Job 23:14
and helps them in * ways. Job 24:22,2
I will give you * illustrations Job 36:
Do you know how * months of Job 39:2,
twice as * as he had before. Job 42:13,14
O LORD, SO * are against me. Ps 3:
against me. So * seek to harm me. Ps 3:
I have so * enemies. Ps 3:
I have so many enemies. So * say Ps 3:
* say that God will never help Ps 4:
his * enemies, including Saul. Ps 18:
the nations. * times you have Ps 18:5
But Lord, my sins! How * they Ps 25:1
See how * enemies I have and how Ps 25:1
* sorrows come to the wicked, but Ps 32:1
to our God. Now * will hear of the Ps 40:
trust in him. * blessings are Ps 40:4
O Lord my God, * and many a time Ps 40:5
O Lord my God, many and * a time Ps 40:5
Meanwhile my sins, too * to Ps 40:12
Walk around and count her * Ps 48:12
against me, for so * are fighting Ps 55:18
* are proud to fight against me; Ps 56:1
full as those of * generations, all Ps 61:6
I promised you * offerings. Ps 66:14
leading * captives in his train. Ps 68:18
My success—at which so * stand Ps 71:7
I recall the * miracles he did Ps 77:11
destroy them all. * and many a time Ps 78:38
Many and * a time he held back Ps 78:38
seen so * of my miracles before. Ps 95:9
the city; and * rulers throughout Ps 102:21,22
He destroyed * a king who tried! Ps 105:14
your * acts of kindness to them. Ps 106:7
big families there, and * cattle. Ps 107:38
* children and much prosperity. Ps 107:41
He will strike down * kings in Ps 110:5
He will crush * heads. Ps 110:6
home of * nations living there. Ps 111:6
My enemies are so *. Ps 119:157
I can't even count how * times a Ps 139:17,18
it will gain you * honors. Pro 1:7,8,9
work returns * blessings to him. Pro 12:14
while the rich have * "friends." Pro 14:20
* counselors bring success. Pro 15:22
* favors are showered on those Pro 16:15
A wealthy man has * "friends"; Pro 19:4
* beg favors from a man who is Pro 19:6
The lazy man longs for * things Pro 21:25,26
with bloodshot eyes and * wounds? Pro 23:29,30
there is safety in * counselors. Pro 24:6
by * people of many nations; Pro 24:24
by many people of * nations; Pro 24:24
faultless despite their * sins. Pro 30:11,12
"There are * fine women in the Pro 31:29
Praise her for the * fine things Pro 31:31
taxes from * kings and provinces. Ecc 2:7,8
And then there were my * beautiful Ecc 2:7,8
sons and as * daughters and lives Ecc 6:3
but being wise has * advantages. Ecc 7:12
they had committed their * crimes! Ecc 8:9,10
Divide your gifts among *, Ecc 11:2
flame of Jehovah. * waters cannot Sol 8:7
Even though you make * prayers, I Is 1:15
and people from * lands will flow Is 2:2
I heard him say, "* a beautiful Is 5:9
Don't you panic as so * of your Is 8:12
Yes, we have finished off * a Is 10:10
But though Israel be now as * as Is 10:22
tumult and the shout of * nations. Is 13:4
of Israel. And * nationalities will Is 14:1
will be blown, and * about to Is 27:13
Does he not finally plant his * Is 28:25
Year after year you make your * Is 29:1
you've dug in * a conquered land, Is 37:25
give her twice as * blessings as he Is 40:2
God has given him victory over * Is 41:2
This was written * years before Is 44:28f
he has chosen to conquer * lands. Is 45:1
And don't forget the * times I Is 46:9
In ancient Babylonia (and in * Is 47:2f
deep terror into * hearts again. Is 47:12
of the world, too * to count, and Is 48:19
exalted. Yet * shall be amazed Is 52:14,15
Or, "So shall he startle * Is 52:14,15f
* nations. Is 52:14,15
a multitude of children, * heirs. Is 53:10
Servant shall make * to be counted Is 53:11
bore the sins of *, and he pled Is 53:12
you the wealth of * lands. Is 60:5
I have reserved the ships of * Is 60:9
to receive the wealth of * lands. Is 60:11
have lain there * generations. Is 61:4
you and will bring you * gifts." Is 62:11

MANY Con't)
idols in * gardens and burning Is 65:3
the slain of the Lord shall be *! Is 66:16
For you have as * gods as there Jer 2:28
me and married * lovers, yet I have Jer 3:1
For their sins are very *; Jer 5:6
for there will be so * slain to Jer 7:32
O my people, you have as * gods Jer 11:13
* foreign rulers have ravaged my Jer 12:10
Now I am sending for * fishermen Jer 16:16
Men from * nations will pass by Jer 22:8
huge rooms and * windows, paneled Jer 22:14
the nations. For * nations and Jer 25:14
to worship from * parts of Judah. Jer 26:2
is up, and then * nations and great Jer 27:7
me spoke against * nations, always Jer 28:8
for you will be there * years. Jer 29:5
for them and have * grandchildren. Jer 29:6
and plan to stay * years, that we Jer 29:28
for your sins are so *, your Jer 30:14
there for * years until you die. Jer 32:5
chief assistant, and * others. Jer 39:3
* places to which they had fled. Jer 40:12
and * shall die of plague. Jer 43:11
Though you have used * medicines, Jer 46:11
It is accompanied by * kings Jer 50:41
kings called by God from * lands. Jer 50:41
Set * watchmen on your walls; Jer 51:12
pieces and to destroy * kingdoms. Jer 51:20
Signal * nations to mobilize for Jer 51:27
the builders from * lands have Jer 51:58
Jerusalem for all her * sins; Lam 1:5
sighs are * and my heart is faint. Lam 1:22
Your "prophets" have said so * Lam 2:14
services—men pay with * gifts. Eze 16:33,34
your lovers—these * nations—to Eze 16:39
you before the eyes of * women. Eze 16:40,41
She insolently worshiped * idols Eze 16:50
a great army and * horses to fight Eze 17:15
again and slaughters * lives. Eze 17:17
They devour * lives; Eze 22:25
came the sound of * men Eze 23:42
you to * nations for devastation. Eze 25:7
Tyre shall become the prey of * Eze 26:5
from Rhodes, and * coastlands are Eze 27:15
her traders to buy your * wares. Eze 27:16
the desires of * nations. Eze 27:33
and silver and * treasures. Eze 28:4
those pierced with * wounds, there Eze 28:8
banish the Egyptians to * lands. Eze 30:23
grief will be in * hearts among Eze 32:9
Yes, terror shall strike in * Eze 32:10
We are *, so we should certainly Eze 33:24
you away as slaves to * lands. Eze 36:3
And I exiled them to * lands; Eze 36:19
north, as well as * others. Eze 38:6
return of its people from * lands. Eze 38:8
capture vast booty and * slaves. Eze 38:12
saying that after * years had Eze 38:17
here so I can show you * things; Eze 40:4
of all the * among you shall enter Eze 44:9
* trees were growing on both Eze 47:7
"those who have read widely in * Dan 1:3,4
But I will give you * wonderful Dan 2:6
are a king over * kings, for the Dan 2:37
he gave him * costly gifts, and Dan 2:48
Devour * people!" Dan 7:5
defeating * by catching them off Dan 8:25
this prophecy is * years away." Dan 10:14
been fulfilled * years later in the Dan 11:6f
dishes and for * years afterward he Dan 11:8
he will have * thousands of his Dan 11:12
the coastal cities and conquer *. Dan 11:18
his army will desert, and * be Dan 11:26
constant danger, * of them dying by Dan 11:33
the governments of * nations. Dan 11:41
* other lands will be occupied. Dan 11:42
"And * of those whose bodies lie Dan 12:2
and those who turn * to Dan 12:3
time of the end. * shall be Dan 12:10
"You must live alone for * days; Hos 3:3
"friends" from * lands, I will Hos 8:10
Ephraim has built * altars, but Hos 8:11
to warn you with * a vision and Hos 12:10
vision and * a parable and dream. Hos 12:10
For * and great are your sins. Amo 5:12
True, * nations have gathered Mic 4:11
trample to pieces * people, and you Mic 4:13
Citizens of * lands will come Mic 7:12
Prepare * bricks for repairing Nah 3:14
have collected * nations, but like Hab 2:5
You have ruined * nations; Hab 2:8
"I have cut off * nations, Zep 3:6
But * commentators prefer this Hag 2:7f
enough for all! * will live outside Zec 2:4
with all their * cattle—and yet Zec 2:4
'At that time * nations will be Zec 2:11,12
hand, accusing Joshua of * things. Zec 3:1
far away represent * others who Zec 6:15
Jerusalem from * foreign cities to Zec 8:20,21
Yes, * people, even strong Zec 8:22
Hebrew text, but * other passages Zec 9:10f
turned * from their lives of sin. Mal 2:6
Your 'guidance' has caused * to Mal 2:8
But when he saw * Pharisees Mt 3:7
Galilee where so * foreigners Mt 4:15,16
* will tell me, 'Lord, Lord, we Mt 7:22
and to do * other great miracles.' Mt 7:22
And I tell you this, that * Mt 8:11
and Jacob. And * an Mt 8:12
there were * notorious Mt 9:10
valuable to him than * sparrows. Mt 10:31
synagogue, with * following him. Mt 12:15
He used * illustrations such as Mt 13:2,3
and your ears, for they hear. * Mt 13:17
Literally, "produces a crop * Mt 13:23f
he would use so *, he never spoke Mt 13:34,35
followed by land from * villages. Mt 14:13
speak, and * others, and laid them Mt 15:30
and was badly mistreated by *. Mt 17:12
This verse is omitted in * of the Mt 17:21f
This verse is omitted in * Mt 18:11f
Omitted here in * manuscripts, but Mt 19:29f
eternal life. But * who are first Mt 19:30
give my life as a ransom for *." Mt 20:28
for his son. * guests were Mt 22:3
For * are called, but few are Mt 22:14
way they keep making up so * laws! Mt 23:2
fool you. For * will come claiming Mt 24:5
Messiah, and will lead * astray. Mt 24:5
and earthquakes in * places. Mt 24:7
you are mine, and * of you shall Mt 24:10
each other. And * false prophets Mt 24:11
will appear and lead * astray. Mt 24:11
and will cool the love of *. Mt 24:12
Literally, "neither the Son." * Mt 24:36f
give you * more responsibilities. Mt 25:21
But even though they found * who Mt 26:60,61
leaders made their * accusations Mt 27:12
tombs opened, and * godly men and Mt 27:52
and appeared to * people there. Mt 27:53
And * women who had come down Mt 27:55
and ordered * demons to come out of Mk 1:34
* from the power of demons. Mk 1:39
tax collectors and * other Mk 2:15
(There were * men of this type Mk 2:15
For there had been * healings Mk 3:10
He used * such illustrations to Mk 4:33
* of us here within this man." Mk 5:9
She had suffered much from * Mk 5:26
And they cast out * demons, and Mk 6:13
demons, and healed * sick people, Mk 6:13
For so * people were coming and Mk 6:31
quieter spot. But * people saw Mk 6:33
them * things they needed to know. Mk 6:34
and as * as touched him were Mk 6:56
This is but one of * examples of Mk 7:4
There are *, many others." Mk 7:12,13
There are many, * others." Mk 7:12,13
Verse 16 is omitted in * of the Mk 7:15,16f
"How * loaves of bread do you Mk 8:5
not. How * more miracles do you Mk 8:12
of bread? How * basketfuls of Mk 8:19
eternal life. But * people who Mk 10:31
then; and * who are considered Mk 10:31
give my life as a ransom for *." Mk 10:45
Then * in the crowd spread out Mk 11:8
* ancient authorities add verse Mk 11:26,f
he said, "for * will come Mk 13:6
Messiah, and will lead * astray. Mk 13:6
in * lands, and famines. Mk 13:8
For there will be * false Mk 13:22
blood, poured out for *, sealing Mk 14:24
were in vain. * false witnesses Mk 14:56
accused him of * crimes, and Pilate Mk 15:3,4
They and * other Galilean women Mk 15:41
and * will rejoice with you. Lk 1:14
And he will persuade * a Jew to Lk 1:16
be rejected by * in Israel, and Lk 2:34,35
be the greatest joy of * others. Lk 2:34,35
And the deepest thoughts of * Lk 2:34,35
He used * such warnings as he Lk 3:18
wife, and for * other wrongs he had Lk 3:19,20
this sin to all his * others. Lk 3:19,20
There were * Jewish widows Lk 4:25,26
* Jewish lepers needing help." Lk 4:27
guest of honor. * of Levi's fellow Lk 5:29
surrounded by * of his followers Lk 6:17,18
And he cast out * demons. Lk 6:17,18
mother, and * mourners from the Lk 7:12
he was curing * sick people of Lk 7:20,21,22
sins—and they are *—are forgiven, Lk 7:47
Susanna, and * others who were Lk 8:3
to hear him—while * others were Lk 8:4
said, "Master, so * are crowding Lk 8:45
you have seen. * a prophet and Lk 10:24
the truth is that * will try to Lk 13:24,25
feast and sent out * invitations. Lk 14:16
return, how * will I find who Lk 18:8
will be repaid * times over now, Lk 18:30
mislead you. For * will come Lk 21:8
and famines in * lands, and Lk 21:11
The courage of * people will Lk 21:26
and * grief-stricken women. Lk 23:27
at last these * Scriptures! Lk 24:45
celebration, * people were Jn 2:23
* from the Samaritan village Jn 4:39
long enough for * of them to Jn 4:40,41
* of the ancient manuscripts omit Jn 5:4f
And a huge crowd, * of them Jn 6:2-5
At this point * of his disciples Jn 6:66
the text of * ancient manuscripts. Jn 7:8f
* among the crowds at the Temple Jn 7:31
Then * of the Jewish leaders who Jn 8:30,31
* a miracle to help the people. Jn 10:32
baptizing. And * followed him. Jn 10:41
And * came to the decision Jn 10:42
Literally, "* believed on him Jn 10:42f
Jerusalem, and * of the Jewish Jn 11:19
And so at last * of the Jewish Jn 11:45
day, was near, and * country people Jn 11:55
of him that * of the Jewish leaders Jn 12:11
they noticed how * prophecies of Jn 12:16
main reason why so * went out to Jn 12:18
But my death will produce * new Jn 12:23,24
However, even * of the Jewish Jn 12:42
There are * homes up there where Jn 14:2,3
Here on earth you will have * Jn 16:33
I have told them * things while I Jn 17:13
there * times with his disciples. Jn 18:2
Greek, so that * people read it. Jn 19:20
Jesus' disciples saw him do * Jn 20:30,31
of the fish, there were so *! Jn 21:6
proved to them in * ways that it Act 1:3
* godly Jews were in Jerusalem Act 2:5
having arrived from * nations. Act 2:5
and the apostles did * miracles. Act 2:43
overnight. But * of the people who Act 4:4
Hall, and they did * remarkable Act 5:12
in Jerusalem; and * of the Jewish Act 6:7
And by means of * remarkable Act 7:36
miracles he did. * evil spirits Act 8:7
their victims, and * who were Act 8:7
been a sorcerer there for * years; Act 8:9,10,11
and * men and women were baptized. Act 8:12
* others to tell him about Jesus. Act 8:35
* ancient manuscripts omit verse Act 8:37f
town, and * believed in the Lord. Act 9:42
year, teaching the * new converts. Act 11:26
John Mark, where * were gathered Act 12:12
and there were * new believers. Act 12:24
And he was seen * times during Act 13:31
next week. And * Jews and godly Act 13:43
and as * as wanted Act 13:48
*—both Jews and Gentiles—believed. Act 14:1
there and making * disciples, they Act 14:21
of God through * tribulations. Act 14:22
every Sabbath for * generations." Act 15:21
* important women of the city. Act 17:4
Some manuscripts read, "* of the Act 17:4f
As a result, * of them believed, Act 17:12
Greek women and * men also. Act 17:12
walking I saw your * altars, and Act 17:23
were * others in Corinth. Act 18:8
one can harm you. * people here in Act 18:10
in * of the ancient manuscripts. Act 18:21f
persuading * to believe in Jesus. Act 19:8
greatly honored. * of the Act 19:18,19
who employed * craftsmen to Act 19:24
Paul has persuaded *, many people Act 19:26
persuaded many, * people that Act 19:26
lighted with * flickering lamps; Act 20:8
and day and my * tears for you. Act 20:31
Paul recounted the * things God had Act 21:19
dear brother, how * thousands of Act 21:20
Jewish affairs for * years, and Act 24:10
around, hurling * serious Act 25:7
So Paul, with * gestures, Act 26:1
* horrible things to the followers Act 26:9
I imprisoned * of the saints in Act 26:10
and about the * other occasions Act 26:16
storm raged unabated * days, Act 27:20
I planned to come * times before Rom 1:13
Yes, being a Jew has * Rom 3:2
Abraham the father of * nations. Rom 4:17
son who would have * descendants Rom 4:18
death to * through his sin. Rom 5:15
to * through God's mercy. Rom 5:15
of death to *, while Christ freely Rom 5:16
freely takes away * sins and gives Rom 5:16
Adam caused * to be sinners Rom 5:19
and Christ caused * to be made Rom 5:19
be the First, with * brothers. Rom 8:29
* will stumble over him (Jesus). Rom 9:33
Now * of the Jews are enemies of Rom 11:28
Just as there are * parts to our Rom 12:4,5
* in their needs, including me. Rom 16:1
have broken Christ into * pieces. 1Co 1:13
there are a great * gods, both in 1Co 8:5
deny yourselves * things that would 1Co 9:25
new and different. * others have 1Co 10:13
No matter how * of us there are, 1Co 10:17
That is why * of you are weak 1Co 11:30

(MANY Con't)
Now God gives us * kinds of 1Co 12:4
There are * ways in which God 1Co 12:6
Our bodies have * parts, but the 1Co 12:12
parts, but the * parts make up only 1Co 12:12
Yes, the body has * parts, not 1Co 12:14
He has made * parts for our 1Co 12:18
So he has made * parts, but 1Co 12:20
but there are * enemies. 1Co 16:9
no matter how * of them there are; 2Co 1:20
there are * of them—whose idea in 2Co 2:17
are leaders in so * ways—you have 2Co 8:7
so much faith, so * good preachers, 2Co 8:7
up * of them to begin helping. 2Co 9:2
I have traveled * weary miles 2Co 11:26
I patiently did * wonders and signs 2Co 12:12
and mourn because * of you who have 2Co 12:21
and the * other Jewish laws Gal 2:12
For I am going to give you * Gal 4:27
Don't drink too much wine, for * Eph 5:18
And because of my imprisonment * Php 1:14
my eyes, there are * who walk along Php 3:18
and for my * other friends who have Col 2:1
God will give us * chances to Col 4:3
trap him with * accusations, and 1Ti 3:7
pierced themselves with * sorrows. 1Ti 6:10
confession before * witnesses. 1Ti 6:12
I pray for you every day, and * 2Ti 1:3
things you and * others have heard 2Ti 2:2
You know how * troubles I have 2Ti 3:11
worse, deceiving *, they themselves 2Ti 3:13
For there are * who refuse to Tit 1:10
became slaves to * evil pleasures Tit 3:3
LONG AGO GOD spoke in * different Heb 1:1
house does. And * people can build Heb 3:4
When a farmer's land has had * Heb 6:7
battle against * kings, Melchizedek Heb 7:1
there had to be * priests, so that Heb 7:23
offering for the sins of * people; Heb 9:28
nation with so * millions of people Heb 11:12
* in their spiritual lives. Heb 12:15
Literally, "Not * (of you) should Jas 3:1f
for we all make * mistakes; Jas 3:1
the forgiveness of his * sins. Jas 5:20
about it, they had * questions as 1Pe 1:10
makes up for * of your faults. 1Pe 4:8
overlooks each other's * faults." 1Pe 4:8f
others God's * kinds of blessings. 1Pe 4:10
is thought by * to be Peter's wife 1Pe 5:13f
us to understand * things that 2Pe 1:19
and terrible end. * will follow 2Pe 2:2
same things in * of his letters. 2Pe 3:15,16
* such persons have appeared. 1Jn 2:18
For there are * false teachers 1Jn 4:1
there are * of them around—who 2Jn 1:7
"He says to you: I know how * Rev 2:2
he rode out to conquer in * Rev 6:2
How * were given this mark? Rev 7:4-8
on the earth and * people died. Rev 8:11
—I heard an announcement of how * Rev 9:16
further about * peoples, nations, Rev 10:11
and people from * nations will Rev 11:8,9
upon the * waters of the world. Rev 17:1
She brewed * a cup of woe for Rev 18:6
and on his head were * crowns. Rev 19:12

MANY-COLORED
wings full of * feathers came to Eze 17:3,4
embroidery and * carpets bound with Eze 27:24

MANY-PEAKED
O splendid * ranges! Ps 68:15,16

MAON
Hebron), Zior, *, Carmel, Ziph, Jos 15:48-62
of * in the south of the desert. 1Sa 23:24,25
A wealthy man from * owned a 1Sa 25:2
Shammai's son was *, the father 1Ch 2:45

MAONITES
the Amalekites, and the *? Ju 10:12

MAP
The scouts will * it into seven Jos 18:5,6
So the scouts went out to * the Jos 18:8
how I need a *—and your commands Ps 119:19
power of man to * his life and plan Jer 10:23
* of the city of Jerusalem on it. Eze 4:1
the center of your * of Jerusalem. Eze 5:2
* and slash at it with a knife. Eze 5:2
"Son of dust, make a * and on it Eze 21:19,20

MARA
Call me *," (Naomi means Ru 1:20
"pleasant"; * means "bitter") Ru 1:20

MARAH
Arriving at *, they couldn't Ex 15:23
was called *, meaning "bitter"). Ex 15:23
It was there at * that the Lord Ex 15:25
Etham wilderness, camping at *. Num 33:8
Leaving *, they came to Elim, Num 33:9

MARAUDERS
When they planted their seed, * Ju 6:3,4
for Philistine * had occupied the 2Sa 23:14
friend spied these * so they 2Ki 13:20,21

MARAUDING
"A * band shall stamp upon Gad, Gen 49:19
new king (for the * bands of Arabs 2Ch 22:1

MARBLE
stones, costly jewels, and *. 1Ch 29:2
rings imbedded in * pillars. Est 1:6
black, red, white, and yellow *. Est 1:6
His legs are as pillars of * set Sol 5:15
and brass and iron and *; Rev 18:12

MARCH
of your exodus, at the end of * Ex 13:4,5
the event annually in late *. Ex 13:10
Forward, *! Ex 14:15
in *, the month you left Egypt; Ex 23:15
dates appointed each year in *; Ex 34:18
to be celebrated at the end of *. Lev 23:5
Next in the line of * was the Num 2:3-31
they were next in the line of *. Num 2:3-31
At the head of the * was the Num 10:14
in the line of *, carrying the Num 10:17
of them as they began their *. Num 10:34
they will * out together against Deu 28:7
You will * out to battle Deu 28:25
miracle occurred on the 25th of *. Jos 4:19
* on, my soul, with strength! Ju 5:21
men began their * upon the city. Ju 9:35
are ready to * against us and I 1Sa 13:12
his entire army to * to Keilah and 1Sa 23:8
long * through the wilderness." 2Sa 17:28,29
arriving on * 25 of the ninth year 2Ki 25:1
* at the head of the procession. 1Ch 15:24
Majesty and honor * before him, 1Ch 16:27
choir leading the *, clothed in 2Ch 20:21
in the middle of * in the seventh Ez 7:7,8,9
at the Ahava River at the end of * Ez 8:31
December 15, and finished by * 15. Ez 10:16-19
attack me, I will * out behind his Ps 118:10
them on as they * against Babylon Is 13:2
Listen as the armies *! Is 13:4
arrows there, nor * outside its Is 37:33
of mankind as they * by? Is 41:4
Yes, * against Babylon, the land Jer 50:21
to * on Babylon and destroy her. Jer 51:11
their long * to distant lands. Eze 12:4
around the middle of *, this Eze 29:17
around the middle of * of the Eze 30:20
I will * against her and destroy Eze 38:11
and * against him and defeat him. Dan 11:7
"The Syrian king will * onward Dan 11:16
Straight forward they *, never Joe 2:7
* across the world and conquer it. Hab 1:6
the east could * their armies Rev 16:12

MARCHED
his army, he * to the frontier with Num 20:20
Then Judah * against the Ju 1:10
And Deborah * with them. Ju 4:10
iron chariots, and * from Ju 4:13
* through the gates! Ju 5:11
Down from Mount Tabor * the Ju 5:13,14
* down against great odds. Ju 5:13,14
So Abimelech and his men * Ju 9:34
* at the rear with King Achish. 1Sa 29:2
Ahab's troops * out of the city. 1Ki 20:16
Syrian army and * out against 1Ki 20:26
the army of Israel * on Jerusalem 2Ki 14:13
They * into Jerusalem 2Ch 20:28
They * against Judah, broke 2Ch 21:17
Judah when she was * away captive, Eze 25:3
You * across the land in awesome Hab 3:12
Your horsemen * across the sea; Hab 3:15

MARCHES
Yes, though a mighty army * Ps 27:3
the invading army * in. Jer 46:22,23
our land and * across our hills, he Mic 5:5
Pestilence * before him; Hab 3:5

MARCHING
When you hear a sound like * 2Sa 5:24
the three armies * against them, 2Ki 3:21
When you hear a sound like * in 1Ch 14:15
"a vast army is * against you from 2Ch 20:2
chariots, * by night, and almost 2Ch 21:9
Who is this in kingly robes, * in Is 63:1
I see great armies * on Jerusalem Jer 2:15
against her, * from their cities of Jer 2:16
the noise of * armies coming near. Jer 4:29
See the armies * from the north—a Jer 6:22
See the armies * from the north! Jer 13:20
riches, first * through Israel and Dan 11:28
20,000 men who are * against him? Lk 14:31

MARDUK
Names of * and Nabu, the two Is 46:1f
her god * will be utterly Jer 50:2

MARE
Literally, "I compare you to my * Sol 1:9f

MAREAL
west, going near * and Dabbesheth Jos 19:11

MARESHAH
Nezib, Keilah, Achzib, and *. Jos 15:37-44
of *, who was the father of 1Ch 2:42
Laadah (the father of *), 1Ch 4:21-22
Gath, *, Ziph, 2Ch 11:5-10
They advanced to the city of *, 2Ch 14:9,10
of Dodavahu from *, prophesied 2Ch 20:37
You people of * will be a prize Mic 1:1

MARITIME
Their descendants became the * Gen 10:

MARK
earth, and * the days and years." Gen 1:14,1
put an identifying * on Cain as a Gen 4:1
in your homes. * this day of your Ex 13:4,
he had branded his * of ownership Ex 13:
anger ends; but * your calendar to Job 14:1
the living. * this well, O Job. Job 33:3
* this well: The Lord has set Ps 4:
He assigned the moon to * the Ps 104:1
months, and the sun to * the days. Ps 104:1
to Israel. * your pathway well. Jer 31:2
arrows go straight to the *; Jer 50:
and put a * on the foreheads of the Eze 9:4
but don't touch anyone with the * Eze 9:6
Implied in * 3:32. Mt 12:46,47
of multitudes. * my words—I will Mt 26:29
implying jealousy, as in * 6:2–6. Mk 6:52
See * 14:29. Jn 21:15
mother of John *, where many were Act 12:12
taking John * with them. Act 12:25
(John * went with them as their Act 13:5
and wanted to take along John *. Act 15:37
Barnabas took * with him and Act 15:39
brand upon us—his * of 2Co 1:22
enemies that * me as his slave. Gal 6:17
so does *, a relative of Barnabas. Col 4:10
And as I said before, give * a Col 4:10
Bring * with you when you come, 2Ti 4:11
So do *, Aristarchus, Demas and Phm 1:24
shaky legs, and * out a straight, Heb 12:13
you, and so does my son *." 1Pe 5:13f
so does my son *. 1Pe 5:13
spiritual death (* 3:29) but can a 1Jn 5:17f
How many were given this *? Rev 7:4-8
the * of God on their foreheads. Rev 9:4
with a certain * on the right hand Rev 13:16
the permit of that *, which was Rev 13:17
and accepting his * on the forehead Rev 14:9
his statue and his * and number. Rev 15:2
who had the * of the Creature and Rev 16:2
*, and who worshiped his statue. Rev 19:20
nor accepted his * on their Rev 20:4

MARKED
Your bodies will thus be * as Gen 17:13
stones that were * in some way and Ex 28:30,31f
everyone whose forehead isn't *. Eze 9:5
Lord—all those * with my name.' Act 15:17
Christ, were * as belonging to Eph 1:13

MARKER
land by moving the boundary *. Deu 19:14
moves the boundary * between his Deu 27:17
he will put up a * beside them so Eze 39:15,16
those who move a boundary *." Hos 5:10f

MARKET
SO BOAZ WENT down to the * place Ru 4:1
the sick in the * plazas and Mk 6:56
come home from the * they must Mk 7:4
turn my Father's House into a *!" Jn 2:16
you want that is sold at the *. 1Co 10:25

MARKETPLACE
them before the judges at the *. Act 16:19

MARKETS
the * of Samaria for a dollar!" 2Ki 7:1
in the * and wherever you look. Ps 55:11
in the streets and *, soliciting at Pro 7:11,12
your *—silver, iron, tin and lead. Eze 27:12
are your captive *, giving payment Eze 27:15
them as they walk through the *. Mk 12:38
as you walk through the *! Lk 11:43

MARKS
him, and if the * of the disease Lev 13:6
nor put tattoo * upon yourselves in Lev 19:28
not move the ancient boundary *. Pro 22:28
*, for their Redeemer is strong; Pro 23:10,11
He measures and * out a block of Is 44:13
them to see [the * of the nails Lk 24:40
Remember, he is the one who * you Eph 4:30
Son is and does * him as God. Heb 1:3
is the blood that * the beginning Heb 9:20

MARKSMEN
who were expert * with their bows. 1Ch 8:40

MAROTH
The people of * vainly hope for Mic 1:12

MARRIAGE
And his mother arranged a * for Gen 21:20,21
for even after many years of * Gen 25:21
More literally, "customary * Ex 22:16f
However such a * was required Lev 20:21f
for the *, Samson threw a party for Ju 14:10,11
bless you with another happy *." Ru 1:9
you what to do concerning *." Ru 3:4
requires your * to Ruth so that she Ru 4:5
he was related to Ahab by *. 2Ki 8:27
Three sons were born from this * 2Ch 11:19
made a * alliance [for his son 2Ch 18:1
your daughter in * to my son.' 2Ch 25:18
happy songs, the * feasts, the Jer 16:9
again, you were old enough for *; Eze 16:8

(MARRIAGE Con't)
you to legally declare my * vow. Eze 16:8
Then, when the * had taken Eze 16:9,10
will be given in * to the king of Dan 11:6
Berenice in * to Antiochus II of Dan 11:6f
him a daughter in *, so that she Dan 11:17
in the resurrection there is no *; Mt 22:30
* feast, and the door was locked. Mt 25:10
joined together permanently in *; Mk 10:6,7
years following seven years of *. Lk 2:36,37
Jesus replied, "* is for people Lk 20:34,35
the laws of * no longer apply to Rom 7:2
from the rights of * for a limited 1Co 7:5
However, * will bring extra 1Co 7:28
Honor your * and its vows, and be Heb 13:4
not broken the * laws by committing Jas 2:11

MARRIAGEABLE
young virgins of * age were saved. Ju 21:10,11,12

MARRIAGES
Jehoiada arranged two * for him, 2Ch 24:3
by these mixed *, and the political Ez 9:2

MARRIED
Lamech * two wives—Adah and Gen 4:19
Meanwhile, Abram * his Gen 11:29
Sarai, while his brother Nahor * Gen 11:29
for that woman you took is *." Gen 20:3
have the same father)—and I * her. Gen 20:11,12
NOW ABRAHAM * again. Gen 25:1
years old when he * Rebekah, the Gen 25:20
Esau, at the age of forty, * a Gen 26:34
and he also * Basemath, daughter Gen 26:34
family and * two additional wives Gen 28:9
Esau * three local girls from Gen 36:2,3
There he met and * a Canaanite Gen 38:2
own, and so, although he * her, Gen 38:9
Joseph thus * into a family of Gen 41:45f
tribe of Levi who * and had a Ex 2:1
* Jochebed, his father's sister; Ex 6:20
Aaron * Elisheba, the daughter of Ex 6:23
Aaron's son Eleazar * one of the Ex 6:25
a slave before he *, then if he Ex 21:3
then if he * afterwards, only he Ex 21:3
but if he was * before he became Ex 21:3
girl who is engaged to be *, they Lev 19:20
If a priest's daughter is * Lev 22:12
of the Cushite woman he had *." Num 12:1f
"If she is * and living in her Num 30:10
'Let them be * to anyone they like, Num 36:6
and Noah, were * to men in their Num 36:11,12
Well, go home and get *! Deu 20:7
a virgin when I * her,' then the Deu 22:13,14
she was not a virgin when she *; Deu 22:17,18
"A newly * man is not to be Deu 24:5
If she were still *, no special Deu 27:23f
and the Israeli girls * their men. Ju 3:6
seventy sons, for he * many wives. Ju 8:30
So she was never *. Ju 11:39
daughters. He * his daughters to Ju 12:9,10
So his wife was * instead to the Ju 14:20
"so I * her to your best man. Ju 15:2
All the men, * women, and Ju 21:10,11,12
* girls of Moab, Orpah and Ruth. Ru 1:4,5
you, and get you happily * again? Ru 3:1
So Boaz * Ruth, and when he slept Ru 4:13
the wedding, Saul * her to Adriel, 1Sa 18:19
David also * Ahino-am from 1Sa 25:43
Jerusalem, David * additional wives 2Sa 5:13
Egypt, and * one of his daughters. 1Ki 3:1
Ben-abinadab (who * Solomon's 1Ki 4:8-19
Ahima-az (who * Princess Basemath, 1Ki 4:8-19
KING SOLOMON * many other girls 1Ki 11:1
the women they * would get them 1Ki 11:2
not enough, he * Jezebel, the 1Ki 16:31
he even * one of Ahab's 2Ki 8:18
After Azubah's death, Caleb * 1Ch 2:19
Hezron * Machir's daughter at the 1Ch 2:21
death, Caleb * Ephrathah, his 1Ch 2:24
Mered * Bithi-ah, an Egyptian 1Ch 4:17
to Jerusalem, he * additional wives 1Ch 14:3
his daughters were * to their 1Ch 23:22
Rehoboam * his cousin 2Ch 11:18
Later he * Maacah, the daughter 2Ch 11:20
very strong. He * fourteen wives 2Ch 13:21
for Jehoram had * one of the 2Ch 21:6
and Barzillai (he * one of the Ez 2:61
The men of Israel had * girls Ez 9:2
for we have * these heathen women. Ez 10:2
"You have sinned, for you have * Ez 10:10
of priests who had * heathen wives Ez 10:16-19
son Jehohanan was * to the daughter Neh 6:18
and Barzillai (he * one of the Neh 7:63
of the Jews had * women from Neh 13:23
But though you have left me and * Jer 3:1
and Jerusalem!) I * them, and they Eze 23:4,5
So Hosea * Gomer, daughter of Hos 1:3
In God's wise plan, when you *, Mal 2:15
was engaged to be * to Joseph. Mt 1:18
The first of these men * and then Mt 22:25
* and died, and left no children. Mk 12:20,21,22
So the second brother * the Mk 12:20,21,22
Then the next brother * her, and Mk 12:20,21,22
be *—they will be like the angels. Mk 12:25
engaged to be * to a man named Lk 1:27
Another had just been * and for Lk 14:20
They ate and drank and * Lk 17:27
The oldest * and then died Lk 20:29
His brother * the widow and he, Lk 20:30
of the seven had * her and died, Lk 20:31
For all of them were * to her!" Lk 20:33
"But I'm not *," the woman Jn 4:17,18
you aren't even * to the man you're Jn 4:17,18
are no longer "* to the law," and Rom 7:4
And now you are "*," so to Rom 7:4
was grown up and *, and Rebecca his Rom 9:10-13
But usually it is best to be *, 1Co 7:2
is her right as a * woman, and the 1Co 7:3
So I say to those who aren't *, 1Co 7:8
Now, for those who are * I have a 1Co 7:10
about girls who are not yet *? 1Co 7:25
Of course, if you already are *, 1Co 7:27
and get * now, it is all right; 1Co 7:28
and if a girl gets * in times 1Co 7:28
But a * man can't do that so 1Co 7:33
A girl who is not * is anxious to 1Co 7:34
But a * woman must consider other 1Co 7:34
it is wrong to be * and wrong to 1Ti 4:3
old and have been * only once. 1Ti 5:9

MARRIES
If he himself * her and then Ex 21:10
If a man * his brother's widow, Lev 20:21
pledge, and later *, and her Num 30:6
"If a man * a girl, then after Deu 22:13,14
bitter woman when she finally *. Pro 30:21,22,23
A servant girl who * her mistress' Pro 30:21,22,23
of a young man who * a virgin; Is 62:5
to commit adultery if she * again. Mt 5:32
And he who * her commits Mt 5:32
and * another, commits adultery." Mt 19:9
"And the man who * a divorced Mt 19:9f
his wife and * someone else commits Lk 16:18
and anyone who * a divorced woman Lk 16:18
Let me illustrate: when a woman * Rom 7:2
for a girl who * no longer has 1Co 7:4
It is the same with a girl who *. 1Co 7:34
So the person who * does well, 1Co 7:38
but only if she * a Christian. 1Co 7:39
and mother when he *, so that he Eph 5:31

MARRY
Why were you willing to let me * Gen 12:19
that our father would let us *. Gen 19:31
not let my son * one of these local Gen 24:3
Isaac * one of the local girls, Gen 24:37
a girl from here to * his son. Gen 24:38
I'd rather die than see Jacob * Gen 27:46
* one of these Canaanite girls. Gen 28:1
Bethuel, and * one of your Gen 28:2
the time came for him to * her. Gen 29:21
"It's not our custom to * off a Gen 29:26
"I want to * her." Gen 34:4
Please let him * her. Gen 34:8
let your daughters * our sons, and Gen 34:9,10
disgrace for her to * such a man. Gen 34:14
for him to * a girl named Tamar. Gen 38:6
Onan, "You must * Tamar, as our Gen 38:8
not to * again at that time, but to Gen 38:11
Shelah was old enough to * her. Gen 38:11
to be permitted to * Shelah, though Gen 38:14
But he did not * her. Gen 38:26
refuses to let her * him, then he Ex 22:17
"None of you shall * Lev 18:6
A girl may not * her father; Lev 18:7
"You shall not * your Lev 18:10
You may not * a half-sister—your Lev 18:11
"You may not * your Lev 18:15
You may not * both a woman and Lev 18:17
You shall not * two sisters, for Lev 18:18
it is all right to * her sister. Lev 18:18
A priest shall not * a Lev 21:7
and he shall not * a divorced Lev 21:7
He must * a virgin. Lev 21:13
He may not * a widow, nor a Lev 21:14,15
But if they * into another Num 36:3
to the tribe into which they *. Num 36:3
are heiresses must * within their Num 36:8
* their sons and daughters. Deu 7:3
someone else would * your fiancée. Deu 20:7
After that you may * her. Deu 21:13
to the girl's father and * her; Deu 22:28,29
husband may not * her again, for Deu 24:4
must not * outside the family; Deu 25:5
must * her and sleep with her. Deu 25:5
refusing to * the widow, then she Deu 25:7
name continue—he refuses to * me.' Deu 25:7
"Someone else will * your Deu 28:30
weeping because I'll never *." Ju 11:37
in thirty girls to * his sons. Ju 12:9,10
mother that he wanted to * her. Ju 14:2
"Why don't you * a Jewish girl?" Ju 14:3
people of Israel you could *?" Ju 14:3
than she is. * her instead." Ju 15:2
their daughters * a man from the Ju 21:1
him, and if he will * you, fine; Ru 3:13
scheduled to * Saul's daughter, 1Sa 17:55f
to * the daughter of a king?" 1Sa 18:23
daughter, to * a man from Gallim 1Sa 25:44
it, for he will let you * me." 2Sa 13:13
Adonijah * Abishag," she replied. 1Ki 2:21
his people not to * into those 1Ki 11:2
let our daughters * their sons, and Ez 9:12
to let our sons * their daughters, Ez 9:12
let our daughters * non-Jewish men Neh 10:30
let our sons * non-Jewish girls. Neh 10:30
we do if someone asks to * her?" Sol 8:8
them and say, "Let us all * you! Is 4:1
You must not * and have children Jer 16:2
there many years. * and have Jer 29:6
He may * only a Jewish maiden, Eze 44:22
he may not * a divorced woman. Eze 44:22
The Lord said to Hosea, "Go and * Hos 1:2
him it was wrong for him to * her. Mt 14:4
it is, it is better not to *!" Mt 19:10
are born without the ability to *, Mt 19:12
and some refuse to * for the sake Mt 19:12
his brother should * the widow and Mt 22:24
for the king to * Herodias, his Mk 6:17,18
his wife to * someone else, he Mk 10:11
brother should * his widow and have Mk 12:19
brother shall * the widow and their Lk 20:28
dead get to heaven, they do not *. Lk 20:34,35
Then she can * someone else if Rom 7:3
that if you do not *, it is good. 1Co 7:1
I'm not saying you must *; 1Co 7:6
yourselves, go ahead and *. 1Co 7:9
It is better to * than to burn 1Co 7:9
But if anyone feels he ought to * 1Co 7:36
let him *. 1Co 7:36
willpower not to * and decides that 1Co 7:37
who doesn't * does even better. 1Co 7:38
dies, then she may * again, but 1Co 7:39
be happier if she doesn't * again; 1Co 7:40
each of you will * in holiness and 1Th 4:3,4
their vow to Christ and * again. 1Ti 5:11
younger widows to * again and have 1Ti 5:14
said you must not * a woman who Jas 2:11

MARRYING
were bitter about his * them. Gen 26:35
warned him against * a Canaanite Gen 28:6,7,8
no longer wanting her after * her. Ex 21:8
However, if after * her you Deu 21:14
in the family by * her off to a Ru 1:11f
you can give Naomi an heir by * me Ru 3:10
* heathen women who worship idols. Mal 2:11
of Galilee, for * Herodias, his Lk 3:19,20
get along without *, just as I do. 1Co 7:7
as God intended, * or not marrying 1Co 7:17
marrying or not * in accordance 1Co 7:17
not to try to keep you from *. 1Co 7:35

MARS
him to the forum at * Hill. Act 17:19
before them at the * Hill forum, Act 17:22

MARSENA
Tarshish, Meres, *, and Est 1:13-15

MARSH
The * hen, Lev 11:13-19

MARSHAL
sent his field *, his chief 2Ki 18:17

MARSHES
rivers, canals, *, and reservoirs, Ex 7:19
porcupines, full of swamps and *. Is 14:23
But the * and swamps will not be Eze 47:11

MART
You were the merchandise * of the Is 23:2,3

MARTHA
* welcomed them into her home. Lk 10:38
But * was the jittery type, and Lk 10:40
But the Lord said to her, "*, Lk 10:41
Literally, "*, Martha." Lk 10:41f
Literally, "Martha, *." Lk 10:41f
Mary and her sister *, was sick. Jn 11:1
Although Jesus was very fond of * Jn 11:5
console * and Mary on their loss. Jn 11:19
When * got word that Jesus was Jn 11:20
* said to Jesus, "Sir, if you Jn 11:21
"Yes," * said, "when everyone Jn 11:24
Do you believe this, *?" Jn 11:26
at the place where * met him. Jn 11:30
But *, the dead man's sister, Jn 11:39
in Jesus' honor. * served, and Jn 12:2

MARTYRED
* among you by Satan's devotees. Rev 2:13
those who had been * for preaching Rev 6:9
* on the earth and joined them. Rev 6:11
prophets have been * and their Rev 16:6
the * prophets and the saints." Rev 18:24

MARTYRS
last the time has come for his * Rev 14:13
of the * of Jesus she had killed. Rev 17:6

MARVEL
They * at the sight and hurry Ps 48:5

MARVELED
How the crowds *! Mt 9:33
The crowds just *, and praised Mt 15:31
All the world * at this miracle Rev 13:3

MARVELING
just stood there, * at what was Lk 2:33
* at his answer, they were silent. Lk 20:26

MARVELOUS
And tell of his * works. 1Ch 16:9
And his * miracles 1Ch 16:12,13
the Lord must be a * structure, 1Ch 22:5
this * rescue from their enemies. 2Ch 20:27
about the * things you do. Ps 9:1
they are a * display of his Ps 19:1
* miracles happen to his people! Ps 66:5
Lord's doing, and it is * to see! Ps 118:23
Your workmanship is *—and how Ps 139:14
* wisdom and defile your splendor! Eze 28:7
For if the * miracles I did in Mt 11:23
* message of God's great kindness. 2Co 6:1
Yet I don't feel that these * 2Co 11:5
thing these other * fellows have 2Co 12:11
into the soil of God's * love; Eph 3:17
He could do these * things Rev 13:14
"Great and * Rev 15:3,4

MARVELS
miracles, * without number. Job 5:9

MARY
in that a virgin (*) conceived and Is 7:14f
was the husband of *, the mother of Mt 1:16
His mother, *, was engaged to be Mt 1:18
hesitate to take * as your wife! Mt 1:20
and brought * home to be his wife, Mt 1:24
where the baby and * his mother Mt 2:11
night he left for Egypt with * Mt 2:14
son, and we know * his mother and Mt 13:55
Among them were * Magdalene and Mt 27:56
Mary Magdalene and * the mother of Mt 27:56
Both * Magdalene and the other Mt 27:61
* were sitting nearby watching. Mt 27:61
day was dawning, * Magdalene and Mt 28:1
the other * went out to the tomb. Mt 28:1
from a distance—* Magdalene, Mary Mk 15:40
Magdalene, * (the mother of James Mk 15:40
(* Magdalene and Mary the mother Mk 15:47
(Mary Magdalene and * the mother Mk 15:47
the Sabbath ended, * Magdalene and Mk 16:1
and Salome and * the mother of Mk 16:1
who saw him was * Magdalene—the Mk 16:9
to a virgin, *, engaged to be Lk 1:27
Confused and disturbed, * tried Lk 1:29
"Don't be frightened, *," the Lk 1:30
* asked the angel, "But how can Lk 1:34
* said, "I am the Lord's Lk 1:38
A few days later * hurried to the Lk 1:39,40
and exclaimed to *, "You are Lk 1:42
* responded, "Oh, how I praise Lk 1:46
* stayed with Elizabeth about Lk 1:56
He took with him *, his fiancée, Lk 2:5
found their way to * and Joseph. Lk 2:16
astonishment, but * quietly Lk 2:19
and so, when * and Joseph arrived Lk 2:27
Joseph and * just stood there, Lk 2:33
but then said to *, "A sword shall Lk 2:34,35
was talking with * and Joseph, and Lk 2:38
among them were * Magdalene Lk 8:2
Her sister * sat on the floor, Lk 10:39
concerned about. * has discovered Lk 10:42
to the tomb were * Magdalene and Lk 24:10
and Joanna and * the mother of Lk 24:10
DO YOU REMEMBER *, who poured Jn 11:1
* and her sister Martha, was sick. Jn 11:1
fond of Martha, *, and Lazarus, he Jn 11:5
Martha and * on their loss. Jn 11:19
to meet him. But * stayed at home. Jn 11:20
and returned to * and, calling her Jn 11:28
So * went to him at once. Jn 11:29
trying to console * saw her leave Jn 11:31
When * arrived where Jesus was, Jn 11:32
who were with * and saw it happen, Jn 11:45
Then * took a jar of costly Jn 12:3
Jesus' mother, *, his aunt, the Jn 19:25
wife of Cleopas, and * Magdalene. Jn 19:25
it was still dark, * Magdalene came Jn 20:1
went on home, and by that time * Jn 20:11
* -Jesus said Jn 20:16
* Magdalene found the disciples Jn 20:18
to the home of *, mother of John Act 12:12
Remember me to *, too, who has Rom 16:6

MARY'S
"He's just a carpenter, * boy, Mk 6:2,3
At the sound of * greeting, Lk 1:41
When the time came for * Lk 2:22

MASCARA
and brighten your eyes with *? Jer 4:30

MASH
were:Uz, Hul, Gether, *. Gen 10:23

MASHAL
gave them Abdon, *, Hukok, and 1Ch 6:74

MASK
they say. They * their faces so no Job 24:14,15
Laughter cannot * a heavy heart. Pro 14:13

MASONS
and * to build a palace for David. 2Sa 5:11
carpenters and * to repair the 2Ki 22:5,6
KING HIRAM OF Tyre sent * and 1Ch 14:1
who hired * and carpenters to 2Ch 24:12
Then they hired * and carpenters, Ez 3:7
And the * and laborers worked Neh 4:17

MASREKAH
Succeeded by: King Samlah, from *. Gen 36:31-39
the city of * came to the throne. 1Ch 1:47

MASS
a shapeless, chaotic *, Gen 1:2
"over the dark, gaseous *." Gen 1:2f
the fatty * above the liver, and Lev 8:15,16
saw the vast * of enemy troops, 1Sa 13:6
with fire, with a * of fire inside Eze 1:4
fire like a tangled * of thorns. Nah 1:10

MASSA
Mishma, Dumah,*, Hadad, Gen 25:12-15
Mishma, Dumah, *, Hadad, Tema, 1Ch 1:28-31
*, addressed to Ithiel and Ucal: Pro 30:1
wise sayings of King Lemuel of *, Pro 31:1

MASSACRE
of Zebulun did not * the people of Ju 1:30
going to come and * all the allied Ju 7:14
And I will send * and famine and Jer 24:10
symbolize the great * they face! Eze 21:14

MASSACRED
Jerusalem, and * its people, Ju 1:8
of Zephath and * all its people. Ju 1:17
is named Hormah (meaning, "*"). Ju 1:17
get in, and they * the entire Ju 1:25

MASSAH
Moses named the place * (meaning Ex 17:7
you complained against him at *. Deu 6:16
and once again at * you angered the Deu 9:22
You tested Levi at * and at Deu 33:8
at Meribah and *. Ps 95:8

MASSES
his teeming *, says the Lord." Eze 31:18
on represent * of people of every Rev 17:15

MASSIVE
confident of a * slaughter just as Ju 20:35-39
AFTERWARDS A * campaign against 2Ch 31:1
mounted a * attack against me. Ps 18:4

MAST
at sea, clinging to a swaying *. Pro 23:34
from Lebanon to make a * for you. Eze 27:5

MASTER
to be the * of all life upon the Gen 1:26
and he shall be your *." Gen 3:16
to * it, until your dying day. Gen 3:19
* and swore to him that ." Gen 24:9f
of everything his * owned, and Gen 24:10
"O Jehovah, the God of my *," Gen 24:12
kindness to my * Abraham and help Gen 24:12
"Thank you, Lord God of my * Gen 24:27
has overwhelmed my * with blessings Gen 24:35
son, and my * has given him Gen 24:36
And my * made me promise not to Gen 24:37
the God of my * Abraham, if you are Gen 24:42
the God of my * Abraham, because he Gen 24:48
kind to my * and do what is right? Gen 24:49
he said, "Send me back to my *!" Gen 24:54
I want to report back to my *." Gen 24:56
Literally, "It is my *." Gen 24:65f
Be the * of your brothers. Gen 27:27,28,29
Isaac: "I have made him your *, Gen 27:37
They are a present for his * Gen 32:18
in the home of his *, so that Gen 39:2
"Look," he told her, "my * Gen 39:8
be slaves forever to your *." Gen 44:9
But if his * gave him a wife Ex 21:4
belong to the *, and he shall go Ex 21:4
'I prefer my *, my wife, and my Ex 21:5
free,' then his * shall bring him Ex 21:6
And if a * knocks out his Ex 21:27
the slave's * shall be given thirty Ex 21:32
of Judah) was the * craftsman, Ex 38:22
"If a slave escapes from his *, Deu 23:15,16
found their * dead on the floor. Ju 3:25
"No," his * said, "we can't Ju 19:12,13
the arrows and ran back to his *. 1Sa 20:38
to talk to our *, but he insulted 1Sa 25:14
be trouble for our * and his whole 1Sa 25:17
So why haven't you guarded your * 1Sa 26:15
himself with his * than by turning 1Sa 29:4
he replied. "My * left me behind 1Sa 30:13
give me back to my *, then I will 1Sa 30:15
"Your father was a hard *," they 1Ki 12:2,3,4
going to take away your * today?" 2Ki 2:5
search the wilderness for your *; 2Ki 2:16
"I wish my * would go to see the 2Ki 5:3
one thing—when my * the king goes 2Ki 5:18
to himself, "My * shouldn't have 2Ki 5:20
"Yes," he said, "but my * has 2Ki 5:22
When he went in to his *, Elisha 2Ki 5:25
"Alas, my *, what shall we do 2Ki 6:15
for his * will soon follow him." 2Ki 6:32
of a Zimri who murdered his *!" 2Ki 9:31
"I conspired against my * and 2Ki 10:9,10
with my *, the king of Assyria! 2Ki 18:23
replied, "Has my * sent me to 2Ki 18:27
speak only to you and to your *? 2Ki 18:27
says, 'Tell your * not to be 2Ki 19:5
of them in all—was a * musician. 1Ch 25:6
"I am sending you a * 2Ch 2:
"Your father was a hard *," 2Ch 10
son, and was a traitor to his *. 2Ch 13
And the Lord said, 'Their * has 2Ch 18:1
slave is free at last from his *. Job 3:1
to * him bring a sharp sword! Job 40:
his eyes upon his * or a slave girl Ps 123.
Or, "like a * workman." Pro 8:3
what fools men are to let it * Pro 20:
The * may get better work from an Pro 26:
Students are wise who * what Ecc 12:1
to a hard, cruel *, to a vicious Is 19:
in Jerusalem? My *, the king of Is 36:8,
But he replied, "My * wants Is 36:1
for I am your * and I will bring Jer 3:1
Jew should be the * of another Jew Jer 34:
"O Belteshazzar, * magician," I Dan 4:
"He will be a * of deception, Dan 8:2
Husband" instead of "My *." Hos 1:1
father, a servant honors his *. Mal 1:
I am your Father and *, yet you Mal 1:
A servant is not above his *. Mt 10:2
And since I, the * of the Mt 10:2
am * even of the Sabbath." Mt 12:
him, "Doesn't your * pay taxes?" Mt 17:2
question: "Good *, what must I do Mt 19:1
just say, 'The * needs them,' and Mt 21:
and to be called 'Rabbi' and '*'! Mt 23:
And don't be called '*,' for Mt 23:1
one is your *, even the Messiah. Mt 23:1
"After a long time their * Mt 25:1
"His * praised him for good Mt 25:2
" 'Good work,' his * said. Mt 25:2
"But his * replied, 'Wicked man! Mt 25:2
So-and-So, and tell him, 'Our * Mt 26:1
to Jesus and said, "Hello, *!" Mt 26:4
"*," they said, "we want you Mk 10:3
just say, 'Our * needs him and will Mk 11:3
the * of the house will come." Mk 13:34
in charge, 'Our * sent us to see Mk 14:14
he walked up to Jesus. "*!" Mk 14:45
am * even of the Sabbath." Lk 6:5
up. "*, Master, we are sinking!" Lk 8:24
"Master, *, we are sinking!" Lk 8:24
and Peter said, "*, so many are Lk 8:45
out, "*, this is wonderful! Lk 9:33
to him and said, "*, we saw Lk 9:49
said to Jesus, "*, shall we order Lk 9:54
sensible man whose * gives him the Lk 12:42,43,44
If his * returns and finds that Lk 12:42,43,44
be a reward—his * will put him in Lk 12:42,43,44
well, his * will return without Lk 12:46
to his * what they had said. Lk 14:21
they had said. His * was angry and Lk 14:21
" 'Well, then,' said his *, 'go Lk 14:23
" 'All right!' his * said. Lk 19:19
*! they exclaimed Lk 21:7
Out in the world the * sits at Lk 22:27
"*," they replied, "we have Lk 22:38
exclaimed, "*, shall we fight? Lk 22:49
take it to the * of ceremonies." Jn 2:7,8
When the * of ceremonies tasted Jn 2:9
John and said, "*, the man you met Jn 3:26
Simon Peter replied, "*, to whom Jn 6:68
"*," his disciples asked him, Jn 9:2
But his disciples objected. * Jn 11:8
"Yes, *," she told him. Jn 11:27
said to him, "*, you shouldn't be Jn 13:6
You call me '*' and 'Lord,' and Jn 13:13
servant is not greater than his *. Jn 13:16
Simon Peter said, "*, where are Jn 13:36
a * doesn't confide in his slaves; Jn 15:15
'A slave isn't greater than his * Jn 15:20
* -she exclaimed Jn 20:16
* which of us will betray you?" Jn 21:20
will never again be your *." Rom 6:14f
never again be your *, for now Rom 6:14
that you can choose your own *? Rom 6:16
your * and you will be his slave. Rom 6:16
you are free from your old *, sin; Rom 6:18
to your new *, righteousness. Rom 6:18
Your "husband," your *, used to Rom 7:4
does just what his * tells him to. 1Co 4:2
because of his * plan of salvation Eph 3:21
Don't work hard only when your * Eph 6:6,7
you have the same * they do, and Eph 6:9
you, too, have a * in heaven who is Col 4:1
and true God only is your *. 1Th 1:9
even their * who bought them; 2Pe 2:1
our only * and Lord, Jesus Christ. Jud 1:4

MASTER-DREAMER
"Here comes that *," they Gen 37:19,20

MASTER'S
to the family of my * relatives." Gen 24:27
"Now when Sarah, my * wife, was Gen 24:36
gave birth to my * son, and my Gen 24:36
to be the wife of my * son.' Gen 24:44
Literally, "my * brother's Gen 24:48f
of my * brother. Gen 24:48

(MASTER'S Con't)
* son, as Jehovah has directed." Gen 24:51
And he replied, "It is my * Gen 24:65
silver or gold from your * house? Gen 44:8
her Egyptian * wife and neighbors. Ex 3:22
"I have given your * grandson 2Sa 9:9
the heads of your * sons to me at 2Ki 10:6
smallest contingent in my * army. 2Ki 18:24
A wise slave will rule his * Pro 17:2
worst contingent of my * troops? Is 36:8,9
The servant shares his *! Mt 10:25
first prepares his * meal and Lk 17:7,8,9

MASTERED
and they soon * all the literature Dan 1:17
later had * most of the Near East. Hab 1:6f

MASTERS
you are * of the fish and birds Gen 1:28
task and served his * with vigor. Gen 49:15
Our * would not let us have Ju 5:8
days who run away from their *. 1Sa 25:10
servants and *, slave girls and Is 24:2
saying, Tell your * that the Lord Jer 27:4
shall no longer be their *! Jer 30:8
former servants have become our *; Lam 5:8
kill to fill their *' homes with Zep 1:9
"You cannot serve two *: God and Mt 6:24
nor anyone else can serve two *. Lk 16:13
and earned much money for her *. Act 16:16
Her *' hopes of wealth were now Act 16:19
of slaves and *, because it is easy Rom 6:19
Slaves, obey your *; Eph 6:5
obey your earthly *, not only Col 3:22
merely for your *, remembering Col 3:23
Urge slaves to obey their * and Tit 2:9
you) should become * (teachers)." Jas 3:1f
Servants, you must respect your * 1Pe 2:18

MASTS
on broken * with useless tackle. Is 33:23

MAT
him a paralyzed boy on a *. Mt 9:2
a paralyzed man on a sleeping *. Lk 5:18,19
*, right in front of Jesus. Lk 5:18,19
his * and went home praising God! Lk 5:25
your sleeping * and go on home!" Jn 5:8
He rolled up the * and began Jn 5:9
to carry that sleeping *!" Jn 5:10

MATATTAH
Mattenai, *, Zabad, Eliphelet, Ez 10:33

MATCH
couldn't win the *, he struck Gen 32:25
And may your strength * the length Deu 33:25
and was obviously the best *! 1Sa 17:11f
that they were no * for Israel. 2Sa 10:15,16
man starts fights as easily as a * Pro 26:21
a burning * among the sheaves; Zec 12:6
and pleasure—* it now with torments Rev 18:7

MATCHED
perfectly *, without one missing. Sol 4:2
Your cheeks are * loveliness Sol 4:3
perfectly * and not one missing. Sol 6:6
Your cheeks are * loveliness Sol 6:7

MATE
* only with Jacob's black rams. Gen 30:39,40
animals to *, and placed the peeled Gen 30:41
told me that I should * the white Gen 31:12
its * on the other long sheet. Ex 36:11,12
to a male animal, to * with it; Lev 18:23
"Obey my laws: Do not * your Lev 19:19
will come, each one with its *. Is 34:15
be there without a *, for the Lord Is 34:16
neighing for his neighbor's *. Jer 5:8

MATED
for that is when they *. Gen 30:38
So the flocks * before the Gen 30:39,40

MATERIAL
made of the same *—threads of gold, Ex 28:8
of wall, and the * must be thrown Lev 14:40
O Lord our God, all of this * 1Ch 29:16
as their source * the reports Lk 1:1,2
omit the * within the parentheses. Jn 5:4f
in return is to give some * aid. Rom 15:27
service to them in * blessings." Rom 15:27f
kind of * each builder has used. 1Co 3:13

MATERIALS
their offerings of * for the Ex 35:21
Moses gave them the * donated by Ex 36:3
more than enough * on hand now to Ex 36:4-7
And King Asa used these * to 1Ki 15:22
to buy the other * needed to repair 2Ki 12:11,12
construction * before his death. 1Ch 22:5
* I have already collected. 1Ch 29:3
purchase building *—stone building 2Ch 34:10,11
carried in the * to the workmen. 2Ch 34:13
palace too, for * to strengthen the Jer 33:4
But there are various kinds of * 1Co 3:12
with the right *, and whose work 1Co 3:14

MATES
and then find * for them and have Jer 29:6

MATHEMATICS
have included *, astronomy and Dan 1:3,4f

MATING
"And at the * season, I had a Gen 31:10
that the he-goats * with the flock Gen 31:10
that all the * males are speckled, Gen 31:12f
sniffing the wind at * time. Jer 2:24

MATRED
of * and granddaughter of Mezahab. Gen 36:31-39
* and granddaughter of Mezahab). 1Ch 1:50

MATRITES
the family of the * was chosen. 1Sa 10:21

MATS
who were with him * to sleep on, 2Sa 17:28,29
folks to him on * and stretchers. Mk 6:55
on beds and * so that at least Act 5:15

MATTAN
images and killing *, the priest of 2Ki 11:18
idols, and killed * the priest of 2Ch 23:15,16,17
BUT WHEN SHEPHATIAH (son of *) Jer 38:1

MATTANAH
through *, Nahaliel, and Bamoth; Num 21:17,18

MATTANIAH
*, to be the next king; 2Ki 24:17
* (the son of Mica, who was the 1Ch 9:15,16
his sons: Bukkiah, *, Uzziel, 1Ch 25:4,5
Ninth, * and twelve of his sons 1Ch 25:9-31
of Je-iel, son of * the Levite, who 2Ch 20:14
the Asaph clan, Zechariah and *; 2Ch 29:12,13,14
*, Zechariah, Jehiel, Ez 10:26
Eli-o-enai, Eliashib, *, Jeremoth, Ez 10:27
*, Bezalel, Binnui, Manasseh. Ez 10:30
Eliashib, *, Mattenai, Jaasu, Bani, Ez 10:34-42
* (son of Mica, son of Zabdi, son Neh 11:15,16,17
Hashabiah, son of *, son of Mica), Neh 11:22,23
Sherebiah, Judah, *—who was the one Neh 12:8
*, Bakbukiah, Obadiah, Neh 12:25
Shemaiah, son of *, son of Micaiah, Neh 12:35,36
son of *) as their assistant. Neh 13:13

MATTATHA
Menna's father was *; Lk 3:23-38

MATTATHA'S
Menna's father was Mattatha;* Lk 3:23-38

MATTATHIAS
Joseph's father was *; Lk 3:23-38
Joseph's father was Mattathias;*' Lk 3:23-38
Maath's father was *; Lk 3:23-38
Maath's father was Mattathias;*' Lk 3:23-38

MATTENAI
*, Matattah, Zabad, Eliphelet, Ez 10:33
Mattaniah, *, Jaasu, Bani, Binnui, Ez 10:34-42
*, leader of the Joiarib clan; Neh 12:12-21

MATTER
claim against me regarding this *. Gen 20:16
feeling in the *, be so kind as to Gen 23:8
you require. No * what dowry or Gen 34:12
"What in the world is the *?" Gen 40:7
And what nation, no * how great, Deu 4:8
in your land, no * how much greater Deu 11:23
"Any Levite, no * where he lives Deu 18:6,7
his duty in this *, refusing to Deu 25:7
If anyone, no * who, rebels Jos 1:17,18
"What's the *, Hannah?" 1Sa 1:8
to discuss the * with Samuel. 1Sa 8:4
to town he asked, "What's the *? 1Sa 11:5
me on a private *," David lied. 1Sa 21:2
my family in this *, for we knew 1Sa 22:15
"I accept all blame in this *, 1Sa 25:24
him, "What's the * with you? 2Sa 11:10
Absalom kept on urging the * 2Sa 13:27
* before you in a different light. 2Sa 14:20
see that you are right in this *; 2Sa 15:3
go, I will go, no * what 2Sa 15:21
but no * how many blankets were 1Ki 1:1
As a * of fact, I have a favor 1Ki 2:14
For no * how much they used, 1Ki 17:16
to clinch the * by exclaiming, 1Ki 20:33
"What in the world is the *?" 1Ki 21:5
the fact of the * is that the Lord 1Ki 22:23
However, what's the *?" 2Ki 6:26-30
"What's the *, sir?" 2Ki 8:12
be wiped out—every male, no * who. 2Ki 9:8
we handled the * improperly—you 1Ch 15:13
defeated no * how well you fight; 2Ch 25:8
agreement in this *, so they sent 2Ch 30:4
the * more thoroughly. Ez 4:21
the * and returned his decision. Ez 5:5
us know your pleasure in this *." Ez 5:17
seriousness of the * and because of Ez 10:9
decide this * for himself. Est 1:8
approached the king about the *. Est 3:8
them that when the * came before Est 9:24,25
"But now my grief remains no * Job 16:6
"The fact of the * is that God Job 19:6
I WILL PRAISE the Lord no * what Ps 34:1
buy him off no * what you offer. Pro 6:35
Wait for the Lord to handle the * Pro 20:22
So discuss the * with him Pro 25:8,9,10
and tiresome. No * how much we see, Ecc 1:8-11
satisfied; no * how much we hear, Ecc 1:8-11
And so the * is lost in red tape Ecc 5:8
no strength for the simplest *. Ecc 10:15
then I could kiss you no * who Sol 8:1
people Israel. No * what I do for Is 1:3
says the Lord; no * how deep the Is 1:18
All is dross. No * how hot the Jer 6:29
cannot charm. No * what you do, Jer 8:17
Don't trust them, no * how Jer 12:6
* where he comes from in Israel. Eze 48:19
What is the *?" Dan 2:15
your music, no * how lovely it is. Amo 5:23
follow you no * where you go!" Mt 8:19
know you tell the truth no * what! Mk 12:14
you no * what the others do!" Mk 14:29
in their homes, no * what their Lk 4:40
follow you no * where you go." Lk 9:57
try to settle the * before it Lk 12:58
"The truth of the * is that you Jn 6:26
always, so that no * what you ask Jn 15:16
But the fact of the * is that it Jn 16:7
promise, a * he had previously Act 1:4
be disturbed no * what is said, and Act 19:36
right, no * who questions them. Rom 3:4
to Christ, no * who we are or what Rom 3:21,22
But the fact of the * is this: Rom 4:15
our heads high no * what happens Rom 5:5
is concerned. No * which way I turn Rom 7:18
of salvation no * how wise they 1Co 1:19
to decide the * instead of taking 1Co 6:1
For instance, take the * of 1Co 6:13
of his body. No * how many of us 1Co 10:17
But there is one * I want to 1Co 11:3
loyal to him no * what the cost. 1Co 13:7
no * how many of them there are; 2Co 1:20
are pure in this *, and I hope 2Co 5:11
no * what your enemies may do. Php 1:28
can keep going no * what Col 1:11
cheat in this * by taking another 1Th 4:6
Always keep on praying. No * 1Th 5:18
you his peace no * what happens. 2Th 3:16
a godly life is not an easy *. 1Ti 3:16
Lord die away, no * what happens. Heb 10:35
that sex sin is not a serious *; Rev 2:20

MATTERS
But the smaller * they can take Ex 18:22
judged the smaller * themselves. Ex 18:26
"yes" or "no" on urgent *. Ex 28:30,31f
Peninnah made * worse by 1Sa 1:6
where Solomon sat to hear legal *; 1Ki 7:7
concerning these * and concerning 2Ch 8:15
in all * of public administration. Neh 11:24
And in all * requiring Dan 1:20
And to make * worse, he couldn't Dan 2:1
*, you won't be in large ones. Lk 16:10
"I have spoken of these * very Jn 16:25
about other *, they can be settled Act 19:39
line with our thinking in these *. Act 21:24
when it comes to these * of faith. Rom 4:16
But be sure in deciding these * 1Co 7:17
I'll talk to you about the other * 1Co 11:34
in understanding * of this kind. 1Co 14:20
has Christ is what *, and he is Col 3:11

MATTHAN
Eleazar was the father of *; Mt 1:15
* was the father of Jacob; Mt 1:15

MATTHAT
Heli's father was *; Lk 3:23-38
Jorim's father was *; Lk 3:23-38

MATTHAT'S
Heli's father was Matthat;* father Lk 3:23-38
Jorim's father was Matthat;* Lk 3:23-38

MATTHEW
Implied. In * 22:41–45, Jesus Ps 110:1f
However, the Gospel of * (1:23) Is 7:14f
* account loses its significance. Is 7:14f
See Exodus 21:32 and * 27:3–9. Zec 11:12f
road, he saw a tax collector, *, Mt 9:9
The * who wrote this book. Mt 9:9f
said to him, and * jumped up and Mt 9:9
* (the tax collector), Mt 10:2,3,4
See * 9:34, where they called him Mt 10:25f
*, Thomas Mk 3:16-19
All include this in * 6:15. Mk 11:26,f
*, Thomas Lk 6:14,15,16
Implied. See * 5:16. Lk 8:16f
Implied. See * 5:16. Lk 8:17f
Prayer as recorded in * 6:9-13. Lk 11:5,6f
a tasteless residue. * 5:13. Lk 14:34f
See * 17:2. Jn 1:14f
This prophecy is recorded in * Jn 18:32f
*, James Act 1:14
in * 8:14, 1 Corinthians 9:5, etc. 1Pe 5:13f
See * 3:16, 17; 1Jn 5:6,7,8f

MATTHEW'S
were eating dinner [at * house Mt 9:10

MATTHIAS
(also called Barsabbas) and *. Act 1:23
and in this manner * was chosen Act 1:26

MATTITHIAH
And * (a Levite and the oldest 1Ch 9:31
Ma-asseiah, *, Eliphelehu, 1Ch 15:18
*, Eliphelehu, Mikneiah, 1Ch 15:21
Jehiel, *, Eliab, Benaiah, 1Ch 16:5
Shime-i, Hashabiah, and *. 1Ch 25:3
Fourteenth, * and twelve of his 1Ch 25:9-31
Je-iel, *, Zabad, Zebina, Jaddai, Ez 10:43

(MATTITHIAH Con't)
To his right stood *, Shema, Neh 8:1

MATURE
Yet when I am among * Christians 1Co 2:6
that you will become * Christians. 2Co 13:9
I hope all of you who are * Php 3:15
things and become * in our Heb 6:1

MATURED
drop their fruit before it is *. Deu 28:40

MATURITY
children grow to * around them, and Job 21:8
to a position of strength and *; Eph 4:12

MAUL
a lion would and * me and drag me Ps 7:2

MAUSOLEUMS
You are like beautiful *—full of Mt 23:27

MAXIMUM
You should be given the * Job 34:36

MAYBE
on the toilet, or * he is away on a 1Ki 18:27
The crowd was amazed. "* Jesus Mt 12:23
they asked. "* he is thinking Jn 7:35
lands, or * even to the Gentiles! Jn 7:35

MAYOR
But when Zebul, the * of the Ju 9:30
"Take him to Amon, the * of the 1Ki 22:26
Joshua, the former * of Jerusalem, 2Ki 23:8
Rephaiah (son of Hur), the * of Neh 3:9
He was the * of the other half of Neh 3:12
the * of the Beth-haccherem area; Neh 3:14
Shallum (son of Colhozeh), the * Neh 3:15
* of half the Beth-zur district; Neh 3:16
Then came Hashabiah, the * of Neh 3:17
of Henadad), the * of the other Neh 3:18
the * of another part of Mizpah; Neh 3:19
At last the * was able to quiet Act 19:35

MAYORS
conference of the * of the five 1Sa 5:8
So they summoned the * again and 1Sa 5:11
and the Philistine * followed 1Sa 6:12
After the five Philistine * had 1Sa 6:16
gifts from the * of the capital 1Sa 6:17
A wise man is stronger than the * Ecc 7:19

ME-ARAH
including * (which belongs to the Jos 13:2-7

ME-JARKON
Gath-rimmon, *, and Rakkon, also Jos 19:41-46

ME-UNIM
Besai, Asnah, *, Nephisim, Bakbuk, Ez 2:43-54
Asnah, *, Nephushesim, Neh 7:46-56

MEADOW
and as far away as Vineyard *. Ju 11:33
He lets me rest in the * grass Ps 23:2,3

MEADOWS
pleasant brooks and * as my share! Ps 16:6
Carmel's pastures and Sharon's *; Is 35:2

MEAL
* and started on toward Sodom; Gen 18:16
After the *, as they were Gen 19:3
* together before the Lord. Ex 18:12
and they had a * together before Ex 24:11
* offerings, or drink offerings. Ex 30:9
offering and a * offering, just as Ex 40:29
a bushel of barley * without oil or Num 5:15
After Boaz had finished a good *, Ru 3:6,7
She brought the * to the king 1Sa 28:25
390 bushels of *, 10 oxen from the 1Ki 4:22
After finishing the *, the old 1Ki 13:23
to cook this last *, and then my 1Ki 17:12
Go ahead and cook that 'last *,' 1Ki 17:13
to Ahab, "Go and enjoy a good *! 1Ki 18:41
"Bring me some *," Elisha said. 2Ki 4:41
Levites prepared a * for themselves 2Ch 35:14
with a hearty *, and to send Neh 8:10
a festive * and to send presents; Neh 8:12
advice satisfies like a good *! Pro 18:20
mourners with a *, or send them a Jer 16:7
even eat a * with them. Jer 16:8
offerings and * offerings and Jer 33:18
ounces at a time, one * a day. Eze 4:10
These are the * offerings, burnt Eze 45:15
burnt offerings, * offerings, drink Eze 45:17
of grain for the * offering—one Eze 45:24
* offering and oil offering. Eze 45:25
He shall present a * offering of Eze 46:5
of flour for a * offering. Eze 46:7
festivals the * offering shall be Eze 46:11
And there must be a * offering Eze 46:14,15
and she got up and prepared a * Mt 8:15
blessing on the *, then broke the Mt 14:19
eat the Passover * with my Mt 26:18
men there for that *, and Mk 6:43,44
up after the *, there were seven Mk 8:8,9
and she got up and prepared a * Lk 4:39
Pharisees asked him home for a *. Lk 11:37,38
his master's * and serves him his Lk 17:7,8,9
place to prepare their Passover *. Lk 22:8
Passover * with his disciples.' Lk 22:11
Go ahead and prepare the * Lk 22:12
eat this Passover * with you before Lk 22:15
his house and set a * before them. Act 16:34
as the oldest son for a single *. Heb 12:16
those who need a * or a place to 1Pe 4:9

MEALS
and began to take her * again. 1Sa 1:18
of duty, for their * were brought 2Ch 35:15
dust, tremble as you eat your *; Eze 12:18
and shared their * with great joy Act 2:46

MEAN
What do you * by this trickery?" Gen 29:25
"What do you * by sneaking off Gen 31:26
one here to tell us what they *." Gen 40:8
"The three branches * three Gen 40:12
"The three baskets * three Gen 40:18,19
as to what the dreams might *; Gen 41:8
"Both dreams * the same thing," Gen 41:25
heads of grain) * that there are Gen 41:26
Ask them, 'What do you * by Gen 44:5
can also * "kid"—a baby goat. Ex 12:3,4f
ask, 'What does all this *? Ex 12:26
"You * you want to sit here Num 32:6
here and what they *, you are to Jos 4:21
Obviously this does not * via Ju 1:24f
"Your dream can * only one thing! Ju 7:14
"What do you *, 'What do I Ju 18:24
* that you must leave immediately. 1Sa 20:22
What do you * by letting him get 2Sa 3:24,25
Apparently we don't * anything to 2Sa 19:6
type does not * that these persons 1Ch 1:1f
* that I denied the God of heaven. Job 31:28
for they will * real life for you, Pro 4:22
though it may * selling everything Pro 6:31
*, so why bother to speak at all? Ecc 6:11
still you won't know what they *.' Is 6:9
so that no one can know what I *. Is 45:19
them up to * a thing I never said? Jer 8:8
you will see what I *. Jer 23:20
"What do you *—Jerusalem Jer 26:9
"This is what I *, the Lord God Eze 15:5,6
said: "What does all this *? Eze 24:19
necessarily * "the end times." Eze 38:15,16f
do you * by doing these things?' Dan 4:35
can also * "predecessor," in this Dan 5:11f
but I will tell you what they *. Dan 5:17
what this could *, suddenly a buck Dan 8:5
"What do you *," he roared, Jon 1:6
by some to * a mournful dirge. Hab 3:1f
"What does this *?" Zec 4:4
" 'What do you *? Mal 3:8
"But you say, 'What do you *? Mal 3:13
understand what I *, he is Elijah, Mt 11:14
"What I * is that the Kingdom of Mt 21:43
him, "What does your story *?" Mk 4:10
"What does he *?" Mk 8:16
to think what the angel could *. Lk 1:29
interpret this to *: "Use your Lk 16:9f
But that doesn't * that the Law Lk 16:17
This may * that God's people will Lk 17:37f
does the Scripture * where it says, Lk 20:17
"What do you *? Jn 3:4
"What do you *?" Jn 3:9
What does he * about our looking Jn 7:36
What does he *, 'You cannot come Jn 8:22
What do you *, 'set free'?" Jn 8:33
other, wondering whom he could *. Jn 13:22
— and by the Comforter I * the Jn 14:26
this is what I * when I say that Jn 16:15
you asking yourselves what I *? Jn 16:19
* their King, or their Messiah?" Jn 18:34f
word "King" to * their religious Jn 18:34f
"What can this *?" Act 2:12
nation, if you * the good deed Act 4:9
What could the vision *? Act 10:17
"we don't know what you *. Act 19:2
* God will break his promises? Rom 3:3
faith, does this * that we no Rom 3:31
That is what the Scriptures * Rom 4:17
Does this * that now we can go Rom 6:15
Does this * that God has rejected Rom 11:11
But that doesn't * we should eat 1Co 6:13
but that doesn't * that you should 1Co 10:23
Lord," and really * it, unless the 1Co 12:3
how will he know what you *? 1Co 14:9
them, but to me they * nothing. 1Co 14:11
Of course, I don't * that those 2Co 8:13
find out what those laws really *? Gal 4:21
Stop being *, bad-tempered and Eph 4:31
Does it * anything to you that we Php 2:1
I don't * to say I am perfect. Php 3:12
such things * nothing. Col 3:11
(By the way, this doesn't * you 1Ti 5:23
Now he will * much more to you Phm 1:16
about does not * the land of Israel Heb 4:8
that his riches * nothing to the Jas 1:10,11
as to what it all could *. 1Pe 1:10
* you are free to do wrong. 1Pe 2:16
letters around to * something quite 2Pe 3:15,16

MEANING
The man named his wife Eve (* Gen 3:20
son, Cain (* "I have created"). Gen 4:1
named him Seth (* "Granted"); Gen 4:2
Lamech named him Noah (* Gen 5:28-3
Peleg (* "Division," for during Gen 10:2
was called Babel (* "confusion"), Gen 11:
was named Zoar, * "Little City." Gen 19:2
and Abraham named him Isaac (* Gen 21:
So they called him Jacob (* Gen 25:2
had a son, Reuben (* "God has Gen 29:3
named him Simeon (* "Jehovah Gen 29:3
named him Levi (* "Attachment") Gen 29:3
named him Judah (* "Praise"), for Gen 29:3
Rachel named him Dan (* Gen 30:
The * is not of the actual Hebrew Gen 30:6
Rachel named him Naphtali (* Gen 30:
Leah named him Gad (* "My luck Gen 30:1
named him Asher (* "Happy"), for Gen 30:1
She named him Issachar (* Gen 30:1
She named him Zebulun (* Gen 30:2
And she named him Joseph (* "May Gen 30:23,2
is called Succoth, * "huts." Gen 33:1
called Perez (* "Bursting Out"). Gen 38:2
had such a good *, he told his Gen 40:1
one of them could tell me the *." Gen 41:2
has revealed the * of the dreams to Gen 41:3
Pharaoh gave him a name * "He Gen 41:4
son Manasseh (* "Made to Gen 41:5
was named Ephraim (* Gen 41:5
(* "Threshing Place of Gen 50:1
Abel-mizraim (* "Egyptian Gen 50:1
She named him Moses (* Ex 2:1
Hebrew word * "to draw out." Ex 2:10
They had a baby named Gershom (* Ex 2:22
The * is not clear. Ex 12:38
was called Marah, * "bitter"). Ex 15:23
as "manna" (* "What is it?" Ex 16:31
Moses named the place Massah (* Ex 17:7
(* "argument" and "strife!" Ex 17:7
(* "Jehovah is my flag"). Ex 17:15,16
two sons, Gershom (* "foreigner," Ex 18:3
and Eliezer (* "God is my help," Ex 18:4
announce to you the * of my name Ex 33:19
and announced the * of his name. Ex 34:5,6
at that time (* "Cluster") Num 13:24
This place was named Meribah (* Num 20:13
Hormah (* "Utterly Destroyed"). Num 21:3
Then Israel traveled to Beer (* Num 21:16
it Havvoth-jair (* 'Jair's Deu 3:14
was called Gilgal (*, "to end" Jos 5:8,9
named Hormah (*, "massacred"). Ju 1:17
called "Bochim" (*, "the place Ju 2:5
a nickname * "Let Baal take care Ju 6:32
Perhaps the * is, "A quick Ju 8:21f
* me, your own flesh and blood!" Ju 9:2
She named him Samuel (* 1Sa 1:19,20
named it Ebenezer (*, "the Stone 1Sa 7:12
the baby Jedidiah (*, "Beloved of 2Sa 12:25
The * of the Hebrew wording is 2Sa 23:20f
the Hebrew word * "distress." 1Ch 4:9f
he called Beriah (* "a tragedy") 1Ch 7:23
The * of the term is uncertain. 1Ch 11:22f
ever since (*, "The Place of 1Ch 14:11
The * of the term is uncertain. 1Ch 15:20f
The * is uncertain. 1Ch 15:21f
His name shall be Solomon (* 1Ch 22:9
and explained the * of the Neh 8:7,8
Possibly the * is that they Est 2:23f
don't even know the * of the word! Ps 58:1
of * in these nuggets of truth." Pro 1:5,6
Some linguists believe the * Pro 30:18,19f
The * is obscure. Sol 8:9f
The * is obscure. Sol 8:9f
used this higher *, "virgin," in Is 7:14f
Immanuel (*, "God is with us"). Is 7:14
Possibly the * is, "the Heir Is 11:10f
Possibly the * is that the Is 21:6,7f
The * is unclear. Is 38:18f
Or perhaps his * is, "Dead Is 38:18f
the Lord without * a word of it, Is 48:1
The * of the Hebrew word is Is 52:14,15f
Perhaps the * is that they are Jer 13:19f
throne" under the * of permanence Jer 36:30f
"There is special * in each Eze 4:3
of the people," * the Syro-Arabian Eze 20:35,36f
so perhaps the * is, "I will Eze 34:29f
now for its *: Dan 2:36
That is the * of the Rock cut Dan 2:45
to tell me the * of my dream, but Dan 4:6
aghast at the * of the dream. Dan 4:19
If you can tell me the * of those Dan 5:16
and asked him the * of all these Dan 7:16
Perhaps the * is, "change Dan 7:25f
to understand the * of this vision, Dan 8:15
tell Daniel the * of his dream." Dan 8:16
Verse 14 is the basis for the * Dan 8:26f
the * of the vision that you saw! Dan 9:23
her Lo-ruhamah (* 'No more mercy') Hos 1:6
him Lo-ammi (* 'Not mine'), for Hos 1:9
Literally, "my Baal," (* "my Hos 1:16f
Zaanan sounds like a verb * "to Mic 1:11f
Zaanan sounds like a verb * "to Mic 1:11f
Zaanan sounds like a verb * "to Mic 1:11f

MEANING Con't)
Haggai then made his * clear. Hag 2:14
name him Jesus (* 'Savior'), for he Mt 1:21
(* "God is with us").' Mt 1:23
the * of this verse of Scripture, Mt 9:13
But if you had known the * of Mt 12:7
they were only stories without *. Mt 13:12,13f
Then Jesus explained his *: Mt 21:31
he would explain his * to them. Mk 4:34
heal yourself '—*, 'Why don't Lk 4:23
you to know the * of these Lk 8:10
"This is its *: The seed is Lk 8:11
—perhaps * that the man could, Lk 9:59f
if you would understand my *." Lk 14:35
Literally, "the Word," * Christ, Jn 1:1f
Literally, "the Word," * Christ, Jn 1:14f
of water" as * the normal process Jn 3:5f
interpret this as * what is Act 27:4f
Perhaps the * is "Their speech Rom 3:13f
Perhaps the * is, "Receive Rom 14:1f
the real * of the Scriptures. 2Co 3:14
For you used to see the * of Gal 3:1
He is quibbling over the * of 1Ti 6:4
heaven to explain the vision's *. Rev 1:1
This is the * of the seven stars Rev 1:20
and only he knew its *. Rev 19:12

MEANINGLESS
sacrifice, but to me it is *! Hos 8:13
play" are * fictions to you! Amo 5:7
faith are *, and faith is foolish. Rom 4:14
who treats Christ's death as *. Gal 2:21
it was not just * chatter to you; 1Th 1:5

MEANINGS
The * of these words are not Ps 9:16f
the * of dreams and visions. Dan 1:17

MEANNESS
him back for all his * to me!" Pro 24:28,29

MEANS
word that * "life-giving." Gen 3:20f
"Edom," which * "Red Stuff." Gen 25:30
"Jacob" * "Cheater." Gen 27:36f
"I know what the dream *," Gen 40:12
these men can tell me what it *. Gen 41:15
God will tell you what it *!" Gen 41:16
Which *, "he to whom it Gen 49:10f
will by no * go out empty-handed! Ex 3:21
to the ephod by * of two twisted Ex 28:22,23,24
of the ephod by * of blue ribbons; Ex 28:28
to be attached by * of a blue Ex 28:37,38
His name, Jehovah, * "I will Ex 33:19f
This * that the following may Lev 11:4-7
"Hoshea" * "salvation"; Num 13:16f
"Joshua" * "Jehovah is Num 13:16f
I will teach you what it * to Num 14:34,35
Call me Mara," (Naomi * Ru 1:20
"pleasant"; Mara * "bitter") Ru 1:20
(Ichabod * "there is no 1Sa 4:21,22
works without regard to human *! 1Sa 17:47
He is a fool—just like his name * 1Sa 25:25
it * life or death." 2Sa 15:21
Jachin * "to establish," and 1Ki 7:16-22f
and Boaz * "strength." 1Ki 7:16-22f
to heaven—by * of a whirlwind! 2Ki 2:1
Italic * that the name has 1Ch 1:5-9f
Eber had two sons: Peleg (which * 1Ch 1:19
a hard time at his birth (Jabez * 1Ch 4:9
Whether this * that he made 1Ch 20:3f
Try to realize what this *—the Ps 100:3
Hard work * prosperity; Pro 12:11
Self-control * controlling the Pro 13:3
A happy face * a glad heart; Pro 15:13
a sad face * a breaking heart. Pro 15:13
wealth gotten by dishonest *. Pro 16:8
despising them * death. Pro 19:16
* that poverty will break in upon Pro 24:34
but to trust in God * safety. Pro 29:25
here sometimes * "virgin" and Is 7:14f
which * 'Your enemies will soon be Is 8:1
his people: Isaiah * "Jehovah will Is 8:18
Shear-jashub * "A remnant shall Is 8:18
* "Your enemies will soon be Is 8:18
*—an altar covered with blood. Is 29:2
nor what it * to be just and good; Is 59:8
who escape" * survivors of the Is 66:19f
right, and it * that I will surely Jer 1:12
who gets his wealth by unjust *. Jer 17:11
His name *, "The Lord will Jer 22:24,25f
the name of which * "Dreamer." Jer 29:24f
consider what this *, even though Eze 12:3
have asked what all this *. Eze 12:9
what this riddle of the eagles *? Eze 17:12,13
even though obeying them * life. Eze 20:13
This is what Ezekiel * by the Eze 30:21f
then we can tell you what it *." Dan 2:4
it was and what it *, I'll have you Dan 2:5
what the dream was and what it *. Dan 2:6
you what the dream * unless you Dan 2:7
you the dream and what it *." Dan 2:16
the understanding of what it *." Dan 2:23
what my dream was and what it *?" Dan 2:26
by supernatural *. Dan 2:34
Tell me what my dream *: Dan 4:9
now tell me what it *. Dan 4:18
be afraid to tell me what it *." Dan 4:19
the ground! This * that you will Dan 4:26
tells me what it *, will be dressed Dan 5:7
tell you what the writing *." Dan 5:12
tell me what it *, but they can't. Dan 5:15
"This is what it *: Dan 5:26
"Mene * 'numbered'—God has Dan 5:26
"Tekel * 'weighed'—you have been Dan 5:27
"Parsin * 'divided'—your kingdom Dan 5:28
no human * could overpower him. Dan 8:25
This number is literal, and * Dan 8:26
to learn will know what it *. Dan 12:10
Call your brother Ammi (which * Hos 1:11
it * to do right," says the Lord. Amo 3:10
rich by evil *, attempting to live Hab 2:9
and peace, to be a * of showing his Mal 2:5
tonight * fair weather tomorrow; Mt 16:2,3
red sky in the morning * foul Mt 16:2,3
'By God's Temple' * nothing—you can Mt 23:16
which *, "My God, my God, why have Mt 27:46
know what it * to really live. Mk 8:35
(Golgotha * skull. Mk 15:22
The name * "one who loves Lk 1:1f
Their careless laughter now * Lk 6:25
from their private * to the support Lk 8:3
when it * forfeiting one's self? Lk 9:25
friends by * of the mammon of Lk 16:9f
the *, an unbiblical idea. Lk 16:9f
some person's God * that person Lk 20:37,38
Some think this * water baptism. Jn 3:5f
"Your approval or disapproval * Jn 5:41,42
Who can tell what he *?" Jn 6:60
(the word "Siloam" * "Sent"). Jn 9:7
"That * he is getting better!" Jn 11:12,13
to the Father except by * of me. Jn 14:6
by * of the commands I gave you. Jn 15:3
We don't know what he *." Jn 16:17,18
And by * of many remarkable Act 7:36
"I must by all * be at Jerusalem Act 18:21
the * of saving us from his wrath. Rom 3:25
after you die, by * of this same Rom 8:11
And trusting * looking forward to Rom 8:24
This * that not all of Abraham's Rom 9:8
understand what the Holy Spirit *. 1Co 2:14
Lord's Table, this *, doesn't it, 1Co 10:16
Christ and what it *, he is eating 1Co 11:29
a * of helping the entire church. 1Co 12:7
"yes" when he really * "no"? 2Co 1:17
My "yes" * "yes." 2Co 1:18
to say "yes" when he * "no." 2Co 1:19
that, of course, * Christ. Gal 3:16
and the Spirit's seal upon us * Eph 1:14
to heaven. This * that he had first Eph 4:9
For to me, living * Php 1:21
* to suffer and to die with him. Php 3:10
to them the Good News is just a * 1Ti 6:5
for Christ it only * that we will 2Ti 2:11
Know what his Word says and *. 2Ti 2:15
Onesimus (whose name * Phm 1:11
Melchizedek's name * "Justice," Heb 7:2
city, Salem, which * "Peace." Heb 7:2
No one can be sure whether this * Heb 7:3f
sons, then it * that you aren't Heb 12:8
By this he * that he will sift Heb 12:27
by * of a small bit in his mouth. Jas 3:3
And by all * don't brag about Jas 3:14
the Scripture * when it says that Jas 4:5
Loving God * doing what he tells 1Jn 5:3
as to whether this * "kept from" Rev 3:10f

MEANT
and wondered what it all *. Gen 37:11
could suggest what his dreams *. Gen 41:8
and he told us what our dreams *. Gen 41:12
Forget"—what he * was that God had Gen 41:51
into good what you * for evil, for Gen 50:20
him even though it * killing your Ex 32:29
is what the Lord * when he said, 'I Lev 10:3
what David *, someone told King 1Sa 17:31
his father really * it when he said 1Sa 20:33
didn't understand what Jonathan *; 1Sa 20:39
that the king * what he said and 1Ki 12:16,17
If she * this literally, she Pro 7:14f
Then he told me what the vision * Eze 37:11
the writing or tell him what it * Dan 5:8
replace it, this * that the Grecian Dan 8:22
he understood what the vision *. Dan 10:1
understand what he *, so I said, Dan 12:8
to explain what he * when he said Mt 15:15
by "yeast" he * the wrong Mt 16:12
to the reader: You know what is *! Mt 24:15
asked him what he * by the Mk 7:17
he * by "rising from the dead." Mk 9:10
were afraid to ask him what he *. Mk 9:32
they didn't understand what he *. Lk 2:50
asked him what the story *. Lk 8:9
know what he *, for their minds had Lk 9:45
what the passages * and what they Lk 24:27
But by "this sanctuary" he * Jn 2:21
with each other about what he *. Jn 6:52
"That is what I * when I said that Jn 6:65
he *, so he explained it to them. Jn 10:6
The disciples, thinking Jesus * Jn 11:12,13
But Jesus * Lazarus had died. Jn 11:12,13
That is what he * when he said, Jn 13:11
at the table knew what Jesus *. Jn 13:28
time of John, and all that it *! Act 18:25,26
His kindness is * to lead you to Rom 2:4
away from them it * that he turned Rom 11:15
That is what the Psalmist * when Rom 15:9
That is what is * by the 1Co 2:9
What I * was that you are not to 1Co 5:11
That is what Isaiah * when he Gal 4:27
If that were what God *, he would Heb 4:8
to obey, when obeying * suffering. Heb 5:8
though it * terrible suffering. Heb 10:32
God, even if it * offering his son Jas 2:21
from what he *, just as they do the 2Pe 3:15,16

MEANTIME
In the * Saul's daughter Michal 1Sa 18:20
In the *, he keeps on reaching Rom 10:21

MEANWHILE
*, the crime rate was rising Gen 6:11
until the earth was dry. * he Gen 8:8
*, Abram married his half-sister Gen 11:29
*, Isaac, whose home was in the Gen 24:62
*, when Leah realized that she Gen 30:9
Laban, *, camped below him in the Gen 31:25
that same day. * Jacob and his Gen 33:17
their return. * King Hamor, Gen 34:6,7
*, in Egypt, the traders sold Gen 37:36
that generation. *, their Ex 1:7
*, Moses stretched his rod over Ex 14:21
of Amalek. * Moses, Aaron, and Hur Ex 17:10
clean. *, the fire on the altar Lev 6:12
Moses and Aaron. *, Korah had Num 16:19
*, a man named Nobah led an army Num 32:42
*, the city gates were kept shut. Jos 2:7
been carried out. *, the people had Jos 4:10
* Ehud had escaped past the Ju 3:26
not one man was left alive. *, Ju 4:17
army of Ammon. * Jephthah had Ju 11:30,31
and two daughters. * Samuel grew up 1Sa 2:21
* LITTLE SAMUEL was helping the 1Sa 3:1
of Gad and Gilead. *, Saul stayed 1Sa 13:7
at Michmash had * been secured by a 1Sa 13:23
* David went down to the 1Sa 25:1
*, one of Nabal's men went and 1Sa 25:14
King Saul, *, had forced David's 1Sa 25:44
(*, Samuel had died and all 1Sa 28:3
* THE PHILISTINES had begun the 1Sa 31:1
for two years; *, David was 2Sa 2:10,11
*, Abner consulted with the 2Sa 3:17
* Joab and the Israeli army were 2Sa 12:26,27
there three years. * David, now 2Sa 13:37,38,39
*, Absalom and his men arrived at 2Sa 16:15
Absalom about it. *, they escaped 2Sa 17:18
*, Ahithophel—publicly disgraced 2Sa 17:23
David soon arrived at Mahanaim. * 2Sa 17:24
*, there was much discussion and 2Sa 19:8,9,10
* Sheba had traveled across 2Sa 20:14
*, Rehoboam the son of Solomon 1Ki 14:21
*, over in Israel, Nadab the son 1Ki 15:25
So Elijah went to tell him. * the 1Ki 18:2
*, the Lord instructed one of the 1Ki 20:35
*, all the prophets continued 1Ki 22:10
*, over in Judah, Jehoshaphat the 1Ki 22:41
*, when the people of Moab heard 2Ki 3:21
* ELISHA HAD summoned one of the 2Ki 9:1
*, King Ahaziah of Judah had fled 2Ki 9:27
*, over in Israel, Jeroboam II 2Ki 14:23
*, King Hezekiah had said to 2Ki 20:8
* the old Tabernacle of the Lord 1Ch 16:39
city of Medeba. *, the mercenary 1Ch 19:9
*, David had stayed in Jerusalem. 1Ch 20:1
coronation. *, friends of Jeroboam 2Ch 10:2,3
* Jeroboam had secretly sent 2Ch 13:13,14
*, King Abijah of Judah became 2Ch 13:21
*, the army of Israel that had 2Ch 25:13
people as slaves. *, the 2Ch 28:17,18
* the Levites and priests praised 2Ch 30:21
by ourselves. *, our enemies were Neh 4:11
*, the other Jews throughout the Est 9:16
*, Queen Esther (daughter of Est 9:29-31
they scoff at. *, the rich mock Job 12:5
* my enemies are trying to kill Ps 38:12
than my head. * my sins, too many Ps 40:12
* (in my vision) Is 21:6,7
Temple to pray. * he sent Eliakim Is 37:2
* the army burned Jerusalem, Jer 39:8
* King Nebuchadnezzar had told Jer 39:11,12
* Ishmael escaped with eight of Jer 41:15
"* continue your demonstration Eze 4:7
"* the king of Syria Dan 11:9
were gathering. *, Peter was Mt 26:58
*, as Peter was sitting in the Mt 26:69
* the chief priests and Jewish Mt 27:20
killing Jesus. *, Jesus and his Mk 3:7,8
* Jesus was in Bethany, at the Mk 14:3
*, all his disciples had fled. Mk 14:50
* Peter was below in the Mk 14:66,67

(MEANWHILE Con't)
before the Lord. *, a great crowd Lk 1:10
* the crowds outside were waiting Lk 1:21
*, as they were exclaiming over Lk 9:43
* THE CROWDS grew until thousands Lk 12:1
"*, the older son was in the Lk 15:25
*, Zacchaeus stood before the Lk 19:8
was no reply. *, the chief priests Lk 23:10
in deep sorrow. *, Jesus' friends, Lk 23:49
*, the disciples were urging Jn 4:31
the Passover?" * the chief Jn 11:57
*, as Simon Peter was standing by Jn 18:25
*, the apostles were meeting Act 5:12
*, Philip found himself at Azotus! Act 8:40
*, the church had peace Act 9:31
*, as Peter was puzzling over the Act 10:19
*, the believers who fled from Act 11:19
* Peter continued knocking. Act 12:16
*, I thought I ought to send Php 2:25

MEASURE
The exact * is not known. Ex 16:16f
into a three-quart *, there was Ex 16:18
The omer—the container used to * Ex 16:36
give full *, for I am Jehovah your Lev 19:35,36
and judges shall * from the body to Deu 21:2
huge, expensive stones, cut to *. 1Ki 7:9
were also cut to *, and were topped 1Ki 7:11
As a temporary * the king 1Ki 8:64
every city as a further safety *. 2Ch 11:12
so richly deserve! * it out to them Ps 28:4
beyond *, high as the heavens. Ps 108:4
moment, in full * in one day: Is 47:9
The man began to * the wall around Eze 40:5
to * the entire Temple area. Eze 42:15
for both liquid and dry *. Eze 45:11
a homer) for dry *, and the bath Eze 45:11
Together they * 8 Eze 48:13
"To * Jerusalem," he said. Zec 2:2
She takes a * of flour and mixes Mt 13:33
up the full * of their evil. Mt 23:32
and overflowing *, pressed down, Lk 6:38
Whatever * you use to give—large Lk 6:38
to * what is given back to you." Lk 6:38
Your care for others is the * of Lk 9:48
is upon him without * or limit. Jn 3:33,34
And here is how to * it—the Jn 15:13
Our goal is to * up to God's plan 2Co 10:13
and told to go and * the temple of Rev 11:1
Literally, "Rise and * the temple Rev 11:1f
"But do not * the outer Rev 11:2
measuring stick to * the city and Rev 21:15

MEASURED
Two-thirds of each row, as * with 2Sa 8:2
so each angel * fifteen feet from 1Ki 6:23-28
degrees as * on Ahaz' sun dial!" Is 38:8
* off the heavens with his ruler? Is 40:12
I have * out especially for you. Jer 13:24,25
Not until the heavens can be * Jer 31:37
upon the seashores *, so the Jer 33:22
* the entry hall of the passage; Eze 40:6
Then he * the entire outside Eze 40:13
Then he * across to the wall on Eze 40:19
the northern wall and * it. Eze 40:20
the south gate and * the various Eze 40:24
He * this passageway and found Eze 40:28
of the inner wall, and * it. Eze 40:32
Then he * the inner court [in Eze 40:47
of the Temple, and * the pillars Eze 41:1
of the nave and * the columns at Eze 41:3
Then he * the wall of the Temple Eze 41:5
Then he * the Temple and its Eze 41:13
to my ankles. He * off another Eze 47:4
When he * it, he found it was a Rev 21:16
Then he * the thickness of the Rev 21:17

MEASUREMENT
shall be your standard unit of * Eze 45:11
The angel used normal units of * Rev 21:17f

MEASUREMENTS
Use accurate *—lengths, weights, Lev 19:35,36
scales and honest *, so that you Deu 25:13,14,15
unjust weights and * are detestable Deu 25:16
side, and all the * were the same Eze 40:21
it had the same * as the Eze 40:28
It too had the same * as the Eze 40:32
wall, and the * there were just Eze 40:35
making these *, he led me out Eze 42:15
"And these are the * of the Eze 43:13
These are the * of the altar to be Eze 43:18
* to me, using standard units). Rev 21:17
Literally, "144 cubits by human * Rev 21:17f

MEASURES
the Ammonites, and * thirteen and a Deu 3:11
as would contain two * of seed." 1Ki 18:32f
checked all the weights and *. 1Ch 23:29
"diverse weights and diverse *." Pro 20:10f
make an idol. He * and marks out a Is 44:13
weighted scales and under-sized *; Amo 8:5

MEASURING
He was a giant of a man, * over 1Sa 17:4-7
It was huge—* 150 feet long, 75 1Ki 7:2
holding in his hand a * tape and Eze 40:3
a measuring tape and a * stick. Eze 40:3
* stick, which was 10½ feet long. Eze 40:5
of the passageway, * across the Eze 40:13
the Temple yard, * 122½ feet wide Eze 41:12
* was still standing beside me). Eze 43:6
* as he went, he took me 1,500 Eze 47:3
"A strip of land * 8 Eze 48:10
of yourselves, * your value by how Rom 12:3
each other, and * themselves 2Co 10:12
NOW I WAS given a * stick and told Rev 11:1
his hand a golden * stick to Rev 21:15

MEAT
the fatty cuts of * from his best Gen 4:4
then she gave him the *, with Gen 27:17
bitter herbs. The * must not be Ex 12:9
The Lord will give you * to eat Ex 16:7,8,9
you will have * and in the morning Ex 16:11,12
boil its * in a sacred area. Ex 29:31
sons shall eat the *, also the Ex 29:32
If any of the * or bread remains Ex 29:34
and none of the * of the Passover Ex 34:25
basins, * hooks, and fire pans. Ex 38:3
bull—the skin, *, head, legs, Lev 4:11,12
priests—may touch this *; Lev 6:27
to him, its * is to be eaten that Lev 7:15
"Any * that comes into contact Lev 7:19
and as for the * that may be Lev 7:19
sons, "Boil the * at the entrance Lev 8:31
Anything left of the * and bread Lev 8:32
the * and hide outside the camp. Lev 9:11
You may not eat their * or even Lev 11:8
You mustn't eat their * or even Lev 11:11
Also, anyone eating its * or Lev 11:40
You must not eat * with undrained Lev 19:26
wept, "Oh, for a few bites of *! Num 11:4,5
Where am I supposed to get * for Num 11:13
weep to me saying, 'Give us *!' Num 11:13
tomorrow they shall have * to eat. Num 11:18
and he is going to give you *. Num 11:18
you will have * until you vomit it Num 11:19,20
and yet you promise them * for Num 11:21
began eating the *, the anger of Num 11:33
had lusted for * and for Egypt. Num 11:34
to the Lord. The * of these Num 18:18
hide, *, blood, and dung. Num 19:5
However, the * you eat may be Deu 12:15
Eat as much of this * as you wish Deu 12:15
shall not eat the life with the *. Deu 12:20-23
the altar, and you will eat the *. Deu 12:26,27
won't get a single bite of the *. Deu 28:31
He gave them milk and *— Deu 32:14
Then, carrying the * in a basket Ju 6:19
him, "Place the * and the bread Ju 6:20
Angel touched the * and bread with Ju 6:21
would demand raw * before it was 1Sa 2:15
choicest cut of *, the piece that 1Sa 9:23
calves, and ate the raw, bloody *. 1Sa 14:32
my water and my * that I've 1Sa 25:11
him bread and * each morning and 1Ki 17:6
He passed around the * to the 1Ki 19:21
the sacrificial * and for the 1Ch 28:17
eating, and the * was yet in their Ps 78:30
They asked for * and he sent Ps 105:40
burns to roast his * and to keep Is 44:16
to bake my bread and roast my *. Is 44:19
and all forbidden *—they will come Is 66:17
Boil the * well, until the flesh Eze 24:5
So take out the * chunk by chunk Eze 24:6
Cook the * well and then empty Eze 24:10
You eat * with the blood; Eze 33:25
Priests may never eat * from any Eze 44:31
priests boil the * of the trespass Eze 46:19,20
neither wine nor *, and of course I Dan 10:3
luxury, eating the * of the Amo 6:4
chop them up like * for the cooking Mic 3:3
or *, will it too become holy?" Hag 2:12
from eating * sacrificed to idols, Act 15:20
unbled * of strangled animals. Act 15:20
unbled * of strangled animals, Act 15:27,28,29
not to eat unbled * from strangled Act 21:25
* that has been offered to idols. Rom 14:2
go without any * at all and eat Rom 14:2
rather than eat that kind of *. Rom 14:2
right to eat such * must not look Rom 14:3
So is the person who eats * that Rom 14:6
won't touch such *, he, too, is Rom 14:6
* that has been offered to idols. Rom 14:14
the work of God for a chunk of *. Rom 14:20
wrong with the *, but it is wrong Rom 14:20
is to quit eating * or drinking Rom 14:21
Should we eat * that has been 1Co 8:4
So if eating * offered to idols 1Co 8:13
laws to eat such *, but that 1Co 10:23
Take any * you want that is sold 1Co 10:25
you that this * has been offered to 1Co 10:28
and wrong to eat *, even though God 1Ti 4:3
and to eat * that has been Rev 2:20

MEBUNNAI
* from Hushath; 2Sa 23:24-39

MECHANICALLY
not in the old way, * obeying a Rom 7:6

MECHERATH
Hepher from *; 1Ch 11:26-

MECONAH
* and its villages, Neh 11:25-

MEDAD
seventy—Eldad and *—were still in Num 11:

MEDAN
Jokshan, *,Midian, Ishbak, Shuah. Gen 25
Jokshan, *, 1Ch 1:

MEDDLE
home and don't * with me, lest you 2Ch 25:
Don't * with God or he will 2Ch 35:2

MEDE
was killed, and Darius the * Dan 5:3
(Darius was a * but became king Dan 9:
* in the first year of his reign. Dan 11:

MEDEBA
As far as Dibon, Nophah, and *. Num 21:27-3
the tableland of * to Dibon; Jos 13:
to beyond the tableland near *. Jos 13:
These forces camped at * where 1Ch 19:
at the gates of the city of *. 1Ch 19:
weep for the fate of Nebo and *; Is 15:

MEDES
and among the cities of the *. 2Ki 17:
Gozan, and in the cities of the *. 2Ki 18:1
a law of the * and Persians that Est 1:1
"law of the * and Persians." Est 8:8
For I will stir up the * against Is 13:1
Elamites and * will take part in Is 21:
The city fell to the * and Is 21:6,7
the kings of the * to march on Jer 51:1
the kings of the * and their Jer 51:2
and given to the * and Persians." Dan 5:28
it will be a 'law of the * and Dan 6:
is 'a law of the * and Persians,' Dan 6:12
and * sacked impregnable Nineveh. Nah 2:1
Here we are—Parthians, *, Act 2:

MEDIA
at Ecbatana, in the province of *. Ez 6:2
of the Kings of * and Persia. Est 10:2
the kings of Zimri, Elam and *; Jer 25:25
saw are the kings of * and Persia; Dan 8:20

MEDIA-PERSIA
emperor of vast *, with its 127 Est 1:1
every part of * for the occasion. Est 1:1
Memucan—seven high officials of *. Est 1:13-15

MEDIATOR
Literally, "The Lord is our * 1Sa 20:23f
man, no * to bring us together. Job 9:32,33
the go-between—the * between the Act 7:38

MEDICAL
healed, and pay any * expenses. Ex 21:19

MEDICINE
of your own *, you murderer!" 2Sa 16:7,8
If they reprove me, it is *! Ps 141:5
A cheerful heart does good like * Pro 17:22
it is a bitter dose of your own * Jer 4:18
They give useless * for my Jer 8:11
Is there no * in Gilead? Jer 8:22
your wound and no * does any good. Jer 30:13
Go up to Gilead for *, O virgin Jer 46:11
give her *; Jer 51:8
be for food and the leaves for *. Eze 47:12
wounds with * and bandaged them. Lk 10:34
sometimes as * for your stomach 1Ti 5:23
and to get * from me to heal your Rev 3:18
the leaves were used for * to Rev 22:2

MEDICINES
Though you have used many *, Jer 46:11

MEDITATE
listed—you will * upon them as you Deu 30:1
"* upon all the laws I have given Deu 32:46
Literally, "* a vain thing." Ps 2:1f
gloomy, but I will * upon your Ps 42:6
Lord, here in your Temple we * Ps 48:9
God's sanctuary to *, and thought Ps 73:17
I search my soul and * upon the Ps 77:6
I will * upon them and give them Ps 119:15
I will * about your glory, Ps 145:5

MEDITATING
out in the fields, *, he looked up Gen 24:63
night are always * on his laws and Ps 1:2
the privilege of * in his Temple, Ps 27:4

MEDITATION
quietly upon your bed in silent *. Ps 4:4

MEDITERRANEAN
down along the coast of the * Sea Num 13:29
down to the * Sea. Num 34:5
be the coastline of the * Sea. Num 34:6
will begin at the * Sea and will Num 34:7,8,9
the * Sea to the Euphrates River. Deu 1:7
the Euphrates River to the * Sea. Deu 11:24
The * coast and the Negeb Deu 33:23
Judah, extending to the * Sea; Deu 34:2
and from the * Sea in the west to Jos 1:4
lived along the * coast—heard that Jos 5:1
the shores of the * as far north as Jos 9:1
and along that to the * Sea. Jos 15:2,3,4
Jabneel and ended at the * Sea. Jos 15:10,11
border was the shoreline of the *. Jos 15:12

MEDITERRANEAN Con't)
extended to the *, and included the Jos 15:46
also the entire * coast from the Jos 15:47
to Gezer and on over to the *. Jos 16:1
Beth-horon, then on to the * Sea. Jos 16:5,6
along Kanah Brook to the * Sea. Jos 16:8
the Brook of Kanah to the * Sea. Jos 17:9
as far west as the * Sea was Jos 17:10
and came to the * Sea at Hosah. Jos 19:29
River to the * Sea shall be yours, Jos 23:4,5
* Sea and build them into rafts. 1Ki 5:9
the coast of the * Sea to Joppa, Ez 3:7
Kings along the * coast—the Ps 72:10
the * Sea to the Euphrates River. Ps 80:11
the Euphrates River to the * Sea. Ps 89:25
Dead Sea just as they do the *! Eze 47:10
will run from the * toward Hethlon, Eze 47:15
will be from the * to Hazar-enon, Eze 47:17
of Egypt (Wadi el-Arish) to the *. Eze 47:19
"On the west side, the * itself Eze 47:20
boundary at the *, across to Eze 48:1
of Egypt (Wadi el-Arish) to the *. Eze 48:27,28
the rest into the *, and then their Joe 2:20
half towards the *, flowing Zec 14:8
and fall into the *,' and your Mk 11:22,23

MEDIUM
"A * or a wizard—whether man or Lev 20:27
a serpent charmer, *, or wizard, or Deu 18:11
to try to find a * so that he could 1Sa 28:7,8
and because he had consulted a *, 1Ch 10:13

MEDIUMS
by consulting * and wizards, for I Lev 19:31
who consults * and wizards instead Lev 20:6
King Saul had banned all * and 1Sa 28:3
* and fortune-tellers executed. 1Sa 28:9
and patronized * and wizards. 2Ki 21:6
Josiah also exterminated the * 2Ki 23:24
by consulting witches and *? Is 8:19
and call upon *, wizards and Is 19:3
dreamers, * and magicians who say Jer 27:9
false prophets and * who are there Jer 29:8

MEDO-PERSIAN
The * Empire, whose first great Dan 2:39f

MEEK
and to defend the * of the earth. Ps 76:9
Proud men end in shame, but the * Pro 11:2
see my plans. The * will be filled Is 29:19
in the dust and kick aside the *. Amo 2:7
The * and lowly are fortunate! Mt 5:5

MEEKLY
*, sitting on a donkey's colt!" Jn 12:15
For if you talk * and courteously 2Ti 2:25

MEET
Sodom came out to * him, and Gen 14:17
He sprang up and ran to * them Gen 18:2
When he saw them he stood up to * Gen 19:1
through the fields to * us?" Gen 24:65
he rushed out to * him and greeted Gen 29:12,13
fields, Leah went out to * him. Gen 30:16
And the angels of God came to * Gen 32:1
* Jacob—with an army of 400 men! Gen 32:6
And then Esau ran to * him and Gen 33:4
our own pace and * you at Seir." Gen 33:14
to Goshen to * his father and they Gen 46:29
into the wilderness to * Moses." Ex 4:27
Stand beside the river bank and * Ex 7:15
in the morning and * Pharaoh as he Ex 8:20
I will * you there at the rock. Ex 17:5,6
Moses went out to * his Ex 18:7
of Israel came to * Jethro, and Ex 18:12
rugged mountain to * with God, and Ex 19:2,3
from the camp to * God, and they Ex 19:17
And I will * with you there and Ex 25:22
* with you and speak with you. Ex 29:42
And I will * with the people of Ex 29:43
I will * with you there. Ex 30:6
I * with you in the Tabernacle; Ex 30:36
left their task to * with Moses and Ex 36:4-7
people to * together for worship; Lev 23:23,24
I * with you, in front of the Ark. Num 17:4
land I will * you with an army!" Num 20:18
and went out to * him at the Arnon Num 22:36
I will see if the Lord will * me; Num 23:3,4
while I go to * the Lord." Num 23:15
to * the Lord as he had earlier. Num 24:1
people went out to * the victorious Num 31:13
cities, he will * with the city Jos 20:4
Jael went out to * Sisera and Ju 4:18
Jael went out to * him and said, Ju 4:22
of his house to * him would be Ju 11:30,31
child—ran out to * him, playing on Ju 11:34
who was delighted to * him. Ju 19:3
As you arrive there you will * a 1Sa 10:5
Saul went out to * him and to 1Sa 13:10
the city came trembling to * him. 1Sa 16:4
David ran out to * him and, 1Sa 17:48,49
I have told my men where to * me 1Sa 21:2
who has sent you to * me today! 1Sa 25:32
not come out to * me, not one of 1Sa 25:34
led David's troops out to * them. 2Sa 2:13
But Michal came out to * him and 2Sa 6:20
come to Gilgal to * him and escort 2Sa 19:15
from Jerusalem to * the king. 2Sa 19:24,25
but when he came down to * me at 1Ki 2:8
and Ahab went out to * him. 1Ki 18:16
"Go to Samaria to * King Ahab. 1Ki 21:18
"Go and * the messengers and ask 2Ki 1:3
came out to * them and asked 2Ki 2:3
And they went to * him and 2Ki 2:15
Run and * her and ask her what 2Ki 4:26
He returned to * Elisha and told 2Ki 4:31
from his chariot and ran to * him. 2Ki 5:21
down from his chariot to * you? 2Ki 5:26
So a soldier rode out to * Jehu. 2Ki 9:18
of Judah rode out to * Jehu. 2Ki 9:21
Rechab, who was coming to * him. 2Ki 10:15
to Damascus to * with King 2Ki 16:10
Before leaving to * the attack, 2Ki 19:9
David went out to * them and 1Ch 12:17
The army of Ammon went out to * 1Ch 19:9
sent his troops to * them there. 2Ch 14:9,10
and he went out to * King Asa as he 2Ch 15:2
lower armor and the breastplate *. 2Ch 18:33
(son of Hanani) went out to * him. 2Ch 19:2
went out to * the returning army. 2Ch 28:9
and Levites to * him at the open 2Ch 29:4,5
asking me to * them in one of the Neh 6:2
around the other way to * them. Neh 12:38
They * together to perfect their Ps 56:6
* in secret to set their traps. Ps 64:5
Let your tenderhearted mercies * Ps 79:8
to * with the Lord in Zion. Ps 84:7
You can safely * a lion or step Ps 91:13
We will * the dawn with song. Ps 108:2
It is safer to * a bear robbed of Pro 17:12
"If I go outside I might * a Pro 22:13
ahead and prepares to * them. Pro 27:12
when the wicked * disaster, good Pro 28:28
"Go out to * King Ahaz, you and Is 7:3
The denizens of hell crowd to * Is 14:9
out of the city to * with him. Is 36:3
for Jeremiah to * him at the side Jer 38:14
city to * them, crying as he went. Jer 41:6
and his men, and ran to * them. Jer 41:13,14
You will agree, when you * them, Eze 14:23
very day I was sent here to * you. Dan 10:12
Prepare to * your God in Amo 4:12
fortresses to * the Lord our God. Mic 7:17
* another angel coming toward him. Zec 2:3
The same day they arrive, * them Zec 6:10,11
But when the king came in to * Mt 22:11
and went to * the bridegroom. Mt 25:1
go to Galilee, and * you there." Mt 26:32
going to Galilee to * them there. Mt 28:7
once for Galilee, to * me there." Mt 28:10
could * Jesus and his disciples. Mk 2:15
* him, and fell down before him. Mk 5:6
go to Galilee and * you there." Mk 14:28
honor or even to come and * you. Lk 7:6,7,8
of Gadara came to * him, a man who Lk 8:27
"If you * your accuser on the Lk 12:58
And he brought Peter to * Jn 1:42
"Come and * a man who told me Jn 4:28,29
was coming, she went to * him. Jn 11:20
to * him, shouting, "The Savior! Jn 12:13
many went out to * him—because they Jn 12:18
said, "Sir, we want to * Jesus." Jn 12:21
myself to * their need for growth Jn 17:19
Stepping forward to * them he Jn 18:4,5
he tried to * with the believers, Act 9:26
Go down and * them and go with Act 10:20
and close friends to * Peter. Act 10:24
to come down to the boat to * him. Act 20:17
us with him to * with James and the Act 21:18
and came to * us at the Forum Act 28:15
who * to worship in their home. Rom 16:5
be with you as you *, and I will be 1Co 5:3,4
is done when you * together for 1Co 11:17
upon himself when you * together. 1Co 11:34
When you * together some will 1Co 14:26
all the others who * in their home 1Co 16:19
a loving handshake when you *. 1Co 16:20
wasn't there to * me and I couldn't 2Co 2:13
and to those who * in his home. Col 4:15
will not rise to * him ahead of 1Th 4:15
the first to rise to * the Lord. 1Th 4:16
in the clouds to * the Lord in the 1Th 4:17
being gathered together to * him? 2Th 2:1
please try to * me at Nicopolis as Tit 3:12

MEETING
hastily called a * of all the Gen 20:8
before * him face to face! Gen 32:20
people of Israel to a council *. Ex 4:29
out from their * with Pharaoh, Ex 5:20
Then Moses and Aaron called a * Ex 16:6
(the "Tent for * with God," he Ex 33:7
NOW MOSES CALLED a * of all the Ex 35:1
and summon all Israel to a * Lev 8:1
and they held a protest *. Num 20:3
called a * under the oak beside the Ju 9:6
anything about her * with David 1Sa 25:36
an open * of all the people; 1Ki 12:20
They called the * and put Naboth 1Ki 21:12
in his house at a * with the elders 2Ki 6:32
Then Jehu called a * of all the 2Ki 10:17
He called a * of all the people. 2Ch 24:20
They dread * me and look the Ps 31:11
the results of the *, he tore his Is 37:1
administrative officials were *. Jer 36:12
call a solemn *. Joe 1:14
people together for a solemn *. Joe 2:15
He called a * of the Jewish Mt 2:4
at this * he found out from them Mt 2:7
Then the Pharisees called a * to Mt 12:14
officials were * at the residence Mt 26:3
had happened. A * of all the Mt 28:12,13
Then the * broke up and everybody Jn 7:53
That evening the disciples were * Jn 20:19
and held a prayer * in an upstairs Act 1:13
those who were present at the *: Act 1:14
This prayer * went on for several Act 1:15
the house where they were *. Act 2:2
the three o'clock daily prayer *. Act 3:1
where they were * shook and they Act 4:31
Meanwhile, the apostles were * Act 5:12
So the Twelve called a * of all Act 6:2
many were gathered for a prayer *. Act 12:12
further * to decide this question. Act 15:6
At the *, after long discussion, Act 15:7
called a general * of the Act 15:30
began a separate * at the lecture Act 19:9
He called a * of his men, Act 19:25
You are to call a * of the 1Co 5:3,4
But now you are * people who 1Co 12:3
become a priest by * the old Heb 7:16
and shrink back from * him. 1Jn 2:28

MEETINGS
they come together in * filled Ps 35:15
your most pious *—all are frauds! Is 1:12,13
In one of these * he told them Act 1:4
and prayer *. Act 2:42
up in one of the * to predict by Act 11:28
at the regular City Council *; Act 19:39
goes on in these *, and the 1Co 11:18
be silent during the church *. 1Co 14:34
11:5), apparently in public *, 1Co 14:34f
their opinions in church *. 1Co 14:35
them be silent in your church *. 1Ti 2:12
Let us not neglect our church *, Heb 10:25

MEETS
kill the murderer when he * him. Num 35:19
Do not rejoice when your enemy * Pro 24:17
whom victory * at every step? Is 41:2
I am his guest, and the church * Rom 16:23
to the church that * in your home, Phm 1:1

MEGIDDO
The king of *; Jos 12:8-24
En-dor, Taanach, * (where there are Jos 17:11
*, with their surrounding towns; Ju 1:27
was Taanach and *, all of 1Ki 4:8-19
the cities of Hazor, *, and Gezer. 1Ki 9:15
He was able to go on as far as *, 2Ki 9:27
but King Neco killed Josiah at * 2Ki 23:29
in a chariot from * to Jerusalem 2Ki 23:30
Beth-shean, Taanach, *, and Dor. 1Ch 7:29
the battle at the Valley of *. 2Ch 35:22
Hadad-rimmon in the valley of *." Zec 12:11f
who was killed in the valley of * Zec 12:11
Armageddon—the Mountain of *. Rev 16:16

MEGIDDO'S
By * springs, Ju 5:19

MEHETABEL
King Hadad's wife was *, daughter Gen 36:31-39
Pai (his wife was *, the daughter 1Ch 1:50
who was the son of *), for he said Neh 6:10

MEHIDA
Harhur, Bazluth, *, Harsha, Barkos, Ez 2:43-54
Bazlith, *, Harsha, Neh 7:46-56

MEHOLATH
to Adriel, a man from *, instead. 1Sa 18:19

MEHUJAEL
of *; Gen 4:18
* was the father Gen 4:18

MEHUMAN
his personal aides—*, Biztha, Est 1:10

MELATIAH
Next to them were * from Gibeon; Neh 3:7

MELCHI
Levi's father was *; Lk 3:23-38
Neri's father was *; Lk 3:23-38

MELCHI'S
Levi's father was Melchi;* father Lk 3:23-38
Neri's father was Melchi;* father Lk 3:23-38

MELCHIZEDEK
to meet him, and *, the king of Gen 14:18
Then * blessed Abram with this Gen 14:19,20
Then Abram gave * a tenth of all Gen 14:19,20
*. God stands beside you to Ps 110:4
with the same rank as *." Heb 5:6
Priest with the same rank as *. Heb 5:10
with the honor and rank of *. Heb 6:20
THIS * WAS king of the city of Heb 7:1
kings, * met him and blessed him; Heb 7:1

(MELCHIZEDEK Con't)
in the battle and gave it to *. Heb 7:2
* had no father or mother Heb 7:3
this means that * was Christ Heb 7:3f
See then how great this * is: Heb 7:4
people, gave * a tenth of the Heb 7:4
would do this if * had been a Heb 7:5
relatives. But * was not a Heb 7:6
(b) * placed a blessing upon Heb 7:6
but we are told that * lives on. Heb 7:8
paid tithes to * through Abraham. Heb 7:9
when Abraham paid the tithes to *. Heb 7:10
with the rank of *, instead of Heb 7:11
with the rank of *, did not become Heb 7:15
forever with the rank of *." Heb 7:17
forever, with the rank of *." Heb 7:21

MELCHIZEDEK'S
* name means "Justice," so he is Heb 7:2
no record of who * father or mother Heb 7:3f

MELEA
Eliakim's father was *; Lk 3:23-38

MELEA'S
Eliakim's father was Melea;* Lk 3:23-38

MELECH
Pithon, *, Tarea, Ahaz. 1Ch 8:35
Micah was the father of Pithon, * 1Ch 9:41

MELODIES
Play joyous * of praise upon the Ps 33:2

MELODIOUS
and mourn. The * chords of the Is 24:8

MELONS
and *, leeks, onions, and garlic! Num 11:4,5
"Stolen * Pro 9:17

MELT
All the people of Canaan * with Ex 15:15
began to * away in all directions. 1Sa 14:16
letting it * in his mouth, sipping Job 20:12
the earth and * copper from stone. Job 28:2
the wind; * them like wax in fire! Ps 68:2
The mountains * like wax before Ps 97:5
I myself will * you in a Is 1:25
the strongest hearts *, and are Is 13:7
the hearts of the Egyptians * Is 19:1
heavens above will * away and Is 34:4
"See, I will * them in a crucible Jer 9:7
boldest heart will * with fear; Eze 21:7
Let their hearts * with terror, Eze 21:15
you, and you will * like silver in Eze 22:22
and more. They * their silver to Hos 13:2
collect all your armies. * your Joe 3:10
They * beneath his feet, and Mic 1:4
mountains quake and hills *; Nah 1:5
hearts * in horror; Nah 2:10
us is going to * away, what holy, 2Pe 3:11
will * and disappear in flames. 2Pe 3:12

MELTED
the food * and disappeared. Ex 16:21
Aaron * the gold, then molded Ex 32:4
He took the calf and * it in the Ex 32:20
their courage * away completely and Jos 5:1
silver, were * down to bullion. 2Ki 25:14,15
(King Solomon later * the bronze 1Ch 18:8

MELTING
Showers soften the earth, * the Ps 65:10
* in the forests of Zalmon. Ps 68:14

MELTS
My heart * like wax; Ps 22:14
speaks, the earth * in submission Ps 46:6
rain that * down an earthen wall. Is 25:4
The snow never * high up in the Jer 18:14
it *, and all its people mourn. Amo 9:5
All opposition * away before the Hab 1:9

MEMBER
For without a son, some other * Gen 15:2,3
by Potiphar, a * of the personal Gen 39:1
No one who is not a * of the Num 18:4
and then each * of the guilty Jos 7:14
Aaron, who was a * of the Kohath Jos 21:9-16
"Are you a * of the tribe of Ju 12:5
Every * will die before his time. 1Sa 2:31
of aging Jesse, a * of the tribe of 1Sa 17:12
honored * of your own household! 1Sa 22:14
son of Gera, a * of Saul's family. 2Sa 16:5
a * of the royal family of Edom. 1Ki 11:14
but he is the only * of your family 1Ki 14:13
Ishmael, who was a * of the royal 2Ki 25:25
Dodo, a * of the subclan of Ahoh. 1Ch 11:12
Levite, choir *, gatekeeper, Temple Ez 7:24
of which I was a *, went around the Neh 12:38
make her a beloved * of your Pro 7:4
a son who is a * of a lawless Pro 28:7
* of a sinful, foul-mouthed race; Is 6:5
Jerahmeel (a * of the royal family Jer 36:26
(It belonged to Malchiah, a * of Jer 38:6
who was a * of the royal family and Jer 41:1
a * of the royal family [Zedekiah Eze 17:12,13
Simon (a * of "The Zealots," a Mt 10:2,3,4
Simon (a * of a political party Mk 3:16-19
an honored * of the Jewish Supreme Mk 15:42,43
Zacharias was a * of the Abijah Lk 1:5
like himself, a * of the priest Lk 1:5
And because Joseph was a * of Lk 2:4
Simon (a * of the Zealots, a Lk 6:14,15,16
in the home of a * of the Jewish Lk 14:1
Then a man named Joseph, a * of Lk 23:50,51,52
named Nicodemus, a * of the sect of Jn 3:1
Among them was Dionysius, a * of Act 17:34
The High Priest or any * of the Act 22:5
Julius, a * of the imperial guard. Act 27:1
and a * of Benjamin's family. Rom 11:1
What's more, I was a * of the Php 3:5

MEMBERS
* of the Assembly, were involved. Num 16:2
For all the * of your families Num 18:11
and all the other * of the Levite Deu 18:1
father-in-law—* of the Kenite Ju 1:16
fear of the other * of his father's Ju 6:27
list of King Solomon's cabinet *: 1Ki 4:1
Jezebel. The * of your family who 1Ki 21:24
the rest of the * of the family of 2Ki 10:11
* of the tribe of Amalek. 1Ch 4:43
of whom were * of the Kohath clan: 1Ch 6:54
Among the * of the tribe of 1Ch 9:7,8
Some * of the Kohath clan were in 1Ch 9:32
(He and twenty-two * of his 1Ch 12:24-37
The choir * from the clan of Ez 2:40,41,42
200 choir *, both men and women. Ez 2:64,65
The choir * from the clan of Neh 7:43,44,45
245 choir *, both men and women. Neh 7:67
the choir *, the Temple attendants, Neh 7:73
the choir *; Neh 10:28
The choir * also came to Neh 12:28
of food for the * of the choir, the Neh 12:47
the Levites, the * of the choir, Neh 13:5
The Sadducees were * of a Jewish Act 4:1f
But one of their *, a Pharisee Act 5:34
and took 4,000 * of the Assassins Act 21:37,38
with those who are * of the church, 1Co 5:12
actually parts and * of Christ? 1Co 6:15
to Adam, being * of his sinful 1Co 15:22
but you are * of God's very own Eph 2:19
and privilege as * of his body. Col 3:15
should not become * of this special 1Ti 5:11
we are now * of God's own family. 1Pe 1:3
people used to be * of our 1Jn 2:19
sin among your *, and you have Rev 2:2

MEMBERSHIP
this man is removed from your *? 1Co 5:2

MEMO
So David dispatched a * to Joab: 2Sa 11:6

MEMORIAL
upright as a * pillar, and poured Gen 28:18
And this * pillar shall become a Gen 28:22
observe this * at the same time. Ex 12:47
This annual * week will brand Ex 13:9
of the ephod, as * stones for the Ex 28:12
Literally, "to be stones of * for Ex 39:6,7f
Literally, "shall burn the * Lev 2:2f
Literally, "the *." Lev 2:9f
This will be a * offering made by Lev 24:5-8
as a * of the people of Israel. Num 31:54
and by lengthening the * fringes Mt 23:5
the * decorations on the walls. Lk 21:5

MEMORIES
We all have happy * of good men Pro 10:7
they don't even have their *. Ecc 9:5

MEMORY
that even the * of the good years Gen 41:31
to the Lord, in * of his Lev 24:5-8
So that even the * of them Deu 32:26
so that the * of what had happened Est 9:28
"All * of his existence will Job 18:17
even the * of them will Ps 9:6
the * of evil men from the earth. Ps 34:16
the very * of her existence. Ps 83:4
off his name from the * of man. Ps 109:15
and in * of my servant David." Is 37:35
incense in your *, just as they did Jer 34:5
wiped out, your * lost in history. Eze 21:32
Have you no * at all of what Mic 6:5
even the * of them will disappear. Zep 1:4
who had no respect for Joseph's *. Act 7:17,18

MEMPHIS
those from * are utterly deluded. Is 19:13
their cities of * and Tahpanhes to Jer 2:16
Tahpanhes and *, and throughout Jer 44:1
cities of Migdol, * and Tahpanhes! Jer 46:14
for the city of * shall be utterly Jer 46:19
and the images at *, and there will Eze 30:13
apart, * will be in daily terror. Eze 30:16
She will gather your dead; * will Hos 9:6

MEMUCAN
Marsena, and *—seven high officials Est 1:13-15
* answered for the others, Est 1:16

MEMUCAN'S
so he followed * counsel, and sent Est 1:21

MEN
Literally, "*." Gen 1:26f
It was during his lifetime that * Gen 4:26
and "daughters of *" to the men Gen 6:1f
to the * of the line of Cain. Gen 6:1f
All of the * listed above Gen 10:32
* and women slaves, and camels. Gen 12:
"This fighting between our * has Gen 13
of Sodom. The * of this area were Gen 13:
One of the * who escaped came Gen 14:
together the * born into his Gen 14:
these young * of mine have eaten; Gen 14:
with all the other * and boys of Gen 17:24-
noticed three * coming toward him. Gen 18
set it before the * and stood Gen 18
Then the * stood up from their Gen 18:
a godly household—* who are just Gen 18:
for the night, the * of the Gen 19
* to us so we can rape them." Gen 19
But leave these * alone, for they Gen 19
worse than with those other *." Gen 19
But the two * reached out and Gen 19:
blinded the * of Sodom so that they Gen 19:1
the * asked. Gen 19:1
But the young * looked at him Gen 19:
and servants—both * and women—and Gen 20:
and two young * who were his Gen 22
told the young *, "and the lad and Gen 22:
So they returned to his young *, Gen 22:1
body, he said to the * of Heth: Gen 23:
"Certainly," the * replied, Gen 23:5,
Abraham bowed again to the * of Gen 23:1
of the * of Heth at the city gate. Gen 23:17,1
by the * of Heth as a burial plot. Gen 23:19,2
* with him stayed there overnight. Gen 24:5
And when the * there asked him Gen 26:
Isaac's * then dug another well, Gen 26:2
So Laban invited all the * of the Gen 29:2
Then, taking several * with him, Gen 31:2
before all these *, I'll give it Gen 31:3
of us, before your * and mine, for Gen 31:36,3
and told his * to gather stones Gen 31:4
many servants, both * and women. Gen 32:
meet Jacob—with an army of 400 *! Gen 32:
He told the * driving the first Gen 32:1
God, you shall prevail with *." Gen 32:28
saw Esau coming with his 400 *. Gen 33:
Esau said. "My * and I will stay Gen 33:1
you some of my * to assist you and Gen 33:1
as wives for your young *. Gen 34:9,1
idea to the other * of the city—for Gen 34:18,1
"Those * are our friends," they Gen 34:2
every one of us * be circumcised, Gen 34:22
So all the * agreed, and all were Gen 34:24
So he asked around of the * of Gen 38:21
the * of the place had told him. Gen 38:22
and when the other * around the Gen 39:14,15
these * can tell me what it means. Gen 41:15
We are all brothers and honest * Gen 42:11
"If you are forthright *." Gen 42:19f
said, 'we are honest *, not spies. Gen 42:31
whether you are spies or honest *; Gen 42:34
* will eat with me this noon. Gen 43:16
you there" ' (you * are witnesses Gen 45:11,12
And I will tell him, 'These * Gen 46:32
They are * of violence and Gen 49:5
that broke out on * and animals Ex 9:10
Everything left in the fields, * Ex 9:25
Let the * go and serve Jehovah Ex 10:7
You that are *, go and serve Ex 10:11
Tell all the * and women of Ex 11:2
of Egypt, both of * and animals; Ex 13:15
The mighty * of Moab tremble; Ex 15:15
So Joshua and his * went out to Ex 17:10
godly, honest * who hate bribes, Ex 18:21
Let these * be responsible to Ex 18:22
He chose able * from all over Ex 18:25
or slaves—whether * or women—or Ex 20:10
the end of six years as the * are. Ex 21:7
"If two * are fighting, and one Ex 21:18
"If two * are fighting, and in Ex 21:22
Then he sent some of the young * Ex 24:5
dedicate these * to their ministry Ex 28:41
So they all did—* and women, boys Ex 32:2,3
three thousand * died that day. Ex 32:28
occasions all the * and boys of Ex 34:23
Both * and women came, all who Ex 35:22
or older, a total of 603,550 *. Ex 38:25,26
fight with one of the * of Israel. Lev 24:10
"Take a census of all the * Num 1:2-15
summoned all the * of Israel who Num 1:17,18,19
in Israel of both * and animals! Num 3:13
Levi, all of the * between the ages Num 4:21,22,23
tribe, all of the * from thirty to Num 4:29
all of the * thirty to fifty years Num 4:35
This applies to * and women Num 5:3
of the tribes, the * who had Num 7:2
are mine, both * and animals; Num 8:17
some of the * had just attended a Num 9:6,7
taken down and the * of the Gershon Num 10:17
are 600,000 * alone [besides all Num 11:21
Some young * ran and told Moses Num 11:27
not one of the * who has seen my Num 14:22
of these wicked *, and don't touch Num 16:26
If these * die a natural death Num 16:29
these * have despised the Lord." Num 16:30
250 * who were offering incense. Num 16:35

MEN Con't)
cen-sers of these * who have sinned Num 16:38
taking some of the * as prisoners. Num 21:1
And the * and women Num 21:27-30
asked him, "Who are these *?" Num 22:9
Balaam told the *, "Go on home! Num 22:13
and go with these *, but be sure to Num 22:20
him, "Go with the *, but say only Num 22:35
some of the young * began going to Num 25:1
gods, and soon the * were not only Num 25:2
But one of the Israeli * Num 25:6
census of all the * of Israel who Num 26:2
and 250 * were destroyed by fire Num 26:5-11
* throughout Israel was 601,730. Num 26:51
Conscript 1,000 * from each Num 31:4,5
* were sent to battle by Moses. Num 31:4,5
priest said to the * who were in Num 31:21
Half of it is for the * who were Num 31:27
for all the * who went out to Num 31:48,49
"If all the * of the tribes of Num 32:29
lived there. The * of Jair, Num 32:41
the names of the * I have appointed Num 34:16-28
These are the names of the * I Num 34:29
the Lord: "The * of the tribe of Num 36:5
were married to * in their own Num 36:11,12
So choose some * from each tribe Deu 1:13
I took the * they selected, some Deu 1:15
until all the *, who thirty-eight Deu 2:14,15
* women, and children alike. Deu 3:6
until their armed * led the other Deu 3:18
nor send his * to Egypt to raise Deu 17:16
he hasn't, both * shall be brought Deu 19:17
" 'Listen to me, all you * of Deu 20:3
shall address the * in this manner: Deu 20:5
this to their *, they will announce Deu 20:9
Then the * of the city shall Deu 21:21
and all the young * of Israel will Deu 21:21
home where the * of the city shall Deu 22:21
"When you are at war, the * in Deu 23:9,10
in Israel, either * or women; Deu 23:17,18
"If two * are fighting and the Deu 25:11
fierce and angry * who will have no Deu 28:50
instructed, "—*, women, children, Deu 31:12
(Ask your father and the aged *; Deu 32:7
Shall terrorize young * and girls Deu 32:25
And aged *. Deu 32:25
They act like * of Sodom and Deu 32:32
in charge, "The * were here Jos 2:4
So the constable and his * went Jos 2:7
Rahab went up to talk to the * Jos 2:8
The * agreed. "If you won't Jos 2:14
days until the * who are searching Jos 2:16
But before they left, the * had Jos 2:17,18
days, until the * who were chasing Jos 2:22
"Now select twelve *, one from Jos 3:12
"Tell the twelve * chosen for a Jos 4:2,3
So Joshua summoned the twelve *, Jos 4:4
So the * did as Joshua told them. Jos 4:8
Egypt all of the * who had been old Jos 5:4,5
until all the * who had been old Jos 5:6
their children—the * who had grown Jos 5:7
the armed * would lead the Jos 6:6-9
in it—* and women, young and old; Jos 6:21
The young * found her and rescued Jos 6:23
sent some of his * to spy on the Jos 7:2
* of Ai as far as the quarries. Jos 7:5
That is why your * are running Jos 7:12
So Joshua sent some * to search Jos 7:22
And the * of Israel stoned them to Jos 7:25
army attacks, the * of Ai will come Jos 8:5
Joshua roused his * and started Jos 8:10
five thousand * to join the troops Jos 8:11,12,13
thousand * already hiding there. Jos 8:11,12,13f
And when the * in ambush saw his Jos 8:19
When the * of Ai looked behind Jos 8:20,21
knew that their * who had been in Jos 8:20,21
So the * of Ai were caught in a Jos 8:22
all the * outside the city, they Jos 8:24
Joshua and the * of Israel, "We Jos 9:6
out—these * were close neighbors. Jos 9:16
its * were known as hard fighters. Jos 10:2
on Gibeon. The * of Gibeon Jos 10:6
in fact, more * died from the Jos 10:11
As the * of Israel were pursuing Jos 10:12
Joshua now instructed his * to Jos 10:22,23
Joshua said to his *. Jos 10:25
city, but Joshua's * killed him and Jos 10:33
Then Joshua and his * did as the Jos 11:9
property as the * of our tribe." Jos 17:4
Select three * from each tribe Jos 18:4
sacred dice. The * did as they Jos 18:9
I brought my people out as free *. Jos 24:5
to Jericho. The * of Jericho fought Jos 24:11
and the other old * who had Jos 24:31
as the old * of his generation were Ju 2:7-9
The young * of Israel took their Ju 3:6
the Israeli girls married their *. Ju 3:6
*, letting not one escape. Ju 3:29
ten thousand * from the tribes of Ju 4:6
When Barak summoned the * of Ju 4:10
ten thousand * volunteered. Ju 4:10

So Barak led his ten thousand * Ju 4:14
Barak and his * chased the enemy Ju 4:16
Among forty thousand * of Israel, Ju 5:8
and for fear of the * of the city; Ju 6:27
and the * of Abiezer came to him. Ju 6:34
Send home any of your * who are Ju 7:3
In Group 1 will be all the * who Ju 7:5,6
Only three hundred of the * drank Ju 7:5,6
only three hundred * with him. Ju 7:8,9
Then he returned to his * and Ju 7:15
He divided the three hundred * Ju 7:16
As soon as I and the * in my Ju 7:18
and the hundred * with him crept to Ju 7:19,20
two hundred of his * did the same, Ju 7:19,20
River with his three hundred *. Ju 8:4
He asked the * of Succoth for Ju 8:5
Literally, "he taught the * of Ju 8:16f
Zalmunna, "The * you killed at Ju 8:18
Now the * of Israel said to Ju 8:22
across to the * of Shechem, "If Ju 9:7
For the * of Shechem set an Ju 9:25
So Abimelech and his * marched Ju 9:34
* began their march upon the city. Ju 9:35
seeing shadows that look like *!" Ju 9:36
be our king?' The * you taunted and Ju 9:38
So Gaal led the * of Shechem into Ju 9:39
and many of the * of Shechem were Ju 9:40
The next day the * of Shechem Ju 9:42
he had divided his * into three Ju 9:43
And when the * of the city went Ju 9:43
attack, he and his * jumped up from Ju 9:43
gate to keep the * of Shechem from Ju 9:44
as I have done," he told his *. Ju 9:47,48
about a thousand * and women. Ju 9:49
When his * saw that he was dead, Ju 9:55
Abimelech and the * of Shechem for Ju 9:56,57
the * of Gilead were mere outcasts Ju 12:4
He married his daughters to * Ju 12:9,10
for thirty young * of the village, Ju 14:10,11
gave the answer to the young *. Ju 14:17
killed thirty *, took their Ju 14:19
it to the young * who had told him Ju 14:19
the * of Judah asked. Ju 15:10
So three thousand * of Judah went Ju 15:11
the * of Judah told him. Ju 15:12,13
I've killed a thousand *, Ju 15:16,17
alerted and many * of the city lay Ju 16:2
Some * were hiding in the next Ju 16:9
I will be as weak as other *." Ju 16:11
him with them. The * were hiding in Ju 16:12
So the * of Dan chose five army Ju 18:2
So the five * went on to the town Ju 18:7
And the * replied, "Let's Ju 18:9,10
So the five * went over to the Ju 18:15,16
all of the armed * standing just Ju 18:15,16
the * of Dan demanded. Ju 18:23
mister," the * of Dan replied. Ju 18:25
So the * of Dan kept going. Ju 18:26
the priest, the * of Dan arrived at Ju 18:27
action against the * of Benjamin Ju 19:30
"That night the * of Gibe-ah Ju 20:5
* have committed a terrible crime. Ju 20:6
Give up these evil * from the Ju 20:13
hundred local * in their defense Ju 20:14,15
were seven hundred * who were Ju 20:16
not counting the * of Benjamin, Ju 20:17
of Benjamin, numbered 400,000 *. Ju 20:17
to attack the * of Benjamin. Ju 20:19,20
But the * defending the village Ju 20:21
So the * of Israel took courage Ju 20:22,23,24
*, all experienced swordsmen. Ju 20:25
The * of Israel asked the Lord, Ju 20:27,28
you defeat the * of Benjamin." Ju 20:27,28
began to kill the * of Israel along Ju 20:31
the ten thousand * in ambush west Ju 20:33
army killed 25,100 * of Benjamin Ju 20:35-39
retreated from the * of Benjamin in Ju 20:35-39
When the * of Benjamin had killed Ju 20:35-39
But then the * in ambush rushed Ju 20:35-39
them, and the * who had set the Ju 20:42
only six hundred * who escaped to Ju 20:46,47
tribe of Benjamin—*, women, Ju 20:48
All the *, married women, and Ju 21:10,11,12
the * of Benjamin at Rimmon Rock. Ju 21:13
They told the * of Benjamin who Ju 21:20
So the * of Benjamin did as they Ju 21:23
These young *, Mahlon and Ru 1:4,5
But later, both * died, so that Ru 1:4,5
I have warned the young * not to Ru 2:8,9
told his young * to let her glean Ru 2:15
ten of the chief * of the village, Ru 4:2
these respected * as witnesses. Ru 4:4
Now the sons of Eli were evil * 1Sa 2:12
So the sin of these young * was 1Sa 2:17
Thirty thousand * of Israel died 1Sa 4:10
Several * of the tribe of Levi 1Sa 6:15
that day by the * of Beth-shemesh. 1Sa 6:15
seventy of the * of Beth-shemesh 1Sa 6:19
SO THE * of Kiriath-jearim came 1Sa 7:1
for his sons were not good *. 1Sa 8:5
So Samuel agreed and sent the * 1Sa 8:22

you will see two * beside Rachel's 1Sa 10:2
you will see three * coming toward 1Sa 10:3
Gibe-ah, a band of * whose hearts 1Sa 10:26
The * of Jabesh then told their 1Sa 11:10
"Where are those * who said that 1Sa 11:12
When the * of Israel saw the vast 1Sa 13:6
I saw that my * were scattering 1Sa 13:11
these six hundred * set up their 1Sa 13:16
Saul and his six hundred * were 1Sa 14:2
Among his * was Ahijah the 1Sa 14:3
about twenty * in all, and their 1Sa 14:14
Then Saul and his six hundred * 1Sa 14:20
Finally even the * hiding in the 1Sa 14:22
his * replied. 1Sa 14:36
Amalek nation—*, women, babies, 1Sa 15:3
to ten thousand * from Judah. 1Sa 15:4
However, Saul and his * kept the 1Sa 15:9
the way you do! * judge by outward 1Sa 16:7
bodies of your * to the birds and 1Sa 17:46
Then Saul instructed his * to say 1Sa 18:22
When Saul's * reported this back 1Sa 18:24
he and his * went out and killed 1Sa 18:27
Saul's * were incredulous! 1Sa 19:24
I have told my * where to meet me 1Sa 21:2
if only your young * have not slept 1Sa 21:4
"I never let my * run wild when 1Sa 21:5
finally King Achish said to his *, 1Sa 21:14,15
leader of about four hundred *. 1Sa 22:2
"Listen here, you * of 1Sa 22:7
there with Saul's *, spoke up. 1Sa 22:9,10
priests' families—*, women, 1Sa 22:19
But David's * said, "We're 1Sa 23:3
and besiege David and his *. 1Sa 23:8
Will the * of Keilah surrender 1Sa 23:11
"And will these * of Keilah 1Sa 23:12
So David and his *—about six 1Sa 23:13
But now the * of Ziph went to 1Sa 23:19
So the * of Ziph returned home. 1Sa 23:24,25
Ziph, he and his * went even 1Sa 23:24,25
As Saul and his * began to close 1Sa 23:26
and his * were hiding in the cave! 1Sa 24:3
David's * whispered to him. 1Sa 24:4
have done it," he said to his *. 1Sa 24:6
persuaded his * not to kill Saul. 1Sa 24:7,8
and some of my * told me to kill 1Sa 24:9,10
and his * went back to their cave. 1Sa 24:22
ten of his young * to Carmel to 1Sa 25:5
Ask your young * and they will 1Sa 25:8
Now I have sent my * to ask for a 1Sa 25:8
The young * gave David's message 1Sa 25:9
Literally, "to * who come from 1Sa 25:11f
Meanwhile, one of Nabal's * went 1Sa 25:14
"David sent * from the wilderness 1Sa 25:14
But David's * were very good to 1Sa 25:15,16
young *, "and I will follow." 1Sa 25:19
if even one of his * remains alive 1Sa 25:22
brought to you and your young *. 1Sa 25:27
not one of Nabal's * would be alive 1Sa 25:34
and followed the * back to David. 1Sa 25:42
NOW THE * from Ziph came back to 1Sa 26:1
"Let one of your young * come 1Sa 26:22
So David took his six hundred * 1Sa 27:2,3
He and his * spent their time 1Sa 27:8
Achish said to David and his *. 1Sa 28:1
accompanied by two of his *. 1Sa 28:7,8
But he refused. The * who were 1Sa 28:23
king and his *, and they ate it. 1Sa 28:25
David and his * marched at the rear 1Sa 29:2
finally summoned David and his *. 1Sa 29:6
some of the finest * I've ever met, 1Sa 29:6
when David and his * arrived home 1Sa 30:1
As David and his * looked at the 1Sa 30:3
* began talking of killing him. 1Sa 30:6
So David and his six hundred * 1Sa 30:9,10
two hundred of the * were too 1Sa 30:9,10
and from the * of Judah. 1Sa 30:16
David and his * rushed in among 1Sa 30:17
young * who fled on camels. 1Sa 30:17
had taken. The * recovered their 1Sa 30:18,19
the two hundred * who had been too 1Sa 30:21
among David's * declared, "They 1Sa 30:22
where David and his * had been: 1Sa 30:27-31
Thousands of * are dead and 2Sa 1:4
David and his * tore their 2Sa 1:11
* of Israel who had died that day. 2Sa 1:12
one of his young *, "Kill him!" 2Sa 1:15
Carmel— and his * and their 2Sa 2:3
When David heard that the * of 2Sa 2:4
sword play between our young *!" 2Sa 2:14
Joab agreed, so twelve * were 2Sa 2:15
day Abner and the * of Israel had 2Sa 2:17
trumpet and his * stopped chasing 2Sa 2:28
That night Abner and his * 2Sa 2:29
Joab and the * who were with him 2Sa 2:30
that only nineteen * were missing, 2Sa 2:30
sixty of Abner's * (all from the 2Sa 2:31
Joab and his * took Asahel's 2Sa 2:32
Twenty * accompanied him, and 2Sa 3:20
May the Lord repay wicked * for 2Sa 3:39
I do to wicked * who kill a good 2Sa 4:11
So David ordered his young * to 2Sa 4:12

(MEN Con't)
After the * who were carrying it 2Sa 6:13
to everyone—* and women alike—of a 2Sa 6:19
of the most famous * in the world! 2Sa 7:9
told him, "These * aren't here to 2Sa 10:3
So Hanun took David's * and 2Sa 10:4
for the * were very embarrassed 2Sa 10:5
We must really act like * today 2Sa 10:12
the enemies' best * were fighting; 2Sa 11:16
the * on the wall attacked us; 2Sa 11:24
and some of our * were killed, 2Sa 11:24
"There were two * in a certain 2Sa 12:1
young * were kept strictly apart. 2Sa 13:2
Absalom told his *, "Wait until 2Sa 13:28
He took two hundred * from 2Sa 15:11
David's instant response to his *. 2Sa 15:14
Go on back with your * to 2Sa 15:19,20
* and their families went along. 2Sa 15:22
fruit are for the young * to eat; 2Sa 16:2
So David and his * continued on, 2Sa 16:13
Meanwhile, Absalom and his * 2Sa 16:15
me twelve thousand * to start out 2Sa 17:1
You know your father and his *; 2Sa 17:8
and a few of your * fall, there 2Sa 17:9
that your * are being slaughtered. 2Sa 17:9
Then Absalom and all the * of 2Sa 17:14
When Absalom's * arrived and 2Sa 17:20
Then the two * crawled out of 2Sa 17:21
the * across the Jordan River. 2Sa 17:24
but his * objected strongly. 2Sa 18:2
were beaten back by David's *. 2Sa 18:7
* laid down their lives that day. 2Sa 18:7
and more * disappeared in the 2Sa 18:8
some of David's * and as he fled 2Sa 18:9
One of David's * saw him and 2Sa 18:10
trumpet, and his * returned from 2Sa 18:16
* of Judah to welcome King David. 2Sa 19:16
A thousand * from the tribe of 2Sa 19:17
But the * of Israel complained 2Sa 19:41
king because only * from Judah had 2Sa 19:41
the * of Judah replied. 2Sa 19:42
and forth, and the * of Judah were 2Sa 19:43
Come on, you * of Israel, let's 2Sa 20:1
But the * of Judah stayed with 2Sa 20:2
of Adri-el. The * of Gibeon 2Sa 21:9
the mother of two of the *, 2Sa 21:10
a request to the * of 2Sa 21:12,13,14
and David and his * were in the 2Sa 21:15
After that David's * declared, 2Sa 21:17
most heroic * in David's army: the 2Sa 23:8
He once killed eight hundred * in 2Sa 23:8
He was one of the three * who, 2Sa 23:9
when all his * deserted him and 2Sa 23:11,12
So the three * broke through the 2Sa 23:16
This is the blood of these * who 2Sa 23:17
Of those three *, Abishai, the 2Sa 23:18,19
the king—800,000 * of conscription 2Sa 24:9
great) than into the hands of *." 2Sa 24:14
and seventy thousand * died 2Sa 24:15
the king and his * coming towards 2Sa 24:20
recruited fifty * to run down the 1Ki 1:5
of two * who were better than he. 1Ki 2:32
of any of the wise * of the East, 1Ki 4:30
and I will send my * to work beside 1Ki 5:6
pay your * whatever wages you ask; 1Ki 5:6
and cypress. My * will bring the 1Ki 5:9
of the Temple. * from Gebal helped 1Ki 5:18
And there were 550 * of Israel 1Ki 9:23
Great * from many lands came to 1Ki 10:24
a gang of bandits—* who fled with 1Ki 11:24
over with the old * who had 1Ki 12:6
young * with whom he had grown up. 1Ki 12:8
And the young * replied, "Tell 1Ki 12:10
and followed that of the young *; 1Ki 12:13,14
to conscript * from the other 1Ki 12:18
the able-bodied * of Judah and 1Ki 12:21
there are 7,000 * in Israel who 1Ki 19:18
I will send my * to search your 1Ki 20:5,6
time, but your * may not search the 1Ki 20:9
the rest of his army of 7,000 *. 1Ki 20:15
chariots, and *, and we will fight 1Ki 20:25
The * were quick to grab this 1Ki 20:33
Then two * who had no conscience 1Ki 21:13
that his * go too, but Jehoshaphat 1Ki 22:49
destroy you and your fifty *!" 2Ki 1:10
captain with fifty * to demand, "O 2Ki 1:11
destroy you and your fifty *." 2Ki 1:12
Once more the king sent fifty *, 2Ki 1:13
Then fifty * searched for three 2Ki 2:17
but there was no water for the * 2Ki 3:9
Then the * of Israel moved 2Ki 3:24
stew for supper for these *." 2Ki 4:38
One of the young * went out into 2Ki 4:39
But after the * had eaten a bite 2Ki 4:40
"Feed one hundred * with only 2Ki 4:43
the servants and sent the * back. 2Ki 5:24
kill the young *, dash their babies 2Ki 8:12
Jehu told the * who were with him, 2Ki 9:15
homes of the chief * of the city, 2Ki 10:6
Jehu shouted to his *. 2Ki 10:14
with eighty of his * and told them, 2Ki 10:24
his officers and *, "Go in and 2Ki 10:25
Then Jehu's * went into the inner 2Ki 10:25
They brought to Jehoiada the * 2Ki 11:9
they were honest and faithful *. 2Ki 12:15
Once some * who were burying a 2Ki 13:20,21
* who had assassinated his father; 2Ki 14:5
him with fifty * from Gilead, and 2Ki 15:25
and the * of Hamath worshiped 2Ki 17:30
*: Eliakam, his business manager; 2Ki 18:18
If you have two thousand * left 2Ki 18:23
that * had made of wood and stone. 2Ki 19:18
him, "What did these * want? 2Ki 20:14
for they were honest *. 2Ki 22:7
He ordered his * to bring out the 2Ki 23:16
And the * of the city told him, 2Ki 23:17
Jericho, and all his * scattered. 2Ki 25:4,5
and their * joined him at Mizpah. 2Ki 25:23
son of Maachathite, and their *. 2Ki 25:23
to Mizpah with ten * and killed 2Ki 25:25
Then all the * of Judah and the 2Ki 25:26
of King Saul, the * of Reuben 1Ch 5:10
Each of these * had a great 1Ch 5:24
and deport the * of Reuben, Gad, 1Ch 5:26
total number of * of war from these 1Ch 7:2
The total number of * available 1Ch 7:5
numbered 36,000 * of war. 1Ch 7:40
These * had 150 sons and 1Ch 8:40
These * were all chiefs of 1Ch 9:9
the bodies of the * killed in 1Ch 10:8
and said to his *, "The first man 1Ch 11:5,6
greatest heroes among David's *. 1Ch 11:11
He once killed 300 * with his 1Ch 11:11
this to his *, these three broke 1Ch 11:17
It is the very blood of these * 1Ch 11:18,19
300 * at one time with his spear. 1Ch 11:20
warriors among David's * were: 1Ch 11:26-47
were "lion-faced *, swift as deer 1Ch 12:8-13
These * were army officers; 1Ch 12:14
Some * from Manasseh deserted the 1Ch 12:19
let David and his * go with them. 1Ch 12:19
that David and his * would imperil 1Ch 12:19
Here is a list of the * from 1Ch 12:20
More * joined David almost every 1Ch 12:22
relatives—all * who understood the 1Ch 12:24-37
All these * came in battle array 1Ch 12:38
assembled * of Israel as follows: 1Ch 13:2
The following * were chosen as 1Ch 15:18
(* and women alike) a loaf of 1Ch 16:3
sent these * to honor your father! 1Ch 19:2,3
let us act like * to save our 1Ch 19:13
came to 1,100,000 * of military age 1Ch 21:5
into the power of *, for God's 1Ch 21:13
and 70,000 * died as a result. 1Ch 21:14
to weigh. The * of Tyre and Sidon 1Ch 22:4
'You have killed too many * in 1Ch 22:8
was taken of the * of the tribe of 1Ch 23:3
In the census, all the * of Levi 1Ch 23:24
were many famous * and high 1Ch 24:5
then appointed * to prophesy to the 1Ch 25:1
These * were from the groups of 1Ch 25:1
all outstanding *, and had 1Ch 26:6,7
Semachiah, were also very able *. 1Ch 26:6,7
outstanding * who were particularly 1Ch 26:8
These * of the Ladan subclan 1Ch 26:20,21,22
For these * dedicated their war 1Ch 26:27
all outstanding *, were placed in 1Ch 26:30
outstanding * of the clan of the 1Ch 26:31,32
These *, all of whom had 1Ch 26:31,32
His 24,000 * were on duty the 1Ch 27:5,6
He had 24,000 * on duty the 1Ch 27:7
Izrah, with 24,000 * on duty the 1Ch 27:8
he had 24,000 * on duty the sixth 1Ch 27:9
with 24,000 * on duty the seventh 1Ch 27:10
who had 24,000 * on duty the eighth 1Ch 27:11
Zerah, with 24,000 * on duty the 1Ch 27:13
with 24,000 * on duty during the 1Ch 27:14
commanded 24,000 * on duty during 1Ch 27:15
These * were King David's 1Ch 27:31
* of authority in his kingdom. 1Ch 28:1
discretion that * are made great 1Ch 29:12
I know, my God, that you test * 1Ch 29:17
for you enjoy good *. 1Ch 29:17
Lebanon, for your * are without 2Ch 2:8
and I will send my * to help them. 2Ch 2:8
I will pay your * 20,000 sacks of 2Ch 2:10
really live upon the earth with *? 2Ch 6:18
Solomon's *, went to Ophir and 2Ch 8:17,18
the size of the * in his bodyguard, 2Ch 9:4
What a privilege for these * of 2Ch 9:7
with the old * who had counseled 2Ch 10:6
young * who had grown up with him. 2Ch 10:8,9
advice of the old *, and followed 2Ch 10:13
courageous * led by King Jeroboam. 2Ch 13:3
the * of Judah to ambush them; 2Ch 13:13,14
The * of Judah began to shout. 2Ch 13:15,16
Abijah and the * of Judah to turn 2Ch 13:15,16
composed of well-trained, brave *. 2Ch 14:8
Don't let mere * defeat you!" 2Ch 14:11
But you * of Judah, keep up the 2Ch 15:7
These * included Ben-hail, 2Ch 17:7,8,9
with an army of 280,000 *. 2Ch 17:14,15
Benjamin supplied 200,000 * 2Ch 17:1
Jehozabad, with 180,000 trained *. 2Ch 17:1
upon one of the * standing 2Ch 20:1
As he and his * were searching 2Ch 22:
These * traveled out across the 2Ch 23:2,
* who had assassinated his father. 2Ch 25:
an army of 300,000 * twenty years 2Ch 25:5,
there killed 10,000 * from Seir. 2Ch 25:1
regiments to which * were drafted 2Ch 26:1
The army consisted of 307,500 *, 2Ch 26:1
by brilliant * to shoot arrows and 2Ch 26:1
*, and demanded that he get out. 2Ch 26:17,1
These * were Azariah the son of 2Ch 28:1
Then the four * already 2Ch 28:1
they are all mere *, while we have 2Ch 32:8
So the * went to Huldah the 2Ch 34:22
killed their young *, even going 2Ch 36:17
even young girls and old *. 2Ch 36:17
choir members, both * and women. Ez 2:64,65
leaders—the old * who remembered Ez 3:12
Babylonians, the * of Erech and Ez 4:8,9
and * from several other nations. Ez 4:10
command that these * must stop Ez 4:21
* who were working on the Temple. Ez 5:4
Parosh—Zechariah, and 150 other *; Ez 8:2-14
of Zerahiah), and 200 other *; Ez 8:2-14
son of Jahaziel, and 300 other *; Ez 8:2-14
(son of Jonathan), and 50 other *; Ez 8:2-14
(son of Athaliah), and 70 other *; Ez 8:2-14
(son of Michael), and 80 other *; Ez 8:2-14
(son of Jehiel), and 218 other *; Ez 8:2-14
of Josiphiah), and 160 other *; Ez 8:2-14
(son of Bebai), and 28 other *; Ez 8:2-14
of Hakkatan), and 110 other *; Ez 8:2-14
* (they arrived at a later time); Ez 8:2-14
Zaccur, and 70 other *. Ez 8:2-14
Elnathan, who were very wise *. Ez 8:16
These 220 * were all listed by Ez 8:20
I consecrated these * to the Ez 8:28
and Amorites. The * of Israel had Ez 9:2
a large crowd of *, women, and Ez 10:1
all the * of Judah and Benjamin Ez 10:9
Then all the * spoke up and said, Ez 10:12
Each of these * had heathen Ez 10:44
some * who had arrived from Judah. Neh 1:2
taking only a few * with me; Neh 2:11,12
and dedicated it. * from the city Neh 3:2
Next were the * from Tekoa, but Neh 3:5
Jadon from Meronoth; and * from Neh 3:7
"the house of the mighty *." Neh 3:16f
and half the * were always on Neh 4:20,21
and homes to these rich *; Neh 5:2,3,4
too, are mortgaged to these *." Neh 5:5
and made these * formally vow to Neh 5:12
And the rich * did as they had Neh 5:13
choir members, both * and women. Neh 7:67
These * were Jeshua, Kadmi-el, Neh 9:4
These * signed on behalf of the Neh 10:28
marry non-Jewish * and not to let Neh 10:30
under the leadership of these *. Neh 11:10-14
There were also 128 stalwart * Neh 11:10-14
These were the * who were active Neh 12:26
On that day * were appointed to Neh 12:44
These * had an excellent Neh 13:13
farm and saw some * treading Neh 13:15
There were also some * from Tyre Neh 13:16
so that all the * could gaze upon Est 1:11
They were * of wisdom who knew Est 1:13-15
These * were Carshena, Shethar, Est 1:13-15
* found guilty, and impaled alive. Est 2:23
They even killed 500 * in Est 9:6
"The Jews have killed 500 * in Est 9:12
killed 300 more *, though again Est 9:15
how much less * made of dust, who Job 4:18,19
frustrates the plans of crafty *. Job 5:12
They grope like blind * in the Job 5:14
sons shall become important *; Job 5:25
like *? Job 10:4-7
And as you say, older * like me Job 12:12
you can fool God as well as *? Job 13:9
harsh with frail *, and demand an Job 14:3
On our side are aged * much Job 15:10
experience of wise * who have been Job 15:17-19
Fair-minded * are astonished Job 17:8
of rich and wicked * who came to Job 21:28
But no doubt you gave * of Job 22:8
Fair and honest * could reason Job 23:7
For wicked * are broken like a Job 24:20
They are evil *. Job 27:7
"* KNOW HOW to mine silver and Job 28:1
from stone. * know how to put Job 28:3,4
shadowed by death, * descend on Job 28:3,4
"* know how to obtain food from Job 28:5
no lion has set his paw there. * Job 28:9
"But though * can do all these Job 28:12
I deride me—young * whose fathers Job 30:1
from civilization. * shouted after Job 30:5
These young *, having humbled me, Job 30:11
THE THREE * refused to reply Job 32:1
is not mere age that makes * wise. Job 32:8,9
on * as they lie on their beds. Job 33:15

MEN Con't)
“Listen to me, you wise *. Job 34:2
time with evil *, for he said, Job 34:7,8
to hide evil * from his eyes, so Job 34:22
*, and puts others in their place. Job 34:24
strikes them down as wicked *. Job 34:26
He does not ignore the good * Job 36:7
time, so that all * everywhere may Job 37:7
No wonder * everywhere fear him! Job 37:24
by the world's wisest *!” Job 37:24
haunts of wicked * and stopped the Job 38:15
and paths of godly *, but the paths Ps 1:6
How strange that * should try to Ps 2:1
The Lord God asks, “Sons of *, Ps 4:2
Go, leave me now, you * of evil Ps 6:8
the hearts of * and examine all Ps 7:9
the prayers of * in trouble when Ps 9:12
they know they are but puny *. Ps 9:20
proud and wicked * who viciously Ps 10:2
Pour upon these * the evil they Ps 10:2
For these * brag of all their Ps 10:3
These wicked *, so proud and Ps 10:4
Break the arms of these wicked * Ps 10:15
GODLY * are fast disappearing. Ps 12:1
world can dependable * be found? Ps 12:1
the reach of evil *, although they Ps 12:7
the godly * and women in the land; Ps 16:3
gone along with cruel and evil *. Ps 17:4
Come and save me from these * of Ps 17:13,14
earthly gain—these * whom you have Ps 17:13,14
For these * plot against you, Ps 21:11
The enemy, this gang of evil *, Ps 22:16
See these * of evil gloat and Ps 22:17
life from all these evil *. Ps 22:20
with tricky, two-faced *; Ps 26:4
When evil * come to destroy me, Ps 27:2
of these arrogant * who are Ps 31:18
accusing honest * of evil deeds.” Ps 31:18
hand, safe from all conspiring *. Ps 31:20
Let everyone in all the world—*, Ps 33:8
memory of evil * from the earth. Ps 34:16
These evil * swear to a lie. Ps 35:11
against innocent * who are minding Ps 35:20
for * and animals alike. Ps 36:6
Don't let these proud * trample Ps 36:11
Don't be envious of evil * who Ps 37:7
Evil * take aim to slay the Ps 37:14
for the strength of evil * shall Ps 37:17
the good deeds done by godly *, Ps 37:18
But evil * shall perish. Ps 37:20
Evil * borrow and “cannot pay Ps 37:21
The steps of good * are directed Ps 37:23
Evil * spy on the godly, waiting Ps 37:32
not let these evil * succeed, nor Ps 37:33
But evil * shall be destroyed, Ps 37:38
them from the plots of evil *. Ps 37:40
of these merciless, deceitful *. Ps 43:1
on life than foolish, stupid *. Ps 49:10
Such is the folly of these *, Ps 49:13
dismayed when evil * grow rich and Ps 49:16
But God says to evil *: Recite my Ps 50:16
your time with evil and immoral *. Ps 50:18
Written by David at the time the * Ps 54:1
For violent * have risen against Ps 54:3
me—ruthless * who care nothing for Ps 54:3
an end to these wicked *, O God. Ps 54:5
These * are born sinners, lying Ps 58:3
fields of slaughtered, wicked *. Ps 58:10
Strong * are out there waiting. Ps 59:3
spare these evil, treacherous *. Ps 59:5
Let these evil * slink back at Ps 59:14,15
* of Edom in the Valley of Salt. Ps 60:1
The greatest of *, or the Ps 62:9
And don't let the rich * be Ps 62:10,11
*, these gangs of criminals. Ps 64:1
Literally, “You caused * to ride Ps 66:12f
*, even those who once were Ps 68:18
They are influential *, these who Ps 69:4
Let these * be blotted from the Ps 69:28
from these unjust and cruel *. Ps 71:4
May all good * flourish in his Ps 72:7
Literally, “* shall pray for him Ps 72:15f
“Look at these * of arrogance; Ps 73:12
about the future of these evil *. Ps 73:17
is full of darkness and cruel *. Ps 74:20
of evil *,” says the Lord, Ps 75:10
power of good * in their place.” Ps 75:10
the finest of Israel's young *. Ps 78:31
were merely mortal *, gone in a Ps 78:39
Their young * were killed by Ps 78:63
needy from the grasp of evil *. Ps 82:4
But in death you are mere *. Ps 82:7
these proud * who hate the Lord? Ps 83:2
O God, proud and insolent * defy Ps 86:14
violent, godless * are trying to Ps 86:14
life you give the sons of *? Ps 89:47
How these * of evil boast! Ps 94:4
God has made the sins of evil * Ps 94:23
dens to rest, and * go off to work Ps 104:23
heaven to consume these wicked *. Ps 106:18
Oh, that these * would praise Ps 107:8
Oh, that these * would praise Ps 107:15
Oh, that these * would praise Ps 107:21
Oh, that these * would praise Ps 107:31
Good * everywhere will see it Ps 107:42
while evil * are stricken silent. Ps 107:42
enemies, for * are useless allies. Ps 108:12
How can * be wise? Ps 111:10
Evil-minded * will be infuriated Ps 112:10
in my alarm, all * are liars.” Ps 116:10,11f
Lord than to put confidence in *. Ps 118:8
Proud * hold me in contempt for Ps 119:51
Evil * have tried to drag me Ps 119:61
Proud * have made up lies about Ps 119:69
These proud * who hate your Ps 119:85,86
Begone, you evil-minded *. Ps 119:115
For these evil * have violated Ps 119:126
me from the oppression of evil *; Ps 119:134
Here come these lawless * to Ps 119:150
Great * have persecuted me, Ps 119:161
these * of Meshech and Kedar. Ps 120:5,6
here among these * who hate peace. Ps 120:5,6
but lead evil * to execution. Ps 125:5
that evil * had bound me with. Ps 129:3,4
silver, made by *— idols with Ps 135:15
proud * must keep their distance. Ps 138:6
Away, bloodthirsty *! Ps 139:19
O LORD, DELIVER me from evil *. Ps 140:1
These proud * have set a trap to Ps 140:5
Don't let these wicked * succeed; Ps 140:6,7,8
then these * will finally listen Ps 141:6,7
these liars, these treacherous *. Ps 144:11
and call on all * everywhere to Ps 145:21
Don't look to * for help; Ps 146:3
For the Lord loves good *. Ps 146:8
judges, young * and maidens, old Ps 148:12
and maidens, old * and children— Ps 148:12
“I want to warn young * about Pro 1:4
Stay far from * like that, for Pro 1:15
it stays away, but not these *; Pro 1:18
away from evil * who want you to Pro 2:11,12,13
partners in crime—* who turn from Pro 2:11,12,13
The * who enter them are doomed. Pro 2:19
None of these * will ever be the Pro 2:19
good * enjoy life to the full; Pro 2:21
evil * lose the good things they Pro 2:22
*, for the Lord is with you; Pro 3:24,25,26
Don't envy violent *. Pro 3:31
For such * are an abomination to Pro 3:32
YOUNG *, LISTEN to me as you would Pro 4:1
else, for evil * don't sleep until Pro 4:16
Young *, listen to me, and never Pro 5:7
corner for * to be her lovers. Pro 7:11,12
Listen to me, young *, and not Pro 7:24
host of * have been her victims. Pro 7:26
to what she says: “Listen, *!” Pro 8:4,5
And so, young *, listen to me, Pro 8:32
whispering to * going by, and to Pro 9:15
Lazy * are soon poor; Pro 10:4
memories of good * gone to their Pro 10:7
of wicked * stink after them. Pro 10:7
* with common sense are admired Pro 10:13
The hope of good * is eternal Pro 10:28
the hopes of evil * are all in Pro 10:28
Proud * end in shame, but the Pro 11:2
God rescues good * from danger Pro 11:8
money to cruel *. Pro 11:16
Godly * are growing a tree that Pro 11:30
The Lord blesses good * and Pro 12:2
kindness of godless * is cruel. Pro 12:10
good * long to help each other. Pro 12:12
wicked * lie Pro 13:5
life, while evil * are being Pro 13:6
Be with wise * and become wise. Pro 13:20
Be with evil * and become evil. Pro 13:20
Evil * shall bow before the Pro 14:19
Wise * are praised for their Pro 14:24
truth saves good * from being Pro 14:25
in the hearts of * of common sense, Pro 14:33
A mocker stays away from wise * Pro 15:12
Take my word for it—proud * shall Pro 16:5
of sensible *, but a fool's goals Pro 17:24
it will bring you before * of Pro 18:16
the consequences. * have died for Pro 18:21
Some * are so lazy they won't Pro 19:24
what fools * are to let it master Pro 20:1
Some * enjoy cheating, but the Pro 20:17
The glory of young * is their Pro 20:29
of old *, their experience. Pro 20:29
God loathes the gifts of evil *, Pro 21:27
short-tempered *, lest you learn to Pro 22:24,25
Don't associate with evil *; Pro 23:6,7,8
Don't envy evil * but continue to Pro 23:17,18
DON'T ENVY GODLESS *; Pro 24:1
When you remove corrupt * from Pro 25:4,5
also it is bad for * to think about Pro 25:27
he is smarter than seven wise *. Pro 26:16
Evil * don't understand the Pro 28:5
Young * who are wise obey the Pro 28:7
prayers of * who flout the law. Pro 28:9
the godly. But * who encourage the Pro 28:10
Rich * are conceited, but their Pro 28:11
Good * will be rescued from harm, Pro 28:18
When the wicked prosper, good * Pro 28:28
meet disaster, good * return. Pro 28:28
With good * in authority, the Pro 29:2
Flattery is a trap; evil * are Pro 29:5,6
good * stay away and sing for joy. Pro 29:5,6
while wise * try to keep peace. Pro 29:8
but good * will live to see the Pro 29:16
Hard liquor is for sick * at the Pro 31:6,7
* have throughout their lives. Ecc 2:3
Next I bought slaves, both * and Ecc 2:7,8
in the hearts of *, even so, man Ecc 3:11
and so that * themselves will see Ecc 3:18
than beasts. For * and animals Ecc 3:19
nothing better for * than that they Ecc 3:22
has given to some * very great Ecc 6:2
Wise * and fools alike spend Ecc 6:7,8
per cent of the * I interviewed Ecc 7:27,28
God has made * upright, each has Ecc 7:29
I have seen wicked * buried and Ecc 8:9,10
evil deeds, these * were praised in Ecc 8:9,10
to treat some good * as though they Ecc 8:14
wicked * as though they were good. Ecc 8:14
and wise * are in God's will; Ecc 9:1
That is why * are not more Ecc 9:2,3
and that wise * are often poor, and Ecc 9:11
* are not necessarily famous; Ecc 9:11
have seen foolish * given great Ecc 10:6
and rich * not given their rightful Ecc 10:6
* of his army surrounding it. Sol 3:7
of Israel, you * of Sodom and Is 1:10
the pride of * will lie in the Is 2:17
criminals sneering at honorable *. Is 3:5
to catch the glances of the *. Is 3:16
AT THAT TIME so few * will be left Is 4:1
Now, * of Jerusalem and Judah, Is 5:3
Your great and honored * will Is 5:13
and putting innocent * in jail. Is 5:23
known as honest *, to watch me as I Is 8:2
to godly * of future generations. Is 8:16
and like that of * dividing up the Is 9:3
joy in their young *, and no mercy Is 9:17
they are proud and haughty *. Is 10:12
small alike, both officers and *. Is 10:33
* will be as scarce as gold—of Is 13:12
Great * and small—all will be Is 19:10
of wise * they have come from? Is 19:11
The “wise *” from Zoan are Is 19:13
Syrians drive the chariots; the * Is 22:6,7
Flee to Tarshish, * of Tyre, Is 23:6
still your lot, O * of the world. Is 24:17
from merciless * who are like a Is 25:4
But for good * the path is not Is 26:7
of * lying drunk in the streets! Is 28:1
* who use any excuse to be unfair. Is 29:21
For these Egyptians are mere *, Is 31:3
destroyed, but not by swords of *. Is 31:8
of as generous, outstanding *! Is 32:5
The smooth tricks of evil * will Is 32:7
But good * will be generous to Is 32:8
No evil-hearted * may walk upon Is 35:8
—that you don't have 2,000 * left Is 36:8,9
carved by * from wood and stone. Is 37:19
For dead * cannot praise you. Is 38:18
He dooms the great * of the Is 40:23
and the young * will all give up. Is 40:30
carpenters—mere *—who claim that Is 44:11
a god—a god for * to worship! Is 44:15
I make wise * give opposite Is 44:25
to me, you stubborn, evil *! Is 46:12
If such * walk in darkness, Is 50:10
fear mere mortal *, who wither like Is 51:12
Let * cast off their wicked deeds; Is 55:7
THE GOOD * perish; Is 57:1
angry and smote these greedy *. Is 57:17
No wonder you grope like blind * Is 59:10
compared with vigorous young *! Is 59:10
no longer will * be considered Is 65:20
e., not *! Is 65:25f
When such * sacrifice an ox on Is 66:3
this degenerate race of evil *? Jer 2:21
herself to other * at every chance, Jer 3:6
The Lord is saying to the * of Jer 4:3
their leaders, the * of importance, Jer 5:5
Their weapons are deadly; the * Jer 5:16
Among my people are wicked * who Jer 5:26
They set their traps for *. Jer 5:26
of young *, and on husbands and Jer 6:11
are all adulterous, treacherous *. Jer 9:2
the young * gather no more in the Jer 9:21
Among all the wise * of the Jer 10:7
The wisest of * who worship idols Jer 10:8
But foolish * without knowledge Jer 10:14
that these * are in, for what they Jer 10:14
Remind the * of Judah and all the Jer 11:1
the * of Judah and Jerusalem. Jer 11:9
the hearts and motives of these *. Jer 11:20
And the Lord replied, The * of Jer 11:21,22
And so their young * shall die in Jer 11:21,22
Why are evil * so happy? Jer 12:1
with mere *—these men of Anathoth Jer 12:5

(MEN Con't)
with mere men—these * of Anathoth Jer 12:5
* and sorrow to their mothers. Jer 15:8
from these wicked * and rescue you Jer 15:21
worthless idols! Can * make God? Jer 16:20
* scoff at me and say, "What is Jer 17:15
priests and wise * and prophets—we Jer 18:18
Let their * die in epidemics and Jer 18:21
And now, Jeremiah, as these * Jer 19:10
and both * and animals shall die. Jer 21:6
them on the fire. * from many Jer 22:8
prophets, all ungodly, wicked *. Jer 23:11
the * of Sodom and Gomorrah were. Jer 23:14
to sweep away these wicked *. Jer 23:19
Then some of the wise old * stood Jer 26:17
several other * to capture Uriah. Jer 26:22
For these * have done a Jer 29:23
and trembling. Do * give birth? Jer 30:6
dance for joy, and * folk—old and Jer 31:13
to all the ways of *, and you Jer 32:19
Babylonians, where * and animals Jer 32:43
enter, and the * of this city are Jer 33:5
Hebrew slaves, both * and women. Jer 34:9
he said, "these * have done a very Jer 38:9
to take thirty * with him and pull Jer 38:10
So Ebedmelech took thirty * and Jer 38:11
to the * who were after his life. Jer 38:16
the guard, and his * sent the Jer 39:9
of a Ma-acathite), and their *. Jer 40:8
in Mizpah, accompanied by ten *. Jer 41:1
and the ten * in league with him Jer 41:2
happened, eighty * approached Jer 41:5
Ishmael and his * killed all but Jer 41:7
the bodies of the * he murdered was Jer 41:9
their * and set out to stop him. Jer 41:12
and his *, and ran to meet them. Jer 41:13,14
* into the land of the Ammonites. Jer 41:15
Then Johanan and his * went to Jer 41:16,17
*, said to Jeremiah, "You lie! Jer 43:2,3
In the crowd were *, women and Jer 43:6
"Call together the * of Judah Jer 43:9
and tell the * of Judah this: The Jer 43:10
and all the * who knew that their Jer 44:15
to all of them, * and women alike, Jer 44:20
before these * from the north. Jer 46:24
Strong * will scream in terror Jer 47:2
are heroes, mighty * of war"? Jer 48:14
is broken for the * of Kir-heres. Jer 48:31
O * of Sibmah, rich in vineyards, Jer 48:32
all your wise * of days gone by? Jer 49:7
Your young * lie dead in the Jer 49:26
all shall be gone—both * and Jer 50:3
Her young * will fall in the Jer 50:30
princes and wise * too. Jer 50:35
Compared to him, all * are Jer 51:17
and young, young * and maidens, Jer 51:22
In their drunken feasts, the * Jer 51:38
armies come and slay her mighty *; Jer 51:56
*, rulers, captains, warriors. Jer 51:57
* of importance found hiding. Jer 52:24,25
Lord has trampled all my mighty *. Lam 1:15
afflicting * and causing sorrow. Lam 3:33
and deprived * of their God-given Lam 3:34,35,36
the finest specimens of *; Lam 4:7
Now these same * are blindly Lam 4:14
Even aged * are treated with Lam 5:12
They take away the young * to Lam 5:13
The old * sit no longer in the Lam 5:14
that looked like *, except that Eze 1:5
Their legs were like those of *, Eze 1:7
and wicked * of pride shall live. Eze 7:10,11
and to wicked * as booty. Eze 7:21
about twenty-five * standing with Eze 8:16
Six * appeared at his call, Eze 9:2
foreheads of the * who weep and Eze 9:4
tell the other *: "Follow him Eze 9:5
the most prominent * of the city, Eze 11:1
these are the * who are responsible Eze 11:1
For these evil * deceive my Eze 13:10
"Son of dust, these * worship Eze 14:3
if these three * were here, the Eze 14:16
if these three * were in the land, Eze 14:18
made statues of * and worshiped Eze 16:17
* instead of her own husband. Eze 16:32
services—* pay with many gifts. Eze 16:33,34
wedlock living with other *. Eze 16:38
he exiled the top * of Israel's Eze 17:12,13
of cruel * skilled in destruction. Eze 21:31
There are * who commit adultery Eze 22:10
attractive young *, captains and Eze 23:6
them—the choicest * of Eze 23:7
those handsome young * on fine Eze 23:12
* pictured, so she sent messengers Eze 23:16
with the lustful * she remembered Eze 23:19,20
young * of high rank, riding their Eze 23:23
side with armored * and I will let Eze 23:24
the sound of many * carousing—lewd Eze 23:42
men carousing—lewd * and drunkards Eze 23:42
lustful * who visit prostitutes. Eze 23:44
your helmsmen are skilled * from Eze 27:8
"Your army includes * from Eze 27:10
it is the ultimate of honor. * Eze 27:11
your towers are manned by * from Eze 27:11
and destroy both * and herds. Eze 29:8
that way, neither * nor animals. Eze 29:11
sell the whole land to wicked *. Eze 30:12
The young * of Heliopolis and Eze 30:17
with all the proud * of the world. Eze 31:14
All these mighty * who once Eze 32:23
is the same as that of ordinary *. Eze 32:24
You are my * and I am your God, Eze 34:31
they will appoint * to search the Eze 39:14
Eat the flesh of mighty * and Eze 39:18
And the * of the tribe of Levi Eze 44:10
These * shall be my ministers; Eze 44:15
as captives—young * of the royal Dan 1:3,4
four of the young * chosen, all Dan 1:6
all the young * to the king for Dan 1:18,19
execute all the wise * of Babylon. Dan 2:12
He gives wise * their wisdom, and Dan 2:21
execute the wise * of Babylon, and Dan 2:24
well as chief over all his wise *. Dan 2:48
of the strongest * of his army to Dan 3:20
throw three * into the furnace?" Dan 3:24
"I see four *, unbound, walking Dan 3:25
I called in all the wise * of Dan 4:6
wants to, even the lowliest of *!' Dan 4:17
all the wisest * of my kingdom Dan 4:18
the kingdoms of *, and gives power Dan 4:25
the kingdoms of * and gives them to Dan 4:32
My wise * and astrologers have Dan 5:15
the kingdoms of *, and that he Dan 5:21
Then the * thronged to Daniel's Dan 6:11
In the evening the * came again Dan 6:15
to bring the * who had accused Dan 6:24
claws that tore * apart and that Dan 7:19
yes, all of us—the * of Judah, Dan 9:7
great vision; the * with me saw Dan 10:7
when he leaves—* who have Dan 11:30,31
and some ungodly * will come, Dan 11:34
I, Daniel, looked and saw two * Dan 12:5
will be born to you from other *. Hos 1:2
they belong to other *. Hos 1:4
run after other * and sell myself Hos 1:5
do not go out with other * nor be Hos 3:3
For you * are doing the same Hos 4:14
The * of Israel finish up their Hos 4:18
listen, all you * of the royal Hos 5:1
"The inspired * are mad." Hos 9:7
Was it not right that the * of Hos 10:9
with skill by the hands of *. Hos 13:2
they say—* kissing calves! Hos 13:2
right, and good * walk along them. Hos 14:9
Listen, you aged * of Israel! Joe 1:2
your old * will dream dreams, and Joe 2:28
and your young * see visions. Joe 2:28
on your slaves, * and women alike, Joe 2:29
with the wickedness of these *. Joe 3:13
of your mighty * will drop their Amo 2:16
sends a thousand * to battle, a Amo 5:3
O evil *, you make "justice" a Amo 5:7
of the Lord. * will wander Amo 8:12
and fine young * alike will grow Amo 8:13
Edom was noted for her wise *; Ob 1:8f
For I will fill the wise * of Ob 1:8
The * were terribly frightened Jon 1:9,10
The * stood there in awe before Jon 1:16
Weep, * of Bakah. Mic 1:10
Where are your wise *? Mic 4:9
Your rich * are wealthy through Mic 6:12
The good * have disappeared from Mic 7:1
everywhere. * stumble over them, Nah 3:3
* who love to argue and to fight. Hab 1:3
"Note this: Wicked * trust Hab 2:4
I will sweep away both * and Zep 1:3
when strong * will weep bitterly. Zep 1:14
and arrogant * from among you; Zep 3:11
"What have these * come to do?" Zec 1:21
sent a group of * headed by Zec 7:2
once again be aged * and women Zec 8:4
In those days ten * from ten Zec 8:23
the young * and girls flourish; Zec 9:16,17
Lord of Hosts, and * should come to Mal 2:7
treachery, for the * of Judah have Mal 2:11
says he hates divorce and cruel *. Mal 2:16
against wicked * who trick the Mal 3:5
treatment of good * and bad, Mal 3:18
how to fish for the souls of *!" Mt 4:19
"Humble * are very fortunate!" Mt 5:3
care for you, O * of little faith? Mt 6:30
give holy things to depraved *. Mt 7:6
And if you hardhearted, sinful * Mt 7:11
But Jesus answered, "O you * of Mt 8:26
two * with demons in them met him. Mt 8:28
And they came out of the * and Mt 8:32
Soon some * brought him a Mt 9:2
associate with * like that?" Mt 9:11
home, two blind * followed along Mt 9:27
good and godly * because of their Mt 10:41
"Truly, of all * ever born, none Mt 11:11
* of violence take it by force." Mt 11:12f
But brilliant * like you can Mt 11:19
How could evil * like you speak Mt 12:3
three nights. The * of Nineveh Mt 12:4
"The farmer's * came and told Mt 13:2
he said to his *, "This must be Mt 14:
(About 5,000 * were in the crowd Mt 14:2
* besides the women and children! Mt 15:37,3
told them, "O * of little faith! Mt 16:
and some are disabled by *, and Mt 19:1
hall and saw some * standing around Mt 20:
and saw some more * standing around Mt 20:
to call the * in and pay them, Mt 20:
beginning with the last * first. Mt 20:8
When the * hired at five o'clock Mt 20:
So when the * hired earlier came Mt 20:1
Two blind * were sitting beside Mt 20:3
"Surely evil * and prostitutes Mt 21:3
very evil * and prostitutes did. Mt 21:3
But the farmers attacked his *, Mt 21:3
group of his * to collect for him, Mt 21:36
put the wicked * to a horrible Mt 21:41
their * along with the Herodians Mt 22:16
The first of these * married and Mt 22:25
You try to look like saintly *, Mt 23:28
of the godly * they destroyed, and Mt 23:29,30
of being the sons of wicked *. Mt 23:31
prophets, and wise *, and inspired Mt 23:34
of murdered godly * from righteous Mt 23:35
"Two * will be working together Mt 24:40
betrayed into the hands of evil *! Mt 26:45
used among * in Eastern lands. Mt 26:49f
One of the * with Jesus pulled Mt 26:51
Finally two * were found who Mt 26:60,61
But after a while the * who had Mt 26:73
and many godly * and women who had Mt 27:52
fishermen for the souls of *!" Mk 1:17
the hired * and went with him. Mk 1:20
Four * arrived carrying a Mk 2:3
(There were many * of this type Mk 2:15
saw him eating with these * of Mk 2:16
what * can do on Sabbath days!" Mk 2:28
Jesus summoned these * and asked Mk 3:23
There were about 5,000 * there Mk 6:43,44
"What about the 5,000 * I fed Mk 8:19
he said, "I see *! Mk 8:24
One of the * in the crowd spoke Mk 9:17
kings and great * of the earth lord Mk 10:42
Off went the two * and found the Mk 11:4,5
them to, and then the * agreed. Mk 11:6
he sent one of his * to collect his Mk 12:2
another of his *, who received the Mk 12:4
and desires of *, but sincerely Mk 12:14
forward—a group of * who say there Mk 12:18
Moses that these *, though dead for Mk 12:27
up the kind of * they really are, Mk 12:40
all those rich * put together! Mk 12:43,44
into the hands of wicked *. Mk 14:41
Finally some * stood up to lie Mk 14:57
"He was counted among evil *." Mk 15:28
will be one of the Lord's great *. Lk 1:15
be fishing for the souls of *!" Lk 5:10
(It seemed that these * showed up Lk 5:17
Then—look! Some * came carrying a Lk 5:18,19
Jesus asked, "Do happy * fast? Lk 5:34
did when he and his * were hungry? Lk 6:3
and I have authority over my *. Lk 7:6,7,8
clothes? No! * who live in luxury Lk 7:25
"What can I say about such *?" Lk 7:31
Then the * at the table said to Lk 7:49
The seed is God's message to *. Lk 8:11
For there were about 5,000 * Lk 9:14
Then two * appeared and began Lk 9:30
and the two * standing with him. Lk 9:32
"You * who are fathers—if your Lk 11:11
"The * of Nineveh, too, shall Lk 11:32
graves in a field. * go by you with Lk 11:44
For you crush * beneath Lk 11:46
those who deny me here among *. Lk 12:9
begins to whip the * and women he Lk 12:45
than other * from Galilee?" Lk 13:2
"And what about the eighteen * Lk 13:4
* who are marching against him? Lk 14:31
even the hired * have food enough Lk 15:17
asked, "Didn't I heal ten *? Lk 17:17
That night two * will be asleep Lk 17:34
and so it will be with * working Lk 17:35,36
"Two * went to the Temple to Lk 18:10
of God belongs to * who have hearts Lk 18:16,17
He replied, "God can do what * Lk 18:27
he called in the * to whom he had Lk 19:15
Literally, "the leading * among Lk 19:47f
he sent one of his * to the farm to Lk 20:10
agents pretending to be honest *. Lk 20:20
Then some Sadducees—* who Lk 20:27
point of view, all * are living." Lk 20:37,38
sentence awaits these *." Lk 20:47
kings and great * order their Lk 22:25
great *) are called 'benefactors.' Lk 22:25f
greeting among * in eastern lands. Lk 22:47f
Suddenly two * appeared before Lk 24:4
Then the * asked, "Why are you Lk 24:5
the power of evil * and be Lk 24:6,7

MEN Con't)
to the *—they didn't believe it. Lk 24:11
Some of our * ran out to see, Lk 24:24
expression of himself to *. Jn 1:1f
expression of himself to *. Jn 1:14f
(One of these * was Andrew, Jn 1:40
Then, going over to the * Jn 2:16
Kingdom of God. * can only Jn 3:6
happen here among *, how can you Jn 3:12
One of the * lying there had been Jn 5:5
count of the * only was 5,000—sat Jn 6:10
Your laws say that if two * Jn 8:17
"He can heal blind *, and yet Jn 9:30
listen to evil *, but he has open Jn 9:31
demon open the eyes of blind *?" Jn 10:21
"In your own Law it says that * Jn 10:34,35,36
for they loved the praise of * Jn 12:43
"I have told these * all about Jn 17:6
of the * broken to hasten death; Jn 19:31
of the two * crucified with Jesus; Jn 19:32
two white-robed * were standing Act 1:10
them, and said, "* of Galilee, Act 1:11
The assembly nominated two *: Act 1:23
show us which of these * you have Act 1:24,25
"For these * are all from Act 2:7
Medes, Elamites, * from Act 2:9
And we all hear these * telling Act 2:11
Some of you are saying these * Act 2:15
and your young * shall see visions, Act 2:17
and your old * dream dreams. Act 2:17
all my servants, * and women alike, Act 2:18
"O * of Israel, listen! Act 2:22
Literally, "* without the Law." Act 2:23f
the crowd. "* of Israel," he Act 3:12
of all to you * of Israel, to bless Act 3:26
a new high of about 5,000 *! Act 4:4
for * to call upon to save them." Act 4:12
"What shall we do with these * Act 4:16
and the younger * covered him with Act 5:6
door are the young * who buried Act 5:9
and the young * came in and, seeing Act 5:10
Lord, crowds both of * and women. Act 5:14
at the jail, the * weren't there, Act 5:22
the news that the * they had jailed Act 5:25
"We must obey God rather than *. Act 5:29
"* of Israel, take care what you Act 5:35
you are planning to do to these *! Act 5:35
my advice is, leave these * alone. Act 5:38
and select seven *, wise and full Act 6:3
But one day some of the * from Act 6:9
So they brought in some * to lie Act 6:11
These * were very jealous of Act 7:9
and saw two * of Israel fighting. Act 7:26
Literally, "devout *." Act 8:2f
and dragging out * and women alike Act 8:3
and many * and women were Act 8:12
found there, both * and women, so Act 9:2
The * with Paul stood speechless Act 9:7
they sent two * to beg him to Act 9:38
Now send some * to Joppa to find Act 10:5,6
Just then the * sent by Cornelius Act 10:17
"Three * have come to see you. Act 10:19
Now send some * to Joppa and Act 10:32
Just then three * who had come Act 11:11
One day as these * were Act 13:2
and prayer, the * laid their hands Act 13:3
and began. "* of Israel," he Act 13:16
few days by the * who had Act 13:31
from Galilee—these * have Act 13:31
street as the two * urged them to Act 13:43
* are gods in human bodies!" Act 14:11
among the people, shouting, "*! Act 14:15
at Antioch, some * from Judea Act 15:1
by some local *, to talk to the Act 15:2
But then some of the * who had Act 15:5
decision. The * chosen were two of Act 15:22
These *—Judas and Silas, who Act 15:26
shouting, "These * are servants of Act 16:17
the jailer, "Let those * go!" Act 16:35
of godly Greek *, and also many Act 17:4
of the wives of the leading *." Act 17:4f
Greek women and many * also. Act 17:12
"* of Athens, I notice that you Act 17:22
as an idol made by * from gold or Act 17:29
of "persuading * to worship God in Act 18:13
prophesied. The * involved were Act 19:7
He called a meeting of his *, Act 19:25
enough to speak. "* of Ephesus," Act 19:35
Yet you have brought these * Act 19:37
Several * were traveling with Act 20:4
told them, "You * know that from Act 20:18
"We suggest this: We have four * Act 21:23
day went with the * to the Temple Act 21:26,27
They grabbed him, yelling, "* Act 21:28
both * and women to prison. Act 22:4
The * with me saw the light but Act 22:9
louder, and the * were tugging at Act 23:10
There are more than forty * Act 23:21
and these * certainly cannot Act 24:13
and I believe, just as these * Act 24:15
Ask these * right here what Act 24:20
me over to these * to kill me. Act 25:10,11
and prominent * of the city, Festus Act 25:23
can bring * back to life again? Act 26:8
and said, "*, you should have Act 27:21
all sinful, evil * who push away Rom 1:18
Since earliest times * have seen Rom 1:20
snakes and puny *. Rom 1:23
And the *, instead of having a Rom 1:27
for each other, * doing shameful Rom 1:27
things with other * and, as a Rom 1:27
* who are lost in darkness to God. Rom 2:19
shown that all * alike are sinners, Rom 3:9
makes * right with God, so that Rom 5:18
Before, sin ruled over all * and Rom 5:21
Literally, "* who know (the) Rom 7:1f
Great * of God were your Rom 9:5
the best ideas of *, even the most 1Co 1:19
So what about these wise *, these 1Co 1:20
to the great * of this world, who 1Co 2:6
But the great * of the world 1Co 2:8
words that we as * might choose. 1Co 2:13
Literally, "Are you not (mere) * 1Co 3:4f
the wise * of this world. 1Co 3:21
Literally, "Let no one glory in * 1Co 3:21f
stared at by * and angels alike. 1Co 4:9
these proud * are just big talkers 1Co 4:19
"Become not bondservants of *." 1Co 7:23f
But if you * decide to go ahead 1Co 7:28
opinions of * as to what is right. 1Co 9:8
hat is a sign of subjection to * 1Co 11:7
But remember that in God's plan * 1Co 11:11
out of man, all * have been born 1Co 11:12
since, and both * and women come 1Co 11:12
evil, but be * of intelligence in 1Co 14:20
God would send * from other lands 1Co 14:21
for they are subordinate to * 1Co 14:34
but not to teach * (1 Tim. 1Co 14:34f
wild beasts—those * of Ephesus—if 1Co 15:32
act like *; 1Co 16:13
the work of such * as these. 1Co 16:18
ourselves, are * of integrity, sent 2Co 2:17
plan that makes * right with God. 2Co 3:9
for me to these * and do for them 2Co 8:24
But I am sending these * just to 2Co 9:3
not those made by *, to knock down 2Co 10:4
built to keep * from finding him. 2Co 10:5
change them into * whose hearts' 2Co 10:5
* who tell you how good they are! 2Co 10:12
God never sent those * at all; 2Co 11:13
Yet those other * keep telling 2Co 11:18
seas and from * who claim to be 2Co 11:26
Did any of the * I sent to you 2Co 12:17
* I could not be Christ's servant. Gal 1:10
* of faith who truly trust in God. Gal 3:7
was given, to show * how guilty Gal 3:19
or slaves or free * or even merely Gal 3:28
men or even merely * or women, but Gal 3:28
he gave generous gifts to *. Eph 4:8
of a slave and becoming like *. Php 2:7
"was made in the likeness of *." Php 2:7f
Watch out for those wicked * Php 3:2
These proud * (though they claim Col 2:18
the rules of * but of God who gives 1Th 4:8
clutches of evil *, for not 2Th 3:2
try to stop the * who are teaching 1Ti 1:3,4
So I want * everywhere to pray 1Ti 2:8
I never let women teach * or lord 1Ti 2:12
of good, steady * as the pastors. 1Ti 3:8
know what kind of * you should 1Ti 3:15
was accepted by * everywhere and 1Ti 3:16
Talk to the younger * as you 1Ti 5:1
Remember that some *, even 1Ti 5:24
out by God to tell * and women 2Ti 1:1
to trustworthy * who will, in turn, 2Ti 2:2
love of argument, are * like that. 2Ti 2:17
that young * often have, but stay 2Ti 2:22
In fact, evil * and false 2Ti 3:13
I gave you. The * you choose must Tit 1:6
must be * of blameless lives Tit 1:7
They must be sensible *, and Tit 1:8
One of their own *, a prophet Tit 1:12
"These * of Crete are all liars; Tit 1:12
and the demands of * who have Tit 1:14
Teach the older * to be serious Tit 2:2
In the same way, urge the young * Tit 2:6
* in their dealings with God. Heb 5:1
gently with other *, though they Heb 5:1
weak and sinful * who could not Heb 7:28
not made by * nor part of this Heb 9:11
And just as it is destined that * Heb 9:27
see it up ahead. * of God in days Heb 11:2
These * of faith I have mentioned Heb 11:13
And these * of faith, though Heb 11:39
a huge crowd of * of faith watching Heb 12:1
* did such terrible things to him. Heb 12:3
So it is with rich *. Jas 1:10,11
God's law for free *, he will not Jas 1:25
usually the rich * who pick on you Jas 2:6
* have trained, or can train, Jas 3:7
against * who are made like God. Jas 3:9
LOOK HERE, YOU rich *, now is the Jas 5:1
and killed good * who had no power Jas 5:6
God's ever-living Message to *. 1Pe 1:23
though * have spurned him, he is 1Pe 2:4
then if * speak against you, 1Pe 3:16
earnest, thoughtful * of prayer. 1Pe 4:7
You younger *, follow the 1Pe 5:5
within these godly * who gave them 2Pe 1:20,21
of ungodly * with the vast flood. 2Pe 2:5
as though they were honest *. 2Pe 2:13
These * are as useless as 2Pe 2:17
when all ungodly * will perish. 2Pe 3:7
of these wicked *, lest you 2Pe 3:17
to you older * because you really 1Jn 2:13
And you young *, I am talking to 1Jn 2:13
and to you young * who are strong, 1Jn 2:14
These * belong to this world, 1Jn 4:5
We believe * who witness in our 1Jn 5:9
including lust of * for other men. Jud 1:7
including lust of men for other *. Jud 1:7
But these * mock and curse at Jud 1:10
When these * join you at the love Jud 1:12
knew about these * and said this Jud 1:14
These * are constant gripers, Jud 1:16
leaders and rich *, and Rev 6:15
officers, and all * great and Rev 6:15
In those days * will try to kill Rev 9:6
But the * left alive after these Rev 9:20
from among the * on the earth as a Rev 14:4
it to scorch all * with its fire. Rev 16:8
slaves—and even the souls of *. Rev 18:13
God is now among *, and he will Rev 21:3
more vile; good * will be better; Rev 22:11

MEN'S
and direction of * lives were only Gen 6:5
to fill the * sacks with grain, but Gen 42:25
"A woman must not wear * Deu 22:5
arranged for the * bones to be 2Sa 21:12,13,14
But Rehoboam refused the old * 1Ki 12:8
He ignored the old * advice and 1Ki 12:13,14
burn incense; and * bones shall be 1Ki 13:2
do not follow evil * advice, who do Ps 1:1
Good News that you forgive * sins. Ps 40:9
* sons have a special heritage. Ps 112:2
flood of these * fury and pride. Ps 124:4,5
to the wise * hall of fame. Pro 15:31,32
by his reaction to * praise. Pro 27:21
arts, I organized * and women's Ecc 2:7,8
constant dread of * oppression, and Is 51:13
found these young * advice ten Dan 1:20
bread won't feed * souls: obedience Mt 4:4
of dead * bones, and of foulness Mt 23:27
For from within, out of * Mk 7:21
someday everything [in * hearts Lk 8:17
* lives, but to save them." Lk 9:55f
God, who knows * hearts, Act 15:8
sinned with other * wives, and 1Co 10:8
no longer counting * sins against 2Co 5:19
and the taking of other * wives. 2Co 12:21
answers built on * thoughts and Col 2:8
cows could cleanse * bodies from Heb 9:13
deep within * hearts, and minds; Rev 2:23
and their faces looked like *. Rev 9:7

MENAHEM
became king, * (the son of Gadi) 2Ki 15:14
* destroyed the city of Tappuah 2Ki 15:16
Name of new king of Israel: * 2Ki 15:17
But * was an evil king. 2Ki 15:18
but King * bought him off with a 2Ki 15:19,20
and returned home. * extorted the 2Ki 15:19,20
history of King * is written in The 2Ki 15:21
Father's name: King * 2Ki 15:23

MEND
I will give him 120 years to * Gen 6:3

MENDED
and as this jar cannot be *, Jer 19:11

MENDING
father Zebedee, * their nets; Mt 4:21
and John, in a boat * their nets. Mk 1:19

MENE
'*,' 'Mene,' 'Tekel,' 'Parsin.' Dan 5:24,25
'Mene,' '*,' 'Tekel,' 'Parsin.' Dan 5:24,25
"* means 'numbered'—God has Dan 5:26

MENELAUS
removed by the Hellenist *. Dan 11:22f
*, the High Priest, who conspired Dan 11:32f

MENNA
Melea's father was *; Lk 3:23-38

MENNA'S
Melea's father was Menna;* father Lk 3:23-38

MENSTRUAL
claiming her * period, which, under Gen 31:35f
"If the * flow continues after Lev 15:25
during her normal * period, and Lev 15:26
the Lord, for her * defilement. Lev 15:30
and for a woman's * period; Lev 15:33

MENSTRUATES
"Whenever a woman *, she shall Lev 15:19

MENSTRUATING
Seven days after the * stops, Lev 15:28
with a woman who is *; Lev 18:19
Literally, "filthy as a * woman's Is 64:6f

MENSTRUATION
the same restrictions as during *. Lev 12:5
her period of *, both shall be Lev 20:18
the purification rites after *. 2Sa 11:4
the time of her *, and is a Eze 18:6
with women in their time of *." Eze 22:10f

MENSTRUOUS
wives and lie with * women. Eze 22:10
Literally, "as a * cloth." Eze 36:17f

MENTAL
Saul's unstable * condition caused 1Sa 17:55f

MENTALLY
my son, for he is * deranged, and Mt 17:15

MENTION
the kindness to *, wherever we Gen 20:13
in his favor, and * me to Pharaoh, Gen 40:14
and remember—never * the name of Ex 23:13
do not even * the names of their Jos 23:7
I would like to * that for the Neh 5:14
"I should *, too, the tremendous Job 41:12
If I were hungry, I would not * Ps 50:12
Nowadays when I * among my Ps 87:4
and * examples of your power. Ps 145:11
For if I say I'll never again * Jer 20:9
don't * the name of the Lord—he Amo 6:10
told them never to * what they had Mk 9:9
Then Peter began to * all that he Mk 10:28
don't even need to * this to you, 2Co 9:1
It would be shameful even to * Eph 5:12
but I won't * how much you owe me! Phm 1:19

MENTIONED
This fact is * in The Book of Num 21:14
is, even those not * in this book, Deu 28:61
if the word Israel is even *. Jos 2:9
areas, besides those already *, Jos 19:15,16
all about it, and * that the owner Ru 2:19
from Boaz, and * his remark that Ru 3:15-18
and found the relative he had *. Ru 4:1
When the messenger * what had 1Sa 4:18
* the scroll found by Hilkiah. 2Ki 22:9,10
gate, and when he * this to his 1Ch 11:17
oil, and wine you *, and we will 2Ch 2:15
Then the four men already * 2Ch 28:15
Then he * the scroll, and how 2Ch 34:18
things I haven't * before, secrets Is 48:6
will scarcely be * any more. Jer 16:14,15
Not the Hazor * in Joshua and Jer 49:30f
the Persian, * in Ezra, Haggai, and Dan 5:31f
of the 490 years * in verse 24, Dan 9:25f
For John is the man * in the Mt 11:10
went from there." * here so Mk 10:1f
* before in one of my letters. Eph 3:2,3
These men of faith I have * died Heb 11:13

MENTIONS
found at Hermopolis in Egypt, * Jer 7:18f

MENU
he ordered a special * for her, Est 2:9

MENUHOTH
ancestor of half of the * tribe. 1Ch 2:52

MEONENIM
the road past the oak of *!" Ju 9:37

MEONOTHAI
Hathath and *; 1Ch 4:13
* was the father of Ophrah; 1Ch 4:14

MEPHA-ATH
Jahaz, Kedemoth, *, Kiriathaim, Jos 13:18
Bezer, Jahaz, Kedemoth, and *. Jos 21:36,37
*, along with their pasturelands. 1Ch 6:78,79
and Jahzah and *, and Dibon and Jer 48:21

MEPHIBOSHETH
King Saul's named *, who was the 2Sa 4:4
So King David sent for * 2Sa 9:5,6
Saul's grandson. * arrived in great 2Sa 9:5,6
* fell to the ground before the 2Sa 9:8
And from that time on, * ate 2Sa 9:10,11
sons. * had a young son, Mica. 2Sa 9:12
servants, but * (who was lame in 2Sa 9:13
"And where is *?" 2Sa 16:3
Now *, Saul's grandson, arrived 2Sa 19:24,25
"Why didn't you come with me, * 2Sa 19:24,25
"Give him all of it," * said. 2Sa 19:30
He spared Jonathan's son *, who 2Sa 21:7
Rizpah—Armoni and *—who were 2Sa 21:8
The son of Jonathan was *; 1Ch 8:34
The son of * 1Ch 8:34
Jonathan was the father of *; 1Ch 9:40
father of *; 1Ch 9:40

MEPHIBOSHETH'S
of Ziba became * servants, but 2Sa 9:12
* household, caught up with him. 2Sa 16:1
Saul was * grandfather. 2Sa 16:3f

MERAB
and two daughters, * and Michal. 1Sa 14:49
my oldest daughter * as your wife. 1Sa 18:17
daughter *, the wife of Adri-el. 2Sa 21:8

MERAIAH
*, leader of the Seraiah clan; Neh 12:12-21

MERAIOTH
*, the father of 1Ch 6:4-15
*, Amariah, Ahitub, 1Ch 6:50-53
Zadok, son of *, son of Ahitub). 1Ch 9:10,11
Amariah was the son of *; Ez 7:1
* was the son of Zerahiah; Ez 7:1
of Zadok, son of *, son of Ahitub Neh 11:10-14
Helkai, leader of the * clan; Neh 12:12-21

MERARI
and his sons: Gershon, Kohath, *. Gen 46:8-14
Gershon, Kohath, *. Ex 6:16
The sons of *:Mahli, Mushi. Ex 6:19
Levi's son * Num 3:31-35
"Now take a census of the * Num 4:29
man by name. The * division will Num 4:33
And of the * division, 3,200. Num 4:42-45
were given to the * division, which Num 7:8
of the Gershon and * divisions of Num 10:17
named after their ancestor *. Num 26:57
The * division received twelve Jos 21:7
of the Levites—the * division—were Jos 21:34,35
So the * division of the Levites Jos 21:40
Gershom, Kohath, *. 1Ch 6:1
Gershom, Kohath, *. 1Ch 6:16
The sons of * were:Mahli, Mushi. 1Ch 6:19,20,21
The subclans of the clan of * 1Ch 6:29,30
clan of *, who stood on his left. 1Ch 6:44-47
Shemer, Mahli, Mushi, *, Levi. 1Ch 6:44-47
The subclans of * received by lot 1Ch 6:63
to the * clan as Cities of Refuge. 1Ch 6:77
who was a descendant of *). 1Ch 9:14
220 from the clan of *; 1Ch 15:4-10
* were the heads of the musicians. 1Ch 15:17
* division. 1Ch 23:6
The sons of * were 1Ch 23:21
The * group was led by his sons: 1Ch 24:26,27
Hosah, one of the * group, 1Ch 26:10
from the clans of Korah and *. 1Ch 26:19
From the * clan, Kish (son of 2Ch 29:12,13,14
Levites of the subclan of *. 2Ch 34:12
and Jeshaiah (the son of *), with Ez 8:19

MERARI'S
stood on his left. * ancestry was 1Ch 6:44-47

MERARITES
The *, named after their ancestor Num 26:57

MERATHAIM
my warriors, against the land of * Jer 50:21

MERCENARIES
thousand Syrian * from the lands of 2Sa 10:6
100,000 experienced * from Israel. 2Ch 25:5,6
Even her famed * have become like Jer 46:20,21

MERCENARY
to enlist * troops, chariots, and 1Ch 19:6
Meanwhile, the * forces were out 1Ch 19:9

MERCHANDISE
gates so that no * could be brought Neh 13:19
Sidon, bringing * from far across Is 23:2,3
You were the * mart of the world. Is 23:2,3
their * and it shall all be yours. Is 45:14
bring in loads of * through these Jer 17:27
and * and break down your walls. Eze 26:12
Your * satisfied the desires of Eze 27:33
all your * and all your crew have Eze 27:34
from bringing in loads of *. Mk 11:16

MERCHANT
King Solomon's * fleet was in 1Ki 10:22
* city, to destroy its strength. Is 23:11
And even if a * lives, his Eze 7:13
gods of that great * land of Eze 16:29
"O mighty seaport city, * center Eze 27:3
Kedar's wealthy * princes bring you Eze 27:21
and the * princes of Tarshish Eze 38:13
is like a pearl * on the lookout Mt 13:45
Thyatira, a * of purple cloth. Act 16:14
captains of the * ships and crews Rev 18:17

MERCHANTS
dealers, and stone *, and to buy 2Ki 12:11,12
balance from the exports of his *. 2Ch 9:13,14
attendants' and *' Guild Hall, Neh 3:31
The other goldsmiths and * Neh 3:32
Sabbath day. The * and tradesmen Neh 13:20
linen garments to sell to the *. Pro 31:24
will thrill, for * from around the Is 60:5
it into a city filled with *. Eze 17:3,4
* from Javan, Tubal and Meshech Eze 27:13
"* come to you from Rhodes, and Eze 27:15
of Israel send * with wheat from Eze 27:17
and goats. The * of Sheba and Eze 27:22
shipwrights and * and soldiers and Eze 27:27
faces. The * of the nations shake Eze 27:36
are like crafty * selling from Hos 12:7
Listen, you * who rob the poor, Amo 8:4
to all your * with their bags Mic 6:11
grasshoppers. *, numerous as Nah 3:16
drove out the *, and knocked over Mt 21:12
thrown out the * the day before. Mt 21:23
to drive out the * and their Mk 11:15
authority to drive out the *?" Mk 11:27,28
to drive out the * from their Lk 19:45
driven out the * from the Temple. Lk 20:2
In the Temple area he saw * Jn 2:14
The * of the earth will weep and Rev 18:11
And so the * who have become Rev 18:15

MERCIES
men, for God's * are very great." 1Ch 21:13
See for yourself the way his * Ps 34:8
hold back your tender * from me! Ps 40:11
And I will wait for your *—for Ps 52:9
Let your tenderhearted * meet our Ps 79:8
from whom your * are removed. Ps 88:5
with lovingkindness and tender *. Ps 103:4
Surround me with your tender *, Ps 119:75,76,77
all the unfailing * and love that I Is 55:3
away my lovingkindness and my *. Jer 16:5
whom I showed my * in the Jer 31:2
It is only the Lord's * that have Lam 3:22
all your faithful *, Lord, please Dan 9:16
the year. My * never fail. Hos 14:8
* waiting for them from the Lord! Jon 2:8
you two * for each of your woes! Zec 9:12
see the * of the Lord and be glad. Zec 10:7
to accept the * God was offering. Act 13:43
May all God's * and peace be Rom 1:6,7
glory to God for his * to them. Rom 15:9

MERCIFUL
the city, for the Lord was *. Gen 19:16
"I am Jehovah, the * and Ex 34:5,6
For the Lord your God is *—he Deu 4:31
anger and be * to you, and have Deu 13:17
your God will be * only if you have Deu 13:18
and may the Lord be * to you." 2Sa 15:19,20
You are * to the merciful; 2Sa 22:26
You are merciful to the *; 2Sa 22:26
and make their captors * to them; 1Ki 8:50
the kings of Israel are very *. 1Ki 20:31
gracious and *, slow to become Neh 9:17
What a gracious and * God you Neh 9:31
and * that he does not destroy us. Job 37:23
Lord, how * you are to those who Ps 18:25
you are to those who are *. Ps 18:25
Be * and send the help I need. Ps 27:7
knows what a * God you are. Ps 52:9
Yet he was * and forgave their Ps 78:38
trusting you. Be *, O Lord, for I Ps 86:3
But you are * and gentle, Lord, Ps 86:15
He is * and tender toward those Ps 103:8
He is kind and *— and all goes Ps 112:4
How good he is! So *, this God of Ps 116:5
Be * just as you promised. Ps 119:58
Jehovah is kind and *, slow to Ps 145:8
But to us, O Lord, be *, for we Is 33:2
come home to me again, for I am *; Jer 3:12
And I will be * to you by making Jer 42:12
and is a * creditor, not holding Eze 18:7
do what you know is right; be * Dan 4:27
"But the Lord our God is *, and Dan 9:9
so * despite our grievous sins. Dan 9:18
God, for he is gracious and *. Joe 2:13
a gracious God, *, slow to get Jon 4:2
fair and just and *, and to walk Mic 6:8
your people, for you love to be *. Mic 7:18
to be * to Jerusalem—I rebuke you. Zec 3:2
to be * and kind to everyone. Zec 7:8,9
Lord to bless us, and be * to us. Zec 8:20,21
Happy are the kind and *, for Mt 5:7
gifts I want—I want you to be *.' Mt 9:13
'I want you to be * more than I Mt 12:7
and how * he has been." Mk 5:19
not forgotten his promise to be *. Lk 1:54
be * to them forever." Lk 1:55
"He has been * to our ancestors, Lk 1:72,73
'God, be * to me, a sinner.' Lk 18:13
gifts God was * to you instead. Rom 11:30
he could be our * and faithful High Heb 2:17
who would be both * to us and Heb 2:17
And I will be * to them in their Heb 8:12
But if you have been *, then Jas 2:13
Or, perhaps, "the Lord will be * 1Jn 3:20f
you. Be * to those who doubt. Jud 1:22
while being * to them as sinners. Jud 1:23

MERCIFULLY
will be treated * by their captors, 2Ch 30:9

MERCILESS
charges of these *, deceitful men. Ps 43:1
of your life to the cruel and *; Pro 5:9
a shelter from * men who are like a Is 25:4
They are a cruel, * people, Jer 6:23
rigid demands and * justice, while Jn 1:17

MERCILESSLY
so they were * killed, as the Jos 11:20
I were your enemy; *, as though I Jer 30:14
the Christians *, hunting them down Gal 1:13

MERCURY
he was the chief speaker, was *! Act 14:12

MERCY
granted me such *, let me flee to Gen 19:18,19,20
May God Almighty give you * Gen 43:14
This is the place of * for your Ex 25:17
Literally, "* seat" or "place Ex 25:17f
with the * place, one at each end. Ex 25:19
upon the place of *, and shall have Ex 25:20
place of * between the cherubim; Ex 25:22
"Now install the * place—the Ex 26:34
near the place of * that is above Ex 30:6
the Ark with the place of * upon Ex 31:7
I show kindness and * to anyone I Ex 33:19

ERCY Con't)
The place of *; Ex 35:10-19
a lid called "the place of *"; Ex 37:6
place of *, looking down upon it. Ex 37:9
The place of *; Ex 39:33-40
the golden lid, the place of *. Ex 40:20
* are, just whenever he chooses. Lev 16:1
in the cloud above the place of *. Lev 16:1
will cover the * place above the Lev 16:13
east side of the * place, and then Lev 16:14
upon the place of * and in front of Lev 16:15
above the place of * over the Ark, Num 7:89
make any treaties or show them *; Deu 7:2
will have no * upon young or old. Deu 28:50
He will have * upon you and come Deu 30:3
He left them to the * of their Ju 2:12-14
the Moabites, at your *!" Ju 3:28
fall to the * of these heathen?" Ju 15:18
in * and have heard their cry." 1Sa 9:16
The Lord placed you at my * back 1Sa 24:9,10
And shows * to his anointed— 2Sa 22:51
the Lord (for his * is great) than 2Sa 24:14
Have * on us! 2Ki 1:14
Lord for his constant love and *. 1Ch 16:41
I will never remove my * and love 1Ch 17:13
the sanctuary for the place of *. 1Ch 28:11
to the Lord for *, and the priests 2Ch 13:13,14
*, and all heaven is disturbed. 2Ch 28:9
of kindness and * and will not 2Ch 30:9
and his love and * toward Israel Ez 3:11
in your love and * you did not Ez 9:9
population at the * of their aides, Neh 5:15
angry, and full of love and *; Neh 9:17
but in your great * you didn't Neh 9:19
and in great * you sent them Neh 9:27
your wonderful * delivered them! Neh 9:28
But in your great * you did not Neh 9:31
I would only plead for *. Job 9:15
me as I call again. Have * on me. Ps 4:1
protected by your * and your love; Ps 5:7
All those who know your *, Lord, Ps 9:10
And now, O Lord, have * on me; Ps 9:13
Or, "His face shines down in * Ps 11:7f
in you and in your * and shall Ps 13:5
through eyes of * and forgiveness, Ps 25:6,7
Come, Lord, and show me your *, Ps 25:16
therefore in * save me. Ps 26:11
because of your *, for you have Ps 31:7
O Lord, have * on me in my Ps 31:9,10
O LOVING AND kind God, have *. Ps 51:1
I trust in the * of God forever Ps 52:8
LORD, HAVE * on me; Ps 56:1
morning about your power and *. Ps 59:16
high tower of safety, my God of *. Ps 59:17
O GOD, IN * bless us; Ps 67:1
is wonderful; your * is so Ps 69:16
our Shield, have * on the one you Ps 84:9
* and truth have met together. Ps 85:10
so full of * for all who ask your Ps 86:5
my pleading hands to you for *. Ps 88:9
Righteousness. * and Truth walk Ps 89:14,15
will come and have * on Ps 102:13
our sins, for his * toward those Ps 103:11
performs—deeds of * and of grace? Ps 111:4
Don't leave me to the * of my Ps 119:121
Come and have * on me as is your Ps 119:132
Lord, how great is your *; Ps 119:156
our God for his * and kindness just Ps 123:2
Have * on us, Lord, have mercy. Ps 123:3,4
Have mercy on us, Lord, have *. Ps 123:3,4
how I implore his *, pouring out my Ps 142:1
* on you in his day of vengeance. Pro 6:34
shall be granted * and quietness. Pro 14:22
Iniquity is atoned for by * and Pro 16:6
young men, and no * upon even the Is 9:17
will have no * on the young people Is 13:18
BUT THE LORD will have * on the Is 14:1
and had no * on his prisoners?" Is 14:17
pity on them or show them his *. Is 27:11
But you showed them no *. Is 47:6
For the Lord in his * will lead Is 49:10
My * and justice are coming soon; Is 51:5
but my justice and * shall last Is 51:8
says the Lord who has * upon you. Is 54:10
that he may have * upon them, and Is 55:7
have * on you through my grace. Is 60:10
in accordance with his * and love. Is 63:7
power, your * and your compassion? Is 63:15
name or pleads with you for *. Is 64:7
Though they cry for *, I will not Jer 11:11
I will not let pity nor * spare Jer 13:14
old which God overthrew without *. Jer 20:16
slaughter them without pity or *. Jer 21:7
the Lord to have * upon them; Jer 26:19
him and surely will have * on him. Jer 31:20
For he is good and his * endures Jer 33:10,11
prosperity and have * on them. Jer 33:25,26
they are cruel and show no *; Jer 50:42
has shown no * even to his Temple. Lam 2:1
The Lord without * has destroyed Lam 2:2
Jerusalem without * and caused her Lam 2:17
you have killed them without *. Lam 2:21
Lord, and slain us without *. Lam 3:43
And though they scream for *, I Eze 8:18
my people and have * upon them and Eze 39:25
to show them his * by telling them Dan 2:18
your promises of * to those who Dan 9:4
(meaning 'No more *') for I will Hos 1:6
will have no more * upon Israel, to Hos 1:6
But I will have * on the tribe Hos 1:7
for now God will have * upon her! Hos 1:11
and justice and love and *. Hos 1:19
O Lord, the fatherless find *." Hos 14:3
have * on his people who remain. Amo 5:15
will have * on us and save us!" Jon 1:6
In your wrath, remember *. Hab 3:2
until you again show * to them?" Zec 1:12
to Jerusalem filled with *; Zec 1:16
I have decreed * to Joshua and Zec 3:2
for God's *, declaring that all was Zec 4:7
have sold them without *. Zec 11:5
" 'God have * on us,' you Mal 1:9
[for my * endures forever Mal 3:6
for they shall be shown *. Mt 5:7
Son of King David, have * on us." Mt 9:27
* on me, O Lord, King David's Son! Mt 15:22
said, "Sir, have * on my son, for Mt 17:15
shouldn't you have * on others, Mt 18:33
others, just as I had * on you?' Mt 18:33
King David's Son, have * on us!" Mt 20:30
things—justice and * and faith. Mt 23:23
Oh, have * on us and do something Mk 9:22
Son of David, have * on me!" Mk 10:47
"O Son of David, have * on me!" Mk 10:48
things to me. His * goes on from Lk 1:50
All this will be because the * Lk 1:78
out, "Jesus, sir, have * on us!" Lk 17:13
Son of David, have * on me!" Lk 18:38
"Son of David, have * on me!" Lk 18:39
But anyone who asks for * from Act 2:21
to many through God's *. Rom 5:15
are free under God's favor and *. Rom 6:14
except for God's * all the Jews Rom 9:29
will share in God's * upon you. Rom 11:31
so that he could have * upon all Rom 11:32
source of every *, and the one who 2Co 1:3,4
IT IS GOD himself, in his *, who 2Co 4:1
in his love and *, invited you to Gal 1:6
May God's * and peace be upon all Gal 6:16
plan he decided on in * long ago; Eph 1:9
But God is so rich in *; Eph 2:4
But God had * on him, and on me Php 2:27
* and kindness to others. Col 3:12
The tender * of our God and of 2Th 1:12
his kindness and * and give you 1Ti 1:2
But God had * on me because I 1Ti 1:13
But God had * on me so that 1Ti 1:16
plead for God's * upon them; 1Ti 2:1
May God's * be upon you. 1Ti 6:21
with his kindness, * and peace. 2Ti 1:2
to receive his * and to find grace Heb 4:16
golden cover, called the * seat. Heb 9:5
sprinkled on the * seat as an Heb 9:7
and sprinkled it on the * seat; Heb 9:12
was killed without * if there were Heb 10:28
who brings God's * to his people. Heb 10:29
for there will be no * to those Jas 2:13
to those who have shown no *. Jas 2:13
then God's * toward you will win Jas 2:13
it is full of * and good deeds. Jas 3:17
he is full of tenderness and *. Jas 5:11
for it is his boundless * that 1Pe 1:3
us with great * and much peace, and 2Jn 1:3
in his * is going to give you. Jud 1:21

MERE
These laws are not * words—they Deu 32:47
the men of Gilead were * outcasts Ju 12:4
when you were a * shepherd, tending 2Sa 7:8
You need more than * promises of 2Ki 18:20,21
Your King Jeroboam is a * 2Ch 13:6
Don't let * men defeat you!" 2Ch 14:11
but they are all * men, while we 2Ch 32:8
" 'Is * man more just than God? Job 4:17
What is * man that you should Job 7:17
for you are no * man as I am. Job 9:32,33
"* man is as likely to be wise Job 11:12
"Is * man of any worth to God? Job 22:2
How can * man stand before God Job 25:4
but it is not * age that makes Job 32:8,9
He becomes thin, * skin and Job 33:21
can bother with * puny man, to pay Ps 8:4
oppressed, so that * earthly man Ps 10:18
be ransomed by * earthly wealth. Ps 49:8,9
him, what can * man do to me? Ps 56:3,4
I am not afraid of anything * man Ps 56:10,11
But in death you are * men. Ps 82:7
What can * man do to me? Ps 118:6
goes to kind and gracious women, * Pro 11:16
* words are not enough—discipline Pro 29:19
two in the bush; * dreaming of nice Ecc 6:9
How much better it is than * Sol 4:10
should you seek a * Shulammite?" Sol 6:13
worship amounts to * words learned Is 29:13
For these Egyptians are * men, Is 31:3
promises worth? * words won't Is 36:5
nothing—* emptiness and froth. Is 40:17
these carpenters—* men—who claim Is 44:11
So what right have you to fear * Is 51:12
with * men—these men of Anathoth Jer 12:5
Why then should we, * humans as Lam 3:39
with a * handful of followers, he Dan 11:23
Their worship is * pretense. Hos 4:15
are * noise to my ears. Amo 5:23
you, a * man, have declared Jn 10:33
them to look like * birds and Rom 1:23
that it is no * pretense when I say Rom 9:1
which say that no * man has ever 1Co 2:9
Literally, "Are you not (*) 1Co 3:4f
responsible to no * man. 1Co 9:1
return, for * food and clothing? 1Co 9:11
real, that it goes beyond * words. 2Co 8:8
on some * human whim or dream. Gal 1:11
Jews by birth, not * Gentile Gal 2:15
Such rules are * human Col 2:22
approach him. No * man has ever 1Ti 6:16
to God, "What is * man that you Heb 2:6
connected with a * earthly model of Heb 8:5
in tents like a * visitor, as did Heb 11:9
that * man can do to me." Heb 13:6
are becoming * moth-eaten rags. Jas 5:2
more precious to God than * gold; 1Pe 1:7
he paid was not * gold or silver, 1Pe 1:18

MERED
*, Epher, Jalon. 1Ch 4:17
* married Bithi-ah, an Egyptian 1Ch 4:17

MERELY
are not to be * separate parts that Ex 30:2
not spread, it is * the scar from Lev 13:23
You are * my tenants and Lev 25:23
being in debt, or * 1Sa 22:2
this Benjaminite is * cursing me. 2Sa 16:11
pointed out to them, it was * a 2Ki 18:4
And * strangers in the Promised 1Ch 16:19
Would he * overpower me with his Job 23:6
he does, * a whisper of his power. Job 26:14
But God in heaven * laughs! Ps 2:4
tender love. He * spoke, and the Ps 33:6
that they were * mortal men, gone Ps 78:39
other nations are * idols, but our Ps 96:5
Their gods are * man-made things Ps 115:4
History * repeats itself. Ecc 1:8-11
He will * think he is attacking Is 10:7
gods at all, but * idols, carved by Is 37:19
who is * stopping for the night? Jer 14:8
You have not * sinned as they Eze 16:47
you will be no god, but * man! Eze 28:9
nations, but you are * a crocodile Eze 32:2
he can divorce her * by giving her Mt 5:31
You are thinking * from a human Mt 16:23
his wife by * writing her a letter Mt 19:7
"But the guests he had invited * Mt 22:5
'Lord,' how can he be * his son?" Mt 22:45
truth, instead of * quoting the Lk 4:32
for * loving those who love you? Lk 6:32
* doing what he is supposed to do. Lk 17:7,8,9
Just so, if you * obey me, you Lk 17:10
by God, or was he * acting under Lk 20:4
John told them, "I * baptize Jn 1:26
who sent me and is not * my own. Jn 5:30
"Why, he is * Jesus the son of Jn 6:42
is from God or is * my own. Jn 7:17
this: "If I am * boasting about Jn 8:54
If what they teach and do is * on Act 5:38
We are * human beings like Act 14:15
but since it is * a bunch of Act 18:15
And I'm not * quoting the 1Co 9:8
For we shall not be * spirits 2Co 5:3
* as a human being like myself. 2Co 5:16
are * those of an ordinary man. 2Co 10:2
free men or even * men or women, Gal 3:28
the Lord and not * for your Col 3:23
THE JEWISH HIGH priest is * a man Heb 5:1
this, for that was * a copy of the Heb 9:24
The blood of bulls and goats * Heb 10:4f
But since you are * lukewarm, I Rev 3:16

MEREMOTH
in the Temple by * (the son of Ez 8:33
Cheluhi, Vaniah, *, Eliashib, Ez 10:34-42
bolts and bars. * (son of Uriah, Neh 3:4
the High Priest. * (son of Uriah, Neh 3:21
Malluch, Harim, *, Neh 10:1
Rehum, *, Iddo, Neh 12:1

MERES
Admatha, Tarshish, *, Marsena, and Est 1:13-15

MERIB-BAAL
Or, "*." 1Ch 8:34f
Or, "*." 1Ch 8:34f
Or, "*." 1Ch 9:40f
Or, "*." 1Ch 9:40f

MERIBAH
referred to it as * (meaning Ex 17:7
This place was named * (meaning Num 20:13
concerning the water at *. Num 20:24

(MERIBAH Con't)
at the waters of * ("Place of Num 27:14
You tested Levi at Massah and at * Deu 33:8
I tested your faith at *, when Ps 81:7
at * and Massah. Ps 95:8
At *, too, Israel angered God, Ps 106:32

MERIBATH-KADESH
of *, in the wilderness of Zin. Deu 32:51
to the springs at * and then follow Eze 47:19
to the Spring at *, and then Eze 48:27,28

MERIT
What have we done to * such Jer 16:10
We don't ask because we * help, Dan 9:18

MERODACH-BALADAN
At that time * (the son of King 2Ki 20:12
king of Babylon (*, the son of Is 39:1
* was at this time planning a Is 39:1f

MEROM
of * as far as one could see; Jos 11:4
their camp at the Springs of *. Jos 11:5
at the Springs of * and attacked. Jos 11:7

MERONOTH
from * had charge of the donkeys. 1Ch 27:30
Jadon from *; Neh 3:7

MEROZ
Put a curse on *. Ju 5:23

MERRILY
and dance * with the timbrels. Jer 31:4

MERRIMENT
would eat and drink with great *. Job 1:4

MERRY
you can go on your * way with the Est 5:14
May he rejoice and be *. Ps 68:3
I SAID TO myself, "Come now, be * Ecc 2:1
eat, drink, and be *, with the hope Ecc 8:15
eat, drink, and be *, for it makes Ecc 9:7
"Let us eat, drink, and be *," Is 22:13
the people in their * feasts. Jer 15:17,18
Literally, "Eat, drink, and be * Lk 12:19f
time: let us eat, drink, and be *. 1Co 15:32

MERRYMAKERS
gone, the * will sigh and mourn. Is 24:7

MESHA
* to the eastern hills of Sephar. Gen 10:26-30
King * of Moab and his people 2Ki 3:4
Caleb (Jerahmeel's brother) was *; 1Ch 2:42
Jobab, Zibia, *, Malcam, 1Ch 8:8,9,10

MESHACH
Misha-el was called *; Dan 1:7
Shadrach, *, and Abednego as Dan 2:49
there—Shadrach, *, and Abednego, Dan 3:12
ordered Shadrach, *, and Abednego Dan 3:13
"Is it true, O Shadrach, *, and Dan 3:14
Shadrach, *, and Abednego Dan 3:16
at Shadrach, *, and Abednego. Dan 3:19
to bind Shadrach, *, and Abednego, Dan 3:20
So Shadrach, *, and Abednego Dan 3:23
"Shadrach, *, and Abednego, Dan 3:26
God of Shadrach, *, and Abednego, Dan 3:28
God of Shadrach, *, and Abednego Dan 3:29
to Shadrach, *, and Abednego, so Dan 3:30

MESHECH
Madai,Javan, Tubal,*, Tiras. Gen 10:2
Javan, Tubal, *, and Tiras. 1Ch 1:5-9
and *. 1Ch 1:17
Lord, these men of * and Kedar. Ps 120:5,6
in North Africa; *, Rosh and Tubal Is 66:19f
Put, Lud, *, Rosh, Tubal, Javan, Is 66:19
Merchants from Javan, Tubal and * Eze 27:13
"The princes of * and Tubal are Eze 32:26
The names of Gog's confederates (* Eze 38:2,3f
king of * and Tubal. Eze 38:2,3
you, Gog, leader of * and Tubal. Eze 39:1

MESHELEMIAH
the son of *, had been responsible 1Ch 9:21
The captain of the guard was *, 1Ch 26:1

MESHELEMIAH'S
for their work. * eighteen sons 1Ch 26:9

MESHES
and hold me helpless in its *. Ps 140:5

MESHEZABEL
of *) and Zadok (son of Baana). Neh 3:4
Meshullam, Hezir, *, Neh 10:14-27
Pethahiah (son of *, a descendant Neh 11:24

MESHILLEMITH
son of *, son of Immer). 1Ch 9:12

MESHILLEMOTH
the son of *, Jehizkiah the son of 2Ch 28:12
of Ahzai, son of *, son of Immer); Neh 11:10-14

MESHOBAB
*, Jamlech, Joshah, Joel, Jehu, 1Ch 4:34-39

MESHULLAM
of Azaliah, son of *) to the Temple 2Ki 22:3,4
*, 1Ch 3:19,20
were Michael, *, Sheba, Jorai, 1Ch 5:13
Zebadiah, *, Hizki, Heber, 1Ch 8:17,18
Sallu (the son of *, the son of 1Ch 9:7,8
* (the son of Shephatiah, the son 1Ch 9:7,8
of Hilkiah, son of *, son of Zadok, 1Ch 9:10,11
Jahzerah, son of *, son of 1Ch 9:12
Zechariah and *, of the subclan 2Ch 34:12
and *, the Levite leaders; Ez 8:16
(son of Tikvah), *, and Shabbethai Ez 10:15
*, Malluch, Adaiah, Jashub, Sheal, Ez 10:29
beyond him were * (son of Neh 3:4
Paseah) and * (son of Besodeiah). Neh 3:6
of Zalaph); and * (son of Neh 3:30
daughter of * (son of Berechiah). Neh 6:18
Hash-baddenah, Zechariah, and *. Neh 8:1
Baruch, *, Abijah, Neh 10:1
*, Hezir, Meshezabel, Neh 10:14-27
Sallu (son of *, son of Joed, son Neh 11:7,8,9
Seraiah (son of Hilkiah, son of *, Neh 11:10-14
*, leader of the Ezra clan; Neh 12:12-21
*, leader of the Ginnethon clan; Neh 12:12-21
*, Talmon, Akkub. Neh 12:25
Azariah, Ezra, *, Judah, Benjamin, Neh 12:33

MESHULLEMETH
His mother's name: * (daughter of 2Ki 21:19,20

MESOPOTAMIA
Beor from Pethor, *, to curse you. Deu 23:4
from *, Aram-maacah, and Zobah. 1Ch 19:6
Elamites, men from *, Judea, Act 2:9
Literally, "*." Act 7:2f

MESOPOTAMIAN
A name by which Ishtar, the * Jer 7:18f
according to * myths, he had been Eze 8:14f

MESS
"The Lord has caused this *," 2Ki 6:33
Lord, don't let me make a * of Ps 119:31
king and take care of this *." Is 3:6

MESSAGE
After this, a * arrived that Gen 22:20-23
with this *: "Hello from Jacob! Gen 32:4
to each driver, with the same *. Gen 32:19
her she sent this * to her Gen 38:25
So they sent him this *: Gen 50:16,17
When Joseph read the *, he Gen 50:16,17
of Israel will accept your *. Ex 3:18
They told him, "We bring you a * Ex 5:1
gave Pharaoh your *, he has only Ex 5:23
Go in and give Pharaoh the * I Ex 6:28,29
So Moses sent a * throughout Ex 36:4-7
They came to Balaam with this *: Num 22:16,17
Then the Lord gave Balaam a * Num 23:5
This was Balaam's *: Num 23:7-10
that his * is from me, shall die. Deu 18:20
a * from other gods must die.' Deu 18:20
the Lord who has given him the *; Deu 18:22
that no one can bring you their *; Deu 30:13
"I have a secret * for you," he Ju 3:17,18,19
to him, "It is a * from God!" Ju 3:20
Sea, they sent a * to the king of Ju 11:17
paid no attention to Jephthah's *. Ju 11:28
and sent this * to Jephthah: "Why Ju 12:1
came to Eli and gave him this * 1Sa 2:27
(Samuel had never had a * from 1Sa 3:7
special * for you from the Lord." 1Sa 9:26,27
and gave them this * from the Lord 1Sa 10:18,19
So they told him about the * from 1Sa 11:5
the city when that * arrived! 1Sa 11:9
Saul sent a * to the Kenites, 1Sa 15:6
But just then a * reached Saul 1Sa 23:27
to give him this *: "May God 1Sa 25:5
The young men gave David's * to 1Sa 25:9
he sent them this *: "May the 2Sa 2:5
David then sent this * to 2Sa 3:14
When the insulting * from the 2Sa 5:8
"Now go and give this * to David 2Sa 7:8
she sent a * to inform him. 2Sa 11:5
trumpets," his * read, "you will 2Sa 15:10
and wait there for a * from you. 2Sa 15:28
Hiram was very pleased with the * 1Ki 5:7
have received your * and I will do 1Ki 5:8
Then the Lord sent this * to 1Ki 6:11,12
But God sent this * to Shemaiah, 1Ki 12:22
proof that his * was from the Lord: 1Ki 13:3
and an angel gave me a * from the 1Ki 13:18
at the table, a * from the Lord 1Ki 13:20
Give your husband this * from 1Ki 14:7
Ben-hadad of Syria, with this *: 1Ki 15:18
A * OF condemnation from the Lord 1Ki 16:1
of the dust," the * said, "to 1Ki 16:2
The * was sent to Baasha and his 1Ki 16:4-7
she sent this * to Elijah: "You 1Ki 19:2
He sent this * into the city to 1Ki 20:2,3
again with another *: "You must 1Ki 20:5,6
Then the Syrian king sent this * 1Ki 20:10
and gave him this * from the Lord: 1Ki 20:13
Israel with this * from the Lord: 1Ki 20:28
Give him this * from me: 'Isn't 1Ki 21:19
Then another * came to Elijah: 1Ki 21:28
* to King Jehoshaphat of Judah: 2Ki 3:6,7,8
the * of the Lord came to Elisha: 2Ki 3:15
then she sent a * to her 2Ki 4:22
* to him: "Why are you so upset? 2Ki 5:8
"I have a * for you, sir," he 2Ki 9:5
of Ahab's sons, sent him this *: 2Ki 10:5
Jehu responded with this *: "If 2Ki 10:6
One day he sent a * to King Joash 2Ki 14:8
Then they sent a * to the king of 2Ki 17:26
and sent this * to the king of 2Ki 18:14
general sent this * to King 2Ki 18:
Amoz), the prophet, with this *: 2Ki 19
sent back this * to King Hezekiah: 2Ki 19
Then Isaiah sent this * to 2Ki 19:2
She gave them this * from the 2Ki 22:15,1
So they took the * to the king. 2Ki 22:2
servant David this *: 'You are not 1Ch 17
So David sent a * of sympathy to 1Ch 19:2
he sent a * to his embarrassed 1Ch 19
When King Asa heard this * from 2Ch 15
Syria, at Damascus, with this *: 2Ch 16
But a prophet arrived with this * 2Ch 25
with this * to King Hezekiah and 2Ch 32
Josiah with this *: "I don't want 2Ch 35:2
that Neco's * was from God. 2Ch 35:2
So King Darius sent this * Ez 6:
to change this * in any way shall Ez 6:1
they sent me a * asking me to meet Neh 6:
by sending back this * to them: Neh 6:
Four times they sent the same *, Neh 6:
he was receiving a * from God. Neh 6:1
to Esther with Mordecai's *. Est 4:
So Hathach gave Esther's * to Est 4:1
Now go ahead and send a * to the Est 8:
Haman's *, too, had been sealed Est 8:8
and sealed the * with the king's Est 8:9,1
* reaches out to all the world. Ps 19:3,
To trust a rebel to convey a * is Pro 26:
THIS IS ANOTHER * to Isaiah from Is 2:
sent this further * to King Ahaz: Is 7:1
AGAIN THE LORD sent me a *: Is 8:1
This is the * that came to me the Is 14:2
HERE IS GOD'S * to Moab: Is 15:1
THIS IS GOD'S * to Damascus, Is 17:1
And this is the * sent to you: Is 18:2
THIS IS GOD'S * concerning Egypt: Is 19:1
THIS IS GOD'S * concerning Is 21:1
This is God's * to Edom: Is 21:1
This is God's * concerning Is 21:13
THIS IS GOD'S * concerning Is 22:1
THIS IS GOD'S * to Tyre: Is 23:1
straightforward * they will stumble Is 28:13
They brought him this * from Is 37:3
So they took the king's * to Is 37:5
Jerusalem to Hezekiah with this *: Is 37:8,9
of Amoz, sent this * to King Is 37:21
and gave him this * from the Lord: Is 38:1
So the Lord sent another * to Is 38:4
to this * from the Lord of Hosts: Is 39:5
THIS IS JEHOVAH'S * to Cyrus, Is 45:1
sent me (with this *): The Lord, Is 48:16
This * from the Lord came to me Jer 3:6
Lord and give this * to the people: Jer 7:2
Judah, listen to this * from God. Jer 7:2
Once again give them this * from Jer 8:4,5
Broadcast this * in Jerusalem's Jer 11:6
Then the Lord's * came to me Jer 13:3
THIS * CAME to Jeremiah from the Jer 14:1
them to speak or give them any *. Jer 14:14
It is your * I've given them, not Jer 17:16
HERE IS ANOTHER * to Jeremiah Jer 18:1
them, This is the * to you from the Jer 19:11
had delivered this *, he stopped in Jer 19:14
Listen to this * from God, O king Jer 22:2
For this is the Lord's * Jer 22:6
I gave them no *, yet they say Jer 23:21
who say, "This * is from God!" Jer 23:30,31
and they have no * at all for my Jer 23:32
ask each other, "What is God's *? Jer 23:35
Jeremiah, "What is the Lord's *? Jer 23:37
Lord," or, "the * of the Lord." Jer 23:38,39f
THIS * FOR all the people of Judah Jer 25:1
Each time the * was this: Turn Jer 25:5
THIS * CAME to Jeremiah from the Jer 26:1
Give them the entire *; Jer 26:2
When Jeremiah had finished his *, Jer 26:7,8
THIS * CAME to Jeremiah from the Jer 27:1
God of Israel, sends you this *: Jer 27:4
Only when his * comes true can it Jer 28:9
the Lord gave this * to Jeremiah: Jer 28:12
Israel, sends this * to all the Jer 29:4
Then the Lord gave this * to Jer 29:30
Listen to this * from the Lord, Jer 31:10
THE FOLLOWING * came to Jeremiah Jer 32:1
Then this * from the Lord came to Jer 32:6,7
Then I knew for sure that the * Jer 32:8
Then this * came to Jeremiah: Jer 32:26
the Lord sent him this second *. Jer 33:1
Then this * came to Jeremiah from Jer 33:19
THIS IS THE * that came to Jer 34:1
So Jeremiah delivered the * to Jer 34:6
This is the * that came to Jer 34:8
gave the following * to Jerusalem. Jer 34:12
THIS IS THE * the Lord gave Jer 35:1
This is apparently an early * to Jer 35:1f
Then the Lord gave this * to Jer 35:12
the Lord gave this * to Jeremiah: Jer 36:1
Begin with the first * back in Jer 36:2
Then the Lord sent this * to Jer 37:6
was any recent * from the Lord. Jer 37:17
The Lord gave the following * to Jer 39:15

MESSAGE Con't)
giving this * from God to all the Jer 43:1
THIS IS THE * God gave to Jeremiah Jer 44:1
THIS IS THE * Jer 45:1
This *, in point of time, follows Jer 45:1f
This * was given against Egypt at Jer 46:2
Then God gave Jeremiah this * Jer 46:13
THIS IS GOD'S * to Jeremiah Jer 47:1
THIS IS THE * of the Lord of Jer 48:1
I have heard this * from the Jer 49:14
Elam God's * against Elam came Jer 49:34
THIS IS THE * from the Lord Jer 50:1
reign, this * came to Jeremiah to Jer 51:59
Then go and give its * to the Eze 3:1
But whenever I give you a *, Eze 3:27
AGAIN A * came from the Lord: Eze 6:1
Israel, hear the * of the Lord God Eze 6:3
THIS FURTHER * came to me from Eze 7:1
Again a * came from the Lord: Eze 11:14
AGAIN A * came to me from the Eze 12:1
The next morning this * came to Eze 12:8
says it is a * to King Zedekiah Eze 12:10
Then this * came to me from the Eze 12:17
Again a * came to me from the Eze 12:21
Then this * came: Eze 12:26
THEN THIS * came to me: Eze 13:1
when you said, 'My * is from God!' Eze 13:6
have said, 'This * is from God,' Eze 13:7
to ask me for a * from the Lord, Eze 14:1
* that came to me to give to them: Eze 14:2
gives him a * anyway, it is a lie. Eze 14:9
Then this * of the Lord came to Eze 14:12
THEN THIS * came to me from the Eze 15:1
THEN AGAIN A * came to me from the Eze 16:1
THEN THIS * came to me from the Eze 17:1
Then this * came to me from the Eze 17:11
THEN THE LORD'S * came to me Eze 18:1
Then the Lord gave me this *: Eze 20:2
not give you any *, though you have Eze 20:31
Then this * came to me from the Eze 20:45
THEN THIS * came to me from the Eze 21:1
Then again this * came to me from Eze 21:8
Then this * came to me. Eze 21:18
NOW ANOTHER * came from the Eze 22:1
Again the * of the Lord came to Eze 22:23
THE LORD'S * came to me again, Eze 23:1
* came to me from the Lord. Eze 24:1
Again a * came to me from the Eze 24:15
THEN THE LORD'S * came to me Eze 25:1
ANOTHER * CAME to me from the Eze 26:1
THEN THIS * came to me from the Eze 27:1
HERE IS ANOTHER * given to me Eze 28:1
Then this further * came to me Eze 28:11
Then another * came to me from Eze 28:20
this * came to me from the Lord: Eze 29:1
this * came to me from the Lord: Eze 29:17
ANOTHER * FROM the Lord! Eze 30:1
captivity, this * came to me: Eze 30:20
this * came to me from the Lord: Eze 31:1
this * came to me from the Lord: Eze 32:1
another * came to me from the Eze 32:17
ONCE AGAIN A * came to me from Eze 33:1
Then this * came to me: Eze 33:23
THEN THIS * came to me from the Eze 34:1
AGAIN A * came from the Lord. Eze 35:1
Tell them: Listen to this * from Eze 36:1
Again a * from the Lord came to Eze 37:15
HERE IS ANOTHER * to me from the Eze 38:1
this * is for you: You are no Dan 4:31
to write this *: 'Mene,' 'Mene,' Dan 5:24,25
Darius wrote this * addressed to Dan 6:25,26
Here is the first *: Hos 1:2
THIS * CAME from the Lord to Joel, Joe 1:1
he rushed a * to Jeroboam, the Amo 7:10
"Now therefore listen to this * Amo 7:16
nations with this *: 'Attention! Ob 1:1
The Lord sent this * to Jonah, the Jon 1:1
nobles sent this * throughout the Jon 3:7
This is God's * to you: The night Mic 3:5
THIS IS THE * that came to the Hab 1:1
SUBJECT: A * from the Lord. Zep 1:1
SUBJECT: A * from the Lord. Hag 1:1
* from the Lord their God; Hag 1:12
(again sending the * through Hag 1:13
sent them this * through Haggai: Hag 2:1
King Darius, this * came from the Hag 2:10
Another * came to Haggai from the Hag 2:20
Darius, another * from the Lord Zec 1:7
"Shout out this * from the Lord of Zec 1:14
Then he said, "This is God's * Zec 4:6
Another * that I received from Zec 4:8
In another * the Lord said: Zec 6:9
ANOTHER * CAME to me from the Zec 7:1
Then this * from the Lord came to Zec 7:8,9
would not listen to this *. Zec 7:11
AGAIN THE LORD'S * came to me: Zec 8:1
Here is another * that came to me Zec 8:18
THIS IS THE * concerning God's Zec 9:1
HERE IS THE Lord's * to Israel, Mal 1:1
This will fulfill God's * Mt 1:22
Then Herod sent a private * to Mt 2:7
Then give him this *, 'Blessed Mt 11:6
man who hears the * and receives it Mt 13:20
man who hears the *, but the cares Mt 13:22
who listens to the * and Mt 13:23
*: "Leave that good man alone; Mt 27:19
That is my * to them." Mt 28:7
to give them the angel's *. Mt 28:8
well, and give my * to them too, Mk 1:38
who brings God's * to others, Mk 4:14
of some of those who hear God's *; Mk 4:15
those who hear the * with joy, Mk 4:16
crowd out God's * from their Mk 4:19
truly accept God's * and produce a Mk 4:20
of me and my * in these days of Mk 8:38
This is my * to you and to Mk 13:35,36,37
Now go and give this * to his Mk 16:7
Tiberius Caesar, a * came from God Lk 3:1
The seed is God's * to men. Lk 8:11
but somehow the * never really gets Lk 8:13
They know the * is true, and sort Lk 8:13
hear the * of God and obey it." Lk 8:21
"If we say his * was from Lk 20:5
and that this * of salvation Lk 24:47
who listens to my * and believes in Jn 5:24
one sent to you with God's *. Jn 5:38
kill me because my * does not find Jn 8:37
gods to whom the * of God came, Jn 10:34,35,36
So the two sisters sent a * to Jn 11:3
But all who reject me and my * Jn 12:48
Then she gave them his *. Jn 20:18
who heard their * believed it, so Act 4:4
and boldly preached God's *. Act 4:31
God's * was preached in Act 6:7
But now they believed Philip's * Act 8:12
*, they sent down Peter and John. Act 8:14
to take my * to the nations and Act 9:15
all creation. This * has spread all Act 10:36,37
also gave their * about the Lord Act 11:20
wanted to hear their * from God. Act 13:6,7
at the power of God's *. Act 13:12
sent them this *: "Brothers, if Act 13:15
glad and rejoiced in Paul's *; Act 13:48
So God's * spread all through Act 13:49
But the Jews who spurned God's * Act 14:2
Lord proved their * was from him by Act 14:3
and gladly listened to the *. Act 17:11
to Beroea with a * for Silas and Act 17:15
But some rejected his * and Act 19:9
and Greeks—heard the Lord's *. Act 19:10
whole area was stirred by God's *. Act 19:20
Paul, also sent a * to him, begging Act 19:31
a farewell * to them, said good-bye Act 20:1
Miletus, he sent a * to the elders Act 20:17
I have had one * for Jews and Act 20:21
from declaring all God's * to you. Act 20:27
You are to take his * Act 22:15
you when you give them my *.' Act 22:17,18
it to heaven. This * was preached Rom 1:16
enough to receive a * from God. Rom 12:6
I have won them by my * and by Rom 15:19
God commands, this * is being Rom 16:25,26,27
simple * of the cross of Christ. 1Co 1:17
saved recognize this * as the 1Co 1:18
who believed his *, which the world 1Co 1:21
ideas to tell you God's *. 1Co 2:1
them that the * was from God. 1Co 2:4
in our * to you from Christ. 1Co 9:12
are re-telling the * of the Lord's 1Co 11:26
else receives a * or idea from the 1Co 14:29,30
a person who has a * from God has 1Co 14:32
you can preach God's * plainly; 1Co 14:39
built upon this wonderful *; 1Co 15:1
the amazing * we preach about the 2Co 4:4
This is the wonderful * he has 2Co 5:19
* of God's great kindness. 2Co 6:1
actually see in my life and my *. 2Co 12:6
*, let him be forever cursed. Gal 1:8
For my * comes from no less a Gal 1:12
* I was preaching to the Gentiles. Gal 2:2
that * doesn't offend anyone. Gal 5:11
now for preaching this * from God. Eph 6:20
to you of the truth of our *. 1Th 1:5
for you received our * with joy 1Th 1:6
repeat the same * to you, even 1Th 2:2
we change his * not one bit to 1Th 2:4
God's *, but our own lives too. 1Th 2:8
Pray first that the Lord's * will 2Th 3:1
This is the * which at the proper 1Ti 2:6
For this wonderful news—the * Heb 4:2
and a voice with a * so terrible Heb 12:19
for the wonderful * we have Jas 1:21
And remember, it is a * to obey, Jas 1:22
God's ever-living * to men. 1Pe 1:23
And his * is the Good News that 1Pe 1:25
He is giving us time to get his * 2Pe 3:15,16
He is God's * of Life. 1Jn 1:1
This is the * God has given us to 1Jn 1:5
for the * to us from the 1Jn 3:11
says it is a * from God: test it 1Jn 4:1
find out if their * is from the 1Jn 4:2
If so, then the * is from God. 1Jn 4:2
If not, the * is not from God 1Jn 4:3
whether a * is really from God; 1Jn 4:6
"I write to inform you of a * Rev 2:1
"Let this * sink into the ears Rev 2:7
"This * is from him who is the Rev 2:8
"This * is from him who wields Rev 2:12
"This is a * from the Son of God, Rev 2:18
"This * is sent to you by the one Rev 3:1
"This * is sent to you by the one Rev 3:7
"This * is from the one who Rev 3:14

MESSAGES
given him Joseph's *, and when he Gen 45:27
to him and heed his * from me. Deu 18:19
urgent * to the following kings: Jos 11:1
by assisting Eli. * from the Lord 1Sa 3:1
Then the Lord began to give * to 1Sa 3:21,4:1
* they were to take to King David. 2Sa 17:17
let us send * to our brothers 1Ch 13:2
who gave him * from the Lord. 2Ch 36:12
Iddo)—who brought * from the God of Ez 5:1
of Ahasuerus with * of good will, Est 9:29-31
These are the * of Agur, son of Pro 30:1
These are the * that came to Is 1:1
In these * God showed him what Is 1:1
"If their * are different than Is 8:20
THESE ARE GOD'S * to Jeremiah the Jer 1:1
The first of these * came to him Jer 1:1
man and all his *," they said. Jer 11:19
I have to give them your * Jer 20:7
who get their * from each Jer 23:30,31
* from God" that I didn't speak. Jer 23:36
God has been sending me his *. Jer 25:2,3
for giving us the * of God, who Jer 26:19
Then send * to the kings of Jer 27:3
THIS IS ANOTHER of the Lord's * to Jer 30:1
order with the other *. Jer 35:1f
write down all my * against Israel, Jer 36:2
* to the people at the Temple. Jer 36:8
Shaphan) heard the * from God, he Jer 36:11
them about the * Baruch was reading Jer 36:13
the * to them too, and Baruch did. Jer 36:14,15
tell us how you got these *. Jer 36:17
listen to your false '* from God'! Jer 44:16
down all God's * as Jeremiah was Jer 45:1
HERE ARE THE * given to Jeremiah Jer 46:1
(This ends Jeremiah's *. Jer 51:64
my *—the messages of the Lord God. Eze 2:4
my messages—the * of the Lord God. Eze 2:4
You must give them my * whether Eze 2:7
to the people of Israel with my *. Eze 3:4
claiming to have * from me when I Eze 13:2,3
the Lord has given them his *. Eze 13:17
and speak false * they claim are Eze 22:28
then he sent * to all the Dan 3:2
years, with your * to our kings and Dan 9:6
THESE ARE THE * from the Lord to Hos 1:1
These are * from the Lord to Mic 1:1
of Judah. The * were addressed to Mic 1:1
that your * were not from God. Mic 3:7
SUBJECT: * FROM the Lord. Zec 1:1
These * from the Lord were given Zec 1:1
(Then you will know these * are Zec 4:9
you will know my * have been from Zec 6:15
miracles that followed their *. Mk 16:20
of Moses and the * of the prophets Lk 16:16
to speak * from the Spirit of God. 1Co 12:3
to be giving God's *—or whether it 1Co 12:10
being able to preach the * of God. 1Co 14:1
preaching the * of God, is helping 1Co 14:3
preaching * from God, helps the 1Co 14:4
preaching God's *, for that is a 1Co 14:5
and special * from God about this, 2Th 2:1
For since the * from angels have Heb 2:2
us that these * are true by signs Heb 2:4
men who gave them true * from God. 2Pe 1:20,21

MESSENGER
Doubtless to tell them that a * Gen 24:28f
As the * from the battlefront 1Sa 4:13
And the * rushed over to Eli and 1Sa 4:14
When the * mentioned what had 1Sa 4:18
When a * came to Gibe-ah, Saul's 1Sa 11:4
he told his *, "If the king is 2Sa 11:19,20,21
So the * arrived at Jerusalem, 2Sa 11:22
A * soon arrived in Jerusalem to 2Sa 15:13
You can be my * some other 2Sa 18:20
As the * came closer, the 2Sa 18:25
The * who went to get Micaiah 1Ki 22:13
Elisha sent a * out to tell him 2Ki 5:10
the king sent a * to summon him. 2Ki 6:32
But before the * arrived Elisha 2Ki 6:32
* arrived [followed by the king 2Ki 6:33
the king that the * had met them 2Ki 9:18
When a * told Jehu that the 2Ki 10:8
King Ahaz sent a * to King 2Ki 16:7
A * rushed to Job's home with Job 1:14,15
While this * was still speaking, Job 1:16
still another * rushed in: "Three Job 1:17
"But if a * from heaven is there Job 33:23,24
An unreliable * can cause a lot Pro 13:17
The anger of the king is a * of Pro 16:14
Literally, "a stern (ruthless) * Pro 17:11f

(MESSENGER Con't)
by telling the * from God that it Ecc 5:6,7
shall I send as a * to my people? Is 6:8
Where is the Lord's * to explain Jer 9:12
Let that * be destroyed like the Jer 20:16
He has sent a * to call the Jer 49:14
and I said to the * from heaven, Dan 10:16
Haggai, his *), "I am with you; Hag 1:13
"LISTEN: I WILL send my * before Mal 3:1
to his Temple—the * of God's Mal 3:1
the Scriptures—a * to precede me, Mt 11:10
to earth, and that a special * Mk 1:2
"This * will live out in the Mk 1:3
This * was John the Baptist. Mk 1:4
I am sending my * ahead of you, Lk 7:27
speaking to her, a * arrived from Lk 8:49
Nor is the * more important than Jn 13:16
"Truly, anyone welcoming my * is Jn 13:20
me as a special * to you Gentiles. Rom 11:13
As God's * I give each of you Rom 12:3
grace, a special * from Jesus Rom 15:15,16
I AM AN apostle, God's *, 1Co 9:1
by God to be Jesus Christ's *; 2Co 1:1
in my flesh, a * from Satan to hurt 2Co 12:7
by God to be Jesus Christ's *. Eph 1:1
*, and from Brother Timothy. Col 1:1
of our blessed God, whose * I am. 1Ti 1:10,11
of God and the * of Jesus Christ. Tit 1:1
Jesus who is God's * and the High Heb 3:1
Moses, the earthly *, how terrible Heb 12:25

MESSENGERS
Jacob now sent * to his brother Gen 32:3
I have sent these * to inform you Gen 32:5
The * returned with the news that Gen 32:6
at Kadesh he sent * to the king of Num 20:14
So King Balak sent * to Balaam Num 22:5,6
The * he sent were some of the Num 22:7
I tell your * that even if you Num 24:12
sent * to several other kings: Jos 10:3
sent * to Joshua at Gilgal. Jos 10:6
He also sent * throughout Ju 6:35
Gideon also sent * throughout Ju 7:24
He sent * to Abimelech in Arumah Ju 9:31
Then Jephthah sent * to the king Ju 11:12
Then Israel sent * to King Sihon Ju 11:19
Then * were sent to the tribe of Ju 20:12
So they sent * to the people at 1Sa 6:21
pieces and sent * to carry them 1Sa 11:7
So he sent the * back to 1Sa 11:9
So Saul sent * to Jesse, asking 1Sa 16:19
So David's * returned and told 1Sa 25:12
But I didn't see the * you sent. 1Sa 25:25
no time in sending * to Abigail to 1Sa 25:39
When the * arrived at Carmel and 1Sa 25:40
Then Abner sent * to David to 2Sa 3:12
Then Joab sent * to catch up with 2Sa 3:26
Joab sent * to tell David, 2Sa 12:26,27
Soon Ben-hadad's * returned again 1Ki 20:5,6
So he told the * from Ben-hadad, 1Ki 20:9
So the * returned to Ben-hadad. 1Ki 20:9
He sent * to the temple of the 2Ki 1:2
"Go and meet the * and ask them, 2Ki 1:3
When Elijah told the * this, they 2Ki 1:4,5
"Why did you send * to 2Ki 1:16
He sent * throughout all Israel 2Ki 10:20,21
letter from the *, read it, and 2Ki 19:14
So the * went from city to city 2Ch 30:10
The * who brought the letters 2Ch 32:18
These * talked about the God of 2Ch 32:19
But the people mocked these * of 2Ch 36:16
They were then sent by * into Est 3:13
him, the king's * arrived to Est 6:14
"If God cannot trust his own * Job 4:18,19
are his *—his servants of fire! Ps 104:4
Let swift * return to you, O Is 18:2
Upon hearing this, he sent * back Is 37:8,9
You have sent your * to mock the Is 37:24
who are designed to be my * of Is 42:19
See, the Lord has sent his * to Is 62:11
and let my true * faithfully Jer 23:28
the city gates. * from every side Jer 51:31
to the men pictured, so she sent * Eze 23:16
At that time I will send swift * Eze 30:9
See, the * come running down the Nah 1:15
The priests are the * of the Lord Mal 2:7
was ready he sent * to notify Mt 22:3
others beat up his * and treated Mt 22:6
talking to her, * arrived from Mk 5:35
One day he sent * ahead to Lk 9:52
of the man who had sent the *. Act 11:12
* to Joppa to find Simon Peter! Act 11:13
The four * went at once to Act 15:30
* you yourselves will choose. 1Co 16:3
these marvelous "* from God," as 2Co 11:5
For we speak as * from God, 1Th 2:4
me as one of his *, and giving me 1Ti 1:12
God speaks of his angels as * Heb 1:7
when she hid those * and sent them Jas 2:25

MESSIAH
Lord and his *, Christ the King. Ps 2:2
Solomon's son to Jesus the *. Ps 72:6f
JEHOVAH SAID TO my Lord the *, Ps 110:1
* (Jeremiah 23:5, Zechariah 3:8). Is 4:2,3,4f
the * in Jerusalem at that time. Is 4:2,3,4f
to the *, the Anointed One. Is 10:27f
Christ, the *. Is 11:1f
Christ, the *. Is 11:1f
who says [to his Servant, the * Is 42:5
here, is the *, our Lord Jesus. Is 52:13f
The *, David's greater Son, whom Jer 30:9f
is used for the * as representative Eze 2:1f
raise up a notable Vine [the * Eze 34:29
"And David, my Servant—the * Eze 37:24
And my Servant David, their *, Eze 37:25
God, and to the *, their King, Hos 3:5
noisy, happy crowd. The * Mic 2:13
Christ, the *. Hag 2:7f
refers to the *, here seen as one Zec 2:8f
e., the *, Christ. Zec 3:8f
e., the *. Zec 10:4f
the mother of Jesus Christ the *). Mt 1:16
us where the * would be born?" Mt 2:4
of the prophets concerning the *, Mt 2:23
birds have nests, but I, the *, Mt 8:20
I, the *, Mt 9:5,6
the miracles the * was doing, so he Mt 11:2
prophets looked forward [to the * Mt 11:13
And I, the *, Mt 11:19
For I, the *, Mt 12:8
"Maybe Jesus is the *!" Mt 12:23
and three nights, so I, the *, Mt 12:39,40
claim of being the * by asking him Mt 16:1
*, the Son of the living God." Mt 16:16
telling others that he was the *. Mt 16:20
must return before the * comes?" Mt 17:10
And I, the * Mt 17:12
And I, the *, Mt 18:11
Jesus replied, "When I, the *, Mt 19:28
must be like my own, for I, the * Mt 20:28
a question: "What about the *? Mt 22:42
one is your master, even the *. Mt 23:10
the *, and will lead many astray. Mt 24:5
tells you, 'The * has arrived at Mt 24:23
"So if someone tells you the * Mt 24:26
shall my coming be, when I, the *, Mt 24:27
"But when I, the *, Mt 25:31
to be the *, the Son of God." Mt 26:63
the future you will see me, the *, Mt 26:64
saying, "Prophesy to us, you *! Mt 26:68
"Are you the Jews' *?" Mt 27:11
you—Barabbas, or Jesus your *?" Mt 27:17
shall I do with Jesus, your *?" Mt 27:22
of Jesus the *, the Son of God. Mk 1:1
I, the *, Mk 2:9,10,11
And I, the *, Mk 2:28
Peter replied, "You are the * Mk 8:29
of unbelief and sin, I, the *, Mk 8:38
return [before the * could come Mk 9:11
when they predicted that the * Mk 9:12,13
He would say to them, "I, the *, Mk 9:30,31
there," he told them, "I, the *, Mk 10:33
For even I, the *, Mk 10:45
claim that the * must be a Mk 12:35
your *, and will lead many astray. Mk 13:6
you, 'This is the *,' or, 'That one Mk 13:21
all mankind will see me, the *, Mk 13:26
"Are you the *, the Son of Mk 14:61
"Hey there, *!" Mk 15:32
the coming of the *, preparing the Lk 1:17
will prepare the way for the *. Lk 1:76
The Savior—yes, the *, the Lk 2:11
and constantly expecting the * Lk 2:25
that the * had finally arrived. Lk 2:38
Everyone was expecting the * to Lk 3:15
I, the *, Lk 5:23,24
ask him, "Are you really the *? Lk 7:19
Peter replied, "The *—the Christ Lk 9:20
"For I, the *, Lk 9:22
"When I, the *, Lk 9:26
I, the *, Lk 9:44
birds have nests, but I, the *, Lk 9:58
to prove his claim of being the *. Lk 11:16
in the skies [to prove I am the * Lk 11:29,30
I assure you of this: I, the *, Lk 12:8
For I, the *, Lk 12:40
the question is: When I, the *, Lk 18:8
sons of Abraham, and I, the *, Lk 19:9,10
"that Christ, the *, is said to be Lk 20:41
to my Lord, the *, "Sit at my Lk 20:42,43
How can the * be both Lk 20:44
announcing themselves as the *, Lk 21:8
But as a result, the * will be Lk 21:13
the *, coming in a cloud with Lk 21:27
this—betray the * with a kiss?" Lk 22:48
or not he claimed to be the *. Lk 22:67,68
time is soon coming when I, the *, Lk 22:69
by claiming he is our *—a King." Lk 23:2
"Are you their *—their King?" Lk 23:3
really God's Chosen One, the *." Lk 23:35
"So you're the *, are you? Lk 23:39
you back in Galilee—that the * Lk 24:6,7
was the glorious * and that he had Lk 24:21
prophets that the * would have to Lk 24:2
long ago that the * must suffer and Lk 24:4
whether he claimed to be the *. Jn 1:1
you aren't the * or Elijah or the Jn 1:24,2
told him, "We have found the *!" Jn 1:4
told him, "We have found the *! Jn 1:4
back and forth to me, the *." Jn 1:5
believed that he really was the *. Jn 2:1
that he was indeed the *. Jn 2:2
For only I, the *, Jn 3:1
you said was the *—he is baptizing Jn 3:2
I told you that I am not the *. Jn 3:2
I know that the * will come—the one Jn 4:2
Then Jesus told her, "I am the * Jn 4:2
Can this be the *?" Jn 4:28,2
he was the * because of the woman's Jn 4:3
believed that Jesus was the *. Jn 4:5
the eternal life that I, the *, Jn 6:2
want us to believe you are the *. Jn 6:30,3
Unless you eat the flesh of the * Jn 6:5
you think if you see me, the *, Jn 6:6
all, that he really is the *? Jn 7:2
do you expect the * to do that this Jn 7:3
who will come just before the *." Jn 7:4
Others said, "He is the *." Jn 7:41,4
Will the * come from Galilee? Jn 7:41,4
state that the * will be born of Jn 7:41,4
who believes he is the *? Jn 7:4
that I am the *, the Son of God, Jn 8:2
"When you have killed the *, Jn 8:2
began believing him to be the *. Jn 8:30,3
was the * would be excommunicated. Jn 9:22,2
said, "Do you believe in the *?" Jn 9:3
If you are the *, tell us Jn 10:24
to the decision that he was the *. Jn 10:42
"I believe you are the *, the Jn 11:27
and believed in Jesus as their *. Jn 12:11
"We understood that the * would Jn 12:34
What * are you talking about?" Jn 12:34
would not believe he was the *. Jn 12:37
him to be the * but wouldn't admit Jn 12:42
*, 'They hated me without reason.' Jn 15:25
you mean their King, or their *?" Jn 18:34f
mean their religious ruler, the *. Jn 18:34f
that he is the *, the Son of God, Jn 20:30,31
descendants would [be the * and Act 2:30
to my Lord, the *, and said to him, Act 2:34
crucified to be the Lord, the *!" Act 2:36
* must suffer all these things. Act 3:18
Jesus your * back to you again. Act 3:20
from Nazareth, the *, the man you Act 4:10
For Jesus the * is (the one Act 4:11
and preach that Jesus is the *. Act 5:42
* whom you betrayed and murdered. Act 7:52
the heavens opened and Jesus the * Act 7:56
often spoke of him as the *. Act 8:9,10,11
that Jesus was the *, and his words Act 8:12
*, who is Lord of all creation. Act 10:36,37
them in the name of Jesus, the *. Act 10:48
asked, 'Do you think I am the *? Act 13:25
sufferings of the * and his coming Act 17:3
and proving that Jesus is the *. Act 17:3
to the Jews that Jesus is the *. Act 18:5
the synagogue, "The * is coming! Act 18:25,26
that Jesus is indeed the *. Act 18:28
to know his will and to see the * Act 22:14
said— that the * would suffer, and Act 26:23
that it is because I believe the * Act 28:20

MESSIAH'S
for at the time of * death. Dan 9:25f
been expecting the * coming and Lk 23:50,51,52
had seen a vision of the * glory. Jn 12:41
and predicting the * resurrection, Act 2:31
saying that the * soul would not be Act 2:31

MESSIAHS
For there will be many false * Mk 13:22

MET
'I am the God you * at Bethel,' Gen 31:13
that when they * Esau and he asked, Gen 32:17
flocks and herds I * as I came?" Gen 33:8
the God who * me here at Bethel" Gen 35:7
There he * and married a Gen 38:2
the Hebrews, has * with us and Ex 3:18
of God, and * Moses there, and they Ex 4:27
"The God of the Hebrews has * Ex 5:3
When they * Moses and Aaron Ex 5:20
* them with his army at Edre-i. Num 21:33
height, and God * him there. Num 23:3,4
And the Lord * Balaam and told Num 23:16
And now the Israeli leaders * at Ju 21:2
Finally the leaders of Israel * 1Sa 8:4
with David, David * Jonathan, the 1Sa 18:1
to find David; he * him at Horesh 1Sa 23:16
she * David coming towards her. 1Sa 25:20
men I've ever *, and I think you 1Sa 29:6
to meet them. They * at the pool of 2Sa 2:13
for the occasion) * him and called 1Ki 11:29
had * them but was not returning. 2Ki 9:18
to meet Jehu. They * him at the 2Ki 9:21
While he was there he * the 2Ki 10:13
As he left the inn, he * 2Ki 10:15

(MET Con't)
bodyguard. He * them in the Temple, 2Ki 11:4
The prophet Shemaiah now * with 2Ch 12:5
So the ships * disaster and 2Ch 20:37
of Ahab, he * King Ahaziah's 2Ch 22:8
The armies * at Beth-shemesh, in 2Ch 25:21
and Levites * with Ezra to go over Neh 8:13
Mercy and truth have * together. Ps 85:10
of deep oppression * his ears. Is 5:7
from him. He * God there at Bethel Hos 12:4
by a lion—and * by a bear, or a man Amo 5:19
two men with demons in them * him. Mt 8:28
Leaving that place, Jesus * a man Mt 9:32
Then the Pharisees * together to Mt 22:15
and Jewish leaders * again to Mt 27:1
There they * him and worshiped Mt 28:17
went away and * with the Mk 3:6
everyone they * to turn from sin. Mk 6:12
shore and * them as they landed. Mk 6:33
* to discuss their next steps. Mk 15:1
I * a man with faith like this." Lk 7:9
hill, a huge crowd * him, and a Lk 9:37
you have never *, who will soon Jn 1:26
the man you * on the other side of Jn 3:26
of his servants * him with the news Jn 4:51
at the place where Martha * him. Jn 11:30
As the believers * together that Act 2:1
And all the believers * together Act 2:44
Temple each day, * in small groups Act 2:46
There he * a man named Aeneas, Act 9:33
Paphos where they * a Jewish Act 13:6,7
Arriving in Jerusalem, they * Act 15:4
Lystra where they * Timothy, a Act 16:1
some people * for prayer; Act 16:13
the river, we * a demon-possessed Act 16:16
Lydia where they * with the Act 16:40
Afterwards they * with him and Act 18:25,26
The upstairs room where we * was Act 20:8
"a place where two seas *." Act 27:41f
And the only other apostle I * Gal 1:19
Melchizedek * him and blessed him; Heb 7:1

METAL
* workers in bronze and iron." Gen 4:22f
Make a bronze grating, with a * Ex 27:4
fire, and when the * cooled, he Ex 32:20
He shall then beat the * into a Num 16:38
into a sheet of * to cover the Num 16:39
had made an idol from molten *. Deu 9:12
cut down the * idols, and leave Deu 12:3
made from molten *—for these Deu 27:15
the backs of two rows of * oxen. 2Ch 4:3
refine them and test them like *. Jer 9:7
court, and the * stands and all the Jer 27:19,20,21
refining precious * and he can Mal 3:2

METALS
will send gifts of precious *. Ps 68:31
you an assayer of *, that you may Jer 6:27

METALSMITH
in terror. The * stands at his Is 44:12

METE
They will * out to them the Eze 23:45

METED
heavy penalties are * out to Ps 34:21
unaided, I * out judgment. Is 63:5

METEORIC
Cyrus began his * rise to power. Is 44:28f

METHOD
This is the * for making Lev 14:53
From the first his * will be Dan 11:23
His usual * of teaching was to Mk 4:2
concerning the * of his execution. Jn 18:32
It is God's powerful * of Rom 1:16
see that God's * changed, for Heb 7:15
certain foods—a * which, by the Heb 13:9
1:1—the ultimate * of God's Rev 19:13f

METHODS
his decisions and his *! Rom 11:33
All such shameful * we forego. 2Co 4:2
plans and * to win my battles. 2Co 10:3

METHUSAEL
of *; Gen 4:18
* was the father Gen 4:18

METHUSELAH
years old when his son * was born. Gen 5:21-24
*: Methuselah was 187 years old Gen 5:25,26,27
Methuselah: * was 187 years old Gen 5:25,26,27
Jared, Enoch, *, Lamech, Noah, 1Ch 1:1
Lamech's father was *; Lk 3:23-38

METHUSELAH'S
Lamech's father was Methuselah;* Lk 3:23-38

METIRE
The eagle, the *, the osprey, Lev 11:13-19

MEUNITES
Ammon, and of the * declared war on 2Ch 20:1
and in his wars with the *. 2Ch 26:7

MEZAHAB
of Matred and granddaughter of *. Gen 36:31-39
of Matred and granddaughter of *). 1Ch 1:50

MEZOBA
Ja-asiel from *. 1Ch 11:26-47

MIBHAR
* (son of Hagri); 1Ch 11:26-47

MIBSAM
Kedar, Abdeel,*, Mishma, Gen 25:12-15
Kedar, Adbeel, *, Mishma, Dumah, 1Ch 1:28-31
was *, and his great-grandson was 1Ch 4:25

MIBZAR
Teman,The clan of *,The clan of Gen 36:40-43
*, Chief Magdi-el, Chief Iram. 1Ch 1:51-54

MICA
Mephibosheth had a young son, *. 2Sa 9:12
Mattaniah (the son of *, who was 1Ch 9:15,16
Pelaiah, Hanan, *, Rehob, Neh 10:9-13
Mattaniah (son of *, son of Zabdi, Neh 11:15,16,17
Mattaniah, son of *), a descendant Neh 11:22,23

MICAH
of Ephraim lived a man named *. Ju 17:1
in Micah's shrine. * had many idols Ju 17:4,5
"Where are you from?" * asked Ju 17:9
"Well, stay here with me," * Ju 17:10,11
Micah's sons. So * consecrated him Ju 17:12
bless me now," * exclaimed, Ju 17:13
his contract with *, and that he Ju 18:4
As they passed the home of *, the Ju 18:13
from Micah's home, * and some of Ju 18:22
'What do I want'!" * retorted. Ju 18:24
kept going. When * saw that there Ju 18:26
Shime-i's son was *; 1Ch 5:5
was *. 1Ch 8:34
The sons of *: 1Ch 8:35
was the father of *; 1Ch 9:40
* was the father of Pithon, 1Ch 9:41
The sons of Uzziel were led by *, 1Ch 23:20
was led by his son * and his 1Ch 24:24,25
Abdon (son of *), Shaphan the 2Ch 34:20
for back in the days when * the Jer 26:18
from the Lord to *, who lived in Mic 1:1
came to * in the form of visions. Mic 1:1
in verses 10–14. * bitterly Mic 1:11f
in verses 10–14. * bitterly Mic 1:11f
in verses 10–14. * bitterly Mic 1:11f
"for this is what the prophet * Mt 2:5
Implied. * 5:2. Mt 2:5f

MICAH'S
from it was placed in * shrine. Ju 17:4,5
He happened to stop at * house as Ju 17:7,8
this, and became as one of * sons. Ju 17:10,11
of Ephraim, they stayed at * home. Ju 18:2
a distance from * home, Micah and Ju 18:22
Then, with * idols and the Ju 18:27
its enemies. So * idols were Ju 18:31
* home town. Mic 1:14f

MICAIAH
His name is *, the son of 1Ki 22:8
to one of his aides, "Go get *. 1Ki 22:9
The messenger who went to get * 1Ki 22:13
But * told him, "This I vow, 1Ki 22:14
king asked him, "*, shall we 1Ki 22:15
Go right ahead!" * told him. 1Ki 22:15
Then * told him, "I saw all 1Ki 22:17
Then * said, "Listen to this 1Ki 22:19
over and slapped * on the face. 1Ki 22:24
And * replied, "You will have 1Ki 22:25
"If you return in peace," * 1Ki 22:28
His mother's name was * (daughter 2Ch 13:1
Zechariah, Nethanel, and *. 2Ch 17:7,8,9
His name is * (son of Imlah)." 2Ch 18:6,7
Go and get * (son of Imlah)," he 2Ch 18:8
The man who went to get * told 2Ch 18:12
But * replied, "I vow by God 2Ch 18:13
king asked him, "*, shall we go to 2Ch 18:14
And * replied, "Sure, go ahead! 2Ch 18:14
Then * told him, "In my vision I 2Ch 18:16
Lord has told me," * continued. 2Ch 18:18
* and slapped him across the face. 2Ch 18:23
out soon enough," * replied, 2Ch 18:24
* replied, "If you return 2Ch 18:27
*, son of Zaccur, son of Asaph), Neh 12:35,36
*, Eli-o-enai, Zechariah, Neh 12:40,41
When * (son of Gemariah, son of Jer 36:11
When * told them about the Jer 36:13

MICAIAH'S
Then King Ahab ordered * arrest. 1Ki 22:26

MICHAEL
Sethur, son of *, from the tribe Num 13:3-15
seven clans, were *, Meshullam, 1Ch 5:13
Jahdo, Jeshishai, *, Gilead, 1Ch 5:14
Berechiah, Shime-a, *, Ba-aseiah, 1Ch 6:39-43
five sons were *, Obadiah, Joel, 1Ch 7:3
Zebadiah, Arad, Eder, *, Ishpah, 1Ch 8:15,16
Adnah, Jozabad, Jedia-el, *, 1Ch 12:20
Over Issachar, Omri (son of *); 1Ch 27:16-22
Azariah, *, and Sheph-atiah. 2Ch 21:2
(son of *), and 80 other men; Ez 8:2-14
blocked my way. Then *, one of Dan 10:13
of Greece. Only *, the angel who Dan 10:20,21
"AT THAT TIME *, the mighty Dan 12:1
Ones. Yet *, one of the mightiest Jud 1:9
Then there was war in heaven; * Rev 12:7

MICHAIAH'S
son), and Achbor (* son) to ask the 2Ki 22:12,13

MICHAL
and two daughters, Merab and *. 1Sa 14:49
Saul's daughter * had fallen in 1Sa 18:20
So Saul gave * to him. 1Sa 18:27
away tonight," * warned him, 1Sa 19:11
Saul demanded of *. 1Sa 19:17
"I had to," * replied. 1Sa 19:17
David's wife *, Saul's daughter, to 1Sa 25:44
me my wife *, Saul's daughter." 2Sa 3:13
me back my wife *, for I bought her 2Sa 3:14
into the city, *, Saul's daughter, 2Sa 6:16
But * came out to meet him and 2Sa 6:20
So * was childless throughout her 2Sa 6:23
adopted sons of * that she brought 2Sa 21:8
David's wife *, the daughter of 1Ch 15:29

MICHMAS
From the subclan of *, 122; Ez 2:3-35
From the subclan of *, 122; Neh 7:8-38

MICHMASH
them with him to * and Mount Bethel 1Sa 13:2
and they camped at * east of 1Sa 13:5
were at *, ready for battle, I 1Sa 13:11
but the Philistines stayed at *. 1Sa 13:16
The mountain pass at * had 1Sa 13:23
was in front of * and the southern 1Sa 14:5
all day from * to Aijalon, growing 1Sa 14:31
Geba, *, Aija, Bethel (and its Neh 11:31-35
at * and crossing over the pass; Is 10:28,29

MICHMETHATH
Sea, ran east past *, then Jos 16:5,6
to *, which is east of Shechem. Jos 17:7
from * to the Spring of Tappu-ah. Jos 17:7

MICHRI
(the son of Uzzi, the son of *); 1Ch 9:7,8

MID-FEBRUARY
IN * OF the twelfth year of King Eze 32:1

MID-MAY
IN * OF the eleventh year of King Eze 31:1

MID-SEPTEMBER
"The Festival of Trumpets: * Lev 23:23,24
NOW, IN *, all the people Neh 8:1

MIDDIN
Beth-arabah, *, Secacah, Nibshan, Jos 15:48-62

MIDDLE
the boat—a bottom, *, and upper Gen 6:16
apart down the *, and to separate Gen 15:10
westward. The * bar, halfway up Ex 26:28
Tabernacle. The * bar of the five Ex 36:33
went through the * of the Red Sea Num 33:8
frontier) to the * of the valley of Deu 3:16
the booty into the * of the street Deu 13:16
dry ground in the * of the Jordan Jos 3:17
standing in the * of the Jordan, Jos 4:2,3
* of the Jordan where the Ark is. Jos 4:5
stones from the * of the Jordan Jos 4:8
stones in the * of the river, at Jos 4:9
Ark stood in the * of the river Jos 4:10
and from the * of the valley of the Jos 12:2
of Arnon in the * of the valley, to Jos 13:16
his blood in the * of the road, and 2Sa 20:12
that lies in the * of the valley of 2Sa 24:5
his ground in the * of the field, 1Ch 11:14
at the * to expose their buttocks; 1Ch 19:4
They left Babylon in the * of Ez 7:7,8,9
between us, no * man, no mediator Job 9:32,33
He has cut me down in * life, Ps 102:23
and sat in triumph at the * gate. Jer 39:3
out from the * of his back. Eze 1:11
lying in the * of your rivers. Eze 29:3
around the * of March, this Eze 29:17
around the * of March of the Eze 30:20
But in the * of your Nah 3:15
were out in the * of the lake, and Mk 6:47
right down the *—the Pharisees Act 23:7

MIDIAN
Jokshan, Medan,*, Ishbak, Shuah. Gen 25:1
army of * when it invaded Moab. Gen 36:31-39
Moses ran away into the land of *. Ex 2:15
of the priest of * came to draw Ex 2:16
the priest of *, out at the edge Ex 3:1
Before Moses left *, Jehovah said Ex 4:19
the priest of *, about all the Ex 18:1
for the land of * from which she Num 12:1f
consulted with the leaders of *. Num 22:4
of the top leaders of Moab and *. Num 22:7
to wage Jehovah's war against *. Num 31:3
And every man of * was killed in Num 31:7
villages of * were then burned. Num 31:9,10,11
*—Evi, Rekem, Zur, Hur, and Reba. Jos 13:21
the people of *, for seven years. Ju 6:1
marauders from *, Amalek, and other Ju 6:3,4
it again, rescuing Israel from *. Ju 6:16f
Soon afterward the armies of *, Ju 6:33
The armies of * were camped north Ju 7:1
The vast armies of *, Amalek, Ju 7:12,13
all the allied forces of *!" Ju 7:14
all the vast armies of *!" Ju 7:15
the outer edge of the camp of *. Ju 7:19,20
and destroy the fleeing army of *. Ju 7:23
two generals of *, were captured. Ju 7:25
the generals of the army of *! Ju 8:2,3
the kings of *," he said. Ju 8:5
for you have saved us from *." Ju 8:22

(MIDIAN Con't)
the troops of *, being Ishmaelites, Ju 8:23,24
That is the true account of how * Ju 8:28
subdued by Israel. * never Ju 8:28
They slipped out of * and went to 1Ki 11:16,17,18
*, Ishbak, and Shuah. 1Ch 1:32
The sons of *: 1Ch 1:33
the army of * in the fields of 1Ch 1:46
Do to them as once you did to *, Ps 83:9
triumphed over * at the rock of Is 10:26
dromedaries from * and Sheba and Is 60:6
of Cushan and of * in mortal fear. Hab 3:7
*, where his two sons were born. Act 7:29

MIDIAN'S
and Leummim. * sons were Ephah, Gen 25:4

MIDIANITE
(son of Reuel, the *), "At last we Num 10:29
* daughter of Reuel (Exodus 2:21); Num 12:1f
brought a * girl into the camp, Num 25:6
killed with the * girl was Zimri, Num 25:14
daughter of Zur, a * prince. Num 25:15
all five of the * kings—Evi, Rekem, Num 31:8
quickly destroy the * hordes!" Ju 6:16
at the * army in surprise raids. Ju 8:11

MIDIANITES
Literally, "*." Gen 37:28f
"Destroy the *, for they are Num 25:16,17
vengeance on the * for leading you Num 31:1
seven years. The * were so cruel Ju 6:2
abject poverty because of the *. Ju 6:6,7
wine—for he was hiding from the *. Ju 6:11
let the * completely ruin us." Ju 6:13
Go and save Israel from the *! Ju 6:14
of you fight the *, for then the Ju 7:2
"I'll conquer the * with these Ju 7:7
During the night, with the * Ju 7:8,9
Take your troops and attack the * Ju 7:8,9
* from escaping by going across. Ju 7:24
first went out to fight the *?" Ju 8:1
you from the *, yet you have Ju 9:17
of the * by Gideon's little band. Is 9:4

MIDNIGHT
"Jehovah says, 'About * I will Ex 11:4
And that night, at *, Jehovah Ex 12:29
It was just after * and the Ju 7:19,20
the girl until *, then went out to Ju 16:3
Suddenly, around *, he wakened Ru 3:8
a land as dark as *, a land of the Job 10:22
the brightest light is dark as *.' Job 10:22
In a moment they die, and at * Job 34:20
At * I will rise to give my Ps 119:62
down to rest until *, when they Mt 25:5,6
will come, at evening, at *, Mk 13:35,36,37
friend's house at *, wanting to Lk 11:5,6
o'clock at night—or even at *. Lk 12:38
Around *, as Paul and Silas were Act 16:25
the next day, he talked until *! Act 20:7
About * on the fourteenth night Act 27:27

MIDST
the * of the siege of your cities. Deu 28:55
fallen in the * of the battle. 2Sa 1:25
be alone in the * of the earth! Is 5:8
the work of my hands, in his *." Is 29:23f
And now in the * of all Lam 1:7
destroyed in the * of the sea? Eze 27:32
island home in the * of the seas. Eze 28:2,3
from the * of the stones of fire. Eze 28:16
the * of the stones of fire." Eze 28:16f
brought fire from the * of you." Eze 28:18f
and I am still in the * of a Php 1:30

MIDWAY
Then, * through the festival, Jn 7:14

MIDWIFE
hard delivery, the * finally Gen 35:17
As they were being born, the * Gen 38:28
Why did the * let me live? Job 3:12

MIDWIVES
the Hebrew * (their names were Ex 1:15,16
But the * feared God and didn't Ex 1:17
And God blessed the *. Ex 1:20
And because the * revered God, Ex 1:21

MIGDAL
the nearby town of * saw what was Ju 9:46

MIGDAL-EL
Enhazor, Yiron, *, Horem, Jos 19:35-39

MIGDAL-GAD
Zenan, Hadashah, *, Dilean, Jos 15:37-44

MIGDOL
between * and the sea, opposite Ex 14:2
camped at the foot of Mount *). Num 33:7
in the cities of *, Tahpanhes and Jer 44:1
publish it in the cities of *, Jer 46:14
of Egypt, from * to Syene, as far Eze 29:10
shall end. From * to Syene they Eze 30:6

MIGHT
"Someone * carelessly have raped Gen 26:10
An example in English * be, Gen 30:6f
as to what the dreams * mean; Gen 41:8
for fear some harm * happen to him Gen 42:4
felt the people * become Ex 13:17,18
he thought they * return to Ex 13:17,18
altar, or someone * look up beneath Ex 20:26
Oh, that my end * be liketheirs!" Num 23:7-10
with all your heart, soul, and *. Deu 6:5
* against the people you fear. Deu 7:19
power and * that made you wealthy. Deu 8:17
and stronger than you they * be. Deu 11:23
begged that you * not have to Deu 18:16
otherwise the angry avenger * Deu 19:6,7
For you * be killed in the Deu 20:5
If so, go home! You * die in Deu 20:6
For you * die in the battle, and Deu 20:7
that you and your children * Deu 30:19
"Israel is destroyed by our own * Deu 32:27
upon anyone who * rebuild Jericho, Jos 6:26
we have heard of the * of the Jos 9:9
the people of Israel * know Ju 3:1f
the pillars with all his *. Ju 16:29
what King Achish * do to him, so 1Sa 21:12
Lord with all his *, and was 2Sa 6:14
me. I * as well have stayed there. 2Sa 14:32
bush and prayed that he * die. 1Ki 19:4
and it * as well be now." 1Ki 19:4
so we * as well go out and 2Ki 7:4
your hand controls power and *, 1Ch 29:12
reign and of his * and all that 1Ch 29:30
finished, you * as well forget Ez 4:16
feared what the Jews * do to them. Est 8:17
any who * try to harm them; Est 9:1
"And how great is his *! Job 12:14
[But I * as well save my breath, Job 30:28,29
If you refuse to answer me, I * Ps 28:1
in so that I * sing glad praises Ps 30:12
Defend me with your *! Ps 54:1
Summon your *; Ps 68:28
of Jacob and of Joseph by your *. Ps 77:15
the good things they * have had, Pro 2:22
Excuses * even be found for a Pro 6:30
"If I go outside I * meet a lion Pro 22:13
"There * be a lion outside!" Pro 26:13
use thinking of what * have been. Ecc 1:12-15
and succeed. He * even become king, Ecc 4:14
and he * Ecc 5:6,7
understanding, counsel and *; Is 11:2
Your * and power are gone; Is 14:11
stand up and show my power and *. Is 33:10
that are near, acknowledge my *! Is 33:13
Others died that you * live; Is 43:4
pounding on it with all his *. Is 44:12
He was chastised that we * have Is 53:5
*, nor the rich man in his riches. Jer 9:23
my power and * and make them Jer 16:21
Oh, that the Lord * look down Lam 3:50
With * and fury I will bring you Eze 20:34
"Because of the way your * Eze 29:6
aggregate military * of the forces Eze 38:2,3f
an alternate rendering * read, Dan 8:23f
rush out to bury him with their *. Dan 11:40
Then she will think, "I * as Hos 1:7
Oh, that we * know the Lord! Hos 6:3
that military * and great armies Hos 10:13
name of the Lord—he * hear you." Amo 6:10
people—your royal * and power will Mic 4:8
be embarrassed at their puny *. Mic 7:16
I will overthrow their armed *, Hag 2:22
'Not by *, nor by power, but by Zec 4:6
And don't think that I * change Zec 8:14,15
hour awaiting him * never come. Mk 14:35
Literally, "that the hour * pass Mk 14:35f
Otherwise he * complete only the Lk 14:29
in this audience * become the same Act 26:29
serve with all my *, telling others Rom 1:9
course, that * be barely possible. Rom 5:7
Literally, "that my name * be Rom 9:17f
that the Jewish people * be saved. Rom 10:1
branches from, we * say, a wild Rom 11:17
Accepting them * cause discord Rom 14:1f
or die as we ourselves * choose. Rom 14:7
of others who * be hurt by it. Rom 14:22
that the Gentiles * be saved and Rom 15:9
not words that we as men * choose. 1Co 2:13
to if I think they * get such a 1Co 6:12
you * fall back into sin. 1Co 7:2
* never come to know the Lord; 1Co 7:14
if we did, you * be less interested 1Co 9:12
the race, I myself * be declared 1Co 9:27
This * be called their 1Co 10:2
* otherwise seem less important. 1Co 12:24
what you mean? You * as well be 1Co 14:9
we die, then we * as well go and 1Co 15:32
life from him—* live no longer for 2Co 5:15
behalf, that we * become the 2Co 5:21f
God * give to them through us. 2Co 8:5
afraid I * be puffed up by them; 2Co 12:7
Christ, that we * be accepted by Gal 2:16
the law, that I * live unto God." Gal 2:19f
that next time it * be one of you Gal 6:1
our evil thoughts * lead us into. Eph 2:3
back up, that he * fill all things Eph 4:10
Literally, "that he * fill all Eph 4:10f
from all that * displease him. Php 2:12
Gentiles for fear some * be saved; 1Th 2:16
because he * be proud of being 1Ti 3:
whether he * change his plans. Heb 6:1
(d) One * even say that Levi Heb 7:
he * bring us safely home to God. 1Pe 3:1
say, "so you * as well be bad. 2Pe 2:1
all dread of what he * do to us. 1Jn 4:1
fear of what he * do to us, and 1Jn 4:1
* take God's place in your hearts. 1Jn 5:2
and power, and *, be to our God Rev 7:12
An alternate rendering * be, "at Rev 7:17

MIGHTIER
far greater and * than they are!" Num 14:12
all greater and * than you are: Deu 7:1
you, * and greater than they are.' Deu 9:13,14
to be * than all the other trees?' Ju 9:13
You are * than all the breakers Ps 93:4
A wise man is * than a strong Pro 24:5
Wisdom is * than strength. Pro 24:5

MIGHTIEST
Joab and the * warriors of Israel. 1Ch 19:8
For God destroys the * warships Ps 48:7
* of our enemies are conquered. Ps 76:5
be compared with God? What * angel Ps 89:6
him the * king in all the earth. Ps 89:27
of the earth and the * mountains; Ps 95:4
refuge in him than in the * king! Ps 118:9
of Solomon with sixty of the * Sol 3:7
World leaders and earth's * Is 14:9
in terror; the * of its soldiers Jer 46:5
not escape, nor the * of warriors. Jer 46:6
and defeat; your * soldiers will Jer 46:12
The hearts of her * warriors fail Jer 48:41
Then the courage of the * Jer 49:22
Babylon, the * hammer in all the Jer 50:23
Panic shall seize her * warriors! Jer 50:36
Her * soldiers no longer fight; Jer 51:30
stupidity. The * soldiers of Teman Ob 1:9
is destined for God's * praise. Lk 1:42
Even Abraham and the * prophets Jn 8:52
Yet Michael, one of the * of the Jud 1:9

MIGHTILY
of the Lord came * upon him and Ju 14:6
the Lord will come * upon you, and 1Sa 10:6
sackcloth and cry * to God, and let Jon 3:8
be * revered among the Gentiles." Mal 1:14
Lord Jesus Christ * bless each one 2Co 1:2

MIGHTY
him, and placed * angels at the Gen 3:24
rain came down in * torrents from Gen 7:10,11,12
He was a * hunter, blessed of Gen 10:9
Or, "a * hunter against the Gen 10:9f
* hunter, blessed of God." Gen 10:9
Or, "a * hunter against the Gen 10:9f
to make you into a * nation. Gen 17:2,3,4
"For Abraham shall become a * Gen 18:18
* blessings promised to Abraham. Gen 28:4
So Jacob took oath before the * Gen 31:53
and may they become a * nation." Gen 48:16
shattered by the * One of Jacob, Gen 49:24
multiply and to become a * nation. Ex 1:20
that I will use my * power and Ex 6:6
of doing * miracles to demonstrate Ex 11:9
brought you out with * miracles. Ex 13:3
you shall tell them, 'With * Ex 13:14
of Israel saw the * miracle the Ex 14:31
They sank as lead in the * waters. Ex 15:10
The * men of Moab tremble; Ex 15:15
such great power and * miracles? Ex 32:11
And the * army of the king of Num 24:21,22
for you with his * miracles, just Deu 1:30
* miracles, war, and terror? Deu 4:34
great power and * miracles—with Deu 6:22
such amazing power and * miracles. Deu 7:8
own eyes—and the * miracles and Deu 7:19
and I will make a * nation of you, Deu 9:13,14
* power and glorious strength. Deu 9:26
your great power and your * arm.' Deu 9:29
He is the great and * God, the Deu 10:17
one who has done * miracles you Deu 10:21
"But you have seen these * Deu 11:7
in Egypt they became a * nation. Deu 26:5
* miracles and a powerful hand. Deu 26:8
great plagues and * miracles that Deu 29:2,3
Jehovah is the * God, and so that Jos 4:24
king and all its * warriors are Jos 6:2
are to give a * shout and the walls Jos 6:5
He is the God who did * miracles Jos 24:17
who had seen the * miracles the Ju 2:7-9
* miracles he had done for Israel. Ju 2:10
fight King Jabin's * army with all Ju 4:7
"* soldier, the Lord is with you!" Ju 6:12
Those who were * are mighty no 1Sa 2:4
Those who were mighty are * no 1Sa 2:4
He gives * strength to his King, 1Sa 2:10
Who can save us from these * 1Sa 4:8
Lord spoke with a * voice of 1Sa 7:10
The Philistines recruited a * 1Sa 13:5
of God to do a * miracle today." 1Sa 14:45
* heroes have fallen. 2Sa 1:19
For there the * Saul has died; 2Sa 1:21
These * heroes have fallen in the 2Sa 1:25

IIGHTY Con't)
The * ones have fallen, 2Sa 1:27
* warriors who surrounded them! 2Sa 16:6
they are * warriors and are 2Sa 17:8
for all Israel knows what a * man 2Sa 17:10
above all gods gave out a * shout. 2Sa 22:14
great name and * miracles) and pray 1Ki 8:41,42
For I hear a * rainstorm 1Ki 18:41
a * windstorm hit the mountain; 1Ki 19:11
demanded of the * cedar tree, 'Give 2Ki 14:9
These five * warriors were chiefs 1Ch 7:7
there were 22,200 * warriors among 1Ch 7:9
Benaiah, whose father was a * 1Ch 11:22
of Ephraim, 20,800 * warriors, each 1Ch 12:24-37
About his * doings. 1Ch 16:8
Remember his * miracles 1Ch 16:12,13
Yours is the * power and glory 1Ch 29:11
powerless against this * army. 2Ch 14:11
earth—you are so powerful, so *. 2Ch 20:6
ourselves against this * army. 2Ch 20:12
Don't be paralyzed by this * 2Ch 20:15
of Assyria or his * army, for there 2Ch 32:7
and before all of his * princes! Ez 7:28
Literally, "the house of the * Neh 3:16f
like stones beneath the * waters. Neh 9:11
for Mordecai was a * name in the Est 9:4
when suddenly a * wind swept in Job 1:19
For God is so wise and so *. Job 9:4
He overthrows the *. Job 12:19
Instead, glorify him for his * Job 36:24
He is like the strong horn of a * Ps 18:2
and a * storm of hail. Ps 18:12
songs to celebrate your * acts! Ps 21:13
The Lord, strong and *, Ps 24:8
Yes, though a * army marches Ps 27:3
Lord spins and topples the * oaks. Ps 29:9
skill, but by your * power and Ps 44:3
Arm yourself, O * One, Ps 45:3
God has ascended with a * shout, Ps 47:5
THE * GOD, the Lord, has summoned Ps 50:1
YOU HIGH and * politicians don't Ps 58:1
With God's help we shall do * Ps 60:12
to the *, towering Rock of safety. Ps 61:2
He formed the mountains by his * Ps 65:6
O * mountains in Bashan! Ps 68:15,16
have done such * things for us. Ps 68:28
* voice thunders from the sky. Ps 68:33
his strength is * in the heavens. Ps 68:34
and * power to his people. Ps 68:35
because you are my * protector. Ps 71:7
too) about all your * miracles. Ps 71:18
HOW WE THANK you, Lord! Your * Ps 75:1
Where is there any other as * as Ps 77:13
them about the * miracles he did. Ps 78:4
the south wind by his * power. Ps 78:26
sleep, and like a * man aroused by Ps 78:65
and use your * power to rescue us. Ps 80:2
we were like the * cedar trees, Ps 80:10
Make their * nobles die as Oreb Ps 83:11
Literally, "the sons of the *." Ps 89:6f
is there any other * One like you? Ps 89:8
The * oceans thunder your praise. Ps 93:3
* Rock where I can hide. Ps 94:21,22
Therefore in * wrath I swore Ps 95:11
Lord telling about his * deeds! Ps 98:1
For he has won a * victory by his Ps 98:1
This * King is determined to give Ps 99:4
Bless the Lord, you * angels of Ps 103:20
There before me lies the * ocean, Ps 104:25
Think of the * deeds he did for Ps 105:5,6
who had done such * miracles in Ps 106:21,22
with * power and rescue me. Ps 108:6
God we shall do * acts of valor. Ps 108:13
thanks to God for his * miracles. Ps 111:1
of the Lord, a Temple for the * Ps 132:2-5
I have decreed for him a * Son. Ps 132:17
* kings— Sihon, king of Amorites; Ps 135:10
Praise him who alone does * Ps 136:4
He brought them out with * power Ps 136:11,12
from the power of * kings, for his Ps 136:17
the heavens he made with * power. Ps 150:1
Praise him for his * works. Ps 150:2
Lord of Hosts, the * One of Israel, Is 1:24
and all the * oaks of Bashan shall Is 2:13
Hovering about him were *, Is 6:2
and Judah—the * king of Assyria Is 7:17
my people with Euphrates' * flood; Is 8:7,8
the king of Assyria and all his * Is 8:7,8
"The * God," "The Everlasting Is 9:6
Only a few from all that * army Is 10:19
of them will return to the * God. Is 10:21
to slay them in a * slaughter like Is 10:26
Look, the * armies of Assyria are Is 10:28,29
to Laish, for the * army comes. Is 10:30
is chopping down the * tree! Is 10:33
He, the * One, will cut down the Is 10:34
sending a * wind to divide it Is 11:15
How * he is!" Is 12:4
For great and * is the Holy One Is 12:6
the palaces of the rich and *. Is 13:2
down to the ground—* though you Is 14:12
will do it by my * power that Is 14:26
me this: Let your * army now Is 18:4
Your * army will be left dead on Is 18:6
that strong and * nation, a terror Is 18:7
the * tribe of Kedar, will end. Is 21:16
You turn * cities into heaps of Is 25:2
For the Lord will send a * army Is 28:2
like a * hailstorm he will burst Is 28:2
crush down his * arm upon his Is 30:30
trusting their * cavalry and Is 31:1
are puny flesh, not * spirits! Is 31:3
shadow of a * rock within a hot and Is 32:2
Edom and make a * slaughter there. Is 34:6
to Hezekiah, "The * king of Is 36:4
You boast, 'I came with my * army Is 37:24
Lord God is coming with * power; Is 40:10
Who has done such * deeds, Is 41:4
Or do some * miracle that makes Is 41:23
the Lord and sing his * power. Is 42:12
The Lord will be a * warrior, Is 42:13
I called forth the * army of Is 43:17
crush the strength of * kings. Is 45:1
Israel from Babylon's * power; Is 47:4
prey from the hands of a * man? Is 49:24
of the most * and most terrible Is 49:25
Redeemer, the * One of Israel." Is 49:26
same today, the * God who dried up Is 51:10
of one who is * and great, because Is 53:12
through his * power and justice. Is 59:16
to your light; * kings will come to Is 60:3
Powerful kings and * nations Is 60:16
and Redeemer, the * One of Israel. Is 60:16
the tiny group shall be a * Is 60:22
I, the Lord, the one who is * to Is 63:1
Where is he whose * power Is 63:12
I will perform a * miracle Is 66:19
on Jerusalem with * shouts Jer 2:15
the Lord—a * nation, an ancient Jer 5:15
the men are all *. Jer 5:16
wisdom, nor the * man in his might, Jer 9:23
in Egypt. That * miracle will Jer 16:14,15
before him, the *, Terrible One, Jer 20:11
do a * miracle as in olden times Jer 21:1
king of Babylon, and his * army. Jer 22:24,25
Is it not like a * hammer that Jer 23:29
you are the great and * God, the Jer 32:18
and do great and * miracles; Jer 32:19
out of Egypt with * miracles and Jer 32:21
What is this * army, rising like Jer 46:7
chariots and * soldiers of Egypt! Jer 46:9
"We are heroes, * men of war"? Jer 48:14
skies their * shouts of victory. Jer 51:14
For see, I am against you, O * Jer 51:25
Babylon; her * voice is stilled as Jer 51:55
armies come and slay her * men; Jer 51:56
The Lord has trampled all my * Lam 1:15
Yes, even our * king, about whom Lam 4:20
or like the shouting of a * army. Eze 1:24
great hailstones and * winds will Eze 13:11
Pharaoh and all his * army shall Eze 17:17
this dirge: 'O * island city, with Eze 26:17
"O * seaport city, merchant Eze 27:3
a hurricane! Your * vessel Eze 27:26
king of Egypt—* dragon lying in the Eze 29:3
was—a great and * nation—like a Eze 31:2,3
the hands of a * nation, to destroy Eze 31:11
* army—the terror of the nations. Eze 32:12
Egypt and for the other * nations. Eze 32:18
to judgment. The * warriors in the Eze 32:21
All these * men who once struck Eze 32:23
and her princes; * as they were, Eze 32:29
in a * battle of the end times. Eze 38:2,3f
you a * host, all fully armed. Eze 38:4
wrath, I promise a * shaking in the Eze 38:19
for a * sacrificial feast. Eze 39:17
Eat the flesh of * men and drink Eze 39:18
It was incredible—a * miracle! Dan 4:3
"I, by my own * power, have built Dan 4:30
a great storm on a * ocean, with Dan 7:2
His power shall be *, but it Dan 8:24
their armies be *, and he will Dan 8:24
But for twenty-one days the * Dan 10:13
"Then a * king will rise in Dan 11:3
will assemble a * army that will Dan 11:10,11
and Egypt, too, will raise a * Dan 11:25
"AT THAT TIME Michael, the * Dan 12:1
Therefore, a * wind Hos 4:19
with fear, for he was a * prince; Hos 13:1
What a * army! Joe 2:2
like a * army moving into battle. Joe 2:5
This is his * army and they Joe 2:11
The Lord has done a * miracle for Joe 2:20
like a whirlwind in a * storm. Amo 1:14
The most courageous of your * Amo 2:16
"I want to see a * flood of Amo 5:24
their own land, a * nation, and the Mic 4:7
Lord, "I will do * miracles for Mic 7:15
O Nineveh, once * lion! Nah 2:12
of Egypt were her * allies, and she Nah 3:9
raging water. The * deep cried out, Hab 3:10
the sea; the * waters piled high. Hab 3:15
He is a * Savior. Zep 3:17,18
with * shouts of thanksgiving for Zec 4:7
Or, "with * shouts, 'How Zec 4:7f
the sword of a * soldier brandished Zec 9:13
They will be * warriors for God, Zec 10:5
They shall be like * warriors. Zec 10:7
them will be as * as King David! Zec 12:8
it will fall with a * crash." Mt 7:27
the sound of a * trumpet blast, and Mt 24:31
he couldn't do any * miracles among Mk 6:5
For he, the * Holy One, has done Lk 1:49
"How powerful is his * arm! Lk 1:51
He is sending us a * Savior from Lk 1:69
to God, "A * prophet has risen Lk 7:16
everyone about Jesus' * miracle. Lk 8:39
But now a * roar rose from the Lk 23:18
miracles and was a * Teacher, Lk 24:19
filled with * joy, and were Lk 24:52
had heard about this * miracle. Jn 12:18
Who will accept God's * miracles Jn 12:38
* miracles you have seen me do. Jn 14:11
If I hadn't done such * miracles Jn 15:24
you so that the * love you have for Jn 17:26
the roaring of a * windstorm in the Act 2:2
about the * miracles of God!" Act 2:11
God's * power supports me. Act 2:25
Then, with * power, God exalted Act 5:31
he became a * prince and orator. Act 7:22
about God's * kindness and love. Act 20:24
proved to be the * Son of God, with Rom 1:4
him, and gave you * promises. Rom 9:4
of diluting the * power there is in 1Co 1:17
the * power of God to save them; 1Co 1:24
He was there with them as a * 1Co 10:3,4
I use God's * weapons, not those 2Co 10:4
and signs and * works among you. 2Co 12:12
you, but is a * power within you. 2Co 13:3
he lives by the * power of God. 2Co 13:4
for doing these * things for us, Eph 1:12
It is that same * power that Eph 1:19
obeying Satan, the * prince of the Eph 2:2
God's promises of * blessings Eph 3:6
will give you the * inner Eph 3:16
Now glory be to God who by his * Eph 3:20
give a * foothold to the devil. Eph 4:27
the Lord's * power within you. Eph 6:10
world, those * satanic beings and Eph 6:12
but laid aside his * power and Php 2:7
to experience the * power that Php 3:10
using the same * power that he will Php 3:21
be filled with his *, glorious Col 1:11
* energy is at work within me. Col 1:29
In him lie hidden all the *, Col 2:3
the Word of the * God who raised Col 2:12
from heaven with a * shout and with 1Th 4:16
fire with his * angels, bringing 2Th 1:7
by the * power of his command. Heb 1:3
he kept right on doing his * Heb 3:9
before the * work at the cross Heb 5:7f
is, and felt the * powers of the Heb 6:5
a blessing upon * Abraham, and as Heb 7:6
And God, in his * power, will 1Pe 1:5
under the * hand of God, in his 1Pe 5:6
And by that same * power he has 2Pe 1:4
against these evil * Ones. 2Pe 2:11
the world with a * flood, long 2Pe 3:5,6
with * shouts of everlasting joy. Jud 1:24,25
sounded like a * trumpet blast, Rev 4:1
seven seals. A * angel with a loud Rev 5:2
fig trees buffeted by * winds. Rev 6:13
And they were shouting with a * Rev 7:10
prepared to blow their * blasts. Rev 8:6
angel, "Release the four * demons Rev 9:14
THEN I SAW another * angel coming Rev 10:1
Then the * angel standing on the Rev 10:5
scroll from the * angel standing Rev 10:8
was shaken by a * earthquake. Rev 11:19
or the rolling of * thunder. Rev 14:2
AND I SAW in heaven another * Rev 15:1
AND I HEARD a * voice shouting Rev 16:1
and a * shout came from the Rev 16:17
He gave a * shout, "Babylon the Rev 18:2
* is the Lord who judges her." Rev 18:8
out, "Alas, Babylon, that * city! Rev 18:10
Then a * angel picked up a Rev 18:21
shore, or like the * rolling of Rev 19:6
who could do * miracles when the Rev 19:20
for battle—a * host, numberless as Rev 20:8

MIGRANT
'My ancestors were * Arameans who Deu 26:5

MIGRANTS
"Justice must be given to * and Deu 24:17
Leave it for the *, orphans, and Deu 24:19
for the *, orphans, and widows. Deu 24:20
any Levites or * living among you. Deu 26:11
to the Levites, *, orphans, and Deu 26:12
the Levites, the *, the orphans, Deu 26:13

MIGRATION
the time of her *, as does the Jer 8:7

MIGRON
around the pomegranate tree at *. 1Sa 14:2

(MIGRON Con't)
Now they are at Aiath, now at *; Is 10:28,29

MIJA-MIN
*, Ma-aziah, Bilgai, Neh 10:1

MIJAMIN
Sixth, the group led by *; 1Ch 24:7-18
Ramiah, Izziah, Malchijah, *, Ez 10:25
Ginnethoi, Abijah, *, Neh 12:1

MIKLOTH
* who was the father of Shimeah. 1Ch 8:30,31,32
Nadab, Gedor, Ahio, Zechariah, *. 1Ch 9:35,36,37
* lived with his son Shime-am in 1Ch 9:38
year. * was his executive officer. 1Ch 27:4

MIKNEIAH
Eliphelehu, *, Obed-edom and 1Ch 15:18
Mattithiah, Eliphelehu, *, 1Ch 15:21

MILALAI
Shemaiah, Azarel, *, Neh 12:35,36

MILCAH
married their orphaned niece *, Gen 11:29
arrived that *, the wife of Gen 22:20-23
and his wife *. Gen 24:15,16
the son of *, the wife of Nahor," Gen 24:24
the son of Nahor and his wife *.' Gen 24:47
Tirzah, Hoglah, *, and Noah, were Num 36:11,12
Noah, Hoglah, *, and Tirzah. Jos 17:3

MILCAH,TIRZAH
Mahlah, Noah, Hoglah, *. Num 26:28-37

MILCOM
the Sidonians, and *, the horrible 1Ki 11:5
and *, the god of the Ammonites. 1Ki 11:33
and for *, the evil god of the 2Ki 23:13
the crown from the head of King * 1Ch 20:2
Why then have you, who worship *, Jer 49:1
for your god * shall be exiled Jer 49:3

MILDEW
your crops, covering them with *. Deu 28:22
"I sent blight and * on your Amo 4:9
labor with rust and * and hail. Hag 2:16,17

MILDEWED
But now it was * and falling Jer 13:7

MILE
However, stay about a half * Jos 3:2,3,4
a tenth of a *. Eze 48:17
their gear for a *, carry it two. Mt 5:41
Bethany was a * or so away, Lk 24:50f
walked the half * back to Jerusalem Act 1:12

MILES
* long and 6 Eze 45:1
* wide. It shall all be holy Eze 45:1
* long and 3 Eze 45:3
* wide. All this section shall Eze 45:3
* long and 3 Eze 45:5
* wide, shall be the residence Eze 45:5
* by 1 Eze 45:6
* for a city open to everyone in Eze 45:6
* long and 6 Eze 48:9
* wide. Eze 48:9
* long by 3 Eze 48:10
* wide, north to south, surrounds Eze 48:10
* by 6 Eze 48:13
*. None of this special land Eze 48:13
* long by 1 Eze 48:15
* wide, south of the Temple Eze 48:15
The city itself is to be 1½ * Eze 48:16
and west for three * alongside the Eze 48:18
* square. Eze 48:20
* square on each side of the Eze 48:21,22
on the 1½ * of the west side, Eze 48:34
of the city is six *. Eze 48:35
five * east of Petra, in Edom. Ob 1:8f
only about eight * in Jon 3:3f
about thirty to sixty * across. Jon 3:3f
a city of sixty * around with walls Zep 2:15f
the country and walked the fifty * Mt 15:21
About fifty * away. Mk 7:24f
Emmaus, seven * out of Jerusalem. Lk 24:13
They were three or four * out Jn 6:18,19
Bethany was only a couple of * Jn 11:18
About forty-three * from Rome. Act 28:15f
About thirty-five * from Rome. Act 28:15f
I have traveled many weary * and 2Co 11:26
in a stream 200 * long and as high Rev 14:20
other dimensions—1,500 * each way. Rev 21:16

MILETUS
and a day later we arrived at *. Act 20:15
But when we landed at *, he sent Act 20:17
and I left Trophimus sick at *. 2Ti 4:20

MILITARY
men available for * service from 1Ch 7:5
1,100,000 men of * age in Israel 1Ch 21:5
stop and all * training will end. Is 2:4
of my anger; his * strength is my Is 10:5,6
of Babylonian * officers, outfitted Eze 23:14,15
the aggregate * might of the forces Eze 38:2,3f
lie—believing that * might and Hos 10:13
peace, and all the * academies and Mic 4:3
If the * demand that you carry Mt 5:41
When the captain of the Roman * Lk 23:47
accompanied by * officers and Act 25:23
and high-ranking * officers, and Rev 6:15

MILITIAMEN
and organized *" (Associated Press Rev 9:16f

MILK
Soon, taking them cheese and * Gen 18:8
ewes,20 rams,30 * camels, with Gen 32:13,14,15
and his teeth are whiter than *. Gen 49:12
land 'flowing with * and honey'—the Ex 3:8
land "flowing with * and honey." Ex 3:17
a land 'flowing with * and honey.' Ex 13:4,5
a young goat in its mother's *. Ex 23:19
It is a land 'flowing with * and Ex 33:3
a young goat in its mother's *." Ex 34:26
It is a land 'flowing with * and Lev 20:24
land 'flowing with * and honey.' Num 13:27
a land 'flowing with * and honey'! Num 14:8
land 'flowing with * and honey,' Deu 6:3
land 'flowing with * and honey'! Deu 11:9
a young goat in its mother's *. Deu 14:21
land "flowing with * and honey!" Deu 26:9
make it a land "flowing with * Deu 26:15
land 'flowing with * and Deu 27:2,3,4
land 'flowing with * and honey'—and Deu 31:20
He gave them * and meat— Deu 32:14
that "flowed with * and honey." Jos 5:6
So she gave him some * and Ju 4:19
And she gave him * in a beautiful Ju 5:25
*, and curdled me like cheese. Job 10:10
and goat's * enough for food for Pro 27:25,26,27
I drink my wine with my *." Sol 5:1
yield plenty of *, and everyone Is 7:21,22
of wine and *—it's all free! Is 55:1
* and honey," as it is today. Jer 11:5
that 'flows with * and honey.' Jer 32:22
snow, whiter than *, more ruddy Lam 4:7f
as it were with * and honey, the Eze 20:5,6
a land full of * and honey, the Eze 20:15
and the hills shall flow with *. Joe 3:18
I have had to feed you with * 1Co 3:2
now you still have to be fed on *. 1Co 3:2
allowed to drink some of the *? 1Co 9:7
*, not old enough for solid food. Heb 5:12,13
is still living on * it shows he Heb 5:12,13
for more, as a baby cries for *. 1Pe 2:2,3f
this as a baby cries for his *. 1Pe 2:2,3

MILLING
* about and crushing each other. Lk 12:1
will be no more * of the grain. Rev 18:22

MILLION
"For a * dollars I wouldn't do 2Sa 18:12
and "a * talents of silver." 1Ch 22:14f
a gift of over a * dollars in gold, 2Ch 9:9
twice: Two * Jews perished in the Zec 13:8f
Roman wars, six * under Hitler. Zec 13:8f

MILLIONS
I will give you * of descendants Gen 17:6
thousands and *, like the stars Gen 22:17
you becomeThe mother of many *! Gen 24:60
O Lord, to the * of Israel." Num 10:36
to me than * in silver and gold! Ps 119:71,72
He can become the leader of * of Ecc 4:16
from before him. * of angels Dan 7:10
and hundreds of * of people stood Dan 7:10
"Though he build his army * Nah 1:12
Jews that though there would be * Rom 9:27
and has become the first of * 1Co 15:20
with so many * of people that, like Heb 11:12
is coming with * of his holy ones. Jud 1:14
of * of angels surrounding the Rev 5:11

MILLO
Then, beginning at the old * 2Sa 5:9
his palace, Fort *, the wall of 1Ki 9:15
Then he built Fort *. 1Ki 9:24
rebuilding Fort *, repairing the 1Ki 11:27,28
at * on the road to Silla. 2Ki 12:20
He also reinforced Fort * in the 2Ch 32:5

MILLSTONE
"It is illegal to take a * as a Deu 24:6
woman on the roof threw down a *. Ju 9:53
woman who threw down a * on 2Sa 11:19,20,21
is hard as rock, just like a *. Job 41:24
that man if a huge * were tied Mk 9:42
shaped like a * and threw it into Rev 18:21

MILLSTONES
Take heavy * and grind the corn; Is 47:2

MIMICKED
"Is it a small thing," they *, Num 16:13

MINCE
Jewish women, who * along, noses in Is 3:16

MIND
go and then changing your *." Ex 8:29
so, even then his * remained Ex 9:7
So the Lord changed his * and Ex 32:14
neither change his * about giving Lev 27:10
out the Lord's * concerning him. Num 15:34
He doesn't change his * like Num 23:18-24
these commandments carefully in *. Deu 11:18
(much on Gideon's *: see verse 13) Ju 6:16f
one * before the Lord at Mizpah. Ju 20:1
your * and give me your counsel!" Ju 20:7
she changed her * and said to her Ru 1:8
had made up her * and could not be Ru 1:18
his *, for he is not a man!" 1Sa 15:
But what Saul had in * was that 1Sa 18:
what you have in *," Nathan 2Sa 7
Give me an understanding * so 1Ki 3
I will give you a wiser * than 1Ki 3:
and a * with broad interests. 1Ki 4:
he changed his * and commanded the 1Ch 21:
and a willing *, for the Lord sees 1Ch 28
the other plans he had in *." 1Ch 28:1
O my God, please keep in * all Neh 5:
"Do you know the * and purposes Job 11
who are you? His * is Job 11
my * tastes truth when I hear it. Job 12:
Nevertheless, his * concerning Job 23:1
and don't * spitting in my face. Job 30:
given understanding to the *?" Job 38:3
and disturbed. My * is filled with Ps 6:
But the Lord has made up his * Ps 34:1
Lord, when doubts fill my *, when Ps 94:1
* that if you are blessing me! Ps 109:2
For he is settled in his * that Ps 112:
keep my * upon your promises. Ps 119:9
of heart and * and do not stumble. Ps 119:16
Lord, if you keep in * our sins Ps 130:3,
Keep these thoughts ever in *; Pro 4:2
corners of your * to warn you of Pro 6:2
always keep it in * and stick to Pro 7:
with half a *—if it is only open! Pro 8:
A good man's * is filled with Pro 12:
an evil man's * is crammed with Pro 12:
a man with a warped * is despised. Pro 12:
From a wise * comes careful and Pro 16:2
few words and settled * is wise; Pro 17:27,2
all that goes on in the king's *! Pro 25:2,
give you happiness and peace of *. Pro 29:1
blinded with dismay. My * reels; Is 21:
people and will not change his *. Is 31:
Your * will think back to this Is 33:1
my * and I will not change it." Jer 4:2
in *—to get what isn't theirs. Jer 8:1
put me out of your * and put your Jer 13:24,2
nation changes its * and turns to Jer 18:1
too will change my * and not bless Jer 18:1
King Zedekiah doubtless had in * Jer 21:1
them one heart and * to worship me Jer 32:3
"What you have in * will not be Eze 20:32
thought will have come to your *. Eze 38:10
He told me to keep in * what I Eze 47:6
But Daniel made up his * not to Dan 1:8
* of an animal instead of a man. Dan 4:16
When my * returned to me, so Dan 4:36
called him—for his * is filled with Dan 5:12
But when his heart and * were Dan 5:20
and a man's * was given to it. Dan 7:4
think that I might change my *. Zec 8:14,15
What was in Peter's * is not Mt 17:4f
later he changed his * and went. Mt 21:29
with all your heart, soul, and *.' Mt 22:37
die, changed his * and deeply Mt 27:3
"He's out of his *," they said. Mk 3:21
and soul and * and strength.' Mk 12:30
through Peter's *: "Before the Mk 14:72
strength, and with all your *. Lk 10:27
replied, "You're out of your *! Jn 7:20
with a gift—peace of * and heart! Jn 14:27
will have peace of heart and *. Jn 16:33
of one heart and *, just as you and Jn 17:21
Now change your * and attitude Act 3:19
of one heart and *, and no one felt Act 4:32
it came into his * to visit his Act 7:23
told Moses to * his own business. Act 7:27
"You're out of your *," they Act 12:15
long studying has broken your *!" Act 26:24
God has had in * for us to be. Rom 5:2
is at war with my * and wins the Rom 7:23,24,25
In my * I want to be God's Rom 7:23,24,25
For who among us can know the * Rom 11:34
and great peace of heart and *. 1Co 1:3
I plead with you to be of one *, 1Co 1:10
the very thoughts and * of Christ. 1Co 2:16
well how the human * reasons, and 1Co 3:20
Hadn't I really made up my * yet? 2Co 1:17
welcome and set his * at ease. 2Co 7:13
Every one must make up his own * 2Co 9:7
you don't * at all when they make 2Co 11:19,20
with one heart and * and purpose. Php 2:2
than the human * can understand. Php 4:7
motives or evil purposes in *; 1Th 2:3
With all these things in *, dear 2Th 2:15
you great peace of heart and *. 1Ti 1:2
for his dirty * and rebellious Tit 1:15
never change his *: You are a Heb 7:21
for a doubtful * will be as Jas 1:6
"Change your * and attitude, or Rev 2:16
I gave her time to change her * Rev 2:21
Neither did they change their * Rev 9:21
* and attitude to give him glory. Rev 16:9

MINDED
were more open * than those in Act 17:11
They must be clean * and level Tit 1:8
sensible and clean *, spending Tit 2:5

MINDING
men who are * their own business. Ps 35:20
and to those * their own business. Pro 9:15
live a quiet life, * your own 1Th 4:11

MINDS
to change their *, and keeping them Job 33:17,18
Their * are dull and stupid, but Ps 119:70
closed their * from understanding. Is 44:18
let them banish from their * the Is 55:7
your * and hearts, not just your Jer 4:4
of hearts and *, let me see your Jer 20:12
They changed their * and made Jer 34:11
of Israel are doing in their *? Eze 8:12
thought that comes into your *. Eze 11:5
For I will punish the * and Eze 14:5
Jesus could read their * and said Mk 2:8
* to the wisdom of faith." Lk 1:17
meant, for their * had been sealed Lk 9:45
Then he opened their * to Lk 24:45
their * and decided he was a god. Act 28:6
* became dark and confused. Rom 1:21
their evil * could think of. Rom 1:28
those with changed hearts and *. Rom 2:29
[with all of your hearts and * Rom 7:6
but his people's * and 2Co 3:14
Jewish hearts and * are covered by 2Co 3:14
present in our *, that we work so 2Co 5:11
And if we are in our right *, it 2Co 5:13,14
changing our * about what we Eph 4:14
have shut their * against him, and Eph 4:17,18
their evil * and reckless lusts. Eph 4:19
and peace-filled hearts and *. 2Th 1:2
and that their * will be clean and 1Ti 1:5
These arguers—their * warped by 1Ti 6:5
They have dirty *, warped and 2Ti 3:8
my laws in their * so that they Heb 8:10
instead of relieving their *. Heb 10:3
my laws into their * so that they Heb 10:16
with tender hearts and humble *. 1Pe 3:8
deep within men's hearts, and *; Rev 2:23
a plan into their *, a plan that Rev 17:17

MINED
which you were *, the rock from Is 51:1

MINES
for they are deep within the *. Job 28:8

MINGLE
* there with wolves and hyenas. Is 34:14
My people * with the heathen, Hos 7:8

MINGLED
of sweetened bread * with oil, and Ex 29:2
yeast, and * with olive oil. Lev 2:5
Literally, "unleavened loaves * Lev 7:12f
offering—flour * with olive oil. Lev 9:4
or frankincense * with it—for it is Num 5:15
of fine flour * with oil, along Num 8:8
of fine flour * with oil shall be Num 29:3,4
of fine flour * with oil for each Num 29:14
there today, * with the Israelis. Ju 1:21
and the weeping * together in a Ez 3:13
told them to, but * in among the Ps 106:35

MINIAMIN
were Eden, *, Jeshua, Shemaiah, 2Ch 31:14,15
of the Moadiah and * Neh 12:12-21
Eliakim, Ma-aseiah, *, Neh 12:40,41

MINIATURE
in the form of * staircases, so 2Ki 20:11f

MINISTER
to be priests, to * to me. Ex 28:1
* to me in the priest's office. Ex 28:3
he goes in to * to the Lord; Ex 28:35
beginning to * in the Tabernacle Ex 29:30
that they can * to me as priests. Ex 30:30
so that they can * as priests; Ex 31:10
him to * to me as a priest. Ex 40:13
that they may * to me as priests; Ex 40:15
been appointed to * to the Lord as Lev 7:35
set apart to * at the Tabernacle. Num 3:3
before the people to * to them? Num 16:8,9
all the tribes, to * to the Lord Deu 18:5
at any time and * in the name of Deu 18:6,7
has chosen them to * before him and Deu 21:5
they are to * to him forever." 1Ch 15:2
of the Levites to * before the Ark 1Ch 16:4
to * regularly at the Tabernacle, 1Ch 16:37
to * to the Lord there. 1Ch 16:39
responsible to * at the Temple. 1Ch 26:12
to * to him and to burn incense." 2Ch 29:11
who * in the Temple of our God. Neh 10:36
the Agagite), as prime *. Est 3:1
Mordecai, [appointing him Prime * Est 8:2
Mordecai the Jew was the Prime * Est 10:3
who was the prime * of Israel, and Is 36:3
the prime *, and Shebna, the royal Is 36:22
Eliakim his prime *, and Shebna his Is 37:2
who * to me will be multiplied. Jer 33:22
near to the Lord to * to him." Eze 40:46
They shall not come near me to * Eze 44:13
and come to my Table to * to me; Eze 44:16
the priests, who * in the Eze 45:4
and human hands can't * to his Act 17:25
worker, God's *, to visit you to 1Th 3:2,3
truth—as God's * and missionary to 1Ti 2:7
But Christ, as a * in heaven, Heb 8:6

MINISTERED
This robe was worn when Aaron * Ex 39:25,26
Millions of angels * to him and Dan 7:10
Literally, "* unto them." Mt 8:15f
his followers had * to him when he Mk 15:41
Literally, "* unto them." Lk 4:39f

MINISTERING
be used when * in the Holy Place; Ex 35:10-19
be used while * in the Holy Place. Ex 39:1
to be worn while * in the Holy Ex 39:41
* to the Lord and to his people. 2Ch 35:3
for use by the * priests, the Neh 10:39,40
they have been * must first be Eze 42:14
they wear while * to me, leaving Eze 44:19

MINISTERS
them as the priests, my *. Ex 28:41
sons who are my *, the priests. Ex 29:44
along with prime * and kings with Job 3:14,15
priests of the Lord, * of our God. Is 61:6
priests, my *, is non-cancelable. Jer 33:20,21
tribe, who are my *, are to be Eze 43:19
These men shall be my *; Eze 44:15
Hear the crying of these * of Joe 1:9
in sackcloth. O * of my God, lie Joe 1:13
The priests, the * of God, will Joe 2:17
He will purify the Levites, the * Mal 3:3
to show that we are true * of God. 2Co 6:4
do it too, and seem like godly *. 2Co 11:15
lives because they are God's *. Tit 1:7
God himself. He * in the temple in Heb 8:2

MINISTRY
these men to their * by anointing Ex 28:41
Levites could carry on their *. Ex 38:21
assigned to the * at the Temple. 1Ch 23:24
Their music * included the 1Ch 25:6,7
this * in the Tabernacle. 1Ch 25:6,7
priests and Levites and their *. Neh 12:44
wide * of teaching in those days. Dan 11:33
about John's * centuries before! Mt 3:3
he began his public * to Israel. Lk 1:80
old when he began his public *. Lk 3:23-38
soon begin his * among you, and I Jn 1:27
Jesus now stopped his public * Jn 11:54
had been doing through their *. Act 15:4
fully accomplished my Gospel *." Rom 15:19f
your share in this * of giving. 2Co 8:6

MINNI
bring out the armies of Ararat, * Jer 51:27

MINNITH
way from Aroer to *, including Ju 11:33
with wheat from * and Pannag, Eze 27:17
Or, "with wheat, * and pannag." Eze 27:17f

MINOR
"These are some of the * things Job 26:14
Tubal were in Asia * and Armenia. Is 66:19f
Regions of Asia *, now in Turkey. Eze 27:13f
Regions of Asia *, now in Turkey. Eze 27:14f
will be an unimportant, * kingdom. Eze 29:14
of Syria and Asia *, and Antipater Dan 8:8f
Those exiled in Asia * shall Ob 1:20
tyrants and each * official lords Mt 20:25

MINT
For you tithe down to the last * Mt 23:23

MINUTE
"I want to talk to you a *." Ru 4:1
Enjoy every * of it! Ecc 11:9
But wait a *! Rom 2:1

MINUTES
*' rest over there in the shade." Ru 2:7
A few * later some Pharisees said Lk 13:31

MIRACLE
believe the first *, they will the Ex 4:8
* to prove that God has sent you; Ex 7:9
and performed the *, as Jehovah had Ex 7:10
saw the mighty * the Lord had done Ex 14:31
But if the Lord does a * and the Num 16:30
"the Lord will do a great *." Jos 3:5
of Israel of this amazing *." Jos 4:7
This * occurred on the 25th of Jos 4:19
of this amazing *—that the nation Jos 4:22
that, then do some * to prove it! Ju 6:17
"Perhaps the Lord will do a * 1Sa 14:6
of God to do a mighty * today." 1Sa 14:45
to Isaiah, "Do a * to prove to me 2Ki 20:8
and the Lord replied with a *. 2Ch 32:24
find out about the * of his being 2Ch 32:31
has done this wonderful * for me. Ps 116:7
Everyone will see this * and Is 41:20
Or do some mighty * that makes us Is 41:23
sprout up. This * will make the Is 55:13
I will perform a mighty * Is 66:19
That mighty * will scarcely be Jer 16:14,15
do a mighty * as in olden times Jer 21:1
It was incredible—a mighty *! Dan 4:3
The Lord has done a mighty * for Joe 2:20
The report of this wonderful * Mt 9:26
heard about the * they said, "He Mt 12:24
Jesus asking him to show them a *. Mt 12:38
the * that happened to Jonah." Mt 16:4
after the * the evening before! Mk 6:52
"Do a * for us," they said. Mk 8:11
the prophet used a * to help the Lk 4:25,26
everyone about Jesus' mighty *. Lk 8:39
give them is a * like that of Lk 11:29,30
hoping to see him perform a *. Lk 23:8
This * at Cana in Galilee was Jn 2:11
God, show us a * to prove it." Jn 2:18
"this is the * I will do for you: Jn 2:19
This was Jesus' second * in Jn 4:54
the Sabbath when this * was done. Jn 5:9
what a great * had happened, they Jn 6:14
done many a * to help the people. Jn 10:32
* from God if you believe?" Jn 11:40
had heard about this mighty *. Jn 12:18
done a tremendous *, and everybody Act 4:16
for this wonderful *— the healing Act 4:21
And by a * 1Co 10:3,4
All the world marveled at this * Rev 13:3

MIRACLE-WORKING
These * demons conferred with Rev 16:14

MIRACLES
I will destroy Egypt with my *, Ex 3:20
perform the * I have shown you." Ex 4:17
Pharaoh and do the * I have shown Ex 4:21
the * they must do before Pharaoh. Ex 4:28
performed the * as they watched. Ex 4:30
and perform great * to deliver them Ex 6:6
my * in the land of Egypt. Ex 7:3
do more * demonstrating my power. Ex 10:1
* to demonstrate my power." Ex 11:9
Aaron did these * right before Ex 11:10
has brought you out with mighty *. Ex 13:3
them, 'With mighty * Jehovah Ex 13:14
such great power and mighty *? Ex 32:11
I will do * such as have never Ex 34:10
all the * I have done among them? Num 14:10,11
my glory and the * I did both in Num 14:22
with his mighty *, just as you saw Deu 1:30
May his * have a deep and Deu 4:9
about the glorious * he did. Deu 4:9
mighty *, war, and terror? Deu 4:34
you out with a great display of *. Deu 5:15
power and mighty *—with terrible Deu 6:22
such amazing power and mighty *. Deu 7:8
the mighty * and wonders, and the Deu 7:19
mighty * you yourselves have seen. Deu 10:21
They weren't there to see the * Deu 11:3
you have seen these mighty *! Deu 11:7
with mighty * and a powerful hand. Deu 26:8
He did great and awesome * before Deu 26:8
plagues and mighty * that the Lord Deu 29:2,3
* which have never been equaled. Deu 34:11,12
He is the God who did mighty * Jos 24:17
* the Lord had done for Israel. Ju 2:7-9
mighty * he had done for Israel. Ju 2:10
And where are all the * our Ju 6:13
thing and done these *." Ju 13:23
watch as the Lord does great *. 1Sa 12:16
You have done great * to destroy 2Sa 7:23
name and mighty *) and pray toward 1Ki 8:41,42
with such tremendous * and power. 2Ki 17:35,36
Remember his mighty * 1Ch 16:12,13
And his marvelous * 1Ch 16:12,13
Tell everyone about his *. 1Ch 16:24
you did glorious * in driving out 1Ch 17:21
You displayed great * against Neh 9:10
to the * you did for them; Neh 9:17
For he does wonderful *, marvels Job 5:9
"He does incredible *, too many Job 9:10
consider the wonderful * of God. Job 37:14
hear of all the * he did for us. Ps 22:31
and telling about your *. Ps 26:7
have done great * for us, and we Ps 40:5
* you did in the days of long ago. Ps 44:1
the greatness of the * of God; Ps 64:9
What marvelous * happen to his Ps 66:5
too) about all your mighty *. Ps 71:18
Your mighty * give proof that you Ps 75:1
I recall the many * he did for Ps 77:11
You are the God of * and Ps 77:14
them about the mighty * he did. Ps 78:4
God and not forget his glorious *. Ps 78:7
the wonderful * God had done for Ps 78:11,12
and refused to believe in *. Ps 78:32
Where are their *? Ps 86:8
For you are great, and do great *. Ps 86:10
Of what use are your * when I am Ps 88:10
Can the darkness speak of your * Ps 88:12
All heaven shall praise your *, O Ps 89:5
Let us see your * again; Ps 90:16
O Lord, what * you do! Ps 92:5
had seen so many of my * before. Ps 95:9
and tell everyone about his *. Ps 105:2
him, to call down * of terror upon Ps 105:27
Who can ever list the glorious * Ps 106:2
the wonder of your * in Egypt, and Ps 106:7
mighty * in Egypt and at the Sea. Ps 106:21,22
thanks to God for his mighty *. Ps 111:1
For his * demonstrate his honor, Ps 111:3
for then I shall see your *. Ps 119:27

(MIRACLES Con't)
He did great * in Egypt before Ps 135:9
alone does mighty *, for his Ps 136:4
I remember the glorious * you did Ps 143:5
glory, splendor, majesty and *. Ps 145:5
They will tell about your * and Ps 145:12
as I perform my *, still you won't Is 6:9
wisdom and do great and mighty *; Jer 32:19
to do great * in Israel and all Jer 32:20
* and great power and terror. Jer 32:21
he does great * in heaven and Dan 6:27
Lord, who does these * for you. Joe 2:26
"I will do mighty * for you, like Mic 7:15
The report of his * spread far Mt 4:24
and to do many other great *.' Mt 7:22
about all the * the Messiah was Mt 11:2
tell him about the * you've seen me Mt 11:4
done most of his *, because they Mt 11:20
For if the * I did in your Mt 11:21
For if the marvelous * I did in Mt 11:23
spreading the news about his *. Mt 12:16
with his wisdom and his *. Mt 13:53,54
only a few great * there, because Mt 13:58
That is why he can do these *." Mt 14:2
these wonderful *, and heard even Mt 21:15
will do wonderful *, so that if it Mt 24:24
For the news about his * had Mk 3:7,8
saying he did his * by Satan's Mk 3:30
the wonderful * Jesus did, and that Mk 5:27
his wisdom and his * because he was Mk 6:2,3
do any mighty * among them except Mk 6:5
* were talked about everywhere. Mk 6:14
"No wonder he can do such *." Mk 6:14
How many more * do you people Mk 8:12
"For no one doing * in my name Mk 9:39
will do wonderful * that would Mk 13:22
* that followed their messages. Mk 16:20
'Why don't you do * here in your Lk 4:23
When reports of Jesus' * reached Lk 9:7
For if the * I did for you had Lk 10:13
* of healing today and tomorrow; Lk 13:32
the wonderful * Jesus had done. Lk 19:36,37
who did incredible * and was a Lk 24:19
"It isn't yet my time for *." Jn 2:4
Because of the * he did in Jn 2:23
Your * are proof enough of this." Jn 3:1
and had seen some of his *. Jn 4:45
me unless I do more and more *?" Jn 4:48
awesome * than this man's healing. Jn 5:20
I refer to the * I do; Jn 5:36
must show us more * if you want us Jn 6:30,31
more people can see your *!" Jn 7:3
they said, "what * do you expect Jn 7:31
an ordinary sinner do such *?" Jn 9:16
"The proof is in the * I do in Jn 10:25
Don't believe me unless I do * Jn 10:37
"John didn't do *," they Jn 10:41
"For this man certainly does *. Jn 11:47
But despite all the * he had Jn 12:37
Who will accept God's mighty * as Jn 12:38
the mighty * you have seen me do. Jn 14:11
shall do the same * I have done, Jn 14:12,13
If I hadn't done such mighty * Jn 15:24
But as it is, they saw these * Jn 15:24
him do many other * besides the Jn 20:30,31
about the mighty * of God!" Act 2:11
* through him, as you well know. Act 2:22
all, and the apostles did many *. Act 2:43
power, and may * and wonders be Act 4:30
remarkable * among the people. Act 5:12
did spectacular * among the Act 6:8
of many remarkable * he led them Act 7:36
to say because of the * he did. Act 8:6
and was amazed by the * he did. Act 8:13
giving them power to do great *. Act 14:3
told about the * God had done Act 15:12
to do unusual *, so that even when Act 19:11
them, and by the * done through me Rom 15:19
He gives power for doing * to 1Co 12:10
Those who do *, 1Co 12:28
everyone have the power to do *? 1Co 12:29
Spirit and work * among you as a Gal 3:5
and will do great *. 2Th 2:9
and various * and by giving certain Heb 2:4
his mighty * for them to see. Heb 3:9
He did unbelievable * such as Rev 13:13
By doing these *, he was Rev 13:14
who could do mighty * when the Rev 19:20
was present—* that deceived all who Rev 19:20

MIRACULOUSLY
Many times you have * rescued Ps 18:50
of Israel were * brought through Zec 10:11f

MIRE
rushes without any * to grow in; Job 8:11-13
the bog and the *, and set my feet Ps 40:2
Deeper and deeper I sink in the * Ps 69:1
Pull me out of this *. Ps 69:14
but always churns up * and dirt. Is 57:20
a thick layer of * at the bottom, Jer 38:6

MIRIAM
Then * the prophetess, the sister Ex 15:20
And * sang this song: Ex 15:21
ONE DAY * and Aaron were Num 12:1
Moses, Aaron, and * to the Num 12:3,4
"Aaron and *, step forward," he Num 12:5
the Tabernacle, * suddenly became Num 12:10
So * was excluded from the camp Num 12:15
and camped at Kadesh, where * Num 20:1
parents of Aaron, Moses, and *. Num 26:58,59
* as you were coming from Egypt. Deu 24:9
She was the mother of *, Shammai, 1Ch 4:17
Aaron, Moses, *. 1Ch 6:3
I gave you Moses, Aaron, and * to Mic 6:4

MIRMAH
Jeuz, Sachia, *. 1Ch 8:8,9,10

MIRROR
* of the skies as he does? Job 37:18
A * reflects a man's face, but Pro 27:19
at his reflection in a poor *; 1Co 13:12
a man looking at his face in a *; Jas 1:23

MIRRORS
the solid bronze * donated by the Ex 38:8
their *, lovely lingerie, Is 3:23
we can be * that brightly reflect 2Co 3:18

MIRTH
lived each day in * and luxury. Lk 16:19

MISAPPLY
A rebel will * an illustration so Pro 26:9

MISCARRIAGE
so that she has a *, but she lives, Ex 21:22
no longer cause death or *." 2Ki 2:21
by the rich, with * of justice Ecc 5:8

MISCARRIAGES
There will be no * nor Ex 23:26
and causes our women to have *." 2Ki 2:19

MISCELLANEOUS
and flocks and a lot of * booty. Num 31:9,10,11
of the labor forces.* Notes: 1Ki 9:23
1,000 * items. Ez 1:9,10

MISCHIEF
"A worthless man devises *; Pro 16:27f

MISDIRECTED
honor of God, but it is * zeal. Rom 10:2

MISERABLE
have been spared this * existence. Job 10:19
What * comforters all of you are. Job 16:2
But my dishonesty made me * and Ps 32:3
I will make your hearts * for all Mic 6:13
I would be utterly *. 1Co 9:16
we are the most * of creatures. 1Co 15:19
* and poor and blind and naked. Rev 3:17

MISERIES
and war and its * are decreed from Dan 9:26

MISERY
and he was grieved by their *. Ju 10:16
" 'Come and put me out of my *,' 2Sa 1:9
their pleasure and are in great *. Neh 9:37
given to those in * and bitterness, Job 3:20,21
not themselves! * comes upon them Job 5:6
Mankind heads for sin and * as Job 5:7
Even when I try to forget my * Job 7:13,14
Only then can you forget your *. Job 11:16
in proportion to our former *! Ps 90:15
death, crushed by * and slavery? Ps 107:10
to forget their poverty and *. Pro 31:6,7
behind a trail of * and death. Is 59:7
the sheep bleat in *. Joe 1:18
but, oh, the * ahead for the man Mk 14:21
was great * for our ancestors. Act 7:11
Wherever they go they leave * and Rom 3:16

MISFORTUNE
overcome by * that strips them bare Ps 35:26
have rejoiced in the day of his *; Ob 1:12

MISFORTUNES
their *, and the Lord heard them. Num 11:1
those who rejoice at others' *. Pro 17:5

MISGUIDED
blithely follow their own * ideas. 2Ti 4:4

MISHA-EL
The sons of Uzziel:*, Elzaphan, Ex 6:22
Then Moses called for * and Lev 10:4
To his left were Pedaiah, *, Neh 8:1
Daniel, Hananiah, *, and Azariah Dan 1:6
Hananiah was called Shadrach;* was Dan 1:7
Daniel, Hananiah, *, and Azariah, Dan 1:11
Daniel, Hananiah, *, and Azariah. Dan 1:18,19
*, and Azariah, his companions. Dan 2:17

MISHAL
Allammelech, Amad, and *. Jos 19:24,25,26
*, Abdon, Helkath, and Rehob. Jos 21:30,31

MISHAM
Eber, *, 1Ch 8:12

MISHMA
Abdeel,Mibsam, *, Dumah,Massa, Gen 25:12-15
Adbeel, Mibsam, *, Dumah, Massa, 1Ch 1:28-31
great-grandson was *. 1Ch 4:25

MISHMA'S
* sons included Hammu-el (the 1Ch 4:26

MISHMANNAH
* was fourth in command; 1Ch 12:8-13

MISHNEH
Asaiah went to the * section of 2Ki 22:14

MISHRAITES
and the * (from whom descended the 1Ch 2:53

MISINTERPRETING
For you are * the whole thing. Job 13:4

MISLEAD
"Don't let anyone * you," he Mk 13:5
He replied, "Don't let anyone * Lk 21:8

MISLEADERS
True leaders? No, *! Is 3:12

MISLED
Don't be *; Gal 6:7
we were * by others and became Tit 3:3
So don't be *, dear brothers. Jas 1:16

MISPAR
Mordecai, Bilshan, *, Bigvai, Ez 2:2

MISPERETH
Mordecai, Bilshan, *; Neh 7:7

MISREAM
Cush, *, Canaan, and 1Ch 1:5-9
named after the sons of * were: 1Ch 1:11,12

MISREPHOTH-MAIM
from Lebanon to *, including all Jos 13:2-7

MISS
"Whose daughter are you, *?" Gen 24:23
"Yes, they will * you tomorrow 1Sa 20:18
I ought to turn to * the traps my Ps 142:3
not one detail will he *; Is 34:16
even the most stupid cannot * the Is 35:8
they do not *! Jer 50:9
His parents didn't * him the Lk 2:43

MISSED
he disappears, he isn't even *! Job 8:18
Like a crooked arrow, they * the Ps 78:57
How we * your presence, Lord! Is 26:17
Those days will not be * or even Jer 3:16
pick what he has *, so the remnant Jer 6:9
But these teachers have * this 1Ti 1:6
Some of these people have * the 1Ti 6:21

MISSES
But the one who * me has injured Pro 8:36
crooked bow that always * targets; Hos 7:16

MISSING
to battle, and not one of us is *! Num 31:48,49
within a hair's breadth, never *! Ju 20:16
that now one of our tribes is *?" Ju 21:3
men were *, in addition to Asahel. 2Sa 2:30
night my lover was * from my bed. Sol 3:1
perfectly matched, without one *. Sol 4:2
perfectly matched and not one *. Sol 6:6
with * arms and legs had new ones; Mt 15:31
that his body was *, and that they Lk 24:22,23
just as we are, with none *. Jn 17:11
no sin in him, no * of God's will 1Jn 3:5

MISSION
you and make your * successful. Gen 24:40
to make my * a success, please Gen 24:42
the Lord has made my * Gen 24:56
Damascus on this *, suddenly a Act 9:3
"I was on such a * to Damascus, Act 26:12

MISSIONARIES
who escape, as * to the Is 66:19
as his "apostles," or "*." Lk 6:13
and * who are passing through. 3Jn 1:5

MISSIONARY
and going as a * among the Jews in Jn 7:35
chosen to be a *, and sent out to Rom 1:1
*, and from brother Sosthenes. 1Co 1:1
FROM: PAUL THE * and all the other Gal 1:1
I was not called to be a * by any Gal 1:1
FROM: PAUL, A * of Jesus Christ, 1Ti 1:1
God's minister and * to teach this 1Ti 2:7
FROM: PAUL, JESUS Christ's *, sent 2Ti 1:1
me to be his *, to preach to the 2Ti 1:11
FROM: PETER, JESUS Christ's *. 1Pe 1:1
FROM: SIMON PETER, a servant and * 2Pe 1:1
to welcome the * travelers himself, 3Jn 1:10

MIST
they are gone like morning * at Is 44:22
He causes * to rise upon the Jer 10:13
like morning *, like dew that Hos 13:3
Instantly * and darkness fell upon Act 13:11

MISTAKE
*, and take your brother and go. Gen 43:12
"If by * you or future Num 15:22
makes the '*,' whether he is a Num 15:30
I think Ahithophel has made a *. 2Sa 17:7
When King Hanun realized his * 1Ch 19:6
see their * and leave him. 2Ch 18:31
this turned out to be a fatal *; 2Ch 22:7
life, and notice every * I make. Job 14:16
it was all a * [to make the vow Ecc 5:6,7
Yes, a small * can outweigh much Ecc 10:1
and discovers his *, he goes back Jer 8:4,5
the diviners make this terrible *? Eze 21:23
a * and I do not feel his sadness? 2Co 11:29

MISTAKEN
Well, you are *! 1Co 14:36

MISTAKENLY
Once I * thought of Christ that 2Co 5:16

MISTAKES
even angels make *), how much less Job 4:18,19

(MISTAKES Con't)
He knows that anger causes *. Pro 14:29
there need be no *. Pro 16:10
Love forgets *; Pro 17:9
A man who refuses to admit his * Pro 28:13
before it, can make serious *. Ecc 11:10
making stupid errors and *. Is 28:7
and honest, and made no *. Dan 6:4
to cover his own * and sins, and Heb 9:7
the * and sins of all the people. Heb 9:7
for we all make many *; Jas 3:1
away by the * of these wicked men, 2Pe 3:17

MISTER
"Be careful how you talk, *," Ju 18:25

MISTREAT
you * your own people like this? Ex 5:22

MISTREATED
But the more the Egyptians * and Ex 1:12
The Egyptians * us and we cried Deu 26:6,7
and was badly * by many. Mt 17:12
And that he had been terribly *, Mk 9:12,13
Share the sorrow of those being * Heb 13:3

MISTREATING
saw an Egyptian * a man of Israel. Act 7:24

MISTREATMENT
Why not just accept * and leave 1Co 6:7

MISTREATS
A son who * his father or mother Pro 19:26
If someone * you because you are Rom 12:14

MISTRESS
and arrogant toward her * Sarai. Gen 16:4
"I am running away from my *." Gen 16:8
The Angel: "Return to your * and Gen 16:9-12
girl said to her *, "I wish my 2Ki 5:3
her * for the slightest signal. Ps 123:2
A servant girl who marries her *' Pro 30:21,22,23
Literally, "who succeeds her *." Pro 30:21,22,23f
faithless city, * of deadly charms, Nah 3:4

MISTRESSES
slave girls and *, buyers and Is 24:2

MISTS
He makes * rise throughout the Ps 135:7

MISUNDERSTAND
"Don't * why I have come—it Mt 5:17
They tried to *, Rom 1:31

MISUNDERSTANDING
for I don't want any * about them. 1Co 12:1
For this veil of * can be removed 2Co 3:14

MISUNDERSTOOD
Some of the bystanders * and Mt 27:47
Greek and Latin, * his first two Mk 15:34f

MISUSE
of the Lord your God to * it." Deu 5:11f

MISUSED
And they * my Sabbaths. Eze 20:13

MITHKAH
From Terah to *; Num 33:15-37
From * to Hashmonah; Num 33:15-37

MITHNA
Joshaphat from *; 1Ch 11:26-47

MITHREDATH
He instructed *, the treasurer Ez 1:8
Bishlam, *, and Tabe-el and their Ez 4:7

MITYLENE
there and we sailed together to *; Act 20:14

MIX
"Quick! * up some pancakes! Gen 18:6
from the altar and * it with some Ex 29:21
He must not * it with olive oil Lev 5:11
in a clay jar and * into it dust Num 5:17
Be sure that you do not * with Jos 23:7
he could watch her * some dough; 2Sa 13:8
and spelt. * the various kinds of Eze 4:9
gallon of oil with which to * it. Eze 46:14,15
for iron and clay don't *. Dan 2:43
I said not to * with evil people. 1Co 5:9
They didn't * it with faith. Heb 4:2
given to him to * with the prayers Rev 8:3

MIXED
Literally, "a * multitude." Ex 12:38f
ground flour * with 2½ pints of Ex 29:40
of fine flour * with olive oil. Lev 2:7
the bruised grain * with oil and Lev 2:16
and the incense * into it, and burn Lev 6:15
offerings, whether * with olive oil Lev 7:10
batter of flour * with olive oil. Lev 7:12
ground flour * with olive oil, and Lev 14:10
fine white flour, * with olive oil, Lev 14:21
of children of * blood—half Lev 21:14,15
ground flour * with olive oil, to Lev 23:13
pancakes made of fine flour * Num 6:15
of fine flour * with oil. Num 7:13
of fine flour * with three pints of Num 15:3,4
of fine flour * with four pints of Num 15:6
of fine flour * with three quarts Num 15:8,9
flour * with three pints of oil. Num 28:5
of fine flour * with oil, and the Num 28:9,10
ground flour * with oil as a grain Num 28:12
ground flour * with oil as a grain Num 28:12
* with oil for a grain offering. Num 28:13
quarts of fine flour * with oil; Num 28:20,21
of fine flour * with oil with each Num 28:28,29
Nine quarts of fine flour * with Num 29:9,10
fried or * with olive oil); 1Ch 23:29
polluted by these * marriages, and Ez 9:2
great banquet, and * the wines, Pro 9:2
and drink the wines that I have *. Pro 9:5
Once like sterling silver; now * Is 1:22
made of flour * from wheat, barley, Eze 4:9
times, they have * their wonderful 2Co 8:2
who are * up concerning the truth. 2Ti 2:25
you yourselves become * up too. 2Pe 3:17
And the perfume of the incense * Rev 8:4
and hail and fire * with blood were Rev 8:7

MIXES
of flour and * in the yeast until Mt 13:33

MIXTURE
This * of iron with clay also Dan 2:43

MIXTURES
in the taverns, trying out new *. Pro 23:29,30

MIZAR
Mount Hermon and Mount * stand. Ps 42:6

MIZPAH
called "The Watchtower" (*). Gen 31:49
of Mount Hermon, in the land of *. Jos 11:1
and eastward into the valley of *; Jos 11:8
to attack Israel's army at *. Ju 10:17
before the Lord in * at a general Ju 11:11
and Manasseh, past * in Gilead, and Ju 11:29
one mind before the Lord at *. Ju 20:1
Israeli forces at * soon reached Ju 20:3
had vowed at * never to let their Ju 21:1
council before the Lord at *?" Ju 21:5
refused to come to *, and Ju 21:8,9
them, "Come to *, all of you, and 1Sa 7:5
So it was at * that Samuel became 1Sa 7:6
great crowds at *, they mobilized 1Sa 7:7
chased them from * to Beth-car, 1Sa 7:11
placed it between * and Jeshanah 1Sa 7:12
Gilgal, and then *, and cases of 1Sa 7:16
of all Israel at *, and gave them 1Sa 10:17
in Benjamin and the city of *. 1Ki 15:22
and their men joined him at *. 2Ki 25:23
line, went to * with ten men and 2Ki 25:25
them to build Geba and * instead. 2Ch 16:6
and men from Gibeon and *, who Neh 3:7
the mayor of the * district, Neh 3:15
the mayor of another part of *; Neh 3:19
at *, where his headquarters were. Jer 40:8
As for me, I will stay at * and Jer 40:10
They stopped at * to discuss Jer 40:12
leaders came to * to warn Gedaliah Jer 40:13,14
in *, accompanied by ten men. Jer 41:1
who were in * with Gedaliah. Jer 41:3
men approached * from Shechem, Jer 41:5
when he fortified * to protect Jer 41:9
at the site of ancient *. Jer 41:9f
Gedaliah's care in * by Jer 41:10
with idols at * and Tabor, and dug Hos 5:1

MIZPEH
Dilean, *, Jokthe-el, Lachish, Jos 15:37-44
Ramah, Be-eroth, *, Chephirah, Jos 18:21-28
(Later David went to * in Moab to 1Sa 22:3

MIZRAIM
The sons of Ham were:Cush, *,Put, Gen 10:6
* was the ancestor Gen 10:13,14

MIZZAH
were:Nahath, Zerah, Shammah, *. Gen 36:13,14
clan of Shammah,The clan of *. Gen 36:17
Nahath, Zerah, Shammah, and *. 1Ch 1:37

MNASON
at the home of *, originally from Act 21:16

MOAB
The older girl's baby was named *; Gen 19:37
army of Midian when it invaded *. Gen 36:31-39
The mighty men of * tremble; Ex 15:15
distance east of *, and from there Num 21:11
the Amorites and the people of *. Num 21:15
in the plateau of *, which Num 21:20
The city of Ar in *, Num 21:27-30
Woe to *! Num 21:27-30
to the plains of * and camped east Num 22:1
When King Balak of * (the son of Num 22:2,3
the top leaders of * and Midian. Num 22:7
King Balak of *," he replied. Num 22:10
with all the princes of *. Num 23:6
"King Balak, king of *, has Num 23:7-10
and the princes of * were standing Num 23:17
Shall smite the people of *, Num 24:15-19
the worship of Baal, the god of *; Num 25:3
in the plains of * beside the Num 26:3,4
in the plains of * beside the Num 26:63
on the plains of * beside the Num 31:12
Iyeabarim (at the border of *). Num 33:44
to the plains of * beside the river Num 33:48
Abel-shittim, on the plains of *. Num 33:49
on the plains of *, opposite Num 35:1
on the plains of * beside the Num 36:13
of *, east of the Jordan River. Deu 1:1
northward toward the * desert. Deu 2:8
the borders of * at Ar, into the Deu 2:18
IT WAS ON the plains of * that Deu 29:1
the land of * across from Jericho. Deu 32:49
from the plains of * to Pisgah Peak Deu 34:1
land of * as the Lord had said. Deu 34:5
near Beth-Peor in *, but no one Deu 34:6
thirty days on the plains of *. Deu 34:8
Then King Balak of * started a Jos 24:9
King Eglon of * to conquer part of Ju 3:12
Jordan River near *, preventing Ju 3:28
one escape. So * was conquered by Ju 3:30
Sidon, *, Ammon and Philistia. Ju 10:6
Then they asked the king of * for Ju 11:17
around Edom and * through the Ju 11:18
boundary of * at the Arnon River; Ju 11:18
they never once crossed into *. Ju 11:18
than King Balak, the king of *? Ju 11:25
famine and moved to the land of *. Ru 1:1
girls of *, Orpah and Ruth. Ru 1:4,5
(Their return from * and arrival Ru 1:22
of * who came back with Naomi. Ru 2:6
Naomi, who came back to us from *. Ru 4:3
the Philistines and the king of *. 1Sa 12:9
direction against *, Ammon, Edom, 1Sa 14:47
(Later David went to Mizpeh in * 1Sa 22:3
They stayed in * during the 1Sa 22:4
He also devastated the land of * 2Sa 8:2
taken from Syria, *, Ammon, the 2Sa 8:11,12
sons of Ariel of *. 2Sa 23:20
—*, Ammon, Edom, Sidon, and from 1Ki 11:1
depraved god of *, and another for 1Ki 11:7
and Chemosh, the god of *; 1Ki 11:33
the nation of * declared its 2Ki 1:1
King Mesha of * and his people 2Ki 3:4
king of * rebelled against Israel. 2Ki 3:5
"The king of * has rebelled 2Ki 3:6,7,8
to let the king of * defeat us." 2Ki 3:10
be destroyed by the king of *!" 2Ki 3:13
you victorious over the army of *! 2Ki 3:18
Meanwhile, when the people of * 2Ki 3:21
and the army of * fled. 2Ki 3:24
into the land of *, destroying 2Ki 3:24
When the king of * saw that the 2Ki 3:26
for Chemosh, the evil god of *; 2Ki 23:13
in the fields of *—became king and 1Ch 1:46
Saraph (who was a ruler in * 1Ch 4:21-22
land of * by Hodesh, his new wife: 1Ch 8:8,9,10
from *. He also killed a lion in 1Ch 11:22
Ithmah from *; 1Ch 11:26-47
He also conquered * and required 1Ch 18:2
nations of Edom, *, Ammon, Amalek, 1Ch 18:11
of the kings of *, Ammon, and of 2Ch 20:1
*, and Mount Seir are doing. 2Ch 20:10
armies of Ammon, *, and Mount Seir 2Ch 20:22
was Shimrith, a woman from *. 2Ch 24:26
Ashdod, Ammon, and *, and that Neh 13:23
great warriors. * shall become my Ps 60:8
Judah is my scepter. But * and Ps 108:9
Literally, "* is my washbasin; Ps 108:9f
nations of Edom and * and Ammon. Is 11:14
HERE IS GOD'S message to *: Is 15:1
The bravest warriors of * cry in Is 15:4
My heart weeps for *! Is 15:5
The whole land of * is a land of Is 15:8
The women of * are left at the Is 16:2
Is this proud *, concerning which Is 16:6
Therefore all * weeps. Is 16:7
Therefore all Moab weeps. Yes, * Is 16:7
'I will weep, weep, weep, for *; Is 16:11
The people of * will pray in Is 16:12
All this concerning * has been Is 16:13,14
fail, the glory of * shall be Is 16:13,14
Jerusalem, and * will be crushed as Is 25:10
The high walls of * will be Is 25:12
the nations of Edom, * and Ammon; Jer 25:21
the kings of Edom, *, Ammon, Tyre Jer 27:3
When the Jews in * and among the Jer 40:11
the God of Israel, against *: Jer 48:1
No one will ever brag of * any Jer 48:2,3,4
for all * is being destroyed. Jer 48:2,3,4
Oh, for wings for * that she Jer 48:9
From her earliest history * has Jer 48:11
Then at last * shall be ashamed Jer 48:13
But now * is to be destroyed; Jer 48:15
Calamity is coming fast to *. Jer 48:16
O friends of *, weep for her and Jer 48:17
those destroying * shall shatter Jer 48:18
*, "What has happened there?" Jer 48:19
And they reply, "* lies in Jer 48:20
the Arnon, that * is destroyed." Jer 48:20
of the land of *, far and near. Jer 48:24
The strength of * is ended—her Jer 48:25
against the Lord. * shall wallow in Jer 48:26
O people of *, flee from your Jer 48:28
pride of *, for it is very great. Jer 48:29
Yes, I wail for *, my heart is Jer 48:31
gladness are gone from fruitful *. Jer 48:33
Sad sings my heart for * and Jer 48:36
* like an old, unwanted bottle. Jer 48:38
See the shame of *! Jer 48:39
the land of *, says the Lord. Jer 48:40
of giving birth. * shall no longer Jer 48:42
be your lot, O *, says the Lord. Jer 48:43

(MOAB Con't)
Woe to you, O *; Jer 48:46
the Lord, I will reestablish *. Jer 48:47
(Here the prophecy concerning * Jer 48:47
eastern flank of *, wiping out her Eze 25:9,10
upon Ammon. And * will no longer Eze 25:9,10
of many nations. *, Edom, and most Dan 11:41
the god of Peor, a city of *. Hos 9:10f
Salaman, king of *, who invaded Hos 10:14f
THE LORD SAYS, "The people of * Amo 2:1
send fire upon *, and it will Amo 2:2
in Kerioth. * shall go down in Amo 2:2
how Balak, king of *, tried to Mic 6:5
of the people of * and Ammon, Zep 2:8
God of Israel, "* and Ammon will Zep 2:9

MOAB'S
* REFUGEES AT Sela send lambs as a Is 16:1
If you let * fugitives settle Is 16:4,5
have put a stop to * worshiping Jer 48:35

MOABITE
parties with the local * girls. Num 25:1
"No Ammonite or * may ever enter Deu 23:3
annual tax money to the * capital. Ju 3:15
every * home and on the streets; Jer 48:38

MOABITES
ancestor of the nation of the *. Gen 19:37
between the * and the Amorites. Num 21:13
'Don't attack the * either, for I Deu 2:9
Rephaim, but the * call them Emim. Deu 2:11
did the *, whose capital is at Ar. Deu 2:29
the Ammonites or the * in any way. Deu 23:6
enemies, the *, at your mercy!" Ju 3:28
Then they attacked the * and Ju 3:29
In those days bandit gangs of * 2Ki 13:20,21
Syrians, *, and Ammonites against 2Ki 24:2
For the Ammonites and * turned 2Ch 20:23
*, Egyptians, and Amorites. Ez 9:1
the Ammonites and * should never be Neh 13:1
and Edomites and * and Hagrites; Ps 83:6
The * and Ammonites were among Ps 83:8f
Ammonites, *, Arabs, and yes, even Jer 9:25,26
The * Jer 48:1
says: Because the * have said that Eze 25:8
judgment upon the *, and they shall Eze 25:11

MOABITESS
purchased Ruth the *, the widow of Ru 4:10

MOADIAH
Piltai, leader of the * and Neh 12:12-21

MOAN
and don't * about it either! Deu 15:10
I think of God and *, Ps 77:3
* with mournful cries like doves. Is 59:11
Weep and *, O evil shepherds; Jer 25:34

MOANED
Israel *. Gen 43:6
in Egypt," they *, "and that the Ex 16:3
"All night I *; Is 38:13

MOANING
headache, and soon was * in pain. 2Ki 4:19
God does not respond to their *. Job 24:12

MOB
Soon a great, sullen * formed; Num 16:42
A great * formed, and they held Num 20:2
"This * will eat us like an ox Num 22:4
But Joash retorted to the whole * Ju 6:31
a great * stoned him to death. 1Ki 12:18
They have plotted to call for a * Jer 12:6
him over to the * to kill him. Jer 26:24
desert for all this * to eat?" Mt 15:33
Then the * led him to the home of Mt 26:57
And the * yelled back, "His Mt 27:25
to touch him for fear of a *. Mk 12:12
arrived with a * equipped with Mk 14:43
Then the * arrested Jesus and Mk 14:46
When the * tried to grab him, he Mk 14:51,52
Now a * began to crowd in toward Mk 15:8
whipped up the * to demand the Mk 15:11
and buy enough for this whole *?" Lk 9:13
the people will * us, for they are Lk 20:6
But even as he said this, a * Lk 22:47
leaders who headed the *. Lk 22:52
and to the * and said, "So? Lk 23:4
good is that with all this *?" Jn 6:8,9
by guiding the * to him, for this Act 1:16
city and incited a * against Paul Act 13:50
a plot to incite a * of Gentiles, Act 14:5,6
into a murderous * that stoned Paul Act 14:19
A * was quickly formed against Act 16:22
to form a * and start a riot. Act 17:5
Then the * Act 18:17
Temple and roused a * against him. Act 21:26,27
When the * saw the troops coming, Act 21:32
the stairs, the * grew so violent Act 21:35

MOBBED
* him, shouting, "Kill him! Jer 26:7,8
sent him, we'll be *, for the crowd Mt 21:26
and jumping up, they * him and Lk 4:29
Then they * him, putting their Act 7:57

MOBILIZATION
(Word of the * of the Israeli Ju 20:3

MOBILIZE
commanded you to * ten thousand men Ju 4:6
and Naphtali to * at Kedesh, ten Ju 4:10
"What I suggest is that you * 2Sa 17:11
Amasa to * the army of Judah within 2Sa 20:4
across Israel to * his own clan of 2Sa 20:14
"We will * our forces at ÇÇ" 2Ki 6:8
to * their troops there!" 2Ki 6:9
* his army and come out and fight. 2Ki 14:8
Remote lands tremble and * for Is 41:5
and Tahpanhes! * for battle, for Jer 46:14
Signal many nations to * for war Jer 51:27
shout to Israel's army, '*!' Eze 7:14
I will * your troops and armored Eze 38:4
*! Mic 5:1

MOBILIZED
Zeboiim, and Bela) * their armies Gen 14:3
as the spies), he * his army and Num 21:1
Instead he * his army and Num 21:23
on us and * his forces at Jahaz. Deu 2:32
He immediately * his army and Deu 3:1
Mount Tabor, he * his entire army, Ju 4:13
The armies of Ammon were * in Ju 10:17
Israel, so he * an army at Jahaz Ju 11:20
THEN THE TRIBE of Ephraim * its Ju 12:1
and the scum of the earth, * his Ju 12:4
they * their army and advanced. 1Sa 7:7
So the entire Israeli army * 1Sa 13:3,4
So Saul * his army at Telaim. 1Sa 15:4
So Saul * his entire army to 1Sa 23:8
THE PHILISTINE ARMY now * at 1Sa 29:1
THEN DAVID * thirty thousand 2Sa 6:1
Meanwhile, Absalom had * the 2Sa 17:24
KING BEN-HADAD OF Syria now * 1Ki 20:1
against them, they * every man who 2Ki 3:21
of Babylon * his entire army and 2Ki 25:1
* their forces to capture him. 1Ch 14:8
reached David, he * all Israel, 1Ch 19:17,18
Rehoboam * the armies of Judah and 2Ch 11:1
and * his armies to attack Israel. 2Ch 16:4
king and * for war against Israel. 2Ch 17:1
Be prepared! Stay *. Eze 38:7

MOBILIZING
he warned, and, * his army, he Num 20:20
All these kings responded by * Jos 11:4

MOBS
"Don't join * intent on evil. Ex 23:2,3
keep out looters. * form in the Is 24:11
jail, faced angry *, worked to 2Co 6:5
I have faced grave dangers from * 2Co 11:26

MOCK
When you * God, shouldn't someone Job 11:3
Meanwhile, the rich * those in Job 12:5
When I stand to speak, they *. Job 19:18
let me speak, and afterwards, * Job 21:2,3
for even fools will * me then. Ps 39:8
when they leave, they laugh and *. Ps 41:6
nations laugh and * at us because Ps 44:13
How they scoff and * me when I Ps 69:10
robbed him while his neighbors *. Ps 89:41
and I'll laugh! * me, will you? Pro 1:26
Mock me, will you?—I'll * you! Pro 1:26
Or, "Fools make a * at sin." Pro 14:9f
They even * the Holy One of Is 5:19
your messengers to * the Lord. Is 37:24
Who is it you *, making faces Is 57:4
No wonder they scoff and * and Jer 20:8
warned you not to * like that, then Jer 23:38,39
shall * at her for all her wounds. Jer 50:13
Near and far they will * you, a Eze 22:5
And all the world will * you for Eze 23:32
For the heathen * at you because Dan 9:16
and drinks with those who * him. Hos 7:5
Yes, so they *, for the nation Hos 9:7
will taunt you and * your dirge of Mic 2:4
Everyone passing that way will *, Zep 2:15
They will * me and spit on me Mk 10:34
they would *. Lk 14:30
But these men * and curse at Jud 1:10

MOCKED
"You have * me again, and told Ju 16:13
Thus the ambassador * the 2Ch 32:16
But the people * these 2Ch 36:16
and insulted and * us and laughed Neh 4:1
O Lord God, for we are being *. Neh 4:4
I am constantly despised, *, Ps 44:15,16
though I am * and cursed and Ps 69:7
How I dread being * for obeying, Ps 119:39
that we won't be * as old maids." Is 4:1
for he has * the Living God. Is 37:16,17
is it you scoffed against and *? Is 37:23
of the city, * by all. Jer 20:7
and they shall be * and taunted and Jer 24:9
and hissed and *, for they refuse Jer 29:18
heaps of ruins, cursed and *; Jer 49:13
for they * my people in their woe. Eze 21:28
was destroyed, and * Israel in her Eze 25:3
You are * and slandered. Eze 36:3
destroyed and * by heathen nations Eze 36:4
I will not let it be * at Eze 39:7
you should not have * in his time Ob 1:12
to my former exiles, * and shamed. Zep 3:19
and I will be * and crucified, and Mt 20:19
and Jewish leaders also * him. Mt 27:41,42,43
the Gentiles to be * and treated Lk 18:32
The soldiers * him, too, by Lk 23:36
the Pharisees *. Jn 7:47
they *, and struck him with Jn 19:3

MOCKER
If you rebuke a *, you will only Pro 9:7,8
a young * doesn't. Pro 13:1
A * never finds the wisdom he Pro 14:6
A * stays away from wise men Pro 15:12
truth, while the * feeds on trash. Pro 15:14
Punish a * and others will learn Pro 19:25
Throw out the *, and you will be Pro 22:10
* is the scourge of all mankind. Pro 24:9

MOCKERS
I am surrounded by *. Job 17:2
The Lord mocks at *, but helps Pro 3:34
* and rebels shall be severely Pro 19:29
* are proud, haughty and Pro 21:24

MOCKERY
"He has made me a * among the Job 17:6
This is absurd, a hollow *, and a Ecc 6:2
and * against his land and people. Is 25:8
do when you make a * of justice, Amo 6:12
scepter and knelt before him in *. Mt 27:29
After the *, they took off the Mt 27:31
by, and wagged their heads in *. Mk 15:29,30

MOCKING
Or, "*"; whether in innocent fun Gen 21:9f
About noontime, Elijah began * 1Ki 18:27
the city began * and making fun of 2Ki 2:23
Don't let them keep on * me! Ps 70:2,3
* the poor is mocking the God who Pro 17:5
Mocking the poor is * the God who Pro 17:5
she had before her * enemy struck Lam 1:7
of Moab and Ammon, * my people and Zep 2:8
in charge of Jesus began * him. Lk 22:63,64
began * and ridiculing Jesus; Lk 23:11
But others in the crowd were *. Act 2:13
him up to * and to public shame. Heb 6:6

MOCKINGLY
used *, "Let Baal be honored!" Ju 6:32f

MOCKS
of Jerusalem scorns and * at you. 2Ki 19:21
Everyone who sees me * and Ps 22:7
The Lord * at mockers, but helps Pro 3:34
A man who * his father and Pro 30:17

MODEL
a mere earthly * of the real Heb 8:5

MODELS
"Send five gold * of the tumor 1Sa 6:4,5
and five gold * of the rats that 1Sa 6:4,5
the gold * of the rats and tumors, 1Sa 6:8
The five gold * of tumors which 1Sa 6:17

MODERATE
Regular, * haircuts are all they Eze 44:20

MODERN
it is spelled in many * versions. Ex 3:15f
This paraphrase is the * 1Sa 20:30f
There is no * parallel to this Hos 4:12f
equivalent to $20 in * times, or Mt 20:2f
straws" would be a * equivalent. Lk 1:8,9f
the equivalent of a * day's wage. Lk 10:35f
The above paraphrase is the * Jn 16:26f

MODESTY
discretion and * is like a fine Pro 11:22

MOIST
Its roots went deep into the * Eze 31:4

MOISTURE
He loads the clouds with * and Job 37:11
olive trees for * and for dew—and Hos 1:21,22
withered and died for lack of *. Lk 8:6

MOLADAH
Amam, Shema, *, Hazar-gaddah, Jos 15:21-32
Beer-sheba, Sheba, *, Hazar-shual, Jos 19:2-7
They lived at Beer-sheba, *, 1Ch 4:28
Jeshua, *, Beth-pelet, Neh 11:25-30

MOLD
for each was cast from the same *. 1Ki 7:37
An idol, made from a *, overlaid Is 40:19
They melt their silver to * into Hos 13:2

MOLDED
Aaron melted the gold, then * Ex 32:4
They have * themselves a calf, Ex 32:8
their five bases were * from Ex 36:38
They were * so that they were Ex 37:8
for the Temple. He * it into the 1Ch 18:8
And he * 100 solid gold bowls. 2Ch 4:8
in place and * all the earth. Is 51:16

MOLDER
and the * helps at the anvil. Is 41:7

MOLDING
with a * of gold all around it. Ex 25:11
Put a * four inches wide around Ex 25:25
ridge along the *, all around. Ex 25:25
a gold * around the entire altar. Ex 30:3
Beneath the *, on each of two Ex 30:4
and out, and had a * of gold all Ex 37:2
a golden * all around the edge. Ex 37:11
with a gold * along the rim. Ex 37:12
close to the *, to hold the Ex 37:14

OLDING Con't)
ınd ran a gold * around the edge. Ex 37:26
, to hold the carrying poles. Ex 37:27

OLDS
he clay, and pack it in the *! Nah 3:14

OLDY
wineskins and dry, * bread. Jos 9:3,4,5
ıow as you see, it is dry and *; Jos 9:12
spoiled and *—too rotten to eat. Jer 24:2
selling them your * wheat— the Amo 8:6

OLE
The *, the rat, Lev 11:29,30

OLECH
to *, burning them upon his altar; Lev 18:21
burnt offering to * shall without Lev 20:1
to *, thus making my Tabernacle Lev 20:3
and another for *, the unutterably 1Ki 11:7
to death on the altars of *; 2Ki 17:17
to death as a sacrifice to *. 2Ki 23:10
prepared for *, the Assyrian god; Is 30:33
and perfume to * as your gift. Is 57:9
as sacrifices to *—something I Jer 32:35
the Lord,' but worship *, too! Zep 1:5

OLES
idols to the * and bats, and crawl Is 2:20

OLEST
site, and don't * the governor of Ez 6:7

OLID
his wife Abihail were Ahban and *. 1Ch 2:29

OLTEN
carved stones, * images, and the Num 33:52
and had made an idol from * metal. Deu 9:12
wood or made from * metal—for these Deu 27:15
capitals of * bronze, each 7½ feet 1Ki 7:16-22
were cast from * bronze, including 1Ki 7:33
and made two calves from * gold. 2Ki 17:16

OMENT
At that * the Angel of God Gen 22:11
The man stood there a * with head Gen 24:26
Be patient with me for a *, for I Gen 44:18
even a *, I would exterminate you. Ex 33:5
for even a *, lest they look at the Num 4:20
From this * you must always Jos 9:23
to God from the * of his birth Ju 13:7
At that * the Spirit of the Lord Ju 14:6
So those he killed at the * of Ju 16:30
pain of death. The * you go beyond 1Ki 2:36,37
At the same * a wide crack 1Ki 13:5
At that very *, the mother of the 2Ki 8:5
For we are here for but a *, 1Ch 29:15
And at that * the glory of the 2Ch 5:13,14
And at the * they began to sing 2Ch 20:22
But now we have been given a * Ez 9:8
You have given us a * of joy and Ez 9:8
*, but then comes sudden disaster. Job 5:3
and test him every * of the day? Job 7:18
may have a little * of comfort Job 10:20,21
He blossoms for a * like a Job 14:2
joy of the godless but for a *? Job 20:5
now, yet in a * they shall be gone Job 24:24
In a * they die, and at midnight Job 34:20
His anger lasts a *; Ps 30:5
that I am here for but a * more. Ps 39:4
My whole lifetime is but a * to Ps 39:5,6
from the * my mother conceived me. Ps 51:5
gone in a * like a breath of wind. Ps 78:39
Every *, you know where I am. Ps 139:3
ends, and in a * all he planned for Ps 146:4
The evil man gets rich for the *, Pro 11:18
in one * it comes crashing down. Is 30:13
upon you in one *, in full measure Is 47:9
For a brief * I abandoned you. Is 54:7
In a * of anger I turned my face Is 54:8
pains come. In a *, just as Is 66:7,8
suddenly, in a *, every house is Jer 4:20
in a * without the hand of man. Lam 4:6
God's plans. The * you began Dan 9:23
he stands still for a *, gazing Hab 3:6
add a single * to your life? Mt 6:27
the woman was well from that *. Mt 9:22
and from that * the boy was well. Mt 17:18
know the date or * of my return. Mt 25:13
At that very * the chief priests Mt 26:3
At that very * while he was still Mt 26:47
Jordan River. The * Jesus came up Mk 1:10
of the world in a * of time; Lk 4:5
And at that * her life Lk 8:55
in the * he arrives and knocks. Lk 12:36
But this is your *—the time when Lk 22:53
At that * Jesus turned and looked Lk 22:61
And at that * he disappeared! Lk 24:31
at Peter for a * and then said, Jn 1:42
it was the same * that Jesus had Jn 4:53
stood there a * and began walking! Act 3:7,8
for only a * as I briefly outline Act 24:4
death at every * of the day—we are Rom 8:36
Yet right up to the present * we 1Co 4:13
It will all happen in a *, in 1Co 15:52
that every * we spend in these 2Co 5:6
them for a single *, for we did not Gal 2:5
At the * I have all I need—more Php 4:18

and at the same * another man comes Jas 2:2
one brief *, to reign with him. Rev 17:12
In one * her judgment fell." Rev 18:10
In one *, all the wealth of the Rev 18:17

MOMENTS
a few * of relief before he dies. Job 14:6
brief are these * before I must go Jn 13:33
He had said just a few * before, Heb 5:7f

MOMMY
to say 'Daddy' or '*,' the king of Is 8:4

MONARCH
his God had made him a powerful *. 2Ch 1:1
proudest—* of all that he sees." Job 41:34

MONARCHS
There are three stately * in the Pro 30:29,30,31

MONARCHY
12:11), and where the *, hated of Hos 9:15f

MONEY
his * in the mouth of the sack! Gen 42:27
"my * is here in my sack." Gen 42:28
each was the * paid for the grain! Gen 42:35
Take double * so that you can Gen 43:12
gifts and double * and went to Gen 43:15
"It's because of the * returned Gen 43:18
our sacks, and the * was there that Gen 43:21
additional * to buy more grain. Gen 43:22
We have no idea how the * got Gen 43:22
we collected your * all right." Gen 43:23
each man's sack the * he had paid! Gen 44:1
sack, along with the grain *. Gen 44:2
Didn't we bring back the * we Gen 44:8
Joseph collected all the * in Gen 47:14
* to Pharaoh's treasure-houses. Gen 47:14
When the people were out of *, Gen 47:15
"Our * is gone," they said, Gen 47:15
and said, "Our * is gone, and our Gen 47:18
That is, "If he owes you * and Ex 21:2f
"If someone gives * or goods to Ex 22:7
then he shall pay the * anyway. Ex 22:17
"If you lend * to a needy Ex 22:25
Use this * for the care of the Ex 30:16
slave with his own *, that slave Lev 22:11
together enough *, then he may Lev 25:26
the * and return the land to him. Lev 25:27
interest on the * you lend him. Lev 25:36
himself if he can find the *. Lev 25:49
shall be stated in standard *. Lev 27:25
So Moses received redemption * Num 3:49
The * collected came to a total Num 3:50
They went to Balaam with * in Num 22:7
the * to the Lord's sanctuary. Deu 14:25
When you arrive, use the * to Deu 14:26
You shall lend * to many nations Deu 15:6
form of *, food, or anything else. Deu 23:19
tax * to the Moabite capital. Ju 3:15
After delivering the * to King Ju 3:17,18,19
They gave him * from the temple Ju 9:4
So they brought the * with them. Ju 16:18
So he returned the * to her. Ju 17:3
him, begging for * and food. 1Sa 2:36
for they were greedy for *. 1Sa 8:3
and brought him annual tribute *. 2Sa 8:6
"Well, * won't do it," the 2Sa 21:4
But he had owed some * when he 2Ki 4:1
will be enough * left for you and 2Ki 4:7
robes, tied up the * in two bags, 2Ki 5:23
Then he hid the * in his house. 2Ki 5:24
Is this the time to receive * and 2Ki 5:26
Now don't use any more * for your 2Ki 12:7
However, the * that was 2Ki 12:16
Menahem extorted the * from the 2Ki 15:19,20
"Collect the * given to the 2Ki 22:3,4
Give this * to the building 2Ki 22:5,6
* that the Pharaoh had demanded. 2Ki 23:35
him a large sum of * every year. 1Ch 18:2
him large amounts of * every year. 1Ch 18:6
large sums of * annually to David. 1Ch 18:13
away loaded with *, garments, and 2Ch 20:25
valuable gifts of * and jewels, 2Ch 21:3,4
and brought the * and placed it in 2Ch 24:10
Priest counted the *, and took the 2Ch 24:11
This went on day after day, and * 2Ch 24:11
The king and Jehoiada gave the * 2Ch 24:12
the remaining * was brought to the 2Ch 24:14
"But the *!" 2Ch 25:9
wine, olive oil, *, and everything 2Ch 31:5,6
the Temple. The * was collected at 2Ch 34:9
of Jerusalem. The * was taken to 2Ch 34:9
recording the * collected at the 2Ch 34:14
"The * chests have been opened 2Ch 34:17
counted, and the * has been put 2Ch 34:17
in Jerusalem. The * that is left Ez 7:18
If you run short of * for the Ez 7:20
I weighed the * as I gave it to Ez 8:26,27
equipment and * and bowls which had Ez 8:28
who ran out of * for food had to Neh 5:2,3,4
slavery to get enough * to live. Neh 5:5
The rest of us are lending * and Neh 5:10
would be enough * to care for the Neh 10:32
telling him, "Keep the *, but Est 3:11
of * could begin to cover." Est 7:4

as others search for food or *? Job 3:20,21
himself, for the * he trusts in Job 15:31
refused to loan * to needy friends Job 22:6
If you give up your lust for *, Job 22:24
they will loan him any * or grain. Job 24:9
"The evil man may accumulate * Job 27:16
"If I have put my trust in *, Job 31:24
him a gift of *, and a gold ring. Job 42:11
whose only goal in life is *. Ps 10:3
to prefer obedience to making *! Ps 119:36
you would for lost * or hidden Pro 2:3,4,5
He has taken a wallet full of * Pro 7:20
* to cruel men. Pro 11:16
Trust in your * and down you go! Pro 11:28
Dishonest * brings grief to all Pro 15:27
He who loves * shall never have Ecc 5:10
leaves so little * at his death Ecc 6:3
either wisdom or *, but being wise Ecc 7:12
happiness, and * gives everything! Ecc 10:19
and drink—even if you have no *! Is 55:1
Why spend your * on foodstuffs Is 55:2
field—paying good * for it before Jer 32:25
some food and * and let him go. Jer 40:5
"Throw away your *! Eze 7:19
of * is the reason for your sin. Eze 7:19
and loans out his * at interest Eze 18:13
and does not loan * at interest, Eze 18:17
when Ahaz paid "protection *" Eze 23:12f
hearts they are loving their *. Eze 33:31
wine they purchased with stolen *. Amo 2:8
try to save your *, it will come to Mic 6:14
build cities with * gained from Hab 2:12
serve two masters: God and *. Mt 6:24
"Don't take any * with you; Mt 10:9
his longing for * choke out God's Mt 13:22
to get enough * to buy the Mt 13:44
give their support * to the church Mt 15:5,6
have and give the * to the poor, Mt 19:21
to give away my * if I want to? Mt 20:15
and loaned them * to invest for him Mt 25:14
and hid the * for safekeeping. Mt 25:18
them to him to account for his *. Mt 25:19
so I hid your * in the earth and Mt 25:24,25
least have put my * into the bank Mt 25:27
Take the * from this man and Mt 25:28
"What a waste of good *," they Mt 26:8,9
and brought back the * to the Mt 27:3
Then he threw the * onto the Mt 27:5
The chief priests picked the * Mt 27:6
to accept * paid for murder." Mt 27:6
no knapsack, no *, not even an Mk 6:8,9
have and give the * to the poor—and Mk 10:21
as the crowds dropped in their *. Mk 12:41
even return for your * or clothes. Mk 13:15,16
and given the * to the poor!" Mk 14:4,5
John replied, "Don't extort * by Lk 3:14
And if you lend * only to those Lk 6:34
"A man loaned * to two Lk 7:41
both, letting them keep the *! Lk 7:42
a beggar's bag, nor food, nor *. Lk 9:3
Don't take any * with you, or a Lk 10:4
of his clothes and * and beat him Lk 10:30
he has enough * to pay the bills? Lk 14:28
out of * before it was finished!' Lk 14:30
his * on parties and prostitutes. Lk 15:13
About the time his * was gone a Lk 15:14
spending your * on prostitutes, you Lk 15:30
each one who owed * to his employer Lk 16:5,6
mean: "Use your * for good, so Lk 16:9f
other people's *, why should you be Lk 16:12
be entrusted with * of your own? Lk 16:12
You cannot serve both God and * Lk 16:13
*, naturally scoffed at all this. Lk 16:14
have and give the * to the poor—it Lk 18:22
he had given the *, to find out Lk 19:15
only the * he had started with. Lk 19:20
you deposit the * in the bank so Lk 19:23
ordered, 'Take the * away from him Lk 19:24
you were without *, duffle bag, or Lk 22:35
bag if you have one, and your *. Lk 22:36
* changers behind their counters. Jn 2:14
scattering the * changers' coins Jn 2:15
and the * given to the poor." Jn 12:5
or to give some * to the poor. Jn 13:29
He bought a field with the * he Act 1:18
by, he asked them for some *. Act 3:3
"We don't have any * for you! Act 3:6
and brought the * to the apostles Act 4:34,35
and brought the * to the apostles Act 4:37
*, claiming it was the full price. Act 5:2
offered * to buy this power. Act 8:18
But Peter replied, "Your * Act 8:20
and earned much * for her masters. Act 16:16
"I have never been hungry for * Act 20:33
to Jerusalem with * to aid the Act 24:17
and then make * your god instead. Rom 2:22
If God has given you *, be Rom 12:8
delivered this * and completed this Rom 15:28
accept the * I am bringing them. Rom 15:31
about the * you are collecting to 1Co 16:1
They begged us to take the * so 2Co 8:4

(MONEY Con't)
be, with your * all collected; 2Co 9:3
anything, for I don't want your *. 2Co 12:14
have made * from us some way." 2Co 12:16
so that you would give us *! 1Th 2:5
for enough * to pay your bills. 1Th 4:12
and night for the * we needed to 2Th 3:8
kind, and not be one who loves *. 1Ti 3:3
and must not be greedy for *. 1Ti 3:8
Then the church can spend its * 1Ti 5:16
News is just a means of making *. 1Ti 6:5
After all, we didn't bring any * 1Ti 6:7
satisfied without * if we have 1Ti 6:8
things to get *, things that hurt 1Ti 6:9
For the love of * is the first 1Ti 6:10
to trust in their *, which will 1Ti 6:17
Tell them to use their * to do 1Ti 6:18
love only themselves and their *; 2Ti 3:2
or fighters or greedy for *. Tit 1:7
teachers are only after your *. Tit 1:11
Stay away from the love of *; Heb 13:5
anything to get hold of your *. 2Pe 2:3
* he could make by doing wrong; 2Pe 2:15
be a Christian has * enough to live 1Jn 3:17
shelter, nor * from those who are 3Jn 1:7
they will do anything for *; Jud 1:11

MONEY-CHANGERS
knocked over the *' tables and the Mt 21:12

MONEYCHANGERS
the tables of the * and the stalls Mk 11:15

MONOPOLY
Do you have a * on wisdom? Job 15:7,8

MONSTER
to rouse the sea *, curse it." Job 3:8f
"O God, am I some *, that you Job 7:12
us like a great * and filled his Jer 51:34,35

MONTH
the first day of the tenth *." Gen 8:5f
*, the first day of the month." Gen 8:13f
month, the first day of the *." Gen 8:13f
been there about a *, Laban said Gen 29:14
now on, this * will be the first Ex 12:2
* of the Jewish calendar. Ex 12:2
tenth day of this * (announce this Ex 12:3,4
day of this *, all these lambs Ex 12:6
day of the * until the evening of Ex 12:18
of the twenty-first day of the *. Ex 12:18
the second * after leaving Egypt. Ex 16:1
in March, the * you left Egypt; Ex 23:15
that was the * you left Egypt. Ex 34:18
on the first day of the first *. Ex 40:2
On the first day of the first *, Ex 40:17
time during the *, the same rules Lev 15:25
*" of the Hebrew calendar. Lev 16:29,30f
*" (of the Hebrew calendar). Lev 23:5f
*" (of the Hebrew calendar). Lev 23:23,24f
*" (of the Hebrew calendar). Lev 23:26,27f
*" (of the Hebrew calendar). Lev 23:33,34f
*" (of the Hebrew calendar). Lev 25:9f
A boy one * to five years old Lev 27:6
*" (of the Jewish calendar). Num 1:1f
*" (of the Jewish calendar). Num 1:17,18,19f
count every male down to one * Num 3:14,15
22,000 males a * old and older. Num 3:39
Israel who are a * old and older, Num 3:40
a * old and older to be 22,273. Num 3:43
during the first * of the second Num 9:1
fourteenth day of this first *, Num 9:2,3
Note: The 14th day of the first * Num 9:2,3f
Passover, but one * later, on the Num 9:10
*, beginning in the evening. Num 9:11
two days, a *, or a year, that is Num 9:22
beginning of each * to rejoice over Num 10:10
the twentieth day of the second * Num 10:11
For one whole * you will have Num 11:19,20
promise them meat for a whole *! Num 11:21
be brought when he is one * old. Num 18:16
Literally, "the first *." Num 20:1f
all the males a * old and upward. Num 26:62
first day of each * there shall be Num 28:11
each * throughout the year. Num 28:14
"Also on the first day of each * Num 28:15
day of the first * of each year, Num 28:16
*" (of the Hebrew calendar). Num 29:1f
*" (of the Hebrew calendar). Num 29:7f
*" (of the Hebrew calendar). Num 29:12f
*" (of the Hebrew calendar). Num 33:3,4f
*" (of the Hebrew calendar). Num 33:38,39f
*" (of the Hebrew calendar). Deu 1:1f
Passover during the * of April, Deu 16:1
Literally, "Abib"—the first * of Deu 16:1f
father and mother for a full *. Deu 21:13
Growing richly * by month, Deu 33:14
Growing richly month by *, Deu 33:14
*" (of the Jewish calendar). Jos 4:19f
evening of the 14th day of the *. Jos 5:10
provisions for one * of the year. 1Ki 4:7
Each * the tax officials 1Ki 4:27
ten thousand a *, so that each man 1Ki 5:14
each man was a * in Lebanon and two 1Ki 5:14
was laid in the * of May in the 1Ki 6:37
Festival in the * of October. 1Ki 8:2
eighth *" of the Hebrew calendar. 1Ki 12:32,33f
This was a * later than the 1Ki 12:32,33f
Length of reign: 1 * 2Ki 15:13
One * after Shallum became king, 2Ki 15:14
day of the last * of the 2Ki 25:27
for active duty one * each year. 1Ch 27:1
on duty the first * of each year. 1Ch 27:2,3
on duty the second * of each year. 1Ch 27:4
on duty the third * of each year. 1Ch 27:5,6
on duty the fourth * of each year. 1Ch 27:7
on duty the fifth * of each year. 1Ch 27:8
on duty the sixth * of each year. 1Ch 27:9
duty the seventh * of each year. 1Ch 27:10
on duty the eighth * of each year. 1Ch 27:11
during the ninth * of each year. 1Ch 27:12
on duty the tenth * of each year. 1Ch 27:13
the eleventh * of each year. 1Ch 27:14
during the twelfth * of each year. 1Ch 27:15
In the very first * of the first 2Ch 29:3
Jerusalem in the * of May for the 2Ch 30:13
DURING THE * of September everyone Ez 3:1
*" of the Hebrew calendar. Ez 3:6f
third day of the * of Adar." Ez 6:15f
first *" of the Hebrew calendar. Ez 6:19f
at Jerusalem in the * of August; Ez 7:7,8,9
first *" of the Hebrew calendar. Ez 8:31f
ninth *" of the Hebrew calendar. Ez 10:9f
Or, "twenty-fifth day of the * Neh 6:15f
But during the * of September, Neh 7:73
of Tabernacles to be held that *. Neh 8:14
day" of the Hebrew *. Neh 9:1f
13th day of the first * " Est 3:12f
to come to him in more than a *." Est 4:11
23rd day of the * of July—and they Est 8:9,10
last days of the *, to celebrate Est 9:21
the days of the * of that year. Job 3:6
from week to week and * to month. Is 66:23
from week to week and month to *. Is 66:23
Two years later, in the * of Jer 39:2
day of the tenth *, Nebuchadnezzar, Jer 52:4
day of the fourth *, when the Jer 52:6
On the tenth day of the fifth * Jer 52:12
first day of the *, in the eleventh Eze 26:1
on the fifteenth day of the *." Eze 32:17f
April was the first * of the Eze 45:18f
day of that * for anyone who has Eze 45:20
day of the same *, you shall Eze 45:21
There will be a new crop every * Eze 47:12
a half years (verse 7) plus one *. Dan 12:11f
today, this 24th day of the *, Hag 2:18,19
during the * of August each year, Zec 7:3
evil shepherds in a single *. Zec 11:8
The following * God sent the Lk 1:26
for that year and * and day and Rev 9:15
fruit, with a fresh crop each *; Rev 22:2

MONTHLY
as during her * periods. Lev 12:2
* burnt offering for that day, Num 29:6
weekly Sabbath and * new moon 2Ch 31:3

MONTHS
was 600 years, two *, and seventeen Gen 7:10,11,12
Three * later, Gen 8:5
About three * later word Gen 38:24
she hid him at home for three *. Ex 2:1
peninsula three * after the night Ex 19:1
friends for two *, weeping because Ju 11:37
fate with her friends for two *. Ju 11:38
and was there about four *. Ju 19:2
where they lived for four *. Ju 20:46,47
country for seven * in all. 1Sa 6:1
Philistines for a year and four *. 1Sa 27:7
It remained there for three *, 2Sa 6:11
The harvest lasted six *, from 2Sa 21:10f
task in nine * and twenty days. 2Sa 24:8
to flee for three * before your 2Sa 24:13
in Lebanon and two * at home. 1Ki 5:14
It took six * to accomplish 1Ki 11:16,17,18
Length of reign: 6 * 2Ki 15:8
Length of his reign: 3 *, in 2Ki 23:31,32
Length of his reign: 3 *, in 2Ki 24:8,9
But seven * later, Ishmael, who 2Ki 25:25
for three *, and the Lord blessed 1Ch 13:14
famine, or three * of destruction 1Ch 21:12
A few * later the Syrian army 2Ch 24:23
to reign, but lasted only three *. 2Ch 36:2
But he lasted only three * and 2Ch 36:9
ONE DAY IN April four * later, as Neh 2:1
The celebration lasted six *, a Est 1:4
would be given six * of beauty Est 2:12,13,14
followed by six * with special Est 2:12,13,14
have been allotted * of Job 7:3
of life—* is all you give him! Job 14:5
Do you know how many * of Job 39:2,3
*, and the sun to mark the days. Ps 104:19
nor worried by long * of drought. Jer 17:8
three brief * in the year 609 B.C. Jer 22:11f
And sure enough, two * later Jer 28:17
It will take seven * for the Eze 39:12
At the end of the seven *, they Eze 39:14
Twelve * after this dream, he Dan 4:29
rain three * before the harvest. Amo
fifth, seventh, and tenth *." Zec 8:1
went into seclusion for five *. Lk 1:
Furthermore, six * ago your Aunt Lk 1:
about three * and then went back to Lk 1:
the summer ends four * from now? Jn 4:
at home for three *, and when at Act 7:
for three *, telling what Act 19
He was in Greece three * and was Act 20
It was three * after the Act 28:
days or * or seasons or years. Gal 4:
for three *, and were not afraid. Heb 11:
them for five * with agony like the Rev 9
for five *, was in their tails. Rev 9:
the Holy City for forty-two *. Rev 11
control the earth for forty-two *. Rev 13

MONUMENT
proud, eternal * to themselves. Gen 11:3
and set it up as a *, and told his Gen 31:4
And Jacob set up a * of stones Gen 35:2
pile them into a * on the other Deu 27:2,3
of these laws plainly [upon the * Deu 27
pile them up as a * at the place Jos 4:2
We will use them to build a * so Jos 4
ask, 'What is this * for?' Jos 4
went across!' The * will be a Jos 4
night and constructed a * there. Jos 4
Joshua also built another * of Jos 4
the Jordan were piled up as a *. Jos 4:2
they built a large * for everyone Jos 22:1
Carmel to erect a * to himself, and 1Sa 15:1
(Absalom had built a * to himself 2Sa 18:1
He called it "Absalom's *," 2Sa 18:1
"What is that * over there?" 2Ki 23:1
horses' hoofs. No * will be given Is 14:2
and a * to the Lord at its border. Is 19:1
before the *, a herald shouted Dan 3:

MONUMENTS
For you build * to the prophets Mt 23:29,3

MOOD
testimony by the * of the majority Ex 23:2,
were in this *, they and the chief Jn 7:3

MOON
the sun and *, to shine down upon Gen 1:1
*, to preside through the night; Gen 1:1
"The sun, *, and eleven stars Gen 37:
"burnt offerings of the new *." Num 29:6
to worship the sun, *, or stars. Deu 4:1
gods, the sun, *, or stars—which I Deu 17:2,
and let the * stand in its place Jos 10:1
And the sun and the * didn't move Jos 10:1
the sun and *—all because of the Jos 10:1
of the celebration of the new *. 1Sa 20:
When the new * celebration began, 1Sa 20:24,2
Baal and the sun, *, and stars. 2Ki 17:1
Heathen altars to the sun god, * 2Ki 21:3,4,
and the sun, *, and stars. 2Ki 23:4
to the sun, *, stars, and planets. 2Ki 23:5
the new * celebrations, and at all 1Ch 23:31
and at the new * celebration and 2Ch 2:4
Sabbaths, on new * festivals, and 2Ch 8:13
and monthly new * festivals, and 2Ch 31:3
and of the sun, *, and stars. 2Ch 33:3
the sun, * and stars—in the very 2Ch 33:4,5
Sabbaths, the new * celebrations, Ez 3:5
* feasts, and the annual feasts. Neh 10:33
that even the * and stars are less Job 25:5
the skies, or the * walking down Job 31:26
your fingers—the * and the stars Ps 8:3
sun and * continue in the skies! Ps 72:5
at full *, new moon and all the Ps 81:3
new * and all the other holidays. Ps 81:3
It shall be eternal as the *, my Ps 89:37
He assigned the * to mark the Ps 104:19
and the * and stars at night, Ps 136:9
Praise him, sun and *, and all Ps 148:3
sun and light and * and stars are Ecc 12:2
dawn, fair as the *, pure as the Sol 6:10
of the new * and the Sabbath, and Is 1:12,13
will shine from stars or sun or *. Is 13:10
sun and * will seem to fade away. Is 24:23
every hill. The * will be as Is 30:26
need the sun or * to give you Is 60:19
Your sun shall never set; the * Is 60:20
* and stars—the gods of my people! Jer 8:2
daytime and the * and stars to Jer 31:35
* shall not give you her light. Eze 32:7
feasts, the new * ceremonies, the Eze 45:17
days of the new * celebrations. Eze 46:1
days of the new * celebrations. Eze 46:3
At the new * celebration, he Eze 46:6
The sun and * are obscured and Joe 2:10
darkness and the * to blood before Joe 2:31
The sun and * will be darkened Joe 3:15
The lofty sun and * began to Hab 3:11
and bow to the sun, * and stars. Zep 1:5
The sun and * and stars will no Zec 14:6
darkened, and the * will not give Mt 24:29
grow dim and the * will not shine, Mk 13:24
portents in the sun, * and stars; Lk 21:25
turn black and the * blood-red Act 2:20

MOON Con't)
sun, * and stars as their gods! Act 7:42
to the sun, *, planets, and stars. 1Co 15:40f
the * and stars have another kind. 1Co 15:41
or new * ceremonies or Sabbaths. Col 2:16
cloth, and the * was blood-red. Rev 6:12
and a third of the * and the stars, Rev 8:12
the sun, with the * beneath her Rev 12:1
no need of sun or * to light it, Rev 21:23

MOORED
they * the boat, and climbed out. Mk 6:53

MORAL
prosper, but the * decay of the Pro 11:11
When there is * rot within a Pro 28:2
of all their * filth by the horrors Is 4:2,3,4

MORALE
will undermine the * of the few Jer 38:4

MORALLY
they have become * rotten, an angry Dan 8:23

MORALS
change all laws, *, and customs. Dan 7:25

MORASTHITE
when Micah the * prophesied in the Jer 26:18

MORDECAI
*, Bilshan, Mispar, Bigvai, Ez 2:2
Azariah, Ra-amiah, Nahamani; *, Neh 7:7
the palace named * (son of Jair, Est 2:5
a Jewess, for * had said not to. Est 2:10
By that time * had become a Est 2:19
One day, as * was on duty at the Est 2:21
assassinate him. * heard about it Est 2:22
crediting * with the information. Est 2:22
commanded. But * refused to bow. Est 3:2
it, to see whether * could get away Est 3:3,4
to lay hands on * alone, but to Est 3:5,6
WHEN * LEARNED what had been Est 4:1
and told her about *, she was Est 4:4
him to go out to * and find out Est 4:5
square, and found * just outside Est 4:6
of the Jews. * also gave Hathach a Est 4:8
Hathach to go back and say to *, Est 4:10
gave Esther's message to *. Est 4:12
Then Esther said to tell *: Est 4:15
So * did as Esther told him to. Est 4:17
But when he saw * there at the Est 5:9
nothing when I see * the Jew just Est 5:13
the king to let you hang * on it; Est 5:14
item telling how * had exposed the Est 6:1
"What reward did we ever give * Est 6:3
the king to hang * from the gallows Est 6:4
you have said—to * the Jew, who Est 6:10
and put them on * and mounted him Est 6:11
Afterwards * returned to his job, Est 6:12
they said, "If * is a Jew, you Est 6:13
to hang *, the man who saved the Est 7:9
Queen Esther. Then * was brought Est 8:1
*, [appointing him Prime Minister Est 8:2
and Esther appointed * to be in Est 8:2
Queen Esther and * the Jew, "I Est 8:7
other decree * can devise that will Est 8:8f
they wrote as * dictated—a decree Est 8:9,10
of the kingdom. * wrote in the name Est 8:9,10
Then * put on the royal robes of Est 8:15
the Jews for fear of *; Est 9:3
of Mordecai; for * was a mighty Est 9:4
* wrote a history of all these Est 9:20
later adopted by * the Jew) had Est 9:29-31
* the Jew and by Queen Esther; Est 9:29-31
the greatness of * and the honors Est 10:2
Media and Persia. * the Jew was Est 10:3

MORDECAI'S
* uncle, who had adopted her." Est 2:15f
still following * orders, just as Est 2:20
against all of * people, the Jews, Est 3:5,6
returned to Esther with * message. Est 4:9
This was * reply to Esther: "Do Est 4:13
So the Jews adopted * suggestion Est 9:23
support behind * letter Est 9:29-31

MORE
and * above the highest peaks. Gen 7:20
Eight * weeks went by. Gen 8:14
This is * consistent with Genesis Gen 11:32f
"What's *," God told him, "I Gen 17:5
I will speak but this once *! Gen 18:32
The servant said no *, but Gen 24:21
What's *, I am with you, and Gen 28:15
So Jacob agreed to work seven * Gen 29:28
and he loved her * than Leah, and Gen 29:30
* literally, "succeeded at his Gen 36:31-39f
loved Joseph * than any of his Gen 37:3
* literally, "an ornamented Gen 37:3f
and said, "She is * in the right Gen 38:26
he himself has no * authority Gen 39:9
The chief jailer had no * Gen 39:23
Then, suddenly, seven * heads Gen 41:6
additional money to buy * grain. Gen 43:22
But the * the Egyptians Ex 1:12
* the Israelis seemed to multiply! Ex 1:12
* the Hebrew slavery * bitter still, Ex 1:13,14
any * straw for making bricks! Ex 5:7,8
to furnish you with no * straw. Ex 5:10,11
he has only been * and more brutal Ex 5:23
only been more and * brutal to Ex 5:23
listen any * because they were too Ex 6:8,9
won't even listen to me any *; Ex 6:12
sinned yet * by their stubborn Ex 9:34
* miracles demonstrating my power. Ex 10:1
will send just one * disaster on Ex 11:1
a lamb for one or * families Ex 12:21
In the morning you will see * of Ex 16:7,8,9
So once * the people growled and Ex 17:2
* literally, "customary marriage Ex 22:16f
Then make two * golden rings and Ex 28:26
The rich shall not give * and Ex 30:15
him, "We have * than enough Ex 36:4-7
that no * donations were needed. Ex 36:4-7
were restrained from bringing *! Ex 36:4-7
spot looks to be * than skin-deep, Lev 13:3
must quarantine him seven days *. Lev 13:5
seems to be * than skin-deep, it is Lev 13:25
then isolated for seven * days. Lev 13:54
times * severely for your sins. Lev 26:18
* plagues because of your sins. Lev 26:21
pay twenty percent * than the value Lev 27:13
* literally, verse 7 reads: "But Num 10:5,6,7f
and what's *, we saw Anakim Num 13:28
What's *, you haven't brought us Num 16:14
of Israel only grumbled the *. Num 17:12,13
number of even * distinguished Num 22:15
tribes to be given * land, the Num 26:54
If he waits * than a day and Num 30:15
total value to be * than $300,000. Num 31:51,52
Only there are * of you, so Num 32:14
if there is * than one witness; Num 35:30
a thousand times *, and bless you Deu 1:11
'Speak of it no *,' he ordered, Deu 3:26
Literally, "and he added no *." Deu 5:22f
you can hold no *, then beware lest Deu 6:10,11,12
so much * powerful than we are?' Deu 7:17
and * powerful than you are! Deu 9:1
told me to cut two * stone tablets Deu 10:1
own possession, * so than any other Deu 14:2
but no * than forty stripes may Deu 25:1
even * than he did your ancestors! Deu 30:5
the Lord, how much * rebellious Deu 31:27
and it won't take * than two or Jos 7:3
in fact, * men died from the hail Jos 10:11
of the Negeb. * specifically, this Jos 15:2,3,4
won't receive any *, for they Jos 18:7
* of war against Reuben and Gad. Jos 22:33
let me make one * test: this time Ju 6:39
of the battle were * important than Ju 8:2,3
* literally, "Are not the last Ju 8:2,3f
I won't save you any *. Ju 10:13
save us once * from our enemies." Ju 10:15
again and give us * instructions Ju 13:8
me again, and told me * lies!" Ju 16:13
"Come just this once *," she Ju 16:18
strengthen me one * time, so that I Ju 16:28
of his death were * than those he Ju 16:30
him to stay one * day, as they were Ju 19:6
the ambush * room for maneuvering. Ju 20:35-39
and two thousand * near Gidom. Ju 20:45
* than she could eat. Ru 2:14
else who is * closely related to Ru 3:12
to worship the Lord once *. 1Sa 1:19,20
who were mighty are mighty no *! 1Sa 2:4
She with many children has no *! 1Sa 2:5
but how much * this sin of yours 1Sa 2:23,24,25
Why have you honored your sons * 1Sa 2:29
* Samuel jumped up and ran to Eli. 1Sa 3:8
by now my father will be * 1Sa 9:5
* we could have slaughtered!" 1Sa 14:30
Aijalon, growing * and more faint. 1Sa 14:31
Aijalon, growing more and * faint. 1Sa 14:31
He is much * interested in your 1Sa 15:22
"What's *," he added, "the 1Sa 16:18
wanted to know * about his family! 1Sa 17:55f
let him return home any *. 1Sa 18:4
But the controversy put David * 1Sa 18:13
he became even * afraid of him; 1Sa 18:15,16
he became even * afraid of him, 1Sa 18:29
hate him * with every passing day. 1Sa 18:29
David was * successful against them 1Sa 18:30
until David could weep no *. 1Sa 20:41
how much * so on this one!" 1Sa 21:5
and give me a * definite report. 1Sa 23:23
What's *, the entire Israeli 1Sa 28:19
wept until they could weep no *. 1Sa 30:4
He is God's appointed king no *. 2Sa 1:21
And how much * shall I do to 2Sa 4:11
to look even * foolish than this, 2Sa 6:22
There will be no * wars against 2Sa 7:10,11
would have given you much, much *. 2Sa 12:8
hated her * than he had loved her. 2Sa 13:15
I want no * bloodshed." 2Sa 14:11
"Please let me ask one * thing 2Sa 14:12
Absalom, as did * and more others. 2Sa 15:12
Absalom, as did more and * others. 2Sa 15:12
countryside, and * men disappeared 2Sa 18:8
replied, "He will have * news." 2Sa 18:26
I am once * king of Israel!" 2Sa 19:22
to hurt us * than Absalom did. 2Sa 20:6
speartip weighed * than twelve 2Sa 21:16
God bless you even * through 1Ki 1:46,47
of which was * than $12,000,000. 1Ki 9:27,28
there was no * spirit in her! 1Ki 10:5
instead, he made * priests than 1Ki 13:33
But you have done * evil than 1Ki 14:9
But he was even * wicked than 1Ki 16:30
idols and did * to anger the Lord 1Ki 16:33
"Now, do it once *!" 1Ki 18:34
up and eat some *, for there is a 1Ki 19:7
"Don't give him anything *," 1Ki 20:8
"May the gods do * to me than I am 1Ki 20:10
The battle became * and more 1Ki 22:35
The battle became more and * 1Ki 22:35
Once * the king sent fifty men, 2Ki 1:13
"There aren't any *!" 2Ki 4:6
Now don't use any * money for 2Ki 12:7
You need * than mere promises of 2Ki 18:20,21
allies will give you * than words? 2Ki 18:20,21
them to do even * evil than the 2Ki 21:9
things and is even * wicked than 2Ki 21:11
these persons were * important; 1Ch 1:1f
Jabez was * distinguished than 1Ch 4:9
And David became * and more 1Ch 11:9
And David became more and * 1Ch 11:9
* men joined David almost every 1Ch 12:22
(for there was * leadership ability 1Ch 24:4
He loved Maacah * than any of 2Ch 11:21
So there was no * war until the 2Ch 15:19
So Jehoshaphat made no * trips to 2Ch 19:4
What's *, Jehoram constructed 2Ch 21:11
to give you much * than this!" 2Ch 25:9
What's *, we have recovered and 2Ch 29:19
finished—and until * priests had 2Ch 29:34
Levites were much * ready to 2Ch 29:34
for not taking a * active part, so 2Ch 30:15
to do even * evil than the nations 2Ch 33:9
instead he sinned * and more. 2Ch 33:23
instead he sinned more and *. 2Ch 33:23
the matter * thoroughly. Ez 4:21
now we are even * deeply under Ez 10:10
revered God * than most people do. Neh 7:2
and for several * hours they took Neh 9:3
again, and once * you let their Neh 9:28
you for help, once * you listened Neh 9:28
And once * all the people of Neh 13:12
And now you are bringing * wrath Neh 13:18
compelled to take * than he wanted, Est 1:8
another queen * worthy than she. Est 1:19
Well, the king loved Esther * Est 2:17
come to him in * than a month." Est 4:11
what's *, who can say but that Est 4:14
he want to honor * than me?" Est 6:6
And now once * Esther came before Est 8:3
he had become * and more powerful. Est 9:4
he had become more and * powerful. Est 9:4
But now, what * do you want? Est 9:12
and killed 300 * men, though again Est 9:15
arrived with * bad news: "The fire Job 1:16
" 'Is mere man * just than God? Job 4:17
God? * pure than his Creator?' Job 4:17
again until the heavens are no *; Job 14:11,12
What do you know * than we do? Job 15:9
* severe than my fault deserves. Job 23:2
enjoyed them * than my daily food. Job 23:12
has planned, and there is * ahead. Job 23:14
No one will remember him any *. Job 24:20
Wisdom is far * valuable than Job 28:17
*, for my counsel satisfied them. Job 29:22
that I dread * than anything Job 31:23
Listen to me, and let me say *. Job 33:31
doesn't pay any * attention to the Job 34:19
and it is even * false to say Job 35:14,15
parents and return to them no *. Job 39:4
his life * than at the beginning. Job 42:12
God also gave him seven * sons Job 42:13,14
more sons and three * daughters. Job 42:13,14
ways to follow him * closely. Ps 1:2
They are * desirable than gold. Ps 19:10
* by my neighbors and friends. Ps 31:11
how I long for my health once *. Ps 38:9
point. The * I mused, the hotter Ps 39:2,3
that I am here for but a moment *. Ps 39:4
Has given you * gladness Ps 45:7
How you love wickedness—far * Ps 52:3
And lying * than truth! Ps 52:3
ever * bold in their wickedness." Ps 52:7
He will destroy them * quickly Ps 58:9
will please him * than sacrificing Ps 69:31
I praise you * and more. Ps 71:14
I praise you more and *. Ps 71:14
city he loves * than any other! Ps 87:1
of the dark any *, nor fear the Ps 91:5
His glory is far * vast than the Ps 108:5
rejoiced in them * than in riches. Ps 119:14
I long for your instructions * Ps 119:20
follow your laws even * closely. Ps 119:32
They are * valuable to me than Ps 119:71,72
* than the finest gold. Ps 119:127
I long for him * than sentinels Ps 130:6

(MORE Con't)
If I fail to love her * than my Ps 137:5,6
For such wisdom is far * valuable Pro 3:13,14,15
Sure, just a little *! Pro 6:10
My instruction is far * valuable Pro 8:10
rebuked, will love you all the *. Pro 9:7,8
a good man, and he will learn *. Pro 9:9
hours of your day * profitable and Pro 9:11
years of your life * fruitful." Pro 9:11
how much * the wicked! Pro 11:31
How much * the hearts of all Pro 15:11
of common sense is * effective than Pro 17:10
how much * his friends! Pro 19:7
Good sense is far * valuable than Pro 20:15
God is * pleased when we are just Pro 21:3
A little * slumber, Pro 24:32,33
HONOR DOESN'T GO with fools any * Pro 26:1
Its intended victim will be no * Pro 26:2
its point will no * be felt than a Pro 26:9
Yanking a dog's ears is no * Pro 26:17
Jealousy is * dangerous and cruel Pro 27:4
You can no * stop her complaints Pro 27:16
frankness * than flattery. Pro 28:23
There is * hope for a fool than Pro 29:20
craving *: no, three things! Pro 30:15,16
she is worth * than precious gems! Pro 31:10
For the * my wisdom, the more my Ecc 1:16-18
For the more my wisdom, the * my Ecc 1:16-18
* than any of the kings before me. Ecc 2:7,8
I did— that wisdom is of * value Ecc 2:13,14
to keep gaining * riches, and to Ecc 4:8
Two can accomplish * than twice Ecc 4:9
happiness! The * you have, the Ecc 5:11
The more you have, the * you Ecc 5:11
The * words you speak, the less Ecc 6:11
A GOOD REPUTATION is * valuable Ecc 7:1
A prostitute is * bitter than Ecc 7:26
That is why men are not * careful Ecc 9:2,3
in anything here on earth any *. Ecc 9:6
no one thought any * about him. Ecc 9:15
THIS SONG OF songs, * wonderful Sol 1:1
The perfume of your love is * Sol 4:10
Don't bring me any * of them. Is 1:11
I want nothing * to do with them. Is 1:12,13
What * could I have done? Is 5:4
clouds not to rain on it any *. Is 5:6
of battle gear; no * the Is 9:5
will not fight each other any *. Is 11:13
the vineyards will be heard no *; Is 16:10
* details of the feast are seen in Is 21:5f
harp and timbrel are heard no *; Is 24:8
the happy days are ended. No * Is 24:9
So scoff no *, lest your Is 28:22
want any * of your reports!" Is 30:10,11
we've heard * than enough about Is 30:10,11
you shall weep no *, for he will Is 30:19
just a little * than a Is 32:10
confidence will reign forever *. Is 32:17
What's *, do you think I have Is 36:10
will let you live fifteen * years. Is 38:5
not be shut against him any *. Is 45:1
to Christ in the * distant future, Is 45:13f
— "you shall do * than restore Is 49:6
winds will not reach them any *. Is 49:10
return and say, 'We need * room! Is 49:20
you shall drink no * of my fury; Is 51:22
for she who was abandoned has * Is 54:1
be remembered no *, for your Is 54:4
Why were you * afraid of them Is 57:11
shall not be heard there any *. Is 65:19
no *! Is 65:25
of God, it is no * acceptable to Is 66:3
Then, when your land is once * Jer 3:16
Pray no * for these people, Jer 7:16
the young men gather no * in the Jer 9:21
rite like theirs, and nothing *. Jer 9:25,26
have to come any * to my Temple? Jer 11:15
ask me any * to bless this people. Jer 14:11
Don't pray for them any *. Jer 14:11
don't you join them any * in Jer 16:8
will scarcely be mentioned any *. Jer 16:14,15
he may speak no * against us, nor Jer 18:18
the Lord—never * speak in his Jer 20:9
nation and once * give kings to sit Jer 22:4
fall and rise no *, for I am Jer 25:27
care anything about you any *; Jer 30:14
land happier and * prosperous than Jer 33:10,11
doomed—will once * see shepherds Jer 33:12
reply: I would no * reject my Jer 33:25,26
* literally, "a large brazier in Jer 36:22f
this time the Lord added a lot *! Jer 36:32
of Babylon any *, for I am with you Jer 42:11
will not obey any * now than you Jer 42:21
and blessing any *, saying, 'O Lord Jer 44:26
And now the Lord has added *! Jer 45:3
brag of Moab any *, for there is a Jer 48:2,3,4
for you even * than for Jazer. Jer 48:32
must suffer, how much * must you! Jer 49:12
to be happy once * on Mount Ephraim Jer 50:19
sink, never * to rise, because of Jer 51:64
about there were a hundred *. Jer 52:23
eleven years later, he took 832 *; Jer 52:29
whiter than milk, * ruddy than Lam 4:7f
any * than they listened to me! Eze 3:7
don't use * than that. Eze 4:11
and has been even * wicked than the Eze 5:5,6,7
I will punish you * terribly than I Eze 5:9
The famine will become * and more Eze 5:16
The famine will become more and * Eze 5:16
There will be no * delays, O Eze 12:25
But you will lie no *; Eze 13:23
your nose and two * for your ears, Eze 16:12
and became * beautiful than ever. Eze 16:13
You have worshiped idols far * Eze 16:51
this proverb any * in Israel, for Eze 18:3
begun, and there is * ahead." Eze 19:14
* important than any daily task. Eze 22:26
and sinned even * than her sister. Eze 23:11
"She was in fact * debased than Eze 23:14,15
you will no * long for Egypt and Eze 23:27
you off from being a nation any *. Eze 25:7
of your songs. No * will there be Eze 26:13
Israel will once * live in their Eze 28:25
will disturb those waters any *. Eze 32:13
save my flock; no * will they be Eze 34:22
I am the Lord. No * will other Eze 34:28
I will do even * for you than I Eze 36:11
But they will not say this any *. Eze 36:14
be crowded once *, and everyone Eze 36:37,38
entrance, there were two * tables. Eze 40:40
I'll give you one * chance. Dan 3:15
The king grew * and more Dan 5:9
The king grew more and * Dan 5:9
Daniel soon proved himself * Dan 6:3
It was far * brutal and vicious Dan 7:7
It will be * brutal than any of Dan 7:23
will arise, * brutal than the Dan 7:24
Three * Persian kings will reign, Dan 11:2
and make it still * powerful. Dan 11:5
(meaning 'No * mercy') for I will Hos 1:6
for I will have no * mercy upon Hos 1:6
not to fear each other any *; Hos 1:18
children. The * my people Hos 4:7
the * they sinned against me. Hos 4:7
it up and lick their lips for *! Hos 4:8
O ISRAEL, REJOICE no * as others Hos 9:1
I will love them no *, for all Hos 9:15
she shall bear no * fruit. Hos 9:16
But the * wealth I give her, the Hos 10:1
I give her, the * she pours it on Hos 10:1
I give her, the * beautiful the Hos 10:1
But the * I called to him, the Hos 11:2
called to him, the * he rebelled, Hos 11:2
And now the people disobey * and Hos 13:2
now the people disobey more and *. Hos 13:2
For there are no * offerings of Joe 1:13
grape vines will flourish once *. Joe 2:22
forgiveness. Once * the autumn Joe 2:23
will pass through her any *. Joe 3:17
not leave her unpunished any *. Amo 1:3
not leave her unpunished any *. Amo 1:6
not leave them unpunished any *. Amo 1:9
not leave him unpunished any *. Amo 1:11
not leave them unpunished any *. Amo 1:13
not leave them unpunished any *. Amo 2:1
not leave them unpunished any *. Amo 2:4
not leave them unpunished any *. Amo 2:6
you the * for all your sins. Amo 3:2
Stupid even to ask, but no * Amo 6:12
* to me than the Ethiopians are? Amo 9:7
history, no longer nations any *. Ob 1:16
my thoughts once * to the Lord. Jon 2:7
This is no * your land and home, Mic 2:10
will be no * fortune-tellers to Mic 5:12
the straightest is * crooked than Mic 7:4
and * prosperous than before. Mic 7:11
They are a fierce people, * Hab 1:8
We are wicked, but they far *! Hab 1:13
What's *, these arrogant Hab 2:5
"Nothing then seemed * improbable Zep 2:15f
Day by day his justice is * Zep 3:5
will be over—you need fear no *. Zep 3:15
once * choose to bless Jerusalem.' Zec 2:11,12
there will be no * grasping Zec 14:21
Then once * the Lord will enjoy Mal 3:4
they are far * important than what Mt 6:25
And you are far * valuable to him Mt 6:26
tomorrow, won't he * surely care Mt 6:30
in heaven even * certainly give Mt 7:11
ask him to recruit * workers for Mt 9:38
how much * will you! Mt 10:25
You are * valuable to him than Mt 10:31
father and mother * than you love Mt 10:37
son or daughter * than me, you are Mt 10:37
Yes, and he is * than just a Mt 11:9
* brightly than John the Baptist. Mt 11:11
you to be merciful * than I want Mt 12:7
And how much * valuable is a Mt 12:12
other spirits * evil than itself, Mt 12:43,44,45
"For to him who has will * be Mt 13:12,13
rejoice over it * than over the Mt 18:13
again and saw some * men standing Mt 20:6
assumed they would receive much *. Mt 20:1
do things like this and much *. Mt 21:2
one dared ask him any * questions. Mt 22:4
"The * lowly your service to Mt 23:1
the * important things undone. Mt 23:2
give you many * responsibilities. Mt 25:2
so now I will give you much *.' Mt 25:2
*, and he shall have abundance. Mt 25:2
no * and to come out of the man. Mk 1:2
*, not even outside the door. Mk 2:
what you hear. The * you do this, Mk 4:2
The more you do this, the * you Mk 4:2
ate until they could hold no *! Mk 6:4
the news, but the * he forbade Mk 7:3
forbade them, the * they made it Mk 7:3
How many * miracles do you people Mk 8:1
For is anything worth * than his Mk 8:3
white, far * glorious than any Mk 9:
oh, help me to have *!" Mk 9:24
this child and enter him no *!" Mk 9:2
in order to spend * time with his Mk 9:30,31
Taking them aside, Jesus once * Mk 10:32
And I know it is far * important Mk 12:33
one dared ask him any * questions. Mk 12:34
widow has given * than all those Mk 12:43,44
and said, "What * do we need? Mk 14:63,64
But Jesus said no *, much to Mk 15:5
"Make sure you collect no * Lk 3:13
are much * important than bread!' Lk 4:4
make room for *, and running over. Lk 6:38
How can a student know * than Lk 6:40
Yes! And * than a prophet. Lk 7:26
has, to him shall be given *; Lk 8:18
to send out * laborers to help you, Lk 10:2
Then, teaching them * about Lk 11:5,6
seven other demons * evil than Lk 11:26
He replied, "Yes, but even * Lk 11:28
and warned them, "* than anything Lk 12:1
Not much * than that. Lk 12:6
Never fear, you are far * Lk 12:7
For life consists of far * than Lk 12:23
And you are far * valuable to him Lk 12:24
" 'Give it one * chance,' the Lk 13:8
For if someone * respected than Lk 14:8
follower must love me far * than Lk 14:26
or sisters—yes, * than his own Lk 14:26
world are * clever [in dishonesty! Lk 16:8
to the Lord, "We need * faith; Lk 17:5
who have, get *, and those who have Lk 19:26
for they dared ask no *! Lk 20:40
widow has given * than all the rest Lk 21:3
as he prayed * and more earnestly. Lk 22:44
as he prayed more and * earnestly. Lk 22:44
said, "Don't resist any *." Lk 22:51
Once *, for the third time, he Lk 23:22
loved the darkness * than the Jn 3:19
unless I do * and more miracles?" Jn 4:48
unless I do more and * miracles?" Jn 4:48
Literally, "sin no *." Jn 5:14f
were all the * eager to kill him Jn 5:18
and the Son will do far * awesome Jn 5:20
"You must show us * miracles if Jn 6:30,31
"Go where * people can see your Jn 7:3
and wrote some * in the dust. Jn 8:8
Go and sin no *." Jn 8:11
to me, and he is * powerful than Jn 10:29
of men * than the praise of God. Jn 12:43
Nor is the messenger * important Jn 13:16
"I don't have much * time to Jn 14:30
Father and you shall see me no *; Jn 16:10
"Oh, there is so much * I want Jn 16:12
be gone, and you will see me no *; Jn 16:16
of this world any * than I am. Jn 17:16
Once * he asked them, "Whom are Jn 18:7
When Pilate heard this, he was * Jn 19:8
you love me * than these others?" Jn 21:15
Literally, "* than these." Jn 21:15f
Once * he asked him, "Simon, son Jn 21:17
for them. And * and more believers Act 5:14
And more and * believers were Act 5:14
Paul became * and more fervent in Act 9:22
Paul became more and * fervent in Act 9:22
So after * fasting and prayer, Act 13:3
back to life again, no * to die. Act 13:34
In another Psalm he explained * Act 13:35
them once * before leaving town. Act 16:40
But the people of Beroea were * Act 17:11
"Come and tell us * about this Act 17:19
things and we want to hear *." Act 17:20
want to hear * about this later." Act 17:32
him the way of God * accurately." Act 18:25,26f
Lord Jesus, 'It is * blessed to Act 20:35
The next morning some forty or * Act 23:12,13
"Pretend you want to ask a few * Act 23:15
want to get some * information. Act 23:20
There are * than forty men hiding Act 23:21
that it was no * than twelve days Act 24:11
Literally, "having * accurate Act 24:22f
to make his stay * comfortable. Act 24:23
when I have a * convenient time, Act 24:25
prisoners listened * to the ship's Act 27:11

IORE Con't)
What's *, God has granted your Act 27:24
For the * we know of God's laws, Rom 3:20
helps us trust God * each time we Rom 5:4
sinners, how much * will he do for Rom 5:9
But the * we see our sinfulness, Rom 5:20
sinfulness, the * we see God's Rom 5:20
keep on showing us * and more Rom 6:1
and * kindness and forgiveness? Rom 6:1
and it has no * control over you. Rom 7:4
and now it is even * wonderful Rom 11:15
he will be far * ready to put the Rom 11:24
don't criticize each other any *. Rom 14:13
And now there is one * thing to Rom 16:17
of God's teachers * than another. 1Co 4:6
It would be far * honoring to the 1Co 6:7
mean we should eat * than we need. 1Co 6:13
themselves * completely to prayer. 1Co 7:5
For it sounds as if * harm than 1Co 11:17
the * important of these gifts. 1Co 12:31
but, even *, I wish you were all 1Co 14:5
is a greater and * useful power 1Co 14:5
* than any of the rest of you. 1Co 14:18
in the Lord. No * than two or 1Co 14:27
After that he was seen by * than 1Co 15:6
is * 1Co 15:45
You can be sure that the * we 2Co 1:5
for Christ, the * he will shower us 2Co 1:5
And that is even * true, if 2Co 1:12
was glorious, much * glorious is 2Co 3:9
us, we become * and more like him. 2Co 3:18
us, we become more and * like him. 2Co 3:18
And the * of you who are won to 2Co 4:15
won to Christ, the * there are to 2Co 4:15
and the * the Lord is glorified. 2Co 4:15
He is not the same any *. 2Co 5:17
That was my purpose even * than 2Co 7:12
He loves you * than ever when he 2Co 7:15
what they could afford, but far *; 2Co 8:3
Don't force anyone to give * than 2Co 9:7
you need and *, so that there will 2Co 9:8
eat, will give you * and more seed 2Co 9:10
give you more and * seed to plant 2Co 9:10
you can give away * and more fruit 2Co 9:10
and * fruit from your harvest. 2Co 9:10
I may seem to be boasting * than 2Co 10:8
But I have served him far *! 2Co 11:23
anyone to think * highly of me than 2Co 12:6
I have, the * I depend on him. 2Co 12:10
it seems that the * I love you, the 2Co 12:15
and power * and more within you? 2Co 13:5
and power more and * within you? 2Co 13:5
What's *, the Scriptures looked Gal 3:8,9
become slaves once * to another Gal 4:9
you will pay * attention to them. Gal 4:17
you many children—* children than Gal 4:27
be persecuted no *—for that message Gal 5:11
This is just one * reason for us Eph 1:14
Yes, his honor is far * glorious Eph 1:21
And I pray that Christ will be * Eph 3:17
will be more and * at home in your Eph 3:17
is able to do far * than we would Eph 3:20
—and so become * and more in every Eph 4:15,16
—and so become more and * in every Eph 4:15,16
things of this life * than God. Eph 5:5
you will overflow * and more with Php 1:9
overflow more and * with love for Php 1:9
they have become * and more bold Php 1:14
become more and * bold in telling Php 1:14
But if living will give me * Php 1:22
be of * help to you by staying! Php 1:24
you must be even * careful to do Php 2:12
So I am all the * anxious to get Php 2:28
What's *, I was a member of the Php 3:5
quarrel no *—be friends again. Php 4:2
which is far * wonderful than the Php 4:7
me say this one * thing: Fix your Php 4:8
At the moment I have all I need—* Php 4:18
learning * and more of what is Col 3:10
learning more and * of what is Col 3:10
constantly to be * and more like Col 3:10
to be more and * like Christ who Col 3:10
to come back to see you once *. 1Th 2:17
* and more closely to that ideal. 1Th 4:1
more and * closely to that ideal. 1Th 4:1
beg you to love them * and more. 1Th 4:10
beg you to love them more and *. 1Th 4:10
* literally, "church leader" or 1Ti 3:1f
exercise is much * important and is 1Ti 4:8
I am * than willing to suffer if 2Ti 2:10
to them they are * likely, with 2Ti 2:25
* literally, "elders." Tit 1:5f
* literally, "elders." Tit 1:7f
After that have nothing * to do Tit 3:10
Now he will mean much * to you Phm 1:16
you will do what I ask and even *! Phm 1:21
has poured out * gladness upon you Heb 1:9
But Jesus has far * glory than Heb 3:3
gets * praise than his house does. Heb 3:3
There is much * I would like to Heb 5:11
with a far * important work than Heb 8:6
contains far * wonderful promises. Heb 8:6
I will remember their sins no *." Heb 8:12
think how much * surely the blood Heb 9:14
with far * precious offerings. Heb 9:23
* sacrifices to get rid of them. Heb 10:18
Think how much * terrible the Heb 10:29
God * than Cain's offering did. Heb 11:4
Well, how much * do I need to Heb 11:32
we not all the * cheerfully submit Heb 12:9
But he gives us * and more Jas 4:6
But he gives us more and * Jas 4:6
* precious to God than mere gold; 1Pe 1:7
a great deal to know * about it. 1Pe 1:12
intelligently to * of God's 1Pe 1:13
for *, as a baby cries for milk. 1Pe 2:2,3f
What's *, you are his holy 1Pe 2:5
join them any * in the wicked 1Pe 4:4
Do you want * and more of God's 2Pe 1:2
Do you want more and * of God's 2Pe 1:2
gifts, you need * than faith; 2Pe 1:5
them deeply. The * you go on in 2Pe 1:8
in this way, the * you will grow 2Pe 1:8
* time for sinners to repent. 2Pe 3:9
will learn to love God * and more. 1Jn 2:5
will learn to love God more and *. 1Jn 2:5
This makes us all the * certain 1Jn 2:18
Lord will surely feel it even *, 1Jn 3:20
love grows * perfect and complete; 1Jn 4:17
Well, I would like to say much *, 2Jn 1:12
May you be given * and more of Jud 1:2
May you be given more and * of Jud 1:2
up your lives ever * strongly upon Jud 1:20
to rise from death, to die no *. Rev 1:5
therefore implies "to die no *." Rev 1:5f
be secure, and will go out no *; Rev 3:12
ends, but there are two * coming! Rev 9:12
there should be no * delay, but Rev 10:6
done to you, and *—give double Rev 18:6
music be there—no * pianos, Rev 18:22
will be no * milling of the grain. Rev 18:22
be seen again. No * joyous wedding Rev 18:23
the nations any * until the Rev 20:3
there shall be no * death, nor Rev 21:4
doing wrong will do it * and more; Rev 22:11
doing wrong will do it more and *; Rev 22:11
the vile will become * vile; Rev 22:11

MOREH
set up camp beside the oak at *. Gen 12:6
Gilgal, where the oaks of * are. Deu 11:30
the valley beside the hill of *. Ju 7:1

MOREOVER
from Laban's. *, he watched for Gen 30:41
Please let him marry her. *, we Gen 34:9,10
be his assistant; *, I have given Ex 31:6
if he had lived. *, this is a Num 27:8
people you fear. *, the Lord your Deu 7:20
I find, *, that there have been Ez 4:20
in their work. *, I decree that Ez 6:8
God of Israel. *, you are to Ez 7:16
*, I notice that throughout the Ecc 3:16
into the skies. *, he further Act 2:34
as the Nazarenes. *, he was trying Act 24:6
Christ, forever. *, because of Eph 1:11

MORESHETH
in the town of * during the reigns Mic 1:1
Write off * Mic 1:14

MORIAH
go to the land of * and sacrifice Gen 22:2
the top of Mount *, where the Lord 2Ch 3:1

MORNING
and there was *, one day (or, Gen 1:4,5f
and there was *, a second day (or, Gen 1:7,8f
and there was *, a third day (or, Gen 1:13f
and there was *, a fourth day (or, Gen 1:19f
and there was *, a fifth day (or, Gen 1:23f
and there was *, a sixth day (or, Gen 1:31f
At dawn the next * the angels Gen 19:15
That * Abraham was up early and Gen 19:27
The next * she said to her Gen 19:34
The king was up early the next *, Gen 20:8
up early the next *, prepared food Gen 21:14
The next * Abraham got up early, Gen 22:3
But early the next * he said, Gen 24:54
In the *, as soon as they were Gen 26:31
The next * he got up very Gen 28:18
But in the *—it was Leah! Gen 29:25
Laban was up early the next * Gen 31:55
The next * Joseph noticed that Gen 40:6
Next *, as he thought about it, Gen 41:8
He devours his enemies in the *, Gen 49:27
to Pharaoh in the *, to be there as Ex 7:15
up early in the * and meet Pharaoh Ex 8:20
The next * all the cattle of the Ex 9:6
up early in the * and stand before Ex 9:13
and when it was *, the east wind Ex 10:13
But in the early * Jehovah Ex 14:24
to normal beneath the * light. Ex 14:27
In the * you will see more of Ex 16:7,8,9
the evening, and bread in the *. Ex 16:7,8,9
meat and in the * you will be Ex 16:11,12
camp, and in the * the desert all Ex 16:13
later in the * it left tiny flakes Ex 16:14
listen, and left it until *; Ex 16:20
So they gathered the food * by Ex 16:21
food morning by *, each home Ex 16:21
And the next * the food was Ex 16:24
each other, from * to evening. Ex 18:13
On the * of the third day there Ex 19:16
left unoffered until the next *. Ex 23:18
and early the next * he built an Ex 24:4
remains until the *, burn it; Ex 29:34
* and the other in the evening. Ex 29:39
libation as in the *, for a Ex 29:41
"Every * when Aaron trims the Ex 30:7
So they were up early the next * Ex 32:6
Be ready in the * to come up Ex 34:2
kept over until the following *. Ex 34:25
gifts were received each *. Ex 36:3
(The next *) the priest shall Lev 6:10
on fresh wood each *, and lay the Lev 6:12
in the * and half in the evening. Lev 6:19,20
to the regular * offering. Lev 9:17
of Holies. Each * and evening Aaron Lev 24:3,4
it until the next *, and must not Num 9:12
the night and moved on the next *. Num 9:20,21
They were up early the next *, Num 14:40
with him, "In the * the Lord will Num 16:5
But the very next * all the Num 16:41
tell you in the * whatever the Lord Num 22:8
The next * Balaam told the men, Num 22:13
So the next * he saddled his Num 22:21
The next * Balak took Balaam to Num 22:41
the *, the other in the evening. Num 28:4
and the first thing in the *. Deu 6:7
shall be left until the next *. Deu 16:4
back to your homes the next *. Deu 16:7
that you will see the * light. Deu 28:66
In the * you will say, 'Oh, that Deu 28:67
will say, 'Oh, that * were here!' Deu 28:67
EARLY THE NEXT * Joshua and all Jos 3:1
In the * Joshua ordered the Jos 3:6
At dawn the next * they went Jos 6:12,13,14
In the * you must come by Jos 7:14
So, early the next *, Joshua Jos 7:16
Early the next * Joshua roused Jos 8:10
out early the next * and attacked Jos 8:14
Early the next *, as the city Ju 6:28
and if, in the *, the fleece is wet Ju 6:37
When he got up the next * he Ju 6:38
and in the *, as soon as it is Ju 9:33
The next * as Gaal sat at the Ju 9:35
"In the *," they thought, "when Ju 16:2
The next * they were up early Ju 19:8
taking turns raping her until *. Ju 19:25
early the next * to go to Gibe-ah, Ju 20:19,20
The next * they were up early and Ju 21:4
She asked me this * if she could Ru 2:7
Stay here tonight, and in the * Ru 3:13
lie down until the *." Ru 3:13
his feet until the * and was up Ru 3:14
up early the next * and went to the 1Sa 1:19,20
Samuel stayed in bed until *, 1Sa 3:15
to see it the next *, Dagon had 1Sa 5:3
but the next * the same thing had 1Sa 5:4
in the * I will tell you what you 1Sa 9:19
At daybreak the next *, Samuel 1Sa 9:26,27
But early the next * Saul 1Sa 11:11
and slaughtered them all *. 1Sa 11:11
Early the next * he went out to 1Sa 15:12
For forty days, twice a day, * 1Sa 17:16
early the next * with the gifts. 1Sa 17:20
"Tomorrow *," he warned him, 1Sa 19:2
The next * 1Sa 19:4
him when he came out in the *. 1Sa 19:11
him, "you'll be dead by *." 1Sa 19:11
The next *, as agreed, Jonathan 1Sa 20:35
men remains alive by tomorrow *!" 1Sa 25:22
men would be alive tomorrow *." 1Sa 25:34
with David until the next *. 1Sa 25:36
Now get up early in the * and 1Sa 29:10
all have gone home tomorrow *." 2Sa 2:27
* until they arrived at Mahanaim. 2Sa 2:29
Finally the next * David wrote a 2Sa 11:14
look so haggard * after morning?" 2Sa 13:4
look so haggard morning after *?" 2Sa 13:4
He got up early every * and went 2Sa 15:2
He shall be as the light of the * 2Sa 23:4
The next * the word of the Lord 2Sa 24:11
*, and it lasted for three days; 2Sa 24:15
And in the * when I tried to 1Ki 3:21
and meat each * and evening, and he 1Ki 17:6
and they called to Baal all *, 1Ki 18:26
the * sacrifice was offered—look! 2Ki 3:20
But early the next * the sun 2Ki 3:22
up early the next * and went 2Ki 6:15
Even if we wait until *, some 2Ki 7:9
leave them there until the next *. 2Ki 10:8
In the * he went out and spoke to 2Ki 10:9,10
all across the landscape in the *. 2Ki 19:35
and they opened the gates each * 1Ch 9:27
to the Lord each * and evening upon 1Ch 16:40
Each * and evening they stood 1Ch 23:30

(MORNING Con't)
offerings each * and evening, and 2Ch 2:4
to the Lord every * and 2Ch 13:11
Early the next * the army of 2Ch 20:20
Early the next *, King Hezekiah 2Ch 29:20
for the daily * and evening burnt 2Ch 31:3
had been busy from * till night 2Ch 35:14
to sacrifice * and evening burnt Ez 3:3
and read from early * until noon. Neh 8:1
and the next * returned to the Est 2:12,13,14
and in the * ask the king to let Est 5:14
up early in the * and offering a Job 1:5
see it, never see the * light. Job 3:9
They are alive in the *, but by Job 4:20
*,' and then I toss till dawn. Job 7:4
inquisitor every *, and test him Job 7:18
darkness will be as bright as *! Job 11:17
The black night is their *; Job 24:17
as the * stars sang together and Job 38:6,7
once commanded the * to appear, and Job 38:12
Each * I will look to you in Ps 5:3
night, but in the * there is joy. Ps 30:5
And "in the *" those who are Ps 49:14
I will pray *, noon, and night, Ps 55:17
But as for me, I will sing each * Ps 59:16
is green in the * but mowed down Ps 90:5,6
darkness, nor disasters in the *. Ps 91:6
Every * tell him, "Thank you for Ps 92:2
be renewed day by day like * dew. Ps 110:3
Early in the *, before the sun Ps 119:147
so hard from early * until late at Ps 127:2
If I ride the * winds to the Ps 139:9
And when I waken in the *, you Ps 139:17,18
in the *, for I am trusting you. Ps 143:8
the dawn gives way to * splendor, Pro 4:18
when you wake up in the *, let Pro 6:22
fill of love until *, for my Pro 7:18
*, he will count it as a curse! Pro 27:14
are already drunk in the *. Ecc 10:16,17
Until the * dawns and the Sol 4:6
up early in the * to go on long Is 5:11
heaven, O Lucifer, son of the *! Is 14:12
on the very * that you plant it, Is 17:11
autumn * during harvest time. Is 18:4
*, all these lay dead before them. Is 37:36
they are gone like * mist at Is 44:22
these weary ones. * by morning he Is 50:4
Morning by * he wakens me and Is 50:4
has come; the * dawns, for your Eze 7:10,11
The next * this message came to Eze 12:8
the people in the *, and in the Eze 24:18
The next * I did all the Lord had Eze 24:18
"Each * a yearling lamb must be Eze 46:13
must be a meal offering each *— Eze 46:14,15
every * for the daily sacrifice. Eze 46:14,15
Very early the next * he hurried Dan 6:19
For your love vanishes like * Hos 6:4
night, and in the * it flames forth Hos 7:6
In one * the king of Israel shall Hos 10:15
They shall disappear like * Hos 13:3
Sacrifice each * and bring your Amo 4:4
he turns the * to darkness and Amo 4:13
darkness into *, and day into Amo 5:8
The next * the worm ate through Jon 4:7
by the Gentiles from * till night. Mal 1:11
About four o'clock in the * Jesus Mt 14:25
red sky in the * means foul Mt 16:2,3
went out early one * to hire Mt 20:1
In the *, as he was returning to Mt 21:18
WHEN IT WAS *, the chief priests Mt 27:1
house that * he asked them, "Which Mt 27:17
that *, one on either side of him. Mt 27:38
EARLY ON SUNDAY *, as the new day Mt 28:1
"Good *!" Mt 28:9
and on Saturday * went into the Mk 1:21
The next * he was up long before Mk 1:35
About three o'clock in the * he Mk 6:48
The next * as they left Bethany, Mk 11:12
Next *, as the disciples passed Mk 11:20
* you will deny me three times." Mk 14:30
EARLY IN THE * the chief priests, Mk 15:1
* when the crucifixion took place. Mk 15:25
crucified that *, their crosses on Mk 15:27
Early the following *, just at Mk 16:1
It was early on Sunday * when Mk 16:9
Early the next * he went out into Lk 4:42
until the * Lot left Sodom. Lk 17:29
early in the * to hear him. Lk 21:37,38
Between now and tomorrow * when Lk 22:34
*, you will deny me three times." Lk 22:61
Early the next * at daybreak the Lk 22:66
BUT VERY EARLY on Sunday * they Lk 24:1
tomb early this * and came back Lk 24:22,23
The next *, back across the lake, Jn 6:22,23
* he was back again at the Temple. Jn 8:2
crows tomorrow *, you will deny Jn 13:38
ended in the early hours of the *. Jn 18:28
*, while it was still dark, Mary Jn 20:1
What you see this * was predicted Act 2:16
Later that * Act 5:21
The next * the judges sent Act 16:35
The next * some forty or more of Act 23:12,13
armory the next *, leaving him with Act 23:32
way to the early * light, Paul Act 27:33
He began lecturing in the * and Act 28:23
as the * fog—now you see it; Jas 4:14
* Star will shine in your hearts. 2Pe 1:19
And I will give you the * Star! Rev 2:28
I am the bright * Star. Rev 22:16

MORNINGS
hundred * and evenings." Dan 8:14f
* which has been told is true." Dan 8:26f

MORROW
literally, "on the *, which is Mt 27:62f

MORSEL
Gossip is a dainty * eaten with Pro 26:22
of this delicious *, Jerusalem. Is 5:14

MORSELS
her * of food in the wine." Ru 2:14f
What dainty * rumors are. Pro 18:8

MORTAL
each side to fight in * combat. 2Sa 2:15
*—born to die—shall worship him. Ps 22:29
they were merely * men, gone in a Ps 78:39
you to fear mere * men, who wither Is 51:12
puts his trust in * man and turns Jer 17:5
The connotation is "* man." Eze 2:1f
against yourselves in * combat! Eze 38:21
of Cushan and of Midian in * fear. Hab 3:7
Literally, "*." Rom 1:23f
(c) The Jewish priests, though *, Heb 7:8

MORTALITY
and your infant * rate will drop Eze 36:14

MORTALLY
* wounded by iceballs from heaven. Ps 78:48
and lie * wounded on the ground. Jer 14:17

MORTAR
and collected bitumen to use as *. Gen 11:3,4
carry heavy loads of * and brick. Ex 1:13,14
* used, and the house replastered. Lev 14:42
timbers, and * shall be carried out Lev 14:45

MORTARS
or pounded it in *, boiled it, and Num 11:8

MORTGAGE
their children or * their fields, Neh 5:2,3,4
"How dare you demand a * as a Neh 5:7
requiring them to * their lands and Neh 5:12

MORTGAGED
fields, too, are * to these men." Neh 5:5

MORTICIANS
Afterwards he commanded his * to Gen 50:2

MORTISE
to * into the next upright piece. Ex 26:17

MOSAIC
under the later * law, caused Gen 31:35f
Under * law, it was illegal to Amo 2:8f
is older than the * law); Jn 7:21,22,23

MOSERAH
of Bene-jaakan to *, where Aaron Deu 10:6

MOSEROTH
From Hashmonah to *; Num 33:15-37
From * to Bene-jaakan; Num 33:15-37

MOSES
She named him * (meaning Ex 2:10
The name * sounds like another Ex 2:10f
when * had grown up and become a Ex 2:11
Hebrew brothers! * looked this way Ex 2:12
When * realized that his deed Ex 2:14
ordered * arrested and executed. Ex 2:15
and executed. But * ran away into Ex 2:15
the girls away. * then came to Ex 2:17
* eventually decided to accept Ex 2:21
ONE DAY AS * was tending the flock Ex 3:1
*' father-in-law goes under two Ex 3:1f
in a bush. When * saw that the bush Ex 3:2
* -Moses! Who is it Ex 3:3,4
"Moses! *!" Ex 3:3,4
"Who is it?" * asked. Ex 3:3,4
and Jacob." (* covered his face Ex 3:6
a job like that!" * exclaimed. Ex 3:11
But * asked, "If I go to the Ex 3:13
BUT * SAID, "They won't believe Ex 4:1
a serpent, and * ran from it! Ex 4:3
But * pleaded, "O Lord, I'm just Ex 4:10
But * said, "Lord, please! Ex 4:13
* returned home and talked it Ex 4:18
"With your permission," * said, Ex 4:18
Before * left Midian, Jehovah Ex 4:19
So * took his wife and sons and Ex 4:20
As * and his family were Ex 4:24
to * and threatened to kill him. Ex 4:24
threw it against *' feet, remarking Ex 4:25,26
into the wilderness to meet *." Ex 4:27
of God, and met * there, and they Ex 4:27
other warmly. * told Aaron what Ex 4:28
So * and Aaron returned to Egypt Ex 4:29
had said to *, and Moses performed Ex 4:30
said to Moses, and * performed the Ex 4:30
* and Aaron went to see Pharaoh. Ex 5:1
But Aaron and * persisted. Ex 5:3
listen to *' and Aaron's lies!" Ex 5:9
When they met * and Aaron Ex 5:20
Then * went back to the Lord. Ex 5:
do to Pharaoh," the Lord told *. Ex 6
So * told the people what God had Ex 6:8
Now the Lord spoke to * again and Ex 6:
"But look," * objected, "my Ex 6:
Then the Lord ordered * and Aaron Ex 6:
and Aaron and * were their sons. Ex 6:2
Aaron and *, included in that Ex 6:2
the same Aaron and * to whom Ex 6:2
This is that * who argued with Ex 6:3
THEN THE LORD said to *, "See, I Ex 7:
So * and Aaron did as the Lord Ex 7:
commanded them. * was eighty years Ex 7:
Then the Lord said to * and Ex 7:
So * and Aaron went in to see Ex 7:1
The Lord pointed this out to *, Ex 7:1
For I have instructed * to hit Ex 7:1
Then the Lord instructed *: Ex 7:1
So * and Aaron did as the Lord Ex 7:2
wouldn't listen to * and Aaron, Ex 7:2
THE LORD SAID to *, "Go in again Ex 8:
Then the Lord said to *, Ex 8:
Then Pharaoh summoned * and Aaron Ex 8:
want them to go," * said, "and I Ex 8:
"All right," * replied, "it Ex 8:1
So * and Aaron went out from the Ex 8:1
of Pharaoh, and * pleaded with the Ex 8:1
And the Lord did as * Ex 8:1
Then the Lord said to *, "Tell Ex 8:1
So * and Aaron did as God Ex 8:1
Next the Lord told *, "Get up Ex 8:2
Pharaoh hastily summoned * and Ex 8:2
But * replied, "That won't do! Ex 8:2
"Yes," * said, "I will ask him Ex 8:29
So * went out from Pharaoh and Ex 8:30
And the Lord did as * asked and Ex 8:31,32
the Lord commanded *, "and tell Ex 9:1
Then Jehovah said to * and Aaron, Ex 9:8
from the kiln. *, toss it into the Ex 9:8
as he watched, * tossed it toward Ex 9:10
stand before * because of the Ex 9:11
as the Lord had predicted to *. Ex 9:12
Then the Lord said to *, "Get up Ex 9:13
Then Jehovah said to *, "Point Ex 9:22
So * held out his hand, and the Ex 9:23
Then Pharaoh sent for * and Ex 9:27
"All right," * replied, "as Ex 9:29
So * left Pharaoh and went out of Ex 9:33
as the Lord had predicted to *. Ex 9:35
THEN THE LORD said to *, "Go back Ex 10:1
So * and Aaron requested another Ex 10:3
Then * stalked out. Ex 10:6
So * and Aaron were brought back Ex 10:8
flocks and herds," * replied. Ex 10:9
Then the Lord said to *, "Hold Ex 10:12
So * lifted his rod and Jehovah Ex 10:13
an urgent call for * and Aaron and Ex 10:16
So * went out from Pharaoh and Ex 10:18
Then Jehovah said to *, "Lift Ex 10:21
So * did, and there was thick Ex 10:22
Then Pharaoh called for * and Ex 10:24
"No," * said, "we must take Ex 10:25
you again," Pharaoh shouted at *. Ex 10:28
"Very well," * replied. Ex 10:29
THEN THE LORD said to *, "I will Ex 11:1
of Israel, and * was a very great Ex 11:3
Now * announced to Pharaoh, Ex 11:4
Then, red-faced with anger, * Ex 11:8
The Lord had told *, "Pharaoh Ex 11:9
So, although * and Aaron did Ex 11:10
THEN THE LORD said to * and Aaron, Ex 12:1
Then * called for all the elders Ex 12:21
So the people of Israel did as * Ex 12:28
And Pharaoh summoned * and Aaron Ex 12:31
of Israel did as * said and asked Ex 12:35
Then Jehovah said to * and Aaron, Ex 12:43
instructions to * and Aaron. Ex 12:50
THE LORD INSTRUCTED *, "Dedicate Ex 13:1
Then * said to the people, "This Ex 13:3
* took the bones of Joseph with Ex 13:19
JEHOVAH NOW INSTRUCTED *, Ex 14:1
And they turned against *, Ex 14:11
But * told the people, "Don't be Ex 14:13
Then the Lord said to *, "Quit Ex 14:15
Meanwhile, * stretched his rod Ex 14:21
the Lord said to *, "Stretch out Ex 14:26
and horsemen." * did, and the sea Ex 14:27
in him and in his servant *. Ex 14:31
THEN * AND the people of Israel Ex 15:1
Then * led the people of Israel Ex 15:22
Then the people turned against *. Ex 15:24
* pleaded with the Lord to help Ex 15:25
bitterly against * and Aaron. Ex 16:2
Then the Lord said to *, "Look, Ex 16:4
Then * and Aaron called a meeting Ex 16:6
And Jehovah said to *, "I have Ex 16:11,12
And * told them, "It is the food Ex 16:15
And * told them, "Don't leave it Ex 16:19
and * was very angry with them. Ex 16:20
came and asked * why this had been Ex 16:22
maggots or odor. * said, "This is Ex 16:25

MOSES Con't)
the Lord asked *. Ex 16:28,29
Then * gave them this further Ex 16:32
them from Egypt. * told Aaron to Ex 16:33
had instructed *, and eventually it Ex 16:34
growled and complained to *. Ex 17:2
"Quiet!" * commanded. Ex 17:2
Then * pleaded with Jehovah. Ex 17:4
Then Jehovah said to *, "Take Ex 17:5,6
for everyone!" * did as he was Ex 17:5,6
water gushed out! * named the Ex 17:7
at Rephidim. * instructed Joshua Ex 17:9
"Tomorrow," * told him, "I will Ex 17:9
Meanwhile *, Aaron, and Hur Ex 17:10
And as long as * held up the rod Ex 17:11
were winning. *' arms finally Ex 17:12
Then the Lord instructed *, Ex 17:14
of Amalek." * built an altar Ex 17:15,16
the banner of the Lord!" * said. Ex 17:15,16
WORD SOON REACHED Jethro, *' Ex 18:1
his people and for *, and how the Ex 18:1
Then Jethro took *' wife, Ex 18:2
home), along with *' two sons, Ex 18:3
"foreigner," for * said when he Ex 18:3
is my help," for * said at his Ex 18:4
They arrived while * and the Ex 18:5,6
to visit you," * was told, "and Ex 18:5,6
* went out to meet his Ex 18:7
went into *' tent to talk further. Ex 18:7
to talk further. * related to his Ex 18:8
The next day * sat as usual to Ex 18:13
When *' father-in-law saw how Ex 18:14
for God's decisions," * told him. Ex 18:15,16
to the people? *, this job is too Ex 18:18
* listened to his father-in-law's Ex 18:24
They brought the hard cases to * Ex 18:26
Soon afterwards * let his Ex 18:27
Sinai and set up camp there. * Ex 19:2,3
* returned from the mountain and Ex 19:7
he asks of us." * reported the Ex 19:8
Then he said to *, "I am going Ex 19:9
So * went down to the people and Ex 19:14
and all the people trembled. * Ex 19:17
louder and louder, * spoke and God Ex 19:19
Sinai and called * up to the top Ex 19:20
mountain, and * ascended to God. Ex 19:20
But the Lord told *, "Go back Ex 19:21
into the mountain!" * protested. Ex 19:23
So * went down to the people and Ex 19:25
They said to *, "You tell us Ex 20:19
"Don't be afraid," * told them, Ex 20:20
in the distance, * entered into the Ex 20:21
And the Lord told * to be his Ex 20:22
THE LORD NOW instructed *, "Come Ex 24:1
All of you except * are to Ex 24:1
at a distance. * alone shall come Ex 24:2
Then * announced to the people Ex 24:3
* wrote down the laws; Ex 24:4
to the Lord. * took half of the Ex 24:6
Then * threw the blood from the Ex 24:8
Then *, Aaron, Nadab, Abihu, and Ex 24:9
And the Lord said to *, "Come up Ex 24:12
So * and Joshua, his Ex 24:13
Then * went up the mountain and Ex 24:15
the seventh day he called to * Ex 24:16
raging fire. And * disappeared Ex 24:18
JEHOVAH SAID TO *, "Tell the Ex 25:1
And Jehovah said to *, "Whenever Ex 30:11,12
And the Lord said to *, "Make a Ex 30:17,18
Then the Lord told * to collect Ex 30:22,23
directions to * concerning the Ex 30:34
THE LORD ALSO said to *, "See, I Ex 31:1
instructions to *: "Tell the Ex 31:12,13
speaking with * on Mount Sinai, he Ex 31:18
WHEN * DIDN'T come back down the Ex 32:1
for this fellow * who brought us Ex 32:1
Then the Lord told *, "Quick! Ex 32:7
and I will make you, *, into a Ex 32:10
But * begged God not to do it. Ex 32:11
Then * went down the mountain, Ex 32:15
he exclaimed to *, "It sounds as Ex 32:17
But * replied, "No, it's not a Ex 32:18
When they came near the camp, * Ex 32:19
fellow * who led us out of Egypt.' Ex 32:23
When * saw that the people had Ex 32:25
Then * told the Levites, "Today Ex 32:29
The next day * said to the Ex 32:30
So * returned to the Lord and Ex 32:31
And the Lord replied to *, Ex 32:33
THE LORD SAID to *, "Lead these Ex 33:1
For the Lord had told * to tell Ex 33:5
* always erected the sacred tent Ex 33:7
Whenever * went to the Ex 33:8
door while the Lord spoke with *. Ex 33:9
the Lord spoke to * face to face, Ex 33:11
Afterwards * would return to the Ex 33:11
* talked there with the Lord and Ex 33:12
For * had said, "If you aren't Ex 33:15
And the Lord had replied to *, Ex 33:17
Then * asked to see God's glory. Ex 33:18
THE LORD TOLD *, "Prepare two Ex 34:1
So * took two tablets of stone Ex 34:4
* fell down before the Lord and Ex 34:8
And the Lord said to *, "Write Ex 34:27
* was up on the mountain with the Ex 34:28
stone tablets. * didn't realize as Ex 34:29
But * called them over to him, Ex 34:31
When * had finished speaking Ex 34:33
NOW * CALLED a meeting of all the Ex 35:1
Then * said to all the people, Ex 35:4
Lord's command to *—brought their Ex 35:29
And * told them, "Jehovah has Ex 35:30,31
Tabernacle." So * told Bezalel and Ex 36:1
work to begin. * gave them the Ex 36:3
task to meet with * and told him, Ex 36:4-7
the job!" So * sent a message Ex 36:4-7
designated by * and was supervised Ex 38:21
with the Lord's instructions to *. Ex 39:1
just as God had directed *. Ex 39:4,5
with the Lord's instructions to *. Ex 39:6,7
All this was commanded to * by the Ex 39:21
just as the Lord had commanded *. Ex 39:25,26
just as Jehovah had commanded *. Ex 39:28,29
of the Lord's instructions to *. Ex 39:32
the entire Tabernacle to *: Ex 39:33-40
all the Lord's instructions to *. Ex 39:42
to Moses. And * inspected all Ex 39:43
THE LORD NOW said to *, "Put Ex 40:1
So * proceeded to do all as the Ex 40:16
was put together. * erected it by Ex 40:18
it for washing. * and Aaron and Ex 40:31
just as the Lord had commanded *. Ex 40:32
So at last * finished the work. Ex 40:33
Lord filled it. * was not able to Ex 40:35
THE LORD NOW spoke to * from the Lev 1:1
these further instructions to *: Lev 4:1
And the Lord said to *, "If Lev 5:14
of a value determined by *. Lev 5:17,18
AND THE LORD said to *, "If Lev 6:1
Then the Lord said to *, "Give Lev 6:8
And Jehovah said to *, "On the Lev 6:19,20
Then the Lord said to *, "Tell Lev 6:24
Then the Lord said to *, "Tell Lev 7:22
And the Lord said to *, "Tell Lev 7:28
were given to * by the Lord on Lev 7:38
THE LORD SAID to *, "Now bring Lev 8:1
assembled, and * said to them, Lev 8:5
crown—as the Lord had commanded *. Lev 8:9
Then * took the anointing oil and Lev 8:10
Next * placed the robes on Lev 8:13
upon its head as * killed it. Lev 8:15,16
camp, as the Lord had commanded *. Lev 8:17
its head, and * killed it and Lev 8:19
* were followed in every detail. Lev 8:21
Then * presented the other ram, Lev 8:22
upon its head. * killed it and Lev 8:23
Literally, "* threw the blood Lev 8:24f
before the altar. * then took it Lev 8:28
the offering. Now * took the Lev 8:29
this was *' portion of the ram of Lev 8:29
Then * said to Aaron and his Lev 8:31
Then * stated again that all he Lev 8:34
all that the Lord had commanded *. Lev 8:36
ceremonies), * summoned Aaron and Lev 9:1
of Israel," * instructed, "to Lev 9:3
For today," * said, "Jehovah Lev 9:4
the Tabernacle, as * had commanded, Lev 9:5
* told them, "When you have Lev 9:6
* then told Aaron to proceed to Lev 9:7
Lord had commanded *, but he Lev 9:10
to him, just as * had commanded. Lev 9:21
from the altar. * and Aaron went Lev 9:23
Then * said to Aaron, "This is Lev 10:3
Then * called for Misha-el and Lev 10:4
their coats as * had told them to. Lev 10:5
Then * said to Aaron and his sons Lev 10:6
And they did as * commanded. Lev 10:7
Jehovah has given through *." Lev 10:11
Then * said to Aaron and to his Lev 10:12
Then * searched everywhere for Lev 10:16
But Aaron interceded with *. Lev 10:19
And when * heard that, he was Lev 10:20
THEN THE LORD said to * and Aaron, Lev 11:1
THE LORD TOLD * to give these Lev 12:1
THE LORD SAID to * and Aaron, "If Lev 13:1
AND THE LORD gave * these Lev 14:1
Then the Lord said to * and Lev 14:33,34
THE LORD TOLD * and Aaron to give Lev 15:1
the Lord said to *, "Warn your Lev 16:1
that the Lord gave to *. Lev 16:35
THE LORD GAVE to * these Lev 17:1
THE LORD THEN told * to tell the Lev 18:1
THE LORD ALSO told * to tell the Lev 19:1
THE LORD GAVE * these further Lev 20:1
THE LORD SAID to *: "Tell the Lev 21:1
And the Lord said to *, "Tell Lev 21:16,17
So * gave these instructions to Lev 21:24
THE LORD TOLD *, "Instruct Aaron Lev 22:1
And the Lord said to *, "Tell Lev 22:17,18
And the Lord said to *, "When a Lev 22:26,27
THE LORD SAID to *, "Announce to Lev 23:1
So * announced these annual Lev 23:44
THE LORD SAID to *, "Tell the Lev 24:1
and was brought to * for Lev 24:11
And the Lord said to *, "Take Lev 24:13,14
died, as Jehovah had commanded *. Lev 24:23
WHILE * WAS on Mount Sinai, the Lev 25:1
Israel, through *, on Mount Sinai. Lev 26:46
THE LORD SAID to *, "Tell the Lev 27:1
the Lord gave to * for the people Lev 27:34
the following instructions to *. Num 1:1
* and Aaron and the above- Num 1:17,18,19
as the Lord had commanded *. Num 1:17,18,19
Lord had said to *, "Exempt the Num 1:47,48,49
Lord to * were put into effect. Num 1:54
instructions to * and Aaron: "Each Num 2:1
by Jehovah's commandment to *). Num 2:32,33
indicated by the Lord to *. Num 2:34
to * on Mount Sinai, Aaron's Num 3:1
the generations of Aaron and *." Num 3:2f
Then the Lord said to *, Num 3:5
And the Lord said to *, "I have Num 3:11,12
The Lord now spoke again to * at Num 3:14,15
So * did: Num 3:16-24
for the tents of * and of Aaron and Num 3:38
as numbered by * and Aaron at the Num 3:39
Then the Lord said to *, "Now Num 3:40
So * took a census of the eldest Num 3:42
Now the Lord said to *, "Give Num 3:44
So * received redemption money Num 3:49
And * gave it to Aaron and his Num 3:51
THEN THE LORD said to * and Aaron, Num 4:1
Then the Lord said to * and Num 4:17,18,19
And the Lord said to *, "Take a Num 4:21,22,23
So * and Aaron and the other Num 4:34
out the Lord's instructions to *. Num 4:37
Thus * and Aaron and the leaders Num 4:46,47,48
to the Lord's instructions to *. Num 4:49
from the Lord to *: "Inform the Num 5:1
Then the Lord said to *, "Tell Num 5:5,6
And the Lord said to *, "Tell Num 5:11,12
THE LORD GAVE * these further Num 6:1
Now the Lord said to *, "Tell Num 6:22,23
* ANOINTED AND sanctified each Num 7:1
the Lord told *, "and use these Num 7:4,5
So * presented the wagons and the Num 7:6
The Lord said to *, "Let each Num 7:11
When * went into the Tabernacle Num 7:89
THE LORD SAID to *, "Tell Aaron Num 8:1
exact design the Lord had shown *. Num 8:4
Then the Lord said to *, "Now Num 8:5,6
So * and Aaron and all the people Num 8:20
Jehovah's instructions to *. Num 8:20
just as the Lord had commanded *. Num 8:22
The Lord also instructed *, "The Num 8:23,24
instructions to * while he and the Num 9:1
So * announced that the Passover Num 9:4,5
They came to * and Aaron and Num 9:6,7
* said he would ask the Lord Num 9:8
and whatever the Lord told * they Num 9:23
NOW THE LORD said to *, "Make Num 10:1
Lord's travel instructions to *. Num 10:13
One day * said to his Num 10:29
"Stay with us," * pleaded, Num 10:31
carried forward, * cried out, Num 10:35
They screamed to * for help, and Num 11:2
* heard all the families standing Num 11:10
hot; * too was highly displeased. Num 11:10
* said to the Lord, "Why pick on Num 11:11
Then the Lord said to *, "Summon Num 11:16
But * said, "There are 600,000 Num 11:21
Then the Lord said to *, "When Num 11:23
So * left the Tabernacle and Num 11:24
and talked with *, and the Lord Num 11:25
that was upon * and put it upon the Num 11:25
Some young men ran and told * Num 11:27
of Nun), one of *' personally Num 11:28
But * replied, "Are you jealous Num 11:29
Then * returned to the camp Num 11:30
* because his wife was a Cushite Num 12:1
is to a second wife of *. Num 12:1f
the Lord spoken only through *? Num 12:2
Immediately he summoned *, Num 12:3,4
* was the humblest man on earth. Num 12:3,4
I communicate with my servant *. Num 12:7,8
he cried out to *, "Oh, sir, do Num 12:11
And * cried out to the Lord, Num 12:13
And the Lord said to *, "If her Num 12:14
JEHOVAH NOW INSTRUCTED *, Num 13:1
at the time.) * did as the Lord had Num 13:3-15
It was at this time that * Num 13:16
* sent them out with these Num 13:17
They made their report to *, Num 13:26
the people as they stood before *. Num 13:30
of complaint against * and Aaron. Num 14:2
Then * and Aaron fell face Num 14:5
the Lord said to *, "How long will Num 14:10,11
it?" * pleaded with the Lord. Num 14:13
Then the Lord added to * and to Num 14:26,27
the camp when * reported God's Num 14:39
But * said, "It's too late. Num 14:41
the Ark nor * left the camp. Num 14:44
THE LORD TOLD * to give these Num 15:1

(MOSES Con't)
The Lord also said to * at this Num 15:17,18
the years through *, then when the Num 15:22
* and Aaron and the other judges. Num 15:33
Then the Lord said to *, "The Num 15:35
The Lord said to *, "Tell the Num 15:37,38
to incite a rebellion against *. Num 16:2
They went to * and Aaron and Num 16:3
When * heard what they were Num 16:4
Then * spoke again to Korah: Num 16:8,9
Then * summoned Dathan and Num 16:11,12
Then * was very angry and said to Num 16:15
And * said to Korah, "Come here Num 16:16
the Tabernacle with * and Aaron. Num 16:18
nation against * and Aaron, and Num 16:19
Jehovah said to * and Aaron, "Get Num 16:20
But * and Aaron fell face Num 16:22
And the Lord said to *, "Then Num 16:23,24
So * rushed over to the tents of Num 16:25
And * said, "By this you shall Num 16:28
And the Lord said to *, "Tell Num 16:36,37
Thus the Lord's directions to * Num 16:40
again against * and Aaron, saying, Num 16:41
Lord was seen. * and Aaron came Num 16:43,44
and the Lord said to *, Num 16:43,44
But * and Aaron fell face Num 16:45
And * said to Aaron, "Quick, Num 16:46
Aaron did as * had told him to, Num 16:47
Then Aaron returned to * at the Num 16:50
THEN THE LORD said to *, "Tell Num 17:1
So * gave the instructions to the Num 17:6
When * brought them out to show Num 17:9
The Lord told * to place Aaron's Num 17:10
* did as the Lord commanded him. Num 17:11
The Lord also said to *, "Tell Num 18:25,26
THE LORD SAID to * and Aaron, Num 19:1
rebelled against * and Aaron. Num 20:2
they shouted at *. Num 20:3
* and Aaron turned away and went Num 20:6
And he said to *, "Get Aaron's Num 20:7
So * did as instructed. Num 20:9
then * and Aaron summoned the Num 20:10
Then * lifted the rod and struck Num 20:11
But the Lord said to * and Aaron, Num 20:12
* struck it, not once, but twice. Num 20:12f
While * was at Kadesh he sent Num 20:14
Then the Lord said to * and Aaron Num 20:23
So * did as the Lord commanded Num 20:27
When they reached the summit, * Num 20:28
of the mountain. * and Eleazar Num 20:28
God and to complain against *. Num 21:5
Then the people came to * and Num 21:7
snakes." * prayed for the people. Num 21:7
So * made the replica, and Num 21:9
the Lord told *, "Summon the Num 21:16
Amorite country, * sent spies to Num 21:31,32
The Lord told * not to fear—that Num 21:34
issued the following command to *: Num 25:4
So * ordered the judges to Num 25:5
before the eyes of * and all the Num 25:6
Then the Lord said to *, Num 25:10,11
Then the Lord said to *, Num 25:16,17
Jehovah said to * and to Eleazar Num 26:1
So * and Eleazar issued census Num 26:3,4
with Korah against * and Aaron, and Num 26:5-11
Then the Lord told * to divide Num 26:52,53
They were the parents of Aaron, * Num 26:58,59
as prepared by * and Eleazar the Num 26:63
give a petition to *, Eleazar the Num 27:1
So * brought their case before Num 27:5
And the Lord replied to *, "The Num 27:6,7
One day the Lord said to *, "Go Num 27:12
Then * said to the Lord, "O Num 27:15
So * did as Jehovah commanded, Num 27:22
As the people watched, * laid Num 27:23
THE LORD GAVE * these instructions Num 28:1
So * gave all of these Num 29:40
NOW * SUMMONED the leaders of Num 30:1
the Lord gave * concerning Num 30:16
THEN THE LORD said to *, "Take Num 31:1
* said to the people, "Some of Num 31:3
men were sent to battle by *. Num 31:4,5
were brought to * and Eleazar the Num 31:12
from Jericho. * and Eleazar the Num 31:13
army, but * was very angry with Num 31:14
Jehovah has given *: 'Anything Num 31:21
And the Lord said to *, "You Num 31:25
So * and Eleazar the priest did Num 31:31
as the Lord had directed *. Num 31:41
people of Israel—* had separated it Num 31:42-46
Lord's directions, * gave two Num 31:47
leaders came to * and said, "We Num 31:48,49
* and Eleazar the priest received Num 31:51,52
So they came to * and Eleazar Num 32:2
do all the fighting?" * demanded. Num 32:6
Then * said, "All right, if you Num 32:20
So * gave his approval by saying Num 32:28
So * assigned the territory of Num 32:33
living there. So * gave Gilead to Num 32:40
* and Aaron led them out of Egypt. Num 33:1
out of Egypt. * had written down Num 33:2
that the Lord told * to tell the Num 33:50,51
THE LORD TOLD * to tell the people Num 34:1
among yourselves by lot," * said. Num 34:13
And the Lord said to *, "These Num 34:16-28
Jericho, the Lord said to *, Num 35:1
And the Lord said to *, "Tell Num 35:9,10
of Joseph) came to * and the Num 36:1
they reminded *, "and to give the Num 36:1
Then * replied publicly, giving Num 36:5
did as the Lord commanded *. Num 36:10
of Israel through *, while they Num 36:13
THIS BOOK RECORDS *' address to Deu 1:1
Here, then, is *' address to Deu 1:1
Then * instructed the people of Deu 4:41
Listed below are the laws * Deu 4:44,45,46
destroyed by * and the Israelis. Deu 4:44,45,46
* CONTINUED SPEAKING to the Deu 5:1
So * told the people, "You must Deu 5:32
THEN * AND the elders of Israel Deu 27:1
Then * and the Levite-priests Deu 27:9
That same day * gave this charge Deu 27:11
of Moab that * restated the Deu 29:1
AFTER * HAD said all these things Deu 31:1
Then * called for Joshua and said Deu 31:7
Then * wrote out the laws he had Deu 31:9
of the Lord. * also gave copies of Deu 31:9
Then the Lord said to *, "The Deu 31:14
instructions." So * and Joshua Deu 31:14
and said to *, "You shall die and Deu 31:16
So, on that very day, * wrote Deu 31:22
When * had finished writing down Deu 31:24
stubborn you are," * told them. Deu 31:27
So * recited this entire song to Deu 31:30
When * and Joshua had recited all Deu 32:44,45
people, * made these comments: Deu 32:46
That same day, the Lord said to * Deu 32:48
THIS IS THE blessing that *, the Deu 33:1
And * said of Judah: Deu 33:7
Then * said concerning the tribe Deu 33:8
the tribe of Benjamin, * said: Deu 33:12
Of the tribe of Zebulun, * said: Deu 33:18
Concerning the tribe of Gad, * Deu 33:20
Of the tribe of Dan, * said: Deu 33:22
Of the tribe of Naphtali, * said: Deu 33:23
THEN * CLIMBED from the plains of Deu 34:1
Promised Land," the Lord told *. Deu 34:4
So *, the disciple of the Lord, Deu 34:5
* was 120 years old when he died, Deu 34:7
for * had laid his hands upon him; Deu 34:9
that the Lord had given to *. Deu 34:9
prophet like *, for the Lord talked Deu 34:10
AFTER THE DEATH of *, the Lord's Jos 1:1
God spoke to *' assistant, whose Jos 1:1
I say to you what I said to *: Jos 1:3
be with you just as I was with *; Jos 1:5
letter every law * gave you, for if Jos 1:7
agreement with *: "The Lord your Jos 1:12,13
Jordan River," * had told them, Jos 1:12,13
just as we obeyed *," they assured Jos 1:17,18
God be with you as he was with *. Jos 1:17,18
am with you just as I was with *. Jos 3:7
Joshua by *, had been carried out. Jos 4:10
armed as * had instructed, and Jos 4:12,13
much as they had *, and respected Jos 4:14
at Mount Ebal, as * had commanded Jos 8:31
Literally, "the law of *." Jos 8:32f
given long before by *. Jos 8:33
and curses that * had written in Jos 8:34
Every commandment * had ever Jos 8:35
his disciple * to conquer this Jos 9:24
as * had commanded long before. Jos 11:12
Lord had commanded his disciple *; Jos 11:15
Moses; and * had passed the Jos 11:15
of the Lord's instructions to *. Jos 11:15
as the Lord had commanded *. Jos 11:20
just as the Lord had instructed *; Jos 11:23
king of Heshbon. * and the people Jos 12:6
these people, and * gave the land Jos 12:6
of the Jordan, for * had previously Jos 13:8
the Rephaim, for * had attacked Jos 13:12
* hadn't assigned any land to the Jos 13:14
* had assigned the following area Jos 13:15
and was killed by * along with the Jos 13:21
* also assigned land to the tribe Jos 13:24
* had assigned the following Jos 13:29
That was how * divided the land Jos 13:32
from Jericho. But * had given no Jos 13:33
(* had already given land to the Jos 14:3,4
with the Lord's directions to *. Jos 14:5
"Remember what the Lord said to * Jos 14:6
at the time, and * had sent us from Jos 14:7
the Lord my God, * told me, 'The Jos 14:9
now as I was when * sent us on that Jos 14:11
"The Lord told * that we were to Jos 17:4
commanded through *, these five Jos 17:5,6
the Jordan where * promised them Jos 18:7
of Refuge, as I instructed *. Jos 20:2
"The Lord instructed * to give Jos 21:2
So the Lord's command to * was Jos 21:8
Lord's disciple * commanded you, Jos 22:2,3
the Lord's servant *, on the other Jos 22:4
of the commandments * gave you. Jos 2
sent them home. (* had assigned Jos 22:
in the book of the laws of *; Jos 2
"Then I sent * and Aaron to Jos 2
the descendants of *' Ju 1
Lord had given to them through *. Ju
the descendants of *' father-in-law Ju 4:
who appeared to * and rescued Ju 6:
(son of Gershom and grandson of *! Ju 18:
"It was the Lord who appointed * 1Sa 1
the Lord, he sent * and Aaron to 1Sa 1
in the law of * so that you will 1Ki
tablets which * had placed there at 1Ki
told your servant * that you had 1Ki 8:
proclaimed by his servant *. 1Ki 8:
through the law of * that fathers 2Ki 14
serpent that * had made, because 2Ki 18
obeyed all of God's commands to *. 2Ki 18
them by * the servant of the Lord. 2Ki 18:
gave them through *, I will never 2Ki 21
and followed all the laws of *; 2Ki 23:
Aaron, *, Miriam. 1Ch 6
commanded by * the servant of God 1Ch 6:
just as the Lord had instructed *. 1Ch 15:
and altar made by * in the 1Ch 21:
through *, you will prosper. 1Ch 22:
was the ancestor of Aaron and *. 1Ch 23:
sons of Amram: Aaron and *." 1Ch 23:1
As for *, the man of God, his 1Ch 23:14,
and grandson of *, was the chief 1Ch 26:23,2
* had built the Tabernacle 500 2Ch 1:2,
Tabernacle constructed by *, the 2Ch 1:2,
tablets which * had put there at 2Ch 5:1
with the instructions * had given; 2Ch 8:1
as prescribed in the law of *. 2Ch 23:1
The tax law enacted by * the 2Ch 24
Lord the tax that * the servant of 2Ch 24
in the law of *, that the fathers 2Ch 25:
by the law of * the man of God; 2Ch 30:1
given to you by *—I won't ever 2Ch 33:
be the laws of God as given to *! 2Ch 34:1
of the Lord through *." 2Ch 35:
as it is written in the law of *. 2Ch 35:1
by the laws of *, they roasted the 2Ch 35:1
in the laws of *, the man of God. Ez 3:
in the laws of *, sacrificing the Ez 3:
as instructed in the laws of *. Ez 6:1
laws which * had given to the Ez 7:
gave us through your servant *. Neh 1:6,
please remember what you told *! Neh 1:
of God which he had given to *. Neh 8:1
out to them the scroll of *' laws. Neh 8:
Jehovah had told * that the people Neh 8:14
as required by the laws of *. Neh 8:18
and you commanded them, through * Neh 9:14
laws as issued by his servant *. Neh 10:29
farms as decreed by the laws of *. Neh 12:44
ON THAT SAME day, as the laws of * Neh 13:1
and olive oil. * had decreed that Neh 13:5
* and Aaron as their shepherds. Ps 77:20
A prayer of *, the man of God. Ps 90:1
When * and Aaron and Samuel, his Ps 99:6
to * and the people of Israel. Ps 103:7
But God sent * as his Ps 105:26
When * spoke, the flies and Ps 105:31
They were envious of *; Ps 106:16
destroy them. But *, his chosen Ps 106:23
God, causing * serious trouble, Ps 106:32
days of old when *, God's servant, Is 63:11
the sea, with * as their shepherd? Is 63:11
before them when * lifted up his Is 63:12
to me, Even if * and Samuel stood Jer 15:1
in the law of * your servant. Dan 9:11
in the law of * has come true; Dan 9:13
I gave you *, Aaron, and Miriam Mic 6:4
* my servant on Mount Horeb. Mal 4:4
cancel the laws of * and the Mt 5:17
"Under the laws of * the rule Mt 5:21
"The laws of * said, 'You shall Mt 5:27
"The law of * says, 'If anyone Mt 5:31
"Again, the law of * says, 'You Mt 5:33
"The law of * says, 'If a man Mt 5:38
of the laws of * in a nutshell. Mt 7:12
required by *' law for lepers who Mt 8:4
read in the law of * how the Mt 12:5
Suddenly * and Elijah appeared Mt 17:3
one for you and one for * and one Mt 17:4
they asked, "did * say a man may Mt 19:7
Jesus replied, "* did that in Mt 19:8
and asked, "Sir, * said that if a Mt 22:24
command in the laws of *?" Mt 22:36
Pharisees were *, the way they keep Mt 23:2
Literally, "sit on *' seat." Mt 23:2f
prescribed by * for a leper who is Mk 1:43,44
For instance, * gave you this law Mk 7:10
Then Elijah and * appeared and Mk 9:4
looked around and * and Elijah were Mk 9:8
"What did * say about divorce?" Mk 10:3
"Teacher, * gave us a law that Mk 12:19
about * and the burning bush? Mk 12:26
God said to *, 'I am the God of Mk 12:26

(MOSES Con't)
"God was telling * that these Mk 12:27
by the laws of * after the birth of Lk 2:22
"Offer the sacrifice *' law Lk 5:14
Pharisees and teachers of *' Law. Lk 7:30
talking with him—* and Elijah! Lk 9:30
with him. As * and Elijah were Lk 9:33
one for * and one for Elijah!" Lk 9:33
One day an expert on *' laws came Lk 10:25
Jesus replied, "What does *' law Lk 10:26
the laws of * and the messages of Lk 16:16
won't listen to * and the prophets, Lk 16:31
"The laws of * state that if a Lk 20:28
writings of * himself prove this. Lk 20:37,38
about me by * and the prophets and Lk 24:44
upon us! For * gave us only the Jn 1:17
—the very person * and the Jn 1:45
And as * in the wilderness Jn 3:14
you of this to the Father—* will! Jn 5:45
Father—Moses will! *, on whose laws Jn 5:45
For you have refused to believe *. Jn 5:46
As the Scriptures say, '* gave Jn 6:30,31
Jesus said, "* didn't give it to Jn 6:32
None of you obeys the laws of *! Jn 7:19
whenever you obey *' law of Jn 7:21,22,23
*' law says to kill her. Jn 8:5
but we are disciples of *. Jn 9:28
We know God has spoken to *, but Jn 9:29
ancient times. *, for instance, Act 3:21,22
Stephen curse *, and even God. Act 6:11
Temple and against the laws of *. Act 6:13
and throw out all of *' laws." Act 6:14
"About that time * was born—a Act 7:20
Israel. So * killed the Egyptian. Act 7:24
So Moses killed the Egyptian. * Act 7:25
"But the man in the wrong told * Act 7:27
"At this, * fled the country, Act 7:29
fire in a bush. * saw it and Act 7:31
Isaac and Jacob.' * shook with Act 7:32
judge over us?' * was sent to be Act 7:35
"* himself told the people of Act 7:37
in the wilderness, * was the Act 7:38
"But our fathers rejected * and Act 7:39
*, who brought us out of Egypt.' Act 7:40
the plan shown to * by the Angel. Act 7:44
from the Books of * and from the Act 13:15
the laws of *, against our Jewish Act 21:21
the prophets and * said— that the Act 26:22
of * and the books of prophecy. Act 28:23
time of Adam until *, God did not Rom 5:13
For God had said to *, "If I Rom 9:15
For * wrote that if a person Rom 10:5
in the time of *, God had said that Rom 10:19
For in the law God gave to * he 1Co 9:9
—as followers of *—their 1Co 10:2
could not bear to look at *' face. 2Co 3:7
as it shone from *' face is worth 2Co 3:10
and not as * did, who put a veil 2Co 3:13
Not only *' face was veiled, but 2Co 3:14
Yes, even today when they read * 2Co 3:15
angels to give to *, who then gave Gal 3:19
angels or * as go-betweens. Gal 3:20
he gave the Ten Commandments to *. Gal 4:24,25
of the laws of * when they haven't 1Ti 1:7
and Jambres fought against *. 2Ti 3:8
Priest, just as * also faithfully Heb 3:2
more glory than *, just as a man Heb 3:3
Well, * did a fine job working in Heb 3:5
out of Egypt with * their leader. Heb 3:16
those who lived in the time of *. Heb 4:2
* had never given them that work. Heb 7:12,13,14
for when * was getting ready to Heb 8:5
For after * had given the people Heb 9:19
to be made pure by * in this way, Heb 9:23
the laws given by * was killed Heb 10:28
*' parents had faith too. Heb 11:23
It was by faith that *, when he Heb 11:24,25
anger. * kept right on going; Heb 11:27
it must die. * himself was so Heb 12:21
to listen to *, the earthly Heb 12:25
with Satan about *' body, did not Jud 1:9
the song of *, the servant of God, Rev 15:3,4

MOST
me out in a * uncivil way." Gen 26:27
now, and expect to die * any day. Gen 27:2,3,4
him, "Swear to me * solemnly that Gen 47:29
be the first and * important month Ex 12:2
that was the * direct route from Ex 13:17,18
Holy Place and the * Holy Place. Ex 26:33
of the Ark—in the * Holy Place. Ex 26:34
be made by the * skilled of the Ex 28:5,6
"Then, using the * careful Ex 28:15
this incense is * holy. Ex 30:36
of the * skilled perfumers. Ex 37:29
for the altar shall then become * Ex 40:10
However, all of it is * holy, Lev 6:17
"This sacrifice is * holy, and Lev 6:25
but only they, for it is * holy. Lev 6:29
the * holy offering for guilt: Lev 7:1
for this is a * holy sacrifice. Lev 7:6
The offering is * holy; Lev 10:12
since it is * holy, and God has Lev 10:17
It is a * holy offering. Lev 14:13
the holy and * holy offerings. Lev 21:22
law of God, and are * holy." Lev 24:9
for they are * holy to the Lord. Lev 27:28
they carry the * holy things: Num 4:17,18,19
All these are * holy offerings. Num 18:9
They are to be eaten only in a * Num 18:10
And has knowledge from the * Num 24:15-19
the Lord hated *, thus provoking Deu 9:18
lie ahead. The * tenderhearted man Deu 28:54
your cities. The * tender and Deu 28:56,57
the strongest and * skillful of Ju 3:29
and killed * of them there. Ju 20:43
His son Saul was the * handsome 1Sa 9:2
of the * famous men in the world! 2Sa 7:9
with him. And * of Judah and half 2Sa 19:40
the Top Three—the * heroic men in 2Sa 23:8
* beautiful girl in all the land. 1Ki 1:3,4
The * famous of the hilltop 1Ki 3:4
of the Temple—the * Holy Place—was 1Ki 6:16
* Holy Place—was sixty feet long. 1Ki 6:17
the entrance to the * Holy Place. 1Ki 6:21,22
in front of the * Holy Place), the 1Ki 7:49
the doors to the * Holy Place, and 1Ki 7:50
of the Temple—the * Holy Place—and 1Ki 8:6
were captured, and * of the Syrian 1Ki 20:21
He was the chief and the * 1Ch 11:21
there were 3,000. (* of that tribe 1Ch 12:24-37
one end, was the * sacred room—the 2Ch 3:8
But for the * part they were 2Ch 30:10
revered God more than * people do. Neh 7:2
Jerusalem (though * of the leaders, Neh 11:3
us go and find the * beautiful Est 2:2
who pleases you * shall be the Est 2:4
and gave her the * luxurious Est 2:9
He was the * powerful official in Est 3:1
of Ahasuerus. The * propitious Est 3:7
one of the king's * noble princes Est 6:9
thing I long for *—to die beneath Job 6:8,9
Literally, "O * High." Ps 9:2f
do you hide when I need you the *? Ps 10:1
helps me do what honors him the *. Ps 23:2,3
the thing I seek * of all, is the Ps 27:4
to one of life's * perplexing Ps 49:4
ears to the * expert of charmers. Ps 58:4,5
hand of the * High has changed." Ps 77:10f
and "sons of the * High." Ps 82:6
Guard my words as your * precious Pro 7:2
and is seen * among the godly. Pro 16:31
* people will tell you what loyal Pro 20:6
* men have throughout their lives. Ecc 2:3
the living. And * fortunate of all Ecc 4:3
than the * expensive perfume. Ecc 7:1
you don't know, O * beautiful woman Sol 1:8
of the * skilled of craftsmen. Sol 7:1
* pious meetings—all are frauds! Is 1:12,13
And so Babylon, the * glorious of Is 13:19
heavens and be like the * High." Is 14:14
even the * stupid cannot miss the Is 35:8
"Even the * desolate parts of Is 49:19
me all these? For * of my children Is 49:21
captives of the * mighty and most Is 49:25
and * terrible shall all be freed; Is 49:25
* precious of their treasures. Jer 2:32
your lovers. The * experienced Jer 2:33
Why do you put on your * Jer 4:30
asks the Lord. * of all they hurt Jer 7:19
The heart is the * deceitful Jer 17:9
the city called '* Beautiful in All Lam 2:15
The nation we expected * to help Lam 4:17
twenty-five of the * prominent men Eze 11:1
the finest and * tender twig from Eze 17:22,23
and all the * tender cuts. Eze 24:4
You say, 'I am the * beautiful Eze 27:3
"This," he told me, "is the * Eze 41:4
shall eat of the * holy offerings Eze 42:13
the * sacred land of all. Eze 48:12
servants of the * High God! Dan 3:26
that the * High God did to me. Dan 4:2
that the * High dominates the Dan 4:17
"Your Majesty, the * High God Dan 4:24
you learn that the * High God Dan 4:25
and worshiped the * High God and Dan 4:34
Your Majesty, the * High God Dan 5:18
he knew that the * High overrules Dan 5:21
the people of the * High God shall Dan 7:18
He will defy the * High God, and Dan 7:25
of the saints of the * High." Dan 7:27f
begin, and the * Holy Place (in the Dan 9:24
"And some who are * gifted in Dan 11:35
Moab, Edom, and * of Ammon will Dan 11:41
or three at the *, he will set us Hos 6:2
to heaven, to the * High God. Hos 7:16
He was called the * fruitful of Hos 13:15
danger then. The * courageous of Amo 2:16
Zion will be the * renowned of all Mic 4:1
had mastered * of the Near East. Hab 1:6f
the tallest and * beautiful of Zec 11:2
things that are * important to me. Mal 2:1
where he had done * of his Mt 11:20
which is the * important command in Mt 22:36
The second * important is Mt 22:38,39
me, Jesus, Son of the * High God? Mk 5:7,8
but not the * ancient. Mk 9:29f
* honored stone in the building! Mk 12:10
which is the * important?" Mk 12:28
not found in the * ancient Mk 16:9f
Literally, "* excellent Lk 1:1f
"I bring you the * joyful news Lk 2:10
Even the * wicked will lend to Lk 6:34
preach—even the * wicked of them Lk 7:29
Which do you suppose loved him * Lk 7:42
owed him the *," Simon answered. Lk 7:43
with me, Jesus, Son of God * High? Lk 8:28
one of the * influential Jews in Lk 19:1
it to the man who earned the *.' Lk 19:24
"You're different from *. Jn 2:10
However, * commentators believe Jn 5:32,33f
* ancient manuscripts omit John Jn 7:53f
he had done, * of the people would Jn 12:37
In fact, * of them didn't even Act 19:32
sorrowing * of all because he said Act 20:38
am not insane, * Excellent Festus. Act 26:25
spend the winter—* of the crew Act 27:12
So this is the situation: * of Rom 11:7
even the * brilliant of them." 1Co 1:19
Now the * important thing about 1Co 4:2
Yet after all this * of them did 1Co 10:5
are really the * necessary. 1Co 12:22
those * gifted is still so poor. 1Co 13:9
at one time, * of whom are still 1Co 15:6
are the * miserable of creatures. 1Co 15:19
I was one of the * religious Gal 1:14
though I am the * useless Christian Eph 3:8
be wise: make the * of every Eph 5:15,16
* of all, let love guide your Col 3:14
Make the * of your chances to Col 4:5
have missed the * important thing 1Ti 6:21
also a priest of the * High God. Heb 7:1
(a) Even Abraham, the first and * Heb 7:4
But * of all, dear brothers, do Jas 5:12
Cornerstone, the * honored and 1Pe 2:7
men of prayer. * important of all, 1Pe 4:8
But since * people don't know 1Jn 3:1
satanic origin, as * commentators Rev 9:1f
ivory goods and * expensive wooden Rev 18:12

MOSTLY
such preaching is * for believers 1Co 14:24
and his work was * to illustrate Heb 3:5

MOTH
For the * shall destroy them Is 51:8
I will destroy her as a * does Hos 5:12
no thief can steal them; no * can Lk 12:33

MOTH-EATEN
rotten tree, like a * coat. Job 13:27,28
clothes are becoming mere * rags. Jas 5:2

MOTH-INFESTED
for he is as fragile as a * cloth; Ps 39:11

MOTHER
his father and * and is joined to Gen 2:24
become the * of all mankind"; Gen 3:20
and make her the * of nations! Gen 17:16
And his * arranged a marriage for Gen 21:20,21
presents to her * and brother. Gen 24:53
her * and brother exclaimed. Gen 24:55
you becomeThe * of many millions! Gen 24:60
to him after the loss of his *. Gen 24:67
Jacob: "But *! Gen 27:11,12
his father and * had sent Jacob to Gen 28:6,7,8
and brought them to his * Leah. Gen 30:14
"Shall I indeed, and your * and Gen 37:10
to them by their *, except for Er, Gen 38:3,4,5
* was a girl from Canaan). Gen 46:8-14
and Ephraim (their * was Asenath, Gen 46:19-22
For your * Rachel died after Gen 48:7
When the baby's * saw that he was Ex 2:1
girl rushed home and called her *! Ex 2:8
*, "and I will pay you well!" Ex 2:9
Shaul (whose * was a Canaanite). Ex 6:15
"Honor your father and *, that Ex 20:12
or * shall surely be put to death. Ex 21:15
or curses his * or father shall Ex 21:17
it with its * for seven days. Ex 22:30
"When a baby boy is born, the * Lev 12:2
nor a son his *, nor any other Lev 18:7
his father or his *, whether born Lev 18:9
she is a close relative of your *; Lev 18:13
his father or * shall surely be put Lev 20:9
with her *, it is a great evil. Lev 20:14
father or of his *, it is a Lev 20:17
the sister of his * or of his Lev 20:19
a near relative—a *, father, son, Lev 21:2,3
person—not even his father or *. Lev 21:11
be left with its * for seven days, Lev 22:26,27
You shall not slaughter a * Lev 22:28
a young man whose * was an Lev 24:10
his father, *, brother, or sister; Num 6:6,7
" 'Honor your father and * Deu 5:16
her father and * for a full month. Deu 21:13
children, and the * of his oldest Deu 21:15
obey his father or *, even though Deu 21:18

(MOTHER Con't)
his father and * shall take him Deu 21:19
in it with the * sitting in the Deu 22:6
don't take the * with the young. Deu 22:6
girl's father and * shall bring the Deu 22:15
who despises his father or *.' Deu 27:16
with my father and *, my brothers Jos 2:12,13
father, *, brothers, and anyone Jos 2:17,18
with her father, *, brothers, and Jos 6:23
Until Deborah became a * to Ju 5:7
The * of Sisera watched through Ju 5:28
only Abimelech's * was from Shechem Ju 9:2f
and they decided that since his * Ju 9:3
but his * was a prostitute. Ju 11:1
and * that he wanted to marry her. Ju 14:2
His father and * didn't realize Ju 14:4
tell his father or * about it. Ju 14:6
some of it to his father and *. Ju 14:9
even told it to my father or *; Ju 14:16
to live with his father and *. Ju 14:19
One day he said to his *, "That Ju 17:2
confessing it," his * replied. Ju 17:2
So his * took a fifth of it to a Ju 17:4,5
your father and * in your own land Ru 2:10,11
Each year his * made a little 1Sa 2:19
now your * shall be childless." 1Sa 15:33
shaming yourself and your *? 1Sa 20:30
for his father and * to live there 1Sa 22:3
as upset as a * bear who has been 2Sa 17:8
and his * was Abigal, the daughter 2Sa 17:25
the sister of Joab's * Zeruiah. 2Sa 17:25
where my father and * are buried. 2Sa 19:37
Then Rizpah, the * of two of the 2Sa 21:10
Adonijah (his * was Haggith) 1Ki 1:5
Solomon's *, and asked her, "Do 1Ki 1:11
to see Solomon's *, Bath-sheba. 1Ki 2:13
for his * be placed beside his; 1Ki 2:19
"What is it, my *?" 1Ki 2:20
who really was the * of the child, 1Ki 3:26
him to live, for she is the *!" 1Ki 3:27
his * was Zeruah, a widow. 1Ki 11:26
(Rehoboam's * was Naamah, an 1Ki 14:21
When Rehoboam died—his * was 1Ki 14:31
(Abijam's * was Maacah, the 1Ki 15:1
downstairs and gave him to his *. 1Ki 17:23
*, and then I'll go with you!" 1Ki 19:20
years. His * was Azubah, the 1Ki 22:42
of his father and * and of 1Ki 22:52,53
as his father and * had been, for 2Ki 3:2
prophets of your father and *!" 2Ki 3:13
"Carry him home to his *." 2Ki 4:19
So he took him home, and his * 2Ki 4:20
But the boy's * said, "I swear 2Ki 4:30
At that very moment, the * of the 2Ki 8:5
in Jerusalem. His * was Athaliah, 2Ki 8:26
* Jezebel are all around us?" 2Ki 9:22
and of the Queen *, Jezebel." 2Ki 10:13
WHEN ATHALIAH, THE * of King 2Ki 11:1
* was Zibiah, from Beer-sheba. 2Ki 12:1
years. (His * was Jeho-addin, a 2Ki 14:2
Name of his *: Jecoliah of 2Ki 15:1
* has no strength to deliver it. 2Ki 19:3
Name of his *: Hephzibah 2Ki 21:1
Name of his *: Jedidah (daughter 2Ki 22:1
Name of his *: Nehushta (daughter 2Ki 24:8,9
the queen * surrendered to him. 2Ki 24:12
and the queen *, to Babylon. 2Ki 24:15
second wife Atarah was the * of 1Ch 2:26
The second was Daniel, whose * was 1Ch 3:1
became the * of his sons Shime-a, 1Ch 3:5
his brothers. His * named him Jabez 1Ch 4:9
She was the * of Miriam, Shammai, 1Ch 4:17
she was the * of Jered, Heber, 1Ch 4:18
King Asa even removed his * 2Ch 15:16
being the queen * because she made 2Ch 15:16
* encouraged him in doing wrong. 2Ch 22:3
were Zabad, whose * was Shime-ath, 2Ch 24:26
and Jehozabad, whose * was 2Ch 24:26
* was Jerushah, daughter of Zadok. 2Ch 27:1
whose father and * were dead, and Est 2:7
and the worm my * and my sister. Job 17:13,14
Even the sinner's own * shall Job 24:20
Who is the * of the ice and Job 38:29
For if my father and * should Ps 27:10
though it were my *, friend or Ps 35:14
from the moment my * conceived me. Ps 51:5
the sins of his father and *. Ps 109:14
so that she becomes a happy *. Ps 113:9
Listen to your father and *. Pro 1:7,8,9
loved by my * as an only child, and Pro 4:3
man, obey your father and your *. Pro 6:20
sad the * of a rebel. Pro 10:1
A rebellious son saddens his *. Pro 15:20
Literally, "despises his *." Pro 15:20f
father and a bitter blow to his *. Pro 17:25
father or * is a public disgrace. Pro 19:26
man who curses his father or *. Pro 20:20
himself, he brings shame to his *. Pro 29:15
their father and *, and feel Pro 30:11,12
and despises his * shall have his Pro 30:17
see the crown with which his * Sol 3:11
tree where your * gave birth to you Sol 8:5
and *, "Why have you produced me? Is 45:10
Can a * forget her little child Is 49:15
Is your * gone because I divorced Is 50:1
And your * was taken in payment Is 50:1
little one is comforted by its *. Is 66:13
and for their * they have an idol Jer 2:26,27
King Jehoiachin and his * Jer 13:18f
suddenly. The * of seven sickens Jer 15:9
"What sadness is mine, my *; Jer 15:10
I will throw you and your * out Jer 22:26
Symbolic * of the northern tribes, Jer 31:15f
yet your * shall be overwhelmed Jer 50:12
an Amorite and your * a Hittite! Eze 16:3
" 'Like *, like daughter'—that Eze 16:44
For your * loathed her husband Eze 16:45
Truly, your * must have been a Eze 16:45
a woman your * was—like a lioness! Eze 19:2
"When Israel, the * lion, saw Eze 19:5
"Your * was like a vine beside Eze 19:10
it is his father, *, child, brother Eze 44:25
Plead with your *, for she has Hos 1:2
For their * has committed Hos 1:5
and I will destroy your *, Hos 4:5
the daughter defies her *; Mic 7:6
own father and * will slay him! Zec 13:3
and Zerah (Tamar was their *); Mt 1:3
father of Boaz (Rahab was his *); Mt 1:5
father of Obed (Ruth was his *); Mt 1:5
(his * was the widow of Uriah); Mt 1:6
* of Jesus Christ the Messiah). Mt 1:16
Jesus Christ: His *, Mary, was Mt 1:18
baby and Mary his * were, they Mt 2:11
the baby and his *," the angel Mt 2:13
the baby and his * back to Israel, Mt 2:20
to Israel with Jesus and his *. Mt 2:21
against her *, and a Mt 10:35
If you love your father and * Mt 10:37
his * and brothers were outside, Mt 12:46,47
he remarked, "Who is my *? Mt 12:48
he said, "these are my * and Mt 12:49
is my brother, sister and *!" Mt 12:50
we know Mary his * and his Mt 13:55
to the girl, who took it to her *. Mt 14:11
law is 'Honor your father and *; Mt 15:4
his father and *, and be forever Mt 19:5,6
your father and *, and love your Mt 19:19
sisters, father, *, wife, Mt 19:29
Then the * of James and John, the Mt 20:20
and Mary the * of James and Joseph, Mt 27:56
Joseph, and the * of James and John Mt 27:56
Now his * and brothers arrived at Mk 3:31,32
"Your * and brothers are outside Mk 3:31,32
He replied, "Who is my *? Mk 3:33
"These are my * and brothers! Mk 3:34
and my sister, and my *." Mk 3:35
girl's father and * and his three Mk 5:40
She went out and consulted her *, Mk 6:24
the girl and she took it to her *. Mk 6:28
God: 'Honor your father and *.' Mk 7:10
against his father or * must die. Mk 7:10
his father and *, and he and his Mk 10:6,7
respect your father and *." Mk 10:19
brothers, sisters, *, father, Mk 10:29
Mary (the * of James the Younger Mk 15:40
(Mary Magdalene and Mary the * of Mk 15:47
and Mary the * of James went out Mk 16:1
the * of my Lord should visit me! Lk 1:43
his * said to him. Lk 2:48
and his * stored away all these Lk 2:51
son of his widowed *, and many Lk 7:12
And Jesus gave him back to his *. Lk 7:15
Once when his * and brothers came Lk 8:19
he remarked, "My * and my Lk 8:21
the little girl's father and *. Lk 8:51
"God bless your *—the womb from Lk 11:27
his son, the other; * and Lk 12:53
he does his own father, *, wife, Lk 14:26
does not hate his father and *." Lk 14:26f
* of James, and several others. Lk 24:10
TWO DAYS LATER Jesus' * was a Jn 2:1
* came to him with the problem. Jn 2:3
But his * told the servants, "Do Jn 2:5
his *, brothers, and disciples. Jn 2:12
whose father and * we know. Jn 6:42
cross were Jesus' *, Mary, his Jn 19:25
When Jesus saw his * standing Jn 19:26
he said, "She is your *!" Jn 19:27
Several women, including Jesus' *, Act 1:14
the home of Mary, * of John Mark, Act 12:12
a believer whose * was a Christian Act 16:1
and also his dear * who has been Rom 16:13
who has been such a * to me. Rom 16:13
you the pains of a * waiting for Gal 4:19
his father and * when he marries, Eph 5:31
Honor your father and *. Eph 6:2
your father and *, yours will be a Eph 6:3
among you as a * feeding and caring 1Th 2:7
Lord, just as your * Eunice and 2Ti 1:5
Melchizedek had no father or * Heb 7:3
father or * were, no record of his Heb 7:3f
able to become a * in spite of her Heb 11:1
the Great, * of Prostitutes and of Rev 17:

MOTHER-CITY
a colony of the *, Sidon. Is 23:
a colony of the *, Sidon. Is 23:
Jerusalem, the * of the Jews, the Gal 4:24,2
But our * is the heavenly Gal 4:2

MOTHER-IN-LAW
*.' And all the people shall Deu 27:2
Orpah kissed her * good-bye, and Ru 1:1
have shown your * since the death Ru 2:10,1
and gave it to her *, with what was Ru 2:1
So Ruth told her * all about Ru 2:1
her *, and laid it on her back. Ru 3:15-1
the bride curses her *. Mic 7:
* was in bed with a high fever. Mt 8:1
against her *— a man's worst Mt 10:3
* sick in bed with a high fever. Mk 1:29,3
* very sick with a high fever. Lk 4:3
* will be spurned by her Lk 12:5

MOTHER-IN-LAW'S
and followed her * instructions. Ru 3:6,7

MOTHER'S
* tent, and she became his wife. Gen 24:67
So Jacob followed his * Gen 27:14
Literally, "your * father." Gen 28:2
Literally, "your * brother." Gen 28:2
Uncle Laban, his * brother—the son Gen 28:5
daughter of his * brother—and Gen 29:10
alone is left of his * children. Gen 42:38
brother Benjamin, his * son." Gen 43:29f
is left of his * children, and his Gen 44:20
boil a young goat in its * milk. Ex 23:19
cook a young goat in its * milk." Ex 34:26
"When a baby girl is born, the * Lev 12:5
nor your aunt—your * Lev 18:13
for judgment. (His * name was Lev 24:11
boil a young goat in its * milk. Deu 14:21
uncles—his * brothers—in Shechem. Ju 9:1
was his grandfather—his * father. 2Sa 13:37,38,39f
* name: Jerusha (daughter of 2Ki 15:32,33
His * name: Abi (daughter of 2Ki 18:1
His * name: Meshullemeth (daughter 2Ki 21:19,20
His * name: Hamutal (the daughter 2Ki 23:31,32
His * name: Zebidah (daughter of 2Ki 23:36,37
His * name: Hamutal (daughter of 2Ki 24:18,19
* name was Naamah the Ammonitess. 2Ch 12:13
He lasted three years. His * name 2Ch 13:1
in Jerusalem. His * name was 2Ch 20:31
in Jerusalem. His * name was 2Ch 22:2
in Jerusalem. His * name was 2Ch 24:1
in Jerusalem. His * name was 2Ch 25:1
in Jerusalem. His * name was 2Ch 26:3
in Jerusalem. His * name was 2Ch 29:1
"I came naked from my * womb," Job 1:21
failure to shut my * womb, for Job 3:10
from their * breasts, and take a Job 24:9
You took me safely from my * womb Ps 22:9,10,11
knit them together in my * womb. Ps 139:13
don't despise an old * experience. Pro 23:22
taught to him at his * knee: Pro 31:1
while it is yet in its * womb. Ecc 11:5
home, into my * old bedroom. Sol 3:4
Literally, "my * house." Sol 8:2f
formed me from my * womb to serve Is 49:5
an infant at a * generous breasts. Is 66:11
were formed within your * womb; Jer 1:5
Oh, that I had died within my * Jer 20:17
in Jerusalem. His * name was Jer 52:1
Consequently, at her * urging, Mt 14:8
his * womb and be born again?" Jn 3:4
* food—it's the other way around; 2Co 12:14

MOTHERLY
grandly, but has no true * love. Job 39:13

MOTHERS
me and these * and my children. Gen 32:11
You must respect your * and Lev 19:1
brothers, fathers, and *. Deu 33:9
the sons of many *, now your mother 1Sa 15:33
young men and sorrow to their *. Jer 15:8
city, and their * and fathers, Jer 16:3
and lame, young * with their little Jer 31:8
upon their *' shrunken breasts. Lam 2:12
Shall * eat their little Lam 2:20
fathers dead, our * widowed. Lam 5:3
Fathers and * are contemptuously Eze 22:7
destroyed; even * and children Hos 10:14
Once when some * Mk 10:13
brothers, sisters, *, children, and Mk 10:30
and to * nursing their children. Mk 13:17
One day some * brought their Lk 18:15
Woe to expectant * in those Lk 21:23
and *, for that pleases the Lord. Col 3:20
their fathers and *, and murder. 1Ti 1:9
Treat the older women as *, and 1Ti 5:2

MOTHS
crushed to death as easily as *! Job 4:18,19
like old clothes eaten up by *! Is 50:9

MOTION
and set in * by my blood. 1Co 11:25

MOTIONED
He * for a piece of paper and to Lk 1:63
Simon Peter * to me to ask him who Jn 13:24
no bounds. He * for them to quiet Act 12:17
* for silence and tried to speak. Act 19:33
and * to the people to be quiet; Act 21:40
The governor * for him to rise Act 24:10

MOTIONLESS
and the boy lay there limp and *, Mk 9:26

MOTIVE
" 'Yet all the time your real * Job 10:13,14
Then I observed that the basic * Ecc 4:4
But whatever their * for doing Php 1:18

MOTIVES
because of wrong * and wrong use of Gen 11:6f
I have done all this with good *, 1Ch 29:17
all their * and their thoughts. Ps 7:9
test my * and affections too. Ps 26:2
searchlight exposing his hidden *. Pro 20:27
every deed but God looks at our *. Pro 21:2
See the hearts and * of these Jer 11:20
examines deepest * so he can give Jer 17:10
their inmost thoughts and *; Rom 2:16
to you with good * and sincere Gal 4:18
But others have purer *, Php 1:15
false * or evil purposes in mind; 1Th 2:3
that you are guided by wrong *. Jas 2:4

MOTTLED
were streaked, speckled, and *. Gen 31:10
are speckled, streaked, and *." Gen 31:12f
speckled, and * he-goats. Gen 31:12

MOTTO
safety and their * will be, "The Jer 33:16

MOUND
* and may never be rebuilt. Deu 13:16
So Ai became a desolate * of Jos 8:28
Abel and built a * to the top of 2Sa 20:15

MOUNDS
built on * except for Hazor. Jos 11:13
See how the siege * have been Jer 32:24
Draw a picture of siege * being Eze 4:1

MOUNT
The Horites in * Seir, as far as Gen 14:5,6
seven days later, at * Gilead. Gen 31:23
from his brother Jacob to * Seir. Gen 36:6,7,8
Edomites, born to him in * Seir: Gen 36:9
So Aaron traveled to * Horeb, Ex 4:27
and * the stones in gold settings. Ex 28:11
with Moses on * Sinai, he gave him Ex 31:18
to come up into * Sinai and present Ex 34:2
early and climbed * Sinai, as the Ex 34:4
by the Lord on * Sinai, to be Lev 7:38
WHILE MOSES WAS on * Sinai, the Lev 25:1
Israel, through Moses, on * Sinai. Lev 26:46
the people of Israel on * Sinai. Lev 27:34
to Moses on * Sinai, Aaron's Num 3:1
three days after leaving * Sinai, Num 10:33
Literally, "the * of Jehovah." Num 10:33f
journeyed from Kadesh to * Hor. Num 20:21,22
and lead them up onto * Hor. Num 20:25
of them went up together into * Num 20:27
Israel returned to * Hor, and from Num 21:4
with * Pisgah in the distance. Num 21:20
to the top of * Bamoth-baal, from Num 22:41
at the top of * Pisgah, and built Num 23:14
of * Peor, overlooking the desert. Num 23:28
"Go up into * Abarim and look Num 27:12
ordained at * Sinai, to be Num 28:6
worship idols on * Peor, and they Num 31:16
camped at the foot of * Migdol). Num 33:7
From Kehelathah to * Shepher; Num 33:15-37
From * Shepher to Haradah; Num 33:15-37
From Kadesh to * Hor (at the edge Num 33:15-37
While they were at the foot of * Num 33:38,39
journeyed from * Hor and camped in Num 33:41
of Abarim, near * Nebo, and Num 33:47
eastward to * Hor, then to Num 34:7,8,9
of Israel left * Horeb—though it Deu 1:1
from * Horeb to Kadesh-barnea, Deu 1:1
going by way of * Seir! Deu 1:1
"It was forty years ago, at * Deu 1:6
"Then we left * Horeb and Deu 1:19,20,21
around in the area of * Seir. Deu 2:1
For I have given them all the * Deu 2:5
of Esau at * Seir, for he destroyed Deu 2:22
valley of the Arnon to * Hermon. Deu 3:8
(The Sidonians called * Hermon Deu 3:9
of * Gilead, including its cities. Deu 3:12
from Chinnereth to * Pisgah and the Deu 3:17
go to the top of * Pisgah where you Deu 3:27
before the Lord at * Horeb, and he Deu 4:10
from the fire at * Horeb, so do Deu 4:15
River valley to * Sirion, or Mount Deu 4:48
Mount Sirion, or * Hermon, as it is Deu 4:48
Sea, below the slopes of * Pisgah. Deu 4:49
with you at * Horeb—not with your Deu 5:2,3
darkness that engulfed * Sinai. Deu 5:22
how angry you made him at * Horeb? Deu 9:8
be proclaimed from * Gerizim, and a Deu 11:29
Gerizim, and a curse from * Ebal! Deu 11:29
begged of God at * Horeb. Deu 18:16
on the other side, at * Ebal. Deu 27:2,3,4
shall stand upon * Gerizim to Deu 27:12
upon * Ebal to proclaim a curse. Deu 27:13
the people of Israel at * Horeb. Deu 29:1
to Moses, "Go to * Nebo in the Deu 32:49
died in * Hor and joined them. Deu 32:50
"The Lord came to us at * Sinai, Deu 33:2
And dawned upon us from * Seir; Deu 33:2
He shone from * Paran, Deu 33:2
in * Nebo, across from Jericho. Deu 34:1
at * Ebal, as Moses had commanded Jos 8:30
Lord had said concerning * Ebal. Jos 8:31
at the foot of * Gerizim and half Jos 8:33
and half at the foot of * Ebal. Jos 8:33
* Hermon, in the land of Mizpah. Jos 11:1
all the way from * Halak, near Jos 11:17
Lebanon, at the foot of * Hermon. Jos 11:17
the Arnon River to * Hermon, Jos 12:1
Sea and the slopes of * Pisgah. Jos 12:3
stretching from * Hermon in the Jos 12:5
to Salecah on * Bashan in the east, Jos 12:5
of Lebanon and * Halak, west of Jos 12:7
Halak, west of * Seir, was allotted Jos 12:7
Baal-gad beneath * Hermon in the Jos 13:2-7
all of * Hermon; Jos 13:11
all of Mount Hermon; * Bashan Jos 13:11
and the slopes of * Pisgah. Jos 13:20
going south of * Akrabbim, on into Jos 15:2,3,4
to the cities of * Ephron before it Jos 15:9
west of Baalah to * Seir, passed Jos 15:10,11
shoulder of * Jearim, and went down Jos 15:10,11
south of Shikkeron and * Baalah. Jos 15:10,11
Kiriath-baal, over * Ephron to the Jos 18:15
To Esau I gave the area around * Jos 24:4
later spread into * Heres, Aijalon, Ju 1:35
of Ephraim, north of * Gaash. Ju 2:7-9
The Hivites living in * Lebanon, Ju 3:1
Lead them to * Tabor, to fight Ju 4:6
were camped at * Tabor, he Ju 4:12
the slopes of * Tabor into battle. Ju 4:14
Yes, even * Sinai quaked Ju 5:5
Down from * Tabor marched the Ju 5:13,14
at the top of * Gerizim and shouted Ju 9:7
led his forces to * Zalmon where he Ju 9:47,48
to Michmash and * Bethel while the 1Sa 13:2
he had gone to * Carmel to erect a 1Sa 15:12
slaughtered wholesale on * Gilboa. 1Sa 31:1
and his three sons on * Gilboa. 1Sa 31:8
"Because I was on * Gilboa and 2Sa 1:6
O * Gilboa, 2Sa 1:21
* of Olives, weeping as he went. 2Sa 15:30
at the top of the * of Olives where 2Sa 15:32
had died in battle on * Gilboa. 2Sa 21:12,13,14
placed there at * Horeb at the time 1Ki 8:9
He even built a temple on the * 1Ki 11:7
of Israel to * Carmel, with all 450 1Ki 18:19
and the prophets to * Carmel. 1Ki 18:20
to the top of * Carmel and got down 1Ki 18:42
forty nights to * Horeb, the 1Ki 19:8
Then he went to * Carmel and 2Ki 2:25
As she approached * Carmel, 2Ki 4:25
tribe of Simeon went to * Seir. 1Ch 4:42
distant as * Nebo and Baal-meon. 1Ch 5:7,8
Baal-hermon, Senir, and * Hermon. 1Ch 5:23
Shechem, in * Ephraim; 1Ch 6:66-69
on the slopes of * Gilboa. 1Ch 10:1
at the top of * Moriah, where the 2Ch 3:1
had put there at * Horeb, when the 2Ch 5:10
Judah arrived at * Zemaraim, in the 2Ch 13:4
Ammon, Moab, and * Seir are doing. 2Ch 20:10
Ammon, Moab, and * Seir to begin 2Ch 20:22
their allies from * Seir and killed 2Ch 20:23
"You came down upon * Sinai and Neh 9:13
It shakes * Lebanon and Mount Ps 29:5,6
It shakes Mount Lebanon and * Ps 29:5,6
* Hermon and Mount Mizar stand. Ps 42:6
Mount Hermon and * Mizar stand. Ps 42:6
He lives upon * Zion in Ps 48:1
What a glorious sight! See * Ps 48:2
for all to see—* Zion, joy of all Ps 48:2
Literally, "* Zion." Ps 48:11f
on * Zion. He comes with the Ps 50:2
the heavens shook. * Sinai quailed Ps 68:8
Well may you look with envy at * Ps 68:15,16
at Mount Zion, the * where God has Ps 68:15,16
Lord moves on from * Sinai and Ps 68:17
his holy temple high upon * Zion. Ps 68:17
they are hiding on * Hermon's Ps 68:22
Literally, "* Zion." Ps 74:2f
He lives upon * Zion. Ps 76:2
Judah—and * Zion which he loved. Ps 78:68
I answered from * Sinai Ps 81:7
You created north and south! * Ps 89:12
Mount Tabor and * Hermon rejoice Ps 89:12
Lord are steady as * Zion, unmoved Ps 125:1
as the dew on * Hermon, on the Ps 133:3
from the top of * Hermon, Sol 4:8
"As * Carmel crowns the Sol 7:5
his fist at Jerusalem on * Zion. Is 10:32
I will preside on the * of Is 14:13
Literally, "I will sit upon the * Is 14:13f
or, "on the slopes of * Is 14:13f
armies will * his throne in Zion Is 24:23
Here on * Zion in Jerusalem, the Is 25:6
in anger, as at * Perazim and Is 28:21
will come and fight upon * Zion. Is 31:4,5
as lovely as * Carmel's pastures Is 35:2
They shall * up with wings like Is 40:31
From Dan and from * Ephraim your Jer 4:15
crags of * Hermon never run dry. Jer 18:14
and prepare to * them—don your Jer 46:4
who is as tall as * Tabor or Mount Jer 46:18
Tabor or * Carmel by the sea! Jer 46:18
on * Ephraim and Mount Gilead. Jer 50:19
on Mount Ephraim and * Gilead. Jer 50:19
"Son of dust, face toward * Seir Eze 35:2
out the people of * Seir, killing Eze 35:7
* Seir and all who live in Edom! Eze 35:15
from Hazar-enon to * Hauran, where Eze 47:18
lair—from his Temple on * Zion. Amo 1:2
lush pastures of * Carmel withered Amo 1:2
BUT IN THE last days * Zion will Mic 4:1
be their King from * Zion forever. Mic 4:7
across the deserts from * Sinai. Hab 3:3
I. from * Paran." Hab 3:3f
stand upon the * of Olives, to the Zec 14:4
Jerusalem, and the * of Olives will Zec 14:4
Moses my servant on * Horeb. Mal 4:4
Bethphage on the * of Olives, Jesus Mt 21:1
You can even say to this * of Mt 21:21
on the slopes of the * of Olives. Mt 24:3
they went out to the * of Olives. Mt 26:30
and came to the * of Olives, Jesus Mk 11:1
can say to this * of Olives, 'Rise Mk 11:22,23
the slopes of the * of Olives Mk 13:3,4
and went out to the * of Olives. Mk 14:26
Bethany, on the * of Olives, he Lk 19:29
down from the * of Olives, the Lk 19:36,37
the night on the * of Olives. Lk 21:37,38
went as usual to the * of Olives. Lk 22:39
the valley on the * of Olives. Lk 24:50f
claim it is here [at * Gerazim Jn 4:20
JESUS RETURNED TO the * of Olives, Jn 8:1
They were at the * of Olives when Act 1:12
in the desert near * Sinai, an Act 7:30
of God—the Living Word—on * Sinai. Act 7:38
He did this on * Sinai, when he Gal 4:24,25
to Moses. * Sinai, by the way, is Gal 4:24,25
way, is called "* Hagar" by the Gal 4:24,25
as shown to him on * Sinai. Heb 8:5
Israelites did at * Sinai when God Heb 12:18
But you have come right up into * Heb 12:22
When he spoke from * Sinai his Heb 12:26
THEN I SAW a Lamb standing on * Rev 14:1

MOUNTAIN
go down, other * peaks appeared. Gen 8:5
for I fear disaster in the *. Gen 19:18,19,20
at the top of the *, and invited Gen 31:54
the night with them on the *. Gen 31:54
near Horeb, the * of God, suddenly Ex 3:1
worship God here upon this *!" Ex 3:12
Mount Horeb, the * of God, and met Ex 4:27
them in and plant them on your *, Ex 15:17
Literally, "the * of God." Ex 18:5,6f
Moses climbed the rugged * to Ex 19:2,3
the * God called to him and said, Ex 19:2,3
Moses returned from the * and Ex 19:7
Do not go up into the *, or even Ex 19:12
Stay away from the * entirely Ex 19:13
then gather at the foot of the * Ex 19:13
came down upon the *, and there was Ex 19:16
they stood at the foot of the *. Ex 19:17
* shook with a violent earthquake. Ex 19:18
the *, and Moses ascended to God. Ex 19:20
people won't come up into the *!" Ex 19:23
around the *, and to declare it off Ex 19:23
billowing from the *, and heard the Ex 20:18
to come up into the * at all." Ex 24:2
at the foot of the *, with twelve Ex 24:4
of Israel went up into the *. Ex 24:9
up to me into the *, and remain Ex 24:12
went up into the * of God. Ex 24:13
Then Moses went up the * and Ex 24:15
Those at the bottom of the * saw Ex 24:17
* top looked like a raging fire. Ex 24:17
the cloud-covered * top, and was Ex 24:18
I am showing you here on the *. Ex 25:40
the manner I showed you in the *. Ex 26:30
just as was shown you on the *. Ex 27:8
come back down the * right away, Ex 32:1
Then Moses went down the *, Ex 32:15
lay broken at the foot of the *. Ex 32:19
to the Lord on the *—perhaps I will Ex 32:30
to me on the top of the *. Ex 34:2
no one must be anywhere on the *. Ex 34:3
or herds feed close to the *." Ex 34:3
Moses was up on the * with the Ex 34:28
came back down the * with the Ex 34:29
the Lord had given him upon the *. Ex 34:32
Aaron died on the top of the *. Num 20:28
up into the *, and there he died. Num 33:38,39
land you will see from the * top.' Deu 3:28

(MOUNTAIN Con't)
You stood at the foot of the *, Deu 4:11
and the * burned with fire; Deu 4:11
of the fire, there at the *. Deu 5:4
and did not go up to him on the *. Deu 5:5
at the top of the *, all your Deu 5:23
I was on the * at the time, Deu 9:9
the fire-covered * while the people Deu 9:10,11
"I came down from the burning *, Deu 9:15
stream that cascaded out of the *. Deu 9:21
in, and to return to God on the *. Deu 10:1
the tablets up on the * to God. Deu 10:3
on the * as you all watched below. Deu 10:4
I stayed on the * before the Lord Deu 10:10
The antelope, and the * sheep. Deu 14:3,4,5
There at the foot of the * you Deu 18:16
fire on the *, lest you die. Deu 18:16
With the finest of * crops Deu 33:15
came down from the * and crossed Jos 2:23
the lowlands, and the * slopes. Jos 10:40
The kings in the * areas of Dor, Jos 11:1
the Arabah, the * slopes, the Jos 12:8-24
and all of the Lebanon * area Jos 13:2-7
on the * above the valley, Jos 13:19
to the top of the * above the Jos 15:8
the top of the * to the spring of Jos 15:9
"Then you shall have the * Jos 17:16,17,18
south, passing the * near Jos 18:14
to the base of the * beside the Jos 18:16
the trail at the top of the *. Ju 9:25
to Zebul, "Look over at that *! Ju 9:36
top of the * across from Hebron! Ju 16:3
Jonathan's. The * pass at Michmash 1Sa 13:23
were now on opposite sides of a *. 1Sa 23:26
They climbed the * slope 1Sa 26:13
and wept as they climbed the *. 2Sa 15:30
them in the * before the Lord. 2Sa 21:9
Like * goats upon the rocks. 2Sa 22:34
and get down the *, or he'll be 1Ki 18:44
Mount Horeb, the * of God, where 1Ki 19:8
me on the *," the Lord told him. 1Ki 19:11
and a mighty windstorm hit the *; 1Ki 19:11
him on some * or in some ravine." 2Ki 2:16
to Elisha at the * she fell to the 2Ki 4:27
of fire everywhere upon the *! 2Ki 6:17
and south of Destruction *. 2Ki 23:13
graves in the side of the *. 2Ki 23:16
valley below the * heard that their 1Ch 10:7
the * as sheep without a shepherd. 2Ch 18:16
had built on the * where the Temple 2Ch 33:15
"DO YOU KNOW how * goats give Job 39:1
* ranges are their pastureland; Job 39:8
making her home in her * fortress. Job 39:28
Literally, "Upon Zion, my holy * Ps 2:6f
Literally, "from his holy *." Ps 3:4f
He is a rugged * where I hide; Ps 18:2
of a * goat upon the crags. Ps 18:33
Who may climb the * of the Lord Ps 24:3
He has made me steady as a *." Ps 30:6,7
your Temple on your holy *, Zion. Ps 43:3
forest fire that roars across a *. Ps 83:14
HIGH ON HIS holy * stands Ps 87:1
* in Jerusalem, for he is holy. Ps 99:9
SHALL I LOOK to the * gods for Ps 121:1
green grass grow in * pastures. Ps 147:8
like water from a * spring. Pro 13:14
and the * grasses are gathered in. Pro 27:25,26,27
I will go to the * of myrrh and to Sol 4:6
*, from the top of Mount Hermon, Sol 4:8
"let us go up the * of the Lord, Is 2:3
in all my holy *, for as the waters Is 11:9
wooded hills and * tops and become Is 17:9
*, let all the world take notice! Is 18:3
* birds and wild animals to eat; Is 18:6
to worship the Lord in his holy *. Is 27:13
trees on the distant * tops. Is 30:17
down each * and every hill. Is 30:25
* of the Lord, the Rock of Israel. Is 30:29
to Jerusalem from the * tops! Is 40:9
And you, too, dwellers in the * Is 42:11
also to my holy * of Jerusalem, and Is 56:7
the land and inherit my Holy *. Is 57:13
* of the Holy One of Israel." Is 60:14
in all my Holy *, says the Lord. Is 65:25
*, to Jerusalem, says the Lord. Is 66:20
as a seasonal * brook—sometimes a Jer 15:17,18
or * goats on inaccessible crags. Jer 16:16
prosper in the * villages and in Jer 33:13
you, O mighty *, Babylon, destroyer Jer 51:25
and leave you, a burnt-out *. Jer 51:25
on every hill and * and under every Eze 6:13
above the * on the east side. Eze 11:23
on the top of Israel's highest *. Eze 17:22,23
For at Jerusalem in my holy *, Eze 20:40
Every * top is filled with idols; Eze 22:9
You had access to the holy * of Eze 28:14
the * of God like a common sinner. Eze 28:16
And the * villages of Israel Eze 33:28
and feed in luscious * pastures. Eze 34:14
me down on a high * where I saw Eze 40:2
* that covered the whole earth. Dan 2:35
Rock cut from the * without human Dan 2:45
your own city, your holy *. Dan 9:16
his holy *, Gabriel, whom I had Dan 9:20
trumpet be heard upon my holy *! Joe 2:1
leaping along the tops of the *! Joe 2:5
Lord your God in Zion, my holy *. Joe 3:17
upon my holy *, and the nations Ob 1:16
"let us visit the * of the Lord, Mic 4:2
pride or haughtiness on my holy *. Zep 3:11
Therefore no *, however high, Zec 4:7
and 'The Holy *,' and 'The Mountain Zec 8:3
and 'The * of the Lord of Hosts.' Zec 8:3
west, for half the * will move Zec 14:4
the valley of my * shall touch Zec 14:5f
of a very high * and showed him the Mt 4:8
As they were going down the *, Mt 17:9
you could say to this *, 'Move!' Mt 17:20
going to the * where Jesus had said Mt 28:16
James and John to the top of a *. Mk 9:2
At the bottom of the * they found Mk 9:14
the slopes of the *, they stood Lk 6:17,18
I could speak to a * and make it 1Co 13:2
animal touched the * it must die. Heb 12:20
there on the holy * when he shone 2Pe 1:17,18
and every * and island shook and Rev 6:14
be a huge burning * was thrown into Rev 8:8,9
Armageddon—the * of Megiddo. Rev 16:16
me to a towering * peak and from Rev 21:10

MOUNTAINOUS
who lived in the * area southeast Eze 38:2,3f

MOUNTAINS
all the high * under the whole Gen 7:19
came to rest upon the * of Ararat. Gen 8:3,4
and the remainder fled to the *. Gen 14:10
Escape to the *. Gen 19:17
of into the *, for I fear disaster Gen 19:18,19,20
in the * with his two daughters. Gen 19:30
* which I'll point out to you!" Gen 22:2
camped below him in the *. Gen 31:25
into coming to the * so that he Ex 32:12
From the eastern *. Num 23:7-10
and on into the * of Abarim, near Num 33:47
(Gerizim and Ebal are * west of Deu 11:30
them—high in the *, up in the Deu 12:2
And setting its * on fire. Deu 32:22
Nebo in the Abarim *, in the land Deu 32:49
to the Lebanon * in the north, and Jos 1:4
"Escape to the *," she told Jos 2:16
The spies went up into the * and Jos 2:22
as the Lebanon *—the Hittites, Jos 9:1
the north side of the * of Gaash. Jos 24:30
the *, living in caves and dens. Ju 6:2
life like a partridge on the *?" 1Sa 26:20
Send your woodsmen to the * of 1Ki 5:6
from the Lebanon * to the 1Ki 5:9
and in the Lebanon * and elsewhere 1Ki 9:19
the * as sheep without a shepherd. 1Ki 22:17
*, yes, the peaks of Lebanon. 2Ki 19:23
men, swift as deer upon the *." 1Ch 12:8-13
from the Lebanon *, as much as you 2Ch 2:16
shrines in the * of Judah, and led 2Ch 21:11
in the Lebanon * a thistle demanded 2Ch 25:18
from the Lebanon * and floated Ez 3:7
"Suddenly he moves the *, Job 9:5
"* wear away and disappear. Job 14:18,19
the showers of the * and live in Job 24:8
how to overturn the roots of *. Job 28:9
and blankets the tops of the *. Job 36:30
sharp sword! The * offer their Job 40:20
to the * for safety," when I am Ps 11:1
reeled, and * shook and trembled. Ps 18:7
justice is as solid as God's *. Ps 36:6
and the * crumble into the sea. Ps 46:2
let the * tremble! Ps 46:3
And all the birds upon the *! Ps 50:10,11
He formed the * by his mighty Ps 65:6
O mighty * in Bashan! Ps 68:15,16
May the * and hills flourish in Ps 72:3
The everlasting * cannot compare Ps 76:4
* were covered with our shadow; Ps 80:10
Before the * were created, Ps 90:2
of the earth and the mightiest *; Ps 95:4
and trembles. The * melt like wax Ps 97:5
of waters covering up the *. Ps 104:6
ocean beds, and * rose and valleys Ps 104:7,8
and streams that gush from the *. Ps 104:10
He sends rain upon the * and Ps 104:13
High in the * are pastures for Ps 104:18
* burst into flame at his touch. Ps 104:32
to cross. The * skipped like rams, Ps 114:4
Why, *, did you skip like rams? Ps 114:6
is from Jehovah who made the *! Ps 121:2
Just as the * surround and Ps 125:2
Mount Hermon, on the * of Israel. Ps 133:3
The * smoke beneath your touch. Ps 144:5
Let the * and hills, the fruit Ps 148:9
before the * and the hills were Pro 8:25
Here he comes, leaping upon the * Sol 2:8
a young stag on the * of spices." Sol 2:17
of the * and cedars of Lebanon. Sol 4:11
the streams from the Lebanon *." Sol 4:15
"As Mount Carmel crowns the *, Sol 7
young deer upon the * of spices." Sol 8:
as the highest of the *." Is 2:
and all the high * and hills, and Is 2:
Hear the tumult on the *! Is 13
Israel and to crush them on my *; Is 14:
graze upon the * where the Is 32:
The rocks of the * will be their Is 33:
the * will flow with their blood. Is 34
as the Lebanon *, as lovely as Is 35
I conquered their highest * and Is 37:
and weighs the * and the hills? Is 40:
enemies apart, making chaff of *. Is 41:
He will level the * and hills Is 42:
break forth into song, O * and Is 44:
and level the * and smash down the Is 45
And I will make my * into level Is 49:
Break forth with song, O *, for Is 49:
How beautiful upon the * are the Is 52
For the * may depart and the Is 54:1
joy and peace. The * and hills, the Is 55:
on the tops of the *, for you Is 57:7
How the * would quake in your Is 64
and how the * quaked! Is 64
* and insulted me upon the hills. Is 65:
the windswept *, crying, crying. Jer 3:2
and of having orgies on the *. Jer 3:2
I looked at the * and saw that Jer 4:2
in the bushes and flee to the *. Jer 4:2
shame and weep alone upon the *; Jer 7:2
I point to their * and pastures, Jer 9:1
stumble and fall upon the dark *; Jer 13:1
tree, high in the * or in the open Jer 17:2,
melts high up in the Lebanon *. Jer 18:1
vineyards upon the * of Samaria and Jer 31:
there in the * of Petra, in the Jer 49:1
then turned them loose in the *. Jer 50:
if we flee to the * they find us. Lam 4:1
over toward the * of Israel and Eze 6:
Say to them, O * of Israel, hear Eze 6:
the *, each weeping for his sins. Eze 7:1
gone out to the * to feast before Eze 18:
idols on the * and commits Eze 18:1
go up on the * to feast before the Eze 18:1
be heard upon the * of Israel. Eze 19:
across the * and valleys and rivers Eze 31:1
the ravines to the tops of the *. Eze 32:
My sheep wandered through the * Eze 34:
feed them upon the * of Israel and Eze 34:1
I will fill your * with the Eze 35:8
OF DUST, prophesy to Israel's *. Eze 36:1
Therefore, O * of Israel, hear Eze 36:4
He says to the hills and *, dales Eze 36:4
to the hills and *, dales and Eze 36:6
multiply. O * of Israel, again you Eze 36:11
presence; * shall be thrown down; Eze 38:20
you toward the * of Israel, Eze 39:2
of your army in the *. Eze 39:2
vast armies will die upon the *. Eze 39:4
Come from far and near to the * Eze 39:17
to idols on the tops of *; Hos 4:13
And the people will cry to the * Hos 10:8
It covers the * like night! Joe 2:2
"Sweet wine will drip from the * Joe 3:18
seats now on the * of Samaria to Amo 3:9
one who formed the * and made the Amo 4:13
crushes down the * underneath his Amo 4:13
the bottoms of the * that rise from Jon 2:6
of all the * of the world, praised Mic 4:1
Let the * and hills be called to Mic 6:1
And now, O *, listen to the Mic 6:2
sea and from distant hills and *. Mic 7:12
In his presence * quake and Nah 1:5
His fury is like fire; the * Nah 1:6
running down the * with glad news: Nah 1:15
people are scattered across the *; Nah 3:18
* and leveling the hills. Hab 3:6
The * watched and trembled. Hab 3:10
and bring me safely over the *. Hab 3:19
Then go up into the * and bring Hag 1:8
looked like two * made of brass. Zec 6:1
destroyed Esau's * and inheritance, Mal 1:2,3
Level the *! Lk 3:5
* to pray, and prayed all night. Lk 6:12
Mankind will beg the * to fall Lk 23:30
he went higher into the * alone. Jn 6:15
and *, hiding in dens and caves. Heb 11:37,38
and rocks of the *, and cried to Rev 6:15
and cried to the * to crush them. Rev 6:16
And islands vanished, and * Rev 16:20

MOUNTAINSIDE
watched, a Rock was cut from the * Dan 2:34
As they descended the * he told Mk 9:9
was feeding on the * nearby, and Lk 8:32
rushed down the * and fell over a Lk 8:33

MOUNTAINSIDES
cry of death echoes from the *. Is 22:5

MOUNTAINTOP
of rubble; the * where the Temple Mic 3:12

MOUNTAINTOPS
comes to earth, walking on the *. Mic 1:3

MOUNTED
* the camels and went with him. Gen 24:61
as attendants, * her donkey, and 1Sa 25:42
army to fifty * troops, ten 2Ki 13:7
I was * on my donkey and the Neh 2:11,12
on Mordecai and * him on the king's Est 6:11
It cannot be bought for jewels * Job 28:17
* a massive attack against me. Ps 18:4
his feet. * on the cherubim, Ps 18:10
people, fully armed, * for war. Jer 6:23
No, lamps are * in the open where Lk 8:16
Take 200 spearmen and 70 * Act 23:23,24
MOUNTING
Keep disobeying—your sins are * Amo 4:4
MOURN
Ithamar, "Do not *—do not let your Lev 10:6
and Abihu, and * because of the Lev 10:6
the city to * over it and bury it. 1Ki 13:29
All of Israel will * for him and 1Ki 14:13
to * them, not even their wives. Job 27:15
as one who comforts those who *. Job 29:25
Why must I * at the oppression of Ps 43:2
when I * and fast before the Lord! Ps 69:10
Yes, Moab, you will * for Is 16:7
to weep and * and shave your heads Is 22:12
the merrymakers will sigh and *. Is 24:7
to * and to confess their sins. Is 57:18
to tell those who * that the time Is 61:2
To all who * in Israel he will Is 61:3
The earth shall *, the heavens Jer 4:28
shall * because of your pride. Jer 13:17
No one shall * for them or bury Jer 16:4
Do not * or weep for them, for I Jer 16:5
No one shall * for them nor Jer 25:33
Anakim, how you will lament and *! Jer 47:5
The roads to Zion *, no longer Lam 1:4
you may not * in public or Eze 24:22
you shall not * or weep. Eze 24:23
for your sins, and * privately for Eze 24:23
I made the oceans * for her and Eze 31:15
"Son of dust, * for Pharaoh, Eze 32:2
the priests and people, too, * Hos 10:5
its doom, and everyone will *. Amo 8:8
it melts, and all its people *. Amo 9:5
listen to them * like doves, and Nah 2:7
they pierced, and * for him as for Zec 12:10
and to sorrow and * for our sins? Mal 3:14,15
Those who * are fortunate! Mt 5:4
friends * and go without food while Mt 9:15
from them, and then they will *. Mk 2:20
I will be sad and * because many of 2Co 12:21
her favors, will * for her as they Rev 18:9
will weep and * for her, for there Rev 18:11
MOURNED
there Abraham * and wept for her. Gen 23:1
on sackcloth and * for his son in Gen 37:34
they * for him for thirty days. Num 20:29
The people of Israel * for him Deu 34:8
And the people * because of the 1Sa 6:19
but he * constantly for him; 1Sa 15:35
Samuel, "You have * long enough 1Sa 16:1
died and all Israel had * for him. 1Sa 28:3
They * and wept and fasted all 2Sa 1:12
husband was dead, she * for him; 2Sa 11:26
Their father Ephraim * for them 1Ch 7:22
and * and fasted for seven days. 1Ch 10:12
the prophet, * for him, as did the 2Ch 35:24,25
When they were ill, I * before Ps 35:13
and * and despised his command. Ps 106:25
like a swallow and * like a dove; Is 38:14
who love her, you who * for her. Is 66:10
dried, and all the shepherds *. Amo 1:2
you fasted and * in August and Zec 7:5
MOURNERS
"Egyptian *") for they said, "It Gen 50:11
as the * go along the streets. Ecc 12:5
of Hosts says: Send for the *! Jer 9:17,18
No one shall comfort the * with Jer 16:7
it is polluted, just as food of * Hos 9:4
call for professional * to wail Amo 5:16
* from the village were with her. Lk 7:12
her aside from the *, told her, Jn 11:28
MOURNFUL
you moan with * cries like doves. Is 59:11
I hear its * cry. Jer 12:11
as a jackal, * as an ostrich crying Mic 1:8
by some to mean a * dirge. Hab 3:1f
MOURNING
son in deepest * for many weeks. Gen 37:34
"I will die in * for my son," he Gen 37:35
After the time of * was over, Gen 38:12
of national * of seventy days. Gen 50:3
Then, when at last the * was Gen 50:4
very deep * by these Egyptians." Gen 50:11
they went into * and stripped Ex 33:4
*, and do not tear your clothes. Lev 10:6
hair hang loose in *, nor tear his Lev 21:10
in your home in * for her father Deu 21:13
while I was in *), nor have I Deu 26:14
dirt on his head as a sign of *. 2Sa 1:1
him, "Go into deep * for Abner." 2Sa 3:31
then, when the period of * was 2Sa 11:27
your * and are eating again." 2Sa 12:21
"Pretend you are in *," Joab 2Sa 14:2,3
"Wear * clothes, and dishevel 2Sa 14:2,3
his feet were bare as a sign of *. 2Sa 15:30
was weeping and * for Absalom. 2Sa 19:1
And there was * for him 1Ki 14:18
for I was * because of the sin of Ez 10:6
permitted to enter in * clothes. Est 4:2
there was great * among the Jews, Est 4:3
and their * into happiness. Est 9:22
joy and gladness has turned to *. Job 30:31
He took away my clothes of * and Ps 30:11
Your people in Dibon go * to Is 15:2
of humility and *, and went over to Is 37:1
sorrow and * will all disappear. Is 51:11
your days of * all will end. Is 60:20
Joy instead of *; Is 61:3
Put on clothes of * and weep Jer 4:8
my people, put on * clothes and sit Jer 6:26
The land itself is *—the pastures Jer 23:10
for I will turn their * into joy Jer 31:13
Put on garments of *; Jer 49:3
grief, she sits alone in her *. Lam 1:1
Literally, "to *." Lam 5:15f
will be lonely as * doves hiding on Eze 7:16
bitterness of heart and deep *. Eze 27:31
been in * for three full weeks. Dan 10:2
Come with fasting, weeping, *. Joe 2:12
into times of *, and your songs of Amo 8:10
garments worn at times of *. Jon 3:4,5
of fasting and * during the month Zec 7:3
fasts and times of * you have kept Zec 8:19
The sorrow and * in Jerusalem at Zec 12:11
* for the godly King Josiah, Zec 12:11
Literally, "Like the * of Zec 12:11f
go into private *, husbands and Zec 12:12,13,14
be deep * all around the earth. Mt 24:30
The home was filled with * Lk 8:52
Why aren't you * in sorrow and 1Co 5:2
of death and * and famine shall Rev 18:8
MOURNS
Judah *; Jer 14:2
MOUSE
The *, the lizard, Lev 11:29,30
there on pork and * and all Is 66:17
MOUTH
at the * of the Persian Gulf. Gen 11:2f
But a heavy stone covered the * Gen 29:2
back over the * of the well again. Gen 29:3
his money in the * of the sack! Gen 42:27
to put into the * of each man's Gen 44:1
we found in the * of our sacks? Gen 44:8
rolled against the * of the cave Jos 10:18
the stone from the * of the cave Jos 10:22,23
was placed at the * of the cave. Jos 10:27
Sea to the * of the Jordan River. Jos 15:5
coast from the * of the Brook of Jos 15:47
"Now where is that big * of Ju 9:38
Eli noticed her * moving as she 1Sa 1:12,13
club and take the lamb from its *. 1Sa 17:35
come directly from the * of God. 2Sa 16:23
Fire leaped from his * 2Sa 22:9
body, placing his * upon the 2Ki 4:34
upon the child's *, and his eyes 2Ki 4:34
a bridle in your * and turn you 2Ki 19:28
* of all of the king's prophets!' 2Ch 18:21
spirit in the * of these prophets 2Ch 18:22
He will yet fill your * with Job 8:21
My own * says no. Job 9:20
Just as my * can taste good Job 12:11
that you are putting in his *? Job 13:7
Your sins are telling your * what Job 15:4,5
Your own * does! Job 15:6
it melt in his *, sipping it Job 20:12
and lay your hand upon your *. Job 21:5
I lay my hand upon my * in Job 40:4
Fire leaps from his *. Job 41:19
coals—flames leap from his *. Job 41:21
Fierce flames leaped from his *, Ps 18:8
my tongue sticks to my *, for you Ps 22:15
a bit in its * to keep it in line! Ps 32:9
shall continually be in my *." Ps 34:1f
I will not open my * to speak one Ps 39:9
Open your * wide and see if I Ps 81:10
Help me, Lord, to keep my * shut Ps 141:3
are scattered at the * of Sheol." Ps 141:6,7f
nor turn from the words of my *." Pro 4:5f
"Put away from you a wayward *." Pro 4:24f
Literally, "but the * of the Pro 10:6f
man says, but the * of the evil man Pro 10:11
keep putting your foot in your *. Pro 10:19
It pays him to keep his * shut. Pro 17:27,28
fights. His * is his undoing! Pro 18:6,7
Keep your * closed and you'll Pro 21:23
In the * of a fool a proverb Pro 26:7
his food from his dish to his *! Pro 26:15
your * with your hand in shame. Pro 30:32
your ears open and your * shut! Ecc 5:1
In that case, your * is making Ecc 5:6,7
scarlet—and how beautiful your *. Sol 4:3
none can rival him. His * is Sol 5:16
open his * to peep against us!" Is 10:14
drink turns bitter in the *. Is 24:9
and a bit in your * and led you Is 37:29
my words in your * and hidden you Is 51:16
Then he touched my * and said, Jer 1:9
I have put my words in your *! Jer 1:9
through your * I will tear down Jer 1:10
pull from his * what he has taken. Jer 51:44
Open your * and eat what I give Eze 2:8
* so that you can't reprove them; Eze 3:26
you will cover your * in silence Eze 16:63
and placed over the * of the den; Dan 6:17
had a man's eyes and a bragging *. Dan 7:8
the loud, bragging *, the one which Dan 7:20
my *, threatening you with death. Hos 6:5
he snatched from the lion's * two Amo 3:12
out of her *, and pull from her Zec 9:7
the * of the first fish you catch. Mt 17:26,27
him foam at the * and grind his Mk 9:18
writhing and foaming at the *. Mk 9:20
so that he foams at the *; Lk 9:39
shearers, so he opened not his *; Act 8:32
to Paul to slap him on the *. Act 23:2
with your own * that Jesus Christ Rom 10:9
and with his * he tells others of Rom 10:10
the breath of his * and destroy by 2Th 2:8
"Never tie up the * of an ox when 1Ti 5:18
out of the * of the lion." 2Ti 4:17f
by means of a small bit in his *. Jas 3:3
come pouring out of the same *. Jas 3:10
double-bladed sword in his *, Rev 1:16
Literally, "coming out from his * Rev 1:16f
them with the sword of my *. Rev 2:16
I will spit you out of my *! Rev 3:16
it was sweet in my * but it gave me Rev 10:10
And from the Serpent's * a vast Rev 12:15
its * and swallowing the flood! Rev 12:16
had bear's feet and a lion's *! Rev 13:2
leap from the * of the Dragon, the Rev 16:13
In his * he held a sharp sword to Rev 19:15
sharp sword in the * of the one Rev 19:21
MOUTHPIECE
idle lips are his *. Pro 16:27
MOUTHS
what was in the * of your sacks, as Gen 43:12
"Who makes *?" Ex 4:11
to their * and lap it like dogs. Ju 7:5,6
with their * in the stream." Ju 7:5,6
all the others drank with their * Ju 7:5,6
in the * of all his prophets.' 1Ki 22:22
spirit in the * of all these 1Ki 22:23
and laid their hands upon their *. Job 29:9
They waited eagerly with open *. Job 29:23
Their * are full of profanity and Ps 10:7
vile language streams from your *. Ps 50:19
was yet in their *, when the anger Ps 78:30
or see, despite their eyes and *! Ps 115:5
with speechless * and sightless Ps 135:16
Their * are filled with lies; Ps 144:8
will turn to gravel in their *. Pro 20:17
the roofs of their * for thirst, Lam 4:3,4
* so that they can't touch me; Dan 6:22
* of those who shake the trees. Nah 3:12
tongues will decay in their *. Zec 14:12
Their * are full of cursing and Rom 3:14
as near as our own hearts and *. Rom 10:8
from their *, killing one-third of Rev 9:17,18
not only in their *, but in their Rev 9:19
of fire shooting from their *. Rev 11:5
MOVABLE
Then he made ten four-wheeled * 1Ki 7:27-30
Each of these * stands had four 1Ki 7:27-30
Ten * stands holding ten vats; 1Ki 7:41-46
MOVE
whether to * this way or that." Gen 24:49
sensitive to every * they made, two Gen 34:25
"* ON TO Bethel now, and settle Gen 35:1
" 'But not a dog shall * his Ex 11:7
let us * a step from this place. Ex 33:15
spot does not * or spread in the Lev 13:28
signal to break camp and * onward. Num 10:5,6,7
* from one tribe to another.' Num 36:9
and you will * in against those Deu 7:23
fall down; then * in upon the city Jos 6:5
And the sun and the moon didn't * Jos 10:13
"I can hardly *!" 1Sa 17:38,39
Lord, "Shall I * back to Judah?" 2Sa 2:1
which they will never have to *. 2Sa 7:10,11
to let his troops * past him to 2Sa 15:17,18
For you watch their every *. 2Sa 22:28
your family and * to some other 2Ki 8:1
the shadow to * ten points backward 2Ki 20:11
the walls to * into Jerusalem so Neh 4:22
alone, but to * against all of Est 3:5,6
the righteous shall * onward and Job 17:9
say, 'and watches every * I make.' Job 33:11
Do not * the ancient boundary Pro 22:28
Lord of Hosts will * against the Is 2:12
and no one can * a finger or open Is 10:14
* from its place in the skies. Is 13:13

(MOVE Con't)
and the Iraqi will * freely back Is 19:23
his god—a god that cannot even *! Is 40:20
much as * from where it is placed. Is 44:13
it stays there, for it cannot *! Is 46:7
and decided to * to Jerusalem. Jer 35:11
most to help us makes no * at all. Lam 4:17
the Lord began to * away, Eze 3:12
property and having to * away." Eze 46:18
Literally, "as those who * a Hos 5:10f
Their cavalry * proudly forward Hab 1:8
* her, they will all be crushed. Zec 12:3
the mountain will * toward the Zec 14:4
I will * swiftly against wicked Mal 3:5
could say to this mountain, '*!' Mt 17:20
Mount of Olives, '* over into the Mt 21:21
days and made no * to go to them. Jn 11:6
For in him we live and * and Act 17:28
to * the hands of God by prayer. 1Co 2:16
and make it *, I would still be 1Co 13:2

MOVED
Then Abram * his tent to the Gen 13:18
NOW ABRAHAM * south to the Negeb, Gen 20:1
(Isaac had now * south to Gen 25:11
time, and so Isaac * to the city of Gen 26:1
So Isaac * to Gerar Valley and Gen 26:17
land of Canaan—and * away from his Gen 36:6,7,8
left home and * to Adullam and Gen 38:1
people scarcely *—but all the Ex 10:23
people of Israel, * the cloud Ex 14:19
Red Sea, and they * out into the Ex 15:22
Whenever the cloud lifted and *, Ex 40:36
stayed, they stayed until it *. Ex 40:37
the Tabernacle is *, the Levites Num 1:51
When the Tabernacle is *, they Num 4:30,31
people of Israel * on to wherever Num 9:17
night and * on the next morning. Num 9:20,21
But day or night, when it *, the Num 9:20,21
but as soon as it *, they moved. Num 9:22
but as soon as it moved, they *. Num 9:22
As the Cloud * from above the Num 12:10
Then they * to the far side of Num 21:13
Then the angel of the Lord * Num 22:26
When the tribe of Judah * into Ju 1:16
Later the man * to Syria and Ju 1:26
Israel, the tribes * into their new Ju 2:6
for the Lord was * to pity by the Ju 2:18
Hobab—had * away from the rest of Ju 4:11
(the son of Ebed) * to Shechem with Ju 9:26
famine and * to the land of Moab. Ru 1:1
and the third * toward the border 1Sa 13:18
Samuel was so deeply * when he 1Sa 15:11
their families all * to Hebron. 2Sa 2:3
lame in both feet) * to Jerusalem 2Sa 9:13
and David was * to harm them by 2Sa 24:1
King Solomon * Pharaoh's daughter 1Ki 9:24
lines, and * into the battle; 1Ki 20:27
troops from Edom, * along a 2Ki 3:9
Then the men of Israel * forward 2Ki 3:24
then he * on toward Jerusalem to 2Ki 12:17
shadow * up and down the steps. 2Ki 20:11f
Then he * the capital to 1Ch 3:4
in war and * into their tents on 1Ch 5:10
After David * to Jerusalem, he 1Ch 14:3
Abishai, * against the Ammonites. 1Ch 19:11
King David was * with deep joy. 1Ch 29:9
Solomon now * his wife (she was 2Ch 8:11
their homes and * to Judah and 2Ch 11:13,14
The people who had * to Judah 2Ch 31:5,6
Some who * to Jerusalem at this Neh 11:2
us—landmarks are *, flocks of sheep Job 24:2
door and my heart was * for him. Sol 5:4
The wild animals and birds have * Jer 12:4
the wheels * forward with them. Eze 1:19,20,21
Then the glory of the Lord * from Eze 10:18
but soon he * to Capernaum, Mt 4:12,13
Jesus was * with pity for them Mt 20:34
And Jesus, * with pity, touched Mk 1:41
farmers and * to another country. Mk 12:1
* away and the entrance was open! Mk 16:4
voice, my baby * in me for joy! Lk 1:44
grass, * by every breath of wind? Lk 7:24
to heaven, he * steadily onward Lk 9:51
with her, he was * with indignation Jn 11:33
And again Jesus was * with deep Jn 11:37,38
These words of Peter's * them Act 2:37
before he * to Syria, Act 7:2
ABOUT THAT TIME King Herod * Act 12:1
cloud that * along ahead of them; 1Co 10:1

MOVEMENT
after every bowel * he must dig a Deu 23:13
He watches every * of the Ps 66:7
for a certain * of the water, for Jn 5:3
the pool at the * of the water. Jn 5:7

MOVEMENTS
Moses had written down their * Num 33:2
and sent out spies to watch his *. 1Sa 26:3,4
I am closely watching their * and Zec 9:8

MOVES
"When the camp *, Aaron and his Num 4:5
" 'Cursed is he who * the Deu 27:17
"The shadow always * forward," 2Ki 20:10
"Suddenly he * the mountains, Job 9:5
He passes by, invisible; he * Job 9:11
* out across the skies as radiant Ps 19:5
chariots, the Lord * on from Mount Ps 68:17
The procession of God my King * Ps 68:24
When his hand *, who can stop Is 14:27

MOVING
praying and get the people *! Ex 14:15
built there. For * the altar, make Ex 27:6
with the Cloud * along ahead of Num 10:34
land by * the boundary marker. Deu 19:14
Eli noticed her mouth * as she 1Sa 1:12,13
After * from Hebron to Jerusalem, 2Sa 5:13
over Israel began * to Jerusalem 2Ch 11:16
orphans by * their ancient boundary Pro 23:10,11
rod strike unless a hand is * it? Is 10:15
the swiftly * serpent, the coiling, Is 27:1
See them * slowly across the Is 30:6
* in on some wild animal! Jer 4:17
like a mighty army * into battle. Joe 2:5
See their glittering chariots * Nah 2:3
I see God * across the deserts Hab 3:3
difficulty and * slowly along the Act 27:7,8

MOWED
in the morning but * down and Ps 90:5,6

MOWER
the *, and no one will bury them. Jer 9:22

MOWING
up after the first *, which went as Amo 7:1

MOZA
Haran, *, and Gazez; 1Ch 2:46
Zimri's son was *. 1Ch 8:36
* was the father of Bine-a, whose 1Ch 8:37
Zimri was the father of *. 1Ch 9:42
* was the father of Bine-a, 1Ch 9:43

MOZAH
Mizpeh, Chephirah, *, Rekem, Jos 18:21-28

MR
"Go into the city and see *. Mt 26:18

MT
Wilderness, between Elim and *. Ex 16:1
you and lead the people out to *. Ex 17:5,6
and the people were camped at *. Ex 18:5,6
Or, "*. Horeb." Literally, "the Ex 18:5,6f
they came to the base of *. Ex 19:2,3
tomorrow, I will come down upon *. Ex 19:11
the foot of the mountain. All *. Ex 19:18
Lord came down upon the top of *. Ex 19:20
glory of the Lord rested upon *. Ex 24:16

MUCH
I will not take so * as a single Gen 14:23
This upset Abraham very *, for Gen 21:11
whom you love so *—and go to the Gen 22:2
He loved her very *, and she was Gen 24:67
without pay. How * do you want?" Gen 29:15
a few days, he was so * in love. Gen 29:20
being here. How * of a raise do Gen 30:28
Shechem was very * in love with Gen 34:18,19
"How * will you pay me?" Gen 38:16
out of her way as * as possible. Gen 39:10
and there was so * that no one kept Gen 41:49
youngest, * to their amazement! Gen 43:33
as * as to any of the others! Gen 43:34
sacks with as * grain as they could Gen 44:1
and his father loves him very *.' Gen 44:20
as * as to those born in the land. Ex 12:19
people, just as * as if his brand Ex 13:16
for they had taken * of the wealth Ex 14:8
and gather as * food as he needs. Ex 16:4
Tell them to gather twice as * Ex 16:5
to gather as * as is needed for his Ex 16:16
gathered twice as * as usual, six Ex 16:22
So cook as * as you want to Ex 16:23
them twice as * on the sixth day, Ex 16:28,29
saw how * time this was taking, he Ex 18:14
half as * of cinnamon and of Ex 30:22,23
encouragement, and * to the Ex 32:25
for burnt offerings give * Lev 1:13
And it will give the Lord * Lev 3:3,4,5
offering that pleases him very *. Lev 6:21
the Lord very *, for Jehovah's Lev 8:21
be told how * to pay instead. Lev 27:11,12
fish we enjoyed so * in Egypt, and Num 11:4,5
I have never stolen so * as a Num 16:15
and will please the Lord very *. Num 28:13
which will give * pleasure to the Num 29:13
so * more powerful than we are?' Deu 7:17
Those nations are * greater and Deu 9:1
and loved them so * that he chose Deu 10:15
no matter how * greater and Deu 11:23
Eat as * of this meat as you wish Deu 12:15
you must lend them as * as they Deu 15:8
"You will sow * but reap little, Deu 28:38
who would not so * as touch her Deu 28:56,57
*, and they shall plague the land. Deu 28:60
and * cattle and wonderful crops; Deu 30:9
the Lord, how * more rebellious Deu 31:27
revered him as * as they had Moses, Jos 4:14
I wanted them so * that I took Jos 7:21
royal cities and * larger than Jos 10:2
were to receive as * property as Jos 17:
of their gods, * less swear by them Jos 23:
'There is * loot to be divided, Ju 5:3
Israel from Egypt (* on Gideon's Ju 6:16
"So *!" Ru 2:1
who loves you so *, and who has Ru 4:1
loved Hannah very *, he could give 1Sa 1:
her cry so * she couldn't eat. 1Sa 1:
replied, "Take as * as you want, 1Sa 2:1
but how * more this sin of yours 1Sa 2:23,24,2
But although I have done so * for 1Sa 10:18,1
and all the people were very * 1Sa 12:1
eaten the honey he felt * better. 1Sa 14:2
See how * better I feel now that 1Sa 14:2
you didn't think * of yourself, God 1Sa 15:1
"Has the Lord as * pleasure in 1Sa 15:22
He is * more interested in your 1Sa 15:22
When the king realized how * the 1Sa 18:28
him as * as he loved himself. 1Sa 20:17
how * more so on this one!" 1Sa 21:5
How * they were loved, how 2Sa 1:23
How * I loved you! 2Sa 1:26
a raid, bringing * loot with them. 2Sa 3:22
And how * more shall I do to 2Sa 4:11
of the Lord with * shouting and 2Sa 6:15
would have given you *, much more. 2Sa 12:8
would have given you much, * more. 2Sa 12:8
if we all came, we would be too * 2Sa 13:25
GENERAL JOAB realized how * 2Sa 14:1
"Why don't you do as * for all 2Sa 14:13
too * of a load to carry around! 2Sa 14:26
Meanwhile, there was * discussion 2Sa 19:8,9,10
for I know very well how * I 2Sa 19:20
and entertainment is not * fun; 2Sa 19:35
as * right in the king as you do; 2Sa 19:43
spent * time in prayer about it. 2Sa 21:1
why the Lord has done so * for me, 2Sa 22:25
as * renown as the Top Three. 2Sa 23:22
so * as by a single scolding! 1Ki 1:6
very *, cried out, "Oh, no, sir! 1Ki 3:26
for Solomon as * cedar and cypress 1Ki 5:10
* less this Temple I have built! 1Ki 8:27
was too small to handle so *. 1Ki 8:64
considered to be of * value! 1Ki 10:21
people, "It's too * trouble to go 1Ki 12:28
For no matter how * they used, 1Ki 17:16
grant me twice as * prophetic power 2Ki 2:9
"How * food do you have in the 2Ki 4:2
If they let us live, so * the 2Ki 7:4
how * I have done for the Lord." 2Ki 10:16
After * discussion they sent them 1Ch 12:19
supplied him with * cedar lumber. 1Ch 14:1
and they smelted so * bronze that 1Ch 22:3
bronze that it was too * to weigh. 1Ch 22:3
and so * iron and bronze that I 1Ch 22:14
a warrior and have shed * blood.' 1Ch 28:3
I have gathered as * as I could for 1Ch 29:2
mountains, as * as you need, and 2Ch 2:16
contain you—how * less this Temple 2Ch 6:18
to count for * in those days! 2Ch 9:20
Then you will realize how * 2Ch 12:8
Be very * afraid to give any 2Ch 19:7
the corpses—so * that it took them 2Ch 20:25
in * better condition than before. 2Ch 24:13
he had done so * good for Israel, 2Ch 24:16
to give you * more than this!" 2Ch 25:9
the Levites were * more ready to 2Ch 29:34
ancestors; how * less your God!' 2Ch 32:15
and each gave as * as he could. Ez 2:69
it will be * to your disadvantage, Ez 4:13
we can't stay out here * longer. Ez 10:13
and there was so * rubble to be Neh 4:10
could have as * as they pleased. Est 1:8
the king very *, and he put the Est 2:4
harem, was very * impressed with Est 2:9
mistakes), how * less men made of Job 4:18,19
with little, you would end with *. Job 8:7
I know as * as you do. Job 13:2
have about as * value as ashes. Job 13:12
On our side are aged men * older Job 15:10
with him! How * less someone like Job 15:16
to him. How * less is man, who is Job 25:6
know as * about him as I do; Job 27:12
He must have spent * time with Job 34:7,8
"You who think you know so *, Job 37:19,20
Tell me, if you know so *. Job 38:4
I have said too * already." Job 40:5
gave him twice as * as before! Job 42:10
and sing his praises with * joy. Ps 27:6
HOW GREAT IS the Lord! How * we Ps 48:1
of you— of how * you have helped Ps 63:7
And I desire no one on earth as * Ps 73:25
forever, for you love me so *! Ps 86:13
You have done so * for me, O Ps 92:4
and our fathers have sinned so *. Ps 106:6
many children and * prosperity. Ps 107:41
Cursing is as * a part of him as Ps 109:18
O Lord, thank you so * for Ps 118:21
I have thought * about your Ps 119:11
and that is why I love them so *. Ps 119:140
pointing out how * I trust in you. Ps 119:147

(MUCH Con't)
Lord, see how * I really love Ps 119:159
and I love them very *; Ps 119:167
seven times as * as he stole, Pro 6:31
Don't talk so *. Pro 10:19
on earth; how * more the wicked! Pro 11:31
Lazy people want * but get Pro 13:4
* more the hearts of all mankind! Pro 15:11
How * better is wisdom than gold, Pro 16:16
how * more his friends! Pro 19:7
you can't do * to help him. Pro 19:19
truth—he enjoys his sinning too *. Pro 19:28
And remember that too * sleep Pro 23:19,20,21
Wisdom is too * for a rebel. Pro 24:7
Don't eat too * of it, or it will Pro 25:16
harmful to eat too * honey, so also Pro 25:27
and a cranky woman are * alike! Pro 27:15
the Lord are * concerned about it. Pro 28:5
No matter how * we see, we are Ecc 1:8-11
no matter how * we hear, we are Ecc 1:8-11
And why is he giving up so * now? Ecc 4:8
more than twice as * as one, for Ecc 4:9
for the results can be * better. Ecc 4:9
he eats little or *, but the rich Ecc 5:12
Yes, a wise man thinks * of Ecc 7:4
can outweigh * wisdom and honor. Ecc 10:1
you yourself may need * help. Ecc 11:2
can see how * he loves me. Sol 2:4
anywhere, this one I love so *?' Sol 3:3
How * better it is than mere wine. Sol 4:10
sound very * alike, as do those for Is 5:7f
that I have done so * for you. Is 5:13
so *—the kings of Israel and Syria Is 7:15,16
concerning which we heard so *? Is 16:6
the night? How * time is left?" Is 21:11
Show them how * you love your Is 26:11
Has God punished Israel as * as Is 27:7,8
and estimating how * they will get Is 33:18
"How * have they seen?" Is 39:4
* as move from where it is placed. Is 44:13
They can be as * mine as anyone. Is 56:3
trying to get as * as he can for Is 56:11
We have done * penance, and you Is 58:3
know how * it longs for you. Jer 12:3
I have had to punish you so *. Jer 30:15
an experience very * like, if not Jer 31:33f
be killed by those you fear so *. Jer 39:17
and sacrifice to her just as * as Jer 44:17
must suffer, how * more must you! Jer 49:12
laziness and too * food, while the Eze 16:49
whose gods she loved so *. Eze 23:9
That is how * regard they have Eze 23:39
you enjoy blood so *, I will give Eze 35:6
one bushel with the ram; as * as Eze 46:11
impressed him as * as Daniel, Dan 1:18,19
But we have sinned so *; Dan 9:5
Though we have sinned so * and Dan 9:15
it was, for God loves you very *. Dan 9:23
"God loves you very *," he Dan 10:19
I wanted so * to bless you! Hos 6:11
No, I will not punish you as * Hos 11:9
be expecting * from him, your God. Hos 12:6
Perhaps he will give you so * Joe 2:14
I am sending you * corn and wine Joe 2:19
done as * for other people, too? Amo 9:7
fig, however * I long for it! Mic 7:1
will be rebuilt, * larger and more Mic 7:11
however * I punish them, they Zep 3:7
Look at the result: You plant * Hag 1:6
"You hope for * but get so Hag 1:9
as * as do the tribes of Israel." Zec 9:1f
Even scoundrels do that *. Mt 5:46
how * more will you! Mt 10:25
And how * more valuable is a Mt 12:12
times as * as he had planted. Mt 13:8
he doesn't have * depth in his Mt 13:21
or even a hundred times as *." Mt 13:23f
Jesus asked them, "How * food do Mt 15:34
a hundred times as * in return, and Mt 19:29
assumed they would receive * more. Mt 20:10
paid them just as * as those of us Mt 20:11,12
do things like this and * more. Mt 21:21
as * as you love yourself.' Mt 22:38,39
so now I will give you * more.' Mt 25:23
and asked, "How * will you pay me Mt 26:15
But Jesus said nothing, * to the Mt 27:14
than I am, so * greater that I am Mk 1:7
thirty times as * as he had Mk 4:8
sixty or a hundred times as *! Mk 4:8
a hundred times as * as was planted Mk 4:20
the people as * as they were ready Mk 4:33
She had suffered * from many Mk 5:26
"How * food do we have?" Mk 6:38
seven loaves, how * was left?" Mk 8:20
how * longer must I be with you Mk 9:19
you believe? How * longer must I be Mk 9:19
If anyone so * as gives you a Mk 9:41
he was very * displeased with his Mk 10:14
were still very * alive, for he Mk 12:27
love others as * as yourself.' Mk 12:31
but I won't be here * longer. Mk 14:7
But Jesus said no more, * to Mk 15:5
my * loved Son, yes, my delight." Lk 3:22
are * more important than bread!' Lk 4:4
leave us—I'm too * of a sinner for Lk 5:8
Even sinners do that *! Lk 6:33
"Try to show as * compassion as Lk 6:36
he works hard, he may learn as *. Lk 6:40
forgiven, for she loved me *; Lk 7:47
must suffer *," he said, "and Lk 9:22
just as * as you love yourself." Lk 10:27
do at least as *, and give the Holy Lk 11:13
A couple of pennies? Not * more Lk 12:6
only lightly. * is required from Lk 12:48
from those to whom * is given, for Lk 12:48
He asked the first one, 'How * do Lk 16:5,6
another one for half that *!' Lk 16:5,6
" 'And how * do you owe him?' Lk 16:7
giving him back four times as *!" Lk 19:8
times as * as the original amount! Lk 19:16
If you knew so * about me and how Lk 19:22
For God loved the world so * Jn 3:16
"How can he know so * when he's Jn 7:15
I could condemn you for * and Jn 8:26
much and teach you *, but I won't, Jn 8:26
"See how * he loved him." Jn 11:36
other just as * as I love you. Jn 13:34
will teach you *, as well as remind Jn 14:26
"I don't have * more time to Jn 14:30
each other as * as I love you. Jn 15:12
"Oh, there is so * more I want Jn 16:12
you love them as * as you love me. Jn 17:23
It isn't true! It's * too early Act 2:15
was yours to decide how * to give. Act 5:4
not being given as * food, in the Act 6:1
will raise up a Prophet * like me Act 7:37
so there was * joy in that city! Act 8:8
And I will show him how * he Act 9:16
each giving as * as he could. Act 11:29
When Herod saw how * this Act 12:3
telling them—* to everyone's Act 15:3
earned * money for her masters. Act 16:16
* dissenting among themselves." Act 28:28,29f
In fact, those heathen will be * Rom 2:27
than you Jews who know so * about Rom 2:27
events with as * certainty as Rom 4:17
was also * too old to have a Rom 4:19
us as sinners, how * more will he Rom 5:9
you didn't bother * with goodness. Rom 6:20
God has given you so *, but Rom 9:4
how very * he wanted to bless you. Rom 9:4
it down, think how * greater a Rom 11:12
for you, is this too * to ask? Rom 12:1
by how * faith God has given you. Rom 12:3
everyone, just as * as possible. Rom 12:18
If you love your neighbor as * Rom 13:9
Spirit—pray * with me for my work. Rom 15:30
Is it too * to ask, in return, 1Co 9:11
agree with them as * as I can, 1Co 9:21
has too * to drink and gets drunk. 1Co 11:21
But in public worship I would * 1Co 14:19
The amount depends on how * the 1Co 16:2
and teach here. So * is happening, 1Co 16:9
for us. For * thanks and praise 2Co 1:11
I can't do * to help your faith, 2Co 1:24
show you how very * I loved you and 2Co 2:4
sorrow to me as * as to all the 2Co 2:5,6
that you still do love him very *. 2Co 2:8
doom was glorious, * more glorious 2Co 3:9
here we are, still very * alive. 2Co 6:9
When he told me how * you were 2Co 7:7
Just see how * good this grief 2Co 7:11
how * you really do care for us. 2Co 7:12
been going through * trouble and 2Co 8:2
ways—you have so * faith, so many 2Co 8:7
good preachers, so * learning, so 2Co 8:7
* enthusiasm, so much love for us. 2Co 8:7
much enthusiasm, so * love for us. 2Co 8:7
important how * you have to give. 2Co 8:12
In this way each will have as * 2Co 8:14
"He that gathered * had nothing 2Co 8:15
I would be very * ashamed—and so 2Co 9:4
if he plants *, he will reap much. 2Co 9:6
if he plants much, he will reap *. 2Co 9:6
mind as to how * he should give. 2Co 9:7
Yes, God will give you * so that 2Co 9:11
you can give away *, and when we 2Co 9:11
has done, it doesn't count for *. 2Co 10:18
You have suffered so * for the Gal 3:4
that child is not * better off than Gal 4:1
he loved us so * that even Eph 2:4
* loved child imitates his father. Eph 5:1
Don't drink too * wine, for many Eph 5:18
Talk with each other * about the Eph 5:19
Tychicus, who is a * loved Eph 6:21
* praise and glory to the Lord. Php 1:11
* happier for me than being here! Php 1:23
Yes, so * so that I greatly Php 3:6
whether I have * or little. Php 4:11
we have heard how * you trust the Col 1:4
and how * you love his people. Col 1:4
I WISH YOU could know how * I have Col 2:1
your children so * that they become Col 3:21
Tychicus, our * loved brother, Col 4:7
a faithful and * loved brother, one Col 4:9
dear brothers, * beloved of God. 1Th 1:4
you, and how * we suffered there. 1Th 2:2
We wanted very * to come and I, 1Th 2:18
Yes, you will bring us * joy as 1Th 2:19
just as * as we want to see you. 1Th 3:6
need to say very *, I'm sure! 1Th 4:9
HERE ARE MY directions: Pray * for 1Ti 2:1
and thinking * about the Lord. 1Ti 2:2
exercise is * more important and is 1Ti 4:8
We work hard and suffer * in 1Ti 4:9,10
as you would to * loved brothers. 1Ti 5:1
something that pleases God very *. 1Ti 5:4
and spending * time in prayer; 1Ti 5:5
everyone knows how * good some 1Ti 5:25
I know how * you trust the Lord, 2Ti 1:5
still trusting him as * as ever. 2Ti 1:5
you how * he helped me at Ephesus. 2Ti 1:18
around to help you very * longer. 2Ti 4:6
coppersmith has done me * harm. 2Ti 4:14
To: Philemon, our * loved fellow Phm 1:1
I myself have gained * joy and Phm 1:7
hasn't been of * use to you in the Phm 1:11
but something * better—a beloved Phm 1:16
Now he will mean * more to you Phm 1:16
I won't mention how * you owe me! Phm 1:19
And since Christ is so * Heb 3:7,8
There is * more I would like to Heb 5:11
and doesn't know * about the Heb 5:12,13
just think how * more surely the Heb 9:14
Think how * more terrible the Heb 10:29
His coming will not be delayed * Heb 10:37
Well, how * more do I need to Heb 11:32
doesn't amount to * in this world Jas 1:9
is best to listen *, speak little, Jas 1:19
and his religion isn't worth *. Jas 1:26
neighbors just as * as you love and Jas 2:8
trusting God so * that he was Jas 2:22
it will bring you * praise and 1Pe 1:7
without so * as trembling, 2Pe 2:10
* and delivering nothing; 2Pe 2:17
SEE HOW VERY * our heavenly Father 1Jn 3:1
God showed how * he loved us by 1Jn 4:9
God loved us as * as that, we 1Jn 4:11
We know how * God loves us 1Jn 4:16
So you can find out how * you 1Jn 5:2
how * you love and obey God. 1Jn 5:2
whom I love so *, as does everyone 2Jn 1:1
* peace, and with truth and love. 2Jn 1:3
Well, I would like to say * more, 2Jn 1:12
I have * to say but I don't want 3Jn 1:13
have * to talk about together. 3Jn 1:14
*, but producing nothing. Jud 1:12
"I know how * you suffer for the Rev 2:9
The horses' heads looked * like Rev 9:17,18
who had tormented them so *! Rev 11:10
for others—give twice as * to her. Rev 18:6
loved so * are gone," they cry. Rev 18:14
so * will never be yours again. Rev 18:14

MUCH-DESIRED
I am seated in his * shade and Sol 2:3

MUCH-LOVED
Epaphras, our * fellow worker, Col 1:7
saying, "This is my * Son; 2Pe 1:17,18

MUD
plunge me into the ditch and *; Job 9:31
God has thrown me into the *. Job 30:19
down like * in the street. Mic 7:10
ground and made * from the spittle Jn 9:6
and smoothed the * over the blind Jn 9:6
call Jesus made * and smoothed it Jn 9:11
Pool of Siloam and wash off the *. Jn 9:11
had smoothed the * over his eyes, Jn 9:15
back and wallow in the * again." 2Pe 2:22

MUDDY
good, and walk the * paths of sin. Jer 18:15
and * the rest with your feet? Eze 34:18

MUDDYING
a fountain or * a spring. Pro 25:26
making bubbles and * the stream. Eze 32:2

MUFFLE
* your face and don't gaze around. Eze 12:6

MUFFLED
with him, with * face, for he won't Eze 12:12
his face * in a head swath. Jn 11:44

MULBERRY
the * trees and attack from there. 1Ch 14:14
in the tops of the * trees, that is 1Ch 14:15
to uproot that * tree over there Lk 17:6

MULE
on his *, it went beneath the 2Sa 18:9
the branches. His * went on, 2Sa 18:9
on my personal *, and Zadok the 1Ki 1:33
riding on King David's own *. 1Ki 1:38
and he rode on the king's own *. 1Ki 1:44,45
senseless horse or * that has to Ps 32:9

MULE-LOADS
But please give me two * of earth 2Ki 5:17

MULES
king jumped on their * and fled. 2Sa 13:29,30

(MULES Con't)
myrrh, spices, horses, and *. 1Ki 10:25
at least some of my horses and *. 1Ki 18:5
on donkeys, camels, *, and oxen. 1Ch 12:40
armor, spices, horses, and *. 2Ch 9:24
*, 435 camels, and 6,720 donkeys. Ez 2:66,67
*, 435 camels, and 6,720 donkeys. Neh 7:68,69
on camels, *, and young dromedaries Est 8:9,10
in litters, and on * and camels, to Is 66:20
come chariot horses, steeds and * Eze 27:14
strike the horses, *, camels, Zec 14:15

MULTIPLIED
crops flourished and his flocks *. Gen 39:5
for the Lord has * you like stars! Deu 1:10
and gold have *, that is the time Deu 8:12,13
for you and has * you, so the Lord Deu 28:63
people of Israel * explosively, Ps 105:24
who minister to me will be *. Jer 33:22
The more my people *, the more Hos 4:7
Jewish people greatly * in Egypt; Act 7:17,18

MULTIPLIES
and * my wounds without a cause. Job 9:17

MULTIPLY
them all. "* and stock the Gen 1:21,22
and told them, "* and fill the Gen 1:28
I will cause him to * and become Gen 17:20
blessings and * your descendants Gen 22:17
do me good, and to * my descendants Gen 32:12
be fertile and to * and to become a Gen 35:11
the more the Israelis seemed to *! Ex 1:12
* and to become a mighty nation. Ex 1:20
refuse, and I will * my miracles in Ex 7:3
own self, 'I will * your posterity Ex 32:13
I will look after you, and * Lev 26:9
And may he * you a thousand Deu 1:11
wild animals would * too quickly Deu 7:22
live, you will * and will go in and Deu 8:1
family and * everything you own. 1Sa 25:6
"If the Lord were to * his 1Ch 21:3
and all the time their riches * Ps 73:12
your own soil and flourish and *. Is 37:31
The smallest family shall * into Is 60:22
Their profits *, and they are Jer 12:2
and have many grandchildren. *! Jer 29:6
and I will * my people and make of Jer 30:19
the population and * the number of Jer 31:27
they * the widows in the land. Eze 22:25
and herds will also greatly *. Eze 36:11
Let them but ask and I will * Eze 36:37,38
I will bless them and * them and Eze 37:26
There is no escape, though you * Nah 3:15

MULTIPLYING
BUT WITH THE believers * rapidly, Act 6:1

MULTITUDE
one nation, but a * of nations!" Gen 17:2,3,4
Literally, "a mixed *." Ex 12:38f
If he has a * of children, it is Job 27:14
have a * of children, many heirs. Is 53:10
bring a * of horses! Jer 51:27
A city named '*' is there! Eze 39:15,16
the roaring of a vast * of people. Dan 10:5,6
soon saw a great * of people Jn 6:2-5
Literally, "This * is accursed." Jn 7:49f

MULTITUDES
This is my blessing on the * of Deu 33:17
them, so that * would stream to Ps 102:21,22
For she has been the ruin of *—a Pro 7:26
Vast * fall in heaps. Jer 46:16
will destroy the * of Egypt. Eze 30:10
will die with the * slain by the Eze 32:20
*, multitudes waiting in the Joe 3:14
Multitudes, * waiting in the Joe 3:14
all the * who choose its easy way. Mt 7:13
until now, ardent * have been Mt 11:12
out to forgive the sins of *. Mt 26:28
And now eager * are pressing in. Lk 16:16
vast * of God's people to heaven; Heb 2:10

MUMBLED
they *. Jn 7:46

MUNCHING
the city * on twigs and branches. Is 27:10

MUPPIM
Ehi, Rosh, *, Gen 46:19-22

MURDER
drained off. And * is forbidden. Gen 9:5,6
"You must not *. Ex 20:13
be presumed to be * and the man who Ex 22:3
is guilty of * and shall be Lev 17:3,4
be presumed to be *, and the Num 35:16
is *, and the murderer shall die. Num 35:17
him, it is not *, for the man Num 35:27
judged guilty of *, he must die—no Num 35:30
be polluted, for * pollutes the Num 35:33
can be made for * except by the Num 35:33
" 'You must not *. Deu 5:17
is guilty of * when there is Deu 17:8
Promised Land, a * victim is found Deu 21:1
one has seen the *, the elders and Deu 21:1
The girl is as innocent as a * Deu 22:25,26,27
Why should you now * an innocent 1Sa 19:5
Therefore * shall be a constant 2Sa 12:10
guilty of *, let him execute me." 2Sa 14:32
you will avenge the * of my 2Ki 9:7
for the * of Naboth and his sons.' 2Ki 9:26
provinces, whether * cases or other 2Ch 19:10
how you abhor all * and Ps 5:6
He who avenges * has an open ear Ps 9:12
of the city and * passersby. Ps 10:8
My enemies encircle me with * in Ps 17:9
while planning to * them. Ps 28:3
and his * of Uriah, her husband. Ps 51:1
There is * and robbery there, Ps 55:11
They * widows, immigrants, and Ps 94:6,7
and polluting the land with *. Ps 106:37,38
of life, and * is their specialty. Pro 1:16
of all who live by violence and *. Pro 1:19
to those who plot *, who shut their Is 33:15
feet run to do evil and rush to *; Is 59:7
Brazenly you * without a cause. Jer 2:34
you can steal, *, commit adultery, Jer 7:9
dishonesty! You * the innocent, Jer 22:17
"Why should we let him come and * Jer 40:15
land is full of * and injustice, Eze 9:9
indict Jerusalem as the City of *. Eze 22:2
City of *, doomed and Eze 22:3
are guilty both of * and idolatry. Eze 22:4
within your walls is bent on *. Eze 22:6
committed both adultery and *; Eze 23:37
you worship idols, and *. Eze 33:25
They polluted the land with * Eze 36:18
to avenge his sister's *. Dan 11:7f
with one * after another. Hos 4:2
packs of priests * along the road Hos 6:9
Jerusalem with * and sin of every Mic 3:10
"Help! *!" Hab 1:2
evil thoughts, *, adultery, Mt 15:19
laws to accept money paid for *." Mt 27:6
of lust, theft, *, adultery, Mk 7:21
for * during an insurrection. Mk 15:7
rage, and began to plot his *. Lk 6:11
for the * of God's servants from Lk 11:50
world— from the * of Abel to the Lk 11:51
of Abel to the * of Zechariah who Lk 11:51
afraid of these who want to * you. Lk 12:4
adultery, don't *, don't steal, Lk 18:20
plotting Jesus' *, trying to find a Lk 22:2
against the government, and for *. Lk 23:19
and *, at their request. Lk 23:25
nail him to the cross and * him. Act 2:23
day and night prepared to * him. Act 9:24
he had argued plotted to * him. Act 9:29
and hate, envy, *, fighting, lying, Rom 1:29
doctrine, envy, *, drunkenness, Gal 5:21
their fathers and mothers, and *. 1Ti 1:9
said you must not *, so even though Jas 2:11
to * has eternal life within. 1Jn 3:15
and he has avenged the * of his Rev 19:2

MURDERED
I would be *," Isaac replied. Gen 26:9
going to die because we * him." Gen 42:22
For in their anger they * a man, Gen 49:6
now called for the * woman's Ju 20:3
You were *— 2Sa 3:33,34
and * him and cut off his head. 2Sa 4:6,7
For you have * Uriah and stolen 2Sa 12:9
So they * Amnon. 2Sa 13:29,30
for they * the Gibeonites." 2Sa 21:1
You know that Joab * my two 1Ki 2:5
You son of a Zimri who * his 2Ki 9:31
of them weie *, and their heads 2Ki 10:7
of Judah, he * great numbers of 2Ki 21:16
into the darkness, lest he be *. Job 15:22
or if I have * its owners to get Job 31:38,39
of the men he * was the large one Jer 41:9
You have * endlessly and filled Eze 11:6
they have worshiped idols and * Eze 23:37
for when they had * their children Eze 23:39
Berenice, * in Antioch by Dan 11:7f
all the blood of * godly men from Mt 23:35
So they caught him and * him Mk 12:8
Messiah whom you betrayed and *. Act 7:52
where he was * on a cross. Act 10:39
adultery, but have * someone, you Jas 2:11
out the blood of those who * them; Rev 16:6

MURDERER
and the * must be executed. Num 35:16
it is murder, and the * shall die. Num 35:17
kill the * when he meets him. Num 35:19
fist so that he dies, he is a *; Num 35:21
and the * shall be executed by Num 35:21
except by the execution of the *. Num 35:33
conscience of a * who took the law 1Sa 25:30,31
"Get out of here, you *, you 2Sa 16:7,8
of your own medicine, you *!" 2Sa 16:7,8
* has sent a man to kill me. 2Ki 6:32
him, "How are you today, you *! 2Ki 9:31
a common sinner or * who plots Ps 26:9,10
is no better than a *. Pro 28:24
who is a robber or * and who Eze 18:10
He was a * from the beginning and Jn 8:44
you demanded the release of a *. Act 3:14
to each other, "A *, no doubt! Act 28:4
brother is really a * at heart; 1Jn 3:1

MURDERER'S
A * conscience will drive him Pro 28:1

MURDERERS
"Also, all * must be executed. Lev 24:1
"All * must be executed, but Num 35:3
Purge all * from Israel! Deu 19:1
They are * who rise in the early Job 24:14,1
of destruction. * and liars will Ps 55:2
me from these criminals, these *. Ps 59:
for your hands are those of *; Is 1:1
Fair Play," but now a gang of *. Is 1:2
earth will no longer hide the *. Is 26:2
For your hands are those of * Is 59:
help, prostrate before their *. Jer 4:31
Hired *, loan racketeers and Eze 22:12
really are—adulteresses and *. Eze 23:45
says: Woe to Jerusalem, City of *; Eze 24:6
"Woe to Jerusalem, City of *. Eze 24:9
I'll let you have the land? *! Eze 33:26
They are all *, turning against Mic 7:1
now they will ruin you. You *! Hab 2:8
the * and burned their city. Mt 22:7
killed the prophets long ago. *! Lk 11:48
the corrupt, and *, and the Rev 21:8
the immoral and * and idolaters, Rev 22:15

MURDERESS
I will punish you as a * is Eze 16:38

MURDERING
them with * an innocent man. Deu 21:8
sin of * Gideon's seventy sons. Ju 9:56,57
has kept you from * and taking 1Sa 25:26
Bless you for keeping me from * 1Sa 25:33
to be executed for * his brother. 2Sa 14:7
for * King Saul and his family; 2Sa 16:7,8
* the son of Jehoiada the priest. 2Ch 24:25
* Pro 6:16-19
And stop your *. Jer 7:6
and widows; stop * the innocent! Jer 22:3
money gained from * and robbery! Hab 2:12
of all your * and violence in Hab 2:17
your suffering for * or stealing or 1Pe 4:15

MURDEROUS
Instead of rain he sent down * Ps 105:32
Lord, you know all their * plots Jer 18:23
And as the * stones came hurtling Act 7:59
the crowds into a * mob that stoned Act 14:19

MURDERS
and any man who * shall be killed; Gen 9:5,6
their just punishment for these *. Ju 9:24
of his senseless * from me and from 1Ki 2:31
for the * of two men who were 1Ki 2:32
guilty of these *, and may the Lord 1Ki 2:33
to all—she boldly *, leaving blood Eze 24:7
Jehu's dynasty to avenge the * Hos 1:4,5
By the * you commit, you have Hab 2:10
The city that * the prophets. Lk 13:34
about all their * and witchcraft, Rev 9:21

MURKY
dense clouds dark as * waters. Ps 18:11

MURMUR
they began to * against God and Num 21:5
humans as we are, * and complain Lam 3:39
appearance dead. A * ran through Mk 9:26
Then the Jews began to * against Jn 6:41
But Jesus replied, "Don't * Jn 6:43
And don't * against God and his 1Co 10:10

MURMURED
"They * and complained in their Deu 1:27
Then she *, "Name the child 1Sa 4:21,22
They * and complained, demanding Ps 78:18

MURMURING
Then at last this * and Num 17:5

MUSCLE
* where it attaches to the hip. Gen 32:32

MUSCLES
See his powerful loins and the * Job 40:16
I will replace the flesh and * Eze 37:6
Then, as I watched, the * and Eze 37:8

MUSED
The more I *, the hotter the Ps 39:2,3

MUSEUM
it to be kept as a * specimen Ex 16:32
His iron bedstead is kept in a * Deu 3:11

MUSHI
The sons of Merari:Mahli, *. Ex 6:19
(clan names) Mahli * Num 3:31-35
The sons of Merari were:Mahli, *. 1Ch 6:19,20,21
Shemer, Mahli, *, Merari, Levi. 1Ch 6:44-47
*. The sons of Mahli were 1Ch 23:21
*. (Ja-aziah's group, led by his 1Ch 24:26,27
The sons of * were Mahli, Eder, 1Ch 24:30

MUSHI'S
the sons of Kish. * sons were 1Ch 23:23

MUSHITES
Mahlites, the *,The Korahites. Num 26:58,59

MUSHKI
be identified as *, Tabal, Eze 38:2,3f

MUSIC
"The harp * will quiet you and 1Sa 16:15,16
Their * ministry included the 1Ch 25:6,7

(MUSIC Con't)
the instruments of * began to play 2Ch 29:27
with * and cymbals day after day. 2Ch 30:21
the Levites of their excellent *. 2Ch 30:22
* while the work progressed. 2Ch 34:12
of ivory, lovely * is being played Ps 45:8
I will praise you with *, telling Ps 71:22
* from the harp and lute and lyre. Ps 92:3
Sing your praise accompanied by * Ps 98:5
You furnish lovely * at your Is 5:12
All the pleasant * in your palace Is 14:11
will rejoice with * and song. Is 30:32
I will stop the * of your songs. Eze 26:13
When the * plays, if you fall Dan 3:15
I will not listen to your *, no Amo 5:23
heard the funeral *, he said, Mt 9:23
he heard dance * coming from the Lk 15:25
* in your hearts to the Lord. Eph 5:19
Never again will the sound of * Rev 18:22

MUSICAL
every sort of * instrument before 2Sa 6:5
the * instruments I have made." 1Ch 23:4,5
playing of other * instruments—all 2Ch 5:13,14
using the * instruments that King 2Ch 7:6
(They used the original * Neh 12:35,36
Even * instruments—the flute, 1Co 14:7

MUSICIAN
Jubal, the first *—the inventor Gen 4:21
of them in all—was a master *. 1Ch 25:6,7

MUSICIANS
The village * Ju 5:11
of Merari were the heads of the *. 1Ch 15:17
The Levites who were skilled * 2Ch 34:12
singers in front, * behind, girls Ps 68:25
be as great * as King David was. Amo 6:5

MUST
Then Jehovah said, "My Spirit * Gen 6:3
Man-killing animals * die, and Gen 9:5,6
Close relatives such as we are * Gen 13:8
posterity. All * be circumcised. Gen 17:13
"You * sleep with me tonight!" Gen 30:16
you feel you * go, and long so Gen 31:30
Onan, "You * marry Tamar, as our Gen 38:8
And if I * bear the anguish of Gen 43:14
of your fathers, * have put it Gen 43:23
And he said, "It * be true! Gen 45:28
I will die. You * bury me with my Gen 49:29,30
This touched her heart. "He * be Ex 2:6
your message. They * go with you to Ex 3:18
God had said they * do, and what Ex 4:28
miracles they * do before Pharaoh. Ex 4:28
go, for they * make a holy Ex 5:1
declared. "We * take a three days' Ex 5:3
but you * produce just as many Ex 5:10,11
given you, and you * deliver the Ex 5:18
"For he * be forced to let my Ex 6:1
* let the people of Israel go." Ex 6:11
will kill us. We * take a Ex 8:27
But I am warning you that you * Ex 8:29
for we * all join in the holy Ex 10:9
"No," Moses said, "we * take Ex 10:25
for we * have sacrifices for the Ex 10:26
The meat * not be eaten raw or Ex 12:9
so it is a law that you * Ex 12:17
For these seven days there * be Ex 12:19
those days you * not eat anything Ex 12:20
yeast, and there * be no yeast in Ex 13:6,7
days each year you * explain to Ex 13:8
However, you * buy back your Ex 13:13
Moses. "* we die of thirst?" Ex 15:24
the Lord when we * refrain from Ex 16:23
boundaries. They * not come up here Ex 19:21
* sanctify themselves, lest Ex 19:22
You * never bow to an image or Ex 20:5
"You * not murder. Ex 20:13
"You * not commit adultery. Ex 20:14
"You * not steal. Ex 20:15
"You * not lie. Ex 20:16
Or, "You * not give false Ex 20:16f
"You * not be envious of your Ex 20:17
Remember, you * not make or Ex 20:23
"The altars you make for me * be Ex 20:24
"HERE ARE OTHER laws you * obey: Ex 21:1
but * treat her as a daughter. Ex 21:9
"A kidnapper * be killed, Ex 21:16
him so that he * be confined to Ex 21:18
except that he * pay for the loss Ex 21:19
the daylight, it * be presumed to Ex 22:3
"If a thief is captured, he * Ex 22:3
if he can't, then he * be sold as Ex 22:3
field to graze, he * pay for all Ex 22:5
then the neighbor * take an oath Ex 22:11
it, and the owner * accept his Ex 22:11
caring for it * repay the owner. Ex 22:12
man who borrowed it * pay for it. Ex 22:14
with her, he * pay the usual dowry Ex 22:16
"You * not oppress a stranger in Ex 22:21
"You * not exploit widows or Ex 22:22
* let him have it back at night. Ex 22:26
"You * be prompt in giving me Ex 22:29
you * take it back to its owner. Ex 23:4
* not go on by, but must help him. Ex 23:5
must not go on by, but * help him. Ex 23:5
religious pilgrimages you * make. Ex 23:14
Or, "feasts you * celebrate." Ex 23:14f
everyone * bring me a sacrifice Ex 23:15
when you * bring to me the first of Ex 23:16
"You * not worship the gods of Ex 23:24
any way, and you * not follow the Ex 23:24
people; you * utterly conquer them Ex 23:24
"You * make no covenant with Ex 23:32
The people of Israel * always Ex 29:28
"Once a year Aaron * sanctify Ex 30:10
to the Lord. They * always wash Ex 30:20
anointing oil. It * never be Ex 30:32
Lord and you * treat it as holy. Ex 30:37
does not obey this command * die; Ex 31:14,15
something * have happened to Ex 32:1
one * be anywhere on the mountain. Ex 34:3
Instead, you * break down their Ex 34:13
For you * worship no other gods, Ex 34:14
* have nothing to do with idols. Ex 34:17
it, then its neck * be broken. Ex 34:20
But your sons * all be redeemed. Ex 34:20
"And you * remember to celebrate Ex 34:22
"You * not use leavened bread Ex 34:25
And you * bring the best of the Ex 34:26
Lord your God. You * not cook a Ex 34:26
the laws of Jehovah you * obey. Ex 35:1
anyone working on that day * die. Ex 35:2
or a goat, it too * be a male, and Lev 1:10
to the Lord, it * be made from Lev 2:4
"Every offering * be seasoned Lev 2:13
but the animal * be entirely Lev 3:1
to the Lord, it * have no defect Lev 3:6
the people, he * offer a young bull Lev 4:3
his attention he * bring as his Lev 4:23
sin offering, it * be a female Lev 4:32
of fine flour. He * not mix it with Lev 5:11
guilty anyway, and * bring his Lev 5:17,18
realizing it. It * be offered as a Lev 5:19
defect, and * be worth whatever Lev 6:6
fire on the altar * be kept Lev 6:12
be kept burning—it * not go out. Lev 6:12
The fire * be kept burning upon Lev 6:13
continually. It * never go out. Lev 6:13
it is baked it * be without yeast. Lev 6:17
it * be washed in a holy place. Lev 6:27
kettle is used, it * be scoured and Lev 6:28
That carcass * be entirely burned Lev 6:30
carcass, and it * be eaten in a Lev 7:6
who eats it * answer for his sin. Lev 7:17,18
to the Lord * bring it personally Lev 7:29
Aaron and his sons * always be Lev 7:34
the meat and bread * be burned." Lev 8:32
therefore you * eat it in the Lev 10:13
"Flying insects with four legs * Lev 11:20
* wash his clothes immediately. Lev 11:25
immediately. He * also quarantine Lev 11:25
anything it touches * be put into Lev 11:32
it is defiled and * be smashed. Lev 11:35
be your God. You * therefore be Lev 11:45
On the eighth day, her son * be Lev 12:3
impurity, she * not touch anything Lev 12:4
boy or girl), she * bring a Lev 12:6
She * take them to the door of the Lev 12:6
a lamb, then she * bring two Lev 12:8
be suspected. He * be brought to Lev 13:1
the priest * declare him a leper. Lev 13:3
* quarantine him seven days more. Lev 13:5
to be examined, he * come back to Lev 13:7
priest * pronounce him a leper. Lev 13:8
priest * pronounce him defiled. Lev 13:11
white, the man * go to the priest Lev 13:19
the priest * declare him a leper. Lev 13:22
the priest * examine the spot. Lev 13:25
priest * pronounce him a leper. Lev 13:25
priest * pronounce him a leper. Lev 13:27
or chin, the priest * examine him; Lev 13:29,30
priest * pronounce him a leper. Lev 13:29,30
then the priest * examine him Lev 13:36
then the priest * pronounce him such. Lev 13:44
to have leprosy * tear his clothes Lev 13:45
and * live outside the camp. Lev 13:46
leprosy, and * be taken to the Lev 13:49
leprosy, and he * burn the Lev 13:52
and * be destroyed by fire. Lev 13:52
it is leprosy and he * burn it. Lev 13:57
however, he * stay outside his Lev 14:8
"Then the priest * offer the sin Lev 14:19
Then he * put some of the olive Lev 14:28
"Then he * offer the two Lev 14:30
and the material * be thrown into a Lev 14:40
until evening, and * wash his Lev 15:5
until evening, and * wash his Lev 15:6
until evening, and * wash his Lev 15:8
until evening, and * wash his Lev 15:10
hands, that person * wash his Lev 15:11
by the defiled man * be broken, and Lev 15:12
utensil * be rinsed in water. Lev 15:12
semen spills on * be washed and Lev 15:17
as well as the man * bathe, and Lev 15:18
entering there: He * bring a young Lev 16:3
offering. He * bathe himself and Lev 16:4
"Then he * go out Lev 16:15
for it. He * smear the blood of the Lev 16:18
"This is a permanent law: You * Lev 16:29,30
but * spend the day in Lev 16:29,30
for food, * pour out the blood and Lev 17:13
eats blood * be excommunicated. Lev 17:14
by wild animals, * wash his clothes Lev 17:15
to take you. You * obey only my Lev 18:4,5
my laws, and you * carry them out Lev 18:4,5
"There * be no sexual Lev 18:19
and a woman * never give herself Lev 18:23
You * strictly obey all of my Lev 18:26
and you * not do any of these Lev 18:26
of Israel, "You * be holy because Lev 19:1
God, am holy. You * respect your Lev 19:1
until the third day * be burned. Lev 19:6
"You * not steal nor lie nor Lev 19:11
nor defraud. You * not swear to a Lev 19:12
"You * not curse the deaf nor Lev 19:14
"Judges * always be just in Lev 19:15
they * always be perfectly fair. Lev 19:15
"I am Jehovah your God! You * Lev 19:26
"You * not trim off your hair on Lev 19:27
They * be treated like any other Lev 19:34
"You * be impartial in judgment. Lev 19:35,36
of Egypt. You * heed all of my Lev 19:37
your God. You * obey all of my Lev 20:8
both the man and the woman * die, Lev 20:11
"You * obey all of my laws and Lev 20:22
You * not follow the customs of Lev 20:23
special garments—* not let his hair Lev 21:10
I am Jehovah. He * marry a Lev 21:13
a prostitute. She * be a virgin Lev 21:14,15
own tribe, for he * not be the Lev 21:14,15
Literally, "he * not profane his Lev 21:14,15f
people of Israel * not be defiled Lev 22:15
without defect; it * be a young Lev 22:19
Anything that has a defect * not Lev 22:20
offering, * sacrifice an animal Lev 22:21
* not be offered to the Lord; Lev 22:22
thanksgiving, you * do it in the Lev 22:29,30
"You * keep all of my Lev 22:31
am the Lord. You * not treat me as Lev 22:32,33
Until this is done you * not eat Lev 23:14
your harvests, you * not thoroughly Lev 23:22
* pay the penalty: he must die. Lev 24:15,16
must pay the penalty: he * die. Lev 24:15,16
the name of Jehovah. He * die. Lev 24:15,16
"Also, all murderers * be Lev 24:17
kills an animal * replace it, and Lev 24:21
it, and whoever kills a man * die. Lev 24:21
to give you, you * let the land Lev 25:1
"You * fear your God and not Lev 25:17,18
of sale there * be a stipulation Lev 25:24
and the owner * accept the money Lev 25:27
but at the Jubilee year it * be Lev 25:28
at any time, and * be returned to Lev 25:33
and they * belong to no one else. Lev 25:34
to you, you * not treat him as an Lev 25:39
the foreigner * treat him as a Lev 25:53
"YOU * HAVE no idols; Lev 26:1
"YOU MUST HAVE no idols; you * Lev 26:1
your God. You * obey my Sabbath Lev 26:2
as a sacrifice, it * be given. Lev 27:9
he * add a fifth to its value. Lev 27:31
"Next they * spread a blue cloth Num 4:7
"Next they * cover with a blue Num 4:9
"They * then spread a blue cloth Num 4:11
but they * not touch the holy Num 4:15
This is what you * do so that Num 4:17,18,19
Otherwise they * never enter the Num 4:20
Israel that they * expel all lepers Num 5:1
it is sin. He * confess his sin Num 5:7
can be made, it * be given to the Num 5:8
a special way, he * not Num 6:3,4
"Throughout that time he * never Num 6:5
that is why he * let his hair Num 6:5
the eighth day, he * bring two Num 6:10
And he * renew his vows that day Num 6:11
longer count. He * begin all over Num 6:12
a new vow, and * bring a male lamb Num 6:12
to the Lord, he * go to the Num 6:13
without defect. He * also offer a Num 6:14
sacrifices he * bring any further Num 6:21
"The people of Israel * Num 9:2,3
They * not leave any of it until Num 9:12
next morning, and * not break a Num 9:12
a bone of it, and * follow all the Num 9:12
proper time; he * bear his guilt. Num 9:13
replied, "No, I * return to my own Num 10:30
tomorrow you * turn back into the Num 14:25
wilderness. You * wander in the Num 14:33
forty days, you * wander in the Num 14:34,35
their sacrifice * be an animal from Num 15:3,4
annual festivals—* be accompanied Num 15:3,4
accompanying it * consist of nine Num 15:8,9
give them, they * present to the Num 15:19,20,21
This loaf * be waved back and Num 15:19,20,21
floor, and * be observed from Num 15:19,20,21

(MUST Con't)
their error, they * offer one young Num 15:23,24
the Lord, and * be offered along Num 15:23,24
to obey his law; he * be executed, Num 15:31
Moses, "The man * die—all the Num 15:35
claiming that we * obey you, and Num 16:3
they pleaded, "* you be angry with Num 16:22
to the Lord. He * also scatter the Num 16:36,37
dies. * we all perish?" Num 17:12,13
The Levites * be careful not to Num 18:2,3
Instead, there * be a payment of Num 18:16
they * be sacrificed to the Lord. Num 18:17
"Then he * wash his clothes, and Num 19:7
burns the animal * wash his Num 19:8
of the heifer * wash his clothes Num 19:10
seven days, and * purify himself Num 19:12
then the defiled person * wash Num 19:19
The man who sprinkles the water * Num 19:21
then you and Aaron * summon the Num 20:8
you rebels! * we bring you water Num 20:10
I tell you that I * say whatever Num 23:26
They too * be destroyed." Num 24:23,24
fine flour. You * also offer a Num 28:22
Pentecost), there * be a special, Num 28:26
There * also be a male goat Num 29:16
the festival, you * sacrifice eight Num 29:29
you * do no hard work that day. Num 29:35
that vow * not be broken: the Num 30:1
* do exactly as he has promised. Num 30:1
Her father * state his Num 30:5
divorced, she * fulfill her vow. Num 30:9
idolatry, and then you * die." Num 31:1
"Some of you * take arms to wage Num 31:3
pure; it * then be further purified Num 31:23
On the seventh day you * wash Num 31:24
* give them the land of Gilead; Num 32:29
but if they refuse, then they * Num 32:30
of Canaan, you * drive out all the Num 33:52
for the slayer * not be killed Num 35:12
piece of iron, it * be presumed to Num 35:16
and the murderer * be executed. Num 35:16
and he * live there until the Num 35:25
"All murderers * be executed, Num 35:30
of murder, he * die—no ransom may Num 35:31
who are heiresses * marry within Num 36:8
said, 'The Lord * hate us, bringing Deu 1:27
He proclaimed the laws you * Deu 4:13
issue the laws you * obey when you Deu 4:14
inheritance. I * die here on this Deu 4:21,22
than him! You * obey these laws Deu 4:40
" 'You * never use my name to Deu 5:11
Literally, "You * not utter the Deu 5:11f
living among you * obey this law. Deu 5:14
Everybody * rest as you do. Deu 5:14
" 'You * not murder. Deu 5:17
" 'You * not commit adultery. Deu 5:18
" 'You * not steal. Deu 5:19
" 'You * not tell lies. Deu 5:20
" 'You * not burn with desire Deu 5:21
So Moses told the people, "You * Deu 5:32
alone. You * love him with all Deu 6:5
And you * think constantly about Deu 6:6
you today. You * teach them to Deu 6:7
"You * not worship the gods of Deu 6:14
of the earth. You * not provoke Deu 6:16
at Massah. You * actively obey him Deu 6:17
you * tell him, 'We were Deu 6:21
"You * break down the heathen Deu 7:5
"You * destroy all the nations Deu 7:16
"YOU * OBEY all the commandments Deu 8:1
(You too * love foreigners, for Deu 10:19
You * fear the Lord your God Deu 10:20
"YOU * LOVE the Lord your God and Deu 11:1
But you * obey all the laws I am Deu 11:32
"THESE ARE THE laws you * obey Deu 12:1
"You * destroy all the heathen Deu 12:2
"You * not make sacrifices to Deu 12:4,5
Rather, you * build a sanctuary Deu 12:4,5
enemies, then you * bring all your Deu 12:11
All these * be brought to the Deu 12:18
you where this altar * be located. Deu 12:18
as they do! You * not insult the Deu 12:31
and soul. You * never worship any Deu 13:4
to lead you astray * be executed, Deu 13:5
given you, you * without fail Deu 13:15
Afterwards you * pile all the Deu 13:16
"You * not boil a young goat in Deu 14:21
"You * tithe all of your crops Deu 14:22
who are poor, you * not shut your Deu 15:7
* lend them as much as they need. Deu 15:8
you as a sin. You * lend him what Deu 15:10
You * lend to them liberally. Deu 15:11
man or woman, you * free him at the Deu 15:12
But when you free a slave you * Deu 15:18
in your homes. It * be eaten at Deu 16:6
of Shelters, * be observed for Deu 16:13
Justice * prevail. Deu 16:20
there * be at least two or three. Deu 17:6
Such sinners * be purged from Deu 17:12
shall choose. He * be an Israelite, Deu 17:15
Egypt again.' He * not have too Deu 17:17

as king, then he * copy these laws Deu 17:18
companion. He * read from it every Deu 17:19
* be given to the priests. Deu 18:3
Promised Land you * be very careful Deu 18:9
to heathen gods, * be killed. Deu 18:10
them. You * walk blamelessly Deu 18:13
* listen and whom you must obey. Deu 18:15
must listen and whom you * obey. Deu 18:15
a message from other gods * die.' Deu 18:20
and homes, you * set apart three Deu 19:2,3
These cities * be scattered so Deu 19:6,7
paths), then you * designate three Deu 19:9
remember that you * never steal a Deu 19:14
There * be at least two, and Deu 19:15
They * be closely questioned, Deu 19:18
peace with you, you * besiege it. Deu 20:12
home with you. She * shave her head Deu 21:12
like her, you * let her go free—you Deu 21:14
wife he loves. He * give the Deu 21:17
overnight. You * bury him the same Deu 21:23
"A woman * not wear men's Deu 22:5
a man * not wear women's clothing. Deu 22:5
"Every new house * have a Deu 22:8
"You * sew tassels on the four Deu 22:12
and such evil * be cleansed from Deu 22:21
the other man's wife * be killed; Deu 22:22
for it * be assumed that she Deu 22:25,26,27
caught in the act, he * pay a fine Deu 22:28,29
loves you. You * never, as long as Deu 23:6
camps * stay away from all evil. Deu 23:9,10
during the night * leave the camp, Deu 23:9,10
Each man * have a spade as part Deu 23:13
after every bowel movement he * Deu 23:13
The camp * be holy, for the Lord Deu 23:14
you * not force him to return; Deu 23:15,16
men or women; you * not bring to Deu 23:17,18
Once you make the vow, you * be Deu 23:23
him, the kidnapper * die, in order Deu 24:7
and guidelines you * obey to the Deu 24:8
another man, you * not enter his Deu 24:10
"Justice * be given to migrants Deu 24:17
orphans and you * never accept a Deu 24:17
* not marry outside the family; Deu 25:5
instead, her husband's brother * Deu 25:5
"In all your transactions you * Deu 25:13,14,15
"You * never forget what the Deu 25:17
living there, you * present to the Deu 26:2,3
"You * wholeheartedly obey all Deu 26:16
that you * obey all of his laws. Deu 26:18
and renown you * be a holy people Deu 26:19
God, so today you * begin to obey Deu 27:10
and you * never worship other Deu 28:14
time has come when you * die. Deu 31:14
said to him, "You * bring the Deu 31:23
After you see the land you * die Deu 32:50
and you yourself * think about them Jos 1:8
fully armed, * lead the other Jos 1:14
* be brought into his treasury." Jos 6:19
"something which * be totally Jos 7:12f
Tell the people, 'Each of you * Jos 7:13
In the morning you * come by Jos 7:14
And that tribe * come by its Jos 7:14
and the clan * come by its Jos 7:14
guilty family * come one by one. Jos 7:14
and we won't. We * let them live, Jos 9:20
From this moment you * always Jos 9:23
happened, and they * let him come Jos 20:4
him come in and * give him a place Jos 20:4
innocent slayer * not be released Jos 20:5
accidental death * stay in that Jos 20:6
by the judges, and * live there Jos 20:6
little that you * rebel again? Jos 22:17,18
said, "then you * destroy all the Jos 24:23
* obey the Lord God of Israel." Jos 24:23
And those who are poor and * walk. Ju 5:10
God, and that you * not worship the Ju 6:10
to Joash. "He * die for insulting Ju 6:30
"They * have been my brothers!" Ju 8:19
And she said, "Father, you * do Ju 11:36
Your son's hair * never be cut, Ju 13:5
me and I think he * be the Angel of Ju 13:6
I gave her. She * not eat grapes or Ju 13:13,14
"Why * you go and get a wife Ju 14:3
then you * give the robes to me!" Ju 14:13
through me today! * I now die of Ju 15:18
anyone who refused to come * die. Ju 21:5
"There * be some way to get Ju 21:17
"You * know I am only a Ru 2:10,11
"* you come here drunk?" 1Sa 1:14
want, but the fat * first be 1Sa 2:16
tribe! You * have the wrong man!" 1Sa 9:21
but now your dynasty * end; 1Sa 13:14
We * find out what sin was 1Sa 14:38
but now I * die." 1Sa 14:43
Saul said, "you * die; 1Sa 14:44
But if I kill him, then you * be 1Sa 17:9
But first you * prove yourself to 1Sa 18:17
warned him, "you * find a hiding 1Sa 19:2
And remember, you * demonstrate 1Sa 20:14
mean that you * leave immediately. 1Sa 20:22
Yes, surely that * be it! 1Sa 20:26

it when he said that David * die. 1Sa 20:
"* you bring me a madman? 1Sa 21:14,
heathen gods. * I die on foreign 1Sa 26:
Israel * hate him bitterly by now. 1Sa 27:
down to Joab, "* our swords 2Sa 2:
Courage! We * really act like 2Sa 10:
All of us * die eventually; 2Sa 14:
"but he * never come here. 2Sa 14:
"Then we * flee at once or it 2Sa 15:
River tonight. He * go across at 2Sa 17:
For they said, "You * be very 2Sa 17:28,
One * be armed to chop them down; 2Sa 23
good man; you * have good news." 1Ki 1:
every man on earth * some day go. 1Ki 2
How the Lord * love Israel—for he 1Ki 10
Benjamin that they * not fight 1Ki 12:23,
son and I * die of starvation." 1Ki 17:
the king said to Obadiah, "We * 1Ki 18
message: "You * not only give me 1Ki 20:5
if he gets away, you * die, or 1Ki 20:
the man I said * die, now you must 1Ki 20:4
must die, now you * die in his 1Ki 20:4
bad enough? * you rob him, too? 1Ki 21:1
"How many times * I tell you to 1Ki 22:1
that you * come down right away." 2Ki 1:1
said, "It's important. I * go." 2Ki 4:2
The entire family of Ahab * be 2Ki 9
the watchman exclaimed. "It * 2Ki 9:2
from now on it * all be spent on 2Ki 12
fathers: everyone * pay the penalty 2Ki 14
For God had said, "You * never 2Ki 17:3
never worship other gods. You * 2Ki 17:3
of this book: you * be very angry 2Ki 22:12,1
Why * you cause Israel to sin?" 1Ch 21
Temple of the Lord * be a marvelous 1Ch 22
of the Presence * be made of gold; 2Ch 4:1
For he said, "She * not live in 2Ch 8:1
How he * love Israel to give them 2Ch 9
But you * pay annual tribute to 2Ch 12
refused to do this * die—whether 2Ch 15:1
"how many times * I tell you to 2Ch 18:1
For there * be no injustice among 2Ch 19
Everyone else * stay in the outer 2Ch 23:5,
of the Lord * be enforced so that 2Ch 24
No, everyone * pay for his own 2Ch 25:
"You * not bring the captives 2Ch 28:1
and sin offering * be sacrificed 2Ch 29:2
that the land * rest for seventy 2Ch 36:2
The Temple of the God of Israel * Ez 4:
that these men * stop building the Ez 4:2
Do not delay, for we * not Ez 4:2
blow you * rush to where I am; Neh 4:1
"Yet we * sell our children into Neh 5:
How often * we redeem them?" Neh 5:
and that they * be on duty at Neh 7:
near the wall * guard the section Neh 7:
You * not be dejected and sad!" Neh 8:1
women and children—* all be killed Est 3:1
letter stated, "* be proclaimed as Est 3:14
this decree, which * be recognized Est 8:1
everywhere as law, * be broadcast Est 8:1
"HOW MANKIND * struggle. Job 7:1
persecuting him? * you be his Job 7:18
Is your life so short that you * Job 10:4-7
"* you go on 'speaking for God' Job 13:7
disappears. * you be so harsh with Job 14:3
For all so soon I * go down that Job 16:22
* you persecute me as God does? Job 19:22
"For instance, you * have Job 22:6
* have stripped them to the bone. Job 22:6
to the bone. You * have refused Job 22:7
* the godly wait for him in vain? Job 24:1
Poor widows * surrender the Job 24:3
aside; they * get out of the way. Job 24:4
desert, the poor * spend all their Job 24:5
grows wild, and * even glean the Job 24:6
That is why they * go about Job 24:10
too, * be punished by the judges. Job 31:28
to burst out! I * speak to find Job 32:20
But first of all we * define Job 34:4
as Job? He * have spent much time Job 34:7,8
"* God tailor his justice to Job 34:33
to your demands? * he change the Job 34:33
The answer * be obvious even to Job 34:33
answers from you, and you * reply. Job 38:3
How long * I be hiding daily Ps 13:2
you * listen to my earnest cry! Ps 17:1
* fear and reverence his name. Ps 22:23
forsaken me? Why * I suffer these Ps 42:9
me aside? Why * I mourn at the Ps 43:2
Wise man! You * die like all the Ps 49:10
You * leave your wealth to others. Ps 49:10
But man with all his pomp * die Ps 49:12
* die like any animal. Ps 49:20
His people * destroy them. Ps 68:23
and so ignorant; I * seem like an Ps 73:22
* drain that cup to the dregs. Ps 75:8
only listen! You * never worship Ps 81:9
fall as any prince—for all * die. Ps 82:7
gods—for every god * bow to him! Ps 97:7
How he * rejoice in all his work! Ps 104:31

MUST Con't)

How long * I wait before you Ps 119:84
proud men * keep their distance. Ps 138:6
for every man * die. Ps 146:4
That is why you * eat the bitter Pro 1:31
For now I * face public Pro 5:14
TO LEARN, YOU * want to be taught. Pro 12:1
A treacherous man * walk a rocky Pro 13:15
sense, but it * shout loudly before Pro 14:33
A short-tempered man * bear his Pro 19:19
If you try once you * try a dozen Pro 19:19
A false witness * be punished; Pro 21:28
IF YOU * choose, take a good name Pro 22:1
A man who assists a thief * Pro 29:24
about this, that I * leave the Ecc 2:18
and skill, I * leave all of it to Ecc 2:20-23
came and to which they * return. Ecc 3:20
rich * worry and suffer insomnia. Ecc 5:12
realize that you * account to God Ecc 11:9
and again? * you forever rebel? Is 1:5,6
* learn to believe what I say." Is 7:9
go ahead and be blind if you *! Is 29:9
half done and I * leave it all. Is 38:10
now I * enter the gates of Sheol. Is 38:10
(The people below * seem to him Is 40:22
and said that you * serve but me Is 41:9
then they * confess that only God Is 43:9
for we * talk about your sins. Is 43:26
After all of this, * you still Is 64:12
How long * this go on? Jer 4:21
How long * I see war and death Jer 4:21
now you * be slaves to foreigners Jer 5:19
wicked ways. I * label them Jer 6:30
Disaster has befallen us! We * Jer 9:19
It cannot speak, and it * be Jer 10:5
My sickness is incurable, but I * Jer 10:19
How long * this land of yours put Jer 12:4
the enemy. They * defend Jer 13:19
those who * die by the sword, to Jer 15:2
You * not marry and have children Jer 16:2
that you * pay for all your sins. Jer 17:2,3
Lord of Hosts says you * drink it! Jer 25:28
on heeding them, I * drive you from Jer 27:15
Therefore the Lord says you * Jer 28:16
but I needed it all, as a calf * Jer 31:18
every Hebrew slave * be freed after Jer 34:14
"We * tell the king," they said. Jer 36:16
said: "Sir, this fellow * die. Jer 38:4
along the sea * be destroyed. Jer 47:7
* suffer, how much more must you! Jer 49:12
must suffer, how much more * you! Jer 49:12
You * drink this cup of judgment! Jer 49:12
of Israel, so * she be killed. Jer 51:49
see what sorrows we * bear! Lam 5:1
We * even pay for water to drink; Lam 5:4
are rebels! You * give them my Eze 2:7
Then I said, "O Lord God, * I be Eze 4:14
Canaan—your father * have been an Eze 16:3
be a prostitute? * you also slay Eze 16:21
Truly, your mother * have been a Eze 16:45
of my holy name * stop! Eze 20:39
me, therefore you * bear the Eze 23:35
"Son of dust, you * accuse Eze 23:36
Yet you * show no sorrow. Eze 24:16
Great care * therefore be taken Eze 28:12f
of the Temple—they * change their Eze 42:14
been ministering * first be Eze 42:14
are holy. They * put on other Eze 42:14
from God to idols * be punished for Eze 44:10
Lord God, that they * be punished. Eze 44:12
things, for they * bear their shame Eze 44:13
"They * wear only linen clothing Eze 44:17
court, for they * wear no wool Eze 44:17
They * wear linen turbans and Eze 44:18
trousers; they * not wear anything Eze 44:18
outer court, they * take off the Eze 44:19
"They * not let their hair grow Eze 44:20
Their decisions * be based upon Eze 44:24
"A priest * not defile himself Eze 44:25
But afterward he * wait seven Eze 44:26
the sanctuary, he * offer a sin Eze 44:27
"You * use honest scales, honest Eze 45:10
half an ounce); it * always be Eze 45:12
"This is the tax you * give to Eze 45:13
With the young bull, he * bring Eze 46:7
feasts, they * go out through the Eze 46:9
Those coming in from the south * Eze 46:9
by the north. They * never go out Eze 46:9
they come in, but * always use the Eze 46:9
"Each morning a yearling lamb * Eze 46:13
And there * be a meal offering Eze 46:14,15
to his sons, it * be from his own Eze 46:18
law that everyone * fall down and Dan 3:10
of every language * obey him. Dan 7:14
* first go by." Dan 8:14
"Son of man," he said, "you * Dan 8:17
* lie desolate for seventy years. Dan 9:2
"You * live alone for many days; Hos 3:3
Therefore, it * be smashed to Hos 8:6
They are guilty and * be Hos 10:2
Samaria * bear her guilt, for Hos 13:16

How weak and helpless he * be!' Joe 2:17
that they * go back to Egypt as Amo 1:5f
That is why I * punish you the Amo 3:2
Everyone * wear sackcloth and Jon 3:8
of Zion, for you * leave this city Mic 4:10
O Lord, how long * I call for Hab 1:2
comes to save. * I forever see Hab 1:3
from their foes? * we be strung up Hab 1:15
about whether they * continue their Zec 7:3
slay him! 'You * die,' they will Zec 13:3
for I * do all that is right." Mt 3:15
was, 'If you kill, you * die.' Mt 5:21
to God, but * fulfill them all.' Mt 5:33
eye, he * pay with his own eye. Mt 5:38
Yes, and you * stand trial Mt 10:18
And I tell you this, that you * Mt 12:36
to his men, "This * be John the Mt 14:2
anyone who reviles his parents * Mt 15:4
insist Elijah * return before the Mt 17:10
Literally, "that Elijah * come Mt 17:10f
Elijah * come and set everything Mt 17:11
* I do to have eternal life?" Mt 19:16
"What else * I do?" Mt 19:20
among you * be your servant. Mt 20:26
the top, you * serve like a slave. Mt 20:27
* be like my own, for I, the Mt 20:28
these * come, but the end is not Mt 24:6
then those in Judea * flee into Mt 24:16
* not even go inside to pack Mt 24:17
For I * die Mt 26:24
that everyone * straighten out his Mk 1:3
But he replied, "We * go on to Mk 1:38
[Satan * be bound before his Mk 3:27
just as a strong man * be tied Mk 3:27
the market they * always sprinkle Mk 7:4
his father or mother * die. Mk 7:10
They finally decided that he * be Mk 8:16
told them, "you * put aside your Mk 8:34
of, that Elijah * return [before Mk 9:11
Jesus agreed that Elijah * come Mk 9:12,13
how much longer * I be with you Mk 9:19
How much longer * I be patient Mk 9:19
to be the greatest * be the Mk 9:35
what * I do to get to heaven?" Mk 10:17
cup of sorrow I * drink from? Mk 10:38
suffering I * be baptized with?" Mk 10:38
great among you * be your servant. Mk 10:43
of all * be the slave of all. Mk 10:44
to God * be given to God!" Mk 12:17
And you * love him with all your Mk 12:30
"The second is: 'You * love Mk 12:31
* be a descendant of King David? Mk 12:35
And the Good News * first be Mk 13:10
* die, as the prophets declared Mk 14:21
Get up! We * go! Mk 14:42
great men. He * never touch wine or Lk 1:15
gestures that he * have seen a Lk 1:22
But Elizabeth said, "No! He * be Lk 1:60
Jesus replied, "We * worship Lk 4:8
But he replied, "I * preach the Lk 4:43
New wine * be put into new Lk 5:38
and you said, 'He * be crazy!' Lk 7:33
* suffer much," he said, "and Lk 9:22
wants to follow me * put aside his Lk 9:23
"that you * love the Lord your God Lk 10:27
And you * love your neighbor just Lk 10:27
follower * love me far more than Lk 14:26
It is worthless and * be thrown Lk 14:35
fattening pen. We * celebrate with Lk 15:23
But first I * suffer terribly Lk 17:25
"Those away from home that day * Lk 17:31
those in the fields * not return Lk 17:31
them that they * keep praying until Lk 18:1
True, wars * come, but the end Lk 21:9
the city * not attempt to return. Lk 21:21
* die. It is part of God's plan. Lk 22:22
said, "You * be one of them!" Lk 22:58
* be betrayed into the power of Lk 24:6,7
replied, "You * be the only person Lk 24:18
in the Psalms * all come true?" Lk 24:44
that the Messiah * suffer and die Lk 24:46
is not enough. You * also be born Jn 3:5f
that you * be born again! Jn 3:7
a pole, even so I * be lifted up Jn 3:14
his success. He * become greater Jn 3:30
and I * become less and less. Jn 3:30
"Sir," the woman said, "you * Jn 4:19
For God is Spirit, and we * have Jn 4:21-24
They replied, "You * show us Jn 6:30,31
All of us * quickly carry out Jn 9:4
"I think he * be a prophet sent Jn 9:17
the wall, * surely be a thief! Jn 10:1
in another fold. I * bring them Jn 10:16
seeing Jesus * report him Jn 11:57
and that "I * fall and die like a Jn 12:23,24
for my servants * be where I am. Jn 12:26
before I * go away and leave you! Jn 13:33
And you also * tell everyone Jn 15:27
"So now we * choose someone else Act 1:21,22
"Each one of you * turn from sin, Act 2:38
Messiah * suffer all these things. Act 3:18

For he * remain in heaven until Act 3:21,22
"We * obey God rather than men. Act 5:29
"You stiff-necked heathen! * you Act 7:51
him how much he * suffer for me." Act 9:16
they decided, "It * be his angel. Act 12:15
[They * have killed him. Act 12:15
them that they * enter into the Act 14:22
Gentile converts * be circumcised Act 15:5
who turn to God * obey our Jewish Act 15:19
"Sirs, what * I do to be saved?" Act 16:30
"I * by all means be at Act 18:21
his baptism * then go on to believe Act 19:4
he said, "I * go on to Rome!" Act 19:21
Jewish believers * continue to Act 21:20
so you * also in Rome." Act 23:11
Gentiles that all * forsake their Act 26:20
what blessings he * have for us now Rom 5:10
of sin, so now you * let yourselves Rom 6:19
not said, "You * not have evil Rom 7:7
we * also share his suffering. Rom 8:17
But if we * keep trusting God Rom 8:25
for his sake we * be ready to face Rom 8:36
But you * be careful not to brag Rom 11:18
for me so I * be pretty good." Rom 11:19
to eat such meat * not look down on Rom 14:3
everyone * decide for himself. Rom 14:5
for we * bear the "burden" of Rom 15:1
But before I come, I * go down to Rom 15:25
the foundation * be very careful. 1Co 3:10
It is the Lord himself who * 1Co 4:4
that you * not have favorites. 1Co 4:6
favorites. You * not be proud of 1Co 4:6
But you yourselves * deal with 1Co 5:13
I'm not saying you * marry; 1Co 7:6
A wife * not leave her husband. 1Co 7:10
And the husband * not divorce his 1Co 7:11
he * not leave her or divorce her. 1Co 7:12
with him, she * not leave him. 1Co 7:13
But a married woman * consider 1Co 7:34
Peter does? And * Barnabas and I 1Co 9:6
he said that you * not put a muzzle 1Co 9:9
of course that I * always do what 1Co 9:21
To win the contest you * deny 1Co 9:25
FOR WE * never forget, dear 1Co 10:1
are warned that we * not desire 1Co 10:6
But why, you may ask, * I be 1Co 10:29
It is because you * do everything 1Co 10:31
that is done * be useful to all, 1Co 14:26
language, and they * speak one at a 1Co 14:27
time, and someone * be ready to 1Co 14:27
they * not speak out loud. 1Co 14:28
out loud. They * talk silently to 1Co 14:28
dead, then Christ * still be dead. 1Co 15:13
This too * be defeated and ended. 1Co 15:26
now that can die, * be transformed 1Co 15:53
But you * help us too, by 2Co 1:11
of yours who * tell you all about 2Co 3:1
We do not tell them that they * 2Co 3:6
* be from God and is not our own. 2Co 4:7
For we * all stand before Christ 2Co 5:10
I am not saying you * do it, but 2Co 8:8
Every one * make up his own mind 2Co 9:7
But if I * brag, I would rather 2Co 11:30
As sure as anything he * have 2Co 12:16
seen a wrong, it * be punished. 2Co 13:1
was that we * always remember to Gal 2:10
being circumcised * always obey Gal 5:3
Each of us * bear some faults Gal 6:5
Now your attitudes and thoughts * Eph 4:23
Yes, you * be a new and Eph 4:24
If anyone is stealing he * stop Eph 4:28
You wives * submit to your Eph 5:22
So you wives * willingly obey Eph 5:24
says, "A man * leave his father Eph 5:31
So again I say, a man * love his Eph 5:33
and the wife * see to it that she Eph 5:33
And you slave owners * treat your Eph 6:9
that your strength * come from the Eph 6:10
whether I live or whether I * die. Php 1:20
And now that I am away you * be Php 2:12
you * be circumcised to be saved. Php 3:2
worship angels, as they say you *. Col 2:18
you, so you * forgive others. Col 3:13
And you husbands * be loving and Col 3:19
You children * always obey your Col 3:20
You slaves * always obey your Col 3:22
YOU SLAVE OWNERS * be just and Col 4:1
But we * forever give thanks to 2Th 2:13
For a pastor * be a good man 1Ti 3:2
spoken against. He * have only one 1Ti 3:2
one wife, and he * be hard working 1Ti 3:2
of good deeds. He * enjoy having 1Ti 3:2
and * be a good Bible teacher. 1Ti 3:2
Bible teacher. He * not be a 1Ti 3:3
but he * be gentle and kind, and 1Ti 3:3
loves money. He * have a 1Ti 3:4
The pastor * not be a new 1Ti 3:6
Also, he * be well spoken of by 1Ti 3:7
The deacons * be the same sort of 1Ti 3:8
the pastors. They * not be heavy 1Ti 3:8
and * not be greedy for money. 1Ti 3:8

(MUST Con't)
They * be earnest, wholehearted 1Ti 3:9
Their wives * be thoughtful, not 1Ti 3:11
only once. She * be well thought 1Ti 5:10
widow's relatives * take care of 1Ti 5:16
All * be treated exactly the same. 1Ti 5:21
For you * teach others those 2Ti 2:2
Christ, then he * turn against us. 2Ti 2:12
God's people * not be 2Ti 2:24
quarrelsome; they * be gentle, 2Ti 2:24
But you * keep on believing the 2Ti 3:14
The men you choose * be well Tit 1:6
good lives; they * have only one Tit 1:6
and their children * love the Lord Tit 1:6
* be men of blameless lives Tit 1:7
They * not be proud or impatient; Tit 1:7
or impatient; they * not be Tit 1:7
They * enjoy having guests in Tit 1:8
homes and * love all that is good. Tit 1:8
They * be sensible men, and fair. Tit 1:8
and fair. They * be clean minded Tit 1:8
have been taught * be strong and Tit 1:9
Christians * obey the Jewish laws. Tit 1:10
the truth, and it * be stopped. Tit 1:11
unruffled; they * be sensible, Tit 2:2
they do. They * not go around Tit 2:3
evil of others and * not be heavy Tit 2:3
These older women * train the Tit 2:4
And here you yourself * be an Tit 2:7
satisfy them. They * not talk back, Tit 2:9
nor steal, but * show themselves Tit 2:10
for others. You * teach these Tit 2:15
They * not speak evil of anyone, Tit 3:2
For our people * learn to help Tit 3:14
SO WE * listen very carefully to Heb 2:1
* explain all that we have done. Heb 4:13
his law * be changed to permit it. Heb 7:12,13,14
Christ * make an offering too. Heb 8:3
in God's sight * live by faith, Heb 10:38
Anyone who wants to come to God * Heb 11:6
touched the mountain it * die. Heb 12:20
good, as God demands that we * be. Jas 1:20
command, "You * love and help your Jas 2:8
For the God who said you * not Jas 2:11
also said you * not murder, so even Jas 2:11
to have faith. You * also do good Jas 2:17
do whatever criticizing * be done Jas 5:9
He himself has said, "You * be 1Pe 1:16
* follow—that they will fall. 1Pe 2:8
Servants, you * respect your 1Pe 2:18
You husbands * be careful of your 1Pe 3:7
peace even if you * run after it to 1Pe 3:11
* have the same attitude he did; 1Pe 4:1
you * be ready to suffer, too. 1Pe 4:1
But just remember that they * 1Pe 4:5
judgment, and it * begin first 1Pe 4:17
who are Christians * be judged, 1Pe 4:17
than faith; you * also work hard to 2Pe 1:5
For then you * learn to know God 2Pe 1:5
he has said, you * live in Christ, 1Jn 2:27
And this is what God says we * 1Jn 3:23
has said that one * love not only 1Jn 4:21
but now I find I * write of Jud 1:3
But you, dear friends, * build up Jud 1:20
I love; so I * punish you, unless Rev 3:19
you what * happen in the future!" Rev 4:1
Then he told me, "You * prophesy Rev 10:11
refusing to worship it * die! Rev 13:15
or the hand, * drink the wine of Rev 14:10

MUSTARD
a tiny * seed planted in a field. Mt 13:31,32
as small as a tiny * seed you could Mt 17:20
It is like a tiny * seed! Mk 4:31,32
It is like a tiny * seed planted Lk 13:19
only the size of a * seed," Jesus Lk 17:6

MUSTER
Guild Hall, opposite the * Gate; Neh 3:31
Man the ramparts! * your Nah 2:1

MUSTERED
had done, they * an army at Shiloh Jos 22:12
* an army under his own command. Ju 3:27
THE PHILISTINES NOW * their army 1Sa 17:1
ABOUT THAT TIME the Philistines * 1Sa 28:1
So he * the troops from the 1Ki 20:15
Israel then * its army, set up 1Ki 20:27
So King Jehoram * the Israeli 2Ki 3:6,7,8
Ben-hadad of Syria * his entire 2Ki 6:24
King Joash of Israel * his army. 2Ki 14:11

MUSTN'T
God says you * eat any of it?" Gen 3:1
God says we * eat it or even Gen 3:2,3
"No, you * ask," the Man told Gen 32:29
to you. You * eat their meat or Lev 11:11
for you * stay here in the Ju 19:20
she * go home without a present. Ru 3:15-18
"You * do it," they said, "for 2Sa 18:3

MUTILATED
or disabled or *, or which has Lev 22:22

MUTTERED
"I am too," the commander *, Act 22:28

MUTTERING
the people began * again against Num 16:41

MUTTERINGS
listen to their whisperings and *. Is 8:19

MUTTON
Fill it with choicest *, the Eze 24:4

MUTUAL
"Let us renew the * security 2Ch 16:3
was *, due to historic reasons. Lk 10:33f

MUTUAL-ASSISTANCE
for there was a * agreement between Ju 4:17

MUTUALLY
They will * agree to give their Rev 17:17

MUZZLE
"Don't * an ox as it treads out Deu 25:4
I loosened his * so he could eat. Hos 11:4
you must not put a * on an ox to 1Co 9:9

MYRA
at *, in the province of Lycia. Act 27:5

MYRIADS
your miracles, O Lord; * of angels Ps 89:5
commanded all the vast * of stars. Is 45:12

MYRRH
*, pistachio nuts, and almonds. Gen 43:11
of pure *; Ex 30:22,23
the same amount of cassia as of *; Ex 30:24
*, spices, horses, and mules. 1Ki 10:25
with oil of *, followed by six Est 2:12,13,14
Your robes are perfumed with *, Ps 45:8
with *, aloes and cinnamon. Pro 7:16,17
My beloved one is a sachet of * Sol 1:13
smelling of * and frankincense and Sol 3:6
* and to the hill of frankincense. Sol 4:6
tree, as well as * and aloes, and Sol 4:13,14
I gather my * with my spices and Sol 5:1
* as I pulled back the bolt. Sol 5:5
lilies, his breath like *. Sol 5:13
gave him gold, frankincense and *. Mt 2:11
ointment made from * and aloes. Jn 19:39

MYRTLE
from olive, *, palm, and fig trees Neh 8:15
I will plant trees—cedars, *, Is 41:19
where briars grew, the * trees Is 55:13
among the * trees beside a river. Zec 1:8

MYSELF
me, though I * gave her the Gen 16:5
"I, the Lord, have sworn by * Gen 22:16
"I said to *, 'He'll take his Gen 31:31
"I can't do it by *," Joseph Gen 41:16
Indeed, I * will take care of you Gen 50:21
to * as though on eagle's wings. Ex 19:4
And the Lord replied, "I * will Ex 33:14
said, 'I will show * holy among Lev 10:3
For I * am present in the cloud Lev 16:1
And I * will turn against that Lev 20:3
to death, then I * will set my Lev 20:5
made you holy to * and rescued you Lev 22:32,33
I took for * all the firstborn in Num 3:13
and I * will personally bless Num 6:27
I claimed them for * the night I Num 8:17
I can't carry this nation by *! Num 11:14
me to carry all by *, for the Lord Deu 1:9
I'll just shake * free." Ju 16:20
kill him rather than doing it *." 1Sa 18:17
Nabal and kept me from doing it *; 1Sa 25:39
and I said to *, 'Perhaps the king 2Sa 14:15,16
And kept * from sin. 2Sa 22:24
but now I have seen it for *! 1Ki 10:7
I will present * to Ahab today." 1Ki 18:15
"I wanted to build it *," David 1Ch 22:7
though I have sanctified it for *. 2Ch 7:20
"I'll disguise * so that no one 2Ch 18:29
walls, and for a house for *." Neh 2:8
Even if I were to wash * with Job 9:30
"And I cannot defend *, for you Job 9:32,33
Well, I know a few things *—you Job 12:3
I would stop defending * and die. Job 13:19
remains no matter how I defend *; Job 16:6
me feel ashamed of * for calling Job 20:3
Even I am frightened when I see *. Job 21:6
get their land for *, then let Job 31:38,39
* and repent in dust and ashes.' Job 42:6
holding * back from doing wrong. Ps 18:23
I said to *, "I will confess Ps 32:5
destroyed. I * have seen it Ps 37:35,36
How constantly I find * upon the Ps 38:17
I SAID TO *, I'm going to quit Ps 39:1
But it was you, a man like *, my Ps 55:13
I saw * so stupid and so Ps 73:22
never have to be ashamed of *. Ps 119:80
I don't think * better than Ps 131:1
I am too stupid even to call * a Pro 30:2
And I applied * to search for Ecc 1:12-15
I said to *, "Look, I am better Ecc 1:16-18
I SAID TO *, "Come now, be merry; Ecc 2:1
and orchards for *, and reservoirs Ecc 2:4,5,6
did not restrain * from any joy. Ecc 2:10
I said to *, "In due season God Ecc 3:17
and to prove to * the wickedness of Ecc 7:25
my enemies! I * will melt you in a Is 1:25
I, *, have risen against him, Is 14:22
I have made Israel for *, and Is 43:21
the heavens. By * I made the earth Is 44:24
I have sworn by * and I will Is 45:2
* will expose you to utter shame. Jer 13:2
this city, and I * will fight Jer 21:
And I * will destroy you for Jer 21:14
God, will unburden * of the burden Jer 23:38,39
I kicked * for my stupidity. Jer 31:19
And I will set * against them to Eze 15:7
"The Lord God says: I, *, will Eze 17:22,23
cedar, and I, *, will plant it on Eze 17:22,23
and revealed * to her in Egypt, I Eze 20:5,6
I have made it for *0,6▮!' Eze 29:3
deserves. I, *, will cut her down. Eze 31:11
pastures. I * will be the Shepherd Eze 34:15,16
So I * will save my flock; Eze 34:22
and sprinkled * with ashes, and Dan 9:3
other men and sell * to them for Hos 1:5
and raise them for *0,6▮! Hos 1:23
eat. I * have stooped and fed him. Hos 11:4
I have gotten it all by *0,6▮!" Hos 12:8
to my land and I, *, will live Zec 8:3
to love others as *, than to offer Mk 12:33
the angels in heaven, nor I *, Mk 13:32
And I'll sit back and say to *, Lk 12:19
I will penalize * by giving him Lk 19:8
You can see that it is I, *0,6▮! Lk 24:39
"When I make claims about * they Jn 5:31
though I make them concerning *. Jn 8:14
no wish to make * great, God wants Jn 8:50
about *, it doesn't count. Jn 8:54
too, and I will reveal * to him." Jn 14:21
I will only reveal * to those who Jn 14:23
of everything I * have told you. Jn 14:26
and I consecrate * to meet their Jn 17:19
I saw all this * and have given Jn 19:35
Council to defend * for believing Act 24:21
"I'd like to hear the man *," Act 25:22
I don't understand * at all, for Rom 7:15
But I can't help *, because I'm Rom 7:17
I turn I can't make * do right. Rom 7:18
I find * still enslaved to sin. Rom 7:23,24,25
Remember that I * am a Jew, a Rom 11:1
As for *, I am perfectly sure on Rom 14:14
I have used Apollos and * as 1Co 4:6
for the blessing I * receive when I 1Co 9:23
for the race, I * might be declared 1Co 9:27
Dear friends, even if I * should 1Co 14:6
"NO," I SAID to *, "I won't do 2Co 2:1
merely as a human being like *. 2Co 5:16
Did I do wrong and cheapen * and 2Co 11:7
and not making me write about *. 2Co 12:11
I am glad to give you * and all 2Co 12:15
up spiritually and not to help *. 2Co 12:19
anyone, including *, who preaches Gal 1:8
with Christ: and I * no longer Gal 2:20
Some people even say that I * am Gal 5:11
to be ashamed of * but that I will Php 1:20
that soon I * may come to see you. Php 2:24
like * is a soldier of the cross. Phm 1:1
Christ Jesus. I * have gained much Phm 1:7
world began, yet I * have seen him 1Jn 1:1
of Demetrius. I * can say the same 3Jn 1:12

MYSIA
the borders of * they headed north Act 16:7
* province to the city of Troas. Act 16:8

MYSTERIES
He reveals profound * beyond Dan 2:22
the Revealer of *, because he has Dan 2:47
that you can solve all kinds of *. Dan 5:16
I will explain * hidden since the Mt 13:34,35

MYSTERIOUS
God's ways are as * as the Ecc 11:5
you work in strange, * ways. Is 45:15
God's veiled plan—* through the Rev 10:7
A * caption was written on her Rev 17:5

MYSTERIOUSLY
*, neither in battle nor in riot. Dan 11:20

MYSTERY
* is too great for you to solve. Dan 4:9
Literally, "the * of lawlessness 2Th 2:7f

MYTHS
to Mesopotamian *, he had been Eze 8:14f
Put an end to their * and fables, 1Ti 1:3,4
ideas and silly * and legends. 1Ti 4:7

NAAM
Elah, *. 1Ch 4:15

NAAMAH
Beth-dagon, *, Makkedah, Libnah, Jos 15:37-44
(Rehoboam's mother was *, an 1Ki 14:21
mother was * the Ammonitess—he was 1Ki 14:31
name was * the Ammonitess. 2Ch 12:13

NAAMAN
Ashbel, Gera, *, Gen 46:19-22
named after their ancestor *. Num 26:38-41
admiration for *, the 2Ki 5:1
* told the king what the little 2Ki 5:4
So * started out, taking gifts of 2Ki 5:5
this letter is my servant *; 2Ki 5:6
you so upset? Send * to me, and he 2Ki 5:8
So * arrived with his horses and 2Ki 5:9
But * was angry and stalked away. 2Ki 5:11
So * went down to the Jordan 2Ki 5:14

NAAMAN Con't)
before him and * said, "I know at 2Ki 5:15
* urged him to take them, but he 2Ki 5:16
"Well," * said, "all right. 2Ki 5:17
"All right," Elisha said. So * 2Ki 5:19
up with him. When * saw him coming, 2Ki 5:21
"Take $4,000," * insisted. 2Ki 5:23
in thought when * stepped down from 2Ki 5:26
Addar, Gera, Abihud, Abishua, *, 1Ch 8:3,4,5
*, Ahijah, 1Ch 8:6,7
Elisha, who healed *, a Syrian, Lk 4:27

NAAMAN'S
been given to * wife as a maid. 2Ki 5:2
Because you have done this, * 2Ki 5:27

NAAMATHITE
the Shuhite, and Zophar the *. Job 2:11
ZOPHAR THE * replies to Job: Job 11:1
THE SPEECH OF Zophar the *: Job 20:1
and Zophar the * did as the Lord Job 42:9

NAAMITES
The *, named after their ancestor Num 26:38-41

NAARAH
to Ataroth and *, and touched Jos 16:7
Helah, and * 1Ch 4:5
* bore him Ahuzzam, Hepher, 1Ch 4:6

NAARAI
* (son of Ezbai); 1Ch 11:26-47

NAARAN
on the east by *, on the west by 1Ch 7:28

NABAIOTH
* (the oldest), Kedar, Adbeel, 1Ch 1:28-31
and the rams of * for my altars, Is 60:7

NABAL
His name was * and his wife, a 1Sa 25:3
When David heard that * was 1Sa 25:4
to * and waited for his reply. 1Sa 25:9
and told him what * had said. 1Sa 25:12
I want to say. * is a bad-tempered 1Sa 25:25
shall be as cursed as * is. 1Sa 25:26
that * had thrown a big party. 1Sa 25:36
When David heard that * was dead, 1Sa 25:39
God has paid back * and kept me 1Sa 25:39
the widow of * from Carmel— and 2Sa 2:2
Abigail, the widow of * of Carmel. 2Sa 3:3

NABAL'S
Meanwhile, one of * men went and 1Sa 25:14
me, not one of * men would be alive 1Sa 25:34
and Abigail of Carmel, * widow. 1Sa 27:2,3

NABONIDUS
Belshazzar was the second under * Dan 5:7f

NABOPOLASSER
from Babylon. * and Jer 4:6f

NABOTH
*, A MAN from Jezreel, had a 1Ki 21:1
He offered cash or, if * 1Ki 21:2
But * replied, "Not on your 1Ki 21:3
"I asked * to sell me his 1Ki 21:6
leaders of Jezreel, where * lived. 1Ki 21:8
Then summon *, and find two 1Ki 21:9
the meeting and put * on trial. 1Ki 21:12
word to Jezebel that * was dead. 1Ki 21:14
the vineyard * wouldn't sell you? 1Ki 21:15
me: 'Isn't killing * bad enough? 1Ki 21:19
as they licked the blood of *!' 1Ki 21:19
They met him at the field of *, 2Ki 9:21
into the field of *, for once when 2Ki 9:25
for the murder of * and his sons.' 2Ki 9:26

NABOTH'S
I'll get you * vineyard!" 1Ki 21:7
He will be at * vineyard, taking 1Ki 21:18
repay him here on * property for 2Ki 9:26
So throw him out on * field, 2Ki 9:26

NABU
Names of Marduk and *, the two Is 46:1f

NACON
threshing floor of *, the oxen 2Sa 6:6

NADAB
Their children were:*, Ex 6:23
here with Aaron, *, Abihu, and Ex 24:1
Then Moses, Aaron, *, Abihu, and Ex 24:9
and his sons *, Abihu, Eleazer, and Ex 28:1
BUT * AND Abihu, the sons of Lev 10:1
the death of * and Abihu, and mourn Lev 10:6
* (his oldest), Abihu, Eleazar, Num 3:2
Tabernacle. But * and Abihu died Num 3:4
To Aaron were born *, Abihu, Num 26:60
and Ithamar. But * and Abihu died Num 26:61
died, his son * took the throne. 1Ki 14:20
Meanwhile, over in Israel, * the 1Ki 15:25
So Baasha replaced * as the king 1Ki 15:28
* and 1Ch 2:28
*, Abihu, Eleazar, Ithamar. 1Ch 6:3
Zur, Kish, Baal, *, Gedor, Ahio, 1Ch 8:30,31,32
Ner, *, Gedor, Ahio, Zechariah, 1Ch 9:35,36,37
* and Abihu were also sons of 1Ch 24:1

NADAB'S
* sons were 1Ch 2:30

NAGGAI
Esli's father was *; Lk 3:23-38

NAGGAI'S
Esli's father was Naggai;* father Lk 3:23-38

NAGGED
She * at him every day until he Ju 16:16,17

NAGGING
Love forgets mistakes; * about Pro 17:9
his father, and a * wife annoys Pro 19:13
and not because of * on my part. 2Co 8:3
Don't keep on scolding and * your Eph 6:4

NAHALAL
included Kattath, *, Shimron, Jos 19:15,16
Jokne-am, Kartah, Dimnah, and *. Jos 21:34,35

NAHALIEL
through Mattanah, *, and Bamoth; Num 21:19

NAHALOL
or *, but made them their slaves; Ju 1:30

NAHAM
Hodiah's wife was the sister of * 1Ch 4:19

NAHAMANI
Azariah, Ra-amiah, *; Neh 7:7

NAHARAI
* from Be-eroth, the armor bearer 2Sa 23:24-39
* from Be-eroth—he was General 1Ch 11:26-47

NAHASH
AT THIS TIME * led the army of the 1Sa 11:1
"All right," * said, "but only 1Sa 11:2
"But when you were afraid of *, 1Sa 12:12
his father * was always so loyal 2Sa 10:2
the daughter of *, who was the 2Sa 17:25
by Shobi (son of * of Rabbah, an 2Sa 17:27
WHEN KING * of Ammon died, his son 1Ch 19:1

NAHATH
Born to her son Reuel were:*, Gen 36:13,14
Canaan:The clan of *,The clan of Gen 36:17
*, Zerah, Shammah, and Mizzah. 1Ch 1:37
Elkanah, Zophai, *, Eliab, 1Ch 6:25,26,27
Jehiel, Azaziah, *, Asahel, 2Ch 31:12,13

NAHBI
*, son of Vophsi, from the tribe Num 13:3-15

NAHOR
years old when his son * was born. Gen 11:22,23
* was twenty-nine years old at Gen 11:24,25
three sons, Abram, *, and Haran. Gen 11:26
Sarai, while his brother * Gen 11:29
*, had borne him eight sons. Gen 22:20-23
father was Bethuel the son of * Gen 24:15,16
the wife of *," she replied. Gen 24:24
the son of * and his wife Milcah.' Gen 24:47
there named Laban, the son of *?" Gen 29:5
God of Abraham and *, and of their Gen 31:53
of Abraham and *, lived east of the Jos 24:2
The son of Serug was *, 1Ch 1:24-27
The son of * was Terah, 1Ch 1:24-27
Terah's father was *; Lk 3:23-38

NAHOR'S
journeyed to Iraq, to * village. Gen 24:10
And she told me, '*. Gen 24:47
Terah's father was Nahor;* father Lk 3:23-38

NAHSHON
of Amminadab and sister of *. Ex 6:23
Judah -* (son of Num 1:2-15
Leader: * (son of Num 2:3-31
So *, the son of Amminadab of the Num 7:12
They were exactly the same as * Num 7:18-23
led by *, the son of Amminadab. Num 10:14
father of *, a leader of Israel. 1Ch 2:10
* was the father of Salma, and 1Ch 2:11
Amminadab was the father of *; Mt 1:4
* was the father of Salmon; Mt 1:4
Salmon's father was *; Lk 3:23-38

NAHSHON'S
Salmon's father was Nahshon;* Lk 3:23-38

NAHUM
THIS IS THE vision God gave to *, Nah 1:1
Amos' father was *; Lk 3:23-38

NAHUM'S
Amos' father was Nahum;* father Lk 3:23-38

NAIL
They * down important truths. Ecc 12:11
unless I see the * wounds in his Jn 20:25
government to * him to the cross Act 2:23

NAILED
of the Gods and * his head to the 1Ch 10:10
to pieces, and * the door of the 2Ch 28:24
A signboard was * to the cross Lk 23:38
Your old evil desires were * to Rom 6:6
Those who belong to Christ have * Gal 5:24
again if you have * the Son of God Heb 6:6

NAILING
it by * it to Christ's cross. Col 2:14

NAILS
All the * used in constructing Ex 38:20
and for all the * used in the Ex 38:29
The cords and *; Ex 39:33-40
head and pare her * and change her Deu 21:12
great quantity of * needed for the 1Ch 22:3
Twenty-six-ounce gold * were 2Ch 3:9
with hammer and *, so that it won't Jer 10:4
and his * were like birds' claws. Dan 4:33
them to see [the marks of the * Lk 24:40

NAIN
to the village of *, with the usual Lk 7:11

NAIOTH
took David with him to live at *. 1Sa 19:18
that David was at * in Ramah, he 1Sa 19:19
Someone told him they were at *. 1Sa 19:22
But on the way to * the Spirit 1Sa 19:23
DAVID NOW FLED from * in Ramah, 1Sa 20:1

NAIVE
"How foolish and * you are! Pro 8:4,5

NAKED
his wife were both *, neither of Gen 2:25
and didn't want you to see me *. Gen 3:10
"Who told you you were *?" Gen 3:11
One day as he was drunk and lay * Gen 9:20,21
*, and in want of everything. Deu 28:47,48
clothes and lay * all day and all 1Sa 19:24
and sent them home half *. 2Sa 10:4
"I came * from my mother's Job 1:21
All night they lie * in the Job 24:7
That is why they must go about * Job 24:10
"The dead stand *, trembling Job 26:5,6
and to walk around * and barefoot. Is 20:2
has been walking * and barefoot for Is 20:3
making them walk * and barefoot, Is 20:4
her stripped * and humiliated. Lam 1:8
yet you were *. Eze 16:6,7
you were * and covered with blood. Eze 16:22
I will make you * before them, that Eze 16:37
and leave you * and ashamed. Eze 16:39
you own, leaving you * and bare. Eze 23:29
will strip her as * as the day she Hos 1:3
I will walk * and barefoot in Mic 1:8
led away as slaves—stripped, * Mic 1:11
is brought out * to the streets, Nah 2:7
your homes; * and you clothed me; Mt 25:36
help you? Or *, and clothe you? Mt 25:38
*, and you wouldn't clothe me; Mt 25:43
or a stranger or * or sick or in Mt 25:44
so that he ran away completely *. Mk 14:51,52
Homeless and *, he lived in a Lk 8:27
of his house * and badly injured. Act 19:16
and poor and blind and *. Rev 3:17
so you won't be * and ashamed; Rev 3:18
not need to walk * and ashamed." Rev 16:15
leave her * and ravaged by fire. Rev 17:16

NAKEDNESS
of their *, and were embarrassed. Gen 3:7
saw his father's * and went outside Gen 9:22
* as they looked the other way. Gen 9:23
of your clothing and see your *. Ex 20:26
Literally, "uncover the * of," Lev 18:6f
"for theirs is your own *." Lev 18:10f
He will expose their * for all to Is 3:17
You shall be in * and shame. Is 47:3
her to cover her *—I will no longer Hos 1:9
Now I will expose her * in Hos 1:10
earth will see your * and shame. Nah 3:5
gloating over their * and shame. Hab 2:15

NAME
he called them, that was their *. Gen 2:19,20
and flesh! Her * is 'woman' because Gen 2:23
His brother's * was Jubal, the Gen 4:21
to invoke the * of Jehovah." Gen 4:26f
and his * became proverbial. Gen 10:9
I will bless you and make your * Gen 12:2
Or, "I will make your * so famous Gen 12:2f
and you are to * him Ishmael ('God Gen 16:9-12
told him, "I am changing your *. Gen 17:5
your wife—her * is no longer Gen 17:15
and you are to * him Isaac Gen 17:19
the Moabites. The * of the younger Gen 19:38
swear to me by God's * that you Gen 21:23
still goes by that * to this day. Gen 22:14
we bless you in the * of the Gen 26:29
previous * of the nearest village Gen 28:19
the actual Hebrew *, but of a Gen 30:6f
a Hebrew word sounding like the *. Gen 30:6f
name. The * given is a Hebrew pun. Gen 30:6f
slur against my *," she said. Gen 30:23,24
me off without a penny to my *. Gen 31:42
"What is your *?" Gen 32:27
"What is your *?" Gen 32:29
its * to the area it occupied. Gen 36:40-43
Pharaoh gave him a * meaning "He Gen 41:45
be an honor to my * and to the Gen 48:16
The * Moses sounds like another Ex 2:10f
Properly the * should be Ex 3:15f
(This is my eternal *, to be Ex 3:15
not reveal my *, Jehovah, to them. Ex 6:2,3
"In the * of God I will not let Ex 10:10
Yes, Jehovah is his *. Ex 15:3
"You shall not use the * of Ex 20:7
Or, "use the * of the Lord your Ex 20:7f
and remember—never mention the * Ex 23:13
Literally, "my * is in him. Ex 23:21f
—he bears my *. Ex 23:21
of Israel and the * of that tribe Ex 28:21
have said you know me by *." Ex 33:12f
Literally, "I know you by *." Ex 33:17f
to you the meaning of my * Ex 33:19
will proclaim before you my *." Ex 33:19f
His *, Jehovah, means "I will Ex 33:19f
announced the meaning of his *. Ex 34:5,6
Literally, "proclaimed the * of Ex 34:5,6f

(NAME Con't)

* and inheritance of the deceased.	Lev 18:16f
never profane the * of your God,	Lev 18:21
* of your God, for I am Jehovah.	Lev 19:12
live in, and insulting my holy *.	Lev 20:3
not dishonor and profane his *;	Lev 21:6
to defile my holy * by desecrating	Lev 22:1
Literally, "blasphemed the *."	Lev 24:11f
(His mother's * was Shelomith,	Lev 24:11
who blasphemes the * of Jehovah.	Lev 24:15,16
and older, and register each *.	Num 3:40
"Assign duties to each man by *.	Num 4:32
Literally, "shall put my * upon	Num 6:27f
So the * of that place was	Num 11:34
changed Hoshea's * to Joshua.	Num 13:16
Joshua is the same * in Hebrew	Num 13:16f
Hebrew as the Greek * "Jesus."	Num 13:16f
But I vow by my own * that just	Num 14:20,21
rod with his * inscribed upon it.	Num 17:1
Aaron's * is to be on the rod of	Num 17:1
* was later changed to Israel.	Num 20:14f
their cities. The * of the region	Num 21:3
you ask. * your own figure!	Num 22:16,17
The * of the man who was killed	Num 25:14
The girl's * was Cozbi, daughter	Num 25:15
Why should the * of our father	Num 27:3,4
* of their area to Havroth-jair.	Num 32:41
the area Nobah, after his own *.	Num 32:42
" 'You must never use my * to	Deu 5:11
must not utter the * of the Lord	Deu 5:11f
* alone to endorse your promises.	Deu 6:13
blot out their * from under heaven,	Deu 9:13,14
his *, just as is done today.	Deu 10:8
him and take oaths by his * alone.	Deu 10:20
all in the * of their religion.	Deu 12:31
minister in the * of the Lord, just	Deu 18:6,7
that his * will not be forgotten.	Deu 25:6
let his brother's * continue—he	Deu 25:7
the * of Amalek from under heaven.	Deu 25:19
and fearful * of Jehovah your God,	Deu 28:58,59
blot out his * from under heaven.	Deu 29:20
assistant, whose * was Joshua (the	Jos 1:1
me by the sacred * of your God that	Jos 2:12,13
his * became famous everywhere.	Jos 6:27
to the honor of your great *?"	Jos 7:9
is another * for Kiriath-jearim).	Jos 15:9
so the * of that place was	Ju 2:5
The same * is used here as in	Ju 6:16f
Gideon—his other *) and his army	Ju 7:1
now known by his *, and Zeeb at the	Ju 7:25
His father (whose * was Gilead)	Ju 11:1
didn't tell me his *, but he told	Ju 13:6
Then Manoah asked him for his *.	Ju 13:17
"Don't even ask my *," the	Ju 13:18
very wealthy man. His * was Boaz.	Ru 2:1
*, and to inherit the land."	Ru 4:5
family * of her dead husband."	Ru 4:10
His father's * was Jeroham,	1Sa 1:1
Then she murmured, "* the child	1Sa 4:21,22
that would dishonor his great *.	1Sa 12:22
I vow by the * of the God who	1Sa 14:39
come to you in the * of the Lord of	1Sa 17:45
And David replied, "His * is	1Sa 17:58
So David's * became very famous	1Sa 18:30
shearing. His * was Nabal and his	1Sa 25:3
He is a fool—just like his *	1Sa 25:25
you swear by God's * that you will	1Sa 30:15
the people in the * of the Lord of	2Sa 6:18
And I will make your * greater	2Sa 7:9
in order to bring glory to your *.	2Sa 7:23
and my husband's * will be	2Sa 14:7
have no sons to carry on my *."	2Sa 18:18
THEN A HOT-HEAD whose * was	2Sa 20:1
And sing praises to your *.	2Sa 22:50
command you in the * of God to stay	1Ki 2:42
this place and confess your *	1Ki 8:35,36
hear of your great * and come from	1Ki 8:41,42
hear of your great * and mighty	1Ki 8:41,42
know and fear your * just as your	1Ki 8:43
built for your *, hear their	1Ki 8:44
built for your *, hear their	1Ki 8:48
and have put my * here forever.	1Ki 9:2,3
hallowed for my * and I will cast	1Ki 9:7
concerning the * of the Lord."	1Ki 10:1f
place for my * to be enshrined.	1Ki 11:36
said, 'Israel shall be your *.'	1Ki 18:31f
So she wrote letters in Ahab's *,	1Ki 21:8
* is Micaiah, the son of Imlah."	1Ki 22:8
cursed them in the * of the Lord;	2Ki 2:24
and call upon the * of the Lord his	2Ki 5:11
alternate form of the * Jehoshaz.	2Ki 8:24,25f
demanded in the * of the king to	2Ki 9:19
and changed its * to Jokthe-el, as	2Ki 14:7
would blot out the * of Israel, so	2Ki 14:27
* of his father: Amaziah, the	2Ki 15:1
* of his mother: Jecoliah of	2Ki 15:1
* of his father: Jeroboam	2Ki 15:8
Father's *: Jabesh	2Ki 15:13
* of new king of Israel: Menahem	2Ki 15:17
* of new king of Israel: Pekahiah	2Ki 15:23
Father's *: King Menahem	2Ki 15:23
Father's *: Remaliah	2Ki 15:27
Father's *: King Uzziah	2Ki 15:32,33
Mother's *: Jerusha (daughter of	2Ki 15:32,33
Father's *: Jotham	2Ki 16:1
Father's *: Elah	2Ki 17:1
* was later changed to Israel).	2Ki 17:34
Father's *: Ahaz	2Ki 18:1
His mother's *: Abi (daughter of	2Ki 18:1
the sake of my own * and for the	2Ki 19:34
glory of my own * and for the sake	2Ki 20:6
* of his mother: Hephzibah	2Ki 21:1
had selected to honor his own *.	2Ki 21:3,4,5
"I will place my * forever in this	2Ki 21:7
* of the new king of Judah: Amon	2Ki 21:19,20
His mother's *: Meshullemeth	2Ki 21:19,20
* of his mother: Jedidah (daughter	2Ki 22:1
His mother's *: Hamutal (the	2Ki 23:31,32
and he changed his * to	2Ki 23:34
His mother's *: Zebidah (daughter	2Ki 23:36,37
* of his mother: Nehushta	2Ki 24:8,9
and he changed his * to Zedekiah.	2Ki 24:17
His mother's *: Hamutal (daughter	2Ki 24:18,19
Italic means that the * has	1Ch 1:5-9f
a daughter, whose * was Achsah.	1Ch 2:48,49
* Reuben as the oldest son.	1Ch 5:1
his brother's * was Sheresh, and	1Ch 7:16
Ephraim's daughter's * was	1Ch 7:24
and his wife's * was Maacah.	1Ch 8:29
the people in the * of the Lord;	1Ch 16:2
Glory in his holy *;	1Ch 16:10
great strength and glory to his *!	1Ch 16:28
The glory due his *!	1Ch 16:29
Then we will thank your holy *,	1Ch 16:35
who were chosen by * to give thanks	1Ch 16:41
I will make your * as great as the	1Ch 17:8
And you made a great * for	1Ch 17:21
honor to your * as everyone	1Ch 17:24
lands. His * shall be Solomon	1Ch 22:9
* of the Lord and for his people.	1Ch 22:18
blessings in his * at all times.	1Ch 23:13
praise your * for ever and ever!	1Ch 29:10
your glorious *, but who am I and	1Ch 29:13
for your holy * comes from you!	1Ch 29:16
where my * will be glorified;	2Ch 6:5,6
the Temple for the * of the Lord	2Ch 6:10
said that you would put your *.	2Ch 6:20,21
worship your great *, and to pray	2Ch 6:32
built for your *, then hear their	2Ch 6:34
* was Naamah the Ammonitess.	2Ch 12:13
His mother's * was Micaiah	2Ch 13:1
your * we attack this vast horde.	2Ch 14:11
His * is Micaiah (son of Imlah)."	2Ch 18:6,7
His mother's * was Azubah, the	2Ch 20:31
His mother's * was Athaliah,	2Ch 22:2
His mother's * was Zibiah, from	2Ch 24:1
His mother's * was Jeho-addan, a	2Ch 25:1
His mother's * was Jecoliah, from	2Ch 26:3
His mother's * was Abijah, the	2Ch 29:1
save their lands! * just one time	2Ch 32:14
(Eliakim's * was changed to	2Ch 36:4
*)—also returned to Jerusalem.	Ez 2:61
220 men were all listed by *.	Ez 8:20
took her family *), whose	Neh 7:63
Praise his glorious *!	Neh 9:5
her, and called for her by *.	Est 2:12,13,14
were signed in the * of King	Est 3:12
to in the king's *, and seal it	Est 8:8
Mordecai wrote in the * of King	Est 8:9,10
for Mordecai was a mighty * in	Est 9:4
Blessed be the * of the Lord."	Job 1:21
of no *, outcasts of civilization.	Job 30:8
I will sing praise to the * of	Ps 7:17
and glory of your * fills all the	Ps 8:1
glory of your * fills the earth.	Ps 8:9
must fear and reverence his *.	Ps 22:23
of all who reverence your *.	Ps 22:25
find him and shall praise his *.	Ps 22:26
them for the honor of your *.	Ps 25:11
glory, the glory of his *.	Ps 29:2
give thanks to his holy *.	Ps 30:4
honor your * by leading me out of	Ps 31:3
We trust his holy *.	Ps 33:21
Lord together, and exalt his *.	Ps 34:3
* that we tread down our enemies;	Ps 44:5
"I will cause your * to be	Ps 45:17
Your * is known throughout the	Ps 48:10
to others. You * your estates	Ps 49:11
Literally, "your *."	Ps 54:1f
I will praise your *, O Lord, for	Ps 54:6
for those who reverence your *.	Ps 61:5
I will praise your * continually,	Ps 61:8
Sing of his glorious *!	Ps 66:2
Jehovah is his *—oh, rejoice in	Ps 68:4
all who love his * shall live	Ps 69:36
His * will be honored forever;	Ps 72:17
Blessed be his glorious *	Ps 72:19
our enemies to dishonor your *?	Ps 74:9,10
nation has blasphemed your *.	Ps 74:18
and needy ones to praise your *!	Ps 74:21
that will not call upon your *!	Ps 79:6
Help us for the honor of your *.	Ps 79:9
your power and *, O Lord.	Ps 83:16
and praise your great and holy *.	Ps 86:9
unite in reverence to your *.	Ps 86:11
I will give glory to your *	Ps 86:12
signed by your * as their maker!	Ps 89:12
great because he trusts in my *.	Ps 91:14
Bless his *.	Ps 96:2
"give glory to his holy *."	Ps 97:12
reverence your great and holy *.	Ps 99:3
thanks to him and bless his *.	Ps 100:4
I BLESS THE holy * of God with all	Ps 103:1
the honor of your * and demonstrate	Ps 106:8
holy * and rejoice and praise you.	Ps 106:47
May his family * be blotted out	Ps 109:12,13
off his * from the memory of man.	Ps 109:15
child, as one who bears your *!	Ps 109:21
a holy, awe-inspiring * that is).	Ps 111:9
Praise his * forever.	Ps 111:10
SERVANTS of Jehovah, praise his *.	Ps 113:1
Blessed is his * forever and	Ps 113:2
GLORIFY YOUR *, not ours, O Lord!	Ps 115:1
and praise his * for saving me.	Ps 116:13
Literally, "in the * of the	Ps 118:26f
we bless you in Jehovah's *."	Ps 129:8
sing to his wonderful *.	Ps 135:3
O Jehovah, your * endures	Ps 135:13
priests of Aaron, bless his *.	Ps 135:19
Oh, bless his *, all of you who	Ps 135:20
backed by all the honor of your *.	Ps 138:2
your Word above all your *."	Ps 138:2f
They blaspheme your * and stand	Ps 139:20
me will bring glory to your *.	Ps 143:11
bless your * each day and forever.	Ps 145:1
his holy * forever and forever.	Ps 145:21
the stars and calls them all by *.	Ps 147:4
Praise his * with dancing,	Ps 149:3
Go and beg to have your * erased.	Pro 6:3
Literally, "The * of the Lord."	Pro 18:10f
IF YOU MUST choose, take a good *	Pro 22:1
other, what is his *—and his son's	Pro 30:4
his son's *—if you know it?	Pro 30:4
and thus insult God's holy *.	Pro 30:9
without even a *, never seeing the	Ecc 6:4
cologne, and how great your *!	Sol 1:3
only let us be called by your *	Is 4:1
Use capital letters! His * will	Is 8:1
This * prophesies that within a	Is 8:4
Praise his *!	Is 12:4
where he has placed his *.	Is 18:7
Just to speak the * of Israel	Is 19:17
be an honor to his family *."	Is 22:23,24
praise your *, for you are my God;	Is 25:1
will obey and glorify your *.	Is 25:3
desire is to glorify your *.	Is 26:8
become as her * "Ariel" means—an	Is 29:2
and rejoice in my *, and praise the	Is 29:23
people from my power? * just one!	Is 36:20
each by its pet *, and counts them	Is 40:26
and call on my *, and I will give	Is 41:25
That is my *, and I will not give	Is 42:8
I have called you by *;	Is 43:1
their hands the * of God or the	Is 44:5
of God or the honored * of Israel.	Is 44:5
the one who calls you by your *.	Is 45:3
I called you by * when you didn't	Is 45:4
shall swear allegiance to my *.	Is 45:23
the Lord of Hosts is his *, the	Is 47:4
the honor of my * I will hold back	Is 48:9
the womb he called me by my *.	Is 49:1
See, I have tattooed your * upon	Is 49:16
exultation, and my * is constantly	Is 52:5
Therefore I will reveal my * to	Is 52:6
shall know the power in that *.	Is 52:6
The Lord of Hosts is his *;	Is 54:5
make the Lord's * very great and be	Is 55:13
within my walls —a * far greater	Is 56:5
For the * that I will give them	Is 56:5
him and love his *, and are his	Is 56:6
the * of God from west to east.	Is 59:19
God will confer on you a new *.	Is 62:2
Your new * will be "The Land	Is 62:4
Yet no one calls upon your * or	Is 64:7
Your * shall be a curse word	Is 65:15
his true servants by another *.	Is 65:15
you out for being loyal to my *.	Is 66:5
a * that shall never disappear.	Is 66:22
will come to me and glorify my *.	Jer 4:2
honored with my *, and see what I	Jer 7:12
called by my *, which you trust for	Jer 7:13,14
A * by which Ishtar, the	Jer 7:18f
when that valley's * will be	Jer 7:32
For you are great and your * is	Jer 10:6
The Lord of Hosts is his *.	Jer 10:16
"Let's kill him so that his *	Jer 11:19
in God's * on pain of death.	Jer 11:21,22
were my people, an honor to my *.	Jer 13:11
among us, and we carry your *;	Jer 14:9
prophets are telling lies in my *.	Jer 14:14
have spoken in my * though I did	Jer 14:15
Lord, for the sake of your own *.	Jer 14:21
How proud I am to bear your *, O	Jer 15:16

NAME Con't)
the Lord has changed your *. Jer 20:3
and make my * a household joke. Jer 20:8
more speak in his *—then his word Jer 20:9
I swear by my own *, says the Lord, Jer 22:5
other names. His * means, "The Jer 22:24,25f
And this is his *: The Lord Our Jer 23:5,6
But can you * even one of these Jer 23:18
then they proceed to lie in my *. Jer 23:25
upon you and your * shall be Jer 23:40
us in the * of the Lord our God." Jer 26:16
they are telling you lies in my *. Jer 27:15
for they prophesy lies in my *. Jer 29:9
lies to you in my *: Look, I am Jer 29:21
wives and have lied in my *. Jer 29:23
the * of which means "Dreamer." Jer 29:24f
* is Lord of Hosts—says this: Jer 31:35
You have made your * very great, Jer 32:20
earth—Jehovah is his *—says this: Jer 33:2
have defiled my * by shrugging off Jer 34:16
sworn by my great *, says the Lord, Jer 44:26
For I have sworn by my own *, Jer 49:13
His * is the Lord of Hosts. Jer 50:34
to it in his own *: Your cities Jer 51:14
the Lord of Hosts is his *. Jer 51:19
His mother's * was Hamutal Jer 52:1
But I called upon your *, O Lam 3:55
the solemn oath he made in my *. Eze 17:19
the honor of my *, lest the Eze 20:9,10
the honor of my *, lest the nations Eze 20:14
them to protect my * among the Eze 20:22
is how it got its *. Eze 20:29
Such desecration of my holy * Eze 20:39
And when I have honored my * by Eze 20:44
* is greatly defiled among them. Eze 22:26
their slaves. Her * was known to Eze 23:10
And I will honor my * in Israel Eze 35:11
upon my holy * because the nations Eze 36:20
to protect my holy * which you Eze 36:22
I will honor my great * that you Eze 36:23
honor upon my *, and all the Eze 38:23
my holy * among my people Israel; Eze 39:7
And they will change the * of the Eze 39:11
not defile my holy * any longer Eze 43:7
Because they sullied my holy * by Eze 43:8
And the * of the city will be Eze 48:35
"Blessed be the * of God forever Dan 2:20
Literally, "Daniel, whose * was Dan 4:19f
honor to your * by removing your Dan 9:15
and your city bear your *." Dan 9:19
And the Lord said, "* the child Hos 1:4,5
And God said to Hosea, "* her Hos 1:6
you are mine"); * your sister Hos 1:11
Jehovah is his *. Hos 12:5
"Everyone who calls upon the * Joe 2:32
temple-girl, corrupting my holy *. Amo 2:7
the God of Hosts, is his *." Amo 4:13
The Lord, Jehovah, is his *. Amo 5:8
sworn by his own *, "I despise the Amo 6:8
don't mention the * of the Amo 6:10
Jehovah, the Lord, is his *. Amo 9:6
the majesty of the * of the Lord Mic 5:4
your * and forfeited your lives. Hab 2:10
will trust in the * of the Lord. Zep 3:12
give you a good *, a name of Zep 3:20
you a good name, a * of distinction Zep 3:20
by my *," says the Lord of Hosts. Zec 5:4
will come, whose * is "The Zec 6:12
lies in the * of the Lord.' Zec 13:3
They will call upon my * and I Zec 13:9
* alone will be worshiped. Zec 14:9
O priests, but you despise my *." Mal 1:6
"When did we ever despise your * Mal 1:6
"But my * will be honored by the Mal 1:11
pure offerings in honor of my *. Mal 1:11
For my * shall be great among the Mal 1:11
of Hosts, "and my * is to be Mal 1:14
give glory to my *, then I will Mal 2:1
"But for you who fear my *, the Mal 4:2
Son, and you shall * him Jesus Mt 1:21
in heaven, we honor your holy *. Mt 6:9
you and used your * to cast out Mt 7:22
And his * shall be the hope Mt 12:21
who comes in the * of the Lord." Mt 21:9f
"And whose * is this beneath the Mt 22:20
Literally, "in the * of the Mt 23:39f
"I demand in the * of the living Mt 26:63
was his *—and forced him to carry Mt 27:32
them into the * of the Father and Mt 28:19
"What is your *?" Mk 5:9
synagogue, whose * was Jairus, came Mk 5:22
like this in my * is welcoming me, Mk 9:37
using your * to cast out demons; Mk 9:38
my * will quickly turn against me. Mk 9:39
who comes in the * of the Lord!" Mk 11:9
have children in his brother's *. Mk 12:19
The * means "one who loves Lk 1:1f
And you are to * him John. Lk 1:13
boy, and you are to * him 'Jesus.' Lk 1:31
They all assumed the baby's * Lk 1:59
in all your family by that *." Lk 1:61
surprise wrote, "His * is John!" Lk 1:63
named Jesus, the * given him by the Lk 2:21
The man's * was Levi. Lk 5:27
smear your * because you are mine! Lk 6:22
"What is your *?" Lk 8:30
using your * to cast out demons. Lk 9:49
obey us when we use your *." Lk 10:17
* be honored for its holiness; Lk 11:2
who comes in the * of the Lord.' Lk 13:35
at Zacchaeus and called him by *! Lk 19:5
And whose *?" Lk 20:24
the dead man, to carry on his *. Lk 20:28
Literally, "will come in my *." Lk 21:8f
are mine and are called by my *. Lk 21:17
Literally, "to believe on his * Jn 1:11,12f
told about! His * is Jesus, the son Jn 1:45
and he calls his own sheep by * Jn 10:3
I do in the * of my Father. Jn 10:25
Philip's * was Greek, though he Jn 12:21f
bring glory and honor to your *." Jn 12:28
anything, using my *, and I will do Jn 14:12,13
Yes, ask anything, using my *, Jn 14:14
disciple with that *) said to him, Jn 14:22
Literally, "in my *." Jn 14:26f
my *, he will give it to you. Jn 15:16
you ask for because you use my *. Jn 16:23
Ask, using my *, and you will Jn 16:24
Literally, "you shall ask in my * Jn 16:26f
Literally, "kept in your * those Jn 17:12f
be baptized in the * of Jesus Act 2:38
I command you in the * of Jesus Act 3:6
"Jesus' * has healed this Act 3:16
Faith in Jesus' *—faith given us Act 3:16
it was done in the * and power of Act 4:10
there is no other * for men to call Act 4:12
* of your holy servant Jesus." Act 4:30
to speak in the * of Jesus, and Act 5:40
to suffer dishonor for his *. Act 5:41
and so do you! * one prophet your Act 7:52
in the * of the Lord Jesus. Act 8:16
preaching in the * of Jesus. Act 9:27
boldly in the * of the Lord. Act 9:29
Literally, "Tabitha," her * in Act 9:40f
sins forgiven through his *." Act 10:43
in the * of Jesus, the Messiah. Act 10:48
But the sorcerer, Elymas (his * Act 13:8
a people to bring honor to his *. Act 15:14
Lord—all those marked with my *.' Act 15:17
"I command you in the * of Jesus Act 16:18
the * of the Lord Jesus. Act 19:5
by using the * of the Lord Jesus. Act 19:13
the city, and the * of the Lord Act 19:17
calling on the * of the Lord.' Act 22:16
Literally, "the *." Act 26:9f
would hear about God's glorious *. Rom 9:17
Literally, "that my * might be Rom 9:17f
Anyone who calls upon the * of Rom 10:13
Gentiles, and sing to your *." Rom 15:9
where the * of Christ has never yet Rom 15:20
never heard the * of Christ before Rom 15:21
calls upon the * of Jesus Christ, 1Co 1:2
I beg you in the * of the Lord 1Co 1:10
Were any of you baptized in my *? 1Co 1:13
this, and in the * of the Lord 1Co 5:3,4
The * given to Jesus' twelve 1Co 15:5f
he is, giving glory to his *. 2Co 1:20
in the * of our Lord Jesus Christ. Eph 5:20
and gave him a * which is above Php 2:9
above every other *, that at the Php 2:9
name, that at the * of Jesus every Php 2:10
of you in the * of the Lord 1Th 4:1
I command you in the * of the 1Th 5:27
be praising the * of the Lord Jesus 2Th 1:12
given in the * of our Lord Jesus 2Th 3:6
In the * of the Lord Jesus 2Th 3:12
used to scoff at the * of Christ. 1Ti 1:13
to bring shame to the * of Christ. 1Ti 1:20
Don't let the * of God or his 1Ti 6:1
them in the * of the Lord not to 2Ti 2:14
I could demand it of you in the * Phm 1:8,9
Onesimus (whose * means Phm 1:11
the fact that his * "Son of God," Heb 1:4
the honor that goes with that *." Heb 1:5,6
an oath in his own *, since there Heb 6:13
Melchizedek's * means "Justice," Heb 7:2
because of the * of his city, Heb 7:2
others of the glory of his *. Heb 13:15
Christ, whose noble * you bear. Jas 2:7
being called by his wonderful *! 1Pe 4:16
the Father. His * is Jesus Christ, 1Jn 2:1
in the * of Jesus our Savior. 1Jn 2:12
do: Believe on the * of his Son 1Jn 3:23
be engraved a new * that no one Rev 2:17
will not erase his * from the Book Rev 3:5
and have not denied my *. Rev 3:8
and I will write my God's * on Rev 3:12
and he will have my new * Rev 3:12
and its rider's * was Death. Rev 6:8
horse whose rider's * was Hell. Rev 6:8
pit whose * in Hebrew is Abaddon, Rev 9:11
all who fear your *, both great and Rev 11:18
blasphemed God's * and his temple Rev 13:6
was either the * of the Creature or Rev 13:17
or the code number of his *. Rev 13:17
the letters in his * add to 666! Rev 13:18
who had his * and his Father's Name Rev 14:1
* written on their foreheads. Rev 14:1
tattooed with the code of his *. Rev 14:11
And glorify your *? Rev 15:3,4
they cursed the * of God who sent Rev 16:9
A * was written on his forehead, Rev 19:12
And if anyone's * was not found Rev 20:15
and his * shall be written on Rev 22:4

NAME-CALLING
which only lead to *, accusations, 1Ti 6:4

NAME'S
kings and governors for my * sake. Lk 21:12

NAMED
Then God * the dry land Gen 1:9,10
One of these was * the Pishon; Gen 2:11,12
The man * his wife Eve (meaning Gen 3:20
him with a baby son * Enoch; Gen 4:17
so when Cain founded a city, he * Gen 4:17
To Adah was born a baby * Jabal. Gen 4:20
* him Seth (meaning "Granted"); Gen 4:25
up, he had a son and * him Enosh. Gen 4:26
Lamech * him Noah (meaning Gen 5:28-31
And Haran had a son * Lot. Gen 11:27
and she had a brother * Iscah. Gen 11:29
an Egyptian girl * Hagar, and gave Gen 16:1
Later that well was * "The Well Gen 16:14
a son, and Abram * him Ishmael. Gen 16:15
* Zoar, meaning "Little City." Gen 19:22
The older girl's baby was * Gen 19:37
and Abraham * him Isaac (meaning Gen 21:3
Abraham * the place "Jehovah Gen 22:14
* Rebekah arrived with a water Gen 24:15,16
when his father had * them. Gen 26:18
So he * the well, "The Well of Gen 26:20
So he * the well, "The Well of Gen 26:33
that grew up there was * "Oath," Gen 26:33
married a girl * Judith, daughter Gen 26:34
oil over it. He * the place Bethel Gen 28:19
"Do you know a fellow there * Gen 29:5
another son and * him Simeon Gen 29:33
and had a son, and * him Levi Gen 29:34
and had a son and * him Judah Gen 29:35
Rachel * him Dan (meaning Gen 30:6
bill the child was * 'Bill'!" Gen 30:6f
Rachel * him Naphtali (meaning Gen 30:8
Leah * him Gad (meaning "My Gen 30:11
son, and Leah * him Asher (meaning Gen 30:13
fifth son. She * him Issachar Gen 30:18
a sixth son. She * him Zebulun Gen 30:20
to a daughter and * her Dinah. Gen 30:21
And she * him Joseph (meaning Gen 30:23,24
They * it "The Witness Gen 31:47,48
So he * the place "God's Gen 32:1
Jacob * the place "Peniel" Gen 32:30
an altar there and * it "The altar Gen 35:7
Jacob * the spot Bethel ("House Gen 35:15
(for she died) she * him Gen 35:18
Esau and Adah had a son * Gen 36:4
Esau and Basemath had a son * Gen 36:4
Esau and Oholibamah had sons * Gen 36:5
And these are the clans * after Gen 36:18,19
in the localities * after Gen 36:40-43
lived there with a man * Hirah. Gen 38:1
for Er, who was * by his father. Gen 38:3,4,5
for him to marry a girl * Tamar. Gen 38:6
was born, and he was * Zerah. Gen 38:30
And he gave him a wife, a girl * Gen 41:45
Joseph * his oldest son Manasseh Gen 41:51
The second boy was * Ephraim Gen 41:52
her son. She * him Moses (meaning Ex 2:10
They had a baby * Gershom Ex 2:22
Moses * the place Massah Ex 17:7
* in the order of their births. Ex 28:10
The Israelis * the valley Num 13:24
This place was * Meribah (meaning Num 20:13
clans, * after Reuben's sons: Num 26:5-11
The Hanochites, * after their Num 26:5-11
The Palluites, * after their Num 26:5-11
The Hezronites, * after their Num 26:5-11
The Carmites, * after their Num 26:5-11
The Nemu-elites, * after their Num 26:12-14
The Jaminites, * after their Num 26:12-14
The Jachinites, * after their Num 26:12-14
The Zerahites, * after their Num 26:12-14
The Shaulites, * after their Num 26:12-14
The Zephonites, * after their Num 26:15-18
The Haggites, * after their Num 26:15-18
The Shunites, * after their Num 26:15-18
The Oznites, * after their Num 26:15-18
The Erites, * after their ancestor Num 26:15-18
The Arodites, * after their Num 26:15-18
The Arelites, * after their Num 26:15-18
following clans * after the sons of Num 26:19-22
The Shelanites, * after their Num 26:19-22
The Perezites, * after their Num 26:19-22
The Zerahites, * after their Num 26:19-22
The Hezronites, * after their Num 26:19-22

(NAMED Con't)
The Hamulites, * after their Num 26:19-22
* after the sons of Issachar: Num 26:23-25
The Tolaites, * after their Num 26:23-25
The Punites, * after their Num 26:23-25
The Jashubites, * after their Num 26:23-25
The Shimronites, * after their Num 26:23-25
clans * after the sons of Zebulun: Num 26:26,27
The Seredites, * after their Num 26:26,27
The Elonites, * after their Num 26:26,27
The Jahleelites, * after their Num 26:26,27
* after their ancestor Machir. Num 26:28-37
* after their ancestor Gilead. Num 26:28-37
The Jezerites, * after their Num 26:28-37
The Helekites, * after their Num 26:28-37
The Asrielites, * after their Num 26:28-37
The Shechemites, * after their Num 26:28-37
The Shemidaites, * after their Num 26:28-37
The Hepherites, * after their Num 26:28-37
* after the sons of Ephraim: Num 26:28-37
The Shuthelahites, * after their Num 26:28-37
was theEranites, * after their Num 26:28-37
The Becherites, * after their Num 26:28-37
The Tahanites, * after their Num 26:28-37
* after the sons of Benjamin: Num 26:38-41
The Bela-ites, * after their Num 26:38-41
Sub-clans * after sons of Bela Num 26:38-41
The Ardites, * after their Num 26:38-41
The Naamites, * after their Num 26:38-41
The Ashbelites, * after their Num 26:38-41
The Ahiramites, * after their Num 26:38-41
The Shuphamites, * after their Num 26:38-41
The Huphamites, * after their Num 26:38-41
* after Shuham, the son of Dan. Num 26:42,43
clans * after the sons of Asher: Num 26:44-47
The Imnites, * after their Num 26:44-47
The Ishvites, * after their Num 26:44-47
The Beriites, * after their Num 26:44-47
Sub-clans * after the sons of Num 26:44-47
The Heberites, * after their Num 26:44-47
The Malchi-elites, * after their Num 26:44-47
Asher also had a daughter * Serah. Num 26:44-47
* after the sons of Naphtali: Num 26:48-50
The Jahzeelites, * after their Num 26:48-50
The Gunites, * after their Num 26:48-50
The Jezerites, * after their Num 26:48-50
The Shillemites, * after their Num 26:48-50
The Gershonites, * after their Num 26:57
The Kohathites, * after their Num 26:57
The Merarites, * after their Num 26:57
Meanwhile, a man * Nobah led an Num 32:42
* Rahab, who was a prostitute. Jos 2:1
* "The Hill of the Foreskins." Jos 5:2,3
had been * after Anak's father. Jos 15:13
The people of Reuben and Gad * Jos 22:34
So now the city is * Hormah Ju 1:17
an altar there and * it "The Altar Ju 6:24
him with a son * Abimelech. Ju 8:31
When her son was born they * him Ju 13:24
Then he * the place "The Spring Ju 15:19
love with a girl * Delilah over in Ju 16:4
of Ephraim lived a man * Micah. Ju 17:1
The city was * "Dan" after Ju 18:29
appointed a man * Jonathan (son of Ju 18:30
a man * Elimelech, from Bethlehem, Ru 1:1
And they * him Obed. Ru 4:16,17
to her. She * him Samuel (meaning 1Sa 1:19,20
She * him this because the Ark 1Sa 4:21,22
the field of a man * Joshua and 1Sa 6:14
and Jeshanah and * it Ebenezer 1Sa 7:12
which had been * Bozez and Seneh. 1Sa 14:4
and find a man * Jesse, for I have 1Sa 16:1
the son of a man * Jesse, who was 1Sa 16:18
intelligent woman, was * Abigail. 1Sa 25:3
Gallim * Palti (the son of Laish). 1Sa 25:44
concubines, a girl * Rizpah. 2Sa 3:7
of King Saul's * Mephibosheth, who 2Sa 4:4
So he * the place "Bursting." 2Sa 5:20
Lord had done, and * the spot "The 2Sa 6:8
He heard about a man * Ziba who 2Sa 9:2
birth to a son and * him Solomon. 2Sa 12:24
had a beautiful sister * Tamar. 2Sa 13:1
All I want is a man * Sheba from 2Sa 20:21
asked for a man * Hiram to come 1Ki 7:13
The one on the south was * the 1Ki 7:16-22
says that a child * Josiah shall be 1Ki 13:2
The clans * after the sons of 1Ch 1:11,12
and Esau's daughter was * Timna. 1Ch 1:38,39
two girls (by the same wife) * 1Ch 2:16
of Ishmael, had a son * Amasa. 1Ch 2:17
but Appa-im had a son * 1Ch 2:31
had two sons * Peleth and Zaza. 1Ch 2:33
And they had a son whom they * 1Ch 2:34,35
Haran had a son * Gazez. 1Ch 2:46
* after Aharhel, the son of Harum. 1Ch 4:8
His mother * him Jabez because 1Ch 4:9
Machir's wife, also * Maacah, 1Ch 7:16
bore him a son whom she * Peresh; 1Ch 7:16
and he had sons * Ulam and Rakem. 1Ch 7:16
His oldest son was * Abdon, 1Ch 8:30,31,32
to Uzza, and he * the place "The 1Ch 13:11
* after the sons of Levi—the 1Ch 23:6
corps were * after his sons 1Ch 23:7
into six groups * after the sons of 1Ch 23:8,9
The subclans of Shime-i were * 1Ch 23:10,11
into four groups * after his sons 1Ch 23:12
divisions * after Aaron's sons, 1Ch 24:1
guards were * after the leaders. 1Ch 26:12
of the divisions * after Amram, 1Ch 26:23,24
of a man * Shesh-bazzar, whom King Ez 5:14
He sent us an outstanding man * Ez 8:18
of my fellow Jews * Hanani came to Neh 1:2
of priests * after Habaiah, Hakkoz, Neh 7:63
Jew at the palace * Mordecai (son Est 2:5
the land of Uz a man * Job—a good Job 1:1
it will be * "The Holy Is 35:8
And why have I * you for this Is 45:4
The older girl was * Oholah; Eze 23:4,5
A city * 'Multitude' is there! Eze 39:15,16
village on this site is so *. Eze 47:15f
"Each city gate will be * in Eze 48:30,31
three gates, one * for Reuben, one Eze 48:30,31
be * for Joseph, Benjamin and Dan. Eze 48:32
be * for Gad, Asher and Naphtali. Eze 48:34
came in—the man I * Belteshazzar Dan 4:8
their country is * 'The Land of Mal 1:4
and Joseph * him "Jesus." Mt 1:25
criminal in jail * Barabbas, and Mt 27:16
man from Arimathea * Joseph, one of Mt 27:57
a blind beggar * Bartimaeus (the Mk 10:46
married to a man * Joseph, a Lk 1:27
He must be * John!" Lk 1:60
ceremony, he was * Jesus, the name Lk 2:21
That day a man * Simeon, a Lk 2:25
And now a man * Jairus, a leader Lk 8:41
where a woman * Martha welcomed Lk 10:38
Jericho, a man * Zacchaeus, one of Lk 19:1
Then a man * Joseph, a member of Lk 23:50,51,52
religious leader * Nicodemus, a Jn 3:1
* the place 'The Field of Blood.' Act 1:19
BUT THERE WAS a man * Ananias Act 5:1
a Pharisee * Gamaliel (an expert on Act 5:34
at the feet of a young man * Paul. Act 7:58
A man * Simon had formerly been a Act 8:9,10,11
in Damascus a believer * Ananias. Act 9:10
the house of a man * Judas and ask Act 9:11
a vision of a man * Ananias coming Act 9:12
There he met a man * Aeneas, Act 9:33
there was a woman * Dorcas Act 9:36
to find a man * Simon Peter, who is Act 10:5,6
and one of them, * Agabus, stood Act 11:28
a girl * Rhoda came to open it. Act 12:13
a fake prophet * Bar-Jesus. Act 13:6,7
and a woman * Damaris, and others. Act 17:34
with a Jew * Aquila, born in Act 18:2,3
As it happened, a Jew * Apollos, Act 18:24
on, a young man * Eutychus, sitting Act 20:9
days, a man * Agabus, who also had Act 21:10
There a man * Ananias, as godly Act 22:12
of an officer * Julius, a member of Act 27:1
a small island * Clauda, where with Act 27:16
on the horse was * "Faithful and Rev 19:11

NAMELY

borders of Edom in the Negeb, *: Jos 15:21-32

NAMES

Many Hebrew * are based on puns. Gen 3:20f
The * of Noah's three sons were Gen 9:18
Their * were:Uz, the oldest,Buz, Gen 22:20-23
twelve tribes that bore their *. Gen 25:16
gave them the same * they had had Gen 26:18
Here are the * of the twelve sons Gen 35:22
Here are the * of Esau's Gen 36:9
Verse 14 is a repetition of the * Gen 36:13,14f
These are the * of the tribes Gen 36:20,21
Verses 29 and 30 repeat the * Gen 36:28,29,30f
These are the * of the kings of Gen 36:31-39
Here are the * of the sub-tribes Gen 36:40-43
These, then, are the * of the Gen 36:40-43
These * were given to them by Gen 38:3,4,5
Here are the * of his sons and Gen 46:8-14
* of my fathers Abraham and Isaac; Gen 48:16
midwives (their * were Shiphrah and Ex 1:15,16
goes under two * in these chapters, Ex 3:1f
These are the * of the heads of Ex 6:14
These are the * of the heads of Ex 6:16
These are all the * of the heads Ex 6:25
the * of the tribes of Israel. Ex 28:9
of Israel. Six * shall be on each Ex 28:10
When engraving these *, use the Ex 28:11
will carry their * before the Lord Ex 28:12
shall carry the * of the tribes of Ex 28:29
engraved with the * of the tribes Ex 39:6,7
* of the twelve tribes of Israel. Ex 39:14
grandsons (clan *) Libni Num 3:16-24
Levi's grandsons (clan *) Num 3:25-30
Levi's grandsons (clan *) Num 3:31-35
Here are the * of his daughters: Num 26:28-37
later changed the * of some of Num 32:37,38
"These are the * of the men I have Num 34:16-28
These are the * of the men I have Num 34:29
* from the face of the earth. Deu 7:24
the * of the battalion leaders. Deu 20:9
three days. (The * of the cities Jos 9:17
daughters whose * were Mahlah, Jos 17:3
do not even mention the * of Jos 23:7
he write down the * of all the Ju 8:14
And he cursed David by the * of 1Sa 17:43
These are the * of the Top 2Sa 23:8
Apparently new * were elected to 2Sa 23:24-39
The * of these twelve officers 1Ki 4:8-19
and deeds and the * of the cities 1Ki 15:23
The * in bold face type are 1Ch 1:1f
Here is a list of the * of the 1Ch 1:43
These * all come from very ancient 1Ch 4:21-22
These are the * of some of the 1Ch 4:34-39
THESE ARE THE * of the sons of 1Ch 6:1
These are the * and ancestries 1Ch 6:33-38
These are the * of some of the 1Ch 11:10
THESE ARE THE * of the famous 1Ch 12:1
These are the * of the sons born 1Ch 14:4-7
These are the * of those given 1Ch 16:4
the * of these clans and subclans; 1Ch 23:24
and wrote down the * and 1Ch 24:6
Here is a list of their * and 1Ch 25:1
Their * were: 1Ch 26:6,7
* of some of his other sons were: 1Ch 26:11
And he gave them *: Jachin (the 2Ch 3:17
under the * of their work corps. 2Ch 31:17,18
for a list of the * of all the men Ez 5:4
And we demanded their * so that Ez 5:10
THESE ARE THE * and genealogies of Ez 8:1
is a list of the * of the Jews who Neh 7:6
put our * to this covenant." Neh 9:38
Following is a list of the * of Neh 11:3
the Levite * were recorded down to Neh 12:23
Their * were Eliphaz the Job 2:11
These were the * of his daughters: Job 42:13,14
out their * forever and ever. Ps 9:5
or even speak the * of their gods. Ps 16:4
my friends the * of Egypt and Ps 87:4
the * of those who were born here. Ps 87:6
* of wicked men stink after them. Pro 10:7
Those whose * are written down to Is 4:2,3,4
me have symbolic * that reveal the Is 8:18
* of Marduk and Nabu, the two Is 46:1f
and Jehoiachin, his other *. Jer 22:24,25f
These are the * of the leaders Jer 40:8
You have heard the vile * they Lam 3:61
I will blot out your * and you Eze 13:9
The * of Gog's confederates Eze 38:2,3f
them Babylonian *, as Dan 1:7
your people whose * are written in Dan 12:1
* will not be spoken anymore. Hos 1:17
* of the idols will be forgotten. Zec 13:2
he recorded the * of those who Mal 3:16
Here are the * of his twelve Mt 10:2,3,4
These are the * of the twelve he Mk 3:16-19
Here are their *: Lk 6:14,15,16
you, but that your * are registered Lk 10:20
have big * or power or wealth. 1Co 1:26
* are written in the Book of Life. Php 4:3
the * and titles of the angels. Heb 1:4
calling you evil *, they will 1Pe 3:16
were blasphemous *, each one Rev 13:1
And all mankind—whose * were not Rev 13:8
Or "those whose * were not Rev 13:8f
and the people of earth, whose * Rev 17:8
And the * of the twelve tribes of Rev 21:12
were written the * of the twelve Rev 21:14
only those whose * are written in Rev 21:27

NAMING

* it after their ancestor. Jos 19:47,48
a city there, * it Luz, too, as it Ju 1:26
our forces at ÇÇ" (* the place). 2Ki 6:8
go near ÇÇ" (* the same place) 2Ki 6:9
shepherd's staffs, * one "Grace" Zec 11:7

NANNY

* goats with streaked, speckled, Gen 31:12
for your ewes and * goats so that Gen 31:38
brother Esau:200 * goats,20 billy Gen 32:13,14,15
or ewe, billy goat or * goat. Lev 3:6
as his sacrifice a * goat without Lev 4:28

NAOMI

With him were his wife, *, and Ru 1:1
and * was left with her two sons. Ru 1:3
men died, so that * was left alone, Ru 1:4,5
But * replied, "It is better for Ru 1:11
Ruth insisted on staying with *. Ru 1:14
"See," * said to her, "your Ru 1:15
And when * saw that Ruth had made Ru 1:18
"Is it really *?" Ru 1:19
she told them, "Don't call me *. Ru 1:20
Call me Mara," (* means Ru 1:20
why should you call me * when the Ru 1:21
NOW * HAD an in-law there in Ru 2:1
One day Ruth said to *, "Perhaps Ru 2:2
And * said, "All right, dear Ru 2:2
land of Moab who came back with *. Ru 2:6
"So much!" * exclaimed. Ru 2:19
dead husband!" * cried excitedly. Ru 2:20
"This is wonderful!" * Ru 2:22
ONE DAY * said to Ruth, "My dear, Ru 3:1
even kinder to * now than before. Ru 3:10

(NAOMI Con't)
can give * an heir by marrying me Ru 3:10
"Well, what happened, dear?" * Ru 3:15-18
She told * everything and gave Ru 3:15-18
Then * said to her, "Just be Ru 3:15-18
*, who came back to us from Moab. Ru 4:3
of the land from * requires your Ru 4:5
and Mahlon, from *, and that with Ru 4:9
the city said to *, "Bless the Ru 4:14
* took care of the baby, and the Ru 4:16,17
"Now at last * has a son again!" Ru 4:16,17

NAOMI'S
Boaz, this relative of * husband. Ru 2:3

NAP
one noon as he was taking a *. 2Sa 4:5
he lay down for a *, and while he Lk 8:23

NAPHATHDOR
The king of Dor in the city of *; Jos 12:8-24

NAPHISH
Hadad, Tema,Jetur, *, Kedemah. Gen 25:12-15
Tema, Jetur, *, and Kedemah. 1Ch 1:28-31

NAPHISHITES
the *, and the Nodabites. 1Ch 5:19

NAPHTALI
Rachel named him * (meaning Gen 30:8
Rachel's servant-girl:Dan, *. Gen 35:25
* and his sons: Jahzeel, Guni, Gen 46:23,24,25
"* is a deer let loose, Gen 49:21
Dan, *,Gad, Asher. Ex 1:1
* -Ahira (son of Enan) Num 1:2-15
* -53,400 Num 1:20-46
Tribe: Dan Asher * Num 2:3-31
tribe of *, with his offerings; Num 7:78-83
and the tribe of *, led by Num 10:27
of Vophsi, from the tribe of *; Num 13:3-15
The tribe of *: 45,400. Num 26:48-50
clans, named after the sons of *: Num 26:48-50
* Pedahel (son of Ammihud Num 34:16-28
Zebulun, Dan, and * shall stand Deu 27:13
Of the tribe of *, Moses said: Deu 33:23
"O *, you are satisfied Deu 33:23
"There is *; Deu 34:2
The Land Given to the Tribe of *: Jos 19:32
its assignment was the tribe of *. Jos 19:32
Galilee in the hill country of *; Jos 20:7
*, and the half-tribe of Manasseh. Jos 21:6
The tribe of * gave: Jos 21:32
And the tribe of * did not drive Ju 1:33
in the land of *, and said to him, Ju 4:6
from the tribes of * and Zebulun. Ju 4:6
men of Zebulun and * to mobilize at Ju 4:10
But the tribes of Zebulun and * Ju 5:18
Zebulun, and *, summoning their Ju 6:35
for the troops of *, Asher, and Ju 7:23
daughters), whose area was *; 1Ki 4:8-19
of the tribe of *, and his father 1Ki 7:14
all the cities in the land of *. 1Ki 15:20
Galilee, and all the land of *; 2Ki 15:29
Joseph, Benjamin, *, Gad, Asher. 1Ch 2:1
Issachar, Asher, *, and Manasseh. 1Ch 6:62
The tribe of * gave them Kedesh 1Ch 6:76
The sons of * (descendants of 1Ch 7:13
From * there were 1,000 officers 1Ch 12:24-37
Zebulun, and * brought food on 1Ch 12:40
Over *, Jeremoth (son of Azriel); 1Ch 27:16-22
all of the supply centers in *. 2Ch 16:4
*, and did the same thing there. 2Ch 34:6
of Zebulun and * are right behind. Ps 68:27
of Zebulun and * will be under Is 9:1
Then comes Manasseh, south of *, Eze 48:4
be named for Gad, Asher and *. Eze 48:34
Galilee, close to Zebulun and *. Mt 4:12,13
and the land of *, beside the Lake, Mt 4:15,16
* 12,000 Rev 7:4-8

NAPHTALI'S
west boundaries. * land lies south Eze 48:3

NAPHTOAH
to the spring of *, and down to Jos 18:15

NAPHTUHIM
Ludim, Anamim, Lehabim, *, Gen 10:13,14
the Lehabim, the *, the Pathrusim, 1Ch 1:11,12

NARCISSUS
Christian slaves over at * House. Rom 16:11

NARD
with the rarest of perfumes; * Sol 4:13,14
from essence of *, and anointed Jn 12:3

NARRATIVES
lee of Cyprus." * from that period Act 27:4f

NARROW
in a place so * that the donkey Num 22:26
Travelers used the *, crooked side Ju 5:6
had to go over a * pass between two 1Sa 14:4
* windows were used throughout. 1Ki 6:4
I try to walk a straight and * Ps 26:11
For a prostitute is a deep and * Pro 23:26,27,28
the blankets are too * to cover Is 28:20
entered only through the * gate! Mt 7:13
is *, and only a few ever find it. Mt 7:14
"The door to heaven is *. Lk 13:24,25

NARROWED
There were windows that * inward Eze 40:16

NARROWER
twenty-one inches * than the base Eze 43:14
Rising from this is a * platform, Eze 43:14
twenty-one inches * on all sides, Eze 43:14
From it a still * platform rises Eze 43:15

NARROWING
to the * of the Temple wall as it Eze 41:7

NASHON
Perez, Hezron, Ram, Amminadab, *, Ru 4:18-22

NATHAN
Shammu-a, Shobab, *, Solomon, 2Sa 5:14,15,16
said to * the prophet, "Look! 2Sa 7:2
have in mind," * replied, "for 2Sa 7:3
But that night the Lord said to * 2Sa 7:4
So * went back to David and told 2Sa 7:17
SO THE LORD sent the prophet * to 2Sa 12:1
Then * said to David, "You are 2Sa 12:7
the Lord," David confessed to *. 2Sa 12:13
Then * replied, "Yes, but the 2Sa 12:13
Then * returned to his home. 2Sa 12:15
sent word by * the prophet." 2Sa 12:25f
and blessings through * the 2Sa 12:25
Igal (son of *) from Zobah; 2Sa 23:24-39
the prophet *, Shime-i, Rei, and 1Ki 1:8
But he didn't invite * the 1Ki 1:10
Then * the prophet went to 1Ki 1:11
aides told him, "* the prophet is 1Ki 1:22,23
* came in and bowed low before the 1Ki 1:22,23
* the prophet, and Benaiah." 1Ki 1:32
the priest and * the prophet are to 1Ki 1:34
So Zadok the priest, * the 1Ki 1:38
the priest and * the prophet and 1Ki 1:44,45
And Zadok and * have anointed him 1Ki 1:44,45
Azariah (son of *) was secretary 1Ki 4:1
Zabud (son of *) was the king's 1Ki 4:1
Attai's son was *; 1Ch 2:36
his sons Shime-a, Shobab, *, and 1Ch 3:5
Joel (brother of *); 1Ch 11:26-47
Shammua, Shobab, *, Solomon, 1Ch 14:4-7
he said to * the prophet, "Look! 1Ch 17:1
And * replied, "Carry out your 1Ch 17:2
But that same night God said to * 1Ch 17:3
So * told King David everything 1Ch 17:15
history written by * the prophet, 1Ch 29:29
in the history of * the prophet and 2Ch 9:29
prophets Gad and *—who had 2Ch 29:25,26
Jarib, Elnathan, *, Zechariah, and Ez 8:16
Shelemiah, *, Adaiah, Machnadebai, Ez 10:34-42
Written after * the prophet had Ps 51:1
Mattatha's father was *; Lk 3:23-38

NATHAN-MELECH
to the quarters of * the eunuch. 2Ki 23:11

NATHAN'S
Attai's son was Nathan; * son was 1Ch 2:36
Mattatha's father was Nathan;* Lk 3:23-38

NATHANAEL
Philip now went off to look for * Jn 1:45
exclaimed *. Jn 1:46
know what I am like?" * demanded. Jn 1:48
* replied, "Sir, you are the Son Jn 1:49
"The Twin," * from Cana in Jn 21:2

NATION
to become the father of a great *; Gen 12:2
But I will punish the * that Gen 15:14
I will make you into a great *. Gen 16:9-12
to make you into a mighty *. Gen 17:2,3,4
*, but a multitude of nations!" Gen 17:2,3,4
to multiply and become a great *. Gen 17:20
become a mighty *, and he will be a Gen 18:18
he became the ancestor of the * Gen 19:37
he became the ancestor of the * Gen 19:38
And I will make a * of the Gen 21:13
a great * from his descendants." Gen 21:18
become a great *—because of my Gen 26:24
may you become a great * of many Gen 28:2
a great *, yes, many nations; Gen 35:11
so that you will become a great *. Gen 45:7
*, ruler of all the land of Egypt. Gen 45:8
that you become a great * there. Gen 46:3,4
make you a great * and I will give Gen 48:4
and may they become a mighty *." Gen 48:16
become a great *, but his younger Gen 48:19
became a large *, and they filled Ex 1:7
multiply and to become a mighty *. Ex 1:20
did, and frogs covered the *. Ex 8:6
the entire *, covering the Ex 8:17
across the * such as there has Ex 9:18
cover the entire * with a thick Ex 10:4,5
of priests to God, a holy *.' Ex 19:6
into a great * instead of them." Ex 32:10
For don't forget that this * is Ex 33:13
"If the entire * of Israel sins Lev 4:13
of the * shall lay their hands Lev 4:15
*, and everyone will be forgiven. Lev 4:20
a sin offering for the entire *. Lev 4:21
be excommunicated from his *. Lev 17:3,4
are born in the * of Israel and to Lev 18:26
be excommunicated from this *. Lev 18:29,30
a permanent law throughout your *. Lev 23:14
firstborn cattle of the whole *." Num 3:41
gift from the entire * of Israel. Num 8:11
I can't carry this * by myself! Num 11:14
make you into a * far greater and Num 14:12
up the entire * against Moses and Num 16:19
From every other *. Num 23:7-10
only a portion of the * of Israel. Num 23:13
(The entire * was camped in the Num 26:3,4
day, as a warning to the entire *. Num 26:5-11
disaster to this entire *!" Num 32:15
THIS IS THE itinerary of the * of Num 33:1
be in various parts of the *; Num 35:8
'What other * is as wise and Deu 4:6
For what other *, great or Deu 4:7
And what *, no matter how great, Deu 4:8
this: An entire * heard the voice Deu 4:33
God's removing a * from its slavery Deu 4:34
become a great * in a glorious land Deu 6:3
you were a larger * than any other, Deu 7:7
you and make you into a great *. Deu 7:13
will make a mighty * of you, Deu 9:13,14
other *, as is evident today. Deu 10:15
make you a great * just as he Deu 13:17
other * on the face of the earth. Deu 14:2
in Egypt they became a mighty *. Deu 26:5
than any other *, allowing you to Deu 26:19
into the greatest * in the world. Deu 28:1
A foreign * you have not even Deu 28:33
will choose, to a * to whom neither Deu 28:36
"The Lord will bring a distant * Deu 28:49
like an eagle; a * whose language Deu 28:49
understand— a * of fierce and Deu 28:50
That * will lay siege to your Deu 28:52
and become a great *, and so that Deu 30:16
Israel is a stupid *; Deu 32:28
That day the entire * crossed the Jos 4:19
miracle—that the * of Israel Jos 4:22
For the * of Israel had traveled Jos 5:6
After the ceremony the entire * Jos 5:8,9
fall upon the entire * of Israel. Jos 6:18
* of Israel because of this. Jos 7:1
and declare our * to be their Jos 9:11
from before the * of Israel, so Jos 13:2-7
and the * of Israel gave a Jos 19:49
Lord, the entire * was punished in Jos 22:20
AFTER JOSHUA DIED, the * of Israel Ju 1:1
So now when the * of Israel went Ju 2:15
of the Philistine * went personally Ju 16:5
"The scourge of our * who killed Ju 16:23,24
Then the entire * was roused to Ju 19:30
THEN THE ENTIRE * of Israel sent Ju 20:1
So the whole * united in this Ju 20:11
all the * of Israel descended! Ru 4:11
He made you a special * for 1Sa 12:22
accounts with the * of Amalek for 1Sa 15:2
the entire Amalek *—men, women, 1Sa 15:3
Thus the whole *, both Judah and 2Sa 3:37
What other * in all the earth 2Sa 7:23
your chosen * in order to bring 2Sa 7:23
so that the entire * was forced to 2Sa 8:14
The leaders of the * pleaded 2Sa 12:17
on all across the *: "Why aren't 2Sa 19:8,9,10
was left of the * of the Amorites. 2Sa 21:2
one end of the * to the other, so 2Sa 24:2
men died throughout the *. 2Sa 24:15
chosen people, a * so great that 1Ki 3:8
the entire *, and all the people 1Ki 3:28
contented * at this time. 1Ki 4:20
the great * of Israel," he said. 1Ki 5:7
has searched every * and kingdom on 1Ki 18:10
the king of that * to swear to the 1Ki 18:10
AFTER KING AHAB'S death the * of 2Ki 1:1
This disaster came upon the * of 2Ki 17:7
told us, 'Go and destroy this *!' 2Ki 18:25
able to save any * from my power? 2Ki 18:35
shall become a great * again; 2Ki 19:30
The death of this * will not 2Ki 22:20
chosen by the * as its new king. 2Ki 23:30
to destroy the *, just as the Lord 2Ki 24:2
was such a troublemaker for his *. 1Ch 2:7
throughout the * and celebrated the 1Ch 10:9
of Israel from all across the * 1Ch 13:5
"And what other * in all the 1Ch 17:21
You have made a unique * and have 1Ch 17:21
children will always rule this *. 1Ch 17:23
leaders of the * such as the 1Ch 26:26
entire * are at your command." 1Ch 28:21
me king over a * as full of people 2Ch 1:9
a great * as this one of yours?" 2Ch 1:10
to some foreign * near or far, and 2Ch 6:36
to be a great, strong * forever." 2Ch 9:8
Kings from every * came to visit 2Ch 9:23
every part of the * (they had fled 2Ch 12:5
that the entire * obey the 2Ch 14:4
Problems troubled the * on every 2Ch 15:5
gave them peace throughout the *. 2Ch 15:15
fortified cities throughout the *. 2Ch 17:19
throughout the * in all the larger 2Ch 19:5
People from all across the * 2Ch 20:4
your * with a great plague. 2Ch 21:14
out across the * secretly, to tell 2Ch 23:2,3
the leaders of the * and sending 2Ch 24:23
for the * and for the Temple. 2Ch 29:21

(NATION Con't)
be sacrificed for the entire *. 2Ch 29:24
every part of the * brought their 2Ch 29:31
But in Judah the entire * felt a 2Ch 30:12
failed to conquer a * we attacked? 2Ch 32:13
I say it again—no god of any * 2Ch 32:15
All the important people of the * 2Ch 36:14
any king and any * that alters this Ez 6:12
They, with the entire *, ate the Ez 6:21,22
oxen for the * of Israel; Ez 8:35
a prosperous * and forever leave Ez 9:12
entire *—for the common people; Neh 10:28
those of any other *, and they Est 3:8
He raises up a * and then Job 12:23
thus saving a * from ruin, and he Job 34:29,30
depose an entire * just as easily. Job 34:29,30
the people of every * shall Ps 22:27
Blessed is the * whose God is the Ps 33:12
I will be honored by every * in Ps 46:10
You have caused this * to Ps 60:2
O Jehovah, an arrogant * has Ps 74:18
out Israel as a *—we will destroy Ps 83:4
"They were a * whose thoughts Ps 95:10
every * sees his glory. Ps 97:6
it to every * by fulfilling his Ps 98:2,3
a greater * than their rulers. Ps 105:24
flashes overwhelmed the *. Ps 105:32
and before the leaders of the *. Ps 107:32
around the world, in every *. Ps 108:3
May our * shout for joy. Ps 132:9
He sends peace across your *, Ps 147:14
he has not done with any other *; Ps 147:20
Without wise leadership, a * is Pro 11:14
a dwindling * is his doom. Pro 14:28
Godliness exalts a *, but sin is Pro 14:34
*, its government topples easily; Pro 28:2
stability to his *, but one who Pro 29:4
for a * to know and keep his laws! Pro 29:18
Oh, what a sinful * they are! Is 1:4
you and on your * and your family. Is 7:17
the whole * will be a pastureland; Is 7:21,22
this godless *, doomed and damned; Is 10:5,6
your * and slain your people. Is 14:20
All your * is doomed. Is 14:31
strong and supple * feared far and Is 18:2
* whose land the upper Nile Is 18:2
strong and mighty *, a terror to Is 18:7
destroying * whose land the rivers Is 18:7
one—you who disgrace your *! Is 22:18
He has made our * very great. Is 26:15
They are a foolish *, a witless, Is 27:11
glory of a * of men lying drunk in Is 28:1
blessed him, he became a great *. Is 51:1
If any * comes to fight you, it Is 54:15
tiny group shall be a mighty *. Is 60:22
* that never called you "Lord"? Is 63:19
For in one day, suddenly, a *, Is 66:7,8
the baby is born; the * begins. Is 66:7,8
from every * as a gift to the Lord, Is 66:20
can find another * anywhere that Jer 2:10,11
Why has Israel become a * of Jer 2:14
my vengeance on such a * as this? Jer 5:9
See, I will bring a distant * Jer 5:15
the Lord—a mighty *, an ancient Jer 5:15
* whose language you don't Jer 5:15
Shouldn't I punish a * such as Jer 5:29
north, coming to destroy this *! Jer 6:1
great * is rising against you. Jer 6:22
Say to them: This is the * that Jer 7:28
And those of this evil * who are Jer 8:3
be avenged on such a * as this?" Jer 9:9
all, and Israel is his chosen *. Jer 10:16
one end of the * to the other; Jer 12:12
But any * refusing to obey me Jer 12:17
This evil * refuses to listen to Jer 13:10
the people of this *, and all you Jer 17:20
this * shall continue forever. Jer 17:25
that a certain * or kingdom is to Jer 18:7
then if that * renounces its evil Jer 18:8
make a certain * strong and great, Jer 18:9
but then that * changes its mind Jer 18:10
that * as I had said I would. Jer 18:10
will deliver this * and once more Jer 22:4
repulsive to every * of the earth, Jer 24:9
it—every * God had sent me to; Jer 25:17
shall go from * to nation—a great Jer 25:32
go from nation to *—a great Jer 25:32
word in every * of the earth. Jer 26:6
the city and the * at the same time Jer 26:20
I will punish any * refusing to Jer 27:8
that * until he has conquered it. Jer 27:8
But the people of any * Jer 27:11
promised to every * that will not Jer 27:13
And in every * where I place them Jer 29:18
of them a great and honored *. Jer 30:19
I will rebuild your *, O virgin Jer 31:4
destroyed the * but now I will Jer 31:28
isn't worthy to be counted as a *. Jer 33:24
will destroy this * that I built; Jer 45:4
will cut her off from being a *." Jer 48:2,3,4
Moab shall no longer be a *, for Jer 48:42
For a * shall come down upon her Jer 50:3
there is, and Israel is his *; Jer 51:19
look in vain. The * we expected Lam 4:17
our own against any * on earth! Lam 4:20
Our homes, our *, now are filled Lam 5:2
sending you to the * of Israel, to Eze 2:3
to a * rebelling against me. Eze 2:3
an entire * in furious rebuke. Eze 5:15
leading the whole * into idolatry, Eze 8:17
the sins of this * from the times Eze 20:4
Temple, the strength of your *. Eze 24:20,21
I will cut you off from being a * Eze 25:7
off than any other *, therefore I Eze 25:8
the glory of the *—Beth-jeshimoth, Eze 25:9,10
great and mighty *—like a cedar of Eze 31:2,3
hands of a mighty *, to destroy her Eze 31:11
let no other * exult with pride Eze 31:14
What * is as beautiful as you, O Eze 32:19
* of sinners, the Lord God says." Eze 36:15
land, to unify them into one *. Eze 37:22
his *, language, or religion Dan 3:7
of any *, language, or religion Dan 3:29
language in every * of the world: Dan 4:1
Then every * under heaven, and Dan 7:27
the shaggy-haired goat is the * Dan 8:21
guard over your *, will stand up Dan 12:1
the * in the Valley of Jezreel." Hos 1:4,5
prosper and become a great *; Hos 1:10
years later and the * disappeared. Hos 4:19f
Yes, so they mock, for the * is Hos 9:7
great armies can make a * safe! Hos 10:13
Literally, "a *." Joe 1:6f
going to happen to his *, Israel. Amo 1:2
against you a * that will bitterly Amo 6:14
our * and is plotting your death. Amo 7:10
that sinful *, and I will root her Amo 9:8
A * southeast of Israel, including Ob 1:1f
own land, a mighty *, and the Lord Mic 4:7
Then the * of Israel will refresh Mic 5:7
a cruel and violent * who will Hab 1:6
you shameless *, while there still Zep 2:1
decreed mercy to Joshua and his *; Zec 3:2
*—and they hated me too. Zec 11:8
I will give this * a shepherd who Zec 11:16
The whole * will be bowed down Zec 12:12,13,14
Two-thirds of all the * of Zec 13:8
And any * anywhere in all the Zec 14:17
your whole * has been robbing me. Mal 3:9
"What shall I say about this *? Mt 11:16
* would ask for further proof; Mt 12:39,40
* at the judgment and condemn you. Mt 12:41
* in the judgment, and condemn it; Mt 12:42
"This evil * is like a man Mt 12:43,44,45
This evil, unbelieving * is Mt 16:4
and given to a * that will give God Mt 21:43
known in every * before the Mk 13:10
should be taken throughout the *. Lk 2:1
and condemn this *, for they Lk 11:32
is here [but this * won't listen Lk 11:32
and be rejected by this whole *. Lk 17:25
immediately— for * shall rise Lk 21:10
shall rise against * and kingdom Lk 21:10
will be great distress upon this * Lk 21:23
religious authorities of the *. Lk 22:66
him out to the * of Israel." Jn 1:31
If we let him alone the whole * Jn 11:48
should the whole * perish?" Jn 11:50
die for the entire * came from Jn 11:51
restore us as an independent *?" Act 1:6
from the evils of their *. Act 2:40
and elders of our *, if you mean Act 4:8
'But I will punish the * that Act 7:7
twelve patriarchs of the Jewish *. Act 7:8
In every * he has those who Act 10:35
"The God of this * Israel chose Act 13:17
Literally, "my own *." Act 26:4f
the founder of our Jewish *. Rom 4:1
* who trust God as Abraham did. Rom 4:17
and become a great *, Abraham Rom 4:18
* who trust in me as you do." Gal 3:8,9
brothers throughout your whole *. 1Th 4:10
the father of a great * of people. Heb 6:14
And so a whole * came from Heb 11:12
even one child—a * with so many Heb 11:12
Abraham a whole * of descendants! Heb 11:18
Lord saved a whole * of people out Jud 1:5
from every * as gifts for God. Rev 5:9
*, tribe, language and people. Rev 14:6
of people of every race and *. Rev 17:15

NATION-WIDE
of administering a * farm program. Gen 41:33

NATION'S
and filled the * homes. Ex 8:13
and turned the * water into blood, Ps 105:29
Have any other * gods ever gained Is 36:18

NATIONAL
of * mourning of seventy days. Gen 50:3
to harm them by taking a * census. 2Sa 24:1
obeyed him. The * leaders, the 1Ch 29:24
of their * fasting and prayer. Est 9:29-31

NATIONALISTIC
but Saul, in his * zeal, had 2Sa 21:2

NATIONALITIES
And many * will come and join Is 14:1

NATIONALITY
What is your *?" Jon 1:8
In this new life one's * or race Col 3:11

NATIONS
Noah came all the * of the earth. Gen 9:19
the maritime * in various lands, Gen 10:5
from Canaan descended these * Gen 10:15-19
lands and *, with many languages. Gen 10:20
* that developed after the flood. Gen 10:32
Or, "The * will bless themselves Gen 12:3f
of the Amorite * living here now Gen 15:16
And I give to them these *: Gen 15:19,20,21
nation, but a multitude of *!" Gen 17:2,3,4
*")—for that is what you will be. Gen 17:5
descendants who will form many *! Gen 17:6
and make her the mother of *! Gen 17:16
for all the * of the earth. Gen 18:18
to all the * of the earth—all Gen 22:18
womb shall become two rival *. Gen 25:23
to all the * of the earth. Gen 26:4
May many * be your slaves. Gen 27:27,28,29
and all the * of the earth will Gen 28:14
a great nation, yes, many *; Gen 35:11
The * heard what happened, and Ex 15:14
from among all the * of the earth; Ex 19:5
of these other *, nor sacrifice to Ex 23:24
For I will drive out the * from Ex 34:24
the * that live there now Lev 18:28
the customs of the * I cast out Lev 20:23
you and the people of other *. Lev 20:24
from the foreign * living around Lev 25:44
you out among the *, destroying you Lev 26:33
You shall perish among the * and Lev 26:38
as all the * watched in wonder. Lev 26:45
your people, the * that have heard Num 14:15
And shall eat up the * that oppose Num 24:3-9
"Amalek was the first of the *, Num 24:20
Don't be afraid of the * there, Deu 3:22
When the surrounding * hear these Deu 4:6
The Lord may permit other * to Deu 4:19
you among the *, and you will be Deu 4:27
He drove away other * greater by Deu 4:38
of the neighboring *, for Jehovah Deu 6:14
following seven *, all greater and Deu 7:1
above all the * of the earth; Deu 7:14
"You must destroy all the * Deu 7:16
ever conquer these * that are so Deu 7:17
"No, do not be afraid of those * Deu 7:21
against those * and destroy them. Deu 7:23
other * in the past to perish. Deu 8:20
the * on the other side. Deu 9:1
Those * are much greater and more Deu 9:1
the other * that he is doing it. Deu 9:4
of the other *, and because of his Deu 9:5
drive out all the * in your land, Deu 11:23
worship the gods of these other *. Deu 11:28
When he destroys the * in the Deu 12:29
Do not ask, 'How do these * Deu 12:30
These * have done horrible things Deu 12:31
other *,' don't listen to him. Deu 13:2
You shall lend money to many * Deu 15:6
You shall rule many *, but they Deu 15:6
like the other * around us'— be Deu 17:14
customs of the * now living there. Deu 18:9
it is because the * do these things Deu 18:12
your God. The * you replace all do Deu 18:14
has destroyed the * you will Deu 19:1
not of the cities of these *." Deu 20:15f
law is that these * did not welcome Deu 23:4
All the * in the world shall see Deu 28:10
and you shall lend to many *, but Deu 28:12
fro among all the * of the earth. Deu 28:25
among all the *, for the Lord will Deu 28:37
you among all the * from one end of Deu 28:64
There among those * you shall Deu 28:65
through the territory of enemy *. Deu 29:16
gods of other *, that day a root Deu 29:18
this to his land?' the * will ask. Deu 29:24
living among the * where the Lord Deu 30:1
you out of all the * where he will Deu 30:3
will destroy the * living there, Deu 31:3
The Lord will destroy the * Deu 31:4
divided up the world among the *, Deu 32:8
To the foolish Gentile * of the Deu 32:21
But the rock of other * Deu 32:31
O Gentile *, Deu 32:40,41
To push against the * everywhere; Deu 33:17
He did this so that all the * of Jos 4:24
WHEN THE * west of the Jordan Jos 5:1
the other nearby * hear about it, Jos 7:9
These were the kings of the * Jos 9:1
whole country—the * and kings of Jos 10:40
are still many * to be conquered. Jos 13:1
the land of the * yet unconquered Jos 23:4,5
out great, strong * from before Jos 23:9
with the * around you, then know Jos 23:12
chase those * from your land. Jos 23:13
other * living here in the land. Jos 24:18
destroy the * living in your land; Ju 2:3

NATIONS Con't)

the idols of the neighboring *.	Ju 2:12-14
evil customs of the * around them.	Ju 2:19
drive out the * left unconquered by	Ju 2:21
Instead, I will use these * to	Ju 2:22
So the Lord left those * in the	Ju 2:23
HERE IS A list of the * the Lord	Ju 3:1
other neighboring * came and	Ju 6:3,4
other neighboring * united in one	Ju 6:33
and the other * of the East were	Ju 7:12,13
the other * have," they pleaded.	1Sa 8:5
want to be like the * around us.	1Sa 8:20
of the * that were torturing you.	1Sa 10:18,19
Lest the heathen * laugh in	2Sa 1:20
the surrounding *, David said to	2Sa 7:1
where the heathen * won't bother	2Sa 7:10,11
If he sins, I will use other * to	2Sa 7:14
As the head of the *.	2Sa 22:44
to you, O Lord, among the *,	2Sa 22:50
among all the surrounding *.	1Ki 4:31
And all the * of the earth will	1Ki 8:43
from among all the * of the earth	1Ki 8:53
a joke to the * and an example and	1Ki 9:7
survived in the * he conquered—the	1Ki 9:20,21
Many of them came from * where	1Ki 11:1
marry into those *, because the	1Ki 11:2
as the heathen * which the Lord	1Ki 14:24
thirty-two allied * and their	1Ki 20:1
customs of the * around	2Ki 16:3
around Judah—* which the Lord	2Ki 16:3
customs of the * which the Lord had	2Ki 17:8
gods of the very * which the Lord	2Ki 17:11
of the * from which they came.	2Ki 17:33
gods of the other * ever delivered	2Ki 18:33
Have the gods of the other *	2Ki 19:12
them—such * as Gozan, Haran,	2Ki 19:12
all those *, and have burned their	2Ki 19:17
So of course the * you conquered	2Ki 19:26
He did the same things the * had	2Ki 21:1
the surrounding * had done, even	2Ki 21:9
destroyed those * for their evil	2Ki 21:9
Lord caused all the * to fear him.	1Ch 14:17
Show his glory to the *!	1Ch 16:24
O people of all * of the earth,	1Ch 16:28
Let all the * say, 'It is the Lord	1Ch 16:31
us safely back from among the *.	1Ch 16:35
the wicked * won't conquer them	1Ch 17:9
out the * from before your people.	1Ch 17:21
he took from the * of Edom, Moab,	1Ch 18:11
the surrounding *, for I have	1Ch 22:18
and to the kings of the nearby *.	1Ch 29:30
of those * which the Israelis had	2Ch 8:7,8
invade those * when Israel left	2Ch 20:10
like the heathen * that were thrown	2Ch 28:3
The gods of those * weren't able	2Ch 32:13
"The gods of all the other *	2Ch 32:17
the surrounding *, and many gifts	2Ch 32:23
of the heathen * destroyed by the	2Ch 33:2
more evil than the * the Lord	2Ch 33:9
of the surrounding *, thus	2Ch 36:14
and men from several other *.	Ez 4:10
from these heathen *, and had taken	Ez 9:2
not to help those * in any way.	Ez 9:12
I will scatter you among the *;	Neh 1:8
enemies among the * around us who	Neh 5:9
the surrounding * heard about it,	Neh 6:16
kingdoms and many *, and you placed	Neh 9:22
You subdued whole * before	Neh 9:24
the heathen * to conquer them.	Neh 9:30
THE * are to rage against the	Ps 2:1
For a summit conference of the *	Ps 2:2
give you all the * of the world.	Ps 2:8
You have rebuked the * and	Ps 9:5
judge justly the * of the world.	Ps 9:7,8
The * fall into the pitfalls they	Ps 9:15
this is the fate of all the *	Ps 9:17
arise and judge and punish the *;	Ps 9:19
put the * in their place until at	Ps 9:20
battle. The * came and served me.	Ps 18:43,44,45
me and subdues the * before me.	Ps 18:47
I will praise you among the *.	Ps 18:49
Some * boast of armies and of	Ps 20:7
Those * will collapse and	Ps 20:8
the Lord is King and rules the *.	Ps 22:28
plans of all the * who oppose him,	Ps 33:10
drove the heathen * from this land	Ps 44:1
pen, and scattered us among the *.	Ps 44:11
The neighboring * laugh and mock	Ps 44:13
among the *, disliked by all.	Ps 44:14
generations; the * of the earth	Ps 45:17
his help. The * rant and rave in	Ps 46:6
He subdues the * before us, and	Ps 47:3
He reigns above the *, sitting	Ps 47:8
sing your praises among the *.	Ps 57:9
the heathen * surrounding us.	Ps 59:5
(And scoff at these surrounding *	Ps 59:8
(And let the * find out too that	Ps 59:12,13
watches every movement of the *.	Ps 66:7
How glad the * will be, singing	Ps 67:4
Literally, "govern the *."	Ps 67:4f
tribute of smaller *, and who	Ps 68:30f
in him; all * will praise him.	Ps 72:17
He drove out the * occupying the	Ps 78:55
been conquered by the heathen *.	Ps 79:1
them. The * all around us scoff.	Ps 79:4
upon the godless *, not on us!	Ps 79:6
Why should the heathen * be	Ps 79:10
vengeance on these * scorning you.	Ps 79:12
us the scorn of the neighboring *.	Ps 80:6
to you. All * are in your hands.	Ps 82:8
All the *—and you made each	Ps 86:9
He punishes the *—won't he also	Ps 94:10
For the gods of other * are	Ps 96:5
O * of the world, confess that	Ps 96:7
Tell the * that Jehovah reigns!	Ps 96:10
He will judge all * fairly.	Ps 96:10
he will judge the * fairly and	Ps 96:13
Let the * tremble!	Ps 99:1
Now let the * and their rulers	Ps 102:15
proclaim them to the *.	Ps 105:1
among the *, and were driven from	Ps 105:13
Nor did Israel destroy the * in	Ps 106:34
That is why he let the heathen *	Ps 106:41,42
Regather us from the * so we can	Ps 106:47
He will punish the *, and fill	Ps 110:6
the home of many * living there.	Ps 111:6
For he is high above the *;	Ps 113:4
Why let the * say, "Their God	Ps 115:2
PRAISE THE LORD, all * everywhere.	Ps 117:1
Though all the * of the world	Ps 118:10
And the other * said, "What	Ps 126:2
He smote great *, slaying mighty	Ps 135:10
execute his punishment upon the *.	Ps 149:6,7
cursed by many people of many *;	Pro 24:24
from even the leaders of the *.	Pro 31:31
all the * will convert their	Is 2:4
He will send a signal to the *	Is 5:26
peace to all the * of the world.	Is 9:7
all the world. The * will rally to	Is 11:10
He will raise a flag among the *	Is 11:12
fly against the * possessing their	Is 11:14
the * of Edom and Moab and Ammon.	Is 11:14
his doings among the *."	Is 12:4f
tumult and the shout of many *.	Is 13:4
loyal allies. The * of the world	Is 14:2
and held the * in your angry grip.	Is 14:6
were against the * of the world.	Is 14:12
The kings of the * lie in stately	Is 14:18
all the * she enslaved will end.	Is 21:2
Or possibly, "throughout the * of	Is 24:13f
proud rulers of the * on earth.	Is 24:21
Therefore strong * will shake	Is 25:3
ruthless * will obey and glorify	Is 25:3
will cool the pride of ruthless *.	Is 25:5
And all the * fighting Jerusalem	Is 29:7
He will sift out the proud * and	Is 30:28
When you stand up, the * flee.	Is 33:3
Listen to what I have done, O *	Is 33:13
COME HERE AND listen, O * of the	Is 34:1
the Lord is enraged against the *;	Is 34:2
all those *, just as the letter	Is 37:18
army against the * of the west.	Is 37:24
All the * are as nothing to him;	Is 40:17
victory over many * and permitted	Is 41:2
he will come against the * and	Is 41:25
he will reveal justice to the *	Is 42:1
be a light to guide the * unto me.	Is 42:6
Gather the * together!	Is 43:9
Gather together and come, you *	Is 45:20
I will make you a Light to the *	Is 49:6
I will rule the *;	Is 51:5
arm before the eyes of all the *;	Is 52:10
far-off foreign * and their kings;	Is 52:14,15
Or, "So shall he startle many *	Is 52:14,15f
many *.	Is 52:14,15
rule the * that took their lands.	Is 54:3
my power by conquering foreign *.	Is 55:4
You also will command the * and	Is 55:5
light shine for all the * to see!	Is 60:1
All * will come to your light;	Is 60:3
For the * refusing to be your	Is 60:12
Powerful kings and mighty *	Is 60:16
* and shall glory in their riches.	Is 61:6
be known and honored among the *;	Is 61:9
The Lord will show the * of the	Is 61:11
* shall see your righteousness.	Is 62:2
I crushed the heathen * in my	Is 63:6
The * would tremble before you;	Is 64:2
Israelites rather than to the *.	Is 65:1f
about me are now seeking me out. *	Is 65:1
Israelites rather than to the *.	Is 65:1f
together all * and people against	Is 66:18
the armies of the *, or survivors	Is 66:19f
to the *—to Tarshish, Put, Lud,	Is 66:19
* and the kingdoms of the world.	Jer 1:10
the Lord, and all * will come to	Jer 3:17
a testimony to the * of the world	Jer 4:2
A lion—a destroyer of *—stalks	Jer 4:7
Warn the other * that the enemy	Jer 4:16
For all these pagan * also	Jer 9:25,26
would not fear you, O King of *?	Jer 10:7
Pour out your fury on the * who	Jer 10:25
this to the evil *, the nations	Jer 12:14
evil nations, the * surrounding the	Jer 12:14
And if these heathen * quickly	Jer 12:16
day of trouble, * from around the	Jer 16:19
Men from many * will pass by the	Jer 22:8
against the other * near you, and I	Jer 25:8,9
by Jeremiah against the *.	Jer 25:13
For many * and great kings shall	Jer 25:14
and make all the * to whom I send	Jer 25:15
and made all the * drink from	Jer 25:17
the * of Edom, Moab and Ammon;	Jer 25:21
against all the *—all mankind.	Jer 25:31
All the * shall serve him and	Jer 27:7
up, and then many * and great kings	Jer 27:7
spoke against many *, always	Jer 28:8
release all the * now in slavery to	Jer 28:11
necks of all these *, forcing them	Jer 28:14
you out of the * where I sent you	Jer 29:14
Even if I utterly destroy the *	Jer 30:11
their * shall be established	Jer 30:20
for Israel, the greatest of the *!	Jer 31:7
from the Lord, you * of the world,	Jer 31:10
me before all the * of the earth!	Jer 33:9
Israel, Judah and the other *.	Jer 36:2
of all the * of the earth.	Jer 44:8
to Jeremiah concerning foreign *.	Jer 46:1
The * have heard of your shame.	Jer 46:12
I will destroy all the * to which	Jer 46:28
to call the * to form a coalition	Jer 49:14
I will make her weak among the *	Jer 49:15
an army of great * from the north	Jer 50:9
the least of the *—a wilderness, a	Jer 50:12
Babylon, all you * round about;	Jer 50:14
Babylon is desolate among the *!	Jer 50:23
the Lord, to break * in pieces and	Jer 51:20
Signal many * to mobilize for war	Jer 51:27
he has taken. The * shall no longer	Jer 51:44
She, once queen of *, is now a	Lam 1:1
She has seen foreign * violate	Lam 1:10
as refuse and garbage among the *.	Lam 3:45
than the * surrounding her."	Eze 5:5,6,7
publicly while all the * watch.	Eze 5:8
the surrounding * and before	Eze 5:14
among the * of the world.	Eze 6:8
exiled among the *, they will	Eze 6:9
the worst of the * to occupy your	Eze 7:24
copied the * all around you."	Eze 11:12
you back from the * where you are	Eze 11:17
them among the *, then they shall	Eze 12:15
to confess to the * how wicked they	Eze 12:16
The Amorites and Hittites were *	Eze 16:3f
great among the * for your beauty;	Eze 16:14
lovers—these many *—to destroy, and	Eze 16:39
Then the * called out their	Eze 19:4
* and ruined their cities;	Eze 19:7
Then the armies of the *	Eze 19:8
my name, lest the * who saw me	Eze 20:14
my name among the * who had seen	Eze 20:22
be like the * all around you,	Eze 20:32
exile, and the * will see the great	Eze 20:41
to all the * of the world.	Eze 22:4
among the *, and you shall know I	Eze 22:16
those very * from which you turned	Eze 23:22
the gods of other *, defiling	Eze 23:30
you to many * for devastation.	Eze 25:7
no longer be counted among the *.	Eze 25:9,10
* against you like ocean waves.	Eze 26:3
the prey of many *, and her	Eze 26:5
satisfied the desires of many *.	Eze 27:33
The merchants of the * shake	Eze 27:36
the terror of the *, shall suddenly	Eze 28:7
other neighbor * prick and tear at	Eze 28:24
I will show the * of the world my	Eze 28:25
When I punish all the bordering *	Eze 28:26
by desolate *, and her cities will	Eze 29:12
* to which they will be banished.	Eze 29:13
will be the lowliest of all the *;	Eze 29:15
raise herself above the other *;	Eze 29:15
a day of despair for the *!	Eze 30:2,3
by desolate *, and her cities shall	Eze 30:7
*—are sent to demolish the land.	Eze 30:11
scatter the Egyptians among the *;	Eze 30:26
All the great * of the world	Eze 31:6
terror of the *—will invade her	Eze 31:12
I made the * shake with fear at	Eze 31:16
nether world—those * that had lived	Eze 31:17
trees of Eden—the * of the world.	Eze 31:18
of hell with all these other *.	Eze 31:18
You will be among the * you	Eze 31:18
*, but you are merely a crocodile	Eze 32:2
I carry you captive among the *."	Eze 32:9f
the distant * you have never seen.	Eze 32:9
mighty army—the terror of the *.	Eze 32:12
Let all the * weep for her and	Eze 32:16
Egypt and for the other mighty *.	Eze 32:18
there beside the * she despised,	Eze 32:21
They scourged the * while they	Eze 32:24
Yes, they terrorized the * while	Eze 32:25
the people and * where they were,	Eze 34:13
No more will other * conquer	Eze 34:28
mocked by heathen * all around: My	Eze 36:4

(NATIONS Con't)
against these *, especially Edom, Eze 36:5
shame before the surrounding *. Eze 36:6
high, that those * are going to Eze 36:7
Now the other * taunt you, saying, Eze 36:13
No longer will those heathen * Eze 36:15
out among the *, then they were a Eze 36:20
name because the * said, 'These are Eze 36:20
which you tarnished among the *. Eze 36:22
the surrounding * be able to scoff Eze 36:30
Then the * all around—all those Eze 36:36
from among the *, and bringing them Eze 37:21
shall they be divided into two *. Eze 37:22
them, then the * shall know that I, Eze 37:28
be, the leader of one of these *. Eze 38:2,3f
from all the *—and I will capture Eze 38:12
all the * will know that I am God. Eze 38:15,16
name, and all the * of the world Eze 38:23
And the * too shall know I am the Eze 39:7
demonstrate my glory among the *; Eze 39:21
And the * will know why Israel Eze 39:23
evident to all the * when I do it. Eze 39:27
my holiness before the *. Eze 39:27
of them remaining among the *. Eze 39:28
"O people of all * and languages, Dan 3:4
that all the * of the world Dan 5:19
glory over all the * of the world, Dan 7:14
*, not even ruled by his sons. Dan 11:4
lost, and other * will join him in Dan 11:14
the governments of many *. Dan 11:41
she lies among the * as a broken Hos 8:8
Jews, homeless among the *. Hos 9:17
I will gather the armies of the * Hos 10:10
Israel spoke, the * shook with Hos 13:1
you a laughingstock among the *. Joe 2:19
the * and dividing up my land. Joe 3:2
Gather together and come, all * Joe 3:11
Collect the *; Joe 3:12
killed innocent people in those *. Joe 3:19
by the other * as grain is sifted Amo 9:9
of all the * that belong to me." Amo 9:12
* with this message: 'Attention! Ob 1:1
to size among the *, Edom, making Ob 1:2
will soon fall upon all Gentile *. Ob 1:15
* round about will drink it, too; Ob 1:16
history, no longer * any more. Ob 1:16
of the world, praised by all *; Mic 4:1
He will arbitrate among the *, Mic 4:3
and dictate to strong * far away. Mic 4:3
pruning-hooks; * shall no longer Mic 4:3
all the * around us worship idols! Mic 4:5
True, many * have gathered Mic 4:11
as a lion. The * will be like Mic 5:8
upon the * who refuse to obey me. Mic 5:15
lion of the *, full of fight and Nah 2:11
back slaves from conquered *; Nah 2:13
enticed the * with her beauty, then Nah 3:4
Literally, "who betrays * with Nah 3:4f
collected many *, but like death Hab 2:5
You have ruined many *; Hab 2:8
that godless *' gains will turn to Hab 2:13
Then he shakes the *, scattering Hab 3:6
trampled down the * in your wrath. Hab 3:12
"I have cut off many *, laying Zep 3:6
stand up and accuse these evil *. Zep 3:8
*, and the Desire of All Nations Hag 2:7
nations, and the Desire of All * Hag 2:7
treasures of the * will pour into Hag 2:7f
strength of the kingdoms of the *. Hag 2:22
with the heathen * sitting around Zec 1:15
my people, but the * afflicted them Zec 1:15
against the * that oppressed you, Zec 2:8
'At that time many * will be Zec 2:11,12
a whirlwind among the far-off *. Zec 7:14
Yes, many people, even strong * Zec 8:22
from ten different * will clutch at Zec 8:23
he shall bring peace among the *. Zec 9:10
seeds among the *, still they will Zec 10:9
to all the nearby * that send their Zec 12:2
And though all the * of the earth Zec 12:3
the neighboring * right and left, Zec 12:6
the * that come against Jerusalem. Zec 12:9
together the * to fight Jerusalem; Zec 14:1
for war, to fight against those *. Zec 14:3
the neighboring * will be Zec 14:14
And so Egypt and the other * Zec 14:19
the *," says the Lord of Hosts. Mal 1:11
"And all * will call you Mal 3:12
and showed him the * of the world Mt 4:8
And he will judge the *. Mt 12:18
is not yet. The * and kingdoms of Mt 24:7
world, so that all * will hear it, Mt 24:14
And the * of the world will see Mt 24:30
And all the * shall be gathered Mt 25:32
Or, "separate the *." Mt 25:32f
all the *, baptizing them into Mt 28:19
of prayer for all *,' but you have Mk 11:17
"For * and kingdoms will Mk 13:8
shine upon the *, and he will be Lk 2:32
to all the * of the world; Lk 21:24
and down here on earth the * will Lk 21:25
to all the *: There is forgiveness Lk 24:47
having arrived from many *. Act 2:5
and the foolish * plan their little Act 4:25,26
the Gentile *, this Tabernacle was Act 7:45
my message to the * and before Act 9:15
Then he destroyed seven * in Act 13:19,20
he permitted the * to go their own Act 14:16
and scattered the * across the Act 17:26
made Abraham the father of many *. Rom 4:17
to the foolish heathen *. Rom 10:19
preached among the *, was accepted 1Ti 3:16
And the * will weep in sorrow and Rev 1:7
me—I will give power over the *. Rev 2:26
to count, from all * and provinces Rev 7:9
peoples, *, tribes, and kings." Rev 10:11
it has been turned over to the *. Rev 11:2
people from many * will crowd Rev 11:8,9
to reign. The * were angry with Rev 11:18
was to rule all * with a heavy Rev 12:5
to rule over all * and language Rev 13:7
she seduced the * of the world and Rev 14:8
read, "King of the *." Rev 15:3,4f
All * will come Rev 15:3,4
For all the * have drunk the Rev 18:3
deceived all * with her sorceries. Rev 18:23
sharp sword to strike down the *; Rev 19:15
could not fool the * any more until Rev 20:3
He will go out to deceive the * Rev 20:8
Its light will light the * of Rev 21:24
the * shall be brought into it. Rev 21:26
used for medicine to heal the *. Rev 22:2

NATIONWIDE
a * religious education program. 2Ch 17:7,8,9

NATIVE
Horite—one of the * families of the Gen 36:20,21
"And anyone—* born or Lev 17:15
all of you who are * Israelites are Lev 23:42
whether he is a * Israeli or a Num 15:30
was living in his * land of Pethor, Num 22:5,6
his mother was a * of their town Ju 9:3
(His mother was Jeho-addin, a * 2Ki 14:2
was Jeho-addan, a * of Jerusalem. 2Ch 25:1
will be to be a * of Jerusalem! Ps 87:5
return to see their * land again. Jer 22:10
speaking all the * languages of the Act 2:8
and told him to leave his * Act 7:3

NATIVE-BORN
apply both to * Israelis and to Num 15:13,14
same law for all, * or foreigner, Num 15:15,16

NATURAL
If these men die a * death or Num 16:29
was a * death, but he had no sons. Num 27:3,4
anything that has died a * death. Deu 14:21
of its size and * divisions so that Jos 18:4
* surroundings, as you can see; 2Ki 2:19
animal that dies a * death or that Eze 44:31
against God's * plan for them and Rom 1:26
For just as there are *, human 1Co 15:44
Adam, was given a *, human body 1Co 15:45
the opposite of our * desires. Gal 5:17
have nailed their * evil desires to Gal 5:24
How * it is that I should feel as Php 1:7
Yes, our * lives will fade as 1Pe 1:24

NATURALIST
He was a great *, with interest 1Ki 4:33

NATURALLY
So Joseph * became quite a Gen 39:4
now than before. * you'd prefer a Ru 3:10
This suggestion * pleased the king Est 2:4
the Samaritans * hated the Jews. Lk 9:53f
money, * scoffed at all this. Lk 16:14
The crowds will * go to the main Jn 3:29
you just * don't believe it! Jn 8:45
So since they persecuted me, * Jn 15:20
For we * love to do evil things Gal 5:17
don't know God, * they don't 1Jn 3:1
world, so, quite *, they are 1Jn 4:5

NATURE
By his fantastic powers in * he Job 36:31
God controls all *, and causes the Job 37:15
sun. All * is within your hands; Ps 74:17
He revealed his will and * to Ps 103:7
Don't fight the facts of *. Ecc 7:13
to do away with these laws of *! Jer 31:36
him how changeable human * is! Jn 2:24,25
with the holy * of God himself. Rom 1:4
of your sinful * was shattered. Rom 6:2,3
Your old sin-loving * was buried Rom 6:4
And since your old sin-loving * Rom 6:8
So look upon your old sin * as Rom 6:11
When your old * was still Rom 7:5
as my old sinful * is concerned. Rom 7:18
so far as my new * is concerned; Rom 7:22
me, in my lower *, that is at war Rom 7:23,24,25
right, but the old * that is still Rom 7:23,24,25
my slavery to this deadly lower *? Rom 7:23,24,25
obey the old evil * within us. Rom 8:4
after the old * leads to death, Rom 8:6
sinful * within us is against God. Rom 8:7
You are controlled by your new * Rom 8:9
* to do what it begs you to do. Rom 8:12
even the things of *, like animals Rom 8:
far as his human * is concerned, he Rom 9
things your evil * wants you to. Gal 5:
off your old evil *—the old you Eph 4:2
Clothe yourself with this new *. Eph 4:2
how your old, evil * died with him Col 2:

NATURES
by their lower * live only to Rom 8:
born with evil *, and were under Eph 2:

NAUGHT
world and brings them all to *. Is 40:2
O Lord, you will take * but Jer 5:
But all for *—it all remains Eze 24:1

NAVAL
city, with your * power that Eze 26:1

NAVE
HE BROUGHT me into the * Eze 41:
8¾ feet deep. The * itself was Eze 41:
at the end of the * and measured Eze 41:
The * of the Temple and the Holy Eze 41:15,1
the doors of the *, and in front of Eze 41:2
Both the * and the Holy of Holies Eze 41:2
The doors leading into the * Eze 41:2
the Holy Place—the * of the Eze 42:1

NAVEL
Your * is lovely as a goblet Sol 7:2

NAVY
his vast army and * will rush out Dan 11:40

NAZARENE
"He shall be called a *." Mt 2:23
"You were with Jesus, the *." Mk 14:66,67
Jesus, the * who was crucified? Mk 16:6

NAZARENES
of the sect known as the *. Act 24:5

NAZARETH
Galilee instead, and lived in *. Mt 2:23
WHILE THEY WERE living in *, Mt 3:1
to * in Galilee; Mt 4:12,13
to his home town, * in Galilee, Mt 13:53,54
prophet from * up in Galilee." Mt 21:11
man was with Jesus—from *." Mt 26:71
Then one day Jesus came from * in Mk 1:9
us, Jesus of *—have you come to Mk 1:24
his disciples to *, his home town. Mk 6:1
that Jesus from * was near, he Mk 10:47
angel Gabriel to *, a village in Lk 1:26
from the Galilean village of *. Lk 2:4
returned home to * in Galilee. Lk 2:39
started home to *, but Jesus stayed Lk 2:43
Then he returned to * with them Lk 2:51
When he came to the village of *, Lk 4:16
to do with you, Jesus from *. Lk 4:34
He was told that Jesus from * Lk 18:37
the Man from *," they said. Lk 24:19
Jesus, the son of Joseph from *!" Jn 1:45
"*!" Jn 1:46
"Jesus of *," they replied. Jn 18:4,5
they replied, "Jesus of *." Jn 18:7
of *, the King of the Jews." Jn 19:19
God publicly endorsed Jesus of * Act 2:22
name of Jesus Christ of *, walk!" Act 3:6
of Jesus from *, the Messiah, the Act 4:10
fellow Jesus of * will destroy the Act 6:14
know that Jesus of * was anointed Act 10:38
And he replied, 'I am Jesus of *, Act 22:8
of Jesus of *. Act 26:9

NAZIRITE
special vow of a *, consecrating Num 6:1
"Then the * shall shave his long Num 6:18
After that the * may again drink Num 6:20
concerning a * and his sacrifices Num 6:21
he took his vow to become a *." Num 6:21
for he shall be a *, a special Ju 13:5
is going to be a *—he will be Ju 13:7
a * to God since before my birth. Ju 16:16,17

NAZIRITES
And I chose your sons to be * Amo 2:11
"But you caused the * to sin by Amo 2:12

NE-ARIAH
(Their leaders were Pelatiah, *, 1Ch 4:42

NEAH
and Rimmon and turned toward *. Jos 19:13

NEAPOLIS
the next day on to *, and finally Act 16:11

NEAR
Admah, and Zeboiim, * Lasha. Gen 10:15-19
came to a place * Shechem, and set Gen 12:6
at a place * the city of Sodom. Gen 13:12
the oaks of Mamre, * Hebron, and Gen 13:18
But he will live * the rest of Gen 16:9-12
at Mach-pelah, * Mamre, and the Gen 23:17,18
cave of Mach-pelah * Mamre, in the Gen 25:9,10
beneath the oak tree * Shechem. Gen 35:4
So Rachel died, and was buried * Gen 35:19
so that you can be * me with all Gen 45:10
As the time drew * for him to Gen 47:29
of the Jordan River, * Jericho. Gen 50:10f
edge of the desert * Horeb, the Ex 3:1
beside the shore * Piha-hiroth, Ex 14:9
priests who come * to Jehovah." Ex 19:22f
Moses alone shall come * to the Ex 24:2

NEAR Con't)
outside the veil, * the place of Ex 30:6
When they came * the camp, Moses Ex 32:19
Israel were afraid to come * him. Ex 34:30
burnt offerings * the entrance, and Ex 40:29
of the ancient * East, the word Lev 2:13f
a * relative, for I am the Lord. Lev 18:6
for they are * relatives, and to do Lev 18:17
his father—for they are * of kin; Lev 20:19
unless it is a * relative—a Lev 21:2,3
the veil, nor come * the altar, Lev 21:23
anyone else who is a * relative. Lev 25:49
They are to live * the Num 1:50
and there is no * relative to Num 5:8
"And he may not go * any dead Num 6:6,7
of Zin to Rehob * Hamath. Num 13:21
of Israel to be * to himself as you Num 16:8,9
* the borders of the Amorites. Num 21:13
of Pethor, * the Euphrates River. Num 22:5,6
and Pihahiroth (* Baal-zephon, Num 33:7
of Abarim, * Mount Nebo, and Num 33:47
defeated at Ashtaroth, * Edre-i. Deu 1:1
"So we remained in the valley * Deu 3:29
River * the city of Beth-peor. Deu 4:44,45,46
in the wasteland * Gilgal, where Deu 11:30
him in a valley * Beth-Peor in Deu 34:6
the city of Adam, * Zarethan, the Jos 3:15,16
from Mount Halak, * Seir, to Jos 11:17
The king of Ai, * Bethel; Jos 12:8-24
to beyond the tableland * Medeba. Jos 13:16
of Ammon as far as Aroer * Rabbah. Jos 13:25
the mountain * Beth-horon and Jos 18:14
to the west, going * Mareal and Jos 19:11
The western boundary began * Jos 19:34
also the territory * Joppa. Jos 19:41-46
the Jordan River * Moab, preventing Ju 3:28
the Oak of Za-anannim, * Kedesh. Ju 4:11
as Beth-shittah * Zererah, and to Ju 7:22
border of Abel-meholah * Tabbath. Ju 7:22
Ephraim hill country, * Shiloh. Ju 19:18
and two thousand more * Gidom. Ju 20:45
Literally, "a * relative, one of Ru 2:20f
in the Temple * the Ark, the Lord 1Sa 3:2,3
The Israeli army was camped * 1Sa 4:1
the valley of Zeboim * the desert. 1Sa 13:18
he had been hiding * the south edge 1Sa 20:41
One day * Horesh he received the 1Sa 23:14,15
there, * the village of Carmel. 1Sa 25:2
who had lived * Shur along the road 1Sa 27:8
at Ammah Hill * Giah, along the 2Sa 2:24
(The well was * the city gate. 2Sa 23:15
of the valley of Gad, * Jazer; 2Sa 24:5
all of Beth-shean * Zarethan below 1Ki 4:8-19
whether far or *, and they come to 1Ki 8:46
and resort cities * Jerusalem and 1Ki 9:19
in Ezion-geber * Eloth on the Red 1Ki 9:26
of Zarephath, * the city of Sidon. 1Ki 17:8,9
of the city * King Ahab's palace. 1Ki 21:1
threshing floor * the city gate. 1Ki 22:10
Israel, "Don't go * ÇÇ" (naming 2Ki 6:9
the road climbs to Gur, * Ibleam. 2Ki 9:27
which was * Joash's hideaway. 2Ki 11:11
on the hills * their cities. 2Ki 17:29
* the conduit of the upper pool. 2Ki 18:17
chariots located * the entrance of 2Ki 23:11
double walls * the king's garden. 2Ki 25:4,5
also lived in or * Etam, Ain, 1Ch 4:32,33
lived together * Jerusalem. 1Ch 8:30,31,32
they lived * the Tabernacle, and 1Ch 9:27
in Jerusalem * his relatives. 1Ch 9:38
Hurai from * the brooks of Gaash; 1Ch 11:26-47
stationed at Jerusalem * the king. 2Ch 1:14
foreign nation * or far, and if in 2Ch 6:36
at an open place * the Samaria 2Ch 18:9
of the fortress * the Temple, and Neh 2:8
who lived * the wall must guard the Neh 7:3
to the Jews * and far, throughout Est 9:20
"I AM SICK and * to death; Job 17:1
They despise me and won't come * Job 30:10
and bones, and draws * to death. Job 33:22
and because he is so *, I never Ps 16:8
for trouble is * and no one else Ps 22:9,10,11
and come * to the Living God. Ps 84:2
Surely his salvation is * to Ps 85:9
of troubles, and death draws *. Ps 88:3
overtake me or any plague come *? Ps 91:10
were gone and death was *. Ps 107:18
but you are *, O Lord; Ps 119:151
Don't go * her house, lest you Pro 5:8
Don't go * her; Pro 7:25
upper reservoir, * the road that Is 7:3
The stream * Dibon will run red Is 15:9
all both far and *, that Is 18:7
And you that are *, acknowledge Is 33:13
He camped * the outlet of the Is 36:2
He who gives me justice is *. Is 50:8
Terror shall not come *. Is 54:14
Call upon him now while he is *. Is 55:6
Peace, peace to them, both * and Is 57:19
noise of marching armies coming *. Jer 4:29
at Benjamin Gate * the Temple. Jer 20:2
the other nations * you, and I will Jer 25:8,9
far and *, one after the other; Jer 25:26
* the door of the New Gate. Jer 36:10
up with him at the pool * Gibeon. Jer 41:12
of Geruth Chimham, * Bethlehem, Jer 41:16,17
of the land of Moab, far and *. Jer 48:24
the two walls * the king's gardens Jer 52:7
in some fields * Jericho—for all Jer 52:8
Our end is *—our days are Lam 4:18
the day draws *. Eze 7:12
of the world. * and far they will Eze 22:5
Come from far and * to the Eze 39:17
Levites may come * to the Lord to Eze 40:46
They shall not come * me to Eze 44:13
Israel, scattered * and far Dan 9:7
For the Day of the Lord is *, in Joe 3:14
you bring the Day of Judgment *. Amo 6:3
the waves, and death was very *. Jon 2:5
had mastered most of the * East. Hab 1:6f
"That terrible day is *. Zep 1:14
"Doomed is Hamath, * Damascus, Zec 9:2
for the Kingdom of heaven is *." Mt 4:17
that the Kingdom of Heaven is * Mt 10:7
and were * the town of Bethphage on Mt 21:1
return is *, even at the doors. Mt 24:33
"God's Kingdom is *! Mk 1:15
from Nazareth was *, he began to Mk 10:47
And wars will break out * and Mk 13:7
*, that I am right at the door. Mk 13:29
army captain was sick and * Lk 7:2
As the time drew * for his return Lk 9:51
Kingdom of God is very * you now.' Lk 10:8,9
were trying to sit * the head of Lk 14:7
For your salvation is *." Lk 21:28
being told that summer is *. Lk 21:30
sure that the Kingdom of God is *. Lk 21:31
was drawing *—the Jewish festival Lk 22:1
He was baptizing at Aenon, * Jn 3:23,24
Inside the city, * the Sheep Jn 5:2
River to stay * the place where Jn 10:40
holy day, was *, and many country Jn 11:55
was crucified was * the city; Jn 19:20
Standing * the cross were Jesus' Jn 19:25
The place of crucifixion was * a Jn 19:41
"As the time drew * when God Act 7:17,18
in the desert * Mount Sinai, an Act 7:30
Those standing * Paul said to Act 23:4
Fair Havens, * the city of Lasea. Act 27:7,8
the sailors suspected land was *. Act 27:27
* the shore where we landed was Act 28:7
in fact, it is as * as our own Rom 10:8
Or, "he brought us * to God." 1Co 1:30f
been brought very * to him because Eph 2:13
him, and to us Jews who were *. Eph 2:17
God, and now we may draw * to him. Heb 7:19
coming back again is drawing *. Heb 10:25
for the coming of the Lord is *. Jas 5:8
that the end of the world is *. 1Jn 2:18
For the time is * when these Rev 1:3
of 6,000,000,000 in the * future. Rev 9:16f
of the world * a place called, in Rev 16:16
for the time of fulfillment is *. Rev 22:10

NEARBY
Egypt, storing them in * cities. Gen 41:48
man appeared * with a drawn sword. Jos 5:13
and the other * nations hear about Jos 7:9
"How do we know you don't live *? Jos 9:7
of Ashdod with their * villages; Jos 15:46
the goddess Asherah that stood *. Ju 6:25
The people at the * town of Ju 9:46
or no contact with the * villages. Ju 18:7
* villages with a plague of boils. 1Sa 5:6
with them on a * hillside, cursing 2Sa 16:13
occupied the * city of Bethlehem. 2Sa 23:14
people standing * and said, "Take 1Ki 22:28
People from * and from as far 1Ch 12:40
road, and two to the * areas. 1Ch 26:18
and to the kings of the * nations. 1Ch 29:30
in Jerusalem and its * villages; Ez 2:70
who lived in the * cities went home Neh 4:12
and its * fields, Azekah Neh 11:25-30
Edom and the other * countries Jer 40:11
returned from the * countries where Jer 43:5
poison to all the * nations that Zec 12:2
town and on the * farms, for the Mt 2:16
Mary were sitting * watching. Mt 27:61
The herdsmen fled to the * towns Mk 5:14
to go away to the * villages and Mk 6:35,36
of the Law were sitting *. Lk 5:17
the mountainside *, and the demons Lk 8:32
rushed away to the * city, Lk 8:34
people away to the * villages and Lk 9:12
with his disciples *, he came over Lk 9:18
from Tiberias were *, so when the Jn 6:22,23
that Peter was * at Lydda, they Act 9:38

NEARED
AS THEY * Bethphage and Bethany on Mk 11:1
sailing, and finally * Cnidus; Act 27:7,8
that Joseph, as he * the end of his Heb 11:22

NEARER
Going *, I saw a man whose face Eze 40:3
is * now than when we first Rom 13:11

NEAREST
the previous name of the * village Gen 28:19
his * relatives may redeem it. Lev 25:25
it shall go to the * relative." Num 27:11
If your * relative or closest Deu 13:6,7
from the body to the * city. Deu 21:2
the city into the * valley until 2Sa 17:13
through the * breach in the wall. Amo 4:3
The herdsmen fled to the * city Mt 8:33

NEARIAH
*, and Shaphat. 1Ch 3:21,22
* had three sons: 1Ch 3:23

NEARING
brother who was sick and * death. Ps 35:14
death's door, and * his everlasting Ecc 12:5
And because Jesus was * Lk 19:11
By this time they were * Emmaus Lk 24:28
"One day as he was * his Act 7:23
As he was * Damascus on this Act 9:3
The next day, as they were * the Act 10:9,10
"As I was on the road, * Act 22:6

NEARLY
and I am not * as old as many of my Gen 47:9
army had killed * every male in the 1Ki 11:15
He was * as great as The Three, 1Ch 11:24,25
* full of water and about to sink. Mk 4:37

NEARS
the day of trouble *. Eze 7:7
last days as the world * its end. 1Co 10:11

NEBAI
Anathoth, *, Magpiash, Neh 10:14-27

NEBAIOTH
Sarah's slave girl:*, Kedar, Gen 25:12-15
the sister of *, and daughter of Gen 28:9
of Ishmael—the sister of *). Gen 36:2,3

NEBALLAT
Hadid, Zeboim, *, Lod, Ono (the Neh 11:31-35

NEBAT
(the son of *), who came from the 1Ki 11:26
(the son of *), who had led the 2Ki 3:3
*) and of Baasha (son of Ahijah). 2Ki 9:9
Jeroboam (son of *), for it 2Ki 10:29
I (the son of *), who had led 2Ki 14:24
Like Jeroboam I (the son of *), 2Ki 15:9
Jeroboam I (son of *) who led 2Ki 15:24
Jeroboam I (son of *), who led all 2Ki 15:28
I (the son of *) as its king. 2Ki 17:21
concerning Jeroboam the son of *. 2Ch 9:29
Jeroboam (son of *) sent word to 2Ch 10:2,3

NEBO
Elealeh, Sebam, *, and Beon. Num 32:3,4
Kiriathaim, *, Num 32:37,38
Abarim, near Mount *, and finally Num 33:47
"Go to Mount * in the Abarim Deu 32:49
in Mount *, across from Jericho. Deu 34:1
distant as Mount * and Baal-meon. 1Ch 5:7,8
From the subclan of *, 52; Ez 2:3-35
From the clan of *: Ez 10:43
From the subclan of *, 52; Neh 7:8-38
weep for the fate of * and Medeba; Is 15:2
THE IDOLS OF Babylon, Bel and *, Is 46:1
Woe to the city of *, for it shall Jer 48:1
and Dibon and * and Jer 48:22

NEBUCHADNEZZAR
* of Babylon attacked Jerusalem. 2Ki 24:1
the armies of King * of Babylon 2Ki 24:10
of Jerusalem. * himself arrived 2Ki 24:11
King * took ten thousand 2Ki 24:14
left in the land. * took King 2Ki 24:15
THEN KING * of Babylon mobilized 2Ki 25:1
year of the reign of King *. 2Ki 25:8
Then King * appointed Gedaliah 2Ki 25:22
Jerusalem into captivity under *). 1Ch 6:4-15
Finally * king of Babylon 2Ch 36:6
to Babylon. * also took some of 2Ch 36:7
was summoned to Babylon by King *. 2Ch 36:10
time, and King * appointed 2Ch 36:10
He rebelled against King *, even 2Ch 36:13
items which King * had taken from Ez 1:7
deported to Babylon by King *. Ez 2:1
them and let King * destroy this Ez 5:12
silver bowls which * had taken from Ez 5:14
Temple of God by * shall be taken Ez 6:5
being exiled by King * of Babylon. Neh 7:6
destroyed by King *, and had been Est 2:6
Nabopolasser and * II soon Jer 4:6f
to help us, for *, king of Babylon, Jer 21:1
and force * to withdraw his Jer 21:1
the hands of King * of Babylon, to Jer 21:7
afraid—to *, king of Babylon, and Jer 22:24,25
AFTER *, KING of Babylon, had Jer 24:1
This was the year *, king of Jer 25:1
of the north under *, king of Jer 25:8,9
* of Babylon, who is my deputy. Jer 27:6
left here by *, king of Babylon, Jer 27:19,20,21
treasures that * carried off to Jer 28:3
in slavery to King * of Babylon." Jer 28:11
slavery to *, king of Babylon. Jer 28:14
to Babylon by *, Jeremiah wrote Jer 29:1
King Zedekiah's ambassadors to *. Jer 29:3

(NEBUCHADNEZZAR Con't)
over to * to execute publicly. Jer 29:21
and to *, king of Babylon; Jer 32:28
from the Lord when *, king of Jer 34:1
But when *, king of Babylon, Jer 35:11
*, KING OF Babylon, did not Jer 37:1
ruler before * captured the city. Jer 37:1f
Judah, that King * and all his army Jer 39:1
and brought him to *, king of Jer 39:5
Meanwhile King * had told Jer 39:11,12
will surely bring *, king of Jer 43:10
over to *, king of Babylon." Jer 44:30
Euphrates River by *, king of Jer 46:2
the coming of *, king of Babylon, Jer 46:13
*, king of Babylon, and his army. Jer 46:26
to be destroyed by *, king of Jer 49:28
for *, king of Babylon, has Jer 49:30
"Go," said the Lord to King *. Jer 49:31
ate them up; then *, the king of Jer 50:17
The Jews in Babylon say, "*, Jer 51:34,35
the tenth month, *, king of Jer 52:4
of the reign of *, king of Jer 52:12
I will tell you. *, king of Eze 17:12,13
and brought them to Babylon. * Eze 17:12,13
many horses to fight against *. Eze 17:15
Israel shall die. (* will pull out Eze 17:16
says: I will bring *, king of Eze 26:7
done to Tyre by *, and foreshadow Eze 26:14f
i.e., * of Babylonia. Eze 27:26f
"Son of dust, the army of King * Eze 29:18
the siege). And * received no Eze 29:18
Tyre capitulated to * at the end Eze 29:18f
the "salary" of *, so the Lord Eze 29:18f
land of Egypt to *, king of Eze 29:19
Tyre capitulated to * at the end Eze 29:20f
the "salary" of *, so the Lord Eze 29:20f
"For the Lord God says: *, king Eze 30:10
the year Jerusalem fell to * and Eze 30:20f
Jerusalem in 588, * withdrew from Eze 30:21f
than an historical figure like *. Eze 38:2,3f
Babylon's King * attacked Jerusalem Dan 1:1
to do. King * had long talks with Dan 1:18,19
year of his reign, * had a Dan 2:1
Then * fell to the ground before Dan 2:46
KING * MADE a golden statue ninety Dan 3:1
Then *, in a terrible rage, Dan 3:13
replied, "O *, we are not worried Dan 3:16
Then * was filled with fury and Dan 3:19
he was watching, * jumped up in Dan 3:24
"Well, look!" * shouted. Dan 3:25
Then * came as close as he could Dan 3:26
Then * said, "Blessed be the God Dan 3:28
THIS IS THE proclamation of * the Dan 4:1
I, *, was living in peace and Dan 4:4
"O King *, listen to me—stop Dan 4:27
all these things happened to *. Dan 4:28
heaven, "O King *, this message is Dan 4:31
was fulfilled. * was chased from Dan 4:33
I, *, looked up to heaven, and my Dan 4:34
"Now, I, *, praise and glorify Dan 4:37
And in the reign of King *, Dan 5:11
Literally, "King * your Dan 5:11f
Daniel that King * brought from Dan 5:13
Most High God gave *, who long ago Dan 5:18

NEBUCHADNEZZAR'S
during the eighth year of * reign. 2Ki 24:12
the eighteenth year of * reign). Jer 32:1
shortly after * victory over the Jer 36:1f
seventh year of * reign was 3,023. Jer 52:28
to worship King * golden statue; Dan 3:5
* reign, and brought to Babylon. Dan 5:2,3,4

NEBUSHAZBAN
of the guard, and *, the chief of Jer 39:13

NEBUZARADAN
General *, the captain of the 2Ki 25:8
taken by General * to the king of 2Ki 25:20
Then *, the captain of the Jer 39:9
had told * to find Jeremiah. Jer 39:11,12
So *, the captain of the Jer 39:13
*, CAPTAIN OF the guard, took Jer 40:1
Then * gave Jeremiah some food and Jer 40:5
Mizpah by *, captain of the guard. Jer 41:10
and all those whom *, the captain Jer 43:6
king of Babylon, *, captain of the Jer 52:12
five years after that he sent *, Jer 52:30

NECESSARILY
and skillful men are not * famous; Ecc 9:11
of my spirit"—not * anger, but Eze 3:14,15f
usage, * mean "the end times." Eze 38:15,16f

NECESSARY
blasts will be * to distinguish Num 10:5,6,7
come from, where irrigation is *. Deu 11:10
that is why this commandment is * Deu 15:11
Hiram also made the * pots, 1Ki 7:40
everything that is * for the 1Ch 28:2
Huramabi also made the * pots, 2Ch 4:11
the other items * for the work of Neh 10:33
will no longer be * to admonish one Jer 31:34
[and it isn't * for you to come Mt 8:8,9
guests, he issued the * orders. Mt 14:9
But Jesus replied, "That isn't * Mt 14:16
17, "For it was * for him to Lk 23:17,f
this will not be * and I will tell Jn 16:25
"Brothers, it was * for the Act 1:16
declared, "It was * that this Good Act 13:46
I felt it *, with no malice against Act 28:19
But I suppose you feel this is * 1Co 11:19
important are really the most *. 1Co 12:22
is a separate and * part of it. 1Co 12:27
was * for salvation, would say; Gal 2:12
are * to the plan of salvation. Gal 5:11
as sternly as * to make them strong Tit 1:13
them when * as one who has every Tit 2:15
And it was * for Jesus to be Heb 2:17
If that had been *, then he Heb 9:26

NECESSITY
They do it here to avoid the * of Eze 46:19,20
Gentiles alike—the * of turning Act 20:21
or about the * of faith in God; Heb 6:1

NECHO
when Pharaoh *, king of Egypt, and Jer 46:2

NECK
a strip of the hide around his *; Gen 27:16
chain about his * and declared, Gen 41:41,42
just as on the * of a coat of mail, Ex 28:32
it, then its * must be broken. Ex 34:20
wringing its *, but not severing Lev 5:8
nor sowed—and there break its *. Deu 21:4
your * until you are destroyed! Deu 28:47,48
the gate and his * was broken by 1Sa 4:18
He has taken me by the * and Job 16:12
his * with a quivering mane? Job 39:19
* strikes terror wherever he goes. Job 41:22
and placed his * in an iron collar, Ps 105:18
"be an ornament to your *." Pro 3:22f
How stately your * with that long Sol 1:10
Your * is stately Sol 4:4
Your * is stately as an ivory Sol 7:4
with silver chains around its *? Is 40:19
*, O captive daughter of Zion. Is 52:2
fasten it on your * with leather Jer 27:2
your * under Babylon's yoke! Jer 27:8
off Jeremiah's * and broke it. Jer 28:10
his *, and become the third ruler Dan 5:7
chain around your *, and make you Dan 5:16
hung around his *, and he was Dan 5:29
I have spared her tender *. Hos 10:11
your * and be thrown into the sea. Mt 18:6
* and he were thrown into the sea. Mk 9:42
rock tied to his *, he would be far Lk 17:2,3

NECKLACE
like a jeweled *, and their Ps 73:6
eyes, by a single bead of your *. Sol 4:9

NECKLACES
*—and gold objects of every kind. Ex 35:22
anklets, rings, earrings, and *. Num 31:50
ornaments, their * and bracelets Is 3:19
and beautiful *, a ring for your Eze 16:11

NECKS
to put their feet on the kings' *. Jos 10:24
ornaments from their camels' *. Ju 8:21
the chains around the camels' *. Ju 8:26
I placed my feet upon their *. Ps 18:38
*, and destroy it as decreed. Is 10:27
Your * are as unbending as iron; Is 48:4
the king of Babylon from your *. Jer 28:2
your * by the king of Babylon." Jer 28:4
have yokes of iron on their *. Jer 28:13
of iron on the * of all these Jer 28:14
yoke from their * and snap their Jer 30:8
We bow our * beneath the Lam 5:5

NECO
In those days King * of Egypt 2Ki 23:29
but King * killed Josiah at 2Ki 23:29
Afterwards King * of Egypt led 2Ch 35:20
But King * sent ambassadors to 2Ch 35:21

NECO'S
Josiah refused to believe that * 2Ch 35:22

NEDABIAH
Shenazzar, Jekamiah, Hoshama, *. 1Ch 3:17,18

NEED
food that they and you will *." Gen 6:21
How much of a raise do you * to Gen 30:28
from Pharaoh and didn't * to sell. Gen 47:22
you won't * to lift a finger!" Ex 14:14
each home according to its *; Ex 16:21
seventh year, and * pay nothing to Ex 21:2
But if the owner is there, he * Ex 22:15
and if it was rented, then he * Ex 22:15
You will * about 107 Ex 25:39
sin, and * not fulfill the vow. Lev 5:6
it was only a scab, and the man * Lev 13:6
income, for I am all that you *. Num 18:20
so they have no * for property." Num 18:24
But first we will * to build Num 32:17
time I told the people, 'I * help! Deu 1:9
* be taken to the central altar. Deu 12:26,27
but will never * to borrow! Deu 15:6
must lend them as much as they *. Deu 15:8
They don't * to own property, Deu 18:2
his right, not just if he is in *. Deu 18:8
They aren't enemies who * to be Deu 20:19
leave what's left for those in *. Deu 24:2
you would never * to make again; Deu 28:6
ancestors. You * only to be strong Jos 1:
If you * the altar because your Jos 22:1
mob, "Does Baal * your help? Ju 6:3
"Because we * you," they Ju 11:
us in our time of *, so I risked Ju 12:
family will be in distress and *. 1Sa 2:3
"What do you *?" 1Sa 3:
"What do you *?" 1Sa 3:
you * a whole army to settle this? 1Sa 17:
* is one hundred dead Philistines! 1Sa 18:2
not * to strike a second time!" 1Sa 26:
"If I * assistance against the 2Sa 10:1
and send us help if we * it." 2Sa 18:
"No, we don't * you now, my 2Sa 18:2
with you is all the honor I *! 2Sa 19:36
He did not * to strike again, and 2Sa 20:8,9,10
the coast to wherever you * them; 1Ki 5:9
If it's rivers I *, I'll wash at 2Ki 5:12
my power! You * more than mere 2Ki 18:20,21
Now the Levites will no longer * 1Ch 23:26
as much as you *, and bring it to 2Ch 2:16
But you will not * to fight! 2Ch 20:17
that they wouldn't * other 2Ch 31:4
and you don't * to carry it back 2Ch 35:3
gates, and didn't * to leave their 2Ch 35:15
Nehemiah is just the man we *!' Neh 6:7
to those in *, for the joy of the Neh 8:10
slander; no * to fear the future. Job 5:21
"You * not worry about your home Job 5:24
me, so that I * no longer live in Job 9:34
quick to despise all those in *. Job 12:5
He will supply your every * Job 12:6
They are wealthy and * deny Job 21:12,13
have encouraged me in my great *! Job 26:2
really, I don't * to, for you Job 27:12
helped the poor in their *, and Job 29:12
You * not be frightened of me. Job 33:7
so there is no * to wait for some Job 34:23
the time when I will * it in war. Job 38:22,23
Why do you hide when I * you the Ps 10:1
the poor or anyone else in *. Ps 10:12
look the other way when I am in *? Ps 13:1
I never * to stumble or to fall. Ps 16:8
All I * to do is cry to him—oh, Ps 18:3
my feet so that I * never slip. Ps 18:36
are pure and * never be changed." Ps 19:9f
Shepherd, I have everything I *! Ps 23:1
Be merciful and send the help I * Ps 27:7
And so we * not fear even if the Ps 46:2
There is no * to fear when times Ps 49:5
No, I don't * your sacrifices of Ps 50:13
I am in deep trouble and I * his Ps 77:2
Thus they did not * to be as Ps 78:8
never * rise against us again. Ps 85:4
Now you don't * to be afraid of Ps 91:5
path, but how I * your help, Ps 101:2
those in *, and hounded Ps 109:16
He gives generously to those in *. Ps 112:9
on earth: how I * a map—and your Ps 119:19
me by giving me the strength I *. Ps 138:3
give them their food as they * it. Ps 145:15
without fear; you * not be afraid Pro 3:24,25,26
it to them in their time of *. Pro 11:26
there * be no mistakes. Pro 16:10
is born to help in time of *. Pro 17:17
be ignored in his own time of *. Pro 21:13
Then you won't * to go to a Pro 27:10
for help in your time of *. Pro 27:10
does that will not * to look back Ecc 5:19,20
you yourself may * much help. Ecc 11:2
If you fear him, you * fear Is 8:13
He who believes * never run away Is 28:16
will have all the water they *. Is 33:16
Did he * instruction as to what Is 40:14
been no * for your destruction. Is 48:19
return and say, 'We * more room! Is 49:20
from relatives who * your help. Is 58:7
All you * to do is to stop Is 58:9
satisfy your every *, and you will Is 60:16
No longer will you * the sun or Is 60:19
for we who belong to you * you so. Is 63:17
Any jack wanting you * not Jer 2:24
course, you don't * to tell us how Jer 13:12
have failed me in my time of *! Jer 15:17,18
prophets—we don't * his advice. Jer 18:18
Help those in * of justice! Jer 22:3
shall not * to be afraid again; Jer 23:4
they * neither walls nor gates. Jer 49:31
to those in *, and grants loans Eze 18:7
For seven years they will * Eze 39:10
weapons will give them all they *. Eze 39:10
We don't * one anyway!" Hos 10:3
and oil, to fully satisfy your *. Joe 2:19
that your brothers * your help. Amo 6:6
deserted Israel in his time of *. Ob 1:11
not have mocked in his time of *. Ob 1:12
he won't * to strike again. Nah 1:9
In this time of our deep *, begin Hab 3:2
that I'll not * to strike again.' Zep 3:7

NEED Con't)
And then you will no longer * to Zep 3:11
will be over—you * fear no more. Zep 3:15
I didn't * to. Mal 1:2,3
every word of God is what we *." Mt 4:4
you * even before you ask him! Mt 6:7,8
to eat—they don't * to sow or reap Mt 6:26
well that you * them, and he will Mt 6:31,32
by its fruit. You * never confuse Mt 7:16
who are well don't * a doctor! Mt 9:12
parents are in *, you may give Mt 15:5,6
* have we for other witnesses? Mt 26:65,66
* the doctor, not healthy ones! Mk 2:17
to human *, he said to the man, Mk 3:5
more miracles do you people *?" Mk 8:12
and they badly * your help, and you Mk 14:7
and said, "What more do we *? Mk 14:63,64
"But why did you * to search?" Lk 2:49
is the sick who * a doctor, not Lk 5:31
I only * to say 'Go!' Lk 7:6,7,8
what does a man * to do to live Lk 10:25
children what they *, don't you Lk 11:13
give you all you * from day to day Lk 12:31
you have and give to those in *. Lk 12:33
to the Lord, "We * more faith; Lk 17:5
illustrate their * for constant Lk 18:1
what they didn't *, but she, poor Lk 21:4
"What * do we have for other Lk 22:71
At that time you won't * to ask Jn 16:23
And I won't * to ask the Father Jn 16:26
* anyone to tell you anything. Jn 16:30
Literally, "and * not that anyone Jn 16:30f
to meet their * for growth in truth Jn 17:19
And so, because of the * for Jn 19:42
and dividing with those in *. Act 2:45
apostles to give to others in *. Act 4:34,35
for distribution to those in *. Act 4:37
preached the * for everyone in Act 13:24
and satisfies every * there is. Act 17:25
of things we would * for the trip. Act 28:10
Then, too, I * your help, for I Rom 1:11,12
we no longer * obey God's laws? Rom 3:31
used for his good purposes. Sin * Rom 6:14
But now you * no longer worry Rom 7:6
something doesn't * to hope and Rom 8:24
says, "You don't * to search the Rom 10:6
and, "You don't * to go among the Rom 10:7
When God's children are in *, Rom 12:13
if they * lodging, for the night. Rom 12:13
For government workers * to be Rom 13:6
It is the only law you *. Rom 13:10
you * is this reminder from me; Rom 15:15,16
given you everything you *. 1Co 3:21
have all the spiritual food you *. 1Co 4:8
mean we should eat more than we *. 1Co 6:13
that he doesn't * to and won't, he 1Co 7:37
plan men and women * each other. 1Co 11:11
not * to be judged and punished. 1Co 11:31
to the hand, "I don't * you." 1Co 12:21
to the feet, "I don't * you." 1Co 12:21
complete, then the * for these 1Co 13:10
of God's Word—that is what you *; 1Co 14:6
examples of the * for speaking in 1Co 14:7
the Christians *, and unbelievers 1Co 14:22
I think you hardly * someone's 2Co 3:1
And we don't * a recommendation 2Co 3:1
The only letter I * is you 2Co 3:2
* not come to you with harshness. 2Co 7:9
can share with you when you * it. 2Co 8:14
also should share with those in *. 2Co 8:15
really don't even * to mention this 2Co 9:1
you everything you * and more, so 2Co 9:8
gifts to those who * them they will 2Co 9:11
gifts—those in * are helped, and 2Co 9:12
I hope I won't * to show you when 2Co 10:2
that is all you *. 2Co 12:9
* to scold and punish when I come; 2Co 13:10
Wouldn't we * to say that faith Gal 2:17
there was no * for Christ to die. Gal 2:21
has come, we don't * those laws any Gal 3:25
eternal life don't * to worry about Gal 5:6
for all we * is faith working Gal 5:6
Holy Spirit you * no longer force Gal 5:18
Then we won't * to look for Gal 5:26
done, and won't * to compare Gal 6:4
so he can give to others in *. Eph 4:28
But to do this, you will * the Eph 6:14
In every battle you will * faith Eph 6:16
And you will * the helmet of Eph 6:17
You sent him to help me in my *; Php 2:25
Not that I was ever in *, for I Php 4:11
At the moment I have all I *—more Php 4:18
I have all I need—more than I *! Php 4:18
We don't * to tell them about it, 1Th 1:8
* to say very much, I'm sure! 1Th 4:9
and you will not * to depend on 1Th 4:12
I really don't * to say anything 1Th 5:1
when they * help, especially those 1Ti 5:8
us all we * for our enjoyment. 1Ti 6:17
to those in *, always being ready 1Ti 6:18
one who does not * to be ashamed 2Ti 2:15
people when they * it, encourage 2Ti 4:2
you when you come, for I * him. 2Ti 4:11
they are given everything they *. Tit 3:13
to help all who * their assistance, Tit 3:14
to help us in our times of *. Heb 4:16
place where you * someone to teach Heb 5:12,13
Surely we don't * to speak Heb 6:1
you don't * further instruction Heb 6:2
sure and never * to wonder whether Heb 6:17
why then did God * to send Christ Heb 7:11
the kind of High Priest we *; Heb 7:26
no * for another to replace it. Heb 8:7
And no one then will * to speak Heb 8:11
there is no * to offer more Heb 10:18
Remember your reward! You * to Heb 10:36
Well, how much more do I * to Heb 11:32
you when you * it, as other fathers Heb 12:8
have with those in *, for such Heb 13:16
I especially * your prayers Heb 13:19
with all you * for doing his will. Heb 13:20,21
If you have a friend who is in * Jas 2:15
then you will not * to fear 1Pe 3:6
with those who * a meal or a place 1Pe 4:9
everything you * for living a truly 2Pe 1:3
But to obtain these gifts, you * 2Pe 1:5
as to those who * to know the 1Jn 2:21
so that you don't * anyone to teach 1Jn 2:27
sees a brother in *, and won't help 1Jn 3:17
We * have no fear of someone who 1Jn 4:18
I don't * a thing!' Rev 3:17
not * to walk naked and ashamed." Rev 16:15
And the city has no * of sun or Rev 21:23
no night there—no * for lamps or Rev 22:5

NEEDED
as much as is * for his Ex 16:16
acacia wood * in the construction. Ex 35:24
in fact, he has every * skill. Ex 35:33
that no more donations were *. Ex 36:4-7
repairs * on any of these items. Num 3:31-35
of the equipment * for their use; Num 3:36,37
would be * to prohibit adultery. Deu 27:23f
He was all they *. Jos 13:33
Benjamin who still * wives, "Go Ju 21:20
So whenever the Israelites * to 1Sa 13:20
flour and oil as long as it was *. 1Ki 17:15
pay for whatever repairs are *." 2Ki 12:4,5
other materials * to repair the 2Ki 12:11,12
doing each day whatever * to be 1Ch 16:37
quantity of nails * for the doors 1Ch 22:3
in whatever way they were *. 1Ch 23:32
* for the lampstands and lamps. 1Ch 28:15
of lumber will be *, for the temple 2Ch 2:9
and children who * it, and gave 2Ch 28:15
Repairs were not * from there to Neh 3:8
and we * a huge supply of all Neh 5:18
for we * supplies of the special Neh 10:33
We also * to purchase the other Neh 10:33
are not enough—discipline is *. Pro 29:19
king that he is * at home at once, Is 37:7
Has he ever * anyone's advice? Is 40:14
but I * it all, as a calf must be Jer 31:18
them many things they * to know. Mk 6:34
All they * to do was to trust him Jn 1:11,12
No one * to tell him how Jn 2:24,25
* to build the church is love. 1Co 8:1
Yes, I am still * down here and Php 1:25
for the money we * to live on, in 2Th 3:8
do whatever was * to help Tit 1:5
a Priest so that no one else is *. Heb 7:24

NEEDING
crafts we will be * in the work. Ex 35:35
There were many Jewish widows * Lk 4:25,26
the many Jewish lepers * help." Lk 4:27
are troubled, * our sympathy and 2Co 1:3,4

NEEDLE
the eye of a * than for a rich man Mt 19:24
the eye of a * than for a rich man Mk 10:25
the eye of a * than for a rich man Lk 18:25

NEEDLESS
Don't get into * fights. Pro 3:30

NEEDN'T
"Tell him he * be frightened by Is 7:4

NEEDS
him, a helper suited to his *." Gen 2:18
give him all the pressure he *! Ex 3:20
and gather as much food as he *. Ex 16:4
and give him what he *, at your Lev 25:37
for whatever * they may have." Num 7:4,5
You must lend him what he *, and Deu 15:10
he is poor he * it right away; Deu 24:14,15
Manasseh in proportion to its *: Jos 13:29
Their * were to be cared for, he 2Sa 20:3
in accordance with our daily *. 1Ki 8:59
is asleep and * to be wakened!" 1Ki 18:27
"The Temple building * repairing. 2Ki 12:4,5
use any more money for your own *; 2Ki 12:7
to care for their personal *. 2Ki 12:8
or for any similar *, you may Ez 7:20
For the * of the needy shall not Ps 9:18
who does this has everything he *. Ps 34:9
mercies meet our *, for we are Ps 79:8
That man shall have the help he * Ps 127:5
A fool thinks he * no advice, but Pro 12:15
If you give to the poor, your * Pro 28:27
me just enough to satisfy my *! Pro 30:8
and she will richly satisfy his *. Pro 31:11
of Jerusalem to see what * repair! Is 22:9,10,11
Anyone who chooses you * to have Is 41:24
they shall care for all your *. Is 49:23
to me about their *, I will go Is 65:24
* until the day of his death. Jer 52:34
"I am the one who * to be Mt 3:14
say, 'The Master * them,' and there Mt 21:3
New wine * fresh wineskins." Mk 2:22
* him and will return him soon.' Mk 11:3
your heavenly Father knows your *. Lk 12:30
doing, just say, 'The Lord * him.' Lk 19:31
replied, "The Lord * him!" Lk 19:34
bathed all over * only to have his Jn 13:10
to his *—for he has no needs! Act 17:25
to his needs—for he has no *! Act 17:25
the * of those who were with me. Act 20:34
bring you and your * in prayer to Rom 1:9
no longer * to be a slave to sin; Rom 6:6
other, and each * all the others. Rom 12:4,5
many in their *, including me. Rom 16:1
our own * without your help. 1Co 9:12
take for their own * some of the 1Co 9:13
each will have as much as he *. 2Co 8:14
for your own *, but plenty left 2Co 9:8
him of your *, and keep praying Eph 6:18
tell God your * and don't forget Php 4:6
supply all your * from his riches Php 4:19
to a brother who * to be warned. 2Th 3:15
He never * the daily blood of Heb 7:27
of their * and honoring them as the 1Pe 3:7

NEEDY
"If you lend money to a * Ex 22:25
the loan and the * man cries out to Deu 15:9
to loan money to * friends unless Job 22:6
a loan. The * are kicked aside; Job 24:4
early dawn to kill the poor and *; Job 24:14,15
They refuse to help the * widows. Job 24:21
Wasn't I deeply grieved for the * Job 30:25
For the needs of the * shall not Ps 9:18
the oppressed, the poor, the *. Ps 12:5
* from those who would rob them? Ps 35:10
I am poor and *, yet the Lord is Ps 40:17
the cries of his * ones, and does Ps 69:33
* and to crush their oppressors. Ps 72:4
May the poor and * revere you Ps 72:5
He feels pity for the weak and * Ps 72:13
Give cause for these poor and * Ps 74:21
Rescue the poor and * from the Ps 82:4
Yes, speak up for the poor and * Pro 31:9
and generously gives to the *. Pro 31:19,20
The * shall lie down in peace. Is 14:30
He presents it to the poor and * Is 26:6
When the poor and * seek water Is 41:17
poor and *, from my oppressors. Jer 20:13
the * and all went well for him. Jer 22:16
and * suffered outside her door. Eze 16:49
the poor and *, and robs his Eze 18:12
and clothes the *, and helps the Eze 18:16
* and cruelly extort from aliens. Eze 22:29
poor and crush the *—you who never Amo 4:1
rob the poor, trampling on the *; Amo 8:4
to disregard his * parents, telling Mk 7:11
at home, supporting * parents. 1Ti 5:4

NEGATIVE
of the spies was *: "The land is Num 13:32
"If the decision is *, then Lk 14:32

NEGEB
to the *, pausing frequently. Gen 12:9
north into the *—Abram with his Gen 13:1
ABRAHAM MOVED south to the *, Gen 20:1
*, had returned to Beer-lahai-roi. Gen 24:62
south to Beer-lahai-roi in the *. Gen 25:11
*, and see what the land is like; Num 13:17
the * and arrived at Hebron. Num 13:22
who lived in the *, in the land of Num 33:40
Arabah, and the *, and all the land Deu 1:7
from the southern * to Lebanon, and Deu 11:24
The Mediterranean coast and the * Deu 33:23
there is the *; Deu 34:3
all the way from * desert in the Jos 1:4
hill country, the *, the lowlands, Jos 10:40
hill country, the *, the land of Jos 11:16
the Judean Desert, and the *. Jos 12:8-24
at the northern edge of the *. Jos 15:1
borders of Edom in the *, namely: Jos 15:21-32
country and in the *, as well as on Ju 1:9
me land in the *, but please give Ju 1:15
new land in the * wilderness south Ju 1:16
Cherethites in the *, and had 1Sa 30:14
forts in the *, and made many water 2Ch 26:10
cities and the * and had already 2Ch 28:17,18
a whirlwind sweeping from the *. Is 21:1
The cities of the * to the south Jer 13:19
and from the * and from the Jer 17:26
plain and in the * too, for some Jer 32:44
the cities of the *, in the land of Jer 33:13

(NEGEB Con't)
it and the forest lands of the *. Eze 20:46
the * to your northern borders. Eze 21:4
Then my people who live in the * Ob 1:19
NEGEB'S
conquer the * outlying villages. Ob 1:20
NEGLECT
My children, don't * your duties 2Ch 29:11
So we agreed together not to * the Neh 10:39,40
Let us not * our church meetings, Heb 10:25
NEGLECTED
"but my own vineyards are *." Sol 1:6f
came in. You * the usual courtesy Lk 7:46
NEGLECTING
for we have been * it ever since 1Ch 13:3
me for * my responsibilities." Dan 1:10
NEGLIGEES
party clothes and * and capes and Is 3:22
NEGOTIATE
"but I will not * with you unless 2Sa 3:13
NEGRO
Ham was not the ancestor of the *, Gen 9:18f
NEHASHTA
King Jehoiachin and his mother *. Jer 13:18f
NEHELAM
Literally, "the Nehelamite." * Jer 29:24f
NEHELAMITE
Literally, "the *." Jer 29:24f
Shemaiah the * has "prophesied" Jer 29:31
NEHEMIAH
Zerubbabel, Jeshua, *, Seraiah, Ez 2:2
THE AUTOBIOGRAPHY OF *, the son Neh 1:1
Next to him was * (son of Neh 3:16
'Look! * is just the man we need!' Neh 6:7
were: Zerubbabel, Jeshua, *; Neh 7:7
I, * THE governor, signed the Neh 10:1
of Zerubbabel and *, the people Neh 12:47
nor with the one in * 12:22. Dan 5:31f
NEHUM
Bigvai, *, Baanah. Neh 7:7
NEHUSHTA
Name of his mother: * (daughter of 2Ki 24:8,9
NEIEL
running north of Beth-emek and *. Jos 19:27
NEIGH
lush pastures, and * like Jer 50:11
NEIGHBOR
"If a man asks his * to keep a Ex 22:10
to it, then the * must take an Ex 22:11
been stolen, the * caring for it Ex 22:12
else) from a *, and it is injured Ex 22:14
by oppressing his *, or by finding Lev 6:2
Don't falsely accuse your * of Lev 19:16
against the blood of your *." Lev 19:16f
but love your * as yourself, for Lev 19:18
forest with his * to chop wood, and Deu 19:5
kills the man's *, he may flee to Deu 19:5
"But if anyone hates his * and Deu 19:11
the baby, and the * women said, Ru 4:16,17
as a man would listen to his *. Job 16:21
never harms his *, speaks out Ps 15:3
Don't plot against your *; Pro 3:29
man slanders his *, the charges Pro 11:9f
To quarrel with a * is foolish; Pro 11:12
Or, "An evil man deceives his * Pro 16:29f
being a good * is out of his Pro 21:10
spitefully against an innocent *. Pro 24:28,29
before your * in shameful defeat. Pro 25:8,9,10
Don't visit your * too often, or Pro 25:17
lying to his * and says, "I was Pro 26:18,19
against brother, * against Is 19:2
neighbor against *, city against Is 19:2
Each man encourages his * and Is 41:6
Beware of your *! Jer 9:4
and Israel's other * nations prick Eze 28:24
and love your * as yourself!" Mt 19:19
* as much as you love yourself.' Mt 22:38,39
And you must love your * just as Lk 10:27
was a * to the bandits' victim?" Lk 10:36
If you love your * as much as Rom 13:9
love your * as you love yourself. Rom 13:9
to his friend or * or brother, Heb 8:11
NEIGHBOR'S
be envious of your * house, or want Ex 20:17
himself has stolen his * property. Ex 22:8
between his land and his *.' Deu 27:17
each neighing for his * mate. Jer 5:8
Adultery with a * wife, a Eze 22:11
NEIGHBORHOOD
visit some of the * girls, but Gen 34:1
another small family in the *; Ex 12:3,4
Wonder fell upon the whole *, and Lk 1:65
NEIGHBORING
the gods of the * nations, for Deu 6:14
before the idols of the * nations. Ju 2:12-14
Amalek, and other * nations came Ju 6:3,4
Amalek, and other * nations united Ju 6:33
and throughout the * lands west of Ez 4:10
at all. The * nations laugh and Ps 44:13
us the scorn of the * nations. Ps 80:6
Israel and her * lands shall Jer 25:11
and the * towns shall be burned. Jer 49:2
and their * towns, says the Lord. Jer 49:18
and Gomorrah and their * towns. Jer 50:40
"Woe to you for making your * Hab 2:15
they will burn up all the * Zec 12:6
The wealth of all the * nations Zec 14:14
Gomorrah and their * towns, all Jud 1:7
NEIGHBORS
her Egyptian master's wife and *. Ex 3:22
ask their Egyptian * for costly Ex 11:2
your brothers, friends, and *.' Ex 32:27
came out—these men were close *. Jos 9:16
and some of his * came chasing Ju 18:22
And one of the * added, "With 1Sa 10:12
pans from your friends and *!" 2Ki 4:3
become a laughingstock to my *. Job 12:4
* while planning to murder them. Ps 28:3
and even more by my * and friends. Ps 31:11
has robbed him while his * mock. Ps 89:41
who secretly slanders his *; Ps 101:5
Even his own * despise the poor Pro 14:20
on someone else, * fighting Is 3:5
neighbors fighting *, youths Is 3:5
as so many of your * are doing when Is 8:12
be frustrated; * and friends shall Jer 6:21
They speak cleverly to their * Jer 9:8
daughters to wail and your * too. Jer 9:20
*' wives and have lied in my name. Jer 29:23
and of scoffing to her * now. Jer 48:39
For all your * shall drive you Jer 49:5
Her children, her brothers, her * Jer 49:9,10
spoken: "Let her * be her foes! Lam 1:17
her * and by all the Philistines. Eze 16:57
the Assyrians, her *, for they Eze 23:4,5
She fawned over her Assyrian *, Eze 23:12
own where you can invite your *.' Zec 3:10
The word spread quickly to her * Lk 1:58
so he asked, "Which *?" Lk 10:29
brothers, relatives, and rich *! Lk 14:12
your friends and * to rejoice with Lk 15:6
friends and * to rejoice with her? Lk 15:9
His * and others who knew him as Jn 9:8
love and help your * just as much Jas 2:8
you behave among your unsaved *; 1Pe 2:12
NEIGHING
each * for his neighbor's mate. Jer 5:8
NEITHER
were both naked, * of them was Gen 2:25
will be * plowing nor harvest. Gen 45:6
all that time he * ate nor drank. Ex 34:28
you shall eat * fat nor blood." Lev 3:17
of Israel, that * they, nor any Lev 17:12
Literally, "* shall you stand Lev 19:16f
for yourselves—* fresh kernels nor Lev 23:14
the donor may * change his mind Lev 27:10
* the Ark nor Moses left the camp. Num 14:44
* see nor hear nor eat nor smell. Deu 4:28
before the Lord, * eating bread nor Deu 9:18
be eaten at home. * the tithe of Deu 12:17
* shall he be excessively rich. Deu 17:17
water—a valley * plowed nor Deu 21:4
blood, * have our eyes seen it. Deu 21:7
a nation to whom * you nor your Deu 28:36
heathen gods that * you nor your Deu 28:64
He will * fail you nor forsake Deu 31:6
boulders that have * been broken Jos 8:31
(That is why to this day * the 1Sa 5:5
it will be * yours nor mine; 1Ki 3:26
"I have * food nor wine to give 2Ki 6:26-30
angry with us, for * we nor our 2Ki 22:12,13
subclan because * had many sons. 1Ch 23:10,11
He will have * son nor grandson Job 18:19
He will fade like a dream. * Job 20:9
away the clouds, * can we gaze at Job 37:22
They boast that * God nor man Ps 10:6
and death are alike in this: * is Pro 27:20
Second, give me * poverty nor Pro 30:8
love, * can the floods drown it. Sol 8:7
away because you * know nor care Is 5:13
help in that day, * will they Is 17:8
for their idols * see nor know. Is 44:9
They shall * hunger nor thirst; Is 49:10
would work out, * are my thoughts Is 55:8
There will be * famine nor war! Jer 5:12
people, Jeremiah. * weep for them Jer 7:16
a god for it can * harm nor help, Jer 10:5
people, * weep nor plead for them; Jer 11:14
I go. I am * a creditor soon to Jer 15:10
foreign land where * you nor your Jer 16:13
idols—idols that * this generation Jer 19:4
jar cannot be mended, * can they. Jer 19:11
* we nor our children forever. Jer 35:6
of Josiah). But * King Zedekiah Jer 37:2
gods—"gods" that * they nor you Jer 44:2,3
they need * walls nor gates. Jer 49:31
It will * satisfy nor feed you, Eze 7:19
I will * pity nor spare. Eze 8:18
and you had been * washed nor Eze 16:4
pass that way, * men nor animals. Eze 29:11
the streams, and * man nor animal Eze 32:13
stone—gods that * see nor hear, nor Dan 5:23
All that time I tasted * wine Dan 10:
desserts. I * washed nor shaved nor Dan 10:
* in battle nor in riot. Dan 11:2
no difference, for * can succeed Dan 11:2
there, but he can * help nor cure. Hos 5:1
and there is * blossom left nor Hab 3:1
Literally, "* the Son." Mt 24:36
do not forgive, * will your Father Mk 11:26,
to the other. But * of them could Lk 7:4
"For * you nor anyone else can Lk 16:1
" 'I fear * God nor man,' he said Lk 18:4,
And Jesus said, "* do I. Jn 8:1
"*," Jesus answered. Jn 9:
so that they can * see nor Jn 12:4
with a yoke that * we nor our Act 15:1
by a curse * to eat nor drink until Act 23:12,1
* eat nor drink till he is dead. Act 23:21
But if I am innocent, * you nor Act 25:10,1
Literally, "* sun nor stars shone Act 27:20
in his kingdom. * will thieves or 1Co 6:9,10
the Lord, and take * food, 3Jn 1:7
"I know you well—you are * hot Rev 3:15
Don't do anything yet—hurt * Rev 7:3
* see nor hear nor walk! Rev 9:20
hear nor walk! * did they change Rev 9:21
NEKODA
Re-aiah, Rezin, *, Gazzam, Uzza, Ez 2:43-54
Tobiah, and *—a total of 652. Ez 2:60
Re-aiah, Rezin, *, Neh 7:46-56
Tobiah, and *—a total of 642. Neh 7:62
NEMU-EL
families of *, Abiram, and Dathan. Num 26:5-11
named after their ancestor *. Num 26:12-14
*, Jamin, Jarib, 1Ch 4:24
NEMU-ELITES
The *, named after their ancestor Num 26:12-14
NEPHEG
The sons of Izhar:Korah, *, Ex 6:21
Ibhar, Elishu-a, *, Japhia, 2Sa 5:14,15,16
Eliphelet, Nogah, *, Japhia, 1Ch 3:6-8
Elpelet, Nogah, *, Japhia, 1Ch 14:4-7
NEPHEW
He took his wife Sarai, his * Gen 12:5
taking with them Lot—Abram's * Gen 14:12
his uncle, *, or anyone else who Lev 25:49
of Kenaz), Caleb's *, was the one Jos 15:17
Caleb's *, Othni-el, son of his Ju 1:13
gave them Caleb's *, Othni-el (son Ju 3:9
"Since you are my *, may God 2Sa 19:13
and David's * Jonathan—the son of 2Sa 21:20,21
but he was killed by David's * 1Ch 20:6,7
But Paul's * got wind of their Act 23:16
NEPHEWS
met King Ahaziah's *, the princes 2Ch 22:8
NEPHISIM
Asnah, Me-unim, *, Bakbuk, Hakupha, Ez 2:43-54
NEPHTOAH
to the spring of *, and from there Jos 15:9
NEPHUSHESIM
Asnah, Me-unim, *, Neh 7:46-56
NER
(Abner's father, *, and Saul's 1Sa 14:50,51
* was the father of Kish, and 1Ch 8:33
*, Nadab, Gedor, Ahio, Zechariah, 1Ch 9:35,36,37
* was the father of Kish, 1Ch 9:39
Abner the son of *, Joab the son of 1Ch 26:28
NER'S
his cousin Abner, his uncle * son. 1Sa 14:50,51
NEREUS
Philologus, Julia, * and his Rom 16:15
NERGAL
from Cuth worshiped their god *; 2Ki 17:30
NERGAL-SHAREZER
the middle gate. * was there, and Jer 39:3
and Sarsechim and * the king's Jer 39:3
the eunuchs, and *, the king's Jer 39:13
NERI
Shealtiel's father was *; Lk 3:23-38
NERI'S
Shealtiel's father was Neri;* Lk 3:23-38
NERIAH
*, who was the son of Mahseiah). Jer 32:12
for Baruch (son of *), and as Jer 36:4
Baruch (son of *) has plotted Jer 43:2,3
to Seraiah (son of *, son of Jer 51:59
NERVE
they lost their * entirely and 1Sa 13:6
NERVES
but eventually she got on his *. Lk 18:4,5
NERVOUS
the Edomites will be *, so be Deu 2:4
renown to make you * and afraid. Job 33:7
NEST
Your * is set in the rocks! Num 24:21,22
"If a bird's * is lying on the Deu 22:6
sitting in the *, don't take the Deu 22:6
in my * after a long, good life.' Job 29:18
up from their * in hunger? Job 38:41
upon the cliffs to make her *? Job 39:27
to come and * among your altars and Ps 84:3
and the birds * beside the streams Ps 104:12

(EST Con't)
a bird that wanders from its *. Pro 27:8
puts his hand in a * of deadly Is 11:8
There the owl will make her * Is 34:15
Like a bird that fills her * with Jer 17:11
that * in the clefts of the rocks. Jer 48:28
and build your * among the stars, I Ob 1:4

ESTED
The birds * in its branches, and Eze 31:6

ESTLE
her young and * them beneath her Is 34:15

ESTLINGS
distance. Her * gulp down blood, Job 39:30

ESTS
There the birds make their *, Ps 104:17
have robbed their * of riches and Is 10:14
hover round their *, and he will Is 31:4,5
to Israel, like doves to their *? Is 60:8
birds have *, but I, the Messiah, Mt 8:20
build their * and be sheltered." Mk 4:31,32
birds have *, but I, the Messiah, Lk 9:58

ET
me and caught me in his *. Job 19:6
in their own *, and destroyed. Ps 35:8
You captured us in your * and Ps 66:11
they wait in ambush with a * to Ps 140:5
a hunter, or a bird from the *. Pro 6:5
He is like a fish caught in a *, Ecc 9:12
as wild goats caught in a *. Is 51:20
I will capture him in my * and Eze 12:13
I will throw my * over him and Eze 17:20
great army to catch you with my *. Eze 32:3
But as she flies, I throw my * Hos 7:12
fishing with a *, for they were Mt 4:18
casts a * into the water and Mt 13:47,48
When the * is full, he drags it Mt 13:47,48
Then he said, "Throw out your * Jn 21:6
draw in the * because of the weight Jn 21:6
pulled the loaded * to the beach, Jn 21:8
went out and dragged the * ashore. Jn 21:11
and yet the * hadn't torn. Jn 21:11

NETHANEL
Issachar -* (son of Zuar Num 1:2-15
Issachar * (son of Zuar) Num 2:3-31
The next day *, the son of Zuar, Num 7:18-23
Issachar, led by *, the son of Num 10:15
his fourth was *, his fifth was 1Ch 2:14
Shebaniah, Joshaphat, *, Amasai, 1Ch 15:24
and the son of *, acted as 1Ch 24:6
* (the fifth), 1Ch 26:4,5
Zechariah, *, and Micaiah. 2Ch 17:7,8,9
Shemaiah, and *, and his brothers 2Ch 35:9
Eli-o-enai, Ma-aseiah, Ishmael, *, Ez 10:22
*, leader of the Jedaiah clan. Neh 12:12-21
Gilalai, Maai, *, Neh 12:35,36

NETHANIAH
included Ishmael, the son of *; 2Ki 25:23
Zaccur, Joseph, *, and Asharelah. 1Ch 25:2
Fifth, * and twelve of his sons 1Ch 25:9-31
Shemaiah, *, Zebadiah, Asahel, 2Ch 17:7,8,9
Jehudi (son of *, son of Shelemiah, Jer 36:14,15
Ishmael (son of *), Johanan and Jer 40:8
(son of *) to assassinate him. Jer 40:13,14
BUT IN OCTOBER, Ishmael (son of *, Jer 41:1

NETHER
long ago the * world of the dead. Eze 26:20
They went down with her to the * Eze 31:17
Send them down to the * world Eze 32:18
The mighty warriors in the * Eze 32:21

NETOPHAH
Maharai from *; 2Sa 23:24-39
Heleb (son of Baanah) from *; 2Sa 23:24-39
Maharai from *; 1Ch 11:26-47
Heled (son of Baanah) from *; 1Ch 11:26-47
was Maharai from * in Zerah, with 1Ch 27:13
was Heldai from * in the area of 1Ch 27:15
From the subclan of *, 56; Ez 2:3-35
subclans of Bethlehem and *, 188; Neh 7:8-38

NETOPHATHITE
the son of Tanhumeth the *; 2Ki 25:23
sons of Ephai (the *), Jezaniah Jer 40:8

NETOPHATHITES
son Bethlehem, the *, 1Ch 2:54
who lived in the area of the *). 1Ch 9:15,16
and from the villages of the *; Neh 12:28

NETS
whose heart is snares and *." Ecc 7:26f
use the * will all be unemployed. Is 19:8
to spread their *, for I have Eze 26:5
for fishermen to spread their *. Eze 26:14
The shores will be filled with * Eze 47:10
in their *, while they rejoice? Hab 1:15
Then they will worship their * Hab 1:16
And they left their * at once Mt 4:20
father Zebedee, mending their *; Mt 4:21
fishing with *, for they were Mk 1:16
At once they left their * and Mk 1:18
John, in a boat mending their *. Mk 1:19
the fishermen washed their *. Lk 5:2
and let down your * and you will Lk 5:4
And this time their * were so Lk 5:6

NETTLES
for shelter beneath the *. Job 30:7
the palaces, and * will grow in its Is 34:13
place of stinging * and salt pits Zep 2:9

NETWORK
intricate bronze * of pomegranates 2Ki 25:17
a * of bronze pomegranates. Jer 52:22
sides, and on the * round about Jer 52:23

NEUTRAL
But empty, since the person is * Lk 11:25f

NEVER
himself, "I will * do it again—I Gen 8:21
do it again—I will * again curse Gen 8:21
vegetables. But * eat animals Gen 9:4
I will * again send another flood Gen 9:9,10,11
every being, that * again will the Gen 9:15
offspring, and I * touched one ram Gen 31:38
"But we've * had a public Gen 38:21
Joseph, * giving him a thought. Gen 40:23
bony—in fact, I've * seen such Gen 41:19
Hebrews and * eat with them. Gen 43:32
them went away and * Gen 44:28
I have * seen him since. Gen 44:28
And Israel said to Joseph, "I * Gen 48:11
May I * be a party to their Gen 49:6
They'll say, 'Jehovah * appeared Ex 4:1
a good speaker. I * have been, and Ex 4:10
you that you must * again lie to us Ex 8:29
* been since Egypt was founded! Ex 9:18
description. * in all the history Ex 9:24
houses of Egypt. * in the history Ex 10:6
"I can see your plot! *! Ex 10:11
and there will * again be another Ex 10:14
"I will * see you again." Ex 10:29
land of Egypt; * before has there Ex 11:6
anguish, and it will * be again. Ex 11:6
The cloud and fire were * out of Ex 13:22
at—you will * see them again. Ex 14:13
You must * bow to an image or Ex 20:5
anyone with evil; * let an innocent Ex 23:7
and remember—* mention the name Ex 23:13
These carrying poles shall * be Ex 25:15
the Lord, so that it * goes out. Ex 27:21
It must * be poured upon an Ex 30:32
and you shall * make any of it Ex 30:32
this incense is most holy. * Ex 30:37
I will do miracles such as have * Ex 34:10
"Be very, very careful * to Ex 34:12
It must * go out. Lev 6:13
people of Israel * to eat fat, Lev 7:23
for other purposes, but * eaten. Lev 7:24
"* eat blood, whether of birds Lev 7:26,27
Aaron, "* drink wine or strong Lev 10:8,9
people of Israel * to eat it, for Lev 17:14
upon his altar; * profane the name Lev 18:21
and a woman must * give herself Lev 18:23
"Tell the priests * to defile Lev 21:1
you must * worship carved images, Lev 26:1
Otherwise they must * enter the Num 4:20
"Throughout that time he must * Num 6:5
Will they * believe me, even Num 14:10,11
I have * stolen so much as a Num 16:15
wrath of God will * again fall upon Num 18:5
However, you may * accept the Num 18:16
defect, one that has * been yoked. Num 19:1
'* favor a man because he is rich; Deu 1:17
Be very careful * to forget what Deu 4:9
" '* worship any god but me. Deu 5:7
" '* make idols; Deu 5:8
" 'You must * use my name to Deu 5:11
He did it so that you would * Deu 8:17
"Don't you remember (oh, * Deu 9:7
children who have * experienced the Deu 11:2
The only restriction is * to eat Deu 12:20-23
You must * worship any God but Deu 13:4
mound and may * be rebuilt. Deu 13:16
the people of God, * cut yourselves Deu 14:1
nations but will * need to borrow! Deu 15:6
part of the land. * twist justice Deu 16:19
a rich man, and * accept bribes. Deu 16:19
"*, under any circumstances, are Deu 16:21
your God. And * set up an obelisk, Deu 16:22
"* SACRIFICE A sick or defective Deu 17:1
However, * put a man to death on Deu 17:6
you, '* return to Egypt again.' Deu 17:16
that you must * steal a man's land Deu 19:14
"* convict anyone on the Deu 19:15
a heifer that has * been yoked, Deu 21:3
his wife and he may * divorce her. Deu 22:19
he may * divorce her. Deu 22:28,29
You must *, as long as you live, Deu 23:6
"* oppress a poor hired man, Deu 24:14,15
and you must * accept a widow's Deu 24:17
"You must * forget what the Deu 25:17
from under heaven. * forget this. Deu 25:19
and you must * worship other Deu 28:14
and will * return to you again. Deu 28:31
you would * need to make again; Deu 28:68
To new gods * before worshiped. Deu 32:17
There has * been another prophet Deu 34:10
which have * been equaled. Deu 34:11,12
You have * before been where we Jos 3:2,3,4
fell, and it was * seen again! Jos 5:11,12
There had * been such a day Jos 10:14
and there has * been another since, Jos 10:14
in Gezer were * driven out, so they Jos 16:10
"We would * forsake the Lord and Jos 24:16
as slaves, but * did force them to Ju 1:28
said that I would * break my Ju 2:1
"You taunted me that I would * Ju 8:15
Midian * recovered, and the land Ju 8:28
armor bearer. "* let it be said Ju 9:54
but they * once crossed into Ju 11:18
weeping because I'll * marry." Ju 11:37
So she was * married. Ju 11:39
Your son's hair must * be cut, Ju 13:5
ropes which have * been used, I Ju 16:11
"My hair has * been cut," he Ju 16:16,17
a hair's breadth, * missing! Ju 20:16
vowed at Mizpah * to let their Ju 21:1
and his hair shall * be cut." 1Sa 1:11
(Samuel had * had a message from 1Sa 3:7
of his sons shall * be forgiven by 1Sa 3:14
"Woe upon us, for we have * had 1Sa 4:7
Fight as you * have before, O 1Sa 4:9
calves—cows that * before have been 1Sa 6:7
"you have * defrauded or oppressed 1Sa 12:4
* taken even one single bribe." 1Sa 12:4
can * accuse me of robbing you." 1Sa 12:5
Samuel * saw Saul again, but he 1Sa 15:35
he had * worn such things before. 1Sa 17:38,39
"He's * done anything to harm 1Sa 19:4
fellow is alive, you'll * be king. 1Sa 20:31
David replied. "I * let my men run 1Sa 21:5
"My father will * find you! 1Sa 23:17
For I said, 'I will * harm him—he 1Sa 24:9,10
do to me, but I will * harm you. 1Sa 24:12
among us, we have * harmed them, 1Sa 25:7
we * suffered any harm from them; 1Sa 25:15,16
and you will * do wrong 1Sa 25:28
years, and I've * found one fault 1Sa 29:3
I could * face your brother Joab 2Sa 2:22
"You'll * come in here," they 2Sa 5:6
For I have * lived in a temple. 2Sa 7:6
And I have * once complained to 2Sa 7:7
which they will * have to move. 2Sa 7:10,11
We have * heard of any other god 2Sa 7:22
I swear that I will * be guilty 2Sa 11:11
I can assure you he will * 2Sa 14:10
"but he must * come here. 2Sa 14:24
King David, had * disciplined him 1Ki 1:6
of Israel—my dynasty will * end. 1Ki 2:4
of Israel and * forsake them." 1Ki 6:13
may he * forsake us. 1Ki 8:57
for his choirs. * before or since 1Ki 10:12
* bowed to Baal nor kissed him!" 1Ki 19:18
for he * prophesies anything good. 1Ki 22:8
He * tells me anything good. 1Ki 22:18
but they * arrived, for they were 1Ki 22:48
* leave the bed he is lying on; 2Ki 1:4,5
from now on I will * again offer 2Ki 5:17
"I would * do that sort of 2Ki 8:13
people of Israel * quit doing the 2Ki 17:22
they were * to worship or make 2Ki 17:35,36
laws and * worship other gods. 2Ki 17:37
For God had said, "You must * 2Ki 17:38
with you; * worship other gods. 2Ki 17:38
He will * be able to save you 2Ki 18:29
Moses, I will * again expel them 2Ki 21:8
and there was * another like it in 2Ki 23:22
(The Egyptian Pharaoh * returned 2Ki 24:7
In all that time I * suggested 1Ch 17:6
I will * remove my mercy and love 1Ch 17:13
In fact, we have * even heard of 1Ch 17:20
his subjects. And * again did the 1Ch 19:19
Joab began the census, but he * 1Ch 27:24
the final total was * put into 1Ch 27:24
that their love for you * changes. 1Ch 29:18
And there will * again be so 2Ch 1:12
For he told him, 'I have * 2Ch 6:5,6
be glorified; and * before have I 2Ch 6:5,6
against you (and who has * sinned? 2Ch 6:36
for the choir. * before had there 2Ch 9:11
evil king, for he * did decide 2Ch 12:14
King Jeroboam of Israel * 2Ch 13:20
he * prophesies anything but evil! 2Ch 18:6,7
"He does it every time. He * 2Ch 18:17
So the ships met disaster and * 2Ch 20:37
before me have * yet failed to 2Ch 32:13
next seven days. * since the time 2Ch 35:18
could * get it done by ourselves. Neh 4:10
Moabites should * be permitted to Neh 13:1
Persians that can * be changed, Est 1:19
that he would * see her again. Est 2:1
rest of her life, * seeing the king Est 2:12,13,14
is a Jew, you will * succeed in Est 6:13
so that it can * be reversed. Est 8:8
they declared they would * fail Est 9:27
* perish from the Jewish race. Est 9:28
God and * anything unpleasant?" Job 2:10
off the calendar, * again to be Job 3:6
Let it long for light, but * see Job 3:9

(NEVER Con't)

see it, * see the morning light.	Job 3:9
—to have * breathed or seen the	Job 3:16
and their home—* to be seen again.	Job 7:10
monster, that you * let me alone?	Job 7:12
shadow of death, * to return— a	Job 10:20,21
for God' when he * once has said	Job 13:7
send him away. He * knows it if his	Job 14:20,21
road from which I shall * return.	Job 16:22
he will * recover.	Job 20:19
every time. They * have trouble,	Job 21:17
dead, then he will * again be able	Job 21:21
who have * known anything good.	Job 21:25
I will *, never agree that you	Job 27:5
I will never, * agree that you	Job 27:5
actually I have * cursed anyone nor	Job 31:30
(actually I have * turned away	Job 31:32
this: God is * wicked or unjust.	Job 34:12
to him, he * replies by instant	Job 35:12
and you will * try it again!	Job 41:8
Their leaves shall * wither, and	Ps 1:3
So many say that God will * help	Ps 3:2
Many say that God will * help us.	Ps 4:6
I will * pray to anyone but you.	Ps 5:1
For you have * yet forsaken those	Ps 9:10
"he'll * know!"	Ps 10:11
For they think that God will *	Ps 10:13
listen to gossip, * harms his	Ps 15:3
and because he is so near, I *	Ps 16:8
my feet so that I need * slip.	Ps 18:36
Foreigners who have * seen me	Ps 18:43,44,45
are pure and need * be changed."	Ps 19:9f
he will * stumble, never fall;	Ps 21:7
he will never stumble, * fall;	Ps 21:7
they were * disappointed when	Ps 22:5
Oh, let it * be said that I	Ps 25:20
For they accuse me of things I *	Ps 27:12
buildings, * to be rebuilt again.	Ps 28:5
Lord will * lack any good thing.	Ps 34:10
They accuse me of things I have *	Ps 35:11
you! * stop giving your salvation	Ps 36:10
* ENVY THE wicked!	Ps 37:1
And in all my years I have * seen	Ps 37:25
he will * abandon his people.	Ps 37:28
"He'll * get out of that bed!"	Ps 41:8
They could * save me.	Ps 44:6
I can * thank you enough!	Ps 44:8
die at birth, who * see the sun.	Ps 58:8
where my enemies can * reach me.	Ps 61:3
"He will * notice them here,"	Ps 64:5
Or, "they * have any pains."	Ps 73:4f
of arrogance; they * have to lift a	Ps 73:12
of things that * really were!	Ps 73:20
Will he * again be favorable?	Ps 77:7
and we will * forsake you again.	Ps 80:18
You must * worship any other	Ps 81:9
O Lord, so that your anger will *	Ps 85:4
my covenant with him will * end.	Ps 89:28
them, but I will * completely take	Ps 89:33
a holy God can * lie), that his	Ps 89:35,36
that they would * enter the	Ps 95:11
His power can * be overthrown.	Ps 96:10
* too busy to heed their requests.	Ps 102:17
But you yourself * grow old.	Ps 102:27
You are forever, and your years *	Ps 102:27
and love. He * bears a grudge, nor	Ps 103:9
so that it would * fall apart.	Ps 104:5
would * again cover the earth.	Ps 104:9
pass he * forgets his promise, his	Ps 105:8,9
now you curse him. He * blessed	Ps 109:17
him; he * forgets his promises.	Ps 111:5
good deeds will * be forgotten.	Ps 112:3
His deeds will * be forgotten.	Ps 112:9
May I * forget your words;	Ps 119:43
* forget your promises to me your	Ps 119:49,50
then I will * have to be ashamed	Ps 119:80
I will * lay aside your laws,	Ps 119:93
to let me live! * let it be said	Ps 119:116
days that your will * changes.	Ps 119:152
He will * let me stumble, slip	Ps 121:3,4
For he is always watching, *	Ps 121:3,4
My enemies have * been able to	Ps 129:2
And surely you will * go back on	Ps 132:11
the dynasty of David shall * end.	Ps 132:12
highest joy, let me * sing again.	Ps 137:5,6
I can * be lost to your Spirit!	Ps 139:7
I can * get away from my God!	Ps 139:7
For your kingdom * ends.	Ps 145:13
His orders will * be revoked.	Ps 148:6
Literally, "* return to the ways	Pro 2:19f
MY SON, * forget the things I've	Pro 3:1
* forget to be truthful and kind.	Pro 3:3
He told me * to forget his	Pro 4:4
Young men, listen to me, and *	Pro 5:7
* has enough of lust and shame.	Pro 9:13
The good shall * lose God's	Pro 10:30
Wickedness * brings real success;	Pro 12:3
be lazy and * succeed.	Pro 12:24
for ransom * worries the poor man!	Pro 13:8
Literally, "but the wicked * get	Pro 13:25f
A truthful witness * lies;	Pro 14:5

A mocker * finds the wisdom he	Pro 14:6
Dishonest gain will * last, so	Pro 21:6
* abandon a friend—either yours	Pro 27:10
The simpleton * looks, and	Pro 27:12
his mistakes can * be successful.	Pro 28:13
broken and * have another chance.	Pro 29:1
First, help me * to tell a lie.	Pro 30:8
* falsely accuse a man to his	Pro 30:10
There are two things * satisfied,	Pro 30:15,16
her household, and is * lazy.	Pro 31:27
sea but the sea is * full, and the	Ecc 1:3-7
much we see, we are * satisfied;	Ecc 1:8-11
are those who have * been born, and	Ecc 4:3
born, and have * seen all the evil	Ecc 4:3
He who loves money shall * have	Ecc 5:10
even a name, * seeing the sun or	Ecc 6:5
food, and * seem to get enough.	Ecc 6:7,8
who is always good and * sins.	Ecc 7:20
A man * knows when he is going	Ecc 9:12
gives everything! * curse the	Ecc 10:20
you will * get anything done.	Ecc 11:4
your seed, for you * know which	Ecc 11:6
They * weary, never stumble,	Is 5:27
They never weary, * stumble,	Is 5:27
weary, never stumble, * stop;	Is 5:27
peaceful government will * end.	Is 9:7
his food, but will * have enough.	Is 9:19,20
Babylon will * rise again.	Is 13:20
the land will * again be lived in.	Is 13:20
it, yet you will * harvest it—your	Is 17:11
not avail, for you * ask for help	Is 22:9,10,11
that this sin will * be forgiven	Is 22:14
He says, "* again, O dishonored	Is 23:12
disappear and * will be rebuilt.	Is 25:2
gone; * again will they return.	Is 26:14
They will * be worshiped again.	Is 27:9
"They can * touch us," you say,	Is 28:15
He who believes need * run away	Is 28:16
a farmer always plow and * sow?	Is 28:23,24
the soil and * planting it?	Is 28:23,24
A sledge is * used on dill, but	Is 28:27
A threshing wheel is * rolled on	Is 28:27
they will claim I * warned them.	Is 30:9
"Oh, no," they'll say, "you *	Is 30:9
* felt destruction for yourselves.	Is 33:1
This judgment on Edom will * end.	Is 34:10
gates of Sheol. * again will I see	Is 38:11
of the living. * again will I see	Is 38:11
Have you * heard nor understood?	Is 40:21
the earth, * grows faint or weary?	Is 40:28
there * was and never will be.	Is 43:10
there never was and * will be.	Is 43:10
and will * think of them again.	Is 43:25
The man * stops to think or	Is 44:19
he is trusting what can * give	Is 44:20
they shall * be disappointed in	Is 45:17
myself and I will * go back on my	Is 45:23
O daughter of Chaldea, * again	Is 47:1
O Babylon; * again will you be	Is 47:5
You thought your reign would *	Is 47:7
You say, "I alone am God! I'll *	Is 47:8
I'll never be a widow; I'll *	Is 47:8
you could * say, "My idol did it;	Is 48:5
*! Can a mother	Is 49:15
Those who wait for me shall * be	Is 49:23
my righteous rule will * die nor	Is 51:6
afflicted, yet he * said a word.	Is 53:7
and had * spoken an evil word.	Is 53:9
swore that I would * again permit	Is 54:9
swear that I will * again pour out	Is 54:9
peace for you will * be broken,	Is 54:10
it will * disappear.	Is 56:5
as greedy as dogs, * satisfied;	Is 56:11
in your search, but you * gave up.	Is 57:10
sea, which is * still, but always	Is 57:20
This kind of fasting will * get	Is 58:4
Your sun shall * set;	Is 60:20
King of kings. * again shall you	Is 62:4
* again give you to your enemies;	Is 62:8
to your enemies; * again shall	Is 62:8
the desert, they * stumbled.	Is 63:13
nation that * called you "Lord"?	Is 63:19
who * before inquired about me	Is 65:1
who * before searched for me are	Is 65:1
asks the Lord your God. No! *!	Is 66:9
a name that shall * disappear.	Is 66:22
me, for their worm shall * die;	Is 66:24
would * turn away from me again.	Jer 3:19
and roar, can * pass those bounds.	Jer 5:22
hotter, but it can * cleanse them,	Jer 6:29
will * let Jerusalem be destroyed.	Jer 7:4
Temple is here, you will * suffer?	Jer 7:8
so horrible I've * even thought of	Jer 7:31
them up to mean a thing I * said?	Jer 8:8
away and I will * see them again.	Jer 10:20
they have * seen nor heard;	Jer 14:14
where you have * been before, for	Jer 15:14
Will they * stop hurting me?	Jer 15:17,18
The snow * melts high up in the	Jer 18:14
crags of Mount Hermon * run dry.	Jer 18:14
thing I * commanded them nor even	Jer 19:5

You have * once let me speak a	Jer 20:
For if I say I'll * again mention	Jer 20:
mention the Lord—* more speak in	Jer 20:
For they will * return to see	Jer 22:1
and * again see his own country.	Jer 22:1
You will * again return to the	Jer 22:2
as they have * known before.	Jer 30:
that your sorrow should * end!	Jer 30:1
it shall * again be captured or	Jer 31:4
Molech—something I * commanded, and	Jer 32:3
them, promising * again to desert	Jer 32:4
me, and they shall * leave me.	Jer 32:4
I will * abandon the Jews, or	Jer 33:25,2
We have * had a drink of wine	Jer 35:
And you will * again see your own	Jer 42:1
Jeremiah concluded: "* forget the	Jer 42:1
said that you will * give up your	Jer 44:2
that will * be broken again."	Jer 50:
of the desert. * again shall it be	Jer 50:3
even your stones shall * be used	Jer 51:2
* to waken again, says the Lord.	Jer 51:3
Babylon sink, * more to rise,	Jer 51:6
For I can * forget these awful	Lam 3:2
of hope: his compassion * ends.	Lam 3:2
My enemies, whom I have * harmed,	Lam 3:5
will end at last, but Edom's *.	Lam 4:2
For I have * been defiled before	Eze 4:14
until now I have * eaten any animal	Eze 4:14
and I have * eaten any of the	Eze 4:14
have * told them anything at all.	Eze 13:2,3
see 'visions' you * saw, and that	Eze 13:7
when I * spoke to you at all?	Eze 13:7
will * see your own country again.	Eze 13:9
'visions' that you * saw, nor	Eze 13:23
There has * been anything like it	Eze 16:16
it seems that you can * find	Eze 16:28
her daughters have * been as wicked	Eze 16:48
his voice could * again be heard	Eze 19:9
everywhere. You * even think of me	Eze 22:12
You will * be rebuilt, for I, the	Eze 26:14
world of the dead. * again will you	Eze 26:20
all the nations; * again will she	Eze 29:15
the other nations; * again will	Eze 29:15
distant nations you have * seen.	Eze 32:9
my people will * again go hungry	Eze 34:29
killed. * again will you revive.	Eze 35:9
your cities will * be rebuilt.	Eze 35:9
and fields, and * again will the	Eze 36:30
You will * reach the cities—you	Eze 39:5
And I will * hide my face from	Eze 39:29
it shall * be opened.	Eze 44:2
Priests may * eat meat from any	Eze 44:31
They must * go out the same way	Eze 46:9
And the prince may * take	Eze 46:18
The leaves will * turn brown and	Eze 47:12
kingdom that will * be destroyed;	Dan 2:44
even then we will * under any	Dan 3:18
kingdom shall * be destroyed and	Dan 6:25,26
and whose power shall * end.	Dan 6:25,26
His power is eternal—it will *	Dan 7:14
his government shall * fall.	Dan 7:14
you would do, for * in all history	Dan 9:12
and do something * done before: he	Dan 11:24
—a god his fathers * knew—and	Dan 11:38
know me then as you * have before.	Hos 1:20
at Acacia. But * forget—I will	Hos 5:2
Her people * seem to recognize	Hos 7:2
the womb, or * even be conceived.	Hos 9:11
I have * put her under a heavy	Hos 10:11
in battle; * again will we call the	Hos 14:3
My mercies * fail.	Hos 14:8
seen before, and * will again	Joe 2:2
Straight forward they march, *	Joe 2:7
They * crowd each other.	Joe 2:8
miracles for you. * again will my	Joe 2:26
And my people shall * again be	Joe 2:27
who * have enough to drink!	Amo 4:1
therefore you will * live in the	Amo 5:11
shall fall and * rise again."	Amo 8:14
"I will * worship anyone but	Jon 2:9
and you will * see them again.	Mic 1:16
nothing can stop me; * again will	Mic 2:3
darkness will cover you, with * a	Mic 3:6
all your idols. * again will you	Mic 5:13
You will eat but * have enough;	Mic 6:14
your sons will * sit upon your	Nah 1:14
from Nineveh will * come again.	Nah 1:15
he will * be seen again.	Nah 1:15
Your finest youth lie dead. *	Nah 2:13
* again will you rule the earth.	Nah 2:13
and hell, they are * satisfied.	Hab 2:5
* loved him and never wanted to."	Zep 1:6
never loved him and * wanted to."	Zep 1:6
they will * have a chance to live	Zep 1:13
They will * drink wine from the	Zep 1:13
It will be as though I had * cast	Zec 10:6
safe at last, * again to be cursed	Zec 14:11
"But you say, 'We have * even	Mal 3:7
where they will * lose their value,	Mt 6:20
You need * confuse grapevines	Mt 7:16
fruit * produces an inedible kind.	Mt 7:18

NEVER Con't)
But I will reply, 'You have * Mt 7:23
Literally, "I * knew you." Mt 7:23f
How the crowds marveled! "* in Mt 9:33
Holy Spirit shall * be forgiven, Mt 12:31,32
use so many, he * spoke to them Mt 13:34,35
* get into the Kingdom of Heaven. Mt 18:3
Then he said to it, "* bear Mt 21:19
* have acted as our fathers did.' Mt 23:29,30
For I tell you this, you will * Mt 23:39
as the world has * before seen in Mt 24:21
its history, and will * see again. Mt 24:21
that one if he had * been born." Mt 26:24
"We've * seen anything like this Mk 2:12
He would * survive. Mk 3:26
the Holy Spirit can * be forgiven. Mk 3:29
Pharisees, will * eat until they Mk 7:3
he told them * to mention what they Mk 9:9
where the worm * dies, and the Mk 9:48
dies, and the fire * goes out— Mk 9:48
to Galilee. He * returned until Mk 10:1f
* be allowed into his Kingdom." Mk 10:15
the man replied, "I've * once Mk 10:20
tied up that has * been ridden. Mk 11:2
"You shall * bear fruit again!" Mk 11:14
you * read in the book of Exodus Mk 12:26
horror as have * been since the Mk 13:19
Oh, that he had * been born!" Mk 14:21
that I shall * again taste wine Mk 14:25
Peter said to him, "I will * Mk 14:29
die with you! I'll * deny you!" Mk 14:31
hour awaiting him might * come. Mk 14:35
He must * touch wine or hard Lk 1:15
his Kingdom shall * end!" Lk 1:33
of marriage. She * left the Temple Lk 2:36,37
your Father does. * criticize or Lk 6:37
it produces. Figs * grow on thorns, Lk 6:44
Turning to the crowd he said, "* Lk 7:9
without food and * took a drop of Lk 7:33
the message * really gets through Lk 8:13
And so they are * able to help Lk 8:14
of your doom. * forget how close Lk 10:11
would * think of trying to keep. Lk 11:46
on your head! * fear, you are far Lk 12:7
Holy Spirit shall * be forgiven. Lk 12:10
Your treasures there will * Lk 12:33
And you will * again see me until Lk 13:35
hard for you and * once refused to Lk 15:29
and in all that time you * gave Lk 15:29
For I * cheat, I don't commit Lk 18:11
come to me! * send them away! Lk 18:16,17
kind of faith will * get within the Lk 18:16,17
"But they would * do a thing like Lk 20:16
And they * die again; Lk 20:36
the darkness can * extinguish it. Jn 1:5
someone you have * met, who will Jn 1:26
* get into the Kingdom of God." Jn 3:3
and obey him shall * see heaven, Jn 3:36
Then I'll * be thirsty again and Jn 4:15
life, and will * be damned for his Jn 5:24
Those believing in me will * Jn 6:35
I will *, never reject them. Jn 6:37
I will never, * reject them. Jn 6:37
will * receive this gift. Jn 6:63
when he's * been to our schools?" Jn 7:15
"We've * heard anything like Jn 7:46
But only he who * sinned may Jn 8:7
* been slaves to any man on earth! Jn 8:33
began there has * been anyone who Jn 9:32
life and they shall * perish. Jn 10:28
in me and shall * perish. Jn 11:26
would live forever and * die. Jn 12:34
"you shall * wash my feet!" Jn 13:8
and he will * leave you. Jn 14:15,16
This is because they have * Jn 16:3
where there was a new tomb, * Jn 19:41
for he * ascended into the Act 2:34
them * again to speak about Jesus. Act 4:18
"Didn't we tell you * again to Act 5:28
and then told them * again to speak Act 5:40
and the eunuch * saw him again, but Act 8:39
"*, Lord," Peter declared, "I Act 10:14
declared, "I have * in all my life Act 10:14
* think of anyone as inferior. Act 10:28
" '*, Lord,' I replied. Act 11:8
'For I have * yet eaten anything Act 11:8
* end your opposition to the Lord? Act 13:10
the Jewish law could * do. Act 13:39
from birth, so he had * walked. Act 14:8
* left himself without a witness; Act 14:17
they want us to leave secretly? *! Act 16:37
He had * heard the rest of the Act 18:25,26
Yet I * shrank from telling you Act 20:20
"I have * been hungry for money Act 20:33
that he would * see them again. Act 20:38
Scriptures say, '* speak evil of Act 23:5
that I have * incited a riot in any Act 24:12
even though they * had God's Rom 2:12-15
and they have * known what it is Rom 3:17
But Abraham * doubted. Rom 4:20
since they themselves had * Rom 5:14
the dead and will * die again. Rom 6:9
Literally, "Sin will * again be Rom 6:14f
* again be your master, for now Rom 6:14
I would * have known the sin in Rom 7:7
is against God. It * did obey God's Rom 8:7
did obey God's laws and it * will. Rom 8:7
evil desires, can * please God. Rom 8:8
that will * be sick again and will Rom 8:23
be sick again and will * die. Rom 8:23
by keeping his laws, * succeeded. Rom 9:31
Those who believe in him will * Rom 9:33
all his life and * sin once, only Rom 10:5
if they have * heard about him? Rom 10:14
and his call can * be withdrawn; Rom 11:29
he will * go back on his Rom 11:29
each other. * be lazy in your work Rom 12:11
* pay back evil for evil. Rom 12:17
Dear friends, * avenge Rom 12:19
for others—* finish paying that! Rom 13:8
way that you will * make your Rom 14:13
name of Christ has * yet been Rom 15:20
those who have * heard the name of Rom 15:21
I can * stop thanking God for all 1Co 1:4
the world would * find God through 1Co 1:21
if they had, they * would have 1Co 2:8
For certainly he has * been one 1Co 2:16
But sexual sin is * right: our 1Co 6:13
and join him to a prostitute? *! 1Co 6:15
might * come to know the Lord; 1Co 7:14
Yet we have * used this right, 1Co 9:12
We have * demanded payment of any 1Co 9:12
Yet I have * asked you for one 1Co 9:15
to anyone, * demanding my rights. 1Co 9:18
heavenly reward that * disappears. 1Co 9:25
FOR WE MUST * forget, dear 1Co 10:1
"Oh, I would * behave like 1Co 10:12
can say is that we * teach anything 1Co 11:16
speak in languages he * learned; 1Co 12:10
The eye can * say to the hand, 1Co 12:21
in languages they have * learned. 1Co 12:28
in languages we've * learned? 1Co 12:30
Love is very patient and kind, * 1Co 13:4
or envious, * boastful or proud, 1Co 13:4
* haughty or selfish or rude. 1Co 13:5
It is * glad about injustice, 1Co 13:6
plainly; and * say it is wrong to 1Co 14:39
of course you * really believed it 1Co 15:2
will * come back to life again? 1Co 15:12
If we will * live again after we 1Co 15:32
all and have * really known God. 1Co 15:34
life again, for they will * die. 1Co 15:42
new bodies that will *, never die; 1Co 15:52
new bodies that will never, * die; 1Co 15:52
feared we would * live through it. 2Co 1:8
when he really means "no"? *! 2Co 1:18
new glory will * go away, we can 2Co 3:12
and so we * give up. 2Co 4:1
fooling anyone. We * try to get 2Co 4:2
We are hunted down, but God * 2Co 4:9
That is why we * give up. 2Co 4:16
We should * regret his sending 2Co 7:10
have * heard a worse preacher!" 2Co 10:10
I have * yet asked you for one 2Co 11:8,9
you for one cent, and I * will. 2Co 11:8,9
God * sent those men at all; 2Co 11:13
that I could * find God's favor by Gal 2:19
the Jewish laws * gave you Gal 3:3
though you * before had a child. Gal 4:27
are * free from their pressures. Gal 5:17
* stopped thanking God for you. Eph 1:16,17
* forget that once you were Eph 2:11
that you will * see the end of it Eph 3:18,19
and of God will * belong to anyone Eph 5:5
hope that I will * do anything that Php 1:20
in the Lord. I * get tired of Php 3:1
died for you, and * shifting from Col 1:23
who have * known me personally. Col 2:1
ready to forgive; * hold grudges. Col 3:13
constantly. We * forget your 1Th 1:3
deepest thoughts. * once did we 1Th 2:5
As for praise, we have * asked 1Th 2:6
And we will * stop thanking God 1Th 2:13
(though our hearts * left you), we 1Th 2:17
will: that you * cheat in this 1Th 4:6
from the Lord, * to see the glory 2Th 1:9
our example: you * saw us loafing; 2Th 3:7
us loafing; we * accepted food 2Th 3:8
* be tired of doing right. 2Th 3:13
ages, the unseen one who * dies; 1Ti 1:17
I * let women teach men or lord 1Ti 2:12
* SPEAK SHARPLY to an older man, 1Ti 5:1
For the Scriptures say, "* tie 1Ti 5:18
exactly the same. * be in a hurry 1Ti 5:22
and respect them; * let it be said 1Ti 6:1
who alone can * die, who lives in 1Ti 6:16
power, you will * be afraid to tell 2Ti 1:8
was * ashamed of my being in jail. 2Ti 1:16
They will be hardheaded and * 2Ti 3:3
but they * understand the truth. 2Ti 3:7
For God * said to any angel, Heb 1:5,6
But you yourself will * change, Heb 1:12
and your years will * end." Heb 1:12
up to me, and they * found the Heb 3:10
oath that he would * let them come Heb 3:11
But now is the time. * forget the Heb 3:15
that they could * go into the land Heb 3:18
believe me will * get in," even Heb 4:3
"They shall * enter my rest." Heb 4:5
therefore let us * stop trusting Heb 4:14
we do, though he * once gave way to Heb 4:15
You will * be able to eat solid Heb 5:14
perfectly sure and * need to wonder Heb 6:17
He was * born and he never died Heb 7:3
He was never born and he * died Heb 7:3
Moses had * given them that work. Heb 7:12,13,14
saving people. It * made anyone Heb 7:19
he * said that of other priests. Heb 7:21
has sworn and will * change his Heb 7:21
in heaven. He * needs the daily Heb 7:27
even so they could * save those who Heb 10:1
that could * take away our sins. Heb 10:11
And then he adds, "I will * Heb 10:17
But we have * turned our backs on Heb 10:39
You can * please God without Heb 11:6
After all, you have * yet Heb 12:4
Whoever heard of a son who was * Heb 12:7
For God has said, "I will *, Heb 13:5
* fail you nor forsake you." Heb 13:5
Jewish laws can * be helped. Heb 13:10
to do wrong it is * God who is Jas 1:13
him, for God * wants to do wrong Jas 1:13
and * tempts anyone else to do it. Jas 1:13
self-confidence * pleases God. Jas 4:16
even though you have * seen him; 1Pe 1:8
church, and I will * disappoint 1Pe 2:6
having * experienced its power. 1Pe 2:15
Follow in his steps: He * 1Pe 2:22
He never sinned, * told a lie, 1Pe 2:22
* answered back when insulted; 1Pe 2:23
who have * believed in the Lord? 1Pe 4:17
made you, for he will * fail you. 1Pe 4:19
you will * stumble or fall away. 2Pe 1:10
false teachers, * speak out 2Pe 2:11
of adultery they * have enough. 2Pe 2:14
It would be better if he had * 2Pe 2:21
He'll * come! 2Pe 3:4
churches, but they * really 1Jn 2:19
in Christ, * to depart from him. 1Jn 2:27
* really known him or become his. 1Jn 3:6
For though we have * yet seen 1Jn 4:12
he love God whom he has * seen? 1Jn 4:20
constant gripers, * satisfied, Jud 1:16
* forgot the horror of it. Rev 1:7f
they will * be hungry again, nor Rev 7:16
so much will * be yours again. Rev 18:14
forever. * again will the sound of Rev 18:22
Its gates * close; Rev 21:25

NEVER-ENDING
This is his * treaty with the Ps 105:10,11
and faced with * Ps 129:2
My eyes flow day and night with * Lam 3:48,49
the chaff with * fire, and storing Mt 3:12
a * share in his glory and honor. 1Pe 5:4

NEVER-FAILING
shown me that his * love protects Ps 31:21

NEVER-TO-BE-FORGOTTEN
because of those * deeds. Neh 9:10

NEVERTHELESS
with Benjamin, but * may have been Gen 31:35f
"*," the Lord said, "go back Ex 7:15
Literally, "*, the heart of Asa 1Ki 15:14f
father had made. * he still clung 2Ki 3:3
Ahab's daughters. *, because God 2Ki 8:19
* the king of Assyria sent his 2Ki 18:17
"*, the Lord God of Israel has 1Ch 28:4
* Edom . 2Ch 21:9f
I expect him to. * I am going to Job 13:15
my daily food. *, his mind Job 23:13
than strength, *, if the wise man Ecc 9:16
*, THAT TIME of darkness and Is 9:1
* the time will come when I will Jer 33:6
through Jeremiah. *, King Zedekiah Jer 37:3
"*, Zedekiah rebelled against Eze 17:15
their idols! *, I spared them. Eze 20:17
"*, again I withdrew my judgment Eze 20:22
For I am your servant. *, Lk 22:28
about them. *, they stayed there a Act 14:3
LET LOVE BE your greatest aim; *, 1Co 14:1

NEW
* possessions I am giving you." Gen 13:17
Keturah was his * wife, and she Gen 25:1
His shepherds also dug a * well Gen 26:19
good harvest of grain, and * wine. Gen 27:27,28,29
One of these * wives was Gen 28:9
gave each of them * clothes—but to Gen 45:22
a * king came to the throne of Ex 1:8
have been removed, * mortar used, Lev 14:42
not throw you out of your * land. Lev 20:22
the * grain of your later crops. Lev 23:15,16
of crops the * owner will get from Lev 25:14,15,16
* owner until the Year of Jubilee; Lev 25:28
permanently to the * owner—it does Lev 25:30

(NEW Con't)

them when the * harvest is ready!	Lev 26:10
traveled to a * campsite.	Num 2:3-31
over again with a * vow, and must	Num 6:12
erected in its * location by the	Num 10:21
of each year's * crops by making	Num 15:19,20,21
please appoint a * leader for	Num 27:16
people to celebrate the * harvest.	Num 28:26
the first of the * crop of grain as	Num 28:26
"burnt offerings of the * moon."	Num 29:6f
of your grain and * wine and olive	Deu 12:17
tithes of grain, * wine, olive oil,	Deu 14:23
of the grain, the * wine, the olive	Deu 18:4
* house, but not yet dedicated it?	Deu 20:5
"Every * house must have a	Deu 22:8
Your grain, * wine, olive oil,	Deu 28:51
afterbirth and the * baby she has	Deu 28:56,57
Joshua is your * commander, as	Deu 31:3
To * gods never before worshiped.	Deu 32:17
[you are the * leader of Israel	Jos 1:2
these wineskins were *, but now	Jos 9:13
As they were leaving for their *	Ju 1:14
moved into its * land in the Negeb	Ju 1:16
moved into their * territories and	Ju 2:6
land to test the * generation of	Ju 3:1
These people were a test to the *	Ju 3:4
When Israel chose * gods,	Ju 5:8
it was gone, and a * altar had been	Ju 6:28
Go and cry to the * gods you	Ju 10:14
they said to his * wife, "Get the	Ju 14:15
So they tied him with two * ropes	Ju 15:12,13
am tied with brand * ropes which	Ju 16:11
Delilah took * ropes and tied him	Ju 16:12
* suit and your board and room."	Ju 17:10,11
Now build a * cart and hitch to	1Sa 6:7
go, God gave him a * attitude, and	1Sa 10:9
of his sons to be the * king."	1Sa 16:1
of the celebration of the * moon.	1Sa 20:5
When the * moon celebration began,	1Sa 20:24,25
appointed me as their * king."	2Sa 2:7
The Ark was placed upon a * cart	2Sa 6:3
who was sporting a * suit of armor,	2Sa 21:16
Apparently * names were elected	2Sa 23:24-39f
But instead, Adonijah is the *	1Ki 1:18
him upon my throne as the * king;	1Ki 1:35
have anointed him as the * king!	1Ki 1:44,45
And Solomon became the * king,	1Ki 2:12
Solomon was the * king of Israel,	1Ki 5:1
Jerusalem—to the * quarters he had	1Ki 9:24
(who had put on a * robe for the	1Ki 11:29
Ahijah tore his * robe into twelve	1Ki 11:30
the * king answered them roughly.	1Ki 12:13,14
it—he caused the * king to do this	1Ki 12:15
became the * king of Judah.	1Ki 15:24
to be the * king of Israel.	1Ki 16:10
of the army, as their * ruler.	1Ki 16:15,16
son became the * king of Israel.	1Ki 22:40
Israel's * king, Ahaziah, had	2Ki 1:2
Jehoram became the * king—for	2Ki 1:17
"Well," he said, "bring me a *	2Ki 2:20
we can build a * one down beside	2Ki 6:1
became the * king during the	2Ki 8:24,25
and his son Jehoahaz became the *	2Ki 10:35
Temple and saw the * king standing	2Ki 11:13,14
his son Amaziah became the * king.	2Ki 12:21
and Jeroboam II became the *	2Ki 13:13
And his son Jeroboam became the *	2Ki 14:16
became the * king at the age of	2Ki 14:21
became the * king of Israel.	2Ki 14:29
* KING OF Judah: Azariah	2Ki 15:1
* king of Israel: Zechariah	2Ki 15:8
* king of Israel: Shallum	2Ki 15:13
Name of * king of Israel: Menahem	2Ki 15:17
son Pekahiah became the * king.	2Ki 15:22
Name of * king of Israel:	2Ki 15:23
So Pekah became the * king.	2Ki 15:25
* king of Israel: Pekah	2Ki 15:27
* king of Israel: Hoshea	2Ki 15:30
* king of Judah: Jotham	2Ki 15:32,33
Then his son Ahaz became the *	2Ki 15:38
* king of Judah	2Ki 16:1
entrance and the * altar), and	2Ki 16:14
on the north side of the * altar.	2Ki 16:14
priest to use the * altar for the	2Ki 16:15
to be sprinkled over the * altar.	2Ki 16:15
son Hezekiah became the * king.	2Ki 16:20
* king of Israel	2Ki 17:1
and teach the * residents the laws	2Ki 17:27,28
* king of Judah	2Ki 18:1
son Esarhaddon became the * king.	2Ki 19:37
son Manasseh became the * king.	2Ki 20:21
* king of Judah	2Ki 21:1
his son Amon became the * king.	2Ki 21:18
Name of the * king of Judah: Amon	2Ki 21:19,20
his son Josiah became the * king.	2Ki 21:26
* king of Judah	2Ki 22:1
by the nation as its * king.	2Ki 23:30
* king of Judah: Jehoahaz	2Ki 23:31,32
* king of Judah: Jehoiakim	2Ki 23:36,37
son Jehoiachin became the * king.	2Ki 24:6
* king of Judah, Jehoiachin	2Ki 24:8,9
* king of Judah: Zedekiah	2Ki 24:18,19
from Bozrah became the * king.	1Ch 1:44
of Rehoboth became the * king.	1Ch 1:48
of Moab by Hodesh, his * wife:	1Ch 8:8,9,10
the house of Abinadab on a * cart.	1Ch 13:7
David was Israel's * king, they	1Ch 14:8
he also built a * Tabernacle to	1Ch 15:1
we transfer the Ark to its * home	1Ch 15:2
of the Ark into the * Tabernacle.	1Ch 15:3
been living in his * palace for	1Ch 17:1
his son Hanun became the * king.	1Ch 19:1
Solomon as the * king of Israel.	1Ch 23:1
sacrifices, the * moon	1Ch 23:31
and at the * moon celebration and	2Ch 2:4
Zion, [to its * home in the Temple	2Ch 5:2
the * palace he had built for her.	2Ch 8:11
the Sabbaths, on * moon festivals,	2Ch 8:13
son Rehoboam became the * king.	2Ch 9:31
his son Abijah became the * king.	2Ch 12:16
ABIJAH BECAME THE * king of	2Ch 13:1
Then his son Asa became the *	2Ch 14:1
gathered at the * court of the	2Ch 20:5
became the * ruler of Judah.	2Ch 21:1
his youngest son, as their * king	2Ch 22:1
his son Amaziah became the * king.	2Ch 24:27
established as the * king, he	2Ch 25:3
Uzziah as their * king.	2Ch 26:1
Then he built * cities in the	2Ch 26:6
his son Jotham became the * king.	2Ch 26:23
his son Ahaz became the * king.	2Ch 27:9
son Hezekiah became the * king.	2Ch 28:27
and monthly * moon festivals, and	2Ch 31:3
crops and grain, * wine, olive oil,	2Ch 31:5,6
for his grain, * wine, and olive	2Ch 32:28,29
son Manasseh became the * king.	2Ch 32:33
his son Amon became the * king.	2Ch 33:20,21
his son Josiah to be the * king.	2Ch 33:25
was selected as the * king.	2Ch 36:1
Jehoahaz, as the * king of Judah.	2Ch 36:4
son Jehoiachin became the * king.	2Ch 36:8
the * king of Judah and Jerusalem.	2Ch 36:10
the Sabbaths, the * moon	Ez 3:5
topped with a layer of * timber.	Ez 6:4
of joy and * life in our slavery.	Ez 9:8
the Sabbaths, the * moon feasts,	Neh 10:33
first of the * wine and olive oil.	Neh 10:37
of grain, * wine, and olive oil to	Neh 10:39,40
During the dedication of the *	Neh 12:27
of grain, * wine, and olive oil.	Neh 13:5
tithes of grain, * wine, and olive	Neh 13:12
You're not telling me anything *.	Job 9:2
and grows tender, * branches.	Job 14:7
touch of water, like a * seedling.	Job 14:8,9
Compose * songs of praise to	Ps 33:3
He has given me a * song to	Ps 40:3
Create in me a *, clean heart, O	Ps 51:10
Give me time to tell this *	Ps 71:18
* moon and all the other holidays.	Ps 81:3
SING A * song to the Lord!	Ps 96:1
SING A * song to the Lord telling	Ps 98:1
a man putting on a * shirt and	Ps 102:26
Then you send your Spirit, and *	Ps 104:30
became God's * home and kingdom.	Ps 114:2
I will sing you a * song, O God,	Ps 144:9
Sing him a * song.	Ps 149:1
guide you into the * day.	Pro 6:22
man is always open to * ideas.	Pro 18:15
taverns, trying out * mixtures.	Pro 23:29,30
harvested, and the * crop appears,	Pro 27:25,26,27
Nothing is truly *;	Ecc 1:8-11
What can you point to that is *?	Ecc 1:8-11
at our doors, the * as well as old,	Sol 7:13
Your holy celebrations of the *	Is 1:12,13
—yes, a * Branch	Is 11:1
though the paths he treads are *.	Is 41:3
for word of Cyrus' * campaigns.	Is 41:5
But they rush to make a *	Is 41:7
You shall be a * and	Is 41:15
Sing a * song to the Lord;	Is 42:10
For I'm going to do a brand *	Is 43:19
Now I will tell you * things I	Is 48:6
things entirely *, for I know so	Is 48:8
the writers of the * Testament and	Is 52:13f
itself, to find * gods to love.	Is 57:9
humble and give * courage to those	Is 57:15
and God will confer on you a *	Is 62:2
Your * name will be "The Land	Is 62:4
For see, I am creating * heavens	Is 65:17
new heavens and a * earth—so	Is 65:17
As surely as my * heavens and	Is 66:22
its old gods for * ones—even though	Jer 2:10,11
but it's all no good—your *	Jer 2:36
and all of those * gods of yours,	Jer 7:9
cause something * and different to	Jer 31:22
when I will make a * contract with	Jer 31:31
But this is the * contract I	Jer 31:33
if not the same as, the * birth.	Jer 31:33f
near the door of the * Gate.	Jer 36:10
son) to be the * king of Judah.	Jer 37:1
and gave him * clothes and fed him	Jer 52:33
give you one heart and a * spirit;	Eze 11:19
you can never find enough * gods.	Eze 16:2
a * heart and a new spirit.	Eze 18:3
a new heart and a * spirit.	Eze 18:3
so that even the * order that	Eze 21:2
And I will give you a * heart—I	Eze 36:2
will give you * and right	Eze 36:2
put a * spirit within you.	Eze 36:2
sin and give you * hearts of love.	Eze 36:2
feasts, the * moon ceremonies, the	Eze 45:1
"The Lord God says: On each *	Eze 45:18
days of the * moon celebrations.	Eze 46:1
days of the * moon celebrations.	Eze 46:3
At the * moon celebration, he	Eze 46:6
There will be a * crop every	Eze 47:12
* birth is offered him, but he is	Hos 13:13
I am raising a * force on the	Hab 1:6
in the * homes they have built.	Zep 1:13
giving you these fine * clothes."	Zec 3:4
into Israel as a * clan: the	Zec 9:7
* king was Herod's son, Archelaus.	Mt 2:22
to store * wine?	Mt 9:17
skins ruined. Only * wineskins are	Mt 9:17
are used to store * wine.	Mt 9:17
Testament as well as from the *!"	Mt 13:52
treasure things both * and old."	Mt 13:52f
missing arms and legs had * ones;	Mt 15:31
my blood, sealing the * Covenant.	Mt 26:28
the day I drink it * with you in my	Mt 26:29
it in his own * rock-hewn tomb, and	Mt 27:60
EARLY ON SUNDAY morning, as the *	Mt 28:1
then teach these * disciples to	Mt 28:20
"What sort of * religion is	Mk 1:27
You know better than to put *	Mk 2:22
* wine needs fresh wineskins."	Mk 2:22
still others claimed he was a *	Mk 6:15
manuscripts read, "* covenant."	Mk 14:24f
the * agreement between God and	Mk 14:24
Literally, "drink it *."	Mk 14:25f
and they shall speak * languages.	Mk 16:17
Literally, "they will speak in *	Mk 16:17f
ancient manuscripts omit "*."	Mk 16:17f
off a piece of a * garment to make	Lk 5:36
Not only will the * garment be	Lk 5:36
look worse with a * patch on it!	Lk 5:36
And no one puts * wine into old	Lk 5:37
wineskins, for the * wine bursts	Lk 5:37
the wine. * wine must be put into	Lk 5:38
New wine must be put into *	Lk 5:38
seems to want the fresh and the *.	Lk 5:39
raised up in * life from the dead.	Lk 20:36
the token of God's * agreement to	Lk 22:20
Literally, "This cup is the *	Lk 22:20f
and laid it in a *, unused tomb	Lk 23:53
Spirit gives * life from heaven;	Jn 3:6
But my death will produce many *	Jn 12:23,24
plentiful harvest of * lives.	Jn 12:23,24
"And so I am giving a *	Jn 13:34
where there was a * tomb, never	Jn 19:41
a * high of about 5,000 men!	Act 4:4
them into their * territory, and	Act 7:45
praying for these * Christians to	Act 8:15
to Antioch to help the * converts.	Act 11:22
teaching the many * converts.	Act 11:26
and there were many * believers.	Act 12:24
to see how the * converts were	Act 15:36
us more about this * religion,"	Act 17:19
discussing the latest * ideas!	Act 17:21
grabbed Sosthenes, the * leader	Act 18:17
to take over his *	Act 25:1
always thinking of * ways of	Rom 1:30
his laws, but by a * way (though	Rom 3:21,22
way (though not *, really, for the	Rom 3:21,22
Now we rejoice in our wonderful *	Rom 5:11
his wonderful * life to enjoy.	Rom 6:4
and now you share his * life, and	Rom 6:5
that you will share his * life.	Rom 6:8
to your * master, righteousness.	Rom 6:18
Christ did, and are a * person.	Rom 7:4
rules, but in the * way, [with all	Rom 7:6
far as my * nature is concerned;	Rom 7:22
So you see how it is: my * life	Rom 7:23,24,25
You are controlled by your *	Rom 8:9
including the * bodies he has	Rom 8:23
world, but be a * and different	Rom 12:2
*, beginning a "Church of Paul."	1Co 1:15
aren't anything * and different.	1Co 10:13
"This cup is the * agreement	1Co 11:25
and an unsaved person or a *	1Co 14:24
it a beautiful * body—just the kind	1Co 15:38
we shall all be given * bodies!	1Co 15:51
become alive, with * bodies that	1Co 15:52
shall suddenly have * bodies too.	1Co 15:52
his * agreement to save them.	2Co 3:6
in the * way, the Holy Spirit	2Co 3:6
glory of the * agreement.	2Co 3:10
of God's * plan for our salvation	2Co 3:11
Since we know that this * glory	2Co 3:12
have wonderful * bodies in heaven,	2Co 5:1
we shall put on like * clothes.	2Co 5:2
We want to slip into our * bodies	2Co 5:4
becomes a brand * person inside.	2Co 5:17

NEW Con't)
He is not the same any more. A * 2Co 5:17
All these * things are from God 2Co 5:18
into * and different people. Gal 6:15
us * lives from Christ Jesus; Eph 2:10
to become one * person, and at last Eph 2:15
Amplified * Testament. Eph 4:15,16f
Yes, you must be a * and Eph 4:24
Clothe yourself with this * Eph 4:24
with him into a * life because you Col 2:12
or * moon ceremonies or Sabbaths. Col 2:16
You are living a brand * kind of Col 3:10
created this * life within you. Col 3:10
In this * life one's nationality Col 3:11
has given you this * kind of life, Col 3:12
The pastor must not be a * 1Ti 3:6
and teach them their * doctrines. 2Ti 3:6
forever following * teachers, but 2Ti 3:7
and giving us the * joy of the Tit 3:5
This * place of rest he is Heb 4:8
save them can take * courage when Heb 6:18
And when God sends a * kind of Heb 7:12,13,14
for Christ, the * High Priest who Heb 7:15
of this * and better arrangement. Heb 7:22
laws, because the * agreement which Heb 8:6
when I will make a * agreement with Heb 8:8
This * agreement will not be Heb 8:9
But this is the * agreement I Heb 8:10
God speaks of these * promises, Heb 8:13
promises, of this * agreement, as Heb 8:13
came with God's * and better way. Heb 9:10
Christ came with this * Heb 9:15
Under this * plan we have been Heb 10:10
This is the fresh, *, Heb 10:20
So take a * grip with your tired Heb 12:12
us his wonderful * agreement; Heb 12:24
be attracted by strange, * ideas. Heb 13:9
when he gave us our * lives, Jas 1:18
first children in his * family. Jas 1:18
For you have a * life. 1Pe 1:23
fade away. This * one will last 1Pe 1:23
God's promise of * heavens and a 2Pe 3:13
new heavens and a * earth 2Pe 3:13
not writing out a * rule for you to 1Jn 2:7
Yet it is always *, and works 1Jn 2:8
disappears and the * light of life 1Jn 2:8
sinning, for this * life has been 1Jn 3:9
will be engraved a * name that no Rev 2:17
city of my God—the * Jerusalem, Rev 3:12
and he will have my * Name Rev 3:12
him a * song with these words: Rev 5:9
a wonderful * song in front of the Rev 14:3
THEN I SAW a * earth (with no Rev 21:1
and a * sky, for the present Rev 21:1
the Holy City, the * Jerusalem, Rev 21:2
"See, I am making all things *!" Rev 21:5

NEWBORN
* Hebrew boys into the Nile River. Ex 1:22
wife and her * son (Isaiah 8:1–4). Is 7:14f
"Where is the * King of the Jews? Mt 2:2

NEWLY
"A * married man is not to be Deu 24:5
sheep's wool, * shorn and washed; Sol 4:2

NEWNESS
a fresh * in all you do and think. Rom 12:2
lives in the fresh * of life of Php 3:11

NEWS
returned with the * that Esau was Gen 32:6
palace, and the * was quickly Gen 45:2
tongues! The * soon reached Gen 45:16
When the * was brought to Joshua Jos 10:17
road to hear the * of the battle, 1Sa 4:13
at Geba. The * spread quickly 1Sa 13:3,4
of Hereth. The * of his arrival in 1Sa 22:6
exclaimed when he heard the *. 1Sa 22:7
ONE DAY * came to David that the 1Sa 23:1
he received the * that Saul was on 1Sa 23:14,15
sent the wonderful * of Saul's 1Sa 31:9
in sorrow when they heard the *. 2Sa 1:11
the *, "Where are you from?" 2Sa 1:13
When the * of the outcome of the 2Sa 4:4
bringing me good *, I killed him; 2Sa 4:10
with the good * that the Lord has 2Sa 18:19
wouldn't be good * to the king that 2Sa 18:20
"There is no further * to 2Sa 18:22
He shouted the * down to David, 2Sa 18:25
"If he is alone, he has *." 2Sa 18:25
replied, "He will have more *." 2Sa 18:26
with good *," the king replied. 2Sa 18:27
have good * for my lord the king. 2Sa 18:31
gates, and as the * spread 2Sa 19:8,9,10
you must have good *." 1Ki 1:42
When * of this reached King 1Ki 2:29
told her, "I have sad * for you. 1Ki 14:6
When Jezebel heard the *, she 1Ki 21:15
This is wonderful *, and we 2Ki 7:9
Then the watchmen shouted the * 2Ki 7:11
When the king heard the *, he 2Ki 8:8,9
will receive bad * from home and 2Ki 19:7
Soon afterwards * reached the 2Ki 19:9
wonderful * before their idols. 1Ch 10:9
When this * reached David, he 1Ch 19:17,18
When this * reached King Rehoboam 2Ch 10:18
shaken by this * and determined to 2Ch 20:3
the * of her son Ahaziah's death. 2Ch 22:10
home with this *: "Your oxen were Job 1:14,15
with more bad *: "The fire of God Job 1:16
when we hear the * of your victory, Ps 20:5
I have told everyone the Good * Ps 40:9
I have not kept this Good * Ps 40:10
the world with the * of your saving Ps 67:2
cry out the happy *: "The armies Ps 68:11,12,13
He does not fear bad *, nor live Ps 112:7
Songs of joy at the * of our Ps 118:15,16
Good * from far away is like cold Pro 25:25
However, when the * came to the Is 7:2
so that I can give you better *. Is 21:12
When Egypt hears the *, there Is 23:5
With this * bring cheer to all Is 35:3
O Crier of Good *, shout to Is 40:9
bring the happy * of peace and Is 52:7
* that the God of Israel reigns. Is 52:7
* to the suffering and afflicted. Is 61:1
father the * that a son was born. Jer 20:15
the sad * from the Lord today?" Jer 23:33
you shall reply, "What sad *? Jer 23:33
You are the sad *, for the Lord Jer 23:33
"today's sad * from God," I will Jer 23:34
using this term, "God's sad *." Jer 23:36
"today's sad * from God," when I Jer 23:38,39
would do when the * reached them Jer 41:18
have heard the * of their doom. Jer 49:23
fearsome * that God has given me. Eze 21:7
"But then * from the east and Dan 11:44
with glad *: "The invaders have Nah 1:15
* about the Kingdom of Heaven. Mt 4:23
the Good * about the Kingdom. Mt 9:35
preaching the Good * to the poor. Mt 11:5
the * about his miracles. Mt 12:16
who hears the Good * about the Mt 13:19
As soon as Jesus heard the *, he Mt 14:13
They landed at Gennesaret. The * Mt 14:35
"And the Good * about the Mt 24:14
wherever the Good * is preached." Mt 26:13
to Galilee to preach God's Good *. Mk 1:14
sins and act on this glorious *!" Mk 1:15
The * of what he had done spread Mk 1:28
the good * that he was healed; Mk 1:45
Capernaum, and the * of his arrival Mk 2:1
For the * about his miracles had Mk 3:7,8
listen to the Good * and receive Mk 4:18
spreading the * as they ran. Mk 5:14
home with the * that it was too Mk 5:35
area to spread the * of his Mk 6:55
For as usual the * of his arrival Mk 7:24
not to spread the *, but the more Mk 7:36
sake of the Good * will ever know Mk 8:35
others the Good *, who won't be Mk 10:29
to tell them the Good *. Mk 13:9
And the Good * must first be Mk 13:10
wherever the Good * is preached Mk 14:9
Good * to everyone, everywhere. Mk 16:15
sent me to you with this good *! Lk 1:19
and the * of what had happened Lk 1:65
"I bring you the most joyful * Lk 2:10
the Good * to the people. Lk 3:18
me to preach Good * to the poor; Lk 4:18,19
preach the Good * of the Kingdom of Lk 4:43
the poor are hearing the Good *. Lk 7:20,21,22
anyone else to believe the Good *. Lk 8:14
city, spreading the * as they ran. Lk 8:34
* that the little girl was dead. Lk 8:49
the Good * and healing the sick. Lk 9:6
But John introduced the Good * Lk 16:16
preaching the Good * in the Temple, Lk 20:1
to preach the Good * and you were Lk 22:35
met him with the * that all was Jn 4:51
The next day, the * that Jesus Jn 12:12
his bowels. The * of his death Act 1:19
Then someone arrived with the * Act 5:25
preaching the Good * about Jesus! Act 8:4
to preach the Good * to them too. Act 8:25
He preached the Good * there and Act 8:40
there the Good * about Jesus—that Act 9:20
The * raced through the town, and Act 9:42
about the Good * for the people of Act 10:36,37
to preach the Good * everywhere and Act 10:42
SOON THE * reached the apostles Act 11:1
them the Good *, but just as I was Act 11:15
the Good *, but only to Jews. Act 11:19
God's Good * was spreading Act 12:24
you this Good *—that God's promise Act 13:32,33
that this Good * from God should be Act 13:46
and preaching the Good * there. Act 14:7
bring you the Good * that you are Act 14:15
After preaching the Good * there Act 14:21
to preach the Good * to the Act 15:7
us to preach the Good * there. Act 16:10
the Good * from the Lord. Act 16:32
others the Good * about God's Act 20:24
sent out to preach God's Good *. Rom 1:1
This Good * was promised long Rom 1:2
It is the Good * about his Son, Rom 1:3
others the Good * about his Son. Rom 1:9
in Rome to preach God's Good *. Rom 1:15
of this Good * about Christ. Rom 1:16
This Good * tells us that God Rom 1:17
who come preaching God's Good *! Rom 10:15
who hears the Good * has welcomed Rom 10:16
Good *—the Good News about Christ. Rom 10:17
Good News—the Good * about Christ. Rom 10:17
the Good * has been told to the Rom 10:18
Because the * about Christ came Rom 15:27
preaching the Good * without 1Co 9:18
Good * I preached to you before. 1Co 15:1
and it is this Good * that saves 1Co 15:2
us apostles to preach the Good *. 2Co 1:21
[of telling his Good * to others 2Co 4:1
If the Good * we preach is hidden 2Co 4:3
joy, but also the * that he brought 2Co 7:7
of the Good * in all the churches. 2Co 8:18
with the Good * concerning Christ. 2Co 10:14
to preach the Good * to other 2Co 10:16
God's Good * to you without 2Co 11:7
show them the Good * about Jesus. Gal 1:16
brought you the Good * of Christ. Gal 4:13
who heard the Good * about how to Eph 1:13
And he has brought this Good * Eph 2:17
accept the Good * about Christ and Eph 3:6
Gentiles the Glad * of the endless Eph 3:8
the Good * of peace with God. Eph 6:15
known the Good * about Christ from Php 1:5
out the Good * concerning Christ. Php 1:12
preaching the Good * because they Php 1:15
that the Good * about Christ is Php 1:18
tell the Good * fearlessly, no Php 1:27
in helping me preach the Good *. Php 2:22
in telling the Good * to others; Php 4:3
The same Good * that came to you Col 1:6
one who brought you this Good *. Col 1:7
of the Good * that Jesus died for Col 1:23
This is the wonderful * that came Col 1:23
to preach the Good * of Christ for Col 4:3
chances to tell others the Good *. Col 4:5
will give you all the latest *. Col 4:9
you the Good *, it was not just 1Th 1:5
preached God's Good * among you. 1Th 2:9
brings the welcome * that your 1Th 3:6
encourage each other with this *. 1Th 4:18
Through us he told you the Good *. 2Th 2:14
the glorious Good * of our blessed 1Ti 1:10,11
to them the Good * is just a 1Ti 6:5
result of my preaching the Good *. 2Ti 3:11
revealed this Good * and permits me Tit 1:3
preaching the Good * about Jesus Phm 1:1
preaching the Good *, and you would Phm 1:13
For this wonderful *—the message Heb 4:2
the Good * and tasted for yourself Heb 6:4
And now at last this Good * has 1Pe 1:12
And his message is the Good * 1Pe 1:25
That is why the Good * was 1Pe 4:6
everlasting Good * to preach to Rev 14:6

NEXT
Her * child was his brother, Gen 4:2
The dove which Noah * dispatched Gen 8:7f
Sarah * year at about this time." Gen 17:21
Then the Lord said, "* year Gen 18:10
Is anything too hard for God? * Gen 18:14
At dawn the * morning the angels Gen 19:15
The * morning she said to her Gen 19:34
The king was up early the * Gen 20:8
So Abraham got up early the * Gen 21:14
The * morning Abraham got up Gen 22:3
oldest,Buz, the * oldest,Kemuel Gen 22:20-23
I'll know what my * step should be, Gen 24:49
But early the * morning he said, Gen 24:54
The * morning he got up very Gen 28:18
So Jacob spent the * seven years Gen 29:20
Laban was up early the * morning Gen 31:55
*, and Rachel and Joseph last. Gen 33:2
low before him. * came Leah with Gen 33:7
had a dream. The * morning Joseph Gen 40:6
was all a dream. * morning, as he Gen 41:8
about to do: The * seven years Gen 41:29
crops of the * seven years, so Gen 41:34,35
And sure enough, for the * seven Gen 41:47
The * year they came again and Gen 47:18
to be used for * year's seed, and Gen 47:24
The * day as he was out visiting Ex 2:13
your robe, * to your chest." Ex 4:6
The following week(continued in * Ex 7:25
* the Lord told Moses, "Get up Ex 8:20
begin the very * day, and it did. Ex 9:5
and it did. The * morning all the Ex 9:6
Don't eat any of it the * day; Ex 12:10
And the * morning the food was Ex 16:24
The * day Moses sat as usual to Ex 18:13
unoffered until the * morning. Ex 23:18
and early the * morning he built Ex 24:4
mortise into the * upright piece. Ex 26:17
"*, make a plate of pure gold Ex 28:36
their robes * to their bodies, Ex 28:42
it upon his head. *, dress his Ex 29:8

(NEXT Con't)
"*, Aaron and his sons shall lay Ex 29:15,16
Whoever is the * High Priest Ex 29:30
So they were up early the * Ex 32:6
The * day Moses said to the Ex 32:30
two clasps joining it to the *. Ex 36:22
* BEZALEL MADE the Ark. Ex 37:1
poles in place. *, using pure Ex 37:15,16
and fire pans. * he made a bronze Ex 38:4
on the under side, * to the ephod. Ex 39:19
* he placed the table at the Ex 40:22
And he placed the lampstand * to Ex 40:24
in the Tabernacle * to the veil, Ex 40:26
* he placed the washbasin between Ex 40:30
(The * morning) the priest shall Lev 6:10
none left to be eaten the * day. Lev 7:15
sacrificed may be eaten the * day. Lev 7:16
for his work. * Moses placed the Lev 8:13
upon the altar. * he quartered the Lev 8:20
his right foot. * he smeared some Lev 8:24
* he took some of the anointing Lev 8:30
* he told them not to leave the Lev 8:33
* he killed the burnt offering Lev 9:12
* he sacrificed the people's Lev 9:15
* he killed the ox and ram—the Lev 9:18
Then, for the * thirty-three Lev 12:4
"The * day, the eighth day, he Lev 14:10
defiled until the * evening. Lev 15:18
it, or the * day at the latest; Lev 19:6
and goes on until the * evening. Lev 23:32
until the * Year of Jubilee. Lev 27:18
Location: * to Judah Num 2:3-31
Tabernacle * to Issachar Num 2:3-31
Zurishaddai * to Reuben Num 2:3-31
* to Simeon Num 2:3-31
Location: Tabernacle * Num 2:3-31
Location: Ephraim * to Num 2:3-31
Location: Tabernacle * to Num 2:3-31
Location: Next to Dan * Num 2:3-31
These three tribes were * in line Num 2:3-31
* in the line of march was the Num 2:3-31
they were * in the line of march. Num 2:3-31
"* they must spread a blue cloth Num 4:7
"* they must cover with a blue Num 4:9
of death. The * day, the eighth Num 6:10
The * day Nethanel, the son of Num 7:18-23
The * day it was Eliasaph's turn, Num 7:42-47
"*, the Levite leaders Num 8:12
of it until the * morning, and must Num 9:12
night and moved on the * morning. Num 9:20,21
son of Amminadab. * came the tribe Num 10:15
tribe of Levi were * in the line of Num 10:17
his people. * was the tribe of Num 10:19
* came the Kohathites carrying Num 10:21
they arrived.) * in line was the Num 10:22
the night and all the * day too! Num 11:32
They were up early the * morning, Num 14:40
But the very * morning all the Num 16:41
he went in the * day, he found that Num 17:8
Israel journeyed * to Oboth and Num 21:10
They * turned their attention to Num 21:33
The * morning Balaam told the Num 22:13
So the * morning he saddled his Num 22:21
sacrifices. The * morning Balak Num 22:41
* was Dophkah, and then Alush; Num 33:12
"* WE TURNED toward King Og's Deu 3:1
His son Eleazar became the * Deu 10:6
shall be left until the * morning. Deu 16:4
back to your homes the * morning. Deu 16:7
EARLY THE * morning Joshua and all Jos 3:1
of the month. The * day they began Jos 5:11,12
At dawn the * morning they went Jos 6:12,13,14
So, early the * morning, Joshua Jos 7:16
Early the * morning Joshua Jos 8:10
went out early the * morning and Jos 8:14
The tribe of Simeon received the * Jos 19:1
and the * generation did not Ju 2:10
For the * eighteen years the Ju 3:14
at peace for the * eighty years. Ju 3:30
The * judge after Ehud was Ju 3:31
Early the * morning, as the city Ju 6:28
When he got up the * morning he Ju 6:38
the city. The * morning as Gaal Ju 9:35
The * day the men of Shechem went Ju 9:42
* to the temple of Baal-berith. Ju 9:46
Abimelech * attacked the city of Ju 9:50
AFTER ABIMELECH'S DEATH, the * Ju 10:1
The * judge was Ibzan, who lived Ju 12:8
The * judge was Elon from Ju 12:11,12
* was Abdon (son of Hillel) from Ju 12:13
judge for the * twenty years, but Ju 15:20
Some men were hiding in the * Ju 16:9
The men were hiding in the * Ju 16:12
This happened in the valley * to Ju 18:28
he gave in. The * morning they Ju 19:8
left early the * morning to go to Ju 20:19,20
* day to fight at the same place. Ju 20:22,23,24
The * morning they were up early Ju 21:4
right to purchase it and I am *." Ru 4:4
was up early the * morning and went 1Sa 1:19,20
The * year Elkanah and Peninnah 1Sa 1:21,22
went to see it the * morning, Dagon 1Sa 5:3
They set him up again, but the * 1Sa 5:4
At daybreak the * morning, 1Sa 9:26,27
But early the * morning Saul 1Sa 11:11
Early the * morning he went out 1Sa 15:12
* Jesse summoned Shammah, but the 1Sa 16:9
the * morning with the gifts. 1Sa 17:20
only thousands. * they'll be making 1Sa 18:8
The very * day, in fact, a 1Sa 18:10
The * morning 1Sa 19:4
tomorrow, or the * day at the 1Sa 20:12
still empty the * day, Saul asked 1Sa 20:27
The * morning, as agreed, 1Sa 20:35
and I will be * to you, as my 1Sa 23:17
with David until the * morning. 1Sa 25:36
the entire * day until evening. 1Sa 30:17
The * day when the Philistines 1Sa 31:8
traveled all the * morning until 2Sa 2:29
Finally the * morning David wrote 2Sa 11:14
Fight harder * time, and conquer 2Sa 11:25
Joab's * to mine," and they did. 2Sa 14:30
asked him, "What shall I do *?" 2Sa 16:20
* in rank was Eleazar, the son of 2Sa 23:9
The * morning the word of the 2Sa 24:11
would be the * king and would sit 1Ki 1:13
would be the * king and would sit 1Ki 1:17
Adonijah to be the * king? 1Ki 1:24
have chosen to be the * king." 1Ki 1:27
shall be the * king and shall sit 1Ki 1:30
expected me to be the * king. 1Ki 2:15
be seen from the * room, but not 1Ki 8:8
And sure enough, the * day at 2Ki 3:20
But early the * morning the sun 2Ki 3:22
to have been the * king, and to the 2Ki 3:27
in the doorway. "* year at about 2Ki 4:15,16
got up early the * morning and went 2Ki 6:15
my son one day and her son the *. 2Ki 6:26-30
ate him, but the * day when I said, 2Ki 6:26-30
made of sackcloth * to his flesh. 2Ki 6:26-30
But the * day Hazael took a 2Ki 8:15
them there until the * morning. 2Ki 10:8
plans and where you are going *; 2Ki 19:27
use it as seed for * year's crop; 2Ki 19:29
of the Temple, * to the quarters of 2Ki 23:11
* he removed the shrines on the 2Ki 23:13
Mattaniah, to be the * king; 2Ki 24:17
went back the * day to strip the 1Ch 10:8
The * war was against the 1Ch 20:4
was *, and Jeush and Beriah were 1Ch 23:10,11
chosen to be the * king of Israel, 1Ch 29:1
The * day they brought a thousand 1Ch 29:21
For the * seven days, they 2Ch 7:8
intended to make him the * king. 2Ch 11:22
General Adnah. * in command was 2Ch 17:14,15
of 280,000 men. * was Amasiah (son 2Ch 17:16
Early the * morning the army of 2Ch 20:20
the Arabs living * to the 2Ch 21:16
so that for the * three years he 2Ch 27:5
Early the * morning, King 2Ch 29:20
Bread for the * seven days. 2Ch 35:17
of Jericho worked * to them, and Neh 3:2
repaired the * section of wall, and Neh 3:4
(son of Baana). * were the men Neh 3:5
bolts and bars. * to them were Neh 3:7
was * down the wall from them. Neh 3:9
his own house, and * to him was Neh 3:10
daughters repaired the * section. Neh 3:12
of Jerusalem. * to him was Neh 3:16
* was a group of Levites working Neh 3:17
his own district. * down the line Neh 3:18
* to them the workers were led by Neh 3:19
the wall turns. * to him was Neh 3:20
sections * to their own houses. Neh 3:23
their own houses. * was Binnui Neh 3:24
* was Pedaiah (son of Parosh). Neh 3:25
rebuilt the wall * to his own Neh 3:29
* was Hananiah (son of Shelemiah); Neh 3:30
who built * to his own house. Neh 3:30
section of wall * to his own home. Neh 7:3
The * day the clan leaders and Neh 8:13
evening and the * morning returned Est 2:12,13,14
the empire * to the king himself. Est 3:1
the kingdom * to the king himself. Est 5:11
together the * day also and killed Est 9:15
February, and the * day they Est 9:17
* day, with feasting and gladness. Est 9:18
with authority * to that of King Est 10:3
*, his heart is full of rebellion. Pro 6:14
* I changed my course again and Ecc 2:3
* I bought slaves, both men and Ecc 2:7,8
* I OBSERVED all the oppression Ecc 4:1
*, he will judge the haughty Is 3:16
* year, and two years from now Is 37:30
when the living wakened the * Is 37:36
known your faithfulness to the *. Is 38:19
as well as the * applies to Is 65:1f
as well as the * applies to Is 65:1f
The * day when Pashhur finally Jer 20:3
This room was located * to the Jer 35:4
the Temple on the * Day of Fasting, Jer 36:6
The * day, before the outside Jer 41:4
looked on. The * morning this Eze 12:
my wife died. The * morning I did Eze 24:1
The north tiers, * to the outer Eze 42:7,
"The strip * to it, 8 Eze 45:
boundary lines. *, to the south, Eze 48:5,6,
land of all. * to it lies the area Eze 48:1
western borders. * is Issachar, Eze 48:2
that for the * thirty days anyone Dan 6:
Very early the * morning he Dan 6:1
* I saw the arrival of a Man—or Dan 7:1
"* to come to power will be an Dan 11:2
a worm! The * morning the worm ate Jon 4:7
produced their * crops: From this Hag 2:18,1
* Satan took him to the peak of a Mt 4:8
until you leave for the * town. Mt 10:11
in one city, flee to the *! Mt 10:23
* to yours?" Mt 20:21
* to mine. Mt 20:23
was passed to the * brother, and so Mt 22:26
"* came the man who had received Mt 25:22
The * day—at the close of the Mt 27:62
The * morning he was up long Mk 1:35
home town. The * Sabbath he went Mk 6:2,3
"We want to sit on the thrones * Mk 10:37
to place you on thrones * to mine. Mk 10:40
The * morning as they left Mk 11:12
left the city. * morning, as the Mk 11:20
The * man he sent was killed; Mk 12:5
Then the * brother married her, Mk 12:20,21,22
to discuss their * steps. Mk 15:1
THE * EVENING, when the Sabbath Mk 16:1
Early the * morning he went out Lk 4:42
Their * complaint was that Jesus' Lk 5:33
The * day as they descended from Lk 9:37
The * day he handed the Lk 10:35
difference the * time I am here.' Lk 10:35
If we get figs * year, fine; Lk 13:9
Yes, today, tomorrow, and the * Lk 13:33
he asked the * man. Lk 16:7
"The * man also reported a Lk 19:18
to go to the * village, and as they Lk 19:30
Early the * morning at daybreak Lk 22:66
The * day John saw Jesus coming Jn 1:29
The * day Jesus decided to go to Jn 1:43
go *, so it is with the Spirit. Jn 3:8
We do not know on whom he will * Jn 3:8
The * morning, back across the Jn 6:22,23
but early the * morning he was Jn 8:2
he was for the * two days and made Jn 11:6
The * day, the news that Jesus Jn 12:12
was sitting * Jn 13:23
John, * to Jesus, was at his Jn 13:23f
of the morning. * he was taken to Jn 18:28
hanging there the * day, which was Jn 19:31
highest honor in heaven, * to God. Act 2:33
The * day it happened that the Act 4:5
* and where all this would end! Act 5:24
"The * day he visited them again Act 7:26
The * day, as they were nearing Act 10:9,10
overnight. The * day he went with Act 10:23
times during the * few days by the Act 13:31
speak to them again the * week. Act 13:42
The * day he left with Barnabas Act 14:20
* they traveled through Phrygia Act 16:6
and the * day on to Neapolis, and Act 16:11
believers! The * morning the Act 16:35
who worshiped God and lived * Act 18:7
So Paul stayed there the * Act 18:11
The * stop was at the port of Cae Act 18:22
This went on for the * two Act 19:10
And since he was leaving the * Act 20:7
the * day we passed Chios; Act 20:15
Chios; the *, we touched at Samos; Act 20:15
to Cos. The * day we reached Rhodes Act 21:1
The * stop after leaving Tyre was Act 21:7
request and the * day went with the Act 21:26,27
The * day the commander freed him Act 22:30
The * morning some forty or more Act 23:12,13
to the armory the * morning, Act 23:32
* day and ordered Paul brought in. Act 25:17
So the * day, after the king and Act 25:23
The * day when we docked at Act 27:3
The * day as the seas grew Act 27:18
Paul lived for the * two years in Act 28:30
of highest honor * to God, pleading Rom 8:34
For God had promised, "* year I Rom 9:9
* IS YOUR question about eating 1Co 8:1
* on my list of items to write 1Co 11:17
send me on to my * destination. 1Co 16:6
sea all night and the whole * day. 2Co 11:25
remembering that * time it might be Gal 6:1
this life, but in the * life too. 1Ti 4:8
greatest honor * to God himself. Heb 8:1
the earth, but, "* time," he Heb 12:26
the * three and one half years! Jas 5:17
the place of honor * to God the 1Pe 3:22
wants you to do. *, learn to put 2Pe 1:6
This will make possible the * 2Pe 1:7

NEZIAH
Barkos, Sisera, Temah, *, Hatipha. Ez 2:43-54
*, Hatipha. Neh 7:46-56

NEZIB	
*, Keilah, Achzib, and Mareshah.	Jos 15:37-44
NIBHAZ	
The gods * and Tartak were	2Ki 17:31
NIBSHAN	
*, The City of Salt, and En-gedi.	Jos 15:48-62
NICANOR	
Philip, Prochorus, *	Act 6:5
NICE	
perfume and some * clothes and go	Ru 3:3
at this * little red-cheeked boy!	1Sa 17:41,42
mere dreaming of * things is	Ecc 6:9
tell us * things;	Is 30:10,11
It's very * to live graciously	Jer 22:23
and lure of * things come in and	Mk 4:19
when people are * to you with good	Gal 4:18
NICELY	
You will be giving thanks very *	1Co 14:17
NICKNAME	
(From this came his * "Edom,"	Gen 25:30
"Jerubbaal," a * meaning "Let	Ju 6:32
a disparaging *—for Jeconiah and	Jer 22:24,25f
but Babylon was the Christian *	1Pe 5:13f
NICKNAMED	
David * the baby Jedidiah	2Sa 12:25
Thomas, * "The Twin," said to	Jn 11:16
apostles * "Barny the Preacher"!	Act 4:36
NICODEMUS	
leader named *, a member of the	Jn 3:1
exclaimed *.	Jn 3:4
"What do you mean?" * asked.	Jn 3:9
Then * spoke up.	Jn 7:50
So he came and took it away. *,	Jn 19:39
NICOLAITANS	
the deeds of the licentious *,	Rev 2:6
*, when translated from Greek to	Rev 2:6f
Literally, "*," Greek form of	Rev 2:15f
NICOLAUS	
* of Antioch (a Gentile convert to	Act 6:5
NICOPOLIS	
try to meet me at * as quickly as	Tit 3:12
NIECE	
married their orphaned * Milcah,	Gen 11:29
NIGH	
Literally, "He is *."	Mt 24:33f
NIGHT	
and to identify the day and the *;	Gen 1:14,15
moon, to preside through the *;	Gen 1:16
over the day and *, and to divide	Gen 1:18
winter and summer, day and *."	Gen 8:22
That * he successfully attacked	Gen 14:15
to my home as my guests for the *;	Gen 19:2
to retire for the *, the men of the	Gen 19:4
So they got him drunk that *,	Gen 19:33
"I slept with my father last *.	Gen 19:34
drunk again that *, and the younger	Gen 19:35
But that * God came to him in a	Gen 20:3
any room to put us up for the *?"	Gen 24:23
to him on the * of his arrival.	Gen 26:24
That *, when he stopped to camp	Gen 28:11
Afterwards, that *, when it was	Gen 29:23
That * God appeared to Laban in	Gen 31:24
to me last * and told me, 'Be	Gen 31:29
Literally, "stolen by day or by *	Gen 31:39f
why he appeared to you last *."	Gen 31:42
the * with them on the mountain.	Gen 31:54
he was for the *, and prepared a	Gen 32:13,14,15
Jacob spent that * in the camp.	Gen 32:21
But during the * he got up and	Gen 32:22,23,24
word to him. One * Joseph had a	Gen 37:5
that *, she told him her story.	Gen 39:16
One * each of them had a dream.	Gen 40:5
had dreams last *, but there is no	Gen 40:8
ONE * TWO years later, Pharaoh	Gen 41:1
and I each had a dream one *.	Gen 41:11
"I had a dream last *," Pharaoh	Gen 41:15
But when they stopped for the *	Gen 42:27
we stopped for the * and opened our	Gen 43:21
During the * God spoke to him in	Gen 46:2
stopped for the *, Jehovah appeared	Ex 4:24
wind to blow all that day and *;	Ex 10:13
roast lamb that *, with unleavened	Ex 12:8
if all is not eaten that *, burn	Ex 12:10
to remind you of this fatal *.	Ex 12:14
of you shall go outside all *.	Ex 12:22
And that *, at midnight, Jehovah	Ex 12:29
people of Egypt got up in the *;	Ex 12:30
during the * and said, "Leave us;	Ex 12:31
That * the people of Israel left	Ex 12:37
This * was selected by the Lord	Ex 12:42
so the same * was selected as the	Ex 12:42
and by a pillar of fire at *.	Ex 13:21
could travel either by day or *.	Ex 13:21
And that *, as it changed to a	Ex 14:20
all that *, drying the sea bottom.	Ex 14:21
* of their departure from Egypt.	Ex 19:1
must let him have it back at *.	Ex 22:26
tending it day and * before the	Ex 27:21
daytime, and at * there was fire in	Ex 40:38
of the altar all *, with the altar	Lev 6:9
day and * for seven days.	Lev 8:35
I claimed them for myself the * I	Num 8:17
eat the Passover lamb that *.	Num 9:6,7
stayed that way throughout the *.	Num 9:15
to the appearance of fire at *.	Num 9:16
* and moved on the next morning.	Num 9:20,21
But day or *, when it moved, the	Num 9:20,21
fell with the dew during the *.	Num 11:9
the * and all the next day too!	Num 11:32
aloud, and they carried on all *.	Num 14:1
you lead and protect us day and *.	Num 14:14
That * God came to Balaam and	Num 22:9
That * God told Balaam, "Get up	Num 22:20
the day after the * of the	Num 33:3,4
killed by the Lord the * before.	Num 33:3,4
all the gods of Egypt that *!	Num 33:3,4
pillar of fire at * and a pillar of	Deu 1:33
God brought you out of Egypt by *.	Deu 16:1
during the * must leave the camp,	Deu 23:9,10
it through the * and bless you;	Deu 24:12,13
You will live * and day in fear,	Deu 28:66
will say, 'Oh, that * were here!'	Deu 28:67
day and every * so that you will be	Jos 1:8
They were planning to spend the *	Jos 2:1
men before they retired for the *.	Jos 2:8
camped for the * and constructed a	Jos 4:8
camp again and spent the * there.	Jos 6:11
So they left that * and lay in	Jos 8:9
of the city. That * Joshua sent	Jos 8:11,12,13
He himself spent the * in the	Jos 8:11,12,13
Joshua traveled all * from Gilgal	Jos 10:9
That * the Lord told Gideon to	Ju 6:25
But he did it at * for fear of	Ju 6:27
as he asked; that * the fleece	Ju 6:40
During the *, with the Midianites	Ju 7:8,9
their torches blazed into the *.	Ju 7:19,20
they fled into the * to places as	Ju 7:22
Come by * with an army and hide	Ju 9:32
through the * and split into four	Ju 9:34
and spent the * with a prostitute.	Ju 16:1
lay in wait all * at the city gate	Ju 16:2
so they went there for the *.	Ju 19:15
us in for the *, even though we	Ju 19:18
abused her all *, taking turns	Ju 19:25
"That * the men of Gibe-ah	Ju 20:5
that * and followed her	Ru 3:6,7
days, but one * after Eli had gone	1Sa 3:2,3
Philistines all * and destroy every	1Sa 14:36
But the Lord made no reply all *.	1Sa 14:37
that he cried to the Lord all *.	1Sa 15:11
to what the Lord told me last *!"	1Sa 15:16
and fled into the *, leaving the	1Sa 19:9,10
all day and all *, prophesying with	1Sa 19:24
in fact, day and * they were like	1Sa 25:15,16
Saul's camp one * to look around.	1Sa 26:5,6,7
He went to the woman's home at *,	1Sa 28:7,8
Then they went out into the *.	1Sa 28:25
them all that * and the entire next	1Sa 30:17
town traveled all * to Beth-shan	1Sa 31:12
That * Abner and his men	2Sa 2:29
then they traveled all * and	2Sa 2:32
the desert that * and escaped.	2Sa 4:6,7
But that * the Lord said to	2Sa 7:4
One * he couldn't get to sleep	2Sa 11:2
He stayed that * at the gateway	2Sa 11:9
* after being away for so long?"	2Sa 11:10
go home that *, but again he slept	2Sa 11:13
food and lay all * before the Lord	2Sa 12:16
spending the * among the troops;	2Sa 17:8
across during the * and were all on	2Sa 17:22
will remain here during the *;	2Sa 19:7
animals from eating them at *.	2Sa 21:10
in a dream that * and told him to	1Ki 3:5
But her baby died during the *	1Ki 3:19
Then she got up in the * and	1Ki 3:20
over this Temple * and day—this	1Ki 8:29
pray, whether by * or by day,	1Ki 8:29
before him day and *, so that he	1Ki 8:59
you by this time tomorrow *."	1Ki 19:2
So one * the king of Syria sent a	2Ki 6:14
and fled into the *, abandoning	2Ki 7:7
Under cover of * he broke through	2Ki 8:21
That very * the angel of the Lord	2Ki 19:35
July 24, and that * the king and	2Ki 25:4,5
But that same * God said to	1Ch 17:3
That * God appeared to Solomon	2Ch 1:7
Look down with favor day and *	2Ch 6:20,21
One * the Lord appeared to	2Ch 7:12
is lighted every *, for we are	2Ch 13:11
marching by *, and almost	2Ch 21:9
from morning till * offering the	2Ch 35:14
Look down and see me praying *	Neh 1:6,7
*, taking only a few men with me;	Neh 2:11,12
day and * to protect ourselves.	Neh 4:9
pillar of fire at * so that they	Neh 9:12
showed them the way through the *.	Neh 9:19
for spending the * with King	Est 2:12,13,14
or drink for three days, * or day;	Est 4:16
THAT * THE king had trouble	Est 6:1
"and the * when I was conceived.	Job 3:2,3
Let that * be bleak and joyless.	Job 3:7
Let the stars of the *	Job 3:9
better in the daytime than at *.	Job 5:14
They say that * is day and day	Job 17:12
that night is day and day is *;	Job 17:12
the wicked. All * they lie naked	Job 24:7
poor and needy; at * they are	Job 24:14,15
They break into houses at * and	Job 24:16
The black * is their morning;	Job 24:17
for the day and for the *	Job 26:10
blown away in the storms of the *.	Job 27:20
the dew lay all * upon my fields	Job 29:19
at my bones. All * long I toss and	Job 30:18
in visions of the * when deep sleep	Job 33:15
do and in a single * he overturns	Job 34:25
gives songs in the *, and makes us	Job 35:9,10
to, and day and * are always	Ps 1:2
every * my pillow is wet with	Ps 6:6
When I look up into the * skies	Ps 8:3
he gives me wisdom in the *.	Ps 16:7
You have come even in the * and	Ps 17:3
Day and * they keep on telling	Ps 19:2
Day and * I keep on weeping,	Ps 22:2
Weeping may go on all *, but in	Ps 30:5
All day and all * your hand was	Ps 32:4
They lie awake at * to hatch	Ps 36:4
Day and * I weep for his help,	Ps 42:3
and through the * I sing his songs	Ps 42:8
deed—it haunts me day and *.	Ps 51:3
Though they patrol their walls *	Ps 55:10
I will pray morning, noon, and *	Ps 55:17
tossing and turning through the *.	Ps 56:8
prowl the city all * before they	Ps 59:14,15
I lie awake at * thinking of you—	Ps 63:6
through the * beneath the	Ps 63:7
Day and * alike belong to you;	Ps 74:16
help so badly. All * long I pray,	Ps 77:2
and at * by a pillar of fire.	Ps 78:14
I have wept before you day and *.	Ps 88:1
Literally, "as a watch in the *	Ps 90:4f
He sends the * and darkness,	Ps 104:20
of flame at * to give them light.	Ps 105:39
I obey them even at * and keep	Ps 119:55
I stay awake through the * to	Ps 119:148
He protects you day and *.	Ps 121:6
until late at *, fearing you will	Ps 127:2
as watchmen in the Temple every *.	Ps 134:1
and the moon and stars at *, for	Ps 136:9
the * becomes light around me.	Ps 139:11
to you the * shines as bright as	Ps 139:12
Every day and all * long their	Pro 6:22
She works far into the *!	Pro 31:18
Also, on a cold *, two under the	Ecc 4:11
activity, day and *.	Ecc 8:16,17
THE GIRL: "One * my lover was	Sol 3:1
against any onslaught in the *.	Sol 3:8
The Girl: "One * as I was	Sol 5:2
in the * and am covered with dew.'	Sol 5:2
clouds of fire at *, covering the	Is 4:5
late at *—woe to you drunken bums.	Is 5:11
In a single * he will burn those	Is 10:17
In one * your cities of Ar and Kir	Is 15:1
All rest at *—so pleasant once—is	Is 21:4
day after day and * after night I	Is 21:8,9
* I have been here at my post.	Is 21:8,9
to me: "Watchman, what of the *?	Is 21:11
Watchman, what of the *?	Is 21:11
All * long I search for you;	Is 26:9
them, and day and * I'll watch to	Is 27:3
the * when holy feasts are held;	Is 30:29
Their howls will fill the *.	Is 34:14
That * the Angel of the Lord went	Is 37:36
"All * I moaned;	Is 38:13
as though it were the darkest *!	Is 59:10
Darkness as black as * shall	Is 60:2
all day and all * for the	Is 62:6,7
their homes. At * they go out	Is 65:4
"Let us attack by * and destroy	Jer 6:5
I would sob day and * for the	Jer 9:1
who is merely stopping for the *?	Jer 14:8
Therefore, tell them this: * and	Jer 14:17
He left him there all *.	Jer 20:3
I had from God last *," they say.	Jer 23:25
stars to light the *, and who stirs	Jer 31:35
day and with the * so that day and	Jer 33:20,21
so that day and * don't come on	Jer 33:20,21
of * and day, of earth and sky.	Jer 33:25,26
fled during the *, going out	Jer 39:4
city during the *, going out by the	Jer 52:7
She sobs through the *;	Lam 1:2
no rest from weeping day or *.	Lam 2:18
Rise in the * and cry to your	Lam 2:19
Day and * his hand is heavy on	Lam 3:3
My eyes flow day and * with	Lam 3:48,49
Then leave the house at *, just	Eze 12:4
and walk away into the *;	Eze 12:6
shall go out at * through a hole in	Eze 12:12
ONE * IN the second year of his	Dan 2:1
And that * in a vision God told	Dan 2:19
when one * I had a dream that	Dan 4:5
That very * Belshazzar, the	Dan 5:30
and didn't sleep all *.	Dan 6:18
ONE * DURING the first year of	Dan 7:1

(NIGHT Con't)
as well as in the *, and so will Hos 4:5
you as surely as day follows *. Hos 6:5
Their plot smolders through the * Hos 7:6
O Israel, ever since that awful * Hos 10:9
O ministers of my God, lie all * Joe 1:13
It covers the mountains like *! Joe 2:2
and day into *, who calls forth the Amo 5:8
had come at * to plunder you—for Ob 1:5
across the desert sands at *. Mic 1:8
WOE TO YOU who lie awake at *, Mic 2:1
to you: The * will close about you Mic 3:6
he pursues them all * long. Nah 1:8
in a vision in the *: I saw a Man Zec 1:7
There will be no normal day and * Zec 14:7
the Gentiles from morning till *. Mal 1:11
* he left for Egypt with Mary and Mt 2:14
glowing in the * for all to see. Mt 5:14
but one * as he slept, his enemy Mt 13:25
the hills to pray. * fell, and out Mt 14:23,24
is that this very *, before the Mt 26:34
nightmare concerning him last *." Mt 27:19
during the * and stole his body. Mt 28:12,13
That * Levi invited his fellow Mk 2:15
All day long and through the * Mk 5:5
During the *, as the disciples Mk 6:47
That * some shepherds were in the Lk 2:8
but stayed there * and day, Lk 2:36,37
last * and didn't catch a thing. Lk 5:5
to pray, and prayed all *. Lk 6:12
find food and lodging for the *. Lk 9:12
where he nursed him through the *. Lk 10:34
The door is locked for the * and Lk 11:7
He may come at nine o'clock at * Lk 12:38
That * two men will be asleep in Lk 17:34
who plead with him day and *? Lk 18:7
the * on the Mount of Olives. Lk 21:37,38
him to stay the * with them, as it Lk 24:29
AFTER DARK ONE * a Jewish Jn 3:1
left before the * falls and all Jn 9:4
Only at * is there danger of a Jn 11:10
would be his last * on earth before Jn 13:1
that this was the * to carry out Jn 13:1
at once, going out into the *. Jn 13:30
man who had come to Jesus at *, Jn 19:39
We did, but caught nothing all *. Jn 21:3
the Lord came at *, opened the Act 5:19
day and * prepared to murder him. Act 9:24
So during the * some of his Act 9:25
The * before he was to be Act 12:6
That * Act 16:9
Literally, "in the *." Act 16:9f
That * the Christians hurried Act 17:10
One * the Lord spoke to Paul in a Act 18:9
Or, "on Saturday *." Act 20:7f
watchcare over you * and day and my Act 20:31
That * the Lord stood beside Paul Act 23:11
So that *, as ordered, the Act 23:31
of Israel strive * and day to Act 26:7
"For last * an angel of the God Act 27:23
on the fourteenth * of the storm, Act 27:27
Day and * I bring you and your Rom 1:9
bitterly day and * because of you. Rom 9:1
if they need lodging, for the *. Rom 12:13
believed. The * is far gone, the Rom 13:12,13
That on the * when Judas betrayed 1Co 11:23
Once I was in the open sea all * 2Co 11:25
worked among you? * and day we 1Th 2:9
for you? For * and day we pray on 1Th 3:10
like a thief in the *. 1Th 5:2
do not belong to darkness and *. 1Th 5:5
and stay sober. * is the time for 1Th 5:7
we worked hard day and * for the 2Th 3:8
or a place to stay for the *. 1Pe 4:9
Day after day and * after night Rev 4:8
Day after day and night after * Rev 4:8
him day and * in his temple. Rev 7:15
them day and * before our God. Rev 12:10
no relief day or *, for they have Rev 14:11
day and * forever and ever. Rev 20:10
all day long—and there is no *! Rev 21:25
And there will be no * there—no Rev 22:5

NIGHT-MONSTERS
There the * will scream at each Is 34:14

NIGHT'S
earth, to end the * wickedness? Job 38:13
was having a good * rest, said, Jn 11:12,13

NIGHTFALL
*, as being ceremonially defiled. Lev 11:25

NIGHTHAWK
The *, the seagull, Lev 11:13-19
The ostrich, the *, Deu 14:11-18

NIGHTMARE
had wakened from a * and was Ju 7:12,13
*, and awoke trembling with fear. Dan 2:1
"I've had a terrible *," he said Dan 2:1
for I had a terrible * concerning Mt 27:19

NIGHTMARES
in sleep, you terrify with *. Job 7:13,14
too busy gives you *, so being a Ecc 5:1

NIGHTS
begin forty days and * of rain; Gen 7:4
the earth for forty days and *. Gen 7:10,11,12
through the cold and sleepless *. Gen 31:40
there for forty days and forty *. Ex 24:18
days and forty *, and in all that Ex 34:28
days and forty *, and all that time Deu 9:9
forty days and * the Lord gave me Deu 9:10,11
forty days and * I lay before the Deu 9:18
for forty days and * when the Lord Deu 9:25
for forty days and * the second Deu 10:10
for three days and *, so they gave 1Sa 30:11,12
days and forty * to Mount Horeb, 1Ki 19:8
and *, no one speaking a word; Job 2:13
these long and weary *. Job 7:3
My weary * are filled with pain Job 30:17
Then my * were filled with Ps 77:6
and grief, and restless, bitter *. Ecc 2:20-23
hot sun and frosty *, and I will Jer 36:30
the fish three days and three *. Jon 1:17
For forty days and forty * he Mt 4:2
and three *, so I, the Messiah, Mt 12:39,40
the earth three days and three *. Mt 12:39,40
through sleepless * of watching, 2Co 11:27
and pain and sleepless *. 2Co 11:27
during the long * I beg my God to 2Ti 1:3
Dark, dark will be her *; Rev 18:23

NIGHTSHIRT
behind, clothed only in a linen *. Mk 14:51,52

NIGHTTIME
and the darkness "*." Gen 1:4,5
beneath the * sky and told him, Gen 15:5
It came in a * vision as others Job 4:13
"Do not desire the *, with its Job 36:20
and the * darkness deepened. Rev 8:12

NILE
on the bank of the * River, when Gen 41:1
the bank of the * River," he said, Gen 41:17
Hebrew boys into the * River. Ex 1:22
water from the * River and pour it Ex 4:9
the water of the * with his rod, Ex 7:17
the surface of the * with the rod, Ex 7:20
to the other. The * River will Ex 8:3,4
—the same one you struck the * Ex 17:5,6
BEYOND the upper reaches of the *, Is 18:1
in fast boats down the *! Is 18:2
nation whose land the upper * Is 18:2
And the waters of the * will Is 19:5
ocean, from Egypt and along the *. Is 23:2,3
slew Egypt, the dragon of the *. Is 51:9
rising like the * at flood time, Jer 46:7
For you have said, 'The * is Eze 29:3
"Because you said: 'The * is Eze 29:10
I will dry up the * and sell the Eze 30:12
of Pathros [along the upper * Eze 30:14
along the banks of the *, making Eze 32:2
It will rise up like the river * Amo 8:8
It rises like the river * in Amo 9:5
straddling the *, protected on Nah 3:8
be held back. The * will become Zec 10:11

NIMRAH
Dibon, Jazer, *, Heshbon, Elealeh, Num 32:3,4

NIMRIM
Even * River is desolate! Is 15:6
The pastures of * are deserted Jer 48:34

NIMROD
of Cush was *, who became the Gen 10:8
as being "like *—a mighty hunter, Gen 10:9
Another of the sons of Cush was * 1Ch 1:10
enter the gates of the land of *. Mic 5:6

NIMSHI
son of Jehoshaphat, the son of *). 2Ki 9:2
of *) rebelled against King Joram. 2Ki 9:14
Jehu (son of *), whom the Lord had 2Ch 22:7

NINE
It was a piece * inches square, Ex 39:9
"The Day of Atonement follows * Lev 23:26,27
it must consist of * quarts of fine Num 15:8,9
Accompany them with * quarts of Num 28:12
grain offering of * quarts of fine Num 28:20,21
grain offering of * quarts of fine Num 28:28,29
A grain offering of * quarts of Num 29:3,4
grain offerings. * quarts of fine Num 29:9,10
grain offerings—* quarts of fine Num 29:14
sacrifice * young bulls, two rams, Num 29:26,27
up among the * and one-half tribes, Num 34:13
the land among the * tribes and the Jos 13:2-7
* and a half tribes of Israel. Jos 14:1
Judah and Simeon gave them the * Jos 21:9-16
He had * hundred iron chariots, Ju 4:2,3
including the * hundred iron Ju 4:13
a man, measuring over * feet tall! 1Sa 17:4-7
task in * months and twenty days. 2Sa 24:8
David also had * other sons: 1Ch 3:6-8
feet high and * feet wide and set Dan 3:1
the other * disciples, as some Mk 9:14
It was about * o'clock in the Mk 15:25
He may come at * o'clock at Lk 12:38
Where are the *? Lk 17:17
for Caesarea at * o'clock tonight! Act 23:23,24

NINE-INCH
the stands. A * rim surrounded the 1Ki 7:35
high, with a * rim around its edge, Eze 43:13

NINETEEN
territory included * cities with Jos 19:35-3
learned that only * men were 2Sa 2:3

NINETEENTH
on July 22 of the * year of the 2Ki 25:
*, the group led by Pethahiah; 1Ch 24:7-1
*, Mallothi and twelve of his sons 1Ch 25:9-3
the fifth month during the * year Jer 52:1

NINETY
Enosh: Enosh was * years old when Gen 5:9,10,1
The Temple was * feet long, 1Ki 6:
The foundation was * feet long 2Ch 3:
The height will be * feet and the Ez 6:
feet and the width will be * feet. Ez 6:
a golden statue * feet high and Dan 3:
again, and found only * feet. Act 27:2
and that Sarah his wife, at *, Rom 4:1

NINETY-EIGHT
(Eli was * years old and was 1Sa 4:1

NINETY-FIVE
9,500 pounds of silver, * pounds Ex 38:2

NINETY-NINE
WHEN ABRAM WAS * years old, God Gen 17:1
Abraham was * years old at that Gen 17:24-27
Won't he leave the * others and Mt 18:12
over the * others safe at home! Mt 18:13
you leave the * others to go and Lk 15:3,4
* others who haven't strayed away! Lk 15:7

NINETY-SIX
for the nation of Israel; * rams; Ez 8:35
There were * pomegranates on the Jer 52:23

NINEVEH
He built *, Rehoboth-Ir, Calah, Gen 10:11,12
is located between * and Calah), Gen 10:11,12
King Sennacherib returned to *; 2Ki 19:36
returned to his own country, to *. Is 37:37
"Go to the great city of *, and Jon 1:2
that great city, *," he said, Jon 3:1
So Jonah obeyed, and went to *. Jon 3:3
to Nineveh. Now * was a very large Jon 3:3
district of * which was about Jon 3:3f
from now * will be destroyed!" Jon 3:4,5
For when the king of * heard what Jon 3:6
a great city like * with its Jon 4:11
the impending doom of *: Nah 1:1
* was the Assyrian capital. Nah 1:1f
What are you thinking of, *, to Nah 1:9
For this enemy from * will never Nah 1:15
*, YOU ARE finished! Nah 2:1
and Medes sacked impregnable *. Nah 2:1f
The queen of * is brought out Nah 2:7
* is like a leaking water tank! Nah 2:8
Where now is that great *, lion Nah 2:11
O *, once mighty lion! Nah 2:12
WOE TO *, City of Blood, full of Nah 3:1
All this because * sold herself Nah 3:4
horror: "* lies in utter ruin." Nah 3:7
*, too, will stagger like a Nah 3:11
its great capital * a desolate Zep 2:13
The men of * shall arise against Mt 12:41
people of * that God had sent him. Lk 11:29,30
"The men of *, too, shall arise Lk 11:32

NINTH
On the * day it was Abidan the Num 7:60-65
Finally, in the * year of King 2Ki 17:6
Hezekiah and the * year of the 2Ki 18:10
on March 25 of the * year of the 2Ki 25:1
Elzabad was * in command; 1Ch 12:8-13
*, the group led by Jeshua; 1Ch 24:7-18
*, Mattaniah and twelve of his 1Ch 25:9-31
The commander of the * Division 1Ch 27:12
during the * month of each year. 1Ch 27:12
* month" of the Hebrew calendar. Ez 10:9f
IT WAS IN January of the * year of Jer 39:1
In the * year of Zedekiah's Jer 52:4
Then finally, on the * day of Jer 52:6
ONE DAY LATE in December of the * Eze 24:1
The * with topaz; Rev 21:18,19,20

NIPPED
of knowledge, * in the bud because Gen 11:6f

NISROCH
temple of his god *, his sons 2Ki 19:37
in the temple of * his god, his Is 37:38

NO-ADIAH
Tobiah, Sanballat, * the Neh 6:14

NO-GODS
be a priest of these * of yours! 2Ch 13:9

NOADIAH
of Jeshua), and * (son of Ez 8:33

NOAH
years old when his son * was born. Gen 5:28-31
Lamech named him * (meaning Gen 5:28-31
*: Noah was 500 years old and had Gen 5:32
Noah: * was 500 years old and had Gen 5:32
But * was a pleasure to the Lord. Gen 6:8
Here is the story of *: He was Gen 6:8
he said to *, "I have decided to Gen 6:12,13
And * did everything as God Gen 6:22
the Lord said to *, "Go into the Gen 7:1
So * did everything the Lord Gen 7:5
female, just as God commanded *. Gen 7:8,9

NOAH Con't)
One week later, when * was 600 Gen 7:10,11,12
and nights. But * had gone into Gen 7:13
all, leaving only * alive, and Gen 7:23
GOD DIDN'T FORGET about * and all Gen 8:1
After another forty days, * Gen 8:6
The dove which * next dispatched Gen 8:7f
and returned to *, for the water Gen 8:9
still too high. So * held out his Gen 8:9
Seven days later * released the Gen 8:10
in her beak. So * knew that the Gen 8:11
* opened the door to look, and Gen 8:13
Then God told *, "You may all Gen 8:15,16
So the boat was soon empty. *, Gen 8:18,19
Then * built an altar and Gen 8:20
GOD BLESSED * and his sons and Gen 9:1
Then God told * and his sons, Gen 9:8
From these three sons of * came Gen 9:19
* became a farmer and planted a Gen 9:20,21
When * awoke from his drunken Gen 9:24,25
* lived another 350 years after Gen 9:28
who were the three sons of *; Gen 10:1
descended from *, through many Gen 10:32
Mahlah, *, Hoglah, Milcah,Tirzah. Num 26:28-37
Milcah, and *, were married to men Num 36:11,12
*, Hoglah, Milcah, and Tirzah. Jos 17:3
Enoch, Methuselah, Lamech, *, 1Ch 1:1
Just as in the time of * I swore Is 54:9
man and beast. If *, Daniel and Eze 14:14
alike, though *, Daniel and Job Eze 14:20
Shem's father was *; Lk 3:23-38
up to the day when * went into the Lk 17:27
* was another who trusted God. Heb 11:7
about the future, * believed him Heb 11:7
in the days of *, had refused to 1Pe 3:20
them while * was building the ark. 1Pe 3:20
the flood except *, the one man who 2Pe 2:5

NOAH'S
The names of * three sons were Gen 9:18
as it was in * time before the Mt 24:37,38
Shem's father was Noah;* father Lk 3:23-38
as the people were in * day. Lk 17:26
saved his family. * belief in God Heb 11:7

NOB
DAVID WENT TO the city of * to see 1Sa 21:1
"When I was at *," he said, "I 1Sa 22:9,10
and all the other priests at *. 1Sa 22:11,12
Then he went to *, the city of 1Sa 22:19
Anathoth, *, Ananiah, Neh 11:31-35
But the enemy stops at * for the Is 10:32

NOBAH
Meanwhile, a man named * led an Num 32:42
the area *, after his own name. Num 32:42
route east of * and Jogbehah, Ju 8:11

NOBILITY
a family of high *, his Gen 41:45f
they are the true *. Ps 16:3
royal family and * of Judah—and to Dan 1:3,4

NOBLE
Tabor marched the * remnant. Ju 5:13,14
by the great and * Osnappar and Ez 4:10
of the king's most * princes to Est 6:9
It shall become a * cedar, Eze 17:22,23
them, "You wear a *, pious Lk 16:15
Christ, whose * name you bear. Jas 2:7

NOBLEMAN
Happy the land whose king is a *, Ecc 10:16,17
"A * living in a certain Lk 19:12

NOBLES
Then the army officers, *, 2Ch 23:20
*, 'You are wicked and unjust'? Job 34:18
Make their mighty * die as Oreb Ps 83:11
And to punish * for being honest! Pro 17:26
He will test its * and find them Is 34:11
Jerusalem. The * send servants for Jer 14:3
children and all the * of Judah. Jer 39:6
And the king and his * sent this Jon 3:7

NOBLEST
his command to crush the * youth. Lam 1:15

NOBODY
know that you want this son of a * 1Sa 20:30
"Jerusalem, the Place * Wants." Jer 30:17
He is really a *. Gal 6:3

NOD
in the land of *, east of Eden. Gen 4:16

NODABITES
the Naphishites, and the *. 1Ch 5:19

NOGAH
Ibhar, Elishama, Eliphelet, *, 1Ch 3:6-8
Elishu-a, Elpelet, *, Nepheg, 1Ch 14:4-7

NOHAH
* the fourth,Rapha, the fifth. 1Ch 8:1

NOISE
When Joshua heard the * below Ex 32:17
"What is all the * about?" 1Sa 4:14
That's what all the * is. 1Ki 1:44,45
When Athaliah heard all the *, 2Ki 11:13,14
heard all the * and commotion, and 2Ch 23:12
For they hate the * of the city Job 39:7
at the * of your waterfalls." Ps 42:7f
He comes with the * of thunder, Ps 50:3
to the shepherd's shouts and *. Is 31:4,5
What is that terrible * from the Is 66:6
* of marching armies coming near. Jer 4:29
for war. The * of their army is Jer 6:23
The * of war resounds from the Jer 8:16
No Power But with Plenty of *!" Jer 46:17
The earth shakes with the * of Jer 49:21
It was the * of the wings of the Eze 3:13
was a rattling * from all across Eze 37:7
Listen to the * they make, like Joe 2:5
praise—they are mere * to my ears. Amo 5:23
closer until the * of the advancing Zep 1:10
When he heard the * of a crowd Lk 18:36
others, I would only be making *. 1Co 13:1
"He sounds big, but it's all *. 2Co 10:10
with a terrible * and the heavenly 2Pe 3:10

NOISY
* celebration all along the way. 1Ki 1:40
in a pasture—a *, happy crowd. Mic 2:12
home and saw the * crowds and heard Mt 9:23

NOMADIC
and of the * tribes of the desert; Jer 25:24
deserts, peopled by * tribes. Eze 20:35,36f

NOMADS
the desert like * for forty years. Num 14:33
The desert * shall bow before Ps 72:9
The * will not even camp there. Is 13:20

NOMINATED
The assembly * two men: Joseph Act 1:23

NON-AGGRESSION
solemn oaths to seal a * pact. Gen 26:31

NON-CANCELABLE
priests, my ministers, is *. Jer 33:20,21

NON-JEWISH
daughters marry * men and not to Neh 10:30
not to let our sons marry * girls. Neh 10:30

NON-JEWS
their children intermarry with *. Neh 13:25

NON-KOSHER
made unholy by eating * food! Mt 15:11
people are not defiled by * food. Mt 15:15

NON-PROFESSIONALS
uneducated *, they were amazed and Act 4:13

NONE
he asked. "* of the fruit in Gen 3:1
There's nothing for us here—* of Gen 31:14
told him, "and * of these men can Gen 41:15
cattle of Egypt; * of the Israeli Ex 9:4
it was true that * of the Israeli Ex 9:7
upon them, and * of you shall go Ex 12:22
be * there for you on that day." Ex 16:26
and remember, * of the ordinary Ex 24:2
to me, and * of the meat of the Ex 34:25
Lord; * of it shall be eaten." Lev 6:22,23
* left to be eaten the next day. Lev 7:15
"* of you shall marry Lev 18:6
Leave * of it for the following Lev 22:29,30
Yes, though * pursue they shall Lev 26:37
Aaron's son. * of the wagons or Num 7:9
In this way * of the land of the Num 36:7
giants, against whom * can stand! Deu 9:1
"But * of the offerings may be Deu 12:17
Keep * of the booty! Deu 13:17
in your homes, and * of the Deu 16:4
* of which will there be a remedy. Deu 28:27
But he appointed * for Israel; Deu 32:9
There is * like the God of Deu 33:26
wilderness, and * of the boys born Jos 5:4,5
all of this. * of the cities was Jos 11:19
their cities. * was left in all Jos 11:22
his time. * shall live to be old. 1Sa 2:31
of Jabesh. "If * of our brothers 1Sa 11:3
So that * can rise again. 2Sa 22:39
In fact, * of the kings before or 2Ki 18:5
six daughters, but * of his 1Ch 4:27
kingdoms so that * of them declared 2Ch 17:10
served the Lord. * of his sons, 2Ch 22:9
During this period * of us—I, Neh 4:23
they turn to their gods, but * Job 5:1
of all the things he dreamed of—* Job 20:20
of the rich; yet * of them cry to Job 35:9,10
he is my Savior, a rock where * Ps 18:2
victory over me. * who have faith Ps 25:3
they fell and * could help them Ps 107:12
them are doomed. * of these men Pro 2:19
the poor man has * left. Pro 19:4
of Lebanon; * can rival him. Sol 5:15
captivity with * to rescue them. Is 5:29
but * will come to save them. Is 16:12
whatever he says will be done; * Is 22:22
and debtors—* will be spared. Is 24:2
but you'll have * of this. Is 30:15
them to see that * are lost or Is 40:26
water and there is * and their Is 41:17
No one else! * other said one Is 41:26
God? No! * that I know about! Is 44:8
works"—* of which will save you. Is 57:12
they have no talent, * at all." Jer 4:22
are closed and * can open them." Jer 13:19f
eat, but there is * to be found. Jer 14:6
as childless, for * of his children Jer 22:30
and his family. * of his Jer 29:32
commanded that * of us should ever Jer 35:6
and disease. * of you will escape Jer 42:17
from your land and * shall help Jer 49:5
surround the city so that * can Jer 50:29
They have no wisdom—* at all! Jer 51:17
there is * to help her. Lam 1:2
in the day of your anger * Lam 2:22
but * will let them stay. Lam 4:15
their climax—* of these rich and Eze 7:10,11
and who fulfills * of his Eze 18:10
* is better than any other. Eze 24:6
to it; * had boughs to compare; Eze 31:8
none had boughs to compare; * Eze 31:8
to save him, then * of his good Eze 33:13
He shall not die. * of his past Eze 33:16
I will leave * of them remaining Eze 39:28
as a sin offering. * are to have Eze 43:25
miles. * of this special land Eze 48:14
each of them, and * of them Dan 1:18,19
But when they came, * of them Dan 5:8
* of them as great as the first. Dan 8:22
But * of these things will happen Dan 8:26
* will be able to stop him. Dan 11:16
and * of them will understand. Dan 12:10
and * cries out to me for help. Hos 7:7
consume her, and * of the idols in Amo 5:6
Lord of Hosts. But * of this will Zec 6:15
"Truly, of all men ever born, * Mt 11:11
further proof; and * will be given Mt 12:39,40
while, seeking rest but finding *. Mt 12:43,44,45
but finding *, it returns to the Lk 11:24
will be full. For * of those I Lk 14:24
such logic that * of your opponents Lk 21:15
to a woman, but * of them asked him Jn 4:27
* of you obeys the laws of Moses! Jn 7:19
* of the others at the table knew Jn 13:28
who sent me; and * of you seems Jn 16:5
of my going; * wonders why. Jn 16:5
Literally, "* of you is asking me Jn 16:5f
just as we are, with * missing. Jn 17:11
Jesus said; and * of us dared Jn 21:12
and Ausia. But * of them were able Act 6:10
"And now I know that * of you Act 20:25
his own. For * of us is perfect! Gal 6:5
we have done, so * of us can take Eph 2:9
time, so that * of you will become Heb 3:13
won his approval, * of them Heb 11:39
rain would fall, * fell for the Jas 5:17

NONSENSE
"Enough of this *," Joab said. 2Sa 18:14
Baal and wasted their time on *. Jer 2:8
their wisdom to be useless *. 1Co 1:20
and the Gentiles say it's all *. 1Co 1:23

NOOK
Every * and cranny will be Ob 1:6
* and cranny until she finds it? Lk 15:8

NOON
men will eat with me this *. Gen 43:16
arrival at *, for they were told Gen 43:25
rescue you before tomorrow *!" 1Sa 11:9
home one * as he was taking a nap. 2Sa 4:5
read from early morning until *. Neh 8:1
I will pray morning, *, and Ps 55:17
Where will you be at *? Sol 1:7
are gone like morning mist at *! Is 44:22
for battle. At * it has begun. Jer 6:4
widows; at * time I will bring Jer 15:8
the sun go down at * and darken the Amo 8:9
of the day. At * and again around Mt 20:5
hours, from * until three o'clock. Mt 27:45
About *, darkness fell across the Mk 15:33
By now it was *, and darkness Lk 23:44
way, and around * as he approached Jn 4:5,6
It was now about * of the day Jn 19:14
Gaza Desert, arriving around *." Act 8:26
It was * and he was hungry, but Act 10:9,10
suddenly about * a very bright Act 22:6
when one day about *, sir, a light Act 26:13

NOONDAY
shining down as from the * sun. Ps 37:6
Literally, "at *." Ps 91:6f

NOONTIME
About *, Elijah began mocking 1Ki 18:27
About *, as Ben-hadad and the 1Ki 20:16
but around * he died. 2Ki 4:20
even at brightest *, as though it Is 59:10
from the scorching * heat. Rev 7:16

NOOSE
Or put a * around his tongue? Job 41:1
to catch me, a * to yank me up and Ps 140:5

NOPHAH
As far as Dibon, *, and Medeba. Num 21:27-30

NORMAL
again, it was *, just as before! Ex 4:7
to * beneath the morning light. Ex 14:27
and everything will be * again. Lev 13:6
after the * time, or at some Lev 15:25
be during her * menstrual period, Lev 15:26
from the * business of the week. Lev 23:3
and * fulfillment of your vows. Lev 23:38

(NORMAL Con't)
with fruit long after the * time! Lev 26:4,5
and the king's arm became * again. 1Ki 13:6
children than was * in Judah. 1Ch 4:27
the weakest was worth a hundred * 1Ch 12:14
without regard to their * duties. 2Ch 5:11,12
rather than at the * time in April, 2Ch 30:2,3
and sedition are * there! Ez 4:19
I am robbed of my * years, and Is 38:10
There will be no * day and Zec 14:7
became *, just like the other one! Mt 12:13
returned to * and she got up and Lk 4:39
did, it became completely * again. Lk 6:10
as meaning the * process observed Jn 3:5f
When he lies, it is perfectly *; Jn 8:44
of having a * sex relationship with Rom 1:27
The angel used * units of Rev 21:17f

NORMALLY
the sacrifices * required for the Lev 14:32

NORTH
SO THEY LEFT Egypt and traveled * Gen 13:1
army to Hobah, * of Damascus, and Gen 14:15
east to west and from * to south; Gen 28:14
On the * side there will also be Ex 26:20
Place and the table on the * side. Ex 26:35
It will be the same on the * Ex 27:11
frames on the * side of the Ex 36:25,26
and rods. The * wall was also 150 Ex 38:11
Next he placed the table at the * Ex 40:22
the Lord on the * side of the Lev 1:11
Location: * side of Num 2:3-31
* side of Tabernacle Num 3:31-35
mountains in the *, and from the Jos 1:4
edge of a valley * of the city. Jos 8:11,12,13
as far * as the Lebanon Jos 9:1
which lies * of the Jabbok River. Jos 12:2
valley as far * as the western Jos 12:3
Hermon in the * to Salecah on Mount Jos 12:5
In the *, Jos 13:2-7
the entrance of Hamath in the *; Jos 13:2-7
Their territory extended * from Jos 13:30
then proceeded * of Beth-arabah to Jos 15:6
of the hill * of Ekron, where it Jos 15:10,11
Turning again to the *, it passed Jos 15:10,11
on the south, to Tyre on the *. Jos 15:47
followed the * bank of the Brook of Jos 17:9
and the land * of the brook and Jos 17:10
Jordan River, went * of Jericho, Jos 18:12
* of the valley of Rephaim. Jos 18:16
along the * edge of the Arabah. Jos 18:18
and ended at the * bay of the Salt Jos 18:19
running * of Beth-emek and Neiel. Jos 19:27
* side of the mountains of Gaash. Jos 24:30
of Ephraim, * of Mount Gaash. Ju 2:7-9
Midian were camped * of them, down Ju 7:1
The crag on the * was in front 1Sa 14:5
the one on the *, the Boaz Pillar. 1Ki 7:16-22
tail, three facing *, three west, 1Ki 7:25
it on the * side of the new altar. 2Ki 16:14
sides: east, west, *, and south. 1Ch 9:24
of the * gate to his son 1Ch 26:14,15
gate, four to the * gate, four to 1Ch 26:17
tail, three facing *, three west, 2Ch 4:4
the *, but cannot find him there; Job 23:9
from the *, the cold. Job 37:9
See Mount Zion rising * of the Ps 48:2
Literally, "on the sides of the * Ps 48:2f
You created * and south! Ps 89:12
As surely as a wind from the * Pro 25:23
The wind blows south and *, here Ecc 1:3-7
whether south or *, the die is Ecc 11:3
The Girl: "Come, * wind, awaken; Sol 4:16
of Assembly far away in the *. Is 14:13
the sides of the *" (Psalm 48:2); Is 14:13f
is coming down from the * against Is 14:31
up (Cyrus) from the * and east; Is 41:25
east and west, from * and south. Is 43:6
away, from * and west and south." Is 49:12
Put and Lud were in * Africa; Is 66:19f
terror from the * will boil out Jer 1:14
kingdoms of the * to come to Jer 1:15
their exile in the *, to the land I Jer 3:18
destruction on you from the *. Jer 4:6
*, coming to destroy this nation! Jer 6:1
marching from the *—a great nation Jer 6:22
all the way from Dan in the *." Jer 8:16f
of great armies coming from the *. Jer 10:22
the armies marching from the *! Jer 13:20
countries of the *, where he had Jer 16:14,15
the armies of the * under Jer 25:8,9
them from the * and from earth's Jer 31:8
were living in the * of Egypt in Jer 44:1
In the *, by the river Euphrates, Jer 46:6
today in the * country beside the Jer 46:10
her running—a gadfly from the *! Jer 46:20,21
girl before these men from the *. Jer 46:24
is coming from the * to overflow Jer 47:2
city * of the Sea of Galilee; Jer 49:30f
upon her from the * with such Jer 50:3
nations from the * and I will bring Jer 50:9
A great army from the *! Jer 50:41
for out of the * shall come Jer 51:48
toward me from the *, driving Eze 1:4
in the south to Riblah in the *. Eze 6:14
* or south—your land is finished. Eze 7:2
entrance of the * gate, where the Eze 8:3
of dust, look toward the *." Eze 8:5
So I looked and, sure enough, * Eze 8:5
He brought me to the * gate of Eze 8:14
* gate, each one with his sword. Eze 9:2
with her daughters * of you; Eze 16:46
you from the * with chariots and Eze 23:24
of kings from the *—against Tyre Eze 26:7
three cities of ancient * Africa. Eze 27:10f
All the princes of the * are Eze 32:30
distant *, as well as many others. Eze 38:6
from all over the * with your vast Eze 38:15,16
bringing you from the distant *. Eze 39:2
Here at the * entry, just as at Eze 40:23
Then he took me around to the * Eze 40:35
going up to the * entrance, there Eze 40:40
the southern entrance, facing *. Eze 40:44
one door faced * and the other Eze 41:11
court to the rooms * of the Temple Eze 42:1
doors of the building facing *. Eze 42:4
The * tiers, next to the outer Eze 42:7,8
Then he told me: "These * and Eze 42:13
Then he brought me through the * Eze 44:4
in through the * passageway to Eze 46:9
the south must go out by the *. Eze 46:9
of sacred chambers that faced *. Eze 46:19,20
the wall through the * passageway Eze 47:2
the * and Damascus to the south. Eze 47:17
to the south and Hamath to the *. Eze 48:1
miles wide, * to south, surrounds Eze 48:10
On the * side, with its 1½-mile Eze 48:30,31
Literally, "the king of the *," Dan 11:6f
from the east and * will alarm him Dan 11:44
from the * and send them far away; Joe 2:20
Teman was in the * of Edom, and Amo 1:12f
strip as far * as Zarephath. Ob 1:20
and so will the lands of the *; Zep 2:13
the land of the *, from Babylon,' Zec 2:6,7
horses will go *, and the one Zec 6:6
"Those who went * have executed my Zec 6:8
the * and half toward the south. Zec 14:4
and from as far * as the seacoasts Lk 6:17,18
Mysia they headed * for the Act 16:7
to go * to Macedonia first. Act 20:3
so we sailed * of Cyprus between Act 27:4
side—*, south, east, and west. Rev 21:13

NORTH-SOUTH
the lucrative * trade routes along Eze 26:2

NORTHEAST
little way to the * of the Egyptian Gen 25:18
boundary proceeded * to En-shemesh Jos 18:17
Tower of Hananel at the * corner, Jer 31:38,39

NORTHEASTER
strength (a "*," they called it) Act 27:14,15

NORTHERN
"Your * border will begin at the Num 34:7,8,9
All the kings of the * hill Jos 11:1
to include the * half of Gilead Jos 12:5
began at the * border of Edom, Jos 15:1
ended at the * edge of the Negeb. Jos 15:1
The * boundary began at the bay Jos 15:5
* end of the Valley of Rephaim. Jos 15:8
of Chesalon on the * shoulder of Jos 15:10,11
Sea. The * boundary began at the Jos 16:5,6
[The western half of the * Jos 16:8
The * boundary of the tribe of Jos 17:7
Manasseh's * boundary was the Jos 17:10
The * boundary began at the Jos 18:12
toward Neah. The * boundary of Jos 19:14
* tribe of Israel for a long time; 2Ch 30:5f
Passover from the * tribes returned 2Ch 31:1
to Judah from the * tribes and the 2Ch 31:5,6
this oracle—ending the * kingdom. Is 7:8f
lands, Galilee and * Transjordan, Is 9:1
of war resounds from the * border. Jer 8:16
Can a man break bars of * iron or Jer 15:12,13
and all the kings of the * Jer 25:26
Symbolic mother of the * tribes, Jer 31:15f
Dedan was in * Arabia and was a Jer 49:8f
from the Negeb to your * borders. Eze 21:4
the * wall and measured it. Eze 40:20
one beside the * entrance, facing Eze 40:44
beside the inner * gate is for the Eze 40:45
"The * boundary will run from Eze 47:15
So the * border will be from the Eze 47:17
point where the * boundary begins. Eze 47:20
him again, and the * king will Dan 11:40
you from your * boundary to your Amo 6:14
All the land from Geba (the * Zec 14:10
at Philippi in * Greece and five Act 20:6

NORTHWARD
Then they continued * toward Gen 13:3,4
instructions: "Go * into the hill Num 13:17
Going *, they passed first Num 13:22
stayed here long enough. Turn *. Deu 2:3
* toward the Moab desert. Deu 2:8
to the Sidonians), stretching * Jos 13:2-7
before it turned * to circle around Jos 15
* toward the present city center. 2Sa 5
"Son of dust, face * Eze 38:2

NORTHWEST
where it turned * toward Gilgal, Jos 15
Turning * again, the boundary Jos 15:10,
to the Corner Gate at the *; Jer 31:38,
For Dan: From the * boundary at Eze 48
only a * and southwest exposure. Act 27:

NOSE
or has a broken * or any extra Lev 21:
put a hook in your * and a bridle 2Ki 19:2
and walk with his * in the air, Job 20
a ring in his * and lead him away. Job 40:2
*, or pierce his jaw with a spike? Job 41
and a blow to the * causes Pro 30:3
of Bath-rabbim. Your * is shapely Sol 7
—I have put a hook in your * and a Is 37:2
a ring for your * and two more for Eze 16:1
you, and cut off your * and ears; Eze 23:2

NOSE-RING
Literally, "*." Gen 24:2

NOSES
until you vomit it from your *; Num 11:19,2
who mince along, * in the air, Is 3:1
thumbing their * at me and arousing Eze 8:1
put hooks in your * and lead you Amo 4:
And you turn up your * at the Mal 1:1

NOSTRILS
Smoke poured from his *; 2Sa 22:
Smoke flows from his *, like Job 41:2
smoke blew from his *. Ps 18:
you bring me is a stench in my *. Is 1:12,1
* of all the nations of the earth. Jer 44:

NOTABLE
"And I will raise up a * Vine Eze 34:2

NOTE
and Manasseh.' " (* that he put Gen 48:2
* that this rule applied to the Lev 21:11
*: The actual value by today's Lev 27:3
of these items. (*: Eleazar, Num 3:31-3
*: The 14th day of the first month Num 9:2,3
*: This was approximately May 5. Num 10:11
on any promissory * he holds Deu 15:
"Take * of what I've said." 1Ki 22:28
"Take * of what I have said." 2Ch 18:27
her many towers! * her walls and Ps 48:1
SON, IF YOU endorse a * for Pro 6:
another's *, to become responsible Pro 17:18
on hand, don't countersign a *. Pro 22:26,27
with the first * of the birds; Ecc 12:4
"Queen of Heaven"; see * on Jer 44:17
can defy me? Take *: The Lord will Jer 49:20
of the Lord. * carefully who may be Eze 44:5
"* this: Wicked men trust Hab 2:4
(A * to the choir director: When Hab 3:19
*: The Great Revival under King Zep 1:1f
*: They were among the exiles who Hag 1:1f
"But now * this: From today, Hag 2:18,19
"Take * that I will rebuke your Mal 2:3
in a holy place (* to the reader: Mt 24:15
Literally, "Let the reader take * Mt 24:15f
And * this: some who are Lk 13:30
said, 'take your * and replace it Lk 16:7
unless each * is sounded clearly. 1Co 14:7
I am sending this * to you 1Pe 5:12
See * on 1:20. Rev 2:8f
See * on 1:20. Rev 2:12f
See * on 1:20. Rev 2:18f
See * on 1:20. Rev 3:1f
See * on 1:4. Rev 3:1f
See * on 1:20. Rev 3:7f
"* this: I will force those Rev 3:9
See * on 1:20. Rev 3:14f
"Take *: I will come as Rev 16:15

NOTED
These clans were * for their 1Ch 4:23
of the gold and silver was *. Ez 8:34
As they studied it, they * that Neh 8:14
You have * each evil act. Ps 10:14
Edom was * for her wise men; Ob 1:8f

NOTES
Miscellaneous *: 1Ki 9:23
play the right *, how will the 1Co 14:8

NOTHING
* will be unattainable for them! Gen 11:6
For I can do * until you are Gen 19:22
(Isaac says * Gen 27:38
There's * for us here—none of our Gen 31:14
I owned * except a walking stick! Gen 32:10
so he did * until their return. Gen 34:5
He has held back * from me except Gen 39:9
jail when I did * to deserve it." Gen 40:15
is * left but our bodies and land. Gen 47:18
those who gathered a lot had * Ex 16:18
need pay * to regain his freedom. Ex 21:2
You must have * to do with Ex 34:17
He may eat * that comes from Num 6:3,4
Is it * to you that he has given Num 16:10
to pass through, and * else." Num 20:19
"There is * to eat here, and Num 21:5

OTHING Con't)
to eat here, and * to drink, and we Num 21:5
gold, I could do * contrary to the Num 22:18
says *, then her vow shall stand. Num 30:4
her vow and says * on the day he Num 30:7
and does *, the vow shall stand; Num 30:11
but if he says * for a day, then Num 30:14
But * I said did any good. Deu 1:32
and you have lacked * in all that Deu 2:7
We left * alive except the Deu 2:33,34
is plentiful, and * is lacking; Deu 8:9
nights, and all that time I ate *. Deu 9:9
* even to remind you of them! Deu 12:3
You have * to fear from him. Deu 18:22
continually, and * will save you. Deu 28:29
as Gaza, leaving * to eat, and Ju 6:3,4
my priest, and I have * left!" Ju 18:24
"My father's family is *!" 1Sa 18:18
it, for there is * else here." 1Sa 21:9
knew * of any plot against you." 1Sa 22:15
and the sheep, and * was stolen 1Sa 25:15,16
for he had eaten * all day. 1Sa 28:20
but David knew * about it. 2Sa 3:26
that he would eat * until sundown. 2Sa 3:35,36
* with these two sons of Zeruiah. 2Sa 3:39
very poor, owning * but a little 2Sa 12:3
but Absalom said * one way or the 2Sa 13:21-24
but they knew * of his intentions. 2Sa 15:11
We have charged him *—he hasn't 2Sa 19:42
"We want * to do with David. 2Sa 20:1
offerings that have cost me *." 2Sa 24:24
There was * in the Ark at that 1Ki 8:9
all her questions; * was too 1Ki 10:3
Literally, "there was * hidden 1Ki 10:3f
"* at all, except a jar of olive 2Ki 4:2
the child's face, but * happened. 2Ki 4:31
king had instructed them to say *. 2Ki 18:36
will be taken—* shall be left. 2Ki 20:17
done for me are * in comparison to 1Ch 17:17
offering that has cost me *!" 1Ch 21:24
of this writing. * was in the Ark 2Ch 5:10
problems. * was hidden from him; 2Ch 9:2
tell you to speak * except what the 2Ch 18:15
as yet I had said * to anyone about Neh 2:16
And they had * to say in their own Neh 5:8
they lacked * in all that time. Neh 9:21
gone through become as * to you. Neh 9:32
for he did * without their advice. Est 1:13-15
"all this is * when I see Mordecai Est 5:13
His courtiers replied, "*!" Est 6:3
man who fears God and will have * Job 1:8
"and I shall have * when I die. Job 1:21
So in all this Job said * Job 2:10
* shall be stolen from your barns. Job 5:24
but there is * there to drink, and Job 6:15-18
My life is but a breath, and * Job 7:7
great, and then reduces it to *. Job 12:23
You are * but a windbag. Job 15:2
they can produce * truly good. Job 15:34
was always greedy, now he has *; Job 20:20
and need deny themselves *; Job 21:12,13
less than * as compared to him. Job 25:5
space, and hangs the earth upon *. Job 26:7
"I am *—how could I ever find Job 40:4
between them, and * can penetrate. Job 41:15-17
Iron is * but straw to him, and Job 41:27,28
There is * else so fearless Job 41:33
things I knew * about and did not Job 42:3
night and found * amiss and know Ps 17:3
end, and * can hide from its heat. Ps 19:6
They care * for God or what he Ps 28:5
is forever; * can stop me now! Ps 30:6,7
will you stand there, doing *? Ps 35:17
I have * to say. Ps 38:13,14
done * against them to deserve it. Ps 38:19
all his busy rushing ends in *. Ps 39:5,6
You valued us at * at all. Ps 44:12
For when they die they carry * Ps 49:17
* for God are seeking my life. Ps 54:3
alike are * in his sight. Ps 62:9
There is * left to show that we Ps 74:9,10
There is * but goodness in him! Ps 92:15
* is perfect except your words. Ps 119:96
because they care * for your laws. Ps 119:158
The speed of a horse is * to Ps 147:10
jewels. * else compares with it. Pro 3:13,14,15
There is * of evil in it. Pro 8:8
rubies; * can be compared with it. Pro 8:11
All our work adds * to it! Pro 10:22
finally have * worthwhile left. Pro 11:29
A worthless witness cares * for Pro 19:28
In my opinion, * is worthwhile; Ecc 1:2
History merely repeats itself. * Ecc 1:8-11
was * really worthwhile anywhere. Ecc 2:11
So I decided that there was * Ecc 2:24-26
first, there is * better for a man Ecc 3:12
* can be added or taken from it; Ecc 3:14
So I saw that there is * better Ecc 3:22
is * left to pass on to one's son. Ecc 5:13,14
back to where he began—with *. Ecc 5:15
all his hard work has been for *; Ecc 5:16
that * is certain in this life. Ecc 7:14
that there was * better in all the Ecc 8:15
is * but death ahead anyway. Ecc 9:2,3
But the dead know * Ecc 9:5
I want * more to do with them. Is 1:12,13
If you fear him, you need fear * Is 8:13
it out unharmed. * will hurt or Is 11:9
Egypt will give you * in return! Is 30:6
and care * for the promises they Is 33:8
You Assyrians will gain * by all Is 33:11
"The Land of *," and its princes Is 34:12
"Don't let Hezekiah fool you—* Is 36:14
had told them to say * in reply. Is 36:21
off to Babylon. * will be left. Is 39:6
of the world are * in comparison Is 40:15
All the nations are as * to him; Is 40:17
in his eyes they are less than * Is 40:17
You are less than *, and can do Is 41:24
than nothing, and can do * at all. Is 41:24
But forget all that—it is * Is 43:18
You are worthless, with * good in Is 48:10
at all, * to make us want him. Is 53:2
In those days * and no one shall Is 65:25
Even their priests cared * for Jer 2:8
ones—even though their gods are *. Jer 2:10,11
her it was * at all that she should Jer 3:9
and act as though * is going on? Jer 5:29
They care * for right and go from Jer 9:3
they care * for me," says the Jer 9:3
rite like theirs, and * more. Jer 9:25,26
to the other; * shall escape. Jer 12:12
as this loincloth—good for *. Jer 13:10
of things they knew * about. Jer 14:18
His life will amount to *. Jer 22:30
of Babylon. And * will change this Jer 28:14
power; * is too hard for you! Jer 32:17
For Israel and Judah have done * Jer 32:30
now it has done * but anger me; Jer 32:31
I will hide * from you." Jer 42:4
rest and * shall make her afraid. Jer 46:27
destroy her; let * be left. Jer 50:26
we could, but * can save her now. Jer 51:9
Idols are *! Jer 51:18
Is it * to you, all you who pass Lam 1:12
There will be * to buy or sell, Eze 7:12
"Is it * to the people of Judah Eze 8:17
as they do—no, that was * to you; Eze 16:47
I swear that I will tell you *. Eze 20:3
For seven years they will need * Eze 39:10
earth are * when compared to him; Dan 4:35
Majesty, there is * you can do. Dan 6:15
the men with me saw *, but they Dan 10:7
ointments, caring * at all that Amo 6:6
you are, when you are less than *! Amo 6:13
[when * that I told them happens Jon 4:3
evil with evil; * can stop me; Mic 2:3
for there will be * to fear. Mic 4:4
it will come to * at the end, and Mic 6:14
"* then seemed more improbable Zep 2:15f
In comparison, it is * now, is Hag 2:3
That proves *. Mt 3:9
he ate * and became very hungry. Mt 4:2
is * to eat here in the desert; Mt 14:15
days now, and have * left to eat; Mt 15:32
and it would go far away. * Mt 17:20
Temple' means *—you can break that Mt 23:16
But Jesus said *, much to the Mt 27:14
He told them to take * with them Mk 6:8,9
food, for there is * to eat here in Mk 6:35,36
days, and have * left to eat. Mk 8:1
He ate * all that time, and was Lk 4:1
We want * to do with you, Jesus Lk 4:34
"For there is * to eat here in Lk 9:12
to crush them. * shall injure you! Lk 10:19
and I've * to give him to eat.' Lk 11:5,6
Flavorless salt is fit for *—not Lk 14:35
you wanted, and Lazarus had *. Lk 16:25
But they could think of *, for Lk 19:48
him back to us—* this man has done Lk 23:15
is—* exists that he didn't make. Jn 1:3
Jesus replied, "The Son can do * Jn 5:19
disapproval means * to me, for as I Jn 5:41,42
"so that * is wasted." Jn 6:12
Literally, "the flesh profits * Jn 6:63f
in public, and they say * to him. Jn 7:26
leaders and teach * in private that Jn 18:20
We did, but caught * all night. Jn 21:3
is said, and should do * rash. Act 19:36
who have stolen * from her temple Act 19:37
But life is worth * unless I use Act 20:24
"We see * wrong with him," they Act 23:9
* worthy of imprisonment or death. Act 23:29
But in my opinion he has done * Act 25:25
I teach * except what the Act 26:22
They replied, "We have heard * Act 28:21
They care * about God nor what he Rom 3:18
to earn our salvation? * at all. Rom 3:27
Yet what we suffer now is * Rom 8:18
For I am convinced that * can Rom 8:38
the deepest ocean—* will ever be Rom 8:39
that there is * really wrong with Rom 14:14
Remember, there is * wrong with Rom 14:20
You may know that there is * Rom 14:22
world, counted as * at all, and 1Co 1:28
to bring down to * those the world 1Co 1:28
be worth * at all without love. 1Co 13:2
them, but to me they mean *. 1Co 14:11
Or, "there are some who know * of 1Co 15:34f
for you know that * you do for the 1Co 15:58
* is written between the lines! 2Co 1:13,14
face is worth * at all in 2Co 3:10
that faded into * was full of 2Co 3:11
We own *, and yet we enjoy 2Co 6:10
"He that gathered much had * 2Co 8:15
see that there is * great about 2Co 10:10
though I am really worth * at all. 2Co 12:11
Literally, "For we can do * 2Co 13:8f
* to add to what I was preaching. Gal 2:6
my hard work for you was worth *. Gal 4:11
There was * unusual about the Gal 4:23
Though I did * to deserve it, and Eph 3:8
They stop at *, being driven by Eph 4:19
it worth less than *, in order that Php 3:8
I know how to live on almost * Php 4:12
before him with * left against Col 1:22
left against you—* left that he Col 1:22
within you; have * to do with Col 3:5
such things mean *. Col 3:11
a great rock, and * can shake it. 2Ti 2:19
and will think * of immorality. 2Ti 3:3
Leave * undone that you ought to 2Ti 4:5
After that have * more to do with Tit 3:10
there is. * is left out." Heb 2:8
of our living God; * can be hidden Heb 4:13
There will be * to look forward Heb 10:27
Since we have a kingdom * can Heb 12:28
his riches mean * to the Lord, for Jas 1:10,11
to God is by faith alone, plus *; Jas 2:18
Once you were less than *; 1Pe 2:10
there is * wrong with sexual sin. 2Pe 2:2
promising much and delivering *; 2Pe 2:17
promising much, but producing *. Jud 1:12
I will ask * further of you; Rev 2:24,25
brought into it. * evil will be Rev 21:27
There shall be * in the city Rev 22:3

NOTHINGNESS
kingdoms into *, but it shall stand Dan 2:44
They will disappear into *, but Heb 1:11

NOTICE
Literally, "* that all the Gen 31:12f
you, whenever you * the tassels, of Num 15:39
Don't * the rebellion and Deu 9:27
* where he lies down to sleep; Ru 3:4
him presents, but he took no *. 1Sa 10:27
Amasa didn't * the dagger in his 2Sa 20:8,9,10
life, and * every mistake I make. Job 14:16
"He will never * them here," Ps 64:5
what is man that you even * him? Ps 144:3
Moreover, I * that throughout the Ecc 3:16
let all the world take *! Is 18:3
and take no * of your majesty. Is 26:10
and you don't even * it!" Is 58:3
and refuse to * their distress. Jer 18:17
And I will * which is plump and Eze 34:22
"Son of dust, * carefully; Eze 44:5
I will bless you. *, I am giving Hag 2:18,19
For he took * of his lowly Lk 1:48
return without * and remove him Lk 12:46
but you refuse to * the warnings Lk 12:56
"* the fig tree, or any other tree. Lk 21:29
"Men of Athens, I * that you are Act 17:22
for people will * how good God is Rom 3:5
* how God is both kind and Rom 11:22
* among yourselves, dear 1Co 1:26
a fact for all the angels to * 1Co 11:10
even * when others do it wrong. 1Co 13:5
and his Child. And * that it Gal 3:16
gifts to men. * that it says he Eph 4:9
* who else lives up to my example. Php 3:17
in this letter, * who he is and 2Th 3:14
* your improvement and progress. 1Ti 4:15

NOTICEABLY
(Isaac begins to tremble *. Gen 27:33

NOTICED
* three men coming toward him. Gen 18:2
But when Sarah * Ishmael—the son Gen 21:9
Then Abraham * a ram caught by Gen 22:13
Rebekah * him and quickly Gen 24:64
(meaning "God has * my trouble"), Gen 29:32
"Jehovah has * my trouble—now my Gen 29:32
Soon Jacob * a considerable Gen 31:2
His brothers of course * their Gen 37:4
A man * him wandering in the Gen 37:15
Suddenly they * a string of Gen 37:25
Judah * her as he went by and Gen 38:15
Potiphar * this and realized Gen 39:3
The next morning Joseph * that Gen 40:6
flocks of sheep) * what wonderful Num 32:1
was in Timnah, he * a certain Ju 14:1
and * how secure everyone felt. Ju 18:7
Eli * her mouth moving as she was 1Sa 1:12,13
over the city, he * a woman of 2Sa 11:2

(NOTICED Con't)
(The people watching * through 2Ki 6:26-30
he was there he * an unusual altar 2Ki 16:10
looking around, he * several graves 2Ki 23:16
"Have you * my servant Job? Job 1:8
"Well, have you * my servant Job 2:3
And yet I * that there was one Ecc 2:13,14
the others and * from far away. Eze 19:11
I * that the Temple was built on Eze 41:8
When Jesus * how large the crowd Mt 8:18
synagogue, and * there a man with Mt 12:10
and * a fig tree beside the road. Mt 21:19
meet the guests he * a man who Mt 22:11
gate, another girl * him and said Mt 26:71
again, and * a man there with a Mk 3:1
him, and * that some of his Mk 7:2
A little way off he * a fig tree Mk 11:13
the High Priest * Peter warming Mk 14:66,67
Word of God. He * two empty boats Lk 5:2
When he * that all who came to Lk 14:7
A servant girl * him in the Lk 22:56
heaven, then they * how many Jn 12:16
He also * the cloth lying there, Jn 20:6
your charities have been * by God! Act 10:31
preached, and Paul * him and Act 14:9
the coastline, but * a bay with a Act 27:39
Christian women should be * for 1Ti 2:9,10

NOTICES
Aaron, "If anyone * a swelling in Lev 13:1
wasn't enough time to get * out. 2Ch 30:2,3

NOTICING
sentences, not * whether a person Lev 19:15
at Micah's home. * the young Ju 18:3

NOTIFIED
the owner had been * and still the Ex 21:29

NOTIFY
So Amasa went out to * the 2Sa 20:5
names so that we could * you. Ez 5:10
sent messengers to * everyone that Mt 22:3
servant around to * the guests that Lk 14:17

NOTORIOUS
They are * for their cruelty. Hab 1:7
there were many * swindlers Mt 9:10
was a particularly * criminal in Mt 27:16
and many other * sinners to be his Mk 2:15
Even tax collectors—* for their Lk 3:12
his eating with such * sinners. Lk 5:30
and other * sinners often came to Lk 15:1
of a * sinner," they grumbled. Lk 19:7
to happen to the * Prostitute, who Rev 17:1

NOUN
collective *, implying plurality. Rev 22:2f

NOURISH
birth, for breasts that cannot *. Hos 9:14

NOURISHED
Your own soul is * when you are Pro 11:17
in the forest to be * by the rain. Is 44:14
and better * than the youths who Dan 1:15

NOURISHMENT
had no * in the shallow soil. Mk 4:5,6
Then Jesus explained: "My * Jn 4:34
* of his own special olive tree. Rom 11:17
into him and draw up * from him. Col 2:7
get our * and strength from God. Col 2:19
manna, the secret * from heaven; Rev 2:17

NOVEMBER
in every detail in * of the 1Ki 6:38
held at Bethel on the first of * 1Ki 12:32,33
prophet) in early * of the second Zec 1:1
the Lord in late * of the fourth Zec 7:1

NOW'S
"* your time!" 1Sa 24:4

NOWADAYS
are told of you! * when I mention Ps 87:4

NOWHERE
the sky, and they had * to go. Jos 8:20,21
gang who suddenly appear from *?" 1Sa 25:11
* on earth, but only from God. Ps 75:6,7
back and forth, getting *. Ecc 1:3-7
all alone and have * else to turn. 1Ti 5:16

NUGGETS
where * of pure gold are found, Gen 2:11,12
of meaning in these * of truth." Pro 1:5,6

NULLIFY
either confirm or * her vow, but Num 30:13
man-made rule, you * the direct Mt 15:5,6

NUMBER
So the total * of those going to Gen 46:26
with the * of their dependents. Gen 47:12
So Joseph went, and a great * of Gen 50:7
So a very great * of chariots, Gen 50:9
So the total * who went with him Ex 1:5
depending upon the * of persons in Ex 12:21
among the people when you * them. Ex 30:11,12
the * of years until the Jubilee. Lev 25:14,15,16
is selling the * of crops the new Lev 25:14,15,16
to the * of harvests until the Lev 25:27
proportion to the * of years left Lev 25:50
a servant for that * of years. Lev 25:50
proportion to the * of years Lev 27:18
not include their * in the census. Num 1:47,48,49
found the total * of eldest sons a Num 3:43
* of Levites, pay five dollars Num 3:46
in excess of the * of Levites. Num 3:49
found that the total * was 2,750. Num 4:36
This time he sent a larger * of Num 22:15
So the total * of the draftable Num 26:51
The total * of Levites in the Num 26:62
and you will be but few in *. Deu 4:27
They were few in *, but in Egypt Deu 26:5
the * of cities assigned to Judah. Jos 15:48-62f
So the total * of cities and Jos 21:26
The total * of cities and Jos 21:41,42
And Joab reported the * of the 2Sa 24:9
table, the great * of servants and 1Ki 10:5
horses with a vast * of chariots 1Ki 10:26
give us the same * of horses, 1Ki 20:25
A great * of the enemy also died 1Ch 5:22
David, the total * of men of war 1Ch 7:2
The total * of men available for 1Ch 7:5
When Israel was few in *—oh, so 1Ch 16:19
the Temple. The * of sacrifices 2Ch 8:13
and a large * of domestic fowls; Neh 5:18
informed of the * of those slain in Est 9:11
miracles, marvels without *. Job 5:9
Who is able to * his hosts of Job 25:3
Who is wise enough to * all the Job 38:37,38
Teach us to * our days and Ps 90:12
were but few in *, very few, and Ps 105:12
the * of cattle here in Israel. Jer 31:27
accomplished. The * of captives Jer 52:28
* is literal, and means just that. Dan 8:26
And he knows the * of hairs on Lk 12:7
it, so that the * of believers now Act 4:4
circles, and the * of disciples Act 6:7
a large * of godly Greek men, and Act 17:4
involved were about twelve in *. Act 19:7
that is the * we had aboard. Act 27:37
of them, only a small * would Rom 9:27
times without *, and faced death 2Co 11:23
I heard the *—it was 144,000, out Rev 7:4-8
and to count the * of worshipers. Rev 11:1
or the code * of his name. Rev 13:17
and his statue and his mark and *. Rev 15:2

NUMBERED
each man who is * shall give a Ex 30:11,12
sentence: "So he * them in the Num 1:17,18,19f
So all the Levites, as * by Moses Num 3:39
of the Levites * in the census: Num 26:57
men of Benjamin, * 400,000 men. Ju 20:17
of King David, * 36,000 troops; 1Ch 7:4
tribe of Issachar * 87,000 1Ch 7:5
genealogy * 36,000 men of war. 1Ch 7:40
Hosah's sons and brothers * 1Ch 26:11
His army of Benjaminites * 2Ch 14:8
of Solomon's officers * 392. Ez 2:58
of Solomon's officers * 392." Neh 7:60
Babylon's days are *; Is 13:22
Our end is near—our days are *. Lam 4:18
"Mene means '*'—God has numbered Dan 5:26
"Mene means 'numbered'—God has * Dan 5:26
very hairs of your head are all *. Mt 10:30
earth are *, and I am soon to die. 2Pe 1:13,14

NUMBERING
They are beyond *. Num 23:7-10

NUMBERLESS
marches in. The * soldiers cut down Jer 46:22,23
the sand of the sea," i.e., *. Rom 9:27f
host, * as sand along the shore. Rev 20:8

NUMBERS
he said, "Let your * increase. Gen 1:21,22
and reproduce in great *." Gen 8:17
fertile, increasing rapidly in *; Ex 1:7
That evening vast * of quail Ex 16:13
and reduce your * so that your Lev 26:22
large * of them with a plague. Num 11:33
situation described in * 25:1-3. Num 24:25f
in Numbers 25:1-3. See * 31:16. Num 24:25f
before you vast * of horses and Deu 20:1
slaughtered great * of them at Jos 10:10
See * 27:5-7. Jos 17:4f
See * 35 and 1 Chronicles 6. Jos 20:2f
The Hebrew, from which the * have 1Sa 13:1f
great * of innocent people. 2Ki 21:16
Implied. See * 26:33. 1Ch 7:15f
* that no one tried to keep count! 2Ch 5:6
* of sheep and oxen for the feast. 2Ch 18:2
large * of his people to Damascus. 2Ch 28:5
slaughtered great * of his troops. 2Ch 28:5
They had not kept it in great * 2Ch 30:5
large * of weapons and shields. 2Ch 32:5
Then frogs invaded in enormous * Ps 105:30
gold, and great * of horses and Is 2:7
a city of Moab. See *, chapter 23. Hos 9:10f
See *, chapter 6. Amo 2:11f
So Jesus healed great * of sick Mk 1:34
* came to see him for themselves. Mk 3:7,8
as a result great * of sick people Mk 3:10
and grew in strength and *. Act 9:31
so that large * of these Gentiles Act 11:21
As a result large * of people Act 11:24
church grew daily in faith and *. Act 16:5
day large * came to his house. Act 28:2
and against huge * of wicked Eph 6:1
(See Revelation 2:14 and * 31:15, Rev 2:

NUMERICAL
this code: the * values of the Rev 13:1

NUMEROUS
to become as * as the stars! Gen 26:
They are as * as dust! Num 23:7-1
before you were as * as stars. Deu 28:6
of camels too * to count and stayed Ju 6:
young woman be as * and honorable Ru 4:1
it because of the * wars going on, 1Ki 5:2,
* altars in the groves of trees. 2Ki 16:
They too were very *. 1Ch 5:2
your descendants shall be as * as Job 5:2
Then you would have become as * Is 48:1
people will be too * to count—like Hos 1:1
It is a terrible army too * to Joe 1:6
Merchants, * as stars, filled Nah 3:16

NUN
Joshua (son of *), stayed behind in Ex 33:1
Joshua (the son of *), one of Num 11:28
son of *, from the half-tribe of Num 13:3-15
Joshua (the son of *), and Caleb Num 14:6
of *) are permitted to enter it. Num 14:30
Jephunneh) and Joshua (son of *). Num 26:64,65
get Joshua (son of *), who has the Num 27:18
and Joshua (son of *)—for they Num 32:12
Joshua (son of *), and one leader Num 34:16-28
son of *), shall lead the people. Deu 1:38
Then he charged Joshua (son of * Deu 31:23
Joshua (son of *) was full of the Deu 34:9
(the son of *), and said to him, Jos 1:1
declared by Joshua, the son of *. 1Ki 16:34
*, the father of 1Ch 7:25,26,27

NURSE
been her childhood *, and blessed Gen 24:59
after this, Rebekah's old * Gen 35:8
women to * the baby for you?" Ex 2:7
"Take this child home and * him Ex 2:9
the child's * grabbed him and fled, 2Sa 4:4
virgin to be your concubine and *. 1Ki 1:2
* in a storeroom of the Temple. 2Ki 11:2,3
He was cared for by his * and by 2Ch 22:12
Why did she * me at her breasts? Job 3:12

NURSED
So she took him home and * him. Ex 2:9
Her children shall be * at her Is 66:12
where he * him through the night. Lk 10:34
And he * them through forty Act 13:18

NURSES
their enemies. He * them when they Ps 41:3

NURSING
me the job of * them along like Num 11:12
The baby * at the breast, Deu 32:25
and to mothers * their children. Mk 13:17
If you are angry, don't sin by * Eph 4:26

NURTURE
plant others and * them and make Jer 1:10

NUTS
myrrh, pistachio *, and almonds. Gen 43:11
the orchard of * and out to the Sol 6:11

NUTSHELL
of the laws of Moses in a *. Mt 7:12

NYMPHAS
Laodicea, and to *, and to those Col 4:15

O'CLOCK
About four * in the morning Jesus Mt 14:25
At noon and again around three * Mt 20:5
"At five * that evening he was Mt 20:6
When the men hired at five * Mt 20:9
hours, from noon until three *. Mt 27:45
About three *, Jesus shouted, Mt 27:46
About three * in the morning he Mk 6:48
It was about nine * in the Mk 15:25
lasting until three * that Mk 15:33
He may come at nine * at Lk 12:38
for three hours, until three *. Lk 23:44
from about four * that afternoon Jn 1:39
at about one * his fever suddenly Jn 4:52
the three * daily prayer meeting. Act 3:1
was about three *—and in this Act 10:3
for Caesarea at nine * tonight! Act 23:23,24

OAK
set up camp beside the * at Moreh. Gen 12:6
living in the * grove at Mamre. Gen 18:1
beneath the * tree near Shechem. Gen 35:4
* tree in the valley below Bethel. Gen 35:8
was called "The * of Weeping." Gen 35:8
at Judah, at the * in Zaanannim, Jos 19:33
it beneath the * tree that was Jos 24:26
the * of Za-anannim, near Kedesh. Ju 4:11
sat beneath the * tree at Ophrah, Ju 6:11
* tree, and presented it to him. Ju 6:19
meeting under the * beside the Ju 9:6
the road past the * of Meonenim!" Ju 9:37
And when you get to the * of 1Sa 10:3
sitting beneath an * tree playing 1Sa 22:6
beneath the * tree at Jabesh and 1Sa 31:13
boughs of a great * tree, and his 2Sa 18:9
as he dangled alive from the *. 2Sa 18:14

OAK Con't)
found him sitting under an * tree. 1Ki 13:14
them beneath the * tree at Jabesh 1Ch 10:12
cypress and the *, he plants the Is 44:14
tree and great * where they offered Eze 6:13

OAKS
his tent to the * of Mamre, near Gen 13:18
camping among the * belonging to Gen 14:13
Gilgal, where the * of Moreh are. Deu 11:30
spins and topples the mighty *. Ps 29:9
in your groves of "sacred" *. Is 1:29
and all the mighty * of Bashan Is 2:13
and graceful * for his own glory. Is 61:3
They made your oars from * of Eze 27:6
* and poplars and terebinth trees. Hos 4:13
as cedar trees, and strong as *! Amo 2:9
Cry in fear, you * of Bashan, as Zec 11:2

OARS
They made your * from oaks of Eze 27:6

OASES
springs and green * will dry away, Hos 13:15

OATH
("Well of the *"), because that Gen 21:31
then you are free from this *; Gen 24:8
You are under * to go and ask. Gen 24:41
the well, "The Well of the *," Gen 26:33
grew up there was named "*," Gen 26:33
So Jacob took * before the mighty Gen 31:53
promise with an * that they would Gen 50:25
must take an * that he has not Ex 22:11
In prayer, or in taking an *. Ex 23:13f
us, then this * will no longer bind Jos 2:20
the agreement with a binding *. Jos 9:14,15
if we break our * the wrath of Jos 9:20
"We promise with a solemn *." Ju 11:10
agreed by solemn * that anyone who Ju 21:5
again of their * to kill anyone who Ju 21:8,9
We have sworn with a solemn * Ju 21:18
But Saul took a solemn * that he 1Sa 28:10
* between himself and Jonathan. 2Sa 21:7
swore with a great *, "May God 1Ki 2:23,24
And his * to Isaac, 1Ch 16:16
They shouted out their * of 2Ch 15:14
he had taken an * of loyalty. 2Ch 36:13
agreed to this * and vowed to Neh 10:29
I have taken an * to establish Ps 89:3,4
his solemn * to care for them. Ps 106:24
Jehovah has taken *, and will Ps 110:4
He has taken an * to do it! Is 14:24
* shall swear by the God of Truth; Is 65:16
Even under *, they lie. Jer 5:2
say when taking an *, "As the Lord Jer 23:7
* and have made them slaves again. Jer 34:16
people—for you have broken your *. Jer 34:18,19
and made him take an * of Eze 17:12,13
the solemn * he made in my name. Eze 17:19
But I took a solemn * against Eze 20:23,24
my hand and taken *, says the Lord Eze 44:12
I promised with hand raised in * Eze 47:14
to heaven, taking * by him who Dan 12:7
but because of his *, and because Mt 14:9
can break that *, but to swear 'By Mt 23:16
And you say that to take an * Mt 23:18
denied it, this time with an *. Mt 26:72
his * in front of his guests. Mk 6:26
an unbreakable * that one of Act 2:30
himself with an * that he would Heb 3:11
he swore with an * that they could Heb 3:18
God took an * in his own name, Heb 6:13
When a man takes an *, he is Heb 6:16
the * ends all argument about it. Heb 6:16
God also bound himself with an * Heb 6:17
promise and his *, two things we Heb 6:18
God took an * that Christ would Heb 7:20
Because of God's *, Christ can Heb 7:22
* his Son who is perfect forever. Heb 7:28

OATHS
* to seal a non-aggression pact. Gen 26:31
him and take * by his name alone. Deu 10:20

OBADIAH
affairs was *, who was a devoted 1Ki 18:3,4
Lord's prophets, * had hidden one 1Ki 18:3,4
the king said to *, "We must 1Ki 18:5
Suddenly * saw Elijah coming 1Ki 18:7
coming toward him! * recognized him 1Ki 18:7
"Oh, sir," * protested, "what 1Ki 18:9
So * went to tell Ahab that 1Ki 18:16
Arnan's son was *; 1Ch 3:21,22
sons were Michael, *, Joel, and 1Ch 7:3
Ishmael, She-ariah, *, Hanan. 1Ch 8:38
* (the son of Shemaiah, son of 1Ch 9:15,16
She-ariah, *, Hanan. 1Ch 9:44
* was second in command; 1Ch 12:8-13
Over Zebulun, Ishmaiah (son of *); 1Ch 27:16-22
These men included Ben-hail, *, 2Ch 17:7,8,9
of Jahath and *, Levites of the 2Ch 34:12
From the clan of Joab—* (son of Ez 8:2-14
*, Daniel, Ginnethon, Neh 10:1
Mattaniah, Bakbukiah, *, Neh 12:25
In a vision the Lord God showed * Ob 1:1

OBADIAH'S
* son was Shecaniah. 1Ch 3:21,22

OBAL
Uzal, Diklah, *, Abima-el, Sheba, Gen 10:26-30

OBBLIGATOS
with trumpet *, the clashing of 2Ch 5:13,14

OBED
And they named him *. Ru 4:16,17
Salmon, Boaz, *, Jesse, David. Ru 4:18-22
Boaz was the father of *, and 1Ch 2:12
and * was the father of Jesse. 1Ch 2:12
Ephlal's son was *; 1Ch 2:37
Eliel; *; 1Ch 11:26-47
*, Elzabad. 1Ch 26:6,7
Azariah (son of *), Maaseiah (son 2Ch 23:1
Boaz was the father of * (Ruth Mt 1:5
* was the father of Jesse; Mt 1:5
Jesse's father was *; Lk 3:23-38

OBED-EDOM
home of *, who had come from Gath. 2Sa 6:10
blessed * and all his household. 2Sa 6:11
it to the home of * the Gittite 1Ch 13:13
with the family of * for three 1Ch 13:14
* and Je-iel, the door keepers. 1Ch 15:18
Mikneiah, *, Je-iel, and Azaziah 1Ch 15:21
And * and Jehiah guarded the Ark. 1Ch 15:24
of * to take the Ark to Jerusalem. 1Ch 15:25
Eliab, Benaiah, *, and Je-iel; 1Ch 16:5
This group included * (the son 1Ch 16:38
The sons of * were also appointed 1Ch 26:4,5
and grandsons of *—all sixty-two of 1Ch 26:8
of the south gate to * and his 1Ch 26:14,15
and he took hostages, including * 2Ch 25:24

OBED'S
Ephlal's son was Obed; * son was 1Ch 2:38
Jesse's father was Obed;* father Lk 3:23-38

OBEDIENCE
GOD tested Abraham's [faith and * Gen 22:1
Because of your *, the Lord your Deu 7:12
depends on your * to all these Deu 19:9
and * Ju 3:1
and sacrifices as in your *? 1Sa 15:22
* is far better than sacrifice. 1Sa 15:22
I was perfect in * 2Sa 22:24
has approached his record of *. 2Ki 23:25
* to him," he told his people. 2Ch 14:7
Help me to prefer * to making Ps 119:36
for * to God, but I stand unmoved. Ps 119:51
I will not give up * to your laws. Ps 119:109
His delight will be * to the Is 11:3
feed men's souls: * to every word Mt 4:4
to the Lord in * to the law, Lk 2:27
to * to Jewish laws and customs. Act 26:5
death) or else * (with acquittal). Rom 6:16
hearts' desire is * to Christ. 2Co 10:5
* to every Jewish law and custom. Php 3:5
and quarrels about * to Jewish Tit 3:9
firm to the end in * to his Rev 14:12

OBEDIENT
if you have been * to him and to Deu 13:18
them faithful and * to his laws. Ps 105:45
for I will remain * to your Word. Ps 119:101
of the Lord, and be * to his laws! Is 2:5
a man spares an * and dutiful son. Mal 3:17
with them and was * to them; Lk 2:51
Literally, "became * unto death, Php 2:8f
should have happy, * families. 1Ti 3:12
being kind and * to their husbands, Tit 2:5
* and ready for any honest work. Tit 3:1
So if we stay close to him, * to 1Jn 3:6

OBELISK
And never set up an *, for the Deu 16:22

OBELISKS
altars, smash the * they worship, Ex 34:13
carved images, *, or shaped stones, Lev 26:1
and shatter the * and cut up the Deu 7:5
Break the altars, smash the *, Deu 12:3
They built shrines and * and 1Ki 14:23
They had placed * and idols at 2Ki 17:10
broke down the *, knocked down the 2Ki 18:4
He smashed the * and cut down 2Ki 23:14
and broke down the *, and chopped 2Ch 14:3
idol altars, the *, shame-images, 2Ch 31:1
knocked apart, the * above the 2Ch 34:4
and chopped down the *. 2Ch 34:7
And he shall break down the * Jer 43:13

OBEY
But if you refuse to *, watch Gen 4:7
* me and live as you should. Gen 17:1
God told him, "is to * its terms. Gen 17:9,10
comes, whom all people shall *. Gen 49:10
God and didn't * the king—they let Ex 1:17
if we don't * him, we face death Ex 5:3
even yet you will not * him." Ex 9:30
be proof that you * me, and when I Ex 12:13
Lord your God, and * it, and do Ex 15:26
will these people refuse to *?" Ex 16:28,29
Now if you will * me and keep Ex 19:5
who love me and * my commandments. Ex 20:6
says and we will *, but don't let Ex 20:19
"HERE ARE OTHER laws you must *: Ex 21:1
"Be sure to * all of these Ex 23:13
Reverence him and * all of his Ex 23:21
But if you are careful to * him, Ex 23:22
in unison, "We will * them all." Ex 24:3
to * every one of these rules." Ex 24:7
Anyone who does not * this Ex 31:14,15
is to * all of my commandments; Ex 34:11
the laws of Jehovah you must *. Ex 35:1
You must * only my laws, and you Lev 18:4,5
If you * them you shall live. Lev 18:4,5
You must strictly * all of my Lev 18:26
So be very sure to * my laws, and Lev 18:29,30
and fathers, and * my Sabbath law, Lev 19:1
"* my laws: Do not mate your Lev 19:19
You must * all of my Lev 20:8
"You must * all of my laws and Lev 20:22
For I am Jehovah. * my laws if Lev 25:17,18
When you *, the land will yield Lev 25:19
You must * my Sabbath laws of Lev 26:2
"If you * all of my Lev 26:3
listen to me or * me, but reject Lev 26:14
"And if even then you will not * Lev 26:21
listen to me or * me, then I will Lev 26:27
to trust me and * me— shall even Num 14:22
deliberately failed to * his law; Num 15:31
that you are to * his laws instead Num 15:39
that we must * you, and acting as Num 16:3
the people of Israel will * him. Num 27:20
I teach you, and * them if you want Deu 4:1
from these; just * them, for they Deu 4:2
"These are the laws for you to * Deu 4:5
If you * them they will give you Deu 4:6
the laws you must *—the Ten Deu 4:13
the laws you must * when you arrive Deu 4:14
You must * these laws that I Deu 4:40
learn them, and be sure to * Deu 5:1
living among you must * this law. Deu 5:14
us, and we will listen and *.' Deu 5:26,27
me, wanting to * my commandments. Deu 5:29
and they will * them in the land Deu 5:31
people, "You must * all the Deu 5:32
which you are to * in the land you Deu 6:1
and be careful to * it, so that all Deu 6:3
If you * these commands you will Deu 6:3
You must actively * him in Deu 6:17
If you * him, all will go well Deu 6:18
And he has commanded us to * all Deu 6:24
with us when we * all the laws of Deu 6:25
love him and who * his commands. Deu 7:9
Therefore, * all these Deu 7:11
"YOU MUST * all the commandments Deu 8:1
or not you would really * him? Deu 8:2
"* the laws of the Lord your Deu 8:6
if you don't * the Lord your God. Deu 8:20
you refused to * him. Deu 9:23
to you, and to * for your own good Deu 10:12,13
and * every one of his commands. Deu 11:1
then, you should * these Deu 11:8
If you * the commandments, you Deu 11:9
"And if you will carefully * all Deu 11:13
to remind you to * them, and tie Deu 11:18
"If you carefully * all the Deu 11:22
There will be blessing if you * Deu 11:27
But you must * all the laws I am Deu 11:32
"THESE ARE THE laws you must * Deu 12:1
"Be careful to * all of these Deu 12:28
* all the commandments I give you. Deu 12:32
God but Jehovah; * only his Deu 13:4
giving you if you * this command. Deu 15:4,5
must listen and whom you must *. Deu 18:15
son who will not * his father or Deu 21:18
and rebellious and won't *; Deu 21:20
you must * to the letter: Remember Deu 24:8
"You must wholeheartedly * all Deu 26:16
have promised to * and keep his Deu 26:17
that you must * all of his laws. Deu 26:18
these further instructions to *: Deu 27:1
you must begin to * all of these Deu 27:10
anyone who does not * these laws.' Deu 27:26
"IF YOU FULLY * all of these Deu 28:1
only * him and walk in his ways. Deu 28:9
If you will only listen and * Deu 28:13
your God and won't * these laws I Deu 28:15-19
"If you refuse to * all the laws Deu 28:58,59
Therefore, * the terms of this Deu 29:9
us and our children to * forever. Deu 29:29
wholeheartedly to * all of the Deu 30:2
"If you return to the Lord and * Deu 30:7,8
He will rejoice if you but * the Deu 30:10
you can't hear and * them, and with Deu 30:12
your lips—so that you can * them. Deu 30:14
on whether you * or disobey. Deu 30:15
your God and to * him and to cling Deu 30:20
the Lord your God and * his laws. Deu 31:12
courageous and to * to the letter Jos 1:7
you are careful to * every one of Jos 1:7
you will be sure to * all of them. Jos 1:8
themselves to * Joshua as their Jos 1:16
"We will * you just as we obeyed Jos 1:17,18
Be sure to continue to * all of Jos 22:5
But if you are unwilling to * Jos 24:15
then decide today whom you will *. Jos 24:15
have chosen to * the Lord." Jos 24:22

(OBEY Con't)
must * the Lord God of Israel." Jos 24:23
worship and * the Lord alone." Jos 24:24
they refused to * God's commands. Ju 2:17
or not they will * the Lord as Ju 2:22
whether they would * the Ju 3:4
Determine to * only the Lord; 1Sa 7:3
Lord wants a man who will * him. 1Sa 13:14
Now be sure that you * him. 1Sa 15:1
he has again refused to * me." 1Sa 15:11
Then why didn't you * the Lord? 1Sa 15:19
you did not * the Lord's 1Sa 28:18
worthy successor. * the laws of 1Ki 2:3
you follow me and * my laws as your 1Ki 3:14
everything, and to * all the 1Ki 8:58
may you always * his laws and 1Ki 8:61
gods and do not * my laws, then I 1Ki 9:6
was always to * me and to do 1Ki 14:8
have refused to * the Lord, and 1Ki 18:18
So you should certainly * him 2Ki 5:13
and are going to * me, bring the 2Ki 10:6
he had warned them to * his 2Ki 17:13
But even Judah refused to * the 2Ki 17:19
of Jacob were to * all of God's 2Ki 17:37
always tried to * you and to please 2Ki 20:3
to the Lord to * him at all times 2Ki 23:3
For if you carefully * the rules 1Ch 22:13
of your being to * the Lord your 1Ch 22:19
And if he continues to * my 1Ch 28:7
Make your people always want to * 1Ch 29:18
he will want to * you in the 1Ch 29:19
to all those who * you, and who are 2Ch 6:14
they will * my laws as you have.' 2Ch 6:16
earnest effort to * the Lord as 2Ch 11:17
was careful to * the Lord his God. 2Ch 14:2
the entire nation * the 2Ch 14:4
desire to * the Lord's direction as 2Ch 30:12
And if you will only * my 2Ch 33:8
to study and * the laws of the Lord Ez 7:10
Anyone refusing to * the law of Ez 7:26
We will * the laws of God. Ez 10:3
kind to those who love and * him! Neh 1:5
but if you return to me and * my Neh 1:9
Moses your servant, to * them all. Neh 9:14
"They refused to * and didn't Neh 9:17
ancestors didn't * your laws or Neh 9:34
who refuses to * the king's orders, Est 1:13-15
they refuse to * the king's laws; Est 3:8
'Why should we * him? Job 21:15
"If they listen and * him, then Job 36:11
give success to those who * them. Ps 19:11
And when we * him, every path he Ps 25:10
joy, all those who try to * him. Ps 32:11
upon my altar have promised to * Ps 50:5
and make me willing to * you. Ps 51:12
has been able to * his laws and to Ps 78:7
because they didn't * his laws. Ps 78:10
my laws and don't * them, then I Ps 89:30,31,32
the Lord, O earth! * him gladly; Ps 100:2
covenant and remember to * him! Ps 103:17,18
You have given us your laws to * Ps 119:4
I will *! Ps 119:8
so that I can continue to * you. Ps 119:17
as I am, to * your laws, for I have Ps 119:29,30
as I live I'll wholeheartedly *. Ps 119:33,34
I long to * them! Ps 119:40,41,42
youth I have tried to * you; Ps 119:52
pilgrimage. I * them even at night Ps 119:55
has been to me—to constantly *. Ps 119:56
And I promise to *! Ps 119:57
I * your laws with all my heart. Ps 119:69
I cling to your laws and * them. Ps 119:83
then I can continue to * you. Ps 119:88
* these wonderful laws of yours. Ps 119:106
I am determined to * you until I Ps 119:112
undecided whether or not to * you; Ps 119:113
then I can continue to * your Ps 119:117
no wonder I love to * your laws! Ps 119:119
and teach me, your servant, to *; Ps 119:124
no wonder I * them. Ps 119:129
then I can * you. Ps 119:134
answer me, O Lord, and I will * Ps 119:145
trust the Lord—on all who * him! Ps 128:1
descendants will * the terms of Ps 132:12
rain, wind and weather, all *. Ps 148:8
Young man, * your father and your Pro 6:20
and stick to it. * me and live! Pro 7:2
men, and not only listen but *; Pro 7:24
in trouble. * it and succeed. Pro 13:13
God blesses those who * him; Pro 16:20
To * the law is to fight evil. Pro 28:4
Young men who are wise * the law; Pro 28:7
* the king as you have vowed to Ecc 8:2,3
Those who * him will not be Ecc 8:5
fear God and * his commandments, Ecc 12:13
only *, then I will make you rich! Is 1:19
us his laws, and we will * them." Is 2:3
ruthless nations will * and Is 25:3
* him, if they were kind and good. Is 28:12
but they do not * me, and since Is 29:13
to * you in everything you said?" Is 38:3
come running to *, not because of Is 55:5
though they would * them—just as Is 58:2
Defiant, you would not * me. Jer 2:20
they still will not *. Jer 2:30
How can they * him?" Jer 5:4
But what I told them was: * me Jer 7:23
that refuses to * the Lord its God, Jer 7:28
nations who don't * the Lord, for Jer 10:25
that if they would * me and do Jer 11:4
And now, Israel, * me, says the Jer 11:5
this day: * my every command! Jer 11:7
Because they refused to *, I did Jer 11:8
But any nation refusing to * me Jer 12:17
but they didn't listen or *. Jer 17:23
But if you * me, says the Lord, Jer 17:24
and refuses to * me, then I too Jer 18:10
listen to me and * the laws I have Jer 26:4
to * you or to follow your laws; Jer 32:23
but they would not listen or *; Jer 32:33
again and you won't listen or *. Jer 35:14
But you wouldn't listen or *. Jer 35:15
hands if only you will * the Lord; Jer 38:20
* whatever he says we should do! Jer 42:5
it or not, we will * the Lord our Jer 42:6
For if we * him, everything will Jer 42:6
"But if you refuse to * the Lord Jer 42:13,14
but you will not * any more now Jer 42:21
to * the Lord and stay in Judah. Jer 43:4
for they would not * the Lord. Jer 43:7
the Lord and refused to * him." Jer 44:23
so that you can * my laws and be Eze 11:20
his promise after swearing to *; Eze 17:18
who refuses to * the laws of God, Eze 18:11
sins and begins to * my laws and do Eze 18:21
They would not * my rules even Eze 20:13
they did not * my laws but scorned Eze 20:23,24
so that you will * my laws and do Eze 36:27
and they shall * my laws and all Eze 37:24
themselves shall * my rules and Eze 44:24
anyone who refuses to * will Dan 3:6
of every language must * him. Dan 7:14
rulers shall serve and * them." Dan 7:27
he does, but we would not *. Dan 9:14
because they will not listen or *. Hos 9:17
laws of God, refusing to * him. Amo 2:4
the nations who refuse to * me. Mic 5:15
humble—all who have tried to *. Zep 2:3
you carefully * the commandments of Zec 6:15
the rules he has given you to *. Mal 1:13
foolish to worship God and * him. Mal 3:14,15
What good does it do to * his Mal 3:14,15
"Remember to * the laws I gave Mal 4:4
only the Lord God. * only him.' Mt 4:10
God's laws and * them shall be Mt 5:19
they * my Father in heaven. Mt 7:21
the winds and the sea * him?" Mt 8:27
am wonderfully pleased with him. * Mt 17:5
and are fulfilled if you * them. Mt 22:40
And of course you should * their Mt 23:3
new disciples to * all the commands Mt 28:20
"Why, even evil spirits * his Mk 1:27
That's why demons * him." Mk 3:22
even the winds and seas * him?" Mk 4:41
people to * their petty rules.' Mk 7:6,7
folk, careful to * all of God's Lk 1:6
words that even demons * him?" Lk 4:36
me 'Lord' when you won't * me? Lk 6:46
and listen and * me are like a man Lk 6:47,48
listen and don't * are like a man Lk 6:49
the message of God and * it." Lk 8:21
even the winds and waves * him?" Lk 8:25
* us when we use your name." Lk 10:17
is not that demons * you, but that Lk 10:20
Just so, if you merely * me, you Lk 17:10
those who don't believe and * him Jn 3:36
too, whenever you * Moses' law of Jn 7:21,22,23
true—I know him and fully * him. Jn 8:55
If anyone hears me and doesn't * Jn 12:47
"If you love me, * me; Jn 14:15,16
to those who love me and * me. Jn 14:23
Anyone who doesn't * me doesn't Jn 14:24
But if you stay in me and * my Jn 15:7
When you * me you are living in Jn 15:10
* my Father and live in his love. Jn 15:10
and you are my friends if you * Jn 15:14
wants us to * you instead of him! Act 4:19
"We must * God rather than men. Act 5:29
given by God to all who * him." Act 5:32
my own heart, for he will * me.' Act 13:22
turn to God must * our Jewish laws, Act 15:19
that you yourself * the Jewish laws Act 21:24
they, too, will believe and * him. Rom 1:5
made, but wouldn't * the blessed Rom 1:25
peace from God for all who * him, Rom 2:10
his written laws but don't * them. Rom 2:12-15
something if you * God's laws; Rom 2:25
And if the heathen * God's laws, Rom 2:26
his promises but don't * his laws. Rom 2:27
we no longer need * God's laws? Rom 3:31
we trust Jesus can we truly * him. Rom 3:31
of their failure to * God's laws. Rom 5:20
So now we can * God's laws if we Rom 8:
* the old evil nature within us. Rom 8
It never did * God's laws and it Rom 8:
* THE GOVERNMENT, for God is Rom 13:
So those who refuse to * the Rom 13:
* God, and punishment will follow. Rom 13:
very purpose. * the laws, then, Rom 13:
duties gladly, * those over you, Rom 13:
have faith in Christ and * him. Rom 16:25,26,2
I am not bound to * anyone just 1Co 9:1
of them did not * God, and he 1Co 10:
must * every law of God or die; 2Co 3:
them God's law to *, his face shone 2Co 3:
to make these Gentiles * them? Gal 2:1
trying—and failing—to * the laws. Gal 2:1
For if trying to * the Jewish Gal 3:
that trying to * them now will make Gal 3:
your trying to * the Jewish laws? Gal 3:
think you have to * the Jewish laws Gal 4:21
was by giving them his laws to *. Gal 4:24,25
by trying to * the Commandments; Gal 4:24,25
must always * every other Jewish Gal 5:3
I advise you to * only the Holy Gal 5:16
force yourself to * Jewish laws. Gal 5:18
and so * our Lord's command. Gal 6:2
So you wives must willingly * Eph 5:24
CHILDREN, * YOUR parents; Eph 6:1
Slaves, * your masters; Eph 6:5
you want to * him, and then helping Php 2:13
and I tried to * every Jewish Php 3:6
if you fully * the truth you have. Php 3:16
You children must always * your Col 3:20
You slaves must always * your Col 3:22
but all the time; * them willingly Col 3:22
If anyone refuses to * what we 2Th 3:14
who * quickly and quietly. 1Ti 3:4
and encourage all to * them. 1Ti 6:2
there are many who refuse to *; Tit 1:10
Christians must * the Jewish laws. Tit 1:10
Urge slaves to * their masters Tit 2:9
REMIND YOUR PEOPLE to * the Tit 3:1
desire to * God at all times. Heb 5:7
*, when obeying meant suffering. Heb 5:8
salvation to all those who * him. Heb 5:9
they will want to * them, and I Heb 8:10
worry of having to * the old rules, Heb 9:14
that they will want to * them." Heb 10:16
A man who refused to * the laws Heb 10:28
refused to *—and because of his Heb 11:7
they refused to * God, for she gave Heb 11:31
So see to it that you * him who Heb 12:25
to *, not just to listen to. Jas 1:22
and doesn't *, he is like a man Jas 1:23
when you truly * our Lord's Jas 2:8
he was willing to * God, even if it Jas 2:21
is right or wrong, but to * it. Jas 4:11
* God because you are his 1Pe 1:14
to God's Word, nor * it, and so 1Pe 2:8
For the Lord's sake, * every law 1Pe 2:13
rule for you to *, for it is an old 1Jn 2:7
and as we * this commandment, to 1Jn 2:8
how much you love and * God. 1Jn 5:2
for every child of God can * 1Jn 5:4
them who did not trust and * him. Jud 1:5
strong, but you have tried to * Rev 3:8

OBEYED
because you have * me and have not Gen 22:16
earth—all because you have * me." Gen 22:18
I will do this because Abraham * Gen 26:5
my promise to Abraham, who * me." Gen 26:24
the Lord, for you * him even though Ex 32:29
kind of man—he has * me fully. Num 14:24
I have * the Lord my God and have Deu 26:14
He * your instructions Deu 33:9
so the people of Israel * him, Deu 34:9
"We will obey you just as we * Jos 1:17,18
they had not * the Lord, and he Jos 5:6
told: he carefully * all of the Jos 11:15
to Moses was *, and the cities and Jos 21:8
you, and have * every order I have Jos 22:2,3
Israel * the Lord throughout the Jos 24:31
Why have you not *? Ju 2:2
for you have not * the Lord's 1Sa 13:14
"But I have * the Lord," Saul 1Sa 15:20
she said, "Sir, I * your command 1Sa 28:21
And I * them. 2Sa 22:23
agreement and * my commandment? 1Ki 2:43
to you, and * your commands. 1Ki 3:6
and have not * my laws, I will tear 1Ki 11:11
my chosen one who * my 1Ki 11:34
but you have not * my commandments 1Ki 14:8
For David had * God during his 1Ki 15:5
you have not * the voice of the 1Ki 20:36
* all of God's commands to Moses. 2Ki 18:6
greatly, and all Israel * him. 1Ch 29:23
So they * the Lord and 2Ch 11:4
worship idols. He * the 2Ch 17:4
ancestors have not * these laws 2Ch 34:21
let it be * with all diligence." Ez 6:12
but I * God and did not act that Neh 5:15
though they should have * them, Neh 9:29

OBEYED Con't)
of God unless we * God's laws as Neh 10:29
Lord, and so I have * your laws. Ps 119:166
we have not * him. Jer 3:25
my commandments and not * my laws. Jer 9:13
things I swore I would if you *. Jer 11:5
all the people had * the king's Jer 34:10
and that if we * we would live Jer 35:7
And we have * him in all these Jer 35:8
and have fully * everything that Jer 35:10
and that if you *, then I would let Jer 35:15
The families of Rechab have * Jer 35:16
because you have * your father in Jer 35:18,19
who have not * me, but rather have Eze 11:12
sons of Zadok who * me and didn't Eze 48:11
So Jonah *, and went to Nineveh. Jon 3:3
in the land * Haggai's message from Hag 1:12
for you have not * me, but you Mal 2:9
"I've always * every one of Mt 19:20
and your command will be *. Mk 11:22,23
The man replied, "I've * Lk 18:21
and they have * you. Jn 17:6
because Abraham * God's laws but Rom 4:13
acceptable to God because he *. Rom 5:19
sin, now you have * with all your Rom 6:17
we * the Jewish laws or not. Gal 2:4
because we have * the Jewish laws. Gal 2:16
commandments which you had not *. Col 2:14
It was by faith that Abel * God Heb 11:4
promised to give him, Abraham *. Heb 11:8
Sarah, for instance, * her 1Pe 3:6
"Because you have patiently * me Rev 3:10

OBEYING
* them, for I am Jehovah." Lev 19:37
Lord your God by * all of his Deu 6:2
comes by * every command of God. Deu 8:3
his God by * all of his commands. Deu 17:19
hearts and souls. * these Deu 30:11
Through * them you will live Deu 32:47
David did, always * me, then I 1Ki 9:4
I consider right, * my commandments 1Ki 11:38
Asa had done, * the Lord in all but 1Ki 22:43
the Lord or * the laws he gave to 2Ki 17:34
King David, * the Lord completely 2Ki 22:1
man so far as * the Lord God of 2Ch 36:13
sin of not * the commandments you Neh 1:6,7
For growth in wisdom comes from * Ps 111:10
don't let them scorn me for * you. Ps 119:22
How I dread being mocked for *, Ps 119:39
Therefore I will keep on * you Ps 119:44,45,46
Don't try to stop me from * God's Ps 119:115
"Save me," I cry, "for I am * Ps 119:146
me, for I am * your commands. Ps 119:153
sinning and begin * the Lord your Jer 26:13
even though * them means life. Eze 20:13
Which of the two was * his Mt 21:31
that you are * all the others." Mt 22:40
No, you are * your real father Jn 8:41
* you will keep a man from dying! Jn 8:52
you could find for * the law, and Act 22:12
it becomes that we aren't * them; Rom 3:20
are saved without * Jewish laws. Rom 4:11
way, mechanically * a set of rules, Rom 7:6
them, you will be * all of God's Rom 13:8
out how far you would go in * me. 2Co 2:9
they think that * the Ten 2Co 3:15
circumcised and by * Jewish laws. Gal 2:5
right with God by * our Jewish Gal 2:16
will ever be saved by * them." Gal 2:16
and * all the other Jewish laws? Gal 2:17
a man is saved by * every law of Gal 3:12
Commandments. If * those laws Gal 3:18
to get to heaven by * God's laws? Gal 4:9
* the Jewish ceremonies or not; Gal 5:6
full of sin, * Satan, the mighty Eph 2:2
* praising and honoring him. Eph 5:33
from being saved, * God with deep Php 2:12
good enough or by * God's laws, but Php 3:9
doing good and * various rules Col 2:20
to obey, when * meant suffering. Heb 5:8
* Jewish laws can never be helped. Heb 13:10
bowing before him and * him. 1Pe 3:22
for because we are * him and doing 1Jn 3:22
the Truth, * God's command. 2Jn 1:4

OBEYS
in Egypt, and how everyone * me. Gen 45:13
and trusts the Lord and * him. Ps 119:63
listens to me and * my instructions Pro 2:1
fears the Lord and * his Servant? Is 50:10
others, and * my laws—that man is Eze 18:9
and * my laws—he shall not die Eze 18:17
his wickedness and * the law, and Eze 18:27
Then he added, "Anyone who * Mt 12:50
None of you * the laws of Moses! Jn 7:19
one who * me shall ever die!" Jn 8:51
The one who * me is the one who Jn 14:21
just as the church * Christ. Eph 5:24

OBIL
in the valleys. *, from the 1Ch 27:30

OBJECT
these things is an * of horror and Deu 18:12
You will become an * of horror, Deu 28:37
Peter asked, "Can anyone * to my Act 10:46,47
as examples—as * lessons to us—to 1Co 10:11
other * of adoration and worship. 2Th 2:4

OBJECTED
"But look," Moses *, "my own Ex 6:12
They * strenuously. Ju 14:3
himself, but his men * strongly. 2Sa 18:2
But Joab *. 1Ch 21:3
So the Jewish leaders *. Jn 5:10
But his disciples *. Jn 11:8

OBJECTIONS
this, all their * were answered and Act 11:18

OBJECTS
designer of * made of gold, silver, Ex 31:4
gold * of every kind. Ex 35:22
This entire group of * shall Num 4:10
at the sacred * there and die." Num 4:20
"If anyone *, bring him to me; 2Sa 14:10
Literally, "the dedicated * of 1Ki 15:15f
King Joash took all the sacred * 2Ki 12:18
He has caused us to be * of 2Ch 29:8

OBLIGATED
slave children, * to the Jewish Gal 4:31

OBLIGATION
the throne of Egypt who felt no * Ex 1:8
and * for the people of Israel. Ex 31:16
has released everyone from his *. Deu 15:2
from that * and that dark battle. Ecc 8:8

OBLIGATIONS
So, dear brothers, you have no * Rom 8:12

OBLIGED
crime, I would be * to listen to Act 18:14

OBOTH
Israel journeyed next to * and Num 21:10
at Punon, then at *, then Num 33:43

OBSCENITIES
hand a golden goblet full of *. Rev 17:4

OBSCURE
The Hebrew is *. Pro 14:9f
The meaning is *. Sol 8:9f
The meaning is *. Sol 8:9f
The Hebrew text is *. Dan 8:12f
of this idea, otherwise *. Jn 16:26f

OBSCURED
The sun and moon are * and the Joe 2:10
began to fade, * by brilliance from Hab 3:11

OBSCURITIES
I do not whisper * in some dark Is 45:19

OBSERVANCE
eat it hurriedly. This * shall be Ex 12:11
concerning the * of the Passover. Ex 12:43
So, for seven days the * 2Ch 30:22
the * for another seven days. 2Ch 30:23
in the Passover *, and this was 2Ch 35:17
the people returned for another * Neh 9:1
Literally, "by the * of which a Neh 9:29f
THE PASSOVER * began two days Mk 14:1

OBSERVATION
*, for he is definitely diseased. Lev 13:11

OBSERVE
* this memorial at the same time. Ex 12:47
you and want to * the Passover with Ex 12:48
"Remember to * the Sabbath as a Ex 20:8
and clans—to * the transferring of 1Ki 8:1
for his people to * the Passover 2Ki 23:21
people refused to * the Sabbath. 2Ch 36:21
no eagle's eye *— for they are Job 28:7
They, too, * the power of God in Ps 107:24
For God will * that land and find Is 34:11
Christians should * the Jewish Rom 14:5

OBSERVED
As God * how bad it was, and saw Gen 6:12,13
which are to be * each year: Lev 23:4
* from generation to generation. Num 15:19,20,21
Shelters, must be * for seven days Deu 16:13
NEXT I * all the oppression and Ecc 4:1
Then I * that the basic motive Ecc 4:4
I also * another piece of Ecc 4:7
In my search for wisdom I * all Ecc 8:16,17
* during every human birth. Jn 3:5f

OBSERVES
Day by day the Lord * the good Ps 37:18

OBSERVETH
Literally, "He that * the wind Ecc 11:4f

OBSERVING
while they are * and carry your Eze 12:5

OBSTACLE
all its armies is no * to you! Is 37:25
I will make an * course of the Jer 6:21
and darkness is no * to him. Dan 2:22

OBSTINATE
your God made him *, so that he Deu 2:30
I knew how hard and * you are. Is 48:4
Literally, "disobedient, *." Rom 10:21f

OBTAIN
to * his forgiveness for you." Ex 32:30
as you are able to * it, because Deu 12:15
"Men know how to * food from the Job 28:5
lest strangers * your wealth, Pro 5:10
could * information from the gods. Eze 21:21f
But to * these gifts, you need 2Pe 1:5

OBVIOUS
It's * what we ought to do!" Ju 18:14
The answer must be * even to you! Job 34:33
read the * signs of the times! Mt 16:2,3
us, then it is * that this would be Gal 3:18

OBVIOUSLY
"The Lord has * brought you here, Gen 24:50
"This is * no friendly visit, Gen 26:27
* as a result of prostitution. Gen 38:24
For he is a man who is * filled Gen 41:38
brick, for they * don't have enough Ex 5:7,8
into the city." * this does not Ju 1:24f
and was * the best match! 1Sa 17:11f
who was * pregnant by this time. Lk 2:5
see that they were * uneducated Act 4:13
lawful for me." *, Paul is not 1Co 6:12f
And quite * when they talked Heb 11:14

OCCASION
a party to celebrate the happy *. Gen 21:8
to warm to the *, a gang of sex Ju 19:22
the happy * by giving presents to 1Sa 1:4
father for this *, but tomorrow 1Sa 20:5
to a feast to celebrate the *. 2Sa 13:21-24
a new robe for the *) met him and 1Ki 11:29
as were required for the *. 1Ch 23:31
prayed by Solomon on that *: 2Ch 6:1
iron horns for the * and 2Ch 18:10
especially for the * so that Neh 8:1
part in the joyous * with their Neh 12:27
part of Media-Persia for the *. Est 1:1
To celebrate the *, he threw Est 2:18
ON YET ANOTHER * God spoke to Jer 16:1
Egypt at the * of the battle of Jer 46:2

OCCASIONS
On each of these three * all the Ex 34:23
"On each of these * bring a gift Deu 16:16
on three * in reconquering the 2Ki 13:25
to celebrate these special *. 2Ch 2:4
On these * they would eat and Job 1:4
Sabbaths and all other similar *. Eze 45:17
with the common people on these *. Eze 46:10
story from those first two *. Dan 11:29
Literally, "because of * of Mt 18:7f
And on these * he talked to them Act 1:3
* when I shall appear to you. Act 26:16

OCCUPATION
you about your *, tell him, 'We Gen 46:33
asked them, "What is your *?" Gen 47:3

OCCUPIED
giving its name to the area it *. Gen 36:40-43
to the land now * by the Ex 3:17
them and * their land from the Num 21:24
and Israel * the land. Num 21:35
tribe of Manasseh, * many of the Num 32:41
villages, and * them, and he called Num 32:42
(This was the land formerly * by Deu 4:44,45,46
a list of the areas still to be *: Jos 13:2-7
* the nearby city of Bethlehem. 2Sa 23:14
king of Babylon * the entire area 2Ki 24:7
the Philistines had * Bethlehem. 1Ch 11:16
from the areas * by the Jews, and 2Ch 34:33
and many other lands will be *. Dan 11:42
and drinking, and * with the Lk 21:34,35

OCCUPY
Now go and * the hill country of Deu 1:7
live in the land you will soon *. Jos 3:10
and they will * the nations of Edom Is 11:14
of the nations to * your homes, Eze 7:24
Horsemen will * every street in Eze 26:11
shall * the hill country of Edom; Ob 1:19
shall return and * the Phoenician Ob 1:20

OCCUPYING
still * our city of Ramoth-gilead? 1Ki 22:3
He drove out the nations * the Ps 78:55

OCCUR
nation will not * until after you 2Ki 22:20
things would not * during their 1Pe 1:12
to * in the life of Jesus Christ. Rev 1:1

OCCURRED
This all * on the third day. Gen 1:13
so that his death * in the year of Gen 11:32f
This incident * about four Ex 1:8f
he died. This * during the fortieth Num 33:38,39
Another similar situation * when Deu 2:23
This miracle * on the 25th of Jos 4:19
This celebration * at the time 1Ki 8:2
(This * during the twenty-seventh 1Ki 16:10
The tragedy * because of the 1Ki 16:13
succeed him. This * in the second 2Ki 1:17
This * during the first year of 2Ki 25:27
Let them try to tell us what * Is 41:22
This * on the Day of Fasting Jer 36:9
This event * six years after this Jer 51:59f
This * when Hezekiah entertained Eze 23:16f
However, it * to me that it Lk 1:3
has * in the Kingdom of God." Lk 22:16
Now as it happened, this all * Jn 9:14
of the dead has already *; 2Ti 2:18

OCCURS
"But before all this *, there Lk 21:12

OCEAN
the * to fulfill your promise!" Num 11:22
nor are they beyond the *, so Deu 30:13
He sets a boundary for the *, Job 26:10
overwhelm me, or the * swallow me; Ps 69:15
into its vast * beds, and mountains Ps 104:7,8
There before me lies the mighty * Ps 104:25
you creatures of the * depths. Ps 148:7
its way across the heaving *. Pro 30:18,19
and all the proud * ships and trim Is 2:16
*, from Egypt and along the Nile. Is 23:2,3
nations against you like * waves. Eze 26:3
The ships of Tarshish are your * Eze 27:25
storm on a mighty *, with strong Dan 7:2
rose up out of the *, too dreadful Dan 7:7
a chip of wood upon an * wave. Hos 10:7
the water from the * and pours it Amo 5:8
the bottom of the *, I will send Amo 9:3
to rise from the * and pours it Amo 9:6
You threw me into the * depths; Jon 2:3
that rise from off the * floor. Jon 2:6
them into the depths of the *! Mic 7:19
over into the *,' and it will. Mt 21:21
or in the deepest *—nothing will Rom 8:39
the sand on the * shores, there is Heb 11:12
the * became as smooth as glass. Rev 7:1
He stood waiting on an * beach. Rev 12:17
seemed to be an * of fire and Rev 15:2
threw it into the * and shouted, Rev 18:21

OCEANS
to form the sky above and the * Gen 1:6
be gathered into * so that the dry Gen 1:9,10
"Multiply and stock the *," he Gen 1:21,22
" 'It's not here,' the * say; Job 28:14
and sets the boundaries of the *. Job 28:25
He is the one who pushed the * Ps 24:2
He made the *, pouring them into Ps 33:7
of wisdom as the * are with water. Ps 36:6
Let the * roar and foam; Ps 46:3
He quiets the raging * and all Ps 65:7
You rule the * when their waves Ps 89:9
The mighty * thunder your Ps 93:3
separated the earth from the *." Ps 136:6f
to the farthest *, even there your Ps 139:9
I lived before the * were Pro 8:24
springs in the depths of the *. Pro 8:27,28,29
the blueprint for the earth and *. Pro 8:27,28,29
and wraps up the * in his cloak? Pro 30:4
Wail, you ships that ply the *, Is 23:14
Who else has held the * in his Is 40:12
the forests and boil the * dry. Is 64:2
so that the *, though they toss and Jer 5:22
fell I made the * mourn for her and Eze 31:15
At his command the * and rivers Nah 1:4
and earth—and the *, too, and the Hag 2:6
to turn rivers and * to blood, and Rev 11:6
his flask upon the *, and they Rev 16:3
and everything in all the * died. Rev 16:3
"The *, lakes and rivers that Rev 17:15
waves of a hundred * crashing on Rev 19:6
he had done. The * surrendered the Rev 20:13
THEN I SAW a new earth (with no *! Rev 21:1

OCHRAN
Pagiel (son of *) Num 1:2-15
Pagiel (son of *) Num 2:3-31
Pagiel, son of *, chief of the Num 7:72-77
led by Pagiel, the son of *; Num 10:26

OCTET
an * accompanied by harps. 1Ch 15:20

OCTOBER
six months, from April until *. 2Sa 21:10f
Festival in the month of *. 1Ki 8:2
This celebration took place in * 2Ch 5:3
Then, on * 7, he sent the people 2Ch 7:10
piles continued to grow until *. 2Ch 31:7,8
ON * 10 Neh 9:1
BUT IN *, Ishmael (son of Jer 41:1
"Early in *, during each of the Eze 45:25
IN EARLY * of the same year, the Hag 2:1
in August and *, were you really in Zec 7:5
in July, August, *, and January Zec 8:19

ODD
their many crimes! How *! Ecc 8:9,10
some parts that seem rather *! 1Co 12:23

ODDS
Marched down against great *. Ju 5:13,14

ODE
When singing this *, the choir is Hab 3:19

ODED
Azariah (son of *), and he went 2Ch 15:1
But *, a prophet of the Lord, was 2Ch 28:9

ODOR
the delicious * and said ." Gen 8:21f
of maggots and had a terrible *; Ex 16:20
and good, without maggots or *. Ex 16:24
Literally, "of a sweet * to the Lev 23:18f
It will be a pleasant * before Num 15:23,24
as a fragrant *, an offering made Num 28:6
It too is a fragrant * to the Num 28:8

OFFEND
not worship him; they * his glory. Is 3:8
However, we don't want to * them, Mt 17:26,27
said to them, "Does this * you? Jn 6:61
that message doesn't * anyone. Gal 5:11

OFFENDED
friendship of an * brother than to Pro 18:19
He killed any who * him, and Dan 5:19
which of them had * the gods and Jon 1:7
* the Pharisees by that remark." Mt 15:12
And they were *! Mk 6:2,3
them, the Jews are * and the 1Co 1:23
one will ever be * or kept back 2Co 6:3

OFFENDERS
leaders were some of the worst *. Ez 9:2

OFFENDING
"not guilty" of * him if we trust Rom 3:24
then you will not need to fear [* 1Pe 3:6

OFFENDS
* your brother or makes him sin. Rom 14:21

OFFENSE
of a Gentile was a serious *. Jn 18:28f

OFFER
altars of earth. * upon them your Ex 20:24
"Each day * two yearling lambs Ex 29:38
With one of them * three quarts Ex 29:40
as a libation. * the other lamb in Ex 29:41
to generation. * no unauthorized Ex 30:9
You may * yeast bread and honey Lev 2:12
them, then * them to the Lord. Lev 2:14
altar, and shall * upon the altar Lev 3:9,10,11
altar, and shall * upon the altar, Lev 3:14
people, he must * a young bull Lev 4:3
it, they shall * a young bull for a Lev 4:14
The priest shall * as the sin Lev 5:8
He shall * the second bird as a Lev 5:10
the altar to * it before the Lord. Lev 6:14
The priest will * upon the altar Lev 7:3
would know how to * their Lev 7:38
and to * them before the Lord. Lev 9:2
the altar and to * the sin offering Lev 9:7
and the priest will * them Lev 12:7
of olive oil and * them to the Lord Lev 14:12
"Then the priest must * the sin Lev 14:19
offering, and * it along with the Lev 14:20
"Then he must * the two Lev 14:30
the priest shall * one for a sin Lev 15:30
to the Lord, * it correctly so that Lev 19:5
the same day you * it, or the next Lev 19:6
The priest is set apart to * the Lev 21:8
may not * the sacrifices to God. Lev 21:16,17
not permitted to * the fire Lev 21:21
When you * the Lord a sacrifice Lev 22:29,30
to him. Also * a drink offering Lev 23:13
And you shall * one male goat Lev 23:19
* a sacrifice by fire to the Lord. Lev 23:25
and they shall * sacrifices by Lev 23:26,27
The priest shall * one of the Num 6:11
Tabernacle and * a burnt sacrifice Num 6:14
He must also * a sin offering, a Num 6:14
bulls and * them before the Lord; Num 8:12
and will * the people's sacrifices, Num 8:19
error, they must * one young bull Num 15:23,24
before the Lord. * the second lamb Num 28:8
month you shall * one male goat for Num 28:15
You shall * as burnt sacrifices Num 28:19
You must also * a male goat as a Num 28:22
Also * one male goat to make Num 28:30
On that day you shall * a burnt Num 29:2
On that day you shall * a burnt Num 29:8
of the festival, * eleven young Num 29:20
Only there may you * your Deu 12:14
against it, first * it a truce. Deu 20:10
and on the altar * burnt offerings Deu 27:5,6
and there you will * to sell Deu 28:68
We can at least * it to him and 1Sa 9:8
They will greet you and * you 1Sa 10:4
was delighted to accept the *. 1Sa 18:26
I don't want to * to the Lord my 2Sa 24:24
the hills and to * incense there. 1Ki 3:3
When they go to Jerusalem to * 1Ki 12:27
common people, to * sacrifices to 1Ki 13:33
but Jehoshaphat had refused the *. 1Ki 22:49
I will never again * any burnt 2Ki 5:17
I will not * a burnt offering 1Ch 21:24
your people * their gifts willingly 1Ch 29:17
service corps to * the burnt 2Ch 31:2
where the Jews * sacrifices. Ez 6:3
Then they will be able to * Ez 6:10
a day if they * enough sacrifices? Neh 4:1
The mountains * their best food Job 40:20
* a burnt offering for yourselves; Job 42:8
and * him pleasing sacrifices. Ps 4:5
I will not * the sacrifices they Ps 16:4
But you have accepted the * of my Ps 40:6
But now what can I * Jehovah for Ps 116:12
I will worship you and * you a Ps 116:17
buy him off no matter what you *. Pro 6:35
king of Assyria's * to you: Give me Is 36:16
animals enough to * to our God. Is 40:16
to * to "The Queen of Heaven" Jer 7:18
have been used to * incense to Jer 32:29
be Levites to * burnt offerings and Jer 33:18
rooms and * them a drink of wine. Jer 35:
They refuse to even * help unless Eze 13:1
For when you * gifts to them and Eze 20:3
there the priests who * up the Eze 42:1
ceremony, * another perfect bullock Eze 43:2
for God—when you * me my food, the Eze 44:
they shall stand before me to * Eze 44:1
sanctuary, he must * a sin offering Eze 44:2
enter and he shall * his sacrifices Eze 46:1
the sacrifices the people *. Eze 46:2
his people to * sacrifices and burn Dan 2:46
pretending to * a helping hand, Dan 11:34
but may not * it to God. Hos 9:4
* you the sacrifice of praise. Hos 14:2
much that you can * your grain and Joe 2:14
and in my own Temple they * Amo 2:8
"When you * polluted sacrifices Mal 1:7
very valuable to * to God!' Mal 1:7
are all right to * on the altar of Mal 1:8
All around the world they will * Mal 1:11
sick animals to * to me on it. Mal 1:12
* me, and throw you out like dung. Mal 2:3
come and * your sacrifice to God. Mt 5:24
as myself, than to * all kinds of Mk 12:33
Jewish priest. "* the sacrifice Lk 5:14
didn't bother to * me water to wash Lk 7:44
How can you * better water than Jn 4:12
we will * it to Gentiles. Act 13:46
Probably a vow to * a sacrifice in Act 18:18f
Probably a vow to * a sacrifice in Act 18:22f
his vow to * a sacrifice seven Act 21:26,27
listen to me as I * my defense." Act 22:1
Jews, and to * a sacrifice to God. Act 24:17
The one to whom you * yourself—he Rom 6:16
a result of God's * of salvation, Rom 11:12
of the world to * his salvation; Rom 11:15
And who could ever * to the Lord Rom 11:35
Those who * comfort to the Rom 12:8
is that those who * food to these 1Co 10:20
is appointed to * gifts and Heb 8:3
is no need to * more sacrifices to Heb 10:18
will continually * our sacrifice of Heb 13:15
—and * to God those things that 1Pe 2:5
But these very teachers who * this 2Pe 2:19
God's people, to * upon the golden Rev 8:3

OFFERED
to Beer-sheba, and * sacrifices Gen 46:1
Jethro * sacrifices Ex 18:12
"No sacrificial blood shall be * Ex 23:18
it shall be * Ex 23:19
the entrance, and * upon it a burnt Ex 40:29
if it is to be * to the Lord! Lev 3:1
It must be * as a guilt Lev 5:19
flour, half to be * in the morning Lev 6:19,20
to the one who brought it to be *; Lev 7:17,18
and the legs, and * these also upon Lev 9:14
he killed the goat and * it in Lev 9:15
and * the incense before the Lord Lev 10:1
and * unholy fire ." Lev 10:1f
handful has been * to the Lord by Lev 10:12
which have been * to the Lord by Lev 10:14
breast that was * when the fat was Lev 10:15
"They * their sin offering and Lev 10:19
have been * to the Lord. Lev 22:15
be *, for it will not be accepted. Lev 22:20
must not be * to the Lord; Lev 22:22
parts, it may be * as a free will Lev 22:23
not be * to the Lord at any time. Lev 22:24
oil, to be * by fire to the Lord; Lev 23:13
kind that may be * as a sacrifice, Lev 27:13
He, too, * the same gifts and Num 7:42-47
the same as those * by the others. Num 7:60-65
This shall be * by fire as a Num 15:10
Lord with sacrifices * by fire; Num 15:13,14
Lord, and must be * along with the Num 15:23,24
people's tithes, * to the Lord by Num 18:24
and he * up a young bull and a Num 23:14
Balaam said, and * a young bull and Num 23:30
* unholy fire before the Lord. Num 26:61
are * as I have instructed you. Num 28:1
Two of them shall be * each day Num 28:3
With them shall be * a grain Num 28:5
to be regularly * as a fragrant Num 28:6
This same sacrifice shall be * Num 28:24
to the Lord, shall be * that day. Num 28:27
with oil shall be * with the bull, Num 29:3,4
which are to be * with the Num 29:6
oil are to be * with the bull; Num 29:9,10
Atonement [* annually on that day Num 29:11
have I * any of it to the dead. Deu 26:14
Then the priests * burnt Jos 8:31
of the city. They * to spare his Ju 1:24
Then they * sacrifices to the Ju 2:5
Who * themselves so willingly! Ju 5:9
* it as a sacrifice to the Lord; Ju 13:19
an altar, and * sacrifices and Ju 21:4
sacrifices were * to the Lord that 1Sa 6:15
suckling lamb and * it to the Lord 1Sa 7:9
Then they * peace offerings to 1Sa 11:15
So I reluctantly * the burnt 1Sa 13:12
has * to anyone who kills him? 1Sa 17:25

(OFFERED Con't)
to the Lord and * burnt offerings 2Sa 24:25
completed, Solomon * burnt 1Ki 9:25
he himself * sacrifices upon the 1Ki 12:32,33
the palace." He * cash or, if 1Ki 21:2
the morning sacrifice was *—look! 2Ki 3:20
They had also * incense to Baal 2Ki 23:5
'The Lord has * you three choices. 1Ch 21:10,11
they also * drink offerings and 1Ch 29:21
burnt offerings have not been *. 2Ch 29:7
and the sacrifices * again. 2Ch 29:35
of the Lord and * sacrifices upon 2Ch 33:16
They also * the special Ez 3:5
of which will be * upon the altar Ez 7:17
Many sacrifices were * on that Neh 12:43
despite the bribes * him—such a man Ps 15:5
for my awful thirst they * me Ps 69:21
and even * sacrifices to the dead! Ps 106:28
buy before it is * to anyone else. Jer 32:6,7
oak where they * incense to their Eze 6:13
and there you * your beauty to Eze 16:25
them, for they * sacrifices and Eze 20:27,28
They roused my fury as they * up Eze 20:27,28
daily sacrifices * to him, and by Dan 8:11
gods and * them choice gifts." Hos 3:1
For no sacrifice that is * there Hos 9:4
New birth is * him, but he is Hos 13:13
For if you * him thousands of Mic 6:7
* to him there, but he refused it. Mk 15:23
parents also * their sacrifice for Lk 2:24
the opportunity God * you." Lk 19:44
* money to buy this power. Act 8:18
from eating food * to idols and Act 15:27,28,29
not to eat food * to idols, not to Act 21:25
eat meat that has been * to idols. Rom 14:2
meat that has been * to idols; Rom 14:6
meat that has been * to idols. Rom 14:14
believed that food * to the idols 1Co 8:7
is really being * to actual gods. 1Co 8:7
So if eating meat * to idols is 1Co 8:13
that has been * to these idols. 1Co 10:20
food * to idols if you want to; 1Co 10:23
Don't ask whether or not it was * 1Co 10:25
this meat has been * to idols, then 1Co 10:28
day when salvation was being *." 2Co 6:2
is now being * to everyone; Tit 2:11
those * by the earthly priests. Heb 8:4
sacrifices were *, but these failed Heb 9:9
Nor has he * himself again and Heb 9:25
and so he * up his son Isaac, and Heb 11:17
And their prayer, if * in faith, Jas 5:15

OFFERING
And the Lord accepted Abel's *, Gen 4:4
there as a burnt * upon one of the Gen 22:2
wood for the burnt * upon Isaac's Gen 22:6
son, as a burnt * on the altar. Gen 22:13
wine over it as an * to God, and Gen 35:13,14
Literally, "a burnt * and Ex 18:12f
may bring me an * from this list: Ex 25:1
the camp and burn it as a sin *. Ex 29:14
it is a burnt * to the Lord, and Ex 29:18
in a gesture of * to the Lord. Ex 29:24
as a fragrant burnt * to him. Ex 29:25
before the Lord in a gesture of *; Ex 29:26
bull as a sin * for atonement; Ex 29:36
a fragrant burnt * to the Lord. Ex 29:41
a perpetual daily * at the door of Ex 29:42
blood of the sin * for atonement. Ex 30:10
a shekel for an * to Jehovah." Ex 30:13f
birthday shall give this *. Ex 30:14
less, for it is an * to the Lord to Ex 30:15
altar, the burnt * altar with all Ex 30:28
the burnt * altar with its Ex 31:9
morning and began * burnt offerings Ex 32:6
and bronze as their * to the Lord; Ex 35:24
the altar of burnt * and its Ex 40:10
upon it a burnt * and a meal Ex 40:29
and a meal *, just as the Lord had Ex 40:29
given as a burnt *, use only a bull Lev 1:2,3
* with which the Lord is pleased. Lev 1:9
"If the animal used as a burnt * Lev 1:10
the altar as an * to the Lord; Lev 1:13
bird as his burnt *, he may choose Lev 1:14
sacrifice a grain * to the Lord is Lev 2:1
the altar, an * made by fire." Lev 2:2f
as a holy burnt * to the Lord. Lev 2:3
is brought as an * to the Lord, it Lev 2:4
oil may also be used as an *. Lev 2:4
If the * is something from the Lev 2:5
upon it—it is a form of grain *. Lev 2:6
If your * is cooked in a pan, it Lev 2:7
bring this grain * to the priest Lev 2:8
of the *, but all of it will be Lev 2:9
as a holy burnt * to the Lord. Lev 2:10
"Every * must be seasoned with Lev 2:13
"If you are * from the first of Lev 2:14
the *, for it is a grain offering. Lev 2:15
the offering, for it is a grain *. Lev 2:15
ANYONE WANTS to give an * Lev 3:1
bladder, as a burnt * to the Lord. Lev 3:9,10,11
a goat as his * to the Lord, he Lev 3:12
altar, as a burnt * to the Lord, Lev 3:14
This burnt * is very pleasing to Lev 3:15,16
defect as a sin * to the Lord. Lev 4:3
the altar of burnt *, just as in Lev 4:10
bull for a sin *, bringing it to Lev 4:14
base of the burnt * altar, at the Lev 4:18
the same procedure as for a sin *; Lev 4:20
it were a sin * for an individual, Lev 4:21
is a sin * for the entire nation. Lev 4:21
This is his sin *. Lev 4:24
blood of this sin * and place it Lev 4:25
Literally, "peace *." Lev 4:26f
the head of the sin * and kill it. Lev 4:29
the horns of the burnt * altar. Lev 4:30
Literally, "peace *." Lev 4:31f
a lamb as his sin *, it must be a Lev 4:32
head and kill it there as a sin *. Lev 4:33
horns of the burnt * altar, and all Lev 4:34
Literally, "peace *." Lev 4:35f
bring his guilt * to the Lord, a Lev 5:6
two young pigeons as his guilt *; Lev 5:7
shall be his sin * and the other Lev 5:7
and the other his burnt *. Lev 5:7
this is the sin *. Lev 5:9
bird as a burnt *, following the Lev 5:10
pigeons as his sin *, then he shall Lev 5:11
on it, because it is a sin *. Lev 5:11
other * to Jehovah made by fire; Lev 5:12
this shall be his sin *. Lev 5:12
was the case with the grain *." Lev 5:13
him, as his guilt * to the Lord. Lev 5:15
guilt *, and he shall be forgiven. Lev 5:16
taken to the priest as a guilt *; Lev 5:17,18
It must be offered as a guilt *, Lev 5:19
his guilt * to the Tabernacle. Lev 6:4,5
His guilt * shall be a ram Lev 6:6
concerning the burnt *: Lev 6:9
"The burnt * shall be left upon Lev 6:9
* and put them beside the altar. Lev 6:10
the daily burnt * on it, and burn Lev 6:12
burn the fat of the daily peace *. Lev 6:12
concerning the grain *: Lev 6:14
* and the entire guilt offering. Lev 6:17
offering and the entire guilt *. Lev 6:17
a regular grain *—a tenth of a Lev 6:19,20
an * that pleases him very much. Lev 6:21
into office by * this same Lev 6:22,23
instructions concerning the sin *: Lev 6:25
may eat this *, but only they, for Lev 6:29
No sin * may be eaten by the Lev 6:30
the most holy * for guilt: Lev 7:1
where the burnt * sacrifices are Lev 7:2
altar as a guilt * to the Lord. Lev 7:5
to both the sin * and the guilt Lev 7:7
and the guilt *—the carcass shall Lev 7:7
(When the * is a burnt Lev 7:8
"If it is an * of thanksgiving, Lev 7:12
This thanksgiving peace * shall Lev 7:13
Lord as a peace * to show special Lev 7:15
simply a voluntary * to the Lord, Lev 7:16
the thanksgiving * anyway, shall be Lev 7:20
eats the peace *, shall be cut off Lev 7:21
Anyone who eats fat from an * Lev 7:25
a thanksgiving * to the Lord must Lev 7:29
He shall bring the * of the fat Lev 7:30
the burnt *, grain offering, sin Lev 7:37
offering, grain *, sin offering, Lev 7:37
offering, sin *, and guilt Lev 7:37
and guilt *, and concerning the Lev 7:37
* and the peace offering; Lev 7:37
offering and the peace *; Lev 7:37
bull for the sin *, the two rams, Lev 8:1
bull for the sin *, and Aaron and Lev 8:14
the Lord the ram for the burnt *. Lev 8:18
it was a burnt * that pleased the Lev 8:21
the altar, along with the burnt * Lev 8:28
Literally, "upon the burnt *." Lev 8:28f
and Jehovah was pleased by the *. Lev 8:28
the herd for a sin *, and a ram Lev 9:2
defect for a burnt *, and to offer Lev 9:2
goat for their sin *, also a Lev 9:3
bodily defect, for their burnt *. Lev 9:3
the Lord a peace * sacrifice—an ox Lev 9:4
*—flour mingled with olive oil. Lev 9:4
to offer the sin * and the burnt Lev 9:7
and the burnt *, making atonement Lev 9:7
from this sin *, as the Lord had Lev 9:10
Next he killed the burnt * Lev 9:12
also upon the altar as a burnt *. Lev 9:14
Next he sacrificed the people's * Lev 9:15
as he had the sin * for himself. Lev 9:15
Thus he sacrificed their burnt * Lev 9:16
Then he presented the grain *, Lev 9:17
addition to the regular morning *. Lev 9:17
people's peace * sacrifice; Lev 9:18
as a gesture of * it to him, just Lev 9:21
the burnt * and fat on the altar; Lev 9:24
"Take the grain *—the food that Lev 10:12
the altar. The * is most holy; Lev 10:12
It is your portion of the peace * Lev 10:14
goat of the sin * and discovered Lev 10:16
"Why haven't you eaten the sin * Lev 10:17
"They offered their sin * and Lev 10:19
offering and burnt * before the Lev 10:19
had eaten the sin * on such a day Lev 10:19
lamb as a burnt *, and a young Lev 12:6
or a turtledove for a sin *. Lev 12:6
One will be for a burnt * and the Lev 12:8
and the other for a sin *. Lev 12:8
Lord as a guilt * by the gesture of Lev 14:12
this guilt * shall then be given Lev 14:13
food, as in the case of a sin *. Lev 14:13
It is a most holy *. Lev 14:13
from this guilt * and smear some of Lev 14:14
did with the blood of the guilt *. Lev 14:17
must offer the sin * and again Lev 14:19
kill the burnt *, and offer it Lev 14:19
with the grain * upon the altar, Lev 14:20
lamb for the guilt *, to be Lev 14:21
grain *, and a pint of olive oil. Lev 14:21
the pair for a sin * and the other Lev 14:22
and the other for a burnt *. Lev 14:22
lamb for the guilt *, and the pint Lev 14:24
as a gesture of * to the Lord. Lev 14:24
lamb for the guilt * and smear some Lev 14:25
did with the blood of the guilt *. Lev 14:28
One of the pair is for a sin * Lev 14:31
other for a burnt *, to be Lev 14:31
sacrificed along with the grain *; Lev 14:31
one for a sin * and the other for a Lev 15:15
and the other for a burnt *; Lev 15:15
one for a sin * and the other for a Lev 15:30
other for a burnt *, and make Lev 15:30
*, and a ram for a burnt offering. Lev 16:3
offering, and a ram for a burnt *. Lev 16:3
for their sin *, and a ram for Lev 16:5
and a ram for their burnt *. Lev 16:5
bull as a sin * for himself, making Lev 16:6
be sacrificed by Aaron as a sin *. Lev 16:9
bull as a sin * for himself and his Lev 16:11
and sacrifice the people's sin * Lev 16:15
his own burnt * and the burnt Lev 16:24
and the burnt * for the people, Lev 16:24
the altar the fat for the sin *. Lev 16:25
used for the sin * (their blood was Lev 16:27
who offers a burnt * or a sacrifice Lev 17:8,9
"When you sacrifice a peace * to Lev 19:5
bring his guilt * to the Lord at Lev 19:21
Tabernacle; the * shall be a ram. Lev 19:21
child as a burnt * to Molech shall Lev 20:1
you offers a burnt * sacrifice to Lev 22:17,18
free will *— it will only be Lev 22:17,18
"Anyone sacrificing a peace * to Lev 22:21
or as a voluntary *, must sacrifice Lev 22:21
it is not a fit burnt * for the Lev 22:22
a free will *, but not for a vow. Lev 22:23
make an * by fire to the Lord. Lev 23:8
in a gesture of *, and it will be Lev 23:9,10,11
lamb without defect as a burnt *. Lev 23:12
A grain * shall accompany it, Lev 23:13
Also offer a drink * consisting Lev 23:13
to the Lord an * of a sample of the Lev 23:15,16
before the Lord in a gesture of *. Lev 23:17
It is an * to the Lord of the Lev 23:17
goat for a sin *, and two male Lev 23:19
male yearling lambs for a peace *. Lev 23:19
an * by fire to the Lord. Lev 23:36
again be an * by fire to the Lord. Lev 23:36
This will be a memorial * made by Lev 24:5-8
the daily grain *, and the Num 4:16
the priest with an * for her of a Num 5:15
suspicion *—to bring out the truth Num 5:15
Literally, "an * for Num 5:15f
the suspicion * in her hands to Num 5:18
take the suspicion * from the Num 5:25
birds for a sin *, and the other Num 6:11
other for a burnt *, and make Num 6:11
lamb a year old for a guilt *. Num 6:12
He must also offer a sin *, a Num 6:14
a peace *, a ram without defect; Num 6:14
and the accompanying grain * and Num 6:15
the sin * and the burnt offering; Num 6:16
the sin offering and the burnt *; Num 6:16
then the ram for a peace *, Num 6:17
and finally the grain * along Num 6:17
offering along with the drink *. Num 6:17
fire under the peace * sacrifice. Num 6:18
before the Lord in a gesture of *; Num 6:20
bring any further * he promised at Num 6:21
a male goat for a sin *; Num 7:16
bull and a grain * of fine flour Num 8:8
another young bull for a sin *. Num 8:8
with a gesture of *, shall present Num 8:11
one for a sin * and the other for Num 8:12
other for a burnt *, to make Num 8:12
to the Lord in a gesture of *. Num 8:21
forbidden from * their sacrifice to Num 9:6,7
Lord with a burnt * or any other Num 15:3,4
or any other * by fire, their Num 15:3,4
or a free-will *, or a special Num 15:3,4
be accompanied by a grain *. Num 15:3,4
three pints of wine for a drink *. Num 15:5

(OFFERING Con't)
four pints of wine for a drink *. Num 15:7
then the grain * accompanying it Num 15:8,9
quarts of wine for the drink *. Num 15:10
in a gesture of * to the Lord. Num 15:19,20,21
It is an annual * from your Num 15:19,20,21
one young bull for a burnt *. Num 15:23,24
the usual grain * and drink Num 15:23,24
offering and drink *, and one male Num 15:23,24
and one male goat for a sin *. Num 15:23,24
the Lord, and by their sin *. Num 15:25
goat for a sin *, and the priest Num 15:27
up the 250 men who were * incense. Num 16:35
fat shall be burned as a fire *; Num 18:17
* to him of grain and wine, as Num 18:27
ashes from the red heifer sin * Num 19:17
"ashes of the burnt sin *." Num 19:17f
* while I go to meet the Lord." Num 23:15
each day as a regular burnt *. Num 28:3
be offered a grain * of three Num 28:5
This is the burnt * ordained at Num 28:6
an * made by fire to the Lord. Num 28:6
shall be the drink *, consisting of Num 28:7
same grain * and drink offering. Num 28:8
same grain offering and drink *. Num 28:8
to the Lord, an * made by fire. Num 28:8
by a grain * of six quarts of fine Num 28:9,10
with oil, and the usual drink *. Num 28:9,10
be an extra burnt * to the Lord of Num 28:11
oil as a grain * with each bull; Num 28:12
with oil as a grain * for the ram; Num 28:12
mixed with oil for a grain *. Num 28:13
This burnt * shall be presented Num 28:13
shall be a drink *—six pints of Num 28:14
This, then, will be the burnt * Num 28:14
male goat for a sin * to the Lord. Num 28:15
burnt * and its drink offering. Num 28:15
burnt offering and its drink *. Num 28:15
shall be a grain * of nine quarts Num 28:20,21
male goat as a sin *, to make Num 28:22
of grain as a grain * to the Lord; Num 28:26
A special burnt *, very pleasant Num 28:27
by your grain * of nine quarts of Num 28:28,29
A grain * of nine quarts of fine Num 29:3,4
sin *, to make atonement for you. Num 29:5
monthly burnt * for that day, Num 29:6
one male goat for a sin *. Num 29:11
This is in addition to the sin * Num 29:11
for a sin *, in addition to the Num 29:16
accompanying grain * and drink Num 29:19
and drink * for a sin offering. Num 29:19
and drink offering for a sin *. Num 29:19
the usual grain * and drink Num 29:21
and drink * with each sacrifice. Num 29:21
goat for a sin *, with its Num 29:22
grain * and drink offering. Num 29:22
grain offering and drink *. Num 29:22
grain * and drink offering; Num 29:24
grain offering and drink *; Num 29:24
also a male goat as a sin * Num 29:25
as a special sin *, in addition to Num 29:28
and drink offerings as a sin *. Num 29:31
also sacrifice an extra sin * of Num 29:34
Sacrifice a burnt *—they are Num 29:36
for a sin *, in addition to the Num 29:38
this special * from the captains Num 31:51,52
The * was taken into the Num 31:54
as a burnt * to Jehovah your God. Deu 13:16
to him a free-will * proportionate Deu 16:10
to the Lord any * from the earnings Deu 23:17,18
And the altar of burnt *. Deu 33:10
the ox as a burnt * to the Lord, Ju 6:26
as a burnt * to the Lord! Ju 11:30,31
an * to sacrifice to the Lord." Ju 13:16
goat and a grain * and offered it Ju 13:19
until evening, * burnt sacrifices Ju 20:26
anyone was * a sacrifice, and while 1Sa 2:13,14
If the man * the sacrifice 1Sa 2:16
"Send a guilt * so that the 1Sa 6:3
"What guilt * shall we send?" 1Sa 6:4,5
them to the Lord as a burnt *. 1Sa 6:14
as a guilt * to the Lord were gifts 1Sa 6:17
as a whole burnt * and pleaded with 1Sa 7:9
the burnt *, the Philistines 1Sa 7:10
* and the peace offerings himself. 1Sa 13:9
offered the burnt * without waiting 1Sa 13:12
in your * the fat of rams to him. 1Sa 15:22
then let him accept my peace *. 1Sa 26:19
While he was * the sacrifice, he 2Sa 15:12
"Here are oxen for the burnt *, 2Sa 24:22
At the customary time for * the 1Ki 18:36
him as a burnt * upon the wall. 2Ki 3:27
As the priests of Baal began * 2Ki 10:24
the burnt *, Jehu went out and told 2Ki 10:25
He even killed his own son by * 2Ki 16:3
inaugurated it with an *. 2Ki 16:11,12
The king presented a burnt * and 2Ki 16:13
and a grain *, poured a drink 2Ki 16:13
poured a drink * over it, and 2Ki 16:13
of burnt *, the evening grain 2Ki 16:15
the evening grain *, the king's 2Ki 16:15
the king's burnt * and grain 2Ki 16:15
offering and grain *, and the 2Ki 16:15
as a burnt * on a heathen altar. 2Ki 21:6
Instead he poured it out as an * 1Ch 11:18,19
Bring an * and come before him; 1Ch 16:29
used in * sacrifices on the altar. 1Ch 18:8
and use the wheat for the grain *. 1Ch 21:23
I will not offer a burnt * that 1Ch 21:24
to burn up the * on the altar. 1Ch 21:26
the altar for Israel's burnt *!" 1Ch 22:1
the burnt * to the Lord as 2Ch 23:18
goats for a sin * for the nation 2Ch 29:21
The male goats for the sin * 2Ch 29:23
and made a sin * with their blood 2Ch 29:24
that the burnt * and sin offering 2Ch 29:24
offering and sin * must be 2Ch 29:24
ordered the burnt * to be placed 2Ch 29:27
the usual drink * with each, and 2Ch 29:35
* the fat of the burnt offerings. 2Ch 35:14
and a freewill * for the Temple." Ez 1:4
* for the twelve tribes of Israel. Ez 6:17
as an * to the God of Israel. Ez 7:15
and twelve goats as a sin *. Ez 8:35
the time of the evening burnt *. Ez 9:4
guilt by * rams as sacrifices): Ez 10:16-19
in the morning and * a burnt Job 1:5
a burnt * for each of them. Job 1:5
offer a burnt * for yourselves; Job 42:8
Bring your * and come to worship Ps 96:8
I will bring him an * of wine Ps 116:13
For I am * you my deliverance; Is 46:13
has been made an * for sin, then he Is 53:10
lamb, or bring an * of grain, it is Is 66:3
and Judah in * incense to Baal that Jer 11:17
You will be to me as an * of Eze 20:41
the flesh of the * was to be laid. Eze 40:43
to be given a bullock for a sin *. Eze 43:19
for the sin * and burn it at the Eze 43:21
cuts or scars—for a sin *. Eze 43:22
salt upon them as a burnt *. Eze 43:24
shall be sacrificed as a sin *. Eze 43:25
* for himself, the Lord God says. Eze 44:27
blood of this sin * and put it on Eze 45:19
bull for a sin * for himself and Eze 45:22
prepare a burnt * to the Lord. Eze 45:23
This daily * will consist of Eze 45:23
be given each day for a sin *. Eze 45:23
grain for the meal *—one bushel for Eze 45:24
for the sin *, burnt offering, meal Eze 45:25
*, meal offering and oil offering. Eze 45:25
offering, meal * and oil offering. Eze 45:25
offering, meal offering and oil *. Eze 45:25
his burnt * and peace offering. Eze 46:2
his burnt offering and peace *. Eze 46:2
"The burnt * which the prince Eze 46:4
He shall present a meal * of one Eze 46:5
of flour for a meal *. Eze 46:7
festivals the meal * shall be one Eze 46:11
an extra burnt * or peace offering Eze 46:12
offering or peace * to be Eze 46:12
as a burnt * to the Lord. Eze 46:13
And there must be a meal * each Eze 46:14,15
lamb, the grain * and the olive oil Eze 46:14,15
of the trespass * and sin offering Eze 46:19,20
offering and sin * and bake the Eze 46:19,20
By * swine on the altar. Dan 11:30,31f
in the Temple, * a sacrifice to Mt 5:23
and take with you the * required Mt 8:4
Take along the * prescribed by Mk 1:43,44
purification * at the Temple, as Lk 2:22
by * him a drink—of sour wine. Lk 23:36
to accept the mercies God was *. Act 13:43
as I was presenting my thank *. Act 24:18
you the Gospel and * you up as a Rom 15:15,16
have taken up an * for those in Rom 15:26
brought by those * it to the Lord. 1Co 9:13
the week, and use it for this *. 1Co 16:2
ready to send an * a year ago. 2Co 9:2
faith which I am * up to God as a Php 2:17
Christ must make an * too. Heb 8:3
mercy seat as an * to God to cover Heb 9:7
an * for the sins of many people; Heb 9:28
If they could have, one * would Heb 10:2
day after day * sacrifices that Heb 10:11
For by that one * he made Heb 10:14
God and brought an * that pleased Heb 11:4
God more than Cain's * did. Heb 11:4
even if it meant * his son Isaac to Jas 2:21
consecrated * to God and the Lamb. Rev 14:4

OFFERINGS

and burnt * to Jehovah our God. Ex 10:25
to me—your burnt * and peace Ex 20:24
and peace * of sheep and oxen. Ex 20:24
* and peace offerings to the Lord. Ex 24:5
offerings and peace * to the Lord. Ex 24:5
the * of the people of Israel. Ex 28:37,38
peace * or thanksgiving Ex 29:28
or thanksgiving *—as their Ex 29:28
incense, burnt *, meal offerings, Ex 30:9
meal *, or drink offerings. Ex 30:9
meal offerings, or drink *. Ex 30:9
the altar to burn * to the Lord. Ex 30:2
offering burnt * and peace Ex 32:
and peace * to the calf-idol; Ex 32:
may bring these * to Jehovah: Ex 35:5-
The altar for the burnt *; Ex 35:10-1
with their * of materials for the Ex 35:2
They brought to the Lord their * Ex 35:2
their freewill * to him. Ex 35:2
burnt * in front of the entrance. Ex 40:
for the burnt * near the entrance, Ex 40:2
for burnt * give much pleasure to Lev 1:1
"Use no yeast with your * of Lev 2:1
permitted in burnt * to the Lord. Lev 2:1
as thanksgiving * at harvest time, Lev 2:1
harvest time, but not as burnt *. Lev 2:1
altar for burnt *, at the entrance Lev 4:7
where the burnt * are killed, and Lev 4:24
the altar of burnt *, and the rest Lev 4:2
animals for burnt * are killed, and Lev 4:29
where the burnt * are killed, and Lev 4:33
part of the burnt * made to me. Lev 6:17
the priests may eat these * made Lev 6:18
These * shall be entirely burned Lev 6:22,23
where the burnt * are killed. Lev 6:25
the people's grain * to the Lord Lev 7:9
All other grain *, whether mixed Lev 7:10
to the Lord as special peace *: Lev 7:11
from the burnt *, and given to all Lev 7:35
the * to Jehovah made by fire; Lev 10:13
the man and his * before the Lord Lev 14:11
place where sin * and burnt Lev 14:13
and burnt * are killed, there at Lev 14:13
* by fire to the Lord their God. Lev 21:6
priests from the * sacrificed to Lev 21:22
from the holy and most holy *. Lev 21:22
she may not eat the sacred *. Lev 22:12
because he has eaten the sacred *; Lev 22:16
am Jehovah who sanctifies the *." Lev 22:16
sacrifice as burnt * to the Lord Lev 23:18
All are fire *, very acceptable Lev 23:18
"The priests shall wave these * Lev 23:20
of all people—when * to the Lord Lev 23:37
For these are * made by fire to Lev 24:9
not respond to your incense *. Lev 26:31
grain offering and drink *. Num 6:15
The priest shall present these * Num 6:16
the census—brought their *. Num 7:2
* of fine flour mixed with oil. Num 7:13
a male yearling lamb as burnt *; Num 7:15
and for the peace * two oxen, Num 7:17
Issachar, brought his gifts and *. Num 7:18-23
the * recorded in verses 13 to 17. Num 7:18-23f
came with his *—the same as those Num 7:24-29
the * recorded in verses 13 to 17. Num 7:24-29f
his gifts and * were the same as Num 7:30-35
the * recorded in verses 13 to 17. Num 7:30-35f
the * recorded in verses 13 to 17. Num 7:36-41f
the * recorded in verses 13 to 17. Num 7:42-47f
the * recorded in verses 13 to 17. Num 7:48-53f
the eighth day with the same *. Num 7:54-59
the * recorded in verses 13 to 17. Num 7:54-59f
the * recorded in verses 13 to 17. Num 7:60-65f
of Dan and his * were the same as Num 7:66-71
the * recorded in verses 13 to 17. Num 7:66-71f
same gifts and * as the others. Num 7:72-77
the * recorded in verses 13 to 17. Num 7:72-77f
the tribe of Naphtali, with his *; Num 7:78-83
the * recorded in verses 13 to 17. Num 7:78-83f
Their combined * were as follows: Num 7:84,85,86
For the burnt * they brought: Num 7:87
grain * that accompanied them). Num 7:87
For sin * they brought: Num 7:87
For the peace * they brought: Num 7:88
your burnt * and peace offerings. Num 10:10
your burnt offerings and peace *. Num 10:10
all these * presented to the Lord Num 18:8
The grain *, the sin offerings, Num 18:9
The grain offerings, the sin *, Num 18:9
and the guilt * are yours, except Num 18:9
All these are most holy *. Num 18:9
people bring as * to the Lord—the Num 18:12
all of these 'wave *' brought by Num 18:19
here by your burnt * and I will see Num 23:3,4
* with all the princes of Moab. Num 23:6
standing beside their burnt *. Num 23:17
of Israel: "The * which you burn Num 28:1
"When you make * by fire, you Num 28:3
—in addition to the regular *. Num 28:9,10
These * shall be in addition to Num 28:23
These special * are in addition Num 28:31
daily burnt * and grain offerings Num 28:31
and grain * and drink offerings. Num 28:31
and grain offerings and drink *. Num 28:31
Literally, "burnt * of the new Num 29:6f
respective grain * and drink Num 29:6
and drink *, as specified by the Num 29:6
and their accompanying grain *. Num 29:9,10
grain *, and drink offerings. Num 29:11
grain offerings, and drink *. Num 29:11
by the usual grain *—nine quarts of Num 29:14
grain * and drink offerings. Num 29:16

FFERINGS Con't)
grain offerings and drink *. Num 29:16
usual grain * and drink offerings. Num 29:18
usual grain offerings and drink *. Num 29:18
grain and drink *) in addition to Num 29:25
usual grain * and drink offerings; Num 29:26,27
usual grain offerings and drink *; Num 29:26,27
grain and drink *, as a special sin Num 29:28
their usual grain and drink *. Num 29:30
and drink * as a sin offering. Num 29:31
its customary grain and drink *; Num 29:33
grain and drink *, in addition to Num 29:34
the customary grain and drink *. Num 29:37
grain and drink * for a sin Num 29:38
These * are compulsory at the Num 29:39
to sacrifices and * you present in Num 29:39
or as free-will *, burnt Num 29:39
sacrifices, grain *, drink Num 29:39
drink *, or peace offerings." Num 29:39
drink offerings, or peace *." Num 29:39
Lord your burnt * and other Deu 12:6
tithes, your * presented by the Deu 12:6
the altar, your * to fulfill your Deu 12:6
your free-will *, and your Deu 12:6
and your * of the firstborn animals Deu 12:6
and other * to his sanctuary, the Deu 12:11
your burnt * just anywhere; Deu 12:13
your sacrifices and bring your *. Deu 12:14
"But none of the * may be eaten Deu 12:17
nor your freewill *, nor the Deu 12:17
offerings, nor the * to be Deu 12:17
the Lord, and the * you have Deu 12:26,27
and your burnt * need be taken to Deu 12:26,27
other * the people bring to him. Deu 18:1
the sacrifices and * as his right, Deu 18:8
burnt * to the Lord your God. Deu 27:5,6
Sacrifice peace * upon it also, Deu 27:7
peace * to the Lord on the altar. Jos 8:31
given the * brought to the Lord. Jos 13:14
to sacrifice burnt * or grain Jos 22:22,23
offerings or grain * or peace Jos 22:22,23
offerings or peace *—may the curse Jos 22:22,23
with our burnt * and peace Jos 22:26,27
and peace * and sacrifices, and Jos 22:26,27
It is not for burnt * or Jos 22:28
*, grain offerings, or sacrifices. Jos 22:29
offerings, grain *, or sacrifices. Jos 22:29
from the temple * of the idol Ju 9:4
accepted our burnt * and wouldn't Ju 13:23
burnt sacrifices and peace *. Ju 20:26
sacrifices and peace * on it. Ju 21:4
for they treated the people's * 1Sa 2:17
the sacrificial * to you priests? 1Sa 2:28
other * which are brought to me? 1Sa 2:29
the best of the * of my people! 1Sa 2:29
be forgiven by sacrifices and *." 1Sa 3:14
And many burnt * and sacrifices 1Sa 6:15
burnt * and peace offerings. 1Sa 10:8
burnt offerings and peace *. 1Sa 10:8
Then they offered peace * to the 1Sa 11:15
offering and the peace * himself. 1Sa 13:9
in your burnt * and sacrifices as 1Sa 15:22
and he sacrificed burnt * and 2Sa 6:17
offerings and peace * to the Lord. 2Sa 6:17
* that have cost me nothing." 2Sa 24:24
burnt * and peace offerings. 2Sa 24:25
burnt offerings and peace *. 2Sa 24:25
sacrificed their * on altars in the 1Ki 3:2
sacrificed one thousand burnt *! 1Ki 3:4
burnt * and peace offerings. 1Ki 3:15
burnt offerings and peace *. 1Ki 3:15
sacrificing peace * to the Lord—a 1Ki 8:62,63
for the burnt *, grain offerings, 1Ki 8:64
offerings, grain *, and the fat of 1Ki 8:64
fat of the peace *: for the bronze 1Ki 8:64
offered burnt * and peace offerings 1Ki 9:25
and peace * three times a year on 1Ki 9:25
and the many * he sacrificed by 1Ki 10:5
offer any burnt * or sacrifices to 2Ki 5:17
and burnt *, Jehu surrounded the 2Ki 10:24
for guilt * and sin offerings was 2Ki 12:16
offerings and sin * was given to 2Ki 12:16
the blood of peace * upon it. 2Ki 16:13
offering, and the * of the people, 2Ki 16:15
people, including their drink *. 2Ki 16:15
The blood from the burnt * and 2Ki 16:15
Literally, "as *." 2Ki 17:17f
sacrificing burnt * and incense, 1Ch 6:49
making the flat cakes for grain *. 1Ch 9:31
* and peace offerings before God. 1Ch 16:1
offerings and peace * before God. 1Ch 16:1
At the conclusion of these * 1Ch 16:2
They sacrificed burnt * to the 1Ch 16:40
"Take the oxen, too, for burnt * 1Ch 21:23
* and peace offerings upon it; 1Ch 21:26
offerings and peace * upon it; 1Ch 21:26
the people's * to the Lord. 1Ch 23:13
for the grain *, and the wafers 1Ch 23:29
of burnt *, the Sabbath sacrifices, 1Ch 23:31
lambs as burnt * to the Lord; 1Ch 29:21
they also offered drink * and 1Ch 29:21
upon it 1,000 burnt * to the Lord. 2Ch 1:5,6
and sacrifice burnt * each 2Ch 2:4
water to wash the *, five to the 2Ch 4:6
sacrificing burnt * to the Lord. 2Ch 7:4,5
Then Solomon sacrificed burnt * 2Ch 8:12
evening—burnt * and sweet incense; 2Ch 13:11
Judah and collect * for the 2Ch 24:5
used in the sacrifices and *. 2Ch 24:14
Burnt * were sacrificed 2Ch 24:14
and burnt * have not been offered. 2Ch 29:7
the altar of burnt * and of its 2Ch 29:18
your sacrifices and thank *." 2Ch 29:31
and thank *, and those who wished 2Ch 29:31
wished to, brought burnt * too. 2Ch 29:31
burnt *, 100 rams, and 200 lambs. 2Ch 29:32,33
prepare the burnt *, so their 2Ch 29:34
abundance of burnt *, and the usual 2Ch 29:35
with each, and many peace *. 2Ch 29:35
brought burnt * into the Temple. 2Ch 30:15
and peace * were sacrificed, and 2Ch 30:22
bulls for *, and 7,000 sheep; 2Ch 30:24
to offer the burnt * and peace 2Ch 31:2
and peace *, and to worship and 2Ch 31:2
and evening burnt *, as well as for 2Ch 31:3
distributing the * to the priests. 2Ch 31:14,15
burnt * in the Valley of Hinnom. 2Ch 33:6
upon it—peace * and thanksgiving 2Ch 33:16
and thanksgiving *—and demanded 2Ch 33:16
bring in their * to the Temple. 2Ch 35:4,5
Passover *, and 3,000 young bulls. 2Ch 35:7
goats, and 300 oxen as Passover *. 2Ch 35:8
the Levites for their Passover *. 2Ch 35:9
boiled the holy * in pots, kettles, 2Ch 35:13
offering the fat of the burnt *. 2Ch 35:14
All the burnt * were sacrificed 2Ch 35:16
and sacrificed burnt * upon it, Ez 3:1
and evening burnt * to the Lord; Ez 3:3
the burnt * specified for each day Ez 3:4
Voluntary * of the people were Ez 3:5
the burnt * to the Lord. Ez 3:6
for burnt * to the God of heaven; Ez 6:9
voluntary Temple * of silver and Ez 7:16
rams, lambs, grain *, and drink Ez 7:17
and drink *, all of which will be Ez 7:17
* to the Lord God of our fathers. Ez 8:28
sacrificed burnt * to the God of Ez 8:35
as well as grain * and burnt Neh 10:33
and burnt * for the Sabbaths, the Neh 10:33
wood for the burnt * at the Temple Neh 10:34
law to bring these * of grain, new Neh 10:39,40
the wave *, the tithes, and Neh 12:44
*, and to collect these from the Neh 12:44
These * were assigned to the Neh 12:44
storing the grain *, frankincense, Neh 13:5
Moses had decreed that these * Neh 13:5
(The wave * were for the priests. Neh 13:5
the grain *, and frankincense. Neh 13:9
and the first * of every harvest. Neh 13:31
him, your sacrifices and burnt *. Ps 20:3
It isn't sacrifices and * which Ps 40:6
You aren't interested in * burned Ps 51:16
in trouble I promised you many *. Ps 66:14
Literally, "Sacrifices of peace * Pro 7:14f
want to see the blood from your *. Is 1:11
their sacrifices and * to him; Is 19:21
you make your many *, but I will Is 29:1
brought me the lambs for burnt *; Is 43:23
Yet my requests for * and incense Is 43:23
sacrifices and *, for my Temple Is 56:7
God will not accept their *. Is 66:3
It will be like * flowing into Is 66:20
I cannot accept your *; Jer 6:20
Away with your * and sacrifices! Jer 7:21
It wasn't * and sacrifices I Jer 7:22
when they present their * and Jer 14:12
with their burnt * and grain Jer 17:26
and grain * and incense, bringing Jer 17:26
* brought to them at the Temple; Jer 31:14
thanksgiving * to the Lord will be Jer 33:10,11
to offer burnt * and meal offerings Jer 33:18
meal * and sacrifices to the Lord. Jer 33:18
and were bringing * and incense. Jer 41:5
children as * to their gods! Eze 20:26
poured out their drink * to them! Eze 20:27,28
* and the finest of your gifts. Eze 20:40
for the burnt *, sin offerings and Eze 40:39
offerings, sin * and guilt Eze 40:39
* to be presented in the Temple. Eze 40:39
of the most holy * and store Eze 42:13
them—the cereal *, sin offerings, Eze 42:13
offerings, sin *, and guilt Eze 42:13
guilt *, for these rooms are holy. Eze 42:13
for the burning of * and the Eze 43:18
altar the burnt * and thank Eze 43:27
and thank * of the people, and I Eze 43:27
brought for burnt * and be present Eze 44:11
people—the cereal *, the sin Eze 44:29
the sin * and the guilt offerings. Eze 44:29
the sin offerings and the guilt *. Eze 44:29
These are the meal *, burnt Eze 45:15
offerings, burnt * and thank Eze 45:15
and thank * to make atonement for Eze 45:15
shall bring their * to the prince. Eze 45:16
public worship—sin *, burnt Eze 45:17
offerings, burnt *, meal offerings, Eze 45:17
offerings, meal *, drink offerings Eze 45:17
offerings, drink * and thank Eze 45:17
and thank *—to make reconciliation Eze 45:17
flour of the flour * into bread. Eze 46:19,20
all their sacrifices and their *; Dan 9:27
I don't want your *—I want you to Hos 6:6
Gone are the * of grain and wine Joe 1:9
For there are no more * of grain Joe 1:13
proper forms and give extra *. Amo 4:5
I will not accept your burnt * Amo 5:22
your burnt offerings and thank *. Amo 5:22
I will not look at your * of Amo 5:22
their wealth as * to the Lord, the Mic 4:13
Lord with * of yearling calves?" Mic 6:6
come with their *, asking me to be Zep 3:10
"and I will not accept your *. Mal 1:10
and pure * in honor of my name. Mal 1:11
lame and sick—as * to God! Mal 1:13
Should I accept such * as Mal 1:13
attention to your * anymore, and Mal 2:13
will enjoy the * brought to him by Mal 3:4
me of the tithes and * due to me. Mal 3:8
than I want your *,' you would not Mt 12:7
pure with far more precious *. Heb 9:23
and burnt before you as * for sin. Heb 10:6
sacrifices and * required under the Heb 10:8

OFFERS
among you who * a burnt offering or Lev 17:8,9
living among you * a burnt offering Lev 22:17,18
while the priest * his burnt Eze 46:2
Whenever the prince * an extra Eze 46:12
And now he * you true Bread from Jn 6:32
honor and eternal life that he *. Rom 2:7
things the world * should make good 1Co 7:31
he * you—be reconciled to God. 2Co 5:20
faith and love Christ Jesus * you. 2Ti 1:13
gifts to God and * to him the blood Heb 5:1
The sacrifice he * is far better Heb 8:4
down here on earth * animal blood Heb 9:25
and all that it * you, for when you 1Jn 2:15

OFFICE
minister to me in the priest's *. Ex 28:3
be inducted into * by offering this Lev 6:22,23
assume this * shall be executed." Num 3:10
in * at the time of the accident. Jos 20:6
were in an * of great trust, for 1Ch 9:26
king's accounting * where the 2Ch 24:11
"Yes, I will drive you out of * Is 22:19
Baruch went to the * of Gemariah Jer 36:10

OFFICER
to Potiphar, an * of the Gen 37:36
so she told the * in charge, "The Jos 2:4
with a baggage * and hurried out to 1Sa 17:22
and made you a commissioned *." 2Sa 18:11
that worn by a commissioned *. 2Sa 18:11f
The * assisting the king said, 2Ki 7:2
The king's * had replied, "That 2Ki 7:19
chief recruiting *, five of the 2Ki 25:19
Each was a high-ranking * of 1Ch 12:20
was the chief * of the treasury. 1Ch 26:23,24
Mikloth was his executive *. 1Ch 27:4
chief financial * in charge of the 1Ch 27:25
empire as his administrative *. Dan 6:3
administrative * of the king, and Zec 7:2
Then the * said, "Sir, I am not Mt 8:8,9
many Gentiles [like this Roman * Mt 8:11
Then Jesus said to the Roman *, Mt 8:13
When the Roman * standing beside Mk 15:39
Roman * in charge and asked him. Mk 15:44
asked him. The * confirmed the Mk 15:45
And the * and his entire Jn 4:53
lived a Roman army *, Cornelius, a Act 10:1
the Roman *, a good and godly man, Act 10:22
Paul said to an * standing there, Act 22:25
The * went to the commander and Act 22:26
So the * did, explaining, "Paul, Act 23:18
the custody of an * named Julius, a Act 27:1
There our * found an Egyptian Act 27:6
and commanding *, "You will all Act 27:31
their commanding * to let them kill Act 27:42

OFFICERS
the senior * of the land, as well Gen 50:7
taskmasters and * he had set over Ex 5:6
So the taskmasters and * informed Ex 5:10,11
chariots driven by Egyptian *. Ex 14:7
the army * and battalion leaders. Num 31:14
Then the * and battalion leaders Num 31:48,49
"Then the * of the army shall Deu 20:5
When the * have finished saying Deu 20:9
administrative *—are standing today Deu 29:10
Now summon all the elders and * Deu 31:28
On the third day, * went through Jos 3:2,3,4
the elders, *, judges, and the Jos 8:33
judges, and *—and said to them, "I Jos 23:2
leaders—the elders, *, and judges. Jos 24:1
than all the rest of Saul's *. 1Sa 18:30
But Achish's * weren't happy 1Sa 21:11

(OFFICERS Con't)
his spear, surrounded by his *. 1Sa 22:6
which King Hadadezer's * had used. 2Sa 8:7
But Hanun's * told him, "These 2Sa 10:3
general and his * are camping out 2Sa 11:11
and the king's * and all the mighty 2Sa 16:6
One of Joab's young * shouted to 2Sa 20:11
when Joab's young * saw that a 2Sa 20:12
top-ranking * of the Israeli 2Sa 23:13
top-ranking * of the army—and was 2Sa 23:18,19
so Joab and the other army * went 2Sa 24:4
army *, or his brother Solomon. 1Ki 1:10
"Take Solomon and my * to Gihon. 1Ki 1:33
The names of these twelve * were: 1Ki 4:8-19
officials, army *, chariot 1Ki 9:22
Ben-hadad commanded his *. 1Ki 20:12
Ben-hadad's * said to him, "The 1Ki 20:23
"Sir," his * said to him, "we 1Ki 20:31
of the king of Israel's * replied. 2Ki 3:11
But his * tried to reason with 2Ki 5:13
he said to his *, "We will 2Ki 6:8
He called together his * and 2Ki 6:11
us, sir," one of the * replied. 2Ki 6:12
his *, "I know what has happened. 2Ki 7:12
One of his * replied, "We'd 2Ki 7:13
around with the other army *. 2Ki 9:5
out and told his * and men, "Go in 2Ki 10:25
summoned the * of the palace 2Ki 11:4
So the * followed Jehoiada's 2Ki 11:9
Jehoiada to the * of the guard. 2Ki 11:15
Then he and the * and the guard 2Ki 11:19
But his * plotted against him 2Ki 12:20
he saw him. His * took his body 2Ki 23:30
the highest-ranking * in the army. 1Ch 11:15f
These men were army *; 1Ch 12:14
were * of the fighting priests. 1Ch 12:24-37
From Naphtali there were 1,000 * 1Ch 12:24-37
all of his army *, he addressed 1Ch 13:1
and the high * of the army went 1Ch 15:25
King Hadadezer's * to Jerusalem, 1Ch 18:7
as the * and generals of the army. 1Ch 26:26
* and administrative staff. 1Ch 27:1
highest-ranking * in David's army. 1Ch 27:5,6
The top political * of the tribes 1Ch 27:16-22
the other army *, those in charge 1Ch 28:1
tribes, the army *, and the 1Ch 29:6,7
the administrative * of the king 1Ch 29:6,7
The national leaders, the army * 1Ch 29:24
He summoned all the army * and 2Ch 1:2,3
*, charioteers, and cavalrymen; 2Ch 8:9
under their *, and stored them with 2Ch 11:11
some of the army * into his 2Ch 23:1
and shields to all the army *. 2Ch 23:9
These *, fully armed, formed a 2Ch 23:10
with the army * and the trumpeters 2Ch 23:12
the priest shouted to the army *. 2Ch 23:13,14
Then the army *, nobles, 2Ch 23:20
So the army * turned over the 2Ch 28:14
commanded by the king and his *. 2Ch 30:12
his princes and * for a council of 2Ch 32:3
army and appointed * and summoned 2Ch 32:6
army with all its * and generals! 2Ch 32:21
At last his own * assassinated 2Ch 33:24
of Solomon's * numbered 392. Ez 2:58
army * and troops to protect me! Neh 2:9
and the old *' Club building. Neh 3:16
friends and the Samaritan army *. Neh 4:1
of Solomon's * numbered 392." Neh 7:60
aides, and army *, bringing them in Est 1:1
For the king had instructed his * Est 1:8
the chief * of the government. Est 1:13-15
elders, army *, businessmen, Is 3:3
and small alike, both * and men. Is 10:33
when the Assyrian * outside your Is 33:18
All the kings of Judah and its * Jer 1:18
and the army * and officials heard Jer 26:21
and the tribal * and craftsmen had Jer 29:1
of their kings, *, priests and Jer 32:32
to the * of the Babylonian army; Jer 38:21,22
fell, and all the * of the Jer 39:3
of the commanding * of the army, Jer 52:24,25
including two *, Ja-azaniah (son of Eze 11:1
steeds, those army * in handsome Eze 23:12
military *, outfitted in striking Eze 23:14,15
My counselors and * came back to Dan 4:36
a thousand of his * to a great Dan 5:1
felt, and his * too were shaken. Dan 5:9
and you and your * and wives and Dan 5:23
Then Michael, one of the top * of Dan 10:13
The king shouts for his *; Nah 2:5
who would get her * as servants. Nah 3:10
of my superior * and I have Mt 8:8,9
palace aides, army *, and the Mk 6:21
of my superior *, and I have Lk 7:6,7,8
priests sent * to arrest Jesus. Jn 7:32
went with his * and arrested them Act 5:26,27
judges sent police * over to tell Act 16:35
The police * reported to the Act 16:38
Some of the Roman * of the Act 19:31
* and ran down among the crowd. Act 21:32
Paul called one of the * and Act 23:17
called two of his * and ordered, Act 23:23,24
by military * and prominent men of Act 25:23
and Paul spoke to the ship's * Act 27:9
But the * in charge of the Act 27:11
Dear brothers, honor the * of 1Th 5:12
should choose as * for the church 1Ti 3:15
government and its *, and always to Tit 3:1
of the king's *, for he has sent 1Pe 2:14
military *, and all men great and Rev 6:15

OFFICES
Aaron and his sons to their *. Ex 29:35

OFFICIAL
of Ahilud) was the * historian and 1Ki 4:1
So the * genealogy doesn't name 1Ch 5:1
were included in the * genealogy: 1Ch 5:7,8
All were included in the * 1Ch 5:17
all included in the * genealogy. 1Ch 7:5
recorded in the * genealogies). 1Ch 7:7
Their descendants in the * 1Ch 7:40
Ahithophel was the king's * 1Ch 27:33
recorded among the * lamentations. 2Ch 35:24,25
was a government *) heard of my Neh 2:10
* and citizen of your empire. Est 1:16
had become a government *. Est 2:19
He was the most powerful * in the Est 3:1
For every * is under orders from Ecc 5:8
used by the palace *, directly Jer 35:4
important palace *, heard that Jer 38:7
* lords it over those beneath him. Mt 20:25
a government *, whose son was very Jn 4:46,47
The * pled, "Sir, please come Jn 4:49
to stone him. The * witnesses—the Act 7:58
to you these two * representatives, Act 15:25

OFFICIALS
all of his * and household staff. Gen 40:20
Or, "Let Pharaoh appoint * to Gen 41:34,35f
and let the * of these districts Gen 41:34,35
happy to hear it, as were his *. Gen 45:16
As Pharaoh and all of his * Ex 7:20
But as for you and your *, I Ex 9:30
this, he and his * sinned yet more Ex 9:34
but I have hardened him and his * Ex 10:1
*, and all the houses of Egypt. Ex 10:6
The court * now came to Pharaoh Ex 10:7
* and the Egyptian people alike. Ex 11:3
All these * of yours will come Ex 11:8
Then Pharaoh and his * and all Ex 12:30
*—your judges and your rulers. Ex 22:28
and administrative * for all the Deu 16:18
were ten high * of Israel, one from Jos 22:14
of Manasseh to these high *: Jos 22:21
and the high * heard this from the Jos 22:30
the king and his * wept with them. 2Sa 13:36
all the royal * of Judah, 1Ki 1:9
Then he invited all of his * to a 1Ki 3:15
There were also twelve * of 1Ki 4:7
supervised these * and their work. 1Ki 4:8-19
Each month the tax * provided 1Ki 4:27
became soldiers, *, army officers, 1Ki 9:22
and a few royal * who took him 1Ki 11:16,17,18
Rezon, one of the * of King 1Ki 11:23
gave them to his * to take to 1Ki 15:18
The city * then sent word to 1Ki 21:14
Ahab said to his *, "Do you 1Ki 22:3
Now a delegation of the city * of 2Ki 2:19
So he directed one of his * to 2Ki 8:6
died there. His * took him by 2Ki 9:28
of his important *, personal 2Ki 10:11
all of his *, and the queen mother 2Ki 24:12
his wives and *, and the queen 2Ki 24:15
* of the Temple in each division. 1Ch 24:5
DAVID AND THE * of the Tabernacle 1Ch 25:1
DAVID NOW SUMMONED all of his * 1Ch 28:1
were government * who administered 2Ch 8:10
He sent out top government * as 2Ch 17:7,8,9
wounded—his own * decided to kill 2Ch 24:25
with the city *, taking seven 2Ch 29:20
*, who laid their hands upon them. 2Ch 29:23
When Hezekiah and his * came and 2Ch 31:7,8
The king's * made willing 2Ch 35:8
descendants of King Solomon's *: Ez 2:55,56,57
the other * sent to King Darius: Ez 5:6
the other * west of the Euphrates: Ez 6:6
judges and other * to govern all Ez 7:25
The city * did not know I had Neh 2:16
against these rich government *. Neh 5:7
I also required my * to spend Neh 5:16
fed 150 Jewish * at my table, Neh 5:17
Solomon's * who returned to Judah: Neh 7:57,58,59
THE ISRAELI * were living in Neh 11:1
of the provincial * who came to Neh 11:3
servants and *—janitors and cabinet Est 1:5
and cabinet * alike—for seven days Est 1:5
high * of Media-Persia. Est 1:13-15
of every one of us * throughout Est 1:18
party for all his * and servants, Est 2:18
Now all the king's * bowed Est 3:2
the governors and * throughout the Est 3:12
Jews and to the *, governors, and Est 8:9,10
governors, *, and aides—helped the Est 9:3
The highest * of the city stood Job 29:10
* look up to their superiors. Ecc 5:
king of Judah, his * and all the Jer 24:
When the high * of Judah heard Jer 26:1
to the * and the people. Jer 26:1
Then the * and people said to the Jer 26:1
army officers and * heard what he Jer 26:2
and the court *, and the tribal Jer 29:
are princes, court *, priests or Jer 34:18,1
of Judah, and his * to the army of Jer 34:2
the administrative * were meeting. Jer 36:1
the people, the * sent Jehudi (son Jer 36:14,1
both hide," the * said to Baruch. Jer 36:1
Then the * hid the scroll in Jer 36:2
to the king as all his * stood by. Jer 36:2
Not another of the king's * Jer 36:24,2
and his * because of their sins. Jer 36:3
Zedekiah nor his * nor the people Jer 37:
took Jeremiah before the city *. Jer 37:1
you or your * or the people? Jer 37:1
And if my * hear that I talked Jer 38:2
all the city * came to Jeremiah and Jer 38:2
and all the * took steps to do as Jer 39:1
of the king's top *, arrived in Jer 41:
all the Jewish * and Babylonian Jer 41:
But some * went to the king and Dan 3:8
this king's own * will rebel Dan 11:5
Your princes and * crowd Nah 3:17
and other Jewish * were meeting at Mt 26:3
priests and Jewish * persuaded the Mt 27:20
Jewish * began yelling, "Crucify! Jn 19:6

OFFICIATING
shall be given to the * priest. Lev 7:32,33

OFFSET
devise that will * the first, Est 8:8f

OFFSPRING
as will all of your * and hers. Gen 3:15
and between your * and hers. Gen 3:15
rods, and their * were streaked and Gen 30:39,40
produced healthy *, and I never Gen 31:38
profane his * among his people." Lev 21:14,15f
animal and her * the same day, Lev 22:28
you * of adulterers and harlots! Is 57:3

OFTEN
* as you like to purchase grain.' Gen 42:34
and the Anakim are * referred to as Deu 2:11
as you wish and as * as you are Deu 12:15
of Jericho, * called "The City of Ju 3:13
How * must we redeem them?" Neh 5:8
"Yes, God * does these things Job 33:29
trusted; how * we ate together. Ps 41:9
Oh, how * they rebelled against Ps 78:40
years are * emptiness and pain; Ps 90:10
I have called you so * but still Pro 1:24
coarse type, seen * in the streets Pro 7:11,12
Don't visit your neighbor too *, Pro 25:17
THE MAN WHO is * reproved but Pro 29:1
For you know how * you yourself Ecc 7:21,22
that wise men are * poor, and Ecc 9:11
of serious punning * used by the Is 5:7f
whose thoughts turn * to the Lord! Is 26:3
later, came * to this Temple. Hag 2:8,9f
Lord spoke * of him to each other. Mal 3:16
the law but * violated its intent. Mt 3:7f
drink wine and * goes without food, Mt 11:18
trouble, for he * falls into the Mt 17:15
asked, "Sir, how * should I Mt 18:21
sends to her! How * I have wanted Mt 23:37
and shackles—as he * was—he snapped Mk 5:3,4
to themselves, but * talked about Mk 9:10
religious leaders * spoke of, that Mk 9:11
and the demon * makes him fall Mk 9:22
heart and * thought about them. Lk 2:19
God by praying and * fasting. Lk 2:36,37
But he * withdrew to the Lk 5:16
This demon had * taken control of Lk 8:29
to help her. How * I have wanted to Lk 13:34
notorious sinners * came to listen Lk 15:1
funds and * dipped into them for Jn 12:6
they had seen so * at The Beautiful Act 3:10
* spoke of him as the Messiah. Act 8:9,10,11
God knows how * I pray for you. Rom 1:9
Jews about it as * as I can, so Rom 11:13
you can—as * as your faith is Rom 12:6
people are * fooled by them. Rom 16:18
and have been * in great danger 2Co 11:26
sleepless nights. * I have been 2Co 11:27
gone without food; * I have 2Co 11:27
For I have told you * before, Php 3:18
faces and do it so * that their 1Ti 4:2
stomach because you are sick so *. 1Ti 5:23
he visited me and encouraged me *. 2Ti 1:16
that young men * have, but stay 2Ti 2:22
kindness has so * refreshed the Phm 1:7
And all too * they are the ones Jas 2:7
upon the earth as * as they wish. Rev 11:6

OFTENER
been put in jail *, been whipped 2Co 11:23

OG
Bashan, but King * of Bashan met Num 21:33
happen to King * as happened to Num 21:34
and killed King *, his sons, and Num 21:35

OG Con't)
and of King * of Bashan—all the Num 32:33
Heshbon, and King * of Bashan had Deu 1:1
fight against King * and his Deu 3:3
"Incidentally, King * of Bashan Deu 3:11
of King *, the Argob region. Deu 3:13
and that of King * of Bashan—they Deu 4:47
Heshbon and King * of Bashan came Deu 29:7
and *, the kings of the Amorites. Deu 31:4
did to Sihon and *, the two Amorite Jos 2:10
of Heshbon, and *, king of Bashan. Jos 9:10
King * of Bashan, the last of the Jos 12:4
and all the territory of King * Jos 13:12
kingdom of King *, and the sixty Jos 13:30
the Amorites and King * of Bashan. 1Ki 4:8-19
of Heshbon and King * of Bashan. Neh 9:22
and *, the king of Bashan; Ps 135:11
continues forever— and *, king Ps 136:20

OG'S
"NEXT WE TURNED toward King * Deu 3:1
Half of Gilead and King * royal Jos 13:31

OHAD
Jemuel, Jamin, *, Jachin, Zohar, Gen 46:8-14
Jemuel, Jamin, *, Ex 6:15

OHEL
Hananiah, Hashubah, *, Berechiah, 1Ch 3:19,20

OHOLAH
The older girl was named *; Eze 23:4,5
But then * turned to other gods Eze 23:4,5

OHOLIAB
"And I have appointed * (son of Ex 31:6
And God has made him and * Ex 35:34
skills to others. (* is the son of Ex 35:34
assist Bezalel and * in Ex 36:1
So Moses told Bezalel and * and Ex 36:1
assisted by * (son of Ahisamach of Ex 38:23

OHOLIBAH
her sister was *. Eze 23:4,5
"But when * (Jerusalem) saw what Eze 23:11
against you, O * (Jerusalem), those Eze 23:22

OHOLIBAMAH
* (daughter of Anah and Gen 36:2,3
Esau and * had sons named Jeush, Gen 36:5
Esau and his wife * (daughter of Gen 36:18,19
The children of Anah:Dishon, * Gen 36:25
clan of *,The clan of Elah,The clan Gen 36:40-43
Jetheth, Chief *, Chief Elah, Chief 1Ch 1:51-54

OIL
and poured olive * over it. Gen 28:18
anointed the pillar with olive *. Gen 35:13,14
acacia wood, olive * for the lamps, Ex 25:1
for the anointing * and for the Ex 25:1
you pure olive * to use in the Ex 27:20
heads with olive *, thus Ex 28:41
bread mingled with *, and Ex 29:2
wafers with * poured over them. Ex 29:2
Then take the anointing * and Ex 29:7
of the anointing * and sprinkle it Ex 29:21
pour olive * upon it to sanctify Ex 29:36
pints of *, pressed from olives; Ex 29:40
and 1½ gallons of olive *. Ex 30:24
all this into a holy anointing *. Ex 30:25
always be my holy anointing *. Ex 30:31
the anointing *; Ex 31:11
Olive * for the lamps; Ex 35:5-9
Spices for the anointing * and for Ex 35:5-9
Lamp holders, with lamps and *; Ex 35:10-19
The anointing * and sweet incense; Ex 35:10-19
and spices, and *—for the light, Ex 35:28
anointing * and the sweet incense. Ex 35:28
he made the sacred * for anointing Ex 37:29
with its lamps, utensils, and *; Ex 39:33-40
The anointing *; Ex 39:33-40
"Take the anointing * and Ex 40:9
Sprinkle the anointing * upon Ex 40:10
pour olive * and incense upon it. Lev 2:1
with olive * but without yeast. Lev 2:4
* may also be used as an offering. Lev 2:4
yeast, and mingled with olive *. Lev 2:5
Break it into pieces and pour * Lev 2:6
of fine flour mixed with olive *. Lev 2:7
Put olive * and incense on the Lev 2:15
grain mixed with * and all of the Lev 2:16
He must not mix it with olive * Lev 5:11
with the olive * and the incense Lev 6:15
using olive *, and should be well Lev 6:21
mixed with olive * or dry, are the Lev 7:10
loaves mingled with *." Lev 7:12f
spread with olive * and loaves from Lev 7:12
of flour mixed with olive *. Lev 7:12
the anointing *, the young bull for Lev 8:1
Then Moses took the anointing * Lev 8:10
Then he poured the anointing * Lev 8:12
spread with olive *, and a slice of Lev 8:26
of the anointing * and some of the Lev 8:30
mingled with olive *. Lev 9:4
* of Jehovah is upon you." Lev 10:7
olive *, and a pint of olive oil; Lev 14:10
olive oil, and a pint of olive *; Lev 14:10
the pint of olive * and offer them Lev 14:12
take the olive * and pour it into Lev 14:15
Some of the * remaining in his Lev 14:17
The remainder of the * in his Lev 14:18
mixed with olive *, for a grain Lev 14:21
offering, and a pint of olive *. Lev 14:21
and the pint of *, and wave them Lev 14:24
pour the olive * into the palm of Lev 14:26
some of the olive * from his hand Lev 14:28
The remaining * in his hand Lev 14:29
special anointing * and wearing the Lev 21:10
* of his God is upon him; Lev 21:12
mixed with olive *, to be offered Lev 23:13
you pure olive * for an eternal Lev 24:1
with fresh * and trim the wicks. Lev 24:3,4
and the reservoir of olive *. Num 4:9
for the * for the light, the sweet Num 4:16
and the anointing *—in fact, the Num 4:16
meal without * or frankincense Num 5:15
of fine flour mixed with olive *; Num 6:15
unleavened wafers spread with *; Num 6:15
of fine flour mixed with *. Num 7:13
flour mingled with *, along with Num 8:8
pancakes fried in vegetable *. Num 11:8
Literally, "olive *." Num 11:8f
three pints of *, accompanied by Num 15:3,4
with four pints of *, and four Num 15:6
three quarts of *, plus three Num 15:8,9
best of the olive *, wine, grain, Num 18:12
flour mixed with three pints of *. Num 28:5
*, and the usual drink offering. Num 28:9,10
flour mixed with * as a grain Num 28:12
* as a grain offering for the ram; Num 28:12
mixed with * for a grain offering. Num 28:13
quarts of fine flour mixed with *; Num 28:20,21
flour mixed with * with each bull, Num 28:28,29
flour mingled with * shall be Num 29:3,4
* are to be offered with the bull; Num 29:9,10
flour mingled with * for each of Num 29:14
grapes for your wine, and olive *. Deu 11:14
new wine and olive *, nor the Deu 12:17
new wine, olive *, and the Deu 14:23
wine, the olive *, and of the Deu 18:4
olive * to anoint yourselves! Deu 28:40
Your grain, new wine, olive *, Deu 28:51
And olive * from stony ground! Deu 32:13
Or, "* from flinty rocks." Deu 32:13f
his feet in soothing olive *. Deu 33:24
the olive * that blesses God and Ju 9:9
a flask of olive * and poured it 1Sa 10:1
Now take a vial of olive * and go 1Sa 16:1
took the olive * he had brought and 1Sa 16:13
a flask of sacred * from the 1Ki 1:39
and 96 gallons of pure olive *. 1Ki 5:11
* in the bottom of the jar. 1Ki 17:12
of flour and * left in your 1Ki 17:14
and * as long as it was needed. 1Ki 17:15
a jar of olive *," she replied. 2Ki 4:2
Then pour olive * from your jar 2Ki 4:4
And then the * stopped flowing! 2Ki 4:6
"Go and sell the * and pay your 2Ki 4:7
"Take this vial of * with you, 2Ki 9:1
and pour the * over his head. 2Ki 9:3
man poured the * over his head and 2Ki 9:6
raisins, wine, *, cattle, and sheep 1Ch 12:40
fried or mixed with olive *); 1Ch 23:29
charge of the supplies of olive *. 1Ch 27:28
and 20,000 barrels of olive *." 2Ch 2:10
barley, olive *, and wine you 2Ch 2:15
them with food, olive *, and wine. 2Ch 11:11
new wine, olive *, money, and 2Ch 31:5,6
wine, and olive *, with many stalls 2Ch 32:28,29
them with food, wine, and olive *. Ez 3:7
and olive * each day without fail. Ez 6:9
first of the new wine and olive *. Neh 10:37
wine, and olive * to the Temple and Neh 10:39,40
of grain, new wine, and olive *. Neh 13:5
olive * to the Temple treasury. Neh 13:12
treatments with * of myrrh, Est 2:12,13,14
out the olive * without tasting it, Job 24:11
out streams of olive * to me! Job 29:6
head with *, my cup runs over." Ps 23:5f
have anointed him with my holy *. Ps 89:20
Literally, "anointed with fresh * Ps 92:10f
glad, and olive * as lotion for his Ps 104:15
fragrant anointing * that was Ps 133:2
* in the dwelling of the wise." Pro 21:20f
the wine and the *, and the healthy Jer 31:12
* and honey they had hidden away. Jer 41:8
And used my * and incense to Eze 16:18
flour and * and honey I gave you; Eze 16:19
* upon a table spread before you. Eze 23:41
and with honey, * and balm. Eze 27:17
as olive *, the Lord God says. Eze 32:14
and one per cent of your olive * Eze 45:14
and twenty-one gallons of olive * Eze 45:24
meal offering and * offering. Eze 45:25
olive * for each bushel of flour. Eze 46:5
is to bring 1½ gallons of olive *. Eze 46:7
and 1½ gallons of * with each Eze 46:11
gallon of * with which to mix it. Eze 46:14,15
and the olive * shall be provided Eze 46:14,15
the grapes, the olive * are gone. Joe 1:10
and *, to fully satisfy your need. Joe 2:19
overflow with olive * and wine. Joe 2:24
of olive *—would that please him? Mic 6:7
you will press out the * from the Mic 6:15
for the olive * that feeds the Zec 4:2
that emptied * into golden bowls Zec 4:12
their lamps with *, while the other Mt 25:2,3,4
Then the five who hadn't any * Mt 25:7,8
anointing them with olive *. Mk 6:13
courtesy of olive * to anoint my Lk 7:46
of olive *,' the man replied. Lk 16:5,6
and pour a little * upon him, Jas 5:14
but there is no olive * or Rev 6:6
Literally, "do not damage the * Rev 6:6f
wine, olive *, and fine flour; Rev 18:13

OIL-SLICK
hold onto anything with * hands. Pro 27:16

OILS
aromatic *, the armory—everything. 2Ki 20:13

OILY
His words were * smooth, but in Ps 55:21

OINTMENT
Literally, "because of *." Is 10:27f
"Make an * of figs and spread it Is 38:21
* made from myrrh and aloes. Jn 19:39
and incense, * and frankincense, Rev 18:13

OINTMENTS
sweet spices and *, and his people 2Ch 16:13,14
with special perfumes and *. Est 2:12,13,14
with sweet *, caring nothing at all Amo 6:6
spices and * to embalm him; Lk 23:56
they took the * to the tomb— and Lk 24:1

OLD
Adam: Adam was 130 years * when Gen 5:3,4,5
Seth: Seth was 105 years * when Gen 5:6,7,8
Enosh: Enosh was ninety years * Gen 5:9,10,11
Kenan: Kenan was seventy years * Gen 5:12,13,14
* when his son Jared was born. Gen 5:15,16,17
Jared: Jared was 162 years * when Gen 5:18,19,20
sixty-five years * when his son Gen 5:21-24
* when his son Lamech was born; Gen 5:25,26,27
Lamech: Lamech was 182 years * Gen 5:28-31
Noah: Noah was 500 years * and Gen 5:32
He was 600 years * when the Gen 7:6
and seventeen days *, the rain came Gen 7:10,11,12
and was 950 years * at his death. Gen 9:29
flood when Shem was 100 years *; Gen 11:10,11
was thirty-five years *, his son Gen 11:12,13
Shelah was thirty years * when Gen 11:14,15
Eber was thirty-four years * when Gen 11:16,17
Peleg was thirty years * when his Gen 11:18,19
Reu was thirty-two years * when Gen 11:20,21
Serug was thirty years * when his Gen 11:22,23
Nahor was twenty-nine years * at Gen 11:24,25
was seventy years *, he had three Gen 11:26
he was 145 years *, so that his Gen 11:32f
Abram was seventy-five years * at Gen 12:4
die in peace, at a ripe * age. Gen 15:15
(Abram was eighty-six years * at Gen 16:16
ABRAM WAS ninety-nine years * Gen 17:1
"Me—100 years *? Gen 17:17
Abraham was ninety-nine years * Gen 17:24-27
were both very *, and Sarah was Gen 18:11
"And with a husband as * as Gen 18:12
Why did she say 'Can an * woman Gen 18:13
young and * from all over the Gen 19:4
And our father will soon be too * Gen 19:31
* age, at the time God had said; Gen 21:1
(Abraham was 100 years * at that Gen 21:4,5
Abraham a child in his * age!" Gen 21:7
WHEN SARAH WAS 127 years *, she Gen 23:1
ABRAHAM WAS NOW a very * man, Gen 24:1
But the * man said, "I don't Gen 24:33
wife, was very *, she gave birth to Gen 24:36
Then Abraham died, at the ripe * Gen 25:7,8
was forty years * when he married Gen 25:20
Isaac was sixty years * when the Gen 25:26
ONE DAY, IN Isaac's * age when he Gen 27:1
Isaac: "I am an * man now, and Gen 27:2,3,4
after this, Rebekah's * nurse Gen 35:8
at the ripe * age of 180. Gen 35:28,29
Joseph was now seventeen years *. Gen 37:2
was born to him in his * age. Gen 37:3
Shelah was * enough to marry her. Gen 38:11
He was thirty years * as he Gen 41:46
"And how is your father—the * Gen 43:27
have a father, an * man, and a Gen 44:20
child of his * age, a little one. Gen 44:20
"How * are you?" Gen 47:8
as * as many of my ancestors." Gen 47:9
years * at the time of his death. Gen 47:28
Joseph was 110 years * when he Gen 50:22
Moses was eighty years * and Ex 7:7
were twenty years * or older, a Ex 38:25,26
A boy one month to five years * Lev 27:6
men twenty years * and older who Num 1:2-15
were twenty years * or older to Num 1:17,18,19
every male down to one month *." Num 3:14,15
22,000 males a month * and older. Num 3:39
who are a month * and older, and Num 3:40
a month * and older to be 22,273. Num 3:43

(OLD Con't)
to fifty years * and who were Num 4:46,47,48
a year * for a guilt offering. Num 6:12
60 male lambs a year *. Num 7:88
you twenty years * and older, who Num 14:29
be brought when he is one month *. Num 18:16
are twenty years * or older, to Num 26:2
the males a month * and upward. Num 26:62
when he was 123 years *. Num 33:38,39
* enough to bear arms, had died. Deu 2:14,15
haven't grown *, and your feet Deu 8:4
have no mercy upon young or *. Deu 28:50
haven't become *, and your shoes Deu 29:5
told them, "I am now 120 years *! Deu 31:2
Moses was 120 years * when he Deu 34:7
men who had been * enough to bear Jos 5:4,5
men who had been * enough to bear Jos 5:6
in it—men and women, young and *; Jos 6:21
on their donkeys, *, patched Jos 9:3,4,5
but now they are * and cracked; Jos 9:13
JOSHUA WAS NOW an * man. Jos 13:1
"You are growing *," the Lord Jos 13:1
"I was forty years * at the Jos 14:7
today I am eighty-five years *. Jos 14:10
south of the * city of Jerusalem Jos 18:16
Joshua was very *, he called for Jos 23:1
to them, "I am an * man now, and Jos 23:2
and the other * men who had Jos 24:31
afterward as the * men of his Ju 2:7-9
Gideon finally died, an *, old Ju 8:32
Gideon finally died, an old, * Ju 8:32
Just then an * man came by on Ju 19:16
"Don't worry," the * man said, Ju 19:20
and yelling at the * man to bring Ju 19:22
rape him. The * man stepped Ju 19:23
for I am too * to have a husband. Ru 1:12
take care of you in your * age; Ru 4:15
Eli was now very *, but he was 1Sa 2:22
None shall live to be *. 1Sa 2:31
(Eli was ninety-eight years * 1Sa 4:15
he died (for he was * and fat). 1Sa 4:18
people, young and *, with the 1Sa 5:9
IN HIS * age, Samuel retired and 1Sa 8:1
I stand here, an *, grey-haired man 1Sa 12:2
years * when he began to reign, 1Sa 13:1f
As that * proverb says, 'Wicked 1Sa 24:13
he will die in battle or of * age. 1Sa 26:10
"He is an * man wrapped in a 1Sa 28:14
Ish-bosheth was forty years * at 2Sa 2:10,11
He was five years * at the time 2Sa 4:4
Then, beginning at the * Millo 2Sa 5:9
And your father is an * soldier 2Sa 17:8
He was very * now, about eighty, 2Sa 19:31,32
"I am far too * for that. 2Sa 19:34
I am eighty years * today, and 2Sa 19:35
IN HIS * age King David was 1Ki 1:1
He was an *, old man now, and 1Ki 1:15
He was an old, * man now, and 1Ki 1:15
When it was three days *, this 1Ki 3:17,18
City of David—the * sector of 1Ki 9:24
Lord, especially in his * age. 1Ki 11:4
it over with the * men who had 1Ki 12:6
But Rehoboam refused the * men's 1Ki 12:8
He ignored the * men's advice and 1Ki 12:13,14
As it happened, there was an * 1Ki 13:11
the * prophet asked. 1Ki 13:12
the donkey," the * man said. 1Ki 13:13
Then the * man said to the 1Ki 13:15
But the * man said, "I am a 1Ki 13:18
But the * man was lying to him. 1Ki 13:18
some water at the * man's home. 1Ki 13:19
Lord came to the * man, and he 1Ki 13:20
After finishing the meal, the * 1Ki 13:23
Bethel where the * prophet lived. 1Ki 13:24,25
He was an * man now, and could no 1Ki 14:4
He was forty-one years * when he 1Ki 14:21
In his * age his feet became 1Ki 15:23
thirty-five years * when he 1Ki 22:42
who could fight, * and young, and 2Ki 3:21
and her husband is an * man." 2Ki 4:14
Jehoram was thirty-two years * 2Ki 8:17
David—the * section of Jerusalem. 2Ki 8:24,25
Ahaziah was twenty-two years * 2Ki 8:26
Joash was seven years * when he 2Ki 11:21
Amaziah was twenty-five years * 2Ki 14:2
beginning of his reign: 16 years * 2Ki 15:1
when he became king: 25 years * 2Ki 15:32,33
Age: 20 years * 2Ki 16:1
Then he removed the * bronze 2Ki 16:14
So the * altar was used only for 2Ki 16:15
"The * bronze altar," he said, 2Ki 16:15
beginning of his reign: 25 years * 2Ki 18:1
beginning of his reign: 22 years * 2Ki 21:19,20
beginning of his reign: 8 years * 2Ki 22:1
when he became king: 23 years * 2Ki 23:31,32
when he became king: 25 years * 2Ki 23:36,37
beginning of his reign: 18 years * 2Ki 24:8,9
when he became king: 21 years * 2Ki 24:18,19
Meanwhile the * Tabernacle of the 1Ch 16:39
BY THIS TIME David was an *, old 1Ch 23:1
BY THIS TIME David was an old, * 1Ch 23:1
were twenty years * or older were 1Ch 23:24
He died at an * age, wealthy and 1Ch 29:28
led them up to the hill to the * 2Ch 1:2,3
in front of the * Tabernacle, and 2Ch 1:5,6
demand with the * men who had 2Ch 10:6
the advice of the * men, and 2Ch 10:13
* or young, man or woman. 2Ch 15:13
thirty-five years *, and reigned 2Ch 20:31
He was thirty-two years * when 2Ch 21:5
He was thirty-two years * when 2Ch 21:20
Ahaziah was twenty-two years * 2Ch 22:2
Literally, "forty-two years *"; 2Ch 22:2f
JOASH WAS SEVEN years * when he 2Ch 24:1
He lived to a very * age, 2Ch 24:15
WAS TWENTY-FIVE years * 2Ch 25:1
men twenty years * and older, all 2Ch 25:5,6
JOTHAM WAS TWENTY-FIVE years * 2Ch 27:1
twenty-five years * when he began 2Ch 27:8
AHAZ WAS TWENTY years * when he 2Ch 28:1
who were sick and * on donkeys, and 2Ch 28:15
WAS TWENTY-FIVE years * 2Ch 29:1
dividing it to young and * alike. 2Ch 31:14,15
from three years * and upward." 2Ch 31:16f
twenty years * and older were 2Ch 31:17,18
WAS ONLY twelve years * 2Ch 33:1
Amon was twenty-two years * when 2Ch 33:20,21
JOSIAH WAS ONLY eight years * when 2Ch 34:1
For when he was sixteen years *, 2Ch 34:3
gates, he found an * scroll which 2Ch 34:14
He was twenty-three years * when 2Ch 36:2
twenty-five years * when he became 2Ch 36:5
Jehoiachin was eight years * when 2Ch 36:9
Zedekiah was twenty-one years * 2Ch 36:11
even young girls and * men. 2Ch 36:17
The altar was rebuilt on its * Ez 3:3
were twenty years * or older were Ez 3:8
other leaders—the * men who Ez 3:12
The * Gate was repaired by Joiada Neh 3:6
and the * Officers' Club building. Neh 3:16
And all who were * enough to Neh 8:1
daughters who were * enough to Neh 10:28
the castle to the * City of David; Neh 12:37
Gate to the * Gate, passed the Fish Neh 12:39
the Jews—young and *, women and Est 3:13
Though its roots have grown * in Job 14:8,9
You make him * and wrinkled, then Job 14:20,21
other relatives. * and young alike Job 18:20
live on to a good * age, and become Job 21:7
young and you are *, so I held back Job 32:6
Then at last he died, an *, old Job 42:17
Then at last he died, an old, * Job 42:17
may indicate that * Testament Ps 6:5f
My eyes are growing * and dim Ps 6:7
them like * buildings, never to be Ps 28:5
I have been young and now I am *. Ps 37:25
God will sweep away both * and Ps 58:9
And now, in my * age, don't set Ps 71:9
And now that I am * and gray, Ps 71:18
I keep thinking of the good * Ps 77:5
before they were * enough to sing Ps 78:63
Young and * shall hear about your Ps 89:1
You have made him * before his Ps 89:45
Even in * age they will still Ps 92:14
They will grow *, like worn-out Ps 102:26
shirt and throwing away the * one! Ps 102:26
But you yourself never grow *. Ps 102:27
men and maidens, * men and Ps 148:12
Hatred stirs * quarrels, but love Pro 10:12
An * man's grandchildren are his Pro 17:6
of * men, their experience. Pro 20:29
despise an * mother's experience. Pro 23:22
dignity, and has no fear of * age. Pro 31:25
than to be an * and foolish king Ecc 4:13
lives to be very *, but leaves so Ecc 6:3
than to be an *, unhappy man. Ecc 6:5
Don't long for "the good * Ecc 7:10
Demolish an * wall—and be bitten Ecc 10:8,9
If a person lives to be very *, Ecc 11:8
are dim to your * eyes, and there Ecc 12:2
withered * man, dragging himself Ecc 12:5
home, into my mother's * bedroom. Sol 3:4
the new as well as *, for I have Sol 7:13
we won't be mocked as * maids." Is 4:1
this child was * enough to talk Is 7:14f
shall know (is * enough) to refuse Is 7:15,16f
and (is * enough to) eat curds Is 7:15,16f
this child is even * enough to say Is 8:4
from the * root. Is 11:1
both young and *, their buttocks Is 20:4
Are we little children, barely * Is 28:9
You have made even the * folks Is 47:6
like * clothes eaten up by moths! Is 50:9
as in the days of * when you slew Is 51:9
those days of * when Moses, God's Is 63:11
think about the * ones anymore. Is 65:17
babies die when only a few days *; Is 65:20
will men be considered * at 100! Is 65:20
has traded in its * gods for new Jer 2:10,11
for "the good * days of long ago" Jer 3:16
history. The * Babylonian Empire Jer 5:15f
of his life become a poor * fool. Jer 17:11
like the cities of * which God Jer 20:16
Then some of the wise * men stood Jer 26:17
joy, and men folk—* and young—will Jer 31:13
There he found some * rags and Jer 38:11
Moab like an *, unwanted bottle. Jer 48:38
both young and * alike shall be Jer 51:3
too, both * and young, young men Jer 51:22
WAS TWENTY-ONE years * Jer 52:1
See them lying in the streets—* Lam 2:21
He has made me * and has broken Lam 3:4
The * men sit no longer in the Lam 5:14
June, when I was thirty years *, Eze 1:1
kill them all—* and young, girls, Eze 9:6
of both young and * alike, by tying Eze 13:18
you were * enough for marriage; Eze 16:8
God says. The * order changes. Eze 21:26
who have become * harlot hags? Eze 23:43
Wise * craftsmen from Gebal do Eze 27:9
a valley full of *, dry bones that Eze 37:1
even realize how weak and * he is. Hos 7:9
prophesy; your * men will dream Joe 2:28
where even the * and feeble, as Nah 2:11
to the site of the * gate, then to Zec 14:10
baby boy two years * and under, Mt 2:16
"And who would patch an * Mt 9:16
And who would use * wineskins Mt 9:17
For the * skins would burst with Mt 9:17
treasures—from the * Testament as Mt 13:52
treasure things both new and *." Mt 13:52f
part of the * way of doing things. Mk 2:21
It is like patching an * garment Mk 2:21
to put new wine into * wineskins. Mk 2:22
(She was twelve years *. Mk 5:41,42
Bartimaeus yanked off his * Mk 10:50
and now they were both very *. Lk 1:7
like Elijah, the prophet of *; Lk 1:17
I'm an * man now, and my wife is Lk 1:18
her—became pregnant in her * age! Lk 1:36
When the baby was eight days *, Lk 1:59
and was very *, for she had been a Lk 2:36,37
When Jesus was twelve years * he Lk 2:41,42
Jesus was about thirty years * Lk 3:23-38
to make a patch for an * one. Lk 5:36
be ruined, but the * garment will Lk 5:36
And no one puts new wine into * Lk 5:37
wine bursts the * skins, ruining Lk 5:37
But no one after drinking the * Lk 5:39
'The * ways are best,' they say." Lk 5:39
a little girl twelve years *. Lk 8:42
Many a prophet and king of * has Lk 10:24
How can an * man go back into his Jn 3:4
*—sure, you've seen Abraham!" Jn 8:57
He is * enough to speak for Jn 9:21
but when you are *, you will Jn 21:18
and your * men dream dreams. Act 2:17
when he was eight days *. Act 7:8
God's prophets in the * Testament. Rom 1:2
that he was too * to be a father, Rom 4:19
was also much too * to have a Rom 4:19
began to grow * and die, Rom 5:12
Your * sin-loving nature was Rom 6:4
Your * evil desires were nailed Rom 6:6
And since your * sin-loving Rom 6:8
So look upon your * sin nature Rom 6:11
And now you are free from your * Rom 6:18
When your * nature was still Rom 7:5
not in the * way, mechanically Rom 7:6
my * sinful nature is concerned. Rom 7:18
do right, but the * nature that is Rom 7:23,24,25
obey the * evil nature within us. Rom 8:4
after the * nature leads to death, Rom 8:6
because the * sinful nature within Rom 8:7
control of their * sinful selves, Rom 8:8
on following their * evil desires, Rom 8:8
whatever to your * sinful nature to Rom 8:12
us the cancerous * life with all 1Co 5:8
Holy Spirit. The * way, trying to 2Co 3:6
Yet that * system of law that led 2Co 3:7
So if the * system that faded 2Co 3:11
to the * life we used to live. 2Co 5:13,14
to follow all the *, traditional Gal 1:14
rebuilding the * systems I have Gal 2:18
throw off your * evil nature—the Eph 4:22
evil nature—the * you that was a Eph 4:22
I was eight days *, having been Php 3:5
of the * original Benjamin family. Php 3:5
you see how your *, evil nature Col 2:12
it was your * life with all its Col 3:9
should be at least sixty years * 1Ti 5:9
you—I, Paul, an * man now, here in Phm 1:8,9
They will become worn out like * Heb 1:11
milk, not * enough for solid food. Heb 5:12,13
LET US STOP going over the same * Heb 6:1
by meeting the * requirement of Heb 7:16
Yes, the * system of priesthood Heb 7:18
Under the * arrangement there had Heb 7:23
Under the * system, even the Heb 7:28
the * Jewish system of sacrifices. Heb 8:4
serve under the * laws, because the Heb 8:6
The * agreement didn't even work. Heb 8:7
fault with the * one, for he said, Heb 8:8

OLD Con't)
not be like the * one I gave to Heb 8:9
as taking the place of the * one; Heb 8:13
for the * one is out of date now Heb 8:13
us that under the * system the Heb 9:8
For under the * system, gifts and Heb 9:9
For the * system dealt only with Heb 9:10
And if under the * system the Heb 9:13
having to obey the * rules, and Heb 9:14
while still under that * system. Heb 9:15
say that under the * agreement Heb 9:22
THE * SYSTEM of Jewish laws gave Heb 10:1
The sacrifices under the * system Heb 10:1
required under the * system, he Heb 10:8
Under the * agreement the Heb 10:11
Men of God in days of * were Heb 11:2
in spite of her * age, for she Heb 11:11
who was too * to have even one Heb 11:12
By faith Jacob, when he was * and Heb 11:21
don't slip back into your * 1Pe 1:14
saintly women of *, who trusted God 1Pe 3:5
him from the * life of sin so that 2Pe 1:9
There is an * saying that "A 2Pe 2:22
obey, for it is an * one you have 1Jn 2:7
FROM: JOHN, THE * Elder of the 2Jn 1:1
friends, of the * rule God gave us 2Jn 1:5
He seized the Dragon—that * Rev 20:2

OLDEN
do a mighty miracle as in * times Jer 21:1
these things. In * times God did Eph 3:5

OLDER
One day the * girl said to her Gen 19:31
night, and the * girl went in and Gen 19:33
The * girl's baby was named Moab; Gen 19:37
and the * shall be a servant of Gen 25:23
*, and her younger sister, Rachel. Gen 29:16
So Joseph's ten * Gen 42:3
upon the head of Manasseh, the *. Gen 48:14
This one over here is the *. Gen 48:18
Later, when he was *, she brought Ex 2:10
old or *, a total of 603,550 men. Ex 38:25,26
years old and * who are able to go Num 1:2-15
years old or * to come and Num 1:17,18,19
22,000 males a month old and *. Num 3:39
old and *, and register each name. Num 3:40
a month old and * to be 22,273. Num 3:43
years old and *, who has complained Num 14:29
years old or *, to find out how Num 26:2
All who at that time were * than Num 26:64,65f
But as for you of the * Deu 1:40
had seven * brothers. 1Sa 17:12
For he is my * brother! 1Ki 2:22
One day when her child was *, he 2Ki 4:18
and some of the * priests to clothe 2Ki 19:2
Levi who were thirty years or *. 1Ch 23:3
years old or * were classified 1Ch 23:24
of Arabs had killed his * sons). 2Ch 22:1
years old and *, all trained and 2Ch 25:5,6
years old and * were listed under 2Ch 31:17,18
years old or * were appointed to Ez 3:8
And as you say, * men like me Job 12:12
On our side are aged men much * Job 15:10
because the others were * than he. Job 32:4
who are * are said to be wiser; Job 32:7
he is * he will remain upon it. Pro 22:6
scribe, and the * priests—all Is 37:2
and some of the * priests with you, Jer 19:1
"Your * sister is Samaria, Eze 16:46
The * girl was named Oholah; Eze 23:4,5
right along behind her * sister. Eze 23:13
A man with two sons told the * Mt 21:28
"Meanwhile, the * son was in the Lk 15:25
"The * brother was angry and Lk 15:28
is * than the Mosaic law); Jn 7:21,22,23
NEVER SPEAK SHARPLY to an * man, 1Ti 5:1
Treat the * women as mothers, 1Ti 5:2
Teach the * men to be serious Tit 2:2
Teach the * women to be quiet and Tit 2:3
These * women must train the Tit 2:4
so that when the * ones died off, Heb 7:23
the leadership of those who are *. 1Pe 5:5
things to you * men because you 1Jn 2:13

OLDEST
Canaan's * son was Sidon, and he Gen 10:15-19
Eber descended from Shem, the * Gen 10:21
Their names were:Uz, the *,Buz, Gen 22:20-23
the next *,Kemuel (father of Gen 22:20-23
who was his * servant, Gen 24:2
he called for Esau his * son. Gen 27:1
Jacob: "It's Esau, your * son. Gen 27:19
Esau, your * son!" Gen 27:32
Reuben, Jacob's * child, Simeon, Gen 35:23
the * son of Esau and Adah. Gen 36:15,16
When his * son Er grew up, Judah Gen 38:6
Joseph named his * son Manasseh Gen 41:51
ages, from the * to the youngest, Gen 43:33
He began searching the * Gen 44:12
Reuben, his * son; Gen 46:8-14
"Reuben, you are my * son, the Gen 49:3
The sons of Reuben, Israel's * Ex 6:14
And all the * sons shall die in Ex 11:5
in Egypt, from the * child of Ex 11:5
the * child of his lowliest slave; Ex 11:5
and kill all the * sons and Ex 12:12
from Pharaoh's * son to the oldest Ex 12:29
oldest son to the * son of the Ex 12:29
redemption payment for your * son. Ex 22:29
Reuben (the * son of Num 1:20-46
Nadab (his *), Abihu, Eleazar, Num 3:2
* sons of the people of Israel. Num 3:11,12
in exchange for all the * sons. Num 3:13
From the day I killed all the * Num 3:13
passed over the * sons of the Num 28:16
the mother of his * son is the wife Deu 21:15
portion to his * son, who is the Deu 21:17
the builder's * son would die, and Jos 6:26
of Manasseh (Joseph's * son): Jos 17:1
The clan of Machir (Manasseh's * Jos 17:1
Then, turning to Jether, his * Ju 8:20
Joel and Abijah, his * sons, 1Sa 8:2
The three *—Eliab, Abinadab, and 1Sa 17:13
But when David's * brother, 1Sa 17:28
my * daughter Merab as your wife. 1Sa 18:17
was at Hebron. The * was Amnon, 2Sa 3:2
his * son, Abiram, died; 1Ki 16:34
Then he took his * son, who was 2Ki 3:27
Nabaioth (the *), Kedar, Adbeel, 1Ch 1:28-31
But the * son, Er, was so wicked 1Ch 2:3
Jerahmeel (the * son of Hezron): 1Ch 2:25
Ram (the *), Bunah, Oren, Ozem, 1Ch 2:25
The * son of 1Ch 2:42
The sons of Hur (who was the * 1Ch 2:50
KING DAVID'S * son was Amnon, who 1Ch 3:1
The son of Hur, the * son of 1Ch 4:3-4
THE * SON of Israel was Reuben, 1Ch 5:1
doesn't name Reuben as the * son. 1Ch 5:1
The * sons of the successive 1Ch 6:4-15
by Samuel's sons:Joel, the *; 1Ch 6:28
was Maacah. His * son was named 1Ch 8:30,31,32
(Shilon's * son) and his sons; 1Ch 9:5
(a Levite and the * son of Shallum 1Ch 9:31
Gibeon, Abdon (the *), Zur, Kish, 1Ch 9:35,36,37
the Rehabiah group, led by his * 1Ch 24:21
group:Jeriah, Hebron's * son; 1Ch 24:23
Zechariah (the *), 1Ch 26:2,3
Shemaiah (the *), 1Ch 26:4,5
his sons, though he was not the *. 1Ch 26:10
to Jehoram because he was the *. 2Ch 21:3,4
We agreed to give to God our * Neh 10:36
* brother's house, tragedy struck. Job 1:12,13
feasting in their * brother's home, Job 1:18
Then he killed the * child in Ps 105:36
Israel, and Ephraim is my * child. Jer 31:9
If you sacrificed your * child, Mic 6:7
him as for an * child who died. Zec 12:10
brothers and the * married and Mk 12:20,21,22
brothers. The * married and then Lk 20:29
not touch the * child in those Heb 11:28
as the * son for a single meal. Heb 12:16

OLIVE
to him with an * leaf in her beak. Gen 8:11
pillar, and poured * oil over it. Gen 28:18
anointed the pillar with * oil. Gen 35:13,14
your vineyards and your * groves. Ex 23:11
acacia wood, * oil for the lamps, Ex 25:1
to bring you pure * oil to use in Ex 27:20
their heads with * oil, thus Ex 28:41
pour * oil upon it to sanctify it. Ex 29:36
and 1½ gallons of * oil. Ex 30:24
* oil for the lamps; Ex 35:5-9
to pour * oil and incense upon it. Lev 2:1
with * oil but without yeast. Lev 2:4
and spread with * oil may also be Lev 2:4
yeast, and mingled with * oil. Lev 2:5
of fine flour mixed with * oil. Lev 2:7
to the Lord. Put * oil and incense Lev 2:15
He must not mix it with * oil or Lev 5:11
flour with the * oil and the Lev 6:15
a griddle, using * oil, and should Lev 6:21
whether mixed with * oil or dry, Lev 7:10
wafers spread with * oil and loaves Lev 7:12
batter of flour mixed with * oil. Lev 7:12
wafer spread with * oil, and a Lev 8:26
offering—flour mingled with * oil. Lev 9:4
* oil, and a pint of olive oil; Lev 14:10
olive oil, and a pint of * oil; Lev 14:10
and the pint of * oil and offer Lev 14:12
shall take the * oil and pour it Lev 14:15
flour, mixed with * oil, for a Lev 14:21
offering, and a pint of * oil. Lev 14:21
then pour the * oil into the palm Lev 14:26
Then he must put some of the * Lev 14:28
flour mixed with * oil, to be Lev 23:13
to bring you pure * oil for an Lev 24:1
trays, and the reservoir of * oil. Num 4:9
of fine flour mixed with * oil; Num 6:15
Literally, "* oil." Num 11:8f
best of the * oil, wine, grain, Num 18:12
and vineyards and * trees you Deu 6:10,11,12
grapes for your wine, and * oil. Deu 11:14
and new wine and * oil, nor the Deu 12:17
grain, new wine, * oil, and the Deu 14:23
your * press, and your wine press. Deu 15:14
the new wine, the * oil, and of the Deu 18:4
olives from your * trees, don't go Deu 24:20
the vines. * trees will be growing Deu 28:40
enough * oil to anoint yourselves! Deu 28:40
Your grain, new wine, * oil, Deu 28:51
And * oil from stony ground! Deu 32:13
He bathes his feet in soothing * Deu 33:24
I gave you vineyards and * groves Jos 24:13
First they asked the * tree, but Ju 9:8
" 'Should I quit producing the * Ju 9:9
grain, and destroying the * trees. Ju 15:5
and vineyards and * groves and give 1Sa 8:14
THEN SAMUEL TOOK a flask of * oil 1Sa 10:1
Now take a vial of * oil and go 1Sa 16:1
Samuel took the * oil he had 1Sa 16:13
and 96 gallons of pure * oil. 1Ki 5:11
made from * wood, each fifteen 1Ki 6:23-28
doorposts of * wood for the 1Ki 6:33
a jar of * oil," she replied. 2Ki 4:2
Then pour * oil from your jar 2Ki 4:4
and clothing and * farms and 2Ki 5:26
grain, wine, * trees, and honey. 2Ki 18:31,32
fried or mixed with * oil); 1Ch 23:29
for the king's * yards and sycamore 1Ch 27:28
charge of the supplies of * oil. 1Ch 27:28
and 20,000 barrels of * oil." 2Ch 2:10
the wheat, barley, * oil, and wine 2Ch 2:15
them with food, * oil, and wine. 2Ch 11:11
grain, new wine, * oil, money, and 2Ch 31:5,6
new wine, and * oil, with many 2Ch 32:28,29
them with food, wine, and * oil. Ez 3:7
and * oil each day without fail. Ez 6:9
get branches from *, myrtle, palm, Neh 8:15
or from our fruit and * trees. Neh 10:35
first of the new wine and * oil. Neh 10:37
new wine, and * oil to the Temple Neh 10:39,40
of grain, new wine, and * oil. Neh 13:5
and * oil to the Temple treasury. Neh 13:12
off his flower as the * tree." Job 15:33f
to press out the * oil without Job 24:11
poured out streams of * oil to me! Job 29:6
But I am like a sheltered * tree Ps 52:8
make him glad, and * oil as lotion Ps 104:15
and healthy as young * trees. Ps 128:3
myrtle, * trees, the cypress, fir Is 41:19
call you his green * tree, Jer 11:16
as * oil, the Lord God says. Eze 32:14
and one per cent of your * oil; Eze 45:14
and twenty-one gallons of * Eze 45:24
of * oil for each bushel of flour. Eze 46:5
is to bring 1½ gallons of * oil. Eze 46:7
offering and the * oil shall be Eze 46:14,15
grapes, and the * trees for Hos 1:21,22
as beautiful as * trees, fragrant Hos 14:6
The grain, the grapes, the * oil Joe 1:10
overflow with * oil and wine. Joe 2:24
the locusts ate your figs and * Amo 4:9
of * oil—would that please him? Mic 6:7
and though the * crops all fail, Hab 3:17
* press, there were only twenty. Hag 2:16,17
reservoir for the * oil that feeds Zec 4:2
And I see two * trees carved Zec 4:3
Then I asked him about the two * Zec 4:11
and about the two * branches that Zec 4:12
people, anointing them with * oil. Mk 6:13
And now they came to an * grove Mk 14:32
usual courtesy of * oil to anoint Lk 7:46
'My debt is 850 gallons of * Lk 16:5,6
and entered a grove of * trees. Jn 18:1
they arrived at the * grove. Jn 18:3
there in the * grove with Jesus?" Jn 18:26
a wild * tree, were grafted in. Rom 11:17
of his own special * tree. Rom 11:17
part of a wild * tree—and graft you Rom 11:24
but there is no * oil or wine." Rev 6:6
These two prophets are the two * Rev 11:4
wine, * oil, and fine flour; Rev 18:13

OLIVE-WOOD
and its two * doors were carved 1Ki 6:32

OLIVES
2½ pints of oil, pressed from *; Ex 29:40
grain, grapes, and *, and great Deu 7:13
trees, pomegranates, *, and honey; Deu 8:8
When you beat the * from your Deu 24:20
Mount of *, weeping as he went. 2Sa 15:30
of the Mount of * where people 2Sa 15:32
on the Mount of *, across the 1Ki 11:7
as a few stray * are left on the Is 17:6
and * and store them away." Jer 40:10
the oil from the *, and not get Mic 6:15
and grapes and * and all your other Hag 1:11
pomegranates and * have produced Hag 2:18,19
upon the Mount of *, to the east of Zec 14:4
and the Mount of * will split Zec 14:4
on the Mount of *, Jesus sent two Mt 21:1
to this Mount of *, 'Move over into Mt 21:21
on the slopes of the Mount of *. Mt 24:3
they went out to the Mount of *. Mt 26:30
to the Mount of *, Jesus sent two Mk 11:1
to this Mount of *, 'Rise up and Mk 11:22,23

(OLIVES Con't)
of the Mount of * across the valley Mk 13:3,4
and went out to the Mount of *. Mk 14:26
on the Mount of *, he sent two Lk 19:29
from the Mount of *, the whole Lk 19:36,37
spend the night on the Mount of *. Lk 21:37,38
went as usual to the Mount of *. Lk 22:39
the valley on the Mount of *. Lk 24:50f
JESUS RETURNED TO the Mount of *, Jn 8:1
They were at the Mount of * when Act 1:12
Can you pick * from a fig tree, Jas 3:12

OLIVEYARDS
fields, vineyards, *, and homes to Neh 5:11
and * and many, many fruit trees; Neh 9:25

OLYMPAS
his sister, and to *, and all the Rom 16:15

OLYMPIC
original * races of Paul's time. 1Co 9:25f

OMAR
Teman, *, Zepho, Gatam, Kenaz, Gen 36:10,11,12
Teman,The clan of *,The clan of Gen 36:15,16
Teman, *, Zephi, Gatam, Kenaz, 1Ch 1:36

OMEGA
Literally, "I am Alpha and *"; Rev 1:8f

OMENS
evil * and portents in the sun, Lk 21:25

OMER
Literally, "an *." Ex 16:16f
crops to eat. The *—the container Ex 16:36

OMINOUSLY
A vulture circles * above the Jer 48:40

OMIT
Many ancient manuscripts * this Mt 24:36f
Some ancient manuscripts * Mk 16:17f
Many of the ancient manuscripts * Jn 5:4f
Most ancient manuscripts * John Jn 7:53f
Many ancient manuscripts * verse Act 8:37f

OMITTED
he has spoiled, or the tithe *, Lev 5:16
and ceremony was * at his funeral. 2Ch 21:19
Verse 30, * in the Septuagint and Eze 40:29,30f
This verse is * in many of the Mt 17:21f
This verse is * in many Mt 18:11f
* here in many manuscripts, but Mt 19:29f
Verse 16 is * in many of the Mk 7:15,16f
with verse 48) are * in some of the Mk 9:43,44f
with verse 48) are * in some of the Mk 9:45,46f
Verse 28 is * in some of the Mk 15:28f
This entire sentence is * in Act 18:21f

OMRI
decided on General *, 1Ki 16:15,16
new ruler. So * led the army of 1Ki 16:17
loyal to General *, and the other 1Ki 16:21
But General * won and Tibni was 1Ki 16:22
so * reigned without opposition. 1Ki 16:22
years when * began his reign over 1Ki 16:23
Then * bought the hill now known 1Ki 16:24
of Shemer. But * was worse than 1Ki 16:25
When * died he was buried in 1Ki 16:28
more wicked than his father *; 1Ki 16:30
granddaughter of King * of Israel. 2Ki 8:26
Eli-o-enai, *, Jeremoth, Abijah, 1Ch 7:8
of Ammihud, son of *, son of Imri, 1Ch 9:4
Over Issachar, * (son of Michael); 1Ch 27:16-22
was Athaliah, granddaughter of *. 2Ch 22:2
commands you keep are those of *; Mic 6:16

OMRI'S
The rest of * history is 1Ki 16:27

ONAM
Manahath, Ebal,Shepho, *. Gen 36:23
Manahath, Ebal, Shephi, and *. 1Ch 1:40
mother of *. 1Ch 2:26

ONAM'S
* sons were 1Ch 2:28

ONAN
had three sons, Er, *, and Shelah. Gen 38:3,4,5
to Er's brother, *, "You must Gen 38:8
But * was not willing to have a Gen 38:9
Judah and his sons: Er, *, Shelah, Gen 46:8-14
(however, Er and * died while still Gen 46:8-14
* who died in the land of Canaan: Num 26:19-22
Er, *, and Shelah. 1Ch 2:3

ONCE
as was * erroneously supposed. Gen 9:18f
I will speak but this * more! Gen 18:32
Instead, go at * to Paddan-aram, Gen 28:2
him three sons!" * again she was Gen 29:35
Then * again she became Gen 30:19
to him * again and blessed him. Gen 35:9
Their father recognized it at *. Gen 37:33
affairs. At * the Lord began Gen 39:5
Pharaoh sent at * for Joseph. Gen 41:14
and I will let you go at *." Ex 9:28
Forgive my sin only this *, and Ex 10:17
'Please leave at *, and take all Ex 11:8
And * again I will harden Ex 14:4
So * more the people growled and Ex 17:2
"* a year Aaron must sanctify Ex 30:10
people of Israel * each year, Lev 16:34
"Let us go up at * and possess Num 13:30
Moses struck it, not *, but Num 20:12f
wants me to go at * and curse them, Num 22:11
Instead, he went at * and looked Num 24:1
he will not do it all at *, for Deu 7:22
"Again at Taberah and * again at Deu 9:22
from vowing!) * you make the vow, Deu 23:23
around the city * a day for six Jos 6:3,4
around the city * that day, after Jos 6:11
the city not *, but seven times. Jos 6:15
The Israeli army set out at * to Jos 9:17
of Israel turned * again to their Ju 3:12
King Eglon stood up at * to Ju 3:20
(son of Anath). He * killed six Ju 3:31
THEN THE PEOPLE of Israel began * Ju 6:1
other gods, and * again the Lord Ju 6:1
listen to me! * upon a time the Ju 9:8
save us * more from our enemies." Ju 10:15
but they never * crossed into Ju 11:18
* AGAIN ISRAEL sinned by Ju 13:1
of God appeared * again to his wife Ju 13:9
"Come just this * more," she Ju 16:18
to worship the Lord * more. 1Sa 1:19,20
third time, and * more Samuel 1Sa 3:8
"Send for him at *," Samuel 1Sa 16:10,11
know at * how he feels about you. 1Sa 20:12
And I have never * complained to 2Sa 7:7
He cut his hair only * a 2Sa 14:26
"Then we must flee at * or it 2Sa 15:14
and his household set out at *. 2Sa 15:16
He must go across at * into the 2Sa 17:16
I am * more king of Israel!" 2Sa 19:22
* when the Philistines were at 2Sa 21:15
beam! And * when the Philistines 2Sa 21:20,21
the Eznite. He * killed eight 2Sa 23:8
Agee from Harar. * during a 2Sa 23:11,12
was the greatest. * he took on 2Sa 23:18,19
* AGAIN THE anger of the Lord 2Sa 24:1
Go at * to King David and ask 1Ki 1:13
King Hiram's, and * every three 1Ki 10:22
* made this same promise to David. 1Ki 11:38
of the Lord. * when Queen Jezebel 1Ki 18:3,4
Obadiah recognized him at * and 1Ki 18:7
"Now, do it * more!" 1Ki 18:34
* more the king sent fifty men, 2Ki 1:13
* when he was resting in the room 2Ki 4:11,12
* when the king of Syria was at 2Ki 6:8
of Naboth, for * when you and I 2Ki 9:25
land each spring. * some men who 2Ki 13:20,21
for his own sins. * Amaziah killed 2Ki 14:7
* killed 300 men with his spear. 1Ch 11:11
on the ground. * he killed an 1Ch 11:23
These had * belonged to King 2Ch 23:9
at * to rebuild the Temple. Ez 1:5
* with the command of King Darius. Ez 6:13
all of this? For * again we have Ez 9:10
They replied at *, "Good! Neh 2:18
to sin again, and * more you let Neh 9:28
to you for help, * more you Neh 9:28
listen. So * again you allowed the Neh 9:30
duties. And * more all the people Neh 13:12
outside Jerusalem * or twice, but Neh 13:20
And now * more Esther came before Est 8:3
God' when he never * has said the Job 13:7
tell us, and we will cease at *.' Job 34:32
"Have you ever * commanded the Job 38:12
me again, so that * again I will Ps 27:13
how I long for my health * more. Ps 38:9
men, even those who * were Ps 68:18
Do to them as * you did to Ps 83:9
I've said it * and I'll say it Ps 119:106
For I, too, was * a son, Pro 4:3
It is hard to stop a quarrel * it Pro 17:14
If you try * you must try a dozen Pro 19:19
that we may see you * again." Sol 6:13
Jerusalem, * my faithful wife! Is 1:21
Running after other gods! * "The Is 1:21
* like sterling silver; Is 1:22
now mixed with worthless alloy! * Is 1:22
hillsides where * the gardens grew, Is 7:25
* again in the land of Israel. Is 14:1
All rest at night—so pleasant * Is 21:4
Stillness reigns where * your Is 23:2,3
that's left of your * joyous land. Is 23:7
O Lord our God, * we worshiped Is 26:13
enemies' feet. * glorious, her Is 28:4
* again enormous crops will come. Is 32:15
needed at home at *, and he will Is 37:7
lived in * again—it shall be done! Is 44:26
Where * were thorns, fir trees Is 55:13
Though * despised and hated Is 60:15
return to me and * again be mine; Jer 3:7
Then, when your land is * more Jer 3:16
* again give them this message Jer 8:4,5
THEN THE LORD spoke to Jeremiah * Jer 11:1
You have never * let me speak a Jer 20:8
this nation and * more give kings Jer 22:4
Yes, fields shall * again be Jer 32:44
is doomed—will * more see shepherds Jer 33:12
sheep and lambs. * again their Jer 33:13
and to be happy * more on Mount Jer 50:19
JERUSALEM'S STREETS, * thronged Lam 1:1
her mourning. She, * queen of Lam 1:1
warning, pass it on to them at *. Eze 3:1
cities in what was * the kingdom of Eze 27:1
"The people of Israel will * Eze 28:2
All these mighty men who * struck Eze 32:2
them idolaters—who * struck terror Eze 32:2
* a terror, now they lie in shame; Eze 32:3
* AGAIN A message came to me from Eze 33:
My people will walk upon you * Eze 36:1
will be crowded * more, and Eze 36:37,3
time, he will * again turn his Dan 11:2
grape vines will flourish * more. Joe 2:2
of forgiveness. * more the autumn Joe 2:2
sent against you. * again you will Joe 2:2
Philistines' land. * they were Amo 6:
my thoughts * more to the Lord. Jon 2:
to be merciful. * again you will Mic 7:1
O Nineveh, * mighty lion! Nah 2:1
That * proud city will become a Zep 2:1
* more choose to bless Jerusalem.' Zec 2:11,1
So they left at *. Zec 6:
that there will * again be aged men Zec 8:
Then * more the Lord will enjoy Mal 3:
And they left their nets at * Mt 4:2
to come too. At * they stopped Mt 4:2
"Sir, that liar * said, 'After Mt 27:6
Go tell my brothers to leave at * Mt 28:1
At * they left their nets and Mk 1:1
power of demons. * a leper came Mk 1:4
at *, "Why does this bother you? Mk 2:
At * the Pharisees Mk 3:6
* AGAIN AN immense crowd gathered Mk 4:1
Satan comes at * to try to make Mk 4:15
the farmer came at * with his Mk 4:29
Jesus realized at * that healing Mk 5:30
But he spoke to them at *. Mk 6:50
recognized him at *, and ran Mk 6:54
* when some mothers Mk 10:13
the man replied, "I've never * Mk 10:20
Taking them aside, Jesus * more Mk 10:32
* as he was teaching in the Lk 4:33
him to go at * without telling Lk 5:14
* when his mother and brothers Lk 8:19
* WHEN JESUS had been out praying, Lk 11:1
*, when Jesus cast out a demon Lk 11:14
you proceed at * to get it out?" Lk 14:5
for you and never * refused to do a Lk 15:29
* a Jewish religious leader asked Lk 18:18
They began at * accusing him: Lk 23:2
* more, for the third time, he Lk 23:22
Those born only *, with physical Jn 6:63
"I told you *; Jn 9:27
* again they started to arrest Jn 10:39
So Mary went to him at *. Jn 11:29
Judas left at *, going out into Jn 13:30
* more he asked them, "Whom are Jn 18:7
* more he asked him, "Simon, son Jn 21:17
days and went at * to the Act 9:20
So I sent for you at *, and you Act 10:33
The four messengers went at * to Act 15:30
them * more before leaving town. Act 16:40
The believers acted at *, Act 17:14
the judges can take the case at *. Act 19:38
to bring Paul to Jerusalem at *. Act 25:3
He died * for all to end sin's Rom 6:10
Thank God that though you * Rom 6:17
And the heathen, of whom it * Rom 9:26
life and never sin *, only then Rom 10:5
on his promises. * you were rebels Rom 11:30
then try to collect it all at *. 1Co 16:2
on the outside. * I mistakenly 2Co 5:16
between us again. * again I can 2Co 7:16
beaten with rods. * I was stoned. 2Co 11:25
Three times I was shipwrecked. * 2Co 11:25
me I didn't go at * and talk it Gal 1:16
and become slaves * more to another Gal 4:9
hurting me! I am * again suffering Gal 4:19
* YOU WERE under God's curse, Eph 2:1
Never forget that * you were Eph 2:11
and though you * were far away from Eph 2:13
For though * your heart was full Eph 5:8
But all these things that I * Php 3:7
This includes you who were * so Col 1:21
Never * did we try to win you 1Th 2:5
to come back to see you * more. 1Th 2:17
old and have been married only *. 1Ti 5:9
* we, too, were foolish and Tit 3:3
* gave way to them and sinned. Heb 4:15
again if you have * understood the Heb 6:4
for he finished all sacrifices, * Heb 7:27
and then only * a year, all alone, Heb 9:7
this world, and * for all took Heb 9:12
He came * for all, at the end of Heb 9:26
that men die only *, and after that Heb 9:27
Christ died only * as an offering Heb 9:28
have been cleansed * for all, and Heb 10:2
dying for us * and for all. Heb 10:10
Now, when sins have * been Heb 10:18
* you were less than nothing; 1Pe 2:10
now you are God's own. * you knew 1Pe 2:10
He died * for the sins of all us 1Pe 3:18
which God gave, * for all, to his Jud 1:3

ONCE Con't)
angels who were * pure and holy, Jud 1:6
that * had caused his death. Rev 5:6

ONCE-DESERTED
road will go through that * land; Is 35:8

ONCE-DESOLATE
I will go to those * cities that Eze 38:12

ONE-BUSHEL
of seed will yield but a * crop! Is 5:10

ONE-FOURTH
They were given control of * of Rev 6:8

ONE-HALF
among the nine and * tribes, for Num 34:13
confederacy for seven and * years. 2Sa 2:10,11
he reigned seven and * years. 1Ch 3:4
who was seven and * feet tall, 1Ch 11:23
rain for three and * years, and Lk 4:25,26

ONE-PIECE
by an elaborate * woven sash made Ex 39:4,5

ONE-ROOM
there were two * buildings, one Eze 40:44

ONE-SIXTH
Literally, "leave * of you." Eze 39:2f

ONE-TENTH
be the ephah (* of a homer) for dry Eze 45:11
bath (* of a homer) for liquid. Eze 45:11

ONE-THIRD
butchered, and * were spared to 2Sa 8:2
pity you at all. * of you will die Eze 5:12
and disease; * will be slaughtered Eze 5:12
by the enemy; and * I will scatter Eze 5:12
upon the earth. * of the earth was Rev 8:7
on fire so that * of the trees were Rev 8:7
mouths, killing * of all mankind. Rev 9:17,18

ONE-YEAR-OLD
shall sacrifice a * female goat for Num 15:27

ONE'S
in any swelling in * skin, or a Lev 14:56
* soul for a piece of bread. Pro 28:21
nothing left to pass on to * son. Ecc 5:13,14
say how * days can best be spent? Ecc 6:12
when it means forfeiting * self? Lk 9:25
In this new life * nationality Col 3:11

ONES
Abraham, the * the Philistines had Gen 26:18
but didn't with the feebler *. Gen 30:42
and the stronger * were Jacob's! Gen 30:42
have the streaked *, then all the Gen 31:8
the skinny cows ate the fat *! Gen 41:4
up the seven fat * that had come Gen 41:20
thin heads swallowed up the fat *! Gen 41:24
we, but you and all our little *. Gen 43:8
*, and to bring your father here. Gen 45:19
with their little * and their Gen 46:5
granddaughters—all his loved *. Gen 46:7
your households and little *." Gen 47:24
"Are these the *?" Gen 48:8
not let you take your little *!" Ex 10:10
like the first * and I will write Ex 34:1
like the first *, and was up early Ex 34:4
these are the * you may not eat: Lev 11:13-19
Literally, "hairy *." Lev 17:7f
and little * will become slaves. Num 14:3
You are the presumptuous *, you Num 16:6,7
their wives and sons and little *. Num 16:27
"These are the very * who Num 31:16
for our little *, but we ourselves Num 32:16
earth to be his own chosen *. Deu 7:6
like the first *, and to make a Deu 10:1
there are young * or eggs in it Deu 22:6
with your little * and your wives Deu 29:11
Literally, "holy *." Deu 33:2f
His holy * are in his hands. Deu 33:3
You are the * who should die for Ju 6:31
show you which * shall go with you Ju 7:4
with you and which * shall not." Ju 7:4
He will protect his godly *, 1Sa 2:9
lot as the guilty *, and the people 1Sa 14:41
The mighty * have fallen, 2Sa 1:27
and his family are the guilty *. 2Sa 3:29
the last * to reinstate the king? 2Sa 19:11,12
the counsel of the younger *. 2Ch 10:14
with their little *, wives, and 2Ch 20:13
condemn the proud and haughty *. Ps 18:27
These are the * who are allowed Ps 24:6
all the wicked * who speak so Ps 28:3
defend and bless your chosen *. Ps 28:9
Hide your loved * in the shelter Ps 31:20
My loved * and friends stay Ps 38:11
cries of his needy *, and does not Ps 69:33
your people—the * you chose in Ps 74:2
and needy * to praise your name! Ps 74:21
plans to slay your precious *. Ps 83:3
"the assembly of the holy *." Ps 89:5f
"the assembly of the holy *." Ps 89:7f
for us, his chosen *—descendants of Ps 105:5,6
"Touch not these chosen * of Ps 105:15
So he brought his chosen * Ps 105:43
Let me share in your chosen *' Ps 106:5
hounded brokenhearted * to death. Ps 109:16
His loved * are very precious to Ps 116:15
You rebuke those cursed proud * Ps 119:21
for God wants his loved * to get Ps 127:2
honoring his godly *—the people of Ps 148:14
O foolish *, let me show you Pro 8:4,5
simple * without good judgment; Pro 9:4
are yet higher * over them." Ecc 5:8f
at all the sweet * he expected. Is 5:2
they are still his special *. Is 14:1
you'll care, O careless *. Is 32:10
bring cheer to all discouraged *. Is 35:3
Israel, you are mine, my chosen *; Is 41:8
my chosen *, can be refreshed. Is 43:20
my servant Israel, O my chosen *: Is 44:1
O Jerusalem, my chosen *, don't Is 44:2
"Don't forget this, O guilty *. Is 46:8
to me, my people, my chosen *! Is 48:12
I should say to all these weary *. Is 50:4
through it for your ransomed *? Is 51:10
to this, afflicted *—full of Is 51:21
We are the * who strayed away Is 53:6
before the * condemning him. Is 53:7
a cluster of bad * (and someone Is 65:8
think about the old * anymore. Is 65:17
old gods for new *—even though Jer 2:10,11
has rejected the * that you trust. Jer 2:37
I have surrendered my dearest * Jer 12:7
the very * they were to care for. Jer 23:1
this Temple, with all our loved *. Jer 28:6
*, those ready to give birth. Jer 31:8
of Lebanon, the * whose roots went Eze 31:16
I will seek my lost *, those who Eze 34:15,16
Watchers, demanded by the Holy *. Dan 4:17
three of the first * were yanked Dan 7:8
* can no longer save themselves. Amo 2:14
Weep, weep for your little *. Mic 1:16
* who hate good and love evil; Mic 3:2
They are the very * whose Zep 1:13
weak and helpless *, and bring Zep 3:19
the two anointed * who assist the Zec 4:14
second by black *, the third by Zec 6:2
care for the dying *, nor look Zec 11:16
feed the healthy *, nor carry the Zec 11:16
instead, he will eat the fat *, Zec 11:16
Literally, "his holy *." Zec 14:5f
even the sick and the blind *.' Mal 1:8
out the edible * into crates and Mt 13:47,48
missing arms and legs had new *; Mt 15:31
of these little * who trusts in me Mt 18:6
of these little * should perish. Mt 18:14
"Which *?" Mt 19:18
* would be deceived. Mt 24:24
gather my chosen * from the Mt 24:31
I will put such faithful * in Mt 24:47
"Then these righteous * will Mt 25:37
you, you cursed *, into the eternal Mt 25:41
need the doctor, not healthy *! Mk 2:17
people to repent, but the bad *." Mk 2:17
summoned certain * he chose, Mk 3:13
like the great * of the past. Mk 6:15
of these little * who believe in me Mk 9:42
But for the sake of his chosen * Mk 13:20
together my chosen * from all over Mk 13:27
scatters the proud and haughty *! Lk 1:51
down my barns and build bigger *! Lk 12:18
matters, you won't be in large *. Lk 16:10
and even greater *, because I am Jn 14:12,13
besides the * told about in this Jn 20:30,31
They even killed the * who Act 7:52
all—except for the * we wrote to Act 21:25
A few have—the * God has picked Rom 11:7
yourselves are the * who do wrong, 1Co 6:8
For our earthly bodies, the * we 1Co 15:53
You are the * to do it, and how 2Co 2:2
sad by the very * who ought to give 2Co 2:3
givers are the * God prizes. 2Co 9:7
there—false *, really—who came to Gal 2:4
these are the * who should take the 1Ti 5:4
and the cheap * are used in the 2Ti 2:20
They were the * who came out of Heb 3:16
when the older * died off, the Heb 7:23
loved * back again from death. Heb 11:35
And all too often they are the * Jas 2:7
even to scoff at the Glorious * 2Pe 2:10
against these evil Mighty *. 2Pe 2:11
even scoffing at the Glorious *. Jud 1:8
with millions of his holy *. Jud 1:14
that you are the * I love. Rev 3:9
"These are the * coming out of Rev 7:14
called and chosen and faithful *. Rev 17:14

ONESIMUS
I am also sending *, a faithful Col 4:9
to my child *, whom I won to the Phm 1:10
in my chains. * (whose name means Phm 1:11

ONESIPHORUS
May the Lord bless * and all his 2Ti 1:16
and those living at the home of *. 2Ti 4:19

ONIONS
and melons, leeks, *, and garlic! Num 11:4,5

ONLOOKERS
his way through the stunned *! Mk 2:12
He spoke here in Aramaic. The *, Mk 15:34f

ONLY
"It's * the fruit from the tree Gen 3:2,3
men's lives were * towards evil, Gen 6:5
Noah: He was the * truly righteous Gen 6:9,10
God destroyed them all, leaving * Gen 7:23
the father of not * one nation, but Gen 17:2,3,4
Suppose there are * forty-five? Gen 18:28
"Suppose there are * forty?" Gen 18:29
"Let me speak: suppose * thirty Gen 18:30
there are * twenty?" Gen 18:31
Suppose * ten are found?" Gen 18:32
"Take with you your * son—yes, Gen 22:2
in fact, have done * good to you Gen 26:29
mate * with Jacob's black rams. Gen 30:39,40
* give me the girl as my wife." Gen 34:12
But they will * consider staying Gen 34:22
and I was * saved by my screams. Gen 39:18
* one of you shall remain in Gen 42:19
starvation—and not * we, but you Gen 43:8
"except that * the one who stole Gen 44:10
"No," Joseph said. "* the man Gen 44:17
go with us. * then may we come.' Gen 44:26
serfs. The * land he didn't buy Gen 47:22
Rachel died after * two children Gen 48:7
message, he has * been more and Ex 5:23
he will not * let them go, but Ex 6:1
But the plague will affect * the Ex 9:4
destroyed. The * spot in all Egypt Ex 9:26
Forgive my sin * this once, and Ex 10:17
with you.' * then will I go!" Ex 11:8
to eat * bread made without yeast. Ex 12:15
after generation. * bread without Ex 12:18
serve * yeastless bread." Ex 12:20
For seven days you shall eat * Ex 13:6,7
Build altars * where I tell you Ex 20:24
use * uncut stones and boulders. Ex 20:25
a Hebrew slave, he shall serve * Ex 21:2
afterwards, * he shall be freed; Ex 21:3
For it is probably his * warmth; Ex 22:27
"Work six days *, and rest the Ex 23:12
shall serve the Lord your God *; Ex 23:25
Or, "shall become holy," or, "* Ex 29:37f
"* what is holy may touch them." Ex 30:29f
Work six days *, for the seventh Ex 31:16
Yet now if you will * forgive Ex 32:32
no other gods, but * Jehovah, for Ex 34:14
times, work * six days, and rest on Ex 34:21
"Work six days *; Ex 35:2
* a bull with no physical defects. Lev 1:2,3
"The priests are to burn * a Lev 2:9
for an individual, * this time it Lev 4:21
generation after generation. But * Lev 6:18
Literally, "(*) whoever is holy Lev 6:18f
the Tabernacle. * those who are Lev 6:27
but * they, for it is most holy. Lev 6:29
to the Lord. * males among the Lev 7:6
it may be eaten * by a person who Lev 7:19
any animal with * semi-parted Lev 11:26
it was * a scab, and the man need Lev 13:6
and the man need * wash his clothes Lev 13:6
spot seems to be * in the skin and Lev 13:31
he shall bring * one, a male lamb Lev 14:21
the altar; and * three quarts of Lev 14:21
This applies not * while the Lev 15:3
You must obey * my laws, and you Lev 18:4,5
This prohibition applied not * Lev 18:14f
offering— it will * be acceptable Lev 22:19
but will receive * houses in their Lev 25:33
and he shall serve you * until Lev 25:40
if the years have passed and * a Lev 25:52
then he will repay * a small part Lev 25:52
this left * Eleazar and Ithamar to Num 3:4
However, * Aaron and his sons Num 3:10
which weighed * about six ounces. Num 7:14
But if it stayed * a few days, Num 9:19
then they remained * a few days; Num 9:19
fire-cloud stayed * during the Num 9:20,21
But if * one is blown, then only Num 10:4
But if only one is blown, then * Num 10:4
south shall go. * the priests are Num 10:8
for my sake? I * wish that all of Num 11:29
the Lord spoken * through Moses? Num 12:2
But the * response of the people Num 14:10,11
the Promised Land. * Caleb (son of Num 14:30
Of all the spies, * Joshua and Num 14:36,37,38
given this task to * you Levites? Num 16:10
But the people of Israel * Num 17:12,13
assistants; but * you and your sons Num 18:2,3
Remember, * the priests are to Num 18:5
They are to be eaten * in a most Num 18:10
a most holy place, and * by males. Num 18:10
guilty and die. * the Levites Num 18:23
demand for it. We * want to pass Num 20:19
Name your own figure! * come and Num 22:16,17
to say * what I tell you to." Num 22:20
say * what I tell you to say." Num 22:35
If * I could die as happy as an Num 23:7-10
there you will see * a portion of Num 23:13
I said that I would say * what Num 24:13
the men were not * attending the Num 25:2
So the plague was stopped, but * Num 25:9

(ONLY Con't)
The * exceptions were Caleb Num 26:64,65
* the little girls may live; Num 31:18
them to. The * exceptions were Num 32:12
the same thing! * there are more of Num 32:14
These are not * for the Num 35:15
be executed, but * if there is more Num 35:30
no man shall die with * one Num 35:30
it takes * eleven days to travel by Deu 1:1
Those were the * commandments he Deu 5:22
laid out for you; * then will you Deu 5:33
he commands. * then will you be Deu 6:18
If you do, you will not * live, Deu 8:1
I say it again, it is * because Deu 9:5
Egypt there were * seventy of them, Deu 10:22
you may * do so in the place the Deu 12:14
one of the tribes. * there may you Deu 12:14
eat it, too. The * restriction is Deu 12:16
may eat them. The * restriction is Deu 12:20-23
your children. * your gifts to the Deu 12:26,27
These may * be sacrificed upon Deu 12:26,27
* his commands and cling to him. Deu 13:4
will be merciful * if you have been Deu 13:18
"* sea animals with fins and Deu 14:9
this command. The * prerequisite Deu 15:4,5
"That is the * way you will be Deu 16:20
on the testimony of * one witness; Deu 17:6
* then will all go well with you. Deu 19:13
These instructions apply * to Deu 20:15
Let her go, and take * the Deu 22:7
the country, * the man shall die. Deu 22:25,26,27
* obey him and walk in his ways. Deu 28:9
If you will * listen and obey Deu 28:13
You need * to be strong and Jos 1:7
them. For * then will you succeed. Jos 1:8
the conquest. * then may you settle Jos 1:15
This is * fair after the way I Jos 2:12,13
and they have not * taken it, Jos 7:10,11
person was dead. * the cattle and Jos 8:27
He had * five daughters whose Jos 17:3
have you given us * one portion of Jos 17:14
to the * true altar of our God. Jos 22:19
or sacrifices. * the altar in front Jos 22:29
"I'll go, but * if you go with Ju 4:8
of them left, and * ten thousand Ju 7:3
* three hundred of the men drank Ju 7:5,6
* three hundred men with him. Ju 7:8,9
"Your dream can mean * one thing! Ju 7:14
But the boy was * a lad and was Ju 8:20
Of all of Gideon's wives, * Ju 9:2f
and Philistia. Not * this, but they Ju 10:6
you think best, * save us once more Ju 10:15
gods and worshiped * the Lord; Ju 10:16
his daughter—his * child—ran out to Ju 11:34
But Samson replied, "I * paid Ju 15:11
that day, leaving * six hundred men Ju 20:46,47
"You must know I am * a Ru 2:10,11
he could give her * one present, 1Sa 1:5
Samuel, though * a child, was the 1Sa 2:18
I will honor * those who honor 1Sa 2:30
in the doorway; * the trunk of his 1Sa 5:4
Determine to obey * the Lord; 1Sa 7:3
and worshiped * the Lord. 1Sa 7:4
Nahash said, "but * on one 1Sa 11:2
* rescue us from our enemies.' 1Sa 12:10
were * about six hundred left! 1Sa 13:15
"A command like that * hurts us. 1Sa 14:29
"It was * a little bit on the 1Sa 14:43
They destroyed * what was 1Sa 15:9
And it was * when my troops 1Sa 15:21
Jesse, who was not * a talented 1Sa 16:18
Jesse responded by sending not * 1Sa 16:20
"I was * asking a question!" 1Sa 17:29
You are * a boy and he has been 1Sa 17:33
bag and, armed * with his 1Sa 17:40
thousands and me with * thousands. 1Sa 18:8
David that the * dowry I need is 1Sa 18:25
discovered that it was * an idol! 1Sa 19:16
But the truth is that I am * a 1Sa 20:3
of the Lord not * to me during my 1Sa 20:14
meant; * Jonathan and David knew. 1Sa 20:39
you can have if * your young men 1Sa 21:4
and sheep. * Abiathar, one of the 1Sa 22:20
he learned that * nineteen men were 2Sa 2:30
It was * Amnon! 2Sa 13:32,33
It was * Amnon." 2Sa 13:32,33
He cut his hair * once a 2Sa 14:26
a year—and then * because it 2Sa 14:26
with me, you will * be a burden; 2Sa 15:33,34
and I will kill * the king, and 2Sa 17:2,3
will be looking * for you. 2Sa 18:3
If * I could have died for you! 2Sa 18:33
For all Israel is ready, and * 2Sa 19:11,12
could expect * death from you, but 2Sa 19:28
I would * be a burden to my lord 2Sa 19:35
the king because * men from Judah 2Sa 19:41
Another time, armed * with a 2Sa 23:21
Let your anger be * against me 2Sa 24:17
of Israel. * the tribe of Judah 1Ki 12:20
him, but he is the * member of your 1Ki 14:13
For this child is the * good 1Ki 14:13
Judah, but he reigned * two years. 1Ki 16:8
But Zimri lasted * seven days; 1Ki 16:15,16
And I have * a handful of flour 1Ki 17:12
"I am the * prophet of the Lord 1Ki 18:22
your prophets, and * I am left; 1Ki 19:10
"You must not * give me your 1Ki 20:5,6
on the plains. * this time replace 1Ki 20:24
say * what the Lord tells me to!" 1Ki 22:14
* what the Lord tells you to?" 1Ki 22:16
* enough to keep him alive 1Ki 22:27
in Edom at that time, * a deputy. 1Ki 22:47
But this is * the beginning, for 2Ki 3:18
finally, * Fort Kir-hareseth was 2Ki 3:25
"Feed one hundred men with * 2Ki 4:43
He is * trying to get an excuse 2Ki 5:7
reigned * one year, in Jerusalem. 2Ki 8:26
her, they found * her skull, her 2Ki 9:35
* those who worship Baal are here; 2Ki 10:23
but * for repairs to the building. 2Ki 12:13,14
now you will be victorious * 2Ki 13:19
So the old altar was used * for 2Ki 16:15
"will be * for my personal use." 2Ki 16:15
his sight until * the tribe of 2Ki 17:18
They were to worship * the Lord 2Ki 17:35,36
You must worship * the Lord; 2Ki 17:39
demand if you will * go away." 2Ki 18:14
speak * to you and to your master? 2Ki 18:27
because they were * things that men 2Ki 19:18
If the people of Israel will * 2Ki 21:8
and smiths. So * the poorest and 2Ki 24:14
Tabernacle. But * Aaron and his 1Ch 6:49
was Zelophehad, who had * 1Ch 7:15
But Benaiah went up to him with * 1Ch 11:23
and Eliezer's * son, Rehabiah, was 1Ch 23:17
no children; so * Eleazar and 1Ch 24:1
* give you what is yours already! 1Ch 29:14
But in the Temple * gold was 2Ch 4:19
measure. For * Judah and Benjamin 2Ch 11:12
not forsaken him. * the descendants 2Ch 13:10
They not * plundered the cities, 2Ch 14:15
to worship * the Lord God of their 2Ch 15:12
"O Lord God of our fathers—the * 2Ch 20:6
and his wives; * his youngest son, 2Ch 21:17
by God's laws. For * the priests 2Ch 23:5,6
God helped him not * with his 2Ch 26:7
for a long time; * a faithful few 2Ch 30:5f
Jerusalem to use * the one altar at 2Ch 32:12
MANASSEH WAS * twelve years old 2Ch 33:1
And if you will * obey my 2Ch 33:8
but * to the Lord their God. 2Ch 33:17
but he lasted for * two years. 2Ch 33:20,21
JOSIAH WAS * eight years old when 2Ch 34:1
I have come * to fight the king 2Ch 35:21
reign, but lasted * three months. 2Ch 36:2
But he lasted * three months and 2Ch 36:9
* to those who had forsaken him! Ez 8:22
You warned us that * if we Ez 9:12
* Jonathan (son of Asahel), Ez 10:15
night, taking * a few men with me; Neh 2:11,12
but from then on, * half worked Neh 4:16
* way you can save yourself!" Neh 6:7
was small; and * a few houses were Neh 7:4
you gave us * what we deserved. Neh 9:33
generous. The * restriction on the Est 1:8
has wronged not * the king but Est 1:16
the queen invited * me and the king Est 5:12
If we were * to be sold as Est 7:4
KING AHASUERUS NOT * laid tribute Est 10:1
I am the * one left." Job 1:14,15
replied; "* spare his life." Job 2:6
Shall we receive * pleasant Job 2:10
For if * I had died at birth, Job 3:13
be born if God is * going to give Job 3:23
commands it so! * he has stretched Job 9:8
I would * plead for mercy. Job 9:15
of death where * confusion reigns, Job 10:22
behind you. * then, without the Job 11:15
* then can you forget your misery. Job 11:16
their * hope is death." Job 11:20
* then will I be able to face you. Job 13:20
For him there is * sorrow and Job 14:22
he trusts in will be his * reward. Job 15:31
possessions. The * thing they can Job 15:35
give birth * to wickedness." Job 15:35
Even the wisest is of value * to Job 22:2
will * admit that you were wrong. Job 22:21
They not * don't know how to get Job 28:13
that line about '* God can convince Job 32:13
evil we have done; * tell us, and Job 34:32
at last, if you will * wait. Job 35:14,15
at the * one who can deliver you. Job 36:18
"* ask, and I will give you Ps 2:8
shield, my glory, and my * hope. Ps 3:3
And yet you have made him * a Ps 8:5
Or, "* a little lower than God!" Ps 8:5f
whose * goal in life is money. Ps 10:3
of the world whose * concern is Ps 17:13,14
help me to stop doing them. * Ps 19:13
* one from the power of the dog!" Ps 22:20f
Who may stand before the Lord? * Ps 24:4
I worship * you; Ps 31:5,6
to save us. * he can help us; Ps 33:2
Don't fret and worry—it * leads Ps 37:
every blessing. * a little while Ps 37:1
And so, Lord, my * hope is in Ps 39:
from me! My * hope is in your love Ps 40:1
For you are God, my * place of Ps 43:
For it is * by your power and Ps 44:
They could never save me. * you Ps 44:
* A FOOL would say to himself, Ps 53:
and save Israel! * when the Lord Ps 53:
You are the * hope of all mankind Ps 65:
Rush to my aid, for * you can Ps 70:
who * does wonderful things! Ps 72:1
Their present life is * a dream! Ps 73:2
nowhere on earth, but * from God. Ps 75:6,
But it was * with their words Ps 78:3
* then shall we be saved. Ps 80:
* then shall we be saved. Ps 80:
and love—* then shall we be saved. Ps 80:1
O Israel, if you will * listen! Ps 81:8
of the land of Egypt. * test me! Ps 81:10
if they will * stop their sinning. Ps 85:8
O Lord, for I worship * you. Ps 86:4
There is * darkness everywhere. Ps 88:18
weeds, there is * eternal Ps 92:7
Worship * him among the gods! Ps 96:4
them to my home. * those who are Ps 101:6
and were * visitors in Canaan. Ps 105:12
How can men be wise? The * way to Ps 111:10
evil, and walking * in his paths. Ps 119:3
If you will * help me to want Ps 119:32
for they are my * hope. Ps 119:43
servant, for they are my * hope. Ps 119:49,50
You are good and do * good; Ps 119:68
Help me, for you love * truth. Ps 119:85,86
And since * your rules can give Ps 119:104
promises are my * source of hope. Ps 119:114
They are * fooling themselves. Ps 119:118
I stand in awe of * your words. Ps 119:161
"Lord," I pled, "you are my * Ps 142:5
of refuge. * you can keep me safe. Ps 142:5
* fools refuse to be taught. Pro 1:7,8,9
* wisdom from the Lord can save a Pro 2:16,17
* good men enjoy life to the full; Pro 2:21
by my mother as an * child, and the Pro 4:3
But afterwards * a bitter Pro 5:4
say, "Oh, if * I had listened! Pro 5:12
* I had not demanded my own way! Pro 5:12
men, and not * listen but obey; Pro 7:24
with half a mind—if it is * open! Pro 8:9
you will * get a smart retort; Pro 9:7,8
he will * hate you for trying to Pro 9:7,8
scorn her, you hurt * yourself. Pro 9:12
A wise man holds his tongue. * a Pro 10:14
* leads to sorrow and trouble. Pro 10:14
The rich man's wealth is his * Pro 10:15
The poor man's poverty is his * Pro 10:15
Day; * righteousness counts then. Pro 11:4
the wicked can expect * wrath. Pro 11:23
success; * the godly have that. Pro 12:3
* a fool idles away his time. Pro 12:11
the evil-minded * wants to fight. Pro 13:2
* the person involved can know Pro 14:10
* a simpleton believes what he is Pro 14:15
* a fool despises his father's Pro 15:5
* the good can give good advice. Pro 15:7
and riches, but * the Lord can give Pro 19:14
* fools insist on quarreling. Pro 20:3
the simpleton can learn * by Pro 21:11
* a stupid prince will oppress Pro 28:16
with a fool. He * rages and scoffs, Pro 29:9
to increase knowledge * increases Ecc 1:16-18
experience the * happiness most men Ecc 2:3
This pleasure was, indeed, my * Ecc 2:10
This is not * foolish, but Ecc 2:20-23
heaven and you are * here on earth, Ecc 5:1
to his country! * he can bring Ecc 5:9
* of having a good time now. Ecc 7:4
(Of course, * God can see Ecc 8:16,17
There is hope * for the living. Ecc 9:4
a small city with * a few people Ecc 9:14
drink, and then * to strengthen Ecc 10:16,17
For the Preacher was not * a Ecc 12:10
he not * taught what he knew to Ecc 12:10
It was * a little while Sol 3:4
one, are the * one among them all, Sol 6:9
THE GIRL: "Oh, if * you were my Sol 8:1
If you will * let me help you, Is 1:19
* obey, then I will make you rich! Is 1:19
food and clothing; * let us be Is 4:1
hiding now. My * hope is in him. Is 8:17
man wastes away. * a few from all Is 10:19
the shore, yet * a few of them will Is 10:22
The desperate refugees take * Is 15:7
harvest it—your * harvest will be a Is 17:11
Kedar, will end. * a few of its Is 21:17
the story is the same—* a remnant Is 24:13
earnestly I seek for God; for * Is 26:9
But they won't listen; the * Is 28:11
* then will they listen to him! Is 28:11
of Israel, says: * in returning to Is 30:15

(ONLY Con't)
But the * swiftness you are Is 30:16
* the redeemed will travel there. Is 35:9
* joy and gladness will be there. Is 35:10
* at the altars here in Jerusalem? Is 36:7
and you will have * volunteer grain Is 37:30
The living, * the living, can Is 38:19
confess that * God can prophesy. Is 43:9
No, you have presented me * with Is 43:24
* God there is, is your God!" Is 45:14
No, for I, Jehovah, speak * truth Is 45:19
For I am God—I *—and there is no Is 46:9
lands today) * harlots were Is 47:2f
was * one when I called him. Is 51:1
they are stupid shepherds who * Is 56:11
your thoughts are * of sinning, Is 59:7
Yes, I will repay them— not * Is 65:7
No longer will babies die when * Is 65:20
* sinners will die that young! Is 65:20
I'm far too young! I'm * a Jer 1:6
Like a thief, the * shame that Jer 2:26,27
was * faked, the Lord God says. Jer 3:10
you. * acknowledge your guilt; Jer 3:13
It is all a farce. * in the Lord Jer 3:23
and weep bitterly as for an * son. Jer 6:26
these conditions *: If you stop Jer 7:5
Then, and * then, will I let you Jer 7:7
are saved!"—* to go right back to Jer 7:10
be my people; * do as I say and all Jer 7:23
health but there was * terror." Jer 8:15
where * jackals have their dens. Jer 9:11
circumcision is * a heathen rite Jer 9:25,26
But the Lord is the * true God, Jer 10:10
you will find * terrible darkness. Jer 13:16
* trouble and terror everywhere. Jer 14:19
talk some sense! * if you return to Jer 15:19
how bad it is! * the Lord knows! Jer 17:10
Am I a God who is * in one place Jer 23:23
you are doing. * then can you Jer 25:5
really sent him. * when his message Jer 28:9
"There is * fear and trembling. Jer 30:5
them, but * to do them good. Jer 32:40
Christ was the true vine, the * Jer 33:15f
usual schedule, * then will my Jer 33:20,21
and Azekah—the * walled cities of Jer 34:7
but the action was * temporary. Jer 34:10
written before, * this time the Jer 36:32
until there was * a handful of Jer 37:10
hands if * you will obey the Lord; Jer 38:20
so well, we are * a tiny remnant of Jer 42:2
"* those who return to Judah (it Jer 44:28
I will punish you, but * enough Jer 46:28
It is * the Lord's mercies that Lam 3:22
That is our * hope! Lam 5:21
And not * famine will come, but Eze 5:17
the wall, taking * what he can Eze 12:12
Those three * would be saved, but Eze 14:16
Lord God says that * they would be Eze 14:20
Of course not! I * want him to Eze 18:23
and let * a small quota return. Eze 20:37
of me, 'He * talks in riddles!' Eze 20:49
will think * of the times the Eze 21:23
tender cuts. Use * the best sheep Eze 24:5
You may sigh, but * quietly. Eze 24:17
But you are * a man, and not a Eze 28:2,3
'Abraham was * one man and yet he Eze 33:24
that you not * keep the best of the Eze 34:18
with people. Not * the people, but Eze 36:11
be their King, their * Shepherd; Eze 37:24
feet wide. The * difference was Eze 40:31
were 87½ feet long—* half as long Eze 42:7,8
beside mine, with * a wall between, Eze 43:8
remain shut. * the prince—because Eze 44:3
But he shall go and come * Eze 44:3
"They must wear * linen clothing Eze 44:17
He may marry * a Jewish maiden, Eze 44:22
It will be a seven-day feast. * Eze 45:21
may keep it * until the Year of Eze 46:17
* gifts to his sons are permanent. Eze 46:17
diet of * vegetables and water; Dan 1:12
steward fed them * vegetables and Dan 1:16
So they concluded, "Our * Dan 6:5
prince of Greece. * Michael, the Dan 10:20,21
over him and not * will her hopes Dan 11:6
will last for * a short while. Dan 11:24
hand, * to take advantage of them. Dan 11:34
but this will * refine and cleanse Dan 11:35
will understand. * those who are Dan 12:10
wild ass. The * friends she has are Hos 8:9
* hatred for those who love God. Hos 9:7
there has been * sin, sin, sin! Hos 10:9
The city that sends a hundred, * Amo 5:3
You say, 'If * the Day of the Amo 5:18
A man's uncle will be the * one Amo 6:10
he will ask the * one still alive Amo 6:10
sorrow, as if your * son had died; Amo 8:10
of which were * about eight miles Jon 3:3f
better days, but * bitterness Mic 1:12
The * commands you keep are those Mic 6:16
those of Omri; the * example you Mic 6:16
* the Lord, as you have vowed. Nah 1:15
* concern is your own fine homes. Hag 1:9
hearts—and not * your sacrifices, Hag 2:14
crop, there were * ten. Hag 2:16,17
olive press, there were * twenty. Hag 2:16,17
favor you if * you return to him. Zec 1:3
at ease, for I was * a little Zec 1:15
think of me, but * of the food and Zec 7:6
am worth; but * if you want to." Zec 11:12
for him as for an * son, and grieve Zec 12:10
day! * the Lord knows how! Zec 14:7
you will * kneel and worship me." Mt 4:9
"The Scriptures say, 'Worship * Mt 4:10
only the Lord God. Obey * him.' Mt 4:10
and tell you that if you are * Mt 5:22
If you love * those who love Mt 5:46
If you are friendly * to your Mt 5:47
are answered * by repeating them Mt 6:7,8
Truly, that is the * reward they Mt 6:16
Anyone who seeks, finds. If * you Mt 7:8
"Heaven can be entered * through Mt 7:13
narrow, and * a few ever find it. Mt 7:14
These leaders * quoted others, Mt 7:29f
If you will * stand here and say, Mt 8:8,9
the skins ruined. * new wineskins Mt 9:17
you will * come and touch her." Mt 9:18
I * touch him, I will be healed." Mt 9:21
she is * sleeping!" Mt 9:24
Samaritans, but * to the people of Mt 10:6
those who can kill * your Mt 10:28
your souls! Fear * God who can Mt 10:28
me by my Father. * the Father knows Mt 11:27
Father is known * by the Son and by Mt 11:27
for I give you * light burdens." Mt 11:29,30
* then can his demons be cast Mt 12:29
But Jesus replied, "* an evil, Mt 12:39,40
Then he explained to them that * Mt 13:11
To others they were * stories Mt 13:12,13f
And so he did * a few great Mt 13:58
And when they looked, * Jesus was Mt 17:8
said. "* those whom God helps. Mt 19:11
fellows worked * one hour, and yet Mt 20:11,12
but they * yelled the louder. Mt 20:31
any figs, but there were * leaves. Mt 21:19
obey them. Keep * these and you Mt 22:40
call you that. For * God is your Mt 23:8
as 'Father,' for * God in heaven Mt 23:9
'Master,' for * one is your master, Mt 23:10
But all this will be * the Mt 24:8
* the Father knows. Mt 24:36
bridegroom. But * five of them Mt 25:2,3,4
Does he think he is God? For * Mk 2:7
* priests were allowed to eat? Mk 2:25,26
In fact, he taught * by Mk 4:34
she is * asleep!" Mk 5:39
And this is * one example. Mk 7:12,13
your heart, but * passes through Mk 7:19
* one loaf of bread in the boat. Mk 8:14
You are looking at this * from a Mk 8:33
you will lose it. * those who throw Mk 8:35
gone, and * Jesus was with them. Mk 9:8
Jesus asked. "* God is truly Mk 10:18
"You lack * one thing," he told Mk 10:21
But he * shouted the louder, again Mk 10:48
But no, there were * leaves, for Mk 11:13
"If you * have faith in God—this Mk 11:22,23
same treatment, * worse, for his Mk 12:4
there was * one left—his only son. Mk 12:6
there was only one left—his * son. Mk 12:6
The Lord our God is the one and * Mk 12:29
there is * one God and no other. Mk 12:32
These herald * the early stages Mk 13:8
will happen; * the Father knows. Mk 13:32
clothed * in a linen nightshirt. Mk 14:51,52
Literally, "wearing * a linen Mk 14:51,52f
This statement is found in * some Mk 14:68f
They * roared the louder, Mk 15:14
saying, "I baptize * with water; Lk 3:16
I wish—if you will * get down on Lk 4:6,7
"Sir," he said, "if you * will, Lk 5:12
an old one. Not * will the new Lk 5:36
For they have their * happiness Lk 6:24
And if you do good * to those Lk 6:33
And if you lend money * to those Lk 6:34
over my men. I * need to say 'Go!' Lk 7:6,7,8
The boy who had died was the * Lk 7:12
with him, for his * child was Lk 8:42
she is * asleep!" Lk 8:52
Be a guest in * one home at each Lk 9:4
"Why, we have * five loaves of Lk 9:13
boy here is my * son, and a demon Lk 9:38
There is really * one thing Lk 10:42
but the * proof I will give Lk 11:29,30
They can * kill the body; Lk 12:4
wrong will be punished * lightly. Lk 12:48
Someone asked him, "Will * a few Lk 13:23
Otherwise he might complete * Lk 14:29
it with one for * 800 bushels!' Lk 16:7
Send Lazarus over here if * to Lk 16:24
"If your faith were * the size Lk 17:6
as being * "half-breed" Hebrews. Lk 17:16f
Does * this foreigner return to Lk 17:18
Jesus asked him. "* God is Lk 18:19
the man, but he * yelled the Lk 18:39
* the money he had started with. Lk 19:20
festival when * bread made without Lk 22:1
to the disciples—* to find them Lk 22:45
"You must be the * person in Lk 24:18
he was * a witness to identify Jn 1:8
was not accepted. * a few would Jn 1:11,12
—the glory of the * Son of the Jn 1:14
For Moses gave us * the Law with Jn 1:17
of course, his * Son has, for he is Jn 1:18
Men can * reproduce human life, Jn 3:6
in heaven? For * I, the Messiah, Jn 3:13
world so much that he gave his * Jn 3:16
for not believing in the * Jn 3:18
He replied, "If you * knew what Jn 4:10
Jerusalem is the * place of Jn 4:20
He does * what he sees the Father Jn 5:19
him, but represent * themselves! Jn 5:43
honor that comes from the * God! Jn 5:44
count of the men * was 5,000—sat Jn 6:10
the Father, for * I have seen him. Jn 6:46
return to heaven again? * the Jn 6:63
Those born * once, with physical Jn 6:63
she dies. But * he who never sinned Jn 8:7
the eldest, until * Jesus was left Jn 8:9
I won't, for I say * what I am told Jn 8:26
"Master," they said, "* a few Jn 11:8
and not stumble. * at night is Jn 11:10
Bethany was * a couple of miles Jn 11:18
again, if you will * ask him to." Jn 11:22
not be for Israel *, but for all Jn 11:52
all over needs * to have his feet Jn 13:10
to reveal yourself * to us Jn 14:22
Jesus replied, "Because I will * Jn 14:23
Instead you are * filled with Jn 16:6
knowing you, the * true God, and Jn 17:3
He * said, "If I want him to live Jn 21:23
and brought * part of the money, Act 5:2
Those who spoke * Greek Act 6:1
For they had * been baptized in Act 8:16
Jews are not God's * favorites! Act 10:34
the Good News, but * to Jews. Act 11:19
Yet * a few days later, some Jews Act 14:19
for we could * conclude that God Act 16:10
go * after they had posted bail. Act 17:8,9
put away idols and worship * him. Act 17:30
And this trend is evident not * Act 19:26
Of course, I am not * talking Act 19:27
worshiped not * throughout this Act 19:27
believers, but stayed * one day. Act 21:7
For I am ready not * to be jailed Act 21:13
your attention for * a moment as I Act 24:4
You are * hurting yourself.' Act 26:14
Phoenix was a good harbor with * Act 27:12
again, and found * ninety feet. Act 27:28
believe, for the * thing we know Act 28:22
for I want not * to share my faith Rom 1:11,12
his laws serve * to make us see Rom 3:20
And does God save * the Jews in Rom 3:29
In fact, * when we trust Jesus Rom 3:31
blessing given * to those who have Rom 4:9
rules, but * trust in Christ? Rom 4:9
to keep them. The * way we can keep Rom 4:15
desires within me! * if there were Rom 7:8
lower natures live * to please Rom 8:5
[For these promises are * to Rom 9:6
the promises apply * to Abraham's Rom 9:7
of God, but * those who believe the Rom 9:8
those who are fit * for Rom 9:22
of them, * a small number would Rom 9:27
never sin once, * then could he be Rom 10:5
Elijah claimed that he was the * Rom 11:2,3
God said, "No, you are not the * Rom 11:4
Remember that you are important * Rom 11:18
you are there * because you do. Rom 11:20
but this will last * until all of Rom 11:25
It is the * law you need. Rom 13:10
and I am not the * one who is Rom 16:4
but * want gain for themselves. Rom 16:18
they believe * what agrees with 1Co 1:22
* of what the Lord has done." 1Co 1:31
that I would speak * of Jesus 1Co 2:2
to him, because * those who have 1Co 2:14
For you are still * baby 1Co 3:3
We are * God's co-workers. 1Co 3:9
that you have * me as your father. 1Co 4:15
to each other. The * exception to 1Co 7:5
but * if she marries a Christian. 1Co 7:39
* his answer is the right one! 1Co 8:1
there is * one God, and no other. 1Co 8:4
But we know that there is * one 1Co 8:6
Do you suppose God was thinking * 1Co 9:9
In a race, everyone runs but * 1Co 9:24
Don't think * of yourself. 1Co 10:24
It is the same and * Holy Spirit 1Co 12:11
many parts make up * one body when 1Co 12:12
I am * an ear, and not an eye"? 1Co 12:16
would be if it had * one part! 1Co 12:19
but still there is * one body. 1Co 12:20
others, I would * be making noise. 1Co 13:1

(ONLY Con't)
see and understand * a little about 1Co 13:12
is of value to us * now in this 1Co 15:19
Ephesus—if it was * for what I gain 1Co 15:32
there * for a little while. 1Co 16:5
a task as this? * those who, like 2Co 2:17
* letter I need is you yourselves! 2Co 3:2
about ourselves * because of our 2Co 3:4
by ourselves. Our * power and 2Co 3:5
Not * Moses' face was veiled, but 2Co 3:14
removed * by believing in Christ. 2Co 3:14
to all that it is * the living 2Co 4:10
of Titus. Not * was his presence a 2Co 7:7
But it hurt you * for a little 2Co 7:8
They gave not * what they could 2Co 8:3
for you were not * the first to 2Co 8:10
come with me, * to find that you 2Co 9:4
few seeds will get * a small crop, 2Co 9:6
there will not * be enough for your 2Co 9:8
will be glad not * because of your 2Co 9:13
Their trouble is that they are * 2Co 10:12
love for one man *, for the one who 2Co 11:2
don't know; * God can answer that. 2Co 12:2,3
I am going to boast * about how 2Co 12:5
among you. The * thing I didn't do 2Co 12:13
And the * other apostle I met at Gal 1:19
the Jews. The * thing they did Gal 2:10
Jewish laws, but * by faith in Gal 2:16
came upon you * after you heard Gal 3:2
him fit for heaven * because he Gal 3:6
has said that the * way we can be Gal 3:11
of law was to last * until the Gal 3:19
its prisoners. The * way out is Gal 3:21,22
wife was born * after God had Gal 4:23
But it takes * one wrong person Gal 5:9
I * wish these teachers who want Gal 5:12
I advise you to obey * the Holy Gal 5:16
from the dead—* by his undeserved Eph 2:5
For us there is * one Lord, one Eph 4:5
Don't use bad language. Say * Eph 4:29
* what is good and right and true. Eph 5:9
Don't work hard * when your Eph 6:6,7
about Christ. * God knows how deep Php 1:8
the privilege not * of trusting him Php 1:29
That is the * true Php 3:3
found it to be the * way to really Php 3:10
leaving Macedonia, * you Php 4:15
you for; the * condition is that Col 1:23
hearts is your * hope of glory. Col 1:26,27
and I can do it * because Christ's Col 1:29
For these were * temporary rules Col 2:17
They were * shadows of the real Col 2:17
sinews and we grow * as we get our Col 2:19
desires. They * make him proud. Col 2:23
masters, not * trying to please Col 3:22
These are the * Jewish Christians Col 4:11
and true God * is your Master. 1Th 1:9
life—and he is our * Savior from 1Th 1:10
we gave you not * God's message, 1Th 2:8
God for you is not * the right 2Th 1:3
This is * one example of the 2Th 1:5
for he can come * when his time 2Th 2:6
Jesus Christ our Lord—* hope. 1Ti 1:1
He must have * one wife, and he 1Ti 3:2
Deacons should have * one wife 1Ti 3:12
will help you not * now in this 1Ti 4:8
* pure thoughts about them. 1Ti 5:2
gossiping, seeking * pleasure and 1Ti 5:6
old and have been married * once. 1Ti 5:9
But in other cases * the judgment 1Ti 5:24
and anger, which * lead to 1Ti 6:4
by the blessed and * Almighty God, 1Ti 6:15
* safe investment for eternity! 1Ti 6:19
and mine, and my * purpose in life 2Ti 1:3
die for Christ it * means that we 2Ti 2:11
arguments which * upset people and 2Ti 2:23
For people will love * 2Ti 3:2
to Dalmatia. * Luke is with me. 2Ti 4:11
they must have * one wife and Tit 1:6
Such teachers are * after your Tit 1:11
* to satisfy their stomachs." Tit 1:12
* right, but it brings results. Tit 3:8
isn't worthwhile; it * does harm. Tit 3:9
no longer * a slave, but something Phm 1:16
because he is not * a servant but Phm 1:16
No, for the angels are * Heb 1:14
in human form; for * as a human Heb 2:14
power of death. * in that way Heb 2:15
houses, but * God made everything. Heb 3:4
house, but he was * a servant; Heb 3:5
with faith. For * we who believe Heb 4:3
of soul to the * one who would save Heb 5:7
who can drink * milk, not old Heb 5:12,13
of other priests. * to Christ he Heb 7:21
their work. But * the high priest Heb 9:7
room, and then * once a year, all Heb 9:7
For the old system dealt * with Heb 9:10
The will goes into effect * Heb 9:17
that men die * once, and after that Heb 9:27
also Christ died * once as an Heb 9:28
Jewish laws gave * a dim foretaste Heb 10:1
says, "I will not * shake the Heb 12:26
* unshakable things will be left. Heb 12:27
men, he will not * remember it but Jas 1:25
that "* believing" is enough? Jas 2:19
that * good deeds will pour forth. Jas 3:13
* what will give you pleasure. Jas 4:3
but to obey it. * he who made the Jas 4:12
These trials are * to test your 1Pe 1:7
world began, but * recently was he 1Pe 1:20
Dear brothers, you are * visitors 1Pe 2:11
to do * God's will at all times. 1Pe 2:16
they tell you—not * if they are 1Pe 2:18
when you have * done what is good. 1Pe 3:16
the ark. Yet * eight persons were 1Pe 3:20
feel like; born * to be caught and 2Pe 2:12
a pig is washed * to come back and 2Pe 2:22
where there will be * goodness. 2Pe 3:13
no sin, we are * fooling ourselves, 1Jn 1:8
for our sins, and not * ours but 1Jn 2:2
good and does * right, we may 1Jn 2:29
that is why * those who have 1Jn 4:6
us by sending his * Son into this 1Jn 4:9
not * God, but his brother too. 1Jn 4:21
—yes, not * at his baptism but 1Jn 5:6,7,8
Literally, "not by water *, but 1Jn 5:6,7,8f
his Son, who is the * true God; 1Jn 5:20
He not * refuses to welcome the 3Jn 1:10
Follow * what is good. 3Jn 1:11
* Master and Lord, Jesus Christ. Jud 1:4
They are not * dead, but doubly Jud 1:12
for others, it is * to get Jud 1:16
further of you; * hold tightly to Rev 2:24,25
* then will you truly be rich. Rev 3:18
Their power of death was not * Rev 9:19
and * he knew its meaning. Rev 19:12
or dishonest—but * those whose Rev 21:27

ONO
Shemed (who built * and Lod and 1Ch 8:12
of Lod, Hadid, and *, 725; Ez 2:3-35
of the villages in the Plain of *. Neh 6:2
of Lod, Hadid, and *, 721; Neh 7:8-38
* (the Valley of the Craftsmen). Neh 11:31-35

ONSLAUGHT
king against any * in the night. Sol 3:8

ONTO
to get his donkey * its feet Ex 23:5
if any blood sprinkles * their Lev 6:27
and lead them up * Mount Hor. Num 20:25
Balaam beat her back * the road. Num 22:22,23
an ox or donkey * its feet when it Deu 22:4
cakes, and packed them * donkeys. 1Sa 25:18
bowels gushed out * the ground. 2Sa 20:8,9,10
running down * the floorboards. 1Ki 22:35
head, and ran down * his beard, and Ps 133:2
and * the border of his robe. Ps 133:2
forth their waters * the earth; Pro 8:24
* anything with oil-slick hands. Pro 27:16
The gods are falling out * the Is 46:1
and drag you out * the land with Eze 29:4
will swoop down * the land of Eze 38:8
walls, opening * this pavement. Eze 40:17
out 10½ feet * the terrace. Eze 41:8
he drags it up * the beach and sits Mt 13:47,48
Then he threw the money * the Mt 27:5
and be driven up * the beach. Act 27:39
heat, fastened itself * his hand! Act 28:3
help him back * the right path, Gal 6:1
and descended * the earth and were Rev 9:3
* the earth with all his army. Rev 12:9
down from heaven * earth—he accused Rev 12:10
fell from the sky * the people Rev 16:21

ONWARD
Israel journeyed *, following it. Ex 40:36
the eighth day * it is acceptable Lev 22:26,27
signal to break camp and move *. Num 10:5,6,7
him great power from that day *. 1Sa 16:13
the righteous shall move * and Job 17:9
God my King moves * to the Ps 68:24
"And from that time *, the Eze 39:22
"The Syrian king will march * Dan 11:16
* swept the raging water. Hab 3:10
from this day *, I will bless you. Hag 2:18,19
he moved steadily * towards Lk 9:51
pressing * toward Jerusalem. Lk 13:22
As they continued * toward Lk 17:11

ONYCHA
spices—stacte, *, galbanum, and Ex 30:34

ONYX
fragrant incense, * stones, stones Ex 25:1
Take two * stones, and engrave Ex 28:9
The fourth row will be an *, a Ex 28:20
settings of the * stones on the Ex 28:25
* stones and stones to be used for Ex 35:5-9
The leaders brought * stones to Ex 35:27
* stones, attached to the [two Ex 39:6,7
In the fourth row, a beryl, an * Ex 39:13
quantities of *, other precious 1Ch 29:2
or precious * stones or sapphires. Job 28:16
chrysolite, *, jasper, sapphire, Eze 28:13

OOZED
over it as the entrails * out. Ju 3:22,23

OPEN
its fruit will * your eyes to make Gen 2:16,1
an * field, waiting to be watered. Gen 29
and the sea will * up a path before Ex 14:1
living bird fly into the * field. Lev 14
into an * field outside the city. Lev 14:5
sacrificing in the * fields, and to Lev 17
and all who have * sores, or who Num 5:
suddenly split * beneath them, and Num 16:3
The man whose eyes are * says, Num 24:3-
Whose eyes are *! Num 24:15-1
He will * to you his wonderful Deu 28:1
the city gates were left wide *. Jos 8:1
are camping out in * fields, and 2Sa 11:1
designs of rosebuds and * flowers. 1Ki 6:1
palm trees, and * flowers were 1Ki 6:2
* flowers, all overlaid with gold. 1Ki 6:3
Angels, palm trees, and * 1Ki 6:3
May your eyes be * and your ears 1Ki 8:5
an * meeting of all the people; 1Ki 12:2
Then Elisha prayed, "Lord, * his 2Ki 6:1
* their eyes and let them see." 2Ki 6:2
the rocks, and rip * the bellies of 2Ki 8:1
"* that eastern window," he 2Ki 13:16,1
and ripped * the pregnant women. 2Ki 15:1
Bend low, O Lord, and listen. * 2Ki 19:1
full regalia at an * place near the 2Ch 18:
to meet him at the * space east of 2Ch 29:4,
in the * space before the Temple; Ez 10:
came with an * letter in his hand Neh 6:5,6
to them not to * the Jerusalem Neh 7:3
My flesh breaks *, full of pus. Job 7:5
"WHY DOESN'T GOD * the court and Job 24:1
They waited eagerly with * Job 29:23
Their young grow up in the * Job 39:4
He who avenges murder has an * Ps 9:12
They come at me with * jaws, Ps 22:13
* up, O ancient gates, and let Ps 24:7
Yes, * wide the gates and let Ps 24:9
me * ground in which to maneuver. Ps 31:8
I will not * my mouth to speak Ps 39:9
* your ears to what I am saying. Ps 78:1
He split * the rocks in the Ps 78:15
the skies to *—he opened the Ps 78:23
* your mouth wide and see if I Ps 81:10
GOD STANDS UP to * heaven's court. Ps 82:1
Go through his * gates with great Ps 100:4
gather it. You * wide your hand to Ps 104:28
* the gates of the Temple Ps 118:19
to obey you. * my eyes to see Ps 119:18
earth were broken * by his Pro 3:20
with half a mind—if it is only *! Pro 8:9
The depths of hell are * to God's Pro 15:11
The intelligent man is always * Pro 18:15
* rebuke is better than hidden Pro 27:5
your ears * and your mouth shut! Ecc 5:1
my bedroom door. '* to me, my Sol 5:2
I jumped up to * it and my hands Sol 5:5
* his mouth to peep against us!" Is 10:14
it lies in an * grave, covered Is 14:19
his salvation!" * the gates to Is 26:2
eyes of Israel will * wide to God; Is 32:3
And when he comes, he will * Is 35:5
of surrender; * the gates and come Is 36:16
I will * up rivers for them on Is 41:18
You will * the eyes of the Is 42:7
God shall * the gates of Babylon Is 45:1
these things. * up, O heavens. Is 45:8
Come to me with your ears wide *. Is 55:3
Your gates will stay wide * Is 60:11
and to * the eyes of the blind. Is 61:1
enemy shall break * the graves of Jer 8:1
If you stumble and fall on * Jer 12:5
are closed and none can * them." Jer 13:19f
or in the * country down below. Jer 17:2,3
be plowed like an * field and this Jer 26:18
Send an * letter to all the Jer 29:31
for your eyes are * to all the Jer 32:19
break * her granaries; Jer 50:26
Don't you be a rebel too! * your Eze 2:8
for your sins are * and unashamed. Eze 21:24
rocks in * view for all to see; Eze 24:7
therefore I will * up the eastern Eze 25:9,10
Those living in the * fields Eze 33:27
My people, I will * your graves of Eze 37:12
will fall upon the * fields; Eze 39:5
of the building * to the public." Eze 42:14
miles for a city * to everyone in Eze 45:6
six work days but * on the Sabbath Eze 46:1
1½ miles square. * land for Eze 48:17
It is * to anyone working in the Eze 48:19
as he could to the * door of the Dan 3:26
with its windows * toward Dan 6:10
and * his court of justice and Dan 7:26
listen to my plea. * your eyes and Dan 9:18
to me, committing * adultery Hos 1:2
women ripped * with a sword. Hos 13:16
crimes, ripping * pregnant women Amo 1:13
and become an * field, her streets Mic 1:6
The river gates are *! Nah 2:6
All her cedar paneling will lie * Zep 2:14

(OPEN Con't)
* YOUR DOORS, O Lebanon, to Zec 11:1
if you do, I will * up the Mal 3:10
you will knock, the door will *. Mt 7:8
and whatever doors you * on earth Mt 16:19
on earth shall be * in heaven!" Mt 16:19
in a line, and * the mouth of the Mt 17:26,27
and rip * the backs of others with Mt 23:34
calling, 'Sir, * the door for us!' Mt 25:11
he saw the heavens * and the Holy Mk 1:10
he sighed and commanded, "*!" Mk 7:34
Why don't you * your ears and Mk 8:18
moved away and the entrance was *! Mk 16:4
No, lamps are mounted in the * Lk 8:16
received him with * arms, for they Lk 8:40
Then you will be ready to * the Lk 12:36
pleading, 'Lord, * the door for Lk 13:24,25
would come and lick his * sores. Lk 16:21
You will even see heaven * and Jn 1:51
welcomed him with * arms, for they Jn 4:45
men, but he has * ears to those who Jn 9:31
* the eyes of someone born blind. Jn 9:32
Can a demon * the eyes of blind Jn 10:21
THEN PILATE LAID * Jesus' back Jn 19:1
burst *, spilling out his bowels. Act 1:18
He saw the sky *, and a great Act 10:11
a girl named Rhoda came to * it. Act 12:13
all the doors flew *—and the chains Act 16:26
prison doors wide *, and assuming Act 16:27
Beroea were more * minded than Act 17:11
the Gentiles to * their eyes to Act 26:18
like the stench from an * grave. Rom 3:13
Literally, "Their throat is an * Rom 3:13f
one who is * to God's knowledge. 1Co 8:3
there is a wide * door for me to 1Co 16:9
Keep your eyes * for spiritual 1Co 16:13
the doors of welcome were wide *. 2Co 6:2
own children. * your hearts to us! 2Co 6:13
Please * your hearts to us 2Co 7:2
Once I was in the * sea all night 2Co 11:25
the way of escape is * to all who Gal 3:21,22
is bare and wide * to the Heb 4:13
their backs cut * with whips, and Heb 11:36
and * up a profitable business." Jas 4:13
And God will * wide the gates of 2Pe 1:11
key of David to * what no one can Rev 3:7
and to shut what no one can *. Rev 3:7
a door standing * in heaven, and Rev 4:1
was permitted to * and read it. Rev 5:3
himself worthy to * the scroll and Rev 5:5
and break its seals and * it; Rev 5:9
second seal, and broke it * too. Rev 6:3
And when he broke * the fifth Rev 6:9
And he held * in his hand a Rev 10:2
in heaven was thrown wide *! Rev 15:5
they stay * all day long—and Rev 21:25

OPEN-AIR
images, and the * sanctuaries in Num 33:52

OPENED
your eyes will be *—you will be Gen 3:5
Tubal-cain. He * the first foundry Gen 4:22
After another forty days, Noah * Gen 8:6
Noah * the door to look, and the Gen 8:13
Then God * her eyes and she saw a Gen 21:19
the world, Joseph * up the Gen 41:56,57
and one of them * his sack to get Gen 42:27
for the night and * our sacks, and Gen 43:21
backs of their donkeys and * them. Gen 44:11
When she * it, there was a baby! Ex 2:6
sea, and the Lord * up a path Ex 14:21
Then the Lord * Balaam's eyes and Num 22:31
I fell, and my eyes were *: Num 24:3-9
He fell, and his eyes were *: Num 24:15-19
But the earth * and swallowed Num 26:5-11
and the earth * up and swallowed Deu 11:6
And when they * the door, they Ju 3:25
When her husband * the door to Ju 19:27
morning, then * the doors of the 1Sa 3:15
seven times and * his eyes! 2Ki 4:35
And the Lord * the young man's 2Ki 6:17
Lord * the windows of heaven!" 2Ki 7:19
Then he * the door and ran. 2Ki 9:10
and they * the gates each morning. 1Ch 9:27
So the crowd * up for them to 2Ch 23:15,16,17
"The money chests have been * 2Ch 34:17
Everyone stood up as he * the Neh 8:1
be * until the Sabbath had ended; Neh 13:19
stranger but have * my doors to Job 31:32
skies to open—he * the windows of Ps 78:23
from heaven. He * up a rock, and Ps 105:41
Because of this the earth * and Ps 106:17
The Jordan River * up a path for Ps 114:3
Praise the Lord who * the Red Ps 136:13
* to my beloved, but he was gone. Sol 5:6
the blossoms have * and whether the Sol 7:12
rooms, too, and * to them all his Is 39:2
The Lord has * his armory and Jer 50:25
the heavens were suddenly * to me Eze 1:1
Two doors * from the tiers of Eze 41:11
it shall never be *. Eze 44:2
gate shall be * up for him to enter Eze 46:12
its session and The Books were *. Dan 7:10
of Days came and * his court and Dan 7:22
The gates of your land will be * Nah 3:13
a Fountain will be * to the people Zec 13:1
Then they * their presents and Mt 2:11
the heavens were * to him and he Mt 3:16
Knock, and the door will be *. Mt 7:7
broke, and tombs *, and many godly Mt 27:52
had * up access to the holy God. Mk 15:38f
the heavens *, and the Holy Spirit Lk 3:21
* it to the place where it says: Lk 4:17
knock and the door will be *. Lk 11:9
and the door is * to everyone who Lk 11:10
eyes were *—they recognized him! Lk 24:31
Then he * their minds to Lk 24:45
"This man who * your eyes—who do Jn 9:17
came at night, * the gates of the Act 5:19
* the gates, no one was there!" Act 5:23
heavens * and Jesus the Messiah Act 7:56
shearers, so he * not his mouth; Act 8:32
and she * her eyes! Act 9:40
this * to them of its own accord! Act 12:10
When they finally went out and * Act 12:16
how God had * the door of faith to Act 14:27
to us, the Lord * her heart and she Act 16:14
in a row he * the Scriptures to the Act 17:2
the following day * Paul's trial. Act 25:6
But God has * the eyes of those 1Co 1:24
which Christ has * up for us by Heb 10:20
Therefore I have * a door to you Rev 3:8
When he * it, smoke poured out Rev 9:2
temple of God was * and the ark of Rev 11:19
Then I saw heaven * and a white Rev 19:11
and The Books were *, including Rev 20:12

OPENING
was sitting in the * of his tent, Gen 18:1
with an * for Aaron's head. Ex 28:32
band around this *, just as on the Ex 28:32
was a five-sided *, and its two 1Ki 6:31
of Israel at the * where the lower 2Ch 18:33
where I made out an * in the wall. Eze 8:7
a 10½-foot doorway * into a 14-foot Eze 40:7-12
the walls, * onto this pavement. Eze 40:17
through an * in the city wall! Act 9:25
but the earth helped her by * Rev 12:16

OPENLY
*, in the sight of all Israel.' 2Sa 12:12
No one rebukes him *. Job 21:30-32
* strikes them down as wicked men. Job 34:26
His pride in other gods has * Hos 7:10
his friend, I will * acknowledge Mt 10:32
denies me, I will * deny him before Mt 10:33
up to the Temple and preached *. Jn 7:14
of sin, and God * displayed to the Col 2:15

OPENS
Literally, "all that * the Ex 34:19f
and the ground * up and swallows Num 16:30
If it accepts the truce and * Deu 20:11
* into the wilderness of Jeruel. 2Ch 20:16
on their beds. He * their ears in Job 33:16
He frees the prisoners, and * Ps 146:8
I am the Lord, who * a way Is 43:16
* my understanding to his will. Is 50:4
"He who * the breach." Mic 2:13f
The gatekeeper * the gate for Jn 10:3
me calling him and * the door, I Rev 3:20

OPERATED
They arrived at an inn * by a Jos 2:1

OPERATING
the * expenses of the Temple. 1Ch 26:27

OPERATION
incredible rescue * God will 2Ch 20:17
not by a bodily * of circumcision Col 2:11
*, the baptism of your souls. Col 2:11

OPHEL
The Temple attendants living in * Neh 3:26
Tower and over to the wall of *. Neh 3:27
Ziha and Gishpa) all lived in *. Neh 11:21

OPHIR
Sheba, *, Havi-lah, Jobab. Gen 10:26-30
and forth from *, bringing gold to 1Ki 9:27,28
to Solomon from *, they also 1Ki 10:11
freighters to sail to * for gold; 1Ki 22:48
Sheba, *, Havilah, and Jobab. 1Ch 1:20-23
worth of gold from * and 1Ch 29:4,5
men, went to * and brought back 2Ch 8:17,18
*, also sandalwood and jewels. 2Ch 9:10
all the gold of * or precious onyx Job 28:16
jewelry of finest gold from *. Ps 45:9
greater value than the gold of *. Is 13:12

OPHNI
Chephar-ammoni, *, Geba, Gibeon, Jos 18:21-28

OPHRAH
Avvim, Parah, *, Chephar-ammoni, Jos 18:21-28
the oak tree at *, on the farm of Ju 6:11
(The altar is still there in * Ju 6:24
from the gold and put it in *, Ju 8:27
*, in the land of the Abiezrites. Ju 8:32
father's home at * and there, upon Ju 9:5
one went toward * in the land of 1Sa 13:17
Meonothai was the father of *; 1Ch 4:14

OPINION
"What is your *?" 2Sa 17:6
Lord's *, just like his ancestors. 2Ki 15:9
was an evil man, in God's *. 2Ki 21:6
and asked the * of the young men 2Ch 10:8,9
the Lord's * of him was concerned. 2Ch 26:4
one in the Lord's *, just as his 2Ch 29:2
me awhile and let me express my *. Job 32:10
Literally, "express his *." Pro 18:2f
Yet in his own * he is smarter Pro 26:16
In my *, nothing is worthwhile; Ecc 1:2
discouraged *, and do not reflect a Ecc 9:5f
discouraged *, and do not reflect a Ecc 9:5f
discouraged *, and do not reflect a Ecc 9:10f
a deep division of * among them. Jn 9:16
divided in their * about them. Act 14:4
But in my * he has done nothing Act 25:25
But in my * she will be happier 1Co 7:40
If in the * of others, I am not 1Co 9:2
"If he disagrees, ignore his *." 1Co 14:38f
in my *, a very faithful brother. 1Pe 5:12

OPINIONS
going to waver between two *?" 1Ki 18:21
no end of * ready to be expressed. Ecc 12:12
You aren't influenced by the * Mk 12:14
the * of others as his authority. Lk 4:32
divided in their * about him. Jn 10:19
And I'm not merely quoting the * 1Co 9:8
their * in church meetings. 1Co 14:35

OPPONENT
Each one grabbed his * by the 2Sa 2:16

OPPONENTS
saves me from these powerful *. Ps 18:48
disputes between powerful *. Pro 18:18
of your * will be able to reply! Lk 21:15

OPPORTUNITIES
nighttime, with its * for crime. Job 36:20
They keep a sharp lookout for * Ps 64:6
our * for doing the Lord's work 1Co 7:29
* without stopping to enjoy them; 1Co 7:31
tremendous * to preach the Gospel. 2Co 2:12
gives us constant * to show forth 2Co 4:11
For to me, living means * for Php 1:21
will give me more * to win people Php 1:22

OPPORTUNITY
give you an * to prove yourselves. Gen 42:18
will give me the * of doing mighty Ex 11:9
For God wanted to give * to the Ju 3:1
"Here's another * to see him 1Sa 18:21
But you have given great * to 2Sa 12:14
and happy for this * of service, 1Ch 29:9
I took the * to inquire about how Neh 1:2
Because he stole at every *, his Job 20:21
lad who sleeps away his hour of *. Pro 10:5
your * is blown away like chaff; Zep 2:2
This will give you the * to tell Mt 10:18
for an * to betray Jesus to them. Mt 26:16
This is your * to tell them the Mk 13:9
looking for an * to arrest Jesus Mk 14:1
rejected the * God offered you." Lk 19:44
Watching their *, they sent Lk 20:20
So he began to look for an * for Lk 22:6
Herod was delighted at the * to Lk 23:8
you another * to believe in me. Jn 11:15
Peter saw his * and addressed the Act 3:12
would have an * for repentance, and Act 5:31
He is given an * to defend Act 25:16
praying for is the *, God willing, Rom 1:10
the Gentiles the * to be acquitted Rom 9:30
you later on when he has the *. 1Co 16:12
be wise: make the most of every * Eph 5:15,16
me and gave me the * to boldly 2Ti 4:17
* for endurance and confidence. Rev 13:10

OPPOSE
eat up the nations that * him; Num 24:3-9
No one will be able to * you as Jos 1:5
Who destroys those who * me 2Sa 22:48
to continue to * him will be Est 6:13
the nations who * him, but his own Ps 33:10
No one can * what I do. Is 43:13
You lie and grumble and * the Is 59:3
Our courts * the righteous man; Is 59:14
What ruler can * my will? Jer 50:44
destroy all who * him, though their Dan 8:24
Antioch I had to * him publicly, Gal 2:11

OPPOSED
Levite * this course of action. Ez 10:15
Jerusalem. So I * them publicly. Neh 13:15
all the forces * to them, and to Est 8:11
Who has ever * him successfully? Job 9:4
crushed everyone who has * them. Is 37:11
of the forces * to God, especially Eze 38:2,3f
But when the Jews * him and Act 18:6
"I have not * the Jewish laws or Act 25:8
I was so violently * to them that Act 26:11
that had been * to each other and Eph 2:15

OPPOSES
For if the majesty of God * me, Job 31:23

OPPOSING
Anyone * you will die. Is 41:11
I know the slander of those * Rev 2:9

OPPOSITE
and the sea, * Baal-zephon, and to Ex 14:2
loops on each side, * each other. Ex 26:4,5
each loop being * its mate on the Ex 36:11,12
of the Jordan River * Jericho. Num 22:1
the Jordan River, * Jericho. Num 26:3,4
the river Jordan, * Jericho. Num 33:48
side of the Jordan, * Jericho." Num 34:14,15
* Jericho, the Lord said to Moses, Num 35:1
toward Gilgal, * the slopes of Jos 15:7
(which is * the slope of Adummim). Jos 18:17
each other on * hills, with the 1Sa 17:3
Jonathan sat * him and Abner was 1Sa 20:24,25
He and David were now on * sides 1Sa 23:26
the mountain slope * the camp until 1Sa 26:13
each other on * sides of the pool. 2Sa 2:13
The two armies camped * each 1Ki 20:29
And across the Jordan River, * 1Ch 6:78,79
* of what they are telling you!" 2Ch 18:22
from a point * the door of Neh 3:21
the section * the Castle Tower and Neh 3:27
immediately * his own house. Neh 3:28
Guild Hall, * the Muster Gate; Neh 3:31
lines to walk in * directions along Neh 12:31,32
I make wise men give * advice to Is 44:25
what appeared to be a city * me. Eze 40:2
On the * side of the Temple a Eze 42:9,10
must always use the * passageway. Eze 46:9
of the wall * the lampstand. Dan 5:5
Just the *! Rom 3:31
that are just the * from the things Gal 5:17
just the * of our natural desires. Gal 5:17
But just the * happened: those Heb 10:3
OPPOSITION
the city without *, and slaughtered Gen 34:25
so Omri reigned without *. 1Ki 16:22
of Ephraim also added their *. 2Ch 28:12
Then all * will be swept away Dan 11:22
their prey. All * melts away Hab 1:9
you never end your * to the Lord? Act 13:10
OPPRESS
"You must not * a stranger in Ex 22:21
"Do not * foreigners; Ex 23:9
"You shall not rob nor * anyone, Lev 19:13
And shall * both Eber and Assyria. Num 24:23,24
he shall choose, and do not * him. Deu 23:15,16
"Never * a poor hired man, Deu 24:14,15
right to you to * and despise me, a Job 10:3
Don't let the proud * me! Ps 119:122
Only a stupid prince will * his Pro 28:16
when they * you just as the Is 10:24
against the wicked who * them. Is 11:4
against those who * them, he will Is 19:20
use to * the poor in the courts. Is 32:7
You murder the innocent, * the Jer 22:17
Even the common people * and rob Eze 22:29
My princes shall no longer * and Eze 45:8
that will bitterly * you from your Amo 6:14
hired hands, or * widows and Mal 3:5
OPPRESSED
will be * as slaves in a foreign Gen 15:13
mistreated and * them, the more the Ex 1:12
the Egyptians have * them with. Ex 3:9
you will be * and robbed Deu 28:29
You will always be * and crushed. Deu 28:33
Have I ever * you? 1Sa 12:3
never defrauded or * us in any way 1Sa 12:4
King Hazael of Syria had * Israel 2Ki 13:22
And Asa * all the people at that 2Ch 16:10
For he has * the poor and Job 20:19
hears the cries of those being *. Job 34:28
profit him. The * may shriek Job 35:9,10
All who are * may come to him. Ps 9:9
and all who are *, so that mere Ps 10:18
defend the *, the poor, the needy. Ps 12:5
hated them and * by their enemies. Ps 106:41,42
and *, and food to the hungry. Ps 146:7
give justice to those who are *. Pro 31:5
tears of the *, and no one helping Ecc 4:1
If you see some poor man being * Ecc 5:8
again, and * without excuse? Is 52:5
He was * and he was afflicted, Is 53:7
and widows are wronged and *. Eze 22:7
a bitter pill for the poor and *. Amo 5:7
severely with all who have * you. Zep 3:19
against the nations that * you, Zec 2:8
OPPRESSES
Anyone who * the poor is Pro 14:31
When a poor man * those even Pro 28:3
adultery, and * the poor and Eze 18:12
OPPRESSING
by robbery, or by * his neighbor, Lev 6:2
the king of Syria was * Israel. 2Ki 13:4
humble when evildoers are * them. Ps 14:6
See them * your people, O Lord, Ps 94:5
He who gains by * the poor or by Pro 22:16
you keep right on * your workers. Is 58:3
is that you stop * those who work Is 58:6
All you need to do is to stop * Is 58:9
Tell them to stop * widows and Zec 7:10
while,' and begin * your fellow Mt 24:49

OPPRESSION
toil, and *, and brought us out of Deu 26:6,7
Why must I mourn at the * of my Ps 43:2
do you ignore our sorrows and *? Ps 44:24
He will save them from * and Ps 72:14
But others become poor through *, Ps 107:39
Rescue me from the * of evil Ps 119:134
NEXT I OBSERVED all the * and Ecc 4:1
the cries of deep * met his ears. Is 5:7
the fire of *, you will not be Is 43:2
dread of men's *, and fear their Is 51:13
into its walls and * into its Jer 22:13
The idolatry and * centering in Mic 1:5
Wherever I look there is * and Hab 1:3
deserts for your * and extortion!' Hab 2:6
OPPRESSIONS
his people under their crushing *; Ju 2:18
OPPRESSORS
poor from the grasp of these *. Job 5:15
of the godless * and made them drop Job 29:17
and needy and to crush their *. Ps 72:4
of their * were powerful allies. Ecc 4:1
exile I asked no fee from your *; Is 52:3
them from the hands of their *. Is 63:4
me, poor and needy, from my *. Jer 20:13
I will not clear their * of Joe 3:21
no foreign * will again overrun Zec 9:8
freed from their *, and that God is Lk 4:18,19
ORACLE
chestpiece to be used as God's *; Ex 28:15
heart (it is God's *) when he goes Ex 28:29
be carrying the * over his heart Ex 28:30,31
Or, "of King Lemuel the *." Pro 31:1f
thirteen years after this * Is 7:8f
ORAL
to the king for * exams, as he had Dan 1:18,19
ORALLY
confirm * what we have decided Act 15:26
ORATOR
I'm no *!" Ex 6:12
he became a mighty prince and *. Act 7:22
Literally, "*." Act 24:1f
ORATORS
He takes away the voice of *, Job 12:20
ORATORY
not with a lot of * and human 1Co 2:4
ORCHARD
A workman may eat from the * he Pro 27:18
the finest in the * as compared Sol 2:3
You are like a lovely * bearing Sol 4:13,14
Literally, "Your shoots are an * Sol 4:13,14f
went down into the * of nuts and Sol 6:11
ORCHARDS
gardens, parks and * for myself, Ecc 2:4,5,6
vineyards and her *—gifts she Hos 1:12
ORCHESTRA
with singing and * and harp? Gen 31:27
singers into an *, and they played 1Ch 15:16
accompanied by an * leading the 2Ch 23:12
Temple, accompanied by the *." Is 38:20
ORCHESTRAL
the Temple into an * group, using 2Ch 29:25,26
ORCHESTRAS
men's and women's choirs and *. Ecc 2:7,8
grand parties; the * are superb! Is 5:12
ORDAIN
the way you shall * Aaron and his Ex 29:35
ORDAINED
"Today you have * yourselves for Ex 32:29
This is the burnt offering * at Num 28:6
on the hills and * priests from the 1Ki 12:31
in Jerusalem, which God had *. 1Ki 12:32,33f
at Bethel that he * priests for the 1Ki 12:32,33
in the manner * by King David. Ez 3:10
Literally, "the Law as it was * Act 7:53f
that Jesus is * of God to be the Act 10:42
Or, "were disposed to," or, "* Act 13:48f
ORDER
placed the wood in *, ready for the Gen 22:9
Here is a list, in the * of their Gen 25:12-15
seated them in the * of their ages, Gen 43:33
Pharaoh sent this * to the Ex 5:6
of Levi, in the * of their ages: Ex 6:16
the Egyptians in * to deliver Ex 18:8
named in the * of their births. Ex 28:10
All was done in the * designated Ex 38:21
in * to make atonement for them. Lev 8:34
the priest shall * the suspected Lev 13:54
The priest shall then * one of Lev 14:5
"The priest shall * the house to Lev 14:36
the priest shall * the removal of Lev 14:40
Then he shall * the inside walls Lev 14:41
Then he shall * the destruction Lev 14:45
That was the * in which the Num 10:28
* to go around the land of Edom. Num 21:4
* water to come out of the rock." Num 27:14
* to get directions from the Lord. Num 27:21
in * to be made ceremonially pure; Num 31:23
must die, in * to purge the evil Deu 24:7
So Joshua issued the *. Jos 4:17
have obeyed every * I have given Jos 22:2,3

you—every * of the Lord your God. Jos 22:2
men of Benjamin in * to give the Ju 20:35-
And he has set the world in *. 1Sa 2
in * to show my joy in the Lord. 2Sa 6:
in * to bring glory to your name. 2Sa 7:
He did it in * to place the 2Sa 14:
wives to keep the palace in *. 2Sa 15:
affairs in *, and hanged himself; 2Sa 17:2
king to do this in * to fulfill his 1Ki 12:1
tents were all in *, but there was 2Ki 7:
"Set your affairs in * and 2Ki 20
against Judah in * to destroy the 2Ki 24
The descendants of Buz, in the * 1Ch 5:1
assigned (by coin-toss) in this *: 1Ch 24:7-1
(God caused him to do it in * to 2Ch 10:1
of Ramah in * to control the road 2Ch 16:
him to himself in * to test him and 2Ch 32:3
He issued this * to the 2Ch 35:
You punished them in * to turn Neh 9:2
of the land in * to serve God. Neh 10:2
guard the gates in * to preserve Neh 13:2
the emperor's * to Queen Vashti, Est 1:1
reversing Haman's * to destroy the Est 8:
to *, who is going to stop him? Job 11:1
yes, he may * them made by his Job 27:1
Must he change the * of the Job 34:3
"Law and * have collapsed," Ps 11:
For you have issued the * to save Ps 71:
Only he can bring * from this Ecc 5:
"Set your affairs in *, for you Is 38:1
* with the other messages. Jer 35:1
"But again I refrained in * to Eze 20:14
The old * changes. Eze 21:26
that even the new * that emerges Eze 21:27
chunk in whatever * it comes—for Eze 24:6
So at last the king gave the * Dan 6:16
Literally, "in * to fulfill the Dan 11:14
must come and set everything in *. Mt 17:11
about Jesus, in * to build a case Mt 26:59
And Pilate issued an * to release Mt 27:58
So we request an * from you Mt 27:64
the law of God in * to protect your Mk 7:12,13
all publicity in * to spend more Mk 9:30,31
their sins, in * to be forgiven. Lk 3:3
They kept begging him not to * Lk 8:31
"Master, shall we * fire down from Lk 9:54
Get your report in *, for you are Lk 16:2
and great men * their slaves Lk 22:25
water in * to point him out to Jn 1:31
"What right have you to * them Jn 2:18
asked Pilate to * the legs of the Jn 19:31
* to deport all Jews from Rome. Act 18:2,3
Possibly in * to arrive in Act 18:20f
truth in * to draw a following. Act 20:30
to Phoenix, in * to winter there; Act 27:12
of little worth in * to shame those 1Co 1:27
I am not giving you an *; 2Co 8:8
be circumcised in * that they can Gal 6:13
than nothing, in * that I can have Php 3:8
to live on, in * that we would not 2Th 3:8
We work hard and suffer much in * 1Ti 4:9,10
care of them in * that we may 3Jn 1:8
ORDERED
Joseph then * his servants to Gen 42:25
Joseph * his household manager to Gen 44:1
he * Moses arrested and executed. Ex 2:15
Then the Lord * Moses and Aaron Ex 6:13
have eaten it there, as I * you." Lev 10:18
So Moses * the judges to execute Num 25:5
'Speak of it no more,' he *, Deu 3:26
In the morning Joshua * the Jos 3:6
out who isn't here," Saul *. 1Sa 14:17
the king shouted. He * his 1Sa 22:17
So David * his young men to kill 2Sa 4:12
*, "but he must never come here. 2Sa 14:24
priest," the king *, "and Nathan 1Ki 1:32
low to her. He * that a throne for 1Ki 2:19
Then King Ahab * Micaiah's 1Ki 22:26
the mountain. He * his men to bring 2Ki 23:16
but David * them burned. 1Ch 14:12
King David also * the Levite 1Ch 15:16
Then David * all the leaders of 1Ch 22:17
Micaiah (son of Imlah)," he *. 2Ch 18:8
son Joash," the king of Israel *. 2Ch 18:25
King Joash himself * him executed 2Ch 24:21
Then King Joash * two hundred 2Ch 25:23
Then Hezekiah * the burnt 2Ch 29:27
Then King Hezekiah * the Levites 2Ch 29:30
I have * a search made of the Ez 4:19
make her happy; he * a special menu Est 2:9
and he * the gallows built. Est 5:14
to read awhile. He * the historical Est 6:1
"Bring him in," the king *. Est 6:5
Haman has just * a 75-foot gallows Est 7:9
"Hang Haman on it," the king *. Est 7:9
the fact that they * God away and Job 21:14
the tree has * it destroyed. Jer 11:17
King Zedekiah had * everyone to Jer 34:9
Then he * Ashpenaz, who was in Dan 1:3,4
exams, as he had been * to do. Dan 1:18,19
who had been * to execute the wise Dan 2:24

RDERED Con't)
a terrible rage, * Shadrach, Dan 3:13
Belshazzar * that these sacred Dan 5:2,3,4
with joy and * that Daniel be Dan 6:23
And the Lord * the fish to spit Jon 2:10
sun was hot, God * a scorching east Jon 4:8
"I have * an end to your dynasty; Nah 1:14
to Bethlehem, he * them to kill Mt 2:16
If you are * to court, and your Mt 5:40
He couldn't pay, so the king * Mt 18:25
that evening and * many demons to Mk 1:34
And he * Jesus flogged with a Mk 15:15
But Jesus * the demon to come Lk 9:42
standing by he *, 'Take the money Lk 19:24
everyone to sit down," Jesus *. Jn 6:10
the angel *. Act 12:8
and the judges * them stripped and Act 16:22
He quickly * out his soldiers Act 21:32
The commander arrested him and * Act 21:33
* Paul to be taken to the armory. Act 21:34
him inside and * him lashed with Act 22:24
he had * him bound and whipped. Act 22:29
his chains and * the chief priests Act 22:30
tear him apart, * his soldiers to Act 23:10
his officers and *, "Get 200 Act 23:23,24
So that night, as *, the soldiers Act 23:31
told him, and * him kept in the Act 23:35
the case. He * Paul to prison but Act 24:23
next day and * Paul brought in. Act 25:17
to Caesar! So I * him back to jail Act 25:21
city, Festus * Paul brought in. Act 25:23
Then he * all who could swim to Act 27:43
unfit and * to stand aside. 1Co 9:27
And he * the people of the world Rev 13:14
Then the statue * that anyone Rev 13:15

RDERING
one who sinned by * the census. 1Ch 21:17
by * me struck like that?" Act 23:3

RDERLY
done properly in a good and * way. 1Co 14:40
*, and full of good deeds. 1Ti 3:2

RDERS
has given * to furnish you with no Ex 5:10,11
* to return to the wilderness. Num 14:41
* to the priests carrying the Ark. Jos 4:15,16
I'm the one who gives the * 2Sa 13:28
given me strict * not to eat 1Ki 13:9
The king then issued * for his 2Ki 23:21
SO KING DARIUS issued * that a Ez 6:1
to obey the king's *, properly sent Est 1:13-15
*, just as she had in his home. Est 2:20
For he * his angels to protect Ps 91:11
who carry out his *, listening for Ps 103:20
He sends his * to the world. Ps 147:15
His * will never be revoked. Ps 148:6
For every official is under * Ecc 5:8
fulfilling their *, I was alone. Eze 9:8
and sent out * to execute all the Dan 2:12
mighty army and they follow his *. Joe 2:11
Then Amaziah sent * to Amos, Amo 7:12
guests, he issued the necessary *. Mt 14:9
even evil spirits obey his *!" Mk 1:27
For you ignore God's specific * Mk 7:8
He gave them strict * not to Lk 9:21
the Lord has given * that those who 1Co 9:14
under his Father's *, so that God 1Co 15:28
I went there with definite * Gal 2:2

ORDINANCE
This is a permanent * for Aaron Ex 28:43
This is a permanent *—the lamb, Eze 46:14,15

ORDINANCES
all of my laws and *, and you must Lev 18:26
commandments and *, carefully Lev 19:37
all of my laws and * so that I will Lev 20:22
These were the laws, *, and Lev 26:46
specified by the * governing them. Num 29:6
These are the commandments and * Num 36:13
commandments and * which the Lord Deu 26:16
keep his laws and *, and to heed Deu 26:17
of the laws and * of God, you are 2Ch 19:10
keep my *; Eze 20:19
Literally, "* by which they could Eze 20:25f

ORDINARY
in an * way, with interest. Ex 22:25
and remember, none of the * Ex 24:2
ceremony). The * people shall not Ex 29:33
be poured upon an * person, and you Ex 30:32
holy and what is *, what is pure Lev 10:10
locusts of all varieties—* Lev 11:21,22
leprosy, but an * infection that Lev 13:39
defile himself as an * person can. Lev 21:4
in verse 1 applied to * priests. Lev 21:11f
Tabernacle like an * house, for the Lev 21:12
blood—half priestly and half *." Lev 21:14,15
must not treat me as common and *. Lev 22:32,33
and all * work shall cease. Lev 23:7
treat him as an * slave, but Lev 25:39
so you may not be sold as * Lev 25:42
* people entered the Tabernacle." Num 8:19
Each sacrifice—whether an * one, Num 15:3,4
death or from some * accident or Num 16:29
God of heaven, not just an * god. Jos 2:11
Lord's people sin. * sin receives 1Sa 2:23,24,25
stay clean even on * trips, how 1Sa 21:5
himself by wearing * clothing 1Sa 28:7,8
in an * soldier's uniform. 1Ki 22:30
Many * people as well as Ez 7:7,8,9
Here is the list of * citizens Ez 10:25
the * citizens, for registration. Neh 7:5
fate is the same as that of * men. Eze 32:24
Others said, "But how could an * Jn 9:16
When the * people of Jerusalem Jn 12:9
but enjoy the company of * folks. Rom 12:16
and also in * language that 1Co 14:15
and also in * language, so that I 1Co 14:15
are merely those of an * man. 2Co 10:2
It is true that I am an *, weak 2Co 10:3
I'm not talking about these * 1Jn 5:17

ORDINATION
is the ram for * of Aaron and his Ex 29:22
breast of Aaron's * ram and wave it Ex 29:26
ram used in the * ceremony—and boil Ex 29:31
This * shall go on for seven days. Ex 29:35

OREB
by going across. * and Zeeb, the Ju 7:25
were captured. * was killed at the Ju 7:25
took the heads of * and Zeeb across Ju 7:25
let you capture * and Zeeb, the Ju 8:2,3
their mighty nobles die as * did, Ps 83:11
at the rock of * or the time God Is 10:26

OREN
Ram (the oldest), Bunah, *, Ozem, 1Ch 2:25

ORGANIZATIONAL
he followed the * chart prepared by 2Ch 8:14

ORGANIZE
Levite leaders to * the singers 1Ch 15:16
Amaziah did was to * the army, 2Ch 25:5,6

ORGANIZED
the men who had * the Num 7:2
He * his army into regiments to 2Ch 26:11
He * Levites at the Temple into 2Ch 29:25,26
Hezekiah now * the priests and 2Ch 31:2
They * a huge work crew to block 2Ch 32:4
as first * by King David of Israel 2Ch 35:4,5
When everything was *, and the 2Ch 35:10
In the cultural arts, I * men's Ecc 2:7,8
armed and * militiamen" Rev 9:16f

ORGANS
of male and female genital *. Ex 34:13f
The internal * and the legs are Lev 1:9
But the internal * and the legs Lev 1:13
the internal *, the two kidneys Lev 3:9,10,11
legs, internal *, and Lev 4:11,12
fat upon the inner *, the gall Lev 8:25
covering the inner *—and the Lev 9:19
the hides and internal *. Lev 16:27

ORGIES
and of having * on the mountains. Jer 3:23

ORIENTAL
Literally, "kiss"—the usual * Mk 14:44f

ORIGEN
Some expositors (*, Jerome, Rev 1:20f

ORIGIN
So that is the * of the 1Sa 10:12
(That is the * of the saying, 2Sa 5:8
is of satanic *, as most Rev 9:1f

ORIGINAL
was included in the * rental fee. Ex 22:15
to the * owners or their heirs. Lev 25:10
home to his * family possession; Lev 25:13
But if the * owner is not able Lev 25:28
* owner in the Year of Jubilee. Lev 25:30
* owner in the Year of Jubilee. Lev 25:31
* owners in the Year of Jubilee; Lev 25:33
* owner from whom it was bought. Lev 27:24
then both the * and the Lev 27:33
The * text repeats the lists of Num 7:18-23f
The * text repeats the lists of Num 7:24-29f
The * text repeats the lists of Num 7:30-35f
The * text repeats the lists of Num 7:36-41f
The * text repeats the lists of Num 7:42-47f
The * text repeats the lists of Num 7:48-53f
The * text repeats the lists of Num 7:54-59f
The * text repeats the lists of Num 7:60-65f
The * text repeats the lists of Num 7:66-71f
The * text repeats the lists of Num 7:72-77f
The * text repeats the lists of Num 7:78-83f
and 62, where the * text indicates Jos 15:48-62f
* manuscript indicates sub-totals. Jos 18:21-28f
6 and 7 of the * manuscript, where Jos 19:2-7f
is indicated in the * text. Jos 21:9-16f
were the * people of that land. Ju 1:31,32
The text is uncertain in the * 2Sa 1:21f
* inhabitants of the land—lived. 1Ch 11:4
to half its * height around the Neh 4:6
(They used the * musical Neh 12:35,36
phrase was part of the * text. Ps 49:20f
and are not in the * text. Sol 1:1f
times as much as the * amount! Lk 19:16
gain—five times the * amount. Lk 19:18
* Olympic races of Paul's time. 1Co 9:25f
of the old * Benjamin family. Php 3:5
Or, "who abandoned their * rank Jud 1:6f

ORIGINALLY
had been assigned * to the tribes Jos 21:4
but it had * been called Laish. Ju 18:29
(He was * from the hill country Ju 19:16
Temple duties as * assigned by God 1Ch 24:19
Tyre was * a colony of the Is 23:1f
Tyre was * a colony of the Is 23:4f
It was * called Lebo-Hamath. Eze 47:15f
was not what God had * intended. Mt 19:8
home of Mnason, * from Cyprus, one Act 21:16

ORION
He made the Bear, * and the Job 9:9
Can you restrain * or Pleiades? Job 38:31
the constellation *, who turns Amo 5:8

ORNAMENT
You will use it as an *! Ps 76:10
Literally, "be an * to your Pro 3:22f
plague of scabs to * their heads! Is 3:17

ORNAMENTED
More literally, "an * tunic," or Gen 37:3f

ORNAMENTS
themselves of their jewelry and *. Ex 33:4
Remove your jewelry and * until I Ex 33:5
the * from their camels' necks. Ju 8:21
With fine clothing and golden *. 2Sa 1:24
rows of * an inch or two apart, 1Ki 7:24
Literally, "*." Sol 1:10f
beauty and their *, their Is 3:18
as jewels to display, as bridal *. Is 49:18
I gave you lovely *, bracelets Eze 16:11
gold and silver * I gave to you and Eze 16:17

ORNAN
threshing-floor of * the Jebusite. 1Ch 21:15
threshing-floor of * the Jebusite. 1Ch 21:18
So David went to see *, who was 1Ch 21:19,20
wheat at the time. * saw the angel 1Ch 21:19,20
Then * saw the king approaching. 1Ch 21:21
David said to *, "Let me buy 1Ch 21:22
it as you wish," * said to David. 1Ch 21:23
So David paid * $4,300 in gold, 1Ch 21:25
of * the Jebusite had been. 2Ch 3:1

ORNAN'S
THEN DAVID SAID, "Right here at * 1Ch 22:1

ORNATE
and capes and * combs and purses; Is 3:22
to pieces; her * idol temples, Mic 1:7

ORPAH
married girls of Moab, * and Ruth. Ru 1:4,5
together, and * kissed her Ru 1:14

ORPHAN
foreigner, the *, and the widow.' Deu 27:19
a helpless *, or selling a friend. Job 6:27
advantage of an * because I thought Job 31:21

ORPHANED
married their * niece Milcah, Gen 11:29

ORPHANS
must not exploit widows or *; Ex 22:22
or to widows and * within your Deu 14:29
foreigners, widows, and *. Deu 16:11
*, and widows of your town. Deu 16:14
to migrants and * and you must Deu 24:17
Leave it for the migrants, *, and Deu 24:19
for the migrants, *, and widows. Deu 24:20
Levites, migrants, *, and widows, Deu 26:12
the migrants, the *, and the Deu 26:13
them, and broke the arms of *. Job 22:9
food to hungry *— (but we have Job 31:17
always cared for * in our home, Job 31:18
You will be with the * and all Ps 10:18
immigrants, and *, for "The Lord Ps 94:6,7
and cares for the * and widows. Ps 146:9
of defenseless * by moving their Pro 23:10,11
and won't defend the widows and *. Is 1:23
the widows and *, for they are all Is 9:17
for the poor, the widows and *. Is 10:2
They refuse justice to * and the Jer 5:28
*, widows and foreigners. Jer 7:6
and immigrants, * and widows; Jer 22:3
We are *—our fathers dead, our Lam 5:3
your 'protection'; * and widows are Eze 22:7
widows and *, foreigners and poor Zec 7:10
oppress widows and *, or defraud Mal 3:5
* in the storm—I will come to you. Jn 14:18
who takes care of * and widows, and Jas 1:27

ORTHODOX
and * Christianity ever since. Is 52:13f

ORTHODOXY
to test Jesus' * by asking him this Lk 10:25

OSNAPPAR
great and noble * and relocated in Ez 4:10

OSPREY
The eagle, the metire, the *, Lev 11:13-19
The *, the buzzard, Deu 14:11-18

OSTENSIBLY
This inquiry was perhaps * to 1Ki 21:9f

OSTRICH
The raven (all kinds), the *, Lev 11:13-19
The *, the nighthawk, Deu 14:11-18
"The * flaps her wings grandly, Job 39:13
mournful as an * crying across the Mic 1:8

OSTRICHES
to jackals and a companion to *. Job 30:28,29
howling creatures. * will live Is 13:21
haunt of jackals and a home for *. Is 34:13
the jackals and * too, for giving Is 43:20
become inhabited by * and jackals; Jer 50:39
They are like cruel desert *, Lam 4:3,4

OTHERWISE
whether in innocent fun or * is Gen 21:9f
one people. * we will take her and Gen 34:17
*, disaster will surely strike." Gen 41:36
be on our way; * we will all die of Gen 43:8
ahead of us. * you will come to Gen 45:11,12
profane his name; * they will be Lev 21:6
food again. But *, no one who is Lev 22:13
each is to carry. * they must Num 4:20
is * dead, or has touched a grave. Num 19:18
away from me; * I would certainly Num 22:33
close to everyone; * the angry Deu 19:6,7
it right away; * he may cry out to Deu 24:14,15
*, she stopped urging her. Ru 1:18
wilderness beyond; * he will die, 2Sa 17:16
how could it be *, for they stand 1Ki 10:8
Can anyone claim *? Job 24:25
Those who declare * are my Job 27:7
* my enemies will conquer me. Ps 5:8
and faithfulness. * I perish, for Ps 40:12
in verse 14, as * the Matthew Is 7:14f
of your hearts; * the good seed Jer 4:3
and live, for * this whole city Jer 27:17
shall be given two sections. *, Eze 47:14
Keep alert and pray. * Mt 26:41
life—* he cannot be my disciple. Lk 14:26
to pay the bills? * he might Lk 14:29
* the statement would be, "He had Lk 20:37,38f
If I said *, I would be as great Jn 8:55
of this idea, * obscure. Jn 16:26f
* you might fall back into sin. 1Co 7:2
Christian husband. *, if the family 1Co 7:14
what it wants to. * I fear that 1Co 9:27
that might * seem less important. 1Co 12:24
and comfort him. * he may become so 2Co 2:7
him in everything. *, if they Heb 10:38
this or that." * you will be Jas 4:16
* would be dark and difficult. 2Pe 1:19

OTHNI
*, Repha-el, 1Ch 26:6,7

OTHNI-EL
Kiriath-sepher. * (son of Kenaz), Jos 15:17
Caleb's nephew, *, son of his Ju 1:13
Caleb's nephew, * (son of Kenaz, Ju 3:9
Then, for forty years under *, Ju 3:11
But when * died, the people of Ju 3:11
* and 1Ch 4:13
in the area of *, who commanded 1Ch 27:15

OTHNI-EL'S
it, so Achsah became * wife. Jos 15:17
* sons were Hathath and 1Ch 4:13

OUGHT
to think, 'We * to have a king like Deu 17:14
It's obvious what we * to do!" Ju 18:14
I swear by the Lord that you * to 1Sa 26:16
Literally, "No such thing * to be 2Sa 13:12f
thinking how I * to build a Ps 132:2-5
know which way I * to turn to miss Ps 142:3
Literally, "standing where he * Mk 13:14f
you * to wash each other's feet. Jn 13:14
They replied, "By our laws he * Jn 19:7
were there (who * to be here if Act 24:19
"I used to believe that I * to Act 26:9
Pay everyone whatever he * to Rom 13:7
blessings, they * also to be of Rom 15:27f
But if anyone feels he * to marry 1Co 7:36
Literally, "For this cause * the 1Co 11:10f
I think you * to know, dear 2Co 1:8
who * to give me greatest joy. 2Co 2:3
you people * to be writing about me 2Co 12:11
Meanwhile, I thought I * to send Php 2:25
For you well know that you * to 2Th 3:7
drinking wine. You * to take a 1Ti 5:23
Leave nothing undone that you * 2Ti 4:5
place of rest—we * to tremble with Heb 4:1
time now, and you * to be teaching Heb 5:12,13
as strong Christians * to be. Heb 6:1
What you * to say is, "If the Jas 4:15
And so we also * to lay down our 1Jn 3:16
surely * to love each other too. 1Jn 4:11

OUNCE
silver shekel (about half an *); Eze 45:12
I promise this with every * of 2Co 11:10

OUNCES
which weighed only about six *. Num 7:14
weighing about four * apiece); Num 7:84,85,86
eight * at a time, one meal a day. Eze 4:10

OURSELVES
—someone like *, Gen 1:26
We will trade * for food, then we Gen 47:19
ones, but we * will go over armed, Num 32:17
we kept the cattle and loot for *. Deu 3:7
plenty of food and wine for *." Ju 19:19
do for you, to rid * of this guilt 2Sa 21:3
We have no way to protect * 2Ch 20:12
we would humble * before our God; Ez 8:21
and rid * of this disgrace!" Neh 2:17
city day and night to protect *. Neh 4:9
we could never get it done by *. Neh 4:10
We also agreed to charge * Neh 10:32
must define among * what is good. Job 34:4
* from all this slavery to God." Ps 2:3
And now we see it for *! Ps 48:8
Let us examine * instead, and Lam 3:40
let's kill him and get it for *!' Mt 21:38
"For we * have heard him say Lk 22:71
we have heard him *, not just Jn 4:42
others such as *, who have been Rom 9:23,24
live or die as we * might choose. Rom 14:7
go ahead and do them to please *; Rom 15:1
other fellow, not *, and do what is Rom 15:1
And why should we * be 1Co 15:30
well go and have * a good time: let 1Co 15:32
how powerless we were to help *; 2Co 1:9
Only those who, like *, are men 2Co 2:17
good things about * only because of 2Co 3:4
do anything of lasting value by *. 2Co 3:5
*, but about Christ Jesus as Lord. 2Co 4:5
All we say of * is that we are 2Co 4:5
Are we trying to pat * on the 2Co 5:12
insane [to say such things about * 2Co 5:13,14
We have proved * to be what we 2Co 6:6
spirit, and purify *, living in the 2Co 7:1
of God, giving * to him alone. 2Co 7:1
right even if we * are despised. 2Co 13:7
to each other we are hurting *. Eph 4:25
that we are helpless to save *. Php 3:3
you about what we * have actually 1Jn 1:3
are only fooling *, and refusing to 1Jn 1:8
By looking within *: are we 1Jn 2:3
So we * should take care of them 3Jn 1:8

OUTBREAK
the place "The * Against Uzza." 1Ch 13:11

OUTCAST
Now you are called "The *" and Jer 30:17
You will die like an * at the Eze 28:10

OUTCASTS
that the men of Gilead were mere * Ju 12:4
of no name, * of civilization. Job 30:8
Let our * stay among you; Is 16:4,5
brings back the * of Israel says, I Is 56:8

OUTCOME
When the news of the * of the 2Sa 4:4
Syria, with the * still uncertain; Ps 60:1
but the final * is in God's hands. Pro 16:1

OUTCROP
rocks, behind an * of the cliff. Sol 2:14

OUTCRY
there was a great * of protest from Neh 5:1

OUTDO
for us, let us * each other in Heb 10:24

OUTDOORSMEN
"Rejoice, O Zebulun, you *, Deu 33:18

OUTER
other on the * side of the veil. Ex 26:35
flame in the * holy room, tending Ex 27:21
the * top edge of the chestpiece. Ex 28:22,23,24
and his linen * garments and clean Lev 6:10
"When we arrive at the * Ju 7:17
the * edge of the camp of Midian. Ju 7:19,20
of the Temple against the * walls. 1Ki 6:5
room, but not from the * court; 1Ki 8:8
his plans for the * court, the 1Ch 28:12
floor facing the * room, with wings 2Ch 3:11,12,13
of the * room of the Temple. 2Ch 4:10
be seen from the * room, but not 2Ch 5:9
the center of the * court, in front 2Ch 6:12,13
Everyone else must stay in the * 2Ch 23:5,6
around the altar in the * court. 2Ch 23:10
had reached the * court, which took 2Ch 29:17
he rebuilt the * wall of the City 2Ch 33:14
"Who is on duty in the * Est 6:4
arrived in the * court of the Est 6:4
of gold, with an * cloak of fine Est 8:15
be heard clear out in the * court. Eze 10:5
"the * court" of the Temple Eze 40:19
as the passageways of the * wall. Eze 40:28
Its entry hall faced the * court Eze 40:34
faced toward the * court, and it Eze 40:37
the terrace. The * wall of these Eze 41:9
overlooking the * court on one Eze 42:3
as those in the * court were, the Eze 42:6
The north tiers, next to the * Eze 42:7,8
entrance from the * court to these Eze 42:9,10
the Temple and the * court, Eze 42:9,10
And there was a door from the * Eze 42:12
before going out to the * court. Eze 42:14
the * wall leading to the east. Eze 43:1
me back to the * wall's eastern Eze 44:1
When they return to the * court, Eze 44:19
through the * court, in case they Eze 46:19,20
Then he brought me out to the * Eze 46:21,22
be cast into * darkness, into the Mt 8:12
him out into the * darkness where Mt 22:13
servant out into * darkness: there Mt 25:30
as long as the * room and the Heb 9:
"But do not measure the * Rev 11:

OUTFITTED
military officers, * in striking Eze 23:14,1

OUTLAWED
Lord shall be * from his people. Lev 7:2
"Sexual intercourse is * between Lev 20:1
in the streets, and justice is *. Is 59:1
or other foods * in Leviticus. Dan 1:8

OUTLET
He camped near the * of the upper Is 36:

OUTLINE
* our case against this man. Act 24:

OUTLINED
handle the situation as * above. Num 5:3

OUTLYING
with all of its * villages. Jos 10:3
conquer the Negeb's * villages. Ob 1:2

OUTNUMBER
for the wicked far * the righteous, Hab 1:4

OUTPOST
at the time; an * of the 1Ch 11:16

OUTPOSTS
to the * of the enemy camp. Ju 7:11

OUTRAGE
it was an * against all of them. Gen 34:6,7

OUTRAGED
and insulted and * the Holy Spirit Heb 10:29

OUTRAN
* Peter and got there first, and Jn 20:3,4

OUTRANK
I alone will * you." Gen 41:40

OUTRUN
horsemen can't * the danger then. Amo 2:15

OUTSIDE
went * and told his two brothers. Gen 9:22
Then God brought Abram * beneath Gen 15:5
or bought from *—and cut off their Gen 17:23
Lot stepped * to talk to them, Gen 19:6
them to safety, * the city, for the Gen 19:16
down * the town, beside a spring. Gen 24:11
why stand here * the city when we Gen 24:31
than to someone * the family." Gen 29:19
in Canaan, and camped * the city. Gen 33:18
the city and * in the fields, and Gen 34:28
waiting for them * the palace, as Ex 5:20
none of you shall go * all night. Ex 12:22
in one house, and not carry it *; Ex 12:46
Overlay it inside and * with Ex 25:11
the rings at the * corner of the Ex 25:26,27
skin and the dung, * the camp and Ex 29:14
Place the altar just * the veil, Ex 30:6
he called it) far * the camp, and Ex 33:7
around the * of the tent, and hang Ex 40:8
side of the room * the veil, and Ex 40:22
and placed the * altar for the Ex 40:29
clean place * the camp—a place Lev 4:11,12
the young bull * the camp and burn Lev 4:21
carry the ashes * the camp to a Lev 6:11
dung, was burned * the camp, as the Lev 8:17
the meat and hide * the camp. Lev 9:11
and carry them * the camp." Lev 10:4
defiled and must live * the camp. Lev 13:46
however, he must stay * his tent Lev 14:8
into a defiled place * the city. Lev 14:40
in a defiled place * the city. Lev 14:41
into an open field * the city. Lev 14:53
shall be carried * the camp and Lev 16:27
is married * the tribe, she may not Lev 22:12
gold which stands * the veil that Lev 24:3,4
Moses, "Take him * the camp and Lev 24:13,14
Let her be confined * the camp Num 12:14
stone him to death * the camp." Num 15:35
So they took him * the camp and Num 15:36
he shall take her * the camp and Num 19:1
purified place * the camp, where Num 19:9
Now stay * of the camp for seven Num 31:19
avenger finds him * and kills him, Num 35:27
shall be taken * the city and shall Deu 17:5
her shall be taken * the gates and Deu 22:23,24
and stay * until the evening; Deu 23:11
The toilet area shall be * the Deu 23:12
Stand *! Deu 24:11
widow must not marry * the family; Deu 25:5
*, the enemies' sword— Deu 32:25
them to live * the camp of Israel. Jos 6:23
all the men * the city, they went Jos 8:24
he started home again. But * the Ju 3:17,18,19
and cursed are right * the city! Ju 9:38
He married his daughters to men * Ju 12:9,10
men standing just * the gate, they Ju 18:15,16
The old man stepped * to talk to Ju 19:23
step * the city on pain of death. 1Ki 2:36,37
took Shime-i * and killed him. 1Ki 2:46
But when it became light *, I saw 1Ki 3:21
decorated on the * with wreaths. 1Ki 7:31
The priests have to go * because 1Ki 8:11
and he was dragged * the city and 1Ki 21:13
lick your blood * the city just as 1Ki 21:19
morning and went *, there were 2Ki 6:15
lepers sitting * the city gates. 2Ki 7:3

UTSIDE Con't)
all and dragged their bodies *. 2Ki 10:25
the Kidron Valley * Jerusalem, and 2Ki 23:4
it * Jerusalem to Kidron Brook; 2Ki 23:6
outer court, the * rooms, the 1Ch 28:12
room, but not from the * doorway. 2Ch 5:9
be made and set * the Temple gate. 2Ch 24:7,8
to plug the springs * the city. 2Ch 32:3
constructing a second wall * it. 2Ch 32:5
and dumped them * the city. 2Ch 33:15
from the plains * the city. Neh 3:22
I told everyone living * the Neh 4:22
charge of the work * the Temple; Neh 11:15,16,17
tradesmen camped * Jerusalem once Neh 13:20
Then he stood * the gate of the Est 4:2
Mordecai just * the palace gates, Est 4:6
children with those * your home? Pro 5:17
gates, or waits for me * my home! Pro 8:34
"If I go * I might meet a lion Pro 22:13
"There might be a lion *!" Pro 26:13
Assyrian officers * your walls are Is 33:18
there, nor march * its gates, nor Is 37:33
And the Babylonians * the walls Jer 32:29
The next day, before the * world Jer 41:4
If you go * the walls, there Eze 7:15
Bring your baggage * your house Eze 12:4
I brought my pack * in the Eze 12:7
and needy suffered * her door. Eze 16:49
wall around the * of the Temple Eze 40:5
Then he measured the entire * Eze 40:13
the * doors of the guardrooms; Eze 40:13
in the Temple. * the entry hall, Eze 40:40
inside and four *, where the Eze 40:41
with a row of rooms along the *. Eze 41:5
appointed place * the Temple area. Eze 43:21
The prince shall enter the * Eze 46:2
Then he brought me * the wall Eze 47:2
a tenth of a mile. * the city, Eze 48:18
of its inhabitants to venture *; Mic 1:11f
of its inhabitants to venture *; Mic 1:11f
dare not show themselves * their Mic 1:11
of its inhabitants to venture *; Mic 1:11f
Many will live * the city walls, Zec 2:4
When the crowd was finally *, Mt 9:25
his mother and brothers were *, Mt 12:46,47
Then, leaving the crowds *, he Mt 13:36
to polish the * of the cup, but the Mt 23:25
they stood *, calling, 'Sir, open Mt 25:11
gathered * the door to watch. Mk 1:32,33
person more, not even * the door. Mk 2:2
"Your mother and brothers are * Mk 3:31,32
are hidden to those * the Kingdom: Mk 4:11,12
in the street, tied * a house. Mk 11:4,5
Meanwhile, a great crowd stood * Lk 1:10
Meanwhile the crowds * were Lk 1:21
were in the fields * the village, Lk 2:8
they were standing * and wanted to Lk 8:20
Pharisees wash the *, but inside Lk 11:39
make the inside as well as the *? Lk 11:40
Then if you stand * knocking, and Lk 13:24,25
teeth as you stand * and see Lk 13:28
escape, and those * the city must Lk 21:21
Now Jesus had stayed * the Jn 11:30
while Peter stood * the gate. Jn 18:16
Pilate went * again and said to Jn 19:4
and was standing * crying. Jn 20:11
Just * that door are the young Act 5:9
were standing *, but when we opened Act 5:23
apostles be sent * the Council Act 5:34
and were standing * at the gate, Act 10:17
was standing * in the street. Act 12:14
went a little way * the city to a Act 16:13
and beat him * the courtroom. Act 18:17
is the Judge of those on the *. 1Co 5:13
Why then go to * judges who are 1Co 6:4
they seem to be like on the *. 2Co 5:16
no rest for us; *, trouble was on 2Co 7:5
of by people * the church—those who 1Ti 3:7
animals were burned * the city. Heb 13:11
suffered and died * the city, where Heb 13:12
walls [that is, * the interests of Heb 13:13
both inside and *, and humbly be Jas 1:21
in the winepress * the city, and Rev 14:20
"* the city are those who have Rev 22:15

OUTSIDERS
As for the Gentiles, the * who Is 56:6
It isn't our job to judge *. 1Co 5:12

OUTSKIRTS
vineyards on the * of the town. Ju 14:5
He arrived at the * of the camp 1Sa 17:20
a vineyard on the * of the city 1Ki 21:1
on the eastern * of Jerusalem. Zec 14:5f
and Bethany on the * of Jerusalem Mk 11:1
located on the * of the city, Act 14:13

OUTSMARTED
is to keep from being * by Satan; 2Co 2:11

OUTSPREAD
They were placed so that their * 1Ki 6:23-28

OUTSTANDING
From the tribe of Simeon, 7,100 * 1Ch 12:24-37
Shemaiah's sons were all * men, 1Ch 26:6,7
of them—were * men who were 1Ch 26:8
from Hebron, all * men, were placed 1Ch 26:30
Twenty-seven hundred * men of 1Ch 26:31,32
He sent us an * man named Ez 8:18
be spoken of as generous, * men! Is 32:5

OUTSTRETCHED
each other, with * wings that Ex 37:9
with his hands * toward heaven. 1Ki 8:54,55

OUTWARD
shall extend * from the city walls Num 35:4
Men judge by * appearance, but I 1Sa 16:7
prayers with great * piety, they Lk 20:47
Don't be concerned about the * 1Pe 3:3

OUTWEAR
often, or you will * your welcome! Pro 25:17

OUTWEIGH
Yes, a small mistake can * much Ecc 10:1

OUTWIT
that men should try to * God! Ps 2:1
His enemies shall not * him, nor Ps 89:22
Thus their attempt to * him Lk 20:26

OVATION
gave him a great *, shouting, "It Act 12:22

OVEN
"If bread baked in the * is Lev 2:4
touches any clay *, it is defiled Lev 11:35
supply so that one * will be large Lev 26:26
as a baker's * is constantly Hos 7:4
ready and the roast is in the *. Mt 22:4

OVENS
They will fill your * and your Ex 8:3,4
This bread was hot from the * Jos 9:12
boiling vats, with * underneath. Eze 46:23

OVERALL
and Rehob—an * total of twenty-two Jos 19:30,31

OVERBOARD
the cargo * to lighten the ship. Jon 1:5
and threw him * into the raging Jon 1:15
crew began throwing the cargo *. Act 27:18
by throwing all the wheat *. Act 27:38
could swim to jump * and make for Act 27:43
you going to just throw it all *? Gal 3:4

OVERCAME
But the king's command * Joab's 2Sa 24:4
—the things that * the world Rom 8:20,21

OVERCAST
from the Lord has * Jerusalem; Lam 2:1

OVERCHARGE
must fear your God and not *! Lev 25:17,18

OVERCHARGED
if I find I have * anyone on his Lk 19:8

OVERCOME
May your descendants* all your Gen 24:60
exit, for he was * with love for Gen 43:30
Terror and dread have * them. Ex 15:16
They shall * their enemies. Num 24:15-19
there, and you shall * them. Deu 31:3
and prepared to * their enemies. Est 8:13
frustration, * by their own anger. Job 5:2
be themselves * by misfortune that Ps 35:26
so that I will not be * by evil. Ps 119:133
my bride; I am * by one glance of Sol 4:9
way, for your eyes have * me! Sol 6:5
and you will be * by my favor Eze 16:61
they were * with utter amazement. Mk 7:37
Her parents were * with Lk 8:56
"Pray God that you will not be * Lk 22:40
but cheer up, for I have * the Jn 16:33
DEAR BROTHERS, IF a Christian is * Gal 6:1
and to * them, and to rule over Rev 13:7

OVERCOMES
attacks and * him and strips him of Lk 11:22
"To every one who *—who to the Rev 2:26

OVERDUE
They will not be * a single day! Hab 2:3

OVEREMPHASIZE
I cannot * this point." Pro 4:5

OVERFED
was soon *; Deu 32:15

OVERFLOW
Let it * against the proud. Job 40:11
blessings *! Ps 23:5
* they shall not reach him." Ps 32:6f
and barley and * your wine vats Pro 3:9,10
This flood will * all its Is 8:7,8
Prosperity shall * Jerusalem Is 66:12
My eyes will * with tears because Jer 13:17
day my eyes shall * with tears; Jer 14:17
to * the land of the Philistines; Jer 47:2
army that will * across Israel Dan 11:10,11
presses * with olive oil and wine. Joe 2:24
Israel will again * with Zec 1:17
Yes, your cup of joy will *! Jn 15:11
and your cup of joy will *. Jn 16:24
I pray that God will help you * Rom 15:13
has been an * of giving to others. 2Co 8:2
and they * with thanks to God. 2Co 9:12
is that you will * more and more Php 1:9
Let your lives * with joy and Col 2:7
love to grow and * to each other 1Th 3:12

OVERFLOWED
again as usual and * the banks of Jos 4:18
her, his heart * with sympathy. Lk 7:13
love for me, well, I * with joy! 2Co 7:7

OVERFLOWING
were full to *, and there was so Gen 41:49
the Jordan was * all its banks; Jos 3:13,14
MY HEART IS * with a beautiful Ps 45:1
Lord, I am * with your blessings, Ps 119:65
at flood time, * all the land? Jer 46:7
for it is full to * with the Joe 3:13
to you in full and * measure, Lk 6:38
*—he couldn't get everything in. Lk 12:17
loved Son. So * is his kindness Eph 1:7

OVERFLOWS
all the earth and * the heavens. Ps 8:1
Whatever is in the heart * into Lk 6:45

OVERGROWN
saw that it was * with thorns, and Pro 24:30,31
it be * with briars and thorns. Is 5:6
stands will be * with brush. Mic 3:12

OVERHANGING
in the valleys, under * rocks. Is 57:5

OVERHEARD
But Rebekah * the conversation. Gen 27:5
had not been * by anyone. Jer 38:27

OVERJOYED
voice, she was so * that she ran Act 12:14

OVERLAID
Make poles from acacia wood * Ex 25:13,14
from acacia wood * with gold. Ex 25:28
acacia pillars * with gold, with Ex 26:32
acacia wood posts, * with gold, Ex 26:37
from acacia wood * with bronze. Ex 27:6
made of acacia wood * with gold. Ex 30:5
The frames and bars were all * Ex 36:34
of acacia wood, * with gold and set Ex 36:36
and rods were * with gold; Ex 36:38
acacia wood, and * them with gold, Ex 37:4
It was * with pure gold, with a Ex 37:11
all one piece. He * it all with Ex 37:26
This altar was * with bronze. Ex 38:2
of acacia wood, * with bronze. Ex 38:6
the tops of the posts were * with Ex 38:17
Its walls and ceiling were * with 1Ki 6:20
Then he * the interior of the 1Ki 6:21,22
and each was * with gold. 1Ki 6:23-28
of both rooms was * with gold. 1Ki 6:30
and open flowers, all * with gold. 1Ki 6:32
doors and carefully * with gold. 1Ki 6:35
throne and * it with pure gold. 1Ki 10:18
doorposts he had * with gold, and 2Ki 18:16
and ceiling * with pure gold! 2Ch 3:4
This too was * with the finest 2Ch 3:8
public court, and * the doors of 2Ch 4:9
ivory throne * with pure gold. 2Ch 9:17
An idol, made from a mold, * with Is 40:19
They are * with gold and silver, Hab 2:19

OVERLAPPING
are terrible. His * scales are his Job 41:15-17

OVERLAY
and 2¼ feet high. * it inside and Ex 25:11
and 2¼ feet high. * it with pure Ex 25:24
the Tabernacle. * the frames with Ex 26:29
and also * the bars with gold. Ex 26:29
and * everything with bronze. Ex 27:2
are attached. * the top, sides, Ex 30:3
the posts and to * their tops, and Ex 38:28

OVERLAYING
for * the walls of the buildings. 1Ch 29:4,5

OVERLOOK
and angry to * the insult, for it Gen 34:6,7
I will not * that. Deu 5:11
Oh, please * the awful wickedness Deu 9:27
I have no hope except in you. * Ps 25:6,7
their sins high and do not * them. Ps 69:27
Don't * the cursing of these Ps 74:23
Don't * them. Ps 109:14
and * you when you do them, too? Rom 2:3
kind of God would he be, to * sin? Rom 3:6
you may * his sins and it will 1Ti 5:22

OVERLOOKING
top of Mount Peor, * the desert. Num 23:28
like the tower of Lebanon * Sol 7:4
The rooms were in three tiers, * Eze 42:3

OVERLOOKS
of Moab, which * the desert with Num 21:20
old quarrels, but love * insults. Pro 10:12
restrains his anger and * insults. Pro 19:11
Or, "love * each other's many 1Pe 4:8f

OVERNIGHT
the men with him stayed there *. Gen 24:54
told them, "Don't leave it *." Ex 16:19
today, and keep what is left *." Ex 16:23
is due them, don't even keep it *. Lev 19:13
"Stay here *," Balaam said, Num 22:8
shall not remain on the tree *. Deu 21:23
and stayed * at a shepherd's inn 2Ki 10:12
they are staying * at Geba. Is 10:28,29
won't let their sheep stay *. Is 13:20
pledged clothing of debtors *. Amo 2:8f
to Bethany, where he stayed *. Mt 21:17
already evening, jailed them *. Act 4:3

(OVERNIGHT Con't)
invited them in and lodged them *. Act 10:23
OVERPOWER
would know how to * and subdue him Ju 16:5
Would he merely * me with his Job 23:6
him, nor shall the wicked * him. Ps 89:22
though no human means could * him. Dan 8:25
Otherwise temptation will * you. Mt 26:41
and pray lest the Tempter * you. Mk 14:38
OVERPOWERED
Save me from being * by my sins, Ps 39:8
OVERPOWERS
Stark fear * me. Ps 55:4
OVERRULES
that the Most High * the kingdoms Dan 5:21
Spirit who * the kingdom of Persia Dan 10:13
OVERRUN
a hunting ground * by wildlife. Is 7:24
Thorns will * the palaces, and Is 34:13
to the east of you * your land. Eze 25:4
will again * my people's land. Zec 9:8
OVERSEE
have appointed to * the dividing of Num 34:29
come here to * my administration. Jer 40:10
by God to * each local church. Rev 1:20f
OVERSEEING
But because the Lord was * the Ez 5:5
OVERSEERS
who were * of the labor forces. 1Ki 9:23
These men were King David's *. 1Ch 27:31
the hand of the * and workmen," he 2Ch 34:17
and Jehiel, the * of the Temple, 2Ch 35:8
is holding you responsible as *. Act 20:28
OVERSHADOW
own, and may a black cloud * it. Job 3:5
and the power of God shall * you; Lk 1:35
OVERSHADOWED
NOW A SEVERE famine * the land, as Gen 26:1
wings that * the place of mercy, Ex 37:9
so now their wings * the Ark and 1Ki 8:7
OVERSHADOWING
I destroyed you, O * cherub, from Eze 28:16
* the earth will be convulsed. Mt 24:29
OVERSIGHT
for the * of the sanctuary. Num 3:31-35
had the * of the king's vineyards; 1Ch 27:27
OVERSPREADS
Even as an eagle * her young. Deu 32:11
OVERTAKE
shall pursue and * you until you Deu 28:45
No, darkness shall * him Job 15:30
Calamity will surely * the Ps 34:21
How then can evil * me or any Ps 91:10
by watching ruin * the wicked. Pro 21:12
That is why disaster shall * you Is 47:11
and famine shall * her in a single Rev 18:8
OVERTAKEN
Let them be * by sudden ruin, Ps 35:8
OVERTAKES
When darkness * him, light will Ps 112:4
OVERTHREW
You * all those who rose against Ex 15:7
of old which God * without mercy. Jer 20:16
won battles, * kingdoms, ruled Heb 11:33
OVERTHROW
* the governments of many nations. Dan 11:41
the earth, and to * thrones and Hag 2:22
I will * their armed might, and Hag 2:22
* of the Roman government), Mk 3:16-19
OVERTHROWN
He has * Pharaoh's chariots and Ex 15:4
has * me and caught me in his net. Job 19:6
His power can never be *. Ps 96:10
Such a man will not be * by evil Ps 112:6
on their own, it will soon be *. Act 5:38
OVERTHROWS
away as slaves. He * the mighty. Job 12:19
OVERTOOK
and the Egyptian army * the Ex 14:9
Then the archers * Saul and 1Sa 31:3,4
OVERTURN
how to * the roots of mountains. Job 28:9
I will *, overturn, overturn the Eze 21:27
I will overturn, *, overturn the Eze 21:27
I will overturn, overturn, * the Eze 21:27
OVERTURNED
his splendor and * his throne. Ps 89:44
OVERTURNING
mountains, * them in his anger. Job 9:5
THE LORD is * the land of Judah Is 24:1
OVERTURNS
a single night he * them, Job 34:25
OVERWHELM
Trembling and horror * me. Ps 55:5
Don't let the floods * me, or the Ps 69:15
therefore I will * my people with Is 8:7,8
OVERWHELMED
"And Jehovah has * my master Gen 24:35
spirit from God * Saul, and he 1Sa 18:10
The unfortunate are * by their Ps 10:10
am helpless, *, in deep distress; Ps 25:16
When my heart is faint and *, Ps 61:2
I think of God and moan, * with Ps 77:3
in upon their enemies and * them. Ps 78:53
Your fierce wrath has * me. Ps 88:16
we are * by your wrath. Ps 90:7
A prayer when * with trouble. Ps 102:1
lightning flashes * the nation. Ps 105:32
For I am * and desperate, and Ps 142:3
and its forts are * and captured. Jer 48:1
mother shall be * with shame, for Jer 50:12
And I sat among them, *, for Eze 3:14,15
They will be * as with a flood, Dan 9:26
We were really crushed and *, and 2Co 1:8
OVERWHELMING
away his enemies with an * flood; Nah 1:8
but despite all this, * victory Rom 8:37
the * glory of the new agreement. 2Co 3:10
OVERWHELMS
Terror * him, and he is blown Job 27:20
OWE
before me? I * no one anything. Job 41:11
back again and * them not a cent! Is 52:3
one, 'How much do you * him?' Lk 16:5,6
" 'And how much do you * him?' Lk 16:7
For I * a great debt to you and Rom 1:14
feel that they * a real debt to the Rom 15:27
I won't mention how much you * me! Phm 1:19
The fact is, you even * me your Phm 1:19
OWED
But he had * some money when he 2Ki 4:1
brought in who * him $10,000,000! Mt 18:24
he went to a man who * him $2,000 Mt 18:28
"I suppose the one who had * him Lk 7:43
"So he invited each one who * Lk 16:5,6
OWES
grumbling, "He * everything he Gen 31:1
That is, "If he * you money and Ex 21:2f
what he * with some extra besides. Ps 37:21
OWL
The hawk (all kinds), the *, Lev 11:13-19
The screech *, the great owl, Deu 14:11-18
The screech owl, the great *, Deu 14:11-18
The horned *, the pelican, Deu 14:11-18
or like an * alone in the desert. Ps 102:6
There the * will make her nest Is 34:15
OWLS
will live, and * and ravens. Is 34:11
the vultures and the * will live Zep 2:14
OWN
"She is part of my * bone and Gen 2:23
Literally, "In his * likeness, Gen 5:3,4,5f
him, "Leave your * country behind Gen 12:1
you, and your * people, and go to Gen 12:1
son to inherit everything you *." Gen 15:4
May you * this land where we now Gen 28:4
"Just think, my very * flesh and Gen 29:14
When should I provide for my * Gen 30:30
So how could I harm my * Gen 31:43
and now I * oxen, donkeys, sheep, Gen 32:5
our * pace and meet you at Seir." Gen 33:14
be counted as his *, and so, Gen 38:9
she was his * daughter-in-law. Gen 38:16
Then Pharaoh placed his * signet Gen 41:41,42
served to them from his * table. Gen 43:34
to put Joseph's * silver cup at the Gen 44:2
to Egypt, of his * descendants, not Gen 46:26
and herds and everything they *.' Gen 46:32
them as my *, and they will inherit Gen 48:5
you shall be your *, and shall Gen 48:6
he gave them children of their *. Ex 1:21
of his * Hebrew brothers! Ex 2:11
your * Hebrew brother like that?" Ex 2:13
mistreat your * people like this? Ex 5:22
objected, "my * people won't even Ex 6:12
brand you as his * unique people, Ex 13:9
Your * homeland, Lord— Ex 15:17
return to his * land. Ex 18:27
you shall be my * little flock from Ex 19:5
wife, or want to * his slaves, Ex 20:17
shall also * half of the dead ox. Ex 21:35
amount of the best of his * crop. Ex 22:5
remember your * experience in the Ex 23:9
hot against your * people whom you Ex 32:11
For you swore by your * self, 'I Ex 32:13
killing your * sons and brothers; Ex 32:29
sins, and accept us as your *." Ex 34:9
priests for their * use, but it is Lev 2:10
it personally with his * hands. Lev 7:29
calf as a sacrifice for his * sin; Lev 9:8
the palm of his * left hand, and Lev 14:26
and sacrifice his * burnt offering Lev 16:24
Literally, "for theirs is your * Lev 18:10f
has cursed his * flesh and blood. Lev 20:9
must die, for it is their * fault. Lev 20:11
They have caused their * doom." Lev 20:27
as her *, shall be burned alive. Lev 21:9
She must be a virgin from his * Lev 21:14,15
a slave with his * money, that Lev 22:11
you from Egypt to be my * people! Lev 22:32,33
you who have no land of their *; Lev 23:22
to his * family and possessions. Lev 25:41
You shall eat your * sons and Lev 26:2
camping area with its * flag. Num 1:5
will have its * tent area, with its Num 2:
together under its * flag, just as Num 2:3-3
tribe under its * banner, in the Num 2:3
return to my * land and kinfolk." Num 10:3
But I vow by my * name that just Num 14:20,2
of following your * desires and Num 15:3
and going your * ways, as you used Num 15:3
I have not done them on my *. Num 16:2
"You priests may * no property, Num 18:2
the Levites shall * no property in Num 18:2
it were from your * property. Num 18:2
* threshing floor and wine press. Num 18:3
Name your * figure! Num 22:16,1
and could not say a word of my *? Num 24:1
Yes, I shall return now to my * Num 24:1
Canaan, but our * land shall be Num 32:3
the area Nobah, after his * name. Num 32:4
may return to his * land and home. Num 35:2
as it is within their * tribe. Num 36:
marry within their * tribe, so that Num 36:
to men in their * tribe of Manasseh Num 36:11,1
may return here to your * land.' Deu 3:2
special people, his * inheritance; Deu 4:2
We saw it all with our * eyes. Deu 6:2
earth to be his * chosen ones. Deu 7:6
saw it with their * eyes—and the Deu 7:19
that it was your * power and might Deu 8:17
God, don't destroy your * people. Deu 9:26
to obey for your * good the Deu 10:12,13
"You will no longer go your * Deu 12:8
for they have no land of their *. Deu 12:12
butchered on your * farms, just as Deu 12:20-23
Execute him! Your * hand shall Deu 13:9
you to be his * possession, more so Deu 14:2
They don't need to * property, Deu 18:2
for it was your * choice, and you Deu 23:23
shall be executed for his * crime. Deu 24:16
you are his very * people, just as Deu 26:18
the flesh of your * sons and Deu 28:53
callous toward his * brother and Deu 28:54
flesh of his * children—because he Deu 28:55
"You have seen with your * eyes Deu 29:2,3
I walk in my * stubborn way!' Deu 29:19
For Israel was God's * personal Deu 32:9
"Israel is destroyed by our * Deu 32:27
Even his * children, brothers, Deu 33:9
return to his * city and home." Jos 20:6
to their * homeland of Gilead. Jos 22:9
by building our * altar for burnt Jos 22:29
the idols you now *, and you must Jos 24:23
their * sections of the country. Jos 24:28
He was buried on his * estate at Jos 24:30
an army under his * command. Ju 3:27
themselves by their * strength! Ju 7:2
me, your * flesh and blood!" Ju 9:2
seemed right in his * eyes. Ju 17:6
But we can't give them our * Ju 21:18
carried them off to their * land. Ju 21:23
you to return to your * people. Ru 1:11
and mother in your * land and have Ru 2:10,11
Or, "that would ruin my * Ru 4:6f
Ark back to its * country, lest the 1Sa 5:11
when we return it to its * land?" 1Sa 6:2
And anyway, you * all the wealth 1Sa 9:20
him ahead of my * sons and now I 1Sa 12:2
the sinner be my * son Jonathan, he 1Sa 14:39
Then Saul gave David his * 1Sa 17:38,39
by the Lord and by your * soul!" 1Sa 20:3
to me during my * lifetime, but 1Sa 20:14
that my * son is on David's side. 1Sa 22:8
Think of it! My * son—encouraging 1Sa 22:8
member of your * household! 1Sa 22:14
I'll protect you with my * life. 1Sa 22:23
and multiply everything you *. 1Sa 25:6
reply as he strapped on his *. 1Sa 25:13
into your * hands, I pray by the 1Sa 25:26
God, and by your * life too, that 1Sa 25:26
who took the law into his * hands! 1Sa 25:30,31
out vengeance with my * hands. 1Sa 25:33
The Lord gives his * reward for 1Sa 26:23
so Saul took his * sword and fell 1Sa 31:3,4
man in his * house and on his bed! 2Sa 4:11
It will be their * land where the 2Sa 7:10,11
though he were one of his * sons. 2Sa 9:10,11
he fed it from his * plate and let 2Sa 12:3
and let it drink from his * cup; 2Sa 12:3
a lamb from his * flocks for food 2Sa 12:4
* household to rebel against you. 2Sa 12:11
gems—and placed it on his * head. 2Sa 12:29,30
to bring home your * banished son. 2Sa 14:13
"He may go to his * quarters," 2Sa 14:24
by God and by your * life that 2Sa 15:21
your * medicine, you murderer!" 2Sa 16:7,8
I to say no? My * son is trying to 2Sa 16:11
Yet you are my * brothers, my own 2Sa 19:11,12
Yet you are my own brothers, my * 2Sa 19:11,12
own tribe, my * flesh and blood!" 2Sa 19:11,12
all those who eat at your * table! 2Sa 19:28
again to die in my * city, where my 2Sa 19:37

(OWN Con't)
"The king is one of our * tribe. 2Sa 19:42
army and the king's * bodyguard. 2Sa 20:7
to mobilize his * clan of Bichri at 2Sa 20:14
If you want to save your * life 1Ki 1:12
riding on King David's * mule. 1Ki 1:38
by the king's * bodyguard; 1Ki 1:44,45
and he rode on the king's * mule. 1Ki 1:44,45
and it will be your * fault." 1Ki 2:36,37
And here I am among your * 1Ki 3:8
and each family had its * home 1Ki 4:25
THEN SOLOMON BUILT his * palace, 1Ki 7:1
just as your * people Israel do; 1Ki 8:43
to be your * special people." 1Ki 8:53
I heard in my * country about your 1Ki 10:6
servants returned to their * land. 1Ki 10:13
palace among Pharaoh's * sons. 1Ki 11:20
Let Rehoboam be king of his * 1Ki 12:16,17
He laid the body in his * grave, 1Ki 13:30
"Well, it's your * fault," the 1Ki 20:40
back in disgust to their * land. 2Ki 3:27
Judah and appointed their * king. 2Ki 8:20
pay for it with your * life." 2Ki 10:24
any more money for your * needs; 2Ki 12:7
to the priests for their * use. 2Ki 12:16
his * hands upon the king's hands. 2Ki 13:16,17
pay the penalty for his * sins. 2Ki 14:6
He even killed his * son by 2Ki 16:3
They even burned their * sons 2Ki 17:17
also worshiped their * gods. 2Ki 17:29
even burned their * children on the 2Ki 17:31
think we have come here on our *? 2Ki 18:25
you to eat their * excrement and 2Ki 18:27
and drink their * urine!" 2Ki 18:27
peace here in your * land until I 2Ki 18:31,32
for the sake of my * name and for 2Ki 19:34
the glory of my * name and for the 2Ki 20:6
Some of your * sons will be 2Ki 20:18
the remainder of my * life!" 2Ki 20:19
had selected to honor his * name. 2Ki 21:3,4,5
shrines upon their * altars, and he 2Ki 23:20
so Saul took his * sword and fell 1Ch 10:4
returned to bless his * household. 1Ch 16:43
me, because of your * great heart. 1Ch 17:19
that he kept for his * use. 1Ch 18:4
and placed it upon his * head. 1Ch 20:2
my * son and I will be his father; 1Ch 22:10
giving all of my * private 1Ch 29:3
not the vats, for their * washing. 2Ch 4:6
your people as their * property. 2Ch 6:27
Temple as well as his * palace. 2Ch 7:11
his * royal palace were completed. 2Ch 8:1
about you in my * country is true! 2Ch 9:5
here and saw it with my * eyes. 2Ch 9:6
retinue returned to their * land. 2Ch 9:12
Let Rehoboam rule his * tribe of 2Ch 10:16
was buried in his * vault that he 2Ch 16:13,14
wounded—his * officials decided to 2Ch 24:25
No, everyone must pay for his * 2Ch 25:4
save their * people from you?" 2Ch 25:15
sacrificed his * children in the 2Ch 28:3
What about your * sins against 2Ch 28:10
returned again to their * homes. 2Ch 31:1
home in deep shame to his * land. 2Ch 32:21
of his * sons killed him there. 2Ch 32:21
And Manasseh sacrificed his * 2Ch 33:6
buried beneath his * palace, and 2Ch 33:20,21
At last his * officers 2Ch 33:24
priests upon their * altars, 2Ch 34:5
to present its * burnt sacrifices 2Ch 35:12
them in his * temple in Babylon. 2Ch 36:7
in the temple of his * gods. Ez 1:7
(They had been taken from their * Ez 4:10
wall beside his * house, and next Neh 3:10
of the wall in his * district. Neh 3:17
sections next to their * houses. Neh 3:23
immediately opposite his * house. Neh 3:28
wall next to his * house, and Neh 3:29
who built next to his * house. Neh 3:30
back upon their * heads, and may Neh 4:4
nothing to say in their * defense. Neh 5:8
of wall next to his * home. Neh 7:3
home to their * towns and villages Neh 7:73
confessing their * sins and those Neh 9:3
to live in their * homes in the Neh 11:3
had built their * villages as Neh 12:29
and raised as his * daughter. Est 2:7
in its * languages and dialects; Est 3:12
and the king's * horse, and the Est 6:7,8
on the king's * horse, shouting Est 6:9
him on the king's * steed, and led Est 6:11
claim it for its *, and may a black Job 3:5
"If God cannot trust his * Job 4:18,19
overcome by their * anger. Job 5:2
They are caught in their * Job 5:13
For your * good, listen to my Job 5:27
Am I righteous? My * mouth says Job 9:20
I condemn you? Your * mouth does! Job 15:6
answer you from my * experience, Job 15:17-19
I even beg him! My * wife and Job 19:17
cast away like his * dung. Job 20:7

Everything they * is cursed. Job 24:18
Even the sinner's * mother shall Job 24:20
them as our * children)— or if I Job 31:18
they weren't her *, and is Job 39:16
that your * strength can save you. Job 40:14
Catch them in their * traps; Ps 5:10
weight of their * transgressions, Ps 5:10
let him fall into his * trap. Ps 7:15
the wicked in their * snares! Ps 9:16
Our lips are our *; Ps 12:3,4
preserve your * from the reach of Ps 12:7
of your * eternal presence. Ps 16:11
by my * people and by all mankind. Ps 22:6
They will receive God's * Ps 24:5
but his * plan stands forever. Ps 33:11
people he has chosen as his *. Ps 33:12
in their * net, and destroyed. Ps 35:8
who are minding their * business. Ps 35:20
"With our * eyes we saw him do Ps 35:21
them bare of everything they *. Ps 35:26
from your * table and let them Ps 36:8
plunged into their * hearts and all Ps 37:15
than to * an evil man's wealth; Ps 37:16
Even my * family stands at a Ps 38:11
They did not conquer by their * Ps 44:3
* brother from the penalty of sin! Ps 49:7
together my * people who by their Ps 50:5
You slander your * brother. Ps 50:20
with their * violence and strife. Ps 55:9
God, even our * God, will bless Ps 67:6,7
Even my * brothers pretend they Ps 69:8
us—the sheep of your * pasture? Ps 74:1
But he led forth his * people Ps 78:52
according to their * desires. Ps 81:12
* use these pasturelands of God!" Ps 83:12
into the Lord's * garden, and are Ps 92:13
He will destroy them by their * Ps 94:23
especially in my * home, where I Ps 101:2
Let them fall into their * Ps 141:10
They lay a booby trap for their * Pro 1:18
of having your * way, and Pro 1:31
your * complacency will kill you. Pro 1:32
conceited, sure of your * wisdom. Pro 3:7,8
If only I had not demanded my * Pro 5:12
Drink from your * well, my son—be Pro 5:15
The wicked man is doomed by his * Pro 5:22
fool, for he destroys his * soul. Pro 6:32
Wisdom is its * reward, and if Pro 9:12
to those minding their * business. Pro 9:15
Your * soul is nourished when you Pro 11:17
but honesty is its * defense. Pro 12:13
tears hers down by her * efforts. Pro 14:1
talk should prick his * pride! Pro 14:3
can know his * bitterness or joy—no Pro 14:10
Even his * neighbors despise the Pro 14:20
and your * best interests. Pro 15:31,32
everything for his * purposes—even Pro 16:4
of conduct by demanding his * way. Pro 18:1
his chances by his * foolishness Pro 19:3
A poor man's * brothers turn away Pro 19:7
He who loves wisdom loves his * Pro 19:8
man must bear his * penalty; Pro 19:19
be ignored in his * time of need. Pro 21:13
Why risk everything you *? Pro 22:26,27
Yet in his * opinion he is Pro 26:16
with her * hands she plants a Pro 31:16
tapestry; her * clothing is Pro 31:22
is appropriate in its * time. Ecc 3:11
to follow his * downward road. Ecc 7:29
choose their * mad course, for they Ecc 9:2,3
Literally, "but my * vineyards Sol 1:6f
else can have, a fountain of my *. Sol 4:12
to be back among my * people." Sol 6:12
But as for my * vineyard, you, O Sol 8:12
We will furnish our * food and Is 4:1
awful fate—with my * ears I heard Is 5:9
wise and shrewd in their * eyes! Is 5:21
will even eat their * children! Is 9:19,20
They boast, "We in our * power Is 10:13
By our * strength we broke down Is 10:13
back to their * land like deer Is 13:14
her far from her * land as though Is 27:7,8
They could have rest in their * Is 28:12
thing—to destroy his * people! Is 28:21
each in its * section of his land? Is 28:25
* eyes you will see your Teacher. Is 30:20
your efforts. Your * breath will Is 33:11
* dung and drink his own urine." Is 36:12
own dung and drink his * urine." Is 36:12
you each have your * farm and Is 36:16
will return to his * land, where I Is 37:7
you back to your * land by the same Is 37:29
* soil and flourish and multiply. Is 37:31
He will return to his * country Is 37:34
For my * honor I will defend it, Is 37:35
to his * country, to Nineveh. Is 37:37
I *, all my priceless treasures." Is 39:4
And some of your * sons will Is 39:7
world is as blind as my * people, Is 42:19
your sins for my * sake and will Is 43:25
Who but a fool would make his * Is 44:10

Yet for my * sake and for the Is 48:9
Yet for my * sake—yes, for my Is 48:11
sake—yes, for my * sake—I will save Is 48:11
you for your * good and leads you Is 48:17
reassign it to its * people again. Is 49:8,9
and not have love for her * son? Is 49:15
enemies with their * flesh and they Is 49:26
with rivers of their * blood. Is 49:26
who live in your * light, and warm Is 50:11
your * fires and not from God's; Is 50:11
from God, for his * sins! Is 53:4
left God's paths to follow our *. Is 53:6
because of your * power or virtue Is 55:5
look after their * interest, each Is 56:11
right into your * homes those who Is 58:7
his * glorious light upon you. Is 58:8
not having your * fun and business Is 58:13
not following your * desires and Is 58:13
plant them there with my * hands; Is 60:21
and graceful oaks for his * glory. Is 61:3
you and will claim you as his *. Is 62:4
He said, "They are my very *; Is 63:8
But my * people—though I have Is 65:2
they follow their * evil paths Is 65:2
not only for their * sins but for Is 65:7
But those who choose their * Is 66:3
Your * wickedness will punish Jer 2:19
leaders after my * heart, who will Jer 3:15
it is a bitter dose of your * Jer 4:18
it will be the fruit of their * Jer 6:18,19
will let you stay in your * land. Jer 7:3
hurt themselves, to their * shame. Jer 7:19
their * stubborn, evil thoughts. Jer 7:24
in my * Temple, polluting it. Jer 7:30
Each followed his * stubborn will Jer 11:8
Even your * brothers, your own Jer 12:6
Even your own brothers, your * Jer 12:6
you home to your * land again, each Jer 12:15
* evil desires and worships idols; Jer 13:10
for the sake of your * reputation! Jer 14:7
out of their * lying hearts. Jer 14:14
Lord, for the sake of your * name. Jer 14:21
I will destroy my * people because Jer 15:7
says: In your * lifetime, before Jer 16:9
message I've given them, not my *. Jer 17:16
We have our * priests and wise Jer 18:18
eat their * children and friends. Jer 19:9
I swear by my * name, says the Jer 22:5
and never again see his * Jer 22:12
back into their * fold, and they Jer 23:3
Jews back to their * land of Israel Jer 23:8
in my * Temple, says the Lord. Jer 23:11
I have begun to punish my * Jer 25:29
shout against his * from his holy Jer 25:30
"You have heard with your * ears Jer 26:11
to stay in their * country and farm Jer 27:11
back home again to your * land. Jer 29:14
and quiet in their * land, and no Jer 30:10
They will have their * ruler Jer 30:21
and eat from your * gardens there. Jer 31:5
will come again to their * land. Jer 31:17
For everyone shall die for his * Jer 31:30
Someday people will again * Jer 32:15
They have even defiled my * Jer 32:34
forever, for their * good and for Jer 32:39
the man after God's * heart. Jer 33:15f
and not to * farms, but always to Jer 35:7
long, good lives in our * land. Jer 35:7
will never again see your * land. Jer 42:18
of Judah, and your * sins, and the Jer 44:9
returning again to their * land. Jer 44:14
I am weary of my * sighing and I Jer 45:3
to your * land, don't be dismayed; Jer 46:27
For I have sworn by my * name, Jer 49:13
Let them rush back to their * Jer 50:16
home again to her * land, to feed Jer 50:19
they will escape back to their * Jer 50:28
Abandon her and return to your * Jer 51:9
sworn to it in his * name: Your Jer 51:14
and cast us out of our * country. Jer 51:34,35
The Lord has rejected his * Lam 2:7
With our * eyes we've seen her Lam 2:16
These are your * people to whom Lam 2:20
My * people laugh at me; Lam 3:14
cooked and eaten their * children; Lam 4:10
our * against any nation on earth! Lam 4:20
sink deep into your * heart first; Eze 3:10
you have saved your * life too." Eze 3:21
Fathers will eat their * sons, Eze 5:10
I will do it in your * Eze 12:25
inventing their * visions and Eze 13:2,3
never see your * country again. Eze 13:9
and save your * souls alive?" Eze 13:18f
will see with your * eyes how Eze 14:22
your * blood, and I said, 'Live! Eze 16:6,7
men instead of her * husband. Eze 16:32
a man's * sins that he will die. Eze 18:4
surely die, and it is his * fault. Eze 18:13
shall die for his * sins because he Eze 18:18
rewarded for his * goodness and the Eze 18:20
each according to your * actions. Eze 18:30

(OWN Con't)
No, I will destroy you in your * Eze 21:30
be spilled in your * country and Eze 21:32
you *, leaving you naked and bare. Eze 23:29
forth fire from your * actions Eze 28:18
more live in their * land, the land Eze 28:25
with pride for its * prosperity, Eze 31:14
if he dies the fault is his *. Eze 33:4
back home to their * land of Eze 34:13
living in their * country, they Eze 36:17
It is not for your * sakes that I Eze 36:32
return home again to your * land. Eze 37:14
the world to their * land, to Eze 37:21
safety in their * land, with no one Eze 39:26
* any, for I am their heritage! Eze 44:28
must be from his * land, for I Eze 46:18
same rights your * children have. Eze 47:22
and wine from his * kitchen during Dan 1:5
or worship any god except their *. Dan 3:28
saying, "I, by my * mighty power, Dan 4:30
and the king sealed it with his * Dan 6:17
strength and not his *. Dan 8:24
he will seal his * doom, for he Dan 8:25
and send us back to our * land Dan 9:3
your * city, your holy mountain. Dan 9:16
sanctuary—for your * glory, Lord. Dan 9:17
Don't delay—for your * sake, O my Dan 9:19
but this king's * officials will Dan 11:5
soon return again to his * land. Dan 11:9
Insurgents among your * people, Dan 11:14
"Those of his * household will Dan 11:26
soil of their * land again." Hos 1:11
*, for they are not my children; Hos 1:4
trap them in their * fortresses. Hos 11:6
return the harm to your * heads. Joe 3:4
took them far from their * land. Joe 3:6
and in my * Temple they offer Amo 2:8
has sworn by his * name, "I Amo 6:8
And priding yourselves on your * Amo 6:13
him for your * good reasons." Jon 1:14
I was there in my * country and you Jon 4:2
of captivity, back to your * land. Mic 2:13
quietly in his * home in peace and Mic 4:4
again in their * land, a mighty Mic 4:7
their brethren in their * land. Mic 5:3
against even their * brothers. Mic 7:1
will be found in his * home. Mic 7:6
Now with my * eyes I see them Mic 7:10
Your * chariots race recklessly Nah 2:4
something in your * lifetime that Hab 1:5
Soon your * glory will be Hab 2:16
You destroyed with their * Hab 3:14
his * land throughout the world. Zep 2:11
are liars seeking their * gain; Zep 3:4
Your only concern is your * fine Hag 1:9
each of you will * a home of your Zec 3:10
own a home of your * where you can Zec 3:10
them—their * shepherds have sold Zec 11:5
clutches of their * wicked leaders, Zec 11:6
* father and mother will slay him! Zec 13:3
I even rejected his very * Mal 1:2,3
returned to their * land, they Mt 2:12
only angry, even in your * home, Mt 5:22
eye, he must pay with his * eye. Mt 5:38
when you have a board in your *? Mt 7:3
because of the board in your *? Mt 7:4
have no home of my *—no place to Mt 8:20
dead care for their * dead." Mt 8:22
Literally, "his * city." Mt 9:1f
shall betray their * children. Mt 10:21
will be right in his * home! Mt 10:36
and destroying his * kingdom. Mt 12:26
what power do your * people use Mt 12:27
except in his * country, and among Mt 13:57
country, and among his * people!" Mt 13:57
against their * people, or against Mt 17:25
must be like my *, for I, the Mt 20:28
question of their * to ask him. Mt 22:34,35
ones in charge of everything I *! Mt 24:47
* clothing, shouting, "Blasphemy! Mt 26:65,66
robe and put his * garment on him Mt 27:31
placed it in his * new rock-hewn Mt 27:60
"Use your * Temple police," Mt 27:65
relatives and by his * family." Mk 6:4
and substitute your * traditions. Mk 7:8
should help my * family—the Jews. Mk 7:27
put aside your * pleasures and Mk 8:34
* the farm when his father dies. Mk 12:7
will betray their * children, and Mk 13:12
possible, even God's * children. Mk 13:22
robe and put his * clothes on him Mk 15:20
and then went back to her * home. Lk 1:56
is accepted in his * home town! Lk 4:24
to their * kind for full return! Lk 6:34
—when a board is in your *? Lk 6:41
must put aside his * desires and Lk 9:23
even * a place to lay my head. Lk 9:58
dead care for their * dead." Lk 9:60f
what about your * followers? Lk 11:19
he does his * father, mother, Lk 14:26
more than his * life—otherwise he Lk 14:26
carry his * cross and follow me. Lk 14:27
be entrusted with money of your *? Lk 16:12
his supper before he eats his *. Lk 17:7,8,9
acting under his * authority?" Lk 20:4
Even in his * land and among his Jn 1:11,12
land and among his * people, the Jn 1:11,12
except in his * country!" Jn 4:43,44
sent me and is not merely my *. Jn 5:30
who sent me, not to have my * way. Jn 6:38
teaching you my * thoughts, but Jn 7:16
is from God or is merely my *. Jn 7:17
Anyone presenting his * ideas is Jn 7:18
telling you my * ideas, but have Jn 8:28
I am not here on my *, but he Jn 8:42
Was it a result of his * sins or Jn 9:2
and he calls his * sheep by name Jn 10:3
and know my * sheep, and they know Jn 10:14
"In your * Law it says that men Jn 10:34,35,36
dipped into them for his * use! Jn 12:6
For these are not my * ideas, Jn 12:49
And God shall give me his * Jn 13:32
The words I say are not my * but Jn 14:10
be presenting his * ideas, but will Jn 16:13
to his * home, leaving me alone. Jn 16:32
Holy Father, keep them in your * Jn 17:11
your * laws," Pilate told them. Jn 18:31
"Your * people and their chief Jn 18:35
to hear their * languages being Act 2:6
men telling in our * languages Act 2:11
one of David's * descendants would Act 2:30
though we by our * power and Act 3:12
felt that what he owned was his *; Act 4:32
*, it will soon be overthrown. Act 5:38
*, not one little tract of land. Act 7:5
adopted him as her * son, and Act 7:21
told Moses to mind his * business. Act 7:27
opened to them of its * accord! Act 12:10
my * heart, for he will obey me.' Act 13:22
come true in our * time, in that Act 13:32,33
to go their * ways, but he never Act 14:16
As one of your * poets says it, Act 17:28
blood be upon your * heads—I am Act 18:6
worked to pay my * way and even to Act 20:34
He took Paul's belt, bound his * Act 21:11
Literally, "his * wife." Act 24:24f
Literally, "my * nation." Act 26:4f
your * people and the Gentiles. Act 26:17
eat something now for your * good! Act 27:34
Or, "at his * expense." Act 28:30f
God's very *—yes, his holy people. Rom 1:6,7
paid within their * souls with the Rom 1:27
their * conscience accuses them, Rom 2:12-15
died it was not for their * sins Rom 5:14
that you can choose your * master? Rom 6:16
good laws for its * evil purposes. Rom 7:13
He sent his * Son in a human body Rom 8:3
like God's very * children, adopted Rom 8:15
us in harmony with God's * will. Rom 8:27
not spare even his * Son for us but Rom 8:32
us whom God has chosen for his *? Rom 8:33
He took you as his * special, Rom 9:4
in fact, it is as near as our * Rom 10:8
others with your * mouth that Jesus Rom 10:9
believe in your * heart that God Rom 10:9
No, God has not discarded his * Rom 11:2,3
of his * special olive tree. Rom 11:17
graft you into his * good tree—a Rom 11:24
Then you will learn from your * Rom 12:2
[Don't take the law into your * Rom 12:19
We are not our * bosses to live Rom 14:7
as one of God's * children, and Rom 16:8
Lord picked out to be his very *; Rom 16:13
thoughts except God's * Spirit. 1Co 2:11
the Lord, but your * desires; 1Co 3:1
by your * desires, not God's. 1Co 3:3
still babies, wanting your * way? 1Co 3:3
be rewarded for his * hard work. 1Co 3:8
man's * brilliance to trap him; 1Co 3:19
he stumbles over his * "wisdom" 1Co 3:19
I don't even trust my * judgment 1Co 4:3
accomplished something on your *? 1Co 4:7
around without homes of our *. 1Co 4:11
others, even your * brothers. 1Co 6:8
sin it is against your * body. 1Co 6:18
* body does not belong to you. 1Co 6:19
man having his * wife, and each 1Co 7:2
woman having her * husband, because 1Co 7:2
full right to her * body, for her 1Co 7:4
full right to his * body, for it 1Co 7:4
to add some suggestions of my *. 1Co 7:12
and made us to be his *; 1Co 8:6
Jesus our Lord with my * eyes. 1Co 9:1
army has to pay his * expenses? 1Co 9:7
our * needs without your help. 1Co 9:12
to take for their * needs some of 1Co 9:13
my services of my * free will, then 1Co 9:17
you are eating, but your *. 1Co 11:21
Love does not demand its * way. 1Co 13:5
Each, however, in his * turn: 1Co 15:23
find the answer in your * garden! 1Co 15:36
letter with my * hand: if anyone 1Co 16:21
his help, and not on our * skills. 2Co 1:1
must be from God and is not our *. 2Co 4:
not for our * profit, but because 2Co 5:13,1
to others. We * nothing, and yet we 2Co 6:1
you truly were my very * children. 2Co 6:1
Every one must make up his * 2Co 9:
be enough for your * needs, but 2Co 9:
against their * little ideas. 2Co 10:1
and from my * people, the Jews, as 2Co 11:2
off my * power and abilities. 2Co 12:
Jews of my * age in the whole Gal 1:14
could adopt us as his very * sons. Gal 4:
longer slaves, but God's * sons. Gal 4:
taken out your * eyes and given Gal 4:1
But when you follow your * wrong Gal 5:1
those in your * little group—and Gal 5:2
some faults and burdens of his *. Gal 6:5
If he sows to please his * wrong Gal 6:8
closing words in my * handwriting. Gal 6:11
everywhere who are really God's *. Gal 6:16
us to be his very *, through what Eph 1:4
adopt us into his * family by Eph 1:5
of God's very * family, citizens of Eph 2:19
each part in its * special way Eph 4:15,16
No one hates his * body but Eph 5:29,30
Don't just think about your * Php 2:4
worrying about his * plans and not Php 2:21
bodies like his *, using the same Php 3:21
all were made by Christ for his * Col 1:16
the cross of his * human body, and Col 1:22
brother, one of your * people. Col 4:9
Here is my * greeting in my own Col 4:18
Here is my own greeting in my * Col 4:18
and caring for her * children. 1Th 2:7
message, but our * lives too. 1Th 2:8
his * children—don't you remember? 1Th 2:11
as being just our *, but you 1Th 2:13
from your * countrymen, just as 1Th 2:14
from their * people the Jews. 1Th 2:14
After they had killed their * 1Th 2:15
in all of our * crushing troubles 1Th 3:7
life, minding your * business and 1Th 4:11
and doing your * work, just as we 1Th 4:11
to work, and earn their * living. 2Th 3:12
am writing with my * hand, as I do 2Th 3:17
This is in my * handwriting. 2Th 3:17
For if a man can't make his * 1Ti 3:5
developing their * confidence and 1Ti 3:13
as though he were your * father. 1Ti 5:1
won't care for his * relatives when 1Ti 5:8
living in his * family, has no 1Ti 5:8
and take care of their * homes; 1Ti 5:14
follow their * misguided ideas. 2Ti 4:4
And now in his * good time he Tit 1:3
One of their * men, a prophet Tit 1:12
but a person whose * heart is Tit 1:15
time in their * homes, being kind Tit 2:5
make us his very * people, with Tit 2:14
and with him comes my * heart. Phm 1:12
it here with my * hand) but I won't Phm 1:19
everything for his * glory, should Heb 2:10
Beware then of your * hearts, Heb 3:12
of the people and his * sins too. Heb 5:1
an oath in his * name, since there Heb 6:13
over first their * sins and then Heb 7:27
God to cover his * mistakes and Heb 9:7
No, he took his * blood, and with Heb 9:12
There he gave his * blood which Heb 10:4f
Christ than to * all the treasures Heb 11:26
man's * evil thoughts and wishes. Jas 1:14
Literally, "Of his * free will he Jas 1:18f
about your * plans, and such Jas 4:16
are now members of God's * family. 1Pe 1:3
you are God's very *—all this so 1Pe 2:9
now you are God's *. 1Pe 2:10
of our sins in his * body when he 1Pe 2:24
first among God's * children. 1Pe 4:17
with my * eyes I saw Christ dying 1Pe 5:1
he even shares his * glory and his 2Pe 1:3
glory and his * goodness with us! 2Pe 1:3
and to give us his * character. 2Pe 1:4
Next, learn to put aside your * 2Pe 1:6
coming again. My * eyes have seen 2Pe 1:16
who follow their * evil, lustful 2Pe 2:10
* eyes and listened to him speak. 1Jn 1:1
I have touched him with my * 1Jn 1:1
And he has put his * Holy Spirit 1Jn 4:13
have seen with our * eyes and now 1Jn 4:14
one of God's very *, and to her 2Jn 1:1
John saw this happen with his * Rev 1:7f
And the Dragon gave him his * Rev 13:2

OWNED
and all that they *, for Abram was Gen 13:1
who lived in Sodom—and all he *. Gen 14:12
his master *, and journeyed to Gen 24:10
Abraham deeded everything he * to Gen 25:5
took everything he * and started Gen 31:17-20
I * nothing except a walking Gen 32:10
over everything he *. Gen 39:6
on the land * by the temples. Gen 47:26
stripped of everything they *! Ex 12:36

(OWNED Con't)
with them, and everything they *. Num 16:32
year you have * him, and don't Deu 15:12
donkeys, and they * thirty cities Ju 10:4
A wealthy man from Maon * a 1Sa 25:2
Solomon * forty thousand chariot 1Ki 4:26
everything she had * was restored 2Ki 8:6
tithe of all they *, as required by 2Ch 31:5,6
for he * 7,000 sheep, 3,000 Job 1:2,3
he *, he couldn't do it." Sol 8:7
We haven't built houses or * Jer 35:9
sold everything he * to get enough Mt 13:44
everything he * to purchase it! Mt 13:46
felt that what he * was his own; Act 4:32
all who * land or houses sold them Act 4:34,35
sold a field he * and brought the Act 4:37
when all you * was taken from you, Heb 10:34

OWNER
not eaten, but the * shall not be Ex 21:28
the past, and the * had been Ex 21:29
and the * also shall be killed. Ex 21:29
into it, the * of the well shall Ex 21:34
damages to the * of the animal, and Ex 21:34
to gore, and its * has not kept it Ex 21:36
but the * of the living ox shall Ex 21:36
by giving the * of the field or Ex 22:5
is lost, and the * believes he has Ex 22:9
stolen it, and the * must accept Ex 22:11
caring for it must repay the *. Ex 22:12
or killed, and the * is not there Ex 22:14
But if the * is there, he need Ex 22:15
you must take it back to its *. Ex 23:4
there, then the * of the house Lev 14:35
of crops the new * will get from Lev 25:14,15,16
Jubilee, and the * must accept the Lev 25:27
But if the original * is not Lev 25:28
new * until the Year of Jubilee; Lev 25:28
to the new *—it does not return to Lev 25:30
original * in the Year of Jubilee. Lev 25:30
original * in the Year of Jubilee. Lev 25:31
a sacrifice, the * shall bring it Lev 27:11,12
* from whom it was bought. Lev 27:24
the Lord, then the * shall pay the Lev 27:27
or if the * does not redeem it, Lev 27:27
take it back to its *. Deu 22:1
If you don't know who the * is, Deu 22:2
it there until the * comes looking Deu 22:2
Keep it for its *. Deu 22:3
guilt to both the house and its *. Deu 22:8
which its * gains his livelihood. Deu 24:6
Stand outside! The * will bring Deu 24:11
that the * of the field was Boaz. Ru 2:19
Samaria from its *, Shemer, for 1Ki 16:24
the ox—know their * and appreciate Is 1:3
"The * of an estate went out Mt 20:1
Finally the * sent his son, Mt 21:37
"When the * returns, what do you Mt 21:40
"The * then sent another of his Mk 12:4
"What do you suppose the * will Mk 12:9
asked Simon, its *, to push out a Lk 5:3
" 'What shall I do?' the * asked Lk 20:13
"What do you think the * will do? Lk 20:15
'So shall the * of this belt be Act 21:11
captain and the * than to Paul. Act 27:11
into slavery with Sin as my *. Rom 7:14
If their * is a Christian, that 1Ti 6:2

OWNERS
dies, then the two * shall sell the Ex 21:35
to the original * or their heirs. Lev 25:10
original * in the Year of Jubilee; Lev 25:33
have murdered its * to get their Job 31:38,39
their * killed or gone." Is 5:9
it, the * demanded an explanation. Lk 19:33
And you slave * must treat your Eph 6:9
YOU SLAVE * must be just and fair Col 4:1
hard for their * and respect them; 1Ti 6:1

OWNERSHIP
his mark of * upon your hands or Ex 13:9
* were placed upon your foreheads. Ex 13:16
jewels, also the * of some of the 2Ch 21:3,4
us—his mark of *—and given us his 2Co 1:22

OWNING
one very rich, * many flocks of 2Sa 12:1
and the other very poor, * 2Sa 12:3

OWNS
has given him everything he *. Gen 24:36
everything he * to our father. Gen 31:1
"The man who * this identification Gen 38:25
And the Lord * every tenth Lev 27:32
donkeys, nor anything else he *.' Deu 5:21
strength and who * the rights of a Deu 21:17
"I give you everything he *." 2Sa 16:4
to buy the farm he * in Anathoth, Jer 32:6,7
taking everything precious she *. Lam 1:10
put him in charge of all he *. Lk 12:42,43,44
back to God, because he * it. 1Co 6:20
* everything his father had. Gal 4:1
you your full portion of all he *. Col 3:24

OX
"If an * gores a man or woman to Ex 21:28
to death, the * shall be stoned and Ex 21:28
held— unless the * was known to Ex 21:29
the * was not kept under control; Ex 21:29
kills someone, the * shall be Ex 21:29
"The same law holds if the * Ex 21:31
But if the * gores a slave, Ex 21:32
silver, and the * shall be stoned. Ex 21:32
cover it, and an * or a donkey Ex 21:33
"If a man's * injures another, Ex 21:35
sell the live * and divide the Ex 21:35
shall also own half of the dead *. Ex 21:35
But if the * was known from past Ex 21:36
but the owner of the living * Ex 21:36
*, and the dead one shall be his. Ex 21:36
"IF A MAN steals an * or sheep Ex 22:1
be returned for each stolen *. Ex 22:1
of stealing a live * or donkey or Ex 22:4
"In every case in which an *, Ex 22:9
to keep a donkey, *, sheep, or any Ex 22:10
"If you come upon an enemy's * Ex 23:4
"If your sacrifice is to be an * Lev 1:2,3
sacrifice—an * and a ram, and a Lev 9:4
Next he killed the * and ram—the Lev 9:18
the fat of the * and the ram—the Lev 9:19
an *, lamb, or goat anywhere Lev 17:3,4
* or sheep, for it is already his. Lev 27:26
two leaders and an * for each one; Num 7:3
"This mob will eat us like an * Num 22:4
has the strength of a wild *. Num 23:18-24
has the strength of a wild *, Num 24:3-9
The *, the sheep, the goat, Deu 14:3,4,5
money to buy an *, a sheep, some Deu 14:26
a lamb or an *, sacrificed to the Deu 16:2
* or sheep to the Lord your God. Deu 17:1
stomach of every * or sheep brought Deu 18:3
"IF YOU SEE someone's * or sheep Deu 22:1
trying to get an * or donkey onto Deu 22:4
"Don't plow with an * and a Deu 22:10
"Don't muzzle an * as it treads Deu 25:4
With the strong horns of a wild * Deu 33:17
with an * goad, thereby saving Ju 3:31
his father's best * to the family Ju 6:25
Then sacrifice the * as a burnt Ju 6:26
* or donkey have I stolen? 1Sa 12:3
For sharpening an * goad, 30Ç) 1Sa 13:21
sacrifice an * and a fat lamb. 2Sa 6:13
instruments and * yokes for wood to 2Sa 24:22
each day were one *, six fat sheep, Neh 5:18
"Will the wild * be your happy Job 39:9
Can you use a wild * to plow Job 39:10
He eats grass like an *. Job 40:15
sacrificing a bullock or an *. Ps 69:31
a statue of an * that eats grass, Ps 106:19,20
He followed her as an * going to Pro 7:22
donkey and the *—know their owner Is 1:3
are being hauled away on * carts! Is 46:1
eat straw as the * does, and Is 65:25
When such men sacrifice an * on Is 66:3
lamb or * on the way to slaughter. Jer 11:19
and the face of an * on his Eze 1:10
faces—the first was that of an *; Eze 10:14
a man would lead his favorite *, Hos 11:4
put a muzzle on an * to keep it 1Co 9:9
up the mouth of an * when it is 1Ti 5:18
the second looked like an *; Rev 4:7

OXEN
of her—sheep, *, donkeys, men and Gen 12:16
took sheep and * and servants—both Gen 20:14
Then Abraham gave sheep and * to Gen 21:27
and now I own *, donkeys, sheep, Gen 32:5
a man, and maimed * just for fun. Gen 49:6
to own his slaves, *, donkeys, or Ex 20:17
peace offerings of sheep and *. Ex 20:24
five to one—five * shall be Ex 22:1
"As to the firstborn of the * Ex 22:30
this is to give your * and Ex 23:12
whether from *, sheep, or goats. Lev 7:23
each drawn by two *—a wagon for Num 7:3
wagons and the * to the Levites. Num 7:6
Two wagons and four * were given Num 7:7
wagons and eight * were given to Num 7:8
offerings two *, five rams, five Num 7:17
Balak sacrificed * and sheep, and Num 22:40
all the captives, *, donkeys, and Num 31:28
72,000 *; Num 31:32-35
36,000 * (of which 72 were given Num 31:36-40
*,30,500 donkeys, and16,000 girls Num 31:42-46
servants, *, donkeys, or cattle; Deu 5:14
land, servants, *, donkeys, nor Deu 5:21
Your * shall be butchered before Deu 28:31
and women, young and old; *; Jos 6:21
his daughters, his *, donkeys, Jos 7:24
all their sheep, *, and donkeys. Ju 6:3,4
He took two * and cut them into 1Sa 11:7
will happen to the * of anyone who 1Sa 11:7
the sheep, *, and calves, and ate 1Sa 14:32
them to bring the * and sheep here 1Sa 14:34
*, sheep, camels, and donkeys.' 1Sa 15:3
of the sheep and * and the fattest 1Sa 15:9
sheep and lowing of * I heard?" 1Sa 15:14
of the sheep and *," Saul 1Sa 15:15
of the sheep and * and loot to 1Sa 15:21
all the *, donkeys, and sheep. 1Sa 22:19
the sheep, *, donkeys, camels, and 1Sa 27:9
of Nacon, the * stumbled and Uzzah 2Sa 6:6
"Here are * for the burnt 2Sa 24:22
for the threshing floor and the * 2Sa 24:24
sacrificed sheep, *, and fat young 1Ki 1:9
by sacrificing *, fat goats, and 1Ki 1:19
by sacrificing * and fat goats and 1Ki 1:25
of meal, 10 * from the fattening 1Ki 4:23
* standing tail to tail, three 1Ki 7:25
with carved lions, *, and angels. 1Ki 7:27-30
Above and below the lions and * 1Ki 7:27-30
One large tank and twelve * 1Ki 7:41-46
sacrificing uncounted sheep and *. 1Ki 8:5
* and 120,000 sheep and goats! 1Ki 8:62,63
Elisha left the * standing there 1Ki 19:20
Elisha then returned to his *, 1Ki 19:21
and sheep and * and servants? 2Ki 5:26
of the bronze * and placed it upon 2Ki 16:17
on donkeys, camels, mules, and *. 1Ch 12:40
Uzza and Ahio drove the *. 1Ch 13:7
of Chidon, the * stumbled and Uzza 1Ch 13:9
"Take the *, too, for burnt 1Ch 21:23
the backs of two rows of metal *. 2Ch 4:3
The tank and * were cast as one 2Ch 4:3
There were twelve of these * 2Ch 4:4
The huge tank and the twelve * 2Ch 4:12-16
sheep and * before the Ark in such 2Ch 5:6
was 22,000 * and 120,000 sheep. 2Ch 7:4,5
Lord seven hundred * and seven 2Ch 15:11
of sheep and * for the feast. 2Ch 18:2
In addition, 600 * and 3,000 2Ch 29:32,33
and 300 * as Passover offerings. 2Ch 35:8
and goats and 500 * to the Levites 2Ch 35:9
They did the same with the *. 2Ch 35:12
the purchase of *, rams, lambs, Ez 7:17
* for the nation of Israel; Ez 8:35
500 teams of *, 500 female donkeys, Job 1:2,3
this news: "Your * were plowing, Job 1:14,15
* do not low when they have food; Job 6:5,6,7
of *, and 1,000 female donkeys. Job 42:12
all sheep and *, and wild animals Ps 8:7
from the horns of these wild *. Ps 22:21
* loaded down with produce. Ps 144:12-15
your cows. The * and young donkeys Is 30:24
and *, captains and rulers; Jer 51:23
Can horses run on rocks? Can * Amo 6:12
of * and wanted to try them out. Lk 14:19
out the sheep and *, scattering the Jn 2:15
to sacrifice * to them at the city Act 14:13
only about * when he said this? 1Co 9:9

OXGOAD
for you to kick against the *!" Act 26:14f

OZEB
Jabez sounds like *, the Hebrew 1Ch 4:9f

OZEM
was *, and his seventh was David. 1Ch 2:15
Ram (the oldest), Bunah, Oren, *, 1Ch 2:25

OZNI
named after their ancestor *. Num 26:15-18

OZNITES
The *, named after their ancestor Num 26:15-18

P.S.
*. Php 4:20

PAARAI
* from Arba; 2Sa 23:24-39

PACE
our own * and meet you at Seir." Gen 33:14
and Shime-i kept * with them on a 2Sa 16:13

PACES
it had gone six *, they stopped and 2Sa 6:13

PACIFIED
did, and the king's wrath was *. Est 7:10

PACK
to load their * animals and return Gen 45:17
for the men or their * animals. 2Ki 3:9
men, circles me like a * of dogs; Ps 22:16
theirs, for it is all a * of lies. Jer 10:2,3
* your bags, he says. Jer 10:17
or Mount Carmel by the sea! * up; Jer 46:19
will be like. * whatever you can Eze 12:3
As they watch, lift your * to Eze 12:6
I brought my * outside in the Eze 12:7
darkness with my * on my shoulder Eze 12:7
the clay, and * it in the molds! Nah 3:14
must not even go inside to * Mt 24:17
that day must not return to *; Lk 17:31

PACKED
So the Kenites * up and left. 1Sa 15:6
cakes, and * them onto donkeys. 1Sa 25:18
their heads were * into baskets and 2Ki 10:7
many generations, all * into one. Ps 61:6
was staying was so * with visitors Mk 2:2
this younger son * all his Lk 15:13
So shortly afterwards, we * our Act 21:15

PACKING
sons have finished * the sanctuary Num 4:15

PACKS
for their victims; * of priests Hos 6:9

PACT
as sacrifices to seal their *. Gen 21:27

(PACT Con't)
oaths to seal a non-aggression *. Gen 26:31
will sign a peace *, you and I, and Gen 31:44
and sealed the * by giving him his 1Sa 18:4
renewed their * of friendship; 1Sa 23:18
mutual security * that there was 2Ch 16:3
* with God, and all of them did. 2Ch 34:32
have broken their peace * Is 33:8
I will make a peace * with them, Eze 34:25
peace with them, an everlasting *. Eze 37:26

PADDAM-ARAM
Aramean from *, sister of Laban. Gen 25:20

PADDAN-ARAM
Instead, go at once to *, to the Gen 28:2
and he went to * to visit his Uncle Gen 28:5
had sent Jacob to *, with his Gen 28:6,7,8
had agreed and had left for *. Gen 28:6,7,8
gotten there at *—and took Gen 31:17-20
en route from *, God appeared to Gen 35:9
All these were born to him at *. Gen 35:26
in *, were thirty-three in all. Gen 46:15
when I came from *, as we were Gen 48:7

PADON
Keros, Siaha, *, Lebanah, Hagabah, Ez 2:43-54
Sia, *, Lebana, Hagaba, Neh 7:46-56

PAGAN
For all these * nations also Jer 9:25,26
the * customs of verses 18 and 26. Eze 20:25f

PAGE
See Diagram 4, * 000. Eze 40:6f
See Diagram 5, * 000. Eze 40:28f
See Diagram 6, * 000. Eze 43:13f
See Diagram 7, * 000. Eze 47:13f
See Diagram 7, * 000. Eze 48:8f

PAGEANT
THEN A GREAT * appeared in heaven, Rev 12:1
another mighty * showing things to Rev 15:1

PAGES
See Diagrams 1, 2, 3, * 000, 000, Eze 40:5f

PAGIEL
Asher -* (son of Ochran Num 1:2-15
Leader: Ammishaddai * Num 2:3-31
*, son of Ochran, chief of the Num 7:72-77
the tribe of Asher, led by *, Num 10:26

PAHATH-MOAB
From the subclan of * (the Ez 2:3-35
From the clan of *—Eli-e-ho-enai Ez 8:2-14
From the clan of *: Ez 10:30
Hasshub (son of *), who repaired Neh 3:11
Joab of the subclan of *, 2,818; Neh 7:8-38
Parosh, *, Elam, Zattu, Neh 10:14-27

PAI
from the city of * (his wife was 1Ch 1:50

PAID
So Abraham * Ephron the price he Gen 23:16
how fully I have * for them with my Gen 30:26
was the money * for the grain! Gen 42:35
there that we had * for the grain. Gen 43:21
man's sack the money he had *! Gen 44:1
* for him two and a half dollars; Lev 27:6
they shall be * for their service Num 18:21
Every creditor shall write "* Deu 15:2
"Now God has * me back." Ju 1:7
But the king of Ammon * no Ju 11:28
But Samson replied, "I only * Ju 15:11
God has * back Nabal and kept me 1Sa 25:39
* him tribute each year. 2Sa 8:2
So David * him 2Sa 24:24
Literally, "* him fifty shekels 2Sa 24:24f
ranchers. They * Israel an annual 2Ki 3:4
Jehoiakim surrendered and * him 2Ki 24:1
So David * Ornan $4,300 in gold, 1Ch 21:25
that * annual tribute to him. 2Ch 9:13,14
He also * $200,000 to hire 2Ch 25:5,6
The Ammonites * annual tribute 2Ch 26:8
All expenses will be * by the Ez 6:4
to understand * close attention. Neh 8:1
And so the Lord has * me with Ps 18:24
He heard my prayer! He * Ps 66:19
He has * a full ransom for his Ps 111:9
this day have I * my vows." Pro 7:14f
Oh, return to me, for I have * Is 44:22
Yet she * no attention, even Jer 3:8
weighed out the silver and * him. Jer 32:10
May she be * in full for all our Jer 51:34,35
when Ahaz * "protection money" Eze 23:12f
and prophesy until you're *. Mic 3:11
they * no attention at all. Zec 1:4
until you have * the last penny. Mt 5:26
until the debt would be * in full. Mt 18:30
he had * every last penny due. Mt 18:34
o'clock were *, each received $20. Mt 20:9
But they, too, were * $20. Mt 20:10
and yet you've * them just as much Mt 20:11,12
How they enjoy the deference * Mt 23:7
to accept money * for murder." Mt 27:6
the Jews and even * personally to Lk 7:5
the last penny is * in full." Lk 12:59
The reapers will be * good wages Jn 4:36
the Passover * a visit to Philip, Jn 12:21
a result, getting * within their Rom 1:27
workers need to be * so that they Rom 13:6
You have been bought and * for 1Co 7:23
should be * by those they help. 1Co 9:10
well should be * well and should be 1Ti 5:17
* well if he raises a large crop. 2Ti 2:6
a relative, and yet Abraham * him. Heb 7:6
receive tithes), * tithes to Heb 7:9
* the tithes to Melchizedek. Heb 7:10
* for their sins with his blood. Heb 7:25
to heaven. God * a ransom to save 1Pe 1:18
and the ransom he * was not mere 1Pe 1:18
But he * for you with the 1Pe 1:19

PAIN
in intense * and suffering; Gen 3:16
a trap to you, a * in your side and Jos 23:13
terrible * but life lingers on.' 2Sa 1:9
outside the city on * of death. 1Ki 2:36,37
and soon was moaning in *. 2Ki 4:19
despite all the *—that I have not Job 6:10
him there is only sorrow and *." Job 14:22
are filled with * as though Job 30:17
"Or, God sends sickness and *, Job 33:19
I am worn out with *; Ps 6:6
* to those who leave your paths. Ps 18:26
feel my *; Ps 25:18
sins I am bent and racked with *. Ps 38:5,6
I am lying there upon my bed of *. Ps 41:6
the * of the one you have pierced. Ps 69:26
me, O God, from my poverty and *. Ps 69:29
years are often emptiness and *; Ps 90:10
A lazy fellow is a * to his Pro 10:26
So banish grief and *, but Ecc 11:10
a pile of grief and incurable *. Is 17:11
constricts and burns with *; Is 21:3
birth, who cries and writhes in *. Is 26:17
My heart, my heart—I writhe in *; Jer 4:19
Fright and * have gripped us like Jer 6:24
in God's name on * of death. Jer 11:21,22
You will writhe in * like a woman Jer 13:21
to Jeremiah, "On * of death, don't Jer 38:24
of terror and * rise from all over Jer 48:34
Babylon trembles and writhes in * Jer 51:29
and made her stagger with the *. Eze 29:7
be racked with *, Thebes will be Eze 30:16
All are gone! * has gripped you Mic 4:9
in your terrible *, O people of Mic 4:10
And whatever their illness and *, Mt 4:24
bed paralyzed and racked with *. Mt 8:5,6
joy and the * is forgotten. Jn 16:21
be released from * and suffering. Rom 8:23
and how can you if I cause you *? 2Co 2:2
because the * turned you to God. 2Co 7:9
and * and sleepless nights. 2Co 11:27
So God sent * and suffering to 1Ti 2:15
and underwent *, you must have the 1Pe 4:1
like the * of scorpion stings. Rev 9:5
screamed in the * of her labor, Rev 12:2
nor sorrow, nor crying, nor *. Rev 21:4

PAINFUL
is, "A quick death is less *." Ju 8:21f
and be freed from his * grip. Job 6:8,9
unhappy with another * visit." 2Co 2:1
how * it would be to you. 2Co 7:8

PAINS
But Rachel's * of childbirth Gen 35:16
dead, her labor * suddenly began. 1Sa 4:19
Or, "because of the * in my Ps 38:8f
and soothes their * and worries. Ps 41:3
Or, "they never have any *." Ps 73:4f
even before the birth * come. Is 66:7,8
women in the * of giving birth. Jer 48:41
for you the * of a mother waiting Gal 4:19
* begin when her child is born. 1Th 5:3
heaven for their * and sores, but Rev 16:11

PAINSTAKINGLY
In the past I * destroyed the Jer 31:28

PAINTED
to Jezreel, she * her eyelids and 2Ki 9:30
cedar and * a lovely red." Jer 22:14
with pictures she saw * on a wall! Eze 23:14,15
You bathed yourself, * your Eze 23:40

PAINTINGS
When she saw these * she longed Eze 23:16

PAIR
Bring a * of every animal—a male Gen 6:19,20
Bring in a * of each kind of bird Gen 6:19,20
Bring in the animals, too—a * of Gen 7:2
And she made him a * of gloves Gen 27:16
stem beneath each * of branches; Ex 37:20,21
also a flower below the bottom * Ex 37:20,21
and above the top *, four in all. Ex 37:20,21
use one of the * for a sin offering Lev 14:22
* he is able to afford). Lev 14:30
One of the * is for a sin Lev 14:31
with a torch between each *. Ju 15:4
altar and with a * of tongs picked Is 6:6
of his back. One * stretched out to Eze 1:11
and the other * covered his body. Eze 1:11
they trade them for a * of shoes. Amo 2:6
of silver or a * of shoes, or Amo 8:6
* of shoes or a change of clothes. Mk 6:8,9
a * of turtledoves or two young Lk 2:24
bag, or even an extra * of shoes. Lk 10:4
just bought five * of oxen and Lk 14:19
a * of balances in his hand. Rev 6:5

PAIRED
and camels were * for the attack. Is 21:6,7f
represented by these * riders. Is 21:6,7f

PAIRS
take seven * of each of them, and Gen 7:2
of each of them, and seven * Gen 7:3
They came into the boat in *, Gen 7:8,9
With them in the boat were * of Gen 7:14,15
left the ark in * and groups. Gen 8:18,19
*, with a torch between each pair. Ju 15:4
When he sees riders in * on Is 21:6,7
troop, horsemen in *, riders on Is 21:6,7f
Here come riders in *!" Is 21:8,9
had four faces and two * of wings! Eze 1:6
Each had two * of wings Eze 1:11
them on ahead in * to all the towns Lk 10:1

PALACE
When the * aides saw her, they Gen 12:15
had her brought to him at his *. Gen 20:2
meeting of all the * personnel and Gen 20:8
Potiphar was captain of the * Gen 37:36
told and took them to Joseph's *. Gen 43:17
entrance to the *, they went over Gen 43:19
conducted into the * and given Gen 43:24
throughout the *, and the news was Gen 45:2
quickly carried to Pharaoh's *. Gen 45:2
them outside the *, as they came Ex 5:20
he returned to his *, unimpressed. Ex 7:23
* and in every home in Egypt. Ex 8:24
They will fill your *, and the Ex 10:6
anger, Moses stomped from the *. Ex 11:8
were to give me a * filled with Num 22:18
if you gave me a * filled with Num 24:13
and masons to build a * for David. 2Sa 5:11
beautiful cedar * while the Ark of 2Sa 7:2
you shall live here at the *!" 2Sa 9:7
to Jerusalem to live at the *. 2Sa 9:13
for a stroll on the roof of the *. 2Sa 11:2
the gateway of the * with the other 2Sa 11:9
So Uriah stayed around the *. 2Sa 11:12
he slept at the entry to the *. 2Sa 11:13
* and she became one of his wives; 2Sa 11:27
I gave you his * and his wives 2Sa 12:8
Then he returned to the * and 2Sa 12:20
wives to keep the * in order. 2Sa 15:16
on the roof of the * where 2Sa 16:22
When he arrived at his * in 2Sa 20:3
building his * and the Temple and 1Ki 3:1
Ahishar was manager of * affairs; 1Ki 4:1
for the * were 195 bushels of fine 1Ki 4:22
THEN SOLOMON BUILT his own *, 1Ki 7:1
One of the rooms in the * was 1Ki 7:2
same size, in the * which he built 1Ki 7:8
the Temple and the porch of the *. 1Ki 7:12
the Temple and the * and all the 1Ki 9:1
the Temple and the *, he gave 1Ki 9:10
construction of the * and Temple. 1Ki 9:11,12
the Temple, his *, Fort Millo, the 1Ki 9:15
he had built for her in the *. 1Ki 9:24
She also saw the beautiful * he 1Ki 10:4
Your people are happy and your * 1Ki 10:8
the Temple and the *, and for harps 1Ki 10:12
And he kept them in his * in the 1Ki 10:16,17
* among Pharaoh's own sons. 1Ki 11:20
"Come to the * with me and rest 1Ki 13:7
your *, I wouldn't go into it; 1Ki 13:8
the Temple and the * and stole 1Ki 14:26
the * guards used these instead. 1Ki 14:27
treasures of the *, and gave them 1Ki 15:18
*, in the capital city of Tirzah. 1Ki 16:9
he went into the * and burned it 1Ki 16:18
men to search your * and the homes 1Ki 20:5,6
* and the homes of the people.' 1Ki 20:9
of the city near King Ahab's *. 1Ki 21:1
it's so convenient to the *." 1Ki 21:2
So Ahab went back to the * angry 1Ki 21:4
story of the ivory * and the cities 1Ki 22:39
porch of his * at Samaria and was 2Ki 1:2
and tell the people at the *." 2Ki 7:9
the news to those in the *. 2Ki 7:11
the gate of the *, she shouted at 2Ki 9:31
Then Jehu went into the * for 2Ki 9:34
So the manager of * affairs and 2Ki 10:5
summoned the officers of the * 2Ki 11:4
on the Sabbath are to guard the *. 2Ki 11:5
So they dragged her to the * 2Ki 11:16
the guardhouse, and into the *. 2Ki 11:19
and the *, and sent it to Hazael. 2Ki 12:18
* treasury, also the gold cups. 2Ki 14:14
him in the * at Samaria (Argob and 2Ki 15:25
between the * and the Temple. 2Ki 16:18
the Temple and in the * treasury. 2Ki 18:15
"What have they seen in your * 2Ki 20:15
* shall be carried to Babylon. 2Ki 20:17
in the * of the king of Babylon." 2Ki 20:18
the garden of his * at Uzza, and 2Ki 21:18
him and killed him in the *. 2Ki 21:23

(PALACE Con't)
in charge of the * tailor shop. 2Ki 22:14
entrance of the * of Joshua, the 2Ki 23:8
on the * roof above the Ahaz Room. 2Ki 23:12
from the Temple and the royal *; 2Ki 24:13
He burned down the Temple, the * 2Ki 25:9
help build David's * and he 1Ch 14:1
living in his new * for some time 1Ch 17:1
in charge of the * treasuries, and 1Ch 27:25
for the Lord and a * for himself. 2Ch 2:1
David when he was building his *. 2Ch 2:3
Temple, and a royal * for himself. 2Ch 2:12
the Temple as well as his own *. 2Ch 7:11
his own royal * were completed. 2Ch 8:1
to the new * he had built for her. 2Ch 8:11
in King David's *, for the Ark of 2Ch 8:11
the beauty of his *, and how 2Ch 9:3
the Temple and the *, and to 2Ch 9:11
Forest of Lebanon Room in his *. 2Ch 9:16
Temple and of the *, also all of 2Ch 12:9
and from the *, and to send it to 2Ch 16:2
in the king's *, including his sons 2Ch 21:17
go over to the *, and a third will 2Ch 23:5,6
they killed her at the * stables. 2Ch 23:15,16,17
Upper Gate to the *, and seated the 2Ch 23:20
well as the treasures from the *; 2Ch 25:24
the * treasures, it did no good. 2Ch 28:21
Then they went back to the * and 2Ch 29:18
beneath his own *, and his son Amon 2Ch 33:20,21
assassinated him in his *. 2Ch 33:24
the Temple and the *, and took with 2Ch 36:18
was found in the * at Ecbatana, in Ez 6:2
when I was at the * at Shushan, Neh 1:1
at Shushan *, to which the emperor Est 1:1
party for the * servants and Est 1:5
in the courtyard of the * garden. Est 1:5
women of the * at the same time. Est 1:9
certain Jew at the * named Mordecai Est 2:5
harem at Shushan *, along with many Est 2:8
girls from the * as her maids, and Est 2:9
So Esther was taken to the * of Est 2:16
was on duty at the *, two of the Est 2:21
were guards at the * gate—became Est 2:21
the gate of the *, for no one was Est 4:2
just outside the * gates, and Est 4:6
*, when all other Jews are killed? Est 4:13
* for just such a time as this?" Est 4:14
royal hall of the *, where the king Est 5:1
watchmen at the * gates, who had Est 6:1
outer court of the * to ask the Est 6:4
went out into the * garden as Haman Est 7:7
king returned from the * garden. Est 7:8
in the *, before my very eyes?" Est 7:8
given Esther the * of Haman and he Est 8:7
was also issued at Shushan *. Est 8:14
name in the king's * and his fame Est 9:4
as they enter in the * gates! Ps 45:15
like the pillars of a * wall. Ps 144:12-15
WISDOM HAS BUILT a * supported on Pro 9:1
king has brought me into his *. Sol 1:4
All the pleasant music in your * Is 14:11
say to Shebna, the * administrator: Is 22:15,16
on a tour of the *, showing them Is 39:2
in the * of the king of Babylon." Is 39:7
including the * of the kings of Jer 19:13
this * shall become a shambles. Jer 22:5
concerning the *: You are as Jer 22:6
for you are building your great * Jer 22:13
a magnificent * with huge rooms and Jer 22:14
But a beautiful * does not Jer 22:15
in a beautiful * among the cedars Jer 22:23
over from the * and sat down at the Jer 26:10
that those in the * of the king of Jer 27:18
her ruins; the * will be Jer 30:18
court of the prison in the *." Jer 32:2f
the *, while the Babylonian army Jer 32:2
and the king's * too, for materials Jer 33:4
one used by the * official, Jer 35:4
went down to the * to the Jer 36:12
part of the * at the time, sitting Jer 36:22
for him to come to the * secretly. Jer 37:17
be placed in the * prison instead, Jer 37:21
So Jeremiah was kept in the * Jer 37:21
an important * official, heard that Jer 38:7
men and went to a * depot for Jer 38:11
the * prison, where he remained. Jer 38:13
women left in your * will be Jer 38:21,22
walls back of the * garden and Jer 39:4
including the *, and tore down the Jer 39:8
of Pharaoh's * here in Tahpanhes, Jer 43:9
the Temple and the * and all the Jer 52:13
was in charge of his * personnel, Dan 1:3,4
poise to look good around the *." Dan 1:3,4
you from your *, and you will live Dan 4:25
roof of the royal * in Babylon, Dan 4:29
You will be forced out of the * Dan 4:32
chased from his * and ate grass Dan 4:33
out of his * into the fields. Dan 5:21
Then the king returned to his * Dan 6:18
to King Hazael's *, destroying the Amo 1:4
The enemy has entered! The * is Nah 2:6
a man dressed as a prince in a *? Mt 11:8
stag party for his * aides, army Mk 6:21
barracks of the *, called out the Mk 15:16,17
out the entire * guard, dressed him Mk 15:16,17
in charge of his * and domestic Lk 8:3
armed, guards his *, it is safe— Lk 11:21
Next he was taken to the * of the Jn 18:28
Then Pilate went back into the * Jn 18:33
He took Jesus back into the * Jn 19:9
of all the affairs of the *. Act 7:10
in the prison at King Herod's *. Act 23:35
those who work in Caesar's *. Php 4:22

PALACES
DAVID NOW BUILT several * for 1Ch 15:1
and burned all the * and destroyed 2Ch 36:19
In your inlaid * of ivory, lovely Ps 45:8
known in her * for a high tower." Ps 48:3f
Note her walls and tour her *, Ps 48:13
Temple of my God than live in * Ps 84:10
walls and prosperity in your *. Ps 122:7
yet are found even in king's *! Pro 30:24-28
the * of the rich and mighty. Is 13:2
and jackals will den within the *. Is 13:22
its * and make it a heap of ruins. Is 23:13
Beautiful * in distant lands Is 25:2
will be gone. * and mansions will Is 32:14
Thorns will overrun the *, and Is 34:13
by night and destroy her *!" Jer 6:5
The fire shall spread to the * Jer 17:27
Judah and in the * in Jerusalem Jer 27:18
shall burn up the * of Benhadad. Jer 49:27
He has destroyed her forts and *. Lam 2:5
he has given their * to their Lam 2:7
Those brought up in * now scratch Lam 4:5
He demolished the * of the Eze 19:7
Israel has built great *; Hos 8:14
those * and burn those fortresses. Hos 8:14
burn down all his forts and *." Amo 1:10
will burn down their forts and *; Amo 1:14
will destroy all the * in Kerioth. Amo 2:2
all Jerusalem's * and forts." Amo 2:5
too—and demolish their ivory *." Amo 3:15
the ruins of her *, hooting from Zep 2:14
in *, not out in the wilderness. Lk 7:25

PALAL
to the corner. * (son of Uzai) Neh 3:25

PALE
Then Haman grew * with fright Est 7:6
is a cup of * and sparkling wine. Ps 75:8
longer * with fear, or be ashamed. Is 29:22
"I'm afraid you will become * and Dan 1:10
be so * and frightened over this. Dan 5:10
and my face was * with fright, but Dan 7:28
and I grew * and weak with fright. Dan 10:8
their faces grow * with fright. Joe 2:6
And now I saw a * horse, and Rev 6:8

PALE-FACED
her people stand aghast, * and Nah 2:10

PALESTINE
living in the desert east of *. Jer 49:28f
coast of * around 1200 B.C. Zep 2:5f
"to the ends of the land" of *. Zec 9:10f

PALL
Over all Israel lies a * of Is 5:30
of gloom, the * of death that hangs Is 25:7

PALLID
city reflect upon your * faces. Is 13:8

PALLU
Reuben's sons: Hanoch, *, Hezron, Gen 46:8-14
son:Hanoch, *,Hezron, Carmi. Ex 6:14
named after their ancestor *. Num 26:5-11
one of the sons of *—were the Num 26:5-11
Hanoch, *, Hezron, Carmi. 1Ch 5:3

PALLUITES
The *, named after their ancestor Num 26:5-11

PALM
springs and seventy * trees; Ex 15:27
pour it into the * of his left Lev 14:15
olive oil into the * of his own Lev 14:26
with fruit, and * fronds, and the Lev 23:40
of water and seventy * trees; Num 33:9
and Jericho, the city of * trees; Deu 34:3
"The City of * Trees," and the Ju 1:16
called "The City of * Trees." Ju 3:13
called "Deborah's * Tree," Ju 4:5
Figures of angels, * trees, and 1Ki 6:29
with cherubim, * trees, and open 1Ki 6:32
Angels, * trees, and open 1Ki 6:35
Cherubim, lions, and * trees 1Ki 7:36
engraved with * trees and chains. 2Ch 3:5
in Jericho, the City of * Trees. 2Ch 28:15
olive, myrtle, *, and fig trees and Neh 8:15
flourish like * trees, and grow Ps 92:12
You are tall and slim like a * Sol 7:7
climb up into the * tree and take Sol 7:8
of the earth; the * of my right Is 48:13
your name upon my * and ever before Is 49:16
The pillars were decorated with * Eze 40:16
entry hall and the * tree Eze 40:22
it, and there were * tree Eze 40:26
It had * tree decorations on the Eze 40:31
and there were * tree decorations Eze 40:34
court, and it had * tree Eze 40:37
two faces, and of * trees Eze 41:17,18
toward the * tree on one side, and Eze 41:19,20
the * tree on the other side. Eze 41:19,20
and * trees, just as on the walls. Eze 41:25
windows and carved * trees on both Eze 41:26
visitors took * branches and went Jn 12:13
with * branches in their hands. Rev 7:9

PALTI
*, son of Raphu, from the tribe of Num 13:3-15
Gallim named * (the son of Laish). 1Sa 25:44
took her away from her husband *. 2Sa 3:15
Helez from *; 2Sa 23:24-39

PALTIEL
Issachar * (son of Azzan) Num 34:16-28

PALTRY
For the sake of a few * handfuls Eze 13:19

PAMPER
* a servant from childhood, and Pro 29:21

PAMPHYLIA
Phrygia, *, Egypt, the Cyrene Act 2:10
Literally, "*." Act 13:13f
through Pisidia to *, preached Act 14:24
since John had deserted them in *. Act 15:38
of Cilicia and *, landing at Myra, Act 27:5

PAN
is cooked in a *, it too shall be Lev 2:7
streams of water and * the gold. Job 28:11

PANCAKES
Mix up some *! Gen 18:6
without yeast; * made of fine flour Num 6:15
lamb, one of the * (made without Num 6:19
it, and then made * from it—they Num 11:8
like * fried in vegetable oil. Num 11:8

PANEL
home and on the * above the door. Ex 12:7
the blood upon the * at the top of Ex 12:23

PANELED
Temple, Solomon * it all, including 1Ki 6:9
to ceiling, was * with cedar, and 1Ki 6:15
Place—was also * from the floor to 1Ki 6:16
it was * with cedar from the 1Ki 7:7
The main part of the Temple was * 2Ch 3:5
and many windows, * throughout with Jer 22:14
entry hall were *, and all three Eze 41:15,16
of the Temple were * with wood Eze 41:15,16
the Holy of Holies was also *. Eze 41:17,18

PANELING
Temple the cedar * laid over the 1Ki 6:18
chopped the carved *, and set the Ps 74:5,6
All her cedar * will lie open to Zep 2:14

PANELS
the two side *, so that there will Ex 12:22
Its * were square, not round. 1Ki 7:31

PANGS
Fear grips you with terrible *, Is 13:8
sharp * of horror are upon me, Is 21:3
upon me, like the * of a woman Is 21:3
at his sides; * of terror gripped Jer 50:43
like the * of a woman in labor. Jer 50:43
hunger * and emptiness will still Mic 6:14

PANIC
sudden terrors and *, and with Lev 26:16
blindness, fear, and * upon you. Deu 28:28
threw them into a * so that the Jos 10:10
the enemy into a *, both the Ju 4:15
in a *, shouting and running away. Ju 7:21
plague, and there was a great *. 1Sa 5:9
Suddenly * broke out throughout 1Sa 14:15
a * and everyone will run away; 2Sa 17:2,3
there will be * among your troops 2Sa 17:9
the banquet table and fled in *; 1Ki 1:49,50
leaders fled in * to Egypt, for 2Ki 25:26
city fell into confusion and *. Est 3:15
they are filled with * like a Ps 48:6
Judah and throw her people into *. Is 7:6
Don't you * as so many of your Is 8:12
They will * and flee, and the Is 31:8
be the shouts of *, "We are Jer 49:29
become fools! * shall seize her Jer 50:36
are burning and the army is in *. Jer 51:32
But don't * when you hear the Jer 51:46
to bring * to the Ethiopians; Eze 30:9
The palace is in *! Nah 2:6
insurrections beginning, don't *. Lk 21:9

PANIC-STRICKEN
I was terrified and *. Ps 30:6,7
with terror, * from the Lord, and Zec 14:13

PANICKED
of the Lord had arrived, they *. 1Sa 4:7
the entire Syrian army * and fled. 1Ki 20:20
So they * and fled into the 2Ki 7:7

PANNAG
with wheat from Minnith and *, Eze 27:17
Or, "with wheat, minnith and *." Eze 27:17f

PANS
* are all to be made of bronze. Ex 27:3
basins, meat hooks, and fire *. Ex 38:3
all the pots and * in the tent, and Num 19:18
"Then borrow many pots and * 2Ki 4:3

(PANS Con't)
into the pots and *, setting them 2Ki 4:4
Her sons brought the pots and * 2Ki 4:5
pots, kettles, and *, and hurried 2Ch 35:13
making pegs to hang up pots and *! Eze 15:3
cleansing for pots, * and dishes. Mk 7:4

PANTED
But Jacob *, "I will not let you Gen 32:26

PANTHEON
gods in the Babylonian *. Is 46:1f

PANTHERS
have their dens, and * prowl. Sol 4:8

PANTING
bare hills * like thirsty jackals. Jer 14:6

PANTS
AS THE DEER * for water, so I long Ps 42:1

PAPER
sets fire to *. Pro 26:21
as quickly gone as * in fire, and Ecc 7:6
He motioned for a piece of * and Lk 1:63

PAPERS
I handed the * to Baruch (son of Jer 32:12
future these * will be valuable. Jer 32:15
Then after I had given the * to Jer 32:16

PAPHOS
they reached * where they met a Act 13:6,7
him left * by ship for Turkey, Act 13:13

PAPYRUS
a little boat from * reeds, Ex 2:3
* dating from the 5th century B.C. Jer 7:18f

PARABLE
King Joash replied with this *: 2Ch 25:18
And now give this * to these Eze 24:3
a vision and many a * and dream. Hos 12:10

PARABLES
prophesied, "I will talk in *; Mt 13:34,35
meaning of these *, for they tell a Lk 8:10

PARADE
he visited the * grounds of the Ju 13:25
for they love to * in dignified Lk 20:46
end of a victor's *, to be stared 1Co 4:9

PARADED
Temple, the guards * before him and 1Ki 14:28

PARADISE
fertile, wonderful place—a real *. Ju 18:9,10
"Today you will be with me in *. Lk 23:43
But anyway, there I was in *, 2Co 12:2,3
the Tree of Life in the * of God. Rev 2:7

PARAH
Bethel, Avvim, *, Ophrah, Jos 18:21-28

PARALLEL
* phrase, "fruit of the land." Is 4:2,3,4f
wing, * to the longer wing. Eze 42:7,8
There is no modern * to this Hos 4:12f
Implied in * passages. Mk 1:12,13f

PARALYZE
in your house, and I will * Eze 3:25
And I will * Eze 4:8

PARALYZED
and they were * with fear. Jos 5:1
The Israeli army was * with fear Jos 7:5
he had a stroke and lay * 1Sa 25:37,38
upon the ground, * with fright 1Sa 28:20
at Hebron, he was * with fear, and 2Sa 4:1
of lions, will be * with fear; 2Sa 17:10
Instantly the king's arm became * 1Ki 13:4
Don't be * by this mighty army! 2Ch 20:15
I am losing all hope; I am * Ps 143:4
becomes as useless as a * leg. Pro 26:7
Your arms lie * with fear; Is 13:7
insane, or *—he healed them all. Mt 4:24
was in bed * and racked with pain. Mt 8:5,6
Soon some men brought him a * boy Mt 9:2
Then, turning to the * man, he Mt 9:5,6
Four men arrived carrying a * Mk 2:3
Then, turning to the * man, he Mk 2:9,10,11
Some men came carrying a * man on Lk 5:18,19
Then, turning to the * man, he Lk 5:23,24
blind, or with * limbs—lay on the Jn 5:3
and many who were * or lame were Act 8:7
* and bedridden for eight years. Act 9:33

PARAN
of *, and became an expert archer. Gen 21:20,21
it stopped in the wilderness of *. Num 10:12
and camped in the wilderness of *. Num 12:16
the wilderness of * at the time. Num 13:3-15
the wilderness of * at Kadesh, and Num 13:26
included Suph, *, Tophel, Laban, Deu 1:1
He shone from Mount *, Deu 33:2
went down to the wilderness of *. 1Sa 25:1
Midian and went to *, where 1Ki 11:16,17,18
from Mount *." Hab 3:3f

PARAPHRASE
In this * "Yahweh" is Ex 3:15f
This * is the modern 1Sa 20:30f
See context for validity of the *. Ps 116:15f
the meaning expressed in the *. Dan 8:26f
The * is of course highly Mt 13:52f
The * relates this to verse 47. Lk 24:49f
This alternate * interprets Jn 3:5f
rendering, or *, of Isaiah 6:10. Jn 12:40f
The above * is the modern Jn 16:26f
A * of this verse—that goes beyond Jn 18:34f
what is indicated in the * above. Act 27:4f
An alternative * of these verses 1Pe 2:2,3f
giving probability to the *; Rev 1:4f

PARAPHRASED
Perhaps this could be *, "Blessed Ps 137:9f

PARAPHRASING
of this book's *—would be, "Do you Jn 18:34f

PARAS
men from far-off *, Lud and Put. Eze 27:10

PARCEL
in Shechem, in the * of ground Jos 24:32
located on the * of ground Jacob Jn 4:5,6

PARCELS
realize that God * out the kingdoms Dan 4:32

PARCHED
kernels nor bread nor * grain. Lev 23:14
Literally, "ate the * grain and Ru 2:14f
and barley flour, * grain, beans, 2Sa 17:28,29
so that the * and barren ground is Job 38:25-27
How I thirst for you in this * Ps 63:1
I thirst for you as * land Ps 143:6
the ditches will be * and dry, Is 19:5
the desert. The * ground will Is 35:7
their tongues are * from thirst, Is 41:17
flow across the dry, * ground. Is 41:18
your thirst and for your * fields. Is 44:3
The ground is * and cracked for Jer 14:4
Then the earth can answer the * Hos 1:21,22
I will turn them back into the * Joe 2:20

PARCHMENTS
the books, but especially the *. 2Ti 4:13

PARDON
he will not * your transgression; Ex 23:21
people, but * our iniquity and our Ex 34:9
Oh, I plead with you, * the sins Num 14:19
will * them as you have requested. Num 14:20,21
For the Lord will not *! Deu 29:20
"* me, sir," Saul replied. 1Sa 9:21
Oh, please * my sin now and go 1Sa 15:25
However, may the Lord * me this 2Ki 5:18
the Lord * me when I bow too." 2Ki 5:18
and the Lord would not * it. 2Ki 24:3,4
the good Lord * everyone who 2Ch 30:17,18,19
always ready to *, gracious and Neh 9:17
Why not just * my sin and take Job 7:21
How many they are. Oh, * them for Ps 25:11
our God, for he will abundantly *! Is 55:7
How can I * you? Jer 5:7
their sins against me, and * them. Jer 33:8
I will * the remnant I preserve. Jer 50:20

PARDONED
refuge in him will be freely *. Ps 34:22
Her sins are *, and the Lord will Is 40:2
will live, for Christ has * it. Rom 8:10
only then could he be * and saved. Rom 10:5

PARDONS
is merciful, and * even those who Dan 9:9
God like you, who * the sins of the Mic 7:18

PARE
She must shave her head and * her Deu 21:12

PARENTHESES
omit the material within the *. Jn 5:4f

PARENTS
home and to her *, and to remain a Gen 38:11
So Tamar went home to her *. Gen 38:11
a bridegroom to the bride's *." Ex 22:16f
They were the * of Aaron, Moses, Num 26:58,59
upon them—your * saw it with their Deu 7:19
while living at home with her *; Deu 22:21
As Samson and his * were going to Ju 14:5
you return to your *' homes instead Ru 1:8
custom of the day. * kept a widowed Ru 1:11f
return to your *' homes, for I am Ru 1:12
Judah, became the * of twin sons, 1Ch 2:4
of Judah, from which their * Ez 2:1
of protest from * against some of Neh 5:1
So I argued with these * and Neh 13:25
* and return to them no more. Job 39:4
your * in your homeland far away. Ps 45:10,11
So give your * joy! Pro 23:24,25
A man who robs his * and says, Pro 28:24
grief for their *' death. Jer 16:7
or not their * are foreigners—are Eze 47:22
their * and cause their deaths. Mt 10:21
anyone who reviles his * must Mt 15:4
But you say, 'Even if your * Mt 15:5,6
God to honor and care for your *. Mt 15:5,6
Her * just couldn't get over it. Mk 5:41,42
his needy *, telling them, 'Sorry, Mk 7:11
will betray their * to be killed. Mk 13:12
of a child, his * took him to Lk 2:22
At that time Jesus' * also Lk 2:24
When Jesus' * had fulfilled all Lk 2:39
he accompanied his * to Jerusalem Lk 2:41,42
in Jerusalem. His * didn't miss him Lk 2:43
His * didn't know what to think. Lk 2:48
he said. Her * were overcome Lk 8:56
lie, honor your *, and so on." Lk 18:20
wife, brothers, *, or children for Lk 18:29
Even those closest to you—your * Lk 21:16
his own sins or those of his *?" Jn 9:2
they called in his * and asked Jn 9:18
His * replied, "We know this is Jn 9:20
our race, forcing * to abandon Act 7:19
divine beauty. His * hid him at Act 7:20
being disobedient to their *. Rom 1:30
born of Jewish * or because you Rom 2:28
* supply food for their children. 2Co 12:14
CHILDREN, OBEY YOUR *; Eph 6:1
And now a word to you *. Eph 6:4
begin at home, supporting needy *. 1Ti 5:4
to their *, ungrateful to them, and 2Ti 3:2
wild or disobedient to their *. Tit 1:6
Moses' * had faith too. Heb 11:23
to you from your *, for the life 1Pe 1:23

PARK
and deer in the *, that you do not Sol 2:7
of the *, not to awake my lover. Sol 3:5

PARKS
gardens, * and orchards for myself, Ecc 2:4,5,6
and *, with a city in the center. Eze 48:15

PARMASHTA
*, Arisai, Est 9:7-10

PARMENAS
Nicanor, Timon, * Act 6:5

PARNACH
Elizaphan (son of *) Num 34:16-28

PARODY
*," says the Lord of Hosts. Mal 2:8

PAROSH
From the subclan of *, 2,172; Ez 2:3-35
From the clan of *—Zechariah, and Ez 8:2-14
From the clan of *: Ez 10:25
Next was Pedaiah (son of *). Neh 3:25
From the subclan of *, 2,172; Neh 7:8-38
*, Pahath-moab, Elam, Zattu, Neh 10:14-27

PARSHANDATHA
*, Dalphon, Aspatha, Poratha, Est 9:7-10

PARSIN
'Mene,' 'Mene,' 'Tekel,' '*.' Dan 5:24,25
"* means 'divided'—your kingdom Dan 5:28

PART
"She is * of my own bone and Gen 2:23
If you want that * over there to Gen 13:9
"Your * of the contract," God Gen 17:9,10
This is a permanent * of this Gen 17:12
and Abraham went with them * of Gen 18:16
me and keep your * of my contract Ex 19:5
Your * of the agreement is to Ex 34:11
were actually a * of the golden Ex 37:8
made as * of the altar so that it Ex 37:25
The main * of the ephod was Ex 39:22
Then the priests shall burn * of Lev 2:16
the priests this * of the burnt Lev 6:17
leavened bread. * of this Lev 7:14
he burned each * upon the altar. Lev 9:13
from the front * of his head, he Lev 13:41
repay only a small * of the amount Lev 25:52
"If a man dedicates any * of his Lev 27:16
but which is not * of his family Lev 27:22
sanctified each * of the Num 7:1
from the choicest * of the tithes Num 18:28,29
God will keep his * of the contract Deu 7:12
justice in every * of the land. Deu 16:18
Each man must have a spade as * Deu 23:13
you go will be * of the land of Jos 1:3
of land—including * of the land Jos 19:1
You have no * in the Lord.' Jos 22:24,25
have no * in the Lord our God.' Jos 22:26,27
if you, on your *, would make no Ju 2:2
conquer * of Israel at that time. Ju 3:12
the girls who took * in the Ju 21:23
a trip to take * in a public 1Sa 9:12,13
Bethlehem to take * in a family 1Sa 20:28,29
the southern * of the wilderness. 1Sa 23:19
so they gave him * of a fig cake, 1Sa 30:11,12
at Ziklag, he sent * of the loot to 1Sa 30:26
to the hottest * of the battle—and 2Sa 11:15
to * them, one of them was killed. 2Sa 14:5,6
spies to every * of Israel to 2Sa 15:10
They were not * of Israel, but 2Sa 21:2
had been cast as * of the stands. 1Ki 7:32
"I want no * of you," Elisha 2Ki 3:13
"Every * of this blueprint," 1Ch 28:19
The main * of the Temple was 2Ch 3:5
they all took * in the ceremonies 2Ch 5:11,12
leaders from every * of the nation 2Ch 12:5
had secretly sent * of his army 2Ch 13:13,14
sheep—it was * of the plunder they 2Ch 15:11
As the people from every * of 2Ch 20:13
So the people from every * of 2Ch 29:31
But for the most * they were 2Ch 30:10
a more active *, so they sanctified 2Ch 30:15
in Jerusalem took * in the Passover 2Ch 35:17
you may have no * in this work. Ez 4:3
forget about this * of your empire Ez 4:16
but you may have no * in this Neh 2:20
the mayor of another * of Mizpah; Neh 3:19
The leaders in this * of the Neh 9:5
to bring the first * of every crop Neh 10:35

PART Con't)
and to take * in the joyous Neh 12:27
them in from every * of Est 1:1
This was * of the famed "law of Est 8:8f
wanted no * of him and his ways. Job 21:14
phrase was * of the original text. Ps 49:20f
every kind, to have no * in them. Ps 101:3
Cursing is as much a * of him as Ps 109:18
him the first * of all your income, Pro 3:9,10
and they have no * in anything here Ecc 9:6
my love, in every * of you. Sol 4:7
my people as * of his plan to Is 10:7
Elamites and Medes will take * in Is 21:2
And after his care, he uses * of Is 44:15
and praise! * of the tree he burns Is 44:16
I planned to give you * of this Jer 3:19
take their * in all the fun; Jer 31:13
The king was in a winterized * Jer 36:22
That is, the wheel was a living * Eze 10:17f
This is * of your punishment for Eze 16:58
its feet * iron and part clay. Dan 2:33
its feet part iron and * clay. Dan 2:33
The feet and toes you saw—* iron Dan 2:41,42
saw—part iron and * clay—show that Dan 2:41,42
Daniel in every * of my kingdom. Dan 6:25,26
they were * of a great wave of Zep 2:5f
Here is your *: Tell the truth. Zec 8:16
this time I was to act the * of a Zec 11:15
Better for * of you to be Mt 5:29
permeates every * of the dough." Mt 13:33
Jesus then left that * of the Mt 15:21
food as * of their religion. Mk 2:18
* of the old way of doing things. Mk 2:21
did during that * of the service Lk 1:10
even the smallest * of your income, Lk 11:42
there in that * of the country.' Lk 17:21
It is * of God's plan. Lk 22:22
because you are not * of my flock. Jn 10:26
They are not * of this world any Jn 17:16
afternoon to take * in the three Act 3:1
and brought only * of the money, Act 5:2
You can have no * in this, for Act 8:21
omit verse 37 wholly or in *. Act 8:37f
throughout this * of Turkey but all Act 19:27
Then Paul thought of something! * Act 23:6
Sadducees, and * were Pharisees! Act 23:6
this is all * of God's great plan Rom 2:16
to become a * of Jesus Christ; Rom 6:2,3
For you have become a * of him, Rom 6:5
with him; that * of you that loves Rom 6:6
Do not let any * of your bodies Rom 6:13
to God—every * of you—for you are Rom 6:13
you are now a * of God's tree; Rom 11:18
from him—being * of a wild olive Rom 11:24
So should I take * of Christ and 1Co 6:15
she becomes a * of him and he 1Co 6:16
of him and he becomes a * of her? 1Co 6:16
So use every * of your body to 1Co 6:20
The wife is * of her husband as 1Co 7:39
Each of us is a * of the one 1Co 12:13
has many parts, not just one *. 1Co 12:14
If the foot says, "I am not a * 1Co 12:15
make it any less a * of the body. 1Co 12:15
say, "I am not * of the body 1Co 12:16
Would that make it any less a * 1Co 12:16
put each * just where he wants it. 1Co 12:18
would be if it had only one *! 1Co 12:19
If one * suffers, all parts 1Co 12:26
it, and if one * is honored, all 1Co 12:26
a separate and necessary * of it. 1Co 12:27
They are not to take * in the 1Co 14:34
lack of love on my *, but because 2Co 6:12
not because of nagging on my *. 2Co 8:3
leading in every * of our lives. Gal 5:25
in, for as * of God's sovereign Eph 1:11
* of this dwelling place of God. Eph 2:22
Gentiles are a * of God's house. Eph 3:1
and living through every * of us. Eph 4:6
and each * in its own special way Eph 4:15,16
Take no * in the worthless Eph 5:11
love his wife as a * of himself; Eph 5:33
But * of my work is to suffer for Col 1:24
life was still * of this world; Col 3:7
* of God's plan for us Christians. 1Th 3:2,3
disown us who are * of himself, and 2Ti 2:13
they did not keep their * in that Heb 8:9
this * was called the Holy Place. Heb 9:1
made by men nor * of this world, Heb 9:11
and poisons every * of the body. Jas 3:6
and important * of the building." 1Pe 2:7
This suffering is all * of the 1Pe 2:21
No one who has become * of God's 1Jn 5:18
of God, sent out into every * of Rev 5:6
do not take * in her sins, or you Rev 18:4
And the world leaders, who took * Rev 18:9
And if anyone subtracts any * of Rev 22:19

PART-TIME
was on Saul's staff on a * basis. 1Sa 17:14,15

PARTAKE
* of me shall live because of me! Jn 6:57

PARTED
and thus he and Abram * company. Gen 13:11
blessing as they *:"Our sister,May Gen 24:60
So they *, David going away and 1Sa 20:42
And the water * and Elisha went 2Ki 2:13,14
smote the rivers and * the sea? Hab 3:8,9

PARTHIANS
Here we are—*, Medes, Elamites, Act 2:9

PARTIAL
a * fulfillment of this prophecy. Dan 9:25f

PARTIALITY
*, and consequently hated Joseph; Gen 37:4
shows no * and takes no bribes. Deu 10:17
no *, no taking of bribes." 2Ch 19:7

PARTICIPANTS
as * in my everlasting covenant. Gen 17:13

PARTICIPATED
Others who * were Governor Ez 4:8,9

PARTICIPATION
worship and into * in their Deu 20:18

PARTICULAR
laws of God to their * disputes." Ex 18:15,16
appointed to their * term of 1Ch 25:8
Each corps will assist * clans of 2Ch 35:4,5
* race that God has set before us. Heb 12:1

PARTICULARLY
* well qualified for their work. 1Ch 26:8
This year there was a * Mt 27:16
died for all, and * for those who 1Ti 4:9,10

PARTIES
denies it, both * to the dispute Ex 22:9
acts is death to both *. Lev 20:13
* with the local Moabite girls. Num 25:1
When these birthday * ended—and Job 1:5
lovely music at your grand *; Is 5:12
*—don't even eat a meal with them. Jer 16:8
joys, her *, holidays, and feasts. Hos 1:11
"And I will turn your * into Amo 8:10
leaders of two different *. Mt 16:1f
—banquets and * and weddings—just Mt 24:37,38
time at drinking * and in Lk 12:45
his money on * and prostitutes. Lk 15:13
Don't spend your time in wild * Rom 13:12,13
*, and all that sort of thing. Gal 5:21
drunk, wild *, drinking bouts, and 1Pe 4:3
other and throw * to celebrate the Rev 11:10

PARTING
was his * shot! Gen 45:24
The prophet left with this * 2Ch 25:16
AFTER * FROM the Ephesian elders, Act 21:1

PARTNER
can't be my *," Jesus replied. Jn 13:8
How can a Christian be a * with 2Co 6:15
say that he is my *, my helper in 2Co 8:23
old you that was a * in your evil Eph 4:22
If you do you will be a * with 2Jn 1:11

PARTNERS
Do fishing * sell him to the Job 41:6
you to be their * in crime—men Pro 2:11,12,13
A shout for help brought their * Lk 5:7
with him, and his * too—James and Lk 5:10
Will you be my prayer *? Rom 15:30
any of you to be * with demons when 1Co 10:20
AS GOD'S * we beg you not to toss 2Co 6:1
my * in giving and receiving. Php 4:15
and your wife are * in receiving 1Pe 3:7
will make you * with Christ in his 1Pe 4:13
* with them in the Lord's work. 3Jn 1:8

PARTNERSHIP
fleet was in * with King Hiram's, 1Ki 10:22
Judah, went into * with Ahaziah, 2Ch 20:35

PARTRIDGE
life like a * on the mountains?" 1Sa 26:20

PARTS
and hated in other * of Egypt. Gen 46:34
Keep four * for yourselves to be Gen 47:24
Literally, "inner *." Ex 12:9f
covers the inner *, also the gall Ex 29:13
separate * that are attached. Ex 30:2
its utensils and *, and all the Ex 40:9
covers the inward *, the two Lev 3:3,4,5
in its body *, it may be offered as Lev 22:23
then divide it into two *. Num 31:27
be in various * of the nation; Num 35:8
body into twelve * and sent one Ju 19:29
All the * of the stands were cast 1Ki 7:33
robe into twelve *, and said to 1Ki 11:30
he also conquered * of Manasseh 2Ki 10:32,33
other * of the Philistine country. 2Ch 26:6
Ephraim, and other * of the remnant 2Ch 34:9
and from all * of Judah, and from 2Ch 35:18
in the inward *, and given Job 38:36f
delicate, inner * of my body, and Ps 139:13
nagging about them * the best of Pro 17:9
caves and thorny *, as well as to Is 7:19
of the farthest * of the earth, Is 40:28
Carefully they join the * Is 41:7
"Even the most desolate * of Is 49:19
to worship from many * of Judah. Jer 26:2
Flee to the remotest * of the Jer 49:8
weigh the hair into three equal *. Eze 5:1
entering the * of the building open Eze 42:14
be divided. Some * of it will be as Dan 2:41,42
Literally, "withdrew into the * Mt 15:21f
handkerchiefs or * of his clothing Act 19:12
Just as there are many * to our Rom 12:4,5
We are all * of it, and it takes Rom 12:4,5
actually * and members of Christ? 1Co 6:15
all * of the one body of Christ. 1Co 10:17
Our bodies have many *, but the 1Co 12:12
but the many * make up only one 1Co 12:12
Yes, the body has many *, not 1Co 12:14
He has made many * for our bodies 1Co 12:18
So he has made many *, but still 1Co 12:20
And some of the * that seem 1Co 12:22
have some * that seem rather odd! 1Co 12:23
of others those * that should not 1Co 12:23
of course the * that may be seen do 1Co 12:24
are given to those * that might 1Co 12:24
among the *, so that the parts have 1Co 12:25
parts, so that the * have the same 1Co 12:25
If one part suffers, all * 1Co 12:26
is honored, all the * are glad. 1Co 12:26
Here is a list of some of the * 1Co 12:28
other and made them * of himself; Eph 2:15
was peace. As * of the same body, Eph 2:16
with Christ as * of a beautiful, Eph 2:21
We are all * of one body, we have Eph 4:4
down to the lowest * of the earth. Eph 4:9
helps the other *, so that the Eph 4:15,16
tell the truth, for we are * of Eph 4:25
loving them as * of themselves. Eph 5:28
the church, of which we are *. Eph 5:29,30
we are * of the body of Christ. Eph 5:32
with all their *, exposing us for Heb 4:12
they do the other * of the 2Pe 3:15,16

PARTY
and Abraham gave a * to celebrate Gen 21:8
celebrate with Jacob at a big *. Gen 29:22
to have a farewell *, with singing Gen 31:27
and he held a * for all of his Gen 40:20
May I never be a * to their Gen 49:6
*, followed by sexual immorality. Ex 32:6
Samson threw a * for thirty young Ju 14:10,11
Were we invited to this * just to Ju 14:15
sandal and hand it to the other *; Ru 4:7
that Nabal had thrown a big *. 1Sa 25:36
As David and his * passed 2Sa 16:5
For my father was no * to the 1Ki 2:32
Then he and his entire * went 2Ki 5:15
Ahab gave a great * for him and his 2Ch 18:2
Then everyone in our * sacrificed Ez 8:35
gave a special * for the palace Est 1:5
Queen Vashti gave a * for the Est 1:9
threw another big * for all his Est 2:18
begin to rot. A * gives laughter, Ecc 10:19
their rings and jewels, and * Is 3:22
get some wine and have a *; Is 56:12
The anti-Babylonian * in Judah Eze 23:17f
a subversive political *), Mt 10:2,3,4
But at a birthday * for Herod, Mt 14:6
were a Jewish political *. Mt 22:16f
A pro-Roman political *. Mk 3:6f
Simon (a member of a political * Mk 3:16-19
and he gave a stag * for his palace Mk 6:21
a subversive political *), Lk 6:14,15,16
So the * began. Lk 15:24

PARTYING
fellow servants, * and getting Mt 24:49

PARUAH
Jehoshaphat (son of *), whose area 1Ki 4:8-19

PARVAIM
the way, was of the best, from *. 2Ch 3:6

PAS-DAMMIM
against the Philistines at *. 1Ch 11:13

PASACH
*, Bimhal, Ashvath. 1Ch 7:33

PASEAH
of Bethrapha, *, and Tehinnah; 1Ch 4:11,12
Gazzam, Uzza, *, Besai, Asnah, Ez 2:43-54
by Joiada (son of *) and Meshullam Neh 3:6
Gazzam, Uzza, *, Besai, Neh 7:46-56

PASHHUR
son of *, son of Malchijah). 1Ch 9:12
From the subclan of *, 1,247; Ez 2:36-39
The sons of *: Ez 10:22
From the subclan of *, 1,247; Neh 7:39-42
Jeremiah, *, Amariah, Neh 10:1
son of *, son of Malchijah). Neh 11:10-14
NOW WHEN * (son of Immer), the Jer 20:1
The next day when * finally Jer 20:3
'*, the Lord has changed your name. Jer 20:3
And as for you, *, you and all Jer 20:6
THEN KING ZEDEKIAH sent * (son of Jer 21:1
Gedaliah (son of *) and Jucal (son Jer 38:1
of Shelemiah) and * (son of Jer 38:1

PASS
May God * on to you and to your Gen 28:4
And I will * on to you the land Gen 35:12
midnight I will * through Egypt. Ex 11:4
For I will * through the land of Ex 12:12
the blood I will * over you and I Ex 12:13
* over you and not destroy you. Ex 12:21
"For Jehovah will * through the Ex 12:23

(PASS Con't)
two side pieces, he will * over Ex 12:23
Will * by them in safety. Ex 15:16
may not *, and tell them, 'Beware! Ex 19:12
"DO NOT * along untrue reports. Ex 23:1
make my goodness * before you, and Ex 33:19
then he would * on to the people Ex 34:34
* on to your children after you; Lev 25:46
as they * by for counting. Lev 27:32
Please let us * through your Num 20:17
We only want to * through, and Num 20:19
to allow Israel to * through their Num 20:21,22
and Eleazar will * on these Num 27:21
Israel, "When you * across the Num 33:50,51
continue south past Scorpion * Num 34:4
had commanded him to * on to them: Deu 1:1
'Let us * through your land,' we Deu 2:27
all we want is permission to * Deu 2:28
He has given them to me to * on Deu 4:5
foreigners that * by from distant Deu 29:22
and * them on to your children. Deu 32:46
ascent of Scorpion *, runs to a Ju 1:36
Gideon returned by way of Heres *. Ju 8:13
permission to * through his land. Ju 11:17
The mountain * at Michmash had 1Sa 13:23
go over a narrow * between two 1Sa 14:4
all who * by will be incredulous. 2Ch 7:21
that I am going to * these Neh 6:7
tradition and to * it on to their Est 9:27
* away, removed by no human hand. Job 34:20
Thus his laws * down from Ps 78:6
Though a thousand generations * Ps 105:8,9
good, and you can * it on to Pro 22:17,18,19
God brings to * again what was in Ecc 3:15
nothing left to * on to one's son. Ecc 5:13,14
days shall * away as quickly as Ecc 8:13
Entrust it to some godly man to * Is 8:16
Michmash and crossing over the *; Is 10:28,29
will cause all this to come to *. Is 37:32
All I say will come to *, for I Is 46:10
stand at attention when you * by; Is 49:7
bring it all to * when it is time. Is 60:22
roar, can never * those bounds. Jer 5:22
good times * him by forever. Jer 17:6
so that all who * by will gasp and Jer 18:16
Men from many nations will * by Jer 22:8
and all who * by shall be appalled Jer 50:13
one lives nor even travelers * by. Jer 51:43
nothing to you, all you who * by? Lam 1:12
All who * by scoff and shake Lam 2:15
warning, * it on to them at once. Eze 3:17
days as they * make liars out of Eze 12:22
it shall come to * and I will do Eze 24:14
not a soul will * that way, neither Eze 29:11
No man shall * through it; Eze 44:2
hundred days to * before the rights Dan 8:26
and try to * the blame to him! Hos 4:4
children about it; * the awful Joe 1:3
will * through her any more. Joe 3:17
will thrive as generations *. Joe 3:20
for I will * through and destroy. Amo 5:17
things will surely come to *. Hab 2:3
"Holiness does not * to other Hag 2:12
They shall * safely through the Zec 10:11
this generation shall * away." Mt 24:34f
Literally, "that the hour might * Mk 14:35f
to * this summary on to you, Lk 1:3
and earth shall * away, yet my Lk 21:33
Or, "Pray for strength to * Lk 21:36f
"But I * no judgment without Jn 5:30
about me. You * judgment on me Jn 8:15
a promise just couldn't come to *! Rom 4:18
we can * on to them this same help 2Co 1:3,4
Do you * the test? 2Co 13:5
* it on to the church at Laodicea? Col 4:16
in turn, * them on to others. 2Ti 2:2
("Let this cup * from me") and Heb 5:7f
the heavens will * away with a 2Pe 3:10
has given us to * on to you: that 1Jn 1:5

PASSAGE
the entrance * through the wall. Ju 1:24
of this confusing * is that Saul's 1Sa 17:55f
of the * that was being read. Neh 8:7,8
of this * by Christ himself, and Is 52:13f
In this * (verses 11–19) some Eze 28:12f
measured the entry hall of the *; Eze 40:6
of the entrance * was 87½ feet from Eze 40:15
went over to the * through the Eze 40:20
through the entry hall of the *." Eze 44:3
the * shall be shut behind him. Eze 46:12
and so also throughout this *. Dan 11:6f
This * evidently refers to the Zec 2:8f
That this is not a * referring Zec 13:6f
Then Jesus quoted them * after Lk 24:27
them passage after * from the Lk 24:27
The * of Scripture he had been Act 8:32
For instance, listen to this * Act 15:15

PASSAGES
but many other * indicate Christ's Zec 9:10f
Implied in parallel *. Mk 1:12,13f
what the * meant and what they said Lk 24:27

PASSAGEWAY
the festive * he had constructed 2Ki 16:18
Then he took me over to the * Eze 40:6
Walking on through the * I saw Eze 40:7-12
inner end of the * was a vestibule Eze 40:7-12
width of the *, measuring across Eze 40:13
* and along the guardroom walls. Eze 40:16
And so we passed through the * to Eze 40:17
the same distance as the * did. Eze 40:18
left the eastern * and went over to Eze 40:20
as for the east *—87½ feet long and Eze 40:21
walked through the * into the Eze 40:23
a * through it to an inner court. Eze 40:23
sections of its * and found they Eze 40:24
walked through the * into the court Eze 40:27
a * through it to the inner court. Eze 40:27
to the inner wall and its south *. Eze 40:28
He measured this * and found that Eze 40:28
entry hall of this * were the same Eze 40:36
each side of the *, and there were Eze 40:37
entry hall of the * there were two Eze 40:39
through the east * to measure the Eze 42:15
out again to the * through the Eze 43:1
the Temple through the eastern *. Eze 43:4
eastern *, but it was closed. Eze 44:1
* to feast there before the Lord. Eze 44:3
* to the front of the Temple. Eze 44:4
they enter the * to the inner Eze 44:17
entry hall of the * and proceed to Eze 46:2
He shall worship inside the * and Eze 46:2
in front of this * on the Sabbaths Eze 46:3
of the * and out the same way; Eze 46:8
through the north * to sacrifice Eze 46:9
must go out through the south *. Eze 46:9
must always use the opposite *. Eze 46:9
side of the main *, he led me Eze 46:19,20
the wall through the north * Eze 47:2
The eastern * was closed. Eze 47:2f
the south side [of the eastern * Eze 47:2

PASSAGEWAYS
The distance between the two * Eze 40:23
And the distance between the * Eze 40:27
as the * of the outer wall. Eze 40:28
those of the other *, and there Eze 40:33

PASSED
flaming torch that * between the Gen 15:17
Literally, "* over this Jordan." Gen 32:10f
over us, for he * over the homes of Ex 12:27
the Egyptians; he * over our houses Ex 12:27
you with my hand until I have *. Ex 33:22
with him, and * in front of him and Ex 34:5,6
Mount Sinai, to be * on to the Lev 7:38
if the years have * and only a Lev 25:52
Going northward, they * first Num 13:22
we have * beyond your borders. Num 21:22
shall be * on to his daughters. Num 27:8
the death angel * over the oldest Num 28:16
or lead— shall be * through fire Num 31:23
"So we * through Edom where our Deu 2:8
He spoke to me and I * on his Deu 5:5
and waited as all the people * by. Jos 3:17
and Moses had * the commandment Jos 11:15
The boundary then * through the Jos 15:8
to Mount Seir, * along to the town Jos 15:10,11
Turning again to the north, it * Jos 15:10,11
Reuben), where it * along the Jos 18:18
of Zebulun * Hannathon and ended at Jos 19:14
It then * to the east of Kabul, Jos 19:27
when we * through their land. Jos 24:17
everyone else who * that way. Ju 9:25
As they * the home of Micah, the Ju 18:13
* them on to the people of Israel. 1Sa 3:21,4:1
and his retinue * by, crossed 2Sa 15:23
the road until everyone had *. 2Sa 15:24
As David and his party * Bahurim, 2Sa 16:5
the city as all the troops * by. 2Sa 18:4
there the Lord * by, and a mighty 1Ki 19:11
their flesh. He * around the meat 1Ki 19:21
As the king * by, the prophet 1Ki 20:39
* that way, he stopped for dinner. 2Ki 4:8
But just then a wild animal * by 2Ki 14:9
The king also * on to Solomon 1Ch 28:13
to the Old Gate, * the Fish Gate Neh 12:39
Mordecai heard about it and * on Est 2:22
whenever he * by, for so the king Est 3:2
as a spirit * before my face—my Job 4:15
they have * this wisdom to us: Job 15:17-19
wrath against your enemies has *. Is 26:20
I have faithfully * them on to Jer 25:2,3
and there judgment was * upon him. Jer 52:9
"Later, when I * by and saw you Eze 16:8
all who * by were shocked to see Eze 36:34
many years had *, I would bring you Eze 38:17
And so we * through the Eze 40:17
keeping them. He * on to the Mal 2:6
and the wife was * to the next Mt 22:26
and * them to his disciples; Mk 8:6
Next morning, as the disciples * Mk 11:20
side of the road and * him by. Lk 10:31
already * out of death into life. Jn 5:24
God and * them out to the people. Jn 6:11
you, for I have * on to them the Jn 17:
They * the first and second cell Act 12:1
So they * through and walked Act 12:1
in all the cities he * through. Act 20:
the next day we * Chios; Act 20:1
island of Cyprus, * it on our left Act 21:
and * along the coast of the Act 27:
Table, and I have * it on to you 1Co 11:2
I * on to you right from the 1Co 15:
God," which was * on to him from Heb 1:
Jesus himself, and * on to us by Heb 2:
It was not * on to you from your 1Pe 1:2

PASSERSBY
alleys of the city and murder *. Ps 10:8

PASSES
At the place where the road * 1Sa 24:3
The lush yield of this land * Neh 9:37
to count. He * by, invisible; Job 9:1
"My life * swiftly away, filled Job 9:25
him, and then he * off the scene. Job 14:20,21
up to run, she * the swiftest horse Job 39:18
Literally, "* through waterless Mt 12:43,44,45f
anything you eat * through the Mt 15:17
* through the digestive system." Mk 7:19
agreement which he * on to us from Heb 8:6

PASSING
of Jehovah's * over us, for he Ex 12:27
that they will be * through the Deu 2:4
bent to the left, * south of Jos 15:10,11
There the border turned south, * Jos 18:14
to hate him more with every * day. 1Sa 18:29
and everyone * by will be amazed 1Ki 9:8
as the shadow of a * cloud, he Job 14:2
I am a traveler * through the Ps 39:12
My life is * swiftly as the Ps 102:11
And may those * by refuse to Ps 129:8
No one gives me a * thought. Ps 142:4
his days are like a * shadow. Ps 144:4
to us, as one * through the land Jer 14:8
the Temple and * to the right of Eze 47:1
Everyone * that way will mock, or Zep 2:15
hours later he was * a hiring hall Mt 20:3
And the people * by hurled Mt 27:39
of the corruption they are *." Lk 11:44
AS JESUS WAS * through Jericho, a Lk 19:1
broke it and was * it over to them, Lk 24:30
be * on to you what he has heard. Jn 16:13
As Peter and John were * by, he Act 3:3
to Crete, * the port of Salmone. Act 27:7,8
a * visit and then go right on; 1Co 16:7
help each other, * on to others 1Pe 4:10
missionaries who are * through. 3Jn 1:5

PASSION
resulting from human * or Jn 1:13
not in lustful * as the heathen 1Th 4:5

PASSIONS
Therefore guard your *! Mal 2:15
Therefore control your *—let Mal 2:16
controlling his *, it is all right, 1Co 7:36
thing that our * or our evil Eph 2:3

PASSOVER
shall be called the Lord's *. Ex 12:11
celebrating the *, and your Ex 12:25
the observance of the *. Ex 12:43
to observe the * with you, let all Ex 12:48
of the meat of the * lamb may be Ex 34:25
"The * of the Lord: This is to Lev 23:5
beginning the day following the *. Lev 23:6
must celebrate the * annually on Num 9:2,3
So Moses announced that the * Num 9:4,5
eat the * lamb that night. Num 9:6,7
are defiled at * time because of Num 9:10
celebrate the *, but one month Num 9:10
instructions concerning the *. Num 9:12
to celebrate the * at the regular Num 9:13
to celebrate the * to the Lord, he Num 9:14
celebrate the *—[when the death Num 28:16
the day after the night of the *. Num 33:3,4
the * during the month of April, Deu 16:1
Your * sacrifice shall be either Deu 16:2
and none of the * lamb shall be Deu 16:4
"The * is not to be eaten in Deu 16:5
celebrated the * during the evening Jos 5:10
to observe the * ceremonies as 2Ki 23:21
There had not been a * 2Ki 23:22
This * was in the eighteenth 2Ki 23:23
festivals—the * celebration, the 2Ch 8:13
for the annual * celebration. 2Ch 30:1
to celebrate the * in May this 2Ch 30:2,3
so they sent a * proclamation 2Ch 30:5
Or, "The * had not been 2Ch 30:5f
of May for the * celebration. 2Ch 30:13
the people killed their * lambs. 2Ch 30:15
killed their * lambs for them, to 2Ch 30:17,18,19
to eat the * anyway, even though 2Ch 30:17,18,19
celebrated the * at Jerusalem for 2Ch 30:21
Jerusalem for the * went out to the 2Ch 31:1
had come to the * from the northern 2Ch 31:1
JOSIAH ANNOUNCED that the * 2Ch 35:1
* lambs were slain that evening. 2Ch 35:1
Kill the * lambs and sanctify 2Ch 35:6

(PASSOVER Con't)
for the people's * offerings, and 2Ch 35:7
and 300 oxen as * offerings. 2Ch 35:8
the Levites for their * offerings. 2Ch 35:9
Levites killed the * lambs and 2Ch 35:11
they roasted the * lambs and boiled 2Ch 35:13
The entire * ceremony was 2Ch 35:16
took part in the * observance, and 2Ch 35:17
there been such a *—not one of the 2Ch 35:18
The * was celebrated on the first Ez 6:19
nation, ate the * feast and Ez 6:21,22
month, you shall celebrate the *. Eze 45:21
On the day of * the prince shall Eze 45:22
"As you know, the * celebration Mt 26:2
"But not during the * Mt 26:5
On the first day of the * Mt 26:17
shall we plan to eat the *?" Mt 26:17
and I will eat the * meal with my Mt 26:18
* celebration—anyone they wanted. Mt 27:15
the first day of the * ceremonies Mt 27:62
THE * OBSERVANCE began two days Mk 14:1
"But we can't do it during the * Mk 14:2
On the first day of the *, the Mk 14:12
to eat the traditional * supper. Mk 14:12
eat the * supper this evening!' Mk 14:14
had said, and prepared the *. Mk 14:16
each year at * time—any prisoner Mk 15:6
for the annual * Festival, which Lk 2:41,42
AND NOW THE * celebration was Lk 22:1
Now the day of the * celebration Lk 22:7
arrived, when the * lamb was killed Lk 22:7
a place to prepare their * meal. Lk 22:8
the * meal with his disciples.' Lk 22:11
said, and prepared the * supper. Lk 22:13
to eat this * meal with you before Lk 22:15
the annual Jewish * celebration, Jn 2:13
Jerusalem at the * celebration, Jn 2:23
Jerusalem at the * celebration and Jn 4:45
for the annual * celebration Jn 6:2-5
Literally, "Now the *, the feast Jn 6:2-5f
The *, a Jewish holy day, was Jn 11:55
ceremony before the * began. Jn 11:55
Will he come for the *?" Jn 11:56
SIX DAYS BEFORE the * ceremonies Jn 12:1
a huge crowd of * visitors took Jn 12:12
the * paid a visit to Philip, Jn 12:20
JESUS KNEW ON the evening of * Day Jn 13:1
be allowed to eat the * lamb. Jn 18:28
from prison each year at *. Jn 18:39
about noon of the day before *. Jn 19:14
for it was the *), so they asked Jn 19:31
days after the * ceremonies, when Act 2:1f
Peter during the * celebration and Act 12:3
Jews for execution after the *. Act 12:4
As soon as the * ceremonies Act 20:6

PAST
was long since * the time when she Gen 18:11
gore people in the *, and the owner Ex 21:29
But if the ox was known from * Ex 21:36
Whenever they walked * the altar Ex 40:32
she squirmed * by pressing against Num 22:25
continue south * Scorpion Pass Num 34:4
other nations in the * to perish. Deu 8:20
the Arnon River, * the city of Jos 13:16
line proceeded * the south of Jos 15:10,11
the Sea, ran east * Michmethath, Jos 16:5,6
on * Taanath-shiloh and Janoah. Jos 16:5,6
Arabah, ran south * Beth-hoglah, Jos 18:19
Heleph and ran * Aznoth-tabor, then Jos 19:34
Meanwhile Ehud had escaped * the Ju 3:26
the road * the oak of Meonenim!" Ju 9:37
and Manasseh, * Mizpah in Gilead, Ju 11:29
his troops move * him to lead the 2Sa 15:17,18
DAVID WAS JUST * the top of the 2Sa 16:1
they stuck out * the angels and 1Ki 8:8
from the Temple, * the guardhouse, 2Ki 11:19
city this has been in the *; Ez 4:15
has in times * been a hotbed of Ez 4:19
speaking out? in the * Job 4:3,4
But the wisdom of the * will Job 8:10
It will all be in the *. Job 11:16
My good days are in the *. Job 17:11
everlasting ages *—and on into Ps 41:13
ages *—will answer them! Ps 55:19
your wings until this storm is *. Ps 57:1
God is my King from ages *; Ps 74:12
days of the *, long since ended. Ps 77:5
times, from the everlasting *. Ps 93:1
In ages * you laid the Ps 102:25
From ages *, I am. Pro 8:23
In the *, haven't I been right? Pro 22:20,21
in the distant * and disappeared. Ecc 3:15
on his *, for God gives him joy. Ecc 5:19,20
For the winter is *, the rain is Sol 2:11
when the terror is *, God will Is 16:4,5
the road going * the field where Is 36:2
lessons from the * and see the ruin Is 42:23
Haven't I proclaimed from ages * Is 44:8
Father, our Redeemer from ages *. Is 63:16
by invading armies as in the *. Is 65:21,22
For the * twenty-three years, Jer 25:2,3
In the * I painstakingly Jer 31:28
* the ruins of your land. Eze 5:14
All his * sins will be Eze 18:22
But if he sins, expecting his * Eze 33:13
None of his * sins shall be Eze 33:16
Then you will remember your * Eze 36:31
and shame will all be in the *; Eze 39:26
Gilead, * the Dead Sea to Tamar. Eze 47:18
way back, * the prince of Persia; Dan 10:20,21
is alive from everlasting ages *! Mic 5:2
They sweep * like wind and are Hab 1:11
"It is already * time for supper, Mt 14:15
like the great ones of the *. Mk 6:15
He started * them, but when they Mk 6:48
can't see * the board in yours? Lk 6:42
*, he asked what was happening. Lk 18:36
walked * them and left the Temple. Jn 8:59
God tolerated man's * ignorance Act 17:30
as though they were already *. Rom 4:17
here, just as I have in the *; Php 1:20
seen me suffer for him in the *; Php 1:30
Forgetting the * and looking Php 3:13
and generations *, but now at last Col 1:26,27
use to you in the *, but now he is Phm 1:11
You have had enough in the * of 1Pe 4:3
The second woe is *, but the Rev 11:14

PASTE
figs and to make a * of them and 2Ki 20:7

PASTOR
that if a man wants to be a * 1Ti 3:1
For a * must be a good man whose 1Ti 3:2
The * must not be a new 1Ti 3:6
duty as a worthy * who is fed by 1Ti 4:6
against the * unless there are two 1Ti 5:19
this whether the * is a special 1Ti 5:21
be in a hurry about choosing a *; 1Ti 5:22

PASTORS
To: The * and deacons and all the Php 1:1
sort of good, steady men as the *. 1Ti 3:8
* who do their work well should 1Ti 5:17
Remember that some men, even *, 1Ti 5:24
how much good some * do, but 1Ti 5:25
and I asked you to appoint * Tit 1:5
These * Tit 1:7

PASTRIES
three baskets of * on my head. Gen 40:16

PASTURE
many animals for the available *. Gen 13:6
for there is no * for our flocks in Gen 47:4
cities and surrounding * lands. Num 35:2
in search of * for their flocks: 1Ch 4:34-39
the entire * country of Sharon. 1Ch 5:16
us—the sheep of your own *? Ps 74:1
the sheep of your *, will thank you Ps 79:13
his people, the sheep of his *. Ps 100:3
his spice beds, to * his flock and Sol 6:2
my vineyard go to * to be trampled Is 5:5
Lambs and calves and kids will * Is 5:17
they shall graze in my *! Is 14:30
Sheep * there, lying quiet and Is 17:2
Achor shall be a place to * herds. Is 65:10
that search for *—helpless game too Lam 1:6
of Rabbah into a * for camels and Eze 25:5
Yes, I will give them good * on Eze 34:14
are my flock, the sheep of my *. Eze 34:31
public use—homes, * and parks, with Eze 48:15
for there is no * for them; Joe 1:18
flock in a *—a noisy, happy crowd. Mic 2:12
The coastland will become a *, a Zep 2:6
Every field will become a lush *. Zec 10:1
with joy like calves let out to *. Mal 4:2

PASTURE-FED
fattening pens, 20 * cattle, 100 1Ki 4:23

PASTURED
Joel was a cattle man, and he * 1Ch 5:9
of the tribe of Judah will be *. Zep 2:7

PASTURELAND
* given to the Levites. Num 35:7
He will give you lush * for your Deu 11:15
and * for our cattle," they said. Jos 21:2
tending your sheep in the *. 2Sa 7:8
Cities of Refuge and * given to 1Ch 6:71
and the surrounding * of each. 1Ch 6:73
The mountain ranges are their *; Job 39:8
the whole nation will be a *; Is 7:21,22
But the abundant * will yield Is 7:21,22
city will become a * for sheep. Zep 2:14

PASTURELANDS
Their * shall extend outward Num 35:4
surrounding * for their cattle. Jos 14:3,4
conquered cities with their *. Jos 21:3
and the cities and * were assigned Jos 21:8
below, with their surrounding *: Jos 21:9-16
these four cities and their *: Jos 21:17,18
cities and * from the tribe of Jos 21:20,21,22
The following four cities and * Jos 21:23,24
with their surrounding *. Jos 21:25
of cities and * given to the Jos 21:26
* from the half-tribe of Manasseh: Jos 21:27
of Asher gave four cities and *: Jos 21:30,31
So thirteen cities with their * Jos 21:33
Gad gave them four cities with *: Jos 21:38,39
The total number of cities and * Jos 21:41,42
Hebron and its surrounding * in 1Ch 6:55,56,57
Refuge with their surrounding *: 1Ch 6:58,59
Cities and * were also assigned 1Ch 6:64,65
* to the subclans of Kohath: 1Ch 6:66-69
Refuge and their * were given to 1Ch 6:70
Hukok, and Rehob, with their *. 1Ch 6:75
Hammon, and Kiriathaim with *. 1Ch 6:76
and Mepha-ath, along with their *. 1Ch 6:78,79
each with their surrounding *. 1Ch 6:81
for our own use these * of God!" Ps 83:12

PASTURES
They found good *, and everything 1Ch 4:40,41
with surrounding *—including Geba, 1Ch 6:60
green, lush * in the wilderness; Ps 65:11,12
with joy. The * are filled with Ps 65:13
High in the mountains are * for Ps 104:18
green grass grow in mountain *. Ps 147:8
He * his flock among the lilies!" Sol 6:3
and with ample * for your cows. Is 30:23
and herds will graze in green *. Is 32:20
Carmel's * and Sharon's meadows; Is 35:2
green * and on the grassy hills. Is 49:8,9
divide your * for their flocks. Jer 6:3
mountains and *, for now they are Jer 9:10
The land itself is mourning—the * Jer 23:10
for the Lord has spoiled their *. Jer 25:36
The * of Nimrim are deserted now. Jer 48:34
that feed in lush *, and neigh like Jer 50:11
and feed in luscious mountain *. Eze 34:14
the best of the * for yourselves, Eze 34:18
Open land for * shall surround Eze 48:17
attempts to lead her in green *. Hos 4:16
For the heat has withered the * Joe 1:19
The creeks are dry and the * are Joe 1:20
the * will turn green again. Joe 2:22
And suddenly the lush * of Mount Amo 1:2
let them enjoy the fertile * of Mic 7:14
the lush * of Bashan and Carmel Nah 1:4
go in and out and find green *. Jn 10:9

PAT
Are we trying to * ourselves on 2Co 5:12

PATARA
reached Rhodes and then went to *. Act 21:1

PATCH
"And who would * an old garment Mt 9:16
For the * would tear away and Mt 9:16
What happens? The * pulls away Mk 2:21
to make a * for an old one. Lk 5:36
look worse with a new * on it! Lk 5:36

PATCHED
long journey, with * shoes, Jos 9:3,4,5
* wineskins and dry, moldy bread. Jos 9:3,4,5

PATCHES
*, and all of the black sheep. Gen 30:35,36
vineyards will become * of briars. Is 7:23
Other seed landed in thistle *, Lk 8:7

PATCHING
It is like * an old garment with Mk 2:21

PATH
* to find a girl from the family Gen 24:48
Jehovah your God put it in my *!" Gen 27:20
He shall be a serpent in the * Gen 49:17
sea will open up a * before you, Ex 14:16
Lord opened up a * through the sea, Ex 14:21
The water covered the * and the Ex 14:28
the Lord made a * through the Red Jos 2:10
enemies, the Lord blocked their *. Ju 2:15
he turned off the * to look at the Ju 14:8
you and walk in my * and do 1Ki 11:38
follow the * of the Lord his God. 2Ch 27:6
There is a booby-trap in every * Job 18:10
God has blocked my * and turned Job 19:8
rain and a * for the lightning. Job 28:26
trip me and lay traps in my *. Job 30:12
Where is the * to the Job 38:24
Who laid out the * for the Job 38:25-27
Show me the * where I should go, Ps 25:4
the proper * to all who go astray; Ps 25:8
And when we obey him, every * he Ps 25:10
narrow * of doing what is right; Ps 26:11
Make their * dark and slippery Ps 35:6
for me and dug a pitfall in my *. Ps 35:7
on a hard, firm * and steadied me Ps 40:2
We have not left your * by a Ps 44:18
They have dug a pitfall in my *. Ps 57:6
And he holds our feet to the *. Ps 66:9
What a slippery * they are Ps 73:18
and then you dried a * for them Ps 74:15
I will try to walk a blameless *, Ps 101:2
The Jordan River opened up a * Ps 114:3
to light the * ahead of me, and Ps 119:105
your *, but I will not turn aside. Ps 119:110
Red Sea to make a * before them, Ps 136:13
You chart the * ahead of me, and Ps 139:3
along the * of everlasting life. Ps 139:24
stay on the right *, for only good Pro 2:20
Stick to the * and be safe. Pro 4:26
For she does not know the * to Pro 5:6
The * of the godly leads to life. Pro 12:28

(PATH Con't)
the good man's * is easy! Pro 15:19
The * of the godly leads away Pro 16:17
he who follows that * is safe. Pro 16:17
choose the right *, and when he is Pro 22:6
and followed the * of folly, so Ecc 2:3
Leading you down the garden * to Is 3:12
The Lord will dry a * through the Is 11:15
But for good men the * is not Is 26:7
and treacherous *, but smooths the Is 26:7
a * they have not seen before. Is 42:16
making a * right through the sea. Is 43:16
the sea, making a * right through Is 51:10
Hosts, who dried a * for you right Is 51:15
evil *, even though I warn them. Jer 8:4,5
pell-mell down the * of sin as Jer 8:6
they have hidden traps along my *. Jer 18:22
burn up everything in its *." Jer 21:14
he has placed a pitfall in my * Lam 1:13
he has filled my * with detours. Lam 3:9
It will block the * of the Eze 39:11
good, to get you on the * again. Mic 2:7
searching for a *, because you have Zep 1:17
out the * where he will walk.' Mt 3:3
*, and the birds came and ate it. Mt 13:4
grain: The hard * where some of Mt 13:19
of it fell on a *, and the birds Mk 4:4
to guide us to the * of peace." Lk 1:79
The hard * where some seed fell Lk 8:12
living light will flood your *." Jn 8:12
That is the * of blessing. Jn 13:17
put a Rock in the * of the Jews, Rom 9:33
onto the right *, remembering that Gal 6:1
for many evils lie along that *; Eph 5:18
that God cleared a * for everything Col 1:20
They have left the * of truth, 2Ti 2:18
a straight, smooth * for your feet Heb 12:13

PATHROS
to the land of * in southern Egypt Eze 29:14
"The cities of * [along the Eze 30:14

PATHRUSIM
Naphtuhim, *, Casluhim (from whom Gen 10:13,14
the Naphtuhim, the *, the 1Ch 1:11,12

PATHS
and walking his *), then you must Deu 19:9
and to follow his * and to keep his Deu 30:16
used the narrow, crooked side *. Ju 5:6
He has not followed my * and has 1Ki 11:33
He followed the evil * of 1Ki 15:34
but you have walked in the evil * 1Ki 16:2
the wicked * of Jeroboam, who had 2Ki 13:2
in the same evil * as Israel had. 2Ki 17:19
He boldly followed the * of 2Ch 17:6
king followed the * of God, he 2Ch 26:5
the ancient * of sin are snatched Job 22:15,16
"I have stayed in God's *, Job 23:11
all the plans and * of godly men, Ps 1:6
the * of the godless lead to doom. Ps 1:6
feet have not slipped from your *. Ps 17:5
pain to those who leave your *. Ps 18:26
Those who walk my * will receive Ps 50:23
would follow me, walking in my *! Ps 81:13
from those who walk along his *. Ps 84:11
This makes us follow his *, and Ps 94:12,13
evil, and walking only in his *. Ps 119:3
Make me walk along the right * Ps 119:35
Teach me your good *. Ps 119:64
I have refused to walk the * of Ps 119:101
Lead me in good *, for your Ps 143:10
down dark and evil *, and exult in Pro 2:11,12,13
* are those of justice and right. Pro 8:20
son, be wise and stay in God's *; Pro 23:19,20,21
have led them down the * of ruin. Is 9:16
And if you leave God's * and go Is 30:21
straighten out the crooked * and Is 40:4
though the * he treads are new. Is 41:3
and I will direct all his *. Is 45:13
the * that you should follow. Is 48:17
mountains into level * for them; Is 49:11
We, who left God's * to follow Is 53:6
they follow their own evil * and Is 65:2
road is, the godly * you used to Jer 6:16
have not tried to follow in my *. Jer 14:10
turn back from your evil * and do Jer 18:11
good, and walk the muddy * of sin. Jer 18:15
Therefore their * will be dark Jer 23:12
walks along the * of right, not Eze 33:15
For the * of the Lord are true Hos 14:9
will follow the * I set for you and Zec 3:7
For you have left God's *. Mal 2:8
make his * straight." Mk 1:3f
God's *, or even truly wanted to. Rom 3:11
the * I wanted them to follow." Heb 3:10

PATHWAY
stepped off God's *, or if my heart Job 31:7,8
down her silver *, and my heart Job 31:26
along the best * for your life; Ps 32:8
steadily along his * and in due Ps 37:34
Your road led by a * through the Ps 77:19
the sea—a * no one knew was there! Ps 77:19
him to make a * for his steps. Ps 85:13
terrors of the * you have chosen. Pro 1:31
them and guarding their *. Pro 2:7,8
be corrected is on the * to life. Pro 10:17
women—the royal * to destruction. Pro 31:3
mysterious as the * of the wind, Ecc 11:5
course of the * of my people; Jer 6:21
Mark your * well. Jer 31:21
The hard *, where some of the Mk 4:15
Widen the * before him! Lk 3:4

PATHWAYS
The sensible stay on the * of Pro 15:21

PATIENCE
"Are you trying to test God's * Ex 17:2
show the great power [of your * Num 14:17,18
him and try his * as you did when Deu 6:16
before. My * was severely tried by Ps 95:9
finally came—how God tested his *! Ps 105:19
testing God's * to the breaking Ps 106:14
starting! * is better than pride! Ecc 7:8
Apparently God's * with their Is 6:10f
aren't satisfied to exhaust my *; Is 7:13
Tell me why your * is exhausted! Mic 6:3
be patient. And * develops Rom 5:4
are to teach us * and to encourage Rom 15:4
May God who gives *, steadiness, Rom 15:5
And don't try the Lord's *—they 1Co 10:9
of the Gospel and by our *. 2Co 6:6
love, joy, peace, *, kindness, Gal 5:22
Somehow my * has encouraged them Php 1:14
about your * and complete faith in 2Th 1:4
of the * that comes from Christ. 2Th 3:5
know my love for you, and my *. 2Ti 3:10
doing everything with love and *. Tit 2:2
though they tried his * sorely; Heb 3:9
of their strong faith and *. Heb 6:12
and let us run with * the Heb 12:1
think about his * as sinful men did Heb 12:3
your * has a chance to grow. Jas 1:3
For when your * is finally in Jas 1:4
For examples of * in suffering, Jas 5:10
I, too, have shared the * Jesus Rev 1:9
watched your hard work and your *; Rev 2:2
love and faith and *, and I can see Rev 2:19

PATIENT
word to you. Be * with me for a Gen 44:18
to her, "Just be * until we hear Ru 3:15-18
You were * with them for many Neh 9:30
How can I be * till I die? Job 6:11
He hates the man who is *. Pro 14:17
Be * and you will finally win, Pro 25:15
I will be * while the Lord Mic 7:9
Just be *! Hab 2:3
But the Lord says, "Be *; Zep 3:8
* with me and I will pay it all.' Mt 18:26
'Be * and I will pay it,' he pled. Mt 18:29
How much longer must I be * with Mk 9:19
Don't you realize how * he is Rom 2:4
for us—they help us learn to be *. Rom 5:3
has been * with for all this time? Rom 9:22
for you. Be * in trouble, and Rom 12:12
We have been * with those who 1Co 4:12
Love is very * and kind, never 1Co 13:4
I HOPE YOU will be * with me as I 2Co 11:1
Be humble and gentle. Be * with Eph 4:2
and be * with everyone. 1Th 5:14
show everyone how * he is with even 1Ti 1:16
others, and to be * and gentle. 1Ti 6:11
they must be gentle, * teachers 2Ti 2:24
But God was * with them forty Heb 3:9
Lord's return, be *, like a farmer Jas 5:7
Yes, be *. Jas 5:8
credit for being * if you are 1Pe 2:20
for it, and are * beneath the 1Pe 2:20
you will become * and godly, gladly 2Pe 1:6

PATIENTLY
Rest in the Lord; wait * for him Ps 37:7
I WAITED * for God to help me; Ps 40:1
Now please listen *! Act 26:3
to those who * do the will of God, Rom 2:7
Literally, "who * do good." Rom 2:7f
For all creation is waiting * Rom 8:19
us to wait * and confidently. Rom 8:25
that you can bear up * against it. 1Co 10:13
We * endure suffering and hardship 2Co 6:4
God himself: for I * did many 2Co 12:12
be ready to suffer quietly and *. Col 3:12
be feeding them * with God's Word. 2Ti 4:2
Then Abraham waited * until Heb 6:15
are eagerly and * waiting for him. Heb 9:28
You need to keep on * doing Heb 10:36
Brethren, please listen * to what Heb 13:22
though he waited * for them while 1Pe 3:20
bless you. Wait * for the eternal Jud 1:21
You have * suffered for me Rev 2:3
"Because you have * obeyed me Rev 3:10
people to endure * every trial and Rev 14:12

PATMOS
I was on the island of *, exiled Rev 1:9

PATRIARCHS
(the days of the Hebrew *), and Jer 5:15f
the twelve * of the Jewish nation. Act 7:8

PATROBAS
Phlegon, Hermes, *, Hermas, and the Rom 16:14

PATROL
Though they * their walls night Ps 55:10
them to * the earth for him." Zec 1:10
to be off, to * back and forth Zec 6:7
Begin your *." Zec 6:7

PATROLING
And Satan replied, "From * the Job 1:7
"From * the earth," Satan Job 2:2

PATROLLED
Lord, "We have * the whole earth, Zec 1:11

PATRON
to you as our *, and we do not want Ez 4:14

PATRONIZED
and * mediums and wizards. 2Ki 21:6

PATTERN
make follows the * I am showing you Ex 25:40
linen, using a checkerboard *; Ex 28:39
They followed this * for six Jos 6:12,13,14
Dear brothers, * your lives after Php 3:17
and live; be a * for them in your 1Ti 4:12
Hold tightly to the * of truth I 2Ti 1:13
follow exactly the * of the Heb 8:5

PATTERNED
* after the altar of Jehovah. Jos 22:28

PAU
King Hadad, from the city of *. Gen 36:31-39

PAUL
the feet of a young man named *. Act 7:58
* is also known as Saul. Act 7:58f
* WAS IN complete agreement with Act 8:1
buried Stephen.) * was like a wild Act 8:3
BUT *, THREATENING with every Act 9:1
heard a voice saying to him, "*! Act 9:4
a voice saying to him, "Paul! *! Act 9:4
"Who is speaking, sir?" * Act 9:5
The men with * stood speechless Act 9:7
saw no one! As * picked himself up Act 9:8,9
and ask there for * of Tarsus. Act 9:11
do what I say. For * is my chosen Act 9:15
So Ananias went over and found * Act 9:17
said, "Brother *, the Lord Jesus, Act 9:17
from his eyes) * could see, and was Act 9:18
* became more and more fervent in Act 9:22
to kill him. But * was told about Act 9:24
and told them how * had seen the Act 9:27
went on to Tarsus to hunt for *. Act 11:25
to Barnabas and * to take to the Act 11:30
Barnabas and * now visited Act 12:25
of King Herod), and *. Act 13:1
Barnabas and * for a special job I Act 13:2
Barnabas and * to visit him, for he Act 13:6,7
attention to what * and Barnabas Act 13:8
Then *, filled with the Holy Act 13:9
Now * and those with him left Act 13:13
But Barnabas and * went on to Act 13:14
So * stood, waved a greeting to Act 13:16
day, they asked * to return and Act 13:42
synagogue followed * and Barnabas Act 13:43
and argued against whatever * Act 13:45
Then * and Barnabas spoke out Act 13:46
a mob against * and Barnabas, and Act 13:50
AT ICONIUM, * and Barnabas went Act 14:1
Gentiles against * and Barnabas, Act 14:2
When * and Barnabas learned of a Act 14:5,6
He was listening as * preached, Act 14:9
Paul preached, and * noticed him Act 14:9
So * called to him, "Stand up!" Act 14:10
crowd saw what * had done, they Act 14:11
Jupiter, and that *, because he was Act 14:12
But when Barnabas and * saw what Act 14:14
But even so, * and Barnabas could Act 14:18
mob that stoned * and dragged him Act 14:19
tribulations. * and Barnabas also Act 14:23
WHILE * AND Barnabas were at Act 15:1
not be saved. * and Barnabas Act 15:2
were present—and * and Barnabas Act 15:4
as Barnabas and * told about the Act 15:12
to Antioch with * and Barnabas, to Act 15:22
with our beloved Barnabas and *. Act 15:25
had sent them. * and Barnabas Act 15:34,35
Several days later * suggested to Act 15:36
John Mark. But * didn't like that Act 15:38
for Cyprus, while * chose Silas Act 15:40,41
* AND SILAS went first to Derbe Act 16:1
and Iconium, so * asked him to Act 16:3
* had a vision. Act 16:9
book, now joined * and accompanied Act 16:10f
accepted all that * was saying. Act 16:14
after day until *, in great Act 16:18
they grabbed * and Silas and Act 16:19
formed against * and Silas, and the Act 16:22
Around midnight, as * and Silas Act 16:25
But * yelled to him, "Don't do Act 16:28
and fell down before * and Silas. Act 16:29
So the jailer told * they were Act 16:36
But * replied, "Oh, no they Act 16:37
* and Silas were Roman citizens. Act 16:38
leave the city. * and Silas then Act 16:40
planning to take * and Silas to the Act 17:5

(PAUL Con't)
Council instead. "* and Silas have Act 17:6
Christians hurried * and Silas to Act 17:10
day to check up on * and Silas' Act 17:11
learned that * was preaching in Act 17:13
at once, sending * on to the coast, Act 17:14
Those accompanying * went on Act 17:15
While * was waiting for them in Act 17:16
So *, standing before them at the Act 17:22
When they heard * speak of the Act 17:32
THEN * LEFT Athens and went to Act 18:1
Jews from Rome. * lived and worked Act 18:2,3
Each Sabbath found * at the Act 18:4
from Macedonia, * spent his full Act 18:5
abuse at Jesus, * shook off the Act 18:6
One night the Lord spoke to * in Act 18:9
So * stayed there the next Act 18:11
action against * and brought him Act 18:12
They accused * of "persuading Act 18:13
But just as * started to make Act 18:14
* stayed in the city several days Act 18:18
At Cenchreae, * had his head Act 18:18
WHILE APOLLOS WAS in Corinth, * Act 19:1
Then * pointed out to them that Act 19:4
Then, when * laid his hands upon Act 19:6
Then * went to the synagogue and Act 19:8
And God gave * the power to do Act 19:11
whom * preaches, to come out!" Act 19:13
and I know *, but who are you?" Act 19:15
Afterwards, * felt impelled by Act 19:21
heard, this man * has persuaded Act 19:26
for trial. * wanted to go in, but Act 19:30
friends of *, also sent a message Act 19:31
WHEN IT WAS all over, * sent for Act 20:1
service, with * preaching. Act 20:7
and as * spoke on and on, a Act 20:9
his death below. * went down and Act 20:10,11,12
together; then * preached another Act 20:10,11,12
* was going by land to Assos, and Act 20:13
* had decided against stopping at Act 20:16
These disciples warned *—the Holy Act 21:4
* not to go on to Jerusalem. Act 21:12
The second day * took us with him Act 21:18
were exchanged, * recounted the Act 21:19
So * agreed to their request and Act 21:26,27
* had taken him into the Temple. Act 21:29
riot followed. * was dragged out of Act 21:30
coming, they quit beating *. Act 21:32
* to be taken to the armory. Act 21:34
soldiers lifted * to their Act 21:35
As * was about to be taken Act 21:37,38
"No," * replied, "I am a Jew Act 21:39
The commander agreed, so * stood Act 21:40
The crowd listened until * came Act 22:22
As they tied * down to lash him, Act 22:25
down to lash him, * said to an Act 22:25
over and asked *, "Tell me, are Act 22:27
when they heard * was a Roman Act 22:29
He had * brought in before them Act 22:30
GAZING INTENTLY AT the Council, * Act 23:1
to * to slap him on the mouth. Act 23:2
* said to him, "God shall slap Act 23:3
Those standing near * said to Act 23:4
brothers," * replied, "for the Act 23:5
Then * thought of something! Act 23:6
jumped up to argue that * was all Act 23:9
were tugging at * from both sides, Act 23:10
* and said, "Don't worry, Paul; Act 23:11
Paul and said, "Don't worry, *; Act 23:11
nor drink until they had killed *! Act 23:12,13
"Ask the commander to bring * Act 23:15
and came to the armory and told *. Act 23:16
* called one of the officers and Act 23:17
did, explaining, "*, the prisoner, Act 23:18
ask you to bring * before the Act 23:20
cavalry. Give * a horse to ride and Act 23:23,24
the soldiers took * to Antipatris. Act 23:31
* and the letter to the governor. Act 23:33
He read it and then asked * Act 23:34
"Cilicia," * answered. Act 23:34
make their accusations against *. Act 24:1
charges against * in the following Act 24:2
* began: "I know, sir, that you Act 24:10
He ordered * to prison but Act 24:23
Sending for *, they listened as Act 24:24
He also hoped that * would bribe Act 24:26
the Jews, he left * in chains. Act 24:27
and gave him their story about *. Act 25:2
They begged him to bring * to Act 25:3
But Festus replied that since * Act 25:4
couldn't prove. * denied the Act 25:8
But * replied, "No! Act 25:10,11
next day and ordered * brought in. Act 25:17
who died, but * insists is alive! Act 25:19
But * appealed to Caesar! Act 25:21
city, Festus ordered * brought in. Act 25:23
THEN AGRIPPA SAID to *, "Go Act 26:1
So *, with many gestures, Act 26:1
Suddenly Festus shouted, "*, you Act 26:24
But * replied, "I am not insane, Act 26:25
And * replied, "Would to God Act 26:29
Rome by ship; so * and several Act 27:1
was very kind to * and let him go Act 27:3
and * spoke to the ship's Act 27:9
captain and the owner than to *. Act 27:11
time, but finally * called the crew Act 27:21
'Don't be afraid, *—for you will Act 27:24
the prow. But * said to the Act 27:31
light, * begged everyone to eat. Act 27:33
wanted to spare *, so he told Act 27:43
As * gathered an armful of sticks Act 28:3
But * shook off the snake into Act 28:5
and dysentery. * went in and prayed Act 28:8
When * saw them, he thanked God Act 28:15
When we arrived in Rome, * was Act 28:16
final word from * ringing in their Act 28:25
* lived for the next two years in Act 28:30
letter is from *, Jesus Christ's Rom 1:1
but * says to welcome them anyway. Rom 14:1f
this letter for *, send my Rom 16:22
Sincerely, * Rom 16:25,26,27
FROM: *, CHOSEN by God to be Jesus 1Co 1:1
saying, "I am a follower of *"; 1Co 1:12
But did I, *, die for your sins? 1Co 1:13
new, beginning a "Church of *." 1Co 1:15
He has given you * and Apollos 1Co 3:22
Obviously, * is not here 1Co 6:12f
Sincerely,* 1Co 16:24
This letter is from me, *, 2Co 1:1
I PLEAD WITH you—yes, I, *—and I 2Co 10:1
fellow, that *, and he fooled us. 2Co 12:16
friendship be yours. * 2Co 13:14
FROM: * THE missionary and all the Gal 1:1
to suppose that * was handicapped Gal 4:15f
Sincerely,* Gal 6:18
the Lord: This is * writing to you, Eph 1:1
I *, THE servant of Christ, am Eph 3:1
Sincerely,* Eph 6:24
FROM: * AND Timothy, slaves of Php 1:1
Sincerely,* Php 4:20
FROM: *, CHOSEN by God to be Jesus Col 1:1
And I, *, have the joy of telling Col 1:23
Sincerely,* Col 4:18
FROM: *, SILAS and Timothy. 1Th 1:1
to come and I, *, tried again and 1Th 2:18
Sincerely,* 1Th 5:28
FROM: *, SILAS and Timothy. 2Th 1:1
Sincerely,* 2Th 3:18
FROM: *, A missionary of Jesus 1Ti 1:1
Sincerely,* 1Ti 6:21
FROM: *, JESUS Christ's 2Ti 1:1
Farewell,* 2Ti 4:22
FROM: *, THE slave of God and the Tit 1:1
Sincerely,* Tit 3:15
FROM: *, IN jail for preaching the Phm 1:1
just to ask you—I, *, an old man Phm 1:8,9
I will pay it back (I, *, Phm 1:19
Jesus Christ be upon your spirit.* Phm 1:25
Our wise and beloved brother * 2Pe 3:15,16

PAUL'S
glad and rejoiced in * message; Act 13:48
As was * custom, he went there Act 17:2
That ended * discussion with Act 17:33
* traveling companions, for trial. Act 19:29
He took * belt, bound his own Act 21:11
But * nephew got wind of their Act 23:16
Now it was * turn. Act 24:10
the following day opened * trial. Act 25:6
On * arrival in court the Jews Act 25:7
discussed * case with the king. Act 25:14
original Olympic races of * time. 1Co 9:25f
Yet some of you are saying, "* 2Co 10:1

PAULUS
governor, Sergius *, a man of Act 13:6,7

PAUSE
Or, "He will * at the door of Ex 12:23f

PAUSED
David * at the edge of the city 2Sa 15:17,18

PAUSING
to the Negeb, * frequently. Gen 12:9

PAVEMENT
seemed to be a * of brilliant Ex 24:10
and placed it upon the stone *. 2Ki 16:17
fell flat on the *, and worshiped 2Ch 7:3
the * right before their eyes; Is 13:16
rocks between the * stones at the Jer 43:9
A stone * ran around the inside Eze 40:17
the walls, opening onto this *. Eze 40:17
This was called "the lower *." Eze 40:18
from crashing to the * below!" Lk 4:9,10,11
The *, but in Hebrew, Gabbatha." Jn 19:13f

PAVEMENTS
benches stood on * of black, red, Est 1:6

PAVILION
shall be a tent *—a Tabernacle. Ex 25:9

PAW
no lion has set his * there. Job 28:8
its * raised, ready to strike. Dan 7:5

PAWN
they want to use you as their *. Pro 23:6,7,8

PAWS
Any animal that walks on * is Lev 11:27

to hear! He * the earth and Job 39:21-23
Fiercely he * the ground and Job 39:24

PAY
I will of course * the full price Gen 23:9
Let me * the full price of the Gen 23:13
for you to work for me without *. Gen 29:15
years working to * for Rachel. Gen 29:20
Whatever it is, I'll * it." Gen 30:28
You made me * for every animal Gen 31:39
you demand, I will * it—only give Gen 34:12
"How much will you * me?" Gen 38:16
so that you can * back what was in Gen 43:12
"Now Joseph will * us back for Gen 50:15
mother, "and I will * you well!" Ex 2:9
* nothing to regain his freedom. Ex 21:2
that he must * for the loss of his Ex 21:19
and * any medical expenses. Ex 21:19
him go free to * for the tooth. Ex 21:27
of the well shall * full damages to Ex 21:34
living ox shall * in full for the Ex 21:36
sells it, he shall * a fine of five Ex 22:1
shall * double value as his fine. Ex 22:4
to graze, he must * for all damages Ex 22:5
shall * double if he is found. Ex 22:7
shall * double to the other. Ex 22:9
man who borrowed it must * for it. Ex 22:14
the owner is there, he need not *; Ex 22:15
then he need not *, because this Ex 22:15
her, he must * the usual dowry Ex 22:16
then he shall * the money anyway. Ex 22:17
This is their *! Lev 7:35
* your hired workers promptly. Lev 19:13
must * the penalty: he must die. Lev 24:15,16
Jubilee, he shall * almost the Lev 25:51
sixty shall * twenty-five dollars; Lev 27:3
to sixty shall * fifteen dollars; Lev 27:4
to twenty shall * ten dollars; Lev 27:5
A man over sixty shall * seven Lev 27:7
is too poor to * this amount, he Lev 27:8
* as the priest shall decide. Lev 27:8
be told how much to * instead. Lev 27:11,12
it, then he shall * twenty percent Lev 27:13
and the man shall * that amount Lev 27:14,15
field, he shall * twenty percent in Lev 27:19
the owner shall * the priest's Lev 27:27
to die may * a fine instead; Lev 27:29
number of Levites, * five dollars Num 3:47,48
In this way you will * for your Num 14:33
we * whatever you demand for it. Num 20:19
of their land. * them for whatever Deu 2:6
in the act, he must * a fine Deu 22:28,29
Literally, "shall * her father Deu 22:28,29f
in your town. * him his wage each Deu 24:14,15
to * crushing taxes to King Eglon. Ju 3:14
so that I may * back the Ju 16:28
and harvest his crops without *; 1Sa 8:12
"But we don't have anything to * 1Sa 9:7
* any attention to what he said. 1Sa 25:25
was forced to * tribute to 2Sa 8:14
* your men whatever wages you ask; 1Ki 5:6
You can * me with food for my 1Ki 5:9
must die, or else * me $2,000!' 1Ki 20:40
"You'll have to *." 1Ki 20:40
to * tribute to Israel any longer. 2Ki 1:1
If she didn't *, he said he would 2Ki 4:1
sell the oil and * your debt, and 2Ki 4:7
* for it with your own life." 2Ki 10:24
gift, use it to * for whatever 2Ki 12:4,5
superintendents to * the 2Ki 12:11,12
* the penalty for his own sins. 2Ki 14:6
* heavy annual taxes to Assyria. 2Ki 17:3
At the same time he refused to * 2Ki 17:4
refused to * tribute any longer. 2Ki 18:7
I will * whatever tribute you 2Ki 18:14
the Edomites to * large sums of 1Ch 18:13
I will * your men 20,000 sacks of 2Ch 2:10
But you must * annual tribute to 2Ch 12:8
they are doing and * them back." 2Ch 24:22
No, everyone must * for his own 2Ch 25:4
by the Levites to * the carpenters 2Ch 34:10,11
refuse to * their taxes to you. Ez 4:13
that you are to * the full Ez 6:8
required to * taxes of any kind.' Ez 7:24
to the limit to * their taxes. Neh 5:2,3,4
to obey and didn't * any attention Neh 9:17
who also set the * scale of the Neh 11:22,23
and I will * $20,000,000 into the Est 3:9
had promised to * into the king's Est 4:7
"Why shouldn't he, when you * Job 1:9
in the Almighty or * any attention Job 27:10
be, and doesn't * any more Job 34:19
man, to * any attention to him! Ps 8:4
their wickedness; * them back for Ps 28:4
Evil men borrow and "cannot * Ps 37:21
well again so I can * them back! Ps 41:10
with burnt-offerings to * my vows. Ps 66:13
* everything I vowed to the Lord. Ps 116:18,19
me to * attention to your laws. Ps 119:71,72
other time," if you can * now. Pro 3:27,28
in his house to * it back. Pro 6:31
It is senseless to * tuition to Pro 17:16

(PAY Con't)
Don't say, "Now I can * him back Pro 24:28,29
agrees to * a stranger's debts. Pro 27:13
treasure to * for Egypt's aid. Is 30:6
* attention, Israel, for you are Is 44:21
you strength? Why * for groceries Is 55:2
I will * them back in full. Is 65:7
We won't * any attention!" Jer 6:17
When they fast, I will not * any Jer 14:12
to *—yet they all curse me. Jer 15:10
that you must * for all your sins. Jer 17:2,3
They stubbornly refused to * Jer 17:23
But if you refuse to * attention Jer 22:5
come, that they * their penalty in Jer 23:12
* for their fathers' sins." Jer 31:29
We must even * for water to Lam 5:4
services—men * with many gifts. Eze 16:33,34
But you had to * them, for no one Eze 16:33,34
'Doesn't the son * for his Eze 18:19
to * you for your 'protection'; Eze 22:7
not * the army for all this work. Eze 29:18
There was little left to * the Eze 29:18f
There was little left to * the Eze 29:20f
but don't * any attention to it! Eze 33:32
God says, I will * back your angry Eze 35:11
to, and I will * you back for all Joe 3:7
and threaten those who will not *! Mic 3:5
give me my *, whatever I am worth; Zec 11:12
the Lord doesn't * attention to Mal 2:13
eye, he must * with his own eye. Mt 5:38
"Doesn't your master * taxes?" Mt 17:24
take it and * them." Mt 17:26,27
He couldn't *, so the king Mt 18:25
with me and I will * it all.' Mt 18:26
'Be patient and I will * it,' he Mt 18:29
He agreed to * them $20 a day Mt 20:2
them he would * them whatever was Mt 20:4
the men in and * them, beginning Mt 20:8
It is my desire to * all the Mt 20:14
others who will * him promptly." Mt 21:41
Now tell us, is it right to * Mt 22:17
much will you * me to get Jesus Mt 26:15
Now tell us, is it right to * Mk 12:14
—reader, * attention! Mk 13:14
one is,' don't * any attention. Mk 13:21
and be content with your *!" Lk 3:14
But neither of them could * him Lk 7:42
he said, 'I'll * the difference the Lk 10:35
is here [and few * any attention Lk 11:31
has enough money to * the bills? Lk 14:28
Now tell us—is it right to * Lk 20:22
them not to * their taxes to the Lk 23:2
had come to * their respects and to Jn 11:19
him to go and * for the food or to Jn 13:29
the governor to * no attention to Act 13:8
of mine worked to * my own way and Act 20:34
too—and * for theirs to be shaved. Act 21:24
Never * back evil for evil. Rom 12:17
* your taxes too, for these same Rom 13:6
serving you. * everyone whatever Rom 13:7
he ought to have: * your taxes and Rom 13:7
whom it is due. * all your debts Rom 13:8
work still stands, will get his *. 1Co 3:14
army has to * his own expenses? 1Co 9:7
this circumstance, what is my *? 1Co 9:18
children don't * for their father's 2Co 12:14
* attention to what I have said. 2Co 13:11
you will * more attention to them. Gal 4:17
Remember, the Lord will * you Eph 6:8
who is going to * you, giving you Col 3:24
for him, he will * you in a way Col 3:25
for enough money to * your bills. 1Th 4:12
who work deserve their *!" 1Ti 5:18
I will * it back (I, Paul, Phm 1:19
whom you have cheated of their *. Jas 5:4
You will do well to * close 2Pe 1:19
That is the * these teachers will 2Pe 2:13
but she refused. * attention now Rev 2:22

PAYING
by * for the loss, plus a twenty Lev 5:16
will be exempted from * taxes!" 1Sa 17:25
"The Lord is * you back for 2Sa 16:7,8
cooperated by * their taxes, so he 2Ch 17:5
of Tyre and Sidon, * for them with Ez 3:7
things— if I were * back evil for Ps 7:4
By not * wages you are building Jer 22:13
So I bought the field, * Hanamel Jer 32:9
to buy the field—* good money for Jer 32:25
* no attention to you or your law. Dan 6:13
become poor from * them, and was no Mk 5:26
for others—never finish * that! Rom 13:8
help their teachers by * them. Gal 6:6

PAYMASTER
"That evening he told the * to Mt 20:8

PAYMENT
* at the top of his sack! Gen 42:25
*, and thus becomes your slave." Ex 21:2f
may leave freely without any *. Ex 21:11
redemption * for your oldest son. Ex 22:29
His * shall be half a dollar. Ex 30:13
to whom the * can be made, it must Num 5:8
Instead, there must be a * of two Num 18:16
great honors plus any * you ask. Num 22:16,17
Nor may a * be accepted from a Num 35:32
sent him an annual * of 125,000 1Ki 5:11
Hiram of Tyre as * for all the 1Ki 9:11,12
it as a * to the Assyrian king. 2Ki 16:8
And your mother was taken in * Is 50:1
giving * in ebony and ivory. Eze 27:15
him to death as * for his sins. Hos 12:14
the throat and demanded instant *. Mt 18:28
Literally, "a denarius," the * Mt 20:2f
We have never demanded * of any 1Co 9:12

PAYMENTS
shall give these * instead: A man Lev 27:1
* to your allies for their love. Eze 16:40,41

PAYS
He is the God who * back those Ps 18:47
It * him to keep his mouth shut. Pro 17:27,28
* wonderful interest on your loan! Pro 19:17
kills a sheep, he * no attention to Is 31:4,5
your proofs that idol-worship *! Is 45:21
The rich man * them off and tells Mic 7:3
just because he * my salary; 1Co 9:19
See that no one * back evil for 1Th 5:15
and the world * attention to them. 1Jn 4:5

PE-ULLETHAI
* (the eighth). 1Ch 26:4,5

PEACE
(But you will die in *, at a Gen 15:15
you and have sent you away in *; Gen 26:29
Come now and we will sign a * Gen 31:44
be * and harmony in the camp." Ex 18:23
and * offerings of sheep and oxen. Ex 20:24
and * offerings to the Lord. Ex 24:5
sacrifices—whether * offerings or Ex 29:28
and * offerings to the calf-idol; Ex 32:6
"No, do not make a * treaty of Ex 34:15
Literally, "* offering." Lev 4:26f
Literally, "* offering." Lev 4:31f
Literally, "* offering." Lev 4:35f
the fat of the daily * offering. Lev 6:12
the Lord as special * offerings: Lev 7:11
This thanksgiving * offering Lev 7:13
to the Lord as a * offering to show Lev 7:15
and then eats the * offering, shall Lev 7:21
offering and the * offering; Lev 7:37
to the Lord a * offering Lev 9:4
people's * offering sacrifice; Lev 9:18
It is your portion of the * Lev 10:14
"When you sacrifice a * offering Lev 19:5
"Anyone sacrificing a * offering Lev 22:21
yearling lambs for a * offering. Lev 23:19
I will give you *, and you will go Lev 26:6
* offering, a ram without defect; Num 6:14
then the ram for a * offering, Num 6:17
under the * offering sacrifice. Num 6:18
his favor, and give you his *.' Num 6:24,25,26
and for the * offerings two Num 7:17
For the * offerings they brought: Num 7:88
burnt offerings and * offerings. Num 10:10
drink offerings, or * offerings." Num 29:39
of Heshbon with a proposal of *. Deu 2:26
* with you, you must besiege it. Deu 20:12
Sacrifice * offerings upon it Deu 27:7
sacrifices and * offerings to the Jos 8:31
to ask for a * treaty with you." Jos 9:6
be their servants, and ask for *.' Jos 9:11
went ahead and signed a * treaty. Jos 9:14,15
leaders because of the * treaty. Jos 9:18
of Gibeon had made * with Israel Jos 10:1
they have made * with Joshua and Jos 10:4
None of the cities was given a * Jos 11:19
Israelis instead of asking for *; Jos 11:20
And the Lord gave them *, just Jos 21:44
grain offerings or * offerings—may Jos 22:22,23
offerings and * offerings and Jos 22:26,27
would make no * treaties with the Ju 2:2
Othni-el, there was * in the land. Ju 3:11
at * for the next eighty years. Ju 3:30
After that there was * in the land Ju 5:31
"The Altar of * with Jehovah." Ju 6:24
the land was at * for forty Ju 8:28
returned home in *, the first Ju 11:30,31
burnt sacrifices and * offerings. Ju 20:26
sacrifices and * offerings on it. Ju 21:4
Then Israel sent a * delegation Ju 21:13
And there was * between Israel 1Sa 7:14
burnt offerings and * offerings. 1Sa 10:8
citizens of Jabesh asked for *. 1Sa 11:1
Then they offered * offerings to 1Sa 11:15
and the * offerings himself. 1Sa 13:9
then let him accept my * offering. 1Sa 26:19
been sent away in *, he rushed to 2Sa 3:23
and * offerings to the Lord. 2Sa 6:17
WHEN THE LORD finally sent * upon 2Sa 7:1
Yes, the king will give us * 2Sa 14:17
me, we will leave the city in *." 2Sa 20:21
burnt offerings and * offerings. 2Sa 24:25
but it was done in a time of *. 1Ki 2:5
what to do—don't let him die in *. 1Ki 2:6
"No," he replied, "I come in *. 1Ki 2:13
burnt offerings and * offerings. 1Ki 3:1
And there was * throughout the 1Ki 4:2
and Israel lived in * and safety; 1Ki 4:2
for the Lord to give him *. 1Ki 5:2,
has given Israel * on every side; 1Ki 5:
made a formal alliance of *. 1Ki 5:1
by sacrificing * offerings to the 1Ki 8:62,6
and the fat of the * offerings: for 1Ki 8:6
offerings and * offerings three 1Ki 9:2
—until I return in *.' 1Ki 22:2
"If you return in *," Micaiah 1Ki 22:2
He also made * with Ahab, the 1Ki 22:4
"Do you come in *?" 2Ki 9:1
"What do you know about *? 2Ki 9:1
the blood of * offerings upon it. 2Ki 16:1
King Hezekiah sued for * and 2Ki 18:14
You can live in * here in your 2Ki 18:31,32
there will be * and security during 2Ki 20:19
*, peace be unto you, 1Ch 12:18
Peace, * be unto you, 1Ch 12:18
And * to all who aid you; 1Ch 12:18
and * offerings before God. 1Ch 16:1
offerings and * offerings upon it; 1Ch 21:26
will be a man of *, for I will give 1Ch 22:9
I will give him * with his enemies 1Ch 22:9
and I will give * and quietness to 1Ch 22:9
"He has given you * with the 1Ch 22:18
has given us *, and he will always 1Ch 23:25
and there was * in the land for the 2Ch 14:1
is why God gave his kingdom *. 2Ch 14:5
blessing us with * because of our 2Ch 14:7
against God there was no *. 2Ch 15:5
And he gave them * throughout the 2Ch 15:15
with each, and many * offerings. 2Ch 29:35
continued, and * offerings were 2Ch 30:22
offerings and * offerings, and to 2Ch 31:2
And now there was * at last 2Ch 32:22
sacrifices upon it—* offerings and 2Ch 33:16
given a moment of *, for you have Ez 9:8
Dangerous animals will be at * Job 5:23
him and you will have * at last! Job 22:21
He enforces * in heaven. Job 25:2
Then I lay down and slept in * Ps 3:5
I will lie down in * and sleep, Ps 4:8
He will bless them with *. Ps 29:11
Try to live in * with everyone; Ps 34:14
They don't talk of * and doing Ps 35:20
and shall have wonderful *. Ps 37:11
the man of *—he has a wonderful Ps 37:37
me—I who was at * with him. Ps 55:20
turn to ashes and their * Ps 69:22
abundance of * to the end of time. Ps 72:7
he speaks * to his people, his Ps 85:8
and * have kissed! Ps 85:10
laws have great * of heart and mind Ps 119:165
here among these men who hate *. Ps 120:5,6
I am for *, but they are for Ps 120:7
Pray for the * of Jerusalem. Ps 122:6
O Jerusalem, may there be * Ps 122:7
and may there be * as a Ps 122:9
let Israel have quietness and *. Ps 125:5
the walls, but * everywhere. Ps 144:12-15
He sends * across your nation, Ps 147:14
live in * and safety, unafraid." Pro 1:33
good lifeRichesHonorPleasure* Pro 3:16,17
Literally, "Sacrifices of * Pro 7:14f
bold reproof leads to *. Pro 10:10
worst enemies to be at * with him. Pro 16:7
A DRY CRUST eaten in * is better Pro 17:1
while wise men try to keep *. Pro 29:8
give you happiness and * of mind. Pro 29:17
A time for *. Ecc 3:8
of war into implements of *. Is 2:4
In that glorious day of * there Is 9:5
Father," "The Prince of *." Is 9:6
He will bring true justice and * Is 9:7
leopard and goats will be at *. Is 11:6
at last we have *." Is 14:8
The needy shall lie down in *. Is 14:30
He will keep in perfect * all Is 26:3
Lord, grant us *; Is 26:12
and beg for * and my protection. Is 27:4,5
the land, and out of justice, *. Is 32:17
has refused their cry for *. Is 33:7
The Assyrians have broken their * Is 33:8
see Jerusalem at *, a place where Is 33:20
At least there will be * during Is 39:8
Then you would have had * flowing Is 48:18
But there is no *, says the Is 48:22
the happy news of * and salvation, Is 52:7
chastised that we might have *; Is 53:5
My promise of * for you will Is 54:10
you will live in *. Is 54:14
You will live in joy and *. Is 55:12
the godly who die shall rest in *. Is 57:2
their sins. *, peace to them, both Is 57:19
Peace, * to them, both near and Is 57:19
There is no *, says my God, for Is 57:21
You don't know what true * is, Is 59:8
won't experience any *, either. Is 59:8
stones for iron. * and Is 60:17

PEACE Con't)
assurances of * when all is war. Jer 6:14
We expected *, but no peace Jer 8:15
We expected peace, but no * Jer 8:15
them *, that you will bless them. Jer 14:13
punishment, will there be no *? Jer 14:19
But no * has come and there is Jer 14:19
protection and my * from them—taken Jer 16:5
who persecute me, but give me *. Jer 17:18
saved and Israel will live in *. Jer 23:5,6
Lord has said you shall have *!" Jer 23:17
So a prophet who foretells * has Jer 28:9
And work for the * and Jer 29:7
for if Babylon has *, so will you. Jer 29:7
"Where shall we find *?" Jer 30:5
live together in * and happiness. Jer 31:24
make them live in * and safety. Jer 32:37
and give her prosperity and *. Jer 33:6
let you live in * here in the land Jer 35:15
O Lord, all * and all prosperity Lam 3:17
You will sue for *, but you won't Eze 7:25
'God will send *,' when that is not Eze 13:10
will have * when there is no peace, Eze 13:16
there is no *, says the Lord God. Eze 13:16
There they will lie down in * and Eze 34:14
lie down in *, the Lord God says. Eze 34:15,16
I will make a * pact with them, Eze 34:25
And I will make a covenant of * Eze 37:26
will be lying in * after the return Eze 38:8
are living in * in their land, then Eze 38:14
they will be home again, in * and Eze 39:26
his burnt offering and * offering. Eze 46:2
burnt offering or * offering to be Eze 46:12
was living in * and prosperity, Dan 4:4
Let your face shine again with * Dan 9:17
king of Syria as a gesture of *, Dan 11:6
of * between their two lands. Dan 11:6f
Then you will lie down in * and Hos 1:18
not look at your offerings of *. Amo 5:22
They will promise * while Ob 1:7
who trusted you, who walk in *. Mic 2:8
You who cry "*" to those who Mic 3:5
There will be universal *, and Mic 4:3
in his own home in * and Mic 4:4
He will be our *. Mic 5:5
make them live in * and Mic 7:14
They will live quietly, in *, and Zep 3:13
And here I will give *,' Hag 2:8,9
* with God through Christ who, 500 Hag 2:8,9f
there is prosperity and *." Zec 1:11
will all live in * and prosperity Zec 3:10
will have * and prosperity so long Zec 8:4
"For I am sowing * and Zec 8:12
Live at * with everyone. Zec 8:16
festivals if you love truth and *! Zec 8:19
shall bring * among the nations. Zec 9:10
give him life and *, to be a means Mal 2:5
Happy are those who strive for * Mt 5:9
I came to bring * to the earth! Mt 10:34
go in *, healed of your Mk 5:34
Live in * with each other." Mk 9:50
to guide us to the path of *." Lk 1:79
"and * on earth for all those Lk 2:14
go in *." Lk 7:50
Go in *." Lk 8:48
have come to give * to the earth? Lk 12:51
truce team to discuss terms of *. Lk 14:32
"Eternal * was within your Lk 19:42
"I am leaving you with a gift—* Jn 14:27
And the * I give isn't fragile Jn 14:27
like the * the world gives. Jn 14:27
you will have * of heart and mind. Jn 16:33
Meanwhile, the church had * Act 9:31
there is * with God through Jesus, Act 10:36,37
and asked for *, for their cities Act 12:20
quietness and * to us Jews and have Act 24:2
May all God's mercies and * be Rom 1:6,7
* from God for all who obey him, Rom 2:10
we can have real * with him because Rom 5:1
leads to life and *, but following Rom 8:6
the Gospel of * with God and bring Rom 10:15
Be at * with everyone, just as Rom 12:18
* and joy from the Holy Spirit. Rom 14:17
full of * as you believe in him. Rom 15:13
And now may our God, who gives *, Rom 15:33
The God of * will soon crush Rom 16:20
and great * of heart and mind. 1Co 1:3
children to live in * and harmony. 1Co 7:15
each one of you, and give you *. 2Co 1:2
Live in harmony and *. 2Co 13:11
And may the God of love and * be 2Co 13:11
the dead. May * and blessing be Gal 1:3
in us: love, joy, *, patience, Gal 5:22
May God's mercy and * be upon all Gal 6:16
May his blessings and * be Eph 1:2
Christ himself is our way of *. Eph 2:14
He has made * between us Jews and Eph 2:14
person, and at last there was *. Eph 2:15
this Good News of * to you Gentiles Eph 2:17
and so be at * with one another. Eph 4:3
the Good News of * with God. Eph 6:15
May God give * to you, my Eph 6:23
* in your hearts and your lives. Php 1:2
experience God's *, which is far Php 4:7
understand. His * will keep your Php 4:7
and the God of * will be with you. Php 4:9
and fill you with his great *. Col 1:2
* with God for all by his blood. Col 1:20
Let the * of heart which comes Col 3:15
May blessing and * of heart be your 1Th 1:1
May the God of * himself make 1Th 5:23
May the Lord of * himself give 2Th 3:16
you his * no matter what happens. 2Th 3:16
you great * of heart and mind. 1Ti 1:2
we can live in * and quietness, 1Ti 2:2
with his kindness, mercy and *. 2Ti 1:2
give you his blessings and his *. Tit 1:4
give you his blessings and his *. Phm 1:3
and he is also the King of * Heb 7:2
city, Salem, which means "*." Heb 7:2
And now may the God of *, who Heb 13:20,21
* and reap a harvest of goodness. Jas 3:18
Try to live in * even if you must 1Pe 3:11
of Christian love. * be to all of 1Pe 5:14
and more of God's kindness and *? 2Pe 1:2
and be at * with everyone so that 2Pe 3:14
much *, and with truth and love. 2Jn 1:3
of God's kindness, *, and love. Jud 1:2
May you have grace and * from God Rev 1:4
* and bring anarchy to the earth; Rev 6:4

PEACE-FILLED
blessings and * hearts and minds. 2Th 1:2

PEACE-LOVING
You are destroying an ancient, * 2Sa 20:19
Then it is * and courteous. Jas 3:17

PEACEABLY
"Give us back our land *," he Ju 11:13

PEACEFUL
and everything was quiet and *; 1Ch 4:40,41
Solomon (meaning "*"), and I will 1Ch 22:9
* because Queen Athaliah was dead. 2Ch 23:21
His ever-expanding, * Is 9:7
is quiet and *"—then, all of a 1Th 5:3

PEACEMAKER
He tried to be a *. Act 7:26

PEACEMAKERS
And those who are * will plant Jas 3:18

PEACOCK
The *. Pro 30:29,30,31

PEACOCKS
* arrived at the Israeli ports. 1Ki 10:22
gold, silver, ivory, apes, and *. 2Ch 9:21

PEAK
of Moab to Pisgah * in Mount Nebo, Deu 34:1
trouble at the * of his powers; Job 20:22
Literally, "Depart from the * of Sol 4:8f
from the * of Senir and Hermon." Sol 4:8f
Next Satan took him to the * of a Mt 4:8
towering mountain * and from there Rev 21:10

PEAKS
feet and more above the highest *. Gen 7:20
down, other mountain * appeared. Gen 8:5
mountains, yes, the * of Lebanon. 2Ki 19:23
But though you live among the * Jer 49:16

PEARL
Heaven is like a * merchant on the Mt 13:45
He discovered a real bargain—a * Mt 13:46
pearls —each gate from a single *! Rev 21:21

PEARLS
Don't give * to swine! Mt 7:6
They will trample the * and turn Mt 7:6
on the lookout for choice *. Mt 13:45
precious gems and *, and held in Rev 17:4
precious stones, *, finest linens, Rev 18:12
gold and precious stones and *! Rev 18:16
The twelve gates were made of * Rev 21:21

PEAS
Then Jacob gave Esau bread, *, Gen 25:34

PEASANT
A leafy plant eaten by * women in Gen 30:14f

PEASANTS
With an army of *! Ju 5:11
extorted from the helpless *. Is 3:14

PEDAHEL
Naphtali * (son of Num 34:16-28

PEDAHZUR
Gamaliel (son of *) Num 2:3-31
Gamaliel, son of *, prince of the Num 7:54-59
led by Gamaliel the son of *; Num 10:23

PEDAIAH
Zebidah (daughter of * of Rumah) 2Ki 23:36,37
*, Shenazzar, Jekamiah, Hoshama, 1Ch 3:17,18
* was the father of 1Ch 3:19,20
of Manasseh, Joel (son of *); 1Ch 27:16-22
Next was * (son of Parosh). Neh 3:25
To his left were *, Misha-el, Neh 8:1
of Joed, son of *, son of Kolaiah, Neh 11:7,8,9
the scribe, and * the Levite in Neh 13:13

PEDESTAL
a bronze basin with a bronze *. Ex 30:17,18
and the washbasin and its *. Ex 30:28
the laver and its *; Ex 31:9
The basin with its *; Ex 35:10-19
and its bronze * were cast from the Ex 38:8
and its *, sanctifying it. Ex 40:11
and its *, to sanctify them. Lev 8:11

PEELED
plane trees, and * white streaks in Gen 30:37
and placed the * branches before Gen 30:41

PEELING
My skin is black and *. Job 30:30

PEEP
open his mouth to * against us!" Is 10:14

PEERED
Stooping, he * in and saw the Lk 24:12

PEERING
now, as if we were * at his 1Co 13:12

PEERS
without fail be stoned by his *. Lev 20:1

PEG
Then Jael took a sharp tent * and Ju 4:21
she drove the * through his temples Ju 4:21
the tent * through his temples. Ju 4:22
and steady * to support my people; Is 22:23,24
out that other * that seems to be Is 22:25
Cornerstone, the * on which all Zec 10:4

PEGS
all the pins and * for hanging the Ex 27:19
and their bases, *, and ropes. Num 3:36,37
with their bases, *, cords, and Num 4:32
making * to hang up pots and pans! Eze 15:3

PEKAH
Then * (son of Remaliah), the 2Ki 15:25
revolt). So * became the new king. 2Ki 15:25
New king of Israel: * 2Ki 15:27
*, too, was an evil king, and he 2Ki 15:28
against * and assassinated him; 2Ki 15:30
Reigning in Israel at this time: * 2Ki 15:32,33
King * of Israel to attack Judah. 2Ki 15:37
at this time: King * (son of 2Ki 16:1
of Syria and King * (son of 2Ki 16:5
On a single day, *, the son of 2Ch 28:6
* of Israel (the son of Remaliah). Is 7:1
those two has-beens, Rezin and *. Is 7:4
Rezin and King * to come and aid Is 8:6

PEKAH'S
The rest of the history of * 2Ki 15:31
King * power will not increase. Is 7:9

PEKAHIAH
When he died, his son * became 2Ki 15:22
Name of new king of Israel: * 2Ki 15:23
But * was an evil king, and he 2Ki 15:24
history of King * is recorded in 2Ki 15:26
Shallum, and *. Hos 7:7f
years: Zechariah, Shallum, *. Hos 13:11f

PEKOD
and against the people of *. Jer 50:21
Chaldeans from * and Shoa and Koa; Eze 23:23

PELAIAH
Hodaviah, Eliashib, *, Akkub, 1Ch 3:24
Jozabad, Hanan, *, and the Levites Neh 8:7,8
*, Hanan, Mica, Rehob, Neh 10:9-13

PELALIAH
of Jeroham, son of *, son of Amzi, Neh 11:10-14

PELATIAH
Hananiah's sons were * and 1Ch 3:21,22
(Their leaders were *, Ne-ariah, 1Ch 4:42
Zadok, Jaddu-a, *, Neh 10:14-27
of Azzur) and * (son of Benaiah). Eze 11:1
* (son of Benaiah) suddenly died. Eze 11:13

PELEG
* (meaning "Division," for Gen 10:25
years old when his son * was born. Gen 11:16,17
* was thirty years old when his Gen 11:18,19
Eber had two sons: * (which means 1Ch 1:19
The son of Eber was *, 1Ch 1:24-27
The son of * was Reu, 1Ch 1:24-27
Reu's father was *; Lk 3:23-38

PELEG'S
and Joktan (* brother). Gen 10:25
Reu's father was Peleg;* father Lk 3:23-38

PELET
Regem, Jotham, Geshan, *, Ephah, 1Ch 2:47
Jezi-el and *, sons of Azmaveth; 1Ch 12:3-7

PELETH
and On (the son of *), all three Num 16:1
had two sons named * and Zaza. 1Ch 2:33

PELETHITES
Literally, "the Cherethites and * 2Sa 8:18f
Gath, and the Cherethites and *. 2Sa 15:17,18
Literally, "the Cherethites and * 2Sa 20:23f
Cherethites and *—and David's sons 1Ch 18:17

PELICAN
The *, Lev 11:13-19
The horned owl, the *, Deu 14:11-18

PELL-MELL
No, all are rushing * down the Jer 8:6

PELON
Helez from *; 1Ch 11:26-47
Ahijah from *; 1Ch 11:26-47

PELONA
was Helez from * in Ephraim, with 1Ch 27:10

PELUSIUM
out my fury upon *, the strongest Eze 30:15

(PELUSIUM Con't)
Yes, I will set fire to Egypt, * Eze 30:16

PEN
an iron * in the rock forever. Job 19:23,24
in a slaughter *, and scattered us Ps 44:11
with an iron * or diamond point Jer 17:1
calf we have in the fattening *. Lk 15:23
It is not a letter written with * 2Co 3:3

PENALIZE
his taxes, I will * myself by Lk 19:8

PENALTIES
made a vow with *, but says Num 30:4
or feels that the * she has agreed Num 30:5
the vow, whatever * to which she Num 30:15
Because he carried out God's * for Deu 33:21
them of the * of sin, and keeping Job 33:17,18
heavy * are meted out to those Ps 34:21
sentence the proud to the * they Ps 94:1
this book—all the * announced by Jer 25:13

PENALTY
brings it, as the * for his sins. Lev 1:4
the loss, plus a twenty percent *; Lev 5:16
Tabernacle under * of death, for Lev 10:7
The * for intrusion is death. Lev 16:1
each other. The * for homosexual Lev 20:13
God must pay the *: he must die. Lev 24:15,16
The * for injuring anyone is to Lev 24:19
not spare that person from the *; Deu 13:8
for this purpose, the * is death. Deu 17:12
is lying, his * shall be the Deu 19:19
a crime, and the * is a beating, Deu 25:1
must pay the * for his own sins. 2Ki 14:6
"What * does the law provide for Est 1:13-15
Let him feel the * himself. Job 21:19
given the maximum * for the wicked Job 34:36
his own brother from the * of sin! Ps 49:7
man must bear his own *; Pro 19:19
* in full for all their sins. Jer 23:12
full * he decrees against them. Jer 23:20
You are under the * of death, Eze 3:18
I have heaped upon you the full * Eze 22:31
You will suffer the full *, and Eze 23:49
has done calls for the death *. Lk 23:15
the * they so richly deserved. Rom 1:27
of God's death * for these crimes, Rom 1:32
Adam's one sin brought the * of Rom 5:16
in my being given the death *. Rom 7:10
them from the * of the sins they Heb 9:15
to the death * from God. Jas 1:15
double * for all her evil deeds. Rev 18:6

PENANCE
You don't want *; Ps 51:16
We have done much *, and you Is 58:3
want—this doing of * and bowing Is 58:5

PENDANTS
the crescents and * or the royal Ju 8:26

PENETRATE
Who can * his hide, or who dares Job 41:13
between them, and nothing can *. Job 41:15-17
let them * deep within your Pro 4:21
They will * to Adullum, the Mic 1:15
of God, whose eyes * like flames of Rev 2:18

PENETRATED
his eyes * like flames of fire. Rev 1:14

PENIEL
Jacob named the place "*" Gen 32:30

PENINNAH
He had two wives, Hannah and *. 1Sa 1:2
and Peninnah. * had some children, 1Sa 1:2
presents to * and her children; 1Sa 1:4
give presents to. * made matters 1Sa 1:6
Every year it was the same—* 1Sa 1:7
The next year Elkanah and * and 1Sa 1:21,22

PENINSULA
in the Sinai * three months after Ex 19:1
Israel on the Sinai * at the time. Num 1:1
Moses at the Sinai *, telling him, Num 3:14,15
were on the Sinai *, during the Num 9:1
*, just as the Lord had commanded. Num 9:4,5

PENIS
the foreskin of his * shall be Gen 17:11
of her young son's *, and threw it Ex 4:25,26
are crushed or his * cut off, he Deu 23:1

PENITENCE
in * and intercession before God. 2Ch 20:3
spirit you want—remorse and *. Ps 51:17

PENNIES
widow came and dropped in two *. Mk 12:42
A couple of *? Lk 12:6

PENNILESS
And if we are hungry, or *, or in Rom 8:35

PENNY
me off without a * to my name. Gen 31:42
"present them without a * lost Ez 8:29
until you have paid the last *. Mt 5:26
Two for a *? Mt 10:29
he had paid every last * due. Mt 18:34
And they handed him a *. Mt 22:19
while she gave up her last *." Mk 12:43,44
the last * is paid in full." Lk 12:59
I have never asked you for one *. 1Co 9:15
carry away a single * when we die. 1Ti 6:7

PENS
with * for his flocks and herds. Gen 33:17
from the fattening *, 20 1Ki 4:23

PENT
For I am * up and full of words, Job 32:18
am * up until it is accomplished! Lk 12:50

PENTATEUCH
The Samaritan * says that Terah Gen 11:32f

PENTECOST
"The Festival of *: Fifty days Lev 23:15,16
of Weeks, or *), there must be a Num 28:26
and the Day of * had now arrived. Act 2:1
for the celebration of *. Act 20:16
the holiday of *, for there is a 1Co 16:8

PENUEL
Then he went up to * and asked Ju 8:8
He also went to * and knocked Ju 8:17
Later he built *. 1Ki 12:25
(his daughter),* (the ancestor of 1Ch 4:3-4
Elam, Anthothijah, Iphdeiah, *. 1Ch 8:22-25

PEOPLE
call themselves "the Lord's *." Gen 4:26
for among all the * of the earth, I Gen 7:1
and his name became proverbial. * Gen 10:9
of the * inhabiting these areas: Gen 10:13,14
his lifetime the * of the world Gen 10:25
The * who lived there began to Gen 11:3,4
you, and your own *, and go to the Gen 12:1
me back my * who were captured; Gen 14:21
terms shall be cut off from his *; Gen 17:14
heard that the * of Sodom and Gen 18:20
Suppose you find fifty godly * Gen 18:24
I find fifty godly * there, I will Gen 18:26
life—*, plants, and animals alike. Gen 19:25
fearful of the * there, and went to Gen 19:30
Here in the presence of my *, I Gen 23:11
that land and my *, and promised to Gen 24:7
great man among the * of his land. Gen 24:35
"and was gathered to his *." Gen 25:17f
(That is why the * of Israel Gen 32:32
"Who are these * with you?" Gen 33:5
unite with you to become one *. Gen 34:16
among all the * of this land—all Gen 34:30
The * began to starve. Gen 41:55
"What kind of * do you think we Gen 44:7
When the * were out of money, Gen 47:15
Thus all the * of Egypt became Gen 47:21
Then Joseph said to the *, "See, Gen 47:23
and soon the * of Israel began to Gen 47:27
"May the * of Israel bless each Gen 48:20
comes, whom all * shall obey. Gen 49:10
"Dan shall govern his * like any Gen 49:16
*—his brothers and their families. Gen 50:8
cavalry, and * accompanied Joseph. Gen 50:9
I could save the lives of many *. Gen 50:20
He told his *, "These Israelis Ex 1:9
So the * of Israel continued to Ex 1:20
all of his * to throw the newborn Ex 1:22
deep sorrows of my * in Egypt, and Ex 3:7
Yes, the wail of the * of Israel Ex 3:9
let you lead my * out of Egypt." Ex 3:10
you have led the * out of Egypt, Ex 3:12
"If I go to the * of Israel and Ex 3:13
'I have visited my *, and have seen Ex 3:16
The elders of the * of Ex 3:18
will be your spokesman to the *. Ex 4:16
so that he will not let the * go. Ex 4:21
* of Israel to a council meeting. Ex 4:29
He says, 'Let my * go, for they Ex 5:1
the * from their work? Ex 5:4,5
had set over the * of Israel: Ex 5:6
"Don't give the * any more straw Ex 5:7,8
informed the *: "Pharaoh has given Ex 5:10,11
So the * scattered everywhere Ex 5:12
Pharaoh and his *," they said, Ex 5:21
you mistreat your own * like this? Ex 5:22
he must be forced to let my * go; Ex 6:1
groanings of the * of Israel, in Ex 6:5
And I will accept them as my * Ex 6:7
It shall belong to my *." Ex 6:8,9
So Moses told the * what God had Ex 6:8,9
he must let the * of Israel go." Ex 6:11
objected, "my own * won't even Ex 6:12
to return to the * of Israel and to Ex 6:13
that the * be permitted to leave. Ex 6:13
"Lead all the * of Israel out of Ex 6:26
to lead the * from the land, and Ex 6:27
demanding that the * of Israel be Ex 7:2
disaster and then lead my * out. Ex 7:4
and force them to let my * go." Ex 7:5
to refuse to let the * go. Ex 7:14
that you let his * go to worship Ex 7:16
"Let my * go and worship me. Ex 8:1
you and your * will be immersed Ex 8:3,4
the * go and sacrifice to him." Ex 8:8
refused to let the * go, just as Ex 8:15
"Let my * go and worship me. Ex 8:20
between your * and my people. Ex 8:23
between your people and my *. Ex 8:23
to let the * go and then changing Ex 8:29
again and did not let the * go! Ex 8:31,3
let his * go to sacrifice to him. Ex 9:
and he refused to let the * go. Ex 9:
to break out upon * and animals Ex 9:
says, "Let my * go to worship me. Ex 9:1
all the Egyptian *, and prove to Ex 9:1
power, and refuse to let my * go? Ex 9:1
upon the *, animals, and trees." Ex 9:2
where the * of Israel lived. Ex 9:2
my * have been wrong all along. Ex 9:2
so Pharaoh refused to let the * Ex 9:3
Let my * go so they can worship Ex 10:
heart and he did not let the * go. Ex 10:2
During all that time the * Ex 10:2
* of Israel had light as usual. Ex 10:2
favorable to the * of Israel, and Ex 11:
and the Egyptian * alike. Ex 11:
against any of the * of Israel, nor Ex 11:
and take all your * with you.' Ex 11:8
wouldn't let the * leave the land. Ex 11:1
this to all the * of Israel) each Ex 12:3,4
the homes of the * of Israel, Ex 12:27
And all the * bowed their Ex 12:27
So the * of Israel did as Moses Ex 12:28
* of Egypt got up in the night; Ex 12:3
urgent upon the * of Israel, to get Ex 12:33
And the * of Israel did as Moses Ex 12:35
That night the * of Israel left Ex 12:37
going on foot. * of various sorts Ex 12:38
It was yeastless because the * Ex 12:39
all of Jehovah's * left the land. Ex 12:40,41
his * out from the land of Egypt; Ex 12:42
So the * of Israel followed all Ex 12:50
brought out the * of Israel from Ex 12:51
Then Moses said to the *, "This Ex 13:3
as his own unique *, just as though Ex 13:9
you as God's *, just as much as if Ex 13:16
So at last Pharaoh let the * go. Ex 13:17,18
that God felt the * might become Ex 13:17,18
Moses, "Tell the * to turn toward Ex 14:2
He pursued the * of Israel, for Ex 14:8
army overtook the * of Israel as Ex 14:9
approached, the * of Israel saw Ex 14:10
But Moses told the *, "Don't be Ex 14:13
praying and get the * moving! Ex 14:15
you, and all the * of Israel shall Ex 14:16
was leading the * of Israel, moved Ex 14:19
the * of Israel and the Egyptians. Ex 14:20
but light to the * of Israel! Ex 14:20
So the * of Israel walked Ex 14:22
The * of Israel had walked Ex 14:29
and the * of Israel saw the Ex 14:30
When the * of Israel saw the Ex 14:31
THEN MOSES AND the * of Israel Ex 15:1
You have led the * you redeemed. Ex 15:13
Fear has gripped the * of Phi- Ex 15:14
All the * of Canaan melt with Ex 15:15
Your * whom you purchased Ex 15:16
While the * of Israel walked Ex 15:19
Then Moses led the * of Israel on Ex 15:22
Then the * turned against Moses. Ex 15:24
There too, the * spoke bitterly Ex 16:2
meeting of all the * of Israel and Ex 16:6
When the * of Israel saw it they Ex 16:15
So the * of Israel went out and Ex 16:17
then the leaders of the * came Ex 16:22
But some of the * went out anyway Ex 16:27
"How long will these * refuse to Ex 16:28,29
So the * rested on the seventh Ex 16:30
So the * of Israel ate the manna Ex 16:35
NOW, AT GOD'S command, the * of Ex 17:1
So once more the * growled and Ex 17:2
with you and lead the * out to Mt. Ex 17:5,6
—for it was there that the * of Ex 17:7
the * of Israel at Rephidim. Ex 17:8
had done for his * and for Moses, Ex 18:1
Moses and the * were camped at Mt. Ex 18:5,6
delivered his * from all of them. Ex 18:8
he delivered his * from the proud Ex 18:11
this alone, with * standing here Ex 18:14
"Well, because the * come to me Ex 18:15,16
you do, what will happen to the *? Ex 18:18
judges, one judge for each 1000 *; Ex 18:21
for the affairs of fifty *; Ex 18:21
the * with justice at all times. Ex 18:22
judges over the *—thousands, Ex 18:25
"Give these instructions to the * Ex 19:2,3
the leaders of the * and told them Ex 19:7
the words of the * to the Lord. Ex 19:8
cloud, so that the * themselves can Ex 19:9
Go down now and see that the * Ex 19:10
Sinai as all the * watch. Ex 19:11
Set boundary lines the * may not Ex 19:12
So Moses went down to the * and Ex 19:14
and all the * trembled. Ex 19:16
the * not to cross the boundaries. Ex 19:21
"But the * won't come up into Ex 19:23
priests and the * break across the Ex 19:24
So Moses went down to the * and Ex 19:25
"And when I punish * for their Ex 20:5
All the * saw the lightning and Ex 20:18

(PEOPLE Con't)
As the * stood in the distance, Ex 20:21
his spokesman to the * of Israel. Ex 20:22
was known to gore * in the past, Ex 21:29
holy—my special *—do not eat any Ex 22:31
the poor among the * harvest any Ex 23:11
as well as the * of your Ex 23:12
And I will destroy those * before Ex 23:23
evil example of these heathen *; Ex 23:24
fall upon all the * whose land you Ex 23:27
you to defeat the * now living in Ex 23:31
of the ordinary * are permitted to Ex 24:2
Then Moses announced to the * all Ex 24:3
and the * answered in unison, Ex 24:3
And he read to the * the Book he Ex 24:7
And the * said again, "We Ex 24:7
basins towards the * and said, Ex 24:8
you can teach the * from them." Ex 24:12
Moses, "Tell the * of Israel that Ex 25:1
For I want the * of Israel to Ex 25:8
commandments for the * of Israel. Ex 25:22
"Instruct the * of Israel to Ex 27:20
rule for the * of Israel. Ex 27:21
stones for the * of Israel: Aaron Ex 28:12
the offerings of the * of Israel. Ex 28:37,38
* will be accepted and forgiven. Ex 28:37,38
and his sons. The * of Israel must Ex 29:28
The ordinary * shall not eat Ex 29:33
And I will meet with the * of Ex 29:43
And I will live among the * of Ex 29:45
a census of the * of Israel, each Ex 30:11,12
among the * when you number them. Ex 30:11,12
it is to bring you, the * of Ex 30:16
And say to the * of Israel, Ex 30:31
Moses: "Tell the * of Israel to Ex 31:12,13
obligation for the * of Israel. Ex 31:16
between me and the * of Israel. Ex 31:17
right away, the * went to Aaron. Ex 32:1
of a calf. The * exclaimed, "O Ex 32:4
When Aaron saw how happy the * Ex 32:5
Go on down, for your * that you Ex 32:7
rebellious lot these * are. Ex 32:9
against your own * whom you brought Ex 32:11
you are planning against your *! Ex 32:12
them, of all the * shouting, he Ex 32:17
the water and made the * drink it. Ex 32:20
"What in the world did the * do Ex 32:21
"You know these * and what a Ex 32:22
When Moses saw that the * had Ex 32:25
The next day Moses said to the *, Ex 32:30
said, "Oh, these * have sinned a Ex 32:31
And now go, lead the * to the Ex 32:34
to visit these *, I will punish Ex 32:34
plague upon the * because they had Ex 32:35
"Lead these * you brought from Ex 33:1
a stubborn, unruly *, and I would Ex 33:3
When the * heard these stern Ex 33:4
"You are an unruly, stubborn *. Ex 33:5
all the * would rise and stand in Ex 33:8
Then all the * worshiped from Ex 33:10
me, 'Take these * to the Promised Ex 33:12
that this nation is your *." Ex 33:13
know that I and my * have found Ex 33:16
* upon the face of the earth?" Ex 33:16
yes, it is an unruly, stubborn *, Ex 34:9
earth, and all the * of Israel Ex 34:10
with the * there in the land where Ex 34:12
any kind with the * living in the Ex 34:15
Aaron and the * of Israel were Ex 34:30
Afterwards, all the * came to Ex 34:32
So that the * would not see the Ex 34:33f
then he would pass on to the * Ex 34:34
the * would see his face aglow. Ex 34:35
meeting of all the * and told them, Ex 35:1
Then Moses said to all the *, Ex 35:4
So all the * went to their tents Ex 35:20
So the * of Israel—every man and Ex 35:29
donated by the * and additional Ex 36:3
Then at last the * were Ex 36:4-7
The * brought gifts of 3,140 Ex 38:24
The * brought 7,540 pounds of Ex 38:29
THEN, FOR THE priests, the * made Ex 39:1
concerning the * of Israel; Ex 39:6,7
So the * of Israel followed all Ex 39:42
and moved, the * of Israel Ex 40:36
all the * of Israel could see it. Ex 40:38
to the * of Israel: "When you Lev 1:2,3
"Tell the * of Israel that these Lev 4:2
guilt upon the *, he must offer a Lev 4:3
not to do, all the * are guilty. Lev 4:13
"If any one of the common * sins Lev 4:27
cut off from his *, for he has Lev 7:20
cut off from his *, for he has Lev 7:21
Moses, "Tell the * of Israel Lev 7:23
Lord shall be outlawed from his *. Lev 7:25
be excommunicated from his *." Lev 7:26,27
Moses, "Tell the * of Israel that Lev 7:29
* of Israel to the sons of Aaron. Lev 7:34
commanded that the * of Israel give Lev 7:36
passed on to the * of Israel so Lev 7:38
So all the * assembled, and Lev 8:4
"And tell the * of Israel," Lev 9:3
In addition, the * are to bring Lev 9:4
commanded, and the * came and stood Lev 9:5
the *, as the Lord had commanded. Lev 9:7
out towards the *, Aaron blessed Lev 9:22
came out again they blessed the *; Lev 9:23
and when the * saw it, they all Lev 9:24
be glorified before all the *.' Lev 10:3
come upon all the * of Israel. Lev 10:6
But the rest of the * of Israel Lev 10:6
arbitrate for the *, to teach them Lev 10:10
sacrifices of the * of Israel. Lev 10:14
The * are to bring the thigh that Lev 10:15
and guilt of the *, to make Lev 10:17
"Tell the * of Israel that the Lev 11:2,3
instructions to the * of Israel: Lev 12:1
Aaron to give the * of Israel these Lev 15:1
shall cleanse the * of Israel from Lev 15:31
and turban. The * of Israel shall Lev 16:5
by the sins of the * of Israel, and Lev 16:16
and for all the * of Israel. Lev 16:17
all the sins of the * of Israel. Lev 16:21
* into a land where no one lives, Lev 16:22
offering for the *, making Lev 16:24
living among the * of Israel; Lev 16:29,30
the altar, the priests, and the *. Lev 16:33
atonement for the * of Israel once Lev 16:34
and for all the * of Israel: Lev 17:1
law is to stop the * of Israel from Lev 17:5
will excommunicate him from his *. Lev 17:10
my decree to the * of Israel, that Lev 17:12
That is why I told the * of Lev 17:14
Moses to tell the * of Israel, Lev 18:1
heathen—like the * of Egypt where Lev 18:3
so long, or the * of Canaan where I Lev 18:3
that is why I am punishing the * Lev 18:25
continually by the * of the land Lev 18:27
Moses to tell the * of Israel, Lev 19:1
excommunicated from Jehovah's *. Lev 19:8
instructions for the * of Israel: Lev 20:1
off from all his *, because he has Lev 20:3
And if the * of the land pretend Lev 20:4
cut that person off from his *. Lev 20:6
be cut off from the * of Israel. Lev 20:17
you and the * of other nations. Lev 20:24
a leader among his * and he may not Lev 21:4
his offspring among his *." Lev 21:14,15f
sons and to all the * of Israel. Lev 21:24
brought by the * or handles the Lev 22:3
brought by the * of Israel must not Lev 22:15
sons and all the * of Israel that Lev 22:17,18
you from Egypt to be my own *! Lev 22:32,33
"Announce to the * of Israel that Lev 23:1
shall gather the * for worship, and Lev 23:7
sacred convocation of all the *; Lev 23:21
is a solemn time for all the * to Lev 23:23,24
All the * are to come together Lev 23:26,27
be excommunicated from his *. Lev 23:29
be a sacred assembly of all the *; Lev 23:35
of all the *, at which time there Lev 23:36
of all *—when offerings to the Lord Lev 23:37
is to remind the * of Israel, Lev 23:43
of the Lord to the * of Israel. Lev 23:44
Moses, "Tell the * of Israel to Lev 24:1
covenant with the * of Israel. Lev 24:5-8
then all the * are to execute him Lev 24:13,14
And tell the * of Israel that Lev 24:15,16
instructions for the * of Israel: Lev 25:1
but your brothers, the * of Lev 25:46
For the * of Israel are my Lev 25:55
your God, and you shall be my *. Lev 26:12
gave to the * of Israel, through Lev 26:46
Moses, "Tell the * of Israel that Lev 27:1
to the Lord—*, animals, or Lev 27:28
the * of Israel on Mount Sinai. Lev 27:34
leaders elected from among the *. Num 1:16
a wall between the * of Israel and Num 1:53
So the * of Israel set up their Num 2:34
on behalf of all the * of Israel. Num 3:7,8,9
of all the * of Israel. Num 3:7,8,9
oldest sons of the * of Israel. Num 3:11,12
on behalf of the * of Israel. Num 3:38
eldest sons of the * of Israel, as Num 3:42
eldest sons of the * of Israel; Num 3:45
cattle of the * of Israel; Num 3:45
"Inform the * of Israel that they Num 5:1
Moses, "Tell the * of Israel that Num 5:5,6
When the * of Israel bring a Num 5:9,10
Moses, "Tell the * of Israel that Num 5:11,12
a curse among your *, for he will Num 5:21,22
she shall be a curse among her *. Num 5:27
for the * of Israel: "When either Num 6:1
blessing to the * of Israel: 'May Num 6:22,23
my name upon the * of Israel." Num 6:27f
upon the * of Israel; Num 6:27
from the other * of Israel. Num 8:5,6
the Tabernacle as all the * watch. Num 8:9
all the * in serving the Lord. Num 8:11
the rest of the * of Israel, and Num 8:14
from among all the * of Israel, and Num 8:16
among the * of Israel are mine, Num 8:17
required of the * of Israel in the Num 8:19
* entered the Tabernacle." Num 8:19
So Moses and Aaron and all the * Num 8:20
"The * of Israel must celebrate Num 9:2,3
"If any of the * of Israel, now Num 9:10
from the * of Israel for refusing Num 9:13
When the Cloud lifted, the * of Num 9:17
the * broke camp and followed. Num 9:20,21
how long the * of Israel stayed; Num 9:22
for summoning the * to assemble and Num 10:1
are blown, the * will know that Num 10:3
the son of Shedeur leading his *. Num 10:18
THE * WERE soon complaining about Num 11:1
discontent of the * of Israel and Num 11:4,5
of a tree. The * gathered it from Num 11:8
me the burden of a * like this? Num 11:11
to get meat for all these *? Num 11:13
the burden of the * along with you, Num 11:17
"And tell the * to purify Num 11:18
reported Jehovah's words to the *; Num 11:24
all of the Lord's * were prophets, Num 11:29
So the * caught and killed quail Num 11:32
rose against the * and he killed Num 11:33
because they buried the * there Num 11:34
days, and the * waited until she Num 12:15
see also what the * are like who Num 13:18
Aaron, and all the * of Israel in Num 13:26
But the * living there are Num 13:28
But Caleb reassured the * as they Num 13:30
"Not against * as strong as they Num 13:31
of warriors, the * are powerfully Num 13:32
THEN ALL THE * began weeping Num 14:1
the ground before the * of Israel; Num 14:5
said to all the *, "It is a Num 14:7
and do not fear the * of the land. Num 14:9
But the only response of the * Num 14:10,11
long will these * despise me? Num 14:10,11
you displayed in rescuing your *. Num 14:13
Now if you kill all your *, the Num 14:15
the sins of this * because of your Num 14:19
But now, since the * of Israel Num 14:25
these wicked * complain about me? Num 14:26,27
slaves of the * of the land. Num 14:31
the hearts of the * were struck Num 14:36,37,38
reported God's words to the *! Num 14:39
to the * of Israel: "When your Num 15:1
"Instruct the * of Israel that Num 15:17,18
then when the * realize their Num 15:23,24
for all of the * of Israel and they Num 15:25
All the * shall be forgiven, Num 15:26
shall be cut off from among his *. Num 15:30
One day while the * of Israel Num 15:32
must die—all the * shall stone him Num 15:35
Moses, "Tell the * of Israel to Num 15:37,38
among all these * of the Lord?" Num 16:3
from among all the * of Israel to Num 16:8,9
before the * to minister to them? Num 16:8,9
to all the *, and Jehovah said to Num 16:19
away from these * so that I may Num 16:21
all the * when one man sins?" Num 16:22
"Then tell the * to get away from Num 16:23,24
he told the *, "get away from Num 16:26
So all the * stood back from the Num 16:27
All of the * of Israel fled at Num 16:34
a reminder to the * of Israel." Num 16:38
a reminder to the * of Israel that Num 16:40
morning all the * began muttering Num 16:41
"You have killed the Lord's *." Num 16:41
"Get away from these * so that I Num 16:45
the * and make atonement for them; Num 16:46
and ran among the *, for the plague Num 16:47
not before 14,700 * had died (in Num 16:49
Moses, "Tell the * of Israel that Num 17:1
to the *, and each of the twelve Num 17:6
it out and show it to the * again Num 17:10
off further catastrophe to the *. Num 17:10
But the * of Israel only grumbled Num 17:12,13
upon any of the * of Israel for Num 18:5
are brought to the Lord by the *; Num 18:8
gifts the * bring as offerings to Num 18:12
sons of the * of Israel, and the Num 18:14,15
by the * of Israel to the Lord; Num 18:19
holy gifts of the * of Israel as Num 18:32
"Tell the * of Israel to bring Num 19:1
be kept for the * of Israel as a Num 19:9
the benefit of the * of Israel and Num 19:10
THE * OF Israel arrived in the Num 20:1
that place, so the * again rebelled Num 20:2
you and Aaron must summon the *. Num 20:8
all the * and all their cattle!" Num 20:8
* to come and gather at the rock; Num 20:10
and the * and their cattle drank. Num 20:11
in the eyes of the * of Israel, you Num 20:12
it was where the * of Israel fought Num 20:13
The * of Edom were descended from Num 20:14f
Esau, while the * of Israel were Num 20:14f
I have given the * of Israel, for Num 20:24
Mount Hor as all the * watched. Num 20:27
and when the * were informed of Num 20:29
Then the * of Israel vowed to Num 21:2
of Arad and his *, they would Num 21:2

(PEOPLE Con't)
Then the * of Israel returned to Num 21:4
Edom. The * were very discouraged; Num 21:4
Then the * came to Moses and Num 21:7
Moses prayed for the *. Num 21:7
the Amorites and the * of Moab. Num 21:15
*, and I will give them water." Num 21:16
that the * sang:Spring up, O well! Num 21:17,18
O * of Chemosh; Num 21:27-30
THE * OF Israel now traveled to Num 22:1
he and his * were terrified. Num 22:2,3
"A vast horde of * has arrived Num 22:5,6
a vast horde of * from Egypt has Num 22:11
Only come and curse these * for Num 22:16,17
* of Israel spread out before him. Num 22:41
A * God has not denounced? Num 23:7-10
These * rise up as a lion; Num 23:18-24
I shall return now to my own *. Num 24:14
are going to do to your *!" Num 24:14
Shall smite the * of Moab, Num 24:15-19
of the * of Amalek and prophesied: Num 24:20
of the Lord was hot against his *. Num 25:3
anger will turn away from the *." Num 25:4
Moses and all the *, as they were Num 25:6
after 24,000 * had already died. Num 25:9
atonement for the * of Israel by Num 25:12,13
figure of the * of Israel, for the Num 26:62
I have given to the * of Israel. Num 27:12
When the * of Israel rebelled, Num 27:14
new leader for the *, a man who Num 27:16
them, so that the * of the Lord Num 27:17
and as all the * watch, charge him Num 27:19
responsibility of leading the *. Num 27:19
all the * of Israel will obey him. Num 27:20
instructions to Joshua and the *. Num 27:21
As the * watched, Moses laid his Num 27:22
to give to the * of Israel: "The Num 28:1
of all the * shall be called, and Num 28:18
of all the *, and during that day Num 28:25
* to celebrate the new harvest. Num 28:26
of all the * on that day, and no Num 29:1
another convocation of all the * Num 29:7
of all the *, and on that day no Num 29:12
"On the eighth day summon the * Num 29:35
instructions to the * of Israel. Num 29:40
Moses said to the *, "Some of Num 31:3
to the rest of the * of Israel who Num 31:12
the leaders of the * went out to Num 31:13
and caused the * of Israel to Num 31:16
including the * and animals; Num 31:26
is to be given to the * of Israel. Num 31:27
that are given to the * of Israel. Num 31:30
assigned to the * of Israel—Moses Num 31:42-46
as a memorial of the * of Israel. Num 31:54
the rest of the * from going across Num 32:7
discouraged the * from going on Num 32:9
* to go on into the Promised Land. Num 32:12
he will make the * stay even longer Num 32:15
for destroying his * and bringing Num 32:15
of the rest of the * of Israel, Num 32:17
here until all the * of Israel have Num 32:18
to the rest of the * of Israel. Num 32:22
the * of Gad and Reuben replied. Num 32:25
The * of Gad built these cities: Num 32:34,35,36
was no water for the * to drink). Num 33:14
the * of Israel had left Egypt. Num 33:38,39
heard that the * of Israel were Num 33:40
Moses to tell the * of Israel, Num 33:50,51
drive out all the * living there Num 33:52
to drive out the * living there, Num 33:55
THE LORD TOLD Moses to tell the * Num 34:1
"Instruct the * of Israel to Num 35:2
Moses, "Tell the * that when they Num 35:9,10
dies, then the * shall judge Num 35:24
then the * shall save the killer Num 35:25
by lot among the * of Israel," Num 36:1
Lord gave to the * of Israel Num 36:13
address to the * of Israel when Deu 1:1
forty years after the * of Israel Deu 1:1
"At that time I told the *, 'I Deu 1:9
and I said to the *, 'The Lord Deu 1:19,20,21
But the * refused to go in, and Deu 1:26
They say that the * of the land Deu 1:28
son of Nun), shall lead the *. Deu 1:38
Inform the * that they will be Deu 2:4
occurred when the * of Caphtor Deu 2:23
Beginning today I will make * Deu 2:25
away from the * of Ammon and from Deu 2:37
'All his * and his land are Deu 3:1
and his *, and we killed them all. Deu 3:3
he shall lead the * across to Deu 3:28
many * for worshiping idols. Deu 4:3
me, 'Summon the * before me and I Deu 4:10
special *, his own inheritance; Deu 4:20
Then Moses instructed the * of Deu 4:41
issued to the * of Israel when they Deu 4:44,45,46
he and his * were destroyed by Deu 4:44,45,46
CONTINUED SPEAKING to the * Deu 5:1
* have said to you, and I agree. Deu 5:28
and you shall teach them to the *; Deu 5:31
So Moses told the *, "You must Deu 5:32
Egypt and Pharaoh and all his *. Deu 6:22
For you are a holy *, dedicated Deu 7:6
He has chosen you from all the * Deu 7:6
same might against the * you fear. Deu 7:19
such fine, upright * that the Lord Deu 9:5
not—you are a wicked, stubborn *. Deu 9:6
while the * had watched below. Deu 9:10,11
because the * I had led out of Deu 9:12
destroy this evil, stubborn *!' Deu 9:13,14
God, don't destroy your own *. Deu 9:26
of these *, but remember instead Deu 9:27
wickedness and sin of these *. Deu 9:27
They are your * and your Deu 9:29
"The * of Israel then journeyed Deu 10:6
and lead the * to the land I Deu 10:11
then the hands of all the *. Deu 13:9
"SINCE YOU ARE the * of God, Deu 14:1
gathering of the * of each city Deu 16:8
and then all the * shall join in. Deu 17:7
offerings the * bring to him. Deu 18:1
he shall be my spokesman to the *. Deu 18:18
death of innocent *, and you will Deu 19:10
its * shall become your servants. Deu 20:11
is to prevent the * of the land Deu 20:18
O Lord, forgive your * Israel Deu 21:8
forget what the * of Amalek did to Deu 25:17
and bless your * and the land you Deu 26:15
are his very own *, just as he Deu 26:18
you must be a holy * to the Lord Deu 26:19
of Israel gave the * these further Deu 27:1
Today you have become the * of Deu 27:9
Moses gave this charge to the *: Deu 27:11
And all the * shall reply, Deu 27:15
And all the * shall reply, Deu 27:16
And all the * shall reply, Deu 27:17
And all the * shall reply, Deu 27:18
And all the * shall reply, Deu 27:19
And all the * shall reply, Deu 27:20
And all the * shall reply, Deu 27:21
And all the * shall reply, Deu 27:22
And all the * shall reply, Deu 27:23
And all the * shall reply, Deu 27:24
And all the * shall reply, Deu 27:25
And all the * shall reply, Deu 27:26
He will change you into a holy * Deu 28:9
the * of Israel at Mount Horeb. Deu 29:1
and his * in the land of Egypt. Deu 29:2,3
All of you—your leaders, the *, Deu 29:10
you today as his *, and to confirm Deu 29:13
told, 'Because the * of the land Deu 29:25
things to the * of Israel, he told Deu 31:1
over to you the * living there, and Deu 31:5
For you shall lead these * into Deu 31:7
delivered to the * and gave them to Deu 31:9
be read to all the * at the end of Deu 31:10,11
After you are gone, these * will Deu 31:16
* of Israel as my warning to them. Deu 31:19
the land, what these * are like." Deu 31:21
must bring the * of Israel into the Deu 31:23
solemn warning to the * of Israel. Deu 31:26
O foolish *, Deu 32:6
As does the Lord his *! Deu 32:11
He was jealous of his *. Deu 32:16
is my special *, Deu 32:34
The Lord will see his * righted, Deu 32:36
Praise his *, Deu 32:40,41
For he will avenge his *, Deu 32:40,41
And his *." Deu 32:40,41
the *, Moses made these comments: Deu 32:44,45
I am giving to the * of Israel. Deu 32:49
me among the * of Israel at the Deu 32:51
I am giving the * of Israel, but Deu 32:52
the * of Israel before his death: Deu 33:1
How he loves his *— Deu 33:3
They shall summon the * Deu 33:19
He led the * Deu 33:21
a young man. The * of Israel Deu 34:8
so the * of Israel obeyed him, Deu 34:9
the * of Israel in the wilderness. Deu 34:11,12
Lead my * across the Jordan River Jos 1:2
be a successful leader of my *; Jos 1:6
Constantly remind the * about Jos 1:8
Israel to tell the * to get ready Jos 1:10,11
and completely destroyed their *. Jos 2:10
"for all the * over there are Jos 2:24
Joshua and all the * of Israel left Jos 3:1
Then Joshua told the * to perform Jos 3:5
Then Joshua summoned all the * Jos 3:9
Jebusites—all the * who now live in Jos 3:10
but as the * set out to cross the Jos 3:13,14
Then all the * crossed at a spot Jos 3:15,16
and waited as all the * passed by. Jos 3:17
WHEN ALL THE * were safely across, Jos 4:1
reminder to the * of Israel of this Jos 4:7
Meanwhile, the * had hurried Jos 4:10
was over, the * watched the priests Jos 4:11
eyes of all the * of Israel, and Jos 4:14
River so the * of Israel could Jos 5:1
the * were afraid of the Israelis; Jos 6:1
blast, all the * are to give a Jos 6:5
Joshua yelled to the *, "Shout! Jos 6:16
So when the * heard the trumpet Jos 6:20
them, and the * of Israel poured Jos 6:20
That is why the * of Israel are Jos 7:12
Tell the *, 'Each of you must Jos 7:13
of Ai and all of his * to you. Jos 8:1
And as the * of Israel watched, Jos 8:32
Then all the * of Jos 8:33
But when the * of Gibeon heard Jos 9:3,4,5
So our elders and our * Jos 9:11
go to the * of Israel and declare Jos 9:11
the Lord God. The * of Israel were Jos 9:18
destroy all the * living in it. Jos 9:24
So Joshua would not allow the * Jos 9:26
for the * of Israel and for the Jos 9:27
and how the * of Gibeon had made Jos 10:1
with Joshua and the * of Israel." Jos 10:4
of Israel was fighting for his *. Jos 10:42
All the * were slaughtered, just Jos 11:12
but they killed all the *. Jos 11:14
and he gave it to the * of Israel Jos 11:23
Moses and the * of Israel had Jos 12:6
destroyed these *, and Moses gave Jos 12:6
and the Negeb. The * who lived Jos 12:8-24
I am ready to drive these * out Jos 13:2-7
However, the * of Israel had not Jos 13:13
and Reba. The * of Israel also Jos 13:22
River where the * were camped at Jos 13:32
us frightened the * and discouraged Jos 14:8
Then he fought against the * Jos 15:15
among the * of Judah to this day. Jos 15:63
as slaves among the * of Ephraim. Jos 16:10
not drive out the * who lived in Jos 17:12
clearing out the * living in the Jos 18:3
its *, and lived there; Jos 19:47,48
"Tell the * of Israel to Jos 20:2
This was the reply of the * of Jos 22:21
between our * and your people! Jos 22:24,25
between our people and your *! Jos 22:24,25
went back to the * of Israel and Jos 22:32
and Gad. The * of Reuben and Gad Jos 22:34
success to the * of Israel against Jos 23:1
drive out all the * living there Jos 23:4,5
* still remaining in the land; Jos 23:7
THEN JOSHUA SUMMONED all the * Jos 24:1
and afterwards I brought my * out Jos 24:5
kings of the Amorites and their *. Jos 24:12
And the * replied, "We would Jos 24:16
But Joshua replied to the *, Jos 24:19
But the * answered, "We choose Jos 24:21
The * replied to Joshua, "Yes, Jos 24:24
Then Joshua said to all the *, Jos 24:27
Then Joshua sent the * away to Jos 24:28
The bones of Joseph, which the * Jos 24:32
"Join us in clearing out the * Ju 1:3
its *, setting the city on fire. Ju 1:8
Zephath and massacred all its *. Ju 1:17
exterminate the * of the hill Ju 1:19
to conquer the * of the valley, who Ju 1:19
to drive out the * living in Ju 1:27
not massacre the * of Kitron or Ju 1:30
were the original * of that land. Ju 1:31,32
not drive out the * of Beth-shemesh Ju 1:33
so these * continue to live among Ju 1:33
announced to the * of Israel, "I Ju 2:1
with the * living in this land; Ju 2:2
The * broke into tears as the Ju 2:4
"the place where * wept"). Ju 2:5
Mount Gaash. The * had remained Ju 2:7-9
But when the * were in this Ju 2:15
Each judge rescued the * of Ju 2:18
groaning of his * under their Ju 2:18
But when the judge died, the * Ju 2:19
He declared, "Because these * Ju 2:20
nations to test my *, to see Ju 2:22
the * of Israel . Ju 3:1f
These * were a test to the new Ju 3:4
them, the * of Israel intermarried Ju 3:6
So the * of Israel were very Ju 3:7
But when Othni-el died, the * of Ju 3:12
eighteen years the * of Israel were Ju 3:14
AFTER EHUD'S DEATH the * of Israel Ju 4:1
for bringing the * back to God, was Ju 4:4
he and all his * were destroyed. Ju 4:24
The * gladly followed! Ju 5:2
The * of the Lord Ju 5:11
The * of the Lord Ju 5:13,14
THEN THE * of Israel began once Ju 6:1
This time it was by the * of Ju 6:1
Then at last the * of Israel Ju 6:6,7
for then the * of Israel will boast Ju 7:2
Doesn't it look like * coming Ju 9:36
"I'm sure I see * coming towards Ju 9:37
*, and leveled it to the ground. Ju 9:45
the ground. The * at the nearby Ju 9:46
So all the * inside died, about a Ju 9:49
Then the * of Israel turned away Ju 10:6
angry with his *, so he immediately Ju 10:7,8
a general assembly of all the *. Ju 11:11
land belonged to the * of Ammon; Ju 11:13
was this: When the * of Israel Ju 11:16
the * of Israel stayed in Kadesh. Ju 11:17

'EOPLE Con't)
Sihon and all your *, so Israel Ju 11:21,22
were subdued by the * of Israel. Ju 11:33
So forty-two thousand * of Ju 12:6
the * of Israel you could marry?" Ju 14:3
a riddle to my * and haven't told Ju 14:16
of Samson. The * made sacrifices to Ju 16:23,24
Half drunk by now, the * Ju 16:25,26
was completely filled with *. Ju 16:27
three thousand * in the balconies Ju 16:27
Philistine leaders and all the * Ju 16:30
yet driven out the * living in the Ju 18:1
So the spies returned to their * Ju 18:8
real paradise. The * aren't even Ju 18:9,10
all the * and burned the city to Ju 18:27
Then the * of the tribe of Dan Ju 18:28
But the * of Benjamin wouldn't Ju 20:13
us against the * of Benjamin?" Ju 20:18
to destroy the * of Jabesh-gilead. Ju 21:10,11,12
So the * of Israel returned to Ju 21:24
* by giving them good crops again. Ru 1:6,7
want to go with you to your *." Ru 1:10
for you to return to your own *. Ru 1:11
back to her * and to her gods; Ru 1:15
you live; your * shall be my Ru 1:16
your people shall be my *, and Ru 1:16
And all the * standing there, and Ru 4:11
from the Lord's * about what you 1Sa 2:23,24,25
thing to make the Lord's * sin. 1Sa 2:23,24,25
* of Israel were slaves in Egypt? 1Sa 2:27
the best of the offerings of my *! 1Sa 2:29
I will give my *, but you and your 1Sa 2:32
was with him and * listened 1Sa 3:19
passed them on to the * of Israel. 1Sa 3:21,4:1
to destroy the * of Ashdod and the 1Sa 5:6
When the * realized what was 1Sa 5:7
destroying its *, young and old, 1Sa 5:9
but when the * of Ekron saw it 1Sa 5:10
Beth-shemesh. The * of 1Sa 6:13
So the * broke up the wood of the 1Sa 6:14
And the * mourned because of the 1Sa 6:19
many * whom the Lord had killed. 1Sa 6:19
So they sent messengers to the * 1Sa 6:21
So Samuel told the * what the 1Sa 8:10
But the * refused to listen to 1Sa 8:19
the Lord what the * had said, and 1Sa 8:21
honor by all the * because 1Sa 9:6
"Let's go and ask the seer," * 1Sa 9:9,10,11
anoint him as the leader of my *. 1Sa 9:16
He will rule my *." 1Sa 9:17
to be the king of his *, Israel! 1Sa 10:1
Then Samuel said to all the *, 1Sa 10:24
And all the * shouted, "Long live 1Sa 10:24
Then Samuel told the * again what 1Sa 10:25
Then Samuel sent the * home 1Sa 10:25
town, and told the * about their 1Sa 11:4
And God caused the * to be afraid 1Sa 11:7
Then the * exclaimed to Samuel, 1Sa 11:12
Then Samuel said to the *, 1Sa 11:14
THEN SAMUEL ADDRESSED the * 1Sa 12:1
and all the * were very much 1Sa 12:18
abandon his chosen *, for that 1Sa 12:22
appointed him as king over his *; 1Sa 13:14
(For the Ark was among the * of 1Sa 14:18
If the * had been allowed to eat 1Sa 14:30
that the * were sinning against the 1Sa 14:33
And the * agreed. 1Sa 14:40
and the * were declared innocent. 1Sa 14:41
So the * rescued Jonathan. 1Sa 14:45
to allow my * to cross their 1Sa 15:2
"For you were kind to the * of 1Sa 15:6
the * and did what they demanded. 1Sa 15:24
and before my * by going with me to 1Sa 15:30
was with all the *, he became even 1Sa 18:28
"Isn't he the one the * honor at 1Sa 21:11
and so the * of Keilah were saved. 1Sa 23:5
you listen to the * who say that I 1Sa 24:9,10
be with the Lord's *, and you have 1Sa 26:19
and the Amalekites—* who had lived 1Sa 27:8
* of Jerahmeel and the Kenites." 1Sa 27:10
thought that the * of Israel must 1Sa 27:12
to the * throughout their land. 1Sa 31:9
But when the * of Jabesh-gilead 1Sa 31:11
and for the Lord's *, and for the 2Sa 1:12
* from chasing their brothers?" 2Sa 2:26
I will save my * from the 2Sa 3:18
with the * of Israel and Benjamin. 2Sa 3:19
of all the * of Israel, and they 2Sa 3:21
Lord that I and my * are innocent 2Sa 3:28
And the king and all the * wept 2Sa 3:32
And all the * wept again for him. 2Sa 3:33,34
This pleased his *, just as 2Sa 3:35,36
And David said to his *, "A 2Sa 3:38
his * too were badly frightened. 2Sa 4:1
in Benjamin. (* from Be-eroth are 2Sa 4:2,3
shepherd and leader of his *." 2Sa 5:2
kindness on Israel, his chosen *. 2Sa 5:12
Then he blessed the * in the 2Sa 6:18
of Israel, the * of the Lord! 2Sa 6:21
leaders, the shepherds of my *. 2Sa 7:7
the leader of my * Israel when you 2Sa 7:8
a homeland for my * from which they 2Sa 7:10,11
did when the judges ruled my *. 2Sa 7:10,11
such blessings as Israel, your *? 2Sa 7:23
You chose Israel to be your * 2Sa 7:24
Israel as your * and have 2Sa 7:26
which will rule your * forever; 2Sa 7:27
Now the * of Ammon realized how 2Sa 10:6
our * and the cities of our God. 2Sa 10:12
He made slaves of the * of the 2Sa 12:31
much for all the * of God as you 2Sa 14:13
the hearts of all the * of Israel. 2Sa 15:6
its * doubtless very proud of him. 2Sa 15:9f
And the * who were with him 2Sa 15:30
of Olives where * worshiped God, 2Sa 15:32
are for your * to ride on, and the 2Sa 16:2
So David and all the * with him 2Sa 17:22
As the * heard of the king's 2Sa 19:2
So all the * crossed the Jordan 2Sa 19:39
Then the woman went to the * with 2Sa 20:22
From the rebels of my *; 2Sa 22:44
census of all the * from one end of 2Sa 24:2
times as many * in your kingdom as 2Sa 24:3
went out to count the * of Israel. 2Sa 24:4
the number of the * to the 2Sa 24:9
blown and all the * shouted, "Long 1Ki 1:39
and all the * are congratulating 1Ki 1:46,47
At that time the * of Israel 1Ki 3:2
your own chosen *, a nation so 1Ki 3:8
are almost too many * to count! 1Ki 3:8
I can govern your * well and know 1Ki 3:9
in governing my *, and haven't 1Ki 3:11
and all the * were awed as they 1Ki 3:28
the * for the king's household. 1Ki 4:7
(This was 480 years after the * 1Ki 6:1
live among the * of Israel and 1Ki 6:13
King Solomon and all the * 1Ki 8:5
* of Israel after they left Egypt. 1Ki 8:9
and faced the * as they stood 1Ki 8:14
'When I brought my * from Egypt, I 1Ki 8:16
Then, as all the * watched, 1Ki 8:22,23
promises to your * if they do their 1Ki 8:22,23
Listen to every plea of the * of 1Ki 8:30
"And when your * sin and their 1Ki 8:33,34
land which you have given your *. 1Ki 8:35,36
cities, or if the * are struck by 1Ki 8:37
is— then when the * realize their 1Ki 8:38
name just as your own * Israel do; 1Ki 8:43
"When you send your * out to 1Ki 8:44
"Forgive your * for all of their 1Ki 8:50
for they are your *—your 1Ki 8:51
earth to be your own special *." 1Ki 8:53
upon all the * of Israel: 1Ki 8:54,55
and given rest to his * Israel; 1Ki 8:56
daily needs. May * all over the 1Ki 8:60
O my *, may you live good and 1Ki 8:61
Then the king and all the * 1Ki 8:62,63
Afterwards Solomon sent the * 1Ki 8:66
servant David and to his * Israel. 1Ki 8:66
will take away the * of Israel from 1Ki 9:7
And the answer will be, 'The * 1Ki 9:9
For the * of Israel had not been 1Ki 9:20,21
Your * are happy and your palace 1Ki 10:8
And you give your * a just, good 1Ki 10:9
instructed his * not to marry into 1Ki 11:2
in getting the * to make certain 1Ki 12:2,3,4
So the * left. 1Ki 12:5
So when Jeroboam and the * 1Ki 12:12
When the * realized that the king 1Ki 12:16,17
When the * of Israel learned of 1Ki 12:20
an open meeting of all the *; 1Ki 12:20
Judah, and all the * of Judah and 1Ki 12:23,24
their brothers, the * of Israel. 1Ki 12:23,24
I'm careful, the * will want a 1Ki 12:26
made and told the *, "It's too 1Ki 12:28
sin, for the * worshiped them. 1Ki 12:30
and file of the *—even those who 1Ki 12:31
from the common *, to offer 1Ki 13:33
* and made you king of Israel. 1Ki 14:7
he will uproot the * of Israel 1Ki 14:15
During his reign the * of 1Ki 14:22
the land, and the * of Judah became 1Ki 14:24
drove out to make room for his *. 1Ki 14:24
for he led the * of Israel into the 1Ki 15:34
"to make you king of my * Israel; 1Ki 16:2
You have made my * sin, and I am 1Ki 16:2
the * of Israel to sin with him. 1Ki 16:19
half the * were loyal to General 1Ki 16:21
Now bring all the * of Israel to 1Ki 18:19
So Ahab summoned all the * and 1Ki 18:20
he asked the *. 1Ki 18:21
And all the * agreed to this 1Ki 18:24
Then Elijah called to the *, 1Ki 18:30
Answer me so these * will know 1Ki 18:37
And when the * saw it, they fell 1Ki 18:39
but the * of Israel have broken 1Ki 19:10
of heaven, but the * have broken 1Ki 19:14
the homes of your *, and they will 1Ki 20:5,6
palace and the homes of the *.' 1Ki 20:9
* shall perish instead of his.' 1Ki 20:42
Amorites did—the * whom the Lord 1Ki 21:26
to make room for the * of Israel. 1Ki 21:26
You and I are brothers; my * are 1Ki 22:4
Then he turned to the * 1Ki 22:28
the hills, so the * sacrificed and 1Ki 22:43
who had led the * of Israel into 2Ki 3:3
King Mesha of Moab and his * were 2Ki 3:4
* and horses are yours to command. 2Ki 3:6,7,8
Meanwhile, when the * of Moab 2Ki 3:21
his clothes. (The * watching 2Ki 6:26-30
and tell the * at the palace." 2Ki 7:9
the king, and the * of Samaria 2Ki 7:16
and killed as the * rushed out. 2Ki 7:17
And he couldn't, for the * 2Ki 7:20
you will do to the * of Israel: you 2Ki 8:12
During Jehoram's reign, the * in 2Ki 8:20
you king of the Lord's *, Israel. 2Ki 9:6
* who were killed by Jezebel. 2Ki 9:7
meeting of all the * of the city 2Ki 10:17
to address the *: "Check to be 2Ki 10:23
the king, and the *, that they 2Ki 11:17
that they would be the Lord's *. 2Ki 11:17
between the king and the *. 2Ki 11:17
guard and all the * led the king 2Ki 11:19
on the hills—the * still sacrificed 2Ki 12:3
he encouraged the * to worship 2Ki 13:11
gracious to the * of Israel, and 2Ki 13:23
the hills, so the * still 2Ki 14:4
* sacrificed and burned incense. 2Ki 15:4
the * of Israel into grievous sin. 2Ki 15:18
and he took the * away to Assyria 2Ki 15:29
* sacrificed and burned incense. 2Ki 15:34,35
the * of Israel entered the land. 2Ki 16:3
offerings of the *, including their 2Ki 16:15
fell and the * of Israel were 2Ki 17:6
Israel because the * worshiped 2Ki 17:7
before them. The * of Israel had 2Ki 17:9
So the * of Israel had done many 2Ki 17:11
listen. The * were as stubborn as 2Ki 17:14
sin, and the * of Israel never 2Ki 17:22
colonies of * from Babylon, Cuthah, 2Ki 17:24
replacing the * of Israel. 2Ki 17:24
Avvites, and the * from Sephar even 2Ki 17:31
* continued to worship other gods. 2Ki 17:40
made, because the * of Israel had 2Ki 18:4
Don't use Hebrew, for the * 2Ki 18:26
Hasn't he sent me to the * on the 2Ki 18:27
in Hebrew to the * on the wall, 2Ki 18:28
their * from the king of Assyria? 2Ki 18:33
But the * on the wall remained 2Ki 18:36
This year my * will eat the 2Ki 19:29
" 'O my * Judah, those of you 2Ki 19:30
A remnant of my * shall become 2Ki 19:31
the leader of my *, and tell him 2Ki 20:5
to make room for the * of Israel 2Ki 21:1
If the * of Israel will only 2Ki 21:8
But the * did not listen to the 2Ki 21:9
the * of Israel entered the land. 2Ki 21:9
he has led the * of Judah into 2Ki 21:11
those few of my * who are left, and 2Ki 21:14
Manasseh led the * of Judah, he 2Ki 21:16
great numbers of innocent *. 2Ki 21:16
Temple when the * come to worship. 2Ki 22:3,4
this city and its *, just as I 2Ki 22:15,16
For the * of Judah have thrown 2Ki 22:17
prophets and the *, small and 2Ki 23:1
in front of the *, and he and they 2Ki 23:3
on the graves of the common *. 2Ki 23:6
orders for his * to observe the 2Ki 23:21
Jehoiakim taxed the * to get the 2Ki 23:35
skilled * were left in the land. 2Ki 24:14
the * of Jerusalem and Judah. 2Ki 24:20
The remainder of the * in the 2Ki 25:11
But the poorest of the * were 2Ki 25:12
governor over the * left in Judah. 2Ki 25:22
lifetime that the * of the earth 1Ch 1:19
of the * whom God had destroyed. 1Ch 5:25
the Lord sent the * of Judah and 1Ch 6:4-15
because the * worshiped idols. 1Ch 9:1
But when the * of Jabesh-gilead 1Ch 10:11
be the shepherd of my * Israel. 1Ch 11:2
But the * of Jebus refused to 1Ch 11:5,6
their arrival. * from nearby and 1Ch 12:40
So David summoned the * of 1Ch 13:5
Then David and all the * danced 1Ch 13:8
reason—to give joy to God's *! 1Ch 14:2
the * in the name of the Lord; 1Ch 16:2
for his blessings upon his *. 1Ch 16:4
'Don't harm my chosen *,' he 1Ch 16:22
O * of all nations of the earth, 1Ch 16:28
And all the * shouted "Amen!" 1Ch 16:36
ended and the * returned to their 1Ch 16:43
to care for my *—that they should 1Ch 17:6
and made you the king of my *. 1Ch 17:7
home to my * Israel, and will plant 1Ch 17:9
I will place him over my * and 1Ch 17:14
that the * could be your people. 1Ch 17:21
that the people could be your *. 1Ch 17:21
the nations from before your *. 1Ch 17:21
You have declared that your * 1Ch 17:22
and required its * to send him a 1Ch 18:2
our * and the cities of our God. 1Ch 19:13
and villages of the * of Ammon. 1Ch 20:1

(PEOPLE Con't)

He drove the * from the city and	1Ch 20:3
to multiply his * a hundred times,	1Ch 21:3
but do not destroy your *."	1Ch 21:17
name of the Lord and for his *.	1Ch 22:18
a population explosion for his *.	1Ch 27:23
"My brothers and my *!	1Ch 28:2
of Israel, the * of God, and in the	1Ch 28:8
I and who are my * that we should	1Ch 29:14
have watched your * offer their	1Ch 29:17
Make your * always want to obey	1Ch 29:18
Then David said to all the *,	1Ch 29:20
with all the * of Israel, and he	1Ch 29:25
of * as the earth is full of dust!	2Ch 1:9
is to help your *, and you haven't	2Ch 1:11
properly guide my *— yes, I am	2Ch 1:11
* that he has made you their king!	2Ch 2:11
covenant with the * of Israel as	2Ch 5:10
around to the * and they stood to	2Ch 6:3
since bringing my * from the land	2Ch 6:5,6
I chosen a king for my * Israel.	2Ch 6:5,6
the Lord and his * Israel."	2Ch 6:11
before the * on a platform in the	2Ch 6:12,13
Now, as all the * watched, he	2Ch 6:12,13
to those of your * Israel when they	2Ch 6:20,21
"If your * Israel are destroyed	2Ch 6:24
themselves your *, and pray to you	2Ch 6:24
*, and teach them what is right;	2Ch 6:27
to your * as their own property.	2Ch 6:27
you, just as your * Israel do;	2Ch 6:33
"If your * go out at your	2Ch 6:34
* who have sinned against you.	2Ch 6:39
All the * had been watching and	2Ch 7:3
Then the king and all the *	2Ch 7:4,5
trumpets, all the * stood again.	2Ch 7:6
7, he sent the * home, joyful and	2Ch 7:10
and Solomon and to his * Israel.	2Ch 7:10
you, then if my * will humble	2Ch 7:14
I will destroy my * from this land	2Ch 7:20
be, 'Because his * abandoned the	2Ch 7:22
some of the * of Israel into them.	2Ch 8:2
So when Jeroboam and the *	2Ch 10:12
When the * realized what the	2Ch 10:16
The * of the tribe of Judah,	2Ch 10:17
Israel, the * stoned him to death.	2Ch 10:18
to the * of Judah and of Benjamin:	2Ch 11:3
who encouraged the * to worship	2Ch 11:15
the * followed him in this sin.	2Ch 12:1
Just like the * of other lands,	2Ch 13:9
against you. O * of Israel, do not	2Ch 13:12
obedience to him," he told his *.	2Ch 14:7
in Israel, the * haven't worshiped	2Ch 15:3
Then he summoned all the * of	2Ch 15:9
Then King Asa and the * of Judah	2Ch 16:6
earth, looking for * whose hearts	2Ch 16:9
And Asa oppressed all the * at	2Ch 16:10
ointments, and his * made a very	2Ch 16:13,14
unlike the * across the border in	2Ch 17:4
All the * of Judah cooperated by	2Ch 17:5
to teach the Scriptures to the *.	2Ch 17:7,8,9
again among the *, traveling from	2Ch 19:4
on Jehoshaphat and the * of Judah.	2Ch 20:1
so he announced that all the * of	2Ch 20:3
before God. * from all across the	2Ch 20:4
in this land when your * arrived?	2Ch 20:7
Your * settled here and built	2Ch 20:8
As the * from every part of Judah	2Ch 20:13
"Listen to me, all you * of	2Ch 20:15
you, O * of Judah and Jerusalem!	2Ch 20:17
earth, and all the * of Judah and	2Ch 20:18
of Judah and the * of Jerusalem did	2Ch 20:18
"Listen to me, O * of Judah and	2Ch 20:20
the leaders of the *, he determined	2Ch 20:21
King Jehoshaphat and his * went	2Ch 20:25
hills, nor had the * as yet really	2Ch 20:33
Judah, and led the * of Jerusalem	2Ch 21:11
in fact, he compelled his * to	2Ch 21:11
and have made the * of Jerusalem	2Ch 21:13
THEN THE * of Jerusalem chose	2Ch 22:1
him, and * from all over the land	2Ch 23:12
the * in a great psalm of praise.	2Ch 23:12
and the * would be the Lord's.	2Ch 23:15,16,17
And all the * rushed over to the	2Ch 23:15,16,17
and all the * escorted the king	2Ch 23:20
So all the * of the land	2Ch 23:21
telling the * to bring to the Lord	2Ch 24:9
And all the leaders and the *	2Ch 24:10
Lord, but the * wouldn't listen.	2Ch 24:19
He called a meeting of all the *.	2Ch 24:20
killing 3,000 * and carrying off	2Ch 25:13
taken from the * of Seir, and set	2Ch 25:14
even save their own * from you?"	2Ch 25:15
God, and how his * conspired	2Ch 25:27
THE * OF Judah now crowned	2Ch 26:1
from his * and from the Temple.	2Ch 26:21
the judging of the * of the land.	2Ch 26:21
even so his * became very corrupt.	2Ch 27:2
numbers of his * to Damascus.	2Ch 28:5
these * from Judah and Jerusalem?	2Ch 28:10
and capturing many * as slaves.	2Ch 28:16
to the gods of the * of Damascus	2Ch 28:23
his ruin, and that of all his *.	2Ch 28:23
So the * from every part of the	2Ch 29:31
And Hezekiah and all the * were	2Ch 29:36
On the first day of May the *	2Ch 30:15
Since many of the * arriving from	2Ch 30:17,18,19
So the * of Israel celebrated the	2Ch 30:21
and the * confessed their sins to	2Ch 30:22
King Hezekiah gave the * 1,000	2Ch 30:24
Then the * of Judah, together	2Ch 30:25
and blessed the *, and the Lord	2Ch 30:27
Then the * who had come to the	2Ch 31:1
In addition, he required the * in	2Ch 31:4
law of God. The * responded	2Ch 31:5,6
great piles. The * who had moved to	2Ch 31:5,6
tribes and the * of Judah living in	2Ch 31:5,6
the Lord and praised his *!	2Ch 31:7,8
for the Lord has blessed his *."	2Ch 31:10
his * from me or my ancestors;	2Ch 32:15
to save their * from my hand, and	2Ch 32:17
language to the * gathered on the	2Ch 32:18
Hezekiah and the * of Jerusalem.	2Ch 32:22
he encouraged his * to worship the	2Ch 33:2
the * of Israel entered the land.	2Ch 33:2
But Manasseh encouraged the * of	2Ch 33:9
by both Manasseh and his *.	2Ch 33:10
demanded that the * of Judah	2Ch 33:16
However, the * still sacrificed	2Ch 33:17
would clear the * of Judah and	2Ch 34:5
Gifts were brought by the *	2Ch 34:9
well as from the * of Jerusalem.	2Ch 34:9
required of God's *, he ripped his	2Ch 34:19
will destroy this city and its *.	2Ch 34:24
For my * have forsaken me and	2Ch 34:25
this city and its *, and have	2Ch 34:27
and its * until after your death.'	2Ch 34:28
and all the * great and small, to	2Ch 34:30
to the Lord and to his *.	2Ch 35:3
clans of the * who bring in their	2Ch 35:4,5
prepare to assist the * who come.	2Ch 35:6
hurried them out to the * to eat.	2Ch 35:13
Levites, and * from Jerusalem and	2Ch 35:18
All the important * of the	2Ch 36:14
on his * and on his Temple.	2Ch 36:15
But the * mocked these	2Ch 36:16
* refused to observe the Sabbath.	2Ch 36:21
who are the Lord's *, return to	2Ch 36:22,23
some of the common * settled in	Ez 2:70
the rest of the * returned to the	Ez 2:70
for the * were fearful of attack.	Ez 3:3
Voluntary offerings of the * were	Ez 3:5
logs from the * of Tyre and Sidon,	Ez 3:7
Then all the * gave a great	Ez 3:11
against the * of Judah and	Ez 4:6
and exile the * to Babylonia.'	Ez 5:12
and the * have been working on it	Ez 5:16
the Levites, and all the *.	Ez 6:16
And some of the heathen * who	Ez 6:21,22
had given to the * of Israel.	Ez 7:6
Many ordinary * as well as	Ez 7:7,8,9
those laws to the * of Israel.	Ez 7:10
the * west of the Euphrates River;	Ez 7:25
* and the priests who had arrived;	Ez 8:15
the leaders and * of Israel had	Ez 8:25
many of the Jewish * and even some	Ez 9:1
of the heathen * who lived in the	Ez 9:1
So the holy * of God were being	Ez 9:2
of this sin of his * came and sat	Ez 9:4
practices of the * living there.	Ez 9:11
with * who do these awful things.	Ez 9:14
and all the * of Israel swear that	Ez 10:5
from the heathen * about you and	Ez 10:11
night and day for your * Israel.	Neh 1:6,7
yes, I and my * have committed	Neh 1:6,7
"We are your servants, the * you	Neh 1:10
The * from Zanoah, led by Hanun,	Neh 3:13
leaders and the * and said to them,	Neh 4:14
like theirs," the * protested.	Neh 5:5
And all the * shouted, "Amen,"	Neh 5:13
assistance from the * of Israel.	Neh 5:14
levy against the *, for they were	Neh 5:18
for these * and bless me for it.	Neh 5:19
revered God more than most * do.	Neh 7:2
and the common * gave $100,000	Neh 7:72
the rest of the * now returned home	Neh 7:73
NOW, IN MID-SEPTEMBER, all the *	Neh 8:1
God, and all the * said, "Amen,"	Neh 8:6
and the Levites went among the *	Neh 8:7,8
Literally, "while the * remained	Neh 8:7,8f
All the * began sobbing when	Neh 8:9
*, telling them, "That's right!	Neh 8:11
So the * went away to eat a	Neh 8:12
Moses that the * of Israel should	Neh 8:14
telling the * to go to the hills to	Neh 8:15
So the * went out and cut	Neh 8:16
the * returned for another	Neh 9:1
called out to the *, "Stand up and	Neh 9:5
Pharaoh and his *, for you knew how	Neh 9:10
You divided the sea for your *	Neh 9:11
* in every corner of the land;	Neh 9:22
the kings and the * of the	Neh 9:24
Your * captured fortified cities	Neh 9:25
going well, your * turned to sin	Neh 9:2
Yet whenever your * returned to	Neh 9:2
entire nation—for the common *;	Neh 10:2
from the heathen * of the land in	Neh 10:2
if the heathen * in the land should	Neh 10:3
areas. The * and the Levites were	Neh 10:39,4
but now a tenth of the * from the	Neh 11:
Levites, and * lived wherever their	Neh 11:2
Some of the towns where the * of	Neh 11:25-3
So the * spread from Beer-sheba to	Neh 11:25-3
The * of the tribe of Benjamin	Neh 11:31-3
the *, the gates, and the wall.	Neh 12:3
* of Jerusalem was heard far away!	Neh 12:4
Levites, for the * of Judah	Neh 12:4
and Nehemiah, the * brought a daily	Neh 12:4
being read, the * found a statement	Neh 13:
been friendly to the * of Israel.	Neh 13:2
And once more all the * of Judah	Neh 13:12
the Sabbath to the * of Jerusalem.	Neh 13:16
wrath upon the * of Israel by	Neh 13:18
all of Mordecai's *, the Jews, and	Est 3:5,6
"There is a certain race of *	Est 3:8
these *—whatever you think best."	Est 3:11
known to all your *, so that they	Est 3:14
go to the king to plead for her *.	Est 4:8
my life and the lives of my *.	Est 7:3
For I and my * have been sold to	Est 7:4
my * butchered and destroyed?"	Est 8:6
of all the * of the kingdom.	Est 8:9,10
to all the * so that the Jews would	Est 8:13
streets filled with shouting *.	Est 8:15
And many of the * of the land	Est 8:17
his best for his *, and was a	Est 10:3
has made me a mockery among the *;	Job 17:6
But I refuse even to deal with *	Job 21:16
"Why don't * exclaim to their	Job 34:31
*, giving them food in abundance.	Job 36:31
What joys he gives to all his *.	Ps 3:8
before all the * at Jerusalem's	Ps 9:14
you know the hopes of humble *.	Ps 10:17
aimed from ambush at the * of God.	Ps 11:2
gently with * who act like that;	Ps 12:3,4
They eat my * like bread and	Ps 14:4
come from Zion now to save his *.	Ps 14:7
by my own * and by all mankind.	Ps 22:6
before all the *.	Ps 22:25
to the Lord; the * of every nation	Ps 22:27
"Come and talk with me, O my *."	Ps 27:8
The Lord protects his * and	Ps 28:8
Defend your *, Lord;	Ps 28:9
He will give his * strength.	Ps 29:11
Lord, all of you who are his *;	Ps 31:23
whose * he has chosen as his own.	Ps 33:12
he will never abandon his *.	Ps 37:28
which you really want from your *.	Ps 40:6
Decree victories for your *.	Ps 44:4
is your lord. The * of Tyre, the	Ps 45:12
Tyre, the richest * of our day,	Ps 45:12
blessings for his Jewish *	Ps 47:4
rejoice! O * of Judah, rejoice!	Ps 48:11
He has come to judge his *.	Ps 50:4
together my own * who by their	Ps 50:5
O my *, listen!	Ps 50:7
your * and protect Jerusalem.	Ps 51:18
deed of yours against God's *.	Ps 52:1
For they devour my * like bread	Ps 53:4
Don't kill them—for my * soon	Ps 59:11
you can deliver your beloved *.	Ps 60:4,5
O my *, trust him all the time.	Ps 62:8
He prepares the earth for his *	Ps 65:9
miracles happen to his *!	Ps 66:5
will give true justice to their *!	Ps 67:4
O God, when you led your *	Ps 68:7
There your * lived, for you gave	Ps 68:9,10
the sea! His * must destroy them.	Ps 68:23
Let all the * of Israel praise	Ps 68:26
and mighty power to his *.	Ps 68:35
of Judah. His * shall live in them	Ps 69:35
to your *, even to the poor.	Ps 72:2
for him. His *	Ps 72:15
may the cities be as full of * as	Ps 72:16
scoff at God and threaten his *.	Ps 73:8
And so God's * are dismayed and	Ps 73:10
have been a traitor to your *.	Ps 73:15
Remember that we are your *—the	Ps 74:2
left to show that we are your *.	Ps 74:9,10
burst forth to give your * water;	Ps 74:15
Save your beloved * from these	Ps 74:19
* be constantly insulted.	Ps 74:21
shakes and all its * live in	Ps 75:3
You led your * along that road	Ps 77:20
O MY *, listen to my teaching.	Ps 78:1
The * of Ephraim, though fully	Ps 78:9
the tents. The * ate their fill.	Ps 78:29
Yet even so the * kept on	Ps 78:32
But he led forth his own * like a	Ps 78:52
was strong and he despised his *.	Ps 78:59
He caused his * to be butchered	Ps 78:62
God presented David to his * as	Ps 78:71,72
The bodies of your * lie	Ps 79:2
For they have destroyed your *	Ps 79:7

EOPLE Con't)
avenge this slaughter of your *! Ps 79:10
Then we your *, the sheep of your Ps 79:13
Listen to me, O my *, while I Ps 81:8
But no, my * won't listen. Ps 81:11
But oh, that my * would listen to Ps 81:13
plot against your *, laying plans Ps 83:3
and Hagrites; * from the lands of Ps 83:7
the sins of your *—yes, covered Ps 85:2
Then your * can rejoice in you Ps 85:6
peace to his *, his saints, if they Ps 85:8
from the common * to be the king— Ps 89:19
Lord, see how all the * are Ps 89:50
Unthinking * do not understand Ps 92:6
See them oppressing your *, O Ps 94:5
The Lord will not forsake his *, Ps 94:14
he protects the lives of his *, Ps 97:10
has seen God's salvation of his *. Ps 98:2,3
He made us—we are his *, the Ps 100:3
For your * love every stone in Ps 102:14
And a * that shall be created Ps 102:18
the groans of his * in slavery—they Ps 102:20
to Moses and the * of Israel. Ps 103:7
treaty with the * of Israel: "I Ps 105:10,11
to save his * from starvation. Ps 105:17
that followed, the * of Israel Ps 105:24
and brought his * safely out from Ps 105:37
are blessing and saving your *. Ps 106:4
Then at last his * believed him. Ps 106:12
breach between the * and their God Ps 106:23
his *, and he abhorred them. Ps 106:40
Let all the * say, "Amen!" Ps 106:48
In that day of your power your * Ps 110:3
before his * my heartfelt thanks to Ps 111:1
great power to his * by giving them Ps 111:6
has paid a full ransom for his *; Ps 111:9
All of you, his *, trust in him. Ps 115:11
He will bless the * of Israel and Ps 115:12
before all the *, I will pay Ps 116:18,19
All Israel—Jehovah's *—have come Ps 122:4
Lord surrounds and protects his *. Ps 125:2
king you chose for your *. Ps 132:10
YES, LET his * praise him as they Ps 135:1
before Pharaoh and all his *. Ps 135:9
an eternal gift to his * Israel. Ps 135:12
For Jehovah will vindicate his * Ps 135:14
him. All * of Jerusalem, Ps 135:21
Praise him who led his * through Ps 136:16
Praise him who saved his * from Ps 136:17
He subdues my * under me. Ps 144:2
Lord, and your * will bless you. Ps 145:10
kings and all the *, with their Ps 148:11
He has made his * strong, Ps 148:14
his godly ones—the * of Israel, the Ps 148:14
of Israel, the * closest to him. Ps 148:14
Sing his praises, all his *. Ps 149:1
in your Maker. O * of Jerusalem, Ps 149:2
For Jehovah enjoys his *; Ps 149:4,5
Let his * rejoice in this honor. Ps 149:4,5
Adore him, O his *! Ps 149:6,7
He is the glory of his *. Ps 149:9
He wrote them to teach his * how Pro 1:2
* curse the man who holds his Pro 11:26
Some * like to make cutting Pro 12:18
Lazy * want much but get little, Pro 13:4
Some rich * are poor, and some Pro 13:7
and some poor * have great wealth! Pro 13:7
The common bond of godly * is Pro 14:9
but sin is a reproach to any *. Pro 14:34
delights in the prayers of his *. Pro 15:8
the king to judge the * fairly; Pro 16:10
The king rejoices when his * are Pro 16:13
Most * will tell you what loyal Pro 20:6
cursed by many * of many nations; Pro 24:24
will oppress his *, but a king will Pro 28:16
treatment to rich * is a clear case Pro 28:21
In the end, * appreciate Pro 28:23
With good men in authority, the * Pro 29:2
When rulers are wicked, their * Pro 29:16
ignorance of God, the * run wild; Pro 29:18
of *, and be very popular. Ecc 4:16
the world, where * have the power Ecc 8:9,10
* feel it is safe to do wrong. Ecc 8:11
with only a few * living in it, and Ecc 9:14
on teaching the * all he knew; Ecc 12:9
he knew to the *, but taught them Ecc 12:10
to be back among my own *." Sol 6:12
"the chariots of my princely *." Sol 6:12f
for them, but not my * Israel. Is 1:3
Oh, my *, haven't you had enough Is 1:5,6
and * from many lands will flow Is 2:2
O my *! Is 3:12
presenting his case against his *! Is 3:13
"How dare you grind my * in the Is 3:15
They will be God's holy *. Is 4:2,3,4
to describe God's *, as explained Is 4:2,3,4f
given you the story of God's *. Is 5:7
the common * will die of thirst. Is 5:13
of the Lord is hot against his *; Is 5:25
bodies of his * will be thrown as Is 5:25
They seize my * and carry them Is 5:29
I send as a messenger to my *? Is 6:8
But tell my * this: 'Though you Is 6:9
the king and his * trembled with Is 7:2
Judah and throw her * into panic. Is 7:6
your land, your crops, your *. Is 7:20
"Since the * of Jerusalem are Is 8:6
my * with Euphrates' mighty flood; Is 8:7,8
Don't let * call you a traitor Is 8:12
armies for his *: Isaiah means Is 8:18
will save (his *)," Shear-jashub Is 8:18
truth in them. My * will be led Is 8:21
with glory. The * who walk in Is 9:2
that bind his * and the whip that Is 9:4
For the leaders of his * have Is 9:16
The * are fuel for the fire. Is 9:19,20
he is attacking my * as part of his Is 10:7
* and carried off their treasures. Is 10:13
rightly decided to destroy his *. Is 10:22
Hosts says, "O my * in Jerusalem, Is 10:24
God will end the bondage of his *. Is 10:27
all the * of Gibeah—the city of Is 10:28,29
scream in terror, O * of Gallim. Is 10:30
There go the * of Madmenah, all Is 10:31
a remnant of his * for the second Is 11:11
Let all the * of Jerusalem shout Is 12:6
mercy on the young * of Babylon or Is 13:18
the Lord gives his * rest from Is 14:3
You persecuted my * with Is 14:6
your nation and slain your *. Is 14:20
* shall no longer be their slaves. Is 14:25
I will shepherd the poor of my * Is 14:30
the poor of his * will find a Is 14:32
Your * in Dibon go mourning to Is 15:2
My heart weeps for Moab! His * Is 15:5
very great. The * of Moab will Is 16:12
of all its * will be left alive. Is 16:13,14
Oh, a very few of her * will be Is 17:6
bare of * except for a few of the Is 17:6
plunder and destroy the * of God. Is 17:14
say, "Blessed be Egypt, my *; Is 19:25
O my *, threshed and winnowed, I Is 21:10
of Arabia. O * of Tema, bring food Is 21:14
resistance. The * slip away but Is 22:3
* as I watch them being destroyed. Is 22:4
the * of Jerusalem and all Judah. Is 22:21
him responsibility over all my *; Is 22:22
and steady peg to support my *; Is 22:23,24
out all its * and scattering them Is 24:1
Priests and *, servants and Is 24:2
suffers for the sins of its *. Is 24:4,5
by crime; the * have twisted the Is 24:4,5
sight of all the elders of his *. Is 24:23
mockery against his land and *. Is 25:8
In that day the * will proclaim, Is 25:9
to punish it will * turn away from Is 26:9
them how much you love your *. Is 26:11
Go home, my *, and lock the Is 26:20
the * of the earth for their sins. Is 26:21
My * are like the dead branches Is 27:11
*, for they turn away from God. Is 27:11
of beauty to his * who are left. Is 28:5
* say, "to speak to us like this! Is 28:9
thing—to destroy his own *! Is 28:21
"Since these * say they are mine Is 29:13
Abraham says: My * will no longer Is 29:22
O my * in Jerusalem, you shall Is 30:19
begins to heal his * and to cure Is 30:26
But the * of God will sing a song Is 30:29
are held; his * will have gladness Is 30:29
smites them, his * will rejoice Is 30:32
* and will not change his mind. Is 31:2
Therefore, O my *, though you are Is 31:6
his * will listen to his voice. Is 32:3
My * will live in safety, quietly Is 32:18
And God will greatly bless his * Is 32:20
The sinners among my * shake Is 33:14
These fierce, violent *, with a Is 33:19
will be divided by the * of God; Is 33:23
their share. The * of Israel will Is 33:24
upon Edom, the * I have doomed. Is 34:5
Don't speak in Hebrew, for the * Is 36:11
delivered their * from my power? Is 36:20
But the * were silent and Is 36:21
or the * of Eden in Telassar? Is 37:12
"The Lord says to him: My *—the Is 37:22
That's why their * had so little Is 37:27
COMFORT, OH, COMFORT my *, says Is 40:1
of the earth. (The * below must Is 40:22
given you to my * as the personal Is 42:6
my covenant with all the *." Is 42:6f
the world is as blind as my own *, Is 42:19
But what a sight his * are—these Is 42:22
* and destroyed them in battle. Is 42:25
the world for my * to go home, and Is 43:19
desert, so that my *, my chosen Is 43:20
and these my * will some day honor Is 43:21
But O my *, you won't ask my Is 43:22
my captive *—and not for a reward! Is 45:13
strength," the * shall declare. Is 45:24
For I was angry with my * Is 47:6
You didn't care a whit about my * Is 47:7
HEAR ME, MY *: you swear Is 48:1
Listen to me, my *, my chosen Is 48:12
restore to him his * Israel, who Is 49:5
reassign it to its own * again. Is 49:8,9
See, my * shall return from far Is 49:12
has comforted his *, and will have Is 49:13
crowded with your *, and your Is 49:19
Listen to me, my *; Is 51:4
a garment, and the * of the earth Is 51:6
who cares for his *: "See, I take Is 51:22
not a cent! My * were tyrannized Is 52:4
Why are my * enslaved again, and Is 52:5
my name to my * and they shall know Is 52:6
Lord God bring his * home again. Is 52:8
for the Lord has comforted his *; Is 52:9
You are the holy * of the Lord; Is 52:11
But who among the * of that day Is 53:8
O my afflicted *, tempest-tossed Is 54:11
who join the * of the Lord and Is 56:6
"A House of Prayer for All *"! Is 56:7
others too besides my * Israel. Is 56:8
of the forest, devour my *. Is 56:9
For the leaders of my *—the Is 56:10
tell my * of their sins! Is 58:1
be known as "The * Who Rebuild Is 58:12
ARISE, MY *! Is 60:1
All your * will be good. Is 60:21
I will faithfully reward my * for Is 61:8
that they are a * God has blessed. Is 61:9
Prepare the roadway for my * to Is 62:10
said, "Tell my *, I, the Lord your Is 62:11
called "The Holy *" and "The Is 62:12
me to avenge my *, to redeem them Is 63:4
servant, led his * out of Egypt and Is 63:11
his Holy Spirit to be among his *? Is 63:11
we weren't your *, as though we Is 63:19
and see that we are all your *. Is 64:9
THE LORD SAYS, * Is 65:1
But my own *—though I have been Is 65:2
* to possess the land of Israel; Is 65:9
As for my * who have sought me, Is 65:10
word among my *, for the Lord God Is 65:15
and her * shall be a joy! Is 65:18
rejoice in Jerusalem, and in my *; Is 65:19
as in the past. My * will plant Is 65:21,22
For my * will live as long as Is 65:21,22
*, and his wrath upon his enemies. Is 66:14
all nations and * against Is 66:18
you always be my *, with a name Is 66:22
the * were taken away as slaves. Jer 1:3
And don't be afraid of the *, Jer 1:8
out upon all the * of this land. Jer 1:14
I will punish my * for deserting me Jer 1:16
and priests and * will not be able Jer 1:18
holy *, the first of my children. Jer 2:3
And yet my * have given up their Jer 2:10,11
For my * have done two evil Jer 2:13
O my *, listen to the words of Jer 2:31
Why then do my * say, "At last Jer 2:31
Yet for years on end my * have Jer 2:32
Israel, my sinful *, come home to Jer 3:12
more filled with *, says the Lord, Jer 3:16
At that time the * of Judah and Jer 3:18
(Then I said, "But Lord, the * Jer 4:10
For my * have rebelled against Jer 4:17
"Until my * leave their Jer 4:22
be a little remnant of my * left. Jer 4:27
decree against my *, but I have Jer 4:28
coming near. The * hide in the Jer 4:29
it is the cry of my * gasping for Jer 4:31
I fed my * until they were fully Jer 5:7
For the * of Israel and Judah are Jer 5:11
up these * like kindling wood. Jer 5:14
And when your * ask, "Why is it Jer 5:19
Listen, O foolish, senseless * Jer 5:21
But my * have rebellious hearts; Jer 5:23,24
Among my * are wicked men who Jer 5:26
prophets, and my * like it so! Jer 5:31
RUN, * OF Benjamin, run for your Jer 6:1
of my * shall be destroyed again. Jer 6:9
For I will punish the * of this Jer 6:12
Were my * ashamed when they Jer 6:15
*: (Listen to it, distant lands; Jer 6:18,19
listen to it, O my * in Jer 6:18,19
I will bring evil upon this *; Jer 6:18,19
course of the pathway of my *; Jer 6:21
They are a cruel, merciless *, Jer 6:23
O Jerusalem, pride of my *, put Jer 6:26
my * and determine their value. Jer 6:27
message to the *: O Judah, listen Jer 7:2
all the wickedness of my * Israel. Jer 7:12
your brothers, the * of Ephraim. Jer 7:15
Pray no more for these *, Jer 7:16
fury on this place—*, animals, Jer 7:20
be your God and you shall be my *; Jer 7:23
and forsaken this * of his wrath. Jer 7:29
For the * of Judah have sinned Jer 7:30
The bodies of my * shall be food Jer 7:33
and prophets and *, and dig out Jer 8:1
moon and stars—the gods of my *! Jer 8:2
But these * keep on along their Jer 8:4,5

(PEOPLE Con't)
but not my *! Jer 8:7
Then the * will say, "Why should Jer 8:14
in it—the cities and * alike. Jer 8:16
Listen to the weeping of my * Jer 8:19
I weep for the hurt of my *; Jer 8:21
and night for the slain of my *! Jer 9:1
Lord replies, "my * have forsaken Jer 9:13
and yes, even you * of Judah. Jer 9:25,26
Don't act like the * who make Jer 10:2,3
The shepherds of my * have lost Jer 10:21
Judah and all the * of Jerusalem Jer 11:1
O my *, you have as many gods as Jer 11:13
no longer for this *, neither weep Jer 11:14
What right do my beloved * have Jer 11:15
Yet the * say, "God won't bring Jer 12:4
abandoned my *, my inheritance; Jer 12:7
their enemies. My * have roared at Jer 12:8
I hated them. My * have fallen. Jer 12:9
nothing shall escape. My * have Jer 12:13
land God gave his * Israel: See, I Jer 12:14
they taught my * to worship), then Jer 12:16
they shall be strong among my *. Jer 12:16
They were my *, an honor to my Jer 13:11
right on down to all the *. Jer 13:13
all the * prostrate themselves to Jer 14:2
we are known as your *. Jer 14:9
will no longer accept you as my *; Jer 14:10
ask me any more to bless this *. Jer 14:11
They tell the * you will surely Jer 14:13
And the * to whom they Jer 14:16
I cannot stop my crying, for my * Jer 14:17
"O Lord," the * will cry, Jer 14:19
pleading for these *, even then I Jer 15:1
destroy my own * because they Jer 15:7
I have not joined the * in their Jer 15:17,18
And when you tell the * all these Jer 16:10
is bringing his * home from the Jer 16:14,15
MY * SIN as though commanded to, Jer 17:1
Lord, I don't want the * crushed Jer 17:16
and say to all the *: Hear the word Jer 17:20
Judah and all the * of this nation, Jer 17:20
splendor among the *, and this city Jer 17:25
west of Judah, the * shall come Jer 17:26
such a thing! My * have done Jer 18:13
But not my *! Jer 18:15
I will scatter my * before their Jer 18:17
Then the * said, "Come, let's Jer 18:18
Take some of the elders of the * Jer 19:1
wickedness. The * burn incense to Jer 19:4
I will shatter the * of Jerusalem; Jer 19:11
said to all the *, The Lord of Jer 19:14
take away these * as slaves to Jer 20:4
"Tell these *, the Lord says: Jer 21:8
and let your servants and your * Jer 22:2
be, "Because the * living here Jer 22:9
the leaders of my *—the shepherds Jer 23:1
In that day * will no longer say Jer 23:7
who rescued the * of Israel from Jer 23:7
Baal and led my * Israel into sin; Jer 23:13
This is my warning to my *, says Jer 23:16
to turn my * from their evil ways. Jer 23:22
trying to get my * to forget me in Jer 23:27
lies that lead my * into sin. Jer 23:32
at all for my *, says the Lord. Jer 23:32
When one of the * or one of their Jer 23:33
and priests and * who joke about Jer 23:34
They shall be my * and I will be Jer 24:7
THIS MESSAGE FOR all the * of Jer 25:1
this land and its * and against the Jer 25:8,9
and his * for their sins; Jer 25:12
just as they enslaved my *; Jer 25:14
to their treatment of my *. Jer 25:14
princes and the *—they too drank Jer 25:19,20
I have begun to punish my own *, Jer 25:29
their pastures. * now living Jer 25:37
to all the * who have come there to Jer 26:2
and all the * in the Temple mobbed Jer 26:7,8
to the officials and the *. Jer 26:11
Then the officials and * said to Jer 26:16
the * standing around and said: Jer 26:17
Judah, he told the * that God said: Jer 26:18
But did King Hezekiah and the * Jer 26:19
But the * of any nation Jer 27:11
insist on dying—you and your *? Jer 27:13
and all the * and told them: "The Jer 27:16
all the important * of Judah and Jer 27:19,20,21
all the priests and * listened. Jer 28:1
of all the priests and *, "Amen! Jer 28:5
in the presence of all these *. Jer 28:7
yoke but these * have yokes of iron Jer 28:13
and the * are believing your lies. Jer 28:15
and prophets, and to all the *. Jer 29:1
plague upon the * left here in Jer 29:16,17
done a terrible thing among my *. Jer 29:23
waiting for my *, for he has taught Jer 29:32
the fortunes of my *, Israel and Jer 30:3
It is a time of trouble for my * Jer 30:7
I will multiply my * and make of Jer 30:19
And you shall be my * and I will Jer 30:22
they shall act like my *. Jer 31:1
O my *, with an everlasting love; Jer 31:3
his *, the remnant of Israel." Jer 31:7
who scattered his * will gather Jer 31:10
I will satisfy my * with my Jer 31:14
build it up. The * shall no longer Jer 31:29
with the * of Israel and Judah. Jer 31:31
then they shall truly be my * and Jer 31:33
I am as likely to reject my * Jer 31:36
Someday * will again own property Jer 32:15
sins of the *, of their kings, Jer 32:32
I will bring my * back again from Jer 32:37
And they shall be my * and I Jer 32:38
of the earth! The * of the world Jer 33:9
my * and will tremble with awe! Jer 33:9
* will sing: "Praise the Lord! Jer 33:10,11
In that day the * of Judah and Jer 33:16
Have you heard what * are saying? Jer 33:24
no more reject my * than I would Jer 33:25,26
quietly among your *, and they will Jer 34:5
The princes and all the * had Jer 34:10
*—for you have broken your oath. Jer 34:18,19
Perhaps when the * of Judah see Jer 36:3
for on that day * will be there Jer 36:6
messages to the * at the Temple. Jer 36:8
(son of Josiah). * came from all Jer 36:9
was reading to the *, the Jer 36:13
and upon all the * of Judah and Jer 36:31
The * of Jerusalem who had Jer 37:1f
officials nor the * who were left Jer 37:2
you or your officials or the *? Jer 37:18
been telling the *— that everyone Jer 38:1
have left, and of all the * too. Jer 38:4
he left a few *, the very poor, and Jer 39:10
his * who were left in the land. Jer 39:14
all the exiled * of Jerusalem and Jer 40:1
For these * have sinned against Jer 40:2,3
Judah with the * left in the land. Jer 40:6
heard that a few * were still left Jer 40:11
and of the * who had been left Jer 41:10
near Gibeon. The * with Ishmael Jer 41:13,14
and all the *, great and small, Jer 42:1
and for all the *, great and small, Jer 42:8
out upon the * of Jerusalem, so it Jer 42:18
God to all the *, Azariah (son of Jer 43:1
and all the * refused to obey the Jer 43:4
carry off the * as his captives. Jer 43:12
and all the * were burning incense Jer 44:21
upon all these *, I will protect Jer 45:5
cut down your * like woodsmen who Jer 46:22,23
But don't you be afraid, O my * Jer 46:27
sit in the dust, O * of Dibon, for Jer 48:18
O * of Moab, flee from your Jer 48:28
to end with all its rebellious *. Jer 48:45
Woe to you, O Moab; the * of the Jer 48:46
parts of the desert, O * of Dedan Jer 49:8
Edom and also the * of Teman—even Jer 49:20
the cry of the * is heard as far Jer 49:21
feeble and all her * turn to flee. Jer 49:24
Go deep into the deserts, O * of Jer 49:30
the * of Elam to the four winds; Jer 49:36
bring the * back, says the Lord. Jer 49:39
Then the * of Israel and Judah Jer 50:4
My * have been lost sheep. Jer 50:6
lead my * home again, for see, I Jer 50:8
plunderers of my *, and are fat as Jer 50:11
and against the * of Pekod. Jer 50:21
But my * will flee; Jer 50:28
For see, I am against you, O * Jer 50:31
The Lord of Hosts says: The * of Jer 50:33
As for the * of Babylon—there is Jer 50:34
It shall smite the * of Jer 50:35
of images, and the * are madly in Jer 50:38
his * and desecrated his Temple. Jer 51:11
have done to my *, says the Lord. Jer 51:24
O my *, flee from Babylon; Jer 51:45
Just as Babylon killed the * of Jer 51:49
until he and the * of Israel were Jer 52:3
gone, the * in the city tore a Jer 52:7
the poorest of the *—along with Jer 52:15
of the poorest * to care for the Jer 52:16
thronged with *, are silent now. Lam 1:1
Her * groan and cry for bread; Lam 1:11
And yet, O * everywhere, behold Lam 1:18
He bends his bow against his * as Lam 2:4
No longer can the * celebrate Lam 2:6
the false "worship" of his *; Lam 2:7
I see what has happened to my *; Lam 2:11
Then the * wept before the Lord. Lam 2:18
These are your own * to whom you Lam 2:20
My own * laugh at me; Lam 3:14
of the destruction of my *. Lam 3:48,49
their young, but not my *, Israel. Lam 4:3,4
For the sin of my * is greater Lam 4:6
the * shout at them. Lam 4:15
Do you rejoice, O * of Edom, in Lam 4:21
are a hardhearted, stiff-necked *. Eze 2:4
its message to the * of Israel." Eze 3:1
the * of Israel with my messages. Eze 3:4
I am sending you to the * of Eze 3:7
Then, afterward, go to your * in Eze 3:11
whenever I send my * a warning, Eze 3:17
For it is a warning to the * of Eze 4:
While all the * are watching, Eze 4:1
the * will drink it with dismay. Eze 4:1
I will cause the * to lack both Eze 4:1
I will chase my * with the sword. Eze 5:
"But I will let a few of my * Eze 6:
against all the * of Israel; Eze 7:1
"Prepare chains for my *, for Eze 7:2
violence, so I will enslave her *. Eze 7:2
in despair. The * will tremble with Eze 7:26,2
Do you see what great sins the * Eze 8:
worshiped by the * of Israel. Eze 8:1
"Is it nothing to the * of Judah Eze 8:17
"The sins of the * of Israel and Eze 9:9
For they say to the *, 'It is Eze 11:
Lord says to the * of Israel: Is Eze 11:5
be my *, and I will be your God. Eze 11:20
All this is a sign to the * of Eze 12:6
my shoulder while the * looked on. Eze 12:7
these rebels, the * of Israel, have Eze 12:9
in Jerusalem and to all the * of Eze 12:10
and say to the *, the Lord God Eze 12:19
God says that the * of Israel and Eze 12:19
"Son of dust, the * of Israel Eze 12:27
For these evil men deceive my * Eze 13:10
my plan at all! My * build a flimsy Eze 13:10
And when the wall falls, the * Eze 13:12
the souls of my *, of both young Eze 13:18
* and save your own souls alive?" Eze 13:18f
will you turn away my * from me? Eze 13:19
to my *—and how they love it! Eze 13:19
my * free like birds from cages. Eze 13:20
veils and save my * from you; Eze 13:21
I will deliver my * out of your Eze 13:23
everyone, whether * of Israel or Eze 14:6,7
him from among my * Israel. Eze 14:9
hypocrites—evil * who say they want Eze 14:10
sins, so that the * of Israel will Eze 14:11
but to be my * and I their God. Eze 14:11
"Son of dust, when the * of this Eze 14:13
not save the * from their doom. Eze 14:16
Lord God says: The * of Jerusalem Eze 15:5,6
no better than the * of Canaan—your Eze 16:3
and all their * will be restored Eze 16:55
this riddle to the * of Israel: Eze 17:2
"Why do * use this proverb about Eze 18:2
Listen to me, O * of Israel. Eze 18:25
"And yet the * of Israel keep Eze 18:29
Lord is unfair!' O * of Israel, it Eze 18:29
So I brought my * out of Egypt Eze 20:9,10
them, that they are truly my *. Eze 20:12
wilderness of the *," meaning the Eze 20:35,36f
and destroy your *, good and bad Eze 21:3
"Sigh and groan before the *, Eze 21:6
slay my * and all their leaders. Eze 21:12
only of the times the * rebelled. Eze 21:23
for they mocked my * in their woe. Eze 21:28
"Son of dust, the * of Israel Eze 22:18,19,20
"Son of dust, say to the * of Eze 22:24
They have not taught my * the Eze 22:26
Even the common * oppress and Eze 22:29
I proclaimed this to the * in the Eze 24:18
Then the * said: "What does all Eze 24:19
me to say to the * of Israel: I Eze 24:20,21
a symbol for these * and they shall Eze 24:27
Ammon and prophesy against its *. Eze 25:2
destruction of my *, therefore I Eze 25:6
says: Because the * of Edom have Eze 25:12
upon the * of Judah, I will smash Eze 25:12
her *, her cattle and her flocks. Eze 25:13
By the hand of my *, Israel, Eze 25:14
they will butcher your *, and Eze 26:11
and all the * sink into the sea on Eze 27:27
"The * of Israel will once more Eze 28:25
the world my holiness among my *. Eze 28:25
Pharaoh her king and all her *. Eze 29:2
and bring her * back to the land of Eze 29:14
I will stamp out the * of Thebes. Eze 30:15
Egypt, and all his *: You are as Eze 31:2,3
the pride of Egypt and all her *; Eze 32:12
and for her *, says the Lord." Eze 32:16
"Son of dust, weep for the * of Eze 32:18
you will be laid beside the * you Eze 32:19
her *, those the sword has slain. Eze 32:22
of Elam lie there with their *. Eze 32:24
by the graves of all their *. Eze 32:25
"Son of dust, tell your *: When Eze 33:2
a country, and the * of that land Eze 33:2
alarm and warn the *, he is Eze 33:6
as a watchman for the * of Israel; Eze 33:7
"O * of Israel, you are saying: Eze 33:10
"And yet your * are saying the Eze 33:17
"Son of dust, your * are Eze 33:30
from among the * and nations where Eze 34:13
"And as for you, O my flock—my * Eze 34:17
all my *, even my Servant, David. Eze 34:23
shall be a Prince among my *. Eze 34:24
land so that my * can safely camp Eze 34:25
I will make my * and their homes Eze 34:26
in Israel so that my * will Eze 34:29
and that they, the * of Israel, are Eze 34:30

(PEOPLE Con't)
are my *, says the Lord God. Eze 34:30
and prophesy against the * saying: Eze 35:2
Because you hate my * Israel, I Eze 35:4,5
You butchered my * when they were Eze 35:4,5
I will utterly wipe out the * of Eze 35:7
Lord, saying, 'His * are helpless; Eze 35:12
You will be wiped out, O * of Eze 35:15
will be rebuilt and filled with *. Eze 36:10
Not only the *, but your flocks Eze 36:11
I am the Lord. My * will walk upon Eze 36:12
is a land that devours her *!' Eze 36:13
"Son of dust, when the * of Eze 36:17
'These are the * of God and he Eze 36:20
by my * throughout the world. Eze 36:21
"Therefore say to the * of Eze 36:22
defiled, and the * of the world Eze 36:23
And you shall be my * and I will Eze 36:28
but for mine. O my * Israel, be Eze 36:32
and walled and filled with *!' Eze 36:35
can these bones become * again?" Eze 37:3
"represent all the * of Israel. Eze 37:11
Lord God says: My *, I will open Eze 37:12
And, then at last, O my *, you Eze 37:13
Tell these * (holding the sticks Eze 37:18,19,20
I am gathering the * of Israel from Eze 37:21
Then they shall truly be my * and Eze 37:23
their God and they shall be my *. Eze 37:27
return of its * from many lands. Eze 38:8
these * living in such confidence! Eze 38:11
now filled with * again—those who Eze 38:12
For the * are rich with cattle Eze 38:12
to Gog: When my * are living in Eze 38:14
I would bring you against my *. Eze 38:17
my holy name among my * Israel; Eze 39:7
"The * of the cities of Israel Eze 39:9
* of Israel to bury the bodies. Eze 39:12
time onward, the * of Israel will Eze 39:22
captivity of my * and have mercy Eze 39:25
Then my * will know I am the Eze 39:28
to return to the * of Israel to Eze 40:4
among the * of Israel forever. Eze 43:7
have shown you to the * of Israel. Eze 43:10
offerings of the *, and I will Eze 43:27
And say to these rebels, the * Eze 44:6
and be present to help the *. Eze 44:11
encouraged the * to worship other Eze 44:12
to assist the * in a general way. Eze 44:14
consecrate the * by touching them Eze 44:19
"He shall teach my * the Eze 44:23
any disagreements among my *. Eze 44:24
the Temple by the *—the cereal Eze 44:29
oppress and rob my *, but shall Eze 45:8
*, giving a portion to each tribe. Eze 45:8
and cheating my * out of their Eze 45:9
All the * of Israel shall bring Eze 45:16
to furnish the * with sacrifices Eze 45:17
for the * of Israel. Eze 45:17
himself and all the * of Israel. Eze 45:22
evening. The * shall worship the Eze 46:3
but when the * come in through Eze 46:9
the common * on these occasions. Eze 46:10
I don't want my * losing their Eze 46:18
in case they sanctify the *. Eze 46:19,20
the sacrifices the * offer. Eze 46:24
into sin when the * of Israel and Eze 48:11
and commanded his * to offer Dan 2:46
shouted out, "O * of all nations Dan 3:4
which he sent to * of every Dan 4:1
happen— that your * will chase you Dan 4:25
All the * of the earth are Dan 4:35
He delivers his *, preserving Dan 6:27
Devour many *!" Dan 7:5
of millions of * stood before him, Dan 7:10
* of every language must obey him. Dan 7:14
But in the end the * of the Most Dan 7:18
against God's * and winning, until Dan 7:21
and vindicated his *, giving them Dan 7:22
God's * will be helpless in his Dan 7:25
shall be given to the * of God; Dan 7:27
Literally, "the * of the saints Dan 7:27f
He fought against the * of God Dan 8:10
is avenged and God's * triumph?" Dan 8:13
and he will devastate God's *. Dan 8:24
my sins and those of my *. Dan 9:4
and princes and to all the *. Dan 9:6
men of Judah, the * of Jerusalem, Dan 9:7
by removing your * from Egypt in a Dan 9:15
* and your city bear your name." Dan 9:19
and the sins of my *, and Dan 9:20
upon Jerusalem and your *. Dan 9:24
treaty with the *, but after half Dan 9:27
roaring of a vast multitude of *. Dan 10:5,6
happen to your *, the Jews, at the Dan 10:14
angel who guards your * Israel, Dan 10:20,21
Insurgents among your own *, the Dan 11:14
and scatter it out among the *. Dan 11:24
But the * who know their God Dan 11:32
And yet every one of your * whose Dan 12:1
"And those who are wise—the * of Dan 12:3
of the holy * comes to an end." Dan 12:7f
after the power of God's * has Dan 12:7
This will illustrate the way my * Hos 1:2
in that day her * will be too Hos 1:10
'You are not my *,' I will tell Hos 1:10
Then the * of Judah and Israel Hos 1:11
God will sow his * in the fertile Hos 1:11
my *," "Now you are my people"; Hos 1:23
my people," "Now you are my *"; Hos 1:23
HEAR THE WORD of the Lord, O * of Hos 4:1
Israel. My * are destroyed because Hos 4:6
The more my * multiplied, the Hos 4:7
rejoice in the sins of the *; Hos 4:8
priests, like *"—because the Hos 4:9
priests are wicked, the * are too. Hos 4:9
and * for all their wicked deeds. Hos 4:9
have robbed my * of their brains. Hos 4:11
For you have deluded the * with Hos 5:1
Her * never seem to recognize Hos 7:2
* constantly aflame with lust. Hos 7:4
My * mingle with the heathen, Hos 7:8
Woe to my * for deserting me; Hos 7:13
descends upon the * of God because Hos 8:1
far away. Her * love the ritual of Hos 8:13
to guard my *, but the people have Hos 9:8
my people, but the * have blocked Hos 9:8
The things my * do are as Hos 9:9
Lord, what shall I ask for your *? Hos 9:14
My God will destroy the * of Hos 9:17
The hearts of her * are false Hos 10:2
of the field. The * of Samaria Hos 10:5
the priests and *, too, mourn Hos 10:5
And the * will cry to the Hos 10:8
rise among your *, and all your Hos 10:14
fate, too, you * of Israel, because Hos 10:15
But my * shall return to Egypt Hos 11:5
For my * are determined to Hos 11:7
For the * shall walk after the Hos 11:10
and my * shall return trembling Hos 11:10
But no, my * are like crafty Hos 12:7
Then the Lord led his * out of Hos 12:13
And now the * disobey more and Hos 13:2
her God. Her * will be killed by Hos 13:16
of Lebanon. Her * will return from Hos 14:7
Gather the elders and all the * Joe 1:14
How great, how powerful these "* Joe 2:2
Fear grips the waiting *; Joe 2:6
Call a fast and gather all the * Joe 2:15
the * and the altar, weeping; Joe 2:17
pray, "Spare your *, O our God; Joe 2:17
Then the Lord will pity his * and Joe 2:18
Fear not, my *; Joe 2:21
"Rejoice, O * of Jerusalem, Joe 2:23
Never again will my * experience Joe 2:26
I am here among my * Israel, and Joe 2:27
And my * shall never again be Joe 2:27
for harming my *, for scattering my Joe 3:2
"They divided up my * as their Joe 3:3
You have sold the * of Judah and Joe 3:6
daughters to the * of Judah and Joe 3:8
But to his * Israel, the Lord Joe 3:16
innocent * in those nations. Joe 3:19
I will avenge the blood of my *; Joe 3:21
with my *." Joe 3:21
The Lord says, "The * of Amo 1:3
For they have threshed my * in Amo 1:3
and kill her * as far away as the Amo 1:5
the * of Syria shall return to Kir Amo 1:5
For she sent my * into exile, Amo 1:6
I will kill the * of Ashdod, and Amo 1:8
The Lord says, "The * of Tyre Amo 1:9
The Lord says, "The * of Ammon Amo 1:13
THE LORD SAYS, "The * of Moab Amo 2:1
The Lord says, "The * of Judah Amo 2:4
The Lord says, "The * of Israel Amo 2:6
crimes. My * have forgotten what Amo 3:10
dry and withered. * from two or Amo 4:8
The Lord says to the * of Israel, Amo 5:4
for the * of Gilgal will be Amo 5:5
How you despise * who tell the Amo 5:10
have mercy on his * who remain. Amo 5:15
and popular among the * of Israel. Amo 6:1
Lord God, please forgive your *! Amo 7:2
And he replied, "I will test my * Amo 7:8
'Go and prophesy to my * Israel.' Amo 7:15
land, and the * of Israel will Amo 7:17
my * Israel—ripe for punishment. Amo 8:2
crashes down upon the * below. Amo 9:1
and it melts, and all its * mourn. Amo 9:5
"O * of Israel, are you any more Amo 9:7
done as much for other *, too? Amo 9:7
the fortunes of my * Israel, and Amo 9:14
Then my * who live in the Negeb Ob 1:19
And the * of Benjamin shall Ob 1:19
began to preach, the * repented. Jon 3:4,5
your plans for destroying these *. Jon 4:2
* in utter spiritual darkness, Jon 4:11
There go the * of Shaphir, Mic 1:11
naked and ashamed. The * of Zaanan Mic 1:11
it stood. The * of Maroth vainly Mic 1:12
and flee, O * of Lachish, for you Mic 1:13
cannot give. You * of Mareshah Mic 1:15
"The * of the Lord" will live Mic 2:5
"Don't say such things," the * Mic 2:6
Yet to this very hour my * rise Mic 2:8
you skin my * and strip them to Mic 3:2
You who lead his * astray! Mic 3:5
by all nations; * from all over the Mic 4:1
back his punished *—sick and lame Mic 4:6
of God's *—your royal might and Mic 4:8
terrible pain, O * of Zion, for you Mic 4:10
the enemies of his * like sheaves Mic 4:12
to pieces many *, and you will give Mic 4:13
God will abandon his * to their Mic 5:3
his God, and his * shall remain Mic 5:4
WHAT the Lord is saying to his *: Mic 6:1
For he has a case against his * Mic 6:2
O my *, what have I done that Mic 6:3
Don't you remember, O my *, how Mic 6:5
Your cities, * of God, will be Mic 7:11
for the great wickedness of her * Mic 7:13
O Lord, come and rule your *; Mic 7:14
sins of the survivors among his *? Mic 7:18
You cannot stay angry with your * Mic 7:18
the earth crumbles and its * are Nah 1:5
"O my *, I have punished you Nah 1:12
For the land of the * of God Nah 2:2
knees quake; her * stand aghast, Nah 2:10
bewitching * everywhere. Nah 3:4
Yet Thebes fell and her * were Nah 3:10
in the dust; your * are scattered Nah 3:18
They are a fierce *, more fierce Hab 1:8
I see the * of Cushan and of Hab 3:7
went out to save your chosen *. Hab 3:13
to come upon the * who invade us. Hab 3:16
slaughter of his * and has chosen Zep 1:7
"Wail in sorrow, you * of Zep 1:11
riddance of all the * of Judah. Zep 1:18
For the Lord God will visit his * Zep 2:7
the taunts of the * of Moab and Zep 2:8
my * and invading their land. Zep 2:8
those of my * who are left will Zep 2:9
at the * of the Lord of Hosts. Zep 2:10
of my returning * to pure Hebrew Zep 3:9
and the few * remaining in the land Hag 1:12
and Joshua and all the *; Hag 2:4
"You *," he said (speaking for Hag 2:14
displeased with my *, but the Zec 1:15
it is big enough for all the *!" Zec 2:2
day be so full of * that she won't Zec 2:4
Lord, and they too shall be my *; Zec 2:11,12
say to all your * and your priests, Zec 7:5
were filled with *, the prophets Zec 7:7
and poor *, and to stop plotting Zec 7:10
I will rescue my * from east and Zec 8:7
they will be my *, and I will be Zec 8:8
given to the * left in the land. Zec 8:12
truth and peace! * from around the Zec 8:20,21
celebrations. * will write their Zec 8:20,21
Yes, many *, even strong Zec 8:22
"Rejoice greatly, O my *! Zec 9:9
including my * in Israel, and he Zec 9:10
The Lord shall lead his * as they Zec 9:14
He will defend his * and they Zec 9:15
God will save his * in that day, as Zec 9:16,17
Red Sea which the * of Israel were Zec 10:11f
and Egypt over my * will end." Zec 10:11
The Lord says, "I will make my * Zec 10:12
the way my * have been bought and Zec 11:5
watch over the * of Judah, but Zec 12:4
themselves, 'The * of Jerusalem Zec 12:5
so that the * of Jerusalem and the Zec 12:7
The Lord will defend the * of Zec 12:8
prayer on all the * of Jerusalem, Zec 12:10
prophet, priest, and *. Zec 12:12,13,14
be opened to the * of Israel and Zec 13:1
clothes to try to fool the * then. Zec 13:4
I will say, 'These are my *,' and Zec 13:9
Yes, you will escape as your * Zec 14:5
on all the * who fought Jerusalem. Zec 14:12
and their * are called 'Those Whom Mal 1:4
You tell the *, 'Lame animals Mal 1:8
and encouraging * to bring cheap, Mal 1:12
He passed on to the * all the Mal 2:6
so the * will learn God's laws. Mal 2:7
in the eyes of all the *; Mal 2:9
to him by the * of Judah and Mal 3:4
will save his * from their sins. Mt 1:21
from you to rule my * Israel.' Mt 2:6
and wild honey. * from Jerusalem Mt 3:5
live—there the * who sat in Mt 4:15,16
wherever he went—* from Galilee, Mt 4:25
so * will feel sorry for them. Mt 6:16
religious are really godly *. Mt 7:21
* were brought to Jesus; Mt 8:16
"Because * who are well don't Mt 9:12
It's the sick * who do!" Mt 9:12
And wherever he went he healed * Mt 9:35
the * of Israel—God's lost sheep. Mt 10:6
me do— the blind * I've healed, Mt 11:5
and the lame * now walking without Mt 11:5
and prepare * to receive me. Mt 11:10
These * are like children Mt 11:16

(PEOPLE Con't)
their * would have repented long Mt 11:21
own * use when they cast them out? Mt 12:27
while the * listened on the beach. Mt 13:2,3
illustrations, so * will hear and Mt 13:12,13
represents the * of the Kingdom; Mt 13:38
the thistles are the * belonging Mt 13:38
the wicked * from the godly, Mt 13:49
the * exclaimed. Mt 13:55
country, and among his own *!" Mt 13:57
the * believed John was a prophet. Mt 14:5
Then he told the * to sit down on Mt 14:19
disciples to place before the *. Mt 14:19
stayed to get the * started home. Mt 14:22
the city, and soon * were rushing Mt 14:35
of you, 'These * say they honor Mt 15:8
when he said that * are not defiled Mt 15:15
"I pity these *—they've been here Mt 15:32
Then Jesus told all of the * to Mt 15:35
Then Jesus sent the * home and Mt 15:39
"Who are the * saying I Mt 16:13
"Oh, you stubborn, faithless *! Mt 17:17
against their own *, or against Mt 17:25
of God's chosen * Mt 24:22
of the flood; * wouldn't believe Mt 24:39
And I will separate the * Mt 25:32
was valued by the * of Israel— and Mt 27:9
of his popularity with the *. Mt 27:18
And the * passing by hurled Mt 27:39
and appeared to many * there. Mt 27:53
* from Jerusalem and from all Mk 1:5
and a huge crowd of * from all Mk 1:32,33
wastelands. And * from everywhere Mk 1:45
told them, "Sick * need the Mk 2:17
I haven't come to tell good * to Mk 2:17
One day some * came to Jesus and Mk 2:18
numbers of sick * were crowding Mk 3:10
was to tell the * stories. Mk 4:2
the hearts of * who listen to the Mk 4:18
to teach the * as much as they were Mk 4:33
He went inside and spoke to the *. Mk 5:39
to teach, and the * were astonished Mk 6:2,3
on a few sick * and heal them. Mk 6:5
*, anointing them with olive oil. Mk 6:13
So the * were saying, "No wonder Mk 6:14
had said to the * they visited. Mk 6:30
For so many * were coming and Mk 6:31
But many * saw them leaving and Mk 6:33
said, "Tell the * to go away to Mk 6:35,36
disciple to place before the *. Mk 6:41
The * standing around there Mk 6:54
he said, 'These * speak very Mk 7:6,7
the * to obey their petty rules.' Mk 7:6,7
the * ran out of food again. Mk 8:1
"I pity these *," he said, "for Mk 8:1
placed them before the *. Mk 8:6
There were about 4,000 * in the Mk 8:8,9
How many more miracles do you * Mk 8:12
at Bethsaida, some * brought a Mk 8:22
them, "Who do the * think I am? Mk 8:27
But many * who seem to be Mk 10:31
of the earth lord it over the *; Mk 10:42
some of the * yelled at him. Mk 10:48
riots because the * were so Mk 11:18
then the * will start a riot." Mk 11:32
(For the * all believed Mk 11:32
Jesus gave to the * at that time: Mk 12:1
was teaching the * in the Temple Mk 12:35
time—any prisoner the * requested. Mk 15:6
the *, released Barabbas to them. Mk 15:15
The * jeered at him as they Mk 15:29,30
Some of the * standing there Mk 15:35
preparing the * for his arrival. Lk 1:17
visit his * and has redeemed them. Lk 1:68
You will tell his * how to find Lk 1:77
be the glory of your * Israel!" Lk 2:32
preaching that * should be baptized Lk 3:3
announced the Good News to the *. Lk 3:18
Here, too, the * were amazed at Lk 4:32
Amazed, the * asked, "What is in Lk 4:36
who had any sick * in their homes, Lk 4:40
by the crowds. For * from all over Lk 6:17,18
curing many sick * of their various Lk 7:20,21,22
money to two *—$5,000 to one and Lk 7:41
* from believing and being saved. Lk 8:12
represents honest, good-hearted *. Lk 8:15
with mourning *, but he said, Lk 8:52
"If the * of a town won't listen Lk 9:5
him to send the * away to the Lk 9:12
"Who are the * saying I am?" Lk 9:18
"O you stubborn faithless *," Lk 9:41
Awe gripped the * as they saw Lk 9:43
But they were turned away! The * Lk 9:53
their * would have sat in deep Lk 10:13
And you * of Capernaum, what Lk 10:15
lack of love for some kinds of *), Lk 10:29
are evil times, with evil *. Lk 11:29,30
proved to the * of Nineveh that God Lk 11:29,30
that God has sent me to these *. Lk 11:29,30
For you hide the truth from the * Lk 11:52
And all the * rejoiced at the Lk 13:17

of God— for * will come from all Lk 13:29
*—even eating with them! Lk 15:2
you honor from the *, but it is an Lk 16:15
as the * were in Noah's day. Lk 17:26
the days of Lot: * went about their Lk 17:28
This may mean that God's * will be Lk 17:37f
justice to his * who plead with him Lk 18:7
But some of his * hated him and Lk 19:14
"the leading men among the *." Lk 19:47f
*—they hung on every word he said. Lk 19:48
sent from God, the * will mob us, Lk 20:6
Now he turned to the * again and Lk 20:9
to outwit him before the * failed; Lk 20:26
"Marriage is for * here on earth, Lk 20:34,35
* as they walk along the street. Lk 20:46
Then let the * of Judea flee to Lk 21:21
and wrath upon this *. Lk 21:23
The courage of many * will Lk 21:26
been leading our * to ruin by Lk 23:2
the *, and announced his verdict: Lk 23:13
"as one who perverts the *." Lk 23:14f
"Father, forgive these *," Lk 23:34
"You are such foolish, foolish *! Lk 24:25
*, the Jews, he was not accepted. Jn 1:11,12
John pointed him out to the *, Jn 1:15
celebration, many * were convinced Jn 2:23
Jesus replied that * soon became Jn 4:13
So the * came streaming from Jn 4:30
great multitude of * climbing the Jn 6:2-5
buy bread to feed all these *?" Jn 6:2-5
God and passed them out to the *. Jn 6:11
When the * realized what a great Jn 6:14
so when the * saw that Jesus Jn 6:24
"Go where more * can see your Jn 7:3
Some of the * who lived there in Jn 7:25
*, "I am the Light of the world. Jn 8:12
done many a miracle to help the *. Jn 10:32
of all these * standing here, so Jn 11:42
man die for the *—why should the Jn 11:50
and many country * arrived in Jn 11:55
When the ordinary * of Jerusalem Jn 12:9
of your King, * of Israel, for he Jn 12:15
done, most of the * would not Jn 12:37
to you! The * of the world will Jn 15:21
"Your own * and their chief Jn 18:35
Then he went out again to the * Jn 18:38
and Greek, so that many * read it. Jn 19:20
effect, to the * in Jerusalem, Act 1:8
day when about 120 * were present, Act 1:15
among all the * of Jerusalem, and Act 1:19
It's much too early for that! * Act 2:15
When the * inside saw him walking Act 3:9
"destroyed from among the *." Act 3:23f
WHILE THEY WERE talking to the *, Act 4:1
But many of the * who heard Act 4:4
you and to all the * of Israel that Act 4:10
well as the * of Israel—are united Act 4:27
Peter asked her, "Did you * Act 5:8
remarkable miracles among the *. Act 5:12
Sick * were brought out into the Act 5:15
in the Temple, preaching to the *! Act 5:25
were afraid the * would kill them Act 5:26,27
so that the * of Israel would have Act 5:31
popular with the *), stood up and Act 5:34
He drew away some * as disciples, Act 5:37
spectacular miracles among the *. Act 6:8
'and afterwards my * will return to Act 7:7
between God and the * of Abraham. Act 7:8
* greatly multiplied in Egypt; Act 7:17,18
his brothers, the * of Israel. Act 7:23
I have seen the anguish of my * Act 7:34
the same man his * had previously Act 7:35
"Moses himself told the * of Act 7:37
between the * of Israel and the Act 7:38
and told the * there about Christ. Act 8:5
the Samaritan * often spoke of him Act 8:9,10,11
heard that the * of Samaria had Act 8:14
I lay my hands on *, they will Act 8:19
of the * of his generation? Act 8:33
as well as to the * of Israel. Act 9:15
Good News for the * of Israel—that Act 10:36,37
As a result large numbers of * Act 11:24
with the * of those two cities, but Act 12:20
At its conclusion the * gave him Act 12:22
"Then the * begged for a king, Act 13:21
As the * left the synagogue that Act 13:42
But the * of the city were Act 14:4
out among the *, shouting, "Men! Act 14:14
the * from sacrificing to them! Act 14:18
a * to bring honor to his name. Act 15:14
understood some * met for prayer; Act 16:13
"They are teaching the * to do Act 16:20,21
Scriptures to the *, explaining Act 17:2
The * of the city, as well as the Act 17:8,9
But the * of Beroea were more Act 17:11
He created all the * of the Act 17:26
can harm you. Many * here in this Act 18:10
placed upon sick *, they were Act 19:12
many, many * that handmade gods Act 19:26
Inside, the * were all shouting, Act 19:32
against our * and tells everybody Act 21:28

permission to talk to these *." Act 21:3
and motioned to the * to be quiet; Act 21:4
Leave Jerusalem, for the * here Act 22:17,1
just as you have told the * about Act 23:1
both your own * and the Gentiles. Act 26:1
along with all * everywhere whose Act 26:1
of Malta. The * of the island were Act 28:
his hand! The * of the island saw Act 28:
was unharmed. The * waited for him Act 28:
Then all the other sick * in the Act 28:
and when the time came to sail, * Act 28:1
world to tell all * everywhere the Rom 1:
be God's very own—yes, his holy *. Rom 1:6,
civilized * and uncivilized alike; Rom 1:1
* you have been talking about!" Rom 2:
good purpose, for * will notice how Rom 3:
(That is the way some * talk. Rom 3:
God will accept all * in every Rom 4:1
because although, of course, * Rom 5:1
OH, ISRAEL, MY *! Rom 9:
special, chosen * and led you along Rom 9:4
"You are not my *," shall be Rom 9:2
that the Jewish * might be saved. Rom 10:
he would make his * jealous and try Rom 10:1
would be found by * who weren't Rom 10:2
and deserted his * the Jews? Rom 11:
discarded his own * whom he chose Rom 11:2,3
has rejected his Jewish * forever? Rom 11:11
It will be like dead * coming Rom 11:15
*, their children will be too. Rom 11:16
of important *, but enjoy the Rom 12:16
frighten * who are doing right; Rom 13:3
along with his * the Jews." Rom 15:10
* are often fooled by them. Rom 16:18
so that * all around the world will Rom 16:25,26,27
to be his * and made acceptable 1Co 1:2
to shame those * considered by the 1Co 1:27
In fact, you are acting like * 1Co 3:3
I said not to mix with evil *. 1Co 5:9
without being with * like that. 1Co 5:10
Or, "Even the least capable * in 1Co 6:4f
Neither will thieves or greedy *, 1Co 6:9,10
According to some *, there are a 1Co 8:5
our * in the wilderness long ago. 1Co 10:1
(The Scriptures tell us, "The * 1Co 10:7
You are intelligent *. 1Co 10:15
And the Jewish *, all who eat 1Co 10:18
But now you are meeting * who 1Co 12:3
I have to poor *, and if I were 1Co 13:3
he can tell * afterwards, plainly. 1Co 14:13
other * present won't be helped. 1Co 14:17
five words that * can understand 1Co 14:19
languages to his *, but even then 1Co 14:21
saying that dead * will never come 1Co 15:12
all his * will become alive again. 1Co 15:23
point is there in * being baptized 1Co 15:29
such glory that * could not bear to 2Co 3:7
We do not try to trick * into 2Co 4:2
for what do the * of God have in 2Co 6:14
have in common with the * of sin? 2Co 6:14
God and they shall be my *." 2Co 6:16
God wants his * to have, so that I 2Co 7:9
of giving. You * there are leaders 2Co 8:7
to you, about helping God's *. 2Co 9:1
these Macedonian * come with me, 2Co 9:4
are Israelites, God's chosen *? 2Co 11:22
and from my own *, the Jews, as 2Co 11:26
My power shows up best in weak * 2Co 12:9
like this—for you * ought to be 2Co 12:11
All they knew was what * were Gal 1:23
who then gave them to the *; Gal 3:19
It is a fine thing when * are Gal 4:18
of God's two ways of helping *. Gal 4:24,25
Some * even say that I myself am Gal 5:11
changed into new and different *. Gal 6:15
this plan with his *, but now he Eph 3:5
ability in winning * to Christ, Eph 4:11
caring for God's * as a shepherd Eph 4:11
It is that God's * will be Eph 4:12
Don't even associate with such * Eph 5:7
fighting against * made of flesh Eph 6:12
to win * to Christ, then I really Php 1:22
of * who are crooked and stubborn. Php 2:15
*—in the city of Colosse. Col 1:2
Lord, and how much you love his *. Col 1:4
made up of his *—that is, his Col 1:18
loved brother, one of your own *. Col 4:9
we go we find * telling us about 1Th 1:8
from their own * the Jews. 1Th 2:14
be among God's *, I don't need to 1Th 4:9
As a result, * who are not 1Th 4:12
When * are saying, "All is 1Th 5:3
And these * will not be able to 1Th 5:3
and the time when * get drunk. 1Th 5:7
he has done for his *, his saints. 2Th 1:10
If you hear of * having visions 2Th 2:1
we appeal to such *—we command 2Th 3:12
* accept God's plan of faith. 1Ti 1:3,4
I hunted down his *, harming them 1Ti 1:13
For some * have disobeyed their 1Ti 1:19
side and all the * on the other 1Ti 2:5

(PEOPLE Con't)
well spoken of by * outside the 1Ti 3:7
much in order that * will believe 1Ti 4:9,10
that Christ's * are poor workers. 1Ti 6:1
and clothing. But * who long to be 1Ti 6:9
kinds of sin. Some * have even 1Ti 6:10
Some of these * have missed the 1Ti 6:21
to be afraid of *, but to be wise 2Ti 1:7
Remind your * of these great 2Ti 2:14
which lead * into the sin of anger 2Ti 2:16
only upset * and make them angry. 2Ti 2:23
God's * must not be quarrelsome; 2Ti 2:24
a Christian. For * will love only 2Ti 3:2
Don't be taken in by * like that. 2Ti 3:5
Correct and rebuke your * when 2Ti 4:2
come a time when * won't listen to 2Ti 4:3
it blinds * to the truth, and it Tit 1:10
In this way they will make * want Tit 2:10
us his very own *, with cleansed Tit 2:14
and encourage your * to do them, Tit 2:15
REMIND YOUR * to obey the Tit 3:1
For our * must learn to help all Tit 3:14
in the Lord Jesus and in his *. Phm 1:5
refreshed the hearts of God's *. Phm 1:7
proved true and * have always been Heb 2:2
multitudes of God's * to heaven; Heb 2:10
in dealing with the sins of the *. Heb 2:17
And many * can build houses, but Heb 3:4
him, as the * of Israel did. Heb 3:7,8
him, as the * of Israel did when Heb 3:15
And who were those * I speak of, Heb 3:16
These same * who sinned and as a Heb 3:17
the land he had promised his *? Heb 3:18
still waiting for the * of God. Heb 4:9
of the * and his own sins too. Heb 5:1
the father of a great nation of *. Heb 6:14
all God's chosen *, gave Heb 7:4
for later on God's * were required Heb 7:5
was weak and useless for saving *. Heb 7:18
sins and then the sins of the *; Heb 7:27
agreement with the * of Israel and Heb 8:8
of Israel and the * of Judah. Heb 8:8
will make with the * of Israel, Heb 8:10
their God and they shall be my *. Heb 8:10
God and his * there were rules for Heb 9:1
mistakes and sins of all the *. Heb 9:7
system the common * could not go Heb 9:8
hearts of the * who brought them. Heb 9:9
this and that. The * had to keep Heb 9:10
away to certain * when he dies—no Heb 9:16
For after Moses had given the * Heb 9:19
and over all the *, using branches Heb 9:19
offering for the sins of many *; Heb 9:28
will make with the * of Israel, Heb 10:16
meetings, as some * do, but Heb 10:25
who brings God's mercy to his *. Heb 10:29
many millions of * that, like the Heb 11:12
the * of Israel out of Egypt; Heb 11:22
with God's * instead of enjoying Heb 11:24,25
God would save his * that he Heb 11:28
The * of Israel trusted God and Heb 11:29
down after the * of Israel had Heb 11:30
These * all trusted God and as a Heb 11:33
ruled their * well, and received Heb 11:33
the * begged God to stop speaking. Heb 12:19
For if the * of Israel did not Heb 12:25
* and look down on poor people? Jas 2:1
people and look down on poor *? Jas 2:1
has chosen poor * to be rich in Jas 2:5
Look here, you * who say, "Today Jas 4:13
you to enjoy other * and to like 2Pe 1:7
spare any of the * who lived in 2Pe 2:5
and there are * who are 2Pe 3:15,16
These "against-Christ" * used 1Jn 2:19
But since most * don't know God, 1Jn 3:1
let us stop just saying we love *; 1Jn 3:18
like ours. Such * are against the 2Jn 1:7
for all, to his * to keep without Jud 1:3
The fate of such * was written Jud 1:4
a whole nation of * out of the land Jud 1:5
He will bring the * of the world Jud 1:15
how to ruin the * of Israel by Rev 2:14
incense—the prayers of God's *! Rev 5:8
blood has bought * from every Rev 5:9
you judge the * of the earth for Rev 6:10
prayers of God's *, to offer upon Rev 8:3
on the earth and many * died. Rev 8:11
woe, woe to the * of the earth Rev 8:13
to attack those * who did not have Rev 9:4
to bury them, and * from many Rev 11:8,9
worldwide holiday—* everywhere will Rev 11:10
and * alike, all who fear your Rev 11:18
But woe to you * of the world, Rev 12:12
him power to fight against God's * Rev 13:7
to fight against God's *." Rev 13:7f
carefully: The * of God who are Rev 13:10
he was deceiving * everywhere. Rev 13:14
And he ordered the * of the world Rev 13:14
nation, tribe, language and *. Rev 14:6
Let this encourage God's * to Rev 14:12
the sky onto the * below, and they Rev 16:21
with her, and the * of the earth Rev 17:2
and the * of earth, whose names Rev 17:8
of kings, and his * are the called Rev 17:14
of * of every race and nation. Rev 17:15
"Come away from her, my *; Rev 18:4
good deeds done by the * of God. Rev 19:8
and surround God's * and the Rev 20:9
with them and they will be his *; Rev 21:3

PEOPLE'S
usual to hear the * complaints Ex 18:13
you: Be these * lawyer—their Ex 18:19,20
The priests who present the * Lev 7:9
Next he sacrificed the * Lev 9:15
* peace offering sacrifice; Lev 9:18
and sacrifice the * sin offering Lev 16:15
the * sacrificing to evil spirits Lev 17:7
by desecrating the * sacred gifts; Lev 22:1
and will offer the * sacrifices, Num 8:19
I promised to this * ancestors. Num 14:23
Israel, for the * tithes, offered Num 18:24
* beginning to worship their gods. Deu 7:4
Joshua recorded the * reply in Jos 24:26
for they treated the * offerings 1Sa 2:17
a man to be my * leader.' 1Ki 8:16
so the king refused the * 1Ki 12:15
The doorkeepers put all of the * 2Ki 12:9
the * offerings to the Lord. 1Ch 23:13
or if your * enemies are in the 2Ch 6:28
and led the * demands on Rehoboam: 2Ch 10:2,3
So the king turned down the * 2Ch 10:15
goats for the * Passover offerings, 2Ch 35:7
"Come," to all his * enemies; Ps 68:22
deciding all the * arguments. Ps 122:5
* scorn or their slanderous talk. Is 51:7
for my * return from captivity. Is 57:14
medicine for my * grievous wounds, Jer 8:11
quickly learn my * ways and claim Jer 12:16
or bronze? This * stubborn will Jer 15:12,13
you hunt my * souls with all your Eze 13:20
to prepare for my * return—and they Eze 36:8
for my * wound is far too deep Mic 1:9
will again overrun my * land. Zec 9:8
with other * money, why should you Lk 16:12
their hands upon * heads—he offered Act 8:18
he accepted the * worship instead Act 12:23
and are upsetting * faith, teaching Rom 16:17
veiled, but his * minds and 2Co 3:14
getting into other * business. 1Ti 5:13
sneak into other * homes and make 2Ti 3:6
and prying into other * affairs. 1Pe 4:15

PEOPLED
deserts, * by nomadic tribes. Eze 20:35,36f

PEOPLES
from all other *, to be mine. Lev 20:26
would displace the * of Canaan, Deu 2:12
The conquered * of those lands 1Ki 4:21
"Tell the * of the world 1Ch 16:8
with all the conquered Ammonite *. 1Ch 20:3
Then all the * of the earth will 2Ch 6:33
Gather all * before you; Ps 7:7,8
May all the * of the earth give Ps 67:5
will bless us. And * from remotest Ps 67:6,7
Praise him, all the * of the Ps 117:1
Literally, "O *." Is 8:9,10f
No, for all the * of the world Is 40:15
cover all the * of the earth, but Is 60:2
will horrify the * of the world. Jer 15:4
against all the * of the earth." Jer 25:29
Literally, "the gate of the *." Eze 26:2f
Tegerama, * who lived in the Eze 38:2,3f
"Of all the * of the earth, I Amo 3:2
Let all the * of the world Mic 1:2
I will change the speech of the * Zep 3:9f
among all the * of the earth, and Zep 3:20
I will disarm all * of the Zec 9:10
Then the * of the earth shall Lk 21:27
*, nations, tribes, and kings." Rev 10:11

PEOR
Mount *, overlooking the desert. Num 23:28
idols on Mount *, and they are the Num 31:16
Was our guilt at *—from which we Jos 22:17,18
of Baal at * and even offered Ps 106:28
Baal-peor, the god of *, a city of Hos 9:10f

PER
used, with twenty * cent added; Lev 22:14
One tenth of one * cent of the men Ecc 7:27,28
and one * cent of your olive Eze 45:14

PERAEA
sovereignty being Galilee and *. Mt 14:1f

PERAS
all fully armed. *, Cush and Put Eze 38:5

PERAZIM
anger, as at Mount * and Gibeon, to Is 28:21

PERCENT
as his tax twenty * of all the Gen 47:26
the loss, plus a twenty * penalty; Lev 5:16
adding a twenty * fine, and give it Lev 6:4,5
shall pay twenty * more than the Lev 27:13
amount plus twenty *, and the house Lev 27:14,15
shall pay twenty * in addition to Lev 27:19
of its worth, plus twenty *; Lev 27:27
adding twenty * and returning it Num 5:7
Also levy a two * tribute of all Num 31:30
two * of these to the Levites. Num 31:47
And I will destroy 85 * Eze 39:2

PERDITION
Literally, "go to *." Rev 17:8f
Literally, "go to *." Rev 17:11f

PERESH
bore him a son whom she named *; 1Ch 7:16

PEREZ
And ever after he was called * Gen 38:29
Er, Onan, Shelah, *, Zerah Gen 46:8-14
The sons of * were Hezron and Gen 46:8-14
named after their ancestor *. Num 26:19-22
also included the sub-clans of *: Num 26:19-22
*, the son of Tamar and Judah." Ru 4:12
beginning with his ancestor *: Ru 4:18-22
*, Hezron, Ram, Amminadab, Nashon, Ru 4:18-22
* and 1Ch 2:4
The sons of * were 1Ch 2:5
*, Hezron, Carmi, Hur, 1Ch 4:1
of the clan of * (son of Judah). 1Ch 9:4
of Mahalelel, a descendant of *); Neh 11:4,5,6
of * who lived in Jerusalem. Neh 11:4,5,6
Judah was the father of * and Mt 1:3
* was the father of Hezron; Mt 1:3
Hezron's father was *; Lk 3:23-38
Hezron's father was Perez;*' Lk 3:23-38

PEREZITES
The *, named after their ancestor Num 26:19-22

PERFECT
His work is *. Deu 32:4
his eyesight was * and he was as Deu 34:7
you're as * as an angel of God. 1Sa 29:9
I was * in obedience 2Sa 22:24
As for God, his way is *; 2Sa 22:31
* lives before the Lord our God; 1Ki 8:61
* toward Jehovah all his days." 1Ki 15:14f
of King Asa was * before God 2Ch 15:17
whose hearts are * toward him, so 2Ch 16:9
Even if I were *, God would prove Job 9:20
be any gain to him if you were *? Job 22:3
And he is * in his understanding. Job 36:5
O GOD, YOU have declared me * in Ps 4:1
What a God he is! How * in every Ps 18:30
God's laws are *. Ps 19:7,8
They meet together to * their Ps 56:6
and in your * righteousness. Ps 89:16
The heavens declare his * Ps 97:6
to judge the world with * justice. Ps 98:8,9
Nothing is * except your words. Ps 119:96
as compared with you, no one is *. Ps 143:2
If you wait for * conditions, Ecc 11:4
but you, my dove, my * one, are Sol 6:9
He will rule with * fairness and Is 9:7
He will keep in * peace all Is 26:3
it was * because of all the gifts Eze 16:14
"You were * in all you did from Eze 28:15
offer another * bullock and a Eze 43:23
and a * ram from the flock. Eze 43:23
one young bull, in * condition; Eze 46:6
with * harmony between the two!' Zec 6:13
But you are to be *, even as Mt 5:48
as your Father in heaven is *. Mt 5:48
you want to be *, go and sell Mt 19:21
God—has caused this * healing. Act 3:16
looked like a * day for the trip; Act 27:13
Does not God have a * right to Rom 9:22
But when we have been made * and 1Co 13:10
Once again I can have * 2Co 7:16
For none of us is *! Gal 6:5
I don't mean to say I am *. Php 3:12
each one to God, * because of what Col 1:28
will stay together in * harmony. Col 3:14
you strong and * and to help you Col 4:12
for his suffering made Jesus a * Heb 2:10
God's * will at the cross. Heb 5:7f
had proved himself * in this Heb 5:9
his oath his Son who is * forever. Heb 7:28
He went into that greater, * Heb 9:11
*, without a single sin or fault. Heb 9:14
he made forever * in the sight of Heb 10:14
in heaven, already made *; Heb 12:23
But whatever is good and * comes Jas 1:17
proves that he has * control over Jas 3:1
He will judge you with * justice 1Pe 1:17
to the Lord with * assurance and 1Jn 3:21
love grows more * and complete; 1Jn 4:17
us perfectly; his * love for us 1Jn 4:18
you, sinless and *, into his Jud 1:24,25

PERFECTED
in me, all being * into one—so that Jn 17:23

PERFECTING
row upon the walls, * your glory. Eze 27:11

PERFECTION
clouds with wonderful * and skill? Job 37:16,17
Literally, "Out of Zion, the * of Ps 50:2f
were the * of wisdom and beauty. Eze 28:12

PERFECTIONS
You show your * 2Sa 22:26
in his incomparable * and glory. Ps 27:4

PERFECTLY
they must always be * fair. Lev 19:15
I instructed them to be * fair Deu 1:16
"I know * well that your God is Jos 2:9
"Your father knows * well about 1Sa 20:3
You know * well that he came to 2Sa 3:24,25
"No," she replied, "I am * 2Ki 4:13
You know * well what the kings 2Ki 19:11
punished us you were being * fair; Neh 9:33
For he knows * all the faults Job 11:11
God is a judge who is * fair, and Ps 7:11
little children to praise you *. Ps 8:2
HAPPY ARE ALL who * follow the Ps 119:1
I've been * fair. Ps 119:121
eternal for your laws are * fair. Ps 119:142
* matched, without one missing. Sol 4:2
* matched and not one missing. Sol 6:6
For a * trained army Is 14:31
We're * safe!" Jer 12:4
already knows * well that you need Mt 6:31,32
Wear my yoke—for it fits *—and Mt 11:29,30
and * sane, they were frightened. Mk 5:15
But you say it is * all right Mk 7:11
Instantly the man could hear * Mk 7:35
When he lies, it is * normal; Jn 8:44
it is * all right after he dies. Rom 7:3
I know * well that what I am Rom 7:16
a person could be * good and hold Rom 10:5
As for myself, I am * sure on the Rom 14:14
It may be * legal, but it may not 1Co 10:23
in heaven how * wise he is when all Eph 3:10
is fitted together *, and each part Eph 4:15,16
so that he can be * joined to his Eph 5:31
we were * straightforward and 1Th 2:3
you know * well that no one knows. 1Th 5:2
to help would be * sure and never Heb 6:17
[And it is * proper for God to do 1Jn 1:9
no fear of someone who loves us *; 1Jn 4:18

PERFORM
* the miracles I have shown you." Ex 4:17
mighty power and * great miracles Ex 6:6
* the rite of atonement for the Lev 14:19
He shall also * the ceremony of Lev 14:49
instructions and * the sacred Num 3:7,8,9
but only you and your sons may * Num 18:2,3
the priests are to * the sacred Num 18:5
Anyone else who attempts to * Num 18:7
Then Joshua told the people to * Jos 3:5
* the ceremonies of purification. 1Ch 23:28
operation God will * for you, O 2Ch 20:17
Though you watch and watch as I * Is 6:9
me the strength to * this task and Is 49:5
I will * a mighty miracle Is 66:19
watching over my word to * it." Jer 1:12f
able to * his Temple duties again. Eze 44:26
hoping to see him * a miracle. Lk 23:8

PERFORMED
* the miracles as they watched. Ex 4:30
see Pharaoh, and * the miracle, as Ex 7:10
ceremony is being *—and upon the Lev 14:25
The rite of atonement shall be * Lev 16:10
shall be * by the anointed High Lev 16:32
He then * the rite of atonement Num 8:21
And at God's command he * Deu 34:11,12
the altar had been *, and he would 1Sa 2:15
And he * the purification rite on 1Sa 16:5
* this ministry in the Tabernacle. 1Ch 25:6,7
around again and * my duties for Dan 8:27
Herodias' daughter * a dance that Mt 14:6
work at the cross could be *. Heb 5:7f

PERFORMING
worshiping God and * the Neh 12:45
For they eat without first * the Mk 7:5
eat without first * the ceremonial Lk 11:37,38

PERFORMS
The priest who * the ceremony Lev 6:26
Who can forget the wonders he * Ps 111:4

PERFUME
and put on some * and some nice Ru 3:3
suggestions are as pleasant as *. Pro 27:9
than the most expensive *. Ecc 7:1
cause even a bottle of * to stink! Ecc 10:1
by the fragrance of my *. Sol 1:12
mere wine. The * of your love is Sol 4:10
and cinnamon, and * from every Sol 4:13,14
waft its lovely * to my beloved. Sol 4:16
hands dripped with *, my fingers Sol 5:5
Instead of smelling of sweet *, Is 3:24
and * to Molech as your gift. Is 57:9
the bucketful and * yourselves with Amo 6:6
*, and poured it over his head. Mt 26:7
She has poured this * on me to Mt 26:12
a beautiful flask of expensive *. Mk 14:3
"Why, she could have sold that * Mk 14:4,5
flask filled with expensive *. Lk 7:37
them and poured the * on them. Lk 7:38
has covered my feet with rare *. Lk 7:46
poured the costly * on Jesus' feet Jn 11:1
Then Mary took a jar of costly * Jn 12:3
"That * was worth a fortune. Jn 12:5
spread the Gospel like a sweet *. 2Co 2:14
Christ we are a life-giving *. 2Co 2:16
for you was like sweet * to him. Eph 5:2
And the * of the incense mixed Rev 8:4

PERFUME-MAKERS
The Lord instructed skilled * to Ex 30:25

PERFUMED
He was laid on a bed * with sweet 2Ch 16:13,14
Your robes are * with myrrh, Ps 45:8
* with myrrh, aloes and cinnamon. Pro 7:16,17
His lips are * lilies, his breath Sol 5:13
as an offering of * incense when I Eze 20:41
and every kind of * wood, and Rev 18:12

PERFUMERS
techniques of the most skilled *. Ex 37:29

PERFUMES
cook and bake and make * for him. 1Sa 8:13
was Hananiah, a manufacturer of *. Neh 3:8
with special * and ointments. Est 2:12,13,14
with the rarest of *; Sol 4:13,14
headbands, earrings, and *; Is 3:20
of silver, gold, spices and *. Is 39:2
Keep your expensive *! Jer 6:20
They brought their * and incense Eze 20:27,28
and spices and * and incense, Rev 18:13

PERGA
landing at the port town of *. Act 13:13
in *, and went on to Attalia. Act 14:25

PERGAMOS
and those in *, Thyatira, Sardis, Rev 1:11
of the church in *: Rev 2:12

PERHAPS
group, * the other can escape." Gen 32:8
face to face! "*," Jacob hoped, Gen 32:20
on the mountain—* I will be able to Ex 32:30
yet another place. * it will please Num 23:27
sad day for you. * you will think Deu 7:17
hiding there. * the additional five Jos 8:11,12,13f
that * he was using the bathroom. Ju 3:24
is his strength." * the meaning Ju 8:21f
One day Ruth said to Naomi, "* I Ru 2:2
the God of Israel, * he will stop 1Sa 6:4,5
let's go and find him and * he 1Sa 9:6
his bodyguard. "* the Lord will do 1Sa 14:6
decide between us. * he will kill 1Sa 24:12
for I said, '* the Lord will be 2Sa 12:22
I said to myself, '* the king will 2Sa 14:15,16
him to do it. And * the Lord will 2Sa 16:12
of your god! * he is talking to 1Ki 18:27
This inquiry was * ostensibly to 1Ki 21:9f
for your master; * the Spirit of 2Ki 2:16
deliver it. Yet * the Lord your 2Ki 19:4
be sold as slaves, * I could remain Est 7:4
For Job said, "* my sons have Job 1:5
so endlessly? But * I'd sermonize Job 16:4
* this could be paraphrased, Ps 137:9f
* the reference is to blackmail, Pro 5:9f
of wealth—except * to watch it as Ecc 5:11
which will grow—* it all will. Ecc 11:6
and Persians, * represented by Is 21:6,7f
* then they will be ashamed! Is 26:11
her for help. But * you say, 'We Is 36:7
not come. But * the Lord your God Is 37:4
The meaning is unclear. * Hezekiah Is 38:18f
57:1,2). Or * his meaning is, Is 38:18f
can open them." * the meaning is Jer 13:19f
war on us! * the Lord will be Jer 21:1
Coniah is an abbreviation—* a Jer 22:24,25f
them to hear. For * they will Jer 26:3
one of them. * when the people of Jer 36:3
all over Judah. * even yet they Jer 36:7
give her medicine; * she can yet Jer 51:8
a wheel," * as in a gyroscope. Eze 1:16f
they can see, for * even yet they Eze 12:3
of renown"; so * the meaning is, Eze 34:29f
be merciful to the poor. * even Dan 4:27
and the law." * the meaning is, Dan 7:25f
* Xerxes (486–465) who launched an Dan 11:2f
* the valiant Maccabees and their Dan 11:32f
Who knows? * even yet he will Joe 2:14
terrible curse. * he will give you Joe 2:14
halls of justice. * even yet the Amo 5:15
Who can tell? * even yet God Jon 3:9
do what is right; * even yet the Zep 2:3
were hardened," * implying Mk 6:52f
board, and then * you can see well Lk 6:42
told him, "or * Elijah or one of Lk 9:19
my father,' "—* meaning that the Lk 9:59f
against—or * the other way around. Lk 12:52
* the reference is to impure salt; Lk 14:34f
He walked away, * a stone's Lk 22:41,42
* twenty to thirty gallons each. Jn 2:6
about it. But * we can stop them Act 4:17
and pray. * God will yet forgive Act 8:22
after God, and * feel their way Act 17:27
they shouted. "* a spirit or angel Act 23:9
ahead if we go on—* shipwreck, loss Act 27:10
But * he is referring here, as Act 28:20f
an open grave." * the meaning is Rom 3:13f
of scruples." * the meaning is, Rom 14:1f
leave him. For * the husband who 1Co 7:14
But * this may refer to the 1Co 15:40f
longer with you, * all winter, and 1Co 16:
I was afraid that * Satan had 1Th 3:
you wanted to. * you could think Phm 1:1
* the reference is to atoms, Heb 11:3
Or, *, "the Lord will be merciful 1Jn 3:20

PERIDA
Sotai, Sophereth, *, Neh 7:57,58,5

PERIL
name by leading me out of this *. Ps 31:

PERILOUS
be rebuilt despite the * times. Dan 9:25

PERIOD
one day (or, '* of time')." Gen 1:4,5
a second day (or, '* of time')." Gen 1:7,8
a third day (or, '* of time')." Gen 1:13f
a fourth day (or, '* of time')." Gen 1:19f
a fifth day (or, '* of time')." Gen 1:23f
a sixth day (or, '* of time')." Gen 1:31f
her menstrual *, which, under the Gen 31:35f
years will be a * of great Gen 41:29
forty days, with a * of national Gen 50:3
with a seven-day * of lamentation Gen 50:10
For that entire * you are to eat Ex 12:15
normal menstrual *, and everything Lev 15:26
and for a woman's menstrual *; Lev 15:33
in her * of defilement afterwards. Lev 15:33
a woman during her * of Lev 20:18
during the entire * of his special Num 6:3,4
during the entire * of his vow, Num 6:6,7
the Lord throughout the entire *. Num 6:8
"At the conclusion of the * of Num 6:13
of his * of special dedication. Num 6:21
During this * Joshua routed all Jos 11:21
during the entire * when David was 1Sa 22:4
then, when the * of mourning was 2Sa 11:27
Egyptian sundials in this * 2Ki 20:11f
During this * none of us—I, nor Neh 4:23
of the Maccabean * were priests as Jer 30:21f
training *, planning to make them Dan 1:5
then, at the end of this trial * Dan 1:13
When the three-year training * Dan 1:18,19
"After this * of 434 years, the Dan 9:26
was active during this same *. Zep 1:1f
Gentiles until the * of Gentile Lk 21:24
The custom of the * was to Jn 13:23f
Narratives from that * Act 27:4f

PERIODS
as during her monthly *. Lev 12:2

PERISH
You shall * among the nations Lev 26:38
Must we all *?" Num 17:12,13
shall certainly *, just as the Deu 8:19
other nations in the past to *. Deu 8:20
you will quickly * from the good Deu 11:17
shall pursue you until you *. Deu 28:22
this day that you shall surely *; Deu 30:18
you, and you will quickly *." Jos 23:15,16
* as Sisera did, Ju 5:31
We will all * along with our god 1Sa 5:7
people shall * instead of his.' 1Ki 20:42
and if I *, I perish." Est 4:16
and if I perish, I *." Est 4:16
never * from the Jewish race. Est 9:28
there to drink, and so they *. Job 6:15-18
existence will * from the earth; Job 18:17
air, yet he shall * forever, cast Job 20:7
ready to * and they blessed me. Job 29:13
to him, they shall * in battle and Job 36:12
his anger is roused and you *. Ps 2:12
My enemies will fall back and * Ps 9:3
Those nations will collapse and *; Ps 20:8
But evil men shall *. Ps 37:20
all who love wickedness shall *. Ps 37:28
Otherwise I *, for problems far Ps 40:12
So let the wicked * at the Ps 68:2
worship God will *, for he destroys Ps 73:27
May they * at your frown. Ps 80:16
They shall *, but you go on Ps 102:26
Let all sinners *—all who refuse Ps 104:35
his hopes all *, for they are Pro 11:7
The wicked shall *; Pro 12:7
The work of the wicked will *; Pro 14:11
(But all sinners shall utterly *, Is 1:28
You will * like a withered tree Is 1:30
Prepare for war against us—and *! Is 8:9,10
war against us—and perish! Yes! *! Is 8:9,10
your plans of attacking us, and *! Is 8:9,10
All crops will *; Is 19:7
and many about to * among their Is 27:13
The strongest will *, young boys Is 34:7
THE GOOD MEN *; Is 57:1
if I did, all mankind would *—the Is 57:16
will *; they shall be destroyed. Is 60:12
to the walled cities and * there. Jer 8:14
be crushed when their makers *. Jer 10:15
Therefore they * and their flocks Jer 10:21
sin, but let them * before you; Jer 18:23
land and send you far away to *. Jer 27:10
behind you and you will * there. Jer 42:16
therefore you shall *. Jer 48:7
she herself will * too. Jer 49:9,10

ERISH Con't)
For you are going to * from war Eze 6:11
city shall * by the sword. Eze 26:6
with them shall * in that war. Eze 30:5
From Migdol to Syene they shall * Eze 30:6
are all destroyed and * with her. Eze 31:17
all will *. Eze 32:12
let them *, for they have sinned Hos 7:13
their leaders will * by the sword Hos 7:16
die at birth, or * in the womb, or Hos 9:11
all Philistines left will *." Amo 1:8
even one house, they too will *. Amo 6:9
and the fish in the sea will *. Zep 1:3
one of these little ones should *. Mt 18:14
are shortened, all mankind will *. Mt 24:22
that you also will * unless you Lk 13:3
And you, too, will * unless you Lk 13:5
not a hair of your head will *! Lk 21:18
shall not * but have eternal life. Jn 3:16
life and they shall never *. Jn 10:28
believing in me and shall never *. Jn 11:26
should the whole nation *?" Jn 11:50
But Peter replied, "Your money * Act 8:20
For they said, 'Look and *, you Act 13:41
a hair of your heads shall *!" Act 27:34
are lost and will *, but if through Rom 8:13
cannot * but will live forever. 1Co 15:53
obey every other Jewish law or * Gal 5:3
day, when all ungodly men will *. 2Pe 3:7
that any should *, and he is giving 2Pe 3:9

ERISHABLE
about * things like food. Jn 6:27
These * bodies of ours are not 1Co 15:50
—is held in a * container, that 2Co 4:7

PERISHED
upon the earth *—birds, domestic Gen 7:21
closed upon them, and they *. Num 16:33
one of those who * in Korah's Num 27:3,4
I would have despaired and * Ps 119:92
than you have * beneath its power. Eze 21:9,10,11
and all your crew have * with you. Eze 27:34
you have forever *.' Eze 27:36
and righteousness *, and evil Dan 8:12
so truth and righteousness *." Dan 8:12f
Cities of the plain that * with Hos 11:8f
Two million Jews * in the Roman Zec 13:8f
of Zechariah who * between the Lk 11:51
I guarded them so that not one *, Jn 17:12
cities of Sodom and Gomorrah *. Rom 9:29

PERIZZITES
and * present in the land. Gen 13:7
Hittites, *, Rephaim, Amorites, Gen 15:19,20,21
land—all the Canaanites and *. Gen 34:30
*, Hivites, and Jebusites live. Ex 3:8
Amorites, *, Hivites, and Ex 3:17
Hittites, *, Canaanites, Hivites, Ex 23:23
*, Hivites, and Jebusites. Ex 33:2
*, Hivites, and Jebusites. Ex 34:11
The *, the Hivites, Deu 7:1
*, the Hivites, and the Jebusites. Deu 20:17
Hittites, Hivites, *, Girgashites, Jos 3:10
*, Hivites, and Jebusites. Jos 9:1
The kings of the *; Jos 11:1
Canaanites, the *, the Hivites, and Jos 12:8-24
where the * and Rephaim live." Jos 17:15
many others—the *, the Canaanites, Jos 24:11
the Canaanites and *, so that ten Ju 1:4,5,6
*, Amorites, and Jebusites. Ju 3:5
*, Hivites, and Jebusites. 1Ki 9:20,21
Amorites, *, Hivites, and 2Ch 8:7,8
Hittites, *, Jebusites, Ammonites, Ez 9:1
*, Jebusites, and Girgashites; Neh 9:8

PERMANENCE
the meaning of * in the Hebrew Jer 36:30f

PERMANENT
This is a * part of this Gen 17:12
a * cemetery for my family." Gen 23:9
They became his * possession, by Gen 23:17,18
year (this is a * law) to remind Ex 12:14
And remember, this is a * law Ex 12:24
this into a * record, to be Ex 17:14
This is a * rule for the people Ex 27:21
This is a * ordinance for Aaron Ex 28:43
their anointing shall be * from Ex 40:15
This is a * law throughout your Lev 3:17
"This is a * law: You must do no Lev 16:29,30
this is a * law. Lev 16:31
This shall be a * law for you, Lev 17:7
This is a * law throughout your Lev 23:14
* law of God, and are most holy." Lev 24:9
these are their * possession, and Lev 25:34
They will be * slaves for you to Lev 25:46
This is a * instruction to be Num 10:8
clothes (this is a * regulation Num 15:37,38
to you and your sons, by * law. Num 18:8
this is a * contract Num 18:19
This is a * law among you, that Num 18:23
this is a * law for the benefit Num 19:10
This is a * law. Num 19:21
These are * laws for all Israel Num 35:29
country as their * possession, and Deu 2:5
deep and * effect upon your lives! Deu 4:9
The monument will be a * Jos 4:7
him Hebron as a * inheritance Jos 14:13,14
them to a * and binding contract Jos 24:25
Make them * guests of the king, 1Ki 2:7
He made * exhibits in the Temple 1Ki 15:15
And I will give a * home to my 1Ch 17:9
into the * records of the realm): Ez 1:1
to build a * home for the Ark Ps 132:2-5
in God's * home here on earth. Ps 132:7
as your home: "This is my * Ps 132:14
yes, a * gift to his servant Ps 136:22
in your heart with * betrothal, for Sol 8:6
we should build * homes and plan to Jer 29:28
This is a * ordinance—the lamb, Eze 46:14,15
Only gifts to his sons are *. Eze 46:17
this rooting out will not be *. Amo 9:8
a * Temple for the God of Jacob. Act 7:46

PERMANENTLY
rings, but are to be left there *. Ex 25:15
is mine, so you may not sell it *. Lev 25:23
it will belong * to the new Lev 25:30
place Aaron's rod * beside the Ark Num 17:10
remain * as it was first allotted. Num 36:7
but if you forsake him, he will * 1Ch 28:9
is that they are * abandoned. Jer 13:19f
be joined together * in marriage; Mk 10:6,7

PERMEATES
it * every part of the dough." Mt 13:33

PERMISSIBLE
Either translation is *, but Eze 34:29f

PERMISSION
"You have my * to punish the Gen 16:6
We request * to live in the land Gen 47:4
Give us your *.' Ex 3:18
"With your *," Moses said, "I Ex 4:18
to Pharaoh to ask * to lead the Ex 6:27
I have given you * to eat and those Lev 20:25
all we want is * to pass through. Deu 2:28
asking * to pass through his land. Ju 11:17
the king of Moab for similar *. Ju 11:17
Heshbon, and asked * to cross Ju 11:19
him that I asked * to go home to 1Sa 20:6
in Moab to ask * of the king for 1Sa 22:3
Pharaoh for * to return to Edom. 1Ki 11:21
"Who gave you * to rebuild this Ez 5:3
'Who has given you * to do this?' Ez 5:9
* to go back again to Jerusalem). Neh 13:6
Now the king is giving * for Est 8:8f
Jews everywhere * to unite in the Est 8:11
against you without the Lord's *? Lam 3:37
He asked the superintendent for * Dan 1:8
When you ask * to stay, be Mt 10:12
And Jesus gave them *. Mk 5:13
let me ask * of those at home." Lk 9:61
for * to take Jesus' body down; Jn 19:38
I request * to talk to these Act 21:39

PERMIT
Ask his majesty to * me to go and Gen 50:5
* the Destroyer to enter ." Ex 12:23f
that home and not * the Destroyer Ex 12:23
animals that I do not * for food. Num 18:16
then refuses to * the vow, whatever Num 30:15
The Lord may * other nations to Deu 4:19
will not * you to do such things. Deu 18:14
Do not delay, for we must not * Ez 4:22
He will not * the godly to slip Ps 55:22
Will you * a corrupt government Ps 94:20
I will not * conceit and pride. Ps 101:5
would never again * the waters of a Is 54:9
"Do you * divorce?" Mt 19:3
asked him, "Do you * divorce?" Mk 10:2
justice will not * him to live!" Act 28:4
his law must be changed to * it. Heb 7:12,13,14
store without the * of that mark, Rev 13:17

PERMITS
Reliable communication * Pro 13:17
they said, "that * no petitions to Dan 6:12
and * me to tell it to everyone. Tit 1:3

PERMITTED
But God has not * him to do me Gen 31:7
not going to be * to marry Shelah, Gen 38:14
that the people be * to leave. Ex 6:13
people are * to come up into the Ex 24:2
for no yeast or honey is * in Lev 2:11
"If an animal which you are * to Lev 11:39
birds of a kind * for food, and Lev 14:4
or bird of a kind * for food, must Lev 17:13
of Aaron—he is not * to offer the Lev 21:21
and no heavy work is *. Lev 23:36
The Levites are not * to sell Lev 25:34
not a kind that is * as a Lev 27:11,12
Only the priests are * to blow Num 10:8
(son of Nun) are * to enter it. Num 14:30
the killer shall be * to stay in Num 35:25
"No prostitutes are * in Israel, Deu 23:17,18
so he immediately * the Philistines Ju 10:7,8
sister Tamar be * to come and cook 2Sa 13:6
be * to give anything to you? 1Ch 29:14
them and they were * to eat the 2Ch 30:17,18,19
for you have * a few of us to Ez 9:8
be * to worship at the Temple. Neh 13:1
* to enter in mourning clothes. Est 4:2
many nations and * him to trample Is 41:2
were * to go without veils. Is 47:2f
of Babylon will be * to stay in Jer 27:11
and said, "We are * to attack them Jer 50:7
Yet God * it because of the sins Lam 4:13
bread * to the priests alone. Mt 12:4
only they were * to understand Mt 13:11
* to eat the crumbs that fall." Mt 15:27
He replied, "You are * to know Mk 4:11,12
So that other disciple was * into Jn 18:15
In bygone days he * the nations Act 14:16
a Greek [and hadn't * this before Act 16:3
return to Ephesus later if God *; Act 18:21
in Rome, Paul was * to live Act 28:16
is eager to leave, it is *. 1Co 7:15
Should they be * to do so? 1Co 7:25
They are * to pray and prophesy 1Co 14:34f
wouldn't even be * to be a priest, Heb 8:4
God * him to reveal these things Rev 1:1
dead was * to open and read it. Rev 5:3
Literally, "It was * to fight Rev 13:7f
He was * to give breath to this Rev 13:15
She is * to wear the cleanest Rev 19:8
Nothing evil will be * in it—no Rev 21:27

PERMITTING
a City of Refuge, * him to return Num 35:32
of Israel by * the Sabbath to be Neh 13:18
* wrong to defeat right? Ps 94:20
Obviously, Paul is not here * 1Co 6:12f
you: You are * that woman Jezebel, Rev 2:20

PERPETRATED
Or, "and great indignities were * Dan 8:12f

PERPETUAL
"This shall be a * daily Ex 29:42
This law is a * covenant and Ex 31:16
This is a * law. Lev 6:22,23
Jehovah will send * plagues upon Deu 28:58,59
consecrating her to * virginity. Ju 11:39f
shut tight, the * flame has been 2Ch 29:7
of the world by * decrees, so that Jer 5:22
said, "becomes a * spring within Jn 4:14

PERPLEXED
the herds stand * for there is no Joe 1:18
be in turmoil, * by the roaring Lk 21:25
They stood there amazed and *. Act 2:12
Peter was very *. Act 10:17
I was * as to how to decide a Act 25:20
We are * because we don't know 2Co 4:8

PERPLEXING
one of life's most * problems: Ps 49:4

PERSECUTE
those who hate you and * you. Deu 30:7,8
Why must you * me as God does? Job 19:22
* me with great power and effect. Job 30:21
men who viciously * the poor. Ps 10:2
But my enemies * with vigor, and Ps 38:19
For they * the one you have Ps 69:26
before you punish those who * me? Ps 119:84
will surely help those they *; Ps 140:12
all who * me, but give me peace. Jer 17:18
Pray for those who * you! Mt 5:44
me, naturally they will * you. Jn 15:20
The people of the world will * Jn 15:21
prophet your ancestors didn't *! Act 7:52

PERSECUTED
shot at him and * him, but their Gen 49:23
to others, and * those in need, and Ps 109:16
Great men have * me, though they Ps 119:161
* FROM MY earliest youth (Israel Ps 129:1
You * my people with unceasing Is 14:6
There is no rest, for those she * Lam 1:3
them, for they * the priests and Lam 4:16
Happy are those who are * Mt 5:10
"When you are reviled and * and Mt 5:11
the ancient prophets were * too. Mt 5:12
"When you are * in one city, Mt 10:23
So since they * me, naturally Jn 15:20
"Isn't this the same man who * Act 9:21
And I * the Christians, hounding Act 22:4
Holy Spirit are * now by those who Gal 4:29
* by Ishmael the slave-wife's son. Gal 4:29
that, I would be * no more—for that Gal 5:11
The fact that I am still being * Gal 5:11
Yes, so much so that I greatly * Php 3:6
and now they have brutally * us 1Th 2:15
You will be * for 'ten days.' Rev 2:10
down to earth, he * the woman who Rev 12:13

PERSECUTING
he will stop * you and your god. 1Sa 6:4,5
you should spend your time * him? Job 7:17
"How dare you go on * me, as Job 19:28
They are * me because I have Jer 15:15
Why are you * me?" Act 9:4
"I am Jesus, the one you are *! Act 9:5
'Saul, Saul, why are you * me?' Act 22:7
of Nazareth, the one you are *.' Act 22:8
'Saul, Saul, why are you * me? Act 26:14
'I am Jesus, the one you are *. Act 26:15

PERSECUTION
the saints with *, and try to Dan 7:25

(PERSECUTION Con't)
trouble comes, or * begins because Mt 13:21
For there will be * such as the Mt 24:21
"Immediately after the * of Mt 24:29
as soon as * begins, they wilt. Mk 4:17
but when the hot winds of * blow, Lk 8:13
a time of special *, and you will Lk 21:12
And a great wave of * of the Act 8:1
who braved the *, or whether they Act 8:2f
cooperation in the * of any Act 9:2
during the * after Stephen's death Act 11:19
spite of all the *, reminding them Act 14:22
and avoid the * they would get if Gal 6:12
in Judea did, * from your own 1Th 2:14
me despite the *, therefore I will Rev 3:10
every trial and *, for they are his Rev 14:12
Verse 12 implies death from * Rev 14:13f

PERSECUTIONS
keep right on with all their *. Jer 15:17,18
be purified by great trials and *. Dan 12:10
children, and land—with *! Mk 10:30
and hardships, * and difficulties; 2Co 12:10

PERSECUTORS
Lord my God, to save me from my *. Ps 7:1
Rescue me from my *, for they are Ps 142:6

PERSIA
kingdom of * conquered Babylon. 2Ch 36:20
of King Cyrus of *, the Lord 2Ch 36:22,23
of King Cyrus of *, the Lord Ez 1:1
"Cyrus, King of *, hereby Ez 1:2
who chose to remain in * gave Ez 1:6
the treasurer of *, to present Ez 1:8
of the reign of King Darius of *. Ez 4:24
and Ar-ta-xerxes, the kings of *. Ez 6:14
reign of King Ar-ta-xerxes of *: Ez 7:1
instead you caused the kings of * Ez 9:9
reign of King Ar-ta-xerxes of *, Neh 1:1
of King Darius of *, in the days of Neh 12:22
of the Kings of Media and *. Est 10:2
Doubtless Cyrus the Great of *. Is 41:2f
saw are the kings of Media and *; Dan 8:20
of Cyrus, king of *, Daniel (also Dan 10:1
who overrules the kingdom of * Dan 10:13
Literally, "the prince of *." Dan 10:13f
through these spirit rulers of *. Dan 10:13
my way back, past the prince of *; Dan 10:20,21

PERSIAN
at the mouth of the * Gulf. Gen 11:2f
this time from the * cities of Ez 2:59
that time from the * cities of Neh 7:61
times as well as * law and justice, Est 1:13-15
"throwing dice" in * is "pur." Est 9:26
was accomplished by later * kings. Jer 51:26f
with Darius the *, mentioned in Dan 5:31f
and in the reign of Cyrus the *. Dan 6:28
Three more * kings will reign, to Dan 11:2
Babylon and the * Gulf, who began Hab 1:6f

PERSIANS
local leaders, the *, the Ez 4:8,9
of the Medes and * that can never Est 1:19
famed "law of the Medes and *." Est 8:8f
The city fell to the Medes and *, Is 21:6,7f
and given to the Medes and *." Dan 5:28
and *' that cannot be revoked." Dan 6:8
of the Medes and *,' that cannot be Dan 6:12

PERSIS
and to dear *, who has worked so Rom 16:12

PERSISTED
But Aaron and Moses *. Ex 5:3
But David *. 1Sa 17:34
David *. 1Sa 23:12

PERSISTENCE
you want—just because of your *. Lk 11:8

PERSON
And man became a living *. Gen 2:7
a way that the two become one *. Gen 2:24
"But I'm not the * for a job Ex 3:11
but no uncircumcised * shall ever Ex 12:48
for each * in his home." Ex 16:16
never let an innocent * be put to Ex 23:7
A bribe hurts the cause of the * Ex 23:8
upon an ordinary *, and you shall Ex 30:32
for the Lord. The * bringing it is Lev 1:4
the Lord, and the * who eats it Lev 7:17,18
by a * who is ceremonially clean. Lev 7:19
a * whose leprosy disappears: Lev 14:1
* being cleansed from his leprosy; Lev 14:19
his hands, that * must wash his Lev 15:11
Afterwards, the * doing the Lev 16:28
whether a * is poor or rich; Lev 19:15
cut that * off from his people. Lev 20:6
by touching a dead *, unless it is Lev 21:1
himself as an ordinary * can. Lev 21:4
*—not even his father or mother. Lev 21:11
who touches a dead *, or who is Lev 22:4
Israelite or other * living among Lev 22:17,18
Israel that when a * makes a Lev 27:1
But if the * is too poor to pay Lev 27:8
been defiled by touching a dead *. Num 5:1
it to the * he took it from. Num 5:7
But if the * he wronged is dead, Num 5:8
no unauthorized *—no one who is not Num 16:40
Anyone who touches a dead * and Num 19:13
Then a * who is not defiled Num 19:18
then the defiled * must wash his Num 19:19
And anything a defiled * touches Num 19:22
Not one * in this entire census Num 26:64,65
not be broken: the * making the vow Num 30:1
of Refuge where a * who has Num 35:6
no man shall die with only one * Num 35:30
He vowed that not one * in that Deu 1:34,35
not spare that * from the penalty; Deu 13:8
a bribe to kill an innocent *.' Deu 27:25
Ai until the last * was dead. Jos 8:26
Not one * in the entire city was Jos 10:28
Every last * was slaughtered, Jos 10:30
Not one * was left alive. Jos 10:37
Every * there was killed and Jos 11:11
peace, the first * coming out of Ju 11:30,31
knows what a wonderful * you are. Ru 3:11
feel and act like a different *. 1Sa 10:6
They didn't leave one * alive in 1Sa 27:9
such an insignificant * as I am? 2Sa 7:18
the very first * in all the tribe 2Sa 19:20
THE FAMILY TREE of every * in 1Ch 9:1
then he gave every * present 1Ch 16:3
* entering the Temple. 2Ch 23:7
is the very * who destroyed all the 2Ch 32:12
and innocent * who was punished? Job 4:7,8
I am not some * of renown to make Job 33:7
cannot really be a good * at all. Ps 14:1
Be sure you know a * well before Pro 11:15
Only the * involved can know his Pro 14:10
Being happy-go-lucky around a * Pro 25:20
gift from God. The * who does that Ecc 5:19,20
that the swiftest * does not always Ecc 9:11
If a * lives to be very old, let Ecc 11:8
a * left—and the whole country is Is 6:11
know it was a * standing there. Is 52:14,15
When a * falls, he jumps up again; Jer 8:4,5
can give to each * his right Jer 17:10
and upon every * living in it; Jer 26:15
his own sins—the * eating sour Jer 31:30
the Edomites the * of my choice. Jer 49:19
The righteous * will be rewarded Eze 18:20
the wicked * for his wickedness. Eze 18:20
But if a wicked * turns away Eze 18:21
However, if a righteous * turns Eze 18:24
And if a wicked * turns away Eze 18:27
if a * keeps them, he shall live. Eze 20:21
repent—that wicked * will die in Eze 33:8
presence of a dead *, unless it is Eze 44:25
than any living * that I know this Dan 2:30
decree, that any * of any nation, Dan 3:29
before me stood a * robed in linen Dan 10:5,6
How can such a * as I even talk Dan 10:17
touches a dead *, and so becomes Hag 2:13
of you became one * in his sight. Mal 2:15
the way to identify a tree or a * Mt 7:20
more valuable is a * than a sheep! Mt 12:12
the heart of a * who hears the Good Mt 13:19
each * according to his deeds. Mt 16:27
* more, not even outside the door. Mk 2:2
and the first * who saw him was Mk 16:9
They told him what a wonderful * Lk 7:4
it returns to the * it left, and Lk 11:24
But empty, since the * is neutral Lk 11:25f
some person's God means that * is Lk 20:37,38
must be the only * in Jerusalem who Lk 24:18
—the very * Moses and the prophets Jn 1:45
and the first * to step down into Jn 5:4
The true Bread is a *—the one Jn 6:33
who sent him is a good and true *. Jn 7:18
for we know Jesus is an evil *." Jn 9:24
is shown when a * lays down his Jn 15:13
Barnabas was a kindly *, full of Act 11:24
resurrection of a * who had been Act 17:32
is a gift; if a * could earn it by Rom 4:4,5
brothers in Christ, that when a * Rom 7:1
when Christ did, and are a new *. Rom 7:4
For Moses wrote that if a * could Rom 10:5
new and different * with a fresh Rom 12:2
So is the * who eats meat that Rom 14:6
And the * who won't touch such Rom 14:6
He was the very first * to become Rom 16:5
like, except that * himself. 1Co 2:11
your hearts. The * who does the 1Co 3:7
that if even one * is allowed to go 1Co 5:6
cancer—this wicked *—from among 1Co 5:7
even eat lunch with such a *. 1Co 5:11
in his sight the two become one *. 1Co 6:16
are joined together as one *. 1Co 6:17
Usually a * should keep on with 1Co 7:20
situation a * is in when he becomes 1Co 7:24
best for a * to remain unmarried. 1Co 7:26
So the * who marries does well, 1Co 7:38
does well, and the * who doesn't 1Co 7:38
But the * who truly loves God is 1Co 8:3
Yes, whatever a * is like, I try 1Co 9:22
but only one * gets first prize. 1Co 9:24
To one * the Spirit gives the 1Co 12:8
Still another * is able to speak 1Co 12:10
So a * "speaking in tongues" 1Co 14
if you talk to a * in some language 1Co 14
mean nothing. A * talking to me in 1Co 14:
Even so, if an unsaved *, or 1Co 14:2
and an unsaved * or a new 1Co 14:2
Remember that a * who has a 1Co 14:3
love the Lord, that * is cursed. 1Co 16:2
is true, I am not that sort of *. 2Co 1:1
he becomes a brand new * inside. 2Co 5:1
from no less a * than Jesus Christ Gal 1:1
But it takes only one wrong * Gal 5:
God will deal with that *, Gal 5:1
*, and at last there was peace. Eph 2:1
and different *, holy and good. Eph 4:2
for a greedy * is really an idol Eph 5:
for this world as a dead * does. Col 3:
Whether a * has Christ is what Col 3:1
Such a * is worse than the 1Ti 5:
his," and "A * who calls himself 2Ti 2:1
me that I am not that kind of *. 2Ti 3:1
A * who is pure of heart sees Tit 1:1
but a * whose own heart is evil Tit 1:1
a * has a wrong sense of values. Tit 3:1
And when a * is still living on Heb 5:12,1
everyone knows, a * who has the Heb 7:
greater than the * he blesses. Heb 7:
the * who wrote the will is dead. Heb 9:16
the death of the * who wrote it. Heb 9:17
For if a * just listens and Jas 1:2
And the * who keeps every law of Jas 2:10
as guilty as the * who has broken Jas 2:10
Truth again, that * who brings him Jas 5:20
And when a * has escaped from 2Pe 2:20
Such a * is antichrist, for he 1Jn 2:22
For a * who doesn't believe in 1Jn 2:23
of the devil. The * who has been 1Jn 3:9
But a * who doesn't have love for 1Jn 3:14
But if a * isn't loving and 1Jn 4:8
it is unclear whether this * is Rev 9:1f

PERSON'S
of Levi, indicating each * clan; Num 3:14,15
be, "He had been that * God." Lk 20:37,38f
some * God means that person is Lk 20:37,38
a * evil thoughts and desires. Col 2:23

PERSONAL
a member of the * staff of Pharaoh, Gen 39:1
stealing my lord's * silver Gen 44:5
(The soldiers had also kept * Num 31:53
receive as his * inheritance some Deu 1:36
will send his * curse upon you. Deu 28:20
For Israel was God's own * Deu 32:9
consecrated him as his * priest. Ju 17:12
and that he was his * priest. Ju 18:4
But you have put aside your * Ru 3:10
use your animals for his * gain. 1Sa 8:16
"If you are, you shall be my * 1Sa 28:2
them under his * command, and took 2Sa 10:9
Ira the Jairite was David's * 2Sa 20:26
Solomon is to ride on my * mule, 1Ki 1:33
* priest and special friend; 1Ki 4:1
* friends, and private chaplains. 2Ki 10:11
to care for their * needs. 2Ki 12:8
"will be only for my * use." 2Ki 16:15
to Gad, David's * prophet, "Go 1Ch 21:9
the Archite was his * advisor. 1Ch 27:33
These * contributions consist of 1Ch 29:4,5
haven't asked for * wealth and 2Ch 1:11
He also made a * contribution of 2Ch 31:3
and Asaiah, the king's * aide. 2Ch 34:20
who were his * aides—Mehuman, Est 1:10
They were his * friends as well Est 1:13-15
garden, and are under his * care. Ps 92:13
chosen Israel as his * possession. Ps 135:4
Then he sent his * Is 36:2
my people as the * confirmation of Is 42:6
they will be under my * care." Zec 10:12
God's * expression of himself to Jn 1:1f
God's * expression of himself to Jn 1:14f
one of his * bodyguard, and told Act 10:7
show you from our * experience how 2Co 1:6,7
This time my * presence is 2Co 10:11
he will have the * satisfaction of Gal 6:4

PERSONALITIES
of semantics and * and your silly Act 18:15

PERSONALLY
its terms. You * and all your Gen 17:9,10
bring it * with his own hands. Lev 7:29
I, even I, will * smite you seven Lev 26:24
and I myself will * bless them." Num 6:27
one of Moses' * chosen assistants, Num 11:28
the priests, shall * handle all the Num 18:7
The avenger of his death shall * Num 35:19
that he * brought you out from Deu 4:37
He will deal with them *. Deu 7:10
the Lord your God * cares for! Deu 11:12
I will * deal with anyone who Deu 18:19
old men who had * witnessed the Jos 24:31
nation went * to her and demanded Ju 16:5
"These are all yours *, as your 1Sa 30:20
was happening, he * led the Israeli 2Sa 10:17
And I think that you should * 2Sa 17:11

PERSONALLY Con't)
Solomon than he has blessed you *! 1Ki 1:46,47
Then Jehovah will hold him * 1Ki 2:32
River, led * by Shophach, King 1Ch 19:16
God who talked * to my father David 2Ch 6:4
* burning incense upon the altar. 2Ch 26:16
He went out * to watch as the 2Ch 34:4
us, and will * select his choicest Ps 47:4
For the God above all gods will * Ps 87:5
heaven and earth will * bless you! Ps 115:15
he was afflicted, and he * Is 63:9
enemy and * fought against them. Is 63:10
I the Lord will * deal with anyone Eze 14:4
I the Lord will * punish Eze 14:6,7
I will * free her from her Hos 1:7
in heaven has * revealed this to Mt 16:17
Supreme Court (who * was eagerly Mk 15:42,43
paid * to build us a synagogue!" Lk 7:5
*, or speaking to you directly. Jn 5:37
Remember, each of us will stand * Rom 14:10
friends who have never known me *. Col 2:1
I will pay it back (I, Paul, * Phm 1:19
judges fairly. He * carried the 1Pe 2:24
eternal glory. He * will come and 1Pe 5:10

PERSONNEL
* and told them what had happened. Gen 20:8
and concerning the treasury *. 2Ch 8:15
and all unauthorized *. 2Ch 23:19
who was in charge of his palace *, Dan 1:3,4

PERSONS
These sixteen * were the sons of Gen 46:18
upon the number of * in the Ex 12:21
him, each counseling ten *. Ex 18:21
by unauthorized *, for these Lev 22:15
And even * who are ceremonially Deu 12:20-23
that these * were more important; 1Ch 1:1f
the gifts dedicated by famous *. 1Ch 28:12
So a total of 42,360 * returned Ez 2:64,65
But just * everywhere will judge Eze 23:45
of about 175,000 *—and the Jon 3:3f
for the * my Father selects." Mt 20:23
"And if even sinful * like Lk 11:13
to Egypt, seventy-five * in all. Act 7:14
blood, but against * without Eph 6:12
Such * claim they know God, but Tit 1:16
Yet only eight * were saved from 1Pe 3:20
already many such * have appeared. 1Jn 2:18

PERSPIRE
that would cause them to *. Eze 44:18

PERSUADE
when he tries to * you that the 2Ki 18:31,32
King Hezekiah is trying to * you 2Ch 32:11
And he will * many a Jew to turn Lk 1:16

PERSUADED
and could not be * otherwise, she Ru 1:18
These words of David * his men 1Sa 24:7,8
and I * some of the leaders of Ez 7:28
the fact that you * me to let you Job 2:3
stood with Jeremiah and * the Jer 26:24
Jewish officials * the crowds to Mt 27:20
to starve. He * a local farmer to Lk 15:15
Some who listened were * and Act 17:4
this man Paul has * many, many Act 19:26

PERSUADING
They accused Paul of "* men to Act 18:13
he believed and why, and * many Act 19:8

PERSUASION
Literally, "with little (*)." Act 26:28f

PERSUASIVE
mind comes careful and * speech. Pro 16:23

PERT
She approached him, saucy and *, Pro 7:10

PERTAINS
Literally, "it * unto Jehovah." Lev 7:20f
* to that final event in history. Dan 8:19

PERUDA
Sotai, Hassophereth, *, Jaalah, Ez 2:55,56,57

PERVERSE
Literally, "son of a *, 1Sa 20:30f

PERVERSION
this is a terrible *. Lev 18:23

PERVERT
the street like a common *!" 2Sa 6:20
how they * the truth! Job 17:12
They take bribes to * justice, Is 5:23

PERVERTED
For they have * justice by Amo 2:6

PERVERTS
a gang of sex * gathered around the Ju 19:22
Literally, "as one who * the Lk 23:14f

PESTILENCE
in his awesome power. * marches Hab 3:5

PET
It was his children's * and he 2Sa 12:3
Can you make a * of him like a Job 41:5
each by its * name, and counts them Is 40:26

PETER
called *, and Andrew—out in a boat Mt 4:18
Simon (also called *), Mt 10:2,3,4
Then * called to him: "Sir, if Mt 14:28
So * went over the side of the Mt 14:29
Then * asked Jesus to explain Mt 15:15
Simon * answered, "The Christ, Mt 16:16
You are *, a stone; Mt 16:18
But * took him aside to Mt 16:22
Jesus turned on * and said, "Get Mt 16:23
SIX DAYS LATER Jesus took *, Mt 17:1
talking with him. * blurted out, Mt 17:4
collectors came to * and asked him, Mt 17:24
"Of course he does," * replied. Mt 17:25
asked him, "What do you think, *? Mt 17:25
"Against the foreigners," * Mt 17:26,27
Then * came to him and asked, Mt 18:21
Then * said to him, "We left Mt 19:27
* declared, "If everyone else Mt 26:33
"I would die first!" * Mt 26:35
He took * with him and Zebedee's Mt 26:37
them asleep. "*," he called, Mt 26:40
Meanwhile, * was following far Mt 26:58
Meanwhile, as * was sitting in Mt 26:69
But * denied it loudly. Mt 26:70
Again * denied it, this time with Mt 26:72
* began to curse and swear. Mt 26:74
Then * remembered what Jesus had Mt 26:75
Simon (he renamed him "*"), Mk 3:16-19
home except * and James and John. Mk 5:37
you think I am?" * replied, "You Mk 8:29
* took him aside and chided him. Mk 8:32
Literally, "* began to rebuke Mk 8:32f
and then said to * very sternly, Mk 8:33
Six days later Jesus took *, Mk 9:2
"Teacher, this is wonderful!" * Mk 9:5
Then * began to mention all that Mk 10:28
Then * remembered what Jesus had Mk 11:21
from Jerusalem, *, James, John, and Mk 13:3,4
* said to him, "I will never Mk 14:29
"*," Jesus said, "before the Mk 14:30
"No!" * exploded. Mk 14:31
He took *, James and John with Mk 14:33
It was *. Mk 14:47f
soon gathered. * followed far Mk 14:54
Meanwhile * was below in the Mk 14:66,67
* warming himself at the fire. Mk 14:66,67
* denied it. Mk 14:68
* denied it again. Mk 14:70
began saying to *, "You are, too, Mk 14:70
to his disciples including *: Mk 16:7
When Simon * realized what had Lk 5:8
Simon (he also called him *), Lk 6:14,15,16
Everyone denied it, and * said, Lk 8:45
the room except *, James, John, and Lk 8:51
* replied, "The Messiah—the Lk 9:20
Eight days later he took *, Lk 9:28
* and the others had been very Lk 9:32
starting to leave, *, all confused Lk 9:33
* asked, "Lord, are you talking Lk 12:41
And * said, "We have left our Lk 18:28
Jesus sent * and John ahead to Lk 22:8
But Jesus said, "*, let me tell Lk 22:34
and * followed at a distance. Lk 22:54
warmth, and * joined them there. Lk 22:55
* denied it. Lk 22:57
"No sir, I am not!" * replied. Lk 22:58
But * said, "Man, I don't know Lk 22:60
Jesus turned and looked at *. Lk 22:61
at Peter. Then * remembered what he Lk 22:61
And * walked out of the Lk 22:62
However, * ran to the tomb to Lk 24:12
He appeared to *!" Lk 24:33,34
find his brother * and told him, Jn 1:41
And he brought * to meet Jn 1:42
Jesus looked intently at * for a Jn 1:42
you shall be called *, the rock!" Jn 1:42
Simon * replied, "Master, to Jn 6:68
When he came to Simon *, Peter Jn 13:6
When he came to Simon Peter, * Jn 13:6
"No," * protested, "you shall Jn 13:8
Simon * exclaimed, "Then wash my Jn 13:9
friend, Simon * motioned to me to Jn 13:24
Simon * said, "Master, where are Jn 13:36
Then Simon * drew a sword and Jn 18:10
But Jesus said to *, "Put your Jn 18:11
Simon * followed along behind, Jn 18:15
while * stood outside the gate. Jn 18:16
at the gate, and she let * in. Jn 18:16
The girl asked *, "Aren't you Jn 18:17
it was cold. And * stood there with Jn 18:18
Meanwhile, as Simon * was Jn 18:25
the man whose ear * had cut Jn 18:26
Again * denied it. Jn 18:27
She ran and found Simon * and me Jn 20:2
Literally, "* and the other Jn 20:3,4f
outran * and got there first, Jn 20:3,4
Then Simon * arrived and went on Jn 20:6
A group of us were there—Simon *, Jn 21:2
Simon * said, "I'm going Jn 21:3
said to *, "It is the Lord!" Jn 21:7
At that, Simon * put on his Jn 21:7
So Simon * went out and dragged Jn 21:11
said to Simon *, "Simon, son of Jn 21:15
"Yes," * replied, "You know I Jn 21:15
"Yes, Lord," * said, "you know Jn 21:16
* was grieved at the way Jesus Jn 21:17
* turned around and saw the Jn 21:20
betray you?" * asked Jesus, Jn 21:21
*, John Act 1:14
were present, * stood up and Act 1:15
Then * stepped forward with the Act 2:14
And * replied, "Each one of you Act 2:38
Then * preached a long sermon, Act 2:40
And those who believed * were Act 2:41
* AND JOHN went to the Temple one Act 3:1
every day. As * and John were Act 3:3
and then * said, "Look here!" Act 3:4
But * said, "We don't have any Act 3:6
Then * took the lame man by the Act 3:7,8
was holding tightly to * and John! Act 3:11
* saw his opportunity and Act 3:12
disturbed that * and John were Act 4:2
Then *, filled with the Holy Act 4:8
the boldness of * and John, and Act 4:13
But * and John replied, "You Act 4:19
As soon as they were freed, * and Act 4:23
But * said, "Ananias, Satan has Act 5:3
had happened. * asked her, "Did Act 5:8
And * said, "How could you and Act 5:9
But * and the apostles replied, Act 5:29
they sent down * and John. Act 8:14
Then * and John laid their hands Act 8:17
But * replied, "Your money Act 8:20
in Samaria, * and John returned to Act 8:25
* traveled from place to place to Act 9:32
* said to him, "Aeneas! Act 9:34
But when they learned that * was Act 9:38
for them. But * asked them all to Act 9:40
And when she saw *, she sat up! Act 9:40
in the Lord. And * stayed a long Act 9:43
a man named Simon *, who is staying Act 10:5,6
nearing the city, * went up on the Act 10:9,10
"Never, Lord," * declared, "I Act 10:14
to heaven. * was very perplexed. Act 10:17
was the place where Simon * lived! Act 10:18
Meanwhile, as * was puzzling over Act 10:19
So * went down. Act 10:21
him to send for * to come and tell Act 10:22
So * invited them in and lodged Act 10:23
and close friends to meet *. Act 10:24
to meet Peter. As * entered his Act 10:25
But * said, "Stand up! Act 10:26
* told them, "You know it is Act 10:28
and summon Simon *, who is staying Act 10:32
Then * replied, "I see very Act 10:34
Even as * was saying these Act 10:44
The Jews who came with * were Act 10:45
* asked, "Can anyone object to my Act 10:46,47
But when * arrived back in Act 11:2
Then * told them the whole story. Act 11:4
to Joppa to find Simon *! Act 11:13
he arrested * during the Passover Act 12:3
was to deliver * to the Jews for Act 12:4
angel of the Lord stood beside *! Act 12:7
So * left the cell, following the Act 12:9
* finally realized what had Act 12:11
tell everyone that * was standing Act 12:14
Meanwhile * continued knocking. Act 12:16
What had happened to *? Act 12:18
long discussion, * stood and Act 15:7
"listen to me. * has told you Act 15:14
they are for Apollos or for *; 1Co 1:12
and Apollos and * as your helpers. 1Co 3:22
Lord's brothers do, and as * does? 1Co 9:5
He was seen by * and later by 1Co 15:5
for a visit with *, and stayed Gal 1:18
In fact, when *, James, and Gal 2:7,8,9
Gentiles, just as * had been Gal 2:7,8,9
But when * came to Antioch I had Gal 2:11
Gospel, I said to * in front of all Gal 2:14
FROM: *, JESUS Christ's 1Pe 1:1
See 1 * 3:19, 20. 1Pe 4:6f
to all of you who are in Christ.* 1Pe 5:14
FROM: SIMON *, a servant and 2Pe 1:1
Good-bye.* 2Pe 3:18

PETER'S
When Jesus arrived at * house, Mt 8:14
at Peter's house, * mother-in-law Mt 8:14
Andrew (* brother), Mt 10:2,3,4
What was in * mind is not Mt 17:4f
flashed through * mind: "Before Mk 14:72
men was Andrew, Simon * brother. Jn 1:40
Bethsaida, Andrew and * home town. Jn 1:44
Then Andrew, Simon * brother, Jn 6:8,9
These words of * moved them Act 2:37
so that at least * shadow would Act 5:15
When she recognized * voice, she Act 12:14
too, following * example, though Gal 2:13
by many to be * wife to whom 1Pe 5:13f

PETHA-HAIAH
*, Judah, Eliezer. Ez 10:23

PETHAHIAH
Nineteenth, the group led by *; 1Ch 24:7-18
Hodiah, Shebaniah, and *. Neh 9:5
* (son of Meshezabel, a Neh 11:24

PETHOR
of *, near the Euphrates River. Num 22:5,6

(PETHOR Con't)
from *, Mesopotamia, to curse you. Deu 23:4
PETHUEL
from the Lord to Joel, son of *: Joe 1:1
PETITION
to give a * to Moses, Eleazar the Num 27:1
of Israel with a *: "The Lord Num 36:1
But their * was denied. Ju 11:17
you your *, whatever it is!" 1Sa 1:17
Hannah, the Lord remembered her *; 1Sa 1:19,20
"What is your *, Queen Esther? Est 7:2
Bring your *. Hos 14:2
PETITIONS
"that permits no * to any God or Dan 6:12
Then you will present your * Jn 16:26
PETRA
of *, in the clefts of the rocks. Jer 49:16
*, the city hewn from rocks; Ob 1:1f
five miles east of *, in Edom. Ob 1:8f
PETTING
and saw Isaac * with Rebekah. Gen 26:8
PETTY
the people to obey their * rules.' Mk 7:6,7
PEWS
the reserved * in the synagogue! Mt 23:6
PHANUEL
She was the daughter of *, of the Lk 2:36,37
PHARAOH
to their king, the *, and she was Gen 12:15
"into the household of *." Gen 12:15f
Then * gave Abram many gifts Gen 12:16
Then * called Abram before him Gen 12:18
And * sent them out of the Gen 12:20
of the *—the king of Egypt. Gen 37:36
staff of *, the king of Egypt. Gen 39:1
Within three days * is going to Gen 40:13
and mention me to *, and ask him to Gen 40:14
bakery goods for *, but the birds Gen 40:17
"Three days from now * will take Gen 40:18,19
ONE NIGHT TWO years later, * Gen 41:1
At which point, * woke up! Gen 41:4
heads! Then * woke up again and Gen 41:7
* sent at once for Joseph. Gen 41:14
of clothes, came in before *. Gen 41:14
"I had a dream last night," * Gen 41:15
So * told him the dream. Gen 41:17
the same thing," Joseph told *. Gen 41:25
farm program. Let * divide Egypt Gen 41:34,35
Or, "Let * appoint officials to Gen 41:34,35f
received by * and his assistants. Gen 41:37
for the job, * said, "Who could do Gen 41:38
Turning to Joseph, * said to Gen 41:39
Then * placed his own signet ring Gen 41:41,42
* also gave Joseph the chariot of Gen 41:43
And * declared to Joseph, "I, Gen 41:44
* gave him a name meaning "He Gen 41:45
Or, "God (or *) says 'He is Gen 41:45f
the presence of *, and began Gen 41:46
They pleaded with * for food, and Gen 41:55
by the life of * that you are not Gen 42:15
as though you were * himself. Gen 44:18
me a counselor to *, and manager of Gen 45:8
The news soon reached * Gen 45:16
have come"; and * was very happy Gen 45:16
Then * said to Joseph, "Tell Gen 45:17
Tell them, '* will assign to you Gen 45:18
So Joseph gave them wagons, as * Gen 45:21
wagons * had provided for them. Gen 46:5
"I'll go and tell * that you are Gen 46:31
So when * calls for you and Gen 46:33
ARRIVAL, Joseph went in to see *. Gen 47:1
with him, and presented them to *. Gen 47:2
* asked them, "What is your Gen 47:3
And * said to Joseph, "Choose Gen 47:5,6
brought his father Jacob to *. Gen 47:7
And Jacob blessed *. Gen 47:7
"How old are you?" * asked him. Gen 47:8
Then Jacob blessed * again Gen 47:10
brothers, just as * had commanded. Gen 47:11
land and we will be serfs to *. Gen 47:19
all the land of Egypt for *; Gen 47:20
from * and didn't need to sell. Gen 47:22
bought you and your land for *. Gen 47:23
everything you get belongs to *. Gen 47:24
will gladly be the serfs of *." Gen 47:25
still the law—that * should have as Gen 47:26
them to speak to * on his behalf. Gen 50:4
* agreed. "Go and bury your Gen 50:6
Then *, the king of Egypt, Ex 1:15,16
Then * commanded all of his Ex 1:22
And sure enough, when * heard Ex 2:15
Now I am going to send you to *, Ex 3:10
you are to go to * and do the Ex 4:21
miracles they must do before *. Ex 4:28
Moses and Aaron went to see *. Ex 5:1
retorted *. Ex 5:2
"Who do you think you are," * Ex 5:4,5
That same day * sent this Ex 5:6
the people: "* has given orders to Ex 5:10,11
These foremen went to * and Ex 5:15
But * replied, "You don't have Ex 5:17
with *, they swore at them. Ex 5:20
us stink before * and his people," Ex 5:21
Ever since I gave * your Ex 5:23
do to *," the Lord told Moses. Ex 6:1
"Go back again to * and tell him Ex 6:11
how can I expect * to? Ex 6:12
of Israel and to *, king of Egypt, Ex 6:13
and who went to * to ask Ex 6:27
Go in and give * the message I Ex 6:28,29
I'm no speaker—why should * Ex 6:30
my ambassador to *, and your Ex 7:1
announce it to *, demanding that Ex 7:2
But I will cause * to stubbornly Ex 7:3
Yet even then * won't listen to Ex 7:4
of their confrontation with *. Ex 7:7
and Aaron, "* will demand that Ex 7:9
went in to see *, and performed the Ex 7:10
his rod before * and his court, and Ex 7:10
Then * called in his Ex 7:11
said, "go back to * in the Ex 7:15
commanded them. As * and all of his Ex 7:20
"Go in again to * and tell him, Ex 8:1
Then * summoned Moses and Aaron Ex 8:8
"Do it tomorrow," * said. Ex 8:10
the presence of *, and Moses Ex 8:12
But when * saw that the frogs Ex 8:15
of God," they exclaimed to *. Ex 8:19
morning and meet * as he comes out Ex 8:20
* hastily summoned Moses and Ex 8:25
"All right, go ahead," * Ex 8:28
So Moses went out from * and Ex 8:30
one remained. But * hardened his Ex 8:31,32
"GO BACK TO *," the Lord Ex 9:1
was even sick. * sent to see Ex 9:7
Moses, toss it into the sky as * Ex 9:8
ashes from the kiln and went to *; Ex 9:10
But Jehovah hardened * in his Ex 9:12
and stand before * and tell him, Ex 9:13
Then * sent for Moses and Aaron. Ex 9:27
So Moses left * and went out of Ex 9:33
When * saw this, he and his Ex 9:34
had promised; so * refused to let Ex 9:35
again and make your demand upon *; Ex 10:1
audience with * and told him: Ex 10:3
The court officials now came to * Ex 10:7
and Aaron were brought back to *. Ex 10:8
your little ones!" * retorted. Ex 10:10
Then * sent an urgent call for Ex 10:16
So Moses went out from * and Ex 10:18
Then * called for Moses and said, Ex 10:24
you again," * shouted at Moses. Ex 10:28
more disaster on * and his land, Ex 11:1
Now Moses announced to *, Ex 11:4
oldest child of *, heir to his Ex 11:5
Literally, "he went out from *." Ex 11:8f
The Lord had told Moses, "* Ex 11:9
Then * and his officials and all Ex 12:30
And * summoned Moses and Aaron Ex 12:31
from our slavery. * wouldn't let Ex 13:15
So at last * let the people go. Ex 13:17,18
the shore. For * will think, Ex 14:3
and glory over * and all his Ex 14:4
* and his staff became bold again. Ex 14:5
they asked. So * led the chase Ex 14:6
get in defeating * and all his Ex 14:17
And of all the army of * that Ex 14:28
The horses of *, his horsemen, Ex 15:19
me from the sword of *"). Ex 18:4
Lord had done to * and the Ex 18:8
from *, and has rescued Israel. Ex 18:10
Egypt and * and all his people. Deu 6:22
to * and to all the land of Egypt. Deu 7:18
Egypt against * and all his land. Deu 11:3
Lord brought upon * and his people Deu 29:2,3
wonders before * and his entire Deu 34:11,12
as * and the Egyptians were. 1Sa 6:6
SOLOMON MADE AN alliance with *, 1Ki 3:1
* had given them homes and 1Ki 11:16,17,18
dead, he asked * for permission to 1Ki 11:21
"Why?" * asked him. 1Ki 11:22
The Egyptian * is totally 2Ki 18:20,21
the money that the * had demanded. 2Ki 23:35
(The Egyptian * never returned 2Ki 24:7
miracles against * and his people, Neh 9:10
Egypt before * and all his people. Ps 135:9
Will they dare tell * about the Is 19:11
to your "wise counselors," O *? Is 19:12
trust in * for his protection. Is 30:2
But in trusting *, you will be Is 30:3
I went to Egypt, and * and his Jer 25:19,20
When the army of * Hophra of Jer 37:5
you here: I will turn * Hophra, Jer 44:30
* Hophra was killed by Amasis, one Jer 44:30f
of Carchemish when * Necho, king of Jer 46:2
Rename * Hophra and call him Jer 46:17
I will punish * too, and all who Jer 46:25
and broke. * and all his mighty Eze 17:17
* her king and all her people. Eze 29:2
I am your enemy, *, king of Eze 29:3
When * Hophra sent an army to Eze 30:21f
of *, king of Egypt, and it has Eze 30:21
says, I am against *, king of Eze 30:2
But I will break the arms of *, Eze 30:2
of * fall useless to his sides. Eze 30:2
"Son of dust, tell *, king of Eze 31:2,
This is the fate of * and all his Eze 31:1
"Son of dust, mourn for *, king Eze 32:
"When * arrives, he will be Eze 32:3
the living. And * and his army Eze 32:3
him favor before *, king of Egypt. Act 7:1
wisdom, so that * appointed him Act 7:1
and they were introduced to *. Act 7:1
*, king of Egypt, was an example Rom 9:1
PHARAOH-NECO
* jailed him at Riblah in Hamath 2Ki 23:3
PHARAOH'S
plague upon * household on account Gen 12:1
I was holding * wine cup in my Gen 40:1
* birthday came three days later, Gen 40:2
had predicted. * wine taster, Gen 40:2
was quickly carried to * palace. Gen 45:
the money to * treasure-houses. Gen 47:14
of Egypt were in * possession. Gen 47:1
And the land became *. Gen 47:2
people of Egypt became * serfs. Gen 47:2
Joseph approached * staff and Gen 50:4
a great number of * counselors and Gen 50:7
A princess, one of * daughters, Ex 2:5
their serpents! * heart was still Ex 7:13
out to Moses, that * heart had been Ex 7:14
into blood; so * heart remained Ex 7:22
to Pharaoh. But * heart was hard Ex 8:19
swarms of flies in * palace and in Ex 8:24
And they were driven out from * Ex 10:11
But the Lord hardened * heart Ex 10:20
So the Lord hardened * heart and Ex 10:27
and was revered by * officials and Ex 11:3
right before * eyes, the Lord Ex 11:10
of Egypt, from * oldest son to the Ex 12:29
And once again I will harden * Ex 14:4
Egypt with them. * entire Ex 14:9
* horses, chariots, and horsemen. Ex 14:23
He has overthrown * chariots and Ex 15:4
you must tell him, 'We were * Deu 6:21
for * daughter—one of his wives. 1Ki 7:8
King Solomon moved * daughter 1Ki 9:24
Hadad became one of * closest 1Ki 11:19
* palace among Pharaoh's own sons. 1Ki 11:20
Pharaoh's palace among * own sons. 1Ki 11:20
his wife (she was * daughter) from 2Ch 8:11
but drowned * army in the sea, for Ps 136:15
my mare harnessed to * chariot." Sol 1:9f
What are the * promises worth? Is 36:5
to happen, that * army, though it Jer 37:7
to engage * army in battle, Jer 37:11
at the entrance of * palace here in Jer 43:9
to abandon him, * daughter found Act 7:21
PHARISEE
When Jesus' host, a *, saw what Lk 7:39
"Simon," he said to the *, "I Lk 7:40
One was a proud, self-righteous * Lk 18:10
The proud * 'prayed' this Lk 18:11
not the *, returned home forgiven! Lk 18:14
But one of their members, a * Act 5:34
am a *, as were all my ancestors! Act 23:6
PHARISEES
But when he saw many * Mt 3:7
is greater than that of the * and Mt 5:20
The * were indignant. Mt 9:11
fast as we do and as the * do?" Mt 9:14
But the * said, "The reason he Mt 9:34
But some * saw them do it and Mt 12:2
a man with a deformed hand. The * Mt 12:10
Then the * called a meeting to Mt 12:14
But when the * heard about the Mt 12:24
including some *, came to Jesus Mt 12:38
SOME * AND other Jewish leaders Mt 15:1
offended the * by that remark." Mt 15:12
ONE DAY THE * and Sadducees Mt 16:1
"beware of the yeast of the * Mt 16:6
the yeast of the * and Sadducees.' Mt 16:11
teaching of the * and Sadducees. Mt 16:12
Some * came to interview him, Mt 19:3
Then the * met together to try to Mt 22:15
by his answers— but not the *! Mt 22:34,35
Then, surrounded by the *, he Mt 22:41
leaders and these * were Moses, the Mt 23:2
"Woe to you, *, and you other Mt 23:13,14
"Yes, woe upon you, *, and you Mt 23:23
"Woe to you, *, and you Mt 23:25
Blind *! Mt 23:26
"Woe to you, *, and you Mt 23:27
"Yes, woe to you, *, and you Mt 23:29,30
—the chief priests and * went to Mt 27:62
Literally, "the scribes of the * Mk 2:16f
At once the * Mk 3:6
The * were a religious sect of the Mk 3:6f
(For the Jews, especially the *, Mk 7:3
of King Herod and of the *." Mk 8:15
Some * came and asked him, "Do Mk 10:2
Literally, "* and Herodians." Mk 12:13f
Literally, "*." Lk 5:17f

'HARISEES Con't)
the * and teachers of the Law Lk 5:21
But the * and teachers of the Law Lk 5:30
so do the disciples of the *. Lk 5:33
But some * said, "That's Lk 6:2
of the Law and the * watched Lk 6:7
Then Jesus said to the * and Lk 6:9
All, that is, except the * and Lk 7:30
One of the * asked Jesus to come Lk 7:36
As he was speaking, one of the * Lk 11:37,38
Then Jesus said to him, "You * Lk 11:39
"But woe to you *! Lk 11:42
"Woe to you *! Lk 11:43
The * and legal experts were Lk 11:53,54
beware of these * and the way they Lk 12:1
A few minutes later some * said Lk 13:31
Council, the * were watching him Lk 14:1
Jesus said to the * and legal Lk 14:3
The *, who dearly loved their Lk 16:14
to convince the *, to whom he gave Lk 16:31f
One day the * asked Jesus, "When Lk 17:20
But some of the * among the crowd Lk 19:39
Then those who were sent by the * Jn 1:24,25
of the sect of the *, came for an Jn 3:1
WHEN THE LORD knew that the * had Jn 4:1
When the * heard that the crowds Jn 7:32
to the chief priests and *. Jn 7:45
the * mocked. Jn 7:47
* who believes he is the Messiah? Jn 7:48
Jewish leaders and * brought a Jn 8:3
The * replied, "You are Jn 8:13
Then they took the man to the *. Jn 9:13
Then the * asked him all about Jn 9:15
Then the * turned on the man who Jn 9:17
The * who were standing there Jn 9:40
But some went away to the * and Jn 11:46
Then the chief priests and * Jn 11:47
chief priests and * had publicly Jn 11:57
Then the * said to each other, Jn 12:19
fear that the * would excommunicate Jn 12:42
The chief priests and * had given Jn 18:3
men who had been * before their Act 15:5
were Sadducees, and part were *! Act 23:6
the middle—the * against the Act 23:7
but the * believe in all of Act 23:8
the strictest of * when it comes to Act 26:5
a member of the * who demand the Php 3:5

PHARPAR
Aren't the Abana River and * 2Ki 5:12

PHI
Fear has gripped the people of * Ex 15:14

PHICOL
Abimelech, and *, commander of his Gen 21:22
Then King Abimelech, and *, Gen 21:32
and also *, his army commander. Gen 26:26

PHILADELPHIA
Sardis, *, and Laodicea." Rev 1:11
of the church in *. Rev 3:7

PHILEMON
See Acts 19:29, 20:4, * 24. Act 27:2f
To: *, our much loved fellow Phm 1:1
for you, dear *, because I keep Phm 1:4

PHILETUS
Hymenaeus and *, in their love of 2Ti 2:17

PHILIP
*, Bartholomew Mt 10:2,3,4
*, Bartholomew Mk 3:16-19
his brother *, over Iturea and Lk 3:1
*, Bartholomew Lk 6:14,15,16
He found * and told him, "Come Jn 1:43
with me." (* was from Bethsaida, Jn 1:44
* now went off to look for Jn 1:45
see for yourself," * declared. Jn 1:46
the fig tree before * found you." Jn 1:48
Turning to * he asked, "Philip, Jn 6:2-5
Turning to Philip he asked, "*, Jn 6:2-5
(He was testing *, for he Jn 6:6
* replied, "It would take a Jn 6:7
the Passover paid a visit to *, Jn 12:21
to meet Jesus." * told Andrew Jn 12:22
* said, "Sir, show us the Father Jn 14:8
yet know who I am, *, even after Jn 14:9
*, Thomas, Act 1:14
*, Prochorus, Nicanor Act 6:5
News about Jesus! *, for instance, Act 8:5
began following * wherever he went, Act 8:13
But as for *, an angel of the Act 8:26
The Holy Spirit said to *, "Go Act 8:29
* ran over and heard what he was Act 8:30
And he begged * to come up into Act 8:31
The eunuch asked *, "Was Isaiah Act 8:34
So * began with this same Act 8:35
"You can," * answered, "if you Act 8:37
into the water and * baptized him. Act 8:38
Lord caught away *, and the eunuch Act 8:39
Meanwhile, * found himself at Act 8:40
at the home of * the Evangelist, Act 21:8

PHILIP'S
his wife Herodias, his brother * Mt 14:3
Herodias, his brother * wife. Mk 6:17,18
* name was Greek, though he was a Jn 12:21f
But now they believed * message Act 8:12

PHILIPPI
When Jesus came to Caesarea *, he Mt 16:13
out to the villages of Caesarea *. Mk 8:27
and finally reached *, a Roman Act 16:12
we boarded ship at * in northern Act 20:6
the Christians in the city of *. Php 1:1
been treated at * just before we 1Th 2:2

PHILIPPIANS
only you * became my partners in Php 4:15

PHILISTIA
Syria, Sidon, Moab, Ammon and *. Ju 10:6
Gebal, Ammon, Amalek, * and Tyre; Ps 83:7
and Babylonia, * and Tyre, or even Ps 87:4
revenge on me, you cities of *? Joe 3:4

PHILISTINE
And Abraham lived in the * Gen 21:34
the Red Sea to the * coast, and Ex 23:31
noticed a certain * girl, and when Ju 14:1
ONE DAY SAMSON went to the * city Ju 16:1
The five heads of the * nation Ju 16:5
she sent for the five * leaders. Ju 16:18
The * leaders declared a great Ju 16:23,24
The five * leaders were there as Ju 16:27
the * leaders and all the people. Ju 16:30
THE ARK REMAINED in the * country 1Sa 6:1
and the * mayors followed them as 1Sa 6:12
After the five * mayors had 1Sa 6:16
God for the other * cities, both 1Sa 6:18
When the * leaders heard about 1Sa 7:7
rescued them from their * captors. 1Sa 7:14
had destroyed the * garrison and 1Sa 13:3,4
to take them to a * blacksmith. 1Sa 13:20
by a contingent of the * army. 1Sa 13:23
To reach the * garrison, 1Sa 14:4
the entire * army, and even among 1Sa 14:15
drafted into the * army revolted 1Sa 14:21
Then Goliath, a * champion from 1Sa 17:4-7
came out of the * ranks to face the 1Sa 17:4-7
and evening the * giant strutted 1Sa 17:16
Soon the Israeli and * forces 1Sa 17:21
step out from the * troops and 1Sa 17:23
for killing this * and ending his 1Sa 17:26
"Who is this heathen * anyway, 1Sa 17:26
"I'll take care of this *!" 1Sa 17:32
it to this heathen * too, for he 1Sa 17:36
bear will save me from this *!" 1Sa 17:37
and hit the * in the forehead. 1Sa 17:48,49
So David conquered the * giant 1Sa 17:50,51
and plundered the deserted * camp. 1Sa 17:53
Whenever the * army attacked, 1Sa 18:30
of Goliath, the *—the fellow you 1Sa 21:9
and the sword of Goliath the *." 1Sa 22:9,10
to fight the whole * army!" 1Sa 23:3
THE * ARMY now mobilized at Aphek, 1Sa 29:1
As the * captains were leading 1Sa 29:2
But the * commanders demanded, 1Sa 29:3
But the * leaders were angry. 1Sa 29:4
the * army went on to Jezreel. 1Sa 29:11
to his rescue and killed the *. 2Sa 21:17
Once during a * attack, when all 2Sa 23:11,12
at the time, for * marauders had 2Sa 23:14
broke through the * ranks and drew 2Sa 23:16
siege to the * city of Gibbethon. 1Ki 15:27
in attacking the * city of 1Ki 16:15,16
* archers shot and wounded him. 1Ch 10:3
through to the * camp, drew some 1Ch 11:18,19
But as it turned out, the * 1Ch 12:19
lowlands bordering * territory, 1Ch 27:28
in other parts of the * country. 2Ch 26:6
Weep, * cities—you are doomed. Is 14:31
army against the * city of Ashdod Is 20:1
the kings of the * cities: Jer 25:19,20
country, in the * plain and in the Jer 32:44
cities east of the * plain, in all Jer 33:13
shall possess the * plains, and Ob 1:19
Ekron—these * cities, too, will be Zep 2:4

PHILISTINE'S
with the * head still in his hand. 1Sa 17:57

PHILISTINES
whom came the *), and Caphtorim. Gen 10:13,14
Abimelech, king of the *, lived. Gen 26:1
king of the *, looked out of a Gen 26:8
And the * became jealous of him. Gen 26:14
the ones the * had filled after his Gen 26:18
the land of the *, although that Ex 13:17,18
All the land of the *; Jos 13:2-7
Five cities of the *: Jos 13:2-7
The * (five cities), Ju 3:1
He once killed six hundred * with Ju 3:31
permitted the * and the Ammonites Ju 10:7,8
the Ammonites, the *, the Ju 10:11
conquered by the *, who kept them Ju 13:1
to rescue Israel from the *." Ju 13:5
get a wife from these heathen *? Ju 14:3
a trap for the *, who at that time Ju 14:4
the fields of the *, burning the Ju 15:5
the * demanded. Ju 15:6
So the * came and got the girl Ju 15:6
rock of Etam. The * in turn sent a Ju 15:9
And the * replied, "To capture Ju 15:10
"Don't you realize that the * Ju 15:11
*," the men of Judah told him. Ju 15:12,13
at Lehi, the * shouted with glee; Ju 15:14
and killed a thousand * with it. Ju 15:15
the * still controlled the land. Ju 15:20
"Samson! The * are here!" Ju 16:9
"Samson! The * have come to Ju 16:12
"The * have come, Samson!" Ju 16:14
Then she screamed, "The * are Ju 16:20
So the * captured him and gouged Ju 16:21
I may pay back the * for the loss Ju 16:28
"Let me die with the *," he Ju 16:30
TIME Israel was at war with the *. 1Sa 4:1
near Ebenezer, the * at Aphek. 1Sa 4:1
And the * defeated Israel, 1Sa 4:2
the * asked. 1Sa 4:6
have before, O *, or we will become 1Sa 4:9
So the * fought desperately and 1Sa 4:10
THE * TOOK the captured Ark of God 1Sa 5:1
five cities of the * to decide how 1Sa 5:8
Then the * called for their 1Sa 6:2
been sent by the * as a guilt 1Sa 6:17
told them that the * had brought 1Sa 6:21
he will rescue you from the *." 1Sa 7:3
that the * were approaching. 1Sa 7:7
offering, the * arrived for battle, 1Sa 7:10
So the * were subdued and 1Sa 7:13
conquered by the *, were now 1Sa 7:14
He will save them from the *, for 1Sa 9:16
where the garrison of the * is. 1Sa 10:5
and by the * and the king of Moab. 1Sa 12:9
the garrison of the * at Geba. 1Sa 13:3,4
the land of the *, and Saul sounded 1Sa 13:3,4
as far as the * were concerned. 1Sa 13:3,4
at Gilgal. The * recruited a 1Sa 13:5
and that the * were at Michmash, 1Sa 13:11
I said, 'The * are ready to march 1Sa 13:12
but the * stayed at Michmash. 1Sa 13:16
soon left the camp of the *; 1Sa 13:17
days, for the * wouldn't allow them 1Sa 13:19
valley to the garrison of the *." 1Sa 14:1
When the * saw them coming they 1Sa 14:11
and knees, and the * fell back as 1Sa 14:13
vast army of the * began to melt 1Sa 14:16
of the * grew louder and louder. 1Sa 14:19
and found the * killing each other, 1Sa 14:20
saw that the * were running away. 1Sa 14:22
and killed the * all day from 1Sa 14:31
"Let's chase the * all night and 1Sa 14:36
God, "Shall we go after the *? 1Sa 14:37
the army, and the * returned home. 1Sa 14:46
the kings of Zobah, and the *. 1Sa 14:47
the * throughout Saul's lifetime. 1Sa 14:52
THE * NOW mustered their army for 1Sa 17:1
So the * and Israelis faced each 1Sa 17:3
I will represent the *, and you 1Sa 17:8
for Saul's army to fight the *. 1Sa 17:13
When the * saw that their 1Sa 17:50,51
rushed after the *, chasing them as 1Sa 17:52
dead and wounded * were strewn all 1Sa 17:52
out against the * and let them kill 1Sa 18:17
to see him killed by the *!" 1Sa 18:21
I need is one hundred dead *! 1Sa 18:25
hundred foreskins of the *." 1Sa 18:25f
killed two hundred * and presented 1Sa 18:27
troops against the * and 1Sa 19:8
to David that the * were at Keilah 1Sa 23:1
I will help you conquer the *." 1Sa 23:4
slaughtered the * and confiscated 1Sa 23:5
Saul that the * were raiding Israel 1Sa 23:27
chase and returned to fight the *. 1Sa 23:28
battle with the *, he was told that 1Sa 24:1
I'll try my luck among the * 1Sa 27:1
the * for a year and four months. 1Sa 27:7
while he was living among the *. 1Sa 27:11
ABOUT THAT TIME the * mustered 1Sa 28:1
The * set up their camp at 1Sa 28:4
vast army of the *, he was frantic 1Sa 28:5,6
"The * are at war with us, and 1Sa 28:15
destroyed by the * tomorrow, and 1Sa 28:19
the land of the * while the 1Sa 29:11
the * and from the men of Judah. 1Sa 30:16
MEANWHILE THE * had begun the 1Sa 31:1
Mount Gilboa. The * closed in on 1Sa 31:2
* capture me and torture me." 1Sa 31:3,4
and the * lived in them. 1Sa 31:7
The next day when the * went out 1Sa 31:8
heard what the * had done, 1Sa 31:11
Don't tell the *, lest they 2Sa 1:20
with the lives of one hundred *." 2Sa 3:14
my people from the * and from all 2Sa 3:18
When the * heard that David had 2Sa 5:17
stronghold. The * arrived and 2Sa 5:18
which had been abandoned by the *. 2Sa 5:21
But the * returned and again 2Sa 5:22
* all the way from Geba to Gezer. 2Sa 5:25
and humbled the * by conquering 2Sa 8:1
the *, Amalek, and King Hadadezer. 2Sa 8:11,12
saved us from our enemies, the *; 2Sa 19:8,9,10
where the * had impaled them 2Sa 21:12,13,14
Once when the * were at war with 2Sa 21:15

(PHILISTINES Con't)
Later, during a war with the * at 2Sa 21:18
And once when the * and the 2Sa 21:20,21
held back the * that time when the 2Sa 23:9
He killed the * until his hand 2Sa 23:10
of lentils and beat back the *; 2Sa 23:11,12
and the invading * were at the 2Sa 23:13
to the land of the *, and down to 1Ki 4:21
the land of the * for seven years. 2Ki 8:2
He also conquered the * as far 2Ki 18:8
Casluhim (the ancestors of the *). 1Ch 1:11,12
THE * ATTACKED and defeated the 1Ch 10:1
And the * came and lived in them. 1Ch 10:7
When the * went back the next 1Ch 10:8
heard what the * had done to Saul, 1Ch 10:11
against the * at Pas-dammim. 1Ch 11:13
it and slaughtered the *; 1Ch 11:14
of Adullam. The * were camped in 1Ch 11:15
an outpost of the * had occupied 1Ch 11:16
with the * against King Saul. 1Ch 12:19
When the * heard that David was 1Ch 14:8
his army. The * were raiding the 1Ch 14:9
*, but David ordered them burned. 1Ch 14:12
Later the * raided the valley 1Ch 14:13
and he cut down the army of the * 1Ch 14:16
DAVID FINALLY SUBDUED the * and 1Ch 18:1
Moab, Ammon, Amalek, and the *. 1Ch 18:11
The next war was against the * 1Ch 20:4
Sippai, and so the * surrendered. 1Ch 20:4
During another war with the *, 1Ch 20:5
to the land of the * and as far 2Ch 9:26
Even some of the * brought him 2Ch 17:11
Then the Lord stirred up the * 2Ch 21:16
He declared war on the * and 2Ch 26:6
wars against the * but also in his 2Ch 26:7
Meanwhile, the * had invaded the 2Ch 28:17,18
shout in triumph over the *." Ps 60:8
shout in triumph over the *." Ps 108:9
with evil spirits, as the * do. Is 2:6
on the east and the * on the west. Is 9:11,12
Don't rejoice, *, that the king Is 14:29
Then how dismayed the * Is 20:5,6
The * Jer 47:1
concerning the * of Gaza, before Jer 47:1
to overflow the land of the *; Jer 47:2
come when all the * and their Jer 47:4
For the Lord is destroying the *, Jer 47:4
who hate you—the *—and even they Eze 16:27
her neighbors and by all the *. Eze 16:57
says: Because the * have acted Eze 25:15
the land of the *, and I will wipe Eze 25:16
all * left will perish." Amo 1:8
and down to Gath in the *' land. Amo 6:2
I brought the * from Caphtor and Amo 9:7
And woe to you * Zep 2:5
With the *, they were part of a Zep 2:5f
of Ashdod, the rich city of the *. Zec 9:6
as a new clan: the * of Ekron will Zec 9:7

PHILOLOGUS
Give my love to *, Julia, Nereus Rom 16:15

PHILOSOPHERS
some of the Epicurean and Stoic *. Act 17:18

PHILOSOPHIES
and joy with their *, their wrong Col 2:8

PHILOSOPHY
their * and seems wise to them. 1Co 1:22

PHINEAS
continued until * executed those Ps 106:30
(For this good deed * will be Ps 106:31

PHINEHAS
and * was one of his children. Ex 6:25
When * (son of Eleazar and Num 25:7
Then the Lord said to Moses, "* Num 25:10,11
battle by Moses. * (son of Eleazar Num 31:6
*, the son of Eleazar the priest. Jos 22:13
When * the priest and the high Jos 22:30
* replied to them, "Today we Jos 22:31
Then * and the ten ambassadors Jos 22:32
which had been given to his son *. Jos 24:33
in those days. *, the son of Ju 20:27,28
the two sons of Eli—Hophni and *. 1Sa 1:3
and *, to die on the same day! 1Sa 2:34
Hophni and *, the sons of Eli, 1Sa 4:4
and Hophni and * were killed. 1Sa 4:11
Hophni and * were killed too, and 1Sa 4:17
Ahitub was the grandson of * and 1Sa 14:3
*, the father of 1Ch 6:4-15
Eleazar, *, Abishua, 1Ch 6:50-53
the Tabernacle. *, the son of 1Ch 9:20
Abishu-a was the son of *; Ez 7:1
* was the son of Eleazar; Ez 7:1
From the clan of *—Gershom; Ez 8:2-14
Eleazar (son of *), Jozabad (son of Ez 8:33

PHINEHAS'S
When Eli's daughter-in-law, * 1Sa 4:19

PHLEGON
to Asyncritus, *, Hermes, Patrobas, Rom 16:14

PHOEBE
*, A DEAR Christian woman from the Rom 16:1

PHOENICIA
traveled as far as *, Cyprus, and Act 11:19
in the cities of * and Samaria to Act 15:3
for the Syrian province of *. Act 21:2

PHOENICIAN
Their manner of life was *, and Ju 18:7
and occupy the * coastal strip as Ob 1:20

PHOENIX
to *, in order to winter there; Act 27:12
to winter there; * was a good Act 27:12

PHONIES
they are "*" who have fooled 2Co 11:13

PHRASE
It is uncertain whether this * Ps 49:20f
parallel *, "fruit of the land." Is 4:2,3,4f
ancient manuscripts omit this *. Mt 24:36f

PHRASES
some descriptive * apply to a human Eze 28:12f

PHRYGIA
*, Pamphylia, Egypt, the Cyrene Act 2:10
Next they traveled through * and Act 16:6
Galatia and * visiting all the Act 18:23

PHYGELLUS
even * and Hermogenes are gone. 2Ti 1:15

PHYLACTERIES
Literally, "enlarge their *." Mt 23:5f

PHYSICAL
use only a bull with no * defects. Lev 1:2,3
a billy goat without any * defect. Lev 4:23
must be a female without * defect. Lev 4:32
male lambs without * defect, one Lev 14:10
ewe-lamb without * defect, ten Lev 14:10
the Lord because of his * defect. Lev 21:21
altar, because of the * defect; Lev 21:23
—not a * rebirth Jn 1:13
Or, "* birth is not enough. Jn 3:5f
Those born only once, with * Jn 6:63
so I was given a * condition 2Co 12:7
causes * death or spiritual death. 1Jn 5:17f
sometimes ends in * death (1 Cor. 1Jn 5:17f

PHYSICALLY
wealth, but don't harm him *." Job 1:12,13

PHYSICIAN
Is there no * there? Jer 8:22
me that proverb, '*, heal Lk 4:23

PIANOS
more *, saxophones, and trumpets. Rev 18:22

PICK
to her, and to * up the pledges he Gen 38:20
will come and * off your flesh!" Gen 40:18,19
followed by the * of Egypt's Ex 14:7
don't go out to * up food from the Ex 16:28,29
fields, and don't * up stray grains Lev 19:9
vines, and don't * up the grapes Lev 19:10
fields, nor * up the fallen grain; Lev 23:22
Moses said to the Lord, "Why * Num 11:11
He will * a place in the Deu 12:14
if she could * up the grains Ru 2:7
at Aphek. Now * up the other 2Ki 13:18
But what is this? They * on me at Ps 62:3,4
each vine to * what he has missed, Jer 6:9
to * the flesh from their corpses. Jer 12:9
will go out and * up your shields Eze 39:9
"* strong, healthy, good-looking Dan 1:3,4
he commanded, "* up your stretcher Mt 9:5,6
he commanded, "* up your stretcher Mk 2:9,10,11
scraps did you * up afterwards?" Mk 8:19
he commanded, "* up your stretcher Lk 5:23,24
So why * on me for breaking them? Jn 7:19
* on you and drag you into court? Jas 2:6
Can you * olives from a fig Jas 3:12
He personally will come and * you 1Pe 5:10

PICKED
And I have * him out to have Gen 18:19
after they are *, but leave what's Deu 24:21
Then he * up a donkey's jawbone Ju 15:15
Then he * up five smooth stones 1Sa 17:40
Then he * up Elijah's cloak and 2Ki 2:13,14
then * up her son and went out. 2Ki 4:37
So the king * them up and struck 2Ki 13:18
After the battle the Israelis * 1Ch 14:12
of tongs * out a burning coal. Is 6:6
bodies shall be * apart by vultures Jer 16:4
no more will they be * on and Eze 34:22
they scale the walls like * and Joe 2:7
Then they * up Jonah and threw Jon 1:15
And when the scraps were * up Mt 14:20
the scraps were * up, there were Mt 15:37,38
The chief priests * the money Mt 27:6
the birds came and * it off the Mk 4:4
of scraps were * up off the grass! Mk 6:43,44
the scraps were * up after the Mk 8:8,9
to his feet, * up his mat and went Lk 5:25
of scraps were * up afterwards! Lk 9:17
leaders * up stones to kill him. Jn 8:59
Then again the Jewish leaders * Jn 10:31
As Paul * himself up off the Act 9:8,9
A few have—the ones God has * Rom 11:7
the Lord * out to be his very own; Rom 16:13
for God has * me out and given me 1Co 9:17
Then a mighty angel * up a Rev 18:21

PICKER
I am just a herdsman and fruit *. Amo 7:14

PICKING
the heathen, * up their evil ways; Hos 7:
trees without any fruit at * time. Jud 1:1

PICKS
labor with saws, *, and axes and 2Sa 12:3
work with saws, iron *, and axes, 1Ch 20:
on the scales. He * up the islands Is 40:1
a shepherd * fleas from his cloak! Jer 43:1

PICTURE
a * of Jerusalem's walls in ruins. Is 49:1
the long-range * of the city's Jer 51:26
Draw a * of siege mounds being Eze 4:
"Whose * is stamped on it?" Mt 22:2
name is this beneath the *?" Mt 22:2
* and title is this on the coin?" Mk 12:1
before you with a * on it of Christ Gal 3:

PICTURED
the men *, so she sent messengers Eze 23:1

PICTURES
The walls were covered with * of Eze 8:1
(son of Shaphan) worshiping the *. Eze 8:1
with * she saw painted on a wall! Eze 23:14,1
They were * of Babylonian Eze 23:14,1
is what baptism * for us: In 1Pe 3:2

PIECE
Please sell me a * of ground for Gen 23:4
They shall be one * with the Ex 25:19
shall be one *—the base, shaft, Ex 25:31
to be one * of pure, beaten gold. Ex 25:36
mortise into the next upright *. Ex 26:17
bases under each * of the frame. Ex 26:18,19
to make one long *, and six others Ex 36:16
six others to make another long *. Ex 36:16
the golden lid—it was all one *. Ex 37:8
almond flowers were all of one *. Ex 37:17
all one * of pure, beaten gold. Ex 37:22
altar so that it was all one *. Ex 37:25
all of one * with the rest. Ex 38:2
it was a skillful and beautiful * Ex 39:3
The chestpiece was a beautiful * Ex 39:8
It was a * nine inches square, Ex 39:9
they brought the animal to him * Lev 9:13
to him piece by *, including the Lev 9:13
or fabric, or in a * of leather or Lev 13:47,48
strip every last * of fruit from Lev 19:10
as are the rib * and shoulder that Num 6:20
and killed by a * of iron, it must Num 35:16
you even a tiny * of their land. Deu 2:5
gave a special * of land to Joshua, Jos 19:49
* of land. Ju 1:14
one * to each tribe of Israel. Ju 19:29
cut of meat, the * that had been 1Sa 9:23
stand was a round * 1½ feet high. 1Ki 7:31
went into each *) and three hundred 1Ki 10:16,17
a single * of bread in the house. 1Ki 17:12
a * of better land in trade. 1Ki 21:2
on every good * of land, stopped up 2Ki 3:25
them, it was merely a * of bronze. 2Ki 18:4
tank and oxen were cast as one *. 2Ch 4:3
Then Job took a broken * of Job 2:8
one's soul for a * of bread. Pro 28:21
I also observed another * of Ecc 4:7
Not a * will be left large enough Is 30:14
of barley or a * of bread will you Eze 13:19
holy portion. This * shall be 8 Eze 45:1
For they are asking a * of wood Hos 4:12
mouth two legs and a * of ear. Amo 3:12
their debt of a * of silver or a Amo 8:6
You want a certain * of land, or Mic 2:2
He motioned for a * of paper and Lk 1:63
one tears off a * of a new garment Lk 5:36
throwing dice for each *. Lk 23:34
They gave him a * of broiled Lk 24:42
all, and broke off a * and ate it. Act 27:35
So use every * of God's armor to Eph 6:13

PIECES
a thousand silver * as damages for Gen 20:16
"Well, the land is worth 400 * Gen 23:14,15
* of silver, as publicly agreed. Gen 23:16
father, for 100 * of silver. Gen 33:19
to them for twenty * of silver, and Gen 37:28
Joseph is without doubt torn in * Gen 37:33
torn to * by some wild animal; Gen 44:28
and three hundred * of silver! Gen 45:22
the two side *, he will pass over Ex 12:23
It dashes the enemy to *. Ex 15:6
be given thirty * of silver, and Ex 21:32
two long *, one for each side. Ex 26:3
two long * together side by side. Ex 26:4,5
of these two wide *, to join them Ex 26:10,11
It will consist of two *, front Ex 28:7
head and the other * of the body, Ex 29:17
will lay the *, with the head and Lev 1:12
Break it into * and pour oil Lev 2:6
the *, the head and the fat. Lev 8:20
He shall break their bones in *, Num 24:3-9
So I cut her body into twelve * Ju 20:6
and sent the * throughout the land Ju 20:6
and cut them into * and sent 1Sa 11:7
And Samuel chopped him in * 1Sa 15:33
Literally, "Given you ten * of 2Sa 18:11f

IECES Con't)
The total weight of these * was 1Ki 7:47
into two hundred * of armor (gold 1Ki 10:16,17
ten of these *, for the Lord God of 1Ki 11:31
and cut it into * and lay it on the 1Ki 18:23
* and laid the pieces on the wood. 1Ki 18:33
pieces and laid the * on the wood. 1Ki 18:33
scattered the * in Kidron Valley. 2Ki 23:12
he sawed them to * is uncertain. 1Ch 20:3f
slashed them to *, and nailed the 2Ch 28:24
There were also two beautiful * Ez 8:26,27
*, then hung me up as his target. Job 16:12
himself with * of silver." Ps 68:30f
to *. Your enemies are scattered Ps 89:10
thousand * of silver from each. Sol 8:11
have my thousand * of silver and I Sol 8:12
* to those who care for it. Sol 8:12
hammer that smashed the rock to *? Jer 23:29
in * and to destroy many kingdoms. Jer 51:20
and gold; its * were crushed as Dan 2:35
I will rip you to * like a bear Hos 13:8
and small should be smashed to *. Amo 6:11
images will be smashed to *; Mic 1:7
will trample to * many people, and Mic 4:13
divided them into *, and gave them Mt 15:36
"They took the thirty * of Mt 27:9
himself with sharp * of stone. Mk 5:5
Breaking the loaves into *, he Mk 6:41
broke them into * and passed them Mk 8:6
it and broke it in * and gave it to Mk 14:22
then he broke off * for his Lk 9:16
have broken Christ into many *. 1Co 1:13
And when we break off * of the 1Co 10:16
clay that is broken into tiny *. Rev 2:27

IERCE
take an awl and * his ear into the Deu 15:17
nose, or * his jaw with a spike? Job 41:2
Their taunts * me like a fatal Ps 42:10
Suddenly his arrow will * them. Ps 64:7
* your hand if you lean on it. Is 36:6
of Babylon and * her warriors in Jer 51:3
arm and * through his right eye; Zec 11:17
"A sword shall * your soul, for Lk 2:34,35

PIERCED
And * Sisera's temples, Ju 5:26
So the young man * him with his Ju 9:54
the blade, and it * him through. 1Sa 31:3,4
away, so Abner * him through the 2Sa 2:23
and the arrow * his heart, and he 2Ki 9:24
and it * his body. 1Ch 10:4
they have * my hands and feet. Ps 22:16
at the pain of the one you have *. Ps 69:26
You shall be * with sharp arrows Ps 120:4
shall die as those * with many Eze 28:8
look on him they *, and mourn for Zec 12:10
However, one of the soldiers * Jn 19:34
shall look on him whom they *." Jn 19:36,37
* themselves with many sorrows. 1Ti 6:10
see him—yes, and those who * him. Rev 1:7

PIERCES
your weight and * your hand. 2Ki 18:20,21
he * the swiftly gliding serpent. Job 26:13

PIERCING
his own eyes—the * of Jesus—and Rev 1:7f

PIETY
of unusual *, with 200,000 troops. 2Ch 17:16
who pretend * by praying publicly Mt 6:5
with great outward *, they are Lk 20:47

PIG
has vomited, and a * is washed only 2Pe 2:22

PIG'S
a fine gold ring in a * snout. Pro 11:22

PIGEON
and a young *, and to slay them Gen 15:9
and a young * or a turtledove for a Lev 12:6

PIGEONS
either turtle-doves or young *. Lev 1:14
two young * as his guilt offering; Lev 5:7
or young * as his sin offering, Lev 5:11
two turtledoves or two young *. Lev 12:8
or two young *—whichever he is able Lev 14:22
or two young * (whichever pair he Lev 14:30
or two young * and come before the Lev 15:14
or two young * and bring them to Lev 15:29
or two young * to the priest at the Num 6:10
*" was the legal requirement. Lk 2:24

PIGPEN
shall slap you, you whitewashed *. Act 23:3

PIGS
cloven hooves. * may not be eaten Deu 14:8
A herd of * was feeding in the Mt 8:30
send us into that herd of *." Mt 8:31
and entered the *, and the whole Mt 8:32
A herd of * was feeding on the Lk 8:32
him to let them enter into the *. Lk 8:32
and went into the *, and Lk 8:33
farmer to hire him to feed his *. Lk 15:15

PIHA-HIROTH
to turn toward * between Migdol and Ex 14:2
near *, across from Baal-zephon. Ex 14:9

PIHAHIROTH
wilderness), and * (near Num 33:7

PILATE
chains to *, the Roman governor. Mt 27:2
Now Jesus was standing before *, Mt 27:11
they are saying?" * demanded. Mt 27:13
Jesus, your Messiah?" * asked. Mt 27:22
"Why?" * demanded. Mt 27:23
When * saw that he wasn't getting Mt 27:24
Then * released Barabbas to them. Mt 27:26
to * and asked for Jesus' body. Mt 27:58
Jesus' body. And * issued an order Mt 27:58
Pharisees went to *, and told him, Mt 27:62
"Use your own Temple police," * Mt 27:65
guard to *, the Roman governor. Mk 15:1
* asked him, "Are you the King Mk 15:2
many crimes, and * asked him, "Why Mk 15:3,4
to crowd in toward *, asking him to Mk 15:8
you the 'King of Jews'?" * asked. Mk 15:9
"But if I release Barabbas," * Mk 15:12
"But why?" * demanded. Mk 15:14
Then *, afraid of a riot and Mk 15:15
to * and asked for Jesus' body. Mk 15:42,43
* couldn't believe that Jesus was Mk 15:44
the fact, and * told Joseph he Mk 15:45
in the deserts. (* was governor Lk 3:1
was informed that * had butchered Lk 13:1
Jesus over to *, the governor. Lk 23:1
So * asked him, "Are you their Lk 23:3
Then * turned to the chief Lk 23:4
"Is he then a Galilean?" * Lk 23:6
When they told him yes, * said to Lk 23:7
on him, they sent him back to *. Lk 23:11
That day Herod and *—enemies Lk 23:12
Then * called together the chief Lk 23:13
and for murder.) * argued with Lk 23:20
So * sentenced Jesus to die as Lk 23:24
* and asked for the body of Jesus. Lk 23:50,51,52
Passover lamb. So *, the governor, Jn 18:29
by your own laws," * told them. Jn 18:31
Then * went back into the palace Jn 18:33
Messiah?" If * was asking as the Jn 18:34f
"Am I a Jew?" * retorted. Jn 18:35
* replied, "But you are a king Jn 18:37
"What is truth?" * exclaimed. Jn 18:38
THEN * LAID open Jesus' back with Jn 19:1
* went outside again and said to Jn 19:4
And * said, "Behold the man!" Jn 19:5
"You crucify him," * said. Jn 19:6
When * heard this, he was more Jn 19:8
"You won't talk to me?" * Jn 19:10
Then * tried to release him, but Jn 19:12
At these words * brought Jesus Jn 19:13
And * said to the Jews, "Here is Jn 19:14
Crucify your king?" * asked. Jn 19:15
Then * gave Jesus to them to be Jn 19:16
between them. And * posted a sign Jn 19:19
Then the chief priests said to *, Jn 19:21
* replied, "What I have written, Jn 19:22
so they asked * to order the legs Jn 19:31
boldly asked * for permission to Jn 19:38
down; and * told him to go ahead. Jn 19:38
rejected before *, despite Pilate's Act 3:13
For Herod the king, and Pontius * Act 4:27
asked * to have him killed anyway. Act 13:28
before Pontius *, that you fulfill 1Ti 6:13

PILATE'S
gathered before * house that Mt 27:17
over the court, * wife sent him Mt 27:19
But Jesus said no more, much to * Mk 15:5
Now, it was * custom to release Mk 15:6
* determination to release him. Act 3:13

PILDASH
Hazo, *, Jidlaph,Bethuel (father of Gen 22:20-23

PILE
together beside the * of rocks. Gen 31:46
They named it "The Witness * Gen 31:47,48
"This * of stones will stand as a Gen 31:47,48
and throw them into the burning *. Num 19:6
Afterwards you must * all the Deu 13:16
and immediately * them into a Deu 27:2,3,4
by a dam, and will * up as though Jos 3:13,14
carry them out and * them up as a Jos 4:2,3
and a great * of stones was Jos 10:27
cave. (The * is still there today. Jos 10:27
Yes, from a * of ashes— 1Sa 2:8
were before, over by the stone *. 1Sa 20:19
in front of the * as though I were 1Sa 20:20
he said to * them in two heaps at 2Ki 10:8
shall be reduced to a * of rubble. Ez 6:11
you have pierced. * their sins Ps 69:27
My troubles * high among these Ps 120:5,6
a * of grief and incurable pain. Is 17:11
"They * evil upon evil, lie upon Jer 9:6
I will * on the fuel beneath her. Eze 24:9
The threshing floors will * high Joe 2:24
Your enemies will * up earth Lk 19:43
* with all the others and burned. Jn 15:6

PILED
They were * into great heaps, Ex 8:14
Jordan were * up as a monument. Jos 4:20
their bodies, and * a great heap Jos 7:26
There he * a great heap of stones Jos 8:29
the bundles were * against the Ju 9:49
* a great heap of stones over it. 2Sa 18:17
around the altar. He * wood upon 1Ki 18:33
Lord and * them up in great heaps. 2Ch 31:5,6
They * up the carcasses for each 2Ch 35:12
for our sins are * higher than our Ez 9:6
solve are * higher than my head. Ps 40:12
it is * high with wood. Is 30:33
the mighty waters * high. Hab 3:15
For her sins are * as high as Rev 18:5

PILES
So they made great * of Gen 11:3,4
* of flax that were drying there. Jos 2:6
was laid out in great *. 2Ch 31:5,6
* continued to grow until October. 2Ch 31:7,8
and saw these huge *, how they 2Ch 31:7,8
into four *, one for each of them. Jn 19:23,24

PILGRIM
I am but a * here on earth: how Ps 119:19
a flutist leads a * band to Is 30:29

PILGRIMAGE
must make a holy * out into the Ex 5:1
we must all join in the holy *." Ex 10:9
"The first is the * of Ex 23:15
Then there is the Harvest *, Ex 23:16
And, finally, the * of Ex 23:16
all these years of my earthly *. Ps 119:54

PILGRIMAGES
annual religious * you must make. Ex 23:14
over the world will make * there. Mic 4:1
world will come on * and pour into Zec 8:20,21

PILGRIMS
And a huge crowd, many of them * Jn 6:2-5

PILHA
*, Shobek, Rehum, Neh 10:14-27

PILING
* up as though against a dam! Jos 3:15,16
unbelievers, thus * up your sins. Is 30:1
For your sins keep * up before Is 59:12

PILL
* for the poor and oppressed. Amo 5:7

PILLAGE
Land' of Israel, and * it. Dan 11:16
king will again * Jerusalem and Dan 11:30,31

PILLAGED
our land and * the countryside. Ps 44:10

PILLAR
him, and became a * of salt. Gen 19:26
*, and poured olive oil over it. Gen 28:18
And this memorial * shall become Gen 28:22
the * and made a vow to serve me. Gen 31:13
Afterwards Jacob built a stone * Gen 35:13,14
anointed the * with olive oil. Gen 35:13,14
The Lord guided them by a * of Ex 13:21
and by a * of fire at night. Ex 13:21
as it changed to a * of fire, it Ex 14:20
and a bronze socket for each *. Ex 26:37
As he entered, the * of cloud Ex 33:9
bowing low to the * of cloud. Ex 33:10
in the form of a * of cloud and Ex 34:5,6
They see the * of cloud and fire Num 14:14
guided them by a * of fire at night Deu 1:33
and a * of cloud during the day. Deu 1:33
great * of fire upon the earth; Deu 4:36
named the Jachin *, and the one on 1Ki 7:16-22
the one on the north, the Boaz *. 1Ki 7:16-22
A capital at the top of each *; 1Ki 7:41-46
bases of the capitals of each *; 1Ki 7:41-46
tore down the * to Baal that his 2Ki 3:2
dragged out the * used for the 2Ki 10:26
beside the *, as was the custom at 2Ki 11:13,14
He stood beside the * in front 2Ki 23:3
Each * was twenty-seven feet 2Ki 25:17
the king by his * at the entrance, 2Ch 23:12
You led our ancestors by a * of Neh 9:12
the day and a * of fire at night so Neh 9:12
wilderness! The * of cloud led them Neh 9:19
by day, and the * of fire showed Neh 9:19
and at night by a * of fire. Ps 78:14
He spoke to them from the * of Ps 99:7
and gave them a * of flame at night Ps 105:39
iron * and heavy gates of brass. Jer 1:18
Or, an eighteen-inch * in front of Eze 40:7-12f
him a * in the temple of my God; Rev 3:12

PILLARS
with twelve * around the altar Ex 24:4
Hang this upon four acacia * Ex 26:32
golden hooks. The * are to rest in Ex 26:32
frames, bars, *, and bases; Ex 35:10-19
The * and their bases; Ex 35:10-19
the two * supporting the roof. Ju 16:25,26
my hands against the two *. Ju 16:25,26
Then Samson pushed against the * Ju 16:29
the beams and *, with cedar. 1Ki 6:9
rested upon four rows of cedar *. 1Ki 7:2
room was called the Hall of *. 1Ki 7:6
a canopy which was supported by *. 1Ki 7:6
He cast two hollow bronze *, each 1Ki 7:15
At the tops of the * he made two 1Ki 7:16-22
Hiram set these * at the entrance 1Ki 7:16-22
Two *; 1Ki 7:41-46

(PILLARS Con't)
algum wood to make * for the Temple 1Ki 10:12
up the bronze * of the Temple and 2Ki 25:13
weight of the two * and the great 2Ki 25:16
capitals at the tops of the * 2Ki 25:17
bronze tank, the *, and the 1Ch 18:8
Temple were two * 52½ feet high, 2Ch 3:15
and placed them on top of the *, 2Ch 3:16
Then he set up the * at the 2Ch 3:17
The construction of the two *, 2Ch 4:12-16
capitals on the tops of the *, 2Ch 4:12-16
silver rings imbedded in marble *. Est 1:6
* of heaven tremble at his rebuke. Job 26:11
turmoil, yet its * are firm, for I Ps 75:3
on two strong *—the one is Justice Ps 89:14,15
like the * of a palace wall. Ps 144:12-15
supported on seven *, and has Pro 9:1
His legs are as * of marble set Sol 5:15
of Hosts says, The * of bronze Jer 27:19,20,21
two large bronze * that stood at Jer 52:17
The weight of the two enormous * Jer 52:20
For the * were each Jer 52:21
your famous, huge * will topple. Eze 26:11
Then he estimated the * on each Eze 40:14
halls. The * were decorated with Eze 40:16
Its guardrooms, * and entrance Eze 40:29,30
on the *, just as the others. Eze 40:31
Its guardrooms, * and entrance Eze 40:33
The guardrooms, * and entry hall Eze 40:36
two *, each of them 8¾ feet thick. Eze 40:48,49
the * that formed its doorway. Eze 41:1
sky—blood and fire and * of smoke. Joe 2:30
the tops of the * and shake the Amo 9:1
Temple until the * crumble and the Amo 9:1
were known as the * of the church, Gal 2:7,8,9

PILLOW
its head on a * of goat's hair. 1Sa 19:13
every night my * is wet with Ps 6:6
is half a chair and a tattered *. Amo 3:12

PILOT
turn wherever the * wants it to go, Jas 3:4

PILOTS
your sailors and *, your Eze 27:27
as your * scream with fright. Eze 27:28

PILTAI
*, leader of the Moadiah and Neh 12:12-21

PIMPLE
a scab or boil or * with Lev 13:1

PIMPLES
in his eye, or has * or scabby Lev 21:20

PIN
Then she took a tent * and a Ju 5:26
She pounded the tent * through his Ju 5:26
intending to * him to the wall. 1Sa 18:11,12
through him. I'll * him to the 1Sa 26:8
they will * their hopes on him Rom 15:12

PINE
Those left shall * away in enemy Lev 26:39
cypress, fir and *—on barren land. Is 41:19
upon us; we * away with guilt. Eze 33:10

PINES
of firs and *, and box trees—to Is 60:13

PINING
sorrow. I am * away with grief; Ps 31:9,10

PINNED
I * them to the ground; Ps 18:38

PINON
Elah,The clan of *,The clan of Gen 36:40-43
Chief Elah, Chief *, Chief Kenaz, 1Ch 1:51-54

PINS
including all the * and pegs for Ex 27:19

PINT
olive oil, and a * of olive oil; Lev 14:10
the lambs and the * of olive oil Lev 14:12
offering, and a * of olive oil. Lev 14:21
offering, and the * of oil, and Lev 14:24
dollars and a * of dove's dung 2Ki 6:25

PINTS
2½ * of oil, pressed from olives; Ex 29:40
also 2½ * of wine, as a libation. Ex 29:40
consisting of three * of wine. Lev 23:13
mixed with three * of oil, Num 15:3,4
* of wine for a drink offering. Num 15:5
mixed with four * of oil, and four Num 15:6
* of wine for a drink offering. Num 15:7
flour mixed with three * of oil. Num 28:5
of three * of strong wine with each Num 28:7
drink offering—six * of wine with Num 28:14
each bull, four * for a ram, and Num 28:14
for a ram, and three * for a lamb. Num 28:14

PIOUS
most * meetings—all are frauds! Is 1:12,13
Yet they act so *! Is 58:2
underneath those * robes of yours Mt 23:28
they pretend to be * by praying Mk 12:40
wear a noble, * expression in Lk 16:15

PIPE
such as handle the harp and *." Gen 4:21f

PIPERS
Literally, "harpers * Rev 18:22f

PIPES
Playing your shepherd *? Ju 5:16

PIRAM
King * of Jarmuth, Jos 10:3

PIRATHON
was Abdon (son of Hillel) from *. Ju 12:13
Then he died and was buried in * Ju 12:15
Benaiah of *; 2Sa 23:24-39
Benaiah from *; 1Ch 11:26-47
was Benaiah from * in Ephraim, with 1Ch 27:14

PISGAH
with Mount * in the distance. Num 21:20
*, and built seven altars there; Num 23:14
to Mount * and the Salt Sea (also Deu 3:17
the top of Mount * where you can Deu 3:27
Sea, below the slopes of Mount *. Deu 4:49
plains of Moab to * Peak in Mount Deu 34:1
Sea and the slopes of Mount *. Jos 12:3
and the slopes of Mount *. Jos 13:20

PISHON
One of these was named the *; Gen 2:11,12

PISIDIA
a city in the province of *. Act 13:14
Then they traveled back through * Act 14:24

PISPA
Jephunneh, *, Ara. 1Ch 7:38

PISTACHIO
myrrh, * nuts, and almonds. Gen 43:11

PIT
of a grape press—a * where grapes Ju 6:11
already hidden in some * or cave. 2Sa 17:9
body into a deep * in the forest 2Sa 18:17
went down into a * and, despite the 2Sa 23:20
lion in a slippery * when there was 1Ch 11:22
his soul from the *, so that he may Job 33:30
He lifted me out of the * of Ps 40:2
that he should not see the *." Ps 49:8,9f
He will send my enemies to the * Ps 55:23
save me from the * that threatens Ps 69:15
down to the * of hell, down to its Is 14:15
will fall into a *, and if you Is 24:18
escape from the * you will step Is 24:18
they have dug a * for me to fall Jer 18:22
trapped him in a * and brought him Eze 19:4
him in a * and captured him. Eze 19:8
I will send you to the * of hell Eze 26:20
They will bring you to the * of Eze 28:8
down to the * of hell with all Eze 31:18
Yet your doom is the *; Eze 32:19
in the *, slain by the sword. Eze 32:25
who have gone down to the *. Eze 32:29
other slain who go down to the *. Eze 32:30
a deep * to trap them at Acacia. Hos 5:2
in a waterless * because of the Zec 9:11
it and dug a * for pressing out the Mk 12:1
order them into the Bottomless *. Lk 8:31
"If your cow falls into a *, Lk 14:5
given the key to the bottomless *. Rev 9:1
of the bottomless * whose name in Rev 9:11
who comes out of the bottomless * Rev 11:7
* and go to eternal destruction; Rev 17:8
* and a heavy chain in his hand. Rev 20:1
the bottomless *, which he then Rev 20:3

PITCH
with burning *, and the ground will Is 34:9
the sea, and there * his royal Dan 11:45

PITCHER
is broken, and the * is broken at Ecc 12:6
along carrying a * of water. Lk 22:10

PITCHERS
dishes, spoons, *, and flagons; Ex 25:29

PITFALL
for me and dug a * in my path. Ps 35:7
They have dug a * in my path. Ps 57:6
he has placed a * in my path and Lam 1:13

PITFALLS
The nations fall into the * they Ps 9:15
it become aware of the * on ahead. Pro 13:14

PITHOM
the store-cities * and Ra-amses. Ex 1:11

PITHON
*, Melech, Tarea, Ahaz. 1Ch 8:35
Micah was the father of *, 1Ch 9:41

PITIED
For God * them, and also he was 2Ki 13:23
no one * you or cared for you. Eze 16:5
name your sister Ruhamah ("*"), Hos 1:11
I will pity those who are "not * Hos 1:23
he * them and healed their sick. Mt 14:14

PITIES
is right, then God * him and says, Job 33:23,24
the hands of someone who * them. Pro 28:8

PITILESS
They are * and arrogant. Ps 17:10
he was * in unrelenting anger. Amo 1:11

PITS
the valley was full of asphalt *. Gen 14:10
slipped into the *, and the Gen 14:10
called the Salt *, and eastward Jos 11:8
have dug deep * for me to fall in. Ps 119:85,86
* from which they can't escape. Ps 140:10
now scratch in garbage * for food. Lam 4:5
Go into the * to trample the Nah 3:14

and salt * and eternal desolation; Zep 2:
They are doomed to the eternal * 2Pe 2:1

PITTANCE
your * has been doled out to you. Lev 26:2
You sold us for a *. Ps 44:1

PITTED
you are a pot that is * with rust Eze 24:

PITY
And please have some * on me Gen 40:1
Have no *, and do not worship Deu 7:1
and have no *: Do not spare that Deu 13:
Don't * him! Deu 19:1
You shall not show * to a false Deu 19:2
hand shall be cut off without *. Deu 25:1
Lord was moved to * by the groaning Ju 2:1
"At last someone has had * on 1Sa 23:2
he stole, and for having no *." 2Sa 12:
Temple, and had no * upon them, 2Ch 36:1
"Oh, my friends, * me, for the Job 19:2
* me, O Lord, for I am weak. Ps 6:
oh, have * and help me." Ps 30:1
have mercy. Have * upon me and take Ps 51:
O GOD, HAVE *, for I am trusting Ps 57:
If even one would show some *, if Ps 69:2
He feels * for the weak and Ps 72:1
so look down in * and grant Ps 86:1
* her—the time you promised help. Ps 102:1
who captured them to * them. Ps 106:4
let no one * his fatherless Ps 109:12,1
Blessed are those who * them. Pro 14:2
* on them or show them his mercy. Is 27:11
love I will have * on you, says the Is 54:8
In his love and * he redeemed Is 63:9
Yet I will look with * on the man Is 66:2
I will not let * nor mercy spare Jer 13:14
slaughter them without * or mercy. Jer 21:7
not * them when they cry for help. Jer 33:5
not spare you nor * you at all. Eze 5:11
turn my eyes away and show no *; Eze 7:4
I will not spare nor * you, and Eze 7:8,9
I will neither * nor spare. Eze 8:18
Spare not nor * them— kill them Eze 9:5
them nor have any * on them, and I Eze 9:10
I will * those who are "not Hos 1:23
Then the Lord will * his people Joe 2:18
And what * he felt for the Mt 9:36
him and said, "I * these Mt 15:32
"Then the king was filled with * Mt 18:27
Jesus was moved with * for them Mt 20:34
And Jesus, moved with *, touched Mk 1:41
and he had * on them because they Mk 6:34
"I * these people," he said, Mk 8:1
when he saw him, he felt deep *. Lk 10:33
"The one who showed him some *." Lk 10:37
filled with loving * and ran and Lk 15:20
he shouted, 'have some *! Lk 16:24
and were heartless—without *. Rom 1:31
And I will take * on anyone I Rom 9:15
God takes * on those he wants to. Rom 9:16
his kindness and *—by washing away Tit 3:5

PLACARD
I had waved a * before you with a Gal 3:1

PLACATE
The gold rats were to * God for 1Sa 6:18

PLACE
and closed up the * from which he Gen 2:21
wandering from * to place." Gen 4:12
wandering from place to *." Gen 4:12
A POPULATION explosion took * Gen 6:1
the dove found no * to light, and Gen 8:9
they came to a * near Shechem, and Gen 12:6
Afterwards Abram left that * and Gen 12:8
* where he had built the altar. Gen 13:3,4
at a * near the city of Sodom. Gen 13:12
(This took * ten years after Gen 16:2,3
"Get them out of this * Gen 19:12
The stench of the * has reached Gen 19:13
hurried out to the * where he had Gen 19:27
figured this to be a godless *. Gen 20:11,12
and choose the * where you want to Gen 20:15
* where they made their covenant. Gen 21:31
* where God had told him to go. Gen 22:3
Abraham saw the * in the distance. Gen 22:4
When they arrived at the * where Gen 22:9
Abraham named the * "Jehovah Gen 22:14
land, with no * to bury my wife. Gen 23:4
and a * prepared for the camels!" Gen 24:31
He named the * Bethel ("House Gen 28:19
shall become a * for worship; Gen 28:22
he continued, 'the * where you Gen 31:13
So he named the * "God's Gen 32:1
Jacob named the * "Peniel" Gen 32:30
(That is why the * is called Gen 33:17
* where God had appeared to him; Gen 35:13,14
the men of the * had told him. Gen 38:22
men around the * came running in to Gen 39:14,15
and found a * where he could weep. Gen 42:24
so he lifted it to * it on Gen 48:17
(meaning "Threshing * of Gen 50:10
renamed the * Abel-mizraim (meaning Gen 50:11
said, "It is a * of very deep Gen 50:11

LACE Con't)

that is why the * was called	Ex 15:23
* from generation to generation.	Ex 16:33
Moses named the * Massah	Ex 17:7
I will appoint a * where he can run	Ex 21:13
When the Ark is finished, *	Ex 25:16
This is the * of mercy for your	Ex 25:17
Literally, "mercy seat" or "*	Ex 25:17f
using beaten gold, and * them at	Ex 25:18
with the mercy *, one at each end.	Ex 25:19
down upon the * of mercy, and shall	Ex 25:20
upon the Ark, and * within the Ark	Ex 25:21
* of mercy between the cherubim;	Ex 25:22
* of God, becomes a single unit.	Ex 26:6
Behind this curtain * the Ark	Ex 26:33
Holy * and the Most Holy Place.	Ex 26:33
Holy Place and the Most Holy *.	Ex 26:33
"Now install the mercy *—the	Ex 26:34
lid of the Ark—in the Most Holy *.	Ex 26:34
Most Holy Place. * the table and	Ex 26:35
* and the table on the north side.	Ex 26:35
Aaron and his sons shall * this	Ex 27:21
golden rings and * them on the two	Ex 28:26
when he goes in to the Holy *;	Ex 28:29
Holy *, so that he will not die.	Ex 28:35
*, lest they be guilty and die.	Ex 28:43
wheat flour.) * the bread in a	Ex 29:3,4
and sash, and * on his head the	Ex 29:6
sashes, and * caps on their heads.	Ex 29:9
the Tabernacle. * its blood upon	Ex 29:12
and the legs; * them with the head	Ex 29:17
Collect the blood and * some of	Ex 29:19,20
before the Lord: * these in the	Ex 29:24
in the Tabernacle and the Holy *.	Ex 29:30
with gold. * the altar just	Ex 30:6
the veil, near the * of mercy that	Ex 30:6
the Ark with the * of mercy upon	Ex 31:7
incense for the Holy *.	Ex 31:11
the people to the * I told you	Ex 32:34
let us move a step from this *.	Ex 33:15
by giving a lamb in its *.	Ex 34:20
The * of mercy;	Ex 35:10-19
The veil to enclose the Holy *;	Ex 35:10-19
when ministering in the Holy *;	Ex 35:10-19
a lid called "the * of mercy";	Ex 37:6
* of mercy, looking down upon it.	Ex 37:9
to hold the carrying poles in *.	Ex 37:14
while ministering in the Holy *.	Ex 39:1
The * of mercy;	Ex 39:33-40
in the Holy *, and the holy	Ex 39:41
In it, * the Ark containing the	Ex 40:3
Then bring in the table and *	Ex 40:4
"* the golden altar for the	Ex 40:5
Tabernacle, and * the altar for	Ex 40:6
the golden lid, the * of mercy.	Ex 40:20
ceremonially clean * outside the	Lev 4:11,12
outside the camp—a * where the	Lev 4:11,12
kill it at the * where the burnt	Lev 4:24
sin offering and * it with his	Lev 4:25
He shall bring it to the * where	Lev 4:29
He shall bring it to the * where	Lev 4:33
to a * that is ceremonially clean.	Lev 6:11
the Lord at the * where the burnt	Lev 6:25
it must be washed in a holy *.	Lev 6:27
to make atonement in the Holy *.	Lev 6:30
be killed at the * where the burnt	Lev 7:2
be eaten in a holy *, for this is a	Lev 7:6
it in the sanctuary, in a holy *.	Lev 10:13
him, may be eaten in any holy *.	Lev 10:14
and the burned * becomes bright	Lev 13:24
examines him shall * the man and	Lev 14:11
the lamb at the * where sin	Lev 14:13
given you, and I * leprosy in some	Lev 14:33,34
into a defiled * outside the city.	Lev 14:40
in a defiled * outside the city.	Lev 14:41
out of the city to a defiled *.	Lev 14:45
into the Holy * behind the veil,	Lev 16:1
the Ark and the * of mercy are,	Lev 16:1
in the cloud above the * of mercy.	Lev 16:1
cover the mercy * above the Ark	Lev 16:13
side of the mercy *, and then seven	Lev 16:14
it upon the * of mercy and in front	Lev 16:15
for the holy * because it is	Lev 16:16
in the Holy *—not until after he	Lev 16:17
for the Holy *, the entire	Lev 16:20
bathe in a sacred *, put on his	Lev 16:24
into the Holy * by Aaron, to make	Lev 16:27
in * of his ancestor Aaron;	Lev 16:32
High Priest shall * twelve loaves	Lev 24:5-8
in a * set apart for the purpose.	Lev 24:9
been given to the Lord in their *.	Num 3:49
a blue cloth, and * the carrying	Num 4:6
is displayed, and * the dishes,	Num 4:7
carrying poles are to be put in *.	Num 4:14
He shall unbind her hair and *	Num 5:18
him from above the * of mercy over	Num 7:89
accepted them in * of all the	Num 8:16
the Levites in * of all the eldest	Num 8:18
to choose a * for them to stop.	Num 10:33
was known as "The * of Burning,"	Num 11:3
So the name of that * was	Num 11:34
* of the Graves Caused by Lust,"	Num 11:34
And from that * they journeyed	Num 11:35
and * fire in it from the altar;	Num 16:46
The Lord told Moses to * Aaron's	Num 17:10
a most holy *, and only by males.	Num 18:10
of the heifer and * them in some	Num 19:9
in some purified * outside the	Num 19:9
This shall take * on the third	Num 19:19
to drink at that *, so the people	Num 20:2
and bring us here to this evil *?	Num 20:5
He took the rod from the * where	Num 20:9
This * was named Meribah (meaning	Num 20:13
This is the * where the Lord told	Num 21:16
Lord stood at a * where the road	Num 22:24
and stood in a * so narrow that the	Num 22:26
him, "Come with me to another *;	Num 23:13
will take you to yet another *.	Num 23:27
of Meribah ("* of Strife") in	Num 27:14
out in the holy * before the Lord.	Num 28:7
you are judging in the * of God.	Deu 1:17
Ammonites lived there in their *.	Deu 2:21
that I should * them in the Ark.	Deu 10:2
for him at a * he himself will	Deu 12:4,5
you arrive in the * of rest the	Deu 12:9
the * he will choose as his home.	Deu 12:11
you may only do so in the * the	Deu 12:14
He will pick a * in the territory	Deu 12:14
land of Egypt, the * of slavery.	Deu 13:10
your God at the * he shall choose	Deu 14:23
If the * the Lord chooses for	Deu 14:24
tithes to that *, then you may	Deu 14:24
It must be eaten at the * the	Deu 16:6
at the * the Lord will designate.	Deu 16:15
But if this deed takes * out in	Deu 22:25,26,27
brought us to this * and given us	Deu 26:9
Then * the samples before the	Deu 26:10
but no one knows the exact *.	Deu 34:6
at the * where you camp tonight."	Jos 4:2,3
They carried them to the * where	Jos 4:8
* where the priests were standing;	Jos 4:9
this purpose. The * where the	Jos 5:2,3
rite took * was named "The Hill of	Jos 5:2,3
So the * where this was done was	Jos 5:8,9
even today that * is called "The	Jos 7:26
* over the valley of Aijalon!"	Jos 10:12
Great Sidon and a * called the Salt	Jos 11:8
give him a * to live among them.	Jos 20:4
could run to that * for a trial,	Jos 20:9
so the name of that * was called	Ju 2:5
"the * where people wept").	Ju 2:5
She held court at a * now called	Ju 4:5
The Angel said to him, "* the	Ju 6:20
These attacks took * east of the	Ju 10:7,8
(The * has been called "Jawbone	Ju 15:16,17
Then he named the * "The Spring	Ju 15:19
him by the hand, "* my hands	Ju 16:25,26
looking for a good * to live.	Ju 17:7,8
I am looking for a * to live."	Ju 17:9
trying to find a * to settle, for	Ju 18:1
wonderful *—a real paradise.	Ju 18:9,10
They camped first at a * west of	Ju 18:12
next day to fight at the same *.	Ju 20:22,23,24
SO BOAZ WENT down to the market *	Ru 4:1
customary * beside the entrance.	1Sa 1:9
to take the * of this one they had	1Sa 2:20
them in the barn. * the Ark of God	1Sa 6:8
his sons as judges in his *.	1Sa 8:1
it in a special * before the Lord.	1Sa 10:25
find a hiding * out in the fields.	1Sa 19:2
when your * at the table is empty.	1Sa 20:18
at his usual * against the wall.	1Sa 20:24,25
Saul, but David's * was empty.	1Sa 20:24,25
But when his * was still empty	1Sa 20:27
to be king in your *, shaming	1Sa 20:30
Ever since that time the * where	1Sa 23:28
At the * where the road passes	1Sa 24:3
of them died. The * has been known	2Sa 2:16
they came to the * where he lay.	2Sa 2:23
So he named the * "Bursting."	2Sa 5:20
the spot "The * of Wrath upon	2Sa 6:8
He did it in order to * the	2Sa 14:20
of my army in * of Joab."	2Sa 19:13
and at the same *, Elhanan killed	2Sa 21:19
king in * of his aged father.	1Ki 1:5
When you bring him back here, *	1Ki 1:35
son, whom I will * upon your	1Ki 5:5
Most Holy *—was also paneled from	1Ki 6:16
Most Holy *—was sixty feet long.	1Ki 6:17
the entrance to the Most Holy *.	1Ki 6:21,22
of the Most Holy *), the flowers,	1Ki 7:49
to the Most Holy *, and the main	1Ki 7:50
Most Holy *—and placed it under the	1Ki 8:6
a * for you to live forever."	1Ki 8:12,13
I didn't appoint a * for my Temple,	1Ki 8:16
And I have prepared a * in the	1Ki 8:21
night and day—this * you have	1Ki 8:29
whenever they face this * to pray;	1Ki 8:30
this * and confess your name.	1Ki 8:35,36
the * for my name to be enshrined.	1Ki 11:36
And I will * you on the throne	1Ki 11:37
his son Rehoboam reigned in his *.	1Ki 11:43
eat or drink even water in this *!	1Ki 13:8
drunk water in the * he told you	1Ki 13:21,22
and his son Asa reigned in his *.	1Ki 15:8
his son Ahab became king in his *.	1Ki 16:28
Cherith Brook at a * east of where	1Ki 17:3
must die in his *, and your people	1Ki 20:42
"I have come to * God's curse upon	1Ki 21:20
* to stay whenever he comes by."	2Ki 4:10
The youth showed him the *, and	2Ki 6:6
our forces at ÇÇ" (naming the *).	2Ki 6:8
(naming the same *) "for the	2Ki 6:9
his chariot at the * where the road	2Ki 9:27
son Ben-hadad reigned in his *.	2Ki 13:24
Temple—the very * which the Lord	2Ki 21:7
he said, "I will * my name forever	2Ki 21:7
which I will bring upon this *."	2Ki 22:20
He had gained his * among The	1Ch 11:20
* "The Outbreak Against Uzza."	1Ch 13:11
That is why the * has been	1Ch 14:11
"The * of Breaking Through").	1Ch 14:11
to the * I have prepared for it.	1Ch 15:12
you die, I will * one of your sons	1Ch 17:11
I will * him over my people and	1Ch 17:14
is the * where I'll build the	1Ch 22:1
its instruments from * to place."	1Ch 23:26
its instruments from place to *."	1Ch 23:26
rest—a * for our God to live in.	1Ch 28:2
the sanctuary for the * of mercy.	1Ch 28:11
his son Solomon reigned in his *.	1Ch 29:28
"It will be a * where I can burn	2Ch 2:4
But it will be a * to worship	2Ch 2:6
Literally, "a * to burn incense	2Ch 2:6f
This celebration took * in	2Ch 5:3
in my father's *, and I have built	2Ch 6:10
Temple—upon this * where you have	2Ch 6:20,21
to you as I face toward this *.	2Ch 6:20,21
the prayers made to you in this *.	2Ch 6:40
enter this resting * of yours where	2Ch 6:41
use that day as a * of sacrifice,	2Ch 7:7
this Temple as the * where I want	2Ch 7:12
to every prayer made in this *.	2Ch 7:15
and they * the Bread of the	2Ch 13:11
regalia at an open * near the	2Ch 18:9
all the debris from the holy *.	2Ch 29:4,5
planning to * them under tribute.	2Ch 32:1
stars—in the very * where the Lord	2Ch 33:4,5
wrath is poured out upon this *.'	2Ch 34:25
For Jerusalem is the * in which I	Neh 1:9
to the Temple and * them in the	Neh 10:39,40
before God in the * where they go.	Job 26:5,6
my * among the honored elders.	Job 29:7
my shoulder be wrenched out of *!	Job 31:22
men, and puts others in their *.	Job 34:24
put the nations in their * until	Ps 9:20
He led me to a * of safety, for	Ps 18:19
You are my hiding * from every	Ps 32:7
For you are God, my only * of	Ps 43:2
for you are my * of safety.	Ps 59:9
tower of refuge, a * of safety in	Ps 59:16
firm, for I have set them in *!"	Ps 75:3
power of good men in their *."	Ps 75:10
its apportioned * as its home.	Ps 78:55
Literally, "in the hiding * of	Ps 81:7f
it will become a * of springs where	Ps 84:6
citizens he will * a checkmark	Ps 87:6
is my refuge, my * of safety;	Ps 91:2
* of rest I planned for them."	Ps 95:11
to safety and a * to live.	Ps 107:7
and follow me, and * your hand of	Ps 139:5
if I go down to the * of the	Ps 139:8
"you are my only * of refuge.	Ps 142:5
she will * a beautiful crown upon	Pro 4:8,9
his children have a * of refuge	Pro 14:26
All go to one *—the dust from	Ecc 3:20
at the right * at the right time.	Ecc 9:11
given their rightful * of dignity!	Ecc 10:6
so others have no * to live.	Is 5:8
he lives will be a glorious *.	Is 11:10
will move from its * in the skies.	Is 13:13
* a just and righteous King."	Is 16:4,5
the harvest will not take *.	Is 32:10
Judah in a safe *, along with	Is 33:6
at peace, a * where God is	Is 33:20
thing in * so it won't fall over!	Is 41:7
put everything in *, and he made	Is 45:18
I planted the stars in * and	Is 51:16
that high and holy * where those	Is 57:15
shall be a * to pasture herds.	Is 65:10
I will recreate Jerusalem as a *	Is 65:18
for help, and this * I gave to you	Jer 7:13,14
my fury on this *—people, animals,	Jer 7:20
it securely in * with hammer and	Jer 10:4
evil upon this *, so terrible that	Jer 19:3
into a * of shame and wickedness.	Jer 19:4
have filled this * with the blood	Jer 19:4
Lord, when I will * a righteous	Jer 23:5,6
Am I a God who is only in one *	Jer 23:23
And you will find no * to hide,	Jer 25:35
And in every nation where I *	Jer 29:18
"Jerusalem, the * Nobody Wants."	Jer 30:17
and who was then crowned in his *.	Jer 44:30f

(PLACE Con't)
and there will be no * to hide. Jer 49:9,10
He has shut me into a * of high, Lam 3:9
equal parts. * a third of it at Eze 5:2
marriage had taken *, I gave you Eze 16:9,10
I said to them: 'What is this * Eze 20:29
And so it is still called 'The * Eze 20:29
uninhabited, a * for fishermen to Eze 26:5
a * for fishermen to spread their Eze 26:14
and * my sword in his hand. Eze 30:24
Yes, when I * my sword into the Eze 30:25
They have a resting * among the Eze 32:25
and you will no longer be a * for Eze 36:12
* to "The Valley of Gog's Army." Eze 39:11
told me, "is the Most Holy *." Eze 41:4
leave the Holy *—the nave of the Eze 42:14
"Son of dust, this is the * of my Eze 43:7
* outside the Temple area. Eze 43:21
rooms, I saw a * where, my guide Eze 46:19,20
will arise to take your *. Dan 2:39
were put in * and the Ancient of Dan 7:9
its * grew four good-sized horns Dan 8:8
take * until the end times come." Dan 8:17
and the Most Holy * (in the Temple) Dan 9:24
Each is right in *. Joe 2:8
When trouble comes, he is the * Nah 1:7
a pasture, a * of shepherd camps Zep 2:6
and become a * of stinging nettles Zep 2:9
she has become a * of utter ruins, Zep 2:15
ruins, a * for animals to live! Zep 2:15
I will fill this * with my glory,' Hag 2:7
"He will grow up in his *." Zec 6:12f
Come to the * of safety, all you Zec 9:12
you give him first * in your life Mt 6:33
the * of weeping and torment." Mt 8:12
have no home of my own—no * to Mt 8:20
Leaving that *, Jesus met a man Mt 9:32
* from your feet as you leave. Mt 10:14
every city and * where he himself Mt 11:1f
disciples to * before the people. Mt 14:19
When Jesus came to the * where Mt 20:32,33
say my Temple is a * of prayer," Mt 21:13
the prophet) standing in a holy * Mt 24:15
at such and such a *, or has Mt 24:23
at a certain *, don't believe it! Mt 24:26
these things take *, this Mt 24:34f
the goats, and * the sheep at my Mt 25:33
curtain secluding the Holiest * Mt 27:51
into the Jewish * of worship—the Mk 1:21
"Please come and * your hands on Mk 5:23
them except to * his hands on a few Mk 6:5
disciple to * before the people. Mk 6:41
to * you on thrones next to mine. Mk 10:40
Temple is to be a * of prayer for Mk 11:17
right time and * to betray Jesus. Mk 14:11
And they brought Jesus to a * Mk 15:22
when the crucifixion took *. Mk 15:25
a * reserved by God for himself; Mk 15:38f
and they will be able to * their Mk 16:18
Then John went from * to place Lk 3:3
Then John went from place to * Lk 3:3
opened it to the * where it says: Lk 4:17
don't even own a * to lay my head. Lk 9:58
but stay in one *, eating and Lk 10:7
him to the * of the unfaithful. Lk 12:46
a better * than this for you!' Lk 14:10
the finest calf we have on the *.' Lk 15:30
in the * of the righteous dead. Lk 16:22
them about this * of torment lest Lk 16:28
begun here in this * or there in Lk 17:21
and that I am in this * or that; Lk 17:23
they reached the * where the road Lk 19:36,37
'My Temple is a * of prayer; Lk 19:46
right hand until I * your enemies Lk 20:42,43
the events taking * that I've Lk 21:31
* to prepare their Passover meal. Lk 22:8
That is the *. Lk 22:12
And he touched the * where the Lk 22:51
him at a * called "The Skull." Lk 23:32,33
This incident took * at Bethany, Jn 1:28
So they went with him to the * Jn 1:39
is the only * of worship, while we Jn 4:20
* where John was first baptizing. Jn 10:40
at the * where Martha met him. Jn 11:30
anguish gives * to rapturous joy Jn 16:21
Judas, the betrayer, knew this * Jn 18:2
judgment seat in a * that is called Jn 19:13f
his cross to the * known as "The Jn 19:17
The * where Jesus was Jn 19:20
of burial. The * of crucifixion Jn 19:41
and foot of the * where the body of Jn 20:12
* my hand into his side." Jn 20:25
named the * 'The Field of Blood.' Act 1:19
to take Judas' * and to join us as Act 1:21,22
who has gone on to his proper *." Act 1:24,25
Peter traveled from * to place to Act 9:32
Peter traveled from place to * to Act 9:32
was the * where Simon Peter lived! Act 10:18
going down to the * of prayer Act 16:16
harbor—a poor * to spend the Act 27:12
to me in the first * and not left Act 27:21
Literally, "a * where two seas Act 27:41f
sight—before the ceremony took *. Rom 4:11
us into this * of highest privilege Rom 5:2
is sitting at the * of highest Rom 8:34
And Isaiah says in another * that Rom 9:29
*, he won't spare you either. Rom 11:21
who were there in the first *? Rom 11:24
And in another *, "Be glad, O Rom 15:10
really believed it in the first *. 1Co 15:2
in the first *, to visit you and 2Co 8:6
me food to eat and a * to stay. 2Co 12:13
life in the first *, why do you Gal 3:3
seated him in the * of honor at Eph 1:20
part of this dwelling * of God. Eph 2:22
should have no * in your lives. Eph 4:31
have a very special * in my heart. Php 1:7
slave, here to help us in your *. Col 1:7
God in the * of honor and power. Col 3:1
will be no * to hide. 1Th 5:3
And in another *, "Those who 1Ti 5:18
all of this take *, but we do see Heb 2:8
let them come to his * of rest. Heb 3:11
all may enter his * of rest—we Heb 4:1
God can enter into his * of rest. Heb 4:3
This new * of rest he is talking Heb 4:8
to go into that * of rest, too, Heb 4:11
back to the * where you need Heb 5:12,13
given the * of honor in heaven. Heb 7:26
in heaven at the * of greatest Heb 8:1
heaven, the true * of worship built Heb 8:2
as taking the * of the old one; Heb 8:13
Inside this * of worship there Heb 9:1
this part was called the Holy *. Heb 9:1
It was not in the earthly * of Heb 9:24
sat down in the * of highest honor Heb 10:12
and now he sits in the * of honor Heb 12:2
sitting in the * of honor next to 1Pe 3:22
or a * to stay for the night. 1Pe 4:9
set you firmly in *, and make you 1Pe 5:10
might take God's * in your hearts. 1Jn 5:21
from its * among the churches. Rev 2:5
just as I took my * with my Father Rev 3:21
* where their Lord was crucified. Rev 11:8,9
God had prepared a * for her, to Rev 12:6
wilderness to the * prepared for Rev 12:14
the world near a * called, in Rev 16:16
away, but they found no * to hide. Rev 20:11
was no longer any * for them." Rev 20:11f

PLACED
to the east, and * in the garden Gen 2:8
At the center of the garden he * Gen 2:9
The Lord God * the man in the Gen 2:15
I have * a curse upon the soil. Gen 3:17
Thus God expelled him, and * Gen 3:24
"for I have * them in your Gen 9:2,3
this sign: I have * my rainbow in Gen 9:13
Abraham * the wood for the burnt Gen 22:6
built an altar and * the wood in Gen 22:9
in them, and * these rods beside Gen 30:38
to mate, and * the peeled branches Gen 30:41
Then Pharaoh * his own signet Gen 41:41,42
clothing and * the royal golden Gen 41:41,42
"See, I have * you in charge of Gen 41:41,42
body was * in a coffin in Egypt. Gen 50:26
blood shall be * on the two Ex 12:7
The blood you have * on the Ex 12:13
were * upon your foreheads. Ex 13:16
* between each set of branches; Ex 25:34,35
On top of these blankets is * a Ex 26:14
to golden rings * at the outer top Ex 28:22,23,24
bread that was * before the Lord: Ex 29:23
of beaten gold and * them at the Ex 37:7
rings of gold and * them into the Ex 37:13
spoons to be * upon this table. Ex 37:15,16
Two gold rings were * on each Ex 37:27
a gold ring was * at the top of Ex 39:15-18
Two other gold rings were * low Ex 39:20
Bells of pure gold were * Ex 39:25,26
Inside the Ark he * the stones Ex 40:20
Next he * the table at the north Ex 40:22
And he * the lampstand next to Ex 40:24
instructions, and * the golden Ex 40:26
Tabernacle, and * the outside Ex 40:29
Next he * the washbasin between Ex 40:30
inside its pouch; and * on Lev 8:9
Next Moses * the robes on Lev 8:13
shoulder, and * on top of these Lev 8:26
had been * there before the Lord. Lev 8:26
All this was * in the hands of Lev 8:27
The fat was * upon the breasts Lev 9:20
the sons of Aaron, * unholy fire in Lev 10:1
Or, "* fire in their censers Lev 10:1f
hand shall then be * by the priest Lev 14:17
his hand shall be * upon the head Lev 14:29
kept alive and * before the Lord. Lev 16:10
shall be * upon a carrying frame. Num 4:10
and * on the carrying frame. Num 4:12
utensils are to be * upon the Num 4:14
and * them around the Tabernacle. Num 11:24
and lit them and * the incense on Num 16:18
No curse can be * on Jacob, Num 23:18-24
Then I came down and * the Deu 10
A yoke of iron shall be * around Deu 28:47,
* there to keep the kings inside. Jos 10:
and a great pile of stones was * Jos 10:
The Lord has * the Jordan River Jos 22:24,
and * it upon his shoulder. Ju 9:47,4
from it was * in Micah's shrine. Ju 17:4
and tumors were * upon the cart. 1Sa 6:
Samuel then took a stone and * 1Sa 7:
the great hall and * them at the 1Sa 9:2
So the chef brought it in and * 1Sa 9:2
Presence that was * before the Lord 1Sa 21
The Lord * you at my mercy back 1Sa 24:9,
when the Lord * you in my power. 1Sa 26:2
His armor was * in the temple of 1Sa 31:1
The Ark was * upon a new cart 2Sa 6:
The Ark was * inside the tent 2Sa 6:1
David * several army garrisons 2Sa 8:
of Salt, and then * garrisons 2Sa 8:1
in his army, * them under his 2Sa 10:
gems—and * it on his own head. 2Sa 12:29,3
A third were * under Joab's 2Sa 18:
house should be * in seclusion. 2Sa 20:
for his mother be * beside his; 1Ki 2:1
of the Covenant of the Lord was *. 1Ki 6:1
Solomon * two statues of angels 1Ki 6:23-2
They were * so that their 1Ki 6:23-2
vats, and * them on the stands. 1Ki 7:3
Holy Place—and * it under the wings 1Ki 8:
the spot where the Ark would be *; 1Ki 8:
which Moses had * there at Mount 1Ki 8:
One of these calf-idols was * in 1Ki 12:2
young bulls and * it on the altar; 1Ki 18:2
the road, having * a bandage over 1Ki 20:3
sitting on thrones * on the 1Ki 22:1
new altar), and * it on the north 2Ki 16:1
and * it upon the stone pavement. 2Ki 16:1
They were * in colonies in the 2Ki 17:
They had * obelisks and idols at 2Ki 17:1
own gods. They * them in the 2Ki 17:2
of the stars were * even in the 2Ki 21:3,4,
the assassins and * Amon's son 2Ki 21:24
of Israel had * in the Temple at 2Ki 24:1
after he had * the Ark in it. 1Ch 6:31
then he * a garrison of his 1Ch 18:6
of Rabbah and * it upon his own 1Ch 20:2
of Aaron) were * into two divisions 1Ch 24:1
Lord and * in the Temple 1Ch 26:20,21,22
men, were * in charge of the 1Ch 26:30
Presence would be * and for the 1Ch 28:16
of Holies, Solomon * two sculptured 2Ch 3:10
to this room he * a veil of blue 2Ch 3:14
and * them on top of the pillars, 2Ch 3:16
lampstands and * them in the 2Ch 4:7
he also built ten tables and * 2Ch 4:8
* it beneath the angels' wings; 2Ch 5:7,8
of Israel, and * the Ark there. 2Ch 6:11
Ark of your strength has been *. 2Ch 6:41
The king * these in the Forest of 2Ch 9:16
Shields and spears were * in 2Ch 11:12
calves which he * on the hills. 2Ch 11:15
Israel. He * garrisons in all of 2Ch 17:2
addition to those * by the king in 2Ch 17:19
little prince and * the crown upon 2Ch 23:11
the money and * it in the chest 2Ch 24:10
offering to be * upon the altar, 2Ch 29:27
Think of it! He * an idol in the 2Ch 33:7
of his chariot and * him in his 2Ch 35:24,25
* in the temple of his own gods. Ez 1:7
had * in the temple of Babylon. Ez 5:14
* in the treasury of the Temple." Ez 8:29
So I * armed guards from each Neh 4:13
nations, and you * your people in Neh 9:22
Temple and * in the storage areas. Neh 10:38
Instantly the death veil was * Est 7:8
man was first * upon the earth, Job 20:4
For God has * my life in Job 30:11
I have * them in the wilderness Job 39:6
and * a crown of glory and honor Ps 8:5
all were helpless before me. I * Ps 18:38
heavens where God * it and moves Ps 19:3,4
He * springs in the valleys, and Ps 104:10
with fetters, and * his neck in an Ps 105:18
where he has * his name. Is 18:7
much as move from where it is *. Is 44:13
I saw two baskets of figs * in Jer 24:2
dungeon, but be * in the palace Jer 37:21
he has * a pitfall in my path and Lam 1:13
Temple of God, and * them in the Dan 1:1
A stone was brought and * over Dan 6:17
on his head, and * a stick in his Mt 27:29
linen cloth, and * it in his own Mt 27:60
A lamp is * on a stand to shine Mk 4:21
and the disciples * them before Mk 8:6
Then Jesus * his hands over the Mk 8:25
Then he * a little child among Mk 9:36
into his arms and * his hands on Mk 10:16
bread that was * before the Lord, Lk 6:4
in adultery and * her out in front Jn 8:3
of thorns and * it on his head and Jn 19:2
when the apostles * their hands Act 8:18

PLACED Con't)
from the cross and * in a tomb. Act 13:29
his clothing were * upon sick Act 19:12
prisoners were * in the custody of Act 27:1
that God has not * in power. Rom 13:1
the parts he has * in his church, 1Co 12:28
has * them in authority over you. Eph 6:1
(b) Melchizedek * a blessing upon Heb 7:6
whom God has * within us, watches Jas 4:5
and a crown was * upon his head; Rev 6:2
and we have * the Seal of God upon the Rev 7:3

PLACES
* and flowed across the land. Gen 2:6
tribes at the * indicated: Gen 14:5,6
the various * where leprosy may Lev 14:54
and destroy your * of worship, and Lev 26:31
And they shall live in many *. Num 24:3-9
camped at various * along the Num 33:49
These Cities will be * of Num 35:12
selected the best * for them to Deu 1:33
cities, the * Jehovah our God had Deu 2:37
grown up to take their fathers' *. Jos 5:7
living in various * as far away as Ju 4:11
into the night to * as far away as Ju 7:22
hiding * and began killing them. Ju 9:43
Discover his hiding * and then 1Sa 23:23
From their hiding *. 2Sa 22:46
Literally, "built them high * in 2Ki 17:9f
"the priests of the high *." 2Ki 23:9f
then he defiled these * by 2Ki 23:14
Literally, "high *." 2Ch 16:1f
in various other * throughout the 2Ch 17:2
Take your *; 2Ch 20:17
standing in their *, and the 2Ch 35:10
were in their *, following 2Ch 35:15
the people remained in their *." Neh 8:7,8f
fallen unto me in pleasant *." Ps 16:6f
assembly * where we worshiped you. Ps 74:8
the many * to which they had fled. Jer 40:12
He buried me in dark *, like Lam 3:6
them from all the * they were Eze 34:12
* and sleep safely in the woods. Eze 34:25
restricted area from the public *. Eze 42:16-20
from all these * you have sold them Joe 3:7
"passes through waterless *." Mt 12:43,44,45f
Those * are reserved for the Mt 20:23
famines and earthquakes in many *. Mt 24:7
and at the * of honor at banquets— Mk 12:39
of God in other * too, for that is Lk 4:43
the world to take their * there. Lk 13:29
over us, or are in * of high 1Ti 2:2
on by others who took their *. Heb 7:23

PLACING
anointed, * them before the altar. Num 7:10
their way again, * their children, Ju 18:21
the child's body, * his mouth upon 2Ki 4:34
from the Temple, * them in his own 2Ch 36:7
but honors them by * them upon Job 36:7
says, See, I am * a Foundation Is 28:16
began to think of * him over the Dan 6:3
imprisoned him, * him under the Act 12:4

PLAGUE
But the Lord sent a terrible * Gen 12:17
we face death by * or sword." Ex 5:3
will send a deadly * to destroy Ex 9:3
But the * will affect only the Ex 9:4
The Lord announced that the * Ex 9:5
This time I am going to send a * Ex 9:14
there been a * like this will be!' Ex 10:6
it was the worst locust * in all Ex 10:14
there will be no * among the people Ex 30:11,12
And the Lord sent a great * upon Ex 32:35
I will send a * among you there; Lev 26:25
There will be no * among the Num 8:19
large numbers of them with a *. Num 11:33
them with a *, and I will make you Num 14:12
them—the * has already begun." Num 16:46
the * had indeed already begun; Num 16:47
the dead, and the * was stopped, Num 16:48
and so the * was stopped. Num 16:50
So the * was stopped, but only Num 25:8
AFTER THE * had ended, Jehovah Num 26:1
cause of the * that destroyed us. Num 31:16
fever, infections, *, and war. Deu 28:22
much, and they shall * the land. Deu 28:60
every sickness and * there is, even Deu 28:61
Inside, the * Deu 32:25
despite the * that tormented us—so Jos 22:17,18
nearby villages with a * of boils. 1Sa 5:6
*, and there was a great panic. 1Sa 5:9
For the * had already begun and 1Sa 5:11
offering so that the * will stop. 1Sa 6:3
send the * upon you after all." 1Sa 6:3
caused by the *, and five gold 1Sa 6:4,5
then we will know that the * was 1Sa 6:9
or to submit to three days of *? 2Sa 24:13
So the Lord sent a * upon Israel 2Sa 24:15
Lord, and he will stop the *." 2Sa 24:21
his prayer, and the * was stopped. 2Sa 24:25
by an epidemic or *—or whatever the 1Ki 8:37
days of deadly * as the angel of 1Ch 21:12
So the Lord sent a * upon Israel 1Ch 21:14
During the * God sent an angel 1Ch 21:15
to the Lord and the * will stop." 1Ch 21:22
your nation with a great *. 2Ch 21:14
by disease and *, with no one to Job 27:15
and protects you from the fatal *. Ps 91:3
overtake me or any * come near? Ps 91:10
Or, "but sent a * to punish Ps 106:15f
him—and so a * broke out upon them Ps 106:29
sins had caused the * to start. Ps 106:30
The Lord will send a * of scabs Is 3:17
Hosts will send a * among your Is 10:16
Lying everywhere, slain by * Is 22:2
And I will send a terrible * on Jer 21:6
warning of war, famine and * Jer 28:8
war, famine and * upon the people Jer 29:16,17
captured, and many shall die of *. Jer 43:11
with locusts in a *, and they shall Jer 51:14
the land, and the * kills man and Eze 14:19
war, famine, ferocious beasts, *. Eze 14:21
Don't send them this *! Amo 7:2
Pestilence marches before him; * Hab 3:5
And the Lord will send a * on all Zec 14:12
(This same * will strike the Zec 14:15
who survive the * will go up to Zec 14:16
will punish her with some other *. Zec 14:18
send every kind of * upon the earth Rev 11:6

PLAGUED
in trouble and * with problems like Ps 73:5

PLAGUES
times more * because of your sins. Lev 26:21
sending terrible *, mighty Deu 4:34
* upon you and upon your children. Deu 28:58,59
own eyes the great * and mighty Deu 29:2,3
to bring terrible * upon Egypt; Jos 24:5
the Egyptians with * when Israel 1Sa 4:8
destroyed them with dreadful *. 1Sa 6:6
in the land, or *, or crop disease, 2Ch 6:28
they forgot the * he sent upon Ps 78:43
them over to * and sickness. Ps 78:50
nor dread the * of darkness, nor Ps 91:6
O Grave, demonstrate your *! Hos 13:14
"I sent you * like those of Amo 4:10
guard them from insects and *. Mal 3:11
* still refused to worship God! Rev 9:20
the seven last *—and then at last Rev 15:1
pour out the seven * then came from Rev 15:6
completed pouring out the seven *. Rev 15:8
God who sent the *—they did not Rev 16:9
* came over and talked with me. Rev 17:1
the seven last *, came and said to Rev 21:9
him the * described in this book. Rev 22:18

PLAGUING
* them with all sorts of trouble. 2Ch 15:6

PLAIN
spread eastward, a * was discovered Gen 11:2
the cities of the *, settling at a Gen 13:12
The Emim in the * of Kiriathaim; Gen 14:5,6
Don't stay down here on the * or Gen 19:17
villages of the *, eliminating all Gen 19:25
He looked out across the * to Gen 19:28
and attacked at the * of Arabah. Jos 8:14
cities on the *—Dibon, Bamoth-baal, Jos 13:17
* robes and thirty fancy robes. Ju 14:12
cut across the * and got there 2Sa 18:23
of the villages in the * of Ono. Neh 6:2
Lord, and make it * because I am Ps 27:11
My words are * and clear to Pro 8:9
hungry will be * for all to see. Is 32:6
in the Philistine * and in the Jer 32:44
of the Philistine *, in all the Jer 33:13
set it up on the * of Dura, in the Dan 3:1
Cities of the * that perished with Hos 11:8f
as far away as the * of Aven, and Amo 1:5
out along the * were filled with Zec 7:7
become one vast *, but Jerusalem Zec 14:10
to light and made * to all. Lk 8:17
want to, it is * where the trouble Rom 7:20
And my preaching was very *, not 1Co 2:4
for speaking in *, simple English 1Co 14:7
God will make it * to you— if you Php 3:15
it *, as, of course, I should. Col 4:4
made all of this * to us by the 2Ti 1:10
across the broad * of the earth and Rev 20:9

PLAINLY
"Well," they said, "we can * Gen 26:28
"But if the man shall * declare, Ex 21:5
Write all of these laws * [upon Deu 27:8
God of Hosts has * told me that he Is 28:22
in uncertainty will speak out *. Is 32:4
I have always told you * what Is 48:16
began to speak * to his disciples Mt 16:21
could hear perfectly and speak *! Mk 7:35
You yourselves know how * I told Jn 3:28
If you are the Messiah, tell us * Jn 10:24
Then he told them *, "Lazarus is Jn 11:14
weren't so, I would tell you *. Jn 14:2,3
tell you * all about the Father. Jn 16:25
"At last you are speaking *," Jn 16:29
Let me say * that no man's blood Act 20:26
But if I speak * what God has 1Co 14:6
he can tell people afterwards, *. 1Co 14:13
you can preach God's message *; 1Co 14:39
So we can * see that God's Heb 7:15
has been * announced to all of us. 1Pe 1:12

PLAINS
at the fertile * of the Jordan Gen 13:10
traveled to the * of Moab and Num 22:1
the *, divided by tribal areas. Num 24:2
was camped in the * of Moab beside Num 26:3,4
the priest, in the * of Moab beside Num 26:63
were camped on the * of Moab beside Num 31:12
and finally to the * of Moab beside Num 33:48
as Abel-shittim, on the * of Moab. Num 33:49
the Jordan on the * of Moab, Num 35:1
were camped on the * of Moab beside Num 36:13
IT WAS ON the * of Moab that Moses Deu 29:1
THEN MOSES CLIMBED from the * of Deu 34:1
for thirty days on the * of Moab. Deu 34:8
army across to the * of Jericho. Jos 4:12,13
at Gilgal on the * of Jericho, they Jos 5:10
as well as on the coastal *. Ju 1:9
were cast at the * of the Jordan 1Ki 7:41-46
we can beat them easily on the *. 1Ki 20:23
will fight against them in the *; 1Ki 20:25
and not of the *,' I will help you 1Ki 20:28
him in the * of Jericho, and all 2Ki 25:4,5
the cattle on the * of Sharon, and 1Ch 27:29
out in the valleys and on the *. 2Ch 26:10
them to the * before the city, and 2Ch 32:6
Then came the priests from the * Neh 3:22
and given them salt * to live in. Job 39:6
high above the * for all to Ps 48:2
the land, even on the highland *; Ps 72:16
Literally, "the * of Zoan." Ps 78:43f
sought me, the * of Sharon shall Is 65:10
he lives on the salt-encrusted * Jer 17:6
caught him on the * of Jericho and Jer 39:5
the Philistine *, and repossess the Ob 1:19

PLAN
"Should I hide my * from Gen 18:17
And do you * to kill me as you Ex 2:14
the construction *, and the details Ex 25:9
Don't go ahead with your * or Num 14:42
"This is the *," he explained Jos 8:5
Love the Lord and follow his * Jos 22:5
Then he explained his *. Ju 7:17
But David learned of Saul's * 1Sa 23:9
told Zadok, "Look, here is my *. 2Sa 15:27
approved of the *, but Absalom 2Sa 17:4
was the better *, so that he could 2Sa 17:14
But Jehu's * was to exterminate 2Ki 10:18,19
"Carry out your * in every detail, 1Ch 17:2
and gave up his * to attack Judah. 2Ch 16:5
So this was the * that was Ez 10:16-19
and the * to which he had agreed. Neh 2:18
Arab heard of our *, they scoffed Neh 2:19
exposed and frustrated their *. Neh 4:15
He claims you * to be their Neh 6:5,6
put the * into immediate effect. Est 2:4
but his own * stands forever. Ps 33:11
your eternal * for all mankind. Ps 67:2
* than yours. Ps 119:37
As your * unfolds, even the Ps 119:130
but those who * good shall be Pro 14:22
To * evil is as wrong as doing Pro 24:8
"But the Lord God says, This * Is 7:7
of his * to conquer the world. Is 10:7
For this is his purpose and *. Is 14:24
This is my * for the whole Is 14:26
me for what I didn't * to give! Is 45:19
Yet it was the Lord's good * to Is 53:10
This * of mine is not what you Is 55:8
are, for we carefully * our lies. Is 59:13
map his life and * his course— so Jer 10:23
The * is yours, not mine. Jer 17:16
Build homes and * to stay; Jer 29:5
homes and * to stay many years, Jer 29:28
or change the * that his Child will Jer 33:25,26
Listen to the * of the Lord Jer 50:45
when that is not my * at all! Eze 13:10
appearance and its * so they will Eze 43:10
But in God's time and *, his Dan 9:27
will * total war against Greece. Dan 11:2
But the * will fail. Dan 11:17
Then the Lord turned from this * Amo 7:6
he abandoned his * to destroy them, Jon 3:10
nor understand my *, for the time Mic 4:12
* in all of this to wipe us out? Hab 1:12
But these things I * won't Hab 2:3
For my * is to destroy all the Zec 12:9
In God's wise *, when you Mal 2:15
shall we * to eat the Passover?" Mt 26:17
They rejected God's * for them Lk 7:30
out in accordance with God's *. Lk 9:31
from the work I * for him is not Lk 9:62
It is part of God's *. Lk 22:22
resulting from human passion or * Jn 1:13
carry out his * to betray Jesus. Jn 13:1
*, let you use the Roman Act 2:23
foolish nations * their little Act 4:25,26
the * shown to Moses by the Angel. Act 7:44

(PLAN Con't)
got wind of their * and came to the Act 23:16
(Their * was to waylay and kill Act 25:3
God's natural * for them and Rom 1:26
this is all part of God's great * Rom 2:16
effect a different * to save us. Rom 8:3
I have been following the * Rom 15:21
This is God's * of salvation for Rom 16:25,26,27
God's wise * for their salvation. 1Co 1:24
This so-called "foolish" * of 1Co 1:25
than the wisest * of the wisest 1Co 1:25
He has chosen a * despised by 1Co 1:28
He showed us God's * of 1Co 1:30
of God's wise * to bring us into 1Co 2:7
of heaven. This * was hidden in 1Co 2:7
may, in God's *, result in the 1Co 7:14
That is the * I follow, too. 1Co 10:33
But remember that in God's * men 1Co 11:11
may be asking, did I change my *? 2Co 1:17
If the * that leads to doom was 2Co 3:9
* that makes men right with God. 2Co 3:9
of God's new * for our salvation 2Co 3:11
up to God's * for us, and this plan 2Co 10:13
for us, and this * includes our 2Co 10:13
necessary to the * of salvation. Gal 5:11
His unchanging * has always been Eph 1:5
* he decided on in mercy long ago; Eph 1:9
of God's sovereign * we were chosen Eph 1:11
me this secret * of his, that the Eph 3:2,3
did not share this * with his Eph 3:5
everyone about this * of his; Eph 3:7
and scope of his * I fall down on Eph 3:14,15
of his master * of salvation for Eph 3:21
tell his secret * to you Gentiles. Col 1:25
of his * are for you Gentiles too. Col 1:26,27
For God's secret *, now at last Col 2:2
part of God's * for us Christians. 1Th 3:2,3
to accept his * to save them 2Th 1:8
people accept God's * of faith. 1Ti 1:3,4
* of salvation through faith. 1Ti 2:7
that was his * long before the 2Ti 1:9
Under this new * we have been Heb 10:10
see how the Lord's * finally ended Jas 5:11
I * to keep on reminding you of 2Pe 1:12
then God's veiled *—mysterious Rev 10:7
eternal * and knowledge of God. Rev 13:8f
For God will put a * into their Rev 17:17
their minds, a * that will carry Rev 17:17

PLANE
almond, and * trees, and peeled Gen 30:37

PLANETS
to the sun, moon, stars, and *. 2Ki 23:5
so God does with stars and *! Is 40:26
to the sun, moon, *, and stars. 1Co 15:40f

PLANK
The altar was hollow, with * Ex 38:7

PLANKS
hollow, made from *, just as was Ex 27:8
* and debris from the broken ship. Act 27:44

PLANNED
I have * this to gain great honor Ex 14:4
now that Jehovah * to bless Israel, Num 24:1
I had * to promote you to great Num 24:11
I had * for you to destroy them." Num 33:56
The king * to lead the army 2Sa 18:2
the presents he had already *. 1Ki 10:13
He completed what he had * to do. 2Ch 7:11
So he will do to me all he has * Job 23:14
men the evil they * for others! Ps 10:2
the place of rest I * for them." Ps 95:11
the very evil they have * for me. Ps 140:9
all he * for himself is ended. Ps 146:4
He is the one who * it long ago. Is 22:9,10,11
things! You * them long ago, and Is 25:1
to happen as I *—that you should Is 37:26
Through it he had * to show the Is 42:21
my children. I * to give you part Jer 3:19
them for all that they have *! Jer 11:20
I will not destroy it as I had *. Jer 18:8
the terrible destruction he has *. Jer 30:24
* against her stands unchanged. Jer 51:29
If he did, they * to arrest him! Mk 3:2
and villages he * to visit later. Lk 10:1
casting out demons * to experiment Act 19:13
Some of the sailors * to abandon Act 27:30
brothers, that I * to come many Rom 1:13
and honors he * to give the Jews? Rom 2:26
and trust that I * to stop and see 2Co 1:15,16
as God our Father *, and rescued us Gal 1:4
to us, for that is the way God *. Gal 4:7
and long ages ago he * that we Eph 2:10
* from the very beginning. Eph 3:9
way he had always * it through Eph 3:11
is what the Lord has * for you. Col 3:18
all that he had * to make. Heb 4:4

PLANNING
if you are * to make my mission a Gen 24:42
was *, and reported it to Rebekah. Gen 27:42
(Reuben was * to get him out Gen 37:21,22
Israelis were not * to return to Ex 14:5
you are * against your people! Ex 32:12
They were * to spend the night Jos 2:1
the house, * to kill me, and they Ju 20:5
Lord was already * to kill them. 1Sa 2:23,24,25
He was * to make you and your 1Sa 13:13
told him what his father was *. 1Sa 19:2
"I'm sure he's not * any such 1Sa 20:2
I'll know that he is * to kill me. 1Sa 20:7
my father was * to kill you?" 1Sa 20:9
heard that Saul is * to come and 1Sa 23:10
So I am * to build a Temple for 1Ki 5:5
the Syrians are * to mobilize their 2Ki 6:9
* to place them under tribute. 2Ch 32:1
Meanwhile, our enemies were * to Neh 4:11
that the Jews are * to rebel, and Neh 6:5,6
neighbors while * to murder them. Ps 28:3
of * how to keep away from wrong. Ps 36:4
their waking hours * treachery. Ps 38:12
joy fills hearts that are * for Pro 12:20
deep in thought, * his evil deeds. Pro 16:30
Any enterprise is built by wise * Pro 24:3,4
*, or knowing, or understanding. Ecc 9:10
are * to refuse my gentle care Is 8:6
I faint when I hear what God is * Is 21:3
was at this time * a revolt in the Is 39:1f
neighbors while * to kill them. Jer 9:8
I didn't know that they were * to Jer 11:19
be punished for * to kill you. Jer 11:21,22
of the Lord. I am * evil against Jer 18:11
See what they are * to do to me! Jer 18:19
training period, * to make them his Dan 1:5
But he knew what they were *, Mt 12:15
* how best to get rid of him. Mk 11:18
piety, they are * schemes to cheat Lk 20:47
"Where is he * to go?" Jn 7:35
The Jews asked, "Is he * Jn 8:22
what you are * to do to these men! Act 5:35
the home of Jason, * to take Paul Act 17:5
Be glad for all God is * for you. Rom 12:12
For I am * to take a trip to Rom 15:24
when it comes to * evil, but be men 1Co 14:20
I am * to send either Artemas or Tit 3:12
I had been * to write you some Jud 1:3

PLANS
be a party to their wicked *. Gen 49:6
about their *, so he had divided Ju 9:42
to fulfill his *—he works without 1Sa 17:47
he * to return and attack us!" 2Sa 3:24,25
Tell them the * that are being 2Sa 15:35,36
about the * from his friends. 1Ki 12:2,3,4
What are your battle *?" 2Ki 3:6,7,8
the king of Israel about my *?" 2Ki 6:11
I know all your * and where you 2Ki 19:27
He also gave Solomon his * for 1Ch 28:12
had given David all these *. 1Ch 28:12
Or, "and the other * he had in 1Ch 28:12f
* and to summon them to Jerusalem. 2Ch 23:2,3
a soul about the * for Jerusalem Neh 2:11,12
to anyone about my *—not to the Neh 2:16
succeed in your * against him; Est 6:13
"He frustrates the * of crafty Job 5:12
over all the * and paths of godly Ps 1:6
He is amused by all their puny *. Ps 2:4
May the violence he * for others Ps 7:16
always boasting of their evil *. Ps 10:7
desire and fulfill all your *. Ps 20:4
he can scatter the * of all the Ps 33:10
meet together to perfect their *; Ps 56:6
their endless evil thoughts and *. Ps 64:6
* to slay your precious ones. Ps 83:3
will destroy them by their own *. Ps 94:23
me, but I will continue in your *. Ps 119:23
I told you my * and you replied. Ps 119:26
for everything serves your *. Ps 119:90,91
The Lord will work out his * for Ps 138:8
But he turns topsy-turvy the * of Ps 146:9
It is pleasant to see * develop. Pro 13:19
* go wrong with too few Pro 15:22
WE CAN MAKE our *, but the final Pro 16:1
We should make *—counting on God Pro 16:9
Don't go ahead with your * Pro 20:18
the upright but ruins the * Pro 22:12
DON'T BRAG ABOUT your * for Pro 27:1
her household, and * the day's work Pro 31:15
* of attacking us, and perish! Is 8:9,10
go along with the * of Judah to Is 8:11
that reveal the * of the Lord of Is 8:18
has spoken—who can change his *? Is 14:27
and while your * are ripening like Is 18:5
Hosts has laid his * against them. Is 19:17
But all your feverish * will not Is 22:9,10,11
try to hide their * from God, who Is 29:15
darkness the blind will see my *. Is 29:18
* which end up in deadly actions. Is 59:5
* and showed me their evil plots. Jer 11:18
For I will upset the battle * Jer 19:7
For I know the * I have for you, Jer 29:11
They are * for good and not for Jer 29:11
to discuss their * with Gedaliah Jer 40:12
In Heshbon, * have been completed Jer 48:2,3,4
about me and their whispered *. Lam 3:62
to help you understand God's *. Dan 9:22
For God's * are unshakable. Dan 11:3
For so the Lord, who * it all, Amo 9:1
THIS CHANGE OF * made Jonah very Jon 4:
* for destroying these people. Jon 4:
to discuss * for killing Jesus. Mk 3:
But Paul was told about their *, Act 9:24
his * made from the beginning. Act 15:18
God and are fitting into his *. Rom 8:2
and don't make * to enjoy evil. Rom 13:14
destroy all human * of salvation no 1Co 1:19
out my present * against some of 2Co 10:
* and methods to win my battles. 2Co 10:
* and not those of Jesus Christ. Php 2:21
them little by little about his *. Heb 1:1
whether he might change his *. Heb 6:17
about your own *, and such Jas 4:16
FIT IN with your husbands' *; 1Pe 3:1
fitted in with their husbands' *. 1Pe 3:5

PLANT
and seed-bearing *, and fruit trees Gen 1:11,12
A leafy * eaten by peasant women Gen 30:14f
a tree, not a * throughout all the Ex 10:15
You will bring them in and * them Ex 15:17
to * or harvest crops that year?' Lev 25:20
trees you didn't *—and when you Deu 6:10,11,12
the fruit of the vineyard you *. Deu 28:30
You will * vineyards and care Deu 28:39
food, though you did not * them.' Jos 24:13
the land caused by * disease or 1Ki 8:37
and will * them in their land. 1Ch 17:9
strong and virile, like a green *; Job 8:16
their fields and * their vineyards, Ps 107:37
A time to *; Ecc 3:2
therefore, even though you * a Is 17:10
morning that you * it, yet you will Is 17:11
Does he not finally * his many Is 28:25
Wherever they *, bountiful crops Is 32:20
Although it is too late now to * Is 37:30
I will * trees—cedars, myrtle, Is 41:19
* them there with my own hands; Is 60:21
My people will * vineyards and Is 65:21,22
destroy them, and * others and Jer 1:10
Why are evil men so happy? You * Jer 12:2
I will * them and not pull them Jer 24:6
Build homes and plan to stay; * Jer 29:5
that we should * fruit trees, for Jer 29:28
Again you will * your vineyards Jer 31:5
to build houses or * crops or Jer 35:7
Thrive like a * in the field!' Eze 16:6,7
I, myself, will * it on the top of Eze 17:22,23
their homes and * their vineyards. Eze 28:26
Literally, "a * of renown"; Eze 34:29f
word for "*" is in the singular. Eze 34:29f
* the good seeds of righteousness Hos 10:12
and they shall * vineyards and Amo 9:14
I will firmly * them there upon Amo 9:15
the stem of the *, so that it Jon 4:7
to be angry because the * died?" Jon 4:9
You will * crops but not harvest Mic 6:15
Look at the result: You * much Hag 1:6
Jesus replied, "Every * not Mt 15:13,14
to * good seed within their lives. Mk 4:14
Look at the ravens—they don't * Lk 12:24
the crops that others *.' Lk 19:21
My work was to * the seed in 1Co 3:6
into a * unless it "dies" first. 1Co 15:36
a different kind of * grows from 1Co 15:38
to the farmer to *, and later on, 2Co 9:10
and more seed to * and will make it 2Co 9:10
peacemakers will * seeds of peace Jas 3:18

PLANTATIONS
hold the water to irrigate my *. Ecc 2:4,5,6

PLANTED
Then the Lord God * a garden in Gen 2:8
The Lord God * all sorts of Gen 2:9
Noah became a farmer and * a Gen 9:20,21
And Abraham * a tamarisk tree Gen 21:33
the land and have * all kinds of Lev 19:23
to go through your * fields, nor Num 20:17
As aloes * by the Lord himself; Num 24:3-9
Has anyone just * a vineyard but Deu 20:6
day a root will be * that will grow Deu 29:18
When they * their seed, Ju 6:3,4
all that I have * be rooted out. Job 31:7,8
and would root out all I have *. Job 31:12
as their blessing from him, * in Ps 24:5
The godly shall be firmly * in Ps 37:29
heathen from your land and * us. Ps 80:8
Protect what you yourself have * Ps 80:15
The Lord * the cedars of Ps 104:16
they ate what others *. Ps 105:44
Praise him who * the water Ps 136:6
But though God has * eternity in Ecc 3:11
all the rocks and * his vineyard Is 5:2
within my hand. I * the stars in Is 51:16
For God has * them like strong and Is 61:3
For when I * you, I chose my seed Jer 2:21
Lord of Hosts who * the tree has Jer 11:17
He is like a tree * along a Jer 17:8
houses or owned farms or * crops. Jer 35:9
There he * it Eze 17:5

PLANTED Con't)
Literally, "* the seed of the Eze 17:5f
He took a seedling and * it in Eze 17:12,13
Now the vine is * in the Eze 19:13
* lush crops in the wilderness. Eze 36:36
from the vineyards they have *." Zep 1:13
hundred times as much as he had *. Mt 13:8
than the amount *—thirty, sixty, or Mt 13:23f
field where you * that choice seed Mt 13:27
a tiny mustard seed * in a field. Mt 13:31,32
"Every plant not * by my Father Mt 15:13,14
certain landowner * a vineyard with Mt 21:33
as much as he had *—some of it even Mk 4:8
much as was * in their hearts." Mk 4:20
"A man * a vineyard and built a Mk 12:1
times as large as he had *." Lk 8:8
"A man * a fig tree in his garden Lk 13:6
It is like a tiny mustard seed * Lk 13:19
story: "A man * a vineyard and Lk 20:9
We have * good spiritual seed in 1Co 9:11
from the seed you first *. 1Co 15:37

PLANTING
their pottery, gardening, and *; 1Ch 4:23
harrowing the soil and never * it? Is 28:23,24
you with rain at * time and with Is 30:23
from the lush vineyards you are *. Amo 5:11
streets plowed up for * grapes! Mic 1:6
about the farmer * grain: The hard Mt 13:18
The person who does the * or 1Co 3:7
it is you are *, then God gives it 1Co 15:37
he will be * seeds of evil and he Gal 6:8

PLANTS
of * and fruits they came from." Gen 1:11,12
the seed-bearing * throughout the Gen 1:29
all the grass and * to the animals Gen 1:30
There were no * or grain Gen 2:5
life—people, *, and animals alike. Gen 19:25
He lies down under the lotus *, Job 40:21
vigorous and tall as growing *. Ps 144:12-15
with her own hands she * a Pro 31:16
up and the tender * are gone. Is 15:6
grass, as tender * you trample down Is 37:27
and the oak, he * the ash in the Is 44:14
young * springing up everywhere. Is 61:11
animals, trees and * will be Jer 7:20
of earth; the * sprang up quickly Mt 13:5
the largest of *, and grows into a Mt 13:31,32
* so that they produced no grain. Mk 4:7
but, like young * in such soil, Mk 4:17
of the largest of *, with long Mk 4:31,32
like animals and *, suffer in Rom 8:22
kinds of seeds and *, so also there 1Co 15:39
A farmer who * just a few seeds 2Co 9:6
if he * much, he will reap much. 2Co 9:6
but if he * the good things of Gal 6:8
hurt the grass or * or trees, but Rev 9:4

PLASTER
Literally, "* them with Deu 27:2,3,4f
Literally, * them with Deu 27:2,3,4f
writing on the * of the wall Dan 5:5

PLASTERING
after the fresh *, then he will Lev 14:48

PLATE
"Next, make a * of pure gold and Ex 28:36
This * is to be attached by Ex 28:37,38
head the turban with the golden *. Ex 29:6
Finally they made the holy * of Ex 39:30
the sacred golden * at its Lev 8:9
you and * it with the silver." Ju 17:3
it from his own * and let it drink 2Sa 12:3
And put an iron * between you Eze 4:3

PLATEAU
then to the valley in the * of Num 21:20
the cities on the *, and all of Deu 3:10
were Bezer, on the * in the Deu 4:43

PLATEAUS
the earth and fields, and high *. Pro 8:26
open up rivers for them on high *! Is 41:18
they be on the * or in the valleys, Jer 48:8

PLATED
It was * with pure gold inside Ex 37:2
some teraphim, and many * idols. Ju 18:14
with cypress wood, * with pure 2Ch 3:5
the Temple were * with gold, with 2Ch 3:7
The upper rooms were also * with 2Ch 3:9
of angels, and * them with gold. 2Ch 3:10

PLATES
Bezalel beat gold into thin * Ex 39:3
scraps from the children's *." Mk 7:28

PLATFORM
the people on a * in the center of 2Ch 6:12,13
of the Lord. The * was made of 2Ch 6:12,13
Standing before them upon a *, he 2Ch 24:20
were on the * praising the Lord God Neh 9:4
altar is a stone * 3½ feet high. Eze 43:14
3½ feet high. This * is twenty-one Eze 43:14
Rising from this is a narrower *, Eze 43:14
From it a still narrower * rises Eze 43:15
This top * of the altar is Eze 43:16
feet square. The * beneath it is Eze 43:17
The entire * extends out from the Eze 43:17
top * and in the curb around it. Eze 43:20
it, and built a * for the watchman, Mt 21:33
bench on the stone-paved *. Jn 19:13

PLATFORMS
* or porches surrounding it. Jn 5:2
limbs—lay on the * (waiting for a Jn 5:3

PLATTER
Jacob carried the * of food into Gen 27:18
It consisted of a silver * Num 7:13

PLATTERS
12 silver * (each weighing about Num 7:84,85,86

PLAY
Literally, "they * the harlot Ex 34:15f
This was a * on words. 1Sa 1:19,20f
"We'll find a good harpist to * 1Sa 16:15,16
Saul, David would * the harp and 1Sa 16:23
sword * between our young men!" 2Sa 2:14
"Now bring me someone to * the 2Ki 3:15
A * on words. 1Ch 4:9f
of music began to * the songs of 2Ch 29:27
to your little girls to * with? Job 41:5
to praise him. * joyous melodies Ps 33:2
whale you made to * in the sea. Ps 104:26
Once "The City of Fair *," but Is 1:21
dance and *, and feast and drink. Is 22:13
There is word * here between Jer 1:12f
Children no longer * in the Jer 9:21
began to *, everyone—whatever his Dan 3:7
begins to *, and that anyone who Dan 3:10
"Righteousness" and "fair *" Amo 5:7
frequent word * in verses 10–14. Mic 1:11f
frequent word * in verses 10–14. Mic 1:11f
frequent word * in verses 10–14. Mic 1:11f
filled with boys and girls at *. Zec 8:5
like it if we * "wedding" and you Lk 7:32
like it if we * "funeral" '! Lk 7:32
And if the army bugler doesn't * 1Co 14:8

PLAYED
Manasseh's son, who * at his feet. Gen 50:23
And as the lute was *, the 2Ki 3:15
and they * loudly and joyously upon 1Ch 15:16
they * the harps and zithers. 1Ch 16:5
and Jahaziel * their trumpets 1Ch 16:6
* the cymbals, lyres, and harps. 2Ch 5:11,12
skilled musicians * background 2Ch 34:12
The priests who * the trumpets Neh 12:35,36
is being * for your enjoyment. Ps 45:8
For they have * the harlot, Hos 4:12
friends, 'We * wedding and you Mt 11:17
we * funeral but you weren't sad.' Mt 11:17
Literally, "We * the flute for Lk 7:32f

PLAYER
a talented harp *, but was 1Sa 16:18

PLAYING
* your shepherd pipes? Ju 5:16
out to meet him, * on a tambourine Ju 11:34
down the hill * a psaltery, a 1Sa 10:5
David began to soothe him by * 1Sa 18:10
listening to David * the harp, 1Sa 19:9,10
an oak tree * with his spear, 1Sa 22:6
juniper trees and * every sort of 2Sa 6:5
loud * on the harps and zithers. 1Ch 15:28
* of cymbals, harps, and zithers; 1Ch 25:6,7
and the loud * of other musical 2Ch 5:13,14
the Levites were * their 2Ch 7:6
girls * the timbrels in between. Ps 68:25
laughing and * in his presence. Pro 8:30
Hard work brings prosperity; * Pro 28:19
Foolish as little children * Is 3:12
upon the children * in the streets, Jer 6:11
These people are like children *, Mt 11:16
I'm not just shadow-boxing or * 1Co 9:26
tune the flute is * unless each 1Co 14:7

PLAYS
voice or * well on an instrument. Eze 33:32
When the music *, if you fall Dan 3:15

PLAZA
assembled at the * in front of the Neh 8:1
Temple, or on the * beside the Neh 8:16
Gate, or at the Ephraim Gate *. Neh 8:16

PLAZAS
sick in the market * and streets, Mk 6:56

PLEA
So God heeded Abraham's * and Gen 19:29
heard my * and given me a son." Gen 30:6
"At that time I made this * to Deu 3:23,24,25
Listen to every * of the people 1Ki 8:30
I will listen to your *. 2Ki 22:18,19
his *, he sacrificed to him again. 1Ch 21:28
and answered his * by returning him 2Ch 33:13
Oh, that I could write my * with Job 19:23,24
listen to my *, O God my King, Ps 5:1
*. Be for me a great Rock of Ps 31:2
listened to my * and answered me. Ps 31:22
and listen to my * and save me. Ps 71:2
Listen to my *! Ps 102:1
answer my *, because you are Ps 143:1
listen to their * and heal them. Is 19:22
to whom we send you with our *. Jer 42:2
down your ear and listen to my *. Dan 9:18
"My * is not for the world but Jn 17:9
Jesus Christ. My * is that you Phm 1:10
that Christ's * was that he be Heb 5:7f
Fellow elders, this is my * to 1Pe 5:1

PLEAD
How can we *? Gen 44:16
and begged, "* with God to take Ex 8:8
Now, hurry and * with God for Ex 8:28
Oh, I * with you, pardon the Num 14:19
"* with God to save us!" 1Sa 7:8
But I have come to * with you 2Sa 14:15,16
O Lord our God, we * with you to 2Ki 19:19
to go there to * before the Lord, 1Ch 21:30
I have built, and * with you with 2Ch 6:37,38
Jerusalem to * unitedly with him. 2Ch 20:4
"Go to the Temple and * with the 2Ch 34:21
to the king to * for her people. Est 4:8
Haman stood up to * for his life to Est 7:7
I would only * for mercy. Job 9:15
I * WITH you to help me, Lord, for Ps 28:1
down your ear and listen as I *. Ps 80:1
O Lord, I * for my life and will Ps 88:13
HOW I * with God, how I implore Ps 142:1
* for advice and help. Is 16:3
what to do; they * with their idols Is 19:3
Listen to me, listen as I *: Does Is 28:23,24
Listen as I *; Is 37:16,17
* your case for my forgiving you. Is 43:26
give you up—I will * for you to Jer 2:9
neither weep nor * for them; Jer 11:14
over again and to * with them not Jer 44:4
He will * for them and see that Jer 50:34
I will * your case; Jer 51:36
lift up your hands to him; * for Lam 2:19
O Lord, you are my lawyer! * my Lam 3:58
Listen as I *! Dan 9:17
* with your mother, for she has Hos 1:2
pot— and then you * with the Lord Mic 3:4
to them: "* with the Lord of the Lk 10:2
who * with him day and night? Lk 18:7
AND SO, DEAR brothers, I * with Rom 12:1
in the church. I * with you to be 1Co 1:10
I * WITH you—yes, I, Paul—and I 2Co 10:1
I, Paul—and I * gently, as Christ 2Co 10:1
Again I *, don't think that I 2Co 11:16
Spirit's wishes. * with him, Eph 6:18
And now I want to * with those Php 4:2
* for God's mercy upon them; 1Ti 2:1
an older man, but * with him 1Ti 5:1
to * for us from his position as Heb 6:20
to * for you before the Father. 1Jn 2:1

PLEADED
don't be angry," Abraham *. Gen 18:30
But he *, "Don't hinder my Gen 24:56
Isaac * with Jehovah to give Gen 25:21
to starve. They * with Pharaoh for Gen 41:55
But Moses *, "O Lord, I'm just Ex 4:10
went to Pharaoh and * with him. Ex 5:15
Pharaoh, and Moses * with the Lord Ex 8:12
Moses * with the Lord to help Ex 15:25
Then Moses * with Jehovah. Ex 17:4
"Lord," he *, "why is your Ex 32:11
"Stay with us," Moses *, "for Num 10:31
Moses * with the Lord. Num 14:13
mankind," they *, "must you be Num 16:22
came to me and *, 'Today the Lord Deu 5:24
But they * with him again and Ju 10:15
why you are so strong," she *. Ju 16:6
Then he * with him to stay one Ju 19:6
the girl's father *, "Stay just Ju 19:8
and * with him to help Israel. 1Sa 7:9
the other nations have," they *. 1Sa 8:5
will be your servants," they *. 1Sa 11:1
And they *, 'We will worship you 1Sa 12:10
Then Saul * again, "I have 1Sa 15:30
to harm you," Jonathan *. 1Sa 19:4
got to talk to a dead man," he *. 1Sa 28:7,8
The leaders of the nation * with 2Sa 12:17
But Ahima-az * with Joab, 2Sa 18:22
before him, and *, "My lord the 2Sa 19:19
before Elijah and * with him, "O 2Ki 1:13
"O Lord," he *, "remember how 2Ki 20:3
O Lord my God, I * with you, and Ps 30:2
I have *, but all in vain. Pro 1:24
So I earnestly * with the Lord Dan 9:3
He wept and * for a blessing from Hos 12:4
"O Jehovah," they *, "don't Jon 1:14
"Lord," he *, "I want to see!" Lk 18:41
wheat, but I have * in prayer for Lk 22:32
here on earth he * with God, Heb 5:7
"Fall on us," they *, "and Rev 6:16

PLEADING
Tabernacle, and * for clemency, 1Ki 1:51
my tears to God, * that he will Job 16:21
has heard my weeping and my *. Ps 6:9
I AM * for your help, O Lord; Ps 17:1
Listen to my *, Lord! Ps 27:7
noon, and night, * aloud with God; Ps 55:17
lifting my hands to heaven, *. Ps 77:2
O Lord, I reach my * hands to you Ps 88:9
and will keep on * day by day. Ps 88:13
return to me, and will keep on *; Jer 2:9

(PLEADING Con't)
for breath, * for help, prostrate Jer 4:31
stood before me * for these people, Jer 15:1
You listened to my *; Lam 3:56
and desperately * with the Lord my Dan 9:20
I will answer the * of the sky for Hos 1:21,22
there came to him, *, "Have mercy Mt 15:22
the crowd began * with Jesus to go Mk 5:17
down before him, * with him to Mk 5:23
So they began * earnestly with Lk 7:4
knocking, and *, 'Lord, open the Lk 13:24,25
Macedonia, Greece, * with him, Act 16:9
to God, * for us there in heaven. Rom 8:34
himself were here * with you, 2Co 5:20
you remember?—* with you, 1Th 2:11

PLEADINGS
his *, but we wouldn't listen." Gen 42:21
their prayers and * from heaven 1Ki 8:49
for what I think, and to my *. Job 13:6
Lord, for he has listened to my *! Ps 28:6
again and prayed, repeating his *. Mk 14:39

PLEADS
"King Balak * with you to come. Num 22:16,17
Ben-hadad *, 'Let me live!' 1Ki 20:32
The poor man * and the rich man Pro 18:23
your name or * with you for mercy. Is 64:7
Yet the Lord * with you still: Jer 6:16
Jerusalem * for help but no one Lam 1:17
Now Israel * with me and says, Hos 8:2
"Sir," the leper *, "if you Mt 8:2
is saying as he * for us in harmony Rom 8:27

PLEAS
have heard their * for freedom from Ex 3:7
to my * and didn't destroy you. Deu 10:10
him added their * to that of the 1Sa 28:23
your ears listening to their *. 1Ki 8:52
I will not listen to their *. Jer 11:11

PLEASANT
was, how * the land, he willingly Gen 49:15
to the Lord, and very * to him. Ex 29:18
this will be very * to him. Lev 23:13
It will be a * odor before the Num 15:23,24
it is very * to the Lord. Num 18:17
they will be very * to the Lord. Num 28:24
A special burnt offering, very * Num 28:27
will be very * to him—of one young Num 29:8
are very * to the Lord—of one young Num 29:36
and enjoys your * home and gets Deu 15:16
and they all had a very * time. Ju 19:4
and we will have a * evening Ju 19:9
Call me Mara," (Naomi means * Ru 1:20
boy, ruddy-faced, and with * eyes. 1Sa 16:12
you give them a * reply and agree 1Ki 12:7
Shall we receive only * things Job 2:10
* valley and to prosper you there. Job 36:16
in a conscious and * hereafter for Ps 6:5f
He sees that I am given * brooks Ps 16:6
are fallen unto me in * places." Ps 16:6f
HOW WONDERFUL IT is, how *, when Ps 133:1
"as a loving hind and a * doe." Pro 5:19f
It is * to see plans develop. Pro 13:19
lies a wide and * road that seems Pro 14:12
* sights and good reports give Pro 15:30
and a * teacher is the best. Pro 16:21
lies a wide and * road he thinks is Pro 16:25
* enough, but don't believe him; Pro 26:24,25,26
Friendly suggestions are as * as Pro 27:9
If you shout a * greeting to a Pro 27:14
It is * to listen to wise words, Ecc 10:12,13
What a lovely, * thing you are, Sol 1:16
how *, O love, for utter delight! Sol 7:6
Israel and Judah are his * Is 5:7
All the * music in your palace Is 14:11
as on a * summer day or a lovely Is 18:4
All rest at night—so * once—is Is 21:4
You have taken * incense and Is 57:9
Israel, the * Land, and overthrow Dan 11:41
incense in the * shade of oaks and Hos 4:13
* Land lay bare and blighted." Zec 7:14

PLEASANTLY
Don't trust them, no matter how * Jer 12:6
prison, and spoke * to him and Jer 52:32

PLEASE
"Sirs," he said, "* don't go Gen 18:3,4
"* don't be angry," Abraham Gen 18:30
behind him. "*, fellows," he Gen 19:7
"Oh no, sirs, *," Lot begged, Gen 19:18,19,20
just a small one. *, please, let me Gen 19:18,19,20
Please, *, let me go there Gen 19:18,19,20
to bury my wife. * sell me a piece Gen 23:4
said to Abraham, "* listen to me. Gen 23:11
mission a success, * guide me in Gen 24:42
"* give me a drink of water!" Gen 24:43
I said to her, '* give me a Gen 24:45
"* don't leave me," Laban Gen 30:27
O Lord, * deliver me from Gen 32:11
"No, but * accept them," Jacob Gen 33:10
* take my gifts. Gen 33:11
just fine. * do as I suggest." Gen 33:15
be his wife. * let him marry her. Gen 34:8
and brothers. "* be kind to me and Gen 34:11
wine taster. And * have some pity Gen 40:14
blame forever.' * sir, let me stay Gen 44:33
But Moses said, "Lord, *! Ex 4:13
low and begging, "* leave at once, Ex 11:8
"Leave us; * go away, all of you; Ex 12:31
If she does not * the man who Ex 21:8
favor before you; *, if this is Ex 33:13
* go with us to the Promised Land; Ex 34:9
me like this, * kill me right now; Num 11:15
"Oh, *, show the great power [of Num 14:17,18
and they want to * the Lord with a Num 15:3,4
you who want to * the Lord with Num 15:13,14
of your land. * let us pass Num 20:17
explained. "* come and curse them Num 22:5,6
Perhaps it will * God to let you Num 23:27
* appoint a new leader for the Num 27:16
and will * the Lord very much. Num 28:13
for our flocks. * let us have this Num 32:5
God: 'O Lord God, * let me cross Deu 3:23,24,25
and Jacob. Oh, * overlook the awful Deu 9:27
* give us springs of water too." Ju 1:15
"* give me some water," he Ju 4:19
Then Gideon said to the Lord, "* Ju 6:39
Then Manoah prayed, "O Lord, * Ju 13:8
to the Angel, "* stay here until Ju 13:15
her his secret. "* tell me, Ju 16:6
You told me a lie! * tell me how Ju 16:10
remember me again—* strengthen me Ju 16:28
will tell them, '* be understanding Ju 21:22
heart to the Lord. * don't think 1Sa 1:15,16
money and food. '*,' they will say, 1Sa 2:36
asked, "Can you * tell me where 1Sa 9:18
demanded. Oh, * pardon my sin now 1Sa 15:25
Then Saul wrote to Jesse, "* let 1Sa 16:22
O Lord God of Israel, * tell 1Sa 23:11
time of holiday. * give us a 1Sa 25:8
"* listen to what I want to say. 1Sa 25:24
boor, but * don't pay any attention 1Sa 25:25
things for you, * remember me!" 1Sa 25:30,31
say no. * don't upset them, but go 1Sa 29:7
fools in Israel. *, just speak to 2Sa 13:13
Then she said, "* swear to me by 2Sa 14:11
"* let me ask one more thing of 2Sa 14:12
prayed, "O Lord, * make Ahithophel 2Sa 15:31
sake, * don't harm young Absalom.' 2Sa 18:12
with Joab, "* let me go, too." 2Sa 18:22
lord the king, * forgive me and 2Sa 19:19
was very wrong. * forgive this 2Sa 24:10
of you; * don't turn me down." 1Ki 2:16
Now * assist me with this 1Ki 5:6
my request: * watch over this 1Ki 8:29
night or by day, * listen to me and 1Ki 8:29
"Oh, *, please," the king cried 1Ki 13:6
"Oh, please, *," the king cried 1Ki 13:6
"O Lord my God, * let this child's 1Ki 17:21
"O man of God, * spare my life and 2Ki 1:13
Then Elijah said to Elisha, "* 2Ki 2:4
"Will you * be quiet?" 2Ki 2:5
Then Elijah said to Elisha, "* 2Ki 2:6,7
And Elisha replied, "* grant me 2Ki 2:9
Israel; now * accept my gifts." 2Ki 5:15
"all right. But * give me two 2Ki 5:17
"*, sir, come with us," someone 2Ki 6:3
"Lord, * make them blind." 2Ki 6:18
said to them, "* speak in Aramaic, 2Ki 18:26
* you in everything I do ." 2Ki 20:3
me in my work; * be with me in all 1Ch 4:10
who has sinned. * forgive me, for I 1Ch 21:8
Yes, Lord God of Israel, * 2Ch 6:17
did decide really to * the Lord. 2Ch 12:14
Joash tried hard to * the Lord 2Ch 24:2
Uzziah was always eager to * God. 2Ch 26:5
Euphrates River. * be informed Ez 4:12
* remember what you told Moses! Neh 1:8
O Lord, * hear my prayer! Neh 1:11
to honor you. * help me now as I go Neh 1:11
I replied, "If it * Your Majesty Neh 2:4
request: "If it * the king, give Neh 2:7
O my God, * keep in mind all Neh 5:19
(O Lord God, * strengthen me! Neh 6:9
If it * the king, issue a decree Est 3:9
And Esther replied, "If it * Est 5:4
honors those who truly * him!' Est 6:9
O king, and if it * Your Majesty, Est 7:3
and said, "If it * Your Majesty, Est 8:5
And Esther said, "If it * Your Est 9:13
"Do with him as you *," the Job 2:6
destroy me. Oh, * remember that Job 10:9
they are doing. Oh, * be quiet! Job 13:5
"As for you—all of you * go Job 17:10
"* LISTEN, JOB, to what I have to Job 33:1
'Why waste time trying to * God?' Job 34:9
who are wise, who want to * God. Ps 14:2
*, Lord, rescue me! Ps 40:13
come quickly, and save me. * Ps 40:17
praise— that will * him more than Ps 69:31
O Lord, * help us. Ps 118:25
When a man is trying to * God, Pro 16:7
showered on those who * the king. Pro 16:15
For God gives those who * him Ecc 2:24-26
and gives it to those who * him. Ecc 2:24-26
May it * God that you escape from Ecc 7:2
up nor awaken love until it *." Sol 2:7
not to awaken him until he *." Sol 8:
to him, "* talk to us in Aramaic Is 36:1
the things that * him, and come to Is 56:
eager you were to * me as a young Jer 2:
correct me, Lord; but * be gentle. Jer 10:2
and said, "* pray for us to the Jer 42:
appoint over them whomsoever I *. Jer 50:4
But if he doesn't, * understand, Dan 3:1
mercies, Lord, * turn away your Dan 9:1
that is offered there can * him; Hos 9:
Then I said, "O Lord God, * Amo 7:
Then I said, "O Lord God, * Amo 7:
"* kill me, Lord; Jon 4:
of olive oil—would that * him? Mic 6:
Then I said, "*, could he also Zec 3:5,6
I'm going! * come with me. Zec 8:20,21
one Jew and say, '* be my friend, Zec 8:2
But Jesus said, "* do it, for I Mt 3:15
in desperation. "* come and place Mk 5:23
and anxious to * the people, Mk 15:15
"* heal her," everyone begged. Lk 4:38
said, "Oh, sir, * leave us—I'm too Lk 5:8
of God Most High? *, I beg you, oh, Lk 8:28
'* don't ask me to get up. Lk 11:7
the crowd, "Sir, * tell my brother Lk 12:13
* take me on as a hired man." Lk 15:19
Abraham, then * send him to my Lk 16:27
you are willing, * take away this Lk 22:41,42
"*, sir," the woman said, Jn 4:15
The official pled, "Sir, * come Jn 4:49
Then Festus, anxious to * the Act 25:9
customs. Now * listen patiently! Act 26:3
he said. "* eat something now for Act 27:34
live only to * themselves, but Rom 8:5
doing those things that * God. Rom 8:5
old evil desires, can never * God. Rom 8:8
to * the Lord, and is thankful. Rom 14:6
ahead and do them to * ourselves; Rom 15:1
Let's * the other fellow, not Rom 15:1
Christ didn't * himself. Rom 15:3
* give my greetings to all those Rom 16:5
I did. * give them my greetings. Rom 16:7
mother to me. And * give my Rom 16:14
work and thinking how to * him. 1Co 7:32
and how to * his wife. 1Co 7:33
* the Lord in all she is and does. 1Co 7:34
I try to * everyone in everything 1Co 10:33
everywhere. * follow their 1Co 16:16
able to recover. * show him now 2Co 2:8
So our aim is to * him always in 2Co 5:9
for themselves, to * themselves, 2Co 5:15
to him alone. * open your hearts 2Co 7:2
* show your love for me to these 2Co 8:24
stay. * forgive me for this wrong! 2Co 12:13
* you by sweet talk and flattery; Gal 1:10
no, I am trying to * God. Gal 1:10
If I were still trying to * men I Gal 1:10
Dear brothers, * feel as I do Gal 4:12
of trying to * God by trying to Gal 4:24,25
If he sows to * his own wrong Gal 6:8
From now on * don't argue with Gal 6:17
So * don't lose heart at what Eph 3:13
and Syntyche. *, please, with the Php 4:2
Please, *, with the Lord's help, Php 4:2
live will always * the Lord and Col 1:10
not only trying to * them when they Col 3:22
and because you want to * him. Col 3:22
* give my greeting to the Col 4:15
know how to * God in your daily 1Th 4:1
to meet him? * don't be upset and 2Th 2:1
for Macedonia, * stay there in 1Ti 1:3,4
only purpose in life is to * him. 2Ti 1:3
Yes, and those who decide to * 2Ti 3:12
* come as soon as you can, for 2Ti 4:9
* say "hello" for me to 2Ti 4:19
As soon as one of them arrives, * Tit 3:12
Everybody here sends greetings. * Tit 3:15
* keep a guest room ready for me, Phm 1:22
You can never * God without Heb 11:6
destroy, let us * God by serving Heb 12:28
Brethren, * listen patiently to Heb 13:22
Christ and making you to * him. 1Pe 1:2
to God those things that * him. 1Pe 2:5
and doing the things that * him. 1Jn 3:22
their love, and * give each of the 3Jn 1:15
doing things that * me—I will give Rev 2:26
"No, sir," I replied. "* tell Rev 7:14

PLEASED
And God was * with it, and Gen 1:4,5
And God was *. Gen 1:9,10
And so it was, and God was *. Gen 1:11,12
And God was *. Gen 1:18
And God was * with what he had Gen 1:25
And Jehovah was * with Gen 8:21
offering with which the Lord is *. Lev 1:9
and the Lord will be fully *. Lev 2:2
it was a burnt offering that * Lev 8:21
and Jehovah was * by the Lev 8:28
this, would it have * the Lord?" Lev 10:19

'LEASED Con't)
sundown. This * his people, just as 2Sa 3:35,36
as everything else he did * them! 2Sa 3:35,36
The Lord was * with his reply and 1Ki 3:10
Hiram was very * with the message 1Ki 5:7
but he wasn't at all * with them. 1Ki 9:11,12
of Abishalom.) He * the Lord like 1Ki 15:11
Azariah was a good king, and he * 2Ki 15:3
could have as much as they *. Est 1:8
This suggestion naturally * the Est 2:4
This * Haman immensely and he Est 5:14
I know you are * with me because Ps 41:11
May he be * by all these Ps 104:34
God is more * when we are just Pro 21:3
nor * me with the sacrificial fat. Is 43:24
done whatever they * and worshiped Jer 9:14
so he could go and come as he *. Jer 37:4
It did as it * and became very Dan 8:4
and I will be * with it and appear Hag 1:8
like that—and see how * he is! Mal 1:8
and I am wonderfully * with him." Mt 3:17
Yes, Father, for it * you to do Mt 11:26
dance that greatly * him, so he Mt 14:6
and I am wonderfully * with him. Mt 17:5
them and greatly * them all. Mk 6:22,23
When Herod saw how much this * Act 12:3
And God was *, for Christ's love Eph 5:2
now at last it has * him to tell it Col 1:26,27
an offering that * God more than Heb 11:4
how * he was with Enoch. Heb 11:5
beneath the blows, God is well *. 1Pe 2:20
I am well * with him." 2Pe 1:17,18
be * with you when he returns. 2Pe 3:14

PLEASES
an offering that * him very much. Lev 6:21
that, the girl who * you most shall Est 2:4
to honor a man who truly * me?" Est 6:6
He does whatever * him Ps 135:6
do exactly as he *, claiming to be Dan 11:36
evil is good, that it * the Lord! Mal 2:17
Learn as you go along what * the Eph 5:10
sacrifice that * God well. Php 4:18
and mothers, for that * the Lord. Col 3:20
This is good and * God our 1Ti 2:3
This is something that * God very 1Ti 5:4
such self-confidence never * God. Jas 4:16
is good and who * God completely. 1Jn 2:1

PLEASING
This burnt offering is very * to Lev 3:15,16
that is a * fragrance to the Lord. Num 15:7
fire as a * fragrance to the Lord. Num 15:10
Lord, and offer him * sacrifices. Ps 4:5
thoughts be * even to you, O Lord Ps 19:14
on earth for all those * him." Lk 2:14
those things that are * to him." Jn 8:29
for you have been made pure and * Rom 15:15,16
whether he is * God and keeping 1Co 7:19
spend their lives * Christ who died 2Co 5:15
such sacrifices are very * to him. Heb 13:16
of Christ all that is * to him. Heb 13:20,21

PLEASURE
And God looked at them with *, Gen 1:21,22
But Noah was a * to the Lord. Gen 6:8
for burnt offerings give much * Lev 1:13
will have * in this sacrifice. Lev 1:15,16,17
And it will give the Lord much *. Lev 3:3,4,5
and it will be received with * by Lev 6:15
me are my food, and are a * to me; Num 28:1
will give much * to the Lord, shall Num 29:13
the Lord as much * in your burnt 1Sa 15:22
the Lord took * in me and has made 1Ch 28:4
and then let us know your * in Ez 5:17
their * and are in great misery. Neh 9:37
bring them to the king for his *. Est 2:2
Is it any * to the Almighty if Job 22:3
I know you get no * from Ps 5:4
May he remember with * the gifts Ps 20:3
good in your good * unto Zion; Ps 51:18f
At his * he could imprison the Ps 105:22
long, good lifeRichesHonor*Peace Pro 3:16,17
A man who loves * becomes poor; Pro 21:17
for joy—what * a wise son is! Pro 23:24,25
I even found great * in hard Ecc 2:10
in hard work. This * was, indeed, Ecc 2:10
Then I realized that even this * Ecc 2:24-26
it, for God has no * in fools. Ecc 5:4
Because you are living in evil * Is 58:3
own desires and *, nor talking Is 58:13
no * in the death of the wicked; Eze 33:11
I have no * in you," says the Mal 1:10
for lustful *, idolatry, spiritism Gal 5:19
* and thus ruining their souls. 1Ti 5:6
back, God will have no * in them. Heb 10:38
want only what will give you *. Jas 4:3
to enjoy the evil * of the unsaved Jas 4:4
* by trusting Christ to help him. 1Jn 5:4
She has lived in luxury and * Rev 18:7

PLEASURE-MAD
O * kingdom, living at ease, Is 47:8

PLEASURES
* of your own eternal presence. Ps 16:11
put aside your own * and shoulder Mk 8:34
responsibilities and * of life. Lk 8:14
Take no part in the worthless * Eph 5:11
mention here those * of darkness Eph 5:12
living and sinful * and to live Tit 2:12
to many evil * and wicked desires. Tit 3:3
of enjoying the fleeting * of sin. Heb 11:24,25
enemies—the evil * of this Jas 4:4
from the evil * of this world; 1Pe 2:11
For they live in evil * day after 2Pe 2:13

PLED
oh, how I *: "What will you Ps 30:8
Then at last I spoke, and * with Ps 39:2,3
IN MY TROUBLES I * with God to Ps 120:1
"Lord," I *, "you are my only Ps 142:5
and he * with God for sinners. Is 53:12
Lord, you know how I have * with Jer 15:11
and Gemariah. They * with the king Jer 36:24,25
The earlier prophets * in vain Zec 1:4
captain came and * with him to come Mt 8:5,6
him and * again, "Sir, help me!" Mt 15:25
patient and I will pay it,' he *. Mt 18:29
can make me well again," he *. Mk 1:40
at his feet, and * with him to Mk 7:26
and the demons * with him to let Lk 8:32
The official *, "Sir, please Jn 4:49
and * with them to leave the city. Act 16:39

PLEDGE
"What * will you give me, so that Gen 38:17
If you take his clothing as a * Ex 22:26
or makes a foolish *, and later Num 30:6
her vow or foolish *, his Num 30:8
a millstone as a *, for it is a Deu 24:6
widow's garment in * of her debt. Deu 24:17
Literally, "take their *." 1Sa 17:18f
and gave him their * of loyalty. 2Sa 5:1
them, he made a * to the Lord to 2Ch 34:31
clothing as a *—yes, you must have Job 22:6
they have as a * to get a loan. Job 24:3
man's baby as a * before they will Job 24:9
to David with a faithful *? Ps 89:49
you as a token and * to Israel, Is 49:8,9
with an eternal * that will never Jer 50:5
I will keep the * I made to you Eze 16:59,60
given to him in * by poor debtors, Eze 18:7
have given him in *, and loves Eze 18:12
the borrower's * and returns what Eze 33:15
he will break his * and stop the Dan 9:27

PLEDGED
Sir, I * my father that I would Gen 44:32
To this they fully agreed, and * Jos 1:16
the king * $145,000,000 in gold; 1Ch 29:6,7
his brothers all * their allegiance 1Ch 29:24
* clothing of debtors overnight. Amo 2:8f

PLEDGES
and to pick up the * he had given Gen 38:20

PLEIADES
Orion and the *, and the Job 9:9
Can you restrain Orion or *? Job 38:31

PLENTIFUL
it is a land where food is *, Deu 8:9
will live long, * lives in the land Deu 32:47
like this one—with * crops, grain, 2Ki 18:31,32
and gold were as * in Jerusalem as 2Ch 1:15
He made silver become as * in 2Ch 9:27
You are ready with a * supply of Ps 69:13
your mercy is so *, so tender and Ps 69:16
also there is a * harvest of Hos 6:11
and produce a * harvest for Mk 4:20
is so * and the workers so few. Lk 10:2
kernels—a * harvest of new lives. Jn 12:23,24

PLENTY
"Yes, we have * of straw and Gen 24:25
May God always give you * of Gen 27:27,28,29
"Brother, I have *," Esau Gen 33:9
So at last the seven years of * Gen 41:53
was * of grain in the storehouses. Gen 41:54
For there we had * to eat. Ex 16:3
Beware that in your * Deu 8:11
and valleys with * of rain— a land Deu 11:11
* to eat and be fully content. Deu 11:15
Then, in *, they forsook their Deu 32:15
our donkeys, and * of food and wine Ju 19:19
will always be * of flour and oil 1Ki 17:14
there was always * left in the 1Ki 17:16
and you will have * for yourselves 2Ki 3:17
says there will be * for all, and 2Ki 4:43
where there are * of logs." 2Ki 6:1
* which you gave to our ancestors! Neh 9:36
I shall again have * of reason to Ps 42:11
to give them * of water, as though Ps 78:15
barns with * of the finest wheat. Ps 147:14
him that she had * of food on hand, Pro 7:14f
hard, and there will be * to eat! Pro 20:13
will yield * of milk, and everyone Is 7:21,22
of grain and grapes, a land of *. Is 36:17
for in those days we had * to eat Jer 44:17
No Power But with * of Noise!" Jer 46:17
in good soil with * of water to Eze 17:8
For I have * of silver and gold Hag 2:8,9
will be fertile, with * of rain; Zec 8:12
them, "and he will have great *; Mt 13:12,13
attention and * of fertilizer. Lk 13:8
And then I'll have * of friends Lk 16:4
there was * of water there. Jn 3:23,24
boat, and you'll get * of them!" Jn 21:6
muttered, "and it cost me *!" Act 22:28
Right now you have * and can help 2Co 8:14
own needs, but * left over to give 2Co 9:8
I have * to boast about and 2Co 12:6
full stomach or hunger, * or want; Php 4:12

PLIED
and from that time on they * him Lk 11:53,54

PLIGHT
about Rachel's *, and answered her Gen 30:22
in this terrible *, the Lord Ju 2:15
*, everyone broke into tears. 1Sa 11:4
king of Israel's *, he sent this 2Ki 5:8
For the Lord saw the bitter * of 2Ki 14:26
our * and care for this your vine! Ps 80:14
"O Lord," she cries, "see my * Lam 1:9

PLODDING
Steady * brings prosperity; Pro 21:5

PLOT
by the men of Heth as a burial *. Gen 23:19,20
"I can see your *! Ex 10:10
warned Abimelech about their *. Ju 9:25
nothing of any * against you." 1Sa 22:15
him in his family * at Ramah. 1Sa 25:1
The victim of a wicked *." 2Sa 3:33,34
very day for this * against me! 1Ki 2:23,24
There was a * against his life 2Ki 14:19
we knew of their *, and that God Neh 4:15
had exposed the * of Bigthana and Est 6:1
stop Haman's * against the Jews. Est 8:3
causing Haman's * to boomerang, and Est 9:24,25
has been called to * against the Ps 2:2
conceives an evil *, labors with Ps 7:14
For these men * against you, Ps 21:11
at those who * against the godly, Ps 37:12,13
to kill me. They * my ruin and Ps 38:12
me with terror and * to kill me. Ps 55:3
is tottering; they * my death and Ps 62:3,4
* to kill me though I am innocent. Ps 69:4
of craftiness and * against your Ps 83:3
the violent, who * and stir up Ps 140:2
Don't * against your neighbor; Pro 3:29
Those who * evil shall wander Pro 14:22
to those who * murder, who shut Is 33:15
How you * and scheme to win your Jer 2:33
for there is a * against her life. Jer 48:2,3,4
This will be his * for Dan 11:17
Their * smolders through the Hos 7:6
of yours who dares to * against Nah 1:11
Don't * harm to others; Zec 8:17
to * Jesus' arrest and death. Mt 12:14
rage, and began to * his murder. Lk 6:11
learned of a * to incite a mob of Act 14:5,6
he discovered a * by the Jews Act 20:3
But when I was informed of a * Act 23:30

PLOTS
or murderer who * against the Ps 26:9,10
doing good, but of * against Ps 35:20
hatch their evil *, instead of Ps 36:4
them from the * of evil men. Ps 37:40
Let their * boomerang! Ps 140:9
of disaster or the * of wicked men, Pro 3:24,25,26
their homes are full of evil *. Jer 5:27
plans and showed me their evil *. Jer 11:18
all their murderous * against me. Jer 18:23
You have seen the * my foes have Lam 3:60
for * against him will succeed. Dan 11:25
* will become public information. Mt 10:26
little * against Almighty God? Act 4:25,26
the * of the Jews against my life. Act 20:19

PLOTTED
tribe of Issachar) * against him 1Ki 15:27
chariot troops, * against him. 1Ki 16:9
But his officers * against him 2Ki 12:20
Then Hoshea (the son of Elah) * 2Ki 15:30
Then the leaders * to kill 2Ch 24:21
They * to lead an army against Neh 4:8
the king and * to assassinate him. Est 2:21
who had * to assassinate him. Est 6:1
all the Jews, had * to destroy them Est 9:24,25
They have * to call for a mob to Jer 12:6
Baruch (son of Neriah) has * Jer 43:2,3
of Babylon, has * against you and Jer 49:30
Your 'prophets' have * against Eze 22:25
This king * against our race, Act 7:19
he had argued * to murder him. Act 9:29

PLOTTERS
Not one of these * of Anathoth Jer 11:23

PLOTTING
Absalom has been * this ever 2Sa 13:32,33
But I realized they were * to Neh 6:2
and all the while are * cruelty. Ps 27:12
for they were * against my life. Ps 31:13
You are sharp as a tack in * Ps 52:2
But those * to destroy me shall Ps 63:9
for they are * against me. Ps 140:4
* evil Pro 6:16-19

(PLOTTING Con't)
Deceit fills hearts that are * Pro 12:20
For they spend their days * Pro 24:2
by being proud or * evil, don't Pro 30:32
and all those * evil will be Is 29:20
you spend your time * evil deeds Is 59:4
will be * against each other at Dan 11:27
to our nation and is * your death. Amo 7:10
They will promise peace while * Ob 1:7
lie awake at night, * wickedness; Mic 2:1
to stop * evil against each other. Zec 7:10
were actively * Jesus' murder, Lk 22:2
Jewish leaders were * his death. Jn 7:1
leaders began * Jesus' death. Jn 11:53

PLOW
"Don't * with an ox and a donkey Deu 22:10
they will be forced to * in the 1Sa 8:12
For sharpening a * point, 60Ç 1Sa 13:21
used wood from the * to build a 1Ki 19:21
Can you use a wild ox to * with? Job 39:10
If you won't * in the cold, you Pro 20:4
a farmer always * and never sow? Is 28:23,24
they shall feed your flocks and * Is 61:5
* up the hardness of your hearts; Jer 4:3
harness her to the * and harrow. Hos 10:11
a crop of my love; * the hard Hos 10:12
Can oxen * the sea? Amo 6:12

PLOW-OX
as you would strap a yoke on a *. Jer 27:2

PLOWED
valley neither * nor sowed—and Deu 21:4
"If you hadn't * with my heifer, Ju 14:18
fertile hill. He * it and took out Is 5:2
hill shall be * like an open field Jer 26:18
streets * up for planting grapes! Mic 1:6
Jerusalem will be * like a field, Mic 3:12

PLOWING
will be neither * nor harvest. Gen 45:6
"Even during * and harvest Ex 34:21
Saul was * in the field, and when 1Sa 11:5
Elisha who was * a field with 1Ki 19:19
"Your oxen were *, with the Job 1:14,15
When a servant comes in from * Lk 17:7,8,9
Those who do the * and threshing 1Co 9:10

PLOWMEN
*, and they all had a great feast. 1Ki 19:21
the crops as vinedressers and *. Jer 52:16

PLOWS
Literally, "As when one * and Ps 141:6,7f

PLOWSHARES
to sharpen their *, discs, axes, or 1Sa 13:20
their swords into * and their Is 2:4f
Melt your * into swords and beat Joe 3:10
their swords into * and their Mic 4:3

PLUCK
Sing, accompanied by drums; * the Ps 81:2
The birds will * off her twigs Eze 31:13

PLUCKED
shall have his eye * out by ravens Pro 30:17
He has * you bare! Jer 48:32
to Lebanon and * off the shoot at Eze 17:3,4
Is not this a brand * out of the Zec 3:2f

PLUG
to * the springs outside the city. 2Ch 32:3

PLUMBLINE
wall built with a *, checking it Amo 7:7
a * to see if it was straight. Amo 7:7
I answered, "A *." Amo 7:8
"I will test my people with a *. Amo 7:8
the * in the hand of Zerubbabel. Zec 4:10

PLUMMET
I will take the line and * of Is 28:17

PLUMMETING
bring you * down, says the Lord. Ob 1:4

PLUMP
every kernel well formed and *. Gen 41:5
up the seven *, well-formed heads! Gen 41:7
all seven heads were * and full. Gen 41:22
gazelles, roebucks, and * fowl. 1Ki 4:23
And I will notice which is * and Eze 34:22

PLUNDER
great amounts of * from the city. 1Ch 20:2
carried off vast quantities of *. 2Ch 14:13
vast quantities of * were collected 2Ch 14:14
* they had captured in the battle. 2Ch 15:11
people went out to * the bodies and 2Ch 20:25
He will vomit the * he gorged. Job 20:15
dividing up the * they have won. Is 9:3
he will enslave them and * them Is 10:5,6
* and destroy the people of God. Is 17:14
Destroying armies * the land; Jer 12:12
And he shall * the land of Egypt Jer 43:12
"They will * all your riches and Eze 26:12
and * those beautiful homes." Amo 3:11
come at night to * you—for they Ob 1:5
full of lies, crammed with *. Nah 3:1
left will * and possess them." Zep 2:9

PLUNDERED
Then the victors * Gen 14:11
sons went over and * the city Gen 34:27
their crops and * the countryside Ju 6:3,4
* the deserted Philistine camp. 1Sa 17:53
out and * the camp of the Syrians. 2Ki 7:16
They not only * the cities, but 2Ch 14:15
I see you * and destroyed. Is 21:2
Bashan and Carmel are *. Is 33:9
Her enemies have * her Lam 1:10
property will be * by the enemy, Zep 1:13

PLUNDERERS
glad, O Chaldeans, * of my people, Jer 50:11

PLUNDERING
and * everything they see. Is 1:7
When they finally stop *, the Is 7:21,22
Literally, "* and despoiling Is 8:1f
off her wealth, * everything she Eze 29:19

PLUNGE
to * it into his son, to slay him. Gen 22:10
would * me into the ditch and mud; Job 9:31
the wicked * ahead—and fall. Pro 12:26

PLUNGED
With that, Joshua * his sword Jos 10:26
* it deep into the king's belly. Ju 3:21
Then he took three daggers and * 2Sa 18:14
But their swords will be * into Ps 37:15
the entire herd * down the steep Mk 5:13
stars, which he * to the earth. Rev 12:4
and his kingdom was * into Rev 16:10

PLUNGES
a fool * ahead with great Pro 14:16
the light and * you into darkness. Lk 11:34

PLURALITY
as a collective noun, implying *. Rev 22:2f

PLUS
frames, * another at each corner. Ex 36:28
by paying for the loss, * a Lev 5:16
pay that amount * twenty percent, Lev 27:14,15
of its worth, * twenty percent; Lev 27:27
quarts of oil, * three quarts of Num 15:10
He promises you great honors * Num 22:16,17
the Arnon River, * half of Mount Deu 3:12
ten dollars a year * a new suit and Ju 17:10,11
The Thirty, * the Top Three, plus 2Sa 23:24-39f
The Thirty, plus the Top Three, * 2Sa 23:24-39f
restored to her, * the value of any 2Ki 8:6
* everything else she asked for! 2Ch 9:12
and history—* a strong dose of Dan 1:3,4f
It will be forty-nine years * 434 Dan 9:25
Three and a half years (verse 7) * Dan 12:11f
God is by faith alone, * nothing; Jas 2:18

PLY
here among us and * their trade. Gen 34:21
Wail, you ships that * the Is 23:14

PLYING
* the trade routes of the world. Ps 107:23

POCHERETH-HAZZEBAIM
Shephatiah, Hattil, *, Ami. Ez 2:55,56,57
*, Amon. Neh 7:57,58,59

POCKET
Insert into the * of the Ex 28:30,31

POCKETS
it into * filled with holes! Hag 1:6

PODS
that even the * he was feeding the Lk 15:16

POEM
referred to King Sihon in this *: Num 21:27-30
I will write a lovely * to the Ps 45:1
wrote this * about his experience: Is 38:9

POETS
The ancient * had referred to Num 21:27-30
As one of your own * says it, 'We Act 17:28

POINT
which I'll * out to you!" Gen 22:2
At which *, Pharaoh woke up! Gen 41:4
"Tell Aaron to * his rod toward Ex 7:19
Aaron to * the rod toward all the Ex 8:5
Then Jehovah said to Moses, "* Ex 9:22
and * out what each is to carry. Num 4:17,18,19
Its southernmost * will be Num 34:4
And the water below that * flowed Jos 3:15,16
there's no * in all of us going Jos 7:3
and the Lord will * out the tribe Jos 7:14
Lord will * out the guilty clan; Jos 7:14
Then the Lord said to Joshua, "* Jos 8:18
From that * it went through the Jos 15:7
For sharpening a plow *, 60Ç 1Sa 13:21
and fell upon the * of the blade, 1Sa 31:3,4
own sword and fell against its *; 1Ch 10:4
But at that * he became proud—and 2Ch 26:16
At that * Manasseh finally 2Ch 33:13
extending from a * opposite the Neh 3:21
Help me! * out my sin to me. Job 13:23
* comes out from his gall. Job 20:25
to say at this *, go ahead. Job 33:32
the trouble to * out to them the Job 36:9
to the distribution * of light? Job 38:24
should go, O Lord; * out the right Ps 25:4
within me grew to the bursting *. Ps 39:2,3
At that * God turned the Ps 105:25
God's patience to the breaking *. Ps 106:14
test my thoughts. * out anything Ps 139:24
I cannot overemphasize this *." Pro 4:5
so that its * will no more be felt Pro 26:9
What can you * to that is new? Ecc 1:8-
But at this * the Assyrian king Is 37:8
Shall I bring to the * of birth Is 66
That was not the * of my command. Jer 7:
Sobbing and weeping, I * to their Jer 9:
pen or diamond * upon their stony Jer 17
At that * Jeremiah walked out. Jer 28:
This message, in * of time, Jer 45:
At that * the water was up to my Eze 47
boundary to the * where the Eze 47:
of attention from this * on. Dan 11:4
Don't * your finger at someone Hos 4:
* of view, and not from God's." Mt 16:2
sadness to the * of death . Mt 26:3
At that *, all the disciples Mt 26:5
not clear on this controversial *. Mk 1:
not clear on this controversial *. Mk 1:
"She is at the * of death," he Mk 5:2
was no * in Jesus' coming now. Mk 5:3
* of view and not from God's." Mk 8:3
by sorrow to the * of death; Mk 14:3
But at this * the chief priests Mk 15:1
add at this * additional portions Lk 11:5,6
shall arise and * her finger at Lk 11:3
To further illustrate the *, he Lk 15:1
its force in even the smallest *. Lk 16:1
So from God's * of view, all men Lk 20:37,3
on this * and find him innocent. Lk 23:1
water in order to * him out to Jn 1:3
And the Scriptures * to me! Jn 5:3
At this * many of his disciples Jn 6:6
At that * the Jewish leaders Jn 8:5
At this * everyone in the Act 6:1
you could * it out to a blind man. Rom 2:1
But from God's * of view Abraham Rom 4:
even from God's * of view, but keep Rom 14:2
trust my own judgment on this *. 1Co 4:
again, then what * is there in 1Co 15:2
for the Scriptures * out very Gal 3:1
And now God can always * to us Eph 2:
Lord—yes, to the * of being filled Eph 4:1
and was at the * of death while Php 2:3
right down to the very last *. Php 3:6
disagree on some *, I believe that Php 3:15
prepared at every *, fully equipped 2Ti 3:17
uses all this to * out to us that Heb 9:8
God the Father's * of view, is the Jas 1:27
what is left is at the * of death. Rev 3:2

POINTED
The Lord * this out to Moses, Ex 7:14
And the Lord * out to him the Deu 34:1
For Joshua kept his spear * Jos 8:26
His father David, Solomon * out 1Ki 5:2,3
* out to them, it was merely a 2Ki 18:4
nor spear nor dart nor * shaft. Job 41:26
He * to his disciples. Mt 12:49
John * him out to the people, Jn 1:15
appointed, and has * him out by Act 17:31
Then Paul * out to them that Act 19:4
Of course I quickly * out to Act 25:16
the Antichrist are * at those who 1Jn 2:26
AND HE * out to me a river of pure Rev 22:1

POINTING
his sword drawn, * toward 1Ch 21:16
and * out how much I trust in you. Ps 119:147
up road signs * back to Israel. Jer 31:21
from slavery by * out your sins. Lam 2:14
* in four directions. Dan 8:8
Look, priest, I am * my finger at Hos 4:4
they knew he was * at them—they Mk 12:12
him glory by * up his honesty in Rom 3:7

POINTLESS
It is all so * and depressing. Ecc 4:8

POINTS
ten * or backward ten points?" 2Ki 20:9
ten points or backward ten *?" 2Ki 20:9
* backward on the sundial of Ahaz! 2Ki 20:11
of God's truth on these *! Ecc 9:5f
of God's truth on these *! Ecc 9:5f
of God's truth on these *! Ecc 9:10f
seek them at the fording * of Jer 22:20
try to prove his * by quoting Mk 1:22
some of these *, knowing that all Rom 15:15,16
And the Psalmist * this out when Heb 7:17

POISE
and have enough * to look good Dan 1:3,4

POISED
fist will still be * to smash you. Is 9:11,12
fist is still * to smash them all. Is 9:17
will still be * to strike you. Is 10:4
Yet the sword is even now * to Jer 4:10
Lord stands * against Jerusalem. Mic 1:12
God's judgment is * to chop down Mt 3:10
The axe of his judgment is * Lk 3:9

POISON
are bitter with *; Deu 32:32
sir, there's * in this stew!" 2Ki 4:40
It is like * and death to him. Job 20:16
For food they gave me *; Ps 69:21
off your feet and drinking *! Pro 26:6
given us a cup of * to drink Jer 8:14

(POISON Con't)
and give them * to drink. Jer 9:15
and give them * to drink. Jer 23:15
like a cup of * to all the nearby Zec 12:2
the sting and * of deadly snakes. Rom 3:13
ready to pour out its deadly *. Jas 3:8

POISONED
he has sent his * arrows deep Job 6:4
tongues aim lies like * spears. Jer 9:8
because it * a third of all the Rev 8:11

POISONING
water into blood, * the fish. Ps 105:29

POISONOUS
So the Lord sent * snakes among Num 21:6
that will grow bitter and * fruit. Deu 29:18
realizing that they were *. 2Ki 4:39
They are * as deadly snakes, Ps 58:4,5
a lion or step on * snakes, yes, Ps 91:13
Their words sting like * snakes. Ps 140:3
For in the end it bites like a * Pro 23:32
Babies will crawl safely among * Is 11:8
ox does, and * snakes shall strike Is 65:25
* snakes which you cannot charm. Jer 8:17
up among them like * weeds in the Hos 10:4
fish, will he be given a * snake? Mt 7:10
anything *, it won't hurt them; Mk 16:18
lay on the fire, a * snake, driven Act 28:3

POISONS
It is full of wickedness, and * Jas 3:6

POLE
your body on a *, and the birds Gen 40:18,19
executed, and impaled on a *." Gen 41:13
to carry it on a * between them! Num 13:23
and attach it to the top of a *; Num 21:8
of a serpent on a *, even so I must Jn 3:14
lifted up upon a *, so that anyone Jn 3:14

POLES
Make * from acacia wood overlaid Ex 25:13,14
gold, and fit the * into the rings Ex 25:13,14
These carrying * shall never be Ex 25:15
these are rings for the * that Ex 25:26,27
Make the * from acacia wood Ex 25:28
For moving the altar, make * Ex 27:6
To carry it, put the * into the Ex 27:7
gold rings to hold the carrying *. Ex 30:4
poles. The * are to be made of Ex 30:5
The Ark and its *; Ex 35:10-19
The table, its carrying *, and all Ex 35:10-19
incense altar and its carrying *; Ex 35:10-19
and its carrying * and utensils; Ex 35:10-19
Then he made * from acacia wood, Ex 37:4
gold, and put the * into the rings Ex 37:5
to hold the carrying * in place. Ex 37:14
molding, to hold the carrying *. Ex 37:27
The carrying * were gold-plated Ex 37:28
grating, to insert the carrying *. Ex 38:5
The carrying * themselves were Ex 38:6
The carrying * were inserted Ex 38:7
The carrying *; Ex 39:33-40
The * and the utensils; Ex 39:33-40
the carrying * to the Ark and Ex 40:20
* of the Ark in their rings. Num 4:6
the carrying * into the table. Num 4:8
the carrying * into the altar. Num 4:11
Finally, the carrying * are to be Num 4:14
the Ark and its carrying *. 1Ki 8:7
poles. The * were so long that 1Ki 8:8
with its carrying *, just as the 1Ch 15:15
over the Ark and its carrying *. 2Ch 5:7,8
These carrying * were so long 2Ch 5:9
totem * erected by their kings. Eze 43:7
away their idols and the totem * Eze 43:9

POLICE
He dispatched a * squadron to Jos 2:3
the city, so the * were alerted and Ju 16:2
and even the * courts are corrupt. Ecc 3:16
in vain. The * stopped me and I Sol 3:3
"Use your own Temple *," Pilate Mt 27:65
some of the Temple * who had been Mt 28:11
to bribe the * to say they had all Mt 28:12,13
So the * accepted the bribe and Mt 28:15
The Temple * who had been sent to Jn 7:45
soldiers and * to accompany him. Jn 18:3
So the Jewish *, with the Jn 18:12
The * and the household servants Jn 18:18
*, and some of the Sadducees Act 4:1
But when the * arrived at the Act 5:22
When the * captain Act 5:24
The * captain went with his Act 5:26,27
the judges sent * officers over to Act 16:35
The * officers reported to the Act 16:38

POLICEMAN
For the * does not frighten Rom 13:3
The * is sent by God to help you. Rom 13:4

POLISH
You are so careful to * the Mt 23:25

POLISHED
for King Solomon, using * bronze. 2Ch 4:12-16
than rubies, * like sapphires." Lam 4:7f
something that shone like * brass. Eze 1:4
they were made of * amber and each Eze 1:16
and * for terrible slaughter. Eze 21:9,10,11
it is sharpened and * and flashes Eze 21:28
his arms and feet shone like * Dan 10:5,6

POLITICAL
according to their * groupings, Gen 10:31
linguistic and * unity, just think Gen 11:6
the seventy-seven * and religious Ju 8:14
a very powerful * leader among the 2Sa 3:6
He summoned all the * and 1Ch 23:2
The top * officers of the tribes 1Ch 27:16-22
to Jerusalem—the * leaders, the 1Ch 28:1
as well as all the * and 2Ch 1:2,3
* leaders to decide what to do. 2Ch 28:14
marriages, and the * leaders were Ez 9:2
plans—not to the * or religious Neh 2:16
The * leaders who signed: Neh 10:14-27
Coniah to Babylon as a * hostage. Jer 37:1f
Using his wealth for * advantage, Dan 11:2
Jewish * leaders. Mt 3:7f
Zealots," a subversive * party), Mt 10:2,3,4
The Herodians were a Jewish * Mt 22:16f
A pro-Roman * party. Mk 3:6f
Simon (a member of a * party Mk 3:16-19
sent other religious and * leaders Mk 12:13
Zealots, a subversive * party), Lk 6:14,15,16

POLITICIANS
Tobiah and the wealthy * of Judah. Neh 6:17
YOU HIGH and mighty * don't even Ps 58:1
lawyers, magicians and *. Is 3:3

POLITICO-RELIGIOUS
Jewish * leaders of two different Mt 16:1f

POLLS
"five shekels apiece by the *; Num 3:47,48f

POLLUTE
am God, I let them * themselves Eze 20:26
you are going to * yourselves just Eze 20:30
Jerusalem and * the sanctuary, Dan 11:30,31
they are what * you and make you Mk 7:23

POLLUTED
land will not be *, for murder Num 35:33
of God were being * by these mixed Ez 9:2
* to the depths of their souls. Ps 55:15
You have * the land with your Jer 3:2
And so the land was greatly * and Jer 3:9
me and not to be * any longer with Eze 14:11
They * the land with murder and Eze 36:18
it is *, just as food of mourners Hos 9:4
"When you offer * sacrifices on Mal 1:7
"* sacrifices? Mal 1:7

POLLUTES
for murder * the land, and no Num 35:33
"It is the thought-life that *. Mk 7:20

POLLUTING
nations, thus * the Temple of the 2Ch 36:14
blood and * the land with murder. Ps 106:37,38
* a fountain or muddying a spring. Pro 25:26
right in my own Temple, * it. Jer 7:30
They shall stop * themselves Eze 37:23

POMEGRANATE
around the * tree at Migron. 1Sa 14:2
Literally, "like halves of a *." Sol 4:3f
"like the halves of a *." Sol 6:7f
wine to drink, sweet * wine. Sol 8:2

POMEGRANATES
*, alternated with gold bells. Ex 28:33,34
would not tear. * were attached to Ex 39:24
placed between the * along the Ex 39:25,26
* alternating all around the edge. Ex 39:25,26
some samples of the * and figs. Num 13:23
vines, and * you told us about? Num 20:5
fig trees, *, olives, and honey; Deu 8:8
and four hundred * in two rows. 1Ki 7:16-22
Four hundred * in two rows on the 1Ki 7:41-46
bronze network of * decorating the 2Ki 25:17
with 100 * attached to the chains. 2Ch 3:16
The 400 * hanging from the two 2Ch 4:12-16
shoots are an orchard of *." Sol 4:13,14f
or the * were blossoming yet. Sol 6:11
whether the * are in flower. Sol 7:12
carvings, a network of bronze *. Jer 52:22
There were ninety-six * on the Jer 52:23
the fig trees are dying; the * Joe 1:12
and figs and * and olives have Hag 2:18,19

POMP
(The customary * and ceremony was 2Ch 21:19
with all their *, and wealthy Job 3:14,15
But man with all his * must die Ps 49:12
For man with all his * Ps 49:20
for your days of glory, * and Is 47:1
princes riding in * and splendor Jer 17:25
with great *, accompanied by Act 25:23

PONDER
All who are thankful should * Ps 111:1

PONTIUS
For Herod the king, and * Pilate Act 4:27
testimony before * Pilate, that 1Ti 6:13

PONTUS
Judea, Cappadocia, *, Ausia, Act 2:9
Aquila, born in *, who had recently Act 18:2,3
throughout *, Galatia, Cappadocia, 1Pe 1:1

POOL
They met at the * of Gibeon, 2Sa 2:13
other on opposite sides of the *. 2Sa 2:13
bodies beside the * in Hebron. 2Sa 4:12
washed beside the * of Samaria, 1Ki 22:38
near the conduit of the upper *. 2Ki 18:17
the * and conduit he made and how 2Ki 20:20
and to the King's *, but my donkey Neh 2:14,15
the wall from the * of Siloam to Neh 3:15
for water from the lower *! Is 22:9,10,11
will become a *, with springs of Is 35:7
of the upper *, along the road Is 36:2
They caught up with him at the * Jer 41:12
Gate, was Bethesda *, with five Jn 5:2
* at the movement of the water. Jn 5:7
and wash in the * of Siloam" (the Jn 9:7
* of Siloam and wash off the mud. Jn 9:11
draw fresh water from a salty *. Jas 3:12

POOLS
streams, and * of Egypt, so that Ex 8:5
land of brooks, *, gushing springs, Deu 8:7
of springs where * of blessing and Ps 84:6
eyes as limpid * in Heshbon by the Sol 7:4
In the deserts will be * of Is 41:18
He will dry up the rivers and *. Is 42:15
and his eyes were * of fire; Dan 10:5,6

POOR
of a man just because he is *. Ex 23:2,3
year, and let the * among the Ex 23:11
give more and the * shall not give Ex 30:15
"If he is too * to bring a lamb Lev 5:7
"If he is too * to bring Lev 5:11
But if she is too * to bring a Lev 12:8
"If he is so * that he cannot Lev 14:21
Leave them for the * and for Lev 19:10
whether a person is * or rich; Lev 19:15
leave it for the * and for Lev 23:22
If anyone becomes * and sells Lev 25:25
"If your brother becomes *, you Lev 25:35
"If a fellow Israelite becomes * Lev 25:39
Israelite becomes * and sells Lev 25:47
But if the person is too * to Lev 27:8
whether the land is rich or *, Num 13:20
No one will become * because of Deu 15:4,5
among you who are *, you must not Deu 15:7
be some among you who are *; Deu 15:11
If the man is * and gives you Deu 24:12,13
"Never oppress a * hired man, Deu 24:14,15
he is * he needs it right away; Deu 24:14,15
Let all Israel, rich and *, Ju 5:10
And those who are * and must walk. Ju 5:10
to this party just to make us *?" Ju 14:15
a younger man, even though *. Ru 3:10
Some he causes to be * 1Sa 2:7
He lifts the * from the dust— 1Sa 2:8
was worthless or of * quality. 1Sa 15:9
But David replied, "How can a * 1Sa 18:23
and the other very *, owning 2Sa 12:3
he took the * man's lamb and 2Sa 12:4
four lambs to the * man for the one 2Sa 12:6
"What does this bunch of *, Neh 4:1
Both rich and * alike are there, Job 3:19
prosperity to the * and humble, and Job 5:11
fatherless and the * from the grasp Job 5:15
And so at last the * have hope, Job 5:16
shall beg from the *, their hard Job 20:10
For he has oppressed the * and Job 20:19
of the * and fatherless are taken. Job 24:3
are taken. * widows must surrender Job 24:3
in the desert, the * must spend all Job 24:5
and take a * man's baby as a pledge Job 24:9
dawn to kill the * and needy; Job 24:14,15
helped the * in their need, and Job 29:12
I was as a father to the *, and Job 29:16
"If I have hurt the * or caused Job 31:16
to the rich than to the *. Job 34:19
* to come to the attention of God. Job 34:28
the hopes of the * shall not Ps 9:18
men who viciously persecute the *. Ps 10:2
waiting to pounce upon the *. Ps 10:9
Don't forget the * or anyone else Ps 10:12
O Lord, the * man trusts himself Ps 10:14
the oppressed, the *, the needy. Ps 12:5
He is the refuge of the * and Ps 14:6
who reverence your name. The * Ps 22:26
A war horse is a * risk for Ps 33:16,17
This * man cried to the Lord—and Ps 34:6
strong, and the * and needy from Ps 35:10
Evil men take aim to slay the *; Ps 37:14
I am * and needy, yet the Lord is Ps 40:17
THOSE who are kind to the *. Ps 41:1
HIGH and low, rich and *, all Ps 49:1
to your people, even to the *. Ps 72:2
Help him to defend the * and Ps 72:4
May the * and needy revere you Ps 72:5
and * when they cry to him; Ps 72:12
Give cause for these * and needy Ps 74:21
Give fair judgment to the * man, Ps 82:3
Rescue the * and needy from the Ps 82:4
But others become * through Ps 107:39
but he rescues the * who are Ps 107:41
For he stands beside the * and Ps 109:31
and lifts the * from the dirt, and Ps 113:7

(POOR Con't)
and satisfy her * with food. Ps 132:15
will maintain the rights of the *. Ps 140:12
justice to the * and oppressed, and Ps 146:7
Lazy men are soon *; Pro 10:4
strength. The * man's poverty is Pro 10:15
Some rich people are *, and some Pro 13:7
some * people have great wealth! Pro 13:7
ransom never worries the * man! Pro 13:8
A * man's farm may have good Pro 13:23
despise the * man, while the rich Pro 14:20
To despise the * is to sin. Pro 14:21
Anyone who oppresses the * is Pro 14:31
To help the * is to honor God. Pro 14:31
Better * and humble than proud Pro 16:19
Mocking the * is mocking the God Pro 17:5
It is * judgment to countersign Pro 17:18
The * man pleads and the rich man Pro 18:23
BETTER BE * and honest than rich Pro 19:1
the * man has none left. Pro 19:4
A * man's own brothers turn away Pro 19:7
When you help the * you are Pro 19:17
And it is better to be * than Pro 19:22
the cries of the * will be ignored Pro 21:13
man who loves pleasure becomes *; Pro 21:17
The rich and the * are alike Pro 22:2
Just as the rich rule the *, so Pro 22:7
man, the one who feeds the *. Pro 22:9
He who gains by oppressing the * Pro 22:16
Don't rob the * and sick! Pro 22:22,23
You are a * specimen if you can't Pro 24:10
It is wrong to sentence the *, Pro 24:23
When a * man oppresses those even Pro 28:3
Better to be * and honest than Pro 28:6
Income from exploiting the * will Pro 28:8
real poverty is evident to the *. Pro 28:11
dangerous to the * as a lion or Pro 28:15
If you give to the *, your needs Pro 28:27
The good man knows the * man's Pro 29:7
Rich and * are alike in this: Pro 29:13
A king who is fair to the * shall Pro 29:14
And if I am too *, I may steal, Pro 30:9
They devour the * with teeth as Pro 30:13,14
Yes, speak up for the * and Pro 31:9
She sews for the *, and Pro 31:19,20
It is better to be a * but wise Ecc 4:13
If you see some * man being Ecc 5:8
problem, yet the * man who is wise Ecc 6:7,8
wise men are often *, and skillful Ecc 9:11
a wise man, very *, and he knew Ecc 9:15
if the wise man is *, he will be Ecc 9:16
the *, the fatherless, and widows. Is 1:17
for they have defrauded the *. Is 3:14
for the *, the widows and orphans. Is 10:2
* Anathoth, what a fate is yours! Is 10:30
defend the * and the exploited. Is 11:4
I will shepherd the * of my Is 14:30
that the * of his people will find Is 14:32
for a few of the * who remain. Is 17:6
But to the *, O Lord, you are a Is 25:4
He presents it to the * and Is 26:6
the Lord, and the * shall exult in Is 29:19
to oppress the * in the courts. Is 32:7
The man too * to buy expensive Is 40:20
When the * and needy seek water Is 41:17
The *, deluded fool feeds on Is 44:20
who are helpless, * and destitute. Is 58:7
blood of the innocent and the *. Jer 2:34
we expect from the * and ignorant? Jer 5:4
orphans and the rights of the *. Jer 5:28
(And I am *, Jer 12:3
of his life become a * old fool. Jer 17:11
For he has delivered me, * and Jer 20:13
were given the * and the needy and Jer 22:16
the * and reign with ruthlessness. Jer 22:17
people, the very *, and gave them Jer 39:10
governor over the * of the land who Jer 40:7
a few for the *, and even thieves Jer 49:9,10
food, while the * and needy Eze 16:49
him in pledge by * debtors, and is Eze 18:7
and oppresses the * and needy, and Eze 18:12
and helps the * and does not loan Eze 18:17
Now the * are exalted, and the Eze 21:26
and rob the * and needy and cruelly Eze 22:29
their goods and make them *?' Eze 38:13
be merciful to the *. Dan 4:27
the * who can't repay their debts; Amo 2:6
They trample the * in the dust Amo 2:7
to rob the * and crush the Amo 4:1
pill for the * and oppressed. Amo 5:7
You trample the * and steal Amo 5:11
you refuse justice to the *. Amo 5:12
rob the *, trampling on the needy; Amo 8:4
you who make slaves of the *, Amo 8:6
Those who are left will be the * Zep 3:12
foreigners and * people, and to Zec 7:10
'May you be as * as Judah,' the Zec 8:13
preaching the Good News to the *. Mt 11:5
good fruit; * varieties don't. Mt 12:33
the money to the *, and you will Mt 19:21
a fortune and given it to the *." Mt 26:8,9
You will always have the * among Mt 26:11
and had become * from paying them, Mk 5:26
the money to the *—and you shall Mk 10:21
Then a * widow came and dropped Mk 12:42
remarked, "That * widow has given Mk 12:43,44
and given the money to the *!" Mk 14:4,5
You always have the * among you, Mk 14:7
he replied, "give one to the *. Lk 3:11
me to preach Good News to the *; Lk 4:18,19
is for you who are *, for the Lk 6:20
from * stock produce choice fruit. Lk 6:43
And the * are hearing the Good Lk 7:20,21,22
And so the * fellow is seven Lk 11:26
Instead, invite the *, the Lk 14:13
the money to the *—it will become Lk 18:22
my wealth to the *, and if I find I Lk 19:8
Then a * widow came by and Lk 21:2
"Really," he remarked, "this * Lk 21:3
need, but she, * as she is, has Lk 21:4
and the money given to the *." Jn 12:5
Not that he cared for the *, Jn 12:6
You can always help the *, but I Jn 12:8
or to give some money to the *. Jn 13:29
for others, especially for the *. Act 9:36
example to you in helping the *; Act 20:35
harbor—a * place to spend the Act 27:12
and even my preaching sounds *, 1Co 1:17
who are * and can bring no food? 1Co 11:22
If I gave everything I have to * 1Co 13:3
those most gifted is still so *. 1Co 13:9
at his reflection in a * mirror; 1Co 13:12
We are *, but we give rich 2Co 6:10
he became so very *, so that by 2Co 8:9
by being * he could make you rich. 2Co 8:9
man gives generously to the *. 2Co 9:9
If I am a * speaker, at least I 2Co 11:6
*, and I, too, was eager for that. Gal 2:10
more to another *, weak, useless Gal 4:9
for widows who are * and alone in 1Ti 5:5
Christ's people are * workers. 1Ti 6:1
people and look down on * people? Jas 2:1
comes in who is * and dressed in Jas 2:2
and say to the * man, "You can Jas 2:3
God has chosen * people to be rich Jas 2:5
you have despised the * man. Jas 2:6
*, your gifts and service to them; Rev 2:19
and * and blind and naked. Rev 3:17
small, rich and *, slave and Rev 13:16

POOR-LOOKING
never seen such * specimens in all Gen 41:19

POORER
while you become * and poorer. Deu 28:43
while you become poorer and *. Deu 28:43
those even *, he is like an Pro 28:3

POOREST
My family is the * in the whole Ju 6:15
So only the * and least skilled 2Ki 24:14
But the * of the people were 2Ki 25:12
The world's * credit risk is the Pro 27:13
some of the * of the people—along Jer 52:15
But he left some of the * people Jer 52:16

POORLY
fuel—and even so, they burn but *! Eze 15:4

POPLAR
fresh shoots from *, almond, and Gen 30:37

POPLARS
of oaks and * and terebinth trees. Hos 4:13

POPULAR
was highly respected and very *. Gen 34:18,19
Two hundred and fifty * leaders, Num 16:2
and how immensely * he was with all 1Sa 18:28
wealthy as well as being very *. 2Ch 17:5
BUT RICH, * King Jehoshaphat of 2Ch 18:1
millions of people, and be very *. Ecc 4:16
and * among the people of Israel. Amo 6:1
law and very * with the people), Act 5:34
that they can be * and avoid the Gal 6:12

POPULARITY
And the Lord gave him great * 1Ch 29:25
the height of his * and power he 2Ch 12:1
because of his * with the people. Mt 27:18
because they envied Jesus' *. Mk 15:10
[What *! 2Co 11:33
for honors and *, which lead to Gal 5:26

POPULATED
and was soon thickly *. Gen 11:2

POPULATION
NOW A * explosion took place upon Gen 6:1
As the * grew and spread Gen 11:2
veritable * explosion among them. Gen 47:27
there was a veritable * explosion Ex 1:7
a time, until your * has increased Ex 23:30
for the entire * is involved in Num 15:26
to their *, as indicated by the Num 26:52,53
to destroy the * of this whole Num 32:3,4
*—men, women, and children alike. Deu 3:6
the entire male * of Israel. Jos 5:2,3
So the entire * of Ai, twelve Jos 8:25
here, too, the entire * was Jos 10:32
slaughtering the entire *. Jos 10:37
of its territory to its size of *, Jos 13:15
of Gad in proportion to its *. Jos 13:24
the entire * except for this man Ju 1:25
Israel's * dwindled, Ju 5:7
and killed the entire male *. Ju 8:17
and the entire * fled into it, Ju 9:51
the entire * of the tribe of Ju 20:48
and burned, killing the Israeli *; 1Ki 9:16
he killed the entire * and ripped 2Ki 15:16
They took away the * of the city 2Ki 16:9
The total * figure which he gave 1Ch 21:5
a * explosion for his people. 1Ch 27:23
and had put the * at the mercy of Neh 5:15
was large, but the * was small; Neh 7:4
You caused a * explosion among Neh 9:23
the entire * of Jerusalem; Ps 79:3
A growing * is a king's glory; Pro 14:28
the foreign * living in his land. Jer 25:19,20
increase the * and multiply the Jer 31:27
the remnant of the * and all those Jer 39:9
I will greatly increase your * Eze 36:10
accommodating a * of about 175,000 Jon 3:3f
* will grow again to former size. Zec 10:8
half the * will be taken away as Zec 14:1
and the entire * came rushing out Mt 8:34
Then the whole * of Lydda and Act 9:35
The whole * of the city was Act 21:30
in view of a world * of Rev 9:16f

POPULATIONS
from the local * as the Israelis Jos 14:15
Lord has given us such large *?" Jos 17:14

POPULOUS
*, contented nation at this time. 1Ki 4:20

PORATHA
Parshandatha, Dalphon, Aspatha, *, Est 9:7-10

PORCH
and escaped across an upstairs *. Ju 3:22,23
Saul up to the * on the roof and 1Sa 9:25
the Temple was a * thirty feet long 1Ki 6:3
feet wide, with a * in front 1Ki 7:6
Temple and the * of the palace. 1Ki 7:12
off the upstairs * of his palace at 2Ki 1:2
A covered * ran along the entire 2Ch 3:4
in front of the * of the Temple. 2Ch 8:12
door, between the * and the bronze Eze 8:16
the * to be about 100 feet high. Eze 40:14
If you are on your rooftop *, Mk 13:15,16

PORCHES
Those on their * Mt 24:17
flat, were used as * at that time. Mt 24:17f
platforms or * surrounding it. Jn 5:2

PORCIUS
then Felix was succeeded by * Act 24:27

PORCUPINES
of *, full of swamps and marshes. Is 14:23
There the hawks and * will live, Is 34:11

PORK
eat * and other forbidden foods. Is 65:4
feasting there on * and mouse and Is 66:17
probably in eating * or other foods Dan 1:8f

PORT
once your hustling * was full of Is 23:2,3
for your home * is destroyed! Is 23:14
O wealthy *, great center of Jer 51:13
seacoast, to the * of Joppa, where Jon 1:3
landing at the * town of Perga. Act 13:13
Arriving at the * of Ephesus, he Act 18:19
The next stop was at the * of Cae Act 18:22
Cnidus was a * on the southeast Act 27:7,8f
Crete, passing the * of Salmone. Act 27:7,8

PORTABLE
* towers, and battering rams Deu 20:20
along with them a * Temple, or Act 7:44

PORTENTS
and * in the sun, moon and stars; Lk 21:25

PORTHOLE
Noah opened a * and released a Gen 8:6

PORTION
the government a * of all the crops Gen 41:48
and Manasseh's * from you. Gen 48:6
brothers, as your * of that land Gen 48:22
contribute this * of their Ex 29:28
burn the memorial * thereof upon Lev 2:2f
to burn only a representative * Lev 2:9
representative * before the Lord. Lev 2:16
a representative *, and burn it on Lev 5:12
a representative * for the Lord; Lev 6:15
to the Lord, any * of the sacrifice Lev 7:16
be given this * of the sacrifice. Lev 7:34
this was Moses' * of the ram of Lev 8:29
It is your * of the peace Lev 10:14
all of it is a holy * for the Num 6:20
to carry their * of the Tabernacle Num 7:9
as the Lord's *, and shall be given Num 18:28,29
there you will see only a * of Num 23:13
for it is the Lord's *." Num 31:30
Literally, "were the Lord's *." Num 31:36-40f
All of the Lord's * was given to Num 31:41
this land as our * instead of the Num 32:5
"the southern * of the country Num 34:3
does not have a * of land reserved Deu 10:9
may sell the tithe * of your crops Deu 14:25

ORTION Con't)
customary double * to his oldest Deu 21:17
given us only one * of land when Jos 17:14
who built the * of the wall from Neh 3:24
The Levites, in turn, gave a * of Neh 12:47
Literally, "Give a * to seven, Ecc 11:2f
have a double * of prosperity and Is 61:7
Sorrows and tears are his * for Lam 2:5
of it to the Lord as his holy *. Eze 45:1
people, giving a * to each tribe. Eze 45:8
It is their special * when the Eze 48:12
have within us a * of the very 1Co 2:16
you your full * of all he owns. Col 3:24

ORTIONED
And the water will be * out in Eze 4:16

ORTIONS
of Israel give these * to them; Lev 7:36
and sip their tiny * of water in Eze 12:19
point additional * of the Lord's Lk 11:5,6f

ORTRAIT
Whose * is this on it? Lk 20:24

ORTRAYING
in heaven, * things to come. Rev 12:1

ORTS
peacocks arrived at the Israeli *. 1Ki 10:22
brought by ship from distant *. Pro 31:14

POSITION
the wine taster to his former *; Gen 40:21
was restored to my * of wine Gen 41:13
me to this high * I have today so Gen 50:20
David's * now became stronger and 2Sa 3:1
He took advantage of his * by 2Sa 3:7
to give up his * as the priest of 1Ki 2:27
arm became paralyzed in that *; 1Ki 13:4
So the Lord strengthened his * 2Ch 17:5
wine, accept his * in life, and Ecc 5:18
pull you down from your high *. Is 22:19
him from his * of trust and assign Lk 12:46
Caiaphas in his * as High Priest—he Jn 11:51
to a * of strength and maturity; Eph 4:12
or social * is unimportant; Col 3:11
to plead for us from his * as Heb 6:20

POSITIONS
Because of their important * 1Ch 9:27
men, and had * of great authority 1Ch 26:6,7
appointing them to * of authority Dan 11:39

POSITIVE
because I am * that you will do Phm 1:21

POSSE
huge * into Judah and raided Lehi. Ju 15:9
Then a * of civilians killed all 2Ki 21:24

POSSESS
I will give it to you to * it. Lev 20:24
"Let us go up at once and * Num 13:30
Israel shall * all Edom and Seir. Num 24:15-19
Go in and * it, for it is the Deu 1:8
Go and * it as he told us to. Deu 1:19,20,21
when you * it, it shall belong to Deu 2:31
and enter into and * the land given Deu 4:1
the land you are to enter and * Deu 5:33
able to go in and * the good land Deu 6:18
It is time to go in and * it.' Deu 10:11
* the land you are about to enter. Deu 11:8
about to enter and * is not like Deu 11:10
into the land to * it, a blessing Deu 11:29
you are about to enter and *. Deu 28:21
You shall * the land again, and Deu 30:5
and the land you are about to *. Deu 30:16
in the land you are going in to *. Deu 30:18
to * across the Jordan River." Deu 32:47
the land we would * was totally Ez 9:11
Literally, "to * the land." Ps 37:34f
they shall * it forever, from Is 34:17
And your descendants will * the Is 54:3
But he who trusts in me shall * Is 57:13
They will * their land forever, Is 60:21
my people to * the land of Israel; Is 65:9
they shall * it and live here Jer 30:3
Should you * the land? Eze 33:26
to * the land of the Amorites. Amo 2:10
and Israel will * what is left of Amo 9:12
lowlands shall * the Philistine Ob 1:19
people of Benjamin shall * Gilead. Ob 1:19
left will plunder and * them." Zep 2:9
the earnestness I * I tell you Jn 3:3
the earnestness I * I tell you Jn 6:53
ounce of truth I *—that I will tell 2Co 11:10

POSSESSED
"We now * all the land of the Deu 3:8
How briefly we * Jerusalem! Is 63:18
you * the Ark of God's covenant. Jer 3:16
or if they were * by demons, or Mt 4:24
* by Satan, the demon king!" Mt 9:34
nation is like a man * by a demon. Mt 12:43,44,45
A man * by a demon was present Mk 1:23
And whenever those * by demons Mk 3:11
he's * by Satan, king of demons. Mk 3:22
The man who had been * by the Mk 5:18
little girl was * by a demon. Mk 7:25
talk because he is * by a demon. Mk 9:17
synagogue, a man * by a demon began Lk 4:33
Some were * by demons; Lk 4:41
this proves they are * by Satan? Lk 11:19
all along you were * by a demon?" Jn 8:48
we know you are * by a demon. Jn 8:52
to us like a man * by a demon! Jn 10:21
sick folk and those * by demons; Act 5:16
* by demons, for God was with him. Act 10:38
tried it on a man * by a demon, the Act 19:15

POSSESSING
of life to those * it, but a fool's Pro 16:22
the nations * their land on the Is 11:14

POSSESSION
They became his permanent *, by Gen 23:17,18
of Egypt were in Pharaoh's *. Gen 47:17
children, for an everlasting *.' Gen 48:4
he is caught in * of his victim or Ex 21:16
found it in the * of someone else Ex 22:9
home to his original family *; Lev 25:13
their permanent *, and they must Lev 25:34
part of his family *, the priest Lev 27:22
shall be your * from the Lord. Num 32:22
as their permanent *, and I will Deu 2:5
and begin to take * of his land. Deu 2:24
you to be his own *, more so than Deu 14:2
Israel was God's own personal *! Deu 32:9
Are your precious *. Deu 33:4
and took * of the land. Ju 2:6
Israelis and took * of Jericho, Ju 3:13
Naboth's vineyard, taking * of it. 1Ki 21:18
and took * of it for themselves. 1Ch 4:40,41
chosen Israel as his personal *. Ps 135:4
my words as your most precious *. Pro 7:2
yet he got * of the whole country! Eze 33:24
We will take * of them. Eze 35:10

POSSESSIONS
wife, and all his household and *. Gen 12:20
the new * I am giving you." Gen 13:17
and all of Lot's *, including the Gen 14:16
So he fled with all of his * Gen 31:21
SO ISRAEL SET out with all his *, Gen 46:1
all their flocks and herds and *. Gen 47:1
return to his own family and *. Lev 25:41
to be rich, or to extend his *. Job 15:29
consumes them with all their *. Job 15:34
and made the choicest of your *. Ps 74:2
put in charge of all the king's *. Ps 105:21
The Lord destroys the * of the Pro 15:25
take only the * they can carry, and Is 15:7
carry your * out through the hole. Eze 12:5
They will use the * of those who Eze 39:10
Who will inherit your * left Hos 9:6
* and dividing with those in need. Act 2:45

POSSESSIVE
I, the Lord your God, am very *. Ex 20:5

POSSIBILITY
pay, because this * was included in Ex 22:15
him beyond the * of reconciliation, 2Sa 16:21
a riot—a * they greatly feared. Lk 22:2
but also of the * that the temple Act 19:27

POSSIBLE
kept out of her way as much as *. Gen 39:10
out of the land as quickly as *. Ex 12:33
as Cush, so it is * that the Num 12:1f
And even if that were *, and I Ru 1:12
"But is it * that God would 1Ki 8:27
This made it * for him to build 2Ch 14:6
It is * to give away and become Pro 11:24,25
It is also * to hold on too Pro 11:24,25
Another * reading is, Sol 6:12f
for himself from every * source. Is 56:11
Either interpretation is * from Zec 9:10f
"How is this *?" Mt 13:55
But with God, everything is *." Mt 19:26
if it were *, even God's chosen Mt 24:24
If it is *, let this cup be taken Mt 26:39
"Anything is * if you have Mk 9:23
But with God everything is *." Mk 10:27
if *, even God's own children. Mk 13:22
that if it were * the awful hour Mk 14:35
said, "everything is * for you. Mk 14:36
And pray that if * you may arrive Lk 21:36
to Jerusalem, if *, for the Act 20:16
*, that I will have a safe trip. Rom 1:10
of course, that might be barely *. Rom 5:7
I can, so that if * I can make Rom 11:14
with everyone, just as much as *. Rom 12:18
Both interpretations are *. 1Co 6:4f
stay as free as * for the Lord; 1Co 7:29
other things as * to distract your 1Co 7:35
And that is even more true, if *, 2Co 1:12
has made all this * for you. 2Th 1:12
For it is not * for the blood of Heb 10:4
This will make * the next step, 2Pe 1:7
of this verse are equally *. 1Jn 5:6,7,8f

POSSIBLY
They said, "We couldn't *. Gen 34:14
lost in antiquity. * they were two Ex 28:30,31f
go on to Gibe-ah, or * Ramah." Ju 19:12,13
time. * there was a co-regency. 2Ki 3:1f
Literally, "hanged on a tree." * Est 2:23f
Lord, but they cannot * succeed. Ps 21:11
near and no one else can * help. Ps 22:9,10,11
Get out of it if you * can! Pro 6:3
Literally, "a man's eyes." * the Pro 27:20f
Root of Jesse." * the meaning is, Is 11:10f
on camels." * the meaning is that Is 21:6,7f
Or *, "throughout the nations of Is 24:13f
* Antiochus III the Great, who was Dan 11:13f
men, how can you * believe if I Jn 3:12
* in order to arrive in Jerusalem Act 18:20f
Or *, "but the Holy Spirit who Rom 8:10f
* his stepmother. 1Co 5:1f
tried as hard as I * could to Gal 1:14
But who could * fight and win 1Jn 5:5

POST
into twenty bronze * holders. Ex 27:9,10
Each * had a bronze base, and Ex 38:17
the stairs to his * at the top of 2Sa 18:24
his * and fled the country. 1Ki 11:23
night I have been here at my *. Is 21:8,9
They call a carved-up wooden * Jer 2:26,27

POSTED
the stone and * guards to protect Mt 27:66
And Pilate * a sign over him Jn 19:19
go only after they had * bail. Act 17:8,9

POSTERITY
be your God and the God of your *. Gen 17:7,8
You personally and all your * Gen 17:9,10
and it applies to all your *. Gen 17:12
Many kings shall be among your * Gen 17:16
princes shall be among his *. Gen 17:20
permanent law for you and your *. Ex 12:24
will multiply your * as the stars Ex 32:13
ruled by my children and their *! 1Ch 17:24
and their * shall be cut off. Ps 37:38
will be able to speak of his *? Act 8:33f

POSTS
five acacia wood *, overlaid with Ex 26:37
held up by twenty *, fitting into Ex 27:9,10
to silver rods, attached to the *. Ex 27:9,10
held up by twenty * fitted into Ex 27:11
wide, with ten * and ten sockets. Ex 27:12
three * imbedded in three sockets. Ex 27:14,15
* imbedded in their four sockets. Ex 27:16
All the * around the court are Ex 27:17
silver hooks, the * being imbedded Ex 27:17
The * of the Tabernacle court, and Ex 35:10-19
set into four * of acacia wood, Ex 36:36
connected by five hooks to five *. Ex 36:38
to five posts. The * and their Ex 36:38
There were twenty * to hold Ex 38:10
with twenty bronze * and bases and Ex 38:11
supported by ten * and bases, and Ex 38:12
each with three * and three bases. Ex 38:14,15
the tops of the * were overlaid Ex 38:17
It was supported by four *, with Ex 38:19
the tops of the * were also Ex 38:19
walls and for the * supporting the Ex 38:27
was used for the * and to overlay Ex 38:28
the bases for the * at the entrance Ex 38:29
the bases for the * supporting the Ex 38:29
*; bases; layers of covering for Ex 39:33-40
court and the * holding them up; Ex 39:33-40
of the Tabernacle building; the *; Num 3:36,37
the bases for the *, and all of Num 3:36,37
for their use; the * around the Num 3:36,37
were supporting * made of bronze 1Ki 7:27-30
establish trading * in Damascus, as 1Ki 20:34
standing at their * of duty, and 2Ch 7:6
priests to their * of duty he 2Ch 8:14
They stood at their * as 2Ch 30:16
to leave their * of duty, for their 2Ch 35:15
of Lebanon. Its * are silver, its Sol 3:10
put it on the door * of the Temple Eze 45:19

POT
Then the clay * in which the Lev 6:28
* held above running water. Lev 14:5
Any earthen * touched by the Lev 15:12
and broth in a *, he took it out to Ju 6:19
fleshhook into the * and demand 1Sa 2:13,14
* that is fired by dry rushes. Job 41:20
like a broken and discarded *. Ps 31:12
than a cooking * can feel the Ps 58:9
glaze covers a common clay *. Pro 26:23
*, and skim off your slag. Is 1:25
Does the * argue with its maker? Is 45:9
or the * exclaim, "How clumsy Is 45:9
And I replied, "I see a * of Jer 1:13
a * of water on the fire to boil. Eze 24:3
fuel on the fire beneath the *. Eze 24:5
you are a * that is pitted with Eze 24:6
let the fire roar and the * boil. Eze 24:10
empty the * and burn the bones. Eze 24:10
among the nations as a broken *. Hos 8:8
for the cooking *— and then you Mic 3:3
towards you carrying a * of water. Mk 14:13
they will be shattered like a * Rev 2:27

POTIPHAR
sold Joseph to *, an officer of the Gen 37:36
king of Egypt. * was captain of the Gen 37:36
from them by *, a member of the Gen 39:1
Now this man * was the captain of Gen 39:1

(POTIPHAR Con't)
he did succeeded. * noticed this Gen 39:3
blessing * for Joseph's sake. Gen 39:5
multiplied. So * gave Joseph the Gen 39:6
in the castle of *, the captain of Gen 40:1
* assigned Joseph to wait on them. Gen 40:4

POTIPHAR'S
administration of * household, and Gen 39:4
One day at about this time * wife Gen 39:7

POTIPHERA
of *, priest of Heliopolis. Gen 41:45
the daughter of *, priest of the Gen 41:50
of *, priest of Heliopolis); Gen 46:19-22

POTS
in bowls and * in the homes will Ex 7:19
with the altar—the *, shovels, Ex 38:3
and upon all the * and pans in the Num 19:18
sleep on, cooking *, serving bowls, 2Sa 17:28,29
Hiram also made the necessary *, 1Ki 7:40
*, shovels, basins 1Ki 7:41-46
"Then borrow many * and pans 2Ki 4:3
your jar into the * and pans, 2Ki 4:4
Her sons brought the * and pans 2Ki 4:5
They also took all the *, 2Ki 25:14,15
made the necessary *, shovels, and 2Ch 4:11
The *, shovels, and fleshhooks. 2Ch 4:12-16
holy offerings in *, kettles, and 2Ch 35:13
smash them like clay *!" Ps 2:9
and used to burn beneath the *. Is 27:11
Go down to the shop where clay * Jer 18:2
all the bronze * and kettles, and Jer 52:18
gold—are treated as earthenware *. Lam 4:2
making pegs to hang up * and pans! Eze 15:3
cleansing for *, pans and dishes. Mk 7:4

POTTER
Isn't he, the *, greater than Is 29:16
He will tread them as a * Is 41:25
We are the clay and you are the * Is 64:8
found the * working at his wheel. Jer 18:3
as this * has done to his clay? Jer 18:6
"Cast it to the *" is the Zec 11:13f

POTTER'S
As the clay is in the * hand, so Jer 18:6

POTTERS
clay was used by *, and to make it Mt 27:7
the * as the Lord directed me." Mt 27:10

POTTERY
If it falls into a * bowl, Lev 11:33
their *, gardening, and planting; 1Ch 4:23
a broken piece of * to scrape Job 2:8
put them into a * jar to preserve Jer 32:14

POUCH
two folds of cloth, forming a *. Ex 28:16
square, doubled over to form a *; Ex 39:9
inside its *; Lev 8:8
An ephod was usually a linen * Ju 8:27f

POUNCE
calamity stands ready to * upon Job 18:12
Don't let them * upon me as a Ps 7:2
waiting to * upon the poor. Ps 10:9
They roar like lions and * upon Is 5:29
the "desert wolves" shall * Jer 5:6
down to * upon their prey. Hab 1:8

POUND
bowl of about one *, both filled Num 7:13
(each weighing about one *); Num 7:84,85,86
terribly, and to * them on the Zec 1:21

POUNDED
it into flour or * it in mortars, Num 11:8
She * the tent pin through his Ju 5:26

POUNDING
* on the seashores of the world! Ps 93:4
so he doesn't keep on * it. Is 28:28
axe, * on it with all his might. Is 44:12
horses' hoofs *, and chariots Nah 3:2

POUNDS
* of pure gold for the lampstand Ex 25:39
the choicest of spices—eighteen * Ex 30:22,23
weighed 107 *, all pure gold. Ex 37:23,24
gifts of 3,140 * of gold, all of Ex 38:24
used was 9,575 *, which came from Ex 38:25,26
* of silver, ninety-five pounds Ex 38:27
pounds of silver, ninety-five * Ex 38:27
The people brought 7,540 * of Ex 38:29
weighing two * and a silver bowl of Num 7:13
(each weighing about two *); Num 7:84,85,86
silver was about thirty-six *); Num 7:84,85,86
weight of gold was about three *). Num 7:84,85,86
it weighed three * and was too much 2Sa 14:26
more than twelve * and who was 2Sa 21:16
* sterling at current value. 1Ch 19:6f
gems and weighed seventy-five *! 1Ch 20:2
my heart * within me. Jer 4:19
came too, bringing a hundred * of Jn 19:39
$20, or three * of barley flour, Rev 6:6
hailstones weighing a hundred * Rev 16:21

POUR
the Nile River and * it upon the Ex 4:9
oil and * it upon his head. Ex 29:7
your finger, and * the rest at the Ex 29:12
atonement for it; * olive oil upon Ex 29:36
* olive oil and incense upon it. Lev 2:1
Break it into pieces and * oil Lev 2:6
Then the priest shall * out the Lev 4:30
the olive oil and * it into the Lev 14:15
"The priest shall then * the Lev 14:26
for food, must * out the blood and Lev 17:13
and tell it to * out its water! Num 20:8
He didn't choose you and * out Deu 7:7
to eat the blood—* it out on the Deu 12:16
Instead, * the blood out upon Deu 12:24,25
But don't eat the blood; * it Deu 15:23
of Israel, to * out upon him all Deu 29:21
there, and * the broth over it." Ju 6:20
God wanted to * out his kindness on 2Sa 5:12
he said, "and * the water over the 1Ki 18:33
behind you. Then * olive oil from 2Ki 4:4
and * the oil over his head. 2Ki 9:3
I will not use Shishak to * out 2Ch 12:7
day, and money continued to * in. 2Ch 24:11
my groans * out like water. Job 3:24
* even greater sorrows upon me. Job 9:28
against me and * out an Job 10:17
My friends scoff at me, but I * Job 16:20
rain, which the skies * down. Job 36:28
the poor. * upon these men the evil Ps 10:2
our light is from your Light. * Ps 36:10
floods of sorrow * upon me like a Ps 42:7
him all the time. * out your Ps 62:8
* out your fury upon them; Ps 69:24
hope is gone? * out your wrath Ps 79:6
in you again. * out your love and Ps 85:7
listen to me! I'll * out the spirit Pro 1:23
* out my anger on you, my enemies! Is 1:24
And I will * out my Spirit and my Is 44:3
Let the skies * out their Is 45:8
I will never again * out my anger Is 54:9
of doom to * out the fury of his Is 66:15
I will * it out over Jerusalem, Jer 6:11
So the Lord God says, I will * Jer 7:20
land and * great troubles down; Jer 10:18
for I would die. * out your fury Jer 10:25
For I will * out terrible Jer 14:16
let the sword * out their blood! Jer 18:21
And now I will * out judgment Jer 23:2
I am ready to * out upon them Jer 26:3
to Baal, and to * out libations to Jer 32:29
I will * out upon them all the Jer 36:31
cry to your God. * out your hearts Lam 2:19
Soon I will * out my fury and Eze 7:8,9
"And when I * out my fury by Eze 14:19
Then I thought, I will * out my Eze 20:8
Then I thought, I will * out my Eze 20:13
Now at last I will * out my fury Eze 20:21
I will * out my fury upon you Eze 21:31
I will * out my anger upon you; Eze 22:31
to the east will * in upon her, Eze 25:9,10
And I will * out my fury upon Eze 30:15
again, for I will * out my Spirit Eze 39:29
sky for clouds, to * down water on Hos 1:21,22
Therefore, I will * my anger down Hos 5:10
* out wine for sacrifice to God. Hos 9:4
* out my Spirit upon all of you! Joe 2:28
And I will * out my Spirit even Joe 2:29
foundations, and * their stones Mic 1:6
And I will * out my vengeance Mic 5:15
of the earth, and * out my fiercest Zep 3:8
the nations will * into this Hag 2:7f
on pilgrimages and * into Jerusalem Zec 8:20,21
"Then I will * out the spirit of Zec 12:10
heaven for you and * out a blessing Mal 3:10
Then he began to * out his Mt 11:20
* out to purchase back your souls. Lk 22:20
God said, 'I will * out my Holy Act 2:17
For God has not chosen to * out 1Th 5:9
It is always ready to * out its Jas 3:8
that only good deeds will * forth. Jas 3:13
pray over him and * a little oil Jas 5:14
were assigned to * out the seven Rev 15:6

POURED
After Abraham's death, God * out Gen 25:11
pillar, and * olive oil over it. Gen 28:18
and he * wine over it as an Gen 35:13,14
And when they * it into a Ex 16:18
wafers with oil * over them. Ex 29:2
It must never be * upon an Ex 30:32
the blood shall be * out at the Lev 4:7
the blood shall be * out at the Lev 4:18
be * out at the base of the altar. Lev 4:25
be * out at the base of the altar. Lev 4:34
Then he * the anointing oil upon Lev 8:12
sanctify it, and * out the rest of Lev 8:15,16
of the altar, and * out the rest at Lev 9:9
with each lamb, * out in the holy Num 28:7
The blood will be * out upon the Deu 12:26,27
out, the water * down again as Jos 4:18
people of Israel * into the city Jos 6:20
they jumped up and * into the city Jos 8:19
And the sky * down its rain. Ju 5:4
well and * it out before the Lord. 1Sa 7:6
of olive oil and * it over Saul's 1Sa 10:1
and * it upon David's head; 1Sa 16:13
like water that is * out on the 2Sa 14:1
Smoke * from his nostrils; 2Sa 22
Instead, he * it out before the 2Sa 23:1
Tabernacle and * it over Solomon; 1Ki 1:3
and the ashes * out, just as the 1Ki 13
and the young man * the oil over 2Ki 9
a grain offering, * a drink 2Ki 16:1
Instead he * it out as an 1Ch 11:18,1
anger has been * out upon us is 2Ch 34:2
wrath is * out upon this place.' 2Ch 34:2
You have already * me from Job 10:1
* out streams of olive oil to me! Job 29
It is his judgment, * out upon Ps 75
The clouds * down their rain, Ps 77:1
Streams * from the rock, flowing Ps 78:1
LORD, YOU HAVE * out amazing Ps 85
oil that was * over Aaron's head, Ps 133
and the skies * down rain. Pro 3:2
they * forth a whispered prayer. Is 26:1
For the Lord has * out upon you Is 29:1
is * down on us from heaven. Is 32:1
That is why God * out such fury Is 42:2
The Lord has * out his fury and Is 51:2
he has * out his soul unto death. Is 53:1
and libations * out to them. Jer 19:1
and fury were * out upon the people Jer 42:1
* out on you when you enter Egypt. Jer 42:1
that has not been * from flask to Jer 48:1
judgment has been * out upon them Jer 48:2
His fury is * out like fire upon Lam 2:
my heart is broken, my spirit * Lam 2:1
his fiercest anger has been * Lam 4:1
and incense and * out their drink Eze 20:27,28
Lord, have * my wrath upon you." Eze 22:2
when the Egyptians * out their Eze 23:8
so I * out my fury upon them. Eze 36:18
be * out upon this Evil One." Dan 9:27
"After I have * out my rains Joe 2:28
a day of the wrath of God * out; Zep 1:15
therefore your blood will be * Zep 1:17
perfume, and * it over his head. Mt 26:7
She has * this perfume on me to Mt 26:12
It is * out to forgive the sins Mt 26:28
Then, breaking the seal, she * it Mk 14:3
my blood, * out for many, sealing Mk 14:24
and God * out his blessings on Lk 2:40
them and * the perfume on them. Lk 7:38
in my blood, * out for you." Lk 22:20f
DO YOU REMEMBER Mary, who * the Jn 11:1
* water into a basin, and began Jn 13:5
* out upon us undeserving sinners; Rom 1:5
anger will be * out upon them. Rom 2:8
is all because God * out such 1Co 15:10
Christ and * into him our sins. 2Co 5:21
Then, in exchange, he * God's 2Co 5:21
favor that he has * out upon us, Eph 1:6
so to speak, to be * out over your Php 2:17
Spirit whom he * out upon us with Tit 3:6
so God, even your God, has * out Heb 1:9
rain, and down it * and the grass Jas 5:18
where the angel had * them out. Rev 8:4
When he opened it, smoke * out Rev 9:2
it is * out undiluted into God's Rev 14:10
the temple and * out his flask over Rev 16:2
The second angel * out his flask Rev 16:3
The third angel * out his flask Rev 16:4
their blood * out upon the earth; Rev 16:6
and now, in turn, you have * out Rev 16:6
Then the fourth angel * out his Rev 16:8
Then the fifth angel * out his Rev 16:10
The sixth angel * out his flask Rev 16:12
Then the seventh angel * out his Rev 16:17
ONE OF THE seven angels who had * Rev 17:1

POURING
and the rain ceased * down. Ex 9:33
come * out, enough for everyone!" Ex 17:5,6
The great cloud of smoke * into Ju 20:35-39
But I am very sad and I was * out 1Sa 1:15,16
He made the oceans, * them into Ps 33:7
speediest writer * out his story. Ps 45:1
* out my troubles before him. Ps 142:1
of Heaven' and * out our libations Jer 44:19
But now she shall have the * out Jer 48:11
in fire, like water * down a hill. Mic 1:4
have been made for * the riches of Rom 9:23,24
come * out of the same mouth. Jas 3:10
by * out his lifeblood for us. Rev 1:5
completed * out the seven plagues. Rev 15:8

POURS
of the elders. He * contempt upon Job 12:21
Yet day by day the Lord also * Ps 42:8
Yes, the Lord * down his Ps 85:12
For God * contempt upon the Ps 107:40
the evil man * out his evil words Pro 15:28
His wrath * out like floods upon Is 30:28
her, the more she * it on the Hos 10:1
* it out as rain upon the land. Amo 5:8
* it down as rain upon the ground. Amo 9:6

POUTED
Instead, they * in their tents Ps 106:25

POVERTY
* along with all your household." Gen 45:11,12

OVERTY (Con't)
'A man's * is no excuse for Ex 23:6
* because of the Midianites. Ju 6:6,7
deep and grinding * who have never Job 21:25
But rescue me, O God, from my * Ps 69:29
And as you sleep, * creeps upon Pro 6:11
bring a man to *, and an adulteress Pro 6:26
The poor man's * is his only Pro 10:15
you will end in * and disgrace; Pro 13:18
talk brings *! Pro 14:23
you love sleep, you will end in *. Pro 20:13
hasty speculation brings *. Pro 21:5
bribing the rich shall end in *. Pro 22:16
for they are on their way to *. Pro 23:19,20,21
means that * will break in upon Pro 24:34
real * is evident to the poor. Pro 28:11
playing around brings *. Pro 28:19
rich quick is evil and leads to *. Pro 28:22
those who close their eyes to *. Pro 28:27
Second, give me neither * nor Pro 30:8
Let them drink to forget their * Pro 31:6,7
become king, though born in *. Ecc 4:14
very dim when * stalks the land. Is 17:4
believers, and no *—for all who Act 4:34,35
with their deep *, and the result 2Co 8:2
* (but you have heavenly riches! Rev 2:9

OWDER
he ground it into * and spread it Ex 32:20
*, and bring it inside the veil. Lev 16:12
altars, ground to * the 2Ch 34:7
though you crush him to *. Pro 27:22
that crushed to * all the iron and Dan 2:45

OWER
them in your *, and they are yours Gen 9:2,3
"It is Israel—one who has * with Gen 32:28
god-like * of life and death!" Gen 41:45
about all my * here in Egypt, and Gen 45:13
will use my mighty * and perform Ex 6:6
I show them my * and force them to Ex 7:5
If you refuse, the * of God Ex 9:3
my * to you and to all the earth. Ex 9:16
*, and refuse to let my people go? Ex 9:17
more miracles demonstrating my *. Ex 10:1
miracles to demonstrate my *." Ex 11:9
us out of Egypt with great *." Ex 13:16
hand, O Lord, is glorious in *; Ex 15:6
O Lord, because of your great * Ex 15:16
you his awesome *, so that from now Ex 20:20
but he has no * to sell her to Ex 21:8
such great * and mighty miracles? Ex 32:11
shall see the * of the Lord—the Ex 34:10
* I will display through you. Ex 34:10
I will break your proud * and Lev 26:19
* to stand before their enemies. Lev 26:37
"They know full well the * you Num 14:13
"Oh, please, show the great * Num 14:17,18
but I have no * to say anything Num 22:38
Jacob shall arise in * Num 24:15-19
and * you have been showing us; Deu 3:23,24,25
Egypt with a great display of *. Deu 4:37
Egypt with great * and mighty Deu 6:21
amazing * and mighty miracles. Deu 7:8
wonders, and the * and strength of Deu 7:19
* and might that made you wealthy. Deu 8:17
God who gives you * to become rich, Deu 8:18
mighty * and glorious strength. Deu 9:26
your great * and your mighty arm.' Deu 9:29
his greatness and his awesome *. Deu 11:2
He will watch their * ebb away, Deu 32:36
No one delivers from my *. Deu 32:39
so many of us is now in our *!" Ju 16:23,24
I demonstrate my * when the people 1Sa 2:27
him great * from that day onward. 1Sa 16:13
your *, to do with as you wish'!" 1Sa 24:4
he will rescue me from your *!" 1Sa 24:15
get away when he had him in his *? 1Sa 24:19
enemy within your * this time for 1Sa 26:8
when the Lord placed you in my *. 1Sa 26:23
had attempted to regain his *. 2Sa 8:3
and saved you from the * of Saul. 2Sa 12:7
By your * I can crush an army; 2Sa 22:30
When they hear of my *. 2Sa 22:45
Hadad the Edomite to grow in *. 1Ki 11:14
whom God raised to * was Rezon, one 1Ki 11:23
Israel, and give you absolute *. 1Ki 11:37
prophetic * as you have had." 2Ki 2:9
did, and his great *, and his wars, 2Ki 14:28
free of Assyria's *, but this 2Ki 17:4
such tremendous miracles and *. 2Ki 17:35,36
'No one can save you from my *! 2Ki 18:19
be able to save you from my *. 2Ki 18:29
able to save any nation from my *? 2Ki 18:35
with you to save us from his *; 2Ki 19:19
conquered had no * against you! 2Ki 19:26
than into the * of men, for God's 1Ch 21:13
Yours is the mighty * and glory 1Ch 29:11
your hand controls * and might, 1Ch 29:12
hear of your *, and come from 2Ch 6:32
his popularity and * he abandoned 2Ch 12:1
never regained his * during 2Ch 13:20
show his great * in helping them. 2Ch 16:9
for God has * to help or to 2Ch 25:8
the * of the kings of Assyria. 2Ch 30:6
Literally, "the * with which I 2Ch 35:21f
you rescued by your great *. Neh 1:10
They have * over our bodies and Neh 9:37
the * of the sword in time of war. Job 5:20
But true wisdom and * are God's. Job 12:13
the rich by his *, and restores Job 24:22,23
And by his * the sea grows calm; Job 26:12
does, merely a whisper of his *. Job 26:14
me with great * and effect. Job 30:21
groan beneath the * of the rich; Job 35:9,10
comprehend the greatness of his *. Job 37:5
everywhere may recognize his *. Job 37:7
We cannot imagine the * of the Job 37:23
O Lord, for all your glorious *. Ps 21:13
only one from the * of the dog!" Ps 22:20f
Deliver my life from their *! Ps 25:20
Now he continues to unveil his *. Ps 29:10
destroys the * of their enemies. Ps 41:2
but by your mighty * and because Ps 44:3
For it is only by your * and Ps 44:5
For the * of their wealth Ps 49:14
my soul from the * of death, for he Ps 49:15
COME WITH GREAT *, Ps 54:1
* and bring them to their knees. Ps 59:11
morning about your * and mercy. Ps 59:16
With dread deeds and awesome * Ps 65:5
How great your *! Ps 66:3
Because of his great * he rules Ps 66:7
of your saving * and your eternal Ps 67:2
* belongs to God! Ps 68:34
and mighty * to his people. Ps 68:35
Your * and goodness, Lord, reach Ps 71:19
Why hold back your *? Ps 74:11
For promotion and * come from Ps 75:6,7
"and increase the * of good men Ps 75:10
still demonstrate your awesome *. Ps 77:14
the south wind by his mighty *. Ps 78:26
They forgot his * and love, and Ps 78:42
of your * by saving them. Ps 79:11
Display your * and radiant glory. Ps 80:1
use your mighty * to rescue us. Ps 80:2
recognize your * and name, O Lord. Ps 83:16
are scattered by your awesome *. Ps 89:10
What glory! Our * is based on Ps 89:17
his life from the * of the grave? Ps 89:48
He rules the world. His * can Ps 96:10
victory by his * and holiness. Ps 98:1
your * to all the world. Ps 106:8
They, too, observe the * of God Ps 107:24
with mighty * and rescue me. Ps 108:6
In that day of your * your Ps 110:3
He has shown his great * to his Ps 111:6
the Ark, the symbol of your *. Ps 132:8
David's * shall grow, for I have Ps 132:17
out with mighty * and upraised fist Ps 136:11,12
people from the * of mighty kings, Ps 136:17
enemies! Your * will save me. Ps 138:7
Keep me out of their *. Ps 140:4
waters, from the * of my enemies. Ps 144:7
and mention examples of your *. Ps 145:11
How great he is! His * is Ps 147:5
the heavens he made with mighty *. Ps 150:1
"in the firmament of his *." Ps 150:1f
of my strength, kings reign in *. Pro 8:14,15
but with the wicked in *, they Pro 29:2
is backed by great *, and no one Ecc 8:4
no one has the * to prevent his Ecc 8:8
have the * of injuring each other. Ecc 8:9,10
King Pekah's * will not increase. Is 7:9
They boast, "We in our own * and Is 10:13
* than the man who uses it? Is 10:15
*, and broken your evil rule." Is 14:5
joyous song: "Your * is broken; Is 14:8
Your might and * are gone; Is 14:11
do it by my mighty * that reaches Is 14:26
The strength of Israel and the * Is 17:3
on "Ethiopia's *" and their Is 20:5,6
says the Lord, "the great * of Is 21:16
For though his * extends to Zoan Is 30:4
stand up and show my * and might. Is 33:10
delivered their people from my *? Is 36:20
you all this * from ancient times? Is 37:26
had so little *, and were such easy Is 37:27
the land; the * of the Lord of Is 37:32
Lord God is coming with mighty *; Is 40:10
He gives * to the tired and worn Is 40:29
the Lord and sing his mighty *. Is 42:12
your idols, I have shown you my *. Is 43:12
if they can, and prove their *. Is 44:7
began his meteoric rise to *. Is 44:28f
Israel from Babylon's mighty *; Is 47:4
are my Servant, a Prince of * Is 49:3
Have I no longer * to deliver? Is 50:2
shall know the * in that name. Is 52:6
whom will God reveal his saving *? Is 53:1
He proved my * by conquering Is 55:4
of your own * or virtue but because Is 55:5
sign [of God's * and love Is 55:13
through his mighty * and justice. Is 59:16
Where is he whose mighty * Is 63:12
*, your mercy and your compassion? Is 63:15
destroy Israel's glory and *. Jer 2:16
great and your name is full of *. Jer 10:6
the earth by his * and wisdom, and Jer 10:12
gods without life or * in them. Jer 10:14
is not within the * of man to map Jer 10:23
my * and might and make them Jer 16:21
evil and their * is used wrongly. Jer 23:10
*—do with me as you think best. Jer 26:14
"By my great * I have made the Jer 27:5
heavens and earth by your great *; Jer 32:17
miracles and great * and terror. Jer 32:21
release you to the * of death by Jer 34:17
No * But with Plenty of Noise!" Jer 46:17
God made the earth by his * and Jer 51:15
over her and boast of their *. Lam 2:17
and * in the attack against her Eze 4:7
* of the Lord God fell upon me. Eze 8:1
who gave him his *, and whose Eze 17:16
* in bringing them out of Egypt. Eze 20:22
and in great anger and with *. Eze 20:33
you have perished beneath its *. Eze 21:9,10,11
with your naval * that terrorized Eze 26:17
and I will reveal my * over you. Eze 28:22
and the pride of her * shall end. Eze 30:6
When I come to break the * of Eze 30:18
and her * shall come to an end. Eze 33:28
THE * OF the Lord was upon me and Eze 37:1
he alone has all wisdom and all *. Dan 2:20
kingdom, *, strength and glory. Dan 2:37
come to an end, another world * Dan 2:39
has fallen, yet a third great * Dan 2:39
and gives * to anyone he chooses. Dan 4:25
by my own mighty *, have built this Dan 4:30
and whose * shall never end. Dan 6:25,26
Daniel from the * of the lions." Dan 6:27
And great * was given to it over Dan 7:6
He was given the ruling * and Dan 7:14
* is eternal—it will never end; Dan 7:14
told me, "is the fourth world * Dan 7:23
and take all * from this vicious Dan 7:26
and all their *, shall be given to Dan 7:27
the height of his *, his horn was Dan 8:8
king shall rise to * with great Dan 8:23
His * shall be mighty, but it Dan 8:24
Literally, "but not with his * Dan 8:24f
Egypt in a great display of *. Dan 9:15
But at the zenith of his *, his Dan 11:4
will increase in *, but this Dan 11:5
"Next to come to * will be an Dan 11:21
He will leave godless Jews in * Dan 11:30,31
when the shattering of the * of Dan 12:7f
after the * of God's people has Dan 12:7
breaking the * of the nation in the Hos 1:4,5
yourselves on your own tiny *! Amo 6:13
But as for me, I am filled with * Mic 3:8
royal might and * will come back to Mic 4:8
when aroused, his * is incredible, Nah 1:3
He shows his * in the terrors of Nah 1:3
restore their honor and * again! Nah 2:2
their * is from their gods." Hab 1:11
Show us your * to save us. Hab 3:2
Or, "He veils his *." Hab 3:4f
in his awesome *. Hab 3:4
His * is just the same as always! Hab 3:6
All saw your *! Hab 3:8,9
'Not by might, nor by *, but by Zec 4:6
my people strong with * from me! Zec 10:12
* goes far beyond our borders!" Mal 1:5
and the * and the glory forever. Mt 6:13f
Satan, then what * do your own Mt 12:27
betrayed into the * of those who Mt 17:22,23
of the Scriptures and of God's *! Mt 22:29
of heaven, with * and great glory. Mt 24:30
many from the * of demons. Mk 1:39
by Satan's * [instead of Mk 3:30
it was by the Holy Spirit's * Mk 3:30
once that healing * had gone out Mk 5:30
by two, with * to cast out demons. Mk 6:7
of God arrive in great *!" Mk 9:1
and don't know the * of God. Mk 12:24
coming in the clouds with great * Mk 13:26
spirit and * like Elijah, the Lk 1:17
the * of God shall overshadow you; Lk 1:35
full of the Holy Spirit's *. Lk 4:14
Now the report of his * spread Lk 5:15
And the Lord's healing * was Lk 5:17
they did healing * went out from Lk 6:19
completely under the demon's *. Lk 8:29
I felt healing * go out from me." Lk 8:46
over all demons—* to cast them Lk 9:1
saw this display of the * of God. Lk 9:43
over all the * of the Enemy, and to Lk 10:19
He gets his * from Satan, Lk 11:15
demons because of * from God, it Lk 11:20
they have no * over your souls. Lk 12:4
* to kill and then cast into hell. Lk 12:5
in a cloud with * and great glory. Lk 21:27
when Satan's * reigns supreme." Lk 22:53
must be betrayed into the * of Lk 24:6,7

(POWER Con't)
fills you with * from heaven." Lk 24:49
the wisdom and * of God and the Jn 1:1f
the wisdom and * of God and the Jn 1:14f
of his heaven-sent *. Jn 2:11
I live by the * of the living Jn 6:57
"But to demonstrate the * of Jn 9:3
For I have the right and * to lay Jn 10:18
the right and * to take it again. Jn 10:18
He has no * over me, but I will Jn 14:30
to keep them safe from Satan's *. Jn 17:15
that I have the * to release you or Jn 19:10
would have no * at all over me Jn 19:11
you will receive * to testify about Act 1:8
God's mighty * supports me. Act 2:25
we by our own * and godliness had Act 3:12
"By what *, or by whose Act 4:7
in the name and * of Jesus from Act 4:10
in your wise * will let them do. Act 4:28
send your healing *, and may Act 4:30
Then, with mighty *, God exalted Act 5:31
of faith and the Holy Spirit's *, Act 6:8
Literally, "full of grace and * Act 6:8f
Literally, "this man is that * of Act 8:9,10,11f
offered money to buy this *. Act 8:18
"Let me have this * too," he Act 8:19
Spirit and with *, and he went Act 10:38
at the * of God's message. Act 13:12
preached with such * that many—both Act 14:1
them * to do great miracles. Act 14:3
And God gave Paul the * to do Act 19:11
his existence and great eternal *. Rom 1:20
For sin's * over us was broken Rom 6:2,3
through his death the * of your Rom 6:2,3
with glorious *, brought him back Rom 6:4
all its allure and its * over you. Rom 6:7
Death no longer has any * over Rom 6:9
all to end sin's *, but now he Rom 6:10
But now you are free from the * Rom 6:22
law no longer holds him in its *? Rom 7:1
For the * of the life-giving Rom 8:2
Spirit—and this * is mine through Rom 8:2
but if through the * of the Holy Rom 8:13
the awesome * of God against him: Rom 9:17
show his fury and * against those Rom 9:22
He has the * to do it. Rom 11:23
Everything lives by his *, and Rom 11:36
that God has not placed in *. Rom 13:1
the Holy Spirit's * within you. Rom 15:13
God—all by the Holy Spirit's *. Rom 15:19
every spiritual gift and * for 1Co 1:7
the mighty * there is in the simple 1Co 1:17
this message as the very * of God. 1Co 1:18
the mighty * of God to save them; 1Co 1:24
have big names or * or wealth. 1Co 1:26
the Holy Spirit's * was in my 1Co 2:4
whether they really have God's *. 1Co 4:19
it is living by God's *. 1Co 4:20
the church—and the * of the Lord 1Co 5:3,4
the dead by his * just as he raised 1Co 6:14
you free from the awful * of sin; 1Co 7:22
temptation's * so that you can bear 1Co 10:13
woman to have * on (her) head." 1Co 11:10f
speaking by the * of the Spirit of 1Co 12:3
The Holy Spirit displays God's * 1Co 12:7
else the * to heal the sick. 1Co 12:9
He gives * for doing miracles to 1Co 12:10
others * to prophesy and preach. 1Co 12:10
He gives someone else the * to 1Co 12:10
* to understand what he is saying. 1Co 12:10
Does everyone have the * to do 1Co 12:29
You will be speaking by the * of 1Co 14:2
and more useful * than to speak in 1Co 14:5
*, but is a sign to the unsaved. 1Co 14:22
from God has the * to stop himself 1Co 14:32
who gave him this * to rule. 1Co 15:27
*, with God's eye upon us. 2Co 2:17
Our only * and success comes from 2Co 3:5
and * that now shine within us 2Co 4:7
that the glorious * within must be 2Co 4:7
to show forth the * of Jesus Christ 2Co 4:11
God's * helping us in all we do. 2Co 6:7
Yet if anyone can claim the * and 2Co 10:7
are beyond a man's * to describe or 2Co 12:4
that is all you need. My * shows 2Co 12:9
of Christ's *, instead of showing 2Co 12:9
off my own * and abilities. 2Co 12:9
you, but is a mighty * within you. 2Co 13:3
he lives by the mighty * of God. 2Co 13:4
* to use in dealing with you. 2Co 13:4
and * more and more within you? 2Co 13:5
God give you the * of the Holy Gal 3:5
the Holy Spirit's *, let us follow Gal 5:25
great his * is to help those who Eph 1:19
It is that same mighty * that Eph 1:19
prince of the * of the air, who is Eph 2:2
and he has given me his * and Eph 3:7
who by his mighty * at work within Eph 3:20
the Lord's mighty * within you. Eph 6:10
aside his mighty * and glory, Php 2:7
the mighty * that brought him back Php 3:10
the same mighty * that he will use Php 3:21
who gives me the strength and *. Php 4:13
* that holds everything together. Col 1:17
with authority over every other *. Col 2:10
took away Satan's * to accuse you Col 2:15
God in the place of honor and *. Col 3:1
the glory of his *, when he comes 2Th 1:9
—rewarding your faith with his *. 2Th 1:11
full of satanic *, and will trick 2Th 2:9
* and dominion forever and ever. 1Ti 6:16
If you will stir up this inner * 2Ti 1:8
who broke the * of death and showed 2Ti 1:10
by the mighty * of his command. Heb 1:3
in dying break the * of the devil Heb 2:14
the devil who had the * of death. Heb 2:14
is full of living *: it is sharper Heb 4:12
person who has the * to bless is Heb 7:7
on the basis of * flowing from a Heb 7:16
* of sin forever by dying for us. Heb 9:26
in God and his *—Rahab the harlot Heb 11:31
Others were given great * in Heb 11:34
in you through the * of Christ all Heb 13:20,21
men who had no * to defend Jas 5:6
has great * and wonderful results. Jas 5:16
And God, in his mighty *, will 1Pe 1:5
It was preached to us in the * of 1Pe 1:12
having never experienced its *. 1Pe 2:15
sin loses its *, and you won't be 1Pe 4:1
be glory and * forever and ever. 1Pe 4:11
To him be all * over all things, 1Pe 5:11
through his great *, everything you 2Pe 1:3
And by that same mighty * he has 2Pe 1:4
to you the * of our Lord Jesus 2Pe 1:16
are far greater in * and strength 2Pe 2:11
us is under Satan's * and control. 1Jn 5:19
* and strength of the Holy Spirit. Jud 1:20
yes, splendor and majesty, all * Jud 1:24,25
and his face shone like the * of Rev 1:16
me—I will give * over the nations. Rev 2:26
the honor and the *, for you have Rev 4:11
He is worthy to receive the *, Rev 5:12
the glory and the * belong to the Rev 5:13
who had been given * to injure Rev 7:2
and honor, and *, and might, be to Rev 7:12
given * to sting like scorpions. Rev 9:3
and their * to hurt, given to them Rev 9:10
Their * of death was not only in Rev 9:19
And I will give * to my two Rev 11:3
They have * to shut the skies so Rev 11:6
great * and have begun to reign. Rev 11:17
God's salvation and the * and the Rev 12:10
And the Dragon gave him his own * Rev 13:2
giving him such *, and they Rev 13:4
The Dragon gave him * to fight Rev 13:7
Just then the angel who has * to Rev 14:18
Literally, "who has * over Rev 14:18f
with smoke from his glory and *; Rev 15:8
kings who have not yet risen to *; Rev 17:12
their * and strength to him. Rev 17:13

POWERFUL
become too rich and * for us." Gen 26:16
living there are *, and their Num 13:28
land are tall and *, and that the Deu 1:28
They were a large and * tribe, Deu 2:21
are so much more * than we are?' Deu 7:17
greater and more * than you are! Deu 9:1
with mighty miracles and a * hand. Deu 26:8
became a very * political leader 2Sa 3:6
He saved me from * enemies, 2Sa 22:18
yet Judah was a * and influential 1Ch 5:2
more famous and *, for the Lord of 1Ch 11:9
his God had made him a * monarch. 2Ch 1:1
the earth—you are so *, so mighty. 2Ch 20:6
even to Egypt, for he was very *. 2Ch 26:8
wonderfully until he was very *. 2Ch 26:15
King Jotham became * because he 2Ch 27:6
He was the most * official in the Est 3:1
for he had become more and more *. Est 9:4
old age, and become great and *. Job 21:7
"God is * and dreadful. Job 25:2
See his * loins and the muscles Job 40:16
saves me from these * opponents. Ps 18:48
the skies. So * is his voice; Ps 29:4
disputes between * opponents. Pro 18:18
as though you were some * prince. Pro 25:6,7
of their oppressors were * allies. Ecc 4:1
Egypt where the * 25th Ethiopian Is 7:18f
Ethiopia was the seat of the * Is 18:1f
will make you so. * kings and Is 60:16
warn everyone that a * army is on Jer 6:1
Though Babylon be as * as Jer 51:53
And I will destroy the *, fat Eze 34:15,16
"O king, you saw a huge and * Dan 2:31
both proud and *, but suddenly, at Dan 8:8
kingdom and make it still more *. Dan 11:5
and capture * strongholds Dan 11:24
How great, how * these "people" Joe 2:2
"How * is his mighty arm! Lk 1:51
me, and he is more * than anyone Jn 10:29
And the apostles preached * Act 4:33
* preaching in the name of Jesus. Act 9:27
heard him—and it was a * sermon. Act 18:25,2
It is God's * method of bringing Rom 1:
What we told you produced a * 1Th 1
the Lord, the All * One who is, and Rev 1

POWERFULLY
the people are * built, and we saw Num 13:3
church, for he * refuted all the Act 18:2

POWERLESS
* against you until this very day! Deu 11
Here we are, * against this 2Ch 14:
people of the Canaanites were *! Neh 9:2
says: You are *, for you do evil! Eze 33:2
Herod's approval she was *. Mk 6:1
how * we were to help ourselves; 2Co 1:
I seem weak and *, but you don't 2Co 10:

POWERS
into trouble at the peak of his *; Job 20:2
By his fantastic * in nature he Job 36:3
The highest of angelic * Ps 89:
them worldwide * of government. Dan 7:2
gods of foreign *, and everyone Zep 2:1
the four world * that have Zec 1:1
by invoking the * of Satan, then Mt 12:2
and all the * of hell shall not Mt 16:1
heavens, and the * overshadowing Mt 24:2
Literally, "the * of the heavens Mt 24:29
The angels won't, and all the * Rom 8:3
these gifts and *, deciding which 1Co 12:1
All the special gifts and * from 1Co 13:
felt the mighty * of the world to Heb 6:
all the angels and * of heaven 1Pe 3:2
the terrifying * of the underworld 2Pe 2:1
with all the demons and * of hell. 2Pe 2:1

PRACTICAL
This arrangement was * because 2Ki 11:2,3

PRACTICALLY
* throw you out of the country. Ex 11:
And the Egyptians were * stripped Ex 12:36

PRACTICE
* any of these horrible customs. Lev 18:29,30
No Israeli may * black magic, or Deu 18:10
It was their regular * to send 1Sa 2:13,14
He began the * that still 2Ch 8:7,8
This was Job's regular *. Job 1:5
who do not * dishonesty and lying. Ps 24:4
from the East who * magic and Is 2:6
you never saw, nor * your magic, Eze 13:23
to this ancient * used by Hos 4:12f
Shechem and * every kind of sin. Hos 6:9
And be sure to put into * what Mk 4:24
Word of God and put it into *." Lk 11:28
crucifixion, a * under Roman law. Jn 18:32f
Keep putting into * all you Php 4:9
you, you should * tenderhearted Col 3:12
are putting into * the things we 2Th 3:4
spiritually and * being a better 1Ti 4:8
does not make a * of sinning, 1Jn 3:9
Dear friends, let us * loving 1Jn 4:7
family makes a * of sinning, for 1Jn 5:18
she urges them to * immorality Rev 2:20

PRACTICED
heathen altar. He * black magic and 2Ki 21:6
With * tongues they fool and Jer 9:5
cuts, as * by false prophets. Zec 13:6f

PRACTICES
their former * instead of truly 2Ki 17:34
* of the people living there. Ez 9:11
through homosexual * and through Eze 22:10f

PRACTICING
who had been * black magic Act 19:18,19
right from wrong by * doing right. Heb 5:14

PRAISE
Judah (meaning "*"), for she Gen 29:35
said, "Now I will * Jehovah!" Gen 29:35
"Judah, your brothers shall * Gen 49:8
He is my God, and I will * him. Ex 15:2
be given to the Lord in * to him. Lev 19:24
He is your * and he is your God, Deu 10:21
to receive *, honor, and renown; Deu 26:19
of your failure to * God for all Deu 28:47,48
* his people, Deu 32:40,41
"* the Lord! Ju 5:2
* the Lord! Ju 5:9
you glean today? * the Lord for Ru 2:19
"* the Lord for a man like that! Ru 2:20
gifts and then * the God of Israel, 1Sa 6:4,5
"Well, * the Lord!" 1Sa 23:21
was dead, he said, "* the Lord! 1Sa 25:39
and no one else received such *. 2Sa 14:25
* to him— 2Sa 22:47
"Amen! * God!" 1Ki 1:36
from Solomon. "* God for giving 1Ki 5:7
have a great celebration to * him. 2Ki 10:18,19
and choirs to * God in the 1Ch 6:31
by giving constant * and thanks to 1Ch 16:4
And triumph in your *.' 1Ch 16:35
four thousand will * the Lord with 1Ch 23:4,5
Lord to sing thanks and * to him. 1Ch 23:30
* your name for ever and ever! 1Ch 29:10
O our God, we thank you and * 1Ch 29:13
"Give * to the Lord your God!" 1Ch 29:20

PRAISE Con't)
as one to * and thank the Lord; 2Ch 5:13,14
made and had used to * the Lord. 2Ch 7:6
to their work of * and of helping 2Ch 8:14
clan stood to * the Lord God of 2Ch 20:19
* that rang out strong and clear. 2Ch 20:19
to sing and to *, the Lord caused 2Ch 20:22
and the shouts of * to the king, 2Ch 23:12
the people in a great psalm of *. 2Ch 23:12
and give thanks and * to the Lord. 2Ch 31:2
thanksgiving and *, for he had 2Ch 32:25
their cymbals to * the Lord in the Ez 3:10
They sang rounds of * and thanks Ez 3:11
Well, * the Lord God of our Ez 7:27
in Jerusalem! And * God for Ez 7:28
"Stand up and * the Lord your God, Neh 9:5
everlasting. * his glorious name! Neh 9:5
the ceremonies of * and Neh 12:24
in hymns of * and thanks to God. Neh 12:46
I will sing * to the name of the Ps 7:17
children to * you perfectly. Ps 8:2
O LORD, I will * you with all my Ps 9:1
Save me, so that I can * you Ps 9:14
is cry to him—oh, * the Lord—and I Ps 18:3
God is alive! * him who is the Ps 18:46
For this, O Lord, I will * you Ps 18:49
flags flying with * to God for all Ps 20:5
Accept our *, O Lord, for all Ps 21:13
I will * you to all my brothers; Ps 22:22
you have done. "* the Lord, each Ps 22:23
Yes, I will stand and * you Ps 22:25
Literally, "* from you." Ps 22:25f
find him and shall * his name. Ps 22:26
I publicly * the Lord for keeping Ps 26:12
Oh, * the Lord, for he has Ps 28:6
I burst out in songs of * to him. Ps 28:7
* THE LORD, you angels of his; Ps 29:1
his; * his glory and his strength. Ps 29:1
and his strength. * him for his Ps 29:2
I WILL * you, Lord, for you have Ps 30:1
How can I * you then to all my Ps 30:9
godly well up in * to the Lord, for Ps 33:1
Lord, for it is right to * him. Ps 33:1
Play joyous melodies of * upon Ps 33:2
Compose new songs of * to him, Ps 33:3
I WILL * the Lord no matter what Ps 34:1
Literally, "His * shall Ps 34:1f
Let us * the Lord together, and Ps 34:3
From the bottom of my heart * Ps 35:10
I will * you all day long. Ps 35:28
I shall yet * him again. Ps 42:4,5
Yes, I shall again * him for his Ps 42:4,5
to * him for all that he will do. Ps 42:11
joy, and * him with my harp. Ps 43:4
I shall again * him for his Ps 43:5
the nations of the earth will * Ps 45:17
How much we should * him. Ps 48:1
But true * is a worthy sacrifice; Ps 50:23
be unsealed—oh, how I will * you. Ps 51:14,15
O Lord, I will * you forever and Ps 52:9
I will * your name, O Lord, for Ps 54:6
I am trusting God—oh, * his Ps 56:10,11
can do to me! Yes, * his promises. Ps 56:10,11
have heard my vows, O God, to * Ps 61:5
me, and I will * your name Ps 61:8
How I * you! Ps 63:3
I will * you with great joy. Ps 63:5
in the Lord, and trust and * him. Ps 64:10
*, and thus fulfill our vow. Ps 65:1
the earth will * the Lord! Ps 67:3
to their people! * God, O world! Ps 67:5
Let all the people of Israel * Ps 68:26
Then I will * God with my Ps 69:30
My thanks will be his *— that Ps 69:30
* him, all heaven and earth! Ps 69:34
heaven and earth! * him, all the Ps 69:34
All day long I'll * and honor Ps 71:8
to help me. I * you more and more. Ps 71:14
I will * you with music, telling Ps 71:22
and there will be constant * Ps 72:15
all nations will * him. Ps 72:17
and needy ones to * your name! Ps 74:21
and * your great and holy name. Ps 86:9
With all my heart I will * you. Ps 86:12
How can I * you then? Ps 88:10
All heaven shall * your miracles, Ps 89:5
will * you for your faithfulness. Ps 89:5
The mighty oceans thunder your * Ps 93:3
Let us sing him psalms of *. Ps 95:2
his glory. * him for the growing Ps 96:12
trees of the forest rustle with *. Ps 96:12
* to God, and sings for utter joy! Ps 98:4
Sing your * accompanied by music Ps 98:5
in all its vastness roar with *! Ps 98:7
enter his courts with *. Ps 100:4
will also * the Lord for all that Ps 102:18
shall be created shall * the Lord. Ps 102:18
in Jerusalem to * him, and his Ps 102:21,22
of the earth. * God forever! Ps 104:31
I will * God to my last breath! Ps 104:33
perish—all who refuse to * him. Ps 104:35
But I will * him. Ps 104:35
Who can ever * him half enough? Ps 106:2
Then they finally sang his *. Ps 106:12
holy name and rejoice and * you. Ps 106:47
Oh, that these men would * the Ps 107:8
Oh, that these men would * the Ps 107:15
Oh, that these men would * the Ps 107:21
Oh, that these men would * the Ps 107:31
Let them * him publicly before Ps 107:32
O GOD, MY heart is ready to * you! Ps 108:1
I will * you everywhere around Ps 108:3
O GOD OF my *, don't stand silent Ps 109:1
his laws. * his name forever. Ps 111:10
* THE LORD! Ps 112:1
O SERVANTS of Jehovah, * his Ps 113:1
* him from sunrise to sunset! Ps 113:3
Hallelujah! * the Lord. Ps 113:9
Cause everyone to * your Ps 115:1
but we can! We * him forever! Ps 115:18
Hallelujah! * the Lord! Ps 115:18
and * his name for saving me. Ps 116:13
I vowed to the Lord. * the Lord. Ps 116:18,19
* THE LORD, all nations Ps 117:1
everywhere. * him, all the peoples Ps 117:1
and his truth endures. * the Lord. Ps 117:2
Let the congregation of Israel * Ps 118:2
give you this thanks and this *. Ps 118:27,28
I will * you seven times a day Ps 119:164
said you would. I * you for Ps 119:171
will let me live, I will * you; Ps 119:175
requires, to thank and * the Lord. Ps 122:4
YES, LET his people * him as they Ps 135:1
* the Lord because he is so good; Ps 135:3
* the Lord, for he lives here in Ps 135:21
forever. * him who alone does Ps 136:4
forever. * him who made the Ps 136:5
forever. * him who planted the Ps 136:6
forever. * him who made the Ps 136:7
forever. * the God who smote the Ps 136:10
continues forever. * the Lord Ps 136:13
* him who led his people through Ps 136:16
forever. * him who saved his Ps 136:17
I WILL * you, my God and King, and Ps 145:1
Greatly * him! Ps 145:3
I will * the Lord and call on all Ps 145:21
* THE LORD! Ps 146:1
Yes, really * him! Ps 146:1
I will * him as long as I live, Ps 146:2
Hallelujah! * the Lord! Ps 146:10
HALLELUJAH! YES, * the Lord! Ps 147:1
* him, O Jerusalem! Ps 147:12
Praise him, O Jerusalem! * your Ps 147:12
Hallelujah! Yes, * the Lord! Ps 147:20
* THE LORD, O heavens! Ps 148:1
PRAISE THE LORD, O heavens! * him Ps 148:1
Praise him from the skies! * Ps 148:2
armies of heaven. * him, sun and Ps 148:3
stars. * him, skies above. Ps 148:4
Praise him, skies above. * him, Ps 148:4
Let everything he has made give * Ps 148:5
And * him down here on earth, you Ps 148:7
all * the Lord together. Ps 148:13
Hallelujah! Yes, * the Lord! Ps 148:14
HALLELUJAH! YES, * the Lord! Ps 149:1
in your King. * his name with Ps 149:3
Hallelujah! * him! Ps 149:9
HALLELUJAH! YES, * the Lord! Ps 150:1
* him in his Temple, and in the Ps 150:1
* him for his mighty works. Ps 150:2
works. * his unequaled greatness. Ps 150:2
greatness. * him with the trumpet Ps 150:3
lute and harp. * him with the Ps 150:4
and processional. * him with Ps 150:4
and horns. * him with the cymbals, Ps 150:5
praises to the Lord! You * him! Ps 150:6
Don't * yourself; Pro 27:2
tested by his reaction to men's *. Pro 27:21
To complain about the law is to * Pro 28:4
greatly praised. * her for the Pro 31:31
and let her works * her in the Pro 31:31f
the queens and concubines * you. Sol 6:9
ON THAT DAY you will say, "* the Is 12:1
say, "Thank the Lord! * his name! Is 12:4
Make known his * around the Is 12:5
of Jerusalem shout his * with joy. Is 12:6
those in the west will * the Is 24:14
in the east will respond with *. Is 24:15,16
O LORD, I will honor and * your Is 25:1
are long forgotten. O * the Lord! Is 26:15
in my name, and * the Holy One of Is 29:23
For dead men cannot * you. Is 38:18
is, "Dead bodies cannot * you." Is 38:18f
living, can * you as I do today. Is 38:19
sing my songs of * in the Temple, Is 38:20
I will not share my * with carved Is 42:8
An idol to fall down before and * Is 44:15
incense to add to the * of God. Is 60:6
and your gates "*." Is 60:18
Joy instead of mourning;* instead Is 61:3
all will * him. Is 61:11
I will * him for all he has done; Is 63:7
to * the Lord in his Temple. Jer 17:26
out in thanks to the Lord! * him! Jer 20:13
Shout out with * and joy: "The Jer 31:7
and be a source of * and glory to Jer 33:9
The people will sing: "* the Jer 33:10,11
and these prophets * them for Eze 13:10
I thank and * you, O God of my Dan 2:23
"Now, I, Nebuchadnezzar, * and Dan 4:37
will offer you the sacrifice of *. Hos 14:2
"* the Lord, who does these Joe 2:26
Away with your hymns of *—they Amo 5:23
and the earth is full of his *! Hab 3:3
and they will * you when I restore Zep 3:20
they will * your heavenly Father. Mt 5:15,16
"* God in highest heaven!" Mt 21:9
'Even little babies shall * him!' Mt 21:16
to the King!" "* God for him who Mk 11:9
"* God for the return of Mk 11:10
is destined for God's mightiest *. Lk 1:42
Mary responded, "Oh, how I * the Lk 1:46
"* the Lord, the God of Israel, Lk 1:68
and said, "I * you, O Father, Lord Lk 10:21
consider yourselves worthy of *. Lk 17:10
is looking for * for himself, but Jn 7:18
for they loved the * of men more Jn 12:43
of men more than the * of God. Jn 12:43
receive great * because of all that Jn 13:31
this will bring * to the Father Jn 14:12,13
He shall * me and bring me great Jn 16:14
* from God, even if not from you. Rom 2:29
over all things. * God forever! Rom 9:5
And then all of us can * the Rom 15:6
he wrote: "I will * you among the Rom 15:9
And yet again, "* the Lord, O Rom 15:11
Gentiles, let everyone * him." Rom 15:11
one whatever * is coming to him. 1Co 4:5
Do you want me to * you? 1Co 11:22
can understand the * I am giving; 1Co 14:15
for if you * and thank God with 1Co 14:16
For much thanks and * will go to 2Co 1:11
and * to God for your help. 2Co 9:11
but they will * God for this proof 2Co 9:13
How we * God, the Father of our Eph 1:3
Now all * to God for his Eph 1:6
was that we should * God and give Eph 1:12
for us to * our glorious God. Eph 1:14
for you are full of * to God! Php 1:3
much * and glory to the Lord. Php 1:11
Think about all you can * God for Php 4:8
How grateful I am and how I * the Php 4:10
As for *, we have never asked 1Th 2:6
comes to receive * and admiration 2Th 1:10
my weary heart will * the Lord. Phm 1:20
gets more * than his house does. Heb 3:3
our sacrifice of * to God by Heb 13:15
bring you much * and glory and 1Pe 1:7
tough and cruel. * the Lord if you 1Pe 2:19
being a Christian. * God for the 1Pe 4:16
all the earth. All * to him who Rev 1:5
heaven, "Hallelujah! * the Lord! Rev 19:1
their voices rang, "* the Lord! Rev 19:3
Hallelujah! * the Lord!" Rev 19:4
voice that said, "* our God, all Rev 19:5
of great thunder, "* the Lord. Rev 19:6

PRAISED
saw her, they * her to their king, Gen 12:15
rejoiced and * God and spoke no Jos 22:33
god Dagon and excitedly * him. Ju 16:23,24
Who is worthy to be *; 2Sa 22:4
is great, and should be highly *; 1Ch 16:25
and * the Lord. 1Ch 16:36
today, and how they * the Lord! 2Ch 20:26
and priests * the Lord with music 2Ch 30:21
blessed the Lord and * his people! 2Ch 31:7,8
shouted, "Amen," and * the Lord. Neh 5:13
vileness is * throughout the land. Ps 12:8
You are * everywhere for the Ps 48:10
description, and greatly to be *. Ps 96:4
Wise men are * for their wisdom; Pro 14:24
reverences God shall be greatly *. Pro 31:30
a wise man than to be * by a fool! Ecc 7:5
these men were * in the very city Ecc 8:9,10
where our fathers * you is burned Is 64:11
and concerning those who * it, I Eze 13:15
Then Daniel * the God of heaven, Dan 2:19
returned, and I * and worshiped the Dan 4:34
But you have not * the God who Dan 5:23
of the world, * by all nations; Mic 4:1
How they * God for giving such Mt 9:8
The crowds just marveled, and * Mt 15:31
"His master * him for good work. Mt 25:21
Then how they * God. Mk 2:12
deed will be remembered and *." Mk 14:9
everyone * him. Lk 4:15
And they * God, remarking over Lk 5:26
is ahead for those * by the Lk 6:26
false prophets have always been *. Lk 6:26
How she * and thanked God! Lk 13:13
And all who saw it happen * God Lk 18:43
They * God but then said, "You Act 21:20
stronger, and he * God for this Rom 4:20

(PRAISED Con't)

him, who is highly * as a preacher	2Co 8:18
who is to be * forever and ever,	2Co 11:31

PRAISES

Join in his *—	Ju 5:10
And sing * to your name.	2Sa 22:50
yes, sing his *	1Ch 16:9
the singers with loud * to God.	1Ch 16:42
trained in singing * to the Lord;	1Ch 25:6,7
expressed his * to the Lord: "O	1Ch 29:10
I will sing your *, O Lord God	Ps 9:2
Oh, sing out your * to the God	Ps 9:11
The * of our fathers surrounded	Ps 22:3,4
Let all Israel sing his *, for	Ps 22:23
and sing his * with much joy.	Ps 27:6
I might sing glad * to the Lord	Ps 30:12
new song to sing, of * to our God.	Ps 40:3
Shout triumphant * to the Lord!	Ps 47:1
Sing out your * to our God, our	Ps 47:6,7
Yes, sing your highest * to our	Ps 47:6,7
Sing thoughtful *!	Ps 47:6,7
No wonder I can sing your *!	Ps 57:7
I will sing your * among the	Ps 57:9
I will sing your *, for you are	Ps 59:9
O my Strength, to you I sing my *;	Ps 59:17
God and sing his *, for he holds	Ps 66:8
help, with * ready on my tongue.	Ps 66:17
Sing * to the Lord!	Ps 68:4
of the earth—sing * to the Lord,	Ps 68:32
I will shout and sing your * for	Ps 71:23
declare the * of the God of Jacob.	Ps 75:9
THE LORD MAKES us strong! Sing *!	Ps 81:1
in your Temple, singing your *.	Ps 84:4
the Lord, to sing * to the God who	Ps 92:1
Sing his *, accompanied by music	Ps 92:3
Sing out his *!	Ps 96:2
I will sing your *!	Ps 101:1
* were sung throughout the city;	Ps 102:21,22
Sing his * and tell everyone	Ps 105:2
The dead cannot sing * to Jehovah	Ps 115:17
I will sing your * before the	Ps 138:1
How good it is to sing his *!	Ps 147:1
to him; sing * to our God,	Ps 147:7
Sing his *, all his people.	Ps 149:1
Let everything alive give * to	Ps 150:6
so does her husband. He * her	Pro 31:28
sing his *, all you who live in	Is 42:10
save, and my * are for you alone.	Jer 17:14
exclaimed with * to God, "A mighty	Lk 7:16
joy and my tongue shouts his *!	Act 2:26
and together we will sing his *."	Heb 2:12
Sometimes it * our heavenly	Jas 3:9
be singing * to the Lord.	Jas 5:13

PRAISING

giving thanks and * the Lord (while	1Ch 25:3
And how the Levites were * the	2Ch 5:11,12
* and thanking the Lord.	2Ch 5:13,14
along * and thanking the Lord!	2Ch 20:21
a great shout, * God because the	Ez 3:11
* the Lord God with songs of joy.	Neh 9:4
glory by * you before my friends.	Ps 6:5
But in his temple all are *,	Ps 29:9
singing with joy, * the Lord?	Ps 42:4,5
the world have joined with us in *	Ps 47:9
him—*	Ps 47:9
my vow of * you each day.	Ps 61:8
wonder I am always * you!	Ps 71:6
and forever, * your greatness from	Ps 79:13
to the Lord, * him to everyone.	Ps 109:30
you shall keep it, * God.	Is 62:9
from them while * gods of silver,	Dan 5:23
speak again, and he began * God.	Lk 1:64
others—the armies of heaven—* God:	Lk 2:13
fields and flocks, * God for the	Lk 2:20
took the child in his arms, * God.	Lk 2:28
up his mat and went home * God!	Lk 5:25
see, and followed Jesus, * God.	Lk 18:43
they walked along, * God for all	Lk 19:36,37
continually in the Temple, * God.	Lk 24:53
joy and thankfulness, * God.	Act 2:47
Then, walking, leaping, and *	Act 3:7,8
and heard him * God, and realized	Act 3:9
For everyone was * God for this	Act 4:21
speaking in tongues and * God.	Act 10:46,47
answered and they began * God!	Act 11:18
you be * God along with you?	1Co 14:16
* and honoring him.	Eph 5:33
And you will be among those *	2Th 1:10
Then everyone will be * the name	2Th 1:12
they will end up * God for your	1Pe 2:12

PRANCING

See the * of his steeds!	Ju 5:22
side by side, pulled by * steeds!	Nah 2:3

PRAY

and he will * for you (for he is a	Gen 20:7
said, "and I will * that the frogs	Ex 8:9
and against you. * to him to take	Num 21:7
I will * to the Lord for you."	1Sa 7:5
I will * for the Lord to send	1Sa 12:17
"* for us lest we die!"	1Sa 12:19
your own hands, I * by the life of	1Sa 25:26
to * this prayer of acceptance.	2Sa 7:27
the Temple and *, whether by night	1Ki 8:29
they face this place to *;	1Ki 8:30
them when they * toward this place	1Ki 8:35,36
their sin and * toward this Temple,	1Ki 8:38
miracles) and * toward this Temple,	1Ki 8:41,42
enemies and they * to you, looking	1Ki 8:44
return to you and * toward this	1Ki 8:48
Then * to your god, and I will	1Ki 18:24
god, and I will * to the Lord;	1Ki 18:24
and went into the Temple to *.	2Ki 19:1
* for the few of us who are left.'	2Ki 19:4
Lord and * to him," they sang.	1Ch 16:8
Now I have the courage to * to	1Ch 17:25
"How I * that you will heed my	2Ch 6:19
the prayers I will * to you as I	2Ch 6:20,21
when they * toward this Temple;	2Ch 6:20,21
your people, and * to you here in	2Ch 6:24
sins, and then we * toward this	2Ch 6:26
great name, and to * toward this	2Ch 6:32
enemies, and they * toward this	2Ch 6:34
themselves and *, and search for	2Ch 7:14
the king told them. "* for all	2Ch 34:21
and to * for me and my sons.	Ez 6:10
You will * to him, and he will	Job 22:27
and my servant Job will * for	Job 42:8
I will never * to anyone but you.	Ps 5:1
Yes, listen as I *.	Ps 17:6
TO YOU, O Lord, I *.	Ps 25:1
and * to God who gives me life.	Ps 42:8
I will * morning, noon, and	Ps 55:17
Literally, "men shall * for him	Ps 72:15f
All night long I *, lifting my	Ps 77:2
I am too distressed even to *!	Ps 77:4
And on kingdoms that refuse to *,	Ps 79:6
by, silent and inactive when we *.	Ps 83:1
I will * as long as I breathe!	Ps 116:2
* for the peace of Jerusalem.	Ps 122:6
When I *, you answer me, and	Ps 138:3
God and my shield—hear me as I *!	Ps 140:6,7,8
The godly * for those who long to	Pro 29:10
From now on, when you * with	Is 1:15
The people of Moab will * in	Is 16:12
and went over to the Temple to *.	Is 37:1
Oh, Isaiah, * for us who are	Is 37:4
see me as I *.	Is 37:16,17
and * to gods that cannot save!	Is 45:20
will not cease to * for her or to	Is 62:1
Take no rest, all you who *, and	Is 62:6,7
* no more for these people,	Jer 7:16
Neither weep for them nor * nor	Jer 7:16
Then they will * to their idols	Jer 11:12
Therefore, Jeremiah, * no longer	Jer 11:14
Don't * for them any more.	Jer 14:11
then let them * to the Lord of	Jer 27:18
of Babylon. * for her, for if	Jer 29:7
In those days when you *, I will	Jer 29:12
to ask Jeremiah to * for them.	Jer 37:3
and said, "Please * for us to the	Jer 42:2
you sent me to * for you and said,	Jer 42:20
the Lord and * for understanding;	Dan 10:12
and they will *, "Spare your	Joe 2:17
GATHER TOGETHER AND *, you	Zep 2:1
But I say: Love your enemies! *	Mt 5:44
When you *, don't be like the	Mt 6:5
But when you *, go away by	Mt 6:6
behind you and * to your Father	Mt 6:6
"* along these lines: 'Our	Mt 6:9
"So * to the one in charge of	Mt 9:38
he went up into the hills to *.	Mt 14:23,24
to lay his hands on them and *.	Mt 19:13
those days. And * that your flight	Mt 24:20
wait while he went on ahead to *.	Mt 26:36
Keep alert and *.	Mt 26:41
alone into the wilderness to *.	Mk 1:35
he went up into the hills to *.	Mk 6:46
You can * for anything, and if	Mk 11:24
children. And * that your flight	Mk 13:18
"Sit here, while I go and *."	Mk 14:32
Watch with me and * lest the	Mk 14:38
to *, and prayed all night.	Lk 6:12
Do good to those who hate you. *	Lk 6:28
John with him into the hills to *.	Lk 9:28
"Two men went to the Temple to *	Lk 18:10
Keep a constant watch. And *	Lk 21:36
Or, "* for strength to pass	Lk 21:36f
There he told them, "* God that	Lk 22:40
"Get up! * God that you will not	Lk 22:46
Shall I *, 'Father, save me from	Jn 12:27
from this great wickedness and *.	Act 8:22
"* for me," Simon exclaimed,	Act 8:24
the flat roof of his house to *.	Act 10:9,10
things and to * instead to the	Act 14:15
God knows how often I * for you.	Rom 1:9
You say, "Don't * to idols,"	Rom 2:22
what we should * for, nor how to	Rom 8:26
for, nor how to * as we should;	Rom 8:26
him; * that God will bless him.	Rom 12:14
So I * for you Gentiles that God	Rom 15:13
believe in him. I * that God will	Rom 15:13
Spirit—* much with me for my work.	Rom 15:30
me for my work. * that I will be	Rom 15:3
not Christians. * also that the	Rom 15:3
Is it right for a woman to * in	1Co 11:1
tongues, he should * also for the	1Co 14:1
For if I * in a language I don't	1Co 14:1
I will * in unknown tongues and	1Co 14:1
They are permitted to * and	1Co 14:34
And they will * for you with	2Co 9:1
I * that you will live good	2Co 13:
God for you. I * for you	Eph 1:16,1
done for you. I * that your hearts	Eph 1:1
given to him! I * that you will	Eph 1:1
on my knees and * to the Father of	Eph 3:14,1
And I * that Christ will be more	Eph 3:1
* all the time.	Eph 6:1
everywhere. * for me, too, and ask	Eph 6:1
from God. But * that I will keep on	Eph 6:2
Yes, I * that God our Father and	Php 1:2
When I * for you, my heart is	Php 1:4
I know that as you * for me, and as	Php 1:19
instead, * about everything;	Php 4:6
Whenever we * for you we always	Col 1:3
Don't forget to * for us too,	Col 4:3
am here in jail. * that I will be	Col 4:4
We always thank God for you and *	1Th 1:2
For night and day we * on and on	1Th 3:10
Dear brothers, * for us.	1Th 5:25
this letter I ask you to * for us.	2Th 3:1
to pray for us. * first that the	2Th 3:1
it came to you. * too that we will	2Th 3:2
HERE ARE MY directions: * much for	1Ti 2:1
* in this way for kings and all	1Ti 2:2
So I want men everywhere to *	1Ti 2:8
you, Timothy. I * for you every	2Ti 1:3
And I * that as you share your	Phm 1:6
for it too. * for us, for our	Heb 13:18
and they should * over him and pour	Jas 5:14
to one another and * for each other	Jas 5:16
* has no favorites when he judges.	1Pe 1:17
Instead, * for God's help for	1Pe 3:9
faith, learning to * in the power	Jud 1:20

PRAYED

an altar to the Lord and * to him.	Gen 12:8
Then Abraham *, asking God to	Gen 20:17
the well, and * there to the Lord,	Gen 21:33
of my master," he *, "show	Gen 24:12
God of my master Abraham," he *;	Gen 24:27
to the spring I * this prayer: 'O	Gen 24:42
Then Jacob *, "O God of Abraham	Gen 32:9
he * for them the fire stopped.	Num 11:2
Moses * for the people.	Num 21:7
but I *, and the Lord spared him.	Deu 9:20
"I * to him, 'O Lord God, don't	Deu 9:26
the foe, Joshua * aloud, "Let the	Jos 10:12
had. They * to heathen gods again,	Ju 2:19
Then Manoah *, "O Lord, please	Ju 13:8
thirsty and he * to the Lord and	Ju 15:18
of the Man Who *," and the spring	Ju 15:19
Then Samson * to the Lord and	Ju 16:28
die with the Philistines," he *.	Ju 16:30
bitterly as she * to the Lord.	1Sa 1:10
the Lord and *, "O Lord God, why	2Sa 7:18
Absalom, David *, "O Lord, please	2Sa 15:31
Now King Solomon * this	1Ki 8:12,13
So he * to the Lord, and the	1Ki 13:6
to the altar and *, "O Lord God of	1Ki 18:36
bush and * that he might die.	1Ki 19:4
door behind him and * to the Lord.	2Ki 4:33
Then Elisha *, "Lord, open his	2Ki 6:17
upon them, Elisha *, "Lord, please	2Ki 6:18
As soon as they arrived Elisha *,	2Ki 6:20
But Jehoahaz * for the Lord's	2Ki 13:4
Then he * this prayer:	2Ki 19:15
He was the one who * to the God	1Ch 4:10
THIS IS THE prayer * by Solomon on	2Ch 6:1
toward heaven, and * this prayer:	2Ch 6:12,13
of the Temple, and * this prayer:	2Ch 20:5
Then King Hezekiah * for them	2Ch 30:17,18,19
sick, and he * to the Lord, and the	2Ch 32:24
and we * that he would give us a	Ez 8:21
Then I *, "Hear us, O Lord God,	Neh 4:4
But we * to our God and guarded	Neh 4:9
"O my God," I *, "don't forget	Neh 6:14
Then Ezra *, "You alone are God.	Neh 9:6
Then, when Job * for his	Job 42:10
I refused to eat; I * for them	Ps 35:13
"O Lord," I *, "be kind and	Ps 41:4
In my distress I * to the Lord	Ps 118:5
LORD, ANSWER me—for I have *.	Ps 141:1
Then I * to Jehovah.	Ps 142:5
the Lord, and *, saying, "O Lord	Is 37:15
turned his face to the wall and *:	Is 38:2
given the papers to Baruch I *:	Jer 32:16
Jerusalem, and * three times a day,	Dan 6:10
As I *, I fasted, and wore rough	Dan 9:3
"O Lord," I *, "you are a great	Dan 9:4
THEN JONAH * to the Lord his God	Jon 2:1
Angel of the Lord * this prayer:	Zec 1:12
And Jesus * this prayer: "O	Mt 11:25
have * and gone without food."	Mt 17:21
on the ground, and *, "My Father!	Mt 26:39

RAYED Con't)

again he left them and *, “My	Mt 26:42
o the ground and * that if it were	Mk 14:35
And he went away again and *,	Mk 14:39
o pray, and * all night.	Lk 6:12
he proud Pharisee ‘*’ this	Lk 18:11
o heaven as he *, but beat upon	Lk 18:13
nd knelt down and * this prayer:	Lk 22:41,42
s he * more and more earnestly.	Lk 22:44
Then they all * for the right	Act 1:24,25
he apostles, who * for them and	Act 6:6
t him, Stephen *, “Lord Jesus,	Act 7:59
hen he knelt and *.	Act 9:40
very church and * for them with	Act 14:23
e knelt and * with them, and they	Act 20:36
where we * and said our farewells.	Act 21:5
rom the stern and * for daylight.	Act 27:29
Paul went in and * for him, and	Act 28:8
So they * to the things God made,	Rom 1:25
*, leaning on the top of his cane.	Heb 11:21
and yet when he * earnestly that no	Jas 5:17
Then he * again, this time that	Jas 5:18

RAYER

I prayed this *: ‘O Jehovah, the	Gen 24:42
In *, or in taking an oath.	Ex 23:13f
because of the * of one man.	Jos 10:14
The Lord answered his *, and	Ju 13:9
and answer my * and give me a son,	1Sa 1:11
THIS WAS HANNAH’S *:	1Sa 2:1
to pray this * of acceptance.	2Sa 7:27
spent much time in * about it.	2Sa 21:1
Then at last God answered * and	2Sa 21:12,13,14
And the Lord answered his *, and	2Sa 24:25
name, hear their * and help them.	1Ki 8:45
As he finished this *, he rose	1Ki 8:54,55
And may these words of my * be	1Ki 8:59
“I have heard your *.	1Ki 9:2,3
And the Lord heard Elijah’s *;	1Ki 17:22
together for fasting and *.	1Ki 21:9
Then he prayed this *:	2Ki 19:15
heard his * and seen his tears.	2Ki 20:5
THIS IS THE * prayed by Solomon on	2Ch 6:1
toward heaven, and prayed this *:	2Ch 6:12,13
Listen to my * that I am praying	2Ch 6:19
every individual’s * concerning his	2Ch 6:29
have heard your * and have chosen	2Ch 7:12
to every * made in this place.	2Ch 7:15
of the Temple, and prayed this *:	2Ch 20:5
* and did not destroy them.	2Ch 30:20
Amoz) cried out in * to God in	2Ch 32:20
deeds, and his * to God, and God’s	2Ch 33:18
of Israel. His *, and the way God	2Ch 33:19
time in * to the God of heaven.	Neh 1:4
Hear my *!	Neh 1:5
O Lord, please hear my *!	Neh 1:11
With a quick * to the God of	Neh 2:4
the thanksgiving services with *;	Neh 11:15,16,17
of their national fasting and *.	Est 9:29-31
he would hear your *, and answer	Job 8:6
“Yet I am innocent, and my * is	Job 16:17
I will accept his * on your behalf,	Job 42:8
accepted Job’s * on their behalf.	Job 42:9
Hear my *.	Ps 4:1
oh, hear our *.	Ps 20:9
Hear my *, O Lord;	Ps 39:12
Oh, listen to my *.	Ps 54:2
LISTEN TO MY *, O God;	Ps 55:1
Hear my *!	Ps 61:1
lifting up my hands to you in *.	Ps 63:4
And because you answer *, all	Ps 65:1
He heard my *!	Ps 66:19
Now answer my * and rescue me as	Ps 69:13
of the heavenly armies, hear my *!	Ps 84:8
BEND DOWN AND hear my *, O	Ps 86:1
Listen closely to my *, O God.	Ps 86:6
A * of Moses, the man of God.	Ps 90:1
A * when overwhelmed with trouble.	Ps 102:1
LORD, HEAR MY *!	Ps 102:1
for answering my * and saving me.	Ps 118:21
Regard my * as my evening	Ps 141:2
But I am in constant * against	Ps 141:5
HEAR MY *, O Lord;	Ps 143:1
Show me where to walk, for my *	Ps 143:8
they poured forth a whispered *.	Is 26:16
my answer to your * against	Is 37:21
full of joy within my House of *.	Is 56:7
“A House of * for All People”!	Is 56:7
our God, hear your servant’s *!	Dan 9:17
Then they shouted out a * to	Jon 1:14
And my earnest * went to you in	Jon 2:7
THIS IS THE * of triumph	Hab 3:1
Lord prayed this *: “O Lord of	Zec 1:12
of grace and * on all the people of	Zec 12:10
“And now about *.	Mt 6:5
“Don’t recite the same * over	Mt 6:7,8
And Jesus prayed this *: “O	Mt 11:25
is a place of *,” he declared,	Mt 21:13
you ask for in *—if you believe.”	Mt 21:22
by wearing on their arms little *	Mt 23:5
so he went back to * the third	Mt 26:44
“Cases like this require *.”	Mk 9:29
to be a place of * for all	Mk 11:17
God has heard your *, and your wife	Lk 1:13
withdrew to the wilderness for *.	Lk 5:16
“Lord, teach us a * to recite	Lk 11:1
And this is the * he taught them:	Lk 11:2
Then, teaching them more about *,	Lk 11:5,6
* as recorded in Matthew 6:9-13.	Lk 11:5,6f
And so it is with *—keep on	Lk 11:9
need for constant * and to show	Lk 18:1
‘prayed’ this *: ‘Thank God, I am	Lk 18:11
‘My Temple is a place of *;	Lk 19:46
I have pleaded in * for you that	Lk 22:32
and prayed this *: “Father, if you	Lk 22:41,42
of these. My * for all of them is	Jn 17:21
and held a * meeting in an	Act 1:13
This * meeting went on for	Act 1:15
and * meetings.	Act 2:42
the three o’clock daily * meeting.	Act 3:1
the believers united in this *:	Act 4:24
After this *, the building where	Act 4:31
Then we can spend our time in *,	Act 6:4
to charity and was a man of *.	Act 10:2
But earnest * was going up to	Act 12:5
were gathered for a * meeting.	Act 12:12
So after more fasting and *,	Act 13:3
understood some people met for *;	Act 16:13
to the place of * beside the river,	Act 16:16
in thanksgiving for answered *.	Act 18:18f
in thanksgiving for answered *.	Act 18:22f
and your needs in * to the one I	Rom 1:9
of my heart and my * is that the	Rom 10:1
Will you be my * partners?	Rom 15:30
or to move the hands of God by *.	1Co 2:16
themselves more completely to *.	1Co 7:5
Our greatest wish and * is that	2Co 13:9
Jesus Christ. My * for you is that	Php 1:9
have struggled in * for you and for	Col 2:1
Don’t be weary in *;	Col 4:2
good by the Word of God and *.	1Ti 4:5
help and spending much time in *;	1Ti 5:5
And their *, if offered in	Jas 5:15
The earnest * of a righteous man	Jas 5:16
be earnest, thoughtful men of *.	1Pe 4:7

PRAYERFUL

Be patient in trouble, and *	Rom 12:12

PRAYERS

And God answered her * and she	Gen 30:17
her * by giving her a child.	Gen 30:22
who answered my * in the day of my	Gen 35:3
* to their gods are valueless.	Deu 32:31
the Lord by ending my * for you;	1Sa 12:23
from heaven and answer their *.	1Ki 8:43
name, hear their * and pleadings	1Ki 8:49
you will heed my *, O Lord my God!	2Ch 6:19
and answer the * I will pray to you	2Ch 6:20,21
Listen to my * and to those of	2Ch 6:20,21
as well as all the public *.	2Ch 6:29
then hear their * from heaven and	2Ch 6:35
the * made to you in this place.	2Ch 6:40
* from his holy temple in heaven.	2Ch 30:27
Heed the * of those of us who	Neh 1:11
And even if my * were answered I	Job 9:16
He will answer all my *.	Ps 6:9
He does not ignore the * of men	Ps 9:12
May he answer all your *!	Ps 20:5
O Jehovah, answer my *, for your	Ps 69:16
you be angry and reject our *?	Ps 80:4
Now hear my *;	Ps 88:2
He will listen to the * of the	Ps 102:17
Count his * as sins.	Ps 109:7
he hears my * and answers them.	Ps 116:1
O Lord, listen to my *;	Ps 119:169
Hear my *;	Ps 119:170
can ever get an answer to his *?	Ps 130:3,4
delights in the * of his people.	Pro 15:8
he hears the * of the righteous.	Pro 15:29
God doesn’t listen to the * of	Pro 28:9
Even though you make many *, I	Is 1:15
Why don’t you hear our *?	Is 58:3
will go ahead and answer their *!	Is 65:24
longer, for I have heard your *	Jer 31:16
and shout, he will not hear my *!	Lam 3:8
that our * do not reach through.	Lam 3:44
to hear Israel’s * for these	Eze 36:37,38
do, who think * are answered only	Mt 6:7,8
your long, public * in the streets,	Mt 23:13,14
pious by praying long * in public.	Mk 12:40
are praying long * with great	Lk 20:47
And the angel replied, “Your *	Act 10:4
He told me, ‘Cornelius, your *	Act 10:31
answers to your * for our safety!	2Co 1:11
*, desires, thoughts, or hopes.	Eph 3:20
All my * for you are full of	Php 1:3
for you with his *, and also for	Col 4:13
* and let me come to you soon.	Phm 1:22
And God heard his * because of	Heb 5:7
I especially need your * right	Heb 13:19
your * will not get ready answers.	1Pe 3:7
children, listening to their *;	1Pe 3:12
incense—the * of God’s people!	Rev 5:8
to mix with the * of God’s people,	Rev 8:3
incense mixed with * ascended up to	Rev 8:4

PRAYING

* and get the people moving!	Ex 14:15
moving as she was * silently and,	1Sa 1:12,13
here that time * to the Lord!	1Sa 1:26
Listen to my prayer that I am *	2Ch 6:19
AS SOLOMON FINISHED *, fire	2Ch 7:1
weeping and * and making this	Ez 10:1
Look down and see me * night and	Neh 1:6,7
O LORD, HEAR me *;	Ps 5:1
requests before you, * earnestly.	Ps 5:3
bread and wouldn’t think of *!	Ps 14:4
Why am I * like this?	Ps 17:6
away when I was *, and didn’t	Ps 66:20
But I keep right on * to you,	Ps 69:13
even while I am * for them, they	Ps 109:4
I am * with great earnestness;	Ps 119:145
sun is up, I was * and pointing out	Ps 119:147
David hears you * and sees your	Is 38:5
* there, asking favors of his God.	Dan 6:11
Even while I was * and confessing	Dan 9:20
The moment you began *, a	Dan 9:23
pretend piety by * publicly on	Mt 6:5
But when you are *, first	Mk 11:25
pious by * long prayers in public.	Mk 12:40
the Temple court, * as they always	Lk 1:10
God by * and often fasting.	Lk 2:36,37
and as he was *, the heavens	Lk 3:21
without food, and *,” they	Lk 5:33
One day as he was alone, *, with	Lk 9:18
And as he was *, his face began	Lk 9:29
ONCE WHEN JESUS had been out *,	Lk 11:1
keep * until the answer comes.	Lk 18:1
I find who have faith [and are *	Lk 18:8
But even while they are * long	Lk 20:47
“I am not * for these alone but	Jn 17:20
they began * for these new	Act 8:15
He is * to me right now, for I	Act 9:11
days ago I was * as usual at this	Act 10:30
“while I was *, I saw a vision—a	Act 11:5
and Silas were * and singing hymns	Act 16:25
while I was * in the Temple, I fell	Act 22:17,18
And one of the things I keep on *	Rom 1:10
our daily problems and in our *.	Rom 8:26
his hat while * or preaching, he	1Co 11:4
prophesying or * publicly in the	1Co 11:16
my spirit is * but I don’t know	1Co 14:14
But you must help us too, by *	2Co 1:11
needs, and keep * earnestly for all	Eph 6:18
we have kept on * and asking God to	Col 1:9
We are *, too, that you will be	Col 1:11
He is always earnestly * for you,	Col 4:12
have given us in our * for you?	1Th 3:9
Always keep on *.	1Th 5:17
And so we keep on * for you that	2Th 1:11
I always thank God when I am *	Phm 1:4
pleaded with God, * with tears and	Heb 5:7
He should keep on * about it.	Jas 5:13
that, there is no use * for him.	1Jn 5:16
Dear friend, I am * that all is	3Jn 1:2

PRAYS

And when he * to God, God will	Job 33:26
it and worships it and * to it.	Is 44:17
And when someone * to it there is	Is 46:7
“Look, O Lord,” she *, “and	Lam 1:11
but the Holy Spirit * for us with	Rom 8:26
woman who publicly * or prophesies	1Co 11:5

PREACH

began to *, the people repented.	Jon 3:4,5
“I’ll * to you the joys of wine	Mic 2:11
* and prophesy until you’re paid.	Mic 3:11
to hear him *, and when they	Mt 3:5
From then on, Jesus began to *,	Mt 4:17
Literally, “to teach and * in	Mt 11:1f
Jesus went to Galilee to * God’s	Mk 1:14
out to * and to cast out demons.	Mk 3:14,15
all the world and * the Good News	Mk 16:15
he has appointed me to * Good	Lk 4:18,19
But he replied, “I must * the	Lk 4:43
came to hear him * and to be healed	Lk 5:15
And all who heard John *—even the	Lk 7:29
Your duty is to come and * the	Lk 9:60
Baptist began to *, the laws of	Lk 16:16
I sent you out to * the Good News	Lk 22:35
Temple and * about this Life!”	Act 5:20
again to * about this Jesus?”	Act 5:28
and * that Jesus is the Messiah.	Act 5:42
to * the Good News to them too.	Act 8:25
And he sent us to * the Good	Act 10:42
to hear them * the Word of God.	Act 13:44
you long ago to * the Good News to	Act 15:7
us to * the Good News there.	Act 16:10
he went there to *, and for three	Act 17:2
they went to the synagogue to *.	Act 17:10
now on I will * to the Gentiles.”	Act 18:6
left, refusing to * to them again.	Act 19:9
and sent out to * God’s Good News.	Rom 1:1
you in Rome to * God’s Good News.	Rom 1:15
some claim that this is what I *!	Rom 3:8
is what we *—is already within easy	Rom 10:8
feet of those who * the Gospel of	Rom 10:15

(PREACH Con't)
to baptize, but to * the Gospel; 1Co 1:17
So when we * about Christ dying 1Co 1:23
You give them to others who * to 1Co 9:12
that those who * the Gospel should 1Co 9:14
to others power to prophesy and *. 1Co 12:10
Prophets—those who * God's Word, 1Co 12:28
able to * the messages of God. 1Co 14:1
you can * God's message plainly; 1Co 14:39
Since you believe what we *, that 1Co 15:12
door for me to * and teach here. 1Co 16:9
us apostles to * the Good News. 2Co 1:21
opportunities to * the Gospel. 2Co 2:12
go away, we can * with great 2Co 3:12
If the Good News we * is hidden 2Co 4:3
amazing message we * about the 2Co 4:4
well they look and *, but don't 2Co 5:12
After that, we will be able to * 2Co 10:16
than the one we *, or a different 2Co 11:4
to heaven which I * is not based on Gal 1:11
the gift of being able to * well; Eph 4:11
* the Good News of peace with God. Eph 6:15
And some * to make me jealous, Php 1:16,17
me in helping me * the Good News. Php 2:22
us many chances to * the Good News Col 4:3
to the church; * God's Word. 1Ti 4:13
* to the Gentiles and teach them. 2Ti 1:11
his kingdom— to * the Word of God 2Ti 4:2
to boldly * a whole sermon for all 2Ti 4:17
Are you called to *? 1Pe 4:11
Are you called to preach? Then * 1Pe 4:11
Good News to * to those on earth—to Rev 14:6

PREACHED
For when Jonah * to them, they Mt 12:41
Kingdom will be * throughout the Mt 24:14
wherever the Good News is *." Mt 26:13
worship—the synagogue—where he *. Mk 1:21
And he * the Word to them. Mk 2:2
again, and * to the crowds that Mk 2:13
the Good News is * throughout the Mk 14:9
in Galilee, and * there in the Lk 4:31
in upon him, he * them this sermon: Lk 11:29,30
(He * this sermon in the Jn 6:59
up to the Temple and * openly. Jn 7:14
known, for I have * regularly in Jn 18:20
Then Peter * a long sermon, Act 2:40
Spirit and boldly * God's message. Act 4:31
And the apostles * powerful Act 4:33
God's message was * in Act 6:7
at Azotus! He * the Good News there Act 8:40
* boldly in the name of the Lord. Act 9:29
to the Jewish synagogue and *. Act 13:5
Afterwards they * from town to Act 13:6,7
John the Baptist * the need for Act 13:24
the synagogue and * with such power Act 14:1
He was listening as Paul *, and Act 14:9
to Pamphylia, * again in Perga, Act 14:25
For these things have been * Act 15:21
* long sermons to the believers, Act 15:32
each city where they had * before, Act 15:36
the believers and * to them once Act 16:40
and * boldly each Sabbath day Act 19:8
of Tyrannus and * there daily. Act 19:9
for the disciples, * a farewell Act 20:1
then Paul * another long Act 20:10,11,12
from heaven! I * first to those in Act 26:20
This message was * first to the Rom 1:16
In this way I have * the full Rom 15:19
message is being * everywhere, so Rom 16:25,26,27
as proof that what is * is true; 1Co 1:22
Christ when I * the Gospel to you. 1Co 4:15
same Good News I * to you before. 1Co 15:1
the important thing is that we * 1Co 15:11
on me because I * God's Good News 2Co 11:7
then when I first * to you, even Gal 4:12
Well, if I * that, I would be Gal 5:11
Christ is being * and I am glad. Php 1:18
the Gospel first was * to you. Col 1:5
as we * God's Good News among you. 1Th 2:9
this: that when we * to you, you 1Th 2:13
by angels, was * among the nations, 1Ti 3:16
It is because I have * these 2Ti 2:9
It was * to us in the power of 1Pe 1:12
the Good News that was * to you. 1Pe 1:25
in prison, and * to them— spirits 1Pe 3:19
That is why the Good News was * 1Pe 4:6
even though they have * to them. 3Jn 1:7

PREACHER
Literally, "the words of the *, Ecc 1:1f
King David's son, "The *." Ecc 1:1
I, the *, was king of Israel, Ecc 1:12-15
This is my conclusion, says the * Ecc 7:27,28
All is futile, says the *; Ecc 12:8
But then, because the * was wise, Ecc 12:9
For the * was not only a wise Ecc 12:10
nicknamed "Barny the *"! Act 4:36
Bible teacher and *, had just Act 18:24
If you are a *, see to it that Rom 12:8
Is everyone a *? 1Co 12:29
praised as a * of the Good News in 2Co 8:18
you have never heard a worse *!" 2Co 10:10

PREACHERS
You can use this on those * of 2Co 5:12
so many good *, so much learning, 2Co 8:7
want reputations as fearless *! Php 1:15

PREACHES
Jesus, whom Paul *, to come out!" Act 19:13
This is the man who * against our Act 21:28
myself, who * any other way to be Gal 1:8
from heaven and * any other Gal 1:8
I will say it again: if anyone * Gal 1:9

PREACHING
encouraged by the * of the prophets Ez 6:14
John the Baptist began * out in Mt 3:1
everywhere * the Good News about Mt 4:23
he went off * in the cities where Mt 11:1
and tell him about my * the Good Mt 11:5
the Baptist began * and baptizing Mt 11:12
Literally, "* a baptism of Mk 1:4f
Here is a sample of his *: Mk 1:7
of Galilee, * in the synagogues and Mk 1:39
went everywhere *, and the Lord was Mk 16:20
the Jordan River, * that people Lk 3:3
Or, "* the baptism of repentance Lk 3:3f
Here is a sample of John's * to Lk 3:7
* in synagogues throughout Judea. Lk 4:44
ONE DAY AS he was * on the shore Lk 5:1
of the villages, * the Good News Lk 9:6
they repented at the * of Jonah; Lk 11:32
was teaching and * the Good News in Lk 20:1
to listen to his *, and I can Jn 5:32,33
But here he is * in public, and Jn 7:26
boldness in their *, and send your Act 4:29
daybreak, and immediately began *! Act 5:21
in the Temple, * to the people! Act 5:25
"We should spend our time *, not Act 6:2
time in prayer, *, and teaching." Act 6:4
* the Good News about Jesus! Act 8:4
After testifying and * in Act 8:25
fervent in his *, and the Damascus Act 9:22
powerful * in the name of Jesus. Act 9:27
there a long time, * boldly, and Act 14:3
area, and * the Good News there. Act 14:7
After * the Good News there and Act 14:21
who were * and teaching there. Act 15:34,35
that Paul was * in Beroea, they Act 17:13
his full time * and testifying to Act 18:5
So he was * boldly and Act 18:25,26
left for Greece, * to the Act 20:2
a communion service, with Paul *. Act 20:7
in the Temple for * this, and tried Act 26:21
those who come * God's Good News! Rom 10:15
go still farther, * where the name Rom 15:20
and even my * sounds poor, for I 1Co 1:17
And my * was very plain, not 1Co 2:4
get from * to you without charge. 1Co 9:15
For just * the Gospel isn't any 1Co 9:16
keep from * it if I wanted to. 1Co 9:16
joy I get from * the Good News 1Co 9:18
praying or *, he dishonors Christ. 1Co 11:4
burned alive for * the Gospel but 1Co 13:3
gifts, and the * of those most 1Co 13:9
But one who prophesies, * the 1Co 14:3
who prophesies, * messages from 1Co 14:4
able to prophesy, * God's messages, 1Co 14:5
However, prophecy (* the deep 1Co 14:22
But if you prophesy, * God's 1Co 14:24
such * is mostly for believers 1Co 14:24
dead, then all our * is useless and 1Co 15:14
We don't go around * about 2Co 4:5
Because of our * we face death, 2Co 4:12
you even if he is * about another 2Co 11:4
enemy is now * the very faith he Gal 1:23
message I was * to the Gentiles. Gal 2:2
nothing to add to what I was *. Gal 2:6
so greatly in his * to the Jews—for Gal 2:7,8,9
right on with our * to the Gentiles Gal 2:7,8,9
that I myself am * that Gal 5:11
that I am still * salvation through Gal 5:11
because of you—for * that you Eph 3:1
I am in chains now for * this Eph 6:20
Some, of course, are * the Good Php 1:15
But others have purer motives, * Php 1:16,17
that we were not * with any false 1Th 2:3
to keep us from * to the Gentiles 1Th 2:16
work hard at both * and teaching. 1Ti 5:17
the path of truth, * the lie that 2Ti 2:18
as a result of my * the Good News. 2Ti 3:11
FROM: PAUL, IN jail for * the Good Phm 1:1
these chains for * the Good News, Phm 1:13
is also here for * Christ Jesus, Phm 1:23
exiled there for * the Word of God, Rev 1:9
been martyred for * the Word of God Rev 6:9

PREARRANGED
But God, following his * plan, Act 2:23

PRECEDE
You both * and follow me, and Ps 139:5
messenger to * me, to announce my Mt 11:10
and he will * the coming of the Lk 1:17

PRECEDED
like the other kings who had * him 2Ki 23:31,32
The ancient prophets who * you Jer 28:8
who long ago * you, a kingdom and Dan 5:1

PRECEDES
A great funeral procession * and Job 21:3

PRECEDING
That is, the * laws in verses Ex 34:2
bought during the * forty-nine Lev 25:14,15,
evil, like the other kings * him 2Ki 23:36,3
deals with events * chapter 9. 1Ch 10
"Jezreel" is implied in the * Hos 1:1

PRECIOUS
Are your * possession. Deu 33:
quantity of spices and * gems; 1Ki 10:1
of onyx, other * stones, costly 1Ch 29:
his silver, gold, * stones, and 2Ch 32:2
of brass which were as * as gold. Ez 8:26,2
he will be your * silver! Job 22:2
the rocks and lay bare * stones. Job 28:1
or * onyx stones or sapphires. Job 28:1
spare my * life from all these Ps 22:2
for men and animals alike. How * Ps 36:
For a soul is far too * to be Ps 49:8,
Egypt will send gifts of * Ps 68:3
for their lives are * to him. Ps 72:1
laying plans to slay your * ones. Ps 83:
His loved ones are very * to him Ps 116:1
Literally, "* in the sight of the Ps 116:15
For harmony is as * as the Ps 133:
How * it is, Lord, to realize Ps 139:17,1
Literally, "how * are your Ps 139:17,18
far more valuable than * jewels. Pro 3:13,14,1
Guard my words as your most * Pro 7:
valuable than gold or * jewels. Pro 20:1
Literally, "There is * treasure Pro 21:20
she is worth more than * gems! Pro 31:1
a lovely orchard bearing * fruit, Sol 4:13,14
firm, tested, * Cornerstone that is Is 28:16
because you are * to me and Is 43:4
of your houses from * jewels. Is 54:11
me—the most * of their treasures. Jer 2:32
the city, with the * jewels and Jer 20:5
She thinks of all the * joys she Lam 1:7
taking everything * she owns. Lam 1:10
with every * stone—ruby, topaz, Eze 28:13
gold and all my * treasures and Joe 3:5
fire refining * metal and he can Mal 3:2
But this * treasure—this light 2Co 4:7
pure with far more * offerings. Heb 9:23
autumn for his * harvest to ripen. Jas 5:7
far more * to God than mere gold; 1Pe 1:7
But he paid for you with the * 1Pe 1:19
him, he is very * to God who has 1Pe 2:4
carefully chosen, * Cornerstone of 1Pe 2:6
Yes, he is very * to you who 1Pe 2:7
quiet spirit which is so * to God. 1Pe 3:4
gives to us. How * it is, and how 2Pe 1:1
made of gold and * gems and pearls, Rev 17:4
gold and silver, * stones, pearls, Rev 18:12
with gold and * stones and pearls! Rev 18:16
* gem, crystal clear like jasper. Rev 21:11

PREDECESSOR
as I took it from Saul, your *. 2Sa 7:15
can also mean "*," in this Dan 5:11f

PREDECESSORS
But like his *, he didn't 2Ki 15:4

PREDESTINED
Then, at the * time, he will Dan 11:29

PREDICAMENT
Daniel, and sympathy for his *. Dan 1:9
way to get Daniel out of this *. Dan 6:14
Oh, what a terrible * I'm in! Rom 7:23,24,25

PREDICT
Which can * a single day ahead? Is 43:9
of the meetings to * by the Spirit Act 11:28

PREDICTABLY
sin and misery as * as flames shoot Job 5:7

PREDICTED
be impaled, just as Joseph had *. Gen 40:22
began, just as Joseph had *. Gen 41:54
listen, just as the Lord had *. Ex 7:13
as the Lord had *, and he returned Ex 7:22
people go, just as the Lord had *. Ex 8:15
to them, just as the Lord had *. Ex 8:19
just as the Lord had * to Moses. Ex 9:12
just as the Lord had * to Moses. Ex 9:35
to tell everyone that you * it!" Ju 13:17
it to David, just as the Lord *." 2Sa 3:9,10
as the Lord had * through Ahijah. 1Ki 14:18
had * through the prophet Jehu. 1Ki 16:12
So Ahaziah died as the Lord had * 2Ki 1:17
year, just as Elisha had *. 2Ki 4:17
This is what Elisha had * on the 2Ki 7:17
speaking for the Lord, had *. 2Ki 10:17
God of Israel had * through Jonah 2Ki 14:25
Jeremiah had * (in Jeremiah 25:12 Ez 1:1f
Who else * this, making you admit Is 41:26
all the evils he *—all have come. Dan 9:13
just as the prophets had *. Mk 9:12,13
about when they * that the Messiah Mk 9:12,13
just as the ancient prophets *. Lk 8:10
Wasn't it clearly * by the Lk 24:26
*: "Lord, who will believe us? Jn 12:38

'REDICTED Con't)
him, for this was * long ago by the Act 1:16
What you see this morning was * Act 2:16
They even killed the ones who * Act 7:52
agrees with what the prophets *. Act 15:15

'REDICTING
the future and * the Messiah's Act 2:31

'REDICTION
to do it in order to fulfill his * 2Ch 10:15
This also fulfilled the * of 2Ch 36:22,23
A * of the Assyrian conquest of Hos 1:4,5f
This fulfilled the prophet's *, Mt 2:15
This fulfilled the * of the Mt 2:23
It was a * that Jesus' death Jn 11:52
when he made this *, for he had Jn 12:41
This fulfilled Jesus' * Jn 18:32
King David's * of this appears Act 1:20

'REDICTIONS
and if his * come true but he Deu 13:2
You have heard my * and seen Is 48:6
Don't be frightened by * such as Jer 10:2,3
of all the false * of safety and Eze 12:24
sorcerers, whose * were based on Hos 4:12f
Fortune-tellers' * are all a Zec 10:2
And when we get there, all the * Lk 18:31
"but all his * concerning this man Jn 10:41

PREDICTS
This chapter * the events of the Nah 2:1f

PREFER
declare, 'I * my master, my wife, Ex 21:5
And * to remain distinct Num 23:7-10
Naturally you'd * a younger man, Ru 3:10
Help me to * obedience to making Ps 119:36
However, some may * to see here Is 4:2,3,4f
But many commentators * this Hag 2:7f
* good times to worshiping God. 2Ti 3:4
but I love you and * just to ask Phm 1:8,9
But some readers may * the Heb 5:7f

PREFERENCE
so that there would be no *, for 1Ch 24:5
him and gave him * over all the Jer 52:32

PREFERENTIAL
and gave him * treatment over all 2Ki 25:28

PREFERRED
He offered cash or, if Naboth * 1Ki 21:2
For they * a statue of an ox Ps 106:19,20
Giving * treatment to rich people Pro 28:21

PREFERRING
beaten to death, * to die rather Heb 11:35

PREFINISHED
of the Temple were * at the quarry, 1Ki 6:7

PREGNANCY
Do you know how many months of * Job 39:2,3

PREGNANT
and when she realized she was *, Gen 16:4
Yes, you are * and your baby will Gen 16:9-12
girls became * from their father. Gen 19:36
and Sarah became * and gave Abraham Gen 21:1
Then at last she became *. Gen 25:21
So Leah became * and had a son, Gen 29:32
She soon became * again and Gen 29:33
Again she became * and had a Gen 29:34
Once again she was * and had a Gen 29:35
* and presented him with a son. Gen 30:5
became * again and gave Jacob a Gen 30:7
she wasn't getting * anymore, she Gen 30:9
this would aid them in becoming *. Gen 30:14f
and she became * again, and gave Gen 30:17
Then once again she became *, Gen 30:19
For she became * and gave birth Gen 30:23,24
Rachel explained, "but I'm *." Gen 31:35
She was * with Benjamin, but Gen 31:35f
and she became * as a result. Gen 38:18
was *, obviously as a result of Gen 38:24
the process hurt a * woman so that Ex 21:22
unharmed and will soon become *. Num 5:28
and I became * tonight, and bore Ru 1:12
wife, who was *, heard that the Ark 1Sa 4:19
he had gotten her * she sent a 2Sa 11:5
open the bellies of the * women!" 2Ki 8:12
and ripped open the * women. 2Ki 15:16
* women ripped open with a sword. Hos 13:16
open * women with their swords. Amo 1:13
she became * by the Holy Spirit. Mt 1:18
"And woe to * women and to those Mt 24:19
"Woe to * women in those days, Mk 13:17
his wife became * and went into Lk 1:24
Very soon now, you will become * Lk 1:31
her—became * in her old age! Lk 1:36
who was obviously * by this time. Lk 2:5
She was * and screamed in the Rev 12:2

PREHISTORIC
O Lord, you have reigned from * Ps 93:1

PREMARITAL
her of having had * intercourse Deu 22:13,14

PREMATURE
I will keep you from * Is 49:8,9
one who would save him from [* Heb 5:7
imminent and * death: for an angel Heb 5:7f

PREMATURELY
Christ should die *, before the Heb 5:7f

PREMISE
when your whole * is so wrong?" Job 21:34
Since he begins with a foolish *, Ecc 10:12,13

PREOCCUPIED
But you are too * with your Job 36:17

PREPARATION
in * for the treaty ceremonies. Gen 26:30
those days except the * of food. Ex 12:16
rites in * for tomorrow, for the Jos 7:13
of the * of the special bread 1Ch 9:32
sanctification in * for bringing 1Ch 15:14
morrow, which is after the *." Mt 27:62f
the day of * for the Sabbath. Lk 23:54
She did it in * for my burial. Jn 12:7

PREPARATIONS
* had been made for their arrival. 1Ch 12:39
so I will begin the * for it 1Ch 22:5
I have made all of these *." 1Ch 29:19
But in the middle of your *, the Nah 3:15

PREPARE
I will * a contract between us, Gen 17:2,3,4
some venison, and * it just the way Gen 27:2,3,4
goats, and I'll * your father's Gen 27:8,9,10
Take them home and * a big Gen 43:16
women of Israel to * to ask their Ex 11:2
THE LORD TOLD Moses, "* two stone Ex 34:1
to their tents to * their gifts. Ex 35:20
altars here, and * seven young Num 23:1
altars, and to * seven young bulls Num 23:29
us, '* for a long journey; Jos 9:11
come and * some food for you. 2Sa 13:5
quarters and * some food for him. 2Sa 13:7
and I will * the other young bull 1Ki 18:23
choose one of the bulls and * it 1Ki 18:25
"* to attack!" 1Ki 20:12
and * to fight for his throne. 2Ki 10:2,3
"Set your affairs in order and * 2Ki 20:1
in Israel to * blocks of squared 1Ch 22:2
too few priests to * the burnt 2Ch 29:34
Hezekiah decided to * storerooms 2Ch 31:11
* to assist the people who come. 2Ch 35:6
to the banquet I shall * for you. Est 5:7,8
Yet they * to kill me. Ps 59:4
Go ahead and * for the conflict, Pro 21:31
She gets up before dawn to * Pro 31:15
* for war against us—and perish! Is 8:9,10
your strategies, * your plans of Is 8:9,10
your shields and * for battle! Is 21:5
rocks and stones. * a glorious Is 57:14
Go out! * the roadway for my Is 62:10
See them * for battle. Jer 6:4
eunuchs, to * to leave for Egypt. Jer 41:16,17
Harness the horses and * to Jer 46:4
Yes, * to fight with Babylon, all Jer 50:14
Temple. * your defenses, Babylon! Jer 51:12
their wine, I will * a different Jer 51:39
* it as you would barley cakes. Eze 4:12
"* chains for my people, for the Eze 7:23
crops of fruit to * for my people's Eze 36:8
* the ground and sow your crops. Eze 36:9
* a burnt offering to the Lord. Eze 45:23
I have spoken of. * to meet your Amo 4:12
Strengthen the forts! * many Nah 3:14
messenger before me to * the way. Mal 3:1
a shout from the wilderness, '* a Mt 3:3
and * people to receive me. Mt 11:10
Literally, "* your way before Mt 11:10f
on me to * my body for burial. Mt 26:12
to * the world for his coming. Mk 1:2
come first and * the way—and that Mk 9:12,13
all set up. * our supper there." Mk 14:15
will * the way for the Messiah. Lk 1:76
wilderness, '* a road for the Lord Lk 3:4
of you, to * the way before you.' Lk 7:27
a place to * their Passover meal. Lk 22:8
Go ahead and * the meal there." Lk 22:12
My work is to * the way for that Jn 3:28
I am here to * the way for Jn 3:28
going to * them for your coming. Jn 14:2,3

PREPARED
the next morning, * food for the Gen 21:14
and a place * for the camels!" Gen 24:31
So Isaac * a great feast for Gen 26:30
* in his father's favorite way. Gen 27:14
He also has * his father's Gen 27:31
for the night, and * a present for Gen 32:13,14,15
clothes on, * for a long journey, Ex 12:11
to the land I have * for you. Ex 23:20
and spinning * blue, purple, and Ex 35:25
"However it is *—whether baked, Lev 2:8
Balaam told the Lord, "I have * Num 23:3,4
census figures as * by Moses and Num 26:63
army at Shiloh and * to go to war Jos 22:12
The people aren't even * to Ju 18:9,10
that the Lord has * the way for you 2Sa 5:24
the tent which David had * for it; 2Sa 6:17
And I have * a place in the 1Ki 8:21
So they * one of the young bulls 1Ki 18:26
So Ahab * a feast. 1Ki 18:42
Other priests * the spices and 1Ch 9:30
troops, all of them * for war. 1Ch 12:24-37
to the place I have * for it. 1Ch 15:12
David had * for it, and the 1Ch 16:1
chart * by his father David; 2Ch 8:14
Afterwards the Levites * a meal 2Ch 35:14
he had * a guest room in the Temple Neh 13:7
banquet I have * for you today." Est 5:4
to the banquet she * for us; Est 5:12
to the banquet Esther had *. Est 6:14
and * to overcome their enemies. Est 8:13
pillars, and has * a great Pro 9:2
Literally, "The horse is * Pro 21:31f
* for Molech, the Assyrian god; Is 30:33
I * for them will soon be gone. Jer 8:13
a great army fully * for attack. Eze 23:24
as well as many others. Be *! Eze 38:7
feast I have * for you. Eze 39:19
the sacrifices were cut up and *. Eze 40:41
crushed us with the calamity he *; Dan 9:14
fire he had * to punish them; Amo 7:4
But God also * a worm! Jon 4:7
he has * a great slaughter of his Zep 1:7
Literally, "He has * a sacrifice Zep 1:7f
the Kingdom was *—shall be cast Mt 8:12
and she got up and * a meal Mt 8:15
of a king who * a great wedding Mt 22:1
"So be *, for you don't know Mt 24:42
"So stay awake and be *, for you Mt 25:13
into the Kingdom * for you from the Mt 25:34
* for the devil and his demons. Mt 25:41
told them, and * the supper there. Mt 26:19
she got up and * dinner for them! Mk 1:31
had said, and * the Passover. Mk 14:16
normal and she got up and * a meal Lk 4:39
"Be *—all dressed and ready— Lk 12:35
"A man * a great feast and sent Lk 14:16
taste of what I had * for them.' Lk 14:24
fattening and has * a great feast Lk 15:27
said, and * the Passover supper. Lk 22:13
Then they went home and * spices Lk 23:56
A banquet was * in Jesus' honor. Jn 12:2
day and night * to murder him. Act 9:24
Her friends * her for burial and Act 9:37
being *, he fell into a trance. Act 10:9,10
of flowers and * to sacrifice oxen Act 14:13
This is what God has * for us 2Co 5:5
of making us well * at every point, 2Ti 3:17
better rewards that were * for us. Heb 11:40
darkness that God has * for them. Jud 1:13
* to blow their mighty blasts. Rev 8:6
where God had * a place for her, to Rev 12:6
to the place * for her, where she Rev 12:14
Lamb, and his bride has * herself. Rev 19:7

PREPARES
Encourage him as he * to take Deu 1:38
man, for God * it for him." Job 20:29
of the cliffs. He * me for battle Ps 18:34
not run dry! He * the earth for his Ps 65:9
difficulties ahead and * for them; Pro 22:3
problems ahead and * to meet them. Pro 27:12
and eat, but first * his master's Lk 17:7,8,9

PREPARING
After the meal, as they were * Gen 19:4
sounds as if they are * for war!" Ex 32:17
But as Abimelech was * to burn Ju 9:52
at that time, * to attack Israel's Ju 10:17
and servant were * to leave, his Ju 19:9
But as the death angel was * to 2Sa 24:16
and in * the stone for the Temple. 1Ki 5:18
citizens of Gebim are * to run. Is 10:31
They are * a great banquet! Is 21:5
you and is * to destroy you. Jer 49:30
and sing with glee, * my doom. Lam 3:63
a vision: He was * a vast swarm of Amo 7:1
* the people for his arrival. Lk 1:17
over the big dinner she was *. Lk 10:40
months and was * to sail for Syria Act 20:3
men here who are * to shave their Act 21:23
same time he is * judgment and 2Th 1:6

PREREQUISITE
The only * for his blessing is Deu 15:4,5

PRESCRIBED
the Lord as * in the law of Moses. 2Ch 23:18
not kept it in great numbers as *. 2Ch 30:5
of Tabernacles as * in the laws of Ez 3:4
Take along the offering * by Mk 1:43,44
within the * thirty days. Act 18:20f

PRESENCE
So Cain went out from the * of Gen 4:16
Here in the * of my people, I Gen 23:11
agreement in the * of the men of Gen 23:17,18
my Lord, in whose * I have walked, Gen 24:40
Joseph went out from the * of Gen 41:46
went out from the * of Pharaoh, and Ex 8:12
were driven out from Pharaoh's *. Ex 10:11
of the * on the table before me. Ex 25:30
in and out of the * of the Lord in Ex 28:35
he goes into the * of the Lord, so Ex 28:37,38
glowed from being in the * of God. Ex 34:29
The Bread of the *; Ex 35:10-19
The Bread of the *; Ex 39:33-40
the Bread of the * upon the table Ex 40:23

(PRESENCE Con't)

So fire blazed forth from the *	Lev 10:2
nor be in the * of any dead	Lev 21:11
the Bread of the * is displayed,	Num 4:7
of being in the * of death.	Num 6:9
be beaten in his * with up to forty	Deu 25:1
over to him in the * of the elders,	Deu 25:9
This was done in the Lord's * at	Jos 19:51
At the * of the God of Israel!	Ju 5:5
him from his * and demoted him to	1Sa 18:13
Bread of the * that was placed	1Sa 21:6
soil, far from the * of Jehovah?	1Sa 26:20
the Bread of the * of God was	1Ki 7:48
heaven, in whose * I stand, that I	1Ki 18:15
you except for the * of King	2Ki 3:14
They provided the Bread of the *	1Ch 23:29
assignments in the * of the king	1Ch 24:6
It was done in the * of King	1Ch 24:31
the Bread of the * would be placed	1Ch 28:16
While still in the * of the whole	1Ch 29:10
Literally, "The Bread of the *."	2Ch 2:4f
of the * must be made of gold;	2Ch 4:19
and they place the Bread of the *	2Ch 13:11
Bread of the * and its equipment.	2Ch 29:18
Bread of the *, as well as grain	Neh 10:33
banished from your * and that you	Est 1:19
went out from the * of the king	Est 8:15
So Satan went out from the * of	Job 2:7
I felt the spirit's *, but	Job 4:16
be rejected instantly from his *.	Job 13:16
terrify me with your awesome *.	Job 13:21
wonder I am so terrified in his *.	Job 23:15
We feel his * in the thunder.	Job 36:33
fall back and perish in your *;	Ps 9:3
pleasures of your own eternal *.	Ps 16:11
Suddenly the brilliance of his *	Ps 18:12
the unquenchable joy of your *.	Ps 21:6
in the fierce fire of your *.	Ps 21:9,10
* of all who reverence your name.	Ps 22:25
for me in the * of my enemies.	Ps 23:5
dazzling splendor of your * lives.	Ps 26:8
living in his * every day of my	Ps 27:4
shelter of your *, safe beneath	Ps 31:20
admitted me forever to your *.	Ps 41:12
banished forever from your *.	Ps 51:11
So let the wicked perish at the *	Ps 68:2
is his name—oh, rejoice in his *.	Ps 68:4
shall walk in the light of your *.	Ps 89:14,15
to the glorious * of God himself.	Ps 106:19,20
Tremble, O earth, at the * of the	Ps 114:7
Yes, in his *—here on earth!	Ps 116:9
the way into the * of the Lord, and	Ps 118:20
for they shall live in your *.	Ps 140:13
laughing and playing in his *.	Pro 8:30
a reference to the * of the Messiah	Is 4:2,3,4f
* among them has endangered them!	Is 8:14,15
How we missed your *, Lord!	Is 26:17
they made in the * of	Is 33:8
live here in the * of this	Is 33:14
dumbfounded, speechless in his *.	Is 52:14,15
Or, "The Angel of his * saved	Is 63:9f
mountains would quake in your *!	Is 64:1
down before the * of the Lord, and	Jer 4:26
you don't even tremble in my *?	Jer 5:22
I will cast you out of my *, you	Jer 23:38,39
you in the * of all these people.	Jer 28:7
publicly, in the * of my cousin	Jer 32:12
from the Lord's * in Jerusalem and	Jer 52:3
shall quake in terror at my *;	Eze 38:20
by being in the * of a dead person,	Eze 44:25
In his * mountains quake and	Nah 1:5
away before the terror of their *.	Hab 1:9
Stand in silence in the * of the	Zep 1:7
and out of my * with these angels.	Zec 3:7
not alive in the * of God, then God	Mt 22:32f
I stand in the very * of God.	Lk 1:19
ready to stand in his * forever.	Lk 1:75
will publicly honor you in the *	Lk 12:8
is joy in the * of the angels of	Lk 15:10
may arrive in my * without having	Lk 21:36
as I stand in your *, the glory we	Jn 17:5
give me wonderful joy in your *.'	Act 2:28
from the * of the Lord and send	Act 3:19
can ever brag in the * of God.	1Co 1:29
We stand in the * of God as we	2Co 4:2
Not only was his * a joy, but	2Co 7:7
This time my personal * is	2Co 10:11
Do you feel Christ's * and power	2Co 13:5
you this in the very * of God.	Gal 1:20
Christians. His * within us is	Eph 1:14
right into God's *, assured of his	Eph 3:12
you into the very * of God, and you	Col 1:22
with him into the * of God the	Col 3:17
destroy by his * when he returns.	2Th 2:8
I solemnly command you in the *	1Ti 5:21
let us into the holy * of God.	Heb 10:20
stand in the very * of the Lord,	2Pe 2:11
the light of God's *, just as	1Jn 1:7
into his glorious * with mighty	Jud 1:24,25
* of the holy angels and the Lamb.	Rev 14:10

PRESENT

and Perizzites * in the land.	Gen 13:7
as we are must * a united front!	Gen 13:8
and prepared a * for his brother	Gen 32:13,14,15
They are a * for his master Esau!	Gen 32:18
marriage * from a bridegroom to the	Ex 22:16f
of the majority *, and do not slant	Ex 23:2,3
Mount Sinai and * yourself to me on	Ex 34:2
the priests, will * the blood	Lev 1:5
to the altar to * it to the Lord.	Lev 2:8
are killed, and * it to the Lord.	Lev 4:24
The priests who * the people's	Lev 7:9
and his sons to * to the Lord by a	Lev 8:27
For I myself am * in the cloud	Lev 16:1
First he shall * to the Lord the	Lev 16:6
* them to Aaron as his assistants.	Num 3:6
The priest shall * these	Num 6:16
of offering, shall * them to the	Num 8:11
and cannot be *, they may still	Num 9:10
them, they must * to the Lord a	Num 15:19,20,21
On that day you are to * the	Num 28:26
and offerings you * in connection	Num 29:39
people of Israel. * this to the	Num 31:30
Give him a large farewell * from	Deu 15:14
there, you must * to the Lord at	Deu 26:2,3
This includes half of the * area	Jos 12:2
additional field as a wedding *.	Jos 15:18,19
she replied, "Give me another *!	Jos 15:18,19
until I go and get a * for you."	Ju 6:18
a young goat as a * to his wife,	Ju 15:1
barley in it as a * for her	Ru 3:15-18
she mustn't go home without a *.	Ru 3:15-18
give her only one *, for the Lord	1Sa 1:5
All right, then, * yourselves	1Sa 10:18,19
Please give us a * of whatever is	1Sa 25:8
And now, here is a * I have	1Sa 25:27
"Here is a * for you, taken from	1Sa 30:26
toward the * city center.	2Sa 5:9
and gave a * to everyone—men and	2Sa 6:19
he sent a * to him at his home.	2Sa 11:8
I am sending you a * of gold and	1Ki 15:19
I will * myself to Ahab today."	1Ki 18:15
Hazael, "Take a * to the man of	2Ki 8:8,9
greetings and a * to Hezekiah, for	2Ki 20:12
so that they could be * when the	1Ch 13:5
were the priests and Levites *:	1Ch 15:4-10
then he gave every person *	1Ch 16:3
his success and to * him with many	1Ch 18:10
as many Levites * as were required	1Ch 23:31
returned, and was * at the	2Ch 10:2,3
for each tribe to * its own burnt	2Ch 35:12
Everyone * in Jerusalem took part	2Ch 35:17
of Persia, to * these gifts to	Ez 1:8
I told them; "* them without a	Ez 8:29
and brought the * evil days upon us	Neh 13:18
came to * themselves before the	Job 1:6
came again to * themselves before	Job 2:1
Have I begged you for a *?	Job 6:22
Their * life is only a dream!	Ps 73:20
Jehovah God is our light. I * to	Ps 118:27,28
me a * as a token of surrender;	Is 36:16
Hezekiah a * and his best wishes,	Is 39:1
when they * their offerings and	Jer 14:12
Then all the women * and all the	Jer 44:15
from the flock. * them before the	Eze 43:24
and be * to help the people.	Eze 44:11
He shall * a meal offering of	Eze 46:5
The * village on this site is so	Eze 47:15f
a * to the great king there.	Hos 10:6
presume to * any fresh revelation.	Mt 7:29f
A man possessed by a demon was *	Mk 1:23
to Jerusalem to * him to the Lord;	Lk 2:22
Joseph arrived to * the baby Jesus	Lk 2:27
Everyone * was gripped with awe	Lk 5:26
* whose right hand was deformed.	Lk 6:6
* who was suffering from dropsy.	Lk 14:1
believe me or let me * my case.	Lk 22:67,68
but I will still be * with you.	Jn 14:19
Then you will * your petitions	Jn 16:26
those who were * at the meeting:	Act 1:14
120 people were *, Peter stood up	Act 1:15
And everyone * was filled with	Act 2:4
and elders were *—and Paul and	Act 15:4
Agrippa and all *," he said,	Act 25:24
"to be able to * my answer before	Act 26:2
He has given you all of the * and	1Co 3:22
Yet right up to the * moment we	1Co 4:13
great dangers to our lives at *.	1Co 7:26
for the world in its * form will	1Co 7:31
other people * won't be helped.	1Co 14:17
But if no one is * who can	1Co 14:28
and * us to him along with you.	2Co 4:14
How weary we grow of our *	2Co 5:2
which is ever * in our minds, that	2Co 5:11
I don't want to carry out my *	2Co 10:2
is the one who marks you to be *	Eph 4:30
in helping me in my * difficulty.	Php 4:14
We want to be able to * each one	Col 1:28
Christ be always * in your hearts	Col 3:15
And if we think that our *	2Ti 2:12
was, and is not, and will be *."	Rev 17:8f
Evil Creature was *—miracles that	Rev 19:20
and a new sky, for the * earth	Rev 21:1

PRESENTATION

AFTER THIS * to the elders, Moses	Ex 5:1

PRESENTED

lambs, and * them to the Lord.	Gen 4:4
Then Cain's wife conceived and *	Gen 4:17
pregnant and * him with a son.	Gen 30:5
and soon Zilpah * him with a son.	Gen 30:10
Then Jacob * a sacrifice to God	Gen 31:54
and * their request.	Gen 34:20
with him, and * them to Pharaoh.	Gen 47:2
sacrifice shall be * to the Lord by	Lev 7:14
of the animal * for the sacrifice.	Lev 7:14
sacrificed and * to the Lord as a	Lev 7:15
which is to be * to the Lord by	Lev 7:30
Then he * to the Lord the ram for	Lev 8:18
Then Moses * the other ram, the	Lev 8:22
Now Moses took the breast and *	Lev 8:29
Then he * the grain offering,	Lev 9:17
and they shall be * before the Lord	Lev 10:15
offering, to be * to the Lord in	Lev 14:21
If the young bull or lamb * to	Lev 22:23
and they * them to the Lord in	Num 7:3
So Moses * the wagons and the	Num 7:6
The leaders also * dedication	Num 7:10
Nahshon had * on the previous day.	Num 7:18-23
as those * on the previous days.	Num 7:24-29
day the gifts were * by Elizur, son	Num 7:30-35
as those * on the previous days.	Num 7:48-53
Then the Levites are to be * to	Num 8:13
them and * them in this way, they	Num 8:15
clothes, and Aaron * them to the	Num 8:21
all these offerings * to the Lord	Num 18:8
for the sample * to the Lord by	Num 18:9
All other gifts * to me by the	Num 18:11
thigh that are * to the Lord by the	Num 18:18
the tithe, to be * to the Lord by	Num 18:25,26
This burnt offering shall be * by	Num 28:13
the priest to be * to the Lord by	Num 31:29
your offerings * by the gesture of	Deu 12:6
offerings to be * to the Lord by	Deu 12:17
So they came and * themselves	Jos 24:1
the oak tree, and * it to him.	Ju 6:19
* him with a son named Abimelech.	Ju 8:31
On the day he * his sacrifice,	1Sa 1:4
seven of his sons * themselves to	1Sa 16:9
* their foreskins to King Saul.	1Sa 18:27
They * the head to David at	2Sa 4:8
Tahpenes. She * him with a son,	1Ki 11:20
baskets and * to Jehu at Jezreel.	2Ki 10:7
The king * a burnt offering and	2Ki 16:13
Ephrath, who * him with a son,	1Ch 2:19
sixty, and she * him with a son,	1Ch 2:21
a fleet * to him by King Hiram.	2Ch 8:17,18
Passover lambs and * the blood to	2Ch 35:11
and twelve male goats were * as a	Ez 6:17
King Ar-ta-xerxes * this letter	Ez 7:11
Israel had * to the Temple of God.	Ez 8:25
law requires; we * them to the	Neh 10:36
with lambs; God * David to his	Ps 78:71,72
No, you have * me only with sins,	Is 43:24
the false prophets * their	Jer 26:11
offerings to be * in the Temple.	Eze 40:39
Ancient of Days and was * to him.	Dan 7:13
disciples who * them to the crowd.	Mt 15:36
Then he * them with a question.	Lk 20:41
These seven were * to the	Act 6:6
in Caesarea, they * Paul and the	Act 23:33
* his defense:	Act 26:1

PRESENTING

gold which we are * as an offering	Ez 7:15
have done and why, * my defense as	Job 31:37
* his case against his people!	Is 3:13
Anyone * his own ideas is	Jn 7:18
for he will not be * his own ideas,	Jn 16:13
and widows, * her to them.	Act 9:41
as I was * my thank offering.	Act 24:18

PRESENTS

and he gave many valuable * to	Gen 24:53
* before meeting him face to face!	Gen 32:20
So the * were sent on ahead,	Gen 32:21
Then they got their * ready for	Gen 43:25
their *, bowing low before him.	Gen 43:26
For example, any Israeli who *	Deu 18:10
* to Peninnah and her children;	1Sa 1:4
so she had no children to give *	1Sa 1:5
him *, but he took no notice.	1Sa 10:27
He gave David * made from silver,	2Sa 8:10
the * he had already planned.	1Ki 10:13
of the land as * for Elisha and	2Ki 8:8,9
brought him * and annual tribute,	2Ch 17:11
valuable * for King Hezekiah, too.	2Ch 32:23
meal, and to send * to those in	Neh 8:10
eat a festive meal and to send *;	Neh 8:12
Let everyone bring him *.	Ps 76:11
crashing down. He * it to the poor	Is 26:6
Then they opened their * and gave	Mt 2:11
with God. He * their gifts to God	Heb 5:1
rejoice and give * to each other	Rev 11:10

PRESERVE

He sent me here ahead of you to *	Gen 45:5
* us alive as he has until now.	Deu 6:24

(PRESERVE Con't)
everything in them. You * it all; Neh 9:6
to * the sanctity of the Sabbath. Neh 13:22
you will forever * your own from Ps 12:7
Literally, "You *." Ps 36:6f
to destroy me. * me from these Ps 59:2
my complaint: Oh, * my life from Ps 64:1
me from evil men. * me from the Ps 140:1
Keep me out of their power. * me Ps 140:4
I will * a remnant of my people Is 65:9
jar to * them for a long time. Jer 32:14
* your life and keep you safe." Jer 39:18
(But I will * your fatherless Jer 49:11
for I will pardon the remnant I *. Jer 50:20

PRESERVED
of Aaron shall be * for the Ex 29:29
wilderness, and * us from our Jos 24:17
You have * me 2Sa 22:44
You have * me 2Sa 22:44
to me, and I was * by your care. Job 10:12
You have * me because I was Ps 41:12
tears and * them in your bottle! Ps 56:8
will be * by your protection. Ps 102:28
That way both are *." Mt 9:17
from me") and * him from seemingly Heb 5:7f

PRESERVES
And * him from every harm." Deu 33:12
it seems as though God * the rich Job 24:22,23
from all evil, and * your life. Ps 121:7
The Lord * the upright but ruins Pro 22:12

PRESERVING
He delivers his people, * them Dan 6:27

PRESIDE
one, the sun, to * over the day and Gen 1:16
the moon, to * through the night; Gen 1:16
the earth, and to * over the day Gen 1:18
I will * on the Mount of Assembly Is 14:13

PRESIDENT
Tell us, as our *, whether we can 2Ki 6:1

PRESIDENTS
understanding of * and kings, and Job 12:24,25
* and kings will send you aid. Is 60:10
to three * (Daniel was one of them) Dan 6:2
than all the other * and governors, Dan 6:3
This made the other * and Dan 6:4
live forever! We *, governors, Dan 6:7

PRESIDING
Just then, as he was * over the Mt 27:19
"church leader" or "* elder." 1Ti 3:1f

PRESS
own threshing floor and wine *. Num 18:30
your olive *, and your wine press. Deu 15:14
your olive press, and your wine *. Deu 15:14
bottom of a grape *—a pit where Ju 6:11
They are forced to * out the Job 24:11
all day long the enemy troops * Ps 56:1
Let us * on to know him, and he Hos 6:3
you will * out the oil from the Mic 6:15
olive *, there were only twenty. Hag 2:16,17
* Release, April 24, 1964). Rev 9:16f

PRESSED
2½ pints of oil, * from olives; Ex 29:40
and the grapes have been *. Deu 16:13
where grapes were * to make Ju 6:11
next morning he * the fleece Ju 6:38
Absalom * him, but he wouldn't 2Sa 13:25
Saul had been hard * with heavy 1Ch 10:3
Then I * further. Neh 5:9
shall drink the wine you *. Is 62:9
ashen-faced, hands * against their Jer 30:6
on ahead and * along behind, Mt 21:9
just then, was * into service to Mk 15:21
great crowds * in on him to listen Lk 5:1
measure, * down, shaken together to Lk 6:38
As the crowd * in upon him, he Lk 11:29,30
We are * on every side by 2Co 4:8

PRESSES
in the wine * has ceased forever. Is 16:10
Moab. The * yield no wine; Jer 48:33
wheat, and the * overflow with Joe 2:24
of Hananel to the king's wine *. Zec 14:10

PRESSING
squirmed past by * against the Num 22:25
"All this crowd * around you, and Mk 5:31
and dug a pit for * out the grape Mk 12:1
always * onward toward Jerusalem. Lk 13:22
And now eager multitudes are * Lk 16:16

PRESSURE
let you go except under heavy *. Ex 3:19
So I will give him all the * he Ex 3:20
can't stand the * of adversity. Pro 24:10
burst with the *, and the wine Mt 9:17
as if it were being given under *. 2Co 9:5
long under such * of spirit as he Heb 5:7f

PRESSURES
able to endure the *, and there Ex 18:23
Eventually these * will subside, Dan 11:34
are never free from their *. Gal 5:17

PRESUME
* to present any fresh revelation. Mt 7:29f

PRESUMED
it must be * to be murder and the Ex 22:3
iron, it must be * to be murder, Num 35:16

PRESUMES
anyone else who * to assume this Num 3:10

PRESUMPTION
"We have had enough of your *; Num 16:3

PRESUMPTUOUS
You are the * ones, you sons of Num 16:6,7

PRETENCE
"I hate your show and *—your Amo 5:21

PRETEND
"He wants to * we stole it and Gen 43:18
And if the people of the land * Lev 20:4
away, don't * you didn't see it; Deu 22:1
Go back to bed and * you are 2Sa 13:5
"* you are in mourning," Joab 2Sa 14:2,3
Even my own brothers * they Ps 69:8
I don't * to "know it all." Ps 131:1
There are "friends" who * to be Pro 18:24
prophets too who * the Lord has Eze 13:17
the hypocrites who * piety by Mt 6:5
And you * to be holy, with all Mt 23:13,14
really are, they * to be pious by Mk 12:40
* to be good when they aren't. Lk 12:1
they requested. "* you want to ask Act 23:15
Don't just * that you love Rom 12:9
Don't just * to be good! 1Pe 2:1

PRETENDED
them instantly, but * he didn't. Gen 42:7
do to him, so he * to be insane! 1Sa 21:13
and Amasa. He * that it was an act 1Ki 2:5
people of the land * to be Jews, Est 8:17
who * to be someone great. Act 5:36

PRETENDING
that the queen, * to be someone 1Ki 14:5
Why are you * to be someone 1Ki 14:6
men will come, * to offer a helping Dan 11:34
secret agents * to be honest men. Lk 20:20
the Council again, * they want to Act 23:20
Or are you just * to be 2Co 13:5
we were not just * to be your 1Th 2:5

PRETENDS
Though he * to be so kind, his Pro 26:24,25,26

PRETENSE
Their worship is mere *. Hos 4:15
evil hearts. Your * brings you Lk 16:15
that it is no mere * when I say Rom 9:1

PRETTIER
But look, her sister is * than Ju 15:2

PRETTIEST
mine, as are your * wives and the 1Ki 20:2,3

PRETTILY
people speak very * about the Lord Mk 7:6,7

PRETTY
So she seduced him with her * Pro 7:21
* words may hide a wicked heart, Pro 26:23
* glaze covers a common clay pot. Pro 26:23
Strip off your * clothes—wear Is 32:11
room for me so I must be * good." Rom 11:19

PREVAIL
with God, you shall * with men." Gen 32:28
Justice must *. Deu 16:20
of anarchy will *—everyone stepping Is 3:5
until truth and righteousness * Is 42:4
He will give a great shout and * Is 42:13
will not be able to * against you. Jer 1:18
* everywhere throughout the earth. Jer 23:5,6
and bribes and trickery *. Hab 1:4
of hell shall not * against it. Mt 16:18

PREVAILED
the roaring floods *, covering the Gen 7:17
he wrestled with the Angel and *. Hos 12:4
Jesus' death, and their voices *. Lk 23:23

PREVAILING
with the sin * everywhere Zec 5:6

PREVAILS
but Israel ('One who * with God'). Gen 35:10
* and treachery is everywhere. Is 24:15,16
for I will see that right *. Is 51:4

PREVENT
to * her from having a baby which Gen 38:9
this will * the chestpiece from Ex 28:28
of God's laws will * him from Deu 17:20
It will also * him from turning Deu 17:20
this command is to * the people of Deu 20:18
flat rooftop to * anyone from Deu 22:8
to * the vultures from tearing at 2Sa 21:10
in Hamath to * his reigning in 2Ki 23:33
Again, he may * a vile man from Job 34:29,30
for it was to * you from getting Job 36:21
no one has the power to * his day Ecc 8:8
and helpless to * the slaughter. Ob 1:9
they will * you from smashing on Mt 4:6
come to me, and don't * them. Mt 19:14
"Just as a man can * trouble Mt 24:43
the third day, to * his disciples Mt 27:64
and you * others from having a Lk 11:52
and does not * eternal death. 2Co 7:10

PREVENTED
It is because you are * from Jn 8:43
before (but was *) so that I could Rom 1:13

PREVENTING
near Moab, * anyone from crossing. Ju 3:28
Beth-barah, thus * the Midianites Ju 7:24

PREVENTS
the words away and * people from Lk 8:12

PREVIOUS
the * name of the nearest village Gen 28:19
begins on the * evening and goes on Lev 23:32
had presented on the * day. Num 7:18-23
as those presented on the * days. Num 7:24-29
same as those given on the * days. Num 7:30-35
as those presented on the * days. Num 7:48-53
the same as those on the * days. Num 7:66-71
had died the * day with Korah). Num 16:49
in the * census taken in the Num 26:64,65
slaughter just as on the * days. Ju 20:35-39
The Lord had told Samuel the * 1Sa 9:15
predicted on the * day when the 2Ki 7:17
appointed by the * kings of Judah, 2Ki 23:5
Implied in * verse. Is 42:22f
destroys him, his * good deeds Eze 3:20
All his * goodness will be Eze 18:24
been upon me the * evening, and he Eze 33:22
any * suffering in Jewish history. Dan 12:1
to the tree on the * day, and Mk 11:21

PREVIOUSLY
with manna, a food * unknown to Deu 8:3
(He had told them *, "Kill Jos 6:17
had * assigned this land to them. Jos 13:8
the territory * assigned to the Jos 18:11
of the land * assigned to Judah. Jos 19:1
And as they had done *, Benjamin Ju 20:31
had * been in the Tabernacle. 1Ki 8:3,4
Italic means that the name has * 1Ch 1:5-9f
As * stated, 1Ch 6:16
The room had * been used for Neh 13:5
he had * discussed with them. Act 1:4
man his people had * rejected by Act 7:35

PREY
that has finished eating its *. Gen 49:9
the eagle that swoops upon its *. Job 9:26
that no bird of * can see, no Job 28:7
Can you stalk * like a lioness, Job 38:39,40
From there she spies her *, from Job 39:29
roaring lions attacking their *. Ps 22:13
like lions and pounce upon the *. Is 5:29
and were such easy * for you. Is 37:27
I will call that swift bird of * Is 46:11
Who can snatch the * from the Is 49:24
my prophets as a lion kills its *. Jer 2:30
his lair like a lion seeking *; Jer 25:38
to catch * and became a man-eater. Eze 19:3
*, and he too became a man-eater. Eze 19:6
against you like lions stalking *. Eze 22:25
Tyre shall become the * of many Eze 26:5
They have become a * to every Eze 34:5
Judah as a lion rips apart its *; Hos 5:14
down to pounce upon their *. Hab 1:8
Israel would be an easy *. Hab 3:14
have left no trace of their *. Zep 3:3

PREYS
other wild animals on which he *. Job 40:20

PRICE
I will of course pay the full * Gen 23:9
Let me pay the full * of the Gen 23:13
So Abraham paid Ephron the * he Gen 23:16
ox and divide the * between Ex 21:35
years, a fair * shall be arrived at Lev 25:14,15,16
years away, the * will be high; Lev 25:14,15,16
if few years, the * will be low; Lev 25:14,15,16
buy it back at a * proportionate to Lev 25:27
the money. The * of his freedom Lev 25:50
than half the * of a hired hand! Deu 15:18
from you at its full *; 1Ch 21:22
"I will buy it for the full *; 1Ch 21:24
get it; its * is far above rubies. Job 28:18
buyer as he haggles over the *. Pro 20:14
Get the facts at any *, and hold Pro 23:23
I have paid the * to set you free. Is 44:22
enemies as the * that you must pay Jer 17:2,3
The * of a slave. Zec 11:12f
of silver—the * at which he was Mt 27:9
"What is the * of five sparrows? Lk 12:6
money, claiming it was the full *. Act 5:2
this was the full *, you were lying Act 5:3
your land for such and such a *?" Act 5:8
God has bought you with a great *. 1Co 6:20

PRICELESS
I own, all my * treasures." Is 39:4
him, along with * gold and silver Dan 11:8
compared with the * gain of knowing Php 3:8
the * gift of eternal life; 1Pe 1:4

PRICES
purchased them at wholesale *. 1Ki 10:28
entire herds at wholesale *. 2Ch 1:16
grain for higher *, but they bless Pro 11:26
is sold to us at the highest of *. Lam 5:4

PRICK
A rebel's foolish talk should * Pro 14:3
will become as foolish as he is! * Pro 26:4,5
neighbor nations * and tear at Eze 28:24
and bother me, and * my pride. 2Co 12:7

PRICKED
will be * by everything he hears. 1Co 14:24

PRICKLE
ears of those who hear it will *. Jer 19:3

PRICKLY
Even the best of them are * as Mic 7:4

PRIDE
O Israel, your * and joy lies 2Sa 1:19
not abate his anger. The * of man Job 9:13
he is skilled at crushing its *! Job 26:12
keeping them from *, and warning Job 33:17,18
Or, "because of man's base *." Job 35:12f
His overlapping scales are his * Job 41:15-17
Literally, "the * of Jacob." Ps 47:4f
lands, he will deflate your *. Ps 66:7
else, so their * sparkles like a Ps 73:6
I will not permit conceit and *. Ps 101:5
home, their * and joy— and brought Ps 105:36
flood of these men's fury and *. Ps 124:4,5
Swallow your *; Pro 6:3
For wisdom hates *, arrogance, Pro 8:13
* leads to arguments; Pro 13:10
talk should prick his own *! Pro 14:3
* disgusts the Lord. Pro 16:5
* goes before destruction and Pro 16:18
* ends in destruction; Pro 18:12
*, lust, and evil actions Pro 21:4
* ends in a fall, while humility Pro 29:23
Patience is better than *! Ecc 7:8
will bow low; the * of men will lie Is 2:17
it to destroy your * and show his Is 23:9
cool the * of ruthless nations. Is 25:5
He will end their * and all their Is 25:11
the * and delight of the drunkards Is 28:1
you direct your violence and *? Is 37:23
O Jerusalem, * of my people, put Jer 6:26
rot the * of Judah and Jerusalem. Jer 13:8,9
shall mourn because of your *. Jer 13:17
We have all heard of the * of Jer 48:29
your fame and your *, living there Jer 49:16
Land of *, you will stumble and Jer 50:32
wickedness and * have run their Eze 7:10,11
and wicked men of * shall live. Eze 7:10,11
I will crush your * by bringing Eze 7:24
Your sister Sodom's sins were * Eze 16:49
Your heart was filled with * Eze 28:17
and the * of her power shall end. Eze 30:6
let no other nation exult with * Eze 31:14
It will smash the * of Egypt and Eze 32:12
the land and her *, and her power Eze 33:28
were hardened in *, God removed him Dan 5:20
Filled with * after this great Dan 11:12
old he is. His * in other gods has Hos 7:10
How you * yourselves and crow Amo 4:5
"I despise the * and false glory Amo 6:8
the Lord, the * of Israel, has Amo 8:7
to Adullum, the "* of Israel." Mic 1:15
the wages of their *, for they have Zep 2:10
In her * she won't listen even Zep 3:2
there will be no * or haughtiness Zep 3:11
be filled with * at their success. Zec 12:7
For they take * in all these Mt 6:31,32
slander, *, and all other folly. Mk 7:22
Abraham had no basis at all for *. Rom 4:1
that is as true as my * in your 1Co 15:31
in you, and my * in you is great. 2Co 7:4
he left me of my * in you—and you 2Co 7:14
and bother me, and prick my *. 2Co 12:7
soon, and * comes before a fall. 1Ti 3:6
be gone, but their * and trust 1Ti 6:17
puffed up with *, and prefer good 2Ti 3:4
to you, and the * that comes from 1Jn 2:16

PRIDES
all these earthly * and fears. 1Co 7:23

PRIDING
than nothing! And * yourselves on Amo 6:13

PRIEST
who was a * of the God of Highest Gen 14:18
of Potiphera, * of Heliopolis. Gen 41:45
* of the sun god Re of Heliopolis. Gen 41:50
of Potiphera, * of Heliopolis); Gen 46:19-22
daughters of the * of Midian came Ex 2:16
the * of Midian, out at the edge Ex 3:1
father-in-law, the * of Midian, Ex 18:1
used by the High * to determine Ex 28:30,31f
Whoever is the next High * after Ex 29:30
not a * shall be excommunicated.' Ex 30:33
for Aaron the *, and the garments Ex 31:10
The holy garments for Aaron the *, Ex 35:10-19
by Ithamar, son of Aaron the *. Ex 38:21
for Aaron the * and those for his Ex 39:41
him to minister to me as a *. Ex 40:13
young pigeons. A * will take the Lev 1:15,16,17
Then the * will remove the crop Lev 1:15,16,17
And the * shall burn it upon the Lev 1:15,16,17
offering to the * and he shall take Lev 2:8
Tabernacle. The * shall throw its Lev 3:13
If a * sins unintentionally, and Lev 4:3
Then the * shall take the Lev 4:5
Then the * shall put some of the Lev 4:7
Then the * shall bring its blood Lev 4:16
in this way the * shall make Lev 4:20
be forgiven. The * shall then cart Lev 4:21
Then the * shall take some of Lev 4:25
thus the * shall make atonement Lev 4:26
And the * shall take some of the Lev 4:30
Then the * shall pour out the Lev 4:30
sacrifice, and the * shall burn Lev 4:31
Thus the * shall make atonement Lev 4:31
sin offering. The * shall take Lev 4:34
lamb—the * shall burn the fat on Lev 4:35
and the * shall make atonement Lev 4:35
or goat, and the * shall make Lev 5:6
offering. The * shall offer as the Lev 5:8
so the * shall make atonement for Lev 5:10
He shall bring it to the * and Lev 5:12
the priest and the * shall take out Lev 5:12
In this way the * shall make Lev 5:13
belong to the *, just as was the Lev 5:13
he shall bring it to the *, and Lev 5:16
priest, and the * shall make Lev 5:16
to the * as a guilt offering; Lev 5:17,18
with it the * shall make Lev 5:17,18
He shall bring it to the *, and Lev 6:6
priest, and the * shall make Lev 6:7
(The next morning) the * shall Lev 6:10
not go out. The * shall put on Lev 6:12
the Lord. The * shall then take Lev 6:15
*, generation after generation. Lev 6:18
are killed. The * who performs the Lev 6:26
the altar. The * will offer upon Lev 7:3
be given to the * who is in charge Lev 7:7
sacrifice, the * who is in charge Lev 7:8
to the assisting *, the one who Lev 7:14
and the * who eats it shall be Lev 7:17,18
clean. Any * who is ceremonially Lev 7:20
Then the * shall burn the fat Lev 7:31
be given to the officiating *. Lev 7:32,33
door of the Tabernacle to the *; Lev 12:6
and the * will offer them before Lev 12:7
sin offering. The * will make Lev 12:8
He must be brought to Aaron the * Lev 13:1
the * must declare him a leper. Lev 13:3
turned white, the * shall Lev 13:4
seventh day, the * will examine him Lev 13:5
the skin, then the * must Lev 13:5
Again on the seventh day the * Lev 13:6
the * shall pronounce him cured; Lev 13:6
he has come to the * to be Lev 13:7
come back to the * again, and the Lev 13:7
again, and the * shall look again, Lev 13:8
the * must pronounce him a leper. Lev 13:8
is brought to the *, the priest is Lev 13:9,10
to the priest, the * is to look to Lev 13:9,10
the * must pronounce him defiled. Lev 13:11
But if the * sees that the Lev 13:12
looks, then the * shall pronounce Lev 13:13
to the * to be examined again. Lev 13:16,17
the * will pronounce him cured. Lev 13:16,17
must go to the * for examination. Lev 13:19
If the * sees that the trouble Lev 13:20
white, then the * shall declare him Lev 13:20
But if the * sees that there are Lev 13:21
is gray, then the * shall Lev 13:21
the * must declare him a leper. Lev 13:22
* shall declare that all is well. Lev 13:23
then the * must examine the spot. Lev 13:25
the * must pronounce him a leper. Lev 13:25
But if the * sees that there are Lev 13:26
and is fading, the * shall Lev 13:26
the * must pronounce him a leper. Lev 13:27
the burn, and the * shall declare Lev 13:28
or chin, the * must examine him; Lev 13:29,30
the * must pronounce him a leper. Lev 13:29,30
itself) and the * shall quarantine Lev 13:33
than the skin, the * shall Lev 13:34
spread, then the * must examine Lev 13:36
the * shall declare him healed. Lev 13:37
In that case the * shall examine Lev 13:43
and the * must pronounce him such. Lev 13:44
be taken to the * to be examined. Lev 13:49
be examined. The * will put it Lev 13:50
not spread, the * shall order the Lev 13:54
But if the * sees that the spot Lev 13:56
"The * shall go out of the camp Lev 14:3
If the * sees that the leprosy is Lev 14:3
is healed. The * shall then order Lev 14:5
Then the * shall sprinkle the Lev 14:7
leprosy, and the * shall pronounce Lev 14:7
then the * who examines him Lev 14:11
Tabernacle. The * shall take one Lev 14:12
be given to the * for food, as in Lev 14:13
offering. The * shall take the Lev 14:14
"Then the * shall take the olive Lev 14:15
be placed by the * upon the tip of Lev 14:17
Thus the * shall make atonement Lev 14:18
"Then the * must offer the sin Lev 14:19
and afterwards the * shall kill Lev 14:19
He shall bring them to the * at Lev 14:23
the Lord. The * shall take the Lev 14:24
"The * shall then pour the olive Lev 14:26
and the * shall make atonement Lev 14:31
and report to the *, 'It seems to Lev 14:35
"The * shall order the house to Lev 14:36
wall, then the * shall order the Lev 14:4
appear again, the * shall come Lev 14:4
"But if, when the * comes again Lev 14:4
and give them to the *. Lev 15:1
the priest. The * shall sacrifice Lev 15:1
thus the * shall make atonement Lev 15:1
bring them to the * at the entrance Lev 15:2
and the * shall offer one for a Lev 15:3
the anointed High *, consecrated in Lev 16:3
sacrifices to the * at the entrance Lev 17:
in this way the * will be able to Lev 17:
be a ram. The * shall make Lev 19:2
For the * is a leader among his Lev 21:4
Lord their God. A * shall not Lev 21:7
man of God. The * is set apart to Lev 21:8
The daughter of any * who Lev 21:9
"The High *—anointed with the Lev 21:10
to the High *, while the contrary Lev 21:11
From now on and forever, if a * Lev 22:3
"No * who is a leper or who has Lev 22:4
And any * who touches a dead Lev 22:4
any reason— that * shall be Lev 22:6
holy sacrifices unless he is a *; Lev 22:10
no one visiting the *, for Lev 22:10
exception—if the * buys a slave Lev 22:11
return to the * the amount he has Lev 22:14
* on the day after the Sabbath. Lev 23:9,10,11
"Every Sabbath day the High * Lev 24:5-8
be brought to the * and the priest Lev 27:8
the priest and the * shall talk it Lev 27:8
shall pay as the * shall decide. Lev 27:8
bring it to the * to value it, and Lev 27:11,12
more than the value set by the *. Lev 27:13
to redeem it, the * will decide its Lev 27:14,15
possession, the * shall estimate Lev 27:23
the * may sell it to someone else. Lev 27:27
(Anyone who was not a * or Num 3:38
be given to the *, along with a Num 5:8
his wife to the * with an offering Num 5:15
"The * shall bring her before Num 5:16
are justified. The * shall stand Num 5:18
Then the * shall write these Num 5:23
"Then the * shall take the Num 5:25
the Lord and the * shall handle the Num 5:30
pigeons to the * at the entrance of Num 6:10
Tabernacle. The * shall offer one Num 6:11
offerings. The * shall present Num 6:16
been shaved, the * shall take the Num 6:19
man's hands. The * shall then wave Num 6:20
portion for the *, as are the rib Num 6:20
And the * shall make atonement Num 15:25
offering, and the * shall make Num 15:28
and whom he has chosen as his *. Num 16:5
son of Aaron the * to pull those Num 16:36,37
So Eleazar the * took the 250 Num 16:39
and shall be given to Aaron the *. Num 18:28,29
Give her to Eleazar the * and he Num 19:1
of Aaron the *) saw this, he jumped Num 25:7
of Aaron the *) has turned away Num 25:10,11
(son of Aaron the *), "Take a Num 26:1
and Eleazar the *, in the plains of Num 26:63
Moses, Eleazar the *, the tribal Num 27:1
him to Eleazar the *, and as all Num 27:19
with Eleazar the * in order to get Num 27:21
and took Joshua to Eleazar the *. Num 27:22
Phinehas (son of Eleazar the *) Num 31:6
and Eleazar the *, and to the rest Num 31:12
Moses and Eleazar the * and all Num 31:13
Then Eleazar the * said to the Num 31:21
and Eleazar the * and the leaders Num 31:26
Give this share to Eleazar the * Num 31:29
So Moses and Eleazar the * did as Num 31:31
*, as the Lord had directed Moses. Num 31:41
Moses and Eleazar the * received Num 31:51,52
and Eleazar the * and the other Num 32:2
Hor, Aaron the * was directed by Num 33:38,39
land: Eleazar the *, Joshua (son of Num 34:16-28
until the death of the High *. Num 35:25
until the death of the High *. Num 35:28
But after the death of the High * Num 35:28
before the death of the High *. Num 35:32
His son Eleazar became the next * Deu 10:6
decision of the * or judge Deu 17:12
Before you begin the battle, a * Deu 20:2
of the * in cases of leprosy, for I Deu 24:8
and hand it to the * on duty and Deu 26:2,3
The * will then take the basket Deu 26:4
Eleazar the *, Joshua, and the Jos 14:1
to Eleazar the * and to Joshua and Jos 17:4
Eleazar the *, Joshua, and the Jos 19:51
death of the High * who was in Jos 20:6
with Eleazar the * and with Joshua Jos 21:1
the son of Eleazar the *. Jos 22:13
When Phinehas the * and the high Jos 22:30
one of his sons as the *. Ju 17:4,5
One day a young * Ju 17:7,8
And he replied, "I am a * Ju 17:9
Micah said, "and you can be my *. Ju 17:10,11
consecrated him as his personal *. Ju 17:12
have a genuine * working for me!" Ju 17:13
Literally, "a Levite as a *." Ju 17:13f

PRIEST Con't)
and that he was his personal *. Ju 18:4
"Yes," the * replied, "all is Ju 18:6
to the young *, and asked him how Ju 18:15,16
the young * demanded when he Ju 18:18
"Be a * to all of us. Ju 18:19
Isn't it better for you to be a * Ju 18:19
The young * was then quite happy Ju 18:20
my *, and I have nothing left!" Ju 18:24
idols and the *, the men of Dan Ju 18:27
and grandson of Aaron, was the *. Ju 20:27,28
Eli the * was sitting at his 1Sa 1:9
helper, for he assisted Eli the *. 1Sa 2:11
brothers to be my *, and to 1Sa 2:28
up a faithful * who will serve me 1Sa 2:35
Among his men was Ahijah the * 1Sa 14:3
Eli, the * of the Lord in Shiloh). 1Sa 14:3
was talking to the *, the shouting 1Sa 14:19
But the * said, "Let's ask God 1Sa 14:36
of Nob to see Ahimelech, the *. 1Sa 21:1
bread," the * replied, "but there 1Sa 21:4
available, the * gave him the holy 1Sa 21:6
"Well," the * replied, "I have 1Sa 21:9
David talking to Ahimelech the *. 1Sa 22:9,10
(Abiathar the * went to Keilah 1Sa 23:6
told Abiathar the * to bring the 1Sa 23:9
Then he said to Abiathar the *, 1Sa 30:7
and Abiathar the * into his 1Ki 1:7
Abiathar the * and General Joab. 1Ki 1:19
General Joab and Abiathar the *; 1Ki 1:25
But Zadok the * and Benaiah and 1Ki 1:26
"Call Zadok the *," the king 1Ki 1:32
and Zadok the * and Nathan the 1Ki 1:34
So Zadok the *, Nathan the 1Ki 1:38
son of Abiathar the *, rushed in. 1Ki 1:42
with Zadok the * and Nathan the 1Ki 1:44,45
He and Abiathar the * and General 1Ki 2:22
to Abiathar the *, "Go back to 1Ki 2:26
position as the * of the Lord, 1Ki 2:27
Zadok as * instead of Abiathar. 1Ki 2:35
(son of Zadok) was the High *; 1Ki 4:1
personal * and special friend; 1Ki 4:1
Anyone who wanted to could be a * 1Ki 13:33
the wife of Jehoiada the High *. 2Ki 11:2,3f
Athaliah's reign, Jehoiada the * 2Ki 11:4
* of Baal, in front of the altar. 2Ki 11:18
the High * instructed him. 2Ki 12:2
Jehoiada the * bored a hole in 2Ki 12:9
and the High * counted it, put it 2Ki 12:10
the * with a detailed description. 2Ki 16:10
He instructed Uriah the * to use 2Ki 16:15
Uriah the * did as King Ahaz 2Ki 16:16
to Hilkiah, the High *: 2Ki 22:3,4
One day Hilkiah the High * went 2Ki 22:8
He commanded Hilkiah the *, and 2Ki 22:12,13
So Hilkiah the *, and Ahikam, and 2Ki 22:14
Hilkiah the High * and the rest of 2Ki 23:4
the * had found in the Temple. 2Ki 23:24
Seraiah, the chief *, his assistant 2Ki 25:18
Azariah (the High * in Solomon's 1Ch 6:4-15
Another * was Maasai (son of 1Ch 9:12
David left Zadok the * and his 1Ch 16:39
leaders: Zadok the *, Ahimelech the 1Ch 24:6
Jehoiada the High *, and was the 1Ch 27:5,6
they anointed Zadok as their *. 1Ch 29:22
Anyone at all can be a * of these 2Ch 13:9
not had a true * to teach them. 2Ch 15:3
Amariah, the High *, to be the 2Ch 19:11
and the wife of Jehoiada the *. 2Ch 22:11
Jehoiada the * got up his courage 2Ch 23:1
* didn't release them to go home. 2Ch 23:8
* shouted to the army officers. 2Ch 23:13,14
the * of Baal before his altar. 2Ch 23:15,16,17
the lifetime of Jehoiada the *. 2Ch 24:2
Jehoiada, the High *, and asked 2Ch 24:6
of the High * counted the money, 2Ch 24:11
the lifetime of Jehoiada the *. 2Ch 24:14
the son of Jehoiada the *. 2Ch 24:25
Azariah the High * went in after 2Ch 26:17,18
And Azariah the High * from the 2Ch 31:10
Hezekiah and Azariah the High *. 2Ch 31:12,13
Hilkiah the High * for accounting, 2Ch 34:9
One day when Hilkiah, the High *, 2Ch 34:14
was the son of Aaron, the chief *. Ez 7:5
*, the student of God's commands: Ez 7:11
"To: Ezra, the *, the teacher of Ez 7:12
you (for he is a * and teacher of Ez 7:21
I also decree that no *, Levite, Ez 7:24
son of Uriah the *), Eleazar (son Ez 8:33
Then I, Ezra the *, arose and Ez 10:10
THEN ELIASHIB THE High * and the Neh 3:1
the home of Eliashib the High *. Neh 3:20
a *, I would forfeit my life. Neh 6:11
So Ezra the * brought out to them Neh 8:1
Then Ezra the *, and I as Neh 8:9
rural towns. A *—a descendant of Neh 10:38
son of Ahitub the chief *). Neh 11:10-14
served under the High * Joiakim: Neh 12:12-21
was the * and teacher of religion. Neh 12:26
Ezra the * led this procession. Neh 12:35,36
the descendants of Aaron the *." Neh 12:47f
Eliashib the *, who had been Neh 13:4
I put Shelemiah the *, Zadok the Neh 13:13
Eliashib the High *) was a Neh 13:28
by God as his *. Ps 106:16
vow, that you are a * forever like Ps 110:4
I asked Uriah the * and Is 8:2
to Jeremiah the * (the son of Jer 1:1
small, prophet and *, have one Jer 8:10
of Immer), the * in charge of the Jer 20:1
and Zephaniah the * (son of Jer 21:1
of Ma-aseiah) the *, and sent Jer 29:25
Jehoiada as * in Jerusalem. Jer 29:26
And I will invite him to be a * Jer 30:21
and Zephaniah the * (son of Jer 37:3
Seraiah the chief *, and Zephaniah Jer 52:24,25
Ezekiel was a * (the son of Buzi) Eze 1:1
are allowed. No * may drink wine Eze 44:21
maiden, or the widow of a *; Eze 44:22
"A * must not defile himself by Eze 44:25
the Temple. The * shall take some Eze 45:19
end while the * offers his burnt Eze 46:2
Menelaus, the High *, who Dan 11:32f
Look, *, I am pointing my finger Hos 4:4
But when Amaziah, the * of Amo 7:10
*—for it was addressed to them. Hag 1:1
the High *, and the few people Hag 1:12
* and everyone left in the land: Hag 2:2
Joshua the High * standing before Zec 3:1
O Joshua the High *, and all you Zec 3:8
(son of Josedech) the High *. Zec 6:10,11
as King and as *, with perfect Zec 6:13
prophet, *, and people. Zec 12:12,13,14
"Oh, to find one * among you who Mal 1:10
last man, whether * or layman, who Mal 2:12
go right over to the * to be Mt 8:4
Caiaphas the High *, to discuss Mt 26:3
Caiaphas the High *, where all the Mt 26:57
Then the High * stood up and said Mt 26:62
Then the High * said to him, "I Mt 26:63
Then the High * tore at his own Mt 26:65,66
immediately by the Jewish *. Mk 1:43,44
was High * then—and they ate the Mk 2:25,26
Then the High * stood up before Mk 14:60
Then the High * asked him. Mk 14:61
Then the High * tore at his Mk 14:63,64
for the High * noticed Peter Mk 14:66,67
My story begins with a Jewish *, Lk 1:5
a member of the * tribe of the Lk 1:5
and be examined by the Jewish *. Lk 5:14
"By chance a Jewish * came Lk 10:31
"Go to the Jewish * and show him Lk 17:14
who was High * that year, said, Jn 11:49
position as High *—he didn't think Jn 11:51
of Caiaphas, the High * that year. Jn 18:13
was acquainted with the High *. Jn 18:15
Inside, the High * began asking Jn 18:19
the way to answer the High *?" Jn 18:22
bound, to Caiaphas the High *. Jn 18:24
slaves of the High *—a relative of Jn 18:26
Annas the High * was there, and Act 4:6
The High * and his relatives and Act 5:17
the High * and his courtiers Act 5:21
the High * demanded. Act 5:28
THEN THE HIGH * asked him, "Are Act 7:1
went to the High * in Jerusalem. Act 9:1
The local * of the Temple of Act 14:13
a Jewish *, were doing this. Act 19:14
The High * or any member of the Act 22:5
Instantly Ananias the High * Act 23:2
the way to talk to God's High *?" Act 23:4
he was the High *, brothers," Paul Act 23:5
FIVE DAYS LATER Ananias the High * Act 24:1
and faithful High * before God, a Heb 2:17
before God, a * who would be both Heb 2:17
and the High * of our faith. Heb 3:1
appointed him High *, just as Moses Heb 3:2
is our great High * who has gone to Heb 4:14
This High * of ours understands Heb 4:15
THE JEWISH HIGH * is merely a man Heb 5:1
* just because he wants to be. Heb 5:4
to the honor of being High *; Heb 5:5
chosen to be a * forever, with the Heb 5:6
him to be a High * with the same Heb 5:10
"having become our High *." Heb 6:20f
our High *, with the honor and Heb 6:20
and also a * of the Most High God. Heb 7:1
of the Son of God—a * forever. Heb 7:3
had been a Jewish *, for later on Heb 7:5
send Christ as a * with the rank of Heb 7:11
a new kind of *, his law must be Heb 7:12,13,14
the new High * who came with the Heb 7:15
did not become a * by meeting the Heb 7:16
"You are a * forever with the rank Heb 7:17
would always be a *, although he Heb 7:20
mind: You are a * forever, with the Heb 7:21
a * so that no one else is needed. Heb 7:24
the kind of High * we need; Heb 7:26
is our High *, and is in heaven at Heb 8:1
And since every high * is Heb 8:3
permitted to be a *, because down Heb 8:4
But only the high * went into Heb 9:7
He came as High * of this better Heb 9:11
again, as the high * down here on Heb 9:25
And since this great High * of Heb 10:21
laws the high * brought the blood Heb 13:11

PRIEST-POLITICIAN
being a major * of the time. Gen 41:45f

PRIEST-TRIBE
who were not from the * of Levi. 1Ki 12:31
not belong to the * of Levi, but Heb 7:12,13,14

PRIEST'S
minister to me in the * office. Ex 28:3
But if the * examination reveals Lev 13:31
If a * daughter is married Lev 22:12
in addition to the * valuation, and Lev 27:19
shall pay the * estimate of its Lev 27:27
little linen robe just like the *. 1Sa 2:18
off the ear of the High * servant. Mt 26:51
of the High * house and went in and Mt 26:58
* servant, cutting off his ear. Mk 14:47
Jesus was led to the High * home Mk 14:53
gates of the High * residence and Mk 14:54
at the High * servant, and cut off Lk 22:50
him to the High * residence, and Lk 22:54
of Malchus, the High * servant. Jn 18:10
others of the High * relatives. Act 4:6

PRIESTHOOD
inducted into the *, they shall Lev 6:19,20
he shall be discharged from the *. Lev 22:3
may carry out the duties of the *; Num 3:10
And now are you demanding the * Num 16:10
* is your special gift of service. Num 18:7
have defiled the * and the promises Neh 13:29
which had not been chosen for *; Heb 7:12,13,14
Yes, the old system of * based on Heb 7:18
Christ, whose * we have just Heb 8:1

PRIESTLY
blood—half * and half ordinary." Lev 21:14,15
the * families may eat this food. Lev 22:13
any impropriety in your * work. Num 18:1
There you shall remove Aaron's * Num 20:26
Moses removed the * garments from Num 20:28
burn incense, and to wear a * robe 1Sa 2:28
in all, all wearing their * robes. 1Sa 22:18
* robes and blew their trumpets; Ez 3:10
Or, "in the * robes." Ps 96:9f

PRIESTS
belonging to the *, for they were Gen 47:22
And you shall be a kingdom of * Ex 19:6
Even the * on duty Ex 19:22
Literally, "The * who come near Ex 19:22f
and don't let the * and the people Ex 19:24
to be *, to minister to me. Ex 28:1
them as the *, my ministers. Ex 28:41
and his sons as *: get a young bull Ex 29:1
They will then be * forever; Ex 29:9
sons who are my ministers, the *. Ex 29:44
that they can minister to me as *. Ex 30:30
so that they can minister as *; Ex 31:10
The beautiful clothing for the *, Ex 35:10-19
for anointing the *, and the pure Ex 37:29
THEN, FOR THE *, the people made Ex 39:1
that they may minister to me as *; Ex 40:15
children shall forever be my *." Ex 40:15
the * could use it for washing. Ex 40:30
where the * will accept your gift Lev 1:2,3
Aaron's sons, the *, will present Lev 1:5
Then the * will skin the animal Lev 1:6,7
washed, then the * will burn them Lev 1:9
Aaron's sons, the *, will sprinkle Lev 1:11
it, and the * will lay the pieces, Lev 1:12
Then the * shall burn it all upon Lev 1:13
to one of the * to burn, and the Lev 2:2
"The * are to burn only a Lev 2:9
The remainder belongs to the * Lev 2:10
Then the * shall burn part of Lev 2:16
Tabernacle; the * shall throw the Lev 3:7,8
I have given to the * this part Lev 6:17
the * may eat these offerings Lev 6:18
As the sons of the * replace Lev 6:22,23
*—may touch this meat; Lev 6:27
Every male among the * may eat Lev 6:29
be eaten by the * if any of its Lev 6:30
sacrificing. The * will burn them Lev 7:5
Only males among the * may then Lev 7:6
The * who present the people's Lev 7:9
as *—to Aaron and to his sons. Lev 7:35
the altar, the *, and the people. Lev 16:33
for Aaron and the * and for all the Lev 17:1
Moses: "Tell the * never to defile Lev 21:1
"The * shall not clip bald spots Lev 21:5
in verse 1 applied to ordinary *. Lev 21:11f
the food of the * from the Lev 21:22
Warn the * to follow these Lev 22:9
"The * shall wave these Lev 23:20
will be given to the * as food. Lev 23:20
and it shall be given to the *. Lev 27:21
All were anointed as * and set Num 3:3
the Lord it shall go to the *." Num 5:9,10
to the Lord is given to the *! Num 8:13
Only the * are permitted to blow Num 10:8
Remember, only the * are to Num 18:5

(PRIESTS Con't)
But you and your sons, the *, Num 18:7
"I have given the * all the gifts Num 18:8
"You * may own no property, nor Num 18:20
other than the * and Levites shall Num 18:22
then give the best tenth to the *. Num 18:32
descendants shall be * forever." Num 25:12,13
your God, to the * and Levites, Deu 17:9
"REMEMBER THAT THE * and all the Deu 18:1
So the * and Levites are to be Deu 18:1
sacrifice must be given to the *. Deu 18:3
In addition, the * shall receive Deu 18:4
brought before the * and judges on Deu 19:17
"Then the * shall come (for the Deu 21:5
shall be confiscated by the *. Deu 22:9
gave them to the *, the sons of Deu 31:9
see the * carrying the Ark of God, Jos 3:2,3,4
Joshua ordered the *, "Take up the Jos 3:6
Instruct the * who are carrying Jos 3:8
When the * who are carrying the Jos 3:13,14
as the feet of the * who were Jos 3:13,14
Jericho, and the * who were Jos 3:17
from where the * are standing in Jos 4:2,3
place where the * were standing; Jos 4:9
to this day. The * who were Jos 4:10
people watched the * carry the Ark Jos 4:11
orders to the * carrying the Ark. Jos 4:15,16
And as soon as the * came out, Jos 4:18
followed by seven * walking ahead Jos 6:3,4
with the * blowing their trumpets. Jos 6:3,4
So Joshua summoned the * and gave Jos 6:6-9
followed by seven * blowing Jos 6:6-9
Behind them would come the * Jos 6:6-9
The seventh time, as the * blew Jos 6:16
Then the * offered burnt Jos 8:31
Between them stood the * with the Jos 8:33
they are * of the Lord. Jos 18:7
These were given to some of the * Jos 21:4
were the *—the descendants of Jos 21:9-16
to the *—the descendants of Aaron. Jos 21:19
pouch worn by * on their chests. Ju 8:27f
and his sons as their *. Ju 18:30
This family continued as * until Ju 18:30
to him. (The * on duty at that time 1Sa 1:3
sacrificial offerings to you *? 1Sa 2:28
could always be my *, it is 1Sa 2:30
that it will no longer serve as *. 1Sa 2:31
shall be * to my kings forever. 1Sa 2:35
me a job among the * so that I will 1Sa 2:36
day neither the * of Dagon nor his 1Sa 5:5
called for their * and diviners and 1Sa 6:2
family and all the other * at Nob. 1Sa 22:11,12
"Kill these *, for they are allies 1Sa 22:17
them, eighty-five * in all, all 1Sa 22:18
the city of the *, and killed the 1Sa 22:19
and killed the *' families—men, 1Sa 22:19
and was wearing *' clothing. 2Sa 6:14
were the High *, and Seraiah was 2Sa 8:17
Literally, "were *." 2Sa 8:18f
Zadok and Abiathar, the *, are 2Sa 15:35,36
and Abiathar, the *, what 2Sa 17:15
and Abiathar the * to say to the 2Sa 19:11,12
and Abiathar were the chief *. 2Sa 20:25
Adonijah were the * Zadok and 1Ki 1:8
Zadok and Abiathar were *; 1Ki 4:1
During the festivities the * 1Ki 8:3,4
Then the * took the Ark into the 1Ki 8:6
As the * are returning from the 1Ki 8:10
the Temple! The * have to go 1Ki 8:11
hills and ordained * from the rank 1Ki 12:31
* for the shrines on the hills. 1Ki 12:32,33
upon you the * from the shrines on 1Ki 13:2
instead, he made more * than ever 1Ki 13:33
the 400 Asherah * left alive by 1Ki 22:6f
Summon all the prophets and * of 2Ki 10:18,19
As the * of Baal began offering 2Ki 10:24
and the other * and asked them, 2Ki 12:7
So the * agreed to set up a 2Ki 12:8
given to the * for their own use. 2Ki 12:16
one of the exiled * from Samaria 2Ki 17:27,28
among themselves * to sacrifice to 2Ki 17:32
some of the older * to clothe 2Ki 19:2
"Collect the money given to the * 2Ki 22:3,4
So all the * and prophets and the 2Ki 23:1
the rest of the * and the guards of 2Ki 23:4
He killed the heathen * who had 2Ki 23:5
to Jerusalem the * of the Lord, who 2Ki 23:8
However, these * 2Ki 23:9
Literally, "the * of the high 2Ki 23:9f
though they ate with the other *. 2Ki 23:9
He executed the * of the heathen 2Ki 23:20
and his descendants were the *. 1Ch 6:49
to the * by the tribe of Benjamin. 1Ch 6:60
and also the *, the Levites, and 1Ch 9:2
The * who returned were: 1Ch 9:10,11
Another of the returning * was 1Ch 9:12
In all, 1,760 * returned. 1Ch 9:13
Other * prepared the spices and 1Ch 9:30
From the *—descendants of 1Ch 12:24-37
were officers of the fighting *. 1Ch 12:24-37
including the * and Levites, 1Ch 13:2
These were the * and Levites 1Ch 15:4-10
Abiathar, the High *, and for the 1Ch 15:11
So the * and the Levites 1Ch 15:14
of whom were *—formed a bugle corps 1Ch 15:24
and zithers. The * Benaiah and 1Ch 16:6
of this choral group of *. 1Ch 16:7
(son of Abiathar) were the head *; 1Ch 18:16
was to assist the *—the descendants 1Ch 23:28
and assisted the * in whatever way 1Ch 23:32
THE * (THE descendants of Aaron) 1Ch 24:1
the heads of the * and Levites. 1Ch 24:6
leaders of the * and the Levites. 1Ch 24:31
various groups of * and Levites; 1Ch 28:13
And these various groups of * 1Ch 28:21
to the left. The * used the tank, 2Ch 4:6
a court for the *, also the public 2Ch 4:9
Then the * carried the Ark into 2Ch 5:7,8
When the * had undergone the 2Ch 5:11,12
* came out of the Holy of Holies! 2Ch 5:11,12
accompanied by 120 * who were 2Ch 5:11,12
* could not continue their work. 2Ch 5:13,14
Let your *, O Lord God, be 2Ch 6:41
so that the * couldn't enter! 2Ch 7:1
sheep. The * were standing at 2Ch 7:6
Then, when the * blew the 2Ch 7:6
In assigning the * to their 2Ch 8:14
the * in each day's duties; 2Ch 8:14
However, the * and Levites from 2Ch 11:13,14
them to stop being * of the Lord. 2Ch 11:13,14
He had appointed other * instead 2Ch 11:15
And you have driven away the * 2Ch 13:9
have appointed heathen * instead. 2Ch 13:9
you accept as * anybody who comes 2Ch 13:9
of Aaron are our *, and the Levites 2Ch 13:10
he is our Leader. His *, 2Ch 13:12
and the * blew the trumpets. 2Ch 13:13,14
also the *, Elishama and Jehoram. 2Ch 17:7,8,9
and * and clan leaders and judges. 2Ch 19:8
A third of you * and Levites who 2Ch 23:4
For only the * and Levites on 2Ch 23:5,6
led a third of the * arriving for 2Ch 23:8
the Levite * as guards, and to 2Ch 23:18
He summoned the * and Levites 2Ch 24:5
with eighty other *, all brave men, 2Ch 26:17,18
"That is the work of the * 2Ch 26:17,18
He summoned the * and Levites to 2Ch 29:4,5
them. The * cleaned up the inner 2Ch 29:16
He instructed the *, the sons of 2Ch 29:21
bulls, and the * took the blood and 2Ch 29:22
Then the * killed the animals 2Ch 29:24
The * formed a trumpet corps. 2Ch 29:25,26
But there were too few * to 2Ch 29:34
until more * had reported to 2Ch 29:34
themselves than the * were. 2Ch 29:34
because not enough * were 2Ch 30:2,3
Then the * and Levites became 2Ch 30:15
and the * sprinkled the blood 2Ch 30:16
Meanwhile the Levites and * 2Ch 30:21
large group of * stepped forward 2Ch 30:24
together with the *, the Levites, 2Ch 30:25
Then the * and Levites stood and 2Ch 30:27
Hezekiah now organized the * and 2Ch 31:2
tithes to the * and Levites, so 2Ch 31:4
Hezekiah asked the * and 2Ch 31:9
the offerings to the *. 2Ch 31:14,15
to the clans of * in their cities, 2Ch 31:14,15
However, the * on duty at the 2Ch 31:16
distribution. The * were listed in 2Ch 31:17,18
registered *, for they had no other 2Ch 31:17,18
One of the * was appointed in 2Ch 31:19
the cities of the * to issue food 2Ch 31:19
supplies to all * in the area, and 2Ch 31:19
of the heathen * upon their own 2Ch 34:5
and the * and Levites and all the 2Ch 34:30
He also reestablished the * in 2Ch 35:2
to the * and Levites. 2Ch 35:8
Temple, gave the * 2,600 sheep and 2Ch 35:8
organized, and the * were standing 2Ch 35:10
the blood to the *, who sprinkled 2Ch 35:11
and for the *, for they had been 2Ch 35:14
so many of the *, Levites, and 2Ch 35:18
including the High *, worshiped the 2Ch 36:14
and to the * and Levites, to return Ez 1:5
concerning the returning *: Ez 2:36-39
Three subclans of *—Habaiah, Ez 2:61
to allow them to continue as *; Ez 2:62,63
them to eat the *' share of food Ez 2:62,63
were descendants of * or not. Ez 2:62,63
silver, and 100 robes for the *. Ez 2:69
So the * and Levites and some of Ez 2:70
with his fellow *, and Zerubbabel Ez 3:1
that the * began sacrificing the Ez 3:6
their fellow * and the Levites. Ez 3:8
of the Temple, the * put on their Ez 3:10
But many of the * and Levites and Ez 3:12
Give the * in Jerusalem young Ez 6:9
great joy by the *, the Levites, Ez 6:16
Then the * and Levites were Ez 6:18
For by that time many of the * Ez 6:20
people as well as *, Levites, Ez 7:7,8,9
including the * and Levites, may Ez 7:13
the Jews and their * in all of the Ez 7:
people and the * who had arrived; Ez 8:
to send us * for the Temple of God Ez 8:
leaders of the *—Sherebiah, Ez 8:
and ten other *— to be in charge Ez 8:
penny lost to the * and the Levite Ez 8:
So the * and the Levites accepted Ez 8:
even some of the * and Levites had Ez 9
our kings and our * were slain by Ez 9
the leaders of the * and the Ez 10
Following is the list of * who had Ez 10:16-
and the other * rebuilt the wall as Neh 3
Then came the * from the plains Neh 3:
of Ophel. The * repaired the wall Neh 3:
Then I summoned the * and made Neh 5:1
concerning the returning *: Neh 7:39-4
subclans of * named after Habaiah, Neh 7:
to continue as * or even to receive Neh 7:64,6
to receive the *' share of food Neh 7:64,6
actually were descendants of *. Neh 7:64,6
530 sets of clothing for the *. Neh 7:7
sets of clothing for the *. Neh 7:7
The *, the Levites, the Neh 7:7
leaders and the * and Levites met Neh 8:1
and princes and * and prophets and Neh 9:3
Our kings, princes, *, and Neh 9:3
and Levites and * put our names to Neh 9:3
above were *. Neh 10:
the common people; the *; Neh 10:2
families of the *, Levites, and Neh 10:3
we presented them to the * who Neh 10:3
by the ministering *, the Neh 10:39,4
the leaders, the *, the Levites, Neh 11:
Leaders from among the *: Neh 11:10-1
In all, there were 822 * doing the Neh 11:10-1
And there were 242 * under the Neh 11:10-1
The other *, Levites, and people Neh 11:2
HERE IS A list of the * who Neh 12:
leaders of the * who served under Neh 12:12-2
the clans of the * and Levites was Neh 12:2
of Jerusalem. The * and Levites Neh 12:3
The * who played the trumpets Neh 12:35,3
joined by the trumpet-playing *— Neh 12:40,4
assigned to the * and Levites, for Neh 12:4
* and Levites and their ministry. Neh 12:4
of what they received to the *. Neh 12:4
wave offerings were for the *. Neh 13:
and vows of the * and Levites. Neh 13:2
tasks to the * and Levites, making Neh 13:3
* are led away as slaves. Job 12:1
eighty-five * and their families. Ps 52:1
songs. The * were slaughtered and Ps 78:6
He is your shield. O * of Aaron, Ps 115:1
of Israel and the * of Aaron, and Ps 115:1
And let the * of Aaron chant, Ps 118:
We will clothe the * in white, Ps 132:9
I will clothe her * with Ps 132:16
O Israel, bless Jehovah! High * Ps 135:19
O Levite *, bless the Lord Ps 135:20
clothes for the * of the Lord! Is 23:18
of the earth. * and people, Is 24:2
led by drunks! Her * and prophets Is 28:7
and the older *—all dressed in Is 37:2
have deposed your * and destroyed Is 43:28
You shall be called * of the Is 61:6
my * and Levites, says the Lord. Is 66:21
its officers and * and people will Jer 1:18
Even their * cared nothing for Jer 2:8
Kings, princes, *, and Jer 2:26,27
on * and idols. Jer 3:24
and the * and the prophets will Jer 4:9
in this land— the * are ruled by Jer 5:31
Yes, even my prophets and *! Jer 6:13
Yet the * and prophets give Jer 6:14
of the princes and * and prophets Jer 8:1
his court and all his evil *? Jer 12:5
throne, and the * and the prophets Jer 13:13
And yet the prophets and * alike Jer 14:18
We have our own * and wise men Jer 18:18
some of the older * with you, and Jer 19:1
And the * are like the prophets, Jer 23:11
"prophets" or * asks you, "Well, Jer 23:33
false prophets and * and people who Jer 23:34
told him to, the * and false Jer 26:7,8
Then the * and the false Jer 26:11
people said to the * and false Jer 26:16
I spoke again and again to the * Jer 27:16
all the * and people listened. Jer 28:1
of all the * and people, "Amen! Jer 28:5
Jewish elders and * and prophets, Jer 29:1
* and to everyone in Jerusalem. Jer 29:25
period were * as well as kings) as Jer 30:21f
I will feast the * with the Jer 31:14
* and prophets—stir me up. Jer 32:32
and my covenant with the Levite * Jer 33:20,21
court officials, * or people—for Jer 34:18,19
Your god Chemosh, with his * and Jer 48:7
along with his princes and *. Jer 49:3
the city gates are silent, her * Lam 1:4
Nor could my * and elders—they Lam 1:19
Kings and * together fall before Lam 2:6

PRIESTS Con't)
Shall * and prophets die within Lam 2:20
her prophets and *, who defiled the Lam 4:13
persecuted the * and elders who Lam 4:16
guide you, but the * and elders and Eze 7:26,27
Your * have violated my laws and Eze 22:26
distant lands for * to come with Eze 23:40
* who supervise the maintenance. Eze 40:45
is for the * in charge of the Eze 40:46
there the * who offer up the Eze 42:13
When the * leave the Holy Eze 42:14
the Lord, and the * shall sprinkle Eze 43:24
day afterward, the * will sacrifice Eze 43:27
not come near me to minister as *; Eze 44:13
continued as my * in the Temple Eze 44:15
And the * themselves shall obey Eze 44:24
gives to the Lord shall be the *'. Eze 44:29
for the Lord shall go to the *. Eze 44:30
be donated to the * too, so that Eze 44:30
bless your homes. * may never eat Eze 44:31
it will be used by the *, who Eze 45:4
guide told me, the * boil the meat Eze 46:19,20
It is for the *, that is, the Eze 48:11
him, including a leader of the *. Dan 11:22
altar, temple, *, or even idols! Hos 3:4
your crimes, you * will stumble in Hos 4:5
your fault, you *, for you Hos 4:6
I refuse to recognize you as my *. Hos 4:6
The * rejoice in the sins of the Hos 4:8
And thus it is: "Like *, like Hos 4:9
* are wicked, the people are too. Hos 4:9
Therefore, I will punish both * Hos 4:9
LISTEN TO THIS, you * and all of Hos 5:1
packs of * murder along the road Hos 6:9
be hurt; the * and people, too, Hos 10:5
of the Lord; the * are starving. Joe 1:9
O *, robe yourselves in Joe 1:13
The *, the ministers of God, will Joe 2:17
take bribes; you * and prophets who Mic 3:11
their idolatrous *, so that even Zep 1:4
own gain; her * defile the Temple Zep 3:4
Ask the * this question about the Hag 2:11
"No," the * replied. Hag 2:12
And the * answered, "Yes." Hag 2:13
and all you other *, you are Zec 3:8
to speak with the * and prophets Zec 7:3
people and your *, 'During those Zec 7:5
O *, but you despise my name." Mal 1:6
LISTEN, YOU *, to this warning Mal 2:1
"*' lips should flow with the Mal 2:7
God's laws. The * are the Mal 2:7
bread permitted to the * alone. Mt 12:4
of Moses how the * on duty in the Mt 12:5
and chief *, and scribes." Mt 16:21f
will be betrayed to the chief * Mt 20:18
But when the chief * and other Mt 21:15
the chief * and other Jewish Mt 21:23
When the chief * and other Jewish Mt 21:45
At that very moment the chief * Mt 26:3
went to the chief *, and asked, Mt 26:14
The chief * and, in fact, the Mt 26:59
WHEN IT WAS morning, the chief * Mt 27:1
chief * and other Jewish leaders. Mt 27:3
The chief * picked the money up. Mt 27:6
But when the chief * and other Mt 27:12
Meanwhile the chief * and Jewish Mt 27:20
And the chief * and Jewish Mt 27:41,42,43
—the chief * and Pharisees went Mt 27:62
* and told them what had happened. Mt 28:11
only * were allowed to eat? Mk 2:25,26
and the Chief * and the other Mk 8:31
before the chief * and the Jewish Mk 10:33
When the chief * and other Jewish Mk 11:18
chief * and other Jewish leaders Mk 11:27,28
The chief * and other Jewish Mk 14:1
went to the chief * to arrange to Mk 14:10
When the chief * heard why he had Mk 14:11
chief * and other Jewish leaders. Mk 14:43
all of the chief * and other Jewish Mk 14:53
Inside, the chief * and the whole Mk 14:55
EARLY IN THE morning the chief *, Mk 15:1
Then the chief * accused him of Mk 15:3,4
by the chief * because they envied Mk 15:10
But at this point the chief * Mk 15:11
The chief * and religious leaders Mk 15:31
Annas and Caiaphas were High *. Lk 3:1
elders, chief *, and teachers of Lk 9:22
but the chief * and other religious Lk 19:47
by the chief * and other religious Lk 20:1
When the chief * and religious Lk 20:19
The chief * and other religious Lk 22:2
over to the chief * and captains of Lk 22:4
Then Jesus addressed the chief * Lk 22:52
the chief * and all the top Lk 22:66
Then Pilate turned to the chief * Lk 23:4
Meanwhile, the chief * and the Lk 23:10
together the chief * and other Lk 23:13
But the chief * and our Lk 24:20
sent * and assistant priests from Jn 1:19
sent priests and assistant * from Jn 1:19
* sent officers to arrest Jesus. Jn 7:32
to the chief * and Pharisees. Jn 7:45
Then the chief * and Pharisees Jn 11:47
Meanwhile the chief * and Jn 11:57
Then the chief * decided to kill Jn 12:10
The chief * and Pharisees had Jn 18:3
their chief * brought you here. Jn 18:35
At sight of him the chief * and Jn 19:6
the chief * shouted back. Jn 19:15
Then the chief * said to Pilate, Jn 19:21
people, the chief *, the captain of Act 4:1
and the chief * heard this, they Act 5:24
and many of the Jewish * were Act 6:7
him from the chief *, authorizing Act 9:14
them in chains to the chief *." Act 9:21
ordered the chief * into session Act 22:30
Then they went to the chief * Act 23:14
where the chief * and other Jewish Act 25:2
the chief * and other Jewish Act 25:15
as authorized by the High *; Act 26:10
of the chief *, when one day about Act 26:12
to help their * because the priests Heb 7:5
the * were their relatives. Heb 7:5
(c) The Jewish *, though mortal, Heb 7:8
of all Jewish *, of all who receive Heb 7:9
(e) If the Jewish * and their Heb 7:11
same rank all other * had? Heb 7:11
he never said that of other *. Heb 7:21
had to be many *, so that when the Heb 7:23
as other * did, to cover over first Heb 7:27
even the high * were weak and Heb 7:28
those offered by the earthly *. Heb 8:4
down here the * still follow the Heb 8:4
Well, when all was ready the * Heb 9:6
Under the old agreement the * Heb 10:11
What's more, you are his holy *; 1Pe 2:5
himself—you are * of the King, you 1Pe 2:9
and made us * of God his Father. Rev 1:6
and made them * of our God; Rev 5:10
for they will be * of God and of Rev 20:6

PRIMARILY
These funds are to be used * for Ez 7:17

PRIMARY
Yes, this is the * law concerning Eze 43:12
the Kingdom of God your * concern. Lk 12:31

PRIME
the Agagite), as * minister. Est 3:1
[appointing him * Minister Est 8:2
Mordecai the Jew was the * Est 10:3
rest, along with * ministers and Job 3:14,15
them down in their *, for there is Ps 55:15
son, who was the * minister of Is 36:3
of Hilkiah), the * minister, and Is 36:22
Meanwhile he sent Eliakim his * Is 37:2

PRIMEVAL
the * source of God's creation: Rev 3:14

PRINCE
are an honored * of God among us; Gen 23:5,6
you think you are our * and judge! Ex 2:14
Gamaliel, son of Pedahzur, * of Num 7:54-59
daughter of Zur, a Midianite *. Num 25:15
The * among his brothers. Deu 33:16
A DAY OR so later, * Jonathan said 1Sa 14:1
(* Jonathan now went to find 1Sa 23:16
who was the son of * Jonathan. 2Sa 4:4
as he had promised * Jonathan. 2Sa 9:1
* ABSALOM, DAVID'S son, had a 2Sa 13:1
named Tamar. And * Amnon (her half 2Sa 13:1
out the young * and put the crown 2Ki 11:12
Israel, and from Judah came a *. 1Ch 5:2
He was a * of the tribe of Reuben 1Ch 5:6
out the little * and placed the 2Ch 23:11
You will fall as any *—for all Ps 82:7
though you were some powerful *. Pro 25:6,7
Only a stupid * will oppress his Pro 28:16
Father," "The * of Peace." Is 9:6
Tirhakah, crown * of Ethiopia, was Is 37:8,9
"You are my Servant, a * of Power Is 49:3
Literally, "to the * in Eze 12:10f
evil * of Israel, your final day Eze 21:25
"Son of dust, say to the * of Eze 28:2,3
shall be a * among my people. Eze 34:24
Messiah, shall be their * forever. Eze 37:25
Only the *—because he is the Eze 44:3
he is the *—may sit inside the Eze 44:3
set apart for the *—one on each Eze 45:7
must give to the *: a bushel of Eze 45:13
bring their offerings to the *. Eze 45:16
"The * shall be required to Eze 45:17
On the day of Passover the * Eze 45:22
And the * shall provide fourteen Eze 45:24
celebrations. The * shall enter Eze 46:2
"The burnt offering which the * Eze 46:4
"The * shall go in at the entry Eze 46:8
passageway. The * shall enter and Eze 46:10
as much as the * is willing to Eze 46:11
Whenever the * offers an extra Eze 46:12
"The Lord God says: If the * Eze 46:16
then the land returns to the *. Eze 46:17
And the * may never take Eze 46:18
of Israel, shall belong to the *. Eze 48:21,22
on the * of Princes in battle; Dan 8:25
Literally, "the * of Persia." Dan 10:13f
my way back, past the * of Persia; Dan 10:20,21
and after him, the * of Greece. Dan 10:20,21
Literally, "your *." Dan 10:20,21f
the mighty angelic * who stands Dan 12:1
without a king or *, and without an Hos 3:4
with fear, for he was a mighty *; Hos 13:1
a man dressed as a * in a palace? Mt 11:8
Literally, "* of this world." Jn 12:31f
the * of this world, shall be Jn 12:31
evil * of this world approaches. Jn 14:30
because the * of this world has Jn 16:11
him to be a * and Savior, so that Act 5:31
he became a mighty * and orator. Act 7:22
Satan, the mighty * of the power of Eph 2:2
Their king is the * of the Rev 9:11

PRINCELY
Literally, "the chariots of my * Sol 6:12f

PRINCES
Twelve * shall be among his Gen 17:20
offerings with all the * of Moab. Num 23:6
the king and the * of Moab were Num 23:17
Listen, O you kings and *, Ju 5:3
Went the * of Issachar Ju 5:15
And treats them as * 1Sa 2:8
including all the * and the best of 2Ki 24:14
of some of the * of wealthy clans 1Ch 4:34-39
of Judah these * invaded the land 1Ch 4:40,41
the * of Judah, and killed them. 2Ch 22:8
and the * donated 1,000 young 2Ch 30:24
summoned his * and officers for a 2Ch 32:3
and took with him all the royal *. 2Ch 36:18
and before all of his mighty *! Ez 7:28
upon our kings and * and priests Neh 9:32
Our kings, *, priests, and Neh 9:34
And we and our * and Levites and Neh 9:38
king's most noble * to robe the man Est 6:9
governors, and * of all the Est 8:9,10
pomp, and wealthy * whose castles Job 3:14,15
He pours contempt upon *, and Job 12:21
at my coming. The * stood in Job 29:9
leads the way. The * and elders of Ps 68:27
of Judah, and the * of Zebulun and Ps 68:27
for he cuts down * and does Ps 76:12
let all their * die like Zebah Ps 83:11
causes * to wander among ruins; Ps 107:40
dump, and sets them among *! Ps 113:8
For even * sit and talk against Ps 119:23
or for a slave to rule over *! Pro 19:10
while * walk like servants! Ecc 10:7
the elders and the *, for they have Is 3:14
every one of his * will soon be a Is 10:8
King is coming, with honest *! Is 32:1
and its * soon will all be gone. Is 34:12
give him victory over kings and *. Is 41:25
when you pass by; * shall bow low Is 49:7
Kings, *, priests and Jer 2:26,27
and the * will tremble in fear; Jer 4:9
Judah and of the * and priests and Jer 8:1
there shall always be kings and * Jer 17:25
along with the * of Judah and the Jer 24:1
their kings and * drank of the cup Jer 25:18
his servants, the * and the Jer 25:19,20
brothers. The * and all the people Jer 34:10
whether you are *, court officials, Jer 34:18,19
and our kings and * have always Jer 44:17
and your kings and * and all the Jer 44:21
his priests and *, shall be taken Jer 48:7
along with his * and priests. Jer 49:3
I will destroy her king and *. Jer 49:38
of Babylon—her * and wise men too. Jer 50:35
I will make drunk her *, wise Jer 51:57
sons and all the * of Judah were Jer 52:10
are gone; her * are like starving Lam 1:6
Her kings and * are enslaved in Lam 2:9
Our * were lean and tanned, Lam 4:7
Our * are hanged by their thumbs. Lam 5:12
and the kings and * will stand Eze 7:26,27
and * [her topmost buds and shoots Eze 17:12,13
wealthy merchant * bring you lambs Eze 27:21
"The * of Assyria lie there Eze 32:22
"The * of Meshech and Tubal are Eze 32:26
is there with her kings and her *; Eze 32:29
All the * of the north are Eze 32:30
and the merchant * of Tarshish Eze 38:13
drink the blood of *—they are the Eze 39:18
his allotment. My * shall no longer Eze 45:8
to all the *, governors, captains, Dan 3:2
Then the *, governors, captains, Dan 3:27
arrived he and his *, wives, and Dan 5:2,3,4
take on the Prince of * in battle; Dan 8:25
kings and * and to all the people. Dan 9:6
O Lord, we and our kings and * Dan 9:8
the * laugh about their lies. Hos 7:3
On the king's birthday, the * get Hos 7:5
She has appointed kings and *, Hos 8:4
And their king and his * will go Amo 1:15
watch over us, eight * to lead us. Mic 5:5
Your * and officials crowd Nah 3:17
O Assyrian king, your * lie dead Nah 3:18
"They scoff at kings and *, and Hab 1:10

(PRINCES Con't)
the leaders and * of Judah, and all Zep 1:8
lions roaring—the * are weeping, Zec 11:3
He has torn * from their thrones Lk 1:52
* of darkness who rule this world; Eph 6:12

PRINCESS
longer 'Sarai' but 'Sarah' ('*'). Gen 17:15
Well, this is what happened: A *, Ex 2:5
approached the * and asked her, Ex 2:7
the * replied. Ex 2:8
him for me," the * instructed the Ex 2:9
to the * and he became her son. Ex 2:10
daughter, the * Taphath), whose 1Ki 4:8-19
Ahima-az (who married * Basemath, 1Ki 4:8-19
girls besides the Egyptian *. 1Ki 11:1
married Bithi-ah, an Egyptian *. 1Ch 4:17
a *, waits within her chamber, Ps 45:13
the lovely *, tender and delicate. Is 47:1

PRINCIPAL
* gods in the Babylonian pantheon. Is 46:1f
The four * successors of Alexander Dan 8:8f

PRINCIPLE
He established this *. Pro 16:11
every sound * of conduct by Pro 18:1
being a man of stern *, Mt 1:19
who live by this * and upon those Gal 6:16

PRINCIPLES
them the * of godly living. Ex 18:19,20
Live by the * of love and Hos 12:6
the very first * in God's Word. Heb 5:12,13

PRISCILLA
from Italy with his wife, *. Act 18:2,3
taking * and Aquila with him. Act 18:18
Get ready to receive him!" * and Act 18:25,26
Tell * and Aquila "hello." Rom 16:3
Aquila and * send you their love 1Co 16:19
Please say "hello" for me to * 2Ti 4:19

PRISON
He threw Joseph into *, where Gen 39:20
over the entire * administration to Gen 39:22
them both in the * where Joseph Gen 40:1
to take you out of * and give you Gen 40:13
were brought to him from the *. Gen 40:20
the rest of you here, bound in *. Gen 42:16
The Lord has rescued you from * Deu 4:20
and made to grind grain in the *. Ju 16:21
So he was brought from the * and Ju 16:25,26
* and in chains for his rebellion. 2Ki 17:4
was released from * on the 2Ki 25:27
to replace his * garb, and for as 2Ki 25:29
put this fellow in * and feed him 2Ch 18:26
king's castle beside the * yard. Neh 3:25
Gate and stopped at the * Gate. Neh 12:39
You send me to * and shut me in Job 13:27,28
There in * they hurt his feet Ps 105:18
For he broke down their * gates Ps 107:16
Bring me out of *, so that I can Ps 142:7
Such a lad could come from * and Ecc 4:14
who sit in * darkness and despair. Is 42:7
From * and trial they led him Is 53:8
Literally, "in the court of the * Jer 32:2f
he would, and visited me in the *. Jer 32:8
deed, and as the * guards watched, Jer 32:12
which had been converted into a *. Jer 37:15,16
in the palace * instead, and that Jer 37:21
Jeremiah was kept in the palace *. Jer 37:21
an empty cistern in the * yard. Jer 38:6
the palace *, where he remained. Jer 38:13
confined to the * yard until the Jer 38:28
out of the *, and put him into the Jer 39:14
arrived, while he was still in *: Jer 39:15
put in * for the rest of his life. Jer 52:11
brought him out of *, and spoke Jer 52:31
who was now in *, heard about all Mt 11:2
chained him in * at the demand of Mt 14:3
So John was beheaded in the *, Mt 14:10
sick and in *, and you visited Mt 25:36
you sick or in *, and visit you?' Mt 25:39
sick, and in *, and you didn't Mt 25:43
sick or in *, and not help you?' Mt 25:44
bodyguards to the * to cut off Mk 6:27
The soldier killed John in the *, Mk 6:27
Herod put John in *, thus adding Lk 3:19,20
(Barabbas was in * for Lk 23:19
the man in * for insurrection and Lk 23:25
John the Baptist was not yet in *. Jn 3:23,24
from * each year at Passover. Jn 18:39
safety all the time he was in *. Act 12:5
guard before the * gate, when Act 12:6
they were thrown into *. Act 16:23
earthquake; the * was shaken to its Act 16:26
The jailer wakened to see the * Act 16:27
both men and women to *. Act 22:4
in the * at King Herod's palace. Act 23:35
He ordered Paul to * but Act 24:23
relatives who were in * with me. Rom 16:7
him even here in *, as I should. Eph 6:20
both when I was in * and when I was Php 1:7
the spirits in *, and preached to 1Pe 3:19
some of you into * to test you. Rev 2:10
* will be arrested and taken away; Rev 13:10
Satan will be let out of his *. Rev 20:7

PRISONER
me a * and said, 'Keep this man; 1Ki 20:39
else, the * disappeared!" 1Ki 20:40
and took him as a * to Jerusalem. 2Ch 25:23
was taken to Egypt as a *. 2Ch 36:4
They took him * and brought him Jer 26:23
and taken as a * before the king of Jer 32:4
"Since I am a * here, you read Jer 36:5
release one Jewish * each year Mt 27:15
release one Jewish * each year at Mk 15:6
time—any * the people requested. Mk 15:6
him to release a * as usual. Mk 15:8
unto them at the feast one (*)." Lk 23:17,f
chains of every * fell off! Act 16:26
"Paul, the *, called me over and Act 23:18
"There is a * here," he told Act 25:14
to send a * to the Emperor without Act 25:27
I BEG YOU—I, a * here in jail for Eph 4:1
with me here as a *, sends you his Col 4:10
Epaphras my fellow *, who is also Phm 1:23

PRISONERS
"Are my daughters *, captured in Gen 31:26
the king's * were kept in chains. Gen 39:20
other * were responsible to him. Gen 39:22
lands as * of war, and slaves. Lev 26:36
taking some of the men as *. Num 21:1
"Do we kill * of war? 2Ki 6:22
were being held as * in Babylon. 2Ki 25:28
There even * are at ease, with Job 3:18
* from jail, singing with joy! Ps 68:6
Listen to the sighing of the * Ps 79:11
He frees the *, and opens the Ps 146:7
you will stumble along as * or Is 10:4
and had no mercy on his *?" Is 14:17
and Ethiopians as *, making them Is 20:4
They will be rounded up like * Is 24:22
They shall follow you as * in Is 45:14
Through you I am saying to the * Is 49:8,9
with him, as his *, Seraiah the Jer 52:24,25
my Sabbaths are ignored. * are Eze 22:9
all you *, for there is yet hope! Zec 9:12
One of the * at that time was Mk 15:7
Lord—and the other * were Act 16:25
and assuming the * had escaped, he Act 16:27
so Paul and several other * were Act 27:1
in charge of the * listened more to Act 27:11
let them kill the * lest any of Act 27:42
of the line, like * soon to be 1Co 4:9
insist we are all its *. Gal 3:21,22

PRISONS
synagogues and * and before kings Lk 21:12
Now God has them chained up in * Jud 1:6

PRIVACY
speak in the * of your bedroom!" 2Ki 6:12
quarters and the bride from her *. Joe 2:16

PRIVATE
of all public and * debts. Lev 25:10
that he could have a * interview. Ju 3:17,18,19
just to one man in his * home?" Ju 18:19
"The king has sent me on a * 1Sa 21:2
was the king's * secretary. 2Sa 8:17
Call him into a * room away from 2Ki 9:2
personal friends, and * chaplains. 2Ki 10:11
Asaph, the king's * prophet, were 1Ch 25:2
Heman, the king's * chaplain, were 1Ch 25:4,5
all of my own * treasures to aid in 1Ch 29:3
concerning his * sorrow, as well as 2Ch 6:29
found even in the king's * rooms. Ps 105:30
"My darling bride is like a * Sol 4:12
Then Johanan had a * conference Jer 40:15
Each family will go into * Zec 12:12,13,14
Then Herod sent a * message to Mt 2:7
from their * means to the support Lk 8:3
* that I have not said in public. Jn 18:20
even entering * homes and dragging Act 8:3

PRIVATELY
gate as if to speak with him *; 2Sa 3:27
So discuss the matter with him *. Pro 25:8,9,10
* for all the evil you have done. Eze 24:23
asked Jesus *, "Why couldn't we Mt 17:19
* and confront him with his fault. Mt 18:15
God that I "speak in tongues" * 1Co 14:18
I talked * to the leaders of the Gal 2:2

PRIVILEGE
gave her the * of being your wife. Gen 16:5
it will be a * to have you choose Gen 23:5,6
What a * for these men of yours 2Ch 9:7
of all, is the * of meditating in Ps 27:4
It is God's * to conceal things, Pro 25:2,3
king's * to discover and invent. Pro 25:2,3
by granting us the * of serving God Lk 1:74
"What a * it would be to get into Lk 14:15
asked for the * of building a Act 7:46
Gentiles, too, the * of turning to Act 11:18
I demand my * of a hearing before Act 25:10,11
place of highest * where we now Rom 5:2
Can't I claim the same * the 1Co 9:4
And God has given us the * of 2Co 5:18
God has given me the wonderful * Eph 3:7
For to you has been given the * Php 1:29
having this * of dying for you. Php 2:1
and * as members of his body. Col 3:1
has given us the * of being born 1Pe 1:
Praise God for the * of being in 1Pe 4:16

PRIVILEGED
quietly, "How * you are to see Lk 10:23

PRIZE
himself is my inheritance, my *. Ps 16:5
his people, for they are his *. Ps 94:14
will be a * to your enemies. Mic 1:15
but only one person gets first *. 1Co 9:24
and receive the * for which God is Php 3:14
or is disqualified and wins no *. 2Ti 2:5
and losing the * that you and I 2Jn 1:8

PRIZED
When we put on our * robes of Is 64:6
Just at that time the highly * Lk 7:2
splendor that you * so much will Rev 18:14

PRIZES
givers are the ones God *. 2Co 9:7

PRO-ROMAN
A * political party. Mk 3:6f

PROBABILITY
4:2–6, giving * to the paraphrase; Rev 1:4f

PROBABLY
* some sort of tortilla. Gen 18:6f
in the distance, * Ishmaelite Gen 37:25
sacks, as it was * someone's Gen 43:12
For it is * his only warmth; Ex 22:27
spot in it, it is * leprosy, and Lev 13:49
If you hurry you can * catch up Jos 2:5
with gold, and *, because of its Ju 8:27f
So hurry, because he'll * be 1Sa 9:12,13
* King Saul was especially 1Sa 17:11f
the true account. * he had found 2Sa 1:10f
warriors and are * as upset as a 2Sa 17:8
he has * already hidden in some 2Sa 17:9
The belt was * that worn by a 2Sa 18:11f
* not the same Shime-i as in verse 1Ch 23:8,9f
The reference * is also to Is 45:13f
This verse * refers to the Jer 30:21f
* in the summer of 605 B.C. Jer 36:1f
The reference is * to Egypt. Lam 1:19f
The reference is * to Egypt. Lam 4:17f
Or, * better, "They exchanged Eze 27:19f
* a symbol of the angels. Eze 28:14f
The defilement was * in eating Dan 1:8f
* the future Antichrist of 2 Dan 7:24f
in intrigues." * a reference to Dan 8:23f
* Jason, treacherously removed by Dan 11:22f
* Antiochus IV and Ptolemy IV. Dan 11:27f
Hebrew: "two others," * angels. Dan 12:5f
Shalman: * Salaman, king of Moab, Hos 10:14f
* an allusion to the kings of Hos 13:11f
* by throwing dice or something Lk 1:8,9f
Then he said, "* you will quote Lk 4:23
Literally, and * ironically, Lk 16:9f
* a vow to offer a sacrifice in Act 18:18f
* a vow to offer a sacrifice in Act 18:22f
Literally, "begotten you." * the Heb 5:5f

PROBLEM
white, and the * seems to be more Lev 13:25
explained their * and protested at Num 9:6,7
But there is one *. Ru 3:12
For the Lord has solved my *. 1Sa 2:1
and expressed interest in his *. 2Sa 15:2
whatever the * is— then when the 1Ki 8:37
"We have a *," they told him. 2Ki 2:19
with the *, but to the doctors. 2Ch 16:12
this exactly King Solomon's *?" Neh 13:26
their real * is internal—wickedness Ps 55:10
There is another serious * I have Ecc 5:13,14
is a very serious *, for all his Ecc 5:16
Both have the same *, yet the Ecc 6:7,8
"That's your *," they retorted. Mt 27:4
Their * was their fear of riots Mk 11:18
He thought about his *, and Lk 12:17
mother came to him with the *. Jn 2:3
Here is the *: We Christians are 1Co 7:26
She faces the same *. 1Co 7:34
You went right to work on the * 2Co 7:11

PROBLEMS
and all the * there had been along Ex 18:8
if there are any * while I am Ex 24:14
to settle all your quarrels and *? Deu 1:12
and she told him all her *. 1Ki 10:2
And Solomon answered all her *. 2Ch 9:2
was no peace. * troubled the nation 2Ch 15:5
my * go from bad to worse. Ps 25:17
Otherwise I perish, for * far Ps 40:12
most perplexing *: There is no Ps 49:4
me sink down deep in desperate *. Ps 71:20
and plagued with * like everyone Ps 73:5
men about some * they will face. Pro 1:4
A sensible man watches for * Pro 27:12
riddles, and solve knotty *. Dan 5:12
because their * were so great and Mt 9:36
occupied with the * of this life, Lk 21:34,35
when we run into * and trials for Rom 5:3
our daily * and in our praying. Rom 8:26
to decide your * down here on earth 1Co 6:3

ROBLEMS Con't)
will bring extra * that I wish you 1Co 7:28
exactly the same * before you. 1Co 10:13
*, and so obey our Lord's command. Gal 6:2
trust him, too, for each day's *; Col 2:6
and understands their * very well. Heb 5:1
don't try to squirm out of your *. Jas 1:4
ROCEDURE
He shall follow the same * as Lev 4:20
as in the * for the thank-offering Lev 4:31
(This * had not been carried out Neh 8:17
ROCEDURES
* that have been set forth; Lev 5:10
"These then, are the * after Lev 12:7
ROCEED
Moses then told Aaron to * to the Lev 9:7
Sea and will * eastward to Mount Num 34:7,8,9
This is how we'll *: A third of 2Ch 23:4
and tell us how to * in setting Ez 10:4
And then they * to lie in my Jer 23:25
the passageway and * to the inner Eze 46:2
you * at once to get it out?" Lk 14:5
ROCEEDED
So Moses * to do all as the Lord Ex 40:16
Then they left the desert and * on Num 21:17,18
Beth-hoglah, then * north of Jos 15:6
the boundary line * past the south Jos 15:10,11
called Bethel) and * down to Jos 18:13
From En-rogel the boundary * Jos 18:17
The army then * to seize the fords Ju 3:28
and trumpets and * to the Temple. 2Ch 20:28
Both choirs then * to the Temple. Neh 12:40,41
Jesus now * to Bethany, to the Mt 26:6
PROCEEDING
can you think of * against even the Is 36:8,9
PROCEEDS
Literally, "what * out of the man Mk 7:15,16f
PROCESS
In the * of time Judah's wife Gen 38:12
The embalming * required forty Gen 50:3
and in the * hurt a pregnant woman Ex 21:22
crushing Balaam's foot in the *. Num 22:25
in the * of time, a baby boy was 1Sa 1:19,20
In the * of time, at the end of 2Ch 21:19
Why continue the * longer? Jer 6:29
In the *, one of his debtors was Mt 18:24
world and loses his soul in the *? Mk 8:36
any earthly * could ever make it! Mk 9:3
torn off in the *, so that he ran Mk 14:51,52
meaning the normal * observed Jn 3:5f
PROCESSION
men would lead the * followed by Jos 6:6-9
(But as the * came into the city, 2Sa 6:16
to march at the head of the *. 1Ch 15:24
Ezra the priest led this *. Neh 12:35,36
A great funeral * precedes and Job 21:33
when you led a great * to the Ps 42:4,5
What a joyful, glad * as they Ps 45:15
The * of God my King moves onward Ps 68:24
He was in the center of the * Mk 11:9
A funeral * was coming out as he Lk 7:12
Olives, the whole * began to shout Lk 19:36,37
PROCESSIONAL
him with the tambourines and *. Ps 150:4
PROCHORUS
Philip, *, Nicanor Act 6:5
PROCLAIM
Literally, "I will * before you Ex 33:19f
be holy, a time to * liberty Lev 25:10
Mount Gerizim to * a blessing, and Deu 27:12
upon Mount Ebal to * a curse. Deu 27:13
I will * the greatness of the Deu 32:3
Can they * your faithfulness? Ps 88:11
he does; * them to the nations. Ps 105:1
I will * your greatness. Ps 145:6
Literally, "* his doings among Is 12:4f
In that day the people will *, Is 25:9
I publicly * bold promises; Is 45:19
faithfully * my every word. Jer 23:28
doom—I dare not refuse to * it. Amo 3:8
O Judah, * a day of Nah 1:15
What I whisper in your ears, * Mt 10:27
said, "and will * that everyone Mk 1:3
"For nations and kingdoms will * Mk 13:8
Literally, "to * the acceptable Lk 4:18,19f
of God's great plan which I *. Rom 2:16
PROCLAIMED
Literally, "* the name of Ex 34:5,6f
see him. He * the laws you must Deu 4:13
blessing shall be * from Mount Deu 11:29
promises * by his servant Moses. 1Ki 8:56
Then Elisha *, "This is the 2Ki 13:16,17
from Judah and * that what you have 2Ki 23:17
the occasion and *, "The Lord says 2Ch 18:10
of the law of God, and * him king. 2Ch 23:11
calf-idol and *, 'This is our God! Neh 9:18
stated, "must be * as law in every Est 3:14
first * in the city of Shushan. Est 3:15
hidden in my heart, but have * Ps 40:10
Haven't I * from ages past [that Is 44:8
I have * your word to them. Jer 15:15
I * this to the people in the Eze 24:18
was * third ruler in the kingdom. Dan 5:29
we * the word of the Lord." Act 15:36f
PROCLAIMING
about Jesus, for * the Word of God, Rev 20:4
PROCLAMATION
Then Abimelech made a public * Gen 26:11
Then King Asa made a * to all 1Ki 15:22
Then a * was sent to all the 2Ch 24:9
sent a Passover * throughout 2Ch 30:5
Cyrus to make this * throughout his 2Ch 36:22,23
to send this * throughout his Ez 1:1
Then a * was made throughout Ez 10:7,8
He had said also that a * should Neh 8:15
THIS IS THE * of Nebuchadnezzar Dan 4:1
PRODDED
They * him into a cage and Eze 19:9
PRODUCE
these seeds will * the kinds of Gen 1:11,12
a gift of his farm *, and Abel Gen 4:3
"Asher shall * rich foods, fit Gen 49:20
but you must * just as many Ex 5:10,11
"A tenth of the * of the land, Lev 27:30
rains that will * wonderful crops Deu 11:14
for him, to * food for his family; 2Sa 9:10,11
of the best * of the land as 2Ki 8:8,9
any grain or other * to be sold on Neh 10:31
They stored the * in the Temple Neh 10:37
and all sorts of * which they took Neh 13:15
they can * nothing truly good. Job 15:34
"Judah shall continue to * Ps 60:6,7
* fruit and be vital and green. Ps 92:14
Oxen loaded down with *. Ps 144:12-15
And the land will * for them its Is 4:2,3,4
An acre of vineyard will not * Is 5:10
to grow and to * seed for the Is 55:10
kind can't * what is good. Mt 7:18
God's message and * a plentiful Mk 4:20
God can * children of Abraham Lk 3:8
Yes, every tree that does not * Lk 3:9
good stock doesn't * scrub fruit Lk 6:43
from poor stock * choice fruit. Lk 6:43
But my death will * many new Jn 12:23,24
off every branch that doesn't *. Jn 15:2
For a branch can't * fruit when Jn 15:4
him shall * a large crop of fruit. Jn 15:5
My true disciples * bountiful Jn 15:8
I appointed you to go and * Jn 15:16
so that you can * good fruit, that Rom 7:4
your lives will * these evil Gal 5:19
our lives he will * this kind of Gal 5:22
with his blood, * in you through Heb 13:20,21
PRODUCED
God, and * sons and daughters; Gen 5:21-24
he * a quarter-ounce gold earring Gen 24:22
Then Zilpah * a second son, and Gen 30:12
then all the flock * speckled; Gen 31:8
goats so that they * healthy Gen 31:38
crops except those * on the land Gen 47:26
So Hiram * for Solomon as much 1Ki 5:10
And he * engines of war 2Ch 26:15
our land *, for the Levites were Neh 10:37
and mother, "Why have you * me? Is 45:10
the eagle and * strong branches and Eze 17:6
and olives have * their next crops: Hag 2:18,19
is by the kind of fruit *. Mt 7:20
on good soil, and * a crop that was Mt 13:8
plants so that they * no grain. Mk 4:7
hearts, so that no crop is *. Mk 4:19
this seed grew and * a crop one Lk 8:8
a fertile farm that * fine crops. Lk 12:16
What we told you * a powerful 1Th 1:5
PRODUCES
I send it out and it always * Is 55:11
A variety that * delicious fruit Mt 7:18
fruit never * an inedible kind. Mt 7:18
A tree from a select variety * Mt 12:33
Literally, "* a crop many times Mt 13:23f
by the kind of fruit it *. Lk 6:44
A good man * good deeds from a Lk 6:45
And an evil man * evil deeds from Lk 6:45
PRODUCING
trees * the choicest of fruit. Gen 2:9
Adam lived another 800 years, * Gen 5:3,4,5
another 807 years, * sons and Gen 5:6,7,8
another 815 years, * sons and Gen 5:9,10,11
another 840 years, * sons and Gen 5:12,13,14
Afterwards he lived 830 years, * Gen 5:15,16,17
another 800 years, * sons and Gen 5:18,19,20
another 782 years, * sons and Gen 5:25,26,27
lived 595 years, * sons and Gen 5:28-31
"Naphtali is a deer let loose, * Gen 49:21
" 'Should I quit * the olive oil Ju 9:9
'Should I quit * sweetness and Ju 9:11
'Shall I quit * the wine that Ju 9:13
right on * all its luscious fruit. Jer 17:8
splendid vine, * leaves and fruit. Eze 17:8
That is why your land is not *; Hos 4:3
And a tree * an inedible kind Mt 7:18
said not to, and * sinful deeds, Rom 7:5
I am confident you are * the good Heb 6:9
promising much, but * nothing. Jud 1:12
PRODUCTION
However, don't reduce their * Ex 5:7,8
for his wine * and storage. 1Ch 27:27
PRODUCTIVE
Their cattle are *, they have Job 21:10
PRODUCTS
Load your donkeys with the best * Gen 43:11
PROFANE
never * the name of your God, for Lev 18:21
guilty, for you * the holiness of Lev 19:8
shall not dishonor and * his name; Lev 21:6
Literally, "he must not * his Lev 21:14,15f
or irreligious, * or godly. Ecc 9:2,3
PROFANING
"Why are you * the Sabbath? Neh 13:17
PROFANITY
Their mouths are full of * and Ps 10:7
PROFESSION
*, too, in what you just said." Lk 11:45
PROFESSIONAL
call for * mourners to wail and Amo 5:16
PROFIT
your cost: don't try to make a *! Lev 25:37
man, or your good deeds may * him. Job 35:8
Work brings *; Pro 14:23
If you * from constructive Pro 15:31,32
who reject making * by fraud, who Is 33:15
help unless they get a * from it. Eze 13:18
and they destroy lives for *. Eze 22:27
"What * was there in worshiping Hab 2:18
What * is there if you gain the Mt 16:26
would demand your *, you should at Mt 25:26
and what * is there in gaining Lk 9:25
not for our own *, but because 2Co 5:13,14
with him, did they make any *? 2Co 12:18
PROFITABLE
of your day more * and the years of Pro 9:11
year, and open up a * business." Jas 4:13
PROFITEERED
from those who * at their expense, Eze 34:27
PROFITEERING
the rich Jews who were * on them. Neh 5:1
PROFITS
sales taxes and * from trade with 1Ki 10:15
common sense, and * wonderfully by Pro 24:3,4
her businesses will give their * Is 23:18
Their * multiply, and they are Jer 12:2
If your * are in heaven your Mt 6:21
with it, and what their * were. Lk 19:15
was afraid [you would demand my * Lk 19:21
Literally, "the flesh * Jn 6:63f
PROFOUND
He reveals * mysteries beyond Dan 2:22
All of Israel will weep in * Zec 12:12,13,14
my sermons with * words and high 1Co 1:17
PROFOUNDLY
The crowds were * impressed by Mt 22:33
PROGENY
Literally, "a *." Ps 132:17f
PROGRAM
a nation-wide farm *. Gen 41:33
nationwide religious education *. 2Ch 17:7,8,9
His public works * was also 2Ch 17:13
great public works *: homes, Ecc 2:4,5,6
and God's * shall prosper in his Is 53:10
a feeding *," they said "Now Act 6:2
PROGRAMS
for local welfare *: Give it to Deu 14:28
PROGRESS
to David his * with the people of 2Sa 3:19
the king about the * of the repairs 2Ki 22:9,10
there was good * being made in the 2Ch 34:15,16
the religious * being made there. Ez 7:14
will advise you and watch your *. Ps 32:8
Reliable communication permits *. Pro 13:17
You have made no * whatever. Hos 10:9
may notice your improvement and *. 1Ti 4:15
PROGRESSED
background music while the work *. 2Ch 34:12
PROHIBIT
law would be needed to * adultery. Deu 27:23f
PROHIBITED
expressly * in verses 8 and 9. 1Co 6:12f
PROHIBITION
This * applied not only while her Lev 18:14f
PROJECT
to be in charge of this entire *. Gen 41:40
general superintendent of the *. Ex 35:30,31
You and Aaron are to direct the * Num 1:2-15
Now please assist me with this *. 1Ki 5:6
to assist his son in this *. 1Ch 22:17
The supervision of the entire * Ez 3:9
should carry this * through to 2Co 8:11
PROJECTING
East Water Gate and the * Tower. Neh 3:26
* out into the hallway. Eze 40:7-12f
with four horns * twenty-one inches Eze 43:15
PROJECTS
the great building * of the Lord's 2Ch 8:1
So they went ahead with these * 2Ch 14:7

(PROJECTS Con't)
when my * prospered, and even Job 29:6

PROLONG
Literally, "He shall * his Is 53:10f

PROLONGS
Literally, "* days." Pro 10:27f

PROMINENT
went to Shunem. A * woman of the 2Ki 4:8
Ulam's sons were * warriors who 1Ch 8:40
The cantors were all * Levites. 1Ch 9:33,34
of the most * men of the city, Eze 11:1
* Greek women and many men also. Act 17:12
officers and * men of the city, Act 25:23

PROMISE
But I * to keep you safe in the Gen 6:18
solemnly * you and your children Gen 9:9,10,11
And I seal this * with this Gen 9:12
as a sign of my * until the end of Gen 9:13
I will remember my * to you and to Gen 9:15
my eternal * to every living being Gen 9:16,17
whom my * will be fulfilled. Gen 21:12
And my master made me * not to Gen 24:37
then you are freed from your *.' Gen 24:41
my * to Abraham, who obeyed me." Gen 26:24
between us. * that you will not Gen 26:29
Rachel too—if you * to work for me Gen 29:27
* to give her to my son Shelah." Gen 38:26
witnesses of my *, and my brother Gen 45:11,12
made his brothers * with an oath Gen 50:25
and remembered his * to Abraham, Ex 2:24
there in Egypt. I * to rescue them Ex 3:17
Egyptians, and I remember my *. Ex 6:5
away this death. I * not to refuse Ex 10:17
"We solemnly * to obey every one Ex 24:7
Remember your * to your Ex 32:13
it is to fulfill a * or is a Lev 22:17,18
and yet you * them meat for a Num 11:21
in the ocean to fulfill your *!" Num 11:22
by what he did—I * that he and his Num 25:12,13
anyone makes a * to the Lord, Num 30:1
harsh, then her * will Num 30:5
he kept his * to your ancestors. Deu 7:8
fulfill his * to your ancestors. Deu 8:18
to the two spies, "Keep your * Jos 6:22
and I no longer * to destroy the Ju 2:3
"We * with a solemn oath." Ju 11:10
Samson said, "but * me that you Ju 15:12,13
Then Jonathan told David, "I * 1Sa 20:12
should he be unfaithful to his *. 1Sa 20:16
lord, didn't you * me that my son 1Ki 1:13
will fulfill the * he gave me, that 1Ki 2:4
But that * doesn't bind you! 1Ki 2:9
Today you have fulfilled your * 1Ki 8:24
your further * to him: that if his 1Ki 8:25
God of Israel, fulfill this * too. 1Ki 8:26
has fulfilled his * and given rest 1Ki 8:56
(I once made this same * to 1Ki 11:38
king unless you * to treat us 1Ki 12:2,3,4
to fulfill his * to Jeroboam, made 1Ki 12:15
they made a solemn * to the Lord to 2Ki 23:3
With an everlasting *: 1Ch 16:17
"And now I accept your *, Lord, 1Ch 17:23
For you have fulfilled your * to 2Ch 1:9
fulfilled the * he made to him. 2Ch 6:4
And you have kept your * to my 2Ch 6:15
out your further * to him that 2Ch 6:16
Israel, please fulfill this * too. 2Ch 6:17
"The Lord's *—that a descendant 2Ch 23:2,3
fail to keep this *," I declared. Neh 5:13
Because of all this, we again * Neh 9:38
The Lord's * is sure. Ps 12:6
the Lord, keeps a * even if it Ps 15:4
Remember your *! Ps 74:20
Has his * failed? Ps 77:8
from them, nor let my * fail. Ps 89:33
his * to be kind to Israel. Ps 98:2,3
never forgets his *, his covenant Ps 105:8,9
was your *—yes, Lord, to save Ps 119:40,41,42
And I * to obey! Ps 119:57
your wonderful * to rescue me. Ps 119:123
I made a solemn * to the Lord. Ps 132:2-5
you will never go back on a *! Ps 132:11
He is the God who keeps every *, Ps 146:6
and rash to make a * to the Lord Pro 20:25
Keep your * to him. Ecc 5:4
Oh, remind me of this * of Is 43:26
not leave you. My * of peace for Is 54:10
"As for me, this is my * to Is 59:21
by forsaking your * to bless us! Jer 14:21
"For I * you: Because you have Eze 5:11
his * after swearing to obey; Eze 17:18
blazing wrath, I * a mighty shaking Eze 38:19
it is a * from the Lord. Hos 11:11
This is a * from the Lord." Joe 3:8
They will * peace while plotting Ob 1:7
Notice, I am giving you this * Hag 2:18,19
is yet hope! I * right now, I will Zec 9:12
To strengthen your * with a vow Mt 5:37
For every * from God shall Lk 1:37
He has not forgotten his * to be Lk 1:54
his sacred * to him, and by Lk 1:72,73
This is a solemn *." Lk 23:43
Literally, "the * of my Lk 24:49f
of the Father's *, a matter he had Act 1:4
and you are included in God's * Act 3:25
is the * God gave to Abraham. Act 3:25
would fulfill his * to Abraham to Act 7:17,18
News—that God's * to our ancestors Act 13:32,33
of God's * made to our ancestors. Act 26:6
It is clear, then, that God's * Rom 4:13
he trusted God to keep his *. Rom 4:13
And this * is from God himself, Rom 4:17
a * just couldn't come to pass! Rom 4:18
who believe the * of salvation Rom 9:8
I never will. I * this with every 2Co 11:10
in everyday life a * made by one Gal 3:15
to say: God's * to save through Gal 3:17
God wrote this * down and signed Gal 3:17
for he simply accepted God's *. Gal 3:18
They were added after the * was Gal 3:19
Child to whom God's * was made. Gal 3:19
but when God gave his * to Gal 3:20
Isaac the child of * was persecuted Gal 4:29
Commandments that ends with a *. Eph 6:2
And this is the *: that if you Eph 6:3
because they broke their first *. 1Ti 5:12
ALTHOUGH GOD'S * still stands—his Heb 4:1
still stands—his * that all may Heb 4:1
Yet the * remains and some get Heb 4:6
For instance, there was God's * Heb 6:13
He has given us both his * and Heb 6:18
to whom God gave the same *. Heb 11:9
who gave her his *, would certainly Heb 11:11
that he made them * to carry his Heb 11:22
for instance, the * to save us 2Pe 1:4
forward to God's * of new heavens 2Pe 3:13

PROMISED
"I have solemnly * Jehovah, the Gen 14:22
I can do for him all I have *." Gen 18:19
THEN GOD DID as he had *, and Gen 21:1
and my people, and * to give me and Gen 24:7
just as I * Abraham your father. Gen 26:3
the mighty blessings * to Abraham. Gen 28:4
again and again just as you * me. Gen 32:10
But you * to do me good, and to Gen 32:12
young goat from my flock," he *. Gen 38:17
And Joseph *. Gen 47:30
your father, as you *," he said. Gen 50:6
to the land he * to the descendants Gen 50:24
under its terms I * to give them Ex 6:4
into the land I * to give to Ex 6:8,9
And the Lord did as Moses *—dead Ex 8:13
refusal to do what they had *; Ex 9:34
you, just as he *, and when you are Ex 12:25
land he * your fathers, a land Ex 13:4,5
into the land he * to your Ex 13:11
route from Egypt to the * Land. Ex 13:17,18
this land I have * to your Ex 32:13
I * Abraham, Isaac, and Jacob; Ex 33:1
people to the * Land,' but you Ex 33:12
please go with us to the * Land; Ex 34:9
I have * you their land; Lev 20:24
offering he * at the time he took Num 6:21
"When you arrive in the * Land Num 10:9
we are on our way to the * Land. Num 10:29
to the land you * their ancestors? Num 11:12
I * to this people's ancestors. Num 14:23
me, shall enter the * Land. Num 14:30
and started towards the * Land. Num 14:40
into the land the Lord has * us." Num 14:40
country you *, nor given us fields Num 16:14
into the land I have * them!" Num 20:12
that God had * the land of the Num 21:24f
Has he ever *, Num 23:18-24
vow must do exactly as he has *. Num 30:1
from going on into the * Land. Num 32:9
see the land he * Abraham, Isaac, Num 32:10,11
people to go on into the * Land. Num 32:12
the southern edge of the * Land. Deu 1:1f
the land the Lord * to your Deu 1:8
bless you as he *, but what can Deu 1:11
[on the border of the * Land Deu 1:19,20,21
good land he had * their fathers, Deu 1:34,35
'You shall not enter the * Land! Deu 1:37
over into the * Land—the good Deu 3:23,24,25
when you arrive in the * Land. Deu 4:14
as the God of your fathers * you. Deu 6:3
into the land he * your ancestors, Deu 6:10,11,12
which the Lord * your ancestors. Deu 6:18
land he had * to our ancestors. Deu 6:23
you into the * Land, as he soon Deu 7:1
he * your fathers to give you. Deu 7:13
* to your fathers by the Lord. Deu 8:1
to the land he * them," or "He Deu 9:28
for it in the * Land, as their Deu 10:9
to the land I * their fathers. Deu 10:11
the land the Lord * to your Deu 11:9
in the land the Lord has * you. Deu 11:21
wherever you go, just as he has *. Deu 11:25
and live in the * Land, and the Deu 12:10
offerings you have * in your vows, Deu 12:26,27
just as he * your ancestors. Deu 13:17
He will bless you as he has *. Deu 1
That is what he * them! Deu 1
"When you arrive in the * Land Deu 1
boundaries as he * your ancestors, Deu 1
all the land he * (whether he does Deu 1
cities, not to those in the * Land Deu 20:
the * Land you are to save no one; Deu 20:
"IF, WHEN YOU arrive in the * Deu 2
you when you arrive in the * Land. Deu 23:
whatever it is you * him, for the Deu 23:
enemies in the * Land, you are Deu 25:
to the land he * our ancestors.' Deu 26:2
given us, as you * our ancestors; Deu 26:
God, and you have * to obey and Deu 26:
people, just as he *, and that you Deu 26:
and go into the * Land—a land Deu 27:2,3
"When you cross into the * Land, Deu 27:
this he has * to do if you will Deu 28
land, just as he *: many children, Deu 28:
ships, a journey I * you would Deu 28:
God, just as he * your ancestors, Deu 29:
the land the Lord * your ancestors, Deu 30:2
* by the Lord to their ancestors; Deu 31
long as you live in the * Land." Deu 31:
foreign gods in the * Land. Deu 31:
into the land I * their ancestors—a Deu 31:2
into the land the Lord * them; Deu 31:2
out to him the * Land, as they Deu 34:
"It is the * Land," the Lord Deu 34
told Moses. "I * Abraham, Isaac, Deu 34:
the Jordan River into the * Land. Jos 1:
the land I * to their ancestors. Jos 1:
family aren't harmed," they *. Jos 2:1
the land he had * to Israel—a land Jos 5:
them from entering the * Land. Jos 14:
hill country which the Lord * me. Jos 14:1
* them that they could settle." Jos 18:
the land he had * to their Jos 21:4
just as he had *, and no one could Jos 21:4
Every good thing the Lord had * Jos 21:4
success and rest as he * he would. Jos 22:
instead, just as he has * you. Jos 23:4,
fights for you, just as he has *. Jos 23:1
the good things he *, just as Jos 23:15,1
given to Caleb as the Lord had *; Ju 1:2
this land which I * to your Ju 2:
save Israel as you *, prove it to Ju 6:3
do whatever you * the Lord, for he Ju 11:3
dollars for this job," they *. Ju 16:
that although I * that your branch 1Sa 2:3
"Has David * you fields and 1Sa 22:
So David *, and Saul went home, 1Sa 24:2
the good things he * you and has 1Sa 25:30,3
As Abner left, he * David, "When 2Sa 3:2
you * to and because you want to! 2Sa 7:2
* concerning me and my family. 2Sa 7:2
and you have * me these good 2Sa 7:28
good things— so do as you have *! 2Sa 7:29
for you, Lord God, have * it. 2Sa 7:29
them, as he had * Prince Jonathan. 2Sa 9:1
God as you have * to do for me?" 2Sa 14:13
River I * I wouldn't kill him. 1Ki 2:8
David and this kingdom he * me." 1Ki 2:23,24
to Solomon just as he had *. 1Ki 5:12
done today what he * my father 1Ki 8:15
now the Lord has done what he *; 1Ki 8:20
place you have * to live in—and as 1Ki 8:29
forever, just as I * your father 1Ki 9:5
as the Lord had * through Elijah! 1Ki 17:16
do what I * during his lifetime; 1Ki 21:29
Nevertheless, because God had * 2Ki 8:19
will do as I have *: This year my 2Ki 19:29
He * Israel 1Ch 16:17
And merely strangers in the * 1Ch 16:19
you have * to do in the future! 1Ch 17:17
God himself has * this good 1Ch 17:26
for the Lord had * a population 1Ch 27:23
has done what he *, for I have 2Ch 6:10
will not send the * evil upon this 2Ch 34:28
the rich men did as they had *. Neh 5:13
and now you have done what you *, Neh 9:8
land you had * to their ancestors. Neh 9:23
And we * to bring to the Levites Neh 10:37
Haman had * to pay into the king's Est 4:7
Lord, lead me as you * me you Ps 5:8
upon my altar have * to obey Ps 50:5
Do as you * and put an end to Ps 54:5
I will surely do what I have *, Ps 56:12
God has * to help us. Ps 60:6,7
For when I was in trouble I * Ps 66:14
my prayer and rescue me as you *. Ps 69:13
from entering the * Land and Ps 78:57
Where is your kindness that you * Ps 89:49
never enter the * Land, the place Ps 95:11
to pity her—the time you * help. Ps 102:13
ones singing into the * Land. Ps 105:43
They refused to enter the * Land, Ps 106:24
He has * to give us all the land Ps 108:7
Be merciful just as you *. Ps 119:58
your blessings, just as you *. Ps 119:65
comfort me, just as you *. Ps 119:75,76,77

ROMISED Con't)
our help, for you have * it. Ps 119:81
ny life again, just as you * me. Ps 119:107
ord, you * to let me live! Ps 119:116
ny life again just as you have *. Ps 119:154
ive me the common sense you *. Ps 119:169
God to help, for he has *. Ps 130:5
For you * me that my son would Ps 132:11
You also * that if my Ps 132:12
give the gift he * is like a cloud Pro 25:14
* to Jacob, your father. Is 58:14
* great blessings on Jerusalem. Jer 4:10
the things they * him they would. Jer 11:6
the evil I have *, because you have Jer 19:15
me when you * me your help. Jer 20:7
the terrors I have * in this Jer 25:13
which the Lord has * to every Jer 27:13
"The Lord has * that within two Jer 28:11
have *, and bring you home again. Jer 29:10
this land that you * their fathers Jer 32:22
I do all the good I have * them. Jer 32:42
and Judah all the good I * them. Jer 33:14
You had solemnly * me in my Jer 34:15
all the evil I *—upon them and upon Jer 36:31
come—for you have * it—when you Lam 1:21
And you have * life to those who Eze 13:19
into the land I * them, for they Eze 20:27,28
home to the land I * your fathers, Eze 20:42
For I, the Lord, have * it, and I Eze 36:36
have done just what I * you." Eze 37:14
an equal share. I * with hand Eze 47:14
as the Lord has *, for he has Joe 2:32
Yet I have * that this rooting Amo 9:8
for she * help she cannot give. Mic 1:14
The Lord himself has * this. Mic 4:4
You will bless us as you * Jacob Mic 7:20
us, as you * our father Abraham! Mic 7:20
'For I * when you left Egypt Hag 2:5
angered me and I * to punish them, Zec 8:14,15
you * to care for and keep. Mal 2:14
it," the Council *, "we'll stand Mt 28:14
and happy and * him a reward. Mk 14:11
For he * our fathers—Abraham and Lk 1:55
David, just as he * through his Lk 1:70
For I have seen him as you * me I Lk 2:29,30,31
to help them and * him a reward. Lk 22:5
upon you, just as my Father *. Lk 24:49
and knew God had * with an Act 2:30
And just as *, the Father gave Act 2:33
For Christ * him to each one of Act 2:39
"However, God * that eventually Act 7:5
who is God's * Savior of Israel! Act 13:23
"For God had * to bring him back Act 13:34
the wonderful thing I * David.' Act 13:34
But he * to return to Ephesus Act 18:21
This Good News was * long ago by Rom 1:2
on, after God had * to bless him Rom 4:11
was well able to do anything he *. Rom 4:21
new bodies he has * us—bodies that Rom 8:23
with himself, and * us his glory. Rom 8:30
For God had *, "Next year I will Rom 9:9
blessing God has * Abraham and his Rom 11:17
away their sins, just as I *." Rom 11:27
* this and will do what he says. 1Co 10:13
gift you * is on hand and waiting. 2Co 9:5
same blessing he * to Abraham; Gal 3:14
* Holy Spirit through this faith. Gal 3:14
had especially * he would come. Gal 4:23
that God *, just as Isaac was. Gal 4:28
been * to all of us Christians. Eph 1:13
really will give us all that he *; Eph 1:14
children and he had * you no help. Eph 2:12
do all this for you, just as he *. 1Th 5:24
life he has * them through faith in 2Ti 1:1
life, which God * them before the Tit 1:1
into the land he had * his people? Heb 3:18
all that God has * them because of Heb 6:12
a son, Isaac, just as he had *. Heb 6:15
to do what he has *, or to punish Heb 6:16
so that those he * to help would be Heb 6:17
them the salvation he has * them. Heb 6:18
all the wonders God has * them. Heb 9:15
any of those things he has * them. Heb 9:17
to the salvation God has * us. Heb 10:23
to do for you all that he has *. Heb 10:36
he * to give him, Abraham obeyed. Heb 11:8
And even when he reached God's * Heb 11:9
receiving all that God had * them; Heb 11:13
whom God had * to give Abraham a Heb 11:18
to suffer for the * Christ than to Heb 11:26
and received what God had * them; Heb 11:33
others were * freedom if they Heb 11:37,38
received all that God had * them; Heb 11:39
that God has * those who love him. Jas 1:12
has * to all those who love him. Jas 2:5
rich and wonderful blessings he *; 2Pe 1:4
"So Jesus * to come back, did he? 2Pe 3:4
slow about his * return, even 2Pe 3:9
And he himself has * us this: 1Jn 2:25

PROMISES
remember again my * to Abraham, Lev 26:42
I will remember my * to their Lev 26:45
has given wonderful * to Israel!" Num 10:29
you to come. He * you great honors Num 22:16,17
"If a woman * the Lord to do or Num 30:3
* he has made to your ancestors. Deu 4:31
his name alone to endorse your *. Deu 6:13
keeps his * and constantly loves Deu 7:9
and because of his * to your Deu 9:5
instead your * to your servants Deu 9:27
"You know very well that God's * Jos 23:14
make us keep our * to each other, 1Sa 20:23
and you keep your * to your people 1Ki 8:22,23
* proclaimed by his servant Moses. 1Ki 8:56
"The Lord * that you will push the 1Ki 22:11
You need more than mere * of 2Ki 18:20,21
me these wonderful * just because 1Ch 17:19
who keeps his kind * to all those 2Ch 6:14
thirst—while he * that "the Lord 2Ch 32:11
God who keeps his * and is so Neh 1:5
formally vow to carry out their *. Neh 5:12
you who keep your * of love and Neh 9:32
priesthood and the * and vows of Neh 13:29
will fulfill all your * to him. Job 22:27
All his * prove true. Ps 18:30
he shares the secrets of his *. Ps 25:14
rescued me, O God who keeps his *. Ps 31:5,6
I want your * fulfilled. Ps 50:14,15
stop claiming my *, for you have Ps 50:16
He broke his *. Ps 55:20
Yes, I will trust the * of God. Ps 56:3,4
am trusting God—oh, praise his *! Ps 56:10,11
Yes, praise his *. Ps 56:10,11
all your *, O Holy One of Israel. Ps 71:22
They did not keep their *. Ps 78:37
His faithful * are your armor. Ps 91:4
for he remembered his sacred * Ps 105:42
he remembered his * to them and Ps 106:45
God has given sacred *; Ps 108:7
he never forgets his *. Ps 111:5
Reassure me that your * are for Ps 119:38
who taunt me, for I trust your *. Ps 119:40,41,42
Never forget your * to me your Ps 119:49,50
straining to see your * come true. Ps 119:82
quietly keep my mind upon your *. Ps 119:95
your * are my only source of hope. Ps 119:114
I have thoroughly tested your * Ps 119:140
the night to think about your *. Ps 119:148
for your * are backed by all the Ps 138:2
you are faithful to your *. Ps 143:1
because you are true to your *. Ps 143:11
*, and abhors those who don't. Pro 12:22
to make rash * to God, for he is in Ecc 5:1
they will make * to God and keep Is 19:21
deliver on his * to save you. Is 30:3
For Egypt's * are worthless! Is 30:7
For the Lord is faithful to his * Is 30:18
* to you, while you betray them! Is 33:1
and care nothing for the * they Is 33:8
What are the Pharaoh's * worth? Is 36:5
I publicly proclaim bold *; Is 45:19
his covenant and *, I will bring Is 56:6
for the fulfillment of his *. Is 62:6,7
other gods. Can * and sacrifices Jer 11:15
carry out your * and vows to her! Jer 44:25
He has fulfilled the * of doom he Lam 2:17
will repay you for your broken *. Eze 16:59,60
But by keeping her *, Israel Eze 17:14
breaking all her * like that? Eze 17:15
you always fulfill your * of Dan 9:4
His * will be worthless. Dan 11:23
They make * they don't intend to Hos 10:4
return she gets their worthless *. Hos 12:1
I will surely fulfill my *. Jon 2:9
what comfort is there in * that Zec 10:2
"Cursed is that man who * a Mal 1:14
God's *, to bring you great joy. Mal 3:1
These are the * of the Lord of Mal 3:12
broke their *, and were Rom 1:31
his * but don't obey his laws. Rom 2:27
they broke their * to God, does Rom 3:3
that mean God will break his *? Rom 3:3
saying that God's * to those who Rom 4:14
we believe the * of God who brought Rom 4:24
by faith in his *, we can have real Rom 5:1
him, and gave you mighty *. Rom 9:4
to fulfill his * to the Jews? Rom 9:6
[For these * are only to those Rom 9:6
For the Scriptures say that the * Rom 9:7
* to Abraham, Isaac, and Jacob. Rom 11:28
he will never go back on his *. Rom 11:29
to his * and to help the Jews. Rom 15:8
all of God's *, no matter how many 2Co 1:20
HAVING SUCH GREAT * as these, 2Co 7:1
only because he believed God's *. Gal 3:6
Now, God gave some * to Abraham Gal 3:16
it doesn't say the * were to his Gal 3:16
and God's * against each other? Gal 3:21,22
of God's * to him belong to us. Gal 3:29
and all of God's * of mighty Eph 3:6
will always carry out his * to us. 2Ti 2:13
God contains far more wonderful *. Heb 8:6
God speaks of these new *, of Heb 8:13
in God and his *, and so he offered Heb 11:17

PROMISING
finished giving you all I am *." Gen 28:15
again lie to us by * to let the Ex 8:29
in fool you by * that Jerusalem Is 37:10
with them, * never again to desert Jer 32:40
letting them go by * to bring him Jer 41:8
the wicked by * life, though they Eze 13:22
* much and delivering nothing; 2Pe 2:17
* much, but producing nothing. Jud 1:12

PROMISSORY
in full" on any * note he holds Deu 15:2

PROMOTE
I had planned to * you to great Num 24:11

PROMOTED
God of Israel: 'I * you from the 1Ki 14:7
The wise are * to honor, but Pro 3:35
honor, but fools are * to shame! Pro 3:35

PROMOTES
God. He * one and deposes another. Ps 75:6,7

PROMOTION
and proud. For * and power come Ps 75:6,7

PROMOTIONS
many children, and * the king had Est 5:11
Then the king gave * to Shadrach, Dan 3:30

PROMPT
"You must be * in giving me the Ex 22:29
to the Lord, be * in doing whatever Deu 23:21
for if you love him you will be * Pro 13:24

PROMPTLY
had a dream and * reported the Gen 37:5
taster, however, * forgot all about Gen 40:23
assure him that I will return * Gen 50:5
shall pay your hired workers *. Lev 19:13
that you * fulfill your vows; Deu 23:21
to others who will pay him *." Mt 21:41

PRONOUNCE
used to * blessings on others." Gen 12:2f
then the priest shall * him cured; Lev 13:6
the priest must * him a leper. Lev 13:8
and the priest must * him defiled. Lev 13:11
the priest shall * him cured of Lev 13:13
then the priest will * him cured. Lev 13:16,17
and the priest must * him a leper. Lev 13:25
Literally, "* him unclean." Lev 13:25f
the priest must * him a leper. Lev 13:27
Literally, "* him unclean." Lev 13:27f
the priest must * him a leper. Lev 13:29,30
the priest shall * him well, and Lev 13:34
and the priest must * him such. Lev 13:44
whether to * it leprous or not. Lev 13:59
the priest shall * him cured, and Lev 14:7
then he will * the house cleansed, Lev 14:48
before him and to * his blessings Deu 21:5
Ark, ready to * their blessing. Jos 8:33
But if he couldn't * the H Ju 12:6
me, he will * me completely Job 23:10
* sentence on them from heaven; Ps 76:8
blast—and he will * their doom. Jer 4:11,12
and he shall * sentence against you Jer 34:3
sit to * judgment on them all. Joe 3:12

PRONOUNCED
Properly the name should be * Ex 3:15f
shall then be * finally cleansed. Lev 14:20
Tanis (or Zoan, as it was * in Num 13:22f
constantly and * blessings in his 1Ch 23:13
for judgment, let him be * guilty. Ps 109:7
And God has * this eternal Ps 133:3
"Now you are * 'Not guilty' Is 6:7
punishment he had * against them. Jer 26:19
of God have been * upon them." Jer 36:7
where he * judgment upon him. Jer 39:5
THIS IS THE fate of Israel, as * Zec 12:1

PRONOUNCEMENTS
and sorrows and * of doom. Eze 2:9,10

PRONOUNCES
He * judgment on the judges. Ps 82:1

PROOF
This will be the * that you and Gen 17:11
and this is the * that I am the one Ex 3:12
doorposts will be * that you obey Ex 12:13
but there is no *, there being no Num 5:13
some fruit we have brought as *. Num 13:27
shall bring the * of her virginity Deu 22:15
yet here is the *.' Deu 22:17,18
Then he gave this * that his 1Ki 13:3
For this was the prophet's * that 1Ki 13:5
And this is the * that I will do 2Ki 19:29
give you a *," Isaiah told him. 2Ki 20:9
a *, they say, of my sins. Job 16:8
Your mighty miracles give * that Ps 75:1
his punishment is * of his love. Pro 3:11,12
"Here is the * that I am the one Is 37:30
pledge to Israel, * that I will Is 49:8,9
has the burden of * on him to prove Jer 28:9
And this is the * I give you Jer 44:29
nation would ask for further *; Mt 12:39,40
but no further * will be given Mt 16:4
have * that you are well again." Mk 1:43,44
but the only * I will give them Lk 11:29,30

(PROOF Con't)
Your miracles are * enough of Jn 3:1
"The * is in the miracles I do Jn 10:25
God's mighty miracles as *0,5▮?" Jn 12:38
* that what is preached is true; 1Co 1:22
but even that isn't final *. 1Co 4:4
God for this * that your deeds are 2Co 9:13
gave you every * that I was truly 2Co 12:12
I will give you all the * you 2Co 13:3
lives were further * to you of the 1Th 1:5
for * that it really is from me. 2Th 3:17
sprinkled [as * of Christ's death Heb 9:18
our hearts as a * to us that we are 1Jn 4:13

PROOFS
your * that idol-worship pays! Is 45:21
You will see greater * than this. Jn 1:50
withstand his * that Jesus was Act 9:22
"With trivial * like these, Act 26:28

PROPAGANDA
stop them from spreading their *. Act 4:17

PROPER
But still there was no * helper Gen 2:19,20
to Jehovah at the * time; Num 9:13
of Joseph have a * complaint. Num 36:5
had been doing it in the * way." 2Ch 30:5f
restored them to their * duties. Neh 13:11
the altar at the * times and cared Neh 13:31
Can you ensure the * sequence of Job 38:32
the * path to all who go astray; Ps 25:8
loved ones to get their * rest. Ps 127:2
Go through all your * forms and Amo 4:5
between the city *—the walls of Jon 3:3f
"This isn't *," he said. Mt 3:14
come true at the * time." Lk 1:20
and at the * time all sat down Lk 22:14
who has gone on to his * place." Act 1:24,25
This is the message which at the * 1Ti 2:6
And it was right and * that God, Heb 2:10
[And it is perfectly * for God to 1Jn 1:9
rank and left their * home." Jud 1:6f

PROPERLY
* the name should be pronounced Ex 3:15f
to rule them *, for who is able to 2Ch 1:10
and knowledge to * guide my people— 2Ch 1:11
* sanctified for the ceremony." 2Ch 30:17,18,19
to all families of * registered 2Ch 31:17,18
* sent through his aides?" Est 1:13-15
We have therefore * used this Is 7:14f
done * in a good and orderly way. 1Co 14:40
I hope you * appreciate the work 1Co 16:18

PROPERTY
He is not going to share your * Gen 21:10
Don't worry about your *, for Gen 45:20
punished—for the slave is his *. Ex 21:21
has stolen his neighbor's *. Ex 22:8
But if the animal or * has been Ex 22:12
the common * of all sons of Aaron. Lev 7:10
rather than as a slave or as *. Lev 25:53
"You priests may own no *, nor Num 18:20
shall own no * in Israel, for the Num 18:23
and so they have no need for *." Num 18:24
as though it were from your own *. Num 18:27
We feel that we should be given * Num 27:3,4
give them the * that would have Num 27:6,7
they have no * or crops as you do. Deu 14:27
be given * like the other tribes. Deu 18:1
They don't need to own *, for Deu 18:2
property, for the Lord is their *! Deu 18:2
much * as the men of our tribe." Jos 17:4
at the edge of his * in Ju 2:7-9
selling our brother Elimelech's *. Ru 4:3
would become an heir to my *, too; Ru 4:6
bought all the * of Elimelech, Ru 4:9
here on Naboth's * for the murder 2Ki 9:26
in charge of his * and livestock 1Ch 28:1
to your people as their own *. 2Ch 6:27
* given to those who killed them. Est 3:13
to them, and to take their *. Est 8:11
did not try to take Haman's *. Est 9:7-10
men, though again they took no *. Est 9:15
his home and his * from all harm. Job 1:10
They leave no * for their Job 24:18
You buy up * so others have no Is 5:8
Someday people will again own * Jer 32:15
to see the * he had bought. Jer 37:12
"As to *, they shall not own Eze 44:28
never take anyone's * by force. Eze 46:18
If he gives * to his sons, it Eze 46:18
their * and having to move away." Eze 46:18
he will take the * and wealth of Dan 11:24
They are the very ones whose * Zep 1:13
on them, "These Are Holy *"; Zec 14:20
children, or *, to follow me, Mt 19:29
would get all the dead man's *. Mt 22:24
can be ransacked and his * robbed. Mk 3:27
children, or *—for love of me and Mk 10:29
to cheat widows out of their *. Lk 20:47
who sold some *, and brought only Act 5:1
Holy Spirit. The * was yours to Act 5:4
but gave him no * of his own, not Act 7:5

PROPHECIES
had finished his * to his sons, he Gen 49:33
He concluded his * by saying: Num 24:23,24
of Samuel's * came true that day. 1Sa 10:9
When Ahab heard these *, he tore 1Ki 21:27
your words and * and turn them into Jer 5:14
Jeremiah repeated all these * to Jer 27:12
May your * come true! Jer 28:6
Baruch wrote down all the *. Jer 36:4
for all these * to be fulfilled.' Eze 12:23
you expect him to fulfill your *. Eze 13:6
These * seem to have been Dan 11:6f
to fulfill the * about me." Mk 14:49
You have seen these * come true. Lk 24:48
noticed how many * of Scripture had Jn 12:16
But God was fulfilling the * Act 3:18
In the book of Amos' * the Lord Act 7:42
fulfilled all the * concerning his Act 13:29
explaining the * about the Act 17:3
any part of these *, God shall take Rev 22:19

PROPHECY
he spoke this * concerning them: Num 24:3-9
So he spoke this * to him: Num 24:15-19
the * is from the Lord or not?' Deu 18:21
Lord revealed this * to me: 'I 2Ki 9:25
prophet and in the * of Ahijah the 2Ch 9:29
the Lord fulfilled Jeremiah's * Ez 1:1
of this *, in that a virgin (Mary) Is 7:14f
chapter 5, as this * was fulfilled Is 21:5f
(Here the * concerning Moab ends. Jer 48:47
Kedar and Hazor This * is about Jer 49:28
occurred six years after this *. Jer 51:59f
it is a lie. His * will not come Eze 14:9
The fulfillment of this sad * has Eze 19:14
That very same hour this * was Dan 4:33
this * indicated for the future; Dan 8:9f
a partial fulfillment of this *. Dan 9:25f
of this * is many years away." Dan 10:14
will join them, thus fulfilling *, Dan 11:14
The * takes a turn here. Dan 11:40f
"But Daniel, keep this * a Dan 12:4
fifty-one years before this *. Nah 3:8f
years after this *, and then, a Zep 1:1f
begins false * again, his own Zec 13:3
fulfilled the * of Jeremiah, Mt 2:17
This fulfilled Isaiah's *: Mt 4:14
This fulfilled the * of Isaiah, Mt 8:17
This fulfilled the * of Isaiah Mt 12:17
"This fulfills the * of Isaiah: Mt 13:14
the ancient *, "Tell Jerusalem Mt 21:4
This fulfilled the * of Jeremiah Mt 27:9
the Holy Spirit and gave this *: Lk 1:67
For the time has come for this * Lk 22:37
remembered this * from the Jn 2:17
This * that Jesus should die for Jn 11:51
fulfilling the * that said: Jn 12:14
that this was a fulfillment of *; Jn 12:16
He did this to carry out the * Jn 18:9
This * is recorded in Matthew Jn 18:32f
fulfilled * by killing Jesus; Act 13:27
daughters who had the gift of *. Act 21:9
had the gift of *, arrived from Act 21:10
written in the books of *; Act 24:14
books of Moses and the books of *. Act 28:23
Remember what the * of Hosea Rom 9:25
If I had the gift of * and knew 1Co 13:2
Someday *, and speaking in 1Co 13:8
the gift of *, being able to preach 1Co 14:1
However, * (preaching the deep 1Co 14:22
have the gift of * can speak, one 1Co 14:31
have the gift of * or any other 1Co 14:37
For no * recorded in Scripture 2Pe 1:20,21
If you read this * aloud to the Rev 1:3
The purpose of all * and of all I Rev 19:10
of Jesus is the spirit of *." Rev 19:10f

PROPHESIED
upon them, they * for some time. Num 11:25
rested upon them, they * there. Num 11:26
of the people of Amalek and *: Num 24:20
other soldiers, but they too *! 1Sa 19:21
from Mareshah, * against 2Ch 20:37
Everything I * came true, and Is 42:9
you lied when you * that everything Jer 20:6
evil, for they * by Baal and led my Jer 23:13
for he has * against this city." Jer 26:11
the Morasthite * in the days of Jer 26:18
Nehelamite has "*" to you when I Jer 29:31
And you have * with clapping Eze 21:17
For it had been *, "I will talk Mt 13:34,35
just as was *, but woe to the man Mt 26:24
shouting as Isaiah *, 'Get ready Jn 1:23
from sin, as * from ancient times. Act 3:21,22
spoke in other languages and *. Act 19:6
meant when he *, "Now you can Gal 4:27

PROPHESIES
If the thing he * doesn't happen, Deu 18:22
him, for he never * anything good. 1Ki 22:8
for he never * anything but evil! 2Ch 18:6,7
He never * anything but evil 2Ch 18:17
This name * that within a couple Is 8:4
publicly prays or * without a 1Co 11:5
But one who *, preaching the 1Co 14:3
but one who *, preaching messages 1Co 14:4

PROPHESY
you, and you will * with them and 1Sa 10
upon him, and he too began to *. 1Sa 10:
them and they also began to *. 1Sa 19:
upon Saul, and he too began to *! 1Sa 19:
appointed men to * to the 1Ch 25
came true, and now I will * again. Is 42
must confess that only God can *. Is 43
They will tell you not to * in Jer 11:21,
any message. They * of visions and Jer 14:
And the people to whom they * Jer 14:
prophets when they * to you, Jer 23:
Therefore * against them. Jer 25:
he said, "to * against this Temple Jer 26:
for they * lies in my name. Jer 29:
for continuing to * that the city Jer 32:
This will * her doom. Eze 4:
of Israel and * against them. Eze 6:
Therefore, son of dust, * Eze 11:
"Son of dust, * against the Eze 13:2,
of the Negeb. * to it and say: Eze 20:4
Jerusalem and * against Israel and Eze 21:
"* to them in this way: Clap Eze 21:1
"Son of dust, * to the Ammonites Eze 21:2
of Ammon and * against its people. Eze 25:
city of Sidon and * against it. Eze 28:2
toward Egypt and * against Pharaoh Eze 29:
"Son of dust, * and say: The Eze 30:2,
"Son of dust, * against the Eze 34:
and * against the people saying: Eze 35:
"SON OF DUST, * to Israel's Eze 36:
"Therefore * and say to the Eze 36:
toward the land of Magog, and * Eze 38:2,
"SON OF DUST, * this also against Eze 39:
Your sons and daughters will *; Joe 2:2
'Go and * to my people Israel.' Amo 7:1
You say, 'Don't * against Amo 7:1
preach and * until you're paid. Mic 3:1
Well did Isaiah * of you, 'These Mt 15:
saying, "* to us, you Messiah! Mt 26:6
daughters shall *, and your young Act 2:17
and women alike, and they shall *. Act 2:18
you the ability to *, then prophesy Rom 12:6
to prophesy, then * whenever you Rom 12:6
to others power to * and preach. 1Co 12:10
were all able to *, preaching God's 1Co 14:5
But if you *, preaching God's 1Co 14:24
Two or three may *, one at a 1Co 14:29,30
permitted to pray and * (1 Cor. 1Co 14:34f
Do not scoff at those who *, 1Th 5:20
Then he told me, "You must * Rev 10:11
my two witnesses to * 1,260 days Rev 11:3
a half years they *, and to turn Rev 11:6

PROPHESYING
and a harp, and * as they come. 1Sa 10:5
When Saul had finished * he 1Sa 10:13
the other prophets *, the Spirit of 1Sa 19:20
night, * with Samuel's prophets. 1Sa 19:24
prophets continued * before the two 1Ki 22:10
"prophets" were * before them. 2Ch 18:9
land of Judah and do your * there! Amo 7:12
* lies in the name of the Lord.' Zec 13:3
Holy Spirit * through them—not to Act 21:4
a covering when * or praying 1Co 11:16
But if, while someone is *, 1Co 14:29,30

PROPHET
he is a *) and you shall live. Gen 20:7
"Even with a *, I would Num 12:6
"IF THERE IS a * among you, or Deu 13:1
"The * who tries to lead you Deu 13:5
raise up for you a * like me, an Deu 18:15
them a *, an Israeli like you. Deu 18:18
But any * who falsely claims Deu 18:20
And any * who claims to give a Deu 18:20
There has never been another * Deu 34:10
reply through the * he sent to them Ju 6:8
One day a * 1Sa 2:27
was going to be a * of the Lord. 1Sa 3:20
There is a * who lives here in 1Sa 9:6
into the city where the * lived. 1Sa 9:9,10,11
ask the *," as we would say now. 1Sa 9:9,10,11
Saul a *?" 1Sa 10:11
the proverb, "Is Saul a *, too?" 1Sa 10:12
so we went to the * Samuel to ask 1Sa 10:14
"Is Saul a *, too?" 1Sa 19:24
One day the * Gad told David to 1Sa 22:5
said to Nathan the *, "Look! 2Sa 7:2
SO THE LORD sent the * Nathan to 2Sa 12:1
sent word by Nathan the *." 2Sa 12:25f
blessings through Nathan the *. 2Sa 12:25
Lord came to the * Gad, who was 2Sa 24:11
and Benaiah, the * Nathan, Shime-i, 1Ki 1:8
invite Nathan the *, Benaiah, the 1Ki 1:10
Then Nathan the * went to 1Ki 1:11
the * is here to see you." 1Ki 1:22,23
"and Nathan the *, and Benaiah." 1Ki 1:32
and Nathan the * are to anoint him 1Ki 1:34
So Zadok the priest, Nathan the * 1Ki 1:38
and Nathan the * and Benaiah, 1Ki 1:44,45
Jerusalem, the * Ahijah from Shiloh 1Ki 11:29
through Ahijah, the * from Shiloh. 1Ki 12:15

(PROPHET Con't)
this message to Shemaiah, the *: 1Ki 12:22
calf-idol, a * of the Lord from 1Ki 13:1
command, the * shouted, "O altar, 1Ki 13:2
angry with the * for saying this. 1Ki 13:4
as the * had said would happen. 1Ki 13:5
cried out to the *, "beg the Lord 1Ki 13:6
Then the king said to the *, 1Ki 13:7
But the * said to the king, 1Ki 13:8
there was an old * living in 1Ki 13:11
told him what the * from Judah had 1Ki 13:11
the old * asked. 1Ki 13:12
he rode after the * and found him 1Ki 13:14
"Are you the * who came from 1Ki 13:14
Then the old man said to the *, 1Ki 13:15
But the old man said, "I am a * 1Ki 13:18
together, and the * ate some food 1Ki 13:19
he shouted at the * from Judah, 1Ki 13:21,22
and the * started off again. 1Ki 13:24,25
in Bethel where the old * lived. 1Ki 13:24,25
"It is the * who disobeyed the 1Ki 13:26
So the * laid the body upon the 1Ki 13:29
the grave where the * is buried. 1Ki 13:31
go to Ahijah the * at Shiloh—the 1Ki 14:2
through Ahijah, the * from Shiloh. 1Ki 15:29
Baasha at this time by the * Jehu: 1Ki 16:1
had predicted through the * Jehu. 1Ki 16:12
THEN ELIJAH, THE * 1Ki 17:1
are a *," she told him afterward, 1Ki 17:24
"I am the only * of the Lord who 1Ki 18:22
to replace you as my *. 1Ki 19:16
Then a * came to see King Ahab 1Ki 20:13
And the * replied, "The Lord 1Ki 20:14
"Yes," the * answered. 1Ki 20:14
Then the * approached King Ahab 1Ki 20:22
Then a * went to the king of 1Ki 20:28
Then the * told him, "Because 1Ki 20:36
Then the * turned to another man 1Ki 20:37
The * waited for the king beside 1Ki 20:38
As the king passed by, the * 1Ki 20:39
Then the * yanked off the bandage 1Ki 20:41
Then the * told him, "The Lord 1Ki 20:42
there a * of the Lord here? 1Ki 22:7
of the Lord told Elijah the *, 2Ki 1:3
"It was Elijah the *!" 2Ki 1:8
there a * of the Lord with us? 2Ki 3:11
When she told the * what had 2Ki 4:7
in from time to time is a holy *. 2Ki 4:9
bed of the * and shut the door; 2Ki 4:21
to the * and come right back." 2Ki 4:22
but the * said, "Let her alone; 2Ki 4:27
Then the * went down and walked 2Ki 4:35
Then the * summoned Gehazi. 2Ki 4:36
would go to see the * in Samaria. 2Ki 5:3
"Go and visit the *," the king 2Ki 5:5
But when Elisha the * heard about 2Ki 5:8
a true * of God here in Israel." 2Ki 5:8
and said, "If the * had told you 2Ki 5:13
times, as the * had told him to. 2Ki 5:14
party went back to find the *; 2Ki 5:15
the * asked. 2Ki 6:6
"Elisha, the *, tells the king 2Ki 6:12
him, and the * had told the king 2Ki 7:18
And the * had said, "You will see 2Ki 7:19
Someone told the king that the * 2Ki 8:7
So the young * did as he was 2Ki 9:4
He told Elijah the * that dogs 2Ki 9:36
for it by the * Hosea (1:4). 2Ki 10:11f
But the * was angry with him. 2Ki 13:19
Amittai) the * from Gath-hepher. 2Ki 14:25
Amoz), the *, with this message: 2Ki 19:2
Isaiah the * went to visit him. 2Ki 20:1
just as the Lord's * had declared 2Ki 23:16
the grave of the * who came from 2Ki 23:17
or those of the * from Samaria. 2Ki 23:18
he said to Nathan the *, "Look! 1Ch 17:1
David's personal *, "Go and tell 1Ch 21:9
the king's private *, were his sons 1Ch 25:2
Lord by Samuel the *, Saul the son 1Ch 26:28
of Samuel the *, the history 1Ch 29:29
by Nathan the *, and in the history 1Ch 29:29
the history written by the * Gad. 1Ch 29:29
of Nathan the * and in the prophecy 2Ch 9:29
But the Lord told Shemaiah the *, 2Ch 11:2
The * Shemaiah now met with 2Ch 12:5
by Shemaiah the * and by Iddo the 2Ch 12:15
in the * Iddo's History of Judah. 2Ch 13:22
About that time the * Hanani came 2Ch 16:7
Asa was so angry with the * for 2Ch 16:10
"Isn't there some * of the Lord 2Ch 18:6,7
uninjured, the * Jehu (son of 2Ch 19:2
Then Elijah the * wrote him this 2Ch 21:12
But a * arrived with this message 2Ch 25:7
And the * replied, "The Lord is 2Ch 25:9
and he sent a * to demand, "Why 2Ch 25:15
The * left with this parting 2Ch 25:16
by the * Isaiah (son of Amoz). 2Ch 26:22
But Oded, a * of the Lord, was 2Ch 28:9
David and of the * Asaph, which 2Ch 29:30
and Isaiah the * (son of Amoz) 2Ch 32:20
of Isaiah (the *, the son of Amoz), 2Ch 32:32
Heman, and Jeduthun the king's *. 2Ch 35:15
time of Samuel the * had there been 2Ch 35:18
even Jeremiah the *, mourned for 2Ch 35:24,25
of Jeremiah the *, who gave him 2Ch 36:12
the prediction of Jeremiah the *. 2Ch 36:22,23
Written after Nathan the * had Ps 51:1
In a vision you spoke to your * Ps 89:19
and Samuel, his *, cried to him for Ps 99:6
Isaiah the *, son of Amoz. Is 37:2
and Isaiah the * (Amoz' son) went Is 38:1
Then Isaiah the * came to the Is 39:3
great and small, * and priest, have Jer 8:10
Another true * of the Lord, Uriah Jer 26:20
of Azzur), a false * from Gibeon, Jer 28:1
So a * who foretells peace has Jer 28:9
Then Hananiah, the false *, took Jer 28:10
the false *, "Listen, Hananiah, Jer 28:15
who claims to be a *, and to put Jer 29:26
this false * Jeremiah of Anathoth? Jer 29:27
Hanan the * (the son of Igdaliah). Jer 35:4
I have sent you * after prophet Jer 35:15
I have sent you prophet after * Jer 35:15
spoken by Jeremiah the *: Jer 50:1
know they have had a * among them. Eze 2:5
You will long for a * to guide Eze 7:26,27
pass make liars out of every *.' Eze 12:22
a * to ask for my help and advice. Eze 14:6,7
against that '*' and destroy him Eze 14:9
know a * has been among them." Eze 33:33
of Jeremiah the *, that Jerusalem Dan 9:2
*, who guided and protected them. Hos 12:13
"Get out of here, you *, you! Amo 7:12
of drunken, lying * that you like! Mic 2:11
* Habakkuk in a vision from God: Hab 1:1
and exile. The * Jeremiah was Zep 1:1f
To: Haggai the *, who delivered Hag 1:1
the Lord through Haggai the *: Hag 2:10
of Iddo the *) in early November of Zec 1:1
of Iddo the *), in a vision in the Zec 1:7
grief—king, *, priest, and people. Zec 12:12,13,14
'I am not a *; Zec 13:5
This is a false * who is lying Zec 13:6f
given through the * Malachi: Mal 1:1
"See, I will send you another * Mal 4:5
Literally, "the * Elijah." Mal 4:5f
"for this is what the * Micah Mt 2:5
Isaiah the * had told about Mt 3:3
If you welcome a * because he is Mt 10:41
be given the same reward a * gets. Mt 10:41
Or a * of God? Mt 11:9
Yes, and he is more than just a * Mt 11:9
what happened to Jonah the *! Mt 12:39,40
Many a * and godly man has Mt 13:17
Then Jesus told them, "A * is Mt 13:57
the people believed John was a *. Mt 14:5
* from Nazareth up in Galilee." Mt 21:11
the crowd all think he was a *." Mt 21:26
for they accepted Jesus as a *. Mt 21:46
the *) standing in a holy place Mt 24:15
In the book written by the * Mk 1:2
Then Jesus told them, "A * is Mk 6:4
*, now returned to life again; Mk 6:15
* like the great ones of the past. Mk 6:15
Isaiah the * described you very Mk 7:6,7
* come back to life again." Mk 8:28
strongly that John was a *. Mk 11:32
"Who hit you that time, you *?" Mk 14:65
he was calling for the * Elijah. Mk 15:34f
he was calling for the * Elijah. Mk 15:35
power like Elijah, the * of old; Lk 1:17
be called the * of the glorious Lk 1:76
In the words of Isaiah the *, Lk 3:4
The book of Isaiah the * was Lk 4:17
to you that no * is accepted in his Lk 4:24
how Elijah the * used a miracle to Lk 4:25,26
Or think of the * Elisha, who Lk 4:27
to God, "A mighty * has risen Lk 7:16
But did you find a *? Lk 7:26
And more than a *. Lk 7:26
that Jesus is no *, for if God had Lk 7:39
ancient * risen from the dead." Lk 9:8
Many a * and king of old has Lk 10:24
For it wouldn't do for a * of God Lk 13:33
are convinced that he was a *." Lk 20:6
"Who hit you that time, *?" Lk 22:63,64
"He was a * who did incredible Lk 24:19
"Are you the *?" Jn 1:21
or Elijah or the *, what right do Jn 1:24,25
the woman said, "you must be a *. Jn 4:19
Jesus used to say, "A * is Jn 4:43,44
is the * we have been expecting!" Jn 6:14
man surely is the * who will come Jn 7:40
"I think he must be a * sent from Jn 9:17
what Isaiah the * had predicted: Jn 12:38
ago by the * Joel— 'In the last Act 2:16
But he was a *, and knew God had Act 2:30
* among you, who will resemble me! Act 3:21,22
"Samuel and every * since have Act 3:24
will raise up a * much like me Act 7:37
Name one * your ancestors didn't Act 7:52
from the book of the * Isaiah. Act 8:28
a fake * named Bar-Jesus. Act 13:6,7
and were followed by Samuel the *. Act 13:19,20
to this passage from the * Amos Act 15:15
when he said through Isaiah the *, Act 28:25
Isaiah the * cried out concerning Rom 9:27
it, for Isaiah the * said, "Lord, Rom 10:16
Elijah the * was complaining to Rom 11:2,3
And the * Isaiah said, "There Rom 15:12
As the * Habakkuk says it, "The Gal 3:11
One of their own men, a * from Tit 1:12
ever thought up by the * himself. 2Pe 1:20,21
the Creature, and his False *. Rev 16:13
and with him the False *, Rev 19:20
and his False *—were thrown alive Rev 19:20
Creature and False * are, and they Rev 20:10

PROPHET'S
For this was the * proof that God 1Ki 13:5
man saddled the * donkey, and the 1Ki 13:23
He found the * body lying in the 1Ki 13:28
Despite the * warning, Jeroboam 1Ki 13:33
dead, lying there upon the * bed. 2Ki 4:32
When the * servant got up early 2Ki 6:15
No one will wear * clothes to try Zec 13:4
This fulfilled the * prediction, Mt 2:15

PROPHETESS
Then Miriam the *, the sister of Ex 15:20
a *, the wife of Lappidoth. Ju 4:4
of Jerusalem to find Huldah the *. 2Ki 22:14
So the men went to Huldah the *, 2Ch 34:22
No-adiah the *, and all the other Neh 6:14
Anna, a *, was also there in the Lk 2:36,37
calls herself a *, to teach my Rev 2:20

PROPHETIC
as much * power as you have had." 2Ki 2:9
the frequent puns in the * books. Jer 29:24f
them, or * vision to guide them. Lam 2:9
determine their * significance. Dan 5:8f
be boasting then of his * gift! Zec 13:4

PROPHETS
Lord's people were *, and that the Num 11:29
(In those days * were called 1Sa 9:9,10,11
meet a band of * coming down the 1Sa 10:5
God they saw the * coming toward 1Sa 10:10
and the other * prophesying, the 1Sa 19:20
prophesying with Samuel's *. 1Sa 19:24
said, 'Is Saul also among the *?' 1Sa 19:24f
or by the *. 1Sa 28:5,6
me and won't reply by * or dreams; 1Sa 28:15
all of the Lord's *, Obadiah had 1Ki 18:3,4
to kill the Lord's *, and I hid a 1Ki 18:13
with all 450 * of Baal and the 400 1Ki 18:19
Baal and the 400 * of Asherah who 1Ki 18:19
people and the * to Mount Carmel. 1Ki 18:20
told them, "but Baal has 450 *. 1Ki 18:22
Now bring two young bulls. The * 1Ki 18:23
Then Elijah turned to the * of 1Ki 18:25
told them to grab the * of Baal. 1Ki 18:40
slaughtered the * of Baal, she 1Ki 19:1
"You killed my *, and now I swear 1Ki 19:2
killed your *, and only I am left; 1Ki 19:10
every one of your * except me; 1Ki 19:14
one of the * to say to another man, 1Ki 20:35
recognized him as one of the *. 1Ki 20:41
the 450 * of Baal were slain. 1Ki 22:6f
* and asked them, "Shall I 1Ki 22:6
Meanwhile, all the * continued 1Ki 22:10
One of the *, Zedekiah (son of 1Ki 22:11
him what the other * were saying, 1Ki 22:13
in the mouths of all his *.' 1Ki 22:22
of all these *, but the fact of the 1Ki 22:23
There the young * of Bethel 2Ki 2:3
young * watched from a distance. 2Ki 2:6,7
When the young * of Jericho saw 2Ki 2:15
"Go to the false * of your 2Ki 3:13
teaching the young *, he said to 2Ki 4:38
to use it to feed the young *. 2Ki 4:42
you that two young * from the hills 2Ki 5:22
HAD summoned one of the young *. 2Ki 9:1
the murder of my * and of all my 2Ki 9:7
Summon all the * and priests of 2Ki 10:18,19
the Lord had sent * to warn both 2Ki 17:13
*, but Israel wouldn't listen. 2Ki 17:13
all his * had warned would happen. 2Ki 17:23
the Lord declared through the *, 2Ki 21:10
So all the priests and * and the 2Ki 23:1
through his * that he would. 2Ki 24:2
'These are my *—touch them not.' 1Ch 16:22
400 of his heathen * and asked 2Ch 18:3,4,5
* were prophesying before them. 2Ch 18:9
and what all the * were saying—that 2Ch 18:12
the mouth of all of the king's *!' 2Ch 18:21
the mouth of these * of yours, when 2Ch 18:22
Believe his *, and everything 2Ch 20:20
God sent * to bring them back to 2Ch 24:19
of David and the * Gad and 2Ch 29:25,26
reply through the *—this is all 2Ch 33:18
recorded in The Annals of the *. 2Ch 33:19
fathers sent his * again and again 2Ch 36:15
scoffing at the * until the anger 2Ch 36:16
BUT THERE WERE * in Jerusalem and Ez 5:1
So they did and the * helped Ez 5:1

(PROPHETS Con't)
preaching of the * Haggai and Ez 6:14
your laws! The * warned us that Ez 9:11
you have appointed * to campaign Neh 6:7
and all the other * who have tried Neh 6:14
law, killed the * who told them to Neh 9:26
You sent your * to warn them Neh 9:30
and priests and * and ancestors Neh 9:32
come, just as all the * foretold. Ps 40:7
your people. The * are gone, and Ps 74:9,10
warned, "and do not hurt my *." Ps 105:15
armies, judges, *, elders, army Is 3:2
often used by the *: the Hebrew Is 5:7f
leaders of Israel and the lying *. Is 9:14,15
Her priests and * reel and Is 28:7
He has closed the eyes of your * Is 29:10
They tell my *, "Shut up—we Is 30:10,11
liars all false * are, by causing Is 44:25
But what my * say, I do; Is 44:26
me, and their * worshiped Baal and Jer 2:8
Kings, princes, priests and *—all Jer 2:26,27
my * as a lion kills its prey. Jer 2:30
and the priests and the * will be Jer 4:9
God's *," they say, "are Jer 5:13
Hosts says to his *: Because of Jer 5:14
false *, and my people like it so! Jer 5:31
Yes, even my * and priests! Jer 6:13
Yet the priests and * give Jer 6:14
sending them my *, day after day. Jer 7:25
and priests and * and people, and Jer 8:1
* right on down to all the people. Jer 13:13
Then I said, O Lord God, their * Jer 14:13
Then the Lord said: The * are Jer 14:14
punish these lying * who have Jer 14:15
And yet the * and priests alike Jer 14:18
and *—we don't need his advice. Jer 18:18
for the false *, full of deceit. Jer 23:9
dried up—for the * do evil and Jer 23:10
And the priests are like the *, Jer 23:11
I knew the * of Samaria were Jer 23:13
but the * of Jerusalem are even Jer 23:14
These * are as thoroughly Jer 23:14
Don't listen to these false * Jer 23:16
even one of these * who lives close Jer 23:18
I have not sent these *, yet they Jer 23:21
If they are "*," they are Jer 23:26
they are * of deceit, inventing Jer 23:26
Let these false * tell their Jer 23:28
So I stand against these "*" Jer 23:30,31
smooth-tongued * who say, "This Jer 23:30,31
or one of their "*" or priests Jer 23:33
And as for the false * and Jer 23:34
*, but you have refused to hear. Jer 25:4
my servants, the *—for I sent them Jer 26:5
priests and false * and all the Jer 26:7,8
Then the priests and the false * Jer 26:11
priests and false *, "This man Jer 26:16
"Do not listen to your false *, Jer 27:9
Don't listen to the false * who Jer 27:14
die—you and all these '*' too." Jer 27:15
listen to your * who are telling Jer 27:16
If they are really God's *, then Jer 27:18
The ancient * who preceded you Jer 28:8
and *, and to all the people. Jer 29:1
let the false * and mediums who are Jer 29:8
accept the false * among you and Jer 29:15
them again and again through my *. Jer 29:19
about your false *, Ahab (son of Jer 29:21
priests and *—stir me up. Jer 32:32
Where are those * now who told Jer 37:19
I sent my servants, the *, to Jer 44:4
Your "*" have said so many Lam 2:14
Shall priests and * die within Lam 2:20
of the sins of her * and priests, Lam 4:13
against the false * of Israel who Eze 13:2,3
"O Israel, these '*' of yours Eze 13:4
O evil *, what have you ever Eze 13:5
wall and these * praise them for Eze 13:10
For they were lying *, claiming Eze 13:16
against the women * too who pretend Eze 13:17
And if one of the false * gives Eze 14:9
False * and hypocrites—evil Eze 14:10
Your magicians and false * have Eze 21:29
Your '*' have plotted against Eze 22:25
Your '*' describe false visions Eze 22:28
ago through the * of Israel, saying Eze 38:17
your servants the *, whom you sent Dan 9:6
us through your servants, the *. Dan 9:10
as the * have declared. Dan 9:24
and so will your false "*" too; Hos 4:5
I sent my * to warn you of your Hos 6:5
"The * are crazy"; Hos 9:7
I appointed the * to guard my Hos 9:8
I sent my * to warn you with Hos 12:10
and *—can you deny this, Amo 2:11
my *, telling them, 'Shut up!' Amo 2:12
of all, I warn you through my *. Amo 3:7
"I am not really one of the *. Amo 7:14
I do not come from a family of *. Amo 7:14
You false *! Mic 3:5
you priests and * who won't Mic 3:11
Her "*" are liars seeking their Zep 3:4
The earlier * pled in vain with Zec 1:4
Your fathers and their * are now Zec 1:5,6
the priests and * about whether Zec 7:3
with people, the * warned them that Zec 7:7
by his Spirit through the early *. Zec 7:12
of the Temple, the * have been Zec 8:9
All false * and fortune-tellers Zec 13:2
cuts, as practiced by false *. Zec 13:6f
God's message through his *— Mt 1:22
"Did the * tell us where the Mt 2:4
of the * concerning the Messiah, Mt 2:23
And remember, the ancient * were Mt 5:12
Moses and the warnings of the *. Mt 5:17
"this is the law and the *." Mt 7:12f
for all the laws and * looked Mt 11:13
the one the * said would come [at Mt 11:14
In fact, because the * said that Mt 13:34,35
Jeremiah or one of the other *." Mt 16:14
the demands of the * stem from Mt 22:40
For you build monuments to the * Mt 23:29,30
"I will send you *, and wise Mt 23:34
that kills the *, and stones all Mt 23:37
And many false * will appear and Mt 24:11
arise, and false *, and will do Mt 24:24
* as recorded in the Scriptures." Mt 26:56
manuscripts read, "the * said." Mk 1:3f
just as the * had predicted. Mk 9:12,13
Then Jesus asked them what the * Mk 9:12,13
Messiahs and false * who will do Mk 13:22
must die, as the * declared long Mk 14:21
through the *, 'I will kill the Mk 14:27
through his holy * long ago— Lk 1:70
* were treated that way too! Lk 6:23
false * have always been praised. Lk 6:26
just as the ancient * predicted. Lk 8:10
ancient * risen from the dead." Lk 9:19
who killed the * long ago. Lk 11:47
you: 'I will send * and apostles to Lk 11:49
Jacob, and all the * within the Lk 13:28
The city that murders the *. Lk 13:34
of the * were your guides. Lk 16:16
to Moses and the *, they won't Lk 16:31
* concerning me will come true. Lk 18:31
* will be abundantly fulfilled. Lk 21:22
me by the * will come true." Lk 22:37
the * wrote in the Scriptures! Lk 24:25
predicted by the * that the Messiah Lk 24:26
writings of the *, beginning with Lk 24:27
by Moses and the * and in the Lk 24:44
—the very person Moses and the * Jn 1:45
* will come from Galilee!" Jn 7:52
Even Abraham and the mightiest * Jn 8:52
And greater than the *, who died? Jn 8:53
This has fulfilled what the * Jn 15:25
You are the children of those *; Act 3:25
his *, 'and earth is my footstool. Act 7:48,49
And all the * have written about Act 10:43
During this time some * came down Act 11:27
AMONG THE * and teachers of the Act 13:1
Moses and from the *, those in Act 13:15
he is the one the * had written Act 13:27
the *' words read every Sabbath. Act 13:27
Don't let the *' words apply to Act 13:40
agrees with what the * predicted. Act 15:15
Or, "*." Act 15:32f
I teach nothing except what the * Act 26:22
Agrippa, do you believe the *? Act 26:27
by God's * in the Old Testament. Rom 1:2
the * and torn down God's altars; Rom 11:2,3
And since Abraham and the * are Rom 11:16
Do you remember what the * said Rom 11:26
But now as the * foretold and as Rom 16:25,26,27
*—those who preach God's Word, 1Co 12:28
Literally, "The spirits of the * 1Co 14:32f
prophets are subject to the *." 1Co 14:32f
long to be * so that you can preach 1Co 14:39
the grave just as the * foretold. 1Co 15:4
on now: the apostles and the *; Eph 2:20
Holy Spirit to his apostles and *. Eph 3:5
killed their own *, they even 1Th 2:15
us through his * that you would. 1Ti 1:18
you through his * when the elders 1Ti 4:14
through the * [in visions, dreams, Heb 1:1
and Samuel and all the other *. Heb 11:32
suffering, look at the Lord's *. Jas 5:10
the * did not fully understand. 1Pe 1:10
that what the * said came true. 2Pe 1:19
truth of the *' words, then the 2Pe 1:19
BUT THERE WERE false *, too, in 2Pe 2:1
from the holy * and from us 2Pe 3:1
servants the *—would be fulfilled. Rev 10:7
These two * are the two olive Rev 11:4
* who had tormented them so much! Rev 11:10
your servants—* and people alike, Rev 11:18
your saints and * have been Rev 16:6
of God and the * and the apostles! Rev 18:20
the martyred * and the saints." Rev 18:24
* for the worship of false gods. Rev 19:2f
God, who tells his * what the Rev 22:6,7
your brothers the * are, as well as Rev 22:9

PROPITIATION
seat" or "place of making *." Ex 25:17
Literally, "to be a *." Rom 3:25

PROPITIOUS
The most * time for this action Est 3:7

PROPORTION
shall be in * to the number of Lev 25:50
Lord, value it in * to its size, as Lev 27:16
value shall be in * to the number Lev 27:18
the tribes in * to their Num 26:52,53
You will be given land in * to Num 33:54
Share with him in * as the Lord Deu 15:14
* to the seriousness of the crime; Deu 25:1
of Gad in * to its population. Jos 13:24
of Manasseh in * to its needs: Jos 13:29
Measure it out to them in * to Ps 28:4
Give us gladness in * to our Ps 90:15
I will punish them in * to their Jer 25:14
* to the vileness of their sins. Eze 39:24
it in * to their abilities—and then Mt 25:15

PROPORTIONATE
it back at a price * to the number Lev 25:27
free-will offering * in size to his Deu 16:10

PROPOSAL
of Heshbon with a * of peace. Deu 2:26
Solomon replied with a * about 1Ki 5:2,3

PROPOSE
only the first to * this idea, but 2Co 8:10

PROPOSED
the city and * Abimelech's scheme; Ju 9:3
Then Saul *, "Jonathan and I 1Sa 14:40
and successor, had * to Jehoshaphat 1Ki 22:49
She replied, "This woman * that 2Ki 6:26-30

PROPOSES
Man *, but God disposes. Pro 19:21

PROPOSITION
"I accept your * and won't destroy Gen 19:21
* and become his son-in-law. 1Sa 18:22

PROPOSITIONED
So he stopped and * her to sleep Gen 38:16

PROPPED
Ahab went back in, * up in his 1Ki 22:35
Ahab went back in, * up in his 2Ch 18:34

PROSECUTE
He will * them to the full. Mic 6:2

PROSECUTING
He is the great * Attorney Is 3:13

PROSECUTION
government for *, even though I had Act 28:17

PROSPER
of Israel began to *, and there was Gen 47:27
For the Lord will * you in Deu 15:10
And the Lord your God will * all Deu 15:18
God will bless and * all you do. Deu 24:19
cattle, and * everything you do Deu 28:8
You shall not * in anything you Deu 28:29
you will * in everything you do. Deu 29:9
curse, 'I shall * even though I Deu 29:19
The Lord your God will * Deu 30:9
O Lord, * the Levites Deu 33:11
"May God * you and your family 1Sa 25:6
so that you will * in everything 1Ki 2:3
be with you and * you as you do 1Ch 22:11
Israel through Moses, you will * 1Ch 22:13
Ramoth-gilead and *, for the Lord 2Ch 18:11
away a good man, nor * evildoers. Job 8:20
For robbers *. Job 12:6
*, it is because you are wicked. Job 18:5
valley and to * you there. Job 36:16
wither, and all they do shall *. Ps 1:3
the land and *, feeding in safety. Ps 37:3
be envious of evil men who * Ps 37:7
May all who love this city *. Ps 122:6
don't let them * and be proud. Ps 140:6,7,8
Don't let liars * here in our Ps 140:11
causes a city to *, but the moral Pro 11:11
Whoever uses it will *! Pro 17:8
Or, "does not *." Pro 17:20f
When the wicked *, good men go Pro 28:28
on this errand and I will * him. Is 48:15
shall *; Is 52:13
and God's program shall * in his Is 53:10
it to, and * everywhere I send it. Is 55:11
Their children shall * as in Jer 30:20
Once again their flocks will * Jer 33:13
Her enemies *, for the Lord has Lam 1:5
and Judah too will * in that day. Eze 16:55
Shall I let this tree grow and *? Eze 17:9
But will Israel * after breaking Eze 17:15
shall * and become a great nation; Hos 1:10
"But Israel will * forever, and Joe 3:20
Your crops will *; Zec 8:12
For those who do evil shall *, Mal 3:14,15

PROSPERED
it, because the Lord has * you. Deu 12:15
and his kingdom *. 1Ki 2:12
So the Lord was with him and * 2Ki 18:7
and he * greatly, and all Israel 1Ch 29:23
of God, he *, for God blessed him. 2Ch 26:5
He * in everything he did. 2Ch 32:30
You have * everything he Job 1:10

ROSPERED Con't)
when my projects *, and even the Job 29:6
for everything I did *; Job 29:19
other trees. It * and grew long Eze 31:5
so that they * greatly there in the Dan 3:30
So Daniel * in the reign of Dan 6:28
and evil triumphed and *. Dan 8:12

ROSPERING
* in a land of corn and wine, Deu 33:28
along and how the war was *. 2Sa 11:7
little, while the diligent are *. Pro 13:4
strength and not his own. * Dan 8:24
gods, and *—until his time is up. Dan 11:36

ROSPERITY
And let him share the * of Shem, Gen 9:26,27
there are seven years of * ahead. Gen 41:26
following the seven years of *. Gen 41:27
a period of great * throughout all Gen 41:29
* will be forgotten and wiped out; Gen 41:30
You will envy the * I will give 1Sa 2:32
Your wisdom and * are far greater 1Ki 10:7
forever leave that * to our Ez 9:12
fields, and gives * to the poor Job 5:11
and to send joy and * to the Job 10:3
his * shall not continue. Job 20:21
They hold me in contempt and my * Job 30:15
with * throughout their lives. Job 36:11
to the throne with success and *. Ps 21:3
In my * I said, "This is Ps 30:6,7
in * because of his good reign. Ps 72:3
For I was envious of the * of Ps 73:3
* of those who hate the Lord. Ps 73:16
your chosen ones' * and rejoice in Ps 106:5
them many children and much *. Ps 107:41
your walls and * in your palaces. Ps 122:7
Their reward shall be * and Ps 128:2
Hard work means *; Pro 12:11
Steady plodding brings *; Pro 21:5
Hard work brings *; Pro 28:19
trusting God leads to *. Pro 28:25
destroy your *. Ecc 5:6,7
Enjoy * whenever you can, and Ecc 7:14
by me, and their * shall be great. Is 54:13
portion of * and everlasting joy. Is 61:7
generous breasts. * shall overflow Is 66:12
and there shall be * for all. Jer 22:4
And work for the peace and * of Jer 29:7
some day I will restore * to them. Jer 32:44
damage and give her * and peace. Jer 33:6
Instead I will restore their * Jer 33:25,26
O Lord, all peace and all * have Lam 3:17
pride for its own *, though it be Eze 31:14
in peace and *, when one night I Dan 4:4
asking them for crops and for *. Hos 7:14
when I restore the * of Judah and Joe 3:1
and *, but darkness and doom! Amo 5:18
home in peace and *, for there will Mic 4:4
make them live in peace and *; Mic 7:14
and restore their * again. Zep 2:7
everywhere there is * and peace." Zec 1:11
overflow with *, and the Lord will Zec 1:17
live in peace and * and each of you Zec 3:10
have peace and * so long that there Zec 8:4
"For I am sowing peace and * Zec 8:12

PROSPEROUS
"He's well and *. Gen 29:6
you as * as Ephraim and Manasseh.' Gen 48:20
shall have a long, * life in the Deu 5:16
you live long and * lives in the Deu 5:33
if you do, you will have long, * Deu 6:2
become full and * and have built Deu 8:12,13
become fat and *, and worship other Deu 31:20
could we become a * nation and Ez 9:12
they are * to the end. Job 21:12,13
are healthy, wealthy, fat, and *; Job 21:23,24
and grandchildren are rich and *. Ps 17:13,14
I will make this city * and Ps 132:15
Why are the wicked so *? Jer 12:1
need to tell us how * we will be! Jer 13:12
When you were * I warned you, Jer 22:21
* than it has ever been before. Jer 33:10,11
HOW * ISRAEL is—a luxuriant vine Hos 10:1
larger and more * than before. Mic 7:11
This is the fate of that vast, * Zep 2:15
when Jerusalem was * and her Zec 7:7
'May you be as * and happy as Zec 8:13
They are fat and * now, but a Lk 6:25

PROSPERS
A rebel who *. Pro 30:21,22,23

PROSTITUTE
he treat our sister like a *?" Gen 34:31
a *, since her face was veiled. Gen 38:15
"Where does the * live who was Gen 38:21
"But we've never had a public * Gen 38:21
by making her a *, lest the land Lev 19:29
A priest shall not marry a *, Lev 21:7
who becomes a *, thus violating her Lev 21:9
a woman who is divorced, nor a *. Lev 21:14,15
crime, being a * while living at Deu 22:21
the earnings of a * or a Deu 23:17,18
a woman named Rahab, who was a *. Jos 2:1
except Rahab the * and anyone in Jos 6:17
Go and rescue the * and everyone Jos 6:22
Thus Joshua saved Rahab the * Jos 6:25
of Gilead, but his mother was a *. Ju 11:1
Gaza and spent the night with a *. Ju 16:1
Spurn the careless kiss of a *. Pro 4:24
For the lips of a * are as sweet Pro 5:3
For a * will bring a man to Pro 6:26
*, from listening to her flattery. Pro 7:5
house of this wayward girl, a *. Pro 7:8,9
A * is loud and brash, and never Pro 9:13
A * is a dangerous trap; Pro 22:14
For a * is a deep and narrow Pro 23:26,27,28
thing too: how a * can sin and then Pro 30:20
A * is more bitter than death. Ecc 7:26
And now a *! Is 1:21
You sit like a * beside the road Jer 3:2
For you are a *, and completely Jer 3:3
and you gave yourself as a * to Eze 16:15
it enough that you should be a *? Eze 16:20
you are a brazen *, building Eze 16:30
You have been worse than a *, so Eze 16:31
"O *, hear the word of the Lord: Eze 16:35
youth when she was a * in Egypt. Eze 23:19,20
a girl who is a *, so that some of Hos 1:2
be a *, and I will wait for you." Hos 3:3
But though Israel is a *, may Hos 4:15
left me as a * leaves her husband; Hos 5:3
they traded a young lad for a *, Joe 3:3
wife will become a * in this city, Amo 7:17
of the streets—a *—heard he was Lk 7:37
of Christ and join him to a *? 1Co 6:15
joins himself to a * she becomes a 1Co 6:16
Rahab, the *, is another example Jas 2:25
to the Notorious *, who sits upon Rev 17:1
He has punished the Great * who Rev 19:2

PROSTITUTES
*, committing adultery against me Ex 34:15
"No * are permitted in Israel, Deu 23:17,18
Soon afterwards two young * came 1Ki 3:16
He executed the male * and 1Ki 15:12
Samaria, where the * bathed, dogs 1Ki 22:38
save a man from the flattery of *; Pro 2:16,17
Why delight yourself with *, Pro 5:20
from * with all their flatteries. Pro 6:24
my advice—stay away from *. Pro 23:26,27,28
hangs around with * disgraces him. Pro 29:3
her own husband. * charge for Eze 16:33,34
So you are different from other * Eze 16:33,34
as young girls became * in Egypt. Eze 23:2,3
zest of lustful men who visit *. Eze 23:44
a big business as *, they shall Hos 4:10
sinning with harlots and temple *. Hos 4:14
evil men and * will get into the Mt 21:31
while very evil men and * did. Mt 21:32
all his money on parties and *. Lk 15:13
your money on *, you celebrate by Lk 15:30
Great, Mother of * and of Idol Rev 17:5

PROSTITUTION
obviously as a result of *. Gen 38:24
the houses of male * that still 1Ki 22:46
the houses of male * around the 2Ki 23:7
the land with your vile *. Jer 3:2
given herself to *, for she has Jer 3:8
and to decorate your bed of *. Eze 16:16
by, in an endless stream of *. Eze 16:25
her spirit of * behind, but was Eze 23:8
She turned to even greater *, Eze 23:19,20
* brought from the land of Egypt; Eze 23:27
And the shame of your * shall be Eze 23:29
There your daughters turn to * and Hos 4:13

PROSTITUTIONS
your * by your alliance with her. Eze 16:26

PROSTRATE
clothing and lay * before the Ark Jos 7:6
robe, and fell * to the ground. 2Sa 13:31
help, * before their murderers. Jer 4:31
all the people * themselves to Jer 14:2

PROTECT
with you, and will * you wherever Gen 28:15
God will help and * me on this Gen 28:20
and God's wrath—to * them from his Num 1:53
'May the Lord bless and * you; Num 6:24,25,26
you lead and * us day and night. Num 14:14
walks among you to * you and to Deu 23:14
And there will be no one to * you. Deu 28:31
walls you will trust to * you. Deu 28:52
He will * his godly ones, 1Sa 2:9
Stay here with me, and I'll * 1Sa 22:23
and he made gold chains to * the 1Ki 6:21,22
as in Jerusalem to * the king. 2Ch 9:25
with walls and gates to * himself: 2Ch 11:5-10
We have no way to * ourselves 2Ch 20:12
a good journey and * us, our Ez 8:21
accompany us and * us from the Ez 8:22
that our God would * all those who Ez 8:22
army officers and troops to * me! Neh 2:9
city day and night to * ourselves. Neh 4:9
* him with your shield of love. Ps 5:12
their foes. * me as you would the Ps 17:8
God's laws are perfect. They * Ps 19:7,8
I expect you to * me and to ransom Ps 25:21
and * me by standing in front. Ps 35:2
Come and * me. Ps 38:15
your people and * Jerusalem. Ps 51:18
from my enemies. * me from these Ps 59:1
O Lord, save me! * your Ps 74:19
this your vine! * what you Ps 80:15
* me from death, for I try to Ps 86:2
I will * and bless him Ps 89:24
For he orders his angels to * Ps 91:11
Who will * me from the wicked? Ps 94:16
God stands beside you to * you. Ps 110:5
surround and * Jerusalem, so the Ps 125:2
Cling to wisdom—she will * you. Pro 4:6
little animals who * themselves by Pro 30:24-28
If you want me to * you, you must Is 7:9
"Give us sanctuary. * us. Is 16:3
for all, with no one to * them. Is 42:22
of Israel, will * you from behind. Is 52:12
the Lord will * you from behind. Is 58:8
* and deliver you, says the Lord. Jer 15:20
Quit your evil deeds! * the Jer 22:3
armpits to * you from the ropes." Jer 38:12
Mizpah to * himself against Baasha, Jer 41:9
people, I will * you wherever you Jer 45:5
and will * us from all harm. Eze 11:3
It will not * you. Eze 11:7
it, for I acted to * the honor of Eze 20:9,10
in order to * the honor of my name, Eze 20:14
against them to * my name among the Eze 20:22
and he couldn't * them from harm!' Eze 36:20
I am doing it to * my holy name Eze 36:22
perhaps even yet the Lord will * Zep 2:3
they have no shepherd to * them. Zec 10:2
and I will not * it from them." Zec 11:6
my contract to lead and * them. Zec 11:10
of angels to * us, and he would Mt 26:53
the stone and posted guards to * Mt 27:66
to * your man-made tradition. Mk 7:12,13
he is supposed to *, and to spend Lk 12:45
their shoulders to * him, and the Act 21:35
And I will * you from both your Act 26:17
And we carefully * from the eyes 1Co 12:23
therefore I will * you from Rev 3:10

PROTECTED
against adultery * her and his Deu 22:30f
God * them in the howling Deu 32:10
May you be * with strong bolts Deu 33:25
in her house, for she * our spies. Jos 6:17
cities and be * from the relatives Jos 20:3
this fellow. We * his flocks in the 1Sa 25:21
* by the king's own bodyguard; 1Ki 1:44,45
and God * us and saved us from Ez 8:31
"You have always * him and his Job 1:10
* by your mercy and your love; Ps 5:7
olive tree * by the Lord himself. Ps 52:8
I follow close behind you, * by Ps 63:8
a prophet, who guided and * them. Hos 12:13
straddling the Nile, * on all Nah 3:8
kill me, but God * me so that I am Act 26:22
Pray that I will be * in Rom 15:31
light keep sober, * by the armor of 1Th 5:8
they will be fully * from the Rev 7:16
was cared for and * from the Rev 12:14

PROTECTING
the childless who have no * sons. Job 24:21
the * shadow of your wings. Ps 63:7
Be to me a great * Rock, where I Ps 71:3
You have broken down the walls * Ps 89:40
He is their shield, * them and Pro 2:7,8
Glorious Land, * it from daytime Is 4:6
God has removed his * care. Is 22:8
of fire * them and all Jerusalem; Zec 2:5

PROTECTION
alone, for they are under my *." Gen 19:8
place where he can run and get *. Ex 21:13
he has removed his * from them! Num 14:9
These Cities will be places of * Num 35:12
These are not only for the * of Num 35:15
You will be safe here in our *. Ju 4:18
there under royal * until David 1Sa 22:3
like a wall of * to us and the 1Sa 25:15,16
Gath under the * of King Achish. 1Sa 27:2,3
sacrifices and the * of the 1Ch 9:19
for the * of the entrance to the 1Ch 9:21
him who is the great rock of *. Ps 18:46
My * and success Ps 62:7
our walls, leaving us without *. Ps 80:12
Yes, our * is from the Lord Ps 89:18
to rule under your *—a government Ps 94:20
will be preserved by your *. Ps 102:28
among the rocks and find * there. Ps 104:18
and may there be peace as a * to Ps 122:9
life, happiness, and * from harm. Pro 19:23
defends all who come to him for *. Pro 30:5
and beg for peace and my *. Is 27:4,5
in exchange for his * against the Is 28:15
your trust in Pharaoh for his *. Is 30:2
of *, and no enemy can cross. Is 33:21
I have removed my * and my peace Jer 16:5
He has withdrawn his * as the Lam 2:3

(PROTECTION Con't)
that under his * we could hold our Lam 4:20
forced to pay you for your "*"; Eze 22:7
when Ahaz paid "* money" to Eze 23:12f
and so he kept him under his *. Mk 6:20

PROTECTIVE
the law, kept in * custody, so to Gal 3:23

PROTECTOR
because you are my mighty *. Ps 71:7
God is our Light and our *. Ps 84:11

PROTECTS
He fills me with strength and * Ps 18:32
The Lord * his people and gives Ps 28:8
* me like the walls of a fort! Ps 31:21
for the Lord * those who are Ps 31:23
Only he can help us; he * us like Ps 33:20
God even * him from accidents. Ps 34:20
Who else * the weak and helpless Ps 35:10
He * them and keeps them alive; Ps 41:2
and * you from the fatal plague. Ps 91:3
who hate evil; he * the lives of Ps 97:10
The Lord * the simple and the Ps 116:6
He * you day and night. Ps 121:6
Lord surrounds and * his people. Ps 125:2
Unless the Lord * a city, Ps 127:1
rescues them. He * all those who Ps 145:20
good men. He * the immigrants, and Ps 146:9
the Lord is with you; he * you. Pro 3:24,25,26
God * the upright but destroys Pro 10:29
anyone should be rewarded who * Pro 27:18
even as a hen * her brood under her Lk 13:34

PROTEST
and they held a * meeting. Num 20:3
come to us in *, we will tell them, Ju 21:22
a great outcry of * from parents Neh 5:1
Let it * on my behalf. Job 16:18
Written by David to * against his Ps 52:1
Why do you * your punishment? Jer 30:15
the prophets, to * over and over Jer 44:4

PROTESTED
"Lord," he *, "how can you Ex 5:22
Moses *. Ex 19:23
their problem and * at being Num 9:6,7
*, "Sir, make them stop!" Num 11:28
"But, sir," * the Israeli Num 20:19
Jonathan *. 1Sa 20:2
"Oh, sir," Obadiah *, "what 1Ki 18:9
just like theirs," the people *. Neh 5:5
And no one * except Elnathan, Jer 36:24,25
saw them do it and *, "Your Mt 12:2
"They *, 'Those fellows worked Mt 20:11,12
among the lot of us," they *; Lk 9:13
like that," his listeners *. Lk 20:16
But the other criminal *. Lk 23:40,41
"No," Peter *, "you shall Jn 13:8
But when the Jews * the Act 28:19

PROUD
*, eternal monument to themselves. Gen 11:3,4
she became very * and arrogant Gen 16:4
from the * and cruel Egyptians." Ex 18:11
I will break your * power and Lev 26:19
you don't become *, and forget the Deu 8:14
Quit acting so * and arrogant! 1Sa 2:3
people doubtless very * of him. 2Sa 15:9f
Edom and are very * about it; 2Ki 14:10
You are very * about your 2Ch 25:19
But at that point he became *—and 2Ch 26:16
for he had become *, and so the 2Ch 32:25
but our ancestors were a * and Neh 9:16
they were * and wouldn't listen, Neh 9:29
Though the godless be * as the Job 20:6
and here shall your * waves stop!' Job 38:11
Let it overflow against the *. Job 40:11
Therefore * sinners will not Ps 5:5
Come and deal with all these * Ps 10:2
These wicked men, so * and Ps 10:4
he will destroy those * liars who Ps 12:3,4
condemn the * and haughty ones. Ps 18:27
Both * and humble together, all Ps 22:29
Don't let these * men trample me. Ps 36:11
seen it happen: a * and evil man, Ps 37:35,36
is but a moment to you. * man! Ps 39:5,6
who are *, or who trust in idols. Ps 40:4
Rich man! * man! Ps 49:10
So many are * to fight against Ps 56:1
They are *, cursing liars. Ps 59:12,13
And don't let the rich men be *. Ps 62:10,11
prosperity of the * and wicked. Ps 73:3
I warned the * to cease their Ps 75:4
and to stop being stubborn and * Ps 75:5
these * men who hate the Lord? Ps 83:2
O God, * and insolent men defy Ps 86:14
sentence the * to the penalties Ps 94:1
You rebuke those cursed * ones Ps 119:21
and revive me! * men hold me in Ps 119:51
* men have made up lies about me, Ps 119:69
Let the * be disgraced, for they Ps 119:78
These * men who hate your truth Ps 119:85,86
Don't let the * oppress me! Ps 119:122
of the scoffing of the rich and *. Ps 123:3,4
LORD, I AM not * and haughty. Ps 131:1
* men must keep their distance. Ps 138:6
These * men have set a trap to Ps 140:5
don't let them prosper and be *. Ps 140:6,7,8
* men end in shame, but the meek Pro 11:2
than to be too * to work—and Pro 12:9
of the * but cares for widows. Pro 15:25
Take my word for it—* men shall Pro 16:5
Better poor and humble than * and Pro 16:19
Mockers are *, haughty and Pro 21:24
They are * beyond description, Pro 30:13,14
a fool by being * or plotting evil, Pro 30:32
your * looks will be brought low; Is 2:11
move against the * and haughty and Is 2:12
wall, and all the * ocean ships Is 2:16
the dust; the * shall be humbled; Is 5:15
they are * and haughty men. Is 10:12
* troops, and strike them down. Is 10:16
arrogance of the * man and the Is 13:11
Is this * Moab, concerning which Is 16:6
* rulers of the nations on earth. Is 24:21
He humbles the * and brings the Is 26:5
the ground. The * city of Is 28:3
He will sift out the * nations Is 30:28
own stubborn will and his * heart. Jer 11:8
Oh, that you were not so * and Jer 13:15
* I am to bear your name, O Lord. Jer 15:16
and all the other * men, said to Jer 43:2,3
You are * of your fertile Jer 49:4
I am against you, O people so *; Jer 50:31
so * of, and defile your Temple. Eze 7:24
In your * days you held Sodom in Eze 16:56
says: You are so * you think you Eze 28:2,3
has made you very rich and very *. Eze 28:5
has become * and arrogant, the Eze 31:10
with all the * men of the world. Eze 31:14
And all the other * trees of Eze 31:16
The victor became both * and Dan 8:8
it, and the * armies of Egypt will Dan 11:15
then you became * and forgot me. Hos 13:6
You are * because you live in Ob 1:3
never again will you be * and Mic 2:3
That once * city will become a Zep 2:14
I will remove all your * and Zep 3:11
glorious like a * steed in battle. Zec 10:3
* and arrogant," says the Lord. Mal 3:13
a furnace. The * and wicked will be Mal 4:1
How he scatters the * and haughty Lk 1:51
dig ditches, and I'm too * to beg. Lk 16:3
One was a *, self-righteous Lk 18:10
collector. The * Pharisee 'prayed' Lk 18:11
For the * shall be humbled, but Lk 18:14
he was a very influential, * man Act 8:9,10,11
of God, insolent, * braggarts, Rom 1:30
You are so * of knowing God's Rom 2:23
Do not be *; Rom 11:20
not feel * and start bragging. Rom 11:25
me to be a little * of all Christ Rom 15:17
So don't be * of following the 1Co 3:21
You must not be * of one of God's 1Co 4:6
will have become *, thinking that I 1Co 4:18
out whether these * men are just 1Co 4:19
For women are * of their long 1Co 11:14,15
never boastful or *, never haughty 1Co 13:4
accept me and be * of me, as you 2Co 1:13,14
break down every * argument against 2Co 10:5
appetite: they are * of what they Php 3:19
These * men (though they claim to Col 2:18
They only make him *. Col 2:23
joy and is our * reward and crown? 1Th 2:19
he might be * of being chosen so 1Ti 3:6
different is both * and stupid. 1Ti 6:4
are rich not to be * and not to 1Ti 6:17
they will be * and boastful, 2Ti 3:2
They must not be * or impatient; Tit 1:7
himself against the * and haughty. Jas 4:6
himself against those who are *. 1Pe 5:5
and those who are * and willful, 2Pe 2:10
about this, but * Diotrephes, who 3Jn 1:9

PROUDEST
Of all the beasts, he is the * Job 41:34

PROUDLY
"Listen to this," he * Gen 37:6
They left *, hurried along by the Num 33:3,4
wrong, or how they have behaved *. Job 36:9
his people. How * they speak! Ps 73:8
"I am the Lord's," they'll * Is 44:5
* and push them into the dust!" Dan 4:37
Their cavalry move * forward from Hab 1:8
They * boast about their sins 2Pe 2:18

PROVE
"What does that *? Gen 42:14
an opportunity to * yourselves. Gen 42:18
if you * to be what you say, then Gen 42:34
How can we * our innocence? Gen 44:16
to * that God has sent you; Ex 7:9
people, and * to you there is no Ex 9:14
This will * to you that the earth Ex 9:29
then do some miracle to * it! Ju 6:17
to prove it! * that it is really Ju 6:17
as you promised, * it to me in Ju 6:37
And to * that what I have said 1Sa 2:34
But first you must * yourself to 1Sa 18:
Isaac, and Israel, * today that you 1Ki 18:
I am your servant; * that I have 1Ki 18:
replied, "it will * that the Lord 1Ki 22:
"Do a miracle to * to me that the 2Ki 20
and could not * that they were Ez 2:
could not * their Jewish ancestry; Neh 7:6
perfect, God would * me wicked. Job 9:
If you could * me wrong I would Job 13:1
I was wrong, you have yet to * it. Job 19:
so great? Then * my guilt! Job 19:
Who can * me a liar and claim Job 24:2
will never help us. * them wrong, Ps 4:
All his promises * true. Ps 18:3
I wash my hands to * my Ps 26:
We can always "*" that we are Pro 16:
For who can * that the spirit of Ecc 3:2
Who can know what will * best for Ecc 6:1
for things, and to * to myself the Ecc 7:2
"Ask me for a sign, Ahaz, to * Is 7:1
me to * that he will heal me?" Is 38:2
if they can, and * their power. Is 44:
to * that God has really sent him. Jer 28:
be my Judge, to * me right. Lam 3:5
Let me * it to you! Mal 3:1
Before being baptized, * that Mt 3:
"It will * you are the Son of Mt 4:
"Jump off," he said, "and * Mt 4:
So I'll * it to you by healing Mt 9:5,
and didn't try to * his points by Mk 1:2
So I'll * it to you by healing Mk 2:9,10,1
First go and * by the way you Lk 3:
"How shall we * to you that we Lk 3:12
"This will * to everyone that Lk 5:14
So I'll * it to you by healing Lk 5:23,24
* his claim of being the Messiah. Lk 11:16
the skies [to * I am the Messiah Lk 11:29,30
My similar experience will * that Lk 11:29,30
writings of Moses himself * this. Lk 20:37,38
Messiah, are you? * it by saving Lk 23:39
God, show us a miracle to * it." Jn 2:18
* that the Father has sent me. Jn 5:36
If you're so great, * it to the Jn 7:4
each other will * to the world that Jn 13:35
"If I lied, * it," Jesus Jn 18:23
and these men certainly cannot * Act 24:13
accusations which they couldn't *. Act 25:7
turn to God—and * their repentance Act 26:20
That God's words will always * Rom 3:4
doesn't that * you are still 1Co 3:3
This is one way to * that your 2Co 8:8
and thus * their lack of it. 1Ti 6:20
You must also do good to * that Jas 2:17
* whether you have faith or not; Jas 2:18
So, dear brothers, work hard to * 2Pe 1:10
* that they are God's children; 3Jn 1:11
and those who continue in evil * 3Jn 1:11
punishment, and to * the terrible Jud 1:15

PROVED
I * to you that I am Jehovah." Ex 10:2
It is * by the raw flesh. Lev 13:14,15
But some of this territory * Jos 19:47,48
My brother, you have * as Job 6:15-18
Is a man * right by all this Job 11:2
is a sinner, or has * that he is. Job 32:11,12
He * my power by conquering Is 55:4
and you have * it by your actions. Jer 44:25
Daniel soon * himself more Dan 6:3
whose experiences * to the people Lk 11:29,30
now you are my friends, * by the Jn 15:15
alive, and * to them in many ways Act 1:3
How true this * to be, for in Act 7:38
and the Lord * their message was Act 14:3
the dead he was * to be the mighty Rom 1:4
We have * ourselves to be what 2Co 6:6
boasting to Titus has also * true! 2Co 7:14
for we have * it again and again. 2Co 11:6
are one body is * by the Scripture Eph 5:31
out the charges * against you, the Col 2:14
as a man, was * spotless and pure 1Ti 3:16
the angels, as * by the fact that Heb 1:4
angels have always * true and Heb 2:2
It was after he had * himself Heb 5:9
until it is * that the person who Heb 9:16
God accepted Abel and * it by Heb 11:4
So we have seen and * that what 2Pe 1:19
When they left us it * that they 1Jn 2:19
has conquered, and * himself worthy Rev 5:5

PROVEN
me, as though I were * guilty? Job 19:28

PROVERB
of horror, a * and a byword among Deu 28:37
So that is the origin of the *, 1Sa 10:12
As that old * says, 'Wicked is 1Sa 24:13
example and * of sudden disaster. 1Ki 9:7
In the mouth of a fool a * Pro 26:7
longer quote this *—"Children pay Jer 31:29
"Son of dust, what is that * Eze 12:22
put an end to this * and they will Eze 12:23
"Why do people use this * about Eze 18:2
will not use this * any more in Eze 18:3

ROVERB Con't)
will quote me that *, 'Physician, Lk 4:23

ROVERBIAL
and his name became *. Gen 10:9
Their fate shall become * of all Jer 29:22

ROVERBS
He was the author of 3,000 * and 1Ki 4:32
THESE ARE THE * of King Solomon of Pro 1:1
These are the * of Solomon: Pro 10:1
Here are some additional *: Pro 24:21,22
THESE * OF Solomon Pro 25:1
and he collected * and classified Ecc 12:9
asked them (using * they all Mk 3:23

ROVES
your son, it * you don't love him; Pro 13:24
Every word of God * true. Pro 30:5
That * nothing. Mt 3:9
to himself, "This * that Jesus is Lk 7:39
Do you think this * they are Lk 11:19
power from God, it * that the Lk 11:20
Since you don't, it * you aren't Jn 8:47
my bad conscience * that I agree Rom 7:16
good or bad. This * that God was Rom 9:10-13
being persecuted * that I am still Gal 5:11
For when he punishes you, it * Heb 12:6
When he whips you it * you are Heb 12:6
his tongue, it * that he has Jas 3:1
If we love other Christians it * 1Jn 3:14

ROVIDE
When should I * for my own Gen 30:30
"What penalty does the law * for Est 1:13-15
You * delicious food for me in Ps 23:5
Then the Lord will * shade on Is 4:5
nations shall * you with the Is 60:16
the prince shall * a young bull for Eze 45:22
And the prince shall * fourteen Eze 45:24
feast, he shall * these same Eze 45:25
* clothing for you, you doubters? Lk 12:28
at all that God will * it for you. Lk 12:29

PROVIDED
the wagons Pharaoh had * for them. Gen 46:5
Each month the tax officials * 1Ki 4:27
They * the Bread of the 1Ch 23:29
olive oil shall be * every morning Eze 46:14,15
the wedding robe [* for him Mt 22:11

PROVIDENCE
using your ignorance to deny my *? Job 38:2
has so foolishly denied your *. Job 42:3
upon the earth: * seems to treat Ecc 8:14
The same * confronts everyone, Ecc 9:2,3

PROVIDES
place "Jehovah *"—and it still Gen 22:14
the jungle? Who * for the ravens Job 38:41
And if God * clothing for the Lk 12:28

PROVINCE
at Ecbatana, in the * of Media. Ez 6:2
who were citizens of the *. Neh 3:7
We will appoint agents in each * Est 2:3
empire, to each * in its own Est 3:12
as law in every *, and made known Est 3:14
And in every city and *, as the Est 8:17
against city, * against province. Is 19:2
against city, province against *. Is 19:2
over the whole * of Babylon, as Dan 2:48
the affairs of the * of Babylon; Dan 2:49
of Dura, in the * of Babylon; Dan 3:1
greatly there in the * of Babylon. Dan 3:30
in the * of Elam, standing beside Dan 8:2
So he traveled throughout the * Mk 1:39
in a certain * was called away to Lk 19:12
to be crowned king of his *. Lk 19:12
and returned to the * of Galilee. Jn 4:3
Literally, "Asia," a * of what Act 2:9f
a city in the * of Pisidia. Act 13:14
Turkish * of Ausia at that time. Act 16:6
north for the * of Bithynia, but Act 16:7
Mysia * to the city of Troas. Act 16:8
in the Turkish * of Ausia—both Jews Act 19:10
but throughout the entire *! Act 19:26
officers of the *, friends of Paul, Act 19:31
for the Syrian * of Phoenicia. Act 21:2
at Myra, in the * of Lycia. Act 27:5
Galatia was a * in what is now Gal 1:1f

PROVINCES
says, 'By the troops from the *.' 1Ki 20:14
troops from the *, 232 of them, 1Ki 20:15
judges out in the *, whether murder 2Ch 19:10
living in the * also brought in the 2Ch 31:5,6
in all of the * of Babylon. Ez 7:16
treasurers in the * west of the Ez 7:21
of all the * west of the Euphrates Ez 8:36
When I arrived in the * west of Neh 2:9
with its 127 * stretching from Est 1:1
to all of his *, in all the local Est 1:22
grants to the * in the form of Est 2:18
through all the * of your Est 3:8
into all the * of the empire, Est 3:13
And throughout all the * there Est 4:3
the Jews throughout the king's *. Est 8:5
princes of all the * from India to Est 8:9,10
throughout all the * of King Est 8:12
all the king's * to defend Est 9:1
And all the rulers of the *—the Est 9:3
throughout all the *, for he had Est 9:4
has happened in the rest of the *! Est 9:12
the king's * had gathered together Est 9:16
Throughout the * this was done Est 9:17
all the king's *, encouraging them Est 9:20
throughout the 127 * of the kingdom Est 9:29-31
as taxes from many kings and *. Ecc 2:7,8
You rule the farthest *, and Dan 2:38
rulers of all the * of his empire, Dan 3:2
into 120 *, each under a governor. Dan 6:1
Turkish * of Cilicia, and Ausia. Act 6:9
the coast of the * of Cilicia and Act 27:5
all nations and * and languages, Rev 7:9

PROVINCIAL
the names of the * officials who Neh 11:3

PROVING
back to him again, * everything you Mt 18:16
and * that Jesus is the Messiah. Act 17:3
was in my words, * to those who 1Co 2:4
* that what we teach is right; 2Co 13:7
you aren't * it by helping others? Jas 2:14

PROVISION
away, but has made * to bring back 2Sa 14:14f
had included this * in his grant. Ez 3:7
with all your bountiful *. Ps 104:28

PROVISIONS
He also gave them * for their Gen 42:25
had commanded, and * for the Gen 45:21
Each of them arranged * for one 1Ki 4:7
countries! The * required for each Neh 5:18

PROVOKE
You must not * him and try his Deu 6:16
and stay home! Why * disaster for 2Ki 14:10
Go ahead and * God—it makes no Job 12:6

PROVOKED
But Ephraim has bitterly * the Hos 12:14

PROVOKES
The fool who * his family to Pro 11:29

PROVOKING
most, thus * him to great anger. Deu 9:18

PROW
to put out anchors from the *. Act 27:30

PROWL
although they * on every side and Ps 12:8
around like dogs that * the city. Ps 59:6
at evening, and * the city all Ps 59:14,15
have their dens, and panthers *. Sol 4:8

PROWLS
"Benjamin is a wolf that *. Gen 49:27
great enemy. He * around like a 1Pe 5:8

PRUDENT
is as wise and * as Israel!' Deu 4:6
what he is told! A * man checks to Pro 14:15
A * man foresees the difficulties Pro 22:3

PRUNE
sow your field and * your vineyards Lev 25:3
Don't sow your crops and don't * Lev 25:4
I won't * it or hoe it, but let Is 5:6

PRUNES
And he * those branches that bear Jn 15:2

PRUNING
and their spears into * hooks." Is 2:4f
you off as though with * shears. Is 18:5
and beat your * hooks into spears. Joe 3:10
He has already tended you by * Jn 15:3

PRUNING-HOOKS
and their spears into *; Mic 4:3

PRYING
and * into other people's affairs. 1Pe 4:15

PSALM
the people in a great * of praise. 2Ch 23:12
A * of David when he fled from his Ps 3:1
A * of David when he was hiding in Ps 63:1
the sides of the north" (* 48:2); Is 14:13f
* 78:2. Mt 13:34,35f
* 22:18. Jn 19:23,24f
* 69:25. Act 1:20f
* 109:8. Act 1:20f
This is what the second * is Act 13:32,33
In another * he explained more Act 13:35
* 51:4. Rom 3:4f
* 14:3. Rom 3:10f
* 32:1-2. Rom 4:8f
just as the * writer did when 2Co 4:13

PSALMIST
David, sweet * of Israel: 2Sa 23:1
As the * said, "He came for the Rom 15:3
That is what the * meant when he Rom 15:9
The * tells about this, for he Eph 4:8
And the * points this out when Heb 7:17

PSALMS
Lord some of the * of David and of 2Ch 29:30
(This ends the * of David, son of Ps 72:20
Let us sing him * of praise. Ps 95:2
in the book of *: 'God said to my Lk 20:42,43
and in the * must all come true?" Lk 24:44
in the Book of *, where he says, Act 1:20
the book of * says about this? Rom 3:4
And again, in the book of *, we 1Co 3:20
the Lord, quoting * and hymns and Eph 5:19
sing them out in * and hymns and Col 3:16
No, for in the book of * David Heb 2:6
For he says in the book of *, Heb 2:12

PSALTERIES
using cymbals, *, and harps. 2Ch 29:25,26

PSALTERY
the hill playing a *, a timbrel, a 1Sa 10:5

PSALTRIES
upon *, harps, and cymbals. 1Ch 15:16
cymbals, *, and harps. Neh 12:27

PSALTRY
harp, sackbut, *, dulcimer, and Dan 3:5f
harp, sackbut, *, dulcimer, and Dan 3:7f
harp, sackbut, *, dulcimer, and Dan 3:10f

PTOLEMAIS
leaving Tyre was * where we greeted Act 21:7

PTOLEMY
the Great were * I of Egypt, Dan 8:8f
Literally, "the southern king"—* Dan 11:5f
In 252 B.C. * II of Egypt gave his Dan 11:6f
was the sister of * III, who now Dan 11:7f
* IV. Dan 11:10,11f
Probably Antiochus IV and * IV. Dan 11:27f

PUAH
were Shiphrah and *) to kill all Ex 1:15,16
(son of * and grandson of Dodo). Ju 10:1
Tola, *, Jashub, Shimron. 1Ch 7:1

PUBIC
and your * hair had grown; Eze 16:6,7

PUBLIC
gift to you as a * confirmation Gen 21:30
Then Abimelech made a * Gen 26:11
"But we've never had a * Gen 38:21
of all * and private debts. Lev 25:10
in a * sacrifice up on the hill. 1Sa 9:12,13
who has been in * service from the 1Sa 12:2
by the army and general * alike. 1Sa 18:5
David more than ever in the * eye. 1Sa 18:13
go to bed with them in * view. 2Sa 12:11
bodies from the * square at 2Sa 21:12,13,14
was superintendent of * works. 1Ki 4:1
* toilet, which it still is today. 2Ki 10:27
* administrators and judges. 1Ch 26:29
and * administration of that area. 1Ch 26:30
the religious and * affairs of the 1Ch 26:31,32
priests, also the * court, and 2Ch 4:9
as well as all the * prayers. 2Ch 6:29
Instead, I will make it a * 2Ch 7:20
who administered all * affairs. 2Ch 8:10
His * works program was also 2Ch 17:13
Then I called a * trial to deal Neh 5:7
all matters of * administration. Neh 11:24
For now I must face * Pro 5:14
father or mother is a * disgrace. Pro 19:26
It will be a * honor to me. Pro 27:11
a great * works program: homes, Ecc 2:4,5,6
home and all its * grounds—a canopy Is 4:5
expose yourself to * view. Is 47:2
"So I will make a * example of Eze 5:14
you may not mourn in * or console Eze 24:22
of the building open to the *." Eze 42:14
restricted area from the * places. Eze 42:16-20
sacrifices for * worship—sin Eze 45:17
section, is for * use—homes, Eze 48:15
belonging to the city, for * use. Eze 48:18
her nakedness in * for all her Hos 1:10
* testimony of your cure." Mt 8:4
plots will become * information. Mt 10:26
all your long, * prayers in the Mt 23:13,14
be baptized as a * announcement of Mk 1:4
in his * teaching, but afterwards, Mk 4:34
by praying long prayers in *. Mk 12:40
he began his * ministry to Israel. Lk 1:80
old when he began his * ministry. Lk 3:23-38
as a * announcement of your doom. Lk 10:11
*, but God knows your evil hearts. Lk 16:15
was Jesus' first * demonstration of Jn 2:11
staying out of the * eye. Jn 7:10
said, "No, he's duping the *." Jn 7:12
out for him in * for fear of Jn 7:13
But here he is preaching in *, Jn 7:26
Jesus now stopped his * ministry Jn 11:54
private that I have not said in *. Jn 18:20
and put them in the * jail. Act 5:18
to the general *, but to us who ate Act 10:40,41
testified to this in * witness. Act 13:31
spoke daily in the * square to all Act 17:17
arguments in * debate, showing by Act 18:28
and burned them at a * bonfire. Act 19:18,19
in * without covering her head? 1Co 11:13
But in * worship I would much 1Co 14:19
11:5), apparently in * meetings, 1Co 14:34f
him up to mocking and to * shame. Heb 6:6
he brought into * view, in these 1Pe 1:20

PUBLIC-SPIRITED
But some * citizens killed all 2Ch 33:25

PUBLICAN
to you as the Gentile and the *." Mt 18:17f

PUBLICANS
e., the *. Lk 7:29f

PUBLICITY
tried to avoid all * in order to Mk 9:30,31
PUBLICIZING
the ceremony, thus * his vow to Act 21:26,27
PUBLICLY
it, whatever is * agreed upon, and Gen 23:9
listened, speaking * before all the Gen 23:10
pieces of silver, as * agreed. Gen 23:16
judges and shall * bore his ear Ex 21:6
and they shall * be cut off from Lev 20:17
the people. * give him your Num 27:20
Then Moses replied *, giving them Num 36:5
shall be punished * and destroyed. Deu 7:10
this * validated the transaction. Ru 4:7
Meanwhile, Ahithophel—* disgraced 2Sa 17:23
So I opposed them *. Neh 13:15
But justify me *; Ps 7:7,8
I can praise you * before all the Ps 9:14
my earnest cry! * acquit me, Lord, Ps 17:2
I will * fulfill my vows in the Ps 22:25
I * praise the Lord for keeping Ps 26:12
to those who * declare that you Ps 31:19
Save me, and I will thank you * Ps 35:18
them alive; he * honors them and Ps 41:2
I will thank you * throughout Ps 57:9
is their God?" * avenge this Ps 79:10
his time and * disgraced him. Ps 89:45
Let them praise him * before the Ps 107:32
Do it *, so all will see that Ps 109:27
I WANT to express * before his Ps 111:1
I will * bring him the sacrifice Ps 116:14
the end of the line, * disgraced! Pro 25:6,7
I * proclaim bold promises; Is 45:19
addressed me * in the Temple while Jer 28:1
to Nebuchadnezzar to execute *. Jer 29:21
copy, and *, in the presence of my Jer 32:12
you * while all the nations watch. Eze 5:8
* denounce her terrible deeds. Eze 22:2
at every turn and * declared their Hos 9:8
he didn't want to * disgrace her. Mt 1:19
DON'T do your good deeds *, to be Mt 6:1
piety by praying * on street Mt 6:5
don't do it *, as the hypocrites Mt 6:16
"If anyone * acknowledges me as Mt 10:32
But if anyone * denies me, I Mt 10:33
that he couldn't * enter a city Mk 1:45
(But after John had * criticized Lk 3:19,20
will * honor you in the presence Lk 12:8
angels if you * acknowledge me here Lk 12:8
and Pharisees had * announced that Jn 11:57
"O men of Israel, listen! God * Act 2:22
They have * beaten us without Act 16:37
his message and * spoke against Act 19:9
truth, either * or in your homes. Act 20:20
And that is why a woman who * 1Co 11:5
or praying * in the church, and all 1Co 11:16
in the unknown language but not *. 1Co 14:28
that I have * boasted you would. 2Co 8:24
had to oppose him *, speaking Gal 2:11
PUBLISH
* his glorious acts throughout Ps 96:3
of the world, and * it abroad: The Jer 31:10
Shout it out in Egypt; * it in Jer 46:14
announcement, and * it throughout Amo 3:13
PUBLISHED
When this decree is * throughout Est 1:20
be * abroad in all the earth." Rom 9:17f
PUBLIUS
to *, the governor of the island. Act 28:7
As it happened, *' father was Act 28:8
PUDENS
and so do *, Linus, Claudia, and 2Ti 4:21
PUFF
A breath can * them away. Is 57:13
have disappeared with a * of wind; Jer 22:22
PUFFED
What are you so * up about? 1Co 4:7
afraid I might be * up by them; 2Co 12:7
they will be hotheaded, * up with 2Ti 3:4
PUL
Then King * of Assyria invaded 2Ki 15:19,20
Also called *, in verse 19 above. 2Ki 15:29f
So God caused King * of Assyria 1Ch 5:26
PULL
to * those censers from the fire; Num 16:36,37
of the elders, * his sandal from Deu 25:9
altar of Baal, and * it down, and Ju 6:25
of purchase to * off his sandal and Ru 4:7
* back and leave him there to die! 2Sa 11:15
he couldn't * it back again! 1Ki 13:4
Will he * the harrow for you? Job 39:10
of this peril. * me from the trap Ps 31:4
you down and * you from your home, Ps 52:5
* me out of this mire. Ps 69:14
Don't sidetrack; * back your Pro 4:27
adders will * it out unharmed. Is 11:8
with food; they * up their chairs Is 21:5
the Lord, "and * you down from Is 22:19
But the Lord will * out that Is 22:25
to those who * out the beard. Is 50:6
Build the roads, * out the Is 62:10
hand, I would * you off and give Jer 22:24,25
I will plant them and not * them Jer 24:6
and * Jeremiah out before he died. Jer 38:10
of Babylon, and * from his mouth Jer 51:44
I will * it out, roots and all! Eze 17:9
It will * out easily enough—it Eze 17:9
(Nebuchadnezzar will * out the Eze 17:16
your jaws and * you to your doom. Eze 38:4
I will reach down and * them up; Amo 9:2
of her mouth, and * from her teeth Zec 9:7
" 'Shall we * out the thistles?' Mt 13:28
He will fall into a ditch and * Lk 6:39
Temptation is the * of man's own Jas 1:14
PULLED
But the two men reached out and * Gen 19:10
got there, they * off his Gen 37:23
came by, his brothers * Joseph Gen 37:28
the man who had his sandal * off!' Deu 25:10
strong left hand, * out the Ju 3:21
he ran over and * Goliath's from 1Sa 17:50,51
but then he * out a dagger and 2Sa 3:27
in his hand and * the spear away 1Ch 11:23
have the beams * from his house and Ez 6:11
my clothing and * hair from my head Ez 9:3
them around and * out their hair; Neh 13:25
The arrow is * from his body—and Job 20:25
lovely myrrh as I * back the bolt. Sol 5:5
was ready, they * him out and Jer 38:13
jumped up, * out their swords and Jer 41:2
its wings were * off so that it Dan 7:4
they shall not be * up again," Amo 9:15
by side, * by prancing steeds! Nah 2:3
Your bow was * from its sheath Hab 3:8,9f
they are like a burning stick * Zec 3:2
The first chariot was * by red Zec 6:2
The chariot * by the black Zec 6:6
north, and the one * by white Zec 6:6
One of the men with Jesus * out a Mt 26:51
* a sword and slashed at the High Mk 14:47
in the boat and * the loaded net to Jn 21:8
by the hand and * him to his feet. Act 3:7,8
Then the sheet was * up again to Act 10:16
so they * up anchor and sailed Act 27:13
for they have been * out, roots and Jud 1:12
aren't * along into their sins. Jud 1:23
PULLING
stones they are * out of the Neh 4:1
gates, * chariots behind them. Eze 26:10
to them again. * out the believers, Act 19:9
sides, * him this way and that. Act 23:10
PULLS
yet anyone who * out the carcass Lev 11:36
If one falls, the other * him Ecc 4:10
The patch * away and leaves the Mk 2:21
PUN
The name given is a Hebrew *. Gen 30:6f
This is a Hebrew *. Jer 23:38,39f
PUNCH
Then he delivered his final * Est 5:12
PUNCHED
cursed them and * a few of them and Neh 13:25
PUNISH
But I will * the nation that Gen 15:14
"You have my permission to * the Gen 16:6
with barrenness to * Abimelech for Gen 20:18
Am I God, to judge and * you? Gen 50:19
"And when I * people for their Ex 20:5
I will * them for their sins." Ex 32:34
do to you: I will * you with sudden Lev 26:16
disobey me, I will * you seven Lev 26:18
sir, do not * us for this sin; Num 12:11
and that you * the father's fault Num 14:17,18
among them to * them, and many of Num 21:6
even though they * him, then his Deu 21:18
"We have sinned. * us in any way Ju 10:15
And may God * you if you hide 1Sa 3:16,17
* whichever one of us is guilty. 1Sa 24:15
other nations to * him, but my 2Sa 7:14
sin I will * the descendants of 1Ki 11:39
Have you come here to * my sins 1Ki 17:18
from heaven and * him if he is 2Ch 6:23
but I will * you with scorpions!" 2Ch 10:14
for God had decided to * Ahaziah 2Ch 22:7
Misery comes upon them to * them Job 5:6
fear, and God does not * them. Job 21:9
least God will * their children!' Job 21:19
But I say that God should * the Job 21:19
DON'T * me in the heat of your Ps 6:1
O Lord, arise and judge and * the Ps 9:19
they have caused. Now * them. Ps 10:14
And you do not * those who run Ps 18:25
Don't * me with all the wicked Ps 28:3
O LORD, DON'T * me while you are Ps 38:1
When you * a man for his sins, Ps 39:11
And Lord, don't * Israel for my Ps 51:18
Israel, arise and * the heathen Ps 59:5
I am ready, I will * the wicked! Ps 75:2
You stand up to * the evil-doers Ps 76:9
them, then I will * them, but I Ps 89:30,31,32
the nations—won't he also * you? Ps 94:10
Or, "but sent a plague to * Ps 106:15f
generation. * the sins of his Ps 109:1
He will * the nations, and fill Ps 110:
you * those who persecute me? Ps 119:8
quickly * them. Ps 140:1
him you will be prompt to * him. Pro 13:2
stop trying, the Lord will * them; Pro 15:9,1
He will * those who rejoice at Pro 17:
And to * nobles for being honest! Pro 17:2
* false witnesses. Pro 19:
* a mocker and others will learn Pro 19:2
If you injure them he will * you. Pro 22:22,2
Because God does not * sinners Ecc 8:1
and dare the Lord to * them. Is 5:19
"Hurry up and * us, O Lord," Is 5:19
the Assyrians and * them too—for Is 10:12
And I will * the world for its Is 13:1
On that day the Lord will * the Is 24:21
on the earth to * it will people Is 26:9
the heavens to * the people of the Is 26:21
swift sword and * leviathan, the Is 27:1
So God will * them by sending Is 28:11
The voice of the Lord shall * Is 30:31
and began to * them a little by Is 47:6
will not be sent by me to * you. Is 54:15
that's why he doesn't * those who Is 59:9
Will you stand silent and still * Is 64:12
For the Lord will * the world by Is 66:16
This is the way I will * my Jer 1:16
Your own wickedness will * you. Jer 2:19
I will * you severely because you Jer 2:35
Shall I not * them for this? Jer 5:9
Shouldn't I * a nation such as Jer 5:29
For I will * the people of this Jer 6:12
Should not I * them for such Jer 9:9
Lord, when I will * all those who Jer 9:25,26
you have done, and * your sins. Jer 14:10
Lord says, I will * these lying Jer 14:15
Jerusalem, I will * you so severely Jer 15:4
I will find you and * you. Jer 16:16
And I will * you doubly for all Jer 16:18
from God," I will * them and their Jer 23:34
of slavery are ended, I will * Jer 25:12
I will * them in proportion to Jer 25:14
I have begun to * my own people, Jer 25:29
I will * any nation refusing to Jer 27:8
I will * him and his family. Jer 29:32
I will * you, yes—you will not go Jer 30:11
that I have had to * you so much. Jer 30:15
I will * anyone who hurts them. Jer 30:20
I had to * him, but I still love Jer 31:20
and I will * him and his family Jer 36:31
I will * them in Egypt just as I Jer 44:13
and that I will * you here: I will Jer 44:29
says: I will * Amon, god of Thebes, Jer 46:25
I will * Pharaoh too, and all who Jer 46:25
I will * you, but only enough to Jer 46:28
I will * you for this, the Lord Jer 49:2
for when I * Edom, I will punish Jer 49:8
for when I punish Edom, I will * Jer 49:8
says: Now I will * the king of Jer 50:18
And I will * Bel, the god of Jer 51:44
coming when I will * this great Jer 51:47
sins, O Lord, and * them as you Lam 1:22
in their sins, but I will * you. Eze 3:18
for his death, and * you. Eze 3:20
you and will * you publicly while Eze 5:8
committed, I will * you more Eze 5:9
For I will * the minds and Eze 14:5
I the Lord will personally * Eze 14:6,7
I will * you as a murderess is Eze 16:38
surely I will * him for despising Eze 17:19
you, O Israel, and * or reward each Eze 18:30
so I will * you with the same Eze 23:31
When I * all the bordering Eze 28:26
And so I will greatly * Egypt Eze 30:19
with mine—I will * you for all your Eze 35:11
I am about to * King Jehu's dynasty Hos 1:4,5
I will * her, says the Lord. Hos 1:13
Therefore, I will * both priests Hos 4:9
But why should I * them? Hos 4:14
I will * her for all her evil Hos 7:12
of their sins and * them; Hos 8:13
He will surely * them. Hos 9:9
to * you for your heaped-up sins. Hos 10:10
No, I will not * you as much as Hos 11:9
and anxious not to * you. Joe 2:13
and * them there for harming my Joe 3:2
That is why I must * you the more Amo 3:2
same day that I * Israel for her Amo 3:14
fire he had prepared to * them; Amo 7:4
at Jerusalem's gates to * her. Mic 1:9
my enemies, and * them for all the Mic 7:9
of Judgment I will * the leaders Zep 1:8
Yes, I will * those who follow Zep 1:9
to find and * those who sit Zep 1:12
however much I * them, they Zep 3:7
and I promised to * them, and I Zec 8:14,15
I will * them—these goats. Zec 10:3
will * her with some other plague. Zec 14:18
Or by saying that God won't * Mal 2:17
* them shall get off scot-free.' Mal 3:14,15

(PUNISH Con't)
to * them without starting a riot. Act 4:21
'But I will * the nation that Act 7:7
in justice, will * anyone who does Rom 2:2
But he will terribly * those who Rom 2:8
He will * sin wherever it is Rom 2:12-15
He will * the heathen when they Rom 2:12-15
And God will * the Jews for Rom 2:12-15
Is it fair, then, for him to * us Rom 3:5
though he did not * those who Rom 3:25
and into Satan's hands, to * him, 1Co 5:5
Like an athlete I * my body, 1Co 9:27
I come ready to * severely and I 2Co 13:2
need to scold and * when I come; 2Co 13:10
to * you but to make you strong. 2Co 13:10
the Lord will * you terribly for 1Th 4:6
over to Satan to * them until they 1Ti 1:20
The Lord will * him, but be 2Ti 4:14
promised, or to * him if he later Heb 6:16
If God doesn't * you when you Heb 12:8
as other fathers * their sons, then Heb 12:8
earth, though they * us, should we Heb 12:9
for God will surely * all those Heb 13:4
has sent them to * all who do 1Pe 2:14
and continue to * the ungodly until 2Pe 2:9
unexpected as a thief, and * you. Rev 3:3
I continually discipline and * Rev 3:19
so I must * you, unless you turn Rev 3:19

PUNISHED
kills Cain will be * seven times, Gen 4:24
should be * seventy-seven times!" Gen 4:24
female—that man shall surely be *. Ex 21:20
*—for the slave is his property. Ex 21:21
a father's sins be * in the sons Ex 34:7
shall be * publicly and destroyed. Deu 7:10
entire nation was * in addition to Jos 22:20
Thus God * both Abimelech and Ju 9:56,57
we have * the village of Gibe-ah. Ju 20:8,9,10
* me in a way that injures you." Ru 1:13
And after you have * them, help 1Ki 8:35,36
He * them by delivering them to 2Ki 17:20
the census and * Israel for it. 1Ch 21:7
because you have * us, then listen 2Ch 6:26
"My father * you with whips, but 2Ch 10:14
the king shall be * immediately by Ez 7:26
(and we have been * far less than Ez 9:13
them! You * them in order to turn Neh 9:29
Every time you * us you were Neh 9:33
and innocent person who was *? Job 4:7,8
him, and he * them, and you begged Job 8:4
sin, a crime that should be *. Job 31:11
too, must be * by the judges. Job 31:28
I am horribly *, even though I Job 34:6
And after you have * me, give me Ps 51:8
They demand that I be * for what Ps 69:4
I will see how the wicked are * Ps 91:8
yet * them when they went wrong. Ps 99:8
He has not * us as we deserve Ps 103:10
The Lord has * me, but not Ps 118:18
I used to wander off until you * Ps 119:67
word for it—proud men shall be *. Pro 16:5
they shall be severely *. Pro 17:11
A false witness shall be * and a Pro 19:9
and rebels shall be severely *. Pro 19:29
learn only by seeing scorners *. Pro 21:11
A false witness must be *; Pro 21:28
Those who obey him will not be * Ecc 8:5
Has God * Israel as much as he Is 27:7,8
as much as he has * her enemies? Is 27:7,8
while he has * Israel but a Is 27:7,8
I have * your children but it Jer 2:30
* them, but they won't change! Jer 5:3
This is the city to be *, for she Jer 6:6
be * for planning to kill you. Jer 11:21,22
groans: "You have * me greatly; Jer 31:18
in Egypt just as I * them in Jer 44:13
land as I * the king of Assyria. Jer 50:18
* Jerusalem for all her many sins; Lam 1:5
them as you have * me, for my sighs Lam 1:22
and complain when * for our sins? Lam 3:39
Israel will be * for 390 years by Eze 4:4,5
words—all will be * for their sins, Eze 14:10
as a murderess is * and as a woman Eze 16:38
are * for their fathers' sins? Eze 18:2
The son shall not be * for his Eze 18:20
I had * them for all their sins. Eze 35:4,5
that is how I * them for the evil Eze 36:19
I turned my face away and * them Eze 39:24
be * for their unfaithfulness. Eze 44:10
the Lord God, that they must be *. Eze 44:12
They are guilty and must be *. Hos 10:2
Judah also will be justly * for Hos 12:2
bring back his * people—sick and Mic 4:6
"O my people, I have * you Nah 1:12
It caught up with them and * Zec 1:5,6
all be * if they refuse to come. Zec 14:19
He will be severely *, for Lk 12:47
punishment will be * only lightly. Lk 12:48
be exposed and they would be *. Jn 3:20
to Jerusalem in chains to be *. Act 22:5
and should be *, you are talking Rom 2:1
be afraid, for he will have you *. Rom 13:4
to keep from being *, and second, Rom 13:5
will not need to be judged and *. 1Co 11:31
Yet, when we are judged and * by 1Co 11:32
He has been * enough by your 2Co 2:5,6
have seen a wrong, it must be *. 2Co 13:1
They will be * in everlasting 2Th 1:9
have always been * for disobeying Heb 2:2
Being * isn't enjoyable while it Heb 12:11
Praise the Lord if you are * for 1Pe 2:19
they will be * for the way they 1Pe 4:5
their bodies were * with death, 1Pe 4:6
is a hell in which sinners are *. Jud 1:7
and she was * to the last drop of Rev 16:19
sins, or you will be * with her. Rev 18:4
He has * the Great Prostitute who Rev 19:2

PUNISHES
that, as a man * his son, the Lord Deu 8:5
son, the Lord * you to help you. Deu 8:5
Rather, he * the sinners. Job 34:11
even return to him when he * them. Job 36:13
in nature he * or blesses the Job 36:31
* the wicked in their own snares! Ps 9:16
* all who haughtily reject him. Ps 31:23
ears and eyes? He * the Ps 94:10
Just as a father * a son he Pro 3:11,12
For the king * those who disobey. Ecc 8:2,3
Lord your God, who * you for your Is 48:17
while the Lord * me, for I have Mic 7:9
be angry when the Lord * you. Heb 12:5
For when he * you, it proves Heb 12:6
one who justly * and makes war. Rev 19:11

PUNISHING
God is * us for our sins. Gen 44:16
that is why I am * the people Lev 18:25
God is doubtless * you far less Job 11:6
you are good that he is * you? Job 22:4
that God had just cause for * him. Job 32:2
understand your * us in the barren Ps 44:19
are, so he helps us by * us. Ps 94:12,13
with you and stop * him! Pro 24:18
of * you for all your evil deeds. Eze 7:8,9
They will burn your homes, * you Eze 16:40,41
I will no longer turn away from * Amo 7:8
this time without * you, to give Rom 2:4
it up [* the man who sinned 2Co 7:11

PUNISHMENT
"This is your *: You are singled Gen 3:14
Cain replied to the Lord, "My * Gen 4:13
times your * to anyone who does." Gen 4:15
will not be ready for * until Gen 15:16
their sins, the * continues upon Ex 20:5
You will not escape * if you do. Ex 20:7
animal, for they deserve their *. Lev 20:16
their * is that they shall bear Lev 20:20
times greater * for your sins. Lev 26:28
they accept the * I send them for Lev 26:40,41
shall accept their * for rejecting Lev 26:43
shall be the * he thought the other Deu 19:19
be given lest the * seem too Deu 25:1
And I decree the * of all her Deu 32:35
their just * for these murders. Ju 9:24
Ordinary sin receives heavy *, 1Sa 2:23,24,25
entire family with * because his 1Sa 3:13
he has received his * for his 1Sa 25:39
And now, even after our * in Ez 9:13
no longer live in terror of his *. Job 9:34
danger of * for your attitude." Job 19:29
bitter one, and my * far more Job 23:2
by instant * of the tyrants. Job 35:12
gives them their full share of *. Job 36:6
as *, or, in his lovingkindness, Job 37:13
They do not see your * awaiting Ps 10:5
Give them the * they so richly Ps 28:4
complaint, for my * is from you. Ps 39:9
now your time of * has come, and I Ps 50:21
you forever and ever for your *. Ps 52:9
This is the Lord's * upon my Ps 109:20
The * you gave me was the best Ps 119:71,72
your * was right and did me good. Ps 119:75,76,77
to execute his * upon the nations. Ps 149:6,7
for his * is proof of his love. Pro 3:11,12
if they rebel against that *, Pro 15:9,10
purposes—even the wicked, for *. Pro 16:4
king stamps out crime by severe *. Pro 20:26
* that hurts chases evil from the Pro 20:30
but * will drive it out of him. Pro 22:15
* will keep them out of hell. Pro 23:13,14
haven't you had enough of *? Is 1:5,6
Your well-earned * is on the Is 3:11
For after all this * you will Is 9:13
When your * was on them, they Is 26:16
language they can understand is *! Is 28:11
So scoff no more, lest your * be Is 28:22
who had been his rod of *. Is 30:31
blessings as he gave her * before. Is 40:2
a * from God, for his own sins! Is 53:4
for—that he was suffering their *? Is 53:8
carry out my threats of *." Jer 1:12
For I will pour out terrible * Jer 14:16
Even after *, will there be no Jer 14:19
he had sent them as slaves for *. Jer 16:14,15
is God's decree of * against King Jer 22:18
No, you shall not evade *. Jer 25:29
Lord of Hosts, the * shall go from Jer 25:32
withhold all the * I am ready to Jer 26:3
* he has announced against you. Jer 26:13
* he had pronounced against them. Jer 26:19
Why do you protest your *? Jer 30:15
For I am sorry for all the * I Jer 42:10
for Egypt, a time of great *. Jer 46:20,21
God gives just * and is giving Jer 51:56
the fact that * was sure to come. Lam 1:9
a year of * ahead for Israel. Eze 4:4,5
to signify the years of Judah's *. Eze 4:6
and to waste away beneath their *. Eze 4:17
then by the lighter * they get. Eze 16:52
Your terrible * will be a Eze 16:54
This is part of your * for all Eze 16:58
And now the time of * has come. Eze 21:24
I will feed them, yes—feed them * Eze 34:15,16
all shall see the * of Gog and Eze 39:21
to exile—it was * for sin, for they Eze 39:23
of further * upon Jerusalem and Dan 9:24
When your day of * comes, you will Hos 5:9
harvest of * waiting—and I wanted Hos 6:11
The time of Israel's * has come; Hos 9:7
Therefore * will spring up among Hos 10:4
harvested and stored away for *. Hos 13:12
Alas, this terrible day of * Joe 1:15
on; your * is well deserved. Amo 3:5
Lord in the dread day of your *. Amo 5:13
You push away all thought of * Amo 6:3
my people Israel—ripe for *. Amo 8:2
I will not defer their * again. Amo 8:2
You drank my cup of * upon my Ob 1:16
God's * on Israel for her sins. Mic 3:8
your time of * is almost here; Mic 7:4
will send terrible * upon you, and Mal 2:1
they shall go away into eternal *; Mt 25:46
Because of this, their * will be Mk 12:40
* on the Judgment Day than you. Lk 10:14
than facing the * in store for Lk 17:2,3
laid his hand of * upon you, and Act 13:11
Silas to the City Council for *. Act 17:5
saving up terrible * for yourselves Rom 2:5
Jesus to take the * for our sins Rom 3:25
Yes, Adam's sin brought * to Rom 5:18
to obey God, and * will follow. Rom 13:2
Shall I come with * and scolding, 1Co 4:21
he won't bring * upon himself when 1Co 11:34
of * their wicked deeds deserve. 2Co 11:15
* for those who are hurting you. 2Th 1:6
but the terrible * of God's awful Heb 10:27
more terrible the * will be for Heb 10:29
do wrong, our * will be greater Jas 3:1
* must follow—that they will fall. 1Pe 2:8
we like without fear of God's *. Jud 1:4
to receive just *, and to prove the Jud 1:15

PUNISHMENTS
the Lord's * or seen his greatness Deu 11:2
lawsuits and *), and shall wash Deu 21:5
And hurl my * upon my enemies! Deu 32:40,41
I fear your *. Ps 119:120
O Lord, you are just and your * Ps 119:137
"And the Lord says: Four great * Eze 14:21
At that time my * will be quick Mal 3:5
your * are just and true." Rev 16:7

PUNITES
The *, named after their ancestor Num 26:23-25

PUNNING
Here is an example of serious * Is 5:7f

PUNON
Zalmonah, then at *, then at Num 33:42

PUNS
Many Hebrew names are based on *. Gen 3:20f
frequent * in the prophetic books. Jer 29:24f
by the use of * their failures. Mic 1:11f
by the use of * their failures. Mic 1:11f
by the use of * their failures. Mic 1:11f

PUNY
He is amused by all their * Ps 2:4
bother with mere * man, to pay any Ps 8:4
last they know they are but * men. Ps 9:20
to him. How * in his sight is the Ps 147:10
to terrify the earth. * man! Is 2:22
Their horses are * flesh, not Is 31:3
be embarrassed at their * might. Mic 7:16
birds and animals and snakes and * Rom 1:23
Do not let sin control your * Rom 6:12

PUPIL
Protect me as you would the * of Ps 17:8

PUPPIES
she replied, "for even the * Mt 15:27
sir, but even the * under the table Mk 7:28

PUR
dice" in Persian is "*." Est 9:26

PURAH
along your servant * if you like— Ju 7:10
So he took * and crept down Ju 7:11

PURCHASE
as often as you like to * grain.' Gen 42:34

(PURCHASE Con't)
"However, you may * slaves from Lev 25:44
you, and you may * the children of Lev 25:45
as we go, but will * every bite we Deu 2:28
You have the first right to * it Ru 4:4
Then Boaz told him, "Your * of Ru 4:5
a right of * to pull off his sandal Ru 4:7
to Egypt to * entire herds at 2Ch 1:16
and to * building materials—stone 2Ch 34:10,11
primarily for the * of oxen, rams, Ez 7:17
We also needed to * the other Neh 10:33
Topaz from Ethiopia cannot * it, Job 28:19
you the first right to * it." Jer 32:8
sealed the deed of * before Jer 32:10
sold everything he owned to * it! Mt 13:46
pour out to * back your souls. Lk 22:20
and gave himself to * our 1Co 1:30
And to * from me white garments, Rev 3:18

PURCHASED
field Abraham had * from Ephron the Gen 25:9,10
traders, he was * from them by Gen 39:1
Abraham * from the sons of Heth." Gen 49:32
slave who has been * may eat it if Ex 12:44
A firstborn donkey may be * back Ex 13:13
Your people whom you * Ex 15:16
with it I have * Ruth the Ru 4:10
agents * them at wholesale prices. 1Ki 10:28
flocks of sheep and goats he *; 2Ch 32:28,29
of wine they * with stolen money. Amo 2:8
of Israel— and * a field from the Mt 27:10
went out and * embalming spices. Mk 16:1
flock—his church, * with his Act 20:28
God has already * us and that he Eph 1:14
They have been * from among the Rev 14:4

PURE
where nuggets of * gold are Gen 2:11,12
and outside with * gold, with a Ex 25:11
"And make a lid of * gold, 3¾ Ex 25:17
Overlay it with * gold, and run Ex 25:24
"Make a lampstand of *, beaten Ex 25:31
to be one piece of *, beaten gold. Ex 25:36
trays are to be made of * gold. Ex 25:38
pounds of * gold for the Ex 25:39
to bring you * olive oil to use in Ex 27:20
Two chains of *, twisted gold Ex 28:13,14
of two twisted cords of * gold. Ex 28:22,23,24
"Next, make a plate of * gold Ex 28:36
of the altar with * gold, and run a Ex 30:3
of * myrrh; half as much of Ex 30:22,23
galbanum, and * frankincense, Ex 30:34
it shall be a * and holy incense. Ex 30:35
instruments; the * gold lampstand Ex 31:8
gold, and the rings were * gold. Ex 36:34
It was plated with * gold inside Ex 37:2
Then, from * gold, he made a lid Ex 37:6
It was overlaid with * gold, Ex 37:11
Next, using * gold, he made the Ex 37:15,16
again using *, beaten gold. Ex 37:17
all one piece of *, beaten gold. Ex 37:22
and the ashtrays, all of * gold. Ex 37:23,24
weighed 107 pounds, all * gold. Ex 37:23,24
He overlaid it all with * gold Ex 37:26
priests, and the * incense, using Ex 37:29
Bells of * gold were placed Ex 39:25,26
the holy plate of * gold to wear on Ex 39:30
The * [gold Ex 39:33-40
what is * and what is impure; Lev 10:10
Keep yourselves * concerning Lev 11:44
will be ceremonially * again." Lev 12:8
to bring you * olive oil for an Lev 24:1
the lampstand of * gold which Lev 24:3,4
a bushel for each. * frankincense Lev 24:5-8
But if she is * and has not Num 5:28
order to be made ceremonially *; Num 31:23
To those who are *, 2Sa 22:27
You show yourself *; 2Sa 22:27
and 96 gallons of * olive oil. 1Ki 5:11
were overlaid with * gold, and 1Ki 6:20
the cedar altar—with * gold; 1Ki 6:21,22
and overlaid it with * gold. 1Ki 10:18
and ceiling overlaid with * gold! 2Ch 3:4
wood, plated with * gold, and 2Ch 3:5
firepans—all were made of * gold. 2Ch 4:22
ivory throne overlaid with * gold. 2Ch 9:17
God? More * than his Creator?' Job 4:17
them— if you were * and good, he Job 8:6
You claim you are * in the eyes Job 11:4
earth can be as * and righteous as Job 15:14
be absolutely * compared with him! Job 15:15
I am innocent, and my prayer is *. Job 16:17
those with * hearts shall become Job 17:9
even sinners by your * hands." Job 22:30
innocent—as * as solid gold! Job 23:10
again— 'I am *, I am innocent; Job 33:9
me for doing right and being *. Ps 18:20
is right, and I am * of heart. Ps 18:24
You give blessings to the * but Ps 18:26
God's laws are *, eternal, just. Ps 19:9
are * and need never be changed." Ps 19:9f
Only those with * hands and Ps 24:4
Let me be * again. Ps 51:2
those whose hearts are *. Ps 73:1
Why take the trouble to be *? Ps 73:13
How can a young man stay *? Ps 119:9
Literally, "but kind words are * Pro 15:26f
what he does is * and right. Pro 20:11
made—a purple gown of * linen. Pro 31:22
fair as the moon, * as the sun, so Sol 6:10
Once so *, but now diluted like Is 1:22
How long before you will be *? Jer 13:27
waters and make them fresh and *. Eze 47:8
them and make them * until the Dan 11:35
of my returning people to * Hebrew Zep 3:9
the peoples to a * speech. " Zep 3:9f
fire and make them *, as gold and Zec 13:9
* offerings in honor of my name. Mal 1:11
their work for God with * hearts. Mal 3:3
are *, for they shall see God. Mt 5:8
"If your eye is *, there will be Mt 6:22
inward being. A * eye lets sunshine Lk 11:34
Make them * and holy through Jn 17:17
for you have been made * and Rom 15:15,16
he made us * and holy 1Co 1:30
among you, so that you can stay *. 1Co 5:7
Let us feast instead upon the * 1Co 5:8
Literally, "* in body and in 1Co 7:34f
we have been * and sincere, quietly 2Co 1:12
that they are * in this matter, and 2Co 5:11
alone, just as a * maiden saves her 2Co 11:2
led away from your * and simple 2Co 11:3
Think about things that are * and Php 4:8
we have been * and honest and 1Th 2:10
you to be holy and *, and to keep 1Th 4:3,4
But concerning the * brotherly 1Th 4:9
you entirely * and devoted to God; 1Th 5:23
that comes from * hearts, and that 1Ti 1:5
spotless and * in his Spirit, was 1Ti 3:16
only * thoughts about them. 1Ti 5:2
love the Lord and have * hearts. 2Ti 2:22
A person who is * of heart sees Tit 1:15
covered on all sides with * gold. Heb 9:4
had to be made * by Moses in this Heb 9:23
copies, were made * with far more Heb 9:23
have been washed with * water. Heb 10:22
marriage and its vows, and be *; Heb 13:4
The Christian who is * and Jas 1:27
* and full of quiet gentleness. Jas 3:17
to make them * and true to him. Jas 4:8
it is kept in heaven for you, * 1Pe 1:4
whether or not it is strong and *. 1Pe 1:7
you are holy and *, you are God's 1Pe 2:9
by your respectful, * behavior. 1Pe 3:1
to stay * because Christ is pure. 1Jn 3:3
to stay pure because Christ is *. 1Jn 3:3
who were once * and holy, but Jud 1:6
"My advice to you is to buy * Rev 3:18
clean and *, so you won't be naked Rev 3:18
undefiled, * as virgins, Rev 14:4
The city itself was *, Rev 21:18,19,20
And the main street was *, Rev 21:21
to me a river of * Water of Life, Rev 22:1

PURE-BLOODED
been born into a * Jewish home that Php 3:5

PURENESS
is no * in them to bring out. Jer 6:29

PURER
Literally, "were * than snow, Lam 4:7f
But others have * motives, Php 1:15

PUREST
worth of * silver to be used for 1Ch 29:4,5
wash myself with * water and Job 9:30
purchase it, nor even the * gold. Job 28:19
all he says is * truth, like Ps 12:6
You set a kingly crown of * gold Ps 21:3
My gifts are better than the * Pro 8:19
His head is * gold, and he has Sol 5:11
statue was made of * gold, its Dan 2:32
with a belt of * gold around his Dan 10:5,6
dishes made of * gold—the very best 2Ti 2:21

PURGE
* the altar by making atonement Ex 29:36
In this way you will * all evil Deu 17:7
Don't pity him! * all murderers Deu 19:13
In this way you will * out evil Deu 19:19
to * the evil from among you. Deu 24:7
them and * Israel of her evil." Ju 20:13
the expenses involved in this *." Est 3:9
Literally, "* me with hyssop." Ps 51:7f
It was to * away Is 27:9
me—I will * from among you. Eze 20:38

PURGED
Such sinners must be * from Deu 17:12
he reformed and * Israel so that Ju 3:10
after he had * the land and cleaned 2Ch 34:8
So I * out the foreigners, and Neh 13:30
with yeast was * from every Jewish Mt 26:17

PURIFICATION
continue in her blood of *." Lev 12:5f
"When these days of * are ended Lev 12:6
to be used for the * ceremony of Lev 14:4
Do this by sprinkling water of * Num 8:7
* ceremonies, for removal of sin. Num 19:9
further purified with the * water. Num 31:
the * ceremony for themselves. Jos 3
you must undergo * rites in Jos 7:
And he performed the * rite on 1Sa 16
at that time for ceremonial *. 1Sa 21
(She had just completed the * 2Sa 11
perform the ceremonies of *. 1Ch 23:
had undergone the * rites for 2Ch 5:11,
not undergone the * rites, the 2Ch 30:17,18,
and performing the * ceremonies as Neh 12:4
When the time came for Mary's * Lk 2:2
sacrifice for *—"either a pair of Lk 2:2
Literally, "about *." Jn 3:2
Literally, "the days of *." Act 21:26,2

PURIFIED
then he shall be * again and may Lev 22:
The Levites * themselves and Num 8:2
place them in some * place outside Num 19:
then he will be *; Num 19:1
To become * again, ashes from Num 19:1
it must then be further * with Num 31:2
shall be * by the water alone.' Num 31:2
clothes and be *, and then you may Num 31:2
The water was *, just as Elisha 2Ki 2:2
You have * us with fire, Ps 66:1
Silver and gold are * by fire, Pro 17:
Many shall be * by great trials Dan 12:1
silver are refined and * by fire. Zec 13:
gold from me, gold * by fire—only Rev 3:1

PURIFIES
by fire, but God * hearts. Pro 17:
tests gold and * it—and your faith 1Pe 1:

PURIFY
of atonement over them to * them. Num 8:2
"And tell the people to * Num 11:1
days, and must * himself the third Num 19:1
and does not * himself in the Num 19:1
and doesn't * himself shall be Num 19:2
a dead body. Then * yourselves and Num 31:1
Remember also to * all your Num 31:2
to the Lord. * yourselves and come 1Sa 16:5
Then I commanded the Levites to * Neh 13:22
of the Lord; * yourselves, all you Is 52:11
no blemishes, to * the Temple. Eze 45:18
He will * the Levites, the Mal 3:3
or spirit, and * ourselves, living 2Co 7:1

PURIFYING
* his land Deu 32:40,41

PURIM
is called "*," because the word Est 9:26
his annual Feast of *. Est 9:29-31
as the Feast of *, decreed by both Est 9:29-31

PURITY
How can you demand * in one born Job 14:4
in white, the symbol of all *. Ps 132:9
The * of silver and gold can be Pro 27:21
as the outside? * is best Lk 11:41
about your *, and yet you let this 1Co 5:6
sees goodness and * in everything; Tit 1:15

PURPLE
blue cloth, * cloth, scarlet cloth, Ex 25:1
wide, dyed blue, *, and scarlet, Ex 26:1
make a veil from blue, *, and Ex 26:31
*, and scarlet fine-twined linen. Ex 26:36
embroidered blue, *, and scarlet Ex 27:16
using blue, *, and scarlet threads Ex 28:5,6
*, and scarlet fine-twined linen. Ex 28:8
use the same gold, blue, *, and Ex 28:15
with blue, *, and scarlet Ex 28:33,34
Blue, *, and scarlet cloth, made Ex 35:5-9
Others brought blue, *, and Ex 35:23
prepared blue, *, and scarlet Ex 35:25
designers in blue, *, and scarlet Ex 35:35
blue, *, and scarlet linen, with Ex 36:8,9
The blue, *, and scarlet inner Ex 36:35
with blue, *, and scarlet. Ex 36:37
with blue, *, and scarlet thread. Ex 38:18
embroidering blue, *, and scarlet Ex 38:23
garments of blue, *, and scarlet Ex 39:1
the blue, *, and scarlet linen; Ex 39:3
same gold, blue, *, and scarlet Ex 39:4,5
gold, blue, *, and scarlet linen. Ex 39:8
with blue, *, and scarlet. Ex 39:24
with blue, *, and scarlet threads, Ex 39:28,29
shall be covered with a * cloth. Num 4:13
and send me weavers to make *, 2Ch 2:7
in the dying of * and blue linen 2Ch 2:14
and blue, fastened with * ribbons Est 1:6
of fine linen and * thread." Est 1:6f
of fine linen and *, and went out Est 8:15
made—a * gown of pure linen. Pro 31:22
its canopy gold, the seat is *; Sol 3:10
* robes that expert tailors make. Jer 10:9
bright with * and scarlet dyes from Eze 27:7
They bring emeralds, * dyes, Eze 27:16
will be dressed in * robes of royal Dan 5:7
will clothe you in * robes, with a Dan 5:16
was robed in *, and a golden chain Dan 5:29
dressed him in a * robe, and made a Mk 15:16,17
they took off the * robe and put Mk 15:20
his head and robed him in royal *. Jn 19:2

PURPLE Con't)
crown of thorns and the * robe. Jn 19:5
Thyatira, a merchant of * cloth. Act 16:14
The woman wore * and scarlet Rev 17:4
linens, * silks, and scarlet; Rev 18:12
clothed in finest * and scarlet Rev 18:16

•URPOSE
for that *. Gen 8:20
me a piece of ground for this *." Gen 23:4
to accomplish the * of my journey. Gen 24:12
his nation. The * of this law is Lev 17:5
shelters. The * of this is to Lev 23:43
in a place set apart for the *. Lev 24:9
a blue cord. The * of this Num 15:39
will live. The * of these laws is Deu 6:2
you, 'What is the * of these laws Deu 6:20
and herds. The * of tithing is to Deu 14:23
for this *, the penalty is death. Deu 17:12
"Here is an example of the * of Deu 19:4
your God. The * of this command is Deu 20:18
Then Joshua explained again the * Jos 4:21
flint knives for this *. Jos 5:2,3
set aside for this * on the east Jos 20:8
and drop them on * for her to Ru 2:16
for that * by his father David. 1Ki 7:51
* of helping David become king. 1Ch 12:24-37
with the single * of making David 1Ch 12:38
God has chosen them for this *; 1Ch 15:2
set aside for that *, just as the 1Ch 16:40
for this * was 22,000 oxen and 2Ch 7:4,5
Levites for this *, including 2Ch 17:7,8,9
And I know that your * for me is Job 30:23
God's * in this is that man Ecc 3:14
to accomplish his *, then he will Is 10:12
For this is his * and plan. Is 14:24
to fulfill my righteous *, and I Is 45:13
priest, have one * in mind—to get Jer 8:10
the Holy Ones. The * of this decree Dan 4:17
"The * of these laws was to Mal 2:5
continue until its * is achieved. Mt 5:18
for a spiritual *, don't do it Mt 6:16
good health. My * is to invite Lk 5:32
has sent me for this very *." Jn 6:27
The thief 's * is to steal, Jn 10:10
and destroy. My * is to give life Jn 10:10
it he said, "The * of his illness Jn 11:4
interested in the * of my going; Jn 16:5
"I was born for that *. Jn 18:37
"His * in all of this is that Act 17:27
sins serve a good *, for people Rom 3:5
Egypt for the very * of displaying Rom 9:17
Of course not! His * was to make Rom 11:11
He is sent by God for that very * Rom 13:4
for this very *, so that he can be Rom 14:9
came for the very * of suffering Rom 15:3
one mind, united in thought and *. 1Co 1:10
to the goal with * in every step. 1Co 9:26
That was my * even more than to 2Co 7:12
and this was his *: that when Eph 1:10
God's * in this was that we Eph 1:12
you for just this *, to let you Eph 6:22
with one strong *—to tell the Good Php 1:27
with one heart and mind and *. Php 2:2
only * in life is to please him. 2Ti 1:3
God chose him for this * long 1Pe 1:20
whose whole * in life is to enjoy Jud 1:18
in Jesus. The * of all prophecy and Rev 19:10

PURPOSED
Literally, "* in the spirit." Act 19:21f

PURPOSELY
He did this *. Gen 48:14

PURPOSES
used for other *, but never eaten. Lev 7:24
was used only for * of divination. 2Ki 16:15
"Do you know the mind and * of Job 11:7
and who can turn him from his *? Job 23:13
"I will reveal the everlasting * Ps 2:7
*—even the wicked, for punishment. Pro 16:4
Jewish ceremonial * and held Jn 2:6
of God, to be used for his good *. Rom 6:13
good laws for its own evil *. Rom 7:13
false motives or evil * in mind; 1Th 2:3
can use you for his highest *. 2Ti 2:21
will carry out his *: They will Rev 17:17

PURSE
though you were safe inside his *! 1Sa 25:29

PURSED
into space with * lips, deep in Pro 16:30

PURSES
and capes and ornate combs and *; Is 3:22
This will fatten your * in Lk 12:33
And the * of heaven have no rips Lk 12:33

PURSUE
Gad, but he shall rob and * them! Gen 49:19
Yes, though none * they shall Lev 26:37
All these devastations shall * Deu 28:22
"All these curses shall * and Deu 28:45

PURSUED
attacked them and * the fleeing Gen 14:15
officers. He * the people of Ex 14:8

PURSUERS
their * and began killing them. Jos 8:20,21

for my * are getting very close. Ps 35:3

PURSUES
flood; he * them all night long. Nah 1:8

PURSUING
they shall fall when no one is * Lev 26:36
As the men of Israel were * and Jos 10:12
with the Angel of the Lord * them. Ps 35:6

PURSUIT
he set out in hot * and caught up Gen 31:23
Wisdom is the main * of sensible Pro 17:24
Go after them in fierce * and Lam 3:66

PUS
My flesh breaks open, full of *. Job 7:5
are festering and full of *. Ps 38:5,6

PUSH
To * against the nations Deu 33:17
that you will * the Syrians around 1Ki 22:11
Gehazi began to * her away, but 2Ki 4:27
stand against them. * them back! Ps 17:13,14
Don't let their wicked hands * me Ps 36:11
God will * them down just as a Is 25:11
here, to * me from my Temple? Eze 8:6
For these shepherds * and butt Eze 34:21
and * them into the dust!" Dan 4:37
at them now. You * away all Amo 6:3
help to * you out of your land. Ob 1:7
built, to * him over the cliff. Lk 4:29
its owner, to * out a little into Lk 5:3
They tried to * through the crowd Lk 5:18,19
who * away the truth from them. Rom 1:18
who loves to * himself forward as 3Jn 1:9

PUSHED
the people were * out of Egypt and Ex 12:39
Then Samson * against the pillars Ju 16:29
Then the girl's husband * her out Ju 19:25
He is the one who * the oceans Ps 24:2
and he * her back into the basket Zec 5:8
the stretcher, and * his way Mk 2:12
First a leaf-blade * through, and Mk 4:28

PUSHES
* down the water with his hands. Is 25:11

PUSHING
Jesus went with him, * through Lk 8:42
"He's * some foreign religion." Act 17:18

PUT
And I will * the fear of you into Gen 3:15
Then the Lord * an identifying Gen 4:15
for, as Eve * it, "God has Gen 4:25
deck—and * a door in the side. Gen 6:16
Ham were:Cush, Mizraim,*, Canaan. Gen 10:6
Literally, "* his hand under the Gen 24:9f
room to * us up for the night?" Gen 24:23
instructed Jacob to * them on. Gen 27:15
your God * it in my path!" Gen 27:20
everything. Now * everything I Gen 31:36,37
and to * on fresh clothing. Gen 35:2
his garments and * on sackcloth and Gen 37:34
Soon he was * in charge of the Gen 39:4
a couple of us and * me and the Gen 41:10
man in Egypt and * him in charge of Gen 41:33
instructions to * each brother's Gen 42:25
fathers, must have * it there, for Gen 43:23
could carry—and to * into the mouth Gen 44:1
He was also told to * Joseph's Gen 44:2
And if any of them are capable, * Gen 47:5,6
older. * your right hand on him!" Gen 48:18
(Note that he * Ephraim Gen 48:20
Let's figure out a way to * an Ex 1:10
slaves of them and * brutal Ex 1:11
it with tar, * the baby in it, and Ex 2:3
"Now * it in again," Jehovah Ex 4:7
wife and sons and * them on a Ex 4:20
a container and * three quarts of Ex 16:33
dies shall surely be * to death. Ex 21:12
mother shall surely be * to death. Ex 21:15
father shall surely be * to death. Ex 21:17
"A sorceress shall be * to Ex 22:18
never let an innocent person be * Ex 23:7
Literally, "* into the Ark the Ex 25:16f
gold around it. * a molding four Ex 25:25
Make four golden rings and * the Ex 25:26,27
To carry it, * the poles into Ex 27:7
Then * Aaron's robe on him, and Ex 29:5
a bronze pedestal. * it between the Ex 30:17,18
Beat some of it very fine and * Ex 30:36
goes by, I will * you in the cleft Ex 33:22
them, he * a veil over his face; Ex 34:33
Afterwards he would * the veil on Ex 34:35
with gold, and * the poles into Ex 37:5
THE LORD NOW said to Moses, "* Ex 40:2
Then bring his sons and * their Ex 40:14
the Tabernacle was * together. Ex 40:17
the framework, and * on the top Ex 40:19
the altar, and * the sections of Lev 1:8
them to the Lord. * olive oil and Lev 2:15
Then the priest shall * some of Lev 4:7
Then he shall * blood upon the Lev 4:18
with olive oil or * any incense on Lev 5:11
the priest shall * on his linen Lev 6:10
and * them beside the altar. Lev 6:10
The priest shall * on fresh wood Lev 6:12

Then he * on him the chestpiece Lev 8:8
anything it touches must be * Lev 11:32
The priest will * it away for Lev 13:50
trouble, it can be * back into Lev 13:58
Then he must * some of the olive Lev 14:28
He must bathe himself and * on Lev 16:4
There before the Lord he shall * Lev 16:13
in a sacred place, * on his clothes Lev 16:24
he shall be the one to * on the Lev 16:32
in a court but not * to death, Lev 19:20
cut yourselves nor * tattoo marks Lev 19:28
and refuse to * him to death, then Lev 20:4
shall surely be * to death—for he Lev 20:9
man and woman shall be * to death. Lev 20:10
And I will * to death anyone who Lev 23:30,31
He was * in jail until the Lord Lev 24:12
he shall surely be * to death. Lev 27:29
be * to death, may be ransomed." Lev 27:29f
Lord to Moses were * into effect. Num 1:54
poles are to be * in place. Num 4:14
These instructions were * into Num 5:4
the hair shall be * in the fire Num 6:18
* them all into the man's hands. Num 6:19
Literally, "shall * my name upon Num 6:27f
you and will * it upon them also; Num 11:17
and * it upon the seventy elders; Num 11:25
* his Spirit upon them all!" Num 11:29
What right do you have to * Num 16:3
light them, and * incense upon them Num 16:6,7
and he * on the incense and made Num 16:47
tribe of Levi. * these rods in the Num 17:4
him a rod. He * them before the Num 17:7
him and * them on Eleazar his son; Num 20:26
and * them on his son Eleazar; Num 20:28
first upon him to * him to death, Deu 13:9
and burn it, then * the entire city Deu 13:16
to * God first in your lives. Deu 14:23
However, never * a man to death Deu 17:6
In this way you will * away the Deu 21:9
In this way you shall * away this Deu 21:21
"Fathers shall not be * to death Deu 24:16
Commandments to * this book of the Deu 31:26
And two * ten thousand to flight, Deu 32:30
* their feet on the kings' necks. Jos 10:24
Each one of you has * to flight Jos 23:10
out to me and I * darkness between Jos 24:7
and truth. * away forever the idols Jos 24:14
were stronger they * the Canaanites Ju 1:28
"for the Lord has * your enemies, Ju 3:28
* a curse on Meroz. Ju 5:23
in this way: I'll * some wool on Ju 6:37
from the gold and * it in Ophrah, Ju 8:27
of the ground. He * them on his Ju 16:3
subdue him and * him in chains. Ju 16:5
tell you—bathe and * on some Ru 3:3
But you have * aside your Ru 3:10
the servant would * a three-pronged 1Sa 2:13,14
I will * an end to your family, 1Sa 2:31
he wrote them in a book and * it 1Sa 10:25
David * it on, strapped the sword 1Sa 17:38,39
from a stream and * them in his 1Sa 17:40
But the controversy * David more 1Sa 18:13
and * to flight their entire army. 1Sa 19:8
and * it in his bed, and covered 1Sa 19:13
"Why should he be * to death?" 1Sa 20:32
'I will certainly * Saul into your 1Sa 24:4
"God has * your enemy within 1Sa 26:8
"Let me go and * that spear 1Sa 26:8
the Lord had * them sound asleep. 1Sa 26:12
" 'Come and * me out of my 2Sa 1:9
* out his hand to steady the Ark. 2Sa 6:6
For when you die, I will * one 2Sa 7:12
The letter instructed Joab to * 2Sa 11:15
like that should be * to death; 2Sa 12:5
So he * her out. 2Sa 13:17,18
Now she tore the robe and * 2Sa 13:19
The man's wife * a cloth over 2Sa 17:19
and have * my name here forever. 1Ki 9:2,3
he was, he * him in charge of his 1Ki 11:27,28
Shiloh (who had * on a new robe for 1Ki 11:29
but don't * any fire under the 1Ki 18:25
Let us wear sackcloth and * ropes 1Ki 20:31
They called the meeting and * 1Ki 21:12
tore his clothing, * on rags, 1Ki 21:27
The Lord has * a lying spirit in 1Ki 22:23
Tell them, 'The king says to * 1Ki 22:27
we can * in a bed, a table, a 2Ki 4:10
Does she want me to * in a good 2Ki 4:13
He shredded them and * them into 2Ki 4:39
the rivers of Israel * together? 2Ki 5:12
don't come will be * to death." 2Ki 10:18,19
young prince and * the crown upon 2Ki 11:12
The doorkeepers * all of the 2Ki 12:9
Priest counted it, * it into bags, 2Ki 12:10
It was not * into the chest. 2Ki 12:16
Then he told the king to * his 2Ki 13:16,17
So the king of Assyria * him in 2Ki 17:4
to Assyria and * them in colonies 2Ki 18:11
his clothes and * on sackcloth 2Ki 19:1
me I am going to * a hook in your 2Ki 19:28
then his eyes were * out and he 2Ki 25:7

(PUT Con't)
they were * to the sword and died. 2Ki 25:21
Misream, Canaan, and *. 1Ch 1:5-9
of Salt. He * garrisons in Edom 1Ch 18:13
* back his sword into its sheath; 1Ch 21:27
the final total was never * into 1Ch 27:24
which Moses had * there at Mount 2Ch 5:10
said that you would * your name. 2Ch 6:20,21
wisdom God had * into his heart. 2Ch 9:23
"Because you have * your trust in 2Ch 16:7
"So you see, the Lord has * a 2Ch 18:22
"Tell them, 'The king says to * 2Ch 18:26
but you * on your royal robes!" 2Ch 18:29
and wine, and * those who were sick 2Ch 28:15
flame has been * out, and the 2Ch 29:7
Conaniah, the Levite, was * in 2Ch 31:12,13
the East Gate, was * in charge of 2Ch 31:14,15
the money has been * into the hand 2Ch 34:17
empire (he also * it into the Ez 1:1
the priests * on their priestly Ez 3:10
to Jerusalem and * into the Temple Ez 6:5
for a great favor—* it into his Neh 1:11
which God had * into my heart. Neh 2:11,12
the desire God had * into my heart, Neh 2:18
in cash, and had * the population Neh 5:15
* our names to this covenant." Neh 9:38
I * Shelemiah the priest, Zadok Neh 13:13
* the plan into immediate effect. Est 2:4
his clothes and * on sackcloth and Est 4:1
THREE DAYS LATER Esther * on her Est 5:1
So Haman took the robes and * Est 6:11
Then Mordecai * on the royal Est 8:15
king were to be * into effect—the Est 9:1
into the air and * earth on their Job 2:12
And your bright flame shall be * Job 18:5
If you return to God and * right Job 22:23
Men know how to * light into Job 28:3,4
"If I have * my trust in money, Job 31:24
Will this * an end to your Job 36:19
Or, "Who has * wisdom in the Job 38:36f
All right then, * on your robes Job 40:10
him off guard or * a ring in his Job 40:24
Or * a noose around his tongue? Job 41:1
Let me * the questions to you! Job 42:4
and their father * them into his Job 42:15
But oh, the joys of those who * Ps 2:12
meditation. * your trust in the Ps 4:5
You have * him in charge of Ps 8:6
everything is * under his Ps 8:6
Make them tremble in fear; * the Ps 9:20
Oh, * God to the test and see how Ps 34:8
attacks on me. * on your armor, Ps 35:2
Come and protect me. * an end to Ps 38:16
Lord, and * their trust in him. Ps 40:3
Do as you promised and * an end Ps 54:5
But when I am afraid, I will * my Ps 56:3,4
He was * in charge of all the Ps 105:21
Lord than to * confidence in men. Ps 118:8
We have * away our lyres, Ps 137:2
In everything you do, * God Pro 3:6
literally, "* away from you a Pro 4:24f
Don't * it off. Pro 6:4
She * her arms around him and Pro 7:13
are * into risky investments that Ecc 5:13,14
no one will be able to * it out. Is 1:31
Don't ever * your trust in him! Is 2:22
the Lord had told me, "* a Is 21:6,7
So I * the watchman on the wall, Is 21:8,9
find aid and have * your trust in Is 30:2
this city will be * under siege Is 36:12
—I have * a hook in your nose and Is 37:29
to * entire armies to the sword. Is 41:2
I have * my Spirit upon him; Is 42:1
seas have * their trust in him. Is 42:4
and earth and * everything in Is 45:18
He will use him to * an end to Is 48:14
And I have * my words in your Is 51:16
But I will * that terrible cup Is 51:23
* on your beautiful clothes, O Is 52:1
bonds and slavery. * Babylon and Is 52:11
and justice. He * on righteousness Is 59:17
When we * on our prized robes of Is 64:6
for I will * aside my anger and Is 65:16
But they shall be * to shame. Is 66:5
* and Lud were in North Africa; Is 66:19f
Tarshish, *, Lud, Meshech, Rosh, Is 66:19
I have * my words in your mouth! Jer 1:9
And no one will be able to * the Jer 4:4
inhabitant. * on clothes of Jer 4:8
Why do you * on your most Jer 4:30
of my people, * on mourning clothes Jer 6:26
* up with all their goings on? Jer 12:4
it—don't * it in water at all. Jer 13:1
So I bought the loincloth and * Jer 13:2
Because you have * me out of Jer 13:24,25
of your mind and * your trust in Jer 13:24,25
able to * out the raging flames. Jer 17:27
him whipped and * in the stocks at Jer 20:2
If you * an end to all these Jer 22:4
Submit to him and serve him—* Jer 27:8
I will surely remove the yoke * Jer 28:4
says: I have * a yoke of iron on Jer 28:14
to * him in the stocks and collar. Jer 29:26
King Zedekiah had * him there Jer 32:3
and the copy and * them into a Jer 32:14
I will * a desire into their Jer 32:40
and * this city to the torch!" Jer 37:10
him flogged and * into the dungeon Jer 37:15,16
of the prison, and * him into the Jer 39:14
your spears, * on your armor. Jer 46:4
Come, all of you from Cush and * Jer 46:9
For the Lord says: I have * a Jer 48:35
and * on clothes of sackcloth. Jer 48:37
Weep, daughter of Rabbah! * on Jer 49:3
I will * her defenders to flight Jer 50:44
to Babylon and * in prison for the Jer 52:11
the walls. And * an iron plate Eze 4:3
brightness. He * out what seemed Eze 8:3
of Jerusalem and * a mark on the Eze 9:4
the cherubim and * them into the Eze 10:7,8
So now * on a demonstration, to Eze 12:3
that his eyes were * out before he Eze 12:12f
that his eyes were * out before he Eze 12:13f
The Lord God says, I will * an Eze 12:23
and after being * in the fire! Eze 15:5,6
is yet time. * them behind you and Eze 18:31
It shall not be * out." Eze 20:48
It will * them all to the Eze 21:13
And * a signpost at the fork in Eze 21:19,20
"And so I will * a stop to your Eze 23:27
* on your finest jewels for them. Eze 23:40
bed and * my incense and my oil Eze 23:41
wilderness, who * bracelets on your Eze 23:42
tell them the Lord God says: * a Eze 24:3
men from far-off Paras, Lud and *. Eze 27:10
heads in grief and * on sackcloth Eze 27:31
I will * hooks into your jaws Eze 29:4
For Cush and * and Lud, Arabia Eze 30:5
not been set nor * into a cast to Eze 30:21
I will * splints and bandages Eze 34:15,16
* a new spirit within you. Eze 36:26
And I will * my Spirit within Eze 36:27
I will * breath into you, and you Eze 37:6
I will * my Spirit into you, and Eze 37:14
* my Temple among them forever. Eze 37:26
I will * hooks into your jaws Eze 38:4
Peras, Cush and * shall join you Eze 38:5
bones, he will * up a marker beside Eze 39:15,16
They must * on other clothes Eze 42:14
Now let them * away their idols Eze 43:9
chambers, and * on other clothes Eze 44:19
sin offering and * it on the door Eze 45:19
So they were * on his regular Dan 1:18,19
whom you have * in charge of Dan 3:12
I watched as thrones were * in Dan 7:9
in fact, I will * an end to Hos 1:4,5
I will * an end to all her joys, Hos 1:11
the times when she * on her Hos 1:13
Israel will be * to shame. Hos 10:6
I have never * her under a heavy Hos 10:11
women alike, and * strange symbols Joe 2:30
come when he will * hooks in your Amo 4:2
the idols in Bethel can * it out. Amo 5:6
from the king on down, everyone * Jon 3:4,5
* on sackcloth and sat in ashes. Jon 3:6
And when God saw that they had * Jon 3:10
you did no work to * it there, and Jon 4:10
I will * an end to all Mic 5:12
as well as * and Libya. Nah 3:9
and you * arrows to the string. Hab 3:8,9f
I will * an end to their Zep 1:4
to, then I will * you in charge of Zec 3:7
and gold. Then * the crown on the Zec 6:10,11
"Then * the crown in the Temple Zec 6:14
They turned stubbornly away and * Zec 7:11
also says not to * the Lord your Mt 4:7
But when you fast, * on festive Mt 6:17
I will * my Spirit upon him, Mt 12:18
and * the wheat in the barn.' Mt 13:30
And he * his hands on their Mt 19:15
replied, "He will * the wicked men Mt 21:41
* your enemies beneath your feet.' Mt 22:44
I will * such faithful ones in Mt 24:47
at least have * my money into the Mt 25:27
"* away your sword," Jesus told Mt 26:52
against Jesus to * him to death." Mt 27:1f
"We can't * it in the Mt 27:6
They stripped him and * a Mt 27:28
long thorns and * it on his head, Mt 27:29
off the robe and * his own garment Mt 27:31
And they * a sign above his Mt 27:37
with sour wine and * it on a stick Mt 27:48
You know better than to * new Mk 2:22
a lamp, does he * a box over it to Mk 4:21
And be sure to * into practice Mk 4:24
whenever he was * into handcuffs Mk 5:3,4
from the crowd and * his fingers Mk 7:33
them, "you must * aside your own Mk 8:34
Some who were rich * in large Mk 12:41
all those rich men * together! Mk 12:43,44
Jesus secretly and * him to death. Mk 14:1
sharp thorns and * it on his head. Mk 15:16,17
purple robe and * his own clothes Mk 15:
he had done, Herod * John in Lk 3:19,
also say, 'Do not * the Lord your Lk 4:
New wine must be * into new Lk 5:
to follow me must * aside his own Lk 9:
We'll * up three shelters—one for Lk 9:
"how long should I * up with Lk 9:4
Then he * the man on his donkey Lk 10:
of God and * it into practice." Lk 11:2
He himself will seat them and * Lk 12:3
* him in charge of all he owns. Lk 12:42,43,4
"When you * on a dinner," he Lk 14:
robe in the house and * it on him. Lk 15:2
so that all who * their trust in me Jn 12:4
After washing their feet he * on Jn 13:
But Jesus said to Peter, "* your Jn 18:1
for us to * any man to death." Jn 18:3
Jesus, they * his garments into Jn 19:23,2
soaked in it and * on a hyssop Jn 19:2
know where they have * him!" Jn 20:
know where they have * him." Jn 20:1
me where you have * him, and I will Jn 20:1
in his hands—and * my fingers into Jn 20:2
Then he said to Thomas, "* your Jn 20:2
hands. * your hand into my side. Jn 20:2
At that, Simon Peter * on his Jn 21:
and * them in the public jail. Act 5:1
and we will * them in charge of Act 6:
dressed and * on your shoes." Act 12:
"Now * on your coat and follow Act 12:
the day arrived he * on his royal Act 12:2
so he took no chances, but * Act 16:2
* away idols and worship only him. Act 17:3
bound for Italy, and * us aboard. Act 27:
to * out anchors from the prow. Act 27:3
to sail, people * on board all Act 28:1
sight—when we * our faith and trust Rom 1:1
God has * this knowledge in their Rom 1:1
are forgiven and * out of sight. Rom 4:
keep them, but God * into effect a Rom 8:
he said, "I have * a Rock in the Rom 9:3
say that God has * them to sleep, Rom 11:
brag about being * in to replace Rom 11:18
the branches he * there in the Rom 11:21
far more ready to * the Jews back Rom 11:24
ability and * you in charge of the Rom 12:
God is the one who has * it there. Rom 13:1
of darkness and * on the armor of Rom 13:12,13
Everyone's work will be * through 1Co 3:13
you had better * this all aside and 1Co 3:18
Sometimes I think God has * us 1Co 4:9
soon to be killed, * on display at 1Co 4:9
man and * him out of your church. 1Co 5:13
situation God has * you into. 1Co 7:17
that you must not * a muzzle on an 1Co 9:9
body when they are all * together. 1Co 12:12
our bodies and * each part just 1Co 12:18
So God has * the body together in 1Co 12:24
I have * away the childish things. 1Co 13:11
* down all enemies of every kind. 1Co 15:24
Son of God, will * himself also 1Co 15:28
When you * a seed into the ground 1Co 15:36
For all you * into the ground is 1Co 15:37
each of you should * aside 1Co 16:2
but that was good, for then we * 2Co 1:9
He has * his brand upon us—his 2Co 1:22
as Moses did, who * a veil over his 2Co 3:13
we shall * on like new clothes. 2Co 5:2
We have been beaten, * in jail, 2Co 6:5
of you, and * on airs, and slap you 2Co 11:19,20
I have worked harder, been * in 2Co 11:23
to describe or * in words (and 2Co 12:4
Let me * it another way. Gal 3:24
And God has * all things under Eph 1:22
power within you. * on all of Eph 6:11
away so that I can * my trust and Php 3:7
I have * aside all else, counting Php 3:8
wrong doctrine. * an end to their 1Ti 1:3,4
head. * these abilities to work; 1Ti 4:15
been * in jail like a criminal. 2Ti 2:9
in the kitchen or to * garbage in. 2Ti 2:20
And you have * him in complete Heb 2:8
he said, "I will * my trust in God Heb 2:13
now and has been * aside forever. Heb 8:13
end of the age, to * away the power Heb 9:26
will, and I will * my laws in their Heb 10:16
has been to you, * away all evil, 1Pe 2:2,3
Next, learn to * aside your own 2Pe 1:6
And he has * his own Holy Spirit 1Jn 4:13
tries to * them out of the church. 3Jn 1:10
For God will * a plan into their Rev 17:17

PUTEOLI
*, where we found some believers! Act 28:13

PUTHITES
the Ithrites, the *, the 1Ch 2:53

PUTI-EL
the daughters of *, and Phinehas Ex 6:25

PUTS
incense like it or * any of it upon Ex 30:33
'And he * my feet in the Job 33:11
men, and * others in their place. Job 34:24

PUTS Con't)
But make everyone rejoice who * Ps 5:11
here on earth. He * the righteous Ps 11:5
happy the man who * his trust in Pro 16:20
God * out the light of the man Pro 20:20
Literally, "The fig tree * forth Sol 2:13f
a little child who * his hand in a Is 11:8
is the man who * his trust in Jer 17:5
a wall—and * his hand on a snake. Amo 5:19
And no one * new wine into old Lk 5:37
Instead, he * it on a lampstand Lk 11:33

PUTTING
of Amalek, * them to the sword. Ex 17:13
without * any fire under the wood; 1Ki 18:23
his kingdom, * it into writing: 2Ch 36:22,23
that you are * in his mouth? Job 13:7
them like a man * on a new shirt Ps 102:26
You keep * your foot in your Pro 10:19
* confidence in an unreliable man Pro 25:19
free and * innocent men in jail. Is 5:23
in the wind and * on sackcloth and Is 58:5
to God as * a dog or the blood of a Is 66:3
in * Jeremiah into the cistern. Jer 38:9
* a stop to the daily sacrifices, Dan 11:30,31
as though you were * it into Hag 1:6
Jesus; and * a kingly robe on him, Lk 23:11
Egypt, as well as * him in charge Act 7:10
Then they mobbed him, * their Act 7:57
hospitality. * to sea from there, Act 27:4
Keep * into practice all you Php 4:9
Lord that you are * into practice 2Th 3:4

PUVAH
Issachar and his sons: Tola, *, Gen 46:8-14
named after their ancestor *. Num 26:23-25

PUZZLE
Here is a * that calls for Rev 13:18

PUZZLED
The king of Syria was *. 2Ki 6:11
he was worried and *, for some Lk 9:7
They stood there *, trying to Lk 24:4
The Jewish leaders were * by this Jn 7:35

PUZZLING
Meanwhile, as Peter was * over Act 10:19

PYRE
The funeral * has long been Is 30:33

PYRRHUS
Sopater of Beroea, the son of *; Act 20:4

QUAIL
That evening vast numbers of * Ex 16:13
wind that brought * from the sea, Num 11:31
there were * flying three or four Num 11:31
caught and killed * all that day Num 11:32
* were spread out all around Num 11:32
My enemies * before me and fall Ps 18:39
and he sent them *, and gave them Ps 105:40

QUAILED
Mount Sinai * before you—the God Ps 68:8

QUAILS
My heart * within me. Ps 40:12

QUAKE
Even their generals will * with Is 31:9
How the mountains would * in your Is 64:1
"The surrounding cities * at the Eze 27:28
All living things shall * in Eze 38:20
In his presence mountains * and Nah 1:5
knees *; Nah 2:10

QUAKED
Yes, even Mount Sinai * Ju 5:5
The foundations of the heavens * 2Sa 22:8
How they *! Ps 18:7
and how the mountains *! Is 64:3

QUAKES
The earth * before them and the Joe 2:10

QUALIFICATIONS
whom had excellent *, were 1Ch 26:31,32

QUALIFIED
well * for their work. 1Ch 26:8
Are you * to judge the Almighty? Job 11:7

QUALIFY
evidently did not * as "sitting on Jer 36:30f

QUALITY
what was worthless or of poor *. 1Sa 15:9
*, and many, many jewels. 2Ch 9:9

QUANTITIES
wood, and great * of onyx, other 1Ch 29:2
Great * of bronze were used, too 2Ch 4:17,18
in gold, and great * of spices of 2Ch 9:9
carried off vast * of plunder. 2Ch 14:13
As a result, additional vast * of 2Ch 14:14
sending back great * of booty to 2Ch 24:23
and carrying off great * of booty. 2Ch 25:13
confiscated—great * of gold and Zec 14:14

QUANTITY
* of spices and precious gems; 1Ki 10:10
into the great * of nails needed 1Ch 22:3
and a great * of incense was Rev 8:3

QUARANTINE
He must also * himself until Lev 11:25
priest shall * him for seven days. Lev 13:4
priest must * him seven days more. Lev 13:5
priest shall * him for seven days. Lev 13:21
the priest shall * him for seven Lev 13:26
* him for another seven days. Lev 13:33

QUARANTINED
The man is not to be * for Lev 13:11
then he shall be * for seven days, Lev 13:31

QUARREL
"Don't * along the way!" Gen 45:24
enemies begin to * among Ps 55:9
"I've decided to forget our *! Pro 7:14
To * with a neighbor is foolish; Pro 11:12
It is hard to stop a * once it Pro 17:14
not shout nor * in the streets. Is 42:2
Don't * with anyone. Rom 12:18
we should be the cause of a *? 1Co 3:5
help, * no more—be friends again. Php 4:2
of anyone, nor *, but be gentle and Tit 3:2

QUARRELING
"Quit * with God! Job 22:21
Only fools insist on *. Pro 20:3
Who is always fighting and *? Pro 23:29,30
when you keep on fighting and *? Is 58:4
and divide up into * groups, 1Co 3:3
There you are, * about whether I 1Co 3:4
I will find you *, and envying each 2Co 12:20
and angry. *, harsh words, and Eph 4:31
And remember, no * among 1Th 5:13

QUARRELS
to settle all your * and problems? Deu 1:12
* and assist them in every way. Deu 1:15
Hatred stirs old *, but love Pro 10:12
wrath, but harsh words cause *. Pro 15:1
THE SELFISH MAN * against every Pro 18:1
be rid of tension, fighting and *. Pro 22:10
bleeding, so anger causes *. Pro 30:33
arguments and *, dear brothers. 1Co 1:11
keep out of arguments and * about Tit 3:9
Try to stay out of all * and seek Heb 12:14
WHAT IS CAUSING the * and fights Jas 4:1

QUARRELSOME
than with a *, complaining woman. Pro 21:19
home with a cranky, * woman. Pro 25:24
A * man starts fights as easily Pro 26:21
He must not be a drinker or *, 1Ti 3:3
God's people must not be *; 2Ti 2:24

QUARRIED
The stonecutters * and shaped 1Ki 5:17

QUARRIES
by the men of Ai as far as the *. Jos 7:5
But outside the city, at the * of Ju 3:17,18,19
had escaped past the * to Se-irah. Ju 3:26

QUARRY
prefinished at the *, so the entire 1Ki 6:7
When working in a *, stones will Ecc 10:8,9
Consider the * from which you Is 51:1

QUARRYMEN
stonemasons, *, timber dealers, and 2Ki 12:11,12

QUART
And use one * of water a day; Eze 4:11

QUARTER
and * it, and build a wood fire Lev 1:6,7
Then the man will * it, and the Lev 1:12

QUARTER-OUNCE
he produced a * gold earring Gen 24:22

QUARTERED
Next he * the ram and burned the Lev 8:20

QUARTERMASTER
(Seraiah was * of Zedekiah's Jer 51:59

QUARTERS
* and prepare some food for him. 2Sa 13:7
woman in her brother Absalom's *. 2Sa 13:20
"He may go to his own *," the 2Sa 14:24
His cedar-paneled living * 1Ki 7:8
(He designed similar living *, 1Ki 7:8
the new * he had built for her in 1Ki 9:24
the * of Nathan-melech the eunuch. 2Ki 23:11
Call the bridegroom from his * Joe 2:16
he said—and left for safer *. Act 12:17

QUARTS
for his household—about three * Ex 16:16
for everyone—three * apiece; Ex 16:18
as usual, six * instead of three; Ex 16:22
were to take three * of it to be Ex 16:32
and put three * of manna in it and Ex 16:33
the manna—held about three *; Ex 16:36
With one of them offer three * Ex 29:40
defect, ten * of finely ground Lev 14:10
and only three * of fine white Lev 14:21
use three * of fine flour mixed Num 15:3,4
is a ram, use six * of fine flour Num 15:6
consist of nine * of fine flour Num 15:8,9
mixed with three * of oil, plus Num 15:8,9
* of wine for the drink offering. Num 15:10
offering of three * of finely Num 28:5
offering of six * of fine flour Num 28:9,10
Accompany them with nine * of Num 28:12
and six * of finely ground flour Num 28:12
and for each lamb, three * of Num 28:13
* of fine flour mixed with oil; Num 28:20,21
with the ram there shall be six * Num 28:20,21
shall be three * of fine flour. Num 28:20,21
offering of nine * of fine flour Num 28:28,29
each bull, six * with the ram, and Num 28:28,29
* with each of the seven lambs. Num 28:28,29
A grain offering of nine * of Num 29:3,4
with the bull, six * with the ram, Num 29:3,4
* with each of the seven lambs. Num 29:3,4
offerings. Nine * of fine flour Num 29:9,10
offerings—nine * of fine flour Num 29:14
six * for each of the two rams; Num 29:14
and three * for each of the Num 29:15

QUARTUS
so does *, a Christian brother. Rom 16:23

QUAVERED
"What is it?" * Ahimelech. 1Sa 22:11,12

QUAVERING
deaf and tuneless, with * voice. Ecc 12:4

QUEEN
cure the king and * and the other Gen 20:17
WHEN THE * of Sheba heard how 1Ki 10:1
the gifts from the * of Sheba, King 1Ki 10:13
a wife—the sister of * Tahpenes. 1Ki 11:19
you as the *, and go to Ahijah the 1Ki 14:2
But the Lord told him that the * 1Ki 14:5
Once when * Jezebel had tried to 1Ki 18:3,4
the time when * Jezebel was trying 1Ki 18:13
WHEN AHAB TOLD * Jezebel what 1Ki 19:1
and of the * Mother, Jezebel." 2Ki 10:13
years while Athaliah reigned as *. 2Ki 11:2,3
In the seventh year of * 2Ki 11:4
the * mother surrendered to him. 2Ki 24:12
and the * mother, to Babylon. 2Ki 24:15
WHEN THE * of Sheba heard of 2Ch 9:1
King Solomon gave the * of Sheba 2Ch 9:12
from being the * mother because she 2Ch 15:16
years while Athaliah reigned as *. 2Ch 22:12
of the reign of * Athaliah, 2Ch 23:1
When * Athaliah heard all the 2Ch 23:12
because * Athaliah was dead. 2Ch 23:21
The king replied, with the * Neh 2:5,6
* Vashti gave a party for the Est 1:9
Carkas— to bring * Vashti to him Est 1:11
to * Vashti, she refused to come. Est 1:12
law provide for a * who refuses to Est 1:13-15
for the others, "* Vashti has Est 1:16
they learn what * Vashti has done. Est 1:17
will hear what the * did and will Est 1:18
be changed, that * Vashti be Est 1:19
another * more worthy than she. Est 1:19
be the * instead of Vashti." Est 2:4
declared her * instead of Vashti. Est 2:17
the information to * Esther, who Est 2:22
And when he saw * Esther Est 5:2
her, "What do you wish, * Esther? Est 5:3
and Esther the * invited only me Est 5:12
"What is your petition, * Esther? Est 7:2
And at last * Esther replied, Est 7:3
with fright before the king and *. Est 7:6
for his life to * Esther, for he Est 7:7
the couch where * Esther was Est 7:8
"Will he even rape the * right Est 7:8
the Jews' enemy, to * Esther. Est 8:1
Then King Ahasuerus said to * Est 8:7
Shushan, he called for * Esther. Est 9:12
Meanwhile, * Esther (daughter of Est 9:29-31
Mordecai the Jew and by * Esther; Est 9:29-31
Standing beside you is the *, Ps 45:9
be called "The * of Kingdoms." Is 47:5
never end, * Kingdom of the world. Is 47:7
to offer to "The * of Heaven" Jer 7:18
mentions the "* of Heaven" among Jer 7:18f
We will burn incense to the '* of Jer 44:17
"* of Heaven"; Jer 44:17f
incense to the '* of Heaven' and Jer 44:18
worshiping the '* of Heaven' and Jer 44:19
sacrifices to the '* of Heaven,' Jer 44:25
She, once * of nations, is now a Lam 1:1
You looked like a *, and so you Eze 16:13
The * of Nineveh is brought out Nah 2:7
The * of Sheba shall rise Mt 12:42
"And at the Judgment Day the * Lk 11:31
Literally, "* of the South." Lk 11:31f
authority under Candace the *. Act 8:27
She boasts, 'I am * upon my Rev 18:7

QUEEN-MOTHER
Say to the king and *, Jer 13:18
THE king, and the *, and the court Jer 29:1
But when the * heard what was Dan 5:10

QUEEN'S
The city fathers followed the * 1Ki 21:11
palace guard and the * bodyguard. 2Ki 11:4

QUEENLY
your tripping feet, O * maiden. Sol 7:1
is held captive in your * tresses. Sol 7:5

QUEENMOTHER
Maacah as * because she had made an 1Ki 15:13

QUEENS
I have sixty other wives, all *, Sol 6:8
the * and concubines praise you. Sol 6:9
Kings and * shall serve you; Is 49:23
of the kings and * of Judah, and Jer 44:9

QUENCH
There the wild donkeys * their Ps 104:11

(QUENCH Con't)
Many waters cannot * the flame Sol 8:7
nor * the dimly burning flame. Is 42:3
upon you like a fire no man can *. Jer 21:12
Or * the smallest hope; Mt 12:20

QUENCHED
their fire shall not be *, and Is 66:24
The terrible flames will not be * Eze 20:47

QUESTION
I'll give it back without *." Gen 31:32
why haven't you answered my *? 1Sa 14:41
"I was only asking a *!" 1Sa 17:29
the answer to your * when you find 1Ki 22:25
"I'd like to ask him the same * 2Ch 18:6,7
even one * of a thousand he asks? Job 9:3
does cry out this * to him, he Job 35:12
Let me ask you a *, and give me Job 40:7
no one can withstand it or * it. Ecc 8:4
right have you to * what I do? Is 45:11
Ask this * of the governor and Hag 2:2
Ask the priests this * about the Hag 2:11
disturbed by their *, and all Mt 2:3
For the decisive * is whether Mt 7:21
Someone came to Jesus with this * Mt 19:16
But to answer your *, you can get Mt 19:17
one * first," Jesus replied. Mt 21:24
I won't answer your * either. Mt 21:27
to ask him this *: "Sir, we know Mt 22:16
a fresh * of their own to ask him. Mt 22:34,35
a *: "What about the Messiah? Mt 22:41
But as for your *—you know the Mk 10:19
tell you if you answer one *! Mk 11:29
I won't answer your * either!" Mk 11:33
Here was their *: Mk 12:18
Temple area, he asked them this *: Mk 12:35
This was the * of the hour, and Lk 3:15
John answered the * by saying, Lk 3:16
of the Law, "I have a * for you. Lk 6:9
When they asked him John's *, Lk 7:20,21,22
* whatever is set before you. Lk 10:7
by asking him this *: "Teacher, Lk 10:25
But the * is: When I, the Lk 18:8
asked him this *: "Good sir, what Lk 18:18
"But as to your *, you know what Lk 18:20
"I'll ask you a * before I Lk 20:3
I won't answer your * either." Lk 20:8
Now here is our *: Whose wife Lk 20:33
"But as to your real *—whether Lk 20:37,38
Then he presented them with a *. Lk 20:41
He asked Jesus * after question, Lk 23:9
He asked Jesus question after *, Lk 23:9
making up this answer to your *! Jn 14:24
The * had been asked before Jn 16:5f
Why are you asking me this *? Jn 18:21
Jesus repeated the *: "Simon, Jn 21:16
Jesus asked the * this third time. Jn 21:17
and elders there about this *. Act 15:2
further meeting to decide this *. Act 15:6
we have decided concerning your *. Act 15:26
this * of being saved by faith? Rom 4:1
Now then, the *: Is this blessing Rom 4:9
For the answer to that *, answer Rom 4:10
I will try to answer your other *. 1Co 7:25
In answer to this *, I have no 1Co 7:25
NEXT IS YOUR * about eating food 1Co 8:1
On this * everyone feels that 1Co 8:1
This is my answer to those who * 1Co 9:3
What a foolish *! 1Co 15:36
then there will be no * about 2Co 10:16
Even that * wouldn't have come up Gal 2:4
Let me ask you this one *: Did Gal 3:2
no * that he will do what he says. Heb 10:23
shouting out this *: "Who is Rev 5:2

QUESTIONED
They must be closely *, and if Deu 19:18
What could I say when he * me Job 31:14
upset you and * your salvation, Act 15:24

QUESTIONS
him their * to decide; Ex 18:19,20
to test him with some hard *. 1Ki 10:1
Solomon answered all her *; 1Ki 10:3
* of Baal-zebub, the god of Ekron. 2Ki 1:6
Jerusalem to test him with hard *. 2Ch 9:1
Let me put the * to you! Job 42:4
trying to fool with your trick *? Mt 22:18
no one dared ask him any more *. Mt 22:46
no one dared ask him any more *. Mk 12:34
discussing deep * with them and Lk 2:46,47
with a host of *, trying to trap Lk 11:53,54
And that ended their *, for they Lk 20:40
merely a bunch of * of semantics Act 18:15
you want to ask a few more *. Act 23:15
and right, no matter who * them. Rom 3:4
belongs to God. On * of this kind Rom 14:5
NOW ABOUT THOSE * you asked in 1Co 7:1
and don't ask any * about it. 1Co 10:27
If they have any * to ask, let 1Co 14:35
ideas that stir up * and arguments 1Ti 1:3,4
over unanswerable * and Tit 3:9
* as to what it all could mean. 1Pe 1:10

QUIBBLE
"And why * about the speck in Lk 6:41

QUIBBLING
He is * over the meaning of 1Ti 6:4

QUICK
the tent and said to Sarah, "*! Gen 18:6
fiancés, "*, get out of the city, Gen 19:14
and after a * shave and change of Gen 41:14
been since Egypt was founded! *! Ex 9:19
Then the Lord told Moses, "*! Ex 32:7
the 250 Israeli leaders. "*!" Num 16:26
And Moses said to Aaron, "*, Num 16:46
Perhaps the meaning is, "A * Ju 8:21f
grew louder and louder. "*! 1Sa 14:19
"*!" 2Sa 17:16
hurried on to King David. "*!" 2Sa 17:21
than Absalom did. *, take my 2Sa 20:6
"*, saddle the donkey," the old 1Ki 13:13
The men were * to grab this straw 1Ki 20:33
Then he said to Gehazi, "*, take 2Ki 4:29
* Get my chariot 2Ki 9:21
his bodyguard, "*, kill me with 1Ch 10:4
called one of his aides. "*! 2Ch 18:8
With a * prayer to the God of Neh 2:4
* to despise all those in need. Job 12:5
Please, Lord, rescue me! *! Ps 40:13
for I am in deep trouble. *! Ps 69:17
*, LORD, ANSWER me—for I have Ps 141:1
yourself by your agreement. *! Pro 6:3
A * retort can ruin everything. Pro 13:3
to get rich * will quickly fail. Pro 28:20
Trying to get rich * is evil and Pro 28:22
a fool than for a man of * temper. Pro 29:20
*, quick, grab your shields Is 21:5
Quick, *, grab your shields and Is 21:5
says: Send for the mourners! *! Jer 9:17,18
of all the evil you are doing. *! Jer 21:12
*! Use your swiftest Mic 1:13
punishments will be * and certain; Mal 3:5
his father said to the slaves, '*! Lk 15:22
he said. "*! Lk 19:5
side to awaken him and said, "*! Act 12:7
They are * to kill, hating anyone Rom 3:15

QUICK-TEMPERED
A fool is *; Pro 12:16
A * man starts fights; Pro 15:18
Don't be *—that is being a fool. Ecc 7:9

QUICKENS
"It is the Spirit who *." Jn 6:63f

QUICKLY
she said, and * lowered the jug for Gen 24:18
She * lifted the jug down from Gen 24:46
Rebekah noticed him and * Gen 24:64
able to find it so *, my son?" Gen 27:20
Rebekah's son. She * ran and told Gen 29:12,13
They * took down their sacks from Gen 44:11
was * carried to Pharaoh's palace. Gen 45:2
And bring him to me *." Gen 45:13
animals and return * to their homes Gen 45:17
* that we can't get there in time! Ex 1:19
the flocks watered so * today?" Ex 2:18
out of the land as * as possible. Ex 12:33
and have * abandoned all my laws. Ex 32:8
lay incense on it, and carry it * Num 16:46
They * consulted with the Num 22:4
be * destroyed from the land. Deu 4:26
his anger may rise * against you, Deu 6:15
too * and become dangerous. Deu 7:22
* conquer them and drive them out. Deu 9:3
He told me to go down * because Deu 9:12
themselves, * turning away from the Deu 9:12
How * you turned away from him! Deu 9:16
and you will * perish from the good Deu 11:17
to Jericho, they * combined their Jos 9:1
"Come * and save us! Jos 10:6
Debir, which they * captured with Jos 10:39
you, and you will * perish." Jos 23:15,16
gods instead. How * they turned Ju 2:17
And you shall * destroy the Ju 6:16
So each of them * cut a bundle Ju 9:49
with her— so she * ran and found Ju 13:10
The news spread * throughout the 1Sa 13:3,4
So the boy * gathered up the 1Sa 20:38
When Abigail saw David, she * 1Sa 25:23
to his request. * getting ready, 1Sa 25:42
And shall * submit to me 2Sa 22:45
decision spread * throughout the 1Ki 3:28
* surrounded by the army of Edom. 2Ki 8:21
They * carpeted the bare steps 2Ki 9:13
He now * returned, and was 2Ch 10:2,3
Ethiopians. He * conquered Judah's 2Ch 12:4
of what God had accomplished so *. 2Ch 29:36
to conduct Haman * to the banquet Est 6:14
like a lion and * finish me off. Job 10:16
Call to me to come—how * I will Job 13:22
a passing cloud, he * disappears. Job 14:2
"But how * they disappear from Job 24:18
Answer * when I cry to you; Ps 31:2
Come *! Ps 38:22
You are my Savior; come *, and Ps 40:17
He will destroy them more * than Ps 58:9
O God, don't stay away! Come * Ps 71:12
* then I would subdue her enemies! Ps 81:14
river, and vanish as * as a dream. Ps 90:5
Yet how * they forgot again! Ps 106:1
The Red Sea saw them coming and * Ps 114:
here in our land; * punish them. Ps 140:1
Come *, Lord, and answer me, for Ps 143:
Wealth from gambling * Pro 13:1
Literally, "* gathered." Pro 20:2
to get rich quick will * fail. Pro 28:2
For a fool's compliment is as * Ecc 7:
shall pass away as * as shadows Ecc 8:1
Come *, my beloved, and be like Sol 8:1
and despoiling (will) come *." Is 8:1
"Yes, I am here," he will * Is 58:
And if these heathen nations * Jer 12:1
would grow as * as a willow tree. Eze 17:
like dew that * dries away, like Hos 13:
a vine to grow up * and spread its Jon 4:
Come to terms * with your enemy Mt 5:2
of fruit trees can * be identified Mt 7:1
the plants sprang up * enough in Mt 13:
arrival spread * throughout the Mt 14:3
did the fig tree wither so *?" Mt 21:2
And now, go * and tell his Mt 28:7
he had done spread * through that Mk 1:2
arrival spread * through the city. Mk 2:1
It grew up * enough, but soon Mk 4:5,6
it, but all too * the attractions Mk 4:19
in my name will * turn against me. Mk 9:39
The word spread * to her Lk 1:58
and told him to go * into the Lk 14:21
He will answer them *! Lk 18:8
All of us must * carry out the Jn 9:4
A mob was * formed against Paul Act 16:22
happened spread * all through Act 19:17
in an uproar. He * ordered out his Act 21:32
ready to lash him, * disappeared Act 22:29
You can * discover that it was Act 24:11
Of course I * pointed out to Act 25:16
upon the earth, * ending his Rom 9:28
Literally, "a wreath that * 1Co 9:25f
you still angry—get over it *; Eph 4:26
children who obey * and quietly. 1Ti 3:4
me at Nicopolis as * as you can, Tit 3:12
is past, but the third * follows: Rev 11:14

QUICKSANDS
to the * of the African coast, Act 27:17

QUIET
* sort who liked to stay at home. Gen 25:27
* -Moses commanded Ex 17:2
shall spend the day in * humility; Lev 16:31
there shall be a * gathering of the Deu 16:8
"Be * and come with us," they Ju 18:19
"The harp music will * you and 1Sa 16:15,16
family who will come to a * end. 1Ki 14:13
* elish snapped 2Ki 2:3
"Will you please be *?" 2Ki 2:5
and everything was * and peaceful; 1Ch 4:40,41
So Jehoshaphat's kingdom was *, 2Ch 20:30
and the city was * and peaceful 2Ch 23:21
the king retorted. "Be * now, 2Ch 25:16
If you keep * at a time like Est 4:14
I could remain *, though even then Est 7:4
then I would be * now, asleep and Job 3:13
answer—then I will keep *. Job 6:24
Oh, please be *! Job 13:5
and leads me beside the * streams. Ps 23:2,3
I'll keep *, especially when the Ps 39:1
O God, my heart is * and Ps 57:7
is in turmoil, * me and give me Ps 94:19
I am * now before the Lord, Ps 131:2
a trustworthy man tries to * them. Pro 11:13
A time to be *; Ecc 3:7
But even so, the * words of a Ecc 9:17
you, don't quit! A * spirit will Ecc 10:4
A quiet spirit will * his bad Ecc 10:4
the water brooks, deep and *. Sol 5:12
whole earth is at rest and is *! Is 14:7
Sheep pasture there, lying * and Is 17:2
worshiped, a city * and unmoved. Is 33:20
They shall have rest and * in Jer 30:10
They shall walk beside the * Jer 31:9
end, and I will be * and not be Eze 16:42
The crowd told them to be *, but Mt 20:31
and said to the sea, "* down!" Mk 4:39
So he spoke to the storm: "* Lk 8:24
He replied, "If they keep *, the Lk 19:40
He motioned for them to * down Act 12:17
At last the mayor was able to * Act 19:35
motioned to the people to be *; Act 21:40
I come with * love and gentleness? 1Co 4:21
and your hearts * and at rest as Php 4:7
to live a * life, minding your own 1Th 4:11
everything is * and 1Th 5:3
command them—to * down, get to 2Th 3:12
be the same way, * and sensible in 1Ti 2:9,10
living *, good, and loving lives. 1Ti 2:15
Teach the older women to be * and Tit 2:3
a * growth in grace and character. Heb 12:11
all pure and full of * gentleness. Jas 3:17
of a gentle and * spirit which is 1Pe 3:4

QUIETED
And the Levites, too, * the Neh 8:11

QUIETED Con't)
their lying lips * at last—the Ps 31:18
judgment and * my anger there." Zec 6:8
QUIETER
So they left by boat for a * Mk 6:32
QUIETLY
and a hammer and, * creeping up to Ju 4:21
They lived *, and were unprepared Ju 18:7
Then Ruth came * and lifted the Ru 3:6,7
"Now stand here * before the 1Sa 12:7
Then David crept forward and * 1Sa 24:4
don't upset them, but go back *." 1Sa 29:7
Return * to the city with your 2Sa 15:27
the lion standing * beside it, 1Ki 13:24,25
that, but remained * at Jerusalem. 2Ch 19:4
stand * and see the incredible 2Ch 20:17
"I was living * until he broke Job 16:12
I shall die * in my nest after a Job 29:18
and do not sin against him. Lie * Ps 4:4
* keep my mind upon your promises. Ps 119:95
O Israel, you too should * trust Ps 131:3
God will watch * from his Temple Is 18:4
My people will live in safety, * Is 32:18
that you will die * among your Jer 34:5
* for the salvation of the Lord. Lam 3:26
You may sigh, but only *. Eze 24:17
Everyone will live * in his own Mic 4:4
I will * wait for the day of Hab 3:16
They will live *, in peace, and Zep 3:13
but to do it *, as he didn't want Mt 1:19
Jesus *, and killing him. Mt 26:4
* in bed, and the demon was gone. Mk 7:30
Mentioned here so *, this was Mk 10:1f
but Mary * treasured these things Lk 2:19
sitting * at Jesus' feet, clothed Lk 8:35
done, he slipped * away with them Lk 9:10
disciples, he said *, "How Lk 10:23
* when the crowds weren't around. Lk 22:6
We have replied * when evil 1Co 4:13
pure and sincere, * depending upon 2Co 1:12
ready to suffer * and patiently. Col 3:12
Women should listen and learn * 1Ti 2:11
children who obey quickly and *. 1Ti 3:4
women to live *, to love their Tit 2:4
you for it. * trust yourself to 1Pe 3:15
QUIETNESS
into * after Athaliah's death. 2Ki 11:20
and * to Israel during his reign. 1Ch 22:9
officials of the city stood in *. Job 29:10
And let Israel have * and peace. Ps 125:5
good shall be granted mercy and *. Pro 14:22
* and confidence is your strength; Is 30:15
of justice, peace. * and confidence Is 32:17
to live again in * in Israel. Jer 50:34
you have given * and peace to us Act 24:2
live in peace and *, spending our 1Ti 2:2
QUIETS
strength. He * the raging oceans Ps 65:7
QUIRINIUS
(This census was taken when * Lk 2:2
QUIT
Then the Lord said to Moses, "* Ex 14:15
do something or to * doing Num 30:1
" 'Should I * producing the olive Ju 9:9
'Should I * producing sweetness Ju 9:11
replied, 'Shall I * producing the Ju 9:13
* acting so proud and arrogant! 1Sa 2:3
again, so Saul * the chase and 1Sa 23:28
to Gath, so he * hunting for him. 1Sa 27:4
of Israel never * doing the evil 2Ki 17:22
"* quarreling with God! Job 22:21
I SAID TO myself, I'm going to * Ps 39:1
man alone, and * trying to cheat Pro 24:15,16
boss is angry with you, don't *! Ecc 10:4
wicked things; * your evil ways. Is 1:16
Tell him to * worrying," the Is 7:4
Even yet, if you * your evil ways I Jer 7:3
And I can't *! Jer 20:9
Help those in need of justice! * Jer 22:3
But ever since we * burning Jer 44:18
to the rulers: * robbing and Eze 45:9
to * giving herself to others. Hos 1:2
Don't *! Act 18:9
coming, they * beating Paul. Act 21:32
will soon be here. So * the evil Rom 13:12,13
The right thing to do is to * Rom 14:21
Get some sense and * your 1Co 15:34
do, but we don't give up and *. 2Co 4:8
become discouraged and * trying. Col 3:21
QUITE
his father gave it * a bit of Gen 37:11
So Joseph naturally became * a Gen 39:4
arrest there for * some time, and Gen 40:4
they stayed there for * a long Num 33:9
Soon he had * a band of Ju 11:3
The young priest was then * happy Ju 18:20
When they were * a distance from Ju 18:22
not * like his ancestor David; 2Ki 14:3
his father's God—* unlike the 2Ch 17:4
This was * a contrast to the Neh 5:15
it turned out * to the contrary—the Est 9:1
of a man who is * alone, without a Ecc 4:8
for we understand it * well. Is 36:11
But among you it is * different. Mt 20:26
by quoting others—* unlike what Mk 1:22
He talked about it * frankly Mk 8:32
"He's * clever at 'saving' Mk 15:31
Lord, for we were * sure of it. Jn 21:12
* small and won't last very long. 2Co 4:17
And we are not afraid, but are * 2Co 5:8
good, I am * happy about "the 2Co 12:10
It is * true that the way to live 1Ti 3:16
down here. And * obviously when Heb 11:14
And have you * forgotten the Heb 12:5
are really getting along * well! 2Pe 1:12
to mean something * different from 2Pe 3:15,16
to this world, so, * naturally, 1Jn 4:5
QUITS
gives up and * hunting for me; 1Sa 27:1
QUITTING
suffered for me without *. Rev 2:3
QUIVER
Happy is the man who has his * Ps 127:5
I am like a sharp arrow in his *. Is 49:2
lots by shaking arrows from the *; Eze 21:21
my lips * with fear. Hab 3:16
QUIVERING
or clothed his neck with a * mane? Job 39:19
QUOTA
"Fulfill your daily * just as Ex 5:13
deliver the regular * of bricks." Ex 5:18
full * of the days of your life. Ex 23:26
and let only a small * return. Eze 20:37
QUOTAS
their production * by a single Ex 5:7,8
* either yesterday or today?" Ex 5:14
were drafted under * set by Je-iel, 2Ch 26:11
QUOTATION
This *, unrecorded in the book Mk 1:3f
The * is from Isaiah 53:12. Mk 15:28f
QUOTE
The people shall no longer * Jer 31:29
that proverb they * in Israel—'The Eze 12:22
you will * me that proverb, Lk 4:23
QUOTED
It is * here from the book, 2Sa 1:17,18
This verse was * by Christ as Ps 40:7f
will be * as having great wisdom. Ps 49:13
These leaders only * others, Mt 7:29f
Then Jesus * them passage after Lk 24:27
that what he had * from the Jn 2:22
"King David * Jesus as saying:'I Act 2:25
he spoke these words I have *, Act 2:29
in these words of his I have * Act 2:34
the words already *, "Today when Heb 4:7
QUOTING
his points by * others—quite unlike Mk 1:22
instead of merely * the opinions of Lk 4:32
He is apparently * some in the 1Co 6:12f
And I'm not merely * the 1Co 9:8
about the Lord, * psalms and hymns Eph 5:19
RA-AMIAH
Azariah, *, Nahamani; Neh 7:7
RA-AMSES
the store-cities Pithom and *. Ex 1:11
RAAMA
Seba, Havilah, Sabta, *, and 1Ch 1:5-9
The sons of * were Sheba and 1Ch 1:5-9
RAAMAH
Havilah, Sabtah,*, Sabteca. Gen 10:7
The sons of * were:Sheba, Dedan. Gen 10:7
The merchants of Sheba and * Eze 27:22
RABBAH
in a museum at *, one of the cities Deu 3:11
of Ammon as far as Aroer near *. Jos 13:25
Kiriath-jearim), *, Beth-arabah, Jos 15:48-62
by laying siege to the city of *. 2Sa 11:1
siege of * the capital of Ammon. 2Sa 12:26,27
to tell David, "* and its 2Sa 12:26,27
So David led his army to * and 2Sa 12:29,30
(son of Nahash of *, an Ammonite) 2Sa 17:27
laid siege to * and conquered it. 1Ch 20:1
of * and placed it upon his own 1Ch 20:2
by destroying your city of *. Jer 49:2
Weep, daughter of *! Jer 49:3
the other to * in Trans-Jordan. Eze 21:19,20
Literally, "* of the Ammonites." Eze 21:19,20f
whether to attack Jerusalem or *. Eze 21:21
And I will turn the city of * Eze 25:5
to the walls of *, and it will burn Amo 1:14
RABBAH'S
took the king of * crown—a $50,000 2Sa 12:29,30
RABBI
As he was saying this, the * of Mt 9:18
and to be called '*' and 'Master'! Mt 23:7
For only God is your * and all of Mt 23:8
Judas, too, had asked him, "*, Mt 26:25
RABBI'S
were going to the * home, a woman Mt 9:19
When Jesus arrived at the * home Mt 9:23
RABBITH
Shion, Anaharath, *, Kishion, Ebez, Jos 19:17-23
RABBLE
some worthless * have led their Deu 13:12,13,14
This * trip me and lay traps in Job 30:12
RACAL
Eshtemoa, *, the cities of the 1Sa 30:27-31
RACE
of the ancient * of giants. Num 13:33
"There is a certain * of people Est 3:8
never perish from the Jewish *. Est 9:28
an athlete looking forward to a *! Ps 19:5
bother at all with the human *? Ps 144:3
not always win the *, nor the Ecc 9:11
of a sinful, foul-mouthed *; Is 6:5
this degenerate * of evil men? Jer 2:21
—has wearied you, how will you * Jer 12:5
human * of which he is the head. Eze 2:1f
Your own chariots * recklessly Nah 2:4
through the Jewish *—that is the Act 3:25
This king plotted against our *, Act 7:19
sin entered the entire human *. Rom 5:12
In a *, everyone runs but only 1Co 9:24
So run your * to win. 1Co 9:24
others for the *, I myself might be 1Co 9:27
of his sinful *, and wherever there 1Co 15:22
the end of the * and receive the Php 3:14
nationality or * or education or Col 3:11
* that God has set before us. Heb 12:1
of people of every * and nation. Rev 17:15
RACED
he did that day * from end to end Lk 7:17
The news * through the town, and Act 9:42
RACES
my heart *; Is 21:4
original Olympic * of Paul's time. 1Co 9:25f
RACHEL
Look, there comes his daughter * Gen 29:6
was going on, * arrived with her Gen 29:9
Then Jacob kissed * and started Gen 29:11
older, and her younger sister, *. Gen 29:16
Leah had lovely eyes, but * was Gen 29:17
Well, Jacob was in love with *. Gen 29:18
if you'll give me * as my wife." Gen 29:18
seven years working to pay for *. Gen 29:20
"I worked for seven years for *. Gen 29:25
and you can have * too—if you Gen 29:27
Then Laban gave him *, too. Gen 29:28
And Laban gave to * a servant Gen 29:29
So Jacob slept with *, too, and Gen 29:30
have a child, while * was barren. Gen 29:31
*, REALIZING SHE was barren, Gen 30:1
Then * told him, "Sleep with my Gen 30:3
a son. * named him Dan (meaning Gen 30:6
a second son. * named him Naphtali Gen 30:8
his mother Leah. * begged Leah to Gen 30:14
* said sadly, "He will sleep with Gen 30:15
birth of Joseph to *, Jacob said to Gen 30:25
So one day Jacob sent for * and Gen 31:4
* and Leah replied, "That's fine Gen 31:14
possessions (and * stole her Gen 31:21
For Jacob didn't know that * Gen 31:32
Rachel's tent. *, remember, was Gen 31:34
* explained, "but I'm pregnant." Gen 31:35
next, and * and Joseph last. Gen 33:2
bowed, and finally * and Joseph Gen 33:7
So * died, and was buried near Gen 35:19
The sons of *:Joseph, Benjamin. Gen 35:24
and descendants of Jacob and *: Gen 46:19-22
given to * by her father, Laban: Gen 46:23,24,25
For your mother * died after Gen 48:7
as fertile as * and Leah, from whom Ru 4:11
Ramah there is bitter weeping, * Jer 31:15
* weeping for her children, Mt 2:18
RACHEL'S
Then Bilhah, * servant-girl, Gen 30:7
Then God remembered about * Gen 30:22
Finally he went into * tent. Gen 31:33
(Bethlehem). But * pains of Gen 35:16
And with * last breath (for Gen 35:18
The sons of Bilhah, * Gen 35:25
see two men beside * tomb at 1Sa 10:2
RACING
And as the enemy was * down the Jos 10:11
as swiftly as a * river, and vanish Ps 90:5,6
they will come * toward Jerusalem. Is 5:26
Like fine stallions * through the Is 63:13
The Lord replied to me: If * with Jer 12:5
RACKED
my sins I am bent and * with pain. Ps 38:5,6
Pelusium will be * with pain, Eze 30:16
in bed paralyzed and * with pain. Mt 8:5,6
RACKETEERS
Hired murderers, loan * and Eze 22:12
RADDAI
his fifth was *, his sixth was 1Ch 2:14
RADIANCE
Because of this * upon his face, Ex 34:30
RADIANT
The earth was * with his 2Sa 22:13
moves out across the skies as * Ps 19:5
I am * with joy because of your Ps 31:7
Others too were * at what he did Ps 34:5

(RADIANT Con't)
Display your power and * glory. Ps 80:1
real life for you, and * health. Pro 4:22
Zion, and shall be * over the Jer 31:12
they will be * with health and Zec 9:16,17
your face will be * too, as though Lk 11:36
face become as * as an angel's! Act 6:15
before me clothed in a * robe! Act 10:30

RADIATE
may the Lord's face * with joy Num 6:24,25,26

RADICALS
king, and don't associate with *. Pro 24:21,22

RAFTERS
cedar from the floor to the *. 1Ki 7:7
leak, and soon the * begin to rot. Ecc 10:18

RAFTS
Sea and build them into *. 1Ki 5:9
then we will break the * apart 1Ki 5:9
great * of cedar logs to David. 1Ch 22:4

RAGE
"Why is your face so dark with * Gen 4:6
Jacob flew into a *. Gen 30:2
King Balak was livid with * by Num 24:10
Saul boiled with *. 1Sa 20:30
So he went away in a *. 2Ki 5:12
He flew into a *, and insulted Neh 4:1
literally, "Why do the heathen * Ps 2:1f
THE nations are to * against the Ps 2:1
mighty armies will * against them. Is 8:7,8
unceasing blows of * and held the Is 14:6
in a terrible *, ordered Shadrach, Dan 3:13
*, and began to plot his murder. Lk 6:11
do the heathen * against the Lord, Act 4:25,26
and ground their teeth in *. Act 7:54

RAGED
Jacob * at Laban. Gen 29:25
The battle * all across the 2Sa 18:8
the way you have * against me. Is 37:28
your anger has * against Jerusalem Zec 1:12
The terrible storm * unabated Act 27:20

RAGES
a great storm * round about him. Ps 50:3
He only * and scoffs, and tempers Pro 29:9
All afternoon it *, until the Jer 6:4

RAGING
mountain top looked like a * fire. Ex 24:17
my enemies like a * flood." 2Sa 5:20
darkness. A * fire will devour his Job 20:26
He is not disturbed by * rivers, Job 40:23
He quiets the * oceans and all Ps 65:7
and turn them into * fire and burn Jer 5:14
be able to put out the * flames. Jer 17:27
like a wild sea in a * storm. Jer 49:23
the land of Israel like a * fire. Lam 2:3
it flames forth like * fire. Hos 7:6
the * sea—and the storm stopped! Jon 1:15
of the cyclone and the * storms; Nah 1:3
Onward swept the * water. Hab 3:10
by fire * through your forests. Zec 11:1

RAGS
clothing, put on *, fasted, slept 1Ki 21:27
much sleep clothes a man with *. Pro 23:19,20,21
we find they are but filthy *. Is 64:6
as a menstruating woman's *." Is 64:6f
There he found some old * and Jer 38:11
"Use these * under your armpits to Jer 38:12
she is tossed away like dirty *. Lam 1:8
her be thrown out like filthy *!" Lam 1:17
worship was as foul as filthy *. Eze 36:17
are becoming mere moth-eaten *. Jas 5:2

RAHAB
named *, who was a prostitute. Jos 2:1
were kept shut. * went up to talk Jos 2:8
everyone except * the prostitute Jos 6:17
Thus Joshua saved * the Jos 6:25
Or, "the helpers of *." Job 9:13f
Literally, "*." Ps 89:10f
Literally, "* who sits still." Is 30:7f
Literally, "*, the dragon." Is 51:9f
Salmon was the father of Boaz (* Mt 1:5
God and his power—* the harlot did Heb 11:31
*, the prostitute, is another Jas 2:25

RAHAB'S
police squadron to * home, Jos 2:3

RAHAM
Shema was the father of *, who 1Ch 2:44

RAID
"Where did you make your * 1Sa 27:10
a *, bringing much loot with them. 2Sa 3:22

RAIDED
huge posse into Judah and * Lehi. Ju 15:9
the Amalekites had * the city and 1Sa 30:1
the Negeb, and had * the south of 1Sa 30:14
Later the Philistines * the 1Ch 14:13
had been sent home * several of the 2Ch 25:13
when the Sabeans * us, drove away Job 1:14,15

RAIDERS
Three companies of * soon left 1Sa 13:17
army, and even among the *. 1Sa 14:15
And after that the Syrian * 2Ki 6:23
against the Amalek * at Ziklag. 1Ch 12:21

RAIDING
Philistines were * Israel again, 1Sa 23:27
spent their time * the Geshurites, 1Sa 27:8
We were on our way back from * 1Sa 30:14
of King Ish-bosheth's * bands. 2Sa 4:2,3
The Philistines were * the 1Ch 14:9

RAIDS
the Midianite army in surprise *. Ju 8:11

RAILED
he insulted them and * at them. 1Sa 25:14

RAIN
the Lord God hadn't sent any *; Gen 2:5
begin forty days and nights of *; Gen 7:4
days old, the * came down in Gen 7:10,11,12
give you plenty of * for your Gen 27:27,28,29
and the * ceased pouring down. Ex 9:33
* down food from heaven for them. Ex 16:4
with plenty of *— a land that the Deu 11:11
will be no * and no harvest, and Deu 11:17
treasury of * in the heavens, to Deu 28:12
dust for lack of *, and dust storms Deu 28:24
Like the gentle * and dew, Deu 32:2
Like * upon the tender grass, Deu 32:2
And the sky poured down its *. Ju 5:4
You know that it does not * at 1Sa 12:17
send thunder and * today, so that 1Sa 12:17
and the Lord sent thunder and *; 1Sa 12:18
Let there be no dew nor * upon 2Sa 1:21
As sunshine after *.' 2Sa 23:4
up and there is no * because of 1Ki 8:35,36
walk, and send * upon the land 1Ki 8:35,36
be any dew or * for several years 1Ki 17:1
*, and the crops grow again!" 1Ki 17:14
that I will soon send * again!" 1Ki 18:1
or he'll be stopped by the *!" 1Ki 18:44
You won't see wind nor *, but 2Ki 3:17
and there is no * because of our 2Ch 6:26
and send * upon this land which 2Ch 6:27
that there is no *, or if I command 2Ch 7:13
He sends the * upon the earth to Job 5:10
He withholds the *, and the Job 12:15
God will * down wrath upon him. Job 20:23
He wraps the * in his thick Job 26:8
He makes the laws of the * and a Job 28:26
those in droughttime long for *. Job 29:23
*, which the skies pour down. Job 36:27
"From the south comes the *; Job 37:9
the valleys for the torrents of *? Job 38:25-27
causing the * to fall upon the Job 38:25-27
"Has the * a father? Job 38:28
shout to the clouds and make it *? Job 38:34
He will * down fire and Ps 11:6
the furrows with abundant *. Ps 65:10
You sent abundant * upon your Ps 68:9,10
The clouds poured down their *, Ps 77:17
He sends * upon the mountains Ps 104:13
Instead of * he sent down Ps 105:32
the lightning to bring down the *; Ps 135:7
you as parched land thirsts for *. Ps 143:6
Let fire and hail, snow, *, wind Ps 148:8
and the skies poured down *. Pro 3:20
a desert without dropping any *. Pro 25:14
Literally, "*." Pro 25:23f
summertime or * with harvest time! Pro 26:1
For the winter is past, the * is Sol 2:11
clouds not to * on it any more. Is 5:6
wither, the skies refuse their *. Is 24:4,5
* that melts down an earthen wall. Is 25:4
Then God will bless you with * at Is 30:23
forest to be nourished by the *. Is 44:14
As the * and snow come down from Is 55:10
one who gives them * each year in Jer 5:23,24
and brings the *, and from his Jer 10:13
why he was holding back the *: Jer 14:1
parched and cracked for lack of *; Jer 14:4
What heathen god can give us * Jer 14:22
the death blows I * upon them." Jer 25:16
lightning with the * and the winds Jer 51:16
wilderness, or a desert without *. Eze 22:24
And I will * down fire on Magog Eze 39:6
earth in answer to its cry for *. Hos 1:21,22
dawn or the * of early spring." Hos 6:3
* three months before the harvest. Amo 4:7
I sent * on one city, but not Amo 4:7
While * fell on one field, Amo 4:7
*, but there wasn't ever enough. Amo 4:8
pours it out as * upon the land. Amo 5:8
it down as * upon the ground. Amo 9:6
welcome showers of *, and Israel Mic 5:7
will be fertile, with plenty of *; Zec 8:12
ASK THE LORD for * in the Zec 10:1
the Lord of Hosts, will have no *. Zec 14:17
good, and sends * on the just and Mt 5:45
Though the * comes in torrents, Mt 7:25
there had been no * for three and Lk 4:25,26
as sending you * and good crops and Act 14:17
and warm us in the * and cold. Act 28:1
earnestly that no * would fall, Jas 5:17
time that it would *, and down it Jas 5:18
without giving *, promising much, Jud 1:12
skies so that no * will fall during Rev 11:6

RAINBOW
I have placed my * in the clouds Gen 9:
the earth, the * will be seen in Gen 9:
For I will see the * in the Gen 9:16,
halo like a * all around him. Eze 1:27,
ruby, and a * glowing like an Rev 4
a cloud, with a * over his head; Rev 1

RAINED
Then the Lord * down fire and Gen 19:
and * down manna for their food. Ps 78:
mighty power. He * down birds as Ps 78:
Then fire and brimstone * down Lk 17:

RAINFALL
was no * anywhere in the land. 1Ki 17
matter and because of the heavy *. Ez 10

RAINING
And it is * so hard that we can't Ez 10:

RAINS
and the torrential * subsided. Gen 8
give you regular *, and the land Lev 26:4
the early and late * that will Deu 11:
While the gentle * descend from Deu 33:2
as the springtime * upon the Ps 72
and refreshment collect after *! Ps 84
When the clouds are heavy, the * Ecc 11
heat and from * and storms. Is 4
even the springtime * have failed. Jer 3
* but send them in their seasons. Eze 34:2
For the * he sends are tokens of Joe 2:2
Once more the autumn * will come, Joe 2:2
"After I have poured out my * Joe 2:2
holding back the * from heaven and Hag 1:1
For when the * and floods come, Mt 7:2

RAINSTORM
For I hear a mighty * coming!" 1Ki 18:4
a heavy wind brought a terrific *. 1Ki 18:4
A heavy * will undermine it; Eze 13:1

RAINY
A constant dripping on a * day Pro 27:1

RAISE
How much of a * do you need to Gen 30:2
"* the banner of the Lord!" Ex 17:15,1
men to Egypt to * horses for him Deu 17:1
"Instead, he will * up for you a Deu 18:1
I will * up from among them a Deu 18:1
I * my hand to heaven Deu 32:40,4
* the baby after he is born?" Ju 13:1
"Then I will * up a faithful 1Sa 2:3
And the Lord will * up a king 1Ki 14:14
Sing praises to the Lord! * your Ps 68:4
How he blesses them! They * big Ps 107:38
He will * a flag among the Is 11:12
When I * my battle flag upon the Is 18:3
boulders, * the flag of Israel." Is 62:10
whom I will * up for them, says Jer 30:9
and no one will * you up, for the Jer 50:32
"The Lord God says: * your hands Eze 6:11
says that he will * against you, O Eze 23:22
never again will she * herself Eze 29:15
"And I will * up a notable Vine Eze 34:29
of Egypt, he will * an army against Dan 11:7
and * a great army against Egypt; Dan 11:25
and Egypt, too, will * a mighty Dan 11:25
and * them for myself! Hos 1:23
to * up children unto Abraham." Mt 3:9f
Heal the sick, * the dead, cure Mt 10:8
He does not * his voice! Mt 12:19
in three days I will * it up!" Jn 2:19
He will even * from the dead Jn 5:21
but that I should * them to eternal Jn 6:39
I should * him at the Last Day." Jn 6:40
and I will * him at the Last Day. Jn 6:54
'The Lord God will * up a Prophet Act 3:21,22
will * up a Prophet much like me Act 7:37
And God is going to * our bodies 1Co 6:14
us, for he can even * the dead. 2Co 1:9
will be afraid to * his voice!" 2Co 10:1

RAISED
On the day the Tabernacle was *, Num 9:15
plight, the Lord * up judges to Ju 2:16
enemies whom God * to power was 1Ki 11:23
they had been * since childhood. 2Ki 10:6
So the Lord * up leaders among 2Ki 13:5
family and * as his own daughter. Est 2:7
and stopped the arm * to strike? Job 38:15
this son you have * for yourself. Ps 80:15
The children I * and cared for so Is 1:2
I have * up Cyrus Is 45:13
Literally, "I have * up him Is 45:13f
the highways shall be * above the Is 49:11
Who bore these? Who * them for Is 49:21
your grain and wine. You * it; Is 62:9
Son, whom God has * up for them. Jer 30:9f
deep sin, I have * my hand and Eze 44:12
I promised with hand * in oath of Eze 47:14
with its paw *, ready to strike. Dan 7:5
and * a thriving crop of sins. Hos 10:13
even care that it was I who * him. Hos 11:3
who hear, and the dead * to life; Mt 11:5
later he would be * to life again. Mt 16:21
But after I am * to life again, Mk 14:28

AISED Con't)
worthy of being * from the dead get Lk 20:34,35
* up in new life from the dead. Lk 20:36
I was born and *, but I am the Jn 7:28
God * back to life again. Act 4:10
* the foresail and headed ashore. Act 27:40
and by being * from the dead he Rom 1:4
Literally, "* for our Rom 4:25f
And if the Spirit of God, who * Rom 8:11
heart that God has * him from the Rom 10:9
as he * up the Lord Jesus Christ. 1Co 6:14
have said that God * Christ from 1Co 15:15
Father who * him from the dead. Gal 1:1
mighty power that * Christ from Eph 1:20
when he * Christ from the Eph 2:5
of this that God * him up to the Php 2:9
God who * Christ from the dead. Col 2:12
can be in God who * Christ from the 1Pe 1:21

AISES
of death. He * up a nation and Job 12:23
"I am the one who * the dead and Jn 11:25
paid well if he * a large crop. 2Ti 2:6

AISIN
grain, one hundred * cakes, and two 1Sa 25:18

AISING
for see, I am * up an army of Jer 50:9
* a roof of shields against it. Eze 26:8
I am * a new force on the world Hab 1:6

AISINS
wine, grape juice, grapes, or *! Num 6:3,4
She must not eat grapes or *, or Ju 13:13,14
two clusters of *, and some water, 1Sa 30:11,12
bread, some wine, and a cake of *. 2Sa 6:19
clusters of *, one hundred bunches 2Sa 16:1
flour, fig cakes, *, wine, oil, 1Ch 12:40
bread, some wine, and a cake of *. 1Ch 16:3
your love—your '*' and your Sol 2:5

AKEM
and he had sons named Ulam and *. 1Ch 7:16

AKKATH
Ziddim, Zer, Hammath, *, Jos 19:35-39

AKKON
*, also the territory near Joppa. Jos 19:41-46

ALLY
have given us a banner to * to; Ps 60:4,5
will * to it; then you can Ps 60:4,5
The nations will * to him, for Is 11:10
the nations for them to * to; Is 11:12
in great anger, will * against Dan 11:10,11

AM
a three-year-old *, a turtle-dove Gen 15:9
Then Abraham noticed a * caught Gen 22:13
So he took the * and sacrificed Gen 22:13
touched one * of yours for food. Gen 31:38
Cut up the * and wash off the Ex 29:17
"Now take the other *, and Aaron Ex 29:19,20
"Then take the fat of the *, Ex 29:22
this is the * for ordination of Ex 29:22
Aaron's ordination * and wave it Ex 29:26
* to Aaron and his sons. Ex 29:27
"Take the * of consecration—the Ex 29:31
consecration—the * used in the Ex 29:31
goats' hair; and * skins dyed red, Ex 35:23
a male or female—* or ewe, billy Lev 3:6
he shall bring a * without defect, Lev 5:15
for him with the * of the guilt Lev 5:16
This sacrifice shall be a * Lev 5:17,18
His guilt offering shall be a * Lev 6:6
Lord the * for the burnt offering. Lev 8:18
Next he quartered the * and Lev 8:20
* was consumed before the Lord; Lev 8:21
Then Moses presented the other *, Lev 8:22
other ram, the * of consecration; Lev 8:22
this was Moses' portion of the * Lev 8:29
offering, and a * without bodily Lev 9:2
ox and a *, and a grain Lev 9:4
Next he killed the ox and *—the Lev 9:18
of the ox and the *—the fat from Lev 9:19
and a * for a burnt offering. Lev 16:3
and a * for their burnt offering. Lev 16:5
the offering shall be a *. Lev 19:21
atonement with the * for the sin Lev 19:22
a peace offering, a * without Num 6:14
then the * for a peace offering, Num 6:17
He brought a young bull, a *, Num 7:15
"If the sacrifice is a *, use Num 15:6
bull, *, lamb, or young goat. Num 15:11,12
a * were sacrificed on each altar. Num 23:2
a young bull and a * on each." Num 23:3,4
young bull and a * on each altar. Num 23:14
a young bull and * on every altar. Num 23:30
young bulls, one *, and seven male Num 28:11
oil as a grain offering for the *; Num 28:12
a *, and three pints for a lamb. Num 28:14
young bulls, one *, and seven Num 28:19
with the * there shall be six Num 28:20,21
*, and seven yearling male lambs. Num 28:27
quarts with the *, and three quarts Num 28:28,29
young bull, one *, and seven Num 29:2
quarts with the *, and three quarts Num 29:3,4
young bull, one *, seven yearling Num 29:8
six with the *; Num 29:9,10
young bull, one *, seven male Num 29:36
Perez, Hezron, *, Amminadab, Ru 4:18-22
were Jerahmeel, *, and Chelubai. 1Ch 2:9
* was the father of Amminadab, 1Ch 2:10
* (the oldest), Bunah, Oren, Ozem, 1Ch 2:25
The sons of *: 1Ch 2:27
of the Clan of *) became angry Job 32:2
and a perfect * from the flock. Eze 43:23
a bullock and a * from the flock Eze 43:25
bushel for each bullock and *; Eze 45:24
lambs and a *, all unblemished. Eze 46:4
to go with the *, and whatever Eze 46:5
six lambs and one *, all without Eze 46:6
With the *, he is to bring one Eze 46:7
one bushel with the *; Eze 46:11
around, I saw a * with two long Dan 8:3
the other. The * butted everything Dan 8:4
furiously at the two-horned *. Dan 8:6
He charged into the * and broke Dan 8:7
Now the * was helpless and the Dan 8:7
"The two horns of the * you saw Dan 8:20
promises a fine * from his flock, Mal 1:14

RAM'S
a * horn sounding one long blast; Ex 19:13
long, loud blast as from a * horn; Ex 19:16
hair, red-dyed * skins, goat-skins, Ex 25:1
a trumpet made from a * horn. Jos 6:3,4

RAMAH
Geba, Gibeon, *, Be-eroth, Mizpeh, Jos 18:21-28
turned toward * and the fortified Jos 19:29
Adamah, *, Hazor, Kedesh, Edre-i, Jos 19:35-39
Tree," between * and Bethel, in Ju 4:5
go on to Gibe-ah, or possibly *." Ju 19:12,13
Then they returned home to *, and 1Sa 1:19,20
So they returned home to * 1Sa 2:11
Then he would come back to *, 1Sa 7:17
built an altar to the Lord at *. 1Sa 7:17
of Israel met in * to discuss the 1Sa 8:4
Then Samuel went home to *, and 1Sa 15:34
Then Samuel returned to *. 1Sa 16:13
away and went to * to see Samuel, 1Sa 19:18
was at Naioth in *, he sent 1Sa 19:19
Then Saul himself went to * and 1Sa 19:22
DAVID NOW FLED from Naioth in *, 1Sa 20:1
him in his family plot at *. 1Sa 25:1
He was buried in *, his home 1Sa 28:3
fortress city of * in an attempt to 1Ki 15:17
city of * and returned to Tirzah. 1Ki 15:21
to help demolish * and haul away 1Ki 15:22
of * in order to control the road 2Ch 16:1
building * and gave up his plan to 2Ch 16:5
Judah went out to * and carried 2Ch 16:6
From the subclans of * and Geba, Ez 2:3-35
From the subclans of * and Geba, Neh 7:8-38
Hazor, *, Gittaim, Hadid, Zeboim, Neh 11:31-35
Fear strikes the city of *; Is 10:28,29
* there is bitter weeping, Rachel Jer 31:15
took Jeremiah to * along with all Jer 40:1
and *, and on over to Beth-aven; Hos 5:8
"Screams of anguish come from *, Mt 2:18
Or, "the region of *." Mt 2:18f

RAMAH-IN-THE-NEGEB
(also known as *) were also given Jos 19:8

RAMATH
And Shime-i from * had the 1Ch 27:27

RAMATH-MIZPEH
from Heshbon to * and Betonim, and Jos 13:26

RAMATHAIM-ZOPHIM
in *, in the hills of Ephraim. 1Sa 1;1

RAMESES
Egypt—the land of *—to his father Gen 47:11
left * and started for Succoth; Ex 12:37
They left the city of *, Egypt, Num 33:3,4
After leaving *, they stayed in Num 33:5,6

RAMIAH
*, Izziah, Malchijah, Mijamin, Ez 10:25

RAMOTH
tribe of Reuben; *, in Gilead, for Deu 4:43
tribe of Reuben; * of Gilead, in Jos 20:8
* (a City of Refuge), Mahanaim, Jos 21:38,39
Bethel, South *, Jattir, Aroer, 1Sa 30:27-31
Kedesh, Daberath, *, and Anem, and 1Ch 6:73
The tribe of Gad gave them * in 1Ch 6:80

RAMOTH-GILEAD
Ben-geber, whose area was *, 1Ki 4:8-19
are still occupying our city of *? 1Ki 22:3
army with mine to recover *?" 1Ki 22:4
"Shall I attack *, or not?" 1Ki 22:6
"Go ahead and attack *," they 1Ki 22:12
shall we attack *, or not?" 1Ki 22:15
entice Ahab to go and die at *?' 1Ki 22:20
of Judah led their armies to *. 1Ki 22:29
Hazael, the king of Syria, at *. 2Ki 8:28
"Get ready to go to *," he told 2Ki 9:1
When he arrived in *, he found 2Ki 9:4
with the army at *, defending 2Ki 9:14
to join forces with him against *. 2Ch 18:2
we go to war with * or not?" 2Ch 18:3,4,5
"go up to * and prosper, for the 2Ch 18:11
we go to war against * or not?" 2Ch 18:14
against * and be killed there?' 2Ch 18:19,20
of Judah led their armies to *. 2Ch 18:28
with King Hazael of Syria at *. 2Ch 22:5

RAMP
nor build a * against its wall, nor 2Ki 19:32

RAMPANT
ever return, for crime was *. Zec 8:10
Sin will be * everywhere and Mt 24:12

RAMPARTS
Therefore the * and walls fell Lam 2:8
Man the *! Nah 2:1

RAMS
them from the *, and let them mate Gen 30:39,40
mate only with Jacob's black *. Gen 30:39,40
goats,200 ewes,20 *,30 milk Gen 32:13,14,15
placed a layer of *' skins, dyed Ex 26:14
young bull and two * with no Ex 29:1
with the young bull and the two *. Ex 29:3,4
of one of the * as it is killed. Ex 29:15,16
Tanned *' skins and specially Ex 35:5-9
roof was made of *' skins, dyed Ex 36:19
roof and sides—the *' skins dyed Ex 39:33-40
offering, the two *, and the basket Lev 8:1
one young bull, and two *. Lev 23:18
two oxen, five *, five male goats, Num 7:17
12 bulls, 12 *, Num 7:87
60 *, 60 male goats, Num 7:88
bulls and seven * for sacrifice." Num 23:1
and seven * for the sacrifice. Num 23:29
young bulls, two *, and fourteen Num 29:13
six quarts for each of the two *; Num 29:14
young bulls, two *, and fourteen Num 29:17
young bulls, two *, fourteen male Num 29:20
young bulls, two *, and fourteen Num 29:23
young bulls, two *, and fourteen Num 29:26,27
young bulls, two *, and fourteen Num 29:29
young bulls, two *, and fourteen Num 29:32
portable towers, and battering * Deu 20:20
Choice Bashan *, and goats— Deu 32:14
your offering the fat of * to him. 1Sa 15:22
lambs and the wool of 100,000 *; 2Ki 3:4
bulls, a thousand *, and a thousand 1Ch 29:21
and seven * for consecration. 2Ch 13:9
7,700 * and 7,700 male goats. 2Ch 17:11
young bulls, seven *, seven lambs, 2Ch 29:21
they killed the * and sprinkled 2Ch 29:22
offerings, 100 *, and 200 lambs. 2Ch 29:32,33
young bulls, *, and lambs for burnt Ez 6:9
*, and 400 lambs were sacrificed; Ez 6:17
purchase of oxen, *, lambs, grain Ez 7:17
ninety-six *; Ez 8:35
by offering * as sacrifices): Ez 10:16-19
bulls and seven * and go to my Job 42:8
these fat he-goats, * and calves. Ps 66:15
The mountains skipped like *, Ps 114:4
mountains, did you skip like *? Ps 114:6
I don't want your fat *; Is 1:11
given you, and the * of Nabaioth Is 60:7
down her trees for battering *; Jer 6:6
the slaughter, like * and goats. Jer 51:40
battering * surrounding the walls. Eze 4:1
With battering * they will go Eze 21:22
He will set up battering * Eze 26:9
bring you lambs and * and goats. Eze 27:21
from kids and * from billy goats! Eze 34:17
are the *, the lambs, the goats and Eze 39:18
bulls and seven * without blemish. Eze 45:23
him thousands of * and ten Mic 6:7

RAN
So Sarai beat her and she * away. Gen 16:6
He sprang up and * to meet them Gen 18:2
Then Abraham * back to the tent Gen 18:6
Then he * out to the herd and Gen 18:7
trough and * down to the spring Gen 24:20
The girl * home to tell her Gen 24:28
She quickly * and told her Gen 29:12,13
And then Esau * to meet him and Gen 33:4
I screamed, he *, and forgot to Gen 39:14,15
everything * smoothly and well. Gen 39:23
But Moses * away into the land of Ex 2:15
a serpent, and Moses * from it! Ex 4:3
* a gold molding around the edge. Ex 37:26
Some young men * and told Moses Num 11:27
told him to, and * among the Num 16:47
for the loot. They * to the tent Jos 7:22
Their territory * from Aroer, on Jos 13:9
of the Salt Sea, * along the road Jos 15:2,3,4
From there it * to Upper Jos 16:5,6
began at the Sea, * east past Jos 16:5,6
The southern border * from the Jos 18:15
into the Arabah, * south past Jos 18:19
Beth-dagon, and * as far as Zebulun Jos 19:27
near Heleph and * past Jos 19:34
only child—* out to meet him, Ju 11:34
The woman * and told her husband, Ju 13:6
so she quickly * and found her Ju 13:10
Manoah * back with his wife and Ju 13:11
angry with him and * away, and Ju 19:2
So they * toward the wilderness, Ju 20:42
He jumped up and * to Eli. 1Sa 3:4,5
Samuel jumped up and * to Eli. 1Sa 3:6

(RAN Con't)
Samuel jumped up and * to Eli. 1Sa 3:8
tribe of Benjamin * from the battle 1Sa 4:12
As Goliath approached, David * 1Sa 17:48,49
Since he had no sword, he * over 1Sa 17:50,51
was dead, they turned and *. 1Sa 17:50,51
So the boy * and Jonathan shot 1Sa 20:36
arrows and * back to his master. 1Sa 20:38
So he * him through with his 2Sa 1:15
running, they * too, and retreated 2Sa 10:14
The man bowed and * off. 2Sa 18:21
not Absalom's) he * to the 1Ki 2:28
and the water * off the altar 1Ki 18:35
standing there and * after Elijah 1Ki 19:20
down the cry * through his troops. 1Ki 22:36,37
his chariot and * to meet him. 2Ki 5:21
Then he opened the door and *. 2Ki 9:10
all the noise, she * into the 2Ki 11:13,14
and his four sons * and hid. 1Ch 21:19,20
A covered porch * along the 2Ch 3:4
that families who * out of money Neh 5:2,3,4
Aaron's head, and * down onto his Ps 133:2
and his men, and * to meet them. Jer 41:13,14
A stone pavement * around the Eze 40:17
A 17½-foot walk * between the Eze 42:4
these walls there * a line of brick Eze 46:23
* to hide, and I was left alone. Dan 10:7
But Jonah was afraid to go and * Jon 1:3
That's why I * away to Tarshish. Jon 4:2
One of them * and filled a Mt 27:48
The women * from the tomb, badly Mt 28:8
man * out from a graveyard, just as Mk 5:1
spreading the news as they *. Mk 5:14
them leaving and * on ahead along Mk 6:33
him at once, and * throughout the Mk 6:55
the people * out of food again. Mk 8:1
them, and then * to greet him. Mk 9:15
A murmur * through the crowd—"He Mk 9:26
that he * away completely naked. Mk 14:51,52
So one man * and got a sponge Mk 15:36
They * to the village and found Lk 2:16
spreading the news as they *. Lk 8:34
'He started that building and * Lk 14:30
* and embraced him and kissed him. Lk 15:20
So he * ahead and climbed into a Lk 19:4
However, Peter * to the tomb to Lk 24:12
Some of our men * out to see, Lk 24:24
The wine supply * out during the Jn 2:3
She * and found Simon Peter and Jn 20:2
* to the tomb to see; Jn 20:3,4
it was, and as he * to see, the Act 7:31
Philip * over and heard what he Act 8:30
overjoyed that she * back inside to Act 12:14
Barnabas, and * them out of town. Act 13:50
in dismay and * out among the Act 14:14
for lights and * to the dungeon and Act 16:29
and * down among the crowd. Act 21:32
too strong, so we * across to Act 27:7,8
and * aground. Act 27:41
this way: that he * away from you Phm 1:15

RANCH
Maon owned a sheep * there, near 1Sa 25:2
and was at his * at this time for 1Sa 25:2

RANCHERS
Moab and his people were sheep *. 2Ki 3:4

RANDOM
shot an arrow at * and it struck 1Ki 22:34

RANG
that * out strong and clear. 2Ch 20:19
Again and again their voices *, Rev 19:3

RANGES
The mountain * are their Job 39:8
O splendid many-peaked *! Ps 68:15,16

RANK
You are the head of the list in * Gen 49:3
demoted him to the * of captain. 1Sa 18:13
Next in * was Eleazar, the son of 2Sa 23:9
priests from the * and file of the 1Ki 12:31
distinction as to age or *. 1Ch 24:31
whatever their *, will be respected Est 1:20
of high *, riding their steeds. Eze 23:23
highest * [in the coming Kingdom Lk 22:24
with the same * as Melchizedek." Heb 5:6
with the same * as Melchizedek. Heb 5:10
the honor and * of Melchizedek. Heb 6:20
a priest with the * of Melchizedek, Heb 7:11
someone with the * of Aaron—the Heb 7:11
same * all other priests had? Heb 7:11
who came with the * of Melchizedek, Heb 7:15
with the * of Melchizedek." Heb 7:17
with the * of Melchizedek." Heb 7:21
* and left their proper home." Jud 1:6f

RANKS
* to face the forces of Israel. 1Sa 17:4-7
out to the * to find his brothers. 1Sa 17:22
will all close * behind you." 2Sa 16:21
the Philistine * and drew water 2Sa 23:16
you from the * of the common people 1Ki 14:7
through their *, but his army 2Ki 8:21
they march, never breaking *. Joe 2:7

RANSACKED
Jerusalem. He * the Temple and the 1Ki 14:26
the enemy, whose homes will be *; Zep 1:13
can be * and his property robbed. Mk 3:27

RANSACKING
from * the cities we had taken. Deu 2:35,36

RANSOM
reads: "But if a * is laid upon Ex 21:30f
shall give a * to the Lord for his Ex 30:11,12
die—no * may be accepted for him. Num 35:31
to * Israel from all her troubles. Ps 25:22
rich as kings, can * his own Ps 49:7
Come, Lord, and rescue me. * me Ps 69:18
He has paid a full * for his Ps 111:9
He himself shall * Israel from Ps 130:8
Being kidnapped and held for * Pro 13:8
Literally, "the wicked is a * for Pro 21:18f
for your freedom, as your *. Is 43:3
Shall I * him from hell? Hos 13:14
You cannot * yourselves with it. Zep 1:18
to give my life as a * for many." Mt 20:28
to give my life as a * for many." Mk 10:45
God paid a * to save you from 1Pe 1:18
to take, and the * he paid was not 1Pe 1:18

RANSOMED
to be put to death, may be *." Lev 27:29f
to be * by mere earthly wealth. Ps 49:8,9
These, the * of the Lord, will Is 35:10
Don't be afraid, for I have * you; Is 43:1
right through it for your * ones? Is 51:10

RANSOMS
He heals me. He * me from hell. Ps 103:4

RANT
The nations * and rave in Ps 46:6

RAPE
men to us so we can * them." Gen 19:5
"He tried to * me, but when I Gen 39:14,15
here tried to * me, and I was only Gen 39:17
with him, so they could * him. Ju 19:22
"Will he even * the queen right Est 7:8
They * the women of Jerusalem Lam 5:11

RAPED
"Someone might carelessly have * Gen 26:10
saw her, he took her and * her. Gen 34:2
they * my wife until she was dead. Ju 20:5
"Is it true that Amnon * you? 2Sa 13:20
this ever since Amnon * Tamar. 2Sa 13:32,33
wives * by the attacking hordes. Is 13:16
that is why you have been * and Jer 13:22
the loot divided, the women *; Zec 14:1

RAPES
If a man * a girl who is not Deu 22:28,29

RAPHA
the fourth,*, the fifth. 1Ch 8:1

RAPHAH
*, Eleasah, Azel. 1Ch 8:37

RAPHU
Palti, son of *, from the tribe of Num 13:3-15

RAPIDLY
rate was rising * across the earth, Gen 6:11
flocks increased * and he became Gen 30:43
that his father was failing *. Gen 48:1
fertile, increasing * in numbers; Ex 1:7
Saul's troops were * slipping away, 1Sa 13:8
The news of his death spread * Act 1:19
multiplying *, there were rumblings Act 6:1
God's Good News was spreading * Act 12:24
will spread * and triumph wherever 2Th 3:1

RAPING
taking turns * her until morning. Ju 19:25

RAPTUROUS
* joy and the pain is forgotten. Jn 16:21

RARE
the Lord were very * in those days, 1Sa 3:1
"O woman of * beauty, what is it Sol 5:9
plant a wonderful, * crop of Is 17:10
covered my feet with * perfume. Lk 7:46

RAREST
with the * of perfumes; Sol 4:13,14
of Jerusalem: "O * of beautiful Sol 6:1
fragrance and the * fruits are at Sol 7:13

RASCAL
admire the * for being so shrewd. Lk 16:8

RASH
"If anyone makes a * vow, Lev 5:4
It is foolish and * to make a Pro 20:25
is sinful to make * promises to Ecc 5:1
is said, and should do nothing *. Act 19:36

RASHLY
That is why I spoke so *. Job 6:3

RAT
The mole, the *, Lev 11:29,30

RATE
Meanwhile, the crime * was rising Gen 6:11
birth * and the expanding economy, Is 29:23
to yourself at the * of eight Eze 4:10
Your birth * will rise and your Eze 36:14
infant mortality * will drop off Eze 36:14
At this * they knew they would Act 27:29

RATED
(a brave warrior * as high or 1Ch 12:3-7

RATES
with high interest *, and refuses Ps 15:5

RATHER
local girls. I'd * die than see Gen 27:4
"I'd * give her to you than to Gen 29:1
and I would * not go free,' then Ex 21:
slave, but * as a hired servant or Lev 25:4
* than as a slave or as property. Lev 25:5
the wilderness, * than be taken Num 14:
we would * have it on this side, Num 32:1
to their gods. *, you must build a Deu 12:4,
in your land; *, they shall be Ju 2:
it; we'd * be killed by a man!" Ju 8:2
against you; *, you have wronged me Ju 11:2
people would say, * than, "Let's 1Sa 9:9,10,1
kill him * than doing it myself." 1Sa 18:1
with you, we would * live in one of 1Sa 27:
hands of the Lord * than into the 1Ch 21:1
in May this time, * than at the 2Ch 30:2,
I would * die of strangulation Job 7:1
out of place! * that than face the Job 31:2
makes men wise. *, it is the spirit Job 32:8,
sin! *, he punishes the sinners. Job 34:11
I would * be a doorman of the Ps 84:10
a good name * than great riches; Pro 22:
for an invitation * than to be sent Pro 25:6,7
Israelites * than to the nations. Is 65:1
Israelites * than to the nations. Is 65:1
shall long to die, * than live Jer 8:3
i.e., * than upon tablets of Jer 31:33f
but *, a group of Arab tribes. Jer 49:30f
not obeyed me, but * have copied Eze 11:12
to be a symbol * than an historical Eze 38:2,3f
willing to die * than serve or Dan 3:28
"Please kill me, Lord; I'd * be Jon 4:3
to the earth! No, *, a sword. Mt 10:34
Naaman, a Syrian, * than the many Lk 4:27
earth? No! *, strife and division! Lk 12:51
"We must obey God * than men. Act 5:29
are saying some * startling things Act 17:20
* than eat that kind of meat. Rom 14:2
yet been heard, * than where a Rom 15:20
and be a fool * than let it hold 1Co 3:18
In fact, I would * die of hunger 1Co 9:15
have some parts that seem * odd! 1Co 12:23
* than in unknown languages. 1Co 14:7
I would much * speak five words 1Co 14:19
But if I must brag, I would * 2Co 11:30
about our Lord. *, we are sinners Gal 2:18
and resentful. *, bring them up Eph 6:4
for slowing down; * they should 1Ti 6:2
preferring to die * than turn from Heb 11:35

RATIFIED
And the leaders of Israel * the Jos 9:14,15
The contract was * before the Ju 11:11

RATION
You are to * this out to Eze 4:10
eat your meals; * out your water as Eze 12:18
Jerusalem shall * their food with Eze 12:19

RATIONED
will be tightly * in Jerusalem. Eze 4:16

RATS
gold models of the * that have 1Sa 6:4,5
gold models of the * and tumors, 1Sa 6:8
the gold * and tumors were placed 1Sa 6:11
the golden * and tumors from the 1Sa 6:15
The gold * were to placate God 1Sa 6:18

RATTLE
though the arrows * against him, or Job 39:21-23

RATTLING
and suddenly there was a * noise Eze 37:7

RAVAGED
and cattle of the * cities were Jos 11:14
the rats that have * the whole 1Sa 6:4,5
Athaliah had * the Temple, and 2Ch 24:7,8
the women, *, shall sit crying on Is 3:25,26
Many foreign rulers have * my Jer 12:10
in this land, now * by the Jer 32:43
and leave her naked and * by fire. Rev 17:16

RAVAGES
have escaped the * of the siege 2Ki 19:30
shall recover from the * of war. Jer 46:26
touched at all by the * of death. Act 13:37

RAVE
and he began to * like a madman. 1Sa 18:10
The nations rant and * in Ps 46:6
hungry they will * and shake their Is 8:21

RAVED
They * all afternoon until the 1Ki 18:29

RAVEN
a * that flew back and forth Gen 8:7
The * (all kinds), the ostrich, Lev 11:13-19
The * (any variety), Deu 14:11-18
gold, and he has wavy, * hair. Sol 5:11

RAVENOUS
Her judges are like * wolves at Zep 3:3

RAVENS
and eat what the * bring you, for I 1Ki 17:4
the brook. The * brought him bread 1Ki 17:6
Who provides for the * when Job 38:41
the young * cry to him for food. Ps 147:9
out by * and eaten by vultures. Pro 30:17
will live, and owls and *. Is 34:11

RAVENS Con't)
the * will croak from her doors. Zep 2:14
Look at the *—they don't plant Lk 12:24
AVINE
on some mountain or in some *." 2Ki 2:16
crossed the Kidron * with his Jn 18:1
AVINES
in frightening *, and in caves, and Job 30:6
* to the tops of the mountains. Eze 32:6
RAVISHED
You have * my heart, my lovely Sol 4:9
The land of Cush has been *. Eze 30:4
RAW
The meat must not be eaten * or Ex 12:9
But if there is * flesh Lev 13:14,15
It is proved by the * flesh. Lev 13:14,15
But if the * flesh later changes Lev 13:16,17
in camp until the * flesh of their Jos 5:8,9
he would demand * meat before it 1Sa 2:15
and ate the *, bloody meat. 1Sa 14:32
their shoulders were * and Eze 29:18
RAW-LEATHER
tied with seven * bowstrings, I Ju 16:7
RAY
darkness without a * of light will Ex 10:21
without one * of light, let them Is 50:10
Yet there is one * of hope: his Lam 3:21
not a * of joy or hope will Amo 5:18
RAYS
From his hands flash * of Hab 3:4
RAZE
"* her to the ground!" Ps 137:7
They will lay siege to it, * its Is 23:13
RAZED
on fire, and * it to the Ps 74:7
city of Jerusalem * into heaps of Jer 26:18
* to the ground and lie in ruins. Jer 47:5
RAZOR
will take this "*"—these Is 7:20
* to shave your head and beard; Eze 5:1
RAZOR-EDGED
it is * for slaughter. Eze 21:15
RE
of the sun god * of Heliopolis. Gen 41:50
RE-AIAH
Shobal's son * was the father of 1Ch 4:2
Giddel, Gahar, *, Rezin, Nekoda, Ez 2:43-54
*, Rezin, Nekoda, Neh 7:46-56
RE-EL-AIAH
Nehemiah, Seraiah, *, Mordecai, Ez 2:2
RE-ESTABLISH
I will * them because I love Zec 10:6
RE-TELLING
this cup you are * the message of 1Co 11:26
REACH
to you. Now * your hand inside Ex 4:6
beyond your strength and *; Deu 30:11
to * their fortified cities. Jos 10:20
had gone. To * the Philistine 1Sa 14:4
city where we can't * him." 2Sa 20:6
within easy * beside them, or with Neh 4:17
dares come within * of his jaws? Job 41:13
your own from the * of evil men, Ps 12:7
can * me, and a tower of safety. Ps 18:2
he holds me safely out of their * Ps 18:48
rock out of * of all my enemies. Ps 27:6
overflow they shall not * him." Ps 32:6f
where my enemies can never * me. Ps 61:3
a Rock where no enemy can * me. Ps 62:7
Your power and goodness, Lord, * Ps 71:19
O Lord, I * my pleading hands to Ps 88:9
of long ago. I * out for you. Ps 143:6
* down from heaven and rescue me; Ps 144:7
For a report from Assyria will * Is 37:7
winds will not * them any more. Is 49:10
That cry of judgment will * the Jer 25:31
that our prayers do not * through. Lam 3:44
against the walls to * the top. Eze 21:22
You will never * the cities—you Eze 39:5
I will * down and pull them up; Amo 9:2
"Who can ever * us way up Ob 1:3
to live beyond the * of danger. Hab 2:9
it will * across to the city gate. Zec 14:5
to the man, "* out your hand." Mk 3:5
crowd to Jesus but couldn't * him. Lk 5:18,19
to the man, "* out your hand." Lk 6:10
and the third day I will * my Lk 13:32
"Reports will * you that I have Lk 17:23
was within your * and you turned it Lk 19:42
within easy * of each of us; Rom 10:8
not * out to me and draw me in. 2Co 6:12
I strain to * the end of the race Php 3:14
beyond the * of change and decay. 1Pe 1:4
God's love can * and bless you. Jud 1:21
REACHED
But the two men * out and pulled Gen 19:10
The stench of the place has * to Gen 19:13
The sun was rising as Lot * the Gen 19:23
* from earth to heaven, and he Gen 28:12
Word soon * Jacob of what had Gen 34:5
months later word * Judah that Gen 38:24
The news soon * Gen 45:16
When word * the king of Egypt Ex 14:5
You * out your hand and the earth Ex 15:12
WORD SOON * Jethro, Moses' Ex 18:1
All who have * their twentieth Ex 30:14
watching until he * its entrance. Ex 33:8
When they * the summit, Moses Num 20:28
and * their cities in three days. Jos 9:17
until it finally * the Brook of Jos 15:2,3,4
it * the brook east of Jeokne-am. Jos 19:11
whereupon Ehud * beneath his robe Ju 3:21
soon * the land of Benjamin. Ju 20:3
army of Israel * Baal-tamar, it Ju 20:33
When they * the city walls Samuel 1Sa 9:26,27
When the report * Saul that 1Sa 19:19
When the boy had almost * the 1Sa 20:37
his arrival in Judah soon * Saul. 1Sa 22:6
Word soon * Saul that David had 1Sa 23:13
But just then a message * Saul 1Sa 23:27
Word soon * Saul that David had 1Sa 27:4
When they * Besor Brook, two 1Sa 30:9,10
When they * Besor Brook and the 1Sa 30:21
night and * Hebron at daybreak. 2Sa 2:32
of the battle * the capital, the 2Sa 4:4
of the city * David, he told his 2Sa 5:8
the report * David: "Absalom has 2Sa 13:29,30
As they * the spot at the top 2Sa 15:32
by the time they * Bahurim, so they 2Sa 16:14
WORD SOON * Joab that the king was 2Sa 19:1
My cry * his ears. 2Sa 22:7
When word * Solomon that 1Ki 1:51
When news of this * King 1Ki 2:29
outspread wings * from wall to 1Ki 6:23-28
This reply of Ahab's * Ben-hadad 1Ki 20:12
Soon afterwards news * the king 2Ki 19:9
* out his hand to steady the Ark. 1Ch 13:9
When this news * David, he 1Ch 19:17,18
he knelt down, * out his arms 2Ch 6:12,13
When this news * King Rehoboam he 2Ch 10:18
Word * Jehoshaphat that "a vast 2Ch 20:2
day they had * the outer court, 2Ch 29:17
my cry * his ears. Ps 18:6
He * down from heaven and took me Ps 18:16
that is why he has * out his hand Is 5:25
joy has * its lowest ebb; Is 24:11
do when the news * them that Jer 41:18
their course and * their Eze 7:10,11
of the cherubim * out his hand (for Eze 10:7,8
And when you * the age of Eze 16:6,7
You have * the limit of your Eze 22:4
will return before you have * Mt 10:23
Instantly Jesus * out his hand Mt 14:31
And so they * Jericho. Mk 10:46
Jesus * out and touched the man Lk 5:13
When reports of Jesus' miracles * Lk 9:7
Jerusalem, they * the border Lk 17:11
him, and as they * the place where Lk 19:36,37
* a new high of about 5,000 men! Act 4:4
SOON THE NEWS * the apostles and Act 11:1
until finally they * Paphos where Act 13:6,7
and finally * Philippi, a Roman Act 16:12
The next day we * Rhodes and then Act 21:1
As they were killing him, word * Act 21:31
As they * the stairs, the mob Act 21:35
And even when he * God's Heb 11:9
Their cries have * the ears of Jas 5:4
REACHES
When the innocent killer * any Jos 20:4
message * out to all the world. Ps 19:3,4
Your faithfulness * beyond the Ps 36:5
Your faithfulness * the skies. Ps 108:4
* everywhere around the world. Is 14:26
AH, LAND BEYOND the upper * of the Is 18:1
floor that * all the way from the Is 27:12
your greatness * up to heaven, Dan 4:22
the advancing army * the very top Zep 1:10
matter before it * the judge, lest Lk 12:58
he * whatever age his father set. Gal 4:2
REACHING
a temple-tower * to the skies—a Gen 11:3,4
flowers, blessings * to the utmost Gen 49:26
sleeveless tunic * from the Ex 28:4f
bodies, * from hips to knees. Ex 28:42
to meet him and, * into his 1Sa 17:48,49
with its roots * deep into the Jer 17:8
above the others, * to the clouds, Eze 31:10
growing so tall, * high into the Dan 4:20
In the meantime, he keeps on * Rom 10:21
REACT
northern king will * with the Dan 11:40
REACTED
the Sadducees * with violent Act 5:17
REACTION
tested by his * to men's praise. Pro 27:21
but indicated here by this *. Eze 3:14,15f
Their *, when he told them about Act 17:18
READ
When Joseph * the message, he Gen 50:16,17
And he * to the people the Book Ex 24:7
He must * from it every day of Deu 17:19
that these laws be * to all the Deu 31:10,11
Joshua then * to them all of Jos 8:34
had ever given was * before the Jos 8:35
his message *, "you will know that 2Sa 15:10
When the king of Israel * it, he 2Ki 5:7
the messengers, * it, and went over 2Ki 19:14
He gave the scroll to Shaphan to * 2Ki 22:8
Then Shaphan * it to the king. 2Ki 22:9,10
as I stated in that book you *. 2Ki 22:15,16
the Lord when you * the book and 2Ki 22:18,19
the king could * to them the entire 2Ki 23:1
If you want to * about the sons 2Ch 24:27
So he * it to the king. 2Ch 34:18
There the king * the scroll to 2Ch 34:30
has been translated and * to me. Ez 4:18
Ar-ta-xerxes was * to Rehum and Ez 4:23
leader, to * to them the law of God Neh 8:1
everyone could see him as he *. Neh 8:1
* from early morning until noon. Neh 8:1
As Ezra * from the scroll, Neh 8:7,8
of the passage that was being *. Neh 8:7,8
Ezra * from the scroll on each Neh 8:18
The laws of God were * aloud to Neh 9:3
Moses were being *, the people Neh 13:1
When this rule was *, all the Neh 13:3
sleeping and decided to * awhile. Est 6:1
"* the history books and see— Job 8:8
When you give it to one who can * Is 29:11
he says, "Sorry, I can't *." Is 29:12
As soon as King Hezekiah had * Is 37:14
and try to * their fate and future Jer 10:2,3
Some versions * "Zedekiah." Jer 27:1f
over to Jeremiah and * it to him! Jer 29:29
Some versions *, "a covenant they Jer 31:32f
here, you * the scroll in the Jer 36:6
told him to, and * all these Jer 36:8
(son of Shaphan) to * the scroll. Jer 36:10
Baruch to come and * the messages Jer 36:14,15
the scribe and * it to the king as Jer 36:21
get to Babylon, * what I have Jer 51:61,62
Some versions *, "190 days." Eze 4:4,5f
Some manuscripts *, "In the Eze 33:21f
"those who have * widely in many Dan 1:3,4
they could * the words but could Dan 5:8f
have tried to * that writing on the Dan 5:15
an alternate rendering might *, Dan 8:23f
so that anyone can * it at a glance Hab 2:2
"Haven't you ever * what King Mt 12:3
And haven't you ever * in the Mt 12:5
* the obvious signs of the times! Mt 16:2,3
"Don't you * the Scriptures?" Mt 19:4
"Didn't you ever * the Mt 21:16
"Didn't you ever * in the Mt 21:42
you ever * the Scriptures? Mt 22:31
Some ancient manuscripts *, "the Mk 1:3f
Jesus could * their minds and Mk 2:8
you never * in the book of Exodus Mk 12:26
Some ancient manuscripts *, Mk 14:24f
It *, "The King of the Jews." Mk 15:26
and stood up to * the Scriptures. Lk 4:16
Jesus replied, "Don't you * the Lk 6:3
Haven't you ever * what King Lk 6:3
Your brothers can * them any time Lk 16:29
they won't bother to * them. Lk 16:30
Greek, so that many people * it. Jn 19:20
prophets' words * every Sabbath. Act 13:27
the church that day as they * it. Act 15:31
Some manuscripts *, "many of the Act 17:4f
the governor. He * it and then Act 23:34
so that we could * about them and 1Co 10:11
Some ancient manuscripts *, 1Co 11:24f
Even now when the Scripture is * 2Co 3:14
Yes, even today when they * 2Co 3:15
By the way, after you have * Col 4:16
And * the letter I wrote to them. Col 4:16
of the Lord to * this letter to all 1Th 5:27
Until I get there, * and explain 1Ti 4:13
these verses could *: "If you have 1Pe 2:2,3f
Eat God's Word—* it, think about 1Pe 2:2,3f
Others believe this should *: 1Pe 5:13f
If you * this prophecy aloud to Rev 1:3
Those who listen to it being * Rev 1:3
was permitted to open and * it. Rev 5:3
Some manuscripts * "616." Rev 13:18f
Some manuscripts *, "King of the Rev 15:3,4f
READER
to the *: You know what is meant! Mt 24:15
Literally, "Let the * take Mt 24:15f
—*, pay attention! Mk 13:14
READERS
But some * may prefer the Heb 5:7f
READILY
she * agreed to his request. 1Sa 25:41
left hands as * as their right! 1Ch 12:2
me, though you * enough receive Jn 5:43
READINESS
They had been kept in * for Rev 9:15
their robes in * and will not need Rev 16:15
READING
This regular * of God's laws Deu 17:20
a favorable *," the man ventured. 2Ch 18:12
man stay pure? By * your Word and Ps 119:9

(READING Con't)
Another possible * is, Sol 6:12f
to hear the * of my laws—just as Is 58:2
Baruch was * to the people, the Jer 36:13
And whenever Jehudi finished * Jer 36:23
Then, when you have finished * Jer 51:63
He replied, "You are good at * Mt 16:2,3
Don't you remember * this verse Mk 12:10
a sign over him *, "Jesus of Jn 19:19
in his chariot, * aloud from the Act 8:28
heard what he was * and asked, "Do Act 8:30
he had been * from was this:"He Act 8:32
for it was through * the Scripture Gal 2:19

READINGS
After the usual * from the Books Act 13:15

READS
Literally, verse 30 *: "But if a Ex 21:30f
More literally, verse 7 *: "But Num 10:5,6,7f
in copying, *: "Saul was . 1Sa 13:1f
The Dead Sea manuscript *, Is 21:16f
manuscripts, *, "There were Eze 40:29,30f
Whoever * that writing on the Dan 5:7
Literally this verse *, "Are you Jn 18:34f
to everyone who * this book: If Rev 22:18

READY
will not be * for punishment Gen 15:16
the wood in order, * for the fire, Gen 22:9
we have a room all * for you, and a Gen 24:31
Then they got their presents * Gen 43:25
WHEN HIS BROTHERS were * to Gen 44:1
For they are almost * to stone Ex 17:4
the people are * for my visit. Ex 19:10
He told them, "Get * for God's Ex 19:15
you broke. Be * in the morning to Ex 34:2
them when the new harvest is *! Lev 26:10
but now we are * to go on into the Num 14:40
He was * to destroy you. Deu 9:8
the Lord was * to destroy you. Deu 9:19
the Lord was * to destroy you. Deu 9:25
get * to cross the Jordan River. Jos 1:10,11
* to pronounce their blessing. Jos 8:33
I am * to drive these people out Jos 13:2-7
were up early, * to leave, but the Ju 19:5
were at Michmash, * for battle, I 1Sa 13:11
Philistines are * to march against 1Sa 13:12
to David, "I am * to give you my 1Sa 18:17
Quickly getting *, she took 1Sa 25:42
For all Israel is *, and only you 2Sa 19:11,12
and said, "Get * for another 1Ki 20:22
"Get * to go to Ramoth-gilead," 2Ki 9:1
Get my chariot *!" 2Ki 9:21
The guards, with weapons *, 2Ki 11:11
and had it * for the king, who, 2Ki 16:11,12
It is as when a child is * to be 2Ki 19:3
were 40,000 trained and * troops. 1Ch 12:24-37
In fact, all of Israel was * for 1Ch 12:38
were much more * to sanctify 2Ch 29:34
always * to pardon, gracious and Neh 9:17
that they will be * to do their Est 3:14
his friends, "get * a 75-foot-high Est 5:14
the Jews would be * and prepared to Est 8:13
the grave is * to receive me. Job 17:1
calamity stands * to pounce upon Job 18:12
I helped those who were * to Job 29:13
My words are * to burst out! Job 32:19
Now get * to fight, for I am Job 38:3
They close in upon me and are * Ps 17:11
they are * to butcher those who Ps 37:14
Literally, "I am * to fall." Ps 38:17f
help, with praises * on my tongue. Ps 66:17
You are * with a plentiful supply Ps 69:13
I am *, I will punish the wicked! Ps 75:2
so good and kind, so * to forgive; Ps 86:5
I have been sickly and * to die. Ps 88:15
O GOD, MY heart is * to praise Ps 108:1
Stand * to help me because I Ps 119:173
sterling * for the silversmith. Pro 25:4,5
I am tired out, O God, and * to Pro 30:2
end of opinions * to be expressed. Ecc 12:12
be before they are * to listen?" Is 6:11
The funeral pyre has long been * Is 30:33
The court is * for your case. Is 41:1
right now! I am * to save you, and Is 46:13
is at stake. I am * to make an Is 55:3
For the enemy is everywhere, * to Jer 6:25
Pack your bags, he says. Get * Jer 10:17
Lord says: I am * to judge you Jer 21:12
punishment I am * to pour out upon Jer 26:3
ones, those * to give birth. Jer 31:8
Then, when Jeremiah was *, Jer 38:12
Pack up; get * to leave for Jer 46:19
you fully * for the battle. Jer 50:42
It is * now to hand to the Eze 21:9,10,11
"The Lord God says: I am * to Eze 36:37,38
with its paw raised, * to strike. Dan 7:5
Announce this far and wide: Get * Joe 3:9
The fact is, I am getting * to Amo 3:4
shows it is * for its food. Amo 3:4
The Lord stands * at Jerusalem's Mic 1:9
and burned. Get * for the siege! Nah 3:14
disciples to get * to cross to the Mt 8:18
the banquet was * he sent Mt 22:3
is * and the roast is in the oven. Mt 22:4
wedding feast is *, and the guests Mt 22:8
until you are * to welcome the one Mt 23:39
being * for my unannounced return. Mt 24:44
and those who were * went in with Mt 25:10
to be * for the Lord's arrival." Mk 1:3
Literally, "make * the way of the Mk 1:3f
have it standing * to rescue him in Mk 3:9
much as they were * to understand. Mk 4:33
the room you have * for us, where Mk 14:14
and acceptable, * to stand in his Lk 1:75
poised over you, * to sever your Lk 3:9
and that God is * to give blessings Lk 4:18,19
"Be prepared—all dressed and *— Lk 12:35
Then you will be * to open the Lk 12:36
are * and waiting for his return. Lk 12:37
be joy for his servants who are *! Lk 12:38
"Everyone would be * for him if Lk 12:39
as they would be * for a thief if Lk 12:39
So be * all the time. Lk 12:40
When all was *, he sent his Lk 14:17
know that he was * to help them and Lk 22:5
to a large room all * for us. Lk 22:12
Simon said, "Lord, I am * to go Lk 22:33
* for the coming of the Lord!' Jn 1:23
us, and are * now for reaping. Jn 4:35
Jesus saw that they were * to Jn 6:15
he asked, "for I am * to die Jn 13:37
When everything is *, then I will Jn 14:2,3
is coming! Get * to receive him!" Act 18:25,26
For I am * not only to be jailed Act 21:13
The soldiers standing * to lash Act 22:29
road * to jump him and kill him. Act 23:21
"Get 200 soldiers * to leave for Act 23:23,24
my ability, I am * to come also to Rom 1:15
that God makes us * for Rom 1:17
sake we must be * to face death at Rom 8:36
will be far more * to put the Jews Rom 11:24
here, and I am * to come after all Rom 15:23
has * for those who love the Lord. 1Co 2:9
unbelievers aren't yet * for it. 1Co 14:22
someone must be * to interpret what 1Co 14:27
Right now God is * to welcome 2Co 6:2
Today he is * to save you. 2Co 6:2
* to send an offering a year ago. 2Co 9:2
you really are *, as I told them 2Co 9:3
* after all I have told them! 2Co 9:4
this time I come * to punish 2Co 13:2
I will always be * to speak out Php 1:20
* to suffer quietly and patiently. Col 3:12
Be gentle and * to forgive; Col 3:13
to make you * for his kingdom, 2Th 1:5
can come only when his time is *. 2Th 2:6
Is she always * to show kindness? 1Ti 5:10
need, always being * to share with 1Ti 6:18
You will be * to suffer with me 2Ti 1:8
and * for any honest work. Tit 3:1
Please keep a guest room * for Phm 1:22
though he has been * and waiting Heb 4:3
We know he is * and waiting Heb 4:4
no good and is * for condemnation Heb 6:8
for when Moses was getting * to Heb 8:5
Well, when all was * the priests Heb 9:6
so you have made * this body of Heb 10:5
son Isaac, and was * to slay him on Heb 11:17
then you will be * for anything, Jas 1:4
for he is always * to give a Jas 1:5
It is always * to pour out its Jas 3:8
hearts are * for the slaughter. Jas 5:5
prayers will not get * answers. 1Pe 3:7
as you do, be * to tell him, and do 1Pe 3:15
you must be * to suffer, too. 1Pe 4:1
to her child, * to eat the baby as Rev 12:4
is * to judge her for her crimes. Rev 18:5

REAFFIRM
I will * my covenant with you, Eze 16:62

REAIAH
his grandson was *; 1Ch 5:5

REAL
and that * life comes by obeying Deu 8:3
wonderful place—a * paradise. Ju 18:9,10
yourself to be a * soldier by 1Sa 18:17
our king you were our * leader. 2Sa 5:2
and brothers, too, were * leaders. 1Ch 26:9
" 'Yet all the time your * Job 10:13,14
to forsake evil is * Job 28:28
invaders, their * problem is Ps 55:10
they will lead you to * living. Pro 4:13
for they will mean * life for you, Pro 4:22
Wickedness never brings * Pro 12:3
No * Pro 12:21
* poverty is evident to the poor. Pro 28:11
So mankind has no * advantage Ecc 3:19
The gods they made are not * gods Jer 16:20
and you were no * shepherds at all, Eze 34:8
always your * interest has been in Amo 5:25,26,27
receives it with * joy, but he Mt 13:20
He discovered a * bargain—a Mt 13:46
them, and they were in * danger. Lk 8:23
don't have. For * life and real Lk 12:15
For real life and * living are Lk 12:1
"But as to your * Lk 20:37,3
—is our worship spiritual and *? Jn 4:21-2
No, you are obeying your * Jn 8:4
has no * concern for the sheep. Jn 10:1
No, your * interest was in your Act 7:4
For there is no * charge against Act 25:2
But the * reason behind their Act 26:
For you are not * Jews just Rom 2:28
No, a * Jew is anyone whose Rom 2:2
we can have * peace with him Rom 5:
that they owe a * debt to the Rom 15:27
Let there be * harmony so that 1Co 1:1
ever lay any other * foundation 1Co 3:1
a * defeat for you as Christians. 1Co 6:7
And this has a * advantage: I am 1Co 9:19
alive and are * gods, and that 1Co 10:19
be of * help to the whole church. 1Co 14:12
at your side with such * devotion. 1Co 16:16
the * meaning of the Scriptures. 2Co 3:14
*, that it goes beyond mere words. 2Co 8:8
* concern for you that I have. 2Co 8:16
I want it to be a * gift and not 2Co 9:5
And the * life I now have within Gal 2:20
You can see from this that the * Gal 3:7
for having a * interest in you; Php 2:20
well, he and I have been * Php 2:25
So I was a * Jew if there ever Php 3:5
Christ with * certainty and clear Col 2:2
They were only shadows of the * Col 2:17
person does. Your * life is in Col 3:3
And when Christ who is our * Col 3:4
will be storing up * treasure for 1Ti 6:19
hearts and * enthusiasm for doing Tit 2:14
to be of * use to both of us. Phm 1:11
of the * tabernacle in heaven; Heb 8:5
But the * things in heaven, of Heb 9:23
a copy of the * temple in heaven. Heb 9:24
was not their * home but that they Heb 11:13
forward to their * home in heaven. Heb 11:14
in good deeds is not * faith. Jas 2:20
Now you can have * love for 1Pe 1:22
Since your * home is in heaven I 1Pe 2:11
We know what * love is from 1Jn 3:16
In this act we see what * love 1Jn 4:10

REALISTIC
be equalled by your * action now. 2Co 8:11

REALIZATION
trembling at the * of what had Mk 5:33
gift comes the * that God wants us Tit 2:12

REALIZE
"Then they will * that Jehovah, Ex 4:5
evening you will * that it was the Ex 16:6
"Don't they * that I am giving Ex 16:28,29
Moses didn't * as he came back Ex 34:29
When they * it, they shall offer Lev 4:14
and doesn't * it, he is guilty. Lev 4:27
But as soon as he does * it, he Lev 4:28
they said. "We * that we have Num 14:40
when the people * their error, they Num 15:23,24
I didn't * you were there. Num 22:34
so you would * that Jehovah is God, Deu 4:35
He did it to help you * that food Deu 8:3
So you should * that, as a man Deu 8:5
so that you would * that it is the Deu 29:6
of the earth will * that Jehovah is Jos 4:24
But of course he didn't * that Jos 8:14
(Manoah didn't yet * that he Ju 13:16
His father and mother didn't * Ju 14:4
"Don't you * that the Ju 15:11
But he didn't * that the Lord Ju 16:20
didn't * the impending disaster. Ju 20:34
so that you will * the extent of 1Sa 12:17
And now I * that you are surely 1Sa 24:20
her, "Do you * that Haggith's son, 1Ki 1:11
when the people * their sin and 1Ki 8:38
did not * that these were wrong. 1Ki 15:14
"Do you * that the Syrians are 1Ki 22:3
him, "Don't you * that I was there 2Ki 5:26
Please forgive me, for I * now 1Ch 21:8
Then you will * how much better 2Ch 12:8
Don't you * that the Lord God of 2Ch 13:5
Don't you * that Hezekiah is the 2Ch 32:12
Don't you * that I and the other 2Ch 32:13
"Yes, I * you know everything! Job 12:2
he will * his failing strength. Job 18:7
"Don't you * that ever since man Job 20:4
"Don't you * that those treading Job 22:15,16
Do you * the extent of the earth? Job 38:17,18
Lord, help me to * how brief my Ps 39:4
at last they will * what amazing Ps 64:9
"Does God * what is going on?" Ps 73:11
Who can * the terrors of your Ps 90:11
Try to * what this means—the Lord Ps 100:3
How precious it is, Lord, to * Ps 139:17,18
and doesn't even * where it leads. Pro 5:6
But they don't * that her Pro 9:18
—but now I * that even this was Ecc 1:16-18
who doesn't even * it is sinful to Ecc 5:1
hard times strike, * that God gives Ecc 7:14
that everyone will * that nothing Ecc 7:14

EALIZE Con't)
ake in everything, but * that Ecc 11:9
No one seems to * that God is Is 57:1
all shall * that they are a Is 61:9
They will * that I alone am God, Eze 6:10
will * that I alone am God. Eze 6:13
until you finally * that God Dan 4:32
She doesn't * that all she has, Hos 1:8
even * how weak and old he is. Hos 7:9
Don't you * that God was speaking Mt 22:31
Don't you * that I could ask my Mt 26:53
For they still didn't * who he Mk 6:52
"Didn't you * that I would be Lk 2:49
don't * what your hearts are like. Lk 9:55f
need, don't you * that your Lk 11:13
And don't you * that you also Lk 13:3
"Do you * what you are saying Lk 18:19
then you will * that I am he and Jn 8:28
be free— (Yes, I * that you are Jn 8:37
(His disciples didn't * at the Jn 12:16
"Don't you * that I have the Jn 19:10
"Dear brothers, I * that what Act 3:17
his brothers would * that God had Act 7:25
recognize him, or * that he is the Act 13:27
"I didn't * he was the High Act 23:5
So I want you to * that this Act 28:28,29
Don't you * how patient he is Rom 2:4
Don't you * that you can choose Rom 6:16
Don't you * that all of you 1Co 3:16
Don't you * that if even one 1Co 5:6
Don't you * that we Christians 1Co 6:3
Don't you * that your bodies are 1Co 6:15
However, some Christians don't * 1Co 8:7
Don't you * that God told those 1Co 9:13
be the first to * that what I am 1Co 14:37
I * THAT I really don't even need 2Co 9:1
as I think you * by now, for we 2Co 11:6
that I came to * that I could never Gal 2:19
I came to * that acceptance with Gal 2:19
I want you to * that God has been Eph 1:18
done for us and * that we are Php 3:3
that others will * that they, too, 1Ti 1:16
us * what is wrong in our lives; 2Ti 3:16
Don't you * that it is usually Jas 2:6
Don't you * that making friends Jas 4:4
Then when you * your Jas 4:10
Now that you * how kind the Lord 1Pe 2:2,3
they should * this: They sin 1Jn 3:6
And you don't * that spiritually Rev 3:17

REALIZED
and when she * she was pregnant, Gen 16:4
Esau * that his father despised Gen 28:6,7,8
Meanwhile, when Leah * that she Gen 30:9
Potiphar noticed this and * that Gen 39:3
Then Pharaoh woke up again and * Gen 41:7
When Moses * that his deed was Ex 2:14
son of Zippor) * how many of them Num 22:2,3
BALAAM * BY now that Jehovah Num 24:1
When Gideon * that it had indeed Ju 6:22
It was then that Manoah finally * Ju 13:21
Delilah * that he had finally Ju 16:18
Then Eli * it was the Lord who had 1Sa 3:8
When the people * what was 1Sa 5:7
No one * that Jonathan had gone. 1Sa 14:3
When it was finally * what David 1Sa 17:31
When the king * how much the Lord 1Sa 18:28
so at last Jonathan * that his 1Sa 20:33
Saul * that it was Samuel and 1Sa 28:14
at the ruins and * what had 1Sa 30:3
David now * why the Lord had 2Sa 5:12
Now the people of Ammon * how 2Sa 10:6
When Joab * that he would have 2Sa 10:9
The Syrians now * that they were 2Sa 10:15,16
he * what had happened. 2Sa 12:19
WHEN GENERAL JOAB * how much 2Sa 14:1
Then Solomon woke up and * it had 1Ki 3:15
were awed as they * the great 1Ki 3:28
She soon * that everything she 1Ki 10:4
When the people * that the king 1Ki 12:16,17
" 'Why haven't you * long before 2Ki 19:25
David now * why the Lord had 1Ch 14:2
When King Hanun * his mistake he 1Ch 19:6
When Joab * that the enemy 1Ch 19:10
When the people * what the king 2Ch 10:16
For as soon as they * he was not 2Ch 18:32
At that point Manasseh finally * 2Ch 33:13
But I * they were plotting to Neh 6:2
Then I * that God had not spoken Neh 6:12,13
and they * that the work had been Neh 6:16
About the same time I * that some Neh 13:23
Then I * that even wisdom is Ecc 2:15
Then I * that even this pleasure Ecc 2:24-26
And then I * that God is letting Ecc 3:18
Then I * that though wisdom is Ecc 9:16
Before I * it I was stricken Sol 6:12
people of that day * it was their Is 53:8
and his soldiers * that the city Jer 39:4
who were watching, * that God was Zec 11:11
Then the disciples * he was Mt 17:13
Jewish leaders * that Jesus was Mt 21:45
Jesus * at once that healing Mk 5:30
Jesus * what they were discussing Mk 8:17
* that Jesus had answered well. Mk 12:28
(For he * by now that this was Mk 15:10
When they finally * who he was, Mk 16:13
to them, and they * from his Lk 1:22
When Simon Peter * what had Lk 5:8
When the woman * that Jesus knew, Lk 8:47
* that he was talking about them. Lk 20:19
saying this and * that what he had Jn 2:22
Then the father * it was the Jn 4:53
When the people * what a great Jn 6:14
Jesus * they wanted to ask him so Jn 16:19
Jesus fully * all that was going Jn 18:4,5
— for until then we hadn't * Jn 20:9
praising God, and * he was the Act 3:10
were amazed and * what being with Act 4:13
Peter finally * what had Act 12:11
and * he had faith to be healed. Act 14:9
But when the crowd * he was a Act 19:34
But when I learned the truth, I * Rom 7:9
old age, for she * that God, who Heb 11:11

REALIZES
as he * that he has touched it. Lev 5:3
or bad, when he * what a foolish Lev 5:4
* that you always do what you say. 1Ch 17:24

REALIZING
RACHEL, * SHE was barren, became Gen 30:1
at Timnah, and * by now that she Gen 38:14
with him, not * of course that she Gen 38:16
sins without * it, and does Lev 4:13
sins without * it and is guilty of Lev 4:22
law of God without * it is guilty Lev 5:17,18
it is he has done without * it. Lev 5:17,18
sacrifices without * it, he shall Lev 22:14
anger, without * it will hit Num 35:22,23
* that they were poisonous. 2Ki 4:39
loss of Vashti, * that he would Est 2:1
* this man's understanding, Jesus Mk 12:34
heavenly bodies, * that every 2Co 5:6
* how painful it would be to you. 2Co 7:8
entertained angels without * it! Heb 13:2

REALLY
serpent came to the woman. "*?" Gen 3:1
you, and be sure it * is Esau!" Gen 27:21
Isaac: "Are you * Esau?" Gen 27:24
(But he didn't * intend for Gen 38:11
and Jacob, has * appeared to you. Ex 4:5
a plague that will * speak to you Ex 9:14
(for you aren't * complaining Ex 16:7,8,9
please, if this is * so, guide Ex 33:13
for what you are * doing is Lev 25:14,15,16
That is what you are * after! Num 16:11,12
or not you would * obey him? Deu 8:2
whether or not you * love him with Deu 13:3
Gideon replied, "If it is * true Ju 6:17
Prove that it is * Jehovah who is Ju 6:17
If Baal is * a god, let him take Ju 6:31
God, "If you are * going to use me Ju 6:36
replied, 'If you * want me, come Ju 9:15
"I * thought you hated her," he Ju 15:2
"Now tell me how you can * be Ju 16:13
"I know the Lord will * bless me Ju 17:13
"Is it * Naomi?" Ru 1:19
them, "If you are * serious about 1Sa 7:3
"I * don't know," Abner said. 1Sa 17:55
that the king * liked him a lot, 1Sa 18:22
that his father * meant it when he 1Sa 20:33
Saul called back, "Is it * you, 1Sa 24:15
Gath and tell where he had * been. 1Sa 27:11
We must * act like men today if 2Sa 10:12
Ahithophel, which * was the better 2Sa 17:14
Then the woman who * was the 1Ki 3:26
that God would * live on earth? 1Ki 8:27
seen it for myself * And *! 1Ki 10:7
"Is it * you, my lord Elijah?" 1Ki 18:7
But he was * thinking, "At 2Ki 20:19
But will God * live upon the 2Ch 6:18
how wise he * was, and how 2Ch 9:3
did decide * to please the Lord. 2Ch 12:14
Do you * think you can defeat 2Ch 13:8
the people as yet * decided to 2Ch 20:33
him and to see what he was * like. 2Ch 32:31
realized that the Lord was * God! 2Ch 33:13
prove that they were * Israelites. Ez 2:59
tell me what you * want, and I will Est 5:6
Does it * seem right to you to Job 10:3
in my hand and say what I * think. Job 13:14
about God— but *, I don't need to, Job 27:12
Do you * think that if you shout Job 36:19
Can anyone * understand the Job 36:29
cannot * be a good person at all. Ps 14:1
Don't they * know any better? Ps 14:4
which you * want from your people. Ps 40:6
and goats that I * want from you. Ps 50:9
sacrifice; this * honors me. Ps 50:23
does right and * seeks for God. Ps 53:2
can they ever be * happy again. Ps 53:6
If I had * said that, I would Ps 73:15
dream of things that never * were! Ps 73:20
I know how delightful they * are. Ps 119:35
Lord, see how much I * love your Ps 119:159
PRAISE THE LORD! Yes, * praise Ps 146:1
or joy—no one else can * share it. Pro 14:10
but what he is * like is shown by Pro 27:19
A man who assists a thief must * Pro 29:24
was nothing * worthwhile anywhere. Ecc 2:11
What does one * get from hard Ecc 3:9
But who can * know what is going Ecc 10:14
bread, and then—he * does —he takes Is 44:15
This is * living; Is 56:12
know at last and * understand that Is 60:16
Do you * think that you can Jer 7:9
No one can * know how bad it is! Jer 17:9
If these threats of yours are * Jer 17:15
If they are * God's prophets, Jer 27:18
to prove that God has * sent him. Jer 28:9
be known that he * is from God." Jer 28:9
and small, shall * know me then, Jer 31:34
I had heard was * from the Lord. Jer 32:8
* are—adulteresses and murderers. Eze 23:45
love, and you will * know me then Hos 1:20
But Amos replied, "I am not * Amo 7:14
Do you * expect him to listen? Mic 3:4
the world how * vile you are." Nah 3:6
"Don't you * know?" Zec 4:5
October, were you * in earnest Zec 7:5
But you retort, "*? Mal 1:2,3
religious are * godly people. Mt 7:21
Jesus, "Are you * the one we are Mt 11:3
"Sir, if it is * you, tell me to Mt 14:28
"You * are the Son of God!" Mt 14:33
them weren't sure it * was Jesus! Mt 28:17
ever know what it means to * live. Mk 8:35
All that's required is that you * Mk 11:22,23
kind of men they * are, they Mk 12:40
you live that you * have repented. Lk 3:8
ask him, "Are you * the Messiah? Lk 7:19
for if God had * sent him, he would Lk 7:39
the message never * gets through to Lk 8:13
and no one * knows the Son except Lk 10:22
Father, and no one * knows the Lk 10:22
There is * only one thing worth Lk 10:42
"*," he remarked, "this poor Lk 21:3
* God's Chosen One, the Messiah." Lk 23:35
words, "The Lord has * risen! Lk 24:33,34
"Why do you doubt that it is * Lk 24:38
that he * was the Messiah. Jn 2:11
the Scriptures * did refer to him, Jn 2:22
If any of you * determines to do Jn 7:17
all, that he * is the Messiah? Jn 7:26
trust me, you are * trusting God. Jn 12:44
If you * love me, you will be Jn 14:28
ask him if he * was the Lord, for Jn 21:12
son of John, do you * love me?" Jn 21:16
was * he himself they were seeing. Act 1:3
we'll * throw the book at them." Act 4:17
didn't believe it was * happening. Act 12:9
"It's * true!" Act 12:11
to see if they were * so. Act 17:11
of God, for you * know his laws, Rom 2:20
No one has ever * followed God's Rom 3:11
(though not new, *, for the Rom 3:21,22
Even if we were good, we * Rom 5:7
and now you can * serve God; Rom 7:6
what the law * demanded. Rom 7:9
at all, for I * want to do what is Rom 7:15
us that we * are God's children. Rom 8:16
they had not been * seeking God. Rom 9:30
how his ways will * satisfy you. Rom 12:2
that you love others: * love them. Rom 12:9
there is nothing * wrong with Rom 14:14
No one can * know what anyone 1Co 2:11
or what he is * like, except that 1Co 2:11
and what was * accomplished. 1Co 3:13
* like, deep down in our hearts. 1Co 4:5
I wish you * were already on your 1Co 4:8
whether they * have God's power. 1Co 4:19
important, what is * needed to 1Co 8:1
an idol is not * a god, and that 1Co 8:4
is * being offered to actual gods. 1Co 8:7
sacrifices are * alive and are real 1Co 10:19
What do you yourselves * think 1Co 11:13
Is this * true? 1Co 11:22
if anyone is * hungry he should 1Co 11:34
whether they are * inspired by God 1Co 12:3
is Lord," and * mean it, unless 1Co 12:3
whether it is * the Spirit of God 1Co 12:10
are * the most necessary. 1Co 12:22
that God is * there among you. 1Co 14:25
of what the Gospel * is, for it has 1Co 15:1
* believed it in the first place. 1Co 15:2
at all and have never * known God. 1Co 15:34
We were * crushed and 2Co 1:8
Hadn't I * made up my mind yet? 2Co 1:17
"yes" when he * means "no"? 2Co 1:17
deep within, you * know it too. 2Co 5:11
how much you * do care for us. 2Co 7:12
If you are * eager to give, then 2Co 8:12
I REALIZE THAT I * don't even need 2Co 9:1
be sure that you * are ready, as I 2Co 9:3
give more than he * wants to, for 2Co 9:7
I am * worth nothing at all. 2Co 12:11

(REALLY Con't)
Are you * Christians? 2Co 13:5
and despised if you are * strong. 2Co 13:9
* doesn't go to heaven at all. Gal 1:6
there—false ones, *—who came to spy Gal 2:4
about what they * believed, and Gal 2:14
find out what those laws * mean? Gal 4:21
He is * a nobody. Gal 6:3
what counts is whether we * have Gal 6:15
everywhere who are * God's own. Gal 6:16
guarantee that he * will give us Eph 1:14
to see clearly and * understand who Eph 1:16,17
deep, and how high his love * is; Eph 3:18,19
If you have * heard his voice Eph 4:21
a greedy person is * an idol Eph 5:5
see how wrong they * are, some of Eph 5:13
now one, a man is * doing himself a Eph 5:28
to Christ, then I * don't know Php 1:22
be the only way to * know Christ Php 3:10
* enemies of the cross of Christ. Php 3:18
He is the one you are * working Col 3:24
I * don't need to say anything 1Th 5:1
because of the * wonderful way your 2Th 1:3
for proof that it * is from me. 2Th 3:17
idea what those laws * show us. 1Ti 1:7
If he has * sinned, then he 1Ti 5:20
those who are * his," and "A 2Ti 2:19
yes, but they won't * believe 2Ti 3:5
I * wanted to keep him here with Phm 1:13
If I am * your friend, give him Phm 1:17
exposing us for what we * are. Heb 4:12
like this I * don't believe that Heb 6:9
It never made anyone * right Heb 7:19
and goats * to take away sins. Heb 10:4
it proves you are * his child." Heb 12:6
that you aren't * God's son at Heb 12:8
you don't * belong in his family. Heb 12:8
so that we can begin * to live? Heb 12:9
be sure that you * expect him to Jas 1:6
so see to it that you * do love 1Pe 1:22
Instead, be * glad—because these 1Pe 4:13
to prove that you * are among those 2Pe 1:10
are * getting along quite well! 2Pe 1:12
He isn't * being slow about his 2Pe 3:9
ourselves: are we * trying to do 1Jn 2:3
men because you * know Christ, the 1Jn 2:13
show that you do not * love God; 1Jn 2:15
but they never * belonged with us 1Jn 2:19
children—think of it—and we * are! 1Jn 3:1
a result of seeing him as he * is. 1Jn 3:2
And everyone who * believes this 1Jn 3:3
never * known him or become his. 1Jn 3:6
brother is * a murderer at heart; 1Jn 3:15
let us * love them, and show it 1Jn 3:18
test it first to see if it * is. 1Jn 4:1
is to ask: Does it * agree that 1Jn 4:2
whether a message is * from God; 1Jn 4:6
convinced that he * loves us. 1Jn 4:18
do, and *, that isn't hard at all; 1Jn 5:3
And if we * know he is listening 1Jn 5:15
of Satan, *), I will ask nothing Rev 2:24,25

REALM
and throughout the entire *. 2Ch 8:6
peace at last throughout his *. 2Ch 32:22
the permanent records of the *): Ez 1:1
"I decree that any Jew in my *, Ez 7:13
and anger throughout your *. Est 1:18
All the Jews throughout the * Est 9:27
I will go on living in the * of Job 33:28
and wise astrologers in his *. Dan 1:20
the nations. His * shall stretch Zec 9:10

REALMS
in the heavenly *—all because of Eph 2:6

REAP
"Sow and * your crops for six Ex 23:10
"As you * each of your crops, Ex 23:19
your crops, don't * the corners of Lev 19:9
will give you and * your first Lev 23:9,10,11
(When you * your harvests, you Lev 23:22
not thoroughly * all the corners of Lev 23:22
Don't even * for yourself the Lev 25:5
"You will sow much but * little, Deu 28:38
let someone else * the crops I have Job 31:7,8
But the godless * his anger. Job 36:13
and * their bumper crops! Ps 107:37
Those who sow tears shall * joy. Ps 126:5
The unjust tyrant will * disaster Pro 22:8
the clouds shall not *." Ecc 11:4f
or barley for every sixty you *; Eze 45:13
and they will * the whirlwind. Hos 8:7
and you will * a crop of my love; Hos 10:12
need to sow or * or store up Mt 6:26
I sent you to * where you didn't Jn 4:38
if he plants much, he will * much. 2Co 9:6
* just the kind of crop he sows! Gal 6:7
and he will surely * a harvest of Gal 6:8
Spirit, he will * the everlasting Gal 6:8
a while we will * a harvest of Gal 6:9
peace and * a harvest of goodness. Jas 3:18
the time has come for you to *; Rev 14:15

REAPED
My people have sown wheat but * Jer 12:13

REAPER
by the *, despised by the binder. Ps 129:6,7
sower and the *, both together! Jn 4:36

REAPERS
behind his *." Ru 2:2
greetings with the * he said to his Ru 2:4,5
dropped by the *, and she has been Ru 2:7
So she sat with his * and he gave Ru 2:14
close behind his * until the entire Ru 2:21
who was working with the *. 2Ki 4:18
joy like that of * when the harvest Is 9:3
I will tell the * to sort out the Mt 13:30
and the * are the angels. Mt 13:39
for reaping. The * will be paid Jn 4:36

REAPING
If, when * your harvest, you Deu 24:19
Beth-shemesh were * wheat in the 1Sa 6:13
Literally, "* where you didn't Mt 25:24,25f
us, and are ready now for *. Jn 4:35

REAPPEARANCE
at his * after being dead. Rev 17:8

REAPPEARED
the spots have not * after the Lev 14:48

REAPPEARS
However, if it then *, it is Lev 13:57

REAPS
that one sows and someone else *. Jn 4:37

REAR
Also five bars for the * of the Ex 26:26,27
which was its *, was made from six Ex 36:27
They brought up the * whenever Num 2:3-31
destroying the enemy from the *. Jos 8:22
and cut them down from the *. Jos 10:19
against the * of the army of Ju 20:34
joined the slaughter from the *. Ju 20:42
marched at the * with King Achish. 1Sa 29:2
far to the *, and came to the Mt 26:58

REARGUARD
carrying the Ark, followed by a *. Jos 6:6-9

REASON
relatives is no * for you to work Gen 29:15
Promised Land. The * was that God Ex 13:17,18
that is the * I abhor them. Lev 20:23
defiled for any *— that priest Lev 22:5
generation. The * for this law is Deu 23:4
and will have no * to believe that Deu 28:66
worn out! The * he hasn't let you Deu 29:6
them of the * for their woes. Deu 31:21
The * for this second Jos 5:4,5
There is no * for it at all!" 1Sa 19:5
But his officers tried to * with 2Ki 5:13
it was for a special *—to give 1Ch 14:2
For this scroll says that the * 2Ch 34:21
Almighty God, or even * with him? Job 9:14
Fair and honest men could * with Job 23:7
out to them the *, what they have Job 36:9
those who fight me without any *! Ps 35:19
have plenty of * to praise him for Ps 42:11
They have no * to hate and fight Ps 109:3
they have no * to, but I stand in Ps 119:161
wisdom and the * for things, and to Ecc 7:25
not understand the * why—that it is Is 42:25
No, that is not the *! Is 50:2
would learn the * for your fame! Is 64:2
The very * all these terrible Jer 44:23
of money is the * for your sin. Eze 7:19
as a lion unless I had a *? Amo 3:4
lying about the * for his scars. Zec 13:6f
But the Pharisees said, "The * Mt 9:34
and for that * couldn't come. Lk 14:20
governor as * for arrest by him. Lk 20:19
I have found no * to sentence him Lk 23:22
That was the main * why so many Jn 12:18
But that is the very * why I Jn 12:27
'They hated me without *.' Jn 15:25
But the real * behind their Act 26:6
Another * for right living is Rom 13:11
In fact that is the very * I Rom 15:22
That is the very * why I am 1Co 4:17
For that * those who have wives 1Co 7:29
truth: the * I haven't come to 2Co 1:23
A further * for forgiveness is 2Co 2:11
and not have to * with you like Gal 4:20
it for just one *: so that they can Gal 6:12
God has told us his secret * for Eph 1:9
This is just one more * for us to Eph 1:14
And his *? Eph 3:10
glad and give you * to glorify Php 1:26
Yet if anyone ever had * to hope Php 3:4
Give them * to report joyfully Heb 13:17
And yet the * you don't have what Jas 4:2
And those who have * to be Jas 5:13
But he is waiting, for the good * 2Pe 3:9

REASONABLE
All I want is a * answer—then I Job 6:24
This sounded * to the whole Act 6:5
For it doesn't seem * to send a Act 25:27
they are kind and *, but even if 1Pe 2:18

REASONABLY
them will be * close to everyone; Deu 19:6,7

REASONED
And as he * with them about Act 24:25
and thought and * as a child does. 1Co 13:1

REASONING
That is the * behind my decree Lev 17:1
(This sort of * delighted the Mk 12:3

REASONS
"Listen to me now, to my * for Job 13:
upon him for your own good *." Jon 1:1
was mutual, due to historic *. Lk 10:3
Obey the laws, then, for two *: Rom 13:
taxes too, for these same two *. Rom 13:
how the human mind *, and how 1Co 3:2

REASSIGN
and * it to its own people again. Is 49:8,

REASSURE
Revive my heart toward you. * me Ps 119:3
to * you of the truth of all you Lk 1:

REASSURED
But Caleb * the people as they Num 13:3
"Don't be frightened," Samuel * 1Sa 12:2
"Don't be afraid," Jonathan * 1Sa 23:1
frightened, but the angel * them. Lk 2:1

REASSURING
spoke very kindly to them, * them. Gen 50:2
the whole country, * everyone that Jer 14:1
immediately spoke to them, * them. Mt 14:2

REBA
kings—Evi, Rekem, Zur, Hur, and *. Num 31:8
Rekem, Zur, Hur, and *. Jos 13:21

REBECCA
and married, and * his wife was Rom 9:10-13

REBEKAH
Jidlaph,Bethuel (father of *). Gen 22:20-23
named * arrived with a water jug Gen 24:15,16
these words, * was coming along Gen 24:45
silver for *, and lovely clothing; Gen 24:53
"But we want * here at least Gen 24:55
So they called *. Gen 24:58
So * and her servant girls Gen 24:61
camels coming. * noticed him and Gen 24:64
And Isaac brought * into his Gen 24:67
when he married *, the daughter of Gen 25:20
Jehovah to give * a child, for even Gen 25:21
*, he said, "She is my sister!" Gen 26:7
and saw Isaac petting with *. Gen 26:8
But Isaac and * were bitter Gen 26:35
But * overheard the conversation. Gen 27:5
*: "Now do exactly as I tell you. Gen 27:8,9,10
*: "Let his curses be on me, Gen 27:13
planning, and reported it to *. Gen 27:42
Then * said to Isaac, "I'm sick Gen 27:46
there they buried Isaac and * his Gen 49:31

REBEKAH'S
home, and * favorite was Jacob. Gen 25:28
and that he was her Aunt * son. Gen 29:12,13
after this, * old nurse Deborah Gen 35:8

REBEL
do not * against him, for he will Ex 23:21
Oh, do not * against the Lord, Num 14:9
Meribah (meaning "* Waters"), Num 20:13
little that you must * again? Jos 22:17,18
For you know that if you * today Jos 22:17,18
But do not * against the Lord by Jos 22:19
the Lord or to * against him by Jos 22:29
and not * against the Lord, and if 1Sa 12:14
But if you * against the Lord's 1Sa 12:15
own household to * against you. 2Sa 12:11
Another * leader was Jeroboam 1Ki 11:26
are planning to *, and that is why Neh 6:5,6
"The wicked * against the light Job 24:13
for they * against you. Ps 5:10
of the nations. O * lands, he will Ps 66:7
they continued to * against him, Ps 106:43
sad the mother of a *. Pro 10:1
good advice, but a * is destroyed Pro 10:21
if they * against that Pro 15:9,10
Truth from a * or lies from a Pro 17:7
hundred lashes on the back of a *. Pro 17:10
a * who has no heart for truth. Pro 17:16
A * doesn't care about the facts. Pro 18:2
The * walks a thorny, treacherous Pro 22:5
Don't waste your breath on a *. Pro 23:9
Wisdom is too much for a *. Pro 24:7
and a * with a rod to his back! Pro 26:3
When arguing with a *, don't use Pro 26:4,5
To trust a * to convey a message Pro 26:6
Honoring a * will backfire like a Pro 26:8
A * will misapply an illustration Pro 26:9
apprentice than from a skilled *! Pro 26:10
You can't separate a * from his Pro 27:22
A * shouts in anger; Pro 29:11
A * who prospers. Pro 30:21,22,23
Must you forever *? Is 1:5,6
I do not * nor turn away. Is 50:5
thing it is to * against the Lord Jer 2:19
taught you to * against the Lord. Jer 29:32
Don't you be a * too! Eze 2:8
own officials will * against him Dan 11:5
was setting up a * government. Jn 18:34f
a king is a * against Caesar." Jn 19:12
against every * who remains after I 2Co 10:6

REBEL'S
A * foolish talk should prick his Pro 14:3

REBEL'S Con't)
It's no fun to be a * father. Pro 17:21
The * schemes are sinful, and the Pro 24:9
A * frustrations are heavier than Pro 27:3

REBELLED
in the thirteenth year, they *. Gen 14:4
again * against Moses and Aaron. Num 20:2
for the two of you * against my Num 20:24
did, for you * against my Num 27:14
When the people of Israel *, you Num 27:14
and * against the Lord's command. Deu 1:26
Instead, they * again against the Deu 1:43
you have constantly * against him. Deu 9:7
had given you, you * and wouldn't Deu 9:23
all those who * against you." 2Sa 18:31
the king of Moab * against Israel. 2Ki 3:5
"The king of Moab has * against 2Ki 3:6,7,8
Libnah also * at that time. 2Ki 8:22
of Nimshi) * against King Joram. 2Ki 9:14
Then he * against the king of 2Ki 18:7
for three years, but then *. 2Ki 24:1
But now King Zedekiah * against 2Ki 24:20
from the Lord. He * against King 2Ch 36:13
instead, they * and appointed a Neh 9:17
disobedient and * against you. Neh 9:26
Oh, how often they * against him Ps 78:40
them, they still * against the God Ps 78:56
Instead they * against you at the Ps 106:7
They * against the Lord, Ps 107:11
for help, and have * against me! Is 36:5
But they * against him and Is 63:10
welcome them all day long—have *; Is 65:2
of those who have * against me, for Is 66:24
admit that you * against the Lord Jer 3:13
For my people have * against me, Jer 4:17
you have * against the Lord." Jer 28:16
for she has * against the Lord. Jer 48:26
it that Zedekiah * against the king Jer 52:3
And the Lord is right, for we *. Lam 1:18
despairs, for I have terribly *. Lam 1:20
we have * against the Lord, and Lam 3:42
"Nevertheless, Zedekiah * Eze 17:15
But they * against me and would Eze 20:8
"But Israel * against me. Eze 20:13
"But their children too * Eze 20:21
only of the times the people *. Eze 21:23
we have * against you and scorned Dan 9:5
even those who have * against him. Dan 9:9
him, the more he *, sacrificing to Hos 11:2
guilt, for she * against her God. Hos 13:16
that they had * and would not Lk 19:14
* against the Roman government." Act 25:8
* against him in the desert." Heb 3:15
to them but then * against him? Heb 3:16

REBELLING
of help before * against me. 2Ki 18:20,21
* against the king like this?" Neh 2:19
on yourselves by * against the Lord Jer 2:17
Israel, to a nation * against me. Eze 2:3

REBELLION
had incited the * against Jehovah Num 14:36,37,38
to incite a * against Moses. Num 16:2
the Ark as a reminder of this *. Num 17:10
Don't notice the * and Deu 9:27
to foment * against the Lord your Deu 13:5
an altar of * against the Lord. Jos 22:16
the altar in * against the Lord. Jos 22:22,23
he will not forgive your * and Jos 24:19
the city to * against you. Ju 9:31
rams to him. For * is as bad as 1Sa 15:23
to incite * against the king. 2Sa 15:10
Here is the story back of his *: 1Ki 11:27,28
And Israel has been in * against 1Ki 12:19
to crush the *: he crossed the 2Ki 8:21
in prison and in chains for his *. 2Ki 17:4
Go home, for I am behind their * 2Ch 11:4
In their times of * against God 2Ch 15:5
in fact, * and sedition are Ez 4:19
For now you have added *, Job 34:37
Yet they kept on with their *, Ps 78:17
Next, his heart is full of *. Pro 6:14
the wicked speak *. Pro 10:32
The wicked live for *; Pro 17:11
is filled with *, but punishment Pro 22:15
chronic * was finally exhausted. Is 6:10f
saw the continued * of Israel. Jer 3:7
their * against me is great. Jer 5:6
It will lead to * all across the Amo 7:10
who led a * a few years ago Act 21:37,38
be a time of great * against God, 2Th 2:3
of * will come—the son of hell. 2Th 2:3
As for the work this man of * and 2Th 2:7
they have done in * against God, Jud 1:15

REBELLIONS
no foreign enemies or internal *. 1Ki 5:4
* against the Roman government. Act 24:5

REBELLIOUS
stubborn, * lot these people are. Ex 32:9
Yes, you have been * against the Deu 9:24
"If a man has a stubborn, * son Deu 21:18
is stubborn and * and won't obey; Deu 21:20
"For I know how * and stubborn Deu 31:27
more * will you be after my death! Deu 31:27
Don't be stubborn and * as 1Sa 6:6
Literally, "son of a perverse, * 1Sa 20:30f
this historically * and evil city; Ez 4:12
* city this has been in the past; Ez 4:15
were—stubborn, *, unfaithful, Ps 78:8
a * teacher spouts foolishness. Pro 15:2
A * son saddens his mother. Pro 15:20
A * son is a grief to his father Pro 17:25
A * son is a calamity to his Pro 19:13
WOE TO MY * children, says the Is 30:1
O my * children, come back to me Jer 3:22
But my people have * hearts; Jer 5:23,24
They are hard and stubborn and * Jer 7:26
end to end with all its * people. Jer 48:45
who hate God, have * hearts, curse 1Ti 1:9
his dirty mind and * heart color Tit 1:15

REBELS
he said to them, "Listen, you *! Num 20:10
you are defiant * against the Lord, Deu 31:27
If anyone, no matter who, * Jos 1:17,18
has destroyed the * who dared to 2Sa 18:28
From the * of my people; 2Sa 22:44
Then a whole gang of worthless * 2Ch 13:7
But for * there is famine and Ps 68:6
men, even those who once were *. Ps 68:18
Remember the insults these * have Ps 74:22
The common bond of * is their Pro 14:9
can give good advice. * can't. Pro 15:7
Mockers and * shall be severely Pro 19:29
Your leaders are *, companions Is 1:23
For they are stubborn *. Is 30:9
wicked *, come, return to God. Is 31:6
traitors you are, * from earliest Is 48:8
We know what * we are and how Is 59:13
Don't come to me—you are all *, Jer 2:29
Are they not the worst of *, Jer 6:28
They keep saying to these * who Jer 23:17
of *, a land that I will judge! Jer 50:21
remember, they are *), they will at Eze 2:5
For remember, they are *! Eze 2:6
for they are utter *). Eze 2:7
even though they are such *." Eze 3:9
for they are *. Eze 3:26
who wants to, for they are *. Eze 3:27
"you live among * who could know Eze 12:2
but they won't, for they are *. Eze 12:3
even though they are such *. Eze 12:3
"Son of dust, these *, the Eze 12:9
There will be no more delays, O * Eze 12:25
"Ask these * of Israel: Don't Eze 17:12,13
and get rid of the *, just as I did Eze 20:35,36
And the others—the * and all Eze 20:38
mock you, a city of infamous *. Eze 22:5
this parable to these *, Israel; Eze 24:3
And say to these *, the people Eze 44:6
more, for all their leaders are *. Hos 9:15
will no longer be * against me. Zep 3:11
Once you were * against God, but Rom 11:30
And now the Jews are the *, but Rom 11:31
I can capture * and bring them back 2Co 10:5

REBIRTH
the time of Israel's spiritual *; Mic 5:3
—not a physical * Jn 1:13

REBORN
All those who believe this are * Jn 1:13

REBUFFED
and hated and * by all, you will be Is 60:15

REBUILD
anyone who might * Jericho, warning Jos 6:26
and used the stones to * the 1Ki 18:32
to Jerusalem to * this Temple of Ez 1:3
Jerusalem at once to * the Temple. Ez 1:5
you permission to * this Temple and Ez 5:3
to * the city of my fathers!" Neh 2:4
Let us * the wall of Jerusalem Neh 2:17
Let's * the wall!" Neh 2:18
his servants, will * this wall; Neh 2:20
For Jehovah will * Jerusalem! Ps 102:16
A time to *; Ecc 3:3
we will * it better than before. Is 9:8,9,10
nor * the cities of the world. Is 14:21
troubled, I will * you on a Is 54:11
I will say, * the road! Is 57:14
Your sons will * the Is 58:12
Who * Their Walls and Cities." Is 58:12
And they shall * the ancient Is 61:4
There is no one left to help me * Jer 10:20
I will * your nation, O virgin Jer 31:4
I will * the cities of both Jer 33:7
'It is time to * Jerusalem, for our Eze 11:3
again to Israel, and * the ruins. Eze 36:33
is given to * Jerusalem, until the Dan 9:25
"Then, at that time, I will * Amo 9:11
and they shall * their ruined Amo 9:14
from Babylon to * Jerusalem. Hag 1:1f
down timber, and * my Temple, and I Hag 1:8
them a desire to * his Temple; Hag 1:14,15
have even begun to * the Temple Hag 2:18,19
lands to * the Temple of the Lord. Zec 6:15
say, 'We will * the ruins,' then Mal 1:4
of God and * it in three days.' Mt 26:60,61
the Temple and * it in three days! Mk 15:29,30
Literally, "* the tabernacle of Act 15:16f

REBUILDERS
Soon your * shall come and chase Is 49:17

REBUILDING
Solomon was * Fort Millo, repairing 1Ki 11:27,28
He now turned his energies to * 2Ch 8:2
also did extensive * of the walls 2Ch 27:3
toward the * of the Temple, and Ez 2:68
returned and were * the Temple, Ez 4:1
from Babylon are * this Ez 4:12
earth and we are * the Temple that Ez 5:11
in the * of the Temple of God. Ez 8:36
assistance in * the Temple of our Ez 9:9
learned that we were * the wall. Neh 4:1
completed the * of the wall—though Neh 6:1
He is * Jerusalem and bringing Ps 147:2
useless as foxes for * your walls! Eze 13:4
the right time for * my Temple?" Hag 1:2
responsibility for * the Temple. Zec 4:6f
Get on with * the Temple! Zec 8:13
if we start * the old systems I Gal 2:18

REBUILDS
he * the cities of Judah. Ps 69:35
Godly skill *. Pro 11:9

REBUILT
cities they had conquered and *. Num 32:37,38
lifeless mound and may never be *. Deu 13:16
Ephraim; he * it and lived there. Jos 19:50
of Dan * the city and lived there. Ju 18:28
Then they * their cities and Ju 21:23
So now Solomon * Gezer along 1Ki 9:17,18
a man from Bethel, * Jericho. 1Ki 16:34
He * the hilltop shrines which 2Ki 21:3,4,5
Joab * the rest of Jerusalem. 1Ch 11:8
He also * and strengthened the 2Ch 11:11
of Ephraim, and he * the altar of 2Ch 15:8
After his father's death, he * 2Ch 26:2
the land. He * the heathen altars 2Ch 33:3
It was after this that he * the 2Ch 33:14
Then he * the altar of the Lord 2Ch 33:16
He now * what earlier kings of 2Ch 34:10,11
* the altar of the God of Israel; Ez 3:1
The altar was * on its old site, Ez 3:3
they have already * its walls and Ez 4:12
if this city is *, it will be much Ez 4:13
if this city is * and the walls Ez 4:16
Temple should be *, and they say Ez 5:13
It is to be *, and the Ez 6:3
Let it be * on its former site, Ez 6:6
the other priests * the wall as far Neh 3:1
then they * the Sheep Gate, hung Neh 3:1
Fountain Gate. He * it, roofed it, Neh 3:15
Zadok (son of Immer) also * the Neh 3:29
What he destroys can't be *. Job 12:14
buildings, never to be * again. Ps 28:5
disappear and never will be *. Is 25:2
and Jerusalem will be * and the Is 44:28
will be * upon her ruins; Jer 30:18
Jerusalem shall be * for the Lord, Jer 31:38,39
You will never be *, for I, the Eze 26:14
your cities will never be *. Eze 35:9
will be * and filled with people. Eze 36:10
The ruined cities are * and Eze 36:35
that I, the Lord, * the ruins and Eze 36:36
be * despite the perilous times. Dan 9:25
of God, will be *, much larger and Mic 7:11
my Temple will be *, says the Zec 1:16

REBUKE
"Don't hate your brother. * Lev 19:17
the living God, and will * him. 2Ki 19:4
"But who can * God, the supreme Job 21:22
of heaven tremble at his *. Job 26:11
Jerusalem. * our enemies, O Lord. Ps 68:30
You * those cursed proud ones who Ps 119:21
If you * a mocker, you will only Pro 9:7,8
WISE YOUTH accepts his father's *; Pro 13:1
A * to a man of common sense is Pro 17:10
on those who * sin fearlessly. Pro 24:25
Open * is better than hidden Pro 27:5
he * you, and you be found a liar. Pro 30:6
Surely God will * him for those Is 37:4
For I can * the sea and make it Is 50:2
out his fury and * upon them. Is 51:20
and his hot * with flames of fire. Is 66:15
an entire nation in furious *. Eze 5:15
to * them for what they have done. Eze 25:17
Literally, "The Lord * you, O Zec 3:2f
who has chosen Jerusalem, * you. Zec 3:2f
be merciful to Jerusalem—I * you. Zec 3:2
"Take note that I will * your Mal 2:3
break the law without *." Mal 2:9
Literally, "Peter began to * Mk 8:32f
"* your brother if he sins, and Lk 17:2,3
crowd said, "Sir, * your followers Lk 19:39
to sadden you with a severe *. 2Co 1:23
but instead, * and expose them. Eph 5:11
Correct and * your people when 2Ti 4:2
simply said, "The Lord * you." Jud 1:9

REBUKED
but his father * him. Gen 37:10
You have * the nations and Ps 9:5
When you * them, God of Jacob, Ps 76:6
But a wise man, when *, will love Pro 9:7,8
Then he stood up and * the wind Mt 8:26
Then Jesus * the demon in the Mt 17:18
Then he * the wind and said to Mk 4:39
crowd was growing he * the demon. Mk 9:25
together. He * them for their Mk 16:14
But Jesus turned and * them, Lk 9:55
then he should be * in front of the 1Ti 5:20

REBUKES
No one * him openly. Job 21:30-32
And then in fierce fury he * Ps 2:5

REBUKING
to the fever, * it, and immediately Lk 4:39
a human voice, scolding and * him. 2Pe 2:16

RECAH
The descendants of * were: 1Ch 4:11,12

RECALL
I * the many miracles he did for Ps 77:11

RECEDED
So the flood gradually * until, Gen 8:3,4
O Lord, the sea * from the shore. Ps 18:15

RECEIPT
"Upon * of this letter, select 2Ki 10:2,3
were Levites. A * was given for Ez 8:34

RECEIVE
tribes, but will * only houses in Lev 25:33
of the tithes they *—a tithe of the Num 18:25,26
of the tithes you * as the Lord's Num 18:28,29
the Lord, would * as his personal Deu 1:36
In addition, the priests shall * Deu 18:4
to * praise, honor, and renown; Deu 26:19
which tribe would * which area was Jos 14:1
that we were to * as much property Jos 17:4
that the Levites won't * any land; Jos 18:7
of Manasseh won't * any more, for Jos 18:7
The third tribe to * its Jos 19:10
The sixth tribe to * its Jos 19:32
First to * their assignment were Jos 21:9-16
to the Lord to * his instructions. Ju 1:1
King Eglon stood up at once to * Ju 3:20
to meet him and to * his blessing, 1Sa 13:10
Let him go with you and * 2Sa 19:37
on you, but may I * God's rich 1Ki 2:45
Is this the time to * money and 2Ki 5:26
For the king of Assyria will * 2Ki 19:7
and they stood to * his blessing: 2Ch 6:3
priests or even to * the priests' Neh 7:64,65
Shall we * only pleasant things Job 2:10
the grave is ready to * me. Job 17:1
and answer and * him with joy, and Job 33:26
They will * God's own goodness Ps 24:5
power of death, for he will * me. Ps 49:15
Those who walk my paths will * Ps 50:23
and afterwards * me into the Ps 73:24
You will * every blessing you can Ps 81:10
and * the glory you give to them. Ps 106:5
It is an honor to * a frank Pro 24:26
* from having sons and daughters. Is 56:5
to * the wealth of many lands. Is 60:11
God of Hosts will * a sacrifice Jer 46:10
Put them behind you and * a new Eze 18:31
be gracious to us and * us, and Hos 14:2
I will see to it that they * evil Amo 9:4
They will * the wages of their Zep 2:10
and you * no blessing from him. Mal 2:13
and prepare people to * me. Mt 11:10
follow me, shall * a hundred times Mt 19:29
assumed they would * much more. Mt 20:10
the Good News and * it, but all Mk 4:18
Yes, Tyre and Sidon will * less Lk 10:14
fail you, they may * you into the Lk 16:9f
Only a few would welcome and * Jn 1:11,12
you readily enough * those who Jn 5:43
will never * this gift. Jn 6:63
I, the Son of God, will * glory Jn 11:4
me—and God shall * great praise Jn 13:31
The world at large cannot * him, Jn 14:17
name, and you will *, and your cup Jn 16:24
told them, "* the Holy Spirit. Jn 20:22
upon you, you will * power to Act 1:8
then you also shall * this gift, Act 2:38
"Lord Jesus, * my spirit." Act 7:59
new Christians to * the Holy Act 8:15
they will * the Holy Spirit!" Act 8:19
Get ready to * him!" Act 18:25,26
"Did you * the Holy Spirit when Act 19:2
more blessed to give than to *.' Act 20:35
'Brother Saul, * your sight!' Act 22:13
so that they may * forgiveness for Act 26:18
friends and * their hospitality. Act 27:3
days also he can * sinners in this Rom 3:26
So now you, too, * the blessing Rom 11:17
enough to * a message from God. Rom 12:6
Literally, "* him that is weak in Rom 14:1f
Perhaps the meaning is, "* Rom 14:1f
the church there. * her as your Rom 16:1
* when I see them come to Christ. 1Co 9:23
Each of us will * whatever he 2Co 5:10
pleading with you, * the love he 2Co 5:20
that those who * your gifts should 2Co 8:13
question: Did you * the Holy Spirit Gal 3:2
of the race and * the prize for Php 3:14
Literally, "* him." Col 4:10f
when he comes to * praise and 2Th 1:10
those who are to * his salvation. Heb 1:14
and stay there to * his mercy and Heb 4:16
of those who * all that God has Heb 6:12
of all who * tithes), paid tithes Heb 7:9
trusting him to * us, because we Heb 10:22
* on that coming day of judgment. Jas 5:3
there safely to * it, because you 1Pe 1:5
in judgment, to * just punishment, Jud 1:15
church, you will * a special Rev 1:3
you are worthy to * the glory and Rev 4:11
He is worthy to * the power, and Rev 5:12

RECEIVED
he sold us, and what he * for us Gen 31:15
Joseph's suggestions were well * Gen 41:37
gifts were * each morning. Ex 36:3
and it will be * with pleasure by Lev 6:15
amount he * when he sold himself; Lev 25:51
amount he * when he sold himself. Lev 25:52
So Moses * redemption money for Num 3:49
after having * the Lord's travel Num 10:13
I have * a command to bless them, Num 23:18-24
Moses and Eleazar the priest * Num 31:51,52
Israel have * their inheritance. Num 32:18
The half-tribe of Manasseh * the Deu 3:13
The tribes of Reuben and Gad * Deu 3:16
They also * the Arabah (or, Deu 3:17
They have * their directions from Deu 33:3
Gad, had already * their Jos 13:8
Judah also * these fortyfour Jos 15:48-62
The tribe of Simeon * the next Jos 19:1
The Gershon division * thirteen Jos 21:6
The Merari division * twelve Jos 21:7
of the Kohath division * four Jos 21:20,21,22
of the Levites, * two cities and Jos 21:27
Then he told him, "I have * a 1Sa 9:26,27
And he * the same reply as 1Sa 17:27
same thing and * the same answer. 1Sa 17:30
One day near Horesh he * the news 1Sa 23:14,15
he has * his punishment for his 1Sa 25:39
all the earth has * such blessings 2Sa 7:23
and no one else * such praise. 2Sa 14:25
Solomon: "I have * your message 1Ki 5:8
of spices King Solomon had ever *. 1Ki 10:10
Each year Solomon * gold worth 1Ki 10:14
When Baasha * word of the 1Ki 15:21
* word that he had left Lachish). 2Ki 19:8
Although Joseph * the birthright, 1Ch 5:2
Kohath, and they * ten cities in 1Ch 6:61
the Gershom clan * by lot thirteen 1Ch 6:62
The subclans of Merari * by lot 1Ch 6:63
Solomon * a billion dollars worth 2Ch 9:13,14
three years he * from them an 2Ch 27:5
and Nathan—who had * their 2Ch 29:25,26
But for the most part they were * 2Ch 30:10
the blood * from the Levites. 2Ch 30:16
* vast tribute, custom, and toll. Ez 4:20
Levites as they * these tithes, and Neh 10:38
of what they * to the priests. Neh 12:47
(though I later * his permission to Neh 13:6
even strangers * a fair trial. Job 29:16
good if a man has * wealth from the Ecc 5:19,20
the Assyrian king * word that Is 37:8,9
You will be * with disgust and Jer 42:18
When the king of Babylon * the Jer 50:43
who had * what she deserved. Eze 23:10
And Nebuchadnezzar * no Eze 29:18
Another message that I * from the Zec 4:8
I * in the house of my friends." Zec 13:6f
they have * all the reward they Mt 6:2
Give as freely as you have *! Mt 10:8
o'clock were paid, each * $20. Mt 20:9
The man who * the $5,000 began Mt 25:16
"But the man who * the $1,000 Mt 25:18
"Next came the man who had * the Mt 25:22
of his men, who * the same Mk 12:4
lake the crowds * him with open Lk 8:40
But to all who * him, he gave the Jn 1:11,12
others did the work, and you * Jn 4:38
Literally, "had *." Jn 19:30f
with the money he * for his Act 1:18
* them from the hands of angels." Act 7:53
and they * the Holy Spirit. Act 8:17
now that they have * the Holy Act 10:46,47
We say that he * these blessings Rom 4:9
And since they * this wonderful Rom 15:27
who live—having * eternal life from 2Co 5:15
so willingly and * him so anxiously 2Co 7:15
Holy Spirit you *, or shows you a 2Co 11:4
share the same blessing Abraham *. Gal 3:8,9
for you * our message with joy 1Th 1:6
* up again to his glory in heaven. 1Ti 3:16
ability you * as a gift from the 2Ti 1:14
priests, though mortal, * tithes; Heb 7:8
and * what God had promised them; Heb 11:33
And some women, through faith, * Heb 11:35
* all that God had promised them; Heb 11:39
message we have *, for it is able Jas 1:21
But you have * the Holy Spirit 1Jn 2:27

RECEIVES
Each man * a girl or two; Ju 5:30
Ordinary sin * heavy punishment, 1Sa 2:23,24,25
in his train. He * gifts for Ps 68:18
For everyone who asks, *. Mt 7:8
the message and * it with real joy, Mt 13:20
Everyone who asks, *; Lk 11:10
someone else * a message or idea 1Co 14:29,30

RECEIVING
at the time, * the contract which Deu 9:9
said he was * a message from God. Neh 6:10
now, as well as * eternal life in Lk 18:30
to him and * eternal life!" Act 11:18
God and that those * his baptism Act 19:4
the law, but on * God's grace! Rom 6:15
my partners in giving and *. Php 4:15
eagerly looking forward to * it. Tit 3:7
* all that God had promised them; Heb 11:13
are partners in * God's blessings, 1Pe 3:7
else knows except the one * it. Rev 2:17

RECENT
was any * message from the Lord. Jer 37:17

RECENTLY
Uncle Laban until *, and now I own Gen 32:4
So they were given some of the * Jos 21:3
a baby daughter. * a guest arrived 2Sa 12:4
the two of us, and * I had a baby. 1Ki 3:17,18
But this was not done. * you Jer 34:15
in Pontus, who had * arrived from Act 18:2,3
began, but only * was he brought 1Pe 1:20

RECEPTION
Soon Levi held a * in his home Lk 5:29

RECEPTIVE
Those who were * to spiritual Mt 13:12,13f

RECESSED
and all three had * windows. Eze 41:15,16
There were * windows and carved Eze 41:26

RECHAB
Baanah and *, who were captains of 2Sa 4:2,3
* and Baanah arrived at King 2Sa 4:5
of *, who was coming to meet him. 2Ki 10:15
Then Jehu and Jehonadab (son of * 2Ki 10:23
the founder of the family of *. 1Ch 2:55
Malchijah (son of *), the mayor of Neh 3:14
all the * families— to the Temple, Jer 35:3
our father (son of *) commanded Jer 35:6
a lesson from the families of *? Jer 35:13
The families of * have obeyed Jer 35:16

RECHABITES
families of the * live and invite Jer 35:2
Then Jeremiah turned to the * and Jer 35:18,19

RECHECK
would be well to * all these Lk 1:3

RECITE
But God says to evil men: * my Ps 50:16
" 'God have mercy on us,' you *; Mal 1:9
"Don't * the same prayer over Mt 6:7,8
"Lord, teach us a prayer to * Lk 11:1

RECITED
So Moses * this entire song to Deu 31:30
When Moses and Joshua had * all Deu 32:44,45
I have * your laws, and Ps 119:13

RECKLESS
by their evil minds and * lusts. Eph 4:19

RECKLESSLY
Your own chariots race * along Nah 2:4

RECKONED
Literally, "faith is * for Rom 4:4,5f

RECKONING
and now your day of * has come. Jer 50:31
your final day of * is here. Eze 21:25
the day of final * has come you Eze 21:29
will you be then, in my day of *? Eze 22:14
Jewish *, from sundown to sundown. Act 20:7f

RECLINE
the period was to * around the Jn 13:23f

RECLINING
Queen Esther was *, just as the Est 7:8
Literally, "* on Jesus' bosom." Jn 13:23f

RECOGNITION
her honor and * from even the Pro 31:31
did that in * of your hard and evil Mt 19:8

RECOGNIZE
Do you * them?" Gen 38:25
so that he didn't * David. 1Sa 17:55f
that no one will * you as the 1Ki 14:2
that no one will * me, but you put 2Ch 18:29
so that the enemy wouldn't * him. 2Ch 35:22
that they could scarcely * him. Job 2:12
wife and brothers refuse to * me. Job 19:17
men everywhere may * his power. Job 37:7
* your power and name, O Lord. Ps 83:16
Teach us to number our days and * Ps 90:12
Everyone will * an evil man when Is 32:6
Then at last they will * that it Is 52:6
of Israel shall * me as the Lord; Jer 31:1
No one can * them. Lam 4:8

(RECOGNIZE Con't)
therefore I refuse to * you as my Hos 4:6
Her people never seem to * that I Hos 7:2
but they didn't * him at first Mk 16:12
How will you * him? Lk 2:12
But they didn't * him, for God Lk 24:16
world didn't * him when he came. Jn 1:10
and they follow him, for they * Jn 10:4
him, for they don't * his voice." Jn 10:5
My sheep * my voice, and I know Jn 10:27
looking for him and doesn't * him. Jn 14:17
It was Jesus, but she didn't * Jn 20:14
for they didn't * him, or realize Act 13:27
When it was day, they didn't * Act 27:39
saved * this message as the very 1Co 1:18
For no one will * the tune the 1Co 14:7

RECOGNIZED
Their father * it at once. Gen 37:33
Joseph * them instantly, but Gen 42:7
Saul * David's voice and said, 1Sa 26:17,18
Obadiah * him at once and fell to 1Ki 18:7
king * him as one of the prophets. 1Ki 20:41
which must be * everywhere as law, Est 8:13
but he wasn't *, and was badly Mt 17:12
The people standing around there * Mk 6:54
their eyes were opened—they * him! Lk 24:31
and how they had * him as he was Lk 24:35
When she * Peter's voice, she Act 12:14
right will become known and *! 1Co 11:19

RECOGNIZES
Son of Man"; John * him from Rev 1:13f

RECOGNIZING
But when they saw him coming, * Gen 37:18

RECOMMENDATION
bring long letters of * with them? 2Co 3:1
And we don't need a * from you, 2Co 3:1

RECOMPENSE
the year of * for what Edom has Is 34:8
the day of * is almost here and Hos 9:7

RECONCILE
way for him to * himself with his 1Sa 29:4

RECONCILED
Meanwhile David, now * to 2Sa 13:37,38,39
apologize and be * to him, and then Mt 5:24
into his favor and be * to him. 2Co 5:18
love he offers you—be * to God. 2Co 5:20
for both of us have been * to God. Eph 2:16

RECONCILIATION
the possibility of *, and they will 2Sa 16:21
make * for the people of Israel. Eze 45:17

RECONDITION
to repair and * the Temple. 2Ch 24:4

RECONFIRM
Gilgal and * Saul as our king." 1Sa 11:14

RECONQUERING
three occasions in * the cities 2Ki 13:25

RECONSIDER
stubborn, but a godly man will *. Pro 21:29

RECONSTRUCTED
Ark will not be *, for the Lord Jer 3:16
the palace will be * as it was Jer 30:18

RECONSTRUCTION
being made in the * of the Temple. 2Ch 34:15,16

RECORD
into a permanent *, to be Ex 17:14
has approached his * of obedience. 2Ki 23:25
This is a * of the cities and 1Ch 6:54
Eventually the * was found in the Ez 6:2
For I had found the * of the Neh 7:5
A genealogical * of the heads of Neh 12:22
sins and God has cleared their *. Ps 32:1
for I will have a clean *. Ps 119:6
side and sets the * straight. Pro 18:17
* this man Coniah as childless, Jer 22:30
the * all that I have said to you. Jer 30:2
us and clear our * of all sin, and Heb 1:3
that there is no * of who Heb 7:3f
were, no * of his birth or death. Heb 7:3f
and there is no * of any of his Heb 7:3

RECORDED
offerings * in verses 13 to 17. Num 7:18-23f
offerings * in verses 13 to 17. Num 7:24-29f
offerings * in verses 13 to 17. Num 7:30-35f
offerings * in verses 13 to 17. Num 7:36-41f
offerings * in verses 13 to 17. Num 7:42-47f
offerings * in verses 13 to 17. Num 7:48-53f
offerings * in verses 13 to 17. Num 7:54-59f
offerings * in verses 13 to 17. Num 7:60-65f
offerings * in verses 13 to 17. Num 7:66-71f
offerings * in verses 13 to 17. Num 7:72-77f
offerings * in verses 13 to 17. Num 7:78-83f
curses (which are * in this book) Deu 29:21
curses (which are * in this book) Deu 29:27
the laws that are * in this book, Deu 31:24
Joshua * the people's reply in Jos 24:26
of his reign—are * in The Annals of 1Ki 14:19
history is * in The Annals of the 1Ki 15:7
Baasha's reign are * in The Annals 1Ki 15:31
The rest of Omri's history is * 1Ki 16:27
Ahaziah's reign is * in The Annals 2Ki 1:18
activities are * in The Annals of 2Ki 10:34
of Joash is * in The Annals of the 2Ki 12:19
of Jehoahaz is * in The Annals of 2Ki 13:8
of Judah are * in The Annals of the 2Ki 14:15
his biography is * in The Annals of 2Ki 14:18
by Judah)—is * in The Annals of the 2Ki 14:28
of Azariah is * in The Annals of the 2Ki 15:6
are * in The Annals of the Kings 2Ki 15:15
King Pekahiah is * in The Annals of 2Ki 15:26
Pekah's reign is * in The Annals of 2Ki 15:31
of King Ahaz is * in The Annals of 2Ki 16:19
into the city—are * in The Annals 2Ki 20:20
sinful reign is * in The Annals of 2Ki 21:17
biography is * in The Annals of the 2Ki 21:25
ceremonies as * by the Lord their 2Ki 23:21
of Jehoiakim is * in The Annals of 2Ki 24:5
(These facts are * in their 1Ch 4:32,33
* in the official genealogies). 1Ch 7:7
was carefully * in The Annals of 1Ch 9:1
of Rehoboam is * in the histories 2Ch 12:15
and speeches are * in the prophet 2Ch 13:22
first to last are * by the prophet 2Ch 26:22
and activities are * in The Annals 2Ch 28:26
* in The Annals of the Prophets. 2Ch 33:19
* among the official lamentations. 2Ch 35:24,25
Levite names were * down to the Neh 12:23
This was all duly * in the book Est 2:23
these dates and it was * as law. Est 9:32
You have * every one in your Ps 56:8
Every day was * in your Book! Ps 139:16
up in which he * the names of those Mal 3:16
prophets as * in the Scriptures." Mt 26:56
Prayer as * in Matthew 6:9-13. Lk 11:5,6f
This prophecy is * in Matthew Jn 18:32f
but these are * so that you will Jn 20:30,31
I saw these events and have * Jn 21:24
For no prophecy * in Scripture 2Pe 1:20,21
name was not found * in the Book of Rev 20:15

RECORDING
Nethanel, acted as * secretary and 1Ch 24:6
office where the * secretary and 2Ch 24:11
was at the Temple * the money 2Ch 34:14
I am * this so that future Ps 102:18

RECORDS
THIS BOOK * Moses' address to the Deu 1:1
was the historian who kept the *. 2Sa 20:24
all come from very ancient *. 1Ch 4:21-22
the permanent * of the realm): Ez 1:1
search the ancient * to discover Ez 4:15
search made of the * and have Ez 4:19
He ordered the historical * of Est 6:1
known from Assyrian * as Hilakku. Eze 27:11f

RECOUNT
It would take too long to * the Heb 11:32

RECOUNTED
exchanged, Paul * the many things Act 21:19

RECOVER
Did he try to * his land after Ju 11:25
Why have you made no effort to * Ju 11:26
you will * everything that was 1Sa 30:8
ask him whether the boy will *." 1Ki 14:3
with mine to * Ramoth-gilead?" 1Ki 22:4
Ekron to ask whether he would * 2Ki 1:2
me to ask you whether he will *." 2Ki 8:8,9
"He told me that you would *." 2Ki 8:14
to rest and * from his wounds. 2Ki 8:29
to Jezreel to * from his wounds. 2Ki 9:15
"The Lord says you won't *." 2Ki 20:1
and returned to Jezreel to *. 2Ch 22:6
he will never *. Job 20:19
Let me * and be filled with Ps 39:13
lying when they say I will *." Ps 116:10,11
you will not * from this Is 38:1
But afterwards the land shall * Jer 46:26
lives are filled with sin will *. Eze 7:13
that he won't be able to *. 2Co 2:7

RECOVERED
of Damascus, and * everything—the Gen 14:16
looked at the bronze snake, he *! Num 21:9
Midian never *, and the land was Ju 8:28
The men * their families and all 1Sa 30:18,19
Jeroboam II * the lost 2Ki 14:25
wars, and how he * Damascus and 2Ki 14:28
* the city of Elath for Syria; 2Ki 16:6
And he *! 2Ki 20:7
of the field, and * it and 1Ch 11:14
What's more, we have * and 2Ch 29:19
that all was well—his son had *. Jn 4:51

RECOVERING
days, while she is * from her Lev 12:4

RECOVERY
days she shall continue her *. Lev 12:5
until the final * of all things Act 3:21,22
*—but the fatal wound was healed! Rev 13:3

RECREATE
I will * Jerusalem as a place of Is 65:18

RECRUIT
with generals! * another army like 1Ki 20:25
and ask him to * more workers for Mt 9:38

RECRUITED
The Philistines * a mighty army 1Sa 13:5
and drivers and * fifty men to run 1Ki 1:5
King Hanun had * from his cities. 1Ch 19:7
1,400 chariots and * 12,000 cavalry 2Ch 1:14
and shields. He * an army and 2Ch 32:6

RECRUITING
Judah, the chief * officer, five of 2Ki 25:19

RECRUITMENT
was in charge of *) and sixty other Jer 52:24,25

RECRUITS
Here is the registry of * who 1Ch 12:23

RED
Give me a bite of that * stuff Gen 25:30
"Edom," which means "* Stuff." Gen 25:30
out into the * Sea, so that there Ex 10:19
through the * Sea wilderness. Ex 13:17,18
Israel on from the * Sea, and they Ex 15:22
from the * Sea to the Philistine Ex 23:31
rams' skins, dyed *, and over them Ex 26:14
and ram skins dyed *, and Ex 35:23
dyed *, and tanned goat skins. Ex 36:19
rams' skins dyed *, the specially Ex 39:33-40
in the direction of the * Sea." Num 14:25
to bring you a * heifer without Num 19:1
through the ashes of the * heifer Num 19:12
from the * heifer sin offering Num 19:17
the road to the * Sea in order to Num 21:4
the middle of the * Sea and on for Num 33:8
camped beside the * Sea, and then Num 33:10
the desert toward the * Sea.' Deu 1:40
toward the * Sea, for so the Lord Deu 2:1
them in the * Sea as they were Deu 11:4
* Sea for you when you left Egypt! Jos 2:10
at the * Sea! Jos 4:23
But when they arrived at the * Jos 24:6
after crossing the * Sea, they Ju 11:16
near Eloth on the * Sea in the land 1Ki 9:26
* as it shone across the water! 2Ki 3:22
their cries from beside the * Sea. Neh 9:9
*, white, and yellow marble. Est 1:6
My eyes are * with weeping and Job 16:16
robed the dawn in *, and disturbed Job 38:14
My eyes are * from weeping; Ps 31:9,10
You divided the * Sea with your Ps 74:13,14
When the * Sea saw you, how it Ps 77:16
rebelled against you at the * Sea. Ps 106:7
You commanded the * Sea to Ps 106:9
The * Sea saw them coming and Ps 114:3
What's wrong, * Sea, that made Ps 114:5
Praise the Lord who opened the * Ps 136:13
And so the matter is lost in * Ecc 5:8
Even if you are stained as * as Is 1:18
will dry a path through the * Sea, Is 11:15
The stream near Dibon will run * Is 15:9
"Why are your clothes so *, as Is 63:2
cedar and painted a lovely *." Jer 22:14
is heard as far away as the * Sea. Jer 49:21
in striking * uniforms, with Eze 23:14,15
Shields flash * in the sunlight! Nah 2:3
a Man sitting on a * horse that was Zec 1:8
Behind him were other horses, * Zec 1:8
Then the rider on the * horse—he Zec 1:10
was pulled by * horses, the second Zec 6:2
The * Zec 6:7
"*" implied. Zec 6:7f
referring to the * Sea which the Zec 10:11f
signs of the skies—* sky tonight Mt 16:2,3
weather tomorrow; * sky in the Mt 16:2,3
and through the * Sea, and back and Act 7:36
through the waters of the * Sea. 1Co 10:1
right through the * Sea as though Heb 11:29
This time a * horse rode out. Rev 6:4
and a third of the sea turned * Rev 8:8,9
Suddenly a * Dragon appeared, Rev 12:3

RED-CHEEKED
at this nice little * boy! 1Sa 17:41,42

RED-DYED
goat's hair, * ram's skins, Ex 25:1

RED-FACED
Then, * with anger, Moses Ex 11:8

REDDENED
'You have * the ground before me 1Ch 22:8

REDDISH
so covered with * hair that one Gen 25:25
spot, sort of * white, the man must Lev 13:19
there is a * white spot, it may be Lev 13:42
and if there is a * white lump that Lev 13:43
is a greenish or a * spot in it, it Lev 13:49
If he finds greenish or * Lev 14:37

REDDISH-WHITE
becomes bright * or white, then Lev 13:24

REDEDICATED
*, as the prophets have declared. Dan 9:24

REDEEM
If you decide not to * it, then Ex 34:20
his nearest relatives may * it. Lev 25:25
If there is no one else to * it, Lev 25:26
is not able to * it, then it shall Lev 25:28
he has up to one year to * it, Lev 25:29
He may also * himself if he can Lev 25:49
but the man wants to * it, then Lev 27:13
and then wishes to * it, the priest Lev 27:14,15
If the man decides to * the Lev 27:19

(REDEEM Con't)
But if he decides not to * the Lev 27:20
or if the owner does not * it, Lev 27:27
I am Jehovah. To * the 273 Num 3:46
Literally, "if you want to * Ru 4:4f
we are helpless to * them, for our Neh 5:5
How often must we * them?" Neh 5:8
serve the Lord, he will * them; Ps 34:22
But as for me, God will * my soul Ps 49:15
my people, to * them from the hands Is 63:4
to let them * what they have given Eze 18:12
I wanted to * them but their hard Hos 7:13
Shall I * him from Death? Hos 13:14
this Bread is my flesh given to * Jn 6:48-51

REDEEMABLE
like farmland, * at any time, and Lev 25:31

REDEEMED
You have led the people you *. Ex 15:13
* by giving a lamb in its place. Ex 34:20
But your sons must all be *. Ex 34:20
Literally, "not yet *, nor given Lev 19:20f
be * at any time by the seller. Lev 25:24
But if it is not * within the Lev 25:30
cities, may be * at any time, and Lev 25:32
family, he may be * by one of his Lev 25:48
If he has not been * by the time Lev 25:54
not be sold or *, for they are most Lev 27:28
(All the others were * because Num 3:49
whom you have *, and do not charge Deu 21:8
nation and have * it from Egypt so 1Ch 17:21
has set apart the * for himself. Ps 4:3
You have * us who are the sons of Ps 77:15
Has the Lord * you? Ps 107:2
who are just and good, shall be *. Is 1:27
That is why the Lord who * Is 29:22
only the * will travel there. Is 35:9
for the Lord * Jacob and is Is 44:23
Lord has * his servants, the Jews. Is 48:20
The time will come when God's * Is 51:11
he has * Jerusalem. Is 52:9
and "The Lord's *," and Jerusalem Is 62:12
In his love and pity he * them Is 63:9
For you have * my life. Lam 3:58
visit his people and has * them. Lk 1:68
and to the spirits of the * in Heb 12:23
who had been * from the earth. Rev 14:3

REDEEMER
"But as for me, I know that my * Job 19:25
to you, O Lord my Rock and my *. Ps 19:14
marks, for their * is strong; Pro 23:10,11
I am the Lord, your *; Is 41:14
The Lord, your *, the Holy One of Is 43:14
it is Israel's *, the Lord of Is 44:6
The Lord, your * who made you, Is 44:24
So speaks our *, who will save Is 47:4
The Lord, your *, the Holy One of Is 48:17
The Lord, the * and Holy One of Is 49:7
and *, the Mighty One of Israel." Is 49:26
he is your *, the Holy One of Is 54:5
on you, says the Lord, your *. Is 54:8
He will come as a * to those in Is 59:20
and *, the Mighty One of Israel. Is 60:16
our Father, our * from ages past. Is 63:16
But their * is strong. Jer 50:34

REDEEMERS
"a near relative, one of our *." Ru 2:20f

REDEEMING
and sing your praises for * me. Ps 71:23

REDEMPTION
shall give for the * of his life Ex 21:30f
the * payment for your oldest son. Ex 22:29
full right of * during that time. Lev 25:29
So Moses received * money for the Num 3:49
Literally, "looking for the * of Lk 2:38f
were sealed unto the day of *." Eph 4:30f

REDUCE
you to * the count of your flock? Gen 31:39
However, don't * their production Ex 5:7,8
wife, he may not * her food or Ex 21:10
your cattle and * your numbers so Lev 26:22
In this way you will * crime Deu 22:25,26,27
and he shall * it to ashes. Jer 21:10

REDUCED
He has * our rights to those of Gen 31:15
And you have * my wages ten Gen 31:41
our tribe will be *, and will not Num 36:3
So Israel was * to abject Ju 6:6,7
Finally the Lord * Jehoahaz's 2Ki 13:7
and his house shall be * to a Ez 6:11
I am * to skin and bones because Ps 102:5
I have * your boundaries and Eze 16:27
* the discrimination against us. Act 24:2

REDUCES
and judges. He * kings to slaves Job 12:18
He makes it great, and then * it Job 12:23

REDUG
And Isaac * the wells of his Gen 26:18

REED
a * whipped about in a stream; 1Ki 14:15
He will not break the bruised *, Is 42:3

REEDS
boat from papyrus *, waterproofed Ex 2:3
the * along the river's edge. Ex 2:3
boat among the * and sent one of Ex 2:5
hidden by the *, covered by their Job 40:21
channels fouled with rotting *. Is 19:6
lived, there will be * and rushes! Is 35:7
and bowing like * in the wind and Is 58:5

REEL
and made us * beneath your blows. Ps 60:3
They * and stagger like Ps 107:27
them * drunkenly down the street! Pro 20:1
Her priests and prophets * and Is 28:7
They shall drink from it and *, Jer 25:16
You will * like a drunkard Eze 23:33
neighboring lands * and stagger Hab 2:15

REELED
Then the earth rocked and *, and Ps 18:7

REELS
My mind *; Is 21:4

REESTABLISH
proof that I will * the land of Is 49:8,9
says the Lord, I will * Moab. Jer 48:47

REESTABLISHED
He also * the priests in their 2Ch 35:2
to me and I was * as head of my Dan 4:36

REFER
This may * to Antiochus IV Dan 11:21f
They may * to me as 'Lord,' but Mt 7:21
Scriptures * when they say, 'Look! Lk 7:27
* to him, and had all come true! Jn 2:22
John. I * to the miracles I do; Jn 5:36
by doing this. I * to the Jesus Act 3:13
which they * to as a sect; Act 24:14
This is what our Scriptures * to Rom 11:8
But perhaps this may * to the 1Co 15:40f

REFERENCE
* is to a second wife of Moses. Num 12:1f
The * seems to look beyond Ps 72:6f
apparently a * to Samuel, who was Ps 89:19f
Perhaps the * is to blackmail, or Pro 5:9f
Possibly the * is to lust. Pro 27:20f
to see here a * to the presence of Is 4:2,3,4f
Some see here a * to the Is 10:27f
The * probably is also to Is 45:13f
The * is to Egypt and Israel's Lam 1:2f
The * is probably to Egypt. Lam 1:19f
The * is probably to Egypt. Lam 4:17f
Apparently a * to the fact that Eze 12:12f
Apparently a * to the fact that Eze 12:13f
Doubtless, the * is to the Eze 20:25f
Probably a * to Antiochus Dan 8:23f
be used in * to the true God. Hos 1:16f
Perhaps the * is to impure salt; Lk 14:34f
* is to the witness of his Father. Jn 5:32,33f
This was not a * to David, for Act 13:36
[No, it was a * to another Act 13:37
Probably the * is to the day of Heb 5:5f
Perhaps the * is to atoms, Heb 11:3f
wife to whom * is made in Matthew 1Pe 5:13f
or whether the * is to Christ. Rev 9:1f

REFERRED
and sometimes they * to it as Ex 17:7
The ancient poets had * to King Num 21:27-30
Anakim are often * to as the Deu 2:11
his house shall be * to as 'the Deu 25:10
The names in bold face type are * 1Ch 1:1f
Whenever a case is * to you by 2Ch 19:10
Benjamin—and so is * to here in 2Ch 28:19f
is (the one * to in the Scriptures Act 4:11

REFERRING
Apparently they were * to his Num 12:1f
He was * to the incident at the Num 27:14
Or, "the Sea of Egypt," * to the Zec 10:11f
That this is not a passage * to Zec 13:6f
Isaiah was * to Jesus when he Jn 12:41
David wasn't * to himself when he Act 2:29
But perhaps he is * here, as in Act 28:20f

REFERS
"sons of God" * to the "godly Gen 6:1f
This * to the custom of the day. Ru 1:11f
Lord," sometimes * to the coming Is 4:2,3,4f
Its immediate use here * to Is 7:14f
streams of Egypt" * to Upper Egypt Is 7:18f
This verse probably * to the Jer 30:21f
here * to, in Leviticus 11. Eze 4:14f
This passage evidently * to the Zec 2:8f

REFILLED
so she * the canteen and gave the Gen 21:19

REFINE
to mine silver and * gold, to dig Job 28:1
I will * them and test them like Jer 9:7
but this will only * and cleanse Dan 11:35

REFINED
Finally, he weighed out the * 1Ch 28:18
truth, like silver seven times *. Ps 12:6
wipe you out. I * you in the Is 48:10
silver are * and purified by fire. Zec 13:9

REFINER
Like a * of silver he will sit Mal 3:3

REFINING
sadness has a * influence on us. Ecc 7:3
The bellows blow fiercely; the * Jer 6:29
For he is like a blazing fire * Mal 3:2
ministers of God, * them like gold Mal 3:

REFLECT
that they * their light forward. Ex 25:37
and do not * a knowledge of God's Ecc 9:5
and do not * a knowledge of God's Ecc 9:5
and do not * a knowledge of God's Ecc 9:10
city * upon your pallid faces. Is 13:8
Your words now * your fate then: Mt 12:37
we can be mirrors that brightly * 2Co 3:18
Let everything you do * your love Tit 2:7

REFLECTED
his face * the terror he felt, Dan 5:9

REFLECTION
peering at his * in a poor mirror; 1Co 13:12

REFLECTS
A mirror * a man's face, but what Pro 27:19

REFORM
"And if even this will not * Lev 26:23

REFORMED
of him and he * and purged Israel Ju 3:10

REFRAIN
must * from doing our daily tasks. Ex 16:23
(But it is not a sin if you * Deu 23:22
write to them to * from eating meat Act 15:20
and wife to * from the rights of 1Co 7:5

REFRAINED
"But again I * in order to Eze 20:14

REFRESH
I get water to * your feet, and a Gen 18:3,4
and given water to * their feet; Gen 43:24
O God, to * it in its weariness! Ps 68:9,10
how they * and revive me! Ps 119:49,50
He will * her as a river in the Is 32:2
and I * the humble and give new Is 57:15
I will * Israel like the dew Hos 14:5
Then the nation of Israel will * Mic 5:7
of God, and we can * each other. Rom 15:32

REFRESHED
on the seventh day, and was *." Ex 31:17
I have been * at many conquered 2Ki 19:24
The caravans turn aside to be *, Job 6:15-18
were constantly * and renewed. Job 29:20
How * I am by your blessings! Ps 92:10
But he himself shall be * from Ps 110:7
May we be * Ps 126:4
people, my chosen ones, can be *. Is 43:20
* us by the arrival of Titus. 2Co 7:6
* the hearts of God's people. Phm 1:7

REFRESHES
The advice of a wise man * like Pro 13:14

REFRESHING
Harmony is as * as the dew on Ps 133:3
But his approval is as * as the Pro 19:12
A faithful employee is as * as a Pro 25:13
of living water, * as the streams Sol 4:15
wilderness! How * was your love! Hos 9:10

REFRESHMENT
and * collect after rains! Ps 84:6
wonderful times of * from the Act 3:19
as a mighty Rock of spiritual *. 1Co 10:3,4

REFUGE
the six Cities of * where a person Num 35:6
land, Cities of * shall be Num 35:11
Three of these six Cities of * Num 35:13,14
to stay in the City of *; Num 35:25
in a City of *, permitting him to Num 35:32
three Cities of * so that anyone Deu 19:2,3
three additional Cities of *. Deu 19:9
of the Cities of *, the elders of Deu 19:11
Arameans who went to Egypt for *. Deu 26:5
rocks they claimed to be their *? Deu 32:37
The eternal God is your *, Deu 33:27
of *, as I instructed Moses. Jos 20:2
The cities chosen as Cities of * Jos 20:7
These Cities of * were for Jos 20:9
as a City of *—it was also called Jos 21:9-16
Shechem (a City of *), Gezer, Jos 21:20,21,22
Golan, in Bashan (a City of *), Jos 21:27
Kedesh, in Galilee (a City of *), Jos 21:32
Ramoth (a City of *), Mahanaim, Jos 21:38,39
happening and took * in the fort Ju 9:46
to take *, bless you for it." Ru 2:12
Who is my rock and my *. 2Sa 22:3
My * and high tower. 2Sa 22:3
Cities of * with their surrounding 1Ch 6:58,59
these Cities of * with the 1Ch 6:66-69
The following Cities of * and 1Ch 6:70
Cities of * and pastureland given 1Ch 6:71
to the Merari clan as Cities of *. 1Ch 6:77
He is a * for them in their times Ps 9:9
He is the * of the poor and Ps 14:6
LORD, WHO MAY go and find * and Ps 15:1
because I have come to you for *. Ps 16:1
Literally, "for you are my *." Ps 31:4f
everyone who takes * in him will Ps 34:22
All humanity takes * in the Ps 36:7
He is their salvation and their * Ps 37:39
you are God, my only place of *. Ps 43:2
GOD IS OUR * and strength, a Ps 46:1
I would flee to some * from all Ps 55:8

REFUGE Con't)
my high tower of *, a place of Ps 59:16
For you are my *, a high tower Ps 61:3
He is my *, a Rock where no enemy Ps 62:7
LORD, YOU ARE my *! Ps 71:1
alone is my *, my place of safety; Ps 91:2
For Jehovah is my *! Ps 91:9
It is better to take * in him Ps 118:9
You are my * and my shield, and Ps 119:114
You are my *. Ps 141:8
"you are my only place of *. Ps 142:5
his children have a place of * Pro 14:26
The godly have a * when they die, Pro 14:32
will find a * within her walls. Is 14:32
O Lord, you are a * from the storm, Is 25:4
and Fortress, my * in the day of Jer 16:19
But our * is your throne, Jer 17:12
He is their * and Strength. Joe 3:16
But Jerusalem will become a *, a Ob 1:17

REFUGEE
be accepted from a * in a City of Num 35:32
on that day a * from Jerusalem Eze 24:26

REFUGEES
The desperate * take only the Is 15:7
MOAB'S * AT Sela send lambs as a Is 16:1
After the fall of Jerusalem the * Jer 7:18f
away as Zoar. Her * will climb the Jer 48:5

REFUSAL
* to do what they had promised; Ex 9:34
without him and reported his *. Num 22:14
stubborn * to believe those who had Mk 16:14

REFUSE
But if you * to obey, watch out. Gen 4:7
to stubbornly *, and I will Ex 7:3
to * to let the people go. Ex 7:14
If you *, I will send vast Ex 8:2
If you * I will send swarms of Ex 8:21
If you *, the power of God will Ex 9:2
power, and * to let my people go? Ex 9:17
long will you * to submit to me? Ex 10:3
If you *, tomorrow I will cover Ex 10:4,5
I promise not to * afterwards to Ex 10:17
"How long will these people * to Ex 16:28,29
I * to clear the guilty, and Ex 34:7
man has done, and * to put him to Lev 20:4
Whom are you trying to fool? We * Num 16:14
but if they *, then they must Num 32:30
But if you * to drive out the Num 33:55
and a curse if you * them and Deu 11:28
Don't * a loan because the year Deu 15:9
If you * to make the loan and the Deu 15:9
* to listen to the Lord your God. Deu 28:45
He will * to give them a share Deu 28:55
to the ground—will * to share with Deu 28:56,57
"If you * to obey all the laws Deu 28:58,59
mound of *, as it still is today. Jos 8:28
If you *, let fire flame forth Ju 9:15
commandments and * to listen to 1Sa 12:15
never come here. I * to see him." 2Sa 14:24
"You know I won't * you." 1Ki 2:20
follow me, if you * the laws I have 2Ch 7:19
then * to pay their taxes to you. Ez 4:13
holy day, we would * to buy it. Neh 10:31
they * to obey the king's laws; Est 3:8
from me in terror and * to help. Job 6:19-21
and to * to forgive my iniquity. Job 10:13,14
nor does it help if I * to speak. Job 16:6
My own wife and brothers * to Job 19:17
But I * even to deal with people Job 21:16
They * to help the needy widows. Job 24:21
I did not * a single one. Ps 18:22
Why do you * to help me or even Ps 22:1
hangouts and * to enter them. Ps 26:5
If you * to answer me, I might as Ps 28:1
You * to let them triumph over me. Ps 30:1
like bread and * to come to God. Ps 53:4
For they * to fear him or even Ps 55:19
didn't * me his kindness and love. Ps 66:20
enemies, for they * to leave their Ps 68:21
And on kingdoms that * to pray, Ps 79:6
How long will you judges * to Ps 82:2
Help me to * the low and vulgar Ps 101:3
Let all sinners perish—all who * Ps 104:35
proud ones who * your commands— Ps 119:21
And may those passing by * to Ps 129:8
Don't let me * it. Ps 141:5
Only fools * to be taught. Pro 1:7,8,9
don't * it—and be wise. Pro 8:33
Those who * me show that they Pro 8:36
Better * than suffer later. Pro 11:15
be taught. To * reproof is stupid. Pro 12:1
If you * criticism you will end Pro 13:18
That is why fools * to give them Pro 13:19
If you * to discipline your son, Pro 13:24
things but his hands * to work. Pro 21:25,26
Don't * to accept criticism; Pro 23:12
perish, for they * to come to me. Is 1:28
be thrown as * in the streets. Is 5:25
(is old enough) to * the evil and Is 7:15,16f
are planning to * my gentle care Is 8:6
wither, the skies * their rain. Is 24:4,5
taking bribes, who * to listen to Is 33:15
but you * to agree it is so. Is 48:6
must you still * to help us, Lord? Is 64:12
for they * to listen to me; Jer 4:22
they * to turn from their sins. Jer 5:3
wicked deeds. They * justice to Jer 5:28
Their ears are closed and they * Jer 6:10
* to come to me," says the Lord. Jer 9:6
Do you still * to listen? Jer 13:17
because they * to turn back to me Jer 15:7
content and * to listen to me. Jer 16:12
says the Lord, and * to work on the Jer 17:24
to me, if you * to keep the Sabbath Jer 17:27
and * to notice their distress. Jer 18:17
But if you * to pay attention to Jer 22:5
And if they * to accept the Jer 25:28
their advice and * to submit to the Jer 27:10
mocked, for they * to listen to me Jer 29:19
But now you * and have defiled Jer 34:16
says: Because you * to listen or Jer 35:17
If you * to surrender, this city Jer 38:18
But if you * to surrender, the Jer 38:21,22
God be on us if we * to obey Jer 42:5
"But if you * to obey the Lord Jer 42:13,14
wrath, but all who * to go back—who Jer 44:28
Their captors hold them and * to Jer 50:33
You have made us as * and Lam 3:45
If you * to warn the wicked when Eze 3:18
on sinning, and * to repent, they Eze 3:19
bad, and you * to warn him of the Eze 3:20
to, and let anyone * who wants to, Eze 3:27
indulgences. They * to even offer Eze 13:18
But if you *, you will be thrown Dan 3:15
But even so we still * to satisfy Dan 9:13
for you yourselves * to know me; Hos 4:6
therefore I * to recognize you as Hos 4:6
Your doom is sealed, for you * to Hos 4:14
doom—I dare not * to proclaim it. Amo 3:8
you take bribes; you * justice to Amo 5:12
upon the nations who * to obey me. Mic 5:15
all be punished if they * to come. Zec 14:19
and * this kind of sacrifice. Mal 1:10
but if you * to forgive them, he Mt 6:14,15
Time enough then for them to * to Mt 9:15
If you * to take up your cross Mt 10:38
is here—and you * to believe him. Mt 12:41
is here—and you * to believe him. Mt 12:42
do to you if you * to truly forgive Mt 18:35
by men, and some * to marry for the Mt 19:12
* to eat at the wedding feast? Mk 2:19
"Do you * to answer this charge? Mk 14:60
But those who * to believe will Mk 16:16
enough, but you * to notice the Lk 12:56
Why do you * to see for Lk 12:57
But if you * to honor God's Son, Jn 5:23
to him, for you * to believe me—the Jn 5:38
my Father and you * to welcome me, Jn 5:43
He wrote about me, but you * to Jn 5:46
him, so you * to believe in me. Jn 5:46
If you * to forgive them, they Jn 20:23
worthy of death, I don't * to die! Act 25:10,11
be, and he makes some * to listen. Rom 9:18
So those who * to obey the laws Rom 13:2
to do them, I'll * to if I think 1Co 6:12
So do not * these rights to each 1Co 7:5
you lost when you * to worship Col 2:18
know God, and who * to accept his 2Th 1:8
For there are many who * to obey; Tit 1:10
our danger if we * to listen to God Heb 12:25
for then if they * to listen when 1Pe 3:1

REFUSED
I am, because I * to keep my Gen 38:26
Joseph *. Gen 39:8
even though he * to listen, and Gen 39:10
But his father *. Gen 48:19
me, but you have *: and now see, I Ex 4:23
his heart and * to let the people Ex 8:15
and he * to let the people go. Ex 9:7
so that he * to listen, just as Ex 9:12
so Pharaoh * to let the people Ex 9:35
years you * to let it lie idle; Lev 26:34,35
ten times * to trust me and obey Num 14:22
of Eliab), but they * to come. Num 16:11,12
Because Edom * to allow Israel Num 20:21,22
But King Sihon *. Num 21:23
* to do what he wanted them to. Num 32:10,11
But the people * to go in, and Deu 1:26
"They * to believe the Lord our Deu 1:32
"But King Sihon * because Deu 2:30
would help you; you * to obey him. Deu 9:23
to the man who * God's verdict, and Deu 17:13
for they * to obey God's commands. Ju 2:17
Zalmunna, and you * to give us food Ju 8:15
asked the olive tree, but it *. Ju 9:9
"But the fig tree also *. Ju 9:11
"I summoned you, but you * to Ju 12:2
At first the man *, but his Ju 19:7
anyone who * to come must die. Ju 21:5
to kill anyone who * to come to Ju 21:8,9
But the people * to listen to 1Sa 8:19
And they despised him and * to 1Sa 10:27
for he has again * to obey me." 1Sa 15:11
fierce anger and * to eat all that 1Sa 20:34
But the soldiers * to harm the 1Sa 22:17
being loyal, and I * to kill you 1Sa 26:23
But the Lord * to answer him, 1Sa 28:5,6
But he *. 1Sa 28:23
But Asahel * and kept on coming. 2Sa 2:21
But he * to turn away, so Abner 2Sa 2:23
David had * to eat anything the 2Sa 3:35,36
up and eat with them, but he *. 2Sa 12:17
living, you wept and * to eat; 2Sa 12:21
tray before him, he * to eat! 2Sa 13:9
because you have * to bring home 2Sa 14:13
him again, but again he * to come. 2Sa 14:29
when Absalom * his advice—saddled 2Sa 17:23
me by saying that I * to come. 2Sa 19:27
But he * to answer. 2Sa 22:42
But he * to drink it! 2Sa 23:16
to King David and * to endorse 1Ki 1:8
clearly wrong and * to follow the 1Ki 11:6
But Rehoboam * the old men's 1Ki 12:8
so the king * the people's 1Ki 12:15
And since you have * to 1Ki 14:9
"For you and your family have * 1Ki 18:18
But the man *. 1Ki 20:35
and sullen. He * to eat and went to 1Ki 21:4
or to trade it, and he *!" 1Ki 21:6
but Jehoshaphat had * the offer. 1Ki 22:49
independence and * to pay tribute 2Ki 1:1
to take them, but he absolutely *. 2Ki 5:16
But Amaziah * to listen, so King 2Ki 14:11
* to accept him as their king; 2Ki 15:16
At the same time he * to pay the 2Ki 17:4
ancestors and * to believe in the 2Ki 17:14
But even Judah * to obey the 2Ki 17:19
and * to pay tribute any longer. 2Ki 18:7
For they had * to listen to the 2Ki 18:12
* to listen to God's instructions. 2Ki 21:22
But the people of Jebus * to let 1Ch 11:5,6
But he * to drink it! 1Ch 11:18,19
generals * to let David and his men 1Ch 12:19
for he * the advice of the old 2Ch 10:13
And Israel has * to be ruled by 2Ch 10:19
So they obeyed the Lord and * 2Ch 11:4
that anyone who * to do this must 2Ch 15:13
Uzziah was furious, and * to set 2Ch 26:19
But Josiah * to turn back. 2Ch 35:22
Josiah * to believe that Neco's 2Ch 35:22
concerned, for he * to take the 2Ch 36:12
concerned, for he * to follow him. 2Ch 36:13
people * to observe the Sabbath. 2Ch 36:21
so the leaders * to allow them to Ez 2:62,63
Temple and * all food and drink; Ez 10:6
that anyone who * to come would be Ez 10:7,8
In fact, I * to eat for several Neh 1:4
of God upon any of them who *. Neh 5:13
wall and * to speculate in land; Neh 5:16
Yet I * to make a special levy Neh 5:18
* to listen to your commandments. Neh 9:16
"They * to obey and didn't pay Neh 9:17
* to turn from their wickedness. Neh 9:35
to Queen Vashti, she * to come. Est 1:12
But Mordecai * to bow. Est 3:2
day after day, but he still *. Est 3:3,4
the sackcloth, but he * it. Est 4:4
"For instance, you must have * Job 22:6
You must have * water to the Job 22:7
I have not * his commandments Job 23:12
to weep, or * food to hungry Job 31:17
so that I * to acknowledge my sin Job 31:34
THE THREE MEN * to reply further Job 32:1
angry because Job * to admit he had Job 32:2
they cried to the Lord, but he * Ps 18:41
him to make them well; I * to eat; Ps 35:13
for you have * my discipline, Ps 50:17
laws. They * to follow his ways. Ps 78:10
and * to believe in miracles. Ps 78:32
and * to follow his commands. Ps 78:56
sword and * to help him in battle. Ps 89:43
from me. They * to accept my laws. Ps 95:10
They * to enter the Promised Ps 106:24
For he * all kindness to others, Ps 109:16
* to yield and disobey your laws. Ps 119:87
I have * to walk the paths of Ps 119:101
But the king *. Is 7:12
Literally, "have * the waters of Is 8:6f
but Israel and Judah have * his Is 8:14,15
Assyria has * their cry for peace. Is 33:7
called them, they * to answer, and Is 66:4
confess that you * to follow me. Jer 3:13
but you * to hear or answer. Jer 7:13,14
Because they * to obey, I did to Jer 11:8
They stubbornly * to pay Jer 17:23
* to listen to the Lord. Jer 19:15
prophets, but you have * to hear. Jer 25:4
in it, but they * to obey you or Jer 32:23
backs upon me and * to return; Jer 32:33
Because you have * the terms of Jer 34:18,19
them to have a drink, but they *. Jer 35:6
but you have * to listen to me. Jer 35:16
and all the people * to obey the Jer 43:4

(REFUSED Con't)
the Lord and * to obey him." Jer 44:23
in immorality, and * to face the Lam 1:9
rights, and * them justice. Lam 3:34,35,36
There in the wilderness they * my Eze 20:13
against me. They * my laws—the laws Eze 20:21
you and you *, remain filthy until Eze 24:13
without dinner. He * his usual Dan 6:18
We have * to listen to your Dan 9:6
broke my covenant; you * my love. Hos 6:7
And yet you * to come. Amo 4:10
Yet, even so, you * to return to Hag 2:16,17
I called but they * to listen, Zec 7:13
happening, you * to repent, and so Mt 21:32
But all *! Mt 22:3
a stranger, and you * me Mt 25:43
"And I will answer, 'When you * Mt 25:45
but when he had tasted it, he *. Mt 27:34
(But he * to allow the demons to Mk 1:34
offered to him there, but he * it. Mk 15:23
for them and * John's baptism. Lk 7:30
her hair. You * me the customary Lk 7:45
The people of the village * to Lk 9:53
he knew his duty he * to do it. Lk 12:47
And when they * to answer, Jesus Lk 14:4
you and never once * to do a single Lk 15:29
For you have * to believe Moses. Jn 5:46
to others if they * to take it Rom 10:19
but when the Jews * his gifts God Rom 11:30
they have * to believe it and 2Th 2:10
A man who * to obey the laws Heb 10:28
of the world—which * to obey—and Heb 11:7
when he grew up, * to be treated as Heb 11:24,25
her city when they * to obey God, Heb 11:31
escape when they * to listen to Heb 12:25
days of Noah, had * to listen to 1Pe 3:20
loyal to me, and * to deny me, even Rev 2:13
her mind and attitude, but she *. Rev 2:21
plagues still * to worship God! Rev 9:20
sores, but they * to repent of all Rev 16:11

REFUSES
Anyone who * these terms shall Gen 17:14
But if her father utterly * to Ex 22:17
on a trip, and yet * to celebrate Num 9:13
But if her father * to let her Num 30:5
But if her husband * to accept Num 30:8
but if he * to allow it on the Num 30:12
a day and then * to permit the vow, Num 30:15
If the defendant * to accept the Deu 17:12
But if it * and won't make peace Deu 20:12
But if the dead man's brother * Deu 25:7
husband's brother * to let his Deu 25:7
name continue—he * to marry me.' Deu 25:7
and if he still *, the widow shall Deu 25:8
* to build his brother's house.' Deu 25:9
oxen of anyone who * to follow Saul 1Sa 11:7
for a queen who * to obey the Est 1:13-15
Anyone who * to slander others, Ps 15:3
rates, and * to testify against the Ps 15:5
A man who * to admit his mistakes Pro 28:13
often reproved but * to accept Pro 29:1
and foolish king who * all advice. Ecc 4:13
Blessed is the man who * to work Is 56:2
is the nation that * to obey the Jer 7:28
Lord its God, and * to be taught. Jer 7:28
This evil nation * to listen to Jer 13:10
turns to evil and * to obey me, Jer 18:10
who * to obey the laws of God, but Eze 18:11
the alarm and * to heed it—well, if Eze 33:4
anyone who * to obey will Dan 3:6
that anyone who * will be thrown Dan 3:11
anything; she * all correction. Zep 3:2
all the world that * to come to Zec 14:17
But if Egypt * to come, God will Zec 14:18
If he still * to listen, then Mt 18:17
that anyone who * to come to God as Mk 10:15
"But if a town * you, go out Lk 10:10
That is why, if a man * to 1Co 11:4
Yes, if she * to wear a head 1Co 11:6
If anyone * to live by these 1Th 4:8
If anyone * to obey what we say 2Th 3:14
punish him if he later * to do it; Heb 6:16
over him and * to listen to me. 3Jn 1:9
He not only * to welcome the 3Jn 1:10

REFUSING
"ANYONE * TO give testimony Lev 5:1
sins against me by * to return a Lev 5:2
or rented, or by * to return Lev 6:2
of Israel for * to sacrifice to Num 9:13
in this matter, * to marry the Deu 25:7
in this book, thus * reverence to Deu 28:58,59
of Amalek for * to allow my people 1Sa 15:2
he said and was * to listen to 1Ki 12:16,17
Anyone * to obey the law of your Ez 7:26
the king's gate, * to bow to me." Est 5:13
But those * to worship God will Ps 73:27
* to give their hearts to God. Ps 78:8
Anyone * has lost his chance. Pro 10:17
your backs and * to listen to me, Is 1:20
For the nations * to be your Is 60:12
of their fathers, * to listen to me Jer 11:10
But any nation * to obey me will Jer 12:17
* to pay—yet they all curse me. Jer 15:10
I will punish any nation * to be Jer 27:8
from your blood, * to do the work Jer 48:10
his debtors by * to let them redeem Eze 18:12
some of the Jews of * to worship! Dan 3:8
have defied you, * to serve your Dan 3:12
"that you are * to serve my gods Dan 3:14
the laws of God, * to obey him. Amo 2:4
You stood aloof, * to lift a Ob 1:11
brothers, you were * help to me.' Mt 25:45
"ANYONE * TO walk through the Jn 10:1
left, * to preach to them again. Act 19:9
in * to turn from your sin; Rom 2:5
and * to come. Rom 10:21
of the land are * to obey God, and Rom 13:2
falsehood, * the Truth, and 2Th 2:12
in laziness, * to work, and wasting 2Th 3:11
and * to accept the truth. 1Jn 1:8
anyone * to worship it must die! Rev 13:15

REFUTED
for he powerfully * all the Jewish Act 18:28

REGAIN
need pay nothing to * his freedom. Ex 21:2
to eat so you'll * your strength 1Sa 28:22
had attempted to * his power. 2Sa 8:3

REGAINED
King Jeroboam of Israel never * 2Ch 13:20

REGALIA
stewards in full *, and saw the 2Ch 9:4
on thrones in full * at an open 2Ch 18:9

REGARD
but those who had no * for the Ex 9:21
works without * to human means! 1Sa 17:47
without * to age or reputation. 1Ch 25:8
gates without * to the reputation 1Ch 26:13
without * to their normal duties. 2Ch 5:11,12
my servants, * me as a stranger. Job 19:15
to you for help! * my prayer as my Ps 141:2
That is how much * they have for Eze 23:39
He will have no * for the gods Dan 11:37
all had the highest * for them. Act 5:13

REGARDED
highly * by both God and man. Lk 24:19
That is, * as slain in the Rev 13:8f

REGARDETH
* the clouds shall not reap." Ecc 11:4f

REGARDING
Then God added, "* Sarai your Gen 17:15
claim against me * this matter. Gen 20:16
with any errors * the offerings as my Ex 28:37,38

REGARDLESS
No one, * of how shrewd or Pro 21:30
teach the truth * of the Mt 22:16
and deceived * of what they say. 2Th 2:3

REGARDS
And give my best * to those Rom 16:10
here send you their best *. 2Co 13:13

REGATHER
O Lord God, save us! * us from Ps 106:47

REGEM
*, Jotham, Geshan, Pelet, Ephah, 1Ch 2:47

REGEM-MELECH
of the king, and *, to the Lord's Zec 7:2

REGENERATION
Literally, "in the *." Mt 19:28f

REGENT
"Rule as my *—I will subdue your Ps 110:1

REGIMENT
a captain of an Italian *. Act 10:1

REGIMENTAL
DAVID NOW APPOINTED * colonels 2Sa 18:1
the units and their * commanders: 1Ch 27:1

REGIMENTS
into twelve *, each with 24,000 1Ch 27:1
He organized his army into * to 2Ch 26:11
clan leaders commanded these *. 2Ch 26:12

REGION
The name of the * was thereafter Num 21:3
the entire Argob * of Bashan. Deu 3:4
kingdom of King Og, the Argob *. Deu 3:13
the whole Argob * (Bashan) to the Deu 3:14
and the * of Argob in Bashan, 1Ki 4:8-19
A * in ancient Cilicia known from Eze 27:11f
Or, "the * of Ramah." Mt 2:18f
of that * and began to tell Mk 5:20
went to the * of Tyre and Sidon, Mk 7:24
and came to the * of Dalmanutha. Mk 8:10
Leaving that * they traveled Mk 9:30,31
all that * for his sermons in the Lk 4:14
wildfire throughout the whole *. Lk 4:37
message spread all through that *. Act 13:49

REGIONAL
was chief of the * treasuries 1Ch 27:25

REGIONS
the kings of the * across the sea; Jer 25:22
* of Asia Minor, now in Turkey. Eze 27:13f
* of Asia Minor, now in Turkey. Eze 27:14f

REGISTER
older to come and *, each man Num 1:17,18,19
old and older, and * each name. Num 3:40
seer, and in The Genealogical *. 2Ch 12:1
the genealogical * by clans, and 2Ch 31:17,1

REGISTERED
from all those * in the census who Ex 38:25,2
The 32,500 * in the half-tribe of Num 26:28-3
of properly * priests, for they had 2Ch 31:17,1
in the area, and to all * Levites. 2Ch 31:1
they are * for earth and not for Jer 17:1
are * as citizens of heaven." Lk 10:2
composed of all those * in heaven; Heb 12:2

REGISTERS
When he * her citizens he will Ps 87:

REGISTRATION
with the ordinary citizens, for *. Neh 7:
to his ancestral home for this *. Lk 2:

REGISTRY
Here is the * of recruits who 1Ch 12:2

REGRET
We should never * his sending it. 2Co 7:1

REGRETS
to express * to Hanun about his 2Sa 10:
Yet no one anywhere * your Nah 3:

REGRETTED
and deeply * what he had done, Mt 27:

REGROUPED
tribe of Benjamin * there at the 2Sa 2:2
So when they *, they were joined 2Sa 10:15,1

REGULAR
deliver the * quota of bricks." Ex 5:1
duties and your * work, but the Ex 20:
event at the * time in March, the Ex 23:1
This shall be a *, annual event Ex 30:1
to the Lord a * grain offering—a Lev 6:19,2
to the * morning offering. Lev 9:17
"(These, then, are the * annual Lev 23:37
your * weekly days of holy rest. Lev 23:38
addition to your * giving and Lev 23:38
I will give you * rains, and the Lev 26:4,5
will have no * responsibilities." Num 8:25,26
follow all the * instructions Num 9:12
Passover at the * time, shall be Num 9:13
each day as a * burnt offering. Num 28:3
—in addition to the * offerings. Num 28:9,10
This is in addition to the * Num 28:15
in addition to the * daily burnt Num 28:31
in addition to the * monthly burnt Num 29:6
and also in addition to the * Num 29:6
and in addition to the * daily Num 29:11
in addition to the * daily burnt Num 29:16
Also, in addition to the * daily Num 29:19
And in addition to the * daily Num 29:22
to the * daily sacrifices. Num 29:25
to the * daily sacrifices. Num 29:34
to the * daily sacrifices. Num 29:38
This * reading of God's laws Deu 17:20
It was their * practice to send 1Sa 2:13,14
"We don't have any * bread," 1Sa 21:4
whether it is a * assessment or 2Ki 12:4,5
* festivals of the Lord our God. 2Ch 2:4
work corps. A * food allotment was 2Ch 31:17,18
other * annual feasts of the Lord. Ez 3:5
must be on duty at * times, and Neh 7:3
to determine when—at * times each Neh 10:34
This was Job's * practice. Job 1:5
And he was given a * allowance Jer 52:34
nor shave it off. *, moderate Eze 44:20
So they were put on his * staff Dan 1:18,19
of them to be his * companions and Mk 3:14,15
other believers in * attendance at Act 2:42
at the * City Council meetings; Act 19:39

REGULARLY
they are brought * and are offered Num 28:1
Mount Sinai, to be * offered as a Num 28:6
brother Levites who work there *. Deu 18:6,7
Mephibosheth ate * with King David, 2Sa 9:10,11
he ate * at the king's table. 2Ki 25:29
their trumpets * before the Ark. 1Ch 16:6
to minister * at the Tabernacle, 1Ch 16:37
the fact that I * fed 150 Jewish Neh 5:17
to my altar, for you bring them *. Ps 50:8
* in the synagogue and Temple; Jn 18:20
They worshiped together * at the Act 2:46
were meeting * at the Temple in the Act 5:12

REGULATES
him as God. He * the universe by Heb 1:3

REGULATION
is a permanent * from generation to Num 15:37,38
The purpose of this * is to Num 15:39
Jewish rule and * right down to the Php 3:6

REGULATIONS
the laws and * God had given him; Ex 24:3
* concerning the burnt offering: Lev 6:9
"These are the * concerning the Lev 6:14
These are the * concerning Lev 13:59
AND THE LORD gave Moses these * Lev 14:1
"These are the * concerning a Num 6:21
out all of these * which the Lord Num 15:22
are the various *: Everyone who Num 19:14
obey the rules and * which he gave 1Ch 22:13
obey my rules and * at all the Eze 44:24
of laws and * they have clung to Mk 7:4

REHABIAH
only son, *, was the leader of his 1Ch 23:17
Jehdeiah; the * group, led by his 1Ch 24:21
went through *, Jesha-iah, Joram, 1Ch 26:25

REHOB
of Zin to * near Hamath. Num 13:21
of Kabul, Ebron, *, Hammon, Kanah, Jos 19:28
Ummah, Aphek, and *—an overall Jos 19:30,31
Mishal, Abdon, Helkath, and *. Jos 21:30,31
Achzib, Helbah, Aphik, or *; Ju 1:31,32
Hadadezer (son of *) of Zobah in a 2Sa 8:3
from the lands of * and Zobah, one 2Sa 10:6
from Zobah, *, Tob, and Maacah 2Sa 10:7,8
and *, with their pasturelands. 1Ch 6:75
Pelaiah, Hanan, Mica, *, Neh 10:9-13

REHOBOAM
and his son * reigned in his 1Ki 11:43
to make certain demands upon *. 1Ki 12:2,3,4
was a hard master," they told *. 1Ki 12:2,3,4
to think this over," * replied. 1Ki 12:5
* talked it over with the old men 1Ki 12:6
But * refused the old men's 1Ki 12:8
Let's go home! Let * be king of 1Ki 12:16,17
and accepted * as their king. 1Ki 12:16,17
When King * sent Adoram (who was 1Ki 12:18
But King * escaped by chariot and 1Ki 12:18
When King * arrived in Jerusalem, 1Ki 12:21
"Tell * the son of Solomon, king 1Ki 12:23,24
to * is according to my wish." 1Ki 12:23,24
will become friendly with King *; 1Ki 12:27
Meanwhile, * the son of Solomon 1Ki 14:21
Afterwards * made bronze shields 1Ki 14:27
There was constant war between * 1Ki 14:30
When * died—his mother was 1Ki 14:31
Literally, "between * and 1Ki 15:6f
*, Abijah, Asa, Jehoshaphat, 1Ch 3:10-14
and his son * became the new king. 2Ch 9:31
and led the people's demands on *: 2Ch 10:2,3
* told them to return in three 2Ch 10:5
Let * rule his own tribe of Judah! 2Ch 10:16
however, remained loyal to *. 2Ch 10:17
Afterwards, when King * sent 2Ch 10:18
When this news reached King * he 2Ch 10:18
UPON ARRIVAL AT Jerusalem, * 2Ch 11:1
"Go and say to King * of Judah, 2Ch 11:3
* stayed in Jerusalem and 2Ch 11:5-10
of Judah, so King * survived for 2Ch 11:17
* married his cousin 2Ch 11:18
BUT JUST WHEN * was at the height 2Ch 12:1
now met with * and the Judean 2Ch 12:5
King * replaced them with bronze 2Ch 12:10
King * reigned seventeen years in 2Ch 12:13
The complete biography of * is 2Ch 12:15
wars between * and Jeroboam. 2Ch 12:15
When * died he was buried in 2Ch 12:16
Solomon's son *, for he was young 2Ch 13:7
Solomon was the father of *; Mt 1:7
* was the father of Abijah; Mt 1:7

REHOBOAM'S
* INAUGURATION WAS at Shechem, 1Ki 12:1
to live in. (* mother was Naamah, 1Ki 14:21
In the fifth year of * reign, 1Ki 14:25
The other events in * reign are 1Ki 14:29
came to Shechem for * coronation. 2Ch 10:1
days to hear King * decision, he 2Ch 10:12
fifth year of King * reign, with 2Ch 12:2

REHOBOTH
*. Gen 26:22f
town of * became the new king. 1Ch 1:48

REHOBOTH-BY-THE-RIVER
Succeeded by: King Shaul, from *. Gen 36:31-39

REHOBOTH-IR
He built Nineveh, *, Calah, and Gen 10:11,12

REHUM
*, Baanah. Ez 2:2
were Governor *, Shimshai (a Ez 4:8,9
reply to Governor * and Shimshai Ez 4:17
was read to * and Shimshai, they Ez 4:23
supervision of * (son of Bani). Neh 3:17
Pilha, Shobek, *, Neh 10:14-27
*, Meremoth, Iddo, Neh 12:1

REI
*, and David's army chiefs. 1Ki 1:8

REIGN
From there he extended his * to Gen 10:11,12
Jehovah shall * forever and Ex 15:18
ensure his having a long, good *. Deu 17:20
to the grapevine, 'You * over us!' Ju 9:12
you wanted a king to * over you. 1Sa 12:12
years old when he began to *, and 1Sa 13:1f
In the second year of his *, he 1Sa 13:1
during David's * that lasted year 2Sa 21:1
* even greater than yours!" 1Ki 1:37
May God make Solomon's * even 1Ki 1:46,47
during my father's *, and you 1Ki 2:26
year of Solomon's * that he began 1Ki 6:1
year of Solomon's *, and the 1Ki 6:37
of the eleventh year of his *. 1Ki 6:38
* for the rest of his life. 1Ki 11:34
will continue to * in Jerusalem, 1Ki 11:36
events of his *—are recorded in The 1Ki 14:19
when he began to *, and he was on 1Ki 14:21
During his * the people of 1Ki 14:22
In the fifth year of Rehoboam's * 1Ki 14:25
The other events in Rehoboam's * 1Ki 14:29
ABIJAM BEGAN HIS three-year * as 1Ki 15:1
year of Jeroboam's * in Israel. 1Ki 15:1
During Abijam's * there was 1Ki 15:6
year of the * of Jeroboam over 1Ki 15:9
of the * of King Asa of Judah. 1Ki 15:25
of the * of King Asa of Judah. 1Ki 15:28
Further details of Baasha's * are 1Ki 15:31
year of the * of King Asa of Judah, 1Ki 16:8
of the * of King Asa of Judah. 1Ki 16:10
history of Elah's * is written in 1Ki 16:14
Omri began his * over Israel, which 1Ki 16:23
(It was during his * that Hiel, a 1Ki 16:34
of the * of King Ahab of Israel. 1Ki 22:41
year of the * of King Jehoshaphat 1Ki 22:51
began to * over Israel in Samaria; 1Ki 22:51
second year of the * of King 2Ki 1:17
of Ahaziah's * is recorded in The 2Ki 1:18
AHAB'S SON JEHORAM began his * 2Ki 3:1
year of the * of King Jehoshaphat 2Ki 3:1
Judah, began his * during the fifth 2Ki 8:16
fifth year of the * of King Joram 2Ki 8:16
During Jehoram's *, the people in 2Ki 8:20
year of the * of King Joram of 2Ki 8:24,25
when he began to * but he reigned 2Ki 8:26
(Ahaziah's * over Judah had 2Ki 9:29
year of the * of King Joram of 2Ki 9:29
Athaliah's *, Jehoiada the priest 2Ki 11:4
year of his * the Temple was still 2Ki 12:6
a seventeen-year * over Israel 2Ki 13:1
of the * of King Joash of Judah. 2Ki 13:1
of the * of King Joash of Judah. 2Ki 13:9,10
The rest of the history of the * 2Ki 13:12
the entire * of King Jehoahaz. 2Ki 13:22
DURING THE SECOND year of the * 2Ki 14:1
Amaziah began his * over Judah. 2Ki 14:1
of the * of King Amaziah of Judah. 2Ki 14:23
Jeroboam's * lasted forty-one 2Ki 14:23
Length of his *: 52 years, in 2Ki 15:1
His age at the beginning of his *: 2Ki 15:1
Length of *: 6 months 2Ki 15:8
of Zechariah's * is found in The 2Ki 15:11
Length of *: 1 month 2Ki 15:13
Length of *: 10 years, in Samaria 2Ki 15:17
Length of *: 3 years, in Samaria 2Ki 15:23
Length of *: 20 years, in Samaria 2Ki 15:27
It was during his * that King 2Ki 15:29
history of Pekah's * is recorded in 2Ki 15:31
Duration of his *: 16 years, in 2Ki 15:32,33
It was during King Jotham's * 2Ki 15:34,35
Duration of *: 16 years, in 2Ki 16:1
Character of his *: evil 2Ki 16:1
The rest of the history of the * 2Ki 16:19
Length of his *: 9 years, in 2Ki 17:1
Character of his *: evil—but not 2Ki 17:1
of King Hoshea's *, Samaria fell 2Ki 17:6
Length of his *: 29 years, in 2Ki 18:1
His age at the beginning of his *: 2Ki 18:1
Character of his *: good (similar 2Ki 18:1
fourth year of his * (which was the 2Ki 18:9
year of the * of King Hoshea in 2Ki 18:9
sixth year of the * of King 2Ki 18:10
ninth year of the * of King Hoshea 2Ki 18:10
year of the * of King Hezekiah, 2Ki 18:13
Length of his *: 55 years, in 2Ki 21:1
Character of his *: evil. 2Ki 21:1
Manasseh's sinful * is recorded in 2Ki 21:17
His age at the beginning of his *: 2Ki 21:19,20
Length of his *: 2 years, in 2Ki 21:19,20
Character of his *: evil 2Ki 21:19,20
His age at the beginning of his *: 2Ki 22:1
Duration of his *: 31 years in 2Ki 22:1
Character of his *: good; 2Ki 22:1
In the eighteenth year of his *, 2Ki 22:3,4
year of the * of King Josiah, and 2Ki 23:23
Length of his *: 3 months, in 2Ki 23:31,32
Character of his *: evil, like the 2Ki 23:31,32
Josiah's sons, to * in Jerusalem; 2Ki 23:34
Length of his *: 11 years, in 2Ki 23:36,37
Character of his *: evil, like the 2Ki 23:36,37
DURING THE * of King Jehoiakim, 2Ki 24:1
His age at the beginning of his *: 2Ki 24:8,9
Length of his *: 3 months, in 2Ki 24:8,9
During his * the armies of King 2Ki 24:10
eighth year of Nebuchadnezzar's *. 2Ki 24:12
Length of his *: 11 years, in 2Ki 24:18,19
Character of his *: evil, like 2Ki 24:18,19
the * of King Zedekiah of Judah. 2Ki 25:1
into the eleventh year of his *. 2Ki 25:2
of the * of King Nebuchadnezzar. 2Ki 25:8
first year of the * of King 2Ki 25:27
So during the * of King Hezekiah 1Ch 4:40,41
During the * of King Saul, the 1Ch 5:10
quietness to Israel during his *. 1Ch 22:9
his descendants to * over every 1Ch 22:10
fortieth year of King David's * 1Ch 26:31,32
seven of them during his * in 1Ch 29:26,27
These accounts tell of his * and 1Ch 29:30
before the * of King Solomon. 2Ch 1:2,3f
During Solomon's *, silver and 2Ch 1:15
fourth year of King Solomon's *. 2Ch 3:2
shall always * over Israel if they 2Ch 6:16
of King Rehoboam's *, with twelve 2Ch 12:2
the * of King Jeroboam of Israel. 2Ch 13:1
Early in his * war broke out 2Ch 13:1
ten years of his *, for Asa was 2Ch 14:1
year of King Asa's *, and 2Ch 15:10
thirty-fifth year of King Asa's *. 2Ch 15:19
year of King Asa's *, King Baasha 2Ch 16:1
year of his *, Asa became seriously 2Ch 16:12
year of his *, and was buried in 2Ch 16:13,14
In the third year of his * he 2Ch 17:7,8,9
The details of Jehoshaphat's * 2Ch 20:34
when he began to *, and he reigned 2Ch 21:5
when he began to * and he reigned 2Ch 21:20
when he began to *, and he 2Ch 22:2
IN THE SEVENTH year of the * of 2Ch 23:1
come for the king's son to *!" 2Ch 23:2,3
The other details of Uzziah's * 2Ch 26:22
when he began to * and he reigned 2Ch 27:8
of Zechariah. His * was a good one 2Ch 29:2
first year of his *, he reopened 2Ch 29:3
But it was an evil *, for he 2Ch 33:2
when he began to * in Jerusalem, 2Ch 33:20,21
It was an evil * like the early 2Ch 33:22
His was a good *, as he 2Ch 34:2
eighth year of his *, he began to 2Ch 34:3
year of his *, after he had purged 2Ch 34:8
year of the * of Josiah. 2Ch 35:19
*, but lasted only three months. 2Ch 36:2
but his * was an evil one. 2Ch 36:5
and it was an evil * as far as the 2Ch 36:9
in Jerusalem. His *, too, was evil 2Ch 36:12
DURING THE FIRST year of the * of Ez 1:1
This went on during his entire * Ez 4:4,5
began to *, they wrote him a letter Ez 4:6
during the * of Ar-ta-xerxes. Ez 4:7
of the * of King Darius of Persia. Ez 4:24
first year of his *, issued a Ez 5:13
first year of the * of King Cyrus, Ez 6:3
in the sixth year of the * of Ez 6:15
during the * of King Ar-ta-xerxes Ez 7:1
year of the * of King Ar-ta-xerxes and Ez 7:7,8,9
during the * of King Ar-ta-xerxes: Ez 8:1
* of King Ar-ta-xerxes of Persia, Neh 1:1
year of the * of King Neh 5:14
during the * of King Darius of Neh 12:22
year of the * of King Ar-ta-xerxes Neh 13:6
IT WAS THE third year of the * of Est 1:1
of the seventh year of his *. Est 2:16
the history of King Ahasuerus' *. Est 2:23
year of the * of Ahasuerus, and Est 3:7
and will * throughout the world. Ps 59:12,13
prosperity because of his good *. Ps 72:3
May the * of this son Ps 72:6
flourish in his *, with abundance Ps 72:7
Let him * from sea to sea, and Ps 72:8
is forever the keynote of your *. Ps 93:5
are glad that you * in majesty over Ps 97:8,9
the majesty and glory of your *. Ps 145:12
The Lord will * forever. Ps 146:10
Because of my strength, kings * Pro 8:14,15
and his * of terror shall end. Pro 22:8
his * will be just and fair. Pro 25:4,5
will have a long * if he hates Pro 28:16
to the poor shall have a long *. Pro 29:14
DURING THE * of Ahaz (the son of Is 7:1
Quietness and confidence will * Is 32:17
of King Hezekiah's *, Sennacherib, Is 36:1
You thought your * would never Is 47:7
year of the * of Amon's son Josiah, Jer 1:1
Others came during the * of Jer 1:3
year of the * of Josiah's son Jer 1:3
to me during the * of King Josiah: Jer 3:6
Why did your father Josiah * so Jer 22:15
the poor and * with ruthlessness. Jer 22:17
fourth year of the * of King Jer 25:1
king of Babylon, began his *. Jer 25:1
year of the * of Josiah (son of Jer 25:2,3
first year of the * of Jehoiakim Jer 26:1
beginning of the * of Jehoiakim Jer 27:1
fourth year of the * of Zedekiah, Jer 28:1
shall prosper as in David's *; Jer 30:20
tenth year of the * of Zedekiah, Jer 32:1
year of Nebuchadnezzar's *). Jer 32:1
have a son to * upon his throne; Jer 33:20,21
of the * of King Jehoiakim of Jer 36:1
fifth year of the * of King Jer 36:9
ninth year of the * of King Jer 39:1
fourth year of the * of King Jer 45:1
fourth year of the * of Jehoiakim Jer 46:2
the * of Zedekiah, king of Judah: Jer 49:34
year of Zedekiah's *, this message Jer 51:59
In the ninth year of Zedekiah's * Jer 52:4
of the * of Nebuchadnezzar, king Jer 52:12
of Nebuchadnezzar's * was 3,023. Jer 52:28
also during the * of Manasseh. Eze 23:16f
during the * of Josiah. Eze 23:19,20f
anarchy shall *! Eze 30:13

(REIGN Con't)
first year of the * of King Cyrus. Dan 1:21
second year of his *, Dan 2:1
*, and brought to Babylon. Dan 5:2,3,4
And in the * of King Dan 5:11
anyone he desires to * over them. Dan 5:21
of your *, and they are ended. Dan 5:26
So Daniel prospered in the * of Dan 6:28
and in the * of Cyrus the Persian. Dan 6:28
of Belshazzar's * over the Dan 7:1
IN THE THIRD year of the * of King Dan 8:1
IT WAS NOW the first year of the * Dan 9:1
In that first year of his *, I, Dan 9:2
IN THE THIRD year of the * of Dan 10:1
Mede in the first year of his *. Dan 11:1
Three more Persian kings will *, Dan 11:2
after a very brief *, he will die Dan 11:20
When: During the * of Josiah (son Zep 1:1
year of the * of King Darius I. Hag 1:1
*, and volunteered their help. Hag 1:14,15
second year of the * of King Hag 2:10
year of the * of King Darius. Zec 1:1
second year of the * of King Zec 1:7
year of the * of King Darius. Zec 7:1
Judea, during the * of King Herod. Mt 2:1
And he shall * over Israel Lk 1:33
IN THE FIFTEENTH year of the * of Lk 3:1
(This was fulfilled during the * Act 11:28
Literally, "* in life." Rom 5:17f
they shall * upon the earth." Rev 5:10
and he shall * forever and Rev 11:15
great power and have begun to *. Rev 11:17
to come, but his * will be brief. Rev 17:10
after his second *, he too, will Rev 17:11
one brief moment, to * with him. Rev 17:12
ten kings who will * with him—all Rev 17:16
shall * with him a thousand years. Rev 20:6
and they shall * forever and Rev 22:5

REIGN:12
beginning of his *: 12 2Ki 21:1

REIGNED
the Amorites, who * in Heshbon, and Jos 13:10
who had * in Ashtaroth and Edre-i. Jos 13:12
BY THIS TIME Saul had * for one 1Sa 13:1
he began to reign, and he *. 1Sa 13:1f
He * in Mahanaim for two years; 2Sa 2:10,11
so he * for forty years 2Sa 5:4,5
David * with justice over Israel 2Sa 8:15
He had * over Israel for forty 1Ki 2:11
and his son Rehoboam * in his 1Ki 11:43
Jeroboam * twenty-two years, and 1Ki 14:20
and his son Asa * in his place. 1Ki 15:8
Israel, and * forty-one years. 1Ki 15:10
become king. He * two years, 1Ki 15:25
Baasha * for twenty-four years, 1Ki 15:32,33
of Judah, but he * only two years. 1Ki 16:8
so Omri * without opposition. 1Ki 16:22
and Ahab * for twenty-two years. 1Ki 16:29
the throne, and he * in Jerusalem 1Ki 22:42
and he * two years. 1Ki 22:51
and he * twelve years. 2Ki 3:1
he * in Jerusalem for eight years. 2Ki 8:17
he * only one year, in Jerusalem. 2Ki 8:26
In all, Jehu * as king of 2Ki 10:36
years while Athaliah * as queen. 2Ki 11:2,3
He * in Jerusalem for forty years. 2Ki 12:1
* in Samaria for sixteen years. 2Ki 13:9,10
his son Ben-hadad * in his place. 2Ki 13:24
the time, and he * in Jerusalem for 2Ki 14:2
kings of Edom who * before the 1Ch 1:43
he * seven and one-half years. 1Ch 3:4
he * another thirty-three years. 1Ch 3:4
David * over all of Israel and 1Ch 18:14
and his son Solomon * in his 1Ch 29:28
So Solomon * in Jerusalem over 2Ch 9:30
King Rehoboam * seventeen years 2Ch 12:13
* twenty-five years, in Jerusalem. 2Ch 20:31
he * eight years, in Jerusalem. 2Ch 21:5
to reign and he * in Jerusalem 2Ch 21:20
when he began to reign, and he * 2Ch 22:2
years while Athaliah * as queen. 2Ch 22:12
he * forty years, in Jerusalem. 2Ch 24:1
* twenty-nine years, in Jerusalem. 2Ch 25:1
In all, he * fifty-two years, in 2Ch 26:3
he * sixteen years, in Jerusalem. 2Ch 27:1
he * sixteen years, in Jerusalem. 2Ch 27:8
he * sixteen years, in Jerusalem. 2Ch 28:1
* twenty-nine years, in Jerusalem. 2Ch 29:1
* fifty-five years, in Jerusalem. 2Ch 33:1
* thirty-one years, in Jerusalem. 2Ch 34:1
he * eleven years, in Jerusalem; 2Ch 36:5
he * eleven years, in Jerusalem. 2Ch 36:11
O Lord, you have * from Ps 93:1
Jehoahaz, or Shallum, * for three Jer 22:11f
he * eleven years in Jerusalem. Jer 52:1
Benjamin, who * for forty years. Act 13:21
* before as one of the seven; Rev 17:11
again and now they * with Christ Rev 20:4

REIGNING
meanwhile, David was * in Hebron 2Sa 2:10,11
Then why is Adonijah *?' 1Ki 1:13
Elah, Baasha's son, began * 1Ki 16:8
* in Israel at this time: King 2Ki 15:1
* in Judah at that time: King 2Ki 15:8
* in Judah at that time: King 2Ki 15:13
* in Israel at this time: Pekah 2Ki 15:32,33
* in Israel at this time: King 2Ki 16:1
* in Judah at this time: King 2Ki 17:1
* in Israel at this time: King 2Ki 18:1
to prevent his * in Jerusalem, and 2Ki 23:33
entered the city and began * at Dan 5:31
we will be there, too, * with you. 1Co 4:8

REIGNS
say, 'It is the Lord who *.' 1Ch 16:31
only confusion *, and where the Job 10:22
Sing thoughtful praises! He * Ps 47:8
Tell the nations that Jehovah *! Ps 96:10
he saw during the * of King Uzziah, Is 1:1
Stillness * where once your Is 23:2,3
the news that the God of Israel *. Is 52:7
help during the * of the last two Eze 23:17f
"During the * of those kings, Dan 2:44
he * forever and ever. Dan 4:3
* of these four kings of Judah: Hos 1:1
during the * of King Jotham, King Mic 1:1
when Satan's power * supreme." Lk 22:53
the sixth now *, and the seventh is Rev 17:10
the Lord our God, the Almighty, *. Rev 19:6

REINED
Then King Joram * the 2Ki 9:23

REINFORCED
to go through, * around the edge so Ex 39:23
He also * Fort Millo in the City 2Ch 32:5

REINSTATE
you the last ones to * the king? 2Sa 19:11,12

REJECT
or obey me, but * my laws, this Lev 26:15
teach you what it means to * me. Num 14:34,35
she cried. "To * me now is a 2Sa 13:16
Then I will * even those few of 2Ki 21:14
The wealth he trusted in shall * Job 18:14
Do not angrily * your servant. Ps 27:9
punishes all who haughtily * him. Ps 31:23
you be angry and * our prayers? Ps 80:4
I will * all selfishness and Ps 101:4
But you have rejected all who * Ps 119:118
Do not * your servant David—the Ps 132:10
But to * criticism is to harm Pro 15:31,32
and fair, who * making profit by Is 33:15
But those who still * me Is 57:20
not listen to me. They * my law. Jer 6:18,19
they broke, forcing me to * them, Jer 31:32
I am as likely to * my people Jer 31:36
I would no more * my people than I Jer 33:25,26
O Samaria, I * this calf—this Hos 8:5
And the Lord said to Satan, "I * Zec 3:2
And those who * you are rejecting Lk 10:16
And those who * me are rejecting Lk 10:16
me—and I will never, never * them. Jn 6:37
for me and judges [those who * me Jn 8:50
But all who * me and my message Jn 12:48
you didn't * me and turn me away. Gal 4:14
and to those who * him, 1Pe 2:7

REJECTED
for you have * the Lord who is Num 11:19,20
for you, you have * me and have 1Sa 10:18,19
And now because you have * the 1Sa 15:23
he has * you from being king." 1Sa 15:23
Since you have * the commandment 1Sa 15:26
the Lord, he has * you from being 1Sa 15:26
I have * him as king of Israel. 1Sa 16:1
themselves to Samuel and were *. 1Sa 16:9
They * his laws and the covenant 2Ki 17:15
So the Lord * all the 2Ki 17:20
But he * their advice and asked 2Ch 10:8,9
be * instantly from his presence. Job 13:16
They are doomed, for God has * Ps 53:5
O GOD, YOU have * us and broken Ps 60:1
Has the Lord * me forever? Ps 77:7
But he * Joseph's family, the Ps 78:67
Then why cast me off, *? Ps 89:38
For you have * me and thrown me Ps 102:9,10
The stone * by the builders has Ps 118:22
But you have * all who reject Ps 119:118
The Lord has * you because you Is 2:6
who is despised, * by mankind, and Is 49:7
We despised him and * him—a man Is 53:3
has * the ones that you trust. Jer 2:37
But they too had utterly * their Jer 5:5
then you shall say, "You * him Jer 5:19
I must label them "Impure, * Jer 6:30
for the Lord has * and forsaken Jer 7:29
they have * the word of the Lord. Jer 8:9
"have you completely * Judah? Jer 14:19
The Lord has * his own altar, for Lam 2:7
Or have you utterly * us? Lam 5:22
For they have * the laws of God, Amo 2:4
Then I said, 'O Lord, you have * Jon 2:4
I even * his very own brother, Mal 1:2,3
'The stone * by the builders has Mt 21:42
that he would be * by the elders Mk 8:31
child shall be * by many in Israel, Lk 2:34,35
Moses' Law. They * God's plan for Lk 7:3
he said, "and be * by the Jewish Lk 9:2
and be * by this whole nation. Lk 17:2
you have * the opportunity God Lk 19:4
says, 'The Stone * by the builders Lk 20:1
I refer to the Jesus whom you * Act 3:1
had previously * by demanding, 'Who Act 7:3
"But our fathers * Moses and Act 7:3
But since you have * it, and Act 13:4
But some * his message and Act 19:
I ASK THEN, has God * and deserted Rom 11:
Does this mean that God has * his Rom 11:1
Stone that was * by the builders 1Pe 2:

REJECTING
punishment for * my laws and for Lev 26:4
the one they are *, not you—they 1Sa 8:
to sinners, to those * God." Job 18:2
do his will, * compromise with Ps 119:
You are simply * God's laws and Mk 7:
And those who reject you are * Lk 10:1
And those who reject me are * God Lk 10:1
the cross again by * him, holding Heb 6:
If anyone sins deliberately by * Heb 10:2

REJECTION
Theirs was no downcast look of *! Ps 34:

REJECTS
grows up around him and * him! Ecc 4:1
among you, who * me for idols, and Eze 14:6,

REJOICE
All who hear about this shall * Gen 21:
of each month to * over your burnt Num 10:1
* in all he has done for you. Deu 12:7
You shall * there before the Deu 12:12
must be located. * before the Lord Deu 12:18
God, and to * with your household. Deu 14:26
It is a time to * before the Deu 16:1
time will * in destroying you; Deu 28:63
for the Lord will again * over Deu 30:9
He will * if you but obey the Deu 30:10
"*, O Zebulun, you outdoorsmen, Deu 33:18
How I * Ju 5:9
prayer: "How I * in the Lord! 1Sa 2:1
How I *! 1Sa 2:1
tell the Philistines, lest they *. 2Sa 1:20
But you have no right to * in 2Sa 24:3
watch over it and * in it. 1Ki 9:2,3
Let all * who seek the Lord. 1Ch 16:10
the heavens be glad, the earth *; 1Ch 16:31
and everything in it *! 1Ch 16:32
your saints * in your kind deeds. 2Ch 6:41
* and send gifts to each other. Est 9:19
reverent fear; * with trembling. Ps 2:11
But make everyone * who puts his Ps 5:11
gates and * that you have rescued Ps 9:14
and shall * in your salvation. Ps 13:5
Their hearts shall * with Ps 22:26
garments to * in so that I might Ps 30:11
* in him, all those who are his, Ps 32:11
But I will * in the Lord. Ps 35:9
Don't let them * Ps 35:19
Don't let my enemies * over me in Ps 35:24
against me and who * at my troubles Ps 35:26
*! O people of Judah, Ps 48:11
O people of Judah, *! Ps 48:11
then you will * in the good that Ps 51:19
The godly shall * in the triumph Ps 58:10
me—and how I * through the night Ps 63:7
will * in God. All who trust in Ps 63:11
And the godly shall * in the Ps 64:10
May he * and be merry. Ps 68:3
Jehovah is his name—oh, * in his Ps 68:4
Then your people can * in you Ps 85:6
Mount Tabor and Mount Hermon * to Ps 89:12
They * all day long in your Ps 89:16
against him and made them *. Ps 89:42
evening * in all his faithfulness. Ps 92:2
just and all the upright will *. Ps 94:15
the heavens be glad, the earth *; Ps 96:11
Let all the earth *! Ps 97:1
How he must * in all his work! Ps 104:31
O worshipers of God, *. Ps 105:3
prosperity and * in all their joys, Ps 106:5
holy name and * and praise you. Ps 106:47
I will sing and * before you. Ps 108:1
We will * and be glad in it. Ps 118:24
your words. I * in your laws like Ps 119:162
The godly will * with me for all Ps 142:7
O Israel, * in your Maker. Ps 149:2
Let his people * in this honor. Ps 149:4,5
* in the wife of your youth. Pro 5:18
He will punish those who * at Pro 17:5
My son, how I will * if you Pro 23:15,16
Do not * when your enemy meets Pro 24:17
men in authority, the people *; Pro 29:2
very old, let him * in every day of Ecc 11:8
Don't *, Philistines, that the Is 14:29
will you *, will you be strong. Is 23:12
then they will fear and * in my Is 29:23
people will * with music and song. Is 30:32
and desert will * in those days; Is 35:1
the world around you—will *. Is 55:12

REJOICE Con't)
and God will * over you as a Is 62:5
I will * in his great goodness to Is 63:7
sad and ashamed, but they shall *. Is 65:13
Be glad; * forever in my Is 65:18
And I will * in Jerusalem, and Is 65:19
* with Jerusalem; Is 66:10
see Jerusalem, your heart will *; Is 66:14
them and make them *, for their Jer 31:13
I will * to do them good and Jer 32:41
Heaven and earth shall *, for Jer 51:48
her enemies to * over her and boast Lam 2:17
Do you *, O people of Edom, in Lam 4:21
"The whole world will * when I Eze 35:14
Now I will * at yours! Eze 35:15
The priests * in the sins of the Hos 4:8
O ISRAEL, * no more as others do, Hos 9:1
be glad now and *, for he has Joe 2:21
"*, O people of Jerusalem, Joe 2:23
Jerusalem, * in the Lord your God! Joe 2:23
Do not * against me, O my enemy, Mic 7:8
out in their nets, while they *? Hab 1:15
empty, yet I will * in the Lord; Hab 3:18
be glad and * with all your Zep 3:14
He will * over you in great Zep 3:17,18
Sing, Jerusalem, and *! Zec 2:10
eyes of the Lord * to see the work Zec 4:10
"* greatly, O my people! Zec 9:9
Their hearts shall * in the Lord. Zec 10:7
And if he finds it, he will * Mt 18:13
birth, and many will * with you. Lk 1:14
How I * in God my Savior! Lk 1:47
When that happens, *! Lk 6:23
and neighbors to * with you because Lk 15:6
and neighbors to * with her? Lk 15:9
Let all heaven *! Lk 19:38
A bridegroom's friends * with Jn 3:29
The world will greatly * over Jn 16:20
see you again and then you will *; Jn 16:22
We can *, too, when we run into Rom 5:3
Now we * in our wonderful new Rom 5:11
all the angels to notice and * in. 1Co 11:10
you can *, O childless woman; Gal 4:27
this, too, and * with me for having Php 2:18
I say it again, *! Php 4:4
everywhere will * and give presents Rev 11:10
them down for him. *, O heavens! Rev 12:12
You citizens of heaven, *! Rev 12:12
But you, O heaven, * over her Rev 18:20
Let us be glad and * and honor Rev 19:7

REJOICED
them, they all * and bowed their Ex 4:31
And yet he * in your fathers and Deu 10:15
"Just as the Lord has * over you Deu 28:63
and all Israel * and praised God Jos 22:33
So all the people of the land *, 2Ch 23:21
The women and children * too, and Neh 12:43
quietness. All * in what I said. Job 29:11
"If I have * at harm to an Job 31:29
I have recited your laws, and * Ps 119:14
"Son of dust, Tyre has * over Eze 26:2
Kings at the ends of the earth * Eze 27:33
You * at Israel's fearful fate. Eze 35:15
you should not have * in the day Ob 1:12
had been to her, and everyone *. Lk 1:58
And all the people * at the Lk 13:17
you benefited and *, but I have a Jn 5:35
Your father Abraham * to see my Jn 8:56
and * in this thing they had made. Act 7:41
very glad and * in Paul's message; Act 13:48
How he and his household * Act 16:34

REJOICES
He paws the earth and * in his Job 39:21-23
when far away. He * at the shouts Job 39:25
HOW THE KING * in your strength, O Ps 21:1
A king * in servants who know Pro 14:35
The king * when his people are Pro 16:13
rays of brilliant light. He * Hab 3:4
but * whenever truth wins out. 1Co 13:6

REJOICING
* before the Lord your God for Lev 23:40
This will be a happy time of * Deu 16:14
whole city is celebrating and *. 1Ki 1:44,45
and everyone was * and blowing 2Ki 11:13,14
all over the land * and blowing 2Ch 23:12
fail, and I shall go right on *! Ps 109:28
I have called those * in their Is 13:3
What a day of *! Is 25:9
And just as stupid is your * in Amo 6:13
They left the Council chamber * Act 5:41
him again, but went on his way *. Act 8:39

REJOIN
of Israel will * their brethren in Mic 5:3

REKEM
kings—Evi, *, Zur, Hur, and Reba. Num 31:8
Midian—Evi, *, Zur, Hur, and Reba. Jos 13:21
Chephirah, Mozah, *, Irpeel, Jos 18:21-28
*, and 1Ch 2:43
* was the father of 1Ch 2:44

RELATED
Moses * to his father-in-law all Ex 18:8
is so closely * to your father; Lev 18:12
more closely * to you than I am. Ru 3:12
he was * to Ahab by marriage. 2Ki 8:27
made known how they were *." Est 8:1f
are not * to how rich we are." Lk 12:15
others employed in * trades, and Act 19:25
all of us are * to Adam, being 1Co 15:22
But all who are * to Christ will 1Co 15:22

RELATES
The paraphrase * this to verse Lk 24:49f

RELATING
all the tasks * to the inner 1Ch 6:49
the tasks * to the annual Day of 1Ch 6:49

RELATIONS
"Anyone having sexual * with an Ex 22:19
(but he had no sexual * with her). 1Ki 1:3,4
and broke off all * with them. Eze 23:17
have had immoral * with her, and Rev 17:2

RELATIONSHIP
"There must be no sexual * with Lev 18:19
* with God that both of us have.' Jos 22:28
a normal sex * with women, burned Rom 1:27
our wonderful new * with God—all Rom 5:11

RELATIONSHIPS
Moses concerning * between a man Num 30:16

RELATIVE
been taken, his * Lot, and all of Gen 14:16
a near *, for I am the Lord. Lev 18:6
daughter—for she is a close *. Lev 18:10
she is a close * of your mother; Lev 18:13
it is a near *—a mother, father, Lev 21:2,3
or anyone else who is a near *. Lev 25:49
and there is no near * to whom Num 5:8
it shall go to the nearest *." Num 27:11
If your nearest * or closest Deu 13:6,7
If a * of the dead man comes to Jos 20:5
king just because he is your *. Ju 9:18
Boaz, this * of Naomi's husband. Ru 2:3
Literally, "a near *, one of our Ru 2:20f
so kind to us, and is a close *. Ru 3:2
law, for you are my close *." Ru 3:9
It's true that I am a close *, Ru 3:12
and found the * he had mentioned. Ru 4:1
Boaz said to his *, "You know Ru 4:3
* for help in your time of need. Pro 27:10
Literally, "*." Lk 1:36f
the High Priest—a * of the man Jn 18:26
Remember me to Herodion my *. Rom 16:11
and so does Mark, a * of Barnabas. Col 4:10
But Melchizedek was not a *, and Heb 7:6

RELATIVES
Close * such as we are must Gen 13:8
"What * do you have here in the Gen 19:12
my homeland, to my *, and find a Gen 24:4
there, to live among your *?" Gen 24:5
to the family of my master's *." Gen 24:27
but to come to his * here in Gen 24:38
Yes, find a girl from among my *, Gen 24:40
May all your * bow low before Gen 27:27,28,29
and all of his * as his servants. Gen 27:37
because we are * is no reason for Gen 29:15
your fathers, and to your * there; Gen 31:3
to the land of my *, and said that Gen 32:9
go back to Egypt and visit my *. Ex 4:18
But the dead man's * may accept Ex 21:30
for they are near *, and to do so Lev 18:17
then his nearest * may redeem it. Lev 25:25
As for the tribe of Levi, your * Num 18:21
* who want to avenge his death; Num 35:12
unless all your *—your father, Jos 2:17,18
and other * who were with her. Jos 6:23
prostitute and her * who were with Jos 6:25
protected from the * of the dead Jos 20:3
wealth with their * back home—their Jos 22:7,8
of Ebed, and his * have come to Ju 9:31
drove Gaal and his * out of Ju 9:41
Later, his brothers and other * Ju 16:31
from their * in Sidon, and had Ju 18:7
man is one of our closest *!" Ru 2:20
and other * soon joined him. 1Sa 22:1
I and all my * could expect only 2Sa 19:28
"Down with David and all his *! 1Ki 12:16,17
He even destroyed distant * and 1Ki 16:11
Ahab's friends and *, just as 2Ki 10:17
His * became heads of clans and 1Ch 5:7,8
Their *, the heads of the seven 1Ch 5:13
Their *—all the other 1Ch 6:48
Jeuel and his *: 690 in all. 1Ch 9:6
He and his close * the Korahites 1Ch 9:19
And their * in the villages were 1Ch 9:25
Shime-am in Jerusalem near his *. 1Ch 9:38
and told him, "We are your *, 1Ch 11:1
tribe with their *—all men who 1Ch 12:24-37
Listen to me and return these * 2Ch 28:11
and *, all of whom were Levites. Ez 3:9
but you and your * will die; Est 4:14
grandson left, nor any other *. Job 18:19
my friends. My * have failed me; Job 19:14
hide from * who need your help. Is 58:7
Jerusalem—on your * who were not Jer 29:16,17
his * and by his own family." Mk 6:4
her neighbors and * of how kind the Lk 1:58
days old, all the * and friends Lk 1:59
for him among their * and friends; Lk 2:44
brothers, *, and rich neighbors! Lk 14:12
parents, brothers, *, and friends Lk 21:16
and others of the High Priest's *. Act 4:6
The High Priest and his * and Act 5:17
good-bye to his * and to start out Act 7:3
* and close friends to meet Peter. Act 10:24
my * who were in prison with me. Rom 16:7
my *, send you their good wishes. Rom 16:21
care for his own * when they need 1Ti 5:8
that a widow's * must take care of 1Ti 5:16
because the priests were their *. Heb 7:5

RELAX
him to go home and *, and he sent a 2Sa 11:8
Now I can *. Ps 116:7

RELAXED
A * attitude lengthens a man's Pro 14:30

RELEASE
may all go out. * all the animals, Gen 8:17
will * Simeon and return Benjamin. Gen 43:14
(This * does not apply to Deu 15:3
year—the Year of *—at the Festival Deu 31:10,11
priest didn't * them to go home. 2Ch 23:8
of the blind, and * those who sit Is 42:7
two years he will * all the nations Jer 28:11
listen to me and * them, I will Jer 34:17
them, I will * you to the power of Jer 34:17
until the Year of * (every seventh Eze 46:17
your chains and * you from the yoke Nah 1:13
custom was to * one Jewish prisoner Mt 27:15
"Which shall I * to you—Barabbas, Mt 27:17
Barabbas' *, and for Jesus' death. Mt 27:20
"Which of these two shall I * to Mt 27:21
And Pilate issued an order to * Mt 27:58
pled with him to * her child from Mk 7:26
Now, it was Pilate's custom to * Mk 15:6
him to * a prisoner as usual. Mk 15:8
* of Barabbas instead of Jesus. Mk 15:11
"But if I * Barabbas," Pilate Mk 15:12
Literally, "*, and you shall be Lk 6:37f
with leaded thongs, and * him." Lk 23:16
for him to * unto them at the feast Lk 23:17,f
him, and * Barabbas to us!" Lk 23:18
them, for he wanted to * Jesus. Lk 23:20
of asking me to * someone from Jn 18:39
So if you want me to, I'll * the Jn 18:39
to * you or to crucify you?" Jn 19:10
Then Pilate tried to * him, but Jn 19:12
told him, "If you * this man, you Jn 19:12
Pilate's determination to * him. Act 3:13
Instead you demanded the * of a Act 3:14
Let them come themselves and * Act 16:37
and wanted to * me, for they found Act 28:18
angel, "* the four mighty demons Rev 9:14
Press *, April 24, 1964). Rev 9:16f

RELEASED
* a raven that flew back and forth Gen 8:7
Seven days later Noah * the dove Gen 8:10
A week later he * the dove Gen 8:12
Then he * Simeon and brought him Gen 43:23
* everyone from his obligation. Deu 15:2
all you do because you have * him! Deu 15:18
slayer must not be * to them, for Jos 20:5
King Jehoiachin was * from prison 2Ki 25:27
of death—and * them, so that Ps 102:20
Soon, soon you slaves shall be * Is 51:14
Pashhur finally * him, Jeremiah Jer 20:3
sent to Babylon, but then * him. Jer 40:1
and * him and forgave his debt. Mt 18:27
Then Pilate * Barabbas to them. Mt 27:26
"Is he the one you want *?" Mk 15:9
the people, * Barabbas to them. Mk 15:15
captives shall be * and the blind Lk 4:18,19
"release, and you shall be *." Lk 6:37f
And he * Barabbas, the man in Lk 23:25
Then God * him from the horrors Act 2:24
to be * from pain and suffering. Rom 8:23
Afterwards he would be * again Rev 20:3

RELEASES
to the lonely, and * prisoners from Ps 68:6

RELEASING
* many from the power of demons. Mk 1:39

RELENT
For I will not *! Hos 13:14

RELENTED
to them and * because of his great Ps 106:45
So the Lord *, and did not Amo 7:3

RELENTLESSLY
were * gnawing at my bones. Job 30:17
me from those who hunt me down *. Ps 31:14,15

RELIABILITY
and Samuel because of their *. 1Ch 9:22

RELIABLE
* communication permits progress. Pro 13:17

RELIED
But you * then on the Lord, and 2Ch 16:8

RELIEF
Noah (meaning "*") because he Gen 5:28-31
"He will bring us * from the hard Gen 5:28-31

(RELIEF Con't)
said, "for what a * it is to see Gen 33:10
BUT THERE WAS no * from the Gen 43:1
What blessed * when at last they Job 3:22
a few moments of * before he dies. Job 14:6
I must speak to find *, so let Job 32:20
covered over! What * for those who Ps 32:1
decided to send * to the Christians Act 11:29
they will have no * day or night, Rev 14:11

RELIEVE
* your shoulder of its burden; Ps 81:6
border of Judah to * the besieged Jer 37:5
sent an army to * Jerusalem in 588, Eze 30:21f

RELIEVING
guilt instead of * their minds. Heb 10:3

RELIGION
hates, all in the name of their *. Deu 12:31
equivalent to our "He got *." 1Sa 10:12f
was the priest and teacher of *. Neh 12:26
his nation, language, or * Dan 3:7
of any nation, language, or * Dan 3:29
"Our only chance is his *!" Dan 6:5
"What sort of new * is this?" Mk 1:27
without food as part of their *. Mk 2:18
But the Jewish teachers of * who Mk 3:22
One of the teachers of * who was Mk 12:28
The teacher of * replied, "Sir, Mk 12:32
"Beware of the teachers of *! Mk 12:38
and teachers of *—the entire Mk 15:1
"Woe to you experts in *! Lk 11:52
these experts in *, for they love Lk 20:46
"He's pushing some foreign *." Act 17:18
about this new *," they said, Act 17:19
of the * of the great Diana, Act 19:35
It was something about their *, Act 25:19
* has made us foolish, you say, 1Co 4:10
the Jewish *—how I went after the Gal 1:13
old, traditional rules of my *. Gal 1:14
weak, useless * of trying to get to Gal 4:9
and his * isn't worth much. Jas 1:26
and when we teachers of *, who Jas 3:1

RELIGIOUS
a * feast, to worship me there.' Ex 5:1
will be special * services for the Ex 12:16
"There are three annual * Ex 23:14
these three annual * festivals: the Ex 34:22
and * leaders of the city. Ju 8:14
of the annual * festival held in Ju 21:19
Saul becoming *, equivalent to our 1Sa 10:12f
"This isn't a * holiday." 2Ki 4:23
to follow the * customs of the 2Ki 17:33
the political and * leaders of 1Ch 23:2
they were responsible for the * 1Ch 26:30
to control the * and public affairs 1Ch 26:31,32
political and * leaders of Israel. 2Ch 1:2,3
A final * service was held on 2Ch 7:9
a nationwide * education program. 2Ch 17:7,8,9
Levites, the * teachers in Israel: 2Ch 35:3
As a Jewish * leader, Ezra was Ez 7:6
the * progress being made there. Ez 7:14
the political or * leaders, or even Neh 2:16
Ezra, their * leader, to read to Neh 8:1
good or bad, * or irreligious, Ecc 9:2,3
at the time of the * feasts, the Eze 45:17
during the * feasts, they must go Eze 46:9
At their * feasts they lounge in Amo 2:8
* feasts and solemn assemblies. Amo 5:21
to end and the * holidays to be Amo 8:5
a meeting of the Jewish * leaders. Mt 2:4
Jewish * leaders who strictly Mt 3:7f
"Not all who sound * are really Mt 7:21
one of the Jewish * teachers Mt 8:19
exclaimed some of the * leaders Mt 9:3
and you other * leaders. Mt 23:13,14
you other * leaders—hypocrites! Mt 23:23
and you * leaders—hypocrites! Mt 23:25
you, Pharisees, and you * leaders! Mt 23:27
and you * leaders—hypocrites! Mt 23:29,30
But some of the Jewish * leaders Mk 2:6
But when some of the Jewish * Mk 2:16
Some of the Jewish * leaders said Mk 2:24
The Pharisees were a * sect of the Mk 3:6f
ONE DAY SOME Jewish * leaders Mk 7:1
So the * leaders asked him, "Why Mk 7:5
the Jewish * leaders often spoke Mk 9:11
But they sent other * and Mk 12:13
"Why do your * teachers claim Mk 12:35
The chief priests and * leaders Mk 15:31
teaching, some Jewish * leaders Lk 5:17
"Sir," said an expert in * law Lk 11:45
beneath impossible * Lk 11:46
from the Jewish * leaders and the Lk 15:2
Once a Jewish * leader asked him Lk 18:18
priests and other * leaders and the Lk 19:47
other * leaders and councilmen. Lk 20:1
When the chief priests and * Lk 20:19
the synagogues and at * festivals! Lk 20:46
The chief priests and other * Lk 22:2
the * leaders who headed the mob. Lk 22:52
top * authorities of the nation. Lk 22:66
and the other * leaders stood there Lk 23:10
But the chief priests and our * Lk 24:20
AFTER DARK ONE night a Jewish * Jn 3:1
for one of the Jewish * holidays. Jn 5:1
mean their * ruler, the Messiah. Jn 18:34f
that day for the * celebrations, Act 2:5
of a Jewish * sect that denied the Act 4:1f
(an expert on * law and very Act 5:34
that you are very *, for as I was Act 17:22
I was one of the most * Jews of Gal 1:14

RELISH
They are eaten with great *! Pro 18:8
dainty morsel eaten with great *. Pro 26:22
my land with *, in utter contempt Eze 36:5

RELOCATED
to him, and he * some of the people 2Ch 8:2
noble Osnappar and * in Jerusalem, Ez 4:10
who had been * in Judah turned from Ez 6:21,22

RELUCTANT
"The * Dragon," Is 30:7

RELUCTANTLY
So I * offered the burnt 1Sa 13:12

RELY
him, who * upon his steady love. Ps 33:18,19
strength, yet you * on him for Is 36:5
Lord, let them * upon their God. Is 50:10
Or, "you * upon the law for your Rom 2:17f

REMAIN
parents, and to * a widow there Gen 38:11
only one of you shall * in chains Gen 42:19
the mountain, and * until I give Ex 24:12
must be washed and * ceremonially Lev 15:17
and only a few * until the Jubilee, Lev 25:52
And prefer to * distinct Num 23:7-10
there, those who * will be as Num 33:55
every tribe is to * permanently as Num 36:7
That city shall forever * a Deu 13:16
was captured, then * in your home Deu 21:13
shall not * on the tree overnight. Deu 21:23
She shall * his wife and he may Deu 22:19
and cattle may * here, but your Jos 1:14
Why did Gilead * across the Ju 5:17
And why did Dan * with his ships? Ju 5:17
let the fleece * dry while the Ju 6:39
for the few who *, since we have Ju 21:7
"Don't kill him, for who can * 1Sa 26:9
them will * here during the night; 2Sa 19:7
and they * there to this day. 1Ki 8:8
Assyria where they * to this day. 2Ki 17:23
River, where they * to this day. 1Ch 5:26
the Jews would * in captivity to Ez 1:1f
who chose to * in Persia gave Ez 1:6
perhaps I could * quiet, though Est 7:4
Should I * silent while you Job 11:3
the things he dreamed of—none *. Job 20:20
I will * obedient to your Word. Ps 119:101
he is older he will * upon it. Pro 22:6
for Damascus will * the capital of Is 7:8
those who escape and those who *. Is 15:9
for a few of the poor who *. Is 17:6
Their hopes * unanswered. Is 44:9
and earth shall *, so surely shall Is 66:22
Even the few who * in Israel Jer 6:9
You may * under these conditions Jer 7:5
and this city shall * forever. Jer 17:25
children who *, and let your widows Jer 49:11
creature will *, and it will be Jer 51:61,62
O Lord, forever you * the same! Lam 5:19
and any who * will die by famine Eze 6:12
and you refused, * filthy until my Eze 24:13
where I shall *, living among the Eze 43:7
"This gate shall * closed; Eze 44:2
here and so it shall * shut. Eze 44:2
wait and * until the 1335th day! Dan 12:12
have mercy on his people who *. Amo 5:15
his people shall * there Mic 5:4
pangs and emptiness will still *. Mic 6:14
that my Spirit would * among you; Hag 2:5
"And my curse shall * upon his Zec 5:4
I will bring the third that * Zec 13:9
disappear, but my words * forever. Mt 24:35
away, yet my words * forever true. Lk 21:33
For he must * in heaven until Act 3:21,22
I want you always to * very clear Rom 16:19
* single or else go back to him. 1Co 7:11
best for a person to * unmarried. 1Co 7:26
There are three things that * 1Co 13:13
we know that you * strong in him. 1Th 3:8
still alive and * on the earth will 1Th 4:17
in the air and * with him forever. 1Th 4:17
but you will * forever. Heb 1:11
for 'ten days.' * faithful even Rev 2:10
are his saints who * firm to the Rev 14:12

REMAINDER
So also throughout the * of the Gen 11:12,13f
and the * fled to the mountains. Gen 14:10
pleased. The * of the flour is to Lev 2:3
by the Lord. The * belongs to the Lev 2:10
Tabernacle; the * of the blood Lev 4:7
But the * of the young bull—the Lev 4:11,12
Lord, and all the * of the blood Lev 4:18
shall pour out the * of the blood Lev 4:30
Implied in * of the verse. Lev 5:1
this handful, the * of the flour Lev 6:1
offering. The * of the oil in his Lev 14:1
received the * of Gilead and all of Deu 3:1
* of the Kohath division was ten. Jos 21:2
The * of the Levites—the Merari Jos 21:34,3
up for the * of the celebration. Ju 14:1
day and the * fled to their tents. 1Sa 4:1
the * of Samuel's lifetime. 1Sa 7:1
judge for the * of his life. 1Sa 7:1
cedar boards. The * of the 1Ki 6:1
interior of the * of the 1Ki 6:21,2
during the * of my own life!" 2Ki 20:1
of Jerusalem. The * of the people 2Ki 25:1
The * of 1 Chronicles deals with 1Ch 10:
The * of his history, including 2Ch 27:
And throughout the * of his 2Ch 34:3
The speaker, as in the * of the Ez 7:28
and give the * of your life to the Pro 5:
at Nob for the * of that day. Is 10:3
* of Israel, says the Lord God. Eze 14:1
assign all the * of the land to the Eze 45:
Implied in * of verse. Mt 1:20
to finish up the * of Christ's Col 1:2

REMAINED
the Lord * with Abraham a while. Gen 18:22,2
They * under arrest there for Gen 40:
so Pharaoh's heart * hard and Ex 7:2
to disappear, so that not one *. Ex 8:31,3
even then his mind * unchanged and Ex 9:
there * not one green thing—not a Ex 10:1
Sea, so that there * not one locust Ex 10:1
through the sea, not one * alive. Ex 14:28
told them to, then * there as long Num 9:18
days, then they * only a few days; Num 9:19
only Joshua and Caleb * alive. Num 14:36,37,38
so that not a single survivor *; Num 21:35
so their inheritance * in their Num 36:11,12
"So we * in the valley near Deu 3:29
the army * in the camp at Jericho. Jos 8:9
still * in Gaza, Gath, and Ashdod. Jos 11:22
in those cities, the Canaanites *. Jos 17:12
The people had * true to the Lord Ju 2:7-9
* who were willing to fight. Ju 7:3
as the Tabernacle * at Shiloh. Ju 18:31
THE ARK * in the Philistine 1Sa 6:1
The Ark * there for twenty 1Sa 7:2
the other thousand * with Jonathan, 1Sa 13:2
* behind to guard their gear. 1Sa 25:13
from Gath. It * there for three 2Sa 6:11
So they * in virtual widowhood 2Sa 20:3
But among those who * loyal to 1Ki 1:8
of Judah, who * loyal and accepted 1Ki 12:16,17
the tribe of Judah * in the land. 2Ki 17:18
But the people on the wall * 2Ki 18:36
The Ark * there with the family 1Ch 13:14
however, * loyal to Rehoboam. 2Ch 10:17
For only Judah and Benjamin * 2Ch 11:12
the economy of Judah * strong. 2Ch 12:12
wiped out so that not one man *; 2Ch 14:13
that, but * quietly at Jerusalem. 2Ch 19:4
Joash * hidden in the Temple for 2Ch 22:12
Literally, "while the people * in Neh 8:7,8f
own brother. I * silent—you Ps 50:21
and with it all I * clear-eyed, so Ecc 2:9
to the palace prison, where he *. Jer 38:13
And Jeremiah * confined to the Jer 38:28
of your anger none escaped or *. Lam 2:22
* a virgin until her Son was born; Mt 1:25
But Jesus * silent. Mt 26:63
against him, Jesus * silent. Mt 27:12
So he * in Galilee. Jn 7:9
while Silas and Timothy * behind. Act 17:14
everything has * exactly as it was 2Pe 3:4
and yet you have * loyal to me, Rev 2:13

REMAINING
and Ithamar, the * sons of Aaron. Lev 10:16
Some of the oil * in his left Lev 14:17
offering. The * oil in his hand Lev 14:29
at the latest; any * until the Lev 19:6
* until the next Year of Jubilee. Lev 27:18
All of the * utensils of the Num 4:12
leave anything * for the Deu 24:20
allotted to the * nine and a half Jos 14:1
people still * in the land; Jos 23:7
Let them take five of the * 2Ki 7:13
assign land to the * descendants of 1Ch 6:61
When all was finished, the * 2Ch 24:14
Oh, let me alone for these few * Job 7:16
that everyone * in Jerusalem would Jer 38:2
sword, and those * in the city will Eze 17:21
I will leave none of them * among Eze 39:28
"The sections given to the * Eze 48:23
and the few people * in the land Hag 1:12
the Temple for the * days of his Lk 1:23
is that our * time is very short, 1Co 7:29
* angels blow their trumpets." Rev 8:13

REMAINS
As long as the earth *, there Gen 8:22
If any of the meat or bread * Ex 29:34
be given whatever * of the Lev 7:9

REMAINS Con't)
food that * after the handful has Lev 10:12
for his vow of consecration * in Num 6:6,7
so he * defiled. Num 19:20
with the * of a sacrifice on it. Ju 6:28
men * alive by tomorrow morning!" 1Sa 25:22
Then they buried their * beneath 1Sa 31:13
"But now my grief * no matter Job 16:6
"The truth * that if you do not Job 18:5
mind concerning me * unchanged, and Job 23:13
my spirits droop, yet God *! Ps 73:26
He never bears a grudge, nor * Ps 103:9
the laughter ends, the grief *. Pro 14:13
Literally, "but the earth * Ecc 1:3-7f
Ekron, and what * of Ashdod, and I Jer 25:19,20
No hope *, for I will loose my Eze 7:3
no strong branch *. Eze 19:14
But all for naught—it all * Eze 24:12
And when my Temple * among them, Eze 37:28
be left in what * of the city. Zec 14:1
the wrath of God * upon them." Jn 3:36
"But your guilt * because you Jn 9:41
every rebel who * after I have 2Co 10:6
doing it, the fact * that the Good Php 1:18
any faith left, he * faithful to us 2Ti 2:13
Yet the promise * and some get Heb 4:6
widows, and who * true to the Jas 1:27
so if your faith * strong after 1Pe 1:7
Strengthen what little *—for even Rev 3:2
smoke rising from her charred *. Rev 18:9

REMALIAH
Then Pekah (son of *), the 2Ki 15:25
Father's name: * 2Ki 15:27
Pekah (son of *), who had been the 2Ki 15:32,33
King Pekah (son of *) who had been 2Ki 16:1
King Pekah (son of *) of Israel 2Ki 16:5
Pekah, the son of *, killed 120,000 2Ch 28:6
Pekah of Israel (the son of *). Is 7:1
"The usurper, the son of *" is Is 7:1f

REMARK
and mentioned his * that she Ru 3:15-18
the Pharisees by that *." Mt 15:12
This * confounded the disciples. Mt 19:25

REMARKABLE
Ask me and I will tell you some * Jer 33:3
how *! Mt 21:42
many * miracles among the people. Act 5:12
And by means of many * miracles Act 7:36
us about your * faith in God. 1Th 1:8

REMARKED
he * that Sarah was his sister! Gen 20:2
Tossing away the jawbone, he *, Ju 15:16,17
David *, "How thirsty I am for 2Sa 23:15
and told him, he *, "That is just 2Ki 9:36
around them, he *, "Take note of 2Ch 18:27
beside him, *, "If even a fox Neh 4:3
there, he *, "Who is my mother? Mt 12:48
to him and *, "That poor widow has Mk 12:43,44
to see him, he *, "My mother and Lk 8:21
"Well said, sir!" * some of the Lk 20:39
"Really," he *, "this poor Lk 21:3
—and she * about this to Jesus. Jn 4:9
And he *, "That is what I meant Jn 6:65
miracles," they * to one another, Jn 10:41

REMARKING
Moses' feet, * disgustedly, "What Ex 4:25,26
And they praised God, * over and Lk 5:26

REMARKS
to glean, and not to make any *. Ru 2:16
to make cutting *, but the words of Pro 12:18
Luke 10:1 *, "The Lord Mt 11:1f
These * stung them to fury; Lk 4:28
begin my * with a bit of history Act 13:16
These * of mine about the 1Jn 2:26

REMARRIES
If she then *, and the second Deu 24:2
a woman who then *, he is not to Jer 3:1
*, she, too, commits adultery." Mk 10:12

REMEDY
none of which will there be a *. Deu 28:27
and there was no longer any *. 2Ch 36:16

REMEMBER
and I will * my promise to you and Gen 9:15
in the cloud and * my eternal Gen 9:16,17
Rachel, *, was the one who had Gen 31:34
"Today I * my sin!" Gen 41:9
the Egyptians, and I * my promise. Ex 6:5
you always to * today as the day Ex 12:17
firstborn. And *, this is a Ex 12:24
"This is a day to * forever—the Ex 13:3
miracles. Now *, during the annual Ex 13:3
And *, when the Lord brings you Ex 13:11
"* to observe the Sabbath as a Ex 20:8
you from heaven. *, you must not Ex 20:23
in any way; *, you yourselves were Ex 22:21
to be a foreigner; * your own Ex 23:9
instructions; and *—never mention Ex 23:13
to the Lord; and *, none of the Ex 24:2
it helps you to * that I am Ex 31:12,13
your people! * your promise to Ex 32:13
"And you must * to celebrate Ex 34:22
love them as yourself, for * that Lev 19:34
before the Lord. * that the first Lev 23:39
And *, the land is mine, so you Lev 25:23
you lend him. *—no interest; Lev 25:37
sins, then I will * again my Lev 26:42
* the land (and its desolation). Lev 26:42
For their sakes I will * my Lev 26:45
Don't you *? Num 14:43
you in any way. *, only the Num 18:5
and seventh days. * also to purify Num 31:20
father and mother (*, this is a Deu 5:16
diseases of Egypt you * so well; Deu 7:15
of them! Just * what the Lord your Deu 7:18
Do you * the terrors the Lord Deu 7:19
Do you * how the Lord led you Deu 8:2
Always * that it is the Lord Deu 8:18
"Don't you * (oh, never forget Deu 9:7
"Don't you * how angry you made Deu 9:8
these people, but * instead your Deu 9:27
and servants; and * to invite the Deu 12:12
has blessed you. * that you were Deu 15:15
not feel bad, for * that for six Deu 15:18
"ALWAYS * TO celebrate the Deu 16:1
* that day all the rest of your Deu 16:3
celebration at the sanctuary. *! Deu 16:12
"* THAT THE priests and all the Deu 18:1
God is giving you, * that you must Deu 19:14
to the letter: * what the Lord Deu 24:9
Always * that you were slaves in Deu 24:18
those in need. * that you were Deu 24:22
came from Egypt. * that they Deu 25:18
"Surely you * how we lived in Deu 29:16
* the days of long ago! Deu 32:7
Banish fear and doubt! For *, the Jos 1:9
"* what the Lord said to Moses Jos 14:6
You will * that as spies we found Jos 14:12
However, * that the Levites Jos 18:7
Don't you * that when Achan, the Jos 22:20
"O Lord Jehovah, * me again—please Ju 16:28
"Sir, do you * me?" 1Sa 1:26
my father. And *, you must 1Sa 20:14
things for you, please * me!" 1Sa 25:30,31
rest of us? And, *, we were the 2Sa 19:43
And do you * Shime-i, the son of 1Ki 2:8
rescue us"—just * that he is the 2Ki 18:22
"O Lord," he pleaded, "* how 2Ki 20:3
* his mighty miracles 1Ch 16:12,13
* his covenant forever— 1Ch 16:15
anointed one. Oh, * your love for 2Ch 6:42
Don't you * what happened to the 2Ch 16:8
Oh, please * what you told Neh 1:8
"Don't be afraid! * the Lord who Neh 4:14
O my God, * this good deed and do Neh 13:14
* this good deed, O my God! Neh 13:22
of the Temple. * them, O my God, Neh 13:29
* me, my God, with your kindness. Neh 13:31
Oh, please * that I'm made of Job 10:9
no one will * him. Job 18:17
No one will * him any more. Job 24:20
you will long * the battle that Job 41:8
May he * with pleasure the gifts Ps 20:3
Do you * those times (but how Ps 42:4,5
your own pasture? * that we are Ps 74:2
these beasts. * your promise! Ps 74:20
our enemies. * the insults these Ps 74:22
like fire? Oh, * how short you Ps 89:47
to his covenant and * to obey him! Ps 103:17,18
* how he destroyed our enemies. Ps 105:5,6
* me too, O Lord, while you are Ps 106:4
LORD, DO YOU * that time when my Ps 132:1
I * the glorious miracles you did Ps 143:5
to poverty. And * that too much Pro 23:19,20,21
We don't * what happened in those Ecc 1:8-11
* what we have done back here. Ecc 1:8-11
but let him also * that eternity is Ecc 11:8
So banish grief and pain, but * Ecc 11:10
then to try to * him, when the sun Ecc 12:2
Yes, * your Creator now while you Ecc 12:6
Don't you * what I did to Hamath Is 36:19
Just * what has happened Is 37:11
"O Lord, don't you * how true Is 38:3
us, Lord, nor forever * our sins. Is 64:9
The Lord says, I * how eager you Jer 2:2
the land and say, * this agreement Jer 11:6
now I will * all the evil you Jer 14:10
Do you * that boast of yours: Jer 48:14
They lost their way and didn't * Jer 50:6
while you can! * the Lord and Jer 51:50
has left me. Oh, * the bitterness Lam 3:19
O LORD, * all that has befallen Lam 5:1
listen or not (for *, they are Eze 2:5
scowls. For *, they are rebels! Eze 2:6
nations, they will * me, for I will Eze 6:9
and you will * with shame all the Eze 16:61
you * that I am the Lord your God. Eze 20:20
* her sin in seeking it before. Eze 29:16
Then you will * your past sins Eze 36:31
But always * this: It is not for Eze 36:32
worse, he couldn't * his dream! Dan 2:1
him, "and I can't * what it was. Dan 2:1
the dream is gone—I can't * it. Dan 2:5
(But *, it's not because I am Dan 2:30
O Israel, how well I * those Hos 9:10
Don't you *, O my people, how Mic 6:5
In your wrath, * mercy. Hab 3:2
survivor to * what happened. Zep 3:6
"Who among you can * the Temple Hag 2:3
now long dead, but * the lesson Zec 1:5,6
will * me and return again to God; Zec 10:9
Lord of Hosts. "* to obey the Mal 4:4
up in heaven. And *, the ancient Mt 5:12
God, and suddenly * that a friend Mt 5:23
again and again. *, your Father Mt 6:7,8
Don't you * at all the 5,000 I Mt 16:9
Don't you * the 4,000 I fed, and Mt 16:10
Don't you * anything at all? Mk 8:18
Don't you * reading this verse Mk 12:10
For example, * how Elijah the Lk 4:25,26
"Listen to me and * what I say. Lk 9:44
But Jesus replied, "*, I don't Lk 9:58
Go now, and * that I am sending Lk 10:3
said to him, 'Son, * that during Lk 16:25
* what happened to Lot's wife! Lk 17:32
Then he said, "Jesus, * me Lk 23:42
Don't you * what he told you back Lk 24:6,7
before, don't you * my telling you Lk 24:44
Then Nicodemus spoke up. (* him? Jn 7:50
DO YOU * Mary, who poured the Jn 11:1
love me. And *, I am not making up Jn 14:24
* what I told you—I am going Jn 14:28
Do you * what I told you? Jn 15:20
happen you will * I warned you. Jn 16:4
Watch out! * the three years I Act 20:31
Do you * what the book of Psalms Rom 3:4
in you. (And * that if anyone Rom 8:9
* what the prophecy of Hosea Rom 9:25
Oh no, not at all. * that I Rom 11:1
Do you * what the Scriptures say Rom 11:2,3
And do you * how God replied? Rom 11:4
were broken off. * that you are Rom 11:18
Watch out! * that those branches, Rom 11:20
Do you * what the prophets said Rom 11:26
look down on him. *, each of us Rom 14:10
a chunk of meat. *, there is Rom 14:20
then God will be glorified. * Rom 15:8
the Jews. And * that he came also Rom 15:9
in Asia. * me to Mary, too, who Rom 16:6
* me to Herodion my relative. Rom 16:11
my relative. * me to the Christian Rom 16:11
I don't * ever baptizing anyone 1Co 1:16
you about Christ, * that you have 1Co 4:15
you are a slave, * that Christ has 1Co 7:22
and you are free, * that you are 1Co 7:22
The important thing to * is that 1Co 7:29
Just * that God doesn't care 1Co 8:8
into sin. But * this—the wrong 1Co 10:13
But * that in God's plan men and 1Co 11:11
Do this to * me." 1Co 11:24
You will * that before you 1Co 12:2
and helped. * that a person who 1Co 14:32
Do you * Stephanas and his 1Co 16:15
* that the man I wrote about, who 2Co 2:5,6
Do you * what the Scriptures say 2Co 8:15
pressure. But * this—if you give 2Co 9:6
we must always * to help the poor, Gal 2:10
BUT * THIS, that if a father dies Gal 4:1
Don't be misled; * that you can't Gal 6:7
of godliness.) * that in those Eph 2:12
the way you live. *, he is the one Eph 4:30
all your hearts. *, the Lord will Eph 6:8
Don't keep threatening them; *, Eph 6:9
But whatever happens to me, * Php 1:27
* that the Lord is coming soon. Php 4:5
never hold grudges. *, the Lord Col 3:13
* what Christ taught and let his Col 3:16
Always * that you, too, have a Col 4:1
watch for God's answers and * to Col 4:2
handwriting: * me here in jail. Col 4:18
Don't you *, dear brothers, how 1Th 2:9
to his own children—don't you *? 1Th 2:11
ever, and that you * our visit with 1Th 3:6
*, no quarreling among yourselves. 1Th 5:13
Don't you * that I told you this 2Th 2:5
* that some men, even pastors, 1Ti 5:24
How happy I would be, for I * 2Ti 1:4
him is hard, just * that some day 2Ti 2:12
Another thing to * is that no one Heb 5:4
who obey him. For * that God has Heb 5:10
and I will * their sins no more." Heb 8:12
* their sins and lawless deeds." Heb 10:17
about Christ. * how you kept right Heb 10:32
what happens. * your reward! Heb 10:35
repentance. So *, and be careful. Heb 12:17
* your leaders who have taught Heb 13:7
who love him. And *, when someone Jas 1:13
And *, it is a message to obey, Jas 1:22
anymore or * what he looks like. Jas 1:24
he will not only * it but he will Jas 1:25
Well, * that the demons believe Jas 2:19
Don't you * that even our father Jas 2:21
*, too, that knowing what is Jas 4:17
And * that your heavenly Father 1Pe 1:17

(REMEMBER Con't)
as the weaker sex. * that you and 1Pe 3:7
what is good. *, if God wants you 1Pe 3:17
suffer, too. For *, when your body 1Pe 4:1
But just * that they must face 1Pe 4:5
Trust the Lord; and * that other 1Pe 5:9
* them long after I have gone. 2Pe 1:15
Why, as far back as anyone can * 2Pe 3:4
And * why he is waiting. 2Pe 3:15,16
Follow only what is good. * that 3Jn 1:11
My answer to them is: * this Jud 1:5
Dear friends, * what the apostles Jud 1:17

REMEMBERED
Then God * about Rachel's plight, Gen 30:22
Then Joseph * the dreams of long Gen 42:8,9
from heaven, and * his promise to Ex 2:24
record, to be * forever, and Ex 17:14
Hannah, the Lord * her petition; 1Sa 1:19,20
sin, the Lord * David's love 1Ki 15:4
old men who * Solomon's beautiful Ez 3:12
Then they * that God was their Ps 78:35
For he * that they were merely Ps 78:39
for he * his sacred promises to Ps 105:42
deed Phineas will be * forever. Ps 106:31
distress; he * his promises to Ps 106:45
He * our utter weakness, for his Ps 136:23
to look for them again and is *. Is 23:15,16
widowhood will be * no more, for Is 54:4
God's covenant with David, here *. Is 55:3f
Then they * those days of old Is 63:11
Egypt—things still * to this day. Jer 32:20
you have not * your youth, but have Eze 16:43
lustful men she * from her youth Eze 23:19,20
none of his good deeds will be *. Eze 33:13
will be * as the king who sent a Dan 11:20
And she will always be * for Mt 26:13
Then Peter * what Jesus had Mt 26:75
Then Peter * what Jesus had said Mk 11:21
deed will be * and praised." Mk 14:9
Then Peter * what he had Lk 22:61
Then they *, and rushed back to Lk 24:8
Then his disciples * this Jn 2:17
the disciples * his saying this and Jn 2:22
for I * the words of the Lord Act 20:35
here want to be * to you, Php 4:22
sins were * in God's thoughts, and Rev 16:19

REMEMBERING
himself, by * his sacred promise to Lk 1:72,73
that you have been * and doing 1Co 11:2
the right path, * that next time it Gal 6:1
for your masters, * that it is the Col 3:24

REMEMBERS
sadness she * happy bygone days. Lam 1:7
than ever when he * the way you 2Co 7:15

REMEMBRANCE
it is a time of *, and is to be Lev 23:23,24
Literally, "an offering for *." Num 5:15f
tradition as a * of the time of Est 9:29-31
And he had a Book of * drawn up Mal 3:16
Eat it in * of me." Lk 22:19
Do this in * of me whenever you 1Co 11:25

REMETH
Kishion, Ebez, *, En-gannim, Jos 19:17-23

REMIND
law) to * you of this fatal night. Ex 12:14
The purpose of this is to * the Lev 23:43
regulation is to * you, whenever Num 15:39
It will * you to be holy to your Num 15:40
Tie them to your hand to * you to Deu 11:18
nothing even to * you of them! Deu 12:3
This is to * you that you left Deu 16:3
this song will * them of the reason Deu 31:21
Constantly * the people about Jos 1:8
you can tell them, 'It is to * Jos 4:7
the Lord as I * you of all the good 1Sa 12:7
and to * them that when the Est 9:24,25
them again. Oh, * me of this Is 43:26
* the men of Judah and all the Jer 11:1
them and me, to * them that it is Eze 20:12
much, as well as * you of Jn 14:26
I lay great stress on this and * Rom 11:13
He will * you of what I teach in 1Co 4:17
matter I want to * you about: that 1Co 11:3
NOW LET ME * you, brothers, of 1Co 15:1
Instead, * each other of God's Eph 5:4
Last of all I want to * you that Eph 6:10
Let me * you again that a widow's 1Ti 5:16
This being so, I want to * you to 2Ti 1:6
* your people of these great 2Ti 2:14
* YOUR PEOPLE to obey the Tit 3:1
always be there to * God that he Heb 7:25
I have tried to * you—if you will 2Pe 3:1
First, I want to * you that in 2Pe 3:3
And now I want to urgently * you, 2Jn 1:5
And I * you of those angels who Jud 1:6

REMINDED
thus Jehovah will be * of them Ex 28:29
And God will be * of his covenant Num 10:10
of Israel," they * Moses, "and to Num 36:1
"At that time I * the tribes of Deu 3:18
of Manasseh and * them of their Jos 1:12,13
the Israeli leaders and * them, Jos 17:4
of Israel and * them that for a 2Sa 3:17
drinking he was * of the gold and Dan 5:2,3,4
the king and * him about his law. Dan 6:12
man, though I have * you about Jn 5:34
water," he * them, "but you Act 1:5
yearly sacrifices * them of their Heb 10:3

REMINDER
It is a * that the Lord brought Ex 13:16
before the Lord as a constant *. Ex 28:12
the Sabbath is a * of the covenant Ex 31:12,13
because the salt is a * of God's Lev 2:13
and the altar sheet shall be a * Num 16:38
altar, to be a * to the people of Num 16:40
the Ark as a * of this rebellion. Num 17:10
seven days as a * of the bread you Deu 16:3
be a permanent * to the people of Jos 4:7
these stones are a * of this Jos 4:22
a huge stone as a * and rolled it Jos 24:26
custom, as a * of the time when Est 9:24,25
all you need is this * from me; Rom 15:15,16

REMINDERS
These stones were * to Jehovah Ex 39:6,7
He gave them as * of his war Ps 81:5
there were always his *—the kind Act 14:17
keep sending these * to you, 2Pe 1:13,14

REMINDING
will speak to you, * you that Job 8:10
the persecution, * them that they Act 14:22
evil desires by * me that such Rom 7:8
Plead with him, * him of your Eph 6:18
I plan to keep on * you of these 2Pe 1:12

REMISSION
in the form of * of taxes. Est 2:18
of repentance for * of sins." Lk 3:3f

REMNANT
except for a tiny * that managed to Jos 10:20
Tabor marched the noble *. Ju 5:13,14
Zalmunna with a * of fifteen Ju 8:10
but a tiny * of their forces. Ju 20:35-39
to the little * of the men of Ju 21:13
all morning. The * of their army 1Sa 11:11
fruit for God. A * of my people 2Ki 19:31
other parts of the * of Israel, as 2Ch 34:9
"Pray for all the * of Israel 2Ch 34:21
not even this little * escapes. Ez 9:14
Yet a tenth—a *—will survive; Is 6:13
means "A * shall return," and Is 8:18
the Assyrians. A * of them will Is 10:21
will bring back a * of his people Is 11:11
Assyria for the * there, just as he Is 11:16
the * of Syria shall be destroyed. Is 17:3
the story is the same—only a * is Is 24:13
For a * shall go out from Is 37:32
I will preserve a * of my people Is 65:9
be a little * of my people left. Jer 4:27
has missed, so the * of my people Jer 6:9
and all the * left in the city into Jer 21:7
And I will gather together the * Jer 23:3
his people, the * of Israel." Jer 31:7
his men sent the * of the Jer 39:9
and stay with the * he rules. Jer 40:5
Why should this * be scattered Jer 40:15
a tiny * of what we were before. Jer 42:2
Lord replies, O * of Judah: The Jer 42:15
For the Lord has said: O * of Jer 42:19
I will take this * of Judah that Jer 44:12
will be but a tiny *) shall escape Jer 44:28
(Then the * of the Jews will say, Jer 46:16
I will pardon the * I preserve. Jer 50:20
this * and destroy all Israel." Eze 5:4
"Son of dust, the * left in Eze 11:15
every * of those who worship Baal; Zep 1:4
There the little * of the tribe Zep 2:7
to you—a *, small, discouraged as Zec 8:6

REMNANTS
"Son of dust, the scattered * of Eze 33:24
then at last the exile * of Mic 5:3

REMODEL
Hate evil and love the good; * Amo 5:15

REMONSTRANCE
king's command overcame Joab's *; 2Sa 24:4

REMONSTRATE
But Peter took him aside to * Mt 16:22

REMORSE
your souls and be filled with *; Lev 23:32
It is a broken spirit you want—* Ps 51:17
made of sackcloth to show your *. Is 22:12
with deep * and say, Alas for all Eze 6:11
shave your heads in sorrow and *. Eze 7:18
Let your * tear at your hearts Joe 2:13
on their heads to show their *. Lk 10:13

REMOTE
new campaigns. * lands tremble and Is 41:5
in a boat to a * area to be alone. Mt 14:13

REMOTEST
And peoples from * lands will Ps 67:6,7
you who live in earth's * corners! Is 42:10
Flee to the * parts of the Jer 49:8

REMOVAL
shall order the * of the spotted Lev 14:40
"for Azazel" or "for *." Lev 16:8
"for Azazel" or "for *." Lev 16:10
"for Azazel" or "for *." Lev 16:26
ceremonies, for * of sin. Num 19:

REMOVE
flocks today and * all the goats Gen 30:31,3
exterminate you. * your jewelry and Ex 33:
Then I will * my hand and you Ex 33:2
Then the priest will * the crop Lev 1:15,16,1
of your harvest, * the kernels from Lev 2:1
and women alike. * them so that Num 5:
There you shall * Aaron's Num 20:2
his men to * the stone from the Jos 10:22,2
This will * the guilt of his 1Ki 2:3
I will never * my mercy and love 1Ch 17:1
When you * dross from silver, you Pro 25:4,
When you * corrupt men from the Pro 25:4,
At that time he will * the cloud Is 25:
and grind the corn; * your veil; Is 47:2
* the foreskin of your hearts." Jer 4:4
I will surely * the yoke put on Jer 28:4
And when you return you will * Eze 11:18
I will * these armies from the Joe 2:20
I will * all your proud and Zep 3:11
For the Lord will * his hand of Zep 3:15
there, "* his filthy clothing." Zec 3:4
I will * the sins of this land in Zec 3:9
without notice and * him from his Lk 12:46
will be affected? * this evil 1Co 5:7
a man refuses to * his hat while 1Co 11:4
or else I will come and * your Rev 2:5

REMOVED
from which he had * it, and made Gen 2:21
* until all the flocks were there. Gen 29:3
"God has * the dark slur against Gen 30:23,24
with the Lord, he * the veil until Ex 34:34
the fat, the tail * close to the Lev 3:9,10,11
All the fat shall be * and Lev 4:19
that have been *, new mortar used, Lev 14:42
"The ashes are to be * from the Num 4:13
The Lord is with us and he has * Num 14:9
the summit, Moses * the priestly Num 20:28
prostitutes and * all the idols his 1Ki 15:12
the hills were not *, for Asa did 1Ki 15:14
Then he * the old bronze altar 2Ki 16:14
in the Temple, * their crosspieces 2Ki 16:17
supported, and * the great tank 2Ki 16:17
of Assyria he also * the festive 2Ki 16:18
He * the shrines on the hills, 2Ki 18:4
and planets. He * the shameful 2Ki 23:6
Next he * the shrines on the 2Ki 23:13
on the scene, he * the crown from 1Ch 20:2
when he * it from Kiriath-jearim. 2Ch 1:4
Also, he * the sun-images from 2Ch 14:5
King Asa even * his mother Maacah 2Ch 15:16
the idol-temples were not * 2Ch 15:17
been * to the temple of Baalam. 2Ch 24:7,8
He also * the foreign gods from 2Ch 33:15
So Josiah * all idols from the 2Ch 34:33
altar as the Levites * the skins. 2Ch 35:11
much rubble to be * that we could Neh 4:10
and * the crown from my head. Job 19:9
pass away, * by no human hand. Job 34:20
from whom your mercies are *. Ps 88:5
He has * our sins as far away Ps 103:12
God has * his protecting care. Is 22:8
crowns are * from your heads. Jer 13:18
them, for I have * my protection Jer 16:5
declares: I have * the yoke of the Jer 28:2
be *, for these robes are holy. Eze 42:14
in this instance, fifth *. Dan 5:11f
in pride, God * him from his royal Dan 5:20
Probably Jason, treacherously * by Dan 11:22f
But God * him and replaced him Act 13:22
man is * from your membership? 1Co 5:2
be * only by believing in Christ. 2Co 3:14

REMOVES
his control. He * kings and sets Dan 2:21

REMOVING
and kept Lot safe, * him from the Gen 19:29
example of God's * a nation from Deu 4:34
his decision by * his ring from his Est 3:10
to your name by * your people from Dan 9:15

RENAME
* Pharaoh Hophra and call him Jer 46:17
* your brother and sister. Hos 1:11

RENAMED
the Canaanites, * the place Gen 50:11
Ma-achthites. They * their country Deu 3:14
Levites (and then *) from the 1Ch 6:64,65
the Chaldeans and * him Abraham. Neh 9:7
Simon (he * him "Peter"), Mk 3:16-19

RENDERING
An alternate * of verse 30 Ps 68:30f
an alternate * might read, Dan 8:23f
prefer this *: "The treasures of Hag 2:7f
The Greek here is a very free * Jn 12:40f
An alternate * might be, "at the Rev 7:17f

RENEW
And he must * his vows that day Num 6:11
"Let us * the mutual security 2Ch 16:3

ENEW Con't)
Therefore in fairness * my life, Ps 119:40,41,42
the Lord shall * their strength. Is 40:31
'I will return and * the broken Act 15:16

ENEWED
So the two of them * their 1Sa 23:18
were constantly refreshed and *. Job 29:20
me and give me * hope and cheer. Ps 94:19
My youth is * like the eagle's! Ps 103:5
And your strength shall be * day Ps 110:3
be given * health and vitality. Pro 3:7,8

ENOUNCE
if they would * their faith, then Heb 11:37,38
They would not * their Rev 9:20

ENOUNCED
Have you * your covenant with Ps 89:39

ENOUNCES
if that nation * its evil ways, I Jer 18:8
then * them all for me. Lk 14:33

ENOUNCING
end without * me shall be saved. Mk 13:13

ENOWN
to receive praise, honor, and *; Deu 26:19
but to attain this honor and * Deu 26:19
almost as much * as the Top Three. 2Sa 23:22
I am not some person of * to make Job 33:7
Literally, "a plant of *"; Eze 34:29f

ENOWNED
will be the most * of all the Mic 4:1

ENT
farmers there, the * being one Sol 8:11
and * the vineyard to others." Lk 20:16

ENTAL
included in the original * fee. Ex 22:15

ENTED
and if it was *, then he need not Ex 22:15
borrowed or *, or by refusing to Lev 6:2
which he * out to some farmers Sol 8:11
a vineyard and * it out to some Lk 20:9
the next two years in his * house Act 28:30

REOCCUPY
Israel will * the land. Ob 1:17

REOPENED
of his reign, he * the doors of the 2Ch 29:3

REPAID
said, "God has * me for giving my Gen 30:18
for you have * me good for evil. 1Sa 24:17
but he has * me bad for good. 1Sa 25:21
That was how King Joash * 2Ch 24:22
May Babylon be * for all she did Jer 51:34,35
For you will be fully * for all Eze 23:49
of God, will be * many times over Lk 18:30

REPAIR
connected with their use and *. Num 4:32
roads to these cities in good *. Deu 19:2,3
set up a special * fund that would 2Ki 12:8
to * the Temple of the Lord. 2Ki 12:11,12
and masons to * the Temple, and to 2Ki 22:5,6
Later on, Joash decided to * and 2Ch 24:4
can maintain the Temple in good *. 2Ch 24:5
city treasurer, to * the Temple. 2Ch 34:8
A time to *; Ecc 3:7
of Jerusalem to see what needs *! Is 22:9,10,11
Thus they * the walls with Eze 22:28

REPAIRED
around him as he * the altar of the 1Ki 18:30
so that the Temple can be *." 2Ch 24:6
doors of the Temple and * them. 2Ch 29:3
* the foundations of the Temple. Ez 4:12
son of Hakkoz) * the next section Neh 3:4
The Old Gate was * by Joiada (son Neh 3:6
Jedaiah (son of Harumaph) * the Neh 3:10
Pahath-moab), who * the Furnace Neh 3:11
his daughters * the next section. Neh 3:12
then they * the 1,500 feet of Neh 3:13
The Dung Gate was * by Malchijah Neh 3:14
district, * the Fountain Gate. Neh 3:15
Then he * the wall from the Pool Neh 3:15
son of Ananiah) * the sections next Neh 3:23
living in Ophel * the wall as far Neh 3:26
Then came the Tekoites, who * Neh 3:27
The priests * the wall beyond Neh 3:28
of the goldsmiths, * as far as the Neh 3:31
were being *, they became furious. Neh 4:7

REPAIRING
Fort Millo, * the walls of this 1Ki 11:27,28
"The Temple building needs *. 2Ki 12:4,5
his defenses by * the wall wherever 2Ch 32:5
the ancient ruins, * cities long Is 61:4
Prepare many bricks for * your Nah 3:14

REPAIRS
* needed on any of these items. Num 3:31-35
pay for whatever * are needed." 2Ki 12:4,5
but only for * to the building. 2Ki 12:13,14
progress of the * at the Temple, he 2Ki 22:9,10
of perfumes. * were not needed from Neh 3:8

REPAY
caring for it must * the owner. Ex 22:12
then he will * only a small part of Lev 25:52
May the Lord * wicked men for 2Sa 3:39
he shall * four lambs to the 2Sa 12:6
to me: 'I will * him here on 2Ki 9:26
hard labor shall * his debts. Job 20:10
They * me evil for good and hate Ps 38:20
If you * evil for good, a curse Pro 17:13
Don't * evil for evil. Pro 20:22
He will * his enemies for their Is 59:18
I will *. Is 65:6
Yes, I will * them— not only for Is 65:6
of these men. * them for all that Jer 11:20
Should they * evil for good? Jer 18:20
before your eyes I will * Jer 51:24
O Lord, * them well for all the Lam 3:64
I will * you in full, and you Eze 7:4
and I will fully * them for all Eze 9:10
who long for idols, I will * them Eze 11:21
do, I will fully * you for all of Eze 16:43
* you for your broken promises. Eze 16:59,60
the poor who can't * their debts; Amo 2:6
I promise right now, I will * you Zec 9:12
who can * you, what good is that? Lk 6:34
about the fact that they won't *. Lk 6:35
inviting those who can't * you." Lk 14:14
he will * those who deserve it. Rom 12:19
I will * them"; Heb 10:30
Don't * evil for evil. 1Pe 3:9
and my reward is with me, to * Rev 22:12

REPAYMENT
as a pledge of his *, you must let Ex 22:26
full * for what he has stolen, Num 5:7
Don't withhold * of your debts. Pro 3:27,28

REPAYS
No one * him for what he has Job 21:30-32

REPEAT
Verses 29 and 30 * the names Gen 36:28,29,30f
Again I *, during those days you Ex 12:20
I'll * it again—any water Lev 11:12
to generation. I *: Anyone, Lev 17:8,9
"To *, whoever kills an animal Lev 24:21
I am not a sinner—I * it again Job 27:6
courage to boldly * the same 1Th 2:2

REPEATED
Lord's specific and * warnings. 2Ki 17:12
But I will give * thanks to the Ps 109:30
Jeremiah * all these prophecies Jer 27:12
Jesus * the question: "Simon, Jn 21:16
The same vision was * three Act 10:16
old system were * again and again, Heb 10:1

REPEATEDLY
*, you won't understand them. Is 6:9

REPEATING
for them again, * it over and over Is 28:13
only by * them again and again. Mt 6:7,8
again and prayed, * his pleadings. Mk 14:39

REPEATS
The original text * the lists of Num 7:18-23f
The original text * the lists of Num 7:24-29f
The original text * the lists of Num 7:30-35f
The original text * the lists of Num 7:36-41f
The original text * the lists of Num 7:42-47f
The original text * the lists of Num 7:48-53f
The original text * the lists of Num 7:54-59f
The original text * the lists of Num 7:60-65f
The original text * the lists of Num 7:66-71f
The original text * the lists of Num 7:72-77f
The original text * the lists of Num 7:78-83f
his vomit, so a fool * his folly. Pro 26:11
History merely * itself. Ecc 1:8-11

REPENT
God, he will be ashamed and *? Job 36:19
myself and * in dust and ashes.' Job 42:6
Unless they *, he will sharpen Ps 7:12
like me—will * and return to you. Ps 51:13
you will not * and turn to him, the Is 9:13
called you to *, to weep and mourn Is 22:12
and lies and won't *, therefore Is 30:12
it is God, wanting them to *. Is 42:25
upon you and will not *." Is 47:3
with faces hard as rock, not to *. Jer 5:3
I will do to them, they will *. Jer 36:3
except those who * of their coming Jer 44:14
and * and turn again to the Lord. Lam 3:40
death, therefore * and save your Eze 3:18
and refuse to *, they will die in Eze 3:19
the Lord God says: * and destroy Eze 14:6,7
that he does not *—that wicked Eze 33:8
But if you warn him to * and he Eze 33:9
water I baptize those who * of Mt 3:11
told you to * and turn to God, and Mt 21:32
to *, and so you couldn't believe. Mt 21:32
people to *, but the bad ones." Mk 2:17
too, will perish unless you *." Lk 13:5
so that they may * and live in the Act 26:18
You cannot bring yourself to * Heb 6:6
giving more time for sinners to *. 2Pe 3:9
to * of all their evil deeds. Rev 16:11

REPENTANCE
spend the day in * and sorrow for Lev 23:29
* for the forgiveness of sins." Mk 1:4
Or, "preaching the baptism of * Lk 3:3f
have sat in deep * long ago, Lk 10:13
an opportunity for *, and for their Act 5:31
prove their * by doing good deeds. Act 26:20
is meant to lead you to *. Rom 2:4
the sorrow of true * and does not 2Co 7:10
though he wept bitter tears of *. Heb 12:17

REPENTANT
courage to those with * hearts. Is 57:15

REPENTED
and began to preach, the people *. Jon 3:4,5
Then at last they *. Zec 1:5,6
their people would have * long Mt 11:21
to them, they * and turned to God Mt 12:41
Literally, "* himself." Mt 27:3f
you live that you really have *. Lk 3:8
they * at the preaching of Jonah; Lk 11:32
So when you have * and turned to Lk 22:32

REPENTING
unless they turn again to me, * Rev 2:22

REPENTS
But if you warn him and he *, he Eze 3:21
if he * and turns from his sins. Eze 33:12
angels of God when one sinner *." Lk 15:10

REPETITION
Verse 14 is a * of the names Gen 36:13,14f

REPHA-EL
Othni, *, 1Ch 26:6,7

REPHAH
*, the father of 1Ch 7:25,26,27

REPHAIAH
Jeshiah's son was * 1Ch 3:21,22
*, and Uzziel—all sons of Ishi. 1Ch 4:42
Uzzi, *, Jeri-el, Jahmai, Ibsam, 1Ch 7:2
Moza was the father of Bine-a, *, 1Ch 9:43
* (son of Hur), the mayor of half Neh 3:9

REPHAIAH'S
* son was Arnan; 1Ch 3:21,22

REPHAIM
The * in Ashteroth-karnaim; Gen 14:5,6
Perizzites, *, Amorites, Gen 15:19,20,21
referred to as the *, but the Deu 2:11
inhabited by the *, called Deu 2:20
was the last of the giant *. Deu 3:11
called 'The Land of the *.' Deu 3:13
the last of the *, who lived at Jos 12:4
(He was the last of the *, for Jos 13:12
northern end of the Valley of *. Jos 15:8
where the Perizzites and * live." Jos 17:15
Hinnom, north of the valley of *. Jos 18:16
spread out across the valley of *. 2Sa 5:18
spread out across the valley of *. 2Sa 5:22
at the valley of *, three of The 2Sa 23:13
in the Valley of *, and David was 1Ch 11:15
the Valley of *, and David asked 1Ch 14:9
grain fields in the Valley of *. Is 17:5

REPHIDIM
desert, going by easy stages to *. Ex 17:1
against the people of Israel at *. Ex 17:8
After breaking camp at *, they Ex 19:2,3
then on to * (where there was no Num 33:14
From * they went to the Num 33:15-37

REPLACE
As the sons of the priests * Lev 6:22,23
be brought to * those that have Lev 14:42
shall * it. Lev 24:18
an animal must * it, and whoever Lev 24:21
Commission Joshua to * you, and Deu 3:28
The nations you * all do these Deu 18:14
"* it with an altar for the Lord Ju 6:26
hall of fame to * those who died. 2Sa 23:24-39f
to * you as my prophet. 1Ki 19:16
Only this time * the kings with 1Ki 20:24
clothing to * his prison garb, and 2Ki 25:29
clothing to him to * the sackcloth, Est 4:4
spring up from the earth to * him! Job 8:19
* the evil years with good. Ps 90:15
let others step forward to * him. Ps 109:8
but we will * them with cedars! Is 9:8,9,10
the son of Hilkiah, to * you. Is 22:20
the Egyptians to * Jehoahaz, whom Jer 22:13f
* Jehoiada as priest in Jerusalem. Jer 29:26
I will * the flesh and muscles Eze 37:6
four smaller horns * it, this meant Dan 8:22
your note and * it with one for Lk 16:7
as an apostle to * Judas the Act 1:24,25
being put in to * the branches that Rom 11:18
own eyes and given them to * mine Gal 4:15
you will fold them up and * them. Heb 1:12
been no need for another to * it. Heb 8:7

REPLACED
It had just been * that day with 1Sa 21:6
king died and his son Hanun * him. 2Sa 10:1
So Baasha * Nadab as the king of 1Ki 15:28
was later * by his son Zebadiah. 1Ch 27:7
King Rehoboam * them with bronze 2Ch 12:10
Soon your own glory will be * by Hab 2:16
But God removed him and * him Act 13:22

REPLACING
as general of the army, * Joab. 2Sa 17:25
the new king, * his father David; 1Ki 2:12
Samaria, * the people of Israel. 2Ki 17:24

REPLANT
them good and will * them in this Jer 32:41

REPLASTERED
new mortar used, and the house *. Lev 14:42
REPLENISH
to * all the living of the earth. Ps 104:30
REPLICA
Lord told him, "Make a bronze * Num 21:8
So Moses made the *, and whenever Num 21:9
REPLIED
And Adam *, "I heard you coming Gen 3:10
"The serpent tricked me," she *. Gen 3:13
Cain * to the Lord, "My Gen 4:13
The Lord *, "They won't kill Gen 4:15
But Abram *, "I have solemnly Gen 14:22
But Abram *, "O Lord Jehovah, Gen 15:2,3
But Abram *, "O Lord Jehovah, Gen 15:8
girl as you see fit," Abram *. Gen 16:6
"No," God *, "that isn't what Gen 17:19
"In the tent," Abraham *. Gen 18:9
And God *, "If I find fifty Gen 18:26
And God *, "I won't destroy it if Gen 18:29
And God *, "I won't do it if Gen 18:30
"Yes, I know," the Lord *. Gen 20:6
Abraham *, "All right, I swear Gen 21:24
And Abraham *, "They are my gift Gen 21:30
"Yes, Lord?" he *. Gen 22:1
see to it, my son," Abraham *. Gen 22:8
"Certainly," the men *, "for Gen 23:5,6
men of Heth, and * to Ephron, as Gen 23:13
the wife of Nahor," she *. Gen 24:24
Then Laban and Bethuel *, "The Gen 24:50
And she *, "Yes, I will go." Gen 24:58
And he *, "It is my master's Gen 24:65
I would be murdered," Isaac *. Gen 26:9
and shepherds are here," they *. Gen 29:8
Laban *. Gen 29:19
of her sister," Laban * smoothly. Gen 29:26
But Leah angrily *, "Wasn't it Gen 30:15
leave me," Laban *, "for a Gen 30:27
Jacob *, "You know how Gen 30:29
Jacob *, "If you will do one Gen 30:31,32
Laban *. Gen 30:34
Rachel and Leah *, "That's fine Gen 31:14
Laban *, "These women are my Gen 31:43
"My children," Jacob *. Gen 33:5
And Jacob *, "They are my gifts, Gen 33:8
But Jacob *, "As you can see, Gen 33:13
"Very good," Joseph *. Gen 37:13,14
and their flocks," Joseph *. Gen 37:16
and your walking stick," she *. Gen 38:18
public prostitute here," they *. Gen 38:21
And they *, "We both had dreams Gen 40:8
is God's business," Joseph *. Gen 40:8
myself," Joseph *, "but God will Gen 41:16
the land of Canaan," they *. Gen 42:7
But Jacob *, "My son shall not Gen 42:38
"Yes," they *. Gen 43:28
"Fair enough," the man *, Gen 44:10
little food,' we *, 'We can't, Gen 44:26
"I am God," the voice *, "the Gen 46:3,4
And they *, "We are shepherds Gen 47:3
Jacob *, "I have lived 130 long, Gen 47:9
"Well then," Joseph *, "give Gen 47:16
the princess *. Ex 2:8
And he *, "A shepherd's rod." Ex 4:2
"Go with my blessing," Jethro *. Ex 4:18
But Pharaoh *, "You don't have Ex 5:17
"All right," Moses *, "it shall Ex 8:10
But Moses *, "That won't do! Ex 8:26
*, "but don't go too far away. Ex 8:28
"All right," Moses *, "as soon Ex 9:29
flocks and herds," Moses *. Ex 10:9
"Very well," Moses *. Ex 10:29
your golden earrings," Aaron *. Ex 32:2,3
But Moses *, "No, it's not a cry Ex 32:18
"Don't get so upset," Aaron *. Ex 32:22
And the Lord * to Moses, Ex 32:33
And the Lord *, "I myself will Ex 33:14
And the Lord had * to Moses, Ex 33:17
The Lord *, "I will make my Ex 33:19
The Lord *, "All right, this is Ex 34:10
But his brother-in-law *, "No, I Num 10:30
But Moses *, "Are you jealous Num 11:29
from King Balak of Moab," he *. Num 22:10
But Balaam *, "If he were to Num 22:18
Balaam *, "I have come, but I Num 22:38
But Balaam *, "Can I say Num 23:12
And he *, Num 23:18-24
But Balaam *, "Didn't I tell you Num 23:26
Balaam *, "Didn't I tell your Num 24:12
And the Lord * to Moses, "The Num 27:6,7
The Lord *, "Go and get Joshua Num 27:18
the people of Gad and Reuben *. Num 32:25
Then Moses * publicly, giving Num 36:5
"But they *, 'First let's send Deu 1:22
"I accept your terms," she *. Jos 2:21
of the Lord's army," he *. Jos 5:14
Achan *, "I have sinned against Jos 7:20
The Israelis * to these Hivites, Jos 9:7
They *, "We will be your Jos 9:8
But the leaders *, "We have Jos 9:19
They *, "We did it because we Jos 9:24
And she *, "Give me another Jos 15:18,19
for you," Joshua *, "and if you Jos 17:15
forests," Joshua *, "and since Jos 17:16,17,18
Phinehas * to them, "Today we Jos 22:31
And the people *, "We would Jos 24:16
But Joshua * to the people, "You Jos 24:19
"Yes," they *, "we are Jos 24:22
The people * to Joshua, "Yes, we Jos 24:24
And she *, "You have been kind Ju 1:15
"All right," she *, "I'll go Ju 4:9
she herself—*, Ju 5:29
"Stranger," Gideon *, "if the Ju 6:13
But Gideon *, "Sir, how can I Ju 6:15
Gideon *, "If it is really true Ju 6:17
"It's all right," the Lord *. Ju 6:23
The other soldier *, "Your dream Ju 7:14
But Gideon *, "God let you Ju 8:2,3
But the leaders of Succoth *, Ju 8:6
They *, "They were dressed just Ju 8:18
But Gideon *, "I will not be Ju 8:23,24
they *, and spread out a sheet Ju 8:25
"But the grapevine *, 'Shall I Ju 9:13
"And the thorn bush *, 'If you Ju 9:15
But the Lord *, "Didn't I save Ju 10:11
"Because we need you," they *. Ju 11:8
"We swear it," they *. Ju 11:10
The king of Ammon * that the Ju 11:13
Jephthah *, "Israel did not Ju 11:14,15
If the man * that he was not, Ju 12:5
"Yes," he *, "I am." Ju 13:11
And the Angel *, "Be sure that Ju 13:13,14
"I'll stay," the Angel *, "but Ju 13:16
Angel *, "for it is a secret." Ju 13:18
a riddle, they * that they would. Ju 14:12
why should I tell you?" he *. Ju 14:16
And the Philistines *, "To Ju 15:10
But Samson *, "I only paid them Ju 15:11
"No," they *, "we won't do Ju 15:12,13
"Well," Samson *, "if I were Ju 16:7
for confessing it," his mother *. Ju 17:2
And he *, "I am a priest Ju 17:9
"Yes," the priest *, "all is Ju 18:6
And the men *, "Let's attack! Ju 18:9,10
talk, mister," the men of Dan *. Ju 18:25
Bethlehem, in Judah," the man *. Ju 19:18
And as one man they *, "Not one Ju 20:8,9,10
And the Lord *, "Judah shall go Ju 20:18
But Naomi *, "It is better for Ru 1:11
But Ruth *, "Don't make me leave Ru 1:16
And the foreman *, "It's that Ru 2:6
"Yes, I know," Boaz *, "and I Ru 2:10,11
"Oh, thank you, sir," she *. Ru 2:13
And Ruth *, "All right. Ru 3:5
"It's I, sir—Ruth," she *. Ru 3:9
The man *, "All right, I'll buy Ru 4:4
"Then I can't do it," the man * Ru 4:6
witnesses *, "We are witnesses. Ru 4:11
she *, "I'm not drunk! 1Sa 1:15,16
the sacrifice *, "Take as much as 1Sa 2:16
Samuel *. 1Sa 3:4,5
And Samuel *, "Yes, I'm 1Sa 3:10
"It is the Lord's will," Eli *; 1Sa 3:18
"Do as they say," the Lord *, 1Sa 8:7
and the Lord * again, "Then do as 1Sa 8:22
to pay him with," Saul *. 1Sa 9:7
"Yes," they *, "stay right on 1Sa 9:12,13
Samuel *. 1Sa 9:19
"Pardon me, sir," Saul *. 1Sa 9:21
And Saul *, "We went to look for 1Sa 10:14
Saul *. 1Sa 10:16
And the Lord *, "He is hiding in 1Sa 10:22
help!" * the elders of Jabesh. 1Sa 11:3
But Saul *, "No one will be 1Sa 11:13
"No," they *, "you have never 1Sa 12:4
"Yes, it is true," they *. 1Sa 12:5
"Well," Saul *, "when I saw 1Sa 13:11
the youth *. 1Sa 14:7
his men *. 1Sa 14:36
Samuel *, "Has the Lord as much 1Sa 15:22
But Samuel *, "It's no use! 1Sa 15:26
you," the Lord *, "and say that 1Sa 16:2
But he *, "All is well. 1Sa 16:5
there is the youngest," Jesse *. 1Sa 16:10,11
David *. 1Sa 17:29
Saul *. 1Sa 17:33
And David *, "His name is Jesse 1Sa 17:58
But David *, "How can a poor man 1Sa 18:23
"I had to," Michal *. 1Sa 19:17
And David *, "Tomorrow is the 1Sa 20:5
the field with me," Jonathan *. 1Sa 20:11
family celebration," Jonathan *. 1Sa 20:28,29
the priest *, "but there is the 1Sa 21:4
"Rest assured," David *. 1Sa 21:5
"Well," the priest *, "I have 1Sa 21:9
David *. 1Sa 21:9
"But sir," Ahimelech *, "is 1Sa 22:14
and the Lord again *, "Go down to 1Sa 23:4
And the Lord *, "Yes, they will 1Sa 23:12
David * to Abigail, "Bless the 1Sa 25:32
"I'll go with you," Abishai *. 1Sa 26:5,6,7
And David *, "Yes, sir, it is. 1Sa 26:17,18
is your spear, sir," David *. 1Sa 26:22
"Bring me Samuel," Saul *. 1Sa 28:11
I am in deep trouble," he *. 1Sa 28:15
But Samuel *, "Why ask me if the 1Sa 28:16
servant of an Amalekite," he *. 1Sa 30:13
The young man *, "If you swear by 1Sa 30:15
"From the Israeli army," he *. 2Sa 1:3
And the man *, "Our entire army 2Sa 1:4
" 'An Amalekite,' I *. 2Sa 1:8
And he *, "I am an Amalekite." 2Sa 1:13
And the Lord *, "Yes." 2Sa 2:1
And the Lord *, "Hebron." 2Sa 2:1
"All right," David *, "but I 2Sa 3:13
But David *, "I swear by the 2Sa 4:9
And the Lord *, "Yes, go ahead, 2Sa 5:19
*, "Don't make a frontal attack. 2Sa 5:23
*, "for the Lord is with you." 2Sa 7:3
"Yes, sir, I am," he *. 2Sa 9:2
"Yes," Ziba *, "Jonathan's lame 2Sa 9:3
twenty servants, *, "Sir, I will 2Sa 9:10,11
Uriah *, "The Ark and the armies 2Sa 11:11
Then Nathan *, "Yes, but the Lord 2Sa 12:13
"Yes," they *, "he is." 2Sa 12:19
David *, "I fasted and wept 2Sa 12:22
The king *, "No, my boy; 2Sa 13:25
"I am a widow," she *, "and my 2Sa 14:5,6
"Oh, thank you, my lord," she * 2Sa 14:9
the king *. 2Sa 14:10
"I vow by God," he *, "that not 2Sa 14:11
"Go ahead," he *. 2Sa 14:12
to know one thing," the king *. 2Sa 14:18
And the woman *, "How can I deny 2Sa 14:19
And Absalom *, "Because I wanted 2Sa 14:32
"We are with you," his aides *. 2Sa 15:15
But Ittai *, "I vow by God and 2Sa 15:21
So David *, "All right, come 2Sa 15:22
And Ziba *, "The donkeys are for 2Sa 16:2
"He stayed at Jerusalem," Ziba * 2Sa 16:3
you, thank you, sir," Ziba *. 2Sa 16:4
Lord and by Israel," Hushai *. 2Sa 16:18
"Well," Hushai *, "this time I 2Sa 17:7
think best," the king finally *. 2Sa 18:4
I wouldn't do it," the man *. 2Sa 18:12
Joab *. 2Sa 18:22
and the king *, "If he is alone, 2Sa 18:25
And the king *, "He will have 2Sa 18:26
with good news," the king *. 2Sa 18:27
And the man *, "May all of your 2Sa 18:32
And he *, "My lord, O king, my 2Sa 19:26
"All right," David *. 2Sa 19:29
"No," he *, "I am far too old 2Sa 19:34
the men of Judah *. 2Sa 19:42
the others *, "so we have ten 2Sa 19:43
And he *, "I am." 2Sa 20:17
And Joab *, "That isn't it at 2Sa 20:20
"All right," the woman *, "we 2Sa 20:21
the Gibeonites *, "and we don't 2Sa 21:4
"Well, then," they *, "give us 2Sa 21:5,6
But Joab *, "God grant that you 2Sa 24:3
decision," David *, "but it is 2Sa 24:14
And David *, "To buy your 2Sa 24:21
She *, "My lord, you vowed to me 1Ki 1:17
Praise God!" * Benaiah, and 1Ki 1:36
clemency, Solomon *, "If he 1Ki 1:52
"No," he *, "I come in peace. 1Ki 2:13
He *, "Speak to King Solomon on 1Ki 2:17
"All right," Bath-sheba *, 1Ki 2:18
Adonijah marry Abishag," she *. 1Ki 2:21
"Do as he says," the king *. 1Ki 2:31
"All right," Shime-i *, 1Ki 2:38
or die? You *, 'Very well, I will 1Ki 2:42
Solomon *, "You were wonderfully 1Ki 3:6
So he *, "Because you have 1Ki 3:11
Solomon * with a proposal about 1Ki 5:2,3
"Everything is wonderful," he *, 1Ki 11:22
to think this over," Rehoboam *. 1Ki 12:5
And they *, "If you give them a 1Ki 12:7
And the young men *, "Tell them, 1Ki 12:10
"Yes," he *, "I am." 1Ki 13:14
"No," he *, "I can't; 1Ki 13:16,17
"Give him to me," Elijah *. 1Ki 17:19
"Yes, it is," Elijah *. 1Ki 18:8
He *, "I have worked very hard 1Ki 19:10
He * again, "I have been working 1Ki 19:14
Elijah *, "Go on back! 1Ki 19:20
"All right, my lord," Ahab *. 1Ki 20:4
And the prophet *, "The Lord 1Ki 20:14
it's your own fault," the king *. 1Ki 20:40
But Naboth *, "Not on your life! 1Ki 21:3
And King Jehoshaphat of Judah *, 1Ki 22:4
one," King Ahab *, "but I hate 1Ki 22:8
Jehoshaphat *. 1Ki 22:8
"And he *, 'I will go as a lying 1Ki 22:22
And Micaiah *, "You will have 1Ki 22:25
peace," Micaiah *, "it will prove 1Ki 22:28
"He was a hairy man," they *, 2Ki 1:8
But Elijah *, "If I am a man of 2Ki 1:10
Elijah *, "If I am a man of God, 2Ki 1:12
But Elisha *, "I swear to God 2Ki 2:1
But Elisha * again, "I swear to 2Ki 2:4
But Elisha * as before, "I swear 2Ki 2:6,7

:PLIED Con't)
.nd Elisha *, "Please grant me 2Ki 2:9
sked a hard thing," Elijah *. 2Ki 2:10
ourse I will," Jehoshaphat *. 2Ki 3:6,7,8
ilderness of Edom," Jehoram *. 2Ki 3:6,7,8
ie king of Israel's officers *. 2Ki 3:11
ut King Jehoram *, "No! 2Ki 3:13
ehoshaphat of Judah," Elisha *. 2Ki 3:14
jar of olive oil," she *. 2Ki 4:2
No," she *, "I am perfectly 2Ki 4:13
ut Elisha *, "I swear by 2Ki 5:16
I haven't been anywhere," he *. 2Ki 5:25
s, sir," one of the officers *. 2Ki 6:12
he *, "This woman proposed that 2Ki 6:26-30
:LISHA *, "THE Lord says that by 2Ki 7:1
ut Elisha *, "You will see it 2Ki 7:2
)ne of his officers *, "We'd 2Ki 7:13
The king's officer had *, "That 2Ki 7:19
And Elisha *, "Tell him, 'Yes.' 2Ki 8:10
Elisha *, "I know the terrible 2Ki 8:12
But Elisha *, "The Lord has shown 2Ki 8:13
And Hazael *, "He told me that 2Ki 8:14
"For you," he *. 2Ki 9:5
was and what he wanted," Jehu *. 2Ki 9:11
Jehu *, "What do you know about 2Ki 9:18
Jehu *, "How can there be 2Ki 9:22
And they *, "We are brothers 2Ki 10:13
'Yes," Jehonadab *. 2Ki 10:15
But King Joash *, "The thistle 2Ki 14:9
But the Assyrian general *, "Has 2Ki 18:27
Isaiah *, "The Lord says, 'Tell 2Ki 19:5,6
moves forward," Hezekiah *; 2Ki 20:10
far away in Babylon," Hezekiah *. 2Ki 20:14
And Hezekiah *, "Everything. 2Ki 20:15
"All right," Hezekiah *, "if 2Ki 20:19
So King Josiah *, "Leave it 2Ki 23:18
Amasai, a leader of The Thirty, *, 1Ch 12:18
And the Lord *, "Yes, I will." 1Ch 14:10
The Lord *, "Go around by the 1Ch 14:14
And Nathan *, "Carry out your 1Ch 17:2
to make," David *, "but let me 1Ch 21:13
"No," the king *, "I will buy 1Ch 21:24
Solomon *, "O God, you have been 2Ch 1:8
God *, "Because your greatest 2Ch 1:11
King Hiram * to King Solomon: 2Ch 2:11
their king," they *, "you will 2Ch 10:7
they *. 2Ch 10:10
King Jehoshaphat *. 2Ch 18:3,4,5
And they *, "Go ahead, for God 2Ch 18:3,4,5
But Micaiah *, "I vow by God 2Ch 18:13
And Micaiah *, "Sure, go ahead! 2Ch 18:14
"He *, 'I will be a lying spirit 2Ch 18:21
enough," Micaiah *, "—when you 2Ch 18:24
Micaiah *, "If you return 2Ch 18:27
And the prophet *, "The Lord is 2Ch 25:9
King Joash * with this parable: 2Ch 25:18
of Zadok *, "These are tithes! 2Ch 31:10
and the Lord * with a miracle. 2Ch 32:24
trouble, she *, "The Lord God of 2Ch 34:23
Jewish leaders *, "No, you may Ez 4:3
"Well," they *, "things are Neh 1:3
I was badly frightened, but I * Neh 2:3
God of heaven, I *, "If it please Neh 2:4
The king *, with the queen Neh 2:5,6
They * at once, "Good! Neh 2:18
But I *, "The God of heaven will Neh 2:20
to kill me, so I * by sending back Neh 6:3
But I *, "Should I, the Neh 6:11
And Esther *, "If it please Your Est 5:4
Esther *, "My request, my Est 5:7,8
His courtiers *, "Nothing!" Est 6:3
So the courtiers * to the king, Est 6:5
So he *, "Bring out some of Est 6:7,8
And at last Queen Esther *, "If Est 7:3
Esther *, "This wicked Haman is Est 7:6
And Satan *, "From patroling the Job 1:7
And the Lord * to Satan, "You Job 1:12,13
patroling the earth," Satan *. Job 2:2
"Skin for skin," Satan *. Job 2:4,5
him as you please," the Lord *; Job 2:6
But he *, "You talk like some Job 2:10
Then Job * to God: Job 40:2
THEN JOB * TO GOD: Job 42:1
I told you my plans and you *. Ps 119:26
And he *, "Not until their cities Is 6:11
But he *, "My master wants Is 36:12
Then Isaiah *, "Tell King Is 37:6
far away in Babylon," Hezekiah *. Is 39:3
And Hezekiah *, "I showed them Is 39:4
"All right," Hezekiah *. Is 39:8
I *, "But my work for them seems Is 49:4
"Don't say that," he *, "for Jer 1:7
And I *, "I see a whip made from Jer 1:11
And the Lord *, "That's right, Jer 1:12
And I *, "I see a pot of boiling Jer 1:13
Then I *, "So be it, Lord!" Jer 11:5
And the Lord *, The men of the Jer 11:21,22
The Lord * to me: If racing with Jer 12:5
Then Jeremiah *, "Lord, you know Jer 15:15
The Lord *: "Stop this Jer 15:19
But they *, "Don't waste your Jer 18:12

Jeremiah *, "Go back to King Jer 21:3,4
but you *, "Don't bother me." Jer 22:21
I *, "Figs, some very good and Jer 24:3
Jeremiah *, "You won't get into Jer 38:20
"All right," Jeremiah *. Jer 42:4
I *, "Lord, you alone know the Eze 37:3
But the king *, "I tell you, the Dan 2:5
The Chaldeans * to the king, Dan 2:10
Daniel *, "No wise man, Dan 2:27
Shadrach, Meshach, and Abednego * Dan 3:16
Daniel *: "Oh, that the events Dan 4:19
"Yes," the king *, "it is 'a Dan 6:12
The other *, "Twenty-three Dan 8:14
He *, "Do you know why I have Dan 10:20,21
He *, with both hands lifted to Dan 12:7
And he *, "I will test my people Amo 7:8
But Amos *, "I am not really one Amo 7:14
I *, "A basket full of ripe Amo 8:2
The Lord *: "Look, and be Hab 1:5
"No," the priests *. Hag 2:12
"I'll tell you," he *. Zec 1:9
He *, "They represent the four Zec 1:19
The angel *, "They have come to Zec 1:21
"A flying scroll!" I *. Zec 5:2
He *, "It is a bushel basket Zec 5:6
He *, "To Babylon Zec 5:11
He *, "These are the four Zec 6:5
Jesus knew their thoughts and *, Mt 12:25
But Jesus *, "Only an evil, Mt 12:39,40
" 'No,' he *. Mt 13:29
But Jesus *, "That isn't Mt 14:16
He *, "And why do your Mt 15:3
Jesus *, "Every plant not Mt 15:13,14
she *, "for even the puppies Mt 15:27
The disciples *, "And where Mt 15:33
And they *, "Seven loaves of Mt 15:34
He *, "You are good at reading Mt 16:2,3
"Well," they *, "some say John Mt 16:14
Jesus *, "They are right. Mt 17:11
Jesus *, "Oh, you stubborn, Mt 17:17
"Of course he does," Peter *. Mt 17:25
the foreigners," Peter *. Mt 17:26,27
Jesus *, "seventy times seven! Mt 18:22
you read the Scriptures?" he *. Mt 19:4
Jesus *, "Moses did that in Mt 19:8
*, "for God alone is truly good. Mt 19:17
And Jesus *, "Don't kill, don't Mt 19:18
every one of them," the youth *. Mt 19:20
And Jesus *, "When I, the Mt 19:28
'Because no one hired us,' they *. Mt 20:7
he asked. She *, "In your Mt 20:21
"Yes," they *, "we are able!" Mt 20:22
And the crowds *, "It's Jesus, Mt 21:11
"Yes," Jesus *. Mt 21:16
one question first," Jesus *. Mt 21:24
So they finally *, "We don't Mt 21:27
They *, "The first, of course." Mt 21:31
The Jewish leaders *, "He will Mt 21:41
"Caesar's," they *. Mt 22:21
Jesus *, " 'Love the Lord your Mt 22:37
"The son of David," they *. Mt 22:42
"But the others *, 'We haven't Mt 25:9
"But his master *, 'Wicked man! Mt 25:26
He *, "Go into the city and see Mt 26:18
He *, "It is the one I served Mt 26:23
"Yes," Jesus *. Mt 27:11
But he *, "We must go on to Mk 1:38
Jesus *, "Do friends of the Mk 2:19
But Jesus *, "Didn't you ever Mk 2:25,26
He *, "Who is my mother? Mk 3:33
He *, "You are permitted to know Mk 4:11,12
Jesus asked, and the demon *, Mk 5:9
Jesus *, "You bunch of Mk 7:6,7
She *, "That's true, sir, but Mk 7:28
"Seven," they *. Mk 8:5
the disciples *, "and others say Mk 8:28
Peter *, "You are the Mk 8:29
And he *, "Since he was very Mk 9:21
The father instantly *, "I do Mk 9:24
Jesus *, "Cases like this Mk 9:29
said it was all right," they *. Mk 10:4
"Teacher," the man *, "I've Mk 10:20
And Jesus *, "Let me assure you Mk 10:29
Jesus *, "I'll tell you if you Mk 11:29
To which Jesus *, "Then I won't Mk 11:33
They *, "The emperor's." Mk 12:16
Jesus *, "Your trouble is that Mk 12:24
Jesus *, "The one that says, Mk 12:29
The teacher of religion *, "Sir, Mk 12:32
Jesus *, "Yes, look! Mk 13:2
He *, "It is one of you twelve Mk 14:20
"Yes," Jesus *, "it is as you Mk 15:2
The angel *, "The Holy Spirit Lk 1:35
The crowd *, "What do you want Lk 3:10
"If you have two coats," he *, Lk 3:11
"By your honesty," he *. Lk 3:13
John *, "Don't extort money by Lk 3:14
But Jesus *, "It is written in Lk 4:4
Jesus *, "We must worship God, Lk 4:8
Jesus *, "The Scriptures also Lk 4:12
But he *, "I must preach the Lk 4:43

"Sir," Simon *, "we worked Lk 5:5
Jesus *, "Don't be afraid! Lk 5:10
and he *, "Why is it blasphemy? Lk 5:22
Jesus *, "Don't you read the Lk 6:3
"All right, Teacher," Simon *, Lk 7:40
He *, "God has granted you to Lk 8:10
"Legion," they *—for the man Lk 8:30
But Jesus *, "You feed them!" Lk 9:13
of about fifty each," Jesus *. Lk 9:14
Peter *, "The Messiah—the Christ Lk 9:20
But Jesus *, "Remember, I don't Lk 9:58
Jesus *, "Let those without Lk 9:60
Jesus *, "What does Moses' law Lk 10:26
"It says," he *, "that you Lk 10:27
Jesus * with an illustration: "A Lk 10:30
The man *, "The one who showed Lk 10:37
He *, "Yes, but even more Lk 11:28
But Jesus *, "Man, who made me a Lk 12:14
And the Lord *, "I'm talking to Lk 12:42,43,44
But the Lord *, "You hypocrite! Lk 13:15
And he *, "The door to heaven is Lk 13:23
Jesus *, "Go tell that fox that Lk 13:32
Jesus * with this illustration: Lk 14:16
him, but he *, 'All these years Lk 15:29
gallons of olive oil,' the man *. Lk 16:5,6
"The rich man *, 'No, Father Lk 16:30
Jesus *, "The Kingdom of God Lk 17:20
Jesus *, "Where the body is, the Lk 17:37
The man *, "I've obeyed every Lk 18:21
He *, "God can do what men Lk 18:27
"Yes," Jesus *, "and everyone Lk 18:29
" 'Yes,' the king *, 'but it is Lk 19:26
And the disciples simply *, "The Lk 19:34
He *, "If they keep quiet, the Lk 19:40
question before I answer," he *. Lk 20:3
Finally they *, "We don't Lk 20:7
They *, "Caesar's—the Roman Lk 20:24
Jesus *, "Marriage is for people Lk 20:34,35
He *, "Don't let anyone mislead Lk 21:8
And he *, "As soon as you enter Lk 22:10
"Fine," they *. Lk 22:35
"Master," they *, "we have two Lk 22:38
Peter *. Lk 22:58
But he *, "If I tell you, you Lk 22:67,68
And he *, "Yes, I am." Lk 22:70
"Yes," Jesus *, "it is as you Lk 23:3
And Jesus *, "Today you will be Lk 23:43
And one of them, Cleopas, *, Lk 24:18
"No," he *. Jn 1:21
He *, "I am a voice from the Jn 1:23
"Sir," they *, "where do you Jn 1:38
And Jesus *, "I could see you Jn 1:48
Nathanael *, "Sir, you are the Jn 1:49
"All right," Jesus *, "this is Jn 2:19
Jesus *, "With all the Jn 3:3
Jesus *, "What I am telling you Jn 3:5
Jesus *, "You, a respected Jn 3:10,11
John *, "God in heaven appoints Jn 3:27
He *, "If you only knew what a Jn 4:10
Jesus * that people soon became Jn 4:13
I'm not married," the woman *. Jn 4:17,18
Jesus *, "The time is coming, Jn 4:21-24
better, and they *, "Yesterday Jn 4:52
But Jesus *, "My Father Jn 5:17
Jesus *, "The Son can do nothing Jn 5:19
Philip *, "It would take a Jn 6:7
Jesus *, "The truth of the Jn 6:26
They *, "What should we do to Jn 6:28
They *, "You must show us more Jn 6:30,31
Jesus *, "I am the Bread of Jn 6:35
But Jesus *, "Don't murmur among Jn 6:43
Simon Peter *, "Master, to whom Jn 6:68
Jesus *, "It is not the right Jn 7:6
The crowd *, "You're out of your Jn 7:20
Jesus *, "I worked on the Jn 7:21,22,23
They *, "Are you a wretched Jn 7:52
The Pharisees *, "You are Jn 8:13
He *, "I am the one I have always Jn 8:25
Jesus *, "You are slaves of sin, Jn 8:34
Jesus *, "for if he were, you Jn 8:39
They *, "We were not born out of Jn 8:41
"I don't know," he *. Jn 9:12
sent from God," the man *. Jn 9:17
His parents *, "We know this is Jn 9:20
or bad," the man *, "but I know Jn 9:25
the man * Jn 9:30
you wouldn't be guilty," Jesus *. Jn 9:41
you don't believe me," Jesus *. Jn 10:25
They *, "Not for any good work, Jn 10:33
it says that men are gods!" he *. Jn 10:34,35,36
Jesus *, "There are twelve hours Jn 11:9
Jesus *, "Let her alone. Jn 12:7
Jesus * that the time had come Jn 12:23,24
Jesus *, "My light will shine Jn 12:35
Jesus *, "You don't understand Jn 13:7
can't be my partner," Jesus *. Jn 13:8
Jesus *, "One who has bathed all Jn 13:10
And Jesus *, "You can't go with Jn 13:36
Jesus *, "Don't you even yet Jn 14:9
Jesus *, "Because I will only Jn 14:23
"Jesus of Nazareth," they *. Jn 18:4,5

(REPLIED Con't)
And again they *, "Jesus of Jn 18:7
Jesus *, "What I teach is widely Jn 18:20
"If I lied, prove it," Jesus *. Jn 18:23
"Of course not," he *. Jn 18:25
Pilate *, "But you are a king Jn 18:37
They *, "By our laws he ought to Jn 19:7
Pilate *, "What I have written, Jn 19:22
my Lord," she *, "and I don't Jn 20:13
the Lord," he *, "I won't believe Jn 20:25
"No," we *. Jn 21:5
"Yes," Peter *, "You know I am Jn 21:15
Jesus *, "If I want him to live Jn 21:22
those dates," he *, "and they are Act 1:7
And Peter *, "Each one of you Act 2:38
But Peter and John *, "You Act 4:19
"Yes," she *, "we did." Act 5:8
But Peter and the apostles *, Act 5:29
But Peter *, "Your money perish Act 8:20
the man *. Act 8:31
And the eunuch *, "I believe that Act 8:37
And the voice *, "I am Jesus, the Act 9:5
"Yes, Lord!" he *. Act 9:10
And the angel *, "Your prayers Act 10:4
Cornelius *, "Four days ago I Act 10:30
Then Peter *, "I see very Act 10:34
" 'Never, Lord,' I *. Act 11:8
They *, "Believe on the Lord Act 16:31
But Paul *, "Oh, no they don't! Act 16:37
"No," they *, "we don't know Act 19:2
And they *, "What John the Act 19:3
a demon, the demon *, "I know Act 19:15
"No," Paul *, "I am a Jew from Act 21:39
And he *, 'I am Jesus of Act 22:8
brothers," Paul *, "for the Act 23:5
"Go away for now," he *, "and Act 24:25
But Festus * that since Paul Act 25:4
But Paul *, "No! Act 25:10,11
advisors and then *, "Very well! Act 25:12
And Festus *, "You Act 25:22
"And the Lord *, 'I am Jesus, the Act 26:15
But Paul *, "I am not insane, Act 26:25
And Paul *, "Would to God that Act 26:29
They *, "We have heard nothing Act 28:21
And do you remember how God *? Rom 11:4
We have * quietly when evil 1Co 4:13
"No, sir," I *. Rev 7:14

REPLIES
Judah were very rough in their *. 2Sa 19:43
BILDAD THE SHUHITE * to Job: Job 8:1
ZOPHAR THE NAAMATHITE * to Job 11:1
there baffled, with no further *. Job 32:15
to him, he never * by instant Job 35:12
His chosen one *, Ps 2:7
The Lord *, "I will arise and Ps 12:5
"Yes," the Lord *, "and when I Ps 75:2
his conceit with silly *! Pro 26:4,5
The watchman *, "Your Is 21:12
the Lord *. Jer 8:19
"Because," the Lord *, "my Jer 9:13
But the Lord *: You have loved to Jer 14:10
And the Lord *: Ephraim is still Jer 31:20
is what the Lord *, O remnant of Jer 42:15
And the Lord *: I will be your Jer 51:36
"Yes," * the Lord, "I will do Mic 7:15
And the Lord *, "I showed my love Mal 1:2,3

REPLY
And she will *, "Certainly! Gen 24:44
At this *, Abraham's servant fell Gen 24:52
— they should *: "These belong Gen 32:18
"Jacob," was the *. Gen 32:27
was the *. Ex 3:14
you will *, 'It is the Ex 12:27
hear his * to your complaints." Ex 16:7,8,9
spoke and God thundered his *. Ex 19:19
about it, and this was God's *: Num 9:9
And all the people shall *, Deu 27:15
And all the people shall *, Deu 27:16
And all the people shall *, Deu 27:17
And all the people shall *, Deu 27:18
And all the people shall *, Deu 27:19
And all the people shall *, Deu 27:20
And all the people shall *, Deu 27:21
And all the people shall *, Deu 27:22
And all the people shall *, Deu 27:23
And all the people shall *, Deu 27:24
And all the people shall *, Deu 27:25
And all the people shall *, Deu 27:26
This was the * of the people of Jos 22:21
our children can *, 'Look at the Jos 22:28
Joshua recorded the people's * Jos 24:26
However, the Lord's * through the Ju 6:8
seventh day they gave him their *. Ju 14:18
"Samson," was the *, "because Ju 15:6
But she did not * or respond in 1Sa 4:20
But the Lord made no * all 1Sa 14:37
And he received the same * as 1Sa 17:27
David shouted in *, "You come to 1Sa 17:45
to Nabal and waited for his *. 1Sa 25:9
was David's * as he strapped on 1Sa 25:13
And David would *, "Against the 1Sa 27:10
and won't * by prophets or dreams; 1Sa 28:15
Ish-bosheth made no *, for he was 2Sa 3:11
The Lord was pleased with his * 1Ki 3:10
Then he sent this * to Solomon: 1Ki 5:8
them a pleasant * and agree to be 1Ki 12:7
But there was no * of any kind. 1Ki 18:26
was no *, no voice, no answer. 1Ki 18:29
This * of Ahab's reached 1Ki 20:12
And this is my * to King 2Ki 19:21
* and treat them with kindness." 2Ch 10:7
to God, and God's * through the 2Ch 33:18
Then the king made this * to Ez 4:17
and each time I gave the same *. Neh 6:4
My * was, "You know you are Neh 6:8
This was Mordecai's * to Esther: Est 4:13
A * TO Job from Eliphaz the Job 4:1
JOB'S *: Job 6:1
JOB'S *: Job 9:1
JOB'S *: Job 12:1
Or let me speak to you, and you * Job 13:22
JOB'S *: Job 16:1
THE FURTHER * of Bildad the Job 18:1
THE * OF Job: Job 19:1
"I hasten to *, for I have the Job 20:2
JOB'S *: Job 21:1
But I *, Ask anyone who has been Job 21:29
But you *, 'That is why he can't Job 22:13
THE * OF Job: Job 23:1
*, and understand what he wants. Job 23:4,5
THE FURTHER * of Bildad the Job 25:1
JOB'S *: Job 26:1
and the seas *, 'Nor is it here.' Job 28:14
THE THREE MEN refused to * further Job 32:1
had no further *, he spoke out Job 32:5
"All right, here is my *: In Job 33:12
answers from you, and you must *. Job 38:3
there is no *— for you are holy. Ps 22:2
is an honor to receive a frank *. Pro 24:26
Literally, "* to a fool as his Pro 26:4,5f
called to him, but there was no *. Sol 5:6
he will *. Is 3:7
The Lord's * to your bragging is Is 9:11,12
This is the * of the Holy One of Is 30:12
had told them to say nothing in *. Is 36:21
I am here," he will quickly *. Is 58:9
And they *, Yes, we will come, for Jer 3:22
But you *, "No, that is not the Jer 6:16
And they will *, Of course, you Jer 13:12
tell them the Lord's * is Jer 16:11
you shall *, "What sad news? Jer 23:33
But this is the Lord's *: I Jer 33:25,26
the Lord gave his * to Jeremiah. Jer 42:7
your request, and this is his *: Jer 42:9
And they *, "Moab lies in ruins; Jer 48:20
and sat before me awaiting his *. Eze 20:1
and they will *, "You are our Hos 1:23
He will *, "See, I am sending Joe 2:19
"The Lord's * is this: Amo 7:17
Is that the right * for you to Mic 2:7
His * to them is this: "Is it Hag 1:3,4
This was the Lord's *: Zec 7:4
But I will *, 'You have never Mt 7:23
was Jesus' *. Mt 9:12
But Jesus gave her no *—not even Mt 15:23
And the man had no *. Mt 22:12
His * surprised and baffled them Mt 22:22
Sadducees with his *, they thought Mt 22:34,35
ones will *, 'Sir, when did we ever Mt 25:37
"Then they will *, 'Lord, when Mt 25:44
the crowd shouted back their *: Mt 27:21
In * Jesus said to the disciples, Mk 11:22,23
"If we * that God sent him, then Mk 11:31
heads in bafflement at his *. Mk 12:17
Jesus launched into an extended *. Mk 13:5
To this Jesus made no *. Mk 14:61
this was his *: "Go back to John Lk 7:20,21,22
he will *, 'I do not know you.' Lk 13:24,25
"And he will *, 'I tell you, I Lk 13:27
bushels of wheat,' was the *. Lk 16:7
your opponents will be able to *! Lk 21:15
question, but there was no *. Lk 23:9
healed me told me to," was his *. Jn 5:11
This was Stephen's lengthy *: Act 7:2
seven thunders crashed their *. Rev 10:3

REPLYING
not * when I call to you for aid. Ps 31:17

REPOPULATE
many children and to * the earth. Gen 9:1
Yes, have many children and * Gen 9:7
out from Jerusalem to * the land; Is 37:32

REPORT
I want to * back to my master." Gen 24:56
no eyewitness to * just what Ex 22:10
shall come and * to the priest, 'It Lev 14:35
The Merari division will also * Num 4:33
They made their * to Moses, Num 13:26
This was their *: "We arrived in Num 13:27
So the majority * of the spies Num 13:32
have frightened us with their *. Deu 1:28
and bring back a * of its size and Jos 18:4
to bring back their * to Joshua. Jos 18:8
standing there to verify the *. 1Sa 17:
When the * reached Saul that 1Sa 19:
and give me a more definite *. 1Sa 23:
When Joab sent a * to David of 2Sa 11:
and gave the * to David. 2Sa 11:
to Jerusalem, the * reached David: 2Sa 13:29,
days and to * back at that time. 2Sa 20
And the * came back, "Elisha is 2Ki 6:
Jezreel to * what we have done." 2Ki 9:
WHEN KING HEZEKIAH heard their * 2Ki 19
This account includes a * of 2Ch 25:
along with his * that there was 2Ch 34:15,
and to send back a * of the Ez 7:
For a * from Assyria will reach Is 37
"We will * you," they say. Jer 20:
wrote in his *), so I approached Dan 7:
This is his * of what he saw and Amo 1
"A * has come from the Lord," he Ob 1:
O Lord, now I have heard your *, Hab 3:
Jerusalem to * to Herod, for God Mt 2:1
and disease. The * of his miracles Mt 4:2
right again! The * of this Mt 9:2
$2,000, with the *, 'Sir, you gave Mt 25:2
They came back to * that there Mk 6:3
Now the * of his power spread Lk 5:1
The * of what he did that day Lk 7:1
Get your * in order, for you are Lk 16:
with an amazing * that his body was Lk 24:22,2
of the woman's *: "He told me Jn 4:3
seeing Jesus must * him immediately Jn 11:5
* so that you also can believe. Jn 19:3
Barnabas, to * on this decision. Act 15:2
good *, and for each one of you. Rom 1:
we are and be encouraged by his *. Eph 6:2
Give them reason to * joyfully Heb 13:1

REPORTED
was planning, and * it to Rebekah. Gen 27:4
But Joseph * to his father some Gen 37:
dream and promptly * the details to Gen 37:
from Canaan," he *, "with all Gen 47:
Moses * the words of the people Ex 19:
* Jehovah's words to the people; Num 11:24
Moses * God's words to the people! Num 14:39
without him and * his refusal. Num 22:14
the river and * to Joshua all that Jos 2:23
land of Canaan. I * what I felt was Jos 14:7
Someone * to Saul what was 1Sa 14:33
When Saul's men * this back to 1Sa 18:24
then he went to Hebron and * to 2Sa 3:19
Then Hushai * to Zadok and 2Sa 17:15
And Joab * the number of the 2Sa 24:9
quietly beside it, * it in Bethel 1Ki 13:24,25
Ben-hadad's scouts * to him, "Some 1Ki 20:17
When Shaphan * to the king about 2Ki 22:9,10
Asaph, Jeduthun, and Heman * 1Ch 25:6,7
to the palace and * to King 2Ch 29:18
more priests had * to work—for the 2Ch 29:34
the writer's case, * back and said, Eze 9:11
Then the other riders * to the Zec 1:11
to Jesus and * what they had done, Lk 9:10
they joyfully * to him, "Even the Lk 10:17
"The servant returned and * to Lk 14:21
"The first man * a tremendous Lk 19:16
"The next man also * a splendid Lk 19:18
that could be * to the Roman Lk 20:19
to the Pharisees and * it to them. Jn 11:46
to the Council and *, "The jail Act 5:22
the believers and * on their trip, Act 14:27
Paul and Barnabas * on what God had Act 15:4
The police officers * to the Act 16:38

REPORTERS
What then shall we tell the *? Is 14:32

REPORTS
whether these * are true or not. Gen 18:21
"DO NOT PASS along untrue *. Ex 23:1
"I have been hearing terrible * 1Sa 2:23,24,25
He also * that you have Neh 6:7
Pleasant sights and good * give Pro 15:30
don't want any more of your *!" Is 30:10,11
material the * circulating among us Lk 1:1,2
When * of Jesus' miracles reached Lk 9:7
he said. "* will reach you that I Lk 17:23
concerned at these * and let them Act 17:8,9
from Judea or * from those arriving Act 28:21
on hearing good * that you are Php 1:27

REPOSSESS
plains, and * the fields of Ephraim Ob 1:19

REPRESENT
Each stone will * one of the Ex 28:21
you, for they * the terms of my Ex 34:27
The Levites will * all the people Num 8:11
I will * the Philistines, and you 1Sa 17:8
choose someone to * you, and we 1Sa 17:8
He took twelve stones, one to * 1Ki 18:31
figs * the exiles sent to Babylon. Jer 24:4,5
"But the rotten figs * Zedekiah, Jer 24:8
Each day will * one year. Eze 4:6
"* all the people of Israel. Eze 37:11
he said, "* four kings who will Dan 7:17
He replied, "They * the four Zec 1:19
For these seven lamps * the eyes Zec 4:10

EPRESENT Con't)
Then he told me, "They * the two Zec 4:14
Iosts says, 'You * the Man who will Zec 6:12
rom so far away * many others who Zec 6:15
rom him, but * only themselves! Jn 5:43
other two brothers * the assemblies 2Co 8:23
which * the seven-fold Spirit Rev 5:6
is seven heads * a certain city Rev 17:9
They also * seven kings. Rev 17:10
s sitting on * masses of people of Rev 17:15
en horns—which * ten kings who Rev 17:16

EPRESENTATIVE
awyer—their * before God—bringing Ex 18:19,20
he is my * Ex 23:21
are to burn only a * portion Lev 2:9
as a * portion before the Lord. Lev 2:16
out a handful as a * portion, and Lev 5:12
altar as a * portion for the Lord; Lev 6:15
was Ethan, a * from the clan of 1Ch 6:44-47
secretary and the * of the High 2Ch 24:11
and to be both his * and yours. Job 33:6
But God sent Moses as his *, and Ps 105:26
Then he sent his personal * with Is 36:2
* as he scoffed at the Living God. Is 37:4
for the Messiah as * of the human Eze 2:1f
but I am the * of one you don't Jn 7:28
let it be as a * of the Lord Jesus, Col 3:17

EPRESENTATIVES
For they are assigned to him as * Num 3:7,8,9
"Let the * of the larger tribes Num 26:55,56
THEN * OF all the tribes of Israel 2Sa 5:1
"And if, as my *, you give even Mt 10:42
these two official *, along with Act 15:25

EPRESENTED
of Israel not * when we held our Ju 21:5
with Zadok, who * the Eleazar clan, 1Ch 24:3
Ahimelech, who * the Ithamar clan; 1Ch 24:3
of the Temple assistants were *: Ez 2:43-54
the following subclans were *: Neh 7:46-56
perhaps * by these paired riders. Is 21:6,7f
—* by the bronze belly of the Dan 2:39

REPRESENTING
Then he is to take a handful, * Lev 2:2
with the loaves * the first Lev 23:20
He shall take a handful, * all Num 5:26
that Aaron's rod, * the tribe of Num 17:8
brothers and sons—* all the Rechab Jer 35:3
I have come to you * my Father and Jn 5:43
lamps * the seven-fold Spirit Rev 4:5

REPRESENTS
Put Babylon and all it * far Is 52:11
Each day you lie there * a year Eze 4:4,5
* Judah and her allied tribes.' Eze 37:16
* all the other tribes of Israel.' Eze 37:16
In any event, he * the aggregate Eze 38:2,3f
and its long horn * the first great Dan 8:21
Then the Lord said, "This fruit * Amo 8:2
—Joshua * my servant The Branch Zec 3:8
"This scroll," he told me, "* Zec 5:3
He said, "She * wickedness," Zec 5:8
of the seeds fell * the heart of a Mt 13:19
The shallow, rocky soil * the Mt 13:20
with thistles * a man who hears the Mt 13:22
The good ground * the heart of a Mt 13:23
seed * the people of the Kingdom; Mt 13:38
of the seed fell, * the hard hearts Mk 4:15
The rocky soil * the hearts of Mk 4:16
"The thorny ground * the hearts Mk 4:18
"But the good soil * the hearts Mk 4:20
some seed fell * the hard hearts of Lk 8:12
The stony ground * those who Lk 8:13
The seed among the thorns * Lk 8:14
"But the good soil * honest, Lk 8:15
until what it * has occurred in the Lk 22:16
slave-wife Hagar * Jerusalem, the Gal 4:24,25
system it * were still in use. Heb 9:8
what the animal she is riding *. Rev 17:7
saw in your vision * the great city Rev 17:18
(Fine linen * the good deeds Rev 19:8

REPRISALS
fear of * from the Jewish leaders. Jn 7:13

REPROACH
thus bringing * upon the name of Lev 19:12
but sin is a * to any people. Pro 14:34
And I will bring * upon you and Jer 23:40
* to all the nations of the world. Eze 22:4
wounded and taken away your *. Zep 3:17,18

REPRODUCE
and * in great numbers." Gen 8:17
Men can only * human life, but Jn 3:6

REPRODUCING
* again after the flood has ended. Gen 7:3

REPROOF
you have spurned my counsel and *. Pro 1:25
to sorrow; bold * leads to peace. Pro 10:10
To refuse * is stupid. Pro 12:1

REPROVE
If they * me, it is medicine! Ps 141:5
from his example. * a wise man and Pro 19:25
mouth so that you can't * them; Eze 3:26

REPROVED
THE MAN WHO is often * but refuses Pro 29:1

REPTILE
kind of bird and animal and *. Gen 6:19,20
or who touches any * or other Lev 22:5
and every kind of * and fish, but Jas 3:7

REPTILES
* and wildlife of every kind." Gen 1:24
of wild animals and cattle and *. Gen 1:25
too, and the * and the birds. Gen 6:7
and * I have made will die." Gen 7:4
were not, and the birds and *. Gen 7:8,9
* and birds of every sort. Gen 7:14,15
wild animals, and * and all Gen 7:21
animals alike, and * and birds. Gen 7:23
birds, and *, so that they will Gen 8:17
all the animals, *, and birds—all Gen 8:18,19
This includes all * that slither Lev 11:41,42
sorts of animals, * and birds Act 11:6

REPULSIVE
* to me, and will not be accepted. Lev 19:7
I will make them * to every Jer 24:9

REPUTATION
a * for wisdom and intelligence. Deu 4:6
of Tekoa who had a * for great 2Sa 14:2,3
that he earned a * equal to The 2Sa 23:18,19
Each of these men had a great * as 1Ch 5:24
without regard to age or *. 1Ch 25:8
regard to the * of their families, 1Ch 26:13
you have a glorious * because of Neh 9:10
These men had an excellent *, and Neh 13:13
GOD'S * IS very great in Judah and Ps 76:1
in your wonderful * and in your Ps 89:16
God and man, and a * for good Pro 3:4,5
because everyone knows his *." Pro 11:9f
A GOOD * is more valuable than the Ecc 7:1
and established his * forever? Is 63:12
he gave himself a magnificent *. Is 63:14
us for the sake of your own *! Jer 14:7
Your * was great among the Eze 16:14
I am concerned about my * that Eze 36:21
for I am concerned about my *! Eze 39:25
the usual * for cheating—sitting at Lk 5:27
and not have a * for being wild or Tit 1:6
"I know your * as a live and Rev 3:1

REPUTATIONS
They want * as fearless Php 1:15

REPUTE
these men of ill *, they said to Mk 2:16

REQUEST
Abraham went further with his *. Gen 18:29
This is my *: When I ask one of Gen 24:14
acting upon this *, for Shechem was Gen 34:18,19
and presented their *. Gen 34:20
bitter there. We * permission to Gen 47:4
last *: do not bury me in Egypt. Gen 47:29
The Lord heeded their * and Num 21:3
"And the Lord agreed to your *, Deu 5:28
However, I have one *. Ju 8:23,24
was behind the *, for God was Ju 14:4
child, and he has given me my *; 1Sa 1:27
and the Lord has answered your *. 1Sa 12:13
she readily agreed to his *. 1Sa 25:41
For you have granted me this *!" 2Sa 14:22
At the same time he sent a * to 2Sa 21:12,13,14
do anything you *) and ask him to 1Ki 2:17
"I have one small * to make of 1Ki 2:20
and answered my *: Please watch 1Ki 8:28
you, then you will get your *. 2Ki 2:10
And God granted him his *. 1Ch 4:10
live, and do what they * of you. 2Ch 6:33
Ben-hadad agreed to King Asa's * 2Ch 16:4
yet completed. We * that you Ez 5:17
and the king granted his *; Ez 7:6
Then I added this to my *: "If Neh 2:7
What is your *? Est 5:3
Esther replied, "My *, my Est 5:7,8
wants to grant my *, that you come Est 5:7,8
life, and you have granted his *; Ps 21:4
The Lord says, "Your * has come Is 49:8,9
your *, and this is his reply: Jer 42:9
Then, at Daniel's *, the king Dan 2:49
Your Majesty, we * your Dan 6:8
Daniel, for your * has been heard Dan 10:12
is large, and your * is granted." Mt 15:28
"What is your *?" Mt 20:21
So we * an order from you Mt 27:64
and murder, at their *. Lk 23:25
you may ask any * you like, and it Jn 15:7
So Paul agreed to their * and the Act 21:26,27
no small town. I * permission to Act 21:39
you to agree to their *." Act 23:21
has granted your * and will save Act 27:24

REQUESTED
staff and * them to speak to Gen 50:4
"Tell his majesty," he * them, Gen 50:5
So Moses and Aaron * another Ex 10:3
I will pardon them as you have *. Num 14:20,21
through your land," they *. Num 21:22
to me, 'I will do as they have *. Deu 18:17
of Shechem," he *, "and ask them Ju 9:2
the Water Gate and * Ezra, their Neh 8:1
time—any prisoner the people *. Mk 15:6

stood up and * that the apostles be Act 5:34
in Jerusalem. He * a letter Act 9:2
to the Council again," they *. Act 23:15

REQUESTING
of Judah, * that they come to his 1Ki 1:9
Hiram at Tyre, * shipments of cedar 2Ch 2:3

REQUESTS
listen to me and answer my *. 1Ki 8:29
Ezra whatever he * of you (for he Ez 7:21
And the king granted these *, for Neh 2:8
* before you, praying earnestly. Ps 5:3
will come to you with their *. Ps 65:1
is never too busy to heed their *. Ps 102:17
Yet my * for offerings and Is 43:23
and to grant them their *. Eze 36:37,38
to grant you these *, for the Jn 16:26
him and make our *, then we can be 1Jn 5:15

REQUIRE
"I will give whatever you *. Gen 34:11
the guilty, and * that a father's Ex 34:7
is gone, he shall * two living Lev 14:4
He shall * her to swear that she Num 5:19
* the woman to drink the water. Num 5:26
the Lord your God * of you except Deu 10:12,13
For you * everyone to worship at 2Ki 18:22
There I will accept you, and * Eze 20:40
"Cases like this * prayer." Mk 9:29
seen do not * this special care. 1Co 12:24
rules of this kind * strong Col 2:23

REQUIRED
Abraham circumcised him, as God *. Gen 21:4,5
The embalming process * forty Gen 50:3
not be * to make restitution. Ex 22:13
the veil * 9,500 pounds of silver, Ex 38:27
* for the ceremony of cleansing. Lev 14:32
However such a marriage was * Lev 20:21f
by the amount of seed * to sow it. Lev 27:16
And the woman shall be * to say, Num 5:21,22
for they were * to carry their Num 7:9
the sacred duties * of the people Num 8:19
of Israel were * to pay crushing Ju 3:14
"The king's business * such 1Sa 21:8
No accounting was * from the 2Ki 12:15
were not * to keep account of their 2Ki 22:7
He also conquered Moab and * its 1Ch 18:2
as were * for the occasion. 1Ch 23:31
This * a force of 70,000 2Ch 2:2
a crime, and is * to swear to his 2Ch 6:22
of the Temple, as * by God's laws. 2Ch 23:5,6
feasts as * in the law of God. 2Ch 31:3
In addition, he * the people in 2Ch 31:4
duties as * in the law of God. 2Ch 31:4
all they owned, as * by law to be 2Ch 31:5,6
what these laws * of God's people, 2Ch 34:19
And he * everyone in Jerusalem 2Ch 34:32
by the Jews, and * all of them to 2Ch 34:33
special sacrifices * for the Ez 3:5
be * to pay taxes of any kind.' Ez 7:24
I also * my officials to spend Neh 5:16
The provisions * for each day Neh 5:18
service as * by the laws of Moses. Neh 8:18
at the Temple as * in the law. Neh 10:34
the Levites were * by law to bring Neh 10:39,40
ceremonies as * by the laws of Neh 12:45
"The prince shall be * to Eze 45:17
and take with you the offering * Mt 8:4
as,* by their ancient traditions. Mk 7:3
All that's * is that you really Mk 11:22,23
Everyone was * to return to his Lk 2:3
at the Temple, as * by the laws of Lk 2:22
washing * by Jewish custom. Lk 11:37,38
Much is * from those to whom much Lk 12:48
that day as * by the Jewish law. Lk 23:56
"and your approval is *." Jn 18:31
be circumcised and * to follow all Act 15:5
head as their laws *, and there was Act 24:18
God's people were * by law to give Heb 7:5
and offerings * under the old Heb 10:8
he * all the world to worship. Rev 13:12
He * everyone—great and small, Rev 13:16

REQUIREMENT
young pigeons" was the legal *. Lk 2:24
by meeting the old * of belonging Heb 7:16

REQUIREMENTS
The daily food * for the palace 1Ki 4:22
they shall fulfill my *. Eze 44:16
fulfilled all the * of the Law of Lk 2:39
—agreed that God's * were right, Lk 7:29
God's laws, fulfilling all his *. Rom 13:8
it fully satisfies all of God's *. Rom 13:10

REQUIRES
our law * of a dead man's brother; Gen 38:8
The eighth day * another sacred Lev 23:36
A section of land that * ten Lev 27:16
(When he * the woman to drink Num 5:24
to the Lord your God, as he *." Deu 26:19
land from Naomi * your marriage to Ru 4:5
first be burned," [as the law * 1Sa 2:16
and flocks, just as the law *; Neh 10:36
*, to thank and praise the Lord. Ps 122:4
to a fool as his folly *." Pro 26:4,5f

(REQUIRES Con't)
A dull axe * great strength; Ecc 10:10
is an impossible thing the king *. Dan 2:11
government * you to." Lk 3:13
Moses' law * for lepers who are Lk 5:14
do what the Father * of me so that Jn 14:31

REQUIRING
brothers without * them to mortgage Neh 5:12
And in all matters * information Dan 1:20
in Damascus, * their cooperation in Act 9:2

REQUISITION
* funds from the royal treasury. Ez 7:20

REQUISITIONED
During those years, Joseph * for Gen 41:48

REQUISITIONING
for * food from the people for the 1Ki 4:7

RESCIND
oath, and will not * his vow, that Ps 110:4

RESCUE
the time had come for their *. Ex 2:25
I promise to * them from the Ex 3:17
and had decided to * them, they all Ex 4:31
way the Lord will * you today. Ex 14:13
hear and * her out in the field. Deu 22:25,26,27
will * you from your captivity! Deu 30:3
Go and * the prostitute and Jos 6:22
left Gilgal and went to * Gibeon. Jos 10:7
and he will begin to * Israel Ju 13:5
then he will * you from the 1Sa 7:3
will * you before tomorrow noon!" 1Sa 11:9
will only * us from our enemies.' 1Sa 12:10
he will * me from your power!" 1Sa 24:15
May he * me from all my 1Sa 26:24
listen to me and * us from those 2Sa 14:15,16
his * and killed the Philistine. 2Sa 21:17
who tries to come to her *." 2Ki 11:15
the Israelis to * them from the 2Ki 13:5
Come and * me.' 2Ki 16:7f
the Lord to * us"—just remember 2Ki 18:22
trusting in the Lord to * you. 2Ki 18:30
Did they * Samaria? 2Ki 18:34
For we trust in you alone to * 2Ch 14:11
and that you will hear us and * 2Ch 20:9
see the incredible * operation God 2Ch 20:17
marvelous * from their enemies. 2Ch 20:27
yet been able to * his people from 2Ch 32:15
drag me away with no one to * me. Ps 7:2
I will * them as they have longed Ps 12:5
Oh, that the time of their * Ps 14:7
help but no one dared to * them; Ps 18:41
it when we see God * him!" Ps 22:8
hurry to my aid. * me from death; Ps 22:20
Yes, God will answer me and * me. Ps 22:21
for help, for he alone can * me. Ps 25:15
I am expecting the Lord to * me Ps 27:13
Don't let my enemies defeat me. * Ps 31:1
my times are in your hands. * me Ps 31:14,15
declare that you will * them. Ps 31:19
He shall * me! Ps 35:9
Act now and * me, for I have but Ps 35:17
Please, Lord, * me! Ps 40:13
God of Jacob, has come to * us. Ps 46:7
God of Jacob, has come to * us! Ps 46:11
* you, and you can give me glory. Ps 50:14,15
O my God, you alone can * me. Ps 51:14,15
are fighting me, yet he will * me. Ps 55:18
He will * me from these liars who Ps 57:3
Use your strong right arm to * Ps 60:4,5
the Lord, waiting for him to * me. Ps 62:1
the Lord, waiting for him to * me. Ps 62:5
Now answer my prayer and * me as Ps 69:13
Don't let me sink in. * me from Ps 69:14
Come, Lord, and * me. Ps 69:18
But * me, O God, from my poverty Ps 69:29
* ME, O God! Ps 70:1
enemies, for you are just! * me! Ps 71:2
order to save me. * me, O God, Ps 71:4
weak and needy, and will * them. Ps 72:13
and use your mighty power to * us. Ps 80:2
the destitute. * the poor and Ps 82:4
Who can * his life from the power Ps 89:48
he loves me, I will * him; Ps 91:14
trouble, and * him and honor him. Ps 91:15
with mighty power and * me. Ps 108:6
at the news of our * are sung in Ps 118:15,16
your wonderful promise to * me. Ps 119:123
overcome by evil. * me from the Ps 119:134
Look down upon my sorrows and * Ps 119:153
Yes, * me and give me back my Ps 119:154
Hear my prayers; * me as you Ps 119:170
for I am very low. * me from my Ps 142:6
Reach down from heaven and * me; Ps 144:7
You are the one who will * your Ps 144:10
will * the children of the godly. Pro 11:21
* those who are unjustly Pro 24:11,12
captivity with none to * them. Is 5:29
for I am coming soon to * you. Is 56:1
Don't let them kill me! * me from Jer 15:15
* you from their ruthless hands." Jer 15:21
Yet God will * them! Jer 30:7
I will find my sheep and * them Eze 34:12
one could * Daniel from the lions. Dan 6:17
for there was no one to * him. Dan 8:7
be able to * her from my hand. Hos 1:10
shepherd tried to * his sheep from Amo 3:12
But there I will * you and free Mic 4:10
You can be sure that I will * my Zec 8:7
would you work to * it that day? Mt 12:11
standing ready to * him in case he Mk 3:9
and that he had come to * Israel. Lk 24:21
the soldiers to * him, for I Act 23:27
so that he could * us from constant Tit 2:14
For Christ died to * them from Heb 9:15
So also the Lord can * you and 2Pe 2:9

RESCUED
and Shechem. They * Dinah from Gen 34:26
to their aid and * them from the Ex 2:17
who has * them from the Egyptians. Ex 6:7
from Pharaoh, and has * Israel. Ex 18:10
holy to myself and * you from Egypt Lev 22:32,33
generation, that I * you from Lev 23:43
all those he had * from Egypt, no Num 32:10,11
The Lord has * you from Deu 4:20
" 'I am Jehovah your God who * Deu 5:6
Egypt and the Lord your God * you! Deu 15:15
and that the Lord your God * you; Deu 24:18
The young men found her and * Jos 6:23
God is the one who * our fathers Jos 24:17
Each judge * the people of Ju 2:18
in Egypt, and * you from the Ju 6:9
to Moses and * Israel from Egypt Ju 6:16f
God, though he had * them from all Ju 8:34
out to me that I haven't * you? Ju 10:12
the Israeli army * them from their 1Sa 7:14
you from Egypt and * you from the 1Sa 10:18,19
for today the Lord has * 1Sa 11:13
So the people * Jonathan. 1Sa 14:45
and David * his two wives. 1Sa 30:18,19
For you have * your chosen nation 2Sa 7:23
Today Jehovah has * you from all 2Sa 18:31
Lord after he had * him from Saul 2Sa 22:1
From above, he * me. 2Sa 22:17
He set me free and * me, 2Sa 22:20
Lord lives who has * me from every 1Ki 1:29
be your gods—they * you from your 1Ki 12:28
Joash was * by his Aunt 2Ki 11:2,3
Joash was * by his Aunt 2Ch 22:11
people you * by your great power. Neh 1:10
gates and rejoice that you have * Ps 9:14
What gladness when the Lord has * Ps 14:7
trials. He * me from deep waters. Ps 18:16
* me, the king you appointed. Ps 18:50
You have * me, O God who keeps his Ps 31:5,6
God has * me from all my trouble, Ps 54:7
have faithfully * me from danger. Ps 71:15
he had * them from their enemies; Ps 78:42
You have * me from deepest hell. Ps 86:13
Thus you * them from their Ps 106:10
in their troubles, and he * them! Ps 107:13
Lord and he answered me and * me. Ps 118:5
Good men will be * from harm, but Pro 28:18
to save the city, and so it was *. Ecc 9:15
and Egypt, will be * and brought Is 27:13
the Lord lives who * the people of Jer 23:7
all those they had *—soldiers, Jer 41:16,17
are finally *—all they will have Amo 3:12
reached out his hand and * him. Mt 14:31
planned, and * us from this evil Gal 1:4
For he has * us out of the Col 1:13
But at the same time the Lord * 2Pe 2:7,8

RESCUER
Yes, he alone is my Rock, my *, Ps 62:2
Yes, he alone is my Rock, my *, Ps 62:6

RESCUERS
them off and chase all * away. Hos 5:14

RESCUES
And * me from my enemies. 2Sa 22:49
He * me from my enemies; Ps 18:48
and * all who reverence him. Ps 34:7
are breaking; he * those who are Ps 34:18
He frees us! He * us from death. Ps 68:20
about the wonderful ways he * me. Ps 73:28
For he * you from every trap, Ps 91:3
and * them from the wicked. Ps 97:10
but he * the poor who are godly Ps 107:41
their cries for help and * them. Ps 145:19
God * good men from danger while Pro 11:8

RESCUING
you displayed in * your people. Num 14:13
do it again, * Israel from Midian. Ju 6:16f

RESEARCHING
this result after * in every Ecc 7:27,28

RESEMBLE
Prophet among you, who will * me! Act 3:21,22

RESEMBLING
images * animals, birds, or fish. Ex 20:4

RESEN
Calah, and * (which is located Gen 10:11,12

RESENT
Young man, do not * it when God Pro 3:11,12
he will not * it. Jas 1:5

RESENTED
was right, but sometimes * it! 2Ch 25:2

RESENTFUL
children, making them angry and *. Eph 6

RESENTMENT
to anger and * will finally have Pro 11:2
he ended the angry * between us, Eph 2:1
free from sin and anger and *. 1Ti 2
Our lives were full of * and Tit 3

RESERVE
the blessings you * for those who Ps 61
ahead to * rooms for them in a Lk 9:5

RESERVED
limits because it is * for God." Ex 19:2
for it is * for the Lord and you Ex 30:3
the Tabernacle was * for the tents Num 3:3
a portion of land * for it in the Deu 10:
Because it is * for a leader. Deu 33:2
that which was * for the Lord's Jos 7:
For I have * it for the time when Job 38:22,2
Friendship with God is * for Ps 25:1
up by the fire * for your enemies. Is 26:1
I have * the ships of many Is 60:
And the wonderful heritage I * Jer 17:
Those places are * for the Mt 20:2
in the * pews in the synagogue! Mt 23:
a place * by God for himself; Mk 15:38
And God has * for his children 1Pe 1:

RESERVOIR
trays, and the * of olive oil. Num 4:
the water *, and the old Officers' Neh 3:16
to the upper *, near the road that Is 7:3
a * for water from the lower pool! Is 22:9,10,1
the top there is a * for the olive Zec 4:2
one on each side of the *. Zec 4:3

RESERVOIRS
marshes, and *, and even the water Ex 7:19
made many water *, for he had great 2Ch 26:10
pouring them into his vast *. Ps 33:7
for myself, and * to hold the water Ecc 2:4,5,6

RESETTLE
and Assyria, and * them in Zec 10:10

RESETTLED
as the Israelis * the land. Jos 14:15
and Sepharvaim and * them in the 2Ki 17:24

RESETTLING
city as captives, * them in Kir, 2Ki 16:9

RESHEPH
*, the father of 1Ch 7:25,26,27

RESIDENCE
During the time of their * Ru 1:3
* at Millo on the road to Silla. 2Ki 12:20
had chosen as his * after 2Ch 12:13
earth, the * of the great King. Ps 48:2
miles wide, shall be the * area Eze 45:5
city as my royal *, and as the Dan 4:30
meeting at the * of Caiaphas the Mt 26:3
the High Priest's * and crouched Mk 14:54
the High Priest's *, and Peter Lk 22:54
hills where this woman has her *. Rev 17:9

RESIDENT
David now drafted all the * 1Ch 22:2
a Jerusalem *, was in the Temple. Lk 2:25

RESIDENTS
local * finally left him alone. Gen 26:22
The local *, the Canaanites, Gen 50:11
drive out the * of Acco, Sidon, Ju 1:31,32
* the laws of the god of the land. 2Ki 17:27,28
from the Lord came upon the *. 2Ch 14:14
the foreign *, and the visitors 2Ch 30:25
But finally Hezekiah and the * 2Ch 32:26
Then the local * tried to Ez 4:4,5
that the guards be * of Jerusalem, Neh 7:3
visitors and * of Jerusalem alike! Act 2:14

RESIDUE
drains out, leaving a tasteless *. Lk 14:34f

RESINOUS
Make a boat from * wood, sealing Gen 6:14

RESIST
was able to * us successfully. 2Ch 32:14
He couldn't * her flattery. Pro 7:21
But I say: Don't * violence! Mt 5:39
But Jesus said, "Don't * any Lk 22:51
Must you forever * the Holy Act 7:51
of God's armor to * the enemy Eph 6:13
humbly to God. * the devil and he Jas 4:7

RESISTANCE
And there was no * from the local Jos 14:15
they surrender without *. Is 22:3

RESISTING
as a heifer, * the Lord's attempts Hos 4:16
child * in the womb—how stubborn! Hos 13:13

RESOLD
Many of these were then * to the 1Ki 10:29
Many of these were then * to the 2Ch 1:17

RESOLVE
"They will serve as judges to * Eze 44:24

RESORT
drivers, and * cities near 1Ki 9:19

RESORTED
* to trickery to save themselves. Jos 9:3,4,5

RESOUND
The wail of death will * Ex 11:6

RESOUNDS
the lightning. It * through the Ps 29:8
The noise of war * from the Jer 8:16

RESOURCE
Using every * at my command, I 1Ch 29:2

RESOURCES
unlimited * he will give you the Eph 3:16

RESPECT
Isaac, to * the boundary line. Gen 31:53
turbans to give them honor and *. Ex 28:40
You must * your mothers and Lev 19:1
"You shall give due honor and * Lev 19:32
he will learn to * the Lord his God Deu 17:19
in the slightest *, and will ensure Deu 17:20
behind, with no * or fear of God. Deu 25:18
the ground before David in deep *. 2Sa 1:1
"I am going to show special * 2Sa 10:2
hard to encourage * for the Temple, 2Ch 31:21
Josiah in this *, involving so many 2Ch 35:18
and stood up in * at my coming. Job 29:8
upon them and give them my full *. Ps 119:15
will listen with interest and *. Ps 119:44,45,46
True humility and * for the Lord Pro 22:4
have * for the Holy One of Israel. Is 17:7
They will no longer have * for Is 17:8
You expect others to * their Is 33:1
have no * for anyone. Is 33:8
have you no * at all for me? Jer 5:22
yet they have no * or fear for me. Jer 5:23,24
father in every *, he shall always Jer 35:18,19
of Edom, with no * for the dead. Amo 2:1
* and awe for me, by keeping them. Mal 2:5
thinking they would surely * him. Mt 21:37
cheat, * your father and mother." Mk 10:19
surely give him their full *. Mk 12:6
Surely they will show * for him.' Lk 20:13
judgment in every *, for I have Jn 8:16
who had no * for Joseph's memory. Act 7:17,18
the same in this *: they all have Rom 10:12
* to all those to whom it is due. Rom 13:7
will trust and * you, and you will 1Th 4:12
rewarded both by * from others and 1Ti 3:13
hard for their owners and * them; 1Ti 6:1
Since we * our fathers here on Heb 12:9
Show * for everyone. 1Pe 2:17
Servants, you must * your masters 1Pe 2:18
and when they show * for others, it Jud 1:16

RESPECTED
he was highly * and very popular. Gen 34:18,19
had Moses, and * him deeply all the Jos 4:14
with these * men as witnesses. Ru 4:4
but I will be * by the girls of 2Sa 6:22
became immensely * among the 2Ch 32:23
rank, will be * by their wives!" Est 1:20
the Jews, and * by all his Est 10:3
But the wise man's speech is *. Pro 14:3
and makes her * and admired Is 62:6,7
be * and maintain her identity. Eze 17:14
her words will be *, and Egypt Eze 29:21
And Herod * John, knowing that Mk 6:20
he sent some * Jewish elders to ask Lk 7:3
For if someone more * than you Lk 14:8
Jesus replied, "You, a * Jewish Jn 3:10,11
They are * by the apostles, and Rom 16:7

RESPECTFUL
synagogues and the * greetings from Lk 11:43
quiet and * in everything they do. Tit 2:3
be won by your *, pure behavior. 1Pe 3:1
and do it in a gentle and * way. 1Pe 3:15

RESPECTFULLY
to meet him and greeted him *. 2Ki 2:15
You may * ask Jeremiah, "What Jer 23:37
them to Jesus and * asked a favor. Mt 20:20
but plead with him * just as though 1Ti 5:1

RESPECTIVE
offered with the * grain offerings Num 29:6
cliffs), with their * villages. Jos 17:11
cities with their * villages: Jos 19:2-7
each famous in his * clan. 1Ch 12:24-37

RESPECTIVELY
who were, *, the ancestors of the 1Ch 4:18

RESPECTS
Yet though he is so great, he * Ps 138:6
If anyone * and fears God, he Pro 8:13
in these * they are like angels, Lk 20:36
come to pay their * and to console Jn 11:19
it that she deeply * her Eph 5:33

RESPITE
and gives us * from our enemies Ps 94:12,13

RESPOND
not * to your incense offerings. Lev 26:31
out how you would *, and whether or Deu 8:2
But she did not reply or * in any 1Sa 4:20
However, Hezekiah didn't * with 2Ch 32:25
yet God does not * to their Job 24:12
he does not instantly * in anger? Job 35:14,15
in the east will * with praise. Is 24:15,16
but don't expect them to *. Jer 7:27
I will give them hearts that * Jer 24:7
down from heaven and * to my cry! Lam 3:50
She will * to me there, singing Hos 1:15
him, and he will * to us as surely Hos 6:3

RESPONDED
They all * in unison, "We will Ex 19:8
All these kings * by mobilizing Jos 11:4
forces, and all of them *. Ju 6:35
And the Lord *. 1Sa 7:9
Jesse * by sending not only 1Sa 16:20
of Judah, and they * as one man. 2Sa 19:14
Jehu * with this message: "If 2Ki 10:6
The people * immediately and 2Ch 31:5,6
Mary *, "Oh, how I praise the Lk 1:46
And Jesus *, "Then I won't Lk 20:8

RESPONDS
And my heart *, "Lord, I am Ps 27:8

RESPONSE
This census was taken in * to Num 4:49
But the only * of the people was Num 14:10,11
was David's instant * to his 2Sa 15:14
Asa's * was to take the silver 2Ch 16:2
my strength for them without *. Is 49:4
In * to all he has done for us, Heb 10:24

RESPONSIBILITIES
*: Num 3:25-30
*: Num 3:31-35
*: Num 3:36,37
but will have no regular *." Num 8:25,26
his *, as the Lord had commanded. Num 27:23
nor given any other special *; Deu 24:5
They were free from other * and 1Ch 9:33,34
and all the others with similar *. Jer 36:12
none of his *, who refuses to obey Eze 18:10
behead me for neglecting my *." Dan 1:10
now I will give you many more *. Mt 25:21
and the * and pleasures of life. Lk 8:14
won't be honest with greater *. Lk 16:10
take over his new *, he left for Act 25:1
* and how to please his wife. 1Co 7:33

RESPONSIBILITY
this continual *: that every male Gen 17:9,10
* over everything he owned. Gen 39:6
sister for whom he has special * Lev 21:2,3
The * of these two clans of Num 3:25-30
The * of these four clans of Num 3:31-35
with special * for the oversight of Num 3:31-35
The * of these two clans was the Num 3:36,37
who had the final * for the Num 3:38
everything in it will be his *." Num 4:16
with the * of leading the people. Num 27:19
street we assume no * whatsoever; Jos 2:19
"And I'll take the * if you are 2Sa 14:9
is able to carry such a heavy *?" 1Ki 3:9
by coin-toss. The * of the east 1Ch 26:14,15
this, you will discharge your *." 2Ch 19:10
now given me the * of building him Ez 1:2
accepted the * of taking it to Ez 8:30
I gave the * of governing Neh 7:2
Don't try to disclaim * by saying Pro 24:11,12
I will give him * over all my Is 22:22
they will load him with *, and he Is 22:23,24
man and the * will lie upon you and Jer 26:15
And it is your * to arrest any Jer 29:26
the * for rebuilding the Temple. Zec 4:6f
* he has shall be taken from him. Mt 25:29
this good man. The * is yours!" Mt 27:24
* of feeding the other servants. Lk 12:42,43,44
is given, for their * is greater. Lk 12:48
of others, take the * seriously. Rom 12:8
are despised. Our * is to 2Co 13:8
for this is your * and privilege as Col 3:15
in places of high *, so that we can 1Ti 2:2
should take the *, for kindness 1Ti 5:4

RESPONSIBLE
"and I have no idea who is *. Gen 21:26
"He is the one who is * for your Gen 30:2
Let's not be * for his death, Gen 37:26,27
the other prisoners were * to him. Gen 39:22
I'll be * for him." Gen 42:37
and we will be * for bringing Gen 44:31
* for the affairs of fifty people; Ex 18:21
Let these men be * to serve the Ex 18:22
poor, you are * to help him; Lev 25:35
"Aaron's son Eleazar shall be * Num 4:16
They are fully * for the Num 4:26
directly * to Aaron's son Ithamar. Num 4:28
horrible disease, for she is *." Num 5:31
your family are * for any Num 18:1
come upon him—he shall be *." Num 30:15
and you will be * for destroying Num 32:15
held * for unjustified bloodshed. Deu 19:10
"We cannot be * for what happens Jos 2:17,18
the one who was * for bringing the Ju 4:4
was in no way * for Abner's death. 2Sa 3:37
him personally * for the murders of 1Ki 2:32
from each tribe—* for 1Ki 4:7
They are still * for the eastern 1Ch 9:17,18
had been * for the protection of 1Ch 9:21
for they were * for the rooms and 1Ch 9:26
Others were * for the furniture, 1Ch 9:29
were * to minister at the Temple. 1Ch 26:12
brothers were also * for the care 1Ch 26:28
they were * for the religious 1Ch 26:30
and Zabdi from Shiphma was * for 1Ch 27:27
Baal-hanan from Gedera was * for 1Ch 27:28
the Levites were * to collect the Neh 10:37
Hegai, who was * for the harem, Est 2:9
O God, hold them *. Ps 5:10
note, to become * for his debts. Pro 17:18
And I will appoint * shepherds Jer 23:4
But I will hold you * for his Eze 3:20
the men who are * for all of the Eze 11:1
people, he is * for their deaths. Eze 33:6
I will hold you * for his death. Eze 33:8
in his sin, and you will not be *. Eze 33:9
I will hold them * for what has Eze 34:9,10
the Lord their God—* for sending Eze 39:28
and * for bringing them home. Eze 39:28
and don't hold us * for his death, Jon 1:14
will be held * for the murder of Lk 11:50
is holding you * as overseers. Act 20:28
Jews, for they are * to keep God's Rom 3:19
They are * to him, not to you. Rom 14:4
it," you will be * for causing 1Co 8:11
God's messenger, * to no mere man. 1Co 9:1
that a wife is * to her husband, 1Co 11:3
her husband is * to Christ, and 1Co 11:3
to Christ, and Christ is * to God. 1Co 11:3
And she was * for the blood of Rev 18:24

REST
to * upon the mountains of Ararat. Gen 8:3,4
But he will live near the * of Gen 16:9-12
Stop awhile and * here in the Gen 18:3,4
I'll keep the * of you here, Gen 42:16
in jail, and the * of you may go on Gen 42:19
And all the * of us will be Gen 44:9
and the * of you can go free." Gen 44:10
be my slave. The * of you can go on Gen 44:17
of seriousness and *, a holy Ex 16:23
seventh day as a day of Sabbath *; Ex 16:28,29
* before the Lord your God. Ex 20:10
day and set it aside for *. Ex 20:11
but let the land * and lie fallow Ex 23:11
leave the * for the animals to Ex 23:11
"Work six days only, and * the Ex 23:12
oxen and donkeys a *, as well as Ex 23:12
The pillars are to * in four Ex 26:32
the * at the base of the altar. Ex 29:12
sprinkle the * of the blood over Ex 29:19,20
of Israel to * on my Sabbath day, Ex 31:12,13
Yes, * on the Sabbath, for it is Ex 31:14,15
day of solemn *, holy to the Lord. Ex 31:16
six days, and * on the seventh. Ex 34:21
is a day of solemn *, a holy day to Ex 35:2
all of one piece with the *. Ex 38:2
offerings, and the * of the blood Lev 4:25
altar, and all the * of the blood Lev 4:34
the altar and the * shall be Lev 5:9
be forgiven. The * of the flour Lev 5:13
and poured out the * of the blood Lev 8:15,16
right feet. The * of the blood he Lev 8:24
the * at the base of the altar. Lev 9:9
But the * of the people of Israel Lev 10:6
It is a Sabbath of solemn * for Lev 16:31
days of solemn * in every home, Lev 23:3
Sabbath of solemn *, and in it you Lev 23:32
regular weekly days of holy *. Lev 23:38
the festival are days of solemn *. Lev 23:39
must let the land * before the Lord Lev 25:1
for it is a year of * for the Lev 25:5
Sabbath laws of *, and reverence Lev 26:2
Then at last the land will * and Lev 26:34,35
Yes, then the land will * and Lev 26:34,35
It will make up for the * you Lev 26:34,35
from among the * of the people of Num 8:14
while he and the * of the Israelis Num 9:1
priest, and to the * of the people Num 31:12
to discourage the * of the people Num 32:7
ahead of the * of the people of Num 32:17
to the * of the people of Israel. Num 32:22
* of you in the land of Canaan." Num 32:30
Everybody must * as you do. Deu 5:14
of * the Lord will give to you). Deu 12:9
the Lord gives you * and keeps you Deu 12:10
Remember that day all the * of Deu 16:3
before you frighten the * of us!' Deu 20:8
God has given you * from all your Deu 25:19
you shall find no *, but the Lord Deu 28:65
him deeply all the * of his life. Jos 4:14
silver buried deeper than the *." Jos 7:21
the silver buried beneath the *. Jos 7:22
but Joshua and the * of the army Jos 8:9
Then Joshua commanded the * of Jos 10:19
Zaphon, and the * of the kingdom of Jos 13:27,28
and * as he promised he would. Jos 22:4
But when the * of Israel heard Jos 22:11
away from the * of his clan, and Ju 4:11
I want to * against them." Ju 16:25,26
us food, and the * of us will Ju 20:8,9,10
defense against the * of Israel. Ju 20:14,15
day's battle. The * of the army Ju 20:45
* over there in the shade." Ru 2:7
for Boaz won't * until he has Ru 3:15-18
The * of the army was sent home. 1Sa 13:2

(REST Con't)
than all the * of Saul's officers. 1Sa 18:30
"* assured," David replied. 1Sa 21:5
Benjamin, and all the * of Israel. 2Sa 2:9
He left the * of the army to his 2Sa 10:10
Now bring the * of the army and 2Sa 12:28
Now the * of the family is 2Sa 14:7
why didn't you invite the * of 2Sa 19:43
the * of the Israeli army fled. 2Sa 23:9
victory. (The * of the army did not 2Sa 23:10
as you for the * of your life! 1Ki 3:13
and given * to his people Israel; 1Ki 8:56
reign for the * of his life. 1Ki 11:34
The * of what Solomon did and 1Ki 11:41
so he joined the * of Israel at 1Ki 12:2,3,4
force the * of Israel to 1Ki 12:21
and * awhile and have some food; 1Ki 13:7
The * of Jeroboam's 1Ki 14:19
The * of Abijam's history is 1Ki 15:7
The * of Asa's biography—his 1Ki 15:23
leading the * of Israel into sin. 1Ki 15:30
The * of Baasha's biography—his 1Ki 16:4-7
about it. The * of the history of 1Ki 16:14
sin with him. The * of the story 1Ki 16:20
So God was very angry. The * of 1Ki 16:27
the * of his army of 7,000 men. 1Ki 20:15
first day. The * fled behind the 1Ki 20:30
The * of Ahab's history—including 1Ki 22:39
of Israel. The * of the deeds of 1Ki 22:45
of Judah. The * of the history of 2Ki 1:18
here and die with the * of us!" 2Ki 7:13
The * of the history of King 2Ki 8:23
to * and recover from his wounds. 2Ki 8:29
Jehu then killed all the * of the 2Ki 10:11
The * of Jehu's activities are 2Ki 10:34
from among the * of the king's 2Ki 11:2,3
The * of the history of Joash is 2Ki 12:19
The * of the history of Jehoahaz 2Ki 13:8
into sin. The * of the history of 2Ki 13:12
The * of the history of Joash and 2Ki 14:15
Joash, and the * of his biography 2Ki 14:18
The * of Jeroboam's biography—all 2Ki 14:28
acting king. The * of the history 2Ki 15:6
himself. The * of the history of 2Ki 15:11
special tax. The * of the history 2Ki 15:21
the new king. The * of the history 2Ki 15:26
The * of the history of Pekah's 2Ki 15:31
was built. The * of Jotham's 2Ki 15:36
The * of the history of the reign 2Ki 16:19
The * of the history of Hezekiah 2Ki 20:20
The * of the history of 2Ki 21:17
the throne. The * of Amon's 2Ki 21:25
Priest and the * of the priests and 2Ki 23:4
The * of the biography of Josiah 2Ki 23:28
The * of the history of the life 2Ki 24:5
with all the * of the gold and 2Ki 25:14,15
allowance for the * of his life. 2Ki 25:30
Joab rebuilt the * of Jerusalem. 1Ch 11:8
May this blessing * upon my 1Ch 17:27
*—a place for our God to live in. 1Ch 28:2
The * of Solomon's biography is 2Ch 9:29
war against the * of Israel in an 2Ch 11:1
The * of the biography of Asa is 2Ch 16:11
for his God had given him *. 2Ch 20:30
The * of the story of Hezekiah 2Ch 32:32
The * of Manasseh's deeds, and 2Ch 33:18
in Babylon. The * of the deeds of 2Ch 36:8
that the land must * for seventy 2Ch 36:21
May his blessings * upon you. Ez 1:3
workers, and the * of the people Ez 2:70
at them, "The * of us are doing Neh 5:8
destroy us? The * of us are Neh 5:10
the Arab, and the * of our enemies Neh 6:1
and the * of the people now Neh 7:73
and all the * who, with their Neh 10:28
lived there the * of her life, Est 2:12,13,14
in the * of the provinces! Est 9:12
now, asleep and at *, along with Job 3:13
and there the weary are at *. Job 3:17
You will take your time, and * in Job 11:18
So give him a little *, won't Job 14:6
We shall * together in the Job 17:16
teach the * of us how we should Job 37:19,20
He lets me * in the meadow grass Ps 23:2,3
* in the Lord; Ps 37:7
You must die like all the *! Ps 49:10
like a dove, to fly away and *! Ps 55:6
place of * I planned for them." Ps 95:11
into their dens to *, and men go Ps 104:22
loved ones to get their proper *. Ps 127:2
I couldn't *, I couldn't sleep, Ps 132:2-5
and tell me where to stop and *. Ps 139:3
They can't * unless they cause Pro 4:16
Don't * until you do. Pro 6:4
and be wise the * of your life. Pro 19:20
A little folding of the hands to * Pro 24:32,33
All the * of his life he is Ecc 5:17
they run without stopping for * Is 5:27
of the Lord shall * upon him, the Is 11:2
gives his people * from sorrow and Is 14:3
whole earth is at * and is quiet! Is 14:7
I am gripped by awful fear. All * Is 21:4
to Cyprus, you will find no *." Is 23:12
For the Lord's good hand will * Is 25:10
They could have * in their own Is 28:12
the demons will come there to *. Is 34:14
does —he takes the * of it and Is 44:15
How can the * of it be a god? Is 44:19
killed and the * were carried away Is 49:21
days of *, but honors them; Is 56:2
For the godly who die shall * in Is 57:2
Take no *, all you who pray, and Is 62:6,7
and give God no * until he Is 62:6,7
Spirit of the Lord gave them *. Is 63:14
But because the * of you have Is 65:11
Travel there, and you will find * Jer 6:16
They shall have * and quiet in Jer 30:10
when Israel sought for *. Jer 31:2
For I have given * to the weary Jer 31:25
of Kareah) and the * of the Jer 41:11
of my own sighing and I find no *. Jer 45:3
return and be at * and nothing Jer 46:27
Lord, when will you be at * again? Jer 47:6
Go back into your scabbard; * and Jer 47:6
of Babylon—there is no * for them! Jer 50:34
in prison for the * of his life. Jer 52:11
There is no *, for those she Lam 1:3
give yourselves no * from weeping Lam 2:18
Sabbath—a day of * every seventh Eze 20:12
but trample down the *? Eze 34:18
and muddy the * with your feet? Eze 34:18
the * of their tribe of Levi did. Eze 48:11
He spent the * of the day trying Dan 6:14
the end of your life and your *; Dan 12:13
far away and * beneath my shadow. Hos 14:7
Dead Sea and the * into the Joe 2:20
They will lie down to * in the Zep 2:7
victory to the * of Judah first, Zec 12:7
Come to me and I will give you * Mt 11:28
you shall find * for your souls; Mt 11:29,30
for a while, seeking * but Mt 12:43,44,45
they lay down to * until midnight, Mt 25:5,6
on now and take your * . Mt 26:45
But the * said, "Leave him Mt 27:49
the crowds for a while and *." Mk 6:31
get your *! Mk 14:41
deserts, searching there for *; Lk 11:24
than all the * of them combined. Lk 21:3
life, like all the * of the world. Lk 21:34,35
a good night's *, said, "That Jn 11:12,13
The * of us stayed in the boat Jn 21:8
have turned the * of the world Act 17:6
He had never heard the * of the Act 18:25,26
for land, and the * to try for it Act 27:44
he turned to the * of the world to Rom 11:15
condemned with the * of the world. 1Co 11:32
more than any of the * of you. 1Co 14:18
later by the * of "the Twelve." 1Co 15:5
the Lord Jesus Christ * upon you. 1Co 16:23
much as to all the * of you—though 2Co 2:5,6
me and I couldn't *, wondering 2Co 2:13
Macedonia there was no * for us; 2Co 7:5
too, and the * of my fellow workers Php 4:3
at * as you trust in Christ Jesus. Php 4:7
God will give you * along with us 2Th 1:7
And to the * of you I say, dear 2Th 3:13
for me to stop fighting and *. 2Ti 4:7
let them come to his place of *. Heb 3:11
enter his place of *—we ought to Heb 4:1
God can enter into his place of *. Heb 4:3
"They shall never enter my *." Heb 4:5
This new place of * he is talking Heb 4:8
So there is a full complete * Heb 4:9
into that place of *, too, being Heb 4:11
disbelief of the * of the Heb 11:7
Now your faith and hope can * in 1Pe 1:21
be spending the * of your life 1Pe 4:2
and that all the * of the world 1Jn 5:19
"As for the * of you in Thyatira Rev 2:24,25
they were told to * a little longer Rev 6:11
out to attack the * of her Rev 12:17
* from all their toils and trials; Rev 14:13
Resurrection. (The * of the dead Rev 20:5

RESTATED
of Moab that Moses * the covenant Deu 29:1

RESTAURANT
eating at a temple *, for you know 1Co 8:10

RESTED
So the people * on the seventh Ex 16:30
but whenever he * his arms at his Ex 17:11
in them, and * the seventh day; Ex 20:11
And the glory of the Lord * upon Ex 24:16
and earth, and * on the seventh Ex 31:17
grating that * upon a ledge about Ex 38:4
The cloud * upon the Tabernacle Ex 40:38
and when the Spirit * upon them, Num 11:25
when the Spirit * upon them, they Num 11:26
the entire nation * in camp until Jos 5:8,9
So the land finally * from its Jos 11:23
He fed their donkeys while they * Ju 19:21
so they stayed there awhile and *. 2Sa 16:14
The great cedar ceiling beams * 1Ki 7:2
the tank. It * on twelve bronze 1Ki 7:
the next day they *, celebrating Est 9:
day also, and * the next day, with Est 9:
had * and stood above the entrance Eze 9
Wild animals * beneath its shade Dan 4:
Sabbath, so they * all that day as Lk 23:
written that God * on the seventh Heb 4

RESTING
of burden * among the saddle bags. Gen 49:
* it upon the ledge built there. Ex 27
worship, and for * from the normal Lev 23
Temple by beams * on blocks built 1Ki 6
Once when he was * in the room he 2Ki 4:11,1
and enter this * place of yours 2Ch 6:4
They have a * place among the Eze 32:2
from heaven and * upon Jesus. Jn 1:3
descending and * upon someone—he is Jn 1:3
He is * from his work, just as Heb 4:1

RESTITUTION
is captured, he must make full *; Ex 22:
the fire shall make full *. Ex 22:
and no * shall be made for it. Ex 22:1
shall not be required to make *. Ex 22:1
And he shall make * for the holy Lev 5:1

RESTLESS
My heart is troubled and *. Job 30:2
and grief, and *, bitter nights. Ecc 2:20-2
are like the * sea, which is Is 57:2
you have done, O * female camel, Jer 2:2

RESTORATION
and about the * of the Temple, see 2Ch 24:2
refers to the * after the Jer 30:21
as to the final * under Christ. Jer 30:21

RESTORE
touch her. Now * her to her Gen 20:
such sin, he shall * what he took, Lev 6:4,
May he * your youth and take Ru 4:1
I will * to you all the land of 2Sa 9:
him live, and * them to you." 2Sa 17:2,
Lord your God to * my arm again." 1Ki 13:
Ben-hadad told him, "I will * 1Ki 20:34
and carpenters to * the Temple; 2Ch 24:12
of usury. * their fields, Neh 5:1
and with gloom. Oh, * me soon. Ps 6:3
Spirit from me. * to me again the Ps 51:12
Lord, * us again to your favor. Ps 60:1
used them to * my joy and health. Ps 119:93
Literally, "* our fortunes, Ps 126:4
will smite Egypt and then * her! Is 19:22
He shall * my city and free my Is 45:13
you, and I will * Jerusalem, and Is 46:13
commissioned me to * to him his Is 49:5
— "you shall do more than * Is 49:6
your slavery and * your fortunes, Jer 29:14
coming when I will * the fortunes Jer 30:3
your captivity and * your fortunes, Jer 30:18
Turn me again to you and * me, Jer 31:18
day I will * prosperity to them. Jer 32:44
and Israel and * their fortunes. Jer 33:7
Instead I will * their prosperity Jer 33:25,26
But afterward I will * the Jer 49:6
(But someday I will * the Eze 16:53
And I will * the fortunes of Eze 29:14
upon them and * their fortunes, for Eze 39:25
"AT THAT TIME, when I * the Joe 3:1
I will * the fortunes of my Amo 9:14
* their honor and power again! Nah 2:2
and * their prosperity again. Zep 2:7
praise you when I * your fortunes Zep 3:20
now and * us as an independent Act 1:6

RESTORED
Then he * the wine taster to his Gen 40:21
as he said: I was * to my position Gen 41:13
she had owned was * to her, plus 2Ki 8:6
he built Elath and * it to Judah. 2Ki 14:22
city of Eloth and * it to Judah. 2Ch 26:2
So it was that the Temple was * 2Ch 29:35
and * them to their proper duties. Neh 13:11
in your home, then you will be *. Job 22:23
Lord * his wealth and happiness! Job 42:10
You have * the fortunes Ps 85:1
Temple *, for I have spoken it. Is 44:28
people will be * again, and Judah Eze 16:55
the daily sacrifice is * again? Dan 8:13
the rights of worship are *, Dan 8:26
was completely *, and he saw Mk 8:25
the man's ear had been and * it. Lk 22:51

RESTORES
by his power, and * them to life Job 24:22,23
streams. He * my failing health. Ps 23:2,3
Only when the Lord himself * them Ps 53:6

RESTORING
For God was in Christ, * the 2Co 5:19

RESTRAIN
Can you * Orion or Pleiades? Job 38:31
and did not * myself from any joy. Ecc 2:10
(Who can * your lust? Jer 2:24
could scarcely * the people from Act 14:18

RESTRAINED
Then at last the people were * Ex 36:4-7
could no longer be *, and there was 2Ch 36:16

RESTRAINED Con't)
However, he * himself and went Est 5:10
he has * himself. Is 42:14
mourn for her and * their tides. Eze 31:15
But the army of heaven was * Dan 8:12

RESTRAINS
A wise man * his anger and Pro 19:11

RESTRAINT
me, now cast off all * before me. Job 30:11
to, free from any *, full of Jer 18:12

RESTRICTED
the * area from the public places. Eze 42:16-20

RESTRICTION
This * applies to the sacrifices Lev 22:25
The only * is that you are not Deu 12:16
The only * is never to eat the Deu 12:20-23
The only * on the drinking was Est 1:8

RESTRICTIONS
* as during her monthly periods. Lev 12:2
the same * as during menstruation. Lev 12:5

RESTS
and a rounded back, with arm *; 1Ki 10:19
spirit of Elijah * upon Elisha!" 2Ki 2:15

RESULT
As a *, Jacob's flocks increased Gen 30:43
and she became pregnant as a *. Gen 38:18
obviously as a * of prostitution. Gen 38:24
As a *, Joshua and his troops Ex 17:13
I want to see the * of all the Deu 3:23,24,25
That would surely * in your Deu 7:4
was weary and faint as a *. 1Sa 14:28
a great victory to Israel as a *? 1Sa 19:5
As a * there was a great famine 2Ki 6:25
Israel and 70,000 men died as a *. 1Ch 21:14
As a *, King Shishak of Egypt 2Ch 12:2
residents. As a *, additional vast 2Ch 14:14
So now, as a * of the king's Est 2:8
Step by step I came to this * Ecc 7:27,28
And the *? Jer 5:27
later as a * of the conquest by Eze 26:14f
As a *, truth and righteousness Dan 8:12
Look at the *: You plant much Hag 1:5
and what has happened as a *! Hag 1:7
that would * in a death sentence. Mt 26:59
was healed; as a *, such throngs Mk 1:45
that day and as a * great numbers Mk 3:10
But as a *, the Messiah will be Lk 21:13
Was it a * of his own sins or Jn 9:2
in faith. As a * large numbers of Act 11:24
As a *, many of them believed, Act 17:12
from Italy as a * of Claudius Act 18:2,3
*, our sales volume is going down! Act 19:26
As a * we were showered with Act 28:10
them to do. The * was that their Rom 1:21
men and, as a *, getting paid Rom 1:27
And what was the *? Rom 6:21
being saved as a * of God's Rom 11:5
became rich as a * of God's offer Rom 11:12
* in the children's salvation. 1Co 7:14
And your changed lives are the * 1Co 9:1
are foolish; the * is that they are 1Co 9:22
of distress will * in God's richest 2Co 4:17
poverty, and the * has been an 2Co 8:2
things happen as a * of your 2Co 9:12
this body is a * of my trusting in Gal 2:20
among you as a * of your trying to Gal 3:5
good things that * from being Php 2:12
body, and now as a * Christ has Col 1:22
This will * in your hearts being 1Th 3:13
As a *, people who are not 1Th 4:12
Satan, but Eve, and sin was the *. 1Ti 2:14
for it, and as a * have pierced 1Ti 6:10
a * of my preaching the Good News. 2Ti 3:11
and as a * died in the wilderness. Heb 3:17
God and as a * won battles, Heb 11:33
But afterwards we can see the *, Heb 12:11
Faith that does not * in good Jas 2:20
the * is disaster for them. 2Pe 3:15,16
a * of seeing him as he really is. 1Jn 3:2
as a * of his loving us first. 1Jn 4:19

RESULTED
This was a great sin, and * in 1Ki 13:34
for it * in all Israel sinning. 2Ki 10:29
me the way of life * instead in my Rom 7:10
to you, for it has * in God's Rom 11:28
it has * in eternal life for you. 2Co 4:12

RESULTING
* from human passion or plan—but Jn 1:13
with God and * in eternal life Rom 5:21

RESULTS
Here are the * of the census: Num 26:3,4
Knowing God * in every other kind Pro 9:10
one, for the * can be much better. Ecc 4:9
WHEN KING HEZEKIAH heard the * Is 37:1
for him, but the * were the same. Mt 21:36
command would bring immediate *! Lk 17:6
Spirit—with the * you are seeing Act 2:33
you and see good *, just as I have Rom 1:13
me—and not without *: for I have 1Co 15:10
wherever there is sin, death *. 1Co 15:22
produce these evil *: impure Gal 5:19

because of the * they see in you; 2Th 1:12
not only right, but it brings *. Tit 3:8
not the kind that * in good deeds. Jas 2:26
has great power and wonderful *. Jas 5:16
the Holy Spirit * in spiritual 1Jn 5:17f

RESUMED
Afterwards she * wearing her Gen 38:19

RESURRECT
day when God will * his children. Rom 8:19

RESURRECTION
say there is no * after death, came Mt 22:23
whose wife will she be in the *? Mt 22:28
For in the * there is no Mt 22:30
whether there is a * of the Mt 22:31
After Jesus' *, they left the Mt 27:53
until after his death and *. Mk 10:1f
of men who say there is no *. Mk 12:18
In the *, whose wife will she be, Mk 12:23
there will be a *—have you never Mk 12:26
Then at the * of the godly, God Lk 14:14
Even Christ's * failed to convince Lk 16:31f
is no *— came to Jesus with this: Lk 20:27
Whose wife will she be in the *? Lk 20:33
or not there is a *—why, even the Lk 20:37,38
everyone else does, on * Day." Jn 11:24
the earth, about my death and *." Act 1:8
join us as witnesses of Jesus' *. Act 1:21,22
Jesus' death and *, and the Day of Act 2:1
the Messiah's *, and saying that Act 2:31
that denied the * of the dead. Act 4:1f
sermons about the * of the Lord Act 4:33
Jesus and his *, was, "He's a Act 17:18
Paul speak of the * of a person who Act 17:32
I believe in the * of the dead!" Act 23:6
say there is no * or angels or even Act 23:8
there will be a * of both the Act 24:15
to believe in the * of the dead? Act 26:8
his belief in the * of the dead. Act 28:20f
For if there is no * of the 1Co 15:13
now there is the * from the dead. 1Co 15:21
as it would be if there were no *. 1Co 15:58
heaven after his * and victory over Eph 4:8
the lie that the * of the dead has 2Ti 2:18
is to the day of Christ's *. Heb 5:5f
be saved out from death, at the *. Heb 5:7f
and the * of the dead and eternal Heb 6:2
death and doom by the * of Christ; 1Pe 3:21
now saves you through the *." 1Pe 3:21f
This is the First *. Rev 20:5
those who share in the First *. Rev 20:6

RETAINED
(Most of that tribe * its 1Ch 12:24-37

RETAKEN
was * by the Babylonians. Jer 38:28

RETARDED
they are dull, * children who Jer 4:22

RETINUE
the king and his * passed by, 2Sa 15:23
A very great * of aides and 2Ch 9:1
Then she and her * returned to 2Ch 9:12

RETIRE
were preparing to * for the night, Gen 19:4
and are to * at the age of fifty. Num 8:23,24

RETIRED
men before they * for the night. Jos 2:8
IN HIS OLD age, Samuel * and 1Sa 8:1

RETIREMENT
After * they can assist with Num 8:25,26
They told him that since his * 1Sa 8:5

RETIRING
after the * army as far as Dan. Gen 14:14

RETORT
you will only get a smart *; Pro 9:7,8
A quick * can ruin everything. Pro 13:3
just as surely a * causes anger! Pro 25:23
But you *, "Really? Mal 1:2,3

RETORTED
Cain *. Gen 4:9
they *. Gen 34:31
"Is that so?" * Pharaoh. Ex 5:2
Pharaoh *. Ex 10:10
But Joash * to the whole mob, Ju 6:31
Jephthah *. Ju 12:2
the answer to my riddle!" he *. Ju 14:18
Micah *. Ju 18:24
But the troops *, "Jonathan, who 1Sa 14:45
David *, "I was dancing before 2Sa 6:21
The king of Israel *, "Don't 1Ki 20:11
help you, what can I do?" he *. 2Ki 6:26-30
the king *. 2Ch 25:16
The king *, "I can see your Dan 2:8,9
Jesus *, "It also says not to Mt 4:7
"That's your problem," they *. Mt 27:4
they *. Jn 18:30
Pilate *. Jn 18:35

RETRACED
So the sun * ten degrees that it Is 38:8

RETREAT
him and cause him to * in shame. Dan 11:18
Angered by having to *, the Dan 11:30,31

RETREATED
the Israeli forces * and Benjamin Ju 20:31

The army of Israel * from the men Ju 20:35-39
That night Abner and his men * 2Sa 2:29
they ran too, and * into the city. 2Sa 10:14

RETREATING
were *, they fled into the city. 1Ch 19:15

RETURN
Then you will * to the ground Gen 3:19
and to the ground you will *." Gen 3:19
they will * here to this land; Gen 15:16
The Angel: "* to your mistress Gen 16:9-12
But if you don't * her to him, Gen 20:7
he pleaded, "Don't hinder my *; Gen 24:56
and told him, "* to the land of Gen 31:3
Now leave this country and * to Gen 31:13
and started out to * to his father Gen 31:17-20
who told me to * to the land of my Gen 32:9
so he did nothing until their *. Gen 34:5
out later and * him to his father. Gen 37:21,22
that time, but to * to her Gen 38:11
release Simeon and * Benjamin. Gen 43:14
let the lad * with his brothers. Gen 44:33
For how shall I * to my father Gen 44:34
"Hurry, * to my father and tell Gen 45:9
pack animals and * quickly to their Gen 45:17
assure him that I will * Gen 50:5
be afraid to * to Egypt, for all Ex 4:19
Moses and Aaron to * to the people Ex 6:13
he thought they might * to Egypt. Ex 13:17,18
not planning to * to Egypt after Ex 14:5
father-in-law * to his own land. Ex 18:27
If you don't * it, and he cries Ex 22:27
sin, but I will * to the Lord on Ex 32:30
Afterwards Moses would * to the Ex 33:11
me by refusing to * a deposit on Lev 6:2
or by refusing to * something Lev 6:2
the leper will * to the priest to Lev 13:16,17
and * to live inside the camp; Lev 14:8
seven days, and * the seventh day Lev 14:39
bathe himself and then * to camp. Lev 16:28
it, he shall * to the priest the Lev 22:14
everyone shall * home to his Lev 25:13
the money and * the land to him. Lev 25:27
owner—it does not * to the original Lev 25:30
his children, and * to his own Lev 25:41
the field shall * to the original Lev 27:24
* to my own land and kinfolk." Num 10:30
down he said, "*, O Lord, to the Num 10:36
Let's get out of here and * to Num 14:3
orders to * to the wilderness. Num 14:41
and afterwards * to the camp and be Num 19:7
Yes, I shall * now to my own Num 24:14
before the Lord, you may *. Num 32:22
may * to his own land and home. Num 35:28
permitting him to * to his home Num 35:32
cattle until you * after the Lord Deu 3:20
you may * here to your own land.' Deu 3:20
you will finally * to the Lord your Deu 4:30
Go and tell them to * to their Deu 5:30
and to * to God on the mountain. Deu 10:1
you, 'Never * to Egypt again.' Deu 17:16
then he shall bathe himself and * Deu 23:11
you must not force him to *; Deu 23:15,16
and will never * to you again. Deu 28:31
If at that time you want to * to Deu 30:2
"If you * to the Lord and obey Deu 30:7,8
Upon their * they told Joshua, Jos 7:3
But then he is free to * to his Jos 20:6
For his *. Ju 5:28
"I'll stay here until you *." Ju 6:18
fail, they'll * and destroy us." Ju 8:6
them to us, I will * and tear your Ju 8:7
* and break down this tower." Ju 8:9
Why, then, should we * it to you? Ju 11:23
one of us will * home until we have Ju 20:8,9,10
She decided to * to Israel with Ru 1:6,7
"Why don't you * to your parents' Ru 1:8
for you to * to your own people. Ru 1:11
No, my daughters, * to your Ru 1:12
(Their * from Moab and arrival in Ru 1:22
it when we * it to its own land?" 1Sa 6:2
if they don't, [but * to their 1Sa 6:9
about wanting to * to the Lord, get 1Sa 7:3
wouldn't let him * home any more. 1Sa 18:4
cave and * to the land of Judah. 1Sa 22:5
AFTER SAUL'S * from his battle 1Sa 24:1
and told her to * home without 1Sa 25:35
And did not * from battle 2Sa 1:22
be loyal to you in *, and reward 2Sa 2:6
So David let Abner * in safety. 2Sa 3:21
he plans to * and attack us!" 2Sa 3:24,25
After his * he destroyed eighteen 2Sa 8:13
tomorrow you may * to the army." 2Sa 11:12
him, but he shall not * to me." 2Sa 12:23
here is my plan. * quietly to the 2Sa 15:27
only be a burden; * to Jerusalem 2Sa 15:33,34
Let's ask David to * and be our 2Sa 19:8,9,10
They sent word to the king, "* 2Sa 19:14
Then let me * again to die in my 2Sa 19:37
(The rest of the army did not * 2Sa 23:10
desired, and in * Solomon sent him 1Ki 5:11
if they honestly * to you and 1Ki 8:48

(RETURN Con't)
for permission to * to Edom. 1Ki 11:21
of Jeroboam's * from Egypt, he was 1Ki 12:20
here, and not to * to Judah by the 1Ki 13:9
and he also told me not to * home 1Ki 13:16,17
this child's spirit * to him." 1Ki 17:21
—until I * in peace.' 1Ki 22:27
"If you * in peace," Micaiah 1Ki 22:28
"It's all over—* home! 1Ki 22:36,37
who, upon his * from Damascus, 2Ki 16:11,12
Samaria should * to Israel and 2Ki 17:27,28
from home and will decide to *; 2Ki 19:7
He shall * by the road he came, 2Ki 19:33
The first to * and live again in 1Ch 9:2
another family to *, including 1Ch 9:5
to * to the one who sent me.' 1Ch 21:12
Rehoboam told them to * in three 2Ch 10:5
afterwards * them to the armory. 2Ch 12:11
until I * safely from the battle!' 2Ch 18:26
Micaiah replied, "If you * 2Ch 18:27
Listen to me and * these 2Ch 28:11
"so that he will * to us who have 2Ch 30:6
will be able to * to this land. 2Ch 30:9
face from you if you * to him." 2Ch 30:9
the Lord's people, * to Israel for 2Ch 36:22,23
kingdom may now * to Jerusalem to Ez 1:3
and Levites, to * to Jerusalem at Ez 1:5
The king instructed him to * the Ez 5:15
He asked to be allowed to * to Ez 7:6
may * to Jerusalem with you. Ez 7:13
Israel to * with me to Jerusalem. Ez 7:28
to * to Jerusalem from our exile. Ez 9:8
let some of us *, we have broken Ez 9:13
but if you * to me and obey my Neh 1:9
When will you *?" Neh 2:5,6
who told them to * to you, and they Neh 9:26
of death, never to *—a land as Job 10:20,21
road from which I shall never *. Job 16:22
If you * to God and put right Job 22:23
with joy, and * him to his duties. Job 33:26
They do not even * to him when he Job 36:13
parents and * to them no more. Job 39:4
shall see it and * to the Lord; Ps 22:27
I do them good, but they * me Ps 35:12
like me—will repent and * to you. Ps 51:13
They * evil for good, and hatred Ps 109:5
Now may those curses * and cling Ps 109:19
* singing, carrying their sheaves. Ps 126:6
Literally, "never * to the ways Pro 2:19f
and won't * for several days." Pro 7:20
wicked meet disaster, good men *. Pro 28:28
came and to which they must *. Ecc 3:20
your gifts will * to you later. Ecc 11:1
The Young Women of Jerusalem: "*, Sol 6:13
* to us, O maid of Shulam. Sol 6:13
Those who * to the Lord, who Is 1:27
"A remnant shall *," and Is 8:18
A remnant of them will * to the Is 10:21
will be left to * at that time; Is 10:22
will help them to *, and those Is 14:2
Let swift messengers * to you, O Is 18:2
she will * again to all her evil Is 23:17
never again will they *. Is 26:14
Egypt will give you nothing in *! Is 30:6
wicked rebels, come, * to God. Is 31:6
once, and he will * to his own Is 37:7
He will * to his own country by Is 37:34
mist at noon! Oh, * to me, for I Is 44:22
See, my people shall * from far Is 49:12
* and say, 'We need more room! Is 49:20
for my people's * from captivity. Is 57:14
the roadway for my people to *! Is 62:10
turn against you? * and help us, Is 63:17
plead for you to * to me, and will Jer 2:9
* to me and once again be mine; Jer 3:7
and of Israel will * together from Jer 3:18
O ISRAEL, IF you will truly * to Jer 4:1
They all * at God's appointed Jer 8:7
but afterwards I will * and have Jer 12:15
The servants *, baffled and Jer 14:3
What I will give them in * is war Jer 14:12
Only if you * to trusting me will Jer 15:19
For they will never * to see Jer 22:10
You will never again * to the Jer 22:27
they shall * to me with great joy. Jer 24:7
For you shall * again, O virgin Jer 31:21
backs upon me and refused to *; Jer 32:33
is about to * in flight to Egypt! Jer 37:7
If you decide to stay, then * to Jer 40:5
they all began to * to Judah from Jer 40:12
no one has wanted to * to me, or Jer 44:14
"Only those who * to Judah (it Jer 44:28
"Come, let us * again to Judah Jer 46:16
O my people who * to your own land, Jer 46:27
Yes, Israel shall * and be at Jer 46:27
Abandon her and * to your own Jer 51:9
Remember the Lord and * to Jer 51:50
And when you * you will remove Eze 11:18
and let only a small quota *. Eze 20:37
and it will not * to its sheath Eze 21:5
Shall I * my sword to its sheath Eze 21:30
will suddenly * to you so that you Eze 24:27
try to escape and all those who *. Eze 35:7
but for Israel, good times will *. Eze 36:8
for my people's *—and they will be Eze 36:8
again and * to the land of Israel. Eze 37:12
and * home again to your own land. Eze 37:14
* of its people from many lands. Eze 38:8
and then you are to * to the Eze 40:4
When they * to the outer court, Eze 44:19
and then * back to the entrance, Eze 46:2
will soon * again to his own land. Dan 11:9
will * with a fully-equipped army Dan 11:13
"The Syrian king will then * Dan 11:28
and he will withdraw and * home. Dan 11:30,31
him and he will * in great anger to Dan 11:44
they will * from exile together; Hos 1:11
"I might as well * to my husband, Hos 1:7
Afterward they will * to the Lord Hos 3:5
I will abandon them and * to my Hos 5:15
"COME, LET US * to the Lord; Hos 6:1
yet he doesn't * to his God, nor Hos 7:10
they shall * to Egypt. Hos 8:13
But my people shall * to Egypt Hos 11:5
because they won't * to me. Hos 11:5
and my people shall * trembling Hos 11:10
their help, and in * she gets their Hos 12:1
O ISRAEL, * to the Lord, your God, Hos 14:1
Her people will * from exile far Hos 14:7
your garments." * to the Lord your Joe 2:13
and * the harm to your own heads. Joe 3:4
the people of Syria shall * to Kir Amo 1:5
Now in * I will send fire upon Amo 2:2
you still would not * to me. Amo 4:6
Yet you wouldn't * to me," says Amo 4:8
And still you wouldn't * to me," Amo 4:9
And still you won't * to me," Amo 4:11
men to battle, a hundred will *. Amo 5:3
in ruins, and * it to its former Amo 9:11
The Israeli exiles shall * and Ob 1:20
Asia Minor shall * to their Ob 1:20
Literally, "they shall * to the Mic 1:7f
Yet, even so, you refused to * to Hag 2:16,17
favor you if only you * to him. Zec 1:3
"Come, * to me," the Lord God Zec 1:4
"When you * to Bethel, say to Zec 7:5
Now I am going to * to my land Zec 8:3
ever *, for crime was rampant. Zec 8:10
remember me and * again to God; Zec 10:9
this warning to * to the laws I Mal 2:4
* to me," says the Lord of Hosts. Mal 3:7
I tell you to *, for King Herod is Mt 2:13
will * before you have reached Mt 10:23
Then it says, 'I will * to the Mt 12:43,44,45
must * before the Messiah comes?" Mt 17:10
in *, and shall have eternal life. Mt 19:29
"What events will signal your *, Mt 24:3
this does not signal my *; Mt 24:6
Those in the fields should not * Mt 24:18
*. And wherever the carcass is, Mt 24:27
* is near, even at the doors. Mt 24:33
being ready for my unannounced *. Mt 24:44
Blessings on you if I * and find Mt 24:46
know the date or moment of my *. Mt 25:13
will be ashamed of him when I * Mk 8:38
* [before the Messiah could come Mk 9:11
later I will * to life again." Mk 9:30,31
needs him and will * him soon.' Mk 11:3
"Praise God for the * of our Mk 11:10
even * for your money or clothes. Mk 13:15,16
be sure that my * is very near, Mk 13:29
Be on the watch [for my * Mk 13:33
the gatekeeper to watch for his *. Mk 13:34
Watch for my *! Mk 13:35,36,37
Everyone was required to * to his Lk 2:3
lend to their own kind for full *! Lk 6:34
Your gift will * to you in full Lk 6:38
As the time drew near for his * Lk 9:51
if not, the blessing will * to Lk 10:6
Lord's * from the wedding feast. Lk 12:36
are ready and waiting for his *. Lk 12:37
exact hour of his *—just as they Lk 12:39
his master will * without notice Lk 12:46
For they will * the invitation. Lk 14:12
Does only this foreigner * to Lk 17:18
For when I *, you will know it Lk 17:24
"[When I * Lk 17:26
right up to the hour of my *. Lk 17:30
home that day must not * to pack; Lk 17:31
those in the fields must not * to Lk 17:31
*, how many will I find who have Lk 18:8
"Upon his * he called in the men Lk 19:15
the city must not attempt to *. Lk 21:21
have come to earth and will * to Jn 3:13
* to heaven again? Jn 6:62
Then I shall * to the one who Jn 7:33
come for him to * to his glory in Jn 12:23,24
come from God and would * to God. Jn 13:1
the world and * to the Father." Jn 16:28
to us since his * from the dead. Jn 21:14
until I *, what is that to you? Jn 21:22
day, just as he went, he will *!" Act 1:11
turn from sin, * to God, and be Act 2
my people will * to this land of Act
Moses and wanted to * to Egypt. Act 7
beg him to * with them to Joppa. Act 9
they asked Paul to * and speak to Act 13
'I will * and renew the broken Act 15
Barnabas that they * again to Act 15
Literally, "* now and visit Act 15:
But he promised to * to Ephesus Act 18
"One day after my * to Act 22:17,
should * with him for the trial. Act 2
is far gone, the day of his * Rom 13:12,
in * is to give some material aid. Rom 15:
the * of our Lord Jesus Christ. 1Co
Is it too much to ask, in *, for 1Co 9:
Open your hearts to us! * our 2Co 6:
safe, when I * to visit you again. Php 1:
forward to his * from there. Php 3:
to the * of our Lord Jesus Christ. 1Th
forward to the * of God's Son from 1Th 1:
Watch for his * and stay sober. 1Th 5
or alive at the time of his *. 1Th 5:
given him until the day of his *. 2Ti 1:
blessing at the day of Christ's *. 2Ti 1:
me on that great day of his *. 2Ti 4
for the Lord's *, be patient, like Jas 5
and honor on the day of his *. 1Pe 1
about his promised *, even though 2Pe 3
to get something from them in *. Jud 1:

RETURNED

to light, and * to Noah, for the Gen 8
evening, the bird * to him with an Gen 8:1
As Abram * from his strike Gen 14:1
And Abraham * to his tent. Gen 18:3
and * Sarah his wife to him. Gen 20:1
of his army, * home again. Gen 21:3
So they * to his young men, and Gen 22:1
Negeb, had * to Beer-lahai-roi. Gen 24:6
and blessed them, and * home. Gen 31:5
The messengers * with the news Gen 32
Jabbok ford, then * again to the Gen 32:22,23,2
house and * to their camp again. Gen 34:2
* to get Joseph out of the well. Gen 37:2
So he * to Judah and told him he Gen 38:2
For we could have gone and * by Gen 43:1
"It's because of the money * to Gen 43:1
donkeys again, and * to the city. Gen 44:1
Sir, we have all * to be your Gen 44:1
So we * to our father and told Gen 44:2
away and never *—doubtless torn to Gen 44:2
And leaving, they * to the land Gen 45:2
Then Joseph * to Egypt with his Gen 50:1
with them when they * to Canaan. Gen 50:2
When they * to their father Reuel Ex 2:1
Moses * home and talked it over Ex 4:1
on a donkey, and * to the land of Ex 4:2
So Moses and Aaron * to Egypt and Ex 4:2
he * to his palace, unimpressed. Ex 7:2
Moses did, and the sea * to Ex 14:27
Moses * from the mountain and Ex 19:7
shall be * for each stolen ox. Ex 22:1
sheep * for each sheep stolen. Ex 22:1
So Moses * to the Lord and said, Ex 32:31
until he * to speak with God. Ex 34:35
by God's Spirit * with their Ex 35:21
her, and has * home to her father's Lev 22:13
to others shall be * to the Lev 25:10
the land before it is * to you. Lev 25:14,15,16
Jubilee year it must be * again. Lev 25:28
and are always * to the original Lev 25:31
time, and must be * to the Lev 25:33
it shall not be * to him again. Lev 27:20
Then Moses * to the camp with Num 11:30
Forty days later they * from Num 13:25
Then Aaron * to Moses at the Num 16:50
Moses and Eleazar *, and when Num 20:28
Then the people of Israel * to Num 21:4
So King Balak's ambassadors * Num 22:14
When Balaam *, the king was Num 23:6
So he * to where the king and Num 23:17
So Balaam and Balak * to their Num 24:25
their survey and * from the valley Num 32:9
not be * at the Year of Jubilee." Num 36:4
* with samples of the local fruit. Deu 1:24,25
Then they * and wept before the Deu 1:45
who are searching for you have *; Jos 2:16
chasing them had * to the city Jos 2:22
which everyone * to the camp again Jos 6:11
again, and * again to the camp. Jos 6:12,13,14
and the Israeli army * to Gilgal. Jos 10:15
Then the Israelis * to their Jos 10:21
Then Joshua and his army * to Jos 10:43
Then they * to Joshua and the Jos 18:9
They stubbornly * to the evil Ju 2:19
on and * alone to the king. Ju 3:17,18,19
When the king's servants * and Ju 3:24
Then he * to his men and shouted, Ju 7:15
Later, Gideon * by way of Heres Ju 8:13
He then * to Succoth. Ju 8:15
lifetime. He * home, and Ju 8:29
disbanded and * to their homes. Ju 9:55

(RETURNED Con't)
then when he * home in peace, the Ju 11:30,31
When Jephthah * home his Ju 11:34
Then she * to her father, who Ju 11:39
When he * for the wedding, he Ju 14:8
So he * the money to her. Ju 17:3
So the spies * to their people Ju 18:8
and ran away, and * to her father's Ju 19:2
Then the Israeli army * and Ju 20:48
wives, and they * to their homes; Ju 21:14
So the people of Israel * to Ju 21:24
and * to her childhood home; Ru 1:14
Then she * to the city. Ru 3:15-18
Then they * home to Ramah, and 1Sa 1:19,20
So they * home to Ramah without 1Sa 2:11
Before they * home Eli would 1Sa 2:20
the army of Israel * to their camp 1Sa 4:3
they * to Ekron that same day. 1Sa 6:16
were now * to Israel, for the 1Sa 7:14
After the feast, when they had * 1Sa 9:25
When Saul * to his home at 1Sa 10:26
field, and when he * to town he 1Sa 11:5
army, and the Philistines * home. 1Sa 14:46
to Ramah, and Saul * to Gibe-ah. 1Sa 15:34
Then Samuel * to Ramah. 1Sa 16:13
Then the Israeli army * and 1Sa 17:53
at Horesh while Jonathan * home. 1Sa 23:18
So the men of Ziph * home. 1Sa 23:24,25
and * to fight the Philistines. 1Sa 23:28
So David's messengers * and told 1Sa 25:12
him that David had * to the 1Sa 26:1
Then David went away and Saul * 1Sa 26:25
water, and his strength soon *. 1Sa 30:11,12
SAUL WAS DEAD and David had * to 2Sa 1:1
who were with him * home too, and 2Sa 2:30
So he *. 2Sa 3:16
of David's troops * from a raid, 2Sa 3:22
well of Sirah and he * with them; 2Sa 3:26
But the Philistines * and again 2Sa 5:22
David * to bless his family. 2Sa 6:20
Afterwards Joab * to Jerusalem. 2Sa 10:14
Then she * home. 2Sa 11:4
Then Nathan * to his home. 2Sa 12:15
Then he * to the palace and ate. 2Sa 12:20
Then David and the army * to 2Sa 12:31
So David's friend Hushai * to the 2Sa 15:37
success and * to Jerusalem. 2Sa 17:20
* from chasing the army of Israel. 2Sa 18:16
and blessed Barzillai, he * home. 2Sa 19:39
they * to the king at Jerusalem. 2Sa 20:22
Then they all * with him to 1Ki 1:40
They have just *, and the whole 1Ki 1:44,45
So Benaiah * to the king for 1Ki 2:30
So Benaiah * to the Tabernacle 1Ki 2:34
gone to Gath and *, he sent for 1Ki 2:41
been a dream. He * to Jerusalem and 1Ki 3:15
Then she and her servants * to 1Ki 10:13
So when Jeroboam and the people * 1Ki 12:12
So Jeroboam's wife * to Tirzah; 1Ki 14:17
the city of Ramah and * to Tirzah. 1Ki 15:21
and the spirit of the child *, 1Ki 17:22
He did, but * to Elijah and told 1Ki 18:43
Elisha then * to his oxen, killed 1Ki 19:21
Soon Ben-hadad's messengers * 1Ki 20:5,6
So the messengers * to Ben-hadad. 1Ki 20:9
they * immediately to the king. 2Ki 1:4,5
"Why have you * so soon?" 2Ki 1:4,5
Elijah's cloak and * to the bank of 2Ki 2:13,14
was still at Jericho when they *. 2Ki 2:18
Carmel and finally * to Samaria. 2Ki 2:25
When she *, he talked to her as 2Ki 4:15,16
So Elisha * with her. 2Ki 4:30
There was no sign of life. He * 2Ki 4:31
Elisha now * to Gilgal, but there 2Ki 4:38
The scouts * and told the king, 2Ki 7:15
After the famine ended, she * to 2Ki 8:3
But he had * to Jezreel to 2Ki 9:15
When they * and told him, he 2Ki 9:36
Then he * to Samaria. 2Ki 14:14
His body was * on horses, and he 2Ki 14:20
so he turned around and * home. 2Ki 15:19,20
So one of them * to Bethel and 2Ki 17:27,28
Then the Assyrian general * to 2Ki 19:8
Then King Sennacherib * to 2Ki 19:36
Finally he * to Jerusalem. 2Ki 23:20
(The Egyptian Pharaoh never * 2Ki 24:7
in Moab before he * to Lehem). 1Ch 4:21-22
of Benjamin who * were these: 1Ch 9:7,8
A total of 956 Benjaminites *. 1Ch 9:9
The priests who * were: 1Ch 9:10,11
In all, 1,760 priests *. 1Ch 9:13
Among the Levites who * was 1Ch 9:14
Other Levites who * included: 1Ch 9:15,16
and the people * to their homes, 1Ch 16:43
* to bless his own household. 1Ch 16:43
Then Joab * to Jerusalem. 1Ch 19:15
Then David and all his army * to 1Ch 20:3
through Israel and * to Jerusalem. 1Ch 21:4
the Tabernacle, * down the hill, 2Ch 1:13
Then she and her retinue * to 2Ch 9:12
He now quickly *, and was present 2Ch 10:2,3
So when Jeroboam and the people * 2Ch 10:12
AS KING JEHOSHAPHAT of Judah * 2Ch 19:1
Then they * to Jerusalem, with 2Ch 20:27
and * to Jezreel to recover. 2Ch 22:6
When King Amaziah * from this 2Ch 25:14
Obed-edom, and * to Samaria. 2Ch 25:24
Then their escorts * to Samaria. 2Ch 28:15
tribes * again to their own homes. 2Ch 31:1
So Sennacherib * home in deep 2Ch 32:21
exiles who now * to Jerusalem and Ez 2:1
Here is a census of those who * Ez 2:2
concerning the Levites who *: Ez 2:40,41,42
Another group * to Jerusalem at Ez 2:59
family name)—also * to Jerusalem. Ez 2:61
So a total of 42,360 persons * to Ez 2:64,65
rest of the people * to the other Ez 2:70
everyone who had * to Judah came to Ez 3:1
all those who had *, and they were Ez 3:8
the exiles had * and were Ez 4:1
the matter and * his decision. Ez 5:5
say King Cyrus * the gold and Ez 5:14
of the sin of the * exiles. Ez 10:6
"—the Jews who * to Jerusalem Neh 1:2
Now we all * to our work on the Neh 4:15
brothers who have * from exile as Neh 5:8
of those who had * to Judah before, Neh 7:5
of the Jews who * to Judah after Neh 7:6
"The others who * at that time Neh 7:7
officials who * to Judah: Neh 7:57,58,59
Another group * to Jerusalem at Neh 7:61
who * to Judah at that time; Neh 7:66
of the people now * home to their Neh 7:73
the people * for another Neh 9:1
Yet whenever your people * to you Neh 9:28
time, for I had * to Babylon in the Neh 13:6
services had * to their farms. Neh 13:10
the next morning * to the second Est 2:12,13,14
So Hathach * to Esther with Est 4:9
Afterwards Mordecai * to his job, Est 6:12
the king * from the palace garden. Est 7:8
Then the water * and covered the Ps 106:11
as their friends * from the Ecc 8:9,10
long ago when they * from Egypt. Is 11:16
* to his own country, to Nineveh. Is 37:37
faithless one "*" to me, but her Jer 3:10
They have * to the sins of their Jer 11:10
As Jeremiah * from Topheth where Jer 19:14
the Temple will be * from Babylon. Jer 27:16
became bold and * to their sins. Jer 34:11f
Jeremiah not be * to the dungeon, Jer 37:21
pulled him out and * him to the Jer 38:13
So Jeremiah * to Gedaliah and Jer 40:6
then to the Jews who have *? Jer 40:15
all those who had * from the nearby Jer 43:5
who have * from all the nations—and Eze 38:12
When he * to Babylon, he took Dan 1:1
and my sanity *, and I praised and Dan 4:34
When my mind * to me, so did my Dan 4:36
Then the king * to his palace and Dan 6:18
you captured the survivors and * Ob 1:14
the exiles who had * from Babylon Hag 1:1f
* to Jerusalem filled with mercy; Zec 1:16
but he * and said, "Look up! Zec 5:5
But when they * to their own Mt 2:12
So he * immediately to Israel Mt 2:21
arrested, he left Judea and * home Mt 4:12,13
illustrations, he * to his home Mt 13:53,54
Jesus now * to the Sea of Mt 15:29
Then he * to Bethany, where he Mt 21:17
When he had * to the Temple and Mt 21:23
the Messiah has * and is out in the Mt 24:26
"Later, when the other five *, Mt 25:11
time their master * from his trip Mt 25:19
Then he * to the three disciples Mt 26:40
He * to them again and found them Mt 26:43
SEVERAL DAYS LATER he * to Mk 2:1
When he * to the house where he Mk 3:20
of the country and * with his Mk 6:1
prophet, now * to life again; Mk 6:15
The apostles now * to Jesus from Mk 6:30
He never * until after his death Mk 10:1f
Then he * to the three disciples Mk 14:37
Again he * to them and found Mk 14:40
The third time when he * to them Mk 14:41
his Temple duties and then * home. Lk 1:23
army of angels had * again to Lk 2:15
* home to Nazareth in Galilee. Lk 2:39
Then he * to Nazareth with them Lk 2:51
Then Jesus * to Galilee, full of Lk 4:14
Then he * to Capernaum, a city in Lk 4:31
her temperature * to normal and she Lk 4:39
And when the captain's friends * Lk 7:10
So he * to the boat and left, Lk 8:37
And at that moment her life * Lk 8:55
After the apostles * to Jesus and Lk 9:10
When the seventy disciples *, Lk 10:17
speak, his voice * to him. Lk 11:14
"The servant * and reported to Lk 14:21
"So he * home to his father. Lk 15:20
mine was dead and has * to life. Lk 15:24
when he * home, he heard dance Lk 15:25
you that I have * and that I am in Lk 17:23
not the Pharisee, * home forgiven! Lk 18:14
And each evening he * to spend Lk 21:37,38
At last he stood up again and * Lk 22:45
Literally, "* from the tomb." Lk 24:9f
And they worshiped him, and * to Lk 24:52
and * to the province of Galilee. Jn 4:3
AFTERWARDS JESUS * to Jerusalem Jn 5:1
not yet * to his glory in heaven. Jn 7:39
sent to arrest him * to the chief Jn 7:45
JESUS * TO the Mount of Olives, Jn 8:1
Then she left him and * to Mary Jn 11:28
but after Jesus * to his glory in Jn 12:16
that time Mary had * to the tomb Jn 20:11
and how he * to heaven after giving Act 1:1
there, so they * to the Council and Act 5:22
Peter and John * to Jerusalem, Act 8:25
their business, * to Antioch, Act 12:25
them and * to Jerusalem. Act 13:13
disciples, they * again to Lystra, Act 14:21
Finally they * by ship to Act 14:26
and then Judas and Silas * to Act 15:33
Paul and Silas then * to the Act 16:40
Athens, and then * to Beroea with a Act 17:15
At the end of the week when we * Act 21:5
Then we went aboard and they * Act 21:6
They * to the armory the next Act 23:32
"After several years away, I * Act 24:17
Eight or ten days later he * to Act 25:6
afterwards when I *, so that I 2Co 1:15,16
that when Christ * triumphantly to Eph 4:8
Notice that it says he * to Eph 4:9
And now Timothy has just * and 1Th 3:6
but now you have * to your 1Pe 2:25

RETURNING
he could weep. *, he selected Gen 42:24
food, as we were * home, we Gen 43:21
adding twenty percent and * it to Num 5:7
Israeli army was * home after David 1Sa 18:6
away and Jonathan * to the city. 1Sa 20:42
clothing before * to their homes. 1Sa 27:9
As the priests are * from the 1Ki 8:10
house a few times; * upstairs, he 2Ki 4:35
had met them but was not *. 2Ki 9:18
"He isn't * either!" 2Ki 9:20
Another of the * priests was 1Ch 9:12
before finally * to Jerusalem. 2Ch 14:15
Asa as he was * from the battle. 2Ch 15:2
he went out to meet the * army. 2Ch 28:9
his plea by * him to Jerusalem and 2Ch 33:13
of Israel before * to Jerusalem. 2Ch 34:7
leader of the exiles * to Judah. Ez 1:8
concerning the * priests: Ez 2:36-39
talk them out of * to Jerusalem. Neh 4:12
concerning the * priests: Neh 7:39-42
the second time, * them to the land Is 11:11
Weep, O ships of Tyre, * home from Is 23:1
says: Only in * to me and waiting Is 30:15
some of those * to be my priests Is 66:21
by * again to their own land. Jer 44:14
in * to Israel from Babylon. Eze 20:35,36f
again, and I felt my strength *. Dan 10:18
of my * people to pure Hebrew Zep 3:9
In the morning, as he was * to Mt 21:18
and * on the clouds of heaven." Mt 26:64
hand of God, and * to earth in the Mk 14:62
on earth before * to his Father. Jn 13:1
each one * to his own home, leaving Jn 16:32
and was now * in his chariot, Act 8:28
to go across to Greece before * Act 19:21
who were * to their homes in Act 20:4
and he himself was * there soon, Act 25:4
along with the others who are *. 1Co 16:11
When Abraham was * home after Heb 7:1

RETURNS
But the good man * what he owes Ps 37:21
hard work * many blessings to him. Pro 12:14
As a dog * to his vomit, so a Pro 26:11
and the water * again to the Ecc 1:3-7
and the dust * to the earth as Ecc 12:7
the spirit * to God who gave it. Ecc 12:7
pledge and * what he has stolen and Eze 33:15
The first day he * to work and Eze 44:27
then the land * to the prince. Eze 46:17
When he * again to Egypt he will Dan 11:8
So it * and finds the man's Mt 12:43,44,45
"When the owner *, what do you Mt 21:40
but finding none, it * to the Lk 11:24
If his master * and finds that he Lk 12:42,43,44
lost sinner who * to God than over Lk 15:7
and guilt on that day when he *. 1Co 1:8
before the Lord * as to whether 1Co 4:5
when our Lord Jesus Christ *. 1Co 5:5
on that day when Jesus Christ *. Php 1:6
you from now until our Lord *. Php 1:10
Then when Christ * how glad I will Php 2:16
Lord Jesus Christ * with all those 1Th 3:13
that when Jesus *, God will bring 1Th 4:14
when the Lord * will not rise to 1Th 4:15
destroy by his presence when he *. 2Th 2:8
now until our Lord Jesus Christ *. 1Ti 6:14

(RETURNS Con't)
to you when Jesus Christ *. 1Pe 1:13
for your good works when Christ *. 1Pe 2:12
his glory and his honor when he *. 1Pe 5:1
be pleased with you when he *. 2Pe 3:14

REU
years old when his son * was born. Gen 11:18,19
* was thirty-two years old when Gen 11:20,21
The son of Peleg was *, 1Ch 1:24-27
The son of * was Serug, 1Ch 1:24-27
Serug's father was *; Lk 3:23-38

REU'S
Serug's father was Reu;* father Lk 3:23-38

REUBEN
and had a son, * (meaning "God has Gen 29:32
harvest, * found some mandrakes Gen 30:14
It was while he was there that * Gen 35:22
*, Jacob's oldest child, Simeon, Gen 35:23
But * hoped to spare Joseph's Gen 37:21,22
touching him!" (* was planning to Gen 37:21,22
Some time later, * (who was away Gen 37:29
tell you not to do it?" * asked. Gen 42:22
Then * said to his father, "Kill Gen 42:37
*, his oldest son; Gen 46:8-14
from me just as * and Simeon will. Gen 48:5
"*, you are my oldest son, the Gen 49:3
their families:*, Simeon, Ex 1:1
The sons of *, Israel's oldest Ex 6:14
* -Elizur (son of Num 1:2-15
* (the oldest son of Num 1:20-46
Tribe: * Elizur (son of Num 2:3-31
Next to * Num 2:3-31
So the total of the * side of the Num 2:3-31
Shedeur, chief of the tribe of *; Num 7:30-35
of the camp of *, with Elizur the Num 10:18
of Zaccur, from the tribe of *; Num 13:3-15
from the tribe of *, to incite a Num 16:1
The tribe of *: 43,730. Num 26:5-11
(* was Israel's eldest son. Num 26:5-11
the tribes of * and Gad (who had Num 32:1
the people of Gad and * replied. Num 32:25
tribes of Gad and * who are Num 32:29
The tribes of Gad and * said Num 32:31
the tribes of Gad, *, and the Num 32:33
The children of * built the Num 32:37,38
for the tribes of * and Gad and Num 34:14,15
to the tribes of *, Gad, and the Deu 3:12
To the tribes of * and Gad I gave Deu 3:12
The tribes of * and Gad received Deu 3:16
the tribes of * and Gad and the Deu 3:18
wilderness, for the tribe of *; Deu 4:43
of *) sinned, and the earth Deu 11:6
and the tribes of *, Gad, Asher, Deu 27:13
to the tribes of * and Gad and to Deu 29:8
Let * live forever Deu 33:6
of the tribes of *, Gad, and the Jos 1:12,13
The troops of *, Gad, and the Jos 4:12,13
* and the half-tribe of Manasseh. Jos 12:6
and the tribes of * and Gad, had Jos 13:8
The Land Given to the Tribe of *: Jos 13:15
to the tribe of *: Their land Jos 13:15
The land of * also included the Jos 13:21
boundary of the tribe of *. Jos 13:23
to the stone of Bohan (son of *). Jos 15:6
tribes of Gad and * and the Jos 18:7
(who was a son of *), where it Jos 18:17
of the land of the tribe of *; Jos 20:8
the tribes of *, Gad, and Zebulun. Jos 21:7
* gave them: Jos 21:36,37
from the tribes of *, Gad, and the Jos 22:1
So the troops of *, Gad, and the Jos 22:9
tribes of *, Gad, and Manasseh. Jos 22:13
to the tribes of *, Gad, and the Jos 22:15
of the people of *, Gad, and the Jos 22:21
from the tribes of *, Gad, and Jos 22:30
no more of war against * and Gad. Jos 22:33
The people of * and Gad named Jos 22:34
(But the tribe of * didn't go. Ju 5:15
Yes, the tribe of * has an uneasy Ju 5:16
well as all of Gilead, Gad, and *; 2Ki 10:32,33
*, Simeon, Levi, Judah, Issachar, 1Ch 2:1
THE OLDEST SON of Israel was *, 1Ch 5:1
doesn't name * as the oldest son. 1Ch 5:1
The sons of *, Israel's son, 1Ch 5:3
He was a prince of the tribe of * 1Ch 5:6
Saul, the men of * defeated the 1Ch 5:10
in the army of *, Gad, and the 1Ch 5:18
deport the men of *, Gad, and the 1Ch 5:26
the tribes of *, Gad, and Zebulun. 1Ch 6:63
the tribe of * gave them Bezer (a 1Ch 6:78,79
from the tribe of *—he was among 1Ch 11:26-47
leaders of the tribe of *; 1Ch 11:26-47
the tribes of * and Gad and the 1Ch 12:24-37
of the tribes of *, Gad, and the 1Ch 26:31,32
Over *, Eliezer (son of Zichri); 1Ch 27:16-22
Ephraim, and then * and then Judah, Eze 48:5,6,7
*, one for Judah and one for Levi. Eze 48:30,31
* 12,000 Rev 7:4-8

REUBEN'S
* sons: Hanoch, Pallu, Hezron, and Gen 46:8-14
clans, named after * sons: Num 26:5-11

REUBENITES
These * 1Ch 5:7,8
So the * lived in the territory 1Ch 5:22

REUEL
and Basemath had a son named *. Gen 36:4
Born to her son * were:Nahath, Gen 36:13,14
the descendants of *, born to Esau Gen 36:17
to their father * he asked, "How Ex 2:18
with them, and * gave him one of Ex 2:21
in these chapters, Jethro and *. Ex 3:1f
(son of *) Num 2:3-31
Hobab (son of *, the Midianite), Num 10:29
daughter of * (Exodus 2:21); Num 12:1f
Eliphaz, *, Jeush, Jalam, and 1Ch 1:35
The sons of *: 1Ch 1:37
the son of *, the son of Ibnijah). 1Ch 9:7,8

REUEL'S
decided to accept * invitation to Ex 2:21

REUMAH
*:Tebah, Gaham,Tahash, Maacah. Gen 22:24

REUNION
Bethlehem for an annual family *. 1Sa 20:6

REUNITE
in an attempt to * the kingdom. 2Ch 11:1

REVEAL
not * my name, Jehovah, to them. Ex 6:2,3
The heavens will * his sins, and Job 20:27
"I will * the everlasting Ps 2:7
I will * these truths to you so Ps 78:4
names that * the plans of the Lord Is 8:18
he will * justice to the nations Is 42:1
Therefore I will * my name to my Is 52:6
To whom will God * his saving Is 53:1
and I will * my power over you. Eze 28:22
whom the Son chooses to * him." Lk 10:22
and I will too, and I will * Jn 14:21
are you going to * yourself only to Jn 14:22
I will only * myself to those who Jn 14:23
the time has come. * the glory of Jn 17:1
And now, Father, * my glory as I Jn 17:5
and grace— to * his Son within me Gal 1:16
day will * the terrible truth. 1Ti 5:24
God permitted him to * these Rev 1:1

REVEALED
"Since God has * the meaning of Gen 41:39
your God has not * to us, but these Deu 29:29
words which he has * are for us and Deu 29:29
For you have * to me, O Lord of 2Sa 7:27
Ahab, the Lord * this prophecy to 2Ki 9:25
to you, for you have * this to me. 1Ch 17:25
the gates of Death been * to you? Job 38:17,18
this victory and * it to every Ps 98:2,3
unfairly. He * his will and nature Ps 103:7
The Lord of Hosts has * to me Is 22:14
I chose Israel and * myself to her Eze 20:5,6
laws he had * to them by his Spirit Zec 7:12
the truth will be *: their secret Mt 10:26
has personally * this to you—this Mt 16:17
For the Holy Spirit had * to him Lk 2:26
of many hearts shall be *." Lk 2:34,35
Then Satan took him up and * to Lk 4:5
Or, "the hour I am *." Lk 17:30f
has the arm of the Lord been *?" Jn 12:38f
And I have * you to them, and Jn 17:26
they went, Joseph * his identity to Act 7:13
of God is * from faith to faith." Rom 1:17f
what God has * to me, and tell you 1Co 14:6
but now he has * it by the Holy Eph 3:5
Christ will be * from heaven by the 1Ti 6:15
good time he has * this Good News Tit 1:3
Their words are not to be *." Rev 10:4

REVEALER
of kings, the * of mysteries, Dan 2:47

REVEALING
and for * it to little children. Mt 11:25
wise and for * them to those who Lk 10:21
and will keep on * you so that the Jn 17:26
against God, * all they have said Jud 1:15
method of God's * himself to man. Rev 19:13f

REVEALS
examination * that the spot seems Lev 13:31
intelligence. He * profound Dan 2:22
God in heaven who * secrets, and he Dan 2:28
He who * secrets was speaking to Dan 2:29
by those to whom the Son * him. Mt 11:27
A good man's speech * the rich Mt 12:35
with venom, and his speech * it. Mt 12:35
That is what the Lord says, who * Act 15:18
and the law, which * our sins, 1Co 15:55,56
who faithfully * all truth to us. Rev 1:5

REVELATION
See also * 20:7-9. Eze 38:2,3f
see verse 27 and the *. Dan 9:25f
presume to present any fresh *. Mt 7:29f
Literally, "waiting for the * of Rom 8:19f
THE * Rev 1:24,25
Literally, "the * of (concerning, Rev 1:1f
also see * 2:7. Rev 1:4f
(See * 2:14 and Numbers 31:15, 16. Rev 2:6f
* 9:11. Rev 11:7f
Implied; * 20:3. Rev 20:10f

REVELATIONS
a man who had special * from God. 2Ch 26
They prophesy of visions and * Jer 14:
I've had, and * from the Lord. 2Co 12

REVELRY
seven days of *, held in the Est 1:
suddenly your * will end. Amo 6

REVENGE
anyone taking * against me for Gen 4:2
I will * the breaking of my Lev 26:2
man, who may try to kill him in *. Jos 20:
to kill him in *, the innocent Jos 20:
a trial, and not be killed in *. Jos 20:
I have full * on my enemies." 1Sa 14:24,2
and killed him in * for the death 2Sa 3:2
Today the Lord has given you * 2Sa 4:
to see Israelites executed in *." 2Sa 21:
May the Lord take * on you, but 1Ki 2:4
nor asked for *)— or if any of my Job 31:3
then we will get our * on him." Jer 20:1
Judah out of * and long-standing Eze 25:1
Are you trying to take * on me, Joe 3:
Herodias wanted John killed in * Mk 6:1

REVERE
and ordinary. * me and hallow me, Lev 22:32,3
and learn how to * the Lord your Deu 31:1
"So * Jehovah and serve him in Jos 24:1
May the poor and needy * you Ps 72:
are for me, for I trust and * you. Ps 119:38

REVERED
And because the midwives * God, Ex 1:2
of Egypt and was * by Pharaoh's Ex 11:3
were afraid and * the Lord, and Ex 14:31
Israel, and they * him as much as Jos 4:14
* God more than most people do. Neh 7:2
Who is as * as he by those Ps 89:7
mightily * among the Gentiles." Mal 1:14

REVERENCE
prepared for you. * him and obey Ex 23:21
"Keep my Sabbath laws and * my Lev 19:30
laws of rest, and * my Tabernacle, Lev 26:2
learn always to * me, and so that Deu 4:10
your grandsons to * the Lord your Deu 6:2
these laws and to * him so that he Deu 6:24
thus refusing * to the glorious and Deu 28:58,59
so that you will * the Lord your Deu 31:12
Literally, "did * to the king." 1Ki 1:31f
always learn to * you as they 1Ki 8:40
Then they will * you forever, 2Ch 6:31
your fame and will * you, just as 2Ch 6:33
before him in deep * whenever he Est 3:2
Have you no fear of God? No * Job 15:4,5
must fear and * his name. Ps 22:23
presence of all who * your name. Ps 22:25
is reserved for those who * him. Ps 25:14
for those who trust and * you. Ps 31:19
guards and rescues all who * him. Ps 34:7
If you belong to the Lord, * Ps 34:9
those of us who * the Lord will Ps 34:10
* him, for he is your lord. Ps 45:10,11
reserve for those who * your name. Ps 61:5
Come and hear, all of you who * Ps 66:16
is near to those who * him; Ps 85:9
my being unite in * to your name. Ps 86:11
Let them * your great and holy Ps 99:3
sympathetic to those who * him. Ps 103:13
everlasting, to those who * him; Ps 103:17,18
The only way to begin is by * for Ps 111:10
both great and small, who * him. Ps 115:13
BLESSINGS ON ALL who * and trust Ps 128:1
to those who * and trust him. Ps 128:4
all of you who trust and * him. Ps 135:20
of those who * and trust him; Ps 145:19
But his joy is in those who * Ps 147:11
The first step is to trust and * Pro 1:7,8,9
did not choose to * and trust the Pro 1:29
the importance of * for the Lord Pro 2:3,4,5
Instead, trust and * the Lord, Pro 3:7,8
For the * and fear of God are Pro 9:10
* for God adds hours to each day; Pro 10:27
* for God gives a man deep Pro 14:26
* for the Lord is a fountain of Pro 14:27
Better a little with * for God, Pro 15:16
Humility and * for the Lord will Pro 15:33
evil is avoided by * for God. Pro 16:6
* for God gives life, happiness, Pro 19:23
but continue to * the Lord all the Pro 23:17,18
and knowledge and * for God. Is 33:6
Then at last they will * and Is 59:19
to generation, to all who * him. Lk 1:50
others here who * God, [let me Act 13:16
Gentiles here who * God—this Act 13:26
God with deep *, shrinking back Php 2:12

REVERENCED
He should be * and feared, for Ps 76:11

REVERENCES
* God shall be greatly praised. Pro 31:30

REVERENT
don't forget to be * to him and to Deu 6:13
Serve the Lord with * fear; Ps 2:11
He was a godly man, deeply *, as Act 10:2

REVERENT Con't)
so act in * fear of him from now 1Pe 1:17
REVERES
Blessed is the man who * God, but Pro 28:14
REVERSE
And I cannot * it! Num 23:18-24
REVERSED
ring, so that it can never be *. Est 8:8
could not be *, even by the king. Est 8:8f
REVERSING
send out a decree * Haman's order Est 8:5
REVILE
of this, Job did not sin or * God. Job 1:22
evil lusts; they * God and Ps 10:3
Whom did you *? Is 37:23
REVILED
hatred—you will be cursed and *. Jer 42:18
"When you are * and persecuted Mt 5:11
REVILES
"Anyone who * or curses his Ex 21:17
anyone who * his parents must Mt 15:4
REVIVAL
Note: The Great * under King Zep 1:1f
REVIVE
you again. * us to trust in you. Ps 80:18
Oh, * us! Ps 85:6
in the dust. * me by your Word. Ps 119:25
plan than yours. * my heart Ps 119:37
how they refresh and * me! Ps 119:49,50
the Lord will * Tyre, but she will Is 23:17
glory of Israel to *, and then at Eze 29:21
Never again will you *. Eze 35:9
REVIVED
Joseph had sent him, his spirit *. Gen 45:27
Samson's spirit was * as he drank. Ju 15:19
dead man * and jumped to his feet! 2Ki 13:20,21
The kingdom of Babylonia, being * Jer 5:15f
Usually believed to be a * Roman Dan 7:23f
His visits * me like a breath of 2Ti 1:16
REVIVING
ago destroyed, * them though they Is 61:4
REVOKED
His orders will never be *. Ps 148:6
and Persians' that cannot be *." Dan 6:8
that cannot be altered or *." Dan 6:12
REVOLT
in Korah's * against the Lord —it Num 27:3,4
Why did you encourage him to * 1Sa 22:13
joined Adonijah's *, though not 1Ki 2:28
Arieh were also slain in the *). 2Ki 15:25
time planning a * in the east Is 39:1f
would not be strong again and *. Eze 17:14
a * against the Roman government. Lk 23:14
REVOLTED
yet you have * against him and Ju 9:18
citizens of Shechem, and they *. Ju 9:22,23
* and joined with the Israelis. 1Sa 14:21
who has * against King David. 2Sa 20:21
the people in Edom * from Judah and 2Ki 8:20
At that time the king of Edom *, 2Ch 21:8
Nevertheless Edom *." 2Ch 21:9f
Libnah * too, because Jehoram had 2Ch 21:10
generals who had * and who was then Jer 44:30f
my treaty and * against my laws. Hos 8:1
of mine who *—bring them in and Lk 19:27
REVOLTING
That is why you are * against Num 16:11,12
neighbors, youths * against Is 3:5
my sickness was * to you, you Gal 4:14
REVOLVES
the whole earth * around them!' Eze 38:12
REWARD
we took as our *, along with the Deu 2:35,36
And may the Lord * you for your Ru 1:8
about the huge * the king has 1Sa 17:25
May the Lord * you well for the 1Sa 24:19
The Lord will surely * you with 1Sa 25:28
The Lord gives his own * for 1Sa 26:23
all yours personally, as your *!" 1Sa 30:20
would * him for killing his rival. 2Sa 1:10f
you in return, and * you with many 2Sa 2:6
David, is this my *—to find fault 2Sa 3:8
and I'll give you a * because you 1Ki 13:7
Now see how they * us! 2Ch 20:11
"What * did we ever give Est 6:3
come, and you would * all I do. Job 14:15
he trusts in will be his only *. Job 15:31
He does not * the wicked with Job 36:6
they are his *. Ps 127:3
Their * shall be prosperity and Ps 128:2
That is God's * to those who Ps 128:4
Wisdom is its own *, and if Pro 9:12
men gone to their *, but the names Pro 10:7
the good man's * lasts forever. Pro 11:18
And he will * everyone according Pro 24:11,12
of himself, and God will * you. Pro 25:21,22
shall be given a worthwhile *. Pro 28:10
to do right will get a rich *. Pro 28:20
my only * for all my labors. Ecc 2:10
you is your best * down here for Ecc 9:9
Tell him, "What a * you are Is 3:10
God will * you for your kindness Is 16:4,5
This is the just * of those who Is 17:14
will tell you your *: In a short Is 32:9
See, his * is with him, to each Is 40:10
my captive people—and not for a *! Is 45:13
leave it all with God for my *." Is 49:4
I will faithfully * my people for Is 61:8
person his right *, according to Jer 17:10
of men, and you * everyone Jer 32:19
As a * for trusting me, I will Jer 39:18
you wherever you go, as your *. Jer 45:5
and punish or * each according to Eze 18:30
the land to them as their *. Dan 11:39
You have earned the full * of Hos 10:13
But the Lord God says, I will * Mic 2:3
for a tremendous * awaits you up Mt 5:12
the * from your Father in heaven. Mt 6:1
all the * they will ever get. Mt 6:2
who knows all secrets will * you. Mt 6:4
Truly, that is all the * they Mt 6:5
knows your secrets, will * you. Mt 6:6
Truly, that is the only * they Mt 6:16
And he will * you. Mt 6:18
given the same * a prophet gets. Mt 10:41
you will be given a * like theirs. Mt 10:41
this solemnly—he won't lose his *. Mk 9:41
and happy and promised him a *. Mk 14:11
For you will have a great * Lk 6:23
Then your * from heaven will be Lk 6:35
there will be a *—his master will Lk 12:42,43,44
godly, God will * you for inviting Lk 14:14
you, and as your *, you shall be Lk 19:17
to help them and promised him a *. Lk 22:5
and * the very angels in heaven? 1Co 6:3
Lord would give me a special *; 1Co 9:17
but we do it for a heavenly * 1Co 9:25
Salvation is not a * for the Eph 2:9
are my joy and my * for my work. Php 4:1
is the well-earned * you will have Php 4:17
joy and is our proud * and crown? 1Th 2:19
so that you will get your full *. Heb 6:11
Remember your *! Heb 10:35
great * that God would give him. Heb 11:26
he will get as his * the crown of Jas 1:12
And your further * for trusting 1Pe 1:9
envied, for God will * you for it. 1Pe 3:14
comes, your * will be a 1Pe 5:4
you will your full * from the Lord. 2Jn 1:8
the dead, and * your Rev 11:18
to enter into their full *. Rev 14:13
it is their just *." Rev 16:6
and my * is with me, to repay Rev 22:12
REWARDED
that is how I * him for his 'glad 2Sa 4:10
"I would have * you handsomely 2Sa 18:11
The Lord * me for my goodness, 2Sa 22:21
discouraged, for you will be *." 2Ch 15:7
His labors shall not be *; Job 20:18
The Lord * me for doing right Ps 18:20
know that good is *, and that there Ps 58:11
Even the godly shall be * here on Pro 11:31
anyone should be * who protects Pro 27:18
"for your work shall be *." Jer 31:16f
The righteous person will be * Eze 18:20
only twenty. I * all your labor Hag 2:16,17
child, you will surely be *." Mt 10:42
will be * for his own hard work. 1Co 3:8
will be well * both by respect from 1Ti 3:13
heaven, has been * with a far more Heb 8:6
REWARDING
be!—* your faith with his power. 2Th 1:11
REWARDS
and gives them eternal *. Ps 37:18
He is loving and kind and * each Ps 62:12
a God and that he * those who Heb 11:6
* that were prepared for us. Heb 11:40
REWRITE
He said he would * on the Deu 10:2
REZEPH
as Gozan, Haran, *, and Eden in the 2Ki 19:12
Gozan, Haran, or *, or the people Is 37:12
REZIN
Lord caused King * of Syria and 2Ki 15:37
Then King * of Syria and King 2Ki 16:5
However, at that time King * of 2Ki 16:6
and King * of Syria was killed. 2Ki 16:9
Gahar, Re-aiah, *, Nekoda, Gazzam, Ez 2:43-54
Re-aiah, *, Nekoda, Neh 7:46-56
attacked by King * of Syria and Is 7:1
those two has-beens, * and Pekah. Is 7:4
about asking King * and King Pekah Is 8:6
REZIN'S
alone, and King * kingdom will not Is 7:8
Or, "* enemies," in some ancient Is 9:11,12f
REZON
to power was *, one of the 1Ki 11:23
entire lifetime, * and Hadad were 1Ki 11:25
RHEGIUM
From there we circled around to *; Act 28:13
RHESA
Joanan's father was *; Lk 3:23-38
RHESA'S
Joanan's father was Rhesa;* father Lk 3:23-38
RHODA
a girl named * came to open it. Act 12:13
RHODES
"Merchants come to you from *, Eze 27:15
The next day we reached * and Act 21:1
RIB
it, and made the * into a woman, Gen 2:22
and run a * of gold around it. Ex 25:24
priest, as are the * piece and Num 6:20
RIBAI
Ittai (son of *) from Gibe-ah, of 2Sa 23:24-39
Ithai (son of *) a Benjaminite 1Ch 11:26-47
RIBALD
the subject of their * song! Job 30:9
all day long they sing their * Lam 3:14
RIBBON
* to the front of Aaron's turban. Ex 28:37,38
rings of the ephod, with a blue *. Ex 39:21
to win a blue * or a silver cup, 1Co 9:25
RIBBONED
You * the earth with rivers." Hab 3:8,9f
RIBBONS
of the ephod by means of blue *; Ex 28:28
Fifty blue * were looped along Ex 36:11,12
and blue, fastened with purple * Est 1:6
Though my back is cut to * with Ps 129:3,4
RIBLAH
on to * at the east side of Ain. Num 34:10,11
Pharaoh-Neco jailed him at * in 2Ki 23:33
He was taken to *, where he was 2Ki 25:6
king of Babylon at *, where they 2Ki 25:20
Babylon who was at *, in the land Jer 39:5
in the city of * in the kingdom of Jer 52:9
king of Babylon at *, where the Jer 52:26
in the south to * in the north. Eze 6:14
RIBS
took one of his * and closed up the Gen 2:21
skinny and all their * stood out. Gen 41:3
brass. His * are like iron bars. Job 40:18
It held three * between its Dan 7:5
RICH
* in livestock, silver, and gold. Gen 13:1
is * because of what I gave him!' Gen 14:23
poured out * blessings upon Isaac. Gen 25:11
too * and powerful for us." Gen 26:16
the meat, with its * aroma, and Gen 27:17
business among us and become *!" Gen 34:9,10
"Asher shall produce * foods, Gen 49:20
offering. The * shall not give Ex 30:15
and * in steadfast love and truth. Ex 34:5,6
whether a person is poor or *; Lev 19:15
among you becomes *, and an Lev 25:47
whether the land is * or poor, Num 13:20
favor a man because he is *; Deu 1:17
power to become *, and he does it Deu 8:18
a * man, and never accept bribes. Deu 16:19
neither shall he be excessively *. Deu 17:17
Let all Israel, * and poor, Ju 5:10
And sit on * carpets, Ju 5:10
And others to be *. 1Sa 2:7
KISH WAS A *, influential man from 1Sa 9:1
city, one very *, owning many 2Sa 12:1
arrived at the home of the * man. 2Sa 12:4
to David, "You are that * man! 2Sa 12:7
I receive God's * blessings, and 1Ki 2:45
world will be as * and famous as 1Ki 3:13
the money from the *, assessing 2Ki 15:19,20
BUT *, POPULAR King Jehoshaphat of 2Ch 18:1
some of the * Jews who were Neh 5:1
and homes to these * men; Neh 5:2,3,4
these * government officials. Neh 5:7
And the * men did as they had Neh 5:13
he does—look how * he is! Job 1:10
castles are full of * treasures. Job 3:14,15
Both * and poor alike are there, Job 3:19
Meanwhile, the * mock those in Job 12:5
"This wicked man is fat and *, Job 15:27,28
But he will not continue to be * Job 15:29
will tell me of * and wicked men Job 21:28
God preserves the * by his power, Job 24:22,23
"He goes to bed *, but wakes up Job 27:19
to the * than to the poor. Job 34:19
groan beneath the power of the *; Job 35:9,10
are * and prosperous. Ps 17:13,14
HIGH and low, * and poor, all Ps 49:1
boast about how * they are, yet Ps 49:6
of them, though * as kings, can Ps 49:7
* man! Ps 49:10
* and build their lovely homes. Ps 49:16
added years of life, as * and Ps 61:6
Don't become * by extortion and Ps 62:10,11
And don't let the * men be proud. Ps 62:10,11
sends them * harvests of grain. Ps 65:9
he drinks, or the * food he eats. Ps 109:18
the scoffing of the * and proud. Ps 123:3,4
than the man who is immensely *! Pro 3:13,14,15
hard workers get *. Pro 10:4
The * man's wealth is his only Pro 10:15
The evil man gets * for the Pro 11:18

(RICH Con't)
- Yes, the liberal man shall be *! — Pro 11:24,25
- Some * people are poor, and some — Pro 13:7
- while the * have many "friends." — Pro 14:20
- poor and humble than proud and *. — Pro 16:19
- The * man thinks of his wealth as — Pro 18:11
- The poor man pleads and the * man — Pro 18:23
- BETTER BE POOR and honest than * — Pro 19:1
- The * and the poor are alike — Pro 22:2
- Just as the * rule the poor, so — Pro 22:7
- the * shall end in poverty. — Pro 22:16
- WHEN DINING WITH a * man, — Pro 23:1
- weary yourself trying to get *. — Pro 23:4,5
- the poor, and let the * go free. — Pro 24:23
- and honest than * and a cheater. — Pro 28:6
- * men are conceited, but their — Pro 28:11
- to do right will get a * reward. — Pro 28:20
- But the man who wants to get * — Pro 28:20
- Giving preferred treatment to * — Pro 28:21
- Trying to get * quick is evil and — Pro 28:22
- * and poor are alike in this: — Pro 29:13
- For if I grow *, I may become — Pro 30:9
- oppressed by the *, with — Ecc 5:8
- * must worry and suffer insomnia. — Ecc 5:12
- To be wise is as good as being *; — Ecc 7:11
- authority, and * men not given — Ecc 10:6
- nor the * man, either; — Ecc 10:20
- only obey, then I will make you *! — Is 1:19
- the palaces of the * and mighty. — Is 13:2
- man and the haughtiness of the *. — Is 13:11
- surrounded by her * valley—Samaria, — Is 28:1
- and the soil made * with fat. — Is 34:7
- a criminal in a * man's grave; — Is 53:9
- Now they are great and *, and — Jer 5:27
- nor the * man in his riches. — Jer 9:23
- profits multiply, and they are *. — Jer 12:2
- O men of Sibmah, * in vineyards, — Jer 48:32
- of these * and wicked men of pride — Eze 7:10,11
- and the * brought very low. — Eze 21:26
- the * variety of goods you make. — Eze 27:18
- made you very * and very proud. — Eze 28:5
- For the people are * with cattle — Eze 38:12
- who ate the king's * food, and — Dan 1:13
- without the * foods and wines! — Dan 1:16
- and wealth of the * and scatter it — Dan 11:24
- no longer give her * harvests of — Hos 1:9
- Ephraim boasts, "I am so *! — Hos 12:8
- You made yourselves * at his — Ob 1:13
- no end of getting * by cheating? — Mic 6:10
- Your * men are wealthy through — Mic 6:12
- demand bribes. The * man pays them — Mic 7:3
- gods who make us *," they'll say. — Hab 1:16
- "Woe to you for getting * by — Hab 2:9
- and become so * that silver is like — Zec 9:3
- the * city of the Philistines. — Zec 9:6
- 'Thank God, now I am *!' — Zec 11:5
- the * treasures within him. — Mt 12:35
- away sadly, for he was very *. — Mt 19:22
- impossible for a * man to get into — Mt 19:23
- needle than for a * man to enter — Mt 19:24
- When evening came, a * man from — Mt 27:57
- sadly away, for he was very *. — Mk 10:22
- impossible for the * to get into — Mk 10:23
- needle than for a * man to enter — Mk 10:25
- can be saved, if not a * man?" — Mk 10:26
- the robes of the * and scholarly, — Mk 12:38
- Some who were * put in large — Mk 12:41
- than all those * men put together! — Mk 12:43,44
- sent the * away with empty hands. — Lk 1:53
- oh, the sorrows that await the *. — Lk 6:24
- are not related to how * we are." — Lk 12:15
- illustration: "A * man had a — Lk 12:16
- * on earth but not in heaven." — Lk 12:21
- relatives, and * neighbors! — Lk 14:12
- his disciples: "A * man hired an — Lk 16:1
- "The * man had to admire the — Lk 16:8
- Or, "Do you think the * man — Lk 16:8f
- "There was a certain * man," — Lk 16:19
- scraps from the * man's table, the — Lk 16:21
- The * man also died and was — Lk 16:22
- "Then the * man said, 'O Father — Lk 16:27
- "The * man replied, 'No, Father — Lk 16:30
- sadly away, for he was very *. — Lk 18:23
- the * to enter the Kingdom of God! — Lk 18:24
- needle than for a * man to enter — Lk 18:25
- of course, a very * man), tried to — Lk 19:1
- was watching the * tossing their — Lk 21:1
- benefited from the * blessings he — Jn 1:16
- Now if the whole world became * — Rom 11:12
- sharing in God's * nourishment of — Rom 11:17
- contented, * kings on your thrones, — 1Co 4:8
- We are poor, but we give * — 2Co 6:10
- he was so very *, yet to help you — 2Co 8:9
- by being poor he could make you *. — 2Co 8:9
- God has been made * because we who — Eph 1:18
- But God is so * in mercy; — Eph 2:4
- of how very, very * his kindness — Eph 2:7
- out of his * storehouse of gifts. — Eph 4:7
- you will have the * experience of — Col 2:2
- your sights on the * treasures and — Col 3:1
- of heart be your * gifts from God — 1Th 1:1
- And may * blessings from our — 1Th 5:28
- Christ give you * blessings and — 2Th 1:2
- Do you want to be truly *? — 1Ti 6:6
- But people who long to be * soon — 1Ti 6:9
- Tell those who are * not to be — 1Ti 6:17
- They should be * in good works — 1Ti 6:18
- But a * man should be glad that — Jas 1:10,11
- So it is with * men. — Jas 1:10,11
- show favoritism to * people and — Jas 2:1
- of fuss over the * man and give him — Jas 2:3
- poor people to be * in faith, and — Jas 2:5
- it is usually the * men who pick on — Jas 2:6
- favor the * and fawn over them; — Jas 2:9
- LOOK HERE, YOU * men, now is the — Jas 5:1
- us all the other * and wonderful — 2Pe 1:4
- "You say, 'I am *, with — Rev 3:17
- then will you truly be *. — Rev 3:18
- world leaders and * men, and — Rev 6:15
- and small, * and poor, slave and — Rev 13:16
- * from all her luxurious living." — Rev 18:3
- She made us all * from her great — Rev 18:19

RICHER
- wealth, and became * and richer. — Gen 26:13
- wealth, and became richer and *. — Gen 26:13
- you shall become * and richer while — Deu 28:43
- become richer and * while you — Deu 28:43
- So King Solomon was * and wiser — 1Ki 10:23
- So King Solomon was * and wiser — 2Ch 9:22
- to give away and become *! — Pro 11:24,25
- far * than the others. — Dan 11:2
- heathen gods; the * the harvests I — Hos 10:1

RICHES
- disappeared. The * God has given — Gen 31:16
- Lo, they taste the * of the sea — Deu 33:19
- for a long life or * for yourself, — 1Ki 3:11
- you didn't ask for—* and honor! — 1Ki 3:13
- of everything. * and honor come — 1Ch 29:12
- And I am also giving you such *, — 2Ch 1:12
- him no longer trust in foolish *, — Job 15:31
- He heaps up * for someone else to — Ps 39:5,6
- and all the time their * — Ps 73:12
- The earth is full of your *. — Ps 104:24
- rejoiced in them more than in *. — Ps 119:14
- Wisdom gives: * — Pro 3:16,17
- Unending *, honor, justice and — Pro 8:18
- wicked man's * continue forever. — Pro 10:3
- Your * won't help you on Judgment — Pro 11:4
- but injustice robs him of its *. — Pro 13:23
- his sons homes and *, but only the — Pro 19:14
- and luxury are not the way to *! — Pro 21:17
- a good name rather than great *; — Pro 22:1
- a man to *, honor and long life. — Pro 22:4
- Why waste your time? For * can — Pro 23:4,5
- Don't covet his *. — Pro 24:19,20
- * can disappear fast. — Pro 27:23,24
- give me neither poverty nor *! — Pro 30:8
- keep gaining more *, and to whom — Ecc 4:8
- Samaria and carry away their *." — Is 8:4
- their nests of * and gathered up — Is 10:14
- hidden in the darkness, secret *; — Is 45:3
- and shall glory in their *. — Is 61:6
- will send it; the * of the Gentiles — Is 66:12
- might, nor the rich man in his *. — Jer 9:23
- he will lose his * and at the end — Jer 17:11
- his belly with our * and cast us — Jer 51:34,35
- "They will plunder all your * — Eze 26:12
- come all kinds of * to your — Eze 27:12
- Everything is lost. Your * and — Eze 27:27
- rejoiced in the * you sent them. — Eze 27:33
- home with great *, first marching — Dan 11:28
- But * can't make up for sin. — Hos 12:8
- it is for those who trust in * — Mk 10:24
- "for those who trust in *." — Mk 10:24f
- out by worry and * and the — Lk 8:14
- you with the true * of heaven? — Lk 16:11
- for pouring the * of his glory — Rom 9:23,24
- gives his * to all those who ask — Rom 10:12
- his wisdom and knowledge and *! — Rom 11:33
- all the * inherited by God's sons; — Eph 3:6
- needs from his * in glory, because — Php 4:19
- for him, and the * and glory of his — Col 1:26,27
- be glad that his * mean nothing to — Jas 1:10,11
- poverty (but you have heavenly *! — Rev 2:9
- the power, and the *, and the — Rev 5:12

RICHEST
- He was, in fact, the * cattleman — Job 1:2,3
- The people of Tyre, the * people — Ps 45:12
- fragrant than all the * spices. — Sol 4:10
- lushest bounty and its * fruit. — Is 4:2,3,4
- He will enter the * areas of the — Dan 11:24
- result in God's * blessing upon us — 2Co 4:17

RICHLY
- Yes, I will bless her *, and make — Gen 17:16
- Growing * month by month, — Deu 33:14
- because he has blessed me so *. — Ps 13:6
- the punishment they so * deserve! — Ps 28:4
- May the Lord * bless both you and — Ps 115:14
- and she will * satisfy his needs. — Pro 31:11
- the penalty they so * deserved. — Rom 1:27
- God who always * gives us all we — 1Ti 6:17
- I beg my God to bless you *. — 2Ti 1:3
- May God bless you * and grant you — 1Pe 1

RICHNESS
- down upon us the * of his grace—for — Eph 1

RID
- * of that slave girl and her son. — Gen 21:1
- the Lord to get * of the flies. — Ex 8:3
- so anxious to get * of you that he — Ex 11:
- wilderness to get * of us, along — Num 20:
- * yourselves of this sin. — Jos 7:1
- to the Lord, get * of your foreign — 1Sa 7:
- I do for you, to * ourselves of — 2Sa 21:
- at home and get * of my leprosy." — 2Ki 5:1
- in that you got * of the — 2Ch 19:
- * ourselves of this disgrace!" — Neh 2:1
- hands to him, get * of your sins — Job 11:13,1
- and you will be * of tension, — Pro 22:1
- her sins, to * her of all her — Is 27:
- "Come, let's get * of Jeremiah. — Jer 18:1
- so I am determined to be * of it. — Jer 32:3
- "Then I said to them: Get * of — Eze 20:
- They didn't get * of their idols, — Eze 20:
- I will judge you there, and get * — Eze 20:35,3
- And I got * of their three evil — Zec 11:
- day I will get * of every vestige — Zec 13:
- anyone wants to be * of his wife, — Mt 5:31
- First get * of the board. — Mt 7:
- they wanted to get * of him, but — Mt 21:4
- planning how best to get * of him. — Mk 11:1
- me help you get * of that speck in — Lk 6:42
- First get * of the board, and — Lk 6:42
- to find some way to get * of him. — Lk 19:47
- anxious to get * of the sin that I — 2Co 7:11
- my best to get * of them all. — Gal 1:13
- more sacrifices to get * of them. — Heb 10:18
- there is no way to get * of it. — Heb 10:26
- So get * of all that is wrong in — Jas 1:21
- SO GET * of your feelings of — 1Pe 2:1
- in an effort to get * of her; — Rev 12:15

RIDDANCE
- He will make a speedy * of all — Zep 1:18

RIDDEN
- tied up that has never been *. — Mk 11:2

RIDDLE
- a *, they replied that they would. — Ju 14:12
- "If you solve my * during these — Ju 14:12
- This was his *: "Food came out — Ju 14:14
- you have told a * to my people and — Ju 14:16
- have found the answer to my *!" — Ju 14:18
- had told him the answer to his *. — Ju 14:19
- "Son of dust, give this * to the — Eze 17:2
- what this * of the eagles means? — Eze 17:12,13

RIDDLED
- a land * with famine and drought. — Hos 1:3

RIDDLES
- say of me, 'He only talks in *!' — Eze 20:49
- *, and solve knotty problems. — Dan 5:12
- Literally, "one who understands * — Dan 8:23f
- He seemed to be talking in *. — Lk 18:34
- disciples said, "and not in *. — Jn 16:29

RIDE
- Those who * on white donkeys — Ju 5:10
- for your people to * on, and the — 2Sa 16:2
- Solomon is to * on my personal — 1Ki 1:33
- men left who can * horses, we'll — 2Ki 18:23
- You sent troops to * across our — Ps 66:12
- Literally, "You caused men to * — Ps 66:12f
- If I * the morning winds to the — Ps 139:9
- you 2,000 horses for them to * on! — Is 36:8,9
- see to it that you * high, and get — Is 58:14
- O Babylon, they * against you — Jer 50:42
- for him to * on. — Mt 21:7
- across its back for him to * on. — Mk 11:7
- Give Paul a horse to * and get — Act 23:23,24

RIDER
- heels, so that the * falls off. — Gen 49:17
- He has thrown both horse and * — Ex 15:1
- The horse and * have been drowned — Ex 15:21
- "Send out a * and find out if he — 2Ki 9:17
- So the king sent out a second *. — 2Ki 9:19
- the swiftest horse with its *. — Job 39:18
- the horse and his *, the chariot — Jer 51:21
- bay and white, each with its *. — Zec 1:8
- Then the * on the red horse—he — Zec 1:10
- a white horse. Its * carried a bow, — Rev 6:2
- rode out. Its * was given a long — Rev 6:4
- horse, with its * holding a pair of — Rev 6:5

RIDER'S
- horse, and its * name was Death. — Rev 6:8
- horse whose * name was Hell. — Rev 6:8

RIDERS
- by swift carriers—* on camels, — Est 8:9,10
- God of Jacob, steeds and * fell. — Ps 76:6
- When he sees * in pairs on — Is 21:6,7
- * on asses, riders on camels." — Is 21:6,7f
- riders on asses, * on camels." — Is 21:6,7f
- represented by these paired *. — Is 21:6,7f
- Here come * in pairs!" — Is 21:8,9
- on horses, * and valiant warriors, — Eze 39:20
- Then the other * reported to the — Zec 1:11
- their * wore fiery-red — Rev 9:17,18
- of horses and *; — Rev 19:18

IDES
Any saddle he * on is defiled. Lev 15:9
song to him who * upon the clouds! Ps 68:4
Lord, to him who * upon the Ps 68:33
The clouds are his chariots. He * Ps 104:3
IDGE
he was camped at the top of a *; Gen 31:25
* along the molding, all around. Ex 25:25
IDICULING
began mocking and * Jesus; Lk 23:11
IDICULOUS
my priests, it is * to think that 1Sa 2:30
"That's *!" 1Sa 14:29
"Don't be *!" 1Sa 17:33
It is all utterly *. Ecc 2:20-23
Don't be *!" Is 36:20
IDING
As Balaam and two servants were * Num 22:22,23
As she was * down the trail on 1Sa 25:20
Gihon, * on King David's own mule. 1Ki 1:38
you and I were * along behind his 2Ki 9:25
I have even seen servants *, Ecc 10:7
against Egypt, * on a swift cloud; Is 19:1
us swift horses for * to battle." Is 30:16
kings and princes * in pomp and Jer 17:25
men of high rank, * their steeds. Eze 23:23
expensive saddlecloths for *. Eze 27:20
Yet he is lowly, * on a donkey's Zec 9:9
* humbly on a donkey's colt!" Mt 21:5
be a colt, not yet broken for *. Lk 19:30
the animal she is * represents. Rev 17:7
mouth of the one * the white horse, Rev 19:21
IFLED
taken, the houses *, the loot Zec 14:1
IFT
"We can't afford to let a * Gen 13:8
IGHT
There is no "*" way to Gen 1:2f
of * and wrong, good and bad. Gen 2:16,17
As for Ishmael, all *, I will Gen 17:20
"All *," they said, "do as you Gen 18:5
That wouldn't be *! Gen 18:25
"All *," the angel said, "I Gen 19:21
Abraham replied, "All *, I swear Gen 21:24
worship, and then come * back." Gen 22:5
"All *," Laban said, "tell us Gen 24:33
me along just the * path to find a Gen 24:48
to my master and do what is *? Gen 24:49
Jacob: "All *, trade me your Gen 25:31
"All *!" Gen 30:34
He is coming * behind us!" Gen 32:18
("Son of my * hand"). Gen 35:18
is more in the * than I am, because Gen 38:26
we collected your money all *." Gen 43:23
Come down to me * away! Gen 45:9
left hand and Manasseh at his *. Gen 48:12,13
heads, so that his * hand was upon Gen 48:14
laid his * hand on Ephraim's head; Gen 48:17
"You've got your * hand on the Gen 48:18
Put your * hand on him!" Gen 48:18
"All *," he said, "your Ex 4:14
bedrooms and * into your beds! Ex 8:3,4
"All *," Moses replied, "it Ex 8:10
and said, "All *, go ahead and Ex 8:25
and if we do this * here before Ex 8:26
"All *, go ahead," Pharaoh Ex 8:28
"Jehovah is *, and I and my Ex 9:27
"All *," Moses replied, "as Ex 9:29
"All *, go and serve Jehovah Ex 10:8
did these miracles * before Ex 11:10
Your * hand, O Lord, is glorious Ex 15:6
it, and do what is *, then I will Ex 15:26
deciding who is * and who is wrong, Ex 18:15,16
"It's not *!" Ex 18:17
the cause of the person who is *. Ex 23:8
the tip of the * ear of Aaron and Ex 29:19,20
and upon their * thumbs and the big Ex 29:19,20
and the big toes of their * feet; Ex 29:19,20
them; and the * thigh—for this is Ex 29:22
* away, the people went to Aaron. Ex 32:1
The Lord replied, "All *, this Ex 34:10
sons, while the * thigh shall be Lev 7:32,33
it is their * forever throughout Lev 7:36
lobe of Aaron's * ear and the thumb Lev 8:23
the thumb of his * hand and upon Lev 8:23
upon the big toe of his * foot. Lev 8:23
the lobes of their * ears, upon Lev 8:24
ears, upon their * thumbs, and upon Lev 8:24
upon the big toes of their * feet. Lev 8:24
their fat, and the * shoulder, and Lev 8:25
but he waved the breasts and * Lev 9:21
the tip of the * ear of the man Lev 14:14
the thumb of his * hand, and upon Lev 14:14
upon the big toe of his * foot. Lev 14:14
hand, and dip his * finger into Lev 14:16
tip of the man's * ear and the Lev 14:17
the thumb of his * hand and the big Lev 14:17
the big toe of his * foot—just as Lev 14:17
tip of the man's * ear—the man on Lev 14:25
the thumb of his * hand and on the Lev 14:25
and on the big toe of his * foot. Lev 14:25
and with his * finger he is to Lev 14:27
tip of the man's * ear, and upon Lev 14:28
the thumb of his * hand, and upon Lev 14:28
the big toe of his * foot, just as Lev 14:28
located * among them and surrounded Lev 16:16
it is all * to marry her sister. Lev 18:18
must do it in the * way, eating the Lev 22:29,30
* of redemption during that time. Lev 25:29
like this, please kill me * now; Num 11:15
Then the Lord said, "All *, I Num 14:20,21
all of us. What * do you have to Num 16:3
the breast and * thigh that are Num 18:18
into the camp, * before the eyes of Num 25:6
Then Moses said, "All *, if you Num 32:20
in Egypt, * before your very eyes. Deu 4:34
is * and good in the Lord's eyes. Deu 6:18
doing whatever he thinks is *; Deu 12:8
If you do what is * in the eyes Deu 12:28
is * in the eyes of the Lord. Deu 13:18
of Israel, has the * to come to the Deu 18:6,7
his *, not just if he is in need. Deu 18:8
" 'All *,' the Lord said to me, Deu 18:17
he is poor he needs it * away; Deu 24:14,15
And with flaming fire at his * Deu 33:2
dried up the river * before our Jos 4:23
actually living * here among us? Jos 9:22
say to ours, 'What * do you have to Jos 22:24,25
"All *," he said, "then you Jos 24:23
turned from doing * and behaved Ju 2:19
strapped against his * thigh. Ju 3:16
against his * thigh, and plunged it Ju 3:21
"All *," she replied, "I'll go Ju 4:9
"All *," the Angel agreed. Ju 6:18
"It's all *," the Lord replied. Ju 6:23
trumpets in their * hands, and Ju 7:19,20
you have done the * thing in making Ju 9:16
that you have done * by Gideon and Ju 9:16
that you have done * by Gideon and Ju 9:19
and cursed are * outside the city! Ju 9:38
of us is *—Israel or Ammon." Ju 11:27
"All *," they agreed, "let's Ju 14:13
"All *," Samson said, "but Ju 15:12,13
gateposts, * out of the ground. Ju 16:3
seemed * in his own eyes. Ju 17:6
man did whatever he thought was *. Ju 21:25
And Naomi said, "All *, dear Ru 2:2
"Stay * here with us to glean; Ru 2:8,9
Stay * behind my women workers; Ru 2:8,9
to let her glean * among the Ru 2:15
Stay with his girls * through the Ru 2:22
And Ruth replied, "All *. Ru 3:5
let me know * away, for if you Ru 4:4
You have the first * to purchase Ru 4:4
The man replied, "All *, I'll buy Ru 4:4
man transferring a * of purchase to Ru 4:7
all * and that the baby was a boy. 1Sa 4:20
"All *," Saul agreed, "let's 1Sa 9:9,10,11
"Yes," they replied, "stay * 1Sa 9:12,13
king instead!' All *, then, present 1Sa 10:18,19
"All *," Nahash said, "but 1Sa 11:2
will gouge out the * eye of every 1Sa 11:2
Tell me and I will make * 1Sa 12:3
your King. All *, here is the king 1Sa 12:13
those things which are good and *. 1Sa 12:23
"All *, then this is what we'll 1Sa 14:8
"Come on, climb * behind me," 1Sa 14:12
lad killed them * and left, about 1Sa 14:13
"This is not the * man either." 1Sa 16:8
"All *," Saul said. 1Sa 16:17
Saul finally consented, "All *, 1Sa 17:37
to which of us is * and punish 1Sa 24:15
lord, if it is all * with you, we 1Sa 27:5
It went * through his body and 2Sa 2:23
"All *," David replied, "but I 2Sa 3:13
*, go and bring back Absalom." 2Sa 14:21
see that you are * in this matter; 2Sa 15:3
"All *," the king told him, 2Sa 15:9
So David replied, "All *, come 2Sa 15:22
And Joab finally said, "All *, go 2Sa 18:23
"Is he all *?" 2Sa 18:29
Is he all *?" 2Sa 18:32
"All *," David replied. 2Sa 19:29
as much * in the king as you do; 2Sa 19:43
his * hand as though to kiss him. 2Sa 20:8,9,10
"All *," the woman replied, "we 2Sa 20:21
"All *," the king said, "I will 2Sa 21:5,6
But you have no * to rejoice in 2Sa 24:3
"All *," Bath-sheba replied, 1Ki 2:18
so she sat at his * hand. 1Ki 2:19
and you suffered * along with him 1Ki 2:26
"All *," Shime-i replied, 1Ki 2:38
what is * and what is wrong. 1Ki 3:9
other. All *, bring me a sword." 1Ki 3:24
But the other woman said, "All *, 1Ki 3:26
entered from the * side of the 1Ki 6:8
him in heaven and do what is *; 1Ki 8:32
gave him the * answers every time. 1Ki 10:3
has not done what I consider *; 1Ki 11:33
I consider *, obeying my 1Ki 11:38
* with God, as King David's was. 1Ki 15:3
"All *, my lord," Ahab replied. 1Ki 20:4
"Why, of course! Go * ahead!" 1Ki 22:15
that you must come down * away." 2Ki 1:11
finally said, "All *, go ahead." 2Ki 2:17
to the prophet and come * back." 2Ki 4:22
See if her husband is all * and 2Ki 4:26
kettle and said, "Now it's all *! 2Ki 4:41
"Well," Naaman said, "all *. 2Ki 5:17
"All *," Elisha said. 2Ki 5:19
"Is everything all *?" 2Ki 5:21
"All *," he told them, "go 2Ki 6:1
see if Elisha was *, and sure 2Ki 6:10
This isn't the * city! 2Ki 6:19
to each other, "This isn't *. 2Ki 7:9
Is everything all *?" 2Ki 9:11
Joash did what was * because 2Ki 12:2
"All *, the Lord will give you a 2Ki 20:9
"All *," Hezekiah replied, "if 2Ki 20:19
left hands as readily as their *! 1Ch 12:2
THEN DAVID SAID, "* here at 1Ch 22:1
the * and the other on the left. 2Ch 3:17
(the one on the *), and Boaz (the 2Ch 3:17
five to the * of the huge tank and 2Ch 4:6
each wall on the * and left. 2Ch 4:8
people, and teach them what is *; 2Ch 6:27
Lord is * in doing this to us!" 2Ch 12:6
and everything will be all *!" 2Ch 20:20
Temple. Stay * beside the king." 2Ch 23:7
Get at it * away. 2Ch 24:5
He did what was *, but sometimes 2Ch 25:2
going after them * into the Temple, 2Ch 36:17
the work was going * ahead and that Neh 4:7
them * back into slavery again. Neh 5:8
To his * stood Mattithiah, Shema, Neh 8:1
people, telling them, "That's *! Neh 8:11
The group which went to the * Neh 12:31,32
"Will he even rape the queen * Est 7:8
difference between * and wrong? Job 6:30
Does it really seem * to you to Job 10:3
Is a man proved * by all this Job 11:2
It isn't * to speak so Job 15:3
If you return to God and put * Job 22:23
with the * and the good. Job 24:13
never, never agree that you are *; Job 27:5
Oh, they have strong backs all * Job 30:2
"All *, here is my reply: In Job 33:12
*, then God pities him and says, Job 33:23,24
should choose to follow what is *. Job 34:4
"Do you think it is * for you to Job 35:2,3
me, so that you can say you are *? Job 40:8
loudly as he? All * then, put on Job 40:10
you have not been * in what you Job 42:7
Then it would be * for you to Ps 7:5
hearts and lives are true and *. Ps 7:10
have done what is *, and you must Ps 17:1
The Lord rewarded me for doing * Ps 18:20
what is *, and I am pure of heart. Ps 18:24
Your * hand, O Lord, supports me; Ps 18:35
Literally, "righteousness," * Ps 24:5f
point out the * road for me to Ps 25:4
the ways that are * and best to Ps 25:9
narrow path of doing what is *; Ps 26:11
the God who always does what is *. Ps 31:1
Lord, for it is * to praise him. Ps 33:1
For all God's words are *, and Ps 33:4
ready to butcher those who do *. Ps 37:14
and fair and knows * from wrong. Ps 37:30,31
hate me for standing for the *. Ps 38:20
Lord is thinking about me * now! Ps 40:17
Literally, "Your * hand is filled Ps 48:10f
with clean thoughts and * desires. Ps 51:10
And when my heart is *, Ps 51:19
does * and really seeks for God. Ps 53:2
shall rejoice in the triumph of *; Ps 58:10
Use your strong * arm to rescue Ps 60:4,5
protected by your strong * arm. Ps 63:8
Zebulun and Naphtali are * behind. Ps 68:27
But I keep * on praying to you, Ps 69:13
You are holding my * hand! Ps 73:23
Literally, "that the * hand of Ps 77:10f
Literally, "the man of your * Ps 80:17f
Strong is your hand! Your * hand Ps 89:13
permitting wrong to defeat *? Ps 94:20
and I shall go * on rejoicing! Ps 109:28
all his laws are *, for they are Ps 111:7
laws, for I have chosen to do *. Ps 119:29,30
Make me walk along the * paths Ps 119:35
for your laws are * and good. Ps 119:39
your decisions are * and that your Ps 119:75,76,77
punishment was * and did me Ps 119:75,76,77
for I have done what is *; Ps 119:121
Every law of God is *, whatever Ps 119:128
Your demands are just and *. Ps 119:138
Literally, "your shade at your * Ps 121:5f
whose hearts are * with the Lord; Ps 125:4
Jerusalem, let my * hand forget its Ps 137:5,6
one—just over there to the *! Ps 142:4
How delightful, and how *! Ps 147:1
He shows how to distinguish * Pro 2:9
to find the * decision every time. Pro 2:9
and stay on the * path, for only Pro 2:20
The man who knows * from wrong Pro 3:13,14,15

(RIGHT Con't)
and doing *—and common sense. Pro 3:21
* is the wisest life there is. Pro 4:11
Everything I say is * and true, Pro 8:6,7
I show the judges who is * and Pro 8:14,15
paths are those of justice and *. Pro 8:20
lasting happiness; * living does. Pro 10:2
To do * honors God; Pro 14:2
that seems * but ends in death. Pro 14:12
is cheerful, everything seems *! Pro 15:15
stay on the pathways of *. Pro 15:21
say the * thing at the right time! Pro 15:23
say the right thing at the * time! Pro 15:23
are *, but is the Lord convinced? Pro 16:2
to do evil. His * to rule depends Pro 16:12
thinks is *, but it ends in death. Pro 16:25
It doesn't seem * for a fool to Pro 19:10
contradicts what you know is *. Pro 19:27
what he does is pure and *. Pro 20:11
Teach a child to choose the * Pro 22:6
In the past, haven't I been *? Pro 22:20,21
The man who wants to do * will Pro 28:20
THERE IS A * time for everything: Ecc 3:1
more you spend, * up to the limits Ecc 5:11
at the * place at the right time. Ecc 9:11
at the right place at the * time. Ecc 9:11
leads him to do *, and a fool's Ecc 10:2
with his * hand he embraces me. Sol 2:6
and his * hand would embrace me. Sol 8:3
They say that what is * is Is 5:20
is wrong, and what is wrong is *; Is 5:20
as well! All * then, the Lord Is 7:14
and knows * from wrong, the two Is 7:15,16
the pavement * before their eyes; Is 13:16
from wickedness and do what is *. Is 26:9
He goes * on and eats. Is 31:4,5
"All *," Hezekiah replied. Is 39:8
as to what is * and best? Is 40:14
you with my victorious * hand. Is 41:10
Or, "with the * hand of my Is 41:10f
I am holding you by your * Is 41:13
making you admit that he was *? Is 41:26
You see and understand what is * Is 42:20
making a path * through the sea. Is 43:16
God shall empower his * hand and Is 45:1
Can't you do anything * at all?" Is 45:10
* have you to question what I do? Is 45:11
not in the distant future, but * Is 46:13
the palm of my * hand spread out Is 48:13
for I will see that * prevails. Is 51:4
Listen to me, you who know the * Is 51:7
sea, making a path * through it for Is 51:10
So what * have you to fear mere Is 51:12
a path for you * through the sea, Is 51:15
sing with joy, for * before their Is 52:8
Do what's * and good, for I am Is 56:1
But they went * on sinning, doing Is 57:17
keep * on oppressing your workers. Is 58:3
hungry and bring * into your own Is 58:7
And the Lord replied, "That's *, Jer 1:12
So you talk, and keep * on Jer 3:4,5
but for doing * they have no Jer 4:22
the least of them * to the top! Jer 6:13
—only to go * back to all these Jer 7:10
They have set up their idols * in Jer 7:30
They care nothing for * and go Jer 9:3
What * do my beloved people have Jer 11:15
* on down to all the people. Jer 13:13
O Lord, you are * here among us, Jer 14:9
You have let them keep * on with Jer 15:17,18
green and it goes * on producing Jer 17:8
to each person his * reward, Jer 17:10
your evil paths and do what is *. Jer 18:11
that everything would be all *." Jer 20:6
bring your enemies * into the heart Jer 21:3,4
Begin doing what is * before my Jer 21:12
Do what is *! Jer 22:3
signet ring on my * hand, I would Jer 22:24,25
despicable acts * here in my own Jer 23:11
What * do you have to say the Jer 26:9
"The decision is *; Jer 26:18
you the first * to purchase it." Jer 32:8
I taught them * from wrong, but Jer 32:33
doing what was *, as I commanded Jer 34:15
"All *," he said. Jer 38:5
"All *," Jeremiah replied. Jer 42:4
they have kept * on with their Jer 44:5
And the Lord is *, for we Lam 1:18
be my Judge, to prove me *. Lam 3:59
with a lion's face on the * Eze 1:10
and lie on your * side for forty Eze 4:6
Then the Lord said, "All *, you Eze 4:15
And begin * here at the Temple." Eze 9:6
was * for me to destroy Jerusalem. Eze 14:22
what is lawful and *, and has not Eze 18:5
For if the son does what is * and Eze 18:19
what is just and *, he shall surely Eze 18:21
the law, and does *, he shall save Eze 18:27
out of Egypt * before the Eze 20:9,10
your idols, go * ahead, but then Eze 20:39
O sword, slash to the * and Eze 21:16
the Man appears who has a * to it. Eze 21:27
difference between * and wrong, and Eze 22:26
sister she went * ahead in the same Eze 23:11
* along behind her older sister. Eze 23:13
what is fair and *— if he gives Eze 33:14
along the paths of *, not doing Eze 33:15
I will take away their * to feed Eze 34:9,10
take away their * to eat. Eze 34:9,10
give you new and * desires—and put Eze 36:26
what is * and what is wrong. Eze 44:23
In such cases it is all *. Eze 44:25
and passing to the * of the altar, Eze 47:1
do what you know is *; Dan 4:27
whose every act is * and good; Dan 4:37
* to wrong and wrong to right." Dan 7:25f
right to wrong and wrong to *." Dan 7:25f
turning from our sins and doing *. Dan 9:13
Was it not * that the men of Hos 10:9
*, and good men walk along them. Hos 14:9
Each is * in place. Joe 2:8
it means to do *," says the Lord. Amo 3:10
all that should be good and *. Amo 6:12
Then the Lord said, "Is it * to Jon 4:4
And God said to Jonah, "Is it * Jon 4:9
it is * for me to be angry enough Jon 4:9
their * hands from their left." Jon 4:11f
Is that the * reply for you to Mic 2:7
For you steal the shirts * off Mic 2:8
children of every God-given *. Mic 2:9
supposed to know * from wrong, yet Mic 3:1
things I plan won't happen * away. Hab 2:3
Walk humbly and do what is *; Zep 2:3
* time for rebuilding my Temple?" Hag 1:2
"Is it then the * time for you to Hag 1:3,4
at the Angel's * hand, accusing Zec 3:1
I promise * now, I will repay you Zec 9:12
arm and pierce through his * eye; Zec 11:17
useless and his * eye blinded." Zec 11:17
nations * and left, while Jerusalem Zec 12:6
animals are all * to offer on the Mal 1:8
it, for I must do all that is *." Mt 3:15
Literally, "your * eye." Mt 5:29f
And if your hand—even your * Mt 5:30
hand what your * hand is doing. Mt 6:3
to anyone; go * over to the Mt 8:4
You have no * to torment us Mt 8:29
"All *," Jesus told them. Mt 8:32
this happen * before their eyes. Mt 9:8
she jumped up and was all * again! Mt 9:25
They went * into the house where Mt 9:28
the * words at the right time. Mt 10:19
the right words at the * time. Mt 10:19
enemies will be * in his own home! Mt 10:36
Yes, it is * to do good on the Mt 12:12
like you speak what is good and *? Mt 12:34
"All *," he said, "I Mt 13:37
"All *," the Lord said, "come Mt 14:29
"It doesn't seem * to take bread Mt 15:26
And her daughter was healed * Mt 15:28
And some of you standing * here Mt 16:28
Jesus replied, "They are *. Mt 17:11
I will be * there among them." Mt 18:20
was * at the end of the day. Mt 20:4
"But I have no * to say who will Mt 20:23
And if you want to be * at the Mt 20:27
Now tell us, is it * to pay Mt 22:17
'God said to my Lord, Sit at my * Mt 22:44
It may be all * to do what they Mt 23:3
The man with $2,000 went * to Mt 25:17
* hand, and the goats at my left. Mt 25:33
say to those at my *, 'Come, Mt 25:34
sitting at the * hand of God and Mt 26:64
a stick in his * hand as a scepter Mt 27:29
and everything will be all *." Mt 28:14
They told Jesus about her * away. Mk 1:29,30
* down in front of Jesus. Mk 2:4
asked, "Is it all * to do kind Mk 3:4
And his sisters live * here among Mk 6:2,3
the Baptist—* now—on a tray!" Mk 6:25
"It's all *," he said. Mk 6:50
petty rules.' How * Isaiah was! Mk 7:6,7
is perfectly all * for a man to Mk 7:11
* away a woman came to him whose Mk 7:25
It isn't * to take the children's Mk 7:27
are standing here * now will live Mk 9:1
and he stood up and was all *! Mk 9:27
"He said it was all *," they Mk 10:4
* and the other at your left!" Mk 10:37
I do not have the * to place you on Mk 10:40
And Jesus said to him, "All *, Mk 10:52
*, why didn't you accept him?' Mk 11:31
Now tell us, is it * to pay taxes Mk 12:14
"All *," he said, "if it is Mk 12:17
my Lord, sit at my * hand until I Mk 12:36
near, that I am * at the door. Mk 13:29
So he began looking for the * Mk 14:11
sitting at the * hand of God, and Mk 14:62
there on the * sat a young man Mk 16:5
and sat down at God's * hand. Mk 16:19
to the * of the altar of incense! Lk 1:11,12
sleeping mat, * in front of Jesus. Lk 5:18,19
present whose * hand was deformed. Lk 6:
Is it * to do good on the Sabbath Lk 6:
*, and they were baptized by him. Lk 7:2
"All *, Teacher," Simon replied, Lk 7:4
trust me, and she'll be all *." Lk 8:5
are standing here * now will not Lk 9:2
"*!" Lk 10:2
Ask them if you are *! Lk 11:1
what they did was *—you would have Lk 11:4
will give you the * words even as Lk 12:1
along all *—for God feeds them. Lk 12:2
And you are *. Lk 12:5
to see for yourselves what is *? Lk 12:5
But it is * to celebrate. Lk 15:3
just as usual * up to the day when Lk 17:2
* up to the hour of my return. Lk 17:3
And Jesus said, "All *, begin Lk 18:4
Kingdom of God would begin * away. Lk 19:1
" 'All *!' Lk 19:1
Now tell us—is it * to pay taxes Lk 20:2
"Sit at my * hand until I place Lk 20:42,43
will give you the * words and such Lk 21:15
now, grant you the * to eat and Lk 22:29
servant, and cut off his * ear. Lk 22:50
Genesis and going * on through the Lk 24:27
the * to become children of God. Jn 1:11,12
what * do you have to baptize?" Jn 1:24,25
water, but * here in the crowd is Jn 1:26
"What * have you to order them Jn 2:18
"All *," Jesus replied, "this Jn 2:19
But those doing * come gladly to Jn 3:21
Jesus replied, "It is not the * Jn 7:6
when it is the * time." Jn 7:8
and you will see that I am *." Jn 7:24
and said, "All *, hurl the stones Jn 8:7
but the Son has every * there is! Jn 8:35
For I have the * and power to lay Jn 10:18
the * and power to take it again. Jn 10:18
the Father has given me this *." Jn 10:18
slashed off the * ear of Malchus, Jn 18:10
Then they all prayed for the * Act 1:24,25
was standing * there beside them! Act 4:14
Jesus standing at God's * hand. Act 7:55
standing beside God, at his * Act 7:56
your heart is not * before God. Act 8:21
He is praying to me * now, for I Act 9:11
isn't * when God declares it is!' Act 11:9
worry," he said, "he's all *!" Act 20:10,11,12
This divided the Council * down Act 23:7
up to argue that Paul was all *. Act 23:9
Ask these men * here what Act 24:20
anyone else has a * to turn me over Act 25:10,11
Holy Spirit was * when he said Act 28:25
heaven—makes us * in God's Rom 1:17
Yes, they knew about him all *, Rom 1:21
yet they went * ahead and did them Rom 1:32
hearts they know * from wrong. Rom 2:12-15
They know what is * but don't do Rom 2:12-15
you know * from wrong and favor Rom 2:18
and favor the * because you have Rom 2:18
anyone whose heart is * with God. Rom 2:29
*, no matter who questions them. Rom 3:4
has kept on doing what is *; Rom 3:12
No one can ever be made * in Rom 3:20
But didn't he earn his * to Rom 4:4,5
again to make us * with God, Rom 4:25
SO NOW, SINCE we have been made * Rom 5:1
came at just the * time and died Rom 5:6
* with God, so that they can live. Rom 5:18
instead, giving us * standing with Rom 5:21
slaves to all that is * and holy. Rom 6:19
is perfectly all * after he dies. Rom 7:3
law itself was wholly * and good. Rom 7:12
want to do what is *, but I can't. Rom 7:15
I turn I can't make myself do *. Rom 7:18
*, I inevitably do what is wrong. Rom 7:21
tells me to do *, but the old Rom 7:23,24,25
goodness, gave us * standing with Rom 8:30
given us * standing with himself. Rom 8:33
doesn't he have a * to use the same Rom 9:21
Does not God have a perfect * to Rom 9:22
And he has a * to take others Rom 9:23,24
so hard to get * with God by Rom 9:31
has died to make them * with God. Rom 10:3
that a man becomes * with God; Rom 10:10
frighten people who are doing *; Rom 13:3
Another reason for * living is Rom 13:11
on the armor of * living, as we who Rom 13:12,13
yours about what is * and wrong. Rom 14:1
Those who think it is all * to Rom 14:3
them whether they are * or wrong. Rom 14:4
he is doing *. Rom 14:6
You have no * to criticize your Rom 14:10
you know that what you do is *. Rom 14:16
stumble. The * thing to do is to Rom 14:21
sin by doing what he knows is *. Rom 14:22
from what he feels is * is sin. Rom 14:23
So it is * for me to be a little Rom 15:17
about what is *, and to stay Rom 16:19
And he guarantees * up to the 1Co 1:8
with the * materials, and whose 1Co 3:14

IGHT Con't)
said about us. Yet * up to the 1Co 4:13
to decide which of you is *? 1Co 6:1
But sexual sin is never *: our 1Co 6:13
all that is her * as a married 1Co 7:3
no longer has full * to her own 1Co 7:4
no longer has full * to his own 1Co 7:4
but they seem * to me: If a 1Co 7:12
and get married now, it is all *; 1Co 7:28
you didn't have to face * now. 1Co 7:28
it is all *, it is not a sin; 1Co 7:36
that only his answer is the * one! 1Co 8:1
"know it is all * to do it," you 1Co 8:11
Literally, "Have we no * to lead 1Co 9:5f
Literally, "Have we no * to lead 1Co 9:5f
have the * to eat some of it? 1Co 9:7
opinions of men as to what is *. 1Co 9:8
we have an even greater * to them? 1Co 9:12
Yet we have never used this *, 1Co 9:12
do what is * as a Christian. 1Co 9:21
Is it * for a woman to pray in 1Co 11:13
you who are always * will become 1Co 11:19
as God sees into my heart * now. 1Co 13:12
doesn't play the * notes, how will 1Co 14:8
I passed on to you * from the 1Co 15:3
not the * kind to live forever. 1Co 15:50
a passing visit and then go * on; 1Co 16:7
So I said good-bye and went * on 2Co 2:13
plan that makes men * with God. 2Co 3:9
at what we can see * now, the 2Co 4:18
And if we are in our * minds, it 2Co 5:13,14
* now God is ready to welcome you. 2Co 6:2
You went * to work on the problem 2Co 7:11
everything you could to make it *. 2Co 7:11
divide with them. * now you have 2Co 8:14
proving that what we teach is *; 2Co 13:7
no, for we want you to do * even 2Co 13:7
to encourage the * at all times, 2Co 13:8
and, I hoped, agree that it was *. Gal 2:2
us to keep * on with our preaching Gal 2:7,8,9
we cannot become * with God by Gal 2:16
can be * in his sight is by faith. Gal 3:11
came to give us * standing with God Gal 3:24
But when the * time came, the Gal 4:4
be there with you * now and not Gal 4:20
laws to make you * with God, then Gal 5:2
our sins and make us * with God. Gal 5:5
him back onto the * path, Gal 6:1
of doing what is *, for after a Gal 6:9
of honor at God's * hand in heaven, Eph 1:20
who is at work * now in the hearts Eph 2:2
Now we can come fearlessly * into Eph 3:12
They don't care anymore about * Eph 4:19
only what is good and * and true. Eph 5:9
this is the * thing to do because Eph 6:1
treat your slaves *, just as I have Eph 6:9
God to give me the * words as I Eph 6:19
you will keep * on helping you grow Php 1:6
difference between * and wrong, and Php 1:10
* down to the very last point. Php 3:6
for God's way of making us * with Php 3:9
on what is true and good and *. Php 4:8
But even so, you have done * in Php 4:14
—why do you keep * on following Col 2:20
more of what is *, and trying Col 3:10
have the * answer for everyone. Col 4:6
had a * to some honor from you. 1Th 2:6
is not only the * thing to do, but 2Th 1:3
we didn't have the * to ask you to 2Th 3:9
never be tired of doing *. 2Th 3:13
clear, doing what you know is *. 1Ti 1:19
Bodily exercise is all *, but 1Ti 4:8
Stay true to what is * and God 1Ti 4:16
will know and do what is *. 1Ti 5:7
has no * to say he is a Christian. 1Ti 5:8
instead at what is * and good, 1Ti 6:11
that makes you want to do *. 2Ti 2:22
us out and helps us do what is *. 2Ti 3:16
them to do *, and all the time be 2Ti 4:2
BUT AS FOR you, speak up for the * Tit 2:1
as one who has every * to do so. Tit 2:15
not only *, but it brings results. Tit 3:8
because it is the * thing for you Phm 1:8,9
commands are always just and *. Heb 1:8
You love * and hate wrong; Heb 1:9
And it was * and proper that Heb 2:10
he kept * on doing his mighty Heb 3:9
difference between * and wrong. Heb 5:12,13
and learn * from wrong by Heb 5:14
from wrong by practicing doing *. Heb 5:14
that you keep * on loving others as Heb 6:11
It never made anyone really * Heb 7:19
honor at God's * hand, waiting for Heb 10:12
now we may walk * into the very Heb 10:19
let us go * in, to God himself, Heb 10:22
Remember how you kept * on with Heb 10:32
Moses kept * on going; Heb 11:27
he could see God * there with him. Heb 11:27
God and went * through the Red Sea Heb 11:29
is always * and for our best good, Heb 12:10
But you have come * up into Mount Heb 12:22
I especially need your prayers * Heb 13:19
brothers, surely this is not *! Jas 3:10
law is * or wrong, but to obey it. Jas 4:11
So what * do you have to judge or Jas 4:12
knowing what is * to do and then Jas 4:17
and to honor those who do *. 1Pe 2:14
if you are punished for doing *! 1Pe 2:19
but if you do * and suffer for 1Pe 2:20
daughters and doing what is *; 1Pe 3:6
Do what is *; 1Pe 3:16
on doing what is * and trust 1Pe 4:19
have always had, * from the start. 1Jn 2:7
anyone to teach you what is *. 1Jn 2:27
good and does only *, we may 1Jn 2:29
those who do * are his children. 1Jn 2:29
God's children, * now, and we can't 1Jn 3:2
his brother who is * there in front 1Jn 4:20
rule God gave us * from the 2Jn 1:5
who do what is * prove that they 3Jn 1:11
carelessly go * on living their Jud 1:8
He held seven stars in his * Rev 1:16
but he laid his * hand on me and Rev 1:17,18
you saw in my * hand, and the seven Rev 1:20
seven stars in his * hand and walks Rev 2:1f
and holds their leaders in his * Rev 2:1
Your deeds are far from * in the Rev 3:2
AND I SAW a scroll in the * hand Rev 5:1
scroll from the * hand of the one Rev 5:7
He set his * foot on the sea and Rev 10:2
land lifted his * hand to heaven, Rev 10:5
on the * hand or on the forehead. Rev 13:16
who had been given the * to judge. Rev 20:4
robes, to have the * to enter in Rev 22:14

RIGHT-HAND
five on the * side of the room. 1Ki 7:39
corner, on the * side of the room. 1Ki 7:39
(five on the * side and five on the 1Ki 7:49
and set it on the * side of the 2Ki 12:9
your net on the * side of the boat, Jn 21:6

RIGHTED
The Lord will see his people *, Deu 32:36
What is wrong cannot be *; Ecc 1:12-15

RIGHTEOUS
was the only truly * man living on Gen 6:9,10
I consider you alone to be *. Gen 7:1
then God considered him * on Gen 15:6
assuming my guilt, for I am *. Job 6:29
"But I? Am I *? Job 9:20
Yes, I, a * man, am now the man Job 12:4
is my case: I know that I am *. Job 13:18
as pure and * as you claim to be? Job 15:14
* shall move onward and forward; Job 17:9
to the Almighty if you are *? Job 22:3
And now the * shall see them Job 22:19
before God and claim to be *? Job 25:4
for you, the * God, look deep Ps 7:9
"What can the * do but flee?" Ps 11:3
He puts the * and the wicked to Ps 11:5
Literally, "you *." Ps 32:11f
Literally, "the *." Ps 37:17f
them the joys of life with the *. Ps 69:28
experienced) your * judgments." Ps 119:7f
while blessings chase the *! Pro 13:21
but he hears the prayers of the *. Pro 15:29
lose; the * will finally win. Pro 21:18
wicked is a ransom for the *." Pro 21:18f
he will place a just and * King." Is 16:4,5
earth, singing glory to the * One! Is 24:15,16
LOOK, A * King is coming, with Is 32:1
to show the world that he is *. Is 42:21
to fulfill my * purpose, and I Is 45:13
my * rule will never die nor end. Is 51:6
experienced, my * Servant shall Is 53:11
many to be counted * before God, Is 53:11
* God, and testify against you. Is 59:12
Our courts oppose the * man; Is 59:14
those who are * and examines the Jer 20:12
* Branch upon King David's throne. Jer 23:5,6
Your lies have discouraged the * Eze 13:22
they seem almost * in comparison Eze 16:51
for his son's. The * person will be Eze 18:20
However, if a * person turns to Eze 18:24
I will not spare even the *. Eze 21:4
For the good works of a * man Eze 33:12
"O Lord, you are *; Dan 9:7
far outnumber the *, and bribes and Hab 1:4
but the * man trusts in me, and Hab 2:4
He is the * One, the Victor! Zec 9:9
living a good and * life, and Mal 2:6
godly men from * Abel to Zechariah Mt 23:35
"Then these * ones will reply, Mt 25:37
but the * into everlasting Mt 25:46
in the place of the * dead. Lk 16:22
Literally, "*." Lk 23:47f
"O * Father, the world doesn't Jn 17:25
want him freed—this holy, * one. Act 3:14
the coming of the * One—the Messiah Act 7:52
guilt and declared *—something the Act 13:39
Literally, "* One." Act 22:14f
of both the * and ungodly. Act 24:15
Literally, "*." Rom 4:6f
the Lord, the * Judge, will give me 2Ti 4:8
The earnest prayer of a * man has Jas 5:16
If the * are barely saved, what 1Pe 4:18
For your * deeds Rev 15:3,4

RIGHTEOUSLY
'One shall come who rules *, 2Sa 23:3
sit on the throne, judging *." Ps 9:4f

RIGHTEOUSNESS
God will count it as * for you. Deu 24:12,13
and honest, for * was my clothing! Job 29:14
of the * of my Maker. Job 36:3
Literally, "God of my *." Ps 4:1f
Literally, "*," right standing Ps 24:5f
"Judge me according to your *." Ps 35:24f
Literally, "your *." Ps 36:10f
Literally, "your *." Ps 40:9f
Literally, "your *." Ps 40:10f
right hand is filled with *." Ps 48:10f
Literally, "*." Ps 51:14,15f
delight in the sacrifice of *." Ps 51:19f
Literally, "will answer us in * Ps 65:5f
Literally, "*." Ps 85:10f
Truth rises from the earth and * Ps 85:11
one is Justice and the other *. Ps 89:14,15
reputation and in your perfect *. Ps 89:16
surround him. * and justice are the Ps 97:2
The heavens declare his perfect *; Ps 97:6
Literally, "his * endures Ps 112:3f
Literally, "his * endures Ps 112:9f
Literally, "the gates of *." Ps 118:19f
me in faithfulness and *." Ps 143:1f
you are, and sing about your *. Ps 145:7
and * are mine to distribute. Pro 8:18
earnings advance the cause of *. Pro 10:16
Judgment Day; only * counts then. Pro 11:4
the throne is established by *." Pro 16:12f
and kind finds life, * and honor. Pro 21:21
He expected *, but the cries of Is 5:7
as do those for "*" and "cry." Is 5:7f
of justice and goodness and *. Is 33:5
Or, "with the right hand of my * Is 41:10f
until truth and * prevail Is 42:4
called you to demonstrate my *. Is 42:6
Let the skies pour out their *. Is 45:8
Let salvation and * sprout up Is 45:8
Jehovah, speak only truth and *. Is 45:19
"In Jehovah is all my * and Is 45:24
river, and great waves of *. Is 48:18
And then there is your "*" and Is 57:12
He put on * as armor, and the Is 59:17
Peace and * shall be your Is 60:17
and draped about me the robe of *. Is 61:10
all will praise him. His * shall Is 61:11
forth in his * and is glorious in Is 62:1
The nations shall see your *. Is 62:2
prized robes of * we find they are Is 64:6
and of * whose love is steadfast; Jer 9:24
justice and cause * to prevail Jer 23:5,6
this is his name: The Lord Our *. Jer 23:5,6
you, O center of *, O holy hill!" Jer 31:23
will be, "The Lord is our *!" Jer 33:16
be saved by their *, and I would Eze 14:14
be saved, because of their *. Eze 14:20
again the wall of * that guards the Eze 22:30
As a result, truth and * Dan 8:12
so truth and * perished." Dan 8:12f
then the kingdom of everlasting * Dan 9:24
* will glitter like stars forever. Dan 12:3
* and justice and love and mercy. Hos 1:19
Plant the good seeds of * and you Hos 10:12
and oppressed. "*" and "fair Amo 5:7
be their God in truth and in *." Zec 8:8f
name, the Sun of * will rise with Mal 4:2
Literally, "to fulfill all *." Mt 3:15f
Literally, "*." Mt 5:20f
world of sin and * and judgment." Jn 16:8f
there is * available because I Jn 16:10
with them about * and self-control Act 24:25
Literally: "(this) * of God is Rom 1:17f
Literally, "A * of God has been Rom 3:21,22f
"faith is reckoned for *." Rom 4:4,5f
all, but Christ's * makes men Rom 5:18
slaves to your new master, *. Rom 6:18
for he has already given you *." Rom 8:10f
the spirit is life because of *." Rom 8:10f
become the * of God in him." 2Co 5:21f
Literally, "wherein * dwells." 2Pe 3:13f

RIGHTFUL
given their * place of dignity! Ecc 10:6

RIGHTLY
* concerning my servant Job." Job 42:8
God has * decided to destroy his Is 10:22
* speak of God as our dear Father. Gal 4:6
Only he who made the law can * Jas 4:12
only right, we may * assume that 1Jn 2:29

RIGHTS
* to his younger brother. Gen 25:33
loss of the * he had thrown away. Gen 25:34
He has reduced our * to those of Gen 31:15
his * to it at the Year of Jubilee Lev 27:20
whether someone's * have been Deu 17:8

(RIGHTS Con't)
and who owns the * of a firstborn Deu 21:17
the * and duties of a king were; 1Sa 10:25
has taken away my *, even the Job 27:2
he will maintain the * of the Ps 140:12
trying to cheat him out of his *. Pro 24:15,16
good man knows the poor man's *; Pro 29:7
to orphans and the * of the poor. Jer 5:28
Protect the * of aliens and Jer 22:3
*, and refused them justice. Lam 3:34,35,36
the same * your own children have. Eze 47:22
the * of worship are restored. Dan 8:26
And slaves don't have *, but the Jn 8:35
give them all the * and honors he Rom 2:26
give us our full * as his children, Rom 8:23
husband then has his * to it, too; 1Co 7:4
So do not refuse these * to each 1Co 7:5
refrain from the * of marriage for 1Co 7:5
answer to those who question my *. 1Co 9:3
Or don't I have any * at all? 1Co 9:4
to anyone, never demanding my *. 1Co 9:18
and cling to his * as God, but Php 2:6
did: he traded his * as the oldest Heb 12:16
he wanted those * back again, it Heb 12:17

RIGID
and grind his teeth and become *. Mk 9:18
the Law with its * demands and Jn 1:17

RIM
the edge. A * four inches high was Ex 37:12
with a gold molding along the *. Ex 37:12
On the underside of the * were 1Ki 7:24
A nine-inch * surrounded the tip 1Ki 7:35
fifteen feet across from * to rim. 2Ch 4:2
fifteen feet across from rim to *. 2Ch 4:2
rim to rim. The * stood 7½ feet 2Ch 4:2
with a nine-inch * around its edge, Eze 43:13

RIMMON
Lebaoth, Shilhim, Ain, and *. Jos 15:21-32
and * and turned toward Neah. Jos 19:13
toward the rock of *, but five Ju 20:45
to the rock of *, where they lived Ju 20:46,47
of the men of Benjamin at * Rock. Ju 21:13
They were the sons of *, who was 2Sa 4:2,3
temple of the god * to worship 2Ki 5:18
Etam, Ain, *, Tochen, and Ashan; 1Ch 4:32,33
of Judah) to * (the southern Zec 14:10

RIMMON-PAREZ
From Rithmah to *; Num 33:15-37
From * to Libnah; Num 33:15-37

RIMMONO
The tribe of Zebulun gave * and 1Ch 6:77

RIMS
the axles, spokes, *, and hubs. 1Ki 7:33
The four wheels had * and Eze 1:18
spokes, and the * were filled with Eze 1:18
eyes, including the * and spokes. Eze 10:9-13

RING
Laban saw the *, and the bracelets Gen 24:29,30
So I gave her the * and the Gen 24:47
his own signet * on Joseph's finger Gen 41:41,42
with a metal * at each corner, and Ex 27:4
as initials are engraved upon a *. Ex 39:6,7
a gold * was placed at the top Ex 39:15-18
sleeping inside a * formed by the 1Sa 26:5,6,7
by removing his * from his finger Est 3:10
Ahasuerus and sealed with his *. Est 3:12
The king took off his *—which he Est 8:2
it with the king's *, so that it Est 8:8
with the king's * and could not be Est 8:8f
with the king's * and sent the Est 8:9,10
a * in his nose and lead him away. Job 40:24
him a gift of money, and a gold *. Job 42:11
a fine gold * in a pig's snout. Pro 11:22
were the signet * on my right hand, Jer 22:24,25
necklaces, a * for your nose and Eze 16:12
his own signet *, and that of his Dan 6:17
like a signet * upon my finger; Hag 2:23
And a jeweled * for his finger; Lk 15:22

RINGED
goats that were * and spotted, and Gen 30:35,36

RINGING
word from Paul * in their ears: Act 28:25
with such a * confession before 1Ti 6:12

RINGLEADER
and was the * in getting the people 1Ki 12:2,3,4
He is a * of the sect known as Act 24:5

RINGS
Cast four * of gold for it and Ex 25:12
lower corners, two * on each side. Ex 25:12
the poles into the * at the sides Ex 25:13,14
be taken from the *, but are to be Ex 25:15
Make four golden * and put the Ex 25:26,27
rings and put the * at the outside Ex 25:26,27
these are * for the poles that Ex 25:26,27
and make gold * to hold the bars; Ex 26:29
the * at each side of the altar. Ex 27:7
attached to golden * placed at the Ex 28:22,23,24
Then make two more golden * and Ex 28:26
also make two other golden * for Ex 28:27
to the bottom * of the ephod by Ex 28:28
gold * to hold the carrying poles. Ex 30:4
jewelry—earrings, * from their Ex 35:22
other at both top and bottom by *. Ex 36:29
gold, and the * were pure gold. Ex 36:34
There were four golden * Ex 37:3
its four feet, two * at each end. Ex 37:3
the poles into the * at the sides Ex 37:5
Then he cast four * of gold and Ex 37:13
Two gold * were placed on each Ex 37:27
Four * were cast for each side Ex 38:5
the * at the side of the altar. Ex 38:7
from these gold *, two strands of Ex 39:15-18
Two gold * were also set at the Ex 39:19
Two other gold * were placed low Ex 39:20
ephod by tying the * of the Ex 39:21
chestpiece to the * of the ephod, Ex 39:21
poles of the Ark in their *. Num 4:6
*, earrings, and necklaces. Num 31:50
tied to silver * imbedded in Est 1:6
their * and jewels, and party Is 3:21
with valuable gold * on his Jas 2:2

RINNAH
Amnon, *, Ben-hanan, Tilon. 1Ch 4:20

RINSED
be scoured and * out thoroughly. Lev 6:28
wooden utensil must be * in water. Lev 15:12
will be washed and * of all their Is 4:2,3,4

RINSING
without first * his hands, that Lev 15:11

RIOT
neither in battle nor in *. Dan 11:20
was afraid of a *, for all the Mt 14:5
"for there would be a *." Mt 26:5
and that a * was developing, he Mt 27:24
then the people will start a *." Mk 11:32
said, "or there will be a *." Mk 14:2
Then Pilate, afraid of a * and Mk 15:15
arrested him there would be a *. Lk 20:19
without starting a *—a possibility Lk 22:2
punish them without starting a *. Act 4:21
to form a mob and start a *. Act 17:5
*, since there is no cause for it. Act 19:40
and a great * followed. Act 21:30
never incited a * in any synagogue Act 24:12

RIOTING
was no crowd around me, and no *! Act 24:18

RIOTOUS
again. The * sound of singing in Amo 8:3

RIOTS
to bring about * and confusion. Neh 4:8
Their problem was their fear of * Mk 11:18
"But he is causing * against the Lk 23:5
entire world to * and rebellions Act 24:5
didn't go around starting *, Act 24:22

RIP
To * them apart with their teeth; Deu 32:24
through the * he tore in them that 2Ki 6:26-30
the rocks, and * open the bellies 2Ki 8:12
I will * you to pieces like a Hos 13:8
crucifixion, and * open the backs Mt 23:34

RIPE
will die in peace, at a * old age. Gen 15:15
Then Abraham died, at the * old Gen 25:7,8
at the * old age of 180. Gen 35:28,29
there were clusters of * grapes. Gen 40:9,10
the barley was *, and the flax was Ex 9:31
and had * almonds hanging from it! Num 17:8
leaves, as * fruit from the trees. Is 34:4
the harvest is * and waiting. Joe 3:13
vision, a basket full of * fruit. Amo 8:1
I replied, "A basket full of * Amo 8:2
my people Israel—* for punishment. Amo 8:2
when the time is * he will gather Eph 1:10
the harvest is * on the earth." Rev 14:15
they are fully * for judgment." Rev 14:18

RIPEN
they *," says the Lord of Hosts. Mal 3:11
for his precious harvest to *. Jas 5:7

RIPENED
back the wine and * corn I Hos 1:9
finally the grain *, and then the Mk 4:28

RIPENING
And grapes will still be * when Lev 26:4,5
your plans are * like grapes, he Is 18:5
Vast fields of human souls are * Jn 4:35

RIPHATH
The sons of Gomer:Ashkenaz, *, Gen 10:3

RIPPED
When Joseph wasn't there, he * at Gen 37:29
They * their clothing in Gen 44:13
son of Jephunneh), * their clothing Num 14:6
had no weapon, he * the lion's jaws Ju 14:6
The king jumped up, * off his 2Sa 13:31
king of Israel. I * the kingdom 1Ki 14:8
and * open the pregnant women. 2Ki 15:16
Athaliah * her clothes and 2Ch 23:12
God's people, he * his clothing in 2Ch 34:19
people, and have * your clothing in 2Ch 34:27
with clothes * to shreds as a sign Is 36:22
women * open with a sword. Hos 13:16
was happening they * at their Act 14:14

RIPPING
cruel crimes, * open pregnant women Amo 1:13

RIPS
Judah as a lion * apart its prey; Hos 5:1
heaven have no * or holes in them. Lk 12:3

RISE
* to take with them on the trip. Ex 12:3
the people would * and stand in Ex 33:
Let your anger * on Israel.' Num 23:7-1
"* up, Balak, and hear: Num 23:18-2
These people * up as a lion; Num 23:18-2
their cities * high into the sky! Deu 1:2
and his anger may * quickly against Deu 6:1
was no time for the bread to *. Deu 16:
Don't let them * again." Deu 33:1
His anger will * hot against you, Jos 23:15,1
So that none can * again. 2Sa 22:3
The sun won't *, the stars won't Job 9:
time, and does not * again until Job 14:11,1
They are murderers who * in the Job 24:14,1
caused the dawn to * in the east? Job 38:1
* up, O Lord my God; Ps 35:2
thrown down and will not * again. Ps 36:1
in the dust. * up, O Lord, and Ps 44:2
Their fury and hatred * to engulf Ps 55:
sacrifice shall * before you. Ps 66:1
the waters * around me. Ps 69:
never need * against us again. Ps 85:4
and none could help them * again. Ps 107:12
the waves * high. Ps 107:25
At midnight I will * to give my Ps 119:62
He makes mists * throughout the Ps 135:7
times, will each time * again? Pro 24:15,16
and hurries around to * again. Ecc 1:3-7
"My beloved said to me, '* up, Sol 2:10
* against them to destroy them." Is 10:25
Babylon will never * again. Is 13:20
Do not let them * and conquer the Is 14:21
fail to * and flood the fields; Is 19:5
It falls and will not * again, Is 24:20
Their bodies shall * again! Is 26:19
He will * against them for the Is 31:2
Its smoke will * up forever. Is 34:10
began his meteoric * to power. Is 44:28f
Awake, O Lord! * up and robe Is 51:9
* from the dust, Jerusalem; Is 52:2
He causes mist to * upon the Jer 10:13
vomit and fall and * no more, for I Jer 25:27
of wrath shall * against the Jer 25:32
other gods, causing my fury to *! Jer 32:29
of terror * from the city below. Jer 48:5
of terror and pain * from all over Jer 48:34
from every side to * against her in Jer 51:2
the vapors to * around the world; Jer 51:16
never more to *, because of the Jer 51:64
* in the night and cry to your Lam 2:19
Your birth rate will * and your Eze 36:14
and cause you to * again and return Eze 37:12
land of Israel, my fury will *! Eze 38:18
statue—will * to rule the world. Dan 2:39
that will * out of his empire; Dan 7:24
angry king shall * to power with Dan 8:23
"Then a mighty king will * in Dan 11:3
and buried will * up, some to Dan 12:2
for you will * again and have Dan 12:13
waits for it to *—so are these Hos 7:4
of war shall * among your people, Hos 10:14
stench will * upon the land. Joe 2:20
upon the ground and cannot *. Amo 5:2
It will * up like the river Nile Amo 8:8
shall fall and never * again." Amo 8:14
He calls for the vapor to * from Amo 9:6
that * from off the ocean floor. Jon 2:6
wickedness; you * at dawn to carry Mic 2:1
Yet to this very hour my people * Mic 2:8
*, thresh, O daughter of Zion; Mic 4:13
for though I fall, I will * again! Mic 7:8
have decreed the * of these Hab 1:12
"Suddenly your debtors will * up Hab 2:7
will * with healing in his wings. Mal 4:2
a Governor shall * from you to rule Mt 2:6
and the floods * and the storm Mt 7:25
And children shall * against Mt 10:21
The Queen of Sheba shall * Mt 12:42
day I will * to life again." Mt 20:19
of the earth will * against each Mt 24:7
* again three days afterwards. Mk 8:31
Mount of Olives, '* up and fall Mk 11:22,23
and the woman * from the dead, they Mk 12:25
When the floodwaters * and break Lk 6:47,48
was sleeping the wind began to *. Lk 8:23
And the third day I will * Lk 18:33
for nation shall * against nation Lk 21:10
he would * again the third day?" Lk 24:6,7
suffer and die and * again from the Lk 24:46
Son, and shall * again—those who Jn 5:29
all such to * again from the dead. Jn 6:44
which should * and fall, and when. Act 17:26
motioned for him to * and speak. Act 24:10
that the dead will * again!' Act 24:21
be the First to * from the dead, to Act 26:23
new life, and shall * as he did. Rom 6:5
did actually * from the dead, and 1Co 15:20

ISE Con't)
elated to Christ will * again. 1Co 15:22
he dead will some day * again? 1Co 15:29
) sleeper, and * up from the dead; Eph 5:14
eturns will not * to meet him 1Th 4:15
he first to * to meet the Lord. 1Th 4:16
to a better life afterwards. Heb 11:35
He was the first to * from death, Rev 1:5
Literally, "* and measure the Rev 11:1f
And they will * to heaven in a Rev 11:12

ISEN
of Israel has * to me in heaven, Ex 3:9
For violent men have * against Ps 54:3
The floods have *. Ps 69:1
I, myself, have * against him, Is 14:22
The sea has * upon Babylon; Jer 51:42
For the wind had * and they were Mt 14:23,24
after he had * from the dead. Mt 17:9
that he has * from the dead, and Mt 28:7
had * from the dead. Mk 9:9
mighty prophet has * among us," Lk 7:16
ancient prophet * from the dead." Lk 9:8
prophets * from the dead." Lk 9:19
until it has * high and light." Lk 13:20,21
words, "The Lord has really *! Lk 24:33,34
saw, and believed [that he had * Jn 20:8
that Jesus had * from the dead. Act 4:2
kings who have not yet * to power; Rev 17:12

ISES
that the eagle * high upon the Job 39:27
he helped me. Joy * in my heart Ps 28:7
of my heart praise * to him. Ps 35:10
Truth * from the earth and Ps 85:11
The sun * and sets and hurries Ecc 1:3-7
when he * to terrify the earth. Is 2:21
and a great cry * from Jerusalem. Jer 14:2
narrower platform * seven feet, and Eze 43:15
people mourn. It * like the river Amo 9:5
for your wickedness * before me; Jon 1:2
though someone * from the dead.' Lk 16:31
The smoke of their torture * Rev 14:11

RISING
Meanwhile, the crime rate was * Gen 6:11
The sun was * as Lot reached the Gen 19:23
furnace, * from the cities there. Gen 19:28
of a man's hand * from the sea." 1Ki 18:44
See Mount Zion * north of the Ps 48:2
surrounded by thick * smoke. Is 30:27
I see the armies of Egypt * Jer 2:16
great nation is * against you. Jer 6:22
to you about it, * up early and Jer 7:13,14
What is this mighty army, * like Jer 46:7
on all sides. * from this is a Eze 43:14
he meant by "* from the dead." Mk 9:10
Literally, "and * up, he went Mk 10:1f
and then began * into the sky, and Lk 24:51
* against the one who hurt him? 2Co 11:29
Creature * up out of the sea. Rev 13:1
smoke * from her charred remains. Rev 18:9

RISK
your command at the * of my life. 1Sa 28:21
Why should we * snuffing out the 2Sa 21:17
for why should we * God's wrath Ez 7:23
A war horse is a poor * for Ps 33:16,17
to rouse his anger is to * your Pro 20:2
never last, so why take the *? Pro 21:6
a note. Why * everything you own? Pro 22:26,27
The world's poorest credit * is Pro 27:13
There is * in each stroke of your Ecc 10:8,9
him not to * his life by entering. Act 19:31
and you won't * having a bad 1Co 10:27

RISKED
fought for you and * his life and Ju 9:17
of need, so I * my life and went Ju 12:3
about the time he * his life to 1Sa 19:5
men who have * their lives." 2Sa 23:17
men who * their lives to get it." 1Ch 11:18,19
Silas, who have * their lives for Act 15:26
In fact, they * their lives for Rom 16:4
for he * his life for the work of Php 2:30

RISKING
for food, * death from enemies. Lam 5:9
be continually * our lives, facing 1Co 15:30

RISKY
It is * to make loans to Pro 20:16
are put into * investments that Ecc 5:13,14

RISSAH
From Libnah to *; Num 33:15-37
From * to Kehelathah; Num 33:15-37

RITE
perform the * of atonement for Lev 14:19
to the Lord in the * of atonement Lev 14:21
the Lord. The * of atonement shall Lev 16:10
"When he has completed the * of Lev 16:20
He then performed the * of Num 8:21
the circumcision * took place was Jos 5:2,3
even before the * of burning the 1Sa 2:15
the purification * on Jesse and his 1Sa 16:5
* like theirs, and nothing more. Jer 9:25,26

RITES
in connection with funeral *; Lev 19:28
purification * in preparation for Jos 7:13
purification * after menstruation. 2Sa 11:4
the purification * for themselves, 2Ch 5:11,12
the purification *, the Levites 2Ch 30:17,18,19
carved idols and strange evil *?" Jer 8:19

RITHMAH
From Hazeroth to *; Num 33:15-37
From * to Rimmon-parez; Num 33:15-37

RITUAL
Her people love the * of their Hos 8:13
"For they ignore our * of Mt 15:2
the * of ceremonial handwashing!" Mt 15:20

RITUALLY
Literally, "clean," i.e., * Gen 8:20f
Literally, "between what is * Eze 44:23f
is ritually clean and * unclean." Eze 44:23f

RITUALS
the usual Jewish * before eating. Mk 7:2
to Jewish laws and * for we thought Gal 4:3
the ceremonies and * of the godly, Eph 2:11
only with certain *—what foods to Heb 9:10

RIVAL
womb shall become two * nations. Gen 25:23
you and given it to your *, David. 1Sa 28:17
reward him for killing his *. 2Sa 1:10f
none can * him. Sol 5:15

RIVALS
two sisters, for they will be *. Lev 18:18

RIVER
Good and Bad. A * from the land of Gen 2:10
afterwards the * divided into Gen 2:10
of the Jordan *, well watered Gen 13:10
Literally, "* of Egypt," at the Gen 15:18f
to the Euphrates *. Gen 15:18
the Euphrates * and headed for the Gen 31:21
across the Jordan * at the Jabbok Gen 32:22,23,24
bank of the Nile *, when suddenly, Gen 41:1
* and began grazing in the grass. Gen 41:2
came up from the *, but they were Gen 41:3
bank of the Nile *," he said, Gen 41:17
came up out of the * and began Gen 41:18
began grazing along the * bank. Gen 41:18
came up from the *, very skinny and Gen 41:19
Located just west of the Jordan *, Gen 50:10f
beyond the Jordan *, they held a Gen 50:10
Hebrew boys into the Nile *. Ex 1:22
to bathe in the *, and as she and Ex 2:5
walking along the * bank, she spied Ex 2:5
from the Nile * and pour it upon Ex 4:9
be there as he goes down to the *. Ex 7:15
Stand beside the * bank and meet Ex 7:15
rod, and the * will turn to blood! Ex 7:17
The fish will die and the * will Ex 7:18
rod, and the * turned to blood. Ex 7:20
wells along the * bank to get Ex 7:24
they couldn't drink from the *. Ex 7:24
The Nile * will swarm with them, Ex 8:3,4
everywhere except in the *." Ex 8:9
except those in the *." Ex 8:11
comes out to the * to bathe, and Ex 8:20
deserts as far as the Euphrates *; Ex 23:31
* valley are the Canaanites." Num 13:29
side of the Arnon *, near the Num 21:13
(The Arnon * is the boundary line Num 21:13
of the Arnon *, and the city of Num 21:14
from the Arnon * to the Jabbok Num 21:24
to the Jabbok *, as far as the Num 21:24
On the heights of the Arnon *. Num 21:27-30
of the Jordan * opposite Jericho. Num 22:1
of Pethor, near the Euphrates *. Num 22:5,6
*, at the border of his land. Num 22:36
the Jordan *, opposite Jericho. Num 26:3,4
the Jordan *, across from Jericho. Num 26:63
look across the * to the land I Num 27:12
the Jordan *, across from Jericho. Num 31:12
the other side of the Jordan *." Num 32:5
the * Jordan, opposite Jericho. Num 33:48
along the Jordan *, from Num 33:49
across the Jordan * into the land Num 33:50,51
*, ending at the Dead Sea." Num 34:12
on the east side of the Jordan *. Num 35:13,14
the Jordan *, across from Jericho. Num 36:13
of Moab, east of the Jordan *. Deu 1:1
Sea to the Euphrates *. Deu 1:7
'Cross the Arnon * into the land of Deu 2:24
edge of the Arnon * valley, and Deu 2:35,36
from the Jabbok * and the hill Deu 2:37
east of the Jordan *—all the land Deu 3:8
Aroer on the Arnon *, plus half of Deu 3:12
from the Jabbok * in Gilead (which Deu 3:16
of the valley of the Arnon *. Deu 3:16
by the Jordan * on the west, from Deu 3:17
across the Jordan *, then you may Deu 3:20
beyond the Jordan * with its Deu 3:23,24,25
you shall not cross the Jordan *. Deu 3:27
go over the Jordan * into the good Deu 4:21,22
die here on this side of the *. Deu 4:21,22
Jordan * and conquer that land. Deu 4:26
east of the Jordan *, where anyone Deu 4:41
* near the city of Beth-peor. Deu 4:44,45,46
edge of the Arnon * valley to Mount Deu 4:48
east of the Jordan * over to the Deu 4:49
cross the Jordan * and begin to Deu 9:1
* to the Mediterranean Sea. Deu 11:24
west of the Jordan *, where the Deu 11:30
But when you cross the Jordan * Deu 12:10
"When you cross the Jordan * and Deu 27:2,3,4
boulders from the * bottom and Deu 27:2,3,4
I shall not cross the Jordan *. Deu 31:2
to possess across the Jordan *." Deu 32:47
Jordan * into the Promised Land. Jos 1:2
to the Euphrates * in the east, Jos 1:4
get ready to cross the Jordan *. Jos 1:10,11
side of the Jordan *," Moses had Jos 1:12,13
across the Jordan * to help them Jos 1:14
to cross the * and check out the Jos 2:1
to the Jordan * looking for them; Jos 2:7
and crossed the * and reported to Jos 2:23
of the Jordan *, where they camped Jos 3:1
Ark and lead us across the *!" Jos 3:6
to stop at the edge of the *." Jos 3:8
earth, will lead you across the *! Jos 3:11
their feet, the * will stop flowing Jos 3:13,14
out to cross the * and as the feet Jos 3:13,14
far up the * at the city of Adam, Jos 3:15,16
a spot where the * was close to the Jos 3:15,16
us that the Jordan * stopped Jos 4:7
of the Jordan *—one for each tribe, Jos 4:8
the middle of the *, at the place Jos 4:9
the middle of the * until all these Jos 4:10
carry the Ark up out of the *. Jos 4:11
the banks of the * as before! Jos 4:18
crossed the Jordan * and camped in Jos 4:19
the Jordan * on dry ground! Jos 4:22
God dried up the * right before our Jos 4:23
west of the Jordan *—the Amorites Jos 5:1
up the Jordan * so the people of Jos 5:1
us over the Jordan * if you are Jos 7:7
west of the Jordan *, along the Jos 9:1
side of the Jordan * whose cities Jos 12:1
of the Arnon * to Mount Hermon, Jos 12:1
of the Arnon * to the Jabbok River, Jos 12:2
to the Jabbok *, which is the Jos 12:2
which lies north of the Jabbok *. Jos 12:2
the Jordan * valley as far north as Jos 12:3
of the Arnon *, included the city Jos 13:9
of the Arnon *, past the city of Jos 13:16
The Jordan * was the western Jos 13:23
The Jordan * was the western Jos 13:27,28
turned east from the Jordan *. Jos 13:27,28
east of the Jordan * where the Jos 13:32
on the east side of the Jordan *. Jos 14:3,4
Sea to the mouth of the Jordan *. Jos 15:5
where the Jordan * empties into the Jos 15:5
from the Jordan * at Jericho Jos 16:1
and ended at the Jordan *. Jos 16:7
[on the east side of the Jordan * Jos 17:1
and Bashan across the Jordan *). Jos 17:5,6
at the Jordan *, went north of Jos 18:12
the southern end of the Jordan *. Jos 18:19
eastern border was the Jordan *. Jos 18:20
of Issachar ended at the Jordan *. Jos 19:17-23
Lakkum, ending at the Jordan *. Jos 19:33
and with the Jordan * at the east. Jos 19:34
the Jordan *, across from Jericho. Jos 20:8
on the other side of the Jordan *. Jos 22:4
* to their own homeland of Gilead. Jos 22:9
They crossed the * and talked to Jos 22:13
on our side of the * where the Lord Jos 22:19
The Lord has placed the Jordan * Jos 22:24,25
All the land from the Jordan * to Jos 23:4,5
lived east of the Euphrates *; Jos 24:2
land across the * and led him into Jos 24:3
"Then you crossed the Jordan * Jos 24:11
the Euphrates * and in Egypt. Jos 24:14
of the Jordan * near Moab, Ju 3:28
them to the Kishon *, and you will Ju 4:7
to the Kishon *. Ju 4:13
The rushing Kishon * Ju 5:21
of the Jordan * at Beth-barah, thus Ju 7:24
Gideon now crossed the Jordan * Ju 8:4
east of the Jordan * in the land of Ju 10:7,8
from the Arnon * to the Jabbok and Ju 11:13
boundary of Moab at the Arnon *; Ju 11:18
from the Arnon * to the Jabbok, and Ju 11:21,22
the wilderness to the Jordan *. Ju 11:21,22
Aroer, and all along the Arnon *. Ju 11:26
tried to cross the *, the Gilead Ju 12:5
crossed the Jordan * and escaped to 1Sa 13:7
crossed the *, and traveled all the 2Sa 2:29
at the Euphrates *, for Hadadezer 2Sa 8:3
the other side of the Euphrates *. 2Sa 10:15,16
ford of the Jordan * and wait there 2Sa 15:28
the ford of the Jordan * tonight. 2Sa 17:16
the men across the Jordan *. 2Sa 17:24
at the Jordan *, it seemed as if 2Sa 19:15
him and escort him across the *! 2Sa 19:15
to conduct the king across the *. 2Sa 19:31,32
Just to go across the * with you 2Sa 19:36
* I promised I wouldn't kill him. 1Ki 2:8
from the Euphrates * to the land of 1Ki 4:21
Euphrates *, from Tiphsah to Gaza. 1Ki 4:24

(RIVER Con't)
* between Succoth and Zarethan. 1Ki 7:41-46
the Euphrates *, for they have 1Ki 14:15
of where it enters the Jordan *. 1Ki 17:3
has sent me to the Jordan *." 2Ki 2:6,7
beside the Jordan * as fifty of the 2Ki 2:6,7
and the * divided and they went 2Ki 2:8
*, and struck the water with it. 2Ki 2:13,14
wash in the Jordan * seven times 2Ki 5:10
Aren't the Abana * and Pharpar 2Ki 5:12
River and Pharpar * of Damascus 2Ki 5:12
down to the Jordan * and dipped 2Ki 5:14
beside the Jordan *, where there 2Ki 6:1
his axhead fell into the *. 2Ki 6:5
way to the Jordan *—thrown away by 2Ki 7:15
crossed the Jordan * and attacked 2Ki 8:21
east of the Jordan *, as well as 2Ki 10:32,33
from the Aroer * in the valley of 2Ki 10:32,33
banks of the Habor * in Gozan, and 2Ki 17:6
banks of the Habor * in Gozan, and 2Ki 18:11
at the Euphrates *, and King Josiah 2Ki 23:29
Brook of Egypt to the Euphrates *. 2Ki 24:7
Shaul from the * town of Rehoboth 1Ch 1:48
to the Euphrates *, for there were 1Ch 5:9
*, where they remain to this day. 1Ch 5:26
And across the Jordan *, opposite 1Ch 6:78,79
They crossed the Jordan * during 1Ch 12:15
side of the Jordan *—where the 1Ch 12:24-37
his grip along the Euphrates *. 1Ch 18:3
of the Euphrates *, led personally 1Ch 19:16
crossed the Jordan *, and engaged 1Ch 19:17,18
of Israel west of the Jordan *; 1Ch 26:30
from the Euphrates * to the land of 2Ch 9:26
at Carchemish on the Euphrates * 2Ch 35:20
lands west of the Euphrates *. Ez 4:10
subjects west of the Euphrates *. Ez 4:11
the area west of the Euphrates *: Ez 4:17
the Euphrates * and have received Ez 4:20
of the Euphrates *: 'You are to Ez 7:21
people west of the Euphrates *; Ez 7:25
We assembled at the Ahava * and Ez 8:15
were at the Ahava * so that we Ez 8:21
We broke camp at the Ahava * at Ez 8:31
of the Euphrates *, and of course Ez 8:36
of the Euphrates * instructing them Neh 2:7
of the Euphrates *, I delivered the Neh 2:9
from a lake, as a * disappears in Job 14:11,12
They are like trees along a * Ps 1:3
and cut off your * of blessings. Ps 30:6,7
where the Jordan * flows and where Ps 42:6
There is a * of joy flowing Ps 46:4
* to the ends of the earth. Ps 72:8
from the rock, flowing like a *! Ps 78:16
Sea to the Euphrates *. Ps 80:11
and Jabin at the * Kishon, and as Ps 83:9
* to the Mediterranean Sea. Ps 89:25
as a racing *, and vanish as Ps 90:5,6
* through the dry and barren land; Ps 105:41
The Jordan * opened up a path for Ps 114:3
What happened, Jordan *, to your Ps 114:5
blow and all the * ice is broken. Ps 147:18
Literally, "the *." Is 11:15f
Even Nimrim * is desolate! Is 15:6
the Arnon * like homeless birds. Is 16:2
sailboats glide along the *! Is 18:1
All green things along the * Is 19:7
* to the Egyptian boundary. Is 27:12
He will refresh her as a * in the Is 32:2
be to us as a wide * of protection, Is 33:21
grass, like willows on a * bank. Is 44:4
like a gentle *, and great waves of Is 48:18
Jerusalem like a *, says the Lord, Is 66:12
to the Euphrates * and hide it in a Jer 13:4
the * again and get the loincloth. Jer 13:6
the Euphrates * by Nebuchadnezzar, Jer 46:2
In the north, by the * Euphrates, Jer 46:6
country beside the * Euphrates! Jer 46:10
I will dry up her *, her water Jer 51:36
into the Euphrates *, and say, 'So Jer 51:63
tears fall down upon you like a *; Lam 2:18
Jewish exiles beside the Chebar *. Eze 3:14,15
beside a broad *, where it would Eze 17:5
beside a broad * and he exiled the Eze 17:12,13
along the course of the Jordan * Eze 26:2
you and your * and I will utterly Eze 29:10
it had become a * so deep I Eze 47:5
growing on both sides of the *! Eze 47:7
He told me: "This * flows east Eze 47:8
the water of this * shall live. Eze 47:9
trees will grow along the * banks. Eze 47:12
For they are watered by the * Eze 47:12
along the Jordan * separating Eze 47:18
* of fire flowed from before him. Dan 7:10
Elam, standing beside the Ulai *. Dan 8:2
long horns standing on the * bank; Dan 8:3
from across the *, "Gabriel, tell Dan 8:16
the great Tigris *, I looked up Dan 10:4
on each bank of a *. Dan 12:5
now above the *, "How long will it Dan 12:6
It will rise up like the * Nile Amo 8:8
It rises like the * Nile in Amo 9:5
But too late! The * gates are Nah 2:6
protected on all sides by the *? Nah 3:8
among the myrtle trees beside a *. Zec 1:8
the * to the ends of the earth. Zec 9:10
he baptized them in the Jordan *. Mt 3:6
* to be baptized there by John. Mt 3:13
beyond the Jordan *, and Upper Mt 4:15,16
and even from across the Jordan *. Mt 4:25
to Judea from across the Jordan *. Mt 19:1
he baptized them in the Jordan *. Mk 1:5
by John there in the Jordan *. Mk 1:9
beyond the Jordan *, and even from Mk 3:7,8
the area east of the Jordan *. Mk 10:1
of the Jordan *, preaching that Lk 3:3
Holy Spirit, left the Jordan *, Lk 4:1
Jordan * where John was baptizing. Jn 1:28
side of the Jordan *—the one you Jn 3:26
beyond the Jordan * to stay near Jn 10:40
the city to a * bank where we Act 16:13
prayer beside the *, we met a Act 16:16
held bound at the great * Rev 9:14
upon the great * Euphrates and it Rev 16:12
AND HE POINTED out to me a * of Rev 22:1
On each side of the * grew Trees Rev 22:2

RIVER'S
among the reeds along the * edge. Ex 2:3
the water at the * edge, suddenly, Jos 3:13,14

RIVERBANK
planted along a *, with its roots Jer 17:8

RIVERBED
Salt Sea until the * was empty. Jos 3:15,16
hurried across the *, and when Jos 4:10
"Come up from the *," the Lord Jos 4:15,16

RIVERS
of Egypt: all its *, canals, Ex 7:19
rod toward all the *, streams, and Ex 8:5
taken from * or from the sea; Lev 11:9
all the * of Israel put together? 2Ki 5:12
If it's * I need, I'll wash at 2Ki 5:12
God blows upon the *, and even Job 37:10
He is not disturbed by raging *, Job 40:23
them drink from your * of delight. Ps 36:8
The * of God will not run dry! Ps 65:9
— how he turned their * into Ps 78:44
He dries up *, and turns the Ps 107:33
WEEPING, WE SAT beside the * of Ps 137:1
The * run into the sea but the Ecc 1:3-7
again to the *, and flows again to Ecc 1:3-7
Literally, "land beyond the * of Is 18:1f
Literally, "whose land the * Is 18:2f
whose land the * divide, will bring Is 18:7
I will open up * for them on Is 41:18
of water, and * fed by springs Is 41:18
He will dry up the * and pools. Is 42:15
When you go through * of Is 43:2
create * for them in the desert! Is 43:19
When I speak to the * and say, Is 44:27
drunk with * of their own blood. Is 49:26
I can turn the * into deserts, Is 50:2
you and against the * and valleys. Eze 6:3
lying in the middle of your *. Eze 29:3
and valleys and * of the land. Eze 31:12
Israel and by the * where the land Eze 34:13
valleys and your * will be filled Eze 35:8
ten thousands of * of olive Mic 6:7
At his command the oceans and * Nah 1:4
the Lord displeased against the *? Hab 3:8,9f
You ribboned the earth with *." Hab 3:8,9f
smote the * and parted the sea? Hab 3:8,9
Those who live far beyond the * Zep 3:10
declare that * of living water Jn 7:38
from flooded *, and from robbers, 2Co 11:26
upon a third of the * and springs. Rev 8:10
and to turn * and oceans to blood, Rev 11:6
his flask upon the * and springs Rev 16:4
"The oceans, lakes and * that Rev 17:15

RIVERSIDE
And fruitful gardens by the *; Num 24:3-9

RIZIA
Arah, Hanniel, *. 1Ch 7:39

RIZPAH
Saul's concubines, a girl named *. 2Sa 3:7
the two sons of *—Armoni and 2Sa 21:8
Then *, the mother of two of the 2Sa 21:10

ROAD
desert spring along the * to Shur. Gen 16:7
buried near the * to Ephrath (also Gen 35:19
and sat beside the * at the Gen 38:14
out beside the * at the entrance of Gen 38:21
her beside the * to Bethlehem." Gen 48:7
stay on the main * and not leave it Num 20:17
stay on the main * and will not Num 20:19
along the * to the Red Sea in order Num 21:4
"We will not leave the * until Num 21:22
to stand in the * to kill him. Num 22:22,23
in the * with a drawn sword. Num 22:22,23
She bolted off the * into a Num 22:22,23
Balaam beat her back onto the *. Num 22:22,23
* went between two vineyard walls. Num 22:24
farther down the * and stood in a Num 22:26
So she lay down in the *! Num 22:27
the Arabah * that goes south to Deu 2
'We will stay on the main * and Deu 2:2
along the * without success. Jos 2:2
Sea, ran along the * going south of Jos 15:2,3,
the * past the oak of Meonenim!" Ju 9:3
east side of the * that goes from Ju 21:1
Eli was waiting beside the * to 1Sa 4:1
straight along the * toward 1Sa 6:1
replied, "stay right on this *. 1Sa 9:12,1
all along the * to Shaaraim. 1Sa 17:5
At the place where the * passes 1Sa 24:
Saul camped along the * at the 1Sa 26:3,
Shur along the * to Egypt ever 1Sa 27:
the * into the Gibeon desert. 2Sa 2:2
the * at the side of the hill. 2Sa 13:3
the * until everyone had passed. 2Sa 15:2
David walked up the * that led to 2Sa 15:3
the middle of the *, and when 2Sa 20:1
him off the * into a field and 2Sa 20:1
to Judah by the * I came on." 1Ki 13:
home by the same * I came on." 1Ki 13:16,1
His body lay there on the *, with 1Ki 13:24,2
body lying in the * and the lion 1Ki 13:24,2
the prophet's body lying in the *; 1Ki 13:2
back by the desert * to Damascus, 1Ki 19:1
king beside the *, having placed a 1Ki 20:3
As he was walking along the *, 2Ki 2:2
fled along the * to Beth-haggan. 2Ki 9:2
the * climbs to Gur, near Ibleam. 2Ki 9:2
at Millo on the * to Silla. 2Ki 12:2
back on the * by which you came. 2Ki 19:28
He shall return by the * he 2Ki 19:3
the upper *, to Shuppim and Hosah. 1Ch 26:16
*, and two to the nearby areas. 1Ch 26:18
in Jerusalem as rocks on the *! 2Ch 1:15
in Jerusalem as stones in the *! 2Ch 9:27
order to control the * to Judah. 2Ch 16:1
* from which I shall never return. Job 16:22
shine upon the * ahead of you. Job 22:28
They block my * and do Job 30:13
point out the right * for me to Ps 25:4
He made a dry * through the sea Ps 66:6
Yes, all through life their * is Ps 73:4
Your * led by a pathway through Ps 77:19
You led your people along that * Ps 77:20
forming a dry * across its bottom. Ps 106:9
the * and drowned their foes; Ps 106:11
Their houses lie along the * to Pro 2:18
If you want to find the * to Pro 7:27
*, and at the door of every house. Pro 8:1
The sinner's * is dark and Pro 13:9
man must walk a rocky *. Pro 13:15
you are on the * to fame. Pro 13:18
wide and pleasant * that seems Pro 14:12
The * of the godly leads upward, Pro 15:24
wide and pleasant * he thinks is Pro 16:25
walks a thorny, treacherous *; Pro 22:5
decided to try the * of drink, Ecc 2:3
away to follow his own downward *. Ecc 7:29
near the * that leads down to the Is 7:3
where lies the * to the sea, will Is 9:1
It lies as a carcass in the *, Is 14:19
Weeping, they climb the upward * Is 15:5
heard all along the * to Horonaim. Is 15:5
but smooths the * before them. Is 26:7
And a main * will go through that Is 35:8
go home along that * to Zion, Is 35:10
pool, along the * going past the Is 36:2
own land by the same * you came." Is 37:29
own country by the * he came on, Is 37:34
shouting, "Make a * for the Lord Is 40:3
make him a straight, smooth * Is 40:3
off the rough spots in the *. Is 40:4
and straighten out the * ahead. Is 42:16
I will make a * through the Is 43:19
I will say, Rebuild the *! Is 57:14
beside the * waiting for a client! Jer 3:2
Ask where the good * is, the godly Jer 6:16
"No, that is not the * we want!" Jer 6:16
when he is on the wrong * and Jer 8:4,5
Turn from the evil * you are Jer 25:5
* signs pointing back to Israel. Jer 31:21
beside the * to watch, and shout to Jer 48:19
at the fork in the * from Babylon. Eze 21:19,20
I'll block the * before her to Hos 1:6
murder along the * to Shechem and Hos 6:9
or a leopard lurking along the *. Hos 13:7
in all the streets and every *. Amo 5:16
'Prepare a * for the Mt 3:3
is small, and the * is narrow, and Mt 7:14
As Jesus was going on down the *, Mt 9:9
or they will faint along the *." Mt 15:32
sitting beside the * and when they Mt 20:30
he stopped in the * and called, Mt 20:32,33
coats along the * ahead of him, and Mt 21:8
noticed a fig tree beside the *. Mt 21:19
them, they will faint along the *! Mk 8:3
you discussing out on the *?" Mk 9:33
the * as Jesus was going by. Mk 10:46
there in the * and said, "Tell him Mk 10:49
and followed Jesus down the *! Mk 10:52

OAD Con't)
:oats along the * before him, while Mk 11:8
. * for the Lord to travel on! Lk 3:4
him lying half dead beside the *. Lk 10:30
side of the * and passed him by. Lk 10:31
the *, begging from travelers. Lk 18:35
beside the *, to watch from there. Lk 19:4
for a donkey tied beside the *. Lk 19:30
robes along the * ahead of him, and Lk 19:36,37
place where the * started down from Lk 19:36,37
the * will burst into cheers!" Lk 19:40
during the walk down the *. Lk 24:32
walking along the * and how they Lk 24:35
Jesus led them out along the * Lk 24:50
of miles down the * from Jerusalem, Jn 11:18
and went down the * to meet him, Jn 12:13
"Go over to the * that runs from Act 8:26
be coming down the * but the Act 8:27
to you on the *, has sent me so Act 9:17
"As I was on the *, nearing Act 22:6
to him [there on the Damascus * Act 23:9
* ready to jump him and kill him. Act 23:21
who is on the * to eternal death. 2Co 4:3
the Christian * who are really Php 3:18
them safely away by a different *. Jas 2:25
the impossible * to heaven which 1Pe 1:18
They have gone off the * and 2Pe 2:15

OADS
so that your * will be deserted. Lev 26:22
and keep the * to these cities in Deu 19:2,3
The main * were deserted. Ju 5:6
the city and the * to seek him, but Sol 3:2
Your * lie in ruins; Is 33:8
travelers detour on back *. Is 33:8
Build the *, pull out the Is 62:10
Don't travel the *! Jer 6:25
The * to Zion mourn, no longer Lam 1:4

ROADWAY
standing in the * with drawn sword, Num 22:31
Israel along the * running between Ju 20:31
Prepare the * for my people to Is 62:10

ROAM
into the hills and * with my girl Ju 11:37

ROAMING
and began * the countryside. 1Sa 23:13

ROAR
Let the vast seas *, 1Ch 16:32
the * of the captain's commands. Job 39:25
Let the oceans * and foam; Ps 46:3
in all its vastness * with praise! Ps 98:7
Then the young lions * for their Ps 104:21
They * like lions and pounce Is 5:29
But though they * like breakers Is 17:13
men! You * like hungry bears; Is 59:11
*, can never pass those bounds. Jer 5:22
And then the * of battle will Jer 48:2,3,4
the men of Babylon * like lions. Jer 51:38
as the waves * in upon her. Jer 51:55
with terror when they heard him *. Eze 19:7
let the fire * and the pot boil. Eze 24:10
was like the * of rushing waters Eze 43:2
I shall * as a lion [at their Hos 11:10
chariots, or the * of fire sweeping Joe 2:5
But now a mighty * rose from the Lk 23:18
was like the * of a lion—and the Rev 10:3

ROARED
they *. Ex 5:14
"Am I a dog," he * at David, 1Sa 17:43
the king *. Est 7:8
Literally, "The lions have * Jer 2:15f
My people have * at me like a Jer 12:8
And as they flew, their wings * Eze 1:24
heard: The Lord *—like a ferocious Amo 1:2
The Lion has *—tremble in fear. Amo 3:8
"What do you mean," he *, Jon 1:6
They only * the louder, Mk 15:14
and wicked slave,' the king *. Lk 19:22
and their wings * like an army of Rev 9:9
crashed and *, and there was a Rev 11:19

ROARING
For forty days the * floods Gen 7:17
He was * drunk, so she didn't 1Sa 25:36
Afterwards comes the * of the Job 37:4
like * lions attacking their prey. Ps 22:13
let the vastness of the * seas Ps 96:11
they blaze against me like a * Ps 118:12
fury is like that of a * lion; Pro 20:2
victims like the * of the sea. Is 5:30
Disaster is * down upon you from Is 21:1
the sea, between the * waves. Is 51:15
gusts but in a * blast—and he will Jer 4:11,12
of their army is like a * sea. Jer 6:23
sea to make the * waves—his name is Jer 31:35
until it becomes a * conflagration, Eze 21:31
fell down bound into the * flames. Dan 3:23
* of a vast multitude of people. Dan 10:5,6
"Would I be * as a lion unless I Amo 3:4
Her leaders are like * lions Zep 3:3
Hear the young lions *—the Zec 11:3
by the * seas and strange tides. Lk 21:25
a sound like the * of a mighty Act 2:2

And when they heard the * in the Act 2:6
He prowls around like a hungry, * 1Pe 5:8
heaven like the * of a great Rev 14:2

ROARS
fire that * across a mountain. Ps 83:14
whirlwind of the Lord * with fury; Jer 30:23
their battle cry * like the surf Jer 50:42

ROAST
and milk and the * veal, he set it Gen 18:8
Everyone shall eat * lamb that Ex 12:8
ear, crush and * them, then offer Lev 2:14
sun goes down. * the lamb and eat Deu 16:7
to build a fire to * their flesh. 1Ki 19:21
Part of the tree he burns to * Is 44:16
it to bake my bread and * my meat. Is 44:19
is ready and the * is in the oven. Mt 22:4

ROASTED
raw or boiled, but *, including the Ex 12:9
shall take the * shoulder of the Num 6:19
They have even * their sons and Deu 12:31
Gideon hurried home and * a young Ju 6:19
this bushel of * grain and these 1Sa 17:17
two bushels of * grain, one hundred 1Sa 25:18
lamb and * it and served it." 2Sa 12:4
of Moses, they * the Passover lambs 2Ch 35:13

ROASTING
so that it could be used for *. 1Sa 2:15

ROB
but he shall * and pursue them! Gen 49:19
"You shall not * nor oppress Lev 19:13
Must you * him, too? 1Ki 21:19
needy from those who would * them? Ps 35:10
"We'll hide and * and kill," Pro 1:11
Don't * the poor and sick! Pro 22:22,23
Yes, it is true that they even * Is 10:2
Those who * you shall be robbed; Jer 30:16
him and doesn't * them, but feeds Eze 18:16
people oppress and * the poor and Eze 22:29
you in hatred, and * you of all Eze 23:29
will ask, 'Who are you to * them Eze 38:13
longer oppress and * my people, but Eze 45:8
sent Heliodorus to * and desecrate Dan 11:20f
your husbands to * the poor and Amo 4:1
Listen, you merchants who * the Amo 8:4
customs and who * and kill to fill Zep 1:9
"Will a man * God? Mal 3:8
When did we ever * you?' Mal 3:8
One cannot * Satan's kingdom Mt 12:29
you would * me of what I earned, Mt 25:24,25
and no one can * you of that joy. Jn 16:22
Literally, "do you * temples?" Rom 2:22f

ROBBED
you will be oppressed and * Deu 28:29
come along, they * everyone else Ju 9:25
bear who has been * of her cubs. 2Sa 17:8
was the man who * God and was such 1Ch 2:7
were captured, *, and disgraced, Ez 9:7
Everyone who comes along has * Ps 89:41
It is safer to meet a bear * of Pro 17:12
when the crop is stripped and *. Is 1:8
In our greatness we have * their Is 10:14
leave it all. I am * of my normal Is 38:10
for they are *, enslaved, Is 42:22
Who let Israel be * and hurt? Is 42:24
This sin has * them of all of Jer 5:25
Those who rob you shall be *; Jer 30:16
For you scorned Israel and * Jer 48:27
Her treasures shall all be *; Jer 50:37
her and * her of her virginity. Eze 23:8
and sword, or being jailed and *. Dan 11:33
Wine, women, and song have * my Hos 4:11
Or if your vineyards were * of Ob 1:5
be searched and *, and every Ob 1:6
And yet you have * me. Mal 3:8
"You have * me of the tithes and Mal 3:8
be ransacked and his property *. Mk 3:27
Instead I "*" other churches 2Co 11:8,9

ROBBER
you like a * and destroys you; Pro 6:11
Like a *, she waits for her Pro 23:26,27,28
a *, and violently like a bandit. Pro 24:34
debtors, and is no *, but gives Eze 18:7
has a son who is a * or murderer Eze 18:10
I some dangerous *, that you come Mk 14:48
"Am I a *," he asked, "that Lk 22:52
Barabbas was a *. Jn 18:40

ROBBERS
all those in need. For * prosper. Job 12:6
He walks into traps, and * will Job 18:8,9
Is my Temple but a den of * in Jer 7:11
I stop them. Like *, they will loot Eze 7:22
Her citizens are gangs of *, Hos 6:9
will taunt them, saying: 'You *! Hab 2:6
Two * were also crucified there Mt 27:38
And the * also threw the same in Mt 27:44
have turned it into a den of *." Mk 11:17
Two * were also crucified that Mk 15:27
And even the two * dying with him, Mk 15:32
came before me were thieves and *. Jn 10:8
drunkards, slanderers, or *. 1Co 6:9,10
rivers, and from *, and from my own 2Co 11:26

ROBBERY
to him, or by *, or by oppressing Lev 6:2
There is murder and * there, and Ps 55:11
become rich by extortion and *. Ps 62:10,11
I hate * and wrong. Is 61:8
money gained from murdering and *! Hab 2:12

ROBBING
can never accuse me of * you." 1Sa 12:5
at Keilah * the threshing floors. 1Sa 23:1
the rulers: Quit * and cheating my Eze 45:9
ways, from his violence and *. Jon 3:8
your whole nation has been * me. Mal 3:9

ROBE
Then Shem and Japheth took a * Gen 9:23
brightly-colored *, and threw him Gen 37:23
your *, next to your chest." Ex 4:6
a *, a checkered tunic, a turban, Ex 28:4
Then put Aaron's * on him, and Ex 29:5
to the bottom edge of the *; Ex 39:24
the edge. This * was worn when Ex 39:25,26
coat, sash, *, and the ephod-jacket Lev 8:7
For I saw a beautiful * imported Jos 7:21
the silver, the *, the wedge of Jos 7:24
beneath his * with his strong left Ju 3:21
linen * just like the priest's. 1Sa 2:18
incense, and to wear a priestly * 1Sa 2:28
to hold him back, and tore his *. 1Sa 15:27
him his *, sword, bow, and belt. 1Sa 18:4
slit off the bottom of Saul's *! 1Sa 24:4
It is the hem of your *! 1Sa 24:11
"He is an old man wrapped in a * 1Sa 28:14
She was wearing a long * with 2Sa 13:17,18
Now she tore the * and put ashes 2Sa 13:19
up, ripped off his *, and fell 2Sa 13:31
had put on a new * for the 1Ki 11:29
tore his new * into twelve parts, 1Ki 11:30
from sight he tore his *. 2Ki 2:12
wearing an inner * made of 2Ki 6:26-30
noble princes to * the man and to Est 6:9
Then Job stood up and tore his * Job 1:20
Literally, "tore his * and shaved Job 1:20f
and onto the border of his *. Ps 133:2
strip off your *; Is 47:2
Rise up and * yourself with Is 51:9
about me the * of righteousness. Is 61:10
the hair and tie it up in your *; Eze 5:3
O priests, * yourselves in Joe 1:13
a tassel of his *, for she Mt 9:20
*, and all who did were healed. Mt 14:36
the wedding * [provided for him Mt 22:11
you are here without a wedding *?' Mt 22:12
and put a scarlet * on him, and Mt 27:28
they took off the * and put his own Mt 27:31
him in a purple *, and made a crown Mk 15:16,17
off the purple * and put his own Mk 15:20
of his *, the bleeding stopped. Lk 8:43,44
Bring the finest * in the house Lk 15:22
and putting a kingly * on him, Lk 23:11
took off his *, wrapped a towel Jn 13:4
feet he put on his * again and sat Jn 13:12
crown of thorns and the purple *. Jn 19:5
up his *," for it was seamless. Jn 19:23,24
them, and cast lots for my *." Jn 19:23,24
before me clothed in a radiant *! Act 10:30
the dust from his * and said, Act 18:6
wearing a long * circled with a Rev 1:13
On his * and thigh was written Rev 19:16

ROBED
Have you ever * the dawn in red, Job 38:14
her chamber, * in beautiful Ps 45:13
He is * in majesty and strength. Ps 93:1
You are * with honor and with Ps 104:1
Daniel was * in purple, and a Dan 5:29
me stood a person * in linen Dan 10:5,6
was not * as well as they are. Lk 12:27
head and * him in royal purple. Jn 19:2

ROBES
"Then, for Aaron's sons, make *, Ex 28:40
worn beneath their * next to their Ex 28:42
Next, dress his sons in their *, Ex 29:8
* were now made for Aaron and his Ex 39:27
sons and put their * upon them, Ex 40:14
Next Moses placed the * on Lev 8:13
And Sisera will get gorgeous *, Ju 5:30
plain * and thirty fancy robes. Ju 14:12
plain robes and thirty fancy *. Ju 14:12
then you must give the * to me!" Ju 14:13
all, all wearing their priestly *. 1Sa 22:18
clothing instead of his royal *. 1Sa 28:7,8
and cut their * off at the buttocks 2Sa 10:4
in their royal * and were sitting 1Ki 22:10
royal *, but I'll not wear mine!" 1Ki 22:30
in his royal *, they thought, 1Ki 22:32,33
He gave him two expensive *, tied 2Ki 5:23
wears one of the special *." 2Ki 10:22
women wove * for the Asherah-idol. 2Ki 23:7
were all dressed in linen *. 1Ch 15:27
and cutting their * off at the 1Ch 19:4
in finespun linen * and standing at 2Ch 5:11,12
me, but you put on your royal *!" 2Ch 18:29
Judah in his royal *, they went for 2Ch 18:31

(ROBES Con't)
(He laid aside his royal * so 2Ch 35:22
silver, and 100 * for the priests. Ez 2:69
* and blew their trumpets; Ez 3:10
put on her royal * and entered the Est 5:1
some of the royal * the king Est 6:7,8
"Hurry and take these * and my Est 6:10
So Haman took the * and put them Est 6:11
Then Mordecai put on the royal * Est 8:15
they tore their * and threw dust Job 2:12
All right then, put on your * of Job 40:10
Your * are perfumed with myrrh, Ps 45:8
Or, "in the priestly *." Ps 96:9f
dressed in holy altar *. Ps 110:3
they'll wear sacks instead of *. Is 3:24
he tore his * and wound himself in Is 37:1
He clothed himself with * of Is 59:17
Who is this in kingly *, marching Is 63:1
When we put on our prized * of Is 64:6
purple * that expert tailors make. Jer 10:9
lay aside their * and beautiful Eze 26:16
The special * in which they have Eze 42:14
be removed, for these * are holy. Eze 42:14
dressed in purple * of royal honor Dan 5:7
you in purple *, with a golden Dan 5:16
the man in linen * who was standing Dan 12:6
aside his royal * and put on Jon 3:6
sacrifice in his *, and happens to Hag 2:12
the memorial fringes of their *. Mt 23:5
those pious * of yours are hearts Mt 23:28
For they love to wear the * of Mk 12:38
spread out their * along the road Lk 19:36,37
in dignified * and to be bowed to Lk 20:46
clothed in shining * so bright Lk 24:4
put on his royal *, sat on his Act 12:21
White * were given to each of Rev 6:11
"they washed their * and Rev 7:14
me, who keep their * in readiness Rev 16:15
are washing their *, to have the Rev 22:14

ROBING
He instructed the head of the * 2Ki 10:22

ROBS
but injustice * him of its riches. Pro 13:23
A man who * his parents and says, Pro 28:24
and needy, and * his debtors by Eze 18:12
he is cruel and * and does wrong. Eze 18:18

ROBUST
became a strong, * lad, and was Lk 2:40

ROCK
he found a * for a headrest and lay Gen 28:11
the Shepherd, the * of Israel. Gen 49:24
I will meet you there at the *. Ex 17:5,6
However, stand here on this * Ex 33:21
the cleft of the * and cover you Ex 33:22
The coney, or * badger (because Lev 11:4-7
As they watch, speak to that * Num 20:8
You will give them water from a * Num 20:8
to come and gather at the *; Num 20:10
we bring you water from this *?" Num 20:10
the * twice, and water gushed out; Num 20:11
Lord had said to speak to the *. Num 20:12f
water to come out of the *." Num 27:14
He gave you water from the *! Deu 8:15
He is the *. Deu 32:4
Honey from the *, Deu 32:13
They shrugged away the * of their Deu 32:15
They spurned the * who had made Deu 32:18
Unless their * had abandoned them, Deu 32:30
But the * of other nations Deu 32:31
Is not like our *; Deu 32:31
a spot called The *, and continues Ju 1:36
bread upon that * over there, and Ju 6:20
up from the * and consumed them! Ju 6:21
Oreb was killed at the * now Ju 7:25
live in a cave in the * of Etam. Ju 15:8
at the cave in the * of Etam. Ju 15:11
toward the * of Rimmon, but five Ju 20:45
who escaped to the * of Rimmon, Ju 20:46,47
the men of Benjamin at Rimmon *. Ju 21:13
Nor any * like our God. 1Sa 2:2
and stopped beside a large *. 1Sa 6:14
the cart and laid them on the *. 1Sa 6:15
(By the way, that large * at 1Sa 6:18
been called, "The * of Escape!" 1Sa 23:28
spread sackcloth upon a * and 2Sa 21:10
"Jehovah is my *, 2Sa 22:2
Who is my * and my refuge. 2Sa 22:3
Literally, "Who is a * save our 2Sa 22:32f
Blessed be my *. 2Sa 22:47
The * of my salvation. 2Sa 22:47
The * of Israel said to me: 2Sa 23:3
from the * when they were thirsty. Neh 9:15
with an iron pen in the * forever. Job 19:23,24
Into the black *, shadowed by Job 28:3,4
and even the * poured out streams Job 29:6
and turns to ice, as hard as *. Job 38:30
His heart is hard as *, just Job 41:24
he is my Savior, a * where none Ps 18:2
Who but he is as a *? Ps 18:31
Praise him who is the great * of Ps 18:46
you, O Lord my * and my Redeemer. Ps 19:14
He will set me on a high * out Ps 27:5
Lord, for you are my * of safety. Ps 28:1
Be for me a great * of safety Ps 31:2
Yes, you are my * and my Ps 31:3
"O God my *," I cry, "why have Ps 42:9
the mighty, towering * of safety. Ps 61:2
Yes, he alone is my *, my Ps 62:2
Yes, he alone is my *, my Ps 62:6
He is my refuge, a * where no Ps 62:7
Be to me a great protecting *, Ps 71:3
Streams poured from the *, Ps 78:16
that God was their *—that their Ps 78:35
Literally, "honey out of the *." Ps 81:16f
my God, and my * of Salvation.' Ps 89:26
mighty * where I can hide. Ps 94:21,22
honor of the * of our salvation! Ps 95:1
He opened up a *, and water Ps 105:41
streams to burst from flinty *. Ps 114:8
THE LORD who is my immovable *. Ps 144:1
How a serpent crawls upon a *. Pro 30:18,19
against the * of their salvation Is 8:14,15
over Midian at the * of Oreb or the Is 10:26
save you—the * who can hide you; Is 17:10
sepulchre in the * for yourself? Is 22:15,16
of the Lord, the * of Israel. Is 30:29
* within a hot and weary land. Is 32:2
There is no other *! Is 44:8
he divided the *, and water Is 48:21
the * from which you were cut! Is 51:1
faces hard as *, not to repent. Jer 5:3
that smashed the * to pieces? Jer 23:29
the scroll, tie a * to it and throw Jer 51:63
in a well and capped it with a *. Lam 3:53
made your forehead as hard as *. Eze 3:9
her soil and make her a bare *! Eze 26:4
I will make your island a bare * Eze 26:14
But as you watched, a * was cut Dan 2:34
But the * that knocked the statue Dan 2:35
That is the meaning of the * cut Dan 2:45
human hands—the * that crushed to Dan 2:45
O God our *, you have decreed the Hab 1:12
who builds his house on solid *. Mt 7:24
collapse, for it is built on *. Mt 7:25
and upon this * I will build my Mt 16:18
for you to have a * tied to your Mt 18:6
All who stumble on this * of Mt 21:44
a cord across the *, the cord being Mt 27:66f
on thin soil with underlying *. Mk 4:5,6
Scriptures? 'The * the builders Mk 12:10
laid upon the underlying *. Lk 6:47,48
on shallow soil with * beneath. Lk 8:6
sea with a huge * tied to his neck, Lk 17:2,3
into the * [at the side of a hill Lk 23:53
shall be called Peter, the *!" Jn 1:42
"I have put a * in the path of the Rom 9:33
of a spiritual * that followed 1Co 10:3,4f
them, and the * was Christ." 1Co 10:3,4f
mighty * of spiritual refreshment. 1Co 10:3,4
great *, and nothing can shake it. 2Ti 2:19
of * upon which God builds; 1Pe 2:4
the * that will make them fall." 1Pe 2:8

ROCK-BADGERS
wild goats, and * burrow in among Ps 104:18

ROCK-HEWN
it in his own new * tomb, and Mt 27:60
and laid it in a * tomb, and rolled Mk 15:46

ROCKED
Then the earth * and reeled, and Ps 18:7

ROCKS
ate together beside the pile of *. Gen 31:46
Your nest is set in the *! Num 24:21,22
Or, "oil from flinty *." Deu 32:13f
The * they claimed to be their Deu 32:37
*, and even in tombs and cisterns. 1Sa 13:6
* and wild goats of the desert. 1Sa 24:2
Like mountain goats upon the *. 2Sa 22:34
blast that the * were torn loose, 1Ki 19:11
babies against the *, and rip open 2Ki 8:12
in Jerusalem as * on the road! 2Ch 1:15
were crushed upon the * below. 2Ch 25:12
tear apart flinty * and how to Job 28:9
They drill tunnels in the * and Job 28:10
and in caves, and among the *. Job 30:6
The wild animals hide in the * Job 37:8
He split open the * in the Ps 78:15
against the * on the trail. Ps 91:12
the * and find protection there. Ps 104:18
and smashes them against the *! Ps 137:9
are heavier than sand and *. Pro 27:3
themselves by living among the *. Pro 30:24-28
"My dove is hiding behind some * Sol 2:14
Crawl into the caves in the * and Is 2:10
the holes in the * and into the Is 2:19
among the jagged * at the tops of Is 2:21
took out all the * and planted his Is 5:2
and cut a winepress in the *. Is 5:2
dwell on high. The * of the Is 33:16
the valleys, under overhanging *. Is 57:5
Clear away the * and stones. Is 57:14
of deserts and *, of drought and Jer 2:6
and hide it in a hole in the *. Jer 13:4
you, bury large * between the Jer 43:
that nest in the clefts of the *. Jer 48:2
of Petra, in the clefts of the *. Jer 49:1
the * in open view for all to see; Eze 24:
Can horses run on *? Amo 6:1
Though they hide among the * at Amo 9:
Petra, the city hewn from *; Ob 1:
from smashing on the * below." Mt 4:
and the earth shook, and * broke, Mt 27:5
and fearing * along the coast, Act 27:2
* and be driven up onto the beach. Act 27:3
in the caves and * of the Rev 6:1

ROCKY
pass between two * crags which had 1Sa 14:
A treacherous man must walk a * Pro 13:1
And some fell on * soil where Mt 13:
The shallow, * soil represents Mt 13:2
forget it. The * soil represents Mk 4:1

ROD
And he replied, "A shepherd's * Ex 4:2
He did, and it became a * in Ex 4:4
And be sure to take your * along Ex 4:17
tightly to the "* of God"! Ex 4:20
*, and it will become a serpent." Ex 7:9
threw down his * before Pharaoh and Ex 7:10
the * that turned into a serpent. Ex 7:15
the Nile with his *, and the river Ex 7:17
Aaron to point his * toward the Ex 7:19
*, and the river turned to blood. Ex 7:20
Aaron to point the * toward all the Ex 8:5
the dust with his *, and it will Ex 8:16
So Moses lifted his * and Jehovah Ex 10:13
Use your *—hold it out over the Ex 14:16
Meanwhile, Moses stretched his * Ex 14:21
Strike it with your * Ex 17:5,6
with the * of God in my hand!" Ex 17:9
Moses held up the * in his hands, Ex 17:11
tired to hold up the * any longer; Ex 17:12
* with his name inscribed upon it. Num 17:1
Aaron's name is to be on the * of Num 17:1
for buds will grow on his *! Num 17:5
(including Aaron) brought him a *. Num 17:6
found that Aaron's *, representing Num 17:8
man except Aaron claimed his *. Num 17:9
to place Aaron's * permanently Num 17:10
Literally, "get the *." Num 20:8f
*; then you and Aaron must summon Num 20:8
He took the * from the place Num 20:9
Then Moses lifted the * and Num 20:11
Rule them with an iron *; Ps 2:9
Literally, "Your * and your staff Ps 23:4f
* of your strength out of Zion." Ps 110:2f
and a rebel with a * to his back! Pro 26:3
Can a * strike unless a hand is Is 10:15
That * is broken, yes; Is 14:29
who had been his * of punishment. Is 30:31
come from the * of God's wrath. Lam 3:1
With a * they shall strike the Mic 5:1
You will rule them with a * of Rev 2:27

RODANIM
Elishah, Tarshish, Kittim, and *. 1Ch 1:5-9

RODE
His thirty sons * around Ju 10:4
who * on seventy donkeys. Ju 12:14
of his life. He * circuit 1Sa 7:16
He * upon the glorious— 2Sa 22:11
and he * on the king's own mule. 1Ki 1:44,45
The stands * on four wheels which 1Ki 7:32
for him, he * after the prophet 1Ki 13:14
into a chariot and * to Jezreel 2Ki 9:16
So a soldier * out to meet Jehu. 2Ki 9:18
a second rider. He * up to them and 2Ki 9:19
of Judah * out to meet Jehu. 2Ki 9:21
Beth-haggan. Jehu * after him, 2Ki 9:27
So Jehonadab * along with him. 2Ki 10:16
sin that you * upon your horses? Hab 3:8,9f
Jesus * along on a young donkey, Jn 12:14
As they * along, they came to a Act 8:36
upon his head; he * out to conquer Rev 6:2
This time a red horse * out. Rev 6:4

RODS
and placed these * beside the Gen 30:38
the white-streaked *, and their Gen 30:39,40
Their * became serpents, too! Ex 7:12
silver *, attached to the posts. Ex 27:9,10
sockets, with silver hooks and *. Ex 27:11
by silver *, using silver hooks, Ex 27:17
and * were overlaid with gold; Ex 36:38
and with silver hooks and *. Ex 38:10
bases and with silver hooks and *. Ex 38:11
and with silver hooks and *. Ex 38:12
all the hooks and * were silver; Ex 38:17
silver, and the * to hold up the Ex 38:17
and with silver hooks and *; Ex 38:19
tops, and for the * and hooks. Ex 38:28
Put these * in the inner room of Num 17:4
I will use these * to identify Num 17:5
is gone out of the * of its Eze 19:14f
as grain is threshed with iron *. Amo 1:3
Again and again the * slashed Act 16:23
Three times I was beaten with *. 2Co 11:25

OEBUCK
The deer, the gazelle, the *, Deu 14:3,4,5
OEBUCKS
deer, gazelles, *, and plump fowl. 1Ki 4:23
OGELIM
and Barzillai (a Gileadite of *). 2Sa 17:27
arrived from * to conduct the king 2Sa 19:31,32
OHGAH
*, Jehubbah, Aram. 1Ch 7:34
OLL
Literally, "This is the * of Gen 5:1f
"We don't * away the stone and Gen 29:8
Literally, "to *" (away). Jos 5:8,9f
Saul said. "* a great stone over 1Sa 14:33
in it himself. * a boulder down on Pro 26:27
and it will * back and crush you. Pro 26:27
The enemy shall * down upon us Jer 4:13
against you and * you down from Jer 51:25
awesome army—will * down upon them Eze 38:9
In Beth-le-aphrah * in the dust Mic 1:10
they could ever * aside the huge Mk 16:3
Jesus told him, "Stand up, * up Jn 5:8
"* the stone aside," Jesus told Jn 11:39
ROLLED
the stone was * back over the mouth Gen 29:3
to the well and * away the stone Gen 29:10
so Aaron and Hur * a stone for Ex 17:12
a great stone be * against the Jos 10:18
as a reminder and * it beneath the Jos 24:26
the night when she * over on it in 1Ki 3:19
"Is this the one who * his Ps 22:8
thunder * and crackled in the sky. Ps 77:17
A threshing wheel is never * on Is 28:27
he has * me in ashes and dirt. Lam 3:16
tomb, and * a great stone across Mt 27:60
* aside the stone and sat on it. Mt 28:2
tomb, and * a stone in front of the Mk 15:46
the entrance had been * aside. Lk 24:2
He * up the mat and began walking! Jn 5:9
a heavy stone * across its door. Jn 11:37,38
So they * the stone aside. Jn 11:41
was * aside from the entrance. Jn 20:1
Jesus' head was * up in a bundle Jn 20:7
as though * up like a scroll and Rev 6:14
Then the thunder crashed and *, Rev 16:18
ROLLED-UP
just like a * scroll, and the stars Is 34:4
ROLLING
with its * hills—and Lebanon. Deu 3:23,24,25
*, fertile fields, Deu 32:13
roar like breakers * upon a beach, Is 17:13
Having started the ball * so 2Co 8:11
or the * of mighty thunder. Rev 14:2
or like the mighty * of great Rev 19:6
ROLLS
of his voice. It * across the Job 37:3
Wave upon wave of destruction * Jer 4:20
ROMAMTI-EZER
Geddalti, *, Joshbekashah, 1Ch 25:4,5
Twenty-fourth, * and twelve of his 1Ch 25:9-31
ROMAN
Apparently the * Empire. Dan 2:40f
Usually believed to be a revived * Dan 7:23f
two occasions. For * warships Dan 11:30,31
* wars, six million under Hitler. Zec 13:8f
in Capernaum, a * army captain came Mt 8:5,6
many Gentiles [like this * officer Mt 8:11
Then Jesus said to the * officer, Mt 8:13
me over to the * government, and I Mt 20:19
to the * government or not?" Mt 22:17
how to induce the * government to Mt 27:1
chains to Pilate, the * governor. Mt 27:2
before Pilate, the * governor. Mt 27:11
he gave him to the * soldiers to Mt 27:26
overthrow of the * government), Mk 3:16-19
guard to Pilate, the * governor. Mk 15:1
Then the * soldiers took him into Mk 15:16,17
When the * officer standing Mk 15:39
* officer in charge and asked him. Mk 15:44
Augustus, the * Emperor, decreed Lk 2:1
collect no more taxes than the * Lk 3:13
the highly prized slave of a * Lk 7:2
Jews in the * tax-collecting Lk 19:1
be reported to the * governor as Lk 20:19
to the * government or not?" Lk 20:22
They replied, "Caesar's—the * Lk 20:24
their taxes to the * government and Lk 23:2
a revolt against the * government. Lk 23:14
When the captain of the * Lk 23:47
him over to the * government to be Lk 24:20
him—and then the * army will come Jn 11:48
to the palace of the * governor. Jn 18:28
a practice under * law. Jn 18:32f
If Pilate was asking as the * Jn 18:34f
plan, let you use the * Act 2:23
IN CAESAREA THERE lived a * army Act 10:1
Cornelius the * officer, a good and Act 10:22
and finally reached Philippi, a * Act 16:12
that are against the * "laws." Act 16:20,21
jailed us—and we are * citizens! Act 16:37
Paul and Silas were * citizens. Act 16:38
ways that are contrary to * law." Act 18:13
Some of the * officers of the Act 19:31
to account by the * government for Act 19:40
commander of the * garrison that Act 21:31
for you to whip a * citizen who Act 22:25
This man is a * citizen!" Act 22:26
"Tell me, are you a * citizen?" Act 22:27
heard Paul was a * citizen, and the Act 22:29
I learned that he was a * citizen. Act 23:27
against the * government. Act 24:5
that he be tried by * law. Act 24:8
against the * government." Act 25:8
out to them that * law does not Act 25:16
handed over to the * government for Act 28:17
ROMANS
But see * 10:20–21. Is 65:1f
But see * 10:20–21. Is 65:1f
defeated by the * at Magnesia. Dan 11:13f
himself with the * and took over. Dan 11:21f
me over to the * to be killed. Mk 10:33
See * 2:12. Act 2:23f
and all the *—as well as the people Act 4:27
and turned over to the *.' Act 21:11
ancestors. The * gave me a trial Act 28:18
ROME
right to pay taxes to *, or not?" Mk 12:14
you going to free Israel [from * Act 1:6
visitors from *—both Jews and Act 2:10
order to deport all Jews from *. Act 18:2,3
he said, "I must go on to *!" Act 19:21
And if * demands an explanation, Act 19:40
so you must also in *." Act 23:11
start us on our way to * by ship; Act 27:1
Then we went on to *. Act 28:14
The brothers in * had heard we Act 28:15
About forty-three miles from *. Act 28:15f
About thirty-five miles from *. Act 28:15f
When we arrived in *, Paul was Act 28:16
DEAR FRIENDS IN *: This letter is Rom 1:1
And you, dear friends in *, are Rom 1:6,7
in * to preach God's Good News. Rom 1:15
I do, I will stop off there in *; Rom 15:24
In fact, when he came to * he 2Ti 1:17
The church here in * 1Pe 5:13
nickname for *, and the "she" is 1Pe 5:13f
ROOF
ship, eighteen inches below the *; Gen 6:16
"The * of the Tabernacle is made Ex 26:7,8
The top layer of the * was made Ex 36:19
layers of covering for the * and Ex 39:33-40
goatskin leather *, and the curtain Num 4:25
them up to the * and hidden them Jos 2:6
to the top of the * to watch. Ju 9:51
on the * threw down a millstone. Ju 9:53
the two pillars supporting the *. Ju 16:25,26
Literally, "on the *." Ju 16:27f
the * and talked with him there. 1Sa 9:25
and went for a stroll on the * of 2Sa 11:2
So a tent was erected on the * of 2Sa 16:22
a little room for him on the *; 2Ki 4:10
the palace * above the Ahaz Room. 2Ki 23:12
gold! The * was 180 feet high. 2Ch 3:4
capital flaring out to the *. 2Ch 3:15
house so that the * fell in on them Job 1:19
as a solitary sparrow on the *. Ps 102:7
Laziness lets the * leak, and Ecc 10:18
stick to the * of your mouth so Eze 3:26
raising a * of shields against it. Eze 26:8
across the * from the outside doors Eze 40:13
strolling on the * of the royal Dan 4:29
crumble and the * crashes down upon Amo 9:1
Jerusalem to the * of the Temple. Mt 4:5
Literally, "* tops" which, being Mt 24:17f
through the clay * above his head Mk 2:4
to a high * of the Temple and said, Lk 4:9,10,11
So they went up on the * above Lk 5:18,19
the flat * of his house to pray. Act 10:9,10
ROOF-COVERING
length of this * hanging down from Ex 26:12
This completes the *. Ex 26:14
ROOF-SHEETS
attached, forming two long *. Ex 36:10
ROOFED
He rebuilt it, * it, hung its Neh 3:15
ROOFS
build huts on the * of their Neh 8:16
burned upon the * to your Jer 19:13
houses where the * have been used Jer 32:29
stick to the * of their mouths for Lam 4:3,4
They go up on their * and bow to Zep 1:5
ROOFTOP
edge of the flat * to prevent Deu 22:8
If you are on your * porch, don't Mk 13:15,16
ROOFTOPS
Why are they running to the *? Is 22:1
incense on the * of their homes. Is 65:3
ROOM
"Would your father have any * to Gen 24:23
for the camels, and a guest *." Gen 24:25
when we have a * all ready for you, Gen 24:31
So he called it, "The Well of * Gen 26:22
* for us and we shall thrive." Gen 26:22
the * where his father was lying. Gen 27:18
Jacob leaves the *, Esau arrives, Gen 27:30
Now he left the * and found a Gen 42:24
across the * from each other on the Ex 26:35
in the outer holy *, tending it day Ex 27:21
north side of the * outside the Ex 40:22
Put these rods in the inner * of Num 17:4
Lord in the inner * of the Num 17:7
in a cool upstairs * and said to Ju 3:20
hiding in the next *, so as soon as Ju 16:9
The men were hiding in the next * Ju 16:12
a new suit and your board and *." Ju 17:10,11
the ambush more * for maneuvering. Ju 20:35-39
and went up to his * over the gate, 2Sa 18:33
Then Joab went to the king's * 2Sa 19:5
The thirty-foot inner * at the 1Ki 6:16
The inner * was where the Ark of 1Ki 6:19
a cedar-wood altar for this *. 1Ki 6:20
each other at the center of the *; 1Ki 6:23-28
Another * was called the Hall of 1Ki 7:6
There was also the Throne * or 1Ki 7:7
of the band wherever there was *. 1Ki 7:36
on the right-hand side of the *. 1Ki 7:39
on the right-hand side of the *. 1Ki 7:39
*, but not from the outer court; 1Ki 8:8
out to make * for his people. 1Ki 14:24
to the guest * where he lived, and 1Ki 17:19
the inner * of one of the houses. 1Ki 20:30
make * for the people of Israel. 1Ki 21:26
yourself hiding in an inner *." 1Ki 22:25
Let's make a little * for him on 2Ki 4:10
Once when he was resting in the * 2Ki 4:11,12
And Gehazi walked from the * a 2Ki 5:27
Call him into a private * away 2Ki 9:2
head of the robing *, "Be sure 2Ki 10:22
to make * for the people of Israel 2Ki 21:1
the palace roof above the Ahaz *. 2Ki 23:12
the most sacred *—the Holy of 2Ch 3:8
Within the innermost *, the Holy 2Ch 3:10
facing the outer *, with wings 2Ch 3:11,12,13
across the *, from wall to wall. 2Ch 3:11,12,13
Across the entrance to this * he 2Ch 3:14
of the outer * of the Temple. 2Ch 4:10
Ark into the inner * of the 2Ch 5:7,8
from the outer *, but not from the 2Ch 5:9
Forest of Lebanon * in his palace. 2Ch 9:16
in the Forest of Lebanon *. 2Ch 9:20
you are hiding in an inner *!" 2Ch 18:24
away in a storage * in the Temple. 2Ch 22:11
by the Lord to make * for Israel. 2Ch 28:3
up the inner * of the Temple, and 2Ch 29:16
Then I went into the * of Ez 10:6
then to the upper * at the Neh 3:31
a storage * into a beautiful guest Neh 13:5
a beautiful guest * for Tobiah. Neh 13:5
for Tobiah. The * had previously Neh 13:5
prepared a guest * in the Temple Neh 13:7
all of his belongings from the *. Neh 13:8
Then I demanded that the * be Neh 13:9
Are you called into his counsel * Job 15:7,8
return and say, 'We need more *! Is 49:20
there won't be * enough for all the Jer 7:32
there won't be * enough for decent Jer 19:11
Temple, into the * assigned for the Jer 35:4
of Igdaliah). This * was located Jer 35:4
directly above the * of Ma-aseiah Jer 35:4
(This * was just off the upper Jer 36:10
to the conference * where the Jer 36:12
the scroll in the * of Elishama the Jer 36:20
uncovered a door to a hidden *. Eze 8:8
hall into a side * where the flesh Eze 40:38
the large main * of the Temple, and Eze 41:1
Then he went into the inner * at Eze 41:3
The inner * was thirty-five feet Eze 41:4
Each * was seven feet wide. Eze 41:5
corner there was a * 70 feet long Eze 46:21,22
out, roots and all, to give it *; Dan 7:8
or a man in a dark * who leans Amo 5:19
she won't have * enough for all! Zec 2:4
there will scarcely be * for all Zec 10:10
won't have * enough to take it in! Mal 3:10
that there wasn't * for a single Mk 2:2
into the * where she was lying. Mk 5:40
sent us to see the * you have ready Mk 14:14
upstairs to a large * all set up. Mk 14:15
in front of the * in the Temple Mk 15:38f
no * for them in the village inn. Lk 2:7
make * for more, and running over. Lk 6:38
anyone into the * except Peter, Lk 8:51
give light to all who enter the *. Lk 11:33
Then I'll have * enough. Lk 12:18
But even then, there was still * Lk 14:22
asleep in the same *, and one will Lk 17:34
show us the guest * where he can Lk 22:11
to a large * all ready for us. Lk 22:12
left the upstairs * and went as Lk 22:39
As soon as Judas left the *, Jn 13:31
in an upstairs * of the house where Act 1:13
and laid her in an upstairs *. Act 9:37
Dorcas lay. The * was filled with Act 9:39

(ROOM Con't)
asked them all to leave the *; Act 9:40
The upstairs * where we met was Act 20:8
broken off to make * for me so I Rom 11:19
as well be talking to an empty *. 1Co 14:9
Please keep a guest * ready for Phm 1:22
was a * called the Holy of Holies. Heb 9:3
In that * there were a golden Heb 9:4
out of the first * whenever they Heb 9:6
into the inner *, and then only Heb 9:7
long as the outer * and the entire Heb 9:8
into that inner *, the Holy of Heb 9:12
There is no longer any * for Heb 10:23

ROOMS
An annex of * was built along the 1Ki 6:5
These * were three stories high, 1Ki 6:6
10½ feet wide. The * were connected 1Ki 6:6
The bottom floor of the side * 1Ki 6:8
the walls of both * of the Temple, 1Ki 6:29
of both * was overlaid with gold. 1Ki 6:30
One of the * in the palace was 1Ki 7:2
for the * and treasuries in the 1Ch 9:26
the upstairs *, the inside rooms, 1Ch 28:11
rooms, the inside *, and the 1Ch 28:11
court, the outside *, the Temple 1Ch 28:12
The upper * were also plated with 2Ch 3:9
even in the king's private *. Ps 105:30
He took them into his jewel *, Is 39:2
palace with huge * and many Jer 22:14
Take them into one of the inner * Jer 35:2
each of these * was 10½ feet Eze 40:7-12
In front of these * was a low Eze 40:7-12
walls, and thirty * were built Eze 40:17
with a row of * along the outside. Eze 41:5
These * were in three tiers, one Eze 41:6
other, with thirty * in each tier. Eze 41:6
the bottom row of * extended out Eze 41:8
The outer wall of these * was 8¾ Eze 41:9
row of * down in the inner court. Eze 41:10
from the tiers of * to the terrace Eze 41:11
inner court to the * north of the Eze 42:1
The rows of * behind this Eze 42:3
of the court. The * were in three Eze 42:3
and the tiers of *, extending the Eze 42:4
The upper two tiers of * were Eze 42:5
court to these * from the east. Eze 42:9,10
* facing the Temple yard are holy; Eze 42:13
offerings, for these * are holy. Eze 42:13
west end of these *, I saw a place Eze 46:19,20
He said these * were where the Eze 46:24
* for them in a Samaritan village. Lk 9:52
in the inner * shall be broadcast Lk 12:3
place of worship there were two *. Heb 9:1

ROOSTER
Just then, a * crowed. Mk 14:68
And immediately the * crowed the Mk 14:72
morning when the * crows, you will Lk 22:34
And as he said the words, a * Lk 22:60
said—"Before the * crows tomorrow Lk 22:61
And immediately a * crowed. Jn 18:27

ROOT
that day a * will be planted that Deu 29:18
would * out all I have planted. Job 31:12
and we took * and filled the land. Ps 80:9
from the old *. Is 11:1
Literally, "the * of Jesse." Is 11:10f
Israel will take * and bud and Is 27:6
in Judah will take * again in your Is 37:31
barely take *, when he blows on Is 40:24
a * in dry and sterile ground. Is 53:2
They take * and their business Jer 12:2
It took * and grew and became a Eze 17:6
as the lily and * deeply in the Hos 14:5
nation, and I will * her up and Amo 9:8
died, for they had so little *. Mt 13:6
the seeds don't * very deeply, and Mt 13:21
them and doesn't take * and grow. Lk 8:13
you are just a branch, not a *. Rom 11:18
bitterness takes * among you, for Heb 12:15
of Judah, the * of David, has Rev 5:5
I am both David's * and his Rev 22:16

ROOTED
In great anger the Lord * them Deu 29:28
you shall be * deeply in the soil 2Ki 19:30
all that I have planted be * out. Job 31:7,8
be * out and left in desolation. Zep 2:4
shall be * up, so ignore them. Mt 15:13,14

ROOTING
Yet I have promised that this * Amo 9:8
huge herd of hogs * around on the Mk 5:11

ROOTS
the garden. His * are in the Job 8:17
Though its * have grown old in Job 14:8,9
He shall die from the * up, and Job 18:16
to overturn the * of mountains. Job 28:9
They eat * and leaves, having Job 30:4
The boar from the forest * Ps 80:13
Their * will rot and their Is 5:24
with its * reaching deep into the Jer 17:8
Or, "the true vine from the * of Jer 33:15f
this tree sent its * and branches Eze 17:7
I will pull it out, * and all! Eze 17:9
will pull out the tree, * and all! Eze 17:16
* went deep into the moist earth. Eze 31:4
because of all the water at its *. Eze 31:5
for its * went deep to water. Eze 31:7
the ones whose * went deep into the Eze 31:16
its stump and * in the ground, Dan 4:15
the stump and the * in the earth Dan 4:23
But the stump and the * were Dan 4:26
out, * and all, to give it room; Dan 7:8
Ephraim is doomed. The * of Hos 9:16
off their fruit and cut their *. Amo 2:9
they will be consumed—* and all. Mal 4:1
died because the * had no Mk 4:5,6
such soil, their * don't go very Mk 4:17
that it was withered from the *! Mk 11:20
to sever your * and cut you down. Lk 3:9
For if the * of the tree are Rom 11:16
May your * go down deep into the Eph 3:17
Let your * grow down into him Col 2:7
out, * and all, to be burned. Jud 1:12

ROPE
them down by a * from a window. Jos 2:15
to you unless this * is hanging Jos 2:17,18
And she left the scarlet * Jos 2:21
Can you tie him with a * through Job 41:2
on a *. They even mock the Holy Is 5:18
and lowered to Jeremiah on a *. Jer 38:11
"But you don't have a * or a Jn 4:11
but I was let down by * and 2Co 11:33

ROPES
altar, and all the * used in tying Num 3:25-30
and their bases, pegs, and *. Num 3:36,37
the *, and all of the accessories. Num 4:26
So they tied him with two new * Ju 15:12,13
Samson, and the * with which he was Ju 15:14
with brand new * which have never Ju 16:11
Delilah took new * and tied him Ju 16:12
But he broke the * from his arms Ju 16:12
and we can take * and drag the 2Sa 17:13
Let us wear sackcloth and put * 1Ki 20:31
on *, swinging back and forth. Job 28:3,4
the * that drew me on to death. Ps 18:5
they are * that catch and hold Pro 5:22
for sashes they'll use *; Is 3:24
and lowered him by * into an empty Jer 38:6
to protect you from the *." Jer 38:12
He wove my sins into * to hitch Lam 1:14
So they bound them tight with * Dan 3:21
so I led Israel with my * of Hos 11:4
Jesus made a whip from some * Jn 2:15
with * to strengthen the hull. Act 27:17
So the soldiers cut the * and Act 27:32

ROSE
As the water * higher and higher Gen 7:18
The sun * as he started on, Gen 32:31
You overthrew all those who * Ex 15:7
anger of the Lord * against the Num 11:33
Their voices * in a great chorus Num 14:2
All those who * against me. 2Sa 22:40
As he finished this prayer, he * 1Ki 8:54,55
and the axhead * to the surface 2Ki 6:6
his kingdom. He * and stood before 1Ch 28:2
and even the aged * and stood up in Job 29:8
anger of the Lord * against them Ps 78:31
Then the Lord * up as though Ps 78:65
and mountains * and valleys sank to Ps 104:7,8
THE GIRL: "I am the * of Sharon, Sol 2:1
For my anger * high against them Jer 44:2,3
the God of Israel * from the Eze 9:3
Then the glory of the Lord * Eze 10:4
and when they * into the air the Eze 10:15,16
the air the wheels * with them, and Eze 10:15,16
their wings and * into the air with Eze 11:22
Then the glory of the Lord * Eze 11:23
of the Temple wall as it * higher. Eze 41:7
At his whim they * or fell. Dan 5:19
a fourth animal * up out of the Dan 7:7
But now a mighty roar * from the Lk 23:18
afterwards that he * into the sky Act 1:9
that Jesus * from the dead. Act 2:32
with him after he * from the dead. Act 10:40,41
Achaia, the Jews * in concerted Act 18:12
He died for our sins and * again Rom 4:25
Christ * from the dead and will Rom 6:9
to the one who * from the dead, so Rom 7:4
Christ died and * again for this Rom 14:9
that Christ * from the dead, why 1Co 15:12
in his own turn: Christ * first; 1Co 15:23
who died and * again for them. 2Co 5:15
that he * again from the dead. 2Ti 2:8
Christ * again from the dead. 1Pe 1:3
Others (Lazarus, etc.) * to die Rev 1:5f

ROSEBUDS
designs of * and open flowers. 1Ki 6:18

ROSH
Ehi, *, Muppim, Gen 46:19-22
Meshech, * and Tubal were in Asia Is 66:19f
Put, Lud, Meshech, *, Tubal, Javan, Is 66:19

ROT
dead bodies to * among your idols; Lev 26:30
thigh * away and your body swell.' Num 5:21,
and her thigh will *, and she shall Num 5:
and your bowels will * away." 2Ch 21:
beloved one to * in the grave. Ps 16:
When there is moral * within a Pro 28
and soon the rafters begin to *. Ecc 10:
Their roots will * and their Is 5:2
beneath his feet and left to *. Is 25:
a tree free from * and hire a man Is 40:2
way that I will * the pride of Jer 13:8
to * and fertilize the soil. Jer 16
the strength of Judah like dry *. Hos 5:1

ROTATED
over Israel, and * them to 1Ki 5:1

ROTE
words learned by *, therefore I Is 29:1

ROTS
jealousy * it away. Pro 14:3
The seed * in the ground; Joe 1:1

ROTTED
body is half * away at birth." Num 12:1

ROTTEN
God, the world was * to the core. Gen 6:1
I am like a fallen, * tree, like Job 13:27,2
straw to him, and brass is * wood. Job 41:27,2
all are * with sin. Ps 14:
and * through and through. Ps 53:
one * apple can spoil a barrelful. Ecc 9:1
childhood, * through and through. Is 48:
spoiled and moldy—too * to eat. Jer 24:
"But the * figs represent Jer 24:
become morally *, an angry king Dan 8:2
I know I am * through and through Rom 7:1
in your evil ways—* through and Eph 4:2
away all these * garments of anger, Col 3:8
They are * and disobedient, Tit 1:16

ROTTENNESS
from the lust and * all around us, 2Pe 1:4

ROTTING
Literally, "Even my bones are * Ps 31:9,10
The hills will tremble, and the * Is 5:25
channels fouled with * reeds. Is 19:6
and the stench of * bodies will Is 34:3
them like * figs, too bad to eat. Jer 29:16,17
* stench will rise upon the land. Joe 2:20
will lie there * on the ground." Zep 1:17
corpses, their flesh * away; Zec 14:12
deeds, the * fruit of death. Rom 7:5
Your wealth is even now * away, Jas 5:2

ROUGH
were very * in their replies. 2Sa 19:43
Is his gentleness too *? Job 15:11
men the path is not uphill and *! Is 26:7
God does not give them a * and Is 26:7
off the * spots in the road. Is 40:4
As I prayed, I fasted, and wore * Dan 9:3
on sackcloth—the *, coarse garments Jon 3:4,5
rowed, and the sea grew very *. Jn 6:18,19
We had several days of * sailing, Act 27:7,8
I come how harsh and * I can be. 2Co 10:2
as * on you as my letters are! 2Co 10:11
They will be * and cruel, and 2Ti 3:3
when the way is *, your patience Jas 1:3
going is * for a while down here. 1Pe 1:6

ROUGHED
kill them if they * up the Act 5:26,27

ROUGHLY
he demanded *. Gen 42:7
spoke very * to us," they told Gen 42:30
the new king answered them *. 1Ki 12:13,14
decision, he spoke * to them; 2Ch 10:13
Lord likes to talk to you so *? Mic 2:7
body, treating it *, training it to 1Co 9:27

ROUND
blood upon the altar * about." Lev 8:24f
Then Hiram cast a * bronze tank, 1Ki 7:23
The top of each stand was a * 1Ki 7:31
Its panels were square, not *. 1Ki 7:31
Then he forged a huge * tank 2Ch 4:2
a great storm rages * about him. Ps 50:3
His arms are * bars of gold set Sol 5:14
as birds hover * their nests, and Is 31:4,5
Babylon, all you nations * about; Jer 50:14
* about there were a hundred more. Jer 52:23
were vestibules * about, and they Eze 40:29,30f
* about will drink it, too; Ob 1:16

ROUNDABOUT
moved along a * route through the 2Ki 3:9

ROUNDED
His troops * up all the flocks 1Sa 30:20
It had six steps and a * back, 1Ki 10:19
maiden. Your * thighs are like Sol 7:1
They will be * up like prisoners Is 24:22
* up with the others to be killed. Dan 2:13

ROUNDS
They sang * of praise and thanks Ez 3:11

ROUSE
as a lion—who will dare to * him? Gen 49:9
to * the sea monster, curse it." Job 3:8f
Waken! * yourself! Ps 44:23
praises! * yourself, my soul! Ps 57:8

ROUSE Con't)
Manasseh see you * yourself and use Ps 80:2
* his anger is to risk your life. Pro 20:2
with strength. * yourself as in the Is 51:9
land, then you will * yourself. Eze 38:14

ROUSED
Early the next morning Joshua * Jos 8:10
Then the entire nation was * to Ju 19:30
he shall not awaken, nor be * Job 14:11,12
before his anger is * and you Ps 2:12
every tree! They * my fury as they Eze 20:27,28
But he * me with a touch, and Dan 8:18
when they were * by the shout, 'The Mt 25:5,6
This accusation * the crowds to Act 6:12
Temple and * a mob against him. Act 21:26,27

ROUSING
For you are * my anger with the Jer 44:8

ROUT
He will utterly * the armies of Is 48:14

ROUTE
at Bethel, en * from Paddan-aram, Gen 35:9
* from Egypt to the Promised Land. Ex 13:17,18
Instead, God led them along a * Ex 13:17,18
traveling the same * as the spies), Num 21:1
discover the best * of entry, and Deu 1:22
by the caravan * east of Nobah and Ju 8:11
along a roundabout * through the 2Ki 3:9
to David as he was en * to Ziklag: 1Ch 12:20

ROUTED
During this period Joshua * all Jos 11:21
and the Israelis * them, and 1Sa 7:10
army will be * and destroyed by the 1Sa 28:19
And * his enemies. 2Sa 22:15
troops had been * and that Saul and 1Ch 10:7
of lightning and * all my enemies. Ps 18:14
by wine, he * his enemies and Ps 78:66
Therefore it will be *, for I am Is 54:15
When they heard that he had * the Mt 22:34,35

ROUTES
plying the trade * of the world. Ps 107:23
All the escape * are blocked; Jer 51:32
on it trace two * for the king of Eze 21:19,20
north-south trade * along the coast Eze 26:2

ROUTING
them, * their entire force. Ju 8:12

ROVE
wanton eyes that * among the crowds Is 3:16

ROW
emerald shall be in the first *. Ex 28:17
The second * will be an emerald, Ex 28:18
The third * will be an amber, an Ex 28:19
The fourth * will be an onyx, a Ex 28:20
In the first * were a sardius, a Ex 39:10
in the second * were an emerald, Ex 39:11
In the third * were a jacinth, Ex 39:12
In the fourth *, a beryl, an Ex 39:13
shall be sprinkled along each * Lev 24:5-8
Two-thirds of each *, as measured 2Sa 8:2
Their shields hang * on row upon Eze 27:11
Their shields hang row on * upon Eze 27:11
a * of rooms along the outside. Eze 41:5
that the bottom * of rooms extended Eze 41:8
was another * of rooms down in the Eze 41:10
just the same. * on row of Hos 12:11
Row on * of altars—like furrows Hos 12:11
They tried harder to * the boat Jon 1:13
Sabbaths in a * he opened the Act 17:2

ROWED
*, and the sea grew very rough. Jn 6:18,19

ROWING
serious trouble, * hard and Mk 6:48

ROWS
Attach to it four * of stones: A Ex 28:17
there were four * of stones Ex 39:10
of bread in two * upon the golden Lev 24:5-8
"Do not sow other crops in the * Deu 22:9
them lie down side by side in *. 2Sa 8:2
upon four * of cedar pillars. 1Ki 7:2
hundred pomegranates in two *. 1Ki 7:16-22
the rim were two * of ornaments an 1Ki 7:24
Four hundred pomegranates in two * 1Ki 7:41-46
the backs of two * of metal oxen. 2Ch 4:3
Go down the * of the vineyards Jer 5:10
feet wide. The * of rooms behind Eze 42:3

ROYAL
gather into the * storehouses all Gen 41:34,35
and placed the * golden chain about Gen 41:41,42
great as the * cities and much Jos 10:2
Half of Gilead and King Og's * Jos 13:31
pendants or the * clothing of the Ju 8:26
to plow in the * fields, and 1Sa 8:12
live there under * protection until 1Sa 22:3
instead of here in the * city." 1Sa 27:5
clothing instead of his * robes. 1Sa 28:7,8
streets before him as * footmen. 1Ki 1:5
David—and all the * officials of 1Ki 1:9
for the * horses in the stables. 1Ki 4:28
a member of the * family of Edom. 1Ki 11:14
Hadad and a few * officials who 1Ki 11:16,17,18
the line of David's * descendants. 1Ki 15:4
in the * cemetery in Jerusalem. 1Ki 15:24
not one of the * family was left, 1Ki 15:29
charge of half the * chariot 1Ki 16:9
killed the entire * family—leaving 1Ki 16:11
dressed in their * robes and were 1Ki 22:10
* robes, but I'll not wear mine!" 1Ki 22:30
Jehoshaphat in his * robes, they 1Ki 22:32,33
He died and was buried in the * 2Ki 8:24,25
they buried him in the * cemetery. 2Ki 9:28
he helped him into the * chariot. 2Ki 10:15
him in his * residence at Millo on 2Ki 12:20
He was buried in the * cemetery 2Ki 12:21
was buried in the * cemetery, in 2Ki 14:20
of Judah in the * cemetery, in the 2Ki 15:38
and from the * vaults and sent it 2Ki 16:8
was buried in the * cemetery, in 2Ki 16:20
and Joah, his * historian. 2Ki 18:18
from the Temple and the * palace; 2Ki 24:13
the captain of the * bodyguard, 2Ki 25:8
a member of the * line, went to 2Ki 25:25
for the eastern * gate. 1Ch 9:17,18
his * line of descent forever. 1Ch 17:12
and a * palace for himself. 2Ch 2:12
his own * palace were completed. 2Ch 8:1
me, but you put on your * robes!" 2Ch 18:29
of Judah in his * robes, they went 2Ch 18:31
but not in the * cemetery. 2Ch 21:20
Even so, Ahaziah was given a * 2Ch 22:9
and buried him in the * cemetery. 2Ch 25:28
was buried in the * cemetery even 2Ch 26:23
but not in the * tombs, and his son 2Ch 28:27
was buried in the * hillside 2Ch 32:33
(He laid aside his * robes so 2Ch 35:22
He was buried there, in the * 2Ch 35:24,25
took with him all the * princes. 2Ch 36:18
you search in the * library of Ez 5:17
funds from the * treasury. Ez 7:20
upon me with your * favor, send me Neh 2:4
he built as far as the * Neh 3:16
an abundance of * wine, for the Est 1:7
to him with the * crown upon her Est 1:11
you issue a * edict, a law of the Est 1:19
young lovelies for the * harem. Est 2:3
that he set the * crown on her head Est 2:17
into the * treasury for the Est 3:9
Esther put on her * robes and Est 5:1
just beyond the * hall of the Est 5:1
was sitting upon his * throne. Est 5:1
out some of the * robes the king Est 6:7,8
own horse, and the * crown, and Est 6:7,8
Then Mordecai put on the * robes Est 8:15
Justice is your * scepter. Ps 45:6
* husband delights in your beauty. Ps 45:10,11
Your * decrees cannot be Ps 93:5
* pathway to destruction. Pro 31:3
news came to the * court, "Syria Is 7:2
These will be his * titles: Is 9:6
THE * LINE of David Is 11:1
In that day he who created the * Is 11:10
"the Heir of David's * line." Is 11:10f
(Asaph's son), the * secretary, Is 36:3
and Shebna, the * scribe, and Joah Is 36:22
of Asaph), the * secretary, went Is 36:22
and Shebna his * scribe, and the Is 37:2
(son of Shaphan), the * secretary, Jer 26:24
(a member of the * family Jer 36:26
a member of the * family. Jer 38:6
a member of the * family and one of Jer 41:1
He shall spread his * canopy over Jer 43:10
a member of the * family [Zedekiah Eze 17:12,13
men of the * family and nobility of Dan 1:3,4
on the roof of the * palace in Dan 4:29
city as my * residence, and as the Dan 4:30
in purple robes of * honor with a Dan 5:7
him from his * throne and took away Dan 5:20
directly in line for * succession. Dan 11:21
there pitch his * tents, but while Dan 11:45
listen, all you men of the * Hos 5:1
and laid aside his * robes and put Jon 3:6
God's people—your * might and power Mic 4:8
To him belongs the * title. Zec 6:13
Jerusalem and the * line of David Zec 12:7
And the * line will be as God, Zec 12:8
Savior from the * line of his Lk 1:69
a member of the * line, he had to Lk 2:4
be born of the * line of David, in Jn 7:41,42
head and robed him in * purple. Jn 19:2
with Blastus, the * secretary, and Act 12:20
he put on his * robes, sat on his Act 12:21
into King David's * family line; Rom 1:3

ROYALTY
you with eternal * for your 1Sa 25:28

RUBBED
nor * with salt nor clothed. Eze 16:4

RUBBING
weather, or * salt in his wounds. Pro 25:20
heads of wheat, * off the husks in Lk 6:1

RUBBISH
out of the * and using again!" Neh 4:1
Toss it out like worthless *, for Eze 7:19

RUBBLE
shall be reduced to a pile of *. Ez 6:11
donkey couldn't get through the *. Neh 2:14,15
and there was so much * to be Neh 4:10
strongest forts are turned to *. Is 25:2
your houses made into heaps of *! Dan 2:5
house knocked into a heap of *. Dan 3:29
you will become a heap of *. Hos 5:9
into a heap of *, and become an Mic 1:6
a field, and become a heap of *; Mic 3:12
will become one vast heap of *." Lk 21:6
the world fell in heaps of *; Rev 16:19

RUBIES
its price is far above *. Job 28:18
value of wisdom is far above *; Pro 8:11
than *, polished like sapphires." Lam 4:7f

RUBY
rows of stones: A *, a topaz, and Ex 28:17
precious stone—*, topaz, diamond, Eze 28:13
or from a shining *, and a rainbow Rev 4:3

RUDDER
And a tiny * makes a huge ship Jas 3:4

RUDDERS
they lowered the *, raised the Act 27:40

RUDDY
than milk, more * than rubies, Lam 4:7f

RUDDY-FACED
He was a fine looking boy, *, and 1Sa 16:12

RUDE
never haughty or selfish or *. 1Co 13:5

RUDIMENTS
Literally, "by the * of the Col 2:20f

RUFFIANS
But some of the * among David's 1Sa 30:22

RUFUS
is the father of Alexander and *. Mk 15:21
Greet * for me, whom the Lord Rom 16:13

RUG
or of clothing, a *, or a sack; Lev 11:32

RUGGED
Moses climbed the * mountain to Ex 19:2,3
stopped there by the * terrain. Num 21:24
He is a * mountain where I hide; Ps 18:2
He will be a man of * Lk 1:17

RUGS
Literally, "spread out the *." Is 21:5f

RUHAMAH
name your sister * ("Pitied"), Hos 1:11

RUIN
the Midianites completely * us." Ju 6:13
Or, "that would * my own Ru 4:6f
* all the good land with stones." 2Ki 3:19
death, and they led him on to *. 2Ch 22:4
But instead, they were his *, and 2Ch 28:23
a nation from *, and he can depose Job 34:29,30
by sudden *, caught in their own Ps 35:8
They plot my * and spend all Ps 38:12
and kingdoms totter into *. Ps 46:6
how he brings * upon the world, Ps 46:8
For she has been the * of Pro 7:26
A quick retort can * everything. Pro 13:3
A man may * his chances by his Pro 19:3
If you don't you will * his life. Pro 19:18
The godly learn by watching * Pro 21:12
is * in a flood of empty words; Ecc 5:6,7
a fool's speech brings him to *. Ecc 10:12,13
will be in utter * because the Jews Is 3:8
have led them down the paths of *. Is 9:16
Iraq, still lies in utter * today. Is 13:20f
This silent * is all that's left Is 23:7
the * that awaits you up ahead? Is 42:23
Your cities will lie in * without Jer 4:7
land, until it lies in utter *; Jer 4:20
an incredible *, cursed, without an Jer 44:22
the sea on the day of your vast *. Eze 27:27
see the extent of * in your land. Eze 36:34
them off and tells them whom to *. Mic 7:3
"Nineveh lies in utter *." Nah 3:7
now they will * you. Hab 2:8
anguish, a day of * and desolation, Zep 1:15
streets in silent * and their Zep 3:6
your cattle, and * everything you Hag 1:11
surely lead to *, as it has.' Zec 7:7
"A divided kingdom ends in *. Mt 12:25
saying something that would * him. Mt 19:3
our people to * by telling them not Lk 23:2
Don't let your eating * someone Rom 14:15
Balak how to * the people of Israel Rev 2:14

RUINED
and how you * their land and Jos 2:10
Then at last, when he had * them, Ps 78:34
grape vines and fig trees were *; Ps 105:33
but they have * Egypt with their Is 19:13
crush walled cities into * heaps. Is 37:26
into heaps of * houses where only Jer 9:11
'We are *! Jer 9:19
valleys, but they will soon be *. Jer 49:4
nations and * their cities; Eze 19:7
surrounded by other * cities. Eze 30:7
living among the * cities keep Eze 33:24
Israel shall be so * that no one Eze 33:28
When I have * the land because Eze 33:29
and to the * farms and the Eze 36:4

(RUINED Con't)
Israel, and the * cities will be Eze 36:10
that was * by my people throughout Eze 36:21
Eden's garden! The * cities are Eze 36:35
of sacrifice. The * cities will be Eze 36:37,38
are * and all your wine is gone! Joe 1:5
They have * my vines and Joe 1:7
return to me. I * your crops by Amo 4:7
rebuild their * cities, and live in Amo 9:14
of despair: "We are finished, *. Mic 2:4
You have * many nations; Hab 2:8
trees, for all the * cedars; Zec 11:2
would be spilled and the skins *. Mt 9:17
spilled out and the wineskins *. Mk 2:22
the new garment be *, but the old Lk 5:36
say that faith in Christ had * us? Gal 2:17

RUINING
"The little foxes are * the Sol 2:15
* the skins and spilling the wine. Lk 5:37
Beware of * each other. Gal 5:15
pleasure and thus * their souls. 1Ti 5:6
feel like, thereby * their souls. Jud 1:10

RUINS
All Egypt lay in *. Ex 9:25
even yet that all Egypt lies in *? Ex 10:7
men looked at the * and realized 1Sa 30:3
become a heap of *, and everyone 1Ki 9:8
are buried is in *, and the gates Neh 2:3
it lies in * and its gates are Neh 2:17
promise even if it * him, does not Ps 15:4
Walk through the awful * of the Ps 74:3
and Jerusalem is a heap of *. Ps 79:1
in * every fort defending him. Ps 89:40
causes princes to wander among *; Ps 107:40
may they be evicted from the * of Ps 109:9,10
the upright but * the plans Pro 22:12
Your country lies in *; Is 1:7
days flocks will feed among the *. Is 5:17
our land lies in * now, we will Is 9:8,9,10
a city—it has become a heap of *! Is 17:1
palaces and make it a heap of *. Is 23:13
The city is left in *; Is 24:12
mighty cities into heaps of *. Is 25:2
Your roads lie in *; Is 33:8
picture of Jerusalem's walls in *. Is 49:16
Let the * of Jerusalem break Is 52:9
the long-deserted * of your cities, Is 58:12
the ancient *, repairing cities Is 61:4
cities in *, burned and desolate. Jer 2:15
all directions everything was *. Jer 4:23
will pass by the * of this city and Jer 22:8
will be rebuilt upon her *; Jer 30:18
razed to the ground and lie in *. Jer 47:5
of Nebo, for it shall lie in *. Jer 48:1
And they reply, "Moab lies in *; Jer 48:20
tableland lie in * too, for God's Jer 48:21
heaps of *, cursed and mocked; Jer 49:13
of * and utterly destroy her; Jer 50:26
become a heap of *, haunted by Jer 51:37
Her cities lie in *—she is a dry Jer 51:43
but wild animals lurking in the *. Lam 5:18
traveling past the * of your land. Eze 5:14
and leave the Temple in *. Eze 7:22
Your city will lie in *, dead, Eze 26:20
cities shall be in *, surrounded by Eze 30:7
Thebes shall lie in * by my hand. Eze 30:14
in the * shall die by the sword. Eze 33:27
to Israel, and rebuild the *. Eze 36:33
Lord, rebuilt the * and planted Eze 36:36
your city lies in * for our sins. Dan 9:16
your city lies in *—for everyone Dan 9:18
thistles will grow up among the *. Hos 9:6
is now lying in *, and return it to Amo 9:11
live among the * of her palaces, Zep 2:14
*, a place for animals to live! Zep 2:15
homes, when the Temple lies in *? Hag 1:3,4
Because my Temple lies in * and Hag 1:9
glorious Jordan valley lies in *. Zec 11:3
will rebuild the *,' then the Lord Mal 1:4
left upon another, except as *." Mk 13:2
it crumbles into a heap of *." Lk 6:49

RULE
Anyone who disobeys this * at any Ex 12:15
The same * applies to your Ex 23:11
This is a permanent * for the Ex 27:21
is completed. This * applies Lev 7:9
and this * applies to your sons Lev 10:8,9
Note that this * applied to the Lev 21:11f
those who hate you will * you; Lev 26:17
my laws and for despising my *. Lev 26:43
You shall * many nations, but Deu 15:6
but they shall not * over you! Deu 15:6
this is your * in such cases. Deu 19:21
They were under his * for eight Ju 3:8
He will * my people." 1Sa 9:17
and Israel shall be yours to *. 1Sa 24:20
and your descendants shall * this 2Sa 7:10,11
Your family shall * my kingdom 2Sa 7:16
which will * your people forever; 2Sa 7:27
and your descendants shall * 1Ki 11:38
will always * this nation. 1Ch 17:23
that will * Israel forever; 1Ch 28:4
may continue to * this good land 1Ch 28:8
it to your children to * forever. 1Ch 28:8
and knowledge to * them properly, 2Ch 1:10
back to Jerusalem to * Israel. 2Ch 1:13
Let Rehoboam * his own tribe of 2Ch 10:16
we followed this * could we become Ez 9:12
When this * was read, all the Neh 13:3
every man should * his home, and Est 1:22
world. * them with an iron rod; Ps 2:9
You * the oceans when their waves Ps 89:9
government to * under your Ps 94:20
"* as my regent—I will subdue Ps 110:1
to * over your enemies. Ps 110:2
For the wicked shall not * the Ps 125:3
the sun to * the day, for his Ps 136:8
You * generation after generation. Ps 145:13
Rulers * well with my help. Pro 8:16
His right to * depends upon his Pro 16:12
A wise slave will * his master's Pro 17:2
or for a slave to * over princes! Pro 19:10
Just as the rich * the poor, so Pro 22:7
is the * for everything she says. Pro 31:26
He will * with perfect fairness Is 9:7
He will * against the wicked who Is 11:4
shall * her enemies! Is 14:2
power, and broken your evil *." Is 14:5
ascend to heaven and * the angels. Is 14:13
throne in Zion and * gloriously in Is 24:23
Then justice will * through all Is 32:16
he will * with awesome strength. Is 40:10
I will * the nations; Is 51:5
my righteous * will never die nor Is 51:6
Those who * them shout in Is 52:5
the exile, and * the nations that Is 54:3
the throne of David or * in Judah. Jer 22:30
He shall be a King who shall * Jer 23:5,6
of David, and he shall * justly. Jer 33:15
Child will someday * these Jer 33:25,26
of all the countries they *. Jer 51:28
Babylon, the land the Chaldeans *! Jer 51:54
your daughters, for you to * over. Eze 16:61
sons alike—and my * is this: It is Eze 18:4
I will * you with an iron fist Eze 20:33
Jehoiakim began to * in Judah, Dan 1:1
and glory. You * the farthest Dan 2:38
statue—will rise to * the world. Dan 2:39
your * to the ends of the earth. Dan 4:22
forever, whose * is everlasting, Dan 4:34
who will someday * the earth. Dan 7:17
High God shall * the governments of Dan 7:18
that will * the earth. Dan 7:23
they shall * all things forever, Dan 7:27
a king who will * a vast kingdom Dan 11:3
don't let the heathen * them, for Joe 2:17
come to Jerusalem and * all Edom. Ob 1:21
They will * Assyria with drawn Mic 5:6
O Lord, come and * your people; Mic 7:14
never again will you * the earth. Nah 2:13
He will * both as King and as Zec 6:13
indicate Christ's universal *. Zec 9:10f
The Nile will become dry—the * of Zec 10:11
from you to * my people Israel.' Mt 2:6
"Under the laws of Moses the * Mt 5:21
But I have added to that *, Mt 5:22
And so, by your man-made *, you Mt 15:5,6
For your * is that to swear 'By Mt 23:16
The only exception to this * 1Co 7:5
This is my * for all the 1Co 7:17
For the * and authority over all 1Co 15:27
Christ does not * over the Father 1Co 15:27
who gave him this power to *. 1Co 15:27
of darkness who * this world; Eph 6:12
obey every Jewish * and regulation Php 3:6
we gave you this *: "He who does 2Th 3:10
This should be your church * so 1Ti 5:7
to sit with him and * with him. 2Ti 2:12
writing out a new * for you to 1Jn 2:7
of the old * God gave us right from 2Jn 1:5
You will * them with a rod of Rev 2:27
gave me the authority to * them; Rev 2:27
Anointed shall now * the world from Rev 11:15f
a boy who was to * all nations with Rev 12:5
the power and the *, and the Rev 12:10
and to overcome them, and to * Rev 13:7

RULED
and Edre-i: He * a territory Jos 12:5
they want to be * by seventy Ju 9:2
LONG AGO WHEN judges * in Israel, Ru 1:1
He then * thirty-three years in 2Sa 5:4,5
did when the judges * my people. 2Sa 7:10,11
King Solomon * the whole area 1Ki 4:21
of Solomon. He * in Jerusalem for 1Ki 11:42
king and * from the city of Avith. 1Ch 1:46
became king and * from the city of 1Ch 1:50
was the father of Jair, who * 1Ch 2:22
before, when the judges * them. 1Ch 17:10
And Israel shall always be * by 1Ch 17:24
the king. He * over all kings and 2Ch 9:26
And Israel has refused to be * 2Ch 10:19
King Ahaz * two tribes of 2Ch 28:19
Jerusalem who have * the entire Ez 4:2
They were * by those who hated Ps 106:41,4
world will be * from Jerusalem. Is 2:
kingdoms had * on Babylonian soil Jer 5:15
the priests are * by false Jer 5:3
with them. He * from 609–598 B.C. Jer 22:13
the kingdoms he *, came and fought Jer 34:
Hophra, or Apries, * Egypt from Jer 44:30
Instead you have * them with Eze 34:
nations, not even * by his sons. Dan 11:
be * by the Lord from Jerusalem! Mic 4:
Judges * for about 450 years, and Act 13:19,2
Before, sin * over all men and Rom 5:2
kingdoms, * their people well, and Heb 11:3
he * them with an iron grip; Rev 19:15

RULER
* of all the land of Egypt. Gen 45:8
"And he is * over all the land Gen 45:26
This * of Israel Num 24:15-19
of the army, as their new *. 1Ki 16:15,16
Saraph (who was a * in Moab before 1Ch 4:21-22
all of Israel and was a just *. 1Ch 18:14
and you are the * of all mankind; 1Ch 29:12
now the undisputed * of Israel, for 2Ch 1:1
of Ishmael), a * in Judah, as the 2Ch 19:11
the heavens, the * of all the 2Ch 20:6
Jehoram became the new * of Judah. 2Ch 21:1
Literally, "a *." Pro 23:1f
A wicked * is as dangerous to the Pro 28:15
A wicked * will have wicked aides Pro 29:12
off the heavens with his *? Is 40:12
He was Judah's last * before the Jer 21:1f
Belshazzar, the last Babylonian *. Jer 25:12f
They will have their own * Jer 30:21
his son Coniah as * before Jer 37:1f
For who is like me? What * can Jer 50:44
whose first great * was Cyrus. Dan 2:39f
the God of gods, * of kings, the Dan 2:47
him to be * over the whole province Dan 2:48
are no longer * of this kingdom. Dan 4:31
neck, and become the third * Dan 5:7
you the third * in the kingdom." Dan 5:16
proclaimed third * in the kingdom. Dan 5:29
battle, the * over all the earth. Zec 10:4
their religious *, the Messiah. Jn 18:34f
'Who made you a * and judge over Act 7:27
made you a * and judge over us?' Act 7:35
Moses was sent to be their * and Act 7:35
king or * or dictator or leader. Eph 1:21
He is the highest *, with Col 2:10
Literally, "dumbfounded at the * Rev 17:8f

RULER'S
Its strongest branch became a * Eze 19:11

RULERS
officials—your judges and your *. Ex 22:28
shall be our *, for you have saved Ju 8:22
at that time were the * of Israel. Ju 14:4
that the Philistines are our *?" Ju 15:11
And all the * of the Est 9:3
O kings and * of the earth, Ps 2:10
The Gentile * of the world have Ps 47:9
supreme above all * of the earth. Ps 99:2
Now let the nations and their * Ps 102:15
and many * throughout the earth Ps 102:21,22
a greater nation than their *. Ps 105:24
people, with their * and their Ps 148:11
wrong. * rule well with my help. Pro 8:16
When * are wicked, their people Pro 29:16
kings and *: For I have seen Ecc 10:5
Can't you see what fools your * Is 3:12
proud * of the nations on earth. Is 24:21
Lord, you scoffing * in Jerusalem: Is 28:14
heel of earthly *: "Kings shall Is 49:7
their * turned against me, and Jer 2:8
Many foreign * have ravaged my Jer 12:10
your allies over you as your *? Jer 13:21
captivity (the * of the Maccabean Jer 30:21f
farmers and oxen, captains and *; Jer 51:23
wise men, *, captains, warriors. Jer 51:57
kingdom to dust, with all its *. Lam 2:2
"Then all the seaport * shall Eze 26:16
For the Lord God says to the *: Eze 45:9
through intermarriage of their *; Dan 2:43
sheriffs, and * of all the Dan 3:2
all * shall serve and obey them." Dan 7:27
at Jerusalem to us and our *. Dan 9:12
through these spirit * of Persia. Dan 10:13
and their slaves will be their *! Zec 2:9
these Jewish * and authorities in Lk 12:11
one of us Jewish * or Pharisees who Jn 7:48
speak evil of any of your *.' Act 23:5
To show to all the * in heaven Eph 3:10
bodies—the evil * of the unseen Eph 6:12
kingdoms, its * and authorities; Col 1:16
with all the * of the world to Rev 16:14
* of earth have enjoyed themselves Rev 18:3
the earth, and the * of the world Rev 21:24

RULES
These same * apply to foreigners Ex 12:19
"These are the * concerning the Ex 12:43

ULES Con't)
'o obey every one of these *." Ex 24:7
month, the same * apply as Lev 15:25
and die for violating these *. Lev 22:9
I have given him * and guidelines Deu 24:8
or forgotten any of your *. Deu 26:13
'One shall come who * righteously, 2Sa 23:3
Who * in the fear of God. 2Sa 23:3
For if you carefully obey the * 1Ch 22:13
this was contrary to God's *. 2Ch 30:17,18,19
he still * from heaven. Ps 11:4
Or, "The * governing the worship Ps 19:9f
For the Lord is King and * the Ps 22:28
out too that God * in Israel and Ps 59:12,13
Because of his great power he * Ps 66:7
Jehovah reigns! He * the world. Ps 96:10
from there he * over everything Ps 103:19
your Word and following its *. Ps 119:9
Blessed Lord, teach me your *. Ps 119:12
for I am ever thinking of your *. Ps 119:99
And since only your * can give Ps 119:104
apply your * to everything I do. Ps 119:125
and stay with the remnant he *. Jer 40:5
They would not obey my * even Eze 20:13
and the * for them to keep. Eze 43:11
and * of the Temple of the Lord. Eze 44:5
shall obey my * and regulations at Eze 44:24
you have learned that heaven *. Dan 4:26
at the * he has given you to obey. Mal 1:13
the people to obey their petty *.' Mk 7:6,7
welcomes you, follow these two *: Lk 10:8,9
*, but only trust in Christ? Rom 4:9
because he also kept the Jewish *? Rom 4:9
do not keep these * are justified Rom 4:11
now God's kindness * instead, Rom 5:21
obeying a set of *, but in the new Rom 7:6
He gave you his * for daily life Rom 9:4
he who now * over all things. Rom 9:5
old, traditional * of my religion. Gal 1:14
in their *, like slaves in chains. Gal 2:4
For these were only temporary * Col 2:17
doing good and obeying various * Col 2:20
bound by such * as not eating, Col 2:20
Such * are mere human teachings, Col 2:22
These * may seem good, for rules Col 2:23
These rules may seem good, for * Col 2:23
to live by these * he is not 1Th 4:8
not disobeying the * of men but of 1Th 4:8
Follow the Lord's * for doing 2Ti 2:5
either follows the * or is 2Ti 2:5
people there were * for worship and Heb 9:1
to eat and drink, * for washing Heb 9:10
and * about this and that. Heb 9:10
The people had to keep these * to Heb 9:10
to obey the old *, and makes us Heb 9:14
those who lived under their *. Heb 10:1
Priest of ours * over God's Heb 10:21
from ceremonial * about eating Heb 13:9
everlasting glory! He * forever! Rev 1:6
* over the kings of the earth." Rev 17:18

RULING
a vile man from *, thus saving a Job 34:29,30
will be like babies, * childishly. Is 3:4
be a king, * a conquered land. Is 10:8
He was given the * power and Dan 7:14

RUMAH
Zebidah (daughter of Pedaiah of *) 2Ki 23:36,37

RUMBLED
and thunder crashed and *, Rev 8:5

RUMBLING
Hear the clattering hoofs and * Jer 47:3
make, like the * of chariots, or Joe 2:5
her, wheels *, horses' hoofs Nah 3:2

RUMBLINGS
there were * of discontent. Act 6:1

RUMOR
the facts to see if the * is true. Deu 13:12,13,14
first check the * very carefully; Deu 17:4
the first * of approaching forces. Jer 51:46
but soon a * went around that the Lk 16:1
So the * spread among the Jn 21:23
brothers, by the * that this day of 2Th 2:1

RUMORS
A gossip goes around spreading *, Pro 11:13
What dainty morsels * are. Pro 18:8
it is gone! The * that you heard in Is 23:1
and spreading vicious *! Is 58:9
* will keep coming year by year. Jer 51:46
all Jerusalem was filled with *. Mt 2:3
These * were circulating all Lk 9:8

RUMP
mutton, the * and shoulder and all Eze 24:4

RUN
affairs began to * smoothly, his Gen 39:5
where he can * and get protection. Ex 21:13
Overlay it with pure gold, and * Ex 25:24
"Make bars of acacia wood to * Ex 26:26,27
pure gold, and * a gold molding Ex 30:3
you will even * when no one is Lev 26:17
days with water [* through the Num 19:12
killed someone can * and be safe, Num 35:6
did before, and we will * away. Jos 8:5
he can * to one of these cities and Jos 20:3
another man could * to that place Jos 20:9
and let the foxes * through the Ju 15:5
in advance to * away so that the Ju 20:32
make them * before his chariots; 1Sa 8:11
army began to * away in fright. 1Sa 17:24
"I never let my men * wild when 1Sa 21:5
who * away from their masters. 1Sa 25:10
Asahel could * like a deer, and 2Sa 2:18
the Syrians began to * away. 2Sa 10:13
fifty footmen to * ahead of him. 2Sa 15:1
a panic and everyone will * away; 2Sa 17:2,3
have to turn and *, and half of us 2Sa 18:3
said, "Let me * to King David with 2Sa 18:19
Turn and * away; 2Sa 22:41
fifty men to * down the streets 1Ki 1:5
They used to * back and forth 1Ki 9:27,28
he was able to * ahead of Ahab's 1Ki 18:46
Shunem is coming. * and meet her 2Ki 4:26
of Israel; then * for your life!" 2Ki 9:3
and had begun to * away, but he 1Ch 11:13
If you * short of money for the Ez 7:20
the governor, * away from danger? Neh 6:11
"He shall * into trouble at the Job 20:22
But whenever she jumps up to *, Job 39:18
and does not * away though the Job 39:21-23
See how they *! Ps 18:14
And you do not punish those who * Ps 18:25
You made them turn and *; Ps 18:40
The rivers of God will not * dry! Ps 65:9
My tears * down into my drink Ps 102:9,10
O Lord, I * to you to hide me. Ps 143:9
not limp or stumble as you *. Pro 4:12
I'm about to say: * from her! Pro 5:8
The godly * to him and are safe. Pro 18:10
or trying to * on a broken foot. Pro 25:19
of God, the people * wild; Pro 29:18
The rivers * into the sea but the Ecc 1:3-7
the long *, it is all so futile. Ecc 4:5,6
he is going to * into bad luck. Ecc 9:12
come, let's *!" Sol 1:4
strong; they * without stopping for Is 5:27
of Gebim are preparing to *. Is 10:31
The armies of Babylon will * Is 13:14
Those who don't * will be Is 13:15
The stream near Dibon will * red Is 15:9
* to the armory for your weapons! Is 22:8
He who believes need never * away Is 28:16
WOE TO THOSE who * to Egypt for Is 31:1
they shall * and not be weary; Is 40:31
Your feet * to do evil and rush Is 59:7
the land. "* for your lives! Jer 4:5
* UP AND down through every street Jer 5:1
*, PEOPLE OF Benjamin, run for Jer 6:1
RUN, PEOPLE OF Benjamin, * for Jer 6:1
people have been * through with a Jer 14:17
Wherever you * to escape my Jer 16:16
crags of Mount Hermon never * dry. Jer 18:14
the mightiest of its soldiers * Jer 46:5
They turn and *, for it is the Jer 46:20,21
the trap shall * into a snare. Jer 48:44
tears * down her cheeks. Lam 1:2
and pride have * their course and Eze 7:10,11
"The northern boundary will * Eze 47:15
"The eastern border will * south Eze 47:18
time will suddenly * out and there Dan 11:45
she said, "I'll * after other men Hos 1:5
tiny horses, and they * as fast. Joe 2:4
They swarm upon the city; they * Joe 2:9
and * for their lives that day." Amo 2:16
Can horses * on rocks? Amo 6:12
Though they *, they will not Amo 9:1
seen him and had * to meet him, and Mk 5:6
for his time had not yet * out. Jn 8:20
stranger but will * from him, for Jn 10:5
A hired man will * when he sees Jn 10:12
let the ship * before the gale. Act 27:14,15
We can rejoice, too, when we * Rom 5:3
That is why I say to * from sex 1Co 6:18
prize. So * your race to win. 1Co 9:24
So I * straight to the goal with 1Co 9:26
Oh, Timothy, you are God's man. * 1Ti 6:11
* from anything that gives you 2Ti 2:22
My time has almost * out. 2Ti 4:6
Everyone had * away. 2Ti 4:16
they made whole armies turn and * Heb 11:34
and let us * with patience the Heb 12:1
* after it to catch and hold it! 1Pe 3:11

RUNAWAY
* servant of King Saul of Israel. 1Sa 29:3

RUNNERS
fail, the swiftest * won't be fast Amo 2:15

RUNNING
Hagar: "I am * away from my Gen 16:8
and his wife Milcah.) * over to Gen 24:17
the place came * in to see what had Gen 39:14,15
of yours will come * to me, bowing Ex 11:8
side, * from one end to the other. Ex 36:33
pot held above * water. Lev 14:5
clothes and bathing in * water. Lev 15:13
leper or who has a * sore may eat Lev 22:4
where there is * water—a valley Deu 21:4
That is why your men are * from Jos 7:12
'The Israelis are * away again just Jos 8:6
* north of Beth-emek and Neiel. Jos 19:27
in a panic, shouting and * away. Ju 7:21
along the roadway * between Bethel Ju 20:31
that the Philistines were * away. 1Sa 14:22
"Start *," he told the boy, 1Sa 20:36
shook hands, tears * down their 1Sa 20:41
they knew he was * away from me, 1Sa 22:17
as she was *, and he became lame. 2Sa 4:4
saw the Syrians *, they ran too, 2Sa 10:14
he saw a lone man * towards them. 2Sa 18:24
saw another man * towards them. 2Sa 18:26
wound * down onto the floorboards. 1Ki 22:35
the brook * through the fields. 2Ch 32:4
Again and again he attacks me, * Job 16:14
around and came * back to you. Ps 119:59,60
And now a prostitute! * after Is 1:21
of Saul—are * for their lives. Is 10:28,29
Why are they * to the rooftops? Is 22:1
You shall not leave in haste, * Is 52:12
and they will come * to obey, not Is 55:5
not search, for you come * to him! Jer 2:24
all this weary * after other gods? Jer 2:25
her *—a gadfly from the north! Jer 46:20,21
every side come * to the king to Jer 51:31
weak to keep on * from their foes. Lam 1:6
Lord, searching, * here and going Amo 8:12
Then he told them he was * away Jon 1:9,10
See, the messengers come * down Nah 1:15
she shouts, but they keep on *. Nah 2:8
them, they'll come *, for I have Zec 10:8
a very wide valley * from east to Zec 14:4
And as they were *, suddenly Mt 28:9
a trip, a man came * to him and Mk 10:17
to make room for more, and * over. Lk 6:38
foundation before * out of funds. Lk 14:29
house, crowds came * to see what it Act 2:6
time is * out. Rom 13:11
their time * around gossiping, 1Ti 5:6

RUNS
up the frames, * all the way from Ex 26:28
* along the ground, or a fish. Deu 4:18
of Scorpion Pass, * to a spot Ju 1:36
my head with oil, my cup * over." Ps 23:5f
Though the tide of battle * Ps 55:18
it as it * through your fingers! Ecc 5:11
The enemy * at the sound of your Is 33:3
its south border * from Tamar to Eze 48:27,28
so that when she * after her Hos 1:7
'If his bill * higher than that,' Lk 10:35
The hired man * because he is Jn 10:13
to the road that * from Jerusalem Act 8:26
In a race, everyone * but only 1Co 9:24

RURAL
the tithes in all our * towns. Neh 10:37

RUSE
(The * convinces Isaac and he Gen 27:23

RUSH
for their dances, * out and catch Ju 21:21
Why did you * for the loot and do 1Sa 15:19
I left in such a * that I came away 1Sa 21:8
blow you must * to where I am; Neh 4:19
They * upon me when I am down. Job 30:14
But I am in deep trouble. * to Ps 70:5
It is dangerous and sinful to * Pro 19:2
Don't be hot-headed and * to Pro 25:8,9,10
But they * to make a new idol; Is 41:7
Your feet run to do evil and * Is 59:7
Let them * back to their own Jer 50:16
his vast army and navy will * out Dan 11:40
as the chariots * forward against Nah 3:2
a glance and * to tell the others. Hab 2:2
But if you aren't, don't * into 1Co 7:27

RUSHED
So Lot * out to tell his Gen 19:14
two daughters and * them to safety, Gen 19:16
her story, he * out to the spring Gen 24:29,30
arrival, he * out to meet him and Gen 29:12,13
you have * them away like this? Gen 31:26
So the little girl * home and Ex 2:8
So Moses * over to the tents of Num 16:25
a spear, and * after the man into Num 25:8
At God's command they * into the Ju 5:15
But then the men in ambush * into Ju 20:35-39
And the messenger * over to Eli 1Sa 4:14
six hundred men * out to the battle 1Sa 14:20
of triumph and * after the 1Sa 17:52
David and his men * in among 1Sa 30:17
away in peace, he * to the king, 2Sa 3:24,25
servants; they * down to the Jordan 2Sa 19:17
son of Abiathar the priest, * in. 1Ki 1:42
Adonijah * into the Tabernacle 1Ki 1:49,50
* out and began killing them; 2Ki 3:24
people of Samaria * out and 2Ki 7:16
and killed as the people * out. 2Ki 7:17
to the king, she * over to the 2Ch 23:12
And all the people * over to the 2Ch 23:15,16,17
the others saw it, they * him out; 2Ch 26:20

(RUSHED Con't)
A messenger * to Job's home with Job 1:14,15
another messenger * in: "Three Job 1:17
was going on, they * over from the Jer 26:10
the cistern, he * out to the Gate Jer 38:8
was happening, she * to the banquet Dan 5:10
So Daniel was * in to see the Dan 5:13
They * back to the king and Dan 6:12
* furiously at the two-horned ram. Dan 8:6
was saying, he * a message to Amo 7:10
and the whole herd * over a cliff Mt 8:32
with joy, and * to find the Mt 28:8
Everyone * out to see for Mk 5:14
who he was, they * back to Mk 16:13
They * over and woke him up. Lk 8:24
broke them and * out into the Lk 8:29
the whole herd * down the Lk 8:33
The herdsmen * away to the Lk 8:34
Then they remembered, and * back Lk 24:9
They all * out to Solomon's Act 3:11
Everyone * to the amphitheater, Act 19:29

RUSHES
They are like * without any mire Job 8:11-13
If he * in and makes an arrest, Job 11:10
the ground and * forward into Job 39:24
swelling Jordan * down upon him. Job 40:23
pot that is fired by dry *. Job 41:20
lived, there will be reeds and *! Is 35:7

RUSHING
You have come * after me as Gen 31:36,37
The * Kishon River Ju 5:21
enemy army began * around in a Ju 7:21
And all his busy * ends in Ps 39:5,6
No, all are * pell-mell down Jer 8:6
as a horse * to the battle! Jer 8:6
wheels as the chariots go * by; Jer 47:3
like the roar of * waters and the Eze 43:2
they stumble in their haste, * to Nah 2:5
population came * out to see Jesus, Mt 8:34
soon people were * around, telling Mt 14:35
an army of chariots * into battle. Rev 9:9

RUST
pitted with * and with wickedness. Eze 24:6
scorch away the * and corruption. Eze 24:11
It is the * and corruption of Eze 24:13
I rewarded all your labor with * Hag 2:16,17

RUSTLE
Ele-ad and Ezer attempted to * 1Ch 7:20,21
Let the trees of the forest * Ps 96:12

RUSTLED
so that not a leaf * in the trees, Rev 7:1

RUTH
girls of Moab, Orpah and *. Ru 1:4,5
* insisted on staying with Naomi. Ru 1:14
But * replied, "Don't make me Ru 1:16
And when Naomi saw that * had Ru 1:18
One day * said to Naomi, Ru 2:2
kind to you." So * told her Ru 2:19
"Well," * told her, "he said Ru 2:21
So * did, and gleaned with them Ru 2:23
ONE DAY NAOMI said to *, "My Ru 3:1
And * replied, "All right. Ru 3:5
to sleep. Then * came quietly and Ru 3:6,7
"It's I, sir—*," she replied. Ru 3:9
your marriage to * so that she can Ru 4:5
I have purchased * the Moabitess, Ru 4:10
So Boaz married *, and when he Ru 4:13
Boaz was the father of Obed (* Mt 1:5

RUTHLESS
risen against me—* men who care Ps 54:3
Literally, "a stern (*) messenger Pro 17:11f
fear before you; * nations will Is 25:3
will cool the pride of * nations. Is 25:5
But suddenly your * enemies will Is 29:5
rescue you from their * hands." Jer 15:21

RUTHLESSNESS
oppress the poor and reign with *. Jer 22:17

RUTS
Smooth out the *! Lk 3:5

S
The thief * purpose is to Jn 10:10

SABACHTHANI
"Eli, Eli, lama *," which means, Mt 27:46
loud voice, "Eli, Eli, lama *?" Mk 15:34

SABBATH
and rest, a holy * to the Lord when Ex 16:23
for today is the * to Jehovah and Ex 16:25
the seventh is a *, and there will Ex 16:26
was the *, but there wasn't any. Ex 16:27
seventh day as a day of * rest; Ex 16:28,29
"Remember to observe the * as a Ex 20:8
* rest before the Lord your God. Ex 20:10
so he blessed the * day and set Ex 20:11
to rest on my * day, for the Ex 31:12,13
day, for the * is a reminder of the Ex 31:12,13
Yes, rest on the *, for it is Ex 31:14,15
It is a * of solemn rest for Lev 16:31
* law, for I am the Lord your God. Lev 19:1
"Keep my * laws and reverence my Lev 19:30
the priest on the day after the *. Lev 23:9,10,11
For this is a * of solemn rest, Lev 23:32
"Every * day the High Priest Lev 24:5-8
You must obey my * laws of Lev 26:2
gathering wood on the * day. Num 15:32
"On the * day, sacrifice two Num 28:9,10
" 'Keep the * day holy. Deu 5:12
day is the * of the Lord your God; Deu 5:14
Why should you keep the *? Deu 5:15
on the * are to guard the palace. 2Ki 11:5
off duty on the * and those who 2Ki 11:9
each *. 1Ch 9:32
offerings, the * sacrifices, the 1Ch 23:31
off duty on the * will stay at the 2Ch 23:4
for duty that *, and a third of 2Ch 23:8
as for the weekly * and monthly new 2Ch 31:3
people refused to observe the *. 2Ch 36:21
the laws about the holy *; Neh 9:14
to be sold on the * or on any other Neh 10:31
winepresses on the *, hauling in Neh 13:15
the * to the people of Jerusalem. Neh 13:16
"Why are you profaning the *? Neh 13:17
* to be desecrated in this way." Neh 13:18
be opened until the * had ended; Neh 13:19
could be brought in on the * day. Neh 13:19
the last time they came on the *. Neh 13:21
to preserve the sanctity of the *. Neh 13:22
Literally, "for the * day." Ps 92:1f
new moon and the *, and your Is 1:12,13
* days of rest, but honors them; Is 56:2
desecrate the *, and have accepted Is 56:6
If you keep the * holy, not Is 58:13
but enjoying the * and speaking of Is 58:13
work on the * day but make it a Jer 17:21,22
to work on the * day and keep it Jer 17:24
refuse to keep the * holy, if on Jer 17:27
holy, if on the * you bring in Jer 17:27
And I gave them the *—a day of Eze 20:12
that the * is kept a sacred day. Eze 44:24
but open on the * and on the days Eze 46:1
to the Lord on the * days shall be Eze 46:4
you who long for the * to end Amo 8:5
It was on the *, the Jewish day Mt 12:1
They are harvesting on the *." Mt 12:2
in the Temple may work on the *? Mt 12:5
am master even of the *." Mt 12:8
to work by healing on the * day?" Mt 12:10
into a well on the *, would you Mt 12:11
it is right to do good on the *." Mt 12:12
not be in winter, or on the *. Mt 24:20
city gates were closed on the *. Mt 24:20f
Another time, on a * day as Jesus Mk 2:23
by harvesting grain on the *." Mk 2:24
But the * was made to benefit Mk 2:27
man, and not man to benefit the *. Mk 2:27
what men can do on * days!" Mk 2:28
Since it was the *, Jesus' Mk 3:2
right to do kind deeds on * days? Mk 3:4
The next * he went to the Mk 6:2,3
all happened the day before the *. Mk 15:42,43
THE NEXT EVENING, when the * Mk 16:1
ONE * AS Jesus and his disciples Lk 6:1
the Jewish law to work on the *." Lk 6:2
am master even of the *." Lk 6:5
On another * he was in the Lk 6:6
man that day, since it was the *. Lk 6:7
Is it right to do good on the * Lk 6:9
One * as he was teaching in a Lk 13:10
Jesus had healed her on the * day. Lk 13:14
come for healing, not on the *!" Lk 13:14
You work on the *! Lk 13:15
the * and lead them out for water? Lk 13:15
because it is the * day, to free Lk 13:16
ONE * AS he was in the home of a Lk 14:1
heal a man on the * day, or not?" Lk 14:3
of you doesn't work on the *?" Lk 14:5
the day of preparation for the *. Lk 23:54
it was the *, so they rested all Lk 23:56
But it was on the * when this Jn 5:9
cured, "You can't work on the *! Jn 5:10
harassing Jesus as a * breaker. Jn 5:16
disobeying their * laws, he had Jn 5:18
"I worked on the * by healing a Jn 7:21,22,23
But you work on the *, too, Jn 7:21,22,23
falls on the *, you go ahead and do Jn 7:21,22,23
a man completely well on the *? Jn 7:21,22,23
this all occurred on a *. Jn 9:14
because he is working on the *." Jn 9:16
day, which was the * (and a very Jn 19:31
a very special * at that, for it Jn 19:31
haste before the *, and because the Jn 19:42
On the * they went into the Act 13:14
the prophets' words read every *. Act 13:27
on every * for many generations." Act 15:21
On the *, we went a little way Act 16:13
Each * found Paul at the Act 18:4
and preached boldly each * day Act 19:8

SABBATHS
(These are in addition to your * Lev 23:3
land will rest and enjoy its *! Lev 26:34,35
For the land shall enjoy its * Lev 26:43
and on the *, and at the new moon 2Ch 2:4
sacrifices on the *, on new moon 2Ch 8:13
required for the *, the new moon Ez 3:
offerings for the *, the new moon Neh 10:3
who keep his * holy and choose the Is 56
celebrate their holy feasts and *. Lam 2:
And they misused my *. Eze 20:1
and violated my *—their hearts were Eze 20:1
hallow my *; Eze 20:2
And they defiled my *. Eze 20:2
and violated my * and longed for Eze 20:23,2
all despised; my * are ignored. Eze 22:
they disregard my *, so my holy Eze 22:2
and ignored my *, for when they Eze 23:3
* and all other similar occasions. Eze 45:1
passageway on the * and on the days Eze 46:
his sacrifices just as on the *. Eze 46:1,
and for three * in a row he opened Act 17:
or new moon ceremonies or *. Col 2:1

SABEANS
them, when the * raided us, drove Job 1:14,1
and * shall be subject to you. Is 45:1
will sell them to the * far away. Joe 3:

SABOTEUR
A lazy man is brother to the *. Pro 18:

SABTA
Seba, Havilah, *, Raama, and 1Ch 1:5-

SABTAH
Havilah, *,Raamah, Sabteca. Gen 10:

SABTECA
Havilah, Sabtah,Raamah, *. Gen 10:7
Seba, Havilah, Sabta, Raama, and * 1Ch 1:5-9

SACAR
* (the fourth), 1Ch 26:4,5

SACHER
Ahiam (son of *) from Harar; 1Ch 11:26-47

SACHET
My beloved one is a * of myrrh Sol 1:13

SACHIA
Jeuz, *, Mirmah. 1Ch 8:8,9,10

SACK
payment at the top of his *! Gen 42:25
of them opened his * to get some Gen 42:27
his money in the mouth of the *! Gen 42:27
"my money is here in my *." Gen 42:28
man's * the money he had paid! Gen 44:1
*, along with the grain money. Gen 44:2
oldest brother's *, going on down Gen 44:12
he in whose * the cup was found." Gen 44:16
or of clothing, a rug, or a *; Lev 11:32
as though to get a * of wheat, but 2Sa 4:6,7
brought Elisha a * of fresh corn 2Ki 4:42
and they shall * your walled Jer 5:17

SACKBUT
flute, harp, *, psaltry, dulcimer, Dan 3:5f
flute, harp, *, psaltry, dulcimer, Dan 3:7f
flute, harp, *, psaltry, dulcimer, Dan 3:10f

SACKCLOTH
and put on * and mourned for his Gen 37:34
spread * upon a rock and stayed 2Sa 21:10
Let us wear * and put ropes on 1Ki 20:31
fasted, slept in *, and went about 1Ki 21:27
robe made of * next to his flesh. 2Ki 6:26-30
clothes and put on * and went into 2Ki 19:1
themselves in * and to go to Isaiah 2Ki 19:2
themselves in * and fell to the 1Ch 21:16
themselves with * and sprinkled Neh 9:1
clothes and put on * and ashes, and Est 4:1
and many lay in * and ashes. Est 4:3
replace the *, but he refused it. Est 4:4
Here I sit in *; Job 16:15
*, asking him to make them well; Ps 35:13
me when I wear * to show my Ps 69:11
They wear * through the streets, Is 15:3
made of * to show your remorse. Is 22:12
clothes—wear * for your grief. Is 32:11
dressed in *—to Isaiah the prophet, Is 37:2
and putting on * and covering Is 58:5
hands and put on clothes of *. Jer 48:37
ground in silence, clothed in *; Lam 2:10
yourselves with *, and horror and Eze 7:18
grief and put on * and weep for you Eze 27:31
and wore rough *, and sprinkled Dan 9:3
O priests, robe yourselves in *. Joe 1:13
everyone put on *—the rough, coarse Jon 3:4,5
and put on * and sat in ashes. Jon 3:6
Everyone must wear * and cry Jon 3:8
ago, clothed in * and throwing Lk 10:13
clothed in *." Rev 11:3

SACKED
their homes will be *, and their Is 13:16
And Babylon shall be * until Jer 50:10
and Medes * impregnable Nineveh. Nah 2:1f

SACKS
to fill the men's * with grain, but Gen 42:25
As they emptied out the *, there Gen 42:35
the mouths of your *, as it was Gen 43:12
to us in our *," they said. Gen 43:18
and opened our *, and the money was Gen 43:21
how the money got into our *." Gen 43:22
fill each of their * with as much Gen 44:1
we found in the mouth of our *? Gen 44:8
They quickly took down their * Gen 44:11

ACKS Con't)
your men 20,000 * of crushed wheat, 2Ch 2:10
in silver, 10,000 * of wheat, and 2Ch 27:5
of wheat, and 10,000 * of barley. 2Ch 27:5
he who invades and * your city." Ps 137:9f
they'll wear * instead of robes. Is 3:24
used for making *, as a sign of Is 37:1

ACRED

to keep it in a * place from Ex 16:33
to make me a * Temple where I can Ex 25:8
across the front of the * tent. Ex 26:9
"The framework of the * tent Ex 26:15,16
south side of the * tent, with Ex 26:18,19
the door of the * tent, make Ex 26:36
"These * garments of Aaron shall Ex 29:29
boil its meat in a * area. Ex 29:31
Moses always erected the * tent Ex 33:7
he made the * oil for anointing the Ex 37:29
used for Aaron's * garments, in Ex 39:1
for he has defiled what is *. Lev 7:20
Apparently a kind of * lot used to Lev 8:8f
turban with the * golden plate at Lev 8:9
*, nor enter the Tabernacle. Lev 12:4
and put on the * linen coat, Lev 16:4
Then he shall bathe in a * Lev 16:24
desecrating the people's * gifts; Lev 22:1
she may not eat the * offerings. Lev 22:12
he has eaten the * offerings; Lev 22:16
* convocation of all the people; Lev 23:21
be a * assembly of all the people; Lev 23:35
The eighth day requires another * Lev 23:36
annual festivals—* convocations of Lev 23:37
and perform the * duties at the Num 3:7,8,9
These are their * duties: Num 4:4
This, then, is the * work of the Num 4:15
at the * objects there and die." Num 4:20
for the * work of the Tabernacle. Num 4:21,22,23
The Levites will carry out the * Num 8:19
* duties in the Tabernacle itself. Num 18:2,3
touch any of the * articles or the Num 18:2,3
are to perform the * duties within Num 18:5
handle all the * service, including Num 18:7
Swear to me by the * name of your Jos 2:12,13
of Judah (as assigned by * lot): Jos 15:1
I will throw the * dice to decide Jos 18:5,6
tribes by the throw of the * dice. Jos 18:8
Joshua by the * lottery which tribe Jos 18:10
supervised the * lottery to divide Jos 19:51
by * lot in the area of Bashan. Jos 21:6
by the toss of the * dice. Jos 21:8
of Benjamin was chosen by * lot. 1Sa 10:20
And finally, the * lot selected 1Sa 10:21
were chosen by * lot as the guilty 1Sa 14:41
If so, I want to fulfill a * vow 2Sa 9:3
took a flask of * oil from the 1Ki 1:39
hold of the horns of the * altar. 1Ki 1:49,50
along with all the * vessels which 1Ki 8:3,4
King Joash took all the * 2Ki 12:18
end, was the most * room—the Holy 2Ch 3:8
with all the other * vessels. 2Ch 5:4,5
involving violation of * affairs; 2Ch 19:11
For today is a * day before the Neh 8:9
place them in the * containers for Neh 10:39,40
Come before him clothed in * Ps 29:2
* home of the God above all gods. Ps 46:4
for he remembered his * promises Ps 105:42
God has given * promises; Ps 108:7
in your groves of "*" oaks. Is 1:29
violate her * Temple—foreigners you Lam 1:10
them in the * chambers, and put on Eze 44:19
at all the * festivals, and they Eze 44:24
that the Sabbath is kept a * day. Eze 44:24
special feasts and * festivals the Eze 46:11
of * chambers that faced north. Eze 46:19,20
the most * land of all. Eze 48:12
"The entire area—including * Eze 48:20
each side of the * and city lands. Eze 48:21,22
along some of the * cups from the Dan 1:1
Belshazzar ordered that these * Dan 5:2,3,4
* as the bowls beside the altar. Zec 14:20
shall be * to the Lord of Hosts; Zec 14:21
is a * vow to God, for the Mt 5:34
it is a * vow, for the earth is Mt 5:35
by remembering his * promise to Lk 1:72,73
this * trust and I have no choice. 1Co 9:17
hymns and singing * songs, making Eph 5:19
himself behind the * curtains of Heb 6:19
was a * tent down here on earth. Heb 9:1
blood on the * tent and on whatever Heb 9:21
That is why the * tent down here Heb 9:23

SACRIFICE

for eating and for *: take seven Gen 7:2
for eating and *, and those that Gen 7:8,9
the * and said to himself, "I Gen 8:21
land of Moriah and * him there as a Gen 22:2
but where is the lamb for the *?" Gen 22:7
Then Jacob presented a * to God Gen 31:54
into the desert to * to him. Ex 3:18
and * there to Jehovah our God; Ex 5:3
'Let us go and * to Jehovah.' Ex 5:17
let the people go and * to him." Ex 8:8
go ahead and * to your God, but do Ex 8:25
the wilderness and * there to Ex 8:27
you let his people go to * to him. Ex 9:1
everyone must bring me a * at Ex 23:15
other nations, nor * to them in any Ex 23:24
the young men to * the burnt Ex 24:5
Every day you shall * a young Ex 29:36
Israel: "When you * to the Lord, Lev 1:2,3
"If your * is to be an ox given Lev 1:2,3
Lord will have pleasure in this *. Lev 1:15,16,17
"ANYONE WHO WISHES to * a grain Lev 2:1
must bring as his * a billy goat Lev 4:23
fat of the * of a thank-offering; Lev 4:26
is to bring as his * a nanny goat Lev 4:28
*, and the priest shall burn it Lev 4:31
other * made to Jehovah by fire; Lev 4:35
offer as the sin * whichever bird Lev 5:8
* of a value determined by Moses. Lev 5:17,18
by Moses. This * shall be a ram Lev 5:17,18
* on the day of their anointing. Lev 6:22,23
"This * is most holy, and shall Lev 6:25
place, for this is a most holy *. Lev 7:6
(When the offering is a burnt *, Lev 7:8
* after the ceremony is completed. Lev 7:9
This rule applies whether the * Lev 7:9
shall be included with the *, Lev 7:12
Part of this * shall be Lev 7:14
of the animal presented for the *. Lev 7:14
"However, if someone brings a * Lev 7:16
any portion of the * that is not Lev 7:16
it will have no value as a *, and Lev 7:17,18
be given this portion of the *. Lev 7:34
a peace offering *—an ox and a ram, Lev 9:4
the calf as a * for his own sin; Lev 9:8
ram—the people's peace offering *; Lev 9:18
The priest shall * them there, Lev 15:15
and * the people's sin offering Lev 16:15
and go out and * his own burnt Lev 16:24
offering or a * anywhere other than Lev 17:8,9
"When you * a peace offering to Lev 19:5
a burnt offering * to the Lev 22:17,18
offering, must * an animal that has Lev 22:21
animal is acceptable for this *." Lev 22:25
as a * by fire to the Lord. Lev 22:26,27
When you offer the Lord a * of Lev 22:29,30
That same day you shall * to the Lev 23:12
wine, you shall * as burnt Lev 23:18
but offer a * by fire to the Lord. Lev 23:25
* an offering by fire to the Lord. Lev 23:36
the Lord as a *, it must be given. Lev 27:9
is permitted as a *, the owner Lev 27:11,12
a kind that may be offered as a *, Lev 27:13
and offer a burnt * to the Lord, a Num 6:14
fire under the peace offering *. Num 6:18
offering their * to the Lord at the Num 9:6,7
* to Jehovah at the proper time; Num 9:13
by fire, their * must be an animal Num 15:3,4
of cattle. Each *—whether an Num 15:3,4
ordinary one, or a * to fulfill a Num 15:3,4
or a special * at any of the annual Num 15:3,4
"If the * is a ram, use six Num 15:6
This will be a * that is a Num 15:7
"If the * is a young bull, then Num 15:8,9
it with their * made by fire before Num 15:25
then he shall * a one-year-old Num 15:27
bulls and seven rams for *." Num 23:1
bulls and seven rams for the *. Num 23:29
"On the Sabbath day, * two Num 28:9,10
Along with each * shall be a Num 28:14
This same * shall be offered on Num 28:24
Make sure that the animals you * Num 28:31
offer a burnt * consisting of one Num 29:2
offer a burnt * to the Lord—it will Num 29:8
You are also to * one male goat Num 29:11
Your special burnt * that day, Num 29:13
daily burnt * with its accompanying Num 29:16
festival you shall * twelve young Num 29:17
daily burnt *, you are to sacrifice Num 29:19
you are to * a male goat with its Num 29:19
and drink offering with each *. Num 29:21
burnt sacrifices, * a male goat for Num 29:22
you are to * ten young bulls, two Num 29:23
of the festival, * nine young Num 29:26,27
also * a male goat with the Num 29:28
festival, you must * eight young Num 29:29
daily sacrifices, * a male goat and Num 29:31
of the festival, * seven young Num 29:32
also * an extra sin offering of Num 29:34
work that day. * a burnt Num 29:36
drink offerings. * also one male Num 29:38
as the heathen * to their gods. Deu 12:4,5
"You are not to * your burnt Deu 12:13
wrong with it, you shall not * it. Deu 15:21
Your Passover * shall be either Deu 16:2
Eat the * with unleavened bread. Deu 16:3
as his sanctuary. * it there on the Deu 16:6
"NEVER * A sick or defective ox Deu 17:1
* must be given to the priests. Deu 18:3
* to heathen gods, must be killed. Deu 18:10
Lord your God. * peace offerings Deu 27:7
built the altar to * burnt Jos 22:22,23
carefully. Then * the ox as a burnt Ju 6:26
with the remains of a * on it. Ju 6:28
an offering to * to the Lord." Ju 13:16
and offered it as a * to the Lord; Ju 13:19
of the heavens and to * to him. 1Sa 1:3
On the day he presented his *, 1Sa 1:4
bull for the *, and a bushel of 1Sa 1:24
After the * they took the child 1Sa 1:25
was offering a *, and while the 1Sa 2:13,14
If the man offering the * 1Sa 2:16
came with her husband for the *. 1Sa 2:19
my priest, and to * upon my altar, 1Sa 2:28
part in a public * up on the hill. 1Sa 9:12,13
will be coming to * burnt offerings 1Sa 10:8
he decided to * the burnt offering 1Sa 13:9
to * them to the Lord your God; 1Sa 15:15
oxen and loot to * to the Lord." 1Sa 15:21
Obedience is far better than *. 1Sa 15:22
have come to make a * to the Lord. 1Sa 16:2
Then call Jesse to the * and I 1Sa 16:3
I have come to * to the Lord. 1Sa 16:5
and come with me to the *." 1Sa 16:5
he could * an ox and a fat lamb. 2Sa 6:13
me go to Hebron to * to the Lord in 2Sa 15:7,8
to Jerusalem, I would * to him." 2Sa 15:7,8
While he was offering the *, he 2Sa 15:12
may the Lord God accept your *." 2Sa 24:23
he continued to * in the hills and 1Ki 3:3
and he shall * upon you the priests 1Ki 13:2
of the evening *, but there was no 1Ki 18:29
the evening *, Elijah walked up to 1Ki 18:36
the morning * was offered—look! 2Ki 3:20
him as a burnt * to the gods, 2Ki 16:3
priests to * to the Lord on the 2Ki 17:32
to death as a * to Molech. 2Ki 23:10
was to be used for worship and *. 1Ch 28:13
and * burnt offerings each 2Ch 2:4
day as a place of *, for there were 2Ch 7:7
place where I want you to * to me. 2Ch 7:12
of God, and to * to carved statues 2Ch 11:15
of their fathers, and * to him. 2Ch 11:16
as guards, and to * the burnt 2Ch 23:18
* them on the altar of the Lord. 2Ch 29:21
altar, and as the * began, the 2Ch 29:27
immediately to * morning and Ez 3:3
who by their * upon my altar have Ps 50:5
made a covenant with me by *." Ps 50:5f
But true praise is a worthy *; Ps 50:23
Literally, "a *." Ps 51:16f
in the * of righteousness." Ps 51:19f
and in the bullocks I bring to * Ps 51:19
The smoke of their * shall rise Ps 66:15
you" as their *, and sing about Ps 107:22
I will publicly bring him the * Ps 116:14
and offer you a * of thanksgiving. Ps 116:17
I present to him my * upon the Ps 118:27,28
Regard my prayer as my evening * Ps 141:2
left from her * at the Temple. Pro 7:14f
for slaying lambs and goats for *. Is 34:6
For the Lord will slay a great * Is 34:6
fuel to consume a * large enough to Is 40:16
When such men * an ox on the Is 66:3
acceptable to him than human *. Is 66:3
If they * a lamb, or bring an Is 66:3
burn their sons in *—a thing I Jer 19:5
and * to her just as much as we Jer 44:17
will receive a * today in the north Jer 46:10
you used it as a lovely * to Eze 16:19
to them: 'What is this place of * Eze 20:29
of *'—that is how it got its name. Eze 20:29
they will * to idols and inspect Eze 21:21
of their *. Eze 21:21
Jerusalem's streets at time of *. Eze 36:37,38
the animals for * were slaughtered Eze 40:39
"The second day, * a young male Eze 43:22
the priests will * on the altar the Eze 43:27
* a young bull with no blemishes, Eze 45:18
passageway to * during the Eze 46:9
every morning for the daily *. Eze 46:14,15
the daily * is restored again? Dan 8:13
of the evening *, and said to me, Dan 9:21
"From the time the daily * is Dan 12:11
They * to idols on the tops of Hos 4:13
in shame, because they * to idols. Hos 4:19
and herds to * to God, but it will Hos 5:6
*, but to me it is meaningless! Hos 8:13
to pour out wine for * to God. Hos 9:4
For no * that is offered there Hos 9:4
the hands of men. "* to these!" Hos 13:2
we will offer you the * of praise. Hos 14:2
Go ahead and * to idols at Bethel Amo 4:4
are mounting up. * each morning and Amo 4:4
Literally, "He has prepared a * Zep 1:7f
is carrying a holy * in his robes, Hag 2:12
doors and refuse this kind of *. Mal 1:10
a sick one to * to God. Mal 1:14
Temple, offering a * to God, and Mt 5:23
you, leave your * there beside the Mt 5:24
then come and offer your * to God. Mt 5:24
also offered their * for Lk 2:24
"Offer the * Moses' law requires Lk 5:14

(SACRIFICE Con't)
and prepared to * oxen to them at Act 14:13
Probably a vow to offer a * in Act 18:18f
Probably a vow to offer a * in Act 18:22f
his vow to offer a * seven Act 21:26,27
the Jews, and to offer a * to God. Act 24:17
himself as a * for our sins. Rom 8:3
Let them be a living *, holy—the Rom 12:1
you up as a fragrant * to God; Rom 15:15,16
has been used as a * to idols, and 1Co 10:27
God as a * to take away your sins. Eph 5:2
up to God as a *—that is, if I am Php 2:17
They are a sweet-smelling * that Php 4:18
offering too. The * he offers is Heb 8:4
and hearts. His * frees us from the Heb 9:14
me to lay as a * upon your altar. Heb 10:5
our sins as one * for all time, and Heb 10:12
to slay him on the altar of *; Heb 11:17
the sanctuary as a * for sin, and Heb 13:11
offer our * of praise to God by Heb 13:15
Or, "atoning *." 1Jn 2:2f

SACRIFICED
Then Noah built an altar and * on Gen 8:20
So he took the ram and * it, Gen 22:13
worshiped it, and * to it, and Ex 32:8
bull or cow * as a thank-offering. Lev 4:10
After the animal has been * and Lev 7:15
it is * may be eaten the next day. Lev 7:16
from an offering * by fire to the Lev 7:25
Next he * the people's offering; Lev 9:15
Thus he * their burnt offering Lev 9:16
* along with the grain offering; Lev 14:31
be * by Aaron as a sin offering. Lev 16:9
"After Aaron has * the young Lev 16:11
where it will be * to the Lord, Lev 17:8,9
from the offerings * to God, both Lev 21:22
that cannot be * because it is not Lev 27:27
If a lamb is being *, use three Num 15:3,4
they must be * to the Lord. Num 18:17
where King Balak * oxen and sheep, Num 22:40
and a ram were * on each altar. Num 23:2
altars, and have * a young bull and Num 23:3,4
One lamb shall be * in the Num 28:4
be a male goat * as a sin offering, Num 29:5
There must also be a male goat * Num 29:16
These may only be * upon the Deu 12:26,27
a lamb or an ox, * to the Lord your Deu 16:2
They * to heathen gods, Deu 32:17
To whom they * their fat and wine? Deu 32:38
* as a burnt offering to the Lord! Ju 11:30,31
the flesh of the * animal was 1Sa 2:13,14
the cows and * them to the Lord as 1Sa 6:14
and he * burnt offerings and 2Sa 6:17
En-rogel where he * sheep, oxen, 1Ki 1:9
people of Israel * their offerings 1Ki 3:2
* one thousand burnt offerings! 1Ki 3:4
of the Lord, he * burnt offerings 1Ki 3:15
many offerings he * by fire to the 1Ki 10:5
people * and burned incense there. 1Ki 22:43
killed him and * him as a burnt 2Ki 3:27
still * and burned incense there. 2Ki 12:3
still * and burned incense there. 2Ki 14:4
the people * and burned incense. 2Ki 15:4
the people * and burned incense. 2Ki 15:34,35
He also * and burned incense at 2Ki 16:4
And he * one of his sons as a 2Ki 21:6
* seven bulls and seven lambs. 1Ch 15:26
leaders of Israel * burnt offerings 1Ch 16:1
They * burnt offerings to the 1Ch 16:40
Lord there, and * burnt offerings 1Ch 21:26
his plea, he * to him again. 1Ch 21:28
before it, as he * upon it 1,000 2Ch 1:5,6
King Solomon and the others * 2Ch 5:6
Then Solomon * burnt offerings to 2Ch 8:12
Asa's reign, and * to the Lord 2Ch 15:11
Burnt offerings were * continually 2Ch 24:14
idols, for he even * his own 2Ch 28:3
Yes, he * and burned incense at 2Ch 28:4
spiritually. He * to the gods of 2Ch 28:23
help him too if he * to them. 2Ch 28:23
must be * for the entire nation. 2Ch 29:24
offerings were *, and the people 2Ch 30:22
And Manasseh * his own children 2Ch 33:6
However, the people still * upon 2Ch 33:17
for Amon * to all the idols just 2Ch 33:22
graves of those who had * to them. 2Ch 34:4
All the burnt offerings were * 2Ch 35:16
God of Israel; and * burnt Ez 3:1
of the people were also *. Ez 3:5
we have * to him ever since King Ez 4:2
200 rams, and 400 lambs were *; Ez 6:17
Then everyone in our party * Ez 8:35
They even * their little Ps 106:37,38
those times you * to idols in your Is 1:29
to me, and * them to your gods; Eze 16:20
shall be * as a sin offering. Eze 43:25
offering to be * to the Lord, the Eze 46:12
* as a burnt offering to the Lord. Eze 46:13
your God and * to other gods on Hos 9:1
"You * to me for forty years Amo 5:25,26,27
* to him and vowed to serve him. Jon 1:16
If you * your oldest child, would Mic 6:7
day the lambs were *, his disciples Mk 14:12
So they made a calf-idol and * Act 7:41
from eating meat * to idols, from Act 15:20
food that has been * to idols. 1Co 8:1
eat meat that has been * to idols? 1Co 8:4
animals that are * to cover the Heb 5:1
when he * himself on the cross. Heb 7:27
where Christ was *—where those who Heb 13:10
eat meat that has been * to idols. Rev 2:20

SACRIFICES
the king, as * to seal their pact. Gen 21:27
and offered * there to the God of Gen 46:1
won't do! Our * to God are hated by Ex 8:26
and herds for * and burnt offerings Ex 10:25
for we must have * for the Lord Ex 10:26
Jethro offered * Ex 18:12
burnt offering and * for God." Ex 18:12f
Offer upon them your * to me—your Ex 20:24
portion of their *—whether peace Ex 29:28
bread with your * to me, and none Ex 34:25
the burnt offering * are slain, and Lev 7:2
concerning the * given to the Lord Lev 7:11
* to God in the Sinai desert. Lev 7:38
* of the people of Israel. Lev 10:14
able to bring the * normally Lev 14:32
"Any Israelite who * Lev 17:3,4
to bring their * to the priest at Lev 17:5
among you—who * his child as a Lev 20:1
apart to offer the * of your God; Lev 21:8
defect may not offer the * to God. Lev 21:16,17
to offer the fire * to the Lord Lev 21:21
defiled * the animals brought by Lev 22:3
may eat the holy * until healed. Lev 22:4
eat of the holy * until after he Lev 22:6
"No one may eat of the holy * Lev 22:10
eat of the holy * without realizing Lev 22:14
for the holy * brought by the Lev 22:15
* have been offered to the Lord. Lev 22:15
applies to the * made by foreigners Lev 22:25
and they shall offer * by fire to Lev 23:26,27
of holy rest. The * made during the Lev 23:38
a Nazirite and his * at the Num 6:21
In addition to these * he must Num 6:21
too, offered the same gifts and *. Num 7:42-47
*, making atonement for them. Num 8:19
the Lord with * offered by fire; Num 15:13,14
the Lord, "Do not accept their *! Num 16:15
and the ambassadors for their *. Num 22:40
them to attend the * to their gods, Num 25:2
You shall offer as burnt * to Num 28:19
in addition to the usual daily *. Num 28:23
These are * which the Lord will Num 29:2
These special * are in addition Num 29:6
daily burnt *, which are to be Num 29:6
daily burnt *, grain offerings, and Num 29:11
daily burnt *, sacrifice a male Num 29:22
addition to the regular daily *. Num 29:25
in addition to the usual daily *. Num 29:28
In addition to the usual daily *. Num 29:31
addition to the regular daily *. Num 29:34
addition to the regular daily *. Num 29:38
are in addition to * and offerings Num 29:39
offerings, burnt *, grain Num 29:39
"You must not make * to your God Deu 12:4,5
and other *—your tithes, your Deu 12:6
all your burnt * and other Deu 12:11
Only there may you offer your * Deu 12:14
supported by the * brought to the Deu 18:1
his share of the * and offerings as Deu 18:8
To celebrate their * with them. Deu 33:19
Then the priests offered burnt * Jos 8:31
offerings and *, and your children Jos 22:26,27
burnt offerings or *, but is a Jos 22:28
offerings, grain offerings, or *. Jos 22:29
Then they offered * to the Lord. Ju 2:5
The people made * to their god Ju 16:23,24
burnt * and peace offerings. Ju 20:26
* and peace offerings on it. Ju 21:4
be forgiven by * and offerings." 1Sa 3:14
And many burnt offerings and * 1Sa 6:15
and * as in your obedience? 1Sa 15:22
Jerusalem to offer * at the Temple, 1Ki 12:27
he himself offered * upon the 1Ki 12:32,33
people, to offer * to idols in the 1Ki 13:33
burnt offerings or * to any other 2Ki 5:17
began offering * and burnt 2Ki 10:24
new altar for the * of burnt 2Ki 16:15
offerings and * was also to be 2Ki 16:15
or make * to any heathen gods. 2Ki 17:35,36
bronze instruments used for the *. 2Ki 25:14,15
in charge of the * and the 1Ch 9:19
vessels used in the * and worship; 1Ch 9:28
used in offering * on the altar. 1Ch 18:8
of Aaron—in the * at the Temple; 1Ch 23:28
They assisted in the special * 1Ch 23:31
the Sabbath *, the new moon 1Ch 23:31
other * on behalf of all Israel. 1Ch 29:21
for use in connection with the *. 2Ch 4:11
from heaven and burned up the *! 2Ch 7:1
were too many * for the bronze 2Ch 7:7
The number of * differed from 2Ch 8:1
there were extra * on the 2Ch 8:1
They burn * to the Lord every 2Ch 13:1
used in the * and offerings. 2Ch 24:1
"Now bring your * and thank 2Ch 29:3
brought their * and thank 2Ch 29:3
service, and the * offered again. 2Ch 29:3
Lord and offered * upon it—peace 2Ch 33:1
its own burnt * to the Lord, as it 2Ch 35:1
of food from the * until the Urim Ez 2:62,6
They also offered the special * Ez 3:
Jerusalem where the Jews offer *. Ez 6:
offer acceptable * to the God of Ez 6:1
guilt by offering rams as *): Ez 10:16-1
in a day if they offer enough *? Neh 4:
of food from the * until the Urim Neh 7:64,6
Many * were offered on that Neh 12:4
and cared for the * and the first Neh 13:3
Lord, and offer him pleasing *. Ps 4:
I will not offer the * they do or Ps 16:4
him, your * and burnt offerings. Ps 20:
Then I will bring him * and sing Ps 27:6
It isn't * and offerings which Ps 40:6
about the * you bring to my altar, Ps 50:8
No, I don't need your * of flesh Ps 50:13
Gladly I bring my * to you; Ps 54:6
and even offered * to the dead! Ps 106:28
Literally, "* of peace offerings Pro 7:14
I am sick of your *. Is 1:11
Who wants your * when you have Is 1:12,13
give their * and offerings to him; Is 19:21
you have not honored me with *. Is 43:23
I will accept their * and Is 56:7
children as human * down in the Is 57:5
Why don't you see our *? Is 58:3
Away with your offerings and *! Jer 7:21
It wasn't offerings and * I Jer 7:22
and daughters as * to their gods—a Jer 7:31
Can promises and * now avert your Jer 11:15
* to me, I will not accept them. Jer 14:12
bringing their * to praise the Lord Jer 17:26
their children as * to Jer 32:35
meal offerings and * to the Lord. Jer 33:18
on with their * to these "gods." Jer 44:5
your devotion and * to the 'Queen Jer 44:25
idols and evil *, therefore I will Eze 5:11
your children as * to your gods, Eze 16:36
for they offered * and incense on Eze 20:27,28
up their * to those 'gods.' Eze 20:27,28
where * were made to the gods. Eze 20:29f
burning them as * on their altars. Eze 23:37
the flesh of the * was washed Eze 40:38
the * were cut up and prepared. Eze 40:41
who offer up the * to the Lord Eze 42:13
blood of the *, says the Lord God. Eze 44:15
be the gifts and * brought to the Eze 44:29
the people with * for public Eze 45:17
provide these same * for the sin Eze 45:25
which the prince * to the Lord on Eze 46:4
his * just as on the Sabbaths. Eze 46:12
of carrying the * through the outer Eze 46:19,20
the * the people offer. Eze 46:24
people to offer * and burn sweet Dan 2:46
the daily * offered to him, and by Dan 8:11
all their * and their offerings; Dan 9:27
putting a stop to the daily *, Dan 11:30,31
I don't want your *—I want your Hos 6:6
all who eat such * are defiled. Hos 9:4
used for * to your idols. Hos 12:11
and in my own Temple they offer * Amo 2:8
contaminating your * by living with Hag 2:14
not only your *, but everything Hag 2:14
her * that she eats with blood. Zec 9:7
free of charge to boil their * in; Zec 14:21
"When you offer polluted * on my Mal 1:7
"Polluted *? Mal 1:7
'It isn't your * and your gifts I Mt 9:13
of * on the altar of the Temple." Mk 12:33
and doves for *, and money changers Jn 2:14
* were given to God at the Temple. Act 18:18f
* were given to God at the Temple. Act 18:22f
eat the *, are united by that act. 1Co 10:18
the heathen bring * are really 1Co 10:19
that these * are of some value? 1Co 10:19
blood of animal *, as other priests Heb 7:27
for he finished all *, once and Heb 7:27
to offer gifts and *, Christ must Heb 8:3
follow the old Jewish system of *. Heb 8:4
system, gifts and * were offered, Heb 9:9
do for us. The * under the old Heb 10:1
those yearly * reminded them of Heb 10:3
with the animal *, slain and burnt Heb 10:6
with the various * and offerings Heb 10:8
after day offering * that could Heb 10:11
offer more * to get rid of them. Heb 10:18
such * are very pleasing to him. Heb 13:16

SACRIFICIAL
* meal together before the Lord. Ex 18:12
"No * blood shall be offered Ex 23:18
leavened bread; no * fat shall be Ex 23:18
"The * animal shall be killed at Lev 7:2

ACRIFICIAL Con't)
* animal the same day it is slain. Lev 22:29,30
* bull, ram, lamb, or young goat. Num 15:11,12
And didn't I assign the * 1Sa 2:28
in handling the * meat and for the 1Ch 28:17
and display the special * bread, 2Ch 2:4
But it isn't * bullocks and Ps 50:9
nor pleased me with the * fat. Is 43:24
together for a mighty * feast. Eze 39:17
this is the * feast I have Eze 39:19

ACRIFICING
the wilderness and * to their God. Ex 5:7,8
"Anyone * to any other god than Ex 22:20
by * to their gods. Ex 34:15
shall be set aside for *. Lev 7:4
of Israel from * in the open Lev 17:5
of the people's * to evil spirits Lev 17:7
"Anyone * a peace offering to Lev 22:21
Just as Samuel was * the burnt 1Sa 7:10
his coronation by * oxen, fat 1Ki 1:19
his coronation by * oxen and fat 1Ki 1:25
Ark, * uncounted sheep and oxen. 1Ki 8:5
the Temple by * peace offerings to 1Ki 8:62,63
incense and * to their gods. 1Ki 11:8
As soon as he had finished * the 2Ki 10:25
Their duties included * burnt 1Ch 6:49
holy service of * the people's 1Ch 23:13
by * burnt offerings to the Lord. 2Ch 7:4,5
the laws of Moses, * the burnt Ez 3:4
that the priests began * the Ez 3:6
more than * a bullock or an ox. Ps 69:31
their evil ways, * to their idols, Ps 106:36
more he rebelled, * to Baal and Hos 11:2
were * at the Temple in Jerusalem. Lk 13:1
it to me you were * during those Act 7:42
the people from * to them! Act 14:18
* to demons, certainly not to God. 1Co 10:20

AD
that they looked dejected and *. Gen 40:6
"You know our * history, how Num 20:14
if you do, it will be a * day for Deu 7:16
(What a * time it was in Israel Ju 21:15
But I am very * and I was pouring 1Sa 1:15,16
Then he told her, "I have * 1Ki 14:6
To this day they still sing * 2Ch 35:24,25
his wine he asked me, "Why so *? Neh 2:1
why shouldn't I be *? Neh 2:3
You must not be dejected and *!" Neh 8:10
Why be discouraged and *? Ps 42:4,5
the face—I was frightened and *. Ps 116:3
me that makes you *, and lead me Ps 139:24
son; * the mother of a rebel. Pro 10:1
a * face means a breaking heart. Pro 15:13
the wicked succeed, everyone is *. Pro 28:12
the world go by, a * situation Ecc 10:5
tell her that her * days are gone. Is 40:2
you shall be * and ashamed, but Is 65:13
As a sign to them of these * days Jer 16:8
the * news from the Lord today?" Jer 23:33
you shall reply, "What * news? Jer 23:33
You are the * news, for the Lord Jer 23:33
about "today's * news from God," Jer 23:34
using this term, "God's * news." Jer 23:36
For what is * is you and your Jer 23:36
about "today's * news from God," Jer 23:38,39
incense to idols. * sings my heart Jer 48:36
The fulfillment of this * Eze 19:14
"Son of dust, sing this * dirge Eze 27:2
Yes, it will be a * day when I Hos 9:12
played funeral but you weren't *.' Mt 11:17
Should they be * while he is with Mk 2:19
If they are *, share their Rom 12:15
I want to make you happy, not *. 2Co 1:24
For if I make you *, who is 2Co 2:2
I will not be made * by the very 2Co 2:3
you and I will be * and mourn 2Co 12:21

SADDEN
to * you with a severe rebuke. 2Co 1:23

SADDENED
before the Lord, * by their sin; Lev 23:26,27

SADDENS
A rebellious son * his mother. Pro 15:20

SADDLE
* and now was sitting on them! Gen 31:34
burden resting among the * bags. Gen 49:14
Any * he rides on is defiled. Lev 15:9
securely in the * as king of 1Sa 14:47
I told him, '* my donkey so that 2Sa 19:26
"Quick, * the donkey," the old 1Ki 13:13
Then he said to his sons, "* my 1Ki 13:27

SADDLEBAGS
shoes, weatherworn * on their Jos 9:3,4,5

SADDLECLOTHS
brings expensive * for riding. Eze 27:20

SADDLED
upon the altar, * his donkey, and Gen 22:3
So the next morning he * his Num 22:21
refused his advice—* his donkey, 2Sa 17:23
they were, he * a donkey and went 1Ki 2:40
And when they had * the donkey 1Ki 13:13
meal, the old man * the prophet's 1Ki 13:23
So she * the donkey and said to 2Ki 4:24

SADDUCEES
and * Mt 3:7
ONE DAY THE Pharisees and * Mt 16:1
yeast of the Pharisees and *." Mt 16:6
the yeast of the Pharisees and *.' Mt 16:11
teaching of the Pharisees and *. Mt 16:12
But that same day some of the *, Mt 22:23
he had routed the * with his reply, Mt 22:34,35
Then the * stepped forward—a Mk 12:18
Then some *—men who believed that Lk 20:27
Temple police, and some of the * Act 4:1
The * were members of a Jewish Act 4:1f
friends among the * reacted with Act 5:17
Part of the Council were *, and Act 23:6
against the *— for the Sadducees Act 23:7
for the * say there is no Act 23:8

SADLY
Rachel said *, "He will sleep Gen 30:15
the field and they * shook hands, 1Sa 20:41
I went about * as though it were Ps 35:14
* I SING this song of grief for Amo 5:1
went away *, for he was very rich. Mt 19:22
went * away, for he was very rich. Mk 10:22
went * away, for he was very rich. Lk 18:23

SADNESS
There was deep * throughout all Ju 21:6
alive will live in * and grief; 1Sa 2:33
There was deep * throughout the 2Sa 15:23
victory was turned into deep *. 2Sa 19:2
is a day of holy joy, not of *." Neh 8:11
"Oh, that my * and troubles were Job 6:2
God, to end my * and be cheerful, Job 9:27
drained away because of *. Ps 31:9,10
the oppression and * throughout the Ecc 4:1
* has a refining influence on us. Ecc 7:3
Then Jeremiah said, "What * is Jer 15:10
* she remembers happy bygone days. Lam 1:7
it is filled with *, and all Hos 4:3
Sorrow and * are everywhere. Joe 1:10
see this sin and * all around me? Hab 1:3
and * to the point of death . Mt 26:38
A great * swept over them, and Mk 14:19
And what * is ahead for those Lk 6:26
They stopped short, * written Lk 24:17
happiness or * or wealth should 1Co 7:30
a mistake and I do not feel his *? 2Co 11:29
Let there be * instead of Jas 4:9

SAFE
But I promise to keep you * in Gen 6:18
plea and kept Lot *, removing him Gen 19:29
to keep them * from attack by the Num 32:17
can run and be *, and forty-two Num 35:6
rest and keeps you * from all your Deu 12:10
to one of those cities and be *. Deu 19:5
You will be * here in our Ju 4:18
your life, you are * in the care of 1Sa 25:29
you were * inside his purse! 1Sa 25:29
until they were at a * distance. 1Sa 26:13
then I will finally be * again." 1Sa 27:1
The Lord has kept us * and helped 1Sa 30:23
For they thought they were *. 2Sa 5:6
He has made me *. 2Sa 22:33
Yes, you hold me * above their 2Sa 22:49
"You will be * from slander; Job 5:21
Their homes are * from every Job 21:9
They are not * on Judgment Day; Ps 1:5
alone, O Lord, you will keep me *. Ps 4:8
fort where I can enter and be *; Ps 18:2
of your presence, * beneath your Ps 31:20
hand, * from all conspiring men. Ps 31:20
They will be kept * forever; Ps 37:28
oh, to be * beneath the shelter Ps 61:4
welcome, * from all attacks. Ps 71:3
He kept them *, so they were not Ps 78:53
Hold me * above the heads of all Ps 119:117
Only you can keep me *. Ps 142:5
They keep you * from defeat and Pro 3:23
Stick to the path and be *. Pro 4:26
he who follows that path is *. Pro 16:17
The godly run to him and are *. Pro 18:10
an honest witness is *. Pro 21:28
those who use God's wisdom are *. Pro 28:26
people feel it is * to do wrong. Ecc 8:11
Where will your treasures be *? Is 10:3
Calves and fat cattle will be * Is 11:6
Cornerstone that is * to build on. Is 28:16
up for Judah in a * place, along Is 33:6
and hidden you * within my hand. Is 51:16
cities that you think are *. Jer 5:17
We're perfectly *!" Jer 12:4
which boasts, 'We are *; Jer 21:13
your life and keep you *." Jer 39:18
* to surrender to the Babylonians. Jer 40:9
shield for you, and you * within. Eze 11:11
great armies can make a nation *! Hos 10:13
been wiped out and we are *!" Nah 1:15
cattle—and yet they will be *. Zec 2:4
be inhabited, * at last, never Zec 14:11
thinking, 'We are * for we are Mt 3:9
value, and are * from thieves. Mt 6:20
the ninety-nine others * at home! Mt 18:13
And don't think you are * because Lk 3:8
his palace, it is *— until someone Lk 11:21
'I've kept it *,' he said, Lk 19:20
I have kept * within your family Jn 17:12
to keep them * from Satan's power. Jn 17:15
that I will have a * trip. Rom 1:10
Christ within [who keeps us * 2Co 4:10
be able to stand * against all Eph 6:11
for keeping me *, when I return to Php 1:26
Thessalonica—kept * in God our 2Th 1:1
only * investment for eternity! 1Ti 6:19
who keeps you * from all attacks. 1Pe 2:25

SAFEKEEPING
delivered into the * of a man named Ez 5:14
ground and hid the money for *. Mt 25:18

SAFELY
the boat floated * upon it; Gen 7:18
bring you back * to this land; Gen 28:15
will bring me back * to my father, Gen 28:21
Then they arrived * at Gen 33:18
you to lead you * to the land I Ex 23:20
if you want to live * in the land. Lev 25:17,18
fill, and live * in the land, for Lev 26:4,5
He will bring us * into the land Num 14:8
Well, instead I will bring them * Num 14:31
them * to their inheritance. Num 32:17
who brought you * out of Egypt! Deu 20:1
we left, we came * through the Deu 29:16
You will then be able to live * Deu 30:20
So Israel dwells *, Deu 33:28
WHEN ALL THE people were * across, Jos 4:1
* out of their slavery in Egypt. 2Ki 17:7
and brought them * back again. 1Ch 11:2
Bring us * back from among the 1Ch 16:35
until I return * from the battle!' 2Ch 18:26
"If you return *, the Lord has not 2Ch 18:27
So at last we arrived * at Ez 8:32
I walked * through the darkness; Job 29:3
peace and woke up *, for the Lord Ps 3:5
He leads me * along the top of Ps 18:33
he holds me * out of their reach Ps 18:48
You took me * from my mother's Ps 22:9,10,11
then you will live * here in the Ps 37:3
love his name shall live there *. Ps 69:36
them * through the wilderness. Ps 78:52
You can * meet a lion or step on Ps 91:13
brought his people * out from Ps 105:37
as he brings them * into harbor! Ps 107:30
and led them * through, for his Ps 136:14
you will bring me * through them. Ps 138:7
Babies will crawl * among Is 11:8
away and goes on *, though the Is 41:3
who brought them * out of Egypt and Jer 2:6
They will live * in Israel, and Eze 28:26
away, and bring them * home again. Eze 34:15,16
that my people can * camp in the Eze 34:25
places and sleep * in the woods. Eze 34:25
allies who live * on the coasts, Eze 39:6
and bring me * over the mountains. Hab 3:19
home again to live * in Jerusalem, Zec 8:8
They shall pass * through the Zec 10:11
"They can guard it * enough." Mt 27:65
Or, "Pray for strength to pass * Lk 21:36f
a man can walk * and not stumble. Jn 11:9
and get him * to Governor Felix." Act 23:23,24
So everyone escaped * ashore! Act 27:44
and he brought them all * through 1Co 10:1
that he is able to * guard all that 2Ti 1:12
them * away by a different road. Jas 2:25
that you get there * to receive it, 1Pe 1:5
he might bring us * home to God. 1Pe 3:18

SAFER
you will be * there than in any Ru 2:22
It is * to meet a bear robbed of Pro 17:12
he said—and left for * quarters. Act 12:17

SAFETY
and rushed them to *, outside the Gen 19:16
I guarantee his *. Gen 43:9
Will pass by them in *. Ex 15:16
and you can eat your fill in *. Lev 25:19
killed someone could flee for *. Deu 4:42
kills someone may flee to *. Deu 19:2,3
And lives in * beside him. Deu 33:12
for the * of the Ark of God. 1Sa 4:13
to save you, and you lived in *. 1Sa 12:11
So David let Abner return in *. 2Sa 3:21
My * and success. 2Sa 23:5
and Israel lived in peace and *; 1Ki 4:25
and then Israel lived in * again 2Ki 13:5
every city as a further * measure. 2Ch 11:12
to Jerusalem for *), and told them, 2Ch 12:5
humble, and takes sufferers to *. Job 5:11
take your time, and rest in *. Job 11:18
to the mountains for *," when I Ps 11:1
can reach me, and a tower of *. Ps 18:2
He led me to a place of *, for Ps 18:19
Lord, for you are my Rock of *. Ps 28:1
Be for me a great Rock of * from Ps 31:2
land and prosper, feeding in *. Ps 37:3
for you are my place of *. Ps 59:9

(SAFETY Con't)
of * in the day of my distress. Ps 59:16
for you are my high tower of *, Ps 59:17
to the mighty, towering Rock of *. Ps 61:2
alone is my refuge, my place of *; Ps 91:2
He led them straight to * and a Ps 107:7
of strength and *, my deliverer. Ps 144:2
live in peace and *, unafraid." Pro 1:33
with good counselors there is *. Pro 11:14
defense, a high wall of *. Pro 18:11
there is * in many counselors. Pro 24:6
trap, but to trust in God means *. Pro 29:25
He will be your *; Is 8:14,15
My people will live in *, quietly Is 32:18
will be their fortress of *; Is 33:16
Instead of leading my flock to * Jer 23:2
and make them live in peace and *. Jer 32:37
shall live in * and their motto Jer 33:16
of * and security for Jerusalem. Eze 12:24
told you lies of * and success—that Eze 21:29
and everyone will live in *. Eze 34:27
They shall live in * and no one Eze 34:28
in peace and * in their own land, Eze 39:26
lie down in peace and *, unafraid; Hos 1:18
and lie down in *, and no one will Zep 3:13
Come to the place of *, all you Zec 9:12
handle snakes with *, and if they Mk 16:18
* all the time he was in prison. Act 12:5
answers to your prayers for our *! 2Co 1:11

SAFFRON
nard and *, calamus and cinnamon, Sol 4:13,14

SAGES
the magicians and * of Egypt and Gen 41:8

SAIL
freighters to * to Ophir for gold; 1Ki 22:48
in Ezion-geber to * to Tarshish. 2Ch 20:36
of mankind. * on, O ships of Is 23:10
and so we set * again. Act 18:21
was preparing to * for Syria when Act 20:3
and when the time came to *, Act 28:10
before we set * again, and this Act 28:11

SAILBOATS
where winged * glide along the Is 18:1

SAILED
to Seleucia and then * for Cyprus. Act 13:4
Barnabas took Mark with him and * Act 15:39
boat at Troas, and * straight Act 16:11
the Christians and * for the coast Act 18:18
and then * on to Antioch. Act 18:22
He joined us there and we * Act 20:14
elders, we * straight to Cos. Act 21:1
on course, so we * north of Cyprus Act 27:4
Literally, "we * under the lee Act 27:4f
so they pulled up anchor and * Act 27:13
We finally * behind a small Act 27:16

SAILING
And then there are the sailors * Ps 107:23
But as the ship was * along, Jon 1:4
There we boarded a ship * for Act 21:2
We had several days of rough *, Act 27:7,8
lives of all those * with you.' Act 27:24

SAILOR
You will stagger like a * tossed Pro 23:34

SAILORS
King Hiram supplied experienced * 1Ki 9:27,28
to Tarshish, using * supplied by 2Ch 9:21
And then there are the * sailing Ps 107:23
depths; the * cringe in terror. Ps 107:26
"Your * come from Sidon and Eze 27:8
Your riches and wares, your * and Eze 27:27
All your * out at sea come to Eze 27:29
the desperate * shouted to their Jon 1:5
the hull. The * were afraid of Act 27:17
the * suspected land was near. Act 27:27
Some of the * planned to abandon Act 27:30

SAILS
The enemies' * hang loose on Is 33:23
Your * are made of Egypt's Eze 27:7

SAINT
Literally, "your *"; Ps 89:19f

SAINTLY
You try to look like * men, but Mt 23:28
was seen in the * women of old, who 1Pe 3:5

SAINTS
your * rejoice in your kind deeds. 2Ch 6:41
that Old Testament * believed in a Ps 6:5f
Oh, sing to him you * of his; Ps 30:4
to his people, his *, if they will Ps 85:8
the Lord is the death of his *." Ps 116:15f
her * shall shout for joy. Ps 132:16
good sense to the godly—his *. Pro 2:7,8
and wear down the * with Dan 7:25
Literally, "the people of the * Dan 7:27f
come, and all his * and angels Zec 14:5
I imprisoned many of the * in Act 26:10
Literally, "with all his *. 1Th 3:13f
he has done for his people, his *. 2Th 1:10
for they are his * who remain firm Rev 14:12
and was, for your * and prophets Rev 16:6
the martyred prophets and the *." Rev 18:24

SAKE
the entire city for their *." Gen 18:26
it for the * of the twenty." Gen 18:31
And God said, "Then, for the * of Gen 18:32
blessing Potiphar for Joseph's *. Gen 39:5
"Are you jealous for my *? Num 11:29
Ittai, "For my *, deal gently with 2Sa 18:5
and Ittai, 'For my *, please don't 2Sa 18:12
However, for the * of your 1Ki 11:12,13
tribe, for David's * and for the 1Ki 11:12,13
* of Jerusalem, my chosen city." 1Ki 11:12,13
for the * of my servant David and 1Ki 11:32
David and for the * of Jerusalem, 1Ki 11:32
for the * of my servant David, my 1Ki 11:34
Literally, "for David's *." 1Ki 15:4f
this city for the * of my own name 2Ki 19:34
for the * of my servant David.' 2Ki 19:34
for the * of my servant David." 2Ki 20:6
and cursed and shamed for your *. Ps 69:7
This I ask for the * of all my Ps 122:8
sins for my own * and will never Is 43:25
For the * of Jacob, my Is 45:4
Yet for my own * and for the Is 48:9
Yet for my own *—yes, for my own Is 48:11
for my own *—I will save you from Is 48:11
Literally, "for your servants' * Is 63:17f
for the * of your own reputation! Jer 14:7
Do not hate us, Lord, for the * Jer 14:21
is for your * that I am suffering. Jer 15:15
For the * of a few paltry Eze 13:19
wisdom for the * of your splendor. Eze 28:17
Don't delay—for your own *, O my Dan 9:19
governors and kings for my *. Mt 10:18
the * of the Kingdom of Heaven. Mt 19:12
for the * of God's chosen Mt 24:22
For God's *, don't torture me!" Mk 5:7,8
your feet for the * of tradition. Mk 7:9
their lives for my * and for the Mk 8:35
sake and for the * of the Good News Mk 8:35
But for the * of his chosen ones Mk 13:20
Whoever loses his life for my * Lk 9:24
children for the * of the Kingdom Lk 18:29
and governors for my Name's *. Lk 21:12
And for your *, I am glad I Jn 11:15
lives for the * of our Lord Jesus Act 15:26
die for the * of the Lord Jesus." Act 21:13
us that for his * we must be ready Rom 8:36
For the Lord Jesus Christ's *, Rom 15:30
eat it for the * of the man who 1Co 10:28
I am here in jail for Christ's *. 2Ti 1:8
in jail for the * of Jesus Christ. Phm 1:8,9
For the Lord's *, obey every law 1Pe 2:13
for the Lord's *, who is writing Rev 1:9
from persecution for Christ's *. Rev 14:13f

SAKES
it, and not spare it for their *? Gen 18:24
For their * I will remember my Lev 26:45
For your * I will send an invading Is 43:14
not for your own * that I will do Eze 36:32

SAKKUTH
heathen gods—in * your king, and Amo 5:25,26,27
your heathen gods—*, and the star Act 7:43

SALA
"* " Lk 3:23-38f

SALAMAN
Shalman: probably *, king of Moab, Hos 10:14f

SALAMIS
There, in the town of *, they Act 13:5

SALARIES
and I accepted no * or other Neh 5:14

SALARY
left to pay the "*" of Eze 29:18f
of Egypt for his *, because he was Eze 29:20
left to pay the "*" of Eze 29:20f
anyone just because he pays my *; 1Co 9:19

SALE
in charge of the * of the grain, it Gen 42:6
"In every contract of * there Lev 25:24

SALECAH
far as the cities of * and Edre-i. Deu 3:10
in the north to * on Mount Bashan Jos 12:5
Mount Bashan with its city of *; Jos 13:11
Gad, who were spread as far as *. 1Ch 5:11

SALEM
the king of * (Jerusalem), who was Gen 14:18
of the city of *, and also a priest Heb 7:1
city, *, which means "Peace." Heb 7:2

SALES
besides * taxes and profits from 1Ki 10:15
As a result, our * volume is Act 19:26

SALESWOMAN
One of them was Lydia, a * from Act 16:14

SALIM
He was baptizing at Aenon, near * Jn 3:23,24

SALLAI
968 descendants of Gabbai and *. Neh 11:7,8,9
Kallai, leader of the * clan; Neh 12:12-21

SALLU
* (the son of Meshullam, the son 1Ch 9:7,8
* (son of Meshullam, son of Joed, Neh 11:7,8,9
Joiarib, Jedaiah, *, Amok, Neh 12:1

SALMA
Nahshon was the father of *, and 1Ch 2:11
and * was the father of Boaz. 1Ch 2:1
* (the father of Bethlehem), and 1Ch 2:5
The descendants of * were his son 1Ch 2:5

SALMON
*, Boaz, Obed, Jesse, David. Ru 4:18-2
Nahshon was the father of *; Mt 1:
* was the father of Boaz (Rahab Mt 1:
Boaz' father was *; Lk 3:23-3

SALMON'S
* father was Nahshon; Lk 3:23-3

SALMONE
to Crete, passing the port of *. Act 27:7,

SALOME
and of Joses), *, and others. Mk 15:4
Mary Magdalene and * and Mary the Mk 16:

SALT
is, the valley of the * Sea). Gen 14:
they were in the * Sea Valley (four Gen 14:8,
him, and became a pillar of *. Gen 19:2
and seasoning it with *; Ex 30:3
offering must be seasoned with *, Lev 2:1
East, the word "*" is a homonym Lev 2:13
because the * is a reminder of Lev 2:1
Literally, "a covenant of *." Num 18:19
Pisgah and the * Sea (also called Deu 3:1
River over to the * Sea, below the Deu 4:4
land is alkali and *, a burned over Deu 29:2
flowed on to the * Sea until the Jos 3:15,16
a place called the * Pits, and Jos 11:8
and as far south as the * Sea and Jos 12:3
south bay of the * Sea, ran along Jos 15:2,3,4
extended along the * Sea to the Jos 15:5
empties into the * Sea, crossed to Jos 15:5
The City of *, and En-gedi. Jos 15:48-62
north bay of the * Sea—which is the Jos 18:19
at the Valley of *, and then 2Sa 8:13
me a new bowl filled with *." 2Ki 2:20
well and threw the * in and 2Ki 2:21
ten thousand Edomites in * Valley; 2Ki 14:7
Edomites in the Valley of *. 1Ch 18:12
from beyond the * Sea, from Syria. 2Ch 20:2
to the Valley of *, and there 2Ch 25:11
and give them wheat, wine, *, and Ez 6:9
any amount of *; Ez 7:22
when there is no * in his food. Job 6:5,6,7
given them * plains to live in. Job 39:6
men of Edom in the Valley of *. Ps 60:1
of the wicked into deserts of *. Ps 107:34
or rubbing * in his wounds. Pro 25:20
nor rubbed with * nor clothed. Eze 16:4
* upon them as a burnt offering. Eze 43:24
and * pits and eternal desolation; Zep 2:9
"Good * is worthless if it loses Mk 9:50
"What good is * that has lost Lk 14:34
the reference is to impure *; Lk 14:34f
when wet, the * dissolves and Lk 14:34f
Flavorless * is fit for Lk 14:35

SALT-ENCRUSTED
he lives on the * plains in the Jer 17:6

SALTED
out— where all are * with fire. Mk 9:49
everyone shall be * with fire." Mk 9:49f

SALTINESS
is worthless if it loses its *; Mk 9:50
good is salt that has lost its *? Lk 14:34

SALTY
it will heal the * waters and make Eze 47:8
they will still be *. Eze 47:11
draw fresh water from a * pool. Jas 3:12

SALU
was Zimri, son of *, a leader of Num 25:14

SALUTE
Literally, "* no one in the Lk 10:4f

SALUTED
Then they *, yelling, "Yea! Mk 15:18

SALUTES
* you, and so does my son Mark." 1Pe 5:13f

SALVATION
I trust in your *, Lord. Gen 49:18
is my strength, my song, and my *. Ex 15:2
"Hoshea" means "*"; Num 13:16f
"Joshua" means "Jehovah is * Num 13:16f
shrugged away the Rock of their *. Deu 32:15
And my *, 2Sa 22:3
But the Lord was my *. 2Sa 22:19
given me the shield of your *; 2Sa 22:36
The Rock of my *. 2Sa 22:47
him, 'Oh, save us, God of our *; 1Ch 16:35
be clothed with *, and let your 2Ch 6:41
For * comes from God. Ps 3:8
mercy and shall rejoice in your *. Ps 13:5
You have given me your * as my Ps 18:35
How he exults in your *. Ps 21:1
you are the God who gives me *. Ps 25:5
THE LORD IS my light and my *; Ps 27:1
Don't forsake me, O God of my *. Ps 27:9
Never stop giving your * Ps 36:10
He is their * and their refuge Ps 37:39
everyone who loves him and his *. Ps 40:16
are praised everywhere for the * Ps 48:10
will receive * from the Lord. Ps 50:23

ALVATION Con't)
he joy of your *, and make me Ps 51:12
ne. For * comes from him alone. Ps 62:1
ne. For * comes from him alone. Ps 62:5
our burdens also gives us our *. Ps 68:19
'in the truth of your *." Ps 69:13f
Let those who love your * Ps 70:4
Help us, God of our *! Ps 79:9
on us, Lord, and grant us your *. Ps 85:7
Surely his * is near to those Ps 85:9
O JEHOVAH, GOD of my *, I have Ps 88:1
Father, my God, and my Rock of *.' Ps 89:26
and give him my *." Ps 91:16
in honor of the Rock of our *! Ps 95:1
The whole earth has seen God's * Ps 98:2,3
reverence him; his * is to Ps 103:17,18
Literally, "the cup of *," i.e. Ps 116:13f
I faint for your *; Ps 119:81
The wicked are far from * for Ps 119:155
I long for your *, Lord, and so Ps 119:166
O Lord, I have longed for your * Ps 119:174
comes to us with armloads of *. Ps 130:7
I will clothe her priests with * Ps 132:16
the Rock of their * and lie fallen Is 8:14,15
will be a banner of * to all the Is 11:10
he is my *. Is 12:2
deeply from the Fountain of *!" Is 12:3
by the walls of his *!" Is 26:1
and our * in the time of trouble. Is 33:2
An abundance of * is stored up Is 33:6
righteousness. Let * and Is 45:8
saved by Jehovah with eternal *; Is 45:17
all the world look to me for *! Is 45:22
world to bring my * to them too." Is 49:6
coming soon; your * is on the way. Is 51:5
But my * lasts forever; Is 51:6
* from generation to generation. Is 51:8
news of peace and *, the news that Is 52:7
earth shall see the * of our God. Is 52:10
and the helmet of * on his head. Is 59:17
Your walls will be "*" and your Is 60:18
with garments of * and draped about Is 61:10
and is glorious in his *. Is 62:1
is I, the Lord, announcing your *; Is 63:1
ever find her help and her *. Jer 3:23
quietly for the * of the Lord. Lam 3:26
he may come and shower * upon you. Hos 10:12
Your chariots were *. Hab 3:8,9f
were sending your chariots of *! Hab 3:8,9
will be happy in the God of my *. Hab 3:18
people how to find * through Lk 1:77
that * has come to this home Lk 19:9,10
For your * is near." Lk 21:28
and that this message of * Lk 24:47
all about him, for * comes to the Jn 4:21-24
There is * in no one else! Act 4:12
God—this * is for all of us! Act 13:26
corners of the earth to my *.' Act 13:47
upset you and questioned your *, Act 15:24
*, which they refer to as a sect; Act 24:14
realize that this * from God is Act 28:28,29
After all, * is not given to Rom 2:12-15
rely upon the law for your *." Rom 2:17f
boast about doing, to earn our *? Rom 3:27
God's blessing and * by keeping his Rom 4:15
(For our * does not depend on Rom 6:15
of * which he made to Abraham. Rom 9:8
but that is not God's way of *. Rom 10:3
But the * that comes through Rom 10:6
For * that comes from trusting Rom 10:8
of his faith, confirming his *. Rom 10:10
"Confession is made unto *." Rom 10:10f
God would give his * to others if Rom 10:19
* to the foolish heathen nations. Rom 10:19
His purpose was to make his * Rom 11:11
to want God's * for themselves. Rom 11:11
of God's offer of *, when the Jews Rom 11:12
rest of the world to offer his *; Rom 11:15
Literally, "our *." Rom 13:11f
Literally, "our *." Rom 13:12,13f
This is God's plan of * for you Rom 16:25,26,27
all human plans of * no matter how 1Co 1:19
of those called to *, both Jews and 1Co 1:24
of God's wise plan for their *. 1Co 1:24
He showed us God's plan of *; 1Co 1:30
gave himself to purchase our *. 1Co 1:30
plan, result in the children's *. 1Co 7:14
bringing you God's comfort and *. 2Co 1:6,7
glory of God's new plan for our * 2Co 3:11
I helped you on a day when * was 2Co 6:2
into thinking that * can be earned Gal 2:5
was necessary for *, would say; Gal 2:12
are necessary to the plan of *. Gal 5:11
am still preaching * through faith Gal 5:11
Or, "* is not of yourselves." Eph 2:8f
it too is a gift from God. * is Eph 2:9
his master plan of * for the church Eph 3:21
alike about our * and about our Eph 4:13
on that day when * from sin will Eph 4:30
need the helmet of * and the sword Eph 6:17
his * is for the Gentiles too. Eph 6:19
as our helmet the happy hope of *. 1Th 5:8
from the very first to give you *, 2Th 2:13
God's plan of * through faith. 1Ti 2:7
for those who have accepted his *. 1Ti 4:9,10
if that will bring * and eternal 2Ti 2:10
* by trusting in Christ Jesus. 2Ti 3:15
For the free gift of eternal * is Tit 2:11
those who are to receive his *. Heb 1:14
to this great * announced by the Heb 2:3
fit to bring them into their *. Heb 2:10
* to all those who obey him. Heb 5:9
that comes along with your *. Heb 6:9
them the * he has promised them. Heb 6:18
made sure of our eternal *. Heb 9:12
This time he will come bringing * Heb 9:28
Now we can look forward to the * Heb 10:23
tell others that * is ours, for Heb 10:23
faith in him assures our souls' *. Heb 10:39
continue to seek * by obeying Heb 13:10
him will be the * of your souls. 1Pe 1:9
This * was something the prophets 1Pe 1:10
up into the fullness of your *; 1Pe 2:2,3
his message of * out to others. 2Pe 3:15,16
thoughts about the * God has given Jud 1:3
a mighty shout, "* comes from our Rev 7:10
God's * and the power and the Rev 12:10
Praise the Lord! * is from our Rev 19:1

SAMARIA
of * shall surely be fulfilled." 1Ki 13:32
hill now known as * from its owner, 1Ki 16:24
calling it * in honor of Shemer. 1Ki 16:24
he was buried in *, and his son 1Ki 16:28
temple and an altar for Baal in *. 1Ki 16:32
had become very severe in *. 1Ki 18:2
besieged *, the Israeli capital. 1Ki 20:1
turn * into handfuls of dust!" 1Ki 20:10
Damascus, as my father did in *." 1Ki 20:34
went home to * angry and sullen. 1Ki 20:43
"Go to * to meet King Ahab. 1Ki 21:18
And his body was taken to * and 1Ki 22:36,37
beside the pool of *, where the 1Ki 22:38
began to reign over Israel in *; 1Ki 22:51
at * and was seriously injured. 2Ki 1:2
Carmel and finally returned to *. 2Ki 2:25
His capital was *. 2Ki 3:1
would go to see the prophet in *. 2Ki 5:3
And he led them to *! 2Ki 6:19
in *, the capital city of Israel! 2Ki 6:20
his entire army and besieged *. 2Ki 6:24
the markets of * for a dollar!" 2Ki 7:1
and the people of * rushed out and 2Ki 7:16
city council of * and to the 2Ki 10:1
Then he set out for *, and 2Ki 10:12
We are going to * to visit the 2Ki 10:13
When he arrived in * he 2Ki 10:17
Jehu died, he was buried in *; 2Ki 10:35
in *, for twenty-eight years. 2Ki 10:36
worship the goddess Asherah at *. 2Ki 13:6
Jehoahaz died and was buried in * 2Ki 13:9,10
reigned in * for sixteen years. 2Ki 13:9,10
Joash died and was buried in * 2Ki 13:13
Then he returned to *. 2Ki 14:14
* with the other kings of Israel. 2Ki 14:16
of Gadi) came to * from Tirzah and 2Ki 15:14
Length of reign: 10 years, in * 2Ki 15:17
Length of reign: 3 years, in * 2Ki 15:23
in the palace at * (Argob and Arieh 2Ki 15:25
Length of reign: 20 years, in * 2Ki 15:27
Length of his reign: 9 years, in * 2Ki 17:1
*, the capital city of Israel. 2Ki 17:5
Hoshea's reign, * fell and the 2Ki 17:6
*, replacing the people of Israel. 2Ki 17:24
So the Assyrians took over * and 2Ki 17:24
priests from * should return to 2Ki 17:27,28
began a siege on the city of *. 2Ki 18:9
of King Hoshea of Israel) * fell. 2Ki 18:10
Did they rescue *? 2Ki 18:34
or those of the prophet from *. 2Ki 23:18
shrines on the hills in all of *. 2Ki 23:19
he went down to * to visit King 2Ch 18:2
place near the * gate, and all the 2Ch 18:9
in the city of *, and brought him 2Ch 22:9
Beth-horon, toward *, killing 3,000 2Ch 25:13
Obed-edom, and returned to *. 2Ch 25:24
of booty which they took to *. 2Ch 28:8
Lord, was there in * and he went 2Ch 28:9
Then their escorts returned to *. 2Ch 28:15
in Jerusalem, *, and throughout the Ez 4:10
living in * and throughout the area Ez 4:17
*, the capital of "Ephraim," Is 7:8f
* is the capital of Ephraim Is 7:9
* and carry away their riches." Is 8:4
and we will destroy * just as we Is 10:9
in Jerusalem and *, so when we Is 10:10
we have defeated * and her idols we Is 10:11
WOE TO THE city of *, surrounded Is 28:1
by her rich valley—*, the pride and Is 28:1
The proud city of *—yes, the joy Is 28:3
And what about Sepharvaim and *? Is 36:19
I knew the prophets of * were Jer 23:13
the mountains of * and eat from Jer 31:5
Shiloh and *, to worship at the Jer 41:5
"Your older sister is *, living Eze 16:46
"Even * has not committed half Eze 16:51
* again, and those of Judah too. Eze 16:53
"Yes, your sisters, Sodom and *, Eze 16:55
take your sisters, * and Sodom, and Eze 16:61
(I am speaking of * and Eze 23:4,5
more debased than *, for she fell Eze 23:14,15
just as your sister * did. Eze 23:33
and * of all their awful deeds. Eze 23:36
They went in to them—to * and Eze 23:44
can even live in * without being a Hos 7:1
O *, I reject this calf—this idol Hos 8:5
The people of * tremble lest Hos 10:5
As for *, her king shall Hos 10:7
die of thirst. * must bear her Hos 13:16
the mountains of * to witness the Amo 3:9
the Israelites in * are finally Amo 3:12
Bashan living in *—you women who Amo 4:1
at Jerusalem and *, so famous and Amo 6:1
the idols of *, Dan, and Beersheba Amo 8:14
the fields of Ephraim and *. Ob 1:19
addressed to both * and Judah, and Mic 1:1
capital cities, * and Jerusalem! Mic 1:5
Therefore the entire city of * Mic 1:6
Galilee and *, and as they entered Lk 17:11
He had to go through * on the Jn 4:4
Judea, in *, and to the ends of the Act 1:8
apostles fled into Judea and *. Act 8:1
to the city of * and told the Act 8:5
that the people of * had accepted Act 8:14
and preaching in *, Peter and John Act 8:25
Judea, Galilee and *, and grew in Act 9:31
of Phoenicia and * to visit the Act 15:3

SAMARITAN
Implied. The * Pentateuch says Gen 11:32f
friends and the * army officers. Neh 4:1
rooms for them in a * village. Lk 9:52
"But a despised * Lk 10:33
Literally, "a *." Lk 10:33f
Kneeling beside him the * Lk 10:34
*. Lk 17:16
Soon a * woman came to draw Jn 4:7
ask a "despised *" for Jn 4:9
Many from the * village believed Jn 4:39
"You *! Jn 8:48
do—in fact, the * people often Act 8:9,10,11
at several * villages along the way Act 8:25

SAMARITANS
Gentiles or the *, but only to the Mt 10:5
The Jews called the * Lk 9:53f
so the * naturally hated the Jews. Lk 9:53f
All * were despised by Jews, Lk 10:33f
Implied. * were despised by Jews Lk 17:16f
worship, while we * claim it is Jn 4:20
But you * know so little about Jn 4:21-24

SAME
will feel the * towards him. Gen 16:9-12
Both were circumcised the * day, Gen 17:24-27
godly and wicked exactly the *! Gen 18:25
the * father)—and I married her. Gen 20:11,12
and gave them the * names they had Gen 26:18
That very * day Isaac's servants Gen 26:32
Jacob gave the * instructions to Gen 32:19
each driver, with the * message. Gen 32:19
started back to Seir that * day. Gen 33:16
be circumcised, the * as they are. Gen 34:22
Then, out of the * stalk, came Gen 41:23
"Both dreams mean the * thing," Gen 41:25
And he did the * with each of Gen 45:15
That * day Pharaoh sent this Ex 5:6
that list, are the * Aaron and Ex 6:26
* thing with their magical arts! Ex 7:11
But the magicians did the * with Ex 8:7
tried to do the * thing with their Ex 8:18
These * rules apply to foreigners Ex 12:19
so the * night was selected as Ex 12:42
this memorial at the * time. Ex 12:47
eat the lamb. The * law applies to Ex 12:49
—the * one you struck the Nile Ex 17:5,6
be freed with him at the * time. Ex 21:3
"The * law holds if the ox gores Ex 21:31
to enjoy. The * rule applies to Ex 23:11
It will be the * on the north Ex 27:11
be made of the * material—threads Ex 28:8
* technique as in making a seal; Ex 28:11
use the * gold, blue, purple, and Ex 28:15
* amount of cassia as of myrrh; Ex 30:24
weighing out the * amounts of each, Ex 30:34
upon them the * commands that were Ex 34:1
wide, just the * as the drapes Ex 38:18
Holy Place. This * cloth was used Ex 39:1
sash made of the * gold, blue, Ex 39:4,5
He shall follow the * procedure Lev 4:20
and on the * day he shall bring Lev 6:4,5
by offering this * sacrifice on the Lev 6:22,23
"The * instructions apply to Lev 7:7
to be eaten that * day, and none Lev 7:15
it in just the * way as he had the Lev 9:15
and under the * restrictions as Lev 12:2
will be under the * restrictions as Lev 12:5

(SAME Con't)
himself. The * instructions apply Lev 15:7
the month, the * rules apply as Lev 15:25
born in the * house or elsewhere. Lev 18:9
Eat it the * day you offer it, or Lev 19:6
It is the * with your grape Lev 19:10
her offspring the * day, whether Lev 22:28
animal the * day it is slain. Lev 22:29,30
You shall do the * on the Lev 23:8
That * day you shall sacrifice Lev 23:12
in exactly the * way: fracture for Lev 24:19
You shall have the * law for the Lev 24:22
* sins as those of their fathers. Lev 26:39
On the * day Num 1:17,18,19
They were exactly the * as Num 7:18-23
his offerings—the * as those Num 7:24-29
offerings were the * as those given Num 7:30-35
tribe of Simeon, with the * gifts. Num 7:36-41
He, too, offered the * gifts and Num 7:42-47
his gifts, the * as those presented Num 7:48-53
eighth day with the * offerings. Num 7:54-59
* as those offered by the others. Num 7:60-65
* as those on the previous days. Num 7:66-71
eleventh day—the * gifts and Num 7:72-77
follow all these * instructions. Num 9:14
Joshua is the * name in Hebrew Num 13:16f
For there is the * law for all, Num 15:15,16
This * law applies to individual Num 15:29
incense, lest the * thing happen to Num 16:40
were traveling the * route as the Num 21:1
"The * thing will happen to King Num 21:34
evening with the * grain offering Num 28:8
This * sacrifice shall be Num 28:24
This is the * kind of thing your Num 32:8
sinners doing exactly the * thing! Num 32:14
shall die. The * is true if he is Num 35:18
You will do the * to all the Deu 3:21
God will use this * might against Deu 7:19
on the tablets the * commandments Deu 10:2
(They were the * commandments he Deu 10:4
Do the * with your women slaves. Deu 15:17
is with you—the * God who brought Deu 20:1
You must bury him the * day, for Deu 21:23
it to him. The * applies to Deu 22:3
It is the * with someone else's Deu 23:25
It is the * for the grapes in Deu 24:21
That * day Moses gave this charge Deu 27:11
That * day, the Lord said to Deu 32:48
It is the * thing the Lord did Jos 4:23
its king, the * as he had done at Jos 10:1
On that * day Joshua destroyed Jos 10:28
kings in this * manner and have fed Ju 1:7
The * name is used here as in Ju 6:16f
God is telling Gideon that the * Ju 6:16f
of his men did the *, blowing the Ju 7:19,20
food there, but got the * answer. Ju 8:8
It was the * story there, so the Ju 11:17
him, "The * man is here again!" Ju 13:10
next day to fight at the * place. Ju 20:22,23,24
you should do the *." Ru 1:15
Every year it was the *—Peninnah 1Sa 1:7
and Phinehas, to die on the * day! 1Sa 2:34
They are the * gods who destroyed 1Sa 4:8
at Shiloh the * day with his 1Sa 4:12
next morning the * thing had 1Sa 5:4
they returned to Ekron that * day. 1Sa 6:16
*, for his sons were not good men. 1Sa 8:5
And now they are giving you the * 1Sa 8:8
In the * way all seven of his 1Sa 16:9
And he received the * reply as 1Sa 17:27
and asked them the * thing and 1Sa 17:30
thing and received the * answer. 1Sa 17:30
The * thing happened a third time! 1Sa 19:21
This is the * man the women of 1Sa 29:5
troops died together that * day. 1Sa 31:6
At the * time he sent a request 2Sa 21:12,13,14
time and at the * place, Elhanan 2Sa 21:19
"we live in the * house, just the 1Ki 3:17,18
quarters, the * size, in the palace 1Ki 7:8
All ten stands were the * size 1Ki 7:37
for each was cast from the * mold. 1Ki 7:37
(I once made this * promise to 1Ki 11:38
At the * moment a wide crack 1Ki 13:5
home by the * road I came on." 1Ki 13:16,17
and led Israel into this * sin. 1Ki 16:26
That * day, while Elijah was on 1Ki 18:5
give us the * number of horses, 1Ki 20:25
and urged him to say the * thing. 1Ki 22:13
ÇÇ" (naming the * place) "for the 2Ki 6:9
At the * time he refused to pay 2Ki 17:4
they too walked in the * evil 2Ki 17:19
their descendants do the * thing. 2Ki 17:41
He did the * things the nations 2Ki 21:1
he worshiped the * idols, and 2Ki 21:21
He also had two girls (by the * 1Ch 2:16
dead, killed himself in the * way. 1Ch 10:5
From the tribe of Benjamin, the * 1Ch 12:24-37
But that * night God said to 1Ch 17:3
Probably not the * Shime-i as in 1Ch 23:8,9f
Sheba gifts of the * value as she 2Ch 9:12
"I'd like to ask him the * 2Ch 18:6,7
did the *, worshiping the Lord. 2Ch 20:18
And he did the * in every city 2Ch 28:25
and did the * with the lambs. 2Ch 29:22
and did the * thing there. 2Ch 34:6
They did the * with the oxen. 2Ch 35:12
and did the * thing during the Ez 4:7
Four times they sent the * Neh 6:4
and each time I gave the * reply. Neh 6:4
ON THAT * day, as the laws of Neh 13:1
About the * time I realized that Neh 13:23
women of the palace at the * time. Est 1:9
to us husbands the * way, and there Est 1:18
and I and my maids will do the *; Est 4:16
ON THAT * day King Ahasuerus gave Est 8:1
This was the * day as was set by Est 8:12f
commandment. The * decree was also Est 8:14
sin and trouble who harvest the *. Job 4:7,8
it is all the * to him, for he Job 9:22
been told this * thing from their Job 15:17-19
But perhaps I'd sermonize the * Job 16:4
Both alike are buried in the * Job 21:26
dust, both eaten by the * worms. Job 21:26
His intentions are the * for Ps 33:11
him with these * words: "His Ps 118:2
men will ever be the * again. Pro 2:19
would come to the * conclusion Ecc 2:12
breathe the * air, and both die. Ecc 3:19
two under the * blanket gain warmth Ecc 4:11
Both have the * problem, yet the Ecc 6:7,8
All is chance! The * providence Ecc 9:2,3
and they shall worship the * God. Is 19:23
Furthermore, the * Lord God of Is 22:15,16
the story is the *—only a remnant Is 24:13
doesn't thresh all grains the *. Is 28:27
own land by the * road you came." Is 37:29
Are you not the * today, the Is 51:10
are my thoughts the * as yours! Is 55:8
* as though they blessed an idol. Is 66:3
I will do the * thing here because Jer 7:13,14
this * land I gave your fathers. Jer 16:14,15
forget me in the * way as their Jer 23:27
at the * time as Jeremiah was. Jer 26:20
ON A DECEMBER day in that * Jer 28:1
if not the * as, the new birth. Jer 31:33f
Now these * men are blindly Lam 4:14
O Lord, forever you remain the *! Lam 5:19
These were the * beings I had Eze 10:15,16
I knew they were the *, for each Eze 10:20
it, dying in the * choice soil Eze 17:10
right ahead in the * way, and Eze 23:11
the * terrors that destroyed her. Eze 23:31
On the * day they defiled my Eze 23:38
then even that * day they actually Eze 23:39
their fate is the * as that of Eze 32:24
* distance as the passageway did. Eze 40:18
were the * as for the east Eze 40:21
just the * as on the east side. Eze 40:22
were just the * as in the others. Eze 40:24
that it had the * measurements as Eze 40:28
It too had the * measurements as Eze 40:32
hall were the * size as those of Eze 40:33
were the * as the others, with a Eze 40:36
the terrace, the * on both sides. Eze 41:9
arranged the * as the other. Eze 42:9,10
the building, the * as in the other Eze 42:11
the court—the * length and width Eze 42:11
and width and the * exits and Eze 42:11
* as those of the tribal sections. Eze 45:7
"On the fourteenth day of the * Eze 45:21
provide these * sacrifices for the Eze 45:25
the passageway and out the * way; Eze 46:8
They must never go out the * way Eze 46:9
* rights your own children have. Eze 47:22
the * east and west boundaries. Eze 48:2
Asher's, with the * boundary lines Eze 48:3
Naphtali, with the * eastern and Eze 48:4
all with the * boundaries on the Eze 48:5,6,7
It has the * eastern and western Eze 48:8
It will be of the * size and Eze 48:13
* eastern and western borders. Eze 48:24
Next is Issachar, with the * Eze 48:25
Then Gad, with the * borders on Eze 48:27,28
The south wall, also the * Eze 48:33
That very * hour this prophecy Dan 4:33
For you men are doing the * Hos 4:14
I am the * Lord, the same God, Hos 12:9
I am the same Lord, the * God, Hos 12:9
of Gilgal flourish just the *. Hos 12:11
father defile the * temple-girl, Amo 2:7
Hosts: "On the * day that I Amo 3:14
At that * time, says the Lord, I Mic 5:10
His power is just the * as Hab 3:6
was active during this * period. Zep 1:1f
IN EARLY OCTOBER of the * year, Hag 2:1
Haggai from the Lord that * day: Hag 2:20
in Babylon. The * day they arrive, Zec 6:10,11
(This * plague will strike the Zec 14:15
We are children of the * father, Mal 2:10
Abraham, all created by the * God. Mal 2:10
That * Mt 2:14
"Don't recite the * prayer over Mt 6:7,8
And the boy was healed that * Mt 8:
given the * reward a prophet gets. Mt 10:4
LATER THAT * day, Jesus left the Mt 13
the afternoon he did the * thing. Mt 20
It is my desire to pay all the *; Mt 20:
him, but the results were the *. Mt 21:3
But that * day some of the Mt 22:2
are on the * level, as brothers. Mt 23:
other disciples said the * thing. Mt 26:3
time, saying the * things again. Mt 26:4
And the robbers also threw the * Mt 27:4
who received the * treatment, only Mk 12.
And all the others vowed the *. Mk 14:3
then they will do the * for you. Lk 6:3
"Yes, now go and do the *." Lk 10:3
"Yes," said Jesus, "the * Lk 11:4
would have done the * yourselves. Lk 11:4
"Well, in the * way heaven will Lk 15:
In the * way there is joy in the Lk 15:1
be asleep in the * room, and one Lk 17:3
Then he sent another, but the * Lk 20:1
A third man was sent and the * Lk 20:1
and David's God at the * time?" Lk 20:4
In the * way, when you see the Lk 21:3
Herod came to the * conclusion Lk 23:1
That * day, Sunday, two of Jesus' Lk 24:1
it was the * moment that Jesus had Jn 4:5
Father doing, and in the * way. Jn 5:1
Afterwards he did the * with the Jn 6:1
me, and in the * way those who Jn 6:5
this the * fellow—that beggar?" Jn 9:
"It can't be the * man," they Jn 9:
And the beggar said, "I am the * Jn 9:
in me shall do the * miracles I Jn 14:12,1
It will be the * joy as that of Jn 16:2
and the * can be said of your Act 3:1
And so God sent back the * man Act 7:3
So Philip began with this * Act 8:3
"Isn't this the * man who Act 9:2
The * vision was repeated three Act 10:1
these Gentiles the * gift he gave Act 11:17
all are saved the * way, by the Act 15:11
That * hour he washed their Act 16:33
day to attain this * hope I have! Act 26:7
might become the * as I am, except Act 26:29
to come to God in this * way. Rom 1:16
for you do these very * things. Rom 2:1
For God treats everyone the *. Rom 2:11
And we all can be saved in this * Rom 3:21,22
sinners in this * way, because Rom 3:26
may come to him in this * manner. Rom 3:29
God treats us all the *; Rom 3:30
accept us in the * way he accepted Rom 4:24
* Holy Spirit living within you. Rom 8:11
And in the * way—by our faith Rom 8:26
a right to use the * lump of clay Rom 9:21
Jew and Gentile are the * in Rom 10:12
they all have the * Lord who Rom 10:12
It is the * today. Rom 11:5
King David spoke of this * thing Rom 11:9
Pay your taxes too, for these * Rom 13:6
a team, with the * aim, though each 1Co 3:8
wife should do the * for her 1Co 7:3
and in the * way the husband no 1Co 7:4
But we are not all the *. 1Co 7:7
and the * may be said to you 1Co 7:16
It is the * with a girl who 1Co 7:34
She faces the * problem. 1Co 7:34
Can't I claim the * privilege the 1Co 9:4
In the * way the Lord has given 1Co 9:14
Literally, "all ate the * . 1Co 10:3,4f
us against doing the * things; 1Co 10:11
exactly the * problems before you. 1Co 10:13
all eat from the * loaf, showing 1Co 10:17
when you eat the * food, along with 1Co 10:20
churches feel the * way about it. 1Co 11:16
In the * way, he took the cup 1Co 11:25
but it is the * Holy Spirit who is 1Co 12:4
it is the * Lord we are serving. 1Co 12:5
but it is the * God who does the 1Co 12:6
is his gift from the * Spirit. 1Co 12:8
It is the * and only Holy Spirit 1Co 12:11
all been given that * Holy Spirit. 1Co 12:13
the parts have the * care for each 1Co 12:25
In the * way, we can see and 1Co 13:12
In the * way, if you talk to a 1Co 14:9
changed—it is the * Good News I 1Co 15:1
In the * way, our earthly bodies 1Co 15:42
will have the * kind of body as 1Co 15:48
(and, by the way, these are the * 1Co 16:1
on to them this * help and comfort 2Co 1:3,4
you undergo these * sufferings. 2Co 1:6,7
We know that the * God who 2Co 4:14
He is not the * any more. 2Co 5:17
Our hearts ache, but at the * 2Co 6:10
given Titus the * real concern for 2Co 8:16
work in just the * way we are. 2Co 11:12
For we have the * Holy Spirit, 2Co 12:18
steps, doing things the * way. 2Co 12:18
to me, for all are the * to God. Gal 2:6
the Jews—for the * God gave us each Gal 2:7,8,9

AME Con't)
Abraham had the * experience—God Gal 3:6
the * blessing Abraham received. Gal 3:8,9
* blessing he promised to Abraham; Gal 3:14
are all the *—we are Christians; Gal 3:28
It is that * mighty power that Eph 1:19
As parts of the * body, our Eph 2:16
body, we have the * Spirit, and we Eph 4:4
called to the * glorious future. Eph 4:4
we all have the * God and Father Eph 4:6
of the earth. The * one who came Eph 4:10
the * way you submit to the Lord. Eph 5:22
of his wife in the * way Christ is Eph 5:23
And you husbands, show the * kind Eph 5:25
you have the * Master they do, Eph 6:9
others, and at the * time keep on Php 1:9
in the Lord, sharing the * Spirit? Php 2:1
his own, using the * mighty power Php 3:21
to you. The * Good News that came Col 1:6
boldly repeat the * message to you, 1Th 2:2
while at the * time he is 2Th 1:6
And the women should be the * 1Ti 2:9,10
The deacons must be the * sort of 1Ti 3:8
All must be treated exactly the * 1Ti 5:21
In the * way, everyone knows how 1Ti 5:25
In the * way, urge the young men Tit 2:6
give him the * welcome you would Phm 1:17
now have the * Father he has. Heb 2:11
These * people who sinned and as Heb 3:17
since he had the * temptations we Heb 4:15
with the * temptations and Heb 5:1
work in the * way God chose Aaron. Heb 5:4
with the * rank as Melchizedek." Heb 5:6
with the * rank as Melchizedek. Heb 5:10
LET US STOP going over the * old Heb 6:1
* rank all other priests had? Heb 7:11
And in the * way he sprinkled Heb 9:21
others suffering the * things. Heb 10:33
to whom God gave the * promise. Heb 11:9
Jesus Christ is the * yesterday, Heb 13:8
and at the * moment another man Jas 2:2
come pouring out of the * mouth. Jas 3:10
the power of the * heaven-sent Holy 1Pe 1:12
him, well—"The * Stone that was 1Pe 2:7
And if you do the *, you will be 1Pe 3:6
must have the * attitude he did; 1Pe 4:1
give this * faith to each of us. 2Pe 1:1
And by that * mighty power he 2Pe 1:4
But at the * time the Lord 2Pe 2:7,8
in the * destruction with them." 2Pe 2:12f
* things in many of his letters. 2Pe 3:15,16
And they all say the * thing: 1Jn 5:6,7,8
I myself can say the * for him, 3Jn 1:12
these very * followers of Balaam Rev 2:15
in heaven, and the * voice I had Rev 4:1
The * hour there will be a Rev 11:13
was exactly the * as its other Rev 21:16
who hears them say the *, 'Come.' Rev 22:17

SAMGAR-NEBO
Nergal-sharezer was there, and * Jer 39:3

SAMLAH
Succeeded by: King *, from Gen 36:31-39
When Hadad died, * from the city 1Ch 1:47
When * died, Shaul from the river 1Ch 1:48

SAMOS
the next, we touched at *; Act 20:15

SAMOTHRACE
straight across to *, and the next Act 16:11

SAMPLE
* of the first day's harvest; Ex 23:19
an offering of a * of the new grain Lev 23:15,16
to the Lord a * of each year's Num 15:19,20,21
except for the * presented to the Num 18:9
the first * from each annual Deu 26:2,3
Here is a * of his preaching: Mk 1:7
Here is a * of John's preaching Lk 3:7

SAMPLES
camels loaded with * of the best of Gen 24:10
some * of the crops you see." Num 13:20
They also took some * of the Num 13:23
with * of the local fruit. Deu 1:24,25
the harvest * brought in Deu 18:4
Then place the * before the Lord Deu 26:10
The first * of each harvest of Eze 44:30

SAMPLING
the first * of your later crops. Lev 23:17
the first * of your later crops. Lev 23:20

SAMSON
they named him *, and the Lord Ju 13:24
ONE DAY WHEN * was in Timnah, he Ju 14:1
But * told his father, "She is Ju 14:3
As * and his parents were going Ju 14:5
lion attacked * in the vineyards on Ju 14:5
for the marriage, * threw a party Ju 14:10,11
When * asked if they would like Ju 14:12
the wheat harvest, * took a young Ju 15:1
* was furious. Ju 15:3
"*," was the reply, "because Ju 15:6
will strike again!" * vowed. Ju 15:7
"To capture * and do to him as he Ju 15:10
* at the cave in the rock of Etam. Ju 15:11
But * replied, "I only paid them Ju 15:11
"All right," * said, "but Ju 15:12,13
led him away. As * and his captors Ju 15:14
the Lord came upon *, and the ropes Ju 15:14
* was Israel's judge for the next Ju 15:20
ONE DAY * went to the Philistine Ju 16:1
* stayed in bed with the girl Ju 16:3
she find out from * what made him Ju 16:5
So Delilah begged * to tell her Ju 16:6
"Please tell me, *, why you are Ju 16:6
"Well," * replied, "if I were Ju 16:7
* the Philistines are Ju 16:9
* the Philistines have Ju 16:12
"The Philistines have come, *!" Ju 16:14
are here to capture you, *!" Ju 16:20
to celebrate the capture of *. Ju 16:23,24
has delivered our enemy * to us!" Ju 16:23,24
"Bring out * so we can have some Ju 16:25,26
the roof. * said to the boy who was Ju 16:25,26
who were watching * and making Ju 16:27
Then * prayed to the Lord and Ju 16:28
Then * pushed against the pillars Ju 16:29
and Barak and * and Jephthah and Heb 11:32

SAMSON'S
So * wife broke down in tears Ju 14:16
had been best man at * wedding. Ju 14:20
* spirit was revived as he drank. Ju 15:19

SAMUEL
She named him * (meaning 1Sa 1:19,20
The word * in Hebrew sounds like 1Sa 1:19,20f
returned home to Ramah without *; 1Sa 2:11
*, though only a child, was the 1Sa 2:18
Meanwhile * grew up in the 1Sa 2:21
Little * was growing in two 1Sa 2:26
MEANWHILE LITTLE * was helping 1Sa 3:1
age by now), and * was sleeping in 1Sa 3:2,3
Ark, the Lord called out, "*! 1Sa 3:4,5
Lord called out, "Samuel! *!" 1Sa 3:4,5
"Yes?" * replied. 1Sa 3:4,5
Then the Lord called again, * 1Sa 3:6
And again * jumped up and ran 1Sa 3:6
(* had never had a message from 1Sa 3:7
more * jumped up and ran to Eli. 1Sa 3:8
So he said to *, "Go and lie 1Sa 3:9
So * went back to bed. 1Sa 3:9
came and called as before, "*! 1Sa 3:10
called as before, "Samuel! *!" 1Sa 3:10
And * replied, "Yes, I'm 1Sa 3:10
Then the Lord said to *, "I am 1Sa 3:11
* stayed in bed until morning, 1Sa 3:15
So * told him what the Lord had 1Sa 3:18
As * grew, the Lord was with him 1Sa 3:19
knew that * was going to be a 1Sa 3:20
At that time * said to them, "If 1Sa 7:3
Then * told them, "Come to 1Sa 7:5
So it was at Mizpah that * became 1Sa 7:6
they begged *. 1Sa 7:8
So * took a suckling lamb and 1Sa 7:9
Just as * was sacrificing the 1Sa 7:10
along the way. * then took a stone 1Sa 7:12
* continued as Israel's judge for 1Sa 7:15
IN HIS OLD age, * retired and 1Sa 8:1
to discuss the matter with *. 1Sa 8:4
* was terribly upset and went to 1Sa 8:6
So * told the people what the 1Sa 8:10
So * told the Lord what the 1Sa 8:21
So * agreed and sent the men home 1Sa 8:22
the gates they saw * coming out 1Sa 9:14
The Lord had told * the previous 1Sa 9:15
When * saw Saul the Lord said, 1Sa 9:17
Just then Saul approached * and 1Sa 9:18
"I am the seer!" * replied. 1Sa 9:19
Then * took Saul and his servant 1Sa 9:22
special guests. * then instructed 1Sa 9:23
"Go ahead and eat it," * said, 1Sa 9:24
So Saul ate with *. 1Sa 9:24
to the city, * took Saul up to the 1Sa 9:25
At daybreak the next morning, * 1Sa 9:26,27
So Saul got up and * accompanied 1Sa 9:26,27
the city walls * told Saul to send 1Sa 9:26,27
THEN * TOOK a flask of olive oil 1Sa 10:1
so we went to the prophet * to 1Sa 10:14
* now called a convocation of all 1Sa 10:17
So * called the tribal leaders 1Sa 10:20
Then * said to all the people, 1Sa 10:24
Then * told the people again what 1Sa 10:25
Then * sent the people home again. 1Sa 10:25
to follow Saul and * to battle!" 1Sa 11:7
Then the people exclaimed to *, 1Sa 11:12
Then * said to the people, 1Sa 11:14
THEN * ADDRESSED the people again: 1Sa 12:1
my witnesses," * declared, "that 1Sa 12:5
Moses and Aaron," * continued. 1Sa 12:6
Jephthah, and * to save you, and 1Sa 12:11
So * called to the Lord, and the 1Sa 12:18
much afraid of the Lord and of *. 1Sa 12:18
they cried out to *. 1Sa 12:19
"Don't be frightened," * 1Sa 12:20
awaited them. * had told Saul 1Sa 13:8
But just as he was finishing, * 1Sa 13:10
his blessing, but * said, "What 1Sa 13:11
"You fool!" * exclaimed. 1Sa 13:13
* then left Gilgal and went to 1Sa 13:15
ONE DAY * said to Saul, "I 1Sa 15:1
Then the Lord said to *, 1Sa 15:10
* was so deeply moved when he 1Sa 15:11
When * finally found him, Saul 1Sa 15:13
of oxen I heard?" * demanded. 1Sa 15:14
Then * said to Saul, "Stop! 1Sa 15:16
And * told him, "When you didn't 1Sa 15:17
* replied, "Has the Lord as much 1Sa 15:22
But * replied, "It's no use! 1Sa 15:26
As * turned to go, Saul grabbed 1Sa 15:27
And * said to him, "See? 1Sa 15:28
So * finally agreed and went with 1Sa 15:31
Then * said, "Bring King Agag 1Sa 15:32
But * said, "As your sword 1Sa 15:33
And * chopped him in pieces 1Sa 15:33
Then * went home to Ramah, and 1Sa 15:34
to Gibe-ah. * never saw Saul 1Sa 15:35
FINALLY THE LORD said to *, "You 1Sa 16:1
But * asked, "How can I do that? 1Sa 16:2
So * did as the Lord had told him 1Sa 16:4
When they arrived, * took one 1Sa 16:6
But the Lord said to *, "Don't 1Sa 16:7
forward and walk in front of *. 1Sa 16:8
themselves to * and were rejected. 1Sa 16:9
any of them," * told Jesse. 1Sa 16:10,11
"Send for him at once," * said, 1Sa 16:10,11
his brothers, * took the olive oil 1Sa 16:13
onward. Then * returned to Ramah. 1Sa 16:13
to Ramah to see *, and told him all 1Sa 19:18
done to him. So * took David with 1Sa 19:18
but when they arrived and saw * 1Sa 19:20
"Where are * and David?" 1Sa 19:22
(See 1 * 10:10–12. 1Sa 19:24f
SHORTLY AFTERWARDS, * died and 1Sa 25:1
(Meanwhile, * had died and all 1Sa 28:3
"Bring me *," Saul replied. 1Sa 28:11
When the woman saw *, she 1Sa 28:12
Saul realized that it was * and 1Sa 28:14
bringing me back?" * asked Saul. 1Sa 28:15
But * replied, "Why ask me if 1Sa 28:16
See 1 * 31:3, 4 for the true 2Sa 1:10f
See 1 * 25:44. 2Sa 3:15f
See 1 * 2:31-35. 1Ki 2:27f
The families of the subclan of * 1Ch 6:28
Joel, *, Elkanah III, Jeroham, 1Ch 6:33-38
* because of their reliability. 1Ch 9:22
See 1 * 28. 1Ch 10:13f
just as the Lord had told *. 1Ch 11:3
Implied in 2 * 23:30. 1Ch 11:26-47f
to the Lord by * the prophet, Saul 1Ch 26:28
in the history of * the prophet, 1Ch 29:29
Never since the time of * the 2Ch 35:18
his enemy Doeg (1 * 22), who later Ps 52:1
to capture and kill him. 1 * 19:11 Ps 59:1
apparently a reference to *, who Ps 89:19f
When Moses and Aaron and *, his Ps 99:6
See 2 * 7 for the terms of God's Is 55:3f
Even if Moses and * stood before me Jer 15:1
God, was instituted (1 * 11:15). Hos 9:15f
"* and every prophet since have Act 3:24
were followed by * the prophet. Act 13:19,20
and * and all the other prophets. Heb 11:32

SAMUEL'S
the remainder of * lifetime. 1Sa 7:13
refused to listen to * warning. 1Sa 8:19
* prophecies came true that day. 1Sa 10:9
prophesying with * prophets. 1Sa 19:24
with fright because of * words. 1Sa 28:20
headed by * sons:Joel, the oldest; 1Ch 6:28

SANAAH
From the subclan of *, 3,930. Neh 7:8-38

SANBALLAT
But when * (the Horonite) and Neh 2:10
But when * and Tobiah and Geshem Neh 2:19
* WAS VERY angry when he learned Neh 4:1
But when * and Tobiah and the Neh 4:7
WHEN *, TOBIAH, Geshem the Arab, Neh 6:1
but Tobiah and * had hired him to Neh 6:12,13
evil of Tobiah, *, No-adiah the Neh 6:14
a son-in-law of * the Horonite, so Neh 13:28

SANBALLAT'S
The fifth time, * servant came Neh 6:5,6

SANCTIFICATION
the ceremonies of * in preparation 1Ch 15:14

SANCTIFIED
to the people and * them and they Ex 19:14
clothing shall be * to the Lord. Ex 29:21
Tabernacle shall be * by my glory. Ex 29:43
Only those who are *—the Lev 6:27
thus he * the altar, making Lev 8:15,16
MOSES ANOINTED AND * each part Num 7:1
After you have * them and Num 8:15
measure the king * the court in 1Ki 8:64
and * it to be my home forever; 2Ch 7:16
though I have * it for myself. 2Ch 7:20
march, clothed in * garments and 2Ch 20:21
the Temple itself, for they are *. 2Ch 23:5,6
fellow Levites and * themselves, 2Ch 29:15
have recovered and * all the 2Ch 29:19

(SANCTIFIED Con't)
priests were * at the earlier date, 2Ch 30:2,3
which he has * forever, and worship 2Ch 30:8
part, so they * themselves and 2Ch 30:15
not properly * for the ceremony." 2Ch 30:17,18,19
stepped forward and * themselves. 2Ch 30:24
He issued this order to the * 2Ch 35:3
before you were born I * you and Jer 1:5
a sacrifice and * his guests." Zep 1:7f
when the one * and sent into the Jn 10:34,35,36
Literally, "* in Christ 1Co 1:2f

SANCTIFIES
for I am the Lord who * you. Lev 20:8
he is holy, for I, the Lord who * Lev 21:8
for it is Jehovah who * it." Lev 21:23
I am the Lord who * them. Lev 22:9
for I am Jehovah who * the Lev 22:16
I, the Lord, who * them, that they Eze 20:12
or the Temple that * the gold? Mt 23:17
the altar itself that * the gift? Mt 23:19

SANCTIFY
for my visit. * them today and Ex 19:10
must * themselves, lest Jehovah Ex 19:22
pour olive oil upon it to * it. Ex 29:36
Yes, I will * the Tabernacle and Ex 29:44
"Once a year Aaron must * Ex 30:10
* them, to make them holy; Ex 30:29
and its pedestal, to * them. Lev 8:11
altar itself, to * it, and poured Lev 8:15,16
his people. So * yourselves and be Lev 20:7
Literally, "did not * me." Num 20:12f
and did not * me in the eyes of Num 20:12
"Now * yourselves with all your 1Ch 15:12
"Listen to me, you Levites. * 2Ch 29:4,5
Sanctify yourselves and * the 2Ch 29:4,5
to clean up and * the Temple, as 2Ch 29:15
much more ready to * themselves 2Ch 29:34
lambs for them, to * them. 2Ch 30:17,18,19
Kill the Passover lambs and * 2Ch 35:6
to him and * them, getting up early Job 1:5
court, in case they * the people. Eze 46:19,20

SANCTIFYING
olive oil, thus * them as the Ex 28:41
and his sons, * them so that they Ex 30:30
offering and its utensils, * it; Ex 40:10
washbasin and its pedestal, * it. Ex 40:11
and anoint him, * him to minister Ex 40:13
and on each item in it, * them. Lev 8:10

SANCTITY
your daughter's * by making her a Lev 19:29
to preserve the * of the Sabbath. Neh 13:22

SANCTUARIES
and the open-air * in the hills Num 33:52
Literally, "against the *." Eze 21:2f

SANCTUARY
The * you made for them to live Ex 15:17
the shekel of the * [the shekel is Ex 30:13f
the frames of the * walls and for Ex 38:27
standard of the shekel of the *." Lev 5:15f
eat it in the *, in a holy place. Lev 10:13
offering in the *, since it is most Lev 10:17
taken inside the *, you should Lev 10:18
for the holy *, the Tabernacle, the Lev 16:33
Literally, "my *." Lev 20:3f
He shall not leave the * [when Lev 21:12
this would defile my *, for it is Lev 21:23
the shekel of the *: twenty gerahs Lev 27:25f
for the oversight of the *. Num 3:31-35
after the shekel of the * shalt Num 3:47,48f
after the shekel of the *." Num 3:50f
packing the * and all the utensils, Num 4:15
never enter the * for even a Num 4:20
the items from the inner *. Num 10:21
desecration of the *," he said, Num 18:1
within the * and at the altar. Num 18:5
not enter the *, lest they be Num 18:22
he has defiled the * of the Lord, Num 19:20
"with the vessels of the *." Num 31:6f
Rather, you must build a * for Deu 12:4,5
offerings to his *, the place he Deu 12:11
place he shall choose as his *; Deu 14:23
chooses for his * is so far away Deu 14:24
take the money to the Lord's *. Deu 14:25
Lord your God each year at his *. Deu 15:20
to the Lord your God at his * Deu 16:2
the Lord shall choose as his *. Deu 16:6
you to the celebration at the *. Deu 16:11
be held at the *, which will be Deu 16:15
year at the * for these festivals: Deu 16:16
the case to the * of the Lord your Deu 17:8
to come to the * at any time and Deu 18:6,7
cut off, he shall not enter the *. Deu 23:1
A bastard may not enter the *, Deu 23:2
may ever enter the *, even after Deu 23:3
Egypt may enter the * of the Lord. Deu 23:8
to the Lord at his * the first Deu 26:2,3
assemble before the Lord at the *. Deu 31:10,11
was claiming * in the Tabernacle, 1Ki 1:51
the Tabernacle for * and caught 1Ki 2:28
This inner * was thirty feet 1Ki 6:20
Within the inner * Solomon placed 1Ki 6:23-28
The doorway to the inner * was a 1Ki 6:31
Ark into the inner * of the 1Ki 8:6
from the inner *, a bright cloud 1Ki 8:10
the front of the *, and surrounded 2Ki 11:11
to the inner *—the Holy of 1Ch 6:49
protection of the *, just as their 1Ch 9:19
the items in the *, and the 1Ch 9:29
and the * for the place of mercy. 1Ch 28:11
the forbidden * of the Temple and 2Ch 26:16
May he send you aid from his * Ps 20:2
could go into your * to see your Ps 63:2
onward to the *— singers in front, Ps 68:24
kneeling here before him in the *. Ps 68:35
Then one day I went into God's * Ps 73:17
what the enemy has done to your *. Ps 74:3
and set the * on fire, and razed Ps 74:7
it to the ground—your *, Lord. Ps 74:7
entire * was filled with smoke. Is 6:4
"Give us *. Is 16:3
and box trees—to beautify my *. Is 60:13
yet I will be a * to you for the Eze 11:16
into my *—those who have no heart Eze 44:7
foreigners to take charge of my *. Eze 44:8
you shall enter my * if he has not Eze 44:9
They shall enter my * and come Eze 44:16
court and the *, he must offer a Eze 44:27
minister in the *, for their homes Eze 45:4
*—for your own glory, Lord. Dan 9:17
shall utterly defile the * of God. Dan 9:27
Jerusalem and pollute the *, Dan 11:30,31
between the altar and the *. Mt 23:35
to enter the inner * and burn Lk 1:8,9
Zacharias was in the * when Lk 1:11,12
between the altar and the *. Lk 11:51
you: Destroy this * and in three Jn 2:19
But by "this *" he meant his Jn 2:21
animals into the * as a sacrifice Heb 13:11

SAND
and hid his body in the *. Ex 2:12
And the treasures of the *." Deu 33:19
like the * upon the seashore—and Ju 7:12,13
as thick as * along the seashore; 1Sa 13:5
For they are heavier than the * Job 6:3
Water grinds the stones to *. Job 14:18,19
are heavier than * and rocks. Pro 27:3
be counted nor the * upon the Jer 33:22
to count—like * along a seashore! Hos 1:10
oceans and rivers become dry *; Nah 1:4
They collect captives like *. Hab 1:9
a man who builds his house on *. Mt 7:26
Literally, "as the * of the Rom 9:27f
of the sky and the * on the ocean Heb 11:12
numberless as * along the shore. Rev 20:8

SANDAL
elders, pull his * from his foot Deu 25:9
the man who had his * pulled off!' Deu 25:10
* and hand it to the other party; Ru 4:7
for yourself," he drew off his *. Ru 4:8
Literally, "of loosing (the * Lk 3:16f

SANDALS
and * made of dolphin hide. Eze 16:9,10

SANDALWOOD
from Ophir, also * and jewels. 2Ch 9:10
The king used the * to make 2Ch 9:11

SANDBAR
But the ship hit a * Act 27:41

SANDS
and like the * along the seashore. Gen 22:17
they become as the * along the Gen 32:12
of them like * along the shore! Ps 78:27
now as many as the * along the Is 10:22
as numerous as the * along the Is 48:19
across the desert * at night. Mic 1:8

SANE
perfectly *, they were frightened. Mk 5:15
at Jesus' feet, clothed and *! Lk 8:35

SANG
of Israel * this song to the Lord: Ex 15:1
And Miriam * this song: Ex 15:21
the people *:Spring up, O well! Num 21:17,18
THEN DEBORAH AND Barak * this Ju 5:1
women of Israel * about in their 1Sa 29:5
DAVID * THIS song to the Lord 2Sa 22:1
Lord and pray to him," they *. 1Ch 16:8
They * with joy as they worked. 2Ch 23:18
singers * and the trumpets blew. 2Ch 29:28
They * rounds of praise and Ez 3:11
They * loudly and clearly under Neh 12:42
the morning stars * together and Job 38:6,7
Then they finally * his praise. Ps 106:12
How we laughed and * for joy. Ps 126:2
chorus they *, "Holy, holy, holy Is 6:3
that Habakkuk * before the Lord: Hab 3:1
Then they * a hymn and went out Mk 14:26
in the highest heaven," they *, Lk 2:14
* a dirge and you didn't weep." Lk 7:32f
Lamb is worthy" (loudly they * Rev 5:12
strong—* a wonderful new song in Rev 14:3

SANITY
to heaven, and my * returned, and I Dan 4:34

SANK
They * as lead in the mighty Ex 15:10
The stone * in, and the man fell 1Sa 17:48,4
and he * down dead in his chariot. 2Ki 9:2
* into the western skies, he died. 2Ch 18:3
of the sea; they * like stones Neh 9:1
* to the levels you decreed. Ps 104:7,
and Jeremiah * down into it. Jer 38:
ocean depths; I * down into the Jon 2:
"I * beneath the waves, and Jon 2:

SANSANNAH
Ziklag, Madmannah, *, Lebaoth, Jos 15:21-3

SAP
I will * away the strength of Hos 5:1

SAPH
killed *, another giant. 2Sa 21:1

SAPHON
or, "on the slopes of Mount *." Is 14:13

SAPPED
My sins have * my strength; Ps 31:9,1
of slavery. He * my strength and Lam 1:1
Worshiping foreign gods has * Hos 7:

SAPPHIRA
(with his wife *) who sold some Act 5:

SAPPHIRE
* stones, as clear as the heavens. Ex 24:1
be an emerald, a *, and a diamond. Ex 28:1
an emerald, a *, and a diamond. Ex 39:1
of beautiful blue * stones, and Eze 1:2
A THRONE of beautiful blue * Eze 10:
onyx, jasper, *, carbuncle, and Eze 28:1
The second with *; Rev 21:18,19,2

SAPPHIRES
"They know how to find * and Job 28:
or precious onyx stones or *. Job 28:16
on a foundation of * and make the Is 54:1
than rubies, polished like *." Lam 4:7

SARAH
'Sarai' but '*' ('Princess'). Gen 17:15
"Me—100 years old? And *, to Gen 17:17
I said. * shall bear you a son; Gen 17:19
* next year at about this time." Gen 17:21
the tent and said to *, "Quick! Gen 18:6
"Where is *, your wife?" Gen 18:9
I will give you and * a son!" Gen 18:10
Sarah a son!" (* was listening Gen 18:10
Now Abraham and * were both Gen 18:11
both very old, and * was long since Gen 18:11
So * laughed silently. Gen 18:12
to Abraham, "Why did * laugh? Gen 18:13
see to it that * has a son." Gen 18:14
But * denied it. Gen 18:15
he remarked that * was his sister! Gen 20:2
and returned * his wife to him. Gen 20:14
Then he turned to *. Gen 20:16
had promised, and * became pregnant Gen 21:1
And * declared, "God has brought Gen 21:6
But when * noticed Ishmael—the Gen 21:9
do as * says, for Isaac is the Gen 21:12
WHEN * WAS 127 years old, she died Gen 23:1
So Abraham buried * there, in Gen 23:19,20
"Now when *, my master's wife, Gen 24:36
*, Abraham's wife was buried. Gen 25:9,10
There they buried Abraham and * Gen 49:31
Abraham and *, from whom you came. Is 51:1
and that * his wife, at ninety, Rom 4:19
I will give you and * a son." Rom 9:9
*, too, had faith, and because of Heb 11:11
*, for instance, obeyed her 1Pe 3:6

SARAH'S
the Egyptian, * slave Gen 25:12-15

SARAI
*, while his brother Nahor Gen 11:29
named Iscah. But * was barren; Gen 11:30
daughter-in-law *, and left Ur of Gen 11:31
He took his wife *, his nephew Gen 12:5
of Egypt, he asked * his wife to Gen 12:11,12,13
BUT * AND Abram had no children. Gen 16:1
no children. So * took her maid, an Gen 16:1
me no children," * said, "you may Gen 16:2,3
arrogant toward her mistress *. Gen 16:4
Then * said to Abram, "It's all Gen 16:5
So * beat her and she ran away. Gen 16:6
Then God added, "Regarding * Gen 17:15
'*' but 'Sarah' ('Princess'). Gen 17:15

SARAI'S
The Angel: "Hagar, * maid, where Gen 16:8

SARAPH
* (who was a ruler in Moab before 1Ch 4:21-22

SARDIS
*, Philadelphia, and Laodicea." Rev 1:11
of the church in * write this Rev 3:1
"Yet even there in * some Rev 3:4

SARDIUS
In the first row were a *, a Ex 39:10

SARDONYX
The fifth with *; Rev 21:18,19,20

SARDUS
The sixth layer with *; Rev 21:18,19,20

SAREA
at the port of Cae * from where he Act 18:22

SARGON
* of Assyria. Is 14:31f

SARGON Con't)
IN THE YEAR when *, king of Is 20:1

SARID
started on the south side of *. Jos 19:10

SARSECHIM
Samgar-nebo and * and Jer 39:3

SASH
tunic, a turban, and a *. Ex 28:4
And the * shall be made of the Ex 28:8
front edge of the ephod at the *. Ex 28:27
and make him an embroidered *. Ex 28:39
chestpiece, and *, and place on Ex 29:5
one-piece woven * made of the same Ex 39:4,5
joined its beautifully woven *. Ex 39:20
beautifully woven * of the ephod by Ex 39:21
the special coat, *, robe, and the Lev 8:7

SASHES
sons, make robes, *, and turbans to Ex 28:40
*, and place caps on their heads. Ex 29:9
stink; for * they'll use ropes; Is 3:24

SAT
* down a hundred yards or so away. Gen 21:16
defilement of all that was * upon. Gen 31:35f
Then they * down for supper. Gen 37:25
herself, and * beside the road at Gen 38:14
his strength and * up in the bed to Gen 48:2
The next day Moses * as usual to Ex 18:13
afterwards they * down to feast Ex 32:6
a seat the man has * upon while Lev 15:6
the Lord came and * beneath the oak Ju 6:11
The next morning as Gaal * at Ju 9:35
met at Bethel and * before God Ju 21:2
So she * with his reapers and he Ru 2:14
he wakened and * up, startled. Ru 3:8
So they * down together. Ru 4:1
began, the king * down to eat at 1Sa 20:24,25
Jonathan * opposite him and Abner 1Sa 20:24,25
and got up and * on the bed. 1Sa 28:23
Gibeon, where they * facing each 2Sa 2:13
the Tabernacle and * before the 2Sa 7:18
So the king went out and * at the 2Sa 19:8,9,10
so she * at his right hand. 1Ki 2:19
Solomon * to hear legal matters; 1Ki 7:7
all day, and * down under a broom 1Ki 19:4
fixed her hair and * at a window. 2Ki 9:30
And he * upon the king's throne. 2Ki 11:19
Then King David went in and * 1Ch 17:16
beard and * down utterly baffled. Ez 9:3
people came and * with me until the Ez 9:4
When I heard this, I * down and Neh 1:4
Then the king and Haman * down Est 3:15
himself, and * among the ashes. Job 2:8
Then they * upon the ground with Job 2:13
WEEPING, WE * beside the rivers of Ps 137:1
the palace and * down at the door Jer 26:10
* in triumph at the middle gate. Jer 39:3
and upon it * someone who appeared Eze 1:26
And I * among them, overwhelmed, Eze 3:14,15
there * women weeping for Tammuz, Eze 8:14
* before me awaiting his reply. Eze 20:1
for them. You * together on a Eze 23:41
* there stunned and silent for an Dan 4:19
Almighty God—* down to judge. Dan 7:9
whitest wool. He * upon a fiery Dan 7:9
All day long he * on the Amo 1:1
put on sackcloth and * in ashes. Jon 3:6
So Jonah went out and * sulking Jon 4:5
the people who * in darkness have Mt 4:15,16
great Light; they * in the land of Mt 4:15,16
and * down and taught them there. Mt 5:1
The disciples just * there, Mt 8:27
The others * there, awestruck. Mt 14:33
and climbed a hill and * there. Mt 15:29
him later, as he * on the slopes of Mt 24:3
That evening as he * eating with Mt 26:20,21
and went in and * with the Mt 26:58
Then they * around and watched Mt 27:36
aside the stone and * on it. Mt 28:2
said to themselves as they * Mk 2:6
and * down and talked from there. Mk 4:1
They just * there, unable to take Mk 6:51
He * down and called them around Mk 9:35
in the Temple and * and watched as Mk 12:41
And as he * on the slopes of the Mk 13:3,4
* a young man clothed in white. Mk 16:5
and * down at God's right hand. Mk 16:19
the attendant and * down, while Lk 4:20
Then the boy * up and began to Lk 7:15
As they * down to eat, a woman Lk 7:36
their people would have * in deep Lk 10:13
Her sister Mary * on the floor, Lk 10:39
When Jesus arrived, he * down to Lk 11:37,38
all * down together at the table; Lk 22:14
the courtyard and * around it for Lk 22:55
As they * down to eat, he asked Lk 24:30
sun and * wearily beside the well. Jn 4:5,6
into the hills and * down with his Jn 6:2-5
5,000—* down on the grassy slopes. Jn 6:10
A crowd soon gathered, and he * Jn 8:2
Martha served, and Lazarus * at Jn 12:2
his robe again and * down and Jn 13:12
to them again and * down at the Jn 19:13
And when she saw Peter, she * up! Act 9:40
his royal robes, * on his throne Act 12:21
us, "The people * down to eat and 1Co 10:7
all sin, and then * down in highest Heb 1:3
all time, and then * down in the Heb 10:12
and the one who * upon it, from Rev 20:11

SATAN
THEN * BROUGHT disaster upon 1Ch 21:1
*, the Accuser, came with them. Job 1:6
the Lord asked *. Job 1:7
And * replied, "From patroling Job 1:7
Then the Lord asked *, "Have you Job 1:8
you pay him so well?" * scoffed. Job 1:9
And the Lord replied to *, "You Job 1:12,13
So * went away; Job 1:12,13
before the Lord, and * with them. Job 2:1
the Lord asked *. Job 2:2
"From patroling the earth," * Job 2:2
"Skin for skin," * replied. Job 2:4,5
So * went out from the presence Job 2:7
Tyre, and some seem to apply to *. Eze 28:12f
of the Lord; and * was there too, Zec 3:1
And the Lord said to *, "I Zec 3:2
"The Lord rebuke you, O * Zec 3:2f
*; yes, I, the Lord, for I have Zec 3:2
Spirit, to be tempted there by *. Mt 4:1
Then * tempted him to get food Mt 4:3
Then * took him to Jerusalem to Mt 4:5
Next * took him to the peak of a Mt 4:8
"Get out of here, *," Jesus Mt 4:10
Then * went away, and angels came Mt 4:11
by *, the demon king!" Mt 9:34
household, have been called '*,' Mt 10:25
cast out demons because he is *, Mt 12:24
And if * is casting out Satan, Mt 12:26
And if Satan is casting out *, Mt 12:26
the powers of *, then what power do Mt 12:27
kingdom without first binding *. Mt 12:29
and doesn't understand it; then * Mt 13:19
are the people belonging to *. Mt 13:38
said, "Get away from me, you *! Mt 16:23
possessed by *, king of demons. Mk 3:22
"How can * cast out Satan? Mk 3:23
"How can Satan cast out *? Mk 3:23
And if * is fighting against Mk 3:26
He would never survive. [* must Mk 3:27
God's message; * comes at once to Mk 4:15
very sternly, "*, get behind me! Mk 8:33
* tempted him for forty days. Lk 4:1
* said, "If you are God's Son, Lk 4:3
Then * took him up and revealed Lk 4:5
Then * took him to Jerusalem to a Lk 4:9,10,11
"Yes," he told them, "I saw * Lk 10:18
He gets his power from *, Lk 11:15
say is true, that * is fighting Lk 11:18
And if I am empowered by *, what Lk 11:19
proves they are possessed by *? Lk 11:19
"For when *, Lk 11:21
bondage in which * has held her for Lk 13:16
Then * entered into Judas Lk 22:3
"Simon, Simon, * has asked to Lk 22:31
has come—and the time when *, Jn 12:31
As soon as Judas had eaten it, * Jn 13:27
But Peter said, "Ananias, * has Act 5:3
will soon crush * under your feet. Rom 16:20
again so that * won't be able to 1Co 7:5
keep from being outsmarted by *; 2Co 2:11
to eternal death. *, who is the 2Co 4:4
by * in the Garden of Eden. 2Co 11:3
Yet I am not surprised! * can 2Co 11:14
a messenger from * to hurt and 2Co 12:7
of sin, obeying *, the mighty Eph 2:2
*, he gave generous gifts to men. Eph 4:8
all strategies and tricks of *. Eph 6:11
fiery arrows aimed at you by *. Eph 6:16
again and again, but * stopped us. 1Th 2:18
I was afraid that perhaps * had 1Th 3:5
I had to give them over to * to 1Ti 1:20
who was fooled by *, but Eve, and 1Ti 2:14
Christians—so that * can't trap him 1Ti 3:7
church and been led astray by *. 1Ti 5:15
having been deceived by *. 2Ti 3:13
attacks from *, your great enemy. 1Pe 5:8
you have won your battle with *. 1Jn 2:13
struggle against *: Stop loving 1Jn 2:14
that you belong to *, who since he 1Jn 3:8
child of God and who belongs to *. 1Jn 3:10
to * and killed his brother. 1Jn 3:12
was arguing with * about Moses' Jud 1:9
to accuse even *, or jeer at him, Jud 1:9
for they support the cause of *. Rev 2:9
them—depths of *, really), I will Rev 2:24,25
of * while claiming to be mine Rev 3:9
the devil, or *, the one deceiving Rev 12:9
The Dragon—*—and the Creature from Rev 17:3f
the devil, *—and bound him in Rev 20:2
When the thousand years end, * Rev 20:7

SATAN'S
One cannot rob * kingdom without Mt 12:29
subjected to * temptations to sin. Mk 1:12,13
his miracles by * power [instead of Mk 3:30
when * power reigns supreme." Lk 22:53
to keep them safe from * power. Jn 17:15
God instead of in * darkness, so Act 26:18
and into * hands, to punish him, 1Co 5:5
Lord's Table and at * table, too. 1Co 10:21
the Lord's Table and at * table. 1Co 10:21
and gloom of * kingdom and brought Col 1:13
In this way God took away * Col 2:15
This man of sin will come as * 2Th 2:9
a fall. (* downfall is an example. 1Ti 3:6
and escape from * trap of slavery 2Ti 2:26
to be made that * great desire was Heb 5:7f
us is under * power and control. 1Jn 5:19
in the city where * throne is, at Rev 2:13
martyred among you by * devotees. Rev 2:13

SATANIC
shall be mighty, but it will be * Dan 8:24
for you in heaven against * forces Dan 12:1
those mighty * beings and great Eph 6:12
tool, full of * power, and will 2Th 2:9
you from * attacks of every kind. 2Th 3:3
is, at the center of * worship; Rev 2:13
this person is of * origin, as most Rev 9:1f

SATED
The sword of the Lord is * with Is 34:6
devour until it is *, yes, drunk Jer 46:10
is * with loot, says the Lord. Jer 50:10

SATELLITES
with her * across the heavens? Job 38:32

SATISFACTION
gives a man great *, and hard work Pro 12:14
as the answer to my search for *. Ecc 2:20-23
than lose the * I get from 1Co 9:15
have the personal * of work well Gal 6:4

SATISFIED
when Moses heard that, he was *. Lev 10:20
so that they can eat and be *; Deu 14:29
"O Naphtali, you are * Deu 33:23
he killed her or * his vow by Ju 11:39f
But Jehoshaphat wasn't *. 2Ch 18:6,7
Why aren't you * with my anguish? Job 19:22
no more, for my counsel * them. Job 29:22
barren ground is * with water, and Job 38:25-27
I will be fully *, for I will see Ps 17:15
shall eat and be *; Ps 22:26
before they are *, howling like Ps 59:14,15
At last I shall be fully *; Ps 63:5
them and they are * with all your Ps 104:28
alike in this: neither is ever *. Pro 27:20
There are two things never *, Pro 30:15,16
how much we see, we are never *; Ecc 1:8-11
aren't * to exhaust my patience; Is 7:13
you will not be *—his fist will Is 9:11,12
anger is not yet *, but his fist is Is 9:17
of this, God's anger is not yet *. Is 9:21
anger will not be *, but my fist Is 10:4
He won't be * Is 42:4
of his soul, he shall be *; Is 53:11
are as greedy as dogs, never *; Is 56:11
they were fully *, and their thanks Jer 5:7
last the anger of the Lord is *; Lam 4:11
you still weren't *, so you Eze 16:28
Babylon—and you still weren't *. Eze 16:29
Your merchandise * the desires Eze 27:33
had eaten and were *, then you Hos 13:6
Would he be *? Mic 6:7
death and hell, they are never *. Hab 2:5
for they shall be completely *. Mt 5:6
He has * the hungry hearts and Lk 1:53
hungry, for you are going to be *! Lk 6:21
us the Father and we will be *." Jn 14:8
So we should be well * without 1Ti 6:8
You were not * with the animal Heb 10:6
about not being * with the various Heb 10:8
of money; be * with what you have. Heb 13:5
gripers, never *, doing whatever Jud 1:16

SATISFIES
For he * the thirsty soul and Ps 107:9
Ability to give wise advice * Pro 18:20
and * every need there is. Act 17:25
That's why it fully * all of Rom 13:10

SATISFY
like a lioness, to * the young Job 38:39,40
He would * you with honey for the Ps 81:16
Turn away your anger from us. * Ps 90:14
I will * him with a full life Ps 91:16
and * her poor with food. Ps 132:15
You constantly * the hunger and Ps 145:16
* you. Let her love alone fill Pro 5:19
good—if it makes you work to * it! Pro 16:26
Give me just enough to * my Pro 30:8
and she will richly * his needs. Pro 31:11
to do this work, to * my anger. Is 13:3
continually, and * you with all Is 58:11
of their goods to * your every Is 60:16
I will * my people with my Jer 31:14
It will neither * nor feed you, Eze 7:19
smite Jerusalem and * my fury." Eze 21:17
But even so we still refuse to * Dan 9:13
and oil, to fully * your need. Joe 2:19

(SATISFY Con't)
"What should we do to * God?" Jn 6:28
how his ways will really * you. Rom 12:2
then you cannot * the one who has 2Ti 2:4
living only to * their stomachs." Tit 1:12
and to try their best to * them. Tit 2:9
and goats cannot * you, so you have Heb 10:5
to * God's anger against our sins. 1Jn 4:10

SATISFYING
If you want a long and * life, Pro 3:1
was your love! How *, like the Hos 9:10
earth having fun, * your every Jas 5:5

SATURATED
a long linen cloth * with the Jn 19:40

SATURDAY
Capernaum and on * morning went Mk 1:21
the synagogue on *, and stood up to Lk 4:16
there in the synagogue every *. Lk 4:31
e., on *, the weekly Jewish holy Jn 9:14f
Or, "on * night." Act 20:7f

SAUCE
the bread dipped in the *." Jn 13:26

SAUCY
She approached him, * and pert, Pro 7:10
him, and with a * look she said, Pro 7:13

SAUL
His son * was the most handsome 1Sa 9:2
* and a servant to look for them. 1Sa 9:3
the land of Zuph, * said to the 1Sa 9:5
to pay him with," * replied. 1Sa 9:7
"All right," * agreed, "let's 1Sa 9:9,10,11
When Samuel saw * the Lord said, 1Sa 9:17
Just then * approached Samuel and 1Sa 9:18
"Pardon me, sir," * replied. 1Sa 9:21
Then Samuel took * and his 1Sa 9:22
the chef to bring * the choicest 1Sa 9:23
it in and placed it before *. 1Sa 9:24
So * ate with Samuel. 1Sa 9:24
city, Samuel took * up to the porch 1Sa 9:25
So * got up and Samuel accompanied 1Sa 9:26,27
* to send the servant on ahead. 1Sa 9:26,27
As * said good-bye and started to 1Sa 10:9
When * and the servant arrived 1Sa 10:10
exclaimed, "What? * a prophet?" 1Sa 10:11
proverb, "Is * a prophet, too?" 1Sa 10:12
concerning worldly * becoming 1Sa 10:12f
When * had finished prophesying 1Sa 10:13
And * replied, "We went to look 1Sa 10:14
had been found!" * replied. 1Sa 10:16
lot selected *, the son of Kish. 1Sa 10:21
When * returned to his home at 1Sa 10:26
* was plowing in the field, and 1Sa 11:5
upon * and he became very angry. 1Sa 11:6
follow * and Samuel to battle!" 1Sa 11:7
But early the next morning * 1Sa 11:11
said that * shouldn't be our king? 1Sa 11:12
But * replied, "No one will be 1Sa 11:13
and reconfirm * as our king." 1Sa 11:14
* and all Israel were very happy. 1Sa 11:15
BY THIS TIME * had reigned for one 1Sa 13:1
in copying, reads: "* was . 1Sa 13:1f
Philistines, and * sounded the call 1Sa 13:3,4
Meanwhile, * stayed at Gilgal, 1Sa 13:7
Samuel had told * earlier to 1Sa 13:8
Samuel arrived. * went out to meet 1Sa 13:10
"Well," * replied, "when I saw 1Sa 13:11
When * counted the soldiers who 1Sa 13:15
six hundred left! * and Jonathan 1Sa 13:16
* and his six hundred men were 1Sa 14:2
"Find out who isn't here," * 1Sa 14:17
"Bring the Ark of God," * 1Sa 14:18
But while * was talking to the 1Sa 14:19
What does God say?" * demanded. 1Sa 14:19
Then * and his six hundred men 1Sa 14:20
* had declared, "A curse upon 1Sa 14:24,25
Someone reported to * what was 1Sa 14:33
"That is very wrong," * said. 1Sa 14:33
And * built an altar to the 1Sa 14:35
Afterwards * said, "Let's chase 1Sa 14:36
So * asked God, "Shall we go 1Sa 14:37
Then * said to the leaders, 1Sa 14:38
Then * proposed, "Jonathan and I 1Sa 14:40
Then * said, "O Lord God of 1Sa 14:41
And Jonathan and * were chosen 1Sa 14:41
Then * said, "Now draw lots 1Sa 14:42
"Tell me what you've done," * 1Sa 14:43
"Yes, Jonathan," * said, "you 1Sa 14:44
Then * called back the army, and 1Sa 14:46
as king of Israel, * sent the 1Sa 14:47
* had three sons, Jonathan, 1Sa 14:49
And whenever * saw any brave, 1Sa 14:52
ONE DAY SAMUEL said to *, "I 1Sa 15:1
So * mobilized his army at 1Sa 15:4
below them. * sent a message to 1Sa 15:6
Then * butchered the Amalekites 1Sa 15:7
However, * and his men kept the 1Sa 15:9
"I am sorry that I ever made * 1Sa 15:11
morning he went out to find *. 1Sa 15:12
When Samuel finally found him, * 1Sa 15:13
sheep and oxen," * admitted, "but 1Sa 15:15
Then Samuel said to *, "Stop! 1Sa 15:16
"What was it?" * asked. 1Sa 15:16
"But I have obeyed the Lord," * 1Sa 15:20
"I have sinned," * finally 1Sa 15:24
As Samuel turned to go, * grabbed 1Sa 15:27
Then * pleaded again, "I have 1Sa 15:30
Ramah, and * returned to Gibe-ah. 1Sa 15:34
Samuel never saw * again, but he 1Sa 15:35
he had ever made * king of Israel. 1Sa 15:35
long enough for *, for I have 1Sa 16:1
can I do that? If * hears about it, 1Sa 16:2
the Lord had left *, and instead, 1Sa 16:14
"All right," * said. 1Sa 16:17
So * sent messengers to Jesse, 1Sa 16:19
From the instant he saw David, * 1Sa 16:21
Then * wrote to Jesse, "Please 1Sa 16:22
from God troubled *, David would 1Sa 16:23
play the harp and * would feel 1Sa 16:23
in Ephes-dammim. * countered with 1Sa 17:2
When * 1Sa 17:11
Probably King * was especially 1Sa 17:11f
(* and the Israeli army were 1Sa 17:19
King *, and the king sent for him. 1Sa 17:31
"Don't be ridiculous!" * 1Sa 17:33
* finally consented, "All right, 1Sa 17:37
Then * gave David his own armor—a 1Sa 17:38,39
As * was watching David go out to 1Sa 17:55
Saul's daughter, * wanted to know 1Sa 17:55f
brought him to * with the 1Sa 17:57
your father, my boy," * said. 1Sa 17:58
AFTER KING * had finished his 1Sa 18:1
King * now kept David at Jerusalem 1Sa 18:4
successfully. So * made him 1Sa 18:5
to cheer for King *, and were 1Sa 18:6
However, this was their song: "* 1Sa 18:7
Of course * was very angry. 1Sa 18:8
So from that time on King * kept 1Sa 18:9
God overwhelmed *, and he began to 1Sa 18:10
this happened. But *, who was 1Sa 18:10
time, too, for * was afraid of him 1Sa 18:11,12
Finally * banned him from his 1Sa 18:13
When King * saw this, he became 1Sa 18:15,16
One day * said to David, "I am 1Sa 18:17
For * thought to himself, 1Sa 18:17
for the wedding, * married her to 1Sa 18:19
with David, and * was delighted 1Sa 18:20
Philistines!" * said to himself. 1Sa 18:21
Then * instructed his men to say 1Sa 18:22
But what * had in mind was that 1Sa 18:25
their foreskins to King *. 1Sa 18:27
Saul. So * gave Michal to him. 1Sa 18:27
* NOW URGED his aides and his son 1Sa 19:1
Finally * agreed, and vowed, "As 1Sa 19:6
Then he took David to * and 1Sa 19:7
But one day as * was sitting at 1Sa 19:9,10
of the wall. * sent troops to 1Sa 19:11
to arrest David and take him to *, 1Sa 19:14
get out of bed. * said to bring 1Sa 19:15
escape?" * demanded of Michal. 1Sa 19:17
him all that * had done to him. 1Sa 19:18
When the report reached * that 1Sa 19:19
When * heard what had happened, 1Sa 19:21
Then * himself went to Ramah and 1Sa 19:22
*, and he too began to prophesy! 1Sa 19:23
they exclaimed. "Is * a 1Sa 19:24
'Is * also among the prophets?' 1Sa 19:24f
*, but David's place was empty. 1Sa 20:24,25
place was empty. * didn't say 1Sa 20:26
the next day, * asked Jonathan, 1Sa 20:27
* boiled with rage. 1Sa 20:30
Then * hurled his spear at 1Sa 20:33
he was fearful of *, and went to 1Sa 21:10
dances, singing, '* has slain his 1Sa 21:11
arrival in Judah soon reached *. 1Sa 22:6
men of Benjamin!" * exclaimed when 1Sa 22:7
King * immediately summoned 1Sa 22:11,12
When they arrived * shouted at 1Sa 22:11,12
against me?" * demanded. 1Sa 22:13
When he told him what * had done, 1Sa 22:21
there, I knew he would tell *. 1Sa 22:22
from the Lord.) * soon learned 1Sa 23:7
So * mobilized his entire army to 1Sa 23:8
have heard that * is planning to 1Sa 23:10
And will * actually come, as I 1Sa 23:11
men of Keilah betray me to *?" 1Sa 23:12
Word soon reached * that David 1Sa 23:13
the news that * was on the way to 1Sa 23:14,15
him and kill him. * hunted him day 1Sa 23:14,15
But now the men of Ziph went to * 1Sa 23:19
"Well, praise the Lord!" * 1Sa 23:21
But when David heard that * was 1Sa 23:24,25
desert. But * followed them there. 1Sa 23:24,25
of a mountain. As * and his men 1Sa 23:26
a message reached * that the 1Sa 23:27
Israel again, so * quit the chase 1Sa 23:28
some sheepfolds, * went into a cave 1Sa 24:3
will certainly put * into your 1Sa 24:4
persuaded his men not to kill *. 1Sa 24:7,8
After * had left the cave and gone 1Sa 24:7,8
And when * looked around, David 1Sa 24:7,8
Then he shouted to *, "Why do 1Sa 24:9,10
* called back, "Is it really you, 1Sa 24:15
So David promised, and * went 1Sa 24:22
King *, meanwhile, had forced 1Sa 25:44
Ziph came back to * at Gibe-ah to 1Sa 26:1
Hachilah Hill. So * took his elite 1Sa 26:2
to hunt him down. * camped along 1Sa 26:3,4
look around. King * and General 1Sa 26:5,6,7
Abner and *, "Wake up, Abner!" 1Sa 26:14
* recognized David's voice and 1Sa 26:17,18
Then * confessed, "I have done 1Sa 26:21
And * said to David, "Blessings 1Sa 26:25
Then David went away and * 1Sa 26:25
"Some day * is going to get me. 1Sa 27:1
Philistines until * gives up and 1Sa 27:1
Word soon reached * that David 1Sa 27:4
home town. King * had banned all 1Sa 28:3
at Shunem, and * and the armies of 1Sa 28:4
When * saw the vast army of the 1Sa 28:5,6
or by the prophets. * then 1Sa 28:7,8
one at Endor. * disguised himself 1Sa 28:7,8
"You know that * has had all of 1Sa 28:9
But * took a solemn oath that he 1Sa 28:10
"Bring me Samuel," * replied. 1Sa 28:11
You are *!" 1Sa 28:12
* realized that it was Samuel and 1Sa 28:14
Samuel asked *. 1Sa 28:15
* now fell full length upon the 1Sa 28:20
servant of King * of Israel. 1Sa 29:3
in their dances: '* has slain his 1Sa 29:5
The Philistines closed in on *, 1Sa 31:2
Then the archers overtook * and 1Sa 31:3,4
was afraid to, so * took his own 1Sa 31:3,4
died with him. So *, his armor 1Sa 31:6
had fled and that * and his sons 1Sa 31:7
the bodies of * and his three sons 1Sa 31:8
down the bodies of * and his sons 1Sa 31:12
* WAS DEAD and David had returned 2Sa 1:1
on the field, and * and his son 2Sa 1:4
Gilboa and saw * leaning against 2Sa 1:6
Probably he had found * dead upon 2Sa 1:10f
fasted all day for * and his son 2Sa 1:12
Then David composed a dirge for * 2Sa 1:17,18
For there the mighty * has died; 2Sa 1:21
Both * and Jonathan slew their 2Sa 1:22
Both * and Jonathan! 2Sa 1:23
O women of Israel, weep for *; 2Sa 1:24
had buried *, he sent them this 2Sa 2:4
subjects, now that * is dead. 2Sa 2:7
the followers of * and of David. 2Sa 3:1
leader among the followers of *. 2Sa 3:6
old at the time * and Jonathan were 2Sa 4:4
enemy * who tried to kill you. 2Sa 4:8
* and upon his entire family!" 2Sa 4:8
someone told me, '* is dead,' 2Sa 4:10
"And even when * was our king 2Sa 5:2
took it from *, your predecessor. 2Sa 7:15
your grandfather *, and you shall 2Sa 9:7
to * and his family," he said. 2Sa 9:9
and saved you from the power of *. 2Sa 12:7
back the kingdom of my father, *.' 2Sa 16:3
* was Mephibosheth's grandfather. 2Sa 16:3f
murdering King * and his family; 2Sa 16:7,8
the servant of *, and Ziba's 2Sa 19:17
of the guilt of * and his family, 2Sa 21:1
to kill them; but *, in his 2Sa 21:2
in Gibeon, the city of King *." 2Sa 21:5,6
grandsons of * by his wife Aiah. 2Sa 21:8
him the bones of * and Jonathan. 2Sa 21:12,13,14
* and from all his other enemies: 2Sa 22:1
During the reign of King *, the 1Ch 5:10
and Kish was the father of *; 1Ch 8:33
Kish was the father of *, 1Ch 9:39
* was the father of Jonathan, 1Ch 9:39
They caught up with * and his 1Ch 10:2
killed them all. * had been hard 1Ch 10:3
to do it, so * took his own sword 1Ch 10:4
seeing that * was dead, killed 1Ch 10:5
the same way. So * and his three 1Ch 10:6
routed and that * and his sons were 1Ch 10:7
the bodies of * and his sons. 1Ch 10:8
had done to *, their heroic 1Ch 10:11
* died for his disobedience to 1Ch 10:13
and even when * was king, you 1Ch 11:2
while he was hiding from King *. 1Ch 12:1
Like King *, they were all of the 1Ch 12:2
the Philistines against King *. 1Ch 12:19
them by deserting to King *. 1Ch 12:19
king instead of *, just as the Lord 1Ch 12:23
* was from, there were 3,000. 1Ch 12:24-37
retained its allegiance to *. 1Ch 12:24-37
it ever since * became king." 1Ch 13:3
daughter of King *, felt a deep 1Ch 15:29
and love from him as I did from *. 1Ch 17:13
the prophet, * the son of Kish, 1Ch 26:28
his many enemies, including *. Ps 18:1
of Ziph tried to betray him to *. Ps 54:1
at the time King * set guards at Ps 59:1
of *—are running for their lives. Is 10:28,29
Paul is also known as *. Act 7:58f
and God gave them * (son of Kish), Act 13:21
saying to me, '*, Saul, why are you Act 22:7
*, why are you persecuting me?' Act 22:7

(SAUL Con't)
'Brother *, receive your sight!' Act 22:13
to me in Hebrew, '*, Saul, why are Act 26:14
*, why are you persecuting me? Act 26:14

SAUL'S

and poured it over * head and 1Sa 10:1
did you go?" * uncle asked him. 1Sa 10:14
came to Gibe-ah, * home town, and 1Sa 11:4
to be afraid of * anger, and they 1Sa 11:7
with Jonathan, * son, in Gibe-ah in 1Sa 13:2
didn't come, and * troops were 1Sa 13:8
day, except for * and Jonathan's. 1Sa 13:22
* lookouts in Gibe-ah saw a 1Sa 14:16
for they all feared * curse. 1Sa 14:26
Merab and Michal. * wife was 1Sa 14:50,51
(Abner's father, Ner, and * 1Sa 14:50,51
Philistines throughout * lifetime. 1Sa 14:52
Some of * aides suggested a 1Sa 16:15,16
* army to fight the Philistines. 1Sa 17:13
on * staff on a part-time basis. 1Sa 17:14,15
scheduled to marry * daughter, Saul 1Sa 17:55f
passage is that * unstable mental 1Sa 17:55f
He was * special assistant, and 1Sa 18:5
In the meantime * daughter 1Sa 18:20
When * men reported this back to 1Sa 18:24
than all the rest of * officers. 1Sa 18:30
prophets. * men were incredulous! 1Sa 19:24
Doeg the Edomite, * chief herdsman, 1Sa 21:7
there with * men, spoke up. 1Sa 22:9,10
But David learned of * plan and 1Sa 23:9
AFTER * RETURN from his battle 1Sa 24:1
slit off the bottom of * robe! 1Sa 24:4
wife Michal, * daughter, to marry a 1Sa 25:44
but David knew of * arrival and 1Sa 26:3,4
David slipped over to * camp one 1Sa 26:5,6,7
So David and Abishai went to * 1Sa 26:5,6,7
They cut off * head and stripped 1Sa 31:9
wonderful news of * death to their 1Sa 31:9
But Abner, * commander-in-chief, 2Sa 2:8
crown * son Ish-bosheth as king. 2Sa 2:8
stronger, while * dynasty became 2Sa 3:1
* concubines, a girl named Rizpah. 2Sa 3:7
me my wife Michal, * daughter." 2Sa 3:13
grandson of King * named 2Sa 4:4
the city, Michal, * daughter, 2Sa 6:16
if any of * family was still 2Sa 9:1
of * servants, and summoned him. 2Sa 9:2
"Is anyone left from * family? 2Sa 9:3
son and * grandson. 2Sa 9:5,6
Then the king summoned * servant 2Sa 9:9
son of Gera, a member of * family. 2Sa 16:5
Now Mephibosheth, * grandson, 2Sa 19:24,25
"give us seven of * sons—the sons 2Sa 21:5,6
who was * grandson, because of the 2Sa 21:7
she brought up for * daughter 2Sa 21:8
in the grave of * father, Kish. 2Sa 21:12,13,14
* sons included: 1Ch 8:33
So they stripped off * armor and 1Ch 10:9

SAVAGE

With * arm and face and head. Deu 33:20

SAVE

could * the lives of many people. Gen 50:20
will hear you and * you from your Num 10:9
* the killer from the avenger; Num 35:25
Promised Land you are to * no one; Deu 20:16
and nothing will * you. Deu 28:29
to trickery to * themselves. Jos 9:3,4,5
"Come quickly and * us! Jos 10:6
to * them from their enemies. Ju 2:16
younger brother) to * them. Ju 3:9
Go and * Israel from the Ju 6:14
"Sir, how can I * Israel? Ju 6:15
going to use me to * Israel as you Ju 6:36
again and begged him to * them. Ju 10:10
"Didn't I * you from the Ju 10:11
I won't * you any more. Ju 10:13
Let them * you in your hour of Ju 10:14
* us once more from our enemies." Ju 10:15
surely * us from our enemies." 1Sa 4:3
Who can * us from these mighty 1Sa 4:8
"Plead with God to * us!" 1Sa 7:8
He will * them from the 1Sa 9:16
"How can this man * us?" 1Sa 10:27
will come and * us, we will agree 1Sa 11:3
to * you, and you lived in safety. 1Sa 12:11
will * me from this Philistine!" 1Sa 17:37
"Yes, go and * Keilah," the Lord 1Sa 23:2
Now may the Lord * my life, even 1Sa 26:24
by whom I will * my people from the 2Sa 3:18
if we are going to * our people and 2Sa 10:12
He will * me from all my enemies. 2Sa 22:4
You will * those in trouble, 2Sa 22:28
Literally, "Who is a rock * our 2Sa 22:32f
If you want to * your own life 1Ki 1:12
enough grass to * at least some of 1Ki 18:5
he used King Jeroboam II to * her. 2Ki 14:27
he will * you from all your 2Ki 17:39
'No one can * you from my power! 2Ki 18:19
He will never be able to * you 2Ki 18:29
What god has ever been able to * 2Ki 18:35
think the Lord can * Jerusalem?' 2Ki 18:35
with you to * us from his power; 2Ki 19:19
I will defend and * this city for 2Ki 19:34
to his life and * him and this city 2Ki 20:6
Cry out to him, 'Oh, * us, God of 1Ch 16:35
us act like men to * our people and 1Ch 19:13
out to the Lord to * him, and the 2Ch 18:31
Temple—and cry out to you to * us; 2Ch 20:9
* their own people from you?" 2Ch 25:15
to do a thing to * their lands! 2Ch 32:13
nations failed to * their people 2Ch 32:17
only way you can * yourself!" Neh 6:7
Your Majesty, * my life and the Est 7:3
"A man will give anything to * Job 2:4,5
no one can * me from your hand? Job 10:4-7
Yes, he will * the humble, and Job 22:29
[But I might as well * my breath, Job 30:28,29
that your own strength can * you. Job 40:14
"Arise, O Lord! * me, O my God!" Ps 3:7
In your kindness * me. Ps 6:4
God, to * me from my persecutors. Ps 7:1
jaws of death. * me, so that I can Ps 9:14
from Zion now to * his people. Ps 14:7
* ME, O God, because I have come Ps 16:1
Come and * me from these men of Ps 17:13,14
"God * the king"—I know he Ps 20:6
* me from these lions' jaws and Ps 22:21
to worse. Oh, * me from them all! Ps 25:17
they hate me! * me from them! Ps 25:20
therefore in mercy * me. Ps 26:11
I am confident that God will * Ps 27:3
Lord, and he will come and * you! Ps 27:14
* me just because you are so kind! Ps 31:16
The best-equipped army cannot * a Ps 33:16,17
is not enough to * anyone. Ps 33:16,17
is strong but it cannot *. Ps 33:16,17
upon the Lord alone to * us. Ps 33:20
say that you will * me from them. Ps 35:3
out to get it. * me, and I will Ps 35:18
* me from being overpowered by my Ps 39:8
come quickly, and * me. Ps 40:17
They could never * me. Ps 44:6
us. * us by your constant love. Ps 44:26
come from Zion now and * Israel! Ps 53:6
O God, and * me! Ps 54:1
upon the Lord to * me—and he will. Ps 55:16
But I am trusting you to * me. Ps 55:23
from heaven to * me, because of his Ps 57:3
O MY GOD, * me from my enemies. Ps 59:1
* ME, O my God. Ps 69:1
ocean swallow me; * me from the pit Ps 69:15
Come and * me. Ps 69:17
For God will * Jerusalem; Ps 69:35
for only you can help and * me. Ps 70:5
Don't let me down! * me from my Ps 71:2
and listen to my plea and * me. Ps 71:2
you have issued the order to * me. Ps 71:3
He will * them from oppression Ps 72:14
O Lord, * me! Ps 74:19
* your beloved people from these Ps 74:19
Oh, * us and forgive our sins. Ps 79:9
all your laws. * me, for I am Ps 86:2
strength to your servant and * me. Ps 86:16
to * his people from starvation. Ps 105:17
O Lord God, * us! Ps 106:47
Help me, O Lord my God! * me Ps 109:26
to * them from their enemies. Ps 109:31
Then I cried, "Lord, * me!" Ps 116:4
O Lord, please help us. * us. Ps 118:25
your promise—yes, Lord, to * me! Ps 119:40,41,42
I am yours! * me! Ps 119:94
obey your laws. "* me," I cry, Ps 119:146
Your power will * me. Ps 138:7
is sincere. * me from my enemies, Ps 143:9
David from the fatal sword. * me! Ps 144:11
he will * the humble. Ps 149:4,5
Only wisdom from the Lord can * a Pro 2:16,17
will lead you and * you from harm; Pro 6:22
* the city, and so it was rescued. Ecc 9:15
not stepped in to * a few of us, we Is 1:9
Assyrians you have hired to * you Is 7:20
"Jehovah will * (his people)," Is 8:18
See, God has come to * me! Is 12:2
but none will come to * them. Is 16:12
* you—the Rock who can hide you; Is 17:10
deliver on his promises to * you. Is 30:3
he will care for us and * us. Is 33:22
He is coming to * you." Is 35:4
you—nothing he can do will * you. Is 36:14
Did their gods * them? Is 36:19
Did their gods * the cities of Is 37:12
O Lord our God, * us so that all Is 37:20
from ages past [that I would * you Is 44:8
and pray to gods that cannot *! Is 45:20
If they cannot even * themselves Is 46:1
* their worshipers from Cyrus? Is 46:1
I am ready to * you, and I will Is 46:13
Redeemer, who will * Israel from Is 47:4
my own sake—I will * you from my Is 48:11
you, and I will * your children. Is 49:25
Was I too weak to * you? Is 50:2
works"—none of which will * you. Is 57:12
you when you cry to them to * you! Is 57:13
THE Lord isn't too weak to * you. Is 59:1
stepped in to * you through his Is 59:16
God, am coming to * you and will Is 62:11
the one who is mighty to *!" Is 63:1
trouble they cry to me to * them! Jer 2:26,27
them go out and * you if they can! Jer 2:28
but that cannot * them from their Jer 11:12
Are you helpless to * us? Jer 14:9
me, you alone can *, and my praises Jer 17:14
For I am with you and I will * Jer 30:11
He will * Israel from those who Jer 31:11
I am with you to * you and to Jer 42:11
for I will * you from far away Jer 46:27
Flee from Babylon! * yourselves! Jer 51:6
could, but nothing can * her now. Jer 51:9
O my people, flee from Babylon; * Jer 51:45
to come and * us, but we look in Lam 4:17
there is no one left to * us. Lam 5:8
repent and * your life—they will Eze 3:18
I will * them to confess to the Eze 12:16
and * your own souls alive?" Eze 13:18f
veils and * my people from you; Eze 13:21
not * the people from their doom. Eze 14:16
right, he shall * his soul, for he Eze 18:27
* you from the king of Babylon. Eze 21:29
will not * him if he turns to sin; Eze 33:12
past goodness to * him, then none Eze 33:13
I will * my flock from being Eze 34:9,10
So I myself will * my flock; Eze 34:22
* them from all this foulness. Eze 37:23
law, and determined to * Daniel. Dan 6:14
if I destroy you, who can * you? Hos 13:9
for them, now let them * you! Hos 13:10
Assyria cannot * us, nor can our Hos 14:3
ones can no longer * themselves. Amo 2:14
will have mercy on us and * us!" Jon 1:6
And though you try and try to * Mic 6:14
I wait for God to * me; Mic 7:7
I cry, but no one comes to *. Hab 1:2
idols to arise and * them, who call Hab 2:19
Show us your power to * us. Hab 3:2
You went out to * your chosen Hab 3:13
Beg him to * you, all who are Zep 2:3
I will * the weak and helpless Zep 3:19
The Lord their God will * his Zec 9:16,17
will * his people from their sins. Mt 1:21
him, shouting, "Lord, * us! Mt 8:25
give it up for me, you will * it. Mt 10:39
and began to sink. "* me, Lord!" Mt 14:30
came to * the lost. Mt 18:11
"but he can't * himself! Mt 27:41,42,43
Elijah will come and * him." Mt 27:49
Is it a day to * lives or to Mk 3:4
If you're so wonderful, * Mk 15:29,30
said, "but he can't * himself!" Mk 15:31
ago— someone to * us from our Lk 1:71
To * life, or to destroy it?" Lk 6:9
for my sake will * it, but whoever Lk 9:24
men's lives, but to * them." Lk 9:55f
whoever loses his life shall * it. Lk 17:33
have come to search for and to * Lk 19:9,10
new agreement to * you—an agreement Lk 22:20
"let's see him * himself if he is Lk 23:35
King of the Jews, * yourself! Lk 23:37
to do was to trust him to * them. Jn 1:11,12
world to condemn it, but to * it. Jn 3:17
those who trust him to * them. Jn 3:18
Son—to * them have eternal life; Jn 3:36
Shall I pray, 'Father, * me from Jn 12:27
* the world and not to judge it. Jn 12:47
his listeners to * themselves from Act 2:40
for men to call upon to * them." Act 4:12
request and will * the lives of all Act 27:24
faith and trust in Christ to * us. Rom 1:17
And does God * only the Jews in Rom 3:29
Christ to * them from God's wrath. Rom 4:4,5
Now he will * us from all of Rom 5:9
effect a different plan to * us. Rom 8:3
damned if that would * you. Rom 9:1
But how shall they ask him to * Rom 10:14
and in that way * some of them. Rom 11:14
hear that Jesus died to * them. 1Co 1:18
Christ dying to * them, the Jews 1Co 1:23
the mighty power of God to * them; 1Co 1:24
about Christ and let Christ * him. 1Co 9:22
on trusting God to * you, and you 1Co 15:17
who alone could * us, for he can 2Co 1:9
about his new agreement to * them. 2Co 3:6
Today he is ready to * you. 2Co 6:2
But what if we trust Christ to * Gal 2:17
Christ and trusted him to * you. Gal 3:2
when God would * the Gentiles also, Gal 3:8,9
the Jewish laws to * them are under Gal 3:10
God's promise to * through Gal 3:17
If obeying those laws could * Gal 3:18
for we thought they could * us. Gal 4:3
God, then Christ cannot * you. Gal 5:2
the cross of Christ alone can *. Gal 6:12
we are helpless to * ourselves. Php 3:3
he could * himself, it would be I. Php 3:4

(SAVE Con't)
but by trusting Christ to * me; Php 3:9
from trusting him to * you. Col 1:23
trusted Christ to * you, trust him, Col 2:6
upon us, but to * us through our 1Th 5:9
accept his plan to * them through 2Th 1:8
it, and let it * them, so God will 2Th 2:10
into the world to * sinners—and I 1Ti 1:15
born, but he will * their souls if 1Ti 2:15
that God wants to * us—has been Heb 4:2
who would * him from [premature Heb 5:7
who flee to him to * them can take Heb 6:18
had been able to * us, why then did Heb 7:11
He is able to * completely all Heb 7:25
they could never * those who lived Heb 10:1
that God would * him from the death Heb 11:23
believed God would * his people Heb 11:28
for it is able to * our souls as it Jas 1:21
Will that kind of faith * anyone? Jas 2:14
He alone decides to * us or Jas 4:12
God paid a ransom to * you from 1Pe 1:18
when you trusted Christ to * you; 1Pe 1:22
for instance, the promise to * us 2Pe 1:4
those who doubt. * some by Jud 1:23

SAVED
so kind to me and * my life, and Gen 19:18,19,20
And my life will be *." Gen 19:18,19,20
Oh, haven't you * even one Gen 27:36
and I was only * by my screams. Gen 39:18
"You have * our lives," they Gen 47:25
Thus Jehovah * Israel that day Ex 14:30
said, "for he has * you from the Ex 18:10
They are your inheritance * from Deu 9:26
Who else has been * by the Lord? Deu 33:29
Thus Joshua * Rahab the Jos 6:25
instead, you have * us from Jos 22:31
Of how the Lord * Israel Ju 5:11
to me that they * themselves by Ju 7:2
for you have * us from Midian." Ju 8:22
of marriageable age were *. Ju 21:10,11,12
So the Lord * Israel that day, 1Sa 14:23
of the God who * Israel that though 1Sa 14:39
who * Israel today, shall die? 1Sa 14:45
the Amalekites and * Israel from 1Sa 14:48
The Lord who * me from the claws 1Sa 17:37
so the people of Keilah were *. 1Sa 23:5
for you * my life today. 1Sa 26:21
even as I have * yours today. 1Sa 26:24
by the Lord who * me from my 2Sa 4:9
and * you from the power of Saul. 2Sa 12:7
the city of Jerusalem will be *." 2Sa 15:14
* him from his enemy Absalom." 2Sa 18:19
said to him, "We * your life today 2Sa 19:5
"For he * us from our enemies, 2Sa 19:8,9,10
He * me from powerful enemies, 2Sa 22:18
he had * him from disaster. 2Ki 6:10
and the Lord * them with a great 1Ch 11:14
That is how the Lord * Hezekiah 2Ch 32:22
and God protected us and * us Ez 8:31
who * the king from assassination! Est 7:9
when the Jews were * from their Est 9:22
I am * from all my enemies! Ps 18:3
their cries for help and * them; Ps 22:5
for you have * me from my enemies. Ps 30:1
him and * him out of his troubles. Ps 34:6
For you have * me from death and Ps 56:13
only then shall we be *. Ps 80:3
only then shall we be *. Ps 80:7
and love—only then shall we be *. Ps 80:19
to me in trouble and I * you; Ps 81:7
and he was kind and * me. Ps 94:18
Even so you * them—to defend the Ps 106:8
Tell others he has * you from Ps 107:2
I was facing death and then he * Ps 116:6
He has * me from death, my eyes Ps 116:8
Praise him who * his people from Ps 136:17
forever. And * us from our foes, Ps 136:24
this trap you have * yourself like Pro 6:5
Egypt cannot be * by anything or Is 19:15
and waiting for me will you be *; Is 30:15
With one word I have * you. Is 43:12
But Israel shall be * by Jehovah Is 45:17
Or, "The Angel of his Presence * Is 63:9f
* them. In his love and pity he Is 63:9
How can such as we be *? Is 64:5
You can yet be * by casting out Jer 4:14
my Temple and chant,"We are *!" Jer 7:10
summer is over and we are not *." Jer 8:20
At that time Judah will be * and Jer 23:5,6
"The Lord has * his people, the Jer 31:7
you have * your own life too." Eze 3:21
alone would be * by their Eze 14:14
Those three only would be *, but Eze 14:16
that they alone would be *. Eze 14:18
*, because of their righteousness. Eze 14:20
warning, he would have * his life. Eze 33:5
the name of the Lord will be *; Joe 2:32
who endure to the end shall be *. Mt 10:22
"Then who in the world can be * Mt 19:25
enduring to the end shall be *. Mt 24:13
mocked him. "He * others," they Mt 27:41,42,43
"Then who in the world can be *, Mk 10:26
without renouncing me shall be *. Mk 13:13
and are baptized will be *. Mk 16:16
the woman, "Your faith has * you; Lk 7:50
people from believing and being *. Lk 8:12
him, "Will only a few be *?" Lk 13:23
that hard, how can anyone be *?" Lk 18:26
you will believe in me and be *. Jn 5:34
the Gate will be * and will go in Jn 10:9
shall have it and shall be *.' Act 2:21
to them all who were being *. Act 2:47
and all your household can be *!' Act 11:14
sent his angel and * me from Herod Act 12:11
circumcision, they could not be *. Act 15:1
Don't you believe that all are * Act 15:11
"Sirs, what must I do to be *?" Act 16:30
be *, and your entire household." Act 16:31
And we all can be * in this same Rom 3:21,22
So it is that we are * Rom 3:28
Well then, if we are * by faith, Rom 3:31
this question of being * by faith? Rom 4:1
No, for being * is a gift; Rom 4:4,5
are * without obeying Jewish laws. Rom 4:11
We aren't * from sin's grasp by Rom 8:3
We are * by trusting. Rom 8:24
a small number would ever be *. Rom 9:27
Because they were trying to be * Rom 9:32
that the Jewish people might be *. Rom 10:1
then could he be pardoned and *. Rom 10:5
him from the dead, you will be *. Rom 10:9
the name of the Lord will be *. Rom 10:13
there are a few being * as a Rom 11:5
And then all Israel will be *. Rom 11:26
Gentiles might be * and give glory Rom 15:9
* recognize this message as the 1Co 1:18
he stepped in and * all those who 1Co 1:21
He himself will be *, but like a 1Co 3:15
his soul will be * when our Lord 1Co 5:5
for them, so that they may be *. 1Co 10:33
And he did help us, and * us 2Co 1:10
* and the unsaved all around us. 2Co 2:15
To those who are not being *, we 2Co 2:16
The old way, trying to be * by 2Co 3:6
Commandments is the way to be *. 2Co 3:15
to be * by keeping the laws of God 2Co 3:17
shows you a different way to be *. 2Co 11:4
* than the one we told you about; Gal 1:8
For no one will ever be * by Gal 2:16
that we cannot be * without being Gal 2:17
of trying to be * by keeping Jewish Gal 2:18
For if we could be * by keeping Gal 2:21
says that a man is * by obeying Gal 3:12
If we could be * by his laws, Gal 3:21,22
Jewish laws to be *: Why don't you Gal 4:21
of his Son, by whom we are *; Eph 1:7
about how to be *, and trusted Eph 1:13
have we ever been *— and lifted us Eph 2:5
been * through trusting Christ. Eph 2:8
result from being *, obeying God Php 2:12
you must be circumcised to be *. Php 3:2
If others could be * by what they Php 3:4
counting on being * by being good Php 3:9
* me for and wants me to be. Php 3:12
ideas of how to be *—by doing good Col 2:20
Gentiles for fear some might be *; 1Th 2:16
Pray too that we will be * out 2Th 3:2
idea of being * by finding favor 1Ti 1:3,4
not made for us, whom God has *; 1Ti 1:9
for all to be * and to understand 1Ti 2:4
It is he who * us and chose us 2Ti 1:9
And he * me from being thrown to 2Ti 4:17
appear, then he * us—not because Tit 3:5
good enough to be *, but because of Tit 3:5
was that he be * out from death, at Heb 5:7f
of trying to be * by being good, or Heb 6:1
This certain hope of being * is a Heb 6:19
he built the ark and * his family. Heb 11:7
So you see, a man is * by what Jas 2:24
She was * because of what she did Jas 2:25
to God will have * a wandering soul Jas 5:20
strong in the Lord and be *." 1Pe 2:2,3f
Yet only eight persons were * 1Pe 3:20
that we have been * from death and 1Pe 3:21
If the righteous are barely *, 1Pe 4:18
"You aren't * by being good," 2Pe 2:19
the Lord * a whole nation of people Jud 1:5

SAVES
each day that he is the one who *! 1Ch 16:23
"God * the fatherless and the Job 5:15
he will defend me. He * those Ps 7:10
of their reach and * me from these Ps 18:48
and * him out of all his troubles. Ps 34:17
The Lord * the godly! Ps 37:39
O God who * us. Ps 65:5
Each day tell someone that he *. Ps 96:2
in their trouble, and he * them. Ps 107:28
A witness who tells the truth * Pro 14:25
The wise man * for the future, Pro 21:20
this ceremony that * them, for Rom 4:12
and it is this Good News that * 1Co 15:2
as a pure maiden * her love for one 2Co 11:2
* you through the Resurrection." 1Pe 3:21
alone is God, who * us through Jud 1:24,25

SAVING
thereby * Israel from disaster. Ju 3:31
said, "for I was * it for you, 1Sa 9:24
For * me from all my enemies. 2Sa 22:3
from ruling, thus * a nation from Job 34:29,30
the news of your * power and your Ps 67:2
greatness of your power by * them. Ps 79:11
are blessing and * your people. Ps 106:4
the thank-offering of wine for * Ps 116:13
and praise his name for * me. Ps 116:13
for answering my prayer and * me. Ps 118:21
Lord, * me will bring glory to Ps 143:11
To whom will God reveal his * Is 53:1
there is no hope of * her. Mic 1:14
If you insist on * your life, Mk 8:35
"He's quite clever at '*' Mk 15:31
Prove it by * yourself—and us, Lk 23:39
and so you are * up terrible Rom 2:5
the means of * us from his wrath. Rom 3:25
It was weak and useless for * Heb 7:18

SAVINGS
seen everywhere—* are put into Ecc 5:13,14

SAVIOR
he sent them a *, Ehud (son of Ju 3:15
My fortress and my *. 2Sa 22:2
Thank you, O my *, 2Sa 22:3
We have no other *. 2Sa 22:32
wonderful ways, O * of all those Ps 17:7
he is my *, a rock where none can Ps 18:2
lives by God himself, their *. Ps 24:5
Help me, O my *. Ps 38:22
You are my *; Ps 40:17
* was the God above all gods. Ps 78:35
Thus they despised their * who Ps 106:21,22
O Jehovah, my Lord and *, my God Ps 140:6,7,8
a *—and he shall deliver them. Is 19:20
your *, the Holy One of Israel. Is 43:3
the Lord, and there is no other *. Is 43:11
Truly, O God of Israel, *, you Is 45:15
me—a just God and a *—no, not one! Is 45:21
carry you along and be your *. Is 46:4
the Lord, am your * and Redeemer, Is 49:26
the Lord, am your * and Redeemer, Is 60:16
And he became their *. Is 63:8
O Hope of Israel, our * in times Jer 14:8
but me, for there is no other *. Hos 13:4
He is a mighty *. Zep 3:17,18
Jesus (meaning '*'), for he will Mt 1:21
How I rejoice in God my *! Lk 1:47
He is sending us a Mighty * from Lk 1:69
for everyone! The *—yes, the Lk 2:11
I have seen the * you have given Lk 2:29,30,31
been awaiting the coming of the * Lk 2:38
shall see the * sent from God.' Lk 3:6
He is indeed the * of the Jn 4:42
to meet him, shouting, "The *! Jn 12:13
to be a Prince and *, so that the Act 5:31
was sent to be their ruler and *. Act 7:35
who is God's promised * of Israel! Act 13:23
we could believe in the coming *. Gal 3:23
that God is the * of the Gentiles Eph 3:9
them to trust him as their *; Eph 4:11
and about our *, God's Son, and all Eph 4:13
to take care of it and be its *! Eph 5:23
our * the Lord Jesus Christ is; Php 3:20
he is our only * from God's 1Th 1:10
command of God our * and by Jesus 1Ti 1:1
pleases God our *, for he longs 1Ti 2:3
the coming of our * Jesus Christ, 2Ti 1:10
By command of God our * I have Tit 1:3
Christ Jesus our * give you his Tit 1:4
want to believe in our * and God. Tit 2:10
our great God and * Jesus Christ. Tit 2:13
love of God our * to appear, then Tit 3:4
Jesus Christ our * did so that he Tit 3:6
by rejecting the * after knowing Heb 10:26
Christ our God and * gives to us. 2Pe 1:1
of our Lord and * Jesus Christ. 2Pe 1:11
about our Lord and * Jesus Christ, 2Pe 2:20
you the words of our Lord and *. 2Pe 3:1
with our Lord and * Jesus Christ. 2Pe 3:18
in the name of Jesus our *. 1Jn 2:12
God sent his Son to be their *. 1Jn 4:14
*—then you are a child of God. 1Jn 5:1

SAVIORS
you sent them * who delivered them Neh 9:27

SAVOR
Literally, "it will be a sweet * Lev 1:9f
Literally, "it will be a sweet * Lev 1:15,16,17f
Literally, "but not for a sweet * Lev 2:12f
burn the fat as a * the Lord will Lev 17:5
burn the fat as a * the Lord will Lev 17:6

SAVORY
the way I like it—* and good—and Gen 27:2,3,4

SAWED
he * them to pieces is uncertain. 1Ch 20:3f
and some by being * in two; Heb 11:37,38

SAWS
them labor with *, picks, and axes 2Sa 12:31

SAWS Con't)
Or, "killed them with * and iron 2Sa 12:31f
work with *, iron picks, and axes, 1Ch 20:3
them labor with * or that he sawed 1Ch 20:3f
saw greater than the man who *? Is 10:15

SAXOPHONES
more pianos, *, and trumpets. Rev 18:22

SCAB
in his skin, or a * or boil or Lev 13:1
it was only a *, and the man need Lev 13:6
a * from a burn, or a bright spot. Lev 14:56

SCABBARD
Go back into your *; Jer 47:6

SCABBY
or has pimples or * skin, or has Lev 21:20

SCABS
The Lord will send a plague of * Is 3:17

SCALE
who also set the pay * of the Neh 11:22,23
Now in your strength I can * any Ps 18:29
infantry; they * the walls like Joe 2:7

SCALES
has fins and *, whether taken from Lev 11:9
fins or * is forbidden to you. Lev 11:12
with fins and * may be eaten; Deu 14:9
must use accurate * and honest Deu 25:13,14,15
His overlapping * are his pride, Job 41:15-17
His belly is covered with * as Job 41:30
They weigh less than air on *. Ps 62:9
Literally, "a just balance and * Pro 16:11f
false *." Pro 20:23f
drop in the bucket, dust on the *. Is 40:15
land with fish sticking to your *. Eze 29:4
"You must use honest *, honest Eze 45:10
dishonest *—they love to cheat. Hos 12:7
* and under-sized measures; Amo 8:5
of ungodly treasures and lying *. Mic 6:10
Instantly (it was as though * Act 9:18

SCANDALOUS
Your sin is so * that your sorrow Jer 30:15
to witness the * spectacle of all Amo 3:9

SCANT
and giving you such * crops. Hag 1:10

SCAPEGOAT
sent out into the desert as a *. Lev 16:10

SCAR
it is merely the * from the boil, Lev 13:23
it is simply a * from the burn, and Lev 13:28

SCARCE
answered I could * believe that he Job 9:16
Men will be as * as gold—of Is 13:12

SCARCELY
time the people * moved—but all the Ex 10:23
bodyguard, she could * believe it! 2Ch 9:4
that they could * recognize him. Job 2:12
My words were * spoken when Is 48:3
one would * know it was a person Is 52:14,15
That mighty miracle will * be Jer 16:14,15
The world can * believe its eyes Jer 51:41
harvest time will * end before the Amo 9:13
You have * enough to eat or Hag 1:6
there will * be room for all of Zec 10:10
going that they * had time to eat. Mk 6:31
and Barnabas could * restrain the Act 14:18

SCARE
You're just trying to * us into Neh 6:9
had hired him to * me and make me Neh 6:12,13
one shall be left to * them away. Jer 7:33
will * him off, and he will Dan 11:30,31

SCARECROW
god like a helpless * in a garden! Jer 10:5

SCARED
over there are * to death of us." Jos 2:24

SCARF
his face in his * and went out and 1Ki 19:13

SCARLET
the midwife tied a * thread around Gen 38:28
the baby with the * thread on his Gen 38:30
purple cloth, * cloth, fine-twined Ex 25:1
blue, purple, and *, with cherubim Ex 26:1
blue, purple, and * cloth, the Ex 26:31
purple, and * fine-twined linen. Ex 26:36
blue, purple, and * fine-twined Ex 27:16
* threads of fine-twined linen. Ex 28:5,6
purple, and * fine-twined linen. Ex 28:8
blue, purple, and * threads of Ex 28:15
blue, purple, and * pomegranates, Ex 28:33,34
Blue, purple, and * cloth, made of Ex 35:5-9
blue, purple, and * cloth made from Ex 35:23
blue, purple, and * thread and Ex 35:25
blue, purple, and * on linen Ex 35:35
blue, purple, and * linen, with Ex 36:8,9
The blue, purple, and * inner Ex 36:35
with blue, purple, and *. Ex 36:37
with blue, purple, and * thread. Ex 38:18
* threads into fine linen cloth. Ex 38:23
blue, purple, and * cloth—garments Ex 39:1
the blue, purple, and * linen; Ex 39:3
blue, purple, and * cloth cut from Ex 39:4,5
gold, blue, purple, and * linen. Ex 39:8
with blue, purple, and *. Ex 39:24
blue, purple, and * threads, just Ex 39:28,29
some cedar wood, a * string, and Lev 14:4
* thread, and the hyssop branch. Lev 14:6
* thread, and hyssop branches. Lev 14:49
hyssop branch, and * thread, as Lev 14:51,52
They will spread a * cloth over Num 4:8
leather on top of the * cloth. Num 4:8
branches and * thread, and throw Num 19:6
And she left the * rope hanging Jos 2:21
Your lips are like a thread of * Sol 4:3
and * dyes from eastern Cyprus. Eze 27:7
See their * uniforms! Nah 2:3
They stripped him and put a * Mt 27:28
and * wool to sprinkle with. Heb 9:19
woman sitting on a * animal that Rev 17:3
The woman wore purple and * Rev 17:4
be brief. The * animal that died Rev 17:11
"The * animal and his ten Rev 17:16
authority to the * animal, so that Rev 17:17
linens, purple silks, and *; Rev 18:12
finest purple and * linens, decked Rev 18:16

SCARS
cuts or *—for a sin offering. Eze 43:22
* on your chest and your back?' Zec 13:6
lying about the reason for his *. Zec 13:6f
on my body the * of the whippings Gal 6:17

SCARVES
Gone shall be their * and ankle Is 3:20

SCATTER
Therefore, I will * their Gen 49:7
"I will * you out among the Lev 26:33
O Lord, and * your enemies; Num 10:35
He must also * the burning Num 16:36,37
Jehovah will * you among the Deu 4:27
* before you in seven directions! Deu 28:7
For the Lord will * you among Deu 28:64
I had decided to * them to Deu 32:26
their fathers and * them beyond the 1Ki 14:15
" 'If you sin, I will * you among Neh 1:8
And with a breath he can * the Ps 33:10
God will * the bones of these, Ps 53:5
ARISE, O GOD, and * all your Ps 68:1
* all who delight in war. Ps 68:30
upon your enemies, and * them. Ps 144:6
Five of them will * you until not Is 30:17
whirlwinds shall * them. Is 41:16
* them, says the Lord of Hosts. Jer 8:3
I will * them around the world, Jer 9:16
false gods, I will * you as chaff Jer 13:24,25
I will * my people before their Jer 18:17
And I will * them around the Jer 29:18
* you, I will not exterminate you; Jer 30:11
where in my fury I will * them. Jer 32:37
And I will * you over all the Jer 34:17
yours, and I will * these heathen Jer 49:32
Elam, and I will * the people of Jer 49:36
burn it there. * another third Eze 5:2
it with a knife. * the last third Eze 5:2
and one-third I will * to the Eze 5:12
coals and * them over the city." Eze 10:2
I will * his servants and guards Eze 12:14
And when I * them among the Eze 12:15
that I would * them, dispersing Eze 20:23,24
I will * you throughout the Eze 22:15
I will * the Egyptians among the Eze 30:26
shake off its leaves, and * its Dan 4:14
and * it out among the people. Dan 11:24
her up and * her across the world. Amo 9:8
and the sheep will *, but I will Zec 13:7
didn't *, and I was afraid ." Mt 25:24,25f
Shepherd, and the sheep will *.' Mk 14:27

SCATTERED
So, in that way, God * them all Gen 11:8
of Ishmael were * across the Gen 25:18
So the people * everywhere to Ex 5:12
living in villages * across the Deu 2:23
These cities must be * so that Deu 19:6,7
nations where he will have * you. Deu 30:3
army was so badly * that no two of 1Sa 11:11
* over about half an acre of land. 1Sa 14:14
I crushed and * them 2Sa 22:43
"I saw all Israel * upon the 1Ki 22:17
her body would be * like manure 2Ki 9:36
he smashed them to bits and * the 2Ki 23:12
of Jericho, and all his men *. 2Ki 25:4,5
He very wisely * his other sons 2Ch 11:23
I saw all Israel * upon the 2Ch 18:16
into dust and * over the graves of 2Ch 34:4
and only a few houses were * Neh 7:4
race of people * through all the Est 3:8
and all their children shall be *. Job 4:11
pen, and * us among the nations. Ps 44:11
you have * throughout the world. Ps 48:10
cover doves! God * their enemies Ps 68:14
Your enemies are * by your Ps 89:10
enemies—all evil-doers—shall be *. Ps 92:9
are * at the mouth of Sheol." Ps 141:6,7f
he will gather the * Israelites Is 11:12
They will flee, * like chaff by Is 17:13
from there, wherever you are *. Jer 3:14
But leave a * few to live. Jer 5:10
be * like dung upon the ground. Jer 8:2
Bodies shall be * across the fields Jer 9:22
perish and their flocks are *. Jer 10:21
you as chaff is * by the fierce Jer 13:24,25
have destroyed and * the very ones Jer 23:1
has come to be slaughtered and *; Jer 25:34
The Lord who * his people will Jer 31:10
Why should this remnant be * and Jer 40:15
all his army was * from him. Jer 52:8
Temple walls are * in the Lam 4:1
and those who survive will be * Eze 5:10
will lie * among the altars. Eze 6:4-7
* among the nations of the world. Eze 6:8
When your slain lie * among your Eze 6:13
Although I have * you in the Eze 11:16
where you are * and give you the Eze 11:17
city will be * to the four winds. Eze 17:21
where you are *, and will bring Eze 20:34
lands where I have * them and I Eze 28:25
Her branches will be * across the Eze 31:12
"Son of dust, the * remnants of Eze 33:24
So they were *, without a Eze 34:5
* in that dark and cloudy day. Eze 34:12
flock until they're * far away. Eze 34:21
But when they were * out among Eze 36:20
* everywhere across the ground. Eze 37:1
and all Israel, * near and far Dan 9:7
Dead bodies will be * everywhere. Amo 8:3
your people are * across the Nah 3:18
* Judah, Israel, and Jerusalem." Zec 1:19
four horns that * Judah so Zec 1:21
exiles there; 'I * you to the winds Zec 2:6,7
I turned away. I * them as with a Zec 7:14
and west, wherever they are *. Zec 8:7
Though I have * them like seeds Zec 10:9
As he * the seed across the Mt 13:4
it falls on will be * as dust." Mt 21:44
the sheep of the flock will be *. Mt 26:31
As he * it across his field, Mk 4:3
As he * the seed on the ground, Lk 8:5
of God * around the world. Jn 11:52
you will be *, each one returning Jn 16:32
he also died, and his followers *. Act 5:37
and * the nations across the face Act 17:26
To: Jewish Christians * Jas 1:1
of Jerusalem and * throughout 1Pe 1:1

SCATTERING
us from * all over the world." Gen 11:3,4
thus widely * them across the face Gen 11:9
that my men were * from me, and 1Sa 13:11
then he defiled these places by * 2Ki 23:14
A time for * stones; Ecc 3:5
* them over the face of the earth. Is 24:1
my people, for * my inheritance Joe 3:2
Then he shakes the nations, * the Hab 3:6
sheep and oxen, * the money Jn 2:15
* the Good News, but only to Jews. Act 11:19

SCATTERS
whiteness, and * the frost upon the Ps 147:16
enemies as the east wind * dust; Jer 18:17
How he * the proud and haughty Lk 1:51
leaps on them and * the flock. Jn 10:12

SCENE
When David arrived on the *, he 1Ch 20:2
him, and then he passes off the *. Job 14:20,21
on the world *, the Chaldeans, Hab 1:6
Then the * changed and I saw a Rev 14:14

SCENT
tongue, and the * of your garments Sol 4:11
is like the * of the mountains and Sol 4:11
clusters, and the * of your breath Sol 7:8

SCENTED
His cheeks are like sweetly * Sol 5:13

SCEPTER
to rouse him? The * shall not Gen 49:10
the king holds out his golden *; Est 4:11
holding out the golden * to her. Est 5:2
held out the golden * to Esther. Est 8:4
Justice is your royal *. Ps 45:6
Judah is my *. Ps 108:8
became a ruler's * and it was very Eze 19:11
* and knelt before him in mockery. Mt 27:29

SCEVA
Seven sons of *, a Jewish Act 19:14

SCHEDULE
(The * of charges was as 1Sa 13:21
on their usual *, only then will my Jer 33:20,21

SCHEDULED
if successful, * to marry Saul's 1Sa 17:55f
will come at the * time with the Ez 10:14
they are * in the laws of Israel. Ps 81:4
I was born and * each day of my Ps 139:16
things God had * against Jer 51:60
cities where they were * to go. Mt 11:1
which was * to make several stops Act 27:2

SCHEME
city and proposed Abimelech's *; Ju 9:3
But if this is simply the * of a 1Sa 26:19
How you plot and * to win your Jer 2:33

SCHEMES
he thwarts their *. Job 5:13

(SCHEMES Con't)
The rebel's * are sinful, and the — Pro 24:9
rise at dawn to carry out your *; — Mic 2:1
they are planning * to cheat widows — Lk 20:47

SCHOLARLY
of the rich and *, and to have — Mk 12:38

SCHOLARS
wisdom, and * their intelligence. — Dan 2:21
wise men, these *, these brilliant — 1Co 1:20

SCHOOLS
when he's never been to our *?" — Jn 7:15

SCIATIC
do not eat the * muscle where it — Gen 32:32

SCIENCE
Language is the basis on which * — Gen 11:6f
the literature and * of the time, — Dan 1:17

SCOFF
man, am now the man they * at. — Job 12:4
My friends * at me, but I pour — Job 16:20
they *. — Job 21:15
they *. — Ps 42:3
again and again they *, "Where — Ps 42:10
Lord, laugh at them! (And * at — Ps 59:8
All who see it happening will * — Ps 64:8
How they * and mock me when I — Ps 69:10
have smitten, and * at the pain of — Ps 69:26
They * at God and threaten his — Ps 73:8
Lord, see how these enemies * at — Ps 74:18
The nations all around us *. — Ps 79:4
to *, "Where is their God?" — Ps 79:10
How long will you * at wisdom and — Pro 1:22
own people! So * no more, lest — Is 28:22
"Glory to God," they *. — Is 66:5
Men * at me and say, "What is — Jer 17:15
No wonder they * and mock and — Jer 20:8
All who pass by * and shake their — Lam 2:15
to * at your land for its famines. — Eze 36:30
"They * at kings and princes, — Hab 1:10
Do not * at those who prophesy, — 1Th 5:20
I used to * at the name of Christ. — 1Ti 1:13
even to * at the Glorious Ones — 2Pe 2:10

SCOFFED
she * to herself. — Gen 18:12
than that," he *, "to catch the — 1Ki 18:27
of our plan, they * and said, — Neh 2:19
Jews think they are doing?" he *. — Neh 4:1
Satan *. — Job 1:9
as he * at the Living God. — Is 37:4
Who is it you * against and — Is 37:23
Because you * when my Temple was — Eze 25:3
for they have * at the people of — Zep 2:10
Then how they all * and sneered — Mt 9:24
"He saved others," they *, — Mt 27:41,42,43
his disciples *. — Mk 8:4
money, naturally * at all this. — Lk 16:14
the Jewish leaders laughed and *. — Lk 23:35
hanging beside him *, "So you're — Lk 23:39
they *. — Jn 7:3
Christ and his way will be * at. — 2Pe 2:2

SCOFFERS
Disgrace these * with their utter — Ps 40:14,15
Bullies will vanish and * will — Is 29:20
there will come * who will do every — 2Pe 3:3
would come these * whose whole — Jud 1:18

SCOFFING
the same—Peninnah * and laughing at — 1Sa 1:7
their words, * at the prophets — 2Ch 36:16
May their * fall back upon their — Neh 4:4
at others lead you into * at God! — Job 36:18
with sinners, * at the things of — Ps 1:1
of the * of the rich and proud. — Ps 123:3,4
Lord, you * rulers in Jerusalem: — Is 28:14
and of * to her neighbors now. — Jer 48:39
This brought * and laughter, — Lk 8:53
them, even * at the Glorious Ones. — Jud 1:8

SCOFFS
He only rages and *, and tempers — Pro 29:9
at you and * and shakes her head at — Is 37:22

SCOLD
I'm not saying this to * or — 2Co 7:3
when I * you in my letters. — 2Co 10:9
need to * and punish when I come; — 2Co 13:10
Fathers, don't * your children — Col 3:21

SCOLDED
wise men because he hates to be *. — Pro 15:12
But the disciples * those who — Mt 19:13

SCOLDING
time—not so much as by a single *! — 1Ki 1:6
* and spanking a child helps him — Pro 29:15
punishment and *, or shall I come — 1Co 4:21
Don't keep on * and nagging your — Eph 6:4
a human voice, * and rebuking him. — 2Pe 2:16

SCOPE
see the whole * of God's work from — Ecc 3:11
When I think of the wisdom and * — Eph 3:14,15

SCORCH
and * them with his burning wind. — Ps 11:6
and they will * the world. — Eze 20:47
to * away the rust and corruption. — Eze 24:11
it to * all men with its fire. — Rev 16:8

SCORCHED
are dry and the pastures are *. — Joe 1:20
the hot sun soon * them and they — Mt 13:6

SCORCHER
you say, 'Today will be a *.' — Lk 12:55

SCORCHING
I worked for you through the * — Gen 31:40
and in his lips there is a * — Pro 16:27f
the searing sun and * desert — Is 49:10
hot, God ordered a * east wind to — Jon 4:8
who worked all day in the * heat.' — Mt 20:11,12
by the * summer sun. — Jas 1:10,11
from the * noontime heat. — Rev 7:16

SCORN
were received with laughter and *! — 2Ch 30:10
shall laugh the wicked to *. — Job 22:19
the * of the neighboring nations. — Ps 80:6
let them * me for obeying you. — Ps 119:22
you * her, you hurt only yourself. — Pro 9:12
and shakes her head at you in *. — Is 37:22
* or their slanderous talk. — Is 51:7
and princes, and * their forts. — Hab 1:10
laugh at you in contempt and *. — 1Pe 4:4

SCORNED
But I am a worm, not a man, * and — Ps 22:6
I am * by all my enemies and — Ps 31:11
Moab shall wallow in her vomit, * — Jer 48:26
For you * Israel and robbed her, — Jer 48:27
are the one who is *—by Edom and — Eze 16:57
obey my laws but * them and — Eze 20:23,24
against you and * your commands. — Dan 9:5
"Though you have * my laws from — Mal 3:7
their virtue and * everyone else: — Lk 18:9

SCORNERS
learn only by seeing * punished. — Pro 21:11

SCORNING
letters * the Lord God of Israel. — 2Ch 32:17
vengeance on these nations * you. — Ps 79:12
against the Lord, * him who is the — Ps 107:11

SCORNS
The daughter of Jerusalem * and — 2Ki 19:21

SCORPION
will continue south past * Pass — Num 34:4
at the ascent of * Pass, runs to a — Ju 1:36
for an egg, do you give him a *? — Lk 11:12
agony like the pain of * stings. — Rev 9:5

SCORPIONS
*, where it was so hot and dry. — Deu 8:15
whips on you, but I'll use *!' — 1Ki 12:11
whips on you, but I'll use *!' — 2Ch 10:11
but I will punish you with *!" — 2Ch 10:14
sharp and barbed and sting like *. — Eze 2:6
serpents and * and to crush them. — Lk 10:19
were given power to sting like *. — Rev 9:3
They had stinging tails like *, — Rev 9:10

SCOT-FREE
to punish them shall get off *.' — Mal 3:14,15

SCOUNDREL
of here, you murderer, you *!" — 2Sa 16:7,8
the * for being so shrewd?" — Lk 16:8f

SCOUNDRELS
and find two * who will accuse him — 1Ki 21:10
good is that? Even * do that much. — Mt 5:46

SCOURED
be * and rinsed out thoroughly. — Lev 6:28

SCOURGE
"The * of our nation who killed — Ju 16:23,24
mocker is the * of all mankind. — Pro 24:9
but his son will be a greater * — Is 14:29
I will therefore * him and let — Lk 23:22

SCOURGED
their people. They * the nations — Eze 32:24
I will therefore have him * with — Lk 23:16

SCOURGES
and the whip that * them, just as — Is 9:4

SCOUT
will send them to * the unconquered — Jos 18:4
The king sent a * to see if — 2Ki 6:10

SCOUTS
it for you. The * will map it into — Jos 18:5,6
So the * went out to map the — Jos 18:8
First they sent *, who captured — Ju 1:22,23
and Eshta-ol as * to go and spy out — Ju 18:2
As they approached, Ben-hadad's * — 1Ki 20:17
"We'd better send out * to see. — 2Ki 7:13
their haste. The * returned and — 2Ki 7:15

SCOWLS
Don't be dismayed by their dark * — Eze 2:6

SCRAMBLE
Men stumble over them, * to their — Nah 3:3

SCRAPE
Then * off some of the blood — Ex 29:21
of pottery to * himself, and sat — Job 2:8
I will * away her soil and make — Eze 26:4

SCRAPED
chariots * along the dry ground. — Ex 14:25
walls of the house * thoroughly, — Lev 14:41
of the city and * them to death — Ju 8:16

SCRAPINGS
and the * dumped in a defiled place — Lev 14:41

SCRAPS
fed them the * under my table!" — Ju 1:7
and live there on * of food. — Hos 9:3
And when the * were picked up — Mt 14:2
And afterwards, when the * were — Mt 15:37,3
of * were picked up off the grass! — Mk 6:43,4
* from the children's plates." — Mk 7:2
day and when the * were picked up — Mk 8:8,
How many basketfuls of * did you — Mk 8:1
still, twelve basketfuls of * — Lk 9:1
As he lay there longing for * — Lk 16:2
"Now gather the *," Jesus told — Jn 6:1

SCRATCH
Those brought up in palaces now * — Lam 4:
And not a * was found on him, — Dan 6:2

SCRATCHED
to be insane! He * on doors and let — 1Sa 21:1
And they * their heads in — Mk 12:1

SCRATCHES
All mankind * for its daily — Lk 12:3

SCRATCHING
spend their lives * for food, and — Ecc 6:7,

SCRAWNY
fat shepherds and their * sheep. — Eze 34:2

SCREAM
because she didn't * for help, and — Deu 22:23,24
I * for help and no one hears me. — Job 19:7
Well may you * in terror, O — Is 10:3
* in terror, for the Lord's time — Is 13:6
There the night-monsters will * — Is 34:14
Strong men will * in terror and — Jer 47:2
And though they * for mercy, I — Eze 8:18
the wounded will * as the — Eze 26:15
as your pilots * with fright. — Eze 27:28
But for now, now you * in terror. — Mic 4:9
It gave a terrible *, shrieking, — Mk 5:7,8
keeps seizing him, making him *; — Lk 9:39

SCREAMED
me, but when I *, he ran, and — Gen 39:14,15
They * to Moses for help, and — Num 11:2
for it must be assumed that she * — Deu 22:25,26,27
just that and then *, "The — Ju 16:14
Then she *, "The Philistines are — Ju 16:20
When the woman saw Samuel, she *, — 1Sa 28:12
she *, and began to tear her — 2Ki 11:13,14
Athaliah ripped her clothes and *, — 2Ch 23:12
In my distress I * to the Lord — Ps 18:6
me. I *, "I'm slipping, Lord!" — Ps 94:18
magicians and astrologers!" he *. — Dan 5:7
They * in terror, for they — Mt 14:26
At that the evil spirit * and — Mk 1:26
beside them they * in terror, — Mk 6:49
Then the demon * terribly and — Mk 9:26
they *. — Lk 8:24
But they * back, "No! — Jn 18:40
She was pregnant and * in the — Rev 12:2

SCREAMING
that he had fled, she began *; — Gen 39:14,15
in battle! Let * be heard from — Jer 18:22
They began * at him, "What do — Mt 8:29
in the wild hills, * and cutting — Mk 5:5
ground before him, *, "What do you — Lk 8:28
were cast out, * as they left their — Act 8:7

SCREAMS
me, and I was only saved by my *. — Gen 39:18
fled at their *, fearing that the — Num 16:34
"* of anguish come from Ramah, — Mt 2:18

SCREECH
The * owl, the great owl, — Deu 14:11-18

SCREEN
"As a * for the door of the — Ex 26:36
set up the veil to * it, just as — Ex 40:21
the courtyard, the * at the — Num 3:25-30

SCRIBE
Literally, "secretary" or "*." — 1Ch 18:16f
Literally, "a *." — 1Ch 27:32f
Rehum, Shimshai (a *), several — Ez 4:8,9
and Shimshai the *, and to their — Ez 4:17
priest, Zadok the *, and Pedaiah — Neh 13:13
Shebna, the king's *, and Joah — Is 36:3
Shebna, the royal *, and Joah (son — Is 36:22
Shebna his royal *, and the older — Is 37:2
of Gemariah the * (son of Shaphan) — Jer 36:10
Elishama (the *) was there, as — Jer 36:12
the * and went to tell the king. — Jer 36:20
from Elishama the * and read it to — Jer 36:21
of Jonathan the *, which had been — Jer 37:15,16
Literally, "a *." — Mt 8:19f

SCRIBES
Literally, "not as the *." — Mt 7:29f
and chief priests, and *." — Mt 16:21f
Literally, "not as the *." — Mk 1:22f
Literally, "*." — Mk 2:6f
Literally, "the * of the — Mk 2:16f
Literally, "* and elders." — Mk 11:27,28f
Literally, "the elders and the * — Act 6:12f
Literally, "*." — Act 23:9f

SCRIPTURE
the meaning of this verse of *, — Mt 9:13
meaning of this * verse, 'I want — Mt 12:7
prayer boxes with * verses inside, — Mt 23:5
And so the * was fulfilled that — Mk 15:28
what does the * mean where it says, — Lk 20:17
"So if the *, which cannot be — Jn 10:34,35,36

SCRIPTURE Con't)
* had come true before their eyes. Jn 12:16
you I chose. The * declares, 'One Jn 13:18
This fulfilled the * that Jn 19:23,24
fulfillment of the * that says, Jn 19:36,37
The passage of * he had been Act 8:32
So Philip began with this same * Act 8:35
This is stated in the * that Act 13:34
As the * says it, "The man who Rom 1:17
In the words of the *, "I chose Rom 9:10-13
For God tells us in the * that in 1Co 6:16
then at last this * will come 1Co 15:54
Even now when the * is read it 2Co 3:14
reading the * that I came to Gal 2:19
For it is written in the *, Gal 3:13
is proved by the * which says, "A Eph 5:31
Literally, "Every *." 2Ti 3:16f
Or what do you think the * means Jas 4:5
As the * says, God gives strength Jas 4:6
For no prophecy recorded in * 2Pe 1:20,21
other parts of the *—and the result 2Pe 3:15,16

SCRIPTURES
to teach the * to the people. 2Ch 17:7,8,9
For the * tell us that bread Mt 4:4
for the * declare, 'God will send Mt 4:6
"The * say, 'Worship only the Mt 4:10
mentioned in the *—a messenger to Mt 11:10
"Don't you read the *?" Mt 19:4
"The * say my Temple is a place Mt 21:13
"Didn't you ever read the *? Mt 21:16
ever read in the *: 'The stone Mt 21:42
of the * and of God's power! Mt 22:29
dead—don't you ever read the *? Mt 22:31
For it is written in the * Mt 26:31
But if I did, how would the * be Mt 26:54
prophets as recorded in the *." Mt 26:56
is written in the *, 'My Temple is Mk 11:17
reading this verse in the *? Mk 12:10
you don't know the *, and don't Mk 12:24
is written in the *, 'Other things Lk 4:4
So it is written in the *." Lk 4:8
For the * say that God will send Lk 4:9,10,11
Jesus replied, "The * also say, Lk 4:12
and stood up to read the *. Lk 4:16
Then he added, "These * came Lk 4:21
replied, "Don't you read the *? Lk 6:3
He is the one to whom the * Lk 7:27
"But Abraham said, 'The * have Lk 16:29
to them, "The * declare, 'My Lk 19:46
and the words of the ancient * Lk 21:22
that the prophets wrote in the *! Lk 24:25
on through the *, explaining what Lk 24:27
* during the walk down the road. Lk 24:32
understand at last these many *! Lk 24:45
prophecy from the *: "Concern for Jn 2:17
quoted from the * really did refer Jn 2:22
"You search the *, for you Jn 5:39
And the * point to me! Jn 5:39
As the * say, 'Moses gave them Jn 6:30,31
As it is written in the *, 'They Jn 6:45
For the * declare that rivers of Jn 7:38
For the * clearly state that the Jn 7:41,42
Search the * and see for Jn 7:52
son of hell, as the * foretold. Jn 17:12
the * said, "I'm thirsty." Jn 19:28
realized that the * said he would Jn 20:9
necessary for the * to come true Act 1:16
referred to in the * when they Act 4:11
and we taught the * to some women Act 16:13
row he opened the * to the people, Act 17:2
They searched the * day by day to Act 17:11
showing by the * that Jesus is Act 18:28
replied, "for the * say, 'Never Act 23:5
Jesus from the *—from the five Act 28:23
No wonder the * say that the Rom 2:24
As the * say, Rom 3:10
for the * told about it long ago). Rom 3:21,22
For the * tell us Abraham Rom 4:3
That is what the * mean when Rom 4:17
No, for the * tell us that for Rom 8:36
For the * say that the promises Rom 9:7
God warned them of this in the * Rom 9:33
For the * tell us that no one Rom 10:11
That is what the * are talking Rom 10:15
Do you remember what the * say Rom 11:2,3
This is what our * refer to when Rom 11:8
written in the * so long ago are to Rom 15:4
spoken of in the * where Isaiah Rom 15:21
As it says in the *, "If anyone 1Co 1:31
That is what is meant by the * 1Co 2:9
as they did. (The * tell us, "The 1Co 10:7
We are told in the ancient * 1Co 14:21
as the * also declare. 1Co 14:34
sins just as the * said he would, 1Co 15:3
The * tell us that the first man, 1Co 15:45
the real meaning of the *. 2Co 3:14
Do you remember what the * say 2Co 8:15
It is as the * say: "The godly 2Co 9:9
As the * say, "If anyone is 2Co 10:17
to visit you. The * tell us that if 2Co 13:1
What's more, the * looked forward Gal 3:8,9
curse, for the * point out very Gal 3:10
* insist we are all its prisoners. Gal 3:21,22
But the * say that God told Gal 4:30
That is why God says in the *, Eph 5:14
and explain the * to the church; 1Ti 4:13
For the * say, "Never tie up 1Ti 5:18
child, you were taught the holy *; 2Ti 3:15
just as the * said that I would.' Heb 10:7
And so it happened just as the * Jas 2:23
As the * express it, "See, I am 1Pe 2:6
And the * also say, "He is 1Pe 2:8

SCROLL
have discovered a * in the Temple, 2Ki 22:8
He gave the * to Shaphan to read. 2Ki 22:8
mentioned the * found by Hilkiah. 2Ki 22:9,10
he found an old * which turned out 2Ch 34:14
Hilkiah gave the * to Shaphan, 2Ch 34:15,16
Then he mentioned the *, and how 2Ch 34:18
For this * says that the reason 2Ch 34:21
All the curses written in the * 2Ch 34:24
There the king read the * to 2Ch 34:30
to do what was written in the *. 2Ch 34:31
out to them the * of Moses' laws. Neh 8:1
stood up as he opened the *. Neh 8:1
As Ezra read from the *, Jeshua, Neh 8:7,8
Ezra read from the * on each of Neh 8:18
like a rolled-up *, and the stars Is 34:4
"Get a * and write down all my Jer 36:2
you read the * in the Temple on Jer 36:6
(son of Shaphan) to read the *. Jer 36:10
them down in ink upon the *. Jer 36:18
Then the officials hid the * Jer 36:20
The king sent Jehudi to get the * Jer 36:21
until the whole * was destroyed. Jer 36:23
*, but he wouldn't listen to them. Jer 36:24,25
After the king had burned the *, Jer 36:27
Get another * and write Jer 36:28
You burned the * because it said Jer 36:29
Then Jeremiah took another * and Jer 36:32
Jeremiah wrote on a * all the Jer 51:60
and gave the *, to Seraiah and said Jer 51:61,62
reading the *, tie a rock to it and Jer 51:63
a *, with writing on both sides. Eze 2:9,10
what I am giving you—eat this *! Eze 3:1
So I took the *. Eze 3:2
I LOOKED UP again and saw a * Zec 5:1
"A flying *!" Zec 5:2
"This *," he told me, Zec 5:3
AND I SAW a * in the right hand of Rev 5:1
on the throne, a * with writing on Rev 5:1
on this *, and to unroll it?" Rev 5:2
* and to break its seven seals." Rev 5:5
and took the * from the right hand Rev 5:7
And as he took the *, the Rev 5:8
* and break its seals and open it; Rev 5:9
seal and began to unroll the *. Rev 6:1
Then he unrolled the * to the Rev 6:3
as though rolled up like a * and Rev 6:14
held open in his hand a small *. Rev 10:2
get the unrolled * from the mighty Rev 10:8
and asked him to give me the *. Rev 10:9
and all else written in the *." Rev 22:6,7

SCRUB
doesn't produce * fruit nor do Lk 6:43

SCRUPLES
faith, not for decisions of *." Rom 14:1f

SCULPTURED
Solomon placed two * statues of 2Ch 3:10

SCUM
and the * of the earth, mobilized Ju 12:4
The wicked are the * you skim Ps 119:119
he stand it, to eat with such *?" Mk 2:16

SCURRY
animals which * about your feet or Lev 11:29,30

SCURRYING
defeat them and send them * home. Jer 37:7

SCURVY
boils, tumors, *, and itch, for Deu 28:27

SE-IRAH
escaped past the quarries to *. Ju 3:26

SE-ORIM
Fourth, the group led by *; 1Ch 24:7-18

SEA
So God created great * Gen 1:21,22
is, the valley of the Salt *). Gen 14:3
were in the Salt * Valley (four Gen 14:8,9
wild waves of the *, and you shall Gen 49:4
the shores of the * and shall be a Gen 49:13
out into the Red *, so that there Ex 10:19
through the Red * wilderness. Ex 13:17,18
Migdol and the *, opposite Ex 14:2
between the desert and the *!' Ex 14:3
the water, and the * will open up a Ex 14:16
his rod over the *, and the Lord Ex 14:21
a path through the *, with walls of Ex 14:21
that night, drying the * bottom. Ex 14:21
through the * on dry ground! Ex 14:22
the bottom of the *—all of Ex 14:23
again over the *, so that the Ex 14:26
Moses did, and the * returned Ex 14:27
the Lord drowned them in the *. Ex 14:27
the *, not one remained alive. Ex 14:28
both horse and rider into the *. Ex 15:1
Drowning them in the *. Ex 15:4
his wind, and the * covered them. Ex 15:10
Tried to follow through the *; Ex 15:19
rider have been drowned in the *. Ex 15:21
on from the Red *, and they moved Ex 15:22
in heaven or earth or in the *." Ex 20:4f
heaven, earth, and *, and Ex 20:11
from the Red * to the Philistine Ex 23:31
taken from rivers or from the *; Lev 11:9
quail from the *, and let them fall Num 11:31
the Mediterranean * and in the Num 13:29
in the direction of the Red *." Num 14:25
road to the Red * in order to go Num 21:4
middle of the Red * and on for Num 33:8
beside the Red *, and then in the Num 33:10
begin at the Dead *, and will Num 34:3
down to the Mediterranean *. Num 34:5
coastline of the Mediterranean *. Num 34:6
the Mediterranean * and will Num 34:7,8,9
tip of the * of Galilee, and then Num 34:10,11
River, ending at the Dead *." Num 34:12
* to the Euphrates River. Deu 1:7
the desert toward the Red *.' Deu 1:40
toward the Red *, for so the Lord Deu 2:1
and the Salt * (also called the Sea Deu 3:17
(also called the * of the Arabah). Deu 3:17
over to the Salt *, below the Deu 4:49
them in the Red * as they were Deu 11:4
River to the Mediterranean *. Deu 11:24
"Only * animals with fins and Deu 14:9
The * gull, the hawk (any Deu 14:11-18
Lo, they taste the riches of the * Deu 33:19
extending to the Mediterranean *; Deu 34:2
the Mediterranean * in the west to Jos 1:4
Red * for you when you left Egypt! Jos 2:10
* until the riverbed was empty. Jos 3:15,16
at the Red *! Jos 4:23
and as far south as the Salt * Jos 12:3
bay of the Salt *, ran along the Jos 15:2,3,4
along that to the Mediterranean *. Jos 15:2,3,4
along the Salt * to the mouth of Jos 15:5
into the Salt *, crossed to Jos 15:5
and ended at the Mediterranean *. Jos 15:10,11
then on to the Mediterranean *. Jos 16:5,6
began at the *, ran east past Jos 16:5,6
Brook to the Mediterranean *. Jos 16:8
of Kanah to the Mediterranean *. Jos 17:9
the Mediterranean * was assigned to Jos 17:10
east of the * went to Manasseh. Jos 17:10
bay of the Salt *—which is the Jos 18:19
to the Mediterranean * at Hosah. Jos 19:29
the Mediterranean * shall be yours, Jos 23:4,5
arrived at the Red *, the Egyptians Jos 24:6
and I brought the * crashing in Jos 24:7
crossing the Red *, they sent a Ju 11:16
Was the * split in two. 2Sa 22:16
The bottom of the * appeared. 2Sa 22:16
* and build them into rafts. 1Ki 5:9
Eloth on the Red * in the land of 1Ki 9:26
"Go and look out toward the *." 1Ki 18:43
a man's hand rising from the *." 1Ki 18:44
and the Dead *, just as the Lord 2Ki 14:25
floats across the * to Joppa, and 2Ch 2:16
beyond the Salt *, from Syria. 2Ch 20:2
the Mediterranean * to Joppa, for Ez 3:7
their cries from beside the Red *. Neh 9:9
You divided the * for your Neh 9:11
enemies in the depths of the *; Neh 9:11
but even on the islands of the *. Est 10:1
who can curse the *, who know how Job 3:8f
rouse the * monster, curse it." Job 3:8f
the earth and wider than the *. Job 11:9
teach you, or the fish of the *. Job 12:7,8,9
And by his power the * grows Job 26:12
One would think the * was made of Job 41:31,32
fish, and all the life in the *. Ps 8:8
the * receded from the shore. Ps 18:15
the mountains crumble into the *. Ps 46:2
the world and far away upon the *. Ps 65:5
He made a dry road through the * Ps 66:6
slopes and deep within the *! Ps 68:22
Let him reign from * to sea, and Ps 72:8
Let him reign from sea to *, and Ps 72:8
You divided the Red * with your Ps 74:13,14
When the Red * saw you, how it Ps 77:16
*—a pathway no one knew was there! Ps 77:19
For he divided the * before them Ps 78:13
But the * closed in upon their Ps 78:53
* to the Euphrates River. Ps 80:11
River to the Mediterranean *. Ps 89:25
He made the * and formed the Ps 95:5
Let the * in all its vastness Ps 98:7
whale you made to play in the *. Ps 104:26
rebelled against you at the Red *. Ps 106:7
You commanded the Red * to Ps 106:9
miracles in Egypt and at the *. Ps 106:21,22
The Red * saw them coming and Ps 114:3
What's wrong, Red *, that made Ps 114:5
who opened the Red * to make a path Ps 136:13

(SEA Con't)
army in the *, for his Ps 136:15
at *, clinging to a swaying mast. Pro 23:34
The rivers run into the * but the Ecc 1:3-7
the sea but the * is never full, Ecc 1:3-7
rivers, and flows again to the *. Ecc 1:3-7
victims like the roaring of the *. Is 5:30
the *, will be filled with glory. Is 9:1
the Egyptian armies in the *. Is 10:26
waters fill the *, so shall the Is 11:9
will dry a path through the Red *, Is 11:15
Literally, "the * of Egypt." Is 11:15f
deserts, and even down to the *. Is 16:8
The Dead * manuscript reads, Is 21:16f
stronghold of the *. Is 23:4
serpent, the dragon of the *. Is 27:1
before me, O lands beyond the *. Is 41:1
The lands beyond the * watch in Is 41:5
Sing, O *! Is 42:10
in distant lands beyond the *! Is 42:10
making a path right through the *. Is 43:16
For I can rebuke the * and make Is 50:2
who dried up the *, making a path Is 51:10
the *, between the roaring waves. Is 51:15
are like the restless *, which is Is 57:20
*, with Moses as their shepherd? Is 63:11
power divided the * before them Is 63:12
them through the bottom of the *? Is 63:13
lands beyond the * that have not Is 66:19
of their army is like a roaring *. Jer 6:23
kings of the regions across the *; Jer 25:22
and who stirs the * to make the Jer 31:35
Tabor or Mount Carmel by the *! Jer 46:18
along the * must be destroyed. Jer 47:7
is heard as far away as the Red *. Jer 49:21
like a wild * in a raging storm. Jer 49:23
city north of the * of Galilee; Jer 49:30f
The * has risen upon Babylon; Jer 51:42
For your wound is deep as the *. Lam 2:13
destroy those along the * coast. Eze 25:16
and even your dust into the *. Eze 26:12
your boundaries out into the *; Eze 27:4
* on the day of your vast ruin. Eze 27:27
All your sailors out at * come Eze 27:29
destroyed in the midst of the *? Eze 27:32
Now you lie broken beneath the * Eze 27:34
Or, "* serpent." Eze 32:2f
of the Black * and southwest of the Eze 38:2,3f
the Travelers, east of the Dead *. Eze 39:11
Valley to the Dead *, where it will Eze 47:8
Fish will abound in the Dead *, Eze 47:9
shores of the Dead *, fishing all Eze 47:10
will fill the Dead * just as they Eze 47:10
tip of the * of Galilee, and down Eze 47:18
Gilead, past the Dead * to Tamar. Eze 47:18
Jerusalem and the *, and there Dan 11:45
into the Dead * and the rest into Joe 2:20
Can oxen plow the *? Amo 6:12
everywhere from * to sea, seeking Amo 8:12
from sea to *, seeking the Word of Amo 8:12
wind over the *, causing a great Jon 1:4
who made the earth and *." Jon 1:9,10
"Throw me out into the *," he Jon 1:12
raging *—and the storm stopped! Jon 1:15
Euphrates, from * to sea and from Mic 7:12
from sea to * and from distant Mic 7:12
waters fill the *, with an Hab 2:14
smote the rivers and parted the *? Hab 3:8,9
horsemen marched across the *; Hab 3:15
and the fish in the * will perish. Zep 1:3
her fortifications into the *; Zec 9:4
His realm shall stretch from * to Zec 9:10
from sea to *, from the river to Zec 9:10
safely through the * of distress, Zec 10:11
Or, "the * of Egypt," referring Zec 10:11f
to the Red * which the people of Zec 10:11f
toward the Dead * and half towards Zec 14:8
the winds and the * obey him?" Mt 8:27
Jesus now returned to the * of Mt 15:29
neck and be thrown into the *. Mt 18:6
the shores of the * of Galilee, he Mk 1:16
and said to the *, "Quiet down!" Mk 4:39
then back to the * of Galilee by Mk 7:31
and he were thrown into the *. Mk 9:42
If he were thrown into the * Lk 17:2,3
and send it hurtling into the *! Lk 17:6
crossed over the * of Galilee, also Jn 6:1
also known as the * of Tiberias. Jn 6:1
rowed, and the * grew very rough. Jn 6:18,19
earth and of the * and everything Act 4:24
through the Red *, and back and Act 7:36
and * and everything in them. Act 14:15
Putting to * from there, we Act 27:4
the ship and blew it out to *. Act 27:14,15
on the Adriatic *, the sailors Act 27:27
them in the *, they lowered the Act 27:40
Though he escaped the *, justice Act 28:4
Literally, "as the sand of the * Rom 9:27f
through the waters of the Red *. 1Co 10:1
both in * and cloud! 1Co 10:2
Once I was in the open * all 2Co 11:25
through the Red * as though they Heb 11:29
as a wave of the * that is driven Jas 1:6
before it was a shiny crystal *. Rev 4:6
earth and in the *, exclaiming, Rev 5:13
to injure earth and *, "Wait! Rev 7:2
neither earth nor * nor trees—until Rev 7:3
thrown into the *, destroying a Rev 8:8,9
and a third of the * turned red Rev 8:8,9
He set his right foot on the * Rev 10:2
standing on the * and land lifted Rev 10:5
contains and the * and its Rev 10:6
there upon the * and land." Rev 10:8
Creature rising up out of the *. Rev 13:1
the * and all its sources." Rev 14:7
worshiping the Creature from the * Rev 14:9
throne of the Creature from the *, Rev 16:10
Creature from the * are also Rev 17:3f

SEA-GOD'S
you crushed the * heads! Ps 74:13,14

SEA-SERPENT
I will send the * after them to Amo 9:3

SEACOAST
He went down to the *, to the Jon 1:3

SEACOASTS
far north as the * of Tyre and Lk 6:17,18

SEAGULL
The nighthawk, the *, Lev 11:13-19

SEAL
And I * this promise with this Gen 9:12
as sacrifices to * their pact. Gen 21:27
oaths to * a non-aggression pact. Gen 26:31
"Your identification * and your Gen 38:18
identification * and walking stick Gen 38:25
same technique as in making a *; Ex 28:11
will be engraved upon it like a *. Ex 28:21
a *, 'Consecrated to Jehovah.' Ex 28:36
engraved like a *, with the names Ex 39:14
them with his *, and addressed them 1Ki 21:8
king's name, and * it with the Est 8:8
making a tight *, so no air can get Job 41:15-17
The Girl: "* me in your heart Sol 8:6
Lord, and * it up for the future. Is 8:16
but in so doing he will * his own Dan 8:25
prophecy a secret; * it up so that Dan 12:4
Then, breaking the *, she poured Mk 14:3
and the Spirit's * upon us means Eph 1:14
* and began to unroll the scroll. Rev 6:1
second *, and broke it open too. Rev 6:3
When he had broken the third *, I Rev 6:5
And when the fourth * was broken, Rev 6:7
open the fifth *, I saw an altar, Rev 6:9
I watched as he broke the sixth * Rev 6:12
the Great * of the Living God. Rev 7:2
we have placed the * of God upon Rev 7:3
broken the seventh *, there was Rev 8:1
Then he instructed me, "Do not * Rev 22:10

SEALED
it, for then your doom is *. Deu 7:26
* as jewels within my treasury. Deu 32:34
Their doom is *. Deu 32:35
for the Lord had * her womb; 1Sa 1:5
brother, and * the pact by giving 1Sa 18:4
His agreement is eternal, final, * 2Sa 23:5
in Ahab's name, * them with his 1Ki 21:8
Ahasuerus and * with his ring. Est 3:12
Haman's message, too, had been * Est 8:8f
King Ahasuerus and * the message Est 8:9,10
keep my mouth shut and my lips *. Ps 141:3
Then I said, "My doom is *, for Is 6:5
events are a * book to them. Is 29:11
he says, "I can't, for it's *." Is 29:11
I signed and * the deed of Jer 32:10
Then I took the * deed Jer 32:11
Take both this * deed and the copy Jer 32:14
signed and * and witnessed—in the Jer 32:44
and the king * it with his own Dan 6:17
Your doom is *, for you refuse to Hos 4:14
but he worshiped Baal and * his Hos 13:1
I made with you, * with blood. Zec 9:11
So they * Mt 27:66
being * at each end with clay. Mt 27:66f
* and they were afraid to ask him. Lk 9:45
you—an agreement * with the blood I Lk 22:20
Literally, "in whom you were * Eph 4:30f
our backs on God and * our fate. Heb 10:39
the back, and * with seven seals. Rev 5:1

SEALING
from resinous wood, * it with tar; Gen 6:14
is my blood, * the New Covenant. Mt 26:28
an order from you * the tomb until Mt 27:64
my blood, poured out for many, * Mk 14:24

SEALS
blood confirms and * the covenant Ex 24:8
the back, and sealed with seven *. Rev 5:1
to break the * on this scroll, and Rev 5:2
scroll and to break its seven *." Rev 5:5
and break its * and open it; Rev 5:9

SEAMLESS
tear up his robe," for it was *. Jn 19:23,24

SEAMS
will soon be bursting at the *! Is 54:3

SEAPORT
Then he went to the * towns of 2Ch 8:17,18
"Then all the * rulers shall Eze 26:16
"O mighty * city, merchant Eze 27:3

SEARCH
Jacob's tent to * there, then into Gen 31:33
"But you will also begin to * Deu 4:29
find him when you * for him with Deu 4:29
upon the earth, * from one end of Deu 4:32
So Joshua sent some men to * for Jos 7:22
to Ziph to * for him and kill him. 1Sa 23:14,15
* every inch of the entire land!" 1Sa 23:23
troops and went to * for him among 1Sa 24:2
and we will * the entire land." 1Ki 18:5
send my men to * your palace and 1Ki 20:5,6
your men may not * the palace and 1Ki 20:9
* the wilderness for your master; 2Ki 2:16
in * of pasture for their flocks: 1Ch 4:34-39
instructing you to * out every 1Ch 28:8
and pray, and * for me, and turn 2Ch 7:14
For the eyes of the Lord * back 2Ch 16:9
reign, he began to * for the God of 2Ch 34:3
We suggest that you * the Ez 4:15
I have ordered a * made of the Ez 4:19
We request that you * in the Ez 5:17
orders that a * be made in the Ez 6:1
it won't come; who * for death as Job 3:20,21
who search for death as others * Job 3:20,21
"But I * in vain. Job 23:8
to * for food for their children. Job 24:5
there they * for every blade of Job 39:8
How I * for you! Ps 63:1
joyous songs. I * my soul and Ps 77:6
* for him and for his strength, Ps 105:4
Happy are all who * for God, and Ps 119:2
* me, O God, and know my heart; Ps 139:23
It will be too late though you * Pro 1:28
Those who * for me shall surely Pro 8:17
If you * for good you will find Pro 11:27
if you * for evil you will find Pro 11:27
And I applied myself to * for Ecc 1:12-15
answer to my * for satisfaction. Ecc 2:20-23
In my * for wisdom I observed all Ecc 8:16,17
All night long I * for you; Is 26:9
* the Book of the Lord and see Is 34:16
You grew weary in your *, but Is 57:10
Any jack wanting you need not *, Jer 2:24
in all Jerusalem; * high and low Jer 5:1
and honest man! * every square, and Jer 5:1
are gone. * for them in Lebanon; Jer 22:20
starving deer that * for Lam 1:6
a dreadful end; no * will be enough Eze 26:21
to * for them or care about them. Eze 34:6
at all, for you didn't * for them. Eze 34:8
"For the Lord God says: I will * Eze 34:11
appoint men to * the land Eze 39:14
She will * for them but not find Hos 1:7
comes, they will * for me and say: Hos 5:15
will * them out and capture them. Amo 9:3
"I will * with lanterns in Zep 1:12
to Bethlehem and * for the child. Mt 2:8
a city or village, * for a godly Mt 10:11
the hills to * for the lost one? Mt 18:12
of wealth, and the * for success Mk 4:19
to Jerusalem to * for him there. Lk 2:45
"But why did you need to *?" Lk 2:49
others to go and * for the lost one Lk 15:3,4
have come to * for and to save Lk 19:9,10
"You * the Scriptures, for you Jn 5:39
You will * for me but not find Jn 7:34
Galilean too? * the Scriptures and Jn 7:52
and you will * for me, and die in Jn 8:21
Then, though you * for me, you Jn 13:33
don't need to * the heavens to find Rom 10:6

SEARCHED
Leah's, and then * the two tents of Gen 31:33
So although Laban * the tents Gen 31:34
and have * through everything. Gen 31:36,37
Then Moses * everywhere for the Lev 10:16
So they * the country from one 1Ki 1:3,4
that the king has * every nation 1Ki 18:10
Then fifty men * for three 2Ki 2:17
and * for him, he has helped them. 2Ch 15:4
* and its deep secrets explored. Job 28:3,4
gone! I * but could not find him! Ps 37:35,36
yes, I have * for them. Ps 119:168
to find. I * everywhere, Ecc 7:25
to seek him, but I * in vain. Sol 3:2
My heart stopped. I * for him but Sol 5:6
who never before * for me are Is 65:1
Every nook and cranny will be * Ob 1:6
The crowds * everywhere for him Lk 4:42
the message. They * the Scriptures Act 17:11
he came to Rome he * everywhere 2Ti 1:17

SEARCHES
Only the Lord knows! He * all Jer 17:10
us, and his Spirit * out and shows 1Co 2:10
that I am he who * deep within Rev 2:23

SEARCHING
He began * the oldest brother's Gen 44:12
who are * for you have returned; Jos 2:16

SEARCHING Con't)
to the city after * everywhere Jos 2:22
Finally, after * in the land of 1Sa 9:5
As he and his men were * for 2Ch 22:9
Will long * make them known to Job 11:7
he sees all sin without *. Job 11:11
not survive your * gaze, for how Ps 5:5
God looks down from heaven, * Ps 53:2
howling like dogs and * for food. Ps 59:14,15
for his strength, and keep on *! Ps 105:4
and are * for them as you would for Pro 2:3,4,5
For though I spend my life * for Ecc 2:20-23
the streets while * through the Lam 1:19
and they began * for some fault in Dan 6:4
Word of the Lord, *, running here Amo 8:12
as a blind man * for a path, Zep 1:17
frantic, * for you everywhere." Lk 2:48
to the deserts, * there for rest; Lk 11:24
them, "Whom are you * for?" Jn 18:7

SEARCHLIGHT
is the Lord's * exposing his Pro 20:27

SEARING
nor thirst; the * sun and scorching Is 49:10

SEAS
"earth," and the water "*." Gen 1:9,10
and in the skies and in the *." Gen 1:26
solid walls to hold the * apart. Ex 15:8
Let the vast * roar, 1Ch 16:32
and the *, and everything in them. Neh 9:6
out and stalked along the *. Job 9:8
and the * reply, 'Nor is it Job 28:14
boundaries of the * when they Job 38:8,9
from which the * come, or walked in Job 38:16
"He has founded it upon the *." Ps 24:2f
Praise him, all the * and Ps 69:34
let the vastness of the roaring * Ps 96:11
of the earth to form the *. Ps 104:3
a boundary for the *, so that they Ps 104:9
sailing the seven *, plying the Ps 107:23
and earth, and in the deepest *. Ps 135:6
the * and everything in them. Ps 146:6
the limits of the * and gave them Pro 8:27,28,29
holds out his hand over the *; Is 23:11
the * have put their trust in him. Is 42:4
how you have vanished from the *! Eze 26:17
Great * shall swallow you. Eze 26:19
are wrecked in the heart of the *! Eze 27:26
island home in the midst of the *. Eze 28:2,3
your island in the heart of the *. Eze 28:8
and they were fighting heavy *. Mt 14:23,24
even the winds and * obey him?" Mk 4:41
the roaring * and strange tides. Lk 21:25
The next day as the * grew Act 27:18
Literally, "a place where two * Act 27:41f
and in the stormy * and from men 2Co 11:26

SEASHORE
and like the sands along the *. Gen 22:17
dead, washed up on the *. Ex 14:30
Upon the *, Ju 5:17
the sand upon the *—and there were Ju 7:12,13
were as thick as sand along the *; 1Sa 13:5
to count—like sand along a *! Hos 1:10
Then Jesus went out to the * Mk 2:13

SEASHORES
than the sand of a thousand *. Job 6:3
pounding on the * of the world! Ps 93:4
sands along the * of the world, too Is 48:19
the sand upon the * measured, so Jer 33:22

SEASON
"And at the mating *, I had a Gen 31:10
In due * the time of her delivery Gen 38:27
In due * Joseph and each of his Ex 1:6
Literally, "in its * from year to Ex 13:10f
at the end of the harvest *. Ex 23:16
end of the harvest *, after the Deu 16:13
to give you fine crops every *. Deu 28:12
Now it was the harvest * and Jos 3:13,14
there through the entire harvest * 2Sa 21:10
(spring was the * when wars usually 1Ch 20:1
fruit each * without fail. Ps 1:3
pathway and in due * he will honor Ps 37:34
I said to myself, "In due * God Ecc 3:17
Literally, "for a * and a time." Dan 7:12f
of grain in its *, or wine at the Hos 1:9
figs of summer in their first *! Hos 9:10
it can't * anything. Mk 9:50
was too early in the * for fruit. Mk 11:13
For in due * Christ will be 1Ti 6:15
get the chance, in * and out, when 2Ti 4:2

SEASONAL
River during its * flooding and 1Ch 12:15
Your help is as uncertain as a * Jer 15:17,18

SEASONED
"Every offering must be * with Lev 2:13
fielded 400,000 * warriors against 2Ch 13:3

SEASONING
incensemaker, and * it with salt; Ex 30:35
"You are the world's *, to make Mt 5:13

SEASONS
they shall bring about the * on Gen 1:14,15
sequence of the *, or guide the Job 38:32
rains but send them in their *. Eze 34:26
days or months or * or years. Gal 4:10

SEAT
Literally, "mercy *" or "place Ex 25:17f
Anyone sitting on a * the man Lev 15:6
backward from his * beside the gate 1Sa 4:18
its canopy gold, the * is purple; Sol 3:10
Ethiopia was the * of the Is 18:1f
Literally, "sit on Moses' *." Mt 23:2f
He himself will * them and put on Lk 12:37
don't always head for the best *. Lk 14:8
to take whatever * is left at the Lk 14:9
Literally, "the judgment * in a Jn 19:13f
before the Judgment * of God. Rom 14:10
golden cover, called the mercy *. Heb 9:5
on the mercy * as an offering to Heb 9:7
and sprinkled it on the mercy *; Heb 9:12
give him the best * in the house Jas 2:3

SEATED
where to sit, and * them in the Gen 43:33
and * the king upon his throne. 2Ch 23:20
other youths. I am * in his Sol 2:3
from the dead and * him in the Eph 1:20

SEATS
Sitting in the * of honor. 1Sa 2:8
"Take your * now on the mountains Amo 3:9
They love to sit in the best * Mk 12:39
For how you love the * of honor Lk 11:43
And how they love the * of honor Lk 20:46

SEAWEED
The waters closed above me; the * Jon 2:5

SEBA
The sons of Cush were:*, Havilah, Gen 10:7
*, Havilah, Sabta, Raama, and 1Ch 1:5-9
from *—all will bring their gifts. Ps 72:10
I gave Egypt and Ethiopia and * Is 43:3

SEBAM
Elealeh, *, Nebo, and Beon. Num 32:3,4

SECACAH
Middin, *, Nibshan, The City of Jos 15:48-62

SECLUDES
veil that * the Holy of Holies. Lev 24:3,4

SECLUDING
The curtain * the Holiest Place Mt 27:51

SECLUSION
keep house should be placed in *. 2Sa 20:3
I was being formed in utter *! Ps 139:15
and went into * for five months. Lk 1:24

SECOND
This all happened on the * day. Gen 1:7,8
a * day (or, 'period of time')." Gen 1:7,8f
lapis lazuli. The * branch is Gen 2:13
her to Abram to be his * wife. Gen 16:2,3
again and gave Jacob a * son. Gen 30:7
Then Zilpah produced a * son, Gen 30:12
asleep again and had a * dream. Gen 41:5
home). The * boy was named Ephraim Gen 41:52
they will the *," the Lord said, Ex 4:8
the * month after leaving Egypt. Ex 16:1
first row. The * row will be an Ex 28:18
Above the ceiling was a * layer Ex 36:14,15
in the * row were an emerald, a Ex 39:11
month, in the * year, the Ex 40:17
He shall offer the * bird as a Lev 5:10
the * shall belong to the Lord! Lev 27:10
first day of the * month" (of the Num 1:1f
of the * year after the Israelis Num 1:1
first day of the * month" (of the Num 1:17,18,19f
of the * year after leaving Egypt: Num 9:1
* month, beginning in the evening. Num 9:11
at the * signal, the tribes on Num 10:5,6,7
the twentieth day of the * month Num 10:11
of the * year of Israel's leaving Num 10:11
reference is to a * wife of Moses. Num 12:1f
Offer the * lamb in the evening Num 28:8
"On the * day of this seven-day Num 29:17
and nights the * time, just as I Deu 10:10
the court's judgment a * time. Deu 17:13
and the * husband also divorces Deu 24:3
your ancestors gave a * thought; Deu 28:36
(It was the * time in Israel's Jos 5:2,3
The reason for this * Jos 5:4,5
Lord gave it to them on the * day; Jos 10:32
In the * year of his reign, he 1Sa 13:1
not need to strike a * time!" 1Sa 26:8
Ahino-am. His * son, Chileab, was 2Sa 3:3
(Amasa was Joab's * cousin; 2Sa 17:25
7½ feet wide, the * floor 9 feet 1Ki 6:6
stairs going up to the * floor; 1Ki 6:8
led from the * to the third. 1Ki 6:8
to him the * time (the first time 1Ki 9:2,3
beginning in the * year of the 1Ki 15:25
This occurred in the * year of 2Ki 1:17
So the king sent out a * rider. 2Ki 9:19
DURING THE * year of the reign of 2Ki 14:1
son was Eliab, his * was Abinadab, 1Ch 2:13
Jerahmeel's * wife Atarah was the 1Ch 2:26
The * was Daniel, whose mother was 1Ch 3:1
Abijah, the *. 1Ch 6:28
Heman's * assistant was Ethan, a 1Ch 6:44-47
Bela, the first,Ashbel, the * 1Ch 8:1
Jeush, the *, 1Ch 8:39
The * of The Top Three was 1Ch 11:12
Obadiah was * in command; 1Ch 12:8-13
Amariah was * in command, 1Ch 23:19
and Isshiah was the * in command. 1Ch 23:20
*, the group led by Jedaiah; 1Ch 24:7-18
Amariah, his * son; 1Ch 24:23
The *, Gedaliah, along with twelve 1Ch 25:9-31
Jedia-el (the *), 1Ch 26:2,3
Jehozabad (the *), 1Ch 26:4,5
Hilkiah, the *; 1Ch 26:11
The commander of the * Division 1Ch 27:4
on duty the * month of each year. 1Ch 27:4
general. His * in command was 2Ch 17:18
constructing a * wall outside it. 2Ch 32:5
tailor, living in the * ward. 2Ch 34:22
placed him in his * chariot and 2Ch 35:24,25
in June of the * year of their Ez 3:8
So the work ended until the * Ez 4:24
returned to the * harem where the Est 2:12,13,14
Later, the king demanded a * bevy Est 2:19
been transferred to the * harem." Est 2:19f
their enemies the * day also, and Est 9:18
celebration on the * day, when they Est 9:19
to tell a lie. *, give me neither Pro 30:8
as he can; and *, that he should Ecc 3:13
his people for the * time, Is 11:11
gave not even a * thought to me? Is 57:11
the Lord sent him this * message: Jer 33:1
with a * wheel crosswise inside. Eze 1:16
for each one had a * wheel Eze 10:9-13
the *, a man's; Eze 10:14
"The * day, sacrifice a young Eze 43:22
ONE NIGHT IN the * year of his Dan 2:1
Belshazzar was the * under Dan 5:7f
given to it. The * animal looked Dan 7:5
When: In late August of the * Hag 1:1
September of the * year of King Hag 1:14,15
In early December, in the * year Hag 2:10
November of the * year of the reign Zec 1:1
still in the * year of the reign of Zec 1:7
by red horses, the * by black ones, Zec 6:2
widow became the * brother's wife. Mt 22:25
commandment. The * most important Mt 22:38,39
So the * brother married the Mk 12:20,21,22
"The * is: 'You must love others Mk 12:31
the cock crows a * time tomorrow Mk 14:30
the rooster crowed the * time. Mk 14:72
This was Jesus' * miracle in Jn 4:54
So for the * time they called in Jn 9:24
to buy some. The * time they Act 7:13
They passed the first and * cell Act 12:10
This is what the * Psalm is Act 13:32,33
The * day Paul took us with him Act 21:18
punished, and *, just because you Rom 13:5
be given a first and * warning. Tit 3:10
THIS IS MY * letter to you, dear 2Pe 3:1
shall not be hurt by the * Death. Rev 2:11
a lion; the * looked like an ox; Rev 4:7
the * seal, and broke it open too. Rev 6:3
And I heard the * Living Being Rev 6:3
Then the * angel blew his Rev 8:8,9
The * woe is past, but the third Rev 11:14
The * angel poured out his flask Rev 16:3
after his * reign, he too, will Rev 17:11
For them the * Death holds no Rev 20:6
This is the * Death—the Lake of Rev 20:14
This is the * Death." Rev 21:8
The * with sapphire; Rev 21:18,19,20

SECOND-CLASS
that I will make them * citizens. Is 56:3

SECOND-IN-COMMAND
the chariot of his *, and wherever Gen 41:43
Azrikam, and the king's * Elkanah. 2Ch 28:7

SECRECY
*, and showed them the king's son. 2Ki 11:4

SECRET
but also gave * instructions to put Gen 42:25
Egypt used their * arts and they, Ex 7:22
same with their * arts, and they, Ex 8:7
* arts, but this time they failed. Ex 8:18
an idol, even in *, whether carved Deu 27:15
"I have a * message for you," he Ju 3:17,18,19
Angel replied, "for it is a *." Ju 13:18
begged Samson to tell her his *. Ju 16:6
and so his * was not discovered. Ju 16:9
longer and finally told her his *. Ju 16:16,17
"This truth was given me in *, Job 4:12
Have you heard the * counsel of Job 15:7,8
They meet in * to set their Ps 64:5
you—our * sins—and see them all. Ps 90:8
hidden in the darkness, * riches; Is 45:3
for no * is hidden from you. Eze 28:2,3
telling them the *, so they would Dan 2:18
that I know this * of your dream, Dan 2:30
because he has told you this *." Dan 2:47
Daniel, keep this prophecy a *; Dan 12:4
your Father who knows every *. Mt 6:18
be revealed: their * plots will Mt 10:26
and tried to keep it a * that he Mk 7:24
they sent * agents pretending to be Lk 20:20

(SECRET Con't)
who had been a * disciple of Jesus Jn 19:38
will judge the * lives of everyone, Rom 2:16
kept * from the beginning of time. Rom 16:25,26,27
the Spirit but it will all be a *. 1Co 14:2
As he listens, his * thoughts 1Co 14:25
and wonderful *: we shall not all 1Co 15:51
God has told us his * reason for Eph 1:9
God himself showed me this * plan Eph 3:2,3
And this is the *: that the Eph 3:6
I have learned the * of Php 4:12
tell his * plan to you Gentiles. Col 1:25
He has kept this * for centuries Col 1:26,27
And this is the *: that Christ in Col 1:26,27
For God's * plan, now at last Col 2:2
the * nourishment from heaven; Rev 2:17

SECRETARIES
Ahijah (sons of Shisha) were *; 1Ki 4:1
Haman called in the king's * and Est 3:12
Immediately the king's * were Est 8:9,10

SECRETARY
Zeruiah), and his * of state was 2Sa 8:16
Seraiah was the king's private *. 2Sa 8:17
Sheva was the *, and Zadok and 2Sa 20:25
Azariah (son of Nathan) was * of 1Ki 4:1
king's financial * and the High 2Ki 12:10
Shebnah, his *; 2Ki 18:18
Shebnah the king's *, and Joah (son 2Ki 18:37
Josiah sent his * Shaphan (son of 2Ki 22:3,4
to Shaphan the * and exclaimed, "I 2Ki 22:8
Literally, "*" or "scribe." 1Ch 18:16f
acted as recording * and wrote down 1Ch 24:6
the recording * and the 2Ch 24:11
set by Je-iel, the * of the army, 2Ch 26:11
to Shaphan, the king's *. 2Ch 34:15,16
son), the royal *, formed a truce Is 36:3
Asaph), the royal *, went back to Is 36:22
(son of Shaphan), the royal *, Jer 26:24
the city, and the * of the Jer 52:24,25
Blastus, the royal *, and asked for Act 12:20

SECRETLY
" 'Cursed is he who * slays Deu 27:24
You did it *, but I will do this 2Sa 12:12
The people of Israel had also * 2Ki 17:9
Meanwhile, Jeroboam had * sent 2Ch 13:13,14
across the nation *, to tell the 2Ch 23:2,3
my heart has been * enticed, and I Job 31:27
I will not tolerate anyone who * Ps 101:5
for him to come to the palace *. Jer 37:17
volunteered to kill Ishmael *. Jer 40:15
to someone, do it *—don't tell your Mt 6:3
to your Father *, and your Father, Mt 6:6
Jesus * and put him to death. Mk 14:1
*, staying out of the public eye. Jn 7:10
who came * to interview Jesus. Jn 7:50
So now they want us to leave *? Act 16:37
* planned from the very beginning. Eph 3:9

SECRETS
"There are * the Lord your God Deu 29:29
searched and its deep * explored. Job 28:3,4
With them alone he shares the * Ps 25:14
Yes, he knows the * of every Ps 44:21
your * to a gossip unless you Pro 20:19
before, * you haven't heard. Is 48:6
some remarkable * about what is Jer 33:3
heaven who reveals *, and he has Dan 2:28
He who reveals * was speaking to Dan 2:29
And your Father who knows all * Mt 6:4
who knows your *, will reward you. Mt 6:6
shows us all of God's deepest * 1Co 2:10
blessings by explaining God's *. 1Co 4:1

SECT
The Pharisees were a religious * Mk 3:6f
a member of the * of the Pharisees, Jn 3:1
a Jewish religious * that denied Act 4:1f
He is a ringleader of the * known Act 24:5
which they refer to as a *; Act 24:14

SECTION
Take your choice of any * of the Gen 13:9
I'll stay here in the western *. Gen 13:9
the whole * was like the Garden Gen 13:10
these tarpaulins into one wide *; Ex 26:9
the other six for another wide *. Ex 26:9
of the spotted * of wall, and the Lev 14:40
to sow it. A * of land that Lev 27:16
told me, 'The * of Canaan you were Jos 14:9
* will be assigned to each tribe. Jos 18:5,6
listing the cities in each *. Jos 18:9
which tribe should have each *: Jos 18:10
The * of land assigned to the Jos 18:11
* had been too large for them. Jos 19:9
at the old Millo * of the city, he 2Sa 5:9
of David—the old * of Jerusalem. 2Ki 8:24,25
the City of David * of Jerusalem. 2Ki 14:20
the City of David * of Jerusalem. 2Ki 15:38
to the Mishneh * of Jerusalem to 2Ki 22:14
repaired the next * of wall, and Neh 3:4
in addition to a * of the wall. Neh 3:11
his daughters repaired the next *. Neh 3:12
the City of David * of Jerusalem. Neh 3:15
they also worked on the * of wall Neh 3:19
of Hakkoz) built a * of the wall Neh 3:21
who repaired the * opposite the Neh 3:27
each one doing the * immediately Neh 3:28
* of wall next to his own home. Neh 7:3
each in its own * of his land? Is 28:25
and slit off the * and throw it Jer 36:23
shall first give a * of it to the Eze 45:1
"A * of this land, 875 feet Eze 45:2
All this * shall be holy land; Eze 45:4
to the holy lands will be a * 8 Eze 45:6
miles wide, south of the Temple * Eze 48:15
Benjamin's * extends across the Eze 48:23
fact, from every * of Judea went Mt 3:5
SOON AFTERWARDS HE left that * of Mk 6:1
while in the * of the Temple known Jn 8:20
the * known as Solomon's Hall. Jn 10:22,23

SECTIONS
and put the * of the animal and Lev 1:8
for the larger *," the Lord Num 26:55,56
tribes draw for the smaller *." Num 26:55,56
The larger * of land will be Num 33:54
and the smaller * will be allotted Num 33:54
came to ten * of land (in addition Jos 17:5,6
map it into seven *, and then I Jos 18:5,6
Then the Lord could assign the * Jos 18:8
into seven *, listing the cities in Jos 18:9
to their own * of the country. Jos 24:28
King Hazael conquered several * 2Ki 10:32,33
the * next to their own houses. Neh 3:23
the various * of its passageway and Eze 40:24
doors, each with two swinging *. Eze 41:24
"Two special * of land shall be Eze 45:7
the same as those of the tribal *. Eze 45:7
shall be given two *. Eze 47:13
This land, lying between the * Eze 48:21,22
"The * given to the remaining Eze 48:23
break into four * with four kings, Dan 8:22
and the central * of their wings Rev 4:8
split into three *, and cities Rev 16:19

SECTOR
of David—the old * of Jerusalem—to 1Ki 9:24
the City of David * of Jerusalem, 2Ki 16:20
the City of David * of Jerusalem to 2Ch 8:11
the City of David * in Jerusalem. 2Ch 32:30

SECU
arrived at the great well in *. 1Sa 19:22

SECULAR
holy and what is *, what is right Eze 44:23

SECUNDUS
Aristarchus and *, from Act 20:4

SECURE
and noticed how * everyone felt. Ju 18:7
grip upon the kingdom became *. 1Ki 2:46
and fair, his kingdom stands *. Pro 20:28
You felt * in all your Is 47:10
bound with cords and made *. Eze 27:24
to feel * or enjoy God's blessing. Rom 3:17
he will be *, and will go out no Rev 3:12

SECURED
had meanwhile been * by a 1Sa 13:23

SECURELY
The chestpiece was held * above Ex 39:21
And now, since he was * in the 1Sa 14:47
and fasten it * in place with Jer 10:4
Son, holds him * and the devil 1Jn 5:18

SECURITY
not enter his house to get his *. Deu 24:10
as *, you are not to sleep in it. Deu 24:12,13
will be peace and * during the 2Ki 20:19
"Let us renew the mutual * pact 2Ch 16:3
If he counts on his home for *, Job 8:15
have a place of refuge and * Pro 14:26
of safety and * for Jerusalem. Eze 12:24
off guard as they bask in false *. Dan 8:25
that lived in such *, that said to Zep 2:15
were no jobs, no wages, no *; Zec 8:10
the inheritance and have some *. Lk 9:59f

SEDITION
long history of * against the kings Ez 4:15
in fact, rebellion and * are Ez 4:19

SEDUCE
Don't let their coyness * you. Pro 6:25
lest she tempt you and * you. Pro 7:25

SEDUCED
If a girl who is engaged is * Deu 22:23,24
and the man who * her shall be Deu 22:23,24
So she * him with her pretty Pro 7:21
a girl will let herself be *." Pro 30:18,19f
city—because she * the nations of Rev 14:8

SEDUCES
"If a man * a girl Ex 22:16
"If a man * a slave Lev 19:20

SEDUCING
that his sons were * the young 1Sa 2:22

SEDUCTIVELY
saucy and pert, and dressed *. Pro 7:10

SEED
Literally, "your *." Gen 9:9,10,11f
for next year's *, and as food for Gen 47:24
it was white, like coriander *, Ex 16:31
falls upon it, the * is defiled. Lev 11:38
your field with two kinds of *; Lev 19:1
amount of * required to sow it. Lev 27:1
bushels of barley * for sowing is Lev 27:1
size of coriander *, and looked Num 11:
When they planted their *, Ju 6:3,
would contain two measures of *." 1Ki 18:32
use it as * for next year's crop; 2Ki 19:2
weeping, carrying * for sowing, and Ps 126:
Keep on sowing your *, for you Ecc 11:
Ten bushels of * will yield but a Is 5:1
give you enough * for a small Is 37:3
and to produce * for the farmer and Is 55:1
my * so carefully—the very best. Jer 2:2
otherwise the good * will be Jer 4:
Literally, "planted the * of the Eze 17:5
God. The * rots in the ground; Joe 1:1
As he scattered the * across the Mt 13:
farmer sowing good * in his field; Mt 13:2
choice * is full of thistles!' Mt 13:2
tiny mustard * planted in a field. Mt 13:31,3
the farmer who sows the choice *. Mt 13:3
the world, and the * represents the Mt 13:3
as a tiny mustard * you could say Mt 17:2
plant good * within their lives. Mk 4:1
where some of the * fell, Mk 4:1
It is like a tiny mustard *! Mk 4:31,3
As he scattered the * on the Lk 8:
Other * fell on shallow soil Lk 8:
rock beneath. This * began to grow, Lk 8:
Other * landed in thistle Lk 8:
fertile soil; this * grew and Lk 8:
"This is its meaning: The * is Lk 8:11
The hard path where some * fell Lk 8:12
interest. The * among the thorns Lk 8:14
It is like a tiny mustard * Lk 13:19
size of a mustard *," Jesus Lk 17:6
I die I will be alone—a single *. Jn 12:23,24
My work was to plant the * in 1Co 3:6
We have planted good spiritual * 1Co 9:11
When you put a * into the ground 1Co 15:36
up out of the *, it is very 1Co 15:37
from the * you first planted. 1Co 15:37
is a dry little * of wheat, or 1Co 15:37
plant grows from each kind of *. 1Co 15:38
For God, who gives * to the 2Co 9:10
you more and more * to plant and 2Co 9:10
born yet, the * from which he came Heb 7:10

SEED-BEARING
sort of grass and * plant, and Gen 1:11,12
I have given you the * plants Gen 1:29

SEEDLING
the touch of water, like a new *. Job 14:8,9
He took a * and planted it in Eze 17:12,13

SEEDS
fruit trees with * inside the Gen 1:11,12
so that these * will produce the Gen 1:11,12
but if the * are wet and the Lev 11:38
vines, not even the * or skins! Num 6:3,4
punish them for sowing * of sin. Job 5:6
* to sprout across the land. Ps 65:10
Plant the good * of righteousness Hos 10:12
them like * among the nations, Zec 10:9
Other * fell among thorns, and Mt 13:7
where some of the * fell represents Mt 13:19
comes and snatches away the * Mt 13:19
his life, and the * don't root very Mt 13:21
It is the smallest of all *, but Mt 13:31,32
Other * fell among thorns that Mk 4:7
But some of the * fell into good Mk 4:8
* grew and grew without his help. Mk 4:27
For the soil made the * grow. Mk 4:28
of the smallest of *, yet it grows Mk 4:31,32
different kinds of * and plants, so 1Co 15:39
A farmer who plants just a few * 2Co 9:6
will be planting * of evil and he Gal 6:8
will plant * of peace and reap a Jas 3:18

SEEK
Don't * vengeance. Lev 19:18
by those who * your life, you are 1Sa 25:29
Let all rejoice who * the Lord. 1Ch 16:10
* the Lord; 1Ch 16:11
Seek the Lord; yes, * his 1Ch 16:11
And * his face untiringly. 1Ch 16:11
If you * him, you will find him; 1Ch 28:9
Literally, "I would * God, and to Job 5:8f
"But I search in vain. I * him Job 23:8
I seek him here, I * him there, Job 23:8
find him. I * him in his workshop Job 23:9
So many * to harm me. Ps 3:1
all who * the Lord shall find him Ps 22:26
God, the thing I * most of all, is Ps 27:4
All who * for God shall live in Ps 69:32
to * him, but I searched in vain. Sol 3:2
The Girl: "Why should you * a Sol 6:13
you better news. * for him, then Is 21:12
earnestly I * for God; Is 26:9
When the poor and needy * water Is 41:17
for deliverance, who * the Lord! Is 51:1
* the Lord while you can find Is 55:6
What bride will * to hide her Jer 2:32
shout for them at Bashan; * them Jer 22:20

SEEK Con't)
you to those who * to kill you, of Jer 22:24,25
You will find me when you * me, Jer 29:13
to happen—Israel shall * him! Jer 31:22
do you no good to * my help and Jer 44:26
who * his life, just as I turned Jer 44:30
for him, to those who * for him. Lam 3:25
to Egypt to * for a great army and Eze 17:15
I will * my lost ones, those who Eze 34:15,16
now is the time to * the Lord, that Hos 10:12
people of Israel, "* me—and live. Amo 5:4
Don't * the idols of Bethel, Amo 5:5
the Lord and live, or else he Amo 5:6
* him who created the Seven Stars Amo 5:8
not trust the Lord, nor * for God. Zep 3:2
at Jerusalem, to * his blessing, Zec 7:2
you ask for. *, and you will find. Mt 7:7
does this generation * a sign?" Mk 8:12f
all who *, find; Lk 11:10
that they should * after God, and Act 17:27
away from sin and * eternal life. 2Co 7:10
all quarrels and * to live a clean Heb 12:14
who continue to * salvation by Heb 13:10

SEEKING
Anyone * to avenge the death Deu 19:6,7
silver, and bronze, * an alliance. 1Ch 18:10
* your help against their foes. Ps 17:7
nothing for God are * my life. Ps 54:3
steadily to my course of * wisdom. Ecc 2:3
Hezekiah was * a defensive Is 30:2f
about me are now * me out. Is 65:1
female camel, * for a male! Jer 2:23
left his lair like a lion * prey; Jer 25:38
Are you * great things for Jer 45:5
weeping and * the Lord their God. Jer 50:4
remember her sin in * it before. Eze 29:16
from sea to sea, * the Word of the Amo 8:12
Her "prophets" are liars * Zep 3:4
for a while, * rest but finding Mt 12:43,44,45
No, spend your energy * the Jn 6:27
but anyone * to honor the one who Jn 7:18
* for the unseen Rom 2:7
they had not been really * God. Rom 9:30
around gossiping, * only pleasure 1Ti 5:6

SEEKS
does right and really * for God. Ps 53:2
Literally, "God * what has been Ecc 3:15f
Anyone who *, finds. Mt 7:8
Literally, "There is one who * Jn 8:50f

SEEM
the skin does not * to be deeper Lev 13:4
infection does not * to be deeper Lev 13:32
of the house which * to be beneath Lev 14:37
Korah: "Does it * a small thing to Num 16:8,9
the punishment * too severe, and Deu 25:1
wrong. You * to love those who 2Sa 19:6
Does it really * right to you to Job 10:3
* to think that God is dead. Ps 10:4
I must * like an animal to you, O Ps 73:22
It doesn't * right for a fool to Pro 19:10
food, and never * to get enough. Ecc 6:7,8
sun and moon will * to fade away. Is 24:23
(The people below must * to him Is 40:22
sisters have; they * almost Eze 16:51
with you, your sisters * innocent! Eze 16:52
and some * to apply to Satan. Eze 28:12f
These prophecies * to have been Dan 11:6f
Her people never * to recognize Hos 7:2
"It doesn't * right to take Mt 15:26
give light, and the stars will * Mt 24:29
But many people who * to be Mk 10:31
"Sir, doesn't it * unfair to you Lk 10:40
"You * to be in a deep Lk 24:17
For it doesn't * reasonable to Act 25:27
Does it * incredible to you that Act 26:8
how wise they * to be, and ignore 1Co 1:19
You * to think you already have 1Co 4:8
the Lord, but they * right to me: 1Co 7:12
When I am with the Jews I * as 1Co 9:20
And some of the parts that * 1Co 12:22
have some parts that * rather odd! 1Co 12:23
might otherwise * less important. 1Co 12:24
being saved, we * a fearful smell 2Co 2:16
they * to be like on the outside. 2Co 5:16
some of you who * to think my deeds 2Co 10:2
look at me and I * weak and 2Co 10:7
I may * to be boasting more than 2Co 10:8
of Eden. You * so gullible: you 2Co 11:4
too, and * like godly ministers. 2Co 11:15
his visits didn't * to cost us 2Co 12:16
Christians here * to have lost Php 1:14
These rules may * good, for Col 2:23
but you don't * to listen, so it's Heb 5:11

SEEMED
And it * as though children were Gen 25:22
But they * to him but a few days, Gen 29:20
more the Israelis * to multiply! Ex 1:12
under his feet there * to be a Ex 24:10
"This * like a good idea, so I Deu 1:23
* right in his own eyes. Ju 17:6
a virgin, and it * impossible to 2Sa 13:2f
Jordan River, it * as if everyone 2Sa 19:15
From his waist up, he * to be all Eze 1:27,28
and from his waist down he * to Eze 1:27,28
He put out what * to be a hand Eze 8:3
into the sky and * to transport me Eze 8:3
of a Man—or so he * to be—brought Dan 7:13
Then the one who * to be a man Dan 10:18
"Nothing then * more improbable Zep 2:15f
nearby. (It * that these men showed Lk 5:17
He * to be talking in riddles. Lk 18:34
So it * wise to us, having Act 15:25
"For it * good to the Holy Act 15:27,28,29
in Athens * to spend all their time Act 17:21
Moses kept right on going; it * Heb 11:27
for what * like half an hour. Rev 8:1
They wore breastplates that * to Rev 9:9
I saw that one of his heads * Rev 13:3
Spread out before me was what * Rev 15:2

SEEMINGLY
the Lord had * abandoned them. 1Sa 7:2
preserved him from * imminent and Heb 5:7f

SEEMS
clothes, and finally * convinced. Gen 27:26
that the trouble * to be down under Lev 13:20
and the problem * to be more than Lev 13:25
if the infection * to be below Lev 13:29,30
that the spot * to be only in the Lev 13:31
to the priest, 'It * to me that Lev 14:35
based on whatever * best under the 1Sa 10:7
in exile. It * but yesterday that 2Sa 15:19,20
let him do what * best to him." 2Sa 15:25,26
At dawn he * so strong and Job 8:16
it * as though God preserves the Job 24:22,23
The reference * to look beyond Ps 72:6f
that * right but ends in death. Pro 14:12
gloomy, everything * to go wrong; Pro 15:15
when he is cheerful, everything * Pro 15:15
Even honey * tasteless to a man Pro 27:7
earth: Providence * to treat some Ecc 8:14
or godly. It * so unfair, that one Ecc 9:2,3
other peg that * to be so firmly Is 22:25
my work for them * all in vain; Is 49:4
no one * to care or wonder why. Is 57:1
No one * to realize that God is Is 57:1
The context * to favor the Is 66:19f
This * to be another of the Jer 29:24f
This change * to describe an Jer 31:33f
it * that you can never find Eze 16:28
It therefore * that Gog was, or Eze 38:2,3f
But from the context Gog * to be Eze 38:2,3f
There * to be no end of Nah 2:9
If it * slow, do not despair, for Hab 2:3
The Lord says, "This * Zec 8:6
* to want the fresh and the new. Lk 5:39
and none of you * interested in Jn 16:5
It * to be a fact of life that Rom 7:21
and silly. It * foolish to the 1Co 1:22
philosophy and * wise to them. 1Co 1:22
But, strange as it *, we 1Co 2:16
And if it * wise for me to go 1Co 16:4
is read it * as though Jewish 2Co 3:14
even though it * that the more I 2Co 12:15
everyone else * to be worrying Php 2:21
though it sometimes * that way. 2Pe 3:9

SEER
knew whether the * was in town. 1Sa 9:9,10,11
"Let's go and ask the *," 1Sa 9:9,10,11
"I am the *!" 1Sa 9:19
of Iddo the * concerning Jeroboam 2Ch 9:29
and by Iddo the *, and in The 2Ch 12:15

SEER'S
tell me where the * house is?" 1Sa 9:18

SEERS
those days prophets were called *. 1Sa 9:9,10,11
your prophets and *, so all of Is 29:10

SEGREGATED
Laban's flock and * them from the Gen 30:39,40

SEGUB
gates, his youngest son, *, died. 1Ki 16:34
*. (Machir was also the father of 1Ch 2:21
* was the father of Jair, who 1Ch 2:22

SEIR
The Horites in Mount *, as far as Gen 14:5,6
in the land of *, with this Gen 32:3
our own pace and meet you at *." Gen 33:14
So Esau started back to * that Gen 33:16
from his brother Jacob to Mount *. Gen 36:6,7,8
Edomites, born to him in Mount *: Gen 36:9
descended from *, the Horite—one of Gen 36:20,21
of the land of *:The tribe of Gen 36:20,21
son of *) were Hori and Heman. Gen 36:22
shall possess all Edom and *. Num 24:15-19
going by way of Mount *! Deu 1:1
and killed them from * to Hormah. Deu 1:44
around in the area of Mount *. Deu 2:1
descendants of Esau who live in *; Deu 2:4
them all the Mount * hill country Deu 2:5
Horites lived in *, but they were Deu 2:12
of Esau at Mount *, for he Deu 2:22
The Edomites at * allowed us to Deu 2:29
And dawned upon us from Mount *; Deu 33:2
Mount Halak, near *, to Baal-gad in Jos 11:17
west of Mount *, was allotted by Jos 12:7
of Baalah to Mount *, passed along Jos 15:10,11
area around Mount * while Jacob and Jos 24:4
When you led us out from *, Ju 5:4
Or, "*." 1Ch 1:38,39f
tribe of Simeon went to Mount *. 1Ch 4:42
Moab, and Mount * are doing. 2Ch 20:10
Moab, and Mount * to begin fighting 2Ch 20:22
* and killed every one of them. 2Ch 20:23
there killed 10,000 men from *. 2Ch 25:11
from the people of *, and set them 2Ch 25:14
face toward Mount * and prophesy Eze 35:2
people of Mount *, killing off all Eze 35:7
Mount * and all who live in Edom! Eze 35:15

SEIZE
we stole it and * us as slaves, Gen 43:18
The army then proceeded to * the Ju 3:28
to * him," the king exclaimed. 2Ki 6:13
Let death * them and cut them Ps 55:15
who said, "Let us * for our own Ps 83:12
May creditors * his entire Ps 109:11
the prey. They * my people and Is 5:29
Panic shall * her mightiest Jer 50:36
They devour many lives; they * Eze 22:25
* their goods and make them poor?' Eze 38:13

SEIZED
the angels * his hand and the hands Gen 19:16
and children, and * the cattle and Num 31:9,10,11
troops who * the fords of the Ju 7:24
So they * them all, and Elijah 1Ki 18:40
armies, and they * him with hooks 2Ch 33:11
You will be * by the king of Jer 38:23
her strongholds are *. Jer 48:41
They will be * with terror, Zec 14:13
So they * him and led him to the Lk 22:54
"This man was * by the Jews and Act 23:27
in his hand. He * the Dragon—that Rev 20:2

SEIZES
Literally, "he *." Job 9:12f

SEIZING
keeps * him, making him scream; Lk 9:39

SELA
he also conquered * and changed 2Ki 14:7
MOAB'S REFUGEES AT * send lambs Is 16:1
you desert cities—Kedar and *! Is 42:11

SELAH
text adds here: "Higgaion. *." Ps 9:16f

SELECT
instructed, "to * a male goat for Lev 9:3
he himself will * as his home. Deu 12:4,5
be sure that you * as king the man Deu 17:15
"Now * twelve men, one from each Jos 3:12
has given to you? * three men from Jos 18:4
"Upon receipt of this letter, * 2Ki 10:2,3
has given you to * and appoint Ez 7:25
each province to * young lovelies Est 2:3
will personally * his choicest Ps 47:4
those I * will inherit it and Is 65:9
to * some of the Jewish youths Dan 1:3,4
A tree from a * variety produces Mt 12:33
Let us * someone who has been Act 1:21,22
dear brothers, and * seven men, Act 6:3

SELECTED
to the herd and * a fat calf and Gen 18:7
the one you have * to be the wife Gen 24:44
Returning, he * Simeon from among Gen 42:24
This night was * by the Lord to Ex 12:42
so the same night was * as the Ex 12:42
Lord shall not be * on the basis of Lev 27:33
the tithe shall be * from the Num 18:28,29
I took the men they *, some from Deu 1:15
the way, and had * the best places Deu 1:33
thirteen cities, * by sacred lot in Jos 21:6
A tenth of the army will be * by Ju 20:8,9,10
And finally, the sacred lot * 1Sa 10:21
I have * him ahead of my own 1Sa 12:2
of his reign, he * three thousand 1Sa 13:2
Jesse, for I have * one of his sons 1Sa 16:1
I have * a homeland for my 2Sa 7:10,11
on two fronts, he * the best 2Sa 10:9
from Shunam, was finally *. 1Ki 1:3,4
Is he the one you have * to sit 1Ki 1:24
of Israel who has * one of my sons 1Ki 1:48
Lord had * to honor his own name. 2Ki 21:3,4,5
buried him in the grave he had *. 2Ki 23:30
and were * by their genealogies. 1Ch 9:33,34
Levites, who was * for his skill. 1Ch 15:22
who were * by my father David. 2Ch 2:7
David had * it as the site for 2Ch 3:1
JOSIAH'S SON JEHOAHAZ was * as 2Ch 36:1
were * by lot to live there too. Neh 11:1
Then he * twelve of them to be Mk 3:14,15
witnesses God had * beforehand—not Act 10:40,41

SELECTING
handpicked grain, * them here and Is 27:12

SELECTIONS
their * were interspersed with 2Ch 5:13,14

SELECTS
He cuts down cedars, he * the Is 44:14
for the persons my Father *." Mt 20:23

SELED
* and 1Ch 2:30
Appa-im. * died without children, 1Ch 2:30

SELEUCIA
to * and then sailed for Cyprus. Act 13:4

SELEUCID
* wars between Egypt and Syria. Dan 11:6f

SELEUCIDS
* to avenge his sister's murder. Dan 11:7f

SELEUCUS
I of Egypt, * of Babylonia, Dan 8:8f
* II. Dan 11:9f
* IV, successor of Antiochus III, Dan 11:20f
when his brother * was Dan 11:21f

SELF
For you swore by your own *, 'I Ex 32:13
I am but a shadow of my former *. Job 17:7
when it means forfeiting one's *? Lk 9:25

SELF-ASSURANCE
they tinkle with * as they walk. Is 3:18

SELF-CONDEMNED
"You die *," David said, "for 2Sa 1:16

SELF-CONFIDENCE
and such * never pleases God. Jas 4:16

SELF-CONTROL
* means controlling the tongue! Pro 13:3
it is better to have * than to Pro 16:32
A man without * is as defenseless Pro 25:28
righteousness and * and the Act 24:25
them because of their lack of *. 1Co 7:5
faithfulness, gentleness and *; Gal 5:23

SELF-EXAMINATION
but must spend the day in * and Lev 16:29,30

SELF-INFLICTED
Evidently * cuts, as practiced by Zec 13:6f

SELF-RIGHTEOUS
sinners, not the *, back to God." Mt 9:13
One was a proud, * Pharisee, and Lk 18:10

SELF-SUFFICIENT
a * fool falls flat on his face. Pro 10:8
that they are *—that they need Jer 49:31

SELFISH
THE * MAN quarrels against every Pro 18:1
You are full of * greed and all Jer 22:17
by living with * attitudes and evil Hag 2:14
never haughty or * or rude. 1Co 13:5
Don't be *; Php 2:3
you are bitter and jealous and *; Jas 3:14
is jealousy or * ambition, there Jas 3:16

SELFISHNESS
I will reject all * and stay Ps 101:4
For jealousy and * are not God's Jas 3:15
been cleansed from * and hatred 1Pe 1:22

SELL
Please * me a piece of ground for Gen 23:4
Zohar's son, to * me the cave of Gen 23:9
he felt sure, * the idea to the Gen 34:18,19
Let's * Joseph to them! Gen 37:26,27
from Pharaoh and didn't need to *. Gen 47:22
but he has no power to * her to Ex 21:8
two owners shall * the live ox and Ex 21:35
so you may not * it permanently. Lev 25:23
not permitted to * the fields of Lev 25:34
priest may * it to someone else. Lev 27:27
You may give it or * it to him, Deu 14:21
then you may * the tithe portion Deu 14:25
free—you may not * her or treat her Deu 21:14
and there you will offer to * Deu 28:68
"I asked Naboth to * me his 1Ki 21:6
vineyard Naboth wouldn't * you? 1Ki 21:15
to her, "Go and * the oil and pay 2Ki 4:7
and barley would * for so little on 2Ki 7:18
for food had to * their children or Neh 5:2,3,4
"Yet we must * our children into Neh 5:5
lands and * them their children. Neh 5:12
Do fishing partners * him to the Job 41:6
garments to * to the merchants. Pro 31:24
THE LORD ASKS, Did I * you to my Is 50:1
There will be nothing to buy or * Eze 7:12
I will dry up the Nile and * the Eze 30:12
other men and * myself to them for Hos 1:5
I will * your sons and daughters Joe 3:8
* them to the Sabeans far away. Joe 3:8
be perfect, go and * everything you Mt 19:21
to buy and * with it and soon Mt 25:16
"go and * all you have and give Mk 10:21
you the Kingdom. * what you have Lk 12:33
Jesus said. "* all you have and Lk 18:22
better * your clothes and buy one! Lk 22:36
The property was yours to * or Act 5:4
"Did you people * your land for Act 5:8

SELLER
be redeemed at any time by the *. Lev 25:24

SELLERS
buyers and *, lenders and Is 24:2

SELLING
And Esau vowed, thereby * all his Gen 25:33
really doing is * the number of Lev 25:14,15,16
She is * our brother Elimelech's Ru 4:3
to him about * him this land. 1Ki 21:2
sorts of wares and * them on the Neh 13:16
a helpless orphan, or * a friend. Job 6:27
though it may mean * everything in Pro 6:31
* one's soul for a piece of bread. Pro 28:21
will be buying and * houses and Jer 32:15
veils and * them indulgences. Eze 13:18
crafty merchants * from dishonest Hos 12:7
exile, * them as slaves in Edom. Amo 1:6
pair of shoes, or * them your moldy Amo 8:6
and the stalls of those * doves. Mt 21:12
stalls of those * doves, and Mk 11:15
buying and *, farming and building— Lk 17:28
he saw merchants * cattle, sheep, Jn 2:14
Then, going over to the men * Jn 2:16
with each other, * their Act 2:45
And after * it, it was yours to Act 5:4
become wealthy by * her these Rev 18:15

SELLS
"If a man * his daughter as a Ex 21:7
and then kills or * it, he shall Ex 22:1
If anyone becomes poor and * Lev 25:25
"If a man * a house in the city, Lev 25:29
becomes poor and * himself to you, Lev 25:39
becomes poor and * himself to the Lev 25:47
If he * himself to a foreigner, Lev 25:53
him as a slave or * him, the Deu 24:7
bless the man who * it to them in Pro 11:26

SELVES
their old sinful *, bent on Rom 8:8

SEMACHIAH
Their brave brothers, Elihu and *, 1Ch 26:6,7

SEMANTICS
of questions of * and personalities Act 18:15

SEMEIN
Mattathias' father was *; Lk 3:23-38

SEMEIN'S
Mattathias' father was Semein;* Lk 3:23-38

SEMEN
"Whenever a man's * goes out Lev 15:16
Any clothing or bedding the * Lev 15:17

SEMI-PARTED
animal with only * hoofs, or any Lev 11:26

SEMINAL
or by a * emission; Lev 15:32
is defiled by a * emission, or who Lev 22:4
because of a * emission during the Deu 23:9,10

SEMINARY
prophets of Bethel * came out to 2Ki 2:3
Then the students at Jericho * 2Ki 2:5
ONE DAY THE wife of one of the * 2Ki 4:1
ONE DAY THE * students came to 2Ki 6:1

SEMITES
Chaldeans: a tribe of * living Hab 1:6f

SENAAH
From the subclan of *, 3,630. Ez 2:3-35

SENATE
and the entire *, they sent for the Act 5:21

SEND
I will never again * another flood Gen 9:9,10,11
When I * clouds over the earth, Gen 9:14
He will * his angel on ahead of Gen 24:7
have walked, will * his angel with Gen 24:40
If they won't * anyone, then you Gen 24:41
said, "* me back to my master!" Gen 24:54
Then I will * for you. Gen 27:45
"I'll * you a young goat from my Gen 38:17
I can be sure you will * it?" Gen 38:17
Judah said to his father, "* the Gen 43:8
Now I am going to * you to Ex 3:10
But Moses said, "Lord, please! * Ex 4:13
Why did you ever * me, if you Ex 5:22
If you refuse, I will * vast Ex 8:2
If you refuse I will * swarms of Ex 8:21
power of God will * a deadly plague Ex 9:3
This time I am going to * a Ex 9:14
this time I will * a hailstorm Ex 9:18
to Moses, "I will * just one more Ex 11:1
the diseases I * on the Egyptians, Ex 15:26
and I will * hornets to drive Ex 23:28
I will * an Angel before you to Ex 33:2
told me whom you will * with me. Ex 33:12
of the goat and * it into the Lev 16:21
to me, I will * you seven times Lev 26:21
I will * wild animals to kill Lev 26:22
I will * a plague among you there; Lev 26:25
my great anger and * you seven Lev 26:28
in the wind will * them fleeing as Lev 26:36
the punishment I * them for their Lev 26:40,41
NOW INSTRUCTED Moses, "* Num 13:2
* one leader from each tribe. Num 13:2
'First let's * out spies to Deu 1:22
Lord your God will * hornets to Deu 7:20
will continue to * both the early Deu 11:14
Lord your God will * fear and dread Deu 11:25
and don't * him away empty-handed! Deu 15:13
for himself, nor * his men to Egypt Deu 17:16
home town shall * for him and shall Deu 19:12
her the letter, and * her away. Deu 24:1
"For the Lord himself will * his Deu 28:20
He will * disease among you Deu 28:21
He will * tuberculosis, fever, Deu 28:22
"He will * upon you Egyptian Deu 28:27
He will * madness, blindness, Deu 28:2
The Lord will * your enemies Deu 28:47,4
then Jehovah will * perpetual Deu 28:58,5
Then the Lord will * you back to Deu 28:6
tribe and I will * them to scout Jos 18:
own strength! * home any of your Ju 7:
the Lord told Gideon. "* all Ju 7:
"Why didn't you * for us when you Ju 8:
practice to * out a servant 1Sa 2:13,1
and begged them to * the Ark back 1Sa 5:1
What sort of gift shall we * with 1Sa 6:
"Yes, * it back with a gift," 1Sa 6:
they were told. "* a guilt 1Sa 6:
* the plague upon you after all." 1Sa 6:
"What guilt offering shall we * 1Sa 6:4,
And they were told, "* five gold 1Sa 6:4,
If you * these gifts and then 1Sa 6:4,
"Where can we * the Ark from 1Sa 6:2
tomorrow I will * you a man from 1Sa 9:1
to know and * you on your way. 1Sa 9:1
Saul to * the servant on ahead. 1Sa 9:26,2
I will pray for the Lord to * 1Sa 12:1
"* for him at once," Samuel 1Sa 16:10,1
he * his son David the shepherd. 1Sa 16:1
I defy the armies of Israel! * 1Sa 17:1
to himself, "I'll * him out 1Sa 18:1
Then I'll * a lad to bring the 1Sa 20:2
were angry. "* them back!" 1Sa 29:
Joab: "* me Uriah the Hittite." 2Sa 11:
"Did Joab * you here?" 2Sa 14:1
me, and they will * their sons 2Sa 15:35,3
and * us help if we need it." 2Sa 18:
"There is no further news to * 2Sa 18:2
with this project. * your woodsmen 1Ki 5:
for me, and I will * my men to work 1Ki 5:
should walk, and * rain upon the 1Ki 8:35,3
"When you * your people out to 1Ki 8:4
that I will soon * rain again!" 1Ki 18:
tomorrow I will * my men to search 1Ki 20:5,
him, "Will you * your army with 1Ki 22:4
is dead; * them to their homes.' 1Ki 22:17
"Why did you * messengers to 2Ki 1:16
to hold the water he will *. 2Ki 3:16
to her husband: "* one of the 2Ki 4:22
"I will * a letter of 2Ki 5:5
are you so upset? * Naaman to me, 2Ki 5:8
he is, and we'll * troops to seize 2Ki 6:13
Give them food and drink and * 2Ki 6:22
"We'd better * out scouts to see. 2Ki 7:13
"* out a rider and find out if he 2Ki 9:17
approval, let us * messages to our 1Ch 13:2
its people to * him a large sum of 1Ch 18:2
were forced to * him large amounts 1Ch 18:6
"So * me skilled 2Ch 2:7
iron workers; and * me weavers to 2Ch 2:7
Also * me cedar trees, fir 2Ch 2:8
and I will * my men to help them. 2Ch 2:8
your father. So * along the wheat, 2Ch 2:15
what is right; and * rain upon this 2Ch 6:27
crops, or if I * an epidemic among 2Ch 7:13
and he didn't * total destruction; 2Ch 12:12
the palace, and to * it to King 2Ch 16:2
has been killed. * them home.' 2Ch 18:16
and I will not * the promised evil 2Ch 34:28
the desire to * this proclamation Ez 1:1
decided to * you this information. Ez 4:14
Jerusalem and to * back a report of Ez 7:14
"I, Ar-ta-xerxes the king, * Ez 7:21
attendants to * us priests for the Ez 8:17
to * them away with our children; Ez 10:3
your royal favor, * me to Judah to Neh 2:4
meal, and to * presents to those in Neh 8:10
a festive meal and to * presents; Neh 8:12
if you love me, * out a decree Est 8:5
Now go ahead and * a message to Est 8:8
rejoice and * gifts to each other. Est 9:19
and to * joy and prosperity to Job 10:3
of my youth. You * me to prison Job 13:27,28
old and wrinkled, then * him away. Job 14:20,21
and they * forth his lightning. Job 37:11
Can you * him out to bring in Job 39:12
May he * you aid from his Ps 20:2
Be merciful and * the help I Ps 27:7
Turn them around and * them Ps 40:14,15
Oh, * out your light and your Ps 43:3
He will * my enemies to the pit Ps 55:23
He will * down help from heaven Ps 57:3
Lord forever. Oh, * your Ps 61:7
* us around the world with the Ps 67:2
Egypt will * gifts of precious Ps 68:31
God will * them sliding over the Ps 73:18
me. * me a sign of your favor. Ps 86:17
Then you * your Spirit, and new Ps 104:30
wilderness and * their children Ps 106:27
Literally, "The Lord will * forth Ps 110:2f
The Lord will * a plague of Is 3:17
Therefore I will * you into Is 5:13
He will * a signal to the nations Is 5:26
I * as a messenger to my people? Is 6:8
And I said, "Lord, I'll go! * Is 6:8
forests, too, and * a vast cloud of Is 9:18

(SEND Con't)
in that day when I * desolation Is 10:3
Lord of Hosts will * a plague among Is 10:16
The Lord of Hosts will * his Is 10:26
MOAB'S REFUGEES AT Sela * lambs Is 16:1
them, he will * them a Savior—and Is 19:20
For the Lord will * a mighty Is 28:2
but I will * heavy judgment upon Is 29:2
In his wisdom, he will * great Is 31:2
guarantee: I will * the sun Is 38:8
For your sakes I will * an Is 43:14
I will strengthen you and * you Is 45:5
the dark. I * good times and bad. Is 45:7
also is my Word. I * it out and it Is 55:11
to, and prosper everywhere I * it. Is 55:11
Presidents and kings will * you Is 60:10
I will * great troubles upon Is 66:4
says the Lord, for I will * it; Is 66:12
them, and I will * those Is 66:19
will go wherever I * you and speak Jer 1:7
gods are nothing. * to the west to Jer 2:10,11
island of Cyprus; * to the east to Jer 2:10,11
cities!" * a signal from Jer 4:6
At that time he will * a burning Jer 4:11,12
So I will * upon them the wild Jer 5:6
Shall I not * my vengeance on Jer 5:9
Sound the alarm in Tekoa; * up a Jer 6:1
And I will * you into exile, Jer 7:15
For I will * these enemy troops Jer 8:17
"The Lord of Hosts says: * for Jer 9:17,18
The nobles * servants for water Jer 14:3
you will surely * them peace, that Jer 14:13
I didn't * them or tell them to Jer 14:14
though I did not * them, who say no Jer 14:15
with a meal, or * them a cup of Jer 16:7
hand, and I will * you away as Jer 17:4
For the Lord will * terror on Jer 20:4
And I will * a terrible plague Jer 21:6
I will * disaster upon the leaders Jer 23:1
I did not * them and they have no Jer 23:32
And I will * massacre and famine Jer 24:10
to whom I * you drink from it. Jer 25:15
Then * messages to the kings of Jer 27:3
I will * war, famine and disease Jer 27:8
land and * you far away to perish. Jer 27:10
stay there until I * for them. Jer 27:22
sent them, I will * war, famine Jer 29:16,17
* an open letter to all the Jer 29:31
you when I didn't * him, and has Jer 29:31
I call, I will * upon Judah and Jer 35:17
them and * them scurrying home. Jer 37:7
I beg you, don't * me back to that Jer 37:20
begged me not to * you back to the Jer 38:26
* him away to Babylon as a slave. Jer 39:7
"* this word to Ebed-melech the Jer 39:16
to whom we * you with our plea. Jer 42:6
said, when he will * troublers to Jer 48:12
I will * against them one who Jer 49:19
Lord will * him to destroy them. Jer 49:28
* out a call for archers to come Jer 50:29
I will * against them an invader Jer 50:44
on your walls; * out an ambush, for Jer 51:12
whenever I * my people a warning, Eze 3:17
winds and * the sword after them. Eze 12:14
God did not * you. Eze 13:6
saying, 'God will * peace,' when Eze 13:10
food supply and * famine to destroy Eze 14:13
"When I * an invasion of Eze 14:15
And I will * my jealousy against Eze 23:25
I will * you to the pit of hell Eze 26:20
kingdom of Israel * merchants with Eze 27:17
and Chilmad all * their wares. Eze 27:23
I will * an epidemic of disease Eze 28:23
At that time I will * swift Eze 30:9
"The Lord God says: I will * a Eze 32:3
mighty nations. * them down to the Eze 32:18
rains but * them in their seasons. Eze 34:26
and * us back to our own land Dan 9:3
lands, I will * her off to exile. Hos 8:10
Therefore, I will * down fire Hos 8:14
the north and * them far away; Joe 2:20
Now in return I will * fire upon Amo 2:2
So I will * them into captivity Amo 5:25,26,27
Don't * them this plague! Amo 7:2
God, "when I will * a famine on Amo 8:11
the ocean, I will * the sea-serpent Amo 9:3
You are to * your armies against Ob 1:1
to * them to the bottom. Jon 1:4
whom I will *. Zec 3:8
nations that * their armies to Zec 12:2
And the Lord will * a plague on Zec 14:12
name, then I will * terrible Mal 2:1
"LISTEN: I WILL * my messenger Mal 3:1
"See, I will * you another Mal 4:5
declare, 'God will * his angels to Mt 4:6
* us into that herd of pigs." Mt 8:31
will * my angels and they will Mt 13:41
in the desert; * the crowds away so Mt 14:15
Then his disciples urged him to * Mt 15:23
I don't want to * them away Mt 15:32
They decided to * some of their Mt 22:16
"I will * you prophets, and wise Mt 23:34
And I shall * forth my angels Mt 24:31
whip you and * you off to the Mt 24:51
us, and he would * them instantly? Mt 26:53
announced that he would * his Son Mk 1:2
to * them to some distant land. Mk 5:10
above the lake. "* us into those Mk 5:12
And if I * them home without Mk 8:3
Don't * them away! Mk 10:14
But if we say God didn't * him, Mk 11:32
And I will * out the angels to Mk 13:27
Their decision was to * Jesus Mk 15:1
say that God will * his angels to Lk 4:9,10,11
and urged him to * the people away Lk 9:12
of the harvest to * out more Lk 10:2
its holiness; * your Kingdom soon. Lk 11:2
about you: 'I will * prophets and Lk 11:49
far away, he will * a truce team to Lk 14:32
'have some pity! * Lazarus over Lk 16:24
then please * him to my father's Lk 16:27
and * it hurtling into the sea! Lk 17:6
Never * them away! Lk 18:16,17
'I know! I'll * my cherished son. Lk 20:13
"And now I will * the Holy Lk 24:49
God did not * his Son into the Jn 3:17
"But I will * you the Jn 15:26
If I do, he will—for I will * him Jn 16:7
the authority to * the Holy Act 2:33
away your sins and * you wonderful Act 3:19
of the Lord and * Jesus your Act 3:20
preaching, and * your healing Act 4:30
Come, I will * you to Egypt.' Act 7:34
So I will * you into captivity Act 7:43
by God! Now * some men to Joppa to Act 10:5,6
instructed him to * for Peter to Act 10:22
by God! Now * some men to Joppa Act 10:32
and told him to * messengers to Act 11:13
So the believers decided to * Act 11:29
voted to * delegates to Antioch Act 15:22
our decision, to * to you these two Act 15:25
* you far away to the Gentiles!' Act 22:21
him, I decided to * him on to you Act 23:30
have no alternative but to * him. Act 25:25
seem reasonable to * a prisoner to Act 25:27
Yes, I am going to * you to the Act 26:17
you can * me on my way again. Rom 15:24
All the churches here * you their Rom 16:16
* you their good wishes. Rom 16:21
letter for Paul, * my greetings Rom 16:22
For Christ didn't * me to 1Co 1:17
that God would * men from other 1Co 14:21
* to the Christians in Jerusalem; 1Co 16:1
When I come I will * your loving 1Co 16:3
* me on to my next destination. 1Co 16:6
but * him back to me happy with 1Co 16:11
The churches here in Asia * you 1Co 16:19
Aquila and Priscilla * you their 1Co 16:19
you could * me on my way to Judea. 2Co 1:15,16
ready to * an offering a year ago. 2Co 9:2
All the Christians here * you 2Co 13:13
told Abraham to * away the Gal 4:30
If the Lord is willing, I will * Php 2:19
I hope to * him to you just as Php 2:23
Meanwhile, I thought I ought to * Php 2:25
been anxious to * what you could, Php 4:10
the brothers with me * their Php 4:21
in Athens and * Timothy, our 1Th 3:2,3
Lord Jesus * us back to you again. 1Th 3:11
and finally * them to hell itself. 1Ti 6:10
I am planning to * either Artemas Tit 3:12
did God need to * Christ as a Heb 7:11
are here with me * you their love. Heb 13:24,25
I am glad when you * them on 3Jn 1:6
Friends here * their love, and 3Jn 1:15
you see, and * your letter to the Rev 1:11
to blood, and to * every kind of Rev 11:6

SENDING
So they told her good-bye, * Gen 24:59
am the one who is * you: When you Ex 3:12
"See, I am * an Angel before you Ex 23:20
its slavery by * terrible plagues, Deu 4:34
from the Midianites! I am * you!" Ju 6:14
Jesse responded by * not only 1Sa 16:20
Then David wasted no time in * 1Sa 25:39
* my brother Amnon instead?" 2Sa 13:26
fathers were. I am * you a present 1Ki 15:19
you that you are * me to my death? 1Ki 18:9
and the god who answers by * fire 1Ki 18:24
who answered by * down fire from 1Ch 21:26
"I am * you a master 2Ch 2:13
of the nation and * back great 2Ch 24:23
frighten them by * agents to tell Ez 4:4,5
by * back this message to them: Neh 6:3
and * us into darkness and death. Ps 44:19
his anger, * sorrow and trouble. Ps 78:49
* a mighty wind to divide it into Is 11:15
hurl you away, * you into Is 22:17
So God will punish them by * Is 28:11
* them my prophets, day after day. Jer 7:25
Now I am * for many fishermen to Jer 16:16
my wrath. I am * for hunters to Jer 16:16
See, the Lord is * a furious Jer 23:19
God has been * me his messages. Jer 25:2,3
I am * terrible wars upon you." Jer 25:27
he said, "I am * you to the nation Eze 2:3
But I am * you to give them my Eze 2:4
of dust, I am * you to the people Eze 3:4
I am not * you to some far-off Eze 3:5
I am * you to the people of Eze 3:7
to the winds, * the sword of the Eze 5:12
out my fury by * an epidemic of Eze 14:19
against Babylon, * ambassadors to Eze 17:15
for * them away to exile, and Eze 39:28
He will reply, "See, I am * you Joe 2:19
For I, the Lord, am * disaster Amo 3:6
the Lord is * them. Mic 6:9
No, you were * your chariots of Hab 3:8,9
Then the Lord told them (again * Hag 1:13
"I am * this curse into the home Zec 5:4
had disobeyed him. * soldiers to Mt 2:16
"I am * you out as sheep among Mt 10:16
He is * us a Mighty Savior from Lk 1:69
say, 'Look! I am * my messenger Lk 7:27
Go now, and remember that I am * Lk 10:3
the world, I am * them into the Jn 17:18
has sent me, even so I am * you." Jn 20:21
he did such as * you rain and good Act 14:17
that God was * us to preach the Act 16:10
The believers acted at once, * Act 17:14
wife, a Jewess. * for Paul, they Act 24:24
and now he is * us out around the Rom 1:5
love for us by * Christ to die for Rom 5:8
am * Timothy—to help you do this. 1Co 4:17
God guided them by * a cloud that 1Co 10:1
We should never regret his * it. 2Co 7:10
I am * another well-known 2Co 8:18
And I am * you still another 2Co 8:22
But I am * these men just to be 2Co 9:3
by * Jesus Christ to die for us. Eph 1:5
secret reason for * Christ, a plan Eph 1:9
I am * him to you for just this Eph 6:22
Now I am * him home again, for Php 2:26
I am also * Onesimus, a faithful Col 4:9
I am * him back to you, and with Phm 1:12
instead of * someone with the rank Heb 7:11
it, "See, I am * Christ to be the 1Pe 2:6
I am * this note to you through 1Pe 5:12
I intend to keep * these reminders 2Pe 1:13,14
he loved us by * his only Son into 1Jn 4:9
"You are just in * this judgment, Rev 16:5

SENDS
time when the Lord * rain, and the 1Ki 17:14
"This man * me a leper to heal! 2Ki 5:7
number. He * the rain upon the Job 5:10
When he * death to snatch a man Job 9:12
a desert; he * the storms, and Job 12:15
he counts me as an enemy. He * Job 19:12
above * calamity on those who do. Job 31:2,3
"Or, God * sickness and pain, Job 33:19
the earth. He * the storms Job 37:13
heaven and * great victories. Ps 20:6
and * them rich harvests of grain. Ps 65:9
of the trees. He * rain upon the Ps 104:13
mark the days. He * the night and Ps 104:20
the earth and * the lightning to Ps 135:7
* the winds from his treasuries. Ps 135:7
with clouds, * down the showers and Ps 147:8
your children. He * peace across Ps 147:14
He * his orders to the world. Ps 147:15
How swiftly his word flies. He * Ps 147:16
Land that * ambassadors in fast Is 18:2
I am the one who * the darkness Is 50:3
and fall and * the harvest times, Jer 5:23,24
upon the earth; he * the lightning Jer 10:13
God of Israel, * you this message: Jer 27:4
the God of Israel, * this message Jer 29:4
but a gadfly * her running—a gadfly Jer 46:20,21
Edom * her traders to buy your Eze 27:16
For the rains he * are tokens of Joe 2:23
"The city that * a thousand men to Amo 5:3
The city that * a hundred, only Amo 5:3
and the good, and * rain on the Mt 5:45
and stones all those God * to her! Mt 23:37
important than the one who * him. Jn 13:16
But when the Father * the Jn 14:26
tell them unless someone * him? Rom 10:15
Erastus, the city treasurer, * Rom 16:23
as a prisoner, * you his love, and Col 4:10
Jesus Justus also * his love. Col 4:11
of Christ Jesus, * you his love. Col 4:12
Dear doctor Luke * his love, and Col 4:14
Eubulus * you greetings, and so 2Ti 4:21
Everybody here * greetings. Tit 3:15
Christ Jesus, * you his greetings. Phm 1:23
And when God * a new kind of Heb 7:12,13,14
—she is your sister in the Lord—* 1Pe 5:13

SENEH
which had been named Bozez and *. 1Sa 14:4

SENIOR
assistants—all the * officers of Gen 50:7

SENIR
while the Amorites called it '*.' Deu 3:9

(SENIR Con't)
Baal-hermon, *, and Mount Hermon. 1Ch 5:23
from the peak of * and Hermon." Sol 4:8f
a ship built of finest fir from *. Eze 27:5

SENNACHERIB
Hezekiah, King * of Assyria 2Ki 18:13
And this is my reply to King *: 2Ki 19:21
Then King * returned to Nineveh; 2Ki 19:36
Hezekiah, King * of Assyria invaded 2Ch 32:1
When it was clear that * was 2Ch 32:2
Then King * of Assyria, while 2Ch 32:9
"King * of Assyria asks, 'Do you 2Ch 32:10
King * also sent letters scorning 2Ch 32:17
and generals! So * returned home in 2Ch 32:21
dynasty against * of Assyria. Is 30:2f
Hezekiah's reign, *, king of Is 36:1
Look at this letter from King *, Is 37:16,17
prayer against *, Assyria's king. Is 37:21
Then *, king of Assyria, Is 37:37
the east against *, so he was Is 39:1f
of Jerusalem from *, king of Jer 21:1f
Assyrian Emperor * invaded Judah Hos 1:7f

SENSE
used here in the * of his created, Gen 6:1f
Thank God for your good *! 1Sa 25:33
this made good *, so he followed Est 1:21
Speak some * if you want us to Job 18:2
because of their lack of good *. Job 36:12
but I have * enough to follow you. Ps 119:70
now give me * to heed your laws. Ps 119:73
therefore give me common * to Ps 119:125
give me the common * you Ps 119:169
will be given wisdom and good *. Pro 2:1
He grants good * to the Pro 2:7,8
You will be given the * to stay Pro 2:11,12,13
*, then trust the Lord completely; Pro 3:4,5
and common * is happier than the Pro 3:13,14,15
and doing right—and common *. Pro 3:21
good judgment and common *! Pro 4:5
common * and good judgment. Pro 4:7
man lacking common *, walking at Pro 7:7
ones, let me show you common *! Pro 8:4,5
give good advice and common *. Pro 8:14,15
Men with common * are admired Pro 10:13
is destroyed by lack of common *. Pro 10:21
a man with good * holds his Pro 11:12
a man with good *, but a man with a Pro 12:8
A man with good * is appreciated. Pro 13:15
easily to the man with common *. Pro 14:6
of men of common *, but it must Pro 14:33
by his common *, and a pleasant Pro 16:21
A rebuke to a man of common * is Pro 17:10
Good * is far more valuable than Pro 20:15
from common * will end up dead! Pro 21:16
if you become a man of common *. Pro 23:15,16
to all the good * you can get. Pro 23:23
through common *, and profits Pro 24:3,4
will be full of * and Is 32:4
this foolishness and talk some *! Jer 15:19
apparently not in this deeper *. Jn 16:5f
A deep * of awe was on them all, Act 2:43
Get some * and quit your 1Co 15:34
a person has a wrong * of values. Tit 3:11

SENSELESS
the guilt of his * murders from me 1Ki 2:31
Don't be like a * horse or mule Ps 32:9
It is * for you to work so hard Ps 127:2
It is * to pay tuition to educate Pro 17:16
Listen, O foolish, * people—you Jer 5:21

SENSES
him as though he had lost his *. Gen 19:14
they come to their * and turn to 1Ki 8:47
Then at last he came to his * 2Ch 33:12
of my people have lost their *; Jer 10:21
"When he finally came to his *, Lk 15:17
Then they will come to their * 2Ti 2:26

SENSIBLE
mouth. Be * and turn off the flow! Pro 10:19
A * son gladdens his father. Pro 15:20
* stay on the pathways of right. Pro 15:21
Wisdom is the main pursuit of * Pro 17:24
I will be if you turn out to be *! Pro 27:11
A * man watches for problems Pro 27:12
but with honest, * leaders there Pro 28:2
alert and *, and have enough poise Dan 1:3,4
to any faithful, * man whose master Lk 12:42,43,44
all such wise and * Christians! 1Co 4:10
as well as *, for then you will Col 4:6
and * in manner and clothing. 1Ti 2:9,10
They must be * men, and fair. Tit 1:8
they must be *, knowing and Tit 2:2
and to be * and clean minded, Tit 2:5
Your conversation should be so * Tit 2:8

SENSITIVE
were sore and * to every move they Gen 34:25

SENT
the Lord God hadn't * any rain; Gen 2:5
of Eden, and * him out to farm the Gen 3:23
in the boat! He * a wind to blow Gen 8:1
Meanwhile he * out a dove to see Gen 8:8
But the Lord * a terrible plague Gen 12:17
And Pharaoh * them out of the Gen 12:20
and God has * us to destroy it." Gen 19:13
Then King Abimelech * for her, Gen 20:2
And when God * me traveling far Gen 20:13
and * her away with their son. Gen 21:14
his concubines and * them off into Gen 25:6
you and have * you away in peace; Gen 26:29
Then Isaac * them happily home Gen 26:31
it to Rebekah. She * for Jacob and Gen 27:42
So Isaac * Jacob away, and he Gen 28:5
and mother had * Jacob to Gen 28:6,7,8
So one day Jacob * for Rachel and Gen 31:4
would have * me off without a penny Gen 31:42
Jacob now * messengers to his Gen 32:3
I have * these messengers to Gen 32:5
So the presents were * on Gen 32:21
to kill her she * this message to Gen 38:25
staff. He * for his wine taster and Gen 40:20
Pharaoh * at once for Joseph. Gen 41:14
for food, and he * them to Joseph. Gen 41:55
for God did it! He * me here ahead Gen 45:5
God has * me here to keep you Gen 45:7
Yes, it was God who * me here, Gen 45:8
of silver! He * his father ten Gen 45:23
So he * his brothers off. Gen 45:24
had * him, his spirit revived. Gen 45:27
Jacob * Judah on ahead to tell Gen 46:28
So they * him this message: Gen 50:16,17
the reeds and * one of the maids to Ex 2:5
fathers' God has * me, they will Ex 3:13
"Just say, 'I Am has * me!' Ex 3:14
and Jacob, has * me to you.' Ex 3:15
that God had * them, and when they Ex 4:31
That same day Pharaoh * this Ex 5:6
to prove that God has * you; Ex 7:9
the Hebrews, has * me back to Ex 7:16
concerning the frogs he had *. Ex 8:12
Pharaoh * to see whether it was Ex 9:7
* thunder and hail and lightning. Ex 9:23
Then Pharaoh * for Moses and Ex 9:27
Then Pharaoh * an urgent call for Ex 10:16
the Lord, and he * a very strong Ex 10:19
You * forth your anger, and it Ex 15:7
to him (for he had * her home), Ex 18:2
Then he * some of the young men Ex 24:5
And the Lord * a great plague Ex 32:35
So Moses * a message throughout Ex 36:4-7
the terrible fire the Lord has *. Lev 10:6
Lord's and which is to be * away. Lev 16:8
it shall then be * out into the Lev 16:10
The Lord * a wind that brought Num 11:31
and * these twelve tribal leaders: Num 13:3-15
Moses * them out with these Num 13:17
in the land you * us to see, and it Num 13:27
that Jehovah has * me to do all Num 16:28
then Jehovah has not * me. Num 16:29
While Moses was at Kadesh he * Num 20:14
he heard us and * an Angel who Num 20:16
So the Lord * poisonous snakes Num 21:6
Israel now * ambassadors to King Num 21:21
country, Moses * spies to look over Num 21:31,32
So King Balak * messengers to Num 22:5,6
The messengers he * were some of Num 22:7
This time he * a larger number of Num 22:15
so he * an angel to stand in the Num 22:22,23
men were * to battle by Moses. Num 31:4,5
fathers did! I * them from Num 32:8
of Kedemoth I * ambassadors to King Deu 2:26
terrors the Lord * upon them—your Deu 7:19
the Lord will have * upon it. Deu 29:22
THEN JOSHUA * two spies from the Jos 2:1
"They have been * by the Israeli Jos 2:3
the spies * to Jericho by Joshua. Jos 6:25
defeat, Joshua * some of his men to Jos 7:2
*—and they were soundly defeated. Jos 7:4
So Joshua * some men to search Jos 7:22
for Ai, Joshua * thirty thousand of Jos 8:3,4
That night Joshua * another five Jos 8:11,12,13
themselves. They * ambassadors to Jos 9:3,4,5
of Jerusalem * messengers to Jos 10:3
The men of Gibeon hurriedly * Jos 10:6
had happened, he * urgent messages Jos 11:1
and Moses had * us from Jos 14:7
I was when Moses * us on that Jos 14:11
So Joshua blessed them and * them Jos 22:6
As Joshua * away these troops, Jos 22:7,8
First, however, they * a Jos 22:13
"Then I * Moses and Aaron to Jos 24:5
And I * hornets ahead of you to Jos 24:12
Then Joshua * the people away to Jos 24:28
First they * scouts, who Ju 1:22,23
to the Lord, he * them a savior, Ju 3:15
of Gilgal, he * his companions on Ju 3:17,18,19
the prophet he * to them was this: Ju 6:8
He also * messengers throughout Ju 6:35
had among them, he * them home, Ju 7:8,9
Then Gideon * for the troops of Ju 7:23
Gideon also * messengers Ju 7:24
was furious. He * messengers to Ju 9:31
The leaders of Gilead * for Ju 11:5
Then Jephthah * messengers to Ju 11:12
the Red Sea, they * a message to Ju 11:1
Then Israel * messengers to King Ju 11:1
army at Zaphon and * this message Ju 12:1
The Philistines in turn * a huge Ju 15:
* for the five Philistine leaders. Ju 16:1
twelve parts and * one piece to Ju 19:2
THEN THE ENTIRE nation of Israel * Ju 20:
twelve pieces and * the pieces Ju 20:6
Then messengers were * to the Ju 20:12
So they * twelve thousand of Ju 21:10,11,12
Then Israel * a peace delegation Ju 21:13
back on me and * such calamity!" Ru 1:21
So they * for the Ark of the Lord 1Sa 4:4
So they * the Ark to Ekron, but 1Sa 5:10
and was not * by God at all." 1Sa 6:9
which had been * by the Philistines 1Sa 6:17
So they * messengers to the 1Sa 6:21
So Samuel agreed and * the men 1Sa 8:22
away, so he * Saul and a servant to 1Sa 9:3
Then Samuel * the people home 1Sa 10:25
into pieces and * messengers to 1Sa 11:7
So he * the messengers back to 1Sa 11:9
to the Lord, he * Moses and Aaron 1Sa 12:8
Then the Lord * Gideon, Barak, 1Sa 12:11
and the Lord * thunder and rain; 1Sa 12:18
The rest of the army was * home. 1Sa 13:2
of Israel, Saul * the Israeli army 1Sa 14:47
Saul * a message to the Kenites, 1Sa 15:6
And he * you on an errand and 1Sa 15:18
So Jesse * for him. 1Sa 16:12
the Lord had * a tormenting spirit 1Sa 16:14
So Saul * messengers to Jesse, 1Sa 16:19
King Saul, and the king * for him. 1Sa 17:31
Saul * troops to watch David's 1Sa 19:11
he * soldiers to capture him; 1Sa 19:20
had happened, he * other soldiers, 1Sa 19:21
"The king has * me on a private 1Sa 21:2
his sheep, he * ten of his young 1Sa 25:5
Now I have * my men to ask for a 1Sa 25:8
Abigail, "David * men from the 1Sa 25:14
I didn't see the messengers you *. 1Sa 25:25
who has * you to meet me today! 1Sa 25:32
Saul's arrival and * out spies to 1Sa 26:3,4
* me away to worship heathen gods. 1Sa 26:19
When he arrived at Ziklag, he * 1Sa 30:26
The gifts were * to the elders 1Sa 30:27-31
off his armor and * the wonderful 1Sa 31:9
buried Saul, he * them this 2Sa 2:5
Then Abner * messengers to David 2Sa 3:12
David then * this message to 2Sa 3:14
king and had been * away in peace, 2Sa 3:23
Then Joab * messengers to catch 2Sa 3:26
Then King Hiram of Tyre * cedar 2Sa 5:11
WHEN THE LORD finally * peace upon 2Sa 7:1
of Hadadezer, he * his son Joram 2Sa 8:10
So King David * for 2Sa 9:5,6
So David * ambassadors to 2Sa 10:2
David has * them to spy out the 2Sa 10:3
and * them home half naked. 2Sa 10:4
about this, he * Joab and the 2Sa 10:7,8
wars begin, David * Joab and the 2Sa 11:1
evening bath. He * to find out who 2Sa 11:3
Then David * for her and when 2Sa 11:4
she * a message to inform him. 2Sa 11:5
he * a present to him at his home. 2Sa 11:8
When Joab * a report to David of 2Sa 11:18
was over, David * for her and 2Sa 11:27
SO THE LORD * the prophet Nathan 2Sa 12:1
the baby, and * congratulations 2Sa 12:25
Literally, "Jehovah * word by 2Sa 12:25f
of Ammon. Joab * messengers to tell 2Sa 12:26,27
David agreed, and * word to 2Sa 13:7
come, though he * his thanks. 2Sa 13:25
see Absalom, he * for a woman of 2Sa 14:2,3
Yes, Joab * me and told me what 2Sa 14:19
So the king * for Joab and told 2Sa 14:21
seen the king, he * for Joab to 2Sa 14:29
Absalom * for him again, but 2Sa 14:29
But while he was there, he * 2Sa 15:10
the sacrifice, he * for Ahithophel, 2Sa 15:12
Then David * Zadok and Abiathar 2Sa 19:11,12
as one man. They * word to the 2Sa 19:14
At the same time he * a request 2Sa 21:12,13,14
So the Lord * a plague upon 2Sa 24:15
"The king * him to Gihon with 1Ki 1:44,45
So King Solomon * Benaiah to 1Ki 2:25
he * Benaiah to execute him. 1Ki 2:29
The king now * for Shime-i and 1Ki 2:36,37
and returned, he * for him and 1Ki 2:42
of those lands * taxes to Solomon 1Ki 4:21
And kings from many lands * 1Ki 4:34
king of Israel, he * ambassadors to 1Ki 5:1
Then he * this reply to Solomon: 1Ki 5:8
in return Solomon * him an annual 1Ki 5:11
Then the Lord * this message to 1Ki 6:11,12
Afterwards Solomon * the people 1Ki 8:66
For Hiram had * gold to Solomon 1Ki 9:14
When King Rehoboam * Adoram (who 1Ki 12:18
But God * this message to 1Ki 12:22
Ben-hadad agreed and * his armies 1Ki 15:20
The message was * to Baasha and 1Ki 16:4-7

NT Con't)
f Baal, she * this message to 1Ki 19:2
apital. He * this message into 1Ki 20:2,3
hen the Syrian king * this 1Ki 20:10
he city officials then * word 1Ki 21:14
njured. He * messengers to the 2Ki 1:2
Then he * an army captain with 2Ki 1:9
o the king * another captain 2Ki 1:11
Once more the king * fifty men, 2Ki 1:13
he Lord has * me to Jericho." 2Ki 2:4
as * me to the Jordan River." 2Ki 2:6,7
sraeli army and * this message to 2Ki 3:6,7,8
hen she * a message to her 2Ki 4:22
light, he * this message to him: 2Ki 5:8
Elisha * a messenger out to tell 2Ki 5:10
ny master has * me to tell you that 2Ki 5:22
he servants and * the men back. 2Ki 5:24
The king * a scout to see if 2Ki 6:10
So one night the king of Syria * 2Ki 6:14
hen * them home to their king. 2Ki 6:23
king * a messenger to summon him. 2Ki 6:32
murderer has * a man to kill me. 2Ki 6:32
found and the king * out two 2Ki 7:14
king of Syria, has * me to ask you 2Ki 8:8,9
So the king * out a second 2Ki 9:19
Ahab's sons, * him this message: 2Ki 10:5
them. He * messengers throughout 2Ki 10:20,21
the palace, and * it to Hazael. 2Ki 12:18
One day he * a message to King 2Ki 14:8
but his enemies * assassins and 2Ki 14:19
he drove out the Jews and * 2Ki 16:6
King Ahaz * a messenger to King 2Ki 16:7
royal vaults and * it as a payment 2Ki 16:8
made a sketch and * it back to 2Ki 16:10
Again and again the Lord had * 2Ki 17:13
arrived, the Lord * lions among 2Ki 17:25
Then they * a message to the king 2Ki 17:26
land, and he has * lions among us 2Ki 17:26
sued for peace and * this message 2Ki 18:14
king of Assyria * his field 2Ki 18:17
but instead he * a truce delegation 2Ki 18:18
Then the Assyrian general * this 2Ki 18:19
The Lord * us and told us, 'Go 2Ki 18:25
"Has my master * me to speak only 2Ki 18:27
Hasn't he * me to the people on 2Ki 18:27
the attack, he * back this message 2Ki 19:9
Then Isaiah * this message to 2Ki 19:20
of Babylon) * ambassadors with 2Ki 20:12
reign, King Josiah * his secretary 2Ki 22:3,4
"Tell the man who * you to me, 2Ki 22:15,16
THEN THE KING * for the elders and 2Ki 23:1
And the Lord * bands of 2Ki 24:2
when the Lord * the people of Judah 1Ch 6:4-15
After much discussion they * them 1Ch 12:19
18,000 were * for the express 1Ch 12:24-37
KING HIRAM OF Tyre * masons and 1Ch 14:1
army, he * his son Hadoram to 1Ch 18:10
So David * a message of sympathy 1Ch 19:2,3
* these men to honor your father! 1Ch 19:2,3
then he * them back to David in 1Ch 19:4
had happened, he * a message to his 1Ch 19:5
his mistake he * $2,000,000 1Ch 19:6
When David learned of this, he * 1Ch 19:8
* one group to engage the Syrians. 1Ch 19:10
to return to the one who * me.' 1Ch 21:12
So the Lord * a plague upon 1Ch 21:14
During the plague God * an angel 1Ch 21:15
Solomon * horse-traders to Egypt 2Ch 1:16
Solomon * an ambassador to King 2Ch 2:3
Then, on October 7, he * the 2Ch 7:10
Every three years the king * his 2Ch 9:21
* word to him of Solomon's death. 2Ch 10:2,3
Afterwards, when King Rehoboam * 2Ch 10:18
themselves he * Shemaiah to tell 2Ch 12:7
had secretly * part of his army 2Ch 13:13,14
* his troops to meet them there. 2Ch 14:9,10
program. He * out top government 2Ch 17:7,8,9
Then a proclamation was * to all 2Ch 24:9
again. God * prophets to bring 2Ch 24:19
So Amaziah * them home again to 2Ch 25:10
that had been * home raided several 2Ch 25:13
very angry and he * a prophet to 2Ch 25:15
KING HEZEKIAH NOW * letters 2Ch 30:1
matter, so they * a Passover 2Ch 30:5
city of Lachish, * ambassadors with 2Ch 32:9
King Sennacherib also * letters 2Ch 32:17
and the Lord * an angel who 2Ch 32:21
So God * the Assyrian armies, 2Ch 33:11
says, Tell the man who * you, 2Ch 34:23
king of Judah who * you to ask me 2Ch 34:26
But King Neco * ambassadors to 2Ch 35:21
of their fathers * his prophets 2Ch 36:15
they * to King Ar-ta-xerxes: Ez 4:11
that the Jews * to Jerusalem from Ez 4:12
The letter you * has been Ez 4:18
other officials * to King Darius: Ez 5:6
a decree has been * out concerning Ez 6:3
So King Darius * this message Ez 6:6
So I * for Eliezer, Ari-el, Ez 8:16
I also * for Joiarib and Ez 8:16
very wise men. I * them to Iddo, Ez 8:17
And God was good! He * us an Ez 8:18
God also * Hashabiah; Ez 8:19
(The king, I should add, had * Neh 2:9
the gates— they * me a message Neh 6:2
Four times they * the same Neh 6:4
and Tobiah * many threatening Neh 6:19
the night. You * your good Spirit Neh 9:20
in great mercy you * them saviors Neh 9:27
many years. You * your prophets to Neh 9:30
in Judah were * to live with the Neh 11:36
and I * some of my servants to Neh 13:19
properly * through his aides?" Est 1:13-15
counsel, and * letters to all of Est 1:22
They were then * by messengers Est 3:13
distressed and * clothing to him to Est 4:4
Then Esther * for Hathach, one Est 4:5
king's ring and * the letters by Est 8:9,10
these events, and * letters to the Est 9:20
In addition, letters were * to Est 9:29-31
he has * his poisoned arrows deep Job 6:4
"He has * away my brothers, and Job 19:13
they chose. You * widows away Job 22:9
They are * into the desert to Job 24:5
than face the judgment * by God; Job 31:23
of evil that God * this suffering. Job 36:21
The wicked shall be * away to Ps 9:17
* by the Angel of the Lord. Ps 35:5
of all the evil you have *. Ps 44:13
on our backs. You * troops to ride Ps 66:12
of Israel. You * abundant rain Ps 68:9,10
they forgot the plagues he * Ps 78:43
drink, and how he * vast swarms of Ps 78:45
back and * them to eternal shame. Ps 78:66
who was * to anoint David as king. Ps 89:19f
Then he * Joseph as a slave to Ps 105:17
Then the king * for him and set Ps 105:20
But God * Moses as his Ps 105:26
and he * thick darkness through the Ps 105:28
Instead of rain he * down Ps 105:32
They asked for meat and he * Ps 105:40
* them leanness in their souls. Ps 106:15
Or, "but * a plague to punish Ps 106:15f
the one who is coming, the one * Ps 118:26
the wines, and * out her maidens Pro 9:3
messenger will be * against him." Pro 17:11f
rather than to be * back to the end Pro 25:6,7
with me and * me out into the sun Sol 1:6
Not long after this, the Lord * Is 7:10
AGAIN THE LORD * me a message: Is 8:1
it is because I have not * them; Is 8:20
not know that it is I who * him. Is 10:7
were when God * fire from heaven; Is 13:19
And this is the message * to you: Is 18:2
The Lord has * a spirit of Is 19:14
king of Assyria, * the Is 20:1
Think of all the colonists you * Is 23:7
Then he * his personal Is 36:2
Meanwhile he * Eliakim his prime Is 37:2
Upon hearing this, he * Is 37:8,9
Then Isaiah, the son of Amoz, * Is 37:21
You have * your messengers to Is 37:24
So the Lord * another message to Is 38:4
For he himself has * this Is 38:15
son of Baladan) * Hezekiah a Is 39:1
he * them nor listen to his laws. Is 42:24
I have * him on this errand and I Is 48:15
his Spirit have * me (with this Is 48:16
I divorced her and * her away? Is 50:1
will not be * by me to punish you. Is 54:15
He has * me to comfort the Is 61:1
He has * me to tell those who Is 61:2
See, the Lord has * his Is 62:11
Where is the God who * his Holy Is 63:11
but now he has * the fury of your Jer 11:16
* them as slaves for punishment. Jer 16:14,15
THEN KING ZEDEKIAH * Pashhur Jer 21:1
wherever I have * them, and bring Jer 23:3
I have not * these prophets, yet Jer 23:21
represent the exiles * to Babylon. Jer 24:4,5
the years, God has * you his Jer 25:4
it—every nation God had * me to; Jer 25:17
the prophets—for I * them again and Jer 26:5
"The Lord * me," he said, "to Jer 26:12
true that the Lord * me to speak Jer 26:15
saying, the king * to kill him. Jer 26:21
Then King Jehoiakim * Elnathan Jer 26:22
I have not * them, says the Jer 27:15
prove that God has really * him. Jer 28:9
the Lord has not * you, and the Jer 28:15
the people. He * the letter with Jer 29:3
I have not * them, says the Lord. Jer 29:9
nations where I * you and bring you Jer 29:14
say the Lord has * them, I will Jer 29:15
the priest, and * copies to all the Jer 29:25
That is why you have * all this Jer 32:23
Just as I have * all these Jer 32:42
Lord * him this second message: Jer 33:1
I have * you prophet after Jer 35:15
So Jeremiah * for Baruch (son of Jer 36:4
the officials * Jehudi (son of Jer 36:14,15
The king * Jehudi to get the Jer 36:21
Nevertheless, King Zedekiah * Jer 37:3
Then the Lord * this message to Jer 37:6
king of Judah, who * you to ask me Jer 37:7
King Zedekiah * for him to come to Jer 37:17
One day King Zedekiah * for Jer 38:14
guard, and his men * the remnant of Jer 39:9
They * soldiers to bring Jer 39:14
who were being * to Babylon, but Jer 40:1
the Ammonites, had * Ishmael (son Jer 40:13,14
to them: "You * me to the Lord, Jer 42:9
For you were deceitful when you * Jer 42:20
ever known. I * my servants, the Jer 44:4
the Lord has * it on an errand? Jer 47:7
He has * a messenger to call the Jer 49:14
five years after that he * Jer 52:30
He has * fire from heaven that Lam 1:13
* his arrows deep within my heart. Lam 3:13
their homes and * away into exile. Eze 12:11
along, this tree * its roots and Eze 17:7
accused and * to their death. Eze 22:9
men pictured, so she * messengers Eze 23:16
"You even * away to distant Eze 23:40
rejoiced in the riches you * them. Eze 27:33
* to demolish the land. Eze 30:11
When Pharaoh Hophra * an army to Eze 30:21f
on every side and * you away as Eze 36:3
why Israel was * away to exile—it Eze 39:23
was furious, and * out orders to Dan 2:12
then he * messages to all the Dan 3:2
Abednego, for he * his angel to Dan 3:28
the king, which he * to people of Dan 4:1
And so God * those fingers to Dan 5:24,25
"My God has * his angel," he Dan 6:22
prophets, whom you * again and Dan 9:6
to you, for God has * me to you." Dan 10:11
that very day I was * here to Dan 10:12
"I WAS THE one * to strengthen Dan 11:1
of Antiochus III, * Heliodorus to Dan 11:20f
as the king who * a tax collector Dan 11:20
like dew. I * my prophets to warn Hos 6:5
Feast. I * my prophets to warn you Hos 12:10
—my great destroying army that I * Joe 2:25
For she * my people into exile, Amo 1:6
"I * you hunger," says the Amo 4:6
the harvest. I * rain on one city, Amo 4:7
"I * blight and mildew on your Amo 4:9
the Lord. "I * you plagues like Amo 4:10
and Israel will be * far away into Amo 7:11
Then Amaziah * orders to Amos, Amo 7:12
"that God has * an ambassador to Ob 1:1
The Lord * this message to Jonah, Jon 1:1
our fault—you have * this storm Jon 1:14
And the king and his nobles * Jon 3:7
our land and * us far away, and Mic 2:4
Lord" will live where they are *. Mic 2:5
you will be * far away into exile Mic 4:10
year, the Lord * them this message Hag 2:1
me, "The Lord has * them to patrol Zec 1:10
"The Lord of Glory has * me Zec 2:8
it was the Lord of Hosts who * me. Zec 2:9
the Lord of Hosts who * me to you. Zec 2:11,12
city of Bethel had * a group of men Zec 7:2
know it was I who * you this Mal 2:4
Then Herod * a private message to Mt 2:7
Jesus * them out with these Mt 10:5
they are welcoming God who * me. Mt 10:40
seventy others and * them two and Mt 11:1f
was doing, so he * his disciples to Mt 11:2
the woman, "I was * to help the Mt 15:24
Then Jesus * the people home and Mt 15:39
"Then the angry king * the man Mt 18:34
and * them out to work. Mt 20:2
for jobs, so he * them also into Mt 20:4
of Olives, Jesus * two of them into Mt 21:1
"Was John the Baptist * from Mt 21:25
And if we deny that God * him, Mt 21:26
grape harvest he * his agents to Mt 21:34
"Then he * a larger group of his Mt 21:36
Finally the owner * his son, Mt 21:37
was ready he * messengers to notify Mt 22:3
So he * other servants to tell Mt 22:4
"Then the angry king * out his Mt 22:7
the one * to you from God." Mt 23:39
clubs, * by the Jewish leaders. Mt 26:47
Then they * him in chains to Mt 27:2
Pilate's wife * him this message: Mt 27:19
was developing, he * for a bowl of Mt 27:24
teaching, and they * word for him Mk 3:31,32
together and * them out two by two, Mk 6:7
For Herod had * soldiers to Mk 6:17,18
So he * one of his bodyguards to Mk 6:27
and afterwards he * them home. Mk 8:8,9
Jesus * him home to his family. Mk 8:26
is welcoming my Father who * me!" Mk 9:37
* two of his disciples on ahead. Mk 11:1
Was he * by God, or not? Mk 11:30
"If we reply that God * him, Mk 11:31
At grape-picking time he * one Mk 12:2
man and * him back empty-handed. Mk 12:3
"The owner then * another of his Mk 12:4
The next man he * was killed; Mk 12:5

(SENT Con't)
He finally * him, thinking they Mk 12:6
But they * other religious and Mk 12:13
supper. He * two of them into Mk 14:13
'Our Master * us to see the room Mk 14:14
swords and clubs, * out by the Mk 14:43
It was he who * me to you with Lk 1:19
The following month God * the Lk 1:26
* the rich away with empty hands. Lk 1:53
shall see the Savior * from God.' Lk 3:6
he has * me to heal the Lk 4:18,19
yet Elijah was not * to them. Lk 4:25,26
too, for that is why I was *." Lk 4:43
about Jesus, he * some respected Lk 7:3
house, the captain * some friends Lk 7:6,7,8
John about it, he * two of his Lk 7:19
if God had really * him, he would Lk 7:39
Then he * them away to tell Lk 9:2
for me is caring for God who * me. Lk 9:48
One day he * messengers ahead to Lk 9:52
disciples and * them on ahead in Lk 10:1
me are rejecting God who * me." Lk 10:16
of Nineveh that God had * him. Lk 11:29,30
that God has * me to these people. Lk 11:29,30
The city that stones those * to Lk 13:34
and healed him and * him away. Lk 14:4
feast and * out many invitations. Lk 14:16
When all was ready, he * his Lk 14:17
But if someone is * to them from Lk 16:30
hated him and * him their Lk 19:14
of Olives, he * two disciples Lk 19:29
"Was John * by God, or was he Lk 20:4
But if we say John was not * Lk 20:6
When harvest time came, he * one Lk 20:10
But the tenants beat him up and * Lk 20:10
Then he * another, but the same Lk 20:11
and * away without collecting. Lk 20:11
A third man was * and the same Lk 20:12
opportunity, they * secret agents Lk 20:20
enemy weapons, or * away as exiles Lk 21:24
Jesus * Peter and John ahead to Lk 22:8
Then Jesus asked them, "When I * Lk 22:35
on him, they * him back to Pilate. Lk 23:11
conclusion and * him back to Lk 23:15
God * John the Baptist as a Jn 1:6,7
* priests and assistant priests Jn 1:19
give an answer to those who * us. Jn 1:22
Then those who were * by the Jn 1:24,25
at the time God * me to baptize he Jn 1:33
that God has * you to teach us. Jn 3:1
For this one—* by God—speaks Jn 3:33,34
* me, and from finishing his work. Jn 4:34
else reaps. I * you to reap where Jn 4:38
God's Son, whom he * to you, then Jn 5:23
in God who * me has eternal life, Jn 5:24
who * me and is not merely my own. Jn 5:30
prove that the Father has * me. Jn 5:36
one * to you with God's message. Jn 5:38
those who aren't * from him, but Jn 5:43
For God the Father has * me for Jn 6:27
you believe in the one he has *." Jn 6:29
a Person—the one * by God from Jn 6:33
who * me, not to have my own way. Jn 6:38
the Father who * me draws him to Jn 6:44
living Father who * me, and in the Jn 6:57
but those of God who * me. Jn 7:16
* him is a good and true person. Jn 7:18
with him, and he * me to you." Jn 7:29
* officers to arrest Jesus. Jn 7:32
shall return to the one who * me. Jn 7:33
The Temple police who had been * Jn 7:45
have with me the Father who * me. Jn 8:16
my Father who * me is the other." Jn 8:18
I am told to by the one who * me; Jn 8:26
And he who * me is with me—he Jn 8:29
I am not here on my own, but he * Jn 8:42
us by the one who * me, for there Jn 9:4
(the word "Siloam" means "*"). Jn 9:7
So the man went where he was * Jn 9:7
"I think he must be a prophet * Jn 9:17
one sanctified and * into the world Jn 10:34,35,36
So the two sisters * a message Jn 11:3
that they will believe you * me. Jn 11:42
you are seeing the one who * me. Jn 12:45
to welcome the Father who * me." Jn 13:20
given by the Father who * me. Jn 14:24
for they don't know God who * me. Jn 15:21
am going away to the one who * me; Jn 16:5
Christ, the one you * to earth! Jn 17:3
you, and they believe you * me. Jn 17:8
As you * me into the world, I am Jn 17:18
the world will believe you * me. Jn 17:21
will know you * me and will Jn 17:23
and these disciples know you * Jn 17:25
Then Annas * Jesus, bound, to Jn 18:24
* me, even so I am sending you." Jn 20:21
to life again, he * him first of Act 3:26
So they * them out of the Act 4:15
Senate, they * for the apostles to Act 5:21
the apostles be * outside the Act 5:34
grain in Egypt, so he * his sons Act 7:12
Then Joseph * for his father Act 7:14
that God had * him to help them, Act 7:25
And so God * back the same man Act 7:35
Moses was * to be their ruler Act 7:35
they * down Peter and John. Act 8:14
on the road, has * me so that you Act 9:17
and then * him to his home Act 9:30
at Lydda, they * two men to beg him Act 9:38
happened and * them off to Joppa. Act 10:8
Just then the men * by Cornelius Act 10:17
All is well, I have * them." Act 10:20
So I came as soon as I was * Act 10:29
So I * for you at once, and you Act 10:33
And he * us to preach the Good Act 10:42
the man who had * the messengers. Act 11:12
had happened, they * Barnabas to Act 11:22
"The Lord has * his angel and Act 12:11
When Herod * for him and found Act 12:19
on them—and * them on their way. Act 13:3
of the service * them this message: Act 13:15
the believers * them to Jerusalem, Act 15:2
to those who had * them. Act 15:33
The next morning the judges * Act 16:35
He * his two assistants, Act 19:22
of Paul, also * a message to him, Act 19:31
WHEN IT WAS all over, Paul * for Act 20:1
at Miletus, he * a message to the Act 20:17
killing him when I * the soldiers Act 23:27
bribe him, so he * for him from Act 24:26
* out to preach God's Good News. Rom 1:1
For God * Christ Jesus to take Rom 3:25
to save us. He * his own Son in a Rom 8:3
The policeman is * by God to Rom 13:4
He is * by God for that very Rom 13:4
because God has * his Spirit to 1Co 2:10
God * them food to eat and water 1Co 10:3,4
God * his Angel to destroy them. 1Co 10:10
men of integrity, * by God, 2Co 2:17
I am no longer sorry that I * 2Co 7:8
Now I am glad I * it, not 2Co 7:9
taking what they * me, and using it 2Co 11:8,9
God never * those men at all; 2Co 11:13
truly an apostle, * to you by God 2Co 12:12
Did any of the men I * to you 2Co 12:17
to visit you, and * our other 2Co 12:18
God decided on, he * his Son, born Gal 4:4
his sons God has * the Spirit of Gal 4:6
peace be yours, * to you from God Eph 1:2
You * him to help me in my need; Php 2:25
in Thessalonica you * help twice. Php 4:16
you * me when Epaphroditus came. Php 4:18
God has * me to help his church Col 1:25
I have * him on this special Col 4:8
no longer I * Timothy to find out 1Th 3:5
of Jesus Christ, * out by the 1Ti 1:1
So God * pain and suffering to 1Ti 2:15
missionary, * out by God to tell 2Ti 1:1
(Tychicus is gone too, as I * 2Ti 4:12
I have been * to bring faith to Tit 1:1
spirit-messengers * out to help and Heb 1:14
for an angel was * to strengthen Heb 5:7f
messengers and * them safely away Jas 2:25
for he has * them to punish all who 1Pe 2:14
for us when he * his Son to satisfy 1Jn 4:10
God * his Son to be their Savior. 1Jn 4:14
I * a brief letter to the church 3Jn 1:9
and then an angel was * from Rev 1:1
"This message is * to you by the Rev 3:1
"This message is * to you by the Rev 3:7
of God, * out into every part of Rev 5:6
name of God who * the plagues—they Rev 16:9
future holds, has * his angel to Rev 22:6,7
I, Jesus, have * my angel to you Rev 22:16

SENTENCE
in the Hebrew text is this * Num 1:17,18,19f
the letter. The * he imposes is to Deu 17:11
The judges shall * the man to be Deu 22:17,18
You saw it all, and your * Ps 51:4
Don't * me to death. Ps 51:14,15
You pronounce * on them from Ps 76:8
Arise and judge the earth; * the Ps 94:1
It is wrong to * the poor, and Pro 24:23
the * of my court upon your sins. Is 47:8
deserve the death *, for he has Jer 26:16
he shall pronounce * against you Jer 34:3
As a * for your crimes, you Hos 4:5
and broken by my * because she is Hos 5:11
The Lord will * him to death as Hos 12:14
This * is added in some ancient Mt 19:9f
that would result in a death *. Mt 26:59
government to * Jesus to death. Mt 27:1
leaders, who will * me to die and Mk 10:33
And the vote for the death * Mk 14:63,64
the judge, lest he * you to jail; Lk 12:58
Therefore God's heaviest * awaits Lk 20:47
I have found no reason to * him Lk 23:22
Their * is based on this fact: Jn 3:19
This entire * is omitted in Act 18:21f
* demanded by the Jewish leaders. Act 28:18
will execute his * upon the earth, Rom 9:28
dictated this * to me: "Blessed Rev 19:9

SENTENCED
but he * the chief baker to be Gen 40:
No one * by the courts to die Lev 27:
and * before the king of Babylon. 2Ki 25
men from being * to death, but a Pro 14:
Rescue those who are unjustly * Pro 24:11,
up the judge who * him, and the men Is 29:
And so I have * them to slavery, Hos 11
have been judged and * to death." Zec 5
So Pilate * Jesus to die as they Lk 23:2
court-martialed and * to death. Act 12:

SENTENCES
be just in their *, not noticing Lev 19:
iron chains, and execute their *. Ps 149
They will mete out to them the * Eze 23:4

SENTENCING
king of Babylon for trial and *. Jer 32:

SENTINELS
I long for him more than * long Ps 130.
are the * upon your walls; Eze 27:1

SENTRIES
protects a city, * do no good. Ps 127:

SENTRY
Benjamin Gate, a * arrested him as Jer 37:1

SEPARATE
And God said, "Let the vapors * Gen 1:
lands, each with a * language. Gen 10:
the land you want, and we will *. Gen 13:
the middle, and to * the halves, Gen 15:1
were served at a * table, and the Gen 43:3
The curtain will * the Holy Place Ex 26:3
merely * parts that are attached. Ex 30:
* camping area with its own flag. Num 1:5
was * from the others in camp. Num 2:3-3
The Lord will * that man from Deu 29:2
had become two * tribes, Manasseh Jos 14:3,4
anything but death to * us." Ru 1:17
what he demands: * yourselves from Ez 10:1
You can't * a rebel from his Pro 27:22
day and keep it *, special and Jer 17:24
all around it to * the restricted Eze 42:16-20
He will * the chaff from the Mt 3:12
and they will * out of the Kingdom Mt 13:41
—the angels will come and * the Mt 13:49
And I will * the people Mt 25:32
Or, "* the nations." Mt 25:32f
And no man may * what God has Mk 10:9
He will * chaff from grain, and Lk 3:17
he began a * meeting at the lecture Act 19:9
can ever * us from his love. Rom 8:38
ever be able to * us from the love Rom 8:39
married, don't * because of this. 1Co 7:27
is a * and necessary part of it. 1Co 12:27
them; * yourselves from them; 2Co 6:17
that used to * us. Eph 2:14

SEPARATED
of the world were * and dispersed), Gen 10:25
itself, * by a distance between. Gen 32:16
Israel—Moses had * it from the half Num 31:42-46
them, "and we are * so widely from Neh 4:19
And the Israelis * themselves Neh 9:1
to understand, had * themselves Neh 10:28
Or, "who * the earth from the Ps 136:6f
Hence it could not be * from the Eze 10:17f
the thistles are * and burned, so Mt 13:40
the veil * him from sinful Mk 15:38f
this was so sharp that they *. Act 15:39
But if she is * from him, let 1Co 7:11
hated him and were * from him by Col 1:21
hell, forever * from the Lord, 2Th 1:9

SEPARATES
gossip * the best of friends. Pro 16:28
as a shepherd * the sheep from Mt 25:32
If anyone * from me, he is Jn 15:6
Otherwise, if the family *, the 1Co 7:14

SEPARATING
between them, * them, and Elijah 2Ki 2:11
the Jordan River * Israel from Eze 47:18
is a great chasm * us, and anyone Lk 16:26

SEPARATION
to indicate his * to God—beautiful Ex 28:2
of his vow of * to the Lord, he Num 6:13
hair—the sign of his vow of *. Num 6:18

SEPHAR
Mesha to the eastern hills of *. Gen 10:26-30
the people from * even burned their 2Ki 17:31

SEPHARVAIM
Avva, Hamath, and * and resettled 2Ki 17:24
Hamath, Arpad, *, Hena, and Ivvah? 2Ki 18:34
What happened to the kings of *, 2Ki 19:13
And what about * and Samaria? Is 36:19
cities of *, Hena, and Ivvah." Is 37:13

SEPTEMBER
work on the twenty-fifth day of * Lev 16:29,30
days later, on the last day of *, Lev 23:33,34
"This last day of *, at the end Lev 23:39
on the fifteenth day of * Num 29:1
DURING THE MONTH of * everyone Ez 3:1
It was on the fifteenth day of * Ez 3:6
was finally finished in early * Neh 6:15
But during the month of *, they Neh 7:73

SEPTEMBER Con't)
so they all gathered in early * Hag 1:14,15

EPTUAGINT
Verse 30, omitted in the * and Eze 40:29,30f

EPULCHER
was buried in the * of his father Ju 8:32

EPULCHRE
* in the rock for yourself? Is 22:15,16

EPULCHRES
the finest of our *, so that you Gen 23:5,6

EQUENCE
Can you ensure the proper * of Job 38:32
These were not in uninterrupted * Dan 9:24f

ERAH
Beriah, and a sister, *. Gen 46:16,17
Asher also had a daughter named *. Num 26:44-47
* (their sister). 1Ch 7:30

SERAIAH
High Priests, and * was the king's 2Sa 8:17
The general took *, the chief 2Ki 25:18
Johanan, the son of Kareah; *, 2Ki 25:23
Othni-el and *. 1Ch 4:13
* was the father of Joab, the 1Ch 4:14
*, the father of 1Ch 6:4-15
Zerubbabel, Jeshua, Nehemiah, *, Ez 2:2
Zedekiah, *, Azariah, Neh 10:1
* (son of Hilkiah, son of Neh 11:10-14
*, Jeremiah, Ezra, Amariah, Neh 12:1
Meraiah, leader of the * clan; Neh 12:12-21
and * (son of Azri-el) and Jer 36:26
(sons of Kareah), * (son of Jer 40:8
to give to * (son of Neriah, son of Jer 51:59
king of Judah. (* was quartermaster Jer 51:59
gave the scroll to * and said to Jer 51:61,62
as his prisoners, * the chief Jer 52:24,25

SERAIAH'S
of Mahseiah), concerning * capture Jer 51:59

SERAPHS
him were mighty, six-winged *. Is 6:2
Then one of the * flew over to Is 6:6

SERE
soil, turning * and yellow when Ps 129:6,7

SERED
Zebulun and his sons: *, Elon, Gen 46:8-14
named after their ancestor *. Num 26:26,27

SEREDITES
The *, named after their ancestor Num 26:26,27

SERENE
in Jerusalem—* as on a pleasant Is 18:4

SERFS
land and we will be * to Pharaoh. Gen 47:19
of Egypt became Pharaoh's *. Gen 47:21
"We will gladly be the * of Gen 47:25

SERGEANT
and their * were terribly Mt 27:54

SERGEANTS
His * were his sons: 1Ch 26:2,3

SERGIUS
to the governor, * Paulus, a man of Act 13:6,7

SERIAH
Ezra was the son of *; Ez 7:1
* was the son of Azariah; Ez 7:1

SERIOUS
and that they were in * trouble. Ju 20:40,41
you are really * about wanting to 1Sa 7:3
"It is a * sin to attack God's 1Sa 24:6
You know what a * crime it is in 2Sa 13:12
No, you will be in * trouble Job 13:10
God, causing Moses * trouble, for Ps 106:32
his debt, you are in * trouble. Pro 6:1
care is headed for * trouble. Pro 28:14
There is another * problem I have Ecc 5:13,14
This, as I said, is a very * Ecc 5:16
YES, BUT THERE is a very * evil Ecc 6:1
a hollow mockery, and a * fault. Ecc 6:2
before it, can make * mistakes. Ecc 11:10
Here is an example of * punning Is 5:7f
it is a * time, as when a woman Is 37:3
the city was very *, with the last Jer 52:6
more and more * until every bit of Eze 5:16
that they were in * trouble, rowing Mk 6:48
You have made a * error." Mk 12:27
of a Gentile was a * offense. Jn 18:28f
hurling many * accusations which Act 25:7
Listen to me, for this is *: if Gal 5:2
Teach the older men to be * and Tit 2:2
that sex sin is not a * matter; Rev 2:20

SERIOUSLY
David was * worried, for in 1Sa 30:6
Ammon realized how * they had 2Sa 10:6
at Samaria and was * injured. 2Ki 1:2
reign, Asa became * diseased in his 2Ch 16:12
you haven't taken * the things that Mal 2:1
I tell you as * as I know how Mk 10:15
worse, for his head was * injured. Mk 12:4
he saw a * handicapped woman who Lk 13:11
others, take the responsibility *. Rom 12:8
behave carefully, taking life *. Tit 2:6

SERIOUSNESS
as a day of * and rest, a holy Ex 16:23
proportion to the * of the crime; Deu 25:1

because of the * of the matter and Ez 10:9

SERMON
such as this one in his *: Mt 13:2,3
surprised at his * because he spoke Mk 1:22
WHEN JESUS HAD finished his * he Lk 7:1
preached them this *: "These are Lk 11:29,30
(He preached this * in the Jn 6:59
So Jesus, in a * in the Temple, Jn 7:28
Then Peter preached a long *, Act 2:40
started with my *, the Holy Spirit Act 11:15
heard him—and it was a powerful *. Act 18:25,26
then Paul preached another long * Act 20:10,11,12
whole * for all the world to hear. 2Ti 4:17

SERMONIZE
But perhaps I'd * the same as Job 16:4

SERMONS
amazed at Jesus' *, for he taught Mt 7:28
for his * in the synagogues; Lk 4:15
Jesus used in his *: "What good is Lk 6:39
enjoy listening to *, but somehow Lk 8:13
often came to listen to Jesus' *; Lk 15:1
preached powerful * about the Act 4:33
preached long * to the believers, Act 15:32
your * are strong and helpful. Rom 12:8
I do not fill my * with profound 1Co 1:17
things, all these * will convince 1Co 14:24

SERPENT
THE * WAS the craftiest of all the Gen 3:1
So the * came to the woman. Gen 3:1
the * hissed. Gen 3:4
"The * tricked me," she replied. Gen 3:13
So the Lord God said to the *, Gen 3:14
He shall be a * in the path that Gen 49:17
became a *, and Moses ran from it! Ex 4:3
his rod, and it will become a *." Ex 7:9
and his court, and it became a *. Ex 7:10
But Aaron's * swallowed their Ex 7:12
hand the rod that turned into a *. Ex 7:15
Literally, "Make a fiery *." Num 21:8f
teller, or be a * charmer, medium, Deu 18:11
They drink the wine of * venom. Deu 32:33
up the bronze * that Moses had 2Ki 18:4
he pierces the swiftly gliding *. Job 26:13
end it bites like a poisonous *; Pro 23:32
How a * crawls upon a rock. Pro 30:18,19
Literally, "If the * bites before Ecc 10:11f
adder, a fiery * to destroy you! Is 14:29
the swiftly moving *, the coiling, Is 27:1
writhing *, the dragon of the sea. Is 27:1
Silent as a * gliding away, Jer 46:22,23
Or, "sea *." Eze 32:2f
bronze image of a * on a pole, even Jn 3:14
This great Dragon—the ancient * Rev 12:9
protected from the *, the Dragon, Rev 12:14
He seized the Dragon—that old *, Rev 20:2

SERPENT'S
fat young goats at the * Stone. 1Ki 1:9
shall be the * food." Is 65:25f
And from the * mouth a vast flood Rev 12:15

SERPENTS
Their rods became *, too! Ex 7:12
Aaron's serpent swallowed their *! Ex 7:12
And deadly * Deu 32:24
Be as wary as * and harmless as Mt 10:16
* and scorpions and to crush them. Lk 10:19
were similar to *' heads that Rev 9:19

SERUG
years old when * was born. Gen 11:20,21
* was thirty years old when his Gen 11:22,23
The son of Reu was *, 1Ch 1:24-27
The son of * was Nahor, 1Ch 1:24-27
Nahor's father was *; Lk 3:23-38

SERUG'S
Nahor's father was Serug;* father Lk 3:23-38

SERVANT
may sleep with my * girl, and her Gen 16:2,3
For now this * girl of mine Gen 16:5
told a * to hurry and butcher it. Gen 18:7
who was his oldest *, Gen 24:2
the * asked. Gen 24:5
So the * vowed Gen 24:9
Running over to her, the * Gen 24:17
had enough. The * said no more, Gen 24:21
"I am Abraham's *," he Gen 24:34
At this reply, Abraham's * fell Gen 24:52
Then they had supper, and the * Gen 24:54
So Rebekah and her * girls Gen 24:61
she asked the *. Gen 24:65
Then the * told Isaac the whole Gen 24:66
and the older shall be a * of the Gen 25:23
(And Laban gave to Leah a * Gen 29:24
And Laban gave to Rachel a * Gen 29:29
"These belong to your * Jacob. Gen 32:18
A hired * or a visiting Ex 12:45
in him and in his * Moses. Ex 14:31
nor a hired *, may eat this food. Lev 22:10
rather as a hired * or as a guest; Lev 25:40
hire a * for that number of years. Lev 25:50
him as a hired * rather than as a Lev 25:53
how I communicate with my * Moses. Num 12:7,8
But my * Caleb is a different Num 14:24

you by the Lord's * Moses, on the Jos 22:4
along your * Purah if you like— Ju 7:10
a special * of God from the time of Ju 13:5
taking along a * and an extra Ju 19:3
and his wife and * were preparing Ju 19:9
His * said to him, "It's getting Ju 19:11
to send out a * whenever anyone was 1Sa 2:13,14
was boiling, the * would put a 1Sa 2:13,14
Sometimes the * would come even 1Sa 2:15
then the * would say, 1Sa 2:16
Saul and a * to look for them. 1Sa 9:3
said to the *, "Let's go home; 1Sa 9:5
But the * said, "I've just 1Sa 9:6
"Well," the * said, "I have a 1Sa 9:8
Then Samuel took Saul and his * 1Sa 9:22
told Saul to send the * on ahead. 1Sa 9:26,27
When Saul and the * arrived at 1Sa 10:10
runaway * of King Saul of Israel. 1Sa 29:3
"I am an Egyptian—the * of an 1Sa 30:13
"Tell my * David not to do it! 2Sa 7:5
Then the king summoned Saul's * 2Sa 9:9
been made for a * girl to carry to 2Sa 17:17
Ziba, the * of Saul, and Ziba's 2Sa 19:17
O king, my * Ziba deceived me. 2Sa 19:26
my father David, who was your *; 1Ki 8:24
you told your * Moses that you had 1Ki 8:53
proclaimed by his * Moses. 1Ki 8:56
* David and to his people Israel. 1Ki 8:66
for the sake of my * David and 1Ki 11:32
for the sake of my * David, my 1Ki 11:34
commandments as my * David did, 1Ki 11:38
my commandments as my * David did. 1Ki 14:8
yet I have been a true * of the 1Ki 18:12
of Israel and that I am your *; 1Ki 18:36
and said to his *, "Go and look 1Ki 18:43
Finally, the seventh time, his * 1Ki 18:44
of Judah, and left his * there. 1Ki 19:3
* Ben-hadad pleads, 'Let me live!' 1Ki 20:32
he said to his * Gehazi, "Tell the 2Ki 4:11,12
donkey and said to the *, "Hurry! 2Ki 4:24
this letter is my * Naaman; 2Ki 5:6
But Gehazi, Elisha's *, said to 2Ki 5:20
When the prophet's * got up 2Ki 6:15
Gehazi, Elisha's *, and saying, 2Ki 8:4
had promised his * David that he 2Ki 8:19
He declared through his * Elijah 2Ki 10:9,10
Literally, "saying, 'I am your * 2Ki 16:7f
them by Moses the * of the Lord. 2Ki 18:12
and for the sake of my * David.' 2Ki 19:34
and for the sake of my * David." 2Ki 20:6
the wife of Jarha, his Egyptian *. 1Ch 2:34,35
* of God were strictly followed. 1Ch 6:49
O descendants of his * Abraham, 1Ch 16:12,13
"Go and give my * David this 1Ch 17:4
"Tell my * David, 'The Lord of 1Ch 17:7
Literally, "David your *." 2Ch 6:15f
Your King Jeroboam is a mere * 2Ch 13:6
by Moses the * of the Lord must be 2Ch 24:6
* of God had assessed upon Israel. 2Ch 24:9
* Hezekiah, heaping up insults. 2Ch 32:16
you gave us through your * Moses. Neh 1:6,7
The fifth time, Sanballat's * Neh 6:5,6
Moses your *, to obey them all. Neh 9:14
laws as issued by his * Moses. Neh 10:29
"Have you noticed my * Job? Job 1:8
"Well, have you noticed my * Job 2:3
I call my *, but he doesn't Job 19:16
For God made me, and made my * Job 31:15
the wild ox be your happy *? Job 39:9
said about me, as my * Job was. Job 42:7
rams and go to my * Job and offer a Job 42:8
and my * Job will pray for you, Job 42:8
rightly concerning my * Job." Job 42:8
Do not angrily reject your *. Ps 27:9
favor shine again upon your *; Ps 31:16
Literally, "*." Ps 35:27f
Moab shall become my lowly *, Ps 60:8
Literally, "your *." Ps 69:17f
He chose his * David, taking him Ps 78:70
strength to your * and save me. Ps 86:16
agreement with my chosen * David. Ps 89:3,4
to be the king— he is my * David! Ps 89:20
of God's * Abraham, and of Jacob. Ps 105:5,6
sacred promises to Abraham his *. Ps 105:42
your *, for they are my only hope. Ps 119:49,50
and teach me, your *, to obey; Ps 119:124
for I am your *; Ps 119:125
kindness just as a * keeps his eyes Ps 123:2
Do not reject your * David—the Ps 132:10
yes, a permanent gift to his * Ps 136:22
for I am your *. Ps 143:12
your * David from the fatal sword. Ps 144:10
He shall be the * of a wiser man. Pro 11:29
the borrower is * to the lender. Pro 22:7
Literally, "for a *." Pro 29:19f
Pamper a * from childhood, and he Pro 29:21
A * girl who marries her mistress' Pro 30:21,22,23
the day's work for her * girls. Pro 31:15
You may hear your * cursing you! Ecc 7:21,22
Then the Lord said, My * Isaiah, Is 20:3
And then I will call my * Is 22:20

(SERVANT Con't)
speech from the * of the king of Is 37:6
it, and in memory of my * David." Is 37:35
SEE MY *, Is 42:1
who says [to his *, the Messiah Is 42:5
Literally, "as my *." Is 42:19f
one," the "* of the Lord"? Is 42:19
LISTEN TO ME, O my * Israel, O my Is 44:1
O * of mine, don't be afraid. Is 44:2
Israel, for you are my *; Is 44:21
For the sake of Jacob, my * Is 45:4
He said to me: "You are my *, a Is 49:3
fears the Lord and obeys his *? Is 50:10
See, my * Is 52:13
The * of the Lord, as the term is Is 52:13f
They shall see my * beaten and Is 52:14,15
my righteous * shall make many to Is 53:11
when Moses, God's *, led his people Is 63:11
So don't be afraid, O Jacob my *; Jer 30:10
with David, my *, be broken so that Jer 33:20,21
of David my * and the line of the Jer 33:22
Jews, or David my *, or change the Jer 33:25,26
here to Egypt, for he is my *. Jer 43:10
Fear not, O Jacob, my *, says Jer 46:28
all my people, even my *, David. Eze 34:23
their God, and my * David shall be Eze 34:24
"And David, my *—the Eze 37:24
lived, the land I gave my * Jacob. Eze 37:25
And my * David, their Messiah, Eze 37:25
his servants, the * may keep it Eze 46:17
"O Daniel, * of the Living God, Dan 6:20
in the law of Moses your *. Dan 9:11
O Zerubbabel my *, and honor you Hag 2:23
—Joshua represents my * The Branch Zec 3:8
"A son honors his father, a * Mal 1:6
through Moses my * on Mount Horeb. Mal 4:4
home and heal his * boy who was in Mt 8:5,6
'Be healed,' my * will get well! Mt 8:8,9
A * is not above his master. Mt 10:24
fate. The * shares his master's! Mt 10:25
"Look at my *. Mt 12:18
a leader among you must be your *. Mt 20:26
To be the greatest, be a *. Mt 23:11
"Are you a wise and faithful * Mt 24:45
'You are a good and faithful *. Mt 25:23
And throw the useless * out into Mt 25:30
the ear of the High Priest's *. Mt 26:51
must be the least—the * of all!" Mk 9:35
be great among you must be your *. Mk 10:43
Priest's *, cutting off his ear. Mk 14:47
Mary said, "I am the Lord's *, Lk 1:38
of his lowly * girl, and now Lk 1:48
And how he has helped his * Lk 1:54
royal line of his * David, just as Lk 1:69
are, and my * boy will be healed! Lk 7:6,7,8
and my * will be well again!" Lk 7:6,7,8
ready, he sent his * around to Lk 14:17
"The * returned and reported to Lk 14:21
When a * comes in from plowing Lk 17:7,8,9
For I am your *. Lk 22:27
*, and cut off his right ear. Lk 22:50
A * girl noticed him in the Lk 22:56
How true it is that a * is not Jn 13:16
of Malchus, the High Priest's *. Jn 18:10
to his * Jesus by doing this. Act 3:13
had brought his * to life again, he Act 3:26
King David, your *, saying, 'Why do Act 4:25,26
your anointed Son, your holy *. Act 4:27
the name of your holy * Jesus." Act 4:30
you as my * and my witness. Act 26:16
be God's willing * but instead I Rom 7:23,24,25
be a * to Jacob, his twin brother. Rom 9:10-13
thing about a * is that he does 1Co 4:2
Have I been a good *? 1Co 4:3
someone is a good * or not. 1Co 4:5
happily become a * of any and all 1Co 9:19
men I could not be Christ's *. Gal 1:10
I PAUL, THE * of Christ, am here Eph 3:1
Epaphras, from your city, a * of Col 4:12
* but also your brother in Christ. Phm 1:16
God's house, but he was only a *; Heb 3:5
FROM: JAMES, A * of God and of the Jas 1:1
FROM: SIMON PETER, a * and 2Pe 1:1
FROM: JUDE, A * of Jesus Christ, Jud 1:1
things to his * John in a vision; Rev 1:1
song of Moses, the * of God, and Rev 15:3,4
For I am a * of God just as you Rev 19:10
I, too, am a * of Jesus as you Rev 22:9

SERVANT-GIRL
"Sleep with my * Bilhah, and her Gen 30:3
Then Bilhah, Rachel's *, Gen 30:7
she gave her * Zilpah to Jacob, to Gen 30:9
The sons of Bilhah, Rachel's * Gen 35:25
The sons of Zilpah, Leah's *:Gad, Gen 35:26

SERVANT'S
"O our God, hear your * prayer! Dan 9:17

SERVANTS
with sheep and cattle and many *. Gen 13:5
his flocks and *, and thus he and Gen 13:11
sheep and oxen and *—both men and Gen 20:14
a well the king's * had taken Gen 21:25
violently away from Abraham's *. Gen 21:25
men who were his *, and started off Gen 22:3
great herds of cattle, and many *. Gen 26:14
by the * of his father Abraham. Gen 26:15
and he settled there, and his * Gen 26:25
That very same day Isaac's * came Gen 26:32
and all of his relatives as his *. Gen 27:37
with many *, camels, and donkeys. Gen 30:43
and many *, both men and women. Gen 32:5
He instructed his * to drive them Gen 32:16
Whose * are you? Gen 32:17
household *, cattle and flocks—all Gen 36:6,7,8
Joseph then ordered his * to Gen 42:25
we did to you. We * of the God of Gen 50:16,17
to you and to your * and to all the Ex 9:14
Remember your promise to your * Ex 32:13
all—for you, your *, your slaves, Lev 25:6,7
land of Egypt, and you are my *; Lev 25:42
For the people of Israel are my *; Lev 25:55
As Balaam and two * were riding Num 22:22,23
*, oxen, donkeys, or cattle; Deu 5:14
his home, land, *, oxen, donkeys, Deu 5:21
your * Abraham, Isaac, and Jacob. Deu 9:27
your sons and daughters and *; Deu 12:12
together with your family and *. Deu 16:14
its people shall become your *. Deu 20:11
to be their *, and ask for peace.' Jos 9:11
So they became * of the Israelis, Jos 9:21
furnish us with * to chop wood and Jos 9:23
"Come and help your *!" Jos 10:6
continue to live among them as *. Ju 1:33
When the king's * returned and Ju 3:24
So Gideon took ten of his * and Ju 6:27
Why should we be his *? Ju 9:28
his friend Zebul should be our *. Ju 9:28
we will be your *," they pleaded. 1Sa 11:1
among all your * who is as faithful 1Sa 22:14
There are lots of * these days 1Sa 25:10
*—they paid him tribute each year. 2Sa 8:2
one of Saul's *, and summoned him. 2Sa 9:2
"You and your sons and * are to 2Sa 9:10,11
sons and twenty *, replied, "Sir, 2Sa 9:10,11
Mephibosheth's *, but Mephibosheth 2Sa 9:12
to David and became his *. 2Sa 10:19
with the other * of the king. 2Sa 11:9
get out of here," he told his *; 2Sa 13:9
So Absalom said to his *, "Go 2Sa 14:30
did your * set my field on fire?" 2Sa 14:31
Ziba's fifteen sons and twenty *; 2Sa 19:17
great number of * and aides who 1Ki 10:5
Then she and her * returned to 1Ki 10:13
the lives of these, your fifty *. 2Ki 1:13
His father said to one of the *, 2Ki 4:19
"Send one of the * and a donkey so 2Ki 4:22
his * to carry back with Gehazi. 2Ki 5:23
Gehazi took the bags from the * 2Ki 5:24
and sheep and oxen and *? 2Ki 5:26
"Jehu, we are your * and will do 2Ki 10:5
Literally, "his *." 2Ki 12:21f
of aides and * accompanied her, 2Ch 9:1
and how many * and aides he had, 2Ch 9:4
Their answer was, 'We are the * Ez 5:11
"We are your *, the people you Neh 1:10
we, his *, will rebuild this wall; Neh 2:20
so that their * could go on guard Neh 4:22
brothers, nor the *, nor the guards Neh 4:23
the Temple *; Neh 10:28
of Solomon's * continued to live in Neh 11:3
and I sent some of my * to guard Neh 13:19
for the palace * and Est 1:5
his officials and *, giving Est 2:18
donkeys, and employed many *. Job 1:2,3
and killed your *, and I alone have Job 1:17
kings to slaves and frees their *. Job 12:18
my *, regard me as a stranger. Job 19:15
"If I have been unfair to my *, Job 31:13
or if any of my * have ever gone Job 31:31
who are truly good shall be my *. Ps 101:6
are his messengers—his * of fire! Ps 104:4
HALLELUJAH! O * of Jehovah, praise Ps 113:1
and have compassion on his *. Ps 135:14
those without it are beaten as *. Pro 10:13
A king rejoices in * who know Pro 14:35
I have even seen * riding, while Ecc 10:7
riding, while princes walk like *! Ecc 10:7
Priests and people, * and Is 24:2
(For Isaiah had told Hezekiah's * Is 38:21
You are my witnesses and my *, Is 43:10
Lord has redeemed his *, the Jews. Is 48:20
This is the heritage of the * of Is 54:17
name, and are his * and don't Is 56:6
Foreigners shall be your *; Is 61:5
Literally, "for your *' sake." Is 63:17f
Israel, for I have true * there. Is 65:8
shall starve, but my * shall eat; Is 65:13
call his true * by another name. Is 65:15
The nobles send * for water from Jer 14:3
wells are dry. The * return, Jer 14:3
and let your * and your people Jer 22:2
Pharaoh and his *, the princes and Jer 25:19,20
not listen to my *, the Jer 26:5
and made their * slaves again. Jer 34:1
I sent my *, the prophets, to Jer 44:
Our former * have become our Lam 5:
I will scatter his * and guards Eze 12:1
land to one of his *, the servant Eze 46:1
Abednego, * of the Most High God! Dan 3:2
his trusting * when they defied the Dan 3:2
to listen to your * the prophets, Dan 9:
us through your *, the prophets. Dan 9:1
and Ethiopians shall be his *. Dan 11:4
who would get her officers as *. Nah 3:1
So he sent other * to tell them, Mt 22:4
And he said to his *, 'The Mt 22:8
"So the * did, and brought in Mt 22:10
your fellow *, partying and getting Mt 24:49
together his * and loaned them Mt 25:14
beside a fire among the *. Mk 14:54
murder of God's * from the founding Lk 11:50
be joy for his * who are ready! Lk 12:38
of feeding the other *. Lk 12:42,43,44
one of the * what was going on. Lk 15:26
the table and is served by his *. Lk 22:27
But his mother told the *, "Do Jn 2:5
Then Jesus told the * to fill Jn 2:7,8
of course, the * did), he called Jn 2:9
way, some of his * met him with the Jn 4:51
me, for my * must be where I am. Jn 12:26
The police and the household * Jn 18:18
come upon all my *, men and women Act 2:18
and grant to your * great boldness Act 4:29
of his household * and a godly Act 10:7
"These men are * of God and they Act 16:17
They are God's *, not yours. Rom 14:4
Why, we're just God's *, each of 1Co 3:5
life and even death are your *. 1Co 3:22
upon as Christ's * who distribute 1Co 4:1
it no wonder his * can do it too, 2Co 11:15
and as * made of flaming fire; Heb 1:7
*, you must respect your masters 1Pe 2:18
to teach my * that sex sin is not a Rev 2:20
brothers, fellow * of Jesus, had Rev 6:11
God upon the foreheads of his *." Rev 7:3
* the prophets—would be fulfilled. Rev 10:7
and reward your *—prophets and Rev 11:18
has avenged the murder of his *." Rev 19:2
God, all you his *, small and Rev 19:5
there, and his * will worship him. Rev 22:3

SERVE
For a time you will * your Gen 27:39,40
the pillar and made a vow to * me. Gen 31:13
Let the men go and * Jehovah Ex 10:7
"All right, go and * Jehovah Ex 10:8
You that are men, go and * Ex 10:11
yeast; * only yeastless bread." Ex 12:20
go and * Jehovah as you said. Ex 12:31
be responsible to * the people with Ex 18:22
a Hebrew slave, he shall * only Ex 21:2
"You shall * the Lord your God Ex 23:25
and he shall * you only until the Lev 25:40
and you will * as eyes for us." Num 10:31f
to him and to * him and to use his Deu 6:13
Cling to him and * him Jos 22:5
"So revere Jehovah and * him in Jos 24:14
my family, we will * the Lord." Jos 24:15
it will no longer * as priests. 1Sa 2:31
priest who will * me and do 1Sa 2:35
to stay here and * me forever!" 1Sa 27:12
Foreigners shall * me 2Sa 22:44
to * him throughout his lifetime. 1Ki 4:21
good to them and * them well, you 1Ki 12:7
whom I worship and *—there won't be 1Ki 17:1
eunuchs who will * in the palace of 2Ki 20:18
did not * at the altar of the 2Ki 23:9
many groups to * at various times. 1Ch 24:3
Worship and * him with a clean 1Ch 28:9
and Levites will * in the Temple. 1Ch 28:21
it is to * me than to serve him!" 2Ch 12:8
it is to serve me than to * him!" 2Ch 12:8
our cattle, and we * them at their Neh 9:37
we again promise to * the Lord! Neh 9:38
of the land in order to * God. Neh 10:28
* the Lord with reverent fear; Ps 2:11
Our children too shall * him, Ps 22:30
But as for those who * the Lord, Ps 34:22
All will * him! Ps 72:11
his angels who * him constantly. Ps 103:21
my bonds and I will * you forever. Ps 116:16
OH, BLESS THE Lord, you who * him Ps 134:1
The delicious food they * will Pro 23:6,7,8
to live in their land will * them. Is 14:2
said that you must * but me alone, Is 41:9
mother's womb to * him who Is 49:5
Kings and queens shall * you; Is 49:23
of the Lord and * him and love his Is 56:6
Literally, "that will not * Is 60:12f
will inherit it and * me there. Is 65:9
lands shall * the king of Babylon Jer 25:11
All the nations shall * him and Jer 27:7
Submit to him and * him—put your Jer 27:8
For they shall * the Lord their Jer 30:9
"Stay here and * the king of Jer 40:9

SERVE Con't)
gods for you to *, and they have Eze 23:40
They * you—it is a feather in Eze 27:10
"They will * as judges to Eze 44:24
you, refusing to * your gods or to Dan 3:12
are refusing to * my gods or to Dan 3:14
any circumstance * your gods or Dan 3:18
to die rather than * or worship any Dan 3:28
rulers shall * and obey them." Dan 7:27
to him and vowed to * him. Jon 1:16
* the Lord and do what he asks.' Mal 1:13
who * him and those who don't. Mal 3:18
"You cannot * two masters: God Mt 6:24
the top, you must * like a slave. Mt 20:27
be served, but to *, and to give my Mt 20:28
and told the disciples to * them. Mk 8:7
and * them as they sit and eat! Lk 12:37
nor anyone else can * two masters. Lk 16:13
You cannot * both God and Lk 16:13
up, and let them * the sun, moon Act 7:42
belong and whom I * stood beside Act 27:23
to the one I * with all my might, Rom 1:9
is good, our sins * a good purpose, Rom 3:5
his laws * only to make us see Rom 3:20
and now you can really * God; Rom 7:6
of serving others, * them well. Rom 12:7
Never be lazy in your work but * Rom 12:11
will help you * the Lord best, with 1Co 7:35
lives because we * the Lord, but 2Co 4:11
that I could * you without cost. 2Co 11:8,9
They say they * Christ? 2Co 11:23
freedom to love and * each other. Gal 5:13
best. * them as you would Christ. Eph 6:5
for we * God alone, who examines 1Th 2:4
than those who * under the old Heb 8:6
makes us want to * the living God. Heb 9:14
you are eager to * the Lord. 1Pe 5:2
And all of you * each other with 1Pe 5:5

SERVED
Then supper was *. Gen 24:33
faithfully I've * you through these Gen 30:29
his brothers were * at a separate Gen 43:32
Their food was * to them from Gen 43:34
task and * his masters with vigor. Gen 49:15
but no leavened bread shall be *. Num 28:17
as he * me? 1Sa 2:28
lamb and roasted it and * it." 2Sa 12:4
to the Lord. He * the Lord 1Ch 23:13
who enthusiastically * the Lord. 2Ch 22:9
* under the High Priest Joiakim: Neh 12:12-21
Drinks were * in golden goblets Est 1:7
my clothing! I * as eyes for the Job 29:15
The nations came and * me. Ps 18:43,44,45
Those we * before are dead and Is 26:14
They worshiped other gods and * Jer 16:11
Daniel * as chief magistrate in Dan 2:49
did not come to be *, but to Mt 20:28
He replied, "It is the one I * Mt 26:23
am not here to be *, but to help Mk 10:45
table and is * by his servants. Lk 22:27
Martha *, and Lazarus sat at the Jn 12:2
after David had * his generation Act 13:36
But I have * him far more! 2Co 11:23
in his Spirit, was * by angels, was 1Ti 3:16
also faithfully * in God's house. Heb 3:2

SERVES
for everything * your plans. Ps 119:90,91
master's meal and * him his supper Lk 17:7,8,9
But among you, the one who * you Lk 22:26
He is a hard worker and * the Col 4:7

SERVICE
paid for them with my * to you." Gen 30:26
as he entered the * of the king. Gen 41:46
and solemn funeral *, with a Gen 50:10
yourselves for the * of the Lord, Ex 32:29
into * after another washing." Lev 13:58
are eligible for the Tabernacle *. Num 4:29
for the Tabernacle *, and found Num 4:35
* and transportation, was 8,580. Num 4:46,47,48
all the sacred *, including the Num 18:7
is your special gift of *. Num 18:7
be paid for their * with the tithes Num 18:21
for their * in the Tabernacle. Num 18:31
water for the * of our God." Jos 9:23
Meanwhile Samuel grew up in the * 1Sa 2:21
* from the time he was a lad. 1Sa 12:2
dining * was made of solid gold. 1Ki 10:21
and my horses are at your *. 1Ki 22:4
for military * from all the clans 1Ch 7:5
apart for the holy * of sacrificing 1Ch 23:13
particular term of * by coin-toss, 1Ch 25:8
opportunity of *, and King David 1Ch 29:9
A final religious * was held on 2Ch 7:9
was restored to *, and the 2Ch 29:35
and Levites into * corps to offer 2Ch 31:2
devoted to the * of the Temple. 2Ch 31:17,18
the traditional * corps of your 2Ch 35:4,5
were formed into * corps as the 2Ch 35:10
into their various * corps, to do Ez 6:18
a solemn closing * as required by Neh 8:18
The leaders in this part of the * Neh 9:5
in charge of the thanksgiving *. Neh 12:8
helped them during the *. Neh 12:9
dromedaries used in the king's *. Est 8:9,10
the offer of my lifelong *. Ps 40:6
else that you did as a '*' to me. Hag 2:14
"The more lowly your * to Mt 23:11
into * to carry Jesus' cross. Mk 15:21
division of the Temple * corps. Lk 1:5
that part of the * when the incense Lk 1:10
will think they are doing God a *. Jn 16:2
in charge of the * sent them this Act 13:15
we gathered for a communion *, Act 20:7
* to them in material blessings." Rom 15:27f
communion *—wait for each other; 1Co 11:33
There are different kinds of * 1Co 12:5
in their home for their church *. 1Co 16:19
that our present * for him is hard, 2Ti 2:12
poor, your gifts and * to them; Rev 2:19

SERVICES
special religious * for the entire Ex 12:16
the thanksgiving * with prayer; Neh 11:15,16,17
* had returned to their farms. Neh 13:10
oh, how they love the Temple *! Is 58:2
the * at the Temple that day. Jer 36:9
Prostitutes charge for their * Eze 16:33,34
sessions and at the Communion * Act 2:42
went into the synagogue for the *. Act 13:14
If I were volunteering my * of my 1Co 9:17
together for your communion *. 1Co 11:17

SERVING
He gave the largest * to Gen 43:34
all the people in * the Lord. Num 8:11
are to begin * in the Tabernacle at Num 8:23,24
as you used to do in * other gods. Num 15:39
along five of her * girls as 1Sa 25:42
But when she set the * tray 2Sa 13:9
on, cooking pots, * bowls, wheat 2Sa 17:28,29
they continued * Jehovah, the God 2Ch 34:33
later, as I was * the king his wine Neh 2:1
and of those * at the Temple was Neh 11:22,23
constantly because of * you! Ps 44:22
he destroys those * other gods. Ps 73:27
Save me, for I am * you and Ps 86:2
must be freed after * six years. Jer 34:14
you, * gods of wood and stone. Eze 20:32
* other gods, deserting me. Hos 4:12
the privilege of * God fearlessly, Lk 1:74
Then Jesus went around * us the Jn 21:13
I follow that system of * the God Act 24:14
If your gift is that of * Rom 12:7
keep on doing God's work, * you. Rom 13:6
but it is the same Lord we are *. 1Co 12:5
and * Christians everywhere. 1Co 16:15
here in jail for * the Lord—to live Eph 4:1
us please God by * him with Heb 12:28
* him day and night in his temple. Rev 7:15

SESSION
Then the court began its * and Dan 7:10
leaders was in * in Jerusalem— Act 4:5
are currently in * and the judges Act 19:38
into * with the Jewish Council. Act 22:30

SESSIONS
* and at the Communion services Act 2:42

SET
And God * them in the sky to Gen 1:17
* up camp beside the oak at Moreh. Gen 12:6
the roast veal, he * it before the Gen 18:8
with him, and he * a great feast Gen 19:3
ewe lambs and * them off by Gen 21:28,29
Then he brought out jewels * in Gen 24:53
up very early and * his stone Gen 28:18
sheep, Jacob * his wives and sons Gen 31:17-20
men with him, he * out in hot Gen 31:23
So Jacob took a stone and * it up Gen 31:45
And Jacob * up a monument of Gen 35:20
SO ISRAEL * out with all his Gen 46:1
officers he had * over the people Ex 5:6
Sinai and * up camp there. Ex 19:2,3
Sinai as all the people watch. * Ex 19:12
You told me to * boundaries Ex 19:23
day and * it aside for rest. Ex 20:11
And I will * your enlarged Ex 23:31
stones to be * in the ephod and in Ex 25:1
placed between each * of branches; Ex 25:34,35
above the top * of branches and one Ex 25:34,35
and one below the bottom *. Ex 25:34,35
the lampstand, and * them so that Ex 25:37
bars with gold. * up this Ex 26:30
garments that will * him apart from Ex 28:3
a jasper—all * in gold settings. Ex 28:20
these things are * apart and holy. Ex 29:33
it shall be * apart for God. Ex 29:37
Or, "shall be * apart for God," Ex 30:29f
he can cut and * stones like a Ex 35:33
to four gold hooks * into four Ex 36:36
gold and * into four silver bases. Ex 36:36
of the ephod, were * in gold, and Ex 39:6,7
a jasper—all * in gold filigree. Ex 39:13
Two gold rings were also * at Ex 39:19
front of the Ark. * up the drapes Ex 40:5
of the entrance. * the washbasin Ex 40:7
the Tabernacle and * up the veil to Ex 40:21
the veil, and * the Bread of the Ex 40:23
and the altar, and * up the Ex 40:33
procedures that have been * forth; Lev 5:10
shall be * aside for sacrificing. Lev 7:4
It is to be * apart from the Lev 7:35
the thigh that was * aside, along Lev 10:15
then I myself will * my face Lev 20:5
"I will * my face against anyone Lev 20:6
holy, and I have * you apart from Lev 20:26
The priest is * apart to offer Lev 21:8
a place * apart for the purpose. Lev 24:9
I will * my face against you and Lev 26:17
than the value * by the priest. Lev 27:13
to take it down and * it up again; Num 1:51
So the people of Israel * up Num 2:34
as priests and * apart to minister Num 3:3
he is to * them so that they will Num 8:2
to Moses, "Now * apart the Levites Num 8:5,6
And when the Ark was * down he Num 10:36
of the brook Zared and * up camp. Num 21:12
Your nest is * in the rocks! Num 24:21,22
of Israel to * apart three cities Deu 4:41
It was there that Jehovah * Deu 10:8
"You shall * aside for God all Deu 15:19
And never * up an obelisk, for Deu 16:22
homes, you must * apart three Deu 19:2,3
hand and * it before the altar. Deu 26:4
"Look, today I have * before you Deu 30:15
that today I have * before you life Deu 30:19
I will * wild beasts upon them, Deu 32:24
but as the people * out to cross Jos 3:13,14
The Lord then told Joshua to * Jos 5:2,3
* up, his youngest son would die. Jos 6:26
* an ambush behind the city." Jos 8:2
give it to you. * the city on Jos 8:8
into the city and * it on fire. Jos 8:19
The Israeli army * out at once Jos 9:17
at Shiloh to * up the Tabernacle. Jos 18:1
three cities be * aside for this Jos 20:8
For the men of Shechem * an Ju 9:25
walls of the fort and * on fire. Ju 9:49
Dan * out from Zorah and Eshta-ol. Ju 18:11
Then they * up the idols and Ju 18:30
So the Israeli army * an ambush Ju 20:29
the third day and * themselves in Ju 20:30
everyone in it, and * it on fire. Ju 20:35-39
the men who had * the ambush came Ju 20:42
And he has * the world in order. 1Sa 2:8
of Jehovah! They * him up again, 1Sa 5:3
* aside for the guest of honor. 1Sa 9:23
six hundred men * up their camp in 1Sa 13:16
The Philistines * up their camp 1Sa 28:4
men * out after the Amalekites. 1Sa 30:9,10
Now Joab and Abishai * out after 2Sa 2:24
from solid gold * with gems—and 2Sa 12:29,30
But when she * the serving tray 2Sa 13:9
servants, "Go and * fire to that 2Sa 14:30
servants * my field on fire?" 2Sa 14:31
So the king and his household * 2Sa 15:16
of God and * it down beside the 2Sa 15:24
to his home town, * his affairs in 2Sa 17:23
So Abishai and Joab * out after 2Sa 20:7
He * me free and rescued me, 2Sa 22:20
in the hall, * in three tiers, one 1Ki 7:3,4
Hiram * these pillars at the 1Ki 7:16-22
and * you on the throne of Israel. 1Ki 10:9
Israel then mustered its army, * 1Ki 20:27
Then he * out for Samaria, and 2Ki 10:12
And Jehoiada * guards at the 2Ki 11:18
So the priests agreed to * up a 2Ki 12:8
a large chest and * it on the 2Ki 12:9
"* your affairs in order and 2Ki 20:1
Manasseh even * up a shameful 2Ki 21:7
Literally, "* to Alamoth." 1Ch 15:20f
(or harps) * to the Sheminith." 1Ch 15:21f
upon the altar * aside for that 1Ch 16:40
from the city and * them to work 1Ch 20:3
Aaron and his sons were * apart 1Ch 23:13
Then he * up the pillars at the 2Ch 3:17
This tank was * on the backs of 2Ch 4:3
Jehoshaphat * up courts in 2Ch 19:8
and * outside the Temple gate. 2Ch 24:7,8
of Seir, and * them up as gods, and 2Ch 25:14
under quotas * by Je-iel, the 2Ch 26:11
and refused to * down the incense 2Ch 26:19
They * to work and destroyed the 2Ch 30:14
on the hills and * up shame-idols 2Ch 33:19
They * up a collection system 2Ch 34:9
And I * a time for my departure! Neh 2:5,6
They laid the beams, * up the Neh 3:6
who also * the pay scale of the Neh 11:22,23
with her that he * the royal crown Est 2:17
This was the same day as was * by Est 8:12f
You have * mankind so brief a Job 14:5
no lion has * his paw there. Job 28:8
'* him free. Job 33:23,24
Mark this well: The Lord has * Ps 4:3
the trap they * has snapped on Ps 9:15
prosperity. You * a kingly crown of Ps 21:3
He will * me on a high rock out Ps 27:5

(SET Con't)
the trap my enemies have * for me. Ps 31:4
and the mire, and * my feet on a Ps 40:2
My enemies have * a trap for me. Ps 57:6
the time King Saul * guards at his Ps 59:1
They meet in secret to * their Ps 64:5
And now, in my old age, don't * Ps 71:9
paneling, and * the sanctuary on Ps 74:7
for I have * them in place!" Ps 75:3
his laws and to * its hope anew on Ps 78:7
Or, "* us in the way of his Ps 85:13f
And then you * a boundary for Ps 104:9
Then the king sent for him and * Ps 105:20
The wicked have * their traps Ps 119:110
These proud men have * a trap to Ps 140:5
traps my enemies have * for me. Ps 142:3
When a bird sees a trap being *, Pro 1:17
I was there when he * the limits Pro 8:27,28,29
round bars of gold * with topaz; Sol 5:14
pillars of marble * in sockets of Sol 5:15
is like a heap of wheat * about Sol 7:2
I, the Lord, have * apart these Is 13:3
I will * them to fighting Is 19:2
a volcano, will * it all on fire. Is 30:33
"* your affairs in order, for you Is 38:1
Yet, though * on fire and burned, Is 42:25
have paid the price to * you free. Is 44:22
and when they * it down it stays Is 46:7
therefore, I have * my face like Is 50:7
Behind closed doors you * your Is 57:7,8
Your sun shall never *; Is 60:20
O Jerusalem, I have * Is 62:6,7
to Jerusalem and * their thrones at Jer 1:15
in my presence? I * the shorelines Jer 5:22
blind. They * their traps for men. Jer 5:26
They shall * up camp around the Jer 6:3
road we want!" I * watchmen over Jer 6:17
They have * up their idols right Jer 7:30
How will you feel when I * your Jer 13:21
then I will * fire to these gates. Jer 17:27
They have * a trap to kill me, Jer 18:20
For I have * my face against Jer 21:10
As you travel into exile, * up Jer 31:21
children's teeth are * on edge." Jer 31:29f
the one whose teeth are * on edge. Jer 31:30
shall come in and * fire to the Jer 32:29
temple doorman. I * cups and jugs Jer 35:5
When the Babylonian army * out Jer 37:11
this city shall be * afire by the Jer 38:18
their men and * out to stop him. Jer 41:12
I will * his throne upon these Jer 43:10
He will * fire to the temples of Jer 43:12
And I will * my throne in Elam, Jer 49:38
O Babylon, I have * a trap for Jer 50:24
* many watchmen on your walls; Jer 51:12
larger homes, and * the Chaldean Jer 52:14
as he spoke, and * me on my feet. Eze 2:2
into me and * me on my feet. Eze 3:24
I will tear off the charms and * Eze 13:20
And I will * myself against them Eze 15:7
worship them! You * before Eze 16:19
children's teeth are * on edge." Eze 18:2f
I will * you on fire, O forest, Eze 20:47
that I, the Lord, have * the fire. Eze 20:48
the bones. Now * it empty on the Eze 24:11
They will * up their encampments Eze 25:4
He will * up battering rams Eze 26:9
Lord when I have * Egypt on fire Eze 30:8
Yes, I will * fire to Egypt, Eze 30:16
it has not been * nor put into a Eze 30:21
Therefore because she has * Eze 31:10
And I will * one Shepherd over Eze 34:23
I, the Lord, have * Israel apart Eze 37:28
land of Israel and * me down on a Eze 40:2
were * back from the ground floor. Eze 42:6
of land shall be * apart for the Eze 45:7
seventh year) when he is * free; Eze 46:17
"South of Judah is the land * Eze 48:8
God of heaven will * up a kingdom Dan 2:44
nine feet wide and * it up on the Dan 3:1
the golden statue you * up." Dan 3:12
worship the golden statue I * up? Dan 3:14
Literally, "they shall * up the Dan 11:30,31f
Horrible Thing is * up to be Dan 12:11
or three at the most, he will * Hos 6:2
and no one shall * them free. Hos 11:7
So I will * fire to King Amo 1:4
So I will * fire to the walls of Amo 1:7
So I will * fire to the walls of Amo 1:10
So I will * fire to Teman, and Amo 1:12
"So I will * fire to the walls Amo 1:14
Your trusted friends will * traps Ob 1:7
Others will * your boundaries Mic 2:5
You will * your love upon us, as Mic 7:20
the walls to * up their defenses. Nah 2:5
enemy and * on fire and burned. Nah 3:13
follow the paths I * for you and do Zec 3:7
facets I have * before Joshua, and Zec 3:9f
and she shall be * on fire and Zec 9:4
I have come to * a man against Mt 10:35
Elijah must come and * everything Mt 17:11
over to him and * the little fellow Mt 18:2
upstairs to a large room all * up. Mk 14:15
disciples to * before the crowd. Lk 9:16
question whatever is * before you. Lk 10:7
(1) Eat whatever is * before you. Lk 10:8,9
Moses, on whose laws you * your Jn 5:45
and the truth will * you free." Jn 8:32
What do you mean, "* free'?" Jn 8:33
and church elders * a further Act 15:6
house and * a meal before them. Act 16:34
For he has * a day for justly Act 17:31
and so we * sail again. Act 18:21
from the day I * foot in Turkey Act 20:18
those who are * apart for himself. Act 20:32
who are * apart by faith in me.' Act 26:18
"He could be * free if he hadn't Act 26:32
before we * sail again, and this Act 28:11
So a time was * and on that day Act 28:23
obeying a * of rules, but in the Rom 7:6
He has * me free. Rom 7:23,24,25
of the Jews have * themselves Rom 11:25
away, and you are * apart for God, 1Co 6:11
that Christ has * you free from the 1Co 7:22
and * in motion by my blood. 1Co 11:25
welcome and * his mind at ease. 2Co 7:13
within the limits * for us, our 2Co 10:15
reaches whatever age his father *. Gal 4:2
When you came to Christ he * you Col 2:11
and this has * you free from Col 2:20
from the dead, now * your sights on Col 3:1
of hard work we * up for you. 2Th 3:6
when he appears to * up his 2Ti 4:1
whom God has * apart for Heb 3:1
our hearts become * against him, as Heb 3:7,8
But he has * another time for Heb 4:7
race that God has * before us. Heb 12:1
A great forest can be * on fire Jas 3:5
And the tongue is * on fire by Jas 3:6
pick you up, and * you firmly in 1Pe 5:10
day when God will * the heavens on 2Pe 3:12
loves us and who * us free from our Rev 1:5
One-third of the earth was * on Rev 8:7
a small scroll. He * his right foot Rev 10:2
Then the furious Dragon * out to Rev 12:17

SETH
named him * (meaning "Granted"); Gen 4:25
When * grew up, he had a son Gen 4:26
the ancestor (of *) was born." Gen 5:3,4,5f
* was born, the very image of his Gen 5:3,4,5
After * was born, Gen 5:3,4,5
this ancestor of * was born." Gen 5:3,4,5f
*: Seth was 105 years old when Gen 5:6,7,8
Seth: * was 105 years old when Gen 5:6,7,8
"godly line" of *, and Gen 6:1f
Adam, *, Enosh, Kenan, Mahalalel, 1Ch 1:1
Enos' father was *; Lk 3:23-38

SETH'S
Enos' father was Seth;* father was Lk 3:23-38

SETHUR
*, son of Michael, from the tribe Num 13:3-15

SETS
Then he made five * of bars from Ex 36:31,32
with seven * of bronze, 1Ki 7:16-22
The two * of chains on the 2Ch 4:12-16
two * of chains on the capitals, 2Ch 4:12-16
530 * of clothing for the priests. Neh 7:70
* of clothing for the priests. Neh 7:72
his clouds. He * a boundary for Job 26:10
He makes the winds blow and * Job 28:25
dump, and * them among princes! Ps 113:8
vinegar that * the teeth on edge. Pro 10:26
side and * the record straight. Pro 18:17
* fire to paper. Pro 26:21
The man who * a trap for others Pro 26:27
The sun rises and * and hurries Ecc 1:3-7
are the spark that * the straw on Is 1:31
He removes kings and * others on Dan 2:21
everything he * out to do. Dan 11:3
Israel will be a fire that * the Ob 1:18
a little fire that * the forest Zec 12:6
So if the Son * you free, you Jn 8:36
"The Father * those dates," he Act 1:7
to the humble, but * himself Jas 4:6
are humble, but * himself against 1Pe 5:5

SETTING
Moses erected it by * its frames Ex 40:18
thus * him apart for his work. Lev 8:12
on the day he finished * it up. Num 7:1
And * its mountains on fire. Deu 32:22
its people, * the city on fire. Ju 1:8
for God was * a trap for the Ju 14:4
The sun was * just as they came Ju 19:14
He rode circuit annually, * up 1Sa 7:16
* fire to the world. 2Sa 22:9
completed it by * up the gates, his 1Ki 16:34
* them aside as they are filled!" 2Ki 4:4
how to proceed in * things Ez 10:4
his mouth, * fire to the earth; Ps 18:8
Jesus was * up a rebel government. Jn 18:34f

SETTINGS
and mount the stones in gold *. Ex 28:11
and a jasper—all set in gold *. Ex 28:2
edges of the two * of the onyx Ex 28:2
in beautiful * of finest gold. Eze 28:1

SETTLE
We let this fellow * among us and Gen 19:
and to * any claim against me Gen 20:1
that they will * here among us." Gen 34:2
"MOVE ON TO Bethel now, and * Gen 35:
They wish to * in the land of Gen 47:
We will not * down here until Num 32:1
* all your quarrels and problems? Deu 1:1
The reason he hasn't let you * Deu 29:
Only then may you * down here on Jos 1:1
promised them that they could *." Jos 18:
to find a place to *, for they had Ju 18:
land they were supposed to * in. Ju 18:
He'll * it today." Ru 3:15-1
'I have decided to * accounts with 1Sa 15:
you need a whole army to * this? 1Sa 17:
we will * this in single combat! 1Sa 17:
'If you want to * an argument, ask 2Sa 20:1
He brings the hungry to * there Ps 107:3
The Lord will * international Is 2:4
He will bring them back to * once Is 14:1
If you let Moab's fugitives * Is 16:4,
my administration. * in any city Jer 40:1
But never forget—I will * up with Hos 5:2
to court, try to * the matter Lk 12:58
its four corners, * to the ground. Act 10:11

SETTLED
of the Lord and * in the land of Gen 4:16
Literally, "and they * there." Gen 11:2f
at the city of Haran and * there. Gen 11:31
and * between Kadesh and Shur. Gen 20:1
and he * there, and his servants Gen 26:25
SO JACOB * again in the land of Gen 37:1
He has * down as a lion—who will Gen 49:9
to the king to have an argument *. 1Ki 3:16
and the city * back into quietness 2Ki 11:20
Your people * here and built 2Ch 20:8
the common people * in Jerusalem Ez 2:70
For he is * in his mind that Ps 112:7
But now it will be * in the Ps 132:7
The man of few words and * mind Pro 17:27,28
When they were * in the house Mk 9:33
the form of a dove * upon him, and Lk 3:22
appeared and * on their heads. Act 2:3
Well, that * it. Act 16:10
they can be * at the regular City Act 19:39

SETTLEMENT
all the men of the * to celebrate Gen 29:22
village is a * without fortifying Lev 25:31
then demanded a * of $1,500,000. 2Ki 18:14
Go to the * where the families of Jer 35:2
to the island * later as a result Eze 26:14f

SETTLES
ends arguments and * disputes Pro 18:18

SETTLING
of the plain, * at a place near the Gen 13:12
could not begin * down until their Deu 3:18

SEVEN
for I will give * times your Gen 4:15
will be punished * times, anyone Gen 4:24
sacrifice: take * pairs of each of Gen 7:2
of each of them, and * pairs Gen 7:3
* days later Noah released the Gen 8:10
But when he took * ewe lambs and Gen 21:28,29
work for you * years if you'll give Gen 29:18
So Jacob spent the next * years Gen 29:20
"I worked for * years for Gen 29:25
to work for me another * years!" Gen 29:27
So Jacob agreed to work * more Gen 29:28
and worked the additional * years. Gen 29:30
* days later, at Mount Gilead. Gen 31:23
he bowed low * times before him. Gen 33:3
when suddenly, * sleek, fat cows Gen 41:2
Then * other cows came up from Gen 41:3
This time he saw * heads of grain Gen 41:5
Then, suddenly, * more heads Gen 41:6
up the * plump, well-formed heads! Gen 41:7
"when suddenly, * fat, Gen 41:18
But then * other cows came up Gen 41:19
cattle ate up the * fat ones that Gen 41:20
This time there were * heads of Gen 41:22
all * heads were plump and full. Gen 41:22
came * withered, thin heads. Gen 41:23
of Egypt. The * fat cows (and also Gen 41:26
cows (and also the * fat, Gen 41:26
are * years of prosperity ahead. Gen 41:26
ahead. The * skinny cows (and also Gen 41:27
cows (and also the * thin and Gen 41:27
that there will be * years of Gen 41:27
the * years of prosperity. Gen 41:27
to do: The next * years will be a Gen 41:29
but afterwards there will be * Gen 41:30
crops of the next * years, so that Gen 41:34,35
when the * years of famine come. Gen 41:36
And sure enough, for the next * Gen 41:47
After * years of this, the Gen 41:49
So at last the * years of plenty Gen 41:53
Then the * years of famine Gen 41:54

SEVEN Con't)

will grow to *, during which there	Gen 45:6
Also in the group were these *	Gen 46:23,24,25
beside a well, * girls who were	Ex 2:16
The celebration shall last *	Ex 12:15
time during the * days of the	Ex 12:15
For these * days there must be	Ex 12:19
For * days you shall eat only	Ex 13:6,7
it with its mother for * days.	Ex 22:30
Bread, when for * days you are not	Ex 23:15
Then make * lamps for the	Ex 25:37
these clothes for * days before	Ex 29:30
This ordination shall go on for *	Ex 29:35
it to God every day for * days.	Ex 29:37
Bread for * days, just as I	Ex 34:18
Then he made the * lamps at the	Ex 37:23,24
and sprinkle it * times before the	Lev 4:6
and sprinkle it * times before the	Lev 4:17
he sprinkled it * times, and also	Lev 8:11
entrance for * days, after which	Lev 8:33
be completed—for it takes * days.	Lev 8:33
day and night for * days.	Lev 8:35
defiled for * days, and under the	Lev 12:2
shall quarantine him for * days.	Lev 13:4
must quarantine him * days more.	Lev 13:5
shall quarantine him for * days.	Lev 13:21
quarantine him for * days, and	Lev 13:26
be quarantined for * days, and	Lev 13:31
quarantine him for another * days.	Lev 13:33
put it away for * days and look at	Lev 13:50
then isolated for * more days.	Lev 13:54
sprinkle the blood * times upon the	Lev 14:7
stay outside his tent for * days.	Lev 14:8
finger * times before the Lord.	Lev 14:16
of it * times before the Lord.	Lev 14:27
up the house for * days, and	Lev 14:38
shall sprinkle the house * times.	Lev 14:51,52
defilement for * days afterwards,	Lev 15:19
defiled for * days, and every bed	Lev 15:24
until evening. * days after the	Lev 15:28
and then * times in front of it.	Lev 16:14
upon the altar * times with his	Lev 16:19
its mother for * days, but from the	Lev 22:26,27
to the Lord * yearling lambs	Lev 23:18
before the Lord for * days.	Lev 23:33,34
On each of the * days of the	Lev 23:36
the Lord your God for * days.	Lev 23:40
During those * days, all of you	Lev 23:42
I will punish you * times more	Lev 26:18
I will send you * times more	Lev 26:21
smite you * times for your sin.	Lev 26:24
anger and send you * times greater	Lev 26:28
A man over sixty shall pay * and	Lev 27:7
beside him, then * days later he	Num 6:9
when he lights the * lamps in the	Num 8:2
face she would be defiled * days.	Num 12:14
the camp for * days, and after that	Num 12:14
from the camp for * days, and the	Num 12:15
been founded * years before Tanis	Num 13:22
and sprinkle it * times towards the	Num 19:4
be defiled for * days, and must	Num 19:11
the time, shall be defiled * days.	Num 19:14
grave, he shall be defiled * days.	Num 19:16
BALAAM SAID TO the king, "Build *	Num 23:1
here, and prepare * young bulls and	Num 23:1
bulls and * rams for sacrifice."	Num 23:1
"I have prepared * altars, and	Num 23:3,4
Pisgah, and built * altars there;	Num 23:14
the king to build * altars, and to	Num 23:29
and to prepare * young bulls and	Num 23:29
and * rams for the sacrifice.	Num 23:29
one ram, and * male yearling	Num 28:11
one ram, and * yearling male	Num 28:19
and with each of the * lambs	Num 28:20,21
each of the * days of the feast;	Num 28:24
ram, and * yearling male lambs.	Num 28:27
quarts with each of the * lambs.	Num 28:28,29
bull, one ram, and * yearling male	Num 29:2
quarts with each of the * lambs.	Num 29:3,4
bull, one ram, * yearling male	Num 29:8
and three with each of the *	Num 29:9,10
sacrifice * young bulls, two rams,	Num 29:32
bull, one ram, * male yearling	Num 29:36
of the camp for * days, all of you	Num 31:19
the following * nations, all	Deu 7:1
Eat unleavened bread for * days	Deu 16:3
your lives! For * days no trace of	Deu 16:4
"* weeks after the harvest	Deu 16:9
be observed for * days at the end	Deu 16:13
before you in * directions!	Deu 28:7
days, followed by * priests walking	Jos 6:3,4
around the city * times, with the	Jos 6:3,4
followed by * priests blowing	Jos 6:6-9
the city not once, but * times.	Jos 6:15
It took * years	Jos 11:18
AFTER THE CONQUEST—although *	Jos 18:1
The scouts will map it into *	Jos 18:5,6
territory into * sections, listing	Jos 18:9
the people of Midian, for * years.	Ju 6:1
He judged Israel for * years	Ju 12:9,10
during these * days of the	Ju 14:12
I were tied with * raw-leather	Ju 16:7
So they brought her the *	Ju 16:8
to join the * hundred local men in	Ju 20:14,15
(Among all these there were *	Ju 20:16
been kinder to you than * sons!"	Ru 4:15
The barren woman now has *	1Sa 2:5
country for * months in all.	1Sa 6:1
Go to Gilgal and wait there *	1Sa 10:8
"Give us * days to see if we can	1Sa 11:3
earlier to wait * days for his	1Sa 13:8
In the same way all * of his	1Sa 16:9
had * older brothers.	1Sa 17:12
at Jabesh and fasted for * days.	1Sa 31:13
for * and one-half years.	2Sa 2:10,11
* years, since the age of thirty.	2Sa 5:4,5
this time leaving * hundred	2Sa 10:18
replied, "give us * of Saul's	2Sa 21:5,6
So all * of them died together at	2Sa 21:9
"Will you choose * years of famine	2Sa 24:13
for forty years, * of them in	1Ki 2:11
So it took * years to build.	1Ki 6:38
Each capital was decorated with *	1Ki 7:16-22
He had * hundred wives and three	1Ki 11:3
But Zimri lasted only * days;	1Ki 16:15,16
and again, and again, * times!"	1Ki 18:43
each other for * days, and on the	1Ki 20:29
through the wilderness for * days;	2Ki 3:9
* times and opened his eyes!	2Ki 4:35
the Jordan River * times and he	2Ki 5:10
and dipped himself * times, as the	2Ki 5:14
that will last for * years."	2Ki 8:1
of the Philistines for * years.	2Ki 8:2
Joash was * years old when he	2Ki 11:21
IT WAS * years after Jehu had	2Ki 12:1
He also took * thousand of the	2Ki 24:16
be exiled. But * months later,	2Ki 25:25
he reigned * and one-half years.	1Ch 3:4
Eli-o-enai had * sons:	1Ch 3:24
the heads of the * clans, were	1Ch 5:13
to time, for * days at a time.	1Ch 9:25
and mourned and fasted for * days.	1Ch 10:12
Egyptian who was * and one-half	1Ch 11:23
* bulls and seven lambs.	1Ch 15:26
seven bulls and * lambs.	1Ch 15:26
of his chariots, * thousand	1Ch 18:4
and he killed * thousand	1Ch 19:17,18
for forty years; * of them during	1Ch 29:26,27
For the next * days, they	2Ch 7:8
and * rams for consecration.	2Ch 13:9
to the Lord * hundred oxen and	2Ch 15:11
hundred oxen and * thousand	2Ch 15:11
JOASH WAS * years old when he	2Ch 24:1
officials, taking * young bulls,	2Ch 29:21
seven young bulls, * rams, seven	2Ch 29:21
bulls, seven rams, * lambs, and	2Ch 29:21
seven lambs, and * male goats for a	2Ch 29:21
for * days with great joy.	2Ch 30:21
So, for * days the observance	2Ch 30:22
the observance for another * days.	2Ch 30:23
Bread for the next * days.	2Ch 35:17
of Unleavened Bread for * days.	Ez 6:21,22
I and my Council of * hereby	Ez 7:14
and his Council of * and before all	Ez 7:28
these huts for the * days of the	Neh 8:17
on each of the * days of the feast,	Neh 8:18
alike—for * days of revelry, held	Est 1:5
wine, he told the * eunuchs who	Est 1:10
* high officials of Media-Persia.	Est 1:13-15
gave her * girls from the palace as	Est 2:9
He had a large family of * sons	Job 1:2,3
him silently for * days and nights,	Job 2:13
Now take * young bulls and seven	Job 42:8
Now take seven young bulls and *	Job 42:8
God also gave him * more sons and	Job 42:13,14
like silver * times refined.	Ps 12:6
sailing the * seas, plying the	Ps 107:23
I will praise you * times a day	Ps 119:164
the Lord hates—no, *	Pro 6:16-19
But even so, he is fined * times	Pro 6:31
supported on * pillars, and has	Pro 9:1
you trip him up * times, will each	Pro 24:15,16
he is smarter than * wise men.	Pro 26:16
Literally, "Give a portion to *,	Ecc 11:2f
be left alive that * women will	Is 4:1
to divide it into * streams that	Is 11:15
the sunlight brighter than * days!	Is 30:26
The mother of * sickens and	Jer 15:9
of the army, * of the king's	Jer 52:24,25
them, overwhelmed, for * days.	Eze 3:14,15
At the end of the * days, the	Eze 3:16
fuel—enough to last them * years.	Eze 39:9
seven years. For * years they will	Eze 39:10
It will take * months for the	Eze 39:12
At the end of the * months, they	Eze 39:14
We climbed the * steps into the	Eze 40:6
And there were * steps leading up	Eze 40:22
It too had a stairway of * steps	Eze 40:26
leading up to it instead of *.	Eze 40:31
of * going up to the entrance.	Eze 40:34
Each room was * feet wide.	Eze 41:5
on all sides, and * feet high.	Eze 43:14
platform rises * feet, and this is	Eze 43:15
"Every day for * days a male	Eze 43:25
Do this each day for * days to	Eze 43:26
But afterward he must wait *	Eze 44:26
On each of the * days of the	Eze 45:23
will consist of * young bulls and	Eze 45:23
bulls and * rams without blemish.	Eze 45:23
during each of the * days of the	Eze 45:25
be heated up * times hotter than	Dan 3:19
wild animals! For * years let him	Dan 4:16
dew of heaven. For * years let him	Dan 4:23
from heaven. For * years this will	Dan 4:25
like the cows for * years until you	Dan 4:32
"At the end of * years	Dan 4:34
verse 24, leaving * years	Dan 9:25f
Seek him who created the * Stars	Amo 5:8
he will appoint * shepherds to	Mic 5:5
this inscription on it * times:	Zec 3:9
Literally, "See the stone with *	Zec 3:9f
lampstand holding * lamps, and at	Zec 4:2
flowing into them through * tubes.	Zec 4:2
For these * lamps represent the	Zec 4:10
Then the demon finds * other	Mt 12:43,44,45
And they replied, "* loaves of	Mt 15:34
and he took the * loaves and the	Mt 15:36
there were * basketfuls left over!	Mt 15:37,38
who sins against me? * times?"	Mt 18:21
Jesus replied, "seventy times *!	Mt 18:22
among us a family of * brothers.	Mt 22:25
For she was the wife of all * of	Mt 22:28
"*," they replied.	Mk 8:5
Then he took the * loaves,	Mk 8:6
* very large basketfuls left over!	Mk 8:8,9
"And when I fed the 4,000 with *	Mk 8:20
"* basketfuls," they said.	Mk 8:20
Well, there were * brothers and	Mk 12:20,21,22
For when these * brothers and	Mk 12:25
whom he had cast out * demons.	Mk 16:9
following * years of marriage.	Lk 2:36,37
had cast out * demons from her),	Lk 8:2
Then it goes and gets * other	Lk 11:26
And so the poor fellow is * times	Lk 11:26
Even if he wrongs you * times a	Lk 17:4
We know of a family of *	Lk 20:29
until each of the * had married her	Lk 20:31
Emmaus, * miles out of Jerusalem.	Lk 24:13
* WEEKS HAD gone by since Jesus'	Act 2:1
and select * men, wise and full of	Act 6:3
These * were presented to the	Act 6:6
Then he destroyed * nations in	Act 13:19,20
to come out!" * sons of Sceva, a	Act 19:14
one of the first * deacons.	Act 21:8
his vow to offer a sacrifice *	Act 21:26,27
The * days were almost ended when	Act 21:26,27
us to stay with them * days.	Act 28:14
I have * thousand others besides	Rom 11:4
* days, as God had commanded them.	Heb 11:30
up for God, and his family of *.	2Pe 2:5
Enoch, who lived * generations	Jud 1:14
To: The * churches in Turkey.	Rev 1:4
Literally, "the * spirits."	Rev 1:4f
to the * churches in Turkey:	Rev 1:11
"The * churches in Asia."	Rev 1:11f
me were * candlesticks of gold.	Rev 1:12
He held * stars in his right	Rev 1:16
This is the meaning of the *	Rev 1:20
hand, and the * golden	Rev 1:20
The * stars are the leaders	Rev 1:20
of the * churches, and the seven	Rev 1:20
of the seven churches, and the *	Rev 1:20
him who holds the * stars in his	Rev 2:1f
Literally, "the * spirits of	Rev 3:1f
of God and the * stars.	Rev 3:1
of his throne were * lighted lamps	Rev 4:5
Literally, "the * spirits of	Rev 4:5f
the back, and sealed with * seals.	Rev 5:1
scroll and to break its * seals."	Rev 5:5
He had * horns and seven eyes,	Rev 5:6
He had seven horns and * eyes,	Rev 5:6
Literally, "the * spirits of	Rev 5:6f
10, where the * eyes are equated	Rev 5:6f
the * lamps and the one Spirit.	Rev 5:6f
And I saw the * angels that	Rev 8:2
and they were given * trumpets.	Rev 8:2
Then the * angels with the seven	Rev 8:6
Then the seven angels with the *	Rev 8:6
* thunders crashed their reply.	Rev 10:3
appeared, with * heads and ten	Rev 12:3
horns, and * crowns on his heads.	Rev 12:3
It had * heads and ten horns, and	Rev 13:1
things to come: * angels were	Rev 15:1
down to earth the * last	Rev 15:1
The * angels who were assigned to	Rev 15:6
to pour out the * plagues then came	Rev 15:6
enter until the * angels had	Rev 15:8
pouring out the * plagues.	Rev 15:8
the temple to the * angels, "Now	Rev 16:1
and empty out the * flasks of the	Rev 16:1
ONE OF THE * angels who had poured	Rev 17:1
that had * heads and ten horns,	Rev 17:3
"And now think hard: his * heads	Rev 17:9

(SEVEN Con't)
built on * hills where this woman Rev 17:9
They also represent * kings. Rev 17:10
reigned before as one of the *; Rev 17:11
Then one of the * angels, who had Rev 21:9
containing the * last plagues, came Rev 21:9

SEVEN-DAY
service, with a * period of Gen 50:10
he shall begin a * cleansing Lev 15:13
this * festival before the Lord. Lev 23:39
This * annual feast is a law Lev 23:41
a great, joyous * festival will Num 28:17
it is the beginning of a * Num 29:12
"On the second day of this * Num 29:17
It will be a * feast. Eze 45:21

SEVEN-FOLD
and from the * Spirit Rev 1:4
by the one who has the * Spirit Rev 3:1
lamps representing the * Spirit Rev 4:5
eyes, which represent the * Spirit Rev 5:6

SEVEN-YEAR
This king will make a * treaty Dan 9:27

SEVENFOLD
O Lord, take * vengeance on Ps 79:12

SEVENS
or "seventy *" (of years). Dan 9:24f

SEVENTEEN
two months, and * days old, the Gen 7:10,11,12
Jacob's son Joseph was now * Gen 37:2
Jacob lived * years after his Gen 47:28
Their inheritance included these * Jos 19:2-7
David captured * hundred cavalry 2Sa 8:4
was on the throne * years in 1Ki 14:21
King Rehoboam reigned * years in 2Ch 12:13
Hanamel * shekels of silver. Jer 32:9

SEVENTEEN-YEAR
of Jehu) began a * reign over 2Ki 13:1

SEVENTEENTH
It was during the * year of the 1Ki 22:51
*, the group led by Hezir; 1Ch 24:7-18
*, Joshbekasha and twelve of his 1Ch 25:9-31
began on the * day of April in the 2Ch 3:2

SEVENTH
So on the * day, having finished Gen 2:2
God blessed the * day and declared Gen 2:3
and again on the * day, there will Ex 12:16
Then, on the * day, a great feast Ex 13:6,7
six days, but the * is a Sabbath, Ex 16:26
For the Lord has given you the * Ex 16:28,29
So the people rested on the * Ex 16:30
work, but the * day is a day of Ex 20:10
in them, and rested the * day; Ex 20:11
be freed in the * year, and need Ex 21:2
fallow during the * year, and let Ex 23:11
six days only, and rest the *; Ex 23:12
it six days; the * day he called to Ex 24:16
Work six days only, for the * Ex 31:16
on the * day, and was refreshed." Ex 31:17
only six days, and rest on the *. Ex 34:21
"Work six days only; the * day Ex 35:2
that time, on the * day, the priest Lev 13:5
Again on the * day the priest Lev 13:6
and examine him again the * day. Lev 13:27
and examined again on the * day. Lev 13:32
again on the * day, and if the spot Lev 13:34
and look at it again on the * day. Lev 13:51
it again on the * day the spot has Lev 13:53
seven days. The * day he shall Lev 14:9
the * day to look at it again. Lev 14:39
* month" of the Hebrew calendar. Lev 16:29,30f
—the * day of every week—which are Lev 23:3
You shall do the same on the * Lev 23:8
first day of the * month" (of the Lev 23:23,24f
tenth day of the * month" (of the Lev 23:26,27f
day of the * month" (of the Hebrew Lev 23:33,34f
rest before the Lord every * year. Lev 25:1
but during the * year the land is Lev 25:4
tenth day of the * month" (of the Lev 25:9f
shall we eat the * year, since we Lev 25:20
* year when you lived upon it. Lev 26:34,35
On the * day, Elishama, the son Num 7:48-53
the third and * days with water Num 19:12
be defiled even after the * day. Num 19:12
place on the third and * days; Num 19:19
On the * day there shall again Num 28:25
first day of the * month" (of the Num 29:1f
tenth day of the * month" (of the Num 29:7f
day of the * month" (of the Hebrew Num 29:12f
"On the * day of the festival, Num 29:32
captives on the third and * days. Num 31:19
On the * day you must wash your Num 31:24
six days, but the * day is the Deu 5:14
"AT THE END of every * year there Deu 15:1
On the * day there shall be a Deu 16:8
the end of every * year—the Year of Deu 31:10,11
On the * day you are to walk Jos 6:3,4
At dawn of the * day they Jos 6:15
seven times. The * time, as the Jos 6:16
At last, on the * day, he told Ju 14:17
So before sunset of the * day Ju 14:18
Then, on the * day, the baby 2Sa 12:18
Finally, the * time, his servant 1Ki 18:44
and on the * day the battle began. 1Ki 20:29
In the * year of Queen Athaliah's 2Ki 11:4
(which was the * year of the reign 2Ki 18:9
was Ozem, and his * was David. 1Ch 2:15
Eliel was * in command; 1Ch 12:8-13
*, the group led by Hakkoz; 1Ch 24:7-18
*, Jesharelah and twelve of his 1Ch 25:9-31
Elie-ho-enai (the *). 1Ch 26:2,3
Issachar (the *), 1Ch 26:4,5
The commander of the * Division 1Ch 27:10
on duty the * month of each year. 1Ch 27:10
IN THE * year of the reign of 2Ch 23:1
* month" of the Hebrew calendar. Ez 3:6f
of March in the * year of the reign Ez 7:7,8,9
do any work every * year and to Neh 10:31
of the * year of his reign. Est 2:16
to Babylon in the * year of Jer 52:28
Literally, "in the * year of Eze 20:1f
day of rest every * day—as a symbol Eze 20:12
Do this also on the * day of Eze 45:20
* year) when he is set free; Eze 46:17
Literally, "fourth, fifth, *, and Zec 8:19f
God rested on the * day of Heb 4:4
WHEN THE LAMB had broken the * Rev 8:1
but that when the * angel blew his Rev 10:7
For just then the * angel blew Rev 11:15
Then the * angel poured out his Rev 16:17
reigns, and the * is yet to come, Rev 17:10
The * with chrysolite; Rev 21:18,19,20

SEVENTY
Kenan: Kenan was * years old when Gen 5:12,13,14
By the time Terah was * years Gen 11:26
there in Egypt totaled *. Gen 46:27
of national mourning of * days. Gen 50:3
* (for Joseph was already there). Ex 1:5
twelve springs and * palm trees; Ex 15:27
and * of the elders of Israel. Ex 24:1
Nadab, Abihu, and * of the elders Ex 24:9
me * of the leaders of Israel; Num 11:16
and he gathered the * elders and Num 11:24
and put it upon the * elders; Num 11:25
But two of the *—Eldad and Num 11:26
springs of water and * palm trees; Num 33:9
there were only * of them, but now Deu 10:22
"I have treated * kings in this Ju 1:7
* sons, for he married many wives. Ju 8:30
to be ruled by * kings—Gideon's Ju 9:2
kings—Gideon's * sons—or by one Ju 9:2
slaughtered all * of his Ju 9:5
killed his * sons upon one stone. Ju 9:18
Gideon's * sons were given their Ju 9:24
sin of murdering Gideon's * sons. Ju 9:56,57
grandsons, who rode on * donkeys. Ju 12:14
But the Lord killed * of the 1Sa 6:19
three days; and * thousand men died 2Sa 24:15
Solomon also had * thousand 1Ki 5:15
of Ahab's * sons—all of whom were 2Ki 10:1
(These * sons of King Ahab were 2Ki 10:6
When the letter arrived, all * 2Ki 10:7
land must rest for * years to make 2Ch 36:21
to the Babylonians for * years. Ez 1:1f
* years are given us! Ps 90:10
For * years Tyre will be Is 23:15,16
Yes, after * years, the Lord Is 23:17
the king of Babylon for * years. Jer 25:11
Literally, "the * years." Jer 25:12f
Literally, "for * years." Jer 29:10f
people of Israel. * elders of Eze 8:11
began by killing the * elders. Eze 9:6
The nave itself was * feet long Eze 41:2
must lie desolate for * years. Dan 9:2
Literally, "* weeks" or Dan 9:24f
or "* sevens" (of years). Dan 9:24f
Lord of Hosts, for * years your Zec 1:12
'During those * years of exile when Zec 7:5
Lord appointed * others and sent Mt 11:1f
Jesus replied, "* times seven! Mt 18:22
THE LORD NOW chose * other Lk 10:1
When the * disciples returned, Lk 10:17

SEVENTY-FIVE
Abram was * years old at that Gen 12:4
the court will be * feet wide, with Ex 27:12
The east side will also be * Ex 27:13
The west side was * feet wide; Ex 38:12
The east side was also * feet Ex 38:13
It was * feet long and forty-five 1Ki 7:6
with gems and weighed * pounds! 1Ch 20:2
come to Egypt, * persons in all. Act 7:14

SEVENTY-SEVEN
should be punished * times!" Gen 4:24
names of all the * political and Ju 8:14
ninety-six rams; * lambs; Ez 8:35

SEVENTY-SIX
all two hundred * of us—for that Act 27:37

SEVER
to * your roots and cut you down. Lk 3:9

SEVERAL
and she bore him * children:Zimran, Gen 25:1
Then, taking * men with him, he Gen 31:23
* years later the king of Egypt Ex 2:23
are to celebrate * annual festivals Lev 2
cities will give * to the Levites, Num 3
sent messengers to * other kings: Jos 1
Sea. (* cities south of the brook Jos 1
was Gilead) had * other sons by his Ju 1
a burnt offering. * men of the 1Sa 6:
a bronze javelin * inches thick, 1Sa 17:4
* sons were born to David while 2Sa 3
David placed * army garrisons in 2Sa 8
with * other Israeli soldiers. 2Sa 11:
* years until I say the word!" 1Ki 17
This happened * times. 2Ki 6:
King Hazael conquered * sections 2Ki 10:32,
around, he noticed * graves in the 2Ki 23:
had no sons, although he had * 1Ch 2:34,
for all five of them had * wives 1Ch 7
DAVID NOW BUILT * palaces for 1Ch 15
Jeduthun, and * others who were 1Ch 16:4
for them to have * wives apiece. 2Ch 11:2
sent home raided * of the cities of 2Ch 25:1
(a scribe), * judges and other Ez 4:8
and men from * other nations. Ez 4:1
In fact, I refused to eat for * Neh 1
There were also * subclans of Neh 7:6
hours, and for * more hours they Neh 9
they lasted * days—Job would summon Job 1
and won't return for * days." Pro 7:2
with * other men to capture Uriah. Jer 26:2
Jeremiah was kept there for * Jer 37:15,1
the Septuagint and * other of the Eze 40:29,3
Susa was one of * capitals of the Dan 8:2
faint and was sick for * days. Dan 8:2
"* years later an alliance will Dan 11:
That evening * demon-possessed Mt 8:1
JESUS TOLD * other stories to show Mt 22:
* DAYS LATER he returned to Mk 2:
* biographies of Christ have Lk 1:1,
distant land to live for * years. Lk 20:
the mother of James, and * others. Lk 24:1
him behind. * small boats from Jn 6:22,2
in Jerusalem * days early so that Jn 11:5
* women, including Jesus' mother, Act 1:1
This prayer meeting went on for * Act 1:1
stopping at * Samaritan villages Act 8:2
him to stay with them for * days. Act 10:4
They stayed * days, Act 15:3
Antioch to assist * others who were Act 15:34,3
* days later Paul suggested to Act 15:36
border, and stayed there * days. Act 16:12
including * prominent Greek women Act 17:12
Paul stayed in the city * days Act 18:18
where he found * disciples. Act 19:1
* men were traveling with him, Act 20:4
During our stay of * days, a man Act 21:10
"After * years away, I returned Act 24:17
During their stay of * days Act 25:14
so Paul and * other prisoners Act 27:1
which was scheduled to make * Act 27:2
We had * days of rough sailing, Act 27:7,8
There we stayed for * days. Act 27:9

SEVERE
NOW A * famine overshadowed the Gen 26:1
So now, with * famine all over Gen 41:56,57
the famine was as * in Canaan as it Gen 42:5
because the famine was so *. Gen 47:20
seem too *, and your brother be Deu 25:1
had become very * in Samaria. 1Ki 18:2
far more * than my fault deserves. Job 23:2
A wise king stamps out crime by * Pro 20:26
Notice how God is both kind and * Rom 11:22
to sadden you with a * rebuke. 2Co 1:23

SEVERED
fruit when * from the vine. Jn 15:4

SEVERELY
He has been * injured by those Gen 49:23
seven times more * for your sins. Lev 26:18
left—leaving Joash * wounded—his 2Ch 24:25
My patience was * tried by their Ps 95:9
they shall be * punished. Pro 17:11
Mockers and rebels shall be * Pro 19:29
I will punish you * because you Jer 2:35
will punish you so * that your fate Jer 15:4
And I will deal * with all who Zep 3:19
unexpected, and * whip you and Mt 24:51
He will be * punished, for Lk 12:47
* and I will not spare them. 2Co 13:2

SEVERING
but not * its head from its body. Lev 5:8

SEW
"You must * tassels on the four Deu 22:12

SEWING
The women skilled in * and Ex 35:25

SEWS
She * for the poor, and Pro 31:19,20

SEX
a gang of * perverts gathered Ju 19:22
into every sort of * sin, and do Rom 1:24
indulged in * sin with each other. Rom 1:26
of having a normal * relationship Rom 1:27
That is why I say to run from * 1Co 6:18
Let there be no * sin, impurity Eph 5:3

EX Con't)
and honoring them as the weaker *. 1Pe 3:7
the godless enjoy—* sin, lust, 1Pe 4:3
craze for *, the ambition to buy 1Jn 2:16
* sin is not a serious matter; Rev 2:20
EXUAL
THEN ADAM HAD * intercourse with Gen 4:1
had * intercourse with her father; Gen 19:33
* intercourse with your wives." Ex 19:15
"Anyone having * relations with Ex 22:19
party, followed by * immorality. Ex 32:6
After * intercourse, the woman Lev 15:18
A man having * intercourse with Lev 15:24
and for anyone who has * Lev 15:33
is, "have * intercourse with." Lev 18:6f
"There must be no * relationship Lev 18:19
A man shall have no * Lev 18:23
And if a man has * intercourse Lev 20:12
If a man has * intercourse with Lev 20:14
"If a man has * intercourse with Lev 20:15
If a woman has * intercourse Lev 20:16
"If a man has * intercourse with Lev 20:17
If a man has * intercourse with Lev 20:18
"* intercourse is outlawed Lev 20:19
women who have had * intercourse. Num 31:17
" 'Cursed is he who has * Deu 27:21
" 'Cursed is he who has * Deu 27:22
" 'Cursed is he who has * Deu 27:23
he had no * relations with her). 1Ki 1:3,4
along: without * desire, standing Ecc 12:5
Then I had * intercourse with my Is 8:3
who live in * sin, or are greedy 1Co 5:10
but indulges in * sins, or is 1Co 5:11
But * sin is never right: our 1Co 6:13
have nothing to do with * sin, Col 3:5
keep clear of all * sin so that 1Th 4:3,4
involved in * sin or becomes Heb 12:16
there is nothing wrong with * sin. 2Pe 2:2
involving them in * sin and Rev 2:14
SEXUALLY
spirit world were * involved with Gen 6:4
SHA-ALABBIN
Zorah, Eshta-ol, Ir-shemesh, *, Jos 19:41-46
SHA-ALBIM
Aijalon, and *, the tribe of Joseph Ju 1:35
Ben-deker, whose area was Makaz, * 1Ki 4:8-19
SHA-ALBON
Eliahba from *; 2Sa 23:24-39
Eliahba from *; 1Ch 11:26-47
SHA-ARAIM
Socoh, Azekah, *, Adithaim, Jos 15:33-36
Hazar-susim, Beth-biri, and *. 1Ch 4:31
SHAALIM
of Shalisha, the * area, and the 1Sa 9:4
SHAAPH
Geshan, Pelet, Ephah, and *. 1Ch 2:47
Sheber, Tirhanah, * (the father of 1Ch 2:48,49
SHAARAIM
strewn all along the road to *. 1Sa 17:52
SHAASHGAZ
There she was under the care of * Est 2:12,13,14
SHABBETHAI
Meshullam, and * the Levite opposed Ez 10:15
Jamin, Akkub, *, Hodiah, Ma-aseiah, Neh 8:7,8
* and Jozabad, who were in Neh 11:15,16,17
SHACK
in some wayside * in the desert, Jer 9:2
SHACKLED
so that even when * with chains he Lk 8:29
SHACKLES
into handcuffs and *—as he often Mk 5:3,4
and smashed the * and walked away. Mk 5:3,4
SHADE
rest here in the * of this tree Gen 18:3,4
His branches * the wall. Gen 49:22
humble yourselves beneath my *! Ju 9:15
rest over there in the *." Ru 2:7
covered by their * among the Job 40:22
Literally, "your * at your right Ps 121:5f
I am seated in his much-desired * Sol 2:3
Then the Lord will provide * on Is 4:5
zeal beneath the * of every tree, Is 57:5
and forest *, with its head high up Eze 31:2,3
and in its * the flocks and herds Eze 31:6
All those who live beneath her * Eze 31:12
that had lived beneath her *. Eze 31:17
Wild animals rested beneath its * Dan 4:12
living in its *, with its branches Dan 4:21
in the pleasant * of oaks and Hos 4:13
a leafy shelter to * him as he Jon 4:5
leaves over Jonah's head to * him. Jon 4:6
SHADED
* by the cedar trees and firs." Sol 1:17
SHADOW
there's not a * of a doubt that 1Ki 20:25
"Do you want the * on the 2Ki 20:9
"The * always moves forward," 2Ki 20:10
and he caused the * to move ten 2Ki 20:11
the * moved up and down the steps. 2Ki 20:11f
our days on earth are like a *, 1Ch 29:15
darkness and the * of death, never Job 10:20,21
a land of the * of death where only Job 10:22
light, even the dark * of death. Job 12:22
as the * of a passing cloud, he Job 14:2
on my eyelids is the * of death. Job 16:16
I am but a * of my former self. Job 17:7
hide me in the * of your wings as Ps 17:8
refuge in the * of your wings. Ps 36:7
Frail as breath! A *! Ps 39:5,6
I will hide beneath the * of your Ps 57:1
the protecting * of your wings. Ps 63:7
mountains were covered with our *; Ps 80:10
WE LIVE WITHIN the * of the Ps 91:1
darkness, in the * of death, Ps 107:10
the darkness and * of death and Ps 107:14
his days are like a passing *. Ps 144:4
in the land of the * of death. Is 9:2
from the storm, a * from the heat, Is 25:4
and as the cooling * of a mighty Is 32:2
He has hidden me in the * of his Is 49:2
of the world lived beneath its *. Eze 31:6
far away and rest beneath my *. Hos 14:7
and death's *, and to guide us to Lk 1:79
at least Peter's * would fall Act 5:15
forever without change or *. Jas 1:17
SHADOW-BOXING
I'm not just * or playing around. 1Co 9:26
SHADOWED
Into the black rock, * by death, Job 28:3,4
SHADOWS
"You're just seeing * that look Ju 9:36
on earth are as transient as *. Job 8:9
before the evening * fall. Ps 90:5,6
passing swiftly as the evening *. Ps 102:11
until the evening * fall again. Ps 104:23
as * because they don't fear God. Ecc 8:13
Before the dawn comes and the * Sol 2:17
dawns and the * flee away, I will Sol 4:6
rages, until the evening * fall. Jer 6:4
They were only * of the real Col 2:17
SHADRACH
Hananiah was called *; Dan 1:7
the king appointed *, Meshach, and Dan 2:49
Jews out there—*, Meshach, and Dan 3:12
rage, ordered *, Meshach, and Dan 3:13
"Is it true, O *, Meshach, and Dan 3:14
*, Meshach, and Abednego replied, Dan 3:16
anger at *, Meshach, and Abednego. Dan 3:19
his army to bind *, Meshach, and Dan 3:20
threw them in! So *, Meshach, and Dan 3:23
and yelled: "*, Meshach, and Dan 3:26
be the God of *, Meshach, and Dan 3:28
against the God of *, Meshach, and Dan 3:29
gave promotions to *, Meshach, and Dan 3:30
SHADY
every hill, beneath every * tree. Jer 3:6
SHAFT
base, *, lamps, and blossoms. Ex 25:31
side of the center *, each branch Ex 25:32,33
The central * itself will be Ex 25:34,35
branches and the * are all to be Ex 25:36
Its base, *, lamp-holders, and Ex 37:17
so that a mine * can be sunk into Job 28:3,4
nor spear nor dart nor pointed *. Job 41:26
SHAFTS
deadly arrows made from * of fire. Ps 7:13
SHAGEE
Jonathan (son of *) from Harar; 1Ch 11:26-47
SHAGGY-HAIRED
and Persia; the * goat is the Dan 8:21
SHAHARAIM
* divorced his wives 1Ch 8:8,9,10
SHAHAZUMAH
Tabor, *, and Beth-shemesh— Jos 19:17-23
SHAKE
* loose from him and be free." Gen 27:39,40
I'll just * myself free." Ju 16:20
that it almost made the ground *! 1Sa 4:5
Then the Lord will * Israel like 1Ki 14:15
Egypt to help him * free of 2Ki 17:4
against you and * my head at you. Job 16:4
If you sin, does that * the Job 35:6
Let the whole earth *. Ps 99:1
when they see me they * their Ps 109:25
from his throne to * up the earth, Is 2:19
trees of a forest * in a storm. Is 7:2
they will rave and * their fists at Is 8:21
For I will * the heavens in my Is 13:13
Therefore strong nations will * Is 25:3
The sinners among my people * Is 33:14
by will gasp and * their heads in Jer 18:16
The whole earth shall * at Jer 50:46
All who pass by scoff and * their Lam 2:15
hands in horror and * your head Eze 6:11
hatred, I will * my fist over the Eze 25:16
your walls will * as the horses Eze 26:10
The whole country will * with Eze 26:15
The merchants of the nations * Eze 27:36
I made the nations * with fear Eze 31:16
lop off its branches; * off its Dan 4:14
and the earth and sky begin to *. Joe 3:16
of the pillars and * the Temple Amo 9:1
mouths of those who * the trees. Nah 3:12
way beneath me and I * in terror. Hab 3:16
mock, or * his head in disbelief. Zep 2:15
I will begin to * the heavens and Hag 2:6
dry land— I will * all nations, Hag 2:7
"I am about to * the heavens and Hag 2:21
and Ekron will * with terror, for Zec 9:5
welcome you—* off the dust of that Mt 10:14
or listen to you, * off the dust Mk 6:11
* hands warmly with each other. Rom 16:16
Dear brothers, pray for us. * 1Th 5:26
great rock, and nothing can * it. 2Ti 2:19
"I will not only * the earth, but Heb 12:26
SHAKEN
Jehoshaphat was badly * by this 2Ch 20:3
Lord, heal it now, for it is * to Ps 60:2
are * to the core. Ps 82:5
to death; I am * off from life as Ps 109:22,23
the world is * beneath you. Is 24:18
felt, and his officers too were *. Dan 5:9
of the heavens shall be *." Mt 24:29f
pressed down, * together to make Lk 6:38
the prison was * to its Act 16:26
was * by a mighty earthquake. Rev 11:19
SHAKES
He * the earth to its foundations. Job 9:6
* Mount Lebanon and Mount Sirion. Ps 29:5,6
and * the wilderness of Kadesh. Ps 29:8
Though the earth * and all its Ps 75:3
of that day. He * his fist at Is 10:32
he * the kingdoms of the earth; Is 23:11
it * like a tent in a storm. Is 24:20
and * her head at you in scorn. Is 37:22
The earth * with the noise of Jer 49:21
Then he * the nations, scattering Hab 3:6
SHAKING
and they stood at a distance, * Ex 20:18
they will cast lots by * arrows Eze 21:21
sit on the ground * with fear at Eze 26:16
I promise a mighty * in the land of Eze 38:19
by hurled abuse, * their heads at Mt 27:39
by * its dust from your feet as Lk 9:5
SHAKY
stand firm on your * legs, and Heb 12:12
SHALISHA
the land of *, the Shaalim area, 1Sa 9:4
SHALLECHETH
of the west gate and the * Gate 1Ch 26:16
SHALLOW
May they be as grass in * soil, Ps 129:6,7
enough in the * soil, but the hot Mt 13:5
his heart. The *, rocky soil Mt 13:20
had no nourishment in the * soil. Mk 4:5,6
Other seed fell on * soil with Lk 8:6
their wrong and * answers built on Col 2:8
SHALLUM
Then * (the son of Jabesh) 2Ki 15:10
New king of Israel: * 2Ki 15:13
One month after * became king, 2Ki 15:14
Additional details about King * 2Ki 15:15
(She was the wife of *—son of 2Ki 22:14
Sismai's son was *; 1Ch 2:40
Jehoiakim, Zedekiah, *. 1Ch 3:15
Shaul's son was *, his grandson 1Ch 4:25
*, the father of 1Ch 6:4-15
Jahzi-el, Guni, Jezer, *. 1Ch 7:13
The gatekeepers were * (the chief 1Ch 9:17,18
the oldest son of * the Korahite) 1Ch 9:31
of *, and Amasa the son of Hadlai. 2Ch 28:12
* (son of Tokhath, son of Hasrah). 2Ch 34:22
son of Hasrah). (* was the king's 2Ch 34:22
(the families of *, Ater, Talmon, Ez 2:40,41,42
Hilkiah was the son of *; Ez 7:1
* was the son of Zadok; Ez 7:1
Of the gatekeepers, *, Telem, and Ez 10:24
Azarel, Shelemiah, Shemariah, *, Ez 10:34-42
of the wall. * (son of Hallohesh) Neh 3:12
* (son of Colhozeh), the mayor of Neh 3:15
From the clans of *, (all of whom Neh 7:43,44,45
Jehoahaz, or *, reigned for three Jer 22:11f
Hanamel (son of *) will soon arrive Jer 32:6,7
of *), who was the temple doorman. Jer 35:4
*, and Pekahiah. Hos 7:7f
years: Zechariah, *, Pekahiah. Hos 13:11f
SHALLUM'S
Sismai's son was Shallum; * son 1Ch 2:41
royal gate. * ancestry went back 1Ch 9:19
SHALMAI
*, Hanan, Giddel, Gahar, Neh 7:46-56
SHALMAN
just as at Beth-arbel, which * Hos 10:14
*: probably Salaman, king of Moab, Hos 10:14f
SHALMANESER
King * of Assyria attacked and 2Ki 17:3
Israel) that King * of Assyria 2Ki 18:9
* V of Assyria. Is 14:29f
SHALT
of the sanctuary * thou take them. Num 3:47,48f
SHAM
and through, full of lust and *. Eph 4:22
SHAMA
* and Je-iel (sons of Hotham) from 1Ch 11:26-47

SHAMAIAH
as Delaiah (son of *), Elnathan Jer 36:12
SHAMBLES
Everything lies in * like a Ps 74:5,6
and made it into a * and demolished Is 14:17
that this palace shall become a *. Jer 22:5
Soon the city is an empty *; Nah 2:10
SHAME
your * of not being circumcised." Jos 5:8,9
Literally, "the * of Egypt." Jos 5:8,9f
Where could I go in my *? 2Sa 13:13
he sent them back to David in *. 1Ch 19:4
home in deep * to his own land. 2Ch 32:21
*, and the wicked destroyed." Job 8:22
can lift my head, now bowed in *. Ps 3:3
turn my glory into * by worshiping Ps 4:2
God will turn them back in *. Ps 6:10
May their example * and silence Ps 8:2
I stoop with sorrow and with *. Ps 31:9,10
"At last we have him!" * them; Ps 35:26
of contempt and * among the Ps 44:14
Confuse them! * them! Ps 70:2,3
back and sent them to eternal *. Ps 78:66
I'll clothe his enemies with *, Ps 132:18
but fools are promoted to *! Pro 3:35
in anguish and in *, when syphilis Pro 5:11
never has enough of lust and *. Pro 9:13
shines, but what a * to see a lad Pro 10:5
Proud men end in *, but the meek Pro 11:2
constantly and come to *. Pro 13:5
What a *—yes, how stupid! Pro 18:13
lawless gang is a * to his father. Pro 28:7
Left to himself, he brings * to Pro 29:15
your mouth with your hand in *. Pro 30:32
to come to me.) * will cover you, Is 1:29
be left to them is * and disgrace. Is 3:24
uncovered, to the * of Egypt. Is 20:4
*—he won't help one little bit! Is 30:5
Israel, leaving her to *. Is 43:28
before the Lord in *, along with Is 44:11
You shall be in nakedness and *. Is 47:3
I do not hide from *—they spit in Is 50:6
you will no longer live in *. Is 54:4
live in shame. The * of your youth Is 54:4
Instead of * and dishonor, you Is 61:7
But they shall be put to *. Is 66:5
Like a thief, the only * that Jer 2:26,27
We lie in * and in dishonor, for Jer 3:25
hurt themselves, to their own *. Jer 7:19
O Jerusalem, shave your head in * Jer 7:29
and your altars of * (your altars Jer 11:13
They shall harvest a crop of *, Jer 12:13
myself will expose you to utter *. Jer 13:26
into a place of * and wickedness. Jer 19:4
been but trouble and sorrow and *. Jer 20:18
The nations have heard of your * Jer 46:12
See the * of Moab! Jer 48:39
overwhelmed with *, for you shall Jer 50:12
Jerusalem hang their heads in *. Lam 2:10
my soul will live in utter *. Lam 3:20
and horror and * shall cover you; Eze 7:18
with * all the evil you have done; Eze 16:61
in silence and in * when I forgive Eze 16:63
And the * of your prostitution Eze 23:29
* in the pit, slain by the sword. Eze 32:25
Once a terror, now they lie in *; Eze 32:30
* before the surrounding nations. Eze 36:6
being covered with *, but for Eze 36:7
Their time of treachery and * Eze 39:26
must bear their * for all the sins Eze 44:13
with * because of all our sins. Dan 9:8
him and cause him to retreat in *. Dan 11:18
to * and everlasting contempt. Dan 12:2
Their love for * is greater than Hos 4:18
they shall die in *, because they Hos 4:19
Israel will be put to *. Hos 10:6
and barefoot in sorrow and *; Mic 1:8
in the dust in your anguish and *. Mic 1:10
here contrasted with their *; Mic 1:11f
here contrasted with their *; Mic 1:11f
here contrasted with their *; Mic 1:11f
your faces in *, and admit that Mic 3:7
will see your nakedness and *. Nah 3:5
over their nakedness and *. Hab 2:15
own glory will be replaced by *. Hab 2:16
no one heeds—the wicked know no *. Zep 3:5
long ago in * and humility. Mt 11:21
worth in order to * those people 1Co 1:27
in sorrow and *, and seeing to it 1Co 5:2
For to your * I say it, some of 1Co 15:34
to bring * to the name of Christ. 1Ti 1:20
him up to mocking and to public *. Heb 6:6
with him there, bearing his *. Heb 13:13
But it is no * to suffer for 1Pe 4:16
All they leave behind them is * Jud 1:13
SHAME-IDOLS
you got rid of the * throughout the 2Ch 19:3
and to worship * instead! 2Ch 24:17,18
hills and set up * and graven 2Ch 33:19
altars and the * on the hills. 2Ch 34:3
down, and the * ground into dust 2Ch 34:4
*, and chopped down the obelisks. 2Ch 34:7
SHAME-IMAGES
the obelisks, *, and other heathen 2Ch 31:1
Baal, and of the *, and of the sun, 2Ch 33:3
SHAMED
But let the wicked be * by what Ps 31:17
and cursed and * for your sake. Ps 69:7
of yours will be * by exile for Jer 8:9
from you shall be disgraced and *; Jer 17:13
they shall be * and thoroughly Jer 20:11
nor be * by heathen conquest. Eze 34:29
commit, you have * your name and Hab 2:10
to my former exiles, mocked and *. Zep 3:19
This * his enemies. Lk 13:17
SHAMEFACED
but as for us, we are always * Dan 9:7
SHAMEFUL
them and break down their * idols. Ex 23:24
and cut down their * idols. Ex 34:13
mother, it is a * thing, and they Lev 20:17
the * images and burn the idols. Deu 7:5
obelisks, burn the * images, cut Deu 12:3
are you to erect * images beside Deu 16:21
has accused her of * things, Deu 22:17,18
father's * behavior toward David. 1Sa 20:34
They made detestable, * idols and 2Ki 17:16
knocked down the * idols of 2Ki 18:4
Baal and made a * Asherah idol, 2Ki 21:3,4,5
Manasseh even set up a * 2Ki 21:7
He removed the * idol of Asherah 2Ki 23:6
cut down the * idols of Asherah; 2Ki 23:14
and burned the * idol of Asherah. 2Ki 23:15
chopped down the * Asherim-idols, 2Ch 14:3
For lust is a * sin, a crime Job 31:11
For I admit my * deed—it haunts Ps 51:3
before your neighbor in * defeat. Pro 25:8,9,10
It is a * business that these men Jer 10:14
She did a * thing when she said, Hos 1:5
other, men doing * things with Rom 1:27
And if it is * for a woman to 1Co 11:6
All such * methods we forego. 2Co 4:2
It would be * even to mention Eph 5:12
sin, impurity, lust and * desires; Col 3:5
He was willing to die a * death Heb 12:2
SHAMEFULLY
me, and how they so * dishonor me. Ps 69:19
them *, even killing some of them. Mt 22:6
mocked and treated * and spat upon, Lk 18:32
SHAMELESS
Jerusalem, these * harlots—with all Eze 23:44
TOGETHER AND pray, you * Zep 2:1
SHAMELESSLY
but they * cheat widows out of Mk 12:40
SHAMGAR
The next judge after Ehud was * Ju 3:31
In the days of * and of Jael, Ju 5:6
SHAMING
to be king in your place, * 1Sa 20:30
the church and * those who are poor 1Co 11:22
SHAMIR
*, Jattir, Socoh, Dannah, Jos 15:48-62
* in the hill country of Ephraim. Ju 10:1
When he died, he was buried in *, Ju 10:2
and his grandsons * and Isshiah, 1Ch 24:24,25
SHAMLAI
Akkub, Hagab, *, Hanan, Giddel, Ez 2:43-54
SHAMMA
Imrah, Bezer, Hod, *, Shilshah, 1Ch 7:36,37
SHAMMAH
were:Nahath, Zerah, *, Mizzah. Gen 36:13,14
clan of *,The clan of Mizzah. Gen 36:17
Next Jesse summoned *, but the 1Sa 16:9
Abinadab, and *—had already 1Sa 17:13
After him was *, the son of Agee 2Sa 23:11,12
* from Harod: 2Sa 23:24-39
* from Harar; 2Sa 23:24-39
Nahath, Zerah, *, and Mizzah. 1Ch 1:37
SHAMMAI
* and Jada. 1Ch 2:28
Father of *. 1Ch 2:44
She was the mother of Miriam, *, 1Ch 4:17
SHAMMAI'S
* sons were 1Ch 2:28
* brother Jada had two sons, 1Ch 2:32
* son was Maon, the father of 1Ch 2:45
SHAMMOTH
* from Harod; 1Ch 11:26-47
SHAMMU-A
*, son of Zaccur, from the tribe Num 13:3-15
*, Shobab, Nathan, Solomon, Ibhar, 2Sa 5:14,15,16
*, leader of the Bilgah clan; Neh 12:12-21
SHAMMUA
*, Shobab, Nathan, Solomon, Ibhar, 1Ch 14:4-7
Bakbukiah and Abda (son of *, Neh 11:15,16,17
SHAMSHERAI
*, Sheshariah, Athaliah, 1Ch 8:26,27
SHAMUTH
Fifth Division was * from Izrah, 1Ch 27:8
SHANTY
like a watchman's * in the field Is 1:8
SHAPE
Don't chip or * the stones with a Ex 20:25
to see, in the * of an altar. Jos 22:
the same size and * as the first. Eze 48:
SHAPED
obelisks, or * stones, for I am the Lev 26
The stonecutters quarried and * 1Ki 5:
its brim was * like a goblet, and 1Ki 7:
up a boulder * like a millstone and Rev 18:
SHAPELESS
a *, chaotic mass, Gen 1
Or, "* and void." Gen 1:
SHAPELY
was *, and in every way a beauty. Gen 29:1
Your nose is * Sol 7
SHAPHAM
by *, also Janai and Shaphat. 1Ch 5:1
SHAPHAN
sent his secretary * (son of 2Ki 22:3,
Priest went to * the secretary and 2Ki 22:
He gave the scroll to * to read. 2Ki 22:
When * reported to the king 2Ki 22:9,1
Then * read it to the king. 2Ki 22:9,1
the priest, and *, and Asaiah, the 2Ki 22:12,1
and Achbor, and *, and Asaiah went 2Ki 22:1
and grandson of *) as governor over 2Ki 25:2
he appointed * (son of Azaliah) and 2Ch 34:
Hilkiah exclaimed to *, the 2Ch 34:15,1
Hilkiah gave the scroll to *, 2Ch 34:15,1
to Shaphan, and * took it to the 2Ch 34:15,1
Ahikam (son of *), Abdon (son of 2Ch 34:2
(son of Micah), * the treasurer, 2Ch 34:2
But Ahikam (son of *), the royal Jer 26:2
Elasah (son of *) and Gemariah (son Jer 29:
(son of *) to read the scroll. Jer 36:1
Gemariah, son of *) heard the Jer 36:1
Gemariah (son of *), Zedekiah (son Jer 36:1
*), to take him back to his home. Jer 39:14
of *) worshiping the pictures. Eze 8:1
SHAPHAN'S
and Ahikam (* son), and Achbor 2Ki 22:12,1
SHAPHAT
*, son of Hori, from the tribe of Num 13:3-15
Elisha (the son of * of 1Ki 19:16
Neariah, and *. 1Ch 3:21,22
by Shapham, also Janai and *. 1Ch 5:12
of Sharon, and * (son of Adlai) had 1Ch 27:29
SHAPHIR
There go the people of *, Mic 1:11
their failures. * sounds like the Mic 1:11f
their failures. * sounds like the Mic 1:11f
their failures. * sounds like the Mic 1:11f
SHAQEDH
There is word play here between * Jer 1:12f
SHARAI
Shashai, *, Azarel, Shelemiah, Ez 10:34-42
SHARAR
Ahiam (the son of *) from Harar; 2Sa 23:24-39
SHARDS
covered with scales as sharp as *; Job 41:30
SHARE
And let him * the prosperity of Gen 9:26,27
but give a * of the booty to Gen 14:24
He is not going to * your Gen 21:10
is small, let it * the lamb with Ex 12:3,4
whether to * in this way depends Ex 12:3,4
you will * the burden with them. Ex 18:22
I will not * your affection with Ex 20:5
If you come, you will * in all Num 10:32
shall have their full * in it. Num 14:24
But first, the Lord gets a * of Num 31:28
by the army. His * is one out of Num 31:28
Give this * to Eleazar the Num 31:29
about the Levites. * with them. Deu 12:19
"Don't forget to * your income Deu 14:27
your wine press. * with him in Deu 15:14
He shall be given his * of the Deu 18:8
He will refuse to give them a * Deu 28:55
refuse to * with her beloved Deu 28:56,57
and told them to * their great Jos 22:7,8
and we will * our land with you. Jos 22:19
talk like this? We * and share 1Sa 30:24
We share and * alike—those who go 1Sa 30:24
eat the priests' * of food from the Ez 2:62,63
the priests' * of food from the Neh 7:64,65
them their full * of punishment. Job 36:6
brooks and meadows as my *! Ps 16:6
are punished but I will not * it. Ps 91:8
Let me * in your chosen ones' Ps 106:5
the street? Why * your children Pro 5:17
joy—no one else can really * it. Pro 14:10
wicked sons and * their estate. Pro 17:2
you now, and * it with others. Pro 22:20,21
even the lame will win their *. Is 33:23
I will not * my praise with Is 42:8
I want you to * your food with Is 58:7
and get your full * of the Is 58:14
each tribe will have an equal *. Eze 47:14
your full * of those last days." Dan 12:13
to the farmers to collect his *. Mt 21:34
will give God his * of the crop. Mt 21:43
the others to * with them, for Mt 25:7,8
men to collect his * of the crop. Mk 12:2

HARE Con't)
ather, 'I want my * of your estate Lk 15:12
o collect his * of the crops. Lk 20:10
his and * it among yourselves. Lk 22:17
want not only to * my faith with Rom 1:11,12
and now you * his new life, and Rom 6:5
know that you will * his new life. Rom 6:8
children, we will * his Rom 8:17
But if we are to * his glory, we Rom 8:17
we must also * his suffering. Rom 8:17
around us will * in the glorious Rom 8:20,21
the world will * in later on when Rom 11:12
will * in God's mercy upon you. Rom 11:31
If they are sad, * their sorrow. Rom 12:15
have come to * in their spiritual Rom 15:27f
have no * in the Kingdom of God? 1Co 6:9,10
have no * in his kingdom. 1Co 6:9,10
expect some * of the harvest. 1Co 9:10
altar of God get a * of the food 1Co 9:13
without waiting to * with the 1Co 11:21
I certainly have my * in it too. 2Co 2:5,6
so they could * in the joy of 2Co 8:4
your * in this ministry of giving. 2Co 8:6
can * with you when you need it. 2Co 8:14
So you also should * with those 2Co 8:15
invited you to * the eternal life Gal 1:6
trust in Christ * the same blessing Gal 3:8,9
is in the wrong. * each other's Gal 6:2
the future he has called you to *. Eph 1:18
In olden times God did not * Eph 3:5
have their full * with the Jews in Eph 3:6
will * my joy with each of you. Php 2:17
has made us fit to * all the Col 1:12
Then he gave you a * in the very Col 2:13
with him and * in all his glories. Col 3:4
into his kingdom to * his glory. 1Th 2:12
Through us he called you to * in 2Th 2:14
being ready to * with others 1Ti 6:18
Take your * of suffering as a 2Ti 2:3
and now we can * in the wealth of Tit 3:7
And I pray that as you * your Phm 1:6
* in all that belongs to Christ. Heb 3:14
king, but chose to * ill-treatment Heb 11:24,25
them to wait and * the even better Heb 11:40
good, that we may * his holiness. Heb 12:10
there yourself. * the sorrow of Heb 13:3
Don't forget to do good and to * Heb 13:16
Cheerfully * your home with 1Pe 4:9
and I, too, will * his glory and 1Pe 5:1
* in his glory and honor. 1Pe 5:4
so that you may * the fellowship 1Jn 1:3
gives, and we shall * his kingdom! Rev 1:9
and made them * the wine of her Rev 14:8
who * in the First Resurrection. Rev 20:6
take away his * in the Tree of Rev 22:19

SHARECROP
some farmers on a * basis, and went Mt 21:33

SHARECROPPERS
You are merely my tenants and *! Lev 25:23

SHARED
this was—and * it with others." Lk 6:4
glory we * before the world began. Jn 17:5
constantly and * everything with Act 2:44
for Communion, and * their meals Act 2:46
We have * together the blessings Php 1:7
of heaven and * in the Holy Spirit, Heb 6:4
I, too, have * the patience Jesus Rev 1:9

SHARES
With them alone he * the secrets Ps 25:14
we'll split with you in equal * Pro 1:14
The student * his teacher's Mt 10:25
The servant * his master's! Mt 10:25
good life: he even * his own glory 2Pe 1:3

SHAREZER
sons Adrammelech and * killed him. 2Ki 19:37
* killed him with their swords; Is 37:38
of men headed by *, the chief Zec 7:2

SHARING
and we aren't * it with anyone! 2Ki 7:9
what they do, * their dainties. Ps 141:4
everyone was *. Act 4:32
and his children, * in God's rich Rom 11:17
who drink it are * together the 1Co 10:16
shows that we are * together in the 1Co 10:16
in the Lord, * the same Spirit? Php 2:1
wonderful joy of * his glory in 1Pe 4:13

SHARKS
all your loan *—all will die. Zep 1:11

SHARON
the entire pasture country of *. 1Ch 5:16
Shitrai from * was in charge of 1Ch 27:29
on the Plains of *, and Shaphat 1Ch 27:29
THE GIRL: "I am the rose of *, Sol 2:1
Lebanon has been destroyed; * has Is 33:9
me, the plains of * shall again be Is 65:10
of Lydda and * turned to the Lord Act 9:35

SHARON'S
Carmel's pastures and * meadows; Is 35:2

SHARP
Then Jael took a * tent peg and a Ju 4:21
to master him bring a * sword! Job 40:19
with scales as * as shards; Job 41:30
Your arrows are * Ps 45:5
You are * as a tack in plotting Ps 52:2
teeth are * as spears and arrows. Ps 57:4
They keep a * lookout for Ps 64:6
You shall be pierced with * Ps 120:4
are like * arrows to defend him. Ps 127:4
is left to you, * as a Pro 5:4
or shooting him with a * arrow. Pro 25:18
poor with teeth as * as knives! Pro 30:13,14
Their arrows are *; Is 5:28
burns with pain; * pangs of horror Is 21:3
* arrows and the terrors of war! Is 21:15
my words of judgment * as swords. Is 49:2
I am like a * arrow in his Is 49:2
their threats are * and barbed and Eze 2:6
"SON OF DUST, take a * sword and Eze 5:1
with teeth as * as those of lions! Joe 1:6
force, and keep a * watch for the Nah 2:1
himself with * pieces of stone. Mk 5:5
"Keep a * lookout! Mk 13:35,36,37
* thorns and put it on his head. Mk 15:16,17
this was so * that they separated. Act 15:39
control his * tongue is just Jas 1:26
right hand and a *, double-bladed Rev 1:16
the * and double-bladed sword. Rev 2:12
head and a * sickle in his hand. Rev 14:14
and he also had a * sickle. Rev 14:17
In his mouth he held a * sword to Rev 19:15
killed with the * sword in the Rev 19:21

SHARP-EYED
even the * birds in the sky Job 28:21

SHARP-TOOTHED
You shall be a new and * Is 41:15

SHARPEN
needed to * their plowshares, 1Sa 13:20
Unless they repent, he will * Ps 7:12
be wise and * the blade. Ecc 10:10
* your spears, put on your armor. Jer 46:4
* the arrows! Jer 51:11

SHARPENED
They cut me down with * tongues; Ps 64:3
She is a * stick that will pierce Is 36:6
A sword is being * and polished for Eze 21:9,10,11
it is * and polished and flashes Eze 21:28

SHARPENING
For * a plow point, 60Ç 1Sa 13:21
For * a disc, 60Ç 1Sa 13:21
For * an axe, 30Ç 1Sa 13:21
For * a sickle, 30Ç 1Sa 13:21
For * an ox goad, 30Ç) 1Sa 13:21

SHARPER
power: it is * than the sharpest Heb 4:12

SHARPEST
sharper than the * dagger, cutting Heb 4:12

SHARPLY
before him and accused him *. Gen 12:18
"Look here," the king said *, 2Ch 18:15
but I spoke * to them and said, Neh 13:21
will drop off *, says the Lord. Eze 36:14
NEVER SPEAK * to an older man, but 1Ti 5:1

SHARPSHOOTERS
men who were left-handed *. Ju 20:16

SHARUHEN
*, En-rimmon, Ether, and Ashan. Jos 19:2-7

SHASHAI
Machnadebai, *, Sharai, Azarel, Ez 10:34-42

SHASHAK
*, Jeremoth. 1Ch 8:14
The sons of * were: 1Ch 8:22-25

SHATTER
heathen altars and * the obelisks Deu 7:5
I will * the people of Jerusalem; Jer 19:11
jar to jar and then * the jars! Jer 48:12
Moab shall * Dibon too, and tear Jer 48:18
It will * all these kingdoms into Dan 2:44
He is surrounding them and will * Amo 3:11

SHATTERED
their weapons were * by the Mighty Gen 49:24
* and the crops were destroyed. Ex 9:25
will not succeed—you will be *. Is 8:9,10
angry enemies lie confused and *. Is 41:11
As this jar lies *, so I will Jer 19:11
the strong, the beautiful is *! Jer 48:17
for I have smashed and * Moab Jer 48:38
all the earth, lies broken and *. Jer 50:23
Your gods will be *; Eze 6:4-7
departed honor of their * gods. Hos 10:5
hopes of wealth were now *; Act 16:19
power of your sinful nature was *. Rom 6:2,3
they will be * like a pot of clay Rev 2:27

SHATTERING
when the * of the power of the Dan 12:7f

SHATTERS
of it, God simply * the greatest of Job 34:24

SHAUL
Succeeded by: King *, from Gen 36:31-39
Jachin, Zohar, and *. (Shaul's Gen 46:8-14
* (whose mother was a Canaanite). Ex 6:15
named after their ancestor *. Num 26:12-14
When Samlah died, * from the 1Ch 1:48
When * died, Baal-hanan the son 1Ch 1:49
Zerah and *. 1Ch 4:24
Assir, Tahath, Uriel, Uzziah, *. 1Ch 6:22,23,24

SHAUL'S
(* mother was a girl from Canaan). Gen 46:8-14
* son was Shallum, his grandson 1Ch 4:25

SHAULITES
The *, named after their ancestor Num 26:12-14

SHAVE
and after a quick * and change of Gen 41:14
skin, he shall * off all the hair Lev 13:33
wash his clothes, * off all his Lev 14:8
The seventh day he shall again * Lev 14:9
later he shall * his defiled head; Num 6:9
"Then the Nazirite shall * his Num 6:18
then having them * their entire Num 8:7
nor * the front halves of your Deu 14:1
She must * her head and pare her Deu 21:12
—and use it on you to * off Is 7:20
and Medeba; they * their heads in Is 15:2
weep and mourn and * your heads in Is 22:12
O Jerusalem, * your head in shame Jer 7:29
cut themselves nor * their heads as Jer 16:6
They * their heads and beards in Jer 48:37
razor to * your head and beard; Eze 5:1
you shall * your heads in sorrow Eze 7:18
They * their heads in grief and Eze 27:31
hair grow too long, nor * it off. Eze 44:20
clothes and * your heads as signs Amo 8:10
lands. * your heads in sorrow. Mic 1:16
* their heads and take some vows. Act 21:23

SHAVED
After the man's head has been *, Num 6:19
So Hanun took David's men and * 2Sa 10:4
Literally, "tore his robe and * Job 1:20f
They had * off their beards, torn Jer 41:5
I neither washed nor * nor combed Dan 10:3
At Cenchreae, Paul had his head * Act 18:18
The head was * thirty days before Act 18:18f
The head was * thirty days before Act 18:22f
and have your head * too—and pay Act 21:24
too—and pay for theirs to be *. Act 21:24
I had * my head as their laws Act 24:18
to have her head *, then she should 1Co 11:6

SHAVEH
at the Valley of * (later called Gen 14:17

SHAVING
ambassadors by * their beards and 1Ch 19:4

SHAVSHA
the head priests; * was the king's 1Ch 18:16

SHAWL
"Bring your *," he told her. Ru 3:15-18

SHE-ALTI-EL
Zerubbabel (son of *) and his clan, Ez 3:1
Zerubbabel (son of *), Jeshua (son Ez 3:8
Zerubbabel (son of *) and Jeshua Ez 5:1
(son of *), governor of Judah; Hag 1:1
Then Zerubbabel (son of *), the Hag 1:12

SHE-ALTIEL
*, Malchiram, 1Ch 3:17,18
Zerubbabel (son of *) and Jeshua: Neh 12:1

SHE-ARIAH
Azrikam, Bocheru, Ishmael, *, 1Ch 8:38
*, Obadiah, Hanan. 1Ch 9:44

SHE'D
ten thousand laws, * say they Hos 8:12

SHE'LL
Just trust me, and * be all Lk 8:50

SHE'S
"* gone," he told her father; Lk 8:49

SHEAF
sheaves, and my * stood up, and Gen 37:7
bring the first * of the harvest to Lev 23:9,10,11
to bring in a * from the field, Deu 24:19

SHEAL
Adaiah, Jashub, *, Jeremoth. Ez 10:29

SHEALTIEL
Jechoniah was the father of *; Mt 1:12
* was the father of Zerubbabel; Mt 1:12
Zerubbabel's father was *; Lk 3:23-38

SHEALTIEL'S
was Shealtiel;* father was Neri; Lk 3:23-38

SHEAR
fields, and do not * the firstborn Deu 15:19

SHEAR-JASHUB
King Ahaz, you and *, your son. Is 7:3
(his people)," * means "A remnant Is 8:18

SHEARED
sheep were being * at Baal-hazor in 2Sa 13:21-24

SHEARERS
slaughtered for my * and give it to 1Sa 25:11
and as a sheep before her * is Is 53:7
the *, so he opened not his mouth; Act 8:32

SHEARING
So one day while Laban was out * Gen 31:17-20
to supervise the * of his sheep. Gen 38:12
oil, and of the fleece at * time. Deu 18:4
at this time for the sheep *. 1Sa 25:2
When David heard that Nabal was * 1Sa 25:4
I am told that you are * your 1Sa 25:7

SHEARS
you off as though with pruning *. Is 18:5

SHEATH
Goliath's from its * and killed him 1Sa 17:50,51
slipped the dagger from its *. 2Sa 20:8,9,10
to put back his sword into its *; 1Ch 21:27
not return to its * again until its Eze 21:5
sword is drawn from its *; Eze 21:28
Shall I return my sword to its * Eze 21:30
Your bow was pulled from its * Hab 3:8,9f

SHEAVES
the field binding *, and my sheaf Gen 37:7
stood up, and your * all gathered Gen 37:7
along with all the * and shocks of Ju 15:5
right among the * without stopping Ru 2:15
hauling in *, and loading their Neh 13:15
return singing, carrying their *. Ps 126:6
like manure, like * after the Jer 9:22
groans that is loaded with *. Amo 2:13
of his people like * upon the Mic 4:12
a burning match among the *; Zec 12:6

SHEBA
The sons of Raamah were:*, Dedan. Gen 10:7
*, Ophir, Havi-lah, Jobab. Gen 10:26-30
Jokshan's two sons were * and Gen 25:3
Beer-sheba, *, Moladah, Jos 19:2-7
A HOT-HEAD whose name was * 2Sa 20:1
and deserted David and followed *! 2Sa 20:2
"That fellow * is going to hurt us 2Sa 20:6
Joab set out after * with an elite 2Sa 20:7
lying there and continued after *. 2Sa 20:8,9,10
went on with Joab to capture *. 2Sa 20:13
Meanwhile * had traveled across 2Sa 20:14
All I want is a man named * from 2Sa 20:21
WHEN THE QUEEN of * heard how 1Ki 10:1
from the queen of *, King Solomon 1Ki 10:13
The sons of Raama were * and 1Ch 1:5-9
*, Ophir, Havilah, and Jobab. 1Ch 1:20-23
Jokshan's sons were * and Dedan. 1Ch 1:32
*, Jorai, Jacan, Zia, and Eber. 1Ch 5:13
WHEN THE QUEEN of * heard of 2Ch 9:1
King Solomon gave the Queen of * 2Ch 9:12
from Tema and from * stop for water Job 6:19-21
those from * and from Seba—all will Ps 72:10
given the gold of *, and there will Ps 72:15
from Midian and * and Ephah, too, Is 60:6
sweet incense from * before me! Jer 6:20
The merchants of * and Raamah Eze 27:22
"But * and Dedan Eze 38:13
The Queen of * shall rise Mt 12:42
at the Judgment Day the Queen of * Lk 11:31

SHEBA'S
* head and threw it out to Joab. 2Sa 20:22

SHEBANIAH
for the Ark. *, Joshaphat, 1Ch 15:24
Kadmi-el, Bani, *, Bunni, Neh 9:4
Hodiah, *, and Pethahiah. Neh 9:5
Malchijah, Hattush, *, Neh 10:1
*, Hodiah, Kelita, Neh 10:9-13
*, Hodiah, Neh 10:9-13
Joseph, leader of the * clan; Neh 12:12-21

SHEBER
Maacah, bore him *, Tirhanah, 1Ch 2:48,49

SHEBNA
Go and say to *, the palace Is 22:15,16
of Israel, and *, the king's Is 36:3
Then Eliakim and * and Joah said Is 36:11
minister, and *, the royal scribe, Is 36:22
minister, and * his royal scribe, Is 37:2

SHEBNAH
manager; *, his secretary; 2Ki 18:18
Then Eliakim, *, and Joah said to 2Ki 18:26
manager, and * the king's 2Ki 18:37
Then he told Eliakim, *, and 2Ki 19:2

SHEBUEL
Gershom's sons were led by *, 1Ch 23:16
Mattaniah, Uzziel, *, Jerimoth, 1Ch 25:4,5
sons of Jehieli. *, son of Gershom 1Ch 26:23,24

SHECANIAH
Obadiah's son was *. 1Ch 3:21,22
Tenth, the group led by *; 1Ch 24:7-18
Jeshua, Shemaiah, Amariah, and *. 2Ch 31:14,15
of David of the clan of *—Hattush; Ez 8:2-14
From the clan of *—the son of Ez 8:2-14
Then * (the son of Jehiel of the Ez 10:2
that they would do as * had said; Ez 10:5
Shemaiah (son of *), the gatekeeper Neh 3:29
father-in-law was * (son of Arah) Neh 6:18
Malluch, Hattush, *, Neh 12:1

SHECANIAH'S
* son was Shemaiah; 1Ch 3:21,22

SHECHEM
to a place near *, and set up camp Gen 12:6
Then they arrived safely at * Gen 33:18
girls, but when *, son of King Gen 34:2
Hamor told Jacob, "My son * is Gen 34:8
Then * addressed Dinah's father Gen 34:11
Her brothers then lied to * and Gen 34:13
what * had done to their sister. Gen 34:13
Hamor and * gladly agreed, and Gen 34:18,19
this request, for * was very much Gen 34:18,19
So Hamor and * appeared before Gen 34:20
man there, including Hamor and *. Gen 34:26
them beneath the oak tree near *. Gen 35:4
flocks to * to graze them there. Gen 37:12
are over in * grazing the flocks. Gen 37:13,14
So he traveled to * from his home Gen 37:13,14
named after their ancestor *. Num 26:28-37
Asri-el, *, Shemida, and Hepher. Jos 17:2
Michmethath, which is east of *. Jos 17:7
*, in the hill country of Ephraim; Jos 20:7
* (a City of Refuge), Gezer, Jos 21:20,21,22
Israel to him at *, along with Jos 24:1
them that day at *, committing them Jos 24:25
were buried in *, in the parcel of Jos 24:32
He also had a concubine in *, Ju 8:31
uncles—his mother's brothers—in *. Ju 9:1
"Go and talk to the leaders of * Ju 9:2
mother was from * (Judges 8:30–31), Ju 9:2f
Then the citizens of * and Ju 9:6
the garrison at *, and Abimelech Ju 9:6
to the men of *, "If you want Ju 9:7
the citizens of * and Beth-millo; Ju 9:20
citizens of *, and they revolted. Ju 9:22,23
the citizens of * who aided him in Ju 9:24
For the men of * set an ambush Ju 9:25
of Ebed) moved to * with his Ju 9:26
During the harvest feast at * Ju 9:27
come to live in *, and now they are Ju 9:31
So Gaal led the men of * into the Ju 9:39
many of the men of * were left Ju 9:40
relatives out of *, and wouldn't Ju 9:41
The next day the men of * went Ju 9:42
to keep the men of * from getting Ju 9:44
and the men of * for their sin of Ju 9:56,57
road that goes from Bethel to *. Ju 21:19
INAUGURATION WAS at *, 1Ki 12:1
rest of Israel at *, and was the 1Ki 12:2,3,4
Jeroboam now built the city of * 1Ki 12:25
*, in Mount Ephraim; 1Ch 6:66-69
The sons of Shemida were Ahian, * 1Ch 7:19
and finally by * and its 1Ch 7:28
to * for Rehoboam's coronation. 2Ch 10:1
No wonder I exult! "*, Succoth, Ps 60:6,7
of *, and also Succoth Valley. Ps 108:7
Mizpah from *, Shiloh and Samaria, Jer 41:5
* and practice every kind of sin. Hos 6:9
All of them were taken to * and Act 7:16

SHECHEM'S
family of Hamor, * father, for 100 Gen 33:19
Meanwhile King Hamor, * father, Gen 34:6,7
They rescued Dinah from * house Gen 34:26
from the sons of Hamor, * father. Act 7:16

SHECHEMITES
The *, named after their ancestor Num 26:28-37

SHED
"we'll * no blood—let's throw Gen 37:21,22
hands have not * this blood, Deu 21:7
You will * bitter tears because 1Sa 8:18
a warrior and have * much blood.' 1Ch 28:3
* his own glorious light upon you. Is 58:8

SHEDDING
idols of Canaan—* innocent blood Ps 106:37,38
the city by * innocent blood. Lam 4:13
and without the * of blood there is Heb 9:22

SHEDEUR
Reuban -Elizur (son of * Num 1:2-15
Elizur (son of *) Num 2:3-31
*, chief of the tribe of Reuben; Num 7:30-35
the son of * leading his people. Num 10:18

SHEEP
because of her—*, oxen, donkeys, Gen 12:16
Lot too was very wealthy, with * Gen 13:5
Then King Abimelech took * and Gen 20:14
Then Abraham gave * and oxen to Gen 21:27
God has given him flocks of * and Gen 24:35
He had large flocks of * and Gen 26:14
three flocks of * lying beside a Gen 29:2
his daughter Rachel with the *." Gen 29:6
*, for she was a shepherdess. Gen 29:9
because the * were his uncle's, Gen 29:10
or spotted, and all the black *. Gen 30:31,32
any white goats or * in my flock, Gen 30:33
patches, and all of the black *. Gen 30:35,36
was out shearing *, Jacob set his Gen 31:17-20
own oxen, donkeys, *, and many Gen 32:5
supervise the shearing of his *. Gen 38:12
* or a goat, without any defects. Ex 12:5
and peace offerings of * and oxen. Ex 20:24
"IF A MAN steals an ox or * and Ex 22:1
stolen ox. For *, the fine shall be Ex 22:1
* returned for each sheep stolen. Ex 22:1
sheep returned for each * stolen. Ex 22:1
ox or donkey or * or whatever it Ex 22:4
an ox, donkey, *, clothing, or Ex 22:9
keep a donkey, ox, *, or any other Ex 22:10
the oxen and the *, give it to me Ex 22:30
is mine—cattle, *, and goats. Ex 34:19
offering is a * or a goat, it too Lev 1:10
"If a goat or * is used as a Lev 3:6
whether from oxen, *, or goats. Lev 7:23
it must be a young bull or a * or Lev 22:19
"When a bullock, *, or goat is Lev 22:26,27
ox or *, for it is already his. Lev 27:26
their flocks of * and goats, or Num 15:
firstborn of cows, *, or goats may Num 18:
oxen and *, and gave animals to Num 22:
not be as * without a shepherd." Num 27:
for themselves) was 675,000 *; Num 31:32-
337,500 * (of which 675 were given Num 31:36-
to:337,500 *,36,000 oxen,30,500 Num 31:42-
large flocks of *) noticed what Num 32
what wonderful * country it was. Num 32
And it is all wonderful * Num 32:
*, and do all you have said." Num 32:
flocks of cattle, *, and goats when Deu 7:
The ox, the *, the goat, Deu 14:3,4
The antelope, and the mountain *. Deu 14:3,4
to buy an ox, a *, some wine, or Deu 14:
of your flocks of * and goats. Deu 15:
ox or * to the Lord your God. Deu 17
of every ox or * brought for Deu 18
"IF YOU SEE someone's ox or * Deu 22
* will be given to your enemies. Deu 28:
oxen; *; Jos 6:
his oxen, donkeys, *, his tent, and Jos 7:
all their *, oxen, and donkeys. Ju 6:3
and butchered the *, oxen, and 1Sa 14:
bring the oxen and * here to kill 1Sa 14:
oxen, *, camels, and donkeys.' 1Sa 15
the best of the * and oxen and the 1Sa 15
of * and lowing of oxen I heard?" 1Sa 15:1
the best of the * and oxen," Saul 1Sa 15:1
the best of the * and oxen and loot 1Sa 15:2
in the fields watching the *." 1Sa 16:10,1
to help his father with the *. 1Sa 17:14,1
So David left the * with another 1Sa 17:2
"What about the * you're 1Sa 17:2
of my father's *," he said, "and 1Sa 17:3
also all the oxen, donkeys, and *. 1Sa 22:1
from Maon owned a * ranch there, 1Sa 25:
He had three thousand * and a 1Sa 25:
at this time for the * shearing. 1Sa 25:
was shearing his *, he sent ten of 1Sa 25:
you are shearing your * and goats. 1Sa 25:
to us and the *, and nothing was 1Sa 25:15,1
wine, five dressed *, two bushels 1Sa 25:1
for themselves the *, oxen, 1Sa 27:
tending your * in the pastureland. 2Sa 7:
flocks of * and herds of goats; 2Sa 12:
when Absalom's * were being sheared 2Sa 13:21-2
What have these * done? 2Sa 24:1
he sacrificed *, oxen, and fat 1Ki 1:
goats, and many * and has invited 1Ki 1:1
fat goats and many *, and has 1Ki 1:2
cattle, 100 *, and, from time to 1Ki 4:2
sacrificing uncounted * and oxen. 1Ki 8:
oxen and 120,000 * and goats! 1Ki 8:62,6
mountains as * without a shepherd. 1Ki 22:17
and his people were * ranchers. 2Ki 3:4
and * and oxen and servants? 2Ki 5:26
camels, 250,000 *, 2,000 donkeys, 1Ch 5:21
oil, cattle, and * were brought to 1Ch 12:40
But what have these * done? 1Ch 21:17
the donkeys. The * were under the 1Ch 27:31
others sacrificed * and oxen before 2Ch 5:6
was 22,000 oxen and 120,000 *. 2Ch 7:4,5
great herds of * and camels before 2Ch 14:15
and seven thousand *—it was part of 2Ch 15:11
of * and oxen for the feast. 2Ch 18:2
mountain as * without a shepherd. 2Ch 18:16
In addition, 600 oxen and 3,000 * 2Ch 29:32,33
bulls for offerings, and 7,000 *; 2Ch 30:24
1,000 young bulls and 10,000 *. 2Ch 30:24
their cattle and *, and brought a 2Ch 31:5,6
of * and goats he purchased; 2Ch 32:28,29
the priests 2,600 * and goats, and 2Ch 35:8
Jozabad—gave 5,000 * and goats and 2Ch 35:9
then they rebuilt the * Gate, Neh 3:1
from that corner to the * Gate. Neh 3:32
one ox, six fat *, and a large Neh 5:18
then we continued on to the * Neh 12:39
for he owned 7,000 *, 3,000 Job 1:2,3
and burned up your * and all the Job 1:16
moved, flocks of * are stolen, and Job 24:2
or fleece from my * to keep him Job 31:19,20
For now he had 14,000 *, 6,000 Job 42:12
authority: all * and oxen, and Ps 8:7
You have treated us like * in a Ps 44:11
We are like * awaiting slaughter. Ps 44:22
with flocks of *, and the valleys Ps 65:13
us—the * of your own pasture? Ps 74:1
like a flock of *, with Moses and Ps 77:20
Their * were killed by lightning. Ps 78:48
him from feeding *, and from Ps 78:70
Then we your people, the * of Ps 79:13
We are his * and he is our Ps 95:7
his people, the * of his pasture. Ps 100:3
have wandered away like a lost *; Ps 119:176
* by the thousands out in our Ps 144:12-15
there feed your * and their lambs. Sol 1:8
to be trampled by cattle and *. Is 5:5
to have a cow and two * left. Is 7:21,22
cattle, * and goats will graze Is 7:25
like * deserted by their shepherd. Is 13:14

IEEP Con't)
he shepherds won't let their * Is 13:20
re deserted. * pasture there, Is 17:2
oung one, kills a *, he pays no Is 31:4,5
eads his *, calling each by its Is 40:26
'hey will be my *, grazing in Is 49:8,9
ne ones who strayed away like *! Is 53:6
nd as a * before her shearers is Is 53:7
ome, tear apart the *; Is 56:9
nd your flocks of * and herds of Jer 5:17
ike helpless * to the slaughter. Jer 12:3
hepherds of my *—for they have Jer 23:1
ee shepherds leading * and lambs. Jer 33:12
ordan stalking the * in the fold. Jer 49:19
My people have been lost *. Jer 50:6
The Israelites are like * the Jer 50:17
hat leaps upon the grazing *. Jer 50:44
Jse only the best * from the Eze 24:5
and where flocks of * can graze. Eze 25:5
Shouldn't shepherds feed the *? Eze 34:2
comes along. My * wandered through Eze 34:6
says: I will search and find my *. Eze 34:11
I will find my * and rescue them Eze 34:12
the Shepherd of my *, and cause Eze 34:15,16
fat shepherds and their scrawny *. Eze 34:20
You are my flock, the * of my Eze 34:31
from each 200 * in all your Eze 45:15
flocks in Israel, give him one *. Eze 45:15
and earned a wife by tending *. Hos 12:12
for them; the * bleat in misery. Joe 1:18
the *, keeping them from straying. Amo 1:1
to rescue his * from a lion, but it Amo 3:12
again like * in a fold, like a Mic 2:12
be like helpless * before her! Mic 5:8
of shepherd camps and folds for *. Zep 2:6
will become a pastureland for *. Zep 2:14
as a Shepherd caring for his *. Zec 9:16,17
led astray and wander like lost *; Zec 10:2
with these *—this nation—and they Zec 11:8
Then those who bought and sold *, Zec 11:11
Shepherd and the * will scatter, Zec 13:7
as harmless *, but are wolves and Mt 7:15
They were like * without a Mt 9:36
the people of Israel—God's lost *. Mt 10:6
"I am sending you out as * among Mt 10:16
you had just one *, and it fell Mt 12:11
valuable is a person than a *! Mt 12:12
* of Israel—not the Gentiles." Mt 15:24
"If a man has a hundred *, and Mt 18:12
as a shepherd separates the * Mt 25:32
and place the * at my right hand, Mt 25:33
* of the flock will be scattered. Mt 26:31
they were like * without a Mk 6:34
Shepherd, and the * will scatter.' Mk 14:27
guarding their flocks of *. Lk 2:8
you had a hundred * and one of them Lk 15:3,4
you because your lost * was found. Lk 15:6
or taking care of *, he doesn't Lk 17:7,8,9
selling cattle, *, and doves for Jn 2:14
and drove out the * and oxen, Jn 2:15
Inside the city, near the * Jn 5:2
* hear his voice and come to him; Jn 10:3
and he calls his own * by name Jn 10:3
"I am the Gate for the *," he Jn 10:7
But the true * did not listen to Jn 10:8
lays down his life for the *. Jn 10:11
and will leave the *, for they Jn 10:12
and has no real concern for the *. Jn 10:13
and know my own *, and they know Jn 10:14
and I lay down my life for the *. Jn 10:15
I have other *, too, in another Jn 10:16
of my flock. My * recognize my Jn 10:27
"Then take care of my *," Jesus Jn 21:16
said, "Then feed my little *. Jn 21:17
was led as a * to the slaughter, Act 8:32
are like * awaiting slaughter; Rom 8:36
care of a flock of * and goats and 1Co 9:7
shepherd does his *, leading and Eph 4:11
Some went about in skins of * and Heb 11:37,38
Shepherd of the * by an everlasting Heb 13:20,21
Like * you wandered away from 1Pe 2:25
wheat, cattle, *, horses, Rev 18:13

SHEEP-SHEARING
had left for the * at Timnah, and Gen 38:13

SHEEP'S
Your teeth are white as * wool, Sol 4:2

SHEEPFOLD
the gate into a *, who sneaks over Jn 10:1

SHEEPFOLDS
"We will build * for our flocks Num 32:16
your families and * for your sheep, Num 32:24
were all fortified cities with *. Num 32:34,35,36
did you sit at home among the *, Ju 5:16
road passes some *, Saul went into 1Sa 24:3
Literally, "among the *." Ps 68:11,12,13f

SHEER
his conclusion is * madness. Ecc 10:12,13

SHEERAH
Ephraim's daughter's name was *. 1Ch 7:24

SHEET
its mate on the other long *. Ex 36:11,12
the metal into a * as a covering Num 16:38
and the altar * shall be a Num 16:38
them out into a * of metal to cover Num 16:39
and spread out a * for everyone to Ju 8:25
now maggots are your *, worms Is 14:11
Joseph bought a long * of linen Mk 15:46
* and took him out and buried him. Act 5:6
*, suspended by its four corners, Act 10:11
In the * were all sorts of Act 10:12
Then the * was pulled up again to Act 10:16
a vision—a huge *, let down by its Act 11:5
Inside the * were all sorts of Act 11:6
times before the * and all it Act 11:10

SHEETS
from ten colored * of fine-twined Ex 26:1
Join five * end to end for each Ex 26:3
yeast, and thin * of sweetened Ex 29:2
first made ten * from finely-twined Ex 36:8,9
Five of these * were attached Ex 36:10
of these two long *, each loop Ex 36:11,12
tying the two long * together to Ex 36:13
lovely, colored * of finest linen Pro 7:16,17
They bring beaten * of silver Jer 10:9

SHEHARIAH
Shamsherai, *, Athaliah, 1Ch 8:26,27

SHEKEL
Literally, "half a * after the Ex 30:13f
a shekel after the * of the Ex 30:13f
the sanctuary [the * is twenty Ex 30:13f
a * for an offering to Jehovah." Ex 30:13f
of the * of the sanctuary." Lev 5:15f
according to the * of the Lev 27:25f
twenty gerahs shall be the *." Lev 27:25f
after the * of the sanctuary Num 3:47,48f
them. (The * is twenty gerahs. Num 3:47,48f
after the * of the sanctuary." Num 3:50f
silver * (about half an ounce); Eze 45:12

SHEKELS
Literally, "five hundred *." Ex 30:22,23f
Literally, "five * apiece by the Num 3:47,48f
Literally, "1,365 * after the Num 3:50f
Literally, "a hundred * of Deu 22:19f
Literally, "paid him fifty * of 2Sa 24:24f
Literally, "six hundred * of gold 1Ch 21:25f
Hanamel seventeen * of silver. Jer 32:9
no less; five * shall be valued at Eze 45:12
be valued at five *, no less; Eze 45:12
and ten * at ten shekels! Eze 45:12
and ten shekels at ten *! Eze 45:12
Fifty * shall always equal one Eze 45:12

SHEKEM
the choice land of * to you instead Gen 48:22

SHELAH
Arpachshad's son was *, and Gen 10:24
of *, and after that ." Gen 11:12,13f
* was born, and after that he Gen 11:12,13
* was thirty years old when his Gen 11:14,15
had three sons, Er, Onan, and *. Gen 38:3,4,5
son * was old enough to marry her. Gen 38:11
really intend for * to do this, for Gen 38:11
permitted to marry *, though he was Gen 38:14
promise to give her to my son *." Gen 38:26
Judah and his sons: Er, Onan, *, Gen 46:8-14
named after their ancestor *. Num 26:19-22
*, and Shelah's son was 1Ch 1:18
the son of Arpachshad was *, 1Ch 1:24-27
The son of * was Eber, 1Ch 1:24-27
Er, Onan, and *. 1Ch 2:3
The sons of * (the son of Judah): 1Ch 4:21-22
Eber's father was *; Lk 3:23-38

SHELAH'S
was Shelah, and * son was Eber. Gen 10:24
Shelah, and * son was 1Ch 1:18
Eber's father was Shelah;* father Lk 3:23-38

SHELAMOTH
the Izhar group, consisting of * 1Ch 24:22

SHELANITES
The *, named after their ancestor Num 26:19-22

SHELEMIAH
east gate went to * and his group; 1Ch 26:14,15
Binnui, Shime-i, *, Nathan, Adaiah, Ez 10:34-42
Azarel, *, Shemariah, Shallum, Ez 10:34-42
Next was Hananiah (son of *); Neh 3:30
I put * the priest, Zadok the Neh 13:13
Nethaniah, son of *, son of Cushi) Jer 36:14,15
of Azri-el) and * (son of Abdeel) Jer 36:26
Jehucal (son of *) and Zephaniah Jer 37:3
(son of *, grandson of Hananiah). Jer 37:13
and Jucal (son of *) and Pashhur Jer 38:1

SHELEPH
Almodad, *, Hazarmaveth, Jerah, Gen 10:26-30
Almodad, *, Hazarmaveth, Jerah, 1Ch 1:20-23

SHELESH
Zophah, Imna, *, Amal. 1Ch 7:35

SHELOMI
Ahihud (son of *) Num 34:16-28

SHELOMITH
(His mother's name was *, Lev 24:11
Jushab-hesed, * (a daughter). 1Ch 3:19,20
The sons of Izhar were led by *. 1Ch 23:18
were Abijah, Attai, Ziza, and *. 2Ch 11:20
From the clan of Bani—* (son of Ez 8:2-14

SHELOMOTH
—*, Haziel, and Haran. 1Ch 23:8,9
Jesha-iah, Joram, Zichri, and *. 1Ch 26:25
and Shelomoth. * and his brothers 1Ch 26:26
of the Temple. * and his brothers 1Ch 26:28

SHELTER
for * beneath the nettles. Job 30:7
find refuge and * in your Ps 15:1
Hide your loved ones in the * of Ps 31:20
oh, to be safe beneath the * of Ps 61:4
They will * you. Ps 91:4
the God above all gods to * me. Ps 91:9
He is my *. Ps 92:15
from the heat, a * from merciless Is 25:4
He will * Israel from the storm Is 32:2
its branches will * every kind of Eze 17:22,23
he made a leafy * to shade him as Jon 4:5
And when the leaves of the * Jon 4:6
yourself when your * is destroyed, Jon 4:10
where birds can come and find *." Mt 13:31,32
food, clothing, *, nor money from 3Jn 1:7
sitting on the throne will * them; Rev 7:15

SHELTERED
But I am like a * olive tree Ps 52:8
of the Almighty, * by the God who Ps 91:1
shade and birds * in its branches, Dan 4:12
can build their nests and be *." Mk 4:31,32

SHELTERS
is the Festival of * Lev 23:33,34
the brooks—and [build * with them Lev 23:40
Israelites are to live in these *. Lev 23:42
and caused you to live in *. Lev 23:43
the Festival of *, must be observed Deu 16:13
The Festival of *. Deu 16:16
you want me to, I'll make three *, Mt 17:4
"We will make three * here, one Mk 9:5
We'll put up three *—one for you Lk 9:33

SHELUMI-EL
Simeon -* (son of Num 1:2-15
Simeon * (son of Num 2:3-31
On the fifth day came *, the son Num 7:36-41
by *, the son of Zuri-shaddai; Num 10:19

SHEM
three sons, *, Ham, and Japheth. Gen 5:32
And he had three sons—*, Ham, and Gen 6:9,10
wife and his sons, *, Ham, and Gen 7:13
sons were *, Ham, and Japheth. Gen 9:18
Then * and Japheth took a robe Gen 9:23
To the descendants of * and Gen 9:24,25
"God bless *, Gen 9:26,27
be Jehovah, the God of * .I.I. Gen 9:26,27f
let him share the prosperity of *, Gen 9:26,27
THESE ARE THE families of *, Ham, Gen 10:1
Eber descended from *, the oldest Gen 10:21
the descendants of *, classified Gen 10:31
flood when * was 100 years old; Gen 11:10,11
*, Ham, and 1Ch 1:1
The sons of *: 1Ch 1:17
of * was Arpachshad, the son of 1Ch 1:24-27
Arphaxad's father was *; Lk 3:23-38

SHEM'S
and may the Canaanites be * Gen 9:26,27f
Here is a list of * other Gen 10:22
* line of descendants included Gen 11:10,11
Arphaxad's father was Shem;* Lk 3:23-38

SHEMA
(or, Hazor), Amam, *, Moladah, Jos 15:21-32
Rekem and * 1Ch 2:43
* was the father of Raham, who 1Ch 2:44
of *, and great-grandson of 1Ch 5:7,8
Beriah and *, chiefs of subclans 1Ch 8:13
To his right stood Mattithiah, *, Neh 8:1

SHEMAAH
Ahi-ezer, son of * from Gibe-ah. 1Ch 12:3-7

SHEMAIAH
But God sent this message to *, 1Ki 12:22
Shecaniah's son was *; 1Ch 3:21,22
* had six sons, including Hattush, 1Ch 3:21,22
Jedaiah, son of Shimri, son of *). 1Ch 4:34-39
Joel's descendants were his son * 1Ch 5:4
who returned was * (son of Hasshub, 1Ch 9:14
Obadiah (the son of *, son of 1Ch 9:15,16
Elizaphan; with * as their leader; 1Ch 15:4-10
Joel, *, Eliel, and Amminadab. 1Ch 15:11
in each division. *, a Levite and 1Ch 24:6
* (the oldest), 1Ch 26:4,5
But the Lord told * the prophet, 2Ch 11:2
The prophet * now met with 2Ch 12:5
themselves he sent * to tell them, 2Ch 12:7
written by * the prophet and by 2Ch 12:15
purpose, including *, Nethaniah, 2Ch 17:7,8,9
From the Jeduthun clan, * and 2Ch 29:12,13,14
Jeshua, *, Amariah, and Shecaniah. 2Ch 31:14,15
The Levite leaders—Conaniah, *, 2Ch 35:9
Jeuel, *, and 60 other men (they Ez 8:2-14
So I sent for Eliezer, Ari-el, * Ez 8:16
Ma-aseiah, Elijah, *, Ez 10:21
Eliezer, Isshijah, Malchijah, *, Ez 10:31,32
and beyond him was * (son of Neh 3:29
I went to visit * (son of Delaiah, Neh 6:10

(SHEMAIAH Con't)
*. (All those listed Neh 10:1
* (son of Hasshub, son of Neh 11:15,16,17
Ma-adiah, Bilgah, *, Neh 12:1
Jehonathan, leader of the * clan; Neh 12:12-21
Judah, Benjamin, *, and Jeremiah. Neh 12:34
Jonathan, son of *, son of Neh 12:35,36
*, Azarel, Milalai, Neh 12:35,36
Ma-aseiah, *, Eleazar, Neh 12:42
Uriah (son of *) from Jer 26:20
And say this to * the dreamer: Jer 29:24
says that because * the Nehelamite Jer 29:31

SHEMAIAH'S
* sons were all outstanding men, 1Ch 26:6,7
Nehelam was * home town, the Jer 29:24f

SHEMARIAH
Bealiah; *; 1Ch 12:3-7
this marriage—Jeush, *, and Zaham. 2Ch 11:19
Shime-on, Benjamin, Malluch, *. Ez 10:31,32
Azarel, Shelemiah, *, Shallum, Ez 10:34-42

SHEMEBER
*, king of Zeboiim, and Gen 14:2

SHEMED
* (who built Ono and Lod and their 1Ch 8:12

SHEMER
from its owner, *, for $4,000 and 1Ki 16:24
calling it Samaria in honor of *. 1Ki 16:24
*, Mahli, Mushi, Merari, Levi. 1Ch 6:44-47
Or, "*." 1Ch 7:34f

SHEMIDA
named after their ancestor *. Num 26:28-37
Asri-el, Shechem, *, and Hepher. Jos 17:2
The sons of * were Ahian, 1Ch 7:19

SHEMIDAITES
The *, named after their ancestor Num 26:28-37

SHEMINITH
zithers (or harps) set to the *." 1Ch 15:21f

SHEMIRAMOTH
Zechariah, Ja-aziel, *, Jehiel, 1Ch 15:18
and Zechariah, Azi-el, *, 1Ch 15:20
Zechariah, Je-iel, *, Jehiel, 1Ch 16:5
Zebadiah, Asahel, *, Jehonathan, 2Ch 17:7,8,9

SHEMUEL
Simeon * (son of Ammihud) Num 34:16-28
Jeri-el, Jahmai, Ibsam, *. 1Ch 7:2

SHENAZZAR
Pedaiah, *, Jekamiah, Hoshama, 1Ch 3:17,18

SHEOL
go down alive into *, then you will Num 16:30
So they went down alive into * Num 16:33
shall be for * to consume." Ps 49:14f
are scattered at the mouth of *." Ps 141:6,7f
and jealousy is as cruel as *. Sol 8:6
Literally, "let it be deep as * Is 7:11f
Literally, "*," "the Is 28:15f
now I must enter the gates of *. Is 38:10
"Though they dig down to *, I Amo 9:2

SHEPH-ATIAH
Azariah, Michael, and *. 2Ch 21:2

SHEPHAM
south to *, then on to Riblah at Num 34:10,11

SHEPHATIAH
to Haggith. Then * was born to 2Sa 3:4
The fifth was *, the son of 1Ch 3:3
Meshullam (the son of *, the son 1Ch 9:7,8
Shemariah; * from Haruph; 1Ch 12:3-7
Over Simeon, * (son of Maacah); 1Ch 27:16-22
From the subclan of *, 372; Ez 2:3-35
Darkon, Giddel, *, Hattil, Ez 2:55,56,57
From the clan of *—Zebadiah (son Ez 8:2-14
From the subclan of *, 372; Neh 7:8-38
*, Hattil, Neh 7:57,58,59
son of *, son of Neh 11:4,5,6
BUT WHEN * (son of Mattan) and Jer 38:1

SHEPHER
From Kehelathah to Mount *; Num 33:15-37
From Mount * to Haradah; Num 33:15-37

SHEPHERD
Abel became a *, while Cain was a Gen 4:2
was to * his father's flocks. Gen 37:2
Jacob, the *, the Rock of Israel. Gen 49:24
not be as sheep without a *." Num 27:17
Playing your * pipes? Ju 5:16
that he send his son David the *. 1Sa 16:19
sheep with another * and took off 1Sa 17:20
the * and leader of his people." 2Sa 5:2
you were a mere *, tending your 2Sa 7:8
mountains as sheep without a *. 1Ki 22:17
be the * of my people Israel. 1Ch 11:2
you from being a * and made you the 1Ch 17:7
the mountain as sheep without a *. 2Ch 18:16
BECAUSE THE LORD is my *, I have Ps 23:1
Lead them like a * and carry them Ps 28:9
Death is the * of all mankind. Ps 49:14
people as their * and he cared for Ps 78:71,72
O * OF Israel who leads Israel Ps 80:1
We are his sheep and he is our *. Ps 95:7
like sheep deserted by their *. Is 13:14
I will * the poor of my people; Is 14:30
He will feed his flock like a *; Is 40:11
created all these stars? As a * Is 40:26
"He is my *," he will certainly Is 44:28
the sea, with Moses as their *? Is 63:11
over them as a * does his flock. Jer 31:10
as a * picks fleas from his cloak! Jer 43:12
What * can defy me? Jer 49:20
they were scattered, without a *. Eze 34:5
I will be like a * looking for Eze 34:12
I myself will be the * of my Eze 34:15,16
And I will set one * over all my Eze 34:23
He shall feed them and be a * to Eze 34:23
be their King, their only *; Eze 37:24
The Lord says, "A * tried to Amo 3:12
there is no * now to gather them. Nah 3:18
of * camps and folds for sheep. Zep 2:6
day, as a * caring for his sheep. Zec 9:16,17
they have no * to protect them. Zec 10:2
and take a job as * of a flock Zec 11:4
"I won't be your * any longer. Zec 11:9
to go again and get a job as a *; Zec 11:15
the part of a worthless, wicked *. Zec 11:15
give this nation a * who will not Zec 11:16
Woe to this worthless * who Zec 11:17
"Awake, O sword, against my *, Zec 13:7
"Strike down the * and the sheep Zec 13:7
They were like sheep without a *. Mt 9:36
as a * separates the sheep from Mt 25:32
that God will smite the *, and Mt 26:31
sheep without a *, and he taught Mk 6:34
*, and the sheep will scatter.' Mk 14:27
For a * comes through the gate. Jn 10:2
"I am the Good *. Jn 10:11
The Good * lays down his life for Jn 10:11
aren't his and he isn't their *. Jn 10:12
"I am the Good * and know my own Jn 10:14
will be one flock with one *. Jn 10:16
Be sure that you feed and * God's Act 20:28
some of it? What * takes care of a 1Co 9:7
God's people as a * does his sheep, Eph 4:11
May he who became the great * of Heb 13:20,21
returned to your *, the Guardian of 1Pe 2:25
and when the Head * comes, your 1Pe 5:4
them and be their * and lead them Rev 7:17

SHEPHERD'S
And he replied, "A * rod." Ex 4:2
put them in his * bag and, armed 1Sa 17:40
only with his * staff and sling, 1Sa 17:40
reaching into his * bag, took out a 1Sa 17:48,49
at a * inn along the way. 2Ki 10:12
to the * shouts and noise. Is 31:4,5
My life is blown away like a * Is 38:12
So I took two * staffs, naming Zec 11:7

SHEPHERDED
the God who has * me all my life, Gen 48:15

SHEPHERDESS
father's sheep, for she was a *. Gen 29:9

SHEPHERDING
ISRAEL IS CHASING the wind, yes, * Hos 12:1

SHEPHERDS
named them. His * also dug a new Gen 26:19
Then the local * came and claimed Gen 26:20
Jacob went over to the * and Gen 29:4
and * are here," they replied. Gen 29:8
I will tell him, 'These men are *. Gen 46:32
him, 'We have been * from our Gen 46:34
For * were despised and hated Gen 46:34
And they replied, "We are * like Gen 47:3
But the * chased the girls away. Ex 2:17
the * and watered their flocks. Ex 2:17
us against the *," they told him; Ex 2:19
While your * have lived among us, 1Sa 25:7
leaders, the * of my people. 2Sa 7:7
of Israel—the * I appointed to care 1Ch 17:6
with Moses and Aaron as their *. Ps 77:20
my flock to the *' tents, and Sol 1:8
camp there. The * won't let their Is 13:20
*—are all blind to every danger. Is 56:10
they are stupid * who only look Is 56:11
They surround Jerusalem like * Jer 4:17
Evil * shall surround you. Jer 6:3
my home. The * of my people have Jer 10:21
of my people—the * of my sheep—for Jer 23:1
And I will appoint responsible * Jer 23:4
Weep and moan, O evil *; Jer 25:34
cries of the * and to the leaders Jer 25:36
and farmers and * alike shall live Jer 31:24
see * leading sheep and lambs. Jer 33:12
Their * led them astray and then Jer 50:6
men and maidens, * and flocks, Jer 51:23
to you: Woe to the * who feed Eze 34:2
against the *, the leaders of Eze 34:2
Shouldn't * feed the sheep? Eze 34:2
"Therefore, O *, hear the word Eze 34:7
you were no real * at all, for you Eze 34:8
therefore I am against the *, Eze 34:9,10
will destroy the powerful, fat *; Eze 34:15,16
to you, O evil *, that you not only Eze 34:18
fat * and their scrawny sheep. Eze 34:20
For these * push and butt and Eze 34:21
and dried, and all the * mourned. Amo 1:2
will appoint seven * to watch over Mic 5:5
"My anger burns against your * Zec 1(
evil *—for their wealth is gone. Zec 1
* have sold them without mercy. Zec 1
three evil * in a single month. Zec 11
That night some * were in the Lk 2
* said to each other, "Come on! Lk 2:
the manger. The * told everyone Lk 2:
All who heard the *' story Lk 2:
Then the * went back again to Lk 2:

SHEPHI
Manahath, Ebal, *, and Onam. 1Ch 1:4

SHEPHO
Manahath, Ebal,*, Onam. Gen 36:2

SHEPHUPHAM
named after their ancestor *. Num 26:38-4

SHEPHUPHAN
Naaman, Ahoah, Gera, *, Huram. 1Ch 8:3,4

SHEREBIAH
man named *, along with eighteen of Ez 8:1
of the priests—*, Hashabiah, and Ez 8:2
Jeshua, Bani, *, Jamin, Akkub, Neh 8:7,
Bunni, *, Bani, and Chenani. Neh 9:
Bani, Hashabneiah, *, Hodiah, Neh 9:
Hashabiah, Zaccur, *, Neh 10:9-1
Jeshua, Binnui, Kadmi-el, *, Neh 12:
Hashabiah, *, and Jeshua (son of Neh 12:2

SHERESH
his brother's name was *, and he 1Ch 7:1

SHERIFFS
counselors, *, and rulers of all Dan 3:

SHESH-BAZZAR
these gifts to *, the leader of the Ez 1:
to * to take back to Jerusalem. Ez 1:1
of a man named *, whom King Cyrus Ez 5:1
as before. So * came and laid the Ez 5:1

SHESHAI
of Anak: Talmai, *, and Ahiman. Jos 15:1
cities of *, Ahiman, and Talmai. Ju 1:1

SHESHAN
*; and Sheshan's son was Ahlai. 1Ch 2:3
* had no sons, 1Ch 2:34,3
Apparently a different * than in 1Ch 2:34,35

SHESHAN'S
Sheshan; and * son was Ahlai. 1Ch 2:3

SHESHITES
There they saw the Ahimanites, *, Num 13:2

SHETH
And destroy the sons of *. Num 24:15-1

SHETHAR
These men were Carshena, *, Est 1:13-1

SHETHAR-BOZENAI
the Euphrates, and *, and their Ez 5:3
governor Tattenai, *, and the other Ez 5:6
to Governor *, and the other Ez 6:6
Governor Tattenai, *, and their Ez 6:13

SHEVA
kept the records. * was the 2Sa 20:25
of Madmannah), and * (the father of 1Ch 2:48,49

SHEWBREAD
Literally, "*." Mk 2:25,26f
and took the *, the special bread Lk 6:4

SHHH
"No," and he will add, "* . Amo 6:10

SHIBAH
*. Gen 26:33f

SHIBBOLETH
then they demanded, "Say '*.' Ju 12:6
instead of "*," he was dragged Ju 12:6

SHIED
donkey saw me and * away from me; Num 22:33

SHIELD
He is your * and your helper! Deu 33:29
A * or spear. Ju 5:8
walked ahead of him with a huge *. 1Sa 17:4-7
David with his * bearer ahead of 1Sa 17:41,42
He is my * 2Sa 22:3
You have given me the * of your 2Sa 22:36
before it with a *, nor build a 2Ki 19:32
They were experts with both * and 1Ch 12:8-13
Armed with his tin *, he Job 15:25,26
But Lord, you are my *, my Ps 3:3
you protect him with your * of Ps 5:12
God is my *; Ps 7:10
He is my *. Ps 18:2
He is a * for everyone who hides Ps 18:30
given me your salvation as my *. Ps 18:35
He is my strength, my * from Ps 28:7
he protects us like a *. Ps 33:20
Put on your armor, take your * Ps 35:2
them to the dust, O Lord our *. Ps 59:11
O God, our Defender and our *, Ps 84:9
He will * you with his wings! Ps 91:4
Who will be my *? Ps 94:16
above them to * them from the Ps 105:39
He is your *. Ps 115:9
he is your *. Ps 115:10
he is your *. Ps 115:11
You are my refuge and my *, and Ps 119:114
my God and my *—hear me as I Ps 140:6,7,8
He stands before me as a *. Ps 144:2
He is their *, protecting them Pro 2:7,8

HIELD Con't)
goodness will be a * before you, Is 58:8
who handle the * and bend the bow! Jer 46:9
city is an iron * and will protect Eze 11:3
You think this city is an iron *? Eze 11:7
* for you, and you safe within. Eze 11:11
need faith as your * to stop the Eph 6:16

HIELDS
David brought the gold * to 2Sa 8:7
He * all who hide behind him. 2Sa 22:31
* ($1,800 worth of gold in each). 1Ki 10:16,17
all the gold * Solomon had made. 1Ki 14:26
made bronze * as substitutes, and 1Ki 14:27
the * back to the guard chamber. 1Ki 14:28
* his grandfather had dedicated, 1Ki 15:15
of spears and * in the Temple that 2Ki 11:10
troops armed with * and spears. 1Ch 12:24-37
troops equipped with * and spears. 1Ch 12:24-37
He brought the gold * of King 1Ch 18:7
to make 200 large *, each worth 2Ch 9:15
smaller *, each worth $140,000. 2Ch 9:16
oil, and wine. * and spears were 2Ch 11:12
also all of Solomon's gold *. 2Ch 12:9
them with bronze * and committed 2Ch 12:10
equipped with light * and spears. 2Ch 14:8
armed with large * and bows. 2Ch 14:8
with bows and * under the command 2Ch 17:17
and * to all the army officers. 2Ch 23:9
Uzziah issued to them *, spears, 2Ch 26:14
large numbers of weapons and *. 2Ch 32:5
and for his * and gold bowls. 2Ch 32:27
the battle * of all the armies of Ps 47:9
jeweled with a thousand heroes' *. Sol 4:4
Quick, quick, grab your * and Is 21:5
the men of Kir hold up the *. Is 22:6,7
Lift up the *! Jer 51:11
raising a roof of * against it. Eze 26:8
have their * hang upon your walls; Eze 27:10
Their * hang row on row upon the Eze 27:11
with their * covering them and Eze 32:27
and pick up your * and bucklers, Eze 39:9
* flash red in the sunlight! Nah 2:3

SHIFT
of the tribe will * to any other Num 36:7
each village—don't * around from Mk 6:10
a village, don't * around from home Lk 10:7

SHIFTED
mountain and island shook and *. Rev 6:14

SHIFTING
* from trusting him to save you. Col 1:23

SHIGIONOTH
Literally, "according to * Hab 3:1f

SHIHOR
Literally, "from *—the Brook of 1Ch 13:5f

SHIHOR-LIBNATH
from Carmel to *, turned east Jos 19:24,25,26

SHIKKERON
south of * and Mount Baalah. Jos 15:10,11

SHILHI
was Azubah, the daughter of *. 1Ki 22:42
was Azubah, the daughter of *. 2Ch 20:31

SHILHIM
Lebaoth, *, Ain, and Rimmon. Jos 15:21-32

SHILLEM
sons: Jahzeel, Guni, Jezer, and *. Gen 46:23,24,25
named after their ancestor *. Num 26:48-50

SHILLEMITES
The *, named after their ancestor Num 26:48-50

SHILOAH
the waters of * that go softly." Is 8:6f

SHILOH
not depart from Judah until * Gen 49:10
at * to set up the Tabernacle. Jos 18:1
to Joshua and the camp at *. Jos 18:9
There at the Tabernacle at * the Jos 18:10
entrance of the Tabernacle at *. Jos 19:51
of Levi came to * to consult with Jos 21:1
army of Israel at * in Canaan and Jos 22:9
an army at * and prepared to go to Jos 22:12
as the Tabernacle remained at *. Ju 18:31
the Ephraim hill country, near *. Ju 19:18
were brought to the camp at * Ju 21:10,11,12
in the fields of *, between Lebonah Ju 21:19
when the girls of * come out for Ju 21:21
the Tabernacle at * to worship the 1Sa 1:3
as they went to *, making her cry 1Sa 1:7
when they were at *, Hannah went 1Sa 1:9
the Tabernacle in *, along with a 1Sa 1:24
when they came to * to worship. 1Sa 2:13,14
the Tabernacle in *, and he passed 1Sa 3:21,4:1
"Let's bring the Ark here from * 1Sa 4:3
and arrived at * the same day with 1Sa 4:12
Eli, the priest of the Lord in *). 1Sa 14:3
of Jehovah at * concerning the 1Ki 2:27
Ahijah from * (who had put on a new 1Ki 11:29
Ahijah, the prophet from *. 1Ki 12:15
the prophet at *—the man who told 1Ki 14:2
wife went to Ahijah's home at *. 1Ki 14:4
Ahijah, the prophet from *. 1Ki 15:29
his Tabernacle at *, where he had Ps 78:60
Go to *, the city I first honored Jer 7:12
as I did in *—this Temple called by Jer 7:13,14
the Tabernacle at *, and I will Jer 26:6
this Temple like the one at *?" Jer 26:9
from Shechem, * and Samaria, to Jer 41:5

SHILON'S
(* oldest son) and his sons; 1Ch 9:5

SHILONITE
of Ahijah the *, and also in the 2Ch 9:29
to Jeroboam by Ahijah, the *. 2Ch 10:15
son of Zechariah, son of the *). Neh 11:4,5,6

SHILONITES
The * were another family to 1Ch 9:5

SHILSHAH
Imrah, Bezer, Hod, Shamma, *, 1Ch 7:36,37

SHIME-A
his sons *, Shobab, Nathan, and 1Ch 3:5
Mahli, Libni, Shime-i, Uzzah, *, 1Ch 6:29,30
Berechiah, *, Michael, Ba-aseiah, 1Ch 6:39-43

SHIME-AH
(the son of David's brother *). 2Sa 13:3
of David's brother *) arrived and 2Sa 13:32,33

SHIME-AM
Mikloth lived with his son * in 1Ch 9:38

SHIME-ATH
mother was *, a woman from Ammon; 2Ch 24:26

SHIME-ATHITES
Tirathites, *, and Sucathites. 1Ch 2:55

SHIME-I
The sons of Gershon were:Libni, * Ex 6:17
grandsons Libni * Num 3:16-24
It was *, the son of Gera, a 2Sa 16:5
continued on, and * kept pace with 2Sa 16:13
Then * (the son of Gera the 2Sa 19:16
As the king was crossing, * fell 2Sa 19:18
Abishai asked, "Shall not * die, 2Sa 19:21
Then, turning to *, he vowed, 2Sa 19:23
of David's brother *—killed him. 2Sa 21:20,21
*, Rei, and David's army chiefs. 1Ki 1:8
And do you remember *, the son 1Ki 2:8
The king now sent for * and told 1Ki 2:36,37
"All right," * replied, 1Ki 2:38
of Gath. When * learned where they 1Ki 2:39
When Solomon heard that * had 1Ki 2:41
took * outside and killed him. 1Ki 2:46
* (son of Ela), whose area was 1Ki 4:8-19
Zerubbabel and *. 1Ch 3:19,20
grandfather of *). 1Ch 4:26
* had sixteen sons and six 1Ch 4:27
and his great-grandson *. 1Ch 5:4
The sons of Gershom were:Libni, * 1Ch 6:17
Mahli, Libni, *, Uzzah, Shime-a, 1Ch 6:29,30
Zimmah, *, Jahath, Gershom, Levi. 1Ch 6:39-43
The sons of * were: 1Ch 8:19,20,21
*. These subdivisions were still 1Ch 23:7
and the sons of * 1Ch 23:8,9f
Probably not the same * as in 1Ch 23:8,9f
The subclans of * were named 1Ch 23:10,11
*, Hashabiah, and Mattithiah. 1Ch 25:3
Tenth, * and twelve of his sons 1Ch 25:9-31
estates. And * from Ramath had the 1Ch 27:27
the Hemanite clan, Jehuel and *; 2Ch 29:12,13,14
brother * and the following aides: 2Ch 31:12,13
Jozabad, *, Ez 10:23
Manasseh, *. Ez 10:33
Bani, Binnui, *, Shelemiah, Nathan, Ez 10:34-42
of *, son of Kish, a Benjaminite). Est 2:5

SHIME-I'S
But three years later two of * 1Ki 2:39
* son was Micah; 1Ch 5:5

SHIME-ON
*, Benjamin, Malluch, Shemariah. Ez 10:31,32

SHIMEA
his third was *, his fourth was 1Ch 2:13
the son of David's brother *. 1Ch 20:6,7

SHIMEAH
Mikloth who was the father of *. 1Ch 8:30,31,32

SHIMEATH
the son of *, and Jehozabad, the 2Ki 12:21

SHIMMERING
bracelets and veils of * gauze. Is 3:19

SHIMON
The sons of *: 1Ch 4:20

SHIMRATH
Eliel, Adaiah, Beraiah, *. 1Ch 8:19,20,21

SHIMRI
son of *, son of Shemaiah). 1Ch 4:34-39
Jedia-el (son of *); 1Ch 11:26-47
group, appointed * as the leader 1Ch 26:10
From the Elizaphan clan, * and 2Ch 29:12,13,14

SHIMRITH
and Jehozabad, whose mother was * 2Ch 24:26

SHIMRON
and his sons: Tola, Puvah, Iob, *. Gen 46:8-14
named after their ancestor *. Num 26:23-25
The king of *; Jos 11:1
included Kattath, Nahalal, *, Jos 19:15,16
Tola, Puah, Jashub, *. 1Ch 7:1

SHIMRON-MERON
The king of *; Jos 12:8-24

SHIMRONITES
The *, named after their ancestor Num 26:23-25

SHIMSHAI
Governor Rehum, * (a scribe), Ez 4:8,9
Governor Rehum and * the scribe, Ez 4:17
read to Rehum and *, they hurried Ez 4:23

SHINAB
*, king of Admah, Gen 14:2

SHINAR
and Calneh in the land of *. Gen 10:10
Literally, "the land of *," Gen 11:2f
Amraphel, king of *, Gen 14:1
of his god in the land of *. Dan 1:1

SHINE
So he let it * for awhile, and Gen 1:4,5
sun and moon, to * down upon the Gen 1:16
* as the sun!" Ju 5:31
won't *, if he commands it so! Job 9:7
And the light of heaven will * Job 22:28
light of your face * down upon us. Ps 4:6
Let your favor * again upon your Ps 31:16
May your glory * throughout the Ps 57:11
Literally, "Cause your face to * Ps 80:3f
Literally, "Cause your face to * Ps 80:7f
belongs, let your glory * out. Ps 94:1
Light that will * on all those who Is 9:2
No light will * from stars or sun Is 13:10
Then your light will * out from Is 58:10
Let your light * for all the Is 60:1
glory of the Lord will * from you. Is 60:2
Your eyes will * with joy, your Is 60:5
Let your face * again with peace Dan 9:17
of God—shall * as brightly as the Dan 12:3
not a ray of joy or hope will *. Amo 5:18
They shall * in his land as Zec 9:16,17
moon and stars will no longer *, Zec 14:6
Let it * for all; Mt 5:15,16
Then the godly shall * as the Mt 13:43
A lamp is placed on a stand to * Mk 4:21
Suddenly his face began to * with Mk 9:2
the moon will not *, and the stars Mk 13:24
He is the Light that will * upon Lk 2:32
was praying, his face began to *, Lk 9:29
Light arrived to * on everyone Jn 1:9
Jesus replied, "My light will * Jn 12:35
I have come as a Light to * in Jn 12:46
and power that now * within us 2Co 4:7
and stubborn. * out among them like Php 2:15
again, you will * with him and Col 3:4
Star will * in your hearts. 2Pe 1:19

SHINES
And his light * down on all the Job 25:3
Or, "His face * down in mercy and Ps 11:7f
God's glory-light * from the Ps 50:2
His majesty * down on Israel; Ps 68:34
to you the night * as bright as Ps 139:12
hay while the sun *, but what a Pro 10:5
behalf until she * forth in his Is 62:1
ever born, none * more brightly Mt 11:11
His life is the light that * Jn 1:5
them, the light * in upon their sin Eph 5:13
God's Son * out with God's glory, Heb 1:3
all light, and he * forever without Jas 1:17
new light of life in Christ * in. 1Jn 2:8

SHINING
looked at the sun * in the skies, Job 31:26
He leaves a * wake of froth Job 41:31,32
* down as from the noonday sun. Ps 37:6
your gates and walls of * gems. Is 54:12
statue of a man, * brilliantly, Dan 2:31
covering it up to keep it from *? Lk 8:16
them, clothed in * robes so bright Lk 24:4
the Gospel that is * upon him, or 2Co 4:4
for, like lights * into dark 2Pe 1:19
diamond, or from a * ruby, and a Rev 4:3

SHINY
Spread out before it was a * Rev 4:6

SHION
Shunem, Hapharaim, *, Anaharath, Jos 19:17-23

SHIP
decks and stalls throughout the *. Gen 6:14
*, eighteen inches below the roof; Gen 6:16
you safe in the *, with your wife Gen 6:18
How a * finds its way across the Pro 30:18,19
brought by * from distant ports. Pro 31:14
You are like a * built of finest Eze 27:5
your * of state into a hurricane! Eze 27:26
he found a * leaving for Tarshish. Jon 1:3
the * to hide there from the Lord. Jon 1:3
But as the * was sailing along, Jon 1:4
cargo overboard to lighten the *. Jon 1:5
him left Paphos by * for Turkey, Act 13:13
Finally they returned by * to Act 14:26
he left us aboard * while he went Act 18:19
ended, we boarded * at Philippi in Act 20:6
Assos, and we went on ahead by *. Act 20:13
accompanied him down to the *. Act 20:38
There we boarded a * sailing for Act 21:2
in Syria, where the * unloaded. Act 21:3
we returned to the *, the entire Act 21:5
start us on our way to Rome by *; Act 27:1
Literally, "a * of Adramyttium." Act 27:2f
to keep the * on course, so we Act 27:4

(SHIP Con't)
found an Egyptian * from Act 27:6
the * and blew it out to sea. Act 27:14,15
and let the * run before the gale. Act 27:14,15
then banded the * with ropes to Act 27:17
even though the * will go down. Act 27:22
to abandon the *, and lowered the Act 27:30
crew lightened the * further by Act 27:38
But the * hit a sandbar Act 27:41
The bow of the * stuck fast, Act 27:41
and debris from the broken *. Act 27:44
* that had wintered at the island. Act 28:11
And a tiny rudder makes a huge * Jas 3:4
SHIP'S
and Paul spoke to the * officers Act 27:9
more to the * captain and the owner Act 27:11
SHIPHI
Ziza (the son of *, son of Allon, 1Ch 4:34-39
SHIPHMA
and Zabdi from * was responsible 1Ch 27:27
SHIPHRAH
(their names were * and Puah) to Ex 1:15,16
SHIPMENTS
Tyre, requesting * of cedar lumber 2Ch 2:3
SHIPOWNERS
And all the * and captains of the Rev 18:17
SHIPS
be a harbor for *, with his borders Gen 49:13
* shall come from the coasts of Num 24:23,24
back to Egypt in *, a journey I Deu 28:68
And why did Dan remain with his *? Ju 5:17
Edom, where he built a fleet of *. 1Ki 9:26
(And when King Hiram's * brought 1Ki 10:11
These *, with King Hiram's 2Ch 8:17,18
the king sent his * to Tarshish, 2Ch 9:21
They made * in Ezion-geber to 2Ch 20:36
So the * met disaster and never 2Ch 20:37
My years disappear like swift *, Job 9:26
See the *! Ps 104:26
Their * are tossed to the Ps 107:26
the proud ocean * and trim harbor Is 2:16
Weep, O * of Tyre, returning home Is 23:1
port was full of * from Sidon, Is 23:2,3
Sail on, O * of Tarshish, for Is 23:10
Wail, you * that ply the oceans, Is 23:14
I have reserved the * of many Is 60:9
Literally, "the * of Tarshish." Is 60:9f
do the calking. * come from every Eze 27:9
made secure. The * of Tarshish are Eze 27:25
destroying a third of all the *; Rev 8:8,9
of the merchant * and crews will Rev 18:17
SHIPTAN
Kemuel (son of *) Num 34:16-28
SHIPWRECK
we go on—perhaps *, loss of cargo, Act 27:10
It was three months after the * Act 28:11
SHIPWRECKED
But we will be * on an island." Act 27:26
Three times I was *. 2Co 11:25
SHIPWRIGHTS
and pilots, your * and merchants Eze 27:27
SHIPYARD
King Solomon had a * in 1Ki 9:26
SHIRK
and then * when he isn't looking; Eph 6:6,7
SHIRKING
favorites who can get away with *. Col 3:25
SHIRT
* and throwing away the old one! Ps 102:26
to court, and your * is taken from Mt 5:40
coat, give him your * besides. Lk 6:29
SHIRTS
For you steal the * right off the Mic 2:8
SHISHA
Elihoreph and Ahijah (sons of *) 1Ki 4:1
SHISHAK
he fled to King * of Egypt and 1Ki 11:40
reign, King * of Egypt attacked and 1Ki 14:25
As a result, King * of Egypt 2Ch 12:2
you and abandoned you to *.' 2Ch 12:5
I will not use * to pour out my 2Ch 12:7
So King * of Egypt conquered 2Ch 12:9
SHISHAK'S
in fact, even after * invasion, 2Ch 12:12
SHITRAI
* from Sharon was in charge of 1Ch 27:29
SHIVERED
often I have * with cold, without 2Co 11:27
SHIZA
Adina (son of *) from the tribe of 1Ch 11:26-47
SHOA
from Pekod and * and Koa; Eze 23:23
SHOBAB
Shammu-a, *, Nathan, Solomon, 2Sa 5:14,15,16
Jesher, *, and Ardon. 1Ch 2:18
his sons Shime-a, *, Nathan, and 1Ch 3:5
Shammua, *, Nathan, Solomon, 1Ch 14:4-7
SHOBACH
the command of *, the 2Sa 10:15,16
cavalrymen, including General *. 2Sa 10:18
SHOBAI
Akkub, Hatita, and *), 139. Ez 2:40,41,42

SHOBAL
Lotan,The tribe of *,The tribe of Gen 36:20,21
The children of *:Alvan, Gen 36:23
Lotan, *, Zibeon, Anah, Dishon, 1Ch 1:38,39
The sons of *: Alian, Manahath, 1Ch 1:40
* (the father of Kiriath-jearim), 1Ch 2:50
Hezron, Carmi, Hur, * 1Ch 4:1
SHOBAL'S
* sons included 1Ch 2:52
* son Re-aiah was the father of 1Ch 4:2
SHOBEK
Pilha, *, Rehum, Neh 10:14-27
SHOBI
warmly greeted by * (son of Nahash 2Sa 17:27
SHOCKED
the fields, too * and angry to Gen 34:6,7
The heavens are * at such a Jer 2:12
all the world will be * at the Jer 25:11
all who passed by were * to see Eze 36:34
Well may you farmers stand so * Joe 1:11
SHOCKING
going to do a * thing in Israel. 1Sa 3:11
It will be a * thing to see. Jer 49:20
one so brutal and *, with its iron Dan 7:19
SHOCKS
field so that the * of grain, or Ex 22:6
the sheaves and * of grain, and Ju 15:5
SHOE
upon Edom I cast my *." Ps 108:9f
(the sandal strap of) his *." Lk 3:16f
SHOES
"Take off your *, for you are Ex 3:5
your walking * and carrying your Ex 12:11
old, and your * haven't worn out! Deu 29:5
"Take off your *," the Jos 5:15
with patched *, weatherworn Jos 9:3,4,5
our clothing and * have become Jos 9:13
it, and gave them *, food, and 2Ch 28:15
including his *, and to walk around Is 20:2
they trade them for a pair of *. Amo 2:6
or a pair of *, or selling them Amo 8:6
I am not worthy to carry his *! Mt 3:11
and *, or even a walking stick; Mt 10:10
Literally, "Whose * I am not Mk 1:7f
pair of * or a change of clothes. Mk 6:8,9
bag, or even an extra pair of *. Lk 10:4
ring for his finger; and *! Lk 15:22
'Take off your *, for you are Act 7:33
"Get dressed and put on your *." Act 12:8
Wear * that are able to speed Eph 6:15
SHOHAM
his brothers *, Zaccur, and Ibri. 1Ch 24:26,27
SHOMER
the son of *—both trusted aides. 2Ki 12:21
Japhlet, *, Hotham, 1Ch 7:32
SHOMER'S
His brother * 1Ch 7:34
SHONE
He * from Mount Paran, Deu 33:2
red as it * across the water! 2Ki 3:22
that * like polished brass. Eze 1:4
feet, and * like burnished brass. Eze 1:7
a man whose face * like bronze, Eze 40:3
his arms and feet * like polished Dan 10:5,6
so that his face * like the sun and Mt 17:2
His face * like lightning and Mt 28:3
and the landscape * bright with the Lk 2:9
John * brightly for a while, and Jn 5:35
light from heaven * around me. Act 22:6
* down on me and my companions. Act 26:13
sun nor stars * upon us." Act 27:20f
to obey, his face * out with the 2Co 3:7
first glory as it * from Moses' 2Co 3:10
mountain when he * out with honor 2Pe 1:17,18
and his face * like the power of Rev 1:16
his face * like the sun and his Rev 10:1
SHOOED
the carcasses, Abram * them away. Gen 15:11
the disciples * them away, telling Mk 10:13
SHOOK
* with a violent earthquake. Ex 19:18
and they sadly * hands, tears 1Sa 20:41
let him, but * his hand instead! 2Sa 15:5
Then the earth * and trembled; 2Sa 22:8
and * his fist at him. 1Ki 13:4
Literally, "then I * out the lap Neh 5:13f
I trembled and * with terror, as Job 4:14
and mountains * and trembled. Ps 18:7
earth trembled and the heavens *. Ps 68:8
The earth trembled and *. Ps 77:18
Such singing it was! It * the Is 6:4
be the one who * the earth and the Is 14:16
Long ago you * off my yoke and Jer 2:20
and saw that they trembled and *. Jer 4:24
everyone in the land * with Eze 19:7
spoke, the nations * with fear, for Hos 13:1
and the earth *, and rocks broke, Mt 27:51
The guards * with fear when they Mt 28:4
they were meeting * and they were Act 4:31
Moses * with terror and dared Act 7:32
But they * off the dust of their Act 13:51

at Jesus, Paul * off the dust from Act 18:
But Paul * off the snake into the Act 28:
special gifts—they * hands with Gal 2:7,8,
that he * with terrible fear. Heb 12:2
Sinai his voice * the earth, but, Heb 12:2
and every mountain and island * Rev 6:1
SHOOT
And shall * them with many arrows. Num 24:3-
And * them down with my arrows. Deu 32:2
I will come out and * three 1Sa 20:2
can find the arrows as I * them." 1Sa 20:3
him, shouting, "* him, too." 2Ki 9:27
* -Elisha commanded 2Ki 13:16,17
wall, nor even * an arrow into it. 2Ki 19:32
brilliant men to * arrows and huge 2Ch 26:1
as flames * upwards from a fire. Job 5:7
They * from ambush at the Ps 64:4
But God himself will * them down. Ps 64:7
but from the stump will grow a * Is 11:1
Jerusalem, nor * their arrows Is 37:33
he was like a tender green *, Is 53:2
bows to * their arrows of untruth. Jer 9:3
let the archers * at her; Jer 50:14
plucked off the * at the top of the Eze 17:3,4
And when the green * comes up 1Co 15:37
SHOOTING
as though I were * at a target. 1Sa 20:20
they know there would be * 2Sa 11:19,20,21
or * him with a sharp arrow. Pro 25:18
of fire * from their mouths. Rev 11:5
SHOOTS
Then Jacob took fresh * from Gen 30:37
Literally, "Your * are an orchard Sol 4:13,14f
princes [her topmost buds and * Eze 17:12,13
SHOP
in charge of the palace tailor *. 2Ki 22:14
every home and * is locked up Is 24:10
Go down to the * where clay pots Jer 18:2
SHOPHACH
led personally by *, King 1Ch 19:16
He also killed *, the 1Ch 19:17,18
SHOPS
Go instead to the * and buy some Mt 25:9
SHOQEDH
in verse 11 and * (watching) in Jer 1:12f
SHORE
and to camp there along the *. Ex 14:2
camped beside the * near Ex 14:9
Lord, the sea receded from the *. Ps 18:15
of them like sands along the *! Ps 78:27
sands along the *, yet only a few Is 10:22
waves against the *, or like the Eze 1:24
upon the mainland *, weeping Eze 27:29
went down to the *, where an Mt 13:1
so go down to the * and throw in a Mt 17:26,27
gathered around him on the *. Mk 5:21
the * and met them as they landed. Mk 6:33
preaching on the * of Lake Lk 5:1
down to the * to wait for him. Jn 6:16
on the * [waiting to see Jesus Jn 6:22,23
down by the *, and ask him to come Act 10:5,6
Simon, a tanner, down by the *.' Act 10:32
and sailed along close to *. Act 27:13
to face back to * but couldn't, so Act 27:14,15
Near the * where we landed was an Act 28:7
like the waves against the *. Rev 1:15
crashing on the *, or like the Rev 19:6
numberless as sand along the *. Rev 20:8
SHORELINE
The western border was the * of Jos 15:12
roars like the surf against the *. Jer 50:42
SHORELINES
I set the * of the world by Jer 5:22
SHORES
along the *—too many to count." Gen 32:12
"Zebulun shall dwell on the * of Gen 49:13
area from the * of the Deu 1:7
River, along the * of the Jos 9:1
western * of the Lake of Galilee; Jos 12:3
by limiting their *, and said, Job 38:10
Fishermen will stand along the * Eze 47:10
to En-eglaim. The * will be filled Eze 47:10
walking along the * of the Sea of Mk 1:16
*, there is no way to count them. Heb 11:12
SHORN
sheep's wool, newly * and washed; Sol 4:2
SHORT
as we were just a * distance from Gen 48:7
thanksgiving, unleavened * bread Lev 7:12
the wilderness, a * distance east Num 21:11
Then Ahima-az took a * cut 2Sa 18:23
If you run * of money for the Ez 7:20
Is your life so * that you must Job 10:4-7
So he cut their lives * and gave Ps 78:33
Oh, remember how * you have made Ps 89:47
have made is far too * to lie on; Is 28:20
your reward: In a * time—in just a Is 32:10
it is cut * as when a weaver Is 38:12
In one * day my life hangs by a Is 38:12
in a very * time you far Eze 16:47
allowed to live a * time longer. Dan 7:12

(SHORT Con't)
this will last for only a * while. Dan 11:24
and Jonah drew the * one. Jon 1:7
Jesus cut him *. Lk 4:35
was too * to see over the crowds. Lk 19:3
They stopped *, sadness written Lk 24:17
all fall * of God's glorious Rom 3:23
dealings, justly cutting them *." Rom 9:28
time is very *, [and so are our 1Co 7:29
Yet this * time of distress will 2Co 4:17
in this letter, for it is a * one. Heb 13:22

SHORT-LIVED
wicked has been *, and the joy of Job 20:5
killed, but his success will be *. Dan 11:12
it there, and it is, at best, *. Jon 4:10

SHORT-SIGHTED
How * to fine the godly for being Pro 17:26

SHORT-TEMPERED
A * man is a fool. Pro 14:17
A * man must bear his own Pro 19:19
Keep away from angry, * men, lest Pro 22:24,25

SHORTCHANGE
You cheat and * everyone. Is 59:6

SHORTCHANGED
up for what he was "*" at Tyre. Eze 29:18f
up for what he was "*" at Tyre. Eze 29:20f

SHORTENED
of the wicked man will be *; Job 18:7
my years are *, drained away Ps 31:9,10
are *, all mankind will perish. Mt 24:22
But they will be * for the sake Mt 24:22

SHORTENING
bread, one cake of * bread, and one Ex 29:23
me down in middle life, * my days. Ps 102:23

SHORTENS
And unless the Lord * that time Mk 13:20

SHORTER
the end of the * wing, parallel to Eze 42:7,8

SHORTLY
War broke out * after that and 1Sa 19:8
* AFTERWARDS, SAMUEL died and 1Sa 25:1
of 605 B.C., * after Jer 36:1f
So * afterwards, we packed our Act 21:15
But * afterwards, the weather Act 27:14,15

SHORTS
linen coat, *, belt, and turban. Lev 16:4

SHORTSIGHTED
or at least very *, and has 2Pe 1:9

SHOT
was his parting *! Gen 45:24
by those who * at him and Gen 49:23
shall be stoned or * to death with Ex 19:13
flames * far into the sky, Deu 4:11
So the boy ran and Jonathan * 1Sa 20:36
He * forth his arrows of 2Sa 22:15
However, someone * an arrow at 1Ki 22:34
and * Joram between the shoulders; 2Ki 9:24
So they * him in his chariot at 2Ki 9:27
archers * and wounded him. 1Ch 10:3
But one of the Syrian soldiers * 2Ch 18:33
among thorns that * up and crowded Mk 4:7

SHOULDER
her * and filled it at the spring. Gen 24:15,16
with her water jug upon her *; Gen 24:45
jug down from her * so that I could Gen 24:46
willingly bent his * to the task Gen 49:15
clasps on the * of the ephod. Ex 28:13,14
onyx stones on the * of the ephod. Ex 28:25
The ephod was held together by * Ex 39:4,5
* straps of the ephod, were set Ex 39:6,7
at the top of each * strap of the Ex 39:15-18
placed low on the * straps of the Ex 39:20
fat, and the right *, and placed Lev 8:25
take the roasted * of the lamb, one Num 6:19
* that were waved before the Lord. Num 6:20
them! The *, the cheeks, and the Deu 18:3
a stone on your *—twelve stones in Jos 4:5
along the southern * of Jebus Jos 15:8
on the northern * of Mount Jearim, Jos 15:10,11
of Timnah to the * of the hill Jos 15:10,11
and placed it upon his *. Ju 9:47,48
Let my * be wrenched out of Job 31:22
will relieve your * of its burden; Ps 81:6
government shall be upon his *. Is 9:6
my * while the people looked on. Eze 12:7
* and all the most tender cuts. Eze 24:4
and wrenched her * out of joint and Eze 29:7
own pleasures and * your cross, and Mk 8:34
She glanced over her * and saw Jn 20:14

SHOULDERS
held it over their * and, walking Gen 9:23
water to Hagar's * and sent her Gen 21:14
upon Isaac's *, while he himself Gen 22:6
and carried them on their *. Ex 12:34
from the * to below the knees. Ex 28:4f
front and back, joined at the *. Ex 28:7
Fasten the two stones upon the * Ex 28:12
breasts and right * slowly before Lev 9:21
of the Tabernacle upon their *. Num 7:9
the Tabernacle upon their *. Num 10:17
He put them on his * and carried Ju 16:3
And he was head and * taller than 1Sa 9:2
head and * above anyone else. 1Sa 10:23
his * and walked away again. 1Ki 19:19
and shot Joram between the *; 2Ki 9:24
the Ark on their * with its 1Ch 15:15
forth upon your *, spend your time 2Ch 35:3
They carry it around on their *, Is 46:7
and your daughters on their *. Is 49:22
* and walk away into the night; Eze 12:6
their * were raw and blistered Eze 29:18
joyfully carry it home on your *. Lk 15:5
Paul to their * to protect him, Act 21:35
You no longer shrugged your *, 2Co 7:11

SHOUT
went the * arose, "Kneel down!" Gen 41:43
them shall * to all Israel, Deu 27:14
to give a mighty * and the walls of Jos 6:5
any of you until I tell you to *; Jos 6:10
I tell you to shout; then *!" Jos 6:10
Joshua yelled to the people, "*! Jos 6:16
of the camp and *, 'We fight for Ju 7:18
Ark coming, their * of joy was so 1Sa 4:5
troops and * his challenge to the 1Sa 17:23
Then the Israelis gave a great * 1Sa 17:52
all gods gave out a mighty *. 2Sa 22:14
Then blow the trumpets and *, 1Ki 1:34
For the Lord told him to * 1Ki 13:32
"You'll have to * louder than 1Ki 18:27
The men of Judah began to *. 2Ch 13:15,16
A great * went up, "Long live the 2Ch 23:11
gave a great *, praising God Ez 3:11
think that if you * loudly enough Job 36:19
Can you * to the clouds and make Job 38:34
and can you * as loudly as he? Job 40:9
and * for joy, all those who try Ps 32:11
They * that they have seen me Ps 35:21
Let them * with delight, "Great Ps 35:27
* triumphant praises to the Lord! Ps 47:1
God has ascended with a mighty *, Ps 47:5
My enemies * against me and Ps 55:3
And I will * in triumph over the Ps 60:8
The dawn and sunset * for joy! Ps 65:8
I will * and sing your praises Ps 71:23
Give a joyous * in honor of the Ps 95:1
Let the cornets and trumpets *! Ps 98:6
on it *, "Glory to the Lord." Ps 98:7
* WITH JOY before the Lord, O Ps 100:1
the sound of your * the water Ps 104:7,8
and I will * in triumph over the Ps 108:9
May our nation * for joy. Ps 132:9
her saints shall * for joy. Ps 132:16
sense, but it must * loudly before Pro 14:33
If you * a pleasant greeting to Pro 27:14
than the * of a king of fools. Ecc 9:17
people of Gallim. * out a warning Is 10:30
Jerusalem * his praise with joy. Is 12:6
enemy attacks. * to them, O Israel, Is 13:2
It is the tumult and the * of Is 13:4
city wall to * out what he sees. Is 21:6,7
Then I heard a Voice * out, Is 21:8,9
But all who are left will * and Is 24:14
could not speak will * and sing! Is 35:6
The voice says, "*!" Is 40:6
"What shall I *?" Is 40:6
"* that man is like the grass Is 40:6
O Crier of Good News, * to Is 40:9
the mountain tops! * louder—don't Is 40:9
He will be gentle—he will not * Is 42:2
He will give a great * and Is 42:13
this wondrous thing. *, O earth; Is 44:23
singing as you go; * to the ends of Is 48:20
Sing for joy, O heavens; *, O Is 49:13
Those who rule them * in Is 52:5
The watchmen * and sing with Is 52:8
* WITH THE voice of a trumpet Is 58:1
Go and * this in Jerusalem's Jer 2:2
* to Jerusalem and to all Judea, Jer 4:5
land and they * against Jerusalem Jer 4:16
Search for them in Lebanon; * for Jer 22:20
Tell them the Lord will * against Jer 25:30
He will * as the harvesters do Jer 25:30
of the nations! * out with praise Jer 31:7
* it out in Egypt; Jer 46:14
road to watch, and * to those who Jer 48:19
* against her from every side. Jer 50:15
Let there be the * of battle in Jer 50:22
land, a * of great destruction. Jer 50:22
And though I cry and *, he will Lam 3:8
the people * at them. Lam 4:15
"The trumpets * to Israel's Eze 7:14
uncovered, to * to me against her Eze 24:8
The Lord leads them with a *. Joe 2:11
the warriors * and trumpets blare. Amo 2:2
will listen? I * to you in vain; Hab 1:2
Sing, O daughter of Zion; *, O Zep 3:14
Then the angel said, "* out this Zec 1:14
"Rejoice greatly, O my people! * Zec 9:9
They will taste victory and * Zec 9:15
a * from the wilderness, 'Prepare Mt 3:3
to a beggar, don't * about it as Mt 6:2
* abroad when daybreak comes. Mt 10:27
He does not fight nor *; Mt 12:19
the *, 'The bridegroom is coming! Mt 25:5,6
way he began to * the good news Mk 1:45
near, he began to * out, "Jesus, Mk 10:47
began to tear! A * for help Lk 5:7
You would * up to him, 'A friend Lk 11:5,6
began to * and sing as they walked Lk 19:36,37
you can * with joy though you Gal 4:27
with a mighty * and with the 1Th 4:16
with a mighty *, "Salvation comes Rev 7:10
and gave a great *—it was like the Rev 10:3
Then a loud voice will * from Rev 11:12
and a mighty * came from the Rev 16:17
He gave a mighty *, "Babylon the Rev 18:2
I heard a loud * from the throne Rev 21:3

SHOUTED
the house and * to Lot, "Bring Gen 19:5
At that moment the Angel of God * Gen 22:11
her out and burn her," Judah *. Gen 38:24
"Joseph is alive," they * to Gen 45:26
you are," Pharaoh *, "distracting Ex 5:4,5
you again," Pharaoh * at Moses. Ex 10:28
camp entrance and *, "All of you Ex 32:26
saw it, they all * and fell flat Lev 9:24
they *. Num 14:4
they * at Moses. Num 20:3
Balaam *. Num 22:29
and disgust he *, "I called you to Num 24:10
they * as loud as they could. Jos 6:20
"Bring out your son," they * to Ju 6:30
Then he returned to his men and * Ju 7:15
Mount Gerizim and * across to the Ju 9:7
"Who is Abimelech," Gaal *, Ju 9:28
for whatever happens now," he *. Ju 15:3
Lehi, the Philistines * with glee; Ju 15:14
Then the army of Benjamin *, Ju 20:32
And all the people *, "Long live 1Sa 10:24
saw them coming they *, "Look! 1Sa 14:11
Then they * to Jonathan, 1Sa 14:12
"Bring the Ark of God," Saul * 1Sa 14:18
He stood and * across to the 1Sa 17:8
David * in reply, "You come to 1Sa 17:45
arrow, Jonathan *, "The arrow is 1Sa 20:37
When they arrived Saul * at him, 1Sa 22:11,12
the king *. 1Sa 22:16
* after him, "My lord the king!" 1Sa 24:7,8
Then he * to Saul, "Why do you 1Sa 24:9,10
Then David * down to Abner and 1Sa 26:14
Again Abner * to him, "Get away 2Sa 2:22
hill, and Abner * down to Joab, 2Sa 2:26
Joab * back, "I swear by God 2Sa 2:27
kicked around like this?" he *. 2Sa 3:8
listen to her. He * for his valet 2Sa 13:17,18
you scoundrel!" he * at David. 2Sa 16:7,8
He * the news down to David, and 2Sa 18:25
towards them. He * down, "Here 2Sa 18:26
One of Joab's young officers * to 2Sa 20:11
*, "Long live King Solomon!" 1Ki 1:39
Jonathan *. 1Ki 1:43
the prophet *, "O altar, the Lord 1Ki 13:2
saying this. He * to his guards, 1Ki 13:4
old man, and he * at the prophet 1Ki 13:21,22
So they * louder and, as was 1Ki 18:28
Then Elijah *, "Hurry to Ahab and 1Ki 18:44
But when Jehoshaphat * out to 1Ki 22:32,33
saw them, he * to Elisha, "Oh, 2Ki 6:21
Then the watchmen * the news to 2Ki 7:11
and *, "Someone is coming." 2Ki 9:17
or foe," King Joram * back. 2Ki 9:17
of the palace, she * at him, "How 2Ki 9:31
and *, "Who is on my side?" 2Ki 9:32
Jehu * to his men. 2Ki 10:14
Then everyone clapped and *, 2Ki 11:12
"Get her out of here," * 2Ki 11:15
Then the Assyrian ambassador * in 2Ki 18:28
And all the people * "Amen!" 1Ch 16:36
they * angrily. 2Ch 10:16
King Abijah * to King Jeroboam and 2Ch 13:4
And as they *, God used King 2Ch 13:15,16
of Judah and Benjamin!" he *. 2Ch 15:2
They * out their oath of loyalty 2Ch 15:14
the priest * to the army officers. 2Ch 23:13,14
the letters * threats in the Jewish 2Ch 32:18
At the trial I * at them, "The Neh 5:8
And all the people *, "Amen," Neh 5:13
Men * after them as after thieves. Job 30:5
and all the angels * for joy? Job 38:6,7
They * for help but no one dared Ps 18:41
There they * their battle cry Ps 74:4
and at last he *, "Sir, day after Is 21:8,9
Then he * in Hebrew to the Jews Is 36:13
The people with Ishmael * for Jer 41:13,14
a herald * out, "O people of all Dan 3:4
Nebuchadnezzar *. Dan 3:25
"He *, 'Cut down the tree; Dan 4:14
desperate sailors * to their gods Jon 1:5
they *. Jon 1:9,10
Then they * out a prayer to Jon 1:14
Jonah * to the crowds that Jon 3:4,5
"Save me, Lord!" he *. Mt 14:30
They *, "Death! Mt 26:65,66

(SHOUTED Con't)
the crowd * back their reply: Mt 27:21
And they *, "Crucify him!" Mt 27:22
About three o'clock, Jesus *, Mt 27:46
Then Jesus * out again, dismissed Mt 27:50
But he only * the louder, again Mk 10:48
They * back, "Crucify him!" Mk 15:13
week to work," he * to the crowd. Lk 13:14
" 'Father Abraham,' he *, 'have Lk 16:24
They all *, "Then you claim you Lk 22:70
they *. Lk 22:71
one voice they *, "Kill him, and Lk 23:18
But they *, "Crucify him! Lk 23:21
But they * louder and louder Lk 23:23
Then Jesus *, "Father, I commit Lk 23:46
holidays, Jesus * to the crowds, Jn 7:37
they *. Jn 9:34
Then he *, "Lazarus, come Jn 11:43
Jesus * to the crowds, "If you Jn 12:44
the chief priests * back. Jn 19:15
apostles, and * to the crowd, Act 2:14
had done, they * (in their local Act 14:11
are corrupting our city," they *. Act 16:20,21
our city," they *, "and Jason Act 17:6
Some * one thing and some Act 21:34
they *, "Away with such a fellow! Act 22:22
So he *, "Brothers, I am a Act 23:6
nothing wrong with him," they *. Act 23:9
when I * out, 'I am here before Act 24:21
Suddenly Festus *, "Paul, you Act 26:24
And he * out to those four angels Rev 7:2
"Fear God," he *, "and extol Rev 14:7
* to the angel with the sickle, Rev 14:18
into the ocean and *, "Babylon, Rev 18:21

SHOUTING

of all the people *, he exclaimed Ex 32:17
in a panic, * and running away. Ju 7:21
"What's all the * about over in 1Sa 4:6
to the priest, the * and the tumult 1Sa 14:19
much * and blowing of trumpets. 2Sa 6:15
will start * that your men are 2Sa 17:9
me to come, there was a lot of *; 2Sa 18:29
and *, 'Long live King Adonijah!' 1Ki 1:25
the commotion and * just as they 1Ki 1:41
them, they began *, "Down with 1Ki 12:16,17
morning, *, "O Baal, hear us!" 1Ki 18:26
the ground *, "Jehovah is God! 1Ki 18:39
a trumpet, *, "Jehu is king!" 2Ki 9:13
around and fled, * to King Ahaziah, 2Ki 9:23
Jehu rode after him, *, "Shoot 2Ki 9:27
while others were * for joy! Ez 3:12
So the * and the weeping mingled Ez 3:13
king's own horse, * before him, Est 6:9
of the city, *, "This is the way Est 6:11
city streets filled with * people. Est 8:15
and want no drivers * at them! Job 39:7
Keep them * for joy because you Ps 5:11
I hear them * insults and Ps 59:7
I hear the voice of someone *, Is 40:3
and to the leaders * in despair, Jer 25:36
Temple mobbed him, *, "Kill him! Jer 26:7,8
There is *, yes, but not the Jer 48:33
yes, but not the * of joy. Jer 48:33
or like the * of a mighty army. Eze 1:24
against the gates, * for the kill; Eze 21:22
wakened him, *, "Lord, save us! Mt 8:25
along behind, *, "O Son of King Mt 9:27
way, they began *, "Sir, King Mt 20:30
*, "God bless King David's Son!" Mt 21:9
in the Temple, * "God bless the Mt 21:15
his own clothing, *, "Blasphemy! Mt 26:65,66
But they kept *, "Crucify! Mt 27:23
present and began *, "Why are you Mk 1:23
Frantically they wakened him, *, Mk 4:38
of them *, "Hail to the King!" Mk 11:9
John was "a voice * from the Lk 3:4
began * at Jesus, "Go away! Lk 4:33
*, "You are the Son of God." Lk 4:41
One of them came back to Jesus, * Lk 17:15
by, so he began *, "Jesus, Son of Lk 18:38
stood there * their accusations. Lk 23:10
barren wilderness, * as Isaiah Jn 1:23
road to meet him, *, "The Savior! Jn 12:13
And he fell to his knees, *, Act 7:60
a great ovation, *, "It is the Act 12:22
out among the people, *, "Men! Act 14:14
She followed along behind us *, Act 16:17
and they began *, "Great is Diana Act 19:28
Inside, the people were all *, Act 19:32
Jew, they started * again and kept Act 19:34
surged behind *, "Away with him, Act 21:36
The * grew louder and louder, and Act 23:10
a loud voice was * out this Rev 5:2
And they were * with a mighty Rev 7:10
were loud voices * down from Rev 11:15
Then I heard a loud voice * Rev 12:10
followed them *, "Anyone Rev 14:9
AND I HEARD a mighty voice * from Rev 16:1
AFTER THIS I heard the * of a vast Rev 19:1
sounded like the * of a huge crowd, Rev 19:6
* loudly to the birds, "Come! Rev 19:17

SHOUTS

with * and battle cries. 1Sa 17:20
to Jerusalem with * of joy, the 1Ch 15:28
commotion, and the * of praise to 2Ch 23:12
and your lips with * of joy. Job 8:21
At the sound of the bugle he *, Job 39:25
He rejoices at the * of battle Job 39:25
May there be * of joy when we Ps 20:5
To heaven and earth he *, Ps 50:4
All the world * with joy, and Ps 65:13
Wisdom * in the streets for a Pro 1:20
A rebel * in anger; Pro 29:11
to the shepherd's * and noise. Is 31:4,5
on Jerusalem with mighty * Jer 2:15
long with battle *, because he did Jer 20:16
no one treads the grapes with * Jer 48:33
around will be the * of panic, "We Jer 49:29
skies their mighty * of victory. Jer 51:14
It is a day of * of anguish, not Eze 7:7
shouts of anguish, not * of joy! Eze 7:7
The Lord * from his Temple in Joe 3:16
there will be wild * of battle Amo 1:14
The king * for his officers; Nah 2:5
"Stop, stop," she *, but they Nah 2:8
with mighty * of thanksgiving for Zec 4:7
Or, "with mighty *, 'How Zec 4:7f
joy and my tongue * his praises! Act 2:26
voice with their *, and dragged Act 7:57
with mighty * of everlasting joy. Jud 1:24,25

SHOVELS

The ash buckets, *, basins, Ex 27:3
altar—the pots, *, basins, meat Ex 38:3
firepans, hooks, *, basins, and Num 4:14
hollowedWith their stavesAnd *. Num 21:17,18
necessary pots, *, and basins and 1Ki 7:40
pots, *, basins 1Ki 7:41-46
as a stable hand * out manure. 1Ki 14:10
They also took all the pots, *, 2Ki 25:14,15
necessary pots, *, and basins for 2Ch 4:11
The pots, *, and fleshhooks. 2Ch 4:12-16
kettles, and ash * used at the Jer 52:18

SHOW

he prayed, "* kindness to my Gen 24:12
animals, did I * them to you and Gen 31:39
indeed God when I * them my power Ex 7:5
demand that you * him a miracle to Ex 7:9
in this way to * you his awesome Ex 20:20
Or, "* me your ways," or, "show Ex 33:13f
Or, "show me your ways," or, "* Ex 33:13f
Jehovah, the Lord. I * kindness Ex 33:19
I, Jehovah, * this steadfast Ex 34:7
peace offering to * special Lev 7:15
he said, 'I will * myself holy Lev 10:3
may he be gracious to you, * you Num 6:24,25,26
"Oh, please, * the great power Num 14:17,18
the Lord will * you who are his, Num 16:5
When Moses brought them out to * Num 17:9
He was to [bring it out and * it Num 17:10
but I will * kindness to a Deu 5:9,10
make any treaties or * them mercy; Deu 7:2
You shall not * pity to a false Deu 19:21
as a symbol to * our children and Jos 22:26,27
family if he would * them the Ju 1:24
"Come, and I will * you the man Ju 4:22
spring and I'll * you which ones Ju 7:4
Nor did they * any kindness to Ju 8:35
but Jehovah the Judge will soon * Ju 11:27
and we'll * you how to fight!" 1Sa 14:12
O Lord God, * us who is guilty." 1Sa 14:41
and I will * you which of his sons 1Sa 16:3
in order to * my joy in the Lord. 2Sa 6:21
"Should the king * kindness to a 2Sa 9:8
"I am going to * special respect 2Sa 10:2
You * your perfections 2Sa 22:26
You * yourself pure; 2Sa 22:27
* his glory to the nations! 1Ch 16:24
"I am going to * friendship to 1Ch 19:2,3
* his great power in helping them. 2Ch 16:9
and told him to * it to Esther and Est 4:8
now let the Almighty * me that I Job 31:35
as a friend, to * him what is Job 33:23,24
"Let me go on and I will * you Job 36:2
Yes, listen as I pray. * me your Ps 17:7
upright you * yourself upright." Ps 18:25f
* me the path where I should go, Ps 25:4
Come, Lord, and * me your mercy, Ps 25:16
* your glory high above the earth. Ps 57:5
wear sackcloth to * my humiliation Ps 69:11
If even one would * some pity, if Ps 69:20
There is nothing left to * that Ps 74:9,10
For I will * you lessons from Ps 78:2,3
* him how it feels! Ps 109:6
I am trusting you. * me where to Ps 143:8
O foolish ones, let me * you Pro 8:4,5
reign in power. I * the judges who Pro 8:14,15
Those who refuse me * that they Pro 8:36
and witches to * them what to do. Is 19:3
anybody—no one can * her the way. Is 19:15
of sackcloth to * your remorse. Is 22:12
your pride and * his contempt for Is 23:9
upraised fist. * them how much you Is 26:11
pity on them or * them his mercy. Is 27:11
to him, so he can * you his love; Is 30:18
stand up and * my power and might. Is 33:10
Let them come and * what they can Is 41:21
Through it he had planned to * Is 42:21
forever, nor always * my wrath; Is 57:16
The Lord will * the nations of Is 61:11
for us you used to *—your power, Is 63:15
to lead you and * you the way! Jer 2:17
come in that spirit, I will * them Jer 16:21
Beg the Lord your God to * us Jer 42:3
they are cruel and * no mercy; Jer 50:42
grief, yet he will * compassion Lam 3:32
days, to * that Israel will be Eze 4:4,5
I will turn my eyes away and * Eze 7:4
But come, and I will * you Eze 8:6
* you greater sins than these!" Eze 8:13
"But I will * you greater evils Eze 8:15
demonstration, to * them what being Eze 12:3
Yet you must * no sorrow. Eze 24:16
When I destroy you and * forth my Eze 28:22
them and I will * the nations of Eze 28:25
Thus will I * my greatness and Eze 38:23
heart everything I * you, for you Eze 40:4
here so I can * you many things; Eze 40:4
God of heaven to * them his mercy Dan 2:18
iron and part clay—* that later on, Dan 2:41,42
But now I will * you what the Dan 11:2
"I hate your * and pretence—your Amo 5:21
dare not * themselves outside Mic 1:11
you with filth and * the world how Nah 3:6
by. * us your power to save us. Hab 3:2
until you again * mercy to them?" Zec 1:12
"Union," to * that the bond of Zec 11:14
should he * you any favor at all? Mal 1:9
with me and I will * you how to Mt 4:19
asking him to * them a miracle. Mt 12:38
by asking him to * them some great Mt 16:1
other stories to * what the Kingdom Mt 22:1
Here, * me a coin." Mt 22:19
they do is done for *. Mt 23:5
He trusted God—let God * his Mt 27:41;42,43
"* me a coin and I'll tell you." Mk 12:15
with a great * of friendliness. Mk 14:45
But when he didn't * up that Lk 2:44
be baptized to * that they had Lk 3:3
"Try to * as much compassion as Lk 6:36
on their heads to * their remorse. Lk 10:13
You will hate one and * loyalty Lk 16:13
and * him that you are healed!" Lk 17:14
prayer and to * them that they must Lk 18:1
Surely they will * respect for Lk 20:13
trickery and said, "* me a coin. Lk 20:24
says for you to * us the guest room Lk 22:11
God, * us a miracle to prove it." Jn 2:18
They replied, "You must * us Jn 6:30,31
blind and to * those who think they Jn 9:39
Philip said, "Sir, * us the Jn 14:8
I say that he will * you my glory. Jn 16:15
know every heart; * us which of Act 1:24,25
And I will * him how much he Act 9:16
was supposed to * me the way of Rom 7:10
a perfect right to * his fury and Rom 9:22
Christ came to * that God is true Rom 15:8
Doesn't this * how little you 1Co 3:4
He said this to * us that 1Co 9:10
He will * you how to escape 1Co 10:13
to help you: to * you from our 2Co 1:6,7
you, but I had to * you how very 2Co 2:4
Please * him now that you still 2Co 2:8
opportunities to * forth the power 2Co 4:11
we do we try to * that we are true 2Co 6:4
so the Lord could * how much you 2Co 7:12
This will glorify the Lord and * 2Co 8:19
Please * your love for me to 2Co 8:24
I hope I won't need to * you when 2Co 10:2
the things that * how weak I am. 2Co 11:30
* them the Good News about Jesus. Gal 1:16
was given, to * men how guilty they Gal 3:19
And his reason? To * to all the Eph 3:10
and your behavior should * it! Eph 5:8
And you husbands, * the same kind Eph 5:25
kind things which * that you are a Php 1:11
great joy, and * your appreciation, Php 2:29
but we wanted to * you, firsthand, 2Th 3:9
Christ our Lord * you his kindness 1Ti 1:2
idea what those laws really * us. 1Ti 1:7
as an example to * everyone how 1Ti 1:16
Gentiles, and to * them God's plan 1Ti 2:7
Is she always ready to * 1Ti 5:10
the world began—to * his love and 2Ti 1:9
those whose lives * that they are 2Ti 4:8
it to others and * those who Tit 1:9
steal, but must * themselves to be Tit 2:10
My plea is that you * kindness Phm 1:10
way you used to * your love for Heb 6:10
has to * you where you are wrong. Heb 12:5
of glory, if you * favoritism to Jas 2:1
Faith that doesn't * itself by Jas 2:17
so that you may * to others how God 1Pe 2:9
* respect for everyone. 1Pe 2:17

(SHOW Con't)
us: In baptism we * that we have 1Pe 3:21
all, continue to * deep love for 1Pe 4:8
* that you do not really love God; 1Jn 2:15
let us really love them, and * it 1Jn 3:18
loving and kind * that they are the 1Jn 4:7
and when they * respect for others, Jud 1:16
up here and I will * you what must Rev 4:1
said, "and I will * you what is Rev 17:1
with me and I will * you the bride, Rev 21:9

SHOW-OFFS
they are loud-mouthed "*," and Jud 1:16

SHOWBREAD
Literally, "*." 1Ch 9:32f

SHOWED
"So God has * you what he is Gen 41:28
them, and the Lord * him a tree to Ex 15:25
manner I * you in the mountain. Ex 26:30
Kadesh, and they * the fruit they Num 13:26
* himself to be holy before them. Num 20:13
I have seen what God Almighty * Num 24:3-9
at Shiloh the Lord * Joshua by the Jos 18:10
So he * them how to get in, and Ju 1:25
The youth * him the place, and 2Ki 6:6
and * them the king's son. 2Ki 11:4
Hezekiah welcomed them and * 2Ki 20:13
I * them all my treasures." 2Ki 20:15
* them the way through the night. Neh 9:19
At the Flood, the Lord * his Ps 29:10
In these messages God * him what Is 1:1
THIS IS THE vision God * Isaiah Is 13:1
And Hezekiah replied, "I * them Is 39:4
But you * them no mercy. Is 47:6
plans and * me their evil plots. Jer 11:18
Egypt, to whom I * my mercies in Jer 31:2
king's officials * any signs of Jer 36:24,25
God * it to me for your benefit. Dan 2:30
THIS IS WHAT the Lord God * me in Amo 7:1
Then the Lord God * me a great Amo 7:4
Then he * me this: The Lord was Amo 7:7
THEN THE LORD God * me, in a Amo 8:1
In a vision the Lord God * Obadiah Ob 1:1
That is the kindness I * you Mic 6:5
Then the Lord * me four Zec 1:20
THEN THE ANGEL * me (in my Zec 3:1
And the Lord replies, "I * my Mal 1:2,3
high mountain and * him the nations Mt 4:8
(By saying this he * that every Mk 7:19
(It seemed that these men * up Lk 5:17
The man replied, "The one who * Lk 10:37
and * them [the wounds in Lk 24:40
After greeting them, he * them Jn 20:20
days later and * him to certain Act 10:40,41
But God * his great love for us Rom 5:8
it was the law that * me my sin. Rom 7:7
He * us God's plan of salvation; 1Co 1:30
other way than the one we * you; Gal 1:7
God himself * me this secret plan Eph 3:2,3
wives as Christ * to the church Eph 5:25
Lord was, for he * me how to trust 1Ti 1:14
power of death and * us the way of 2Ti 1:10
But the Lord Jesus Christ has * 2Pe 1:13,14
God * how much he loved us by 1Jn 4:9
the angel who * them to me; Rev 22:8

SHOWER
* down on all who trust in him. Ps 34:8
of our day, will * you with gifts Ps 45:12
How long will you * special Ps 82:2
"I will * you with deadly arrows Eze 5:16
may come and * salvation upon you. Hos 10:12
west, you say, 'Here comes a *.' Lk 12:54
the more he will * us with his 2Co 1:5
May God our Father * you with Col 1:2
Jesus our Lord * you with his 2Ti 1:2

SHOWERED
God, why have you * your blessings 2Sa 7:18
great goodness you * upon them. Neh 9:35
Many favors are * on those who Pro 16:15
but blessings shall be * on Pro 24:25
As a result we were * with Act 28:10
and he has * down upon us the Eph 1:8

SHOWERS
Like * on the hillside. Deu 32:2
They are wet with the * of the Job 24:8
For he directs the snow, the *, Job 37:6
abundant rain. * soften the earth, Ps 65:10
grass—like * that water the earth! Ps 72:6
sends down the * and makes the Ps 147:8
And there shall be *, showers of Eze 34:26
And there shall be showers, * of Eze 34:26
dew or the welcome * of rain, and Mic 5:7
will answer with lightning and *. Zec 10:1
land has had many * upon it and Heb 6:7

SHOWING
double impact, * that what I have Gen 41:32
* wealth and extravagance. Gen 49:11f
God's laws, and * them the Ex 18:19,20
I am * you here on the mountain. Ex 25:40
by forgiving our sins and * us Num 14:17,18
and power you have been * us; Deu 3:23,24,25
of the palace, * them his treasure Is 39:2

i.e., * their desire for foreign Zep 1:8f
snapped it in two, * that I had Zec 11:10
to be a means of * his respect and Mal 2:5
split from above, * that Christ's Mk 15:38f
me great honor by * you my glory. Jn 16:14
widows who were * one another the Act 9:39
in public debate, * by the Act 18:28
God can keep on * us more and more Rom 6:1
he is just * his ignorance. 1Co 8:2
the same loaf, * that we are all 1Co 10:17
* off my own power and abilities. 2Co 12:9
But if instead of * love among Gal 5:15
special work of * God's favor to Eph 3:2,3
mighty pageant * things to come: Rev 15:1

SHOWN
loving kindnesses * me again and Gen 32:10
the miracles I have * you." Ex 4:17
miracles I have * you, but I will Ex 4:21
just as was * you on the mountain. Ex 27:8
exact design the Lord had * Moses. Num 8:4
He sees what Almighty God has * Num 24:15-19
has * us his glory and greatness; Deu 5:24
kindness you have * your Ru 2:10,11
the kindness you have * me today. 1Sa 24:19
that the Lord had * to his servant 1Ki 8:66
But the Lord has * me that he 2Ki 8:10
"The Lord has * me that you are 2Ki 8:13
The Lord has * me his favor. Ps 30:6,7
Lord, for he has * me that his Ps 31:21
He has * his great power to his Ps 111:6
is really like is * by the kind of Pro 27:19
your idols, I have * you my power. Is 43:12
has * no mercy even to his Temple. Lam 2:1
everything the Lord had * me. Eze 11:25
* you to the people of Israel. Eze 43:10
"Thus the great God has * what Dan 2:45
for they shall be * mercy. Mt 5:7
greatest love is * when a person Jn 15:13
the plan * to Moses by the Angel. Act 7:44
now, for I have * him a vision of Act 9:12
But God has * me in a vision that Act 10:28
rejected it, and * yourselves Act 13:46
we have already * that all men Rom 3:9
But now God has * us a different Rom 3:21,22
look foolish, and * their wisdom to 1Co 1:20
grace of God * through you. 2Co 9:14
kindness is, as * in all he has Eph 2:7
the kind that was * us by Jesus Php 2:5
and that he was God, as * by the 2Ti 2:8
God always has * us that these Heb 2:4
as * to him on Mount Sinai. Heb 8:5
to those who have * no mercy. Jas 2:13
from God has been * to us and we 1Jn 1:2
the Father and then was * to us. 1Jn 1:2
and what will soon be * to you. Rev 1:19
* you is to tell about Jesus." Rev 19:10

SHOWS
God of terror who * no partiality Deu 10:17
And * mercy to his anointed— 2Sa 22:51
their pathway. He * how to Pro 2:9
gives them away and * their guilt. Is 3:9
I am the one who * what liars all Is 44:25
with clay also * that these Dan 2:43
with sin, and * only hatred for Hos 9:7
* it is ready for its food. Amo 3:4
easily forgive. He * his power in Nah 1:3
a vow * that something is wrong. Mt 5:37
but one who is forgiven little, * Lk 7:47
respected than you * up, the host Lk 14:8
Jesus told him, "This * Lk 19:9,10
But God * his anger from heaven Rom 1:18
* us all of God's deepest secrets. 1Co 2:10
together, this * that we are 1Co 10:16
* you a different way to be saved. 2Co 11:4
My power * up best in weak 2Co 12:9
upon their sin and * it up, and Eph 5:13
living on milk it * he isn't very Heb 5:12,13
man by his wealth * that you are Jas 2:4
But if you keep on sinning, it * 1Jn 3:8
* that he is not in God's family; 1Jn 3:10
and kind, it * that he doesn't know 1Jn 4:8
do to us, and * that we are not 1Jn 4:18

SHRANK
Yet I never * from telling you Act 20:20

SHRED
crops, without a * of Deu 29:23

SHREDDED
wild gourds. He * them and put them 2Ki 4:39

SHREDS
clothes ripped to * as a sign of Is 36:22

SHREWD
No one, regardless of how * or Pro 21:30
Woe to those who are wise and * Is 5:21
and Zidon, too, * though they be. Zec 9:2
admire the rascal for being so *. Lk 16:8
the scoundrel for being so *?" Lk 16:8f

SHREWDNESS
with great * and intelligence. Dan 8:23

SHRIEK
hears me. I *, but get no justice. Job 19:7
The oppressed may * beneath Job 35:9,10

SHRIEKED
As soon as he saw Jesus he * and Lk 8:28

SHRIEKING
him *, "You are the Son of God!" Mk 3:11
It gave a terrible scream, *, Mk 5:7,8

SHRINE
from it was placed in Micah's *. Ju 17:4,5
"There is a * in there with an Ju 18:14
spies entered the * and took the Ju 18:17
down the altar and * at Bethel 2Ki 23:15
Lord, I love your home, this * Ps 26:8
Literally, "Your innermost *," Ps 28:2f

SHRINES
He also made * on the hills and 1Ki 12:31
priests for the * on the hills. 1Ki 12:32,33
priests from the * on the hills who 1Ki 13:2
curse against the * in the cities 1Ki 13:32
to idols in the * on the hills. 1Ki 13:33
They built * and obelisks and 1Ki 14:23
However, the * on the hills were 1Ki 15:14
not destroy the * on the hills, so 1Ki 22:43
didn't destroy the * on the 2Ki 12:3
However, he didn't destroy the * 2Ki 14:4
didn't destroy the * on the hills 2Ki 15:4
But he didn't destroy the * on 2Ki 15:34,35
incense at the * on the hills and 2Ki 16:4
They placed them in the * on the 2Ki 17:29
He removed the * on the hills, 2Ki 18:4
He rebuilt the hilltop * which 2Ki 21:3,4,5
incense in the * on the hills 2Ki 23:5
tore down all the * on the hills 2Ki 23:8
He also destroyed the * at the 2Ki 23:8
Next he removed the * on the 2Ki 23:13
(Solomon had built these * for 2Ki 23:13
Josiah demolished the * on the 2Ki 23:19
of the heathen * upon their own 2Ki 23:20
destroy the idol * on the hills, 2Ch 20:33
constructed idol * in the mountains 2Ch 21:11
at the idol * on the hills and 2Ch 28:4
for making idol * and to decorate Eze 16:16
the heathen * from among you, and Mic 5:14
* of the Greek goddess Diana. Act 19:24

SHRINK
and * back in horror and dismay. Jer 2:12
All who see you will * back in Nah 3:7
for I didn't * from declaring all Act 20:27
Otherwise, if they * back, God Heb 10:38
and * back from meeting him. 1Jn 2:28

SHRINKING
deep reverence, * back from all Php 2:12

SHRIVEL
the apples * on the trees; Joe 1:12
their eyes will * in their Zec 14:12
Your grapes won't * away before Mal 3:11

SHRIVELED
* and withered by the east wind. Gen 41:6
I am * like a wineskin in the Ps 119:83

SHRIVELING
They were like grass * beneath 2Ki 19:26

SHROUDED
Let it be lost even to God, * in Job 3:4

SHROUDS
He * his throne with his clouds. Job 26:9

SHRUB
He is like a stunted * in the Jer 17:6

SHRUGGED
They * away the Rock of their Deu 32:15
You no longer * your shoulders, 2Co 7:11

SHRUGGING
defiled my name by * off your oath Jer 34:16

SHRUGS
sees me mocks and sneers and *. Ps 22:7

SHRUNKEN
upon their mothers' * breasts. Lam 2:12

SHUA
Canaanite girl—the daughter of *. Gen 38:2
* (their sister). 1Ch 7:32

SHUAH
Jokshan, Medan,Midian, Ishbak, *. Gen 25:1
Midian, Ishbak, and *. 1Ch 1:32

SHUAL
in the land of *, another went to 1Sa 13:17
Suah, Harnepher, *, Beri, Imrah, 1Ch 7:36,37

SHUBA-EL
his descendant *; 1Ch 24:20
Thirteenth, * and twelve of his 1Ch 25:9-31

SHUBA-EL'S
his descendant Shuba-el; and * 1Ch 24:20

SHUDDER
Horror takes hold upon me and I * Job 21:6
They shall * with terror when I Eze 32:10

SHUHAH
Chelub (the brother of *), whose 1Ch 4:11,12

SHUHAM
named after *, the son of Dan. Num 26:42,43

SHUHAMITES
the clan of the *, named after Num 26:42,43

SHUHITE
the *, and Zophar the Naamathite. Job 2:11
BILDAD THE * replies to Job: Job 8:1
THE FURTHER REPLY of Bildad the *: Job 18:1

(SHUHITE Con't)
THE FURTHER REPLY of Bildad the *: Job 25:1
and Bildad the *, and Zophar the Job 42:9

SHULAM
return to us, O maid of *. Sol 6:13

SHULAMMITE
"Why should you seek a mere *?" Sol 6:13

SHUMATHITES
the Puthites, the *, and the 1Ch 2:53

SHUNAM
Abishag, from *, was finally 1Ki 1:3,4

SHUNAMMITE
me Abishag, the *, as my wife." 1Ki 2:17

SHUNEM
Jezreel, Chesulloth, *, Hapharaim, Jos 19:17-23
up their camp at *, and Saul and 1Sa 28:4
One day Elisha went to *. 2Ki 4:8
that woman from * is coming. 2Ki 4:25

SHUNI
and his sons: Ziphion, Haggi, *, Gen 46:16,17
named after their ancestor *. Num 26:15-18

SHUNITES
The *, named after their ancestor Num 26:15-18

SHUNNED
but the liar's counsel is *. Pro 10:31

SHUPHAMITES
The *, named after their ancestor Num 26:38-41

SHUPPIM
The sons of Ir were * and Huppim. 1Ch 7:12
who found wives for Huppim and *. 1Ch 7:15
on the upper road, to * and Hosah. 1Ch 26:16

SHUR
desert spring along the road to *. Gen 16:7
and settled between Kadesh and *. Gen 20:1
from Havilah to * (which is a Gen 25:18
the wilderness of * and were there Ex 15:22
all the way to *, east of Egypt. 1Sa 15:7
who had lived near * along the road 1Sa 27:8

SHUSHAN
when I was at the palace at *, Neh 1:1
celebration at * Palace, to which Est 1:1
king's harem at * Palace, along Est 2:8
first proclaimed in the city of *. Est 3:15
all the Jews of * and fast for me; Est 4:16
was also issued at * Palace.. Est 8:14
They even killed 500 men in *. Est 9:6
in *, he called for Queen Esther. Est 9:11
killed 500 men in * alone," he Est 9:12
who are here at * do again tomorrow Est 9:13
was announced at *, and they hung Est 9:14
Then the Jews at * gathered Est 9:15
But the Jews at * went on Est 9:18

SHUT
closed the door and * them in. Gen 7:16
you, and he will * the Deu 11:17
* your heart or hand against them; Deu 15:7
the city gates were kept *. Jos 2:7
were kept tightly * because the Jos 6:1
been yoked—and * their calves away 1Sa 6:7
calves were * up in the barn. 1Sa 6:10
"And when the skies are * up and 1Ki 8:35,36
sons and * the door behind you. 2Ki 4:4
bed of the prophet and * the door; 2Ki 4:21
He went in and * the door behind 2Ki 4:33
When he arrives, * the door and 2Ki 6:32
"When the skies are * and there 2Ch 6:26
If I * up the heavens so that 2Ch 7:13
door of the Temple * so that no one 2Ch 28:24
The doors have been * tight, the 2Ch 29:7
of the city be * as darkness fell Neh 13:19
Curse it for its failure to * my Job 3:10
You send me to prison and * me Job 13:27,28
Help me, Lord, to keep my mouth * Ps 141:3
It pays him to keep his mouth *. Pro 17:27,28
your ears open and your mouth *! Ecc 5:1
close their ears and * their eyes. Is 6:10
They tell my prophets, "* up—we Is 30:10,11
plot murder, who * their eyes to Is 33:15
God has * their eyes so that they Is 44:18
the gates shall not be * against Is 45:1
He has * me into a place of Lam 3:9
for I will not * off the rains but Eze 34:26
here and so it shall remain *. Eze 44:2
the passage shall be * behind him. Eze 46:12
he said, "to * the lions' mouths Dan 6:22
my prophets, telling them, '* up!' Amo 2:12
A trap doesn't snap * unless it Amo 3:5
you who would * the doors and Mal 1:10
all alone, and * the door behind Mt 6:6
a box over it to * out the light? Mk 4:21
"* up!" Mk 10:48
Literally, "* up all unto Rom 11:32f
trying to do is to * you off from Gal 4:17
because they have * their minds Eph 4:17,18
what no one can * and to shut what Rev 3:7
and to * what no one can open. Rev 3:7
a door to you that no one can *. Rev 3:8
They have power to * the skies Rev 11:6
pit, which he then * and locked, so Rev 20:3

SHUTHELAH
named after their ancestor *. Num 26:28-37
their ancestor Eran, a son of *. Num 26:28-37
*, Bered, Tahath, Eleadah, Tahath, 1Ch 7:20,21
Tahath, Eleadah, Tahath, Zabad, *, 1Ch 7:20,21

SHUTHELAHITES
The *, named after their ancestor Num 26:28-37
(A sub-clan of the * was Num 26:28-37

SHUTS
His anger * you out like iron Pro 18:19
He who * his ears to the cries of Pro 21:13
A lustful eye * out the light and Lk 11:34

SHUTTING
to them, * the door behind him. Gen 19:6
deepest darkness, * out all light. Lam 3:2
put them to sleep, * their eyes and Rom 11:8

SIA
*, Padon, Lebana, Hagaba, Neh 7:46-56

SIAHA
Ziha, Hasupha, Tabbaoth, Keros, *, Ez 2:43-54

SIBBECAI
at Gob, * the Hushathite killed 2Sa 21:18
* from Hushath; 1Ch 11:26-47
at Gezer. But *, a man from 1Ch 20:4
Division was * of the Hushite 1Ch 27:11

SIBBOLETH
the H and said, "*" instead of Ju 12:6

SIBMAH
Baal-meon, *. Num 32:37,38
Kiriathaim, *, Zereth-shahar on Jos 13:19
of Heshbon and the vineyards at *. Is 16:8
for Jazer and the vineyards of *. Is 16:9
O men of *, rich in vineyards, I Jer 48:32

SIBRAIM
then to Berothah and *, which Eze 47:16

SICK
* and tired of these local girls. Gen 27:46
of the Israeli herds was even *. Ex 9:6
"NEVER SACRIFICE A * or defective Deu 17:1
she told them he was * and 1Sa 19:14
three days ago because I was *. 1Sa 30:13
made Bath-sheba's baby deathly *. 2Sa 12:15
the baby being *," they said, 2Sa 12:18
back to bed and pretend you are *; 2Sa 13:5
SON ABIJAH now became very *. 1Ki 14:1
about her son, for he was very *. 1Ki 14:5
is * and all those who are well. 1Ki 14:10
the woman's son became * and died. 1Ki 17:17
where King Ben-hadad lay *. 2Ki 8:7
HEZEKIAH NOW BECAME deathly *, 2Ki 20:1
put those who were * and old on 2Ch 28:15
became deathly *, and he prayed to 2Ch 32:24
You aren't *, are you? Neh 2:1
"I AM * and near to death; Job 17:1
Heal me, for my body is *, and I Ps 6:2
who was * and nearing death. Ps 35:14
anger my body is *, my health is Ps 38:3,4
He nurses them when they are *, Ps 41:3
come to visit me while I am *; Ps 41:6
is broken and my heart is *; Ps 102:3,4
there were no * and feeble folk Ps 105:37
Hope deferred makes the heart *; Pro 13:12
but a broken spirit makes one *. Pro 17:22
Don't rob the poor and *! Pro 22:22,23
much of it, or it will make you *! Pro 25:16
Hard liquor is for * men at the Pro 31:6,7
tell him that I am * with love." Sol 5:8
From head to foot you are * and Is 1:5,6
I am * of your sacrifices. Is 1:11
body, as when a * man wastes away. Is 10:18
they make Egypt stagger like a * Is 19:14
say, "We are * and helpless," for Is 33:24
became deathly * and Isaiah the Is 38:1
very * and now was well again. Is 39:1
He has left me * and desolate the Lam 1:13
nor tended the * nor bound up the Eze 34:4
their broken limbs and heal the *. Eze 34:15,16
butt and crowd my * and hungry Eze 34:21
Then I grew faint and was * for Dan 8:27
all living things grow * and die; Hos 4:3
When Ephraim and Judah see how * Hos 5:13
punished people—* and lame and Mic 4:6
even the * and the blind ones.' Mal 1:8
* animals to offer to me on it. Mal 1:12
Stolen animals, lame and *—as Mal 1:13
a * one to sacrifice to God. Mal 1:14
of Galilee so that * folk were soon Mt 4:24
and all the * were healed. Mt 8:16
to the * boy, "Cheer up, son! Mt 9:2
It's the * people who do!" Mt 9:12
woman who had been * for twelve Mt 9:20
Heal the *, raise the dead, cure Mt 10:8
He healed all the * among them, Mt 12:15
he pitied them and healed their *. Mt 14:14
to bring in their * to be healed. Mt 14:35
to be healed. The * begged him to Mt 14:36
him, and he healed their *. Mt 19:2
naked and you clothed me; * and Mt 25:36
When did we ever see you * or in Mt 25:39
clothe me; *, and in prison, and Mt 25:43
* or in prison, and not help you?' Mt 25:44
* in bed with a high fever. Mk 1:29,30
filled with the * and Mk 1:32,33
great numbers of * folk that Mk 1:34
and lowered the * man on his Mk 2:4
Jesus said to the * man, "Son, Mk 2:5
he told them, "* people need the Mk 2:17
great numbers of * people were Mk 3:10
woman who had been * for twelve Mk 5:25
on a few * people and heal them. Mk 6:5
and healed many * people, anointing Mk 6:13
and began carrying * folks to him Mk 6:55
laid the * in the market plazas and Mk 6:56
hands on the * and heal them." Mk 16:18
very * with a high fever. Lk 4:38
who had any * people in their Lk 4:40
and lowered the * man down into the Lk 5:18,19
them, "It is the * who need a Lk 5:31
army captain was * and near Lk 7:2
he was curing many * people of Lk 7:20,21,22
Kingdom of God and to heal the *. Lk 9:2
the Good News and healing the *. Lk 9:6
(2) Heal the *; Lk 10:8,9
Jesus took the * man by the hand Lk 14:4
whose son was very *, heard that Jn 4:46,47
Crowds of * folks—lame, blind, Jn 5:3
had been * for thirty-eight years. Jn 5:5
"I can't," the * man said, Jn 5:7
he went, to watch him heal the *. Jn 6:2-5
Mary and her sister Martha, was *. Jn 11:1
good friend is very, very *." Jn 11:3
of men and women. * people were Act 5:15
bringing their * folk and those Act 5:16
were placed upon * people, they Act 19:12
Then all the other * people in Act 28:9
be * again and will never die. Rom 8:23
and *, and some have even died. 1Co 11:30
else the power to heal the *. 1Co 12:9
Can everyone heal the *? 1Co 12:30
us for they become * and die; 1Co 15:43
even though I was * when I first Gal 4:13
Has she helped those who are * 1Ti 5:10
because you are * so often. 1Ti 5:23
and I left Trophimus * at Miletus. 2Ti 4:20
after they had been weak or *. Heb 11:34
They were hungry and * and Heb 11:37,38
Is anyone *? Jas 5:14
he was a good man, * of the 2Pe 2:7,8

SICKBED
lay her upon a * of intense Rev 2:22

SICKENS
The mother of seven * and Jer 15:9

SICKLE
handfuls of it, but don't use a *. Deu 23:25
For sharpening a *, 30Ç 1Sa 13:21
Now let the * do its work; Joe 3:13
with his * and harvested it." Mk 4:29
head and a sharp * in his hand. Rev 14:14
"Begin to use the *, for the time Rev 14:15
cloud swung his * over the earth, Rev 14:16
heaven, and he also had a sharp *. Rev 14:17
shouted to the angel with the *, Rev 14:18
sickle, "Use your * now to cut off Rev 14:18
So the angel swung his * on Rev 14:19

SICKLES
discs, axes, or *, they had to take 1Sa 13:20

SICKLY
From my youth I have been * and Ps 88:15
withered, *, with no grain; Hos 8:7

SICKNESS
I will take away * from among you. Ex 23:25
take away all your * and will not Deu 7:15
upon you every * and plague there Deu 28:61
of Ekron, to ask about your *?" 2Ki 1:16
for he had learned of his *. 2Ki 20:12
Touch his body with * and he will Job 2:4,5
"Or, God sends * and pain, even Job 33:19
"You make all his bed in his *." Ps 41:3f
handed them over to plagues and *. Ps 78:50
For he himself has sent this *. Is 38:15
* and wounds are ever before me. Jer 6:7
My grief is great. My * is Jer 10:19
* or that I found injured or dead; Eze 4:14
defects—without *, deformities, Eze 43:22
And he healed every kind of * and Mt 4:23
tell his * to go—and it will go!" Mt 8:8,9
heal every kind of * and disease. Mt 10:1
you are healed of your *!" Lk 13:12
Herod with a * so that he was Act 12:23
plants, suffer in * and death as Rom 8:22
But even though my * was Gal 4:14
and if his * was caused by some Jas 5:15

SICKNESSES
our * and bore our diseases." Mt 8:17

SIDDIM
their armies in * Valley (that is, Gen 14:3

SIDE
deck—and put a door in the *. Gen 6:16
on her father's *, and that he was Gen 29:12,13
in Egypt with Joseph at your *." Gen 46:3,4
against the two * panels, so that Ex 12:22
two * pieces, he will pass over Ex 12:23
with walls of water on each *; Ex 14:21
Israelites were on the other *, Ex 14:26

(SIDE Con't)
walled up on either * of them. Ex 14:29
they stood on each *, holding up Ex 17:12
corners, two rings on each *. Ex 25:12
out from each * of the center Ex 25:32,33
to end for each * of the tent, Ex 26:3
two long pieces, one for each *. Ex 26:3
long pieces together * by side. Ex 26:4,5
long pieces together side by *. Ex 26:4,5
on each *, opposite each other. Ex 26:4,5
grooves on each * to mortise into Ex 26:17
form the south * of the sacred Ex 26:18,19
On the north * there will also Ex 26:20
On the west * there will be six Ex 26:22
bars on each * of the Tabernacle. Ex 26:26,27
other on the outer * of the veil. Ex 26:35
be on the south * of the Holy Place Ex 26:35
and the table on the north *. Ex 26:35
the rings at each * of the altar. Ex 27:7
On the south * the curtains will Ex 27:9,10
same on the north * of the Ex 27:11
The west * of the court will be Ex 27:12
The east * will also be Ex 27:13
On each * of the entrance there Ex 27:14,15
*, come over here and join me." Ex 32:26
on the south *, with the bottoms Ex 36:23
on the north * of the Tabernacle, Ex 36:25,26
The west * of the Tabernacle, Ex 36:27
So, on the west *, there were a Ex 36:30
five for each * of the Tabernacle. Ex 36:31,32
frames, along each *, running from Ex 36:33
six branches, three from each *. Ex 37:18
placed on each *, beneath this Ex 37:27
Four rings were cast for each * Ex 38:5
the rings at the * of the altar. Ex 38:7
The west * was seventy-five feet Ex 38:12
The east * was also seventy-five Ex 38:13
The drapes at either * of the Ex 38:14,15
on the under *, next to the ephod. Ex 39:19
table at the north * of the room Ex 40:22
on the south * of the Tabernacle. Ex 40:24
Lord on the north * of the altar, Lev 1:11
drained out at the * of the altar. Lev 1:15,16,17
* of the altar with the ashes. Lev 1:15,16,17
the blood at the * of the altar and Lev 5:9
upon the east * of the mercy place, Lev 16:14
East * of the Tabernacle Num 2:3-31
South * of the Tabernacle Num 2:3-31
west * of Tabernacle Num 2:3-31
North * of Tabernacle Num 2:3-31
Judah's * of the camp was 186,400. Num 2:3-31
So the total of the Reuben * of Num 2:3-31
So the total on the Ephraim * of Num 2:3-31
So the total on Dan's * of the Num 2:3-31
West * of Tabernacle Num 3:16-24
North * of Tabernacle Num 3:31-35
camped on the east * of the Num 10:5,6,7
your border on the other *." Num 20:17
Then they moved to the far * of Num 21:13
the other * of the Jordan River." Num 32:5
land on the other * of the Jordan; Num 32:19
we would rather have it on this * Num 32:19
And the land on the eastern * Num 32:22
be here on this * of the Jordan." Num 32:32
on to Riblah at the east * of Ain. Num 34:10,11
land on the east * of the Jordan, Num 34:14,15
on the east * of the Jordan River. Num 35:13,14
off into the fields on either *. Deu 2:27
on the other * of the Jordan. Deu 3:21
I must die here on this * of the Deu 4:21,22
the nations on the other *. Deu 9:1
on the other *, at Mount Ebal. Deu 27:2,3,4
here on the east * of the Jordan Jos 1:12,13
their territory on the other *; Jos 1:14
on the east * of the Jordan." Jos 1:15
other *, especially at Jericho. Jos 2:1
city from every * and captured it! Jos 6:20
Why didn't we stay on the other * Jos 7:7
Bethel and the west * of Ai; Jos 8:9
ambush on the west * of the city. Jos 8:11,12,13
kings on the east * of the Jordan Jos 12:1
on the west * of the Jordan. Jos 12:7
on the east * of the Jordan, for Jos 13:8
on the east * of the Jordan River. Jos 14:3,4
on the south * of the valley. Jos 15:7
[on the east * of the Jordan River Jos 17:1
So now, land on the west * of Jos 17:2
land on the east * of the Jordan Jos 18:7
started on the south * of Sarid. Jos 19:10
The boundary on the west * went Jos 19:24,25,26
on the east * of the Jordan River, Jos 20:8
the other * of the Jordan River. Jos 22:4
land on the west * of the Jordan. Jos 22:7,8
join us on our * of the river where Jos 22:19
a pain in your * and a thorn in Jos 23:13
on the other * of the Jordan; Jos 24:8
north * of the mountains of Gaash. Jos 24:30
used the narrow, crooked * paths. Ju 5:6
who live around you on every *. Ju 6:10
from all their enemies on every *. Ju 8:34
living on the far * of the hill Ju 19:1
along the east * of the road that Ju 21:19
'They're on this *,' then you will 1Sa 20:21
that my own son is on David's *. 1Sa 22:8
When the Israelis on the other * 1Sa 31:7
each * to fight in mortal combat. 2Sa 2:15
*, so that all of them died. 2Sa 2:16
them lie down * by side in rows. 2Sa 8:2
them lie down side by * in rows. 2Sa 8:2
other * of the Euphrates River. 2Sa 10:15,16
the road at the * of the hill. 2Sa 13:34
with a dagger strapped to his *. 2Sa 20:8,9,10
has given Israel peace on every *; 1Ki 5:4
The bottom floor of the * rooms 1Ki 6:8
from the right * of the Temple, and 1Ki 6:8
an annex on each * of the building, 1Ki 6:10
decorated with wreaths on each *. 1Ki 7:27-30
on the right-hand * of the room. 1Ki 7:39
on the right-hand * of the room. 1Ki 7:39
on the right-hand * and five on the 1Ki 7:49
and a lion standing on each *. 1Ki 10:19
When they arrived on the other * 2Ki 2:9
and shouted, "Who is on my *?" 2Ki 9:32
"If you are on my * and are going 2Ki 10:6
on the right-hand * of the altar at 2Ki 12:9
on the north * of the new altar. 2Ki 16:14
* as one enters the city gate. 2Ki 23:8
graves in the * of the mountain. 2Ki 23:16
to the east * of Gedor Valley in 1Ch 4:34-39
bounded on one * by Bethel and its 1Ch 7:28
We are on your *, son of Jesse. 1Ch 12:18
From the other * of the Jordan 1Ch 12:24-37
at the east * of the altar. 2Ch 5:11,12
Gold lions also stood at each * 2Ch 9:19
a line from one * to the other in 2Ch 23:10
to the west * of the City of David 2Ch 32:30
house to the * of the house. Neh 3:21
prison and shut me in on every *. Job 13:27,28
On our * are aged men much older Job 15:10
He has broken me down on every * Job 19:10
Then he will be on my *! Job 19:27
I would tell him all about my * Job 23:4,5
try to see my * of this argument. Job 31:35
me on every *, I am not afraid. Ps 3:6
prowl on every * and vileness is Ps 12:8
Though a thousand fall at my *, Ps 91:7
The Lord is on my *, he will Ps 118:7
IF THE LORD had not been on our * Ps 124:1
not been on our *, we would have Ps 124:1
I was always at his * like a Pro 8:30
* and sets the record straight. Pro 18:17
them, while on the * of their Ecc 4:1
be routed, for I am on your *. Is 54:15
Yet on every * I hear their Jer 20:10
Gate on the east * of the city; Jer 31:40
at the * entrance of the Temple. Jer 38:14
them on every *, says the Lord. Jer 46:5
Shout against her from every *. Jer 50:15
they shall come from every * to Jer 51:2
Messengers from every * come Jer 51:31
face on the right * [of his head Eze 1:10
an ox on his left *, and the face Eze 1:10
beings on each *, and the other Eze 1:11
"Now lie on your left * for 390 Eze 4:4,5
lie on your right * for forty days, Eze 4:6
turn over from one * to the other Eze 4:8
a writer's case strapped to his *. Eze 9:2
above the mountain on the east *. Eze 11:23
coming from every *, and trapped Eze 19:8
They will surround you on every * Eze 23:24
your streets by troops on every *. Eze 28:23
you on every * and sent you away as Eze 36:3
were three guardrooms on each *; Eze 40:7-12
pillars on each * of the porch to Eze 40:14
wall on the other * of this court Eze 40:19
guardrooms on each *, and all the Eze 40:21
and 43¾ feet from * to side across Eze 40:21
feet from side to * across the top Eze 40:21
just the same as on the east *. Eze 40:22
the walls of each * of the Eze 40:37
entry hall into a * room where the Eze 40:38
on each * of the entry hall of Eze 40:39
hall, on each * of the stairs going Eze 40:40
Its walls extended up on either * Eze 40:48,49
A stairway at the * of the Temple Eze 41:7
palm tree on one *, and the other Eze 41:19,20
the palm tree on the other *. Eze 41:19,20
outer court on one *, and having a Eze 42:3
On the opposite * of the Temple a Eze 42:9,10
was on the south * of the inner Eze 42:9,10
feet long on each *, with a wall Eze 42:16-20
On the east * are steps to climb Eze 43:17
each * of the holy lands and city; Eze 45:7
the wall at the * of the main Eze 46:19,20
altar, that is, on its south *. Eze 47:1
south * [of the eastern passageway Eze 47:2
"On the west *, the Eze 47:20
miles square on each * of the Eze 48:21,22
On the north *, with its 1½-mile Eze 48:30,31
On the east *, with its 1½-mile Eze 48:32
on the 1½ miles of the west *, Eze 48:34
and win them over to his *. Dan 11:32
deeds give them away on every *; Hos 7:2
them and follows them on every *! Joe 2:3
on the east * of the city, and he Jon 4:5
moving forward * by side, pulled by Nah 2:3
by *, pulled by prancing steeds! Nah 2:3
one on each * of the reservoir. Zec 4:3
trees on each * of the lampstand, Zec 4:11
cross to the other * of the lake. Mt 8:18
When they arrived on the other * Mt 8:28
cross to the other * of the lake Mt 14:22
So Peter went over the * of the Mt 14:29
morning, one on either * of him. Mt 27:38
to the other * of the lake." Mk 4:35
WHEN THEY ARRIVED at the other * Mk 5:1
boat to the other * of the lake, a Mk 5:21
on the other * of the lake they Mk 6:53
to the other * of the lake. Mk 8:13
their crosses on either * of his. Mk 15:27
cross to the other * of the lake. Lk 8:22
So they arrived at the other *, Lk 8:26
back to the other * of the lake. Lk 8:37
On the other * of the lake the Lk 8:40
* of the road and passed him by. Lk 10:31
working * by side in the fields." Lk 17:35,36
working side by * in the fields." Lk 17:35,36
and the two criminals on either *. Lk 23:32,33
into the rock [at the * of a hill Lk 23:53
on the other * of the Jordan River Jn 1:28
met on the other * of the Jordan Jn 3:26
John, next to Jesus, was at his * Jn 13:23f
either *, with Jesus between them. Jn 19:18
pierced his * with a spear, and Jn 19:34
a bundle and was lying at the *. Jn 20:7
he showed them his hands and *. Jn 20:20
place my hand into his *." Jn 20:25
Put your hand into my *. Jn 20:27
on the right-hand * of the boat, Jn 21:6
The angel slapped him on the * to Act 12:7
gave me their * of the story and Act 25:15
If God is on our *, who can ever Rom 8:31
Stand on the * of the good. Rom 12:9
at your * with such real devotion. 1Co 16:16
We are pressed on every * by 2Co 4:8
you are standing * by side with one Php 1:27
standing side by * with one strong Php 1:27
working and battling * by side. Php 2:25
working and battling side by *. Php 2:25
for they worked * by side with me Php 4:3
worked side by * with me in telling Php 4:3
That God is on one * and all the 1Ti 2:5
on the other *, and Christ Jesus, 1Ti 2:5
in foul sin on the * while they 2Pe 2:13
we are on God's *, and our 1Jn 3:19
directly in front, not to one *. Rev 7:17f
on every *. Rev 20:9
There were three gates on each * Rev 21:13
On each * of the river grew Trees Rev 22:2

SIDE-FRAMES
placed on the two * of the door of Ex 12:7

SIDES
his arms at his *, the soldiers of Ex 17:11
at the * of the Ark, to carry it. Ex 25:13,14
Overlay the top, *, and horns of Ex 30:3
on each of two *, construct two Ex 30:4
on both * of two stone tablets. Ex 32:15
For the * of the Tabernacle he Ex 36:20
together along the *, five for each Ex 36:31,32
of gold all the way around the *. Ex 37:2
at the * of the Ark, to carry it. Ex 37:5
for the roof and *—the rams' skins Ex 39:33-40
it upon all * of the altar at the Lev 1:5
blood against the * of the altar. Lev 3:2
blood against the * of the altar, Lev 3:7,8
blood against the * of the altar, Lev 3:13
in your eyes and thorns in your *. Num 33:55
be thorns in your *, and their gods Ju 2:3
blow yours on all * of the camp and Ju 7:18
now on opposite * of a mountain. 1Sa 23:26
other on opposite * of the pool. 2Sa 2:13
length of both * of the Temple 1Ki 6:5
three east. The * of the tank were 1Ki 7:26
*: east, west, north, and south. 1Ch 9:24
or with swords belted to their *. Neh 4:18
Literally, "on the * of the Ps 48:2f
banked up along both * of them! Ps 78:13
the * of the north" (Psalm 48:2); Is 14:13f
their * like women in labor?" Jer 30:6
his hands fell helpless at his *; Jer 50:43
on the *, and on the network round Jer 52:23
a scroll, with writing on both *. Eze 2:9,10
of Pharaoh fall useless to his *. Eze 30:25
walls along both * of the Eze 40:16
the terrace, the same on both *. Eze 41:9
terrace, on both * of the Temple, Eze 41:10
its corners, base and * were all Eze 41:22
palm trees on both * of the entry Eze 41:26
inches beyond the altar on all *. Eze 43:13
than the base block on all *. Eze 43:14
on all *, and seven feet high. Eze 43:14
top twenty-one inches on all *. Eze 43:17
many trees were growing on both * Eze 47:7

(SIDES Con't)
"The land on both * of this Eze 48:21,22
protected on all * by the river? Nah 3:8
to place on both * of the Jordan Lk 3:3
*, pulling him this way and that. Act 23:10
covered on all * with pure gold. Heb 9:4
stood at the throne's four *. Rev 4:6

SIDETRACK
Don't *; Pro 4:27

SIDING
altar was hollow, with plank *. Ex 38:7

SIDON
Canaan's oldest son was *, and he Gen 10:15-19
Canaan spread from * all the way to Gen 10:15-19
with his borders extending to *. Gen 49:13
as far as Great * and a place Jos 11:8
Hammon, Kanah, and Greater *. Jos 19:28
residents of Acco, *, Ahlab, Ju 1:31,32
*, Moab, Ammon and Philistia. Ju 10:6
their relatives in *, and had Ju 18:7
too far away from *, and they had Ju 18:28
and to Dan-jaan and around to *; 2Sa 24:6
—Moab, Ammon, Edom, *, and from 1Ki 11:1
of Zarephath, near the city of *. 1Ki 17:8,9
* (his firstborn) and Heth. 1Ch 1:13-16
The men of Tyre and * brought 1Ch 22:4
people of Tyre and *, paying for Ez 3:7
a colony of the mother-city, *. Is 23:1f
full of ships from *, bringing Is 23:2,3
Be ashamed, O *, Is 23:4
a colony of the mother-city, *. Is 23:4f
daughter of *, will you rejoice, Is 23:12
and all the kings of Tyre and *, Jer 25:22
Ammon, Tyre and *, through their Jer 27:3
from Tyre and * will be destroyed. Jer 47:4
"Your sailors come from * and Eze 27:8
city of * and prophesy against it. Eze 28:21
I am your enemy, O *, and I will Eze 28:22
Tyre and *, don't you try to Joe 3:4
had been done in wicked Tyre and * Mt 11:21
Truly, Tyre and * will be better Mt 11:22
into the parts of Tyre and *." Mt 15:21f
to Tyre and *. Mt 15:21
from as far away as Tyre and *. Mk 3:7,8
went to the region of Tyre and *, Mk 7:24
From Tyre he went to *, then back Mk 7:31
foreigner from the land of *. Lk 4:25,26
of Tyre and * had come to hear him Lk 6:17,18
done in the cities of Tyre and *, Lk 10:13
Yes, Tyre and * will receive Lk 10:14
Tyre and * arrived to see him. Act 12:20
The next day when we docked at *, Act 27:3

SIDONIANS
(The * called Mount Hermon Deu 3:9
to the *), stretching northward Jos 13:2-7
including all the land of the *. Jos 13:2-7
The *, Ju 3:1
Philistines, the *, the Ju 10:12
can cut timber like you *!" 1Ki 5:6
the goddess of the *, and Milcom, 1Ki 11:5
Ashtoreth, the goddess of the *; 1Ki 11:33
Ethbaal of the *, and then began 1Ki 16:31
the evil goddess of the *; 2Ki 23:13
are there, and the *, all slain. Eze 32:30

SIEGE
Use them for the * [to make Deu 20:20
That nation will lay * to your Deu 28:52
terrible days of * that lie ahead. Deu 28:53
the midst of the * of your cities. Deu 28:55
hunger during the * and the awful Deu 28:56,57
They began by laying * to the 2Sa 11:1
* of Rabbah the capital of Ammon. 2Sa 12:26,27
army laying * to the Philistine 1Ki 15:27
though the city were under *." 1Ki 22:27f
began a * on the city of Samaria. 2Ki 18:9
the ravages of the * shall become a 2Ki 19:30
arrived during the *, and King 2Ki 24:11
army and laid * to Jerusalem, 2Ki 25:1
of Judah. The * continued into the 2Ki 25:2
After destroying them, he laid * 1Ch 20:1
Judah and laid * to the fortified 2Ch 32:1
you can survive my * of Jerusalem? 2Ch 32:10
and Medes will take part in the *. Is 21:2
They will lay * to it, raze its Is 23:13
Jerusalem and lay * against it, and Is 29:3
will be put under * until everyone Is 36:12
he will abandon his *. Is 37:30
Get ready now to leave; the * Jer 10:17
your enemies lay * to the city Jer 19:9
See how the * mounds have been Jer 32:24
walls against the * guns of the Jer 33:4
When the * was temporarily lifted Jer 34:11f
laid * to the city for two years. Jer 52:5
thus they survived the *. Lam 4:10
Draw a picture of * mounds being Eze 4:1
of the * of Jerusalem; Eze 4:7
completed all the days of your *. Eze 4:8
After your *, burn it there. Eze 5:2
remain will die by famine and *. Eze 6:12
of Babylon lays * to Jerusalem Eze 17:17
they will build * towers and make Eze 21:22
city by building a * wall and Eze 26:8
burdens of stones for the *). Eze 29:18f
end of a 13-year * (587–574 B.C.). Eze 29:18f
end of a 13-year * (587–574 B.C.). Eze 29:20f
withdrew from the * just long Eze 30:21f
will come and lay * to a fortified Dan 11:15
THE ENEMY lays * to Jerusalem! Mic 5:1
Get ready for the *! Nah 3:14

SIEVE
is sifted in a *, yet not one true Amo 9:9

SIFT
He will * out the proud nations Is 30:28
I will * you at the gates of Jer 15:7
to have you, to * you like wheat, Lk 22:31
means that he will * out everything Heb 12:27

SIFTED
that Israel be * by the other Amo 9:9
as grain is * in a sieve, yet not Amo 9:9

SIGH
You hear my every *. Ps 38:9
the merrymakers will * and mourn. Is 24:7
men who weep and * because of all Eze 9:4
"* and groan before the people, Eze 21:6
* with grief and broken heart. Eze 21:6
You may *, but only quietly. Eze 24:17
make us groan and *, but we 2Co 5:4

SIGHED
Then, looking up to heaven, he * Mk 7:34
He * deeply when he heard this Mk 8:12

SIGHING
I cannot eat for *; Job 3:24
Listen to the * of the prisoners Ps 79:11
All our days are filled with *. Ps 90:9
For them all sorrow and all * Is 35:10
I am weary of my own * and I find Jer 45:3

SIGHS
* are many and my heart is faint. Lam 1:22

SIGHT
when we are out of each other's *. Gen 31:49
and fire were never out of *. Ex 13:22
saw the awesome *: the glory of the Ex 24:17
favor in your *, O Lord, then Ex 34:9
very evil in God's *, for they Ju 3:7
saw a strange *—the vast army of 1Sa 14:16
openly, in the * of all Israel.' 2Sa 12:12
and I will cast them out of my *; 1Ki 9:7
is evil in the * of the Lord." 1Ki 21:20f
As they disappeared from * he tore 2Ki 2:12
king in the Lord's *, though not 2Ki 14:3
He swept them from his * until 2Ki 17:18
Judah out of his * because of the 2Ki 24:3,4
of God, and in the * of our God, I 1Ch 28:8
fair in the * of the Lord his God. 2Ch 31:20
man, who is but a worm in his *?" Job 25:6
What a glorious *! Ps 48:2
They marvel at the * and hurry Ps 48:5
at my sins—erase them from your *. Ps 51:9
alike are nothing in his *. Ps 62:9
was adultery in the * of God. Ps 106:39
Literally, "Precious in the * of Ps 116:15f
How puny in his * is the strength Ps 147:10
I can't stand the * of them. Is 1:14
* of all the elders of his people. Is 24:23
But what a * his people Is 42:22
be a disgusting * to all mankind. Is 66:24
Get them out of my *! Jer 15:1
be appalled, and gasp at the *. Jer 49:17
the * of all those watching you. Eze 28:18
They ate everything in *. Amo 7:2
of you became one person in his *. Mal 2:15
by demons caught * of him they Mk 3:11
intently, his * was completely Mk 8:25
is an abomination in the * of God. Lk 16:15
the world to give * to those who Jn 9:39
At * of him the chief priests and Jn 19:6
Holy Spirit and get your * back." Act 9:17
'Brother Saul, receive your *!' Act 22:13
us right in God's *—when we put our Rom 1:17
* by doing what the law commands. Rom 3:20
to be good in his * if they have Rom 4:4,5
are forgiven and put out of *. Rom 4:7
*—before the ceremony took place. Rom 4:11
right in God's * by faith in his Rom 5:1
his * the two become one person. 1Co 6:16
can be right in his * is by faith. Gal 3:11
taking them out of * for hundreds Heb 10:4f
perfect in the * of God all those Heb 10:14
them good in God's * must live by Heb 10:38
frightened at the * that he shook Heb 12:21
for he is great in the Lord's *. Jas 1:9
him good in God's *, and he was Jas 2:23
far from right in the * of God. Rev 3:2
eyes and give you back your *. Rev 3:18
It was a glorious *, beautiful as Rev 21:2

SIGHTED
of Phoenicia. We * the island of Act 21:3

SIGHTLESS
* eyes and ears that cannot hear; Ps 135:16

SIGHTS
Pleasant * and good reports give Pro 15:30
drinking in the * around him. Mk 8:25
dead, now set your * on the rich Col 3:1

SIGN
promise with this *: I have placed Gen 9:12
in the clouds as a * of my promise Gen 9:13
and I will * my covenant with him Gen 17:19
Come now and we will * a peace Gen 31:44
hang loose as a * of your mourning, Lev 10:6
* of his vow of separation. Num 6:18
as a * of sorrow for their sins. 1Sa 7:6
on his head as a * of mourning. 2Sa 1:1
feet were bare as a * of mourning. 2Sa 15:30
There was no * of life. 2Ki 4:31
to snuff out any * of life. Job 16:9
Look, I will * my signature to my Job 31:35
Send me a * of your favor. Ps 86:17
"Ask me for a *, Ahaz, to prove Is 7:11
will choose the *—a child shall be Is 7:14
God's * was that before this Is 7:14f
This will be for a * of loyalty Is 19:20
to shreds as a * of their despair Is 36:22
making sacks, as a * of humility Is 37:1
had asked, "What * will the Lord Is 38:22
* [of God's power and love Is 55:13
As a * to them of these sad days Jer 16:8
For she is a * of horror and of Jer 48:39
All this is a * to the people of Eze 12:6
on this law; * it so that it cannot Dan 6:8
for some strange * in the heavens, Mt 16:4
And they put a * above his head, Mt 27:37
it is a * that you have abandoned Mk 6:11
does this generation seek a *?" Mk 8:12f
sought of him a * from heaven." Lk 11:16f
And Pilate posted a * over him Jn 19:19
The circumcision ceremony was a * Rom 4:11
they want a * from heaven as proof 1Co 1:22
is a * of her subjection to him 1Co 11:5
hat is a * of subjection to men 1Co 11:7
on her head as a * that she is 1Co 11:10
tongues" is not a * to God's 1Co 14:22
power, but is a * to the unsaved. 1Co 14:22
themselves as a * of godliness. Eph 2:11
They will see this as a * of Php 1:28
it will be a clear * from God that Php 1:28
there was then no * of a flood, and Heb 11:7
They will all * a treaty giving Rev 17:13

SIGNAL
* to break camp and move onward. Num 10:5,6,7
When the travel * is blown, the Num 10:5,6,7
at the second *, the tribes on Num 10:5,6,7
in ambush saw his *, they jumped up Jos 8:19
the sky was the * for the Israeli Ju 20:35-39
for it will be God's * that he 1Sa 14:10
drunk, then, at my *, kill him! 2Sa 13:28
that is your * to attack, for God 1Ch 14:15
her mistress for the slightest *. Ps 123:2
He will send a * to the nations Is 5:26
I will give a * to the Gentiles and Is 49:22
Send a * from Jerusalem: Jer 4:6
send up a smoke * at Jer 6:1
* many nations to mobilize for Jer 51:27
"What events will * your return, Mt 24:3
this does not * my return; Mt 24:6
"And then at last the * of my Mt 24:30
this is not the * of the end-time. Mk 13:7
that will * the end of the age. Mk 13:30

SIGNALING
and for * the breaking of camp. Num 10:1

SIGNALS
constant liar; he * his true Pro 6:12,13

SIGNATURE
Look, I will sign my * to my Job 31:35
Your Majesty, we request your * Dan 6:8
present your petitions over my *! Jn 16:26

SIGNBOARD
"Make a large * and write on it Is 8:1
A * was fastened to the cross Mk 15:26
A * was nailed to the cross above Lk 23:38
and the * was written in Hebrew, Jn 19:20

SIGNED
went ahead and * a peace treaty. Jos 9:14,15
I, NEHEMIAH THE governor, * the Neh 10:1
The others who * it were: Neh 10:1
These were the Levites who *: Neh 10:9-13
The political leaders who *: Neh 10:14-27
These men * on behalf of the Neh 10:28
these letters were * in the name Est 3:12
conference—they * a treaty to ally Ps 83:5
be * by your name as their maker! Ps 89:12
of silver. I * and sealed the deed Jer 32:10
witnesses who had * the deed, and Jer 32:12
and sold—deeds * and sealed and Jer 32:44
my marriage vow. I * a covenant Eze 16:8
So King Darius * the law. Dan 6:9
"Haven't you * a decree," they Dan 6:12
you can do. You * the law and it Dan 6:15
'Yes, here is the contract you * Lk 16:5,6
down and *, cannot be changed. Gal 3:15
promise down and * it—could not be Gal 3:17
God and you, * with his blood, Heb 13:20,21

SIGNET
Then Pharaoh placed his own * Gen 41:41,42

(SIGNET Con't)
if you were the * ring on my right Jer 22:24,25
it with his own * ring, and that of Dan 6:17
you like a * ring upon my finger; Hag 2:23

SIGNIFICANCE
the Matthew account loses its *. Is 7:14f
not determine their prophetic *. Dan 5:8f

SIGNIFICANT
with today's world is *. Gen 11:6f

SIGNIFY
For it will * that the Lord has 2Sa 5:24
* the years of Judah's punishment. Eze 4:6
your arm bared [to * great strength Eze 4:7

SIGNING
with himself for * the law, and Dan 6:14

SIGNPOST
And put a * at the fork in the Eze 21:19,20

SIGNS
after these two *, then take water Ex 4:9
their heads as * of sorrow (as is Jer 16:6
up road * pointing back to Israel. Jer 31:21
showed any * of fear or anger at Jer 36:24,25
your heads as * of sorrow, as if Amo 8:10
the weather * of the skies—red sky Mt 16:2,3
read the obvious * of the times! Mt 16:2,3
isn't ushered in with visible *. Lk 17:20
done through me as * from God—all Rom 15:19
and * and mighty works among you. 2Co 12:12
are true by * and wonders and Heb 2:4

SIHN
* Wilderness, between Elim and Mt. Ex 16:1
of Israel left the * desert, going Ex 17:1
and then in the wilderness of *. Num 33:11

SIHON
to King * of the Amorites. Num 21:21
But King * refused. Num 21:23
referred to King * in this poem: Num 21:27-30
By King * of the Amorites. Num 21:27-30
happened to King * at Heshbon," Num 21:34
territory of King * of the Num 32:33
this address, King * of the Deu 1:1
* the Amorite, king of Heshbon. Deu 2:24
to King * of Heshbon with a Deu 2:26
"But King * refused because Deu 2:30
he could destroy * by the hands of Deu 2:30
to give you the land of King *; Deu 2:31
"King * then declared war on us Deu 2:32
* of the Amorites, at Heshbon.' Deu 3:1
King *, whose capital was Heshbon; Deu 4:44,45,46
"When we came here, King * of Deu 29:7
as he destroyed * and Og, the kings Deu 31:4
And we know what you did to * and Jos 2:10
of the Amorites—*, king of Heshbon, Jos 9:10
King * of the Amorites, who lived Jos 12:2
the Jabbok River. * also Jos 12:3
the kingdom of *, king of Heshbon. Jos 12:5
the cities of King * of the Jos 13:10
tableland and the kingdom of *. Jos 13:21
kingdom of Sihon. * was the king Jos 13:21
the kingdom of King * of Heshbon. Jos 13:27,28
messengers to King * of the Ju 11:19
But King * didn't trust Israel, Ju 11:20
Israel defeat King * and all your Ju 11:21,22
of King * of the Amorites and King 1Ki 4:8-19
the land of King * of Heshbon and Neh 9:22
kings— *, king of Amorites; Ps 135:11
continues forever: *, king of Ps 136:19

SIHON'S
which had been King * capital. Num 21:25,26
King * capital, Num 21:27-30
had destroyed King * kingdom at Deu 3:6
But a fire comes from Heshbon—* Jer 48:45

SILAS
(also called Barsabbas) and *. Act 15:22
These men—Judas and *, who have Act 15:26
Then Judas and *, both being Act 15:32
and then Judas and * returned to Act 15:33
while Paul chose * and, with the Act 15:40,41
PAUL AND * went first to Derbe and Act 16:1
they grabbed Paul and * and Act 16:19
against Paul and *, and the judges Act 16:22
Around midnight, as Paul and * Act 16:25
and fell down before Paul and *. Act 16:29
Paul and * were Roman citizens. Act 16:38
Paul and * then returned to the Act 16:40
to take Paul and * to the City Act 17:5
"Paul and * have turned the rest Act 17:6
and * to Beroea, and, as usual, Act 17:10
up on Paul and *' statements to see Act 17:11
* and Timothy remained behind. Act 17:14
with a message for * and Timothy to Act 17:15
And after the arrival of * and Act 18:5
FROM: PAUL, * and Timothy. 1Th 1:1
FROM: PAUL, * and Timothy. 2Th 1:1

SILENCE
"Let there be complete * except Jos 6:10
Then out of the dreadful * came Job 4:16
The princes stood in * and laid Job 29:9
* and I will teach you wisdom!" Job 33:33
I lay my hand upon my mouth in *. Job 40:4
May their example shame and * Ps 8:2
of lying in * in the grave. Ps 30:12
Literally, "when I kept *." Ps 32:3f
"comes, and does not keep *." Ps 50:3f
upon a beach, God will * them. Is 17:13
Deathly * is everywhere. Is 23:2,3
LISTEN IN * before me, O lands Is 41:1
Sit in darkness and *, O Babylon; Is 47:5
Let's * him that he may speak no Jer 18:18
ground in *, clothed in sackcloth; Lam 2:10
to sit apart in * beneath the Lam 3:28
you will cover your mouth in * Eze 16:63
be carried out of the city in *." Amo 8:3
Stand in * in the presence of the Zep 1:7
He motioned for * and tried to Act 19:33
soon a deep * enveloped the Act 21:40
in Hebrew, the * was even greater. Act 22:2
good lives should * those who 1Pe 2:15
seal, there was * throughout all Rev 8:1

SILENCED
But the wicked shall be * in 1Sa 2:9
him exult, while liars shall be *. Ps 63:11
An angry man is * by giving him a Pro 21:14
your wine, and you * my prophets, Amo 2:12

SILENT
the wall remained *, for the king 2Ki 18:36
Should I remain * while you Job 11:3
"Be * now and let me alone, that Job 13:13
advice, and were * until I spoke. Job 29:21
continue to wait when you are *? Job 32:16
Lie quietly upon your bed in * Ps 4:4
Without a sound or word, * in Ps 19:3,4
Don't stay *! Ps 35:22
threats; I am * before them as a Ps 38:13,14
"Stand *! Ps 46:10
I remained *—you thought I Ps 50:21
wait before you in * praise, and Ps 65:1
O GOD, DON'T sit idly by, * and Ps 83:1
while evil men are stricken *. Ps 107:42
O GOD OF my praise, don't stand * Ps 109:1
thought to be wise when he is *. Pro 17:27,28
This * ruin is all that's left Is 23:7
Her walled cities will be * and Is 27:10
But the people were * and Is 36:21
Long has he been *; Is 42:14
Is that why the house is * and Is 50:2
* before the ones condemning him. Is 53:7
Will you stand * and still punish Is 64:12
out before me: I will not stand *; Is 65:6
I stand amazed, *, dumb with Jer 8:21
homes shall lie in * darkness. Jer 25:10
great punishment. * as a serpent Jer 46:22,23
In Madmen all is *. Jer 48:2,3,4
Your cities will become as * as Jer 49:18
thronged with people, are * now. Lam 1:1
the city gates are *, her priests Lam 1:4
sat there stunned and * for an Dan 4:19
They will stand in * awe, deaf to Mic 7:16
Your chariots stand there, * and Nah 2:13
Should you be * while the wicked Hab 1:13
let all the earth be * before Hab 2:20
I have left their streets in * Zep 3:6
"Be *, all mankind, before the Zec 2:13
But Jesus remained *. Mt 26:63
against him, Jesus remained *. Mt 27:12
are to be stricken *, unable to Lk 1:20
Jesus cut him short. "Be *!" Lk 4:35
them and told them to be *. Lk 4:41
at his answer, they were *. Lk 20:26
and as a lamb is * before the Act 8:32
Women should be * during the 1Co 14:34
Let them be * in your church 1Ti 2:12

SILENTLY
So Sarah laughed *. Gen 18:12
as she was praying * and, hearing 1Sa 1:12,13
ground with him * for seven days Job 2:13
Like lions they crouch *, Ps 10:9
let them lie * in their graves, Ps 31:17
But as I stood there * the Ps 39:2,3
I STAND * before the Lord, waiting Ps 62:1
But I stand * before the Lord, Ps 62:5
the earth trembles and stands * Ps 76:8
They must talk * to themselves 1Co 14:28

SILK
of linens and *, embroidered, and Eze 16:9,10
your clothes were * and linen and Eze 16:13

SILKEN
as the * tents of Solomon!" Sol 1:5

SILKS
linens, purple *, and scarlet; Rev 18:12

SILL
on the window *, went fast asleep Act 20:9

SILLA
at Millo on the road to *. 2Ki 12:20

SILLY
worshiping these * idols, when Ps 4:2
against you—how * can they be? Ps 139:20
will say foolish, * things that Pro 23:33
his conceit with * replies! Pro 26:4,5
For it is * to be laughing all Ecc 2:1
and it is * to be impressed by it. Ecc 7:6
In this * life I have seen Ecc 7:15-17
up their glorious God for * idols! Jer 2:10,11
All are worthless, *; Jer 10:15
Ephraim is a *, witless dove, Hos 7:11
are all a bunch of * lies; Zec 10:2
and your * Jewish laws, you take Act 18:15
began to think up * ideas of what Rom 1:21
the world calls foolish and *. 1Co 1:21
ideas and * myths and legends. 1Ti 4:7
friendships with *, sin-burdened 2Ti 3:6

SILOAM
from the Pool of * to the king's Neh 3:15
when the Tower of * fell on them? Lk 13:4
in the Pool of *" (the word Jn 9:7
(the word "*" means "Sent"). Jn 9:7
Pool of * and wash off the mud. Jn 9:11

SILVANUS
Timothy and * and I have been 2Co 1:19
the courtesy of * who is, in my 1Pe 5:12

SILVER
rich in livestock, *, and gold. Gen 13:1
a thousand * pieces as damages for Gen 20:16
400 pieces of *," Ephron said, Gen 23:14,15
pieces of *, as publicly agreed. Gen 23:16
and a fortune in * and gold, and Gen 24:35
in solid gold and * for Rebekah, Gen 24:53
father, for 100 pieces of *. Gen 33:19
twenty pieces of *, and they took Gen 37:28
put Joseph's own * cup at the top Gen 44:2
my lord's personal * drinking cup, Gen 44:5
Why would we steal * or gold from Gen 44:8
and three hundred pieces of *! Gen 45:22
ask for jewels, *, gold, and the Ex 3:22
for costly gold and * jewelry." Ex 11:2
the Egyptians for * and gold Ex 12:35
of * or gold or of anything else! Ex 20:23
of *, and the ox shall be stoned. Ex 21:32
Gold, *, bronze, blue cloth, Ex 25:1
tent, with forty * bases for the Ex 26:18,19
with their forty * bases, two Ex 26:21
with sixteen * bases for the Ex 26:25
The pillars are to rest in four * Ex 26:32
be held up with * hooks attached to Ex 27:9,10
to * rods, attached to the posts. Ex 27:9,10
sockets, with * hooks and rods. Ex 27:11
to be connected by * rods, using Ex 27:17
silver rods, using * hooks, the Ex 27:17
made of gold, *, and bronze. Ex 31:4
Gold, *, and bronze; Ex 35:5-9
Others brought * and bronze as Ex 35:24
from gold, *, and bronze; Ex 35:32
fitting into forty * bases. Ex 36:24
forty * bases, two for each frame. Ex 36:25,26
with sixteen * bases beneath them, Ex 36:30
gold and set into four * bases. Ex 36:36
bronze and with * hooks and rods. Ex 38:10
bases and with * hooks and rods. Ex 38:11
bases, and with * hooks and rods. Ex 38:12
and all the hooks and rods were *; Ex 38:17
were overlaid with *, and the rods Ex 38:17
hold up the drapes were solid *. Ex 38:17
bases, and with * hooks and rods; Ex 38:19
the tops of the posts were also * Ex 38:19
The amount of * used was 9,575 Ex 38:25,26
pounds of *, ninety-five pounds Ex 38:27
Literally, "a [*] talent." Ex 38:27f
for each socket. The * left over Ex 38:28
It consisted of a * platter Num 7:13
two pounds and a * bowl of about Num 7:13
12 * platters (each weighing about Num 7:84,85,86
12 * bowls (each weighing about Num 7:84,85,86
(so the total weight of the * was Num 7:84,85,86
trumpets of beaten * to be used for Num 10:1
palace filled with * and gold, I Num 22:18
palace filled with * and gold, I Num 24:13
heat—such as gold, *, bronze, iron, Num 31:22
the * or gold they are made of. Deu 7:25
large, and your * and gold have Deu 8:12,13
"a hundred shekels of *." Deu 22:19f
pay her father fifty of *." Deu 22:28,29f
made of wood, stone, *, and gold. Deu 29:17
But all the * and gold and the Jos 6:19
it except that the * and gold and Jos 6:24
Babylon, and some * worth $200, and Jos 7:21
* buried deeper than the rest." Jos 7:21
the * buried beneath the rest. Jos 7:22
took Achan, the *, the robe, the Jos 7:24
booty of cattle, *, gold, bronze, Jos 22:7,8
for you and plate it with the *." Ju 17:3
made from *, gold, and bronze. 2Sa 8:10
along with the * and gold he had 2Sa 8:11,12
you ten pieces of * and a belt." 2Sa 18:11f
way of knowing the value of the *. 2Sa 18:11f
"paid him fifty shekels of *." 2Sa 24:24f
of the Temple the *, the gold, and 1Ki 7:51
of solid gold. (* wasn't used 1Ki 10:21
load of gold, *, ivory, apes, and 1Ki 10:22
annual tribute of * and gold 1Ki 10:25
at Jerusalem. * was as common as 1Ki 10:27
along with the * and gold vessels 1Ki 15:15
Then Asa took all the * and gold 1Ki 15:18
you a present of gold and *. 1Ki 15:19

(SILVER Con't)
of Israel: "Your * and gold are 1Ki 20:2,3
only give me your *, gold, wives, 1Ki 20:5,6
* and gold, just as he demanded." 1Ki 20:7
of $20,000 in *, $60,000 in gold, 2Ki 5:5
* and two suits to give to them." 2Ki 5:22
and carrying out * and gold and 2Ki 7:8
It was not used to buy * cups, 2Ki 12:13,14
all the gold and * from the Temple 2Ki 14:14
Ahaz took the * and gold from 2Ki 16:8
used all the * stored in the Temple 2Ki 18:15
his treasures—the *, gold, spices, 2Ki 20:13
The gold and * bowls, with all 2Ki 25:14,15
*, were melted down to bullion. 2Ki 25:14,15
gifts of gold, *, and bronze, 1Ch 18:10
as he did the * and gold he took 1Ch 18:11
talents of *," approximately 1Ch 19:6f
bullion, $2,000,000 worth of *, 1Ch 22:14
and "a million talents of *." 1Ch 22:14f
They are expert gold and * 1Ch 22:16
enough gold and * to make these 1Ch 28:14
He also weighed out enough * for 1Ch 28:15
silver for the * candlesticks and 1Ch 28:15
the * for the silver tables. 1Ch 28:16
the silver for the * tables. 1Ch 28:16
cups, and bowls of gold and *. 1Ch 28:17
it—enough gold, *, bronze, iron, 1Ch 29:2
worth of purest * to be used for 1Ch 29:4,5
made of gold and * and for the 1Ch 29:4,5
$30,000,000 in *; 1Ch 29:6,7
During Solomon's reign, * and 2Ch 1:15
of Lebanon Room. * was too cheap to 2Ch 9:20
*, ivory, apes, and peacocks. 2Ch 9:21
annual tribute of * and gold bowls, 2Ch 9:24
He made * become as plentiful in 2Ch 9:27
the Temple the * and gold bowls 2Ch 15:18
Asa's response was to take the * 2Ch 16:2
See, here is * and gold to induce 2Ch 16:3
the gold and * spoons and bowls 2Ch 24:14
of $200,000 in *, 10,000 sacks of 2Ch 27:5
buildings for his *, gold, precious 2Ch 32:27
1,000 * trays, Ez 1:9,10
2,410 * bowls (of various Ez 1:9,10
5,469 gold and * items turned over Ez 1:11
*, and 100 robes for the priests. Ez 2:69
the gold and * bowls which Ez 5:14
And the gold and * bowls which Ez 6:5
to Jerusalem the * and gold which Ez 7:15
offerings of * and gold from the Ez 7:16
of heaven), up to $200,000 in *; Ez 7:22
transporting the *, gold, the Ez 8:25
found it to total $1,300,000 in *; Ez 8:26,27
$200,000 in * utensils; Ez 8:26,27
our arrival the *, gold, and other Ez 8:33
of the gold and * was noted. Ez 8:34
$100,000 in gold and $77,000 in *; Neh 7:71
gold, $70,000 in *, and sixty-seven Neh 7:72
tied to * rings imbedded in Est 1:6
Gold and * benches stood on Est 1:6
he will be your precious *! Job 22:25
and shall divide his * among them. Job 27:17
"MEN KNOW HOW to mine * and Job 28:1
bought for gold or *, nor for all Job 28:15
walking down her * pathway, and my Job 31:26
truth, like * seven times refined. Ps 12:6
O Lord, like * in a crucible. Ps 66:10
See them sparkle with jewels of * Ps 68:11,12,13
himself with pieces of *." Ps 68:30f
Egypt, loaded with * and gold; Ps 105:37
man-made things of * and of gold. Ps 115:4
to me than millions in * and gold! Ps 119:71,72
idols of gold and *, made by men— Ps 135:15
more valuable than * or gold." Pro 8:10
the purest gold or sterling *! Pro 8:19
gold, and understanding than *! Pro 16:16
* and gold are purified by fire, Pro 17:3
esteem is better than * and gold. Pro 22:1
When you remove dross from *, you Pro 25:4,5
as golden apples in a * basket. Pro 25:11
The purity of * and gold can be Pro 27:21
I collected * and gold as taxes Ecc 2:7,8
* lining left among your clouds. Ecc 12:2
young, before the * cord of life Ecc 12:6
you golden earrings and * beads." Sol 1:11
Its posts are *, its canopy Sol 3:10
build upon her a battlement of *, Sol 8:9
thousand pieces of * from each. Sol 8:11
thousand pieces of * and I will Sol 8:12
Once like sterling *; Is 1:22
Israel has vast treasures of * Is 2:7
their gold and * idols to the moles Is 2:20
of * or gold will buy them off. Is 13:17
destroy all your * idols and golden Is 30:22
golden idols and * images—which in Is 31:7
of *, gold, spices and perfumes. Is 39:2
and with * chains around its neck? Is 40:19
lavishly with * and with gold? Is 46:6
affliction, but found no * there. Is 48:10
your iron for *, your wood for Is 60:17
*," and I have discarded them. Jer 6:30
it with gold and * and fasten it Jer 10:4
They bring beaten sheets of * Jer 10:9
and gold and * of your kings, shall Jer 20:5
Hanamel seventeen shekels of *. Jer 32:9
weighed out the * and paid him. Jer 32:10
* candlesticks and cups and bowls. Jer 52:19
with gold and *, and your clothes Eze 16:13
and gold and * ornaments I gave to Eze 16:17
slag left when * is smelted. Eze 22:18,19,20
you will melt like * in fierce Eze 22:22
markets—*, iron, tin and lead. Eze 27:12
and * and many treasures. Eze 28:4
you to rob them of * and gold and Eze 38:13
* shekel (about half an ounce); Eze 45:12
and arms were of *, its belly and Dan 2:32
of iron, clay, brass, *, and gold; Dan 2:35
the clay, the *, and the gold. Dan 2:45
of the gold and * cups taken long Dan 5:2,3,4
*, brass and iron, wood and stone. Dan 5:2,3,4
praising gods of *, gold, brass, Dan 5:23
priceless gold and * dishes and for Dan 11:8
all the gold and * that she used in Hos 1:8
they made from their * and gold. Hos 8:4
They melt their * to mold into Hos 13:2
"You have taken my * and gold Joe 3:5
debt of a piece of * or a pair of Amo 8:6
Loot the *! Nah 2:9
They are overlaid with gold and * Hab 2:19
Your * and gold will be of no use Zep 1:18
For I have plenty of * and gold Hag 2:8,9
bring gifts of * and gold from the Zec 6:10,11
them a crown from the * and gold. Zec 6:10,11
so rich that * is like dirt to her, Zec 9:3
counted out thirty little * coins Zec 11:12
pure, as gold and * are refined and Zec 13:9
of gold and * and fine clothing. Zec 14:14
Like a refiner of * he will sit Mal 3:3
them like gold or *, so that they Mal 3:3
And they gave him thirty * Mt 26:15
"They took the thirty pieces of * Mt 27:9
valuable * coins and loses one. Lk 15:8
gold or * or chipped from stone. Act 17:29
to manufacture * shrines of the Act 19:24
Some use gold and * and jewels; 1Co 3:12
to win a blue ribbon or a * cup, 1Co 9:25
made of gold and * as well as some 2Ti 2:20
The value of your gold and * is Jas 5:3
gold or *, as you very well know. 1Pe 1:18
made of gold and *, brass, stone, Rev 9:20
for gold and *, precious stones, Rev 18:12

SILVERSMITH
a fifth of it to a *, and the idol Ju 17:4,5
He is a skillful goldsmith and *, 2Ch 2:14
you have sterling ready for the *. Pro 25:4,5
at all! The * is dulled by the Jer 51:17
It began with Demetrius, a * who Act 19:24

SILVERSMITHS
and *, brass and iron workers; 2Ch 2:7

SIMEON
son and named him * (meaning Gen 29:33
Dinah's brothers, * and Levi, took Gen 34:25
Then Jacob said to Levi and *, Gen 34:30
Reuben, Jacob's oldest child, *, Gen 35:23
Returning, he selected * from Gen 42:24
didn't come back, * is gone, and Gen 42:36
release * and return Benjamin. Gen 43:14
Then he released * and brought him Gen 43:23
* and his sons: Jemuel, Jamin, Gen 46:8-14
from me just as Reuben and * will. Gen 48:5
"* and Levi are two of a kind. Gen 49:5
That is, the tribes of * and Levi Gen 49:7f
families:Reuben, *, Levi,Judah, Ex 1:1
of the clans of the tribe of *: Ex 6:15
* -Shelumi-el (son of Num 1:2-15
* -59,300 Num 1:20-46
Tribe: Reuben * Gad Num 2:3-31
Next to * Num 2:3-31
tribe of *, with the same gifts. Num 7:36-41
Next was the tribe of * headed Num 10:19
son of Hori, from the tribe of *; Num 13:3-15
Salu, a leader of the tribe of *. Num 25:14
The tribe of *: 22,200. Num 26:12-14
* Shemuel (son of Ammihud Num 34:16-28
the tribes of *, Levi, Judah, Deu 27:12
THE LAND GIVEN to the Tribe of *: Jos 19:1
The tribe of * received the next Jos 19:1
were also given to the tribe of *. Jos 19:8
So the * tribe's inheritance Jos 19:9
tribes of Judah, *, and Benjamin. Jos 21:4
The tribes of Judah and * gave Jos 21:9-16
asked help from the tribe of *. Ju 1:3
So the army of * went with the Ju 1:3
Reuben, *, Levi, Judah, Issachar, 1Ch 2:1
The sons of *: 1Ch 4:24
the tribe of * went to Mount Seir. 1Ch 4:42
tribes of Judah, *, and Benjamin. 1Ch 6:64,65
From the tribe of *, 7,100 1Ch 12:24-37
Over *, Shephatiah (son of 1Ch 27:16-22
Manasseh, and *, in Israel, when 2Ch 15:9
Ephraim, and *, even to distant 2Ch 34:6
area lies that of *, also extending Eze 48:24
gates of *, Issachar and Zebulun; Eze 48:33
That day a man named *, a Lk 2:25
to the law, * was there and took Lk 2:28
* blessed them but then said to Lk 2:34,35
She came along just as * was Lk 2:38
Levi's father was *; Lk 3:23-38
* 12,000 Rev 7:4-8

SIMEON'S
clans, founded by * sons: Num 26:12-14
of Judah joined * and they fought Ju 1:17
Levi's father was Simeon;* father Lk 3:23-38

SIMILAR
for Eve sounds * to a Hebrew word Gen 3:20f
on is in a * state of defilement. Lev 15:26
to Moses. A * census of the Num 4:38-41
Another * situation occurred Deu 2:23
the king of Moab for * permission. Ju 11:17
(He designed * living quarters, 1Ki 7:8
and were * to chariot wheels. 1Ki 7:33
upon himself), * to the annual 1Ki 12:32,33
trumpets, or * articles, but only 2Ki 12:13,14
Character of his reign: good (* to 2Ki 18:1
Temple or for any * needs, you may Ez 7:20
to a country very * to this one—a Is 36:17
others with * responsibilities. Jer 36:12
of the Temple a * building composed Eze 42:9,10
and all other * occasions. Eze 45:17
had another dream * to the first. Dan 8:1
The second most important is *: Mt 22:38,39
dice or something *—"drawing Lk 1:8,9f
had sent him. My * experience will Lk 11:29,30
their tails were * to serpents' Rev 9:19

SIMILARITY
knowledge gained. * with today's Gen 11:6f

SIMILARLY
then five others * attached, Ex 36:10
the lampstand was * decorated with Ex 37:20,21
The Lord had * helped the Deu 2:22

SIMON
saw two brothers—*, also called Mt 4:18
* (also called Peter), Mt 10:2,3,4
* (a member of "The Zealots," a Mt 10:2,3,4
Joseph, *, and Judas. Mt 13:55
* Peter answered, "The Christ, Mt 16:16
"God has blessed you, *, son of Mt 16:17
to the home of * the leper. Mt 26:6
Cyrene, in Africa—* was his Mt 27:32
of Galilee, he saw * and his Mk 1:16
went over to * and Andrew's home, Mk 1:29,30
Later, * and the others went out Mk 1:36,37
* (he renamed him "Peter"), Mk 3:16-19
* (a member of a political party Mk 3:16-19
of James and Joseph, Judas and *. Mk 6:2,3
at the home of * the leper; Mk 14:3
*! He said Mk 14:37
* of Cyrene, who was coming in Mk 15:21
Jesus' cross. (* is the father of Mk 15:21
boats, Jesus asked *, its owner, to Lk 5:3
he said to *, "Now go out where it Lk 5:4
"Sir," * replied, "we worked Lk 5:5
When * Peter realized what had Lk 5:8
* (he also called him Peter), Lk 6:14,15,16
* (a member of the Zealots, a Lk 6:14,15,16
his thoughts. "*," he said to the Lk 7:40
"All right, Teacher," * replied, Lk 7:40
owed him the most," * answered. Lk 7:43
the woman and said to *, "Look! Lk 7:44
"*, Simon, Satan has asked to Lk 22:31
"Simon, *, Satan has asked to Lk 22:31
* said, "Lord, I am ready to go Lk 22:33
away to his death, * of Cyrene, who Lk 23:26
(One of these men was Andrew, * Jn 1:40
said, "You are *, John's son—but Jn 1:42
Then Andrew, * Peter's brother, Jn 6:8,9
* Peter replied, "Master, to Jn 6:68
of Judas, son of * Iscariot, one of Jn 6:71
When he came to * Peter, Peter Jn 13:6
* Peter exclaimed, "Then wash my Jn 13:9
closest friend, * Peter motioned Jn 13:24
it to Judas, son of * Iscariot. Jn 13:26
* Peter said, "Master, where are Jn 13:36
Then * Peter drew a sword and Jn 18:10
die for all." * Peter followed Jn 18:15
Meanwhile, as * Peter was Jn 18:25
She ran and found * Peter and me Jn 20:2
Then * Peter arrived and went on Jn 20:6
A group of us were there—* Peter, Jn 21:2
* Peter said, "I'm going Jn 21:3
At that, * Peter put on his Jn 21:7
Jesus said. So * Peter went out Jn 21:11
After breakfast Jesus said to * Jn 21:15
to Simon Peter, "*, son of John, Jn 21:15
Jesus repeated the question: "*, Jn 21:16
Once more he asked him, "*, son Jn 21:17
* (also called "The Zealot"), Act 1:14
A man named * had formerly been a Act 8:9,10,11
Then * himself believed and was Act 8:13
When * saw this—that the Holy Act 8:18
"Pray for me," * exclaimed, Act 8:24
Joppa, living with *, the tanner. Act 9:43
find a man named * Peter, who is Act 10:5,6
is staying with *, the tanner, down Act 10:5,6

SIMON Con't)
was the place where * Peter lived! Act 10:18
Joppa and summon * Peter, who is Act 10:32
*, a tanner, down by the shore.' Act 10:32
to Joppa to find * Peter! Act 11:13
FROM: * PETER, a servant and 2Pe 1:1

SIMON'S
where they found * mother-in-law Mk 1:29,30
day, he went to * home where he Lk 4:38
where he found * mother-in-law very Lk 4:38
Andrew (* brother), Lk 6:14,15,16
to Judas Iscariot, * son, that this Jn 13:1

SIMPLE
for me must be * altars of earth. Ex 20:24
* "Yes" or "No" alternatives. Lev 8:8f
The Lord protects the * and the Ps 116:6
As your plan unfolds, even the * Ps 119:130
you * ones without good judgment; Pro 9:4
at a time and in such * words!" Is 28:10
over in * words whenever he can; Is 28:13
yet over this *, straightforward Is 28:13
Say just a * 'Yes, I will' or Mt 5:37
understand this * illustration, Mk 4:13
But this is the * truth—some of Lk 9:27
you can guide the * and teach even Rom 2:20
* message of the cross of Christ. 1Co 1:17
for speaking in plain, * English 1Co 14:7
from your pure and * devotion to 2Co 11:3
just say a * yes or no, so that Jas 5:12

SIMPLE-MINDED
"I want to make the * wise!" Pro 1:4
day, and saw a * lad, a young man Pro 7:7
They are good speakers, and * Rom 16:18

SIMPLEST
has no strength for the * matter. Ecc 10:15

SIMPLETON
Only a * believes what he is Pro 14:15
The * is crowned with folly; Pro 14:18
by listening; the * can learn only Pro 21:11
for them; the * goes blindly on and Pro 22:3
to meet them. The * never looks, Pro 27:12

SIMPLETONS
in all the land: "You *!" Pro 1:22
home with me," she urges *. Pro 9:16

SIMPLY
of a vow or is * a voluntary Lev 7:16
is fading, it is * a scar from the Lev 13:28
of his head, he * has a bald Lev 13:41
shall live if he * looks at it!" Num 21:8
the plague was * a coincidence and 1Sa 6:9
But if this is * the scheme of a 1Sa 26:19
Zimri * walked in and struck him 1Ki 16:10
* to go and wash and be cured!" 2Ki 5:13
it is * a way of easier 1Ch 1:1f
case of it, God * shatters the Job 34:24
their forts. They * heap up dirt Hab 1:10
You are * rejecting God's laws Mk 7:9
with chains he * broke them and Lk 8:29
For you have * done your duty!" Lk 17:10
And the disciples * replied, Lk 19:34
for he * accepted God's promise. Gal 3:18
chains * because I am a Christian. Php 1:13
in human form, or * that there is Heb 7:3f
* said, "The Lord rebuke you." Jud 1:9

SIN
obey, watch out. * is waiting to Gen 4:7
my kingdom guilty of this great *? Gen 20:9,10
It would be a great * against Gen 39:9
"Today I remember my *!" Gen 41:9
"I confess my * against Jehovah Ex 10:16
Forgive my * only this once, and Ex 10:17
will be afraid to * against him!" Ex 20:20
you with their * of worshiping Ex 23:33
camp and burn it as a * offering. Ex 29:14
as a * offering for atonement; Ex 29:36
upon its horns the blood of the * Ex 30:10
such a terrible * upon them?" Ex 32:21
sinned a great *, but I will return Ex 32:30
sinned a great *, and have made Ex 32:31
only forgive their *—and if not, Ex 32:32
and transgression and *." Ex 34:7f
as a * offering to the Lord. Lev 4:3
a young bull for a * offering, Lev 4:14
procedure as for a * offering; Lev 4:20
though it were a * offering for an Lev 4:21
* offering for the entire nation. Lev 4:21
This is his * offering. Lev 4:24
the blood of this * offering and Lev 4:25
his *, and he shall be forgiven. Lev 4:26
without defect to atone for his *. Lev 4:28
of the * offering and kill it. Lev 4:29
a lamb as his * offering, it must Lev 4:32
and kill it there as a * offering. Lev 4:33
man, and his * shall be forgiven. Lev 4:35
shall confess his * and bring his Lev 5:5
*, and need not fulfill the vow. Lev 5:6
one of the birds shall be his * Lev 5:7
The priest shall offer as the * Lev 5:8
this is the * offering. Lev 5:9
his * and he shall be forgiven. Lev 5:10
pigeons as his * offering, then he Lev 5:11
on it, because it is a * offering. Lev 5:11
this shall be his * offering. Lev 5:12
for him for any * of this kind, and Lev 5:13
guilty of any such *, he shall Lev 6:4,5
as is the entire * offering and the Lev 6:17
concerning the * offering: Lev 6:25
is most holy. No * offering may be Lev 6:30
apply to both the * offering and Lev 7:7
who eats it must answer for his *. Lev 7:17,18
grain offering, * offering, and Lev 7:37
young bull for the * offering, the Lev 8:1
young bull for the * offering, and Lev 8:14
the herd for a * offering, and a Lev 9:2
goat for their * offering, also a Lev 9:3
and to offer the * offering and the Lev 9:7
calf as a sacrifice for his own *; Lev 9:8
bladder from this * offering, as Lev 9:10
he had the * offering for himself. Lev 9:15
the goat of the * offering and Lev 10:16
"Why haven't you eaten the * Lev 10:17
"They offered their * offering Lev 10:19
if I had eaten the * offering on Lev 10:19
or a turtledove for a * offering. Lev 12:6
and the other for a * offering. Lev 12:8
at the place where * offerings and Lev 14:13
as in the case of a * offering. Lev 14:13
offer the * offering and again Lev 14:19
of the pair for a * offering and Lev 14:22
One of the pair is for a * Lev 14:31
there, one for a * offering and the Lev 15:15
offer one for a * offering and the Lev 15:30
a young bull for a * offering, and Lev 16:3
goats for their * offering, and a Lev 16:5
young bull as a * offering for Lev 16:6
by Aaron as a * offering. Lev 16:9
young bull as a * offering for Lev 16:11
and sacrifice the people's * Lev 16:15
altar the fat for the * offering. Lev 16:25
goat used for the * offering (their Lev 16:27
for it is an enormous *. Lev 18:22
the ram for the * the man has Lev 19:22
bear their * and die childless. Lev 20:20
male goat for a * offering, and two Lev 23:19
the Lord, saddened by their *; Lev 23:26,27
and sorrow for * shall be Lev 23:29
smite you seven times for your *. Lev 26:24
by betraying a trust, it is *. Num 5:5,6
He must confess his * and make Num 5:7
of the birds for a * offering, and Num 6:11
He must also offer a * offering, Num 6:14
* offering and the burnt offering; Num 6:16
a male goat for a * offering; Num 7:16
For * offerings they brought: Num 7:87
young bull for a * offering. Num 8:8
one for a * offering and the Num 8:12
sir, do not punish us for this *; Num 12:11
that you don't let * go unpunished, Num 14:17,18
one male goat for a * offering. Num 15:23,24
the Lord, and by their * offering. Num 15:25
female goat for a * offering, and Num 15:27
and die in his *." Num 15:31
The grain offerings, the * Num 18:9
ceremonies, for removal of *. Num 19:9
from the red heifer * offering Num 19:17
Literally, "ashes of the burnt * Num 19:17f
He has not seen * in Jacob. Num 23:18-24
goat for a * offering to the Lord. Num 28:15
a male goat as a * offering, to Num 28:22
sacrificed as a * offering, to make Num 29:5
one male goat for a * offering. Num 29:11
This is in addition to the * Num 29:11
sacrificed for a * offering, in Num 29:16
drink offering for a * offering. Num 29:19
a male goat for a * offering, with Num 29:22
also a male goat as a * offering Num 29:25
as a special * offering, in Num 29:28
drink offerings as a * offering. Num 29:31
also sacrifice an extra * Num 29:34
offerings for a * offering, in Num 29:38
your * will catch up with you. Num 32:23
because of your *, heaven and Deu 4:25
* against the Lord your God. Deu 9:16
I took your *—the calf you had Deu 9:21
wickedness and * of these people. Deu 9:27
be counted against you as a *. Deu 15:9
it is a * if you don't. Deu 23:21
(But it is not a * if you Deu 23:22
be counted as a * against you. Deu 24:14,15
because of the * of forsaking him. Deu 28:20
He is faithful, without *. Deu 32:4
Smeared with *. Deu 32:5
BUT THERE WAS * among the Jos 7:1
rid yourselves of this *. Jos 7:12
until you deal with this *. Jos 7:13
Shechem for their * of murdering Ju 9:56,57
So the * of these young men was 1Sa 2:17
thing to make the Lord's people *. 1Sa 2:23,24,25
Ordinary * receives heavy 1Sa 2:23,24,25
how much more this * of yours 1Sa 2:23,24,25
me that I should * against the Lord 1Sa 12:23
But if you continue to *, you 1Sa 12:25
them, and not to * against the Lord 1Sa 14:34
We must find out what * was 1Sa 14:38
or is the * among the others? 1Sa 14:41
For rebellion is as bad as the * 1Sa 15:23
Oh, please pardon my * now and 1Sa 15:25
"It is a serious * to attack 1Sa 24:6
his punishment for his *." 1Sa 25:39
you, and you won't die for this *. 2Sa 12:13
And kept myself from *. 2Sa 22:24
"And when your people * and 1Ki 8:33,34
because of their *, hear them from 1Ki 8:35,36
realize their * and pray toward 1Ki 8:38
"If they * against you (and who 1Ki 8:46
But because of Solomon's * I 1Ki 11:39
This was of course a great *, 1Ki 12:30
This was a great *, and resulted 1Ki 13:34
all of Israel * along with him." 1Ki 14:16
Lord with their *, for it was even 1Ki 14:22
But despite Abijam's *, the Lord 1Ki 15:4
and led all of Israel into *. 1Ki 15:26
leading the rest of Israel into *. 1Ki 15:30
into the * of worshiping idols. 1Ki 15:34
You have made my people *, and I 1Ki 16:2
people of Israel to * with him. 1Ki 16:19
and led Israel into this same *. 1Ki 16:26
and have led all of Israel into *. 1Ki 21:22
into the * of worshiping idols. 1Ki 22:52,53
clung to the great * of Jeroboam 2Ki 3:3
was the great * of Jeroboam (son of 2Ki 10:29
cause of such great * in Israel. 2Ki 10:31
offerings and * offerings was given 2Ki 12:16
who had caused Israel to *. 2Ki 13:2
But they continued to *, 2Ki 13:6
worship idols and led them into *. 2Ki 13:11
into the * of worshiping idols. 2Ki 14:24
in the * of worshiping idols. 2Ki 15:9
people of Israel into grievous *. 2Ki 15:18
into the * of worshiping idols. 2Ki 15:28
He made them * a great sin, and 2Ki 17:21
He made them sin a great *, and 2Ki 17:21
made when he led Israel into *. 2Ki 23:15
Why must you cause Israel to *?" 1Ch 21:3
"If they * against you (and who 2Ch 6:36
the people followed him in this *. 2Ch 12:1
be angry, and this * will be added 2Ch 28:13
a deep * before the Lord our God; 2Ch 29:6
male goats for a * offering for the 2Ch 29:21
The male goats for the * 2Ch 29:23
animals and made a * offering with 2Ch 29:24
burnt offering and * offering must 2Ch 29:24
guilt of their * of idol-worship. 2Ch 34:5
presented as a * offering for the Ez 6:17
and twelve goats as a * offering. Ez 8:35
because of this * of his people Ez 9:4
whole history has been one of *; Ez 9:7
acknowledge our * against our God, Ez 10:2
of the * of the returned exiles. Ez 10:6
Confess your * to the Lord God Ez 10:11
the horrible * of not obeying the Neh 1:6,7
" 'If you *, I will scatter you Neh 1:8
Do not ignore their *. Neh 4:5
me * by fleeing to the Temple; Neh 6:12,13
people turned to * again, and once Neh 9:28
listen, and continued to *. Neh 9:29
In all of this, Job did not * or Job 1:22
is those who sow * and trouble who Job 4:7,8
punish them for sowing seeds of *. Job 5:6
Mankind heads for * and misery Job 5:7
chastening of the Lord when you *. Job 5:17
"Has my * harmed you, O God, Job 7:20
Why not just pardon my * and Job 7:21
he sees all * without searching. Job 11:11
the spots of * to defile you, can Job 11:15
Point out my * to me. Job 13:23
in * as a sponge soaks up water! Job 15:16
can 'conceive' is *, and their Job 15:35
ancient paths of * are snatched Job 22:15,16
of any other *, then let someone Job 31:7,8
For lust is a shameful *, a Job 31:11
to acknowledge my * and do not go Job 31:34
can convince the sinner of his *.' Job 32:13
the penalties of *, and keeping Job 33:17,18
everyone knows that God doesn't *! Job 34:10
If you *, does that shake the Job 35:6
Even if you * again and again, Job 35:6
to turn away from their *. Job 36:10
because of your *, your failure to Job 42:8
and do not * against him. Ps 4:4
cannot tolerate the slightest *. Ps 5:4
full of the stench of * and death. Ps 5:9
all are rotten with *. Ps 14:3
speaks out against *, criticizes Ps 15:4
Turn from all known * and spend Ps 34:14
* LURKS DEEP in the hearts of the Ps 36:1
I find myself upon the verge of *; Ps 38:17
own brother from the penalty of *! Ps 49:7
His life is corroded with *. Ps 53:1
they are filthy with *—corrupt Ps 53:3
for there is * in their homes, and Ps 55:15
were finally destroyed by their *. Ps 106:43
and let me slip back into * again. Ps 119:8

(SIN Con't)
they would hold me back from *. Ps 119:11
to drag me into *, but I am firmly Ps 119:61
Israel from her slavery to *. Ps 130:8
not go unpunished for this *. Pro 6:29
Winking at * leads to sorrow; Pro 10:10
The evil man squanders his on *. Pro 10:16
To do right honors God; to * is Pro 14:2
Or, "Fools make a mock at *." Pro 14:9f
To despise the poor is to *. Pro 14:21
Godliness exalts a nation, but * Pro 14:34
company—and leads others into *. Pro 16:29
* brings disgrace. Pro 18:3
are all *. Pro 21:4
on those who rebuke * fearlessly. Pro 24:25
lest he curse you for your *. Pro 30:10
a prostitute can * and then say, Pro 30:20
case, your mouth is making you *. Ecc 5:6,7
will not forgive you for this *. Is 2:9
And they boast that their * is Is 3:9
sin is equal to the * of Sodom; Is 3:9
its evil, the wicked for their *; Is 13:11
to me that this * will never be Is 22:14
an offering for *, then he shall Is 53:10
Because of * he has turned his Is 59:2
your fingers are filthy with *. Is 59:3
you do is filled with *; Is 59:6
to find no steps taken against *. Is 59:15
Zion who have turned away from *. Is 59:20
made us * and turn against you? Is 63:17
all infected and impure with *. Is 64:6
desert me? What * did they find in Jer 2:4,5
it into a land of * and corruption Jer 2:7
and the judgment that follows *. Jer 5:5
from them. This * has robbed them Jer 5:25
fruit of their own *, because they Jer 6:18,19
Is anyone sorry for *? Jer 8:6
down the path of * as swiftly as a Jer 8:6
by exile for this *, for they have Jer 8:9
What is our * against the Lord Jer 16:10
watching you and I see every *. Jer 16:17
MY PEOPLE * as though commanded Jer 17:1
Their youths do not forget to *, Jer 17:2,3
and walk the muddy paths of *. Jer 18:15
*, but let them perish before you; Jer 18:23
and led my people Israel into *; Jer 23:13
lies that lead my people into *. Jer 23:32
For your * is an incurable Jer 30:12
punishment? Your * is so scandalous Jer 30:15
In Jeremiah 17:1 their * was Jer 31:33f
causing Judah to * so greatly! Jer 32:35
says the Lord, no * shall be found Jer 50:20
is filled with * against the Holy Jer 51:5
For the * of my people is Lam 4:6
help him—he shall die in his *. Eze 3:20
are filled with * will recover. Eze 7:13
of money is the reason for your *. Eze 7:19
any longer with *, but to be my Eze 14:11
of this land * against me, then I Eze 14:13
of adultery and * you have not Eze 16:22
so eager for * that you have not Eze 16:31
and stays away from *, and is Eze 18:8
and all those who * against me—I Eze 20:38
you do, all is filled with *. Eze 21:24
the consequence of all your *. Eze 23:35
her * in seeking it before. Eze 29:16
he will die in his *, and you will Eze 33:9
not save him if he turns to *; Eze 33:12
* and give you new hearts of love. Eze 36:26
was punishment for *, for they Eze 39:23
burnt offerings, * offerings and Eze 40:39
cereal offerings, * offerings, and Eze 42:13
given a bullock for a * offering. Eze 43:19
Then take the bullock for the * Eze 43:21
cuts or scars—for a * offering. Eze 43:22
be sacrificed as a * offering. Eze 43:25
to fall into deep *, I have raised Eze 44:12
he must offer a * offering for Eze 44:27
offerings, the * offerings and the Eze 44:29
for public worship—* offerings, Eze 45:17
the blood of this * offering and Eze 45:19
a young bull for a * offering for Eze 45:22
given each day for a * offering. Eze 45:23
sacrifices for the * offering, Eze 45:25
offering and * offering and bake Eze 46:19,20
and didn't go into * when the Eze 48:11
with *, just as you see us now; Dan 9:7
and confessing my * and the sins of Dan 9:20
to stay away from *, and their Dan 9:24
and practice every kind of *. Hos 6:9
They are altars of *! Hos 8:11
is weighted with *, and shows only Hos 9:7
there has been only *, sin, sin! Hos 10:9
there has been only sin, *, sin! Hos 10:9
there has been only sin, sin, *! Hos 10:9
But riches can't make up for *. Hos 12:8
the Nazirites to * by urging them Amo 2:12
die for this man's *, and don't Jon 1:14
Israel in her * of idol worship. Mic 1:13
with * and it will vomit you out. Mic 2:10
with murder and * of every kind— Mic 3:10
For how you stink with *!" Nah 1:14
Must I forever see this * and Hab 1:3
Will you, who cannot allow * in Hab 1:13
Was your wrath against their * Hab 3:8,9f
filled with the * prevailing Zec 5:6
turned many from their lives of *. Mal 2:6
has caused many to stumble in *. Mal 2:8
from * by doing worthy deeds. Mt 3:8
"Turn from *, and turn to God, for Mt 4:17
*, cut it off and throw it away. Mt 5:30
forgive those who * against you; Mt 6:14,15
or any other *, can be Mt 12:31,32
*, cut it off and throw it away. Mt 18:8
And if your eye causes you to *, Mt 18:9
every sort of hypocrisy and *. Mt 23:28
* and betray and hate each other. Mt 24:10
lead many astray. * will be Mt 24:12
*, so that God could forgive them. Mk 1:4
to Satan's temptations to *. Mk 1:12,13
"I solemnly declare that any * Mk 3:28
It is an eternal *." Mk 3:29
everyone they met to turn from *. Mk 6:12
of unbelief and *, I, the Messiah, Mk 8:38
death, for man's *, had opened up Mk 15:38f
this * to all his many others. Lk 3:19,20
be temptations to *," Jesus said Lk 17:1
God who takes away the world's *! Jn 1:29
they wanted to * in the darkness. Jn 3:20
don't * as you did before, Jn 5:14
Literally, "* no more." Jn 5:14f
all judgment of * to his Son, so Jn 5:22
because I accuse it of * and evil. Jn 7:7
Go and * no more." Jn 8:11
are slaves of *, every one of you. Jn 8:34
accuse me of one single *? Jn 8:46
"You were altogether born in *." Jn 9:34f
they have no excuse for their *. Jn 15:22
the world of its *, and of the Jn 16:8
the world of * and righteousness Jn 16:8f
The world's * is unbelief in me; Jn 16:9
me to you have the greater *." Jn 19:11
you must turn from *, return to Act 2:38
of all things from *, as prophesied Act 3:21,22
don't charge them with this *!" Act 7:60
and * in your heart." Act 8:23
in Israel to turn from * to God. Act 13:24
to turn from * to God and that Act 19:4
of turning from * to God through Act 20:21
every sort of sex *, and do Rom 1:24
indulged in sex * with each other. Rom 1:26
of wickedness and *, of greed and Rom 1:29
give you time to turn from your *? Rom 2:4
in refusing to turn from your *; Rom 2:5
He will punish * wherever it is Rom 2:12-15
heathen when they *, even though Rom 2:12-15
of God would he be, to overlook *? Rom 3:6
When Adam sinned, * entered the Rom 5:12
human race. His * spread death Rom 5:12
Literally, "* entered into the Rom 5:12f
the world, and death through *." Rom 5:12f
[We know that it was Adam's * Rom 5:13
man's * and God's forgiveness! Rom 5:15
death to many through his *. Rom 5:15
Adam's one * brought the penalty Rom 5:16
life instead. The * of this one Rom 5:17
Yes, Adam's * brought punishment Rom 5:18
Before, * ruled over all men and Rom 5:21
that part of you that loves to * Rom 6:6
longer needs to be a slave to *; Rom 6:6
for when you are deadened to * Rom 6:7
So look upon your old * nature Rom 6:11
unresponsive to *, and instead be Rom 6:11
Do not let * control your puny Rom 6:12
for his good purposes. * need Rom 6:14
Literally, "* will never again be Rom 6:14f
to the law where * enslaves you, Rom 6:14
and * and not worry about it? Rom 6:15
You can choose * (with death) or Rom 6:16
to be slaves of *, now you have Rom 6:17
are free from your old master, *; Rom 6:18
to all kinds of *, so now you must Rom 6:19
you were slaves of * you didn't Rom 6:20
from the power of * and are slaves Rom 6:22
For the wages of * is death, but Rom 6:23
was the law that showed me my *. Rom 7:7
I would never have known the * in Rom 7:7
But * used this law against Rom 7:8
death penalty. * fooled me by Rom 7:11
No, it was *, devilish stuff that Rom 7:13
into slavery with * as my owner. Rom 7:14
It is * inside me that is Rom 7:17
* still has me in its evil grasp. Rom 7:20
to the * that is still within me. Rom 7:23,24,25
I find myself still enslaved to *. Rom 7:23,24,25
is still inside me loves to *. Rom 7:23,24,25
the vicious circle of * and death. Rom 8:2
your body will die because of *; Rom 8:10
and thistles, *, death, and decay Rom 8:20,21
from * which God's children enjoy. Rom 8:20,21
his life and never * once, only Rom 10:5
For God has given them all up to * Rom 11:32
And you won't * with his wife or Rom 13:
your brother or makes him *. Rom 14:2
* by doing what he knows is right. Rom 14:2
from what he feels is right is *. Rom 14:2
when God will conquer * and death. Rom 15:
free from all * and guilt on that 1Co 1:
Or, "to free us from slavery to * 1Co 1:30
in * with his father's wife. 1Co 5:
who live in sexual *, or are greedy 1Co 5:1
But sexual * is never right: our 1Co 6:1
is why I say to run from sex *. 1Co 6:1
No other * affects the body as 1Co 6:1
When you * this sin it is against 1Co 6:1
When you sin this * it is against 1Co 6:1
you might fall back into *. 1Co 7:
free from the awful power of *; 1Co 7:2
in times like these, it is no *. 1Co 7:2
it is all right, it is not a *; 1Co 7:3
brother to * whose conscience 1Co 8:
And it is a * against Christ to 1Co 8:1
against Christ to * against your 1Co 8:1
to make my brother *, I'll not eat 1Co 8:1
For you too may fall into *. 1Co 10:1
he is guilty of * against the body 1Co 11:2
there is *, death results. 1Co 15:2
Where then your sting? For *—the 1Co 15:55,5
Literally, "Him who knew no *, he 2Co 5:21
no sin, he made * on our behalf, 2Co 5:21
in common with the people of *? 2Co 6:14
away from * and seek eternal life. 2Co 7:10
of the * that I wrote you about. 2Co 7:11
out of the grip of *—for the Gal 3:21,22
overcome by some *, you who are Gal 6:1
others, full of *, obeying Satan, Eph 2:2
If you are angry, don't * by Eph 4:26
on that day when salvation from * Eph 4:30
Let there be no sex *, impurity Eph 5:3
in upon their * and shows it up, Eph 5:13
to accuse you of *, and God openly Col 2:15
have nothing to do with sexual *, Col 3:5
God's terrible anger against *. 1Th 1:10
of all sexual * so that each of you 1Th 4:3,4
This man of * will come as 2Th 2:9
from * and anger and resentment. 1Ti 2:8
but Eve, and * was the result. 1Ti 2:14
you yourself stay away from all *. 1Ti 5:22
minds warped by *—don't know how to 1Ti 6:5
first step toward all kinds of *. 1Ti 6:10
the * of anger with each other. 2Ti 2:16
If you stay away from * you will 2Ti 2:21
trap of slavery to * which he uses 2Ti 2:26
was the * of Jannes and Jambres. 2Ti 3:9
falling into * and make us his very Tit 2:14
our record of all *, and then sat Heb 1:3
of *. For if we are faithful to Heb 3:13
unstained by *, undefiled by Heb 7:26
men's bodies from *, just think Heb 9:13
without a single * or fault. Heb 9:14
of * forever by dying for us. Heb 9:26
before you as offerings for *. Heb 10:6
forgiveness, this * is not covered Heb 10:26
two or three witnesses to his *. Heb 10:28
contrast to the * and disbelief of Heb 11:7
the fleeting pleasures of *. Heb 11:24,25
struggled against * and temptation Heb 12:4
involved in sexual * or becomes Heb 12:16
as a sacrifice for *, and then the Heb 13:11
it is *. Jas 2:9
to do and then not doing it is *. Jas 4:17
not * and be condemned for it. Jas 5:12
some *, the Lord will forgive him. Jas 5:15
be finished with * and live a good 1Pe 2:24
innocent of any * at any time, that 1Pe 3:18
him to cleanse our hearts from *. 1Pe 3:21
your body suffers, * loses its 1Pe 4:1
godless enjoy—sex *, lust, getting 1Pe 4:3
the old life of * so that now he 2Pe 1:9
is nothing wrong with sexual *. 2Pe 2:2
teachers will have for their *. 2Pe 2:13
by living in foul * on the side 2Pe 2:13
lure back into * those who have 2Pe 2:18
slaves to * and destruction. 2Pe 2:19
tangled up with * and becomes its 2Pe 2:20
those who turn again to their *. 2Pe 2:22
darkness and *, we are lying. 1Jn 1:6
his Son cleanses us from every *. 1Jn 1:7
If we say that we have no *, we 1Jn 1:8
so that you will stay away from *. 1Jn 2:1
But if you *, there is someone to 1Jn 2:1
around in darkness and *. 1Jn 2:10
* is done against the will of God. 1Jn 3:4
that there is no * in him, no 1Jn 3:5
realize this: They * because they 1Jn 3:6
to * has kept steadily at it. 1Jn 3:8
Whoever is living a life of * and 1Jn 3:10
him, defeating * and evil pleasure 1Jn 5:4
he has sinned that one fatal *. 1Jn 5:16
But there is that one * which 1Jn 5:16
Every wrong is a *, of course. 1Jn 5:17
about what * this is, and whether 1Jn 5:17f
a Christian ever * in such a way? 1Jn 5:17f

(SIN Con't)
holy, but turned to a life of *. Jud 1:6
Hate every trace of their * while Jud 1:23
I know you don't tolerate * among Rev 2:2
them in sexual * and encouraging Rev 2:14
sex * is not a serious matter; Rev 2:20
me, repenting of their * with her; Rev 2:22
of her intense impurity and *." Rev 14:8
corrupted the earth with her *; Rev 19:2

SIN-BURDENED
with silly, * women and teach them 2Ti 3:6

SIN-LOVING
Your old * nature was buried Rom 6:4
so that your * body is no longer Rom 6:6
And since your old * nature Rom 6:8

SIN'S
don't have to? For * power over us Rom 6:2,3
is no longer under * control, no Rom 6:6
He died once for all to end * Rom 6:10
We aren't saved from * grasp by Rom 8:3
destroyed * control over us by Rom 8:3

SINAI
Elim and Mt. *, arriving there on Ex 16:1
the people were camped at Mt. *. Ex 18:5,6
THE ISRAELIS ARRIVED in the * Ex 19:1
of Mt. * and set up camp there. Ex 19:2,3
Mt. * as all the people watch. Ex 19:11
All Mt. * was covered with smoke Ex 19:18
the top of Mt. * and called Moses Ex 19:20
rested upon Mt. * and the cloud Ex 24:16
Moses on Mount *, he gave him the Ex 31:18
come up into Mount * and present Ex 34:2
and climbed Mount *, as the Lord Ex 34:4
the Lord on Mount *, to be passed Lev 7:38
sacrifices to God in the * desert. Lev 7:38
WHILE MOSES WAS on Mount *, the Lev 25:1
Israel, through Moses, on Mount *. Lev 26:46
the people of Israel on Mount *. Lev 27:34
on the * peninsula at the time. Num 1:1
them in the wilderness of *." Num 1:17,18,19f
to Moses on Mount *, Aaron's Num 3:1
of * when they used unholy fire. Num 3:4
to Moses at the * peninsula, Num 3:14,15
were on the * peninsula, during the Num 9:1
there in the * peninsula, just as Num 9:4,5
so the Israelites left the * Num 10:12
three days after leaving Mount *, Num 10:33
taken in the wilderness of *! Num 26:64,65
ordained at Mount *, to be Num 28:6
they went to the wilderness of *; Num 33:15-37
from the wilderness of * to Num 33:15-37
darkness that engulfed Mount *. Deu 5:22
"The Lord came to us at Mount *, Deu 33:2
Yes, even Mount * quaked Ju 5:5
"You came down upon Mount * and Neh 9:13
Mount * quailed before you—the Ps 68:8
on from Mount * and comes to his Ps 68:17
I answered from Mount * Ps 81:7
across the deserts from Mount *. Hab 3:3
desert near Mount *, an Angel Act 7:30
of God—the Living Word—on Mount *. Act 7:38
He did this on Mount *, when he Gal 4:24,25
Mount *, by the way, is called Gal 4:24,25
as shown to him on Mount *. Heb 8:5
* when God gave them his laws. Heb 12:18
When he spoke from Mount * his Heb 12:26

SINCE
"* the Lord has given me no Gen 16:2,3
and Sarah was long * past the time Gen 18:11
Then Abraham spoke again. "* I Gen 18:27
Then Abraham said, "* I have Gen 18:31
Lot begged, "* you've been so Gen 19:18,19,20
them and said, "* this is your Gen 23:8
no friendly visit, * you kicked me Gen 26:27
* I have given him three sons!" Gen 29:34
prostitute, * her face was veiled. Gen 38:15
said to him, "* God has revealed Gen 41:39
everywhere else. * Joseph was Gen 42:6
I have never seen him *. Gen 44:28
Ever * I gave Pharaoh your Ex 5:23
never been * Egypt was founded! Ex 9:18
her to foreigners, * he has wronged Ex 21:8
"And * you yourselves are Ex 22:31
in the sanctuary, * it is most Lev 10:17
he demanded. "* its blood was Lev 10:18
* she has no husband. Lev 21:2,3
the seventh year, * we are not Lev 25:20
unholy fire. And * they had no Num 3:4
But now, * the people of Israel Num 14:25
" '* the spies were in the land Num 14:34,35
"* YOU ARE the people of God, Deu 14:1
* he had not killed deliberately. Deu 19:6,7
* she belonged to his father. Deu 22:30
before sunset, for * he is poor he Deu 24:14,15
Then, * her house was on top of Jos 2:15
* that time had been circumcised. Jos 5:4,5
never been another *, when the Lord Jos 10:14
Promised Land. But * I had followed Jos 14:8
forty-five years * crisscrossing Jos 14:10
villages. But * the descendants of Jos 17:12
replied, "and * you are such a Jos 17:16,17,18
And now * you have broken the Ju 2:3
and they decided that * his Ju 9:3
upon him and * he had no weapon, he Ju 14:6
called "Jawbone Hill" ever *. Ju 15:16,17
Nazirite to God * before my birth. Ju 16:16,17
a horrible crime * Israel left Ju 19:30
few who remain, * we have sworn by Ju 21:7
for the others, * all the women of Ju 21:16
been at it ever * except for a few Ru 2:7
your mother-in-law * the death of Ru 2:10,11
They told him that * his 1Sa 8:5
Ever * I brought them from Egypt 1Sa 8:8
And now, * he was securely in 1Sa 14:47
"It's no use! * you have rejected 1Sa 15:26
been in the army * he was a boy!" 1Sa 17:33
sling and a stone. * he had no 1Sa 17:50,51
son is this?" * David was, if 1Sa 17:55f
an expedition, and * they stay 1Sa 21:5
So, * there was no other food 1Sa 21:6
Philistines. Ever * that time the 1Sa 23:28
Sir, * the Lord has kept you 1Sa 25:26
to Egypt ever * ancient times. 1Sa 27:8
one fault in him * he arrived." 1Sa 29:3
The place has been known ever * 2Sa 2:16
seven years, * the age of thirty. 2Sa 5:4,5
My home has been a tent ever * 2Sa 7:6
listen to her; and * he was 2Sa 13:14
Don't be so upset, * it's all in 2Sa 13:20
this ever * Amnon raped Tamar. 2Sa 13:32,33
in the field, and * no one was 2Sa 14:5,6
to tell Amasa, "* you are my 2Sa 19:13
* the day the king left Jerusalem. 2Sa 19:24,25
Never before or * has there been 1Ki 10:12
said to him, "* you have not kept 1Ki 11:11
gold calves. And * you have refused 1Ki 14:9
in Israel? Now, * you have done 2Ki 1:6
"* you want me to be king," Jehu 2Ki 9:15
they had been raised * childhood. 2Ki 10:6
of Israel. But * these Assyrian 2Ki 17:25
angered me ever * I brought their 2Ki 21:15
like that * the days of the judges 2Ki 23:22
and no king * the time of Josiah 2Ki 23:25
And they have lived there ever *. 1Ch 4:43
was Reuben, but * he dishonored his 1Ch 5:1
"* you think that I should be 1Ch 13:2
be your king, and * the Lord our 1Ch 13:2
it ever * Saul became king." 1Ch 13:3
Baal-perazim ever * (meaning, "The 1Ch 14:11
have never before, * bringing my 2Ch 6:5,6
IT WAS NOW twenty years * Solomon 2Ch 8:1
"* when have I asked your 2Ch 25:16
for he felt that * these gods had 2Ch 28:23
* many of the people arriving 2Ch 30:17,18,19
like this one * the days of King 2Ch 30:26
"* the Ark is now in Solomon's 2Ch 35:3
Never * the time of Samuel the 2Ch 35:18
we have sacrificed to him ever * Ez 4:2
taxes to you. * we are grateful to Ez 4:14
*, though it is not yet completed. Ez 5:16
carried out * the days of Joshua. Neh 8:17
"Don't you realize that ever * Job 20:4
I have depended upon you * birth; Ps 22:9,10,11
of God. And * I am trusting him, Ps 56:3,4
days of the past, long * ended. Ps 77:5
than honey. And * only your rules Ps 119:104
* the Lord is directing our Pro 20:24
him to ruin. * he begins with a Ecc 10:12,13
has not been known * the division Is 7:17
"* the people of Jerusalem are Is 8:6
And so the Lord says, "* these Is 29:13
not obey me, and * their worship Is 29:13
Let them do as I have done * Is 44:7
and cared for you * you were born. Is 46:3
and orthodox Christianity ever *. Is 52:13f
quaked! For * the world began no Is 64:4
you and say that * the Temple of Jer 7:4
Ever * the day your fathers left Jer 7:25
bother me." * childhood you have Jer 22:21
but wrong * their earliest days; Jer 32:30
a drink of wine * then, nor our Jer 35:8
said to Baruch, "* I am a prisoner Jer 36:5
But ever * we quit burning Jer 44:18
No one has lived in them *, and Jer 50:40
have long * gone, for you have Lam 3:17
As I live, the Lord God says, * Eze 35:6
beside them. And * the building Eze 42:6
* the writing was in familiar Dan 5:8f
you as my priests. * you have Hos 4:6
O Israel, ever * that awful night Hos 10:9
* I brought you out from Egypt. Hos 13:4
long enough! For * you began laying Zec 8:9
his master's! And * I, the master Mt 10:25
I will explain mysteries hidden * Mt 13:34,35
* David called him 'Lord,' how Mt 22:45
Lazy slave! * you knew I would Mt 25:26
they said, "* it's against our Mt 27:6
* it was the Sabbath, Jesus' Mk 3:2
And he replied, "* he was very Mk 9:21
your footstool.' * David called Mk 12:37
as have never been * the beginning Mk 13:19
only the Father knows. And * you Mk 13:33
that day, * it was the Sabbath. Lk 6:7
But empty, * the person is neutral Lk 11:25f
laws * I was a small child." Lk 18:21
in me. And * you don't believe Jn 5:47
And * I am telling you the Jn 8:46
the words of God. * you don't, it Jn 8:47
and do his will. * the world began Jn 9:32
it is true. And * I, the Lord and Jn 13:14
wondering whom he could mean. * I Jn 13:23
Some thought that * Judas was Jn 13:29
his master!' So * they persecuted Jn 15:20
And all of them, * they are Jn 17:10
"and * I am the one you are Jn 18:8
to us * his return from the dead. Jn 21:14
SEVEN WEEKS HAD gone by * Jesus' Act 2:1
"Samuel and every prophet * have Act 3:24
They arrested them and * it was Act 4:3
And * it was God who gave these Act 11:17
to you Jews. But * you have Act 13:46
that idea at all, * John had Act 15:38
in it, and * he is Lord of heaven Act 17:24
to you, but * it is merely a bunch Act 18:15
happened to Jesus * the time of Act 18:25,26
us from heaven. * this is an Act 19:36
riot, * there is no cause for it. Act 19:40
preaching. And * he was leaving the Act 20:7
But Festus replied that * Paul Act 25:4
And * Fair Havens was an exposed Act 27:12
in their hearts. * earliest times Rom 1:20
SO NOW, * we have been made right Rom 5:1
sinners. And * by his blood he did Rom 5:9
to come. And *, when we were his Rom 5:10
* they themselves had never Rom 5:14
over you. And * your old Rom 6:8
Evidently not good, * you are Rom 6:21
on the cross; and * you are Rom 7:4
children. And * we are his Rom 8:17
be against us? * he did not spare Rom 8:32
back to life. And * Abraham and Rom 11:16
in Jerusalem. And * they received Rom 15:27
from women ever *, and both men and 1Co 11:12
but not to others, * they won't be 1Co 14:2
stranger to him. * you are so 1Co 14:12
But tell me this! * you believe 1Co 15:12
So, my dear brothers, * future 1Co 15:58
* we know that this new glory 2Co 3:12
controls us now. * we believe that 2Co 5:13,14
and abilities. * I know it is all 2Co 12:10
long * discarded the Jewish laws; Gal 2:14
own sons. And * we are his sons, Gal 4:7
That is why, ever * I heard of Eph 1:15
of themselves. For * a man and his Eph 5:28
and have been ever * the Gospel Col 1:5
So ever * we first heard about Col 1:9
* you died, as it were, with Col 2:20
* YOU BECAME alive again, so to Col 3:1
* you have been chosen by God who Col 3:12
have no hope. For * we believe 1Th 4:14
from them. For * the messages from Heb 2:2
* we, God's children, are human Heb 2:14
the people. For * he himself has Heb 2:18
And * Christ is so much superior, Heb 3:7,8
for them * the world began. Heb 4:3
our weaknesses, * he had the same Heb 4:15
in his own name, * there was no one Heb 6:13
God through him. * he will live Heb 7:25
And * every high priest is Heb 8:3
and again, ever * the world began. Heb 9:26
And * this great High Priest of Heb 10:21
* WE HAVE such a huge crowd of men Heb 12:1
in his family. * we respect our Heb 12:9
* we have a kingdom nothing can Heb 12:28
the events which, * then, have 1Pe 1:11
visitors here. * your real home is 1Pe 2:11
* CHRIST SUFFERED and underwent 1Pe 4:1
was * the first day of creation." 2Pe 3:4
And so * everything around us is 2Pe 3:11
from meeting him. * we know that 1Jn 2:29
we really are! But * most people 1Jn 3:1
to Satan, who * he first began to 1Jn 3:8
Dear friends, * God loved us as 1Jn 4:11
in the church. * the Truth is in 2Jn 1:2
or the other! But * you are merely Rev 3:16
the ages ever * it was announced by Rev 10:7

SINCERE
a blameless life and is truly *. Ps 15:2
where to walk, for my prayer is *. Ps 143:8
* and sit before you listening. Eze 33:31
have been pure and *, quietly 2Co 1:12
have been straightforward and *; 2Co 1:13,14
became earnest and *, and very 2Co 7:11
good motives and * hearts, Gal 4:18
Jewish law and custom. And *? Php 3:6
perfectly straightforward and *. 1Th 2:3
and straightforward and *. Jas 3:17
Let there be sorrow and * grief. Jas 4:9

SINCERELY
"Trust the Lord and * worship 1Sa 12:24
is close to all who call on him *. Ps 145:18
men, but * teach the ways of God. Mk 12:14
Jesus Christ our Lord. Amen.*, Rom 16:25,26,27

(SINCERELY Con't)
all belong to Christ Jesus.*,Paul 1Co 16:24
Christ be with you all.*,Paul Gal 6:18
who * love our Lord Jesus Christ. Eph 6:24
love our Lord Jesus Christ.*,Paul Eph 6:24
forever and ever. Amen.*,Paul Php 4:20
*,Paul Col 4:18
*,Paul 1Th 5:28
*,Paul 2Th 3:18
*,Paul 1Ti 6:21
blessings be with you all.*,Paul Tit 3:15
rewards those who * look for him. Heb 11:6
of his many sins.*,James Jas 5:20
place in your hearts. Amen.*,John 1Jn 5:21
choice child of God.*,John 2Jn 1:13
a special greeting from me.*,John 3Jn 1:15

SINCERITY
and serve him in * and truth. Jos 24:14
I will speak the truth with all *. Job 33:3
There is no * left. Ps 12:2
yes, utter * and truthfulness. Ps 51:6
bread of honor and * and truth. 1Co 5:8

SINEWS
and knit together bones and *. Job 10:11
as a cedar. The * of his thighs are Job 40:17
by his strong * and we grow only as Col 2:19

SINFUL
Therefore, cleanse your * hearts Deu 10:16
again to their * ways, so God Ju 3:12
of Manasseh's * reign is recorded 2Ki 21:17
of us involved in this * affair. Ez 10:13
you get away with this * deed?" Neh 13:27
who is corrupt and *, drinking in Job 15:16
were ill because of their * ways. Ps 107:17
It is dangerous and * to rush Pro 19:2
The rebel's schemes are *, and Pro 24:9
world go on its * way so that he Ecc 3:18
even realize it is * to make rash Ecc 5:1
Oh, what a * nation they are! Is 1:4
member of a *, foul-mouthed race; Is 6:5
O Israel, my * people, come home to Jer 3:12
to follow me. O * children, come Jer 3:14
"But if this * man has, in turn, Eze 18:14
Their * deeds give them away on Hos 7:2
Israel, that * nation, and I will Amo 9:8
WOE TO FILTHY, * Jerusalem, city Zep 3:1
And if you hardhearted, * men Mt 7:11
"And if your eye is *, gouge it Mk 9:47
the veil separated him from * Mk 15:38f
"And if even * persons like Lk 11:13
heaven against all *, evil men who Rom 1:18
* things with each other's bodies. Rom 1:24
of your * nature was shattered. Rom 6:2,3
do not give in to its * desires. Rom 6:12
was still active, * desires were at Rom 7:5
to, and producing * deeds, the Rom 7:5
No, the law is not * but it was Rom 7:7
as my old * nature is concerned. Rom 7:18
that ours are *—and destroyed sin's Rom 8:3
* nature within us is against God. Rom 8:7
of their old * selves, bent on Rom 8:8
to your old * nature to do what it Rom 8:12
members of his * race, and wherever 1Co 15:22
You were dead in sins, and your * Col 2:13
Away then with *, earthly things; Col 3:5
* lives and everyone knows it. 1Ti 5:24
godless living and * pleasures and Tit 2:12
were weak and * men who could not Heb 7:28
his patience as * men did such Heb 12:3
No woman can escape their * 2Pe 2:14

SINFULNESS
* of Israel, and making it holy. Lev 16:19
in your * you have made. Is 31:7
you for your *, says the Lord. Jer 21:14
But the more we see our *, the Rom 5:20

SING
I will * to the Lord, for he has Ex 15:1
* to the Lord, for he has Ex 15:21
up, O well!* of the water! Num 21:17,18
For I shall * about the Lord, Ju 5:3
To * of the triumphs of the Lord. Ju 5:11
Again and again they * the ballad Ju 5:11
Awake, O Deborah, and *! Ju 5:12
And * praises to your name. 2Sa 22:50
to * thanksgiving to the Lord. 1Ch 16:7
* to him; yes, sing his praises 1Ch 16:9
Sing to him; yes, * his praises 1Ch 16:9
* to the Lord, O earth, 1Ch 16:23
Let the trees in the woods * for 1Ch 16:33
to * thanks and praise to him. 1Ch 23:30
they began to * and to praise, the 2Ch 20:22
the Levites to * before the Lord 2Ch 29:30
To this day they still * sad 2Ch 35:24,25
the widows' hearts to * for joy. Job 29:13
I will * praise to the name of Ps 7:17
I will * your praises, O Lord God Ps 9:2
Oh, * out your praises to the God Ps 9:11
I will * to the Lord because he Ps 13:6
Let all Israel * his praises, Ps 22:23
and * his praises with much joy. Ps 27:6
Oh, * to him you saints of his; Ps 30:4
so that I might * glad praises to Ps 30:12
on the harp; * joyfully. Ps 33:3
He has given me a new song to *, Ps 40:3
the night I * his songs and pray to Ps 42:8
trumpets blaring. * out your Ps 47:6,7
our King. Yes, * your highest Ps 47:6,7
the earth. * thoughtful praises! Ps 47:6,7
Then I will * of your Ps 51:14,15
No wonder I can * your praises! Ps 57:7
I will * your praises among the Ps 57:9
I will * your praises, for you Ps 59:9
But as for me, I will * each Ps 59:16
O my Strength, to you I * my Ps 59:17
* TO THE Lord, all the earth! Ps 66:1
earth! * of his glorious name! Ps 66:2
worship you and * of your glories. Ps 66:4
Let everyone bless God and * his Ps 66:8
May he rejoice and be merry. * Ps 68:4
God in adoration. * to the Lord, O Ps 68:32
of the earth—* praises to the Lord, Ps 68:32
I will shout and * your praises Ps 71:23
enough to * their wedding songs. Ps 78:63
THE LORD MAKES us strong! * Ps 81:1
Sing praises! * to Israel's God! Ps 81:1
*, accompanied by drums; Ps 81:2
And in the festivals they'll *, Ps 87:7
FOREVER AND EVER I will * about Ps 89:1
A song to * on the Lord's Day Ps 92:1
to the Lord, to * praises to the Ps 92:1
his faithfulness. * his praises, Ps 92:3
No wonder I am glad! I * for joy. Ps 92:4
OH, COME, LET us * to the Lord! Ps 95:1
Let us * him psalms of praise. Ps 95:2
* A NEW song to the Lord! Ps 96:1
SING A NEW song to the Lord! * it Ps 96:1
the world! * out his praises! Ps 96:2
* A NEW song to the Lord telling Ps 98:1
* your praise accompanied by Ps 98:5
and the hills * out their songs of Ps 98:8,9
I WILL * about your lovingkindness Ps 101:1
I will * your praises! Ps 101:1
* among the branches of the trees. Ps 104:12
I will * to the Lord as long as I Ps 104:33
proclaim them to the nations. * Ps 105:2
and * about his glorious deeds. Ps 107:22
I will * and rejoice before you. Ps 108:1
The dead cannot * praises to Ps 115:17
I will * about their wonder, for Ps 119:172
so good; * to his wonderful name. Ps 135:3
willow trees, for how can we *? Ps 137:3,4
demand that we * for them the happy Ps 137:3,4
highest joy, let me never * again. Ps 137:5,6
I will * your praises before the Ps 138:1
Yes, they shall * about Ps 138:5
I will * you a new song, O God, Ps 144:9
and * about your righteousness. Ps 145:7
How good it is to * his praises! Ps 147:1
dust. * out your thanks to him; Ps 147:7
Sing out your thanks to him; * Ps 147:7
YES, PRAISE the Lord! * him a new Ps 149:1
Sing him a new song. * his Ps 149:1
Let them * for joy as they lie Ps 149:4,5
good men stay away and * for joy. Pro 29:5,6
NOW I WILL * a song about his Is 5:1
How mighty he is!" * to the Is 12:5
All the world begins to *! Is 14:7
cedars of Lebanon—* out this joyous Is 14:8
But instead, you * and dance and Is 22:13
she will * sweet songs as a Is 23:15,16
are left will shout and * for joy; Is 24:14
land of Judah will * this song: Is 26:1
dust shall awake and * for joy! Is 26:19
But the people of God will * a Is 30:29
could not speak will shout and *! Is 35:6
from now on I will * my songs of Is 38:20
* a new song to the Lord; Is 42:10
Sing a new song to the Lord; * Is 42:10
remotest corners! *, O sea! Is 42:10
Sing, O sea! *, all you who live Is 42:10
the Lord and * his mighty power. Is 42:12
*, O heavens, for the Lord has Is 44:23
* for joy, O heavens; Is 49:13
The watchmen shout and * with Is 52:8
*, O CHILDLESS woman! Is 54:1
and despair, while they * for joy. Is 65:14
Therefore I will * out in thanks Jer 20:13
For the Lord says, * with joy Jer 31:7
They shall come home and * songs Jer 31:12
The people will *: "Praise the Jer 33:10,11
all day long they * their ribald Lam 3:14
See how they laugh and * with Lam 3:63
the young no longer dance and *. Lam 5:14
"* THIS DEATH dirge for the Eze 19:1
"Son of dust, * this sad dirge Eze 27:2
* together that "God sows!" Hos 1:21,22
SADLY I * this song of grief for Amo 5:1
calves. You * idle songs to the Amo 6:5
*, O daughter of Zion; Zep 3:14
me. *, Jerusalem, and rejoice! Zec 2:10
began to shout and * as they walked Lk 19:36,37
Gentiles, and * to your name." Rom 15:9
I will * in unknown tongues and 1Co 14:15
together some will *, another will 1Co 14:26
teach them to each other and * Col 3:16
together we will * his praises." Heb 2:12
and no one could * this song Rev 14:3

SINGED
a hair of their heads was *; Dan 3:27

SINGERS
to organize the * into an 1Ch 15:16
the Ark, the *, and Chenaniah the 1Ch 15:27
the * with loud praises to God. 1Ch 16:42
musician. The * were appointed to 1Ch 25:8
of Holies! The * were Asaph, Heman, 2Ch 5:11,12
trumpets, and the * singing, 2Ch 23:12
the * sang and the trumpets blew. 2Ch 29:28
The * (the sons of Asaph) were in 2Ch 35:15
and the *, the gatekeepers, the Ez 2:70
priests, Levites, *, gatekeepers, Ez 7:7,8,9
Of the *, there was Eliashib. Ez 10:24
the gatekeepers, *, and Levites, I Neh 7:1
the gatekeepers, and the choir *. Neh 10:39,40
clan became the Tabernacle *. Neh 11:22,23
also set the pay scale of the *. Neh 11:22,23
Azmaveth, for the * had built their Neh 12:29
and by the *— Neh 12:42
the work of the * and gatekeepers, Neh 12:45
they and the choir * who were Neh 13:10
to the sanctuary— * in front, Ps 68:25

SINGING
with * and orchestra and harp? Gen 31:27
cry of victory or defeat, but *." Ex 32:18
Saul, and were * and dancing for 1Sa 18:6
at their dances, *, 'Saul has slain 1Sa 21:11
accompanied by * and by zithers, 1Ch 13:8
trained in * praises to the Lord; 1Ch 25:6,7
garments and * the song "His 2Ch 20:21
and the singers *, accompanied by 2Ch 23:12
and thanks to God, * this song: Ez 3:11
spend their time * and dancing. Job 21:12,13
your altar, * a song of Ps 26:7
* with joy, praising the Lord? Ps 42:4,5
How glad the nations will be, * Ps 67:4
prisoners from jail, * with joy! Ps 68:6
Then I will praise God with my * Ps 69:30
in your Temple, * your praises. Ps 84:4
come before him, * with joy. Ps 100:2
So he brought his chosen ones * Ps 105:43
source of joy and * through all Ps 119:54
return *, carrying their sheaves. Ps 126:6
time of the * of birds has come. Sol 2:12
Such * it was! Is 6:4
The happy * in the vineyards will Is 16:10
Hear them * to the Lord from the Is 24:15,16
* glory to the Righteous One! Is 24:15,16
LISTEN TO THEM *! Is 26:1
of flowers and * and joy! Is 35:2
* the songs of everlasting joy. Is 35:10
Leave Babylon, * as you go; Is 48:20
They shall come with * to Is 51:11
I will end the happy * and Jer 7:34
And they shall wail for you, * Eze 26:17
She will respond to me there, * Hos 1:15
The riotous sound of * in the Amo 8:3
director: When * this ode, the Hab 3:19
were praying and * hymns to the Act 16:25
and hymns and * sacred songs, Eph 5:19
spiritual songs, * to the Lord with Col 3:16
be * praises to the Lord. Jas 5:13
before the throne, *, "O Lord, Rev 4:10
They were * Rev 5:9
Then in my vision I heard the * Rev 5:11
It was the * of a choir Rev 14:2
and they were * the song of Moses, Rev 15:3,4

SINGLE
AT THAT TIME all mankind spoke a * Gen 11:1
take so much as a * thread from Gen 14:23
If you find a * thing we've Gen 31:32
quotas by a * brick, for they Ex 5:7,8
place of God, becomes a * unit. Ex 26:6
they cut down a * cluster of grapes Num 13:23
Not a * one of you twenty years Num 14:29
"If the error is made by a * Num 15:27
so that not a * survivor remained; Num 21:35
won't get a * bite of the meat. Deu 28:31
How could one * enemy chase a Deu 32:30
"Not a * word from any of you Jos 6:10
Not a * one of them will be able Jos 10:8
without having lost a * man! Jos 10:21
never taken even one * bribe." 1Sa 12:4
So there was not a * sword or 1Sa 13:22
we will settle this in * combat! 1Sa 17:8
you don't, not a * one of them will 2Sa 19:7
so much as by a * scolding! 1Ki 1:6
in fact, it was the largest * 1Ki 10:10
family—leaving not a * male child. 1Ki 16:11
a * piece of bread in the house. 1Ki 17:12
"Don't let a * one escape," he 1Ki 18:40
he will not let a * one of your 1Ki 21:21
Don't let a * one escape." 2Ki 10:25
to Hebron with the * purpose of 1Ch 12:38
combined into a * subclan because 1Ch 23:10,11

SINGLE Con't)
a * one of the enemy had escaped. 2Ch 20:24
On a * day, Pekah, the son of 2Ch 28:6
to try to find a * fault, and so to Job 33:10
they do and in a * night he Job 34:25
I did not refuse a * one. Ps 18:22
We have not left your path by a * Ps 44:18
see if there is a * one who does Ps 53:2
A * day spent in your Temple is Ps 84:10
They are like a * hour! Ps 90:4
be blotted out in a * generation. Ps 109:12,13
And there is not a * man in all Ecc 7:20
by a * bead of your necklace. Sol 4:9
destroy them. In a * night he will Is 10:17
Which can predict a * day ahead? Is 43:9
Is there a * spot in all the Jer 3:2
Are they even as valuable as a * Eze 15:2
Not a cluster to eat, not a * Mic 7:1
They will not be overdue a * day! Hab 2:3
deserted without a * survivor to Zep 3:6
the sins of this land in a * day. Zec 3:9
three evil shepherds in a * month. Zec 11:8
Will all your worries add a * Mt 6:27
and when he spoke a * word, all Mt 8:16
a * one of these little children. Mt 18:10
wasn't room for a * person more, Mk 2:2
broken a * one of those laws." Mk 10:20
Yet God does not forget a * one Lk 12:6
Will it add a * day to your life? Lk 12:25
and there hasn't been a * fig!' Lk 13:7
to do a * thing you told me to; Lk 15:29
to be with you even for a * day, Lk 17:22
"Is there a * one of us Jewish Jn 7:48
truthfully accuse me of one * sin? Jn 8:46
Unless I die I will be alone—a * Jn 12:23,24
have not lost a * one of those you Jn 18:9
remain * or else go back to him. 1Co 7:11
one of which could speak a * word. 1Co 12:2
There isn't a * thing these other 2Co 12:11
to them for a * moment, for we did Gal 2:5
any time breaks a * one of these Gal 3:10
eyes, without a * fault—we who Eph 1:4
church without a * spot or wrinkle Eph 5:27
being holy and without a * fault. Eph 5:27
carry away a * penny when we die. 1Ti 6:7
perfect, without a * sin or fault. Heb 9:14
as the oldest son for a * meal. Heb 12:16
overtake her in a * day, and she Rev 18:8
And now in a * hour all is Rev 18:19
pearls —each gate from a * pearl! Rev 21:21

SINGLED
You are * out from among all the Gen 3:14
and the clan of Zerah was * out. Jos 7:17
The honored guest was thus * Jn 13:26f

SINGLEHANDED
the enemy * and killed them all. 2Sa 23:18,19

SINGLEMINDED
but kept on, *, after Abner alone. 2Sa 2:19

SINGS
the world shouts with joy, and *. Ps 65:13
to God, and * for utter joy! Ps 98:4
songs as a harlot * who, long Is 23:15,16
to idols. Sad * my heart for Moab Jer 48:36
like someone who * lovely songs Eze 33:32

SINGULAR
word for "plant" is in the *. Eze 34:29f

SINITES
Arkites, *,Arvadites, Zemarites, Gen 10:15-19
Hivites, Arkites, *, Arvadites, 1Ch 1:13-16

SINK
Deeper and deeper I * in the Ps 69:1
Don't let me * in. Ps 69:14
You have let me * down deep in Ps 71:20
heavens and * again to the depths; Ps 107:26
'So shall Babylon *, never more to Jer 51:64
* deep into your own heart first; Eze 3:10
You will * beneath the terrible Eze 26:19
and all the people * into the sea Eze 27:27
toss about, and * again. Amo 8:8
he was terrified and began to *. Mt 14:30
full of water and about to *. Mk 4:37
"Let this message * into the Rev 2:7

SINKING
me harm. I am * down to death. Ps 35:12
We're *!" Mt 8:25
with fish and on the verge of *. Lk 5:7
"Master, Master, we are *!" Lk 8:24

SINKS
Nile in Egypt, and then * again. Amo 9:5

SINLESS
Even if I were * I wouldn't say Job 9:15
have cleansed my heart; I am *"? Pro 20:9
For God took the * Christ and 2Co 5:21
being made strong, * and holy by 1Th 3:13
like ours (except that his was *). Heb 5:7f
the *, spotless Lamb of God. 1Pe 1:19
and to bring you, * and perfect, Jud 1:24,25

SINNED
and * greatly against Jehovah. Gen 13:13
and his officials * yet more by Ex 9:34
people, "You have * a great sin, Ex 32:30
these people have * a great sin, Ex 32:31
"Whoever has * against me will be Ex 32:33
"We realize that we have *, but Num 14:40
have * at the cost of their lives. Num 16:38
out, "We have *, for we have Num 21:7
Then Balaam confessed, "I have * Num 22:34
then you will have * against the Num 32:23
"Then they confessed, 'We have * Deu 1:41
of Reuben) *, and the earth Deu 11:6
Israel has * and disobeyed my Jos 7:10,11
Achan replied, "I have * against Jos 7:20
the son of Zerah, * against the Jos 22:20
to the one man who had *?" Jos 22:20
* against the Lord as we thought; Jos 22:31
of Israel again * against the Lord, Ju 4:1
"We have * against you and have Ju 10:10
him again and said, "We have *. Ju 10:15
No, I have not * against you; Ju 11:27
ONCE AGAIN ISRAEL * by worshiping Ju 13:1
that they had * by turning away 1Sa 12:10
"I have *," Saul finally 1Sa 15:24
Saul pleaded again, "I have *; 1Sa 15:30
yourself if I have * against your 1Sa 20:8
that I have not * against you, even 1Sa 24:11
"I have * against the Lord," 2Sa 12:13
for I know very well how much I *. 2Sa 19:20
"Look, I am the one who has *! 2Sa 24:17
'We have *, we have done wrong'; 1Ki 8:47
because Jeroboam * and made all of 1Ki 14:16
For he, too, had * like 1Ki 16:19
to God, "I am the one who has *. 1Ch 21:8
one who * by ordering the census. 1Ch 21:17
because they have * against you, 2Ch 6:24
against you (and who has never *? 2Ch 6:36
people who have * against you. 2Ch 6:39
corrupt. He * against the Lord his 2Ch 26:16
had, however, * by invading the 2Ch 27:2
and brothers who * against the Lord 2Ch 30:7
instead he * more and more. 2Ch 33:23
"You have *, for you have married Ez 10:10
I confess that we have * against Neh 1:6,7
They * in so many ways, but in Neh 9:18
we have * so greatly that you Neh 9:33
have * and turned away from God Job 1:5
Would I not admit it if I had *? Job 6:30
If your children * against him, Job 8:4
me was to destroy me if I *; Job 10:13,14
to admit he had * and to Job 32:2
I have not *.' Job 33:9
* by speaking of God that way. Job 33:12
friends, 'I *, but God let me go. Job 33:27
even though I have not *.' Job 34:6
'We have *, but we will stop'? Job 34:31
claim, 'I haven't *, but I'm no Job 35:2,3
and have not * by turning back from Ps 18:21
I *, and did this terrible thing. Ps 51:4
Both we and our fathers have * so Ps 106:6
It is the Lord they * against, Is 42:24
your ancestors * against me—all Is 43:27
You deliberately * before my very Is 65:12
because you say, "I haven't *!" Jer 2:35
our fathers have * from childhood Jer 3:25
For the people of Judah have * Jer 7:30
O Lord, we have * against you Jer 14:7
For these people have * against Jer 40:2,3
burned incense and * against the Jer 44:23
for they have * against the Lord, Jer 50:7
spare no arrows, for she has * Jer 50:14
For Jerusalem * so horribly; Lam 1:8
to him in heaven, for we have *; Lam 3:42
Our fathers * but died before the Lam 5:7
of yours you have * with, both Eze 16:37
You have not merely * as they Eze 16:47
And so she * with them—the Eze 23:7
and * even more than her sister. Eze 23:11
of Edom have * so greatly by Eze 25:12
with internal turmoil and you *. Eze 28:16
O Israel, you have * greatly, by Eze 44:6
for anyone who has * through error Eze 45:20
But we have * so much; Dan 9:5
Though we have * so much and are Dan 9:15
the more they * against me. Hos 4:7
let them perish, for they have * Hos 7:13
where Israel * will crumble. Hos 10:8
of Damascus have * again and again, Amo 1:3
The Lord says, "Gaza has * again Amo 1:6
of Tyre have * again and again and Amo 1:9
The Lord says, "Edom has * again Amo 1:11
of Ammon have * again and again, Amo 1:13
of Moab have * again and again, and Amo 2:1
of Judah have * again and again, Amo 2:4
hearts and * as their fathers did. Amo 2:4
of Israel have * again and again, Amo 2:6
me, for I have * against him; Mic 7:9
you have * against the Lord; Zep 1:17
those who have * against us. Mt 6:12
"I have *," he declared, "for Mt 27:4
forgiven those who * against us. Lk 11:4
"Father, I have * against both Lk 15:18
'Father, I have * against heaven Lk 15:21
But only he who never * may throw Jn 8:7
Yes, all have *; Rom 3:23
those who * in former times. Rom 3:25
When Adam *, sin entered the Rom 5:12
for all *. Rom 5:12
when some of them * with other 1Co 10:8
it up [punishing the man who * 2Co 7:11
who *, or his father 2Co 7:12
of you who have * became sinners 2Co 12:21
If he has really *, then he 1Ti 5:20
These same people who * and as a Heb 3:17
never once gave way to them and *. Heb 4:15
Follow in his steps: He never *, 1Pe 2:22
the angels who *, but threw them 2Pe 2:4
If we claim we have not *, we 1Jn 1:10
God a liar, for he says we have *. 1Jn 1:10
he has * that one fatal sin. 1Jn 5:16

SINNER
that though the * be my own son 1Sa 14:39
He was as great a * as his 1Ki 15:3
now you have declared I am a *. Job 19:3
for calling you a *, but my spirit Job 20:3
I am not a *—I repeat it again Job 27:6
is a *, or has proved that he is. Job 32:11,12
can convince the * of his sin.' Job 32:13
Don't treat me as a common * or Ps 26:9,10
I wouldn't admit what a * I was. Ps 32:3
But I was born a *, yes, from Ps 51:5
but when a * dies, his wealth is Pro 13:22
but if a * becomes wealthy, God Ecc 2:24-26
am a foul-mouthed *, a member of a Is 6:5
Slay the children of this *. Is 14:21
He was counted as a *, and he Is 53:12
*, should he be allowed to live? Eze 18:24
in the land as a * who had received Eze 23:10
mountain of God like a common *. Eze 28:16
of a * for you to have around." Lk 5:8
over one lost * who returns to God Lk 15:7
of God when one * repents." Lk 15:10
God, I am not a * like everyone Lk 18:11
'God, be merciful to me, a *.' Lk 18:13
I tell you, this *, not the Lk 18:14
of a notorious *," they grumbled. Lk 19:7
an ordinary * do such miracles?" Jn 9:16
condemn me as a * if my dishonesty Rom 3:7
* who is declared "not guilty" Rom 4:6
law and was a *, doomed to die. Rom 7:9
fact that he is a *, and his 1Co 14:24

SINNER'S
Even the * own mother shall Job 24:20
The * road is dark and gloomy. Pro 13:9

SINNERS
But here you are, a brood of * Num 32:14
Such * must be purged from Israel. Deu 17:12
[and destroyed many * Deu 33:9
destroy the *, the Amalekites, 1Sa 15:18
*, into the hands of the wicked. Job 16:11
Yes, that is what happens to *, Job 18:21
help even * by your pure hands." Job 22:30
Death consumes * as drought and Job 24:19
Rather, he punishes the *. Job 34:11
May all * be warned. Job 36:33
hang around with *, scoffing at the Ps 1:1
But for *, what a different Ps 1:4
Therefore proud * will not Ps 5:5
I hate the *' hangouts and Ps 26:5
your ways to other *, and Ps 51:13
These men are born *, lying from Ps 58:3
Let all * perish—all who refuse Ps 104:35
don't let me want to be with *, Ps 141:4
Curses chase *, while blessings Pro 13:21
* love to fight; Pro 17:19
her, but * don't evade her snares. Ecc 7:26
Because God does not punish * Ecc 8:11
(But all * shall utterly perish, Is 1:28
destroyed, and all the * with it. Is 13:9
* among my people shake with fear. Is 33:14
Holy City; for *—those who turn Is 52:1
many, and he pled with God for *. Is 53:12
You children of * and liars! Is 57:4
Yes, we know what * we are. Is 59:12
we are constant * and have been Is 64:5
100! Only * will die that young! Is 65:20
nation of *, the Lord God says." Eze 36:15
Gilead is a city of *, tracked Hos 6:8
them. But * trying it will fail. Hos 14:9
But all these * who say, 'God Amo 9:10
They will not be *, full of lies Zep 3:13
For I have come to urge *, not Mt 9:13
around with the worst sort of *!' Mt 11:19
other notorious * to be his dinner Mk 2:15
his eating with such notorious *. Lk 5:30
My purpose is to invite * to Lk 5:32
so wonderful? Even * do that much! Lk 6:33
a friend of tax gatherers and *." Lk 7:34f
"Do you think they were worse * Lk 13:2
Were they the worst * in Lk 13:4
other notorious * often came to Lk 15:1
poured out upon us undeserving *; Rom 1:5
are *, whether Jews or Gentiles. Rom 3:9
only to make us see that we are *. Rom 3:20
he can receive * in this same way, Rom 3:26

(SINNERS Con't)
For God declares * to be good in — Rom 4:4,5
for us * who had no use for him. — Rom 5:6
die for us while we were still *. — Rom 5:8
all this for us as *, how much more — Rom 5:9
Adam caused many to be * because — Rom 5:19
have sinned became * and don't even — 2Co 12:21
not mere Gentile *, and yet we — Gal 2:15
Rather, we are * if we start — Gal 2:18
about God's great kindness to *. — Col 1:6
they are for * who hate God, have — 1Ti 1:9
to identify as * all who are — 1Ti 1:10,11
the world to save *—and I was the — 1Ti 1:15
even the worst *, so that others — 1Ti 1:16
sin, undefiled by *, and to him has — Heb 7:26
Wash your hands, you *, and let — Jas 4:8
of all us guilty *, although he — 1Pe 3:18
giving more time for * to repent. — 2Pe 3:9
is a hell in which * are punished. — Jud 1:7
while being merciful to them as *. — Jud 1:23

SINNING
I held you back from * against me; — Gen 20:6
customs, thus * deeply against the — Deu 20:18
know why you are * against the God — Jos 22:16
the people were * against the Lord — 1Sa 14:33
God of Israel by * and leading the — 1Ki 15:30
for it resulted in all Israel *. — 2Ki 10:29
other gods, thus * against the Lord — 2Ki 17:7
their rebellion, * against the God — Ps 78:17
Yet even so the people kept on * — Ps 78:32
if they will only stop their *. — Ps 85:8
truth—he enjoys his * too much. — Pro 19:28
But they went right on *, doing — Is 57:17
your thoughts are only of *, and — Is 59:7
themselves out with all their *. — Jer 9:5
But if you stop your * and begin — Jer 26:13
* against me until this very hour. — Eze 2:3
and they keep on *, and refuse to — Eze 3:19
person turns to * and acts like any — Eze 18:24
good and begins * and dies in his — Eze 18:26
prostitution, * with the lustful — Eze 23:19,20
listen to me—stop *; — Dan 4:27
the same thing, * with harlots and — Hos 4:14
of new ways of * and continually — Rom 1:30
and Gentiles alike who keep on *. — Rom 2:9
the Jews for * because they have — Rom 2:12-15
people were * from the time of Adam — Rom 5:13
WELL THEN, SHALL we keep on * so — Rom 6:1
Should we keep on * when we don't — Rom 6:2,3
of wickedness, to be used for *; — Rom 6:13
laws to break would there be no *. — Rom 7:8
on *, soon all will be affected? — 1Co 5:6
and who are * in these ways. — 1Co 5:12
Get some sense and quit your *. — 1Co 15:34
had been * when I was there last; — 2Co 13:2
He is *, and he knows it. — Tit 3:11
come, try hard to live without *; — 2Pe 3:14
But those who keep on * are — 1Jn 3:4
to him, we won't be * either; — 1Jn 3:6
but as for those who keep on *, — 1Jn 3:6
But if you keep on *, it shows — 1Jn 3:8
make a practice of *, because now — 1Jn 3:9
so he can't keep on *, for this — 1Jn 3:9
If you see a Christian * in a way — 1Jn 5:16
a practice of *, for Christ, God's — 1Jn 5:18

SINS
God is punishing us for our *. — Gen 44:16
people for their *, the punishment — Ex 20:5
is the place of mercy for your *. — Ex 25:17
I will punish them for their *." — Ex 32:34
thousands by forgiving their *; — Ex 34:7
that a father's * be punished in — Ex 34:7
*, and accept us as your own." — Ex 34:9
it, as the penalty for his *. — Lev 1:4
If a priest * unintentionally, — Lev 4:3
nation of Israel * without — Lev 4:13
"If one of the leaders * without — Lev 4:22
the common people * and doesn't — Lev 4:27
"If anyone * by unintentionally — Lev 5:15
"If anyone * against me by — Lev 6:2
is defiled by the * of the people — Lev 16:16
all the * of the people of Israel. — Lev 16:21
He shall lay all their * upon the — Lev 16:21
carry all the * of the people into — Lev 16:22
Lord's eyes from all of your *. — Lev 16:29,30
each year, because of their *." — Lev 16:34
Rebuke anyone who *; — Lev 19:17
times more severely for your *. — Lev 26:18
more plagues because of your *. — Lev 26:21
greater punishment for your *. — Lev 26:28
because of their *, the same sins — Lev 26:39
same * as those of their fathers. — Lev 26:39
confess their * and their fathers' — Lev 26:40,41
* of treachery against me. — Lev 26:40,41
them for their *, then I will — Lev 26:40,41
fierce anger against their *." — Num 1:53
by forgiving our * and showing — Num 14:17,18
you, pardon the * of this people — Num 14:19
day, bearing the burden of your *. — Num 14:34,35
all the people when one man *?" — Num 16:22
* [and be destroyed with them — Num 16:26
of a father's * upon even the third — Deu 5:9,10
to death for the * of their sons — Deu 24:16
sons for the * of their fathers; — Deu 24:16
their * in worshiping other gods. — Deu 31:18
not forgive your rebellion and *. — Jos 24:19
So I have vowed that the * of — 1Sa 3:14
as a sign of sorrow for their *. — 1Sa 7:6
other * by asking for a king." — 1Sa 12:19
If he *, I will use other nations — 2Sa 7:14
descendants for their *. — 1Ki 16:4-7
the * of Baasha and his son Elah; — 1Ki 16:13
Have you come here to punish my * — 1Ki 17:18
whose * had caused the famine. — 1Ki 21:9f
children for the * of their — 2Ki 14:6
pay the penalty for his own *. — 2Ki 14:6
of the many * of Manasseh, for he — 2Ki 24:3,4
and forgive their * and give them — 2Ch 6:25
because of our *, and then we pray — 2Ch 6:26
and turn from our * because you — 2Ch 6:26
and forgive the * of your people, — 2Ch 6:27
their * and heal their land. — 2Ch 7:14
confessed their * and exclaimed, — 2Ch 12:6
for the children's *, nor the — 2Ch 25:4
the children for the father's *. — 2Ch 25:4
everyone must pay for his own *. — 2Ch 25:4
What about your own * against the — 2Ch 28:10
confessed their * to the Lord God — 2Ch 30:22
account of his * and errors, — 2Ch 33:19
to you, for our * are piled higher — Ez 9:6
* and those of their ancestors. — Neh 9:3
*, but still they wouldn't listen. — Neh 9:30
to conquer us because of our *. — Neh 9:37
this: Go to God and confess your * — Job 5:8
must hound me for * you know full — Job 10:4-7
all the faults and * of mankind; — Job 11:11
get rid of your * and leave all — Job 11:13,14
No reverence for him? Your * are — Job 15:4,5
a proof, they say, of my *. — Job 16:8
The heavens will reveal his *, — Job 20:27
the man who *, not his children! — Job 21:19
to disaster because of their *. — Job 21:28
wickedness! Your * are endless! — Job 22:5
tried to hide my *, fearing the — Job 31:33
and blasphemy to your other *." — Job 34:37
Your * may hurt another man, or — Job 35:8
high above them, judging their *. — Ps 7:7,8
But how can I ever know what * — Ps 19:12
Overlook my youthful *, O Lord! — Ps 25:6,7
But Lord, my *! — Ps 25:11
forgive my *. — Ps 25:18
My * have sapped my strength; — Ps 31:9,10
What joys when * are covered — Ps 32:1
confessed their * and God has — Ps 32:1
admitted all my * to you and — Ps 32:5
should confess his * to God when he — Ps 32:6
who are humbly sorry for their *. — Ps 34:18
my health is broken beneath my *. — Ps 38:3,4
Because of my * I am bent and — Ps 38:5,6
I confess my *; — Ps 38:18
overpowered by my *, for even fools — Ps 39:8
When you punish a man for his *, — Ps 39:11
News that you forgive men's *. — Ps 40:9
Meanwhile my *, too many to — Ps 40:12
me, for I have confessed my *." — Ps 41:4
Don't keep looking at my *—erase — Ps 51:9
Israel for my *—help your people — Ps 51:18
Though * fill our hearts, you — Ps 65:3
if I had not confessed my *. — Ps 66:18
I am, and you know all my *. — Ps 69:5
humiliation and sorrow for my *! — Ps 69:11
Pile their * high and do not — Ps 69:27
* and didn't destroy them all. — Ps 78:38
hold us guilty for our former *! — Ps 79:8
Oh, save us and forgive our *. — Ps 79:9
of Israel, and forgiven the * of — Ps 85:2
You spread out our * before — Ps 90:8
you—our secret *—and see them all. — Ps 90:8
God has made the * of evil men — Ps 94:23
and forgave their *, yet punished — Ps 99:8
He forgives all my *. — Ps 103:3
for all our *, for his mercy — Ps 103:10
He has removed our * as far away — Ps 103:12
* had caused the plague to start. — Ps 106:30
Count his prayers as *. — Ps 109:7
Punish the * of his father and — Ps 109:14
Lord, if you keep in mind our * — Ps 130:3,4
for they thoroughly enjoy their *. — Pro 2:14
wicked man is doomed by his own *; — Pro 5:22
fall beneath their load of *. — Pro 11:5
the wicked are crushed by their *. — Pro 14:32
faultless despite their many *. — Pro 30:11,12
who is always good and never *. — Ecc 7:20
But though a man * a hundred — Ecc 8:12
you have no sorrow for your *? — Is 1:12,13
the stain of your *, I can take it — Is 1:18
Woe to those who drag their * — Is 5:18
lips. Your * are all forgiven." — Is 6:7
in sorrow for your *, and to wear — Is 22:12
The land suffers for the * of — Is 24:4,5
the * of the earth are very great. — Is 24:20
people of the earth for their *. — Is 26:21
her *, to rid her of all her idol — Is 27:9
thus piling up your *. — Is 30:1
them their * and bless them. — Is 33:24
you have forgiven all my *. — Is 38:17
days are gone. Her * are pardoned, — Is 40:2
me only with *, and wearied me with — Is 43:24
blots away your * for my own sake — Is 43:25
for we must talk about your *. — Is 43:26
I've blotted out your *; — Is 44:22
sentence of my court upon your *. — Is 47:8
then to cleanse away your *. — Is 47:11
you sold yourselves for your *. — Is 50:1
from God, for his own *! — Is 53:4
was wounded and bruised for our *. — Is 53:5
guilt and * of every one of us! — Is 53:6
it was their * that he was dying — Is 53:8
for he shall bear all their *. — Is 53:11
and he bore the * of many, and he — Is 53:12
to mourn and to confess their *. — Is 57:18
tell my people of their *! — Is 58:1
But the trouble is that your * — Is 59:2
For your * keep piling up before — Is 59:12
And our *, like the wind, sweep — Is 64:6
us and turned us over to our *. — Is 64:7
Lord, nor forever remember our *. — Is 64:9
only for their own * but for those — Is 65:7
delighting in their *, are cursed. — Is 66:3
Face the awful * that you have — Jer 2:23
and I will heal you from your *. — Jer 3:22
to a crisp because of all your *. — Jer 4:4
they refuse to turn from their *. — Jer 5:3
For their * are very many; — Jer 5:6
to drink because of all our *. — Jer 8:14
They have returned to the * of — Jer 11:10
of the grossness of your *; — Jer 13:22
you have done, and punish your *. — Jer 14:10
punishment upon them for their *. — Jer 14:16
So, because of all your * against — Jer 15:12,13
burst with indignation at their *. — Jer 15:17,18
for all your * because you have — Jer 16:18
that you must pay for all your *. — Jer 17:2,3
penalty in full for all their *. — Jer 23:12
of turning them back from their *. — Jer 23:14
and his people for their *; — Jer 25:12
for your * are so many, your — Jer 30:14
pay for their fathers' *." — Jer 31:29
die for his own *—the person eating — Jer 31:30
I will forgive and forget their *. — Jer 31:34
them away forever for their *! — Jer 31:37
suffer for their fathers' *; — Jer 32:18
The * of Israel and Judah—the — Jer 32:32
and Judah—the * of the people, of — Jer 32:32
* against me, and pardon them. — Jer 33:8
bold and returned to their *. — Jer 34:11f
his officials because of their *. — Jer 36:31
Have you forgotten the * of your — Jer 44:9
fathers, and the * of the kings and — Jer 44:9
and your own *, and the sins of — Jer 44:9
own sins, and the * of your wives — Jer 44:9
vengeance on all of Babylon's *. — Jer 51:6
Jerusalem for all her many *; — Lam 1:5
He wove my * into ropes to hitch — Lam 1:14
Look also on their *, O Lord, and — Lam 1:22
slavery by pointing out your *. — Lam 2:14
complain when punished for our *? — Lam 3:39
it because of the * of her prophets — Lam 4:13
Israel's exile for her * will — Lam 4:22
Woe upon us for our *. — Lam 5:16
in their *, but I will punish you. — Eze 3:18
will die in their *, but you are — Eze 3:19
Because of the terrible * you — Eze 5:9
mountains, each weeping for his *. — Eze 7:16
Do you see what great * the — Eze 8:6
show you greater * than these!" — Eze 8:6
show you greater * than these!" — Eze 8:13
these terrible *, leading the whole — Eze 8:17
all the * they see around them." — Eze 9:4
But he said to me, "The * of the — Eze 9:9
for their *," the Lord God says. — Eze 11:21
despair because of all their *. — Eze 12:19
though they continue in their *. — Eze 13:22
punished for their *, so that the — Eze 14:10
Jerusalem about her loathsome *. — Eze 16:2
I see your filthy *, your adultery — Eze 16:36
for all of your *, says the Lord. — Eze 16:43
Your sister Sodom's * were pride — Eze 16:49
has not committed half your *. — Eze 16:51
For your * are so awful that in — Eze 16:52
for all your *, says the Lord. — Eze 16:58
are punished for their fathers' *? — Eze 18:2
a man's own * that he will die. — Eze 18:4
not die because of his father's *; — Eze 18:17
die for his own * because he is — Eze 18:18
the son pay for his father's *?' — Eze 18:19
The one who * is the one who — Eze 18:20
*, nor the father for his son's. — Eze 18:20
away from all his * and begins to — Eze 18:21
All his past * will be — Eze 18:22
and he shall die for his *. — Eze 18:24
and dies in his *, he dies for the — Eze 18:26
from his * and live a good life. — Eze 18:28

SINS Con't)
Oh, turn from your * while there Eze 18:30
tell them of all the * of this Eze 20:4
back at all your * and loathe Eze 20:43
for your * are open and unashamed. Eze 21:24
the full penalty for all your *." Eze 22:31
another for your *, and mourn Eze 24:23
They will die in their *, but I Eze 33:6
will die in his *, but I will hold Eze 33:8
saying: 'Our * are heavy upon us; Eze 33:10
and the * of an evil man will not Eze 33:12
he repents and turns from his *. Eze 33:12
But if he *, expecting his past Eze 33:13
I will destroy him for his *. Eze 33:13
he turns from his * and does what Eze 33:14
None of his past * shall be Eze 33:16
because of their *, then they shall Eze 33:29
had punished them for all their *. Eze 35:4,5
I will cleanse away your *. Eze 36:29
remember your past * and loathe Eze 36:31
you from your *, I will bring you Eze 36:33
and their other *, for I will save Eze 37:23
to the vileness of their *. Eze 39:24
will be ashamed of all their *. Eze 43:10
in addition to all your other *. Eze 44:7
for all the * they have committed. Eze 44:13
my * and those of my people. Dan 9:4
with shame because of all our *. Dan 9:8
from our * and doing right. Dan 9:13
your city lies in ruins for our *. Dan 9:16
merciful despite our grievous *. Dan 9:18
my sin and the * of my people, and Dan 9:20
The priests rejoice in the * of Hos 4:8
Israel, but her * were far too Hos 7:1
of their * and punish them; Hos 8:13
punish you for your heaped-up *. Hos 10:10
and raised a thriving crop of *. Hos 10:13
But the * of Gilgal flourish Hos 12:11
him to death as payment for his *. Hos 12:14
Ephraim's * are harvested and Hos 13:12
you have been crushed by your *. Hos 14:1
say, "O Lord, take away our *; Hos 14:2
you the more for all your *. Amo 3:2
together with your * between us? Amo 3:3
Israel for her *, I will also Amo 3:14
Keep disobeying—your * are Amo 4:4
For many and great are your *. Amo 5:12
Now your * will be exposed for Ob 1:10
Because of the * of Israel and Mic 1:5
sins of Israel and Judah. What *? Mic 1:5
punishment on Israel for her *. Mic 3:8
Then would he forgive your *? Mic 6:7
For your * are very great—is Mic 6:10
hearts miserable for all your *. Mic 6:13
who pardons the * of the survivors Mic 7:18
You will tread our * beneath your Mic 7:19
and correct us for our awful *. Hab 1:12
contented in their *, indifferent Zep 1:12
taken away your *, and now I am Zec 3:4
I will remove the * of this land Zec 3:9
* behind, and coming back to me? Zec 7:5
and yet forgiving them their *!" Zec 8:8
all their * and uncleanness." Zec 13:1
and to sorrow and mourn for our *? Mal 3:14,15
will save his people from their *. Mt 1:21
was, "Turn from your *. Mt 3:2
confessed their *, he baptized them Mt 3:6
those who repent of their *; Mt 3:11
and forgive us our *, just as we Mt 6:12
For I have forgiven your *!" Mt 9:2
authority on earth to forgive *. Mt 9:5,6
to God from your * and become as Mt 18:3
"If a brother * against you, go Mt 18:15
a brother who * against me? Mt 18:21
It is poured out to forgive the * Mt 26:28
for the forgiveness of *." Mk 1:4f
confessed their * he baptized them Mk 1:5
Turn from your * and act on this Mk 1:15
man, "Son, your * are forgiven!" Mk 2:5
For only God can forgive *." Mk 2:7
authority on earth to forgive *. Mk 2:9,10,11
God, or be forgiven for their *.' Mk 4:11,12
will forgive you your * too." Mk 11:25
through forgiveness of their *. Lk 1:77
their *, in order to be forgiven. Lk 3:3
repentance for remission of *." Lk 3:3f
that we have abandoned our *?" Lk 3:12
friend, your * are forgiven!" Lk 5:20
Who but God can forgive *?" Lk 5:21
authority on earth to forgive *. Lk 5:23,24
to turn from their *, not to spend Lk 5:32
Therefore her *—and they are Lk 7:47
And he said to her, "Your * are Lk 7:48
he is, going around forgiving *?" Lk 7:49
And forgive our *—for we have Lk 11:4
then they will turn from their *.' Lk 16:30
"Rebuke your brother if he *, and Lk 17:2,3
of * for all who turn to me. Lk 24:47
for fear their * would be exposed Jn 3:20
be damned for his *, but has Jn 5:24
and to judge the * of all mankind Jn 5:27
search for me, and die in your *. Jn 8:21
said that you will die in your *; Jn 8:24
of God, you will die in your *." Jn 8:24
Was it a result of his own * or Jn 9:2
If you forgive anyone's *, they Jn 20:23
for the forgiveness of your *; Act 2:38
cleanse away your * and send you Act 3:19
by turning you back from your *." Act 3:26
and for their * to be forgiven. Act 5:31
* forgiven through his name." Act 10:43
there is forgiveness for your *! Act 13:38
you how to have your * forgiven." Act 16:17
cleansed from your *, calling on Act 22:16
for their * and God's inheritance Act 26:18
everywhere whose * are cleansed Act 26:18
must forsake their * and turn to Act 26:20
God is good, our * serve a good Rom 3:5
us when our * are helping him?" Rom 3:5
Jesus Christ to take away our *. Rom 3:21,22
kindness freely takes away our *. Rom 3:24
punishment for our * and to end all Rom 3:25
would come and take away those *. Rom 3:25
because Jesus took away their *. Rom 3:26
in Jesus who took away their *. Rom 3:26
* and declared him "not guilty." Rom 4:3
"are those whose * are forgiven Rom 4:7
for anyone whose * are no longer Rom 4:8
* and declared him "not guilty." Rom 4:22
He died for our * and rose again Rom 4:25
our *—making us friends of God. Rom 5:11
died it was not for their own * Rom 5:14
* and gives glorious life instead. Rom 5:16
himself as a sacrifice for our *. Rom 8:3
their *, just as I promised." Rom 11:27
do it. He * if he does, for he Rom 14:23
But did I, Paul, die for your *? 1Co 1:13
indulges in sexual *, or is greedy, 1Co 5:11
that but now your * are washed 1Co 6:11
here permitting * such as have just 1Co 6:12f
Corinth who were excusing their *. 1Co 6:12f
died for our * just as the 1Co 15:3
under condemnation for your *; 1Co 15:17
and the law, which reveals our *, 1Co 15:55,56
*, then the veil is taken away. 2Co 3:16
counting men's * against them but 2Co 5:19
Christ and poured into him our *. 2Co 5:21
He died for our * just as God Gal 1:4
Jesus Christ to take away our *. Gal 2:16
our * and make us right with God. Gal 5:5
took away all our * through the Eph 1:7
curse, doomed forever for your *. Eph 2:1
*, he gave us back our lives again Eph 2:5
a sacrifice to take away your *. Eph 5:2
to excuse these *, for the terrible Eph 5:6
blood and forgave us all our *. Col 1:14
You were dead in *, and your Col 2:13
forgave all your *, and blotted Col 2:13
He took this list of * and Col 2:14
where your * were all taken away. Col 2:15
and so their * continue to grow. 1Th 2:16
the Truth, and enjoying their *. 2Th 2:12
you may overlook his * and it 1Ti 5:22
against our *, so that he could Tit 2:14
washing away our * and giving us Tit 3:5
dealing with the * of the people. Heb 2:17
to cover the * of the people and Heb 5:1
of the people and his own * too. Heb 5:1
paid for their * with his blood. Heb 7:25
* and then the sins of the people; Heb 7:27
sins and then the * of the people; Heb 7:27
I will remember their * no more." Heb 8:12
own mistakes and *, and the Heb 9:7
mistakes and * of all the people. Heb 9:7
God to die for our *—he being Heb 9:14
the penalty of the * they had Heb 9:15
there is no forgiveness of *. Heb 9:22
offering for the * of many people; Heb 9:28
but not to deal again with our *. Heb 9:28
and goats really to take away *. Heb 10:4
covered over the *, taking them out Heb 10:4f
which forever took those * away. Heb 10:4f
that could never take away our *. Heb 10:11
to God for our * as one sacrifice Heb 10:12
their * and lawless deeds." Heb 10:17
Now, when * have once been Heb 10:18
If anyone * deliberately by Heb 10:26
especially those * that wrap Heb 12:1
where his blood washed our * away. Heb 13:12
the forgiveness of his many *. Jas 5:20
the load of our * in his own body 1Pe 2:24
He died once for the * of all us 1Pe 3:18
of idols, and other terrible *. 1Pe 4:3
They proudly boast about their * 2Pe 2:18
But if we confess our * to him, 1Jn 1:9
Literally, "if we confess our * 1Jn 1:9f
Christ died to wash away our *. 1Jn 1:9
wrath against our * upon himself, 1Jn 2:2
for our *, and not only ours but 1Jn 2:2
because your * have been forgiven 1Jn 2:12
take away our *, and that there is 1Jn 3:5
satisfy God's anger against our *. 1Jn 4:10
talking about these ordinary *; 1Jn 5:17
aren't pulled along into their *. Jud 1:23
us free from our * by pouring out Rev 1:5
and so all of "Babylon's" * Rev 16:19
do not take part in her *, or you Rev 18:4
For her * are piled as high as Rev 18:5

SIP
utmost care and * their tiny Eze 12:19

SIPHMOTH
Jattir, Aroer, *, Eshtemoa, Racal, 1Sa 30:27-31

SIPPAI
sons of the giant, *, and so the 1Ch 20:4

SIPPING
* it slowly, lest it disappear. Job 20:13

SIR
of the town: "*," he said to Gen 23:11
"Certainly, *," she said, and Gen 24:18
me, 'Certainly, *, and I will water Gen 24:46
all brothers and honest men, *! Gen 42:11
"*," they said, "there are Gen 42:13
said to him, "O *, after our first Gen 43:20
us for our sins. *, we have all Gen 44:16
and said, "O *, let me say just Gen 44:18
"*, you asked us if we had a Gen 44:19
But we said to you, '*, the lad Gen 44:22
And now, *, if I go back to my Gen 44:30
to the grave. *, I pledged my Gen 44:32
Please *, let me stay here as a Gen 44:33
"*," they told him, "the Ex 1:19
protested, "*, make them stop!" Num 11:28
*, do not punish us for this sin; Num 12:11
"But, *," protested the Israeli Num 20:19
to him, "Come into my tent, *. Ju 4:18
But Gideon replied, "*, how can Ju 6:15
"Oh, thank you, *," she Ru 2:13
"It's I, *—Ruth," she replied. Ru 3:9
"Oh, no, *!" 1Sa 1:15,16
"Oh, thank you, *!" 1Sa 1:18
"*, do you remember me?" 1Sa 1:26
"Pardon me, *," Saul replied. 1Sa 9:21
"But *," Ahimelech replied, 1Sa 22:14
Come on down, *, and we will 1Sa 23:20
you sent. *, since the Lord has 1Sa 25:26
And David replied, "Yes, *, it 1Sa 26:17,18
"Here is your spear, *," David 1Sa 26:22
was, she said, "*, I obeyed your 1Sa 28:21
"Yes, *, I am," he replied. 2Sa 9:2
replied, "*, I will do all that 2Sa 9:10,11
"Thank you, thank you, *," Ziba 2Sa 16:4
and exclaimed, "Oh, thank you, * 1Ki 1:31
"*," one of them began, "we 1Ki 3:17,18
very much, cried out, "Oh, no, *! 1Ki 3:26
"Oh, *," Obadiah protested, 1Ki 18:9
*, if I do that, I'm dead!" 1Ki 18:14
"*," his officers said to him, 1Ki 20:31
out to him, "*, I was in the 1Ki 20:39
"*," they said, "just say the 2Ki 2:16
*, there's poison in this stew!" 2Ki 4:40
"Please, *, come with us," 2Ki 6:3
"Oh, *," he cried, "it was 2Ki 6:5
"It's not us, *," one of the 2Ki 6:12
"Oh, *, shall I kill them? 2Ki 6:21
"Oh, *!" 2Ki 8:5
"What's the matter, *?" 2Ki 8:12
"I have a message for you, *," 2Ki 9:5
from the Lord: "*, do not hire 2Ch 25:7
"*: Greetings from your loyal Ez 4:11
frightened, but I replied, "*, Neh 2:3
aides, said, "*, Haman has just Est 7:9
last he shouted, "*, day after day Is 21:8,9
said: "*, this fellow must die. Jer 38:4
to the king, "*, tell us the dream Dan 2:4
please understand, *, that even Dan 3:18
God, nor, *, have I wronged you." Dan 6:22
from heaven, "*, I am terrified by Dan 10:16
*, for you have strengthened me." Dan 10:19
"*, how will this all come out?" Dan 12:8
and I asked him, "*, what are all Zec 1:9
What is it, *?" Zec 4:4
"No, *," I said, "I don't." Zec 4:5
"No, *," I said. Zec 4:13
"And what are these, *?" Zec 6:4
him, worshiping. "*," the leper Mt 8:2
Then the officer said, "*, I am Mt 8:8,9
disciples said, "*, when my father Mt 8:21
and told him, "*, the field where Mt 13:27
Then Peter called to him: "*, if Mt 14:28
and pled again, "*, help me!" Mt 15:25
"Heaven forbid, *," he said. Mt 16:22
Peter blurted out, "*, it's Mt 17:4
Jesus and said, "*, have mercy on Mt 17:15
him and asked, "*, how often Mt 18:21
and said, 'Oh, *, be patient with Mt 18:26
began shouting, "*, King David's Mt 20:30
"*," they said, "we want to Mt 20:32,33
and he said, 'Yes, *, I will.' Mt 21:30
to ask him this question: "*, we Mt 22:16
him and asked, "*, Moses said Mt 22:24
spoke up: "*, which is the most Mt 22:36
'*, open the door for us!' Mt 25:11
with the report, '*, you gave me Mt 25:22

(SIR Con't)
came and said, '*, I knew you were Mt 25:24,25
ones will reply, '*, when did we Mt 25:37
and told him, "*, that liar once Mt 27:63
She replied, "That's true, *, Mk 7:28
replied, "*, you have spoken a Mk 12:32
"*," Simon replied, "we worked Lk 5:5
and said, "Oh, *, please leave Lk 5:8
"*," he said, "if you only Lk 5:12
friends to say, "*, don't Lk 7:6,7,8
She came to Jesus and said, "*, Lk 10:40
"*," said an expert in Lk 11:45
from the crowd, "*, please tell my Lk 12:13
"Jesus, *, have mercy on us!" Lk 17:13
question: "Good *, what shall I do Lk 18:18
Lord and said, "*, from now on I Lk 19:8
" 'But, *,' they said, 'he has Lk 19:25
the crowd said, "*, rebuke your Lk 19:39
They said to Jesus, "*, we know Lk 20:21
"Well said, *!" Lk 20:39
"No *, I am not!" Lk 22:58
"*," they replied, "where do Jn 1:38
Nathanael replied, "*, you are Jn 1:49
with Jesus. "*," he said, "we Jn 3:1
"Please, *," the woman said, Jn 4:15
"*," the woman said, "you must Jn 4:19
The official pled, "*, please Jn 4:49
said, "*, how did you get here?" Jn 6:25
"*," they said, "give us that Jn 6:34
"No, *," she said. Jn 8:11
The man answered, "Who is he, *, Jn 9:36
telling him, "*, your good friend Jn 11:3
Martha said to Jesus, "*, if you Jn 11:21
feet, saying, "*, if you had been Jn 11:32
"*, we want to meet Jesus." Jn 12:21
Philip said, "*, show us the Jn 14:8
said to him, "*, why are you going Jn 14:22
the gardener. "*," she said, "if Jn 20:15
"Who is speaking, *?" Act 9:5
"What do you want, *?" Act 10:4
" 'Who is it speaking to me, *?' Act 22:8
Paul began: "I know, *, that you Act 24:10
day about noon, *, a light from Act 26:13
" 'Who are you, *?' Act 26:15
"No, *," I replied. Rev 7:14

SIRAH
They found him at the well of * 2Sa 3:26

SIRION
Mount Hermon '*,' while the Deu 3:9
valley to Mount *, or Mount Hermon, Deu 4:48
shakes Mount Lebanon and Mount *. Ps 29:5,6

SIRS
"*," he said, "please don't go Gen 18:3,4
"*," he said, "come to my home Gen 19:2
"Oh no, *, please," Lot begged, Gen 19:18,19,20
"*, what must I do to be saved?" Act 16:30
"*," he said, "I believe there Act 27:10

SISERA
of his army was *, who lived in Ju 4:2,3
of conquering * will go to a woman Ju 4:9
When General * was told that Ju 4:12
He has already delivered * into Ju 4:14
charioteers, and * leaped from his Ju 4:15
Meanwhile, * had escaped to the Ju 4:17
Jael went out to meet * and said Ju 4:18
When Barak came by looking for *, Ju 4:22
the tent and found * lying there Ju 4:22
Fought *. Ju 5:20
The mother of * watched through Ju 5:28
And * will get gorgeous robes, Ju 5:30
Perish as * did, Ju 5:31
be conquered by *, the general of 1Sa 12:9
Barkos, *, Temah, Neziah, Hatipha. Ez 2:43-54
Barkos, *, Temah, Neh 7:46-56
or as you did to * and Jabin at the Ps 83:9

SISERA'S
chariots, under General * command. Ju 4:7
until all of * army was destroyed; Ju 4:16
And pierced * temples, Ju 5:26

SISMAI
Ele-asah's son was *; 1Ch 2:40

SISMAI'S
Ele-asah's son was Sismai; * son 1Ch 2:40

SISTER
tell everyone that she was his *! Gen 12:11,12,13
But if you say you are my *, Gen 12:11,12,13
marry her, saying she was your *? Gen 12:19
girl said to her *, "There isn't a Gen 19:31
to her younger *, "I slept with my Gen 19:34
he remarked that Sarah was his *! Gen 20:2
He told me, 'She is my *,' and Gen 20:5
And besides, she is my *—or at Gen 20:11,12
we come, that you are my *.' Gen 20:13
they parted:"Our *,May you Gen 24:60
from Paddam-aram, * of Laban. Gen 25:20
Rebekah, he said, "She is my *!" Gen 26:7
Why did you say she is your *?" Gen 26:9
was Mahalath, the * of Nebaioth, Gen 28:9
older, and her younger *, Rachel. Gen 29:16
her *," Laban replied smoothly. Gen 29:26
barren, became envious of her *. Gen 30:1
with my * and I am winning!" Gen 30:8
what Shechem had done to their *. Gen 34:13
their * had been dishonored there. Gen 34:27
"Should he treat our * like a Gen 34:31
of Ishmael—the * of Nebaioth). Gen 36:2,3
(Lotan had a *, Timna. Gen 36:22
Beriah, and a *, Serah. Gen 46:16,17
The baby's * watched from a Ex 2:4
Then the baby's * approached the Ex 2:7
married Jochebed, his father's *; Ex 6:20
of Amminadab and * of Nahshon. Ex 6:23
Then Miriam the prophetess, the * Ex 15:20
wives, nor his * or half-sister, Lev 18:9
nor your aunt—your father's * Lev 18:12
nor your aunt—your mother's * Lev 18:13
it is all right to marry her *. Lev 18:18
with his *, whether the daughter of Lev 20:17
aunt—whether the * of his mother or Lev 20:19
* for whom he has special Lev 21:2,3
his father, mother, brother, or *; Num 6:6,7
with his *, whether she be a full Deu 27:22
she be a full * or a half-sister.' Deu 27:22
But look, her * is prettier than Ju 15:2
had a beautiful * named Tamar. 2Sa 13:1
in love with Tamar, my half *." 2Sa 13:4
favor—that his * Tamar be permitted 2Sa 13:6
of what he had done to his *. 2Sa 13:21-24
the * of Joab's mother Zeruiah. 2Sa 17:25
a wife—the * of Queen Tahpenes. 1Ki 11:19
who was a * of King Ahaziah (for 2Ki 11:2,3
Hodiah's wife was the * of Naham. 1Ch 4:19
Machir's * was Maacah. 1Ch 7:15
Hammolecheth, Machir's *, bore 1Ch 7:18
Serah (their *). 1Ch 7:30
Shua (their *). 1Ch 7:32
who was King Ahaziah's * 2Ch 22:11
and the worm my mother and my *. Job 17:13,14
The Girl: "We have a little * Sol 8:8
And her faithless * Judah saw the Jer 3:7
"Your older * is Samaria, living Eze 16:46
your younger * is Sodom and her Eze 16:46
Your * Sodom's sins were pride Eze 16:49
a half *—this is common. Eze 22:11
named Oholah; her * was Oholibah. Eze 23:4,5
happened to her * she went right Eze 23:11
and sinned even more than her *. Eze 23:11
right along behind her older *. Eze 23:13
as I despised her *, because she Eze 23:18
just as your * Samaria did. Eze 23:33
child, brother or unmarried *. Eze 44:25
Laodice, was the * of Ptolemy III, Dan 11:7f
RENAME your brother and *. Hos 1:11
name your * Ruhamah ("Pitied"), Hos 1:11
is my brother, * and mother!" Mt 12:50
and my *, and my mother." Mk 3:35
her home. Her * Mary sat on the Lk 10:39
to you that my * just sits here Lk 10:40
Mary and her * Martha, was sick. Jn 11:1
But Martha, the dead man's *, Jn 11:39
She was his *. Act 25:13f
Receive her as your * in the Rom 16:1
Nereus and his *, and to Olympas, Rom 16:15
and to Apphia our *, and to Phm 1:1
read: "Your * church here in 1Pe 5:13f
—she is your * in the Lord—sends 1Pe 5:13
*—another choice child of God. 2Jn 1:13

SISTER-IN-LAW
to her, "your * has gone back to Ru 1:15

SISTER'S
bracelets on his * wrists, and Gen 24:29,30
You have followed in your * Eze 23:31
Seleucids to avenge his * murder. Dan 11:7f

SISTERS
You shall not marry two *, for Lev 18:18
and *, and all their families. Jos 2:12,13
* to his home for a celebration. Job 1:4
Then all of his brothers, *, and Job 42:11
And you are exactly like your *, Eze 16:45
idols far more than your * have; Eze 16:51
with you, your * seem innocent! Eze 16:52
"Yes, your *, Sodom and Samaria, Eze 16:55
when I take your *, Samaria and Eze 16:61
"Son of dust, there were two * Eze 23:2,3
And his *—they all live here. Mt 13:56
brothers, *, father, mother, wife, Mt 19:29
And his * live right here among Mk 6:2,3
brothers, *, mother, father, Mk 10:29
homes, brothers, *, mothers, Mk 10:30
brothers, or *—yes, more than his Lk 14:26
So the two * sent a message to Jn 11:3
the girls as your *, thinking only 1Ti 5:2
brothers and * in the Lord—by how 1Jn 5:2

SIT
you wanted. * up and eat it, so Gen 27:19
with the venison. * up and eat it Gen 27:31
He told each of them where to *, Gen 43:33
a stone for him to * on, and they Ex 17:12
"You mean you want to * here Num 32:6
And * on rich carpets, Ju 5:10
Why did you * at home among the Ju 5:16
And why did Asher * unmoved Ju 5:17
and asked them to * as witnesses. Ru 4:2
* down to eat until he arrives." 1Sa 16:10,11
king and would * upon your throne? 1Ki 1:13
king and would * upon your throne. 1Ki 1:17
selected to * upon your throne? 1Ki 1:24
king and shall * upon my throne, 1Ki 1:30
one of my sons to * upon my throne 1Ki 1:48
always * upon this throne." 1Ki 2:45
* upon the throne of Israel. 1Ki 8:25
"Why * here until we die?" 2Ki 7:3
Here I * in sackcloth; Job 16:15
"You * there baffled, with no Job 32:15
Gather all peoples before you; * Ps 7:7,8
Literally, "You * on the throne, Ps 9:4f
Don't * back, unmindful of my Ps 39:12
They shall * on thrones around Ps 45:16
O GOD, DON'T * idly by, silent and Ps 83:1
Who are these who * in darkness, Ps 107:10
For even princes * and talk Ps 119:23
There they * around the dinner Ps 128:3
* on my throne and succeed me. Ps 132:11
You know when I * or stand. Ps 139:2
desire to * beside my beloved in Sol 6:12f
the women, ravaged, shall * Is 3:25,26
Literally, "I will * upon the Is 14:13f
* in prison darkness and despair. Is 42:7
BABYLON, THE unconquered, come * Is 47:1
* in darkness and silence, O Is 47:5
Theirs is no fire to * beside to Is 47:14
You * like a prostitute beside Jer 3:2
for a client! You * alone like a Jer 3:2
Should I * back and act as Jer 5:29
clothes and * in ashes and weep Jer 6:26
your thrones and * in the dust, for Jer 13:18
I * alone beneath the hand of God. Jer 15:17,18
more give kings to * on David's Jer 22:4
shall ever * upon the throne of Jer 22:30
Judah: He shall have no one to * Jer 36:30
Come down from your glory and * Jer 48:18
The elders of Jerusalem * upon Lam 2:10
it causes him to * apart in silence Lam 3:28
The old men * no longer in the Lam 5:14
garments and * on the ground Eze 26:16
and * before you listening. Eze 33:31
is the prince—may * inside the Eze 44:3
for there I will * to pronounce Joe 3:12
When I * in darkness, the Lord Mic 7:8
your sons will never * upon your Nah 1:14
punish those who * contented in Zep 1:12
of silver he will * and closely Mal 3:3
over the world and * down in the Mt 8:11
Then he told the people to * down Mt 14:19
of the people to * down on the Mt 15:35
shall * upon my glorious throne Mt 19:28
shall certainly * on twelve thrones Mt 19:28
let my two sons * on two thrones Mt 20:21
to say who will * on the thrones Mt 20:23
'God said to my Lord, * at my Mt 22:44
Literally, "* on Moses' seat." Mt 23:2f
And how they love to * at the Mt 23:6
I shall * upon my throne of glory. Mt 25:31
and told them to * down and wait Mt 26:36
and helped her to * up, the fever Mk 1:31
Then Jesus told the crowd to * Mk 6:39,40
So he told the crowd to * down Mk 8:6
"We want to * on the thrones Mk 10:37
said to my Lord, * at my right hand Mk 12:36
They love to * in the best seats Mk 12:39
"* here, while I go and pray." Mk 14:32
light to those who * in darkness Lk 1:79
so that he could * in the boat and Lk 5:3
"Just tell them to * down on the Lk 9:14
And I'll * back and say to Lk 12:19
and serve them as they * and eat! Lk 12:37
were trying to * near the head of Lk 14:7
'Let this man * here instead.' Lk 14:9
he doesn't just * down and eat, but Lk 17:7,8,9
across its back for Jesus to * on. Lk 19:35
the Messiah, "* at my right hand Lk 20:42,43
and you will * on thrones judging Lk 22:30
"Tell everyone to * down," Jn 6:10
* on David's throne. Act 2:30
and said to him, * here in honor Act 2:34
into the chariot and * with him. Act 8:31
Christ, where we * with him in the Eph 2:6
He will go in and * as God in the 2Th 2:4
to * with him and rule with him. 2Ti 2:12
does to his Son, "* here beside me Heb 1:13
you like, or else * on the Jas 2:3
one who conquers * beside me on my Rev 3:21
has come when he will * as Judge. Rev 14:7

SITE
any other tool at the building *. 1Ki 6:7
David had selected it as the * 2Ch 3:1
rebuilt on its old *, and it was Ez 3:3
the construction * of the Temple of Ez 5:8
Let it be rebuilt on its former * Ez 6:6
at the * of ancient Mizpah. Jer 41:9f
The present village on this * is Eze 47:15f
* is with difficulty discovered." Zep 2:15f
be on an elevated *, covering the Zec 14:10

TE Con't)
ver to the * of the old gate, then Zec 14:10
THRI
f Uzziel:Misha-el, Elzaphan, *. Ex 6:22
TNAH
Gen 26:21f
TS
nything he * on is contaminated; Lev 15:4
Anything she lies on or * on Lev 15:20
r anything she * upon shall wash Lev 15:21,22,23
nd everything she * on is in a Lev 15:26
r anything she * on shall be Lev 15:27
een crowned and * upon his throne Deu 17:18
n forever; he * upon his throne to Ps 9:7,8
Jehovah * in majesty in Zion, Ps 99:2
nd shame. She * at the door of Pro 9:14
well known, for he * in the council Pro 31:23
Literally, "Rahab who * still." Is 30:7f
It is God who * above the circle Is 40:22
t is yet day. She * childless now, Jer 15:9
n the king who * on David's Jer 29:16,17
she * alone in her mourning. Lam 1:1
Now she * in exile far away. Lam 1:3
onto the beach and * down and sorts Mt 13:47,48
* here while I do all the work? Lk 10:40
unless he first * down and counts Lk 14:33
Out in the world the master * at Lk 22:27
"And now he * on the throne of Act 2:33
of heaven where he * beside God in Col 3:1
and now he * in the place of Heb 12:2
Prostitute, who * upon the many Rev 17:1
TTING
as he was * in the opening of his Gen 18:1
Lot was * there as they arrived. Gen 19:1
Ephron was * there among the Gen 23:10
saddle and now was * on them! Gen 31:34
As he was * there beside a well, Ex 2:15
Anyone * on a seat the man has Lev 15:6
Talk about them when you are * at Deu 11:19
it with the mother * in the nest, Deu 22:6
to him as he was * in a cool Ju 3:20
wife as she was * in the field. Ju 13:9
Eli the priest was * at his 1Sa 1:9
* in the seats of honor. 1Sa 2:8
But one day as Saul was * at 1Sa 19:9,10
him and Abner was * beside Saul, 1Sa 20:24,25
He was in Gibe-ah at the time, * 1Sa 22:6
David was * at the gate of the 2Sa 18:24
Solomon is * on the throne, and 1Ki 1:46,47
and found him * under an oak tree. 1Ki 13:14
Then, suddenly, while they were * 1Ki 13:20
someone, or is out * on the toilet, 1Ki 18:27
And we're * here without doing a 1Ki 22:3
robes and were * on thrones placed 1Ki 22:10
I saw the Lord * on his throne, 1Ki 22:19
They found him * on top of a 2Ki 1:9
Elisha was * in his house at a 2Ki 6:32
Now there were four lepers * 2Ki 7:3
he found Jehu * around with the 2Ki 9:5
"O Lord God of Israel, * on your 2Ki 19:15
The two kings were * on thrones 2Ch 18:9
arrived and were * in the open Ez 10:9
with the queen * beside him, "How Neh 2:5,6
king was * upon his royal throne. Est 5:1
the Jew just * there in front of Est 5:13
He reigns above the nations, * Ps 47:8
A king * as judge weighs all the Pro 20:8
He was * on a lofty throne, and Is 6:1
from ever * on his throne. Is 14:22
the king * on David's throne, and Jer 13:13
* on the throne here in Jerusalem; Jer 17:25
of Judah, * on David's throne; Jer 22:2
an heir * on the throne of Israel. Jer 33:17
time, * in front of a fireplace, Jer 36:22
not qualify as "* on the throne" Jer 36:30f
think you are God, * on the throne Eze 28:2,3
I saw a Man * on a red horse that Zec 1:8
heathen nations * around at ease, Zec 1:15
see a woman * inside the basket! Zec 5:7
James and John, * in a boat with Mt 4:21
* at a tax collection booth. Mt 9:9
Two blind men were * beside the Mt 20:30
* at the right hand of God and Mt 26:64
Meanwhile, as Peter was * in the Mt 26:69
other Mary were * nearby watching. Mt 27:61
* at his tax collection booth. Mk 2:14
but as they saw the man * there, Mk 5:15
each were * on the green grass. Mk 6:39,40
of Timaeus) was * beside the road Mk 10:46
and as they were * around the Mk 14:18
* at the right hand of God, and Mk 14:62
He was in the Temple, * among the Lk 2:46,47
and teachers of the Law were * Lk 5:17
* at a tax collection booth. Lk 5:27
demon-possessed * quietly at Jesus' Lk 8:35
to where you are * and say, 'Let Lk 14:9
Hearing this, a man * at the Lk 14:15
war without first * down with his Lk 14:31
a blind man was * beside the road, Lk 18:35
But here at this table, * among Lk 22:21
meekly, * on a donkey's colt!" Jn 12:15
was * next Jn 13:23
A jar of sour wine was * Jn 19:29
white-robed angels * at the head Jn 20:12
named Eutychus, * on the window Act 20:9
for us and is * at the place of Rom 8:34
And now Christ is in heaven, * 1Pe 3:22
—a throne and someone * on it! Rev 4:2
with twenty-four Elders * on them; Rev 4:4
thanks to the one * on the throne, Rev 4:9
of the one who was * on the throne, Rev 5:1
hand of the one * upon the throne. Rev 5:7
belong to the one * on the throne, Rev 5:13
face of the one * on the throne, Rev 6:16
The one * on the throne will Rev 7:15
And the twenty-four Elders * on Rev 11:16
cloud, and someone * on it who Rev 14:14
So the one * on the cloud Rev 14:16
There I saw a woman * on a Rev 17:3
that the woman is * on represent Rev 17:15
God, who was * upon the throne, and Rev 19:4
and the one * on the horse was Rev 19:11
one * on the horse and his army. Rev 19:19
Then I saw thrones, and * on them Rev 20:4
And the one * on the throne said, Rev 21:5
SITUATED
"Yes, you are strongly *, Num 24:21,22
The cities of Judah which were * Jos 15:21-32
The following cities * in the Jos 15:33-36
cities which were * in the areas Jos 17:11
the hill where the Temple was *. 2Ch 27:3
SITUATION
that they were indeed in a bad *. Ex 5:19
handle the * as outlined above. Num 5:30
Let me out of this impossible * Num 11:15
the * described in Numbers 25:1–3. Num 24:25f
Another similar * occurred when Deu 2:23
and check out the * on the other Jos 2:1
and cleaned up the * at the Temple, 2Ch 34:8
the * to get out of control!" Ez 4:22
the entire *, our enemies did not Ez 5:5
be decided and the * will be Ez 10:14
Then as I looked over the *, I Neh 4:14
"What shall we do about this *?" Est 1:13-15
world go by, a sad * concerning Ecc 10:5
Daniel handled the * with great Dan 2:14
his disciples to discuss the *. Mk 8:1
to come and discuss the *. Lk 16:5,6
will receive glory from this *." Jn 11:4
a council to discuss the *. Jn 11:47
aspects of this * and our loss of Act 19:27
So this is the *: Most of the Rom 11:7
In this *, happy is the man who Rom 14:22
whatever * God has put you into. 1Co 7:17
So, dear brothers, whatever * a 1Co 7:24
but that is not the *, for God 1Co 9:17
in every *, whether it be a full Php 4:12
SITUATIONS
In such * you can do something 1Ti 5:24
SIX
me, for I have given him * sons." Gen 30:20
and * years to get the flock! Gen 31:41
there were * hundred thousand of Ex 12:37
usual, * quarts instead of three; Ex 16:22
Gather the food for * days, but Ex 16:26
as a holy day. * days a week are Ex 20:9
For in * days the Lord made the Ex 20:11
shall serve only * years and be Ex 21:2
the end of * years as the men are. Ex 21:7
"Sow and reap your crops for * Ex 23:10
"Work * days only, and rest the Ex 23:12
Sinai and the cloud covered it * Ex 24:16
feet long and * feet wide, dyed Ex 26:1
feet across and * feet wide. Ex 26:7,8
and use the other * for another Ex 26:9
On the west side there will be * Ex 26:22
tribes of Israel. * names shall be Ex 28:10
Work * days only, for the Ex 31:16
For in * days the Lord made Ex 31:17
* days, and rest on the seventh. Ex 34:21
"Work * days only; Ex 35:2
feet long and * feet wide). Ex 36:14,15
long piece, and * others to make Ex 36:16
was made from * frames, plus Ex 36:27
The lampstand had * branches, Ex 37:18
seventh year. For * years you may Lev 25:3
They brought * covered wagons, Num 7:3
which weighed only about * ounces. Num 7:14
is a ram, use * quarts of fine Num 15:6
grain offering of * quarts of fine Num 28:9,10
each bull; and * quarts of finely Num 28:12
a drink offering—* pints of wine Num 28:14
with the ram there shall be * Num 28:20,21
with each bull, * quarts with the Num 28:28,29
with the bull, * quarts with the Num 29:3,4
with the bull; * with the ram; Num 29:9,10
* quarts for each of the two rams; Num 29:14
the Levites the * Cities of Refuge Num 35:6
Three of these * Cities of Num 35:13,14
a half feet long by * feet wide. Deu 3:11
Work the other * days, but the Deu 5:13
remember that for * years he has Deu 15:18
For the following * days you Deu 16:8
once a day for * days, followed by Jos 6:3,4
They followed this pattern for * Jos 6:12,13,14
He once killed * hundred Ju 3:31
Jephthah was Israel's judge for * Ju 12:7
So * hundred armed troops of the Ju 18:11
day, leaving only * hundred men who Ju 20:46,47
thousand chariots, * thousand 1Sa 13:5
were only about * hundred left! 1Sa 13:15
Saul and Jonathan and these * 1Sa 13:16
Saul and his * hundred men were 1Sa 14:2
Then Saul and his * hundred men 1Sa 14:20
So David and his men—about * 1Sa 23:13
So David took his * hundred men 1Sa 27:2,3
So David and his * hundred men 1Sa 30:9,10
it had gone * paces, they stopped 2Sa 6:13
to lead the way—* hundred Gittites 2Sa 15:17,18
the captain of the * hundred 2Sa 15:19,20
Then Ittai and his * hundred 2Sa 15:22
The harvest lasted * months, from 2Sa 21:10f
Gath, a giant with * fingers on 2Sa 21:20,21
on each hand and * toes on each 2Sa 21:20,21
Each vat was * feet square and 1Ki 7:38
It had * steps and a rounded 1Ki 10:19
It took * months to accomplish 1Ki 11:16,17,18
twelve years, * of them in Tirzah. 1Ki 16:23
They lived there for * years 2Ki 11:2,3
the floor five or * times," he 2Ki 13:19
distance of about * hundred feet. 2Ki 14:13
These * were born to him in 1Ch 3:4
Shemaiah had * sons, including 1Ch 3:21,22
Shime-i had sixteen sons and * 1Ch 4:27
Azel had * sons: 1Ch 8:38
Azel had * sons: 1Ch 9:44
Gath, a giant with * fingers on 1Ch 20:6,7
on each hand and * toes on each 1Ch 20:6,7
Literally, "* hundred shekels of 1Ch 21:25f
instructed, "* thousand are to be 1Ch 23:4,5
divided into * groups named after 1Ch 23:8,9
zither), were his * sons: Gedaliah, 1Ch 25:3
and Hosah. * guards were assigned 1Ch 26:17
the storehouses. * guards were 1Ch 26:18
It had * gold steps and a 2Ch 9:18
in the Temple for * years while 2Ch 22:12
day were one ox, * fat sheep, and a Neh 5:18
The celebration lasted * months, Est 1:4
would be given * months of beauty Est 2:12,13,14
myrrh, followed by * months with Est 2:12,13,14
For there are * things the Lord Pro 6:16-19
be freed after serving * years. Jer 34:14
This event occurred * years after Jer 51:59f
* men appeared at his call, Eze 9:2
LATE IN JULY, * Eze 20:1
closed during the * work days but Eze 46:1
days shall be * lambs and a ram, Eze 46:4
perfect condition; * lambs and one Eze 46:6
of the city is * miles. Eze 48:35
wars, * million under Hitler. Zec 13:8f
* DAYS LATER Jesus took Peter, Mt 17:1
* days later Jesus took Peter, Mk 9:2
Furthermore, * months ago your Lk 1:36
"There are * days of the week to Lk 13:14
* stone waterpots were standing Jn 2:6
* DAYS BEFORE the Passover Jn 12:1
These * brothers here accompanied Act 11:12
Living Beings had * wings, and the Rev 4:8
SIX-WINGED
about him were mighty, * seraphs. Is 6:2
SIXTEEN
These * persons were the sons of Gen 46:18
the building with * silver bases Ex 26:25
eight frames with * silver bases Ex 36:30
* cities in all, each with its Jos 19:17-23
reigned in Samaria for * years. 2Ki 13:9,10
the new king at the age of *. 2Ki 14:21
Shime-i had * sons and six 1Ch 4:27
were divided into * groups and 1Ch 24:4
twenty-two sons and * daughters. 2Ch 13:21
he reigned * years, in Jerusalem. 2Ch 27:1
he reigned * years, in Jerusalem. 2Ch 27:8
he reigned * years, in Jerusalem. 2Ch 28:1
job was completed in * days. 2Ch 29:17
For when he was * years old, in 2Ch 34:3
him under the guard of * soldiers. Act 12:4
there, he had the * guards Act 12:19
SIXTEEN-YEAR-OLD
THE PEOPLE OF Judah now crowned * 2Ch 26:1
SIXTEENTH
*, the group led by Immer; 1Ch 24:7-18
*, Hananiah and twelve of his sons 1Ch 25:9-31
SIXTH
This ended the * day. Gen 1:31
a * day (or, 'period of time')." Gen 1:31f
she became pregnant, with a * son. Gen 30:19
usual on the * day of each week." Ex 16:5
On the * day they gathered twice Ex 16:22
as much on the * day, so that there Ex 16:28,29
wide section. (The * tarpaulin will Ex 26:9
bumper crops the * year that will Lev 25:21,22
"On the * day of the festival, Num 29:29
at the end of the * year you have Deu 15:12

(SIXTH Con't)
The * tribe to receive its Jos 19:32
Three years later (during the * 2Ki 18:10
was Raddai, his * was Ozem, and 1Ch 2:15
The * was Ithream, the son of his 1Ch 3:3
Attai was * in command; 1Ch 12:8-13
*, the group led by Mijamin; 1Ch 24:7-18
*, Bukkiah and twelve of his sons 1Ch 25:9-31
Jeho-hanan (the *), 1Ch 26:2,3
Ammi-el (the *), 1Ch 26:4,5
The commander of the * Division 1Ch 27:9
he had 24,000 men on duty the * 1Ch 27:9
in the * year of the reign of Ez 6:15
Hanun (the * son of Zalaph); Neh 3:30
THEN, LATE IN August of the * year Eze 8:1
I watched as he broke the * seal, Rev 6:12
The * angel blew his trumpet and Rev 9:13
saying to the * angel, "Release Rev 9:14
The * angel poured out his flask Rev 16:12
Five have already fallen, the * Rev 17:10
The * layer with sardus; Rev 21:18,19,20

SIXTY
Isaac was * years old when the Gen 25:26
* shall pay twenty-five dollars; Lev 27:3
to * shall pay fifteen dollars; Lev 27:4
A man over * shall pay seven and Lev 27:7
We conquered all * of his Deu 3:4
the * cities of Jair in Bashan. Jos 13:30
But three hundred and * of 2Sa 2:31
* walled cities with bronze gates; 1Ki 4:8-19
Most Holy Place—was * feet long. 1Ki 6:17
counselors, and * farmers, all of 2Ki 25:19
at the age of *, and she presented 1Ch 2:21
and its * surrounding villages. 1Ch 2:23
eighteen wives and * 2Ch 11:21
sons and * daughters). 2Ch 11:21
hundred chariots, * thousand 2Ch 12:3
of Solomon with * of the Sol 3:7
I have * other wives, all Sol 6:8
recruitment) and * other men of Jer 52:24,25
or barley for every * you reap; Eze 45:13
about thirty to * miles across. Jon 3:3f
empire, a city of * miles around Zep 2:15f
that was thirty, *, and even a Mt 13:8
and brings thirty, *, or even a Mt 13:23
planted—thirty, *, or even a Mt 13:23f
even * or a hundred times as much! Mk 4:8
for God—thirty, *, or even a Mk 4:20
should be at least * years old 1Ti 5:9

SIXTY-EIGHT
* of their colleagues as guards. 1Ch 16:38

SIXTY-FIVE
Mahalalel: Mahalalel was * years Gen 5:15,16,17
Enoch: Enoch was * years old when Gen 5:21-24
And within * years Ephraim, too, Is 7:8

SIXTY-SEVEN
in silver, and * sets of clothing Neh 7:72

SIXTY-SIX
the wives of Jacob's sons, was *. Gen 46:26
Then for a further * days she Lev 12:5

SIXTY-TWO
of Obed-edom—all * of them—were 1Ch 26:8
began reigning at the age of *. Dan 5:31

SIZE
depends on the * of the families). Ex 12:3,4
proportion to its *, as indicated Lev 27:16
The manna was about the * of Num 11:7
to the * of your tribes. Num 33:54
proportionate in * to his blessing Deu 16:10
Fitting the * of its territory to Jos 13:15
territory to its * of population, Jos 13:15
a report of its * and natural Jos 18:4
quarters, the same *, in the palace 1Ki 7:8
All ten stands were the same * 1Ki 7:37
cloud about the * of a man's hand 1Ki 18:44
to whittle down the * of Israel. 2Ki 10:32,33
Don't be frightened by the * of 1Ch 28:20
and saw the * of the men in his 2Ch 9:4
of heaven, the * of the earth, or Pro 25:2,3
hall were the same * as those of Eze 40:33
It will be of the same * and Eze 48:13
I will cut you down to * among Ob 1:2
will grow again to former *. Zec 10:8
For he was awestruck by the * Lk 5:9
"If your faith were only the * Lk 17:6

SIZING
As Joshua was * up the city of Jos 5:13

SKELETONS
for any * left and bury them, so Eze 39:14

SKETCH
and made a * and sent it back to 2Ki 16:10
A thumbnail * of King 2Ch 20:31

SKIES
life, and let the * be filled with Gen 1:20
and in the * and in the seas." Gen 1:26
reaching to the *—a proud, eternal Gen 11:3,4
Why, even the * and the highest 1Ki 8:27
"And when the * are shut up and 1Ki 8:35,36
"When the * are shut and there 2Ch 6:26
sank into the western *, he died. 2Ch 18:34
You have made the * and the Neh 9:6
sun shining in the *, or the moon Job 31:26
into rain, which the * pour down. Job 36:28
mirror of the * as he does? Job 37:18
When I look up into the night * Ps 8:3
silent in the *, their message Ps 19:3,4
moves out across the * as radiant Ps 19:5
of glory thunders through the *. Ps 29:3
faithfulness is higher than the *. Ps 57:10
as sun and moon continue in the *! Ps 72:5
he commanded the * to open—he Ps 78:23
Your faithfulness reaches the *. Ps 108:4
Praise him from the *! Ps 148:1
Praise him, * above. Ps 148:4
and the * poured down rain. Pro 3:20
will move from its place in the *. Is 13:13
wither, the * refuse their rain. Is 24:4,5
Let the * pour out their Is 45:8
the darkness out across the *. Is 50:3
Look high in the * and watch the Is 51:6
beneath, for the * shall disappear Is 51:6
the * and made the earth. Is 51:13
forth from the * and come down! Is 64:1
earth and *, and they are mine. Is 66:2
* their mighty shouts of victory. Jer 51:14
great demonstrations in the *. Mt 16:1
signs of the *—red sky tonight Mt 16:2,3
the * [to prove I am the Messiah Lk 11:29,30
that flashes across the *. Lk 17:24
events in the *—warnings, evil Lk 21:25
bread from the *, they all died. Jn 6:48-51
windstorm in the * above them and Act 2:2
for he never ascended into the *. Act 2:34
They have power to shut the * so Rev 11:6
the * while everyone was watching. Rev 13:13
him through the *, saying, Rev 14:8
descending out of the * from God. Rev 21:10

SKILL
have given special * as tailors to Ex 28:3
ability, and * in constructing the Ex 31:3
moreover, I have given special * Ex 31:6
used their special * to spin the Ex 35:26
in fact, he has every needed *. Ex 35:33
He gives me * in war 2Sa 22:35
who was selected for his *. 1Ch 15:22
with wonderful perfection and *? Job 37:16,17
own strength and *, but by your Ps 44:3
hand forget its * upon the harp. Ps 137:5,6
He gives me strength and * in Ps 144:1
Godly * rebuilds. Pro 11:9
knowledge, and *, I must leave all Ecc 2:20-23
you trusted in your wealth and *; Jer 48:7
formed with * by the hands of men. Hos 13:2

SKILLED
made by the most * of the workmen, Ex 28:5,6
The Lord instructed * Ex 30:25
He is *, too, as a jeweler and Ex 31:5
"Come, all of you who are * Ex 35:10-19
The women * in sewing and Ex 35:25
The * weavers first made ten Ex 36:8,9
of the most * perfumers. Ex 37:29
he too was a * craftsman and also Ex 38:23
was a * craftsman in bronze work. 1Ki 7:13
So only the poorest and least * 2Ki 24:14
were all * warriors and chiefs. 1Ch 7:40
And you have many * stonemasons 1Ch 22:15
"So send me * 2Ch 2:7
blue cloth; and * engravers to work 2Ch 2:7
* in the use of spear and sword. 2Ch 25:5,6
The Levites who were * musicians 2Ch 34:12
he is * at crushing its pride! Job 26:12
apprentice than from a * rebel! Pro 26:10
They are all * swordsmen and Sol 3:8
work of the most * of craftsmen. Sol 7:1
of Judah and the * tradesmen—the Jer 24:1
of cruel men * in destruction. Eze 21:31
your helmsmen are * men from Eze 27:8
that of all the * magicians and Dan 1:20
might read, "* in intrigues." Dan 8:23f
and how * they are in using them! Mic 7:3

SKILLFUL
As the boys grew, Esau became a * Gen 25:27
it was a * and beautiful piece of Ex 39:3
strongest and most * of their Ju 3:29
He is a * goldsmith and 2Ch 2:14
This * craftsman, Huramabi, made 2Ch 4:12-16
with a true heart and * hands. Ps 78:71,72
* men are not necessarily famous; Ecc 9:11
* goldsmiths who make their idols; Jer 10:9

SKILLFULLY
curtain from * embroidered blue, Ex 26:36
cherubim * embroidered upon them. Ex 36:8,9
cherubim * embroidered into it. Ex 36:35
to him, accompanied * on the harp; Ps 33:3

SKILLS
teachers of their * to others. Ex 35:34
both with unusual * as jewelers, Ex 35:35
Others with * of every kind will 1Ch 28:21
his help, and not on our own *. 2Co 1:12

SKIM
The wicked are the scum you * Ps 119:119
smelting pot, and * off your slag. Is 1:25

SKIN
Esau is, and how smooth my * is! Gen 27:11,
from the hairy * of the young Gen 27:1
including the * and the dung, Ex 29:1
Then the priests will * the Lev 1:6
shall * ." Lev 1:6,
the young bull—the *, meat, head, Lev 4:11,
a swelling in his *, or a scab or Lev 13
*, leprosy is to be suspected. Lev 13
"But if the white spot in the * Lev 13
be deeper than the *, and the hair Lev 13
not spread in the *, then the Lev 13
But if the spot spreads in the * Lev 13
swelling in the * with white hairs Lev 13:9,
has a boil in his * which heals, Lev 13:1
be down under the *, and if the Lev 13:2
be deeper than the *, and if the Lev 13:2
no deeper than the * and is fading, Lev 13:2
If the spot spreads in the *, the Lev 13:2
or spread in the *, and is fading, Lev 13:2
to be below the * and yellow hair Lev 13:29,3
to be only in the * and that there Lev 13:3
be deeper than the *, he shall Lev 13:3
no deeper than the *, the priest Lev 13:3
areas in the *, but these spots Lev 13:3
that has broken out in the *. Lev 13:3
anything made of * or leather, Lev 13:5
swelling in one's *, or a scab from Lev 14:5
pimples or scabby *, or has Lev 21:2
itch or any other * disease, must Lev 22:2
a leper, his * as white as snow. 2Ki 5:2
"* for skin," Satan replied. Job 2:4,
"Skin for *," Satan replied. Job 2:4,
"My * is filled with worms and Job 7:
You gave me * and flesh and knit Job 10:1
O God, you have turned me to * Job 16:
him. His * is eaten by disease. Job 18:1
I am * and bones and have Job 19:2
death by the * of my teeth. Job 19:2
My * is black and peeling. Job 30:3
He becomes thin, mere * and Job 33:21
I am reduced to * and bones Ps 102:5
*, and bread to give him strength. Ps 104:15
from fasting and I am * and bones. Ps 109:24
change the color of his *? Jer 13:23
Their * sticks to their bones; Lam 4:8
Our * was black from famine. Lam 5:10
on you and cover you with *. Eze 37:6
the bones, and * covered them, but Eze 37:8
waist, and glowing, lustrous *! Dan 10:5,6
and love evil; you * my people and Mic 3:2

SKIN-DEEP
to be more than *, it is leprosy, Lev 13:3
to be more than *, it is leprosy Lev 13:25

SKINNY
* and all their ribs stood out. Gen 41:3
Then the * cows ate the fat Gen 41:4
the river, very *—in fact, Gen 41:19
And these * cattle ate up the Gen 41:20
they were still as * as before! Gen 41:21
The seven * cows (and also the Gen 41:27

SKINS
garments made from * of animals. Gen 3:21
red-dyed ram's *, goat-skins, Ex 25:1
a layer of rams' *, dyed red, and Ex 26:14
Tanned rams' * and specially Ex 35:5-9
and ram * dyed red, and specially Ex 35:23
was made of rams' *, dyed red, and Ex 36:19
dyed red, and tanned goat *. Ex 36:19
sides—the rams' * dyed red, the Ex 39:33-40
goat *, and the entrance drape; Ex 39:33-40
vines, not even the seeds or *! Num 6:3,4
as the Levites removed the *. 2Ch 35:11
For the old * would burst with Mt 9:17
would be spilled and the * ruined. Mt 9:17
bursts the old *, ruining the skins Lk 5:37
the * and spilling the wine. Lk 5:37
Some went about in * of sheep and Heb 11:37,38

SKIP
They leap and * before him like Ps 29:5,6
Why, mountains, did you * like Ps 114:6

SKIPPED
The mountains * like rams, the Ps 114:4

SKIPS
trouble, and God * them when he Job 21:17

SKIRT
bottom edge of the *, with bells Ex 39:25,26

SKIRTS
up beneath the * of your clothing Ex 20:26

SKULL
Abimelech's head, crushing his *. Ju 9:53
her *, her feet, and her hands. 2Ki 9:35
that is, "* Hill," where the Mt 27:33
(Golgotha means *. Mk 15:22
him at a place called "The *." Lk 23:32,33
*," in Hebrew, "Golgotha." Jn 19:17

SKY
to form the * above and the Gen 1:6
So God made the *, dividing Gen 1:7,8
water beneath the * be gathered Gen 1:9,10
lights in the * to give light to Gen 1:14,15

KY Con't)
And God set them in the * to Gen 1:17
torrents from the *, and the Gen 7:10,11,12
the nighttime * and told him, Gen 15:5
from the *, "Hagar, what's wrong? Gen 21:17
above you in the *, and like the Gen 22:17
Moses, toss it into the * as Ex 9:8
it toward the *, and it became Ex 9:10
the smoke billowed into the * as Ex 19:18
their cities rise high into the *! Deu 1:28
flames shot far into the *, Deu 4:11
And do not look up into the * to Deu 4:19
you as many as the stars in the *! Deu 10:22
long as there is * above the earth, Deu 11:21
the *, and they had nowhere to go. Jos 8:20,21
And the * poured down its rain. Ju 5:4
up toward the *, and as Manoah and Ju 13:20
pouring into the * was the signal Ju 20:35-39
And sure enough, the * was soon 1Ki 18:45
the Lord made windows in the *!" 2Ki 7:2
birds in the * cannot discover it. Job 28:21
Look up there into the *, high Job 35:5
mighty voice thunders from the *. Ps 68:33
rolled and crackled in the *. Ps 77:17
my faithful witness in the *!" Ps 89:37
or swallow flitting through the *. Pro 26:2
How an eagle glides through the *. Pro 30:18,19
of night and day, of earth and *. Jer 33:25,26
The * spreading out above them Eze 1:22
came a voice from the crystal * Eze 1:25
For high in the * above them was Eze 1:26
me up into the * and seemed to Eze 8:3
appeared in the * above the heads Eze 10:1
higher into the * until it could be Dan 4:10,11
pleading of the * for clouds, to Hos 1:21,22
her down like a bird from the *. Hos 7:12
in the earth and *—blood and fire Joe 2:30
the earth and * begin to shake. Joe 3:16
splendor fills the earth and *; Hab 3:3
is traveling through the *!" Zec 5:5
flew off with it, high in the *. Zec 5:9
looked up into the * and asked Mt 14:19
of the skies—red * tonight means Mt 16:2,3
tomorrow; red * in the morning Mt 16:2,3
flashes across the * from east to Mt 24:27
"Make something happen in the *. Mk 8:11
up into the * and gave thanks; Lk 9:16
to happen in the * to prove his Lk 11:16
You interpret the * well enough, Lk 12:56
into the *, and went on to heaven. Lk 24:51
he rose into the * and disappeared Act 1:9
standing here staring at the *? Act 1:11
the roaring in the * above the Act 2:6
He saw the * open, and a great Act 10:11
by its four corners from the *. Act 11:5
seen the earth and * and all God Rom 1:20
are—high above the *, or in the Rom 8:39
will be a trumpet blast from the * 1Co 15:52
the stars of the * and the sand on Heb 11:12
Literally, "the * departed." Rev 6:14f
fell from the * onto the people Rev 16:21
face the earth and * fled away, but Rev 20:11
and a new *, for the present Rev 21:1
earth and * had disappeared. Rev 21:1

SKY-BLUE
some were * and others yellow. Rev 9:17,18

SKYLIGHT
Construct a * all the way around Gen 6:16

SLAG
smelting pot, and skim off your *. Is 1:25
* left when silver is smelted. Eze 22:18,19,20

SLAIN
sacrifices are *, and its blood Lev 7:2
animal the same day it is *. Lev 22:29,30
And have drunk the blood of the * Num 23:18-24
Or if the * man was struck down Num 35:17
Of all the * and captives. Deu 32:40,41
of the enemy were * at Bezek. Ju 1:4,5,6
and children were *, but the young Ju 21:10,11,12
song: "Saul has * his thousands, 1Sa 18:7
singing, 'Saul has * his thousands 1Sa 21:11
dances: 'Saul has * his thousands 1Sa 29:5
Jonathan is * upon the hills. 2Sa 1:25
the 450 prophets of Baal were *. 1Ki 22:6f
were waiting to be *, and hid him 2Ki 11:2,3
Arieh were also * in the revolt). 2Ki 15:25
The Passover lambs were * that 2Ch 35:1
our priests were * by the heathen Ez 9:7
number of those * in Shushan, he Est 9:11
for she goes wherever the * are." Job 39:30
to die, like those * on Ps 88:5
as prisoners or lie among the *. Is 10:4
dead bodies of those * in battle. Is 14:19
your nation and * your people. Is 14:20
Lying everywhere, * by plague Is 22:2
the * of the Lord shall be many! Is 66:16
they shall lie among the *. Jer 6:15
for there will be so many * to Jer 7:32
and night for the * of my people! Jer 9:1
On that day those the Lord has * Jer 25:33
They shall fall down * in the Jer 51:4
Lord, and * us without mercy. Lam 3:43
When your * lie scattered among Eze 6:13
It will not protect you. Your * Eze 11:7
Literally, "Your * Eze 11:7f
the wounded shall be * in your Eze 28:23
the * shall cover the ground. Eze 30:4
and cover the ground with the *. Eze 30:11
the multitudes * by the sword, for Eze 32:20
her people, those the sword has *. Eze 32:22
place among the *, surrounded by Eze 32:25
shame in the pit, * by the sword. Eze 32:25
those who are * by the sword. Eze 32:28
whom the sword has *, with the Eze 32:29
there, and the Sidonians, all *. Eze 32:30
other * who go down to the pit. Eze 32:30
all his army *, says the Lord God. Eze 32:31
who are * by the sword." Eze 32:32
breathe upon these * bodies, that Eze 37:9
I have * you with the words of my Hos 6:5
You Ethiopians, too, will be * by Zep 2:12
been bought and * by wicked Zec 11:5
of Barachiah), * by you in the Mt 23:35
Christ, God's Lamb, has been * 1Co 5:7
animal sacrifices, * and burnt Heb 10:6
the blood of the * animals into the Heb 13:11
for you were *, and your blood Rev 5:9
"—the Lamb who was *. Rev 5:12
the founding of the world in the * Rev 13:8
Life of the Lamb * before the Rev 13:8f
That is, regarded as * in the Rev 13:8f

SLAKES
and their wealth * the thirst of Job 5:5

SLAMMED
Has he * the door in anger on his Ps 77:9

SLANDER
"You will be safe from *; Job 5:21
Anyone who refuses to * others, Ps 15:3
filled with * against me—I didn't Ps 35:15
mouths. You * your own brother. Ps 50:20
You love to *—you love to say Ps 52:4
wicked * me and tell their lies. Ps 109:2
To hate is to be a liar; to * is Pro 10:18
he accuse you of * and you can't Pro 25:8,9,10
fornication, theft, lying and *. Mt 15:19
*, pride, and all other folly. Mk 7:22
I know the * of those opposing Rev 2:9

SLANDERED
But Ziba has * me by saying that 2Sa 19:27
You are mocked and *. Eze 36:3

SLANDERERS
people, drunkards, *, or robbers. 1Co 6:9,10

SLANDEROUS
of people's scorn or their * talk. Is 51:7
another and spread their * lies. Jer 9:4

SLANDERS
I heard the lies about me, the * Ps 31:13
who secretly * his neighbors; Ps 101:5
Or, "When a godless man * his Pro 11:9f

SLANT
and do not * your testimony in Ex 23:2,3

SLAP
to swallow me; they * my cheek. Job 16:10
And he will * them in the face, Ps 3:7
cheek, let him * the other too! Lk 6:29
to Paul to * him on the mouth. Act 23:2
Paul said to him, "God shall * Act 23:3
on airs, and * you in the face. 2Co 11:19,20

SLAPPED
over and * Micaiah on the face. 1Ki 22:24
Micaiah and * him across the face. 2Ch 18:23
If you are * on one cheek, turn Mt 5:39
him and some * him, saying, Mt 26:67
The angel * him on the side to Act 12:7

SLAPS
"If someone * you on one cheek, Lk 6:29

SLASH
in anguish, and * their hands and Jer 48:37
your map and * at it with a knife. Eze 5:2
O sword, * to the right and Eze 21:16
to the right and * to the left, Eze 21:16

SLASHED
the Temple and * them to pieces, 2Ch 28:24
* to death in her streets. Jer 51:4
out a sword and * off the ear of Mt 26:51
pulled a sword and * at the High Mk 14:47
And one of them * at the High Lk 22:50
drew a sword and * off the right Jn 18:10
Again and again the rods * down Act 16:23

SLAUGHTER
allies arrived and the * began. Gen 14:5,6
You shall not * a mother animal Lev 22:28
army continued the * and wiped out Jos 10:20
with a terrible * all the way from Ju 11:33
* just as on the previous days. Ju 20:35-39
and joined the * from the rear. Ju 20:42
There was a great * and twenty 2Sa 18:7
army was killed in a great *. 1Ki 20:21
returned from this * of the 2Ch 25:14
are doomed to destruction and *. Est 7:4
us like sheep in a * pen, and Ps 44:11
We are like sheep awaiting *. Ps 44:22
Publicly avenge this * of your Ps 79:10
them in a mighty * like the time Is 10:26
them and deliver them to *. Is 34:2
in Edom and make a mighty * there. Is 34:6
He was brought as a lamb to the * Is 53:7
to the "Valley of *"; Jer 7:32
as a lamb or ox on the way to *. Jer 11:19
off like helpless sheep to the *. Jer 12:3
Valley," but "The Valley of *." Jer 19:6
can they. The * shall be so great Jer 19:11
to * them without pity or mercy. Jer 21:7
He will * all the wicked. Jer 25:31
get away from all this * here!" Jer 46:16
are doomed to *, says the King, the Jer 48:15
They are fully armed for *; Jer 50:42
to the *, like rams and goats. Jer 51:40
and polished for terrible *. Eze 21:9,10,11
it is razor-edged for *. Eze 21:15
the wounded will scream as the * Eze 26:15
70 by Titus and the subsequent * Dan 9:25f
forced to lead their sons to *. Hos 9:13
and helpless to prevent the *. Ob 1:9
he has prepared a great * of his Zep 1:7
They will * their foes, leaving Zec 9:15
as a sheep to the *, and as a lamb Act 8:32
day—we are like sheep awaiting *; Rom 8:36
fat hearts are ready for the *. Jas 5:5

SLAUGHTERED
opposition, and * every man there, Gen 34:25
But Israel * them and occupied Num 21:24
Egypt to be * by these Amorites. Deu 1:27
aren't enemies who need to be *! Deu 20:19
the army of Israel * great numbers Jos 10:10
Every last person was *, just as Jos 10:30
was *, just as at Libnah. Jos 10:32
All the people were *, just as Jos 11:12
* its people, and lived there; Jos 19:47,48
one stone, they * all seventy of Ju 9:5
they went in and * all the people Ju 18:27
the village and * everyone in it, Ju 20:35-39
army returned and * the entire Ju 20:48
Ammonites and * them all morning. 1Sa 11:11
how many more we could have *!" 1Sa 14:30
Philistines and * many of them, and 1Sa 19:8
They went to Keilah and * the 1Sa 23:5
my meat that I've * for my shearers 1Sa 25:11
in among them and * them all that 1Sa 30:17
were * wholesale on Mount Gilboa. 1Sa 31:1
He also * twenty-two thousand 2Sa 8:5
that your men are being *. 2Sa 17:9
and that he had * the prophets of 1Ki 19:1
So they * them all and dragged 2Ki 10:25
* on the slopes of Mount Gilboa. 1Ch 10:1
it and * the Philistines; 1Ch 11:14
Israel, and they * 500,000 elite 2Ch 13:17
The armies from Israel also * 2Ch 28:5
appointed day and * their enemies. Est 9:5
22), who later * eighty-five Ps 52:1
fields of *, wicked men. Ps 58:10
of his forces, * 12,000 men of Edom Ps 60:1
The priests were * and their Ps 78:64
Stay here in Jerusalem and die—* Jer 21:9
has come to be * and scattered; Jer 25:34
Then they went out and * all the Jer 41:3
one-third will be * by the enemy; Eze 5:12
but you will be dragged out and *. Eze 11:7
You will be * all the way to the Eze 11:10
in Judea will be * by the sword. Eze 24:20,21
for sacrifice were * for the burnt Eze 40:39

SLAUGHTERING
had finished * all the men outside Jos 8:24
villages, * the entire population. Jos 10:37
had commanded, * them from Jos 10:41
to Ziklag after * the Amalekites. 2Sa 1:1

SLAUGHTERS
Literally, "*." Lev 17:3,4f
Jerusalem again and * many lives. Eze 17:17

SLAVE
And may Canaan be his *. Gen 9:26,27
And let Canaan be his *." Gen 9:26,27
every foreign-born * as well as to Gen 17:12
rid of that * girl and her son. Gen 21:10
Egyptian, Sarah's * girl:Nebaioth, Gen 25:12-15
in this Hebrew * to insult us!" Gen 39:14,15
"That Hebrew * you've had around Gen 39:17
there who was a * of the captain of Gen 41:12
stole it will be a *, and the rest Gen 44:10
stole the cup, he shall be my *. Gen 44:17
me stay here as a * instead of the Gen 44:33
oldest child of his lowliest *; Ex 11:5
the lamb, but any * who has been Ex 12:44
and thus becomes your *." Ex 21:2f
a Hebrew *, he shall serve only Ex 21:2
"If he sold himself as a * Ex 21:3
before he became a *, then his wife Ex 21:3
while he was a *, and they have Ex 21:4
after that he will be a * forever. Ex 21:6
his daughter as a *, she shall not Ex 21:7
or has already sold him as a *. Ex 21:16
"If a man beats his * to Ex 21:20
death—whether the * is male or Ex 21:20

(SLAVE Con't)
However, if the * does not die Ex 21:21
the * is his property. Ex 21:21
"If a man hits his * in the eye, Ex 21:26
blinded, then the * shall go free Ex 21:26
But if the ox gores a *, whether Ex 21:32
must be sold as a * for his debt. Ex 22:3
"If a man seduces a * Lev 19:20
the priest buys a * with his own Lev 22:11
own money, that * may eat it, and Lev 22:11
eat it, and any * children born in Lev 22:11
him as an ordinary *, but rather Lev 25:39
rather than as a * or as property. Lev 25:53
"If you buy a Hebrew *, whether Deu 15:12
"But if your Hebrew * doesn't Deu 15:16
that he shall be your * forever. Deu 15:17
But when you free a * you must Deu 15:18
You were a * in Egypt, so be sure Deu 16:12
a *, for you have humiliated her. Deu 21:14
"If a * escapes from his master, Deu 23:15,16
treats him as a * or sells him, the Deu 24:7
Both * and free. Deu 32:36
And now you have chosen his * Ju 9:18
while others will be * laborers; 1Sa 8:12
of conscripting as * laborers the 2Ch 8:7,8
* is free at last from his master. Job 3:19
long and hard, like that of a *. Job 7:1
let you make him your * for life? Job 41:4
my lowly servant, and Edom my *. Ps 60:8
Then he sent Joseph as a * to Ps 105:17
his master or a * girl watches her Ps 123:2
and you become a * of foreigners. Pro 5:10
A wise * will rule his master's Pro 17:2
or for a * to rule over princes! Pro 19:10
A * who becomes a king. Pro 30:21,22,23
and masters, * girls and Is 24:2
take off the * bands from your Is 52:2
Babylon and make him their *. Jer 27:7
any nation refusing to be his *; Jer 27:8
I told them that every Hebrew * Jer 34:14
send him away to Babylon as a *. Jer 39:7
once queen of nations, is now a *. Lam 1:1
Why is Judah led away, a *? Lam 1:3
and led away, a *, with all her Nah 2:7
The price of a *. Zec 11:12f
comes, and to my * boy, 'Do this or Mt 8:8,9
the top, you must serve like a *. Mt 20:27
replied, 'Wicked man! Lazy *! Mt 25:26
I am not even worthy to be his *. Mk 1:7
of all must be the * of all. Mk 10:44
am not even worthy of being his *. Lk 3:16
the highly prized * of a Roman Lk 7:2
to ask him to come and heal his *. Lk 7:3
and to my *, 'Do this or that,' Lk 7:6,7,8
found the * completely healed. Lk 7:10
'You vile and wicked *,' the Lk 19:22
I am not even fit to be his *." Jn 1:27
* isn't greater than his master!' Jn 15:20
and sold him to be a * in Egypt. Act 7:9
a demon-possessed * girl who was a Act 16:16
Jesus Christ's *, chosen to be a Rom 1:1
no longer needs to be a * to sin; Rom 6:6
your master and you will be his *. Rom 6:16
and makes me a * to the sin that Rom 7:23,24,25
Are you a *? 1Co 7:21
you, and you are a *, remember that 1Co 7:22
that you are now a * of Christ. 1Co 7:22
better off than a * until he grows Gal 4:1
that system, are her * children. Gal 4:24,25
and she is not a * to Jewish laws. Gal 4:26
Dear brothers, we are not * Gal 4:31
enemies that mark me as his *. Gal 6:17
you do, whether you are * or free. Eph 6:8
And you * owners must treat your Eph 6:9
of a * and becoming like men. Php 2:7
He is Jesus Christ's faithful *, Col 1:7
YOU * OWNERS must be just and fair Col 4:1
FROM: PAUL, THE * of God and the Tit 1:1
no longer only a *, but something Phm 1:16
For a man is a * to whatever 2Pe 2:19
and becomes its * again, he is 2Pe 2:20
great and small, * and free, hid Rev 6:15
rich and poor, * and free—to be Rev 13:16
great and small, * and free." Rev 19:18

SLAVE-GIRL
upset over the boy or your * wife; Gen 21:12
for giving my * to my husband." Gen 30:18
and Zilpah, the * given to Leah by Gen 46:18
and Bilhah, the * given to Rachel Gen 46:23,24,25
between a Hebrew * and his son, Ex 21:9
treat her as a *, but must treat Ex 21:9

SLAVE-GIRL'S
descendants of the * son, too, Gen 21:13

SLAVE-WIFE
* and one from his freeborn wife. Gal 4:22
Abraham's * Hagar represents Gal 4:24,25
children than the * has." Gal 4:27
to send away the * and her son, for Gal 4:30

SLAVE-WIFE'S
about the birth of the * baby. Gal 4:23
persecuted by Ishmael the * son. Gal 4:29
her son, for the * son could not Gal 4:30

SLAVE-YOKE
He will break the * off their Is 10:27

SLAVE'S
And if a master knocks out his * Ex 21:27
or female, the * master shall be Ex 21:32

SLAVERY
in this land of my *," he said). Gen 41:52
made the Hebrew * more bitter Ex 1:13,14
because of their *, and weeping Ex 2:23
of Israel, in * now to the Ex 6:5
them from *, and make them free. Ex 6:6
day of leaving Egypt and your *; Ex 13:3
us out of Egypt from our *. Ex 13:14
you from your * in Egypt. Ex 20:2
a nation from its * by sending Deu 4:34
who rescued you from * in Egypt. Deu 5:6
the land of Egypt, the land of *. Deu 6:10,11,12
brought you out of * in Egypt with Deu 7:8
of your * in the land of Egypt. Deu 8:14
you out of * in the land of Egypt. Deu 13:5
the land of Egypt, the place of *. Deu 13:10
from their * in the land of Egypt. Jos 24:17
brought you out of * in Egypt, and Ju 6:8
of Israel left their * in Egypt. 1Ki 6:1
safely out of their * in Egypt. 2Ki 17:7
of joy and new life in our *. Ez 9:8
mercy you did not abandon us to *; Ez 9:9
* to get enough money to live. Neh 5:5
them right back into * again. Neh 5:8
to take them back into * in Egypt! Neh 9:17
from all this * to God." Ps 2:3
ancient times from * and made the Ps 74:2
of his people in *—they were Ps 102:20
them from their *, but they Ps 106:43
of death, crushed by misery and *? Ps 107:10
ransom Israel from her * to sin. Ps 130:8
and fear, from * and chains, you Is 14:3
Go now, leave your bonds and *. Is 52:11
them out of * in Egypt that if they Jer 11:4
I brought you out from * in Egypt. Jer 16:14,15
of * are ended, I will punish the Jer 25:12
the nations now in * to King Jer 28:11
forcing them into * to Jer 28:14
I will end your * and restore your Jer 29:14
them from their * in Egypt. Jer 34:13
ropes to hitch me to a yoke of *. Lam 1:14
from * by pointing out your sins. Lam 2:14
their chains of * and delivered Eze 34:27
So I bought her [back from her * Hos 3:2
And so I have sentenced them to * Hos 11:7
delivered you from * in Egypt, and Hos 12:9
him, and led him into * to Edom. Amo 1:9
and sold into * the poor who can't Amo 2:6
sent far away into exile and *." Amo 7:11
Egypt, and cut your chains of *. Mic 6:4
I brought you out of * in Egypt. Mic 7:15
yoke of * to this Assyrian king." Nah 1:13
them out of * the first time. Zec 10:11f
descendants from *, the Jewish Act 7:17,18
leading them out of their *. Act 13:17
sold into * with Sin as my owner. Rom 7:14
Who will free me from my * to Rom 7:23,24,25
Or, "to free us from * to sin." 1Co 1:30f
* to Jewish laws and ceremonies. Gal 5:1
Satan's trap of * to sin which he 2Ti 2:26

SLAVES
"May they be the lowest of * Gen 9:24,25
may the Canaanites be Shem's *." Gen 9:26,27f
cattle and * he had gotten in Gen 12:5
men and women *, and camels. Gen 12:16
* in a foreign land for 400 years. Gen 15:13
whether born there or bought as *. Gen 17:24-27
and many * and camels and donkeys. Gen 24:35
May many nations be your *. Gen 27:27,28,29
seize us as *, with our donkeys." Gen 43:18
And all the rest of us will be * Gen 44:9
to be your *, both we and he in Gen 44:16
him and said, "We are your *." Gen 50:18
So the Egyptians made * of them Ex 1:11
cattle and * in from the fields; Ex 9:20
letting all these * get away?" Ex 14:5
we were *, to leave us alone? Ex 14:12
be better to be * to the Egyptians Ex 14:12
son, daughter, or *—whether men or Ex 20:10
or want to own his *, oxen, Ex 20:17
household—your * and visitors. Ex 23:12
servants, your *, and any Lev 25:6,7
ordinary *, or treated harshly; Lev 25:42
"However, you may purchase * Lev 25:44
They will be permanent * for you Lev 25:46
intention that you be * no longer; Lev 26:13
lands as prisoners of war, and *. Lev 26:36
and little ones will become *. Num 14:3
* of the people of the land. Num 14:31
and became * of the Egyptians. Num 20:15
It is because you were * in Deu 5:15
'We were Pharaoh's * in Egypt, and Deu 6:21
Remember that you were * in the Deu 15:15
Do the same with your women *. Deu 15:17
Always remember that you were * Deu 24:18
Remember that you were * in the Deu 24:2
and daughters are taken away as *. Deu 28:3
be snatched away from you as *. Deu 28:4
You will become * to your enemies Deu 28:47,4
to your enemies as *—but no one Deu 28:6
They replied, "We will be your * Jos 9:
as * among the people of Ephraim. Jos 16:1
the Canaanites to work as *. Jos 17:1
to work as *, but never did force Ju 1:2
or Nahalol, but made them their *; Ju 1:3
them and made them their *. Ju 1:3
people of Israel were * in Egypt? 1Sa 2:2
* just as they have been ours." 1Sa 4:
He will demand your * and the 1Sa 8:16
flocks, and you shall be his *. 1Sa 8:17
kill me, then we will be your *. 1Sa 17:9
kill him, then you must be our *! 1Sa 17:9
He made * of the people of the 2Sa 12:31
* escaped to King Achish of Gath. 1Ki 2:39
And when he had found his *, he 1Ki 2:40
and they continue as * even today. 1Ki 9:20,21
would take her two sons as his *. 2Ki 4:1
us and make * of us and get in." 2Ki 7:12
However, he didn't make * of any 2Ch 8:9
And now are you going to make * 2Ch 28:10
and capturing many people as *. 2Ch 28:16
away to Babylon as * to the king 2Ch 36:20
in addition to 7,337 * and 200 Ez 2:64,65
For we were *, but in your love Ez 9:9
from exile as * in distant lands, Neh 5:8
also, 7,337 * and 245 choir Neh 7:67
"So now we are * here in the Neh 9:36
* among all this abundance! Neh 9:36
If we were only to be sold as *, Est 7:4
and deceived are both his *. Job 12:16
He reduces kings to * and frees Job 12:18
Priests are led away as *. Job 12:19
be the * of those who are good. Ps 49:14
where we were * on foreign soil. Ps 81:5
Next I bought *, both men and Ecc 2:7,8
all taken away as * to other Is 6:12
people shall no longer be their *. Is 14:25
Assyrians will be taken away as *. Is 31:8
sons will become *, yes, eunuchs, Is 39:7
I have not treated you as *. Is 43:23
enemies shall come and be your *. Is 49:18
Soon, soon you * shall be Is 51:14
the people were taken away as *. Jer 1:3
has Israel become a nation of *? Jer 2:14
now you must be * to foreigners Jer 5:19
flock shall be carried away as *. Jer 13:17
Judah shall be taken away as *. Jer 13:19
take you as * to a land where you Jer 15:14
had sent them as * for punishment. Jer 16:14,15
send you away as * to your enemies Jer 17:4
as * to Babylon and kill them. Jer 20:4
shall become * in Babylon and die Jer 20:6
your friends are taken off as *. Jer 22:22
and all your enemies shall be *. Jer 30:16
taken away by the Assyrians as *. Jer 31:15f
had freed all the * in Jerusalem— Jer 34:8
his Hebrew *, both men and women. Jer 34:9
and freed their *, but the action Jer 34:10
and made their servants * again. Jer 34:11
I commanded you, and freed your *. Jer 34:15
oath and have made them * again. Jer 34:16
kill you or make * of you but will Jer 42:12
or carried off to Babylon as *." Jer 43:2,3
and daughters are taken away as *. Jer 48:46
will be dragged away as *! Jer 49:20
shall be dragged away as *; Jer 50:45
did to others, making them her *. Lam 1:3
captured and taken far away as *. Lam 1:5
far away as * to distant lands. Lam 1:18
took away her children as their *. Eze 23:10
be taken away as *, and everything Eze 23:25
bring * and bronze dishes, while Eze 27:13
the women will be taken away as *. Eze 30:17
sent you away as * to many lands. Eze 36:3
capture vast booty and many *. Eze 38:12
are carried off to Assyria as *? Hos 9:6
when they go as * to Assyria, a Hos 10:6
even on your *, men and women Joe 2:29
divided up my people as their *; Joe 3:3
go back to Kir as * was like saying Amo 1:5f
back to Egypt as *, for the Syrians Amo 1:5f
as *." The Lord has spoken. Amo 1:5
exile, selling them as * in Edom. Amo 1:6
be the first to be taken as *; Amo 6:7
* in exile, far from their land.' Amo 7:17
you who make * of the poor, Amo 8:6
led away as *—stripped, naked and Mic 1:11
They have gone as * to distant Mic 1:16
homes with captured goods and *. Nah 2:12
Never again will you bring back * Nah 2:13
and her people were led off as *; Nah 3:10
and their * will be their rulers! Zec 2:9
be taken away as *, and half will Zec 14:1
"But his father said to the *, Lk 15:22
men order their * around, and the Lk 22:25
* have no choice but to like it! Lk 22:25

(SLAVES Con't)
never been * to any man on earth! Jn 8:33
Jesus replied, "You are * of Jn 8:34
one of you. And * don't have Jn 8:35
As the lowliest of * would dress. Jn 13:4f
I no longer call you *, for a Jn 15:15
a master doesn't confide in his *; Jn 15:15
But one of the household * of the Jn 18:26
and there become * for 400 years. Act 7:6
once chose to be * of sin, now you Rom 6:17
and you have become * to your new Rom 6:18
illustration of * and masters, Rom 6:19
as you used to be * to all kinds of Rom 6:19
* to all that is right and holy. Rom 6:19
In those days when you were * of Rom 6:20
of sin and are * of God, and his Rom 6:22
cringing, fearful *, but we should Rom 8:15
Remember me to the Christian * Rom 16:11
some are * and some are free. 1Co 12:13
that we are your * because of what 2Co 4:5
make you their * and take 2Co 11:19,20
in their rules, like * in chains. Gal 2:4
Jews or Greeks or * or free men or Gal 3:28
We were * to Jewish laws and Gal 4:3
for us who were * to the law so Gal 4:5
Now we are no longer *, but Gal 4:7
knew God you were * to so-called Gal 4:8
again and become * once more to Gal 4:9
*, obey your masters; Eph 6:5
must treat your * right, just as I Eph 6:9
remember, you yourselves are * to Eph 6:9
FROM: PAUL AND Timothy, * of Jesus Php 1:1
You * must always obey your Col 3:22
be just and fair to all your *. Col 4:1
CHRISTIAN * SHOULD work hard for 1Ti 6:1
Urge * to obey their masters and Tit 2:9
others and became * to many evil Tit 3:3
lives as * to constant dread. Heb 2:15
* to sin and destruction. 2Pe 2:19
and *—and even the souls of men. Rev 18:13

SLAY
pigeon, and to * them and to cut Gen 15:10
will you * an innocent man? Gen 20:4
plunge it into his son, to * him. Gen 22:10
see, I will * your eldest son." Ex 4:23
Jehovah to * us"), and sometimes Ex 17:7
against God and tempted him to * Ex 17:7
so that he could * them, destroying Ex 32:12
into the wilderness to * them." Deu 9:28
Or, "Though he * me, yet will I Job 13:15f
will sharpen his sword and * them. Ps 7:12
no one can follow me in and * me. Ps 18:2
Evil men take aim to * the poor; Ps 37:14
plans to * your precious ones. Ps 83:3
Surely you will * the wicked, Ps 139:19
Don't let them * me. Ps 141:8
send his angel to * them in a Is 10:26
* the children of this sinner. Is 14:21
For the Lord will * a great Is 34:6
of every tree, and * your children Is 57:5
the Lord God will * you and call Is 65:15
Destroying armies come and * her Jer 51:56
the sword of the enemy will * you; Eze 5:17
Must you also * my children in Eze 16:21
* my people and all their leaders. Eze 21:12
they may * the animals brought Eze 44:11
And if she gives birth, I will * Hos 9:16
and * all the leaders under him." Amo 2:3
leaders, and they will * them. Zec 11:6
own father and mother will * him! Zec 13:3
* him on the altar of sacrifice; Heb 11:17
yes, to * even Isaac, through Heb 11:18

SLAYER
for the * must not be killed Num 35:12
"If the * leaves the City, and Num 35:26
kill the innocent *, even though he Deu 19:6,7
the innocent * must not be released Jos 20:5

SLAYING
He smote great nations, * mighty Ps 135:10
* lambs and goats for sacrifice. Is 34:6
of idols—and the * of your children Eze 16:36

SLAYS
" 'Cursed is he who secretly * Deu 27:24

SLEDGE
grains the same. A * is never used Is 28:27
* hammers demolish your forts. Eze 26:9

SLEDGEHAMMERS
They came with their axes and * Ps 74:5,6

SLEEK
suddenly, seven *, fat cows came up Gen 41:2
They grow * and fat. Ps 73:4
Egypt is * as a heifer, but a Jer 46:20,21

SLEEP
fall into a deep *, and took one of Gen 2:21
going down, a deep * fell upon Gen 15:12
said, "you may * with my servant Gen 16:2,3
and then we will * with him, so Gen 19:32
*, and dreamed that a staircase Gen 28:11
wife, so that I can * with her." Gen 29:21
Then Rachel told him, "* with my Gen 30:3
Rachel said sadly, "He will * Gen 30:15
"You must * with me tonight!" Gen 30:16
whenever he went in to * with Gen 38:9
her to * with him, not realizing of Gen 38:16
she let him come and * with her; Gen 38:18
that he come and * with her. Gen 39:7
sleeve demanding, "* with me." Gen 39:12
house, or want to * with his wife, Ex 20:17
or fail to * with her as his wife. Ex 21:10
how can he * without it? Ex 22:27
and you will go to * without fear. Lev 26:6
A man shall not * with his Deu 22:30
security, you are not to * in it. Deu 24:12,13
must marry her and * with her. Deu 25:5
his wife, intending to * with her; Ju 15:1
She lulled him to * with his Ju 16:19
Notice where he lies down to *; Ru 3:4
a heap of grain and went to *. Ru 3:6,7
One night he couldn't get to * 2Sa 11:2
wine and dine and * with my wife? 2Sa 11:11
Ahithophel told him, "Go and * 2Sa 16:21
with him mats to * on, cooking 2Sa 17:28,29
longer * with them as his wives. 2Sa 20:3
on it in her * and smothered it. 1Ki 3:19
and took mine to * beside her. 1Ki 3:20
in *, you terrify with nightmares. Job 7:13,14
awaken, nor be roused from his *. Job 14:11,12
at night and * in the daytime—they Job 24:16
night when deep * falls on men as Job 33:15
I will lie down in peace and *, Ps 4:8
Don't *, O Lord! Ps 44:23
They lie before us in the * of Ps 76:5
I cannot * until you act. Ps 77:4
awakening from *, and like a mighty Ps 78:65
I couldn't rest, I couldn't *, Ps 132:2-5
With them on guard you can * Pro 3:24,25,26
for evil men don't * until they've Pro 4:16
But you—all you do is *. Pro 6:9
"Let me * a little longer!" Pro 6:10
And as you *, poverty creeps Pro 6:11
If you love *, you will end in Pro 20:13
And remember that too much * Pro 23:19,20,21
"A little extra *, Pro 24:32,33
Let him *!" Sol 2:7
Let him *." Sol 3:5
stopping for rest or for *. Is 5:27
out upon you a spirit of deep *. Is 29:10
All my * has fled because of my Is 38:15
They love to lie there, love to * Is 56:10
"Such * is very sweet!" Jer 31:26
to the floor, to * forever, never Jer 51:39
They shall * and not wake up Jer 51:57
places and * safely in the woods. Eze 34:25
and didn't * all night. Dan 6:18
closed their eyes in *, Mt 13:15
* on now and take your rest . Mt 26:45
returned to them he said, "* on; Mk 14:41
The time for * has ended! Mk 14:41
has gone to *, but now I will go Jn 11:11
has put them to *, shutting their Rom 11:8
Night is the time for * and the 1Th 5:7

SLEEPER
O *, and rise up from the dead; Eph 5:14

SLEEPING
a girl, then after * with her Deu 22:13,14
and Samuel was * in the Temple near 1Sa 3:2,3
General Abner were * inside a ring 1Sa 26:5,6,7
of his position by * with one of 2Sa 3:7
But as he was *, an angel touched 1Ki 19:5
his father by * with one of his 1Ch 5:1
THAT NIGHT THE king had trouble * Est 6:1
he is always watching, never *. Ps 121:3,4
The Girl: "One night as I was *, Sol 5:2
roared, "* at a time like this? Jon 1:6
she is only *!" Mt 9:24
and found them *, for their eyes Mt 26:43
Don't let me find you *. Mk 13:35,36,37
them *, for they were very tired. Mk 14:40
a paralyzed man on a * mat. Lk 5:18,19
* mat, right in front of Jesus. Lk 5:18,19
he was * the wind began to rise. Lk 8:23
up your * mat and go on home!" Jn 5:8
It's illegal to carry that * Jn 5:10

SLEEPLESS
and through the cold and * nights. Gen 31:40
They lie there * with anxiety, Hos 7:14
awake through * nights of watching, 2Co 6:5
weariness and pain and * nights. 2Co 11:27

SLEEPS
to anyone, and * with her, he must Ex 22:16
If a man * with his father's Lev 20:11
Israel * as a lion or a lioness— Num 24:3-9
* away his hour of opportunity. Pro 10:5
A lazy man * soundly—and goes Pro 19:15
The man who works hard * well Ecc 5:12

SLEEVE
* demanding, "Sleep with me." Gen 39:12

SLEEVELESS
Apparently a sort of * tunic Ex 28:4f

SLEEVES
a long robe with *, as was the 2Sa 13:17,18
clutch at the coat * of one Jew and Zec 8:23

SLENDER
You grew up and became tall, * Eze 16:6,7

SLEPT
So he * with Hagar, and she Gen 16:4
"I * with my father last night. Gen 19:34
But Abimelech hadn't * with her Gen 20:4
Leah to Jacob, and he * with her. Gen 29:23
So Jacob * with Rachel, too, and Gen 29:30
his wife, and he * with her, and Gen 30:4
there that Reuben * with Bilhah, Gen 35:22
I am demoting you, for you * with Gen 49:4
'If no man has * with you except Num 5:19
up to him as he *, she drove the Ju 4:21
seven bowstrings, and while he * Ju 16:8
So that time, as he *, Ju 16:12
So while he *, she did just that Ju 16:14
Ruth, and when he * with her, the Ru 4:13
and when Elkanah * with Hannah, 1Sa 1:19,20
not * with any women for awhile." 1Sa 21:4
and when she came he * with her. 2Sa 11:4
he * at the entry to the palace. 2Sa 11:13
and when he * with her, she 2Sa 12:24
Then he lay down and * beneath 1Ki 19:5
on rags, fasted, * in sackcloth, 1Ki 21:27
in a nighttime vision as others *. Job 4:13
Then I lay down and * in peace Ps 3:5
but one night as he *, his enemy Mt 13:25

SLEW
Both Saul and Jonathan * their 2Sa 1:22
Literally, "* Goliath of Gath." 2Sa 21:19f
* Egypt, the dragon of the Nile. Is 51:9

SLICE
olive oil, and a * of bread, all Lev 8:26

SLIDING
God will send them * over the edge Ps 73:18

SLIGHTEST
I hadn't the * intention of Gen 20:5
God's laws in the * respect, and Deu 17:20
me without the * fear of God. Job 6:14
Have I ever asked you for one * Job 6:22
Just the * wickedness, and I am Job 10:15
and cannot tolerate the * sin. Ps 5:4
her mistress for the * signal. Ps 123:2
No one had the * interest in Eze 16:5
they haven't the * idea what those 1Ti 1:7

SLIGHTING
But because Jacob was * Leah, Gen 29:31

SLIM
You are tall and * like a palm Sol 7:7
The Girl: "I am *, tall, Sol 8:10

SLIME
be as snails that dissolve into *; Ps 58:8

SLING
and *, started across to Goliath. 1Sa 17:40
hurled it from his *, and hit the 1Sa 17:48,49
giant with a * and a stone. 1Sa 17:50,51
disappear like stones from a *! 1Sa 25:29

SLINGERS
Literally, "the * surrounded and 2Ki 3:25f
expert archers and *, and they 1Ch 12:2

SLINGSHOT
backfire like a stone tied to a *! Pro 26:8

SLINGSTONES
coats of mail, bows, and *. 2Ch 26:14
Arrows cannot make him flee. * Job 41:27,28

SLINK
Let these evil men * back at Ps 59:14,15
At dawn they * back into their Ps 104:22
and * away, their hopes thwarted. Ps 112:10

SLINKING
At evening they come to spy, * Ps 59:6

SLIP
compassion on them when they *. Deu 32:36
my feet so that I need never *. Ps 18:36
He will not permit the godly to * Ps 55:22
Oh, don't forsake me and let me * Ps 119:8
He will never let me stumble, * Ps 121:3,4
Don't let them * away, for they Pro 3:21
but a crook will * and fall. Pro 10:9
The people * away but they are Is 22:3
days shall * away and disappear, Is 47:15
for you will * out of your hand, Jer 17:4
me, waiting for a fatal *. Jer 20:10
Her soldiers * away, deserting Nah 2:8
We want to * into our new bodies 2Co 5:4
every law of God, without one *. Gal 3:12
makes one little *, is just as Jas 2:10
don't * back into your old 1Pe 1:14

SLIPPED
fled, some * into the pits, and the Gen 14:10
* off and she was left holding it Gen 39:12
when it has * beneath its load, Deu 22:4
David * over to Saul's camp one 1Sa 26:5,6,7
* the dagger from its sheath. 2Sa 20:8,9,10
at the time). They * out of 1Ki 11:16,17,18
My feet have not * from your Ps 17:5
behind and then * inside the gates Mk 14:54
they had done, he * quietly away Lk 9:10
And the Jewish leaders * away Jn 8:9
Dear brothers, if anyone has * Jas 5:19

SLIPPERY
and, despite the * snow on the 2Sa 23:20

(SLIPPERY Con't)
He also killed a lion in a * pit 1Ch 11:22
Make their path dark and * Ps 35:6
What a * path they are Ps 73:18
their paths will be dark and *; Jer 23:12

SLIPPING
were rapidly * away, he decided to 1Sa 13:8
To keep them from *. 2Sa 22:37
for keeping me from * and falling. Ps 26:12
and my feet from *, so that I can Ps 56:13
My feet were * and I was almost Ps 73:2
I screamed, "I'm *, Lord!" Ps 94:18
I am * down the hill to death; Ps 109:22,23
And he is able to keep you from * Jud 1:24,25

SLIT
* off the bottom of Saul's robe! 1Sa 24:4
his knife, and * off the section Jer 36:23

SLITHER
This includes all reptiles that * Lev 11:41,42

SLOPE
is opposite the * of Adummim). Jos 18:17
They climbed the mountain * 1Sa 26:13

SLOPES
Sea, below the * of Mount Pisgah. Deu 4:49
the lowlands, and the mountain *. Jos 10:40
the cities on the * of Mount Jos 11:1
Sea and the * of Mount Pisgah. Jos 12:3
the mountain *, the Judean Desert, Jos 12:8-24
and the * of Mount Pisgah. Jos 13:20
opposite the * of Adummim on the Jos 15:7
the * of Mount Tabor into battle. Ju 4:14
no crops of grain grow on your *. 2Sa 1:21
on the * of Mount Gilboa. 1Ch 10:1
them coming up the * of Ziz at the 2Ch 20:16
highest * and deep within the sea! Ps 68:22
that frisk across the * of Gilead. Sol 4:1
frisking down the * of Gilead. Sol 6:5
or, "on the * of Mount Saphon." Is 14:13f
on the * of the Mount of Olives. Mt 24:3
And as he sat on the * of the Mk 13:3,4
When they came down the * of the Lk 6:17,18
5,000—sat down on the grassy *. Jn 6:10

SLOW
They are not * like the Egyptian Ex 1:19
Literally, "my speech is * and Ex 4:10f
God," he said, "* to anger and Ex 34:5,6
Don't * down for my comfort 2Ki 4:24
and merciful, * to become angry, Neh 9:17
and gentle, Lord, * in getting Ps 86:15
he is * to get angry and full of Ps 103:8
Jehovah is kind and merciful, * Ps 145:8
those who die of * starvation. Lam 4:9
God, merciful, * to get angry, and Jon 4:2
He is * in getting angry, but Nah 1:3
If it seems *, do not despair, Hab 2:3
He isn't really being * about 2Pe 3:9

SLOW-TEMPERED
It is better to be * than famous; Pro 16:32

SLOWING
that is no excuse for * down; 1Ti 6:2

SLOWLY
Thus he continued * southward to Gen 12:9
right shoulders * before the Lord Lev 9:21
sipping it *, lest it disappear. Job 20:13
See them moving * across the Is 30:6
One of these, growing * at Dan 8:9
happen right away. *, steadily, Hab 2:3
for she had been * bleeding for Lk 8:43,44
and moving * along the southern Act 27:7,8

SLOWS
off anything that * us down or Heb 12:1

SLUMBER
A little more *, Pro 24:32,33

SLUMBERING
a ring formed by the * soldiers. 1Sa 26:5,6,7

SLUR
"God has removed the dark * Gen 30:23,24

SMALL
close by and it is just a * one. Gen 19:18,19,20
Don't you see how * it is? Gen 19:18,19,20
some of the children are *, and Gen 33:13
(or, if a family is *, let it Ex 12:3,4
* family in the neighborhood; Ex 12:3,4
as * as hoarfrost on the ground. Ex 16:14
"THEN MAKE A * altar for burning Ex 30:1
each, and fifty * bronze clasps to Ex 36:18
"These are the forbidden * Lev 11:29,30
will repay only a * part of the Lev 25:52
"Does it seem a * thing to you Num 16:8,9
"Is it a * thing," they Num 16:13
be fair to great and * alike. Deu 1:17
nation, great or *, has God among Deu 4:7
animal, bird, a * animal that runs Deu 4:18
Joshua, "It's a * city and it Jos 7:3
Then, though he was still so *, 1Sa 1:24
of grapes, and a * barrel of wine. 2Sa 16:1
But now I have just a * favor to 1Ki 2:16
"I have one * request to make of 1Ki 2:20
altar was too * to handle so much. 1Ki 8:64
was a very * child at the time). 1Ki 11:16,17,18
can see, our dormitory is too *. 2Ki 6:1
cities both large and *. 2Ki 18:8
And with an army as * as yours, 2Ki 18:24
and the people, * and great, of 2Ki 23:1
*, to accompany him to the Temple. 2Ch 34:30
items, great and *, used in the 2Ch 36:18
large, but the population was *; Neh 7:4
midnight great and * shall suddenly Job 34:20
of every kind, both great and *. Ps 104:25
great and *, who reverence him. Ps 115:13
There are four things that are * Pro 30:24-28
There was a * city with only a few Ecc 9:14
Yes, a * mistake can outweigh Ecc 10:1
* and great, all bow before them; Is 2:9
Her great and * shall be Is 5:14
* alike, both officers and men. Is 10:33
Great men and *—all will be Is 19:10
enough seed for a * harvest next Is 37:30
You worry at being so * and few, Is 51:1
for all of them, great and *, Jer 8:10
Both great and * shall die in Jer 16:6
For everyone, both great and *, Jer 31:34
that he be given a * loaf of fresh Jer 37:21
people, great and *, came to Jer 42:1
people, great and *, and said to Jer 42:8
and let only a * quota return. Eze 20:37
"Is it a * thing to you, O evil Eze 34:18
its pieces were crushed as * as Dan 2:35
suddenly another * horn appeared Dan 7:8
Therefore your harvests will be * Hos 9:2
and * should be smashed to pieces. Amo 6:11
For Israel is so *!" Amo 7:2
For Israel is so *!" Amo 7:5
Edom, making you * and despised. Ob 1:2
you are but a * Judean village, yet Mic 5:2
Do not despise this * Zec 4:10
to you—a remnant, *, discouraged as Zec 8:6
But the Gateway to Life is *, Mt 7:14
"We have exactly five * loaves Mt 14:17
of bread and a few * fish!" Mt 15:34
"For if you had faith even as * Mt 17:20
Jesus called a * child over to Mt 18:2
in handling this * amount,' he told Mt 25:21
faithful over this * amount, so now Mt 25:23
Jesus took a * loaf of bread and Mt 26:26
A few * fish were found, too, so Mk 8:7
he was very *, and the demon often Mk 9:21
to give—large or *—will be used to Lk 6:38
For unless you are honest in * Lk 16:10
laws since I was a * child." Lk 18:21
and dropped in two * copper coins. Lk 21:2
and then took a * loaf of bread and Lk 24:30
Several * boats from Tiberias Jn 6:22,23
each day, met in * groups in homes Act 2:46
they came to a * body of water, and Act 8:36
in Cilicia which is no * town. Act 21:39
to everyone, both great and *. Act 26:22
We finally sailed behind a * Act 27:16
of them, only a * number would Rom 9:27
quite * and won't last very long. 2Co 4:17
your love is too * and does not 2Co 6:12
will get only a * crop, but if he 2Co 9:6
You know how, when you were a * 2Ti 3:15
great and *, will know me already. Heb 8:11
by means of a * bit in his mouth. Jas 3:3
So also the tongue is a * thing, Jas 3:5
all men great and *, slave and Rev 6:15
And he held open in his hand a * Rev 10:2
both great and *—and to destroy Rev 11:18
He required everyone—great and *, Rev 13:16
* and great, who fear him." Rev 19:5
great and *, slave and free." Rev 19:18
I saw the dead, great and *, Rev 20:12

SMALLER
the day and the * one, the moon, to Gen 1:16
But the * matters they can take Ex 18:22
judged the * matters themselves. Ex 18:26
more land, the * tribes less land. Num 26:54
"and let the * tribes draw for the Num 26:55,56
tribes draw for the * sections." Num 26:55,56
tribes, and the * sections will be Num 33:54
will be allotted to the * tribes. Num 33:54
the * tribes will give fewer." Num 35:8
* shields, each worth $140,000. 2Ch 9:16
the tribute of * nations, and who Ps 68:30f
and dry measure. * units shall be Eze 45:11
off, and four * horns replace it, Dan 8:22
Twenty-four * thrones surrounded Rev 4:4

SMALLEST
other, for you were the * of all! Deu 7:7
of Benjamin, the * in Israel, and 1Sa 9:21
* contingent in my master's army. 2Ki 18:24
to obey you in the * detail, and 1Ch 29:19
against even the * and worst Is 36:8,9
this will bring me glory. The * Is 60:22
and steal their * crumb by all your Amo 5:11
Or quench the * hope; Mt 12:20
It is the * of all seeds, but Mt 13:31,32
Though this is one of the * of Mk 4:31,32
to tithe even the * part of your Lk 11:42
will get even the * taste of what I Lk 14:24
its force in even the * point. Lk 16:17

SMART
you will only get a * retort; Pro 9:7,
They are * enough at doing wrong, Jer 4:2

SMARTER
Yet in his own opinion he is * Pro 26:1

SMASH
heathen altars, * the obelisks they Ex 34:1
defiled, and you shall * the bowl. Lev 11:3
Break the altars, * the Deu 12:
Rule them with an iron rod; * Ps 2:
reached out his hand to * them. Is 5:2
will still be poised to * you. Is 9:11,1
is still poised to * them all. Is 9:1
God will * you like a broken Is 30:1
the mountains and * down the city Is 45:
* down the walls of Jerusalem. Jer 6:
And I will * fathers and sons Jer 13:1
these men watch, * the jar you Jer 19:1
of Judah, I will * Edom with my Eze 25:1
And I will * the idols of Egypt Eze 30:1
It will * the pride of Egypt and Eze 32:1
you and I will * you with my fist Eze 35:
heathen altars and * their idols. Hos 10:
altar, saying, "* the tops of the Amo 9:
" 'I will * them with my fist Zec 2:

SMASHED
oven, it is defiled and must be *. Lev 11:3
ground! I * them before your eyes! Deu 9:1
the tablets I had *, and that I Deu 10:
of the Temple; he * them to bits 2Ki 23:1
Ammonites.) He * the obelisks and 2Ki 23:1
sledgehammers and * and chopped the Ps 74:5,
hammer that * the rock to pieces? Jer 23:2
for I have * and shattered Moab Jer 48:3
All your cities will be * and Eze 6:4-
Therefore, it must be * to bits. Hos 8:6
and small should be * to pieces. Amo 6:1
All her carved images will be * Mic 1:7
* the shackles and walked away. Mk 5:3,4

SMASHES
and * them against the rocks! Ps 137:9

SMASHING
of iron and clay, * them to bits. Dan 2:34
will be strong as iron—*, Dan 2:40
they will prevent you from * on Mt 4:6

SMEAR
his finger and * it upon the horns Lev 4:30
his finger and * it upon the horns Lev 4:34
guilt offering and * some of it Lev 14:14
guilt offering and * some of its Lev 14:25
He must * the blood of the young Lev 16:18
of its blood and * it on the four Eze 43:20
* your name because you are mine! Lk 6:22

SMEARED
killed it. He * some of the blood Lev 8:15,16
of its blood and * it upon the lobe Lev 8:23
Next he * some of the blood upon Lev 8:24
finger in it and * it upon the Lev 9:9
* with sin. Deu 32:5

SMEARING
of the altar, * it on with your Ex 29:12
the altar, * Ex 30:10

SMEARS
they are evil * among you, laughing Jud 1:12

SMELL
Isaac: "The * of my son is the Gen 27:27,28,29
my son is the good * of the earth Gen 27:27,28,29
see nor hear nor eat nor *. Deu 4:28
Nor can they hear, nor *, nor Ps 115:6
How delicious they *! Sol 2:13
and they didn't even * of smoke! Dan 3:27
stench of death was terrible to *. Amo 4:10
said, "By now the * will be Jn 11:39
big ear, how could you * anything? 1Co 12:17
we seem a fearful * of death and 2Co 2:16

SMELLED
Literally, "and Jehovah * the Gen 8:21f

SMELLING
along the ground, * of myrrh and Sol 3:6
Instead of * of sweet perfume, Is 3:24

SMELLS
He * the battle when far away. Job 39:25
me; it * to highest heaven.' Jon 1:2

SMELT
* you with the heat of my wrath. Eze 22:18,19,20

SMELTED
and they * so much bronze that it 1Ch 22:3
slag left when silver is *. Eze 22:18,19,20

SMELTING
I myself will melt you in a * Is 1:25

SMILE
it is to see your friendly *! Gen 33:10
he will make me * again, Ps 43:5

SMILED
When they were discouraged, I * Job 29:24
you * upon them and favored them. Ps 44:3

SMILES
Agag arrived all full of *, for 1Sa 15:32
righteousness * down from heaven. Ps 85:11

SMITE
when I * the land of Egypt. Ex 12:13

SMITE Con't)
* you seven times for your sin. Lev 26:24
Shall * the people of Moab, Num 24:15-19
Let the godly * me! Ps 141:5
The Lord will * Egypt and then Is 19:22
The "sword of God" will * them. Is 31:8
The sword of destruction shall * Jer 50:35
It shall * the people of Jer 50:35
* Jerusalem and satisfy my fury." Eze 21:17
that God will * the Shepherd, and Mt 26:31

SMITES
And when the Lord * them, his Is 30:32

SMITH
I have created the * who blows Is 54:16

SMITHS
of the soldiers, craftsmen, and *. 2Ki 24:14
craftsmen and *, all of whom were 2Ki 24:16
* and bronze and iron workers. 1Ch 22:16

SMITTEN
the one you have *, and scoff at Ps 69:26

SMOKE
and saw columns of * and fumes, as Gen 19:28
Sinai was covered with * because Ex 19:18
form of fire; the * billowed into Ex 19:18
lightning and the * billowing from Ex 20:18
behind them, * from the city was Jos 8:20,21
with him saw the *, they knew that Jos 8:20,21
The great cloud of * pouring into Ju 20:35-39
* poured from his nostrils; 2Sa 22:9
Fire leaps from his mouth. * Job 41:20
* blew from his nostrils. Ps 18:8
like grass, and disappear like *. Ps 37:20
and calves. The * of their Ps 66:15
Drive them off like * before the Ps 68:2
for my days disappear like *. Ps 102:3,4
in the *, exhausted with waiting. Ps 119:83
The mountains * beneath your Ps 144:5
his employers—like * in their eyes Pro 10:26
like a cloud of * along the ground, Sol 3:6
canopy of * and cloud throughout Is 4:5
sanctuary was filled with *. Is 6:4
* billowing up from their burning. Is 9:18
surrounded by thick rising *. Is 30:27
end. Its * will rise up forever. Is 34:10
disappear like *, the earth shall Is 51:6
send up a * signal at Jer 6:1
cloud of * above their heads. Eze 8:11
and they didn't even smell of *! Dan 3:27
by the wind, like a cloud of *. Hos 13:3
and fire and pillars of *. Joe 2:30
and fire and clouds of *; Act 2:19
When he opened it, * poured out Rev 9:2
and air were darkened by the *. Rev 9:2
Then locusts came from the * and Rev 9:3
like lions', and * and fire and Rev 9:17,18
and the Lamb. The * of their Rev 14:11
The temple was filled with * Rev 15:8
* rising from her charred remains. Rev 18:9
as they watch the * ascend, and Rev 18:18
the Lord! The * from her burning Rev 19:3

SMOKING
dark, Abram saw a * fire-pot and a Gen 15:17

SMOLDERS
Their plot * through the night, Hos 7:6

SMOOTH
Esau is, and how * my skin is! Gen 27:11,12
Then he picked up five * stones 1Sa 17:40
His words were oily *, but in Ps 55:21
all through life their road is *! Ps 73:4
* flattery is her stock in trade. Pro 5:3
Don't let the sparkle and the * Pro 23:31
best of wine, * and sweet, Sol 7:9
all to see. The * tricks of evil Is 32:7
make him a straight, * road Is 40:3
* off the rough spots in the road. Is 40:4
before them and * and straighten Is 42:16
Your gods are the * stones in Is 57:6
to flask, and is fragrant and *. Jer 48:11
me into a place of high, * walls Lam 3:9
Straighten the curves! * out the Lk 3:5
someone may fool you with * talk. Col 2:4
out a straight, * path for your Heb 12:13
the ocean became as * as glass. Rev 7:1

SMOOTH-TONGUED
each other—these * prophets who Jer 23:30,31

SMOOTHED
the spittle and * the mud over the Jn 9:6
Jesus made mud and * it over my Jn 9:11
So he told them how Jesus had * Jn 9:15

SMOOTHLY
of her sister," Laban replied *. Gen 29:26
began to run *, his crops Gen 39:5
so that everything ran * and well. Gen 39:23
* as olive oil, the Lord God says. Eze 32:14

SMOOTHS
path, but * the road before them. Is 26:7

SMOTE
his people. He * great nations, Ps 135:10
Praise the God who * the Ps 136:10
that the king who * you is dead. Is 14:29
I was angry and * these greedy Is 57:17
Was it in anger, Lord, you * the Hab 3:8,9

SMOTHER
Do not * the Holy Spirit. 1Th 5:19

SMOTHERED
over on it in her sleep and * it. 1Ki 3:19
king's face until he * to death. 2Ki 8:15

SMYRNA
the one in *, and those in Rev 1:11
of the church in * write this Rev 2:8

SNAIL
The *, the chameleon. Lev 11:29,30

SNAILS
Let them be as * that dissolve Ps 58:8

SNAKE
at the bronze *, he recovered! Num 21:9
an old wall—and be bitten by a *! Ecc 10:8,9
From the * will be born an adder, Is 14:29
a wall—and puts his hand on a *. Amo 5:19
will he be given a poisonous *? Mt 7:10
for fish, do you give him a *? Lk 11:11
fire, a poisonous *, driven out by Act 28:3
But Paul shook off the * into the Act 28:5
did, and died from * bites. 1Co 10:9

SNAKES
So the Lord sent poisonous * Num 21:6
Pray to him to take away the *." Num 21:7
of one of these * and attach it Num 21:8
with the dangerous * and scorpions, Deu 8:15
in animals, birds, *, fish, and 1Ki 4:33
They are poisonous as deadly *, Ps 58:4,5
step on poisonous *, yes, even Ps 91:13
words sting like poisonous *. Ps 140:3
and cattle, the * and birds, the Ps 148:10
among poisonous *, and a little Is 11:8
and swift venomous * live—and Egypt Is 30:6
does, and poisonous * shall strike Is 65:25
* which you cannot charm. Jer 8:17
of all kinds of *, lizards and Eze 8:10
birds, and *, not to fear each Hos 1:18
They will see what * they are, Mic 7:17
"You sons of *!" Mt 3:7
You brood of *! Mt 12:34
full measure of their evil. *! Mt 23:33
even to handle * with safety, and Mk 16:18
for baptism: "You brood of *! Lk 3:7
sorts of animals, * and birds Act 10:12
birds and animals and * and puny Rom 1:23
the sting and poison of deadly *. Rom 3:13

SNAP
her, and to * off some heads of Ru 2:16
their necks and * their chains, and Jer 30:8
"But now I * my fingers and call Eze 22:13
I will * the bars that locked Amo 1:5
A trap doesn't * shut unless it Amo 3:5
Don't * back at those who say 1Pe 3:9

SNAPPED
which he was tied * like thread and Ju 15:14
Then he * the bowstrings like Ju 16:9
Elisha *. 2Ki 2:3
the trap they set has * on them. Ps 9:15
of death and * their chains. Ps 107:14
For he has * the chains that evil Ps 129:3,4
cracked staff, you * beneath her Eze 29:7
"Grace" and * it in two, showing Zec 11:10
he often was—he * the handcuffs Mk 5:3,4

SNAPS
tow * when it touches the fire." Ju 16:9f
cord of life *, and the golden bowl Ecc 12:6

SNARE
Do not take it or it will be a * Deu 7:25
Instead, they will be a * and a Jos 23:13
lives as a bird from a hunter's *. Ps 124:7
The * is broken and we are free! Ps 124:7
He was as a bird flying into a *, Pro 7:23
in a net, or a bird caught in a *. Ecc 9:12
from the trap shall run into a *. Jer 48:44
be captured in my *, and I will Eze 17:20

SNARES
the wicked in their own *! Ps 9:16
Let them fall into their own *, Ps 141:10
woman whose heart is * and nets." Ecc 7:26f
but sinners don't evade her *. Ecc 7:26
anointed—was captured in their *. Lam 4:20

SNARL
yes, he will * at you. Pro 9:7,8

SNARLED
"Get out of here!" he * at her. 2Sa 13:15
* at King Jehoram of Israel. 2Ki 3:13
they *. Mk 14:4,5
the Jewish leaders *. Jn 8:48

SNATCH
When he sends death to * a man Job 9:12
"The wicked * fatherless Job 24:9
Lord, * me back from the jaws of Ps 9:13
Who can * the prey from the hands Is 49:24
No one shall * them away from me, Jn 10:28

SNATCHED
will be * away from you as slaves. Deu 28:41
paths of sin are * away in youth, Job 22:15,16
He spoke, and they were healed—* Ps 107:20
be gone, greedily * away as an Is 28:4
fig is hungrily * and gobbled up! Is 28:4
was too late; he * from the lion's Amo 3:12
firebrands * away from fire. Amo 4:11
But, O Lord my God, you have * me Jon 2:6
For they are * away and you will Mic 1:16

SNATCHES
comes and * away the seeds from Mt 13:19

SNATCHING
Save some by * them as from the Jud 1:23

SNEAK
They are the kind who craftily * 2Ti 3:6

SNEAKED
"I * away because I was Gen 31:31
of wheat, but then * into his 2Sa 4:6,7

SNEAKING
"What do you mean by * off like Gen 31:26

SNEAKS
a sheepfold, who * over the wall, Jn 10:1

SNEAKY
but he is a * fellow, that Paul, 2Co 12:16

SNEER
heathen nations *, for you will no Eze 36:15
who see you will snicker and *! Mic 6:16
and * at those who try to be good. 2Ti 3:3

SNEERED
"Your enemies have * at you and Eze 36:2
Then how they all scoffed and * Mt 9:24

SNEERING
ahead of him, * in contempt at this 1Sa 17:41,42
criminals * at honorable men. Is 3:5
They are * and saying that Israel Jer 33:24
and boastful, * at God, disobedient 2Ti 3:2

SNEERS
be troubled by the * these 2Ki 19:5,6
Everyone who sees me mocks and * Ps 22:7

SNEEZED
This time the little boy * seven 2Ki 4:35

SNEEZES
"When he *, the sunlight Job 41:18

SNICKER
all who see you will * and sneer! Mic 6:16

SNIFFING
You are a wild donkey, * the Jer 2:24

SNIFFS
Isaac * his clothes, and finally Gen 27:26

SNIP
He will * the spreading tendrils. Is 18:5

SNORTING
His majestic * is something to Job 39:20
Literally, "The * of their war Jer 8:16f

SNOUT
a fine gold ring in a pig's *. Pro 11:22

SNOW
the slippery * on the ground, took 2Sa 23:20
a leper, his skin as white as *. 2Ki 5:27
when there was * on the ground. 1Ch 11:22
it floods when there is ice and * Job 6:15-18
as drought and heat consume *. Job 24:19
For he directs the *, the Job 37:6
treasuries of the *, or seen where Job 38:22,23
me and I shall be whiter than *. Ps 51:7
He sends the * in all its lovely Ps 147:16
Let fire and hail, *, rain, wind Ps 148:8
Literally, "*." Pro 25:13f
any more than * with summertime or Pro 26:1
you as clean as freshly fallen *. Is 1:18
As the rain and * come down from Is 55:10
understand. The * never melts high Jer 18:14
Literally, "were purer than *, Lam 4:7f
His clothing was as white as *, Dan 7:9
was white as wool or *, and his Rev 1:14

SNOWFLAKES
their enemies like * melting in the Ps 68:14

SNUFF
watched to * out any sign of life. Job 16:9

SNUFFED
Their candle of life is * out. Job 4:21
his light will be * out. Pro 24:19,20
lives * out like candlewicks. Is 43:17

SNUFFERS
forward. The * and trays are to be Ex 25:38
the branches, the *, and the Ex 37:23,24
the lamps, *, trays, and the Num 4:9
tongs, cups, *, basins, spoons, 1Ki 7:50
silver cups, gold *, bowls, 2Ki 12:13,14
shovels, firepans, *, spoons, and 2Ki 25:14,15
tongs, lamp *, basins, spoons, and 2Ch 4:22
the altar, and the *, spoons, Jer 52:18

SNUFFING
Why should we risk * out the 2Sa 21:17

SO-AND-SO
city and see Mr. *, and tell him, Mt 26:18

SO-CALLED
The other * gods are demons, 1Ch 16:26
other gods: Your * gods, who have Jer 10:11
This * "foolish" plan of God 1Co 1:25
up except for some * "Christians" Gal 2:4
to * gods that did not even exist. Gal 4:8

SOAKED
The land will be * with blood, Is 34:7
so a sponge was * in it and put on Jn 19:29

SOAKS
in sin as a sponge * up water! Job 15:16
SOAP
No amount of * or lye can make Jer 2:22
SOAR
Though you * as high as eagles, Ob 1:4
SOARS
"Do you know how a hawk * and Job 39:26
SOB
(Esau begins to * with deep and Gen 27:34
I would * day and night for the Jer 9:1
SOBBED
"Yes," he *, "it is my son's Gen 37:33
she *. Gen 39:14,15
SOBBING
and burst into tears, * wildly. Gen 21:16
They soon arrived, weeping and *, 2Sa 13:36
All the people began * when they Neh 8:9
* and weeping, I point to their Jer 9:10
Son of dust, with *, beat upon Eze 21:12
SOBER
By that time he was *, and when 1Sa 25:37,38
would embarrass you no end when *. Pro 23:33
I speak words of * truth. Act 26:25
Watch for his return and stay *. 1Th 5:6
in the light keep *, protected by 1Th 5:8
SOBERLY
So now you can look forward * 1Pe 1:13
SOBS
to sob with deep and bitter *. Gen 27:34
Then he wept aloud. His * could Gen 45:2
Then he broke down with great * Is 38:3
She * through the night; Lam 1:2
SOCIAL
or * position is unimportant; Col 3:11
SOCIETY
darkness, all the foundations of * Ps 82:5
SOCKET
knocked it out of joint at the *. Gen 32:25
and a bronze * for each pillar. Ex 26:37
for each *. Ex 38:27
let my arm be torn from its *! Job 31:22
SOCKETS
*, with silver hooks and rods. Ex 27:11
wide, with ten posts and ten *. Ex 27:12
three posts imbedded in three *. Ex 27:14,15
posts imbedded in their four *. Ex 27:16
of marble set in * of finest gold, Sol 5:15
shrivel in their *, and their Zec 14:12
SOCO
Beth-zur, *, Adullam, 2Ch 11:5-10
Aijalon, Gederoth, *, Timnah, and 2Ch 28:17,18
SOCOH
Jarmuth, Adullam, *, Azekah, Jos 15:33-36
Shamir, Jattir, *, Dannah, Jos 15:48-62
and camped between * in Judah and 1Sa 17:1
* and all the land of Hepher; 1Ki 4:8-19
SOCOITES
the Gedorites, *, and Zanoahites. 1Ch 4:18
SODA
Literally, "like vinegar upon * Pro 25:20f
SODI
Gaddiel, son of *, from the tribe Num 13:3-15
SODOM
and to *, Gomorrah, Admah, and Gen 10:15-19
Jehovah destroyed * and Gomorrah); Gen 13:10
at a place near the city of *. Gen 13:12
Bera, king of *, Gen 14:2
These kings (of *, Gomorrah, Gen 14:3
of the kings of *, Gomorrah, Admah, Gen 14:8,9
And as the army of the kings of * Gen 14:10
* and Gomorrah and carried off Gen 14:11
who lived in *—and all he owned. Gen 14:12
the king of * came out to meet him, Gen 14:17
The king of * told him, "Just Gen 14:21
meal and started on toward *; Gen 18:16
that the people of * and Gomorrah Gen 18:20
two went on toward *, but the Lord Gen 18:22,23
of the city of *, and Lot was Gen 19:1
blinded the men of * so that they Gen 19:11
from heaven upon * and Gomorrah, Gen 19:24
the plain to * and Gomorrah and saw Gen 19:28
like * and Gomorrah and Admah and Deu 29:23
They act like men of * and Deu 32:32
wiped out as * and Gomorrah were. Is 1:9
* and Gomorrah, as I call you now. Is 1:10
sin is equal to the sin of *; Is 3:9
destroyed as * and Gomorrah were Is 13:19
as the men of * and Gomorrah were. Jer 23:14
as silent as * and Gomorrah and Jer 49:18
as he destroyed * and Gomorrah and Jer 50:40
than that of *, where utter Lam 4:6
your younger sister is * and her Eze 16:46
"As I live, the Lord God says, * Eze 16:48
the fortunes of * and Samaria Eze 16:53
"Yes, your sisters, * and Eze 16:55
In your proud days you held * in Eze 16:56
Samaria and *, and make them your Eze 16:61
that perished with * and Gomorrah Hos 11:8f
cities, as I did * and Gomorrah; Amo 4:11
be destroyed like * and Gomorrah, Zep 2:9
Truly, the wicked cities of * Mt 10:15
I did in you had been done in *, Mt 11:23
Truly, * will be better off at Mt 11:24
Even wicked * will be better Lk 10:12
until the morning Lot left *. Lk 17:29
cities of * and Gomorrah perished. Rom 9:29
Later, he turned the cities of * 2Pe 2:6
rescued Lot out of * because he was 2Pe 2:7,8
And don't forget the cities of * Jud 1:7
described as "*" or Rev 11:8,9
SODOM'S
Your sister * sins were pride Eze 16:49
SODOMITES
of the city—yes, *, young and old Gen 19:4
SOFT
him as the * earth covers him. Job 21:33
is hard and firm, not * and fat. Job 41:23
A * ANSWER turns away wrath, but Pro 15:1
a * tongue can break hard bones. Pro 25:15
Your eyes are * as doves'. Sol 1:15
SOFTEN
Showers * the earth, melting the Ps 65:10
He will * adult hearts to become Lk 1:17
SOFTENING
Wisdom lights up a man's face, * Ecc 8:1
SOFTLY
the waters of Shiloah that go *." Is 8:6f
but it is beaten * with a flail. Is 28:27
SOIL
was there anyone to farm the *. Gen 2:5
Or, "from a lump of *," or, Gen 2:7f
*," or, "from a clod of clay." Gen 2:7f
formed from the * every kind of Gen 2:19,20
I have placed a curse upon the *. Gen 3:17
Must I die on foreign *, far 1Sa 26:20
worship Jehovah on Israel's *. 2Ki 5:17f
in the * and bear fruit for God. 2Ki 19:30
He was a man who loved the * and 2Ch 26:10
Torrents tear away the *. Job 14:18,19
and tilled the * and we took root Ps 80:9
where we were slaves on foreign *. Ps 81:5
decaying corpses fertilized the *. Ps 83:10
grass in shallow *, turning sere Ps 129:6,7
A poor man's farm may have good * Pro 13:23
Is he forever harrowing the * and Is 28:23,24
and the * made rich with fat. Is 34:7
own * and flourish and multiply. Is 37:31
Babylonian * as early as 3000 B.C. Jer 5:15f
ground to rot and fertilize the *. Jer 16:4
already in good * with plenty of Eze 17:8
* where it had grown so well." Eze 17:10
I will scrape away her * and make Eze 26:4
* of their own land again." Hos 1:11
in the * like cedars in Lebanon. Hos 14:5
I am a farmer. The * has been my Zec 13:5
And some fell on rocky * where Mt 13:5
in the shallow *, but the hot sun Mt 13:5
But some fell on good *, and Mt 13:8
The shallow, rocky * represents Mt 13:20
Some fell on thin * with Mk 4:5,6
no nourishment in the shallow *. Mk 4:5,6
fell into good * and yielded thirty Mk 4:8
The rocky * represents the Mk 4:16
plants in such *, their roots don't Mk 4:17
"But the good * represents the Mk 4:20
For the * made the seeds grow. Mk 4:28
Other seed fell on shallow * Lk 8:6
Still other fell on fertile *; Lk 8:8
"But the good * represents Lk 8:15
the * of God's marvelous love; Eph 3:17
SOILED
my feet, and should I get them *?' Sol 5:3
to the Lord—not * and dirtied by Jas 1:27
some haven't * their garments with Rev 3:4
SOLD
foreign women; he * us, and what he Gen 31:15
of the well and * him to them for Gen 37:28
Egypt, the traders * Joseph to Gen 37:36
storehouses and * grain to the Gen 41:56,57
brother whom you * into Egypt! Gen 45:4
all the Egyptians * him their Gen 47:20
"If he * himself as a slave Ex 21:3
or has already * him as a slave. Ex 21:16
if he can't, then he must be * as Ex 22:3
the family estates * to others Lev 25:10
if he has * it, it shall be his Lev 25:13
if the land is * or bought during Lev 25:14,15,16
so you may not be * as ordinary Lev 25:42
he received when he * himself; Lev 25:51
he received when he * himself. Lev 25:52
or if he has * the field to someone Lev 27:20
not be * or redeemed, for they are Lev 27:28
you have * yourself to the devil. 1Ki 21:20
because you have * yourself to that 1Ki 21:20f
No one else was so completely * 1Ki 21:25
a donkey's head * for fifty dollars 2Ki 6:25
grain will be * in the markets of 2Ki 7:1
of barley were * that day for one 2Ki 7:16
magic and * themselves to evil. 2Ki 17:17
At that time Egyptian chariots * 2Ch 1:17
We have already * some of our Neh 5:5
produce to be * on the Sabbath or Neh 10:
For I and my people have been * Est
If we were only to be * as Est
nations. You * us for a pittance. Ps 44:
say, and * yourselves to the devil Is 28:
No, you * yourselves for your Is 5
For the Lord says, When I * you Is 52
Fields will again be bought and * Jer 32:
be bought and *—deeds signed and Jer 32:
they have * all they have for Lam 1:
our fuel is * to us at the Lam 5
land shall ever be * or traded or Eze 48:
You have * the people of Judah Joe 3
places you have * them to, and I Joe 3
bribes, and * into slavery the poor Amo 2
All this because Nineveh * Nah 3
have * them without mercy. Zec 11
Then those who bought and * Zec 11:
In his excitement, he * Mt 13:4
of great value—and * everything he Mt 13:4
king ordered him * for the debt, Mt 18:2
"Why, she could have * it for a Mt 26:8
"Why, she could have * that Mk 14:4
It should have been * and the Jn 12
land or houses * them and brought Act 4:34,3
He was one of those who * a Act 4:3
wife Sapphira) who * some property, Act 5
and * him to be a slave in Egypt. Act 7
me, because I am * into slavery Rom 7:1
Take any meat you want that is * 1Co 10:2
SOLDER
Now we can * on the arms." Is 41
SOLDIER
there was not a * left in Ai or Jos 8:1
*, the Lord is with you!" Ju 6:1
The other * replied, "Your dream Ju 7:1
to be a real * by fighting the 1Sa 18:1
And your father is an old * and 2Sa 17
a heroic * from Kabzeel. 2Sa 23:2
Each one killed a Syrian *, and 1Ki 20:2
So a * rode out to meet Jehu. 2Ki 9:1
sword of a mighty * brandished Zec 9:1
it to him. The * killed John in the Mk 6:2
and a godly *, one of his personal Act 10:
wanted to, though guarded by a *. Act 28:1
What * in the army has to pay 1Co 9:
as a good * of Jesus Christ, just 2Ti 2:
and as Christ's * do not let 2Ti 2:
like myself is a * of the cross. Phm 1:
SOLDIER'S
in an ordinary * uniform. 1Ki 22:3
SOLDIERS
the * of Amalek were winning. Ex 17:1
which the * kept for themselves) Num 31:32-3
(The * had also kept personal Num 31:5
So approximately three thousand * Jos 7:4
and all the * in the city were Jos 8:16
a panic, both the * and the Ju 4:1
of their best * to destroy the Ju 21:10,11,12
and so many * that they were as 1Sa 13:5
When Saul counted the * who were 1Sa 13:15
the * were asking. 1Sa 17:25
When the * came to arrest David 1Sa 19:14
Ramah, he sent * to capture him; 1Sa 19:20
other *, but they too prophesied! 1Sa 19:21
But the * refused to harm the 1Sa 22:17
a ring formed by the slumbering *. 1Sa 26:5,6,7
with several other Israeli *. 2Sa 11:17
is and how courageous his * are. 2Sa 17:10
they became *, officials, army 1Ki 9:22
of some Israeli * who had died in 1Ki 11:15
with fifty * to arrest him. 2Ki 1:9
of the *, craftsmen, and smiths. 2Ki 24:14
were killed by David and his *. 1Ch 20:8
but used them as *, officers, 2Ch 8:9
with companies of * under their 2Ch 11:11
But one of the Syrian * shot an 2Ch 18:33
of his bravest * because they had 2Ch 28:6
ask the king for * and cavalry to Ez 8:22
courage to your * who are battling Is 28:6
Assyrians and killed 185,000 *; Is 37:36
never again shall foreign * come Is 62:8
homes as troops of * come suddenly Jer 18:22
morale of the few * we have left, Jer 38:4
When King Zedekiah and his * Jer 39:4
They sent * to bring Jeremiah Jer 39:14
and Babylonian * who were in Mizpah Jer 41:3
they had rescued—*, women, children Jer 41:16,17
the mightiest of its * run Jer 46:5
chariots and mighty * of Egypt! Jer 46:9
your mightiest * will stumble Jer 46:12
The numberless * cut down your Jer 46:22,23
Her mightiest * no longer fight; Jer 51:30
wall and all the * fled from the Jer 52:7
But the Chaldean * chased them Jer 52:8
And all the best * of Israel Eze 17:21
and merchants and * and all the Eze 27:27
against Tyre. The *' heads were Eze 29:18
the * as they threw them in! Dan 3:22
These "*" charge like Joe 2:7
Conscript your best *; Joe 3:9

(SOLDIERS Con't)
The mightiest * of Teman will be Ob 1:9
Her * slip away, deserting her; Nah 2:8
of the streets. * drew straws to Nah 3:10
Sending * to Bethlehem, he Mt 2:16
authority over my *, and I say to Mt 8:8,9
and sat with the *, and waited to Mt 26:58
Roman * to take away and crucify. Mt 27:26
* gave him drugged wine to drink; Mt 27:34
After the crucifixion, the * Mt 27:35
The * at the crucifixion and Mt 27:54
For Herod had sent * to arrest Mk 6:17,18
Then the Roman * took him into Mk 15:16,17
"And us," asked some *, "what Lk 3:14
a distance. The * lit a fire in Lk 22:55
Now Herod and his * began mocking Lk 23:11
And the * gambled for his Lk 23:34
The * mocked him, too, by Lk 23:36
of * and police to accompany him. Jn 18:3
So the Jewish police, with the * Jn 18:12
One of the * standing there Jn 18:22
whip, and the * made a crown of Jn 19:2
When the * had crucified Jesus, Jn 19:23,24
So the * came and broke the legs Jn 19:32
However, one of the * pierced Jn 19:34
The * did this in fulfillment of Jn 19:36,37
him under the guard of sixteen *. Act 12:4
between two * with others standing Act 12:6
He quickly ordered out his * and Act 21:32
violent that the * lifted Paul to Act 21:35
The * standing ready to lash him, Act 22:29
apart, ordered his * to take him Act 23:10
ordered, "Get 200 * ready to leave Act 23:23,24
when I sent the * to rescue him, Act 23:27
So that night, as ordered, the * Act 23:31
But Paul said to the * and Act 27:31
So the * cut the ropes and let Act 27:32
The * advised their commanding Act 27:42
how will the * know that they are 1Co 14:8
including all the * over at the Php 1:13

SOLEMN
up, they each took * oaths to seal Gen 26:31
a very great and * funeral service, Gen 50:10
And I entered into a * covenant Ex 6:4
day of * rest, holy to the Lord. Ex 31:16
the seventh day is a day of * Ex 35:2
It is a Sabbath of * rest for Lev 16:31
are always days of * rest in every Lev 23:3
is a * time for all the people to Lev 23:23,24
For this is a Sabbath of * rest, Lev 23:32
the festival are days of * rest. Lev 23:39
be a holy and * assembly of all the Num 28:25
must be a special, * assembly of Num 28:26
there shall be a * assembly of Num 29:1
This will be a day of * humility Num 29:7
the people to another * assembly; Num 29:35
* warning to the people of Israel. Deu 31:26
"We promise with a * oath." Ju 11:10
it was agreed by * oath that anyone Ju 21:5
We have sworn with a * oath that Ju 21:18
So they went to Gilgal and in a * 1Sa 11:15
But Saul took a * oath that he 1Sa 28:10
he and they made a * promise to the 2Ki 23:3
Then Jehoiada made a * contract 2Ch 23:15,16,17
day there was a * closing service Neh 8:18
"I have made a * agreement with Ps 89:3,4
his * oath to care for them. Ps 106:24
I made a * promise to the Lord. Ps 132:2-5
sing a song of * joy, like songs in Is 30:29
But listen now to the * words I Jer 28:7
You lightly broke your * vows to Eze 16:59,60
the * oath he made in my name. Eze 17:19
But I took a * oath against them Eze 20:23,24
call a * meeting. Joe 1:14
people together for a * meeting. Joe 2:15
religious feasts and * assemblies. Amo 5:21
And I tell you this in * truth, Mk 14:9
This is a * promise." Lk 23:43
"In * truth I tell you, anyone Jn 14:12,13
and a * fear descended on the Act 19:17
It is because of this * fear of 2Co 5:11
years of their * testimony, the Rev 11:7

SOLEMNIZE
between its halves to * your vows. Jer 34:18,19

SOLEMNLY
* promise you and your children Gen 9:9,10,11
But Abram replied, "I have * Gen 14:22
"Swear to me most * that you will Gen 47:29
And the people said again, "We * Ex 24:7
For I * said to your fathers Jer 11:7
You had * promised me in my Jer 34:15
Lord spoke very * to Joshua and Zec 3:5,6
"I * declare that any sin of man Mk 3:28
said to them very *, "Beware of Mk 8:15
this *—he won't lose his reward. Mk 9:41
Jesus said, "I * declare that one Mk 14:18
God and man. I * declare that I Mk 14:25
But I * declare to you that no Lk 4:24
"I * declare to you that when Lk 21:32
And I * declare that the time is Jn 5:25
Dear friends, I * swear that the Gal 1:11
as we have * told you before. 1Th 4:6
I * command you in the presence 1Ti 5:21
AND SO I * urge you before God and 2Ti 4:1
And I * declare to everyone who Rev 22:18

SOLICITING
live who was * out beside the road Gen 38:21
and markets, * at every corner for Pro 7:11,12

SOLID
out jewels set in * gold and silver Gen 24:53
They stood as * walls to hold the Ex 15:8
being imbedded in * bronze bases. Ex 27:17
were cast from the * bronze mirrors Ex 38:8
hold up the drapes were * silver. Ex 38:17
strong, and had good, * judgment. 1Sa 16:18
treasure made from * gold set with 2Sa 12:29,30
in the Temple were made of * gold. 1Ki 7:48
Each of these was made of * gold. 1Ki 7:50
cups were of * gold, and in the 1Ki 10:21
dining service was made of * gold. 1Ki 10:21
the gold for the * gold hooks used 1Ch 28:17
And he molded 100 * gold bowls. 2Ch 4:8
cups were * gold, as were all the 2Ch 9:20
30 bowls of * gold, Ez 1:9,10
innocent—as pure as * gold! Job 23:10
Your justice is as * as God's Ps 36:6
towering temple, * and enduring as Ps 78:69
firepans and the * gold and silver Jer 52:19
who builds his house on * rock. Mt 7:24
milk and not with * food, because 1Co 3:2
milk, not old enough for * food. Heb 5:12,13
You will never be able to eat * Heb 5:14
everything without * foundations, Heb 12:27
the Lord to give you any * answer. Jas 1:7,8
with a crown of * gold upon his Rev 14:14

SOLIDLY
But when Jehoram had become * 2Ch 21:3,4

SOLITARY
Literally, "a * land." Lev 16:22f
I lie awake, lonely as a * Ps 102:7
As I watched, I saw a * eagle Rev 8:13

SOLOMON
Shammu-a, Shobab, Nathan, *, 2Sa 5:14,15,16
birth to a son and named him *. 2Sa 12:24
army officers, or his brother *. 1Ki 1:10
of your son *—do exactly as I say! 1Ki 1:12
me that my son * would be the next 1Ki 1:13
God that my son * would be the next 1Ki 1:17
But he didn't invite *. 1Ki 1:19
If you don't act, my son * and I 1Ki 1:21
and * and I weren't invited. 1Ki 1:26
that your son * shall be the next 1Ki 1:30
"Take * and my officers to Gihon. 1Ki 1:33
officers to Gihon. * is to ride on 1Ki 1:33
and shout, 'Long live King *!' 1Ki 1:34
the Lord be with * as he has been 1Ki 1:37
bodyguard took * to Gihon, riding 1Ki 1:38
Tabernacle and poured it over *; 1Ki 1:39
shouted, "Long live King *!" 1Ki 1:39
David has declared * as king!" 1Ki 1:43
That's what all the noise is. * 1Ki 1:46,47
even more through * than he has 1Ki 1:46,47
When word reached * that 1Ki 1:51
for clemency, * replied, "If he 1Ki 1:52
So King * summoned him, and 1Ki 1:53
and then * curtly dismissed him. 1Ki 1:53
he gave this charge to his son *: 1Ki 2:1
in Jerusalem. And * became the new 1Ki 2:12
He replied, "Speak to King * on 1Ki 2:17
went to ask the favor of King *. 1Ki 2:19
Then King * swore with a great 1Ki 2:23,24
So King * sent Benaiah to execute 1Ki 2:25
So * forced Abiathar to give up 1Ki 2:27
When news of this reached King * 1Ki 2:29
When * heard that Shime-i had 1Ki 2:41
* MADE AN alliance with Pharaoh, 1Ki 3:1
(* loved the Lord and followed 1Ki 3:3
* replied, "You were wonderfully 1Ki 3:6
glad that * had asked for wisdom. 1Ki 3:10
Then * woke up and realized it 1Ki 3:15
King * ruled the whole area from 1Ki 4:21
sent taxes to * and continued to 1Ki 4:21
Throughout the lifetime of *, all 1Ki 4:25
* owned forty thousand chariot 1Ki 4:26
food for King * and his court; 1Ki 4:27
God gave * great wisdom and 1Ki 4:29
that David's son * was the new king 1Ki 5:1
and good wishes. * replied with a 1Ki 5:2,3
His father David, * pointed out 1Ki 5:2,3
"But now," * said to Hiram, 1Ki 5:4
pleased with the message from *. 1Ki 5:7
Then he sent this reply to *: 1Ki 5:8
So Hiram produced for * as much 1Ki 5:10
and in return * sent him an annual 1Ki 5:11
to * just as he had promised. 1Ki 5:12
And Hiram and * made a formal 1Ki 5:12
Then * drafted thirty thousand 1Ki 5:13
this labor camp. * also had 1Ki 5:15
After completing the Temple, * 1Ki 6:9
this message to * concerning the 1Ki 6:11,12
pure gold, and * made a cedar-wood 1Ki 6:20
Within the inner sanctuary * 1Ki 6:23-28
THEN * BUILT his own palace, which 1Ki 7:1
where * sat to hear legal matters; 1Ki 7:7
King * then asked for a man named 1Ki 7:13
So he came to work for King *. 1Ki 7:14
been assigned to him by King *. 1Ki 7:40
finally finished, * took into the 1Ki 7:51
THEN * CALLED a convocation at 1Ki 8:1
King * and all the people 1Ki 8:5
Now King * prayed this 1Ki 8:12,13
people watched, * stood before the 1Ki 8:22,23
* had been kneeling with his 1Ki 8:54,55
Afterwards * sent the people 1Ki 8:66
WHEN * HAD finished building the 1Ki 9:1
years during which * built the 1Ki 9:10
For Hiram had sent gold to * 1Ki 9:14
* had conscripted forced labor to 1Ki 9:15
So now * rebuilt Gezer along 1Ki 9:17,18
* conscripted his labor forces 1Ki 9:20,21
even today. * didn't conscript any 1Ki 9:22
King * moved Pharaoh's daughter 1Ki 9:24
After the Temple was completed, * 1Ki 9:25
King * had a shipyard in 1Ki 9:26
gold to King *, the total value of 1Ki 9:27,28
Lord had blessed * with wisdom, 1Ki 10:1
of the fame of * concerning the 1Ki 10:1f
* answered all her questions; 1Ki 10:3
spices King * had ever received. 1Ki 10:10
brought gold to * from Ophir, they 1Ki 10:11
trees and gems. * used the algum 1Ki 10:12
of Sheba, King * gave her 1Ki 10:13
Each year * received gold worth 1Ki 10:14
territories. * had some of the 1Ki 10:16,17
So King * was richer and wiser 1Ki 10:23
* built up a great stable of 1Ki 10:26
KING * MARRIED many other girls 1Ki 11:1
their gods. Yet * did it anyway. 1Ki 11:2
David had done. * worshiped 1Ki 11:5
Thus * did what was clearly 1Ki 11:6
of the Ammonites. * built temples 1Ki 11:8
Jehovah was very angry with * 1Ki 11:9,10
this, for now * was no longer 1Ki 11:9,10
grow in power. And * became 1Ki 11:14
of his rebellion: * was rebuilding 1Ki 11:27,28
able, and when * saw how 1Ki 11:27,28
from the hand of * and give ten of 1Ki 11:31
of Israel. For * has forsaken me 1Ki 11:33
* reign for the rest of his life. 1Ki 11:34
* tried to kill Jeroboam, but he 1Ki 11:40
stayed there until the death of *. 1Ki 11:40
The rest of what * did and said 1Ki 11:41
written in the book The Acts of *. 1Ki 11:41
had fled from King *, heard about 1Ki 12:2,3,4
who had counseled his father *. 1Ki 12:6
"Tell Rehoboam the son of *, 1Ki 12:23,24
Meanwhile, Rehoboam the son of * 1Ki 14:21
all the gold shields * had made. 1Ki 14:26
to David and * about when he said, 2Ki 21:7
Mountain. (* had built these 2Ki 23:13
bowls which King * of Israel had 2Ki 24:13
King *—because they were so heavy. 2Ki 25:16
Nathan and *. 1Ch 3:5
are the descendants of King *: 1Ch 3:10-14
Then, when * built the Temple at 1Ch 6:32
Shammua, Shobab, Nathan, *, Ibhar, 1Ch 14:4-7
(King * later melted the bronze 1Ch 18:8
"* my son is young and tender," 1Ch 22:5
He now commanded his son * to 1Ch 22:6
His name shall be * (meaning 1Ch 22:9
son * as the new king of Israel. 1Ch 23:1
has chosen * to succeed me on the 1Ch 28:5
He has told me, 'Your son * 1Ch 28:6
Then David turned to * and said: 1Ch 28:8
to rule forever. *, my son, get to 1Ch 28:9
Then David gave * the blueprint 1Ch 28:11
He also gave * his plans for the 1Ch 28:12
The king also passed on to * the 1Ch 28:13
David told *, "was given to me in 1Ch 28:19
and said: "My son *, whom God has 1Ch 29:1
Give my son * a good heart 1Ch 29:19
they crowned King David's son * 1Ch 29:22
So God appointed * to take the 1Ch 29:23
their allegiance to King *. 1Ch 29:24
and his son * reigned in his 1Ch 29:28
KING DAVID'S SON * was now the 2Ch 1:1
years before the reign of King *. 2Ch 1:2,3f
and now * and those he had invited 2Ch 1:5,6
That night God appeared to * and 2Ch 1:7
* replied, "O God, you have been 2Ch 1:8
* then left the Tabernacle, 2Ch 1:13
common sycamore! * sent 2Ch 1:16
* NOW DECIDED that the time had 2Ch 2:1
3,600 foremen. * sent an 2Ch 2:3
the Lord my God," * told Hiram. 2Ch 2:4
King Hiram replied to King *: 2Ch 2:11
* now took a census of all 2Ch 2:17
Holy of Holies, * placed two 2Ch 3:10
work assigned to him by King *: 2Ch 4:11
for King *, using polished bronze. 2Ch 4:12-16
gold was used. For * commanded that 2Ch 4:19
finished. Then * brought in the 2Ch 5:1
* now summoned to Jerusalem all 2Ch 5:2

(SOLOMON Con't)
King * and the others sacrificed 2Ch 5:6
THIS IS THE prayer prayed by * on 2Ch 6:1
As he spoke, * was standing 2Ch 6:12,13
AS * FINISHED praying, fire 2Ch 7:1
stood again. * consecrated the 2Ch 7:7
and * and to his people Israel. 2Ch 7:10
So * finished building the Temple 2Ch 7:11
One night the Lord appeared to * 2Ch 7:12
IT WAS NOW twenty years since * 2Ch 8:1
It was at this time, too, that * 2Ch 8:3
* now moved his wife (she was 2Ch 8:11
Then * sacrificed burnt offerings 2Ch 8:12
to their gates. * did not deviate 2Ch 8:15
Thus * successfully completed 2Ch 8:16
And * answered all her problems. 2Ch 9:2
King * gave the Queen of Sheba 2Ch 9:12
* received a billion dollars 2Ch 9:13,14
So King * was richer and wiser 2Ch 9:22
In addition, * had 4,000 stalls 2Ch 9:25
So * reigned in Jerusalem over 2Ch 9:30
he had gone to escape from King *. 2Ch 10:2,3
who had counseled his father *. 2Ch 10:6
as King David and King * had done. 2Ch 11:17
in the way of David and *." 2Ch 11:17f
the days of King David's son *. 2Ch 30:26
David and his son *, "I will be 2Ch 33:7
David of Israel and by his son *. 2Ch 35:4,5
the laws of David and his son *. Neh 12:45
THESE ARE THE proverbs of King * Pro 1:1
These are the proverbs of *: Pro 10:1
THESE PROVERBS OF * Pro 25:1
Hezekiah lived 200 years after *. Pro 25:1f
THE AUTHOR: * Ecc 1:1
THE SONG OF * Sol 1:1
was composed by King *:The Girl: Sol 1:14
King *: "But lovely as the silken Sol 1:1
lovely as the silken tents of *!" Sol 1:5
King *: "If you don't know, O Sol 1:5
King *: "My beloved is a bouquet Sol 1:7
King *: "Yes, a lily among Sol 1:13
of * with sixty of the mightiest Sol 2:1
For King * made himself a Sol 3:7
The Girl: "Go out and see King * Sol 3:9
KING *: "How beautiful you are, Sol 3:11
KING *: "I am here in my garden, Sol 4:1
King *: "O my beloved, you are Sol 5:1
King *: "Because you dance so Sol 6:3
KING *: "How beautiful your Sol 6:13
King *: "Under the apple tree Sol 7:1
King *: "If she has no breasts Sol 8:5
my lover's eyes. * had a vineyard Sol 8:8
vineyard, you, O *, shall have my Sol 8:11
been made in the days of King *. Sol 8:12
David was the father of * (his Jer 52:20
* was the father of Rehoboam; Mt 1:6
Yet King * in all his glory was Mt 1:7
land to hear the wisdom of *; Mt 6:29
and now a greater than * is Mt 12:42
to listen to the wisdom of *; Mt 12:42
but one far greater than * is Lk 11:31
and spin, and yet * in all his Lk 11:31
But it was * who actually built Lk 12:27
Act 7:47

SOLOMON'S
to Bath-sheba, * mother, and asked 1Ki 1:11
* reign even greater than yours!" 1Ki 1:37
May God make * reign even greater 1Ki 1:46,47
came to see * mother, Bath-sheba. 1Ki 2:13
So * grip upon the kingdom became 1Ki 2:46
HERE IS A list of King * cabinet 1Ki 4:1
officials of * court—one man from 1Ki 4:7
Ben-abinadab (who married * 1Ki 4:8-19
another of * daughters), whose area 1Ki 4:8-19
Men from Gebal helped * and 1Ki 5:18
the fourth year of * reign that he 1Ki 6:1
the fourth year of * reign, and 1Ki 6:37
as dowry—she was one of * wives. 1Ki 9:16
sailors to accompany * crews. 1Ki 9:27,28
All of King * cups were of solid 1Ki 10:21
King * merchant fleet was in 1Ki 10:22
common sycamore! * horses were 1Ki 10:28
Another of * enemies whom God 1Ki 11:23
During * entire lifetime, Rezon 1Ki 11:25
and Benjamin were left to * son. 1Ki 11:32f
But because of * sin I will 1Ki 11:39
Azariah (the High Priest in * 1Ch 6:4-15
During * reign, silver and gold 2Ch 1:15
had appeared to * father, King 2Ch 3:1
the fourth year of King * reign. 2Ch 3:2
to the Lord. King * contribution 2Ch 7:4,5
working alongside * men, went to 2Ch 8:17,18
THE QUEEN of Sheba heard of * 2Ch 9:1
King Hiram's and King * crews 2Ch 9:10
All of King * cups were solid 2Ch 9:20
The rest of * biography is 2Ch 9:29
sent word to him of * death. 2Ch 10:2,3
Rehoboam of Judah, * son, and to 2Ch 11:3
also all of * gold shields. 2Ch 12:9
him, defying * son Rehoboam, for he 2Ch 13:7
"Since the Ark is now in * Temple 2Ch 35:3
descendants of King * officials: Ez 2:55,56,57
of * officers numbered 392. Ez 2:58
men who remembered * beautiful Ez 3:12
* officials who returned to Judah: Neh 7:57,58,59
of * officers numbered 392." Neh 7:60
the descendants of * servants Neh 11:3
"Wasn't this exactly King * Neh 13:26
beyond * son to Jesus the Messiah. Ps 72:6f
These statements are * discouraged Ecc 9:5f
These statements are * discouraged Ecc 9:5f
These statements are * discouraged Ecc 9:10f
the division of * empire into Is 7:17
the section known as * Hall. Jn 10:22,23
They all rushed out to * Hall, Act 3:11
the area known as * Hall, and they Act 5:12

SOLVE
"If you * my riddle during these Ju 14:12
But if you can't * it, then you Ju 14:13
* are piled higher than my head. Ps 40:12
mystery is too great for you to *. Dan 4:9
riddles, and * knotty problems. Dan 5:12
I am told that you can * all Dan 5:16
calls for careful thought to * it. Rev 13:18

SOLVED
For the Lord has * my problem. 1Sa 2:1

SOMEBODY'S
of Dan replied. "* apt to get Ju 18:25

SOMEDAY
countries. But * the highest honor Ps 87:5
I thought that * she would Jer 3:7
* people will again own property Jer 32:15
his Child will * rule these Jer 33:25,26
(But * I will restore the Eze 16:53
kings who will * rule the earth. Dan 7:17
"All that is now hidden will * Mk 4:22
This illustrates the fact that * Lk 8:17
from God will * come to an end, but 1Co 13:8
goes on forever. * prophecy, and 1Co 13:8
a poor mirror; but * we are going 1Co 13:12
very well (I hope * you will), I 2Co 1:13,14

SOMEHOW
them down—* they'll find a way! Ps 10:6
to sermons, but * the message never Lk 8:13
fear of chains! * my patience has Php 1:14

SOMEONE
—* like ourselves, Gen 1:26
People would speak of * as being Gen 10:9
"I thought * would kill me to Gen 26:9
Abimelech exclaimed. "* might Gen 26:10
But * got wind of what he was Gen 27:42
than to * outside the family." Gen 29:19
and * told Israel about it. Gen 35:22
When * told Tamar that her Gen 38:13
"Lord, please! Send * else." Ex 4:13
for the altar, or * might look up Ex 20:26
in that case, if it kills *, the Ex 21:29
"If * deliberately lets his Ex 22:5
"If * gives money or goods to Ex 22:7
the possession of * else who denies Ex 22:9
any of it upon * who is not a Ex 30:33
"However, if * brings a Lev 7:16
"If * should eat of the holy Lev 22:14
"If * donates his home to the Lev 27:14,15
sold the field to * else [and has Lev 27:20
the priest may sell it to * else. Lev 27:27
If he is defiled by having * Num 6:9
* shall kill her as he watches. Num 19:1
Then * shall burn the heifer as Num 19:5
Then * who is not ceremonially Num 19:9
"If * out in a field touches the Num 19:16
the corpse of * who has been killed Num 19:16
bone, or touching * who has been Num 19:18
killed * can run and be safe, and Num 35:6
if he has killed * accidentally. Num 35:11
"But if * is struck and killed Num 35:16
killed * could flee for safety. Deu 4:42
instance, whether * is guilty of Deu 17:8
kills * may flee to safety. Deu 19:2,3
he has seen * do wrong when he Deu 19:16
and * else would dedicate it! Deu 20:5
You might die in battle and * Deu 20:6
* else would marry your fiancée. Deu 20:7
"If you see * trying to get an Deu 22:4
It is the same with * else's Deu 23:25
"* else will marry your fiancée; Deu 28:30
your fiancée; * else will live in Deu 28:30
house you build; * else will eat Deu 28:30
night there, but * informed the Jos 2:2
Israel says that * has stolen from Jos 7:13
If a man is guilty of killing * Jos 20:3
began to stir, * discovered that Ju 6:28
that way.) But * warned Abimelech Ju 9:25
However, * had told Abimelech Ju 9:42
Suddenly * thought of the annual Ju 21:19
but there is * else who is more Ru 3:12
Then * told him that his father 1Sa 14:28
raw, bloody meat. * reported to 1Sa 14:33
out to find Saul. * said that he 1Sa 15:12
and you choose * to represent you, 1Sa 17:8
what David meant, * told King Saul, 1Sa 17:31
* told him they were at Naioth. 1Sa 19:22
"At last * has had pity on me! 1Sa 23:21
the king when * came to kill him? 1Sa 26:1
"Go after * else!" 2Sa 2:2
that when * told me, 'Saul is 2Sa 4:1
When * told David that 2Sa 15:3
your family and give it to * else. 1Ki 11:1
pretending to be * else, would come 1Ki 14:
Why are you pretending to be * 1Ki 14:
Perhaps he is talking to *, or is 1Ki 18:2
However, * shot an arrow at 1Ki 22:3
"Now bring me * to play the 2Ki 3:1
"Please, sir, come with us," * 2Ki 6:
lay sick. * told the king that the 2Ki 8:
and shouted, "* is coming." 2Ki 9:17
Afterwards he said, "* go and 2Ki 9:34
You speak as though I were * very 1Ch 17:17
"Whenever * commits a crime, and 2Ch 6:22
"We'll get * else to be our 2Ch 10:16
army, for there is * with us who is 2Ch 32:7
"Shouldn't * stem this torrent Job 11:2
When you mock God, shouldn't * Job 11:3
How much less * like you, who is Job 15:16
is * who will lift you up again. Job 22:29
sin, then let * else reap the crops Job 31:7,8
and * else become her husband. Job 31:10
that there were * who would listen Job 31:35
lest I insult *, and don't make me Job 32:21,22
were wishing for, * to stand Job 33:6
She forgets that * may step on Job 39:15
He heaps up riches for * else to Ps 39:5,6
distant Ethiopia, * boasts that he Ps 87:4
Each day tell * that he saves. Ps 96:2
they cause * to stumble and fall. Pro 4:16
SON, IF YOU endorse a note for * Pro 6:1
It is better to eat soup with * Pro 15:17
love than steak with * you hate. Pro 15:17
Any story sounds true until * Pro 18:17
Telling lies about * is as Pro 25:18
Roll a boulder down on *, and it Pro 26:27
in the hands of * who pities them. Pro 28:8
leave all of it to * who hasn't Ecc 2:20-23
What shall we do if * asks to Sol 8:8
stepping on * else, neighbors Is 3:5
* from among you keeps calling, Is 21:11
I hear the voice of * shouting, Is 40:3
And when * prays to it there is Is 46:7
up and worship * other than me. Is 57:7,8
of bad ones (and * will say, Is 65:8
wants to curse * he will say, "The Jer 29:22
it sat * who appeared to be a Man. Eze 1:26
the voice of * speaking to me: Eze 1:27,28
to them, like * who sings lovely Eze 33:32
or give them to * else, but I will Dan 5:17
Then *—he looked like a Dan 10:16
Don't point your finger at * Hos 4:4
they applied to * far away. Hos 8:12
piece of land, or * else's house Mic 2:2
Then Haggai asked, "But if * Hag 2:13
"And if * asks, 'Then what are Zec 13:6
of their sins; but * else is Mt 3:11
But when you do a kindness to *, Mt 6:3
with him. When * told him they were Mt 12:46,47
* came to Jesus with this Mt 19:16
"So if * tells you the Messiah Mt 24:26
"* is coming soon who is far Mk 1:7
Then he asked them, "When * Mk 4:21
But if * causes one of these Mk 9:42
his wife to marry * else, he Mk 10:11
Jesus and held him fast. But * Mk 14:47
long ago— * to save us from our Lk 1:71
with water; but * is coming soon Lk 3:16
"If * slaps you on one cheek, Lk 6:29
the other too! If * demands your Lk 6:29
in * else's eye—his little fault Lk 6:41
"Who ever heard of * lighting a Lk 8:16
him, "No, it was * who Lk 8:46
"Master, we saw * using your name Lk 9:49
As they were walking along * said Lk 9:57
it is safe— until * stronger and Lk 11:22
of Jonah; and * far greater than Lk 11:32
Then * called from the crowd, Lk 12:13
* asked him, "Will only a few be Lk 13:23
For if * more respected than you Lk 14:8
wife and marries * else commits Lk 16:18
But if * is sent to them from the Lk 16:30
though * rises from the dead.' Lk 16:31
After a while * else looked at Lk 22:58
About an hour later * else flatly Lk 22:59
in a tomb for * who is alive? Lk 24:5
when I said, '* is coming who is Jn 1:15
in the crowd is * you have never Jn 1:26
and resting upon *—he is the one Jn 1:33
One day * began an argument with Jn 3:25
that one sows and * else reaps. Jn 4:37
While I am trying to get there, * Jn 5:7
but * else, yes, John the Baptist, Jn 5:32,33
open the eyes of * born blind. Jn 9:32
or did * else say it about me?" Jn 18:34f
me to release * from prison each Jn 18:39
and saw * standing behind her. Jn 20:14
work be given to * else to do.' Act 1:20
"So now we must choose * else to Act 1:21,22

OMEONE Con't)
Let us select * who has been with Act 1:21,22
Then * arrived with the news Act 5:25
who pretended to be * great. Act 5:36
talking about himself or * else?" Act 8:34
* to take his hand and lead him. Act 13:11
—* God brought back to life, Act 13:37
While he was in Egypt, * had Act 18:25,26
a public bonfire. (* estimated the Act 19:18,19
and about * called Jesus who died, Act 25:19
Then she can marry * else if she Rom 7:3
I want to be kind to *, I will. Rom 9:15
given just because * decides to Rom 9:16
about him unless * tells them? Rom 10:14
and tell them unless * sends him? Rom 10:15
If * mistreats you because you Rom 12:14
But if * believes it is wrong, Rom 14:14
Don't let your eating ruin * for Rom 14:15
already been started by * else. Rom 15:20
* is a good servant or not. 1Co 4:5
what may happen: * who thinks it is 1Co 8:10
If * who isn't a Christian asks 1Co 10:27
But if * warns you that this 1Co 10:28
and limited by what * else thinks? 1Co 10:29
enjoy it, why let * spoil 1Co 10:30
give wise advice; * else may be 1Co 12:8
* else the power to heal the sick. 1Co 12:9
He gives * else the power to know 1Co 12:10
If you love * you will be loyal 1Co 13:7
If * is given the gift of 1Co 14:13
unsaved person, or * who doesn't 1Co 14:23
or tell what * else is saying who 1Co 14:26
one at a time, and * must be ready 1Co 14:27
But if, while * is prophesying, 1Co 14:29,30
is prophesying, * else receives a 1Co 14:29,30
But * may ask, "How will the 1Co 15:35
When * becomes a Christian he 2Co 5:17
work * else has done among you. 2Co 10:15
about being in * else's field. 2Co 10:16
When * boasts about himself 2Co 10:18
to compare himself with * else. Gal 6:4
we believe because * has told us Eph 4:14
* may fool you with smooth talk. Col 2:4
where you need * to teach you all Heb 5:12,13
he is calling upon * greater than Heb 6:16
instead of sending * with the rank Heb 7:11
Now, if * dies and leaves a Heb 9:16
And remember, when * wants to do Jas 1:13
but have murdered *, you have Jas 2:11
But * may well argue, "You say Jas 2:18
the Lord, and * helps him Jas 5:19
But if you sin, there is * to 1Jn 2:1
* may say, "I am a Christian; 1Jn 2:4
But if * who is supposed to be a 1Jn 3:17
hear just because * says it is a 1Jn 4:1
because there is * in your hearts 1Jn 4:4
We need have no fear of * who 1Jn 4:18
—a throne and * sitting on it! Rev 4:2
a white cloud, and * sitting on it Rev 14:14

SOMEONE'S
as it was probably * mistake, and Gen 43:12
or whether * rights have been Deu 17:8
"IF YOU SEE * ox or sheep Deu 22:1
sound of * voice but saw no one! Act 9:7
I think you hardly need * letter 2Co 3:1

SOMETHING
we are beaten for * that isn't our Ex 5:16
tiny flakes of * as small as Ex 16:14
witness stand * you know is false. Ex 23:1
* must have happened to him." Ex 32:1
to lead us, for * has happened to Ex 32:23
If the offering is * from the Lev 2:5
it, and does * that Jehovah has Lev 4:13
a deposit on * borrowed or rented, Lev 6:2
refusing to return * entrusted to Lev 6:2
promptly. If * is due them, don't Lev 19:13
Lord, either to do * or to quit Num 30:1
or to quit doing *, that vow must Num 30:1
to do or not do *, and she is still Num 30:3
hatred by throwing * at him, or Num 35:20
case in which * is thrown Num 35:22,23
"IF A MAN doesn't like * about Deu 24:1
* beyond your strength and reach; Deu 30:11
Literally, they have become "* Jos 7:12f
until we can get you * to eat." Ju 13:15
However, if you wish to bring *, Ju 13:16
"We've got to do * about it." Ju 19:30
said, "I've just thought of *! 1Sa 9:6
public alike. But * had happened 1Sa 18:6
wouldn't hide * like this from me. 1Sa 20:2
he supposed that * had happened so 1Sa 20:26
let me give you * to eat so you'll 1Sa 28:22
cook a little * for him to eat. 2Sa 13:6
as though we had done * wrong. 2Sa 19:5
"If a man is accused of doing * 1Ki 8:31
But while I was busy doing * 1Ki 20:40
He always has * gloomy to say. 1Ki 22:8
"Let her alone; * is deeply 2Ki 4:27
I will chase after him and get * 2Ki 5:20
horses—if * happens to the animals 2Ki 7:13
This is at least a beginning, * 1Ch 22:14
But this isn't * that can be Ez 10:13
Death speak of knowing * about it! Job 28:22
pain as though * were relentlessly Job 30:17
His majestic snorting is * to Job 39:20
to Israel— * he has not done with Ps 147:20
If a man enjoys folly, * is Pro 15:21
You may start * you can't finish Pro 25:8,9,10
If he is thirsty, give him * to Pro 25:21,22
that you will do *, don't delay in Ecc 5:4
to say you'll do * than to say you Ecc 5:5
are, by causing * else to happen Is 44:25
Why doesn't God do *? Jer 8:22
My people have done * too Jer 18:13
Why haven't you done * about Jer 29:27
For the Lord will cause * new and Jer 31:22
to Molech—* I never commanded, and Jer 32:35
"I want to ask you *," the king Jer 38:14
and in the fire there was * that Eze 1:4
warning and do * never done before: Dan 11:24
For I am going to do * in your Hab 1:5
*, does it become contaminated?" Hag 2:13
* is traveling through the sky!" Zec 5:5
don't swear that * is true when Zec 8:17
telling them * through what I did. Zec 11:11
that a friend has * against you, Mt 5:23
with a vow shows that * is wrong. Mt 5:37
into saying * that would ruin him. Mt 19:3
* for which they could arrest him. Mt 22:15
told them to give her * to eat. Mk 5:43
but when they saw * walking along Mk 6:49
"Make * happen in the sky. Mk 8:11
Now they began asking him about * Mk 9:11
Oh, have mercy on us and do * if Mk 9:22
saying * he could be arrested for. Mk 12:13
trying to find * against Jesus that Mk 14:55
asked him, "Why don't you say *? Mk 15:3,4
Probably by throwing dice or * Lk 1:8,9f
"I have * to say to you." Lk 7:40
"Give her * to eat!" Lk 8:55
Others asked for * to happen Lk 11:16
him into saying * for which they Lk 11:53,54
up space we can use for * else.' Lk 13:7
So they tried to get him to say * Lk 20:19
said, "Peter, let me tell you *. Lk 22:34
discussion about *," he said. Lk 24:17
or * even worse may happen to Jn 5:14
him into saying * they could use Jn 8:6
two men agree on * that has Jn 8:17
But I'll give you * else! Act 3:6
If he says * is kosher, then it Act 10:15
* the Jewish law could never do. Act 13:39
for I am doing * in your Act 13:41
in your day—* that you won't Act 13:41
Then Paul thought of *! Act 23:6
He has * important to tell him." Act 23:17
young man to you to tell you *." Act 23:18
I soon discovered it was * about Act 23:29
If I have done * worthy of death, Act 25:10,11
It was * about their religion, Act 25:19
accusations is * else—it is because Act 26:6
"Please eat * now for your own Act 27:34
Being a Jew is worth * if you Rom 2:25
If so, then he would have * to Rom 4:1
but there is * else deep within Rom 7:23,24,25
forward to getting * we don't yet Rom 8:24
who already has * doesn't need to Rom 8:24
trusting God for * that hasn't Rom 8:25
If he is thirsty give him * to Rom 12:20
But if you are doing * wrong, of Rom 13:4
you doing * he thinks is wrong. Rom 14:13
But anyone who believes that * Rom 14:23
trying to start * new, beginning a 1Co 1:15
have accomplished * on your own? 1Co 4:7
there among you, * so evil that 1Co 5:1
HOW IS IT that when you have * 1Co 6:1
him to do * he thinks is wrong. 1Co 8:12
is * else I cannot agree with. 1Co 11:17
me tell you about * else that is 1Co 12:31
should put aside * from what you 1Co 16:2
to be able to do * about your joy: 2Co 1:24
first to begin doing * about it. 2Co 8:10
Such bragging isn't * the Lord 2Co 11:17
That experience is * worth 2Co 12:5
But then * happened! Gal 1:15
afterward to do * else instead. Gal 3:15
that you can see * of the future he Eph 1:18
has told us * different, or has Eph 4:14
This is * that pleases God very 1Ti 5:4
In such situations you can do * 1Ti 5:24
only a slave, but * much better—a Phm 1:16
that * we want is going to happen. Heb 11:1
This salvation was * the prophets 1Pe 1:10
around to mean * quite different 2Pe 3:15,16
I must write of * else instead, Jud 1:3
only to get * from them in return. Jud 1:16

SOMETHING'S
said to the leaders, "* wrong! 1Sa 14:38

SOMETIME
attractive. But * later, King Gen 26:8
today and leave * this evening." Ju 19:8
I've got to die *, and it might 1Ki 19:4
Try it on your governor *—give Mal 1:8

SOMETIMES
to slay us"), and * they referred Ex 17:7
instructed them. * the fire-cloud Num 9:20,21
which she came was * called Cush. Num 12:1f
(Bashan is * called 'The Land of Deu 3:13
Mount Hermon, as it is * called; Deu 4:48
of Kiriath-baal (* called Jos 18:14
to worship. * the servant would 1Sa 2:15
Judah and Benjamin were * (as in 1Ki 12:20f
He did what was right, but * 2Ch 25:2
parties ended—and * they lasted Job 1:5
"Yet * Job 24:22,23
Even strong young lions * go Ps 34:10
* mere words are not Pro 29:19
of the Lord," * refers to the Is 4:2,3,4f
word used here * means "virgin" Is 7:14f
"virgin" and * "young woman." Is 7:14f
mountain brook—* a flood, Jer 15:17,18
a flood, * as dry as a bone." Jer 15:17,18
the Jewish leaders * fasted, that Mk 2:18
accuses them, or * excuses them. Rom 2:12-15
with you. * I think God has put us 1Co 4:9
For God * uses sorrow in our 2Co 7:10
to live or die! * I want to live Php 1:23
You ought to take a little * as 1Ti 5:23
pastors do, but * their good deeds 1Ti 5:25
suffering. * you were laughed at Heb 10:33
at and beaten, and * you watched Heb 10:33
deadly poison. * it praises our Jas 3:9
Father, and * it breaks out into Jas 3:9
even though it * seems that way. 2Pe 3:9
* ends in physical death (1 Cor. 1Jn 5:17f

SOMEWHERE
the country. "Go * else," he Gen 26:16
with God, and from * in the Ex 19:2,3
away, go * else, for evil men Pro 4:15
and leave your home—go * else. Eze 12:3
always looking * else instead of up Heb 3:10

SON
gave birth to a *, Cain (meaning Gen 4:1
him with a baby * named Enoch; Gen 4:17
he named it Enoch, after his *. Gen 4:17
birth to another * and named him Gen 4:25
* for the one Cain killed." Gen 4:25
When Seth grew up, he had a * Gen 4:26
Adam was 130 years old when his * Gen 5:3,4,5
Or, by Hebrew usage, "When his *, Gen 5:3,4,5f
old when his * Enosh was born. Gen 5:6,7,8
old when his * Kenan was born. Gen 5:9,10,11
old when his * Mahalalel was born. Gen 5:12,13,14
old when his * Jared was born. Gen 5:15,16,17
old when his * Enoch was born. Gen 5:18,19,20
when his * Methuselah was born. Gen 5:21-24
old when his * Lamech was born; Gen 5:25,26,27
old when his * Noah was born. Gen 5:28-31
Ham, his younger *, had done, he Gen 9:24,25
Or, "the * of Cush." Gen 10:8f
Canaan's oldest * was Sidon, and Gen 10:15-19
Arpachshad's * was Shelah, and Gen 10:24
Shelah, and Shelah's * was Eber. Gen 10:24
was thirty-five years old, his * Gen 11:12,13
years old when his * Eber was born, Gen 11:14,15
old when his * Peleg was born. Gen 11:16,17
years old when his * Reu was born. Gen 11:18,19
old when his * Nahor was born. Gen 11:22,23
old at the birth of his * Terah. Gen 11:24,25
And Haran had a * named Lot. Gen 11:27
Then Terah took his * Abram, his Gen 11:31
grandson Lot (his * Haran's child), Gen 11:31
Literally, "Abram's brother's * Gen 14:12f
your blessings when I have no *? Gen 15:2,3
For without a *, some other Gen 15:2,3
* to inherit everything you own." Gen 15:4
baby will be a *, and you are to Gen 16:9-12
your woes. This * of yours will be Gen 16:9-12
So Hagar gave Abram a *, and Gen 16:15
her and give you a * from her! Gen 17:16
Sarah shall bear you a *; Gen 17:19
took Ishmael his * and every other Gen 17:23
I will give you and Sarah a *!" Gen 18:10
see to it that Sarah has a *." Gen 18:14
Abraham a baby * in his old age, at Gen 21:1
Ishmael—the * of Abraham and the Gen 21:9
rid of that slave girl and her *. Gen 21:10
to share your property with my *. Gen 21:10
after all, Ishmael too was his *. Gen 21:11
for Isaac is the * through whom my Gen 21:12
the slave-girl's *, too, because he Gen 21:13
and sent her away with their *. Gen 21:14
defraud me or my * or my grandson, Gen 21:23
"Take with you your only *—yes, Gen 22:2
took with him his * Isaac and two Gen 22:3
"God will see to it, my *," Gen 22:8
plunge it into his *, to slay him. Gen 22:10
even your beloved * from me." Gen 22:12
it, instead of his *, as a burnt Gen 22:13
even your beloved * from me, I Gen 22:16
Ephron, Zohar's *, to sell me the Gen 23:8
will not let my * marry one of Gen 24:3
are you to take my * there." Gen 24:8

(SON Con't)
(Her father was Bethuel the * of Gen 24:15,16
"My father is Bethuel, the * of Gen 24:24
to my master's *, and my master has Gen 24:36
a girl from here to marry his *. Gen 24:38
to be the wife of my master's *.' Gen 24:44
My father is Bethuel, the * of Gen 24:47
*, as Jehovah has directed." Gen 24:51
replied, "It is my master's *!" Gen 24:65
from Ephron the * of Zohar, the Gen 25:9,10
who was the * of Abraham and Gen 25:12-15
he called for Esau his oldest *. Gen 27:1
Isaac: "My *?" Gen 27:1
to you, my first-born *, Gen 27:2,3,4
she called her * Jacob and told Gen 27:6,7
"Let his curses be on me, dear *. Gen 27:13
Who is it, my *—Esau or Jacob?" Gen 27:18
Jacob: "It's Esau, your oldest * Gen 27:19
to find it so quickly, my *?" Gen 27:20
"Come here and kiss me, my *!" Gen 27:26
Isaac: "The smell of my * is the Gen 27:27,28,29
Esau, your oldest *!" Gen 27:32
* of Bethuel the Aramean. Gen 28:5
daughter of Ishmael, Abraham's *. Gen 28:9
named Laban, the * of Nahor?" Gen 29:5
that he was her Aunt Rebekah's *. Gen 29:12,13
pregnant and had a *, Reuben Gen 29:32
and had another * and named him Gen 29:33
so he has given me another *." Gen 29:33
pregnant and had a *, and named him Gen 29:34
pregnant and had a * and named him Gen 29:35
and presented him with a *. Gen 30:5
heard my plea and given me a *." Gen 30:6
again and gave Jacob a second *. Gen 30:7
Zilpah presented him with a *. Gen 30:10
Then Zilpah produced a second *, Gen 30:12
some mandrakes my * has found!" Gen 30:16
and gave birth to her fifth *. Gen 30:17
became pregnant, with a sixth *. Gen 30:19
pregnant and gave birth to a *. Gen 30:23,24
"May Jehovah give me another *." Gen 30:23,24
but when Shechem, * of King Hamor Gen 34:2
Hamor told Jacob, "My * Shechem Gen 34:8
"Ben-oni" ("* of my sorrow"); Gen 35:18
("* of my right hand"). Gen 35:18
Esau and Adah had a * named Gen 36:4
Esau and Basemath had a * named Gen 36:4
Adah, born to her * Eliphaz were: Gen 36:10,11,12
Born to her * Reuel were:Nahath, Gen 36:13,14
the oldest * of Esau and Adah. Gen 36:15,16
The children of Lotan (the * of Gen 36:22
King Bela (* of Beor), from Gen 36:31-39
by: King Jobab (* of Zerah), from Gen 36:31-39
Succeeded by: King Hadad (* of Gen 36:31-39
Succeeded by: King Baal-hanan (* Gen 36:31-39
Jacob's * Joseph was now Gen 37:2
mourned for his * in deepest Gen 37:34
"I will die in mourning for my * Gen 37:35
When his oldest * Er grew up, Gen 38:6
until his youngest * Shelah was old Gen 38:11
to give her to my * Shelah." Gen 38:26
Joseph named his oldest * Gen 41:51
But Jacob replied, "My * shall Gen 42:38
Benjamin, his mother's *." Gen 43:29f
How are you, my *? Gen 43:29
tell him, 'Your * Joseph says, Gen 45:9
Joseph my * is alive! Gen 45:28
Reuben, his oldest *; Gen 46:8-14
Dan and his *: Hushim. Gen 46:23,24,25
he called for his * Joseph and said Gen 47:29
"I know what I'm doing, my *," Gen 48:19
"Reuben, you are my oldest *, Gen 49:3
the birth of his * Ephraim's Gen 50:23
*, who played at his feet. Gen 50:23
and a baby * was born to them. Ex 2:1
the princess and he became her *. Ex 2:10
is my eldest *, and I have Ex 4:22
see, I will slay your eldest *." Ex 4:23
*:Hanoch, Pallu,Hezron, Carmi. Ex 6:14
Aaron's * Eleazar married one of Ex 6:25
Pharaoh's oldest * to the oldest Ex 12:29
* of the captive in the dungeon; Ex 12:29
nor shall your *, daughter, or Ex 20:10
slave-girl and his *, then he may Ex 21:9
payment for your oldest *. Ex 22:29
of his * who succeeds him, from Ex 29:29
appointed Bezalel (* of Uri, and Ex 31:1
"And I have appointed Oholiab (* Ex 31:6
him, Joshua (* of Nun), stayed Ex 33:11
Bezalel (the * of Uri and grandson Ex 35:30,31
(Oholiab is the * of Ahisamach, Ex 35:34
by Ithamar, * of Aaron the priest. Ex 38:21
Bezalel (* of Uri and grandson Ex 38:22
by Oholiab (* of Ahisamach of the Ex 38:23
On the eighth day, her * must be Lev 12:3
nor a * his mother, nor any Lev 18:7
of either your * or your Lev 18:10
*, daughter, brother, or unmarried Lev 21:2,3
and has no * to support her, and Lev 22:13
the fight the Egyptian man's * Lev 24:11
"the Israelite woman's *." Lev 24:11f

Reuben -Elizur (* of Num 1:2-15
Simeon -Shelumi-el (* of Num 1:2-15
Judah -Nahshon (* of Num 1:2-15
Issachar -Nethanel (* of Num 1:2-15
Zebulun -Eliab (* of Num 1:2-15
Ephraim (* of Joseph) Num 1:2-15
Elishama (* of Ammihud) Num 1:2-15
Manassh (* of Joseph) Num 1:2-15
Gamaliel (* of Dedahzur) Num 1:2-15
Benjamin -Abidan (* of Num 1:2-15
Dan -Ahiezer (* of Num 1:2-15
Asher -Pagiel (* of Num 1:2-15
Gad -Eliasaph (* of Num 1:2-15
Naphtali -Ahira (* of Num 1:2-15
* of Joseph) Num 1:20-46
Reuben (the oldest * of Num 1:20-46
* of Joseph) Num 1:20-46
Nahshon (* of Amminadab) Num 2:3-31
Nethanel (* of Zuar) Num 2:3-31
Eliab (* of Helon) Num 2:3-31
Elizur (* of Shedeur) Num 2:3-31
(* of Zurishaddai) Num 2:3-31
Eliasaph (* of Reuel) Num 2:3-31
Elishama (* of Ammihud) Num 2:3-31
Gamaliel (* of Pedahzur) Num 2:3-31
Abidan (* of Gideoni) Num 2:3-31
Ahiezer (* of Ammishaddai Num 2:3-31
Pagiel (* of Ochran) Num 2:3-31
Ahira (* of Enan) Num 2:3-31
Levi's * Gershon Num 3:16-24
Elisaph (* of Lael) Num 3:16-24
Levi's * Kohath Num 3:25-30
Elizaphan (* of Uzziel) Num 3:25-30
(Note: Eleazar, Aaron's *, shall Num 3:31-35
Levi's * Merari Num 3:31-35
Zuriel (* of Abihail) Num 3:31-35
"Aaron's * Eleazar shall be Num 4:16
responsible to Aaron's * Ithamar. Num 4:28
report to Aaron's * Ithamar." Num 4:33
leadership of Ithamar, Aaron's *. Num 7:8
So Nahshon, the * of Amminadab of Num 7:12
The next day Nethanel, the * of Num 7:18-23
On the third day Eliab, the * of Num 7:24-29
by Elizur, * of Shedeur, chief of Num 7:30-35
Shelumi-el, the * of Zuri-shaddai, Num 7:36-41
Eliasaph's turn, * of Deuel, chief Num 7:42-47
day, Elishama, the * of Ammihud, Num 7:48-53
Gamaliel, * of Pedahzur, prince Num 7:54-59
it was Abidan the * of Gideoni, Num 7:60-65
Ahiezer, the * of Ammishaddai, Num 7:66-71
Pagiel, * of Ochran, chief of the Num 7:72-77
On the twelfth day came Ahira, * Num 7:78-83
by Nahshon, the * of Amminadab. Num 10:14
by Nethanel, the * of Zuar, and Num 10:15
led by Eliab, the * of Helon. Num 10:16
* of Shedeur leading his people. Num 10:18
Shelumi-el, the * of Zuri-shaddai; Num 10:19
led by Eliasaph, the * of Deuel. Num 10:20
led by Elishama, the * of Ammihud; Num 10:22
led by Gamaliel the * of Pedahzur; Num 10:23
led by Abidan the * of Gideoni. Num 10:24
of Ahiezer, the * of Ammishaddai; Num 10:25
led by Pagiel, the * of Ochran; Num 10:26
led by Ahira, the * of Enan. Num 10:27
Hobab (* of Reuel, the Midianite), Num 10:29
and Joshua (the * of Nun), one of Num 11:28
Shammu-a, * of Zaccur, from the Num 13:3-15
Shaphat, * of Hori, from the tribe Num 13:3-15
Caleb, * of Jephunneh, from the Num 13:3-15
Igal, * of Joseph, from the tribe Num 13:3-15
* of Nun, from the half-tribe of Num 13:3-15
Palti, * of Raphu, from the tribe Num 13:3-15
Gaddiel, * of Sodi, from the tribe Num 13:3-15
Gaddi, * of Susi, from the tribe Num 13:3-15
Ammiel, * of Gemalli, from the Num 13:3-15
Sethur, * of Michael, from the Num 13:3-15
Nahbi, * of Vophsi, from the tribe Num 13:3-15
Geuel, * of Machi, from the tribe Num 13:3-15
two of the spies, Joshua (the * Num 14:6
and Caleb (the * of Jephunneh), Num 14:6
Only Caleb (* of Jephunneh) and Num 14:30
and Joshua (* of Nun) are permitted Num 14:30
ONE DAY KORAH (* of Izhar, Num 16:1
Eliab) and On (the * of Peleth), Num 16:1
"Tell Eleazar the * of Aaron the Num 16:36,37
Now take Aaron and his * Eleazar Num 20:25
him and put them on Eleazar his *; Num 20:26
and put them on his * Eleazar; Num 20:28
When King Balak of Moab (the * Num 22:2,3
to Balaam (* of Beor) who was Num 22:5,6
Listen to me, you * of Zippor. Num 23:18-24
"Balaam the * of Beor says that Num 24:3-9
"Balaam the * of Beor is the man Num 24:15-19
When Phinehas (* of Eleazar and Num 25:7
Moses, "Phinehas (* of Eleazar and Num 25:10,11
girl was Zimri, * of Salu, a leader Num 25:14
and to Eleazar (* of Aaron the Num 26:1
(Reuben was Israel's eldest *. Num 26:5-11
(Hepher's *, Zelophehad, had no Num 26:28-37
ancestor Eran, a * of Shuthelah. Num 26:28-37
named after Shuham, the * of Dan. Num 26:42,43

the wife of Amram, * of Kohath. Num 26:58,
were Caleb (* of Jephunneh) and Num 26:64,
Jephunneh) and Joshua (* of Nun). Num 26:64,
of Manasseh (a * of Joseph). Num 27
Their ancestor was Machir, * of Num 27
Manasseh's * Gilead was their Num 27
his * Hepher was their grandfather, Num 27
his * Zelophehad was their father. Num 27
just because he had no *? Num 27:3
and get Joshua (* of Nun), who has Num 27:1
Phinehas (* of Eleazar the Num 31
Balaam, the * of Beor, was also Num 31
were Caleb (* of Jephunneh the Num 32:1
and Joshua (* of Nun)—for they Num 32:1
of Manasseh (* of Joseph). Num 32:3
priest, Joshua (* of Nun), and one Num 34:16-2
Caleb (* of Jephunneh) Num 34:16-2
Shemuel (* of Ammihud) Num 34:16-2
Elidad (* of Chislon) Num 34:16-2
Dan Bukki (* of Jogli) Num 34:16-2
Hanniel (* of Ephod) Num 34:16-2
Kemuel (* of Shiptan) Num 34:16-2
Elizaphan (* of Parnach) Num 34:16-2
Paltiel (* of Azzan) Num 34:16-2
Ahihud (* of Shelomi) Num 34:16-2
Pedahel (* of Ammihud) Num 34:16-2
tribe of Manasseh (* of Joseph); Num 36:11,1
except Caleb (the * of Jephunneh), Deu 1:3
* of Nun), shall lead the people. Deu 1:3
to come when your * asks you, 'What Deu 6:2
a man punishes his *, the Lord Deu 8:
* Eleazar became the next priest. Deu 10:
even a brother, *, daughter, or Deu 13:6,
of his oldest * is the wife he Deu 21:1
*, the son of the wife he loves. Deu 21:1
son, the * of the wife he loves. Deu 21:1
to his oldest *, who is the Deu 21:1
of a firstborn *, even though he is Deu 21:1
though he is the * of the wife his Deu 21:1
rebellious * who will not obey his Deu 21:1
and declare, 'This * of ours is Deu 21:2
hire Balaam, the * of Beor from Deu 23:4
dies without a *, his widow must Deu 25:5
The first * she bears to him Deu 25:6
be counted as the * of the dead Deu 25:6
beloved husband, *, and daughter. Deu 28:56,57
Then he charged Joshua (* of Deu 31:23
"Asher is a favorite *, Deu 33:24
Joshua (* of Nun) was full of the Deu 34:9
(the * of Nun), and said to him, Jos 1:1
builder's oldest * would die, and Jos 6:26
set up, his youngest * would die. Jos 6:26
For Achan (the * of Carmi, Jos 7:1
Joshua said to Achan, "My *, Jos 7:19
the magician, the * of Beor. Jos 13:22
clan Machir, who was Manasseh's *. Jos 13:31
the stone of Bohan (* of Reuben). Jos 15:6
to Caleb (* of Jephunneh), so he Jos 15:13
Othni-el (* of Kenaz), Caleb's Jos 15:17
of Manasseh (Joseph's oldest *): Jos 17:1
(Manasseh's oldest * who was the Jos 17:1
However, Hepher's * Zelophehad Jos 17:3
Bohan (who was a * of Reuben), Jos 18:17
to Caleb, the * of Jephunneh; Jos 21:9-16
the * of Eleazar the priest. Jos 22:13
when Achan, the * of Zerah, sinned Jos 22:20
descendants through Isaac his *. Jos 24:3
the * of Beor, to curse you. Jos 24:9
Eleazar, the * of Aaron, also Jos 24:33
had been given to his * Phinehas. Jos 24:33
Caleb's nephew, Othni-el, * of Ju 1:13
nephew, Othni-el (* of Kenaz, Ju 3:9
a savior, Ehud (* of Gera, a Ju 3:15
Ehud was Shamgar (* of Anath). Ju 3:31
One day she summoned Barak (* of Ju 4:6
O * of Abino-am, lead away your Ju 5:12
Joash's *, Gideon, had been Ju 6:11
it was Gideon, the * of Joash. Ju 6:29
"Bring out your *," they Ju 6:30
Gideon, the * of Joash, the Ju 7:14
*, he instructed him to kill them. Ju 8:20
not be your king, nor shall my *; Ju 8:23,24
him with a * named Abimelech. Ju 8:31
ONE DAY GIDEON'S * Abimelech Ju 9:1
his slave girl's *, Abimelech, to Ju 9:18
At that time Gaal (the * of Ju 9:26
him, "Gaal, * of Ebed, and his Ju 9:31
of Jotham, Gideon's *, came true. Ju 9:56,57
(* of Puah and grandson of Dodo). Ju 10:1
"You * of a whore!" Ju 11:1
Next was Abdon (* of Hillel) from Ju 12:13
will soon conceive and have a *! Ju 13:2,3
When her * was born they named Ju 13:24
ancestor, Israel's *, but it had Ju 18:29
named Jonathan (* of Gershom and Ju 18:30
Phinehas, the * of Eleazar and Ju 20:27,28
"For her * would become an heir Ru 4:6
she can have a * to carry on the Ru 4:10
Perez, the * of Tamar and Judah." Ru 4:12
with her, the Lord gave her a *. Ru 4:13
for he is the * of your Ru 4:15

ON Con't)
t last Naomi has a * again!" Ru 4:16,17
and give me a *, then I will give 1Sa 1:11
"No, I didn't call you, my *," 1Sa 3:6
"My *," he said, "what did the 1Sa 3:16,17
and installed his * Eleazar to be 1Sa 7:1
He was the * of Abiel, grandson 1Sa 9:1
of Aphiah. His * Saul was the most 1Sa 9:2
asking, 'How am I to find my *?' 1Sa 10:2
ot selected Saul, the * of Kish. 1Sa 10:21
Jonathan, Saul's *, in Gibe-ah in 1Sa 13:2
* of Ahitub, Ichabod's brother; 1Sa 14:3
* Jonathan, he shall surely die!" 1Sa 14:39
cousin Abner, his uncle Ner's *. 1Sa 14:50,51
Then Jesse told his * Abinadab to 1Sa 16:8
in Bethlehem, the * of a man named 1Sa 16:18
he send his * David the shepherd. 1Sa 16:19
David (the * of aging Jesse, a 1Sa 17:12
David was the youngest *, and 1Sa 17:14,15
Literally, "Whose * is this?" 1Sa 17:55f
the king's *, and there was an 1Sa 18:1
SAUL NOW URGED his aides and his * 1Sa 19:1
"You * of a bitch!" 1Sa 20:30
Literally, "* of a perverse, 1Sa 20:30f
that you want this * of a nobody 1Sa 20:30
Literally, "* of Jesse." 1Sa 20:30f
that my own * is on David's side. 1Sa 22:8
My own *—encouraging David to 1Sa 22:8
"Listen to me, you * of Ahitub!" 1Sa 22:11,12
"Is it really you, my * David?" 1Sa 24:15
"Who does this * of Jesse think 1Sa 25:10
named Palti (the * of Laish). 1Sa 25:44
brother and the * of Zeruiah). 1Sa 26:5,6,7
said, "Is that you, my * David?" 1Sa 26:17,18
Come back home, my *, and I'll no 1Sa 26:21
"Blessings on you, my * David. 1Sa 26:25
his * Jonathan have been killed." 2Sa 1:4
for Saul and his * Jonathan, and 2Sa 1:12
Saul's * Ish-bosheth as king. 2Sa 2:8
General Joab (the * of Zeruiah) led 2Sa 2:13
His second *, Chileab, was born 2Sa 3:3
who was the * of Prince Jonathan. 2Sa 4:4
Ish-bosheth, the * of your enemy 2Sa 4:8
his father and he shall be my *. 2Sa 7:14
of King Hadadezer (* of Rehob) of 2Sa 8:3
he sent his * Joram to 2Sa 8:10
his army was Joab (* of Zeruiah), 2Sa 8:16
was Jehoshaphat (* of Ahilud). 2Sa 8:16
Zadok (* of Ahitub) and 2Sa 8:17
and Ahimelech (* of Abiathar) were 2Sa 8:17
Benaiah (* of Jehoiada) was 2Sa 8:18
lame * is still alive." 2Sa 9:3
* and Saul's grandson. 2Sa 9:5,6
Mephibosheth had a young *, 2Sa 9:12
died and his * Hanun replaced him. 2Sa 10:1
and she gave birth to his *. 2Sa 11:27
to a * and named him Solomon. 2Sa 12:24
PRINCE ABSALOM, DAVID'S *, had a 2Sa 13:1
* of David's brother Shime-ah. 2Sa 13:3
Why should the * of a king look 2Sa 13:4
But just then Jonadab (the * of 2Sa 13:32,33
(the * of Ammihud) and stayed 2Sa 13:37,38,39
for fellowship with his * Absalom. 2Sa 13:37,38,39
surrender my other * to them to be 2Sa 14:7
you won't let anyone harm my *. 2Sa 14:11
to bring home your own banished *. 2Sa 14:13
bring your * back from his exile. 2Sa 14:14
with you for my * because my life 2Sa 14:15,16
the city with your * Ahima-az and 2Sa 15:27
and Abiathar's * Jonathan. 2Sa 15:27
It was Shime-i, the * of Gera, a 2Sa 16:5
has given it to your * Absalom! 2Sa 16:7,8
My own * is trying to kill me, 2Sa 16:11
greeted by Shobi (* of Nahash of 2Sa 17:27
and Machir (* of Ammiel of Lodebar) 2Sa 17:27
Abishai (the * of Zeruiah); 2Sa 18:2
by killing his * (and the king 2Sa 18:13
Then Zadok's * Ahima-az said, 2Sa 18:19
to the king that his * is dead. 2Sa 18:20
* of Zadok," the watchman said. 2Sa 18:27
"O my * Absalom, my son, my son 2Sa 18:33
"O my son Absalom, my *, my son 2Sa 18:33
"O my son Absalom, my son, my * 2Sa 18:33
O Absalom, my *, my son." 2Sa 18:33
O Absalom, my son, my *." 2Sa 18:33
deep grief for his *, the joy of 2Sa 19:2
kept on weeping, "O my * Absalom! 2Sa 19:4
O Absalom my *, my son!" 2Sa 19:4
O Absalom my son, my *!" 2Sa 19:4
Then Shime-i (the * of Gera the 2Sa 19:16
Chimham was Barzillai's *. 2Sa 19:37f
name was Sheba (* of Bichri, a 2Sa 20:1
He spared Jonathan's * 2Sa 21:7
But Abishai the * of Zeruiah 2Sa 21:17
Jonathan—the * of David's brother 2Sa 21:20,21
"David, the * of Jesse, speaks. 2Sa 23:1
Next in rank was Eleazar, the * 2Sa 23:9
After him was Shammah, the * of 2Sa 23:11,12
(* of Zeruiah), was the greatest. 2Sa 23:18,19
There was also Benaiah (* of 2Sa 23:20
Elhanan (* of Dodo) from 2Sa 23:24-39
Ira (* of Ikkesh) from Tekoa; 2Sa 23:24-39
Heleb (* of Baanah) from Netophah; 2Sa 23:24-39
Ittai (* of Ribai) from Gibe-ah, 2Sa 23:24-39
Ahiam (the * of Sharar) from 2Sa 23:24-39
Eliphelet (* of Ahasbai) from 2Sa 23:24-39
Eliam (the * of Ahithophel) from 2Sa 23:24-39
Igal (* of Nathan) from Zobah; 2Sa 23:24-39
bearer of Joab (* of Zeruiah); 2Sa 23:24-39
At about that time, David's * 1Ki 1:5
that Haggith's *, Adonijah, is now 1Ki 1:11
* Solomon—do exactly as I say! 1Ki 1:12
promise me that my * Solomon would 1Ki 1:13
your God that my * Solomon would be 1Ki 1:17
If you don't act, my * Solomon 1Ki 1:21
I decree that your * Solomon shall 1Ki 1:30
Jonathan, the * of Abiathar the 1Ki 1:42
gave this charge to his * Solomon: 1Ki 2:1
Shime-i, the * of Gera the 1Ki 2:8
One day Adonijah the * of Haggith 1Ki 2:13
by giving him a * to succeed him. 1Ki 3:6
night and took my * from beside me 1Ki 3:20
saw that it wasn't my * at all." 1Ki 3:21
*, and the living child is mine." 1Ki 3:22
Azariah (* of Zadok) was the High 1Ki 4:1
Jehoshaphat (* of Ahilud) was the 1Ki 4:1
Benaiah (* of Jehoiada) was 1Ki 4:1
Azariah (* of Nathan) was 1Ki 4:1
Zabud (* of Nathan) was the king's 1Ki 4:1
Adoniram (* of Abda) was 1Ki 4:1
Baana (* of Ahilud), whose area 1Ki 4:8-19
(the * of Manasseh) in Gilead; 1Ki 4:8-19
Ahinadab (the * of Iddo), whose 1Ki 4:8-19
Baana (* of Hushai), whose areas 1Ki 4:8-19
Jehoshaphat (* of Paruah), whose 1Ki 4:8-19
Shime-i (* of Ela), whose area was 1Ki 4:8-19
Geber (* of Uri), whose area was 1Ki 4:8-19
that David's * Solomon was the new 1Ki 5:1
For the Lord told him, 'Your *, 1Ki 5:5
David a wise * to be king of the 1Ki 5:7
He was half Jewish, being the * 1Ki 7:14
said, 'but your * is the one who 1Ki 8:19
take the kingdom away from your *. 1Ki 11:12,13
She presented him with a *, 1Ki 11:20
was Jeroboam (the * of Nebat), who 1Ki 11:26
Benjamin were left to Solomon's *. 1Ki 11:32f
kingdom from his * and give ten of 1Ki 11:35
to you. His * shall have the other 1Ki 11:36
and his * Rehoboam reigned in his 1Ki 11:43
"Tell Rehoboam the * of Solomon, 1Ki 12:23,24
JEROBOAM'S * ABIJAH now became 1Ki 14:1
about her *, for he was very sick. 1Ki 14:5
died, his * Nadab took the throne. 1Ki 14:20
Meanwhile, Rehoboam the * of 1Ki 14:21
and his * Abijam took the throne. 1Ki 14:31
his * Asa reigned in his place. 1Ki 15:8
Then his * Jehoshaphat became the 1Ki 15:24
the * of Jeroboam had become king. 1Ki 15:25
Then Baasha (the * of Ahijah, 1Ki 15:27
Elah, Baasha's *, began reigning 1Ki 16:8
the sins of Baasha and his * Elah; 1Ki 16:13
followed Tibni, the * of Ginath. 1Ki 16:21
* Ahab became king in his place. 1Ki 16:28
his oldest *, Abiram, died; 1Ki 16:34
his youngest *, Segub, died. 1Ki 16:34
as declared by Joshua, the * of 1Ki 16:34
* and I must die of starvation." 1Ki 17:12
be enough food for you and your *. 1Ki 17:13
and Elijah and her * continued to 1Ki 17:15
But one day the woman's * became 1Ki 17:17
punish my sins by killing my *?" 1Ki 17:18
you killed the * of this widow with 1Ki 17:20
Then anoint Jehu (* of Himshi) 1Ki 19:16
anoint Elisha (the * of Shaphat of 1Ki 19:16
His name is Micaiah, the * of 1Ki 22:8
One of the prophets, Zedekiah (* 1Ki 22:11
Then Zedekiah (* of Chenaanah) 1Ki 22:24
of the city, and to my * Joash. 1Ki 22:26
* became the new king of Israel. 1Ki 22:40
Jehoshaphat the * of Asa had become 1Ki 22:41
Ahaziah, King Ahab's * and 1Ki 22:49
and his * Jehoram took the 1Ki 22:50
Ahaziah, Ahab's *, began to reign 1Ki 22:51
did not have a * to succeed him. 2Ki 1:17
(* of Jehoshaphat) of Judah. 2Ki 1:17
AHAB'S * JEHORAM began his reign 2Ki 3:1
of Jeroboam (the * of Nebat), who 2Ki 3:3
Then he took his oldest *, who 2Ki 3:27
doesn't have a *, and her husband 2Ki 4:14
this time you shall have a *!" 2Ki 4:15,16
was you who said I'd have a *. 2Ki 4:28
in, he said, "Here's your *!" 2Ki 4:36
then picked up her * and went out. 2Ki 4:37
my * one day and her son the next. 2Ki 6:26-30
my son one day and her * the next. 2Ki 6:26-30
So we boiled my * and ate him, 2Ki 6:26-30
I said, 'Kill your * so we can eat 2Ki 6:26-30
HAD TOLD the woman whose * 2Ki 8:1
and this is her *—the very one 2Ki 8:5
to him, "Your * Ben-hadad, the 2Ki 8:8,9
King Jehoram, the * of King 2Ki 8:16
Joram of Israel, the * of Ahab. 2Ki 8:16
Then his * Ahaziah 2Ki 8:24,25
Joram of Israel, the * of Ahab. 2Ki 8:24,25
He joined King Joram of Israel (* 2Ki 8:28
(* of Jehoram) came to visit him. 2Ki 8:29
and find Jehu (the * of 2Ki 9:2
of Jehoshaphat, the * of Nimshi). 2Ki 9:2
of Jeroboam (* of Nebat) and of 2Ki 9:9
and of Baasha (* of Ahijah). 2Ki 9:9
That is how Jehu (* of 2Ki 9:14
of Jehoshaphat, * of Nimshi) 2Ki 9:14
you murderer! You * of a Zimri who 2Ki 9:31
met Jehonadab, the * of Rechab, who 2Ki 10:15
Then Jehu and Jehonadab (* of 2Ki 10:23
sin of Jeroboam (* of Nebat), for 2Ki 10:29
I will cause your *, your grandson, 2Ki 10:30
and his * Jehoahaz became the new 2Ki 10:35
learned that her * was dead, she 2Ki 11:1
* Joash. Joash was rescued by his 2Ki 11:2,3
and showed them the king's *. 2Ki 11:4
were Jozachar, the * of Shimeath, 2Ki 12:21
* of Shomer—both trusted aides. 2Ki 12:21
his * Amaziah became the new king. 2Ki 12:21
JEHOAHAZ (THE * of Jehu) began a 2Ki 13:1
his * Ben-hadad to conquer them. 2Ki 13:3
Samaria, and his * Joash reigned in 2Ki 13:9,10
* Ben-hadad reigned in his place. 2Ki 13:24
(the * of Jehoahaz) was 2Ki 13:25
of Israel (the * of Jehoahaz and 2Ki 14:8
daughter to be a wife for my *.' 2Ki 14:9
And his * Jeroboam became the new 2Ki 14:16
Then his * Azariah 2Ki 14:21
as Jeroboam I (the * of Nebat), who 2Ki 14:24
through Jonah (* of Amittai) the 2Ki 14:25
of Israel, and his * Zechariah 2Ki 14:29
And his * Jotham was the acting 2Ki 15:5
and his * Jotham became king. 2Ki 15:7
Like Jeroboam I (the * of Nebat), 2Ki 15:9
Then Shallum (the * of Jabesh) 2Ki 15:10
true, that Jehu's *, grandson, and 2Ki 15:12
king, Menahem (the * of Gadi) came 2Ki 15:14
When he died, his * Pekahiah 2Ki 15:22
by Jeroboam I (* of Nebat) who led 2Ki 15:24
Then Pekah (* of Remaliah), the 2Ki 15:25
of Jeroboam I (* of Nebat), who led 2Ki 15:28
Then Hoshea (the * of Elah) 2Ki 15:30
Concurrent with: Jotham (* of 2Ki 15:30
this time: Pekah (* of Remaliah), 2Ki 15:32,33
Then his * Ahaz became the new 2Ki 15:38
time: King Pekah (* of Remaliah) 2Ki 16:1
He even killed his own * by 2Ki 16:3
and King Pekah (* of Remaliah) of 2Ki 16:5
'I am your servant and your *. 2Ki 16:7f
* Hezekiah became the new king. 2Ki 16:20
I (the * of Nebat) as its king. 2Ki 17:21
time: King Hoshea (* of Elah), who 2Ki 18:1
Then Eliakim (* of Hilkiah) the 2Ki 18:37
and Joah (* of Asaph) the historian 2Ki 18:37
to go to Isaiah (* of Amoz), the 2Ki 19:2
* Esarhaddon became the new king. 2Ki 19:37
(the * of King Baladan of Babylon) 2Ki 20:12
When he died, his * Manasseh 2Ki 20:21
his * Amon became the new king. 2Ki 21:18
Amon's * Josiah upon the throne. 2Ki 21:24
his * Josiah became the new king. 2Ki 21:26
secretary Shaphan (* of Azaliah, 2Ki 22:3,4
(son of Azaliah, * of Meshullam) to 2Ki 22:3,4
Ahikam (Shaphan's *), and Achbor 2Ki 22:12,13
Achbor (Michaiah's *) to ask the 2Ki 22:12,13
(She was the wife of Shallum—* of 2Ki 22:14
of Tikvah, * of Harhas—who was in 2Ki 22:14
use it to burn his * or daughter to 2Ki 23:10
And his * Jehoahaz was chosen by 2Ki 23:30
When he died, his * Jehoiachin 2Ki 24:6
Gedaliah (the * of Ahikam and 2Ki 25:22
These included Ishmael, the * of 2Ki 25:23
Johanan, the * of Kareah; 2Ki 25:23
Seraiah, the * of Tanhumeth the 2Ki 25:23
and Ja-azaniah, * of Maachathite, 2Ki 25:23
Arpachshad's * was 1Ch 1:18
Shelah, and Shelah's * was 1Ch 1:18
So the * 1Ch 1:24-27
of the word "*" could also be 1Ch 1:24-27f
of Shem was Arpachshad, the * of 1Ch 1:24-27
The * of Shelah was Eber, 1Ch 1:24-27
The * of Eber was Peleg, 1Ch 1:24-27
The * of Peleg was Reu, 1Ch 1:24-27
The * of Reu was Serug, 1Ch 1:24-27
The * of Serug was Nahor, 1Ch 1:24-27
The * of Nahor was Terah, 1Ch 1:24-27
The * of Terah was Abram (later 1Ch 1:24-27
Abraham's * Isaac had two sons, 1Ch 1:34
Anah's * was 1Ch 1:41
Bela (the * of Beor), who lived in 1Ch 1:43
When Bela died, Jobab the * of 1Ch 1:44
When Husham died, Hadad the * of 1Ch 1:46
When Shaul died, Baal-hanan the * 1Ch 1:49
But the oldest *, Er, was so 1Ch 2:3
(Achan, the * of Carmi, was the 1Ch 2:7
Ethan's * was Azariah. 1Ch 2:8
Jesse's first * was Eliab, his 1Ch 2:13
of Ishmael, had a * named Amasa. 1Ch 2:17

(SON Con't)
Caleb (the * of 1Ch 2:18
who presented him with a *, 1Ch 2:19
Hur's * was 1Ch 2:20
Uri, and Uri's * was Bezalel. 1Ch 2:20
and she presented him with a *, 1Ch 2:21
Jerahmeel (the oldest * of 1Ch 2:25
but Appa-im had a * named 1Ch 2:31
Ishi's * was 1Ch 2:31
and Sheshan's * was Ahlai. 1Ch 2:31
And they had a * whom they named 1Ch 2:34,35
Attai's * was Nathan; 1Ch 2:36
Nathan's * was Zabad; 1Ch 2:36
Zabad's * was Ephlal; 1Ch 2:37
Ephlal's * was Obed; 1Ch 2:37
Obed's * was Jehu; 1Ch 2:38
Jehu's * was Azariah; 1Ch 2:38
Azariah's * was Helez; 1Ch 2:39
Helez's * was Ele-asah; 1Ch 2:39
Ele-asah's * was Sismai; 1Ch 2:40
Sismai's * was Shallum; 1Ch 2:40
Shallum's * was Jekamiah; 1Ch 2:41
Jekamiah's * was Elishama. 1Ch 2:41
The oldest * of 1Ch 2:42
Shammai's * was Maon, the father 1Ch 2:45
Haran had a * named Gazez. 1Ch 2:46
Hur (who was the oldest * of Caleb 1Ch 2:50
of Salma were his * Bethlehem, the 1Ch 2:54
KING DAVID'S OLDEST * was 1Ch 3:1
The third was Absalom, the * of 1Ch 3:2
The fourth was Adonijah, the * of 1Ch 3:2
The fifth was Shephatiah, the * 1Ch 3:3
The sixth was Ithream, the * of 1Ch 3:3
Jeshiah's * was Rephaiah 1Ch 3:21,22
Rephaiah's * was Arnan; 1Ch 3:21,22
Arnan's * was Obadiah; 1Ch 3:21,22
Obadiah's * was Shecaniah. 1Ch 3:21,22
Shecaniah's * was Shemaiah; 1Ch 3:21,22
Shobal's * Re-aiah was the father 1Ch 4:2
The * of Hur, the oldest son of 1Ch 4:3-4
The son of Hur, the oldest * of 1Ch 4:3-4
after Aharhel, the * of Harum. 1Ch 4:8
whose * was Mahir, the father of 1Ch 4:11,12
The sons of Caleb (the * of 1Ch 4:15
The sons of Shelah (the * of 1Ch 4:21-22
Shaul's * was Shallum, his 1Ch 4:25
Benaiah, Ziza (the * of Shiphi, son 1Ch 4:34-39
son of Shiphi, * of Allon, son of 1Ch 4:34-39
son of Allon, * of Jedaiah, son of 1Ch 4:34-39
* of Shimri, son of Shemaiah). 1Ch 4:34-39
son of Shimri, * of Shemaiah). 1Ch 4:34-39
THE OLDEST * of Israel was Reuben, 1Ch 5:1
name Reuben as the oldest *. 1Ch 5:1
The sons of Reuben, Israel's *, 1Ch 5:3
Joel's descendants were his * 1Ch 5:4
Shime-i's * was Micah; 1Ch 5:5
Baal's * was Beerah. 1Ch 5:6
Bela (the * of Azaz, grandson of 1Ch 5:7,8
Ahi, the * of Abdi-el and 1Ch 5:15
given to Caleb the * of Jephunneh), 1Ch 6:55,56,57
Uzzi's * was Izrahiah among whose 1Ch 7:3
The * of Jedia-el was 1Ch 7:10
him a * whom she named Peresh; 1Ch 7:16
Ulam's * was Bedan. 1Ch 7:17
and bore a * whom he called Beriah 1Ch 7:23
of Joseph the * of Israel, 1Ch 7:29
His oldest * was named Abdon, 1Ch 8:30,31,32
The * of Jonathan was 1Ch 8:34
The * of Mephibosheth 1Ch 8:34
Zimri's * was Moza. 1Ch 8:36
that of Uthai (the * of Ammihud, 1Ch 9:4
son of Ammihud, * of Omri, son of 1Ch 9:4
son of Omri, * of Imri, son of 1Ch 9:4
Omri, son of Imri, * of Bani) of 1Ch 9:4
of the clan of Perez (* of Judah). 1Ch 9:4
(Shilon's oldest *) and his sons; 1Ch 9:5
Sallu (the * of Meshullam, the son 1Ch 9:7,8
Sallu (the son of Meshullam, the * 1Ch 9:7,8
of Hodaviah, the * of Hassenuah); 1Ch 9:7,8
Ibneiah (the * of Jeroham); 1Ch 9:7,8
Elah (the * of Uzzi, the son of 1Ch 9:7,8
Elah (the son of Uzzi, the * of 1Ch 9:7,8
Meshullam (the * of Shephatiah, 1Ch 9:7,8
* of Reuel, the son of Ibnijah). 1Ch 9:7,8
son of Reuel, the * of Ibnijah). 1Ch 9:7,8
Azariah (the * of Hilkiah, son of 1Ch 9:10,11
Azariah (the son of Hilkiah, * of 1Ch 9:10,11
son of Meshullam, * of Zadok, son 1Ch 9:10,11
* of Meraioth, son of Ahitub). 1Ch 9:10,11
son of Meraioth, * of Ahitub). 1Ch 9:10,11
was Adaiah (* of Jeroham, son of 1Ch 9:12
* of Pashhur, son of Malchijah). 1Ch 9:12
son of Pashhur, * of Malchijah). 1Ch 9:12
Another priest was Maasai (* of 1Ch 9:12
(son of Adi-el, * of Jahzerah, son 1Ch 9:12
son of Jahzerah, * of Meshullam, 1Ch 9:12
* of Meshillemith, son of Immer). 1Ch 9:12
son of Meshillemith, * of Immer). 1Ch 9:12
was Shemaiah (* of Hasshub, son of 1Ch 9:14
(son of Hasshub, * of Azrikam, son 1Ch 9:14
son of Azrikam, * of Hashabiah, who 1Ch 9:14
Mattaniah (the * of Mica, who was 1Ch 9:15,16
Mica, who was the * of Zichri, who 1Ch 9:15,16
Zichri, who was the * of Asaph). 1Ch 9:15,16
Obadiah (the * of Shemaiah, son of 1Ch 9:15,16
Obadiah (the son of Shemaiah, * of 1Ch 9:15,16
son of Galal, * of Jeduthun). 1Ch 9:15,16
Berechiah (the * of Asa, son of 1Ch 9:15,16
Berechiah (the son of Asa, * of 1Ch 9:15,16
Phinehas, the * of Eleazar, was 1Ch 9:20
At that time Zechariah, the * of 1Ch 9:21
and the oldest * of Shallum the 1Ch 9:31
Mikloth lived with his * Shime-am 1Ch 9:38
kingdom to David, the * of Jesse. 1Ch 10:14
Joab, the * of Zeruiah, was the 1Ch 11:5,6
Jashobeam (the * of a man from 1Ch 11:11
was Eleazar, the * of Dodo, a 1Ch 11:12
Elhanan, the * of Dodo from 1Ch 11:26-47
Ira (* of Ikkesh) from Tekoa; 1Ch 11:26-47
Heled (* of Baanah) from 1Ch 11:26-47
Ithai (* of Ribai) a Benjaminite 1Ch 11:26-47
Jonathan (* of Shagee) from Harar; 1Ch 11:26-47
Ahiam (* of Sacher) from Harar; 1Ch 11:26-47
Eliphal (* of Ur); 1Ch 11:26-47
Naarai (* of Ezbai); 1Ch 11:26-47
Mibhar (* of Hagri); 1Ch 11:26-47
Zabad (* of Ahlai); 1Ch 11:26-47
Adina (* of Shiza) from the tribe 1Ch 11:26-47
Hanan (* of Maacah); 1Ch 11:26-47
Jedia-el (* of Shimri); 1Ch 11:26-47
Literally, "the * of Kish." 1Ch 12:1f
Their chief was Ahi-ezer, * of 1Ch 12:3-7
We are on your side, * of Jesse. 1Ch 12:18
Heman (* of Joel), Asaph (son of 1Ch 15:17
Heman (son of Joel), Asaph (* of 1Ch 15:17
and Ethan (* of Kushaiah) from the 1Ch 15:17
Obed-edom (the * of Jeduthun), 1Ch 16:38
his father, and he shall be my *; 1Ch 17:13
army, he sent his * Hadoram to 1Ch 18:10
Abishai (* of Zeruiah) then 1Ch 18:12
Joab (* of Zeruiah) was 1Ch 18:15
Jehoshaphat (* of Ahilud) was the 1Ch 18:15
Zadok (* of Ahitub) and 1Ch 18:16
and Ahimelech (* of Abiathar) were 1Ch 18:16
Benaiah (* of Jehoiada) was in 1Ch 18:17
his * Hanun became the new king. 1Ch 19:1
Elhanan (the * of Jair) killed 1Ch 20:5
the * of David's brother Shimea. 1Ch 20:6,7
"Solomon my * is young and 1Ch 22:5
He now commanded his * Solomon 1Ch 22:6
But I will give you a *,' he 1Ch 22:9
my own * and I will be his father; 1Ch 22:10
"So now, my *, may the Lord be 1Ch 22:11
to assist his * in this project. 1Ch 22:17
and appointed his * Solomon as the 1Ch 23:1
and Eliezer's only *, Rehabiah, was 1Ch 23:17
Shemaiah, a Levite and the * of 1Ch 24:6
Ahimelech the * of Abiathar, and 1Ch 24:6
led by his oldest * Isshiah; 1Ch 24:21
group:Jeriah, Hebron's oldest *; 1Ch 24:23
Amariah, his second *; 1Ch 24:23
Jahaziel, his third *; 1Ch 24:23
Jekameam, his fourth *. 1Ch 24:23
The Uzziel group was led by his * 1Ch 24:24,25
and by Isshiah's * Zechariah. 1Ch 24:24,25
(Ja-aziah's group, led by his * 1Ch 24:26,27
was Meshelemiah, the * of Kore. 1Ch 26:1
of the north gate to his * 1Ch 26:14,15
Shebuel, * of Gershom and 1Ch 26:23,24
prophet, Saul the * of Kish, Abner 1Ch 26:28
of Kish, Abner the * of Ner, Joab 1Ch 26:28
of Ner, Joab the * of Zeruiah, and 1Ch 26:28
(He was the * of Jehoiada the 1Ch 27:5,6
David's army.) His * Ammizabad 1Ch 27:5,6
later replaced by his * Zebadiah. 1Ch 27:7
Ira, the * of Ikkesh from Tekoa; 1Ch 27:9
Over Reuben, Eliezer (* of 1Ch 27:16-22
Over Simeon, Shephatiah (* of 1Ch 27:16-22
Over Levi, Hashabiah (* of 1Ch 27:16-22
Over Issachar, Omri (* of 1Ch 27:16-22
Over Zebulun, Ishmaiah (* of 1Ch 27:16-22
Over Naphtali, Jeremoth (* of 1Ch 27:16-22
Over Ephraim, Hoshea (* of 1Ch 27:16-22
of Manasseh, Joel (* of Pedaiah); 1Ch 27:16-22
in Gilead, Iddo (* of Zechariah); 1Ch 27:16-22
Over Benjamin, Ja-asiel (* of 1Ch 27:16-22
Over Dan, Azarel (* of Jeroham). 1Ch 27:16-22
Azmaveth (* of Adi-el) was the 1Ch 27:25
and Jonathan (* of Uzziah) was 1Ch 27:25
Ezri (* of Chelub) was manager of 1Ch 27:26
and Shaphat (* of Adlai) had charge 1Ch 27:29
Jehiel (the * of Hachmoni) was 1Ch 27:32
* of Benaiah) and by Abiathar. 1Ch 27:34
He has told me, 'Your * Solomon 1Ch 28:6
for I have chosen him as my * and 1Ch 28:6
Solomon, my *, get to know the 1Ch 28:9
and said: "My * Solomon, whom God 1Ch 29:1
Give my * Solomon a good heart 1Ch 29:19
they crowned King David's * 1Ch 29:22
and his * Solomon reigned in his 1Ch 29:28
KING DAVID'S * Solomon was now the 2Ch 1:1
made by Bezalel (* of Uri, son of 2Ch 1:5,6
(son of Uri, * of Hur) still stood 2Ch 1:5
and understanding * to build God's 2Ch 2:1
He is a brilliant man, the * of 2Ch 2:1
his * was chosen for that task. 2Ch 6
Jeroboam the * of Nebat. 2Ch 9:2
* Rehoboam became the new king. 2Ch 9:3
of Jeroboam (* of Nebat) sent word 2Ch 10:2
Judah, Solomon's *, and to the 2Ch 11
She was the daughter of David's * 2Ch 11:1
Maacah's * Abijah was his 2Ch 11:2
his * Abijah became the new king. 2Ch 12:1
servant of David's *, and was a 2Ch 13
defying Solomon's * Rehoboam, for 2Ch 13
Then his * Asa became the new 2Ch 14
came upon Azariah (* of Oded), and 2Ch 15
THEN HIS * Jehoshaphat became the 2Ch 17
Next was Amasiah (* of Zichri), 2Ch 17:1
a marriage alliance [for his * 2Ch 18
His name is Micaiah (* of 2Ch 18:6,
Go and get Micaiah (* of 2Ch 18
One of them, Zedekiah (* of 2Ch 18:1
Then Zedekiah (* of Chenaanah) 2Ch 18:2
Amon and to my * Joash," the king 2Ch 18:2
(* of Hanani) went out to meet him. 2Ch 19
and Zebadiah (* of Ishmael), a 2Ch 19:1
there—Jahaziel (* of Zechariah, son 2Ch 20:1
(son of Zechariah, * of Benaiah, 2Ch 20:1
son of Benaiah, * of Je-iel, son of 2Ch 20:1
son of Je-iel, * of Mattaniah the 2Ch 20:1
of Jehu the * of Hanani, which is 2Ch 20:3
Then Eliezer, * of Dodavahu from 2Ch 20:3
Jerusalem, and his * Jehoram became 2Ch 21:
only his youngest *, Jehoahaz, 2Ch 21:1
his youngest *, as their new king 2Ch 22:
of Israel (the * of Ahab), who was 2Ch 22:
to challenge Jehu (* of Nimshi), 2Ch 22:
the news of her * Ahaziah's death. 2Ch 22:1
Azariah (* of Jeroham), Ishmael 2Ch 23:
Jeroham), Ishmael (* of Jehohanan), 2Ch 23:
Azariah (* of Obed), Maaseiah (son 2Ch 23:
Obed), Maaseiah (* of Adaiah), and 2Ch 23:
and Elishaphat (* of Zichri). 2Ch 23:
come for the king's * to reign!" 2Ch 23:2,
came upon Zechariah, Jehoiada's *. 2Ch 24:2
love and loyalty—by killing his *. 2Ch 24:2
the * of Jehoiada the priest. 2Ch 24:2
When Joash died, his * Amaziah 2Ch 24:2
(* of Jehoahaz, grandson of Jehu). 2Ch 25:1
daughter in marriage to my *.' 2Ch 25:1
the Temple. His * Jotham became 2Ch 26:2
by the prophet Isaiah (* of Amoz). 2Ch 26:2
his * Jotham became the new king. 2Ch 26:2
his * Ahaz became the new king. 2Ch 27:9
On a single day, Pekah, the * of 2Ch 28:6
killed the king's * Ma-aseiah, and 2Ch 28:7
These men were Azariah the * of 2Ch 28:12
Berechiah the * of Meshillemoth, 2Ch 28:12
Jehizkiah the * of Shallum, and 2Ch 28:12
and Amasa the * of Hadlai. 2Ch 28:12
* Hezekiah became the new king. 2Ch 28:27
From the Kohath clan, Mahath (* 2Ch 29:12,13,14
Amasai) and Joel (* of Azariah); 2Ch 29:12,13,14
From the Merari clan, Kish (* of 2Ch 29:12,13,14
and Azariah (* of Jehallelel); 2Ch 29:12,13,14
From the Gershon clan, Joah (* 2Ch 29:12,13,14
of Zimmah) and Eden (* of Joah). 2Ch 29:12,13,14
days of King David's * Solomon. 2Ch 30:26
Kore (* of Imnah, the Levite), 2Ch 31:14,15
the prophet (* of Amoz) cried out 2Ch 32:20
(the prophet, the * of Amoz), and 2Ch 32:32
Then his * Manasseh became the 2Ch 32:33
told David and his * Solomon, "I 2Ch 33:7
his * Amon became the new king. 2Ch 33:20,21
his * Josiah to be the new king. 2Ch 33:25
appointed Shaphan (* of Azaliah) 2Ch 34:8
and Joah (* of Joahaz), the city 2Ch 34:8
Hilkiah, Ahikam (* of Shaphan), 2Ch 34:20
Shaphan), Abdon (* of Micah), 2Ch 34:20
(* of Tokhath, son of Hasrah). 2Ch 34:22
(son of Tokhath, * of Hasrah). 2Ch 34:22
of Israel and by his * Solomon. 2Ch 35:4,5
JOSIAH'S * JEHOAHAZ was selected 2Ch 36:1
and his * Jehoiachin became the 2Ch 36:8
Then Jeshua (* of Jozadak) with Ez 3:1
and Zerubbabel (* of She-alti-el) Ez 3:1
of Zerubbabel (* of She-alti-el), Ez 3:8
Jeshua (* of Jozadak), and their Ez 3:8
and Zechariah (the * of Iddo)—who Ez 5:1
to Zerubbabel (* of She-alti-el) Ez 5:1
and Jeshua (* of Jozadak), Ez 5:1
Haggai and Zechariah (* of Iddo). Ez 6:14
Ezra was the * of Seriah; Ez 7:1
Seriah was the * of Azariah; Ez 7:1
Azariah was the * of Hilkiah; Ez 7:1
Hilkiah was the * of Shallum; Ez 7:1
Shallum was the * of Zadok; Ez 7:1
Zadok was the * of Ahitub; Ez 7:1
Ahitub was the * of Amariah; Ez 7:1
Amariah was the * of Meraioth; Ez 7:1
Meraioth was the * of Zerahiah; Ez 7:1
Zerahiah was the * of Uzzi; Ez 7:1

ON Con't)

Uzzi was the * of Bukki;	Ez 7:1
Bukki was the * of Abishu-a;	Ez 7:1
Abishu-a was the * of Phinehas;	Ez 7:1
Phinehas was the * of Eleazar;	Ez 7:1
Eleazar was the * of Aaron, the	Ez 7:1
(* of Zerahiah), and 200 other men;	Ez 8:2-14
From the clan of Shecaniah—the *	Ez 8:2-14
From the clan of Adin—Ebed (* of	Ez 8:2-14
From the clan of Elam—Jeshaiah (*	Ez 8:2-14
(* of Michael), and 80 other men;	Ez 8:2-14
From the clan of Joab—Obadiah (*	Ez 8:2-14
From the clan of Bani—Shelomith (*	Ez 8:2-14
(* of Bebai), and 28 other men;	Ez 8:2-14
From the clan of Azgad—Johanan (*	Ez 8:2-14
* of Levi and grandson of Israel.	Ez 8:18
and Jeshaiah (the * of Merari),	Ez 8:19
by Meremoth (the * of Uriah the	Ez 8:33
priest), Eleazar (* of Phinehas),	Ez 8:33
Jozabad (* of Jeshua), and Noadiah	Ez 8:33
and Noadiah (* of Binnui)—all of	Ez 8:33
Then Shecaniah (the * of Jehiel	Ez 10:2
Only Jonathan (* of Asahel),	Ez 10:15
Asahel), Jahzeiah (* of Tikvah),	Ez 10:15
OF Nehemiah, the * of Hecaliah:	Neh 1:1
crew led by Zaccur (* of Imri).	Neh 3:2
Meremoth (* of Uriah, son of	Neh 3:4
Meremoth (son of Uriah, * of	Neh 3:4
were Meshullam (* of Berechiah, son	Neh 3:4
(son of Berechiah, * of Meshezabel)	Neh 3:4
and Zadok (* of Baana).	Neh 3:4
by Joiada (* of Paseah) and	Neh 3:6
and Meshullam (* of Besodeiah).	Neh 3:6
Uzziel (* of Harhaiah) was a	Neh 3:8
Rephaiah (* of Hur), the mayor of	Neh 3:9
Jedaiah (* of Harumaph) repaired	Neh 3:10
was Hattush (* of Hashabneiah).	Neh 3:10
Then came Malchijah (* of Harim)	Neh 3:11
and Hasshub (* of Pahath-moab), who	Neh 3:11
Shallum (* of Hallohesh) and his	Neh 3:12
by Malchijah (* of Rechab), the	Neh 3:14
Shallum (* of Colhozeh), the	Neh 3:15
Next to him was Nehemiah (* of	Neh 3:16
supervision of Rehum (* of Bani).	Neh 3:17
led by Bavvai (* of Henadad), the	Neh 3:18
were led by Ezer (* of Jeshua), the	Neh 3:19
Next to him was Baruch (* of	Neh 3:20
Meremoth (* of Uriah, son of	Neh 3:21
Meremoth (son of Uriah, * of	Neh 3:21
and Azariah (* of Ma-aseiah, son of	Neh 3:23
(son of Ma-aseiah, * of Ananiah)	Neh 3:23
Next was Binnui (* of Henadad),	Neh 3:24
Palal (* of Uzai) carried on the	Neh 3:25
Next was Pedaiah (* of Parosh).	Neh 3:25
Zadok (* of Immer) also rebuilt	Neh 3:29
him was Shemaiah (* of Shecaniah),	Neh 3:29
Next was Hananiah (* of	Neh 3:30
Hanun (the sixth * of Zalaph);	Neh 3:30
and Meshullam (* of Berechiah),	Neh 3:30
to visit Shemaiah (* of Delaiah,	Neh 6:10
who was the * of Mehetabel), for he	Neh 6:10
was Shecaniah (* of Arah) and	Neh 6:18
and because his * Jehohanan was	Neh 6:18
of Meshullam (* of Berechiah).	Neh 6:18
Jeshua (* of Azaniah), Binnui	Neh 10:9-13
(* of Henadad), Kadmi-el,	Neh 10:9-13
Athaiah (* of Uzziah, son of	Neh 11:4,5,6
Athaiah (son of Uzziah, * of	Neh 11:4,5,6
son of Zechariah, * of Amariah, son	Neh 11:4,5,6
son of Amariah, * of	Neh 11:4,5,6
Shephatiah, * of	Neh 11:4,5,6
Ma-aseiah (* of Baruch, son of	Neh 11:4,5,6
Ma-aseiah (son of Baruch, * of	Neh 11:4,5,6
son of Col-hozeh, * of Hazaiah, son	Neh 11:4,5,6
son of Hazaiah, * of Adaiah, son of	Neh 11:4,5,6
son of Adaiah, * of Joiarib, son of	Neh 11:4,5,6
son of Joiarib, * of Zechariah, son	Neh 11:4,5,6
of Zechariah, * of the Shilonite).	Neh 11:4,5,6
Sallu (* of Meshullam, son of	Neh 11:7,8,9
Sallu (son of Meshullam, * of	Neh 11:7,8,9
son of Joed, * of Pedaiah, son of	Neh 11:7,8,9
son of Pedaiah, * of Kolaiah, son	Neh 11:7,8,9
son of Kolaiah, * of Ma-aseiah, son	Neh 11:7,8,9
* of Ithi-el, son of Jeshaiah).	Neh 11:7,8,9
son of Ithi-el, * of Jeshaiah).	Neh 11:7,8,9
Their chief was Joel, * of	Neh 11:7,8,9
by Judah, * of Hassenu-ah.	Neh 11:7,8,9
Jedaiah (* of Joiarib);	Neh 11:10-14
Seraiah (* of Hilkiah, son of	Neh 11:10-14
Seraiah (son of Hilkiah, * of	Neh 11:10-14
son of Meshullam, * of Zadok, son	Neh 11:10-14
son of Zadok, * of Meraioth, son of	Neh 11:10-14
* of Ahitub the chief priest).	Neh 11:10-14
of Adaiah (* of Jeroham, son of	Neh 11:10-14
(son of Jeroham, * of Pelaliah, son	Neh 11:10-14
son of Pelaliah, * of Amzi, son of	Neh 11:10-14
son of Amzi, * of Zechariah, son of	Neh 11:10-14
* of Pashhur, son of Malchijah).	Neh 11:10-14
son of Pashhur, * of Malchijah).	Neh 11:10-14
of Amashsai (* of Azarel, son of	Neh 11:10-14
(son of Azarel, * of Ahzai, son of	Neh 11:10-14

* of Meshillemoth, son of Immer);	Neh 11:10-14
son of Meshillemoth, * of Immer);	Neh 11:10-14
who was assisted by Zabdiel (* of	Neh 11:10-14
Shemaiah (* of Hasshub, son of	Neh 11:15,16,17
Shemaiah (son of Hasshub, * of	Neh 11:15,16,17
* of Hashabiah, son of Bunni);	Neh 11:15,16,17
son of Hashabiah, * of Bunni);	Neh 11:15,16,17
Mattaniah (* of Mica, son of	Neh 11:15,16,17
Mattaniah (son of Mica, * of	Neh 11:15,16,17
son of Zabdi, * of Asaph) was the	Neh 11:15,16,17
Bakbukiah and Abda (* of	Neh 11:15,16,17
(son of Shammua, * of Galal, son	Neh 11:15,16,17
son of Galal, * of Jeduthun) were	Neh 11:15,16,17
Temple was Uzzi (* of Bani, son of	Neh 11:22,23
Uzzi (son of Bani, * of Hashabiah,	Neh 11:22,23
son of Hashabiah, * of Mattaniah,	Neh 11:22,23
son of Mattaniah, * of Mica), a	Neh 11:22,23
Pethahiah (* of Meshezabel, a	Neh 11:24
of Zerah, a * of Judah) assisted in	Neh 11:24
(* of She-altiel) and Jeshua:	Neh 12:1
of Johanan, the * of Eliashib.	Neh 12:23
and Jeshua (* of Kadmi-el).	Neh 12:24
time of Joiakim (* of Jeshua, son	Neh 12:26
(son of Jeshua, * of Jozadak), and	Neh 12:26
were Zechariah (* of Jonathan, son	Neh 12:35,36
(son of Jonathan, * of Shemaiah,	Neh 12:35,36
son of Shemaiah, * of Mattaniah,	Neh 12:35,36
son of Mattaniah, * of Micaiah, son	Neh 12:35,36
* of Zaccur, son of Asaph)	Neh 12:35,36
son of Zaccur, * of Asaph),	Neh 12:35,36
laws of David and his * Solomon.	Neh 12:45
and I appointed Hanan (* of	Neh 13:13
(son of Zaccur, * of Mattaniah) as	Neh 13:13
of Jehoiada (the * of Eliashib the	Neh 13:28
named Mordecai (* of Jair, son of	Est 2:5
(son of Jair, * of Shime-i, son of	Est 2:5
* of Kish, a Benjaminite).	Est 2:5
appointed Haman (* of Hammedatha	Est 3:1
Literally, "Haman, * of	Est 3:10f
(* of Hammedatha), the Jews' enemy—	Est 9:7-10
time when Haman (* of Hammedatha	Est 9:24,25
He will have neither * nor	Job 18:19
Then Elihu (* of Barachel, the	Job 32:2
has said to me, 'You are my *.	Ps 2:7
Fall down before his * and kiss	Ps 2:12
when he fled from his * Absalom	Ps 3:1
help his * to walk in godliness.	Ps 72:1
May the reign of this *	Ps 72:6
Solomon's * to Jesus the Messiah.	Ps 72:6f
(This ends the psalms of David, *	Ps 72:20
Then he killed the eldest *	Ps 78:51
* you have raised for yourself.	Ps 80:15
the * of your choice,	Ps 80:17
Literally, "the * of man you made	Ps 80:17f
as my firstborn *, and make him the	Ps 89:27
For you promised me that my *	Ps 132:11
I have decreed for him a mighty *.	Ps 132:17
Literally, "or the * of man that	Ps 144:3f
King Solomon of Israel, David's *:	Pro 1:1
Don't do it, *!	Pro 1:15
MY *, NEVER forget the things I've	Pro 3:1
Just as a father punishes a * he	Pro 3:11,12
For I, too, was once a *,	Pro 4:3
your head. My *, listen to me and	Pro 4:10
Listen, * of mine, to what I say.	Pro 4:20
LISTEN TO ME, my *!	Pro 5:1
Drink from your own well, my *—be	Pro 5:15
*, IF YOU endorse a note for	Pro 6:1
FOLLOW MY ADVICE, my *;	Pro 7:1
IS THE man with a level-headed *;	Pro 10:1
*, it proves you don't love him;	Pro 13:24
a wise * considers each	Pro 15:5
A sensible * gladdens his father.	Pro 15:20
A rebellious * saddens his	Pro 15:20
A rebellious * is a grief to his	Pro 17:25
A rebellious * is a calamity to	Pro 19:13
Discipline your * in his early	Pro 19:18
A * who mistreats his father or	Pro 19:26
My *, how I will rejoice if you	Pro 23:15,16
O my *, be wise and stay in	Pro 23:19,20,21
for joy—what pleasure a wise * is!	Pro 23:24,25
O my *, trust my advice—stay	Pro 23:26,27,28
My *, honey whets the appetite,	Pro 24:13,14
My *, watch your step before the	Pro 24:21,22
My *, how happy I will be if you	Pro 27:11
obey the law; a * who is a member	Pro 28:7
A wise * makes his father happy,	Pro 29:3
Discipline your * and he will	Pro 29:17
expect you to treat him as a *!	Pro 29:21
These are the messages of Agur, *	Pro 30:1
O my *, whom I have dedicated to	Pro 31:2
the Preacher, the * (or descendant)	Ecc 1:1f
of Jerusalem, King David's *,	Ecc 1:1
And who can tell whether my *	Ecc 2:19
alone, without a * or brother, yet	Ecc 4:8
left to pass on to one's *.	Ecc 5:13,14
But, my *, be warned: there is no	Ecc 12:12
came to Isaiah, * of Amoz, in the	Is 1:1
DURING THE REIGN of Ahaz (the *	Is 7:1
of Israel (the * of Remaliah).	Is 7:1
"The usurper, the * of Remaliah"	Is 7:1f

you and Shear-jashub, your *.	Is 7:3
the * of Tabeel as their king.'	Is 7:6
and her newborn * (Isaiah 8:1–4).	Is 7:14f
bore a *, Immanuel, the Christ.	Is 7:14f
of the * I am going to give you.	Is 8:1
and Zechariah the * of Jeberechiah,	Is 8:2
and bore me a *, and the Lord said,	Is 8:3
unto us a * is given;	Is 9:6
God showed Isaiah (* of Amoz)	Is 13:1
O Lucifer, * of the morning!	Is 14:12
your people. Your * will not	Is 14:20
but his * will be a greater	Is 14:29
told Isaiah, the * of Amoz, to take	Is 20:2
the * of Hilkiah, to replace you.	Is 22:20
Then Eliakim, Hilkiah's *, who	Is 36:3
and Joah (Asaph's *), the royal	Is 36:3
Then Eliakim (* of Hilkiah), the	Is 36:22
scribe, and Joah (* of Asaph), the	Is 36:22
Isaiah the prophet, * of Amoz.	Is 37:2
Then Isaiah, the * of Amoz, sent	Is 37:21
and Esar-haddon his * became king.	Is 37:38
the prophet (Amoz' *) went to visit	Is 38:1
the * of Baladan) sent Hezekiah a	Is 39:1
and not have love for her own *?	Is 49:15
the priest (the * of Hilkiah) who	Jer 1:1
of Amon's * Josiah, king of Judah.	Jer 1:1
reign of Josiah's * Jehoiakim, king	Jer 1:3
reign of Josiah's * Zedekiah, king	Jer 1:3
weep bitterly as for an only *.	Jer 6:26
that Manasseh, * of Hezekiah, king	Jer 15:4
NOW WHEN PASHHUR (* of Immer),	Jer 20:1
father the news that a * was born.	Jer 20:15
KING ZEDEKIAH sent Pashhur (*	Jer 21:1
the priest (* of Ma-aseiah) to	Jer 21:1
* of Jehoiakim king of Judah—even	Jer 22:24,25
enslaved Jeconiah (* of Jehoiakim),	Jer 24:1
Jehoiakim of Judah (* of Josiah).	Jer 25:1
reign of Josiah (* of Amon) king of	Jer 25:2,3
(* of Josiah), king of Judah:	Jer 26:1
the Lord, Uriah (* of Shemaiah)	Jer 26:20
sent Elnathan (* of Achbor) to	Jer 26:22
But Ahikam (* of Shaphan), the	Jer 26:24
(* of Josiah), king of Judah:	Jer 27:1
serve him and his * and his	Jer 27:7
with Jeconiah (* of Jehoiakim),	Jer 27:19,20,21
of Judah—Hananiah (* of Azzur), a	Jer 28:1
* of Jehoiakim, king of Judah,	Jer 28:4
with Elasah (* of Shaphan) and	Jer 29:3
and Gemariah (* of Hilkiah) when	Jer 29:3
prophets, Ahab (* of Kolaiah) and	Jer 29:21
and Zedekiah (* of Maaseiah), who	Jer 29:21
to Zephaniah (* of Ma-aseiah) the	Jer 29:25
The Messiah, David's greater *,	Jer 30:9f
is still my *, my darling child.	Jer 31:20
cousin Hanamel (* of Shallum) will	Jer 32:6,7
papers to Baruch (* of Neriah, who	Jer 32:12
who was the * of Mahseiah).	Jer 32:12
bring to the throne the true *	Jer 33:15
have a * to reign upon his throne;	Jer 33:20,21
when Jehoiakim (* of Josiah) was	Jer 35:1
to see Ja-azaniah (* of Jeremiah,	Jer 35:3
who was the * of Habazziniah), and	Jer 35:3
the prophet (the * of Igdaliah).	Jer 35:4
room of Ma-aseiah (* of Shallum),	Jer 35:4
our father (* of Rechab) commanded	Jer 35:6
of Judah (* of Josiah) the Lord	Jer 36:1
So Jeremiah sent for Baruch (* of	Jer 36:4
of King Jehoiakim (* of Josiah).	Jer 36:9
(* of Shaphan) to read the scroll.	Jer 36:10
When Micaiah (* of Gemariah, son	Jer 36:11
When Micaiah (son of Gemariah, *	Jer 36:11
well as Delaiah (* of Shamaiah),	Jer 36:12
Elnathan (* of Achbor), Gemariah	Jer 36:12
Achbor), Gemariah (* of Shaphan),	Jer 36:12
Zedekiah (* of Hananiah), and all	Jer 36:12
sent Jehudi (* of Nethaniah, son of	Jer 36:14,15
(son of Nethaniah, * of Shelemiah,	Jer 36:14,15
son of Shelemiah, * of Cushi) to	Jer 36:14,15
"a * of the king."	Jer 36:26f
and Seraiah (* of Azri-el) and	Jer 36:26
and Shelemiah (* of Abdeel) to	Jer 36:26
by his * Jehoiachin (also called	Jer 36:30f
*) to be the new king of Judah.	Jer 37:1
appointed his * Coniah as ruler	Jer 37:1f
Instead he chose Zedekiah (* of	Jer 37:1
sent Jehucal (* of Shelemiah) and	Jer 37:3
the priest (* of Ma-aseiah) to ask	Jer 37:3
arrest was Irijah (* of Shelemiah,	Jer 37:13
BUT WHEN SHEPHATIAH (* of	Jer 38:1
and Gedaliah (* of Pashhur) and	Jer 38:1
and Jucal (* of Shelemiah) and	Jer 38:1
and Pashhur (* of Malchiah) heard	Jer 38:1
care of Gedaliah (* of Ahikam, son	Jer 39:14
(son of Ahikam, * of Shaphan), to	Jer 39:14
who came: Ishmael (* of Nethaniah),	Jer 40:8
Kareah), Seraiah (* of Tanhumeth),	Jer 40:8
Jezaniah (* of a Ma-acathite), and	Jer 40:8
But soon afterwards Johanan (* of	Jer 40:13,14
had sent Ishmael (* of Nethaniah)	Jer 40:13,14
BUT IN OCTOBER, Ishmael (* of	Jer 41:1
(son of Nethaniah, * of Elishama),	Jer 41:1

(SON Con't)
But when Johanan (* of Kareah) Jer 41:11
people, Azariah (* of Hoshaiah) Jer 43:2,3
and Johanan (* of Kareah) and all Jer 43:2,3
Baruch (* of Neriah) has plotted Jer 43:2,3
of King Jehoiakim (* of Josiah), Jer 45:1
(* of Josiah), king of Judah: Jer 46:2
give to Seraiah (* of Neriah, son Jer 51:59
(son of Neriah, * of Mahseiah), Jer 51:59
Ezekiel was a priest (the * of Eze 1:1
AND HE SAID to me: "Stand up, * Eze 2:1
Or, "* of man" Eze 2:1f
"* of dust," he said, "I am Eze 2:3
"* of dust, don't be afraid of Eze 2:6
Listen, * of dust, to what I say Eze 2:8
AND HE SAID to me: "* of dust, Eze 3:1
Then he said: "* of dust, I am Eze 3:4
Then he added: "* of dust, let Eze 3:10
"* of dust, I have appointed you Eze 3:17
"AND NOW, * of dust, take a large Eze 4:1
Then he told me, "* of dust, Eze 4:16
"* OF DUST, take a sharp sword Eze 5:1
"* of dust, look over toward the Eze 6:2
He said to me, "* of dust, look Eze 8:5
And he said: "* of dust, do you Eze 8:6
with Ja-azaniah (* of Shaphan) Eze 8:11
Then the Lord said to me: "* of Eze 8:12
Ja-azaniah (* of Azzur) and Eze 11:1
and Pelatiah (* of Benaiah). Eze 11:1
Then the Spirit said to me, "* of Eze 11:1
Therefore, * of dust, prophesy Eze 11:4
(* of Benaiah) suddenly died. Eze 11:13
"* of dust, the remnant left in Eze 11:15
"* of dust," he said, "you Eze 12:2
"* of dust, these rebels, the Eze 12:9
"* of dust, tremble as you eat Eze 12:18
"* of dust, what is that proverb Eze 12:22
"* of dust, the people of Israel Eze 12:27
"* of dust, prophesy against the Eze 13:2,3
"* of dust, speak out against Eze 13:17
"* of dust, these men worship Eze 14:3
"* of dust, when the people of Eze 14:13
"* of dust, what good are vines Eze 15:2
"* of dust," he said, "speak Eze 16:2
"* of dust, give this riddle to Eze 17:2
"But if that man has a * who is Eze 18:10
has, in turn, a * who sees all his Eze 18:14
'Doesn't the * pay for his Eze 18:19
For if the * does what is right Eze 18:19
one who dies. The * shall not be Eze 18:20
"* of dust, say to the elders of Eze 20:3
Judge them, * of dust; Eze 20:4
"* of dust, tell them that the Eze 20:27,28
"* of dust, look toward Eze 20:46
"* of dust, face toward Eze 21:2
* of dust, in your bitter anguish; Eze 21:6
"* of dust, tell them this: A Eze 21:9,10,11
the executioner. * of dust, with Eze 21:12
"* of dust, make a map and on it Eze 21:19,20
"* of dust, prophesy to the Eze 21:28
"* of dust, indict Jerusalem as Eze 22:2
"* of dust, the people of Israel Eze 22:18,19,20
"* of dust, say to the people of Eze 22:24
"* of dust, there were two Eze 23:2,3
"* of dust, you must accuse Eze 23:36
"* of dust," he said, "write Eze 24:2
"* of dust, I am going to take Eze 24:16
"* of dust, on the day I finish Eze 24:25
"* of dust, look toward the land Eze 25:2
"* of dust, Tyre has rejoiced Eze 26:2
"* of dust, sing this sad dirge Eze 27:2
"* of dust, say to the prince of Eze 28:2,3
"* of dust, weep for the king of Eze 28:12
"* of dust, look toward the city Eze 28:21
"* of dust, face toward Egypt Eze 29:2
"* of dust, the army of King Eze 29:18
"* of dust, prophesy and say: Eze 30:2,3
"* of dust, I have broken the Eze 30:21
"* of dust, tell Pharaoh, king Eze 31:2,3
"* of dust, mourn for Pharaoh, Eze 32:2
"* of dust, weep for the people Eze 32:18
"* of dust, tell your people: Eze 33:2
"So with you, * of dust. Eze 33:7
"* of dust, the scattered Eze 33:24
"* of dust, your people are Eze 33:30
"* of dust, prophesy against the Eze 34:2
"* of dust, face toward Mount Eze 35:2
"* OF DUST, prophesy to Israel's Eze 36:1
"* of dust, when the people of Eze 36:17
"* of dust, can these bones Eze 37:3
"* of dust, face northward Eze 38:2,3
"* OF DUST, prophesy this also Eze 39:1
"And now, * of dust, call all Eze 39:17
He said to me: "* of dust, watch Eze 40:4
"* of dust, this is the place of Eze 43:7
"* of dust, describe the Temple Eze 43:10
"* of dust, the Lord God says: Eze 43:18
"* of dust, notice carefully; Eze 44:5
Literally, "looks like a * of the Dan 3:25f
to the ground. "* of man," he Dan 8:17
King Darius, the * of Ahasuerus. Dan 9:1
the Lord to Hosea, * of Beeri, Hos 1:1
of Israel, Jeroboam, * of Joash. Hos 1:1
she conceived and bore him a *. Hos 1:3
and this time gave birth to a *. Hos 1:8
a * and brought him out of Egypt. Hos 11:1
the Lord to Joel, * of Pethuel: Joe 1:1
while Jeroboam (* of Joash) was Amo 1:2
as if your only * had died; Amo 8:10
to Jonah, the * of Amittai: Jon 1:1
curse of Balaam, * of Beor, but I Mic 6:5
For the * despises his father; Mic 7:6
To: Zephaniah (* of Cushi, Zep 1:1
Josiah (* of Amon) king of Judah. Zep 1:1
it to Zerubbabel (* of Hag 1:1
and to Joshua (* of Josedech), Hag 1:1
Then Zerubbabel (* of Hag 1:12
Judah, and Joshua (* of Josedech), Hag 1:12
to Zechariah (* of Berechiah, and Zec 1:1
came to Zechariah (* of Berechiah Zec 1:7
home of Josiah (* of Zephaniah), Zec 6:10,11
(* of Josedech) the High Priest. Zec 6:10,11
him as for an only *, and grieve Zec 12:10
"A * honors his father, a Mal 1:6
spares an obedient and dutiful *. Mal 3:17
"Joseph, * of David," the angel Mt 1:20
And she will have a *, and you Mt 1:21
She shall give birth to a *, and Mt 1:23
a virgin until her * was born; Mt 1:25
"I have called my * from Egypt." Mt 2:15
new king was Herod's *, Archelaus. Mt 2:22
is my beloved *, and I am Mt 3:17
"It will prove you are the * of Mt 4:3
"and prove you are the * of God; Mt 4:6
Literally, "the * of Man." Mt 8:20f
do you want with us, O * of God? Mt 8:29
to the sick boy, "Cheer up, *! Mt 9:2
Literally, "the * of Man." Mt 9:5,6f
shouting, "O * of King David, have Mt 9:27
James (Zebedee's *), Mt 10:2,3,4
James (Alphaeus' *), Mt 10:2,3,4
Literally, "the * of Man." Mt 10:23f
or if you love your * or daughter Mt 10:37
Literally, "the * of Man." Mt 11:19f
Only the Father knows the *, and Mt 11:27
known only by the * and by those to Mt 11:27
those to whom the * reveals him. Mt 11:27
Literally, "the * of Man." Mt 12:8f
Literally, "the * of David." Mt 12:23f
Literally, "the * of Man." Mt 12:31,32f
Literally, "the * of Man." Mt 12:39,40f
Literally, "the * of Man." Mt 13:37f
Literally, "the * of Man." Mt 13:41f
"He's just a carpenter's *, and Mt 13:55
"You really are the * of God!" Mt 14:33
on me, O Lord, King David's *! Mt 15:22
Literally, "the * of Man." Mt 16:13f
the * of the living God." Mt 16:16
"God has blessed you, Simon, * Mt 16:17
For I, the * of Mankind, shall Mt 16:27
is my beloved *, and I am Mt 17:5
Literally, "the * of Man." Mt 17:12f
have mercy on my *, for he is Mt 17:15
Literally, "the * of Man." Mt 18:11f
Literally, "the * of Man." Mt 19:28f
Literally, "the * of Man." Mt 20:18f
Literally, "the * of Man." Mt 20:28f
David's *, have mercy on us!" Mt 20:30
"God bless King David's *!" Mt 21:9
"God bless the * of David," they Mt 21:15
the older boy, '*, go out and work Mt 21:28
Finally the owner sent his *, Mt 21:37
farmers saw the * coming they said Mt 21:38
a great wedding dinner for his *. Mt 22:1
Whose * is he?" Mt 22:42
"The * of David," they Mt 22:42
how can he be merely his *?" Mt 22:45
the * of hell you are yourselves. Mt 23:15
Abel to Zechariah (* of Barachiah), Mt 23:35
Literally, "the * of Man." Mt 24:27f
"of the coming of the * of Man." Mt 24:30f
No, nor even God's *. Mt 24:36
Literally, "neither the *." Mt 24:36f
Literally, "the * of Man." Mt 25:31f
Literally, "the * of Man." Mt 26:2f
Literally, "the * of Man goes." Mt 26:24f
Literally, "the * of Man." Mt 26:45f
to be the Messiah, the * of God." Mt 26:63
Literally, "the * of Man." Mt 26:64f
cross if you are the * of God!" Mt 27:40
Didn't he say, 'I am God's *'?" Mt 27:41,42,43
"Surely this was God's *." Mt 27:54
Father and of the * and of the Holy Mt 28:19
Jesus the Messiah, the * of God. Mk 1:1
announced that he would send his * Mk 1:2
said, "You are my beloved *; Mk 1:11
I know who you are—the holy * of Mk 1:24
"*, your sins are forgiven!" Mk 2:5
Literally, "* of Man." Mk 2:9,10,11f
he saw Levi, the * of Alphaeus, Mk 2:14
Literally, "the * of Man." Mk 2:28f
"You are the * of God!" Mk 3:11
James (the * of Alphaeus), Mk 3:16-1
me, Jesus, * of the Most High God? Mk 5:7,
Literally, "the * of Man." Mk 8:31
Literally, "the * of Man." Mk 8:38
said, "This is my beloved *. Mk 9:
Literally, "the * of Man." Mk 9:9
Literally, "the * of Man." Mk 9:12,13
I brought my * for you to heal—he Mk 9:1
Literally, "the * of Man." Mk 9:30,31
Literally, "the * of Man." Mk 10:33
Literally, "the * of Man." Mk 10:45
Bartimaeus (the * of Timaeus) was Mk 10:46
* of David, have mercy on me!" Mk 10:47
* of David, have mercy on me!" Mk 10:48
was only one left—his only *. Mk 12:6
his Lord, how can he be his *?" Mk 12:37
Literally, "the * of Man." Mk 13:26
Literally, "the *." Mk 13:32
Literally, "the * of Man." Mk 14:21,
Literally, "the * of Man." Mk 14:21
Literally, "the * of Man." Mk 14:41
"Are you the Messiah, the * of Mk 14:61
Literally, "the * of Man." Mk 14:62f
"Truly, this was the * of God!" Mk 15:39
wife Elizabeth will bear you a *! Lk 1:13
and shall be called the * of God. Lk 1:32
will be utterly holy—the * of God. Lk 1:35
"And you, my little *, shall be Lk 1:76
birth to her first child, a *. Lk 2:7
didn't know what to think. "*!" Lk 2:48
God to John (the * of Zacharias), Lk 3:1
much loved *, yes, my delight." Lk 3:22
Jesus was known as the * of Lk 3:23-38
Satan said, "If you are God's *, Lk 4:3
you are the * of God, jump off! Lk 4:9,10,11
"Isn't this Joseph's *?" Lk 4:22
I know who you are—the Holy * of Lk 4:34
"You are the * of God." Lk 4:41
Literally, "the * of Man." Lk 5:23,24f
Literally, "the * of Man." Lk 6:5f
James (the * of Alphaeus), Lk 6:14,15,16
Judas (* of James), Lk 6:14,15,16
Literally, "on account of the * Lk 6:22f
died was the only * of his widowed Lk 7:12
me, Jesus, * of God Most High? Lk 8:28
Literally, "the * of Man." Lk 9:22f
Literally, "the * of Man." Lk 9:26f
"This is my *, my Chosen One; Lk 9:35
here is my only *, and a demon Lk 9:38
Literally, "the * of Man." Lk 9:44f
For the * of Man has not come to Lk 9:55f
Literally, "the * of Man." Lk 9:58f
and no one really knows the * Lk 10:22
Father except the * and those to Lk 10:22
the * chooses to reveal him." Lk 10:22
Literally, "the * of Man." Lk 12:8f
Literally, "the * of Man." Lk 12:10f
Literally, "the * of Man." Lk 12:40f
way about me; his *, the other; Lk 12:53
"A few days later this younger * Lk 15:13
worthy of being called your *. Lk 15:19
"His * said to him, 'Father, I Lk 15:21
worthy of being called your *—' Lk 15:21
a feast, for this * of mine was Lk 15:24
"Meanwhile, the older * was in Lk 15:25
Yet when this * of yours comes Lk 15:30
" 'Look, dear *,' his father Lk 15:31
"But Abraham said to him, '*, Lk 16:25
Or, "long for the * of Man." Lk 17:22f
Literally, "the * of Man." Lk 18:8f
* of David, have mercy on me!" Lk 18:38
"* of David, have mercy on me!" Lk 18:39
Literally, "the * of Man." Lk 19:9,10f
I'll send my cherished *. Lk 20:13
"But when the tenants saw his *, Lk 20:14
be both David's * and David's God Lk 20:44
Literally, "the * of Man." Lk 21:27f
Literally, "the * of Man." Lk 22:22f
Literally, "the * of Man." Lk 22:69f
you claim you are the * of God?" Lk 22:70
Literally, "the * of Man." Lk 24:6,7f
—the glory of the only * of the Jn 1:14
Or, "his unique *." Jn 1:14f
course, his only * has, for he is Jn 1:18
testify that he is the * of God." Jn 1:34
are Simon, John's *—but you shall Jn 1:42
His name is Jesus, the * of Jn 1:45
honest man—a true * of Israel." Jn 1:47
the * of God—the King of Israel!" Jn 1:49
Literally, "the * of Man." Jn 1:51f
Literally, "the * of Man." Jn 3:13f
Or, "the unique * of God." Jn 3:16f
* so that anyone who believes in Jn 3:16
God did not send his * into the Jn 3:17
Or, "the unique * of God." Jn 3:18f
* of God. Their sentence is Jn 3:18
because he is his *, and God has Jn 3:35
And all who trust him—God's *—to Jn 3:36
ground Jacob gave to his * Joseph. Jn 4:5,6
official, whose * was very sick, Jn 4:46,47
*, who was now at death's door. Jn 4:46,47

N Con't)
ack home. Your * is healed!" Jn 4:50
I was well—his * had recovered. Jn 4:51
ld him, "Your * is healed." Jn 4:53
esus replied, "The * can do Jn 5:19
or the Father loves the *, and Jn 5:20
nd the * will do far more Jn 5:20
f sin to his *, so that everyone Jn 5:22
, just as they honor the Father. Jn 5:23
honor God's *, whom he sent to Jn 5:23
oice of the * of God—and those who Jn 5:25
as granted his * to have life in Jn 5:26
ecause he is the * of Man. Jn 5:27
e voice of God's *, and shall Jn 5:28
iterally, "the * of Man." Jn 6:27f
ho sees his * and believes on him Jn 6:40
Why, he is merely Jesus the * Jn 6:42
iterally, "* of Man." Jn 6:53f
iterally, "the * of Man." Jn 6:62f
now you are the holy * of God." Jn 6:69
e was speaking of Judas, * of Jn 6:71
he Messiah, the * of God, you will Jn 8:24
ou have lifted up the * of Man." Jn 8:28f
he * has every right there is! Jn 8:35
o if the * sets you free, you Jn 8:36
nd asked them, "Is this your *? Jn 9:19
now this is our * and that he was Jn 9:20
iterally, "the * of Man." Jn 9:35f
ather says, 'I am the * of God'? Jn 10:34,35,36
, the * of God, will receive Jn 11:4
he Messiah, the * of God, the one Jn 11:27
scariot, Simon's *, that this was Jn 13:1
to Judas, * of Simon Iscariot. Jn 13:26
f what I, the *, will do for you. Jn 14:12,13
Reveal the glory of your * so Jn 17:1
except the * of hell, as the Jn 17:12
e called himself the * of God." Jn 19:7
e said to her, "He is your *." Jn 19:26
the Messiah, the * of God, and that Jn 20:30,31
Peter, "Simon, * of John, do you Jn 21:15
question: "Simon, * of John, do Jn 21:16
him, "Simon, * of John, are you Jn 21:17
James (* of Alphaeus), Act 1:14
Judas (* of James), Act 1:14
let the body of your Holy * decay. Act 2:27
against the anointed * of God!' Act 4:25,26
anointed *, your holy servant. Act 4:27
And so Isaac, Abraham's *, was Act 7:8
him as her own *, and taught him Act 7:21
Literally, "the * of Man." Act 7:56f
Jesus Christ is the * of God." Act 8:37
he is indeed the * of God! Act 9:20
and said, "You * of the devil, Act 13:10
gave them Saul (* of Kish), a man Act 13:21
God said, 'David (* of Jesse) is a Act 13:22
I have honored you as my *.' Act 13:32,33
of Beroea, the * of Pyrrhus; Act 20:4
It is the Good News about his *, Rom 1:3
to be the mighty * of God, with the Rom 1:4
others the Good News about his *. Rom 1:9
would give him a * who would have Rom 4:18
the death of his *, what blessings Rom 5:10
He sent his own * in a human body Rom 8:3
to his * Jesus is now ours too. Rom 8:17
become like his *, so that his Son Rom 8:29
Son, so that his * would be the Rom 8:29
spare even his own * for us but Rom 8:32
only to Abraham's * Isaac and Rom 9:7
I will give you and Sarah a *." Rom 9:9
And years later, when this *, Rom 9:10-13
with his *, even Christ our Lord. 1Co 1:9
then he, the * of God, will put 1Co 15:28
about Jesus Christ the * of God. 2Co 1:19
Thank God for his *—his Gift too 2Co 9:15
to reveal his * within me so that Gal 1:16
my trusting in the * of God, who Gal 2:20
for his little *, that child is not Gal 4:1
on, he sent his *, born of a woman, Gal 4:4
the Spirit of his * into our Gal 4:6
by Ishmael the slave-wife's *. Gal 4:29
slave-wife and her *, for the Gal 4:30
the slave-wife's * could not Gal 4:30
along with the free woman's *. Gal 4:30
we belong to his dearly loved *. Eph 1:6
of his *, by whom we are saved; Eph 1:7
our Savior, God's *, and all become Eph 4:13
He has been just like a * to me Php 2:22
of his dear *, who bought our Col 1:13
all of himself to be in his *. Col 1:19
It was through what his * did Col 1:20
return of God's * from 1Th 1:10
rebellion will come—the * of hell. 2Th 2:3
Timothy, you are like a * to me in 1Ti 1:2
Now, Timothy, my *, here is my 1Ti 1:18
To: Timothy, my dear *. 2Ti 1:2
OH, TIMOTHY, MY *, be strong with 2Ti 2:1
To: Titus, who is truly my * in Tit 1:4
to us through his * to whom he has Heb 1:2
God's * shines out with God's Heb 1:3
* is and does marks him as God. Heb 1:3
that his name "* of God," which Heb 1:4
"You are my *, and today I have Heb 1:5,6
am his Father and he is my *." Heb 1:5,6
his firstborn * came to earth—God Heb 1:5,6
but of his * he says, "Your Heb 1:8
as he does to his *, "Sit here Heb 1:13
And who is this * of Man you Heb 2:6
But Christ, God's faithful *, is Heb 3:6
But Jesus the * of God is our Heb 4:14
God said to him, "My *, today I Heb 5:5
And even though Jesus was God's * Heb 5:8
have nailed the * of God to the Heb 6:6
and give him a * and make him the Heb 6:14
*, Isaac, just as he had promised. Heb 6:15
of the * of God—a priest forever. Heb 7:3
oath his * who is perfect forever. Heb 7:28
underfoot the * of God and treated Heb 10:29
he offered up his * Isaac, and was Heb 11:17
He said, "My *, don't be angry Heb 12:5
Whoever heard of a * who was Heb 12:7
really God's * at all—that you Heb 12:8
as the oldest * for a single meal. Heb 12:16
his * Isaac to die on the altar? Jas 2:21
you, and so does my * Mark." 1Pe 5:13f
so does my * Mark. 1Pe 5:13
saying, "This is my much-loved *; 2Pe 1:17,18
like Balaam, the * of Beor, who 2Pe 2:15
and with Jesus Christ his *. 1Jn 1:3
his * cleanses us from every sin. 1Jn 1:7
in God the Father and in his *. 1Jn 2:22
in Christ, God's *, can't have God 1Jn 2:23
But he who has Christ, God's *, 1Jn 2:23
both God the Father and his *. 1Jn 2:24
But the * of God came to destroy 1Jn 3:8
on the name of his * Jesus Christ, 1Jn 3:23
Christ, God's *, actually became 1Jn 4:2
sending his only * into this wicked 1Jn 4:9
when he sent his * to satisfy God's 1Jn 4:10
God sent his * to be their Savior. 1Jn 4:14
that Jesus is the * of God has God 1Jn 4:15
he is God's * and your Savior—then 1Jn 5:1
that Jesus is truly the * of God? 1Jn 5:5
that Jesus Christ is the * of God. 1Jn 5:6,7,8
God declares that Jesus is his *. 1Jn 5:9
what God has said about his *. 1Jn 5:10
and that this life is in his *. 1Jn 5:11
So whoever has God's * has life; 1Jn 5:12
whoever does not have his *, does 1Jn 5:12
who believe in the * of God so that 1Jn 5:13
for Christ, God's *, holds him 1Jn 5:18
And we know that Christ, God's * 1Jn 5:20
his *, who is the only true God; 1Jn 5:20
Jesus Christ his * will bless us 2Jn 1:3
have both the Father and the *. 2Jn 1:9
who called himself the * of Man, Rev 1:13
Literally, "like unto a * of Rev 1:13f
"This is a message from the * of Rev 2:18
who was called "The * of Man," Rev 14:14
Literally, "one like a * of Rev 14:14f
be his God and he will be my *. Rev 21:7

SON-IN-LAW
I that I should be the king's *?" 1Sa 18:18
"You can be my * after all, for I 1Sa 18:21
proposition and become his *. 1Sa 18:22
is as faithful as David your *? 1Sa 22:14
High Priest) was a * of Sanballat Neh 13:28

SON'S
a girl from there to be my * wife. Gen 24:7
And now will you steal my * Gen 30:15
"Yes," he sobbed, "it is my * Gen 37:33
of her young * penis, and threw it Ex 4:25,26
your daughter-in-law—your * wife; Lev 18:15
Your * hair must never be cut, Ju 13:5
your * head shall be disturbed!" 2Sa 14:11
my life and my * life have been 2Sa 14:15,16
his * name—if you know it? Pro 30:4
sins, nor the father for his *. Eze 18:20

SONG
of Israel sang this * to the Lord: Ex 15:1
The Lord is my strength, my *, Ex 15:2
And Miriam sang this *: Ex 15:21
described in this * that the people Num 21:17,18
the words of this *, and teach it Deu 31:19
them, then this * will remind them Deu 31:21
(For this * will live from Deu 31:21
* and taught it to the Israelites. Deu 31:22
So Moses recited this entire * to Deu 31:30
the words of this * to the people, Deu 32:44,45
DEBORAH AND Barak sang this * Ju 5:1
However, this was their *: "Saul 1Sa 18:7
DAVID SANG THIS * to the Lord 2Sa 22:1
The * leader was Chenaniah, the 1Ch 15:22
and Chenaniah the * leader were all 1Ch 15:27
their thanksgiving * "His 2Ch 7:6
and singing the * "His 2Ch 20:21
God, singing this *: "He is good, Ez 3:11
the subject of their ribald * Job 30:9
This * of David was written at a Ps 18:1
altar, singing a * of thanksgiving Ps 26:7
He has given me a new * to sing, Ps 40:3
I will tell in * accompanied by Ps 49:4
Let us greet the dawn with *! Ps 57:8
Raise your voice in * to him who Ps 68:4
town and the * of the drunkards. Ps 69:12
A * to sing on the Lord's Day Ps 92:1
SING A NEW * to the Lord! Ps 96:1
SING A NEW * to the Lord telling Ps 98:1
We will meet the dawn with *. Ps 108:2
He is my strength and * in the Ps 118:14
I will sing you a new *, O God, Ps 144:9
Sing him a new *. Ps 149:1
THE * OF SOLOMON Sol 1:14
THIS * OF songs, more wonderful Sol 1:1
NOW I WILL sing a * about his Is 5:1
for the Lord is my strength and *; Is 12:2
joyous *: "Your power is broken; Is 14:8
more are the joys of wine and *; Is 24:9
land of Judah will sing this *: Is 26:1
let this anthem be their *: Is 27:2
of God will sing a * of solemn joy, Is 30:29
will rejoice with music and *. Is 30:32
Sing a new * to the Lord; Is 42:10
break forth into *, O mountains Is 44:23
Break forth with *, O mountains, Is 49:13
break into joyous *, for the Lord Is 52:9
Break out into loud and joyful *, Is 54:1
and the joyous * of those bringing Jer 33:10,11
"And this is the * of their Eze 27:32
Wine, women, and * have robbed my Hos 4:11
SADLY I SING this * of grief for Amo 5:1
exulting over you in happy *: Zep 3:17,18
Wine, women, and * for you!" Lk 12:19
him a new * with these words: Rev 5:9
a wonderful new * in front of the Rev 14:3
and no one could sing this * Rev 14:3
were singing the * of Moses, the Rev 15:3,4
of God, and the * of the Lamb: Rev 15:3,4

SONGLEADERS
King David appointed * and choirs 1Ch 6:31

SONGS
3,000 proverbs and wrote 1,005 *. 1Ki 4:32
God of Israel with * of praise that 2Ch 20:19
began to play the * of the Lord, 2Ch 29:27
To this day they still sing sad * 2Ch 35:24,25
death, for these * of sorrow were 2Ch 35:24,25
the Lord God with * of joy. Neh 9:4
my Maker who gives * in the night, Job 35:9,10
We will write * to celebrate your Ps 21:13
I burst out in * of praise to him. Ps 28:7
You surround me with * of Ps 32:7
Compose new * of praise to him, Ps 33:3
night I sing his * and pray to God Ps 42:8
nights were filled with joyous *. Ps 77:6
enough to sing their wedding *. Ps 78:63
sing out their * of joy before the Ps 98:8,9
me the victory. * of joy at the Ps 118:15,16
sing for them the happy * of Zion! Ps 137:3,4
THIS SONG OF *, more wonderful Sol 1:1
she will sing sweet * as a harlot Is 23:15,16
solemn joy, like * in the night Is 30:29
singing the * of everlasting joy. Is 35:10
on I will sing my * of praise in Is 38:20
there, thanksgiving and lovely *. Is 51:3
land—the happy *, the marriage Jer 16:9
* of bridegrooms and of brides. Jer 16:9
They shall come home and sing * Jer 31:12
day long they sing their ribald *. Lam 3:14
I will stop the music of your *. Eze 26:13
who sings lovely * with a beautiful Eze 33:32
You sing idle * to the sound of Amo 6:5
mourning, and your * of joy will be Amo 8:10
and singing sacred *, making music Eph 5:19
and spiritual *, singing to the Col 3:16

SONS
years, producing * and daughters, Gen 5:3,4,5
years, producing * and daughters, Gen 5:6,7,8
years, producing * and daughters, Gen 5:9,10,11
years, producing * and daughters, Gen 5:12,13,14
years, producing * and daughters, Gen 5:15,16,17
years, producing * and daughters, Gen 5:18,19,20
God, and produced * and daughters; Gen 5:21-24
years, producing * and daughters, Gen 5:25,26,27
years, producing * and daughters, Gen 5:28-31
three *, Shem, Ham, and Japheth. Gen 5:32
Literally, "* of God" used here Gen 6:1f
the expression "* of God" refers Gen 6:1f
And he had three *—Shem, Ham, and Gen 6:9,10
wife and your * and their wives. Gen 6:18
with his wife and * and their Gen 7:7
his wife and his *, Shem, Ham, and Gen 7:13
Noah, his wife, and his * and Gen 8:18,19
GOD BLESSED NOAH and his * and Gen 9:1
Then God told Noah and his *, Gen 9:8
The names of Noah's three * were Gen 9:18
From these three * of Noah came Gen 9:19
who were the three * of Noah; Gen 10:1
sons of Noah; for * were born to Gen 10:1
The * of Japheth were Gen 10:2
The * of Gomer:Ashkenaz, Riphath, Gen 10:3
The * of Javan:Elishah, Gen 10:4
The * of Ham were:Cush, Gen 10:6
The * of Cush were:Seba, Havilah, Gen 10:7
The * of Raamah were:Sheba, Dedan. Gen 10:7

(SONS Con't)

Aram's *	Gen 10:23
Two * were born to Eber:	Gen 10:25
and had many * and daughters.	Gen 11:10,11
and had many * and daughters.	Gen 11:12,13
and had many * and daughters.	Gen 11:14,15
and had many * and daughters.	Gen 11:16,17
and had many * and daughters.	Gen 11:18,19
that, with many * and daughters.	Gen 11:20,21
with many * and daughters.	Gen 11:22,23
and had * and daughters.	Gen 11:24,25
three *, Abram, Nahor, and Haran.	Gen 11:26
*, daughters, or anyone else.	Gen 19:12
Nahor, had borne him eight *.	Gen 22:20-23
Jokshan's two * were Sheba and	Gen 25:3
Dedan's * were Asshurim,	Gen 25:3
Midian's * were Ephah, Epher,	Gen 25:4
however, he gave gifts to the *	Gen 25:6
of 175, and his * Isaac and	Gen 25:9,10
These twelve * of his became the	Gen 25:16
And he told her, "The * in your	Gen 25:23
since I have given him three *!"	Gen 29:34
me, for I have given him six *."	Gen 30:20
He gave them to Jacob's * to take	Gen 30:35,36
BUT JACOB LEARNED that Laban's *	Gen 31:1
set his wives and * on camels, and	Gen 31:17-20
happened, but his * were out in the	Gen 34:5
just as Jacob's * came in from the	Gen 34:6,7
marry our *, and we will give our	Gen 34:9,10
Then all of Jacob's * went over	Gen 34:27
Here are the names of the twelve *	Gen 35:22
The * of Leah:	Gen 35:23
The * of Rachel:Joseph, Benjamin.	Gen 35:24
The * of Bilhah, Rachel's	Gen 35:25
The * of Zilpah, Leah's	Gen 35:26
And his * Esau and Jacob buried	Gen 35:28,29
Esau and Oholibamah had * named	Gen 36:5
All these * were born to Esau in	Gen 36:5
named after the * of Esau and his	Gen 36:18,19
half-brothers, the * of his	Gen 37:2
had three *, Er, Onan, and Shelah.	Gen 38:3,4,5
so that her * from you will be	Gen 38:8
arrived and she had twin *.	Gen 38:27
famine years, two * were born to	Gen 41:50
he said to his *, "Why are you	Gen 42:1
So it was that Israel's *	Gen 42:5
We are twelve brothers, * of one	Gen 42:32
"Kill my two * if I don't bring	Gen 42:37
my wife had two *, and that one of	Gen 44:27
and his * brought him to Egypt,	Gen 46:5
all his children, * and daughters,	Gen 46:7
Here are the names of his * and	Gen 46:8-14
Reuben's *: Hanoch, Pallu, Hezron,	Gen 46:8-14
Simeon and his *: Jemuel, Jamin,	Gen 46:8-14
Levi and his *: Gershon, Kohath,	Gen 46:8-14
Judah and his *: Er, Onan, Shelah,	Gen 46:8-14
The * of Perez were Hezron and	Gen 46:8-14
Issachar and his *: Tola, Puvah,	Gen 46:8-14
Zebulun and his *: Sered, Elon,	Gen 46:8-14
Gad and his *: Ziphion, Haggi,	Gen 46:16,17
Asher and his *: Imnah, Ishvah,	Gen 46:16,17
Beriah's * were Heber and	Gen 46:16,17
These sixteen persons were the *	Gen 46:18
these fourteen * and descendants of	Gen 46:19-22
Joseph's *, born in the land of	Gen 46:19-22
Benjamin's *: Bela, Becher,	Gen 46:19-22
were these seven * and	Gen 46:23,24,25
Naphtali and his *: Jahzeel, Guni,	Gen 46:23,24,25
wives of Jacob's *, was sixty-six.	Gen 46:26
With Joseph's two * included,	Gen 46:27
So, taking with him his two *,	Gen 48:1
And now, as to these two * of	Gen 48:5
"these are my * whom God has given	Gen 48:9
together all his * and said,	Gen 49:1
Listen to me, O * of Jacob;	Gen 49:2
Your father's * shall bow before	Gen 49:8
father blessed his twelve * with.	Gen 49:28
purchased from the * of Heth."	Gen 49:32
prophecies to his *, he lay back in	Gen 49:33
So his * did as Israel	Gen 50:12,13
THIS IS THE list of the * of Jacob	Ex 1:1
You will clothe your * and	Ex 3:22
So Moses took his wife and * and	Ex 4:20
The * of Reuben, Israel's oldest	Ex 6:14
The * of Gershon were:Libni,	Ex 6:17
The * of Kohath:Amram,	Ex 6:18
The * of Merari:Mahli, Mushi.	Ex 6:19
and Aaron and Moses were their *.	Ex 6:20
The * of Izhar:Korah, Nepheg,	Ex 6:21
The * of Uzziel:Misha-el,	Ex 6:22
The * of Korah:Assir, Elkanah,	Ex 6:24
"We will go with our * and	Ex 10:9
And all the oldest * shall die	Ex 11:5
all the oldest * and firstborn male	Ex 12:12
all the firstborn * in the land of	Ex 12:29
The * of Jacob and their	Ex 12:40,41
to me all of the firstborn *	Ex 13:1
all firstborn * and firstborn male	Ex 13:12
must buy back your firstborn *.	Ex 13:13
eldest * are always bought back.'	Ex 13:15
had made the * of Israel vow before	Ex 13:19
with Moses' two *, Gershom (meaning	Ex 18:3
your wife and your two *."	Ex 18:5,6
and they have * or daughters, the	Ex 21:4
Aaron and his * shall place this	Ex 27:21
brother, and his * Nadab, Abihu,	Ex 28:1
special garments for Aaron's *.	Ex 28:4
"Then, for Aaron's *, make	Ex 28:40
Clothe Aaron and his * with	Ex 28:41
Aaron and his * go into the	Ex 28:43
ordinance for Aaron and his *.	Ex 28:43
of Aaron and his * as priests: get	Ex 29:1
"Bathe Aaron and his * there at	Ex 29:3,4
Next, dress his * in their	Ex 29:8
shall consecrate Aaron and his *.	Ex 29:9
and Aaron and his * shall lay their	Ex 29:10
"Next, Aaron and his * shall lay	Ex 29:15,16
and Aaron and his * shall lay their	Ex 29:19,20
of Aaron and his *, and upon their	Ex 29:19,20
and his * and upon their clothes;	Ex 29:21
of Aaron and his *— and one loaf	Ex 29:22
of Aaron and his *, to wave them in	Ex 29:24
ram to Aaron and his *.	Ex 29:28
Aaron and his * shall eat the	Ex 29:32
Aaron and his * to their offices.	Ex 29:35
and Aaron and his * who are my	Ex 29:44
Aaron and his * shall wash their	Ex 30:19
* from generation to generation."	Ex 30:21
Use it to anoint Aaron and his *	Ex 30:30
garments for his *, so that they	Ex 31:10
killing your own * and brothers;	Ex 32:29
be punished in the * and grandsons,	Ex 34:7
as wives for your *—and then your	Ex 34:16
sons—and then your * would commit	Ex 34:16
But your * must all be redeemed.	Ex 34:20
Aaron the priest, and for his *."	Ex 35:10-19
* from fine-twined linen thread.	Ex 39:27
his *, to be worn when on duty.	Ex 39:41
"Now bring Aaron and his * to	Ex 40:12
Then bring his * and put their	Ex 40:14
Moses and Aaron and Aaron's *	Ex 40:31
Lord, and Aaron's *, the priests,	Lev 1:5
altar, and Aaron's *, the priests,	Lev 1:11
to Aaron and his * as their food;	Lev 2:3
Then Aaron's * shall throw the	Lev 3:2
Aaron and his * these regulations	Lev 6:9
"Aaron's * shall stand in front	Lev 6:14
to Aaron and his * for their food;	Lev 6:16
day Aaron and his * are anointed	Lev 6:19,20
As the * of the priests replace	Lev 6:22,23
Aaron and his * that these are the	Lev 6:25
common property of all * of Aaron.	Lev 7:10
to Aaron and his *, while the	Lev 7:31
of Israel to the * of Aaron.	Lev 7:34
Aaron and his * must always be	Lev 7:34
as priests—to Aaron and to his *.	Lev 7:35
Aaron and his * to the entrance of	Lev 8:1
Then he took Aaron and his * and	Lev 8:6
robes on Aaron's *, with the belts	Lev 8:13
and Aaron and his * laid their	Lev 8:14
Aaron and his * laid their hands	Lev 8:18
Aaron and his * laid their hands	Lev 8:22
blood upon Aaron's *—upon the lobes	Lev 8:24
of Aaron and his * to present to	Lev 8:27
and upon his * and upon their	Lev 8:30
Aaron and his * and their clothes.	Lev 8:30
to Aaron and his *, "Boil the meat	Lev 8:31
Aaron and his * to stay at the	Lev 8:35
So Aaron and his * did all that	Lev 8:36
Aaron and Aaron's * and the elders	Lev 9:1
his own sin; his * caught the	Lev 9:9
animal, and his * caught the blood	Lev 9:12
and Aaron's * brought the blood	Lev 9:18
BUT NADAB AND Abihu, the * of	Lev 10:1
cousins, the * of Uzziel, and told	Lev 10:4
to Aaron and his * Eleazar and	Lev 10:6
and this rule applies to your *	Lev 10:8,9
Aaron and to his * who were left,	Lev 10:12
It belongs to you and to your *,	Lev 10:13
It belongs to you and to your *	Lev 10:14
Ithamar, the remaining * of Aaron.	Lev 10:16
* for the spot to be examined.	Lev 13:1
AFTER AARON'S TWO * died before	Lev 16:1
* and to all the people of Israel.	Lev 21:24
Aaron and his * to be very careful	Lev 22:1
Aaron and his * and all the people	Lev 22:17,18
by Aaron and his *, in a place set	Lev 24:9
You shall eat your own * and	Lev 26:29
* were:	Num 3:2
However, only Aaron and his *	Num 3:10
oldest * of the people of Israel.	Num 3:11,12
in exchange for all the oldest *.	Num 3:13
all the oldest * of the Egyptians,	Num 3:13
of Aaron and his *, who had the	Num 3:38
of all the eldest * in Israel who	Num 3:40
for the eldest * of Israel;	Num 3:41
of the eldest * of the people of	Num 3:42
number of eldest * a month old and	Num 3:43
eldest * of the people of Israel;	Num 3:45
To redeem the 273 eldest * in	Num 3:46
for each one to Aaron and his *	Num 3:47,48
for the 273 eldest * of Israel who	Num 3:49
his * as the Lord had commanded.	Num 3
Aaron and his * will enter the	Num
When Aaron and his * have	Num 4
sacred work of the * of Kohath.	Num 4
Aaron and his * shall go in with	Num 4:17,18
Aaron or any of his * may assign	Num 4
Aaron and his * that they are to	Num 6:22
This is how Aaron and his *	Num 6
to Aaron and his *, just as any	Num 8
of all the eldest * of Israel.	Num 8
as a gift to Aaron and his *.	Num 8
as assistants to Aaron and his *;	Num 8
and Abiram (the * of Eliab) and On	Num 1
ones, you * of Levi."	Num 16:
and Abiram (the * of Eliab), but	Num 16:11,
their wives and * and little ones.	Num 16
"You and your * and your family	Num 1
but only you and your * may	Num 18:
But you and your *, the priests,	Num 1
you and your *, by permanent law.	Num 1
families, * and daughters alike.	Num 18:
the firstborn * of the people of	Num 18:14,
the firstborn *, nor the firstborn	Num 18:
Aaron and his * and their	Num 18:
His * have fled,	Num 21:27-
King Og, his *, and his subjects,	Num 21:
And destroy the * of Sheth.	Num 24:15-
clans, named after Reuben's *:	Num 26:5-
was one of the * of Pallu—were the	Num 26:5-
clans, founded by Simeon's *:	Num 26:12-
clans founded by the * of Gad:	Num 26:15-
named after the * of Judah—but not	Num 26:19-
named after the * of Issachar:	Num 26:23-
named after the * of Zebulun:	Num 26:26,
son, Zelophehad, had no *.	Num 26:28-
named after the * of Ephraim:	Num 26:28-
named after the * of Benjamin:	Num 26:38-
Sub-clans named after * of Bela	Num 26:38-
clans named after the * of Asher:	Num 26:44-
Sub-clans named after the * of	Num 26:44-
named after the * of Naphtali:	Num 26:48-
a natural death, but he had no *.	Num 27:3
dies and has no *, then his	Num 27
over the oldest * of the Israelites	Num 28:
all their eldest *, killed by the	Num 33:3
one of the * of Joseph) came to	Num 36
household—your *, daughters,	Deu 5:
to cause you, your *, and your	Deu 6
them, nor let your * and daughters	Deu 7
marry their * and daughters.	Deu 7
(the * of Eliab, descendants	Deu 11
Literally, "*."	Deu 11:
your * and daughters and servants;	Deu 12:
They have even roasted their *	Deu 12:3
good reign. His * will then follow	Deu 17:2
the sins of their * nor the sons	Deu 24:
* for the sins of their fathers;	Deu 24:
You will watch as your * and	Deu 28:3
Your * and daughters will be	Deu 28:4
flesh of your own * and daughters	Deu 28:5
the priests, the * of Levi, who	Deu 31:
His * and daughters were insulting	Deu 32:1
wedge of gold, his *, his	Jos 7:2
of the three * of Anak: Talmai,	Jos 15:1
of Manasseh) had no *.	Jos 17:
for $200 from the * of Hamor.	Jos 24:3
of the three * of Anak.	Ju 1:2
just like you—like * of kings!"	Ju 8:1
You and your * and all your	Ju 8:2
*, for he married many wives.	Ju 8:3
seventy *—or by one man—meaning me,	Ju 9:
his seventy * upon one stone.	Ju 9:1
Gideon's seventy * were given their	Ju 9:2
of murdering Gideon's seventy *.	Ju 9:56,5
His thirty * rode around	Ju 10:
had several other * by his	Ju 11:
He had thirty * and thirty	Ju 12:9,1
in thirty girls to marry his *.	Ju 12:9,1
He had forty * and thirty	Ju 12:1
one of his * as the priest.	Ju 17:4,
and became as one of Micah's *.	Ju 17:10,1
and his * as their priests.	Ju 18:3
Now then, * of Israel, express	Ju 20:
and his two *, Mahlon and Chilion.	Ru 1:
and Naomi was left with her two *.	Ru 1:
alone, without her husband or *.	Ru 1:4,
Do I have younger * who could	Ru 1:1
tonight, and bore *, would you	Ru 1:1
been kinder to you than seven *!"	Ru 4:1
two * of Eli—Hophni and Phinehas.	1Sa 1:
me better than having ten *?"	1Sa 1:
Now the * of Eli were evil men	1Sa 2:1
it brought up be given to Eli's *.	1Sa 2:13,1
And the Lord gave Hannah three *	1Sa 2:2
He knew, for instance, that his *	1Sa 2:2
you are doing," Eli told his *.	1Sa 2:23,24,2
Why have you honored your * more	1Sa 2:2
cause your two *, Hophni and	1Sa 2:3
because his * are blaspheming God,	1Sa 3:1
of Eli and of his * shall never be	1Sa 3:1
Hophni and Phinehas, the * of	1Sa 4:

ONS Con't)
his * as judges in his place. 1Sa 8:1
Joel and Abijah, his oldest *, 1Sa 8:2
same, for his * were not good men. 1Sa 8:5
conscript your * and make them run 1Sa 8:11
ahead of my own * and now I stand 1Sa 12:2
Saul had three *, Jonathan, 1Sa 14:49
both were the * of Abiel. 1Sa 14:50,51
has killed the * of many mothers, 1Sa 15:33
one of his * to be the new king." 1Sa 16:1
you which of his * to anoint." 1Sa 16:3
and his *, and invited them too. 1Sa 16:5
all seven of his * presented 1Sa 16:9
Only Abiathar, one of the * of 1Sa 22:20
and your * will be here with me." 1Sa 28:19
and killed his * Jonathan, 1Sa 31:2
bearer, his three *, and his troops 1Sa 31:6
that Saul and his * were dead, they 1Sa 31:7
and his three * on Mount Gilboa. 1Sa 31:8
of Saul and his * from the wall and 1Sa 31:12
Several * were born to David 2Sa 3:2
with these two * of Zeruiah. 2Sa 3:39
They were the * of Rimmon, who 2Sa 4:2,3
and had many * and daughters. 2Sa 5:13
It was driven by Abinadab's *, 2Sa 6:3
put one of your * upon your throne 2Sa 7:12
and David's * were his 2Sa 8:18
"You and your * and servants 2Sa 9:10,11
Ziba, who had fifteen * and twenty 2Sa 9:10,11
though he were one of his own *. 2Sa 9:10,11
of his * attend, including Amnon. 2Sa 13:27
Then the other * of the king 2Sa 13:29,30
*, and not one is left alive!" 2Sa 13:29,30
No, no! Your * aren't all dead! 2Sa 13:32,33
"There they are now! Your * are 2Sa 13:35
"and my two * had a fight out in 2Sa 14:5,6
He had three * and one daughter, 2Sa 14:27
will send their * Ahima-az and 2Sa 15:35,36
have no * to carry on my name." 2Sa 18:18
the lives of your *, your 2Sa 19:5
fifteen * and twenty servants; 2Sa 19:17
us seven of Saul's *—the sons of 2Sa 21:5,6
of Saul's sons—the * of the man who 2Sa 21:5,6
But he gave them the two * of 2Sa 21:8
the five adopted * of Michal that 2Sa 21:8
* of Ariel of Moab. 2Sa 23:20
The * of Jashen; 2Sa 23:24-39
brothers—the other * of King 1Ki 1:9
invited all your * and Abiathar the 1Ki 1:19
your * to attend the festivities. 1Ki 1:25
to which of your * you have chosen 1Ki 1:27
selected one of my * to sit upon my 1Ki 1:48
But be kind to the * of 1Ki 2:7
Elihoreph and Ahijah (* of Shisha) 1Ki 4:1
Calcol, and Darda, the * of Mahol; 1Ki 4:31
him, 'One of your * shall always be 1Ki 9:5
palace among Pharaoh's own *. 1Ki 11:20
in Bethel, and his * went home and 1Ki 13:11
Then he said to his *, "Saddle 1Ki 13:27
Afterwards he said to his *, 1Ki 13:31
all of your *—this boy who is sick 1Ki 14:10
the tribes of the * of Jacob to 1Ki 18:31f
it will happen to his *; 1Ki 21:29
take her two * as his slaves. 2Ki 4:1
"Go into your house with your * 2Ki 4:4
So she did. Her * brought the 2Ki 4:5
another jar," she said to her *. 2Ki 4:6
for you and your * to live on!" 2Ki 4:7
the murder of Naboth and his *.' 2Ki 9:26
*—all of whom were living there. 2Ki 10:1
best one of Ahab's * to be your 2Ki 10:2,3
Ahab's *, sent him this message: 2Ki 10:5
king instead of one of Ahab's *." 2Ki 10:5
of your master's * to me at Jezreel 2Ki 10:6
(These seventy * of King Ahab were 2Ki 10:6
of the king's * had arrived, he 2Ki 10:8
him, but I didn't kill his *! 2Ki 10:9,10
to visit the * of King Ahab and of 2Ki 10:13
They even burned their own * and 2Ki 17:17
god Nisroch, his * Adrammelech and 2Ki 19:37
Some of your own * will be taken 2Ki 20:18
And he sacrificed one of his * 2Ki 21:6
the Valley of the * of Hinnom, so 2Ki 23:10
Josiah's *, to reign in Jerusalem; 2Ki 23:34
He was forced to watch as his * 2Ki 25:7
The * of Japheth 1Ch 1:5-9
The * of Gomer: 1Ch 1:5-9
The * of Javan: 1Ch 1:5-9
The * of Ham: 1Ch 1:5-9
The * of Cush were: 1Ch 1:5-9
The * of Raama were Sheba and 1Ch 1:5-9
Another of the * of Cush was 1Ch 1:10
The clans named after the * of 1Ch 1:11,12
Among Canaan's * were: 1Ch 1:13-16
The * of Shem: 1Ch 1:17
Eber had two *: Peleg (which 1Ch 1:19
The * of Joktan: 1Ch 1:20-23
Abraham's * were 1Ch 1:28-31
The * of Ishmael: 1Ch 1:28-31
Abraham also had * by his 1Ch 1:32
Jokshan's * were Sheba and Dedan. 1Ch 1:32
The * of Midian: 1Ch 1:33
Abraham's son Isaac had two *, 1Ch 1:34
The * of Esau: 1Ch 1:35
The * of Eliphaz: 1Ch 1:36
The * of Reuel: 1Ch 1:37
The * of Esau 1Ch 1:38,39
Lotan's *: Hori and Homam. 1Ch 1:38,39
The * of Shobal: Alian, Manahath, 1Ch 1:40
Zibeon's * were Aiah and 1Ch 1:40
The * of Dishon: Hamran, Eshban, 1Ch 1:41
The * of Ezer: Bilhan, Zaavan, 1Ch 1:42
Dishan's * were Uz and Aran. 1Ch 1:42
THE * OF Israel were: 1Ch 2:1
Judah had three * by Bath-shua, a 1Ch 2:3
became the parents of twin *, 1Ch 2:4
So Judah had five *. 1Ch 2:4
The * of Perez were 1Ch 2:5
The * of Zerah were: 1Ch 2:6
The * of Hezron were Jerahmeel, 1Ch 2:9
Zeruiah's * were Abishai, Joab, 1Ch 2:16
These are the * of 1Ch 2:25
The * of Ram: 1Ch 2:27
Onam's * were 1Ch 2:28
Shammai's * were 1Ch 2:28
The * of Abishur and his wife 1Ch 2:29
Nadab's * were 1Ch 2:30
Shammai's brother Jada had two *, 1Ch 2:32
had two * named Peleth and Zaza. 1Ch 2:33
had no *, although he had several 1Ch 2:34,35
The * of Hebron: Korah, Tappuah, 1Ch 2:43
The * of Jahdai: 1Ch 2:47
The * of Hur (who was the oldest 1Ch 2:50
Shobal's * included 1Ch 2:52
* Shime-a, Shobab, Nathan, and 1Ch 3:5
David also had nine other *: 1Ch 3:6-8
(This list does not include the * 1Ch 3:9
The * of Josiah were: 1Ch 3:15
The * of Jehoiakim: 1Ch 3:16
These are the * who were born to 1Ch 3:17,18
Hananiah's * were Pelatiah and 1Ch 3:21,22
Shemaiah had six *, including 1Ch 3:21,22
Neariah had three *: 1Ch 3:23
Eli-o-enai had seven *: 1Ch 3:24
THESE ARE THE * of Judah: 1Ch 4:1
The * of Kenaz were 1Ch 4:13
Othni-el's * were Hathath and 1Ch 4:13
The * of Caleb (the son of 1Ch 4:15
The * of Elah included Kenaz. 1Ch 4:15
Jehallelel's * were:Ziph, Ziphah, 1Ch 4:16
Ezrah's * were:Jether, 1Ch 4:17
One of her * was the father of 1Ch 4:19
The * of Shimon: 1Ch 4:20
The * of Ishi:Zoheth, Ben-zoheth. 1Ch 4:20
The * of Shelah (the son of 1Ch 4:21-22
The * of Simeon: 1Ch 4:24
Mishma's * included Hammu-el (the 1Ch 4:26
Shime-i had sixteen * and six 1Ch 4:27
and Uzziel—all * of Ishi. 1Ch 4:42
The * of Reuben, Israel's son, 1Ch 5:3
THESE ARE THE names of the * of 1Ch 6:1
Kohath's * were: 1Ch 6:2
Aaron's * were: 1Ch 6:3
The oldest * of the successive 1Ch 6:4-15
the * of Levi were: 1Ch 6:16
The * of Gershom were:Libni, 1Ch 6:17
The * of Kohath were:Amram, 1Ch 6:18
The * of Merari were:Mahli, 1Ch 6:19,20,21
into the families of his *: 1Ch 6:25,26,27
by Samuel's *:Joel, the oldest; 1Ch 6:28
of Merari were headed by his *: 1Ch 6:29,30
THE * OF Issachar: 1Ch 7:1
The * of Tola, each of whom was 1Ch 7:2
among whose five * were Michael, 1Ch 7:3
them had several wives and many *. 1Ch 7:4
The * of Benjamin were: 1Ch 7:6
The * of Bela: 1Ch 7:7
The * of Becher were: 1Ch 7:8
The * of Bilhan were: 1Ch 7:10
The * of Ir were Shuppim and 1Ch 7:12
Hushim was one of the * of Aher. 1Ch 7:12
The * of Naphtali (descendants of 1Ch 7:13
The * of Manasseh, born to his 1Ch 7:14
and he had * named Ulam and Rakem. 1Ch 7:16
So these were the * of Gilead, 1Ch 7:17
The * of Shemida were Ahian, 1Ch 7:19
The * of Ephraim: 1Ch 7:20,21
The * of Beriah were: 1Ch 7:31
Japhlet's * were: 1Ch 7:33
* were: 1Ch 7:34
The * of his brother Hotham 1Ch 7:35
The * of Zophah were: 1Ch 7:36,37
The * of Ithran 1Ch 7:38
The * of Ulla were: 1Ch 7:39
THE * OF Benjamin, according to 1Ch 8:1
The * of Bela were: 1Ch 8:3,4,5
The * of Ehud, chiefs of the 1Ch 8:6,7
These * all became chiefs of 1Ch 8:8,9,10
The * of Elpaal were: 1Ch 8:12
His other * were 1Ch 8:13
Elpaal's * also included: 1Ch 8:14
The * of Beriah were: 1Ch 8:15,16
The * of Elpaal also included: 1Ch 8:17,18
The * of Shime-i were: 1Ch 8:19,20,21
The * of Shashak were: 1Ch 8:22-25
The * of Jeroham were: 1Ch 8:26,27
Saul's * included: 1Ch 8:33
The * of Micah: 1Ch 8:35
father of Bine-a, whose * were: 1Ch 8:37
Azel had six *: 1Ch 8:38
Azel's brother Eshek had three *: 1Ch 8:39
Ulam's * were prominent warriors 1Ch 8:40
These men had 150 * and 1Ch 8:40
(Shilon's oldest son) and his *; 1Ch 9:5
there were also the * of Zerah, 1Ch 9:6
*, including: 1Ch 9:35,36,37
Azel had six *: 1Ch 9:44
Saul and his three *, Jonathan, 1Ch 10:2
So Saul and his three * died 1Ch 10:6
that Saul and his * were dead, they 1Ch 10:7
the bodies of Saul and his *. 1Ch 10:8
and the bodies of his three *. 1Ch 10:12
The * 1Ch 11:26-47
Shama and Je-iel (* of Hotham) 1Ch 11:26-47
Jeribai and Joshaviah (* of 1Ch 11:26-47
Jezi-el and Pelet, * of Azmaveth; 1Ch 12:3-7
Jo-elah and Zebadiah (* of 1Ch 12:3-7
father of many * and daughters. 1Ch 14:3
These are the names of the * born 1Ch 14:4-7
O chosen * of Jacob, 1Ch 16:12,13
And Jeduthun's * were appointed 1Ch 16:42
one of your * upon your throne; 1Ch 17:11
David's * were his chief aides. 1Ch 18:17
killed one of the * of the giant, 1Ch 20:4
and his four * ran and hid. 1Ch 21:19,20
and I will cause his * and his 1Ch 22:10
named after the * of Levi—the 1Ch 23:6
corps were named after his * 1Ch 23:7
named after the * of Ladan: Jehiel 1Ch 23:8,9
and the * of Shime 1Ch 23:8,9
four *: Jahath was greatest, Zizah 1Ch 23:10,11
because neither had many *. 1Ch 23:10,11
four groups named after his * 1Ch 23:12
Literally, "the * of Amram: Aaron 1Ch 23:13f
Aaron and his * were set apart 1Ch 23:13
for Moses, the man of God, his * 1Ch 23:14,15
Gershom's * were led by Shebuel, 1Ch 23:16
The * of Izhar were led by 1Ch 23:18
The * of Hebron were led by 1Ch 23:19
The * of Uzziel were led by 1Ch 23:20
The * of Merari were 1Ch 23:21
Mushi. The * of Mahli were 1Ch 23:21
Eleazar died without any *, and 1Ch 23:22
to their cousins, the * of Kish. 1Ch 23:22
Mushi's * were Mahli, Eder, and 1Ch 23:23
divisions named after Aaron's *, 1Ch 24:1
Nadab and Abihu were also * of 1Ch 24:1
The Merari group was led by his * 1Ch 24:26,27
who had no *, and Kish, among 1Ch 24:28
Kish, among whose * was Jerahmeel. 1Ch 24:29
Jerahmeel. The * of Mushi were 1Ch 24:30
prophet, were his * Zaccur, Joseph, 1Ch 25:2
were his six *: Gedaliah, Zeri, 1Ch 25:3
chaplain, were his *: Bukkiah, 1Ch 25:4,5
fourteen * and three daughters. 1Ch 25:4,5
with twelve of his * and brothers; 1Ch 25:9-31
and twelve of his * and brothers; 1Ch 25:9-31
and twelve of his * and brothers; 1Ch 25:9-31
and twelve of his * and brothers; 1Ch 25:9-31
Sixth, Bukkiah and twelve of his * 1Ch 25:9-31
and twelve of his * and brothers; 1Ch 25:9-31
and twelve of his * and brothers; 1Ch 25:9-31
and twelve of his * and brothers; 1Ch 25:9-31
Tenth, Shime-i and twelve of his * 1Ch 25:9-31
and twelve of his * and brothers; 1Ch 25:9-31
and twelve of his * and brothers; 1Ch 25:9-31
and twelve of his * and brothers; 1Ch 25:9-31
and twelve of his * and brothers; 1Ch 25:9-31
and twelve of his * and brothers; 1Ch 25:9-31
and twelve of his * and brothers; 1Ch 25:9-31
and twelve of his * and brothers; 1Ch 25:9-31
and twelve of his * and brothers; 1Ch 25:9-31
and twelve of his * and brothers; 1Ch 25:9-31
and twelve of his * and brothers; 1Ch 25:9-31
and twelve of his * and brothers; 1Ch 25:9-31
and twelve of his * and brothers; 1Ch 25:9-31
and twelve of his * and brothers; 1Ch 25:9-31
and twelve of his * and brothers. 1Ch 25:9-31
His sergeants were his *: 1Ch 26:2,3
The * of Obed-edom were also 1Ch 26:4,5
God gave him with all those *! 1Ch 26:4,5
Shemaiah's * were all outstanding 1Ch 26:6,7
All of these * and grandsons of 1Ch 26:8
Meshelemiah's eighteen * and 1Ch 26:9
*, though he was not the oldest. 1Ch 26:10
The names of some of his other * 1Ch 26:11
Hosah's * and brothers numbered 1Ch 26:11
and his group (his * were given 1Ch 26:14,15
Zetham and Joel, the * of Jehieli. 1Ch 26:20,21,22
Chenaniah and his * (from the 1Ch 26:29
The attendant to the king's * was 1Ch 27:32
and from among his *, the Lord 1Ch 28:4
And from among my *—the Lord has 1Ch 28:5

(SONS Con't)
and all their * and brothers, 2Ch 5:11,12
Three * were born from this 2Ch 11:19
* and sixty daughters). 2Ch 11:21
his other * in the fortified cities 2Ch 11:23
* and sixteen daughters. 2Ch 13:21
who was one of the * of Asaph). 2Ch 20:14
His brothers—other * of 2Ch 21:2
including his * and his wives; 2Ch 21:17
of Arabs had killed his older *). 2Ch 22:1
None of his *, however, except 2Ch 22:9
as Jehoiada and his * anointed 2Ch 23:11
him, and he had * and daughters. 2Ch 24:3
If you want to read about the * 2Ch 24:27
priests alone, the * of Aaron who 2Ch 26:17,18
in war, and our * and daughters and 2Ch 29:9
He instructed the priests, the * 2Ch 29:21
of his own * killed him there. 2Ch 32:21
The singers (the * of Asaph) were 2Ch 35:15
the king and his * until the 2Ch 36:20
Henadad, and their * and relatives, Ez 3:9
and to pray for me and my *. Ez 6:10
wrath against the king and his *? Ez 7:23
eighteen of his * and brothers; Ez 8:18
with twenty of his * and brothers; Ez 8:19
taken them as wives for their *. Ez 9:2
marry their *, and not to let our Ez 9:12
and not to let our * marry their Ez 9:12
The * of Immer: Ez 10:20
The * of Harim: Ez 10:21
The * of Pashhur: Ez 10:22
The Fish Gate was built by the * Neh 3:3
their wives and * and daughters who Neh 10:28
let our * marry non-Jewish girls. Neh 10:30
to God our oldest * and the Neh 10:36
One of the * of Jehoiada (the son Neh 13:28
They also killed the ten * of Est 9:7-10
"and also Haman's ten *. Est 9:12
* be hanged upon the gallows." Est 9:13
up the bodies of Haman's ten *. Est 9:14
his * were hanged on the gallows. Est 9:24,25
He had a large family of seven * Job 1:2,3
Every year when each of Job's * Job 1:4
For Job said, "Perhaps my * have Job 1:5
Literally, "the * of God." Job 1:6f
not long afterwards when Job's * Job 1:12,13
to say, "Your * and daughters were Job 1:18
Literally, "* of God." Job 2:1f
"Your * shall become important Job 5:25
He never knows it if his * are Job 14:20,21
who have no protecting *. Job 24:21
These * of theirs have also Job 30:8
God also gave him seven more * Job 42:13,14
The Lord God asks, "* of men, Ps 4:2
Literally, "all you * of Jacob." Ps 22:23f
* and daughters, come and listen Ps 34:11
"Your * will some day be kings Ps 45:16
us who are the * of Jacob and of Ps 77:15
and "* of the Most High." Ps 82:6
Literally, "the * of the Ps 89:6f
futile life you give the * of men? Ps 89:47
Egypt and lived there with his *. Ps 105:23
men's * have a special heritage. Ps 112:2
* vigorous and tall as growing Ps 144:12-15
wicked * and share their estate. Pro 17:2
A father can give his * homes and Pro 19:14
Even if a man has a hundred * and Ecc 6:3
his god, his * Adrammelech and Is 37:38
And some of your own * will Is 39:7
I will bring my * and daughters Is 43:6
carry your little * back to you in Is 49:22
Not one of her * is left alive Is 51:18
For your * have fainted and lie Is 51:20
from having * and daughters. Is 56:5
But you—come here, you witches' * Is 57:3
Your * will rebuild the Is 58:12
For your * and daughters are Is 60:4
to bring the * of Israel home Is 60:9
The * of anti-Semites will come Is 60:14
It is the * of Israel who have Jer 3:21
and herds and * and Jer 3:24
fathers and * shall be Jer 6:21
death their little * and daughters Jer 7:31
And I will smash fathers and * Jer 13:14
Husbands, wives, * and Jer 14:16
faints, for all her * are dead. Jer 15:9
they burn their * in sacrifice—a Jer 19:5
his brothers and *—representing all Jer 35:3
for the use of the * of Hanan the Jer 35:4
or our * or daughters either. Jer 35:8
and Jonathan (* of Kareah), Seraiah Jer 40:8
of Tanhumeth), the * of Ephai (the Jer 40:8
and your * and daughters are taken Jer 48:46
watch while his * and all the Jer 52:10
despair, for my * and daughters are Lam 1:18
Fathers will eat their own *, Eze 5:10
and * will eat their fathers; Eze 5:10
And you took my * and daughters Eze 16:20
judge—fathers and * alike—and my Eze 18:4
give your little * to be burned to Eze 20:31
and they bore me * and daughters. Eze 23:4,5
they will butcher their * and Eze 23:47
And your * and daughters in Eze 24:20,21
wives and their * and their Eze 24:25
"However, the * of Zadok, of the Eze 44:15
*, it will belong to him forever. Eze 46:16
Only gifts to his * are Eze 46:17
If he gives property to his *, it Eze 46:18
that is, the * of Zadok who obeyed Eze 48:11
nations, not even ruled by his *. Dan 11:4
However, the * of this Syrian Dan 11:10,11
my *, children of the Living God.' Hos 1:10
In my vision I have seen the * of Hos 9:13
to lead their * to slaughter. Hos 9:13
* and daughters will prophesy; Joe 2:28
I will sell your * and daughters Joe 3:8
And I chose your * to be Amo 2:11
city, and your * and daughters will Amo 7:17
* will never sit upon your throne. Nah 1:14
against the * of Greece." Zec 9:13
"You * of snakes!" Mt 3:7
shall be called the * of God. Mt 5:9
true * of your Father in heaven. Mt 5:45
and John, the * of Zebedee, brought Mt 20:20
let my two * sit on two thrones Mt 20:21
A man with two * told the older Mt 21:28
of being the * of wicked men. Mt 23:31
Snakes! * of vipers! Mt 23:33
and Zebedee's two * James and John, Mt 26:37
James and John (the * of Zebedee). Mt 27:56
he saw Zebedee's *, James and John, Mk 1:19
James and John (the * of Zebedee, Mk 3:16-19
called them "* of Thunder"), Mk 3:16-19
Then James and John, the * of Mk 10:35
and John, the * of Zebedee. Lk 5:10
truly be acting as * of God: for he Lk 6:35
this story: "A man had two *. Lk 15:11
divide his wealth between his *. Lk 15:12
Literally, "* of the light." Lk 16:8f
This man was one of the lost * of Lk 19:9,10
angels, and are * of God, for they Lk 20:36
he and his * and cattle enjoyed?" Jn 4:12
Literally, "* of light." Jn 12:36f
Literally, "the * of Zebedee." Jn 21:2f
mankind, and your * and daughters Act 2:17
grain in Egypt, so he sent his * Act 7:12
where he died, and all his *. Act 7:15
the * of Hamor, Shechem's father. Act 7:16
Midian, where his two * were born. Act 7:29
"Brothers—you * of Abraham, and Act 13:26
says it, 'We are the * of God.' Act 17:28
Seven * of Sceva, a Jewish Act 19:14
by the Spirit of God are * of God. Rom 8:14
the revelation of the * of God." Rom 8:19f
be called "* of the Living God." Rom 9:26
you will be my * and daughters." 2Co 6:18
would if all his *—all the Gal 3:16
could adopt us as his very own *. Gal 4:5
And because we are his * God has Gal 4:6
no longer slaves, but God's own *. Gal 4:7
And since we are his *, Gal 4:7
Abraham had two *, one from his Gal 4:22
the riches inherited by God's *; Eph 3:6
to his two *, Jacob and Esau. Heb 11:20
of Joseph's two * as he stood and Heb 11:21
punish their *, then it means that Heb 12:8

SONS-IN-LAW
"Get them out of this place—*, Gen 19:12

SOON
So the boat was * empty. Gen 8:18,19
and was * thickly populated. Gen 11:2
and butcher it. *, taking them Gen 18:8
And our father will * be too old Gen 19:31
He was * a man of great wealth, Gen 26:13
In the morning, as * as they Gen 26:31
(As * as Isaac has blessed Jacob, Gen 27:30
"My father will * be gone, and Gen 27:41
Laban, and as * as he heard of Gen 29:12,13
She * became pregnant again Gen 29:33
* Zilpah presented him with a son. Gen 30:10
* after the birth of Joseph to Gen 30:25
expense." * Jacob noticed a Gen 31:2
Word * reached Jacob of what had Gen 34:5
* after this Rebekah's Gen 35:8
Isaac died * afterwards, at the Gen 35:28,29
Then, * afterwards, the baby Gen 38:30
favorite with him. * he was put in Gen 39:4
In fact, the jailer * handed Gen 39:22
and blossom, and * there were Gen 40:9,10
* he fell asleep again and had a Gen 41:5
it, and it is going to happen *. Gen 41:32
The news * reached Gen 45:16
* arrive in Goshen—which they did. Gen 46:28
exchange for food. * all the Gen 47:17
in Egypt, and * the people of Gen 47:27
And Joseph did. * afterwards Gen 47:31
Then he told them, "* I will Gen 49:29,30
"* I will die," Joseph told his Gen 50:24
so that they * became a large Ex 1:7
all Hebrew boys as * as they were Ex 1:15,16
replied, "as * as I have left the Ex 9:29
WORD * REACHED Jethro, Moses' Ex 18:1
* afterwards Moses let his Ex 18:2
* be following their evil ways. Ex 34:1
of God's laws, as * as it is Lev 4:2
But as * as he does realize it, Lev 4:2
becomes guilty as * as he realizes Lev 5:
and will * become pregnant. Num 5:2
but as * as it moved, they moved. Num 9:2
THE PEOPLE WERE * complaining Num 11:
* a great, sullen mob formed; Num 16:4
to their gods, and * the men were Num 25:
from the land. *, now, you will Deu 4:2
the land you will * be entering, Deu 6:
Land, as he * will, he will destroy Deu 7:
was * overfed; Deu 32:1
in the land you will * occupy. Jos 3:1
And as * as the priests came Jos 4:1
* after Jericho's defeat, Joshua Jos 7:
"* I will be going the way of Jos 23:1
* after this he died at the age Jos 24:2
the Israeli army * captured him and Ju 1:4,5,
their men. And * Israel was Ju 3:
* afterward the armies of Midian, Ju 6:3
just as I do. As * as I and the Ju 7:1
But all Israel * began worshiping Ju 8:2
But as * as Gideon was dead, the Ju 8:3
Make me your king and you'll * Ju 9:2
and in the morning, as * as it Ju 9:3
the land of Tob. * he had quite a Ju 11:
but Jehovah the Judge will * show Ju 11:2
will * conceive and have a son! Ju 13:2,
Word * spread that he had been Ju 16:
next room, so as * as she had tied Ju 16:
* reached the land of Benjamin. Ju 20:
But they * forgot about the Lord 1Sa 12:
Three companies of raiders * 1Sa 13:1
you and you'll * be well again." 1Sa 16:15,1
and battle cries. * the Israeli 1Sa 17:2
of Israel. As * as they saw him 1Sa 17:2
As * as he was gone, David came 1Sa 20:4
and other relatives * joined him. 1Sa 22:
arrival in Judah * reached Saul. 1Sa 22:
Saul * learned that David was 1Sa 23:
countryside. Word * reached Saul 1Sa 23:1
Word * reached Saul that David 1Sa 27:
"You will * see what a help we 1Sa 28:
and leave as * as it is light." 1Sa 29:1
and his strength * returned. 1Sa 30:11,1
They * arrived, weeping and 2Sa 13:3
the king. "As * as you hear the 2Sa 15:1
A messenger * arrived in 2Sa 15:1
David * arrived at Mahanaim. 2Sa 17:24
WORD * REACHED Joab that the king 2Sa 19:1
criminals as * as you are dead." 1Ki 1:21
* afterwards two young 1Ki 3:16
She * realized that everything 1Ki 10:4
that I will * send rain again!" 1Ki 18:1
But as * as I leave you, the 1Ki 18:12
And sure enough, the sky was * 1Ki 18:45
* Ben-hadad's messengers returned 1Ki 20:5,6
kill you as * as you leave me." 1Ki 20:36
"Why have you returned so *?" 2Ki 1:4,5
and * there was water everywhere. 2Ki 3:20
after another! * every container 2Ki 4:6
the woman * conceived and had a 2Ki 4:17
and * was moaning in pain. 2Ki 4:19
As * as they arrived Elisha 2Ki 6:20
his master will * follow him." 2Ki 6:32
As * as he had finished 2Ki 10:25
And as * as the body touched 2Ki 13:20,21
As * as he had a firm grip on the 2Ki 14:5
left Lachish). * afterwards news 2Ki 19:9
* after his father Hezron's 1Ch 2:24
God, and you will * be bringing the 1Ch 22:19
gone so *, without a trace. 1Ch 29:15
cities and * arrived at Jerusalem. 2Ch 12:4
in Naphtali. As * as King Baasha 2Ch 16:5
"You'll find out * enough," 2Ch 18:24
For as * as they realized he was 2Ch 18:32
their companions * arrived in Ez 5:3
* AFTERWARDS KING Ahasuerus Est 3:1
long. * you'll look upon me dead. Job 7:8
For all so * I'll lie down in the Job 7:21
change me back again to dust so *? Job 10:9
are good days they will * be gone. Job 15:21
For all so * I must go down that Job 16:22
I am warning you—his wrath will * Ps 2:12
Oh, restore me *. Ps 6:3
against him will * be fulfilled!" Ps 35:25
NEVER ENVY THE wicked! * they Ps 37:2
But my enemies say, "May he * Ps 41:5
come to God. But * unheard-of Ps 53:5
Don't kill them—for my people * Ps 59:11
* my hands would be upon her foes! Ps 81:14
* it will be too late! Ps 88:10
* they disappear, and we are gone. Ps 90:10
in Egypt, and * forgot your many Ps 106:7
you will * learn the importance Pro 2:3,4,5
Lazy men are * poor; Pro 10:4
lies are * exposed. Pro 12:19
turn sour, and * there is nothing Ecc 5:13,14
The man who speculates is * back Ecc 5:15

SOON Con't)
and * the rafters begin to rot. Ecc 10:18
Ethiopian Dynasty would * arise. Is 7:18f
enemies will * be destroyed.' Is 8:1
enemies will * be destroyed." Is 8:18
Though * the land of Zebulun and Is 9:1
his princes will * be a king, Is 10:8
her time of doom will * be here. Is 13:22
*—and it will not be very Is 29:17
of yours that will * be gone, and Is 32:12
But * they will all be gone. Is 33:19
its princes * will all be gone. Is 34:12
As * as King Hezekiah had read Is 37:14
* AFTERWARDS, THE king of Babylon Is 39:1
walls in ruins. * your rebuilders Is 49:17
land shall * be crowded with your Is 49:19
My mercy and justice are coming *; Is 51:5
all day long? *, soon you slaves Is 51:14
Soon, * you slaves shall be Is 51:14
For you will * be bursting at Is 54:3
for I am coming * to rescue you. Is 56:1
tries a better life is * attacked. Is 59:15
and Nebuchadnezzar II * attacked. Jer 4:6f
prepared for them will * be gone. Jer 8:13
the siege will * begin. Jer 10:17
I am neither a creditor * to Jer 15:10
and which will * desert her and fly Jer 17:11
of Lebanon, but * you will cry and Jer 22:23
telling you that * the golden Jer 27:16
* afterwards, the Lord gave this Jer 28:12
of Shallum) will * arrive to ask Jer 32:6,7
But * afterwards Johanan (son of Jer 40:13,14
of the guard. * after he took them Jer 41:10
The time is coming *, the Lord Jer 48:12
but they will * be ruined. Jer 49:4
shouts of joy! * I will pour out Eze 7:8,9
and they will * stop saying it. Eze 12:23
they will be coming home again *! Eze 36:8
to learn and they * mastered all Dan 1:17
Daniel * proved himself more Dan 6:3
slowly at first, * became very Dan 8:9
* return again to his own land. Dan 11:9
* Gomer had another child—this Hos 1:6
* after defeating Israel, the Hos 1:7f
help again, for as * as trouble Hos 5:15
is almost here and * Israel will Hos 9:7
and * you were as foul as they. Hos 9:10
The Lord's vengeance will * fall Ob 1:15
* the city is an empty shambles; Nah 2:10
and shame. * your own glory will Hab 2:16
the time is coming * when I will Zep 3:8
THE day of the Lord is coming *! Zec 14:1
Kingdom of Heaven is coming *." Mt 3:2
After his baptism, as * as Jesus Mt 3:16
to Nazareth in Galilee; but * he Mt 4:12,13
sick folk were * coming to be Mt 4:24
* some men brought him a Mt 9:2
where an immense crowd * gathered. Mt 13:2,3
but the hot sun * scorched them Mt 13:6
As * as Jesus heard the news, he Mt 14:13
the city, and * people were rushing Mt 14:35
And * Mt 21:19
it and * earned another $5,000. Mt 25:16
"Someone is coming * who is far Mk 1:7
as a result, such throngs * Mk 1:45
through the city. * the house Mk 2:2
gather again, and * it was so full Mk 3:20
It grew up quickly enough, but * Mk 4:5,6
get along fine, as * as persecution Mk 4:17
But * a terrible storm arose. Mk 4:37
And a large crowd * gathered Mk 5:15
And sure enough, as * as she Mk 5:29
* AFTERWARDS HE left that section Mk 6:1
King Herod * heard about Jesus, Mk 6:14
to sit down, and * colorful groups Mk 6:39,40
needs him and will return him *.' Mk 11:3
the widow, but * he died too, and Mk 12:20,21,22
So as * as they arrived he Mk 14:45
other Jewish leaders * gathered. Mk 14:53
returned home. * afterwards Lk 1:24
Very * now, you will become Lk 1:31
to come *. Lk 2:25
Messiah to come *, and eager to Lk 3:15
but someone is coming * who has Lk 3:16
Spirit's power. * he became well Lk 4:14
the other boat and * both boats Lk 5:7
And as * as they landed, they Lk 5:11
* Levi held a reception in his Lk 5:29
One day * afterwards he went out Lk 6:12
John the Baptist * heard of all Lk 7:18
This seed began to grow, but * Lk 8:6
grain stalks were * choked out. Lk 8:7
to others who also * believe." Lk 8:15
the tombs. As * as he saw Jesus he Lk 8:28
* a crowd came out to see for Lk 8:35
send your Kingdom *. Lk 11:2
in a garden; * it grows into a tall Lk 13:19
his affairs, but * a rumor went Lk 16:1
the Kingdom of God would come *. Lk 16:16
who have little, * lose even that. Lk 19:26
And he replied, "As * as you Lk 22:10
But the time is * coming when I, Lk 22:69
met, who will * begin his ministry Jn 1:27
when I said, '* a man far greater Jn 1:30
* a Samaritan woman came to draw Jn 4:7
Jesus replied that people * Jn 4:13
around him, he * saw a great Jn 6:2-5
Capernaum. But * a gale swept down Jn 6:18,19
his death. But * it was time for Jn 7:2
A crowd * gathered, and he sat Jn 8:2
me,' and this will * come true. Jn 13:18
As * as Judas had eaten it, Satan Jn 13:27
As * as Judas left the room, Jn 13:31
the glory of God will * surround Jn 13:31
his own glory, and this so very *. Jn 13:32
And as * as God had brought his Act 3:26
As * as they were freed, Peter Act 4:23
As * as Ananias heard these Act 5:5
own, it will * be overthrown. Act 5:38
him, and they were * joined by Jews Act 6:9
and John. As * as they arrived, Act 8:15
This he did; as * as he arrived, Act 9:39
As * as the angel was gone, Act 10:7
So I came as * as I was sent Act 10:29
you have done well to come so *. Act 10:33
* THE NEWS reached the apostles Act 11:1
me, and we * arrived at the home of Act 11:12
Jerusalem and, as * as they had Act 12:25
But he is coming *—and in Act 13:25
As * as they heard this, they Act 19:5
A crowd began to gather and * the Act 19:29
us at Troas. As * as the Passover Act 20:6
to be quiet; * a deep silence Act 21:40
he had done. I * discovered it was Act 23:29
returning there *, those with Act 25:4
they would * be driven ashore; Act 27:29
WE * LEARNED that we were on the Act 28:1
will * be here. Rom 13:12,13
As * as I have delivered this Rom 15:28
will be coming to see you *. Rom 16:1
The God of peace will * crush Rom 16:20
like prisoners * to be killed, put 1Co 4:9
But I will come, and *, if the 1Co 4:19
sinning, * all will be affected? 1Co 5:6
its present form will * be gone. 1Co 7:31
to seeing him *, along with the 1Co 16:11
The troubles will * be over, but 2Co 4:18
turning away so * from God who, in Gal 1:6
I will send Timothy to see you *. Php 2:19
him to you just as * as I find out Php 2:23
* I myself may come to see you. Php 2:24
that the Lord is coming *. Php 4:5
suffering would * come—and it did. 1Th 3:4
It isn't surprising that * they 1Ti 1:19
*, and pride comes before a fall. 1Ti 3:6
to be with you *, so that if I 1Ti 3:14
But people who long to be rich * 1Ti 6:9
money, which will * be gone, but 1Ti 6:17
run out. Very * now I will be on my 2Ti 4:6
Please come as * as you can, for 2Ti 4:9
to you. As * as one of them Tit 3:12
prayers and let me come to you *. Phm 1:22
if he comes here *, I will come Heb 13:23
Lord, for he will * be gone, like a Jas 1:10,11
They will * die and leave behind Jas 1:10,11
in a mirror; as * as he walks Jas 1:24
fog—now you see it; * it is gone. Jas 4:14
The end of the world is coming *. 1Pe 4:7
are numbered, and I am * to die. 2Pe 1:13,14
to come to see you * and then we 2Jn 1:12
I hope to see you * and then we 3Jn 1:14
future activities * to occur in the Rev 1:1
and what will * be shown to you. Rev 1:19
the devil will * throw some of you Rev 2:10
Look, I am coming *! Rev 3:11
things that will * happen when the Rev 8:13
eat the baby as * as it was born. Rev 12:4
And yet, * he will come up out of Rev 17:8
and true: 'I am coming *!' Rev 22:6,7
to tell you this will happen *. Rev 22:6,7
"See, I am coming *, Rev 22:12

SOONER
by unjust means. * or later he will Jer 17:11
so that I can come back to you *. Heb 13:19

SOOT
now their faces are as black as *. Lam 4:8

SOOTHE
David began to * him by playing 1Sa 18:10
the words of the wise * and heal. Pro 12:18

SOOTHED
him the Samaritan * his wounds with Lk 10:34

SOOTHES
and * their pains and worries. Ps 41:3

SOOTHING
He bathes his feet in * olive oil. Deu 33:24

SOOTHSAYERS
Chaldeans and * of Babylon. Dan 5:11

SOP
shall dip the * and give it him." Jn 13:26f

SOPATER
they were * of Beroea, the son of Act 20:4

SOPHERETH
Sotai, *, Perida, Neh 7:57,58,59

SORCERER
been a * there for many years; Act 8:9,10,11
*, a fake prophet named Bar-Jesus. Act 13:6,7
But the *, Elymas (his name in Act 13:8
angrily at the * and said, "You Act 13:9

SORCERERS
Then Pharaoh called in his *—the Ex 7:11
and *, and encouraged every sort of 2Ch 33:6
incantationists, *, and Dan 2:1
practice used by *, whose Hos 4:12f
from God, and the * and the immoral Rev 22:15

SORCERESS
"A * shall be put to death. Ex 22:18

SORCERIES
deceived all nations with her *. Rev 18:23

SORE
their wounds were * and sensitive Gen 34:25
"If a man or woman has a * on Lev 13:29,30
is found in the *, the priest must Lev 13:29,30
who has a running * may eat the Lev 22:4
chewing with a * tooth, or trying Pro 25:19

SOREK
Delilah over in the valley of *. Ju 16:4

SORELY
though they tried his patience *; Heb 3:9

SORES
or which has * or itch or any other Lev 22:22
all who have open *, or who have Num 5:1
would come and lick his open *. Lk 16:21
malignant * broke out on everyone Rev 16:2
their pains and *, but they refused Rev 16:11

SORROW
him "Ben-oni" ("Son of my *"); Gen 35:18
befalls him, I shall die with *.' Gen 44:29
gray hairs with * to the grave. Gen 44:31
in repentance and * for sin shall Lev 23:29
What * there was throughout the Num 14:39
and bodies wasted from * and fear. Deu 28:65
look down upon my * and answer my 1Sa 1:11
all Israel was in * because the 1Sa 7:2
day as a sign of * for their sins. 1Sa 7:6
in * when they heard the news. 2Sa 1:11
their clothes in horror and *. 2Sa 13:31
been in deep * for a long time." 2Sa 14:2,3
his private *, as well as all the 2Ch 6:29
for these songs of * were recorded 2Ch 35:24,25
when their * was turned to gladness Est 9:22
heads to demonstrate their *. Job 2:12
I will speak in my * and Job 10:1
For him there is only * and Job 14:22
him for all his *, and comforting Job 42:11
gods shall all be filled with *; Ps 16:4
Then he turned my * into joy! Ps 30:11
my health is broken from *. Ps 31:9,10
I stoop with * and with shame. Ps 31:9,10
this source of * always stares me Ps 38:17
me, and floods of * pour upon me Ps 42:7
my humiliation and * for my sins! Ps 69:11
his anger, sending * and trouble. Ps 78:49
You have fed us with * and Ps 80:5
through oppression, trouble and *. Ps 107:39
my heart is heavy with *; Ps 119:28
Winking at sin leads to *; Pro 10:10
that only leads to * and trouble. Pro 10:14
Or, "and he adds no * Pro 10:22f
is filled with anguish and *? Pro 23:29,30
Days full of * and grief, and Ecc 2:20-23
to look back with * on his past, Ecc 5:19,20
is still time. * is better than Ecc 7:3
when you have no * for your sins? Is 1:12,13
and * and the heavens are black. Is 5:30
people rest from * and fear, from Is 14:3
they shave their heads in * and Is 15:2
and my * for Kir-haresh will be Is 16:11
your heads in * for your sins, and Is 22:12
the news, there will be great *. Is 23:5
and there will be weeping and *. Is 29:2
Beat your breasts in * for those Is 32:12
For them all * and all sighing Is 35:10
compassion upon them in their *. Is 49:13
* and mourning will all disappear. Is 51:11
You shall cry in * and vexation Is 65:14
to me, but her "*" was only Jer 3:10
young men and * to their mothers. Jer 15:8
of * (as is their heathen custom). Jer 16:6
been but trouble and * and shame. Jer 20:18
that your * should never end! Jer 30:15
Crying and * will be in every Jer 48:38
Fear, anguish and * have gripped Jer 49:24
Look and see if there is any * Lam 1:12
any sorrow like my *, because of Lam 1:12
upon their heads in * and despair. Lam 2:10
world has there ever been such *? Lam 2:13
afflicting men and causing *. Lam 3:33
you shall shave your heads in * Eze 7:18
the awful blows of * and distress, Eze 23:33
Yet you must show no *. Eze 24:16
But you will * to one another for Eze 24:23
"And this is the song of their * Eze 27:32
Weep with *, as a virgin weeps Joe 1:8
The fields are bare of crops. * Joe 1:10

(SORROW Con't)
There will be * and crying in Amo 5:17
*, as if your only son had died; Amo 8:10
naked and barefoot in * and shame; Mic 1:8
Shave your heads in *. Mic 1:16
"Wail in *, you people of Zep 1:11
who died. The * and mourning in Zec 12:11
of Israel will weep in profound *. Zec 12:12,13,14
apart, to face their * alone. Zec 12:12,13,14
and to * and mourn for our sins? Mal 3:14,15
were filled with * and dread. Mt 17:22,23
* chilled their hearts, and each Mt 26:22
bitter cup of * I must drink from? Mk 10:38
by * to the point of death; Mk 14:34
laughter now means * then. Lk 6:25
upon his chest in *, exclaiming, Lk 18:13
dead, they went home in deep *. Lk 23:48
you are only filled with *. Jn 16:6
You have * now, but I will see Jn 16:22
came and with great * buried Act 8:2
There will be * and suffering Rom 2:9
If they are sad, share their *. Rom 12:15
Why aren't you mourning in * and 1Co 5:2
has not caused * to me as much as 2Co 2:5,6
It was a good kind of * you felt, 2Co 7:9
felt, the kind of * God wants his 2Co 7:9
For God sometimes uses * in our 2Co 7:10
But the * of the man who is not a 2Co 7:10
is not the * of true repentance and 2Co 7:10
Don't cause the Holy Spirit * by Eph 4:30
this * on top of everything else. Php 2:27
*, as those are who have no hope. 1Th 4:13
Share the * of those being Heb 13:3
Lord and not with *, for then you Heb 13:17
Let there be * and sincere grief. Jas 4:9
continued to trust the Lord in *; Jas 5:11
And the nations will weep in * Rev 1:7
I will not experience *.' Rev 18:7
heads in their * and say, "Alas, Rev 18:19
nor *, nor crying, nor pain. Rev 21:4

SORROWFUL
soul is exceeding * unto death." Heb 5:7f

SORROWING
They bring joy to my * heart and Jer 15:16
to the weary and joy to all the *. Jer 31:25
him in farewell, * most of all Act 20:38
Those who offer comfort to the * Rom 12:8

SORROWS
have seen the deep * of my people Ex 3:7
and had seen their *, and had Ex 4:31
"You saw the troubles and * of Neh 9:9
but fills me with bitter *. Job 9:18
would pour even greater * upon me. Job 9:28
he distributes his * and anger. Job 21:17
See my *; Ps 25:18
Many * come to the wicked, but Ps 32:10
Why do you ignore our * and Ps 44:24
Look down upon my * and rescue Ps 119:153
you will live among *. Is 50:11
him—a man of *, acquainted with Is 53:3
bore, our * that weighed him down. Is 53:4
The shame of your youth and the * Is 54:4
and all their * shall be gone. Jer 31:12
all its * will be behind them. Jer 31:13
forts and palaces. * and tears are Lam 2:5
me a cup of deepest * to drink. Lam 3:15
see what * we must bear! Lam 5:1
and * and pronouncements of doom. Eze 2:9,10
Yes, cry for the * of Egypt. Eze 32:16
and *, and this time he understood Dan 10:1
"But, oh, the * that await the Lk 6:24
you will have many trials and *; Jn 16:33
will add to my * here in jail! Php 1:16,17
the trials and * it brought you. 1Th 1:6
pierced themselves with many *. 1Ti 6:10
it now with torments and with *. Rev 18:7
Therefore the * of death and Rev 18:8

SORRY
evil, he was * he had made them. Gen 6:6
For I am * I made them." Gen 6:7
"I am * that I ever made Saul 1Sa 15:11
and the Lord was * that he had 1Sa 15:35
You're not even * for me. 1Sa 22:8
the Lord was * for what was 2Sa 24:16
But because you were * and 2Ki 22:18,19
'Because you are * and have 2Ch 34:27
he rescues those who are humbly * Ps 34:18
I confess my sins; I am * for Ps 38:18
he says, "*, I can't read." Is 29:12
Is anyone * for sin? Jer 8:6
Who will feel * for you, Jer 15:5
from God but I was * afterwards. Jer 31:19
For I am * for all the punishment Jer 42:10
Then the Lord said, "You feel * Jon 4:10
And why shouldn't I feel * for a Jon 4:11
so people will feel * for them. Mt 6:16
Then the king was *, but he was Mk 6:26
them, '*, I can't help you! Mk 7:11
sins, and forgive him if he is *. Lk 17:2,3
my visit, and how * you were about 2Co 7:7
I am no longer * that I sent that 2Co 7:8
though I was very * for a time, 2Co 7:8

SORT
forth with every * of grass and Gen 1:11,12
* of fish and every kind of bird. Gen 1:21,22
reptiles and birds of every *. Gen 7:14,15
Probably some * of tortilla. Gen 18:6f
quiet * who liked to stay at home. Gen 25:27
"What * of trick is this?" Gen 29:25
Apparently a * of sleeveless tunic Ex 28:4f
or a bright spot, * of reddish Lev 13:19
Ark of God? What * of gift shall we 1Sa 6:2
"Abner, what * of family does this 1Sa 17:55
and playing every * of musical 2Sa 6:5
"What * of deal is this, my 1Ki 9:13
him to do every * of evil. 1Ki 21:25
"I would never do that * of 2Ki 8:13
encouraged every * of evil, making 2Ch 33:6
fathers did this * of thing and Neh 13:18
And the worst * of anarchy will Is 3:5
Animals of every * will gather Eze 17:22,23
and every other * of instrument." Dan 3:5f
and every other * of instrument." Dan 3:7f
and every other * of instrument." Dan 3:10f
become the lowest * of thieves. Hos 5:10
It's disgraceful, that * of talk. Mic 2:6
How I hate all that * of thing!" Zec 8:17
people of every * of illness. Mt 9:35
with the worst * of sinners!' Mt 11:19
the reapers to * out the thistles Mt 13:30
with every * of hypocrisy and sin. Mt 23:28
"What * of new religion is Mk 1:27
(This * of reasoning delighted the Mk 12:37
And has the lowest * of friends!' Lk 7:34
true, and * of believe for awhile; Lk 8:13
What * of death will he die?" Jn 21:21
full of every * of trickery and Act 13:10
ahead into every * of sex sin, and Rom 1:24
yet you let this * of thing go on. 1Co 5:6
true, I am not that * of person. 2Co 1:18
parties, and all that * of thing. Gal 5:21
anyone living that * of life will Gal 5:21
that did that * of thing; Col 3:9
The deacons must be the same * of 1Ti 3:8
that is the worst * of lie. Jas 3:14

SORTS
God made all * of wild animals Gen 1:25
The Lord God planted all * of Gen 2:9
People of various * Ex 12:38
them with all * of trouble. 2Ch 15:6
figs, and all * of produce which Neh 13:15
in fish and all * of wares and Neh 13:16
for sheep. All * of wild animals Zep 2:14
and sits down and * out the edible Mt 13:47,48
And they threw all * of other Lk 22:65
In the sheet were all * of Act 10:12
Inside the sheet were all * of Act 11:6
all * of evil things about them. Act 14:2
put on board all * of things we Act 28:10

SOSIPATER
and Jason and *, my relatives, send Rom 16:21

SOSTHENES
grabbed *, the new leader of the Act 18:17
missionary, and from brother *. 1Co 1:1

SOTAI
*, Hassophereth, Peruda, Jaalah, Ez 2:55,56,57
*, Sophereth, Perida, Neh 7:57,58,59

SOUGHT
Even kings were killed who * to 1Ch 16:21
disappointed when they * your aid. Ps 22:5
Or, "I * to learn about composure Ecc 1:16-18f
Lord, in their distress they * Is 26:16
As for my people who have * me, Is 65:10
when Israel * for rest. Jer 31:2
literally, "Others, tempting, * Lk 11:16f
Then the Jewish leaders * to Jn 7:30

SOUL
O my *, stay away from them. Gen 49:6
the Lord for his *, so that there Ex 30:11,12
Not another * shall be inside Lev 16:17
Literally, "that * shall be Num 15:31f
with all your heart, *, and might. Deu 6:5
him with all your heart and *. Deu 13:3
March on, my *, with strength! Ju 5:21
I'm with you heart and *, 1Sa 14:7
by the Lord and by your own *!" 1Sa 20:3
but there was not a * around. 2Ki 7:10
all his heart and *, and to do what 2Ch 34:31
for I hadn't told a * about the Neh 2:11,12
you have told many a troubled * Job 4:3,4
out of the bitterness of my *. Job 7:11
For the * of every living thing Job 12:10
to keep * and body together. Job 24:5
has embittered my *, that as long Job 27:2
brings back his * from the pit, so Job 33:30
Heart, body, and * are filled Ps 16:9
Literally, "Deliver my * from the Ps 22:20f
and have seen the crisis in my *. Ps 31:7
Take courage, my *! Ps 42:4,5
But O my *, don't be Ps 42:11
O my *, why be so gloomy and Ps 43:5
For a * is far too precious to Ps 49:8,9
one *, to keep it out of hell. Ps 49:8,
God will redeem my * from the power Ps 49:1
is of them that uphold my *." Ps 54:4
Rouse yourself, my *! Ps 57:
I search my * and meditate upon Ps 77:
For he satisfies the thirsty * Ps 107:
and fills the hungry * with good. Ps 107:
Literally, "David's *." Ps 132:1
fool, for he destroys his own *. Pro 6:3
Your own * is nourished when you Pro 11:1
the man who values his * will Pro 22:
be like them and endanger your *. Pro 22:24,2
one's * for a piece of bread. Pro 28:2
The Lord will destroy them, * and Is 10:1
But when his * has been made an Is 53:1
of his *, he shall be satisfied; Is 53:1
has poured out his * unto death. Is 53:1
good food that fattens up the *! Is 55:
Listen, for the life of your * Is 55:
I have heard, O my *, the blast of Jer 4:1
"Shall not my * be avenged on Jer 9:
are desolate, without a living *. Jer 9:1
they are food to my hungry *. Jer 15:16
left desolate without a living *. Jer 34:22
"Don't tell a * where you are!" Jer 36:19
and ashes, without a living *. Jer 44:2,3
and left without a * alive. Jer 46:19
shall be left without a living *. Jer 48:9
left desolate without a living *. Jer 51:29
incredible, without a living *. Jer 51:37
my heart is broken and my * Lam 1:20
always my * will live in utter Lam 3:20
each day. My * claims the Lord as Lam 3:24
he shall save his *, for he has Eze 18:27
For forty years not a * will Eze 29:11
there will be sunshine in your *. Mt 6:22
destroy both * and body in hell. Mt 10:28
He is my Beloved, in whom my * Mt 12:18
with all your heart, *, and mind.' Mt 22:37
Then he told them, "My * is Mt 26:38
what you eat won't harm your *? Mk 7:18
and loses his * in the process? Mk 8:36
is anything worth more than his *? Mk 8:37
and * and mind and strength.' Mk 12:30
a * in all the earth will survive. Mk 13:20
And he said to them, "My * is Mk 14:34
shall pierce your *, for this child Lk 2:34,35
and with all your *, and with all Lk 10:27
eye lets sunshine into your *. Lk 11:34
buried, and his * went into hell. Lk 16:23
Now my * is deeply troubled. Jn 12:27
'You will not leave my * in hell Act 2:27
that the Messiah's * would not be Act 2:31
"Don't let a * know you told me Act 23:22
in the hope that his * will be 1Co 5:5
Literally, "was made a living * 1Co 15:45f
and may your spirit and * and 1Th 5:23
is, you even owe me your very *! Phm 1:19
tears and agony of * to the only Heb 5:7
before, "My * is exceeding Heb 5:7f
saved a wandering * from death, Jas 5:20
is as healthy as I know your * is. 3Jn 1:2

SOUL-STIRRING
shout and with the * cry of the 1Th 4:16

SOUL'S
fled because of my * bitterness. Is 38:15

SOULS
altar as an atonement for your *; Lev 17:11
your * and be filled with remorse; Lev 23:32
for our * before the Lord." Num 31:50
him with all your hearts and *. Deu 4:29
him with all your hearts and *? Deu 10:12,13
your hearts and *, and will worship Deu 11:13
your hearts and *, and Israel shall Deu 30:6
God with all your hearts and *. Deu 30:10
polluted to the depths of their *. Ps 55:15
but sent them leanness in their *. Ps 106:15
fruit, and all who win * are wise. Pro 11:30
Or, "He that is wise wins *." Pro 11:30f
and trampled your * to the dust and Is 51:23
very * that I have made. Is 57:16
and you will find rest for your *. Jer 6:16
are damning the * of my people, of Eze 13:18
Literally, "Will you hunt the * Eze 13:18f
and save your own * alive?" Eze 13:18f
* with all your magic charms. Eze 13:20
Israel, for all * are mine to Eze 18:4
won't feed men's *: obedience to Mt 4:4
how to fish for the * of men!" Mt 4:19
bodies—but can't touch your *! Mt 10:28
you shall find rest for your *; Mt 11:29,30
you fishermen for the * of men!" Mk 1:17
Your * aren't harmed by what you Mk 7:15,16
be fishing for the * of men!" Lk 5:10
they have no power over your *. Lk 12:4
harm these little children's *. Lk 17:2,3
for and to save such * as his." Lk 19:9,10
stand firm, you will win your *. Lk 21:19
pour out to purchase back your *. Lk 22:20
Vast fields of human * are Jn 4:35
* into the granaries of heaven! Jn 4:36

)ULS Con't)
.iterally, "subverted your *." Act 15:24f
/ithin their own * with the penalty Rom 1:27
.ood spiritual seed in your *. 1Co 9:11
peration, the baptism of your *. Col 2:11
e will save their * if they trust 1Ti 2:15
leasure and thus ruining their *. 1Ti 5:6
.nchor for our *, connecting us Heb 6:19
n him assures our *' salvation. Heb 10:39
o watch over your *, and God will Heb 13:17
· as it takes hold of our hearts. Jas 1:21
vill be the salvation of your *. 1Pe 1:9
ecause your * have been cleansed 1Pe 1:22
hey fight against your very *. 1Pe 2:11
Guardian of your * who keeps you 1Pe 2:25
vill dawn in your * and Christ the 2Pe 1:19
ke, thereby ruining their *. Jud 1:10
t all the * of those who had been Rev 6:9
nd slaves—and even the * of men. Rev 18:13
And I saw the * of those who had Rev 20:4

)UND
That evening they heard the * of Gen 3:8
constant fear. The * of a leaf Lev 26:36
out you shall not * the alarm." Num 10:5,6,7f
* the alarm with these trumpets. Num 10:9
Why don't we hear the * of the Ju 5:28
*, thought she had been drinking. 1Sa 1:12,13
the Lord had put them * asleep. 1Sa 26:12
When you hear a * like marching 2Sa 5:24
built without the * of hammer, axe, 1Ki 6:7
was the * of a gentle whisper. 1Ki 19:12
When you hear a * like marching 1Ch 14:15
chosen to * the bronze cymbals; 1Ch 15:19
The trumpeter stayed with me to * Neh 4:18
They * like animals among the Job 30:7
At the * of the bugle he shouts, Job 39:25
Without a * or word, silent in Ps 19:3,4
pluck the sweet lyre and harp. * Ps 81:3
You spoke, and at the * of your Ps 104:7,8
against every * principle of Pro 18:1
in his heart may * pleasant Pro 26:24,25,26
and "bloodshed" * very much Is 5:7f
every home comes the * of weeping. Is 15:3
to you at the * of your cry. Is 30:19
The enemy runs at the * of your Is 33:3
* the alarm throughout the land. Jer 4:5
Flee from Jerusalem! * the alarm Jer 6:1
"Listen for the * of the trumpet! Jer 6:17
Hear the terrible * of great Jer 10:22
war on Babylon. * the battle cry; Jer 51:27
by the * of a great earthquake. Eze 3:12
me the * of a great earthquake." Eze 3:12f
the * of their wheels beside them. Eze 3:13
And the * of the wings of the Eze 10:5
From your apartment came the * Eze 23:42
No more will there be the * of Eze 26:13
quake at the * as your pilots Eze 27:28
with fear at the * of her fall, for Eze 31:16
coming and doesn't * the alarm and Eze 33:6
from the east. The * of his coming Eze 43:2
will disappear. * the alarm! Hos 5:8
* THE ALARM! Hos 8:1
* THE ALARM in Jerusalem! Joe 2:1
* the trumpet in Zion! Joe 2:15
You sing idle songs to the * of Amo 6:5
The riotous * of singing in the Amo 8:3
And all this time Jonah was * Jon 1:5
by enemy armies! * the alarm! Nah 2:1
the Lord God shall * the trumpet Zec 9:14
"Not all who * religious are Mt 7:21
my angels with the * of a mighty Mt 24:31
At the * of Mary's greeting, Lk 1:41
Others said, "This doesn't * to Jn 10:21
there was a * like the roaring of a Act 2:2
for they heard the * of someone's Act 9:7
teaches us. They * foolish to him, 1Co 2:14
and made the lie * like the truth. Eph 4:14
but they are the *, wholesome 1Ti 6:3
And I heard a * from heaven like Rev 14:2
Never again will the * of music Rev 18:22

SOUNDED
and Saul * the call to arms 1Sa 13:3,4
of this detail, * the cymbals. 1Ch 16:5
The alarm has *—listen and fear! Amo 3:6
The Lord God has * your doom—I Amo 3:8
But the story * like a fairy Lk 24:11
This * reasonable to the whole Act 6:5
They *, and found 120 feet of Act 27:28
A little later they * again, and Act 27:28
unless each note is * clearly. 1Co 14:7
me, a voice that * like a trumpet Rev 1:10
heard before, that * like a mighty Rev 4:1
* like thunder, said, "Come!" Rev 6:1
Then I heard again what * like Rev 19:6

SOUNDING
of a Hebrew word * like the name. Gen 30:6f
a ram's horn * one long blast; Ex 19:13
with trumpets blaring and horns *. 2Ch 15:14
words and high * ideas, for fear of 1Co 1:17

SOUNDLY
sent—and they were * defeated. Jos 7:4

A lazy man sleeps *—and goes Pro 19:15

SOUNDS
word for Eve * similar to a Hebrew Gen 3:20f
Which * a little like the Hebrew Gen 25:25f
The name Moses * like another Ex 2:10f
to Moses, "It * as if they are Ex 32:17
The word Samuel in Hebrew * like 1Sa 1:19,20f
the * of a great army approaching. 2Ki 7:6
Jabez * like ozeb, the Hebrew 1Ch 4:9f
We can choose the * we want to Job 34:3
Any story * true until someone Pro 18:17
Her streets echo with the * of Jer 6:7
Shaphir * like the Hebrew word Mic 1:11f
Zaanan * like a verb meaning "to Mic 1:11f
Beth-ezel * like a word for Mic 1:11f
Shaphir * like the Hebrew word Mic 1:11f
Zaanan * like a verb meaning "to Mic 1:11f
Beth-ezel * like a word for Mic 1:11f
Shaphir * like the Hebrew word Mic 1:11f
Zaanan * like a verb meaning "to Mic 1:11f
Beth-ezel * like a word for Mic 1:11f
and even my preaching * poor, for 1Co 1:17
I know very well how foolish it * 1Co 1:18
For it * as if more harm than 1Co 11:17
"He * big, but it's all noise. 2Co 10:10

SOUP
It is better to eat * with Pro 15:17

SOUR
he has eaten turns * within him. Job 20:14
serve will turn * in your stomach Pro 23:6,7,8
that turn *, and soon there is Ecc 5:13,14
grew were wild and * and not at all Is 5:2
Literally, "The fathers eat the * Jer 31:29f
person eating * grapes is the one Jer 31:30
fathers have eaten * grapes and the Eze 18:2f
and corrupt and * all that should Amo 6:12
a sponge with * wine and put it on Mt 27:48
and filled it with * wine and held Mk 15:36
by offering him a drink—of * wine. Lk 23:36
A jar of * wine was sitting Jn 19:29
it, it will make your stomach *!" Rev 10:9

SOURCE
and he will be a * of blessing for Gen 18:18
food, for it is his * of life. Lev 22:7
of Israel as a * of water for the Num 19:9
they had no other * of income 2Ch 31:17,18
from some other *, but you and your Est 4:14
its boundaries, or go to its *? Job 38:20
this * of sorrow always stares me Ps 38:17
for he is the * of all my joy. Ps 104:34
yours have been my * of joy and Ps 119:54
promises are my only * of hope. Ps 119:114
for himself from every possible *. Is 56:11
me joy and be a * of praise and Jer 33:9
you—this is not from any human *. Mt 16:17
using as their * material the Lk 1:1,2
Holy Spirit, the * of all truth. Jn 15:26
Spirit who is the * of them all. 1Co 12:4
Jesus Christ, the * of every mercy, 2Co 1:3,4
is the hidden * of their faith. 1Ti 3:9
the primeval * of God's Rev 3:14

SOURCES
subterranean water * ceased their Gen 8:2
walked in the * of their depths? Job 38:16
Literally, "* of the streams of Is 7:18f
earth, the sea and all its *." Rev 14:7

SOUTH
NOW ABRAHAM MOVED * to the Gen 20:1
(Isaac had now moved * to Gen 25:11
east to west and from north to *; Gen 28:14
will form the * side of the sacred Ex 26:18,19
The lampstand will be on the * Ex 26:35
On the * side the curtains will Ex 27:9,10
frames on the * side, with the Ex 36:23
The * wall was 150 feet long; Ex 38:9
on the * side of the Tabernacle. Ex 40:24
Location: * side of the Num 2:3-31
the tribes on the * shall go. Num 10:5,6,7
The Amalekites live in the *, Num 13:29
will continue * past Scorpion Pass Num 34:4
be from Hazar-enan * to Shepham, Num 34:10,11
first going * and then westward Num 34:10,11
Road that goes * to Elath and Deu 2:8
desert in the * to the Lebanon Jos 1:4
The kings in the Arabah, * of Jos 11:1
and as far * as the Salt Sea and Jos 12:3
His kingdom also stretched * to Jos 12:5
The land of the Avvim in the *; Jos 13:2-7
Hermon in the * to the entrance of Jos 13:2-7
began at the * bay of the Salt Sea, Jos 15:2,3,4
the road going * of Mount Akrabbim, Jos 15:2,3,4
of Zin to Hezron (* of Jos 15:2,3,4
on the * side of the valley. Jos 15:7
proceeded past the * of Timnah to Jos 15:10,11
* of Shikkeron and Mount Baalah. Jos 15:10,11
on the *, to Tyre on the north. Jos 15:47
On the * the boundary went from Jos 17:7
(Several cities * of the brook Jos 17:9
The land * of the brook and as Jos 17:10
From there the boundary went * Jos 18:13
country * of Lower Beth-horon. Jos 18:13
There the border turned *, Jos 18:14
* of the old city of Jerusalem Jos 18:16
the Arabah, ran * past Jos 18:19
The cities as far * as Jos 19:8
Its boundary started on the * Jos 19:10
boundary in the *, and with the Jos 19:34
Negeb wilderness * of Arad, the Ju 1:16
hiding near the * edge of the field 1Sa 20:41
of Maon in the * of the desert. 1Sa 23:24,25
"Against the * of Judah and the 1Sa 27:10
and had raided the * of Judah and 1Sa 30:14
Bethel, * Ramoth, Jattir, Aroer, 1Sa 30:27-31
camped at Aroer, * of the city that 2Sa 24:5
* to Judah as far as Beer-sheba. 2Sa 24:7
The one on the * was named the 1Ki 7:16-22
west, three *, and three east. 1Ki 7:25
and * of Destruction Mountain. 2Ki 23:13
sides: east, west, north, and *. 1Ch 9:24
of the * gate to Obed-edom and 1Ch 26:14,15
gate, four to the * gate, and two 1Ch 26:17
west, three *, and three east. 2Ch 4:4
nor can I find him in the *; Job 23:9
"From the * comes the rain; Job 37:9
warm when the * wind is blowing and Job 37:16,17
and spreads her wings to the *? Job 39:26
the * wind by his mighty power. Ps 78:26
You created north and *! Ps 89:12
The wind blows * and north, here Ecc 1:3-7
when a tree falls, whether * or Ecc 11:3
come, * wind, blow upon my garden Sol 4:16
an army against him [from the * Is 37:8,9
east and west, from north and *. Is 43:6
away, from north and west and *." Is 49:12
The cities of the Negeb to the * Jer 13:19
in the * to Riblah in the north. Eze 6:14
north or *—your land is finished. Eze 7:2
standing at the * end of the Temple Eze 10:3
Sodom and her daughters, in the *. Eze 16:46
far * as the border of Ethiopia. Eze 29:10
Then he took me around to the * Eze 40:24
inner wall and its * passageway. Eze 40:28
entrance, facing *, and one beside Eze 40:44
door faced north and the other *. Eze 41:11
tiers was on the * side of the Eze 42:9,10
"These north and * tiers of rooms Eze 42:13
go out through the * passageway. Eze 46:9
Those coming in from the * must Eze 46:9
the altar, that is, on its * side. Eze 47:1
* side [of the eastern passageway Eze 47:2
the north and Damascus to the *. Eze 47:17
"The eastern border will run * Eze 47:18
to the * and Hamath to the north. Eze 48:1
Asher's territory lies * of Eze 48:2
Naphtali's land lies * of Eze 48:3
Then comes Manasseh, * of Eze 48:4
Next, to the *, is Ephraim, and Eze 48:5,6,7
"* of Judah is the land set Eze 48:8
miles wide, north to *, surrounds Eze 48:10
miles wide, * of the Temple Eze 48:15
western border. * of Benjamin's Eze 48:24
west, while its * border runs from Eze 48:27,28
and Dan. The * wall, also the same Eze 48:33
and attacked the * and east, and Dan 8:9
the king of the * will attack him Dan 11:40
of Edom, and Bozrah in the *. Amo 1:12f
Then all the cities of the * Mic 1:13
while the dappled-greys will go * Zec 6:6
off the desert from the *. Zec 9:14
the north and half toward the *. Zec 14:4
Literally, "Queen of the *." Lk 11:31f
"When the * wind blows you say, Lk 12:55
blowing from the *, and it looked Act 27:13
a day later a * wind began Act 28:13
side—north, *, east, and west. Rev 21:13

SOUTHEAST
The tank was in the * corner, on 1Ki 7:39
The huge tank was in the * 2Ch 4:10
across to Goah on the *. Jer 31:38,39
mountainous area * of the Black Sea Eze 38:2,3f
A nation * of Israel, including Ob 1:1f
Cnidus was a port on the * coast Act 27:7,8f

SOUTHERN
Egypt," at the * border of Judah. Gen 15:18f
and from the * deserts as far as Ex 23:31
homeland), "the * portion of the Num 34:3
edge of Edom. The * boundary will Num 34:3
Kadesh-barnea was at the * edge of Deu 1:1f
stretch from the * Negeb to Deu 11:24
Egypt to the * boundary of Ekron; Jos 13:2-7
Judah's * boundary began at the Jos 15:1
Hinnom, along the * shoulder of Jos 15:8
THE * BOUNDARY of the Tribes of Jos 16:1
The * border ran from the edge of Jos 18:15
is the * end of the Jordan River. Jos 18:19
the * one was in front of Geba. 1Sa 14:5
in the * part of the wilderness. 1Sa 23:19
him from Egypt and * Turkey, where 1Ki 10:28
constellations of the * Zodiac. Job 9:9
appeared at the * border of Judah Jer 37:5
and throughout * Egypt as well: Jer 44:1
in * Egypt) answered Jeremiah: Jer 44:15

(SOUTHERN Con't)
In * Babylonia. Jer 50:21f
from the * coast of Cyprus. Eze 27:6
land of Pathros in * Egypt where Eze 29:14
the * entrance, facing north. Eze 40:44
The building beside the inner * Eze 40:46
the Jordan at the * tip of the Sea Eze 47:18
"The * border will go west from Eze 47:19
boundary, from the * boundary to Eze 47:20
Literally, "the * king"—Ptolemy Dan 11:5f
boundary to your * tip, all the way Amo 6:14
from rocks; her * boundary was on Ob 1:1f
immigrants to the * coast of Zep 2:5f
prosperous and her * suburbs out Zec 7:7
to Rimmon (the * border) will Zec 14:10
slowly along the * coast, we Act 27:7,8

SOUTHERNMOST
in the direction of Zin. Its * Num 34:4
it touches the * tip of the Sea of Num 34:10,11

SOUTHSIDE
* of the Tabernacle Num 3:25-30

SOUTHWARD
left that place and traveled * Gen 12:8
Thus he continued slowly * to Gen 12:9
there continued * along the road to Num 21:4
From Janoah it turned * to Jos 16:7
Manasseh extended * from the border Jos 17:7
tipping *, spilling over Judah." Jer 1:13
turn his armies *, as he had Dan 11:29
and went * to the Judean borders Mk 10:1

SOUTHWEST
from the Hill of Gareb at the *, Jer 31:38,39
the Black Sea and * of the Caspian, Eze 38:2,3f
only a northwest and * exposure. Act 27:12

SOVEREIGN
" 'The * God,' " Ex 3:14
as part of God's * plan we were Eph 1:11
Lord and said, "O * Lord, holy and Rev 6:10

SOVEREIGNTY
his * being Galilee and Peraea. Mt 14:1f

SOW
Go and * the land. Gen 47:23
"* and reap your crops for six Ex 23:10
don't * your field with two kinds Lev 19:19
For six years you may * your Lev 25:3
Don't * your crops and don't Lev 25:4
In it you shall not *, nor gather Lev 25:11
you will * your crops in vain, Lev 26:16
amount of seed required to * it. Lev 27:16
"Do not * other crops in the Deu 22:9
"You will * much but reap Deu 28:38
it is those who * sin and trouble Job 4:7,8
their cities, to * their fields Ps 107:37
Those who * tears shall reap joy. Ps 126:5
the wind shall not * and he that Ecc 11:4f
a farmer always plow and never *? Is 28:23,24
the ground and * your crops. Eze 36:9
day when God will * his people in Hos 1:11
At that time I will * a crop of Hos 1:23
starts again to * another crop, and Amo 9:13
don't need to * or reap or store up Mt 6:26
where you didn't *, and gathering Mt 25:24,25f
A farmer decided to * some grain. Mk 4:3
went out to his field to * grain. Lk 8:5
you to reap where you didn't *; Jn 4:38

SOWED
times the grain he *. Gen 26:12
nor *—and there break its neck. Deu 21:4
and * thistles among the wheat. Mt 13:25
The enemy who * the thistles Mt 13:39
"A farmer * his field, and went Mk 4:26

SOWER
What joys await the * and the Jn 4:36

SOWING
ripening when * time comes again. Lev 26:4,5
of barley seed for * is valued at Lev 27:16
to punish them for * seeds of sin. Job 5:6
carrying seed for *, and return Ps 126:6
witness* discord among brothers Pro 6:16-19
Keep on * your seed, for you Ecc 11:6
"For I am * peace and Zec 8:12
"A farmer was * grain in his Mt 13:2,3
a farmer * good seed in his field; Mt 13:24

SOWN
grain to be * in the field, it is Lev 11:37
the crops I have * and let all that Job 31:7,8
Light is * for the godly and joy Ps 97:11
My people have * wheat but Jer 12:13
They have * the wind and they Hos 8:7

SOWS
An evil man * strife; Pro 16:28
"the day of Jezreel ('God *')"; Hos 1:11f
sing together that "God *!" Hos 1:21,22
am the farmer who * the choice Mt 13:37
For it is true that one * and Jn 4:37
reap just the kind of crop he *! Gal 6:7
If he * to please his own wrong Gal 6:8

SPACE
a clear * between you and the Ark; Jos 3:2,3,4
him at the open * east of the 2Ch 29:4,5
in the open * before the Temple; Ez 10:9
heaven over empty *, and hangs the Job 26:7
all the universe and *. Pro 3:19
The wicked man stares into * with Pro 16:30
* and stretched out the heavens. Jer 10:12
leaving a free * of 8¾ feet out to Eze 41:9
the windows. The * above the door Eze 41:17,18
It's taking up * we can use for Lk 13:7

SPACES
in the cleared * behind the walls. Neh 4:13

SPACIOUS
God— you built a * brothel for Eze 16:24

SPADE
Each man must have a * as part Deu 23:13
the * and cover the excrement. Deu 23:13

SPAIN
to take a trip to *, and when I do, Rom 15:24
come to see you on my way to *. Rom 15:28

SPAN
mankind so brief a * of life—months Job 14:5

SPANKING
Scolding and * a child helps him Pro 29:15

SPARE
because of you, and * my life!" Gen 12:11,12,13
it, and not * it for their sakes? Gen 18:24
there, I will * the entire city for Gen 18:26
But Reuben hoped to * Joseph's Gen 37:21,22
and if you are, I will * you." Gen 42:20
troughs into their * clothes, and Ex 12:34
* that person from the penalty; Deu 13:8
They offered to * his life and Ju 1:24
David begged him to * the child, 2Sa 12:16
man of God, please * my life and 2Ki 1:13
"only * his life." Job 2:6
Rescue me from death; * my Ps 22:20
* me, Lord! Ps 39:13
Do not * these evil, treacherous Ps 59:5
anger and did not * the Egyptians' Ps 78:50
to save me! Now * me by your Ps 119:40,41,42
In your kindness, * my life; Ps 119:88
I will not let pity nor mercy * Jer 13:14
you to * these enemies of mine." Jer 15:11
let the archers shoot at her; * Jer 50:14
not * you nor pity you at all. Eze 5:11
I will not * nor pity you, and Eze 7:8,9
I will neither pity nor *. Eze 8:18
isn't marked. * not nor pity them— Eze 9:5
And so I will not * them nor Eze 9:10
But I will * a few of them from Eze 12:16
I will not * even the righteous. Eze 21:4
Perhaps even yet God will * Dan 4:27
and they will pray, "* your Joe 2:17
And I won't * them either," Zec 11:6
And I will * them as a man spares Mal 3:17
*, and here I am, dying of hunger! Lk 15:17
wanted to * Paul, so he told them Act 27:43
Since he did not * even his own Rom 8:32
For if God did not * the Rom 11:21
place, he won't * you either. Rom 11:21
severely and I will not * them. 2Co 13:2
For God did not * even the 2Pe 2:4
And he did not * any of the 2Pe 2:5

SPARED
to face, and yet my life is *." Gen 32:30
Lord changed his mind and * them. Ex 32:14
killed you by now, and * her." Num 22:33
but I prayed, and the Lord * him. Deu 9:20
"It's true that the army * the 1Sa 15:15
worst is over and I have been *!" 1Sa 15:32
told me to kill you, but I * you. 1Sa 24:9,10
and one-third were * to become 2Sa 8:2
he vowed, "Your life is *." 2Sa 19:23
He * Jonathan's son Mephibosheth, 2Sa 21:7
'Because you have * the man I said 1Ki 20:42
Then I would have been * this Job 10:19
man is usually * in the day of Job 21:30-32
and debtors—none will be *. Is 24:2
your life will be * and all will Jer 38:20
No one shall be *; Jer 51:3
Nevertheless, I * them. Eze 20:17
offended him, and * any he liked. Dan 5:19
I have * her tender neck. Hos 10:11

SPARES
And I will spare them as a man * Mal 3:17

SPARING
appear among you, not * the flock. Act 20:29

SPARINGLY
he will not act *. Is 30:14

SPARK
your evil deeds are the * that Is 1:31
can be set on fire by one tiny *. Jas 3:5

SPARKLE
See them * with jewels of silver Ps 68:11,12,13
Don't let the * and the smooth Pro 23:31

SPARKLED
crosswise within, * like Eze 10:9-13

SPARKLES
"When he sneezes, the sunlight * Job 41:18
so their pride * like a jeweled Ps 73:6

SPARKLING
They drank the * wine. Deu 32:14
there is a cup of pale and * wine. Ps 75:8
I will make your towers of * Is 54:
will be a land * with happiness. Mal 3:

SPARKS
His eyes glow like *. Job 41:
* that fly when iron strikes iron. Pro 27:
their bows are bent; * fly from Is 5:

SPARROW
as a solitary * on the roof. Ps 102
by it than by a * or swallow Pro 26
Not one * (What do they cost? Mt 10:

SPARROWS
Even the * and swallows are Ps 84
more valuable to him than many *. Mt 10:
"What is the price of five *? Lk 12
to him than a whole flock of *. Lk 12

SPAT
Then they * in his face and Mt 26:
And they * on him and grabbed Mt 27:
man's ears, then * and touched the Mk 7:
the village, and * upon his eyes, Mk 8:
* upon, and lashed and killed. Lk 18:
Then he * on the ground and made Jn 9

SPATTERED
killed a goat and * its blood on Gen 37:
and her blood * against the wall 2Ki 9:

SPEAK
People would * of someone as Gen 10
let me go on and * further to the Gen 18:
"Let me *: suppose only thirty Gen 18:
I have dared to * to God, let me Gen 18:
I will * but this once more! Gen 18:
to * to Pharaoh on his behalf. Gen 50
Who makes a man so that he can * Ex 4:
can speak or not *, see or not see, Ex 4:
I will help you to * well, and I Ex 4:1
both of you to * well, and I will Ex 4:1
that will really * to you and to Ex 9:1
but don't let God * directly to us, Ex 20:1
will meet with you and * with you. Ex 29:4
the Tabernacle to * with the Lord, Ex 34:
until he returned to * with God. Ex 34:
the Tabernacle to * with God, he Num 7:8
With him I * face to face! Num 12:7
As they watch, * to that rock Num 20
The Lord had said to * to the Num 20:1
the Lord caused the donkey to *! Num 22:2
and that is what I shall *." Num 22:3
The Lord will * to Eleazar Num 27:2
me cross over. '* of it no more,' Deu 3:2
Now we know that a man may * to Deu 5:2
so that I can * to them, and call Deu 31:2
She got off her donkey to * to Jos 15:18,1
her donkey to * to Caleb about it. Ju 1:1
Or, "to listen to her * to them Ju 4:
I felt that I should * to you Ru 4:
as if to * with him privately; 2Sa 3:2
* of giving me an eternal dynasty! 2Sa 7:1
Please, just * to the king about 2Sa 13:1
"Go ahead," he replied. "*!" 2Sa 14:1
If not, * up." 2Sa 17:
were the first to * of bringing him 2Sa 19:4
He replied, "* to King Solomon 1Ki 2:1
must I tell you to * only what the 1Ki 22:1
the Lord leave me and * to you?" 1Ki 22:2
the woman I want to * to her." 2Ki 4:11,1
even the words you * in the privacy 2Ki 6:1
come out to * to them, but instead 2Ki 18:1
to them, "Please * in Aramaic, for 2Ki 18:2
* only to you and to your master? 2Ki 18:2
kings too! You * as though I were 1Ch 17:1
must I tell you to * nothing except 2Ch 18:1
* the language of Judah at all. Neh 13:2
"It is wonderful to * the truth, Job 6:25,2
Let me be free to * out of the Job 7:1
The experience of others will * Job 8:1
Then I could * without fear to Job 9:3
I will * in my sorrow and Job 10:
Oh, that God would * and tell Job 11:
Oh, how I long to * directly to Job 13:
alone, that I may *—and I am Job 13:1
Or let me * to you, and you Job 13:2
It isn't right to * so Job 15:
What have I said that makes you * Job 16:
I would * in such a way that it Job 16:
nor does it help if I refuse to * Job 16:
"Who are you trying to fool? * Job 18:
When I stand to *, they mock. Job 19:1
let me *, and afterwards, mock Job 21:2,
my lips shall * no evil, my tongue Job 27:4
evil, my tongue shall * no lies. Job 27:4
"But Destruction and Death * of Job 28:2
They longed for me to * as those Job 29:2
Elihu had waited until now to * Job 32:4
I must * to find relief, so let Job 32:20
I have begun to *; Job 33:2
I will * the truth with all Job 33:3
Yet when he chooses not to *, Job 34:29,30
'Listen and I will *! Job 42:4
your failure to * rightly Job 42:8
For they cannot * one truthful Ps 5:9
or even * the names of their gods. Ps 16:4

SPEAK Con't)
wicked ones who * so sweetly to Ps 28:3
How can my dust in the grave * Ps 30:9
I will constantly * of his Ps 34:1
before them as a man who cannot *. Ps 38:13,14
I will not open my mouth to * one Ps 39:9
How proudly they *! Ps 73:8
Can the darkness * of your Ps 88:12
storms; you *, and they lie still. Ps 89:9
You *, and man turns back to Ps 90:3
the Lord redeemed you? Then * out! Ps 107:2
use their hands or feet! Nor *! Ps 115:7
I will * to kings about their Ps 119:44,45,46
Literally, "when they * with Ps 127:5f
Listen, and grow wise, for I * Pro 4:1
The upright * what is helpful; Pro 10:32
the wicked * rebellion. Pro 10:32
Yes, * up for the poor and needy Pro 31:9
A time to * up; Ecc 3:7
The more words you *, the less Ecc 6:11
mean, so why bother to * at all? Ecc 6:11
of those who are asleep to *." Sol 7:9
Just to * the name of Israel Is 19:17
begin to * the Hebrew language. Is 19:18
say, "to * to us like this! Is 28:9
who * strange gibberish! Is 28:11
in uncertainty will * out plainly. Is 32:4
could not * will shout and sing! Is 35:6
Don't * in Hebrew, for the people Is 36:11
says your God. * tenderly to Is 40:2
Come now and *. Is 41:1
When I * to the rivers and say, Is 44:27
No, for I, Jehovah, * only truth Is 45:19
you and * whatever I tell you to. Jer 1:7
of importance, and * to them, for Jer 5:5
spears. They * cleverly to their Jer 9:8
It cannot *, and it must be Jer 10:5
no matter how pleasantly they *. Jer 12:6
to * or give them any message. Jer 14:14
nor heard; they * foolishness Jer 14:14
Let's silence him that he may * Jer 18:18
with you, and * to them whatever Jer 19:1
You have never once let me * a Jer 20:8
Lord—never more * in his name—then Jer 20:9
to me: Go over and * directly to Jer 22:1
They do not * for me! Jer 23:16
yet they claim to * for me; Jer 23:21
from God" that I didn't *. Jer 23:36
Lord sent me to * every word that Jer 26:15
the solemn words I * to you in the Jer 28:7
tongue and let you *, and you shall Eze 3:27
"Son of dust, * out against the Eze 13:17
"Son of dust," he said, "* to Eze 16:2
Jerusalem and * out against it and Eze 20:46
false visions and * false messages Eze 22:28
me so that I could * again by the Eze 33:22
Then he told me to * to the bones Eze 37:4
looking down, unable to * a word. Dan 10:15
can go ahead and *, sir, for you Dan 10:19
and * to her tenderly there. Hos 1:14
Can images * for God? Hab 2:19
blessing, and to * with the Zec 7:3
* because a demon was inside him. Mt 9:32
so that he could both * and see. Mt 12:22
How could evil men like you * Mt 12:34
Day for every idle word you *. Mt 12:36
those who couldn't *, and many Mt 15:30
From then on Jesus began to * Mt 16:21
he had a chance to *, Jesus asked Mt 17:25
*, because they knew who he was. Mk 1:34
Don't stop to * to anyone along Mk 1:43,44
'These people * very prettily about Mk 7:6,7
hear perfectly and * plainly! Mk 7:35
Literally, "will be able to * Mk 9:39f
and they shall * new languages. Mk 16:17
Literally, "they will * in new Mk 16:17f
to * until the child is born. Lk 1:20
out, he couldn't * to them, and Lk 1:22
Instantly Zacharias could * Lk 1:64
and * to the crowds from there. Lk 5:3
and meet you. Just * a word from Lk 7:6,7,8
orders not to * of this to anyone. Lk 9:21
*, his voice returned to him. Lk 11:14
(Yet those who * against me Lk 12:10
may be forgiven—while those who * Lk 12:10
they wouldn't even * to them! Jn 4:9
had the courage to * out for him in Jn 7:13
He is old enough to * for Jn 9:21
when they * of) a 'stone discarded Act 4:11
them never again to * about Jesus. Act 4:18
never again to * in the name of Act 5:40
be able to * of his posterity? Act 8:33f
and * to them again the next week. Act 13:42
When they heard Paul * of the Act 17:32
him, "Don't be afraid! * out! Act 18:9
for silence and tried to *. Act 19:33
to quiet them down enough to *. Act 19:35
and hear him *. Act 22:14
* evil of any of your rulers.' Act 23:5
motioned for him to rise and *. Act 24:10
Festus. I * words of sober truth. Act 26:25
these things. I * frankly for I am Act 26:26
with him, so to *, when he died Rom 6:5
I * this way, using the Rom 6:19
"married," so to *, to the one Rom 7:4
He has helped you * out for him 1Co 1:5
For I decided that I would * 1Co 2:2
Christians I do * with words of 1Co 2:6
of which could * a single word. 1Co 12:2
* messages from the Spirit of God. 1Co 12:3
Still another person is able to * 1Co 12:10
Those who * in languages they have 1Co 12:28
us the ability to * in languages 1Co 12:30
of being able to * in other 1Co 13:1
them, and could * in every language 1Co 13:1
so that I could * to a mountain and 1Co 13:2
of being able to "* in tongues," 1Co 14:2
that is, to * in languages you 1Co 14:2
power than to * in unknown 1Co 14:5
But if I * plainly what God has 1Co 14:6
I thank God that I "* in 1Co 14:18
would much rather * five words that 1Co 14:19
other lands to * in foreign 1Co 14:21
being able to "* in tongues" is 1Co 14:22
has given him, or * in an unknown 1Co 14:26
or three should * in an unknown 1Co 14:27
and they must * one at a time, and 1Co 14:27
they must not * out loud. 1Co 14:28
of prophecy can *, one after the 1Co 14:31
"They are not authorized to *." 1Co 14:34f
and never say it is wrong to "* 1Co 14:39
of God as we * and so we tell the 2Co 4:2
"I believe and therefore I *." 2Co 4:13
God is using us to * to you: we 2Co 5:20
custody, so to *, until we could Gal 3:23
* of God as our dear Father. Gal 4:6
always be ready to * out boldly for Php 1:20
can * a word of blame against you. Php 2:15
And if my lifeblood is, so to *, Php 2:17
alive again, so to *, when Christ Col 3:1
And they * of how you are 1Th 1:10
For we * as messengers from God, 1Th 2:4
as an enemy, but * to him as you 2Th 3:15
NEVER * SHARPLY to an older man, 1Ti 5:1
many others have heard me * about. 2Ti 2:2
And this is true. So * to the Tit 1:13
BUT AS FOR you, * up for the right Tit 2:1
They must not * evil of anyone, Tit 3:2
on to us by those who heard him *? Heb 2:3
the living God. * to each other Heb 3:13
And who were those people I * of, Heb 3:16
he is chosen to * for all other men Heb 5:1
Surely we don't need to * further Heb 6:1
And no one then will need to * Heb 8:11
* little, and not become angry; Jas 1:19
Don't criticize and * evil about Jas 4:11
Your godly lives will * to them 1Pe 3:1
then if men * against you, 1Pe 3:16
The faith I * of is the kind that 2Pe 1:1
teachers, never * out 2Pe 2:11
my own eyes and listened to him *. 1Jn 1:1
him, and you know I * the truth. 3Jn 1:12
the Creature to * great blasphemies Rev 13:5
to this statue and even make it *! Rev 13:15

SPEAKER
"O Lord, I'm just not a good *. Ex 4:10
is a good *. Ex 4:14
I'm no *—why should Pharaoh Ex 6:30
The *, as in the remainder of the Ez 7:28f
he was the chief *, was Mercury! Act 14:12
If I am a poor *, at least I 2Co 11:6

SPEAKERS
The headings identifying the * are Sol 1:1f
and Silas, both being gifted *, Act 15:32
They are good *, and Rom 16:18

SPEAKING
others listened, * publicly before Gen 23:10
As he was still * to the Lord Gen 24:15,16
"Well, while I was still * these Gen 24:45
* among themselves, they said, Gen 42:21
* to them through an interpreter. Gen 42:23
Then, as God finished * with Ex 31:18
When Moses had finished * with Ex 34:33
he heard the Voice * to him from Num 7:89
He had hardly finished * the Num 16:31
the voice of God * to it from fire, Deu 4:33
MOSES CONTINUED * to the people Deu 5:1
of the living God * from the heart Deu 5:26,27
tears as the Angel finished *; Ju 2:4
While she was *, the king's aides 1Ki 1:22,23
And while he was still *, 1Ki 1:42
that God had been * through him. 1Ki 13:5
* for the Lord, had predicted. 2Ki 10:17
Generally *, Jotham was a good 2Ki 15:34,35
For now, O Lord God, you are * of 1Ch 17:17
the king (who was * for the Lord) 2Ch 29:15
While this messenger was still *, Job 1:16
As he was still *, another Job 1:18
days and nights, no one * a word; Job 2:13
For who could keep from * out? Job 4:2
"Must you go on '* for God' when Job 13:7
have sinned by * of God that way. Job 33:12
that you, Job, are * like a fool. Job 34:34,35
After the Lord had finished * Job 42:7
youth (Israel is *), and faced Ps 129:1
the Sabbath and * of it with Is 58:13
that all was well, * of things they Jer 14:18
the voice of someone * to me: Eze 1:27,28
While I was still * and telling Eze 11:13
(I am * of Samaria and Jerusalem! Eze 23:4,5
And I heard the Lord * to me Eze 43:6
Then the astrologers (* in Dan 2:4
He who reveals secrets was * to Dan 2:29
While he was still * these words, Dan 4:31
"You people," he said (* for Hag 2:14
* words of comfort and assurance. Zec 1:13
heavenly Father * through you! Mt 10:20
except one: * against the Holy Mt 12:31,32
As Jesus was * in a crowded house Mt 12:46,47
when * to the crowds. Mt 13:34,35
he was * of John the Baptist. Mt 17:13
and said, "Humanly *, no one. Mt 19:26
Don't you realize that God was * Mt 22:31
"Then why does David, * under Mt 22:43
while he was still *, Judas, one of Mt 26:47
But while he was still * these Mk 9:7
Holy Spirit was * through him when Mk 12:36
Then you will not be *, but the Mk 13:11
while he was still *, Judas (one of Mk 14:43
When he had finished *, he said Lk 5:4
Whether the demons were * Lk 8:30f
While he was still * to her, a Lk 8:49
and they were * of his death at Lk 9:31
As he was *, a woman in the crowd Lk 11:27
As he was *, one of the Pharisees Lk 11:37,38
personally, or * to you directly. Jn 5:37
He was * of Judas, son of Jn 6:71
(He was * of the Holy Spirit, Jn 7:39
As he was *, the Jewish leaders Jn 8:3
said, "and he is * to you!" Jn 9:37
"At last you are * plainly," Jn 16:29
Holy Spirit, * through King David. Act 1:16
* in languages they didn't know, Act 2:4
yet we hear them * all the native Act 2:8
He was * of Jesus, and we all Act 2:32
"[No, David was not * of himself Act 2:34
who was constantly * against the Temple Act 6:13
"Who is *, sir?" Act 9:5
for they heard them * in tongues Act 10:46,47
When he had finished *, he knelt Act 20:36
(When they heard him * in Act 22:2
" 'Who is it * to me, sir?' Act 22:8
I heard a voice * to me in Hebrew, Act 26:14
ABRAHAM WAS, HUMANLY *, the Rom 4:1
Here is the test: no one * by the 1Co 12:3
evil spirits are * through those 1Co 12:10
really the Spirit of God who is *. 1Co 12:10
Someday prophecy, and * in 1Co 13:8
You will be * by the power of the 1Co 14:2
So a person "* in tongues" 1Co 14:4
had the gift of "* in tongues" 1Co 14:5
for * in plain, simple English 1Co 14:7
If someone is given the gift of * 1Co 14:13
the spirit alone, * in another 1Co 14:16
words while "* in tongues" in an 1Co 14:19
is saying who is * in the unknown 1Co 14:26
the one who is * should stop. 1Co 14:29,30
sent by God, * with Christ's power, 2Co 2:17
him publicly, * strongly against Gal 2:11
truth at all times—* truly, dealing Eph 4:15,16
Let me say this, then, * for the Eph 4:17,18
But pray that I will keep on * Eph 6:20
They must not go around * evil of Tit 2:3
hear God's voice * to you, do not Heb 3:15
heard God's voice * to them but Heb 3:16
And to whom was God * when he Heb 3:18
He was * to all those who Heb 3:18
the people begged God to stop *. Heb 12:19
that you obey him who is * to you. Heb 12:25
God himself were * through you. 1Pe 4:11
* of Christ, who is eternal Life. 1Jn 1:2
* of that one that ends in death. 1Jn 5:17
When I turned to see who was *, Rev 1:12
I heard a voice * from the four Rev 9:13

SPEAKS
to face, as a man * to his friend. Ex 33:11
but we will surely die if he * Deu 5:25
"David, the son of Jesse, *. 2Sa 23:1
"For God * again and again, in Job 33:14
is sure. He * no careless word; Ps 12:6
his neighbor, * out against sin, Ps 15:4
anger—but when God *, the earth Ps 46:6
The Lord *. Ps 68:11,12,13
is saying—for he * peace to his Ps 85:8
When a good man *, he is worth Pro 10:20
A good man thinks before he *; Pro 15:28
When she *, her words are wise, Pro 31:26
So * our Redeemer, who will save Is 47:4
it is I, yes, I, who * to them. Is 52:6
When he * there is thunder in Jer 51:16
God when he * and could be heard Eze 10:5
of the world, the Lord God *. Eze 27:3
who * a word against the God of Dan 3:29

(SPEAKS Con't)
And he said that anyone who * Mk 7:10
burning bush, he * of God as 'the Lk 20:37,38
For this one—sent by God—* God's Jn 3:33,34
Those the Father * to, who learn Jn 6:45
cannot be untrue, * of those as Jn 10:34,35,36
* evil of God because of you. Rom 2:24
live again and * of future events Rom 4:17
For his Holy Spirit * to us Rom 8:26
you want that Christ * through me. 2Co 13:3
God * of his angels as messengers Heb 1:7
God * of these new promises, of Heb 8:13
to God who * to us from heaven! Heb 12:25
And Hebrews 6:4-8 * of the 1Jn 5:17f
itself, * highly of Demetrius. 3Jn 1:12

SPEAR
up, grabbed a *, and rushed after Num 25:7
He thrust the * all the way Num 25:8
"Point your * toward Ai, for I Jos 8:18
For Joshua kept his * pointed Jos 8:26
A shield or *. Ju 5:8
a single sword or * in the entire 1Sa 13:22
with a sword and a *, but I come to 1Sa 17:45
fiddling with his *, suddenly 1Sa 18:10
He had his * in his hand, and 1Sa 19:9,10
night, leaving the * imbedded in 1Sa 19:9,10
Then Saul hurled his * at 1Sa 20:33
he had a * or sword he could use. 1Sa 21:8
his *, surrounded by his officers. 1Sa 22:6
* in the ground beside his head. 1Sa 26:5,6,7
"Let me go and put that * 1Sa 26:8
take his * and his jug of water and 1Sa 26:11
So David took the * and jug of 1Sa 26:12
Where is the king's * and the jug 1Sa 26:16
"Here is your *, sir," David 1Sa 26:22
against his * with the enemy 2Sa 1:6
belly with the butt end of his *. 2Sa 2:23
warrior who was armed with a *; 2Sa 23:21
he wrenched the * from the 2Sa 23:21
He once killed 300 men with his * 1Ch 11:11
300 men at one time with his *. 1Ch 11:20
* was as thick as a weaver's beam. 1Ch 11:23
and pulled the * away from him and 1Ch 11:23
both shield and * and were 1Ch 12:8-13
the handle of his * was like a 1Ch 20:5
skilled in the use of * and sword. 2Ch 25:5,6
or the flashing * and javelin. Job 39:21-23
No sword can stop him, nor * nor Job 41:26
Lift your * in my defense, for Ps 35:3
the flashing of your glittering *. Hab 3:11
*, and blood and water flowed out. Jn 19:34

SPEARHANDLE
whose * was as huge as a weaver's 2Sa 21:19

SPEARHEAD
iron *, and his armor bearer walked 1Sa 17:4-7

SPEARMEN
Take 200 * and 70 mounted Act 23:23,24

SPEARS
swords and * for the Hebrews. 1Sa 13:19
from the supply of * and shields in 2Ki 11:10
troops armed with shields and *. 1Ch 12:24-37
equipped with shields and *. 1Ch 12:24-37
Shields and * were placed in 2Ch 11:12
equipped with light shields and *. 2Ch 14:8
Then Jehoiada issued * and 2Ch 23:9
Uzziah issued to them shields, * 2Ch 26:14
teeth are sharp as * and arrows. Ps 57:4
and their * into pruning hooks." Is 2:4f
tongues aim lies like poisoned *. Jer 9:8
sharpen your *, put on your armor. Jer 46:4
javelins and *, to use for Eze 39:9
beat your pruning hooks into *. Joe 3:10
and their * into pruning-hooks; Mic 4:3
and glittering * in the upraised Nah 3:3

SPEARTIP
Ishbi-benob, a giant whose * 2Sa 21:16

SPECIAL
and she was a * comfort to him Gen 24:67
So one day Jacob gave him a * Gen 37:3
was with Joseph in a very * way. Gen 39:3
day, there will be * religious Ex 12:16
are holy—my * people—do not eat any Ex 22:31
and always keep the * Bread of Ex 25:30
Make * clothes for Aaron, to Ex 28:2
whom I have given * skill as Ex 28:3
They shall also make * garments Ex 28:4
moreover, I have given * skill to Ex 31:6
seventh day is a * day of solemn Ex 31:16
craftsmen having * talents, and Ex 35:10-19
gladly used their * skill to spin Ex 35:26
to the Lord as * peace offerings: Lev 7:11
offering to show * appreciation and Lev 7:15
Aaron with the * coat, sash, robe, Lev 8:7
sister for whom he has * Lev 21:2,3
with the * anointing oil and Lev 21:10
and wearing the * garments—must not Lev 21:10
day, for it is a * day for making Lev 23:28
a person makes a * vow to give Lev 27:1
the Levites, with * responsibility Num 3:31-35
a woman takes the * vow of a Num 6:1
to the Lord in a * way, he must Num 6:1
period of his * consecration to the Num 6:3,4
of his period of * dedication. Num 6:21
are to give this * blessing to the Num 6:22,23
offering, or a * sacrifice at any Num 15:3,4
is your * gift of service. Num 18:7
there must be a *, solemn assembly Num 28:26
on that day. A * burnt offering, Num 28:27
These * offerings are in Num 28:31
These * sacrifices are in Num 29:6
Your * burnt sacrifice that day, Num 29:13
offerings, as a * sin offering, in Num 29:28
So we have brought a * Num 31:50
received this * offering from the Num 31:51,52
his * people, his own inheritance; Deu 4:20
any other * responsibilities; Deu 24:5
"Every third year is a year of * Deu 26:12
If she were still married, no * Deu 27:23f
is my * people, Deu 32:34
one from each tribe, for a * task. Jos 3:12
men chosen for a * task, one from Jos 4:2,3
and the nation of Israel gave a * Jos 19:49
be a Nazirite, a * servant of God Ju 13:5
you give us any * instructions Ju 13:12
them above the thirty * guests. 1Sa 9:22
* message for you from the Lord." 1Sa 9:26,27
it in a * place before the Lord. 1Sa 10:25
He made you a * nation for 1Sa 12:22
three thousand * troops and took 1Sa 13:2
He was Saul's * assistant, and 1Sa 18:5
so he took three thousand * 1Sa 24:2
thirty thousand * troops and led 2Sa 6:1
"I am going to show * respect 2Sa 10:2
then she baked some * bread for 2Sa 13:8
personal priest and * friend; 1Ki 4:1
earth to be your own * people." 1Ki 8:53
Benjamin: 180,000 * troops—to force 1Ki 12:21
and the Lord gave * strength to 1Ki 18:46
The king appointed his * 2Ki 7:17
wears one of the * robes." 2Ki 10:22
assessment or some * gift, use it 2Ki 12:4,5
agreed to set up a * repair fund 2Ki 12:8
one $2,000 in the form of a * tax. 2Ki 15:19,20
of the preparation of the * bread 1Ch 9:32
it was for a * reason—to give joy 1Ch 14:2
Shavsha was the king's * 1Ch 18:16
They assisted in the * 1Ch 23:31
display the * sacrificial bread, 2Ch 2:4
to celebrate these * occasions. 2Ch 2:4
Zechariah was a man who had * 2Ch 26:5
He had to construct * treasury 2Ch 32:27
They also offered the * Ez 3:5
Yet I refused to make a * levy Neh 5:18
for we needed supplies of the * Neh 10:33
the king gave a * party for the Est 1:5
he ordered a * menu for her, Est 2:9
with * perfumes and ointments. Est 2:12,13,14
Burnt animals bring no * joy to Ps 40:6
How long will you shower * favors Ps 82:2
good men's sons have a * heritage. Ps 112:2
Sabbath, and your * days for Is 1:12,13
they are still his * ones. Is 14:1
keep it separate, * and holy, then Jer 17:24
of the king's * counselors Jer 52:24,25
"There is * meaning in each Eze 4:3
Israel apart for * blessings." Eze 37:28
outer court. The * robes in which Eze 42:14
"Two * sections of land shall be Eze 45:7
"To summarize: At the * feasts Eze 46:11
It is their * portion when the Eze 48:12
None of this * land shall ever Eze 48:14
superintendent a * appreciation for Dan 1:9
God gave to Daniel * ability in Dan 1:17
He was driven off by * Hos 1:7f
And I will not give * favors to Hos 1:4
and they ate the * bread permitted Mt 12:4
to earth, and that a * messenger Mk 1:2
then—and they ate the * bread Mk 2:25,26
surely upon him in some * way." Lk 1:66
the shewbread, the * bread that was Lk 6:4
and I'll give it * attention and Lk 13:8
will be a time of * persecution. Lk 21:12
(and a very * Sabbath at that, for Jn 19:31
for a * job I have for them." Act 13:2
you brag that you are his * Rom 2:17
Are there any * benefits for them Rom 3:1
disobeyed God's * law against Rom 5:14
He took you as his own *, chosen Rom 9:4
as a * messenger to you Gentiles. Rom 11:13
of his own * olive tree. Rom 11:17
Jewish holidays as * days to Rom 14:5
If you have * days for Rom 14:6
for I am, by God's grace, a * Rom 15:15,16
of us with certain * abilities, and 1Co 3:5
* command for them from the Lord. 1Co 7:25
Gospel isn't any * credit to me—I 1Co 9:16
the Lord would give me a * reward; 1Co 9:17
It is the * joy I get from 1Co 9:18
to write about the * abilities the 1Co 12:1
Now God gives us many kinds of * 1Co 12:4
He gives * faith to another, and 1Co 12:9
seen do not require this * care. 1Co 12:24
All the * gifts and powers from 1Co 13:8
languages, and * knowledge—these 1Co 13:8
even with our * gifts, and the 1Co 13:9
these inadequate * gifts will come 1Co 13:10
nevertheless, ask also for the * 1Co 14:1
so anxious to have * gifts from the 1Co 14:12
or tell some * information God has 1Co 14:26
or any other * ability from the 1Co 14:37
gave us each our * gifts—they shook Gal 2:7,8,9
has given me this * work of showing Eph 3:2,3
power and * ability to do it well. Eph 3:7
chosen for this * joy of telling Eph 3:8
given each of us * Eph 4:7
Some of us have been given * Eph 4:11
some have * ability in winning Eph 4:11
he gives us these * abilities to do Eph 4:12
part in its own * way helps the Eph 4:15,16
have a very * place in my heart. Php 1:7
like—for he has no * favorites who Col 3:25
I have sent him on this * trip Col 4:8
having visions and * messages from 2Th 2:1
become one of the * church workers 1Ti 5:9
members of this * group because 1Ti 5:11
is a * friend of yours or not. 1Ti 5:21
May the Lord give him a * 2Ti 1:18
by giving certain * abilities from Heb 2:4
* loaves of holy bread upon it; Heb 9:1
God has given each of you some * 1Pe 4:10
for God gives * blessings to those 1Pe 5:5
folks there a * greeting from me. 3Jn 1:15
a * blessing from the Lord. Rev 1:3

SPECIALLY
Tanned rams' skins and * treated Ex 35:5-9
and ram skins dyed red, and * Ex 35:23
dyed red, the * tanned goat skins, Ex 39:33-40
for I have * chosen you," says Hag 2:23

SPECIALTY
of life, and murder is their *. Pro 1:16

SPECIFIC
The Hebrew word is not *. Gen 39:12f
Lord's * and repeated warnings. 2Ki 17:12
as well as the * amount of gold 1Ch 28:15
For you ignore God's * orders Mk 7:8

SPECIFICALLY
"But the man * asked us about Gen 43:7
"Jehovah has * appointed Bezalel Ex 35:30,31
More *, this boundary began at Jos 15:2,3,4
* against worshiping other gods. 1Ki 11:9,10

SPECIFICATIONS
and he gave * for each item in 1Ch 28:13

SPECIFIED
in the manner *, has defiled the Num 19:13
offerings, as * by the ordinances Num 29:6
the king had * that the burnt 2Ch 29:24
* for each day of the feast. Ez 3:4

SPECIFY
at the time you *, everywhere Ex 8:9

SPECIMEN
kept as a museum * forever, so that Ex 16:32
such a handsome * of manhood as 2Sa 14:25
You are a poor * if you can't Pro 24:10

SPECIMENS
* in all the land of Egypt. Gen 41:19
the finest * of men; Lam 4:7

SPECK
And why worry about a * in the Mt 7:3
help you get that * out of your Mt 7:4
"And why quibble about the * in Lk 6:41
get rid of that * in your eye,' Lk 6:42
well enough to deal with his *! Lk 6:42

SPECKLED
the goats that are * or spotted, Gen 30:31,32
females that were * and spotted Gen 30:35,36
For if he said the * animals Gen 31:8
then all the flock produced *; Gen 31:8
were streaked, *, and mottled. Gen 31:10
are *, streaked, and mottled." Gen 31:12f
nanny goats with streaked, *, and Gen 31:12

SPECTACLE
* of all Israel's crimes. Amo 3:9
What a * it was! Mt 15:31

SPECTACULAR
when she saw their * uniforms and 2Ch 9:4
did * miracles among the people. Act 6:8

SPECTER
"I see a * coming up out of the 1Sa 28:13

SPECULATE
the wall and refused to * in land; Neh 5:16

SPECULATES
The man who * is soon back to Ecc 5:15

SPECULATION
hasty * brings poverty. Pro 21:5

SPED
he * swiftly to my aid with wings Ps 18:10

SPEECH
me, for I have a * impediment." Ex 4:10
Literally, "my * is slow and Ex 4:10f
The * was given on February 15, Deu 1:1
THE * OF Zophar the Naamathite: Job 20:1
with her pretty *, her coaxing and Pro 7:21
But the wise man's * is Pro 14:3

PEECH Con't)
omes careful and persuasive *. Pro 16:23
ut a fool's * brings him to ruin. Ecc 10:12,13
isturbed by this * from the Is 37:6
will change the * of my returning Zep 3:9
will change the * of the Zep 3:9f
he peoples to a pure *." Zep 3:9f
man's heart determines his *. Mt 12:34
A good man's * reveals the rich Mt 12:35
with venom, and his * reveals it. Mt 12:35
A deaf man with a * impediment Mk 7:32
s in the heart overflows into *. Lk 6:45
his throne and made a * to them. Act 12:21
s "Their * injures others." Rom 3:13f
who have that gift of foreign *? 1Co 12:30

PEECHES
His complete biography and * are 2Ch 13:22

PEECHLESS
Or, "you will be * with Ex 14:14f
And Aaron was *. Lev 10:3
Lord, I am * before you. Ps 39:9
men— idols with * mouths and Ps 135:16
they shall stand dumbfounded, * Is 52:14,15
* stone to tell them what to do. Hab 2:19
deaf as well as *, and had not Lk 1:62f
The men with Paul stood * with Act 9:7

PEED
* of a horse is nothing to him. Ps 147:10
With blinding * and violence he Amo 5:9
will give me the * of a deer and Hab 3:19
Wear shoes that are able to * Eph 6:15

PEEDED
and * by the king's commandment. Est 8:14

PEEDIEST
out by the king's * couriers, after Est 3:15
* writer pouring out his story. Ps 45:1

PEEDING
in the distance, * after them, and Ex 14:10
the clatter of * chariots and a 2Ki 7:6

PEEDY
Bend down your ear and give me * Ps 102:2
He will make a * riddance of all Zep 1:18

PELL
So the Lord will * it out for Is 28:13
you and cast an evil * upon you? Gal 3:1

SPELLED
it is * in many modern versions. Ex 3:15f

SPELT
barley, beans, lentils, and *. Eze 4:9

SPEND
but must * the day in Lev 16:29,30
shall * the day in quiet humility; Lev 16:31
Anyone who does not * the day in Lev 23:29
They were planning to * the night Jos 2:1
Should he * his time chasing one 1Sa 24:14
your shoulders, * your time 2Ch 35:3
I also required my officials to * Neh 5:16
* your time persecuting him? Job 7:17
* their time singing and dancing. Job 21:12,13
the poor must * all their time just Job 24:5
Turn from all known sin and * Ps 34:14
town and * their time cursing me. Ps 35:16
They plot my ruin and * all their Ps 38:12
up riches for someone else to *. Ps 39:5,6
and help him, and * your time with Ps 50:18
of crime. They * long hours with Ps 64:6
help us to * them as we should. Ps 90:12
For they * their days plotting Pro 24:2
the Lord, do not * your time with Pro 31:3
For though I * my life searching Ecc 2:20-23
have, the more you *, right up to Ecc 5:11
Wise men and fools alike * their Ecc 6:7,8
It is better to * your time at Ecc 7:2
Then I decided to * my time Ecc 8:15
all free! Why * your money on Is 55:2
based on lies; you * your time Is 59:4
doing them. You * your time and Is 59:5
in order to * more time with his Mk 9:30,31
their sins, not to * my time with Lk 5:32
to protect, and to * his time at Lk 12:45
And each evening he returned to * Lk 21:37,38
like food. No, * your energy Jn 6:27
"We should * our time preaching, Act 6:2
Then we can * our time in Act 6:4
Athens seemed to * all their time Act 17:21
harbor—a poor place to * the Act 27:12
Don't * your time in wild parties Rom 13:12,13
An unmarried man can * his time 1Co 7:32
every moment we * in these earthly 2Co 5:6
themselves, but to * their lives 2Co 5:15
* these lives in helping others. Eph 2:10
don't * your time worrying about Col 3:2
whole idea and * their time arguing 1Ti 1:6
myths and legends. * your time and 1Ti 4:7
to be lazy and * their time 1Ti 5:13
Then the church can * its money 1Ti 5:16

SPENDING
be * the night among the troops; 2Sa 17:8
turn came for * the night with King Est 2:12,13,14
comes back after * your money on Lk 15:30
After * some time there, he left Act 18:23
and they are * their lives helping 1Co 16:15
and quietness, * our time in godly 1Ti 2:2
help and * much time in prayer; 1Ti 5:5
but not if they are * their time 1Ti 5:6
and clean minded, * their time in Tit 2:5
and you won't be * the rest of 1Pe 4:2

SPENDS
And he * his time thinking of all Pro 6:14
but the foolish man * whatever he Pro 21:20
It is the one who * long hours in Pro 23:29,30
any Christian who * his days in 2Th 3:6

SPENT
brother's fury is *, and he Gen 27:44
So Jacob * the next seven years Gen 29:20
and afterwards * the night with Gen 31:54
Jacob * that night in the camp. Gen 32:21
Your strength shall be * in Lev 26:20
camp again and * the night there. Jos 6:11
He himself * the night in the Jos 8:11,12,13
and * the night with a prostitute. Ju 16:1
He and his men * their time 1Sa 27:8
* much time in prayer about it. 2Sa 21:1
from now on it must all be * on 2Ki 12:7
days, for I * the time in prayer to Neh 1:4
He must have * much time with Job 34:7,8
A single day * in your Temple is Ps 84:10
say how one's days can best be *? Ecc 6:12
I have * my strength for them Is 49:4
to save Daniel. He * the rest of Dan 6:14
* everything she had on doctors Lk 8:43,44
Literally, "* some time." Act 15:33f
Macedonia, Paul * his full time Act 18:5
bodies is time * away from our 2Co 5:6
You have * your years here on Jas 5:5

SPERM
her, he spilled the * on the bed Gen 38:9

SPICE
every other * that can be bought? Sol 3:6
aloes, and every other lovely *. Sol 4:13,14
his garden, to his * beds, to Sol 6:2

SPICED
I would give you * wine to drink, Sol 8:2

SPICES
*, and herbs from Gilead to Egypt. Gen 37:25
gifts—balm, honey, *, myrrh, Gen 43:11
oil for the lamps, * for the Ex 25:1
shall burn sweet * on the altar, Ex 30:7
the choicest of *—eighteen pounds Ex 30:22,23
"Use sweet *—stacte, onycha, Ex 30:34
* for the anointing oil and for Ex 35:5-9
chestpiece; and *, and oil—for the Ex 35:28
Then, from sweet *, he made the Ex 37:29
*, just as the Lord had commanded. Ex 40:27
carrying *, gold, and jewels; 1Ki 10:2
quantity of * and precious gems; 1Ki 10:10
* King Solomon had ever received. 1Ki 10:10
myrrh, *, horses, and mules. 1Ki 10:25
silver, gold, *, aromatic oils, the 2Ki 20:13
fine flour, wine, incense, and *. 1Ch 9:29
Other priests prepared the * and 1Ch 9:30
incense and sweet * before God, and 2Ch 2:4
of *, gold, and jewels. 2Ch 9:1
quantities of * of incomparable 2Ch 9:9
armor, *, horses, and mules. 2Ch 9:24
with sweet * and ointments, and his 2Ch 16:13,14
stones, and *, and for his shields 2Ch 32:27
stag on the mountains of *." Sol 2:17
fragrant than all the richest *. Sol 4:10
I gather my myrrh with my * and Sol 5:1
like sweetly scented beds of *. Sol 5:13
deer upon the mountains of *." Sol 8:14
of silver, gold, * and perfumes. Is 39:2
all kinds of *, jewels and gold. Eze 27:22
out and purchased embalming *. Mk 16:1
* and ointments to embalm him; Lk 23:56
saturated with the *, as is the Jn 19:40
and marble; and * and perfumes and Rev 18:13

SPIDER
is as fragile as a * web, as full Job 27:18

SPIDER'S
God is trusting in a * web. Job 8:14

SPIDERWEBS
the ropes from his arms like *! Ju 16:12

SPIED
river bank, she * the little boat Ex 2:5
So they * out the land all the Num 13:21
Our brothers who * out the land Deu 1:28
burying a friend * these marauders 2Ki 13:20,21

SPIES
But he said to them, "You are *. Gen 42:8,9
We are not *!" Gen 42:11
"It is as I said: you are *." Gen 42:14f
You are *. Gen 42:14
then I'll know you are *." Gen 42:16
told him, "and took us for *. Gen 42:30
said, 'we are honest men, not *. Gen 42:31
whether you are * or honest men; Gen 42:34
Moses, "Send * into the land of Num 13:2
the other * said. Num 13:31
So the majority report of the * Num 13:32
two of the *, Joshua (the son of Num 14:6
" 'Since the * were in the land Num 14:34,35
Then the ten * who had incited Num 14:36,37,38
Of all the *, only Joshua and Num 14:36,37,38
same route as the *), he mobilized Num 21:1
* to look over the Jazer area; Num 21:31,32
let's send out * to discover the Deu 1:22
twelve *, one from each tribe. Deu 1:23
THEN JOSHUA SENT two * from the Jos 2:1
suspected of being * had arrived in Jos 2:2
"They are *," he explained. Jos 2:3
but I didn't know they were *. Jos 2:4
the window. The * went up into the Jos 2:22
Then the two * came down from Jos 2:23
house, for she protected our *. Jos 6:17
Then Joshua said to the two *, Jos 6:22
the * sent to Jericho by Joshua. Jos 6:25
You will remember that as * we Jos 14:12
So the * returned to their Ju 18:8
the five * told the others. Ju 18:14
Then the five * entered the Ju 18:17
sent out * to watch his movements. 1Sa 26:3,4
was there, he sent * to every part 2Sa 15:10
From there she * her prey, from Job 39:29
"Teacher," these * said, "we Mk 12:14
gave a friendly welcome to the *. Heb 11:31

SPIKE
nose, or pierce his jaw with a *? Job 41:2

SPILL
on it will * to the ground." 1Ki 13:3
send troublers to * her out from Jer 48:12

SPILLED
her, he * the sperm on the bed Gen 38:9
Literally, "* it on the ground." Gen 38:9f
in full for all our blood she *!" Jer 51:34,35
your blood will be * in your own Eze 21:32
would be * and the skins ruined. Mt 9:17
The wine would be * out and the Mk 2:22

SPILLING
tipping southward, * over Judah." Jer 1:13
ruining the skins and * the wine. Lk 5:37
he burst open, * out his bowels. Act 1:18

SPILLS
bedding the semen * on must be Lev 15:17

SPIN
to * the goats' hair into cloth. Ex 35:26
of their chariots * like the wind. Is 5:28
They don't toil and *, and yet Lk 12:27

SPINNING
The women skilled in sewing and * Ex 35:25
time and energy in * evil plans Is 59:5

SPINS
The voice of the Lord * and Ps 29:9
wool and flax and busily * it. Pro 31:13

SPIRIT
with the * of God brooding over Gen 1:2
time that beings from the * world Gen 6:1
Then Jehovah said, "My * must Gen 6:3
beings from the * world were Gen 6:4
filled with the * of God." Gen 41:38
had sent him, his * revived. Gen 45:27
broken * and the cruel bondage." Ex 6:8,9f
him with the * of God, giving him Ex 31:3
stirred by God's * returned with Ex 35:21
I will take of the * which is on Num 11:17
Lord took of the * that was upon Num 11:25
and when the * rested upon them, Num 11:25
camp, and when the * rested upon Num 11:26
would put his * upon them all!" Num 11:29
Then the * of God came upon him, Num 24:2
Nun), who has the * in him, and Num 27:18
was full of the * of wisdom, for Deu 34:9
to save them. The * of the Lord Ju 3:10
Then the * of the Lord came upon Ju 6:34
At that time the * of the Lord Ju 11:29
And the * of the Lord began to Ju 13:25
At that moment the * of the Lord Ju 14:6
Then the * of the Lord came upon Ju 14:19
* was revived as he drank. Ju 15:19
"At that time the * of the Lord 1Sa 10:6
them, and the * of God came upon 1Sa 10:10
Then the * of God came strongly 1Sa 11:6
and the * of Jehovah came upon 1Sa 16:13
But the * of the Lord had left 1Sa 16:14
sent a tormenting * that filled him 1Sa 16:14
* is bothering you," they said. 1Sa 16:15,16
And whenever the tormenting * 1Sa 16:23
and the evil * would go away. 1Sa 16:23
fact, a tormenting * from God 1Sa 18:10
* from the Lord attacked him. 1Sa 19:9,10
prophesying, the * of God came upon 1Sa 19:20
But on the way to Naioth the * 1Sa 19:23
"Will you bring his * up?" 1Sa 28:7,8
The * of the Lord spoke by me, 2Sa 23:2
there was no more * in her! 1Ki 10:5
this child's * return to him." 1Ki 17:21
and the * of the child returned, 1Ki 17:22
I leave you, the * of the Lord will 1Ki 18:12
will go as a lying * in the mouths 1Ki 22:22
The Lord has put a lying * in the 1Ki 22:23
"When did the * of the Lord leave 1Ki 22:24
* of Elijah rests upon Elisha!" 2Ki 2:15

(SPIRIT Con't)
perhaps the * of the Lord has 2Ki 2:16
Then the Holy * came upon them, 1Ch 12:18
For the Holy * had given David 1Ch 28:12
The word in the Hebrew for * 1Ch 28:12f
THEN THE * of God came upon 2Ch 15:1
but finally a * stepped forward 2Ch 18:19,20
'I will be a lying * in the mouth 2Ch 18:21
has put a lying * in the mouth of 2Ch 18:22
"When did the * of the Lord 2Ch 18:23
and children, the * of the Lord 2Ch 20:14
Then the * of God came upon 2Ch 24:20
stirred up the * of Cyrus to make 2Ch 36:22,23
You sent your good * to instruct Neh 9:20
with terror, as a * passed before Job 4:15
comparison? His * is broader than Job 11:9
is buried, where does his * go? Job 14:10
but my * won't let me stop. Job 20:3
no wonder my * is so troubled. Job 21:4
are made beautiful by his *; Job 26:13
Rather, it is the * in a man, the Job 32:8,9
and the * within me urges me on. Job 32:18
For the * of God has made me, Job 33:4
If God were to withdraw his *, Job 34:14
Into your hand I commit my *. Ps 31:5,6
Don't take your Holy * from me. Ps 51:11
It is a broken * you Ps 51:17
my heart; my * is heavy within me. Ps 69:20
Then you send your *, and new Ps 104:30
I can never be lost to your *! Ps 139:7
Lead me in good paths, for your * Ps 143:10
I'll pour out the * of wisdom Pro 1:23
but a broken * makes one sick. Pro 17:22
Literally, "*." Pro 18:14f
Literally, "*." Pro 20:27f
For who can prove that the * of Ecc 3:21
upward and the * of animals goes Ecc 3:21
No one can hold back his * from Ecc 8:8
A quiet * will quiet his bad Ecc 10:4
in which a human * is infused into Ecc 11:5
the * returns to God who gave it. Ecc 12:7
And the * of the Lord shall rest Is 11:2
rest upon him, the * of wisdom, Is 11:2
and might; the * of knowledge and Is 11:2
The Lord has sent a * of Is 19:14
out upon you a * of deep sleep. Is 29:10
until at last the * is poured down Is 32:15
his * will make it all come true. Is 34:16
Who can advise the * of the Lord Is 40:13
I have put my * upon him; Is 42:1
and breath and * to everyone in all Is 42:5
And I will pour out my * and my Is 44:3
And now the Lord God and his * Is 48:16
Lord: "My Holy * shall not leave Is 59:21
THE * OF the Lord God is upon me, Is 61:1
him and grieved his Holy *. Is 63:10
his Holy * to be among his people? Is 63:11
the * of the Lord gave them rest Is 63:14
in body but not in *—the Egyptians, Jer 9:25,26
And when they come in that *, Jer 16:21
For the Lord has stirred up the * Jer 51:11
my heart is broken, my * poured Lam 2:11
Wherever their * Eze 1:12
Literally, "the *." Eze 1:12f
For the * of the four living Eze 1:19,20,21
so wherever their * went, the Eze 1:19,20,21
And the * entered into me as he Eze 2:2
Then the * lifted me up and the Eze 3:12
The * lifted me up and took me Eze 3:14,15
in the heat of my *"—not Eze 3:14,15f
Then the * entered into me and Eze 3:24
And the * lifted me up into the Eze 8:3
so did the wheels, for the * Eze 10:17
THEN THE * lifted me and brought Eze 11:1
Then the * said to me, "Son of Eze 11:1
Then the * of the Lord came upon Eze 11:5
give you one heart and a new *; Eze 11:19
Afterwards the * of God carried Eze 11:24
receive a new heart and a new *. Eze 18:31
Every * will faint; Eze 21:7
did not leave her * of prostitution Eze 23:8
put a new * within you. Eze 36:26
And I will put my * within you Eze 36:27
away by the * of the Lord to a Eze 37:1
the four winds, O *, and breathe Eze 37:9
I will put my * into you, and Eze 37:14
* upon them, says the Lord God." Eze 39:29
Then the * took me up and brought Eze 43:5
man in whom is the * of the holy Dan 4:8
"I know that the * of the holy Dan 4:9
But you can tell me, for the * of Dan 4:18
within him the * of the holy gods. Dan 5:11
I have heard that you have the * Dan 5:14
the mighty Evil * who overrules the Dan 10:13
through these * rulers of Persia. Dan 10:13
God again, for the * of adultery is Hos 5:4
pour out my * upon all of you! Joe 2:28
And I will pour out my * even on Joe 2:29
Do you think the * of the Lord Mic 2:7
power, with the * of the Lord, Mic 3:8
that my * would remain among you; Hag 2:5
power, but by my *, says the Lord Zec 4:6
*, though you are few and weak.' Zec 4:6
his * through the early prophets. Zec 7:12
formed the * of man within him: Zec 12:1
"Then I will pour out the * of Zec 12:10
she became pregnant by the Holy *. Mt 1:18
has been conceived by the Holy *. Mt 1:20
Or, "in the Holy * and in fire." Mt 3:11f
the Holy * and with fire. Mt 3:11
him and he saw the * of God coming Mt 3:16
*, to be tempted there by Satan. Mt 4:1
will be the * of your heavenly Mt 10:20
I will put my * upon him, Mt 12:18
out demons by the * of God, then Mt 12:28
against the Holy * shall never be Mt 12:31,32
of the Holy *, call him 'Lord'?" Mt 22:43
For the * indeed is willing, but Mt 26:41
again, dismissed his *, and died. Mt 27:50
and of the Holy *, and then teach Mt 28:19
God's Holy *!" Mk 1:8
open and the Holy * in the form of Mk 1:10
Immediately the Holy * urged Mk 1:12,13
At that the evil * screamed and Mk 1:26
but blasphemy against the Holy * Mk 3:29
said, "Come out, you evil *." Mk 5:7,8
said—and the Holy * was speaking Mk 12:36
be speaking, but the Holy * will. Mk 13:11
For though the * is willing Mk 14:38
loud cry, and dismissed his *. Mk 15:37
he dismissed his *, he exclaimed, Mk 15:39
laws in * as well as in letter. Lk 1:6
*, even from before his birth! Lk 1:15
* and power like Elijah, the Lk 1:17
The angel replied, "The Holy * Lk 1:35
she was filled with the Holy *. Lk 1:41
the Holy * and gave this prophecy: Lk 1:67
Literally, "became strong in *." Lk 1:80f
with the Holy * and constantly Lk 2:25
For the Holy * had revealed to Lk 2:26
The Holy * had impelled him to Lk 2:27
you with fire—with the Holy *. Lk 3:16
and the Holy * in the form of a Lk 3:22
THEN JESUS, FULL of the Holy *, Lk 4:1
being urged by the * out into the Lk 4:1
"The * of the Lord is upon me; Lk 4:18,19
joy of the Holy * and said, "I Lk 10:21
Holy * to those who ask for him?" Lk 11:13
Holy * shall never be forgiven. Lk 12:10
for the Holy * will give you the Lk 12:12
in such agony of * that he broke Lk 22:44
I commit my * to you," and with Lk 23:46
Literally, "yielded up the *." Lk 23:46f
"And now I will send the Holy * Lk 24:49
until the Holy * comes and fills Lk 24:49
seeing the Holy * in the form of a Jn 1:32
you see the Holy * descending and Jn 1:33
the Holy *.' Jn 1:33
and the *, he cannot enter the Jn 3:5
Holy * gives new life from heaven; Jn 3:6
will go next, so it is with the *. Jn 3:8
words, for God's * is upon him Jn 3:33,34
For God is *, and we must have Jn 4:21-24
Only the Holy * gives eternal Jn 6:63
Literally, "It is the * who Jn 6:63f
(He was speaking of the Holy * Jn 7:39
but the * had not yet been given, Jn 7:39
great anguish of * and exclaimed, Jn 13:21
He is the Holy *, the Spirit who Jn 14:17
He is the Holy Spirit, the * who Jn 14:17
I mean the Holy *—he will teach you Jn 14:26
Holy *, the source of all truth. Jn 15:26
When the Holy *, who is truth, Jn 16:13
his head and dismissed his *. Jn 19:30
told them, "Receive the Holy *. Jn 20:22
instructions from the Holy *. Act 1:1
until the Holy * came upon them in Act 1:4
the Holy * in just a few days." Act 1:5
But when the Holy * has come Act 1:8
*, speaking through King David. Act 1:16
with the Holy * and began speaking Act 2:4
for the Holy * gave them this Act 2:4
pour out my Holy * upon all Act 2:17
Yes, the Holy * shall come upon Act 2:18
to send the Holy *—with the results Act 2:33
receive this gift, the Holy *. Act 2:38
with the Holy *, said to them, Act 4:8
ago by the Holy * through our Act 4:25,26
with the Holy * and boldly preached Act 4:31
you were lying to the Holy *. Act 5:3
to test the * of God's ability to Act 5:9
"to try the * of the Lord." Act 5:9f
and so is the Holy *, who is given Act 5:32
full of the Holy *, who are well Act 6:3
full of faith and the Holy *), Act 6:5
against Stephen's wisdom and *. Act 6:10
you forever resist the Holy *? Act 7:51
But Stephen, full of the Holy *, Act 7:55
"Lord Jesus, receive my *." Act 7:59
receive the Holy *, for as yet he Act 8:15
and they received the Holy *. Act 8:17
this—that the Holy * was given when Act 8:18
they will receive the Holy *!" Act 8:
The Holy * said to Philip, "Go Act 8:
of the water, the * of the Lord Act 8:
Holy * and get your sight back." Act 9:
and in the comfort of the Holy *. Act 9:
vision, the Holy * said to him, Act 10:
God with the Holy * and with power, Act 10:
* fell upon all those listening! Act 10:
* would be given to Gentiles too! Act 10:
the Holy * just as we did?" Act 10:46,
The Holy * told me to go with Act 11:
sermon, the Holy * fell on them, Act 11:
the Holy *.' Act 11:
of the Holy * and strong in faith. Act 11:2
to predict by the * that a great Act 11:2
fasting the Holy * said, "Dedicate Act 13
Directed by the Holy * they went Act 13
Then Paul, filled with the Holy * Act 13
with joy and with the Holy *. Act 13:5
Holy *, just as he gave him to us. Act 15
good to the Holy * and to us to Act 15:27,28,2
because the Holy * had told them Act 16
but again the * of Jesus said no. Act 16
"Did you receive the Holy * Act 19
What is the Holy *?" Act 19
heads, the Holy * came on them, and Act 19
Paul felt impelled by the Holy * Act 19:2
Literally, "purposed in the *." Act 19:2
there irresistibly by the Holy *, Act 20:2
that the Holy * has told me in city Act 20:2
blood—for the Holy * is holding you Act 20:2
Paul—the Holy * prophesying through Act 21:
said, "The Holy * declares, 'So Act 21:1
or even eternal * within us, Act 23:
Literally, "nor *." Act 23:8
"Perhaps a * or angel spoke to Act 23:
ears: "The Holy * was right when Act 28:2
given us the Holy * to fill our Rom 5:
of the life-giving *—and this power Rom 8:
after the Holy * and no longer obey Rom 8:
after the Holy * find themselves Rom 8:
Following after the Holy * leads Rom 8:
have the * of God living in you. Rom 8:
doesn't have the * of Christ living Rom 8:
but your * will live, for Christ Rom 8:1
Or possibly, "but the Holy * who Rom 8:10
Literally, "but the * is life Rom 8:10
And if the * of God, who raised Rom 8:1
same Holy * living within you. Rom 8:1
power of the Holy * you crush it Rom 8:1
For all who are led by the * of Rom 8:14
For his Holy * speaks to us Rom 8:16
we have the Holy * within us as a Rom 8:23
—the Holy * helps us with our Rom 8:26
but the Holy * prays for us with Rom 8:26
course, what the * is saying as he Rom 8:27
Christ knows and the Holy * knows Rom 9:1
and peace and joy from the Holy *. Rom 14:17
and pleasing to him by the Holy *. Rom 15:15,16
*—pray much with me for my work. Rom 15:30
God has sent his * to tell us, and 1Co 2:10
tell us, and his * searches out and 1Co 2:10
God's thoughts except God's own *. 1Co 2:11
given us his * (not the world's 1Co 2:12
(not the world's *) to tell us 1Co 2:12
to us by the Holy *, not words that 1Co 2:13
God, which the Holy * teaches us. 1Co 2:14
who have the Holy * within them can 1Co 2:14
understand what the Holy * means. 1Co 2:14
who are filled with the *. 1Co 3:1
God, and that the * of God lives 1Co 3:16
I will be there in *— and cast out 1Co 5:3,4
* of our God have done for you. 1Co 6:11
home of the Holy * God gave you, 1Co 6:19
Literally, "pure in body and in * 1Co 7:34f
from God's * when I say this. 1Co 7:40
abilities the Holy * gives to each 1Co 12:1
speak messages from the * of God. 1Co 12:3
the power of the * of God can curse 1Co 12:3
unless the Holy * is helping him. 1Co 12:3
* who is the source of them all. 1Co 12:4
The Holy * displays God's power 1Co 12:7
To one person the * gives the 1Co 12:8
this is his gift from the same *. 1Co 12:8
the * of God who is speaking. 1Co 12:10
It is the same and only Holy * 1Co 12:11
But the Holy * has fitted us all 1Co 12:13
body by the one *, and have all 1Co 12:13
all been given that same Holy *. 1Co 12:13
abilities the Holy * gives, and 1Co 14:1
the * but it will all be a secret. 1Co 14:2
from the Holy *, ask him for the 1Co 14:12
understand, my * is praying but I 1Co 14:14
thank God with the * alone, 1Co 14:16
from the Holy * should be the first 1Co 14:37
that, for he was life-giving *. 1Co 15:45
given us his Holy * in our hearts 2Co 1:22
but by the * of the living God; 2Co 3:3
is life for them from the Holy *. 2Co 3:6
in the new way, the Holy * gives 2Co 3:6
when the Holy * is giving life? 2Co 3:8

PIRIT Con't)
The Lord is the * who gives them 2Co 3:17
And as the * of the Lord works 2Co 3:18
he has given us his Holy *. 2Co 5:5
loving and filled with the Holy *. 2Co 6:6
whether of body or *, and purify 2Co 7:1
also in the * of cheerful giving. 2Co 8:7
or a different * than the Holy 2Co 11:4
than the Holy * you received, or 2Co 11:4
or just my *, for I don't know; 2Co 12:2,3
For we have the same Holy *, and 2Co 12:18
receive the Holy * by trying to Gal 3:2
Of course not, for the Holy * Gal 3:2
power of the Holy * and work Gal 3:5
Holy * through this faith. Gal 3:14
God has sent the * of his Son into Gal 4:6
Where is that happy * that we Gal 4:15
born of the Holy * are persecuted Gal 4:29
But we by the help of the Holy * Gal 5:5
that the Holy * tells us to do; Gal 5:17
to do when the * has his way with Gal 5:17
guided by the Holy * you need no Gal 5:18
But when the Holy * controls our Gal 5:22
good things of the *, he will reap Gal 6:8
life which the Holy * gives him. Gal 6:8
Christ by the Holy *, who long ago Eph 1:13
each other by the *, and are part Eph 2:22
* to his apostles and prophets. Eph 3:5
inner strengthening of his Holy *. Eph 3:16
by the Holy *, and so be at peace Eph 4:3
we have the same *, and we have all Eph 4:4
Don't cause the Holy * sorrow by Eph 4:30
be filled instead with the Holy * Eph 5:18
of wicked spirits in the * world. Eph 6:12
of the *—which is the Word of God. Eph 6:17
and as the Holy * helps me, this is Php 1:19
in the Lord, sharing the same *? Php 2:1
which the Holy * has given you. Col 1:8
we can't; the * world with its Col 1:16
you, for the Holy * gave you great 1Th 1:5
joy from the Holy * in spite of the 1Th 1:6
God who gives his Holy * to you. 1Th 4:8
Do not smother the Holy *. 1Th 5:19
and may your * and soul and body 1Th 5:23
work of the Holy * and by your 2Th 2:13
and pure in his *, was served by 1Ti 3:16
BUT THE HOLY * tells us clearly 1Ti 4:1
For the Holy *, God's gift, does 2Ti 1:7
the Holy * who lives within you. 2Ti 1:14
Lord Jesus Christ be with your *. 2Ti 4:22
indwelling Holy * whom he poured Tit 3:5
Lord Jesus Christ be upon your *. Phm 1:25
the Holy * to those who believe; Heb 2:4
superior, the Holy * warns us to Heb 3:7,8
such pressure of * as he underwent Heb 5:7f
shared in the Holy *, and know how Heb 6:4
And the Holy * uses all this to Heb 9:8
the eternal Holy *, Christ Heb 9:14
And the Holy * testifies that Heb 10:15
outraged the Holy * who brings Heb 10:29
when there is no * in it, so faith Jas 2:26
says that the Holy *, whom God has Jas 4:5
And the Holy * has been at work 1Pe 1:2
They wondered what the * of 1Pe 1:11
Holy * who spoke to them; 1Pe 1:12
* which is so precious to God. 1Pe 3:4
But though his body died, his * 1Pe 3:18
and it was in the * that he 1Pe 3:19
that happens the * of God will come 1Pe 4:14
Or, "the glory of the * of God is 1Pe 4:14f
It was the Holy * within these 2Pe 1:20,21
that, for the Holy * has come upon 1Jn 2:20
But you have received the Holy * 1Jn 2:27
* he has given us tells us so. 1Jn 3:24
is from the Holy * is to ask: Does 1Jn 4:2
And he has put his own Holy * 1Jn 4:13
And the Holy *, forever truthful, 1Jn 5:6,7,8
voice of the Holy * in our hearts, 1Jn 5:6,7,8
Literally, "the *, and the water, 1Jn 5:6,7,8f
Blasphemy against the Holy * 1Jn 5:17f
they do not have the Holy * Jud 1:19
power and strength of the Holy *. Jud 1:20
and from the seven-fold * Rev 1:4
of the Holy * are described, and Rev 1:4f
to what the * is saying to the Rev 2:7
listen to what the * is saying to Rev 2:11
listen to what the * is saying to Rev 2:17
what the * says to the churches. Rev 2:29
the one who has the seven-fold * Rev 3:1
the * is saying to the churches. Rev 3:6
the * is saying to the churches. Rev 3:13
the * is saying to the churches." Rev 3:22
And instantly I was, in *, there Rev 4:2
representing the seven-fold * Rev 4:5
lamps are equated with the one *. Rev 4:5f
which represent the seven-fold * Rev 5:6
the seven lamps and the one *. Rev 5:6f
a half days, the * of life from God Rev 11:11
Yes, says the *, they are blest Rev 14:13
So the angel took me in * into Rev 17:3
devils and every kind of evil *. Rev 18:2
of Jesus is the * of prophecy." Rev 19:10f
The * and the bride say, 'Come.' Rev 22:17

SPIRIT-MEDIUMS
He consulted *, too, and 2Ch 33:6

SPIRIT-MESSENGERS
No, for the angels are only * Heb 1:14

SPIRIT'S
I felt the * presence, but Job 4:16
it was by the Holy * power Mk 3:30
Galilee, full of the Holy * power. Lk 4:14
Do we have the Holy * help? Jn 4:21-24
of faith and the Holy * power, Act 6:8
the Holy * power within you. Rom 15:13
from God—all by the Holy * power. Rom 15:19
but the Holy * power was in my 1Co 2:4
So we use the Holy * words to 1Co 2:13
words to explain the Holy * facts. 1Co 2:13
May God's love and the Holy * 2Co 13:14
obey only the Holy * instructions. Gal 5:16
now by the Holy * power, let us Gal 5:25
us follow the Holy * leading in Gal 5:25
and the * seal upon us means that Eph 1:14
with the Holy * help because of Eph 2:18
in line with the Holy * wishes. Eph 6:18

SPIRITISM
idolatry, * (that is, encouraging Gal 5:20

SPIRITS
the people's sacrificing to evil * Lev 17:7
the God of the * of all mankind, Num 27:16
call on the evil * for aid, or be a Deu 18:10
or call forth the * of the dead. Deu 18:11
them, and lightened their *. Job 29:24
My health fails; my * droop, yet Ps 73:26
Literally, "*." Ps 104:4f
evil *, as the Philistines do. Is 2:6
are puny flesh, not mighty *! Is 31:3
with contrite, humble * dwell; Is 57:15
to worship evil *, and they eat Is 65:4
the four heavenly * who stand Zec 6:5
to cast out evil * and to heal Mt 10:1
finds seven other * more evil than Mt 12:43,44,45
"Why, even evil * obey his Mk 1:27
Then the evil * came out of the Mk 5:13
the blind and casting out evil *. Lk 7:20,21,22
Many evil * were cast out, Act 8:7
know whether evil * are speaking 1Co 12:10
Literally, "The * of the prophets 1Co 14:32f
For we shall not be merely * 2Co 5:3
of wicked * in the spirit world. Eph 6:12
it is worshiping him with our *. Php 3:3
Lord Jesus Christ be upon your *. Php 4:23
and to the * of the redeemed in Heb 12:23
he visited the * in prison, and 1Pe 3:19
preached to them— * of those who, 1Pe 3:20
live in their * as God lives. 1Pe 4:6
other with humble *, for God gives 1Pe 5:5
Literally, "the seven *." Rev 1:4f
Literally, "the seven * of God." Rev 3:1f
Literally, "the seven * of God." Rev 4:5f
Literally, "the seven * of God"; Rev 5:6f
And I saw three evil * disguised Rev 16:13

SPIRITUAL
land, for they are * prostitutes, Ex 34:15
for he had destroyed the * fiber 2Ch 28:19
"Those with * understanding will Dan 11:33
people in utter * darkness, Jon 4:11
the time of Israel's * rebirth; Mic 5:3
your food for a * purpose, don't do Mt 6:16
you are in deep * darkness. Mt 6:23
Those who were receptive to * Mt 13:12,13f
but there is no * defilement from Mt 15:20
—is our worship * and real? Jn 4:21-24
you how to get this true * life. Jn 6:63
Literally, "some * gift . Rom 1:11,12f
So Abraham is the * father of Rom 4:11
And Abraham is also the * father Rom 4:12
this wonderful * gift of the Gospel Rom 15:27
to share in their * blessings, they Rom 15:27f
every * gift and power for doing 1Co 1:7
Or, "interpreting * truth in 1Co 2:13f
spiritual truth in * language." 1Co 2:13f
But the * man has insight into 1Co 2:15
have all the * food you need. 1Co 4:8
you still so conceited, so "*"? 1Co 5:2
for causing great * damage to a 1Co 8:11
We have planted good * seed in 1Co 9:11
Literally, "For they drank of a * 1Co 10:3,4f
as a mighty Rock of * refreshment. 1Co 10:3,4
are also supernatural, * bodies. 1Co 15:44
God gives us *, heavenly bodies. 1Co 15:46
Keep your eyes open for * danger; 1Co 16:13
We are poor, but we give rich * 2Co 6:10
I have for your * good, even though 2Co 12:15
never gave you * life in the first Gal 3:3
a harvest of * decay and death; Gal 6:8
keep on growing in * knowledge and Php 1:9
to make you wise about * things; Col 1:9
but by a * operation, the baptism Col 2:11
and hymns and * songs, singing to Col 3:16
is all right, but * exercise is 1Ti 4:8
able to eat solid * food and Heb 5:14
about baptism and * gifts Heb 6:2
hurting many in their * lives. Heb 12:15
new ideas. Your * strength comes as Heb 13:9
Obey your * leaders and be Heb 13:17
But grow in * strength and 2Pe 3:18
* darkness and sin, we are lying. 1Jn 1:6
is wandering in * darkness and 1Jn 2:11
causes physical death or * death. 1Jn 5:17f
Spirit results in * death (Mark 1Jn 5:17f

SPIRITUALLY
deep trial, King Ahaz collapsed *. 2Ch 28:22
Let those who are * Mt 8:22
Or, "Let those who are * dead Lk 9:60f
You must also be born *." Jn 3:5f
to those who are * blind and to Jn 9:39
You are full and * contented, 1Co 4:8
helps himself grow *, but one who 1Co 14:4
Who is * hurt without my fury 2Co 11:29
you up * and not to help myself. 2Co 12:19
though we were * dead and doomed by Eph 2:5
in the exercise of keeping * fit. 1Ti 4:7
So exercise yourself * and 1Ti 4:8
nor become * dull and indifferent, Heb 6:12
will grow strong * and become 2Pe 1:8
And you don't realize that * you Rev 3:17
For they are * undefiled, pure Rev 14:4

SPIT
her father had but * in her face Num 12:14
from his foot and * in his face. Deu 25:9
me alone—even long enough to *? Job 7:19
the people; they * in my face. Job 17:6
I do not hide from shame—they * Is 50:6
the fish to * up Jonah on the Jon 2:10
They will mock me and * on me Mk 10:34
Then some of them began to * at Mk 14:65
with a cane, and * on him and went Mk 15:19
I will * you out of my mouth! Rev 3:16

SPITE
But there is hope for Israel in * Ez 10:2
in the faith in * of all the Act 14:22
you have made me so happy in * of 2Co 7:4
the Holy Spirit in * of the trials 1Th 1:6
faith in God, in * of all the 2Th 1:4
become a mother in * of her old Heb 11:11

SPITEFULLY
Don't testify * against an Pro 24:28,29

SPITS
Anyone he * on is ceremonially Lev 15:8

SPITTING
me, and don't mind * in my face. Job 30:10

SPITTLE
doors and let his * flow down his 1Sa 21:13
the man's tongue with the *. Mk 7:33
made mud from the * and smoothed Jn 9:6

SPLASHED
The other half he * against the Ex 24:6

SPLENDID
stood around in * uniforms, his 1Ki 10:5
in all the world so * as that one. 1Ki 10:20
O mighty mountains in Bashan! O * Ps 68:15,16
and said, "I have chosen a * Ps 89:19
* crown for the King of kings. Is 62:3
water to become a * vine, producing Eze 17:8
give you all these * kingdoms and Lk 4:6,7
They were * in appearance, Lk 9:31
"The next man also reported a * Lk 19:18
here and are * examples of those 2Co 8:23
Guard well the *, God-given 2Ti 1:14
To him be all glory and * honor, 2Pe 3:18

SPLENDIDLY
said, "who was * clothed and lived Lk 16:19

SPLENDOR
Who is so awesome in *, Ex 15:11
is a young bull in strength and *, Deu 33:17
In majestic * to help you. Deu 33:26
heaven, clothed in dazzling *. Job 37:22
of state, your majesty and *. Job 40:10
You have clothed him with * and Ps 21:5
dazzling * of your presence lives. Ps 26:8
You have ended his * and Ps 89:44
glory, *, majesty and miracles. Ps 145:5
the dawn gives way to morning *, Pro 4:18
riding in pomp and * among the Jer 17:25
wisdom and defile your *! Eze 28:7
wisdom for the sake of your *. Eze 28:17
His brilliant * fills the earth Hab 3:3
and I will fill it with *." Hag 2:7f
'The future * of this Temple Hag 2:8,9
than the * of the first one! Hag 2:8,9
My own eyes have seen his * and 2Pe 1:16
our Lord; yes, * and majesty, all Jud 1:24,25
the earth grew bright with his *. Rev 18:1
"The dainty luxuries and * that Rev 18:14

SPLINTS
I will put * and bandages upon Eze 34:15,16

SPLIT
ground suddenly * open beneath Num 16:31
the night and * into four groups, Ju 9:34
Was the sea * in two. 2Sa 22:16
"This altar will * apart, and the 1Ki 13:3

(SPLIT Con't)
kingdom of Israel was * in two; 1Ki 16:21
For Israel * off from the 2Ki 17:21
clouds are not * by the weight. Job 26:8
of fire. He * open the rocks in Ps 78:15
we'll * with you in equal Pro 1:14
of Olives will * apart, making a Zec 14:4
in the Temple was * apart from Mt 27:51
Now this veil was * from above, Mk 15:38f
in the Temple was * apart from Mk 15:38
From now on families will be * Lk 12:52
hanging in the Temple * apart. Lk 23:45
The great city of "Babylon" * Rev 16:19

SPLITS
It breaks down the cedars. It * Ps 29:5,6
there won't be * in the church. 1Co 1:10

SPOIL
in the evening divides the *." Gen 49:27
rotten apple can * a barrelful. Ecc 9:18
and treasures as * to the enemy. Jer 15:12,13
Literally, "then will he * his Mt 12:29f
why let someone * everything just 1Co 10:30
Don't let others * your faith and Col 2:8

SPOILED
he has *, or the tithe omitted, Lev 5:16
* and moldy—too rotten to eat. Jer 24:2
I will treat them like * figs, Jer 24:8
for the Lord has * their pastures. Jer 25:36

SPOILS
Melchizedek a tenth of all the *. Gen 14:19,20
The captives and other * of war Num 31:12
they flew upon the * of battle 1Sa 14:32
If anyone defiles and * God's 1Co 3:17
a tenth of the * he took from the Heb 7:4

SPOKE
AT THAT TIME all mankind * a Gen 11:1
in Egypt everyone * of her beauty. Gen 12:14
AFTERWARDS JEHOVAH * to Abram Gen 15:1
Hagar * of Jehovah—for it was he Gen 16:13
Then Abraham * again. Gen 18:27
others, and now he * up, answering Gen 23:10
Jehovah now * to Jacob and told Gen 31:3
Then he * to his father about it. Gen 34:4
Then the king's wine taster * Gen 41:9
"The king's chief assistant * Gen 42:30
father—the old man you * about? Gen 43:27
up with them and * to them along Gen 44:6
During the night God * to him in Gen 46:2
And he * very kindly to them, Gen 50:21
Now the Lord * to Moses again and Ex 6:10
There too, the people * bitterly Ex 16:2
* and God thundered his reply. Ex 19:19
door while the Lord * with Moses. Ex 33:9
Inside the tent the Lord * to Ex 33:11
THE LORD NOW * to Moses from the Lev 1:1
AT THE TIME when the Lord * to Num 3:1
The Lord now * again to Moses at Num 3:14,15
Then Moses * again to Korah: Num 16:8,9
THE LORD NOW * to Aaron: "You Num 18:1
* this prophecy concerning them: Num 24:3-9
So he * this prophecy to him: Num 24:15-19
And the Lord * to you from the Deu 4:12
God that day as he * to you from Deu 4:15
alive today. He * with you face to Deu 5:4
the mountain. He * to me and I Deu 5:5
disciple, God * to Moses' Jos 1:1
praised God and * no more of war Jos 22:33
but the Lord * with a mighty voice 1Sa 7:10
together, he * well of David and 1Sa 19:4
there with Saul's men, * up. 1Sa 22:9,10
by the girls of whom you *!" 2Sa 6:22
for every word Ahithophel * was 2Sa 16:23
The Spirit of the Lord * by me, 2Sa 23:2
happen when he * through Ahijah, 1Ki 15:29
Then Elijah * again. 1Ki 18:22
In the morning he went out and * 2Ki 10:9,10
the Lord * to him again. 2Ki 20:4
As he *, Solomon was standing 2Ch 6:12,13
decision, he * roughly to them; 2Ch 10:13
(King Hezekiah * very 2Ch 30:22
Then all the men * up and said, Ez 10:12
so after thinking about it I * Neh 5:7
Mount Sinai and * with them from Neh 9:13
or twice, but I * sharply to them Neh 13:21
of their children * in the language Neh 13:24
Finally they * to Haman about it, Est 3:3,4
AT LAST JOB *, and cursed the day Job 3:1
That is why I * so rashly. Job 6:3
All who saw me * well of me. Job 29:11
advice, and were silent until I *. Job 29:21
And after I *, they spoke no Job 29:22
And after I spoke, they * no Job 29:22
further reply, he * out angrily, Job 32:5
Then the Lord * to Job again from Job 40:6
of a fort! I * too hastily when I Ps 31:22
He merely *, and the heavens Ps 33:6
For when he but *, the world Ps 33:9
Then at last I *, and pled with Ps 39:2,3
destroyed by those they * against. Ps 64:8
They even * against God himself. Ps 78:19,20
In a vision you * to your prophet Ps 89:19
answered them. He * to them from Ps 99:7
mountains. You *, and at the sound Ps 104:7,8
When Moses *, the flies and Ps 105:31
on the ground. He *, and hordes of Ps 105:34
he became angry and * foolishly. Ps 106:33
them. He *, and they were Ps 107:20
They are the vineyard that I * Is 5:7
Then the Lord * to me again and Is 8:5
I * and they came into being. Is 48:13
when I *, you wouldn't listen. Is 65:12
I * to them, they would not hear. Is 66:4
AGAIN THE LORD * to me and said: Jer 2:1
Again and again I * to you about Jer 7:13,14
THEN THE LORD * to Jeremiah once Jer 11:1
Again the Lord * to me and said: Jer 11:9
ON YET ANOTHER occasion God * to Jer 16:1
to kill me, yet I * well of them to Jer 18:20
Then the Lord * to them and said: Jer 19:3
Then Jeremiah * in his defense. Jer 26:12
old men stood and * to all the Jer 26:17
I * again and again to the Jer 27:16
you and me * against many nations, Jer 28:8
to me though I * to them again and Jer 29:19
The Lord * to me again, saying: Jer 31:15
The Lord * to Jeremiah again and Jer 33:23
Then at Tahpanhes, the Lord * to Jer 43:8
of prison, and * pleasantly to him Jer 52:32
me as he *, and set me on my feet. Eze 2:2
Then the Lord * to the man in Eze 10:2
when I never * to you at all? Eze 13:7
"Then I * to their children and Eze 20:18
each evil word you * against the Eze 35:12
So I * these words from God, just Eze 37:7
So I * to the winds as he Eze 37:10
You are the one I * of long ago Eze 38:17
Then he * to me, and I fell to Dan 10:9
Suddenly, as he * these words, I Dan 10:19
face to face. God * to him— the Hos 12:4
IT USED TO be when Israel *, the Hos 13:1
THEN THE LORD * to Jonah again: Jon 3:1
Then the Angel of the Lord * very Zec 3:5,6
Lord * often of him to each other. Mal 3:16
and when he * a single word, all Mt 8:16
Jesus turned around and * to her. Mt 9:22
so many, he never * to them without Mt 13:34,35
But Jesus immediately * to them, Mt 14:27
One of them, a lawyer, * up: Mt 22:34,35
Then Jesus * to the crowd. Mt 26:55
Then the angel * to the women. Mt 28:5
sermon because he * as an Mk 1:22
Then Jesus * to the demon within Mk 5:7,8
He went inside and * to the Mk 5:39
But he * to them at once. Mk 6:50
leaders often * of, that Elijah Mk 9:11
One of the men in the crowd * up Mk 9:17
over and * to him in a low voice. Mk 10:35
He * here in Aramaic. Mk 15:34f
The onlookers, who * Greek and Mk 15:34f
All who were there * well of him Lk 4:22
For he * as one who knew the Lk 4:32
Standing at her bedside he * to Lk 4:39
Then Jesus * up and answered his Lk 7:40
So he * to the storm: "Quiet Lk 8:24
Finally she *: "This man was Lk 22:56
As he *, he held out his hands Lk 24:40
Simon Peter's brother, * up. Jn 6:8,9
Then Nicodemus * up. Jn 7:50
Then a voice * from heaven saying, Jn 12:28
Then the other disciple * to the Jn 18:16
He * to them again and said, "As Jn 20:21
he * these words I have quoted, Act 2:29
stated, 'God * to my Lord, the Act 2:34
in them— you * long ago by the Act 4:25,26
Those who * only Greek complained Act 6:1
as the widows who * Hebrew. Act 6:1
often * of him as the Messiah. Act 8:9,10,11
The Lord * to him in a vision, Act 9:10
The voice * again, "Don't Act 10:15
Then Paul and Barnabas * out Act 13:46
and * to the demon within her. Act 16:18
Gentiles, and * daily in the public Act 17:17
One night the Lord * to Paul in a Act 18:9
on them, and they * in other Act 19:6
and publicly * against Christ, so Act 19:9
and as Paul * on and on, a young Act 20:9
"Perhaps a spirit or angel * to Act 23:9
and Paul * to the ship's officers Act 27:9
leaders and * to them as follows: Act 28:17
King David * of this, describing Rom 4:6
King David * of this same thing Rom 11:9
I was a child I * and thought and 1Co 13:11
of the words we * as being just our 1Th 2:13
LONG AGO GOD * in many different Heb 1:1
life, confidently * of God bringing Heb 11:22
words God * to you, his child? Heb 12:5
When he * from Mount Sinai his Heb 12:26
Holy Spirit who * to them; 1Pe 1:12
the one man who * up for God, and 2Pe 2:5
when his donkey * to him with a 2Pe 2:16
trumpet blast, * to me and said, Rev 4:1
Then the voice from heaven * to Rev 10:8

SPOKEN
my fathers has come and * to me. Gen 3
because God had * to him there. Gen 35:
after you have * to me, for I have Ex 4:
the Lord * only through Moses? Num 1:
Hasn't he * through us, too?" Num 1.
I, Jehovah, have *. Num 14:34,
* against Jehovah and against you. Num 2
he had * from the fire-covered Deu 9:10,
the Lord who had * to the child. 1Sa
even if you hadn't *, we would all 2Sa 2:
the Lord has not * through me." 1Ki 22:
which the Lord had * to David and 2Ki 2
* to Jeroboam by Ahijah, the 2Ch 10:
the Lord has not * through me." 2Ch 18:
Thus the word of the Lord * 2Ch 36:
that God had not * to him, but Neh 6:12,
Job, you have * like a fool." Job 35:
the God above all gods has *—oh, Ps 18:
May my * words and unspoken Ps 19:
I, the Lord, have *. Is 1:
the Jews have * out against their Is 3
The Lord has * out against that Is 9:8,9,
has *—who can change his plans? Is 14:
Lord, the God of Israel, has *. Is 21:
fall with it, for the Lord has *. Is 22:
he has * out against this great Is 23:
The Lord has *. Is 24
The Lord has *—he will surely do Is 25
Wealthy cheaters will not be * of Is 32
The Lord has *—it shall be. Is 40
Temple restored, for I have * it. Is 44:
My words were scarcely * when Is 48
The Lord God has * to me and I Is 50
and had never * an evil word. Is 53
The Lord has *. Is 58:1
In accord with my words * through Jer 1:
listen to the Lord, for he has *. Jer 13:
prophets who have * in my name Jer 14:1
every word of all that I have *. Jer 26:1
for he has * to us in the name of Jer 26:
But I have * to you again and Jer 35:1
* by Jeremiah the prophet: Jer 50:
For the Lord has *: "Let her Lam 1:1
All our enemies have * out Lam 3:4
I, the Lord, have * it! Eze 5:1
I, the Lord, have * it!" Eze 5:1
gone, for God has * against all the Eze 7:1
I, the Lord, have * these words. Eze 17:2
For I, the Lord, have * it." Eze 21:3
For I, the Lord, have *, and I Eze 22:1
hasn't * one word to them at all. Eze 22:2
For I have *, says the Lord. Eze 23:3
I, the Lord, have * it; Eze 24:1
I have * it, says the Lord God. Eze 26:
for I, the Lord, have * it. Eze 26:1
For I have * it, the Lord God Eze 28:1
I, the Lord, have * it. Eze 30:1
I, the Lord, have * it. Eze 34:2
for I have *, the Lord God says. Eze 39:
their names will not be * anymore. Hos 1:1
The Lord has *. Amo 1:
The Lord has *. Amo 1:8
The Lord has *. Amo 1:1
The Lord has *. Amo 2:
The Lord God has *. Amo 2:1
It is * by the Lord against both Amo 3:
these further evils I have * of. Amo 4:1
The Lord has *. Amo 8:
no survivors, for the Lord has *. Ob 1:18
"Sir, you have * a true word in Mk 12:32
laws, he had * of God as his Jn 5:18
have * what the Father taught me. Jn 8:28
We know God has * to Moses, but Jn 9:29
declared an angel had * to him. Jn 12:29
Judgment by the truths I have *. Jn 12:48
if I had not come and * to them. Jn 15:22
"I have * of these matters very Jn 16:25
being * by the disciples. Act 2:6
* about what is going on today. Act 3:24
I have been following the plan * Rom 15:21
Jews—were being * of, but to his Gal 3:16
whose life cannot be * against. 1Ti 3:2
Also, he must be well * of by 1Ti 3:7
* against by those who know them. Tit 2:5
But now in these days he has * to Heb 1:2
he would not have * long afterwards Heb 4:8

SPOKES
the axles, *, rims, and hubs. 1Ki 7:33
The four wheels had rims and *, Eze 1:18
eyes, including the rims and *. Eze 10:9-13

SPOKESMAN
He will be your * to the people. Ex 4:16
brother Aaron shall be your *. Ex 7:1
be his * to the people of Israel. Ex 20:22
he shall be my * to the people. Deu 18:18
you as my * to the world." Jer 1:5
will I let you continue as my *. Jer 15:19

SPONGE
in sin as a * soaks up water! Job 15:16
One of them ran and filled a * Mt 27:48

(SPONGE Con't)
So one man ran and got a * and Mk 15:36
there, so a * was soaked in it and Jn 19:29

SPONTANEOUS
a promise or is a * free will Lev 22:17,18

SPOONS
And make golden dishes, *, Ex 25:29
* to be placed upon this table. Ex 37:15,16
place the dishes, *, bowls, cups, Num 4:7
snuffers, basins, *, firepans, the 1Ki 7:50
snuffers, *, and other bronze 2Ki 25:14,15
snuffers, basins, *, and 2Ch 4:22
gold and silver * and bowls used 2Ch 24:14
and the snuffers, *, bowls, and all Jer 52:18

SPORT
tired of their *, they took off the Mk 15:20

SPORTING
pounds and who was * a new suit of 2Sa 21:16

SPOT
Jacob named the * Bethel Gen 35:15
The only * in all Egypt without Ex 9:26
sons for the * to be examined. Lev 13:3
If the hair in this * turns Lev 13:3
white, and if the * looks to be Lev 13:3
"But if the white * in the skin Lev 13:4
the hair in the * has not turned Lev 13:4
again, and if the * has not changed Lev 13:5
But if the * spreads in the skin Lev 13:7
again, and if the * has spread, Lev 13:8
in the *, and an ulcer developing. Lev 13:9,10
If the * has indeed turned Lev 13:16,17
or a bright *, sort of reddish Lev 13:19
if the hair at the * has turned Lev 13:20
hairs in this *, and the spot does Lev 13:21
this spot, and the * does not Lev 13:21
If during that time the * Lev 13:22
But if the bright * grows no Lev 13:23
the priest must examine the *. Lev 13:25
If the hair in the bright * turns Lev 13:25
in the bright *, and the brightness Lev 13:26
If the * spreads in the skin, the Lev 13:27
But if the bright * does not Lev 13:28
reveals that the * seems to be only Lev 13:31
If the * has not spread and no Lev 13:32
hair around the * (but not on the Lev 13:33
(but not on the * itself) and the Lev 13:33
day, and if the * has not spread, Lev 13:34
But if, later on, this * begins Lev 13:35
are found in the *, then he is Lev 13:37
*, it may be leprosy breaking out. Lev 13:42
or a reddish * in it, it is Lev 13:49
If the * has spread, it is a Lev 13:51
seventh day the * has not spread, Lev 13:53
If after that time the * has not Lev 13:55
sees that the * has faded after the Lev 13:56
a scab from a burn, or a bright *. Lev 14:56
the * between the two cherubim. Num 7:89
crossed at a * where the river was Jos 3:15,16
Pass, runs to a * called The Rock, Ju 1:36
and named the * "The Place of 2Sa 6:8
So Joab assigned Uriah to a * 2Sa 11:16
As they reached the * at the 2Sa 15:32
* where the Ark would be placed; 1Ki 8:7
Is there a single * in all the Jer 3:2
the choicest * on earth, because Eze 20:15
they left by boat for a quieter *. Mk 6:32
*, and it is getting late." Mk 6:35,36
in this deserted *," they said. Lk 9:12
When Jesus arrived at the *, he Lk 18:40
without a single * or wrinkle or Eph 5:27

SPOTLESS
a man, was proved * and pure in his 1Ti 3:16
the sinless, * Lamb of God. 1Pe 1:19

SPOTLESSLY
temple, clothed in * white linen, Rev 15:6

SPOTS
skin, but these * are growing Lev 13:39
If the * have spread in the wall, Lev 14:39
"But if the * appear again, the Lev 14:43
he sees that the * have spread, it Lev 14:44
again to look, the * have not Lev 14:48
not clip bald * in their hair or Lev 21:5
Only then, without the * of sin Job 11:15
off the rough * in the road. Is 40:4
or a leopard take away his *? Jer 13:23

SPOTTED
or *, and all the black sheep. Gen 30:31,32
were ringed and *, and the females Gen 30:35,36
were speckled and * with any white Gen 30:35,36
were streaked and *, and Jacob Gen 30:39,40
the removal of the * section of Lev 14:40
light from heaven * down upon him! Act 9:3
Alexander was * among the crowd Act 19:33

SPOUT
I would * off my criticisms Job 16:4

SPOUTS
a rebellious teacher * Pro 15:2
She * evil like a fountain! Jer 6:7

SPRANG
toward him. He * up and ran to meet Gen 18:2
the main crop that * up after the Amo 7:1
the plants * up quickly enough in Mt 13:5
So Levi left everything, * up Lk 5:28

SPRAWLING
Turn them around and send them * Ps 40:14,15

SPREAD
of Canaan * from Sidon all the way Gen 10:15-19
of Ham, * abroad in many lands and Gen 10:20
As the population grew and * Gen 11:2
It will * like fine dust over Ex 9:9
the city I will * out my hands to Ex 9:29
wings * out above the gold lid. Ex 25:20
it into powder and * it upon the Ex 32:20
Then he * the coverings over the Ex 40:19
Wafers made without yeast and * Lev 2:4
unleavened wafers * with olive oil Lev 7:12
wafer, one wafer * with olive oil, Lev 8:26
Then, with hands * out towards Lev 9:22
and has not * in the skin, then the Lev 13:5
and have not *, then the priest Lev 13:6
if the spot has *, then the priest Lev 13:8
has erupted and * all over his body Lev 13:12
and does not *, it is merely the Lev 13:23
does not move or * in the skin, and Lev 13:28
If the spot has not * and no Lev 13:32
the spot has not *, and it appears Lev 13:34
spot begins to *, then the priest Lev 13:35
If the spot has *, it is a Lev 13:51
the spot has not *, the priest Lev 13:53
though it has not *, it is leprosy Lev 13:55
If the spots have * in the wall, Lev 14:39
the spots have *, it is leprosy, Lev 14:44
"Next they must * a blue cloth Num 4:7
They will * a scarlet cloth over Num 4:8
"They must then * a blue cloth Num 4:11
leather will be * over them. Num 4:14
unleavened wafers * with oil; Num 6:15
Quail were * out all around Num 11:32
people of Israel * out before him. Num 22:41
I see them * before me as green Num 24:3-9
And they shall * the garment Deu 22:17,18
You will see * out before you Deu 32:52
but when the Amorites later * Ju 1:35
they replied, and * out a sheet Ju 8:25
for all that time, * across the Ju 11:26
Word soon * that he had been Ju 16:2
The news * quickly throughout the 1Sa 13:3,4
They were * out across the 1Sa 30:16
The Philistines arrived and * 2Sa 5:18
returned and again * out across the 2Sa 5:22
and as the news * throughout the 2Sa 19:8,9,10
* sackcloth upon a rock and 2Sa 21:10
Word of the king's decision * 1Ki 3:28
that their wings * out over the 1Ki 8:7
with his hands * out towards heaven 1Ki 8:22,23
and * it out before the Lord. 2Ki 19:14
of them and * it on the boil. 2Ki 20:7
Gad, who were * as far as Salecah. 1Ch 5:11
The half-tribe of Manasseh * 1Ch 5:23
for joy had * throughout the land. 1Ch 12:40
David's fame * everywhere, and 1Ch 14:17
their wings * over the Ark and 2Ch 5:7,8
him, and his fame * even to Egypt, 2Ch 26:8
"The work is so * out," I Neh 4:19
So the people * from Beer-sheba to Neh 11:25-30
his branches * across the garden. Job 8:16
Can you * out the gigantic Job 37:18
the daylight to * to the ends of Job 38:13
your wrath. You * out our sins Ps 90:8
He * out a cloud above them to Ps 105:39
My bed is * with lovely, colored Pro 7:16,17
not to * beyond their boundaries. Pro 8:27,28,29
their armies * out as far as Is 16:8
Literally, "* out the rugs." Is 21:5f
Lord of Hosts will * a wondrous Is 25:6
to the Temple and * it out before Is 37:14
of figs and * it over the boil, and Is 38:21
the palm of my right hand * out Is 48:13
him, the one who * the stars Is 51:13
build on additions; * out your Is 54:2
their bones and * them out on the Jer 8:2
and * their slanderous lies. Jer 9:4
The fire shall * to the palaces Jer 17:27
He shall * his royal canopy over Jer 43:10
will * his wings against Bozrah. Jer 49:22
my oil upon a table * before you. Eze 23:41
for fishermen to * their nets, for Eze 26:5
a place for fishermen to * their Eze 26:14
Her branches will * out, as Hos 14:6
up quickly and * its broad leaves Jon 4:6
and I will * on your faces the Mal 2:3
The report of his miracles * far Mt 4:24
they * his fame all over the town. Mt 9:31
The news of their arrival * Mt 14:35
trees and * them out before him. Mt 21:8
Their story * widely among the Mt 28:15
The news of what he had done * Mk 1:28
* quickly through the city. Mk 2:1
his miracles had * far and wide and Mk 3:7,8
the whole area to * the news of his Mk 6:55
the news of his arrival * fast. Mk 7:24
Jesus told the crowd not to * the Mk 7:36
Then many in the crowd * out Mk 11:8
The word * quickly to her Lk 1:58
* through the Judean hills. Lk 1:65
what he had done * like wildfire Lk 4:37
Now the report of his power * Lk 5:15
them and steadily * them to others Lk 8:15
Then the crowds * out their robes Lk 19:36,37
So the rumor * among the Jn 21:23
The news of his death * rapidly Act 1:19
This message has * all through Act 10:36,37
So God's message * all through Act 13:49
The story of what happened * Act 19:17
His sin * death throughout all Rom 5:12
* the Gospel like a sweet perfume. 2Co 2:14
of the Lord has * out from you to 1Th 1:8
message will * rapidly and triumph 2Th 3:1
of God. * out before it was a Rev 4:6
wings * out as though in flight. Rev 4:7
I saw their horses * out before Rev 9:17,18
* out before me was what seemed Rev 15:2

SPREADING
But if it appears that the * has Lev 13:37
understand the * of the clouds, and Job 36:29
gave it all to us, * Israel from Ps 44:1
A gossip goes around * rumors, Pro 11:13
They will come in vast hordes, * Is 7:19
He will snip the * tendrils. Is 18:5
accusations and * vicious rumors! Is 58:9
I have been * out my arms to Is 65:2
has cut off your * tendrils and Jer 48:32
Each had two pairs of wings * Eze 1:11
The sky * out above them looked Eze 1:22
became a low but * vine that turned Eze 17:6
* the news about his miracles. Mt 12:16
* the news as they ran. Mk 5:14
city, * the news as they ran. Lk 8:34
stop them from * their propaganda. Act 4:17
God's Good News was * rapidly and Act 12:24
and is now * all over the world. Col 1:23

SPREADS
But if the spot * in the skin Lev 13:7
If during that time the spot *, Lev 13:22
If the spot * in the skin, the Lev 13:27
He * his wings over them, Deu 32:11
See how he * the lightning Job 36:30
and * her wings to the south? Job 39:26

SPREE
for a drinking * as the city fell Est 3:15

SPRING
a desert * along the road to Shur. Gen 16:7
down outside the town, beside a *. Gen 24:11
beside this *, and the girls of the Gen 24:13
shoulder and filled it at the *. Gen 24:15,16
ran down to the * again and kept Gen 24:20
rushed out to the * where the man Gen 24:29,30
when I came to the * I prayed this Gen 24:42
Here I am, standing beside this *. Gen 24:43
and she went down to the * and Gen 24:45
and found a gushing underground *. Gen 26:19
If the body falls into a * or Lev 11:36
are to be added to * water in a Num 19:17
that the people sang:* up, O well! Num 21:17,18
mountain to the * of Nephtoah, and Jos 15:9
Michmethath to the * of Tappu-ah. Jos 17:7
From the * of Tappu-ah the Jos 17:9
Ephron to the * of Naphtoah, and Jos 18:15
and went as far as the * of Harod. Ju 7:1
Bring them down to the * and I'll Ju 7:4
Then he named the place "The * Ju 15:19
and the * is still there today. Ju 15:19
IN THE * of the following year, at 2Sa 11:1
IT WAS IN the * of the fourth year 1Ki 6:1
used to invade the land each *. 2Ki 13:20,21
THE FOLLOWING * (spring was the 1Ch 20:1
THE FOLLOWING SPRING (* was the 1Ch 20:1
He dammed up the Upper * of 2Ch 32:30
from west of the * of Gihon in the 2Ch 33:14
The following * he was summoned 2Ch 36:10
And others * up from the earth to Job 8:19
water, as though gushing from a *. Ps 78:15
weather, and the * winds blow and Ps 147:18
like water from a mountain *. Pro 13:14
a fountain or muddying a *. Pro 25:26
of birds has come. Yes, * is here. Sol 2:12
private garden, a * that no one Sol 4:12
leads from Gihon * to the upper Is 7:3
crops will * up, and their flocks Is 32:20
garden, like an ever-flowing *. Is 58:11
a garden in early *, full of young Is 61:11
rain each year in * and fall and Jer 5:23,24
from Tamar to the * at Eze 48:27,28
of dawn or the rain of early *." Hos 6:3
Therefore punishment will * up Hos 10:4
will come, as well as those of *. Joe 2:23
sprout, you know that * has come. Mk 13:28
a perpetual * within them, watering Jn 4:14
Does a * of water bubble out Jas 3:11

SPRINGING
The flowers are * up and the Sol 2:12
of young plants * up everywhere. Is 61:11

SPRINGS
discovered a hot * in the wasteland Gen 36:24

(SPRINGS Con't)
twelve * and seventy palm trees; Ex 15:27
they camped there beside the *. Ex 15:27
* of water and seventy palm trees; Num 33:9
gushing *, valleys, and hills; Deu 8:7
his neighbor and * out of hiding Deu 19:11
of Israel at the * of Deu 32:51
around the * of Merom as far as one Jos 11:4
their camp at the * of Merom. Jos 11:5
at the * of Merom and attacked. Jos 11:7
extended to the * at En-shemesh and Jos 15:7
Give us some *, too!" Jos 15:18,19
he gave her the upper and lower *. Jos 15:18,19
please give us * of water too." Ju 1:15
gave her the upper and lower *. Ju 1:15
By Megiddo's *, Ju 5:19
camped at the * in Jezreel. 1Sa 29:1
* forth upon the earth; 2Sa 23:4
to plug the * outside the city. 2Ch 32:3
"Have you explored the * from Job 38:16
with water, and tender grass * up? Job 38:25-27
At your command the * burst Ps 74:15
become a place of * where pools of Ps 84:6
He placed * in the valleys, and Ps 104:10
be refreshed from * along the way. Ps 110:7
before the * bubbled forth their Pro 8:24
* in the depths of the oceans. Pro 8:27,28,29
shout and sing! * will burst forth Is 35:6
* of water in the thirsty land. Is 35:7
and rivers fed by * shall flow Is 41:18
wilderness, yes, * in the desert, Is 43:20
from Tamar to the * at Eze 47:19
All his flowing * and green oases Hos 13:15
All saw your power! Then * burst Hab 3:8,9
you, for as it * up it causes deep Heb 12:15
as dried-up * of water, promising 2Pe 2:17
to the * of the Water of Life. Rev 7:17
upon a third of the rivers and *. Rev 8:10
and * and they became blood. Rev 16:4
I will give to the thirsty the * Rev 21:6

SPRINGTIME
there will be * and harvest, cold Gen 8:22
fruitful as the * rains upon the Ps 72:6
valley to see the * there, to see Sol 6:11
That is why even the * rains Jer 3:3
ASK THE LORD for rain in the *, Zec 10:1

SPRINKLE
their right feet; * the rest of the Ex 29:19,20
anointing oil and * it upon Aaron Ex 29:21
"Take the anointing oil and * it Ex 40:9
and it shall become holy. * the Ex 40:10
the priests, will * its blood back Lev 1:11
in the blood and * it seven times Lev 4:6
in the blood and * it seven times Lev 4:17
Then he shall * some of the Lev 5:9
Then the priest shall * the Lev 14:7
into it, and * it with his finger Lev 14:16
finger he is to * some of it seven Lev 14:27
and shall * the house seven times. Lev 14:51,52
the young bull and * it with his Lev 16:14
the veil, and * it upon the place Lev 16:15
of the altar, and * blood upon the Lev 16:19
will be able to * the blood upon Lev 17:6
you the blood to * upon the altar Lev 17:11
his finger and * it seven times Num 19:4
into the water and * the water upon Num 19:18
* me with the cleansing blood Ps 51:7
the priests shall * salt upon them Eze 43:24
they must always * themselves in Mk 7:4
bushes and scarlet wool to * with. Heb 9:19
told them to and * the blood on the Heb 11:28

SPRINKLED
be collected and * upon the altar. Ex 29:15,16
* back and forth upon the altar. Lev 7:2
anointing oil and * it upon the Lev 8:10
When he came to the altar he * Lev 8:11
times, and also * the utensils of Lev 8:11
killed it and * the blood back and Lev 8:19
The rest of the blood he * back Lev 8:24
that had been * upon the altar, and Lev 8:30
the altar, and * it upon Aaron and Lev 8:30
the blood and he * it back and Lev 9:12
to him and he * it back and forth Lev 9:18
Pure frankincense shall be * Lev 24:5-8
Their blood is to be * upon the Num 18:17
The cleansing water was not * Num 19:13
him has not been * upon him; Num 19:20
over it, and * the blood of peace 2Ki 16:13
also to be * over the new altar. 2Ki 16:15
took the blood and * it on the 2Ch 29:22
the rams and * their blood upon the 2Ch 29:22
and the priests * the blood 2Ch 30:16
the priests, who * it upon the 2Ch 35:11
and * dirt in their hair. Neh 9:1
be as though I had * clean water on Eze 36:25
sackcloth, and * myself with ashes, Dan 9:3
have * their arms to the elbows, Mk 7:3
blood which he * on the mercy seat Heb 9:7
and * it on the mercy seat; Heb 9:12
That is why blood was * [as proof Heb 9:18
with water, and * the blood over Heb 9:19
And in the same way he * blood Heb 9:21
being * with the blood of animals. Heb 9:23
we have been * with Christ's blood Heb 10:22
and to the * blood which Heb 12:24

SPRINKLES
if any blood * onto their Lev 6:27
the one who * the blood of the Lev 7:14
The man who * the water must Num 19:21

SPRINKLING
before the Lord, * it upon all Lev 1:5
Do this by * water of Num 8:7
and the * of blood upon it. Eze 43:18
was cleansed by * it with blood, Heb 9:22

SPROUT
my help and my desire to *." 2Sa 23:5f
decays, it may * and bud again at Job 14:8,9
seeds to * across the land. Ps 65:10
Let salvation and righteousness * Is 45:8
grew, the myrtle trees will * up. Is 55:13
leaves begin to *, you know that Mt 24:32
*, you know that spring has come. Mk 13:28

SPROUTING
There were no plants or grain * Gen 2:5
green shoot, * from a root in dry Is 53:2

SPROUTS
it's cut down it * again, and grows Job 14:7

SPUR
are like goads that * to action. Ecc 12:11

SPURN
I am very angry with those who * Ps 119:53
in your life. * the careless kiss Pro 4:24

SPURNED
They * the Rock who had made Deu 32:18
For you have * my counsel and Pro 1:25
mother-in-law will be * by her Lk 12:53
But the Jews who * God's message Act 14:2
though men have * him, he is very 1Pe 2:4

SPURNING
your back on me, * my advice. Pro 1:30

SPY
he entered as a *, and his Num 14:24
Kadesh-barnea to * out the land, Num 32:8
ground, or if you * one in a tree, Deu 22:6
some of his men to * on the city of Jos 7:2
to * out the land of Canaan. Jos 14:7
scouts to go and * out the land Ju 18:2
that he came to * on us and that he 2Sa 3:24,25
David has sent them to * out the 2Sa 10:3
They are here to * out the land 1Ch 19:2,3
Evil men * on the godly, waiting Ps 37:32
At evening they come to *, Ps 59:6
really—who came to * on us and see Gal 2:4

SPYING
You are * on me." 1Sa 28:9

SQUAD
had given Judas a * of soldiers and Jn 18:3

SQUADRON
He dispatched a police * to Jos 2:3

SQUALLS
being born who * to his father and Is 45:10

SQUANDERED
daughters—* on priests and idols. Jer 3:24

SQUANDERS
The evil man * his on sin. Pro 10:16

SQUARE
"USING ACACIA WOOD, make a * Ex 27:1
It is to be eighteen inches * Ex 30:2
It was eighteen inches * and Ex 37:25
it was 7½ feet * at the top, and Ex 38:1
It was a piece nine inches *, Ex 39:9
in, they camped in the village *. Ju 19:15
camped in the *, he asked them Ju 19:17
you mustn't stay here in the *. Ju 19:20
from the public * at Beth-shan 2Sa 21:12,13,14
Then he made * doorposts of olive 1Ki 6:33
and windows had a * frame. 1Ki 7:5
each 6 feet * and 4½ feet high. 1Ki 7:27-30
with undercarriages braced with * 1Ki 7:27-30
Its panels were *, not round. 1Ki 7:31
Each vat was six feet * and 1Ki 7:38
Holy of Holies—thirty feet *. 2Ch 3:8
7½ feet * and 4½ feet high. 2Ch 6:12,13
He faced the * in front of the Neh 8:1
out to the city *, and found Est 4:6
Search every *, and if you find Jer 5:1
rooms was 10½ feet *, with a Eze 40:7-12
These tables were about 2⅝ feet * Eze 40:42
and found it to be 175 feet *, Eze 40:47
They were 10½ feet *. Eze 41:1
inner room was thirty-five feet *. Eze 41:4
The area was 175 feet *. Eze 41:13
There were * doorposts at the Eze 41:21
This altar was 3½ feet *, and 5¼ Eze 41:22
in the form of a *, 875 feet long Eze 42:16-20
of the altar is twenty-one feet *. Eze 43:16
it is 24½ feet * with a 10½-inch Eze 43:17
land, 875 feet *, shall be Eze 45:2
city itself is to be 1½ miles *. Eze 48:16
miles *. Eze 48:20
miles * on each side of the Eze 48:21,22
* to all who happened to be there. Act 17:17
it was a * as wide as it was long; Rev 21:1

SQUARED
blocks of * stone for the Temple. 1Ch 22:

SQUARELY
bow and aimed it * at me, and sent Lam 3:1
for your faith is * built upon this 1Co 15:

SQUARES
young men gather no more in the *. Jer 9:2
and through the *, darting like Nah 2:

SQUEEZED
the grapes and * the juice into it, Gen 40:1
terror and * out the last drops. Is 51:17

SQUIRM
try to * out of your problems. Jas 1:4

SQUIRMED
there, she * past by pressing Num 22:25

STABBED
hand, and Joab * him in the stomach 2Sa 20:8,9,10

STABILITY
sensible leaders there is *. Pro 28:2
A just king gives * to his Pro 29:4
the earth, for the * of the very Lk 21:26

STABLE
build up a large * of horses for Deu 17:16
Solomon built up a great * of 1Ki 10:26
as a * hand shovels out manure. 1Ki 14:10
An empty * stays clean—but there Pro 14:4
is no income from an empty *. Pro 14:4

STABLES
for the royal horses in the *. 1Ki 4:28
the palace * and killed her there. 2Ki 11:16
they killed her at the palace *. 2Ch 23:15,16,17

STACHYS
our fellow worker, and beloved *. Rom 16:9

STACTE
"Use sweet spices—*, onycha, Ex 30:34

STAFF
* of Pharaoh, the king of Egypt. Gen 39:1
of his officials and household *. Gen 40:20
Pharaoh's * and requested them to Gen 50:4
and his * became bold again. Ex 14:5
"if he walks abroad with his *." Ex 21:19f
Balaam beat her again with his *. Num 22:27
and bread with his *, and fire Ju 6:21
my *, for I am very fond of him." 1Sa 16:22
on Saul's * on a part-time basis. 1Sa 17:14,15
his shepherd's * and sling, started 1Sa 17:40
armed only with a *, he killed an 2Sa 23:21
to Gehazi, "Quick, take my *! 2Ki 4:29
Lay the * upon the child's 2Ki 4:29
ahead and laid the * upon the 2Ki 4:31
* from Lachish with a great army; 2Ki 18:17
officers and administrative *. 1Ch 27:1
Literally, "Your rod and your * Ps 23:4f
will have wicked aides on his *. Pro 29:12
like a cracked *, you snapped Eze 29:7
So they were put on his regular * Dan 1:18,19
Literally, "their *." Hos 4:12f
And I took my * called "Grace" Zec 11:10
Then I broke my other *, Zec 11:14

STAFFS
based on how their * landed on the Hos 4:12f
So I took two shepherd's *, Zec 11:7

STAG
butcher, or as a * that is trapped, Pro 7:22
* on the mountains of spices." Sol 2:17
and he gave a * party for his Mk 6:21

STAGE
few steps upon the * of life, and Job 14:16
The first * of the altar is a Eze 43:14

STAGES
going by easy * to Rephidim. Ex 17:1
These herald only the early * of Mk 13:8

STAGGER
such lessons—but * them with your Ps 59:11
They will * backward, destroyed Ps 64:8
They reel and * like drunkards Ps 107:27
You will * like a sailor tossed Pro 23:34
they make Egypt * like a sick Is 19:14
prophets reel and *, making stupid Is 28:7
either! *, and not from wine! Is 29:9
them * and fall to the ground." Is 63:6
I awake with fear and * as a Jer 23:9
yet they would * out and defeat you Jer 37:10
Let her * and fall like a Jer 48:26
* beneath their heavy loads. Lam 5:13
and made her * with the pain. Eze 29:7
yes, drink and * back and Ob 1:16
Nineveh, too, will * like a Nah 3:11
lands reel and * like drunkards Hab 2:15
on yourselves. * and fall! Hab 2:16

STAGGERED
be * [by all that lies ahead. Jn 16:1
They * back under God's command Heb 12:20

STAGGERING
Now these same men are blindly * Lam 4:14

STAGGERS
path to life. She * down a crooked Pro 5:6
The world * like a drunkard; Is 24:20

STAIN
the awful * of my transgressions. Ps 51:1

AIN Con't)
o matter how deep the * of your Is 1:18
hey are a disgrace and a * among 2Pe 2:13
AINED
ven if you are * as red as Is 1:18
'ou are * with guilt that cannot Jer 2:22
'our clothing is * with the Jer 2:34
AIRCASE
o sleep, and dreamed that a * Gen 28:12
AIRCASES
orm of miniature *, so that the 2Ki 20:11f
AIRS
t the top of the * stood the Gen 28:13
When the watchman climbed the * 2Sa 18:24
' going up to the second floor; 1Ki 6:8
nother flight of * led from the 1Ki 6:8
arden and the * that descend from Neh 3:15
nd climbed the * which go up Neh 12:37
ach side of the * going up to the Eze 40:40
As they reached the *, the mob Act 21:35
Paul stood on the * and motioned to Act 21:40
'AIRWAY
t too had a * of seven steps Eze 40:26
t rose higher. A * at the side of Eze 41:7
TAKE
for the life of your soul is at *. Is 55:3
TALK
of grain on one *, with every Gen 41:5
appeared on the *, but these were Gen 41:6
of grain on one *, and all seven Gen 41:22
Then, out of the same *, came Gen 41:23
Can you * prey like a lioness, Job 38:39,40
disease and war will * your land, Eze 5:17
TALKED
Then Moses * out. Ex 10:6
But Naaman was angry and * away. 2Ki 5:11
heavens out and * along the seas. Job 9:8
years, and hunger * the land; Lk 4:25,26
TALKING
of Jordan * the sheep in the fold. Jer 49:19
against you like lions * prey. Eze 22:25
TALKS
very dim when poverty * the land. Is 17:4
A lion—a destroyer of nations—* Jer 4:7
grain * were soon choked out. Lk 8:7
TALL
You're trying to * for time until Dan 2:8,9
TALLIONS
Like fine * racing through the Is 63:13
They are well-fed, lusty *, each Jer 5:8
and neigh like *, yet your mother Jer 50:11
TALLS
and construct decks and * Gen 6:14
In addition, Solomon had 4,000 * 2Ch 9:25
oil, with many * for his animals, 2Ch 32:28,29
and the * of those selling doves. Mt 21:12
and the * of those selling doves, Mk 11:15
cattle from their * on the Sabbath Lk 13:15
from their *, saying to them, Lk 19:45
STALWART
These were the 468 * descendants Neh 11:4,5,6
There were also 128 * men under Neh 11:10-14
Only a few of its * archers will Is 21:17
STAMMER
and those who * in uncertainty will Is 32:4
STAMMERING
he even corrects deafness and * Mk 7:37
STAMP
"A marauding band shall * upon Gen 49:19
Literally, "clap your hands and * Eze 6:11f
I will * out the people of Thebes. Eze 30:15
STAMPED
you clapped and * and cheered with Eze 25:6
* others to death with its feet. Dan 7:19
"Whose picture is * on it?" Mt 22:20
STAMPING
Hear the * Ju 5:22
STAMPS
A wise king * out crime by severe Pro 20:26
STAND
"* back," they yelled. Gen 19:9
why * here outside the city when Gen 24:31
"This pile of stones will * as a Gen 31:47,48
JOSEPH COULD * it no longer. Gen 45:1
down to the river. * beside the Ex 7:15
And the magicians couldn't * Ex 9:11
in the morning and * before Pharaoh Ex 9:13
be afraid. Just * where you are and Ex 14:13
told him, "I will * at the top of Ex 17:9
* something you know is false. Ex 23:1
When on the witness *, don't be Ex 23:2,3
I will not * for this. Ex 23:7
would rise and * in their tent Ex 33:8
come down and * at the door while Ex 33:9
However, * here on this rock Ex 33:21
"Aaron's sons shall * in front of Lev 6:14
Literally, "neither shall you * Lev 19:16f
power to * before their enemies. Lev 26:37
then the whole estimate shall *; Lev 27:17
The priest shall * before her Num 5:18
Tabernacle, to * there with you. Num 11:16
of Jehovah, and to * before the Num 16:8,9
so he sent an angel to * in the Num 22:22,23
Then Balaam said to the king, "* Num 23:3,4
Then Balaam said to the king, "* Num 23:15
nothing, then her vow shall *. Num 30:4
he hears of it, her vow shall *. Num 30:7
and does nothing, the vow shall *; Num 30:11
that will * heat—such as gold, Num 31:22
But anything that won't * heat Num 31:23
Then you come back and * here Deu 5:31
No one will be able to * against Deu 7:24
giants, against whom none can *! Deu 9:1
of Jehovah, and to * before the Deu 10:8
No one will be able to * against Deu 11:25
to tell lies on the witness *. Deu 19:20
* before the Israeli army and say, Deu 20:2
to get his security. * outside! Deu 24:11
and Benjamin shall * upon Mount Deu 27:12
and Naphtali shall * upon Mount Deu 27:13
the Lord, and they will * in awe. Deu 28:10
you alone as you * before him Deu 29:14,15
will be able to * up to you." Jos 10:8
"Let the sun * still over Gibeon, Jos 10:12
and let the moon * in its place Jos 10:12
and no one could * against them; Jos 21:44
"* in the door of the tent," he Ju 4:20
was just * there worshiping God! Ju 7:15
until he couldn't * it any longer Ju 16:16,17
prison and made to * at the center Ju 16:25,26
"Who is able to * before 1Sa 6:20
own sons and now I * here, an old, 1Sa 12:2
Now tell me as I * before the 1Sa 12:3
"Now * here quietly before the 1Sa 12:7
and I will * over here, and all of 1Sa 14:40
and all of you * over there." 1Sa 14:40
who dared to * against you." 2Sa 18:28
The top of each * was a round 1Ki 7:31
tip of each *, banded with lugs. 1Ki 7:35
was cast as one unit with the *. 1Ki 7:35
for they * here day after day 1Ki 10:8
whose presence I *, that I will 1Ki 18:15
"Go out and * before me on the 1Ki 19:11
"Two kings couldn't * against 2Ki 10:4
The other two-thirds shall * 2Ki 11:6,7,8
He shall not * before it with a 2Ki 19:32
to * here and listen to you talk! 2Ch 9:7
and couldn't * up to them. 2Ch 13:7
and he will * beside you and help 2Ch 19:6
"Be fearless in your * for truth 2Ch 19:11
Who can * against you? 2Ch 20:6
or famine—we can * here before this 2Ch 20:9
Take your places; * quietly and 2Ch 20:17
us justice as we * here before you Ez 9:15
He stood on a wooden * made Neh 8:1
to the people, "* up and praise Neh 9:5
When I * to speak, they mock. Job 19:18
he will * upon the earth at last. Job 19:25
How can mere man * before God Job 25:4
"The dead * naked, trembling Job 26:5,6
don't answer me. I * before you and Job 30:20
from sunburn. I * up and cry to the Job 30:28,29
for, someone to * between you and Job 33:6
"* up like a man and brace Job 40:7
down the wicked where they *. Job 40:12
And if no one can * before him, Job 41:10
before him, who can * before me? Job 41:10
they shall not * among the godly. Ps 1:5
to him. * before the Lord in awe, Ps 4:4
a man shall * firm forever. Ps 15:5
Lord, arise and * against them. Ps 17:13,14
we will arise to * firm and sure! Ps 20:8
I will * up before the Ps 22:22
Yes, I will * and praise you Ps 22:25
Who may * before the Lord? Ps 24:3
who are allowed to * before the Ps 24:6
the Lord and * in awe of him. Ps 33:8
Lord, how long will you * there, Ps 35:17
he did for me, and * in awe before Ps 40:3
find him to come and * before him? Ps 42:2
Mount Hermon and Mount Mizar *. Ps 42:6
burning every weapon. "* silent! Ps 46:10
I * SILENTLY before the Lord, Ps 62:1
But I * silently before the Ps 62:5
Then everyone shall * in awe and Ps 64:9
My success—at which so many * Ps 71:7
Who can * before an angry God? Ps 76:7
before you. You * up to punish the Ps 76:9
* up, O God, and judge the earth. Ps 82:8
I * helpless before your terrors. Ps 88:15
* in dread and awe of him. Ps 89:7
O GOD OF my praise, don't * silent Ps 109:1
and goodness, and * firm forever. Ps 111:8
obedience to God, but I * unmoved. Ps 119:51
but I * in awe of only your words. Ps 119:161
of them is just. * ready to help Ps 119:173
as they * in his Temple courts. Ps 135:1
You know when I sit or *. Ps 139:2
They blaspheme your name and * Ps 139:20
Who can * before his freezing Ps 147:17
What you learn from them will * Pro 1:7,8,9
don't let embarrassment * in the Pro 6:3
the godly shall *. Pro 12:7
he is, can * against the Lord. Pro 21:30
He shall be successful and * Pro 22:29
can't * the pressure of adversity. Pro 24:10
don't * back and let them die. Pro 24:11,12
tremble—no, four it cannot *: Pro 30:21,22,23
Her children * and bless her; Pro 31:28
can * back-to-back and conquer; Ecc 4:12
they see. You * there helpless and Is 1:8
I can't * the sight of them. Is 1:14
of Israel, and * in awe of him. Is 29:23
so that it will * until the end of Is 30:8
When you * up, the nations flee. Is 33:3
But the Lord says, I will * up Is 33:10
Word of our God shall * forever." Is 40:8
All that worship these will * Is 44:11
Together they will * in terror. Is 44:11
* at attention when you pass by; Is 49:7
they shall * dumbfounded, Is 52:14,15
Will you * silent and still Is 64:12
before me: I will not * silent; Is 65:6
then come here and * before me in Jer 7:10
* amazed, silent, dumb with grief. Jer 8:21
The wild donkeys * upon the bare Jer 14:6
said to me, Go and * in the gates Jer 17:19
So I * against these Jer 23:30,31
* out in front of the Temple of Jer 26:2
Then why do they * there, Jer 30:6
Those in Aroer * anxiously Jer 48:19
Don't * and watch—flee while you Jer 51:50
AND HE SAID to me: "* up, son of Eze 2:1
* helpless, weeping in despair. Eze 7:26,27
true, and I will * against that Eze 14:9
land, who could * in the gap and Eze 22:30
Lord God says: I * against you, Eze 26:3
finest linens; you * beneath Eze 27:7
I * against you, Gog, leader of Eze 39:1
they shall * before me to offer Eze 44:15
Fishermen will * along the Eze 47:10
shall * forever, indestructible. Dan 2:44
* against it or help its victims. Dan 8:4
too frightened to *, and fell down Dan 8:17
God," he said, "* up and listen Dan 10:11
your nation, will * up [and fight Dan 12:1
Their cornstalks * there barren, Hos 8:7
Well may you farmers * so shocked Joe 1:11
the herds * perplexed for there Joe 1:18
of God, will * between the people Joe 2:17
And he shall * and feed his flock Mic 5:4
She will * up to her foes; Mic 5:9
cities where your idol temples *. Mic 5:14
* up and state your case against Mic 6:1
All the world will * amazed at Mic 7:16
They will * in silent awe, deaf Mic 7:16
they will * in awe. Mic 7:17
Who can * before an angry God? Nah 1:6
her people * aghast, pale-faced Nah 2:10
Your chariots * there, silent and Nah 2:13
"No wonder I * against you," Nah 3:5
sin in any form, * idly by while Hab 1:13
you * trembling and helpless. Hab 2:7
* in silence in the presence of Zep 1:7
soon when I will * up and accuse Zep 3:8
high, can * before Zerubbabel! Zec 4:7
spirits who * before the Lord of Zec 6:5
That day his feet will * upon Zec 14:4
If you will only * here and say, Mt 8:8,9
Yes, and you must * trial before Mt 10:18
divided against itself cannot *. Mt 12:25
promised, "we'll * up for you and Mt 28:14
he * it, to eat with such scum?" Mk 2:16
Jesus asked the man to come and * Mk 3:3
A lamp is placed on a * to shine Mk 4:21
But when you are arrested and * Mk 13:11
but my words * sure forever. Mk 13:31
I * in the very presence of God. Lk 1:19
to * in his presence forever. Lk 1:75
* here where everyone can see." Lk 6:8
the blessing, the blessing will *; Lk 10:6
instantly she could * straight. Lk 13:13
Then if you * outside knocking, Lk 13:24,25
of teeth as you * outside and see Lk 13:28
And Jesus said to the man, "* up Lk 17:19
For if you * firm, you will win Lk 21:19
to happen, * straight and look up! Lk 21:28
Jesus told him, "* up, roll up Jn 5:8
my glory as I * in your presence, Jn 17:5
But none of them were able to * Act 6:10
But Peter said, "* up! Act 10:26
So Paul called to him, "* up!" Act 14:10
Jerusalem and * trial before me?" Act 25:9
be willing to * trial on these Act 25:20
you are persecuting. Now * up! Act 26:16
will surely * trial before Caesar! Act 27:24
they * before God at Judgment Day Rom 1:20
where we now *, and we confidently Rom 5:2
Hate what is wrong. * on the side Rom 12:9
Remember, each of us will * Rom 14:10
But everyone knows that you * Rom 16:19
your faith to * firmly upon God, 1Co 2:5
unfit and ordered to * aside. 1Co 9:27

(STAND Con't)
that you can't * up against it, for 1Co 10:13
* your ground in defending him. 1Co 13:7
danger; * true to the Lord; 1Co 16:13
we forego. We * in the presence of 2Co 4:2
For we must all * before Christ 2Co 5:10
We * true to the Lord whether 2Co 6:8
fault—we who * before him covered Eph 1:4
What a foundation you * on now: Eph 2:20
will be able to * safe against all Eph 6:11
us much joy as we * together before 1Th 2:19
FINALLY, WHEN I could * it no 1Th 3:1
so that you may * before him 1Th 3:13
dear brothers, * firm and keep a 2Th 2:15
And so they will * condemned 1Ti 5:12
* steady, and don't be afraid of 2Ti 4:5
your tired hands, * firm on your Heb 12:12
You have not had to * face to Heb 12:18
man, "You can * over there if you Jas 2:3
and * utterly guilty before him. Jas 2:11
* against all such evil longings. Jas 4:6
fast, yet it will * as evidence Jas 5:3
apart. * firm when he attacks. 1Pe 5:9
help you to * firmly in his love. 1Pe 5:12
in heaven who * in the very 2Pe 2:11
even when we * before the Lord. 1Jn 3:19
seven angels that * before God, and Rev 8:2
enter them and they will * up! Rev 11:11
They will * far off, trembling Rev 18:10
these things shall * at a distance, Rev 18:15
and crews will * a long way off, Rev 18:17

STANDARD
Literally, "using the * of the Lev 5:15f
shall be stated in * money. Lev 27:25
is far beyond any human *! 2Sa 7:19
shall be your * unit of Eze 45:11
to me, using * units). Rev 21:17

STANDARDS
value by today's * is uncertain. Lev 27:3f
by this world's *, you had better 1Co 3:18
are living by the * of the Gospel. 3Jn 1:3

STANDING
the whole heaven, * twenty-two Gen 7:20
Then, * beside her body, he said Gen 23:3
See, here I am, * beside this Gen 24:13
the man was still * beside his Gen 24:29,30
Here I am, * beside this spring. Gen 24:43
that he was * on the bank of the Gen 41:1
"I was * upon the bank of the Gen 41:17
* around looking at one another? Gen 42:1
them as he was * there, for he had Gen 42:23
for you are * on holy ground. Ex 3:5
alone, with people * here all day Ex 18:14
of grain, or the * grain, are Ex 22:6
and 2¼ feet wide, * upright, with Ex 26:15,16
frames of acacia wood * on end. Ex 36:20
the cloud was * there, and the Ex 40:35
Moses heard all the families * Num 11:10
of cloud and fire * above us, and Num 14:14
friends who were * with them, and Num 16:32
* in the road with a drawn sword. Num 22:22,23
When the donkey saw him * there, Num 22:25
he saw the angel * in the roadway Num 22:31
the king was * beside the burnt Num 23:6
* beside their burnt offerings. Num 23:17
Then the Levites * between Deu 27:14
officers—are * today before the Deu 29:10
You are * here to enter into a Deu 29:12
the priests are * in the middle of Jos 4:2,3
place where the priests were *; Jos 4:9
half of them * at the foot of Mount Jos 8:33
of the armed men * just outside the Ju 18:15,16
and to the crowd * around, "You Ru 4:9
And all the people * there, and Ru 4:11
David talked to some others * 1Sa 17:26
Then Doeg the Edomite, who was * 1Sa 22:9,10
But as she was * there before 2Sa 13:11
oxen * tail to tail, three facing 1Ki 7:25
wrong and then, * here before your 1Ki 8:31
and a lion * on each side. 1Ki 10:19
donkey and the lion * beside it. 1Ki 13:24,25
road and the lion * quietly beside 1Ki 13:24,25
lion were still * there beside it, 1Ki 13:28
Elisha left the oxen * there and 1Ki 19:20
Then he turned to the people * 1Ki 22:28
saw the new king * beside the 2Ki 11:13,14
* on the walls will hear you." 2Ki 18:26
(The angel of the Lord was * at 1Ch 21:15
angel of the Lord * between heaven 1Ch 21:16
of these oxen * tail to tail, three 2Ch 4:4
* at the east side of the altar. 2Ch 5:11,12
As he spoke, Solomon was * before 2Ch 6:12,13
The priests were * at their 2Ch 7:6
one of the men * there—Jahaziel 2Ch 20:14
of all the people. * before them 2Ch 24:20
the priests were * in their places, 2Ch 35:10
Tobiah, who was * beside him, Neh 4:3
And when he saw Queen Esther * Est 5:2
at the gate, not * up or trembling Est 5:9
but couldn't see it * there. Job 4:16
good life; like * grain, you'll not Job 5:26
LORD, WHY ARE you * aloof and far Ps 10:1
right * with God. Ps 24:5f
and protect me by * in front. Ps 35:2
and hate me for * for the right. Ps 38:20
Yet I am * here depressed and Ps 42:6
* beside you is the queen, Ps 45:9
Now we are * here inside the Ps 122:2,3
She is * at the city gates and at Pro 8:1
And one * alone can be attacked Ecc 4:12
sexual desire, * at death's door, Ecc 12:5
know it was a person * there. Is 52:14,15
all the people * around and said: Jer 26:17
pillars of bronze * before the Jer 27:19,20,21
walled cities of Judah still *. Jer 34:7
down the obelisks * in the city of Jer 43:13
Seventy elders of Israel were * Eze 8:11
twenty-five men * with their backs Eze 8:16
The cherubim were * at the south Eze 10:3
bronze, * beside the Temple gate, Eze 40:3
court, * in front of the Temple. Eze 40:47
measuring was still * beside me). Eze 43:6
arrived and were * before the Dan 3:3
and it was left * on the ground, on Dan 7:4
one of those * beside the throne Dan 7:16
in the province of Elam, * beside Dan 8:2
long horns * on the river bank; Dan 8:3
suddenly a man was * in front of Dan 8:15
in April, as I was * beside the Dan 10:4
robes who was * now above the Dan 12:6
this: The Lord was * beside a wall Amo 7:7
I SAW THE Lord * beside the altar, Amo 9:1
red horse that was * among the Zec 1:8
* before the Angel of the Lord; Zec 3:1
said to the others * there, Zec 3:4
that Joshua is * beside, and I will Zec 3:9
and saw an angel * beside him. Mt 1:20
to them again, * over Bethlehem. Mt 2:9
"So if you are * before the Mt 5:23
And some of you * right here now Mt 16:28
and saw some men * around waiting Mt 20:3
saw some more men * around and Mt 20:6
the prophet) * in a holy place Mt 24:15
and said to those * around, "This Mt 26:71
men who had been * there came over Mt 26:73
Now Jesus was * before Pilate, Mt 27:11
and to have it * ready to rescue Mk 3:9
The people * around there Mk 6:54
of you who are * here right now Mk 9:1
and found the colt * in the street, Mk 11:4,5
it, some who were * there demanded, Mk 11:4,5
religion who was * there listening Mk 12:28
the horrible thing * in the Temple Mk 13:14
Literally, "* where he ought Mk 13:14f
The maid saw him * there and Mk 14:69
A little later others * around the Mk 14:70
also * around joking about Jesus. Mk 15:31
Some of the people * there Mk 15:35
When the Roman officer * beside Mk 15:39
an angel appeared, * to the right Lk 1:11,12
* at her bedside he spoke to the Lk 4:39
He noticed two empty boats * at Lk 5:2
When Jesus heard they were * Lk 8:20
of you who are * here right now Lk 9:27
glory, and the two men * with him. Lk 9:32
law who was * there, "you have Lk 11:45
words even as you are * there." Lk 12:12
and legal experts * around, "Well, Lk 14:3
"Then turning to the others * by Lk 19:24
the Jewish law who were * there. Lk 20:39
was suddenly * there among them, Lk 24:36
The following day as John was * Jn 1:35
Six stone waterpots were * there; Jn 2:6
The Pharisees who were * there Jn 9:40
all these people * here, so that Jn 11:42
servants were * around a fire they Jn 18:18
One of the soldiers * there Jn 18:22
Meanwhile, as Simon Peter was * Jn 18:25
* near the cross were Jesus' Jn 19:25
When Jesus saw his mother * Jn 19:26
Literally, "* by the disciple Jn 19:26f
and was * outside crying. Jn 20:11
and saw someone * behind her. Jn 20:14
Jesus was * there among them! Jn 20:19
* among them and greeting them. Jn 20:26
At dawn we saw a man * on the Jn 21:4
men were * there among them, and Act 1:10
are you * here staring at the sky? Act 1:11
was * right there beside them! Act 4:14
the guards were * outside, but when Act 5:23
for you are * on holy ground. Act 7:33
and Jesus * at God's right hand. Act 7:55
* beside God, at his right Act 7:56
the house and were * outside at the Act 10:17
suddenly a man was * before me Act 10:30
with others * guard before the Act 12:6
Peter was * outside in the street. Act 12:14
So Paul, * before them at the Act 17:22
came to me, and * beside me said, Act 22:13
was killed, I was * there Act 22:20
said to an officer * there, "Is it Act 22:25
The soldiers * ready to lash him, Act 22:29
Those * near Paul said to him, Act 2
giving us right * with God and Rom 5:
gave us right * with himself, and Rom 8:
and given us right * with himself. Rom 8:
* with God through our faith. Gal 3:
all over, you will still be * up. Eph 6:
that you are * side by side with Php 1:
God, and you are * there before him Col 1:
believe the Truth, * in it Col 1:
know you are * true to the Lord. 1Th 3
of gold. And * among them was one Rev 1:
I have been * at the door and I Rev 3:
THEN AS I looked, I saw a door * Rev 4
I looked and saw a Lamb * there Rev 5
THEN I SAW four angels * at the Rev 7
and languages, * in front of the Rev 7
For the Lamb * in front of Rev 7:1
Then the mighty angel * on the Rev 10
* there upon the sea and land." Rev 10
and two candlesticks * before the Rev 11:
THEN I SAW a Lamb * on Mount Zion Rev 14:
opened and a white horse * there; Rev 19:1
Then I saw an angel * in the Rev 19:1
great and small, * before God; Rev 20:1

STANDS
Laban continued, "* between us as Gen 31:51,5
of pure gold which * outside the Lev 24:3,
table that * before the Lord. Lev 24:5-
movable *, each 6 feet square and 1Ki 7:27-3
Each of these movable * had four 1Ki 7:27-3
each corner of the * were 1Ki 7:27-3
The * rode on four wheels which 1Ki 7:3
had been cast as part of the *. 1Ki 7:3
All the parts of the * were cast 1Ki 7:3
corners of the *, and these, too, 1Ki 7:3
these, too, were cast with the *. 1Ki 7:3
All ten * were the same size and 1Ki 7:3
vats, and placed them on the *. 1Ki 7:3
Ten movable * holding ten vats; 1Ki 7:41-4
the wheeled * in the Temple, 2Ki 16:1
The world * unmoved. 1Ch 16:3
It * in Haman's courtyard." Est 7:
calamity * ready to pounce upon Job 18:1
When he * up, the strongest are Job 41:2
him, but his own plan * forever. Ps 33:1
Even my own family * at a Ps 38:1
therefore it * unmoved despite Ps 46:
the earth trembles and * silently Ps 76:
GOD * UP to open heaven's court. Ps 82:
HIGH ON HIS holy mountain * Ps 87:1
For he * beside the poor and Ps 109:3
Melchizedek. God * beside you to Ps 110:
Forever, O Lord, your Word * firm Ps 119:89
He * before me as a shield. Ps 144:2
of her house or * at the street Pro 9:14
Truth * the test of time; Pro 12:19
and fair, his kingdom * secure. Pro 20:28
When the Lord * up from his Is 2:19
The Lord * up! Is 3:13
The metalsmith * at his forge to Is 44:12
over, and there * their god like a Jer 10:5
But the Lord * beside me like a Jer 20:11
top where the great Temple now *!' Jer 26:18
and the metal * and all the other Jer 27:19,20,21
planned against her * unchanged. Jer 51:29
there * the enemy to kill you. Eze 7:15
For the king of Babylon * at a Eze 21:21
angelic prince who * guard over Dan 12:1
The Lord * ready at Jerusalem's Mic 1:9
Lord * poised against Jerusalem. Mic 1:12
* will be overgrown with brush. Mic 3:12
He stops; he * still for a Hab 3:6
left, while Jerusalem * unmoved. Zec 12:6
* firm, for it is strongly built. Lk 6:47,48
that this man * here healed! Act 4:10
in fact, all the world * hushed Rom 3:19
work still *, will get his pay. 1Co 3:14
But God's truth * firm like a 2Ti 2:19
GOD'S PROMISE still *—his Heb 4:1
is from the one who * firm, Rev 3:14
golden altar that * before the Rev 9:13
where the altar *, and to count the Rev 11:1

STANK
troops that they * to high heaven 1Sa 13:3,4

STAR
That there shall come a * from Num 24:15-19
for we have seen his * in far-off Mt 2:2
time when they first saw the *. Mt 2:7
And look! The * appeared to them Mt 2:9
had told him the * first appeared Mt 2:16
and the * god Kaiway, and in all Act 7:43
* will shine in your hearts. 2Pe 1:19
And I will give you the Morning *! Rev 2:28
a great flaming * fell from heaven Rev 8:10
The * was called "Bitterness" Rev 8:11
Literally, "a * fallen from Rev 9:1f
I am the bright Morning *. Rev 22:16

STAR-GODS
the roofs to your *, and libations Jer 19:13

STARE
around to * at him, they dragged 2Sa 20:12

ARE Con't)
ee these men of evil gloat and * Ps 22:17
veryone there will * at you and Is 14:16
iracle that makes us *, amazed. Is 41:23
eir sinful *, and of adultery 2Pe 2:14

ARED
e others, they * in disbelief! Num 17:9
lisha * at Hazael until he 2Ki 8:11
eath * me in the face—I was Ps 116:3
s I * at all of this, I saw four Eze 1:15
nd as the man * intently, his Mk 8:25
ornelius * at him in terror. Act 10:4
e * at by men and angels alike. 1Co 4:9
ad killed. I * at her in horror. Rev 17:6

ARES
is source of sorrow always * me Ps 38:17
he wicked man * into space with Pro 16:30

ARGAZERS
strologers and *, who try to tell Is 47:13

ARING
e firelight and began * at him. Lk 22:56
er out in front of the * crowd. Jn 8:3
cloud, leaving them * after him. Act 1:9
ou standing here * at the sky? Act 1:11

ARK
within me. * fear overpowers me. Ps 55:4

ARLIGHT
ou made the * and the sun. Ps 74:16

ARRY
You stretched out the * curtain Ps 104:1
of heaven" and "the * host." Dan 8:10f
of heaven" and "the * host." Dan 8:10f
And the * heavens disappeared Rev 6:14

ARS
e also made the *. Gen 1:16
and count the * if you can. Gen 15:5
millions, like the * above you in Gen 22:17
to become as numerous as the *! Gen 26:4
"The sun, moon, and eleven * Gen 37:9
posterity as the * of heaven, and I Ex 32:13
Lord has multiplied you like *! Deu 1:10
to worship the sun, moon, or *. Deu 4:19
you as many as the * in the sky! Deu 10:22
the sun, moon, or *—which I have Deu 17:2,3
before you were as numerous as *. Deu 28:62
The very * of heaven Ju 5:20
Baal and the sun, moon, and *. 2Ki 17:16
the gods of the * were placed even 2Ki 21:3,4,5
Asherah, and the sun, moon, and *. 2Ki 23:4
to the sun, moon, *, and planets. 2Ki 23:5
Israel like to the * of heaven." 1Ch 27:23f
and of the sun, moon, and *. 2Ch 33:3
the sun, moon and *—in the very 2Ch 33:4,5
Let the * of the night Job 3:9
The sun won't rise, the * won't Job 9:7
the heavens, higher than the *. Job 22:12
even the moon and * are less than Job 25:5
as the morning * sang together and Job 38:6,7
"Can you hold back the *? Job 38:31
moon and the * you have made— I Ps 8:3
formed, and all the galaxies of *. Ps 33:6
and the moon and * at night, for Ps 136:9
He counts the * and calls them Ps 147:4
and moon, and all you twinkling *. Ps 148:3
light and moon and * are dim to Ecc 12:2
No light will shine from * or sun Is 13:10
Literally, "the * of God." Is 14:13f
scroll, and the * will fall as Is 34:4
Who created all these *? Is 40:26
so God does with * and planets! Is 40:26
all the vast myriads of *. Is 45:12
one who spread the * throughout the Is 51:13
I planted the * in place and Is 51:16
moon and *—the gods of my people! Jer 8:2
their fate and future in the *! Jer 10:2,3
he hung the * in space and Jer 10:12
and the moon and * to light the Jer 31:35
And as the * cannot be counted Jer 33:22
veil the heavens and darken the *. Eze 32:7
bright * will be dark above you. Eze 32:8
will glitter like * forever. Dan 12:3
are obscured and the * are hid. Joe 2:10
and the * withdraw their light. Joe 3:15
Seek him who created the Seven * Amo 5:8
your god of the *, and in all the Amo 5:25,26,27
nest among the *, I will bring you Ob 1:4
Merchants, numerous as *, filled Nah 3:16
and bow to the sun, moon and *. Zep 1:5
The sun and moon and * will no Zec 14:6
give light, and the * will seem Mt 24:29
Literally, "the * shall fall from Mt 24:29f
shine, and the * will fall—the Mk 13:25
portents in the sun, moon and *; Lk 21:25
the sun, moon and * as their gods! Act 7:42
Literally, "neither sun nor * Act 27:20f
to the sun, moon, planets, and *. 1Co 15:40f
the moon and * have another kind. 1Co 15:41
And the * differ from each other 1Co 15:41
the world and the *—in fact, all Heb 11:3
that, like the * of the sky and the Heb 11:12
as bright as *, but ahead of them Jud 1:13
He held seven * in his right Rev 1:16
of the seven * you saw in my right Rev 1:20
The seven * are the leaders Rev 1:20
holds the seven * in his right hand Rev 2:1f
of God and the seven *. Rev 3:1
Then the * of heaven appeared to Rev 6:13
Literally, "the * of heaven fell Rev 6:13f
the moon and the *, so that the Rev 8:12
a crown of twelve * on her head. Rev 12:1
*, which he plunged to the earth. Rev 12:4

START
and called them Man from the *. Gen 5:2
Don't * a fight! Deu 2:5
and eat it, then * back to your Deu 16:7
army got an early * and went as far Ju 7:1
"* running," he told the boy, 1Sa 20:36
men to * out after David tonight. 2Sa 17:1
and everyone will * shouting that 2Sa 17:9
something with which to *. 1Ch 22:14
queen did and will * talking to us Est 1:18
If I * to get up off the ground, Job 10:16
is this going to * an earthquake? Job 18:4
sins had caused the plague to *. Ps 106:30
You may * something you can't Pro 25:8,9,10
Fools * fights everywhere while Pro 29:8
to doing evil now * being good. Jer 13:23
And I will * a fire at the edge Jer 49:27
way to Zion and * back home again. Jer 50:5
Jerusalem will * on a journey to Eze 24:26
can get out and * cheating Amo 8:5
then the people will * a riot." Mk 11:32
"Do this instead—* at the foot; Lk 14:10
relatives and to * out for a Act 7:3
to form a mob and * a riot. Act 17:5
* us on our way to Rome by ship; Act 27:1
This is accomplished from * to Rom 1:17
not feel proud and * bragging. Rom 11:25
been trying to * something new, 1Co 1:15
hint that I would like to * now. 1Co 9:15
If you listen to them you will * 1Co 15:33
idea at the * be equalled by your 2Co 8:11
Rather, we are sinners if we * Gal 2:18
afford it, so you * a fight to take Jas 4:2
have always had, right from the *. 1Jn 2:7

STARTED
their meal and * on toward Sodom; Gen 18:16
his servants, and * off to the Gen 22:3
Then Jacob kissed Rachel and * Gen 29:11
he owned and * out to return to his Gen 31:17-20
* on again. Gen 32:1
The sun rose as he * on, and Gen 32:31
So Esau * back to Seir that same Gen 33:16
Then they * on again. Gen 35:5
with the grain and * for home. Gen 42:26
left Rameses and * for Succoth; Ex 12:37
the one who * the fire shall make Ex 22:6
and * towards the Promised Land. Num 14:40
his donkey and * off with them. Num 22:21
And so they * out. Jos 3:6
seventh day they * out again, but Jos 6:15
roused his men and * toward Ai, Jos 8:10
Its boundary * on the south side Jos 19:10
Then King Balak of Moab * a war Jos 24:9
was very fat!) he * home again. Ju 3:17,18,19
They * on their way again, Ju 18:21
So they * into the city where the 1Sa 9:9,10,11
As Saul said good-bye and * to 1Sa 10:9
and sling, * across to Goliath. 1Sa 17:40
Four hundred of them * off with 1Sa 25:13
So the king * back to Jerusalem. 2Sa 19:15
get them * worshiping their gods. 1Ki 11:2
and the prophet * off again. 1Ki 13:24,25
So Naaman * out, taking gifts of 2Ki 5:5
So Naaman * home again. 2Ki 5:19
and then Elisha * crying. 2Ki 8:11
and * off to Jerusalem; Ez 8:31
And though you * with little, Job 8:7
They hardly get *, barely take Is 40:24
it into a lump and * again. Jer 18:4
battle, Jeremiah * to leave the Jer 37:12
they had fled, now * off for Egypt Jer 43:5
poured out. He * a fire in Lam 4:11
So Gabriel * toward me. Dan 8:17
the astrologers * out again. Mt 2:9
Then he got into a boat and * Mt 8:23
stayed to get the people * home. Mt 14:22
just as he was and * out, leaving Mk 4:36
So the man * off to visit the Ten Mk 5:20
good-bye and get them * home. Mk 6:45
on the water. He * past them, but Mk 6:48
was over they * home to Nazareth, Lk 2:43
that evening, they * to look for Lk 2:44
they would mock. 'He * that Lk 14:30
back only the money he had * with. Lk 19:20
where the road * down from the Lk 19:36,37
the man believed Jesus and * home. Jn 4:50
Once again they * to arrest him. Jn 10:39
"The Freedmen" * an argument with Act 6:9
as I was getting * with my sermon, Act 11:15
leaped to his feet and * walking! Act 14:10
But just as Paul * to make his Act 18:14
he was a Jew, they * shouting again Act 19:34
already been * by someone else. Rom 15:20
finish what you * to do a year ago, 2Co 8:10
Having * the ball rolling so 2Co 8:11
lead us into. We * out bad, being Eph 2:3

STARTING
Finishing is better than *! Ecc 7:8
As he was * out on a trip, a man Mk 10:17
As Moses and Elijah were * to Lk 9:33
kill him without * a riot—a Lk 22:2
(Barabbas was in prison for * Lk 23:19
to punish them without * a riot. Act 4:21
didn't go around * riots, Act 24:22

STARTLE
acts of God shall * everyone. Ps 65:8
Or, "So shall he * many Is 52:14,15f

STARTLED
he wakened and sat up, *. Ru 3:8
The women were *, but the angel Mk 16:5
Zacharias was * and terrified. Lk 1:11,12

STARTLING
saying some rather * things and we Act 17:20

STARTS
A quick-tempered man * fights; Pro 15:18
hard to stop a quarrel once it *, Pro 17:14
A quarrelsome man * fights as Pro 26:21
A hot-tempered man * fights and Pro 29:22
anguish *, the baby is born; Is 66:7,8
before the farmer * again to sow Amo 9:13

STARVATION
Esau: "When a man is dying of *, Gen 25:32
otherwise we will all die of * Gen 43:8
wilderness to kill us with *." Ex 16:3
of *, or be killed by the sword!" 2Sa 3:29
then my son and I must die of *." 1Ki 17:12
Egypt to save his people from *. Ps 105:17
dungeon, * and death are not your Is 51:14
lie those dead from * and disease. Jer 14:18
those doomed to *, to famine; Jer 15:2
enemies, killed by * and disease—or Jer 21:9
die by sword, * or disease, but Jer 38:2
off than those who die of slow *. Lam 4:9

STARVE
The people began to *. Gen 41:55
for us before we all * to death." Gen 42:2
"We will * if we stay here and 2Ki 7:4
* if we go back into the city; 2Ki 7:4
lions they shall *, and all their Job 4:11
will die in war, or * to death. Job 27:14
fearing you will * to death; Ps 127:2
not let a good man * to death, nor Pro 10:3
to be too proud to work—and *. Pro 12:9
Your great and honored men will * Is 5:13
*, but my servants shall eat; Is 65:13
their boys and girls shall *. Jer 11:21,22
Now, Lord, let their children * Jer 18:21
but you let your flocks *. Eze 34:3
You fed yourselves and let them * Eze 34:8
He will * out all those gods of Zep 2:11
a drought to * both you and all Hag 1:11
over the land, and he began to *. Lk 15:14

STARVED
Esau: "Boy, am I *! Gen 25:30

STARVES
The fool won't work and almost * Ecc 4:5,6

STARVING
land of Egypt and Canaan were *. Gen 47:13
he is * in the midst of the siege Deu 28:55
Those who were well are now *; 1Sa 2:5
Those who were * are fed. 1Sa 2:5
The Syrians know we are *, so 2Ki 7:12
the thirsty, and bread to the *. Job 22:7
to carry food while they are *. Job 24:10
thief, if he steals when he is *! Pro 6:30
her princes are like * deer that Lam 1:6
elders—they were * in the streets Lam 1:19
the priests are *. Joe 1:9

STATE
she shall be in a * of ceremonial Lev 15:19
is in a similar * of defilement. Lev 15:26
Her father must * his Num 30:5
* was Jehoshaphat (son of Ahilud). 2Sa 8:16
of Nathan) was secretary of *; 1Ki 4:1
of *, your majesty and splendor. Job 40:10
Arise, O God, and * your case Ps 74:22
Know the * of your flocks and Pro 27:23,24
your case and * your proofs that Is 45:21
your ship of * into a hurricane! Eze 27:26
Stand up and * your case against Mic 6:1
"The laws of Moses * that if a Lk 20:28
and instructed to * whether or not Lk 22:67,68
For the Scriptures clearly * that Jn 7:41,42
"Therefore I clearly * to Act 2:36
let me clearly * to you and to all Act 4:10
as head of the *, and those of the 1Pe 2:13

STATED
Then Moses * again that all he Lev 8:34
All the valuations shall be * in Lev 27:25
where it is * that the valley of Num 21:14
AS HAS ALREADY been *, there was Ju 18:1
As already *, there was an annex 1Ki 6:10

(STATED Con't)
just as I * in that book you read. 2Ki 22:15,16
As previously *. 1Ch 6:16
the letter *, "must be proclaimed Est 3:14
It further * that a copy of this Est 8:13
all the evils * in the contract. Jer 11:8
else flatly *, "I know this fellow Lk 22:59
Moreover, he further *, 'God Act 2:34
This is * in the Scripture that Act 13:34
added, "God himself has * this." Rev 19:9
who heed the truth * in this Book. Rev 22:9

STATELY
There are three * monarchs in the Pro 30:29,30,31
falling down upon them! How * Sol 1:10
Your neck is * Sol 4:4
Your neck is * as an ivory Sol 7:4
The kings of the nations lie in * Is 14:18

STATEMENT
(So the Lord's * to Jehu came 2Ki 15:12
the people found a * which said Neh 13:1
There is no truer * than this: Job 34:12
"Not everyone can accept this * Mt 19:11
Let anyone who can, accept my * Mt 19:12
meant by the * he had just made. Mk 7:17
This * is found in only some of Mk 14:68f
Otherwise the * would be, "He had Lk 20:37,38f
so don't be surprised at my * Jn 3:7
leaders were puzzled by this *. Jn 7:35
Now this wonderful *—that he was Rom 4:23
a true * of the way God blesses. 1Pe 5:12

STATEMENTS
to them all of the * of blessing Jos 8:34
These tremendous * you have made Job 13:12
These * are Solomon's discouraged Ecc 9:5f
These * are Solomon's discouraged Ecc 9:5f
These * are Solomon's discouraged Ecc 9:10f
Jesus made these * while in the Jn 8:20
* to see if they were really so. Act 17:11

STATESMEN
"But now your * bring your ship Eze 27:26

STATING
address to Israel, * all the laws Deu 1:1
may write a letter * that he has Deu 24:1
of independence, * that they had Lk 19:14

STATIONED
* themselves along their frontier. 2Ki 3:21
were * at Jerusalem near the king. 2Ch 1:14
12,000 cavalrymen * in the chariot 2Ch 9:25
army * at Jerusalem, his capital. 2Ch 17:13
And he * his army generals in all 2Ch 33:14

STATIONING
* themselves around the city. Ju 9:34

STATISTICS
Here are the * concerning the Ez 2:36-39
Here are the * concerning the Ez 2:40,41,42
"Here are the * concerning the Neh 7:39-42
"Here are the * concerning the Neh 7:43,44,45

STATUE
trying to make a * of God—an idol Deu 4:16,17
For they preferred a * of an ox Ps 106:19,20
huge and powerful * of a man, Dan 2:31
The head of the * was made of Dan 2:32
It came hurtling toward the * and Dan 2:34
Then the whole * collapsed into Dan 2:35
But the Rock that knocked the * Dan 2:35
the *—will rise to rule the world. Dan 2:39
MADE a golden * ninety feet high Dan 3:1
come to the dedication of his *. Dan 3:2
King Nebuchadnezzar's golden *; Dan 3:5
to the ground and worshiped the *. Dan 3:7
worship the golden * when the band Dan 3:10
worship the golden * you set up." Dan 3:12
to worship the golden * I set up? Dan 3:14
worship the *, all will be well. Dan 3:15
the golden * you have erected." Dan 3:18
to make a great * of the first Rev 13:14
to this * and even make it speak! Rev 13:15
Then the * ordered that anyone Rev 13:15
and his * and accepting his mark Rev 14:9
Creature and his *, and have been Rev 14:11
and his * and his mark and number. Rev 15:2
Creature and was worshiping his *. Rev 16:2
mark, and who worshiped his *. Rev 19:20
Creature or his *, nor accepted his Rev 20:4

STATUES
These were carved * of male and Ex 34:13f
Solomon placed two * of angels 1Ki 6:23-28
He tore down the * of horses and 2Ki 23:11
two sculptured * of angels, and 2Ch 3:10
to carved * of goats and calves 2Ch 11:15
to you and made * of men and Eze 16:17
the * and idols she erects. Hos 10:1
Above the golden chest were * of Heb 9:5

STATUS
I was given great * because the Ez 7:28

STAVES
It was hollowedWith their *And Num 21:17,18

STAY
* here in the western section. Gen 13:9
strengthen you. Do * awhile before Gen 18:5
Don't * down here on the plain or Gen 19:17
"* here with the donkey," Gen 22:5
"Come and * with us, friend; Gen 24:31
quiet sort who liked to * at home. Gen 25:27
Do as I say and * here in this Gen 26:3
Laban in Haran. * there with him Gen 27:44
raise do you need to get you to *? Gen 30:28
"My men and I will * with you Gen 33:12
Please sir, let me * here as a Gen 44:33
O my soul, * away from them. Gen 49:6
let your flocks and herds * here; Ex 10:24
of Sabbath rest; * in your tents Ex 16:28,29
man or animal.' * away from the Ex 19:13
He told the elders, "* here and Ex 24:14
and his sons to * at the entrance Lev 8:35
however, he must * outside his Lev 14:8
"* with us," Moses pleaded, Num 10:31
wells, but will * on the main road Num 20:17
But the king of Edom said, "* Num 20:18
"we will * on the main road and Num 20:19
of Edom was adamant. "* out!" Num 20:20
"* here overnight," Balaam Num 22:8
However, * here tonight so that Num 22:19
yourselves. Now * outside of the Num 31:19
make the people * even longer in Num 32:15
* here in the cities of Gilead. Num 32:26
to * in the City of Refuge; Num 35:25
'We will * on the main road and Deu 2:27
camps must * away from all evil. Deu 23:9,10
and * outside until the evening; Deu 23:11
the other side; * with them until Jos 1:15
However, * about a half mile Jos 3:2,3,4
Why didn't we * on the other Jos 7:7
I will not * with you any longer Jos 7:12
death must * in that city until he Jos 20:6
to me! But * here until I go and Ju 6:18
"I'll * here until you return." Ju 6:18
Angel, "Please * here until we can Ju 13:15
"I'll *," the Angel replied, Ju 13:16
"Well, * here with me," Micah Ju 17:10,11
Her father urged him to * Ju 19:4
Then he pleaded with him to * Ju 19:6
father pleaded, "* just today and Ju 19:8
it's getting late. * just tonight, Ju 19:9
let's * here tonight." Ju 19:11
said, "we can't * in this heathen Ju 19:12,13
for you mustn't * here in the Ju 19:20
"* right here with us to glean; Ru 2:8,9
* right behind my women workers; Ru 2:8,9
to come back and * close behind his Ru 2:21
"Do as he has said. * with his Ru 2:22
to you than I am. * here tonight, Ru 3:13
"Yes," they replied, "* right 1Sa 9:12,13
us, if they say, '* where you are 1Sa 14:9
in the field and * there until the 1Sa 20:5
and since they * clean even on 1Sa 21:5
father's family. * here with me, 1Sa 22:23
"Now he will have to * here and 1Sa 27:12
he told them to * at Jericho until 2Sa 10:5
"Well, * here tonight," David 2Sa 11:12
urge him not to * at the ford of 2Sa 17:16
is better that you * here in the 2Sa 18:3
of God to * in Jerusalem or die? 1Ki 2:42
left Gilgal, "* here, for the Lord 2Ki 2:1
Elisha, "Please * here in Bethel, 2Ki 2:4
Elisha, "Please * here, for the 2Ki 2:6,7
place to * whenever he comes by." 2Ki 4:10
"We will starve if we * here 2Ki 7:4
loss than if they * here and die 2Ki 7:13
* with the king at all times." 2Ki 11:6,7,8
with your glory and * home! 2Ki 14:10
telling them to * at Jericho until 1Ch 19:5
"The Lord will * with you as 2Ch 15:2
you as long as you * with him! 2Ch 15:2
will * at the entrance as guards. 2Ch 23:4
Everyone else must * in the outer 2Ch 23:5,6
Temple. * right beside the king." 2Ch 23:7
my advice is to * home and don't 2Ch 25:19
we can't * out here much longer. Ez 10:13
Will he * beside your feeding Job 39:9
O Lord, don't * away. Ps 22:19
Don't * silent! Ps 35:22
My loved ones and friends * Ps 38:11
the far off deserts and * there. Ps 55:7
O God, don't * away! Ps 71:12
and * away from every evil. Ps 101:4
deceive and lie to * in my house. Ps 101:7
How can a young man * pure? Ps 119:9
I trust in you. I * awake through Ps 119:148
Don't do it, son! * far from men Pro 1:15
You will be given the sense to * Pro 2:11,12,13
godly instead, and * on the right Pro 2:20
* far from her. Pro 4:24
Don't go near her; * away from Pro 7:25
If you are looking for advice, * Pro 14:7
The sensible * on the pathways of Pro 15:21
It is an honor for a man to * out Pro 20:3
end in poverty. * awake, work hard, Pro 20:13
and you'll * out of trouble. Pro 21:23
who values his soul will * away. Pro 22:5
O my son, be wise and * in God's Pro 23:19,20,21
O my son, trust my advice—* Pro 23:26,27,28
And the king's crown doesn't * in Pro 27:23,
good men * away and sing for joy. Pro 29:5
leader, they * together in swarms. Pro 30:24-
the fields and * in the villages. Sol 7:
won't let their sheep * overnight. Is 13:
Let our outcasts * among you; Is 16:4
Your enemies will * far away; Is 54:
from heaven and * upon the ground Is 55:
Your gates will * wide open Is 60:
I will let you * in your own land. Jer 7
will I let you * in this land that Jer 7
Its leaves * green and it goes Jer 17
of life or death! * here in Jer 21
be permitted to * in their own Jer 27:1
* there until I send for them. Jer 27:2
Build homes and plan to *; Jer 29
homes and plan to * many years, Jer 29:2
If you decide to *, then return Jer 40
and * with the remnant he rules. Jer 40
"* here and serve the king of Jer 40
As for me, I will * at Mizpah Jer 40:1
"* here in this land. Jer 42:1
will let you * here in your land. Jer 42:1
say, 'We will not * here,'—and Jer 42:13,1
so that we will * here and be Jer 43:2,
to obey the Lord and * in Judah. Jer 43:
If you *, you will be destroyed Jer 51:
fight; they * in their barracks. Jer 51:3
but none will let them *. Lam 4:1
If you * inside, famine and Eze 7:1
Be prepared! * mobilized. Eze 38:
Then at last they will learn to *. Dan 9:2
may Judah * far from such a life. Hos 4:1
green pastures. * away from her, Hos 4:1
You may no longer * here in this Hos 9:
O Ephraim! * away from idols! Hos 14:8
You cannot * angry with your Mic 7:1
belongs and where she will *!" Zec 5:11
of Zephaniah), where they will *. Zec 6:10,1
angel said, "and * there until I Mt 2:1
for you will * there until you Mt 5:26
a godly man and * in his home until Mt 10:1
When you ask permission to *, be Mt 10:12
"So * awake and be prepared, for Mt 25:13
point of death * here Mt 26:38
stay here * awake with Mt 26:38
you even * awake with me one hour? Mt 26:40
to * out in the barren wastelands. Mk 1:45
"* at one home in each Mk 6:10
He himself would * and tell the Mk 6:45
where they were to * he asked them, Mk 9:33
know when it will happen, * alert. Mk 13:33
death; * here and watch with me." Mk 14:34
leave them, but to * at Capernaum. Lk 4:42
home to home, but * in one place, Lk 10:7
they begged him to * the night with Lk 24:29
yet—* here in the city until the Lk 24:49
begged him to * at their village; Jn 4:40,41
At the end of the two days' * he Jn 4:43,44
for he wanted to * out of Judea Jn 7:1
Jordan River to * near the place Jn 10:40
But if you * in me and obey my Jn 15:7
'Would I * in it? Act 7:48,49
to * with them for several days. Act 10:48
the believers to * close to the Act 11:23
said, "come and * at my home." Act 16:15
They asked him to * for a few Act 18:20
During our * of several days, a Act 21:10
to make his * more comfortable. Act 24:23
During their * of several days Act 25:14
They begged us to * with them Act 28:14
I end this letter. * away from Rom 16:17
and to * innocent of any wrong. Rom 16:19
among you, so that you can * pure. 1Co 5:7
being able to * happily unmarried. 1Co 7:7
widows—better to * unmarried if you 1Co 7:8
but she wants to * with him anyway, 1Co 7:12
he wants her to * with him, she 1Co 7:13
that the other *, for God wants his 1Co 7:15
will be converted if they *; 1Co 7:16
Christian, let him * there, for now 1Co 7:24
have wives should * as free as 1Co 7:29
It could be that I will * longer 1Co 16:6
I want to come and * awhile, if 1Co 16:7
me food to eat and a place to *. 2Co 12:13
Now make sure that you * free and Gal 5:1
In everything you do, * away from Php 2:14
My beloved friends, * true to the Php 4:1
* together in perfect harmony. Col 3:14
I decided to * alone in Athens and 1Th 3:1
Watch for his return and * sober. 1Th 5:6
by his authority: * away from any 2Th 3:6
who he is and * away from him, that 2Th 3:14
Macedonia, please * there in 1Ti 1:3,4
you do and think. * true to what is 1Ti 4:16
Be sure that you yourself * away 1Ti 5:22
If you * away from sin you will 2Ti 2:21
often have, but * close to anything 2Ti 2:22
decided to * there for the winter. Tit 3:12
throne of God and * there to Heb 4:16
Try to * out of all quarrels and Heb 12:14

TAY Con't)
* away from the love of money; Heb 13:5
and God bless you; * warm and eat Jas 2:16
and such a town, * there a year, Jas 4:13
or a place to * for the night. 1Pe 4:9
so that you will * away from sin. 1Jn 2:1
And now, my little children, * in 1Jn 2:28
to * pure because Christ is pure. 1Jn 3:3
So if we * close to him, 1Jn 3:6
* always within the boundaries Jud 1:21
Its gates never close; they * Rev 21:25

TAYED
For Abram * in the land of Gen 13:12
men with him * there overnight. Gen 24:54
So Isaac * in Gerar. Gen 26:6
than Leah, and * and worked the Gen 29:30
* and cared for Laban's flock. Gen 30:35,36
Jacob * where he was for the Gen 32:13,14,15
Nun), * behind in the Tabernacle. Ex 33:11
But if the cloud *, they stayed Ex 40:37
But if the cloud stayed, they * Ex 40:37
When traveling, each tribe * Num 2:3-31
* that way throughout the night. Num 9:15
there as long as the Cloud *. Num 9:18
If it * a long time, then they Num 9:19
time, then they * a long time. Num 9:19
But if it * only a few days, then Num 9:19
Sometimes the fire-cloud * only Num 9:20,21
If the Cloud * above the Num 9:22
how long the people of Israel *; Num 9:22
to Hazeroth, where they * awhile. Num 11:35
to visit Egypt and * there so long, Num 20:15
After leaving Rameses, they * in Num 33:5,6
* there for quite a long time. Num 33:9
man should have * inside the City Num 35:28
us, 'You have * here long enough. Deu 1:6
So they * there at Kadesh for a Deu 1:46
" 'You have * here long enough. Deu 2:3
However, we * away from the Deu 2:37
"As I said before, I * on the Deu 10:10
the mountains and * there three Jos 2:22
in the heavens and * there for Jos 10:13
so the Canaanites * there. Ju 1:27
to count and * until the land was Ju 6:5
that night the fleece * dry, but Ju 6:40
the people of Israel * in Kadesh. Ju 11:17
Samson * in bed with the girl Ju 16:3
Ephraim, they * at Micah's home. Ju 18:2
stay awhile, so he * three days, Ju 19:4
So she * home until the baby was 1Sa 1:23
Samuel * in bed until morning, 1Sa 3:15
Meanwhile, Saul * at Gilgal, and 1Sa 13:7
but the Philistines * at 1Sa 13:16
They * in Moab during the entire 1Sa 22:4
and David * at Horesh while 1Sa 23:18
But David * in Jerusalem. 2Sa 11:1
But Uriah didn't go there. He * 2Sa 11:9
So Uriah * around the palace. 2Sa 11:12
(the son of Ammihud) and * there 2Sa 13:37,38,39
I might as well have * there. 2Sa 14:32
back into the city and * there. 2Sa 15:29
"He * at Jerusalem," Ziba 2Sa 16:3
so they * there awhile and rested. 2Sa 16:14
But the men of Judah * with their 2Sa 20:2
upon a rock and * there through the 2Sa 21:10
of Egypt and * there until the 1Ki 11:40
* away from the land of Israel. 2Ki 6:23
for Samaria, and * overnight at a 2Ki 10:12
Meanwhile, David had * in 1Ch 20:1
Rehoboam * in Jerusalem and 2Ch 11:5-10
The trumpeter * with me to sound Neh 4:18
act that way. I * at work on the Neh 5:16
man who feared God and * away Job 1:1
"I have * in God's paths, Job 23:11
now than she whose husband *! Is 54:1
and elders who * true to God. Lam 4:16
and * beside them as they flew. Eze 10:15,16
* there until King Herod's death. Mt 2:15
* to get the people started home. Mt 14:22
to Bethany, where he * overnight. Mt 21:17
in the Temple. He * on at the Lk 1:23
Mary * with Elizabeth about three Lk 1:56
She never left the Temple but * Lk 2:36,37
but Jesus * behind in Jerusalem. Lk 2:43
the darkness. They * away from that Jn 3:20
left Jerusalem and * for a while in Jn 3:22
and Lazarus, he * where he was for Jn 11:6
But Mary * at home. Jn 11:20
Now Jesus had * outside the Jn 11:30
and * there with his disciples. Jn 11:54
The rest of us * in the boat and Jn 21:8
strengthened. He * with the Act 9:19
And Peter * a long time in Act 9:43
and both of them * there for a Act 11:26
Nevertheless, they * there a Act 14:3
And they * there with the Act 14:28
They * several days, Act 15:33
Paul and Barnabas * on at Act 15:34,35
border, and * there several days. Act 16:12
After that he * with Titus Act 18:7
So Paul * there the next year Act 18:11
Paul * in the city several days Act 18:18
he * awhile longer in Turkey. Act 19:22
Troas, Turkey, where we * a week. Act 20:6
believers and * with them a week. Act 21:4
the believers, but * only one day. Act 21:7
on to Caesarea and * at the home of Act 21:8
There we * for several days. Act 27:9
Syracuse, where we * three days. Act 28:12
to exhaustion, * awake through 2Co 6:5
* there with him for fifteen days. Gal 1:18
Erastus * at Corinth, and I left 2Ti 4:20
now because they * true to him Jas 5:11
with us or else they would have *. 1Jn 2:19

STAYING
But they will only consider * Gen 34:22
the man who was * with him, so they Ju 19:22
but Ruth insisted on * with Ru 1:14
of where he is * and who has seen 1Sa 23:22
Jonathan and Ahima-az had been * 2Sa 17:17
of this widow with whom I am *?" 1Ki 17:20
commit suicide by * there—to die by 2Ch 32:11
you a traitor for * true to God. Is 8:12
they are * overnight at Geba. Is 10:28,29
of Babylon who was * in the city of Jer 52:9
house where he was *, and Jesus Mt 9:28
Soon the house where he was * Mk 2:2
house where he was *, the crowds Mk 3:20
place where he was * and were with Jn 1:39
secretly, * out of the public eye. Jn 7:10
of the house where they were *. Act 1:13
Peter, who is * with Simon, the Act 10:5,6
Peter, who is * in the home of Act 10:32
at the house where I was *! Act 11:11
* there only for a little while. 1Co 16:5
I will be * here at Ephesus 1Co 16:8
I can be of more help to you by *! Php 1:24
certain I will be * on earth a Php 1:25
in your faith; my * will make you Php 1:26

STAYS
it * away, but not these men; Pro 1:17
a wise man * cool when insulted. Pro 12:16
An empty stable * clean—but there Pro 14:4
A mocker * away from wise men Pro 15:12
it * there, for it cannot move! Is 46:7
and * away from sin, and is Eze 18:8
written. It * exactly as it is." Jn 19:22
die unless everyone * aboard." Act 27:31
me that your life * clean and true, 3Jn 1:3

STEAD
them will stand you in good *; Pro 1:7,8,9

STEADFAST
and rich in * love and truth. Ex 34:5,6
I, Jehovah, show this * love to Ex 34:7
sins and showing us your * love. Num 14:17,18
your magnificent, * love, just as Num 14:19
for he depends upon the * love of Ps 21:7
Your * love, O Lord, is as great Ps 36:5
also pours out his * love upon me, Ps 42:8
of righteousness whose love is *; Jer 9:24
standing in it * and firm, strong Col 1:23
must be strong and *, so that they Tit 1:9

STEADIED
path and * me as I walked along. Ps 40:2

STEADILY
* forward to God without fear. Job 11:15
Keep traveling * along his Ps 37:34
* to my course of seeking wisdom. Ecc 2:3
Slowly, *, surely, the time Hab 2:3
cling to them and * spread them to Lk 8:15
heaven, he moved * onward towards Lk 9:51
Holy Spirit, gazed * upward into Act 7:55
But if anyone keeps looking * Jas 1:25
began to sin has kept * at it. 1Jn 3:8

STEADINESS
May God who gives patience, *, Rom 15:5

STEADY
put out his hand to * the Ark. 2Sa 6:6
He causes the good to walk a * 2Sa 22:34
reached out his hand to * the Ark. 1Ch 13:9
But the Lord held me *. Ps 18:18
He has made me * as a mountain." Ps 30:6,7
him, who rely upon his * love. Ps 33:18,19
I will * him and make him Ps 89:21
They will * you with their hands Ps 91:12
THOSE WHO TRUST in the Lord are * Ps 125:1
* plodding brings prosperity; Pro 21:5
and * peg to support my people; Is 22:23,24
hope and faith are strong and *. Rom 5:4
you strong and * in the Lord, just Rom 16:25,26,27
be strong and *, always abounding 1Co 15:58
strong faith and * looking forward 1Th 1:3
of good, * men as the pastors. 1Ti 3:8
Stand *, and don't be afraid of 2Ti 4:5
If you are wise, live a life of * Jas 3:13

STEAK
love than * with someone you hate. Pro 15:17
is better than * every day along Pro 17:1

STEAL
it enough to * my husband? Gen 30:15
And now will you * my son's Gen 30:15
Why would we * silver or gold Gen 44:8
"You must not *. Ex 20:15
"You must not * nor lie nor Lev 19:11
We will not * food as we go, but Deu 2:28
" 'You must not *. Deu 5:19
you must never * a man's land by Deu 19:14
"Israel did not * the land. Ju 11:14,15
Don't * the land of defenseless Pro 23:10,11
And if I am too poor, I may *, Pro 30:9
his brother to * his food, but will Is 9:19,20
think that you can *, murder, Jer 7:9
fruit and * your dairy cattle. Eze 25:4
You swear and lie and kill and * Hos 4:2
You trample the poor and * their Amo 5:11
For you * the shirts right off Mic 2:8
It says that all who * and lie Zec 5:3
adultery, don't *, don't lie, Mt 19:18
adultery, don't *, don't lie, don't Mk 10:19
no thief can * them; Lk 12:33
murder, don't *, don't lie, honor Lk 18:20
The thief 's purpose is to *, Jn 10:10
You tell others not to *—do you Rom 2:21
tell others not to steal—do you *? Rom 2:21
him, or kill him or * from him. Rom 13:9
They must not talk back, nor *, Tit 2:10

STEALING
Ask them, 'What do you mean by * Gen 44:5
"If he is caught in the act of * Ex 22:4
That is *. Pro 22:28
heavy is as bad as * his jacket in Pro 25:20
from coming and * his body and then Mt 27:64
this I hear about your * from me? Lk 16:2
If anyone is * he must stop it Eph 4:28
for murdering or * or making 1Pe 4:15

STEALS
"IF A MAN * an ox or sheep and Ex 22:1
if he * when he is starving! Pro 6:30
devil comes and * the words away Lk 8:12

STEALTHILY
to greet Amasa, he * slipped the 2Sa 20:8,9,10

STEAM
his nostrils, like * from a boiling Job 41:20

STEAMROLLER
drags across the ground like a *! Job 41:30

STEED
He has chained his * to the Gen 49:11
on the king's own *, and led him Est 6:11
glorious like a proud * in battle. Zec 10:3

STEEDS
See the prancing of his *! Ju 5:22
God of Jacob, * and riders fell. Ps 76:6
his * are swifter than eagles. Jer 4:13
young men on fine *, those army Eze 23:12
men of high rank, riding their *. Eze 23:23
come chariot horses, * and mules. Eze 27:14
by side, pulled by prancing *! Nah 2:3

STEELED
Israel did. They * themselves Heb 3:7,8

STEEP
plunged down the * hillside into Mk 5:13

STEER
says and means. * clear of foolish 2Ti 2:16

STELLAE
Literally, "*." Eze 43:9f

STEM
The main * of the lampstand was Ex 37:20,21
* beneath each pair of branches; Ex 37:20,21
"Shouldn't someone * this Job 11:2
ate through the * of the plant, so Jon 4:7
of the prophets * from these two Mt 22:40

STENCH
completely. The * of the place has Gen 19:13
a terrible * throughout the land. Ex 8:14
full of the * of sin and death. Ps 5:9
The incense you bring me is a * Is 1:12,13
unburied, and the * of rotting Is 34:3
you a curse and a * in the nostrils Jer 44:8
rotting * will rise upon the land. Joe 2:20
* of death was terrible to smell. Amo 4:10
like the * from an open grave. Rom 3:13

STEP
know what my next * should be, Gen 24:49
let us move a * from this place. Ex 33:15
"Aaron and Miriam, * forward," Num 12:5
blessed you every * of the way for Deu 2:7
son Abinadab to * forward and walk 1Sa 16:8
Goliath the giant * out from the 1Sa 17:23
it, and took a * or two to see what 1Sa 17:38,39
I am only a * away from death! 1Sa 20:3
watch their * and are faithful to 1Ki 2:4
and don't * outside the city on 1Ki 2:36,37
two lions on each *—twelve in all. 1Ki 10:20
home, and when you * into the city, 1Ki 14:12
also stood at each side of each *. 2Ch 9:19
"Watch your *—I have not 2Ch 19:6
I do, and every * I take. Job 31:4
She forgets that someone may * Job 39:15
knows, for he watches my every *. Ps 18:24
He delights in each * they take. Ps 37:23
not left your path by a single *. Ps 44:18
You can safely meet a lion or * Ps 91:13
let others * forward to replace Ps 109:8

(STEP Con't)
The first * is to trust and Pro 1:7,8,9
the first * toward becoming wise! Pro 4:7
Watch your *. Pro 4:26
My son, watch your * before the Pro 24:21,22
says the Preacher. * by step I came Ecc 7:27,28
Step by * I came to this result Ecc 7:27,28
the pit you will * into a trap, for Is 24:18
whom victory meets at every *? Is 41:2
first person to * down into it Jn 5:4
a wrong *, because of the dark." Jn 11:10
the goal with purpose in every *. 1Co 9:26
first * toward all kinds of sin. 1Ti 6:10
possible the next *, which is for 2Pe 1:7

STEPHANAS
and I baptized the family of *. 1Co 1:16
Do you remember * and his family? 1Co 16:15
I am so glad that *, Fortunatus, 1Co 16:17

STEPHEN
* (a man unusually full of faith Act 6:5
converted too. *, the man so full Act 6:8
heard * curse Moses, and even God. Act 6:11
against *, and the Jewish leaders Act 6:12
again that * was constantly Act 6:13
in rage. But *, full of the Holy Act 7:55
hurtling at him, * prayed, "Lord Act 7:59
agreement with the killing of *. Act 8:1
and with great sorrow buried *. Act 8:2
And when your witness * was Act 22:20

STEPHEN'S
stand against * wisdom and spirit. Act 6:10
chamber saw * face become as Act 6:15
This was * lengthy reply: "The Act 7:2
stung to fury by * accusation, and Act 7:54
persecution after * death traveled Act 11:19

STEPMOTHER
Possibly his *. 1Co 5:1f

STEPPED
Lot * outside to talk to them, Gen 19:6
Then Judah * forward and said, Gen 44:18
The old man * outside to talk to Ju 19:23
So Ahima-az * aside. 2Sa 18:30
As he * forward to greet Amasa, 2Sa 20:8,9,10
when Naaman * down from his chariot 2Ki 5:26
passed by and * on the thistle and 2Ki 14:9
old man, so he * down from the 1Ch 23:1
finally a spirit * forward before 2Ch 18:19,20
and * on the thistle, crushing it! 2Ch 25:18
group of priests * forward and 2Ch 30:24
The young saw me and * aside, Job 29:8
or if I have * off God's pathway, Job 31:7,8
But Moses, his chosen one, * into Ps 106:23
If the Lord of Hosts had not * in Is 1:9
Therefore he himself * in to save Is 59:16
So they * out of the fire. Dan 3:26
snap shut unless it is * on; Amo 3:5
was saying, he * down from his Jon 3:6
was there as he * from the boat; Mk 6:34
Then the Sadducees * forward—a Mk 12:18
Then Peter * forward with the Act 2:14
and then he * in and saved all 1Co 1:21
of the world. He * forward and Rev 5:7

STEPPING
prevail—everyone * on someone else, Is 3:5
their nets. * into one of the Lk 5:3
to happen to him. * forward to meet Jn 18:4,5

STEPS
And don't make * for the altar, Ex 20:26
This summarizes the various * in Ex 38:21
They followed in your *, O Lord. Deu 33:3
You have made wide * for my feet, 2Sa 22:37
It had six * and a rounded back, 1Ki 10:19
They quickly carpeted the bare * 2Ki 9:13
Or, "on the * of Ahaz." 2Ki 20:11f
shadow moved up and down the *. 2Ki 20:11f
for he followed in the * of his 2Ki 22:1
to make terraced * for the Temple 2Ch 9:11
It had six gold * and a 2Ch 9:18
you give me so few * upon the stage Job 14:16
in God's paths, following his *. Job 23:11
You have made wide * beneath my Ps 18:36
The * of good men are directed by Ps 37:23
for my *, waiting to kill me. Ps 56:6
above all else to follow your *. Ps 84:5
him to make a pathway for his *. Ps 85:13
Or, "set us in the way of his * Ps 85:13f
Follow the * of the godly Pro 2:20
Since the Lord is directing our * Pro 20:24
In that day when God * in to Is 30:25
to find no * taken against sin. Is 59:15
* to do as the king had commanded. Jer 39:13
We climbed the seven * into the Eze 40:6
And there were seven * leading up Eze 40:22
It too had a stairway of seven * Eze 40:26
that it had eight * leading up to Eze 40:31
there were eight * instead of seven Eze 40:34
* leading up to the entrance. Eze 40:37
of the Temple. Ten * led up to it Eze 40:48,49
On the east side are * to climb Eze 43:17
And you are following in their * Mt 23:32
Court—met to discuss their next *. Mk 15:1

*, doing things the same way. 2Co 12:18
holding him back * out of the way. 2Th 2:7
Follow in his *: He never 1Pe 2:21
following in her * like good 1Pe 3:6

STERILE
be lepers, or be *, or die of 2Sa 3:29
from a root in dry and * ground. Is 53:2

STERLING
800,000 pounds * at current value. 1Ch 19:6f
than the purest gold or * silver! Pro 8:19
have * ready for the silversmith. Pro 25:4,5
Once like * silver; Is 1:22

STERN
When the people heard these * Ex 33:4
despite the Lord's * warnings. 2Ki 17:15
while I give you * warnings. Ps 81:8
Literally, "a * (ruthless) Pro 17:11f
being a man of * principle, Mt 1:19
the * and prayed for daylight. Act 27:29
fast, while the * was exposed to Act 27:41

STERNLY
Jesus * warned them not to tell Mt 9:30
Jesus then told him *, "Go and Mk 1:43,44
very *, "Satan, get behind me! Mk 8:33
there as * as necessary to make Tit 1:13

STEW
One day Jacob was cooking * when Gen 25:29
gave Esau bread, peas, and *; Gen 25:34
some * for supper for these men." 2Ki 4:38
sir, there's poison in this *!" 2Ki 4:40

STEWARD
Daniel talked it over with the * Dan 1:11
trial period the * could see how Dan 1:13
The * finally agreed to the test. Dan 1:14
So after that the * fed them Dan 1:16

STEWARDS
uniforms and his * in full regalia, 2Ch 9:4

STICK
owned nothing except a walking *! Gen 32:10
and your walking *," she replied. Gen 38:18
* is the father of my child. Gen 38:25
so he dipped a * into a 1Sa 14:27
a little bit on the end of a *; 1Sa 14:43
"that you come at me with a *?" 1Sa 17:43
a * and threw it into the water; 2Ki 6:6
find her to be a * that breaks 2Ki 18:20,21
Watch your step. * to the path Pro 4:26
always keep it in mind and * to Pro 7:1
the charges won't * because Pro 11:9f
They won't die if you use a * on Pro 23:13,14
happiness would * with him in all Ecc 8:15
dill, but it is beaten with a *. Is 28:27
She is a sharpened * that will Is 36:6
The children's tongues * to the Lam 4:3,4
and I will make your tongue * to Eze 3:26
"Take a * and carve on it these Eze 37:16
these words: 'This * represents Eze 37:16
Then take another * and carve Eze 37:16
words on it: 'This * represents all Eze 37:16
together in your hand as one *. Eze 37:17
and make them one * in my hand. Eze 37:18,19,20
measuring tape and a measuring *. Eze 40:3
*, which was 10½ feet long. Eze 40:5
they are like a burning * pulled Zec 3:2
and shoes, or even a walking *; Mt 10:10
head, and placed a * in his right Mt 27:29
and grabbed the * and beat him on Mt 27:30
* and held it up to him to drink. Mt 27:48
wine and held it up to him on a *. Mk 15:36
along a walking *," he instructed Lk 9:3
NOW I WAS given a measuring * and Rev 11:1
a golden measuring * to measure the Rev 21:15

STICKING
faces and * out your tongues? Is 57:4
land with fish * to your scales. Eze 29:4

STICKS
your walking * in your hands; Ex 12:11
city he saw a widow gathering *; 1Ki 17:10
I was just gathering a few * to 1Ki 17:12
my tongue * to my mouth, for you Ps 22:15
who * closer than a brother. Pro 18:24
he says. He * to his bed like Pro 26:14
Their skin * to their bones; Lam 4:8
Tell these people (holding the * Eze 37:18,19,20
you * his finger in Jehovah's eye! Zec 2:8
their walking *—no food, no Mk 6:8,9
As Paul gathered an armful of * Act 28:3
and some build with *, and hay, 1Co 3:12

STIFF-NECKED
For they are a hardhearted, * Eze 2:4
"You * heathen! Act 7:51

STIFLE
They * me. Is 65:5

STIGMA
shall have a * upon them forever. Jer 20:11

STILL
their name. But * there was no Gen 2:19,20
for the water was * too high. Gen 8:9
When Lot * hesitated, the angels Gen 19:16
* goes by that name to this day. Gen 22:14
As he was * speaking to the Lord Gen 24:15,16

where the man was * standing beside Gen 24:29,
"Well, while I was * speaking Gen 24:
people of Israel * do not eat the Gen 32:
while they were * a long way away. Gen 35:
they were * as skinny as before! Gen 41:
our father was * living and he Gen 4
Is he * alive?" Gen 43:
and the Egyptians at * another; Gen 43:
Joseph was * home when Judah and Gen 44:
"Is my father * alive?" Gen 4
' "for there are * five years of Gen 45:11,
Onan died while * in Canaan, before Gen 46:8-
of Egypt—and it is * the law—that Gen 47:
more bitter *, forcing them to toil Ex 1:13,
know whether they are * alive." Ex 4:
Pharaoh's heart was * hard and Ex 7:
So you * think you are so great, Ex 9:
and children shall * belong to the Ex 21
been notified and * the ox was not Ex 21:
The other bird, * living, shall Lev 14
If there are * many years until Lev 25:
And grapes will * be ripening Lev 26:4
"And if you * disobey me, I will Lev 26:
and you will * be hungry after Lev 26:2
"And if you * won't listen to me Lev 26:2
present, they may * celebrate the Num 9:1
and Medad—were * in the camp, and Num 11:2
and she is * a girl at home in her Num 30
Villages') as it is * known today. Deu 3:1
Lord your God are * alive today. Deu 4:
him, and if he * refuses, the Deu 25:
If she were * married, no special Deu 27:2
and his children who are * alive. Deu 28:5
land, where they * live today!' Deu 29:2
"If even today, while I am * Deu 31:2
and is * called that today. Jos 5:8,
house, and they * live among the Jos 6:2
The stones are * there to this Jos 7:2
mound of refuse, as it * is today. Jos 8:2
over it, which can * be seen. Jos 8:2
This arrangement is * in force at Jos 9:2
the sun stand * over Gibeon, and Jos 10:1
(The pile is * there today. Jos 10:2
though some * remained in Gaza, Jos 11:2
* many nations to be conquered. Jos 13:
Here is a list of the areas * to Jos 13:2-
Ma-acathites, who * live there Jos 13:1
journey, and I can * travel and Jos 14:1
out, so they * live as slaves among Jos 16:1
while they were * in Canaan, they Jos 22:1
people * remaining in the land; Jos 23:
Jerusalem, so they * live there Ju 1:2
Luz, too, as it is * known today. Ju 1:26
* live among the tribe of Ephraim. Ju 1:29
so the Israelis * live among the Ju 1:31,32
generation were * living—those who Ju 2:7-9
a long time, he * didn't come out, Ju 3:25
(The altar is * there in Ophrah Ju 6:24
Gideon, "There are * too many! Ju 7:4
They were very tired, but * Ju 8:4
* called "The Cities of Jair." Ju 10:4
Three days later they were * Ju 14:14
and the spring is * there today. Ju 15:19
Philistines * controlled the land. Ju 15:20
times now, and you * haven't told Ju 16:15
in Judah (which is * called "The Ju 18:12
of Benjamin, who * didn't realize Ju 20:34
of Benjamin who * needed wives, Ju 21:20
Then, though he was * so small, 1Sa 1:24
* be seen in the field of Joshua. 1Sa 6:18
"Even so, we * want a king," 1Sa 8:19
but when he * didn't come, and 1Sa 13:8
soldiers who were * with him, he 1Sa 13:15
Philistine's head * in his hand. 1Sa 17:57
arrows are * ahead of you,' then it 1Sa 20:22
But when his place was * empty 1Sa 20:27
"The arrow is * ahead of you. 1Sa 20:37
him Ziklag (which * belongs to the 1Sa 27:6
of Israel, and it is * followed. 1Sa 30:25
it is * called to this day). 2Sa 6:8
Saul's family was * living, for he 2Sa 9:1
lame son is * alive." 2Sa 9:3
"While the baby was * living, 2Sa 12:21
as it is * known today. 2Sa 18:18
another giant. At * another time 2Sa 21:19
And while you are * talking 1Ki 1:14
And while he was * speaking, 1Ki 1:42
while I am * alive to see it.' 1Ki 1:48
(And they are * known as "The 1Ki 9:13
do this while you are * alive. 1Ki 11:12,13
Jeroboam, who was * in Egypt 1Ki 12:2,3,4
and the donkey and lion were * 1Ki 13:28
and afterwards there will * be 1Ki 17:13
allied kings were * drinking 1Ki 20:16
"Oh, is he * alive?" 1Ki 20:32
the Syrians are * occupying our 1Ki 22:3
prostitution that * continued from 1Ki 22:46
Elisha was * at Jericho when they 2Ki 2:18
Nevertheless he * clung to the 2Ki 3:3
told him, "The child is * dead." 2Ki 4:31
While Elisha was * saying this, 2Ki 6:33

TILL Con't)
toilet, which it * is today. 2Ki 10:27
hills—the people * sacrificed and 2Ki 12:3
the Temple was * in disrepair. 2Ki 12:6
And this is * true. 2Ki 13:23
so the people * sacrificed and 2Ki 14:4
And this is * going on among 2Ki 17:34
But the Lord * did not hold back 2Ki 23:26
They are * responsible for the 1Ch 9:17,18
And it is * called that today. 1Ch 13:11
These subdivisions were * 1Ch 23:8,9
king of Israel, is * young and 1Ch 29:1
While * in the presence of the 1Ch 29:10
Uri, son of Hur) * stood in front 2Ch 1:5,6
The Ark is * there at the time of 2Ch 5:9
He began the practice that * 2Ch 8:7,8
who was * in hiding at the Temple. 2Ch 23:2,3
of Assyria, while * besieging the 2Ch 32:9
However, the people * sacrificed 2Ch 33:17
to the workmen. * others assisted 2Ch 34:13
To this day they * sing sad songs 2Ch 35:24,25
the wall of Jerusalem is * torn Neh 1:3
while the guards were * on duty. Neh 7:3
sins, but * they wouldn't listen. Neh 9:30
Esther * hadn't told anyone she Est 2:20
for she was * following Mordecai's Est 2:20
day after day, but he * refused. Est 3:3,4
While they were * discussing it Est 6:14
While this messenger was * Job 1:16
Before this man finished, * Job 1:17
As he was * speaking, another Job 1:18
His wife said to him, "Are you * Job 2:9
trust in God * be your confidence? Job 4:6
Though * a young man, his bones Job 20:11
"My complaint today is * a Job 23:2
when the Almighty was * with me Job 29:5
is blowing and everything is *? Job 37:16,17
"Do you * want to argue with the Job 40:2
But the Lord is * in his holy Ps 11:4
temple; he * rules from heaven. Ps 11:4
with the outcome * uncertain; Ps 60:1
Gilead, Manasseh—* are mine!" Ps 60:6,7
* demonstrate your awesome power. Ps 77:14
for them, they * rebelled against Ps 78:56
you speak, and they lie *. Ps 89:9
Even in old age they will * Ps 92:14
with waiting. But * I cling to your Ps 119:83
morning, you are * thinking of me! Ps 139:17,18
I have called you so often but * Pro 1:24
of drink, while * holding steadily Ecc 2:3
about it while there is * time. Ecc 7:2
hundred times and * lives, I know Ecc 8:12
I do for them, they * don't care. Is 1:3
his hand is heavy on them *. Is 5:25
* you won't know what they mean.' Is 6:9
stump * lives to grow again." Is 6:13
will * be poised to smash you. Is 9:11,12
is * poised to smash them all. Is 9:17
His hand is * heavy upon them, to Is 9:21
will * be poised to strike you. Is 10:4
Babylon, in Iraq, * lies in utter Is 13:20f
they are * his special ones. Is 14:1
Will they * boast of their Is 19:11
grief, for evil * prevails and Is 24:15,16
* your lot, O men of the world. Is 24:17
of eating, but is * hungry, and as Is 29:8
drinking, but is * faint from Is 29:8
Literally, "Rahab who sits *." Is 30:7f
Yet the Lord * waits for you to Is 30:18
grain this fall, * it will give you Is 37:30
But those who * reject me Is 57:20
which is never *, but always churns Is 57:20
Surely you are * our Father! Is 63:16
would disown us, * you would be our Is 63:16
After all of this, must you * Is 64:12
Will you stand silent and * Is 64:12
While they are * talking to me Is 65:24
no good; they * will not obey. Jer 2:30
I cannot be * because I have Jer 4:19
Yet the Lord pleads with you *: Jer 6:16
nation who are * left alive shall Jer 8:3
Do you * refuse to listen? Jer 13:17
the golden dishes * here in the Jer 27:18
is * my son, my darling child. Jer 31:20
I had to punish him, but I * love Jer 31:20
* remembered to this day. Jer 32:20
WHILE JEREMIAH WAS * in jail, the Jer 33:1
walled cities of Judah * standing. Jer 34:7
arrived, while he was * in prison: Jer 39:15
a few people were * left in Judah, Jer 40:11
rest and be *! Jer 47:6
But how can it be * when the Jer 47:7
He is * their God, but the land Jer 51:5
Are you angry with us *? Lam 5:22
When the cherubim stood *, so Eze 10:17
While I was * speaking and Eze 11:13
After your adultery there, you * Eze 16:28
you * weren't satisfied. Eze 16:29
them while they are * in Egypt. Eze 20:8
And so it is * called 'The Place Eze 20:29
behind, but was * as lewd as in her Eze 23:8
around—all those * left—will know Eze 36:36
was * standing beside me). Eze 43:6
From it a * narrower platform Eze 43:15
they will * be salty. Eze 47:11
While he was * speaking these Dan 4:31
But even so we * refuse to Dan 9:13
his kingdom * unrealized Dan 9:26
me and lifted me, * trembling, to Dan 10:10
So I stood up, * trembling with Dan 10:11
and make it * more powerful. Dan 11:5
For the Lord * loves Israel Hos 3:1
They will eat and * be hungry. Hos 4:10
deceit, but Judah * trusts in God Hos 11:12
you * would not return to me. Amo 4:6
olive trees. And * you wouldn't Amo 4:9
from fire. And * you won't return Amo 4:11
ask the only one * alive inside, Amo 6:10
hunger pangs and emptiness will * Mic 6:14
he stands * for a moment, gazing Hab 3:6
while there * is time—before Zep 2:2
The following February, * in the Zec 1:7
among the nations, * they will Zec 10:9
evening time it will * be light. Zec 14:7
time, yet you may * return to me," Mal 3:7
But while she was * a virgin she Mt 1:18
'Lord,' but * won't get to heaven. Mt 7:21
it would * be here today. Mt 11:23
One day while they were * in Mt 17:22,23
If he * refuses to listen, then Mt 18:17
while he was * speaking, Judas, one Mt 26:47
* used among men in Eastern lands. Mt 26:49f
That is why the cemetery is * Mt 27:8
the Jews, and is * believed by them Mt 28:15
When Jesus was * far out on the Mk 5:6
While he was * talking to her, Mk 5:35
to life again; * others claimed he Mk 6:15
For they * didn't realize who he Mk 6:52
for centuries, and * follow, such Mk 7:4
But while he was * speaking these Mk 9:7
and * there were no children; Mk 12:20,21,22
were * very much alive, for he Mk 12:27
leaders were * looking for an Mk 14:1
And immediately, while he was * Mk 14:43
* later he appeared to the eleven Mk 16:14
into the crowd, * on his sleeping Lk 5:18,19
many others were * on the way, Lk 8:4
* other fell on fertile soil; Lk 8:8
While he was * speaking to her, a Lk 8:49
And everyone ate and ate; *, Lk 9:17
but inside you are * dirty—full of Lk 11:39
But even then, there was * room. Lk 14:22
enemy troops are * far away, he Lk 14:32
And while he was * a long Lk 15:20
"There is * one thing you Lk 18:22
and he, too, died. * no children. Lk 20:30
This is * the traditional Lk 22:47f
* they stood there undecided, Lk 24:41
But as darkness fell and Jesus * Jn 6:17
* others, "But he can't be! Jn 7:41,42
But they * didn't understand Jn 8:27
But while I am * here in the Jn 9:5
my brother would * be alive." Jn 11:32
the Light while there is * time; Jn 12:36
but I will * be present with you. Jn 14:19
things now while I am * with you. Jn 14:25
MORNING, while it was * dark, Jn 20:1
and his tomb is * here among us. Act 2:29
that there was * grain in Egypt, so Act 7:12
me so that I am * alive today to Act 26:22
So if you * claim that God's Rom 4:14
for us while we were * sinners. Rom 5:8
When your old nature was * Rom 7:5
of death. But *, you see, the law Rom 7:12
sin * has me in its evil grasp. Rom 7:20
to the sin that is * within me. Rom 7:23,24,25
I find myself * enslaved to sin. Rom 7:23,24,25
that is * inside me loves to sin. Rom 7:23,24,25
That's why those who are * under Rom 8:8
God has given you so much, but * Rom 9:4
all the land who * loved God, and Rom 11:2,3
besides you who * love me and have Rom 11:4
Yet the Jews are * beloved of God Rom 11:28
do these things, * we cannot just Rom 15:1
has been to go * farther, preaching Rom 15:20
as though you were * just babies in 1Co 3:1
And even now you * have to be fed 1Co 3:2
For you are * only baby 1Co 3:3
* babies, wanting your own way? 1Co 3:3
work * stands, will get his pay. 1Co 3:14
And are you * so conceited, so 1Co 5:2
the time he * feels it is wrong. 1Co 8:10
who is speaking. * another person 1Co 12:10
So he has made many parts, but * 1Co 12:20
it move, I would * be worth nothing 1Co 13:2
of those most gifted is * so poor. 1Co 13:9
But if anyone * disagrees—well, 1Co 14:38
You welcomed it then and * do 1Co 15:1
saves you if you * firmly believe 1Co 15:2
disciples, and * used after Judas 1Co 15:5f
most of whom are * alive, though 1Co 15:6
dead, then Christ must * be dead. 1Co 15:13
And if he is * dead, then all 1Co 15:14
If they don't, then Christ is * 1Co 15:16
you, and you are * under 1Co 15:17
and then we who are * alive shall 1Co 15:52
Please show him now that you * 2Co 2:8
here we are, * very much alive. 2Co 6:9
Any coldness * between us is not 2Co 6:12
were made happier * by Titus' joy 2Co 7:13
And I am sending you * another 2Co 8:22
to find that you * aren't ready 2Co 9:4
grow and that, * within the limits 2Co 10:15
and I was getting hungry I * 2Co 11:8,9
and it is * not going to cost you 2Co 12:14
If I were * trying to please men Gal 1:10
and Cilicia. And * the Christians Gal 1:22
The fact that I am * being Gal 5:11
proves that I am * preaching Gal 5:11
(But their hearts, too, were * Eph 2:11
as their Savior; * others have a Eph 4:11
you * angry—get over it quickly; Eph 4:26
over, you will * be standing up. Eph 6:13
Yes, I am * needed down here and Php 1:25
and I am * in the midst of a Php 1:30
No, dear brothers, I am * not all Php 3:13
them anyway, * bound by such rules Col 2:20
life was * part of this world; Col 3:7
Even while we were * with you we 1Th 3:4
whether your faith was * strong. 1Th 3:5
that we who are * living when the 1Th 4:15
Then we who are * alive and 1Th 4:17
Even while we were * there with 2Th 3:10
and I feel sure you are * 2Ti 1:5
And * another time—when his Heb 1:5,6
And at * another time, "See, Heb 2:13
day while there is * time, so that Heb 3:13
ALTHOUGH GOD'S PROMISE * Heb 4:1
* waiting for the people of God. Heb 4:9
And when a person is * living on Heb 5:12,13
He is * a baby-Christian! Heb 5:12,13
* do—by helping his children? Heb 6:10
the system could * be carried on by Heb 7:23
here the priests * follow the old Heb 8:4
it represents were * in use. Heb 9:8
while * under that old system. Heb 9:15
While he is * alive no one can Heb 9:17
long dead, we can * learn lessons Heb 11:4
him, Abraham * trusted in God and Heb 11:17
Are there * some among you who Jas 2:19
death, they could * live in their 1Pe 4:6
As long as I am * here I intend 2Pe 1:13,14
his fellow man, is * in darkness. 1Jn 2:9
plagues * refused to worship God! Rev 9:20

STILL-BORN
Oh, to have been *! Job 3:16

STILLED
Yes, my begging has been *. Ps 131:2
her mighty voice is * as the Jer 51:55

STILLNESS
What a blessing is that *, as he Ps 107:30
Deathly silence is everywhere. * Is 23:2,3

STILLS
He calms the storm and * the Ps 107:29

STIMULATING
A friendly discussion is as * as Pro 27:17

STING
Their words * like poisonous Ps 140:3
you, like bees to * and to kill. Is 7:18
and barbed and * like scorpions. Eze 2:6
the * and poison of deadly snakes. Rom 3:13
Where then your *? 1Co 15:55,56
For sin—the * that causes 1Co 15:55,56
given power to * like scorpions. Rev 9:3

STINGING
become a place of * nettles and Zep 2:9
They had * tails like scorpions, Rev 9:10

STINGS
serpent; it * like an adder. Pro 23:32
agony like the pain of scorpion *. Rev 9:5

STINK
"You have made me * among all the Gen 34:30
you for making us * before Pharaoh Ex 5:21
and the river will *, so that the Ex 7:18
names of wicked men * after them. Pro 10:7
even a bottle of perfume to *! Ecc 10:1
of sweet perfume, they'll *; Is 3:24
For how you * with sin!" Nah 1:14

STIPULATION
there must be a * that the land can Lev 25:24

STIR
the city began to *, someone Ju 6:28
No one dares to * him up, let Job 41:10
and * up trouble all day long. Ps 140:2
Literally, "that you * not up nor Sol 2:7f
For I will * up the Medes Is 13:17
priests and prophets—* me up. Jer 32:32
THE LORD SAYS: I will * up a Jer 51:1
Then he will * up his courage Dan 11:25
ideas that * up questions and 1Ti 1:3,4
to remind you to * into flame the 2Ti 1:6
Literally, "* up the gift of 2Ti 1:6f
If you will * up this inner 2Ti 1:8

(STIR Con't)
They * up arguments; Jud 1:19

STIRRED
Those whose hearts were * by Ex 35:21
Meanwhile, Korah had * up the Num 16:19
Three years later God * up Ju 9:22,23
village was * by their arrival. Ru 1:19
If the Lord has * you up against 1Sa 26:19
Then the Lord * up the 2Ch 21:16
Persia, the Lord * up the spirit of 2Ch 36:22,23
Who has * up this one from the Is 41:2
But I have * up (Cyrus) from the Is 41:25
For the Lord has * up the spirit Jer 51:11
of Jerusalem was * as he entered. Mt 21:10
Then the Jewish leaders * up both Act 13:50
God's message * up distrust among Act 14:2
they went over and * up trouble. Act 17:13
whole area was * by God's message. Act 19:20
of yours that * up many of them to 2Co 9:2

STIRRING
"He is * up trouble despite the 1Ki 20:7
he can do, and * up discontent. Pro 6:14
eat or drink but * up goodness and Rom 14:17
Christ's words and * up arguments 1Ti 6:4

STIRS
Hatred * old quarrels, but love Pro 10:12
the night, and who * the sea to Jer 31:35

STOCK
"Multiply and * the oceans," he Gen 1:21,22
smooth flattery is her * in trade. Pro 5:3
had forgotten to * up on food Mk 8:14
"A tree from good * doesn't Lk 6:43
from poor * produce choice fruit. Lk 6:43

STOCKS
'And he puts my feet in the *,' Job 33:11
and put in the * at Benjamin Gate Jer 20:2
to put him in the * and collar. Jer 29:26
and clamped their feet into the *. Act 16:24

STOIC
the Epicurean and * philosophers. Act 17:18

STOLE
(and Rachel * her father's Gen 31:21
Now put everything I * out here Gen 31:36,37
"He wants to pretend we * it and Gen 43:18
only the one who * it will be a Gen 44:10
a man as I would know who * it?" Gen 44:15
"Only the man who * the cup, he Gen 44:17
were cursing about—well, I * it!" Ju 17:2
he *, and for having no pity." 2Sa 12:6
So in this way Absalom * the 2Sa 15:6
his family; you * his throne and 2Sa 16:7,8
and the palace and * everything, 1Ki 14:26
father). She * him away from among 2Ki 11:2,3
at Jerusalem I * out during the Neh 2:11,12
He shall not enjoy the goods he *; Job 20:17
Because he * at every Job 20:21
me because I * the fruit it bears, Job 31:38,39
as much as he *, though it may mean Pro 6:31
during the night and * his body. Mt 28:12,13

STOLEN
keep for yourself the booty * Gen 14:21
and now he has * my blessing. Gen 27:36
that I have * them from you!" Gen 30:33
home—why have you * my idols?" Gen 31:30
single thing we've * from you, I Gen 31:32
was the one who had * the idols; Gen 31:34
for every animal * from the flocks, Gen 31:39
Literally, "* by day or by Gen 31:39f
shall be returned for each * ox. Ex 22:1
sheep returned for each sheep *. Ex 22:1
for him, and it is *, the thief Ex 22:7
has * his neighbor's property. Ex 22:8
that he has not * it, and the owner Ex 22:11
property has been *, the neighbor Ex 22:12
full repayment for what he has *, Num 5:7
I have never * so much as a Num 16:15
that someone has * from him, and Jos 7:13
And the one who has * that which Jos 7:15
tent and found the * goods hidden Jos 7:22
it had been * from them, he said, Ju 11:13
you thought was * from you, and you Ju 17:2
king—whose ox or donkey have I *? 1Sa 12:3
harmed them, nor * anything from 1Sa 25:7
and nothing was * from us the whole 1Sa 25:15,16
thing was lost or *, but he has 1Sa 25:21
For you have murdered Uriah and * 2Sa 12:9
They had * their bodies from the 2Sa 21:12,13,14
Their harvests are * and their Job 5:5
nothing shall be * from your Job 5:24
of sheep are *, and even the Job 24:2
she urges simpletons. "* melons Pro 9:17
are the sweetest; * apples Pro 9:17
When the horse is *, it is too Ecc 10:11
what he has * and walks along the Eze 33:15
in clothing * from their debtors, Amo 2:8
wine they purchased with * money. Amo 2:8
Think of it! * animals, lame and Mal 1:13
they can erode away or may be *. Mt 6:19
men here who have * nothing from Act 19:37
you in any way or * anything from Phm 1:18

STOMACH
the man's body and into her *. Num 25:8
cheeks, and the * of every ox or Deu 18:3
stabbed him in the * with it, so 2Sa 20:8,9,10
turn sour in your * and you will Pro 23:6,7,8
* constricts and burns with pain; Is 21:3
full * or hunger, plenty or want; Php 4:12
* because you are sick so often. 1Ti 5:23
it, it will make your * sour!" Rev 10:9
me a * ache when I swallowed it. Rev 10:10

STOMACHS
for food and * to digest it. 1Co 6:13
will do away with both * and food. 1Co 6:13
living only to satisfy their *." Tit 1:12

STOMPED
anger, Moses * from the palace. Ex 11:8

STONE
early and set his * headrest Gen 28:18
But a heavy * covered the mouth Gen 29:2
(The custom was that the * was Gen 29:3
After watering them, the * was Gen 29:3
"We don't roll away the * and Gen 29:8
* and watered his uncle's flock. Gen 29:10
So Jacob took a * and set it up Gen 31:45
Afterwards Jacob built a * pillar Gen 35:13,14
But Jacob's heart was like a *; Gen 45:26
down into the depths like a *. Ex 15:5
For they are almost ready to * Ex 17:4
so Aaron and Hur rolled a * for Ex 17:12
You may also build altars from * Ex 20:25
the other with a * or with his fist Ex 21:18
on tablets of *, so that you can Ex 24:12
it the tablets of * I will give Ex 25:16
the tablets of * I shall give you. Ex 25:21
Ark containing the * tablets Ex 26:33
Six names shall be on each *, so Ex 28:10
Each * will represent one of the Ex 28:21
the two tablets of * on which the Ex 31:18
on both sides of two * tablets. Ex 32:15
"Prepare two * tablets like the Ex 34:1
So Moses took two tablets of * Ex 34:4
the two * tablets in his hands. Ex 34:4
Ten Commandments—on the * tablets. Ex 34:28
(containing the * tablets of the Lev 16:13
All the congregation shall * him; Lev 24:15,16
* him to death outside the camp." Num 15:35
down with a large *, it is murder, Num 35:17
or in which a * is thrown without Num 35:22,23
wrote them on two * tablets. Deu 4:13
made from wood and *, idols that Deu 4:28
and he wrote them out on two * Deu 5:22
is as common as *, and copper is Deu 8:9
made with you—the * tablets with Deu 9:9
me to cut two more * tablets like Deu 10:1
and hewed out two * tablets like Deu 10:3
all the people. * him to death Deu 13:10
of the city shall * him to death. Deu 21:21
of the city shall * her to death. Deu 22:21
shall worship gods of wood and *! Deu 28:36
known, gods made of wood and *! Deu 28:64
made of wood, *, silver, and gold. Deu 29:17
each to take a * from where the Jos 4:2,3
Each of you is to carry out a * Jos 4:5
that a great * be rolled against Jos 10:18
men to remove the * from the mouth Jos 10:22,23
to the * of Bohan (son of Reuben). Jos 15:6
Then it went down to the * of Jos 18:17
and took a huge * as a reminder and Jos 24:26
the people, "This * has heard Jos 24:27
there, upon one *, they slaughtered Ju 9:5
his seventy sons upon one *. Ju 9:18
Samuel then took a * and placed 1Sa 7:12
(meaning, "the * of Help"), for 1Sa 7:12
"Roll a great * over here, and 1Sa 14:33
bag, took out a *, hurled it from 1Sa 17:48,49
the forehead. The * sank in, and 1Sa 17:48,49
giant with a sling and a *. 1Sa 17:50,51
were before, over by the * pile. 1Sa 20:19
within him and he became as *." 1Sa 25:37,38f
until every * is torn down." 2Sa 17:13
As they arrived at the great * 2Sa 20:8,9,10
young goats at the Serpent's *. 1Ki 1:9
huge blocks of *—a very expensive 1Ki 5:17
in preparing the * for the Temple. 1Ki 5:18
laid over the * walls was carved 1Ki 6:18
* and one layer of cedar beams. 1Ki 6:36
courses of hewn * in its walls, 1Ki 7:12
except the two * tablets which 1Ki 8:9
dealers, and * merchants, and to 2Ki 12:11,12
and placed it upon the * pavement. 2Ki 16:17
that men had made of wood and *. 2Ki 19:18
Temple, and to buy lumber and *." 2Ki 22:5,6
of squared * for the Temple. 1Ch 22:2
I have also gathered timber and * 1Ch 22:14
Ark except the two * tablets which 2Ch 5:10
building materials—* building 2Ch 34:10,11
Am I unfeeling, like *? Job 6:12
the earth and melt copper from *. Job 28:2
For your people love every * in Ps 102:14
The * rejected by the builders Ps 118:22
like a * tied to a slingshot! Pro 26:8
some down for * for fixing walls. Is 22:9,10,11
a Foundation * in Zion—a firm, Is 28:16
carved by men from wood and *. Is 37:
have an idol chiseled out from *. Jer 2:26,
worship idols made of wood and *. Jer 3
into heaps of *, and a forest shall Jer 26:
rather than upon tablets of *, Jer 31:3
walled up my ways with hewn *." Lam 3:
you your hearts of * and give you Eze 11:
you, serving gods of wood and *. Eze 20:3
For their enemies will * them Eze 23:4
every precious *—ruby, topaz, Eze 28:1
in contrast to "hearts of *." Eze 36:2
court inside. A * pavement ran Eze 40:
There were also four * tables Eze 40:4
is a * platform 3½ feet high. Eze 43:
brass and iron, wood and *. Dan 5:2,3,
iron, wood, and *—gods that neither Dan 5:2
threw him in. A * was brought and Dan 6:1
in the beautiful * houses you are Amo 5:1
* to tell them what to do. Hab 2:1
He will be the Foundation * of Zec 3:
Literally, "See the * with seven Zec 3:9
Jerusalem will be a heavy * Zec 12:
will he be given a * instead? Mt 7:
You are Peter, a *; Mt 16:1
Scriptures: 'The * rejected by the Mt 21:4
Literally, "on this *." Mt 21:44
one * left on top of another!" Mt 24:
* across the entrance as he left. Mt 27:6
the * and posted guards to Mt 27:6
rolled aside the * and sat on it. Mt 28:
himself with sharp pieces of *. Mk 5:
most honored * in the building! Mk 12:1
For not one * will be left upon Mk 13:
a * in front of the entrance. Mk 15:4
the huge * from the entrance. Mk 16:
and saw that the *—a very heavy Mk 16:4
Zacharias was apparently * deaf as Lk 1:62
* to become a loaf of bread." Lk 4:
for bread, do you give him a *? Lk 11:11
your enemies will not leave one * Lk 19:44
it says, 'The * rejected by the Lk 20:17
over that * shall be broken; Lk 20:18
* will be left on top of another; Lk 21:6
that the huge * covering the Lk 24:2
Six * waterpots were standing Jn 2:6
It was a cave with a heavy * Jn 11:37,38
"Roll the * aside," Jesus told Jn 11:39
So they rolled the * aside. Jn 11:41
and found that the * was rolled Jn 20:1
they speak of) a "* discarded by Act 4:11
In it they kept the * tablets Act 7:44
him out of the city to * him. Act 7:58
to attack and * them, they fled for Act 14:5,6
gold or silver or chipped from *. Act 17:29
they took wood and * and made idols Rom 1:23
over the great stumbling *. Rom 9:32
not one carved on *, but in human 2Co 3:3
It is a foundation * with these 2Ti 2:19
the tablets of * with the Ten Heb 9:4
well—"The same * that was rejected 1Pe 2:7
say, "He is the * that some will 1Pe 2:8
and I will give to each a white * Rev 2:17
stone, and on the * will be Rev 2:17
and silver, brass, *, and Rev 9:20
thrown away this *, and she shall Rev 18:21

STONE-FACED
Knock them into the dust, * in Job 40:13

STONE-PAVED
judgment bench on the * platform. Jn 19:13

STONE'S
He walked away, perhaps a * Lk 22:41,42

STONECUTTERS
eighty thousand * in the hill 1Ki 5:15
foremen. The * quarried and shaped 1Ki 5:17
* in the hills, and 3,600 foremen. 2Ch 2:2

STONED
but he shall be * or shot to death Ex 19:13
the ox shall be * and its flesh not Ex 21:28
the ox shall be * and the owner Ex 21:29
of silver, and the ox shall be *. Ex 21:32
without fail be * by his peers. Lev 20:1
woman—shall surely be * to death. Lev 20:27
of the camp and * him until he Lev 24:23
the city and shall be * to death. Deu 17:5
the gates and * to death—the girl Deu 22:23,24
And the men of Israel * them to Jos 7:25
a great mob * him to death. 1Ki 12:18
outside the city and * to death. 1Ki 21:13
Israel, the people * him to death. 2Ch 10:18
one, killed one and * another. Mt 21:35
murderous mob that * Paul and Act 14:19
they laid aside as they * him.' Act 22:20
Once I was *. 2Co 11:25

STONEMASONS
the carpenters, *, quarrymen, 2Ki 12:11,12
And you have many skilled * and 1Ch 22:15
the carpenters and *, and to 2Ch 34:10,11

STONES
his men to gather * and make a Gen 31:46
"This pile of * will stand as a Gen 31:47,48
And Jacob set up a monument of * Gen 35:20

(STONES Con't)
use only uncut * and boulders. Ex 20:25
Don't chip or shape the * with a Ex 20:25
*, as clear as the heavens. Ex 24:10
incense, onyx *, stones to be set Ex 25:1
onyx stones, * to be set in the Ex 25:1
Take two onyx *, and engrave on Ex 28:9
and mount the * in gold settings. Ex 28:11
Fasten the two * upon the Ex 28:12
ephod, as memorial * for the people Ex 28:12
Attach to it four rows of *: A Ex 28:17
* on the shoulder of the ephod. Ex 28:25
Possibly they were two * that Ex 28:30,31f
Onyx * and stones to be used for Ex 35:5-9
Onyx stones and * to be used for Ex 35:5-9
The leaders brought onyx * to be Ex 35:27
he can cut and set * like a Ex 35:33
onyx *, attached to the [two Ex 39:6,7
in gold, and the * were engraved Ex 39:6,7
These * were reminders to Jehovah Ex 39:6,7
Literally, "to be * of memorial Ex 39:6,7f
there were four rows of * across Ex 39:10
filigree. The * were engraved like Ex 39:14
Inside the Ark he placed the * Ex 40:20
Other * shall be brought to Lev 14:42
the house—all its *, timbers, and Lev 14:45
*, for I am the Lord your God. Lev 26:1
idols—their carved *, molten Num 33:52
throw the first *, and then all the Deu 17:7
Face the * with a coating of lime Deu 27:2,3,4
shoulder—twelve * in all, one for Jos 4:5
They took twelve * from the Jos 4:8
monument of twelve * in the middle Jos 4:9
and there the twelve * from the Jos 4:20
the purpose of the *: "In the Jos 4:21
ask you why these * are here and Jos 4:21
them that these * are a reminder of Jos 4:22
piled a great heap of * upon them. Jos 7:26
upon them. The * are still there to Jos 7:26
There he piled a great heap of * Jos 8:29
carved upon the * of the altar each Jos 8:32
and a great pile of * was placed Jos 10:27
this hill, laying the * carefully. Ju 6:26
Then he picked up five smooth * 1Sa 17:40
disappear like * from a sling! 1Sa 25:29
He threw * at the king and the 2Sa 16:6
went and throwing * at David and 2Sa 16:13
piled a great heap of * over it. 2Sa 18:17
The * used in the construction of 1Ki 6:7
huge, expensive *, cut to measure. 1Ki 7:9
The foundation * were twelve to 1Ki 7:10
The huge * in the walls were 1Ki 7:11
Silver was as common as * in 1Ki 10:27
and haul away its * and timbers. 1Ki 15:22
He took twelve *, one to 1Ki 18:31
and used the * to rebuild the 1Ki 18:32
the wood, the *, the dust, and even 1Ki 18:38
on hot *, and a jar of water! 1Ki 19:6
ruin all the good land with *." 2Ki 3:19
the cities, threw * on every good 2Ki 3:25
He crushed the * to dust and 2Ki 23:15
*, costly jewels, and marble. 1Ch 29:2
in Jerusalem as * in the road! 2Ch 9:27
away the building * and timbers and 2Ch 16:6
* from the towers and battlements. 2Ch 26:15
gold, precious *, and spices, and 2Ch 32:27
It is being built with huge *, Ez 5:8
layers of huge * in the foundation, Ez 6:4
And look at those charred * they Neh 4:1
they sank like * beneath the Neh 9:11
in the stream, down among the *. Job 8:17
Water grinds the * to sand. Job 14:18,19
the rocks and lay bare precious *. Job 28:10
or precious onyx * or sapphires. Job 28:16
A time for scattering *; Ecc 3:5
A time for gathering *; Ecc 3:5
When working in a quarry, * will Ecc 10:8,9
Your gods are the smooth * in Is 57:6
Clear away the rocks and *. Is 57:14
wood for brass, your * for iron. Is 60:17
heads upon the *, for their time Jer 25:34
the pavement * at the entrance of Jer 43:9
upon these * that I have hidden. Jer 43:10
even your * shall never be used Jer 51:26
blue sapphire *, and upon it sat Eze 1:26
and dump your * and timber and even Eze 26:12
You walked among the * of fire. Eze 28:14
from the midst of the * of fire. Eze 28:16
from the midst of the * of fire." Eze 28:16f
(from burdens of * for the siege). Eze 29:18
their * into the valleys below. Mic 1:6
against the * of the streets. Nah 3:10
The very * in the walls of your Hab 2:11
God can change these * here into Mt 3:9
is able of these * to raise up Mt 3:9f
changing * into loaves of bread. Mt 4:3
and * all those God sends to her! Mt 23:37
of Abraham from these desert *! Lk 3:8
The city that * those sent to Lk 13:34
keep quiet, the * along the road Lk 19:40
hurl the * at her until she dies. Jn 8:7
leaders picked up * to kill him. Jn 8:59
leaders picked up * to kill him. Jn 10:31
And as the murderous * came Act 7:59
silver, precious *, pearls, finest Rev 18:12
gold and precious * and pearls! Rev 18:16
twelve foundation *, and on them Rev 21:14
of foundation * inlaid with gems: Rev 21:18,19,20

STONEWORK
about *, carpentry, and weaving; 2Ch 2:14
Look at the decorated * on the Mk 13:1
the beautiful * of the Temple and Lk 21:5

STONING
people are to execute him by *. Lev 24:13,14
the people was to talk of * them. Num 14:10,11
Some died by * and some by being Heb 11:37,38

STONY
And olive oil from * ground! Deu 32:13
point upon their * hearts or on the Jer 17:1
I will take out your * hearts of Eze 36:26
being saved. The * ground Lk 8:13

STOOD
before the men and * beneath the Gen 18:8
Then the men * up from their meal Gen 18:16
When he saw them he * up to meet Gen 19:1
where he had * before the Lord. Gen 19:27
The man * there a moment with Gen 24:26
At the top of the stairs * the Gen 28:13
and my sheaf * up, and your sheaves Gen 37:7
skinny and all their ribs * out. Gen 41:3
They went over and * beside the Gen 41:3
to Egypt, and * before Joseph. Gen 43:15
them, and it * between the people Ex 14:20
They * as solid walls to hold the Ex 15:8
sit on, and they * on each side, Ex 17:12
* at the foot of the mountain. Ex 19:17
and they * at a distance, shaking Ex 20:18
As the people * in the distance, Ex 20:21
their enemies— he * at the camp Ex 32:26
of cloud and * there with him, and Ex 34:5,6
came and * there before the Lord. Lev 9:5
So they * before the Lord. Num 12:3,4
in the Cloud and * at the entrance Num 12:5
the people as they * before Moses. Num 13:30
on them, and * at the entrance of Num 16:18
So all the people * back from the Num 16:27
came out and * at the entrances of Num 16:27
Moses and Aaron came and * at Num 16:43,44
And he * between the living and Num 16:48
Now the angel of the Lord * at a Num 22:24
down the road and * in a place so Num 22:26
about the day you * before the Lord Deu 4:10
You * at the foot of the Deu 4:11
the mountain. I * as an Deu 5:5
So Moses and Joshua came and * Deu 31:14
carrying the Ark * on dry ground in Jos 3:17
carrying the Ark * in the middle of Jos 4:10
Between them * the priests with Jos 8:33
King Eglon * up at once to receive Ju 3:20
the goddess Asherah that * nearby. Ju 6:25
Then they just * and watched as Ju 7:21
about this, he * at the top of Ju 9:7
"I am the woman who * here that 1Sa 1:26
him out, and he * head and 1Sa 10:23
So as David * there among his 1Sa 16:13
He * and shouted across to the 1Sa 17:8
Philistine forces * facing each 1Sa 17:21
So he * at the gate of the city 2Sa 18:4
him and fled, he * alone at the 2Sa 23:11,12
So she came back in and * before 1Ki 1:28
The king * up from his throne as 1Ki 2:19
And as he * before the Ark of the 1Ki 3:15
* before him, and blessed them. 1Ki 8:14
watched, Solomon * before the altar 1Ki 8:22,23
and aides who * around in splendid 1Ki 10:5
And as Elijah * there the Lord 1Ki 19:11
and * at the entrance of the cave. 1Ki 19:13
the armies of heaven * around him. 1Ki 22:19
So they went on together and * 2Ki 2:6,7
to her as she * in the doorway. 2Ki 4:15,16
* at the door of Elisha's home. 2Ki 5:9
the prophet; they * humbly before 2Ki 5:15
weapons ready, * across the front 2Ki 11:11
the Temple (it had * between the 2Ki 16:14
in the Temple. He * beside the 2Ki 23:3
clan of Merari, who * on his left. 1Ch 6:44-47
Each morning and evening they * 1Ch 23:30
He rose and * before them and 1Ch 28:2
son of Hur) still * in front of the 2Ch 1:5,6
They * on the floor facing the 2Ch 3:11,12,13
The rim * 7½ feet above the 2Ch 4:2
they * to receive his blessing: 2Ch 6:3
trumpets, all the people * again. 2Ch 7:6
Gold lions also * at each side 2Ch 9:19
Jehoshaphat * among them as they 2Ch 20:5
part of Judah * before the Lord 2Ch 20:13
and the Korah clan * to praise the 2Ch 20:19
going on—and there * the king by 2Ch 23:12
They * at their posts as 2Ch 30:16
Then the priests and Levites * 2Ch 30:27
where the Temple *, and the altars 2Ch 33:15
As the king * before them, he 2Ch 34:31
Finally I * before the Lord in Ez 9:5
So I * up and demanded that the Ez 10:5
other half * guard behind them. Neh 4:16
of Moses' laws. He * on a wooden Neh 8:1
Everyone * up as he opened the Neh 8:1
To his right * Mattithiah, Shema, Neh 8:1
Gold and silver benches * on Est 1:6
Then he * outside the gate of Est 4:2
garden as Haman * up to plead for Est 7:7
So she arose and * before him, Est 8:4
together and * for their lives and Est 9:16
Then Job * up and tore his robe Job 1:20
my face—my hair * up on end. Job 4:15
and * up in respect at my coming. Job 29:8
The princes * in silence and Job 29:9
of the city * in quietness. Job 29:10
But as I * there silently the Ps 39:2,3
The water * banked up along both Ps 78:13
the city *. Is 7:1
is dumb, so he * silent before the Is 53:7
Moses and Samuel * before me Jer 15:1
Then some of the wise old men * Jer 26:17
* with Jeremiah and persuaded the Jer 26:24
king as all his officials * by. Jer 36:21
pillars that * at the entrance of Jer 52:17
*, and carted them off to Babylon. Jer 52:17
gate, in the entrance, * the idol. Eze 8:5
and * beside the bronze altar. Eze 9:2
rested and * above the entrance Eze 9:3
man went in and * beside one of the Eze 10:6
When the cherubim * still, so Eze 10:17
Temple and * above the cherubim. Eze 10:18
of the God of Israel * above them. Eze 11:22
over the city and * above the Eze 11:23
they lived, and * up—a very great Eze 37:10
A large building * on the west, Eze 41:12
he said as they * before him, "and Dan 2:1
millions of people * before him, Dan 7:10
there before me * a person robed in Dan 10:5,6
So I * up, still trembling with Dan 10:11
time of need. You * aloof, refusing Ob 1:11
his expense. You * at the Ob 1:14
The men * there in awe before Jon 1:16
very ground on which it *. Mic 1:11
An angel * beside me, and I asked Zec 1:9
the angel who * beside me, speaking Zec 1:13
he * before the Angel of the Lord. Zec 3:3
and * over where the baby was." Mt 2:9f
Jesus * there amazed! Mt 8:10
Then he * up and rebuked the Mt 8:26
returned, they * outside, calling, Mt 25:11
Then the High Priest * up and Mt 26:62
and he * up and was all right! Mk 9:27
Finally some men * up to lie Mk 14:57
Then the High Priest * up before Mk 14:60
Meanwhile, a great crowd * Lk 1:10
Joseph and Mary just * there, Lk 2:33
and * up to read the Scriptures. Lk 4:16
the mountain, they * with Jesus on Lk 6:17,18
thoughts, so he * a little child Lk 9:47
there, ten lepers * at a distance, Lk 17:12
"But the corrupt tax collector * Lk 18:13
Meanwhile, Zacchaeus * before the Lk 19:8
AS HE * in the Temple, he was Lk 21:1
Nevertheless, because you have * Lk 22:28
At last he * up again and Lk 22:45
religious leaders * there shouting Lk 23:10
* in the distance watching. Lk 23:49
They * there puzzled, trying to Lk 24:4
Still they * there undecided, Lk 24:41
an answer, so he * up again and Jn 8:7
Then Jesus * up again and said to Jn 8:10
while Peter * outside the gate. Jn 18:16
And Peter * there with them, Jn 18:18
present, Peter * up and addressed Act 1:15
They * there amazed and Act 2:12
up with a leap, * there a moment Act 3:7,8
Everyone * there awed by the Act 3:11
with the people), * up and Act 5:34
The men with Paul * speechless Act 9:7
named Agabus, * up in one of the Act 11:28
angel of the Lord * beside Peter! Act 12:7
So Paul *, waved a greeting to Act 13:16
But as the believers * around Act 14:20
their conversion * to their feet Act 15:5
discussion, Peter * and addressed Act 15:7
The commander agreed, so Paul * Act 21:40
That night the Lord * beside Paul Act 23:11
and all the others * and left. Act 26:30
and whom I serve * beside me, and Act 27:23
agree that I have * that test and 2Co 13:6
But the Lord * with me and gave 2Ti 4:17
the priests * before the altar day Heb 10:11
two sons as he * and prayed, Heb 11:21
* at the throne's four sides. Rev 4:6
censer came and * at the altar; Rev 8:3
to the earth. He * before the woman Rev 12:4
He * waiting on an ocean beach. Rev 12:17
glass, and on it * all those who Rev 15:2

STOOP
I * with sorrow and with shame. Ps 31:9,10

(STOOP Con't)
* to this, he is fooling himself. Gal 6:3

STOOPED
I myself have * and fed him. Hos 11:4
him, but Jesus * down and wrote in Jn 8:6
Then he * down again and wrote Jn 8:8
there first, and * and looked in Jn 20:5
And as she wept, she * and looked Jn 20:11

STOOPING
the tomb to look. *, he peered in Lk 24:12

STOOPS
and the earth; he * to look, and Ps 113:6

STOP
our men has got to *," he said. Gen 13:8
go any further. * awhile and rest Gen 18:3,4
"They'll be hungry if you * so Gen 29:7
after them and * them and ask them Gen 44:4
and the thunder and hail will *. Ex 9:29
The purpose of this law is to * Lev 17:5
to choose a place for them to *. Num 10:33
protested, "Sir, make them *!" Num 11:28
complaining against you will *!" Num 17:5
"I have come to * you because Num 22:32
hearts and * your stubbornness. Deu 10:16
to * at the edge of the river." Jos 3:8
the river will * flowing as though Jos 3:13,14
our children * worshiping him. Jos 22:24,25
He happened to * at Micah's house Ju 17:7,8
after them, yelling at them to *. Ju 18:23
brother Benjamin, or shall we *?" Ju 20:27,28
God, and he doesn't * them. 1Sa 3:13
so that the plague will *. 1Sa 6:3
* persecuting you and your god. 1Sa 6:4,5
then we will * and wait for 1Sa 14:9
Then Samuel said to Saul, "*! 1Sa 15:16
He wouldn't * for anything, but 2Sa 2:19
I will * at the ford of the 2Sa 15:28
I did not * till all were gone. 2Sa 22:38
was happening and told him to *. 2Sa 24:16
Lord, and he will * the plague." 2Sa 24:21
the destroying angel, "*! 1Ch 21:15
the Lord and the plague will *." 1Ch 21:22
to * being priests of the Lord. 2Ch 11:13,14
O our God, won't you * them? 2Ch 20:12
these men must * building the Ez 4:21
and forced the Jews to * building. Ez 4:23
not force us to * building, but let Ez 5:5
I beg you, gentlemen, * this Neh 5:10
Why should I * to come and visit Neh 6:3
and you did not * giving them bread Neh 9:20
* Haman's plot against the Jews. Est 8:3
* and think! Job 4:7,8
and from Sheba * for water there, Job 6:19-21
Would I lie to your face? * Job 6:29
who can * him? Job 9:12
Oh, let him * beating me, so Job 9:34
to order, who is going to * him? Job 11:10
would * defending myself and die. Job 13:19
Won't you ever * your flow of Job 16:3
but my spirit won't let me *. Job 20:3
'We have sinned, but we will *'? Job 34:31
"Listen, O Job, * and consider Job 37:14
here shall your proud waves *!' Job 38:11
No sword can * him, nor spear Job 41:26
and that no one can * you. Job 42:2
who can * us?" Ps 12:3,4
help me to * doing them. Ps 19:13
nothing can * me now! Ps 30:6,7
Never * giving your salvation Ps 36:10
* your anger! Ps 37:8
no longer, and * claiming my Ps 50:16
Shame them! * them! Ps 70:2,3
and to * being stubborn and Ps 75:5
I cannot * thinking about them. Ps 77:12
if they will only * their sinning. Ps 85:8
Don't try to * me from obeying Ps 119:115
and tell me where to * and rest. Ps 139:3
If they * trying, the Lord will Pro 15:9,10
a cool-tempered man tries to * Pro 15:18
It is hard to * a quarrel once it Pro 17:14
* listening to teaching that Pro 19:27
with you and * punishing him! Pro 24:18
You can no more * her complaints Pro 27:16
than you can * the wind or hold Pro 27:16
Don't * him! Pro 28:17
Then at the last all wars will * Is 2:4
weary, never stumble, never *; Is 5:27
When they finally * plundering, Is 7:21,22
When his hand moves, who can * Is 14:27
none will be able to * him. Is 22:22
"*, you're doing it wrong!" Is 45:9
I want is that you * oppressing Is 58:6
All you need to do is to * Is 58:9
the weak, and to * making false Is 58:9
and I can't * loving them now!" Jer 2:25
only: If you * your wicked thoughts Jer 7:5
to others, and * exploiting Jer 7:6
foreigners. And * your murdering. Jer 7:6
And stop your murdering. And * Jer 7:6
I cannot * my crying, for my Jer 14:17
Will they never * hurting me? Jer 15:17,18
The Lord replied: "* this Jer 15:19
widows; * murdering the innocent! Jer 22:3
But * using this term, "God's Jer 23:36
But if you * your sinning and Jer 26:13
wicked ways and to * worshiping Jer 35:15
"Do as you like—I can't * you." Jer 38:5
their men and set out to * him. Jer 41:12
For the Lord says: I have put a * Jer 48:35
they defile it, nor will I * them. Eze 7:22
and they will soon * saying it. Eze 12:23
* worshiping them in your hearts. Eze 14:6,7
And I will see to it that you * Eze 16:40,41
of my holy name must *! Eze 20:39
"And so I will put a * to your Eze 23:27
I will * the music of your Eze 26:13
They shall * polluting Eze 37:23
listen to me—* sinning; Dan 4:27
No one can * him or challenge Dan 4:35
his pledge and * the Jews from all Dan 9:27
none will be able to * him. Dan 11:16
But a general will * him and Dan 11:18
putting a * to the daily Dan 11:30,31
Beg her to * her harlotry, to Hos 1:2
No weapon can * them. Joe 2:8
"What should we do to you to * Jon 1:11
they had put a * to their evil Jon 3:10
nothing can * me; Mic 2:3
He will * you with one blow; Nah 1:9
she cannot hold them back. "*, Nah 2:8
"Stop, *," she shouts, but they Nah 2:8
Tell them to * oppressing widows Zec 7:10
people, and to * plotting evil Zec 7:10
that Tyre would * the enemies' Zec 9:5
Then Jesus says to him, "Don't * Mt 8:4
Temple and you didn't * me then. Mt 26:55
Don't * to speak to anyone along Mk 1:43,44
but he said, "* the weeping! Lk 8:52
But perhaps we can * them from Act 4:17
We cannot * telling about the Act 4:20
They won't * at anything that Act 4:28
not be able to * them, lest you Act 5:39
The next * was at the port of Cae Act 18:22
The next * after leaving Tyre was Act 21:7
Our first * was Syracuse, where Act 28:12
and no one tried to * him. Act 28:31
I do, I will * off there in Rome; Rom 15:24
I can never * thanking God for 1Co 1:4
to * arguing among yourselves. 1Co 1:10
* fooling yourselves. 1Co 3:18
I can't easily * when I want to. 1Co 6:12
the one who is speaking should *. 1Co 14:29,30
to * himself or wait his turn. 1Co 14:32
that I planned to * and see you on 2Co 1:15,16
for them. So * evaluating 2Co 5:16
impure ways. They * at nothing. Eph 4:19
* lying to each other; Eph 4:25
If anyone is stealing he must * Eph 4:28
* being mean, bad-tempered and Eph 4:31
as your shield to * the fiery Eph 6:16
And we will never * thanking God 1Th 2:13
Ephesus and try to * the men who 1Ti 1:3,4
for me to * fighting and rest. 2Ti 4:7
the faith, and to * them from Tit 1:14
therefore let us never * trusting Heb 4:14
LET US * going over the same old Heb 6:1
people begged God to * speaking. Heb 12:19
against Satan: * loving this evil 1Jn 2:15
Little children, let us * just 1Jn 3:18
cause of Satan. * being afraid of Rev 2:10
said to me, "* crying, for look! Rev 5:5

STOPPED
but they * instead at the city of Gen 11:31
That night, when he * to camp at Gen 28:11
And then she * having children. Gen 29:35
So he * and propositioned her to Gen 38:16
But when they * for the night Gen 42:27
returning home, we * for the night Gen 43:21
along and had * for the night, Ex 4:24
thunder and hail *, and the rain Ex 9:33
When they * to eat, they baked Ex 12:39
Tabernacle, they * and washed, just Ex 40:32
the spreading has * and black hairs Lev 13:37
wherever it *, and camped there. Num 9:17
of the Lord and * where he told Num 9:18
it * in the wilderness of Paran. Num 10:12
he prayed for them the fire *. Num 11:2
and the plague was *, but not Num 16:48
and so the plague was *. Num 16:50
but they were * there by the Num 21:24
So the plague was *, but only Num 25:8
so I have * destroying all Israel Num 25:10,11
the Jordan River * flowing when the Jos 4:7
of Israel, and * at the edge of a Jos 8:11,12,13
So the sun * in the heavens and Jos 10:13
when the Lord * the sun and Jos 10:14
otherwise, she * urging her. Ru 1:18
Joshua and * beside a large rock. 1Sa 6:14
and everyone * when they came to 2Sa 2:23
* chasing the troops of Israel. 2Sa 2:28
six paces, they * and waited so 2Sa 6:13
is dead, you have * your mourning 2Sa 12:21
his prayer, and the plague was *. 2Sa 24:2
or he'll be * by the rain!" 1Ki 18:4
piece of land, * up the wells, and 2Ki 3:2
And then the oil * flowing! 2Ki 4
passed that way, he * for dinner. 2Ki 4
and my anger can't be *. 2Ki 22:1
of Israel, they * chasing him. 2Ch 18:3
On the way Jehoshaphat * and 2Ch 20:2
Gate and * at the Prison Gate. Neh 12:3
and * the arm raised to strike? Job 38:1
to you and * trying to hide them. Ps 32:
The police * me and I said to Sol 3:
My heart *. Sol 5:
anger of the Lord has not * yet. Jer 4:
this message, he * in front of the Jer 19:1
had fled. They * at Mizpah to Jer 40:1
of Heaven' and * worshiping her we Jer 44:1
When the living beings *, the Eze 1:19,20,2
beings stopped, the wheels *. Eze 1:19,20,2
When they * they let down their Eze 1:2
And every time they *, there Eze 1:2
the raging sea—and the storm *! Jon 1:1
At once they * their work and, Mt 4:2
back into the boat, the wind *. Mt 14:3
where they were he * in the road Mt 20:32,3
* and she knew she was well! Mk 5:2
into the boat and the wind *! Mk 6:5
When Jesus heard him he * there Mk 10:4
doves, and * everyone from Mk 11:1
* them and told them to be silent. Lk 4:4
and touched it, and the bearers *. Lk 7:14
edge of his robe, the bleeding *. Lk 8:43,44
to you from here is * at its edge; Lk 16:26
Jesus arrived at the spot, he *. Lk 18:40
They * short, sadness written Lk 24:17
Jesus now * his public ministry Jn 11:54
He * the chariot, and they went Act 8:38
have never * thanking God for you. Eph 1:16,17
again and again, but Satan * us. 1Th 2:18
to the truth, and it must be *. Tit 1:11
but Balaam was * from his mad 2Pe 2:16

STOPPING
sheaves without * her, and to snap Ru 2:15
to scare us into * our work." Neh 6:9
they run without * for rest or Is 5:27
who is merely * for the night? Jer 14:8
to Jerusalem, * at several Act 8:25
on to Jerusalem, * along the way in Act 15:3
Paul had decided against * at Act 20:16
without * to enjoy them; 1Co 7:31

STOPS
"When the discharge *, he shall Lev 15:13
the menstruating *, she is no Lev 15:28
sure this man who * in from time to 2Ki 4:9
Man's work * at such a time, so Job 37:7
His breathing *, life ends, and Ps 146:4
tensions disappear when gossip *. Pro 26:20
But the enemy * at Nob for the Is 10:32
weaver * his working at the loom. Is 38:12
The man never * to think or Is 44:19
follows close behind. He *; Hab 3:6
several * along the Turkish coast. Act 27:2

STORAGE
He also built cities for grain * 1Ki 9:19
for his wine production and *. 1Ch 27:27
rooms, the Temple * areas, and the 1Ch 28:12
and was hidden away in a * room 2Ch 22:11
Temple and placed in the * areas. Neh 10:38
had converted a * room into a Neh 13:5

STORE
and reptile. * away in the boat Gen 6:21
Listen to his instructions and * Job 22:22
Ants: they aren't strong, but * up Pro 30:24-28
and olives and * them away." Jer 40:10
holy offerings and * them—the Eze 42:13
Get ready for the siege! * up Nah 3:14
"Don't * up treasures here on Mt 6:19
or may be stolen. * them in heaven Mt 6:20
to sow or reap or * up food—for Mt 6:26
to * new wine? Mt 9:17
Only new wineskins are used to * Mt 9:17
one to his farm, another to his *; Mt 22:5
fire and * away the grain." Lk 3:17
or have barns to * away their food, Lk 12:24
the punishment in * for those who Lk 17:2,3
even buy in any * without the Rev 13:17

STORE-CITIES
the * Pithom and Ra-amses. Ex 1:11

STORED
and even the water * in bowls and Ex 7:19
but * his armor in his tent. 1Sa 17:54
all the silver * in the Temple and 2Ki 18:15
They were * in the Temple 2Ch 5:1
officers, and * them with food, 2Ch 11:11
David and were * in the Temple. 2Ch 23:9
archives, where documents were *. Ez 6:1
They * the produce in the Temple Neh 10:37
or seen where hail is made and *? Job 38:22,23
For you have * up great blessings Ps 31:19
your words, and * them in my heart Ps 119:11
his wealth is * up for the godly. Pro 13:22

(STORED Con't)
I have * them up for my beloved." Sol 7:13
An abundance of salvation is * Is 33:6
the treasures * up by your Is 39:6
and * away for punishment. Hos 13:12
and his mother * away all these Lk 2:51
enough * away for years to come. Lk 12:19
That is what you have * up for Jas 5:3
and the heavens be * away for a 2Pe 3:7

STOREHOUSE
Bring all the tithes into the * Mal 3:10
have out of his rich * of gifts. Eph 4:7

STOREHOUSES
into the royal * all the excess Gen 41:34,35
was plenty of grain in the *. Gen 41:54
opened up the * and sold grain to Gen 41:56,57
sons were given charge of the *); 1Ch 26:14,15
gate, and two to each of the *. 1Ch 26:17
He also built many * for his 2Ch 32:28,29
of the administration of the *; Neh 13:13

STOREROOM
his nurse in a * of the Temple. 2Ki 11:2,3

STOREROOMS
Hezekiah decided to prepare * in 2Ch 31:11
of the Temple * and who was also a Neh 13:4

STORES
captured * of clothing to the women 2Ch 28:15
We have been eating from these * 2Ch 31:10

STORIES
What * you can tell your Ex 10:2
These rooms were three * high, 1Ki 6:6
"Tell me some * of the great 2Ki 8:4
from our history, * handed down to Ps 78:2,3
were, the upper * were set back Eze 42:6
The upper * of his home are in Amo 9:6
To others they were only * Mt 13:12,13f
JESUS TOLD SEVERAL other * to Mt 22:1
teaching was to tell the people *. Mk 4:2
they didn't get their * straight! Mk 14:59
whom I hear such strange *?" Lk 9:9
fell three * to his death below. Act 20:9
Dirty *, foul talk and coarse Eph 5:4
to recount the * of the faith of Heb 11:32

STORING
Egypt, * them in nearby cities. Gen 41:48
been used for * the grain Neh 13:5
they are * some of their Is 10:28,29
you succeed in * up I'll give to Mic 6:14
fire, and * away the grain." Mt 3:12
These were leather bags for * Mt 9:17f
By doing this they will be * up 1Ti 6:19

STORK
The vulture, the *, Lev 11:13-19
The *, the heron (any variety), Deu 14:11-18
the battle! The * knows the time Jer 8:7
us, with wings like those of a *. Zec 5:9

STORKS
their nests, the * in the firs. Ps 104:17

STORM
of Jehovah left them out in the *. Ex 9:21
had there been a * like that. Ex 9:24
and lightning *, and a huge cloud Ex 19:16
as it is daylight, * the city. Ju 9:33
Are they carried away by the *? Job 21:18
are broken like a tree in the *. Job 24:20
and dissolve me in the *. Job 30:22
(warn us) of the coming *." Job 36:33f
and * to fall upon the earth. Job 37:6
and a mighty * of hail. Ps 18:12
hiding place from every * of life; Ps 32:7
a great * rages round about him. Ps 50:3
to some refuge from all this *. Ps 55:8
your wings until this * is past. Ps 57:1
He calls to the * winds; Ps 107:25
He calms the * and stills the Ps 107:29
When a * of terror surrounds Pro 1:27
trees of a forest shake in a *. Is 7:2
like whirling dust before a *. Is 17:13
it shakes like a tent in a *. Is 24:20
a refuge from the *, a shadow from Is 25:4
blown away in a * from the east. Is 27:7,8
a * of hail will knock it down! Is 28:17
Israel from the * and wind. Is 32:2
roll down upon us like a * wind; Jer 4:13
in the thunder of the * clouds. Jer 10:13
like a wild sea in a raging *. Jer 49:23
I saw, in this vision, a great * Eze 1:4
it away with a * of indignation and Eze 13:13
* and cover the land like a cloud. Eze 38:9
In my dream I saw a great * on a Dan 7:2
like a whirlwind in a mighty *. Amo 1:14
causing a great * that threatened Jon 1:4
gods and caused this terrible *; Jon 1:7
"to bring this awful * upon us? Jon 1:8
we do to you to stop the *?" Jon 1:11
For I know this terrible * has Jon 1:12
* was too fierce to fight against. Jon 1:13
have sent this * upon him for your Jon 1:14
the raging sea—and the * stopped! Jon 1:15
rise and the * winds beat against Mt 7:25
floods come, and * winds beat Mt 7:27
Suddenly a terrible * came up, Mt 8:24
the * subsided and all was calm. Mt 8:26
But soon a terrible * arose. Mk 4:37
A fierce * developed that Lk 8:23
So he spoke to the *: "Quiet Lk 8:24
in the *—I will come to you. Jn 14:18
The terrible * raged unabated Act 27:20
night of the *, as we were being Act 27:27
and a terrible *, as the Israelites Heb 12:18
as clouds driven by the * winds. 2Pe 2:17

STORMED
Abimelech * the city gate to Ju 9:44
the village * out and killed Ju 20:21
caused this mess," the king *. 2Ki 6:33

STORMS
and dust * shall destroy you. Deu 28:24
he sends the *, and floods the Job 12:15
blown away in the * of the night. Job 27:20
He sends the * Job 37:13
Chase them with your fiery *, Ps 83:15
their waves arise in fearful *; Ps 89:9
daytime heat and from rains and *. Is 4:6
terrible * and huge hailstones. Is 30:30
of the cyclone and the raging *; Nah 1:3

STORMY
covered by your wild and * waves. Jon 2:3
deserts and in the * seas and from 2Co 11:26

STORY
Here is the * of Noah: He was Gen 6:8
and heard her *, he rushed out to Gen 24:29,30
servant told Isaac the whole *. Gen 24:66
This is the * of Isaac's Gen 25:19
Then Jacob told him his *. Gen 29:12,13
that night, she told him her *. Gen 39:17
his wife's *, he was furious. Gen 39:19
I will test your *: I swear by the Gen 42:15
out whether your * is true or not. Gen 42:16
It was the same * there, so the Ju 11:17
THIS IS THE * of Elkanah, a man of 1Sa 1:1
Nathan to tell David this *: 2Sa 12:1
* of the annex was 7½ feet high. 1Ki 6:10
Here is the * back of his 1Ki 11:27,28
The rest of the * of Zimri and 1Ki 16:20
the * of the ivory palace and the 1Ki 22:39
The rest of the * of Hezekiah and 2Ch 32:32
one bit of truth to the whole *. Neh 6:8
and heard the whole * from him; Est 4:7
for sinners, what a different *! Ps 1:4
the good man—what a different *! Ps 37:37
writer pouring out his *. Ps 45:1
Any * sounds true until someone Pro 18:17
I have given you the * of God's Is 5:7
the * is the same—only a remnant Is 24:13
* from those first two occasions. Dan 11:29
pass the awful * down from Joe 1:3
city with the * of what had Mt 8:33
explanation of the * I told about Mt 13:18
"Just as in this * the thistles Mt 13:40
"Now listen to this *: A certain Mt 21:33
the farmers in his *— they wanted Mt 21:45
illustrated by the * of a king who Mt 22:1
by the * of ten bridesmaids Mt 25:1
illustrated by the * of a man going Mt 25:14
for this deed. The * of what she Mt 26:13
Their * spread widely among the Mt 28:15
HERE BEGINS THE wonderful * of Mk 1:1
him, "What does your * mean?" Mk 4:10
"Here is another * illustrating Mk 4:26
* shall I use to illustrate it? Mk 4:30
and they were awestruck by his *. Mk 5:20
were the wicked farmers in his *. Mk 12:12
My * begins with a Jewish priest, Lk 1:5
All who heard the shepherds' * Lk 2:18
The * of what he had done Lk 4:37
Then Jesus told him this *: "A Lk 7:41
His apostles asked him what the * Lk 8:9
this *: "A man had two sons. Lk 15:10
JESUS NOW TOLD this * to his Lk 16:1
his disciples a * to illustrate Lk 18:1
Then he told this * to some who Lk 18:9
he told a * to correct the Lk 19:11
After telling this *, Jesus went Lk 19:28
and told them this *: "A man Lk 20:9
heard about this * he had told, Lk 20:19
But the * sounded like a fairy Lk 24:11
Emmaus told their * of how Jesus Lk 24:35
Then Peter told them the whole *. Act 11:4
had never heard the rest of the *! Act 18:25,26
The * of what happened spread Act 19:17
and gave him their * about Paul. Act 25:2
* and asked me to have him killed. Act 25:15
Tell us your *." Act 26:1
Now this true * is an Gal 4:24,25

STORY-ILLUSTRATIONS
HERE ARE SOME of the * Jesus gave Mk 12:1
Here are some of the * Jesus used Lk 6:39

STOUTHEARTED
numbered 87,000 * warriors, all 1Ch 7:5
Be brave, * and courageous. Ps 27:14

STOUTLY
urging you to * defend the truth Jud 1:3

STRADDLING
* the Nile, protected on all Nah 3:8

STRAIGHT
and for leading me * to the family Gen 24:27
And sure enough, the cows went * 1Sa 6:12
get the facts *: both of you claim 1Ki 3:23
*, and we will fully cooperate." Ez 10:4
Gate they went * ahead and climbed Neh 12:37
His tail is as * as a cedar. Job 40:17
His vertebrae lie * as a tube of Job 40:18
see your arrows aimed * at them. Ps 21:12
I try to walk a * and narrow path Ps 26:11
words like arrows * at my heart. Ps 64:3
He led them * to safety and a Ps 107:7
Look * ahead; Pro 4:25
other side and sets the record *. Pro 18:17
make him a *, smooth road through Is 40:3
The enemies' arrows go * to the Jer 50:9
flew * forward without turning. Eze 1:9
went they went, going * forward Eze 1:12
Each being's wings stretched * Eze 1:23
the cherubim could go * forward Eze 10:9-13
* ahead, just as the others did. Eze 10:22
the court, and * across it, he came Eze 40:23
into the court and * across it, he Eze 40:27
trained commandos. * forward they Joe 2:7
a plumbline to see if it was *. Amo 7:7
So now Judas came * to Jesus and Mt 26:49
make his paths *." Mk 1:3f
they didn't get their stories *! Mk 14:59
and instantly she could stand *. Lk 13:13
to happen, stand * and look up! Lk 21:28
And the Lord said, "Go over to * Act 9:11
Troas, and sailed * across to Act 16:11
elders, we sailed * to Cos. Act 21:1
So I run * to the goal with 1Co 9:26
tell lies with * faces and do it so 1Ti 4:2
and mark out a *, smooth path for Heb 12:13

STRAIGHTEN
level the hills; * out the Is 40:4
smooth and * out the road ahead. Is 42:16
road for the Lord—* out the path Mt 3:3
that everyone must * out his life Mk 1:3
Fill up the valleys! * the Lk 3:5
years and was unable to * herself. Lk 13:11

STRAIGHTENED
get things * out before I come. 2Co 2:3

STRAIGHTENS
in our lives; it * us out and helps 2Ti 3:16

STRAIGHTEST
as briars; the * is more crooked Mic 7:4

STRAIGHTFORWARD
yet over this simple, * message Is 28:13
My letters have been * and 2Co 1:13,14
we were perfectly * and sincere. 1Th 2:3
It is wholehearted and * and Jas 3:17

STRAIGHTWAY
Literally, "and * the boat was at Jn 6:21f

STRAIN
jackals. They * their eyes looking Jer 14:6
Blind guides! You * out a gnat Mt 23:24
lies ahead, I * to reach the end Php 3:14

STRAINING
My eyes are * to see your Ps 119:82
As they were * their eyes for Act 1:10
because they are * to help you. 1Th 5:13

STRANDED
and all the fish * in the desert to Eze 29:5
leave you * on the land to die. Eze 32:4

STRANDS
gold rings, two * of twined gold Ex 39:15-18

STRANGE
This is a * way to act. Gen 31:28
"I had this * dream," he was Ju 7:12,13
and the Angel did a * and Ju 13:19
in Gibe-ah saw a * sight—the vast 1Sa 14:16
the Lord! How * that men should try Ps 2:1
There is a * thing happening here Ecc 8:14
foreigners who speak * gibberish! Is 28:11
Gibeon, to do a *, unusual thing—to Is 28:21
people, with a *, jabbering Is 33:19
you work in *, mysterious ways. Is 45:15
or seen anything as * as this? Is 66:7,8
ever heard so * a thing as this. Jer 2:10,11
carved idols and * evil rites?" Jer 8:19
of the cloud, four * forms appeared Eze 1:5
tribes with *, difficult tongues. Eze 3:6
children in the fires of * altars? Eze 16:21
to know about the * thing that the Dan 4:2
The third of these * animals Dan 7:6
alike, and put * symbols in the Joe 2:30
is asking for some * sign in the Mt 16:4
"We have seen * things today." Lk 5:26
whom I hear such * stories?" Lk 9:9
They keep asking for some * Lk 11:29,30
"Then there will be * events in Lk 21:25
by the roaring seas and * tides. Lk 21:25
"Why, that's very *!" Jn 9:30
And I will cause * Act 2:19
But, * as it seems, we Christians 1Co 2:16
What a * thing a body would be 1Co 12:19

(STRANGE Con't)
But I am telling you this * and 1Co 15:51
everyone with * demonstrations, and 2Th 2:9
So do not be attracted by *, new Heb 13:9
and it is all so * and wonderful 1Pe 1:12
for this is no *, unusual thing 1Pe 4:12
AND NOW, IN my vision, I saw a * Rev 13:1
and they worshiped the * Creature. Rev 13:4
Then I saw another * animal, this Rev 13:11

STRANGELY
hearts had felt * warm as he talked Lk 24:32

STRANGER
"I am a * in a foreign land." Ex 2:22
"You must not oppress a * in any Ex 22:21
"*," Gideon replied, "if the Ju 6:13
my servants, regard me as a *. Job 19:15
Yes, I shall see him, not as a *, Job 19:27
turned away even a * but have Job 31:32
why are you as a * to us, as one Jer 14:8
I was a * and you invited me into Mt 25:35
Or a *, and help you? Mt 25:38
*, and you refused me hospitality; Mt 25:43
or thirsty or a * or naked or sick Mt 25:44
They won't follow a * but will Jn 10:5
will be a * to me and I will be a 1Co 14:11
to me and I will be a * to him. 1Co 14:11

STRANGER'S
man who agrees to pay a * debts. Pro 27:13

STRANGERS
have come here to live among *. Ru 2:10,11
And merely * in the Promised Land; 1Ch 16:19
for but a moment, * in the land as 1Ch 29:15
that even * received a fair trial. Job 29:16
and * take all he has earned. Ps 109:11
lest * obtain your wealth, and Pro 5:10
It is risky to make loans to *! Pro 20:16
I've fallen in love with these * Jer 2:25
world, to be * in distant lands; Jer 9:16
or defraud *, and do not fear me," Mal 3:5
Now you are no longer * to God Eph 2:19
Has she been kind to * as well as 1Ti 5:10
were just * visiting down here. Heb 11:13
Don't forget to be kind to *. Heb 13:2
And yet, of the two *, you have Jas 2:6

STRANGLED
eating unbled meat of * animals. Act 15:20
and from unbled meat of * Act 15:27,28,29
unbled meat from * animals, and not Act 21:25

STRANGULATION
I would rather die of * than go Job 7:15

STRAP
of each shoulder * of the ephod, Ex 39:15-18
you would * a yoke on a plow-ox. Jer 27:2
(the sandal * of his shoe." Lk 3:16f

STRAPPED
the journey, and * a canteen of Gen 21:14
So they * on their weapons and Deu 1:41
* against his right thigh. Ju 3:16
dagger * against his right thigh, Ju 3:21
David put it on, * the sword over 1Sa 17:38,39
was David's reply as he * on 1Sa 25:13
with a dagger * to his side. 2Sa 20:8,9,10
a writer's case * to his side. Eze 9:2

STRAPS
by shoulder * at the top, and was Ex 39:4,5
shoulder * of the ephod, were Ex 39:6,7
on the shoulder * of the ephod, Ex 39:20

STRATEGIES
war, develop your *, prepare your Is 8:9,10
against all * and tricks of Satan. Eph 6:11

STRATEGY
Jacob's * was to appease Esau Gen 32:20

STRAW
"Yes, we have plenty of * and Gen 24:25
and Laban gave him * to bed down Gen 24:32
any more * for making bricks! Ex 5:7,8
to furnish you with no more *. Ex 5:10,11
scattered everywhere to gather *. Ex 5:12
"We are given no * and told to Ex 5:16
Get back to work. No * will be Ex 5:18
consumed them as fire consumes *. Ex 15:7
also the barley and * for the 1Ki 4:28
The men were quick to grab this * 1Ki 20:33
driven before the wind like *? Job 21:18
Iron is nothing but * to him, Job 41:27,28
are as ineffective as *. Job 41:27,28
you will disappear like burning *; Is 1:31
that sets the * on fire, and no one Is 1:31
They will disappear like * on Is 5:24
will be crushed as * beneath his Is 25:10
the wind carries them off like *. Is 40:24
the lion shall eat * as the ox Is 65:25
They burst into flames like *. Nah 1:10
wicked will be burned up like *; Mal 4:1
with sticks, and hay, or even *! 1Co 3:12

STRAWS
Will you chase dry, useless *? Job 13:25
Then the crew decided to draw * Jon 1:7
Soldiers drew * to see who would Nah 3:10
*" would be a modern equivalent. Lk 1:8,9f
Then they drew *. Act 1:26

STRAY
* grains of wheat from the ground. Lev 19:9
just as a few * olives are left on Is 17:6

STRAYED
or donkey that has * away, you must Ex 23:4
One day Kish's donkeys * away, so 1Sa 9:3
But no, all have * away; Ps 14:3
none are lost or *, so God does Is 40:26
We are the ones who * away like Is 53:6
ones, those who * away, and bring Eze 34:15,16
me when Israel * away from God to Eze 44:10
and one of them * away and was lost Lk 15:3,4
others who haven't * away! Lk 15:7
are those who have * away from God. Rev 22:15

STRAYING
the sheep, keeping them from *. Amo 1:1

STRAYS
The man who * away from common Pro 21:16
A man who * from home is like a Pro 27:8

STREAKED
offspring were * and spotted, and Gen 30:39,40
I could have the * ones, then all Gen 31:8
ones, then all the lambs were *! Gen 31:8
were *, speckled, and mottled. Gen 31:10
are speckled, *, and mottled." Gen 31:12f
nanny goats with *, speckled, and Gen 31:12

STREAKS
and peeled white * in them, and Gen 30:37
or reddish * in the walls of the Lev 14:37

STREAM
threw it into the * that cascaded Deu 9:21
with their mouths in the *." Ju 7:5,6
drank with their mouths to the *. Ju 7:5,6
stones from a * and put them in his 1Sa 17:40
like a reed whipped about in a *; 1Ki 14:15
must check every * and brook to see 1Ki 18:5
His roots are in the *, down Job 8:17
the willows there beside the *. Job 40:22
multitudes would * to the Temple in Ps 102:21,22
to the other. The * near Dibon Is 15:9
Tears of joy shall * down their Jer 31:9
in an endless * of prostitution. Eze 16:25
making bubbles and muddying the *. Eze 32:2
I saw a * flowing eastward from Eze 47:1
where I saw the * flowing along on Eze 47:2
the * and told me to go across. Eze 47:3
Water will fill the dry * beds of Joe 3:18
flowed out in a * 200 miles long Rev 14:20

STREAMING
For the glory of the Lord is * Is 60:1
So the people came * from the Jn 4:30

STREAMLETS
It grew luxuriantly and gave * of Eze 31:4

STREAMS
all the rivers, *, and pools of Ex 8:5
They dam up * of water and pan Job 28:11
poured out * of olive oil to me! Job 29:6
and leads me beside the quiet *. Ps 23:2,3
vile language * from your mouths. Ps 50:19
from a spring, * poured from the Ps 78:16
* that gush from the mountains. Ps 104:10
nest beside the * and sing among Ps 104:12
For he caused gushing * to burst Ps 114:8
as by * in the desert. Ps 126:4
A wise man's words express deep * Pro 18:4
* from the Lebanon mountains." Sol 4:15
Literally, "sources of the * of Is 7:18f
* that can easily be crossed. Is 11:15
he will give you * of water flowing Is 30:25
to Israel. The * of Edom will be Is 34:9
wilderness, and * in the desert. Is 35:6
The cold, flowing * from the Jer 18:14
the quiet * and not stumble. Jer 31:9
with never-ending * of tears Lam 3:48,49
graze beside the *, and neither man Eze 32:13

STREET
stretch out here along the *." Gen 19:2
the middle of the * and burn it, Deu 13:16
If they go out into the * we Jos 2:19
the * like a common pervert!" 2Sa 6:20
crowds along Main *, and to the Pro 1:21
children with women of the *? Pro 5:16
twilight down the * to the house of Pro 7:8,9
or stands at the * corners of the Pro 9:14
them reel drunkenly down the *! Pro 20:1
a lion in the * and be killed!" Pro 22:13
by the way he walks down the *! Ecc 10:3
RUN UP AND down through every * in Jer 5:1
are along every * in Jerusalem. Jer 11:13
altars on every *, and there you Eze 16:24
altars, your brothels, on every *. Eze 16:31
Horsemen will occupy every * in Eze 26:11
trampled down like mud in the *. Mic 7:10
publicly on * corners and in the Mt 6:5
Now go out to the * corners and Mt 22:9
in the *, tied outside a house. Mk 11:4,5
people as they walk along the *. Lk 20:46
carried along the * and laid beside Act 3:2
over to Straight * and find the Act 9:11
iron gate to the *, and this opened Act 12:10
was standing outside in the *. Act 12:14

Barnabas down the * as the two men Act 13:
And the main * was pure, Rev 21:
down the center of the main *. Rev 22

STREETS
Like dust along the *. 2Sa 22:
the * before him as royal footmen. 1Ki 1
him through the * on the king's own Est 6
him through the * of the city, Est 6:
* filled with shouting people. Est 8:
for every grain of dust in her *. Ps 102:
No crime in our *. Ps 144:12-
Wisdom shouts in the * for a Pro 1:
seen often in the * and markets, Pro 7:11,
as the mourners go along the *. Ecc 12
I went out into the * of the Sol 3
will be thrown as refuse in the *. Is 5:
through the *, and from every home Is 15
lovers, walks the * to look for Is 23:15,
Mobs form in the *, crying for Is 24:
houses abandoned, * grown up with Is 27:1
of men lying drunk in the *! Is 28:
not shout nor quarrel in the *. Is 42:
and lie in the *, helpless as wild Is 51:2
Truth falls dead in the *, and Is 59:1
in Jerusalem's *: The Lord says, I Jer 2:
a fountain! Her * echo with the Jer 6:
playing in the *, upon the Jer 6:1
Judah and in the * of Jerusalem? Jer 7:1
laughter in the * of Jerusalem and Jer 7:3
Children no longer play in the *; Jer 9:2
in Jerusalem's *—go from city to Jer 11:
out into the * of Jerusalem, Jer 14:1
and if I walk in the *, there lie Jer 14:1
Judah and into the * of Jerusalem, Jer 44:
Judah and in the * of Jerusalem; Jer 44:1
Judah and in the * of Jerusalem? Jer 44:2
every Moabite home and on the *; Jer 48:3
Your young men lie dead in the * Jer 49:2
Her young men will fall in the * Jer 50:3
slashed to death in her *. Jer 51:
her dead shall lie in the *. Jer 51:4
JERUSALEM'S *, ONCE thronged with Lam 1:
starving in the * while searching Lam 1:1
In the * the sword awaits me; Lam 1:2
are fainting and dying in the *. Lam 2:1
they faint with hunger in the *. Lam 2:1
See them lying in the *—old and Lam 2:21
dead upon the * before the enemy. Lam 2:22
walls are scattered in the *! Lam 4:1
in the * for anything at all. Lam 4:5
through the *, covered with blood, Lam 4:14
We can't go into the * without Lam 4:18
"Walk through the * of Jerusalem Eze 9:4
and filled your * with the dead. Eze 11:6
in your * by troops on every side. Eze 28:23
* at time of sacrifice. Eze 36:37,38
Jerusalem's * and walls will be Dan 9:25
in all the * and every road. Amo 5:16
* plowed up for planting grapes! Mic 1:6
along the * and through the Nah 2:4
out naked to the *, and led away, a Nah 2:7
as they bump wildly through the *! Nah 3:2
The dead are lying in the * Nah 3:3
death against the stones of the *. Nah 3:10
I have left their * in silent Zep 3:6
through her * on canes, and the Zec 8:4
on canes, and the * will be filled Zec 8:5
like dust in the *, yet the Lord Zec 9:3
the synagogues and * to call Mt 6:2
I did in your * had been done in Mt 11:21
paid them on the *, and to be Mt 23:7
prayers in the *, while you are Mt 23:13,14
market plazas and *, and begged him Mk 6:56
a woman of the *—a Lk 7:37
go out into its * and say, 'We Lk 10:10
taught in our *,' you will say. Lk 13:26
quickly into the * and alleys of Lk 14:21
out into the * on beds and mats so Act 5:15
* to form a mob and start a riot. Act 17:5
synagogue or on the * of any city; Act 24:12
be exposed in the * of Jerusalem Rev 11:8,9

STRENGTH
he gathered his * and sat up in the Gen 48:2
The Lord is my *, my song, and my Ex 15:2
Your * shall be spent in vain; Lev 26:20
But now our * is gone, and day Num 11:6
Israel has the * of a wild ox. Num 23:18-24
Israel has the * of a wild ox, Num 24:3-9
and the power and * of Almighty God Deu 7:19
your mighty power and glorious *. Deu 9:26
you may have the * to go in and Deu 11:8
beginning of his * and who owns the Deu 21:17
something beyond your * and reach; Deu 30:11
He is a young bull in * and Deu 33:17
And may your * match the length of Deu 33:25
So lead on with courage and *!" Jos 1:17,18
March on, my soul, with *! Ju 5:21
saved themselves by their own *! Ju 7:2
as the man is, so is his *." Ju 8:21f
but then the * of the Lord came Ju 15:14
If my hair were cut, my * would Ju 16:16,17

TRENGTH Con't)
see that his * was leaving him. Ju 16:19
No one shall succeed by * alone. 1Sa 2:9
He gives mighty * to his King, 1Sa 2:10
regain your * for the trip back." 1Sa 28:22
But David took * from the Lord. 1Sa 30:6
water, and his * soon returned. 1Sa 30:11,12
By your * I leap over a wall. 2Sa 22:30
And * to bend a bow of bronze. 2Sa 22:35
For you have given me * for the 2Sa 22:40
no right to rejoice in their *." 2Sa 24:3
establish," and Boaz means "*." 1Ki 7:16-22f
Lord gave special * to Elijah so 1Ki 18:46
gave him enough * to travel forty 1Ki 19:8
bow with his full * and shot Joram 2Ki 9:24
You are the * of Israel!" 2Ki 13:14
the mother has no * to deliver it. 2Ki 19:3
* of Egypt just by walking by!" 2Ki 19:24
yes, seek his * 1Ch 16:11
* and gladness walk beside him. 1Ch 16:27
Ascribe great * and glory to his 1Ch 16:28
men are made great and given *. 1Ch 29:12
the Ark of your * has been placed. 2Ch 6:41
for the joy of the Lord is your *. Neh 8:10
Oh, why does my * sustain me? Job 6:11
Yes, with him is * and wisdom. Job 12:16
he will realize his failing *. Job 18:7
God gives them confidence and *, Job 24:22,23
"Have you given the horse *, or Job 39:19
rejoices in his *, and when he goes Job 39:21-23
you that your own * can save you. Job 40:14
the tremendous * in his limbs, and Job 41:12
"The tremendous * in his neck Job 41:22
* and fall beneath their blows. Ps 10:10
Now in your * I can scale any Ps 18:29
He fills me with * and protects Ps 18:32
and gives me * to draw an iron Ps 18:34
HOW THE KING rejoices in your *, O Ps 21:1
their prey. My * has drained away Ps 22:14
My heart melts like wax; my * Ps 22:15
O God my *, hurry to my aid. Ps 22:19
He is my *, my shield from every Ps 28:7
praise his glory and his *. Ps 29:1
He will give his people *. Ps 29:11
My sins have sapped my *; Ps 31:9,10
heavy on me. My * evaporated like Ps 32:4
* is not enough to save anyone. Ps 33:16,17
for the * of evil men shall be Ps 37:17
My heart beats wildly, my * Ps 38:10
by their own * and skill, but by Ps 44:3
GOD IS OUR refuge and *, a tested Ps 46:1
O God my *! Ps 59:9
O my *, to you I sing my Ps 59:17
to see your * and glory, for your Ps 63:2
the mountains by his mighty *. Ps 65:6
display your *, O God, for you Ps 68:28
his * is mighty in the heavens. Ps 68:34
The God of Israel gives * and Ps 68:35
Don't forsake me now when my * is Ps 71:9
I walk in the * of the Lord God. Ps 71:16
He is the * of my heart; Ps 73:26
divided the Red Sea with your *; Ps 74:13,14
"I will cut off the * of evil Ps 75:10
the beginning of its * and joy. Ps 78:51
They will grow constantly in * Ps 84:7
so look down in pity and grant * Ps 86:16
hand is lifted high in glorious *. Ps 89:13
You are their *. Ps 89:17
He is robed in majesty and *. Ps 93:1
* and beauty are in his Temple. Ps 96:6
his skin, and bread to give him *. Ps 104:15
Search for him and for his *, and Ps 105:4
Who but God can give me * to Ps 108:10
the rod of your * out of Zion." Ps 110:2f
And your * shall be renewed day Ps 110:3
He is my * and song in the heat Ps 118:14
They give me * in all my Ps 119:49,50
me by giving me the * I need. Ps 138:3
guide me, your * will support me. Ps 139:10
He gives me * and skill in Ps 144:1
he is my fortress, my tower of * Ps 144:2
How puny in his sight is the * of Ps 147:10
Because of my *, kings reign in Pro 8:14,15
*. The poor man's poverty is his Pro 10:15
the other kind corrodes his * and Pro 12:4
for God gives a man deep *; Pro 14:26
The glory of young men is their * Pro 20:29
Wisdom is mightier than *. Pro 24:5
She is a woman of * and dignity, Pro 31:25
is better than *, nevertheless, if Ecc 9:16
A dull axe requires great *; Ecc 10:10
has no * for the simplest matter. Ecc 10:15
his military * is my weapon upon Is 10:5,6
By our own * we broke down the Is 10:13
for the Lord is my * and song; Is 12:2
rejoicing in their * to do this Is 13:3
them away. The * of Israel and the Is 17:3
merchant city, to destroy its *. Is 23:11
Jehovah is your everlasting *. Is 26:4
and confidence is your *; Is 30:15
Be our * each day and our Is 33:2
Mere words won't substitute for * Is 36:5
he will rule with awesome *. Is 40:10
and worn out, and * to the weak. Is 40:29
upon the Lord shall renew their *. Is 40:31
shall crush the * of mighty kings. Is 45:1
and *," the people shall declare. Is 45:24
I have spent my * for them Is 49:4
has given me the * to perform this Is 49:5
Rise up and robe yourself with *. Is 51:9
clothe yourselves with * [from God Is 52:1
foodstuffs that don't give you *? Is 55:2
in the greatness of his *? Is 63:1
O Lord, my * and Fortress, my Jer 16:19
The * of Moab is ended—her horns Jer 48:25
crushed us and emptied out our *; Jer 51:34,35
she increase her * immeasurably, Jer 51:53
have for food to give a little *. Lam 1:11
He sapped my * and gave me to my Lam 1:14
All the * of Israel vanishes Lam 2:3
were an enemy. His * is used Lam 2:4
All hope is gone; my * has Lam 3:18
[to signify great * and power in Eze 4:7
with fear; all * will disappear. Eze 21:7
Temple, the * of your nation. Eze 24:20,21
your kingdom, power, * and glory. Dan 2:37
* and not his own. Dan 8:24
vision my * left me, and I grew Dan 10:8
by your appearance and have no *. Dan 10:16
For my * is gone and I can hardly Dan 10:17
again, and I felt my * returning. Dan 10:18
the * and fury of a whirlwind; Dan 11:40
I will sap away the * of Judah Hos 5:12
their *, but they don't know it. Hos 7:9
save us, nor can our * in battle; Hos 14:3
He is their Refuge and *. Joe 3:16
his flock in the * of the Lord, in Mic 5:4
The Lord God is my *, and he Hab 3:19
* of the kingdoms of the nations. Hag 2:22
have found * in the Lord of Hosts, Zec 12:5
and had such * that whenever he was Mk 5:3,4
heart and soul and mind and *.' Mk 12:30
understanding and *, and to love Mk 12:33
your *, and with all your mind. Lk 10:27
and I haven't the * to go out and Lk 16:3
Or, "Pray for * to pass safely Lk 21:36f
back for greater * and usefulness Jn 15:3
and grew in * and numbers. Act 9:31
I try with all my * to always Act 24:16
wind of typhoon * (a Act 27:14,15
And patience develops * of Rom 5:4
live again they will be full of *. 1Co 15:43
He will give you the * to endure. 2Co 1:6,7
dying, our inner * in the Lord is 2Co 4:16
to a position of * and maturity; Eph 4:12
you that your * must come from the Eph 6:10
who gives me the * and power. Php 4:13
mighty, glorious * so that you can Col 1:11
our nourishment and * from God. Col 2:19
and giving me the * to be faithful 1Ti 1:12
stir into flame the * and boldness 2Ti 1:6
he will give you * in suffering. 2Ti 1:8
with the * Christ Jesus gives you. 2Ti 2:1
Your spiritual * comes as a gift Heb 13:9
But he gives us more and more * Jas 4:6
says, God gives * to the humble, Jas 4:6
Do it with all the * and energy 1Pe 4:11
in power and * than these false 2Pe 2:11
But grow in spiritual * and 2Pe 3:18
power and * of the Holy Spirit. Jud 1:20
Hold tightly to the little * you Rev 3:11
wisdom, and the *, and the honor, Rev 5:12
giving their power and * to him. Rev 17:13

STRENGTHEN
feet, and a bite to eat to * you. Gen 18:5
me again—please * me one more time, Ju 16:28
(O Lord God, please * me! Neh 6:9
May they perish at your frown. * Ps 80:17
* themselves for the tasks ahead! Ecc 10:16,17
I will * you; Is 41:10
I will * you and send you out to Is 45:5
for materials to * the walls Jer 33:4
you ever done to * the walls of Eze 13:5
And I will * the arms of the Eze 30:24
I will * the hands of the king Eze 30:25
will try to * themselves by forming Dan 2:43
"I WAS THE one sent to * and help Dan 11:1
Store up water! * the forts! Nah 3:14
"I will * Judah, yes, and Israel Zec 10:6
Your word is enough. To * your Mt 5:37
to me again, * and build up the Lk 22:32
used of God to * the church, for Act 18:27
the ship with ropes to * the hull. Act 27:17
to visit you to * your faith and 1Th 3:2,3
was needed to help * each of its Tit 1:5
angel was sent to * him so that he Heb 5:7f
Now wake up! * what little Rev 3:2

STRENGTHENED
all who are with you will be *." 2Sa 16:21f
He also rebuilt and * the forts, 2Ch 11:11
This * the kingdom of Judah, so 2Ch 11:17
So the Lord * his position as 2Ch 17:5
Then Hezekiah further * his 2Ch 32:5
Literally, "* himself in his Ps 52:7f
You have * his enemies against Ps 89:42
up. You * yourself and went on. Is 57:10
speak, sir, for you have * me." Dan 10:19
appeared and * him, for he was in Lk 22:43
were healed and * so that he came Act 3:7,8
Then he ate and was *. Act 9:19

STRENGTHENING
enemies—by * Israel in the Lord? Eze 13:5
to the believers, * their faith. Act 15:32
mighty inner * of his Holy Spirit. Eph 3:16

STRENGTHENS
* us in our hardships and trials. 2Co 1:3,4

STRENUOUSLY
They objected *. Ju 14:3

STRESS
the Tabernacle. (* this Lev 6:17
I lay great * on this and remind Rom 11:13

STRESSING
local languages, * that every man Est 1:22

STRETCH
* out here along the street." Gen 19:2
the Lord said to Moses, "* out Ex 14:26
the curtains will * for 150 feet, Ex 27:9,10
Your frontiers will * from the Deu 11:24
"Before you turn to God and * Job 11:13,14
the days of his life * on and on Ps 21:4
Ethiopia will * out her hands to Ps 68:31
His realm shall * from sea to Zec 9:10
Then he said to the man, "* Mt 12:13
but when you are old, you will * Jn 21:18

STRETCHED
his arms as he * them out to lay Gen 48:14
Meanwhile, Moses * his rod over Ex 14:21
of Israel which * away across the Num 24:2
(The area involved * all the way Jos 12:1
His kingdom also * south to Jos 12:5
And he * himself upon the child 1Ki 17:21
returning upstairs, he * himself 2Ki 4:35
whose wings were * over the Ark of 1Ch 28:18
room, with wings * wingtip to 2Ch 3:11,12,13
Only he has * the heavens out Job 9:8
and light! You * out the starry Ps 104:1
with your hands * out to heaven, I Is 1:15
the heavens and * them out and Is 42:5
I alone * out the heavens. Is 44:24
With my hands I have * out the Is 45:12
in space and * out the heavens. Jer 10:12
and wisdom. He * out the heavens by Jer 51:15
One pair * out to attach to the Eze 1:11
Each being's wings * straight out Eze 1:23
by the Lord, who * out the heavens Zec 12:1
Literally, "* forth his hand." Act 26:1f
their wings * out over the ark's Heb 9:5

STRETCHER
"Pick up your * and go on home, Mt 9:5,6
carrying a paralyzed man on a *. Mk 2:3
*, right down in front of Jesus. Mk 2:4
"Pick up your * and go on home, Mk 2:9,10,11
The man jumped up, took the *, Mk 2:12
"Pick up your * and go on home, Lk 5:23,24

STRETCHERS
sick folks to him on mats and *. Mk 6:55

STRETCHES
they go. God * out heaven over Job 26:7
as one who falls * out his hand or Job 30:24
He is the one who * out the Is 40:22

STRETCHING
ruled a territory * from Mount Jos 12:5
to the Sidonians), * northward Jos 13:2-7
* from India to Ethiopia. Est 1:1
Outside the city, * east and Eze 48:18

STREWN
* all along the road to Shaaraim. 1Sa 17:52
bones are * across the ground, Ps 141:6,7

STRICKEN
for God had * all the women with Gen 20:18
You will be * with an intestinal 2Ch 21:15
glad, while evil men are * silent. Ps 107:42
Before I realized it I was * Sol 6:12
Yes, Moab, you will mourn for * Is 16:7
prophets will be * with horror. Jer 4:9
and Arpad are * with fear, for they Jer 49:23
farmers stand so shocked and *; Joe 1:11
me, you are to be * silent, unable Lk 1:20
happened, he was * with awe before Lk 23:47
will be * awhile with blindness." Act 13:11

STRICT
of the land was in * accordance Jos 14:5
For the Lord has given me * 1Ki 13:9
He gave them * orders not to Lk 9:21

STRICTEST
always been the * of Pharisees when Act 26:5
who demand the * obedience to every Php 3:5

STRICTLY
and that they had * warned him Gen 28:6,7,8
creatures are * forbidden to you. Lev 11:10
You must * obey all of my laws Lev 18:26
stars—which I have * forbidden— Deu 17:2,3
and young men were kept * apart. 2Sa 13:2

(STRICTLY Con't)
The Lord * warned me against it; 1Ki 13:16,17
servant of God were * followed. 1Ch 6:49
and then, though it is * Est 4:16
Jewish religious leaders who * Mt 3:7f
But he * warned them not to Mk 3:12

STRIDE
"The confident * of the wicked Job 18:7

STRIFE
(meaning "argument" and "*!" Ex 17:7
("Place of *") in Kadesh, in the Num 27:14
with their own violence and *. Ps 55:9
seen violence and * in the city." Ps 55:9f
An evil man sows *; Pro 16:28
day along with argument and *. Pro 17:1
A home filled with * and Mk 3:25
a home filled with argument and *. Lk 11:17
Rather, * and division! Lk 12:51

STRIKE
He shall * you on your head, Gen 3:15
while you will * at his heel." Gen 3:15
As Abram returned from his * Gen 14:17
Otherwise, disaster will surely * Gen 41:36
"Tell Aaron to * the dust with his Ex 8:16
lamb's blood, and * the hyssop Ex 12:22
at the rock. * it with your rod Ex 17:5,6
If you do, God will * you dead Lev 10:6
"Now my vengeance will * Ju 15:7
may God * me dead if you are not 1Sa 14:44
not need to * a second time!" 1Sa 26:8
Surely God will * him down some 1Sa 26:10
"Let me go over and * off his 2Sa 16:9
my nephew, may God * me dead if I 2Sa 19:13
He did not need to * again, and 2Sa 20:8,9,10
oath, "May God * me dead if 1Ki 2:23,24
man, "* me with your sword!" 1Ki 20:35
said, "* me with your sword." 1Ki 20:37
and * them against the floor." 2Ki 13:18
Doesn't his majesty * terror to Job 13:11
frank, lest God should * me dead. Job 32:21,22
and stopped the arm raised to *? Job 38:15
cause it to * as you direct it? Job 38:35
But God will * you down and pull Ps 52:5
He will * down many kings in the Ps 110:5
upraised fist to * their enemies, Ps 136:11,12
when hard times *, realize that God Ecc 7:14
will still be poised to * you. Is 10:4
Can a rod * unless a hand is Is 10:15
proud troops, and * them down. Is 10:16
of Israel will * deep terror in Is 19:17
Call on them to help you * deep Is 47:12
does, and poisonous snakes shall * Is 65:25
even now poised to * them dead!" Jer 4:10
The arrows of the enemy shall * Jer 51:3
cheek to those who * him, and Lam 3:30
Disease will * down those in Eze 6:12
Yes, terror shall * in many Eze 32:10
with its paw raised, ready to *. Dan 7:5
my judgment will * you as surely as Hos 6:5
Beware, for I will * back Joe 3:4
With a rod they shall * the Judge Mic 5:1
he won't need to * again. Nah 1:9
terror will * you because of all Hab 2:17
so that I'll not need to * again.' Zep 3:7
Lord of Hosts. "* down the Zec 13:7
(This same plague will * the Zec 14:15
into the boat and * out across the Mk 6:45
and I will * her children dead. Rev 2:23
sharp sword to * down the nations; Rev 19:15

STRIKES
"Anyone who * his father or Ex 21:15
But now, when trouble *, you Job 4:5
openly * them down as wicked men. Job 34:26
neck * terror wherever he goes. Job 41:22
trouble *, and you will help me. Ps 86:7
Disaster * like a cyclone and the Pro 10:25
sparks that fly when iron * iron. Pro 27:17
at Geba. Fear * the city of Ramah; Is 10:28,29
* up, you are to fall flat on the Dan 3:5

STRIKING
knife and the flint for * a fire. Gen 22:6
against Jehovah by * fear into the Num 14:36,37,38
with rage by now. * his hands Num 24:10
him, or angrily * him with his Num 35:21
and Jogbehah, * at the Midianite Ju 8:11
* deep within your hearts. Jer 4:18
outfitted in * red uniforms, with Eze 23:14,15

STRING
Suddenly they noticed a * of Gen 37:25
wood, a scarlet *, and some hyssop Lev 14:4
Literally, "like a * of tow snaps Ju 16:9f
neck with that long * of jewels. Sol 1:10
and you put arrows to the *. Hab 3:8,9f

STRINGED
Praise him with * instruments and Ps 150:4
be accompanied by * instruments. Hab 3:19

STRINGING
This was done by * a cord across Mt 27:66f

STRIP
the way to Gerar, in the Gaza *; Gen 10:15-19
a * of the hide around his neck; Gen 27:16
grape crop—don't * every last piece Lev 19:10
went out to * the dead, they found 1Sa 31:8
the next day to * the bodies of the 1Ch 10:8
For the Lord will * away their Is 3:18
throw off your unconcern. * off Is 32:11
Just as locusts * the fields and Is 33:4
will * the fallen army of Assyria! Is 33:4
* off your robe; Is 47:2
few to live. * the branches from Jer 5:10
but I will * bare the land of Esau, Jer 49:9,10
idol altars, and * you and take Eze 16:39
They will * you of your Eze 23:26
* of inner court on the other. Eze 42:3
An additional 87½-foot * all Eze 45:2
"The * next to it, 8 Eze 45:5
"A * of land measuring 8 Eze 48:10
"The * of land 8 Eze 48:15
If she doesn't, I will * her as Hos 1:3
* as far north as Zarephath. Ob 1:20
you skin my people and * them to Mic 3:2
let us * off anything that slows us Heb 12:1

STRIPES
with up to forty * in proportion to Deu 25:1
but no more than forty * may be Deu 25:1
That same hour he washed their * Act 16:33

STRIPPED
* of everything they owned! Ex 12:36
into mourning and * themselves of Ex 33:4
was completely * and devastated. Ju 6:5
They cut off Saul's head and * 1Sa 31:9
* of their weapons, and dead. 2Sa 1:27
He even * off the gold from the 2Ki 18:16
So they * off Saul's armor and 1Ch 10:9
and jewels * from the corpses—so 2Ch 20:25
He has * me of my glory and Job 19:9
you must have * them to the bone. Job 22:6
when the crop is * and robbed. Is 1:8
and Israel—* bare of people except Is 17:6
seen her * naked and humiliated. Lam 1:8
They * her and killed her and Eze 23:10
They have ruined my vines and * Joe 1:7
led away as slaves—*, naked and Mic 1:11
their homes, and * their children Mic 2:9
Her vast, uncounted wealth is * Nah 2:9
They * him and put a scarlet Mt 27:28
by bandits. They * him of his Lk 10:30
tunic (for he was * to the waist) Jn 21:7
* and beaten with wooden whips. Act 16:22

STRIPPER-LOCUSTS
And then the *, too! Joe 1:4

STRIPS
It * the forests bare. Ps 29:9
by misfortune that * them bare of Ps 35:26
overcomes him and * him of his Lk 11:22

STRIVE
Happy are those who * for Mt 5:9
The twelve tribes of Israel * Act 26:7

STRODE
Joshua * over to him and Jos 5:13

STROKE
he had a * and lay paralyzed 1Sa 25:37,38
There is risk in each * of your Ecc 10:8,9

STROLL
and went for a * on the roof of 2Sa 11:2

STROLLING
this dream, he was * on the roof of Dan 4:29

STRONG
Because you have been * with God, Gen 32:28
"Issachar is a * beast of burden Gen 49:14
and he sent a very * west wind that Ex 10:19
and a * east wind blew all that Ex 14:21
drink wine or * drink when you go Lev 10:8,9
to the Lord, taste * drink or wine Num 6:3,4
they are * or weak, many or few; Num 13:18
"Not against people as * as they Num 13:31
He wasn't * enough to bring them Num 14:16
of the children of Ammon was *." Num 21:24f
of three pints of * wine with each Num 28:7
Not one city was too * for us, Deu 2:35,36
some wine, or some * drink, to Deu 14:26
for wine and * drink, is so that Deu 29:6
as I have commanded you. Be *! Deu 31:6
as all Israel watched, "Be *! Deu 31:7
(son of Nun) to be * and Deu 31:23
established you and made you *? Deu 32:6
With the * horns of a wild ox Deu 33:17
May you be protected with * bolts Deu 33:25
and he was as * as a young man. Deu 34:7
"Be * and brave, for you will be Jos 1:6
You need only to be * and Jos 1:7
Yes, be bold and *! Jos 1:9
and forty thousand *—led the other Jos 4:12,13
to his men. "Be * and courageous, Jos 10:25
I am as * now as I was when Jos 14:11
Israelis became * enough, they Jos 17:13
chariots and are too * for us." Jos 17:16,17,18
are such a large, * tribe you will Jos 17:16,17,18
are * and have iron chariots." Jos 17:16,17,18
He has driven out great, * Jos 23:9
his robe with his * left hand, Ju 3:21
him and said, "I will make you *! Ju 6:14
eater, and sweetness from the *!" Ju 14:1
what made him so *, so that they Ju 16
why you are so *," she pleaded. Ju 16
told me what makes you so *!" Ju 16:1
in the area * enough to try it. Ju 18
Those who were weak are now *. 1Sa 2:
saw any brave, * young man, he 1Sa 14:5
*, and had good, solid judgment. 1Sa 16:1
And now I ask you to be my * and 2Sa 2.
and I will make his kingdom *. 2Sa 7:1
"And if the Ammonites are too * 2Sa 10:1
So the conspiracy became very *. 2Sa 15:1
And from those who were too * for 2Sa 22:1
God is my * fortress; 2Sa 22:3
I am counting on you to be a * 1Ki 2:
shall become * in Jerusalem. 2Ki 19:3
of whom were * and fit for war. 2Ki 24:1
and I will make his kingdom *. 1Ch 17:1
"If the Syrians are too * for 1Ch 19:1
"and if the Ammonites are too * 1Ch 19:1
will prosper. Be * and courageous, 1Ch 22:1
Be * and do as he commands." 1Ch 28:1
Then he continued, "Be * and 1Ch 28:2
He wants them to be a great, * 2Ch 9:
Benjamin, 180,000 *, and declared 2Ch 11:
the economy of Judah remained *. 2Ch 12:1
Israeli troops—*, courageous men 2Ch 13:
Abijah of Judah became very *. 2Ch 13:2
army was 300,000 *, equipped with 2Ch 14:
So Jehoshaphat became very *, 2Ch 17:1
praise that rang out * and clear. 2Ch 20:1
nation felt a *, God-given desire 2Ch 30:1
"Be *, be brave, and do not be 2Ch 32:
At dawn he seems so * and Job 8:1
He alone is * and just. Job 9:1
upon princes, and weakens the *. Job 12:2
Oh, they have * backs all right, Job 30:2
as a cloud before a * wind. Job 30:15
Because he is so *, will you Job 39:11
Are you as * as God, and can you Job 40:9
Show me your * love in wonderful Ps 17:7
He is like the * horn of a mighty Ps 18:2
He delivered me from my * enemy, Ps 18:17
For you have armed me with * Ps 18:39
* as the giant bulls from Bashan. Ps 22:12
The Lord, * and mighty, Ps 24:8
For you alone are * enough. Ps 31:4
is * but it cannot save. Ps 33:16,17
Even * young lions sometimes go Ps 34:10
helpless from the *, and the poor Ps 35:10
life. * men are out there waiting. Ps 59:3
Use your * right arm to rescue Ps 60:4,5
in triumph into Edom's * cities? Ps 60:9,10
protected by your * right arm. Ps 63:8
was * and he despised his people. Ps 78:59
of man you made * for yourself." Ps 80:17f
THE LORD MAKES us *! Ps 81:1
Happy are those who are * in the Ps 84:5
as their maker! * is your arm! Ps 89:13
Strong is your arm! * is your Ps 89:13
Your throne is founded on two * Ps 89:14,15
I will steady him and make him * Ps 89:21
But you have made me as * as a Ps 92:10
that God alone is glorious and *. Ps 96:7
of the godly. The * arm of the Lord Ps 118:15,16
for they are too * for me. Ps 142:6
He has made his people *, Ps 148:14
But the good man has a * anchor. Pro 10:25
is a * fortress. Pro 18:10
The wise man conquers the * man Pro 21:22
marks, for their Redeemer is *; Pro 23:10,11
taste of * wine deceive you. Pro 23:31
planning, becomes * through common Pro 24:3,4
A wise man is mightier than a * Pro 24:5
Ants: they aren't *, but store up Pro 30:24-28
with age, and your * legs will Ecc 12:3
for love is * as death and jealousy Sol 8:6
are tight, their bootstraps *; Is 5:27
return to you, O * and supple Is 18:2
come when that * and mighty nation, Is 18:7
you into captivity, O * man! Is 22:17
I will make of him a * and Is 22:23,24
will you rejoice, will you be *. Is 23:12
* drink turns bitter in the mouth. Is 24:9
Therefore * nations will shake Is 25:3
"Our city is *! Is 26:1
and flee, and the * young Assyrians Is 31:8
Tell them, "Be *, fear not, for Is 35:4
For God has planted them like * Is 61:3
them and make them * and great." Jer 1:10
You are * like a fortified city Jer 1:18
they shall be * among my people. Jer 12:16
a certain nation * and great, but Jer 18:9
from those who are too * for them! Jer 31:11
in them. * men will scream in Jer 47:2
See how the *, the beautiful is Jer 48:17
But their Redeemer is *. Jer 50:34
but the hand of the Lord was * Eze 3:14,15
* branches and luxuriant leaves. Eze 17:6
would not be * again and revolt. Eze 17:14
grew into a * young lion, and Eze 19:3

TRONG Con't)
)y a * wind from the east; Eze 19:12
ıo * branch remains. Eze 19:14
Every spirit will faint; * knees Eze 21:7
ɔloodshed. How * and courageous Eze 22:14
ıt * enough to hold a sword again. Eze 30:21
both his arms—the * one and the one Eze 30:22
It was * and beautiful, for its Eze 31:7
of yourself as a * young lion among Eze 32:2
a * dose of alchemy and magic! Dan 1:3,4f
"Pick *, healthy, good-looking Dan 1:3,4
will be * as iron—smashing, Dan 2:40
Some parts of it will be as * as Dan 2:41,42
For you have grown * and great; Dan 4:22
mighty ocean, with * winds blowing Dan 7:2
to describe and incredibly *. Dan 7:7
soon became very * and attacked the Dan 8:9
Calm yourself; be *—yes, Dan 10:19
be strong—yes, *!" Dan 10:19
of followers, he will become *. Dan 11:23
shall be * and do great things. Dan 11:32
*, yet now they turn against me. Hos 7:15
I am living and *! Hos 14:8
Let the weak be *. Joe 3:10
the * fortress of Ben-hadad. Amo 1:4
as cedar trees, and * as oaks! Amo 2:9
in flight. The * will all be weak, Amo 2:14
on the *, breaking all defenses. Amo 5:9
and dictate to * nations far away. Mic 4:3
and make them * again in their own Mic 4:7
and Israel will be as * as a lion. Mic 5:8
his army millions *," the Lord Nah 1:12
Swiftly it comes—a day when * men Zep 1:14
Yes, many people, even * Zec 8:22
I will make them * and glorious Zec 10:3
my people * with power from me! Zec 10:12
Literally, "the *." Mt 12:29f
just as a * man must be tied up Mk 3:27
No one was * enough to control Mk 5:3,4
Literally, "became * in spirit." Lk 1:80f
There the child became a *, Lk 2:40
a house on a * foundation laid upon Lk 6:47,48
Literally, "the *." Lk 11:21f
* and fully armed, guards his Lk 11:21
army of 10,000 is * enough to Lk 14:31
It is as * and unshakable as Lk 16:17
Your * love for each other will Jn 13:35
of the Holy Spirit and * in faith. Act 11:24
are trivial or *, both you and Act 26:29
but the winds had become too *, Act 27:7,8
that will help your church grow * Rom 1:11,12
And because his faith was *, he Rom 4:19
hope and faith are * and steady. Rom 5:4
as your faith is * enough to Rom 12:6
your sermons are * and helpful. Rom 12:8
able to make you * and steady in Rom 16:25,26,27
upon him and grow * in the 1Co 5:8
from becoming so * that you can't 1Co 10:13
is sure, be * and steady, always 1Co 15:58
act like men; be *; 1Co 16:13
faith, for it is * already, I want 2Co 1:24
I'm not * and daring like that! 2Co 11:21
for when I am weak, then I am * 2Co 12:10
we live and are *, as he is, and 2Co 13:4
and despised if you are really *. 2Co 13:9
to punish you but to make you *. 2Co 13:10
I heard of your * faith in the Lord Eph 1:15
you will need the * belt of truth Eph 6:14
by side with one * purpose—to tell Php 1:27
and firm, * in the Lord, convinced Col 1:23
knit together by * ties of love, Col 2:2
because of your * faith in Christ. Col 2:5
Lord, and become * and vigorous in Col 2:7
together by his * sinews and we Col 2:19
this kind require * devotion and Col 2:23
God to make you * and perfect and Col 4:12
you, and your * faith and steady 1Th 1:3
whether your faith was still *. 1Th 3:5
and love are as * as ever, and that 1Th 3:6
we know that you remain * in him. 1Th 3:8
hearts being made *, sinless and 1Th 3:13
Indeed, your love is already * 1Th 4:10
and body be kept * and blameless 1Th 5:23
firm and keep a * grip on the truth 2Th 2:15
he will make you * and guard you 2Th 3:3
will be clean and their faith *. 1Ti 1:5
but to be wise and *, and to love 2Ti 1:7
OH, TIMOTHY, MY son, be * with the 2Ti 2:1
taught must be * and steadfast, so Tit 1:9
to make them * in the faith, and Tit 1:13
There is a * case to be made that Heb 5:7f
* desire to obey God at all times. Heb 5:7
as * Christians ought to be. Heb 6:1
of their * faith and patience. Heb 6:12
being saved is a * and trustworthy Heb 6:19
bring him to that * heavenly city Heb 11:10
Some were made * again after they Heb 11:34
and hurt themselves, but become *. Heb 12:13
* in character, full and complete. Jas 1:4
go, even though the winds are *. Jas 3:4
whether or not it is * and pure. 1Pe 1:7
so if your faith remains * after 1Pe 1:7
grow * in the Lord and be saved." 1Pe 2:2,3f
more you will grow * spiritually 2Pe 1:8
live a *, good life for the Lord. 2Pe 1:9
young men who are *, with God's 1Jn 2:14
you aren't *, but you have tried Rev 3:8
This tremendous choir—144,000 * Rev 14:3

STRONGER
One will be * than the other; Gen 25:23
Moreover, he watched for the * Gen 30:41
and the * ones were Jacob's! Gen 30:42
and * than you they might be. Deu 11:23
the Israelis were * they put the Ju 1:28
on Israel became * and stronger Ju 4:24
stronger and * against King Jabin, Ju 4:24
they asked, "and what is * Ju 14:18
They were swifter than eagles, * 2Sa 1:23
David's position now became * and 2Sa 3:1
stronger and *, while Saul's 2Sa 3:1
and since he was * than she, he 2Sa 13:14
shall become * and stronger. Job 17:9
shall become stronger and *. Job 17:9
A wise man is * than the mayors Ecc 7:19
because you are * than I am, but Jer 20:7
For those far * than you have Eze 21:9,10,11
one which was * than the others. Dan 7:20
words, I felt * and said to him, Dan 10:19
until someone * and better-armed Lk 11:22
trust grew ever *, and he praised Rom 4:20
It is sin inside me that is * Rom 7:17
the cross—is far * than any man. 1Co 1:25
you couldn't digest anything *. 1Co 3:2
Are you * than he is? 1Co 10:22
now will make you * Christians? Gal 3:3
place, and make you * than ever. 1Pe 5:10
your hearts who is * than any evil 1Jn 4:4
his love within us grows ever *. 1Jn 4:12

STRONGEST
thousand of the * and most skillful Ju 3:29
and Jonathan slew their * foes, 2Sa 1:22
When he stands up, the * are Job 41:25
the race, nor the * man the battle, Ecc 9:11
water. The * among you will Is 1:31
The Lord has said in * terms: Do Is 8:11
* hearts melt, and are afraid. Is 13:7
The * forts are turned to rubble. Is 25:2
there. The * will perish, young Is 34:7
Bring your * arguments. Is 41:1
the water. Its * branch became a Eze 19:11
upon Pelusium, the * fortress of Eze 30:15
for some of the * men of his army Dan 3:20
success against the * fortresses. Dan 11:39
down go the walled cities and * Zep 1:16

STRONGHOLD
and captured the * of Zion, now 2Sa 5:7
So David made the * of Zion (also 2Sa 5:9
were coming and went into the *. 2Sa 5:17
David was in the * at the time, 2Sa 23:14
and then to the * of Tyre, and 2Sa 24:7
David was in the * at the time; 1Ch 11:16
* of the sea. Is 23:4

STRONGHOLDS
They come trembling from their *. Ps 18:43,44,45
Her cities are fallen; her * are Jer 48:41
capture powerful * throughout his Dan 11:24
men, to knock down the devil's *. 2Co 10:4

STRONGLY
"Yes, you are * situated, Num 24:21,22
Then the Spirit of God came * 1Sa 11:6
himself, but his men objected *. 2Sa 18:2
He trusted very * in the Lord 2Ki 18:5
the foundations are to be * laid. Ez 6:3
Though the tide of battle runs * Ps 55:18
When Jesus saw how * they Mk 2:5
(For the people all believed * Mk 11:32
it stands firm, for it is * built. Lk 6:47,48
about Jesus and * urging all his Act 2:40
to judge and deal * with those who 1Co 5:12
publicly, speaking * against what Gal 2:11
* that they tremble in terror! Jas 2:19
lives ever more * upon the Jud 1:20

STRUCK
win the match, he * Jacob's hip, Gen 32:25
—the same one you * the Nile Ex 17:5,6
were * dead before the Lord. Num 14:36,37,38
Then Moses lifted the rod and * Num 20:11
Moses * it, not once, but twice. Num 20:12f
"But if someone is * and killed Num 35:16
Or if the slain man was * down Num 35:17
they will be * down before their Deu 1:42
with you and * down those who were Deu 25:18
if the people are * by an epidemic 1Ki 8:37
Zimri simply walked in and * him 1Ki 16:10
at random and it * King Ahab 1Ki 22:34
Then lightning * them and 2Ki 1:10
together and * the water with it; 2Ki 2:8
River, and * the water with it. 2Ki 2:13,14
So the king picked them up and * 2Ki 13:18
"You should have * the floor 2Ki 13:19
the Lord * him with leprosy, 2Ki 15:5
the land and * down the tents and 1Ch 4:40,41
the Lord * him and he died. 2Ch 13:20
troops, and it * the king of Israel 2Ch 18:33
Literally, "Jehoram * down 2Ch 21:9f
all that you have will be * down. 2Ch 21:14
It was after this that Jehovah * 2Ch 21:18
out, because the Lord had * him. 2Ch 26:20
The enemy archers * King Josiah 2Ch 35:23
oldest brother's house, tragedy *. Job 1:12,13
of the Lord and * Job with a Job 2:7
and lazy, yet trouble * me down." Job 3:26
For the Lord has * me down with Job 6:4
He will be chased and * down. Job 20:24
Your arrows have * deep; Ps 38:2
You have * down his sword and Ps 89:43
The guards found me and * and Sol 5:7
You have * a bargain with Death, Is 28:15
her mocking enemy * her down—and Lam 1:7
utter disaster * in a moment Lam 4:6
All these mighty men who once * Eze 32:23
* terror to the hearts of all; Eze 32:26
Then they spat in his face and * Mt 26:67
Messiah! Who * you that time?" Mt 26:68
there * Jesus with his fist. Jn 18:22
they mocked, and * him with Jn 19:3
Instantly, an angel of the Lord * Act 12:23
by ordering me * like that?" Act 23:3
that * and bit with fatal wounds. Rev 9:19

STRUCTURE
so the entire * was built without 1Ki 6:7
be a marvelous *, famous and 1Ch 22:5
The whole * was supported by Eze 41:6
rebuild the Temple *, and before Hag 2:18,19

STRUCTURES
This group of * was 175 feet Eze 42:2

STRUGGLE
All your life you will * to Gen 3:17
"HOW MANKIND MUST *. Job 7:1
to * up from their nest in hunger? Job 38:41
* now, as you know so well. Php 1:30
and have won your * against Satan: 1Jn 2:14

STRUGGLED
Trapped and helpless, I * Ps 18:5
When he was born, he * with his Hos 12:3
how much I have * in prayer for you Col 2:1
After all, you have never yet * Heb 12:4

STRUGGLING
and * against the wind and waves. Mk 6:48

STRUNG
So they * fig leaves together to Gen 3:7
He has bent and * his bow and Ps 7:12
For the wicked have * their bows, Ps 11:2
Must we be * up on their hooks Hab 1:15

STRUT
their words * through the earth. Ps 73:9

STRUTTED
* before the armies of Israel. 1Sa 17:16

STUBBORN
I will make him * so that he will Ex 4:21
was still hard and *, and he Ex 7:13
remained hard and *, and he Ex 7:22
heart was hard and *, and he Ex 8:19
yet more by their * refusal to do Ex 9:34
have seen what a *, rebellious lot Ex 32:9
you, for you are a *, unruly Ex 33:3
"You are an unruly, * people. Ex 33:5
yes, it is an unruly, * people, Ex 34:9
not—you are a wicked, * people. Deu 9:6
may destroy this evil, * people!' Deu 9:13,14
"If a man has a *, rebellious Deu 21:18
* and rebellious and won't obey; Deu 21:20
though I walk in my own * way!' Deu 29:19
"For I know how rebellious and * Deu 31:27
They are a *, twisted generation. Deu 32:5
For they are a *, faithless Deu 32:20
Don't be * and rebellious as 1Sa 6:6
churlish, *, and ill-mannered. 1Sa 25:3
family—he's such a * lout that no 1Sa 25:17
The people were as * as their 2Ki 17:14
Do not be *, as they were, but 2Ch 30:8
Zedekiah was a hard and * man so 2Ch 36:13
were a proud and * lot, and they Neh 9:16
to leave their guilty, * ways. Ps 68:21
and to stop being * and proud. Ps 75:5
their fathers were—*, rebellious, Ps 78:8
go their blind and * way, living Ps 81:12
The Lord hates the * but delights Pro 11:20
An evil man is *, but a godly man Pro 21:29
For they are * rebels. Is 30:9
Listen to me, you *, evil men! Is 46:12
their own *, evil thoughts. Jer 7:24
They are hard and * and Jer 7:26
Each followed his own * will and Jer 11:8
that you were not so proud and *! Jer 13:15
This people's * will can't be Jer 15:12,13
of them are hard, impudent and *. Eze 3:7
and * too—as tough as they are. Eze 3:8
Don't be like Israel, * as a Hos 4:16
child resisting in the womb—how *! Hos 13:13
Jesus replied, "Oh, you *, Mt 17:17
unbelief—their * refusal to believe Mk 16:14
"O you * faithless people," Lk 9:41

(STUBBORN Con't)
of people who are crooked and *. Php 2:15

STUBBORNLY
But I will cause Pharaoh to * Ex 7:3
worship. They * returned to the Ju 2:19
the Almighty, * assaulting him. Job 15:25,26
* follow their evil desires. Jer 3:17
or obey. They * refused to pay Jer 17:23
* refused to listen to the Lord. Jer 19:15
They turned * away and put their Zec 7:11

STUBBORNNESS
Pharaoh in his *, so that he Ex 9:12
Don't notice the rebellion and * Deu 9:27
sinful hearts and stop your * Deu 10:16
* is as bad as worshiping idols. 1Sa 15:23
full of * and wickedness!" Jer 18:12
because of your * in refusing to Rom 2:5

STUCK
so long that they * out past the 1Ki 8:8
The bow of the ship * fast, while Act 27:41

STUDENT
priest, the * of God's commands: Ez 7:11
* is not greater than his teacher. Mt 10:24
The * shares his teacher's fate. Mt 10:25
How can a * know more than his Lk 6:40

STUDENTS
Then the * at Jericho Seminary 2Ki 2:5
of the seminary * came to Elisha to 2Ki 4:1
ONE DAY THE seminary * came to 2Ki 6:1
important truths. * are wise who Ecc 12:11

STUDIED
As they * it, they noted that Neh 8:14

STUDY
had determined to * and obey the Ez 7:10
Now I began a * of the Ecc 2:12

STUDYING
to be expressed. * them can go on Ecc 12:12
Your long * has broken your Act 26:24
especially good at * and teaching, 1Co 12:8

STUFF
Give me a bite of that red * Gen 25:30
"Edom," which means "Red *." Gen 25:30
All kinds of *! Pro 1:13
be on your guard and don't * Pro 23:1
"This is wonderful *!" Jn 2:10
No, it was sin, devilish * that Rom 7:13

STUFFED
she had * them into her camel Gen 31:34
you will be * with bread, and you Ex 16:11,12

STUFFING
on, gorging and * themselves Jud 1:12

STUMBLE
pursue they shall * over each other Lev 26:37
I never need to * or to fall. Ps 16:8
Lord, he will never *, never fall: Ps 21:7
destroy me, they will * and fall! Ps 27:2
of heart and mind and do not *. Ps 119:165
He will never let me *, slip or Ps 121:3,4
you'll not limp or * as you run. Pro 4:12
they cause someone to * and fall. Pro 4:16
They never weary, never *, never Is 5:27
you will * along as prisoners or Is 10:4
message they will * and fall and be Is 28:13
them, they will * and fall among Is 31:3
like blind men and * along in broad Is 59:10
If you * and fall on open ground, Jer 12:5
you so that you * and fall upon the Jer 13:16
Terrible One, they shall *. Jer 20:11
the quiet streams and not *. Jer 31:9
your mightiest soldiers will * Jer 46:12
Land of pride, you will * and Jer 50:32
things of God will * in those days Dan 11:35
you priests will * in broad Hos 4:5
She will * under her load of Hos 5:5
Your swiftest warriors will * in Amo 2:14
his officers; they * in their Nah 2:5
everywhere. Men * over them, Nah 3:3
has caused many to * in sin. Mal 2:8
Literally, "cause to *." Mt 18:6f
All who * on this rock of truth Mt 21:44
a man can walk safely and not *. Jn 11:9
and many will * over him (Jesus). Rom 9:33
make your brother * by letting him Rom 14:13
to eat it if it makes another *. Rom 14:20
that some will * over, and the Rock 1Pe 2:8
They will * because they will 1Pe 2:8
you will never * or fall away. 2Pe 1:10

STUMBLED
"I've * into his home! Gen 28:16,17
out his back. He * to the ground 2Sa 2:23
of Nacon, the oxen * and Uzzah put 2Sa 6:6
Chidon, the oxen * and Uzza reached 1Ch 13:9
care and thereby * against the Rock Is 8:14,15
through the desert, they never *. Is 63:13
Euphrates, they have * and fallen. Jer 46:6
They have * over the great Rom 9:32
when the Jews * over it and turned Rom 11:12

STUMBLES
evil man gropes and * in the dark. Pro 4:19
And he added, "Whoever * over Lk 20:18
to trap him; he * over his own 1Co 3:19

STUMBLING
* block to those who trust in you. Ps 69:6
* against the rocks on the trail. Ps 91:12
eyes from tears, my feet from *. Ps 116:8
ahead of me, and keep me from *. Ps 119:105
disaster and from * off the trail. Pro 3:23
away captive, *, weary and hungry. Is 8:21
The beasts are *! Is 46:1
"because of occasions of *." Mt 18:7f
is he who keeps from * over me." Lk 7:23f
me, you won't be * through the Jn 8:12
stumbled over the great * stone. Rom 9:32
So don't be a * block to anyone, 1Co 10:32
* around in darkness and sin. 1Jn 2:10

STUMP
the earth, and its * decays, it may Job 14:8,9
* still lives to grow again." Is 6:13
but from the * will grow a Shoot Is 11:1
but leave its * and roots in the Dan 4:15
it, but leave the * and the roots Dan 4:23
But the * and the roots were Dan 4:26

STUNG
These remarks * them to fury; Lk 4:28
The Jewish leaders were * to fury Act 7:54

STUNNED
they were so * with surprise. Gen 45:3
sat there * and silent for an Dan 4:19
his way through the * onlookers! Mk 2:12
about, and were * to hear their own Act 2:6

STUNTED
He is like a * shrub in the Jer 17:6

STUPID
Israel is a * nation; Deu 32:28
I'm not *. Job 13:2
like animals to you, * and dumb? Job 18:3
but they are useless, * fools. Job 30:2
lease on life than foolish, * men. Ps 49:10
O God, you know so well how * I Ps 69:5
I saw myself so * and so Ps 73:22
Their minds are dull and *, but Ps 119:70
Why was I so *? Pro 5:13
To refuse reproof is *. Pro 12:1
What a shame—yes, how *! Pro 18:13
Only a * prince will oppress his Pro 28:16
I am too * even to call myself a Pro 30:2
of Egypt is utterly * and wrong. Is 19:11
nation, a witless, * people, for Is 27:11
making * errors and mistakes. Is 28:7
You are *—and not from drinking, Is 29:9
How * can they be! Is 29:16
even the most * cannot miss the Is 35:8
they are * shepherds who only Is 56:11
are altogether * and foolish. Jer 10:8
Compared to him, all men are * Jer 51:17
Can oxen plow the sea? * even to Amo 6:12
Stupid even to ask, but no more * Amo 6:12
And just as * is your rejoicing Amo 6:13
These * crowds do, yes; Jn 7:49
year, said, "You * idiots— let Jn 11:49
different is both proud and *. 1Ti 6:4
are deliberately *, and always 2Pe 3:15,16

STUPIDITY
How you have enlightened my *! Job 26:3
Such * and ignorance! Is 44:18
I kicked myself for my *. Jer 31:19
fill the wise men of Edom with *. Ob 1:8
their own little ideas. What *! 2Co 10:12

STUPOR
from his drunken *, and learned Gen 9:24,25
troubles and in a * (but not from Is 51:21

SUAH
*, Harnepher, Shual, Beri, Imrah, 1Ch 7:36,37

SUB-CLAN
(In the * of Eliab—who was one of Num 26:5-11
The * of the Machirites was the Num 26:28-37
Shuthelah. (A * of the Num 26:28-37
THEN THE HEADS of the * of Gilead Num 36:1

SUB-CLANS
This census also included the * of Num 26:19-22
* named after sons of Bela were: Num 26:38-41
* named after the sons of Beriah Num 26:44-47

SUB-TOTAL
Implied in verse 16, where a * is Jos 21:9-16f

SUB-TOTALS
text indicates * of the number of Jos 15:48-62f
original manuscript indicates *. Jos 18:21-28f
manuscript, where * are indicated. Jos 19:2-7f

SUB-TRIBES
Here are the names of the * of Gen 36:40-43
the names of the * of Edom, each Gen 36:40-43

SUBCLAN
The * of Elkanah was further 1Ch 6:25,26,27
The families of the * of Samuel 1Ch 6:28
each of whom was the head of a *: 1Ch 7:2
Dodo, a member of the * of Ahoh. 1Ch 11:12
200 from the * of Elizaphan; 1Ch 15:4-10
80 from the * of Hebron; 1Ch 15:4-10
112 from the * of Uzziel; 1Ch 15:4-10
* because neither had many sons. 1Ch 23:10,11
These men of the Ladan * from 1Ch 26:20,21,22
his sons (from the * of Izhar) were 1Ch 26:29
of the Hushite * from Zerah, who 1Ch 27:
Levites of the * of Merari. 2Ch 34:
Zechariah and Meshullam, of the * 2Ch 34:
From the * of Parosh, 2,172; Ez 2:3-35
From the * of Shephatiah, 372; Ez 2:3-35
From the * of Arah, 775; Ez 2:3-35
From the * of Pahath-moab (the Ez 2:3-35
From the * of Elam, 1,254; Ez 2:3-35
From the * of Zattu, 945; Ez 2:3-35
From the * of Zaccai, 760; Ez 2:3-35
From the * of Bani, 642; Ez 2:3-35
From the * of Bebai, 623; Ez 2:3-35
From the * of Azgad, 1,222; Ez 2:3-35
From the * of Adonikam, 666; Ez 2:3-35
From the * of Bigvai, 2,056; Ez 2:3-35
From the * of Adin, 454; Ez 2:3-35
From the * of Ater (the Ez 2:3-35
From the * of Bezai, 323; Ez 2:3-35
From the * of Jorah, 112; Ez 2:3-35
From the * of Hashum, 223; Ez 2:3-35
From the * of Gibbar, 95; Ez 2:3-35
From the * of Bethlehem, 123; Ez 2:3-35
From the * of Netophah, 56; Ez 2:3-35
From the * of Anathoth, 128; Ez 2:3-35
From the * of Azmaveth, 42; Ez 2:3-35
From the * of Michmas, 122; Ez 2:3-35
From the * of Nebo, 52; Ez 2:3-35
From the * of Magbish, 156; Ez 2:3-35
From the * of Elam, 1,254; Ez 2:3-35
From the * of Harim, 320; Ez 2:3-35
From the * of Jericho, 345; Ez 2:3-35
From the * of Senaah, 3,630. Ez 2:3-35
Jedaiah of the * of Jeshua, 973; Ez 2:36-39
From the * of Immer, 1,052; Ez 2:36-39
From the * of Pashhur, 1,247; Ez 2:36-39
From the * of Harim, 1,017. Ez 2:36-39
Kedmi-el of the * of Hodaviah, 74; Ez 2:40,41,42
From the * of David of the clan of Ez 8:2-14
From the * of Parosh, 2,172; Neh 7:8-38
From the * of Shephatiah, 372; Neh 7:8-38
From the * of Arah, 652; Neh 7:8-38
of the * of Pahath-moab, 2,818; Neh 7:8-38
From the * of Elam, 1,254; Neh 7:8-38
From the * of Zattu, 845; Neh 7:8-38
From the * of Zaccai, 760; Neh 7:8-38
From the * of Binnui, 648; Neh 7:8-38
From the * of Bebai, 628; Neh 7:8-38
From the * of Azgad, 2,322; Neh 7:8-38
From the * of Adonikam, 667; Neh 7:8-38
From the * of Bigvai, 2,067; Neh 7:8-38
From the * of Adin, 655; Neh 7:8-38
of Hezekiah of the * of Ater, 98; Neh 7:8-38
From the * of Hashum, 328; Neh 7:8-38
From the * of Bezai, 324; Neh 7:8-38
From the * of Hariph, 112; Neh 7:8-38
From the * of Gibeon, 95; Neh 7:8-38
From the * of Anathoth, 128; Neh 7:8-38
From the * of Beth-azmaveth, 42; Neh 7:8-38
From the * of Michmas, 122; Neh 7:8-38
From the * of Nebo, 52; Neh 7:8-38
From the * of Elam, 1,254; Neh 7:8-38
From the * of Harim, 320; Neh 7:8-38
From the * of Jericho, 345; Neh 7:8-38
From the * of Sanaah, 3,930. Neh 7:8-38
From the family of Jeshua of the * Neh 7:39-42
From the * of Immer, 1,052; Neh 7:39-42
From the * of Pashhur, 1,247; Neh 7:39-42
From the * of Harim, 1,017. Neh 7:39-42
of Kadmi-el of the * of Hodevah of Neh 7:43,44,45

SUBCLANS
The * of the Levites were: 1Ch 6:19,20,21
The * of the clan of Merari were 1Ch 6:29,30
The * of the Gershom clan 1Ch 6:62
The * of Merari received by lot 1Ch 6:63
pasturelands to the * of Kohath: 1Ch 6:66-69
were given to the * of the 1Ch 6:70
and Isshiah, all chiefs of *. 1Ch 7:3
were chiefs of * and were the 1Ch 7:7
They were the chiefs of the * of 1Ch 7:11
were heads of * and were all 1Ch 7:40
The sons of Ehud, chiefs of the * 1Ch 8:6,7
These sons all became chiefs of *. 1Ch 8:8,9,10
Beriah and Shema, chiefs of * 1Ch 8:13
These were the chiefs of the * 1Ch 8:28
These men were all chiefs of *. 1Ch 9:9
The * of Shime-i were named after 1Ch 23:10,11
the names of these clans and *; 1Ch 23:24
those who returned (listed by *): Ez 2:2
From the * of Kiriatharim, Ez 2:3-35
From the * of Ramah and Geba, 621; Ez 2:3-35
From the * of Bethel and Ai, 223; Ez 2:3-35
From the * of Lod, Hadid, and Ono, Ez 2:3-35
This group included the * of Ez 2:60
Three * of priests—Habaiah, Ez 2:61
From the * of Bethlehem and Neh 7:8-38
From the * of Kiriath-jearim, Neh 7:8-38
From the * of Ramah and Geba, 621; Neh 7:8-38
From the * of Bethel and Ai, 123; Neh 7:8-38
From the * of Lod, Hadid, and Ono, Neh 7:8-38
the following * were represented: Neh 7:46-56
these were the * of Delaiah, Neh 7:62

UBCLANS Con't)
There were also several * of Neh 7:63
UBDIVIDED
The division of Kohath was * into 1Ch 23:12
He has surveyed and * the land Is 34:17
UBDIVISIONS
* of the Gershom corps were named 1Ch 23:7
These * were still further 1Ch 23:8,9
UBDUE
and fill the earth and * it; Gen 1:28
repopulate the earth and * it." Gen 9:7
Israel to * King Jabin of Canaan. Ju 4:23
and * him and put him in chains. Ju 16:5
And have caused me to * 2Sa 22:40
I will * all of your enemies. 1Ch 17:10
managed to * him. 2Ch 21:9
How quickly then I would * her Ps 81:14
"Rule as my regent—I will * your Ps 110:1
and they will * their enemies, Zec 9:15
UBDUED
* before the Lord, you may return. Num 32:22
of how Midian was * by Israel. Ju 8:28
Thus the Ammonites were * by the Ju 11:33
So the Philistines were * and 1Sa 7:13
AFTER THIS DAVID * and humbled 2Sa 8:1
DAVID FINALLY * the Philistines 1Ch 18:1
ancestors. You * whole nations Neh 9:24
UBDUES
me and * the nations before me. Ps 18:47
all the earth. He * the nations Ps 47:3
a shield. He * my people under me. Ps 144:2
UBJECT
they had all been * to King Gen 14:4
We suggest that, * to your Est 1:19
"And now I have become the * of Job 30:9
and Sabeans shall be * to you. Is 45:14
Then Jeremiah broached the * of Jer 37:18
*: A MESSAGE from the Lord. Zep 1:1
*: A MESSAGE from the Lord. Hag 1:1
*: MESSAGES FROM the Lord. Zec 1:1
they brought up the * again. Mk 10:10
prophets are * to the prophets." 1Co 14:32f
UBJECTED
* to Satan's temptations to sin. Mk 1:12,13
UBJECTION
kept them in * for forty years. Ju 13:1
your enemies into complete *.' Act 2:35
covering is a sign of her * to him 1Co 11:5
for his hat is a sign of * to men 1Co 11:7
UBJECTS
his sons, and his *, so that not a Num 21:35
loyal *, now that Saul is dead. 2Sa 2:7
became David's * and brought him 2Sa 8:6
to King David and became his *. 1Ch 19:19
"Sir: Greetings from your loyal * Ez 4:11
when he dies. His * will not even Jer 22:18
And his * gnawed their tongues in Rev 16:10
UBMERGING
Immanuel, * it from end to end." Is 8:7,8
UBMISSION
* and kingdoms totter into ruin. Ps 46:6
UBMISSIVE
Bring them—*, tax in hand. Ps 68:30
and they shall come trembling, * Hos 3:5
UBMIT
long will you refuse to * to me? Ex 10:3
And shall quickly * to me 2Sa 22:45
or to * to three days of plague? 2Sa 24:13
themselves up and * to the 2Ki 25:24
have never seen me * instantly. Ps 18:43,44,45
him their slave. * to him and Jer 27:8
and refuse to * to the king of Jer 27:10
"If you want to live, * to the Jer 27:12
that will not * to Babylon's king? Jer 27:13
He will honor those who * to him, Dan 11:39
And even those teachers who * to Gal 6:13
You wives must * to your Eph 5:22
in the same way you * to the Lord. Eph 5:22
You wives, * yourselves to your Col 3:18
more cheerfully * to God's training Heb 12:9
SUBMITTING
Literally, "everyone * himself Ps 68:30f
But the people of any nation * Jer 27:11
Honor Christ by * to each other. Eph 5:21
SUBORDINATE
discussion, for they are * to men 1Co 14:34
SUBSCRIBE
and Benjamin to * to this pact with 2Ch 34:32
SUBSEQUENT
The * usage of the word "son" 1Ch 1:24-27f
70 by Titus and the * slaughter Dan 9:25f
SUBSIDE
pressures will *, and some ungodly Dan 11:34
SUBSIDED
and the torrential rains *. Gen 8:2
and the storm * and all was calm. Mt 8:26
wind and waves * and all was calm! Lk 8:24
SUBSTITUTE
then becomes his *: the death of Lev 1:4
* good for bad or bad for good; Lev 27:10
him die, for I have found a *.' Job 33:23,24
Mere words won't * for strength, Is 36:5
orders and * your own traditions. Mk 7:8
SUBSTITUTES
* for the eldest sons of Israel; Num 3:41
cattle are mine as * for the Num 3:41
have taken the Levites as their *. Num 8:16
bronze shields as *, and the palace 1Ki 14:27
* a sick one to sacrifice to God. Mal 1:14
SUBSTITUTION
original and the * shall belong to Lev 27:33
the Levites in * for all the oldest Num 3:11,12
SUBSTITUTIONS
or bad, and there shall be no *; Lev 27:33
SUBTERRANEAN
the sky, and the * waters burst Gen 7:10,11,12
for the * water sources ceased Gen 8:2
SUBTRACT
Do not add other laws or * from Deu 4:2
Do not add to or * from them. Deu 12:32
SUBTRACTS
And if anyone * any part of Rev 22:19
SUBURBS
as Gaza and its *, destroying 2Ki 18:8
the fields and * were given to 1Ch 6:55,56,57
Jeshanah, Ephron, and their *. 2Ch 13:18,19
own villages as * of Jerusalem. Neh 12:29
First he will destroy your *; Eze 26:8
with extensive *—so large that it Jon 3:3
and her southern * out along the Zec 7:7
from the Jerusalem *, bringing Act 5:16
SUBVERSIVE
Zealots," a * political party), Mt 10:2,3,4
the Zealots, a * political party), Lk 6:14,15,16
SUBVERTED
Literally, "* your souls." Act 15:24f
SUCATHITES
Tirathites, Shime-athites, and *. 1Ch 2:55
SUCCEED
But if you don't *, then you are Gen 24:8
For only then will you *. Jos 1:8
No one shall * by strength alone. 1Sa 2:9
David continued to * in 1Sa 18:14
the one you have chosen to * you. 1Ki 1:20
him by giving him a son to * him. 1Ki 3:6
you will *. 1Ki 22:22
did not have a son to * him. 2Ki 1:17
chosen Solomon to * me on the 1Ch 28:5
fathers, for you will not *!" 2Ch 13:12
Joash, lived to * him as king, for 2Ch 22:9
never * in your plans against him; Est 6:13
Lord, but they cannot possibly *. Ps 21:11
Don't let my enemies *. Ps 25:2
let these evil men *, nor let the Ps 37:33
would sit on my throne and * me. Ps 132:11
Don't let these wicked men *; Ps 140:6,7,8
be lazy and never *. Pro 12:24
Obey it and *. Pro 13:13
work to the Lord, then it will *. Pro 16:3
for a fool to * or for a slave to Pro 19:10
When the wicked *, everyone is Pro 28:12
lad could come from prison and *. Ecc 4:14
This plan will not *, for Damascus Is 7:7
but you will not *—you will be Is 8:9,10
Your son will not * you as the Is 14:20
against you shall *, and you will Is 54:17
You will not * despite their aid. Jer 2:37
Will she *? Eze 17:15
emerges will not * until the Man Eze 21:27
but this will not *, for iron and Dan 2:43
but they will not *. Dan 11:14
for plots against him will *. Dan 11:25
for neither can * until God's Dan 11:27
what little you * in storing up Mic 6:14
Will they * forever in their Hab 1:17
of Hosts—you will * because of my Zec 4:6
Or, "that I will finally * in Rom 1:10f
SUCCEEDED
* Gen 36:31-39
More literally, "* at his death Gen 36:31-39f
* by: King Husham, from the land Gen 36:31-39
* by: King Hadad (son of Bedad), Gen 36:31-39
* by: King Samlah, from Masrekah. Gen 36:31-39
* by: King Shaul, from Gen 36:31-39
* by: King Baal-hanan (son of Gen 36:31-39
* by: King Hadad, from the city of Gen 36:31-39
so that everything he did *. Gen 39:2
Shamir, and was * by Jair, a man Ju 10:3
His son Ammizabad * him as 1Ch 27:5,6
says this about Jehoahaz who * Jer 22:11
Jehoiakim, who * his father Josiah Jer 22:18
will reign, to be * by a fourth, Dan 11:2
then Felix was * by Porcius Act 24:27
God by keeping his laws, never *. Rom 9:31
SUCCEEDING
on and on to each * generation. Ps 100:5
SUCCEEDS
of his son who * him, from Ex 29:29
Literally, "who * her mistress." Pro 30:21,22,23f
SUCCESS
make my mission a *, please guide Gen 24:42
will go with you and give you *." Ex 33:14
along the road without *. Jos 2:22
God has given us * and rest as he Jos 22:4
the Lord had given * to the people Jos 23:1
They looked for them without * 2Sa 17:20
to whom God gave such wonderful *; 2Sa 23:1
My safety and *. 2Sa 23:5
King David on his * and to present 1Ch 18:10
from heaven and give them *. 2Ch 6:35
your God, and you shall have *! 2Ch 20:20
forward with great energy and *. Ez 5:8
Yet there is * in everything Ps 10:5
and give * to those who obey them. Ps 19:11
the throne with * and prosperity. Ps 21:3
loudly applauds *— yet in the end Ps 49:18
My protection and * Ps 62:7
praising you! My *—at which so Ps 71:7
our God favor us and give us *. Ps 90:17
Give us *. Ps 118:25
you and crown your efforts with *. Pro 3:6
a good man's *—and also the godless Pro 11:10
Wickedness never brings real *; Pro 12:3
many counselors bring *. Pro 15:22
own best interest and will be a *. Pro 19:8
basic motive for * is the driving Ecc 4:4
lies of safety and *—that your gods Eze 21:29
but his * will be short-lived. Dan 11:12
With great * he will besiege and Dan 11:24
he will have great * against the Dan 11:39
be filled with pride at their *. Zec 12:7
and the search for * and lure of Mk 4:19
and I am filled with joy at his *. Jn 3:29
Our only power and * comes from 2Co 3:5
that their * will add to my sorrows Php 1:16,17
forever the * of this new and Heb 7:22
SUCCESSFUL
with you and make your mission *. Gen 24:40
the Lord has made my mission *, Gen 24:56
way you will be * in the land which Deu 16:20
will be a * leader of my people; Jos 1:6
will be * in everything you do. Jos 1:7
or not our trip will be *." Ju 18:5
May you be a great and * man in Ru 4:11
And wherever he turned, he was *. 1Sa 14:47
Since David was, if *, 1Sa 17:55f
David was more * against them than 1Sa 18:30
(the son of Jehoahaz) was * on 2Ki 13:25
Israeli army in * attacks against 1Ch 20:1
But to this day Edom has been * 2Ch 21:10
the Ammonites was *, so that for 2Ch 27:5
and godly living, and was very *. 2Ch 31:21
Those who turn from God may be * Job 5:3
He shall be * and stand before Pro 22:29
When the godly are *, everyone is Pro 28:12
admit his mistakes can never be *. Pro 28:13
SUCCESSFULLY
and earth were * completed, with Gen 2:1
That night he * attacked them Gen 14:15
hope that he can battle them *." Num 22:11
carried out his assignments *. 1Sa 18:5
Israeli army were * ending their 2Sa 12:26,27
Thus Solomon * completed the 2Ch 8:16
ahead with these projects very *. 2Ch 14:7
anywhere, was able to resist us *. 2Ch 32:14
Who has ever opposed him *? Job 9:4
SUCCESSION
not directly in line for royal *. Dan 11:21
SUCCESSIVE
The oldest sons of the * 1Ch 6:4-15
SUCCESSOR
you to be a strong and worthy *. 1Ki 2:2
Ahaziah, King Ahab's son and *, 1Ki 22:49
"And you, his *, O Dan 5:22
"His * Dan 11:20
Seleucus IV, * of Antiochus III, Dan 11:20f
SUCCESSORS
The four principal * of Alexander Dan 8:8f
SUCCOTH
his household went as far as *. Gen 33:17
is called *, meaning "huts." Gen 33:17
left Rameses and started for *; Ex 12:37
Leaving *, they camped in Etham Ex 13:20
they stayed in *, Etham (at the Num 33:5,6
and Beth-nimrah, *, Zaphon, and the Jos 13:27,28
He asked the men of * for food. Ju 8:5
But the leaders of * replied, Ju 8:6
young fellow from * and demanded Ju 8:14
He then returned to *. Ju 8:15
"he taught the men of *." Ju 8:16f
River between * and Zarethan. 1Ki 7:41-46
valley between * and Zeredah. 2Ch 4:17,18
"Shechem, *, Gilead, Ps 60:6,7
of Shechem, and also * Valley. Ps 108:7
SUCCOTH-BENOTH
worshiped idols of their god *; 2Ki 17:30
SUCH
to his wife in * a way that the two Gen 2:24
"How could you do * a thing?" Gen 3:13
* as handle the harp and pipe." Gen 4:21f
not alight on * floating carrion, Gen 8:7f
though he does * wicked things. Gen 8:21
Close relatives * as we are must Gen 13:8

(SUCH Con't)
Surely you wouldn't do * a thing, Gen 18:25
"don't do * a wicked thing. Gen 19:7
you've granted me * mercy, let Gen 19:18,19,20
disgrace for her to marry * a man. Gen 34:14
How can I do * a wicked thing as Gen 39:9
first dream had * a good meaning, Gen 40:16
I've never seen * poor-looking Gen 41:19
us of * a terrible thing as that? Gen 44:7
"Didn't you know * a man as I Gen 44:15
making * unreasonable demands." Ex 5:16
across the nation * as there has Ex 9:18
never before has there been * Ex 11:6
* great power and mighty miracles? Ex 32:11
* a terrible sin upon them?" Ex 32:21
I will do miracles * as have Ex 34:10
unclean—* as the dead body of an Lev 5:2
guilty of any * sin, he shall Lev 6:4,5
sin offering on * a day as this, Lev 10:19
the dead body of * an animal shall Lev 11:27
"If the dead body of * an animal Lev 11:35
the priest must pronounce him *. Lev 13:44
However * a marriage was Lev 20:21f
of leafy trees—* as willows that Lev 23:40
You will have * a surplus of Lev 26:10
we were fools to do * a thing. Num 12:11
in * error and forgiveness. Num 15:26
will stand heat—* as gold, silver, Num 31:22
would always have * a heart for me, Deu 5:29
in Egypt with * amazing power and Deu 7:8
because you are * fine, upright Deu 9:5
* wickedness as this among you. Deu 13:11
it is certain that * a horrible Deu 13:12,13,14
the dead bodies of * animals. Deu 14:8
has any defect * as being lame or Deu 15:21
you left Egypt in * a hurry that Deu 16:3
He doesn't feel honored by * Deu 17:1
penalty is death. * sinners must be Deu 17:12
not permit you to do * things. Deu 18:14
this is your rule in * cases. Deu 19:21
her parents; and * evil must be Deu 22:21
you and has done * wonderful things Deu 28:63
There had never been * a day Jos 10:14
given us * large populations?" Jos 17:14
since you are * a large, strong Jos 17:16,17,18
has lasted for * a long time. Jos 22:2,3
care of you for * a long time." Jos 24:20
have told us about—* as when God Ju 6:13
have given Israel * a wonderful Ju 15:18
as they were having * a good time. Ju 19:6
"No, my brothers, don't do * a Ju 19:23
don't do * a thing to this man." Ju 19:24
"There hasn't been * a horrible Ju 19:30
back on me and sent * calamity!" Ru 1:21
Why make * a fuss over having no 1Sa 1:8
he had never worn * things before. 1Sa 17:38,39
not planning any * thing, for he 1Sa 20:2
"The king's business required * 1Sa 21:8
and I left in * a rush that I came 1Sa 21:8
Should * a fellow as this be my 1Sa 21:14,15
kind of trouble, * as being in 1Sa 22:2
whole family—he's * a stubborn lout 1Sa 25:17
* an insignificant person as I am? 2Sa 7:18
eternal dynasty! * generosity is 2Sa 7:19
earth has received * blessings as 2Sa 7:23
Literally, "No * thing ought to 2Sa 13:12f
Now no one in Israel was * a 2Sa 14:25
and no one else received * praise. 2Sa 14:25
David, the man to whom God gave * 2Sa 23:1
It was by * feats that he earned 2Sa 23:18,19
"Why is the city in * an 1Ki 1:41
carry * a heavy responsibility?" 1Ki 3:9
constructed in * a manner that 1Ki 8:7
has the Lord done * things to this 1Ki 9:8
been * a supply of beautiful wood. 1Ki 10:12
it was * a terrible blast that 1Ki 19:11
cause of * great sin in Israel. 2Ki 10:31
* tremendous miracles and power. 2Ki 17:35,36
delivered them—* nations as Gozan, 2Ki 19:12
I will bring * evil upon Jerusalem 2Ki 21:12
* a troublemaker for his nation. 1Ch 2:7
because she had * a hard time at 1Ch 4:9
and the supplies * as fine flour, 1Ch 9:29
but then he felt * compassion 1Ch 21:15
of the nation * as the officers and 1Ch 26:26
govern by himself * a great nation 2Ch 1:10
And I am also giving you * 2Ch 1:12
of cedar lumber * as Hiram had 2Ch 2:3
has given to David * a wise, 2Ch 2:12
before the Ark in * numbers that no 2Ch 5:6
" 'Why has the Lord done * a 2Ch 7:21
Never before had there been * 2Ch 9:11
with any calamity * as war, 2Ch 20:9
had there been * a Passover—not one 2Ch 35:18
King Cyrus ever made * a decree; Ez 5:17
* lovingkindness to me Ez 7:28
"Don't cry on * a day as this! Neh 8:9
for just * a time as this?" Est 4:14
"At * a time as this should not Job 4:6
many instances * as you describe. Job 13:1
What good do * words do? Job 15:3
I would speak in * a way that it Job 16:5
Literally, "and many * things are Job 23:14f
For if I had done * things, it Job 31:28
Man's work stops at * a time, so Job 37:7
* a man shall stand firm forever. Ps 15:5
For you have done * tremendous Ps 18:1
Who else can do * glorious Ps 40:5
like any animal. * is the folly of Ps 49:13
heaven who does * wonders for me. Ps 57:2
people soon forget * lessons—but Ps 59:11
have done * mighty things for us. Ps 68:28
You have done * wonderful things. Ps 71:19
who had done * mighty miracles in Ps 106:21,22
* a man will not be overthrown by Ps 112:6
their own lives. * is the fate of Pro 1:19
rich! For * wisdom is far more Pro 3:13,14,15
Don't copy their ways. For * men Pro 3:32
cake they buy with * ill-gotten Pro 20:17
all advice. * a lad could come Ecc 4:14
in every way. *, O women of Sol 5:16
his glory." * singing it was! Is 6:4
There will be terror, * as has Is 7:17
of war; all * will be burned. Is 9:5
of his people. * glory there will Is 24:23
you do * wonderful things! Is 25:1
at a time and in * simple words!" Is 28:10
He goes right on and eats. In * Is 31:4,5
though you are * wicked rebels, Is 31:6
* as these shall dwell on high. Is 33:16
and were * easy prey for you. Is 37:27
Who has done * mighty deeds, Is 41:4
Can your idols make * claims as Is 41:21
That is why God poured out * Is 42:25
idols ever has foretold * things? Is 43:9
* stupidity and ignorance! Is 44:18
themselves from * a fall, how can Is 46:1
his Servant? If * men walk in Is 50:10
seen or heard of * a God as ours, Is 64:4
How can * as we be saved? Is 64:5
offerings. When * men sacrifice an Is 66:3
The heavens are shocked at * a Jer 2:12
surely you won't be angry about * Jer 3:4,5
vengeance on * a nation as this? Jer 5:9
Isn't * a God to be feared and Jer 5:22
Shouldn't I punish a nation * as Jer 5:29
Should not I punish them for * Jer 9:9
avenged on * a nation as this?" Jer 9:9
by predictions * as theirs, for it Jer 10:2,3
Don't be afraid of * a god for it Jer 10:5
our God, can do * things as this? Jer 14:22
* terrible things against us? Jer 16:10
What have we done to merit * Jer 16:10
one has ever heard of * a thing! Jer 18:13
Why did he destroy * a great Jer 22:8
of terror * as in that coming day? Jer 30:7
—* as they have never known before. Jer 30:7
(Then Jeremiah wakened. "* sleep Jer 31:26
whatever of doing any * thing!" Jer 37:14
you to do any * thing, for you are Jer 40:16
the north with * destruction that Jer 50:3
has there ever been * sorrow? Lam 2:13
even though they are * rebels." Eze 3:9
even though they are * rebels. Eze 12:3
Lord God, to do * things as these; Eze 16:30
to me as well! * desecration of my Eze 20:39
was there ever * a wondrous city as Eze 27:32
treated them with * contempt, then Eze 28:26
people living in * confidence! Eze 38:11
my holy name by * wickedness, I Eze 43:8
In * cases it is all right. Eze 44:25
the world who would ask * a thing! Dan 2:10
can tell the king * things, but Dan 2:27
had demanded * a hot fire in the Dan 3:22
with fear, and * terror gripped him Dan 5:6
He gave him * majesty that all Dan 5:19
How can * a person as I even Dan 10:17
may Judah stay far from * a life. Hos 4:15
all who eat * sacrifices are Hos 9:4
you ever heard of * a thing as I am Joe 1:2
experience disaster * as this. Joe 2:26
when there will be * abundance of Amo 9:13
"Don't say * things," the Mic 2:6
that sort of talk. * evils surely Mic 2:6
city that lived in * security, that Zep 2:15
and giving you * scant crops. Hag 1:10
That is why * great wrath came Zec 7:12
Should I accept * offerings as Mal 1:13
are you thinking * evil thoughts? Mt 9:4
How they praised God for giving * Mt 9:8
He used many illustrations * as Mt 13:2,3
For of * is the Kingdom of Mt 19:14
For there will be persecution * Mt 24:21
has arrived at * and such a place, Mt 24:23
at such and * a place, or has Mt 24:23
I will put * faithful ones in Mt 24:47
as a result, * throngs soon Mk 1:45
he stand it, to eat with * scum?" Mk 2:16
young plants in * soil, their roots Mk 4:17
He used many * illustrations to Mk 4:33
and had * strength that whenever he Mk 5:3,4
wonder he can do * miracles." Mk 6:14
and still follow, * as their Mk 7:
of God belongs to * as they. Mk 10:1
For those will be days of * Mk 13:1
He used many * warnings as he Lk 3:1
eating with * notorious sinners. Lk 5:3
not worthy of any * honor or even Lk 7:6,7,
"What can I say about * men?" Lk 7:3
whom I hear * strange stories?" Lk 9:
than * a city on the Judgment Day. Lk 10:1
they aren't. But * hypocrisy cannot Lk 12:
you to decide * things as that? Lk 12:1
And if worry can't even do * Lk 12:2
associating with * despicable Lk 15:
for and to save * souls as his." Lk 19:9,1
right words and * logic that none Lk 21:1
of them would ever do * a thing. Lk 22:2
for he was in * agony of spirit Lk 22:4
For if * things as this are done Lk 23:3
are * foolish, foolish people! Lk 24:2
I tell you about * things as these Jn 3:1
"Who said * a thing as that?" Jn 5:1
all * to rise again from the dead. Jn 6:4
"He says * wonderful things!" Jn 7:4
ordinary sinner do * miracles?" Jn 9:1
If I hadn't done * mighty Jn 15:2
land for * and such a price?" Act 5:
land for such and * a price?" Act 5:
all my life eaten * creatures, for Act 10:1
and preached with * power that Act 14:
kind things he did * as sending you Act 14:1
but they had no * instructions Act 15:2
thirty days before * gifts and Act 18:18
thirty days before * gifts and Act 18:22
shouted, "Away with * a fellow! Act 22:2
"I was on * a mission to Act 26:1
anyone who does * things as these. Rom 2:
of those who say * things is just. Rom 3:
God even though * a promise just Rom 4:1
reminding me that * desires are Rom 7:
prays for us with * feeling that it Rom 8:2
What can we ever say to * Rom 8:3
to take others * as ourselves, who Rom 9:23,2
Do things in * a way that Rom 12:1
all right to eat * meat must not Rom 14:
And the person who won't touch * Rom 14:
Try instead to live in * a way Rom 14:1
are going through * hard times. Rom 15:26
who has been * a mother to me. Rom 16:1
have been taught. * teachers are Rom 16:18
* wise and sensible Christians! 1Co 4:10
Don't even eat lunch with * a 1Co 5:1
To have * lawsuits at all is a 1Co 6:7
Don't you know that those doing * 1Co 6:9,10
permitting sins * as have just been 1Co 6:12
they might get * a grip on me that 1Co 6:12
is permitted. In * cases the 1Co 7:15
other things * as housekeeping and 1Co 7:34
So when they eat * food it 1Co 8:7
God's laws to eat * meat, but that 1Co 10:23
body together in * a way that extra 1Co 12:24
Word, [even though * preaching is 1Co 14:24
God poured out * kindness and grace 1Co 15:10
fooled by those who say * things. 1Co 15:33
at your side with * real devotion. 1Co 16:16
the work of * men as these. 1Co 16:18
But who is adequate for * a task 2Co 2:16
death began with * glory that 2Co 3:7
All * shameful methods we forego. 2Co 4:2
Are we insane [to say * things 2Co 5:13,14
We try to live in * a way that no 2Co 6:3
HAVING * GREAT promises as these, 2Co 7:1
when you gave him * a fine welcome 2Co 7:13
anxiously and with * deep concern. 2Co 7:15
as they do. * bragging isn't 2Co 11:17
to use * weakness for his glory. 2Co 12:5
to think * things about our Lord. Gal 2:17
* wonderful blessings as these. Eph 4:1
to accuse you of any * things. Eph 5:3
Don't even associate with * Eph 5:7
IS THERE ANY * thing as Christians Php 2:1
still bound by * rules as not Col 2:20
certain foods? * rules are mere Col 2:22
is upon those who do * things. Col 3:6
* things mean nothing. Col 3:11
(But of course you know that * 1Th 3:2,3
we appeal to * people—we command 2Th 3:12
who are teaching * wrong doctrine. 1Ti 1:3,4
he is a Christian. * a person is 1Ti 5:8
knows it. In * situations you can 1Ti 5:24
confessed with * a ringing 1Ti 6:12
things. * arguments are confusing 2Ti 2:14
the grace of God. * teachers are Tit 1:11
sees and hears. * persons claim Tit 1:16
do with him, for * a person has a Tit 3:11
yes, God has assigned * gifts to Heb 2:4
live long under * pressure of Heb 5:7f
they hear * assurances from God; Heb 6:18
But enough of * details. Heb 9:5
SINCE WE HAVE * a huge crowd of Heb 12:1
men did * terrible things to him. Heb 12:3
those in need, for * sacrifices are Heb 13:16

UCH Con't)
kind of wisdom. * things are Jas 3:15
stand against all * evil longings. Jas 4:6
we are going to * and such a town, Jas 4:13
going to such and * a town, stay Jas 4:13
own plans, and * self-confidence Jas 4:16
just escaped from * wicked living. 2Pe 2:18
many * persons have appeared. 1Jn 2:18
is not Christ. * a person is 1Jn 2:22
a Christian ever sin in * a way? 1Jn 5:17f
a body like ours. * people are 2Jn 1:7
hear * things about my children. 3Jn 1:4
The fate of * people was written Jud 1:4
for giving him * power, and they Rev 13:4
He did unbelievable miracles * Rev 13:13
is there another city * as this?" Rev 18:18

UCK
and the breasts that gave you *!" Lk 11:27

UCKLING
So Samuel took a * lamb and 1Sa 7:9

UDDEN
punish you with * terrors and Lev 26:16
example and proverb of * disaster. 1Ki 9:7
moment, but then comes * disaster. Job 5:3
by traps and * fears, and darkness Job 22:10,11
Let them be overtaken by * ruin, Ps 35:8
down with them to * disaster, and Pro 24:21,22
before the * coming of the flood; Mt 24:37,38
Don't let my * coming catch you Lk 21:34,35
so why, all of a *, are you Gal 2:14
all of a *, disaster will fall upon 1Th 5:3

UDDENLY
And as they ate it, * they Gen 3:7
of his tent, he * noticed three Gen 18:2
Then they sat down for supper. * Gen 37:25
Nile River, when *, seven sleek, Gen 41:2
Then, *, seven more heads Gen 41:6
he said, "when *, seven fat, Gen 41:18
mountain of God, * the Angel of Ex 3:2
God commanded, and * lice infested Ex 8:17
them together and *, out toward the Ex 16:10
* became white with leprosy. Num 12:10
when the ground * split open Num 16:31
sullen mob formed; *, as they Num 16:42
Balaam's donkey * saw the angel of Num 22:22,23
the river's edge, *, far up the Jos 3:15,16
as they could. And * the walls of Jos 6:20
his troops arrived * at the Springs Jos 11:7
them! And * the Angel was gone! Ju 6:21
* they blew their trumpets and Ju 7:19,20
* someone thought of the annual Ju 21:19
and lay there. *, around midnight, Ru 3:8
dead, her labor pains * began. 1Sa 4:19
an acre of land. * panic broke out 1Sa 14:15
with his spear, * hurled it at 1Sa 18:11,12
playing the harp, * the tormenting 1Sa 19:9,10
gang who * appear from nowhere?" 1Sa 25:11
Then * his love turned to hate, 2Sa 13:15
But * the king turned to Ittai, 2Sa 15:19,20
Then, *, while they were sitting 1Ki 13:20
So they did, each going alone. * 1Ki 18:7
Then, *, fire flashed down from 1Ki 18:38
soldier, and * the entire Syrian 1Ki 20:20
along, talking, * a chariot of 2Ki 2:11
But look! *—leprosy appeared in 2Ch 26:19
home, when * a mighty wind swept Job 1:19
others slept. *, fear gripped me; Job 4:14
to keep it alive. * it begins to Job 8:11-13
"* he moves the mountains, Job 9:5
"But * the food he has eaten Job 20:14
and small shall * pass away, Job 34:20
All my enemies shall be * Ps 6:10
as murky waters. * the brilliance Ps 18:12
* my courage was gone; Ps 30:6,7
at the innocent. * the deed is Ps 64:4
* his arrow will pierce them. Ps 64:7
path they are on—* God will send Ps 73:18
But he will be destroyed *, Pro 6:15
break in upon you * like a robber, Pro 24:34
criticism will * be broken and Pro 29:1
foundations, and * the entire Is 6:4
valley will * be gone, greedily Is 28:4
The Lord will come * and in Is 28:21
But * your ruthless enemies will Is 29:5
will come upon you *, as upon a Is 30:13
* you'll care, O careless ones. Is 32:10
shall overtake you *—so suddenly Is 47:11
you suddenly—so * that you won't Is 47:11
when * I did just what I said. Is 48:3
For in one day, *, a nation, Is 66:7,8
in utter ruin; *, in a moment, Jer 4:20
an only son. For * the destroying Jer 6:26
the siege will soon begin. For * Jer 10:18
and terror to fall upon them *. Jer 15:8
of soldiers come * upon them, for Jer 18:22
* the devastating whirlwind of Jer 30:23
in league with him * jumped up, Jer 41:2
sheep in the fold. * Edom shall be Jer 49:19
come upon them *, like a lion from Jer 50:44
But now, * Babylon too has Jer 51:8
the heavens were * opened to me Eze 1:1
Lord so angry. * the glory of the Eze 8:4
* A THRONE of beautiful blue Eze 10:1
Pelatiah (son of Benaiah) * died. Eze 11:13
your lovely wife. *, she will die. Eze 24:16
your voice will * return to you so Eze 24:27
the nations, shall * draw their Eze 28:7
he told me to; and * there was a Eze 37:7
to the east. And * the glory of Eze 43:2
But *, as he was watching, Dan 3:24
*, as they were drinking from Dan 5:5
As I was looking at the horns, * Dan 7:8
this could mean, * a buck goat Dan 8:5
and powerful, but *, at the height Dan 8:8
of this vision, * a man was Dan 8:15
I looked up and * there before me Dan 10:5,6
but they were * filled with Dan 10:7
*, as he spoke these words, I felt Dan 10:19
his time will * run out and there Dan 11:45
that aren't his. * they and all Hos 5:7
you with death. *, without warning, Hos 6:5
on Mount Zion. And * the lush Amo 1:2
slaves; * your revelry will end. Amo 6:7
was sailing along, * the Lord flung Jon 1:4
"* your debtors will rise up in Hab 2:7
* the heavy lead cover on the Zec 5:7
you are looking for will come * Mal 3:1
to God, and * remember that a Mt 5:23
his disciples. * a terrible storm Mt 8:24
And * they could see! Mt 9:30
* Moses and Elijah appeared and Mt 17:3
* there was a great earthquake; Mt 28:2
And as they were running, * Mt 28:9
sit up, the fever * left, and she Mk 1:31
* his face began to shine with Mk 9:2
Then * they looked around and Mk 9:8
the second time. * Jesus' words Mk 14:72
the sanctuary when * an angel Lk 1:11,12
flocks of sheep. * an angel Lk 2:9
*, the angel was joined by a vast Lk 2:13
light from the sun was gone—and * Lk 23:45
happened to it. * two men appeared Lk 24:4
death, when * Jesus himself came Lk 24:15
to them, when *—it was as though Lk 24:31
Jesus himself was * standing there Lk 24:36
o'clock his fever * disappeared!" Jn 4:52
miles out when * they saw Jesus Jn 6:18,19
But your weeping shall * be Jn 16:20
leaders, when * Jesus was standing Jn 20:19
The doors were locked; but *, as Jn 20:26
another glimpse, * two white-robed Act 1:10
that day, * there was a sound like Act 2:2
on this mission, * a brilliant Act 9:3
afternoon, when * a man was Act 10:30
prison gate, when * there was a Act 12:7
* there was a great earthquake; Act 16:26
nearing Damascus, * about noon a Act 22:6
* Festus shouted, "Paul, you are Act 26:24
piece and ate it. * everyone felt Act 27:36
to begin swelling or * fall dead; Act 28:6
who have died will * become alive, 1Co 15:52
alive shall * have new bodies too. 1Co 15:52
fall upon them as * as a woman's 1Th 5:3
Lord Jesus appears * from heaven in 2Th 1:7
without dying; * he was gone Heb 11:5
worshiping, when * I heard a loud Rev 1:10
I will come to you * and fight Rev 2:16
Unless you do, I will come * upon Rev 3:3
Or, "*," "unexpectedly." Rev 3:11f
* a red Dragon appeared, with Rev 12:3
Or, "*," "unexpectedly." Rev 22:6,7f
Or, "*," "unexpectedly." Rev 22:12f

SUE
You will * for peace, but you Eze 7:25

SUED
King Hezekiah * for peace and 2Ki 18:14

SUES
But, instead, one Christian * 1Co 6:6

SUFFER
will not make you * the diseases I Ex 15:26
he shall * the consequence." Lev 17:16
will not let you * any of the Deu 7:15
grape juice as they * from thirst. Job 24:11
see how I * at the hands of those Ps 9:13
Why must I * these attacks from Ps 42:9
Better refuse than * later. Pro 11:15
Those who love to talk will * the Pro 18:21
rich must worry and * insomnia. Ecc 5:12
Temple is here, you will never *? Jer 7:8
* for their fathers' sins; Jer 32:18
must *, how much more must you! Jer 49:12
You will * the full penalty, and Eze 23:49
he would * at the hands of the Mt 16:21
shall also * at their hands." Mt 17:12
would *, and that he would be Mk 8:31
would * and be treated with utter Mk 9:12,13
must * much," he said, "and be Lk 9:22
Literally, "But he said, 'Lord, * Lk 9:59f
But first I must * terribly and Lk 17:25
would have to * all these things Lk 24:26
the Messiah must * and die and rise Lk 24:46
Messiah must * all these things. Act 3:18
worthy to * dishonor for his name. Act 5:41
him how much he must * for me." Act 9:16
the Messiah would *, and be the Act 26:23
Yet what we * now is nothing Rom 8:18
and plants, * in sickness and death Rom 8:22
If one part suffers, all parts * 1Co 12:26
You have seen me * for him in the Php 1:30
it means to * and to die with him. Php 3:10
But part of my work is to * for Col 1:24
ready to * quietly and patiently. Col 3:12
We work hard and * much in order 1Ti 4:9,10
You will be ready to * with me 2Ti 1:8
I am more than willing to * if 2Ti 2:10
that when we * and die for Christ 2Ti 2:11
But if we give up when we *, and 2Ti 2:12
godly lives will * at the hands of 2Ti 3:12
allow Jesus to *, for in doing this Heb 2:10
it is like when we * and are Heb 2:18
it was better to * for the promised Heb 11:26
those in jail. * with them as Heb 13:3
to * with him there, bearing his Heb 13:13
for then you will * for it too. Heb 13:17
but if you do right and * for it, 1Pe 2:20
Remember, if God wants you to *, 1Pe 3:17
it is better to * for doing good 1Pe 3:17
you must be ready to *, too. 1Pe 4:1
But it is no shame to * for 1Pe 4:16
"I know how much you * for the Rev 2:9
you are about to *—for the devil Rev 2:10

SUFFERED
and we never * any harm from them; 1Sa 25:15,16
reign, and you * right along with 1Ki 2:26
Literally, "He * no man to do Ps 105:14f
presence, Lord! We * as a woman Is 26:17
poor and needy * outside her door. Eze 16:49
fury because you * shame before the Eze 36:6
who has not * from your cruelty? Nah 3:19
She had * much from many doctors Mk 5:26
"Is that why they *? Lk 13:2
of you has * any wrong from us. 2Co 7:2
You have * so much for the Gal 3:4
to you, and how much we * there. 1Th 2:2
And then, dear brothers, you * 1Th 2:14
* from their own people the Jews. 1Th 2:14
faith in Christ and how I have *. 2Ti 3:10
honor because he * death for us. Heb 2:9
same things. You * with those Heb 10:34
That is why Jesus * and died Heb 13:12
even though they * greatly for it. Jas 5:11
Christ, who * for you, is your 1Pe 2:21
when he * he did not threaten to 1Pe 2:23
Christ also *. 1Pe 3:18
SINCE CHRIST * and underwent pain, 1Pe 4:1
After you have * a little while, 1Pe 5:10
You have patiently * for me Rev 2:3

SUFFERER
John, a fellow * for the Lord's Rev 1:9

SUFFERERS
and humble, and takes * to safety. Job 5:11

SUFFERING
children in intense pain and *; Gen 3:16
out and he died in terrible *. 2Ch 21:19
for they saw that his * was too Job 2:13
Don't let your * embitter you at Job 36:18
life of evil that God sent this *. Job 36:21
he was * their punishment? Is 53:8
good news to the * and afflicted. Is 61:1
people for their * and make an Is 61:8
it is for your sake that I am *. Jer 15:15
and * you have dealt to me! Lam 3:19
any previous * in Jewish history. Dan 12:1
of * I must be baptized with?" Mk 10:38
was present who was * from dropsy. Lk 14:1
meal with you before my * begins. Lk 22:15
city that jail and * lie ahead. Act 20:23
There will be sorrow and * for Rom 2:9
glory, we must also share his *. Rom 8:17
to be released from pain and *. Rom 8:23
very purpose of * under the insults Rom 15:3
We patiently endure * and hardship 2Co 6:4
me so happy in spite of all my *. 2Co 7:4
I am once again * for you the Gal 4:19
It is for you I am * and you Eph 3:13
him but also of * for him. Php 1:29
that * would soon come—and it did. 1Th 3:4
troubles and * here, now that we 1Th 3:7
say to you who are *, God will give 2Th 1:7
So God sent pain and * to women 1Ti 2:15
he will give you strength in *. 2Ti 1:8
That is why I am * here in jail 2Ti 1:12
Take your share of * as a good 2Ti 2:3
don't be afraid of * for the Lord. 2Ti 4:5
for his * made Jesus a perfect Heb 2:10
now been through * and temptation, Heb 2:18
to obey, when obeying meant *. Heb 5:8
even though it meant terrible *. Heb 10:32
with others * the same things. Heb 10:33
For examples of patience in *, Jas 5:10
Is anyone among you *? Jas 5:13
*, and his great glory afterwards. 1Pe 1:11
This * is all part of the work 1Pe 2:21

(SUFFERING Con't)
with Christ in his *, and 1Pe 4:13
Don't let me hear of your * for 1Pe 4:15
So if you are * according to 1Pe 4:19
SUFFERINGS
about the * of the Messiah and his Act 17:3
more we undergo * for Christ, the 2Co 1:5
you when you undergo these same *. 2Co 1:6,7
These * of ours are for your 2Co 4:15
These troubles and * of ours 2Co 4:17
* for his body, the church. Col 1:24
he is using your * to make you 2Th 1:5
are going through these * too. 1Pe 5:9
SUFFERS
blindly on and * the consequences. Pro 22:3
The simpleton never looks, and * Pro 27:12
The land * for the sins of its Is 24:4,5
Kingdom of Heaven * violence and Mt 11:12f
If one part *, all parts suffer 1Co 12:26
For remember, when your body *, 1Pe 4:1
SUFFICIENT
do not contain * fuel to consume a Is 40:16
Literally, "* unto the day is the Mt 6:34f
be * to condemn him to death. Mk 14:55
SUGGEST
Please do as I *." Gen 33:15
could * what his dreams meant. Gen 41:8
"What I * is that you mobilize 2Sa 17:11
information. We * that you search Ez 4:15
Ar-ta-xerxes! I * that you come and Neh 6:7
your realm. We * that, subject to Est 1:19
"We * this: We have four men Act 21:23
I want to * that you finish what 2Co 8:10
The only thing they did * was Gal 2:10
to illustrate and * those things Heb 3:5
SUGGESTED
One day Cain * to his brother, Gen 4:8
the price he had *—400 pieces of Gen 23:16
* that he come and sleep with her. Gen 39:7
Some of Saul's aides * a cure. 1Sa 16:15,16
Then Abner * to Joab, "Let's 2Sa 2:14
and what he himself had * instead. 2Sa 17:15
So King Ben-hadad did as they * 1Ki 20:25
He *, "She doesn't have a son, 2Ki 4:14
sir, come with us," someone *. 2Ki 6:3
In all that time I never * to 1Ch 17:6
other leaders and *, "Let us work Ez 4:2
So his aides *, "Let us go and Est 2:2
"Well," * Zeresh his wife and Est 5:14
Follow every detail you have *." Est 6:10
and Azariah, and * a ten-day diet Dan 1:12
Then Jesus *, "Let's get away Mk 6:31
out in a boat, he * that they cross Lk 8:22
devil had already * to Judas Jn 13:1
Several days later Paul * to Act 15:36
SUGGESTING
commanded, and cannot imagine *. Jer 32:35
Well then, am I * that these laws Rom 7:7
SUGGESTION
happen soon. My * is that you find Gen 41:33
advice, and followed this *. Ex 18:24
don't conceal his horrible *. Deu 13:8
astray with the * that they Deu 13:12,13,14
This * naturally pleased the king Est 2:4
So the Jews adopted Mordecai's * Est 9:23
I WAS GLAD for the * of going to Ps 122:1
a wise son considers each *. Pro 15:5
But he was alarmed by Daniel's * Dan 1:10
I have a command, not just a *. 1Co 7:10
He is glad to follow my * that 2Co 8:17
SUGGESTIONS
But she kept on with her * day Gen 39:10
Joseph's * were well received by Gen 41:37
"Various * were made, until one 1Ki 22:20
"There were many *, but finally a 2Ch 18:19,20
Their * are full of the stench of Ps 5:9
Friendly * are as pleasant as Pro 27:9
so that all their * are wrong; Is 19:14
Here I want to add some * of my 1Co 7:12
approves, with * and godly advice. Eph 6:4
SUICIDE
you to commit * by staying there—to 2Ch 32:11
Jews asked, "Is he planning *? Jn 8:22
SUIT
a new * and your board and room." Ju 17:10,11
was sporting a new * of armor, 2Sa 21:16
of the universe to * your whims? Job 34:33
* or a bride with her jewels. Is 61:10
* the taste of those who hear it; 1Th 2:4
SUITED
him, a helper * to his needs." Gen 2:18
SUITOR
shall court a *," or, "a woman Jer 31:22f
SUITS
in gold, and ten * of clothing. 2Ki 5:5
and two * to give to them." 2Ki 5:22
SUKKIIM
Libyans, *, and Ethiopians. 2Ch 12:3
SULKING
So Jonah went out and sat * Jon 4:5
SULLEN
Soon a great, * mob formed; Num 16:42
went home to Samaria angry and *. 1Ki 20:43
back to the palace angry and *. 1Ki 21:4
or fear their *, angry looks, even Eze 3:9
SULLIED
Because they * my holy name by Eze 43:8
SULPHUR
fire and flaming * billowed from Rev 9:17,18
fire and burning * in the presence Rev 14:10
Lake of Fire that burns with *. Rev 19:20
Fire burning with * where the Rev 20:10
Lake that burns with fire and *. Rev 21:8
SUM
him a large * of money every year. 1Ch 18:2
—this magnificent * they value you Zec 11:13
SUMMARIZE
"To *: At the special feasts and Eze 46:11
SUMMARIZES
This * the various steps in Ex 38:21
SUMMARY
Here is a * of the events in the Gen 2:4
traveled. In *, the armies of Num 2:32,33
* of the Battle: Ju 20:35-39
and Judah. In *, then, he was 2Ch 27:8
to pass this * on to you, Lk 1:3
SUMMED
For the whole Law can be * up in Gal 5:14
SUMMER
winter and *, day and night." Gen 8:22
happened: One hot * afternoon as he Gen 18:1
and the bread and * fruit are for 2Sa 16:2
you make the * and the winter Ps 74:17
*, gathering food for the winter. Pro 6:8
upon their * fruits and harvests. Is 16:9
as on a pleasant * day or a lovely Is 18:4
tear bodies all *, and the wild Is 18:6
"The harvest is finished; the * Jer 8:20
Probably in the * of 605 B.C. Jer 36:1f
Harvest the grapes and * fruits Jer 40:10
your grapes and * fruits. Jer 48:32
figs of * in their first season! Hos 9:10
mansions and their * houses, Amo 3:15
both in winter and in *. Zec 14:8
you know that * is almost here. Mt 24:32
without being told that * is near. Lk 21:30
the * ends four months from now? Jn 4:35
by the scorching * sun. Jas 1:10,11
SUMMERTIME
in the hot *. Pro 25:13
with * or rain with harvest time! Pro 26:1
SUMMIT
When they reached the *, Moses Num 20:28
For a * conference of the Ps 2:2
decision at their * conference—they Ps 83:5
We will look down from the * of Sol 4:8
SUMMON
* all Israel to a meeting there." Lev 8:1
Then the Lord said to Moses, "* Num 3:6
Then the Lord said to Moses, "* Num 11:16
then you and Aaron must * the Num 20:8
Lord told Moses, "* the people, Num 21:16
"On the eighth day * the people Num 29:35
and he told me, '* the people Deu 4:10
the city will then * him and talk Deu 25:8
when you must die. * Joshua and Deu 31:14
my death! Now * all the elders and Deu 31:28
They shall * the people Deu 33:19
Then * Naboth, and find two 1Ki 21:9
king sent a messenger to * him. 2Ki 6:32
I am going to! * all the prophets 2Ki 10:18,19
plans and to * them to Jerusalem. 2Ch 23:2,3
days—Job would * his children to Job 1:5
* your might; Ps 68:28
I will * the Babylonian armies Jer 34:22
I will * every kind of terror Eze 38:21
Now send some men to Joppa and * Act 10:32
SUMMONED
The king * them before him and Ex 1:18
to Egypt and * the elders of the Ex 4:29
Then Pharaoh * Moses and Aaron Ex 8:8
Pharaoh hastily * Moses and Aaron Ex 8:25
And Pharaoh * Moses and Aaron Ex 12:31
ceremonies), Moses * Aaron and Lev 9:1
leaders * all the men of Israel Num 1:17,18,19
Immediately he * Moses, Aaron, Num 12:3,4
Then Moses * Dathan and Abiram Num 16:11,12
then Moses and Aaron * the Num 20:10
NOW MOSES * the leaders of the Num 30:1
Mount Horeb. He * all Israel Deu 29:2,3
Then he * the leaders of the Jos 1:12,13
Then Joshua * all the people and Jos 3:9
So Joshua * the twelve men, and Jos 4:4
So Joshua * the priests and gave Jos 6:6-9
Joshua * their leaders and Jos 9:22
THEN JOSHUA * all the people of Jos 24:1
One day she * Barak (son of Ju 4:6
When Barak * the men of Zebulun Ju 4:10
"I * you, but you refused to Ju 12:2
So they * the mayors again and 1Sa 5:11
Next Jesse * Shammah, but the 1Sa 16:9
King Saul immediately * Ahimelech 1Sa 22:11,12
So Achish finally * David and his 1Sa 29:6
one of Saul's servants, and * him. 2Sa 9:
Then the king * Saul's servant 2Sa 9:
Syrian troops * by Hadadezer from 2Sa 10:15,1
Uriah had done, he * him and asked 2Sa 11:1
Then at last David * Absalom, and 2Sa 14:3
So King David * the Gibeonites. 2Sa 21:
Then he * all of his brothers—the 1Ki 1:
So King Solomon * him, and 1Ki 1:5
in Jerusalem, he * his army—all the 1Ki 12:2
So Ahab * all the people and the 1Ki 18:2
Then Ahab * his advisors. 1Ki 20:
So King Ahab * his four hundred 1Ki 22:
Then the prophet * Gehazi. 2Ki 4:3
MEANWHILE ELISHA HAD * one of 2Ki 9:
* the officers of the palace 2Ki 11:
So David * the people of Israel 1Ch 13:
Then David * all Israel to 1Ch 15:
After their defeat, the Syrians * 1Ch 19:1
of Israel. He * all the political 1Ch 23:
DAVID NOW * all of his officials 1Ch 28:
monarch. He * all the army 2Ch 1:2,
Solomon now * to Jerusalem all of 2Ch 5:
Then he * all the people of Judah 2Ch 15:
So King Ahab * 400 of his heathen 2Ch 18:3,4,
the Temple. He * the priests and 2Ch 24:
repaired them. He * the priests 2Ch 29:4,
They in turn * their fellow 2Ch 29:1
Hezekiah * his princes and 2Ch 32:
officers and * them to the plains 2Ch 32:
in despair, and * Hilkiah, Ahikam 2Ch 34:2
Then the king * all the elders 2Ch 34:2
The following spring he was * to 2Ch 36:1
Then I * the priests and made Neh 5:12
THE MIGHTY GOD, the Lord, has * Ps 50:1
Then the Lord * me and said, Zec 6:8
into the hills and * certain ones Mk 3:13
Jesus * these men and asked them Mk 3:23
SUMMONING
to be used for * the people to Num 10:1
and Naphtali, * their fighting Ju 6:35
country of Ephraim * troops who Ju 7:24
Israel * those who worshiped Baal; 2Ki 10:20,21
SUMMONS
between the * to assemble and the Num 10:5,6,7
court without his * is doomed to Est 4:11
SUMS
* of money annually to David. 1Ch 18:13
SUN
huge lights, the * and moon, to Gen 1:16
larger one, the *, to preside over Gen 1:16
That evening as the * was going Gen 15:12
As the * went down and it was Gen 15:17
The * was rising as Lot reached Gen 19:23
The * rose as he started on, Gen 32:31
"The *, moon, and eleven stars Gen 37:9
of the * god Re of Heliopolis. Gen 41:50
* so that the land was darkened; Ex 10:15
and when the * became hot upon Ex 16:21
When the * is down, then he Lev 22:7
to worship the *, moon, or stars. Deu 4:19
evening just as the * goes down. Deu 16:6
other gods, the *, moon, or Deu 17:2,3
With the best of what the * makes Deu 33:14
but as the * was going down, he Jos 8:29
aloud, "Let the * stand still over Jos 10:12
And the * and the moon didn't Jos 10:13
So the * stopped in the heavens Jos 10:13
Lord stopped the * and moon—all Jos 10:14
As the * was going down, Joshua Jos 10:27
Shine as the *!" Ju 5:31
So they went on. The * was Ju 19:14
after Abner. The * was just going 2Sa 2:24
Literally, "under this *." 2Sa 12:11f
with grain on it to dry in the *; 2Sa 17:19
Just as the * was going down the 1Ki 22:36,37
But early the next morning the * 2Ki 3:22
Baal and the *, moon, and stars. 2Ki 17:16
beneath the hot *, and like grain 2Ki 19:26
Heathen altars to the * god, moon 2Ki 21:3,4,5
and the *, moon, and stars. 2Ki 23:4
the *, moon, stars, and planets. 2Ki 23:5
kings of Judah to the * god. 2Ki 23:11
but just as the * sank into the 2Ch 18:34
and of the *, moon, and stars. 2Ch 33:3
for worshiping the *, moon and 2Ch 33:4,5
foundations. The * won't rise, the Job 9:7
have looked at the * shining in the Job 31:26
For as we cannot look at the * Job 37:21
all the world. The * lives in the Ps 19:3,4
to a race! The * crosses the Ps 19:6
down as from the noonday *. Ps 37:6
die at birth, who never see the *. Ps 58:8
* and moon continue in the skies! Ps 72:5
it will continue as the *; Ps 72:17
you made the starlight and the *. Ps 74:16
Literally, "his throne as the * Ps 89:35,36f
and the * to mark the days. Ps 104:19
from the burning *, and gave them a Ps 105:39
before the * is up, I was praying Ps 119:147
forever: the * to rule the day, Ps 136:8
Praise him, * and moon, and all Ps 148:3

(SUN Con't)
hay while the * shines, but what a Pro 10:5
The * rises and sets and hurries Ecc 1:3-7
never seeing the * or even knowing Ecc 6:5
him, when the * and light and moon Ecc 12:2
is so dark—the * has tanned me. Sol 1:6
with me and sent me out into the * Sol 1:6
as the *, so utterly captivating?' Sol 6:10
shine from stars or * or moon. Is 13:10
Heliopolis, "The City of the *." Is 19:18
* and moon will seem to fade away. Is 24:23
as bright as the *, and the Is 30:26
housetops, burnt yellow by the *. Is 37:27
I will send the * backwards ten Is 38:8
as measured on Ahaz' * dial!" Is 38:8
So the * retraced ten degrees that Is 38:8
the searing * and scorching Is 49:10
No longer will you need the * or Is 60:19
Your * shall never set; Is 60:20
ground before the * and moon and Jer 8:2
sons are dead. Her * is gone down Jer 15:9
out to the hot * and frosty nights, Jer 36:30
facing east, worshiping the *! Eze 8:16
I will cover the * with a cloud, Eze 32:7
filled with nets drying in the *. Eze 47:10
tremble. The * and moon are Joe 2:10
"The * will be turned into Joe 2:31
The * and moon will be darkened Joe 3:15
At that time I will make the * Amo 8:9
Then, when the * was hot, God Jon 4:8
on Jonah, and the * beat down upon Jon 4:8
word from God. The * will go down Mic 3:6
* comes up and warms the earth. Nah 3:17
The lofty * and moon began to Hab 3:11
and bow to the *, moon and stars. Zep 1:5
The * and moon and stars will no Zec 14:6
fear my name, the * of Mal 4:2
soil, but the hot * soon scorched Mt 13:6
the * in their Father's Kingdom. Mt 13:43
shone like the * and his clothing Mt 17:2
of those days the * will be Mt 24:29
beneath the hot * and died because Mk 4:5,6
blotting out the *, and a voice Mk 9:7
ends, then the * will grow dim and Mk 13:24
As the * went down that evening, Lk 4:40
portents in the *, moon and stars; Lk 21:25
The light from the * was Lk 23:45
* and sat wearily beside the well. Jn 4:5,6
of smoke; the * shall turn black Act 2:20
*, moon and stars as their gods! Act 7:42
brighter than the * shone down on Act 26:13
Literally, "neither * nor stars Act 27:20f
the *, moon, planets, and stars. 1Co 15:40f
of ours. The * has one kind of 1Co 15:41
Don't let the * go down with you Eph 4:26
by the scorching summer *. Jas 1:10,11
of the * in unclouded brilliance. Rev 1:16
and the * became dark like black Rev 6:12
a third of the * was blighted and Rev 8:12
furnace, and the * and air were Rev 9:2
his face shone like the * and his Rev 10:1
I saw a woman clothed with the *, Rev 12:1
his flask upon the *, causing it to Rev 16:8
And the city has no need of * or Rev 21:23
need for lamps or *—for the Lord Rev 22:5

SUN-BAKED
my strength has dried up like * Ps 22:15

SUN-IDOLS
the images of Ashtaroth and the *. Is 17:8

SUN-IMAGES
Also, he removed the * from the 2Ch 14:5

SUN'S
as brightly as the * brilliance, Dan 12:3

SUNBURN
I am black, but not from *. Job 30:28,29

SUNDAY
EARLY ON * morning, as the new day Mt 28:1
It was early on * morning when Mk 16:9
BUT VERY EARLY on * morning they Lk 24:1
That same day, *, two of Jesus' Lk 24:13
EARLY * Jn 20:1
On *, Act 20:7

SUNDIAL
"Do you want the shadow on the * 2Ki 20:9
points backward on the * of Ahaz! 2Ki 20:11

SUNDIALS
Egyptian * in this period were 2Ki 20:11f

SUNDOWN
stopped to camp at *, he found a Gen 28:11
Take it back to him at * so that Deu 24:12,13
that he would eat nothing until *. 2Sa 3:35,36
reckoning, from * to sundown. Act 20:7f
reckoning, from sundown to *. Act 20:7f

SUNG
that it be * throughout Israel. 2Sa 1:17,18
were * throughout the city; Ps 102:21,22
are * in the homes of the godly. Ps 118:15,16
And when they had * a hymn, they Mt 26:30

SUNK
mine shaft can be * into the earth, Job 28:3,4

SUNLIGHT
You shall grope in the bright * Deu 28:29
"When he sneezes, the * sparkles Job 41:18
the * brighter than seven days! Is 30:26
The Lord who gives us * in the Jer 31:35
Shields flash red in the *! Nah 2:3
For he gives his * to both the Mt 5:45

SUNNY
like water on a * day until I Ps 32:4

SUNRISE
A cloudless * 2Sa 23:4
We worked early and late, from * Neh 4:20,21
until well after *, and to close Neh 7:3
Praise him from * to sunset! Ps 113:3
morning, just at *, they carried Mk 16:1

SUNSET
holding up his hands until *. Ex 17:12
bathe himself and return at *. Deu 23:11
each day before *, for since he is Deu 24:14,15
So before * of the seventh day Ju 14:18
early and late, from sunrise to *; Neh 4:20,21
The dawn and * shout for joy! Ps 65:8
Praise him from sunrise to *! Ps 113:3
By * the courtyard was filled Mk 1:32,33

SUNSHINE
As * after rain.' 2Sa 23:4
there will be * in your soul. Mt 6:22
A pure eye lets * into your soul. Lk 11:34
So watch out that the * isn't Lk 11:35
standing in the *, shouting loudly Rev 19:17

SUPERB
the orchestras are *! Is 5:12

SUPERFLUOUS
Lord has anything * or lacking in Lev 22:23

SUPERHUMAN
to life they will be * bodies. 1Co 15:44

SUPERINTENDED
Other Levites * the unskilled 2Ch 34:13

SUPERINTENDENT
as general * of the project. Ex 35:30,31
Adoniram (son of Abda) was * of 1Ki 4:1
Adoniram was the general * of 1Ki 5:14
home of Arza, the * of the palace, 1Ki 16:9
However, their * gave them Dan 1:7
He asked the * for permission to Dan 1:8
God had given the * a special Dan 1:9
appointed by the * to look after Dan 1:11
was completed, the * brought all Dan 1:18,19

SUPERINTENDENTS
the construction * to pay the 2Ki 12:11,12
the construction *, for they were 2Ki 12:15
to the building * so that they can 2Ki 22:5,6
(The building * were not required 2Ki 22:7
to the building *, who hired masons 2Ch 24:12
of Kohath, were the building *. 2Ch 34:12

SUPERIOR
by their * strength and fall Ps 10:10
authority of my * officers and I Mt 8:8,9
authority of my * officers, and I Lk 7:6,7,8
And since Christ is so much *, Heb 3:7,8

SUPERIORS
officials look up to their *. Ecc 5:8

SUPERNATURAL
of his created, * beings, but no Gen 6:1f
by * means. It came hurtling Dan 2:34
Literally, "all ate the same * 1Co 10:3,4f
are also *, spiritual bodies. 1Co 15:44

SUPERVISE
to * the shearing of his sheep. Gen 38:12
of them will * the work at the 1Ch 23:4,5
were appointed to * the workmen. Ez 3:8
the priests who * the maintenance. Eze 40:45

SUPERVISED
by Moses and was * by Ithamar, son Ex 38:21
the tribal leaders * the lottery. Jos 14:1
tribes of Israel * the sacred Jos 19:51
A general manager * these 1Ki 4:8-19
He then * the Babylonian army in 2Ki 25:10
had * and guarded the Tabernacle. 1Ch 9:19
district, who * the building of the Neh 3:17

SUPERVISING
He gave each of them a * angel! Deu 32:8

SUPERVISION
oil—in fact, the * of the entire Num 4:16
under the * of Jerijah, were 1Ch 26:31,32
the workmen. The * of the entire Ez 3:9
the * of Rehum (son of Bani). Neh 3:17

SUPERVISOR
The * of the Levites in Jerusalem Neh 11:22,23

SUPERVISORS
as accountants, *, and carriers. 2Ch 34:13

SUPH
(Cities in the area included *, Deu 1:1

SUPPER
Then * was served. Gen 24:33
Then they had *, and the servant Gen 24:54
Then they sat down for *. Gen 37:25
Invite him home for *." Ex 2:20
and afterward they had * together. Ju 19:21
you until he has finished his *. Ru 3:3
One evening after *, when they 1Sa 1:9
begged him to take a bite of *. 2Sa 3:35,36
some stew for * for these men." 2Ki 4:38
past time for *, and there is Mt 14:15
them, and prepared the * there. Mt 26:19
during * a woman came in with a Mk 14:3
to eat the traditional Passover *. Mk 14:12
eat the Passover * this evening!' Mk 14:14
Prepare our * there." Mk 14:15
him his * before he eats his own. Lk 17:7,8,9
said, and prepared the Passover *. Lk 22:13
After * he gave them another Lk 22:20
During * the devil had already Jn 13:1
So he got up from the * table, Jn 13:4
'One who eats * with me will betray Jn 13:18
leaned around at * that time to ask Jn 21:20
"the Lord's *." Act 2:42f
and ate the Lord's * together; Act 20:10,11,12
* you are eating, but your own. 1Co 11:20
cup of wine after *, saying, "This 1Co 11:25
for the Lord's *—the communion 1Co 11:33
Gather together for the * of the Rev 19:17

SUPPLE
you, O strong and * nation feared Is 18:2
and *, a jewel among jewels. Eze 16:6,7

SUPPLIED
King Hiram * experienced sailors 1Ki 9:27,28
he * him with much cedar lumber. 1Ch 14:1
such as Hiram had * to David when 2Ch 2:3
using sailors * by King Hiram, to 2Ch 9:21
Benjamin * 200,000 men equipped 2Ch 17:17
were * directly from there, so 2Ch 31:16
They * wood for the altar at the Neh 13:31
to the poor, your needs will be *! Pro 28:27
food will be * to them and they Is 33:16
eating the food * by the king! Dan 1:15
corn I constantly *, and the Hos 1:9
I am generously * with the gifts Php 4:18

SUPPLIES
Even if Egypt * you with horses 2Ki 18:24
sanctuary, and the * such as fine 1Ch 9:29
and oxen. Vast * of flour, fig 1Ch 12:40
had charge of the * of olive oil. 1Ch 27:28
All the dedicated * were brought 2Ch 31:12,13
food and other * to all priests in 2Ch 31:19
transportation, * for the journey, Ez 1:4
for we needed * of the special Neh 10:33
and water * and kill her leaders; Is 3:1
* where used clothing was kept. Jer 38:11
energy that God *, so that God will 1Pe 4:11

SUPPLY
Aaron shall * it with fresh oil and Lev 24:3,4
I will destroy your food * so Lev 26:26
by lot as a * line to bring us Ju 20:8,9,10
I can * both cedar and cypress. 1Ki 5:8
a great * of algum trees and gems. 1Ki 10:11
been such a * of beautiful wood. 1Ki 10:12
to eat from her * of flour and oil 1Ki 17:15
its army, set up * lines, and moved 1Ki 20:27
them from the * of spears and 2Ki 11:10
cities in Hamath as * centers. 2Ch 8:4
both being * centers, building 2Ch 8:5
Baalath and other * centers at this 2Ch 8:6
all of the * centers in Naphtali. 2Ch 16:4
and * cities throughout Judah. 2Ch 17:12
who do, and also * them with Ez 1:4
and we needed a huge * of all Neh 5:18
and leaders should * the wood for Neh 10:34
brought a daily * of food for the Neh 12:47
He will * your every need anyway! Job 12:6
You are ready with a plentiful * Ps 69:13
You * it, and they gather it. Ps 104:28
of Canaan, cutting off its food *. Ps 105:16
even her water * will fail. Jer 50:38
river, her water *, and Babylon Jer 51:36
off their food * and send famine to Eze 14:13
The wine * ran out during the Jn 2:3
way and even to * the needs of Act 20:34
living, while you * these others? 1Co 9:6
* our own needs without your help. 1Co 9:12
parents * food for their 2Co 12:14
And it is he who will * all your Php 4:19
* of wisdom to all who ask him; Jas 1:5

SUPPORT
But the land could not * both Gen 13:6
not land enough to * them both Gen 36:6,7,8
and has no son to * her, and has Lev 22:13
as well as the * of the king of 1Ch 19:7
their war loot to * the operating 1Ch 26:27
throwing her full * behind Est 9:29-31
guide me, your strength will * me. Ps 139:10
and steady peg to * my people; Is 22:23,24
I will guard and * you, for I Is 42:6
attached to the Temple wall for *. Eze 41:6
give their * money to the church Mt 15:5,6
the * of Jesus and his disciples. Lk 8:3
for they * the cause of Satan. Rev 2:9

SUPPORTED
the walls were made from drapes * Ex 38:12
It was * by four posts, with Ex 38:19
Levites are to be * by the Deu 18:1
a canopy which was * by pillars. 1Ki 7:6
of Asherah who are * by Jezebel." 1Ki 18:19
water vats they *, and removed the 2Ki 16:17

(SUPPORTED Con't)
WISDOM HAS BUILT a palace * on Pro 9:1
The whole structure was * by Eze 41:6
be * by those who accept it. 1Co 9:14

SUPPORTING
and for the posts * the veil Ex 38:27
for the posts * the drapes Ex 38:29
the two pillars * the roof. Ju 16:25,26
of the stands were * posts made of 1Ki 7:27-30
One large tank and twelve oxen * 1Ki 7:41-46
begin at home, * needy parents. 1Ti 5:4
"Note this: I will force those * Rev 3:9

SUPPORTS
There were * at each of the four 1Ki 7:34
What * its foundations, and who Job 38:6,7
Your right hand, O Lord, * me; Ps 18:35
The Lord * the humble, but Ps 147:6
and everything it * will fall with Is 22:25
God's mighty power * me. Act 2:25

SUPPOSE
and bad alike? * you find fifty Gen 18:24
* there are only forty-five? Gen 18:28
"* there are only forty?" Gen 18:29
"Let me speak: * only thirty are Gen 18:30
*there are only twenty?" Gen 18:31
once more! * only ten are found?" Gen 18:32
"But * I can't find a girl who Gen 24:5
'But * I can't find a girl who Gen 24:39
the man demanded. "I * you Ex 2:14
added, "do you * that we were Jer 44:19
Do you * I'll let you have the Eze 33:25
"What do you * the owner will do Mk 12:9
Which do you * loved him most Lk 7:42
"I * the one who had owed him Lk 7:43
he used this illustration: "* Lk 11:5,6
don't you * that he will provide Lk 12:28
And I * that if all the other Jn 21:25
Do you * God was thinking only 1Co 9:9
But I * you feel this is 1Co 11:19
part of the body? * the whole body 1Co 12:17
I * that there are hundreds of 1Co 14:10
I * you think I am saying all 2Co 12:19
It is traditional to * that Paul Gal 4:15f

SUPPOSED
"Am I * to keep track of him Gen 4:9
Negro, as was once erroneously *. Gen 9:18f
Where am I * to get meat for all Num 11:13
the land they were * to settle in. Ju 18:2
"What about the sheep you're * 1Sa 17:28
that day, for he * that something 1Sa 20:26
singers who were * to conduct the Neh 13:10
"You are * to be a wise man, and Job 15:2
of Israel—you are * to know right Mic 3:1
"Are we * to find food for them Mk 8:4
and women he is * to protect, and Lk 12:45
merely doing what he is * to do. Lk 17:7,8,9
Moses * his brothers would Act 7:25
What was he * to do? Act 10:17
at all what I * they would be. Act 25:18
good law which was * to show me the Rom 7:10
What am I * to say about these 1Co 11:22
letters that are * to have come 2Th 2:1
But if someone who is * to be a 1Jn 3:17

SUPPOSING
they went for him, * that he was 2Ch 18:31

SUPREME
"The blessing of the * God, Gen 14:19,20
Jehovah, the * God, Creator of Gen 14:22
your God is the * God of heaven, Jos 2:11
"But who can rebuke God, the * Job 21:22
gods in * charge of all the earth. Ps 83:18
* above all rulers of the earth. Ps 99:2
the entire Jewish * Court assembled Mt 26:59
the whole Jewish * Court were Mk 14:55
entire * Court—met to discuss their Mk 15:1
of the Jewish * Court (who Mk 15:42,43
when Satan's power reigns *." Lk 22:53
the Jewish * Court assembled, Lk 22:66
of the Jewish * Court, from the Lk 23:50,51,52
everything else will be utterly *. 1Co 15:28
and made him the * Head of the Eph 1:22

SUPREMELY
this is the Lord's * holy altar." Ex 30:10

SURE
And * enough, when they Gen 12:14
* that you will give it to me?" Gen 15:8
And * enough, she had twins. Gen 25:24
I want to feel you, and be * it Gen 27:21
"We * do." Gen 29:5
and could, he felt *, sell the idea Gen 34:18,19
I can be * you will send it?" Gen 38:17
And * enough, for the next seven Gen 41:47
way and that to be * no one was Ex 2:12
frightened. And * enough, when Ex 2:15
And be * to take your rod along Ex 4:17
of Egypt—as he was * God would. Ex 13:19
"Be * to obey all of these Ex 23:13
"Be * that everything you make Ex 25:40
"Be * to celebrate the Feast of Ex 34:18
on the altar—make * there is no Lev 10:12
So be very * to obey my laws, and Lev 18:29,30
beginning in the evening. Be * to Num 9:2,3
Aaron will be here too. Be * to Num 16:17
assured him. And * enough, Israel Num 21:35
these men, but be * to say only Num 22:20
offerings. Make * that the animals Num 28:31
and you may be * that your sin will Num 32:23
learn them, and be * to obey Deu 5:1
so be * to carry out this command. Deu 16:12
around us'— be * that you select Deu 17:15
a foreigner. Be * that he doesn't Deu 17:16
you will be * to obey all of them. Jos 1:8
* that you don't get any closer." Jos 3:2,3,4
going to know for * that the living Jos 3:10
And I'm * you can drive out the Jos 17:16,17,18
Jordan River. Be * to continue to Jos 22:5
"But be very * to follow all the Jos 23:6
little bit. Be * that you do not Jos 23:7
"Now make * that you have done Ju 9:16
If you are * that you have done Ju 9:19
"I'm * I see people coming Ju 9:37
"*!" Ju 11:9
And the Angel replied, "Be * Ju 13:13,14
the cart. And * enough, the cows 1Sa 6:12
wrong, but make * now that you 1Sa 12:20
Now be * that you obey him. 1Sa 15:1
"I'm * he's not planning any 1Sa 20:2
Go and check again to be * of 1Sa 23:22
*," Abishai whispered to David. 1Sa 26:8
concubines; and * enough, they 1Ki 11:3
"Now I know for * that you are a 1Ki 17:24
And * enough, the sky was soon 1Ki 18:45
And * enough, as he turned to 1Ki 20:36
be * of what he wants us to do." 1Ki 22:5
And * enough! 2Ki 2:22
And * enough, the next day at 2Ki 3:20
She said to her husband, "I'm * 2Ki 4:9
And * enough, there was, just as 2Ki 4:44
was right, and * enough, he had 2Ki 6:10
robing room, "Be * that every 2Ki 10:22
"Check to be * that only those who 2Ki 10:23
And Micaiah replied, "*, go 2Ch 18:14
"You can be very * that I am Neh 6:7
So Satan went away; and * enough, Job 1:12,13
"*, I know all that. Job 9:2
The Lord's promise is *. Ps 12:6
we will arise to stand firm and * Ps 20:8
Don't be conceited, * of your own Pro 3:7,8
longer!" *, just a little more! Pro 6:10
Be * you know a person well Pro 11:15
You can be very * that the evil Pro 11:21
And you can also be very * that Pro 11:21
to the wicked, "Your doom is *. Is 3:11
anger God. I'm * he isn't angry!" Jer 2:35
But there is one thing *, if you Jer 26:15
And * enough, two months later Jer 28:17
Then I knew for * that the Jer 32:8
And * enough, it wasn't long Jer 38:27
that punishment was * to come. Lam 1:9
So I looked and, * enough, Eze 8:5
your dream is as * and certain as Dan 2:45
And now I know for * that his Dan 4:3
You can be * that I will rescue Zec 8:7
weren't * it really was Jesus! Mt 28:17
and be * of this—that I am with Mt 28:20
And be * to put into practice Mk 4:24
And * enough, as soon as she Mk 5:29
you can be * that my return is very Mk 13:29
but my words stand * forever. Mk 13:31
they yelled at him. "*, you Mk 15:29,30
"Make * you collect no more Lk 3:13
But I am * you can always Lk 7:35
Jesus said, and * enough, as they Lk 19:33
* that the Kingdom of God is near. Lk 21:31
out to see, and * enough, Jesus' Lk 24:24
Touch me and make * that I am not Lk 24:39
old—*, you've seen Abraham!" Jn 8:57
Lord, for we were quite * of it. Jn 21:12
to him. I'm * you have heard about Act 10:36,37
"And now beware! Be * that you Act 20:28
I speak frankly for I am * these Act 26:26
You are so * of the way to God Rom 2:19
He was completely * that God was Rom 4:21
As for myself, I am perfectly * Rom 14:14
And I am * that when I come the Rom 15:29
comes you can be * that we will be 1Co 4:8
But be * in deciding these 1Co 7:17
however, be * that everything is 1Co 14:40
future victory is *, be strong and 1Co 15:58
as I am * they were to you, too. 1Co 16:18
You can be * that the more we 2Co 1:5
It was because I was so * of 2Co 1:15,16
I felt * that your happiness was 2Co 2:3
am * all is well between us again. 2Co 7:16
men just to be * that you really 2Co 9:3
he fooled us. As * as anything he 2Co 12:16
Now make * that you stay free and Gal 5:1
Let everyone be * that he is Gal 6:4
You can be * of this: The kingdom Eph 5:5
And I am * that God who began Php 1:6
And say to Archippus, "Be * Col 4:17
need to say very much, I'm *! 1Th 4:9
that is said to be * it is true. 1Th 5:21
Teach these things and make * 1Ti 4:11
Be * to use the abilities God has 1Ti 4:14
of them. Be * that you yourself 1Ti 5:22
and I feel * you are still 2Ti 1:5
I trust, and I am * that he is able 2Ti 1:12
When you come, be * to bring 2Ti 4:13
would be perfectly * and never need Heb 6:17
No one can be * whether this means Heb 7:3f
made * of our eternal salvation. Heb 9:12
and he was so * of it that he Heb 11:22
But when you ask him, be * that Jas 1:6
power, will make * that you get 1Pe 1:5
abilities; be * to use them to help 1Pe 4:10
And how can we be * that we 1Jn 2:3
comes you will be * that all is 1Jn 2:28
Then we will know for *, by our 1Jn 3:19
And we are * of this, that he 1Jn 5:14
can be * that he will answer us. 1Jn 5:15

SUREFOOTEDNESS
He gives me the * of a mountain Ps 18:33

SURELY
That wouldn't be right! * you Gen 18:25
the same! * you wouldn't do that! Gen 18:25
for she said, "* now my husband Gen 29:34
Otherwise, disaster will * Gen 41:36
"but God will * come and get you, Gen 50:24
he dies shall * be put to death. Ex 21:12
or mother shall * be put to death. Ex 21:15
or father shall * be put to death. Ex 21:17
man shall * be punished. Ex 21:20
me for my help, I will * give it. Ex 22:23
or mother shall * be put to Lev 20:9
woman—shall * be stoned to death. Lev 20:27
he shall * be put to death. Lev 27:29
but we will * die if he speaks Deu 5:25
That would * result in your Deu 7:4
you and he would * destroy you. Deu 7:4
"* you remember how we lived in Deu 29:16
this day that you shall * perish; Deu 30:18
tribe you will * be able to clear Jos 17:16,17,18
will * save us from our enemies." 1Sa 4:3
son Jonathan, he shall * die!" 1Sa 14:39
for he thought, "* the worst is 1Sa 15:32
and thought, "* this is the man 1Sa 16:6
impure. Yes, * that must be it! 1Sa 20:26
And now I realize that you are * 1Sa 24:20
The Lord will * reward you with 1Sa 25:28
chosen king? * God will strike him 1Sa 26:10
cases. I * wish I were the judge; 2Sa 15:4
of Samaria shall * be fulfilled." 1Ki 13:32
King Ahab, "As * as the Lord God 1Ki 17:1
he will * die.' 2Ki 1:4,5
you will * die.' 2Ki 1:6
you will * die." 2Ki 1:16
has shown me that he will * die!" 2Ki 8:10
awful things, * your anger will Ez 9:14
And God * knows where it is to Job 28:23,24
"I thought, '* I shall die Job 29:18
understanding, * everyone knows Job 34:10
of humble people. * you will hear Ps 10:17
Calamity will * overtake the Ps 34:21
I will * do what I have Ps 56:12
their sinning. * his salvation is Ps 85:9
about us and he will * bless us. Ps 115:12
succeed me. And * you will never go Ps 132:11
* you will slay the wicked, Lord! Ps 139:19
But the Lord will * help those Ps 140:12
of the poor. * the godly are Ps 140:13
Those who search for me shall * Pro 8:17
all the time, for * you have a Pro 23:17,18
As * as a wind from the north Pro 25:23
just as * a retort causes anger! Pro 25:23
The Lord has spoken—he will * do Is 25:8
more, for he will * be gracious to Is 30:19
at the Living God. * God won't let Is 37:4
away with this. * God will rebuke Is 37:4
* they will not be false again." Is 63:8
Where are they now? * you are Is 63:16
As * as my new heavens and earth Is 66:22
shall remain, so * shall you always Is 66:22
means that I will * carry out my Jer 1:12
been my Friend; * you won't be Jer 3:4,5
* you will just forget it?" Jer 3:4,5
They tell the people you will * Jer 14:13
off as slaves. * at last you will Jer 22:22
I will * remove the yoke put on Jer 28:4
I long for him and * will have Jer 31:20
of Jerusalem would * be captured by Jer 38:3
says: I will * bring Jer 43:10
For the time is * coming when I Jer 51:47
And yet, O Lord, the time will * Lam 1:21
Yes, it will * fall. Eze 13:13
"The Lord God says: As I live, * Eze 17:19
the Lord, and he shall * live. Eze 18:9
He shall * die, and it is his own Eze 18:13
he shall * live. Eze 18:17
keeps my laws, he shall * live. Eze 18:19
he shall * live and not die. Eze 18:21
He shall * live—he shall not die. Eze 18:28
For the Lord God says: I will * Eze 23:28

(SURELY Con't)
not doing evil—he shall * live. Eze 33:15
to the good and shall * live. Eze 33:16
says: As I live, * those living in Eze 33:27
God says: I will * judge between Eze 34:20
it will * happen— that your people Dan 4:24
respond to us as * as the coming of Hos 6:3
you as * as day follows night. Hos 6:5
He will * punish them. Hos 9:9
of Bethel shall * come to grief." Amo 5:5
The time is * coming," says the Amo 8:11
I will * fulfill my promises. Jon 2:9
Such evils * will not come our Mic 2:6
all of this to wipe us out? * not! Hab 1:12
Slowly, steadily, *, the time Hab 2:3
these things will * come to pass. Hab 2:3
I thought, '* they will listen Zep 3:7
listen to me now—* they will heed Zep 3:7
would * lead to ruin, as it has.' Zec 7:7
Yes, he is * coming," says the Mal 3:1
"Will a man rob God? * not! Mal 3:8
won't he more * care for you, O men Mt 6:30
child, you will * be rewarded." Mt 10:42
his meaning: "* evil men and Mt 21:31
thinking they would * respect him. Mt 21:37
They exclaimed, "* this was Mt 27:54
* give him their full respect. Mk 12:6
from God shall * come true." Lk 1:37
For the hand of the Lord is * Lk 1:66
Yes, it will * be charged against Lk 11:51
that God will * give justice to his Lk 18:7
I'll send my cherished son. * Lk 20:13
said, "* this man was innocent." Lk 23:47
they exclaimed, "*, he is the Jn 6:14
"This man * is the prophet who Jn 7:40
"but he * looks like him!" Jn 9:9
the wall, must * be a thief ! Jn 10:1
will * stand trial before Caesar! Act 27:24
The day will * come when at Rom 2:16
he also * give us everything else? Rom 8:32
God will * do this for you, for 1Co 1:9
Never! As * as God is true, I am 2Co 1:18
evil and he will * reap a harvest Gal 6:8
And he * was; Php 2:27
ought to be. * we don't need to Heb 6:1
how much more * the blood of Christ Heb 9:14
for God will * punish all those Heb 13:4
Dear brothers, * this is not Jas 3:10
The day of the Lord is * coming, 2Pe 3:10
the Lord will * feel it even more, 1Jn 3:20
we * ought to love each other too. 1Jn 4:11
our courts, and so * we can believe 1Jn 5:9

SURF
their battle cry roars like the * Jer 50:42

SURFACE
Aaron hit the * of the Nile with Ex 7:20
to be beneath the * of the wall, Lev 14:37
and the axhead rose to the * and 2Ki 6:6
food from the * of the earth, while Job 28:5
* of the earth to form the seas. Ps 104:3
but you don't look beneath the *. 2Co 10:7

SURGE
of battle will * against Horonaim, Jer 48:2,3,4

SURGED
a vast crowd * along behind. Mt 20:29
Then the crowds * on ahead and Mt 21:9
and the crowd * behind shouting, Act 21:36

SURGING
For when they see the * birth Is 29:23

SURPASSED
in a very short time you far * Eze 16:47

SURPLUS
You will have such a * of crops Lev 26:10
Literally, "out of their *." Mk 12:43,44f

SURPRISE
word, they were so stunned with *. Gen 45:3
and took the enemy armies by *. Jos 10:9
at the Midianite army in * raids. Ju 8:11
This was an expression of * 1Sa 10:12f
and launched a * attack against the 1Sa 11:11
And now, to my *, Eze 47:7
you ask in fake *. Mal 2:17
nothing, much to the governor's *. Mt 27:14
* wrote, "His name is John!" Lk 1:63
speechless with *, for they heard Act 9:7
the door, their * knew no bounds. Act 12:16

SURPRISED
throughout the land, don't be *! Ecc 5:8
Don't be * then by the lighter Eze 16:52
His reply * and baffled them and Mt 22:22
The congregation was * at his Mk 1:22
the angel said, "Don't be so *. Mk 16:6
This greatly * his host. Lk 11:37,38
so don't be * at my statement Jn 3:7
The woman was * that a Jew would Jn 4:9
They were * to find him talking Jn 4:27
Don't be so *! Jn 5:28
The Jewish leaders were * when Jn 7:15
by healing a man, and you were *. Jn 7:21,22,23
Gate, they were inexpressibly *! Act 3:10
the commander asked, *. Act 21:37,38
Yet I am not *! 2Co 11:14
and you won't be * as by a thief 1Th 5:4
will be very * when you don't 1Pe 4:4
be bewildered or * when you go 1Pe 4:12
So don't be *, dear friends, if 1Jn 3:13
"Why are you so *?" Rev 17:7

SURPRISING
said, "what is so * about this? Act 3:12
It isn't * that soon they lost 1Ti 1:19

SURRENDER
and I'll * them to you to do with Gen 19:8
home, demanding that she * them. Jos 2:3
then told their enemies, "We *. 1Sa 11:10
Will the men of Keilah * me to 1Sa 23:11
discuss a deal—to * the kingdom of 2Sa 3:12
demanding that I * my other son to 2Sa 14:7
so we might as well go out and * 2Ki 7:4
Don't listen to King Hezekiah. * 2Ki 18:31,32
to him. The * was accepted, and 2Ki 24:12
Poor widows must * the little Job 24:3
No wonder your enemies *! Ps 66:3
of Judah to * to Syria and Israel. Is 8:11
All your leaders flee; they * Is 22:3
enemies of mine * and beg for peace Is 27:4,5
that if you don't *, this city will Is 36:12
Give me a present as a token of *; Is 36:16
* to the Chaldean army and live. Jer 21:9
Don't listen to them. * to the Jer 27:17
You can't win! * now!" Jer 32:5
And I will * Zedekiah, king of Jer 34:21
says: If you will * to Babylon, you Jer 38:17
If you refuse to *, this city Jer 38:18
"But I am afraid to *," the Jer 38:19
But if you refuse to *, the Lord Jer 38:21,22
be safe to * to the Babylonians. Jer 40:9
out, announcing its * to the Lord. Hab 3:10
yourselves, and you * to Christ. 2Co 10:6

SURRENDERED
defeated, they * to David and 2Sa 10:19
Jehoiakim * and paid him tribute 2Ki 24:1
and the queen mother * to him. 2Ki 24:12
Then King Hadadezer's troops * 1Ch 19:19
Sippai, and so the Philistines *. 1Ch 20:4
he * his glory into enemy hands. Ps 78:61
I have * my dearest ones to their Jer 12:7
The oceans * the bodies buried Rev 20:13

SURRENDERING
but anyone * to the Babylonians Jer 38:2

SURRENDERS
Look! She *! Jer 50:15

SURROUND
it, they will * us and attack us Jos 7:9
chariots and horses to * the city. 2Ki 6:14
at the Temple; * the king, weapons 2Ki 11:6,7,8
His archers * me, letting fly Job 16:13
He sends his troops to * my Job 19:12
His favor will * you if you will Job 22:21
thousand enemies * me on every Ps 3:6
You * me with songs of victory. Ps 32:7
your constant love * us, for our Ps 33:22
with death. They * me with terror Ps 55:3
constantly and * him with my love; Ps 89:24
Honor and majesty * him; Ps 96:6
Clouds and darkness * him. Ps 97:2
Yes, they * and attack me; Ps 118:11
as you promised. * me with your Ps 119:75,76,77
Just as the mountains * and Ps 125:2
I will * Jerusalem and lay siege Is 29:3
They * Jerusalem like shepherds Jer 4:17
Evil shepherds shall * you. Jer 6:3
Yes, terror shall * them on every Jer 46:5
come to Babylon; * the city so that Jer 50:29
They will * you on every side Eze 23:24
Open land for pastures shall * Eze 48:17
thistles will grow up to * them. Hos 10:8
And I will * my Temple like a Zec 9:8
send their armies to * Jerusalem. Zec 12:2
the glory of God will soon * Jn 13:31
May God's blessings * you. Col 4:18
temptations that * us, and continue 2Pe 2:9
waters to form the earth and * it. 2Pe 3:5,6
of the earth and * God's people and Rev 20:9

SURROUNDED
all over the city—* the house and Gen 19:4
them and * by their defilement. Lev 16:16
flames shot far into the sky, * Deu 4:11
heart of the fire, * by the clouds Deu 5:22
* by ten thousands of holy angels, Deu 33:2
the men of Gibe-ah * the house, Ju 20:5
with his spear, * by his officers. 1Sa 22:6
the mighty warriors who * them! 2Sa 16:6
* Absalom and finished him off. 2Sa 18:15
The waves of death * me; 2Sa 22:5
Darkness * him, 2Sa 22:12
* a courtyard behind this hall. 1Ki 7:8
A nine-inch rim * the tip of 1Ki 7:35
and palm trees * by wreaths were 1Ki 7:36
Literally, "the slingers * and 2Ki 3:25f
was quickly * by the army of Edom. 2Ki 8:21
offerings, Jehu * the building with 2Ki 10:24
the sanctuary, and * the altar, 2Ki 11:11
of coronation, * by her bodyguard 2Ki 11:13,14
so Judah was *, with the enemy 2Ch 13:13,14
"I saw him upon his throne * by 2Ch 18:18
He is * by terrors, and if there Job 15:21
I am * by mockers. Job 17:2
That is why you are now * by Job 22:10,11
The praises of our fathers * your Ps 22:3,4
I am * by fearsome enemies, Ps 22:12
because I am * by waiting enemies. Ps 27:11
come, even though * by enemies! Ps 49:5
* by devastating fire; Ps 50:3
I am * by fierce lions—hotheads Ps 57:4
to live forever. * by unnumbered Ps 68:17
Though I am * by troubles, you Ps 138:7
We are * by the walls of his Is 26:1
WOE TO THE city of Samaria, * by Is 28:1
her fading beauty * by a fertile Is 28:4
wrath, * by thick rising smoke. Is 30:27
(of panic, "We are * and doomed!" Jer 49:29
(for the city was * by the Jer 52:7
* me with anguish and distress. Lam 3:5
Then the armies of the nations * Eze 19:8
I will make Egypt desolate, * by Eze 29:12
She shall be desolate, * by Eze 30:7
ruins, * by other ruined cities. Eze 30:7
Assyria lie there * by the graves Eze 32:22
depths of hell, * by their allies. Eze 32:23
among the slain, * by the graves of Eze 32:25
Tubal are there, * by the graves of Eze 32:26
and brass, * by the tender grass. Dan 4:15
roots in the earth * by tender Dan 4:23
You lie on ivory beds * with Amo 6:4
You are already * by enemy Nah 2:1
Then, * by the Pharisees, he Mt 22:41
as a result, such throngs soon * Mk 1:45
large, level area, * by many of his Lk 6:17,18
in turn, were * by the crowds. Lk 6:17,18
"But when you see Jerusalem * by Lk 21:20
The Jewish leaders * him and Jn 10:24
even though we were * by enemies. 1Th 2:2
for he, too, is * with the same Heb 5:1
He is arriving, * by clouds; Rev 1:7
Twenty-four smaller thrones * Rev 4:4
down from heaven, * by a cloud, Rev 10:1

SURROUNDING
in all the * countries too, but in Gen 41:54
and the fat * them, and the right Ex 29:22
Then he erected the enclosure * Ex 40:33
in their cities, and the * fields. Lev 25:33
of common land * their cities, for Lev 25:34
covering the fence * the courtyard, Num 3:25-30
of the courtyard * the Tabernacle, Num 3:25-30
to Kenath and its * villages, and Num 32:42
cities and * pasture lands. Num 35:2
homes, and the * lands for their Num 35:3
cities with the * pastureland given Num 35:7
When the * nations hear these Deu 4:6
of the awesome horrors * you. Deu 28:67
WHEN THE KINGS of the * area heard Jos 9:1
it and all of its * villages, Jos 10:37
* pasturelands for their cattle. Jos 14:3,4
cities with their * villages. Jos 15:21-32
cities with their * villages. Jos 15:33-36
country with their * villages: Jos 15:48-62
All of these cities and their * Jos 18:21-28
and each of their * villages. Jos 19:15,16
in all, each with its * villages. Jos 19:17-23
cities and their * villages. Jos 19:30,31
cities with their * villages. Jos 19:35-39
cities listed below, with their * Jos 21:9-16
the city and the * villages were Jos 21:9-16
with their * pasturelands. Jos 21:25
and Ekron, with their * villages. Ju 1:18
Megiddo, with their * towns; Ju 1:27
cities from all the * territory. 1Sa 7:16
at war with the * nations, David 2Sa 7:1
and he was famous among all the * 1Ki 4:31
and the other * territories. 1Ki 10:15
of Tappuah and the * countryside, 2Ki 15:16
more evil than the * nations had 2Ki 21:9
The Babylonian troops * the city 2Ki 25:4,5
Kenath and its sixty * villages. 1Ch 2:23
Hebron and its * pasturelands in 1Ch 6:55,56,57
Refuge with their * pasturelands: 1Ch 6:58,59
Thirteen other cities with * 1Ch 6:60
of Refuge with the * pasturelands 1Ch 6:66-69
and the * pastureland of each. 1Ch 6:73
each with their * pasturelands. 1Ch 6:81
by Bethel and its * towns, on the 1Ch 7:28
by Shechem and its * villages as 1Ch 7:28
cities and their * areas: 1Ch 7:29
Ono and Lod and their * villages). 1Ch 8:12
conquered Gath and its * towns. 1Ch 18:1
with his enemies in the * lands. 1Ch 22:9
you peace with the * nations, for I 1Ch 22:18
fell upon all the * kingdoms so 2Ch 17:10
before, when the * kingdoms heard 2Ch 20:29
and the trumpeters * him, and 2Ch 23:12
* villages, and were living there. 2Ch 28:17,18
among the * nations, and many gifts 2Ch 32:23
idols of the * nations, thus 2Ch 36:14

(SURROUNDING Con't)
When our enemies and the * Neh 6:16
Jekabzeel (and their * villages), Neh 11:25-30
* villages), Ziklag, Neh 11:25-30
* villages), Lachish Neh 11:25-30
Aija, Bethel (and its * villages), Neh 11:31-35
Jerusalem from the * villages and Neh 12:28
punish the heathen nations * us. Ps 59:5
(And scoff at these * nations Ps 59:8
as revered as he by those * him? Ps 89:7
mightiest men of his army * it. Sol 3:7
must I see war and death * me? Jer 4:21
the nations * the land God gave his Jer 12:14
this city and her * towns all the Jer 19:15
and battering rams * the walls. Eze 4:1
wicked than the nations * her." Eze 5:5,6,7
you before all the * nations and Eze 5:14
* nations and ruined their cities; Eze 19:7
"The * cities quake at the sound Eze 27:28
shame before the * nations. Eze 36:6
again will the * nations be able to Eze 36:30
and its immediately * yards. Eze 41:13
He is * them and will shatter Amo 3:11
a great crowd * the other nine Mk 9:14
covered platforms or porches * it. Jn 5:2
Derbe, and the * area, and Act 14:5,6
of millions of angels * the Rev 5:11

SURROUNDINGS
natural *, as you can see; 2Ki 2:19
the Temple and its * —the 1Ch 28:11

SURROUNDS
* the altar and the Tabernacle. Num 4:26
God * him with his loving care, Deu 33:12
* those who trust in the Lord. Ps 32:10
He ransoms me from hell. He * me Ps 103:4
Lord * and protects his people. Ps 125:2
When a storm of terror * you, Pro 1:27
miles wide, north to south, * the Eze 48:10
Israel * me with lies and deceit, Hos 11:12

SURVEY
finished their * and returned from Num 32:9

SURVEYED
He has * and subdivided the land Is 34:17

SURVEYING
determined, and who did the *? Job 38:5

SURVIVE
one of your male descendants *! 1Ki 21:21
you can * my siege of Jerusalem? 2Ch 32:10
Those who * shall be brought Job 27:15
sinners will not * your searching Ps 5:5
Yet a tenth—a remnant—will *; Is 6:13
of its stalwart archers will *." Is 21:17
of Anathoth shall *, for I will Jer 11:23
and those who * will be scattered Eze 5:10
for he has chosen some to *. Joe 2:32
In the end, those who * the Zec 14:16
He would never *. Mk 3:26
a soul in all the earth will *. Mk 13:20
his demons, how can his kingdom *? Lk 11:18
has come, and who can * it?" Rev 6:17

SURVIVED
and was * by his father. Gen 11:28
not one man * or escaped, except Jos 8:22
so not one enemy troop * the Jos 11:8
from those who * in the nations he 1Ki 9:20,21
so King Rehoboam * for three years 2Ch 11:17
Those who * were taken away to 2Ch 36:20
not one *. Ps 106:11
with those who * the city's Jer 52:15
thus they * the siege. Lam 4:10

SURVIVING
There they destroyed the few * 1Ch 4:43

SURVIVOR
so that not a single * remained; Num 21:35
destroyed and not one *?" Jer 26:9
* to remember what happened. Zep 3:6

SURVIVORS
Lions will hunt down the *, both Is 15:9
who escape" means * of the armies Is 66:19f
or * of the Jews in Israel. Is 66:19f
only a handful of * and they lay Jer 37:10
If there are * and they come Eze 14:22
and ears; your * will be killed; Eze 23:25
you captured the * and returned Ob 1:14
There will be no *, for the Lord Ob 1:18
sins of the * among his people? Mic 7:18

SUSA
men of Erech and *, and men from Ez 4:8,9
This time I was at *, the capital Dan 8:2
* was one of several capitals of Dan 8:2f

SUSANNA
domestic affairs), *, and many Lk 8:3

SUSI
Gaddi, son of *, from the tribe of Num 13:3-15

SUSPECT
Who would * that you would do a Gen 20:9,10
that no one will * you are hungry, Mt 6:18

SUSPECTED
skin, leprosy is to be *. Lev 13:1
"When anyone * of having leprosy Lev 13:9,10
"If leprosy is * in a woolen or Lev 13:47,48
shall order the * article to be Lev 13:54
Israelis who were * of being spies Jos 2:2
so no one * they were there. 2Sa 17:19
Sea, the sailors * land was near. Act 27:27

SUSPENDED
sheet, * by its four corners, Act 10:11

SUSPENSE
are you going to keep us in *? Jn 10:24
I could bear the * no longer I sent 1Th 3:5

SUSPICION
* offering—to bring out the truth Num 5:15
hair and place the * offering in Num 5:18
shall take the * offering from the Num 5:25
guard against any *, for we are 2Co 8:20

SUSPICIONS
not her husband's * are justified. Num 5:18
a husband's * against his wife— to Num 5:29
accusations, and evil *. 1Ti 6:4

SUSPICIOUS
he is jealous and *, the man shall Num 5:14
An evil man is * of everyone Pro 17:20
for then, even if they are * of 1Pe 2:12

SUSTAIN
Oh, why does my strength * me? Job 6:11
can * his broken body, but when Pro 18:14
Your words are what * me; Jer 15:16

SUSTAINED
For forty years you * them in Neh 9:21

SWADDLING
Literally, "* clothes." Lk 2:7f
Literally, "* clothes." Lk 2:12f

SWALLOW
that the earth would * them too. Num 16:34
have gaping jaws to * me; Job 16:10
overwhelm me, or the ocean * me; Ps 69:15
if you possibly can! * your pride; Pro 6:3
or * flitting through the sky. Pro 26:2
he will * up death forever. Is 25:8
Delirious, I chattered like a * Is 38:14
and the crane, and the *. Jer 8:7
Great seas shall * you. Eze 26:19
for a great fish to * Jonah. Jon 1:17
stand idly by while they * us up? Hab 1:13
You strain out a gnat and * a Mt 23:24
way to be saved. You * it all. 2Co 11:4
but when you * it, it will make Rev 10:9

SWALLOWED
And these thin heads * up the Gen 41:7
And the thin heads * up the fat Gen 41:24
But Aaron's serpent * their Ex 7:12
your hand and the earth * them. Ex 15:12
a great fissure * them up, along Num 16:32
But the earth opened and * them; Num 26:5-11
opened up and * them, with their Deu 11:6
Well, does a man wish to be * Job 37:19,20
* Dathan, Abiram and his friends; Ps 106:17
we would have been * alive by our Ps 124:2,3
Her great and small shall be * Is 5:14
he has * us like a great monster Jer 51:34,35
true—"Death is * up in victory." 1Co 15:54
were, be * up by everlasting life. 2Co 5:4
me a stomach ache when I * it. Rev 10:10

SWALLOWING
opening its mouth and * the flood! Rev 12:16

SWALLOWS
opens up and * them and everything Num 16:30
Even the sparrows and * are Ps 84:3

SWAM
into the water [and * ashore Jn 21:7

SWAMP
that threatened to * them, and they Lk 8:23

SWAMPS
porcupines, full of * and marshes. Is 14:23
But the marshes and * will not Eze 47:11

SWARM
The Nile River will * with them, Ex 8:3,4
And he found a * of bees in it, Ju 14:8
They * around me like bees; Ps 118:12
and of Assyria too, to * down Is 7:18
They * upon the city; Joe 2:9
preparing a vast * of locusts to Amo 7:1
* like locusts and carry it away. Nah 3:16

SWARMED
and other insects * in vast clouds Ps 105:31

SWARMER-LOCUSTS
the * will take what's left! Joe 1:4

SWARMS
If you refuse I will send * of Ex 8:21
were terrible * of flies in Ex 8:24
cause the * of flies to disappear. Ex 8:29
and caused the * to disappear, so Ex 8:31,32
command the locust * to eat up all 2Ch 7:13
how he sent vast * of flies to fill Ps 78:45
leader, they stay together in *. Pro 30:24-28
I will bring upon them * of Jer 12:9

SWATH
his face muffled in a head *. Jn 11:44
there, while the * that had Jn 20:7

SWAY
They whirl and * beneath the Ps 29:9
He will hold * from the Ps 89:25

SWAYED
stand, don't be * in your testimony Ex 23:2,3

SWAYING
at sea, clinging to a * mast. Pro 23:34

SWEAR
you do; * to me by God's name that Gen 21:23
Abraham replied, "All right, I * Gen 21:24
"* by Jehovah, the God of heaven Gen 24:3
stolen from you, I * before all Gen 31:32
the king of Egypt, * that you shall Gen 41:44
test your story: I * by the life of Gen 42:15
and said to him, "* to me most Gen 47:29
And Joseph promised. "* that Gen 47:31
father made Joseph * to take his Gen 50:5
the Lord your God to * falsely." Ex 20:7f
nor use it to * to a falsehood. Ex 20:7
You must not * to a falsehood, Lev 19:12
He shall require her to * that Num 5:19
Now I beg for this one thing: * Jos 2:12,13
but we * that no one inside this Jos 2:19
"We * by Jehovah, the God of Jos 22:22,23
less * by them or worship them. Jos 23:7
Gideon exclaimed. "I * that if Ju 8:19
"We * it," they replied. Ju 11:10
but if he won't, then I will, I * Ru 3:13
away from death! I * it by the Lord 1Sa 20:3
But Jonathan made David * to it 1Sa 20:17
to rule. Oh, * to me by the Lord 1Sa 24:21
For I * by the Lord, the God of 1Sa 25:34
This isn't good at all! I * by 1Sa 26:16
"I * by the Lord," he told them, 1Sa 29:6
The young man replied, "If you * 1Sa 30:15
Joab shouted back, "I * by God 2Sa 2:27
But David replied, "I * by the 2Sa 4:9
with my wife? I * that I will never 2Sa 11:11
David was furious. "I * by the 2Sa 12:5
Then she said, "Please * to me 2Sa 14:11
the troops, for I * by Jehovah that 2Sa 19:7
plot against me! I * it by the 1Ki 2:23,24
But she said, "I * by the Lord 1Ki 17:12
For I * by God that the king has 1Ki 18:10
to * to the truth of his claim. 1Ki 18:10
But Elijah said, "I * by the 1Ki 18:15
and now I * by the gods that I am 1Ki 19:2
But Elisha replied, "I * to God 2Ki 2:1
But Elisha replied again, "I * to 2Ki 2:4
* to God that I won't leave you." 2Ki 2:6,7
"I * by the Lord God that I 2Ki 3:14
But the boy's mother said, "I * 2Ki 4:30
But Elisha replied, "I * by 2Ki 5:16
and is required to * to his 2Ch 6:22
people of Israel * that they would Ez 10:5
These evil men * to a lie. Ps 35:11
* to the truth of what is false. Ps 144:8
shall * allegiance to my name. Is 45:23
HEAR ME, MY people: you * Is 48:1
its life, so now I * that I will Is 54:9
oath shall * by the God of Truth; Is 65:16
and if you will * by me alone, the Jer 4:2
to this warning, I * by my own Jer 22:5
I * that I will tell you nothing. Eze 20:3
in your land. You * and lie and Hos 4:2
don't * that something is true Zec 8:17
And don't * 'By Jerusalem!' Mt 5:35
Don't even * 'By my head!' Mt 5:36
For your rule is that to * 'By Mt 23:16
that oath, but to * 'By the gold in Mt 23:16
be broken, but to * 'By the gifts Mt 23:18
When you * 'By the altar' you Mt 23:20
it, and when you * 'By the Temple' Mt 23:21
And when you * 'By heavens' you Mt 23:22
Peter began to curse and *. Mt 26:74
He began to curse and *. Mk 14:71
Dear friends, I solemnly * that Gal 1:11
hearts, curse and *, attack their 1Ti 1:9
no one greater to * by, that he Heb 6:13
brothers, do not * either by heaven Jas 5:12

SWEARING
lying about it, * that he doesn't Lev 6:3
broke his promise after * to obey; Eze 17:18
the altar' you are * by it and Mt 23:20
Temple' you are * by it, and by God Mt 23:21
heavens' you are * by the Throne of Mt 23:22

SWEARS
before your altar, * that he didn't 1Ki 8:31
here, the Lord God * that it would Eze 14:16
and everyone who * falsely by my Zec 5:4

SWEAT
All your life you will * to Gen 3:19
them with work and make them *; Ex 5:9
he broke into a * of blood, with Lk 22:44
until you * great drops of blood. Heb 12:4

SWEATED
Night and day we toiled and * to 1Th 2:9

SWEATING
caused * of great drops of blood? Heb 5:7f

SWEEP
Or, "God does not * life away, 2Sa 14:14f
I will * away your family as a 1Ki 14:10
great harm to you and * you away; 1Ki 21:21
has used me to * away my enemies 1Ch 14:11

(SWEEP Con't)
God will * away both old and Ps 58:9
its channels and * into your land Is 8:7,8
I will * the land with the broom Is 14:23
like a flood and * it away, and you Is 28:17
upon them all, to * them all away. Is 30:28
And our sins, like the wind, * us Is 64:6
to * away these wicked men. Jer 23:19
The Lord God says: I will * it Eze 13:13
I will make a clean * throughout Eze 21:4
shall * them away; Hos 4:19
or else he will * like fire through Amo 5:6
They * past like wind and are Hab 1:11
"I will * away everything in all Zep 1:2
I will * away both men and Zep 1:3
When the floods * down against Lk 6:49
of the house and * every nook and Lk 15:8

SWEEPING
great fear was * across the city. 1Sa 5:11
flood * away their last hope. Pro 28:3
"Who is this * in from the Sol 3:6
like a whirlwind * from the Negeb. Is 21:1
the roar of fire * across a field, Joe 2:5
began that day, * over the church Act 8:1

SWEEPINGS
I threw them away like * from the Ps 18:42

SWEEPS
is gone. It * him into eternity. Job 27:21
But he * away his enemies with Nah 1:8

SWEET
the water, and the water became *. Ex 15:25
he shall burn * spices on the Ex 30:7
half as much of cinnamon and of * Ex 30:22,23
the incense: "Use * spices—stacte, Ex 30:34
The anointing oil and * incense; Ex 35:10-19
anointing oil and the * incense. Ex 35:28
Then, from * spices, he made the Ex 37:29
The * incense; Ex 39:33-40
incense made from * spices, just as Ex 40:27
Literally, "it will be a * savor Lev 1:9f
Literally, "it will be a * savor Lev 1:15,16,17f
Literally, "but not for a * savor Lev 2:12f
his hands with * incense beaten Lev 16:12
Literally, "of a * odor to the Lev 23:18f
for the light, the * incense, the Num 4:16
David, * psalmist of Israel: 2Sa 23:1
burn incense and * spices before 2Ch 2:4
offerings and * incense; 2Ch 13:11
bed perfumed with * spices and 2Ch 16:13,14
anguish I eagerly await * death! Job 14:14
His words were *, but underneath Ps 55:21
pluck the * lyre and harp. Ps 81:2
prostitute are as * as honey, and Pro 5:3
necklace. How * is your love, my Sol 4:10
His mouth is altogether *, Sol 5:16
wine, smooth and *, causing the Sol 7:9
to drink, * pomegranate wine. Sol 8:2
Instead of smelling of * Is 3:24
not at all the * ones he expected. Is 5:2
give me wild grapes instead of *? Is 5:4
bitter is * and sweet is bitter. Is 5:20
bitter is sweet and * is bitter. Is 5:20
she will sing * songs as a harlot Is 23:15,16
There is no use now in burning * Jer 6:20
they have no * fragrance for me. Jer 6:20
"Such sleep is very *!" Jer 31:26
And when I ate it, it tasted * as Eze 3:3
and burn * incense before him. Dan 2:46
"* wine will drip from the Joe 3:18
yourselves with * ointments, caring Amo 6:6
hills of Israel will drip * wine! Amo 9:13
they will offer * incense and pure Mal 1:11
the Gospel like a * perfume. 2Co 2:14
there is a *, wholesome fragrance 2Co 2:15
please you by * talk and flattery; Gal 1:10
for you was like * perfume to him. Eph 5:2
And just as he had said, it was * Rev 10:10

SWEET-SMELLING
You have brought me no * incense Is 43:24
They are a * sacrifice that Php 4:18

SWEET-SPICE
and the * incense for the Holy Ex 31:11

SWEETENED
and thin sheets of * bread mingled Ex 29:2

SWEETER
"What is * than honey?" Ju 14:18
They are * than honey dripping Ps 19:10
your words are * than honey. Ps 119:102,103
for your love is * than wine. Sol 1:2

SWEETEST
are the *; Pro 9:17

SWEETHEART
Love wisdom like a *; Pro 7:4

SWEETLY
Worms shall feed * on him. Job 24:20
ones who speak so * to their Ps 28:3
His cheeks are like * scented Sol 5:13
they talk very * about loving the Eze 33:31

SWEETNESS
'Should I quit producing * and Ju 9:11
eater, and * from the strong!" Ju 14:14

SWELL
thigh rot away and your body *.' Num 5:21,22
and her body will * and her thigh Num 5:27
wear out and their feet didn't *! Neh 9:21

SWELLING
anyone notices a * in his skin, or Lev 13:1
there is a white * in the skin with Lev 13:9,10
leaves a white * or a bright spot, Lev 13:19
house, or in any * in one's skin, Lev 14:56
the * Jordan rushes down upon him. Job 40:23
to begin * or suddenly fall dead; Act 28:6

SWEPT
And great fear * through the Gen 20:8
The idea * the camp. Num 14:4
* them away. Ju 5:21
So the Lord was very angry. He * 2Ki 17:18
the Lord finally * them away, just 2Ki 17:23
a mighty wind * in from the desert, Job 1:19
gods shall be * from his land. Ps 10:16
It is all * away. Ecc 5:16
Then all opposition will be * Dan 11:22
are * away—the very ground on Mic 1:11
Onward * the raging water. Hab 3:10
A chill of fear * through the Mt 9:8
miracle * the entire countryside. Mt 9:26
A great sadness * over them, and Mk 14:19
A great fear * the crowd, and Lk 7:16
wave of fear had * over them). Lk 8:37
former home is all * and clean. Lk 11:25
a great famine * over the land, and Lk 15:14
But soon a gale * down upon them Jn 6:18,19
way to Jerusalem * through the Jn 12:12
What a wave of awesome joy * Act 20:10,11,12
gushed out and * toward the woman Rev 12:15

SWERVED
but I have not * from your will. Ps 119:157

SWIFT
* as deer upon the mountains." 1Ch 12:8-13
the letters by * carriers—riders on Est 8:9,10
My years disappear like * ships, Job 9:26
down the Nile! Let * messengers Is 18:2
Egypt, riding on a * cloud; Is 19:1
take his terrible, * sword and Is 27:1
where lions and * venomous snakes Is 30:6
they will give us * horses for Is 30:16
I will call that * bird of prey Is 46:11
with fire and with * chariots of Is 66:15
the Lord. The * will not escape, Jer 46:6
come will fly as * as a vulture and Jer 49:22
darted to and fro, * as lightning. Eze 1:14
At that time I will send * Eze 30:9
as messengers * as the wind and as Heb 1:7
dagger, cutting * and deep into our Heb 4:12
but theirs will be a * and 2Pe 2:1

SWIFTER
They were * than eagles, stronger 2Sa 1:23
his steeds are * than eagles. Jer 4:13
Our enemies are * than the Lam 4:19
Their horses are * than Hab 1:8

SWIFTEST
passes the * horse with its rider. Job 39:18
and saw that the * person does not Ecc 9:11
Your * warriors will stumble in Amo 2:14
aim will fail, the * runners won't Amo 2:15
Use your * chariots and flee, O Mic 1:13

SWIFTLY
So the mail went out *, carried Est 8:14
"My life passes * away, filled Job 9:25
he pierces the * gliding serpent. Job 26:13
he sped * to my aid with wings of Ps 18:10
tides of time as * as a racing Ps 90:5,6
My life is passing * as the Ps 102:11
the world. How * his word flies. Ps 147:15
leviathan, the * moving serpent, Is 27:1
the path of sin as * as a horse Jer 8:6
from the west, so * that it didn't Dan 8:5
vision, flew * to me at the time of Dan 9:21
Beware, for I will strike back *, Joe 3:4
But your judgment day is coming * Mic 7:4
"That terrible day is near. * it Zep 1:14
I will move * against wicked men Mal 3:5

SWIFTNESS
But the only * you are going to Is 30:16
the * of your enemies chasing you! Is 30:16

SWIM
to get across unless I were to *. Eze 47:5
any of them * ashore and escape. Act 27:42
Then he ordered all who could * Act 27:43

SWIMMER
down just as a * pushes down the Is 25:11

SWIMS
and whatever * in the water or Lev 11:46

SWINDLER
is greedy, or is a *, or worships 1Co 5:11

SWINDLERS
They are * and liars, from the Jer 6:13
there were many notorious * Mt 9:10

SWINE
The * (because although it has Lev 11:4-7
or the blood of a * on his altar! Is 66:3
By offering * on the altar. Dan 11:30,31f
Don't give pearls to *! Mt 7:6
feeding the * looked good to him. Lk 15:16

SWINGING
on ropes, * back and forth. Job 28:3,4
doors, each with two * sections. Eze 41:24

SWINGS
of Babylon, and he * it over the Eze 30:25

SWIRL
For thick clouds * about him so Job 22:14
War will * through their cities; Hos 11:6

SWOLLEN
feet haven't been blistered or *. Deu 8:4
my eyes are * with weeping, Ps 69:3

SWOOP
were planning to * down upon us and Neh 4:11
In distant years you will * down Eze 38:8

SWOOPING
* down upon you like an eagle; Deu 28:49
like eagles they come * down to Hab 1:8

SWOOPS
the eagle that * upon its prey. Job 9:26

SWORD
with a flaming * to guard the Gen 3:24
shall hew your way with your *. Gen 27:39,40
with my * and with my bow." Gen 48:22
we face death by plague or *." Ex 5:3
I will cut them apart with my * Ex 15:9
of Amalek, putting them to the *. Ex 17:13
me from the * of Pharaoh"). Ex 18:4
though chased by a man with a *; Lev 26:36
in the road with a drawn *. Num 22:22,23
"I wish I had a * with me, for I Num 22:29
roadway with drawn *, and he fell Num 22:31
Outside, the enemies' *— Deu 32:25
I will whet the lightning of my *! Deu 32:40,41
My * devours the flesh and blood Deu 32:40,41
He is your excellent *! Deu 33:29
appeared nearby with a drawn *. Jos 5:13
With that, Joshua plunged his * Jos 10:26
him with his *, and he died. Ju 9:54
their children shall die by the *. 1Sa 2:33
So there was not a single * or 1Sa 13:22
But Samuel said, "As your * 1Sa 15:33
David put it on, strapped the * 1Sa 17:38,39
come to me with a * and a spear, 1Sa 17:45
Since he had no *, he ran over 1Sa 17:50,51
him his robe, *, bow, and belt. 1Sa 18:4
he had a spear or * he could use. 1Sa 21:8
"I have the * of Goliath, the 1Sa 21:9
the * of Goliath the Philistine." 1Sa 22:9,10
and a * and talk to God for him? 1Sa 22:13
me with your * before these heathen 1Sa 31:3,4
Saul took his own * and fell upon 1Sa 31:3,4
fell upon his * and died with him. 1Sa 31:5
through with his * and he died. 2Sa 1:15
* play between our young men!" 2Sa 2:14
and thrust his * into the other's 2Sa 2:16
been known ever since as * Field. 2Sa 2:16
or be killed by the *!" 2Sa 3:29
"The * kills one as well as 2Sa 11:25
Literally, "the * devours now one 2Sa 11:25f
hand was too tired to hold his *; 2Sa 23:10
him, and he killed him with a *. 1Ki 2:25
All right, bring me a *." 1Ki 3:24
So a * was brought to the king. 1Ki 3:24
man, "Strike me with your *!" 1Ki 20:35
said, "Strike me with your *." 1Ki 20:37
they were put to the * and died. 2Ki 25:21
kill me with your * before these 1Ch 10:4
own * and fell against its point; 1Ch 10:4
and earth with his * drawn, 1Ch 21:16
to put back his * into its sheath; 1Ch 21:27
drawn * of the angel of Jehovah. 1Ch 21:30
skilled in the use of spear and *. 2Ch 25:5,6
the power of the * in time of war. Job 5:20
to master him bring a sharp *! Job 40:19
Terror grips them. No * can stop Job 41:26
will sharpen his * and slay them. Ps 7:12
my soul from the *, my only one Ps 22:20f
They are doomed to die by the *, Ps 63:10
You have struck down his * and Ps 89:43
servant David from the fatal *. Ps 144:10
And take a double-edged * to Ps 149:6,7
to you, sharp as a double-edged *. Pro 5:4
him with a *, or shooting him with Pro 25:18
Each one has his * upon his thigh Sol 3:8
you out with famine and the *. Is 14:30
and not by *. Is 22:2
terrible, swift * and punish Is 27:1
The "* of God" will smite them. Is 31:8
And when my * has finished its Is 34:5
* of the Lord is sated with blood; Is 34:6
and to put entire armies to the *. Is 41:2
Yes, famine and the *. Is 51:19
you to the *, and your "fate" Is 65:12
by fire and by his *, and the slain Is 66:16
Yet the * is even now poised to Jer 4:10
and even there the * of Jer 9:16
the land; the * of the Lord devours Jer 12:12
run through with a * and lie Jer 14:17
bodies of those the * has killed; Jer 14:18

(SWORD Con't)
those who must die by the *, to Jer 15:2
must die by the sword, to the *; Jer 15:2
says the Lord—the * to kill, the Jer 15:3
let the * pour out their blood! Jer 18:21
him with a * and had him buried in Jer 26:23
the city by *, famine and disease. Jer 32:24
would die by *, starvation or Jer 38:2
Yes, you will die from *, famine Jer 42:17
you will die by *, famine and Jer 42:22
in Egypt, killed by famine and *; Jer 44:12
by *, famine and disease. Jer 44:13
been destroyed by * and famine." Jer 44:18
his enemies. The * shall devour Jer 46:10
Mobilize for battle, for the * of Jer 46:14
O * of the Lord, when will you be Jer 47:6
for them! The * of destruction Jer 50:35
is God's battleaxe and *. Jer 51:20
Go, you who escaped the *! Jer 51:50
In the streets the * awaits me; Lam 1:20
Those killed by the * are far Lam 4:9
"SON OF DUST, take a sharp * and Eze 5:1
I will chase my people with the *. Eze 5:2
* of the enemy chasing after you. Eze 5:12
the * of the enemy will slay you; Eze 5:17
north gate, each one with his *. Eze 9:2
winds and send the * after them. Eze 12:14
be killed by the *, and those Eze 17:21
I will unsheath my * and destroy Eze 21:3
I, the Lord. His * is in his hand, Eze 21:5
tell them this: A * is being Eze 21:9,10,11
thigh, for that * shall slay my Eze 21:12
then take a * and brandish it Eze 21:14
for a * glitters at every gate; Eze 21:15
for slaughter. O *, slash to the Eze 21:16
"Against you also my glittering * Eze 21:28
Shall I return my * to its Eze 21:30
will be slaughtered by the *. Eze 24:20,21
her flocks. The * will destroy Eze 25:13
city shall perish by the *. Eze 26:6
nations! A * shall fall on Egypt; Eze 30:4
Syene they shall perish by the *. Eze 30:6
shall die by the * and the women Eze 30:17
strong enough to hold a * again. Eze 30:21
make his * clatter to the ground. Eze 30:22
and place my * in his hand. Eze 30:24
Yes, when I place my * into the Eze 30:25
you despise, killed by the *. Eze 31:18
when I brandish my * before them. Eze 32:10
"For the Lord God says: The * of Eze 32:11
slain by the *, for the sword is Eze 32:20
the sword, for the * is drawn Eze 32:20
despised, all victims of the *. Eze 32:21
her people, those the * has slain. Eze 32:22
shame in the pit, slain by the *. Eze 32:25
those who are slain by the *. Eze 32:28
others whom the * has slain, with Eze 32:29
who are slain by the *." Eze 32:32
in the ruins shall die by the *. Eze 33:27
with those the * has killed. Eze 35:8
I will fight you with *, Eze 38:22
and *, or being jailed and robbed. Dan 11:33
will perish by the * of the enemy Hos 7:16
women ripped open with a *. Hos 13:16
his brother, Israel, with the *; Amo 1:11
of King Jeroboam by the *." Amo 7:9
command the * to kill them there. Amo 9:4
not touch us,' will die by the *. Amo 9:10
you; the * will cut you down; Nah 3:15
be slain by his *, and so will the Zep 2:12
Both of you will be my *, like Zec 9:13
my sword, like the * of a mighty Zec 9:13
God's * will cut his arm and Zec 11:17
"Awake, O *, against my Zec 13:7
No, rather, a *. Mt 10:34
Jesus pulled out a * and slashed Mt 26:51
"Put away your *," Jesus told Mt 26:52
pulled a * and slashed at the Mk 14:47
said to Mary, "A * shall pierce Lk 2:34,35
And if you don't have a *, better Lk 22:36
Then Simon Peter drew a * and Jn 18:10
said to Peter, "Put your * away. Jn 18:11
he drew his * to kill himself. Act 16:27
salvation and the * of the Eph 6:17
faith, escaped death by the *. Heb 11:34
then were killed with the *. Heb 11:37,38
double-bladed * in his mouth, Rev 1:16
the sharp and double-bladed *. Rev 2:12
them with the * of my mouth. Rev 2:16
Its rider was given a long * and Rev 6:4
In his mouth he held a sharp * to Rev 19:15
with the sharp * in the mouth of Rev 19:21

SWORDS
Levi, took their *, entered the Gen 34:25
says, 'Get your * and go back and Ex 32:27
they will die beneath your *. Lev 26:7
than by the * of the Israelis. Jos 10:11
It was not your * or bows that Jos 24:12
* and spears for the Hebrews. 1Sa 13:19
"Get your *!" 1Sa 25:13
Joab, "Must our * continue to kill 2Sa 2:26
and * until the blood gushed out. 1Ki 18:28
or with * belted to their sides. Neh 4:18
But their * will be plunged into Ps 37:15
Their tongues are like *. Ps 57:4
Literally, "beat their * into Is 2:4f
They have fled from drawn * and Is 21:15
be destroyed, but not by * of men. Is 31:8
Sharezer killed him with their *; Is 37:38
my words of judgment sharp as *. Is 49:2
die by the * of their enemies. Jer 20:4
out their * and killed Gedaliah. Jer 41:2
withholding their * from your Jer 48:10
girls, killed by the enemies' *. Lam 2:21
stone them and kill them with *; Eze 23:47
draw their * against your marvelous Eze 28:7
their * beneath their heads. Eze 32:27
Melt your plowshares into * and Joe 3:10
open pregnant women with their *. Amo 1:13
They will beat their * into Mic 4:3
Assyria with drawn * and enter the Mic 5:6
See the flashing * and Nah 3:3
crowd armed with * and clubs, sent Mt 26:47
"Those using * will get killed. Mt 26:52
yourselves with * and clubs before Mt 26:55
mob equipped with * and clubs, sent Mk 14:43
"we have two * among us." Lk 22:38
We brought along the *!" Lk 22:49
armed with * and clubs to get me? Lk 22:52

SWORDSMEN
thousand men, all experienced *. Ju 20:25
he led 700 of his * in a last 2Ki 3:26
They are all skilled * and Sol 3:8

SWORE
curse upon the Canaanites," he *. Gen 9:24,25
master and * to him that Gen 24:9f
with Pharaoh, they * at them. Ex 5:21
For you * by your own self, 'I Ex 32:13
the land he * he would give them.' Num 14:16
them, and he * that of all those he Num 32:10,11
Jonathan * to be his blood 1Sa 18:1
David, and David * to it with a 1Sa 20:16
throne, just as I * to you before 1Ki 1:30
Then King Solomon * with a 1Ki 2:23,24
He met them in the Temple, * them 2Ki 11:4
Lord God of Israel * that David's 2Ch 13:5
On arrival they * allegiance to 2Ch 23:2,3
Therefore in mighty wrath I * Ps 95:11
Therefore he * that he would Ps 106:26
Just as in the time of Noah I * Is 54:9
things I * I would if you obeyed. Jer 11:5
So King Zedekiah * before Jer 38:16
to her in Egypt, I * to her and her Eze 20:5,6
But I * to them in the Eze 20:15
speaking when he * with an oath Heb 3:18
to heaven, and * by him who lives Rev 10:6

SWORN
"I, the Lord, have * by myself Gen 22:16
replied, "We have * before the Jos 9:19
since we have * by the Lord that we Ju 21:7
We have * with a solemn oath that Ju 21:18
Do this for me as my * brother. 1Sa 20:8
Israel had * not to kill them; 2Sa 21:2
For many in Judah had * Neh 6:18
the land you had * to give them; Neh 9:15
For I have * to David (and a Ps 89:35,36
But the Lord of Hosts has * your Is 5:9
I have * by myself and I will Is 45:23
The Lord has * to Jerusalem with Is 62:8
of Egypt: I have * by my great Jer 44:26
For I have * by my own name, Jer 49:13
this vow, and * to it in his own Jer 51:14
and has * to defend Jerusalem! Eze 21:23
Therefore I have * with hand Eze 36:7
The Lord God has * by his Amo 4:2
God of Hosts, has * by his own Amo 6:8
*: "I won't forget your deeds! Amo 8:7
He has said, "I have * in my Heb 4:3
"The Lord has * and will never Heb 7:21

SWUNG
Then they * around to Enmishpat Gen 14:7
on the cloud * his sickle over the Rev 14:16
So the angel * his sickle on Rev 14:19

SYCAMORE
greater value than the common *! 1Ki 10:27
olive yards and * trees in the 1Ch 27:28
lumber was used like common *! 2Ch 1:15
used as though it were common *. 2Ch 9:27
than before. The * trees are cut Is 9:8,9,10
and climbed into a * tree beside Lk 19:4

SYCAMORES
grapevines and their * with hail. Ps 78:47

SYCHAR
the village of *, he came to Jn 4:5,6

SYENE
from Migdol to *, as far south as Eze 29:10
From Migdol to * they shall Eze 30:6

SYMBOL
It is an eternal * of the Ex 31:17
the altar as a * to show our Jos 22:26,27
but is a * of the relationship with Jos 22:28
I am a * of failure to all Ps 109:25
with the Ark, the * of your power. Ps 132:8
in white, the * of all purity. Ps 132:9
three years, is a * of the terrible Is 20:3
seventh day—as a * between them and Eze 20:12
for they are a * of the contract Eze 20:20
and you will be a * for these Eze 24:27
Probably a * of the angels. Eze 28:14f
Gog seems to be a * rather than an Eze 38:2,3f
become a *, the center of world Zec 5:11f

SYMBOLIC
has given me have * names that Is 8:18
* mother of the northern tribes, Jer 31:15f

SYMBOLICALLY
It was used * for "goodness" Lev 2:13f
the word used * through the Rev 19:2f

SYMBOLIZE
to * the great massacre they face! Eze 21:14

SYMBOLS
and put strange * in the earth and Joe 2:30

SYMEON
were Barnabas and * (also called Act 13:1

SYMPATHETIC
and * to those who reverence him. Ps 103:13
food brought to you by * friends. Eze 24:22
they were godly and * Jews. Act 8:2f
Are your hearts tender and * at Php 2:1

SYMPATHIZE
And who is left to *? Is 51:19

SYMPATHIZED
you watched and * with others Heb 10:33

SYMPATHIZERS
the valiant Maccabees and their *. Dan 11:32f

SYMPATHY
So David sent a message of * to 1Ch 19:2,3
No, he would listen with *. Job 23:6
her walls and feel * for every Ps 102:14
Daniel, and * for his predicament. Dan 1:9
her, his heart overflowed with *. Lk 7:13
needing our * and encouragement, we 2Co 1:3,4
family, full of * toward each 1Pe 3:8

SYMPHONY
Make a joyful * before the Lord, Ps 98:6

SYMPTOMS
If he finds these *, it is an Lev 13:11

SYNAGOGUE
local * came and worshiped him. Mt 9:18
Then he went over to the *, and Mt 12:9
the *, with many following him. Mt 12:15
and taught there in the * and Mt 13:53,54
and in the reserved pews in the *! Mt 23:6
worship—the *—where he preached. Mk 1:21
Then, leaving the *, he and his Mk 1:29,30
went over to the * again, and Mk 3:1
The leader of the local *, whose Mk 5:22
he went to the * to teach, and the Mk 6:2,3
as usual to the * on Saturday, and Lk 4:16
in the * gazed at him intently. Lk 4:20
there in the * every Saturday. Lk 4:31
Once as he was teaching in the *, Lk 4:33
After leaving the * that day, he Lk 4:38
he was in the * teaching, and a man Lk 6:6
paid personally to build us a *!" Lk 7:5
leader of a Jewish *, came and fell Lk 8:41
was teaching in a *, he saw a Lk 13:10
in charge of the * was very angry Lk 13:14
this sermon in the * in Capernaum. Jn 6:59
excommunicate them from the *; Jn 12:42
regularly in the * and Temple; Jn 18:20
at once to the * to tell everyone Act 9:20
went to the Jewish * and preached. Act 13:5
went into the * for the services. Act 13:14
As the people left the * that Act 13:42
worshiped at the * followed Paul Act 13:43
together to the * and preached with Act 14:1
where there was a Jewish *. Act 17:1
they went to the * to preach. Act 17:10
He went to the * for discussions Act 17:17
Each Sabbath found Paul at the *, Act 18:4
God and lived next door to the *. Act 18:7
the leader of the *, and all his Act 18:8
new leader of the *, and beat him Act 18:17
* for a discussion with the Jews. Act 18:19
in the *, "The Messiah is coming! Act 18:25,26
Then Paul went to the * and Act 19:8
in every * who believed on you. Act 22:19
* or on the streets of any city; Act 24:12

SYNAGOGUES
in the Jewish *, everywhere Mt 4:23
trumpets in the * and streets to Mt 6:2
the * where everyone can see them. Mt 6:5
in the Jewish * and announcing the Mt 9:35
and tried, and whipped in the *. Mt 10:17
with whips in your *, and hound Mt 23:34
preaching in the * and releasing Mk 1:39
best seats in the *, and at the Mk 12:39
and beaten in the *, and accused Mk 13:9
region for his sermons in the *; Lk 4:15
preaching in * throughout Judea. Lk 4:44
of honor in the * and the Lk 11:43
authorities in the *, don't be Lk 12:11
the * and at religious festivals! Lk 20:46

(SYNAGOGUES Con't)
be dragged into * and prisons and Lk 21:12
from the *, and indeed the time is Jn 16:2
addressed to * in Damascus, Act 9:2
against in Jewish * in every city Act 15:21

SYNTYCHE
two dear women, Euodias and *. Php 4:2

SYPHILIS
in anguish and in shame, when * Pro 5:11

SYRACUSE
Our first stop was *, where we Act 28:12

SYRIA
Later the man moved to * and Ju 1:26
of eastern * conquer them. Ju 3:8
and the gods of *, Sidon, Moab, Ju 10:6
he had taken from *, Moab, Ammon, 2Sa 8:11,12
Ben-hadad of *, with this message: 1Ki 15:18
anoint Hazael to be king of *. 1Ki 19:15
KING BEN-HADAD OF * now 1Ki 20:1
another attack by the king of *." 1Ki 20:22
was no war between * and Israel. 1Ki 22:1
For the king of * had commanded 1Ki 22:31
THE KING OF * had high admiration 2Ki 5:1
Once when the king of * was at 2Ki 6:8
The king of * was puzzled. 2Ki 6:11
So one night the king of * sent a 2Ki 6:14
King Ben-hadad of * mustered his 2Ki 6:24
*), where King Ben-hadad lay sick. 2Ki 8:7
the king of *, has sent me to ask 2Ki 8:8,9
are going to be the king of *." 2Ki 8:13
the king of *, at Ramoth-gilead. 2Ki 8:28
the forces of King Hazael of *. 2Ki 9:14
About this time, King Hazael of * 2Ki 12:17
King Hazael of * and his son 2Ki 13:3
king of * was oppressing Israel. 2Ki 13:4
for the king of * had destroyed 2Ki 13:7
arrow, full of victory over *; 2Ki 13:16,17
would have beaten * until they were 2Ki 13:19
King Hazael of * had oppressed 2Ki 13:22
Then King Hazael of * died, and 2Ki 13:24
King Rezin of * and King Pekah of 2Ki 15:37
Then King Rezin of * and King 2Ki 16:5
time King Rezin of * recovered the 2Ki 16:6
recovered the city of Elath for *; 2Ki 16:6
attacking armies of * and Israel. 2Ki 16:7
Damascus, the capital of *. 2Ki 16:9
and King Rezin of * was killed. 2Ki 16:9
the kings of the Hittites and *. 2Ch 1:17
*, at Damascus, with this message: 2Ch 16:2
in the king of * instead of in the 2Ch 16:7
king of * has escaped from you. 2Ch 16:7
Now the king of * had issued 2Ch 18:30
from beyond the Salt Sea, from *. 2Ch 20:2
King Hazael of * at Ramoth-gilead. 2Ch 22:5
the king of * to defeat him and 2Ch 28:5
the kings of *, they would help him 2Ch 28:23
he was at war with *, with the Ps 60:1
by King Rezin of * and King Pekah Is 7:1
the royal court, "* is allied with Is 7:2
Yes, the kings of * and Israel Is 7:5
the capital of * alone, and King Is 7:8
so much—the kings of Israel and * Is 7:15,16
Do your worst, O * and Israel, Is 8:9,10
to surrender to * and Israel. Is 8:11
of * and Israel attacking you. Is 8:12
message to Damascus, capital of *: Is 17:1
remnant of * shall be destroyed. Is 17:3
Antigonus of * and Asia Minor, and Dan 8:8f
be formed between the king of * Dan 11:6
Seleucid wars between Egypt and *. Dan 11:6f
king of * as a gesture of peace, Dan 11:6
to Antiochus II of * to conclude a Dan 11:6f
the king of *, and march against Dan 11:7
"Meanwhile the king of * Dan 11:9
vast forces of * and defeat them. Dan 11:10,11
Jacob fled to * and earned a Hos 12:12
people of * shall return to Kir Amo 1:5
Or, "for the cities of * belong Zec 9:1f
be healed from as far away as *. Mt 4:24
when Quirinius was governor of *. Lk 2:2
before he moved to *, Act 7:2
city in the area we now know as *. Act 7:2f
in *, until his father died. Act 7:4
in Antioch, * and Cilicia. Act 15:23
left for * and Cilicia, to Act 15:40,41
for the coast of *, taking Act 18:18
to sail for * when he discovered a Act 20:3
in *, where the ship unloaded. Act 21:3
visit I went to * and Cilicia. Gal 1:21

SYRIAC
The translation here follows the * Zec 11:13f

SYRIAN
twenty thousand * mercenaries from 2Sa 10:6
by additional * troops summoned by 2Sa 10:15,16
resold to the Hittite and * kings. 1Ki 10:29
Then the * king sent this message 1Ki 20:10
Each one killed a * soldier, and 1Ki 20:20
entire * army panicked and fled. 1Ki 20:20
and most of the * army was killed 1Ki 20:21
he called up the * army and marched 1Ki 20:26
to the vast * forces that filled 1Ki 20:27
And the Israelis killed 100,000 * 1Ki 20:29
As the * army advanced upon them, 2Ki 6:18
And after that the * raiders 2Ki 6:23
out and surrender to the * army. 2Ki 7:4
had made the whole * army hear the 2Ki 7:6
the * camp and no one was there! 2Ki 7:10
troops in Damascus, the * capital. 1Ch 18:6
commander-in-chief of the * army. 1Ch 19:17,18
So when the * charioteers saw 2Ch 18:31
But one of the * soldiers shot 2Ch 18:33
A few months later the * army 2Ch 24:23
for the tiny * army, but the Lord 2Ch 24:24
Helbon, and white * wool to trade Eze 27:18
he will leave the * king alone. Dan 11:8
However, the sons of this * king Dan 11:10,11
"A few years later the * king Dan 11:13
Then the * king and his allies Dan 11:15
"The * king will march onward Dan 11:16
"The * king will then return Dan 11:28
to retreat, the * king will again Dan 11:30,31
healed Naaman, a *, rather than the Lk 4:27
for the * province of Phoenicia. Act 21:2

SYRIANS
thousand * from Damascus when they 2Sa 8:5
Damascus, and the * became David's 2Sa 8:6
Literally, "*." 2Sa 8:13f
city while the * from Zobah, Rehob, 2Sa 10:7,8
out to fight the * in the fields. 2Sa 10:9
against the *, come out and help 2Sa 10:11
attacked, the * began to run away. 2Sa 10:13
Ammonites saw the * running, they 2Sa 10:14
to Jerusalem. The * now realized 2Sa 10:15,16
Helam, where the * attacked him. 2Sa 10:17
But again the * fled from the 2Sa 10:18
saw that the * had been defeated, 2Sa 10:19
And the * were afraid to help the 2Sa 10:19
"Because the * have declared, 'The 1Ki 20:28
realize that the * are still 1Ki 22:3
you will push the * around with 1Ki 22:11
Bands of * had invaded the land 2Ki 5:2
place) "for the * are planning to 2Ki 6:9
the *, but there was no one there! 2Ki 7:5
has happened. The * know we are 2Ki 7:12
to see where the * had gone. 2Ki 7:14
away by the * in their haste. 2Ki 7:15
and plundered the camp of the *. 2Ki 7:16
them from the tyranny of the *; 2Ki 13:5
completely conquer the * at Aphek. 2Ki 13:16,17
he drove out the Jews and sent * 2Ki 16:6
of Chaldeans, *, Moabites, and 2Ki 24:2
When the * arrived from Damascus 1Ch 18:5
So the *, too, were forced to 1Ch 18:6
sent one group to engage the *. 1Ch 19:10
"If the * are too strong for me, 1Ch 19:12
attacked the *, and the Syrians 1Ch 19:14
and the * turned and fled. 1Ch 19:14
saw that the * were retreating, 1Ch 19:15
After their defeat, the * 1Ch 19:16
But the * again fled from David, 1Ch 19:17,18
And never again did the * aid the 1Ch 19:19
gore the * to death with these!" 2Ch 18:10
to fight the *, but just as the sun 2Ch 18:34
When the * left—leaving Joash 2Ch 24:25
enemies against you—the * on the Is 9:11,12
Elamites are the archers; * Is 22:6,7
Decreeing that the * should go Amo 1:5f
as slaves, for the * had made their Amo 1:5f
from Caphtor and the * out of Kir. Amo 9:7

SYRO-ARABIAN
meaning the * deserts, peopled by Eze 20:35,36f

SYROPHOENICIAN
(But she was *—a "despised Mk 7:26

SYRTIS
they should be cast upon the *." Act 27:17f

SYSTEM
They set up a collection * for 2Ch 34:9
passes through the digestive *." Mk 7:19
I follow that * of serving the Act 24:14
Yet that old * of law that led to 2Co 3:7
So if the old * that faded into 2Co 3:11
of that impossible * by taking the Gal 3:13
But this * of law was to last Gal 3:19
the center of that * of trying to Gal 4:24,25
that *, are her slave children. Gal 4:24,25
annul that whole * of Jewish laws. Eph 2:15
Yes, the old * of priesthood Heb 7:18
ones died off, the * could still be Heb 7:23
Under the old *, even the high Heb 7:28
the old Jewish * of sacrifices. Heb 8:4
that under the old * the common Heb 9:8
* it represents were still in use. Heb 9:8
For under the old *, gifts and Heb 9:9
For the old * dealt only with Heb 9:10
this better * which we now have. Heb 9:11
And if under the old * the blood Heb 9:13
while still under that old *. Heb 9:15
THE OLD * of Jewish laws gave only Heb 10:1
The sacrifices under the old * Heb 10:1
*, he then added, "Here I am. Heb 10:8
He cancels the first * in favor of Heb 10:9
Under the * of Jewish laws the Heb 13:11

SYSTEMATICALLY
to search the land * for any Eze 39:14

SYSTEMS
rebuilding the old * I have been Gal 2:18

TAANACH
The king of *; Jos 12:8-24
Dor, En-dor, *, Megiddo (where Jos 17:11
gave the cities of * and Jos 21:25
in Beth-shean, *, Dor, Ibleam, Ju 1:27
The kings of Canaan fought in * Ju 5:19
whose area was * and Megiddo, all 1Ki 4:8-19
Beth-shean, *, Megiddo, and Dor. 1Ch 7:29

TAANATH-SHILOH
continued on past * and Janoah. Jos 16:5,6

TABAL
as Mushki, *, Gimaraya, Tegerama, Eze 38:2,3f

TABBAOTH
Ziha, Hasupha, *, Keros, Siaha, Ez 2:43-54
Ziha, Hasupha, *, Keros, Neh 7:46-56

TABBATH
the border of Abel-meholah near *. Ju 7:22

TABE-EL
Bishlam, Mithredath, and * and Ez 4:7

TABEEL
the son of * as their king.' Is 7:6

TABERAH
Literally, "*." Num 11:3f
"Again at * and once again at Deu 9:22

TABERNACLE
it was kept in the Ark in the *. Ex 16:34
mine shall be a tent pavilion—a *. Ex 25:9
so that the *, the dwelling place Ex 26:6
"The roof of the * is made of Ex 26:7,8
five bars on each side of the *. Ex 26:26,27
the way from end to end of the *. Ex 26:28
"[Inside the * Ex 26:31
"Then make a courtyard for the * Ex 27:9,10
in the work of the *, including all Ex 27:19
the *, to burn there continually. Ex 27:20
sons go into the * or to the altar Ex 28:43
entrance of the *, along with the Ex 29:3,4
young bull to the *, and Aaron and Ex 29:10
Lord, at the entrance of the *. Ex 29:11
in the * and the Holy Place. Ex 29:30
the basket, at the door of the *. Ex 29:32
at the door of the * before the Ex 29:42
* shall be sanctified by my glory. Ex 29:43
Yes, I will sanctify the * and Ex 29:44
this money for the care of the *; Ex 30:16
Put it between the * and the Ex 30:17,18
they go into the * to appear before Ex 30:20
"to anoint the *, the Ark, the Ex 30:26,27
where I meet with you in the *; Ex 30:36
the * and everything it contains. Ex 31:3
instructed you to make: the *; Ex 31:7
all the furnishings of the *; Ex 31:7
Whenever Moses went to the *, all Ex 33:8
of Nun), stayed behind in the *. Ex 33:11
to the * of the Lord your God. Ex 34:26
but whenever he went into the * Ex 34:34
The * tent, and its coverings, Ex 35:10-19
The curtain for the door of the *; Ex 35:10-19
The posts of the * court, and Ex 35:10-19
materials for the *, its equipment, Ex 35:21
and furnishing the *." Ex 36:1
to form the ceiling of the *. Ex 36:13
For the sides of the * he used Ex 36:20
north side of the *, with forty Ex 36:25,26
The west side of the *, which Ex 36:27
five for each side of the *. Ex 36:31,32
drapery for the entrance to the *; Ex 36:37
at the entrance to the *. Ex 38:8
the * and court were bronze. Ex 38:20
in building the * to house the Ark, Ex 38:21
which was used throughout the *. Ex 38:24
entrance to the *, and for the Ex 38:29
of the * and the court. Ex 38:29
And so at last the * was Ex 39:32
Then they brought the entire * to Ex 39:33-40
The curtain-door of the *; Ex 39:33-40
used there in the work of the *. Ex 39:33-40
"Put together the * on the first Ex 40:2
entrance of the *, and place the Ex 40:5
and there upon the * and everything Ex 40:9
of the * and wash them with water; Ex 40:12
year, the * was put together. Ex 40:17
the Ark into the * and set up the Ex 40:21
table, on the south side of the *. Ex 40:24
altar in the * next to the veil, Ex 40:26
entrance of the *, and placed the Ex 40:28
altar to enter the *, they stopped Ex 40:32
Then the cloud covered the * and Ex 40:34
glory of the Lord filled the *. Ex 40:35
The cloud rested upon the * Ex 40:38
to Moses from the *, and commanded Lev 1:1
entrance of the * where the priests Lev 1:2,3
altar at the entrance of the *. Lev 1:5
and kill it at the door of the *. Lev 3:2
kill it at the entrance of the *; Lev 3:7,8
kill it at the entrance of the *. Lev 3:13
to the door of the *, and shall lay Lev 4:4

(TABERNACLE Con't)
blood into the *, and shall dip Lev 4:5
altar before the Lord in the *; Lev 4:7
at the entrance to the *. Lev 4:7
it to the * where the leaders Lev 4:14
its blood into the *, and shall Lev 4:16
altar there in the * before the Lev 4:18
altar, at the entrance to the *. Lev 4:18
bring his guilt offering to the *. Lev 6:4,5
yeast in the courtyard of the *. Lev 6:16
eat it in the courtyard of the *. Lev 6:26
is taken into the *, to make Lev 6:30
entrance of the *, together with Lev 8:1
it upon the * itself and on each Lev 8:10
entrance of the *, and eat it along Lev 8:31
not to leave the * entrance for Lev 8:33
* day and night for seven days. Lev 8:35
entrance of the *, as Moses had Lev 9:5
Moses and Aaron went into the *. Lev 9:23
from before the *, and carry them Lev 10:4
But you are not to leave the * Lev 10:7
you go into the *, lest you die; Lev 10:8,9
anything sacred, nor enter the *. Lev 12:4
the door of the * to the priest; Lev 12:6
the Lord at the entrance of the *. Lev 14:11
are killed, there at the *; Lev 14:13
entrance of the * on the eighth Lev 14:23
*, and give them to the priest. Lev 15:14
entrance of the *, and the priest Lev 15:29
my * that is among them." Lev 15:31
entrance of the *, and cast lots Lev 16:7
and for the *, located right among Lev 16:16
be inside the * when Aaron enters Lev 16:17
Place, the entire *, and the altar. Lev 16:20
"Then Aaron shall go into the * Lev 16:23
and leave them there in the *. Lev 16:23
sanctuary, the *, the altar, the Lev 16:33
except at the * is guilty of murder Lev 17:3,4
entrance of the *, and to burn the Lev 17:5
entrance of the *, and to burn the Lev 17:6
entrance of the *, where it will be Lev 17:8,9
the Lord at the entrance of the *; Lev 19:21
reverence my *, for I am the Lord. Lev 19:30
child to Molech, thus making my * Lev 20:3
nor treat my * like an ordinary Lev 21:12
reverence my *, for I am the Lord. Lev 26:2
(He was in the * at the camp of Num 1:1
with the * and its transportation. Num 1:50
They are to live near the *, and Num 1:50
and whenever the * is moved, the Num 1:51
around the * as a wall between the Num 1:53
tribal compounds will be the *." Num 2:1
East of the * Num 2:3-31
side of the * Num 2:3-31
west side of * Num 2:3-31
North side of * Num 2:3-31
march was the *, with the Levites. Num 2:3-31
set apart to minister at the *. Num 3:3
duties at the * on behalf of all Num 3:7,8,9
and maintenance of the *. Num 3:7,8,9
West side of * Num 3:16-24
the care of the *: its coverings, Num 3:25-30
surrounding the *, the altar, and Num 3:25-30
used in tying the * together. Num 3:25-30
Southside of the * Num 3:25-30
used in the *, the veil, and any Num 3:31-35
North side of * Num 3:31-35
of the frames of the * building; Num 3:36,37
The area east of the * was Num 3:38
for the * on behalf of the people Num 3:38
into the *, was to be executed. Num 3:38
who are able to work in the *. Num 4:3
will enter the * first and take Num 4:5
utensils of the * are to be wrapped Num 4:12
of the entire * and everything in Num 4:16
for the sacred work of the *. Num 4:21,22,23
curtains of the *, the Tabernacle Num 4:25
Tabernacle, the * itself with its Num 4:25
the curtain for the * entrance. Num 4:25
surrounds the altar and the *. Num 4:26
are eligible for the * service. Num 4:29
When the * is moved, they are to Num 4:30,31
the frames of the *, the bars, the Num 4:30,31
eligible for the * service, and Num 4:35
eligible for the * service and Num 4:46,47,48
it dust from the floor of the *. Num 5:17
priest at the entrance of the *. Num 6:10
entrance of the * and offer a Num 6:13
entrance of the *, after which the Num 6:18
each part of the *, including the Num 7:1
to the Lord in front of the *. Num 7:3
wagons for the work of the *. Num 7:4,5
of the * upon their shoulders. Num 7:9
When Moses went into the * to Num 7:89
of the * as all the people watch. Num 8:9
and out of the * to do their work. Num 8:15
of Israel in the *, and will offer Num 8:19
ordinary people entered the *." Num 8:19
After that they went into the * Num 8:22
serving in the * at the age of Num 8:23,24
duties in the *, but will have no Num 8:25,26
On the day the * was raised, the Num 9:15
If the Cloud stayed above the * Num 9:22
gather at the entrance of the *. Num 10:3
side of the * shall leave first; Num 10:5,6,7
The Cloud lifted from the * on Num 10:11
The * was taken down and the men Num 10:17
the * upon their shoulders. Num 10:17
sanctuary. (The * was already Num 10:21
bring them to the *, to stand Num 11:16
So Moses left the * and reported Num 11:24
and placed them around the *. Num 11:24
and Miriam to the *: "Come here, Num 12:3,4
stood at the entrance of the *. Num 12:5
from above the *, Miriam suddenly Num 12:10
as you work in the * of Jehovah, Num 16:8,9
of the * with Moses and Aaron. Num 16:18
looked toward the *, the Cloud Num 16:42
the *, and the Lord said to Moses, Num 16:43,44
to Moses at the entrance of the *; Num 16:50
inner room of the * where I meet Num 17:4
inner room of the *, and when he Num 17:7
even comes close to the * dies. Num 17:12,13
the sacred duties in the * itself. Num 18:2,3
assistants for the work of the *. Num 18:6
for their service in the *. Num 18:31
times towards the front of the *. Num 19:4
has defiled the * of the Lord, and Num 19:13
entrance of the *, where they fell Num 20:6
were weeping at the door of the *. Num 25:6
entrance of the * to give a Num 27:1
*, for it is the Lord's portion." Num 31:30
was taken into the * and kept there Num 31:54
Summon Joshua and come into the * Deu 31:14
great cloud at the * entrance, and Deu 31:15
at Shiloh to set up the *. Jos 18:1
There at the * at Shiloh the Jos 18:10
the entrance of the * at Shiloh. Jos 19:51
among us in his *, and we will Jos 22:19
Only the altar in front of the * Jos 22:29
oak tree that was beside the *. Jos 24:26
long as the * remained at Shiloh. Ju 18:31
journeyed to the * at Shiloh to 1Sa 1:3
Shiloh, Hannah went over to the *. 1Sa 1:9
* to worship the Lord once more. 1Sa 1:19,20
annual trip to the * without 1Sa 1:21,22
to the * and leave him there." 1Sa 1:21,22
took him to the * in Shiloh, along 1Sa 1:24
So she left him there at the * 1Sa 1:28
assisted at the entrance to the *. 1Sa 2:22
him there at the * in Shiloh, and 1Sa 3:21,4:1
placed before the Lord in the *. 1Sa 21:6
Then David went into the * and 2Sa 7:18
into the * and worshiped the Lord. 2Sa 12:20
to see the Ark and the * again. 2Sa 15:25,26
the * and poured it over Solomon; 1Ki 1:39
Adonijah rushed into the * and 1Ki 1:49,50
sanctuary in the *, and pleading 1Ki 1:51
he ran to the * for sanctuary and 1Ki 2:28
Benaiah went into the * and said 1Ki 2:30
So Benaiah returned to the * and 1Ki 2:34
to Jerusalem and went into the *. 1Ki 3:15
the Lord from the * in Zion, the 1Ki 8:1
at the time of the * Festival in 1Ki 8:2
had previously been in the *. 1Ki 8:3,4
that the annual * Festival would be 1Ki 12:32,33
praise God in the * after he had 1Ch 6:31
to various other tasks in the *. 1Ch 6:48
had supervised and guarded the *. 1Ch 9:19
of the entrance to the *. 1Ch 9:21
were in charge of the Lord's *. 1Ch 9:23
and treasuries in the * of God. 1Ch 9:26
lived near the *, and they opened 1Ch 9:27
also built a new * to house the Ark 1Ch 15:1
of the Ark into the new *. 1Ch 15:3
ARK of God was brought into the *. 1Ch 16:1
choirs in the * to sing 1Ch 16:7
to minister regularly at the *, 1Ch 16:37
Meanwhile the old * of the Lord 1Ch 16:39
to him again. The * and altar made 1Ch 21:29
need to carry the * and its 1Ch 23:26
And they took care of the * and 1Ch 23:32
DAVID AND THE officials of the * 1Ch 25:1
performed this ministry in the *. 1Ch 25:6,7
Moses had built the * 500 years 2Ch 1:2,3f
* constructed by Moses, the 2Ch 1:2,3
(There was a later * in 2Ch 1:4
front of the old *, and now Solomon 2Ch 1:5,6
Solomon then left the *, returned 2Ch 1:13
the Ark from the [* in the 2Ch 5:2
it out of the *, along with all the 2Ch 5:4,5
celebrated the * Festival, with 2Ch 7:8
whose clan became the * singers. Neh 11:22,23
in your * up on your holy hill? Ps 15:1
the Holy of Holies within the *. Ps 28:2f
I shall live forever in your *; Ps 61:4
with you within the holy * courts! Ps 65:4
Then he abandoned his * at Ps 78:60
as I destroyed the * at Shiloh, and Jer 26:6
you do each year at the * Feast. Hos 12:9
But soon it was time for the * Jn 7:2
or *, through the wilderness. Act 7:44
nations, this * was taken with them Act 7:45
Literally, "rebuild the * of Act 15:16f
model of the real * in heaven; Heb 8:5
ready to build the *, God warned Heb 8:5
* as shown to him on Mount Sinai. Heb 8:5
greater, perfect * in heaven, not Heb 9:11

TABERNACLE-TENT
"MAKE THE * from ten colored Ex 26:1
Set up this * in the manner I Ex 26:30
Set the washbasin between the * Ex 40:7

TABERNACLES
"The Festival of *: Five days Lev 23:33,34
Or, "Feast of *." Lev 23:33,34f
the Festival of *, when all Israel Deu 31:10,11
at the annual Festival of *. 2Ch 5:3
of Weeks, and the Festival of *. 2Ch 8:13
the Feast of * as prescribed in the Ez 3:4
of * to be held that month. Neh 8:14
Literally, "We will go into his * Ps 132:7f
Literally, "the Feast of *" or Zec 14:16f
Literally, "three *" or Mt 17:4f
receive you into the eternal *!" Lk 16:9f

TABITHA
Literally, "*," her name in Act 9:40f

TABLE
at a separate *, and the Egyptians Gen 43:32
was served to them from his own *. Gen 43:34
"Then make a * of acacia wood Ex 25:23
that will be used to carry the *. Ex 25:26,27
the Presence on the * before me. Ex 25:30
Place the * and lampstand across Ex 26:35
Place and the * on the north side. Ex 26:35
the Ark, the * and all its Ex 30:26,27
the * and its instruments; Ex 31:8
The *, its carrying poles, and all Ex 35:10-19
Then he made a *, using acacia Ex 37:10
the edges of the *, with a gold Ex 37:12
them into the four * legs, close Ex 37:13
spoons to be placed upon this *. Ex 37:15,16
The * and all its utensils; Ex 39:33-40
Then bring in the * and place Ex 40:4
Next he placed the * at the north Ex 40:22
Presence upon the * before the Ex 40:23
next to the *, on the south side of Ex 40:24
* that stands before the Lord. Lev 24:5-8
of the Ark, the *, the lampstand, Num 3:31-35
cloth over the * where the Bread of Num 4:7
the carrying poles into the *. Num 4:8
fed them the scraps under my *!" Ju 1:7
at the head of the *, honoring them 1Sa 9:22
when your place at the * is empty. 1Sa 20:18
Jonathan left the * in fierce 1Sa 20:34
all those who eat at your own *! 2Sa 19:28
the banquet * and fled in panic; 1Ki 1:49,50
This included the altar, the * 1Ki 7:48
foods on his *, the great number of 1Ki 10:5
sitting at the *, a message from 1Ki 13:20
we can put in a bed, a *, a 2Ki 4:10
he ate regularly at the king's *. 2Ki 25:29
the gold for the * on which the 1Ch 28:16
the altar, and the * for the Bread 2Ch 4:19
of the Presence upon the holy *. 2Ch 13:11
also the * of the Bread of the 2Ch 29:18
officials at my *, besides visitors Neh 5:17
from your own * and let them drink Ps 36:8
Literally, "their *." Ps 69:22f
around the dinner * as vigorous and Ps 128:3
my oil upon a * spread before you. Eze 23:41
Feast at my banquet *—feast on Eze 39:20
"This," he told me, "is the * Eze 41:22
Literally, "the * which is before Eze 41:22f
come to my * to minister to me; Eze 44:16
at the conference *, attempting to Dan 11:27
beneath the * are permitted to eat Mt 15:27
to sit at the head * at banquets, Mt 23:6
puppies under the * are given some Mk 7:28
Some of those at the * were Mk 14:4,5
sitting around the * eating, Jesus Mk 14:18
Then the men at the * said to Lk 7:49
the head of the *, he gave them Lk 14:7
seat is left at the foot of the *! Lk 14:9
man sitting at the * with Jesus Lk 14:15
the rich man's *, the dogs would Lk 16:21
all sat down together at the *; Lk 22:14
But here at this *, sitting Lk 22:21
* and is served by his servants. Lk 22:27
and drink at my * in that Kingdom; Lk 22:30
and Lazarus sat at the * with him. Jn 12:2
So he got up from the supper *, Jn 13:4
"There was one at the *." Jn 13:23f
the *, leaning on the left elbow. Jn 13:23f
to Jesus at the *, being his Jn 13:23
None of the others at the * knew Jn 13:28
wine at the Lord's *, this means, 1Co 10:16
* and at Satan's table, too. 1Co 10:21
Table and at Satan's *, too. 1Co 10:21
the Lord's * and at Satan's table. 1Co 10:21
the Lord's Table and at Satan's *. 1Co 10:21
Eat whatever is on the * and 1Co 10:27
has said about his *, and I have 1Co 11:23
candlestick and a * with special Heb 9:1

TABLE Con't)
Impenitence at the Communion * 1Jn 5:17f
TABLELAND
crossed the * of Medeba to Dibon; Jos 13:9
to beyond the * near Medeba. Jos 13:16
of the * and the kingdom of Sihon. Jos 13:21
All the cities of the * lie in Jer 48:21
TABLES
But the * are turned, and 1Ki 2:15
for the other gold *, and he 1Ch 28:16
the silver for the silver *. 1Ch 28:16
he also built ten * and placed 2Ch 4:8
the food at his *, and how many 2Ch 9:4
They load the * with food; Is 21:5
Their * are covered with vomit; Is 28:8
there were two * where the animals Eze 40:39
entrance, there were two more *. Eze 40:40
So, in all, there were eight *, Eze 40:41
There were also four stone * Eze 40:42
These * were about 2⅝ feet square Eze 40:42
hall, and on the * the flesh of the Eze 40:43
money-changers' * and the stalls of Mt 21:12
knocked over the * of the Mk 11:15
floor and turning over their *! Jn 2:15
TABLETS
I have written on * of stone, so Ex 24:12
inside it the * of stone I will Ex 25:16
the * of stone I shall give you. Ex 25:21
stone * engraved with God's laws. Ex 26:33
gave him the two * of stone on Ex 31:18
on both sides of two stone *. Ex 32:15
written the commandments on the *. Ex 32:16
anger he threw the * to the ground Ex 32:19
two stone * like the first ones and Ex 34:1
that were on the * you broke. Ex 34:1
So Moses took two * of stone like Ex 34:4
the two stone * in his hands. Ex 34:4
Ten Commandments—on the stone *. Ex 34:28
mountain with the * that his face Ex 34:29
stone * of the Ten Commandments); Lev 16:13
wrote them on two stone *. Deu 4:13
two stone * and gave them to me. Deu 5:22
with you—the stone * with the laws Deu 9:9
the contract, the * on which he had Deu 9:10,11
* inscribed with the laws of God. Deu 9:15
I lifted the * high above my Deu 9:17
cut two more stone * like the first Deu 10:1
rewrite on the * the same Deu 10:2
that were on the * I had smashed, Deu 10:2
out two stone * like the first two, Deu 10:3
the * up on the mountain to God. Deu 10:3
and placed the * in the Ark I had Deu 10:5
the two stone * which Moses had 1Ki 8:9
the two stone * which Moses had put 2Ch 5:10
rather than upon * of stone, as Jer 31:33f
Literally, "on the *." Hab 2:2f
In it they kept the stone * with Act 7:44
Inside the ark were the * of Heb 9:4
TABOR
*, Shahazumah, and Beth-shemesh— Jos 19:17-23
Lead them to Mount *, to fight Ju 4:6
camped at Mount *, he mobilized Ju 4:12
the slopes of Mount * into battle. Ju 4:14
Down from Mount * marched the Ju 5:13,14
killed at *—what were they like?" Ju 8:18
get to the oak of * you will see 1Sa 10:3
gave Rimmono and * to the Merari 1Ch 6:77
Mount * and Mount Hermon rejoice Ps 89:12
* or Mount Carmel by the sea! Jer 46:18
at Mizpah and *, and dug a deep Hos 5:1
TABULATION
Here is the final *: Num 1:20-46
TACK
You are sharp as a * in plotting Ps 52:2
TACKLE
* every task that comes along, Ecc 7:18
on broken masts with useless *. Is 33:23
they threw out the * and anything Act 27:19
TADMOR
He built * in the desert, and 2Ch 8:4
TAH-CHEMON
from *, known also as Adino, the 2Sa 23:8
TAHAN
named after their ancestor *. Num 26:28-37
*, the father of 1Ch 7:25,26,27
TAHANITES
The *, named after their ancestor Num 26:28-37
TAHASH
Reumah:Tebah, Gaham,*, Maacah. Gen 22:24
TAHATH
From Makheloth to *; Num 33:15-37
From * to Terah; Num 33:15-37
Elkanah, Ebiasaph, Assir, *, 1Ch 6:22,23,24
Zephaniah, *, Assir, Ebiasaph, 1Ch 6:33-38
Shuthelah, Bered, *, Eleadah, 1Ch 7:20,21
Eleadah, *, Zabad, Shuthelah, 1Ch 7:20,21
TAHPANHES
of Memphis and * to utterly destroy Jer 2:16
at the city of *, for they would Jer 43:7
Then at *, the Lord spoke to Jer 43:8
palace here in *, and tell the men Jer 43:9
cities of Migdol, * and Memphis, Jer 44:1
cities of Migdol, Memphis and *! Jer 46:14
TAHPENES
him a wife—the sister of Queen *. 1Ki 11:19
TAHRE-A
of Pithon, Melech, *, and Ahaz; 1Ch 9:41
TAHTIM-HODSHI
in the land of * and to Dan-jaan 2Sa 24:6
TAIL
told him, "Grab it by the *!" Ex 4:4
including the fat * and the fat Ex 29:22
altar the fat, the * removed close Lev 3:9,10,11
fat, including the *, the fat that Lev 7:3
Then he took the fat, the *, the Lev 8:25
head and not the *, and you shall Deu 28:13
the head and you shall be the *! Deu 28:44
oxen standing * to tail, three 1Ki 7:25
oxen standing tail to *, three 1Ki 7:25
oxen standing * to tail, three 2Ch 4:4
standing tail to *, three facing 2Ch 4:4
His * is as straight as a cedar. Job 40:17
on his heads. His * drew along Rev 12:4
TAILOR
in charge of the palace * shop. 2Ki 22:14
(Shallum was the king's *, living 2Ch 34:22
them made by his *, but the Job 27:17
"Must God * his justice to your Job 34:33
TAILORED
the beautifully * garments to be Ex 39:41
TAILORS
special skill as * to make the Ex 28:3
purple robes that expert * make. Jer 10:9
TAILS
fat from their * and the fat Lev 9:19
and tied their * together in pairs, Ju 15:4
They had stinging * like Rev 9:10
for five months, was in their *. Rev 9:10
but in their * as well, for their Rev 9:19
as well, for their * were similar Rev 9:19
TAINTED
but this was a * word because Hos 1:16f
TAKE
and for sacrifice: * seven pairs of Gen 7:2
Here, * her and be gone!" Gen 12:19
I'll tell you what we'll do. * Gen 13:9
that I will not * so much as a Gen 14:23
Then Jehovah told him to * a Gen 15:9
"Hurry," they said to Lot, "* Gen 19:15
"* with you your only son—yes, Gen 22:2
"Then shall I * Isaac there, to Gen 24:5
are you to * my son there." Gen 24:8
so what can we say? * her and go! Gen 24:51
die 'most any day. * your bow and Gen 27:2,3,4
from them. Then * it to your Gen 27:8,9,10
Let me * my wives and Gen 30:26
He gave them to Jacob's sons to * Gen 30:35,36
"I said to myself, 'He'll * his Gen 31:31
my daughters, or * other wives, I Gen 31:50
Please * my gifts. Gen 33:11
Otherwise we will * her and be Gen 34:17
the Adullamite to * the young goat Gen 38:20
ran, and forgot to * his jacket." Gen 39:14,15
is going to * you out of prison and Gen 40:13
now Pharaoh will * off your head Gen 40:18,19
I'm going to * a chance that you Gen 42:19
here with me and * grain for your Gen 42:33
now you want to * Benjamin too! Gen 42:36
of the land. * them to the man as Gen 43:11
and almonds. * double money so Gen 43:12
and * your brother and go. Gen 43:13
with me this noon. * them home and Gen 43:16
And if you * away his brother Gen 44:29
that I would * care of the lad. Gen 44:32
I will * care of you there" ' Gen 45:11,12
And tell your brothers to * Gen 45:19
he couldn't * it in. Gen 45:26
But when I am dead, * me out of Gen 47:30
Joseph swear to * his body back to Gen 50:5
Indeed, I myself will * care of Gen 50:21
land of Egypt and * you back to the Gen 50:24
that they would * his body back Gen 50:25
"* this child home and nurse him Ex 2:9
God told him. "* off your shoes, Ex 3:5
Egyptians and to * them out of Ex 3:8
undergoing, and to * them to the Ex 3:17
two signs, then * water from the Ex 4:9
And be sure to * your rod along Ex 4:17
"We must * a three days' trip Ex 5:3
with God to * the frogs away, and I Ex 8:8
We must * a three-day trip into Ex 8:27
Aaron, "* ashes from the kiln. Ex 9:8
"We will * everything with us; Ex 10:9
not let you * your little ones!" Ex 10:10
your God to * away this death. Ex 10:17
you can even * your children with Ex 10:24
"No," Moses said, "we must * Ex 10:25
and * all your people with you.' Ex 11:8
a basin, and then * a cluster of Ex 12:22
as you said. * your flocks and Ex 12:32
rise to * with them on the trip. Ex 12:39
that they would * his bones with Ex 13:19
Lord: they were to * three quarts Ex 16:32
did you ever * us out of Egypt? Ex 17:3
Then Jehovah said to Moses, "* Ex 17:5,6
going to * care of us or not?" Ex 17:7
they can * care of themselves. Ex 18:22
the neighbor must * an oath that he Ex 22:11
If you * his clothing as a Ex 22:26
you must * it back to its owner. Ex 23:4
"* no bribes, for a bribe makes Ex 23:8
* away sickness from among you. Ex 23:25
linen. * two onyx stones, and Ex 28:9
Then * the anointing oil and Ex 29:7
Then * all the fat that covers Ex 29:13
Then * the body, including the Ex 29:14
"Now * the other ram, and Aaron Ex 29:19,20
"Then * the fat of the ram, Ex 29:22
Afterwards, * them from their Ex 29:25
Then * the breast of Aaron's Ex 29:26
"* the ram of consecration—the Ex 29:31
"Whenever you * a census of the Ex 30:11,12
been telling me, '* these people to Ex 33:12
"* the anointing oil and Ex 40:9
A priest will * the bird to the Lev 1:15,16,17
Then he is to * a handful, Lev 2:2
and he shall * it to the altar to Lev 2:8
Then the priest shall * the Lev 4:5
Then he shall * all the fat on Lev 4:8
Then the priest shall * some of Lev 4:25
And the priest shall * some of Lev 4:30
The priest shall * some of the Lev 4:34
the priest shall * out a handful as Lev 5:12
The priest shall then * out a Lev 6:15
and told Aaron to * a bull calf Lev 9:2
and Ithamar, "* the grain Lev 10:12
given it to you to * away the Lev 10:17
She must * them to the door of the Lev 12:6
food, and shall * some cedar wood, Lev 14:4
day, he shall * two male lambs Lev 14:10
The priest shall * one of the Lev 14:12
The priest shall * the blood Lev 14:14
"Then the priest shall * the Lev 14:15
The priest shall * the lamb for Lev 14:24
On the eighth day he shall * two Lev 15:14
from him, he shall * a complete Lev 15:16
"On the eighth day, she shall * Lev 15:29
family, he shall * a censer full Lev 16:12
again and * off the linen garments Lev 16:23
Canaan where I am going to * you. Lev 18:3
"Do not * advantage of Lev 19:33
On the first day, * boughs of Lev 23:40
And the Lord said to Moses, "* Lev 24:13,14
"* a census of all the men Num 1:2-15
to * it down and set it up again; Num 1:51
telling him, "* a census of the Num 3:14,15
to Moses, "Now * a census of all Num 3:40
the sanctuary shalt thou * them. Num 3:47,48f
Moses and Aaron, "* a census of Num 4:1
first and * down the veil and cover Num 4:5
And the Lord said to Moses, "* a Num 4:21,22,23
"Now * a census of the Merari Num 4:29
the Lord, and * holy water in a Num 5:17
"Then the priest shall * the Num 5:25
He shall * a handful, Num 5:26
the priest shall * the roasted Num 6:19
there and I will * of the Spirit Num 11:17
"Let's elect a leader to * us Num 14:4
* care of them in the wilderness. Num 14:16
those with you, * censers tomorrow Num 16:6,7
to Aaron, "Quick, * a censer and Num 16:46
and he shall * her outside the camp Num 19:1
Eleazar shall * some of her Num 19:4
Eleazar shall * cedar wood and Num 19:6
not defiled shall * hyssop branches Num 19:18
This shall * place on the third Num 19:19
at Meribah. Now * Aaron and his Num 20:25
Pray to him to * away the Num 21:7
will * you to yet another place. Num 23:27
the priest), "* a census of all Num 26:2
in him, and * him to Eleazar the Num 27:19
THEN THE LORD said to Moses, "* Num 31:1
"Some of you must * arms to wage Num 31:3
I have given the land to you; * Num 33:53
Encourage him as he prepares to * Deu 1:38
War against him and begin to * Deu 2:24
And the Lord will * away all Deu 7:15
Do not * it or it will be a snare Deu 7:25
and will go in and * over the land Deu 8:1
I didn't even * a drink of water. Deu 9:9
him and * oaths by his name alone. Deu 10:20
and herds and * the money to the Deu 14:25
with you— then * an awl and pierce Deu 15:17
violated—you shall * the case to Deu 17:8
of that city shall * a heifer that Deu 21:3
your wife, * her home with you. Deu 21:12
and mother shall * him before the Deu 21:19
see it; * it back to its owner. Deu 22:1
who the owner is, * it to your farm Deu 22:2
don't * the mother with the young. Deu 22:6
Let her go, and * only the Deu 22:7
the judges shall * the girl to the Deu 22:21
You may * interest from a Deu 23:20

(TAKE Con't)
For if you * interest from a Deu 23:20
do not * any away in a container. Deu 23:24
"It is illegal to * a millstone Deu 24:6
to sleep in it. * it back to him at Deu 24:12,13
The priest will then * the Deu 26:4
milk and honey'—* out boulders from Deu 27:2,3,4
Lord your God will * his curses and Deu 30:7,8
the priests, "* up the Ark and Jos 3:6
tribe, each to * a stone from where Jos 4:2,3
up to * their fathers' places. Jos 5:7
"* off your shoes," the Jos 5:15
Don't * any loot, for everything Jos 6:18
city and it won't * more than two Jos 7:3
or discouraged; * the entire army Jos 8:1
He would * care of them in other Jos 13:33
a god, let him * care of himself Ju 6:31
Baal * care of himself!" Ju 6:32
Gideon, "Get up! * your troops and Ju 7:8,9
to the camp alone—* along your Ju 7:10
the Lord and I cannot * it back." Ju 11:35
to capture you and * you to the Ju 15:12,13
Here, * my virgin daughter and Ju 19:24
and catch them and * them home with Ju 21:21
to * refuge, bless you for it." Ru 2:12
for if you don't * it, I will. Ru 4:4
May he restore your youth and * Ru 4:15
and began to * her meals again. 1Sa 1:18
and then I will * him to the 1Sa 1:21,22
replied, "* as much as you want, 1Sa 2:16
"No, give it to me now or I'll * 1Sa 2:16
other children to * the place of 1Sa 2:20
The decision was to * it to Gath. 1Sa 5:8
He will * your daughters from 1Sa 8:13
He will * away the best of your 1Sa 8:14
He will * a tenth of your 1Sa 8:15
from a trip to * part in a public 1Sa 9:12,13
* them to a Philistine blacksmith. 1Sa 13:20
of Israel. Now * a vial of olive 1Sa 16:1
"* a heifer with you," the Lord 1Sa 16:2
One day Jesse said to David, "* 1Sa 17:17
Literally, "* their pledge." 1Sa 17:18f
"I'll * care of this 1Sa 17:32
and * the lamb from its mouth. 1Sa 17:35
to arrest David and * him to Saul, 1Sa 19:14
go to Bethlehem to * part in a 1Sa 20:28,29
him to * them back to the city. 1Sa 20:40
* that if you want it, for there 1Sa 21:9
Should I * my bread and my water 1Sa 25:11
But I'll tell you what—we'll * 1Sa 26:11
I can to * away the entire kingdom 2Sa 3:9,10
begged him to * a bite of supper. 2Sa 3:35,36
a command. * courage and do it!" 2Sa 13:28
"And I'll * the responsibility 2Sa 14:9
Go on back and * your troops with 2Sa 15:19,20
and we can * ropes and drag the 2Sa 17:13
they were to * to King David. 2Sa 17:17
"I will * care of you there." 2Sa 19:33
Quick, * my bodyguard and chase 2Sa 20:6
of his army, "* a census of all 2Sa 24:2
he said to them, "* Solomon and my 1Ki 1:33
and General Joab would * over!" 1Ki 2:22
May the Lord * revenge on you, 1Ki 2:44
laws, then I will * away the 1Ki 9:7
I will * them from this Temple 1Ki 9:7
I will * the kingdom away from 1Ki 11:12,13
to Jeroboam, "* ten of these 1Ki 11:31
I will not * the kingdom from 1Ki 11:34
" 'But I will * away the kingdom 1Ki 11:35
I am to * you home with me and 1Ki 13:18
become king. * him a gift of ten 1Ki 14:3
his officials to * to Damascus, to 1Ki 15:18
told the Lord. "* away my life. 1Ki 19:4
will * away whatever they like!" 1Ki 20:5,6
"* them alive," Ben-hadad 1Ki 20:18
Then * him out and execute him." 1Ki 21:10
"* him to Amon, the mayor of the 1Ki 22:26
"* note of what I've said." 1Ki 22:28
"* me out of the battle, for I am 1Ki 22:34
for the Lord to * Elijah to 2Ki 2:1
to * Elijah away from you today?" 2Ki 2:3
to * away your master today?" 2Ki 2:5
* her two sons as his slaves. 2Ki 4:1
Gehazi, "Quick, * my staff0,6ı! 2Ki 4:29
Naaman urged him to * them, but he 2Ki 5:16
of earth to * back with me, for 2Ki 5:17
"* $4,000," Naaman insisted. 2Ki 5:23
Follow me and I will * you to the 2Ki 6:19
Let them * five of the remaining 2Ki 7:13
back to life, "* your family and 2Ki 8:1
said to Hazael, "* a present to 2Ki 8:8,9
he told him. "* this vial of oil 2Ki 9:1
own land until I * you to another 2Ki 18:31,32
the best course for Israel to *. 1Ch 12:24-37
Finally he decided to * it to the 1Ch 13:13
to * the Ark to Jerusalem. 1Ch 15:25
made David decide to * a census. 1Ch 21:1
"* a complete census throughout 1Ch 21:2
"* it, my lord, and use it as 1Ch 21:23
said to David. "* the oxen, too, 1Ch 21:23
I cannot * what is yours and give 1Ch 21:24
So God appointed Solomon to * 1Ch 29:23
can * them inland to Jerusalem." 2Ch 2:16
defeat them and * them away as 2Ch 6:36
Asa's response was to * the 2Ch 16:2
"Arrest this man and * him back 2Ch 18:25
"* note of what I have said." 2Ch 18:27
not need to fight! * your places; 2Ch 20:17
"* her out and kill her," 2Ch 23:13,14
up for them to * her out and they 2Ch 23:15,16,17
"* me out of the battle," he 2Ch 35:23
for he refused to * the counsel of 2Ch 36:12
to * back to Jerusalem. Ez 1:11
instruct you to * a copy of God's Ez 7:14
We also commission you to * with Ez 7:15
of your God. And * with you the Ez 7:19
So we fasted and begged God to * Ez 8:23
We will obey the laws of God. * Ez 10:4
* them back into slavery in Egypt! Neh 9:17
ceremonies and to * part in the Neh 12:27
be compelled to * more than he Est 1:8
"Hurry and * these robes and my Est 6:10
to them, and to * their property. Est 8:11
But they did not try to * Haman's Est 9:7-10
but they did not * their goods. Est 9:16
But just * away his wealth, and Job 1:11
had, and they were his to * away. Job 1:21
Why not just pardon my sin and * Job 7:21
You will * your time, and rest in Job 11:18
Yes, I will * my life in my hand Job 13:14
I would try to * away your grief. Job 16:5
breasts, and * a poor man's baby as Job 24:9
I do, and every step I *. Job 31:4
"* a look at the behemoth! Job 40:15
Job was. Now * seven young bulls Job 42:8
So cheer up! * courage if you Ps 31:24
Let all who are discouraged * Ps 34:2
Put on your armor, * your shield Ps 35:2
Evil men * aim to slay the poor; Ps 37:14
He delights in each step they *. Ps 37:23
* courage, my soul! Ps 42:4,5
they cannot * it with them. Ps 49:14
Have pity upon me and * away the Ps 51:1
Don't * your Holy Spirit from me. Ps 51:11
He will * care of the helpless Ps 72:12
Why * the trouble to be pure? Ps 73:13
O Lord, * sevenfold vengeance on Ps 79:12
never completely * away my Ps 89:33
I will not * back one word of Ps 89:34
and strangers * all he has earned. Ps 109:11
that Jehovah will * care of him. Ps 112:7
It is better to * refuge in him Ps 118:9
* away my lust for evil things; Ps 141:4
man that you * account of him?" Ps 144:3f
Adore him, O his people! And * a Ps 149:6,7
Oh, why wouldn't I * advice? Pro 5:13
* a lesson from the ants, you Pro 6:6
* to heart all of their advice. Pro 6:21
Come on, let's * our fill of Pro 7:18
be humble, * advice and become Pro 13:10
Pride disgusts the Lord. * my Pro 16:5
never last, so why * the risk? Pro 21:6
IF YOU MUST choose, * a good name Pro 22:1
They'll even * your bed! Pro 22:26,27
it, and have to * back your words Pro 23:6,7,8
Do all you want to; * in Ecc 11:9
girls love you! * me with you; Sol 1:4
and * hold of its branches. Sol 7:8
your sins, I can * it out and make Is 1:18
all of them * bribes and won't Is 1:23
king and * care of this mess." Is 3:6
They * bribes to pervert Is 5:23
In that day the Lord will * this Is 7:20
I will * the highest throne. Is 14:13
The desperate refugees * only Is 15:7
let all the world * notice! Is 18:3
son of Amoz, to * off his clothing, Is 20:2
For the king of Assyria will * Is 20:4
Elamites and Medes will * part in Is 21:2
away all tears and * away forever Is 25:8
they keep on doing wrong and * no Is 26:10
IN THAT DAY the Lord will * his Is 27:1
when Israel will * root and bud and Is 27:6
I will * the line and plummet Is 28:17
therefore I will * awesome Is 29:14
the harvest will not * place. Is 32:10
Lord's telling me to * this land? Is 36:10
I can arrange to * you to a country Is 36:17
left in Judah will * root again in Is 37:31
started, barely * root, when he Is 40:24
They hire a goldsmith to * your Is 46:6
and delicate. * heavy millstones Is 47:2
I will * vengeance upon you and Is 47:3
people: "See, I * from your hands Is 51:22
Rise from the dust, Jerusalem; * Is 52:2
now I can * you back again and Is 52:3
Come, * your choice of wine and Is 55:1
of his promises. * no rest, all you Is 62:6,7
and * away your grain and wine. Is 62:8
a blessing or * an oath shall swear Is 65:16
he is not to * her back again, for Jer 3:1
O Lord, you will * naught but Jer 5:3
like this I'll * your words and Jer 5:14
and * their fields and wives. Jer 6:12
Beware of your brother! All * Jer 9:4
You plant them. They * root and Jer 12:2
This time he said, * the Jer 13:4
flock I gave you to * care of? Jer 13:20
or a leopard * away his spots? Jer 13:23
of your cities and * from you all Jer 15:7
I will have your enemies * you Jer 15:14
The Lord says: * warning and Jer 17:21,22
Buy a clay jar and * it out into Jer 19:1
gate of the city. * some of the Jer 19:1
Lord, and he shall * away these Jer 20:4
* your choice of life or death! Jer 21:8
I will * away your joy, your Jer 25:10
For the Lord God said to me: "* Jer 25:15
* their part in all the fun; Jer 31:13
"He shall * you to Babylon and Jer 32:5
of Israel, says: * both this sealed Jer 32:14
to the Temple. * them into one of Jer 35:2
the king would * his knife, and Jer 36:23
Ebedmelech to * thirty men with him Jer 38:10
to * him back to his home. Jer 39:14
Now I am going to * off your Jer 40:4
I will * this remnant of Judah Jer 44:12
Then Israel shall come and * back Jer 49:2
even thieves don't * everything, Jer 49:9,10
What shepherd can defy me? * Jer 49:20
They * away the young men to Lam 5:13
"AND NOW, SON of dust, * a large Eze 4:1
Each day * flour from the barrel Eze 4:12
"SON OF DUST, * a sharp sword and Eze 5:1
then * a few hairs out and throw Eze 5:4
me, for I will * away their Eze 6:9
Therefore I will * it all away Eze 7:20
the cherubim and * a handful of Eze 10:2
the cherubim and * some burning Eze 10:6
God, and I will * you from Eze 11:9
I will * from you your hearts of Eze 11:19
I could * into exile—and in the Eze 12:7
and strip you and * your beautiful Eze 16:39
by my favor when I * your sisters, Eze 16:61
enough—it won't * a big crew or a Eze 17:9
and made him * an oath of Eze 17:12,13
I, myself, will * the finest and Eze 17:22,23
vigorously, then * a sword and Eze 21:14
is here. * off your jeweled crown, Eze 21:26
wickedness. So * out the meat chunk Eze 24:6
"Son of dust, I am going to * Eze 24:16
I will * away their right to feed Eze 34:9,10
* away their right to eat. Eze 34:9,10
That you * the best water for Eze 34:18
We will * possession of them. Eze 35:10
for me, to * it for themselves. Eze 36:5
I will * out your stony hearts of Eze 36:26
"* a stick and carve on it these Eze 37:16
Then * another stick and carve Eze 37:16
God says: I will * the tribes of Eze 37:18,19,20
It will * seven months for the Eze 39:12
will see them and * them to the Eze 39:15,16
and listen and * to heart Eze 40:4
You shall * some of its blood Eze 43:20
Then * the bullock for the sin Eze 43:21
to * charge of my sanctuary. Eze 44:8
court, they must * off the clothes Eze 44:19
The priest shall * some of the Eze 45:19
And the prince may never * Eze 46:18
"Don't kill them. * me to the king Dan 2:24
will arise to * your place. Dan 2:39
for he is able to * those who Dan 4:37
of justice and * all power from Dan 7:26
vision will not * place until the Dan 8:17
that he will even * on the Prince Dan 8:25
against him and * away his kingdom Dan 11:5
But during a crisis he will * Dan 11:21
before: he will * the property and Dan 11:24
hand, only to * advantage of them. Dan 11:34
But now I will * back the wine Hos 1:9
grow, I will * them from you; Hos 9:12
say, "O Lord, * away our sins; Hos 14:2
will * what's left! Joe 1:4
Are you trying to * revenge on Joe 3:4
leaders, saying, "* your seats now Amo 3:9
of everything good; you * bribes; Amo 5:12
they would not * everything! Ob 1:5
* three days to walk around it. Jon 3:3
all he has); you * it by fraud and Mic 2:2
kind— you leaders who * bribes; Mic 3:11
turn on you and * all you have, Hab 2:7
now, is it? But * courage, O Hag 2:4
all the people; * courage and work, Hag 2:4
But when that happens, I will * Hag 2:23
have come to * hold of the four Zec 1:21
fair—and not to * bribes—and to be Zec 7:8,9
"Foreigners will * over the city Zec 9:6
to me, "Go and * a job as shepherd Zec 11:4
"* note that I will rebuke your Mal 2:3
won't have room enough to * it in! Mal 3:10
hesitate to * Mary as your wife! Mt 1:20
him, "Get up and * the baby and Mt 2:20
"* CARE! Mt 6:1

TAKE Con't)
For they * pride in all these Mt 6:31,32
God will * care of your tomorrow Mt 6:34
be examined; and * with you the Mt 8:4
"Don't * any money with you; Mt 10:9
If you refuse to * up your cross Mt 10:38
men of violence * it by force." Mt 11:12f
"It doesn't seem right to * Mt 15:26
and * up his cross and follow me. Mt 16:24
both of us; * it and pay them." Mt 17:26,27
But if not, then * one or two Mt 18:16
to listen, then * your case to the Mt 18:17
all day for $20? * it and go. Mt 20:14
And you say that to * an oath Mt 23:18
and wanted to * him on a tour of Mt 24:1
Literally, "Let the reader * Mt 24:15f
Or, "after all these things * Mt 24:34f
some interest. * the money from Mt 25:28
and said, "* it and eat it, for Mt 26:26
on now and * your rest Mt 26:45
soldiers to * away and crucify. Mt 27:26
along the way. * along the offering Mk 1:43,44
to try to * him home with them. Mk 3:21
He told them to * nothing with Mk 6:8,9
"It would * a fortune Mk 6:37
They just sat there, unable to * Mk 6:51
It isn't right to * the Mk 7:27
Are your hearts too hard to * it Mk 8:17
* care! Mk 13:23
He will * you upstairs to a Mk 14:15
for you. * away this cup from me. Mk 14:36
Then you can * him easily." Mk 14:44
Elijah will come and * him down!" Mk 15:36
exclaimed, "to * away my disgrace Lk 1:25
them and doesn't * root and grow. Lk 8:13
"Don't even * along a walking Lk 9:3
Don't * any money with you, or a Lk 10:4
and told him to * care of the Lk 10:35
I won't * it away from her!" Lk 10:42
for years to come. Now * it easy! Lk 12:19
the world to * their places there. Lk 13:29
will have to * whatever seat is Lk 14:9
"Or * another illustration: A Lk 15:8
Please * me on as a hired man." Lk 15:19
to * care of me when I leave!' Lk 16:4
'Here,' the accountant said, '* Lk 16:7
by he ordered, '* the money away Lk 19:24
He will * you upstairs to a Lk 22:12
for it, he said, "* this and share Lk 22:17
"But now," he said, "* a Lk 22:36
* away this cup of horror from me. Lk 22:41,42
Pilate said to * him to King Herod, Lk 23:7
"Dip some out and * it to the Jn 2:7,8
Philip replied, "It would * a Jn 6:7
they were ready to * him by force Jn 6:15
the right and power to * it again. Jn 10:18
* over the Jewish government." Jn 11:48
I gave you. * care to live in me, Jn 15:4
I'm not asking you to * them out Jn 17:15
"Then * him away and judge him Jn 18:31
permission to * Jesus' body down; Jn 19:38
"Then * care of my sheep," Jesus Jn 21:16
direct you and * you where you Jn 21:18
someone else to * Judas' place and Act 1:21,22
one afternoon to * part in the Act 3:1
"Men of Israel, * care what you Act 5:35
"And the Lord said to him, '* Act 7:33
instrument to * my message to the Act 9:15
them all and * them in chains to Act 9:21
who had come to * me with them to Act 11:11
and Paul to * to the elders of the Act 11:30
to * his hand and lead him. Act 13:11
the Gentiles to * from them a Act 15:14
Barnabas agreed, and wanted to * Act 15:37
Jason, planning to * Paul and Silas Act 17:5
Jewish laws, you * care of it. Act 18:15
the judges can * the case at once. Act 19:38
shave their heads and * some vows. Act 21:23
You are to * his message Act 22:15
his soldiers to * him away from Act 23:10
"* this boy to the commander. Act 23:17
o'clock tonight! * 200 spearmen and Act 23:23,24
cavalry to * him on to Caesarea. Act 23:32
in Caesarea to * over his new Act 25:1
sailing with you.' So * courage! Act 27:25
Jesus Christ to * away our sins. Rom 3:21,22
For God sent Christ Jesus to * Rom 3:25
would come and * away those sins. Rom 3:25
but all who will * God's gift of Rom 5:17
yourself—he will * you and be your Rom 6:16
And I will * pity on anyone I Rom 9:15
And he has a right to * others Rom 9:23,24
to others if they refused to * it Rom 10:19
For if God was willing to * you Rom 11:24
At that time I will * away their Rom 11:27
* the responsibility seriously. Rom 12:8
* delight in honoring each other. Rom 12:10
[Don't * the law into your own Rom 12:19
For I am planning to * a trip to Rom 15:24
to Jerusalem to * a gift to the Rom 15:25
Others just can't * it in. 1Co 2:14
For instance, * the matter of 1Co 6:13
So should I * part of Christ and 1Co 6:15
you get a chance to be free, * it. 1Co 7:21
in his temple to * for their own 1Co 9:13
Here's what you should do. * any 1Co 10:25
and said, "* this and eat it. 1Co 11:24
They are not to * part in the 1Co 14:34
They begged us to * the money so 2Co 8:4
me to * the gift to Jerusalem. 2Co 8:19
much, and when we * your gifts to 2Co 9:11
their slaves and * everything you 2Co 11:19,20
you have, and * advantage of you, 2Co 11:19,20
I sent to you * advantage of you? 2Co 12:17
Jesus Christ to * away our sins. Gal 2:16
of us can * any credit for it. Eph 2:9
a sacrifice to * away your sins. Eph 5:2
* no part in the worthless Eph 5:11
(He gave his very life to * care Eph 5:23
When he comes back he will * Php 3:21
are frightened; * tender care of 1Th 5:14
The church should * loving care 1Ti 5:3
ones who should * the 1Ti 5:4
and * care of their own homes; 1Ti 5:14
relatives must * care of her, and 1Ti 5:16
You ought to * a little sometimes 1Ti 5:23
* your share of suffering as a 2Ti 2:3
We have not yet seen all of this * Heb 2:8
to save them can * new courage when Heb 6:18
and goats really to * away sins. Heb 10:4
that could never * away our sins. Heb 10:11
It would * too long to recount Heb 11:32
So * a new grip with your tired Heb 12:12
you love and * care of yourself." Jas 2:8
a fight to * it away from them. Jas 4:2
Yes, be patient. And * courage, Jas 5:8
fathers tried to *, and the ransom 1Pe 1:18
so that he could * away our sins, 1Jn 3:5
* God's place in your hearts. 1Jn 5:21
for the Lord, and * neither food, 3Jn 1:7
So we ourselves should * care of 3Jn 1:8
no one will * away your crown. Rev 3:11
are worthy to * the scroll and Rev 5:9
"Yes, * it and eat it," he Rev 10:9
to * care of her for 1,260 days. Rev 12:6
"* note: I will come as Rev 16:15
do not * part in her sins, or you Rev 18:4
God shall * away his share in the Rev 22:19

TAKEN
because she was * out of a man." Gen 2:23
ground from which he had been *. Gen 3:23
and she was * into his harem. Gen 12:15
loot that had been *, his relative Gen 14:16
servants had * violently away from Gen 21:25
know that Rachel had * them. Gen 31:32
they saw where they were being *. Gen 43:18
for they had * much of the wealth Ex 14:8
shall never be * from the rings, Ex 25:15
All the fat shall be * off, just Lev 4:31
vow he has *, he is guilty. Lev 5:4
without blemish * to the priest as Lev 5:17,18
of its blood is * into the Lev 6:30
of bread, all * from the basket Lev 8:26
"Since its blood was not * Lev 10:18
* from rivers or from the sea; Lev 11:9
be * to the priest to be examined. Lev 13:49
(their blood was * into the Holy Lev 16:27
he has * what belongs to his Lev 20:20
for he has * what belongs to his Lev 20:21
This census was * in response to Num 4:49
Israelites: I have * the Levites as Num 8:16
The Tabernacle was * down and the Num 10:17
* into this country ahead of us. Num 14:3
He was arrested and * before Num 15:33
his tent, where he had * the girl. Num 25:8
in the previous census * in the Num 26:64,65
all mankind, [before I am * away Num 27:16
The offering was * into the Num 31:54
ransacking the cities we had *. Deu 2:35,36
need be * to the central altar. Deu 12:26,27
or woman shall be * outside the Deu 17:5
her shall be * outside the gates Deu 22:23,24
daughters are * away as slaves. Deu 28:32
But actually she had * them up to Jos 2:6
and has * loot when I said it was Jos 7:10,11
when I said it was not to be *; Jos 7:10,11
and they have not only * it, they Jos 7:10,11
their bodies be * down and thrown Jos 10:27
cities were * by the Israelis for Jos 11:14
even though he has * care of you Jos 24:20
He was * to Jerusalem, and died Ju 1:7
"You've * away all my gods and Ju 18:24
But no one has * us in for the Ju 19:18
Have I ever * a bribe? 1Sa 12:3
never * even one single bribe." 1Sa 12:4
he would and has * the kingdom from 1Sa 28:17
everything that was * from you!" 1Sa 30:8
of loot they had * from the 1Sa 30:16
got back everything they had *. 1Sa 30:18,19
"Here is a present for you, * 1Sa 30:26
a new cart and * from the hillside 2Sa 6:3
and gold he had * from Syria, Moab, 2Sa 8:11,12
"I have * the City of Waters." 2Sa 12:26,27f
the wine is to be * with you into 2Sa 16:2
But after he had * the census, 2Sa 24:10
the city had been *, he went into 1Ki 16:18
And his body was * to Samaria and 1Ki 22:36,37
I grant you before I am * away?" 2Ki 2:9
"If you see me when I am * from 2Ki 2:10
will be *—nothing shall be left. 2Ki 20:17
Some of your own sons will be * 2Ki 20:18
He was * to Riblah, where he was 2Ki 25:6
with chains and * away to Babylon. 2Ki 25:7
were all * as exiles to Babylon. 2Ki 25:11
in the city, were * by General 2Ki 25:20
of Reuben and was * into captivity 1Ch 5:6
It was * from the house of 1Ch 13:7
At this time a census was * of 1Ch 23:3
Another 10,000 were * alive to 2Ch 25:12
with him idols * from the people of 2Ch 25:14
The money was * to Hilkiah the 2Ch 34:9
Jehoahaz was * to Egypt as a 2Ch 36:4
the Temple were * away to Babylon 2Ch 36:10
he had * an oath of loyalty. 2Ch 36:13
Those who survived were * away 2Ch 36:20
Nebuchadnezzar had * from the Ez 1:7
(They had been * from their own Ez 4:10
want to see you * advantage of and Ez 4:14
Nebuchadnezzar had * from the Ez 5:14
bowls which were * from the Temple Ez 6:5
shall be * back to Jerusalem and Ez 6:5
and Levites had * up the horrible Ez 9:1
* them as wives for their sons. Ez 9:2
that before being * to the king's Est 2:12,13,14
She was * to the king's apartment Est 2:12,13,14
So Esther was * to the palace of Est 2:16
ring—which he had * back from Est 8:2
me down, and * away my family. Job 16:7
He has * me by the neck and Job 16:12
of the poor and fatherless are *. Job 24:3
For they have * advantage of the Job 24:21
God, who has * away my rights, even Job 27:2
or if I have * advantage of an Job 31:21
For I have * your lovingkindness Ps 26:3
I have * an oath to establish his Ps 89:3,4
Jehovah has * oath, and will not Ps 110:4
He has * a wallet full of money Pro 7:20
can be added or * from it; Ecc 3:14
and they are all * away as slaves Is 6:12
But it was not *; Is 7:1
He has * an oath to do it! Is 14:24
will be * away as slaves. Is 31:8
And your mother was * in payment Is 50:1
You have * pleasant incense and Is 57:9
to find no steps * against sin. Is 59:15
the people were * away as slaves. Jer 1:3
And so I have * away these Jer 5:25
my children have been * away and Jer 10:20
and all Judah shall be * away as Jer 13:19
my peace from them—* away my Jer 16:5
kingdom is to be * up and Jer 18:7
his father King Josiah, and was * Jer 22:11
all your friends are * off as Jer 22:22
the golden dishes * from the Temple Jer 27:16
* away by the Assyrians as slaves. Jer 31:15f
be caught and * as a prisoner Jer 32:4
you shall be captured and * Jer 34:3
of Babylon had not * them all away, Jer 40:11
shall be * away to distant lands! Jer 48:7
daughters are * away as slaves. Jer 48:46
* over Gad and all its cities? Jer 49:1
Their camels will be * away, and Jer 49:29
The Lord has * vengeance. Jer 50:15
The Lord of Hosts has * this Jer 51:14
pull from his mouth what he has *. Jer 51:44
* away as captives to Babylon. Jer 52:3
out and he was * in chains to Jer 52:11
The number of captives * to Jer 52:28
captured and * far away as slaves. Lam 1:5
and daughters are * far away as Lam 1:18
gone, for you have * them away. Lam 3:17
was * to Babylon, Jeremiah 52:11. Eze 12:12f
was * to Babylon, Jeremiah 52:11. Eze 12:13f
Then, when the marriage had * Eze 16:9,10
your children will be * away as Eze 23:25
was * away to captivity). Eze 26:1
Great care must therefore be * to Eze 28:12f
Her wealth is * away, her Eze 30:4
women will be * away as slaves. Eze 30:17
will be * away as captives. Eze 30:18
You haven't * care of the weak Eze 34:4
I will save my flock from being * Eze 34:9,10
before being * to the altar; Eze 40:38
raised my hand and * oath, says the Eze 44:12
and silver cups * long before from Dan 5:2,3,4
and he was * to the den of lions. Dan 6:16
kingdoms were * from them, but they Dan 7:12
daily sacrifice is * away and the Dan 12:11
cubs have been * away, and like a Hos 13:8
"You have * my silver and gold Joe 3:5
be the first to be * as slaves; Amo 6:7
and every treasure found and *. Ob 1:6
which had been * away from them. Mic 1:11f

(TAKEN Con't)
which had been * away from them. Mic 1:11f
which had been * away from them. Mic 1:11f
wounded and * away your reproach. Zep 3:17,18
"See, I have * away your sins, and Zec 3:4
the city will be *, the houses Zec 14:1
half the population will be * Zec 14:1
you haven't * seriously the things Mal 2:1
is * from you, give your coat too. Mt 5:40
will be * from them. Mt 9:15
the little he has will be * away. Mt 13:12,13
of God shall be * away from you. Mt 21:43
and one will be *, the other left. Mt 24:40
one will be *, the other left. Mt 24:41
he has shall be * from him. Mt 25:29
let this cup be * away from me. Mt 26:39
But some day he will be * away Mk 2:20
from him who has not shall be * Mk 4:25
will be arrested and * before the Mk 10:33
with them, he was * up into heaven Mk 16:19
should be * throughout the nation. Lk 2:1
(This census was * when Lk 2:2
Literally, "* away from them." Lk 5:35f
and when things are * away from Lk 6:30
he has shall be * away from him." Lk 8:18
This demon had often * control of Lk 8:29
will be * away, the other left. Lk 17:34
one will be *, the other left; Lk 17:35,36
"Lord, where will they be *?" Lk 17:37
people will be * out to the Lk 17:37f
As the body was * away, the women Lk 23:55
should be * from Jerusalem to all Lk 24:47
Next he was * to the palace of Jn 18:28
last, and he was * out of the city, Jn 19:17
then their bodies could be * Jn 19:31
and said, "They have * the Jn 20:2
"Because they have * away my Jn 20:13
"if you have * him away, tell me Jn 20:15
he was * from us into heaven." Act 1:21,22
All of them were * to Shechem Act 7:16
Tabernacle was * with them into Act 7:45
For his life is * from the Act 8:33
his death, he was * from the cross Act 13:29
Jewish custom, for he had * a vow. Act 18:18
Paul had * him into the Temple. Act 21:29
Paul to be * to the armory. Act 21:34
As Paul was about to be * inside, Act 21:37,38
and Achaia have * up an offering Rom 15:26
Jerusalem, to be * there by 1Co 16:3
his sins, then the veil is * away. 2Co 3:16
we live in now is * down—when we 2Co 5:1
We have cheated no one nor * 2Co 7:2
was * up to heaven 2Co 12:2,3
would gladly have * out your own Gal 4:15
where your sins were all * away. Col 2:15
Don't be * in by people like 2Ti 3:5
all you owned was * from you, Heb 10:34
up like a scroll and * away; Rev 6:14
will be arrested and * away; Rev 13:10

TAKES
(Jacob * it over to him and Isaac Gen 27:25
her and then * another wife, he may Ex 21:10
be completed—for it * seven days. Lev 8:33
a man or a woman * the special vow Num 6:1
"If she * a vow or makes a Num 30:6
Horeb—though it * only eleven days Deu 1:1
no partiality and * no bribes. Deu 10:17
But if this deed * place out in Deu 22:25,26,27
" 'Cursed is he who * advantage Deu 27:18
And it * time. Ju 5:30
humble, and * sufferers to safety. Job 5:11
He overthrows the mighty. He * Job 12:20
it to nothing. He * away the Job 12:24,25
a booby-trap in every path he *. Job 18:10
Horror * hold upon me and I Job 21:6
cuts him off and * away his life? Job 27:8
then he * the trouble to point out Job 36:9
everyone who * refuge in him will Ps 34:22
All humanity * refuge in the Ps 36:7
* care of those he has forgiven. Ps 37:17
Blessed is the man who * your Ps 137:9
wealthy, God * the wealth away from Ecc 2:24-26
Then the woodcarver * the axe Is 44:13
really does —he * the rest of it Is 44:15
destroyed when God * his vengeance Jer 51:6
* over as king of Egypt, he will Dan 11:7
The prophecy * a turn here. Dan 11:40f
that is why he * vengeance on Nah 1:2
making bread. She * a measure of Mt 13:33
them, "Anyone who * care of a Lk 9:48
There is the Lamb of God who * Jn 1:29
kindness freely * away our sins. Rom 3:24
Christ freely * away many sins and Rom 5:16
They are given because God * pity Rom 9:16
We are all parts of it, and it * Rom 12:4,5
What shepherd * care of a flock 1Co 9:7
But it * only one wrong person Gal 5:9
So, whatever it *, I will be one Php 3:11
When a man * an oath, he is Heb 6:16
Watch out that no bitterness * Heb 12:15
souls as it * hold of our hearts. Jas 1:21
is the one who * care of orphans Jas 1:27

TAKING
times, anyone * revenge against me Gen 4:24
* with them Lot—Abram's nephew Gen 14:12
Soon, * them cheese and milk and Gen 18:8
Abimelech for * Abraham's wife. Gen 20:18
One evening as he was * a walk Gen 24:63
Then, * several men with him, he Gen 31:23
traders who were * gum, spices, and Gen 37:25
But as they were * her out to Gen 38:25
rapidly. So, * with him his two Gen 48:1
much time this was *, he said, Ex 18:14
In prayer, or in * an oath. Ex 23:13f
had told him to, * the two stone Ex 34:4
After * out this handful, the Lev 6:16
grain offering, * a handful and Lev 9:17
am * you, and the land is defiled. Lev 18:27
* some of the men as prisoners. Num 21:1
* vengeance on his enemies, Deu 32:40,41
to eat, and * away all their sheep, Ju 6:3,4
The Lord is * care of you." Ju 18:6
it is ours for the *—a broad, Ju 18:9,10
Then her husband, * along a Ju 19:3
* turns raping her until morning. Ju 19:25
you're supposed to be * care of? 1Sa 17:28
"When I am * care of my father's 1Sa 17:34
Keilah with David, * his ephod with 1Sa 23:6
from murdering and * vengeance into 1Sa 25:26
home one noon as he was * a nap. 2Sa 4:5
cut off his head. * his head with 2Sa 4:6,7
So he decided against * it 2Sa 6:10
unusual beauty * her evening bath. 2Sa 11:2
insulted me by * Uriah's wife. 2Sa 12:10
on to Gilgal, * Chimham with him. 2Sa 19:40
harm them by * a national census. 2Sa 24:1
vineyard, * possession of it. 1Ki 21:18
So Naaman started out, * gifts of 2Ki 5:5
get away without * his gifts. 2Ki 5:20
no partiality, no * of bribes." 2Ch 19:7
city officials, * seven young 2Ch 29:21
themselves for not * a more active 2Ch 30:15
* it to God's Temple in Jerusalem. Ez 8:30
night, * only a few men with me; Neh 2:11,12
He chose his servant David, * Ps 78:70
satisfy you with honey for the *. Ps 81:16
their hands from * bribes, who Is 33:15
* them away from evil days ahead. Is 57:1
It is the voice of the Lord * Is 66:6
no longer say when * an oath, "As Jer 23:7
near Bethlehem, * with them all Jer 41:16,17
* everything precious she owns. Lam 1:10
hole in the wall, * only what he Eze 12:12
the day I finish * from them in Eze 24:25
lifted to heaven, * oath by him who Dan 12:7
"Where are they * her?" Zec 5:10
all to leave, and * the little Mk 5:40
* her by the hand he said to her, Mk 5:41,42
among them; and * the child in his Mk 9:36
* them aside, Jesus once more Mk 10:32
linen cloth and, * Jesus' body down Mk 15:46
and wondered why he was * so long. Lk 1:21
any longer? It's * up space we can Lk 13:7
in from plowing or * care of sheep, Lk 17:7,8,9
man to deal with, * what isn't Lk 19:21
you see the events * place that Lk 21:31
* John Mark with them. Act 12:25
to Jerusalem * greetings and Act 15:33
* Priscilla and Aquila with him. Act 18:18
Sin fooled me by * the good laws Rom 7:11
matter instead of * it to other 1Co 6:1
other churches by * what they sent 2Co 11:8,9
and the * of other men's wives. 2Co 12:21
system by * the curse for our Gal 3:13
power and glory, * the disguise of Php 2:7
in this matter by * another man's 1Th 4:6
carefully, * life seriously. Tit 2:6
as * the place of the old one; Heb 8:13
over the sins, * them out of sight Heb 10:4f
work for God in * care of the 3Jn 1:5

TALE
like a fairy * to the men—they Lk 24:11

TALENT
Literally, "a [gold] *." Ex 25:39f
Literally, "a [silver] *." Ex 38:27f
they have no *, none at all." Jer 4:22

TALENTED
who was not only a * harp player, 1Sa 16:18

TALENTS
having special *, and construct Ex 35:10-19
Literally, "a thousand * of 1Ch 19:6f
Literally, "a hundred thousand * 1Ch 22:14f
and "a million * of silver." 1Ch 22:14f
Literally, "10,000 *." Mt 18:24f

TALES
O city of God, what wondrous * Ps 87:3
to Jewish folk * and the demands of Tit 1:14
telling you fairy * when we 2Pe 1:16

TALK
there began to * about building a Gen 11:3,4
Lot stepped outside to * to them, Gen 19:6
to * things over with them. Gen 31:5
father, went to * with Jacob, Gen 34:6,7
into Moses' tent to * further. Ex 18:7
can hear me when I * with you, and Ex 19:9
with you there and * with you from Ex 25:22
the priest shall * it over with Lev 27:8
I will come down and * with you Num 11:17
people was to * of stoning them. Num 14:10,11
that you * with her face to face. Num 14:14
your children and * about them when Deu 6:7
Teach them to your children. * Deu 11:19
summon him and * it over with him, Deu 25:8
Rahab went up to * to the men Jos 2:8
"Go and * to the leaders of Ju 9:2
"Be careful how you *, mister," Ju 18:25
The old man stepped outside to * Ju 19:23
the morning I'll * to him, and if Ru 3:13
"I want to * to you a minute." Ru 4:1
me, and I'll * to him about you; 1Sa 19:3
the latest, I will * to my father 1Sa 20:12
and a sword and * to God for him? 1Sa 22:13
the wilderness to * to our master, 1Sa 25:14
that no one can even * to him!" 1Sa 25:17
"I've got to * to a dead man," 1Sa 28:7,8
to you when you * like this? 1Sa 30:24
"Don't * to me like that!" 2Sa 19:22
Come over here so I can * to 2Sa 20:16
and called him aside to * to him. 1Ki 11:29
"Don't * like that!" 1Ki 22:8
Don't * to anyone along the way. 2Ki 4:29
he would come out and * to me! 2Ki 5:11
to stand here and listen to you *! 2Ch 9:7
"Oh, come now, don't * like 2Ch 18:6,7
enemies tried to * them out of Neh 4:12
I suggest that you come and * it Neh 6:7
But he replied, "You * like some Job 2:10
a man proved right by all this *? Job 11:2
I want to * this over with God Job 13:3
you give us all this foolish *. Job 15:2
his throne and * with him there. Job 23:3
and * with me, O my people." Ps 27:8
They don't * of peace and doing Ps 35:20
How they * about me when I wear Ps 69:11
I am the * of the town and the Ps 69:12
You know how they * about me, Ps 69:19
I will * to others all day long Ps 71:24
Forgetfulness * about your help? Ps 88:12
They can't * or see, despite Ps 115:5
For even princes sit and * Ps 119:23
They will * together about the Ps 145:11
Don't * so much. Pro 10:19
A rebel's foolish * should prick Pro 14:3
Work brings profit; * brings Pro 14:23
Those who love to * will suffer Pro 18:21
So when you * to God and vow to Ecc 5:4
Come, let's * this over! Is 1:18
was old enough to * (verse 4) the Is 7:14f
children, barely old enough to *? Is 28:9
him, "Please * to us in Aramaic Is 36:11
Don't let him * you into Is 36:15
for we must * about your sins. Is 43:26
scorn or their slanderous *. Is 51:7
So you *, and keep right on Jer 3:4,5
Because of * like this I'll take Jer 5:14
full of evil * against the Lord? Jer 6:28
this foolishness and * some sense! Jer 15:19
made and I will * to you there. Jer 18:2
That kind of * will undermine the Jer 38:4
and I will * to you." Eze 2:1
valley and I will * to you there"— Eze 3:22
no longer will you * of seeing Eze 13:23
to you so that you can * with him; Eze 24:27
your back. They * about you in Eze 33:30
tell them to; they * very sweetly Eze 33:31
lips and I could * again, and I Dan 10:16
such a person as I even * to you? Dan 10:17
It's disgraceful, that sort of *. Mic 2:6
Lord likes to * to you so roughly? Mic 2:7
says to him, "Don't stop to * Mt 8:4
* is cheap—anybody could say that. Mt 9:5,6
and instantly the man could *. Mt 9:33
and unable to *—was brought to Mt 12:22
outside, wanting to * with him. Mt 12:46,47
"I will * in parables; Mt 13:34,35
Then he went into the house to * Mt 17:25
WHEN JESUS HAD finished this * Mt 26:1
* is cheap—anybody could say that. Mk 2:9,10,11
him to come out and * with them. Mk 3:31,32
to heal—he can't * because he is Mk 9:17
to * with him and try to trap him Mk 12:13
bewildered, too frightened to *. Mk 16:8
* is cheap—anybody could say that. Lk 5:23,24
began to * to those around him! Lk 7:15
much more time to * to you, for the Jn 14:30
"You won't * to me?" Jn 19:10
some local men, to * to the Act 15:2
I request permission to * to Act 21:39
way to * to God's High Priest?" Act 23:4
(That is the way some people *. Rom 3:5
Their * is foul and filthy like Rom 3:13
I cannot * to you as I would to 1Co 3:1
I'll * to you about the other 1Co 11:34

ALK Con't)
- n the same way, if you * to a 1Co 14:9
- 'hey must * silently to 1Co 14:28
- ave lost my wits to * like this; 2Co 11:16
- ou by sweet * and flattery; Gal 1:10
- nd * it over with anyone else; Gal 1:16
- Dirty stories, foul * and coarse Eph 5:4
- with each other much about the Eph 5:19
- o everywhere we go we * about Col 1:28
- nay fool you with smooth *. Col 2:4
- oving deeds as we * to our God and 1Th 1:3
- our own father. * to the younger 1Ti 5:1
- 'or if you * meekly and 2Ti 2:25
- But this is foolish *; Tit 1:10
- They must not * back, nor steal, Tit 2:9
- Psalms, "I will * to my brothers Heb 2:12
- of you and * against you, they will 1Pe 2:12
- o listen when you * to them about 1Pe 3:1
- istening when we * to him and make 1Jn 5:15
- and then we can * over these things 2Jn 1:12
- have much to * about together. 3Jn 1:14

ALKED
- Then Abram * it over with Lot. Gen 13:8
- in the dust as God * with him. Gen 17:2,3,4
- Moses returned home and * it over Ex 4:18
- Moses * there with the Lord and Ex 33:12
- congregation came and * with him. Ex 34:31
- in the Cloud and * with Moses, and Num 11:25
- the Lord * to him face to face. Deu 34:10
- They crossed the river and * to Jos 22:13
- who * to my wife the other day?" Ju 13:11
- Upon arriving at Timnah he * Ju 14:7
- the gate, they * to the young Ju 18:15,16
- Boaz went over and * to her. Ru 2:8,9
- on the roof and * with him there. 1Sa 9:25
- David * to some others standing 1Sa 17:26
- Abner also * to the leaders of 2Sa 3:19
- Rehoboam * it over with the old 1Ki 12:6
- Then Elijah * to them. 1Ki 18:21
- One day the king * to him about 1Ki 21:2
- When she returned, he * to her as 2Ki 4:15,16
- "—the God who * personally to my 2Ch 6:4
- These messengers * about the God 2Ch 32:19
- wicked way you have * about God. Job 34:36
- hear that I * with you and they Jer 38:25
- The ten had * Ishmael into Jer 41:8
- me on my feet. He * to me and said: Eze 3:24
- Daniel * it over with the steward Dan 1:11
- aside, and * to them about what Mt 20:18
- They * it over among themselves. Mt 21:25
- They * it over and finally Mt 27:7
- and sat down and * from there. Mk 4:1
- "The farmer I * about is anyone Mk 4:14
- miracles were * about everywhere. Mk 6:14
- Herod was disturbed whenever he * Mk 6:20
- afterwards. He * about it quite Mk 8:32
- but often * about it, and wondered Mk 9:10
- They * it over among themselves. Mk 11:31
- After they left, Jesus * to the Lk 7:24
- floor, listening to Jesus as he *. Lk 10:39
- Later he * again about this with Lk 17:22
- They * it over among themselves. Lk 20:5
- warm as he * with them and Lk 24:32
- and he sat down and * to them. Jn 8:2
- And on these occasions he * to Act 1:3
- the Council chamber while he *. Act 5:34
- So he got up and they * together Act 10:27
- the next day, he * until midnight! Act 20:7
- from time to time and * with him. Act 24:26
- As they * it over afterwards Act 26:31
- I go I hear you being * about! Rom 1:8
- to the Gentiles. I * privately to Gal 2:2
- one of you. We * to you as a 1Th 2:11
- And quite obviously when they * Heb 11:14
- brother Paul has * about these same 2Pe 3:15,16
- and * with God will listen to us. 1Jn 4:6
- plagues came over and * with me. Rev 17:1

TALKERS
- men are just big * or whether they 1Co 4:19

TALKING
- "What in the world are you * Gen 44:7
- ask, 'Which God are you * about?' Ex 3:13
- they wouldn't be * about going out Ex 5:7,8
- I am not * now to your children Deu 11:2
- is really Jehovah who is * to me! Ju 6:17
- But while Saul was * to the 1Sa 14:19
- As he was * with them, he saw 1Sa 17:23
- David * like that, he was angry. 1Sa 17:28
- as Jonathan and his father were * 1Sa 19:4
- David * to Ahimelech the priest. 1Sa 22:9,10
- "Today is the day the Lord was * 1Sa 24:4
- his men began * of killing him. 1Sa 30:6
- He had no way of * to her, for 2Sa 13:2
- * about bringing the king back?" 2Sa 19:8,9,10
- And while you are still * with 1Ki 1:14
- "You're * about yourself," 1Ki 18:18
- Perhaps he is * to someone, or is 1Ki 18:27
- As they were walking along, *, 2Ki 2:11
- in, the king was * with Gehazi, 2Ki 8:4
- did and will start * to us husbands Est 1:18
- "What are you * about?" Est 7:5
- I was * about things I knew Job 42:3
- and pleasure, nor * idly— then the Is 58:13
- While they are still * to me Is 65:24
- word of the Lord you keep * about? Jer 17:15
- as I was * with the elders of Eze 8:1
- the holy angels * to each other. Dan 8:13
- Then the angel who was * to me Zec 2:3
- THEN THE ANGEL who had been * Zec 4:1
- For it won't be you doing the * Mt 10:20
- began * about him to the crowds. Mt 11:7
- a word before were * excitedly, and Mt 15:31
- How could you even think I was * Mt 16:11
- appeared and were * with him. Mt 17:3
- that Jesus was * about them—that Mt 21:45
- * about," he angrily declared. Mt 26:70
- While he was still * to her, Mk 5:35
- that he must be * about their Mk 8:16
- appeared and began * with Jesus! Mk 9:4
- He said this just to be *, for he Mk 9:6
- could have been * about when they Mk 9:12,13
- "I don't know what you're * Mk 14:68
- fellow you are * about," he said. Mk 14:71
- Jesus had finished * with them, he Mk 16:19
- father, * to him by gestures. Lk 1:62
- just as Simeon was * with Mary and Lk 2:38
- began * with him—Moses and Elijah! Lk 9:30
- Peter asked, "Lord, are you * Lk 12:41
- And the Lord replied, "I'm * to Lk 12:42,43,44
- He seemed to be * in riddles. Lk 18:34
- realized that he was * about them. Lk 20:19
- Some of his disciples began * Lk 21:5
- don't know what you are * about." Lk 22:60
- As they walked along they were * Lk 24:14
- is the one I was * about when I Jn 1:15
- He is the one I was * about when Jn 1:30
- They were surprised to find him * Jn 4:27
- that he was * to them about God. Jn 8:27
- What Messiah are you * about?" Jn 12:34
- WHILE THEY WERE * to the people, Act 4:1
- * about himself or someone else?" Act 8:34
- second Psalm is * about when it Act 13:32,33
- Of course, I am not only * about Act 19:27
- people you have been * about!" Rom 2:1
- punished, you are * about Rom 2:1
- That is what the Scriptures are * Rom 10:15
- what we are * about when we tell Rom 11:8
- DEAR BROTHERS, I have been * to 1Co 3:1
- The Kingdom of God is not just * 1Co 4:20
- EVERYONE IS * about the terrible 1Co 5:1
- But when I said that I wasn't * 1Co 5:10
- you will be * to God but not to 1Co 14:2
- should come to you * in some 1Co 14:6
- You might as well be * to an 1Co 14:9
- A person * to me in one of these 1Co 14:11
- and hears you all * in other 1Co 14:23
- I am * to you now as if you 2Co 6:13
- me as I keep on * like a fool. 2Co 11:1
- I know what I am * about, as I 2Co 11:6
- boast about—I'm * like a fool 2Co 11:21
- to those you are * to, and what Eph 4:29
- time arguing and * foolishness. 1Ti 1:6
- And the future world we are * Heb 2:5
- This new place of rest he is * Heb 4:8
- Dear friends, even though I am * Heb 6:9
- within them was * about, for he 1Pe 1:11
- * about others behind their backs. 1Pe 2:1
- And you young men, I am * to you 1Jn 2:13
- I'm not * about these ordinary 1Jn 5:17

TALKS
- Anyone who * like that is Ps 14:1
- say of me, 'He only * in riddles!' Eze 20:49
- King Nebuchadnezzar had long * Dan 1:18,19
- Later, in one of his *, Jesus Jn 8:12
- He even * against the Temple and Act 21:28

TALL
- before them, they were so *!" Num 13:33
- of the land are * and powerful, and Deu 1:28
- tribe, * as the giants of Anakim; Deu 2:10
- tribe, as * as the Anakim; Deu 2:21
- a man, measuring over nine feet *! 1Sa 17:4-7
- and one-half feet *, whose spear 1Ch 11:23
- grow * as the cedars of Lebanon. Ps 92:12
- They are * and flourishing. Ps 104:16
- Sons vigorous and * as growing Ps 144:12-15
- You are * and slim like a palm Sol 7:7
- The Girl: "I am slim, *, Sol 8:10
- All the * cedars of Lebanon and Is 2:13
- Egypt who is as * as Mount Tabor or Jer 46:18
- You grew up and became *, slender Eze 16:6,7
- "I saw a very * tree out in a Dan 4:10,11
- you saw growing so *, reaching high Dan 4:20
- Amorites, as * as cedar trees, and Amo 2:9
- So Jesus grew both * and wise, Lk 2:52
- soon it grows into a * bush, and Lk 13:19

TALLER
- was getting *, and he was becoming 1Sa 2:26
- And he was head and shoulders * 1Sa 9:2
- This tree was * than any other Eze 31:8

TALLEST
- for he was the * of the Israelites, 1Sa 17:11f
- I have cut down the * cedars and 2Ki 19:23
- I cut down the * cedars and Is 37:24
- at the top of the * cedar tree and Eze 17:3,4
- ruined cedars; the * and most Zec 11:2

TALMAI
- of Anak: *, Sheshai, and Ahiman. Jos 15:14
- cities of Sheshai, Ahiman, and *. Ju 1:10
- the daughter of King * of Geshur. 2Sa 3:3
- Absalom fled to King * of Geshur 2Sa 13:37,38,39
- King * was his grandfather—his 2Sa 13:37,38,39f
- the daughter of King * of Geshur. 1Ch 3:2

TALMITES
- Sheshites, and *, all families Num 13:22

TALMON
- Akkub, *, and Ahiman—all Levites. 1Ch 9:17,18
- of Shallum, Ater, *, Akkub, Hatita, Ez 2:40,41,42
- *, and others of their clan. Neh 11:19
- Meshullam, *, Akkub. Neh 12:25

TAMAR
- for him to marry a girl named *. Gen 38:6
- "You must marry *, as our law Gen 38:8
- Then Judah told *, his Gen 38:11
- So * went home to her parents. Gen 38:11
- When someone told * that her Gen 38:13
- reached Judah that *, his Gen 38:24
- Perez, the son of * and Judah." Ru 4:12
- had a beautiful sister named *. 2Sa 13:1
- in love with *, my half sister." 2Sa 13:4
- ask him to let * come and prepare 2Sa 13:5
- his sister * be permitted to come 2Sa 13:6
- David agreed, and sent word to * 2Sa 13:7
- Then he said to *, "Now bring me 2Sa 13:10
- it to me." So * took it to him. 2Sa 13:10
- So * lived as a desolate woman in 2Sa 13:20
- this ever since Amnon raped *. 2Sa 13:32,33
- *, who was a very beautiful girl. 2Sa 14:27
- Baalath, and *, a desert city. 1Ki 9:17,18
- Then Er's widow, *, and her 1Ch 2:4
- David also had a daughter *. 1Ch 3:9
- Gilead, past the Dead Sea to *. Eze 47:18
- will go west from * to the springs Eze 47:19
- border runs from * to the Spring at Eze 48:27,28
- and Zerah (* was their mother); Mt 1:3

TAMARISK
- And Abraham planted a * tree Gen 21:33

TAMBOURINE
- on a * and dancing for joy. Ju 11:34

TAMBOURINES
- for joy with * and cymbals. 1Sa 18:6
- harps, *, castanets, and cymbals. 2Sa 6:5
- harps, *, cymbals, and trumpets. 1Ch 13:8
- Praise him with the * and Ps 150:4

TAME
- no human being can * the tongue. Jas 3:8

TAMMUZ
- and there sat women weeping for *, Eze 8:14
- The women wept for *, the god of Eze 8:14f

TAMMUZ-ADONIS
- See Ezekiel 18:14. *, a Babylonian Dan 11:37f

TANGLED
- the fire like a * mass of thorns. Nah 1:10
- and then gets * up with sin and 2Pe 2:20

TANHUMETH
- Seraiah, the son of * the 2Ki 25:23
- Seraiah (son of *), the sons of Jer 40:8

TANIS
- been founded seven years before * Num 13:22
- * (or Zoan, as it was pronounced Num 13:22f
- he sent upon the Egyptians in * Ps 78:43

TANK
- Then Hiram cast a round bronze *, 1Ki 7:23
- which were cast along with the *. 1Ki 7:24
- The sides of the * were four 1Ki 7:26
- of the room. The * was in the 1Ki 7:39
- One large * and twelve oxen 1Ki 7:41-46
- removed the great * from the backs 2Ki 16:17
- and the bronze * and its bases and 2Ki 25:13
- and the great * and its bases—all 2Ki 25:16
- He molded it into the bronze *, 1Ch 18:8
- Then he forged a huge round * 2Ch 4:2
- This * was set on the backs of 2Ch 4:3
- * and oxen were cast as one piece. 2Ch 4:3
- The walls of the * were five 2Ch 4:5
- the huge * and five to the left. 2Ch 4:6
- The priests used the *, and not 2Ch 4:6
- The huge * was in the southeast 2Ch 4:10
- The huge * and the twelve oxen 2Ch 4:12-16
- Nineveh is like a leaking water *! Nah 2:8

TANNED
- * rams' skins and specially Ex 35:5-9
- skins, dyed red, and * goat skins. Ex 36:19
- red, the specially * goat skins, Ex 39:33-40
- * as the dark tents of Kedar." Sol 1:5
- is so dark—the sun has * me. Sol 1:6
- The Girl: "My beloved one is * Sol 5:10
- Our princes were lean and *, Lam 4:7

TANNER
- Joppa, living with Simon, the *. Act 9:43
- with Simon, the *, down by the Act 10:5,6
- of Simon, a *, down by the shore.' Act 10:32

TAPE
- as measured with a *, were 2Sa 8:2

(TAPE Con't)
is lost in red * and bureaucracy. Ecc 5:8
holding in his hand a measuring * Eze 40:3

TAPESTRY
She also upholsters with finest *; Pro 31:22

TAPHATH
the princess *), whose area was the 1Ki 4:8-19

TAPPU-AH
The king of *; Jos 12:8-24
Zanoah, En-gannim, *, Enam, Jos 15:33-36
went from *, and followed along Jos 16:8
Michmethath to the Spring of *. Jos 17:7
(The land of * belonged to Jos 17:8
but the city of *, on the border of Jos 17:8
From the spring of * the border Jos 17:9

TAPPUAH
Menahem destroyed the city of * 2Ki 15:16
The sons of Hebron: Korah, *, 1Ch 2:43

TAR
resinous wood, sealing it with *; Gen 6:14
fire and flaming * from heaven upon Gen 19:24
it with *, put the baby in it, and Ex 2:3

TARALAH
Rekem, Irpeel, *, Zela, Ha-eleph, Jos 18:21-28

TAREA
Pithon, Melech, *, Ahaz. 1Ch 8:35

TARGET
They could hit a * within a Ju 20:16
as though I were shooting at a *. 1Sa 20:20
Why have you made me your *, and Job 7:20
pieces, then hung me up as his *. Job 16:12
He hurls each at its *. Job 36:32
they missed the * of God's will. Ps 78:57

TARGETS
crooked bow that always misses *; Hos 7:16

TARNISHED
which you * among the nations. Eze 36:22

TARPAULIN
(The sixth * will hang down to Ex 26:9

TARPAULINS
is made of goat's hair *. Ex 26:7,8
There are to be eleven of these * Ex 26:7,8
Connect five of these * into one Ex 26:9

TARRY
Literally, "*." Jn 21:22f
Literally, "*." Jn 21:23f

TARSHISH
The sons of Javan:Elishah, * Gen 10:4
Elishah, *, Kittim, and Rodanim. 1Ch 1:5-9
Chenaanah, Zethan, *, Ahishahar. 1Ch 7:10
sent his ships to *, using sailors 2Ch 9:21
ships in Ezion-geber to sail to *. 2Ch 20:36
disaster and never arrived at *. 2Ch 20:37
Shethar, Admatha, *, Meres, Est 1:13-15
coast—the kings of * and the Ps 72:10
Flee to *, men of Tyre, weeping Is 23:6
Sail on, O ships of *, for your Is 23:10
Literally, "the ships of *." Is 60:9f
to the nations—to *, Put, Lud, Is 66:19
of silver from * and gold from Jer 10:9
"From * come all kinds of riches Eze 27:12
The ships of * are your ocean Eze 27:25
and the merchant princes of * Eze 38:13
he found a ship leaving for *. Jon 1:3
That's why I ran away to *. Jon 4:2

TARSUS
Judas and ask there for Paul of *. Act 9:11
in *. Act 9:30
Then Barnabas went on to * to Act 11:25
"I am a Jew from * in Cilicia Act 21:39
he said, "born in *, a city in Act 22:3
from my earliest childhood in * Act 26:4

TARTAK
The gods Nibhaz and * were 2Ki 17:31

TASK
finished his *, God ceased from Gen 2:2
shoulder to the * and served his Gen 49:15
all left their * to meet with Moses Ex 36:4-7
led by a man appointed for the *. Lev 16:21
you will not have the * alone. Num 11:17
given this * to only you Levites? Num 16:10
from each tribe, for a special *. Jos 3:12
for a special *, one from each Jos 4:2,3
the whole nation united in this *. Ju 20:11
* in nine months and twenty days. 2Sa 24:8
Ithamar were assigned to each *. 1Ch 24:6
by the size of the *, for the Lord 1Ch 28:20
it: his son was chosen for that *. 2Ch 6:9
*, and the Lord be with you." 2Ch 36:22,23
My daily * will be to ferret out Ps 101:8
Tackle every * that comes along, Ecc 7:18
set apart these armies for this *; Is 13:3
* and honored me for doing it! Is 49:5
more important than any daily *. Eze 22:26
Have I given you the * of Mt 24:45
and, oh, that my * were completed! Lk 12:49
But who is adequate for such a * 2Co 2:16
grace until his * within you is Php 1:6

TASKMASTERS
and put brutal * over them to wear Ex 1:11
for freedom from their harsh *. Ex 3:7
this order to the * and officers he Ex 5:6
So the * and officers informed Ex 5:10,11
The * were brutal. Ex 5:13
the fault of your * for making such Ex 5:16
and righteousness shall be your *! Is 60:17

TASKS
seen the heavy * the Egyptians have Ex 3:9
refrain from doing our daily *. Ex 16:23
the Gershonites' * to them, but Num 4:27
various other * in the Tabernacle. 1Ch 6:48
handling all the * relating to the 1Ch 6:49
of Holies—and the * relating to the 1Ch 6:49
All * were assigned to the 1Ch 24:5
and assigned * to the priests and Neh 13:30
your hands from their heavy *." Ps 81:6
themselves for the * ahead! Ecc 10:16,17
be going about their household *; Mt 24:41
Begin the joyous * I have Mt 25:21
working together at household *; Lk 17:35,36
carry out the * assigned us by the Jn 9:4
throw yourself into your * so 1Ti 4:15

TASSEL
him and touched a * of his robe. Mt 9:20
touch even the * of his robe, and Mt 14:36

TASSELS
of Israel to make * for the hems of Num 15:37,38
and to attach the * to their Num 15:37,38
you notice the *, of the Num 15:39
"You must sew * on the four Deu 22:12

TASTE
to the Lord, * strong drink or wine Num 6:3,4
Lo, they * the riches of the sea Deu 33:19
At last you will * some of your 2Sa 16:7,8
Just as my mouth can * good Job 12:11
"He enjoyed the * of his Job 20:12
a man loses all * and appetite for Job 33:20
we can choose the * we want in Job 34:3
* the best!" Pro 9:17
* of strong wine deceive you. Pro 23:31
They will * victory and shout Zec 9:15
shall never again * wine until the Mk 14:25
even the smallest * of what I had Lk 14:24
suit the * of those who hear it; 1Th 2:4
"At first it will * like honey, Rev 10:9

TASTED
and flat, and * like honey bread. Ex 16:31
from it—they * like pancakes fried Num 11:8
"I * a little honey," Jonathan 1Sa 14:43
And when I ate it, it * sweet as Eze 3:3
All that time I * neither wine Dan 10:3
but when he had * it, he refused. Mt 27:34
When the master of ceremonies * Jn 2:9
When Jesus had * Jn 19:30
kindness, Jesus * death for Heb 2:9
the Good News and * for yourself Heb 6:4
"If you have * the Lord's goodness 1Pe 2:2,3f

TASTELESS
And how * is the uncooked white Job 6:5,6,7
My food is *, and I have lost my Ps 102:3,4
Even honey seems * to a man who Pro 27:7
drains out, leaving a * residue. Lk 14:34f

TASTER
baker and his wine *, so he jailed Gen 40:1
The wine * told his dream first. Gen 40:9,10
you back your job as his wine *. Gen 40:13
He sent for his wine * and chief Gen 40:20
Then he restored the wine * to Gen 40:21
Pharaoh's wine *, however, Gen 40:23
Then the king's wine * spoke up. Gen 41:9
position of wine *, and the chief Gen 41:13

TASTES
so my mind * truth when I hear it. Job 12:11
yourself, though it all * so good; Pro 23:1

TASTING
olive oil without * it, and to Job 24:11
forth your terrors for his *! Hos 13:14
*, or even touching certain foods? Col 2:21

TASTY
Food and wine are no longer *, 2Sa 19:35

TATTENAI
But *, the governor of the lands Ez 5:3
which governor *, Shethar-bozenai, Ez 5:6
Governor *, Shethar-bozenai, and Ez 6:13

TATTERED
is half a chair and a * pillow. Amo 3:12

TATTOO
yourselves nor put * marks upon Lev 19:28
say, or, "I am a Jew," and * Is 44:5

TATTOOED
See, I have * your name upon my Is 49:16
and free—to be * with a certain Rev 13:16
been * with the code of his name. Rev 14:11

TAUGHT
song and * it to the Israelites. Deu 31:22
Literally, "he * the men of Ju 8:16f
to Bethel and * the colonists from 2Ki 17:27,28
You have * the little children Ps 8:2
to me, for it * me to pay attention Ps 119:71,72
turned away from what you * me; Ps 119:102,103
Only fools refuse to be *. Pro 1:7,8,9
forget the things I've * you. Pro 3:1
TO LEARN, YOU must want to be *. Pro 12
* to him at his mother's knee: Pro 31
he not only * what he knew to the Ecc 12:
* them in an interesting manner. Ecc 12:
will be willing to be *! Is 29:2
And all your citizens shall be * Is 54:1
Lord its God, and refuses to be *. Jer 7:2
of Baal (whom they * my people to Jer 12:1
refused to pay attention and be *. Jer 17:2
* you to rebel against the Lord. Jer 29:3
year after year, I * them right Jer 32:3
and * him to be 'king of the Eze 19:
They have not * my people the Eze 22:2
I trained him from infancy, I * Hos 11:
her beauty, then * them all to Nah 3:
and sat down and * them there. Mt 5:
sermons, for he * as one who had Mt 7:2
He got into a boat and * from it Mt 13:2,
and * there in the synagogue and Mt 13:53,5
He lived in the wilderness and * Mk 1:
In fact, he * only by Mk 4:3
a shepherd, and he * them many Mk 6:3
and as usual he * them. Mk 10:
things he * them at this time: Mk 12:3
of the truth of all you were *. Lk 1:
just as John * one to his Lk 11:
And this is the prayer he * them: Lk 11:
* in our streets,' you will say. Lk 13:2
After that he * daily in the Lk 19:4
'They shall all be * of God.' Jn 6:4
have spoken what the Father * me. Jn 8:2
her own son, and * him all the Act 7:2
and we * the Scriptures to some Act 16:1
"What John the Baptist *." Act 19:
Kingdom of God and * them about Act 28:2
* his laws from earliest youth. Rom 2:1
contrary to what you have been *. Rom 16:1
God, in his kindness, has * me 1Co 3:1
and doing everything I * you. 1Co 11:2
No one else has * me. Gal 1:12
Those who are * the Word of God Gal 6:6
But that isn't the way Christ * Eph 4:20
vigorous in the truth you were *. Col 2:7
Remember what Christ * and let Col 3:16
the truth that we * you in our 2Th 2:15
* you, and that you always will. 2Th 3:4
pattern of truth I * you, 2Ti 1:13
the things you have been *. 2Ti 3:14
trust those of us who have * you. 2Ti 3:14
you were * the holy Scriptures; 2Ti 3:15
they have been * must be strong and Tit 1:9
Remember your leaders who have * Heb 13:7
have been * from the beginning. 1Jn 2:24
what Christ *, don't even invite 2Jn 1:10
Balaam did when he * Balak how to Rev 2:14

TAUNT
Then Jephthah, furious at the * Ju 12:4
and all the while my enemies * me. Ps 42:3
My enemies * me day after day and Ps 102:8
* me, for I trust your promises. Ps 119:40,41,42
and these women will * you with Jer 38:21,22
the other nations * you, saying, Eze 36:13
Then your enemies will * you and Mic 2:4
will * them, saying: 'You robbers! Hab 2:6

TAUNTED
"You * me that I would never Ju 8:15
The men you * and cursed are Ju 9:38
David *. 1Sa 26:15
also a giant) defied and * Israel; 1Ch 20:6,7
despised, mocked, * and cursed by Ps 44:15,16
It was not an enemy who * me—then Ps 55:12
be mocked and * and cursed wherever Jer 24:9

TAUNTING
Peninnah made matters worse by * 1Sa 1:6
and be ashamed for * me, "Where is Mic 7:10

TAUNTS
Their * pierce me like a fatal Ps 42:10
disgraced by the * of the heathen Joe 2:17
"I have heard the * of the Zep 2:8

TAVERNS
in the *, trying out new mixtures. Pro 23:29,30
Others joined us at The Three * Act 28:15

TAX
should have as his * twenty percent Gen 47:26
fifty-cent head * collected from Ex 38:25,26
* money to the Moabite capital. Ju 3:15
Each month the * officials 1Ki 4:27
$2,000 in the form of a special *. 2Ki 15:19,20
* against Judah totaling $230,000. 2Ki 23:33
Jerusalem? The * law enacted by 2Ch 24:6
to the Lord the * that Moses the 2Ch 24:9
with a Temple * so that there would Neh 10:32
Bring them—submissive, * in hand. Ps 68:30
"This is the * you must give to Eze 45:13
king who sent a * collector into Dan 11:20
he saw a * collector, Matthew, Mt 9:9
sitting at a * collection booth. Mt 9:9
Matthew (the * collector), Mt 10:2,3,4
the Temple * collectors came to Mt 17:24
sitting at his * collection booth. Mk 2:14
invited his fellow * collectors and Mk 2:15

AX Con't)
Even * collectors—notorious for Lk 3:12
the town he saw a * collector—with Lk 5:27
at a * collection booth. Lk 5:27
Many of Levi's fellow * Lk 5:29
Literally, "even the * Lk 7:29f
Literally, "is a friend of * Lk 7:34f
DISHONEST * COLLECTORS and Lk 15:1
the other a cheating * collector. Lk 18:10
like that * collector over there! Lk 18:11
"But the corrupt * collector Lk 18:13

AX-COLLECTING
Jews in the Roman * business (and, Lk 19:1

AXATION
Ben-hur, whose area for this * was 1Ki 4:8-19
"After him, at the time of the * Act 5:37

AXED
Jehoiakim * the people to get 2Ki 23:35

AXES
to pay crushing * to King Eglon. Ju 3:14
will be exempted from paying *!" 1Sa 17:25
those lands sent * to Solomon and 1Ki 4:21
besides sales * and profits from 1Ki 10:15
to pay heavy annual * to Assyria. 2Ki 17:3
by paying their *, so he became 2Ch 17:5
collect the Temple * from the 2Ch 24:6
then refuse to pay their * to you. Ez 4:13
my * collected in your territory. Ez 6:8
be required to pay * of any kind.' Ez 7:24
to the limit to pay their *. Neh 5:2,3,4
in the form of remission of *. Est 2:18
I collected silver and gold as * Ecc 2:7,8
by all your *, fines, and usury; Amo 5:11
which went as * to the king. Amo 7:1
"Doesn't your master pay *?" Mt 17:24
to cover the * for both of us; Mt 17:26,27
is it right to pay * to the Roman Mt 22:17
Now tell us, is it right to pay * Mk 12:14
"Make sure you collect no more * Lk 3:13
anyone on his *, I will penalize Lk 19:8
Now tell us—is it right to pay * Lk 20:22
not to pay their * to the Roman Lk 23:2
Pay your * too, for these same Rom 13:6
to have: pay your * and import Rom 13:7

EA
comes to them through * leaves! Hos 4:12

EACH
that will * them to listen to Ex 5:9
you can * the people from them." Ex 24:12
for the people, to * them the Lev 10:10
and to * them all the laws Lev 10:11
I will * you what it means to Num 14:34,35
to these laws I * you, and obey Deu 4:1
can * my laws to their children.' Deu 4:10
you shall * them to the people;' Deu 5:31
You must * them to your children Deu 6:7
eyes! * them to your children. Deu 11:19
The purpose of tithing is to * Deu 14:23
of this song, and * it to the Deu 31:19
The Levites shall * God's laws to Deu 33:10
and I will continue to * you 1Sa 12:23
to Israel and * the new residents 2Ki 17:27,28
people, and * them what is right; 2Ch 6:27
not had a true priest to * them. 2Ch 15:3
to * the Scriptures to the people. 2Ch 17:7,8,9
of your God, you are to * them. Ez 7:25
the wisdom of the past will * you. Job 8:10
or let the earth * you, or the Job 12:7,8,9
"I will * you about God— but Job 27:11
Keep silence and I will * you Job 33:33
* the rest of us how we should Job 37:19,20
Lead me; * me; Ps 25:5
The Lord is good and glad to * Ps 25:8
he will * the ways that are Ps 25:9
God will * him how to choose the Ps 25:12
listen and let me * you the Ps 34:11
Then I will * your ways to other Ps 51:13
our fathers to * them to their Ps 78:5
turn could * their children too. Ps 78:6
* us to number our days and Ps 90:12
aides and * the king's advisors. Ps 105:22
Blessed Lord, * me your rules. Ps 119:12
* me your good paths. Ps 119:64
you promised. Now * me good Ps 119:66
Accept my grateful thanks and * Ps 119:108
and * me, your servant, to obey; Ps 119:124
Look down in love upon me and * Ps 119:135
He wrote them to * his people how Pro 1:2
you all the more. * a wise man, Pro 9:9
will be the wiser; * a good man, Pro 9:9
* a child to choose the right Pro 22:6
and there you would * me. Sol 8:2
there he will * us his laws, and Is 2:3
be with you to * you—with your own Is 30:20
O women who wail. * your daughters Jer 9:20
"He shall * my people the Eze 44:23
of Judah—and to * them the Chaldean Dan 1:3,4
But those who * God's laws and Mt 5:19
Literally, "to * and preach in Mt 11:1f
fits perfectly—and let me * you; Mt 11:29,30
for they * their man-made laws Mt 15:9
very honest and * the truth Mt 22:16
Spirit, and then * these new Mt 28:20
illustrations to * the people as Mk 4:33
the synagogue to *, and the people Mk 6:2,3
but sincerely * the ways of God. Mk 12:14
"Lord, * us a prayer to recite Lk 11:1
think, but * the ways of God. Lk 20:21
to the Temple to *, and the crowds Lk 21:37,38
that God has sent you to * us. Jn 3:1
you for much and * you much, but I Jn 8:26
"Are you trying to * us?" Jn 9:34
Spirit—he will * you much, as well Jn 14:26
Jesus replied, "What I * is Jn 18:20
Jewish leaders and * nothing in Jn 18:20
If what they * and do is merely Act 5:38
they continued to * and preach that Act 5:42
and began to * the believers that Act 15:1
great and small. I * nothing except Act 26:22
the simple and * even children the Rom 2:20
Yes, you * others—then why don't Rom 2:21
why don't you * yourselves? Rom 2:21
so long ago are to * us patience Rom 15:4
able to * others all about them. Rom 15:14
thousand others to * you about 1Co 4:15
He will remind you of what I * in 1Co 4:17
Doesn't even instinct itself * 1Co 11:14,15
is that we never * anything else 1Co 11:16
sing, another will *, or tell some 1Co 14:26
meetings, but not to * men (1 Tim. 1Co 14:34f
door for me to preach and * here. 1Co 16:9
proving that what we * is right; 2Co 13:7
and make you wise; * them to each Col 3:16
and missionary to * this truth to 1Ti 2:7
I never let women * men or lord 1Ti 2:12
* these things and make sure 1Ti 4:11
let them follow the way you * and 1Ti 4:12
* these truths, Timothy, and 1Ti 6:2
preach to the Gentiles and * them. 2Ti 1:11
For you must * others those 2Ti 2:2
me speak about. * these great 2Ti 2:2
you are trying to * those who are 2Ti 2:25
and * them their new doctrines. 2Ti 3:6
and is useful to * us what is true 2Ti 3:16
has chosen and to * them to know Tit 1:1
will be able to * it to others and Tit 1:9
Christianity. * the older men to Tit 2:2
* the older women to be quiet and Tit 2:3
You must * these things and Tit 2:15
need someone to * you all over Heb 5:12,13
anyone to * you what is right. 1Jn 2:27
If anyone comes to * you, and he 2Jn 1:10
a prophetess, to * my servants that Rev 2:20

TEACHER
to become a Bible *, teaching those Ez 7:10
"To: Ezra, the priest, the * of Ez 7:12
he is a priest and * of the laws of Ez 7:21
was the priest and * of religion. Neh 12:26
Who is a * like him? Job 36:22
A wise * makes learning a joy; Pro 15:2
a rebellious * spouts Pro 15:2
and a pleasant * is the best. Pro 16:21
not only a wise man, but a good *; Ecc 12:10
* and gives the farmer wisdom. Is 28:29
your own eyes you will see your *. Is 30:20
or be his * or give him counsel? Is 40:13
said to him, "*, I will follow Mt 8:19
"Why does your * associate with Mt 9:11
student is not greater than his *. Mt 10:24
him, shouting, "*, don't you even Mk 4:38
"*, this is wonderful!" Mk 9:5
up and said, "*, I brought my son Mk 9:17
him one day, "*, we saw a man Mk 9:38
and asked, "Good *, what must I do Mk 10:17
"*," the man replied, "I've Mk 10:20
"O *," the blind man said, "I Mk 10:51
day, and exclaimed, "Look, *! Mk 11:21
"*," these spies said, "we Mk 12:14
"*, Moses gave us a law that Mk 12:19
The * of religion replied, "Sir, Mk 12:32
disciples said, "*, what beautiful Mk 13:1
a student know more than his *? Lk 6:40
"All right, *," Simon replied, Lk 7:40
"there's no use troubling the * Lk 8:49
out to him, "*, this boy here is Lk 9:38
this question: "*, what does a man Lk 10:25
we know what an honest * you are. Lk 20:21
lives there, 'Our * says for you to Lk 22:11
and was a mighty *, highly Lk 24:19
a respected Jewish *, and yet you Jn 3:10,11
"*," they said to Jesus, "this Jn 8:4
And since I, the Lord and *, Jn 13:14
a wonderful Bible * and preacher, Act 18:24
If you are a *, do a good job of Rom 12:7
The Jewish laws were our * and Gal 3:24
home, and must be a good Bible *. 1Ti 3:2
any evil * in this wicked world. 1Jn 4:4

TEACHER'S
The student shares his * fate. Mt 10:25

TEACHERS
* of their skills to others. Ex 35:34
as * in all the cities of Judah. 2Ch 17:7,8,9
the religious * in Israel: 2Ch 35:3
Yes, wiser than my *, for I am Ps 119:99
who master what their * tell them. Ecc 12:11
laws," when your * have twisted Jer 8:8
These wise * of yours will be Jer 8:9
"Beware of false * who come Mt 7:15
one of the Jewish religious * Mt 8:19
But the Jewish * of religion who Mk 3:22
One of the * of religion who was Mk 12:28
"Why do your religious * claim Mk 12:35
"Beware of the * of religion! Mk 12:38
elders and * of religion—the entire Mk 15:1
sitting among the * of Law, Lk 2:46,47
and * of the Law were sitting Lk 5:17
the Pharisees and * of the Law Lk 5:21
But the Pharisees and * of the Lk 5:30
was deformed. The * of the Law and Lk 6:7
the Pharisees and * of the Law, "I Lk 6:9
the Pharisees and * of Moses' Law. Lk 7:30
and * of the Law—and be killed; Lk 9:22
AMONG THE PROPHETS and * of the Act 13:1
I leave you, false *, like vicious Act 20:29
Such * are not working for our Rom 16:18
one of God's * more than another. 1Co 4:6
*, Those who do miracles 1Co 12:28
Are all *? 1Co 12:29
like those false * of yours who 2Co 3:1
Those false * who are so anxious Gal 4:17
I only wish these * who want you Gal 5:12
help their * by paying them. Gal 6:6
Those * of yours who are trying Gal 6:12
And even those * who submit to Gal 6:13
But these * have missed this 1Ti 1:6
They want to become famous as * 1Ti 1:7
of * with devil-inspired ideas. 1Ti 4:1
These * will tell lies with 1Ti 4:2
they must be gentle, patient * of 2Ti 2:24
following new *, but they never 2Ti 3:7
And these * fight truth just as 2Ti 3:8
In fact, evil men and false * 2Ti 3:13
around looking for * who will tell 2Ti 4:3
Such * are only after your money. Tit 1:11
but they should be * of goodness. Tit 2:3
you) should become masters (*)." Jas 3:1f
and when we * of religion, who Jas 3:1
there will be false * among you. 2Pe 2:1
These * in their greed will tell 2Pe 2:3
than these false *, never speak out 2Pe 2:11
But false * are fools—no better 2Pe 2:12
That is the pay these * will have 2Pe 2:13
But these very * who offer this 2Pe 2:19
For there are many false * 1Jn 4:1
of the traveling * and missionaries 3Jn 1:5
some godless * have wormed their Jud 1:4
Yet these false * carelessly go Jud 1:8

TEACHES
Experience * that it is those who Job 4:7,8
commandment, and * others to, he Mt 5:19
happened yet, it * us to wait Rom 8:25
God, which the Holy Spirit * us. 1Co 2:14
that the Bible * what it doesn't. 2Co 4:2
For he * you all things, and he 1Jn 2:27

TEACHING
his decisions, * them God's laws, Ex 18:19,20
One day as he was * the young 2Ki 4:38
a Bible teacher, * those laws to Ez 7:10
O MY PEOPLE, listen to my *. Ps 78:1
no wonder I hate every false *. Ps 119:104
Stop listening to * that Pro 19:27
went on * the people all he knew; Ecc 12:9
wide ministry of * in those days. Dan 11:33
through Galilee * in the Jewish Mt 4:23
This is the * of the laws of Mt 7:12
of that area, * in the Jewish Mt 9:35
* of the Pharisees and Sadducees. Mt 16:12
the Temple and was *, the chief Mt 21:23
I was with you * daily in the Mt 26:55
house where he was *, and they sent Mk 3:31,32
beach as he was *, so he got into a Mk 4:1
His usual method of * was to Mk 4:2
in his public *, but afterwards, Mk 4:34
he went out among the villages, *. Mk 6:6
time with his disciples, * them. Mk 9:30,31
so enthusiastic about Jesus' *. Mk 11:18
Later, as Jesus was * the people Mk 12:35
I was there * every day. Mk 14:49
Once as he was * in the Lk 4:33
One day while he was *, some Lk 5:17
in the synagogue *, and a man was Lk 6:6
he was *, because of the crowds. Lk 8:19
And he welcomed them, * them Lk 9:11
Then, * them more about prayer, Lk 11:5,6
One Sabbath as he was * in a Lk 13:10
Now he began * them again about Lk 13:18
to village, * as he went, always Lk 13:22
ON ONE OF those days when he was * Lk 20:1
So Jesus told them, "I'm not * Jn 7:16
* is from God or is merely my own. Jn 7:17
* them your words of truth. Jn 17:17
and what he had been * them. Jn 18:19
at the apostles' * sessions and at Act 2:42

(TEACHING Con't)
with your * and intend to bring the — Act 5:28
in prayer, preaching, and *." — Act 6:4
year, * the many new converts. — Act 11:26
who were preaching and * there. — Act 15:34,35
"They are * the people to do — Act 16:20,21
and a half, * the truths of God. — Act 18:11
whom I went about * the Kingdom — Act 20:25
* to which God has committed you. — Rom 6:17
are a teacher, do a good job of *. — Rom 12:7
people's faith, * things about — Rom 16:17
at studying and *, and this is his — 1Co 12:8
what I had been * and, I hoped, — Gal 2:2
and * them in the ways of God. — Eph 4:11
and * them as well as we know how. — Col 1:28
For God himself is * you to love — 1Th 4:9
men who are * such wrong doctrine. — 1Ti 1:3,4
by the true * you have followed. — 1Ti 4:6
work hard at both preaching and *. — 1Ti 5:17
* be laughed at because of this. — 1Ti 6:1
you ought to be * others, but — Heb 5:12,13
and again, always * those first — Heb 6:1
Many will follow their evil * — 2Pe 2:2
For if you wander beyond the * — 2Jn 1:9
this false * ('deeper truths,' as — Rev 2:24,25

TEACHINGS
Jesus' life and * and how he — Act 1:1
Such rules are mere human *, for — Col 2:22
sound, wholesome * of the Lord — 1Ti 6:3
Christ's *, you will have God too. — 2Jn 1:9

TEAM
end of the line with the last *. — 1Ki 19:19
formed a truce * and went out of — Is 36:3
truce * to discuss terms of peace. — Lk 14:32
A * of itinerant Jews who were — Act 19:13
Apollos and I are working as a * — 1Co 3:8

TEAMED
Don't be * with those who do not — 2Co 6:14

TEAMMATE
And I ask you, my true *, to — Php 4:3

TEAMS
None of the wagons or * was — Num 7:9
horses except for one hundred *. — 2Sa 8:4
with eleven other * ahead of him; — 1Ki 19:19
He crippled all the chariot * — 1Ch 18:4
3,000 camels, 500 * of oxen, 500 — Job 1:2,3
camels, 1,000 * of oxen, and 1,000 — Job 42:12

TEAR
the edge so that it would not *. — Ex 39:23
* it apart, but not completely. — Lev 1:15,16,17
and do not * your clothes. — Lev 10:6
have leprosy must * his clothes and — Lev 13:45
in mourning, nor * his clothing, — Lev 21:10
I will return and * your flesh with — Ju 8:7
For they * the hand that touches — 2Sa 23:6
my laws, I will * the kingdom away — 1Ki 11:11
says, 'I will * the kingdom from — 1Ki 11:31
of Jezreel shall * apart the body — 1Ki 21:23
she screamed, and began to * — 2Ki 11:13,14
Torrents * away the soil. — Job 14:18,19
Just because you * your clothes — Job 18:4
Men know how to * apart flinty — Job 28:9
They are like lions eager to * — Ps 17:12
God, before I * you apart—and no — Ps 50:22
O God, break off their fangs. * — Ps 58:6
A time to *; — Ecc 3:7
I will * down the fences and let — Is 5:5
the vultures will * bodies all — Is 18:6
You check over the houses and * — Is 22:9,10,11
instrument to * all enemies apart, — Is 41:15
come, * apart the sheep; — Is 56:9
your mouth I will * down some and — Jer 1:10
kill, the dogs to *, and the — Jer 15:3
They will * out all of your fine — Jer 22:7
too, and * down all her towers. — Jer 48:18
I will * off the charms and set — Eze 13:20
I will * off the magic veils and — Eze 13:21
like wolves, who * apart their — Eze 22:27
of Tyre and * down her towers. — Eze 26:4
nations prick and * at Israel like — Eze 28:24
I will * Ephraim and Judah as a — Hos 5:14
Let your remorse * at your — Joe 2:13
The Lord will * down her wall and — Mic 1:6
depend on, and * down your walls — Mic 5:11
are wolves and will * you apart. — Mt 7:15
For the patch would * away and — Mt 9:16
were so full that they began to *! — Lk 5:6
'I know—I'll * down my barns and — Lk 12:18
told him. '* it up and write — Lk 16:5,6
But they said, "Let's not * up — Jn 19:23,24
fearing they would * him apart, — Act 23:10
god there is, and * down every — 2Th 2:4
for some victim to * apart. — 1Pe 5:8

TEARFUL
has heard your * complaints about — Num 11:18

TEARING
to prevent the vultures from * at — 2Sa 21:10
in * down the walls of Jerusalem. — 2Ki 25:10
king insulted, * down his temples — Is 36:7
work * down the walls of the city. — Jer 52:14
of its victims by * them apart with — Dan 7:7
fat ones, even * off their feet. — Zec 11:16
up for us by * the curtain—his — Heb 10:20

TEARS
and burst into *, sobbing wildly. — Gen 21:16
and both of them were in *! — Gen 33:4
The people broke into * as the — Ju 2:4
So Samson's wife broke down in * — Ju 14:16
You will shed bitter * because — 1Sa 8:18
plight, everyone broke into *. — 1Sa 11:4
sadly shook hands, * running down — 1Sa 20:41
Then the king broke into *, and — 2Sa 18:33
heard his prayer and seen his *. — 2Ki 20:5
begging him with * to stop Haman's — Est 8:3
God hates me and angrily * at my — Job 16:9
but I pour out my * to God, — Job 16:20
night my pillow is wet with *. — Ps 6:6
Don't sit back, unmindful of my * — Ps 39:12
You have collected all my * and — Ps 56:8
us with sorrow and *, and have — Ps 80:5
of bread. My * run down into my — Ps 102:9,10
from *, my feet from stumbling. — Ps 116:8
Those who sow * shall reap joy. — Ps 126:5
and * down everything he does. — Pro 12:4
* hers down by her own efforts. — Pro 14:1
the earth—the * of the oppressed, — Ecc 4:1
of Sibmah. My * shall flow for — Is 16:9
The Lord God will wipe away all * — Is 25:8
and sees your * and will let you — Is 38:5
THAT MY eyes were a fountain of *; — Jer 9:1
Let the * flow from your eyes. — Jer 9:17,18
My eyes will overflow with * — Jer 13:17
day my eyes shall overflow with *; — Jer 14:17
who comes. * of joy shall stream — Jer 31:9
She sobs through the night; * run — Lam 1:2
For all these things I weep; * — Lam 1:16
Sorrows and * are his portion for — Lam 2:5
I have cried until the * no — Lam 2:11
O walls of Jerusalem, let * fall — Lam 2:18
streams of * because of the — Lam 3:48,49
let there be no *. — Eze 24:16
altar with your * because the Lord — Mal 2:13
"No one * off a piece of a new — Lk 5:36
her * falling down upon his feet; — Lk 7:38
* and wiped them with her hair. — Lk 7:44
and see." * came to Jesus' eyes. — Jn 11:35
and with *—and have faced grave — Act 20:19
and day and my many * for you. — Act 20:31
it again now with * in my eyes, — Php 3:18
your * as we left each other. — 2Ti 1:4
God, praying with * and agony of — Heb 5:7
he wept bitter * of repentance. — Heb 12:17
Let there be * for the wrong — Jas 4:9
And God will wipe their * away." — Rev 7:17
He will wipe away all * from — Rev 21:4

TEASING
and the Egyptian girl Hagar—* — Gen 21:9

TEBAH
Reumah:*, Gaham,Tahash, Maacah. — Gen 22:24

TEBALIAH
*, the third; — 1Ch 26:11

TECHNIQUE
the same * as in making a seal; — Ex 28:11

TECHNIQUES
using the usual * of the — Ex 30:35
* of the most skilled perfumers. — Ex 37:29

TEEM
Then God said, "Let the waters * — Gen 1:20
though the land * with them. — Lev 20:25

TEEMING
the mighty ocean, * with life of — Ps 104:25
all his * masses, says the Lord." — Eze 31:18

TEETH
and his * are whiter than milk. — Gen 49:12
To rip them apart with their *; — Deu 32:24
from the claws and * of the lion — 1Sa 17:37
he has gnashed upon me with his * — Job 16:9
escaped death by the skin of my *. — Job 19:20
For his * are terrible. — Job 41:14
them and breaking off their *. — Ps 3:7
* are sharp as spears and arrows. — Ps 57:4
Tear out the * of these young — Ps 58:6
they will gnash their * in anger — Ps 112:10
vinegar that sets the * on edge. — Pro 10:26
They devour the poor with * as — Pro 30:13,14
weak, and your * will be too few to — Ecc 12:3
eating, when your * are gone! — Ecc 12:4
Your * are white as sheep's — Sol 4:2
Your * are white as freshly — Sol 6:6
children's * are set on edge." — Jer 31:29f
the one whose * are set on edge. — Jer 31:30
They hiss and grind their * and — Lam 2:16
me eat gravel and broken my *; — Lam 3:16
children's * are set on edge." — Eze 18:2f
It held three ribs between its *, — Dan 7:5
with its huge iron *, and others it — Dan 7:7
with its iron * and brass claws — Dan 7:19
with * as sharp as those of lions! — Joe 1:6
and pull from her * her sacrifices — Zec 9:7
be weeping and gnashing of *. — Mt 13:42
be weeping and gnashing of *. — Mt 13:50
is weeping and gnashing of *.' — Mt 22:13
will be weeping and gnashing of *. — Mt 24:5
be weeping and gnashing of *.' — Mt 25:3
also threw the same in his *. — Mt 27:4
and grind his * and become rigid. — Mk 9:1
armed to the * to capture me? — Mk 14:4
and gnashing of * as you stand — Lk 13:2
and ground their * in rage. — Act 7:5
and their * were those of lions. — Rev 9:

TEGERAMA
Tabal, Gimaraya, *, peoples who — Eze 38:2,3

TEHAPHNEHES
it will be a dark day for * too; — Eze 30:1

TEHINNAH
of Bethrapha, Paseah, and *; — 1Ch 4:11,1
* was the father of Irnahash. — 1Ch 4:11,1

TEKEL
'Mene,' 'Mene,' '*,' 'Parsin.' — Dan 5:24,2
"* means 'weighed'—you have been — Dan 5:2

TEKOA
for a woman of * who had a — 2Sa 14:2,
Ira (son of Ikkesh) from *; — 2Sa 23:24-3
birth to Ashhur, the father of *. — 1Ch 2:2
Ashhur, the father of *, had two — 1Ch 4:
Ira (son of Ikkesh) from *; — 1Ch 11:26-4
was Ira, the son of Ikkesh from *; — 1Ch 27:
Bethlehem, Etam, *, — 2Ch 11:5-1
went out into the wilderness of *. — 2Ch 20:2
Next were the men from *, but — Neh 3:
Sound the alarm in *; — Jer 6:
living in the village of *. — Amo 1:

TEKOITES
Then came the *, who repaired — Neh 3:27

TEL
took me away to * Abib, another — Eze 3:14,1

TEL-HARSHA
*, Cherub, Addan, and Immer. — Ez 2:59
*, Cherub, Addon, and Immer. — Neh 7:61

TEL-MELAH
Persian cities of *, Tel-harsha, — Ez 2:59
Persian cities of *, Tel-harsha, — Neh 7:61

TELAH
*, the father of — 1Ch 7:25,26,27

TELAIM
So Saul mobilized his army at *. — 1Sa 15:4

TELASSAR
Rezeph, and Eden in the land of *? — 2Ki 19:12
or the people of Eden in *? — Is 37:12

TELEM
Ithnan, Ziph, *, Be-aloth, — Jos 15:21-32
Of the gatekeepers, Shallum, *, — Ez 10:24

TELL
Sarai his wife to * everyone that — Gen 12:11,12,13
"Why didn't you * me she was — Gen 12:18
I'll * you what we'll do. — Gen 13:9
"I saw God and lived to * it." — Gen 16:13
now he tries to * us what to do! — Gen 19:9
So Lot rushed out to * his — Gen 19:14
Why didn't you * me before?" — Gen 21:26
The girl ran home to * her folks, — Gen 24:28
Doubtless to * them that a — Gen 24:28f
"All right," Laban said, "* us — Gen 24:33
of my master's brother. So * me, — Gen 24:49
When you * me, then I'll know — Gen 24:49
servants came to * him, "We have — Gen 26:32
Rebekah: "Now do exactly as I * — Gen 27:8,9,10
Just do what I * you. — Gen 27:13
grandchildren and * them good-bye? — Gen 31:28
I'll * you what we'll do—if — Gen 34:15
into a well and * father that a — Gen 37:19,20
one here to * us what they mean." — Gen 40:8
replied. "* me what you saw." — Gen 40:8
these men can * me what it means. — Gen 41:15
God will * you what it means!" — Gen 41:16
of them could * me the meaning." — Gen 41:24
"Didn't I * you not to do it?" — Gen 42:22
"Why did you ever * him you had — Gen 43:6
to my father and * him, 'Your son — Gen 45:9
household." ' * our father about — Gen 45:13
Then Pharaoh said to Joseph, "* — Gen 45:17
to Egypt to live. * them, 'Pharaoh — Gen 45:18
And * your brothers to take — Gen 45:19
Jacob sent Judah on ahead to * — Gen 46:28
"I'll go and * Pharaoh that you — Gen 46:31
And I will * him, 'These men are — Gen 46:32
your occupation, * him, 'We have — Gen 46:34
When you * him this, he will let — Gen 46:34
me and I will * you what is going — Gen 49:1
"* his majesty," he requested — Gen 50:5
instructed us to * you to forgive — Gen 50:16,17
of Israel and * them that their — Ex 3:13
What shall I * them?" — Ex 3:13
Yes, * them, 'Jehovah, — Ex 3:15
him, "and * them about Jehovah — Ex 3:16
king of Egypt and * him, 'Jehovah, — Ex 3:18
They won't do what I * them to. — Ex 4:1
Now go ahead and do as I * you, — Ex 4:12
and I will * you what to say." — Ex 4:12
So I will * you what to tell — Ex 4:15
So I will tell you what to * — Ex 4:15
well, and I will * you what to do. — Ex 4:15
Then you are to * him, 'Jehovah — Ex 4:22

ELL Con't)

"Therefore * the descendants of	Ex 6:6
to Pharaoh and * him that he must	Ex 6:11
your spokesman. * Aaron everything	Ex 7:2
Moses: "* Aaron to point his rod	Ex 7:19
to Pharaoh and * him, 'Jehovah	Ex 8:1
"Be so kind as to * me when you	Ex 8:9
Then the Lord said to Moses, "*	Ex 8:16
Moses, "and * him, 'Jehovah, the	Ex 9:1
before Pharaoh and * him, 'Jehovah	Ex 9:13
What stories you can * your	Ex 10:2
am doing in Egypt! * them what	Ex 10:2
of the country. * all the men and	Ex 11:2
you shall * them, 'With mighty	Ex 13:14
NOW INSTRUCTED Moses, "*	Ex 14:2
or not. * them to gather twice as	Ex 16:5
their complaints. * them, 'In the	Ex 16:11,12
you will * them his decisions,	Ex 18:19,20
people of Israel. * them, 'You	Ex 19:2,3
may not pass, and * them, 'Beware!	Ex 19:12
They said to Moses, "You * us	Ex 20:19
Build altars only where I * you	Ex 20:24
JEHOVAH SAID TO Moses, "* the	Ex 25:1
There I will * you my	Ex 25:22
to Moses: "* the people of Israel	Ex 31:12,13
For the Lord had told Moses to *	Ex 33:5
"* the people of Israel that	Lev 4:2
Then the Lord said to Moses, "*	Lev 6:25
Then the Lord said to Moses, "*	Lev 7:23
And the Lord said to Moses, "*	Lev 7:29
"And * the people of Israel,"	Lev 9:3
"* the people of Israel that the	Lev 11:2,3
THE LORD THEN told Moses to * the	Lev 18:1
THE LORD ALSO told Moses to * the	Lev 19:1
THE LORD SAID to Moses: "* the	Lev 21:1
And the Lord said to Moses, "*	Lev 21:16,17
And the Lord said to Moses, "*	Lev 22:17,18
THE LORD SAID to Moses, "* the	Lev 24:1
the camp and * all who heard him to	Lev 24:13,14
by stoning. And * the people of	Lev 24:15,16
THE LORD SAID to Moses, "* the	Lev 27:1
Then the Lord said to Moses, "*	Num 5:5,6
And the Lord said to Moses, "*	Num 5:11,12
Now the Lord said to Moses, "*	Num 6:22,23
THE LORD SAID to Moses, "* Aaron	Num 8:2
"And * the people to purify	Num 11:18
have meat to eat. * them, 'The Lord	Num 11:18
have been saying. * them, 'The	Num 14:28
The Lord said to Moses, "* the	Num 15:37,38
to Moses, "Then * the people to	Num 16:23,24
And the Lord said to Moses, "*	Num 16:36,37
THEN THE LORD said to Moses, "*	Num 17:1
The Lord also said to Moses, "*	Num 18:25,26
"* the people of Israel to bring	Num 19:1
and * it to pour out its water!	Num 20:8
said, "and I'll * you in the	Num 22:8
to say only what I * you to."	Num 22:20
say only what I * you to say."	Num 22:35
and I will * you what he says to	Num 23:3,4
But Balaam replied, "Didn't I *	Num 23:26
Balaam replied, "Didn't I * your	Num 24:12
But first, let me * you what the	Num 24:14
Lord told Moses to * the people of	Num 33:50,51
THE LORD TOLD Moses to * the	Num 34:1
And the Lord said to Moses, "*	Num 35:9,10
"But the Lord said to me, "*	Deu 1:42
upon your lives! * your children	Deu 4:9
miracles he did. * them especially	Deu 4:10
laws that I will * you today, so	Deu 4:40
" 'You must not * lies.	Deu 5:20
then come and * us, and we will	Deu 5:26,27
Go and * them to return to their	Deu 5:30
you must * him, 'We were	Deu 6:21
He will * you where this altar	Deu 12:18
I will * him what to say, and he	Deu 18:18
to * lies on the witness stand.	Deu 19:20
"Her father shall * them, 'I	Deu 22:16
They will * you all about it.	Deu 32:7
of Israel to * the people to get	Jos 1:10,11
"* the twelve men chosen for a	Jos 4:2,3
you can * them, 'It is to	Jos 4:7
mean, you are to * them that these	Jos 4:22
on dry ground! * them how the Lord	Jos 4:23
any of you until I * you to shout;	Jos 6:10
"Get up! * the people, 'Each of	Jos 7:13
* me what you have done."	Jos 7:19
"* the people of Israel to	Jos 20:2
me, * them that no one is here."	Ju 4:20
to Abimelech! I'll * Abimelech,	Ju 9:29
and he didn't * me his name, but	Ju 13:6
certainly want to * everyone that	Ju 13:17
But he didn't * his father or	Ju 14:6
But he didn't * them where he had	Ju 14:9
why should I * you?"	Ju 14:16
So Delilah begged Samson to * her	Ju 16:6
"Please * me, Samson, why you	Ju 16:6
Please * me how you can be	Ju 16:10
"Now * me how you can really be	Ju 16:13
protest, we will * them, 'Please be	Ju 21:22
Now do what I * you—bathe and	Ru 3:3
there, and he will * you what to do	Ru 3:4
me and do whatever I * him to do.	1Sa 2:35
he was afraid to * Eli what the	1Sa 3:15
Lord say to you? * me everything.	1Sa 3:16,17
can * us where the donkeys are."	1Sa 9:6
* me where the seer's house is?"	1Sa 9:18
in the morning I will * you what	1Sa 9:19
they will * you that the donkeys	1Sa 10:2
(But he didn't * him that he had	1Sa 10:16
he was a lad. Now * me as I stand	1Sa 12:3
Have I ever taken a bribe? * me	1Sa 12:3
But he didn't * his father that	1Sa 14:1
the troops and * them to bring the	1Sa 14:34
But no one would * him what the	1Sa 14:39
"* me what you've done," Saul	1Sa 14:43
"* me about your father, my	1Sa 17:58
he told them, "* David that the	1Sa 18:25
then I'll * you everything I can	1Sa 19:3
* Jonathan—why should I hurt him?'	1Sa 20:3
"* me what I can do," Jonathan	1Sa 20:4
asks where I am, * him that I asked	1Sa 20:6
* you, so you can escape and live.	1Sa 20:13
If you hear me * him, 'They're on	1Sa 20:21
But if I * him, 'Go farther—the	1Sa 20:22
"He told me not to * anybody why	1Sa 21:2
from me, but they didn't * me!"	1Sa 22:17
there, I knew he would * Saul.	1Sa 22:22
O Lord God of Israel, please *	1Sa 23:11
* you whether or not this is true.	1Sa 25:8
But she didn't * her husband	1Sa 25:19
so she didn't * him anything about	1Sa 25:36
Saul at Gibe-ah to * him that David	1Sa 26:1
But I'll * you what—we'll take	1Sa 26:11
and * where he had really been.	1Sa 27:11
"Can you * me where they went?"	1Sa 30:15
children and * them to be gone."	1Sa 30:22
David demanded. "* me how the	2Sa 1:4
Don't * the Philistines, lest	2Sa 1:20
with Abner and * him to come back.	2Sa 3:26
"* my servant David not to do it!	2Sa 7:5
—then * him, 'Uriah was killed,	2Sa 11:19,20,21
"Well, * Joab not to be	2Sa 11:25
city; * him he is doing well."	2Sa 11:25
Nathan to * David this story:	2Sa 12:1
David's aides were afraid to *	2Sa 12:18
when we * him the child is dead?"	2Sa 12:18
Joab sent messengers to * David,	2Sa 12:26,27
"Well," Jonadab said, "I'll *	2Sa 13:5
some food for you. * him you'll	2Sa 13:5
in Jerusalem to * King David, "All	2Sa 15:13
return to Jerusalem and *	2Sa 15:33,34
are there. * them the plans that	2Sa 15:35,36
me and * me what is going on."	2Sa 15:35,36
* the king what you have seen."	2Sa 18:21
was afraid to * the king what	2Sa 18:29f
And he told them to * Amasa,	2Sa 19:13
"Just * me and I will do it for	2Sa 21:4
The Lord said to Gad, "* David	2Sa 24:12
"If you do as I * you to and	1Ki 6:11,12
If you listen to what I * you	1Ki 11:38
And the young men replied, "*	1Ki 12:10
"* Rehoboam the son of Solomon,	1Ki 12:23,24
people of Israel. * them to disband	1Ki 12:23,24
And the Lord told him what to *	1Ki 14:5
Elijah, "Go and * King Ahab that I	1Ki 18:1
So Elijah went to * him.	1Ki 18:2
"Now go and * the king I am	1Ki 18:8
And now you say, 'Go and * him	1Ki 18:11
And now you say, 'Go * the king	1Ki 18:14
So Obadiah went to * Ahab that	1Ki 18:16
to Ahab and * him to get into his	1Ki 18:44
from Ben-hadad, "* my lord the	1Ki 20:9
"How many times must I * you to	1Ki 22:16
I * you this would happen?	1Ki 22:18
to my son Joash. * them, 'The king	1Ki 22:27
to the king and * him, 'The Lord	2Ki 1:6
"Didn't I * you not to go?"	2Ki 2:18
to * him of her husband's death.	2Ki 4:1
servant Gehazi, "* the woman I	2Ki 4:11,12
said to Gehazi, "* her that we	2Ki 4:13
my comfort unless I * you to."	2Ki 4:24
Elisha sent a messenger out to *	2Ki 5:10
has sent me to * you that two young	2Ki 5:22
is too small. * us, as our	2Ki 6:1
come on, let's go back and * the	2Ki 7:9
and saying, "* me some stories of	2Ki 8:4
the man of God and * him to ask the	2Ki 8:8,9
And Elisha replied, "* him,	2Ki 8:10
asked him, "What did he * you?"	2Ki 8:14
oil over his head. * him that the	2Ki 9:3
"No, we don't," they said. "*	2Ki 9:12
no one could * whose it was."	2Ki 9:36
and will do anything you * us to.	2Ki 10:5
I'll * you what: Make a bet	2Ki 18:23
"The Lord says, "* your master not	2Ki 19:5,6
of my people, and * him that the	2Ki 20:5
"* the man who sent you to me,	2Ki 22:15,16
"* the peoples of the world	1Ch 16:8
And * of his marvelous works.	1Ch 16:9
* everyone about his miracles.	1Ch 16:24
"* my servant David, 'The Lord	1Ch 17:7
prophet, "Go and * David, 'The	1Ch 21:10,11
These accounts * of his reign	1Ch 29:30
walk where you * them to go.	2Ch 6:31
"What shall I * them?"	2Ch 10:6
they replied. "* them, 'If you	2Ch 10:10
I'll be like!' * them, 'My little	2Ch 10:10
sent Shemaiah to * them, "Because	2Ch 12:7
many times must I * you to speak	2Ch 18:15
"Didn't I * you?"	2Ch 18:17
Israel ordered. "* them, 'The	2Ch 18:26
secretly, to * the Levites and clan	2Ch 23:2,3
says, * the man who sent you,	2Ch 34:23
ask me about this: * him, the Lord	2Ch 34:26
* lies about them to King Cyrus.	Ez 4:4,5
leaders came to * me that many of	Ez 9:1
Take courage and * us how to	Ez 10:4
to Esther and to * her what was	Est 4:8
Then Esther said to * Mordecai:	Est 4:15
The king turned to his aides. "*	Est 5:5
to Esther, "Now * me what you	Est 5:6
It will be granted to you. * me	Est 9:12
I alone have escaped to * you."	Job 1:16
I alone have escaped to * you."	Job 1:17
and I alone escaped to * you."	Job 1:19
* me, what have I done wrong?	Job 6:24
* him boldly that I am not guilty.	Job 9:35
me—* me why you are doing it.	Job 10:2
Oh, that God would speak and *	Job 11:5
ask the birds—they will * you;	Job 12:7,8,9
* me, what have I done wrong?	Job 13:23
to say— you will * me of rich and	Job 21:28
around and he can * you the truth,	Job 21:29
I would * him all about my side	Job 23:4,5
Then I would * him exactly what	Job 31:37
did not dare to * you what I think,	Job 32:6
* us, and we will cease at once.'	Job 34:32
earth? * me, if you know so much.	Job 38:4
earth? * me about it if you know!	Job 38:17,18
there? Or * me about the darkness.	Job 38:19
will conquer me. * me clearly what	Ps 5:8
all my heart, and * everyone about	Ps 9:1
* the world about his	Ps 9:11
HOW DARE YOU * me, "Flee	Ps 11:1
* me what to do, O Lord, and make	Ps 27:11
speak out and * the world about	Ps 30:9
And I will * everyone how great	Ps 35:28
There isn't time to * of all your	Ps 40:5
so that you can * your children.	Ps 48:13
I will * in song accompanied by	Ps 49:4
Sing of his glorious name! * the	Ps 66:2
Lord, and I will * you what he did	Ps 66:16
I will * everyone how good you	Ps 71:15
of the Lord God. I * everyone that	Ps 71:16
Give me time to * this new	Ps 71:18
I have chosen him and I will *	Ps 73:28
your children, and * them about the	Ps 78:4
* me where you want me to go and	Ps 86:11
Every morning * him, "Thank you	Ps 92:2
Each day * someone that he saves.	Ps 96:2
the earth. * everyone about the	Ps 96:3
* the nations that Jehovah reigns!	Ps 96:10
Let all the earth rejoice! * the	Ps 97:1
praise the Lord. * them that God	Ps 102:19
Sing his praises and * everyone	Ps 105:2
Then speak out! * others he has	Ps 107:2
Let them * him "Thank you" as	Ps 107:22
slander me and * their lies.	Ps 109:2
my enemies who * lies about me and	Ps 109:20
I shall not die, but live to *	Ps 118:17
instructions more than I can *.	Ps 119:20
Just * me what to do and I will	Ps 119:33,34
and * me where to stop and rest.	Ps 139:3
Let each generation * its	Ps 145:4
Everyone will * about how good	Ps 145:7
They will * about your miracles	Ps 145:12
If young toughs * you, "Come and	Pro 1:10
Most people will * you what loyal	Pro 20:6
Don't *	Pro 20:19
Don't * anyone else, lest he	Pro 25:8,9,10
First, help me never to * a lie.	Pro 30:8
And who can * whether my son	Ecc 2:19
for a little bird will * them	Ecc 10:20
master what their teachers * them.	Ecc 12:11
The Girl: "* me, O one I love,	Sol 1:7
* him that I am sick with love."	Sol 5:8
for the godly man. * him, "What a	Is 3:10
And he said, "Yes, go. But * my	Is 6:9
bleaching field. * him to quit	Is 7:4
the Lord said. "* him he needn't	Is 7:4
Praise his name! * the world	Is 12:4
What then shall we * the	Is 14:32
the reporters? * them that the Lord	Is 14:32
Will they dare * Pharaoh about	Is 19:11
If they are wise, let them * you	Is 19:12
* him, 'This is it!'	Is 21:6,7
They * my prophets, "Shut up—we	Is 30:10,11
Or they say, "Don't * us the	Is 30:10,11
us the truth; * us nice things;	Is 30:10,11
tell us nice things; * us lies.	Is 30:10,11
Because you despise what I * you	Is 30:12
listen to me and I will * you	Is 32:9
I will * you who can live	Is 33:15

(TELL Con't)

who are afraid. * them, "Be	Is 35:4
Then Isaiah replied, "* King	Is 37:6
"Go and * Hezekiah that the Lord	Is 38:5
* her that her sad days are gone.	Is 40:2
Shout louder—don't be afraid—*	Is 40:9
Let them try to * us what	Is 41:22
If you are gods, * what will	Is 41:23
I was the first to * Jerusalem,	Is 41:27
I will * you the future before it	Is 42:9
Who else can * you what is going	Is 44:7
Let them * you if they can, and	Is 44:7
And I didn't * Israel to ask me	Is 45:19
can * you what is going to happen.	Is 46:10
to * you what the future holds.	Is 47:13
Now I will * you new things I	Is 48:6
Yes, I'll * you things entirely	Is 48:8
alive to help or * her what to do.	Is 51:18
Listen and I'll * you where to	Is 55:2
blast; * my people of their sins!	Is 58:1
I'll * you why!	Is 58:3
He has sent me to * those who	Is 61:2
Let me * you how happy God has	Is 61:10
land and said, "* my people, I,	Is 62:11
I will * of the lovingkindnesses	Is 63:7
you and speak whatever I * you to.	Jer 1:7
* them whatever I tell you to say.	Jer 1:17
tell them whatever I * you to say.	Jer 1:17
* them everything that I will do	Jer 7:27
* them this, says the Lord:	Jer 9:22
They will * you not to prophesy	Jer 11:21,22
* them this: The Lord God of	Jer 13:12
to * us how prosperous we will be!	Jer 13:12
Then * them: You're getting the	Jer 13:13
will come. They * the people you	Jer 14:13
I didn't send them or * them to	Jer 14:14
Therefore, * them this: Night and	Jer 14:17
where can we go? * them the Lord	Jer 15:2
And when you * the people all	Jer 16:10
Lord our God?" * them the Lord's	Jer 16:11
King Zedekiah and * him the Lord	Jer 21:3,4
"* these people, the Lord says:	Jer 21:8
Let these false prophets * their	Jer 23:28
* them, "The Lord of Hosts, the	Jer 25:27
to accept the cup, * them, "The	Jer 25:28
against them. * them the Lord will	Jer 25:30
their evil deeds. * them the Lord	Jer 26:4
saying, * your masters that the	Jer 27:4
Go and * Hananiah that the Lord	Jer 28:13
in Babylon and * them this: The	Jer 29:31
Ask me and I will * you some	Jer 33:3
Go * Zedekiah, king of Judah,	Jer 34:2
after prophet to * you to turn back	Jer 35:15
"We must * the king," they	Jer 36:16
"But first, * us how you got	Jer 36:17
"Don't * a soul where you are!"	Jer 36:19
the scribe and went to * the king.	Jer 36:20
of Israel, says: * the king of	Jer 37:7
"What crime have I committed? *	Jer 37:18
Jeremiah said, "If I * you the	Jer 38:15
don't * anyone you told me this!	Jer 38:24
death unless you * them what we	Jer 38:25
"I will ask him and I will * you	Jer 42:4
and said, 'Just * us what God says	Jer 42:20
you to * us not to go to Egypt!	Jer 43:2,3
in Tahpanhes, and * the men of	Jer 43:10
find no rest. But * Baruch this,	Jer 45:4
weep and wail. * it by the banks	Jer 48:20
* all the world that Babylon will	Jer 50:2
own country to * how the Lord their	Jer 50:28
to the king to * him all is lost!	Jer 51:31
they will listen, * them: This is	Eze 3:11
when I want you to * them, You are	Eze 3:18
"* Israel, Wherever you	Eze 7:2
given the city! * them to bring	Eze 9:1
Then I heard the Lord * the other	Eze 9:5
"But * the exiles that the Lord	Eze 11:16
all this means. * them the Lord	Eze 12:10
"* these evil builders that	Eze 13:11
* us that it wasn't good enough?	Eze 13:12
his messages. * them the Lord God	Eze 13:18
ask me anything? * them, the Lord	Eze 14:4
that land and * the armies of the	Eze 14:17
loathsome sins. * her, the Lord	Eze 16:3
I will * you.	Eze 17:12,13
I swear that I will * you	Eze 20:3
condemn them; * them of all the	Eze 20:4
until now. * them the Lord God	Eze 20:5,6
"Son of dust, * them that the	Eze 20:27,28
When they ask you why, * them:	Eze 21:7
"Son of dust, * them this: A	Eze 21:9,10,11
people in their woe. * them this:	Eze 21:28
rebels, Israel; * them the Lord God	Eze 24:3
What are you trying to * us?"	Eze 24:19
to * you what has happened.	Eze 24:26
its people. * them: Listen to what	Eze 25:3
* him, the Lord God says: You	Eze 28:12
all her people. * them that the	Eze 29:3
"Son of dust, * Pharaoh, king of	Eze 31:2,3
"Son of dust, * your people:	Eze 33:2
and you don't * him what I say,	Eze 33:8
How can we live?' * them: As I	Eze 33:11
And when I * the wicked he will	Eze 33:14
to * me, "The city has fallen!"	Eze 33:21
"* them: The Lord God says: As I	Eze 33:27
Let's go hear him * us what the	Eze 33:30
of doing what I * them to;	Eze 33:31
mountains. * them: Listen to this	Eze 36:1
But * them, the Lord God says:	Eze 37:12
as one stick. * these people	Eze 37:18,19,20
king of Meshech and Tubal. * him	Eze 38:2,3
this also against Gog. * him:	Eze 39:1
to * them all you have seen."	Eze 40:4
people of Israel. * them its	Eze 43:10
Listen to all I * you about the	Eze 44:5
* him what his dream had been.	Dan 2:1
what it was. * me, for I fear some	Dan 2:1
the king, "Sir, * us the dream and	Dan 2:4
then we can * you what it means."	Dan 2:4
But the king replied, "I * you,	Dan 2:5
And if you won't * me what it was	Dan 2:5
and honors if you * me what the	Dan 2:6
They said again, "How can we *	Dan 2:7
unless you * us what it was?"	Dan 2:7
But if you don't * me the dream,	Dan 2:8,9
* others what they have dreamed!	Dan 2:10
No one except the gods can * you	Dan 2:11
said, "and I will * you the dream	Dan 2:16
Take me to the king and I will *	Dan 2:24
who will * you your dream!"	Dan 2:25
Can you * me what my dream was	Dan 2:26
or wizard can * the king such	Dan 2:27
men of Babylon to * me the meaning	Dan 4:6
solve. * me what my dream means:	Dan 4:9
my dream; now * me what it means.	Dan 4:18
But you can * me, for the spirit	Dan 4:18
be afraid to * me what it means."	Dan 4:19
the writing or * him what it	Dan 5:8
He will * you what the writing	Dan 5:12
on the wall, and * me what it	Dan 5:15
If you can * me the meaning of	Dan 5:16
but I will * you what they mean.	Dan 5:17
river, "Gabriel, * Daniel the	Dan 8:16
"I am here," he said, "to *	Dan 8:19
don't * anyone about them yet."	Dan 8:26
I am here to * you what it was,	Dan 9:23
Now I am here to * you what will	Dan 10:14
I am here to * you what is	Dan 10:20,21
my people,' I will * them, 'You are	Hos 1:10
of wood to * them what to do.	Hos 4:12
a thing as I am going to * you?	Joe 1:2
In years to come, * your	Joe 1:3
How you despise people who * the	Amo 5:10
Who can *?	Jon 3:9
he will * us what to do, and we	Mic 4:2
turn away from me? * me why your	Mic 6:3
their tongues can't * the truth!	Mic 6:12
a glance and rush to * the others.	Hab 2:2
stone to * them what to do.	Hab 2:19
No one can * her anything;	Zep 3:2
* Zerubbabel, the governor of	Hag 2:21
"I'll * you," he replied.	Zec 1:9
"Go * this young man," said the	Zec 2:4
you and do all I * you to, then I	Zec 3:7
the High Priest. * him that the	Zec 6:12
to Zechariah. "* them to be honest	Zec 7:8,9
kind to everyone. * them to stop	Zec 7:10
Here is your part: * the truth.	Zec 8:16
'You must die,' they will * him,	Zec 13:3
You * the people, 'Lame animals	Mal 1:8
you cry. I'll * you why;	Mal 2:14
"Did the prophets * us where the	Mt 2:4
him, come back and * me so that I	Mt 2:8
stay there until I * you to return,	Mt 2:13
For the Scriptures * us that	Mt 4:4
and * you that if you are only	Mt 5:22
acts of charity! I * you in all	Mt 6:2
it secretly—don't * your left hand	Mt 6:3
many will * me, 'Lord, Lord, we	Mt 7:22
Literally, "See you * no man."	Mt 8:4f
have authority to * his sickness to	Mt 8:8,9
And I * you this, that many	Mt 8:11
warned them not to * anyone about	Mt 9:30
the opportunity to * them about me,	Mt 10:18
"What I * you now in the gloom,	Mt 10:27
back to John and * him about the	Mt 11:4
to life; and * him about my	Mt 11:5
And I * you this, that you must	Mt 12:36
and I will * the reapers to sort	Mt 13:30
came to * Jesus what had happened.	Mt 14:12
it is really you, * me to come over	Mt 14:28
send her away. "* her to get	Mt 15:23
them not to * anyone what they had	Mt 17:9
For I * you that in heaven their	Mt 18:10
And I * you this—whatever you	Mt 18:18
"I also * you this—if two of you	Mt 18:19
And I * you this, that anyone	Mt 19:9
prophecy, "* Jerusalem her King	Mt 21:5
"I'll * you if you answer one	Mt 21:24
So he sent other servants to *	Mt 22:4
or favor. Now * us, is it right to	Mt 22:17
For they don't do what they * you	Mt 23:3
For I * you this, you will never	Mt 23:3
"And I, the King, will * them,	Mt 25:4
So-and-So, and * him, 'Our Master	Mt 26:1
God that you * us whether you claim	Mt 26:6
for we can * by your Galilean	Mt 26:7
And now, go quickly and * his	Mt 28:
be frightened! Go * my brothers to	Mt 28:1
I haven't come to * good people	Mk 2:1
was to * the people stories.	Mk 4:
all the others I am going to *?	Mk 4:1
you will understand what I * you.	Mk 4:2
he told him, "and * them what	Mk 5:1
of that region and began to *	Mk 5:2
earnestly not to * what had	Mk 5:4
to him and said, "* the people to	Mk 6:35,3
He himself would stay and * the	Mk 6:4
But Jesus warned them not to *	Mk 8:3
Then he began to * them about the	Mk 8:3
"I'll * you why—it was a	Mk 10:
Don't send them away! I * you as	Mk 10:1
love of me and to * others the Good	Mk 10:2
and said, "* him to come here."	Mk 10:4
Jesus replied, "I'll * you if	Mk 11:2
you * the truth no matter what!	Mk 12:1
ways of God. Now * us, is it right	Mk 12:1
"Show me a coin and I'll * you."	Mk 12:1
This is your opportunity to *	Mk 13:
And I * you this in solemn	Mk 14:
At the house he enters, * the	Mk 14:1
to Jerusalem to * the others, but	Mk 16:1
For I have come to * you that God	Lk 1:1
You will * his people how to	Lk 1:7
you are God's Son, * this stone to	Lk 4:
back to John and * him all you	Lk 7:20,21,22
Good News. And * him, 'Blessed is	Lk 7:2
parables, for they * a great deal	Lk 8:1
he told him, "and * them what a	Lk 8:39
that they not * anyone the details	Lk 8:56
Then he sent them away to *	Lk 9:2
"Just * them to sit down on the	Lk 9:14
They didn't * anyone what they	Lk 9:36
work? * her to come and help me."	Lk 10:40
"But I'll * you this—though he	Lk 11:8
But I'll * you whom to fear—fear	Lk 12:5
"Sir, please * my brother to	Lk 12:13
"And he will reply, 'I * you, I	Lk 13:27
Jesus replied, "Go * that fox	Lk 13:32
But shall I * you to act that	Lk 16:9
more faith; * us how to get it."	Lk 17:5
me, a sinner.' I * you, this	Lk 18:14
I'll * you—he will come and kill	Lk 20:16
You always * the truth and don't	Lk 20:21
ways of God. Now * us—is it right	Lk 20:22
For I * you now that I won't eat	Lk 22:16
But Jesus said, "Peter, let me *	Lk 22:34
But he replied, "If I * you, you	Lk 22:67,68
to * his eleven disciples—and	Lk 24:9
"Then who are you? * us, so we	Jn 1:22
No one needed to * him how	Jn 2:24,25
I possess I * you this: Unless you	Jn 3:3
the wind but can't * where it comes	Jn 3:8
believe me when I * you about such	Jn 3:12
* you what is going on in heaven?	Jn 3:12
But say, * me, why is it that	Jn 4:20
"* everyone to sit down," Jesus	Jn 6:10
"How earnestly I * you	Jn 6:47
I possess I * you this: Unless you	Jn 6:53
Who can * what he means?"	Jn 6:60
"* us who you are," they	Jn 8:25
if you live as I * you to, and you	Jn 8:30,31
And so when I * the truth, you	Jn 8:45
I have I * you this—no one who	Jn 8:51
If you are the Messiah, * us	Jn 10:24
"But didn't I * you that you	Jn 11:40
want to be my disciples, * them	Jn 12:26
you what the Father said to * you.	Jn 12:49
soon come true. I * you this now	Jn 13:19
If this weren't so, I would * you	Jn 14:2,3
"In solemn truth I * you, anyone	Jn 14:12,13
and will * you all about me.	Jn 15:26
And you also must * everyone	Jn 15:27
I didn't * you earlier because I	Jn 16:4
more I want to * you, but you can't	Jn 16:12
He will * you about the future.	Jn 16:13
and I will * you plainly all about	Jn 16:25
need anyone to * you anything.	Jn 16:30
taken him away, * me where you have	Jn 20:15
But go find my brothers and *	Jn 20:17
We'll * them that if they do it	Act 4:17
"Didn't we * you never again to	Act 5:28
many others to * him about Jesus.	Act 8:35
the synagogue to * everyone there	Act 9:20
* him what God wanted him to do.	Act 10:22
for. Now * me what you want."	Act 10:29
what he has told you to * us!"	Act 10:33
'He will * you how you and all	Act 11:14
ran back inside to * everyone that	Act 12:14
him out of jail. "* James and the	Act 12:17
they have come to * you how to have	Act 16:17
officers over to * the jailer,	Act 16:35
"Come and * us more about this	Act 17:19

(TELL Con't)
and now I wish to * you about him. Act 17:23
"* me, are you a Roman citizen?" Act 22:27
He has something important to * Act 23:17
man to you to * you something." Act 23:18
is it you want to * me, lad?" Act 23:19
on to you and will * his accusers Act 23:30
him and then * me what to write. Act 25:26
"Go ahead. * us your story." Act 26:1
You are to * the world about this Act 26:16
alive today to * these facts to Act 26:22
and I could * you that it is Act 28:20
the world to * all people Rom 1:5
yourselves? You * others not to Rom 2:21
For the Scriptures * us Abraham Rom 4:3
No, for the Scriptures * us that Rom 8:36
For if you * others with your Rom 10:9
For the Scriptures * us that no Rom 10:11
And how will anyone go and * Rom 10:15
about when we * them of Christ. Rom 11:8
Let him * them whether they are Rom 14:4
* Priscilla and Aquila "hello." Rom 16:3
ideas to * you God's message. 1Co 2:1
sent his Spirit to * us, and his 1Co 2:10
world's spirit) to * us about the 1Co 2:12
be glad to * you what I think. 1Co 7:25
he will let me * him about Christ 1Co 9:22
(The Scriptures * us, "The 1Co 10:7
Well, I'll * you why. 1Co 10:31
First, however, let me * you about 1Co 12:31
of course, you can * everyone 1Co 14:5
to me, and * you the things I know, 1Co 14:6
can * people afterwards, plainly. 1Co 14:13
will teach, or * some special 1Co 14:26
language, or * what someone else is 1Co 14:26
But * me this! 1Co 15:12
The Scriptures * us that the 1Co 15:45
I * you this, my brothers: an 1Co 15:50
It almost broke my heart and I * 2Co 2:4
go he uses us to * others about the 2Co 2:14
of yours who must * you all about 2Co 3:1
letter to * you about us, do you? 2Co 3:1
who has helped us * others about 2Co 3:6
We do not * them that they must 2Co 3:6
but we * them there is life for 2Co 3:6
we speak and so we * the truth, as 2Co 4:2
he has given us to * others. 2Co 5:19
NOW I WANT to * you what God in 2Co 8:1
men who * you how good they are! 2Co 10:12
* everyone in Greece about it! 2Co 11:10
and ever, knows I * the truth. 2Co 11:31
Let me * about the visions I've 2Co 12:1
not allowed to * them to others). 2Co 12:4
That isn't it at all. I * you, 2Co 12:19
The Scriptures * us that if two 2Co 13:1
and managers * him to, until he Gal 4:2
enemy because I * you the truth? Gal 4:16
He will * you where to go and Gal 5:16
Let me * you again as I have Gal 5:21
Stop lying to each other; * the Eph 4:25
words as I boldly * others about Eph 6:19
Lord's work, will * you all about Eph 6:21
strong purpose—to * the Good News Php 1:27
instead, pray about everything; * Php 4:6
* his secret plan to you Gentiles. Col 1:25
has pleased him to * it to those Col 1:26,27
Don't * lies to each other; Col 3:9
be bold enough to * it freely and Col 4:4
chances to * others the Good News. Col 4:5
will * you how I am getting along. Col 4:7
We don't need to * them about it, 1Th 1:8
trusted by him to * the truth; 1Th 2:4
I can * you this directly from 1Th 4:15
We are happy to * other churches 2Th 1:4
These teachers will * lies with 1Ti 4:2
sin—don't know how to * the truth; 1Ti 6:5
* those who are rich not to be 1Ti 6:17
our enjoyment. * them to use their 1Ti 6:18
sent out by God to * men and women 2Ti 1:1
never be afraid to * others about 2Ti 1:8
And you know better than I can * 2Ti 1:18
teachers who will * them just what 2Ti 4:3
permits me to * it to everyone. Tit 1:3
is impossible for God to * a lie. Heb 6:18
doubt, and we can * others that Heb 10:23
and he will gladly * you, for he is Jas 1:5
expect him to * you, for a doubtful Jas 1:6
eager to * others their faults, Jas 3:1
do whatever they * you—not only if 1Pe 2:18
do, be ready to * him, and do it in 1Pe 3:15
They will cleverly * their lies 2Pe 2:1
their greed will * you anything to 2Pe 2:3
So now we can * who is a child of 1Jn 3:10
own eyes and now * all the world 1Jn 4:14
When I come I will * you some of 3Jn 1:10
of the church at Ephesus and * Rev 2:1
no one could * us what it said. Rev 5:4
"Please * me." Rev 7:14
"I'll * you who she is and what Rev 17:7
shown you is to * about Jesus." Rev 19:10
down, for what I * you is Rev 21:5
to * you this will happen soon. Rev 22:6,7
* the churches all these things. Rev 22:16

TELLER

or be a fortune *, or be a serpent Deu 18:10

TELLING

without * Laban his intentions. Gen 31:17-20
"God was * you what he is going Gen 41:25
whether you are * me the truth; Gen 42:20
cup, which he uses for fortune *? Gen 44:5
And you will be as God to him, * Ex 4:16
"You have been * me, 'Take these Ex 33:12
nor use fortune * or witchcraft. Lev 19:26
Sinai peninsula, * him, "Take a Num 3:14,15
God is * Gideon that the same one Ju 6:16f
and was * his tent-mate about it. Ju 7:12,13
in Arumah * him, "Gaal, son of Ju 9:31
to the Kenites, * them to get out 1Sa 15:6
And Gehazi was * the king 2Ki 8:5
emissaries, * them to stay at 1Ch 19:5
had fired them, * them to stop 2Ch 11:13,14
opposite of what they are * you!" 2Ch 18:22
Jehoshaphat, * him, "Because you 2Ch 20:37
Jerusalem * the people to bring to 2Ch 24:9
people, * them, "That's right! Neh 8:11
in Jerusalem, * the people to go to Neh 8:15
* him, "Keep the money, but go Est 3:10
across the item * how Mordecai had Est 6:1
to the Jews, * them whatever you Est 8:8
You're not * me anything new. Job 9:2
Your sins are * your mouth what Job 15:4,5
I am * you the honest truth, for Job 36:4
THE HEAVENS ARE * the glory of Ps 19:1
Day and night they keep on * Ps 19:2
and * about your miracles. Ps 26:7
I will praise you with music, * Ps 71:22
SING A NEW song to the Lord * Ps 98:1
literally, she was * him that she Pro 7:14f
* the truth gives a man great Pro 12:14
are, but are they * the truth? Pro 20:6
Then believe what I am * you now, Pro 22:20,21
* lies about someone is as Pro 25:18
Don't try to defend yourself by * Ecc 5:6,7
Hear what he is * you! Is 1:10
God is * me what he is going to Is 21:2
the Lord's * me to take this land? Is 36:10
in the Lord by * you the Lord won't Is 36:15
and to all Judea, * them to sound Jer 4:5
their prophets are * them that all Jer 14:13
prophets are * lies in my name. Jer 14:14
they say. By * these false dreams Jer 23:27
prophets who keep * you the king of Jer 27:14
they are * you lies in my name. Jer 27:15
prophets who are * you that soon Jer 27:16
you will understand what I am * Jer 30:24
Jeremiah had been * the people— Jer 38:1
While I was still speaking and * Eze 11:13
them his mercy by * them the Dan 2:18
my prophets, * them, 'Shut up!' Amo 2:12
prophets have been * you about the Zec 8:9
that God was * them something Zec 11:11
rushing around, * everyone to bring Mt 14:35
* others that he was the Messiah. Mt 16:20
into his fields, * them he would Mt 20:4
* everyone he came back to life! Mt 27:64
what happened were * everyone about Mk 5:16
So the disciples went out, * Mk 6:12
* them, 'Sorry, I can't help you! Mk 7:11
away, * them not to bother him. Mk 10:13
"God was * Moses that these men, Mk 12:27
began * the others, "There he is! Mk 14:69
thanking God and * everyone in Lk 2:38
go at once without * anyone what Lk 5:14
So he went all through the city * Lk 8:39
After * this story, Jesus went on Lk 19:28
people to ruin by * them not to pay Lk 23:2
They began * each other how their Lk 24:32
And just as they were * about Lk 24:36
you remember my * you that Lk 24:44
Don't begin * others Lk 24:49
out to the people, * the crowds, Jn 1:15
Jesus replied, "What I am * you Jn 3:5
these things? I am * you what I Jn 3:10,11
John's disciples, * them that Jn 3:25
I have not been * you my own ideas, Jn 8:28
I am * you what I saw when I was Jn 8:38
And since I am * you the truth, Jn 8:46
a message to Jesus * him, "Sir, Jn 11:3
back to life were * all about it. Jn 12:17
Jesus was * him to go and pay for Jn 13:29
I am * you these things now Jn 14:25
Yes, I'm * you these things now Jn 16:4
"Should you hit a man for * the Jn 18:23
When they kept * him, "We have Jn 20:25
And we all hear these men * in Act 2:11
a long sermon, * about Jesus and Act 2:40
We cannot stop * about the Act 4:20
"Well, I began * them the Good Act 11:15
on their trip, * how God had opened Act 14:27
the believers, * them—much to Act 15:3
there, * them to welcome him. Act 18:27
for three months, * what Act 19:8
Yet I never shrank from * you Act 20:20
Jesus—the work of * others the Good Act 20:24
* what you have seen and heard. Act 22:15
who visited him, * them with all Act 28:31
with all my might, * others the Rom 1:9
about the Jews, * God how they had Rom 11:2,3
they are from God, * of God's wise 1Co 2:7
has given us. In * you about these 1Co 2:13
I'm * you what God's law says. 1Co 9:8
Everyone keeps * me about the 1Co 11:18
But I am * you this strange and 1Co 15:51
and I have been * you about Jesus 2Co 1:19
me if I am not * the absolute 2Co 1:23
work [of * his Good News to others 2Co 4:1
Yet those other men keep * you 2Co 11:18
saying, for I am * you this in the Gal 1:20
* everyone about this plan of his; Eph 3:7
special joy of * the Gentiles the Eph 3:8
truth and * others about Christ. Php 1:7
bold in * others about Christ. Php 1:14
can cheer me up by * me all about Php 2:19
I never get tired of * you this Php 3:1
me in * the Good News to others; Php 4:3
And I, Paul, have the joy of * it Col 1:23
go we find people * us about your 1Th 1:8
it, for they keep * us about the 1Th 1:9
* them little by little about Heb 1:1
do without my even * them, and Heb 8:10
* others of the glory of his name. Heb 13:15
and guard your lips from * lies. 1Pe 3:10
For we have not been * you fairy 2Pe 1:16
Again I say, we are * you about 1Jn 1:3
MY LITTLE CHILDREN, I am * you 1Jn 2:1
me very happy by * me that your 3Jn 1:3
* what I knew about Jesus Christ. Rev 1:9

TELLS

"Do whatever he * you to," he Gen 41:55
except what God * me to say; Num 22:38
except what Jehovah * me to?" Num 23:12
say whatever Jehovah * me to?" Num 23:26
God and listen to what he * you. Deu 4:30
and to heed all he * you to do. Deu 26:17
for he always * me everything he's 1Sa 20:2
say only what the Lord * me to!" 1Ki 22:14
only what the Lord * you to?" 1Ki 22:16
He never * me anything good. 1Ki 22:18
"Elisha, the prophet, * the king 2Ki 6:12
except what the Lord * you to?" 2Ch 18:15
decision than what God * you to. 2Ch 19:7
"Geshem * me that everywhere he Neh 6:5,6
in the night. He * me what to do. Ps 16:7
A witness who * the truth saves Pro 14:25
true until someone * the other side Pro 18:17
future and * everyone in detail! Ecc 10:14
of Matthew (1:23) * us that there Is 7:14f
to talk? He * us everything over Is 28:10
out who * the truth, I or they! Jer 44:28
on the wall, and * me what it Dan 5:7
much as my fierce anger * me to. Hos 11:9
The rich man pays them off and * Mic 7:3
"Then if anyone * you, 'The Mt 24:23
"So if someone * you the Messiah Mt 24:26
Just say what God * you to. Mk 13:11
"And then if anyone * you, 'This Mk 13:21
"Do whatever he * you to." Jn 2:5
of earth. He * what he has seen Jn 3:32
how few believe what he * them! Jn 3:32
and * him everything he is doing; Jn 5:20
so whatever he * me to say, I Jn 12:50
carefully to everything he * you. Act 3:21,22
our people and * everybody to Act 21:28
This Good News * us that God Rom 1:17
it is: my new life * me to do Rom 7:23,24,25
in our hearts, and * us that we Rom 8:16
and with his mouth he * others of Rom 10:10
about him unless someone * them? Rom 10:14
just what his master * him to. 1Co 4:2
For God * us in the Scripture 1Co 6:16
whatever anyone * you even if he is 2Co 11:4
that the Holy Spirit * us to do; Gal 5:17
The Psalmist * about this, for he Eph 4:8
BUT THE HOLY Spirit * us clearly 1Ti 4:1
Christ * him to, he is a liar. 1Jn 2:4
But those who do what Christ * 1Jn 2:5
Spirit he has given us * us so. 1Jn 3:24
he * us that he loves us dearly. 1Jn 4:16
Loving God means doing what he * 1Jn 5:3
we will do whatever he * us to. 2Jn 1:6
himself, but * others not to, and 3Jn 1:10
God, who * his prophets what the Rev 22:6,7

TEMA

Hadad, *,Jetur, Naphish, Kedemah. Gen 25:12-15
*, Jetur, Naphish, and Kedemah. 1Ch 1:28-31
When caravans from * and from Job 6:19-21
O people of *, bring food and Is 21:14
Dedan and * and Buz, and the Jer 25:23

TEMAH

Sisera, *, Neziah, Hatipha. Ez 2:43-54
Barkos, Sisera, *, Neh 7:46-56

TEMAN

*, Omar, Zepho, Gatam, Kenaz, Gen 36:10,11,12

(TEMAN Con't)
here:The clan of *,The clan of Gen 36:15,16
Kenaz,The clan of *,The clan of Gen 36:40-43
*, Omar, Zephi, Gatam, Kenaz, 1Ch 1:36
Chief Kenaz, Chief *, Chief Mibzar, 1Ch 1:51-54
Is there not one left in all of * Jer 49:7
also the people of *—even little Jer 49:20
everything from * to Dedan. Eze 25:13
So I will set fire to *, and it Amo 1:12
* was in the north of Edom, and Amo 1:12f
friends, was from *, five miles Ob 1:8f
The mightiest soldiers of * will Ob 1:9
Literally, "from * . Hab 3:3f

TEMANITE
Their names were Eliphaz the *, Job 2:11
A REPLY TO Job from Eliphaz the *: Job 4:1
THE ANSWER OF Eliphaz the *: Job 15:1
Job, he said to Eliphaz the *: Job 42:7
So Eliphaz the *, and Bildad the Job 42:9

TEMANITES
Husham, from the land of the *. Gen 36:31-39
country of the * became the king. 1Ch 1:45

TEMENI
Hepher, *, and Haahashtari; 1Ch 4:6

TEMPER
In a great fit of * Balaam beat Num 22:27
who understood the * of the times 1Ch 12:24-37
who knew the * of the times as well Est 1:13-15
A wise man controls his *. Pro 14:29
a wise man holds his * in and Pro 29:11
a fool than for a man of quick *. Pro 29:20
quiet spirit will quiet his bad *. Ecc 10:4

TEMPERATURE
immediately her * returned to Lk 4:39

TEMPERS
He only rages and scoffs, and * Pro 29:9

TEMPEST-TOSSED
O my afflicted people, * and Is 54:11

TEMPESTS
your fiery storms, * and tornados. Ps 83:15

TEMPESTUOUS
during her last * years: Zechariah, Hos 13:11f

TEMPLE
* where I can live among them. Ex 25:8
They gave him money from the * Ju 9:4
year, held in the * of the local Ju 9:27
fort next to the * of Baal-berith. Ju 9:46
the center of the *, between the Ju 16:25,26
By then the * was completely Ju 16:27
And the * crashed down upon the Ju 16:30
sleeping in the * near the Ark, 1Sa 3:2,3
the doors of the * as usual, for he 1Sa 3:15
at Ebenezer to the * of their idol 1Sa 5:1
of the * of Dagon in Ashdod. 1Sa 5:5
His armor was placed in the * of 1Sa 31:10
For I have never lived in a *. 2Sa 7:6
you built me a beautiful cedar *?' 2Sa 7:7
is the one who shall build me a *. 2Sa 7:13
And he heard me from his *. 2Sa 22:7
* and the wall around the city. 1Ki 3:1
the hills, for the * of the Lord 1Ki 3:2
* of the Lord he wanted to build. 1Ki 5:2,3
So I am planning to build a * 1Ki 5:5
your throne, shall build me a *.' 1Ki 5:5
job—for the foundation of the *. 1Ki 5:17
in preparing the stone for the *. 1Ki 5:18
the actual construction of the *. 1Ki 6:1
The * was ninety feet long, 1Ki 6:2
All along the front of the * was 1Ki 6:3
of the * against the outer walls. 1Ki 6:5
the walls of the * by beams resting 1Ki 6:6
of the * were prefinished at the 1Ki 6:7
right side of the *, and there were 1Ki 6:8
After completing the *, Solomon 1Ki 6:9
to the * walls by cedar timbers. 1Ki 6:10
concerning the * he was building: 1Ki 6:11,12
At last the * was finished. 1Ki 6:14
the far end of the *—the Most Holy 1Ki 6:16
The remainder of the *—other 1Ki 6:17
Throughout the * the cedar 1Ki 6:18
remainder of the *—including the 1Ki 6:21,22
both rooms of the *, and the floor 1Ki 6:29
wood for the entrance to the *. 1Ki 6:33
The foundation of the * was laid 1Ki 6:37
the * and the porch of the palace. 1Ki 7:12
pillars at the entrance of the *. 1Ki 7:16-22
the work in the * of the Lord which 1Ki 7:40
in the * were made of solid gold. 1Ki 7:48
the main entrance doors of the *. 1Ki 7:50
When the * was finally finished, 1Ki 7:51
treasury of the * the silver, the 1Ki 7:51
Zion, the City of David, to the *. 1Ki 8:1
the Ark to the *, along with all 1Ki 8:3,4
sanctuary of the *—the Most Holy 1Ki 8:6
a bright cloud fills the *! 1Ki 8:10
a place for my *, but I appointed a 1Ki 8:16
He wanted to build a * for the 1Ki 8:17
is the one who shall build my *.' 1Ki 8:19
and now this * has been built for 1Ki 8:20
a place in the * for the Ark which 1Ki 8:21
much less this * I have built! 1Ki 8:27
watch over this * night and 1Ki 8:29
I face toward the * and pray, 1Ki 8:29
pray toward this *, hear them from 1Ki 8:38
pray toward this *, hear them from 1Ki 8:41,42
will know that this is your *. 1Ki 8:43
and toward this * which I have 1Ki 8:44
and toward this *, which I have 1Ki 8:48
dedicated the * by sacrificing 1Ki 8:62,63
in front of the * for the burnt 1Ki 8:64
building the * and the palace and 1Ki 9:1
I have hallowed this * which you 1Ki 9:2,3
I will take them from this * 1Ki 9:7
This * will become a heap of 1Ki 9:8
things to this land and this *?' 1Ki 9:8
Solomon built the * and the palace, 1Ki 9:10
construction of the palace and *. 1Ki 9:11,12
labor to build the *, his palace, 1Ki 9:15
After the * was completed, 1Ki 9:25
pillars for the * and the palace, 1Ki 10:12
He even built a * on the Mount 1Ki 11:7
sacrifices at the *, they will 1Ki 12:27
He ransacked the * and the 1Ki 14:26
Whenever the king went to the *, 1Ki 14:28
exhibits in the * of the bronze 1Ki 15:15
gold left in the * treasury and all 1Ki 15:18
First he built a * and an altar 1Ki 16:32
He sent messengers to the * of 2Ki 1:2
king goes into the * of the god 2Ki 5:18
and filled the * of Baal from one 2Ki 10:20,21
went into the * to address the 2Ki 10:23
into the inner *, dragged out the 2Ki 10:25
They wrecked the * and converted 2Ki 10:27
his nurse in a storeroom of the *. 2Ki 11:2,3
He met them in the *, swore them 2Ki 11:4
shall stand guard at the *; 2Ki 11:6,7,8
* that had belonged to King David. 2Ki 11:10
she ran into the * and saw the new 2Ki 11:13,14
"Don't kill her here in the *. 2Ki 11:15
Everyone went over to the * of 2Ki 11:18
And Jehoiada set guards at the * 2Ki 11:18
the king from the *, past the 2Ki 11:19
"The * building needs repairing. 2Ki 12:4,5
the * was still in disrepair. 2Ki 12:6
you done anything about the *? 2Ki 12:7
the * into good condition." 2Ki 12:7
of the altar at the * entrance. 2Ki 12:9
to repair the * of the Lord. 2Ki 12:11,12
treasuries of the * and the palace, 2Ki 12:18
silver from the * and palace 2Ki 14:14
of the * of the Lord was built. 2Ki 15:34,35
and gold from the * and from the 2Ki 16:8
an unusual altar in a heathen *. 2Ki 16:10
the front of the * (it had stood 2Ki 16:14
stood between the * entrance and 2Ki 16:14
stands in the *, removed their 2Ki 16:17
between the palace and the *. 2Ki 16:18
the * and in the palace treasury. 2Ki 18:15
the gold from the * doors, and from 2Ki 18:16
and went into the * to pray. 2Ki 19:1
went over to the * and spread it 2Ki 19:14
worshiping in the * of his god 2Ki 19:37
will be out of bed and at the *! 2Ki 20:5
the * again three days from now." 2Ki 20:8
placed even in the * of the Lord—in 2Ki 21:3,4,5
in the *—the very place which the 2Ki 21:7
forever in this *, and in 2Ki 21:7
Meshullam) to the * to give 2Ki 22:3,4
* when the people come to worship. 2Ki 22:3,4
*, and to buy lumber and stone." 2Ki 22:5,6
a scroll in the *, with God's laws 2Ki 22:8
the repairs at the *, he also 2Ki 22:9,10
Jerusalem to go to the * with him. 2Ki 23:1
there at the * so that the king 2Ki 23:1
had been discovered in the *. 2Ki 23:1
the guards of the * to destroy all 2Ki 23:4
Asherah from the * and took it 2Ki 23:6
around the *, where the women wove 2Ki 23:7
entrance of the *, next to the 2Ki 23:11
built in the two courts of the *; 2Ki 23:12
the priest had found in the *. 2Ki 23:24
and the * that I said was mine." 2Ki 23:27
from the * and the royal palace; 2Ki 24:13
in the * at the Lord's directions. 2Ki 24:13
He burned down the *, the 2Ki 25:9
pillars of the * and the bronze 2Ki 25:13
made for the * by King 2Ki 25:16
* guards to Babylon as captives. 2Ki 25:18
* at Jerusalem), the father of 1Ch 6:4-15
Then, when Solomon built the * 1Ch 6:32
the Levites, and the * assistants. 1Ch 9:2
was the chief custodian of the *. 1Ch 9:10,11
They lived in Jerusalem at the * 1Ch 9:33,34
the walls of the * of the Gods and 1Ch 10:10
his head to the wall of Dagon's *. 1Ch 10:10
'You are not to build my *! 1Ch 17:4
should build me a cedar-lined *.' 1Ch 17:6
shall build me a *, and I will 1Ch 17:12
the bronze and used it for the *. 1Ch 18:8
I'll build the * of the Lord and 1Ch 22:1
blocks of squared stone for the *. 1Ch 22:2
said, "and the * of the Lord must 1Ch 22:5
a * for the Lord God of Israel. 1Ch 22
so you are not to build my *. 1Ch 22
He shall build my *, and he 1Ch 22:
to do and build the * of the Lord. 1Ch 22:
worship into the * of the Lord!" 1Ch 22:
the work at the *," David 1Ch 23:4
thousand will be * guards, and four 1Ch 23:4
assigned to the ministry at the *. 1Ch 23:2
Aaron—in the sacrifices at the *; 1Ch 23:2
Tabernacle and the * and assisted 1Ch 23:3
of the * in each division. 1Ch 24:
Each group carried out the * 1Ch 24:1
THE * GUARDS were from the Asaph 1Ch 26:
were also appointed as * guards: 1Ch 26:4,
The divisions of the * guards 1Ch 26:1
responsible to minister at the *. 1Ch 26:1
nearby areas. The * guards were 1Ch 26:1
Lord and placed in the * treasury. 1Ch 26:20,21,2
the operating expenses of the *. 1Ch 26:2
It was my desire to build a * in 1Ch 28:
not to build my *, for you are a 1Ch 28:
son Solomon shall build my *; 1Ch 28:
chosen you to build his holy *. 1Ch 28:1
blueprint of the * and its 1Ch 28:1
outside rooms, the * storage areas, 1Ch 28:1
each item in the * which was to be 1Ch 28:1
and Levites will serve in the *. 1Ch 28:2
for the * he will build is not 1Ch 29:
my devotion to the * of God, I am 1Ch 29:
deposited at the * treasury with 1Ch 29:
to build a * for your holy name 1Ch 29:1
building of your *, for which I 1Ch 29:1
come to build a * for the Lord and 2Ch 2:
"I am about to build a * for the 2Ch 2:
It is going to be a wonderful * 2Ch 2:
be allowed to build a * for God? 2Ch 2:
be needed, for the * I am going to 2Ch 2:
*, and a royal palace for himself. 2Ch 2:1
construction of the * began. 2Ch 3:
selected it as the site for the *. 2Ch 3:
The main part of the * was 2Ch 3:
throughout the * were plated with 2Ch 3:
Within the *, at one end, was the 2Ch 3:
At the front of the * were two 2Ch 3:1
the front of the *, one on the 2Ch 3:17
in the *, five against each wall; 2Ch 4:7
corner of the outer room of the *. 2Ch 4:10
But in the * only gold was used. 2Ch 4:19
Even the doorway of the *, the 2Ch 4:22
SO THE * was finally finished. 2Ch 5:1
They were stored in the * 2Ch 5:1
as Zion, [to its new home in the * 2Ch 5:2
inner room of the *—the Holy of 2Ch 5:7,8
cloud, filled the * so that the 2Ch 5:13,14
But I have made a * for you, O 2Ch 6:1
* where my name will be glorified; 2Ch 6:5,6
this *, but the Lord said not to. 2Ch 6:7
I have built the * for the Name of 2Ch 6:10
less this * which I have built! 2Ch 6:18
night upon this *—upon this place 2Ch 6:20,21
when they pray toward this *; 2Ch 6:20,21
you here in this *, then listen to 2Ch 6:24
pray toward this * and claim you as 2Ch 6:26
pray toward this *, hear them from 2Ch 6:32
* I have built is truly yours. 2Ch 6:33
chosen, and this * which I have 2Ch 6:34
this city and your * I have built, 2Ch 6:37,38
Lord filled the *, so that the 2Ch 7:1
dedicated the * by sacrificing 2Ch 7:4,5
inner court of the * for use that 2Ch 7:7
the * as well as his own palace. 2Ch 7:11
have chosen this * as the place 2Ch 7:12
For I have chosen this * and 2Ch 7:16
them, and this * shall be destroyed 2Ch 7:20
thing to this land and to this *?' 2Ch 7:21
of the Lord's * and his own royal 2Ch 8:1
in front of the porch of the *. 2Ch 8:12
the construction of the *. 2Ch 8:16
steps for the * and the palace, and 2Ch 9:11
treasures of the * and of the 2Ch 12:9
Whenever the king went to the *, 2Ch 12:11
of the Lord in front of the *. 2Ch 15:8
He brought back into the * the 2Ch 15:18
and gold from the * and from the 2Ch 16:2
of the *, and prayed this prayer: 2Ch 20:5
and built this * for you, truly 2Ch 20:8
here before this * and before 2Ch 20:9
*—and cry out to you to save us; 2Ch 20:9
trumpets and proceeded to the *. 2Ch 20:28
away in a storage room in the *. 2Ch 22:11
Joash remained hidden in the * 2Ch 22:12
who was still in hiding at the *. 2Ch 23:2,3
the *, as required by God's laws. 2Ch 23:5,6
* itself, for they are sanctified. 2Ch 23:5,6
person entering the *. 2Ch 23:7
David and were stored in the *. 2Ch 23:9
in front of the * and around the 2Ch 23:10
rushed over to the * to see what 2Ch 23:12
"Don't do it here at the *. 2Ch 23:13,14
rushed over to the * of Baal and 2Ch 23:15,16,17
The guards at the * gates kept 2Ch 23:19

EMPLE Con't)	
the king from the *, wending their	2Ch 23:20
to repair and recondition the *.	2Ch 24:4
can maintain the * in good repair.	2Ch 24:5
and collect the * taxes from the	2Ch 24:6
so that the * can be repaired."	2Ch 24:6
had ravaged the *, and everything	2Ch 24:7,8
been removed to the * of Baalam.	2Ch 24:7,8
made and set outside the * gate.	2Ch 24:7,8
the chest back to the * again.	2Ch 24:11
and carpenters to restore the *;	2Ch 24:12
and finally the * was in much	2Ch 24:13
Israel, for God, and for the *.	2Ch 24:16
him to abandon the * of the God of	2Ch 24:17,18
executed in the court of the *.	2Ch 24:21
*, see The Annals of the Kings.	2Ch 24:27
bowls from the *, as well as the	2Ch 25:24
sanctuary of the * and personally	2Ch 26:16
from his people and from the *.	2Ch 26:21
by invading the *—but even so his	2Ch 27:2
He built the Upper Gate of the *,	2Ch 27:3
the hill where the * was situated.	2Ch 27:3
had given him the * gold and the	2Ch 28:21
bowls from the * and slashed them	2Ch 28:24
the door of the * shut so that no	2Ch 28:24
doors of the * and repaired them.	2Ch 29:3
of the *, and addressed them thus:	2Ch 29:4,5
and sanctify the * of the Lord God	2Ch 29:4,5
they abandoned the Lord and his *	2Ch 29:6
and sanctify the *, as the king	2Ch 29:15
inner room of the *, and brought	2Ch 29:16
cleansing of the * and of the altar	2Ch 29:18
by King Ahaz when he closed the *.	2Ch 29:19
went to the * with the city	2Ch 29:20
for the nation and for the *.	2Ch 29:21
He organized Levites at the *	2Ch 29:25,26
So it was that the * was restored	2Ch 29:35
to come to the * at Jerusalem for	2Ch 30:1
and come to his * which he has	2Ch 30:8
burnt offerings into the *.	2Ch 30:15
prayers from his holy * in heaven.	2Ch 30:27
to prepare storerooms in the *.	2Ch 31:11
duty at the * and their families	2Ch 31:16
devoted to the service of the *.	2Ch 31:17,18
respect for the *, the law, and	2Ch 31:21
one altar at the *, and to burn	2Ch 32:12
And when he arrived at the * of	2Ch 32:21
both courts of the * of the Lord,	2Ch 33:4,5
He placed an idol in the very *	2Ch 33:7
here in this *, and in	2Ch 33:7
his idol from the * and tore down	2Ch 33:15
mountain where the * stood, and the	2Ch 33:15
situation at the *, he appointed	2Ch 34:8
city treasurer, to repair the *.	2Ch 34:8
system for gifts for the *.	2Ch 34:9
The money was collected at the *	2Ch 34:9
Priest, was at the * recording the	2Ch 34:14
"See what I have found in the *!	2Ch 34:15,16
in the reconstruction of the *.	2Ch 34:15,16
"Go to the * and plead with the	2Ch 34:21
small, to accompany him to the *.	2Ch 34:30
of God that was found in the *.	2Ch 34:30
begin their work at the * again.	2Ch 35:2
now in Solomon's * and you don't	2Ch 35:3
bring in their offerings to the *.	2Ch 35:4,5
overseers of the *, gave the	2Ch 35:8
for him, as did the * choirs.	2Ch 35:24,25
items from the *, placing them in	2Ch 36:7
them in his own * in Babylon.	2Ch 36:7
Many treasures from the * were	2Ch 36:10
the * of the Lord in Jerusalem.	2Ch 36:14
on his people and on his *.	2Ch 36:15
right into the *, and had no pity	2Ch 36:17
small, used in the *, and treasures	2Ch 36:18
from both the * and the palace, and	2Ch 36:18
Then his army burned the * and	2Ch 36:19
all the valuable * utensils.	2Ch 36:19
me to build him a * in Jerusalem,	2Ch 36:22,23
of building him a * in Jerusalem,	Ez 1:2
to rebuild this * of Jehovah, who	Ez 1:3
a freewill offering for the *."	Ez 1:4
at once to rebuild the *.	Ez 1:5
could, as well as gifts for the *.	Ez 1:6
had taken from the * at Jerusalem	Ez 1:7
placed in the * of his own gods.	Ez 1:7
The following families of the *	Ez 2:43-54
The * assistants and the	Ez 2:58
rebuilding of the *, and each gave	Ez 2:68
gatekeepers, the * workers, and the	Ez 2:70
building the foundation of the *.	Ez 3:6
The actual construction of the *	Ez 3:8
foundation of the *, the priests	Ez 3:10
foundation of the * had been laid.	Ez 3:11
beautiful *—wept aloud, while	Ez 3:12
rebuilding the *, they approached	Ez 4:1
in this work. The * of the God of	Ez 4:3
repaired the foundations of the *.	Ez 4:12
stop building the * until I have	Ez 4:21
this * and finish these walls?"	Ez 5:3
the men who were working on the *.	Ez 5:4
the * of the great God of Judah.	Ez 5:8
are rebuilding the * that was	Ez 5:11
destroy this * and exile the people	Ez 5:12
a decree that the * should be	Ez 5:13
had taken from the * in Jerusalem	Ez 5:14
had placed in the * of Babylon.	Ez 5:14
* of God be built there as before.	Ez 5:15
foundations of the * at Jerusalem;	Ez 5:16
out concerning the * of God at	Ez 6:3
taken from the * of God by	Ez 6:5
into the * as they were before."	Ez 6:5
disturb the construction of the *.	Ez 6:6
commandment and destroys this *.	Ez 6:12
The * was finally finished, as had	Ez 6:14
The * was then dedicated with	Ez 6:16
in the construction of the *.	Ez 6:21,22
and * workers traveled with him.	Ez 7:7,8,9
collect voluntary * offerings of	Ez 7:16
* when you arrive in Jerusalem.	Ez 7:17
the * of your God at Jerusalem.	Ez 7:19
of the * or for any similar needs,	Ez 7:20
God of heaven demands for his *;	Ez 7:23
gatekeeper, * attendant, or other	Ez 7:24
worker in the * shall be required	Ez 7:24
the * of the Lord in Jerusalem!	Ez 7:27
brothers and the * attendants to	Ez 8:17
for the * of God at Jerusalem.	Ez 8:17
and 220 * attendants.	Ez 8:20
attendants. (The * attendants were	Ez 8:20
classification of * employees first	Ez 8:20
had presented to the * of God.	Ez 8:25
placed in the treasury of the *."	Ez 8:29
taking it to God's * in Jerusalem.	Ez 8:30
weighed in the * by Meremoth (the	Ez 8:33
in the rebuilding of the * of God.	Ez 8:36
in rebuilding the * of our God and	Ez 9:9
in front of the *, weeping and	Ez 10:1
* and refused all food and drink;	Ez 10:6
in the open space before the *;	Ez 10:9
fortress near the *, and for the	Neh 2:8
The * attendants living in Ophel	Neh 3:26
as far as the * attendants' and	Neh 3:31
"Let us hide in the * and bolt	Neh 6:10
And if I go into the *, not being	Neh 6:11
make me sin by fleeing to the *;	Neh 6:12,13
"Of the * assistants, the	Neh 7:46-56
"In all, the * assistants and	Neh 7:60
choir members, the * attendants,	Neh 7:73
the court of the *, or on the plaza	Neh 8:16
the choir members; the *	Neh 10:28
annually with a * tax so that there	Neh 10:32
to care for the * of our God;	Neh 10:32
* and for the atonement of Israel.	Neh 10:33
at the * as required in the law.	Neh 10:34
every crop to the *—whether it be a	Neh 10:35
who minister in the * of our God.	Neh 10:36
They stored the produce in the *	Neh 10:37
* and placed in the storage areas.	Neh 10:38
olive oil to the * and place them	Neh 10:39,40
not to neglect the * of our God.	Neh 10:39,40
the Levites, the * assistants, and	Neh 11:3
the work at the * under the	Neh 11:10-14
charge of the work outside the *;	Neh 11:15,16,17
However, the * workers (whose	Neh 11:21
serving at the * was Uzzi (son of	Neh 11:22,23
choirs then proceeded to the *.	Neh 12:40,41
be permitted to worship at the *.	Neh 13:1
custodian of the * storerooms and	Neh 13:4
guest room in the * for Tobiah— I	Neh 13:7
I brought back the * bowls, the	Neh 13:9
"Why has the * been forsaken?"	Neh 13:11
and olive oil to the * treasury.	Neh 13:12
all that I have done for the *.	Neh 13:14
so I chased him out of the *.	Neh 13:28
heard me from his * in Jerusalem.	Ps 3:4
come into your * protected by your	Ps 5:7
the Lord is still in his holy *;	Ps 11:4
Literally, "out of his *."	Ps 18:6f
meditating in his *, living in his	Ps 27:4
But in his * all are praising,	Ps 29:9
procession to the * on festival	Ps 42:4,5
Let them lead me to your * on	Ps 43:3
Lord, here in your * we meditate	Ps 48:9
shines from the beautiful *	Ps 50:2
to the * of the Lord on holy days.	Ps 55:14
Now I have come to your * with	Ps 66:13
his holy * high upon Mount Zion.	Ps 68:17
gifts to your * in Jerusalem.	Ps 68:29
There he built his towering *,	Ps 78:69
nations. Your * is defiled and	Ps 79:1
HOW LOVELY IS your *, O Lord of	Ps 84:1
in your *, singing your praises.	Ps 84:4
A single day spent in your * is	Ps 84:10
* of my God than live in palaces	Ps 84:10
strength and beauty are in his *.	Ps 96:6
down from his * in heaven, and	Ps 102:19
stream to the * in Jerusalem to	Ps 102:21,22
Here in the courts of the * in	Ps 116:18,19
Open the gates of the *	Ps 118:19
We bless you from the *.	Ps 118:26
Jerusalem, to the * of the Lord.	Ps 122:1
a protection to the * of the Lord.	Ps 122:9
of the Lord, a * for the mighty	Ps 132:2-5
be settled in the *, in God's	Ps 132:7
Arise, O Lord, and enter your *	Ps 132:8
as watchmen in the * every night.	Ps 134:1
him as they stand in his * courts.	Ps 135:1
I face your * as I worship,	Ps 138:2
Praise him in his *, and in the	Ps 150:1
left from her sacrifice at the *.	Pro 7:14f
AS YOU ENTER the *, keep your ears	Ecc 5:1
Jerusalem and the * of the Lord	Is 2:2
to the * of the God of Israel;	Is 2:3
the * was filled with his glory.	Is 6:1
It shook the * to its	Is 6:4
God will watch quietly from his *	Is 18:4
and went over to the * to pray.	Is 37:1
went over to the * and spread it	Is 37:14
worshiping in the * of Nisroch his	Is 37:38
*, accompanied by the orchestra."	Is 38:20
* restored, for I have spoken it.	Is 44:28
offerings, for my * shall be called	Is 56:7
They come to the * every day and	Is 58:2
oh, how they love the * services!	Is 58:2
glorify my glorious * in that day.	Is 60:7
sanctuary. My * will be glorious.	Is 60:13
Within the * courts you	Is 62:9
Our holy, beautiful * where our	Is 64:11
the Lord and his * and worship gods	Is 65:11
my footstool: What * can you build	Is 66:1
is that terrible noise from the *?	Is 66:6
flowing into the * of the Lord at	Is 66:20
Go over to the entrance of the *	Jer 7:2
say that since the * of the Lord is	Jer 7:4
You think that because the * is	Jer 7:8
my * and chant,"We are saved!"	Jer 7:10
Is my * but a den of robbers in	Jer 7:11
Yes, I will destroy this *, as I	Jer 7:13,14
did in Shiloh—this * called by my	Jer 7:13,14
right in my own *, polluting it.	Jer 7:30
have to come any more to my *?	Jer 11:15
to praise the Lord in his *.	Jer 17:26
in front of the * of the Lord and	Jer 19:14
in charge of the * of the Lord,	Jer 20:1
at Benjamin Gate near the *.	Jer 20:2
here in my own *, says the Lord.	Jer 23:11
in front of the * in Jerusalem.	Jer 24:2
own from his holy * in heaven, and	Jer 25:30
Stand out in front of the * of	Jer 26:2
will destroy this * as I destroyed	Jer 26:6
the people in the * mobbed him,	Jer 26:7,8
this * like the one at Shiloh?"	Jer 26:9
the door of the * to hold court.	Jer 26:10
against this * and this city.	Jer 26:12
top where the great * now stands!'	Jer 26:18
* will be returned from Babylon.	Jer 27:16
still here in the *, left from	Jer 27:18
before the *, and the great bronze	Jer 27:19,20,21
basin in the * court, and the metal	Jer 27:19,20,21
me publicly in the * while all the	Jer 28:1
bring back all the * treasures that	Jer 28:3
this *, with all our loved ones.	Jer 28:6
brought to them at the *;	Jer 31:14
They have even defiled my own *	Jer 32:34
me in my * that you would do it.	Jer 34:15
live and invite them to the *.	Jer 35:2
families— to the *, into the room	Jer 35:4
Shallum), who was the * doorman.	Jer 35:4
the scroll in the * on the next Day	Jer 36:6
messages to the people at the *.	Jer 36:8
the services at the * that day.	Jer 36:9
*, near the door of the New Gate.	Jer 36:10
him at the side entrance of the *.	Jer 38:14
to worship at the * of the Lord.	Jer 41:5
upon those who destroyed his *.	Jer 50:28
his people and desecrated his *.	Jer 51:11
"We are ashamed because the * of	Jer 51:51
and burned the * and the palace	Jer 52:13
entrance of the *, and the bronze	Jer 52:17
all the other items used in the *.	Jer 52:18
the three chief * guards, one of	Jer 52:24,25
come to celebrate the * feasts;	Lam 1:4
violate her sacred *—foreigners you	Lam 1:10
has shown no mercy even to his *.	Lam 2:1
broken down his * as though it were	Lam 2:6
who carouse in the * as Israel used	Lam 2:7
lands, without a *, without a	Lam 2:9
die within the * of the Lord?	Lam 2:20
* walls are scattered in the	Lam 4:1
Jerusalem and the * of the Lord	Lam 5:18
have defiled my * with idols and	Eze 5:11
in decorating the *, and you used	Eze 7:20
They shall defile my *.	Eze 7:21
and leave the * in ruins.	Eze 7:22
so proud of, and defile your *.	Eze 7:24
doing here, to push me from my *?	Eze 8:6
to the door of the * court, where I	Eze 8:7
north gate of the *, and there sat	Eze 8:14
inner court of the * and there at	Eze 8:16
their backs to the * of the Lord,	Eze 8:16
They all went into the * and	Eze 9:2
to the *.	Eze 9:3
And begin right here at the *."	Eze 9:6

(TEMPLE Con't)
And he said, "Defile the *! Eze 9:7
end of the * when the man went in. Eze 10:3
went over to the door of the *. Eze 10:4
of the Temple. The * was filled Eze 10:4
the court of the * was filled with Eze 10:4
* and stood above the cherubim. Eze 10:18
them to the east gate of the *. Eze 10:19
east gate of the *, where I saw Eze 11:1
against Israel and against my *! Eze 21:2
and defiled my * and my holiness. Eze 22:26
they defiled my * and ignored my Eze 23:38
came into my * to worship! Eze 23:39
*, the strength of your nation. Eze 24:20,21
Because you scoffed when my * was Eze 25:3
and put my * among them forever. Eze 37:26
And when my * remains among Eze 37:28
standing beside the * gate, Eze 40:3
the outside of the * area with his Eze 40:5
"the outer court" of the * Eze 40:19
to be presented in the *. Eze 40:39
the inner court [in front of the * Eze 40:47
court, standing in front of the *. Eze 40:47
me to the entrance hall of the *. Eze 40:48,49
main room of the *, and measured Eze 41:1
the wall of the * and found that it Eze 41:5
to the * wall for support. Eze 41:6
of the * wall as it rose higher. Eze 41:7
A stairway at the side of the * Eze 41:7
I noticed that the * was built on Eze 41:8
both sides of the *, was another Eze 41:10
west, facing the * yard, measuring Eze 41:12
Then he measured the * and its Eze 41:13
at the east of the * was also 175 Eze 41:14
of the *, including its two walls. Eze 41:15,16
The nave of the * and the Holy of Eze 41:15,16
The inner walls of the * were Eze 41:15,16
around the inner wall of the *. Eze 41:19,20
beside the *, and on the canopy Eze 41:26
THEN HE LED me out of the *, back Eze 42:1
* yard, and to another building. Eze 42:1
* court, which was 175 feet long. Eze 42:7,8
On the opposite side of the * a Eze 42:9,10
court, between the * and the outer Eze 42:9,10
rooms facing the * yard are holy; Eze 42:13
nave of the *—they must change Eze 42:14
to measure the entire * area. Eze 42:15
* through the eastern passageway. Eze 43:4
glory of the Lord filled the *. Eze 43:5
me from within the * (the man who Eze 43:6
"Son of dust, describe the * I Eze 43:10
the basic law of the *: Holiness! Eze 43:12
hill where the * is built is holy. Eze 43:12
place outside the * area. Eze 43:21
passageway to the front of the *. Eze 44:4
Lord filled the * of the Lord, and Eze 44:4
and rules of the * of the Lord. Eze 44:5
be admitted to the *, and who is to Eze 44:5
They may be * guards and Eze 44:11
They are the * caretakers, to do Eze 44:14
my priests in the * when Israel Eze 44:15
in the inner court or in the *. Eze 44:17
to perform his * duties again. Eze 44:26
brought to the * by the people—the Eze 44:29
shall be designated for the *. Eze 45:2
left empty. The * shall be built Eze 45:3
for their homes and for my *. Eze 45:4
for the Levites who work at the *. Eze 45:5
no blemishes, to purify the *. Eze 45:18
door posts of the * and upon the Eze 45:19
and so the * will be cleansed. Eze 45:20
were where the * assistants—the Eze 46:24
me back to the door of the *. Eze 47:1
from beneath the * and passing to Eze 47:1
by the river flowing from the *. Eze 47:12
is the land set aside for the *. Eze 48:8
units, with the * in the center. Eze 48:8
This * area will be 8 Eze 48:9
north to south, surrounds the *. Eze 48:10
miles wide, south of the * Eze 48:15
cups from the * of God, and placed Dan 1:1
before from the * in Jerusalem Dan 5:2,3,4
here these cups from his *; Dan 5:23
to him, and by defiling his *. Dan 8:11
against the * ceremonies, so truth Dan 8:12f
destruction of the * is avenged and Dan 8:13
Holy Place (in the *) will be Dan 9:24
will destroy the city and the *. Dan 9:26
and desecrate the * in Jerusalem. Dan 11:20f
and worshiping idols inside the *. Dan 11:30,31
altar, *, priests, or even idols! Hos 3:4
with harlots and * prostitutes. Hos 4:14
hatred, even in the * of the Lord. Hos 9:8
to bring to the * of the Lord; Joe 1:9
people into the * of the Lord your Joe 1:14
will be ended in the * of our God. Joe 1:16
The Lord shouts from his * in Joe 3:16
forth from the * of the Lord to Joe 3:18
his lair—from his * on Mount Zion. Amo 1:2
and in my own * they offer Amo 2:8
the * will turn to weeping then. Amo 8:3

and shake the * until the pillars Amo 9:1
I ever again see your holy *?' Jon 2:4
prayer went to you in your holy *. Jon 2:7
For the Lord in his holy * has Mic 1:2
the mountaintop where the * Mic 3:12
see the * of the God of Israel; Mic 4:2
"But the Lord is in his holy *; Hab 2:20
her priests defile the * by their Zep 3:4
right time for rebuilding my *?" Hag 1:2
homes, when the * lies in ruins? Hag 1:3,4
and rebuild my *, and I will be Hag 1:8
Because my * lies in ruins and Hag 1:9
them a desire to rebuild his *; Hag 1:14,15
remember the * as it was before? Hag 2:3
pour into this *, and I will fill Hag 2:7f
shall come to this *, and I will Hag 2:7
'The future splendor of this * Hag 2:8,9
years later, came often to this *. Hag 2:8,9f
you have begun to build the *. Hag 2:15
as the foundation of the Lord's * Hag 2:18,19
to rebuild the * structure, and Hag 2:18,19
with mercy; my * will be rebuilt, Zec 1:16
charge of my *, to keep it holy; Zec 3:7
Stone of the * that Joshua is Zec 3:9
for rebuilding the *. Zec 4:6f
will finish building this * Zec 4:7
this *, and he will complete it. Zec 4:9
—and will build the * of the Lord. Zec 6:12
"Then put the crown in the * of Zec 6:14
to rebuild the * of the Lord. Zec 6:15
to the Lord's * at Jerusalem, to Zec 7:2
foundation of the *, the prophets Zec 8:9
Get on with rebuilding the *! Zec 8:13
And I will surround my * like a Zec 9:8
me, 'Toss it into the * treasury Zec 11:13
and the trash cans in the * of Zec 14:20
in the * of the Lord of Hosts! Zec 14:21
holy and beloved * by marrying Mal 2:11
suddenly to his *—the Messenger of Mal 3:1
there will be food enough in my *; Mal 3:10
to Jerusalem to the roof of the *. Mt 4:5
the altar in the *, offering a Mt 5:23
He went into the * and they ate Mt 12:4
in the * may work on the Sabbath? Mt 12:5
is here who is greater than the *! Mt 12:6
in Capernaum, the * tax collectors Mt 17:24
Jesus went into the *, drove out Mt 21:12
"The Scriptures say my * is a Mt 21:13
and he healed them there in the *. Mt 21:14
children in the * shouting, "God Mt 21:15
When he had returned to the * and Mt 21:23
to swear 'By God's *' means Mt 23:16
'By the gold in the *' is binding! Mt 23:16
or the * that sanctifies the gold? Mt 23:17
you swear 'By the *' you are Mt 23:21
by you in the * between the altar Mt 23:35
AS JESUS WAS leaving the * Mt 24:1
a tour of the various * buildings. Mt 24:1
the * and you didn't stop me then. Mt 26:55
to destroy the * of God and rebuild Mt 26:60,61
* and went out and hanged himself. Mt 27:5
You can destroy the * and build Mt 27:40
in the * was split apart from top Mt 27:51
"Use your own * police," Pilate Mt 27:65
city, some of the * police who had Mt 28:11
Jerusalem and went into the *. Mk 11:11
he went to the * and began to drive Mk 11:15
Scriptures, 'My * is to be a place Mk 11:17
through the * area, the chief Mk 11:27,28
on the altar of the *." Mk 12:33
the people in the * area, he asked Mk 12:35
boxes in the * and sat and watched Mk 12:41
AS HE WAS leaving the * that day, Mk 13:1
all this going to happen to the *? Mk 13:3,4
horrible thing standing in the * Mk 13:14
Why didn't you arrest me in the *? Mk 14:49
will destroy this * made with human Mk 14:58
"Sure, you can destroy the * and Mk 15:29,30
of the room in the * called "The Mk 15:38f
in the * was split apart from top Mk 15:38
division of the * service corps. Lk 1:5
his work in the *—for his division Lk 1:8,9
outside in the * court, praying as Lk 1:10
must have seen a vision in the *. Lk 1:22
He stayed on at the * for the Lk 1:23
* duties and then returned home. Lk 1:23
offering at the *, as required by Lk 2:22
Jerusalem resident, was in the *. Lk 2:25
him to go to the * that day; Lk 2:27
was also there in the * that day. Lk 2:36,37
She never left the * but stayed Lk 2:36,37
He was in the *, sitting among Lk 2:46,47
at the *, in my Father's House?" Lk 2:49
a high roof of the * and said, "If Lk 4:9,10,11
He went into the * and took the Lk 6:4
sacrificing at the * in Jerusalem. Lk 13:1
"Two men went to the * to pray. Lk 18:10
Then he entered the * and began Lk 19:45
'My * is a place of prayer; Lk 19:46
daily in the *, but the chief Lk 19:47
Good News in the *, he was Lk 20:1

out the merchants from the *. Lk 2
AS HE STOOD in the *, he was Lk 2
stonework of the * and the memorial Lk 2
Every day Jesus went to the * to Lk 21:37,
captains of the * guards to discuss Lk 22
captains of the * guards and the Lk 22:
Why didn't you arrest me in the *? Lk 22:
the thick veil hanging in the * Lk 23:
in the *, praising God. Lk 24:
In the * area he saw merchants Jn 2:
to build this *, and you can do it Jn 2:
found him in the * and told him, Jn 5:
up to the * and preached openly. Jn 7:
So Jesus, in a sermon in the *, Jn 7:
Many among the crowds at the * Jn 7:
The * police who had been sent to Jn 7:
he was back again at the *. Jn 8
of the * known as the Treasury. Jn 8:
walked past them and left the *. Jn 8:
of the cleansing of the *. Jn 10:22,2
He was at the *, walking through Jn 10:22,2
gossiped in the *, they asked each Jn 11:5
regularly in the synagogue and *; Jn 18:2
regularly at the * each day, met in Act 2:4
PETER AND JOHN went to the * one Act 3:
As they approached the *, they Act 3:
laid beside the * gate—the one Act 3:
God, he went into the * with them. Act 3:7,
the captain of the * police, and Act 4:
regularly at the * in the area Act 5:1
* and preach about this Life!" Act 5:2
They arrived at the * about Act 5:2
arrived at the *, and, convening Act 5:2
Literally, "the captain of the * Act 5:24
in the *, preaching to the people! Act 5:2
And every day, in the * and in Act 5:4
* and against the laws of Moses. Act 6:1
will destroy the *, and throw out Act 6:1
them a portable *, or Tabernacle, Act 7:4
permanent * for the God of Jacob. Act 7:4
to worship at the *, and was now Act 8:2
The local priest of the * of Act 14:1
were given to God at the *. Act 18:18
were given to God at the *. Act 18:22
that the * of the great goddess Act 19:2
her * and have not defamed her. Act 19:3
Go with them to the * and have Act 21:2
the men to the * for the ceremony, Act 21:26,2
* and roused a mob against him. Act 21:26,2
He even talks against the * and Act 21:28
Paul had taken him into the *. Act 21:29
Paul was dragged out of the *, Act 21:30
was praying in the *, I fell into a Act 22:17,18
defile the * when we arrested him. Act 24:6
to worship at the *, and you will Act 24:1
My accusers saw me in the * as I Act 24:18
or desecrated the * or rebelled Act 25:8
The Jews arrested me in the * Act 26:2
you eating at a * restaurant, for 1Co 8:10
working in his * to take for their 1Co 9:13
be between God's * and idols? 2Co 6:16
For you are God's *, the home of 2Co 6:16
constantly growing * for God. Eph 2:21
sit as God in the * of God, 2Th 2:4
He ministers in the * in heaven, Heb 8:2
a copy of the real * in heaven. Heb 9:24
him a pillar in the * of my God; Rev 3:12
him day and night in his *. Rev 7:15
go and measure the * of God, Rev 11:1
and measure the * of God, and the Rev 11:1f
Then, in heaven, the * of God was Rev 11:19
* and all those living in heaven. Rev 13:6
Then an angel came from the * and Rev 14:15
came from the * in heaven, and he Rev 14:17
* in heaven was thrown wide open! Rev 15:5
then came from the *, clothed in Rev 15:6
and forever. The * was filled with Rev 15:8
shouting from the * to the seven Rev 16:1
So the first angel left the * and Rev 16:2
the throne of the * in heaven, Rev 16:17
No * could be seen in the city, Rev 21:22
Literally, "are its *." Rev 21:22f

TEMPLE-ASSISTANT
A Jewish * Lk 10:32

TEMPLE-GIRL
same *, corrupting my holy name. Amo 2:7

TEMPLE-KEEPER
Literally, "is the *." Act 19:35f

TEMPLE-TOWER
great city, with a * reaching to Gen 11:3,4

TEMPLES
on the land owned by the *. Gen 47:26
your hair on your * or clip the Lev 19:27
through his * and into the ground; Ju 4:21
with the tent peg through his *. Ju 4:22
And pierced Sisera's *, Ju 5:26
Solomon built * for these 1Ki 11:8
mourning to their * to weep for the Is 15:2
gods in their idol *, but none will Is 16:12
tearing down his * and altars in Is 36:7
He will set fire to the * of the Jer 43:12

EMPLES Con't)
lown the * of the gods of Egypt." Jer 43:13
They built their idol * beside Eze 43:8
hem off to your heathen *. Joe 3:5
The idol altars and * of Israel Amo 7:9
ier ornate idol *, built with the Mic 1:7
cities where your idol * stand. Mic 5:14
gods and *, and I will bury you! Nah 1:14
However, God doesn't live in * Act 7:48,49
ie doesn't live in man-made *; Act 17:24
Literally, "do you rob *?" Rom 2:22f

EMPORARILY
the door, and * blinded the men of Gen 19:11
When the siege was * lifted Jer 34:11f

EMPORARY
As a * measure the king 1Ki 8:64
slaves, but the action was only *. Jer 34:10
For these were only * rules that Col 2:17

EMPT
lest she * you and seduce you. Pro 7:25
won't be able to * them because of 1Co 7:5

EMPTATION
will be a constant * to you." Ju 2:3
you fall to her * and lose your Pro 5:9
Don't bring us into *, but Mt 6:13
the Kingdom every * and all who are Mt 13:41
* to do wrong is inevitable, but Mt 18:7
Otherwise * will overpower you. Mt 26:41
have continued with me in my *." Lk 22:28f
"that you enter not into *." Lk 22:40f
by *." Lk 22:40
hold out against * all his life and Rom 10:5
And no * is irresistible. 1Co 10:13
You can trust God to keep the * 1Co 10:13
suffering and *, he knows what it Heb 2:18
against sin and * until you sweat Heb 12:4
else to do it. * is the pull of Jas 1:14
Tribulation and *, which will come Rev 3:10

EMPTATION'S
He will show you how to escape * 1Co 10:13

EMPTATIONS
was subjected to Satan's * to sin. Mk 1:12,13
had ended all the *, he left Jesus Lk 4:13
"THERE WILL ALWAYS be * to sin," Lk 17:1
he had the same * we do, though he Heb 4:15
with the same * and understands Heb 5:1
life full of difficulties and *? Jas 1:2
and me from the * that surround us, 2Pe 2:9

TEMPTED
against God and * him to slay Ex 17:7
* to destroy you along the way." Ex 33:3
the ground or are * to despair. Job 4:3,4
turned away and * God to kill them, Ps 78:41
fainthearted, those * to despair. Is 42:3
Spirit, to be * there by Satan. Mt 4:1
Then Satan * him to get food by Mt 4:3
where Satan * him for forty days. Lk 4:1
And don't allow us to be *." Lk 11:4
will not fall when you are *." Lk 22:46
we suffer and are *, and he is Heb 2:18
wrong when he is *, for afterwards Jas 1:12

TEMPTER
and pray lest the * overpower you. Mk 14:38

TEMPTING
Massah (meaning "* Jehovah to slay Ex 17:7
but woe to the man who does the *. Mt 18:7
literally, "Others, *, sought of Lk 11:16f
woe to the man who does the *. Lk 17:1
Are you * the Lord to be angry 1Co 10:22
never God who is * him, for God Jas 1:13

TEMPTS
and never * anyone else to do it. Jas 1:13

TEN
(This took place * years after Gen 16:2,3
Suppose only * are found?" Gen 18:32
of the *, I won't destroy it." Gen 18:32
He took with him * of Abraham's Gen 24:10
at least another * days or so!" Gen 24:55
And you have reduced my wages * Gen 31:41
So Joseph's * older Gen 42:3
He sent his father * Gen 45:23
of Egypt, and * donkeys loaded with Gen 45:23
he in turn will have * judges Ex 18:21
him, each counseling * persons. Ex 18:21
* Commandments engraved on them. Ex 25:16
THE TABERNACLE-TENT from * Ex 26:1
with * posts and ten sockets. Ex 27:12
with ten posts and * sockets. Ex 27:12
Ark containing the * Commandments. Ex 30:6
stone on which the * Commandments Ex 31:18
in his hands the * Commandments Ex 32:15
wrote out the Covenant—the * Ex 34:28
The skilled weavers first made * Ex 36:8,9
supported by * posts and bases, and Ex 38:12
the Ark with the * Commandments Ex 39:33-40
Ark containing the * Commandments; Ex 40:3
stones with the * Commandments Ex 40:20
physical defect, * quarts of finely Lev 14:10
tablets of the * Commandments); Lev 16:13
and a hundred of you, * thousand! Lev 26:8
available for * entire families; Lev 26:26
to twenty shall pay * dollars; Lev 27:5
A section of land that requires * Lev 27:16
two, or five or * or even twenty! Num 11:19,20
the wilderness—and * times refused Num 14:22
Then the * spies who had incited Num 14:36,37,38
"* days later Num 29:7
are to sacrifice * young bulls, two Num 29:23
you must obey—the * Deu 4:13
He again wrote the * Deu 10:4
Ark containing the * Commandments Deu 10:8
his descendants for * generations. Deu 23:2
the * Commandments of the Lord. Deu 31:9
Ark containing the * Commandments Deu 31:25
And two put * thousand to flight, Deu 32:30
Surrounded by * thousands of holy Deu 33:2
altar each of the * Commandments. Jos 8:32
came to * sections of land (in Jos 17:5,6
were given * cities from the Jos 21:5
of the Kohath division was *. Jos 21:26
In this delegation were * high Jos 22:14
* tribes, and each a clan leader. Jos 22:14
Then Phinehas and the * Jos 22:32
so that * thousand of the enemy Ju 1:4,5,6
and killed about * thousand of the Ju 3:29
you to mobilize * thousand men from Ju 4:6
* thousand men volunteered. Ju 4:10
So Barak led his * thousand men Ju 4:14
So Gideon took * of his servants Ju 6:27
left, and only * thousand remained Ju 7:3
He judged Israel for * years and Ju 12:11,12
I will give you * dollars a year Ju 17:10,11
attacked, and the * thousand men in Ju 20:33
Then Boaz called for * of the Ru 4:2
me better than having * sons?" 1Sa 1:8
to * thousand men from Judah. 1Sa 15:4
grain and these * loaves of bread 1Sa 17:17
and David his * thousands!" 1Sa 18:7
"They credit David with * 1Sa 18:8
and David his * thousands'?" 1Sa 21:11
sheep, he sent * of his young men 1Sa 25:5
for about * days, then died, for 1Sa 25:37,38
and David his * thousands!' 1Sa 29:5
* thousand from the land of Tob. 2Sa 10:6
He left no one behind except * of 2Sa 15:16
You are worth * thousand of us, 2Sa 18:3
Literally, "Given you * pieces of 2Sa 18:11f
from the oak. * of Joab's young 2Sa 18:15
"But there are * tribes in 2Sa 19:43
"so we have * times as much right 2Sa 19:43
that his * wives he had left to 2Sa 20:3
them to Lebanon, * thousand a 1Ki 5:14
Literally, "* in a cubit." 1Ki 7:24f
Then he made * four-wheeled 1Ki 7:27-30
was room. All * stands were the 1Ki 7:37
Then he made * brass vats, and 1Ki 7:38
* movable stands holding ten vats; 1Ki 7:41-46
Ten movable stands holding * vats; 1Ki 7:41-46
Jeroboam, "Take * of these pieces, 1Ki 11:31
and give * of the tribes to you! 1Ki 11:31
and give * of the tribes to you. 1Ki 11:35
Take him a gift of * loaves of 1Ki 14:3
in gold, and * suits of clothing. 2Ki 5:5
him a copy of the * Commandments, 2Ki 11:12
mounted troops, * chariots, and ten 2Ki 13:7
chariots, and * thousand infantry; 2Ki 13:7
Once Amaziah killed * thousand 2Ki 14:7
* points or backward ten points?" 2Ki 20:9
ten points or backward * points?" 2Ki 20:9
the shadow to move * points 2Ki 20:11
King Nebuchadnezzar took * 2Ki 24:14
to Mizpah with * men and killed 2Ki 25:25
and they received * cities in the 1Ch 6:61
He also constructed * vats for 2Ch 4:6
he then cast * gold lampstands and 2Ch 4:7
he also built * tables and 2Ch 4:8
land for the first * years of his 2Ch 14:1
three months and * days, and it was 2Ch 36:9
Hashabiah, and * other priests— to Ez 8:24
all kinds of wines every * days. Neh 5:18
They also killed the * sons of Est 9:7-10
"and also Haman's * sons. Est 9:12
and let Haman's * sons be hanged Est 9:13
up the bodies of Haman's * sons. Est 9:14
with your words? * times now you Job 19:3
he had before. (* were in heaven. Job 42:13,14f
And now, although * thousand Ps 3:6
at my side, though * thousand are Ps 91:7
than the mayors of * big cities! Ecc 7:19
better than * thousand others! Sol 5:10
a gallon of juice! * bushels of Is 5:10
the sun backwards * degrees as Is 38:8
So the sun retraced * degrees that Is 38:8
stone, as were the * Commandments. Jer 31:33f
in Mizpah, accompanied by * men. Jer 41:1
Ishmael and the * men in league Jer 41:2
men killed all but * of them and Jer 41:7
a cistern. The * had talked Jer 41:8
* days later the Lord gave his Jer 42:7
of the Temple. * steps led up to it Eze 40:48,49
and * shekels at ten shekels! Eze 45:12
and ten shekels at * shekels! Eze 45:12
Well, at the end of the * days, Dan 1:15
young men's advice * times better Dan 1:20
other animals, and it had * horns. Dan 7:7
I asked, too, about the * horns Dan 7:20
before it. His * horns are ten Dan 7:24
His ten horns are * kings that Dan 7:24
*, and will destroy three of them. Dan 7:24
Even if I gave her * thousand Hos 8:12
only * will come back alive." Amo 5:3
If there are as few as * of them Amo 6:9
of rams and * thousands of rivers Mic 6:7
followed about * years after this Zep 1:1f
crop, there were only *. Hag 2:16,17
In those days * men from ten Zec 8:23
In those days ten men from * Zec 8:23
Galilee, and the * Cities, and Mt 4:25
The other * disciples were Mt 20:24
by the story of * bridesmaids Mt 25:1
started off to visit the * Towns Mk 5:20
of Galilee by way of the * Towns. Mk 7:31
A woman has * valuable silver coins Lk 15:8
a village there, * lepers stood at Lk 17:12
Jesus asked, "Didn't I heal * Lk 17:17
you know what the * commandments Lk 18:20
he called together * assistants and Lk 19:13
a tremendous gain—* times as much Lk 19:16
shall be governor of * cities.' Lk 19:17
* Commandments written on them. Act 7:44
Eight or * days later he returned Act 25:6
The * Commandments were given so Rom 5:20
the * Commandments say is wrong. Rom 13:9
say is wrong. All * are wrapped up Rom 13:9
For although you may have * 1Co 4:15
be helped by, than * thousand words 1Co 14:19
the * Commandments, ends in death; 2Co 3:6
that obeying the * Commandments is 2Co 3:15
when God gave the * Commandments. Gal 3:17
gave the * Commandments to Moses. Gal 4:24,25
This is the first of God's * Eph 6:2
of stone with the * Commandments Heb 9:4
You will be persecuted for "* Rev 2:10
seven heads and * horns, and seven Rev 12:3
It had seven heads and * horns, Rev 13:1
and * crowns upon its horns. Rev 13:1
that had seven heads and * horns, Rev 17:3
His * horns are ten kings who Rev 17:12
His ten horns are * kings who Rev 17:12
"The scarlet animal and his * Rev 17:16
represent * kings who will reign Rev 17:16

TEN-DAY
and suggested a * diet of only Dan 1:12

TEN-STRINGED
a new song, O God, with a * harp. Ps 144:9

TENANT
Then he leased the farm to * Mk 12:1

TENANTS
You are merely my * and Lev 25:23
But the * beat him up and sent Lk 20:10
"But when the * saw his son, Lk 20:14
They were the wicked * in his Lk 20:19

TEND
gardener, to * and care for it. Gen 2:15
to * the vineyards, but see what Sol 1:6
I, the Lord, will * the fruitful Is 27:3
your fields and * your vineyards. Is 61:5

TENDED
of the weak nor * the sick nor Eze 34:4
He has already * you by pruning Jn 15:3

TENDER
* love, he made with your fathers. Deu 7:12
The most * and delicate woman Deu 28:56,57
Like rain upon the * grass, Deu 32:2
When the * grass 2Sa 23:4
"Solomon my son is young and * 1Ch 22:5
again, and grows *, new branches. Job 14:7
water, and * grass springs up? Job 38:25-27
the earth is filled with his * Ps 33:5
O Lord, don't hold back your * Ps 40:11
your mercy is so plentiful, so * Ps 69:16
though we were a * vine and drove Ps 80:8
about the * kindness of the Lord! Ps 89:1
with lovingkindness and * mercies. Ps 103:4
He is merciful and * toward those Ps 103:8
He is like a father to us, * and Ps 103:13
with fruit. The * grass grows up Ps 104:14
Surround me with your * mercies, Ps 119:75,76,77
and * embrace Pro 5:19
up and the * plants are gone. Is 15:6
as the grass, as * plants you Is 37:27
lovely princess, * and delicate. Is 47:1
he was like a * green shoot, Is 53:2
stone and give you * hearts of love Eze 11:19
finest and most * twig from the top Eze 17:22,23
shoulder and all the most * cuts. Eze 24:4
brass, surrounded by the * grass. Dan 4:15
surrounded by * grass, banded with Dan 4:23
I have spared her * neck. Hos 10:11
the young and *, lived unafraid? Nah 2:11
thorns choked out the * blades. Mt 13:7
When her branch is * and the Mt 24:32
When its buds become * and its Mk 13:28

(TENDER Con't)
of our God is very *, and heaven's Lk 1:78
and hurts their * consciences. 1Co 8:7
* conscience for whom Christ died. 1Co 8:11
Are your hearts * and sympathetic Php 2:1
take * care of those who are weak; 1Th 5:14
belong to him. The * mercy of our 2Th 1:12
watches over us with * jealousy? Jas 4:5
with * hearts and humble minds. 1Pe 3:8

TENDER-HEARTED
slow starvation. * women have Lam 4:10

TENDEREST
* lambs and the choicest calves. Amo 6:4

TENDERHEARTED
The most * man among you will be Deu 28:54
Let your * mercies meet our Ps 79:8
to each other, *, forgiving one Eph 4:32
* mercy and kindness to others. Col 3:12

TENDERLY
For I, too, was once a son, * Pro 4:3
long and * have turned against me. Is 1:2
Speak * to Jerusalem and tell Is 40:2
and speak to her * there. Hos 1:14
how God will * comfort you when you 2Co 1:6,7

TENDERNESS
you—with the * of Jesus Christ. Php 1:8
for he is full of * and mercy. Jas 5:11

TENDING
ONE DAY AS Moses was * the flock Ex 3:1
outer holy room, * it day and night Ex 27:21
* your sheep in the pastureland. 2Sa 7:8
and earned a wife by * sheep. Hos 12:12

TENDRILS
He will snip the spreading *. Is 18:5
off your spreading * and harvested Jer 48:32

TENDS
may eat from the orchard he *; Pro 27:18
with long hair * to be ashamed. 1Co 11:14,15

TENS
hundreds, fifties, and *. Ex 18:25
fifties, and * to decide their Deu 1:15

TENSE
Why then should I be * with fear Ps 62:2
be * with fear when troubles come? Ps 62:6

TENSION
rid of *, fighting and quarrels. Pro 22:10

TENSIONS
and * disappear when gossip stops. Pro 26:20

TENT
lay naked in his *, Ham, the Gen 9:20,21
backwards into the *, let it fall Gen 9:23
Then Abram moved his * to the Gen 13:18
the opening of his *, he suddenly Gen 18:1
Then Abraham ran back to the * Gen 18:6
"In the *," Abraham replied. Gen 18:9
(Sarah was listening from the * Gen 18:10
And Abraham returned to his *. Gen 18:33
*, and she became his wife. Gen 24:67
Laban went first into Jacob's * Gen 31:33
Finally he went into Rachel's *. Gen 31:33
into Moses' * to talk further. Ex 18:7
"This home of mine shall be a * Ex 25:9
each side of the *, forming two Ex 26:3
across the front of the sacred *. Ex 26:9
the back of the *, and a 1½-foot Ex 26:12
"The framework of the sacred * Ex 26:15,16
side of the sacred *, with forty Ex 26:18,19
door of the sacred *, make another Ex 26:36
Moses always erected the sacred * Ex 33:7
sacred tent (the "* for Meeting Ex 33:7
and stand in their * doors watching Ex 33:8
from their * doors, bowing low to Ex 33:10
Inside the * the Lord spoke to Ex 33:11
The Tabernacle *, and its Ex 35:10-19
the outside of the *, and hang the Ex 40:8
between the * and the altar, and Ex 40:30
surrounding the * and the altar, Ex 40:33
stay outside his * for seven days. Lev 14:8
will have its own * area, with its Num 2:1
around their * doors weeping, and Num 11:10
"When a man dies in a *, these Num 19:14
who enters the *, and those who are Num 19:14
Any container in the * without a Num 19:15
the water upon the * and upon all Num 19:18
and pans in the *, and upon anyone Num 19:18
by being in the *, or by touching a Num 19:18
*, where he had taken the girl. Num 25:8
ground beneath my *, with the Jos 7:21
They ran to the * and found the Jos 7:22
sheep, his *, and everything he Jos 7:24
had escaped to the * of Jael, the Ju 4:17
to him, "Come into my *, sir. Ju 4:18
So he went into her * and she Ju 4:18
"Stand in the door of the *," Ju 4:20
Then Jael took a sharp * peg and Ju 4:21
So he followed her into the * and Ju 4:22
the * peg through his temples. Ju 4:22
Then she took a * pin and a Ju 5:26
She pounded the * pin through his Ju 5:26
It hit our * and knocked it Ju 7:12,13
but stored his armor in his *. 1Sa 17:54
The Ark was placed inside the * 2Sa 6:17
the Ark of God is out in a *!" 2Sa 7:2
My home has been a * ever since 2Sa 7:6
So a * was erected on the roof of 2Sa 16:22
* to lie with his father's wives. 2Sa 16:22
they went into one * after another, 2Ki 7:8
of God is out there in a *!" 1Ch 17:1
I've gone from * to tent as my 1Ch 17:5
I've gone from tent to * as my 1Ch 17:5
sends his troops to surround my *. Job 19:12
it shakes like a * in a storm. Is 24:20
is blown away like a shepherd's *; Is 38:12
curtain and makes his * from them. Is 40:22
FOR WE KNOW that when this * we 2Co 5:1
was a sacred * down here on earth. Heb 9:1
on the sacred * and on whatever Heb 9:21
That is why the sacred * down Heb 9:23

TENT-MATE
and was telling his * about it. Ju 7:12,13

TENTH
the first day of the * month." Gen 8:5f
Then Abram gave Melchizedek a * of Gen 14:19,20
and I will give you back a * of Gen 28:22
Annually, on the * day of this Ex 12:3,4
Literally, "the * day of Abib." Ex 13:4,5f
it is approximately a * of a Ex 16:36
a * of a bushel of fine flour. Lev 5:11
grain offering—a * of a bushel of Lev 6:19,20
Literally, "on the * day of the Lev 16:29,30f
Literally, "on the * day of the Lev 23:26,27f
Literally, "the * day of the Lev 25:9f
"A * of the produce of the land, Lev 27:30
And the Lord owns every * animal Lev 27:32
for counting. The * given to the Lev 27:33
for her of a * of a bushel of Num 5:15
brought his gifts on the * day. Num 7:66-71
give to the Lord a * of the tithes Num 18:25,26
give the best * to the priests. Num 18:32
Literally, "on the * day of the Num 29:7f
even after the * generation. Deu 23:3
Literally, "The * day of the Jos 4:19f
of Gibe-ah. A * of the army will be Ju 20:8,9,10
He will take a * of your harvest 1Sa 8:15
He will demand a * of your 1Sa 8:17
Jeremiah was * in command; 1Ch 12:8-13
*, the group led by Shecaniah; 1Ch 24:7-18
*, Shime-i and twelve of his sons 1Ch 25:9-31
The commander of the * Division 1Ch 27:13
on duty the * month of each year. 1Ch 27:13
to the Levites a * of everything Neh 10:37
tithes, and a * of all that was Neh 10:38
but now a * of the people from Neh 11:1
direction: One * of one per cent of Ecc 7:27,28
Yet a *—a remnant—will survive; Is 6:13
the Lord in the * year of the reign Jer 32:1
reign, on the * day of the tenth Jer 52:4
tenth day of the * month, Jer 52:4
On the * day of the fifth month Jer 52:12
LATE IN DECEMBER of the * year (of Eze 29:1
a * of a mile. Eze 48:17
fifth, seventh, and * months." Zec 8:19f
to God a * of everything I earn.' Lk 18:12
then Abraham took a * of all he Heb 7:2
gave Melchizedek a * of the spoils Heb 7:4
* of the city, leaving 7,000 dead. Rev 11:13
The * with chrysoprase; Rev 21:18,19,20

TENTMAKERS
for they were * just as he was. Act 18:2,3

TENTS
cattlemen and those living in *. Gen 4:20
Literally, "many *." Gen 13:5f
searched the two * of the Gen 31:33
So although Laban searched the * Gen 31:34
stay in your * and don't go out Ex 16:28,29
So all the people went to their * Ex 35:20
The Levites' * shall be Num 1:53
reserved for the * of Moses and of Num 3:38
* of Korah, Dathan, and Abiram." Num 16:23,24
So Moses rushed over to the * of Num 16:25
away from the * of these wicked Num 16:26
* of Korah, Dathan, and Abiram. Num 16:27
entrances of their * with their Num 16:27
along with their * and families and Num 16:32
in their * and said, 'The Lord must Deu 1:27
tell them to return to their *. Deu 5:30
households and * and all their Deu 11:6
And Issachar, you lovers of your * Deu 33:18
Above all women who live in *. Ju 5:24
Gideon crept up to one of the * Ju 7:12,13
and the remainder fled to their *. 1Sa 4:10
as they were drinking in their *. 1Ki 20:12
abandoning their *, horses, 2Ki 7:7
tethered and the * were all in 2Ki 7:10
struck down the * and houses of the 1Ch 4:40,41
* on the eastern edge of Gilead. 1Ch 5:10
the cattle * and captured great 2Ch 14:15
should live in * during the Neh 8:14
to fall to the ground among the *. Ps 78:28
Literally, "*." Ps 84:10f
Instead, they pouted in their * Ps 106:25
tanned as the dark * of Kedar." Sol 1:5
as the silken * of Solomon!" Sol
the shepherds' *, and there feed Sol
farms, but always to live in *; Jer 3
We have lived in * and have Jer 35
wounded in their *, yet they would Jer 37
Their flocks and their * will be Jer 49
pitch his royal *, but while he is Dan 11
you to living in * again, as you do Hos 1
"three tabernacles" or "*." Mt 17
land, he lived in * like a mere Heb 1

TERAH
old at the birth of his son *. Gen 11:24
By the time * was seventy years Gen 11
Then * took his son Abram, his Gen 11
And there * died at the age of Gen 11
says that * died when he was 145 Gen 11:
From Tahath to *; Num 33:15-
From * to Mithkah; Num 33:15-
including * the father of Abraham Jos 2
The son of Nahor was *, 1Ch 1:24-
The son of * was Abram (later 1Ch 1:24-
Abraham's father was *; Lk 3:23-

TERAH'S
Abraham's father was Terah;* Lk 3:23-

TERAPHIM
an ephod and some *, and he Ju 17:
some *, and many plated idols. Ju 18:
the idols, the ephod, and the *. Ju 18:
the ephod, the *, and the idols. Ju 18:
Literally, "*." 1Sa 19:1

TEREBINTH
of oaks and poplars and * trees. Hos 4:

TERESH
Bigthan and *—who were guards at Est 2:
of Bigthana and *, two of the Est 6

TERM
The meaning of the * is 1Ch 11:2
The meaning of the * is 1Ch 15:
their particular * of service by 1Ch 25
The * used here, "branch of the Is 4:2,3,
The Servant of the Lord, as the * Is 52:1
But stop using this *, "God's Jer 23:

TERMS
God told him, "is to obey its *. Gen 17:9,
Anyone who refuses these * shall Gen 17:
be on friendly * with my country, Gen 21:
and I, and will live by its *." Gen 31:
under its * I promised to give Ex 6
they represent the * of my covenant Ex 34:
Therefore, obey the * of this Deu 29
"I accept your *," she replied. Jos 2:
us, we will agree to your *." 1Sa 11
will obey the * of your contract Ps 132:
The Lord has said in strongest *: Is 8:
See 2 Samuel 7 for the * of God's Is 55:
containing the * and conditions, Jer 32:1
Because you have refused the * Jer 34:18,
Come to * quickly with your Mt 5:2
truce team to discuss * of peace. Lk 14:3

TERRACE
was built on a * and that the Eze 41
extended out 10½ feet onto the *. Eze 41
of the *, the same on both sides. Eze 41
Thirty-five feet away from the *, Eze 41:1
* yard, which was 8¾ feet wide; Eze 41:1

TERRACED
sandalwood to make * steps for the 2Ch 9:1

TERRACES
crop, and the * of grapes upon the Amo 9:1

TERRAIN
stopped there by the rugged *. Num 21:2

TERRIBLE
There was at that time a * famine Gen 12:1
But the Lord sent a * plague upon Gen 12:1
and a vision of * foreboding, Gen 15:1
The famine will be so * that Gen 41:3
BUT THERE WAS no relief from the * Gen 43:
us of such a * thing as that? Gen 44:
the * conditions they were under. Ex 2:1
a * stench throughout the land. Ex 8:1
so that there were * swarms of Ex 8:2
It was * beyond description. Ex 9:2
full of maggots and had a * odor; Ex 16:2
Turn away from this * evil you Ex 32:1
dancing, and in * anger he threw Ex 32:1
bring such a * sin upon them?" Ex 32:2
of the Lord—the * power I will Ex 34:1
of the * fire the Lord has sent. Lev 10:
this is a * perversion. Lev 18:2
Whoever does any of these * Lev 18:29,3
us here in this * wilderness, and Num 16:1
the great and * desert, finally Deu 1:19,20,2
slavery by sending * plagues, Deu 4:3
and saw the * fire at the top of Deu 5:2
miracles—with * blows against Egypt Deu 6:2
the great and * wilderness with the Deu 8:1
* sin against the Lord your God. Deu 9:1
* days of siege that lie ahead. Deu 28:5
can eat them: so * will be the Deu 28:56,57
be destroyed. * trouble will come Deu 31:17
Then Joshua declared a * curse Jos 6:26

ERRIBLE Con't)
o bring * plagues upon Egypt; Jos 24:5
vere in this * plight, the Lord Ju 2:15
Ammonites with a * slaughter all Ju 11:33
nen have committed a * crime. Ju 20:6
* thing that was done among you? Ju 20:12
May the Lord do * things to me if Ru 1:17
'I have been hearing * reports 1Sa 2:23,24,25
here was * confusion everywhere. 1Sa 14:20
swore to it with a * curse against 1Sa 20:16
am in * pain but life lingers on.' 2Sa 1:9
me and forget the * thing I did 2Sa 19:19
He cursed me with a * curse as I 1Ki 2:8
it was such a * blast that the 1Ki 19:11
morning, some * calamity will 2Ki 7:9
Elisha replied, "I know the * 2Ki 8:12
"This is a * decision to make," 1Ch 21:13
" 'Why has the Lord done such a * 2Ch 7:21
out and he died in * suffering. 2Ch 21:19
and they did many other * things. Neh 9:26
* case of boils from head to foot. Job 2:7
can we gaze at the * majesty of God Job 37:22
For his teeth are *. Job 41:14
I sinned, and did this * thing. Ps 51:4
Literally, "You are * as an Sol 6:4f
Literally, "* as an army with Sol 6:10f
was stricken with * homesickness Sol 6:12
reading is, "* desire to sit Sol 6:12f
the Lord will bring a * curse on Is 7:17
Fear grips you with * pangs, like Is 13:8
is coming, the * day of his wrath Is 13:9
is a symbol of the * troubles I Is 20:3
upon you from the * desert, like a Is 21:1
The whole city is in * uproar. Is 22:2
Lord will take his *, swift sword Is 27:1
devil, so when the * enemy floods Is 28:18
slowly across the * desert to Is 30:6
and * storms and huge hailstones. Is 30:30
and most * shall all be freed; Is 49:25
I take from your hands the * cup; Is 51:22
But I will put that * cup into Is 51:23
What is that * noise from the Is 66:6
Does anyone say, "What a * thing Jer 8:6
approach of the * army, for the Jer 8:16
Hear the * sound of great armies Jer 10:22
you will find only * darkness. Jer 13:16
For I will pour out * punishment Jer 14:16
shall die from * diseases. Jer 16:4
decreed such * things against us? Jer 16:10
the people crushed by * calamity. Jer 17:16
says, I will bring * evil upon this Jer 19:3
this place, so * that the ears of Jer 19:3
Mighty, * One, they shall stumble. Jer 20:11
And I will send a * plague on Jer 21:6
If you put an end to all these * Jer 22:4
wicked men. The * anger of the Jer 23:20
drank from that * cup, along with Jer 25:19,20
I am sending * wars upon you." Jer 25:27
and the Lord held back the * Jer 26:19
For these men have done a * Jer 29:23
is an incurable bruise, a * wound. Jer 30:12
the * destruction he has planned. Jer 30:24
sent all this * evil upon them. Jer 32:23
in writing all the * things I will Jer 36:3
The very reason all these * Jer 44:23
a scroll all the * things God had Jer 51:60
Because of the * sins you have Eze 5:9
they commit these * sins, leading Eze 8:17
* example of him, destroying him; Eze 14:8
Your * punishment will be a Eze 16:54
and dry alike. The * flames will Eze 20:47
and polished for * slaughter. Eze 21:9,10,11
the diviners make this * mistake? Eze 21:23
Publicly denounce her * deeds. Eze 22:2
I will execute * vengeance upon Eze 25:17
You will sink beneath the * waves Eze 26:19
for the * day is almost here; Eze 30:2,3
But when all these * things Eze 33:33
vindicated in your * destruction Eze 38:15,16
"I've had a * nightmare," he Dan 2:1
brilliantly, frightening and *. Dan 2:31
Then Nebuchadnezzar, in a * rage, Dan 3:13
then, as a climax to all his * Dan 9:27
It is a * army too numerous to Joe 1:6
Alas, this * day of punishment Joe 1:15
the Lord is an awesome, * thing. Joe 2:11
a blessing instead of his * curse. Joe 2:14
and * Day of the Lord shall come. Joe 2:31
The stench of death was * to Amo 4:10
* the darkness will be for you; Amo 5:18
in that * time of his distress. Ob 1:14
the gods and caused this * storm; Jon 1:7
For I know this * storm has come Jon 1:12
Writhe and groan in your * pain, Mic 4:10
But first comes * destruction to Mic 7:13
"That * day is near. Zep 1:14
it is a day of * distress and Zep 1:15
and the * day of his wrath begins. Zep 2:2
The Lord will do * things to Zep 2:11
then I will send * punishment upon Mal 2:1
Suddenly a * storm came up, with Mt 8:24
* cup I am about to drink from?" Mt 20:22
for I had a * nightmare Mt 27:19
But soon a * storm arose. Mk 4:37
It gave a * scream, shrieking, Mk 5:7,8
to tell them about the * things he Mk 8:31
There is a * baptism ahead of Lk 12:50
stood true to me in these * days, Lk 22:28
heard about the * things that Lk 24:18
the smell will be *, for he has Jn 11:39
it was who would do this * deed. Jn 13:24
* things won't happen to me." Act 8:24
heard about the * things this man Act 9:13
* storm raged unabated many days, Act 27:20
be saying, "what * people you have Rom 2:1
and so you are saving up * Rom 2:5
Oh, what a * predicament I'm in! Rom 7:23,24,25
EVERYONE IS TALKING about the * 1Co 5:1
What a * thing it is that you are 1Co 5:6
us, and saved us from a * death; 2Co 1:10
me their * thirty-nine lashes. 2Co 11:24
sins, for the * wrath of God is Eph 5:6
of a great and * struggle now, as Php 1:30
God's * anger is upon those who Col 3:6
from God's * anger against sin. 1Th 1:10
day will reveal the * truth. 1Ti 5:24
lives in light so * that no human 1Ti 6:16
forward to but the * punishment of Heb 10:27
Think how much more * the Heb 10:29
even though it meant * suffering. Heb 10:32
so that God's * Angel of Death Heb 11:28
men did such * things to him. Heb 12:3
darkness and a * storm, as the Heb 12:18
with a message so * that the people Heb 12:19
sight that he shook with * fear. Heb 12:21
messenger, how * our danger if we Heb 12:25
all the * troubles ahead of you. Jas 5:1
from drowning in that * flood. 1Pe 3:20
of idols, and other * sins. 1Pe 4:3
be judged, what * fate awaits those 1Pe 4:17
but theirs will be a swift and * 2Pe 2:1
man, sick of the * wickedness he 2Pe 2:7,8
pass away with a * noise and the 2Pe 3:10
And Hebrews 6:4-8 speaks of the * 1Jn 5:17f
and to prove the * things they have Jud 1:15
and there was a * earthquake. Rev 8:5
because of the * things that will Rev 8:13
The same hour there will be a * Rev 11:13
filled with the * wrath of the Rev 15:7
cursed God because of the * hail. Rev 16:21

TERRIBLY
I am frightened—* afraid that he is Gen 32:11
and they were * frightened, and Ex 14:10
Samuel was * upset and went to 1Sa 8:6
for the Lord saw how * the king 2Ki 13:4
despairs, for I have * rebelled. Lam 1:20
punish you more * than I have ever Eze 5:9
kings shall be * afraid because of Eze 32:10
The men were * frightened when Jon 1:9,10
scattered Judah so *, and to pound Zec 1:21
to the ground, * frightened. Mt 17:6
sergeant were * frightened by the Mt 27:54
and they were all * frightened. Mk 9:6
And that he had been * Mk 9:12,13
Then the demon screamed * and Mk 9:26
But first I must suffer * and be Lk 17:25
But the whole group was * Lk 24:37
But he will * punish those who Rom 2:8
will punish you * for this, as we 1Th 4:6

TERRIFIC
day there was a * thunder and Ex 19:16
heavy wind brought a * rainstorm. 1Ki 18:45
the Lord flung a * wind over the Jon 1:4

TERRIFIED
Some of the Egyptians, * by this Ex 9:20
he and his people were *. Num 22:2,3
everyone is * if the word Israel Jos 2:9
them and were * to discover that Ju 20:40,41
Lord, for he was * by the drawn 1Ch 21:30
"No wonder I am so * in his Job 23:15
he, the Almighty, has * me with Job 23:16,17
I was * and panic-stricken. Ps 30:6,7
let them be ashamed and * until Ps 83:17
I am *, blinded with dismay. Is 21:3
"Sir, I am * by your appearance Dan 10:16
be cut down! You * the wild animals Hab 2:17
waves, he was * and began to sink. Mt 14:30
Zacharias was startled and *. Lk 1:11,12
The women were * and bowed low Lk 24:5
They were *, but he called out Jn 6:18,19
Everyone was *, and the younger Act 5:5
the judgment to come, Felix was *. Act 24:25

TERRIFY
in sleep, you * with nightmares. Job 7:13,14
And don't * me with your awesome Job 13:21
earthly man will * them no longer. Ps 10:18
when he rises to * the earth. Is 2:21
without mercy. * him all day long Jer 20:16

TERRIFYING
Beg God to end this * thunder Ex 9:28
to listen to the * voice of God Deu 18:16
He did great and * wonders before Deu 34:11,12
had a * nightmare, and awoke Dan 2:1
* things happening in the heavens. Lk 21:11
at the * powers of the underworld 2Pe 2:12

TERRITORIAL
The * Assignments Jos 13:14

TERRITORIES
killed all the kings of those *. Jos 11:17
cities from the * of Ephraim, Dan, Jos 21:5
* and took possession of the land. Ju 2:6
including the * of King Sihon of 1Ki 4:8-19
and the other surrounding *. 1Ki 10:15
Jeroboam II recovered the lost * 2Ki 14:25
had come from the * of Ephraim, 2Ch 15:9

TERRITORY
and headed for the * of Gilead. Gen 31:21
So he named the place "God's * Gen 32:1
very best * in the land of Egypt. Gen 45:18
So Moses assigned the * of King Num 32:33
"This is the * you are to Num 34:13
He will pick a place in the * Deu 12:14
through the * of enemy nations. Deu 29:16
conquer their * on the other side; Jos 1:14
The Israeli * now extended all Jos 11:17
He ruled a * stretching from Mount Jos 12:5
The * now belonging to the Jos 13:2-7
include all this * when you divide Jos 13:2-7
Their * ran from Aroer, on the Jos 13:9
It included Gilead; the * of the Jos 13:11
and all the * of King Og of Jos 13:12
Fitting the size of its * to its Jos 13:15
This * included Jazer, all the Jos 13:25
Moses had assigned the following * Jos 13:29
Their * extended north from Jos 13:30
some of Judah's * to Caleb (son of Jos 15:13
The * of the tribe of Judah also Jos 15:45
Ataroth, in the * of the Archites; Jos 16:1
* of the half-tribe of Manasseh. Jos 16:9
they were located in Manasseh's *. Jos 17:9
boundary was the * of Asher and the Jos 17:10
boundary was the * of Issachar. Jos 17:10
the unconquered * and bring back a Jos 18:4
divided the entire * into seven Jos 18:9
lay between the * previously Jos 18:11
Sea at Hosah. The * also included Jos 19:29
cities included in this * were: Jos 19:35-39
So altogether the * included Jos 19:35-39
and Rakkon, also the * near Joppa. Jos 19:41-46
But some of this * proved Jos 19:47,48
Ramoth of Gilead, in the * of the Jos 20:8
(The land was located in the * Jos 24:32
living in the * allotted to us," Ju 1:3
the whole * from the Arnon River Ju 11:13
it was in the * of Benjamin. Ju 19:16
cities from all the surrounding *. 1Sa 7:16
* when Israel came from Egypt. 1Sa 15:2
as king. His * included Gilead, 2Sa 2:9
and all the * from Beth-shean to 1Ki 4:8-19
So the Reubenites lived in the * 1Ch 5:22
* of the half-tribe of Manasseh. 1Ch 6:61
in charge of the * of Israel west 1Ch 26:30
Philistine *, while Joash had 1Ch 27:28
Obil, from the * of Ishmael, had 1Ch 27:30
from my taxes collected in your *. Ez 6:8
tribes and the * each is to get. Eze 48:1
Asher's * lies south of Dan's Eze 48:2
into their new *, and used until Act 7:45

TERROR
he exclaimed in *. Gen 28:16,17
And the * of God was upon all the Gen 35:5
We saw his * and anguish and Gen 42:21
They were filled with *. Gen 42:28
for the grain! * gripped them, as Gen 42:35
* and dread have overcome them. Ex 15:16
"The * of the Lord shall fall Ex 23:27
mighty miracles, war, and *? Deu 4:34
God, the God of * who shows no Deu 10:17
earthquake, increasing the *. 1Sa 14:15
in it, he tore his clothes in *. 2Ki 22:11
in that area, and * from the Lord 2Ch 14:14
I trembled and shook with *, as Job 4:14
from me in * and refuse to help. Job 6:19-21
live in * of his punishment. Job 9:34
Doesn't his majesty strike * to Job 13:11
When I think of it, * grips me. Job 23:15
wealth is gone. * overwhelms him, Job 27:20
"I live in * now. Job 30:15
neck strikes * wherever he goes. Job 41:22
are afraid. * grips them. Job 41:25
* shall grip them, for God is Ps 14:5
But soon unheard-of * will fall Ps 53:5
They surround me with * and plot Ps 55:3
their happiness, an eternity of *. Ps 73:19
gave them years of * and disaster. Ps 78:33
of * upon the land of Egypt. Ps 105:27
the sailors cringe in *. Ps 107:26
When a storm of * surrounds you, Pro 1:27
and his reign of * shall end. Pro 22:8
rocks and hide in * from his Is 2:10
get away from the * of the Lord and Is 2:21
There will be *, such as has not Is 7:17
Well may you scream in *, O Is 10:30

(TERROR Con't)
Scream in *, for the Lord's time Is 13:6
warriors of Moab cry in utter *. Is 15:4
then, when the * is past, God will Is 16:4,5
In the evening Israel waits in * Is 17:14
mighty nation, a * to all both far Is 18:7
will strike deep * in their hearts, Is 19:17
What a day of confusion and * Is 22:5
is everywhere. * and the captivity Is 24:17
When you flee in * you will fall Is 24:18
will quake with * and flee when Is 31:9
to this time of * when the Assyrian Is 33:18
Together they will stand in *. Is 44:11
deep * into many hearts again. Is 47:12
* and squeezed out the last drops. Is 51:17
you will live in peace. * shall Is 54:14
"Yes," he said, "for * from Jer 1:14
All the cities flee in * at the Jer 4:29
are abandoned—all have fled in *. Jer 4:29
for health but there was only *." Jer 8:15
is only trouble and * everywhere. Jer 14:19
I will cause anguish and * to Jer 15:8
call you 'The Man Who Lives in *.' Jer 20:3
For the Lord will send * on you Jer 20:4
of * such as in that coming day? Jer 30:7
miracles and great power and *. Jer 32:21
The Egyptian army flees in *; Jer 46:5
glance. Yes, * shall surround them Jer 46:5
Apis, your bull god, fled in *? Jer 46:15
Strong men will scream in * and Jer 47:2
of * rise from the city below. Jer 48:5
Instead the awful cries of * and Jer 48:34
But see, I will bring * upon Jer 49:5
his enemies. The * that befalls Jer 50:25
pangs of * gripped him like the Jer 50:43
oh, the *. Jer 50:45
another in frantic *, and to waste Eze 4:17
everyone in the land shook with * Eze 19:7
Let their hearts melt with *, Eze 21:15
drain that cup of * to the very Eze 23:34
an enemy army, the * of the Eze 28:7
great * shall befall them at that Eze 30:9
He and his armies—the * of the Eze 30:11
apart, Memphis will be in daily *. Eze 30:16
(from Babylon)—the * of the Eze 31:12
Yes, * shall strike in many Eze 32:10
They shall shudder with * when I Eze 32:10
mighty army—the * of the nations. Eze 32:12
who once struck * into the hearts Eze 32:23
struck * to the hearts of all; Eze 32:26
They were a * to all while they Eze 32:27
Once a *, now they lie in shame; Eze 32:30
For I have caused my * to fall Eze 32:32
shall quake in * at my presence; Eze 38:20
I will summon every kind of * Eze 38:21
fear, and such * gripped him that Dan 5:6
his face reflected the * he felt, Dan 5:9
the coming time of *—for what you Dan 8:19
with unreasoning * and ran to hide, Dan 10:7
But for now, now you scream in *. Mic 4:9
confusion, destruction, and * Mic 7:4
before the * of their presence. Hab 1:9
in your traps—now * will strike you Hab 2:17
way beneath me and I shake in *. Hab 3:16
will shake with *, for their hopes Zec 9:5
They will be seized with *, Zec 14:13
They screamed in *, for they Mt 14:26
they screamed in *, thinking it was Mk 6:49
they were filled with * and dread. Mk 10:32
cloud formed above them; and * Lk 9:34
her husband. * gripped the entire Act 5:11
Moses shook with * and dared not Act 7:32
Cornelius stared at him in *. Act 10:4
face to face with *, flaming fire, Heb 12:18
strongly that they tremble in *! Jas 2:19
in sorrow and in * when he comes. Rev 1:7
One * now ends, but there are two Rev 9:12
will, in their *, give glory to the Rev 11:13

TERROR-STRICKEN
dishonored, *, and disgraced. Ps 6:10

TERRORIZE
Shall * young men and girls alike; Deu 32:25

TERRORIZED
we are * at every turn. Jer 6:25
naval power that * the mainland, Eze 26:17
Yes, they * the nations while Eze 32:25

TERRORS
you with sudden * and panic, and Lev 26:16
Do you remember the * the Lord Deu 7:19
All God's * are arrayed against Job 6:4
He is surrounded by *, and if Job 15:21
be brought down to the King of *. Job 18:14
gall. The * of death are upon him. Job 20:25
they ally themselves with the * Job 24:17
I stand helpless before your *. Ps 88:15
me. Your * have cut me off. Ps 88:16
Who can realize the * of your Ps 90:11
* of the pathway you have chosen. Pro 1:31
and sharp arrows and the * of war! Is 21:15
I will bring upon them all the * Jer 25:13
Just as I have sent all these * Jer 32:42

the same * that destroyed her. Eze 23:31
Yes, the * that fell upon her Eze 23:32
accomplished all its * upon you! Eze 24:13
it be until all these * end?" Dan 12:6
Therefore the * of war shall rise Hos 10:14
O Death, bring forth your * for Hos 13:14
He shows his power in the * of Nah 1:3
Death holds no *, for they will be Rev 20:6

TERTIUS
good wishes. I, *, the one who is Rom 16:22

TERTULLUS
*, to make their accusations Act 24:1
When * was called forward, he Act 24:2
that everything * said was true. Act 24:9

TEST
This is the way I will * your Gen 42:15
conditions, to * their commitment Ex 15:25
And I will * them in this, to see Ex 16:4
"Are you trying to * God's Ex 17:2
these nations to * my people, to Ju 2:22
in the land to * the new generation Ju 3:1
These people were a * to the new Ju 3:4
me make one more *: this time let Ju 6:39
she decided to * him with some 1Ki 10:1
all the people agreed to this *. 1Ki 18:24
I know, my God, that you * men 1Ch 29:17
to * him with hard questions. 2Ch 9:1
in order to * him and to see what 2Ch 32:31
and * him every moment of the day? Job 7:18
righteous and the wicked to the *; Ps 11:5
* my motives and affections too. Ps 26:2
Oh, put God to the * and see how Ps 34:8
of the land of Egypt. Only * me! Ps 81:10
and know my heart; * my thoughts. Ps 139:23
Truth stands the * of time; Pro 12:19
way so that he can * mankind, and Ecc 3:18
He will * its nobles and find Is 34:11
that you may * this my people and Jer 6:27
I will refine them and * them Jer 9:7
It will put them all to the * Eze 21:13
steward finally agreed to the *. Dan 1:14
balances and have failed the *. Dan 5:27
And he replied, "I will * my Amo 7:8
Lord your God to a foolish *!" Mt 4:7
came to * Jesus' claim of being Mt 16:1
Literally, "to * him." Mk 8:11f
the Lord your God to a foolish *.' Lk 4:12
laws came to * Jesus' orthodoxy by Lk 10:25
together to * the Spirit of God's Act 5:9
Here is the *: no one speaking by 1Co 12:3
Do you pass the *? 2Co 13:5
* and truly belong to the Lord. 2Co 13:6
who prophesy, but * everything 1Th 5:21
in the church as a * of their 1Ti 3:10
These trials are only to * your 1Pe 1:7
being tried in the * tube of fiery 1Pe 1:7
* it first to see if it really is. 1Jn 4:1
some of you into prison to * you. Rev 2:10
the world to * everyone alive. Rev 3:10

TESTAMENT
indicate that Old * saints believed Ps 6:5f
writers of the New * and orthodox Is 52:13f
Old * as well as from the New!" Mt 13:52
by God's prophets in the Old *. Rom 1:2
Amplified New *. Eph 4:15,16f

TESTED
LATER ON, GOD * Abraham's [faith Gen 22:1
You * Levi at Massah and at Deu 33:8
You have * me and seen that I am Ps 17:3
a * help in times of trouble. Ps 46:1
where the thunder hides. I * your Ps 81:7
came—how God * his patience! Ps 105:19
I have thoroughly * your Ps 119:140
and gold can be * in a crucible, Pro 27:21
* by his reaction to men's praise. Pro 27:21
in Zion—a firm, *, precious Is 28:16
It is being * as fire tests gold 1Pe 1:7

TESTICLES
or has imperfect *— although he is Lev 21:20
"IF A MAN'S * are crushed or his Deu 23:1
by grabbing the * of the other man, Deu 25:11

TESTIFIED
I have constantly * to others of Ps 71:17
himself has also * about me, though Jn 5:37
The lying witnesses * again that Act 6:13
* to this in public witness. Act 13:31

TESTIFIES
The very arrogance of Israel * Hos 5:5
And the Holy Spirit * that this Heb 10:15

TESTIFY
be a witness to * against you if Jos 24:27
and refuses to * against the Ps 15:5
congregation and * of the wonderful Ps 22:22
Don't * spitefully against an Pro 24:28,29
so they could * that I had written Is 8:2
righteous God, and * against you. Is 59:12
* that he is the Son of God." Jn 1:34
receive power to * about me with Act 1:8
everywhere and to * that Jesus is Act 10:42
the Council can * that this is so. Act 22:5
and I can * that they did it 2Co 8:3

who * of their faith in Jesus. Rev 19:

TESTIFYING
only one person * against him. Num 35:
After * and preaching in Samaria, Act 8:
time preaching and * to the Jews Act 18

TESTIMONY
Or, "You must not give false * in Ex 20:1
be swayed in your * by the mood of Ex 23:2
do not slant your * in favor of a Ex 23:2
the * which I shall give you." Ex 25:1
"ANYONE REFUSING TO give * Lev 5
on the * of only one witness; Deu 17
"Never convict anyone on the * Deu 19:
the earth will give * against him. Job 20:2
then you will be a * to the nations Jer 4:
healed—a public * of your cure." Mt 8
Literally, "as a * against Lk 9:
shall turn out unto you for a *." Lk 21:1
to me because of the * of these. Jn 17:2
gave a fearless * before Pontius 1Ti 6:1
of their solemn *, the tyrant who Rev 11:
blood of the Lamb, and by their *; Rev 12:1
Literally, "The * of Jesus is the Rev 19:10
beheaded for their * about Jesus, Rev 20:

TESTING
humbling you and * you to find out Deu 8:
For the Lord is * you to find out Deu 13:
* God's patience to the breaking Ps 106:1
(He was * Philip, for he Jn 6.
to come a time of * at Christ's 1Co 3:1
in the desert while he was * them. Heb 3:7,
While God was * him, Abraham Heb 11:1
failing in the hour of *." Rev 3:10

TESTS
It is being tested as fire * gold 1Pe 1:

TETHERED
The horses and donkeys were * and 2Ki 7:1

TETRARCH
Literally, "the *"—he was one of Mt 14:1
Literally, "Herod the *." Lk 9:7

TEXT
otherwise is not clear in the *. Gen 21:9
The * adds, "all these were the Gen 25:4
Added in the Hebrew * is this Num 1:17,18,19
The original * repeats the lists Num 7:18-23
The original * repeats the lists Num 7:24-29
The original * repeats the lists Num 7:30-35
The original * repeats the lists Num 7:36-41
The original * repeats the lists Num 7:42-47
The original * repeats the lists Num 7:48-53
The original * repeats the lists Num 7:54-59
The original * repeats the lists Num 7:60-65
The original * repeats the lists Num 7:66-71
The original * repeats the lists Num 7:72-77
The original * repeats the lists Num 7:78-83
It is indeterminate from the * as Num 12:1
Implied in other *. Jos 11:18
where the original * indicates Jos 15:48-62
is indicated in the original *. Jos 21:9-16f
where the total appears in the *. Jos 21:20,21,22f
The * is uncertain in the original 2Sa 1:21
Here is the * of the letter they Ez 4:11
The Hebrew * adds here: Ps 9:16f
Implied in *. Ps 49:7f
phrase was part of the original *. Ps 49:20f
and are not in the original *. Sol 1:1f
The * here is uncertain. Eze 27:19f
The Hebrew * is obscure. Dan 8:12f
The Hebrew * is uncertain. Hos 4:18f
The Hebrew * makes no distinction Jon 3:3f
The Hebrew * of this verse is very Hab 1:11f
from the Hebrew *, but many other Zec 9:10f
the * of many ancient manuscripts. Jn 7:8f

THADDAEUS
*, Simon Mt 10:2,3,4
*, Simon Mk 3:16-19

THANK
Jehovah. "* you, Lord God of my Gen 24:27
he prayed; "* you for being so Gen 24:27
"Oh, * you, sir," she replied. Ru 2:13
"* God for a girl like you!" Ru 3:10
"Oh, * you, sir!" 1Sa 1:18
today! * God for your good sense! 1Sa 25:33
"Oh, * you, my lord," she 2Sa 14:9
"* you, thank you, sir," Ziba 2Sa 16:4
"Thank you, * you, sir," Ziba 2Sa 16:4
* you, O my Savior, 2Sa 22:3
and exclaimed, "Oh, * you, sir. 1Ki 1:31
Then we will * your holy name, 1Ch 16:35
O our God, we * you and praise 1Ch 29:13
as one to praise and * the Lord; 2Ch 5:13,14
"Now bring your sacrifices and * 2Ch 29:31
sacrifices and * offerings, and 2Ch 29:31
Save me, and I will * you Ps 35:18
I can never * you enough! Ps 44:8
Lord, and * you for your help. Ps 56:12
I will * you publicly throughout Ps 57:9
HOW WE * you, Lord! Ps 75:1
your pasture, will * you forever Ps 79:13
IT IS GOOD to say, "* you" to Ps 92:1
Every morning tell him, "* you Ps 92:2

HANK Con't)
THE LORD for all the glorious Ps 105:1
ALLELUJAH! * YOU, Lord! Ps 106:1
ations so we can * your holy name Ps 106:47
AY "* YOU" to the Lord for Ps 107:1
et them tell him "* you" as Ps 107:22
)H, * THE Lord, for he's so good! Ps 118:1
) Lord, * you so much for Ps 118:21
ne I will * you by living as I Ps 119:7
o * and praise the Lord. Ps 122:4
ORD, WITH ALL my heart I * you. Ps 138:1
ny mother's womb. * you for making Ps 139:14
f prison, so that I can * you. Ps 142:7
All living things shall * you, Ps 145:10
ood eyesight and good hearing, * Pro 20:12
ay you will say, "* the Lord! Is 12:4
n the fields will * me, the Is 43:20
They say, "* God!" Jer 12:2
fferings and * offerings of the Eze 43:27
fferings and * offerings to make Eze 45:15
fferings and * offerings—to make Eze 45:17
o him. I * and praise you, O God Dan 2:23
urnt offerings and * offerings. Amo 5:22
For how can I * you enough for Jon 2:9
* God, now I am rich!' Zec 11:5
heaven and earth, * you for hiding Mt 11:25
Yes, * you, Father, for that is Lk 10:21
his prayer: '* God, I am not a Lk 18:11
'Father, * you for hearing me. Jn 11:41
as I was presenting my * offering. Act 24:18
How I * God through Jesus Christ Rom 1:8
even * him for all his daily care. Rom 1:21
be his slave. * God that though Rom 6:17
this deadly lower nature? * God! Rom 7:23,24,25
Literally, "I * God through Rom 7:23,24,25f
If I can * God for the food and 1Co 10:30
for if you praise and * God with 1Co 14:16
I * God that I "speak in 1Co 14:18
How we * God for all of this! 1Co 15:57
more there are to * him for his 2Co 4:15
* God for his Son—his Gift too 2Co 9:15
forget to * him for his answers. Php 4:6
We always * God for you and pray 1Th 1:2
How can we * God enough for you 1Th 3:9
How I * God for you, Timothy. 2Ti 1:3
I always * God when I am praying Phm 1:4

HANK-OFFERING
sheep is used as a * to the Lord, Lev 3:6
a bull or cow sacrificed as a *. Lev 4:10
the fat of the sacrifice of a *; Lev 4:26
just as in the procedure for the * Lev 4:31
be used just as in the case of a * Lev 4:35
So we have brought a special * Num 31:50
e., the * of wine for saving me. Ps 116:13f

HANKED
She * him warmly. Ru 2:10,11
and worshiped and * the Lord. 2Ch 7:3
Then he took the seven loaves, * Mk 8:6
How she praised and * God! Lk 13:13
And he is not even *, for he is Lk 17:7,8,9
and when he had * God for it, he Lk 22:19
When Paul saw them, he * God and Act 28:15

HANKFUL
Oh, how grateful and * I am to Ps 7:17
Come before him with * hearts. Ps 95:2
All who are * should ponder them Ps 111:1
he is * to the Lord for it; Rom 14:6
to please the Lord, and is *. Rom 14:6
only one who is * to them: so are Rom 16:4
I am so * now that I didn't 1Co 1:14
I am * to God that he has given 2Co 8:16
other of God's goodness and be *. Eph 5:4
for I know how * you will be to see Php 2:28
Lord, and always * to the Father Col 1:12
And always be *. Col 3:15
singing to the Lord with * hearts. Col 3:16
remember to be * when they come. Col 4:2
happens, always be *, for this is 1Th 5:18
How * I am to Christ Jesus our 1Ti 1:12
Christians to enjoy and be * for. 1Ti 4:3
gladly if we are * for it, and if 1Ti 4:4
serving him with * hearts, and with Heb 12:28
And those who have reason to be * Jas 5:13

THANKFULNESS
great joy and *, praising God. Act 2:46

THANKING
praising and * the Lord. 2Ch 5:13,14
along praising and * the Lord! 2Ch 20:21
O Lord my God, I will keep on * Ps 30:12
Surely the godly are * you, for Ps 140:13
and she also began * God and Lk 2:38
dust, * him for what he had done. Lk 17:16
I can never stop * God for all 1Co 1:4
have never stopped * God for you. Eph 1:16,17
And we will never stop * God for 1Th 2:13

THANKLESS
For you are * in addition to all Eze 16:43

THANKS
"Oh, no *," they said, "we'll Gen 19:2
come, though he sent his *. 2Sa 13:25
No wonder I give * to you, O 2Sa 22:50
praise and * to the Lord God of 1Ch 16:4
"Oh, give * to the Lord and pray 1Ch 16:8
Oh, give * to the Lord, for he is 1Ch 16:34
by name to give * to the Lord for 1Ch 16:41
Lord to sing * and praise to him. 1Ch 23:30
who led in giving * and praising 1Ch 25:3
and give * and praise to the Lord. 2Ch 31:2
They sang rounds of praise and * Ez 3:11
the wall, giving * as they went. Neh 12:31,32
in hymns of praise and * to God. Neh 12:46
the grave, who shall give you *?" Ps 6:5f
of his; give * to his holy name. Ps 30:4
I want from you is your true *; Ps 50:14,15
of the earth give * to you. Ps 67:5
my singing! My * will be his Ps 69:30
Give * to him and bless his name. Ps 100:4
But I will give repeated * to Ps 109:30
* to God for his mighty miracles. Ps 111:1
—I will go in and give him my *. Ps 118:19
give you this * and this praise. Ps 118:27,28
Oh, give * to the Lord, for he Ps 118:29
my * to you for your good laws. Ps 119:62
Accept my grateful * and teach Ps 119:108
OH, GIVE * to the Lord, for he is Ps 136:1
Give * to the God of gods, for Ps 136:2
Give * to the Lord of lords, for Ps 136:3
Oh, give * to the God of heaven, Ps 136:26
I worship, giving * to you for all Ps 138:2
shall give you *, O Lord, for all Ps 138:4
Sing out your * to him; Ps 147:7
and their * was to commit adultery Jer 5:7
Therefore I will sing out in * Jer 20:13
always had, giving * to his God. Dan 6:10
the fish, and gave * to God for Mt 15:36
of wine and gave * for it and gave Mt 26:27
up to heaven, gave * for the food. Mk 6:41
of wine and gave * to God for it Mk 14:23
looked up into the sky and gave *; Lk 9:16
when he had given * for it, he Lk 22:17
loaves and gave * to God and passed Jn 6:11
hardtack and gave * to God before Act 27:35
when he had given * to God for it, 1Co 11:24
How can they join you in giving * 1Co 14:16
You will be giving * very 1Co 14:17
For much * and praise will go to 2Co 1:11
But * be to God! 2Co 2:14
and they overflow with * to God. 2Co 9:12
Always give * for everything to Eph 5:20
begin by giving * to God the Father Col 1:3
God the Father to give him your *. Col 3:17
Dear brothers, giving * to God 2Th 1:3
But we must forever give * to 2Th 2:13
upon them; give * for all he is 1Ti 2:1
and honor and * to the one sitting Rev 4:9
saying, "We give *, Lord God Rev 11:17

THANKSGIVING
peace offerings or * offerings—as Ex 29:28
bread and honey as * offerings at Lev 2:12
an offering of * to the Lord, he Lev 3:1
"If it is an offering of *, Lev 7:12
This * peace offering shall be Lev 7:13
appreciation and * to him, its meat Lev 7:15
that is not for *, but is because Lev 7:16
but eats the * offering anyway, Lev 7:20
anyone bringing a * offering to the Lev 7:29
a sacrifice of *, you must do it in Lev 22:29,30
It is a time of deep * to the Deu 16:15
samples brought in * to the Deu 18:4
Tabernacle to sing * to the Lord. 1Ch 16:7
were playing their * song, "His 2Ch 7:6
respond with true * and praise, for 2Ch 32:25
offerings and * offerings—and 2Ch 33:16
began the * services with prayer; Neh 11:15,16,17
one in charge of the * service. Neh 12:8
of praise and *, just as commanded Neh 12:24
*, cymbals, psaltries, and harps. Neh 12:27
* and telling about your miracles. Ps 26:7
his open gates with great *; Ps 100:4
and offer you a sacrifice of *. Ps 116:17
found there, * and lovely songs. Is 51:3
with joy and great *, and I will Jer 30:19
of those bringing * offerings to Jer 33:10,11
O Judah, proclaim a day of *, Nah 1:15
with mighty shouts of * for God's Zec 4:7
of *. And any nation anywhere in Zec 14:16
in * for answered prayer. Act 18:18f
in * for answered prayer. Act 18:22f
* and praise to God for your help. 2Co 9:11
joy and * for all he has done. Col 2:7
and wisdom, and *, and honor, and Rev 7:12

THAT'S
"* a lie!" Gen 3:4
Rachel and Leah replied, "* fine Gen 31:14
"* the man I told you about! 1Sa 9:17
"* ridiculous!" 1Sa 14:29
"* not true!" 1Sa 20:2
* what all the noise is. 1Ki 1:44,45
"* the man we're after." 1Ki 22:32,33
people, telling them, "* right! Neh 8:11
claim * made for them is false?" Ps 4:2
This silent ruin is all * left Is 23:7
ruined heaps. * why their people Is 37:27
a face on it, and * his god—a god Is 40:20
Yes, * it! Is 41:23
God's blessings; * why he doesn't Is 59:9
And the Lord replied, "* right, Jer 1:12
to Jerusalem. * why we are here." Jer 35:11
"* not true," Jeremiah said. Jer 37:14
your feet? All * left for my flock Eze 34:19
* why I ran away to Tarshish. Jon 4:2
"* your problem," they retorted. Mt 27:4
demons. * why demons obey him." Mk 3:22
She replied, "* true, sir, but Mk 7:28
be obeyed. All * required is that Mk 11:22,23
Look, * where his body was lying. Mk 16:6
But some Pharisees said, "* Lk 6:2
'Hard, am I? * exactly how I'll Lk 19:22
"Why, * very strange!" Jn 9:30
"They're drunk, * all!" Act 2:13
it never will. * why those who are Rom 8:8
Love does no wrong to anyone. * Rom 13:10
But when the Lord commends him, * 2Co 10:18
and give up. * why whenever we can Gal 6:10
and dying—well, * better yet! Php 1:21

THEBES
Amon, god of *, and all the other Jer 46:25
and Zoan and * shall lie in Eze 30:14
I will stamp out the people of *. Eze 30:15
racked with pain, * will be torn Eze 30:16
Are you any better than *, Nah 3:8
* was conquered by the Assyrians Nah 3:8f
and Libya. Yet * fell and her Nah 3:10

THEBEZ
the city of *, and captured it. Ju 9:50
Wasn't Abimelech killed at * by a 2Sa 11:19,20,21

THEERANITES
Shuthelahites was *, named after Num 26:28-37

THEFT
fornication, *, lying and slander. Mt 15:19
thoughts of lust, *, murder, Mk 7:21
their immorality and *. Rev 9:21

THEFTS
loot from their * and banditry. Amo 3:10

THEIRS
Literally, "for * is your own Lev 18:10f
"For our army is bigger than * 2Ki 6:16
like *," the people protested. Neh 5:5
These sons of * have also turned Job 30:8
he did for them. * was no downcast Ps 34:5
and great feebleness be *. Ps 69:23
lift a finger—* is a life of ease; Ps 73:12
glory departed, so *, too, will Is 17:3
from them at all. * is no fire to Is 47:14
in mind—to get what isn't *. Jer 8:10
rite like *, and nothing more. Jer 9:25,26
*, for it is all a pack of lies. Jer 10:2,3
I will demand your blood for *. Eze 3:18
for it will be greater than *. Eze 16:54
ancient heights as *, and Eze 36:2
who say, 'Where is this God of *? Joe 2:17
for the Kingdom of Heaven is *. Mt 5:10
They don't worry about *. Mt 6:28
you will be given a reward like *. Mt 10:41
came to get *, they assumed they Mt 20:10
too—and pay for * to be shaved. Act 21:24
this good deed of *, I will come to Rom 15:28
of Jesus Christ, our Lord and *. 1Co 1:2
of Heaven is *, for that is the Jas 2:5
bought them; but * will be a swift 2Pe 2:1

THEME
Their * was "He is so good! 2Ch 5:13,14
His constant * was, "Turn from Mt 3:1

THEOLOGICAL
and controversial * ideas; Tit 3:9

THEOPHILUS
Literally, "most excellent *." Lk 1:1f

THEREAFTER
* Hagar spoke of Jehovah Gen 16:13
way, he must not *, during the Num 6:3,4
The name of the region was * Num 21:3

THEREBY
And Esau vowed, * selling all his Gen 25:33
* saving Israel from disaster. Ju 3:31
of the Lord, * fulfilling the 1Ki 2:27
his care and * stumbled against the Is 8:14,15
* making himself equal with God. Jn 5:18
feel like, * ruining their souls. Jud 1:10

THEREFORE
fierce and cruel. *, I will scatter Gen 49:7
"* tell the descendants of Ex 6:6
The offering is most holy; * you Lev 10:13
for I am holy; * do not defile Lev 11:44
You must * be holy, for I am Lev 11:45
is its blood. *, anyone who eats Lev 17:14
"You shall * make a distinction Lev 20:25
ahead of you. *, O Israel, listen Deu 6:3
"Understand, *, that the Lord Deu 7:9
them personally. *, obey all these Deu 7:11
is evident today. *, cleanse your Deu 10:16
or fear of God. *, when the Lord Deu 25:19
inheritance. *, obey the terms of Deu 29:9
"*, I, the Lord God of Israel, 1Sa 2:30

(THEREFORE Con't)
stolen his wife. * murder shall be 2Sa 12:10
told you not to, * your body shall 1Ki 13:21,22
not been offered. * the wrath of 2Ch 29:8
for their deeds. *, my unquenchable 2Ch 34:25
custom, and toll. *, I command Ez 4:21
the king's laws; *, it is not in Est 3:8
I * looked for good to come. Job 30:26
for himself. * he will listen to me Ps 4:3
slightest sin. * proud sinners Ps 5:5
what is right; * in mercy save me. Ps 26:11
what he has made; * God will Ps 28:5
* God, your God, Ps 45:7
in that City; * it stands unmoved Ps 46:5
accept my laws. * in mighty wrath Ps 95:11
his command. * he swore that he Ps 106:26
I long to obey them! * in Ps 119:40,41,42
for they are my only hope. * I Ps 119:44,45,46
for I am your servant; * give me Ps 119:125
mind is wise; *, even a fool is Pro 17:27,28
and orphans. * the Lord of Hosts, Is 1:24
thought or care. * I will send you Is 5:13
men in jail. * God will deal with Is 5:24
We have * properly used this Is 7:14f
and aid them, * I will overwhelm Is 8:7,8
heaven's armies. * the Lord, in Is 9:14,15
* the Lord God of Hosts says, "O Is 10:24
all gone now! * all Moab weeps. Is 16:7
who can hide you; *, even though Is 17:10
* the curse of God is upon them; Is 24:6
will be rebuilt. * strong nations Is 25:3
away from God. *, he who made them Is 27:11
* hear the word of the Lord, you Is 28:14
learned by rote, * I will take Is 29:14
and won't repent, * calamity will Is 30:13
*, O my people, though you are Is 31:6
not be dismayed; *, I have set my Is 50:7
day by day. * I will reveal my Is 52:6
all their sins. * I will give him Is 53:12
me to punish you. * it will be Is 54:15
no one intervened. * he himself Is 59:16
* your wrath is heavy on us. Is 64:5
you for mercy. * you have turned Is 64:7
and "Destiny," * I will Is 65:12
know I despise. * the Lord God Is 65:13
* go and say to Israel, O Israel, Jer 3:12
* this is what the Lord God of Jer 5:14
* they shall lie among the slain. Jer 6:15
* the Lord of Hosts says this: Jer 9:7
told them to. * this is what the Jer 9:15
nor ask his will. * they perish and Jer 10:21
and canceled. *, the Lord says, I Jer 11:11
*, Jeremiah, pray no longer for Jer 11:14
worships idols; * it shall become Jer 13:10
own lying hearts. *, the Lord Jer 14:15
*, tell them this: Night and day Jer 14:17
things as this? * we will wait for Jer 14:22
backs upon me. * I will clench my Jer 15:6
to listen to me. * I will throw Jer 16:13
Literally, "*, behold, I will Jer 16:21f
* go and warn all Judah and Jer 18:11
paths of sin. * their land shall Jer 18:16
my cause to you. * I will sing out Jer 20:13
* this is God's decree of Jer 22:18
says the Lord. * their paths will Jer 23:12
* the Lord of Hosts says: I will Jer 23:15
* prophesy against them. Jer 25:30
* the Lord says you must die. Jer 28:16
* listen to the word of God, all Jer 29:20
Now * the Lord God of Israel says Jer 32:36
*, says the Lord, because you Jer 34:17
to listen to me. * the Lord God of Jer 35:17
the other times. * know for a Jer 42:22
* the Lord of Hosts, the God of Jer 44:11
and skill; * you shall perish. Jer 48:7
their bones. * the Lord of Hosts, Jer 50:18
* this city of Babylon shall Jer 50:39
so horribly; * she is tossed away Lam 1:8
of destruction. * the ramparts and Lam 2:8
inheritance; * I will hope in him. Lam 3:24
penalty of death, * repent and save Eze 3:18
her." * the Lord God says, I, Eze 5:8
evil sacrifices, * I will not spare Eze 5:11
to make idols! * I will take it all Eze 7:20
* I will deal with them in fury. Eze 8:18
*, son of dust, prophesy against Eze 11:4
"* the Lord God says: You think Eze 11:7
long, long time.' * say to them: Eze 12:28
"* the Lord God says: I will Eze 13:8
"* warn them that the Lord God Eze 14:6,7
"* I have crushed you with my Eze 16:27
as I watched. * I crushed her. Eze 16:50
to obey; * he shall not escape. Eze 17:18
iron and the lead. * the Lord God Eze 22:18,19,20
backs upon me, * you must bear the Eze 23:35
away captive, * I will let the Eze 25:4
of my people, * I will lay my hand Eze 25:7
any other nation, * I will open up Eze 25:9,10
"* the Lord God says: I stand Eze 26:3
"* the Lord God says: Because Eze 28:6
Great care must * be taken to Eze 28:12f
and you sinned. *, I cast you out Eze 28:16
of your splendor. * I have cast you Eze 28:17
* I brought forth fire from your Eze 28:18
with the pain. * the Lord God Eze 29:8
I made it!' * I am against you Eze 29:10
*, the Lord God says, I will Eze 29:19
the Lord God says. * because she Eze 31:10
waters any more. * the waters of Eze 32:14
people of Israel; * listen to what Eze 33:7
"*, O shepherds, hear the word Eze 34:7
let them starve; * I am against Eze 34:9,10
"* the Lord God says: I will Eze 34:20
God is there!' * as I live, the Eze 35:11
You are mocked and slandered. *, Eze 36:4
"* prophesy and say to the hills Eze 36:6
nations. * I have sworn with hand Eze 36:7
"* say to the people of Israel: Eze 36:22
central Turkey. It * seems that Gog Eze 38:2,3f
against their God. * I turned my Eze 39:23
except their own. *, I make this Dan 3:29
refuse to know me; * I refuse to Hos 4:6
people are too. *, I will punish Hos 4:9
*, a mighty wind Hos 4:19
*, I will pour my anger down upon Hos 5:10
It is not God! *, it must be Hos 8:6
their Maker. *, I will send down Hos 8:14
* your harvests will be small; Hos 9:2
intend to keep. * punishment will Hos 10:4
* the terrors of war shall rise Hos 10:14
"* I will make you groan as a Amo 2:13
and banditry. *," the Lord God Amo 3:11
"* I will bring upon you all Amo 4:12
fines, and usury; * you will never Amo 5:11
to the poor. * those who are wise Amo 5:13
* the Lord God of Hosts says Amo 5:16
need your help. * you will be the Amo 6:7
"Now * listen to this message to Amo 7:16
* the entire city of Samaria will Mic 1:6
promised this. (* we will follow Mic 4:5
* I will wound you! Mic 6:13
is that of Ahab! * I will make an Mic 6:16
against the Lord; * your blood will Zep 1:17
their land. * as I live," says Zep 2:9
my intentions. * the Lord Zec 1:16
few and weak.' * no mountain, Zec 4:7
Lord of Hosts. "* I have made you Mal 2:9
Godly children from your union. * Mal 2:15
and cruel men. * control your Mal 2:16
of Heaven. * anyone who humbles Mt 18:4
earth. * go and make disciples in Mt 28:19
in marriage; * a man is to leave Mk 10:6,7
rare perfume. * her sins—and they Lk 7:47
and strife. *, if what you say is Lk 11:18
of their property. * God's heaviest Lk 20:47
*, don't be concerned about how Lk 21:14
I will * have him scourged with Lk 23:16
I will * scourge him and let him Lk 23:22
to this man, and I * testify that Jn 1:34
Literally, "that disciple * whom Jn 21:7f
"* I clearly state to everyone Act 2:36
said, "I believe and * I speak." 2Co 4:13
*, DEAR BROTHERS whom God has Heb 3:1
* let us never stop trusting him. Heb 4:14
He is, *, exactly the kind of Heb 7:26
is coming soon. * be earnest, 1Pe 4:7
As used here the expression * Rev 1:5f
and have not denied my Name. * I Rev 3:8
* I will protect you from Rev 3:10
I will not experience sorrow.' * Rev 18:8

THEREIN
altar, and them that worship *." Rev 11:1f

THEREOF
memorial portion * upon the altar, Lev 2:2f
* or in the forehead thereof." Lev 13:55f
thereof or in the forehead *." Lev 13:55f
fruit * as their uncircumcision." Lev 19:23f
unto the day is the evil *." Mt 6:34f

THEREWITH
Or, "and he adds no sorrow *." Pro 10:22f

THESSALONIANS
future Antichrist of 2 * 2:3, 4. Dan 7:24f

THESSALONICA
and came to *, where there was a Act 17:1
than those in *, and gladly Act 17:11
But when the Jews in * learned Act 17:13
Aristarchus and Secundus, from *; Act 20:4
a Greek from *, was with us. Act 27:2
Even when I was over in * you Php 4:16
To: The Church at *—to you who 1Th 1:1
To: The church of *—kept safe in 2Th 1:1
things of this life and went to *. 2Ti 4:10

THEUDAS
was that fellow *, who pretended to Act 5:36

THEY'LL
Jacob asked. "* be hungry if Gen 29:7
I tell them to. * say, 'Jehovah Ex 4:1
If we feed you and you fail, * Ju 8:6
Next * be making him their king!" 1Sa 18:8
battle with us—* turn against us. 1Sa 29:4
them down—somehow * find a way! Ps 10:6
And in the festivals * sing, Ps 87:7
Why risk everything you own? * Pro 22:26,
of sweet perfume, * stink; Is 3:
for sashes * use ropes; Is 3:
* wear sacks instead of robes. Is 3:
"Oh, no," * say, "you never Is 30
"I am the Lord's," * proudly Is 44
'Fine friends you have,' * say, Jer 38:21,
gods who make us rich," * say. Hab 1:1
and happy as Judah is,' * say. Zec 8:1
When I whistle to them, * come Zec 10

THEY'RE
If you hear me tell him, '* on 1Sa 20:2
flock until * scattered far away. Eze 34:2
mocking. "* drunk, that's all!" Act 2:1

THEY'VE
don't sleep until * done their evil Pro 4:1
pity these people—* been here with Mt 15:3
the earth for what * done to us? Rev 6:1

THICK
nation with a * layer of locusts so Ex 10:4,
So Moses did, and there was * Ex 10:2
covered with them, three feet *!" Num 11:3
by the clouds and * darkness that Deu 5:2
as * as sand along the seashore; 1Sa 13:
several inches *, tipped with a 1Sa 17:4-
went beneath the * boughs of a 2Sa 18:
men were in the * of the battle, 2Sa 21:1
And clouds were * around him; 2Sa 22:1
of the tank were four inches *; 1Ki 7:2
he would live in the * darkness; 1Ki 8:12,1
spear was as * as a weaver's beam. 1Ch 11:2
were five inches *, flaring out 2Ch 4:
he would live in the * darkness, 2Ch 6:
How can he judge through the * Job 22:1
darkness? For * clouds swirl about Job 22:1
all around me, *, impenetrable Job 23:16,1
He wraps the rain in his * Job 26:
No darkness is * enough to hide Job 34:2
with clouds and * darkness, and Job 38:8,
* darkness was beneath his feet. Ps 18:
He rained down birds as * as Ps 78:2
and he sent * darkness through the Ps 105:2
surrounded by * rising smoke. Is 30:2
but there was a * layer of mire at Jer 38:
so there was a * cloud of smoke Eze 8:1
Lebanon, full of * branches and Eze 31:2,
It prospered and grew long * Eze 31:
pillars, each of them 8¾ feet *. Eze 40:48,4
and found them to be 3½ feet *; Eze 41:
it was 10½ feet *, with a row of Eze 41:
rooms was 8¾ feet *, leaving a free Eze 41:
Its walls were 8¾ feet *. Eze 41:12
of black clouds and * darkness. Joe 2:2
feet high and so * that three Zep 2:15
the * veil hanging in the Temple Lk 23:45
are covered by a * veil, because 2Co 3:14

THICKER
is * than my father's loins! 2Ch 10:10

THICKEST
and destroyed their * forests.' Is 37:24
as you watch the * forests felled. Zec 11:2

THICKETS
to hide in caves, *, coverts, among 1Sa 13:6

THICKLY
and was soon * populated. Gen 11:2

THICKNESS
Then he measured the * of the Rev 21:17

THIEF
"If a * is caught in the act of Ex 22:2
"If a * is captured, he must make Ex 22:3
* shall pay double if he is found. Ex 22:7
But if no * is found, then the Ex 22:8
You see a * and help him, and Ps 50:18
be found for a *, if he steals when Pro 6:30
A man who assists a * must really Pro 29:24
Like a *, the only shame that Jer 2:26,27
being a liar, *, and bandit! Hos 7:1
the home of every * and everyone Zec 5:4
disappear; no * can steal them; Lk 12:33
* if they knew when he was coming. Lk 12:39
the wall, must surely be a *! Jn 10:1
pastures. The *'s purpose is Jn 10:10
like a * in the night. 1Th 5:2
* when that day of the Lord comes. 1Th 5:4
unexpectedly as a *, and then the 2Pe 3:10
unexpected as a *, and punish you. Rev 3:3
come as unexpectedly as a *! Rev 16:15

THIEVES
at night they are * and Job 24:14,15
Men shouted after them as after * Job 30:5
are rebels, companions of *; Is 1:23
the poor, and even * don't take Jer 49:9,10
have become the lowest sort of *. Hos 5:10
coming like * through the windows. Joe 2:9
be for you if * had come at night Ob 1:5
their value, and are safe from *. Mt 6:20
have turned it into a den of *." Mt 21:13
trouble from * by keeping watch for Mt 24:43
have turned it into a den of *.' Lk 19:46
came before me were * and robbers. Jn 10:8
cheats and * and idol worshipers. 1Co 5:10

HIEVES Con't)
Neither will * or greedy people, 1Co 6:9,10

HIGH
his hand under the * of Abraham his Gen 24:9f
and the right *—for this is the ram Ex 29:22
'Give the breast and * of the Ex 29:27
while the right * shall be given Lev 7:32,33
the breast and * as donations from Lev 7:34
But the breast and the *, which Lev 10:14
The people are to bring the * Lev 10:15
* rot away and your body swell.' Num 5:21,22
will swell and her * will rot, and Num 5:27
breast and right * that are Num 18:18
strapped against his right *. Ju 3:16
against his right *, and plunged it Ju 3:21
Each one has his sword upon his * Sol 3:8
beat upon your *, for that sword Eze 21:12
On his robe and * was written Rev 19:16

HIGHS
The sinews of his * are tightly Job 40:17
Your rounded * are like jewels, Sol 7:1
its belly and * of brass, its legs Dan 2:32

HIN
And these * heads swallowed up Gen 41:7
came seven withered, * heads. Gen 41:23
And the * heads swallowed up the Gen 41:24
also the seven * and withered heads Gen 41:27
without yeast, and * sheets of Ex 29:2
Bezalel beat gold into * plates Ex 39:3
He becomes *, mere skin and Job 33:21
is plump and which is *, and why! Eze 34:22
become pale and * compared with the Dan 1:10
Some fell on * soil with Mk 4:5,6

HING
"How could you do such a *?" Gen 3:13
Surely you wouldn't do such a *, Gen 18:25
"don't do such a wicked *. Gen 19:7
you would do a * like this to me? Gen 20:9,10
*, I'll go back to work for you. Gen 30:31,32
If you find a single * we've Gen 31:32
How can I do such a wicked * as Gen 39:9
"Both dreams mean the same *," Gen 41:25
What a wicked * you have done!" Gen 44:5
us of such a terrible * as that? Gen 44:7
same * with their magical arts! Ex 7:11
to do the same * with their secret Ex 8:18
there remained not one green * Ex 10:15
for the holy * he has spoiled, or Lev 5:16
No crawling * with many feet may Lev 11:41,42
it is a shameful *, and they shall Lev 20:17
or other forbidden *, or who Lev 22:5
we were fools to do such a *. Num 12:11
it seem a small * to you that the Num 16:8,9
"Is it a small *," they Num 16:13
lest the same * happen to him as Num 16:40
"The same * will happen to King Num 21:34
This is the same kind of * your Num 32:8
sinners doing exactly the same *! Num 32:14
at bedtime and the first * in the Deu 6:7
detest it, for it is a cursed *. Deu 7:26
such a horrible * is happening Deu 13:12,13,14
to know: If the * he prophesies Deu 18:22
destroy every living *. Deu 20:16
Now I beg for this one *: Swear Jos 2:12,13
It is the same * the Lord did Jos 4:23
Every good * the Lord had Jos 21:45
"Your dream can mean only one *! Ju 7:14
done the right * in making Ju 9:16
and wonderful *, for as the flames Ju 13:19
* and done these miracles." Ju 13:23
don't do such a * to this man." Ju 19:24
* that was done among you? Ju 20:12
Now don't worry about a *, my Ru 3:11
"It is an awful * to make the 1Sa 2:23,24,25
to do a shocking * in Israel. 1Sa 3:11
morning the same * had happened—the 1Sa 5:4
we don't have a * to give him." 1Sa 9:7
* and received the same answer. 1Sa 17:30
"Don't worry about a *," David 1Sa 17:32
The same * happened a third time! 1Sa 19:21
planning any such *, for he always 1Sa 20:2
"Just the *!" 1Sa 21:9
so that not one * was lost or 1Sa 25:21
man who would do a * like that 2Sa 12:5
Literally, "No such * ought to be 2Sa 13:12f
"Please let me ask one more * of 2Sa 14:12
"I want to know one *," the 2Sa 14:18
* I did when you left Jerusalem; 2Sa 19:19
lord the king delight in this *?" 2Sa 24:3f
is the only good * which the Lord 1Ki 14:13
Literally, "this * I cannot do." 1Ki 20:9f
here without doing a * about it!" 1Ki 22:3
and urged him to say the same *. 1Ki 22:13
in all but one *: he did not 1Ki 22:43
"You have asked a hard *," 2Ki 2:10
*, wouldn't you have done it? 2Ki 5:13
pardon me this one *—when my master 2Ki 5:18
"I would never do that sort of * 2Ki 8:13
their descendants do the same *. 2Ki 17:41
has promised this good * to me! 1Ch 17:26
such a terrible * to this land and 2Ch 7:21
Another * Amaziah did was to 2Ch 25:5,6
to do a * to save their lands! 2Ch 32:13
and did the same * there. 2Ch 34:6
and did the same * during the Ez 4:7
they did the whole *—cut the Neh 3:3
did this sort of * and brought the Neh 13:18
"Oh, that God would grant the * Job 6:8,9
asked you for one slightest *? Job 6:22
For the soul of every living * Job 12:10
are misinterpreting the whole *. Job 13:4
How can you do this *? Job 13:11
told this same * from their Job 15:17-19
The only * they can 'conceive' Job 15:35
that I should say a * like that. Job 22:18
In this very *, you have sinned by Job 33:12
Literally, "meditate a vain *." Ps 2:1f
The one * I want from God, the Ps 27:4
want from God, the * I seek most of Ps 27:4
Lord will never lack any good *. Ps 34:10
I sinned, and did this terrible *. Ps 51:4
This one * I know: God is for me! Ps 56:9
No good * will he withhold from Ps 84:11
would not let one * be done to them Ps 105:14
me was the best * that could have Ps 119:71,72
What an awesome * this is! Ps 130:3,4
He gives food to every living *, Ps 136:25
and thirst of every living *. Ps 145:16
say the right * at the right time! Pro 15:23
It is a horrible * for a king to Pro 16:12
have died for saying the wrong *! Pro 18:21
who finds a wife finds a good *; Pro 18:22
There is one * worse than a fool, Pro 26:12
but what a wonderful * it is for Pro 29:18
There is another * too: how a Pro 30:20
that there was one * that happened Ecc 2:13,14
Well, one *, at least, is good: Ecc 5:18
and it is a good * to think about Ecc 7:2
There is a strange * happening Ecc 8:14
Here is another * that has made a Ecc 9:13
It is a wonderful * to be alive! Ecc 11:7
every hidden *, good or bad. Ecc 12:14
What a lovely, pleasant * you Sol 1:16
*—to destroy his own people! Is 28:21
* in place so it won't fall over! Is 41:7
For I'm going to do a brand new *. Is 43:19
to ask, "Is this *, this idol that Is 44:20
the Lord has done this wondrous *. Is 44:23
my inheritance into an evil *. Jer 2:7
ever heard so strange a * as this. Jer 2:10,11
shocked at such a * and shrink back Jer 2:12
an evil, bitter * it is to rebel Jer 2:19
How can you say a * like that? Jer 2:23
"I haven't done a * to anger God. Jer 2:35
be angry about such a little *! Jer 3:4,5
A horrible * has happened in this Jer 5:30
I will do the same * here because Jer 7:13,14
"What a terrible * I have done?" Jer 8:6
them up to mean a * I never said? Jer 8:8
The heart is the most deceitful * Jer 17:9
no one has ever heard of such a *! Jer 18:13
in sacrifice—a * I never commanded Jer 19:5
But there is one * sure, if you Jer 26:15
done a terrible * among my people. Jer 29:23
they have hardly done one * you Jer 32:23
whatever of doing any such *!" Jer 37:14
done a very evil * in putting Jer 38:9
you to do any such *, for you are Jer 40:16
do this horrible * I hate, but Jer 44:4
It will be a shocking * to see. Jer 49:20
"Is it a small * to you, O evil Eze 34:18
the world who would ask such a *! Dan 2:10
This is an impossible * the king Dan 2:11
about the strange * that the Most Dan 4:2
and the Horrible * is set up to be Dan 12:11
She did a shameful * when she Hos 1:5
For you men are doing the same *, Hos 4:14
Yes, I have seen a horrible * in Hos 6:10
This idol—this calf-god *—will Hos 10:6
a * as I am going to tell you? Joe 1:2
not one * escapes. Joe 2:3
Lord is an awesome, terrible *. Joe 2:11
are—but it is no great * for me. Zec 8:6
How I hate all that sort of *!" Zec 8:17
When have we ever done a * like Mal 1:7
or layman, who has done this *! Mal 2:12
the afternoon he did the same *. Mt 20:5
what an amazing * the Lord has Mt 21:42
"So, when you see the horrible * Mt 24:15
For she has done a good * to me. Mt 26:10
other disciples said the same *. Mt 26:35
"You lack only one *," he told Mk 10:21
and it is an amazing * to see.' Mk 12:11
"When you see the horrible * Mk 13:14
why berate her for doing a good * Mk 14:6
Let's see this wonderful * that Lk 2:15
last night and didn't catch a *. Lk 5:5
* God has done for you." Lk 8:39
However, the important * is not Lk 10:20
There is really only one * worth Lk 10:42
to do a single * you told me to; Lk 15:29
I know just the *! Lk 16:4
"There is still one * you Lk 18:22
But they didn't understand a * he Lk 18:34
another, but the same * happened; Lk 20:11
was sent and the same * happened. Lk 20:12
"But they would never do a * like Lk 20:16
of them would ever do such a *. Lk 22:23
man hasn't done one * wrong." Lk 23:40,41
"Who said such a * as that?" Jn 5:12
Abraham wouldn't do a * like Jn 8:40
apart from me you can't do a *. Jn 15:5
the wonderful * that had happened. Act 3:11
How could you do a * like this? Act 5:4
think of doing a * like Act 5:9
rejoiced in this * they had made. Act 7:41
the wonderful * I promised David.' Act 13:34
shouting, some one * and some Act 19:32
Some shouted one * and some Act 21:34
"But one * I do confess, that I Act 24:14
that I said one * I shouldn't Act 24:21
for the only * we know about these Act 28:22
Should the * made say to the one Rom 9:20
King David spoke of this same * Rom 11:9
very unusual * to do—don't you see Rom 11:24
you are doing a good *. Rom 14:6
For, after all, the important * Rom 14:17
The right * to do is to quit Rom 14:21
And now there is one more * to Rom 16:17
Now the most important * about a 1Co 4:2
about the terrible * that has 1Co 5:1
What a terrible * it is that you 1Co 5:6
yet you let this sort of * go on. 1Co 5:6
That is the important *. 1Co 7:19
The important * to remember is 1Co 7:29
For the earth and every good * 1Co 10:26
it is the important *, not yours. 1Co 10:29
What a strange * a body would be 1Co 12:19
the important * is that we 1Co 15:11
There isn't a single * these 2Co 12:11
The only * I didn't do for you, 2Co 12:13
The only * they did suggest was Gal 2:10
It is a fine * when people are Gal 4:18
parties, and all that sort of *. Gal 5:21
doing every wicked * that our Eph 2:3
this is the right * to do because Eph 6:1
you for each good * you do, whether Eph 6:8
IS THERE ANY such * as Christians Php 2:1
bear on this one *: Forgetting the Php 3:13
say this one more *: Fix your Php 4:8
of the real *—of Christ himself. Col 2:17
that did that sort of *; Col 3:9
not only the right * to do, but it 2Th 1:3
in every good * you say and do. 2Th 2:17
* in life—they don't know God. 1Ti 6:21
this kind of * isn't worthwhile; Tit 3:9
it is the right * for you to do, Phm 1:8,9
Another * to remember is that no Heb 5:4
It is a fearful * to fall into Heb 10:31
So also the tongue is a small *, Jas 3:5
* that is going to happen to you. 1Pe 4:12
And they all say the same *: that 1Jn 5:6,7,8
"Yet there is one * wrong; Rev 2:4
I don't need a *!' Rev 3:17

THINGS
And all living * upon the earth Gen 7:21
all living *, even though man's Gen 8:21
even though he does such wicked *. Gen 8:21
flocks, to talk * over with them. Gen 31:5
some of the bad * they were doing. Gen 37:2
of the good * of Egypt, and ten Gen 45:23
incredible * I am doing in Egypt! Ex 10:2
all the wonderful * God had done Ex 18:1
any of these three *, then she may Ex 21:11
these * are set apart and holy. Ex 29:33
can make all the * I have Ex 31:6
So they brought all these * to Lev 9:5
All other * that fly and have Lev 11:23
*, and be holy, for I am holy; Lev 11:44
these * that crawl upon the earth. Lev 11:44
these are the * the heathen do; Lev 18:24
not do any of these abominable *; Lev 18:26
Do not do these * or I will Lev 18:28
these * I have warned you against; Lev 20:23
"the elevation of the holy *." Lev 22:12f
the most holy *: Aaron and his Num 4:17,18,19
the good * the Lord does for us." Num 10:32
to long for the good * of Egypt. Num 11:4,5
me to do all these * that I have Num 16:28
He did these * so you would Deu 4:35
full of good *—cities you didn't Deu 6:10,11,12
have done horrible * that he hates, Deu 12:31
Anyone doing these * is an Deu 18:12
nations do these * that the Lord Deu 18:12
all do these evil *, but the Lord Deu 18:14
will not permit you to do such *. Deu 18:14
her of shameful *, claiming that Deu 22:17,18
all the good * he has given you. Deu 26:11
abundance of good * in the land, Deu 28:11
such wonderful * for you and has Deu 28:63
"WHEN ALL THESE * have happened Deu 30:1
AFTER MOSES HAD said all these * Deu 31:1
him after hearing * like that, for Jos 2:11

(THINGS Con't)
given you the good * he promised, Jos 23:15,16
They did many * which the Lord Ju 2:11
May the Lord do terrible * to me Ru 1:17
the dreadful * I warned Eli about. 1Sa 3:12
his retirement * hadn't been the 1Sa 8:5
of all the good * he has done for 1Sa 12:7
those * which are good and right. 1Sa 12:23
think of all the tremendous * he 1Sa 12:24
he had never worn such * before. 1Sa 17:38,39
to do, even little *, and I know he 1Sa 20:2
done all the good * he promised you 1Sa 25:30,31
* for you, please remember me!" 1Sa 25:30,31
You are doing all these * just 2Sa 7:21
*— so do as you have promised! 2Sa 7:28
good * you want to give him." 2Sa 19:37
And what about all the wicked * 1Ki 2:44
* to this land and this Temple?' 1Ki 9:8
* going on here is all true. 1Ki 10:6
of the great * Elisha has done." 2Ki 8:4
know the terrible * you will do to 2Ki 8:12
secretly done many * that were 2Ki 17:9
*, and the Lord was very angry. 2Ki 17:11
doing the evil * that Jeroboam led 2Ki 17:22
they were only * that men had made 2Ki 19:18
the Lord, who lets you do these *? 2Ki 19:25
and I also know the evil * you 2Ki 19:27
He did the same * the nations had 2Ki 21:1
done these evil * and is even more 2Ki 21:11
He did all the evil * his father 2Ki 21:21
For all the great * you have 1Ch 17:17
kind * his father did for me." 1Ch 19:2,3
last * David did before his death. 1Ch 23:27
But there are some good * about 2Ch 19:3
of the dedicated * to give to the 2Ch 31:5,6
all of the good * he did are 2Ch 32:32
with people who do these awful *. Ez 9:14
proceed in setting * straight, and Ez 10:4
how * were going in Jerusalem. Neh 1:2
"Well," they replied, "* are Neh 1:3
full of good *, with cisterns and Neh 9:25
they did many other terrible *. Neh 9:26
the wonderful * you did for them Neh 9:35
Shall we receive only pleasant * Job 2:10
Well, I know a few * myself—you Job 12:3
And who doesn't know these * Job 12:3
that the Lord does * like that? Job 12:7,8,9
once has said the * that you are Job 13:7
"O God, there are two * I beg Job 13:20
"You write bitter * against me Job 13:26
say all these evil * against him. Job 15:13
of all the * he dreamed of—none Job 20:20
filled their homes with good *. Job 22:18
Literally, "and many such * are Job 23:14f
What wise * you have said! Job 26:3
"These are some of the minor * Job 26:14
saying all these useless * to me. Job 27:12
the light the * that are hidden." Job 28:11f
can do all these *, they don't know Job 28:12
done any of these *, then let my Job 31:22
For if I had done such *, it Job 31:28
"Yes, God often does these * for Job 33:29
Everyone has seen these * from a Job 36:25
I was talking about * I knew Job 42:3
* far too wonderful for me. Job 42:3
scoffing at the * of God: But they Ps 1:1
I were doing evil *— if I were Ps 7:3
about the marvelous * you do. Ps 9:1
done such tremendous * for me. Ps 18:1
of the wonderful * you have done. Ps 22:22
For they accuse me of * I never Ps 27:12
They accuse me of * I have never Ps 35:11
of the glorious * he did for me, Ps 40:3
Who else can do such glorious *? Ps 40:5
Come, see the glorious * that Ps 46:8
we shall do mighty *, for he will Ps 60:12
realize what amazing * he does. Ps 64:9
us among all the good * there. Ps 65:4
Come, see the glorious * God has Ps 66:5
have done such mighty * for us. Ps 68:28
others of the wonderful * you do. Ps 71:17
You have done such wonderful *. Ps 71:19
Israel, who only does wonderful *! Ps 72:18
dream of * that never really were! Ps 73:20
* to the kings of the earth. Ps 76:12
let our children see glorious *, Ps 90:16
Tell everyone about the amazing * Ps 96:3
me to refuse the low and vulgar *; Ps 101:3
the glorious * he does for me. Ps 103:2
He fills my life with good *! Ps 103:5
for all the glorious * he does; Ps 105:1
With all these * they angered Ps 106:29
about the evil * he has done, and Ps 109:15
Their gods are merely man-made * Ps 115:4
of the Lord has done glorious *! Ps 118:15,16
Open my eyes to see wonderful * Ps 119:18
don't let me make a mess of *. Ps 119:31
* the Lord has done for them." Ps 126:2
Yes, glorious *! Ps 126:3
Take away my lust for evil *; Ps 141:4
children what glorious * he does. Ps 145:4

All living * shall thank you, Ps 145:10
evil men lose the good * they Pro 2:22
MY SON, NEVER forget the * I've Pro 3:1
For there are six * the Lord Pro 6:16-19
The lazy man longs for many * but Pro 21:25,26
say foolish, silly * that would Pro 23:33
to conceal *, and the king's Pro 25:2,3
There are two * never satisfied, Pro 30:15,16
forever craving more: no, three *! Pro 30:15,16
There are three * too wonderful Pro 30:18,19
There are three * that make the Pro 30:21,22,23
There are four * that are small Pro 30:24-28
Praise her for the many fine * Pro 31:31
that I could evaluate all these *. Ecc 2:9
mere dreaming of nice * is Ecc 6:9
All * are decided by fate; Ecc 6:10
See the way God does * and fall Ecc 7:13
and the reason for *, and to prove Ecc 7:25
to understand *, to be able to Ecc 8:1
see you doing all these wicked *; Is 1:16
Write down all these * I am Is 8:16
Lord, for he has done wonderful *. Is 12:5
All green * along the river bank Is 19:7
you do such wonderful *! Is 25:1
tell us nice *; Is 30:10,11
like filthy * you hate to touch. Is 30:22
they are all foolish, worthless *; Is 41:29
idols ever has foretold such *? Is 43:9
you, says, All * were made by me; Is 44:24
to happen than the * they say. Is 44:25
Jehovah, am he who does these *. Is 45:7
Who but God has said that these * Is 45:21
Well, those two * shall come Is 47:9
Now I will tell you new * I Is 48:6
Yes, I'll tell you * entirely Is 48:8
These two * have been your lot: Is 51:19
and choose the * that please him, Is 56:4
If you do these *, God will shed Is 58:8
good *, and keep you healthy too; Is 58:11
you did awesome * beyond our Is 64:3
all the * of beauty are destroyed. Is 64:11
upon them—all the * they feared, Is 66:4
have done two evil *: They have Jer 2:13
them of all of these good *. Jer 5:25
back to all these evil * again? Jer 7:10
and all the good * I prepared for Jer 8:13
punish them for such * as this?" Jer 9:9
* I swore I would if you obeyed. Jer 11:5
* they promised him they would. Jer 11:6
of * they knew nothing about. Jer 14:18
our God, can do such * as this? Jer 14:22
Because of the wicked * that Jer 15:4
people all these * and they ask, Jer 16:10
such terrible * against us? Jer 16:10
worse! The * they do are horrible; Jer 23:14
and from the evil * you are doing. Jer 25:5
and I give these * of mine to Jer 27:5
you all the good * I have promised, Jer 29:10
You have done incredible * in Jer 32:20
* still remembered to this day. Jer 32:20
we have obeyed him in all these *. Jer 35:8
all the terrible * I will do to Jer 36:3
bear all the evil * you were doing Jer 44:22
all these terrible * have befallen Jer 44:23
Are you seeking great * for Jer 45:5
all the terrible * God had Jer 51:60
had been. * became so bad at last Jer 52:3
For all these * I weep; Lam 1:16
many foolish *, false to the core. Lam 2:14
* are being done to Israel." Eze 14:23
You used the lovely * I gave you Eze 16:16
Lord God, to do such * as these; Eze 16:30
by all these evil * you do, I will Eze 16:43
The * of God are all despised; Eze 22:8
To them the * of God are no more Eze 22:26
But when all these terrible * Eze 33:33
All living * shall quake in Eze 38:20
here so I can show you many *; Eze 40:4
any of my holy *, for they must Eze 44:13
permission to eat other * instead. Dan 1:8
He knows all hidden *, for he is Dan 2:22
tell the king such *, but there is Dan 2:27
But all these * happened to Dan 4:28
do you mean by doing these *?' Dan 4:35
*, and he explained them to me. Dan 7:16
they shall rule all * forever, Dan 7:27
But none of these * will happen Dan 8:26
those who hate the * of God, Dan 11:32
shall be strong and do great *. Dan 11:32
most gifted in the * of God will Dan 11:35
me: for all these * I will punish Hos 1:13
all living * grow sick and die; Hos 4:3
of the Lord. The * my people do Hos 9:9
wise, let him understand these *. Hos 14:9
for he has done amazing * for you. Joe 2:21
him some of the * that were going Amo 1:2
"Don't say such *," the people Mic 2:6
"Don't harp on * like that. Mic 2:6
Are we but creeping * that have Hab 1:14
But these * I plan won't happen Hab 2:3
these * will surely come to pass. Hab 2:3

the fearful * you are going to do. Hab 3
The Lord will do terrible * to Zep 2:1
not pass to other * that way." Hag 2:
hand, accusing Joshua of many *. Zec 3
of the good * to come. Zec 3:
* that are most important to me. Mal 2:
Literally, "until all * be Mt 5:1
about *—food, drink, and clothes. Mt 6:2
pride in all these * and are deeply Mt 6:31,3
"Don't give holy * to depraved Mt 7.
his treasure * both new and old." Mt 13:5
can do * like this and much more. Mt 21:2
authority do you do these *?" Mt 21:2
*—justice and mercy and faith. Mt 23:2
leave the more important * undone. Mt 23:2
you see all these * beginning to Mt 24:3
Or, "after all these * take Mt 24:34
time, saying the same * again. Mt 26:4
is part of the old way of doing *. Mk 2:2
and lure of nice * come in and Mk 4:1
wonderful * God has done for you; Mk 5:1
great * Jesus had done for him; Mk 5:2
them many * they needed to know. Mk 6:3
All these vile * come from Mk 7:2
tell them about the terrible * he Mk 8:3
"You shouldn't say * like Mk 8:3
Here are some of the other * he Mk 12:3
But when these * begin to Mk 13:
And when you see these * Mk 13:2
or hour when these * will happen; Mk 13:3
But these * are happening to Mk 14:4
Literally, "after these *." Mk 16:12
Literally, "an account of the * Lk 1:3
Holy One, has done great * to me. Lk 1:4
treasured these * in her heart and Lk 2:1
away all these * in her heart. Lk 2:5
Scriptures, 'Other * in life are Lk 4:4
were amazed at the * he said. Lk 4:32
"We have seen strange * today." Lk 5:26
and when * are taken away from Lk 6:30
all the wonderful * he was doing, Lk 9:43
themselves with * like that. Lk 9:60
for hiding these * from the Lk 10:21
not leave these other * undone. Lk 11:42
over you to decide such * as that? Lk 12:14
do such little * as that, what's Lk 12:26
the use of worrying over bigger *? Lk 12:26
at the wonderful * he did. Lk 13:17
be [as indifferent to the * of God Lk 17:26
for saying * like that!" Lk 19:39
when all these * you are admiring Lk 21:6
* happening in the heavens. Lk 21:11
So when all these * begin to Lk 21:28
* happen, the end of this age Lk 21:32
For if such * as this are done Lk 23:31
* that happened there last week." Lk 24:18
"What *?" Lk 24:19
"The * that happened to Jesus, Lk 24:19
suffer all these * before entering Lk 24:26
God and the first cause of all *; Jn 1:1f
God and the first cause of all *; Jn 1:14f
them, "Get these * out of here. Jn 2:16
yet you don't understand these *? Jn 3:10,11
you about such * as these that Jn 3:12
is limited to the * of earth. Jn 3:31
about perishable * like food. Jn 6:27
"He says such wonderful *!" Jn 7:46
* that are pleasing to him." Jn 8:29
him say these * began believing him Jn 8:30,31
you love to do the evil * he does. Jn 8:44
saying these glorious * about me. Jn 8:54
When he said these *, the Jewish Jn 10:19
After saying these *, Jesus went Jn 12:36
You know these *—now do them! Jn 13:17
"I am not saying these * to all Jn 13:18
I am telling you these * now Jn 14:25
I have told you these * before Jn 14:29
"I HAVE TOLD you these * so that Jn 16:1
Yes, I'm telling you these * now Jn 16:4
saying all these * he looked up to Jn 17:1
I have told them many * while I Jn 17:13
AFTER SAYING THESE * Jesus Jn 18:1
Literally, "all *." Jn 21:17f
my account of these * is accurate. Jn 21:24
Messiah must suffer all these *. Act 3:18
recovery of all * from sin, as Act 3:21,22
the wonderful * we saw Jesus do and Act 4:20
And we are witnesses of these *, Act 5:32
of the amazing * he could do—in Act 8:9,10,11
terrible * won't happen to me." Act 8:24
about the terrible * this man has Act 9:13
always doing kind * for others, Act 9:36
Even as Peter was saying these *, Act 10:44
saw the wonderful * God was doing, Act 11:23
all sorts of evil * about them. Act 14:2
of these foolish * and to pray Act 14:15
reminders—the kind * he did such as Act 14:17
For these * have been preached Act 15:21
the people to do * that are against Act 16:20,21
* and we want to hear more." Act 17:20
about these *, but now he commands Act 17:30

THINGS Con't)
our * and left for Jerusalem. Act 21:15
recounted the many * God had Act 21:19
the * they accuse me of doing. Act 24:13
many horrible * to the followers Act 26:9
King Agrippa knows about these *. Act 26:26
of * we would need for the trip. Act 28:10
the great * God has done for them, Rom 1:5
And one of the * I keep on Rom 1:10
sinful * with each other's bodies. Rom 1:24
So they prayed to the * God made, Rom 1:25
the blessed God who made these *. Rom 1:25
do all these evil *, so that even Rom 1:26
men doing shameful * with other men Rom 1:27
for you do these very same *. Rom 2:1
anyone who does such * as these. Rom 2:2
of those who say such * is just. Rom 3:8
instead of doing all these evil *; Rom 3:19
and not by the good * we do. Rom 3:28
heaven by all the good * he did? Rom 4:4,5
think about those * you used to do, Rom 6:21
am that makes me do these evil *. Rom 7:17
doing those * that please God. Rom 8:5
—the * that overcame the world Rom 8:20,21
For we know that even the * of Rom 8:22
say to such wonderful * as these? Rom 8:31
he who now rules over all *. Rom 9:5
what shall we say about these *? Rom 9:30
bring glad tidings of good *." Rom 10:15
Let these good * boomerang on Rom 11:9
the ability to do certain * well. Rom 12:6
evil for evil. Do * in such a way Rom 12:17
* others have no doubts about." Rom 14:1f
we do these *, still we cannot just Rom 15:1
those who feel these * are wrong. Rom 15:1
These * that were written in Rom 15:4
you know these * so well that you Rom 15:14
faith, teaching * about Christ that Rom 16:17
what wonderful * God has ready for 1Co 2:9
But we know about these * 1Co 2:10
he is the one who makes * grow. 1Co 3:7
evil * have been said about us. 1Co 4:13
I am not writing about these * to 1Co 4:14
these little * among yourselves? 1Co 6:2
able to decide these * for you." 1Co 6:4f
those doing such * have no share in 1Co 6:9,10
Literally, "All * are lawful for 1Co 6:12f
but some of these * aren't good 1Co 6:12
with the exciting * the world 1Co 7:31
consider other * such as 1Co 7:34
with as few other * as possible to 1Co 7:35
God, the Father, who created all * 1Co 8:6
Literally, "of whom are all *." 1Co 8:6f
yourselves many * that would keep 1Co 9:25
not desire evil * as they did, nor 1Co 10:6
All these * happened to them as 1Co 10:11
warn us against doing the same *; 1Co 10:11
I supposed to say about these *? 1Co 11:22
I have put away the childish *. 1Co 13:11
There are three * that 1Co 13:13
and tell you the * I know, and what 1Co 14:6
in your understanding of these *. 1Co 14:20
about these *, all these sermons 1Co 14:24
God is not one who likes * to be 1Co 14:33
authority over all * has been given 1Co 15:27
be fooled by those who say such *. 1Co 15:33
* straightened out before I come. 2Co 2:3
We dare to say these good * about 2Co 3:4
we don't know why * happen as they 2Co 4:8
We know these * are true by 2Co 5:7
* he has done in his earthly body. 2Co 5:10
Are we insane [to say such * 2Co 5:13,14
All these new * are from God who 2Co 5:18
don't touch their filthy *, and I 2Co 6:17
So, two good * happen as a 2Co 9:12
the * that show how weak I am. 2Co 11:30
and heard * so astounding that 2Co 12:4
steps, doing * the same way. 2Co 12:18
and saying wicked * about each 2Co 12:20
the wicked, impure * you have done: 2Co 12:21
to think such * about our Lord. Gal 2:17
I do about these *, for I am as Gal 4:12
believing as I do about these *. Gal 5:10
* your evil nature wants you to. Gal 5:16
love to do evil * that are just the Gal 5:17
opposite from the * that the Holy Gal 5:17
and the good * we want to do when Gal 5:17
but if he plants the good * of Gal 6:8
all the attractive * of the world Gal 6:14
me about these *, for I carry on my Gal 6:17
to be his, and all * happen just as Eph 1:11
doing these mighty * for us, who Eph 1:12
And God has put all * under his Eph 1:22
to you how I know about these *. Eph 3:4
as he who made all * had secretly Eph 3:9
he might fill all * everywhere with Eph 4:10
"that he might fill all *." Eph 4:10f
abilities to do certain * best? Eph 4:12
able to accuse you of any such *. Eph 5:3
good * of this life more than God. Eph 5:5
those good, kind * which show that Php 1:11
to do the good * that result from Php 2:12
to do for me the * you couldn't do Php 2:30
But all these * that I once Php 3:7
with me on these *, and if you Php 3:15
Think about * that are pure and Php 4:8
on the fine, good * in others. Php 4:8
make you wise about spiritual *; Col 1:9
doing good, kind * for others, Col 1:10
all the wonderful * that belong to Col 1:12
and earth, the * we can see and the Col 1:16
we can see and the * we can't; Col 1:16
to come to him—all * in heaven and Col 1:20
time worrying about * down here. Col 3:2
Away then with sinful, earthly *; Col 3:5
don't worship the good * of life, Col 3:5
anger is upon those who do such *. Col 3:6
unimportant; such * mean nothing. Col 3:11
dark about these *, and you won't 1Th 5:4
just way God does *, for he is 2Th 1:5
not come until two * happen: first, 2Th 2:3
With all these * in mind, dear 2Th 2:15
into practice the * we taught you, 2Th 3:4
a son to me in the * of the Lord. 1Ti 1:2
all others who do * that contradict 1Ti 1:10,11
I am writing these * to you now, 1Ti 3:14
God gave these * to well-taught 1Ti 4:3
Teach these * and make sure 1Ti 4:11
Some may deny these *, but they 1Ti 6:3
all kinds of wrong * to get money, 1Ti 6:9
to get money, * that hurt them and 1Ti 6:9
Run from all these evil * and 1Ti 6:11
these * that God entrusted to you. 1Ti 6:20
teach others those * you and many 2Ti 2:2
not to argue over unimportant *. 2Ti 2:14
with each other. * will be said 2Ti 2:17
not be doing * that are wrong." 2Ti 2:19
the * you have been taught. 2Ti 3:14
He loved the good * of this life 2Ti 4:10
for doing kind * for others. Tit 2:14
You must teach these * and Tit 2:15
These * I have told you are all Tit 3:8
the wealth of good * in you that Phm 1:6
* that would happen later on. Heb 3:5
other about these * every day while Heb 3:13
the deeper * of God's Word until Heb 5:14
Let us go on instead to other * Heb 6:1
we will go on now to other *. Heb 6:3
yourself the good * of heaven and Heb 6:4
and his oath, two * we can Heb 6:18
a will—a list of * to be given away Heb 9:16
of those * he has promised them. Heb 9:17
it—all copied from * in heaven—all Heb 9:23
But the real * in heaven, of Heb 9:23
the good * Christ would do for us. Heb 10:1
with others suffering the same *. Heb 10:33
that better * were awaiting you in Heb 10:34
* that would be yours forever. Heb 10:34
all *—were made at God's command; Heb 11:3
made from * that can't be seen. Heb 11:3
back to the good * of this world. Heb 11:15
men did such terrible * to him. Heb 12:3
only unshakable * will be left. Heb 12:27
of wisdom. Such * are earthly, Jas 3:15
for the wrong * you have done. Jas 4:9
told that these * would not occur 1Pe 1:12
—and offer to God those * that 1Pe 2:5
those who say unkind * about you. 1Pe 3:9
past of the evil * the godless 1Pe 4:3
more in the wicked * they do, and 1Pe 4:4
To him be all power over all *, 1Pe 5:11
you of these * even though you 2Pe 1:12
to understand many * that otherwise 2Pe 1:19
Literally, "the * they do not 2Pe 2:12f
waiting for these * to happen and 2Pe 3:14
same * in many of his letters. 2Pe 3:15,16
I am writing these * to all of 1Jn 2:12
I am saying these * to you older 1Jn 2:13
you love these * you show that you 1Jn 2:15
for all these worldly *, these 1Jn 2:16
evil, forbidden * will go with it, 1Jn 2:17
For he teaches you all *, and he 1Jn 2:27
and doing the * that please him. 1Jn 3:22
* together and have a joyous time. 2Jn 1:12
to hear such * about my children. 3Jn 1:4
you some of the * he is doing and 3Jn 1:10
and what wicked * he is saying 3Jn 1:10
prove the terrible * they have done Jud 1:15
they love the evil * of the Jud 1:19
* to his servant John in a vision; Rev 1:1
For the time is near when these * Rev 1:3
the Ending of all *," says God, Rev 1:8
how many good * you are doing. Rev 2:2
"And yet I have a few * against Rev 2:14
improvement in all these *. Rev 2:19
end keeps on doing * that please Rev 2:26
enthusiastic about the * of God. Rev 3:19
power, for you have created all *. Rev 4:11
of the terrible * that will soon Rev 8:13
in heaven, portraying * to come. Rev 12:1
He could do these marvelous * Rev 13:14
pageant showing * to come: Seven Rev 15:1
"All the fancy * you loved so Rev 18:14
selling her these * shall stand at Rev 18:15
according to the * written in The Rev 20:12
"See, I am making all * new!" Rev 21:5
heard all these *, and fell down to Rev 22:8
to tell the churches all these *. Rev 22:16

THINK

just * of what they will do later! Gen 11:6
"Who do you * you are? Gen 19:9
Whatever made you * of this vile Gen 20:9,10
would * he was wearing a fur coat! Gen 25:25
* how hairy Esau is, and how Gen 27:11,12
He'll * I'm making a fool of him, Gen 27:11,12
"Just *, my very own flesh and Gen 29:14
The other women will * me blessed Gen 30:13
"What kind of people do you * we Gen 44:7
"I suppose you * you are our Ex 2:14
"Who do you * you are," Pharaoh Ex 5:4,5
So you still * you are so great, Ex 9:17
For Pharaoh will *, 'Those Ex 14:3
"But what will the Egyptians * Num 14:13
And you must * constantly about Deu 6:6
Perhaps you will * to yourself, Deu 7:17
it, and begin to *, 'We ought to Deu 17:14
"Let no one blithely *, when he Deu 29:19
you yourself must * about them Jos 1:8
you will soon occupy. * of it! Jos 3:11
Punish us in any way you * best, Ju 10:15
And besides, just who do you * Ju 11:25
to me and I * he must be the Angel Ju 13:6
"I don't * anyone could ever Ju 16:6
don't * of going to any other Ru 2:8,9
Please don't * that I am just 1Sa 1:15,16
"Well, whatever you * best," 1Sa 1:23
is ridiculous to * that what you 1Sa 2:30
worship him; * of all the 1Sa 12:24
"Do as you * best; 1Sa 14:7
among our enemies, * how many more 1Sa 14:30
"Do as you * best." 1Sa 14:36
"When you didn't * much of 1Sa 15:17
"Do you * I don't know that you 1Sa 20:30
You're not even sorry for me. * 1Sa 22:8
"Who does this son of Jesse * he 1Sa 25:10
You'd better * fast, for there 1Sa 25:17
ever met, and I * you should go 1Sa 29:6
Do you * that anyone will listen 1Sa 30:24
"Do as you * best." 2Sa 15:15
I * Ahithophel has made a mistake. 2Sa 17:7
And I * that you should 2Sa 17:11
"Well, whatever you * best," 2Sa 18:4
of God, so do what you * best. 2Sa 19:27
days of plague? * this over and let 2Sa 24:13
"Give me three days to * this 1Ki 12:5
"What do you * I should do?" 1Ki 12:6
"What do you * I should do?" 1Ki 12:9
them, 'If you * my father was hard 1Ki 12:10
And do you * we have come here 2Ki 18:25
So what makes you * the Lord can 2Ki 18:35
"Since you * that I should be 1Ch 13:2
to the land. * it over and let me 1Ch 21:12
"What do you fellows * I should 2Ch 10:8,9
"Tell them, 'If you * my father 2Ch 10:10
Do you really * you can defeat 2Ch 13:8
asks, 'Do you * you can survive my 2Ch 32:10
What makes you * your God can do 2Ch 32:14
* of it! 2Ch 33:7
feeble Jews * they are doing?" Neh 4:1
"Do they * they can build the Neh 4:1
It is far greater than we can * Neh 9:5
Do you * that we will let you Neh 13:27
people—whatever you * best." Est 3:11
Esther: "Do you * you will escape Est 4:13
Stop and *! Job 4:7,8
When I go to bed I *, 'Oh, that Job 7:4
innocent, I dare not * of it. Job 9:21
for what I *, and to my pleadings. Job 13:6
Or do you * you can fool God as Job 13:9
my hand and say what I really *. Job 13:14
but mark your calendar to * of me Job 14:13
it. You * yourselves so great? Job 19:5
When I * of it, terror grips me. Job 23:15
How did you ever * of all these Job 26:4
to tell you what I *, for those Job 32:6
"Do you * it is right for you to Job 35:2,3
Do you really * that if you Job 36:19
"You who * you know so much, Job 37:19,20
It is frightening even to * about Job 41:9
One would * the sea was made of Job 41:31,32
seem to * that God is dead. Ps 10:4
They wouldn't * of looking for Ps 10:4
For they * that God will never Ps 10:13
bread and wouldn't * of praying! Ps 14:4
conceit, they * they can hide their Ps 36:2
"No one will hear us," they *. Ps 59:7
until he acts. I * of God and Ps 77:3
* of the mighty deeds he did for Ps 105:5,6
what I am saying. * about the Ps 107:43
Don't overlook them. * Ps 109:15
Oh, how I love them. I * about Ps 119:97
night to * about your promises. Ps 119:148
I don't * myself better than Ps 131:1

(THINK Con't)
It is amazing to * about. Ps 139:14
don't let yourself * about her. Pro 7:25
is bad for men to * about all the Pro 25:27
is a good thing to * about it while Ecc 7:2
you will blush to * of all those Is 1:29
doing when they * of Syria and Is 8:12
He will merely * he is attacking Is 10:7
Then at last they will * of God Is 17:7
"And who do you * you are, Is 22:15,16
What a history was yours! * of Is 23:7
"Who does Isaiah * he is," the Is 28:9
Your mind will * back to this Is 33:18
you are a fool to * that the king Is 36:4
army, how can you * of proceeding Is 36:8,9
What's more, do you * I have Is 36:10
And do you * this God of yours Is 36:20
Do you * you will be any Is 37:11
to the next. * of it! Is 38:20
and will never * of them again. Is 43:25
The man never stops to * or Is 44:19
about my people or * about the fate Is 47:7
Then you will * to yourself, Is 49:21
you were cut! Yes, * about your Is 51:1
don't let them * that I will make Is 56:3
even * about the old ones anymore. Is 65:17
walled cities that you * are safe. Jer 5:17
You * that because the Temple is Jer 7:8
Do you really * that you can Jer 7:9
power—do with me as you * best. Jer 26:14
to Egypt where you * you will be Jer 42:13,14
"Do you * the Lord didn't know Jer 44:21
O Lord, *! Lam 2:20
everything you *—every thought that Eze 11:5
You * this city is an iron shield? Eze 11:7
"Do you * I like to see the Eze 18:23
But (the king of Babylon) will * Eze 21:23
You never even * of me and my Eze 22:12
are so proud you * you are God, Eze 28:2,3
say to him: You * of yourself as a Eze 32:2
the king began to * of placing him Dan 6:3
the day trying to * of some way to Dan 6:14
Then she will *, "I might as Hos 1:7
"Yet * of all I did for them! Amo 2:9
Do you * the Spirit of the Lord Mic 2:7
"* it over," says the Lord of Hag 1:7
Hosts: Don't you * I care about Zec 1:14
to God, you don't * of me, but only Zec 7:6
And don't * that I might change Zec 8:14,15
he has given you to obey. * of it! Mal 1:13
him and loved to * about him. Mal 3:16
heathen do, who * prayers are Mt 6:7,8
from those who * themselves so Mt 11:25
It is what you say and * Mt 15:11
How could you even * I was Mt 16:11
asked them, "Who do you * I am?" Mt 16:15
asked him, "What do you *, Peter? Mt 17:25
crowd all * he was a prophet." Mt 21:26
"But what do you * about this? Mt 21:28
* he will do to those farmers?" Mt 21:40
together to try to * of some way to Mt 22:15
"You would * these Jewish leaders Mt 23:2
But those who * themselves great Mt 23:12
Does he * he is God? Mk 2:7
eat, but by what you * and say!" Mk 7:15,16
"And yet you * I'm worried that Mk 8:21
them, "Who do the people * I am? Mk 8:27
"Some of them * you are John the Mk 8:28
Then he asked, "Who do you * I Mk 8:29
to * what the angel could mean. Lk 1:29
His parents didn't know what to * Lk 2:48
And don't * you are safe because Lk 3:8
sent to them. Or * of the prophet Lk 4:27
"Who does this fellow * he is?" Lk 5:21
with those who * themselves already Lk 5:32
"Do you * you deserve credit for Lk 6:32
How can you * of saying to him, Lk 6:42
does this man * he is, going around Lk 7:49
asked them, "Who do you * I am?" Lk 9:20
Do you * this proves they are Lk 11:19
would never * of trying to keep. Lk 11:46
"But if the man begins to *, 'My Lk 12:45
"Do you * I have come to give Lk 12:51
"Do you * they were worse Lk 13:2
Or, "Do you * the rich man Lk 16:8f
that, don't you * that God will Lk 18:7
But they could * of nothing, for Lk 19:48
"What do you * the owner will do? Lk 20:15
*, but teach the ways of God. Lk 20:21
* what could have happened to it. Lk 24:4
Some * this means water baptism. Jn 3:5f
Do you * the work of harvesting Jn 4:35
Then what will you * if you see Jn 6:62
on the Sabbath? * this through and Jn 7:24
Who do you * you are?" Jn 8:53
"I * he must be a prophet sent Jn 9:17
* they see that they are blind." Jn 9:39
Priest—he didn't * of it by Jn 11:51
asked each other, "What do you *? Jn 11:56
* they are doing God a service. Jn 16:2
"Dear brothers, *! Act 2:29
your husband even * of doing a Act 5:9
never * of anyone as inferior. Act 10:28
asked, 'Do you * I am the Messiah? Act 13:25
If this is true, we shouldn't * Act 17:29
And after awhile they began to * Rom 1:21
their evil minds could * of. Rom 1:28
Do you * that God will judge and Rom 2:3
You Jews * all is well between Rom 2:17
a blind man. You * of yourselves as Rom 2:19
to God. You * that you can guide Rom 2:20
now even to * about those things Rom 6:21
turned it down, * how much greater Rom 11:12
When you * of what he has done Rom 12:1
fresh newness in all you do and *. Rom 12:2
And don't * you know it all! Rom 12:16
is weaker; they * it is wrong, and Rom 14:2
Those who * it is all right to Rom 14:3
Some * that Christians should Rom 14:5
For now no one can * that I have 1Co 1:15
over what you * about this, or what 1Co 4:3
You seem to * you already have 1Co 4:8
Sometimes I * God has put us 1Co 4:9
refuse to if I * they might get 1Co 6:12
Don't * of eating as important, 1Co 6:13
will be glad to tell you what I *. 1Co 7:25
In times like these I * it is 1Co 7:26
he has to * about his earthly 1Co 7:33
and I * I am giving you counsel 1Co 7:40
Don't * only of yourself. 1Co 10:24
Try to * of the other fellow, 1Co 10:24
What do you yourselves really * 1Co 11:13
And what would you * if you 1Co 12:16
he is likely to * you are crazy. 1Co 14:23
And do you * that the knowledge 1Co 14:36
I * you ought to know, dear 2Co 1:8
with them? I * you hardly need 2Co 3:1
and not because we * we can do 2Co 3:5
are blind and they * that obeying 2Co 3:15
wouldn't like to * of dying and 2Co 5:4
you again—but I * he would have 2Co 8:17
of you who seem to * my deeds and 2Co 10:2
that you will not * I am just 2Co 10:9
about, as I * you realize by now, 2Co 11:6
Again I plead, don't * that I 2Co 11:16
here I go: (You * you are so 2Co 11:19,20
want anyone to * more highly of me 2Co 12:6
I suppose you * I am saying all 2Co 12:19
to * such things about our Lord. Gal 2:17
place, why do you * that trying to Gal 3:3
Listen to me, you friends who * Gal 4:21
Just *! Eph 3:8
When I * of the wisdom and scope Eph 3:14,15
Don't just * about your own Php 2:4
and all they * about is this life Php 3:19
good and right. * about things that Php 4:8
things in others. * about all you Php 4:8
to you, you didn't * of the words 1Th 2:13
that is wrong. * highly of them 1Th 5:13
Don't * of him as an enemy, but 2Th 3:15
Don't let anyone * little of you 1Ti 4:12
a close watch on all you do and *. 1Ti 4:16
So I * it is better for these 1Ti 5:14
a large crop. * over these three 2Ti 2:7
And if we * that our present 2Ti 2:12
and will * nothing of immorality. 2Ti 3:3
Don't let anyone * that what you Tit 2:15
Perhaps you could * of it this Phm 1:15
what makes us * that we can escape Heb 2:3
want you to * now about this Jesus Heb 3:1
from sin, just * how much more Heb 9:14
to his sin. * how much more Heb 10:29
and weary, * about his patience as Heb 12:3
the Word of God. * of all the good Heb 13:7
watch what you do and what you *; Jas 2:12
Or what do you * the Scripture Jas 4:5
Eat God's Word—read it, * about 1Pe 2:2,3f
can * of, and laugh at the truth. 2Pe 3:3
* of it—and we really are! 1Jn 3:1
you don't love me as at first! * Rev 2:5
"And now * hard: his seven heads Rev 17:9

THINKING
they waited, * that perhaps he was Ju 3:24
The man I'm * of is Boaz! Ru 3:2
BUT DAVID KEPT * to himself, 1Sa 27:1
'Saul is dead,' * he was bringing 2Sa 4:10
in the fields, * that we will be 2Ki 7:12
But he was really *, "At least 2Ki 20:19
so after * about it I spoke out Neh 5:7
on his laws and * about ways to Ps 1:2
I am always * of the Lord; Ps 16:8
the Lord is * about me right now! Ps 40:17
I lie awake at night * of you— Ps 63:6
I keep * of the good old days of Ps 77:5
I cannot stop * about them. Ps 77:12
Jehovah is constantly * about us Ps 115:12
for I am ever * of your rules. Ps 119:99
I couldn't sleep, * how I ought to Ps 132:2-5
rivers of Babylon * of Jerusalem. Ps 137:1
you are * about me constantly! Ps 139:17,18
morning, you are still * of me! Ps 139:17,18
And he spends his time * of all Pro 6:14
and there is no use * of what Ecc 1:12-1
So, after a lot of *, I decided Ecc 2:
The foolishness of * that wealth Ecc 5:1
I know what they are *, so I will Is 66:1
What are you * of, Nineveh, to Nah 1:
* Israel would be an easy prey. Hab 3:1
to God, * he will let them alone. Zep 1:1
get by as you are, *, 'We are safe Mt 3:
Jesus knew what they were * and Mt 9:
are you * such evil thoughts? Mt 9:
Jesus knew what they were * and Mt 16:
You are * merely from a human Mt 16:2
* they would surely respect him. Mt 21:3
Jesus knew what they were *, and Mt 26:1
in terror, * it was a ghost, for Mk 6:4
He finally sent him, * they would Mk 12:
Jesus knew what they were *, and Lk 5:2
* they were seeing a ghost! Lk 24:3
"Maybe he is * of leaving the Jn 7:3
The disciples, * Jesus meant Jn 11:12,1
for * God's gift can be bought! Act 8:2
Apollos had been * about going to Act 18:2
line with our * in these matters. Act 21:2
braggarts, always * of new ways of Rom 1:3
trap them into * all is well Rom 11:
anyone else is *, or what he is 1Co 2:1
have become proud, * that I am 1Co 4:1
you, I have been * a lot about 1Co 5:3,
work and * how to please him. 1Co 7:3
have been used to * of idols as 1Co 8:
Do you suppose God was * only 1Co 9:
Wasn't he also * about us? 1Co 9:1
If you are *, "Oh, I would never 1Co 10:1
unworthily, not * about the body of 1Co 11:2
into * they are Christ's apostles. 2Co 11:1
confuse you into * that salvation Gal 2:5
make me jealous, * that their Php 1:16,17
Be humble, * of others as better Php 2:3
living and * much about the Lord. 1Ti 2:2
* only pure thoughts about them. 1Ti 5:2
for he is always * about you and 1Pe 5:7

THINKS
the girl and ask her what she *." Gen 24:57
doing whatever he * is right; Deu 12:8
"let him do what he * best." 1Sa 3:18
Archite what he * about this." 2Sa 17:5
speak and tell you what he *! Job 11:5
A fool * he needs no advice, but Pro 12:15
A wise man * ahead; Pro 13:16
A good man * before he speaks; Pro 15:28
* is right, but it ends in death. Pro 16:25
The rich man * of his wealth as Pro 18:11
Yes, a wise man * much of death, Ecc 7:4
* only of having a good time now. Ecc 7:4
bygone days. She * of all the Lam 1:7
Whenever she * of asking for it, Eze 29:16
he does whatever he * best among Dan 4:35
have, even what he * he has shall Lk 8:18
about God nor what he * of them. Rom 3:18
you doing something he * is wrong. Rom 14:13
He sins if he does, for he * it Rom 14:23
about this, or what anyone else *. 1Co 4:3
If anyone * he knows all the 1Co 8:2
Someone who * it is wrong to eat 1Co 8:10
him to do something he * is wrong. 1Co 8:12
limited by what someone else *? 1Co 10:29
just because he * I am wrong? 1Co 10:30
by what the world * about them or 2Co 5:16
If anyone * he is too great to Gal 6:3

THIRD
This all occurred on the * day. Gen 1:13
a * day (or, 'period of time')." Gen 1:13f
land of Cush. The * branch is the Gen 2:14
On the * day of the journey Gen 22:4
The * day Joseph said to them, Gen 42:18
On the morning of the * day there Ex 19:16
a diamond. The * row will be an Ex 28:19
In the * row were a jacinth, an Ex 39:12
until the * day shall be burned. Lev 7:17,18
it is eaten on the * day, the Lord Lev 7:17,18
any remaining until the * day Lev 19:6
For any of it eaten on the * day Lev 19:7
If you eat it on the * day you Lev 19:8
On the * day Eliab, the son of Num 7:24-29
to the * and fourth generation. Num 14:17,18
purify himself the * and seventh Num 19:12
not do this on the * day, he will Num 19:12
This shall take place on the * Num 19:19
"On the * day of the festival, Num 29:20
on the * and seventh days. Num 31:19
sins upon even the * and fourth Deu 5:9,10
"Every * year you are to use Deu 14:28
"Every * year is a year of Deu 26:12
On the * day, officers went Jos 3:2,3,4
The * tribe to receive its Jos 19:10
out again on the * day and set Ju 20:30
So now the Lord called the * 1Sa 3:8
the * will have a bottle of wine. 1Sa 10:3
and the * moved toward the border 1Sa 13:18
The same thing happened a * time! 1Sa 19:21
until the evening of the * day. 1Sa 20:5

'HIRD Con't)
of Carmel. The * was Absalom, born 2Sa 3:3
his troops. A * were placed under 2Sa 18:2
and a * under Ittai, the Gittite. 2Sa 18:2
led from the second to the *. 1Ki 6:8
Tirzah, during the * year of the 1Ki 15:28
But during the * year, while 1Ki 22:2
instructions: "A * of those who 2Ki 11:5
and in the * year they will have 2Ki 19:29
was Abinadab, his * was Shimea, 1Ch 2:13
The * was Absalom, the son of his 1Ch 3:2
second,Aharah, the *,Nohah, the 1Ch 8:1
Eliphelet, the *. 1Ch 8:39
Eliab was * in command; 1Ch 12:8-13
was *, and Jekameam was fourth. 1Ch 23:19
*, the group led by Harim; 1Ch 24:7-18
Jahaziel, his * son; 1Ch 24:23
The *, Zaccur and twelve of his 1Ch 25:9-31
Zebadiah (the *), 1Ch 26:2,3
Joah (the *), 1Ch 26:4,5
Tebaliah, the *; 1Ch 26:11
The commander of the * Division 1Ch 27:5,6
His 24,000 men were on duty the * 1Ch 27:5,6
In the * year of his reign he 2Ch 17:7,8,9
This is how we'll proceed: A * 2Ch 23:4
Another * will go over to the 2Ch 23:5,6
and a * will be at the Lower Gate. 2Ch 23:5,6
Each of the three leaders led a * 2Ch 23:8
Sabbath, and a * of those whose 2Ch 23:8
Literally, "the * day of the Ez 6:15f
IT WAS THE * year of the reign of Est 1:1
The * harvest from then would Is 37:30f
Place a * of it at the center of Eze 5:2
Scatter another * across your map Eze 5:2
Scatter the last * to the wind, Eze 5:2
the second, a man's; the *, a Eze 10:14
has fallen, yet a * great power Dan 2:39
his neck, and become the * ruler Dan 5:7
you the * ruler in the kingdom." Dan 5:16
proclaimed * ruler in the kingdom. Dan 5:29
The * of these strange animals Dan 7:6
IN THE * year of the reign of King Dan 8:1
IN THE * year of the reign of Dan 10:1
black ones, the * by white horses Zec 6:3
but a * will be left in the land. Zec 13:8
I will bring the * that remain Zec 13:9
me, and on the * day afterwards I Mt 17:22,23
* day I will rise to life again." Mt 20:19
back to prayer the * time, saying Mt 26:44
the tomb until the * day, to Mt 27:64
The * time when he returned to Mk 14:41
and the * day I will reach my Lk 13:32
And the * day I will rise Lk 18:33
"But the * man brought back only Lk 19:20
collecting. A * man was sent and Lk 20:12
Once more, for the * time, he Lk 23:22
he would rise again the * day?" Lk 24:6,7
again from the dead on the * day; Lk 24:46
This was the * time Jesus had Jn 21:14
asked the question this * time. Jn 21:17
Literally, "the * heaven." 2Co 12:2,3f
coming to you again, the * time; 2Co 12:14
THIS IS THE * time I am coming to 2Co 13:1
[Well, this is my * warning, as I 2Co 13:1
ox; the * had the face of a man; Rev 4:7
When he had broken the * seal, I Rev 6:5
the * Living Being say, "Come!" Rev 6:5
destroying a * of all the ships; Rev 8:8,9
and a * of the sea turned red as Rev 8:8,9
and a * of the fish were killed. Rev 8:8,9
The * angel blew, and a great Rev 8:10
a * of the rivers and springs. Rev 8:10
because it poisoned a * of all Rev 8:11
and immediately a * of the sun was Rev 8:12
darkened, and a * of the moon and Rev 8:12
was dimmed by a *, and the Rev 8:12
loose to kill a * of all mankind. Rev 9:15
The second woe is past, but the * Rev 11:14
along behind him a * of the stars, Rev 12:4
Then a * angel followed them Rev 14:9
The * angel poured out his flask Rev 16:4
The * with chalcedony; Rev 21:18,19,20

THIRST
"Must we die of *?" Ex 15:24
But, tormented by *, they cried Ex 17:3
Must I now die of *, and fall to Ju 15:18
die by famine and *—while he 2Ch 32:11
from heaven or water for their *. Neh 9:20
* of many others, not themselves! Job 5:5
grape juice as they suffer from *. Job 24:11
God. I * for God, the living God. Ps 42:2
How I * for you in this parched Ps 63:1
for my awful * they offered me Ps 69:21
quench their *, and the birds nest Ps 104:11
I reach out for you. I * for you Ps 143:6
and * of every living thing. Ps 145:16
the common people will die of *. Is 5:13
still faint from * when he wakes Is 29:8
are parched from *, then I will Is 41:17
* and for your parched fields. Is 44:3
They shall neither hunger nor *; Is 49:10
their mouths for *, for there is Lam 4:3,4
away and die of * as in a land Hos 1:3
dry away, and he will die of *. Hos 13:15
believing in me will never *. Jn 6:35

THIRSTING
and weary, * for the Word of God. Amo 8:13

THIRSTS
you as parched land * for rain. Ps 143:6

THIRSTY
will be hungry, *, naked, and in Deu 28:47,48
he said, "for I am very *." Ju 4:19
But now he was very * and he Ju 15:18
when you are *, go and help Ru 2:8,9
and hungry and * after your long 2Sa 17:28,29
David remarked, "How * I am for 2Sa 23:15
from the rock when they were *. Neh 9:15
the *, and bread to the starving. Job 22:7
like water into * ground. Ps 58:7
desert, hungry and * and faint. Ps 107:5
For he satisfies the * soul and Ps 107:9
If he is *, give him something to Pro 25:21,22
away is like cold water to the *. Pro 25:25
hungry, and as a * man dreams of Is 29:8
springs of water in the * land. Is 35:7
is so hungry and * that he will eat Is 36:12
He grows hungry and *, weak and Is 44:12
They were not * when he led them Is 48:21
IS anyone *? Is 55:1
you shall be * while they drink; Is 65:13
bare hills panting like * jackals. Jer 14:6
in that dry and * land. Hos 13:5
I was * and you gave me water; Mt 25:35
* and give you anything to drink? Mt 25:37
wouldn't feed me; *, and you Mt 25:42
see you hungry or * or a stranger Mt 25:44
* again after drinking this water. Jn 4:13
Then I'll never be * again and Jn 4:15
*, let him come to me and drink. Jn 7:37
the Scriptures said, "I'm *." Jn 19:28
If he is * give him something to Rom 12:20
gone hungry and *, without even 1Co 4:11
Often I have been hungry and * 2Co 11:27
hungry again, nor *, and they will Rev 7:16
I will give to the * the springs Rev 21:6
Let the * one come—anyone who Rev 22:17

THIRTEEN
at that time, and Ishmael was *. Gen 17:24-27
the Lord, shall be * young bulls, Num 29:13
oil for each of the * young bulls; Num 29:14
and measures * and a half feet long Deu 3:11
pasturelands. * of these cities Jos 21:4
The Gershon division received * Jos 21:6
So in all, * cities were given to Jos 21:19
So * cities with their Jos 21:33
which took * years to construct. 1Ki 7:1
* other cities with surrounding 1Ch 6:60
received by lot * cities in the 1Ch 6:62
and brothers numbered * in all. 1Ch 26:11
in 722 B.C., * years after this Is 7:8f
me during those * years at Tyre, Eze 29:20

THIRTEENTH
now in the * year, they rebelled. Gen 14:4
*, the group led by Huppah; 1Ch 24:7-18
*, Shuba-el and twelve of his sons 1Ch 25:9-31
came to him in the * year of the Jer 1:1
said, from the * year of the reign Jer 25:2,3

THIRTIETH
Literally, "in the * year." Eze 1:1f

THIRTY
Shelah was * years old when his Gen 11:14,15
Peleg was * years old when his Gen 11:18,19
Serug was * years old when his Gen 11:22,23
"Let me speak: suppose only * Gen 18:30
do it if there are * there." Gen 18:30
He was * years old as he entered Gen 41:46
shall be given * pieces of silver, Ex 21:32
It was * feet long and 7½ feet Ex 38:18
males from ages * to fifty who are Num 4:3
the ages of * and fifty who are Num 4:21,22,23
of the men from * to fifty who are Num 4:29
all of the men * to fifty years of Num 4:35
Levites who were * to fifty years Num 4:46,47,48
they mourned for him for * days. Num 20:29
for * days on the plains of Moab. Deu 34:8
Ai, Joshua sent * thousand of his Jos 8:3,4
additional to the * thousand men Jos 8:11,12,13f
years. His * sons rode around Ju 10:4
around together on * donkeys, and Ju 10:4
and they owned * cities in the land Ju 10:4
He had * sons and thirty Ju 12:9,10
He had thirty sons and * Ju 12:9,10
in * girls to marry his sons. Ju 12:9,10
He had forty sons and * Ju 12:14
threw a party for * young men of Ju 14:10,11
"I'll give you * plain robes and Ju 14:12
plain robes and * fancy robes. Ju 14:12
Ashkelon, killed * men, took their Ju 14:19
so that about * of them died. Ju 20:31
had killed about * of the Israelis, Ju 20:35-39
defeated again. * thousand men of 1Sa 4:10
them above the * special guests. 1Sa 9:22
addition to * thousand from Judah. 1Sa 11:8
seven years, since the age of *. 2Sa 5:4,5
THEN DAVID MOBILIZED * thousand 2Sa 6:1
three of The *—the top-ranking 2Sa 23:13
But he was the greatest of The * 2Sa 23:18,19
of The *, but was not actually 2Sa 23:23
of Joab, was also one of The *. 2Sa 23:24-39
The *, plus the Top Three, plus 2Sa 23:24-39f
Then Solomon drafted * thousand 1Ki 5:13
ninety feet long, * feet wide, and 1Ki 6:2
* feet long and fifteen feet deep. 1Ki 6:3
This inner sanctuary was * feet 1Ki 6:20
* feet wide, and thirty feet high. 1Ki 6:20
thirty feet wide, and * feet high. 1Ki 6:20
Another time, three of The * 1Ch 11:15
"The *" were the highest-ranking 1Ch 11:15f
brother, was commander of The *. 1Ch 11:20
place among The * by killing 300 1Ch 11:20
most famous of The *, but he was 1Ch 11:21
he was very famous among The *. 1Ch 11:24,25
as high or higher than The *); 1Ch 12:3-7
a leader of The *, replied, 1Ch 12:18
of Levi who were * years or older. 1Ch 23:3
the chief of the * highest-ranking 1Ch 27:5,6
ninety feet long and * feet wide. 2Ch 3:3
Holy of Holies—* feet square. 2Ch 3:8
HE ALSO MADE a bronze altar * feet 2Ch 4:1
thirty feet long, * feet wide, and 2Ch 4:1
Ebedmelech to take * men with him Jer 38:10
So Ebedmelech took * men and Jer 38:11
One day late in June, when I was * Eze 1:1
of the walls, and * rooms were Eze 40:17
other, with * rooms in each tier. Eze 41:6
that for the next * days anyone who Dan 6:7
God or man—except you—for * days? Dan 6:12
was about * to sixty miles across. Jon 3:3f
"It appears to be about * feet Zec 5:2
So they counted out * little Zec 11:12
So I took the * coins and threw Zec 11:13
a crop that was *, sixty, and even Mt 13:8
out and brings *, sixty, or even a Mt 13:23
the amount planted—*, sixty, or Mt 13:23f
And they gave him * silver Mt 26:15
"They took the * pieces of Mt 27:9
soil and yielded * times as much as Mk 4:8
harvest for God—*, sixty, or even a Mk 4:20
Jesus was about * years old when Lk 3:23-38
perhaps twenty to * gallons each. Jn 2:6
The head was shaved * days before Act 18:18f
within the prescribed * days. Act 18:20f
The head was shaved * days before Act 18:22f
four hundred and * years later when Gal 3:17

THIRTY-EIGHT
"So it took us * years to Deu 2:14,15
all the men, who * years earlier Deu 2:14,15
been on the throne * years when 1Ki 16:29
there had been sick for * years. Jn 5:5

THIRTY-FIFTH
the * year of King Asa's reign. 2Ch 15:19

THIRTY-FIVE
When Arpachshad was * years old, Gen 11:12,13
Jehoshaphat was * years old when 1Ki 22:42
Judah when he was * years old, and 2Ch 20:31
was seventy feet long by * feet. Eze 41:2
The inner room was * feet Eze 41:4
* feet away from the terrace, on Eze 41:10
About * miles from Rome. Act 28:15f

THIRTY-FOOT
boards. The * inner room at the 1Ki 6:16
along the entire * width of the 2Ch 3:4

THIRTY-FOOT-WIDE
court will be a * curtain, made of Ex 27:16

THIRTY-FOUR
Eber was * years old when his son Gen 11:16,17

THIRTY-NINE
gave me their terrible * lashes. 2Co 11:24

THIRTY-NINTH
In the * year of his reign, Asa 2Ch 16:12

THIRTY-ONE
So in all, * kings and their Jos 12:8-24
been on the throne * years when 1Ki 16:23
* leaders of the tribe of Reuben; 1Ch 11:26-47
He reigned * years, in Jerusalem. 2Ch 34:1

THIRTY-SECOND
until the * year of the reign of Neh 5:14
to Babylon in the * year of the Neh 13:6

THIRTY-SEVEN
Uriah the Hittite—* 2Sa 23:24-39

THIRTY-SEVENTH
He came to the throne in the * 2Ki 13:9,10
of the * year of his captivity. 2Ki 25:27

THIRTY-SIX
of the silver was about * pounds); Num 7:84,85,86
About * of the Israelis were Jos 7:5

THIRTY-SIXTH
IN THE * year of King Asa's reign, 2Ch 16:1

THIRTY-THREE
in Paddan-aram, were * in all. Gen 46:15
Then, for the next * days, while Lev 12:4
He then ruled * years in 2Sa 5:4,5
them in Hebron and * in Jerusalem. 1Ki 2:11

(THIRTY-THREE Con't)
country, and * hundred foremen. 1Ki 5:16
where he reigned another * years. 1Ch 3:4
in Hebron and * in Jerusalem. 1Ch 29:26,27

THIRTY-TWO

Reu was * years old when Serug Gen 11:20,21
his army and, with * allied nations 1Ki 20:1
Ben-hadad and the * allied kings 1Ki 20:16
had commanded his * chariot 1Ki 22:31
Jehoram was * years old when he 2Ki 8:17
He hired * thousand chariots, as 1Ch 19:7
He was * years old when he began 2Ch 21:5
He was * years old when he 2Ch 21:20

THISTLE

But King Joash replied, "The * 2Ki 14:9
the * and trod it into the ground! 2Ki 14:9
mountains a * demanded of a cedar 2Ch 25:18
and stepped on the *, crushing it! 2Ch 25:18
Other seed landed in * patches, Lk 8:7

THISTLES

It will grow thorns and * for Gen 3:18
myself, then let * grow on that Job 31:40
And thorns and * will grow up Hos 9:6
Thorns and * will grow up to Hos 10:8
with thorn bushes or figs with *. Mt 7:16
The ground covered with * Mt 13:22
came and sowed * among the wheat. Mt 13:25
began to grow, the * grew too. Mt 13:26
that choice seed is full of *!' Mt 13:27
" 'Shall we pull out the *?' Mt 13:28
to sort out the * and burn them, Mt 13:30
of the * and the wheat. Mt 13:36
the Kingdom; the * are the people Mt 13:38
The enemy who sowed the * among Mt 13:39
"Just as in this story the * are Mt 13:40
For on that day thorns and *, Rom 8:20,21
on having crops of * and thorns, Heb 6:8

THOMAS

*, Matthew Mt 10:2,3,4
*, James Mk 3:16-19
*, James (the son of Lk 6:14,15,16
*, nicknamed "The Twin," said Jn 11:16
"No, we don't," * said. Jn 14:5
One of the disciples, *, "The Jn 20:24
and this time * was with them. Jn 20:26
Then he said to *, "Put your Jn 20:27
"My Lord and my God!" * said. Jn 20:28
there—Simon Peter, *, "The Twin," Jn 21:2
Philip, *, Act 1:14

THONGS

neck with leather * as you would Jer 27:2
with leaded *, and release him." Lk 23:16

THORN

in your side and a * in your eyes, Jos 23:13
finally turned to the * bush. Ju 9:14
"And the * bush replied, 'If you Ju 9:15
a * in the hand of a drunkard. Pro 26:9
* bushes or figs with thistles. Mt 7:16
which has been a * in my flesh, a 2Co 12:7
happy about "the *," and about 2Co 12:10

THORNBUSHES

fence her in with briars and *; Hos 1:6

THORNFIELD

All the land will be one vast *, Is 7:24

THORNS

It will grow * and thistles for Gen 3:18
in your eyes and * in your sides. Num 33:55
rather, they shall be * in your Ju 2:3
* and briars of the wilderness." Ju 8:7
with wild * and briars. Ju 8:16
But the godless are as * to be 2Sa 23:6
the blazing fire of * beneath it. Ps 58:9
with *, and covered with weeds; Pro 24:30,31
a lily among *, so is my beloved as Sol 2:2
it be overgrown with briars and *. Is 5:6
grew, for * will cover them; Is 7:25
wickedness, these * and briars; Is 9:18
he will burn those * and briars, Is 10:17
If I find * and briars bothering Is 27:4,5
will thrive with * and briars; Is 32:13
* cut down and tossed in the fire. Is 33:12
will all be gone. * will overrun Is 34:13
Where once were *, fir trees Is 55:13
seed will be wasted among the *. Jer 4:3
have sown wheat but reaped *; Jer 12:13
at Israel like * and briars, though Eze 28:24
Memphis will bury them. And * and Hos 9:6
will crumble. * and thistles will Hos 10:8
is more crooked than a hedge of *. Mic 7:4
the fire like a tangled mass of *. Nah 1:10
Other seeds fell among *, and Mt 13:7
* choked out the tender blades. Mt 13:7
a crown from long * and put it on Mt 27:29
Other seeds fell among * that Mk 4:7
sharp * and put it on his head. Mk 15:16,17
Figs never grow on *, or grapes Lk 6:44
The seed among the * represents Lk 8:14
made a crown of * and placed it on Jn 19:2
crown of * and the purple robe. Jn 19:5
For on that day * and thistles, Rom 8:20,21
of thistles and *, the land is Heb 6:8

THORNY

The rebel walks a *, treacherous Pro 22:5
and caves and * parts, as well as Is 7:19
"The * ground represents the Mk 4:18

THOROUGH

to last and after * investigation Lk 1:3
I was given a * Jewish training Act 26:4

THOROUGHLY

the tents *, he didn't find them. Gen 31:34
time until he is * healed, and pay Ex 21:19
must be scoured and rinsed out *. Lev 6:28
the house scraped *, and the Lev 14:41
you must not * reap all the corners Lev 23:22
investigated the matter more *. Ez 4:21
that the room be * cleaned, and I Neh 13:9
established it and examined it *. Job 28:27
I have * tested your promises Ps 119:140
for they * enjoy their sins. Pro 2:14
they shall be shamed and * Jer 20:11
These prophets are as * depraved Jer 23:14
I was * ashamed of all I did in Jer 31:19
the accountant was * dishonest. Lk 16:1
I have examined him * on this Lk 23:14
ungrateful to them, and * bad. 2Ti 3:2

THOU

the sanctuary shalt * take them. Num 3:47,48f
Literally, "* hast instructed Job 4:3,4f

THOUGHT

upon me," for she *, "I saw God Gen 16:13
and will kill me to get her,' I *. Gen 20:11,12
Isaac replied. "I * someone would Gen 26:9
* and wondered what it all meant. Gen 37:11
as he went by and * she was a Gen 38:15
Joseph, never giving him a *. Gen 40:23
Next morning, as he * about it, Gen 41:8
Joseph, "I never * that I would Gen 48:11
he * they might return to Egypt. Ex 13:17,18
their weapons and * it would be Deu 1:41
This is your wonderful * for the Deu 4:39
he * the other man would get. Deu 19:19
your ancestors gave a second *; Deu 28:36
But then I *, Deu 32:27
sinned against the Lord as we *; Jos 22:31
least * of in the entire family!" Ju 6:15
"I really * you hated her," he Ju 15:2
"In the morning," they *, "when Ju 16:2
And he woke up and *, "I will Ju 16:20
dollars you * was stolen from you, Ju 17:2
Then they * again of their oath Ju 21:8,9
Suddenly someone * of the annual Ju 21:19
man did whatever he * was right. Ju 21:25
no sound, * she had been drinking. 1Sa 1:12,13
said, "I've just * of something! 1Sa 9:6
of smiles, for he *, "Surely the 1Sa 15:32
look at Eliab and *, "Surely this 1Sa 16:6
For Saul * to himself, "I'll 1Sa 18:17
all loved him and * he should 1Sa 18:22
Achish believed David and * that 1Sa 27:12
the king *. 1Sa 27:12
upon the field and * David would 2Sa 1:10f
For they * they were safe. 2Sa 5:6
Jeroboam *, "Unless I'm 1Ki 12:26
*, "That's the man we're after." 1Ki 22:32,33
"Look," he said, "I * at least 2Ki 5:11
I was there in * when Naaman 2Ki 5:26
and understands and knows every *. 1Ch 28:9
The king and all his aides * this Est 1:21
Haman * to himself, "Whom would Est 6:6
with hardly a * from anyone. Job 4:20
I gag at the * of eating it! Job 6:5,6,7
live again? This * gives me hope, Job 14:14
"I *, 'Surely I shall die Job 29:18
orphan because I * I could get away Job 31:21
IS overflowing with a beautiful *! Ps 45:1
I remained silent—you * I didn't Ps 50:21
Literally, "And the inward * and Ps 64:6f
to meditate, and * about the future Ps 73:17
In my discouragement I *, "They Ps 116:10,11
I have * much about your words, Ps 119:11
you promised. I * about the wrong Ps 119:59,60
When far away you know my every * Ps 139:2
No one gives me a passing *. Ps 142:4
out his evil words without a *. Pro 15:28
in *, planning his evil deeds. Pro 16:30
therefore, even a fool is * to be Pro 17:27,28
words express deep streams of *. Pro 18:4
I have * about this in Ecc 3:10
I have * deeply about all that Ecc 8:9,10
But afterwards no one * any more Ecc 9:15
But for the Lord you have no * or Is 5:12
burdens. You * your reign would Is 47:7
And we * his troubles were a Is 53:4
minds the very * of doing wrong! Is 55:7
gave not even a second * to me? Is 57:11
shady tree. I * that someday she Jer 3:7
be missed or even * about, and the Jer 3:16
And I * how wonderful it would Jer 3:19
me "Father," and * that you would Jer 3:19
I've never even * of it, let alone Jer 7:31
be no peace? We *, Now at last he Jer 14:19
commanded them nor even * of! Jer 19:5
and * no one could ever harm you. Jer 49
my head. I *, This is the end! Lam 3:5
* that comes into your minds. Eze 11
"But you * you could get along Eze 16:1
sin you have not * of those days Eze 16:2
soul, for he has * it over and Eze 18:2
Then I *, I will pour out my fury Eze 20:
Then I *, I will pour out my fury Eze 20:1
by which ancients * they could Eze 21:2
For at that time an evil * will Eze 38:1
the winds, and knows your every *; Amo 4:1
You push away all * of Amo 6:
is exactly what I * you'd do, Lord, Jon 4:
to Shigionoth"—* by some to mean a Hab 3:1
what happened. I *, 'Surely they Zep 3:
his robe, for she *, "If I only Mt 9:2
terror, for they * he was a ghost. Mt 14:2
They * he was saying this because Mt 16:
his reply, they * up a fresh Mt 22:34,3
and * he was calling for Elijah. Mt 27:4
For she * to herself, "If I can Mk 5:2
The king * Jesus was John the Mk 6:1
Others * Jesus was Elijah the Mk 6:1
Eloi") and * he was calling for Mk 15:34
standing there * he was calling for Mk 15:3
who heard about it * long thoughts Lk 1:6
her heart and often * about them. Lk 2:1
everything in. He * about his Lk 12:1
and some who are highly * of now Lk 13:3
"The accountant * to himself, Lk 16:
We had * he was the glorious Lk 24:2
same man," they *, "but he surely Jn 9:
some of them * it was thunder, Jn 12:2
Some * that since Judas was Jn 13:2
She * he was the gardener. Jn 20:1
who are well * of by everyone; Act 6:
of him. They * he was faking! Act 9:2
godly man, well * of by the Jews, Act 10:2
Then I * of the Lord's words Act 11:1
But all the time he * it was a Act 12:
After a little * he went to Act 12:1
Timothy was well * of by the Act 16:
the law, and well * of by all the Act 22:1
Then Paul * of something! Act 23:
one mind, united in * and purpose. 1Co 1:1
You are well * of, while we are 1Co 4:1
* and reasoned as a child does. 1Co 13:1
the others, but he * that it was 1Co 16:1
Once I mistakenly * of Christ 2Co 5:1
for we * they could save us. Gal 4:
Meanwhile, I * I ought to send Php 2:2
things that I once * very Php 3:7
She must be well * of by 1Ti 5:1
be well * of for their good lives; Tit 1:6
of sin. He * that it was better to Heb 11:26
and the "she" is * by many to be 1Pe 5:13
ever * up by the prophet himself. 2Pe 1:20,21
themselves without a * for others. Jud 1:12
calls for careful * to solve it. Rev 13:18

THOUGHT-LIFE

And then he added, "It is the * Mk 7:20

THOUGHTFUL

of all the earth. Sing * praises! Ps 47:6,7
the godly man is *." Pro 21:29f
will thrill to your *, wise words. Pro 23:15,16
hard working and *, orderly, and 1Ti 3:2
Their wives must be *, not heavy 1Ti 3:11
your wives, being * of their needs 1Pe 3:7
Therefore be earnest, * men of 1Pe 4:7

THOUGHTLESSLY

Don't act *, but try to find out Eph 5:17

THOUGHTS

at a man's * and intentions." 1Sa 16:7
all their motives and their *. Ps 7:9
words and unspoken * be pleasing Ps 19:14
for us, and we are ever in your *. Ps 40:5
with clean * and right desires. Ps 51:10
All their * are how to harm me. Ps 56:5
their endless evil * and plans. Ps 64:6
deeds are constantly in my *. Ps 77:12
And how deep are your *! Ps 92:5
and futile the * of mankind are, Ps 94:11
"They were a nation whose * and Ps 95:10
May he be pleased by all these * Ps 104:34
and keep my *, O Lord, on you. Ps 119:55
But I will concentrate my * upon Ps 119:78
a day your * turn towards me. Ps 139:17,18
"how precious are your * to me." Ps 139:17,18f
test my *. Ps 139:23
Keep these * ever in mind; Pro 4:21
mind is filled with honest *; Pro 12:5
The Lord hates the * of the Pro 15:26
so the Lord directs the king's *. Pro 21:1
the king, not even in your *; Ecc 10:20
whose * turn often to the Lord! Is 26:3
are my * the same as yours! Is 55:8
than yours, and my * than yours. Is 55:9
to murder; your * are only of Is 59:7
follow their own evil paths and *. Is 65:2
saved by casting out your evil *. Jer 4:14
stop your wicked * and deeds, and Jer 7:5

(THOUGHTS Con't)
their own stubborn, evil *. Jer 7:24
the deepest * of hearts and minds, Jer 20:12
the fields. His * and feelings Dan 5:21
turned my * once more to the Lord. Jon 2:7
But they do not know my * nor Mic 4:12
clouded with evil * and desires, Mt 6:23
are you thinking such evil *? Mt 9:4
Jesus knew their * and replied, Mt 12:25
For from the heart come evil *, Mt 15:19
hearts, come evil * of lust, theft, Mk 7:21
it thought long * and asked, "I Lk 1:66
And the deepest * of many hearts Lk 2:34,35
How well he knew their *! Lk 6:8
Jesus spoke up and answered his *. Lk 7:40
But Jesus knew their *, so he Lk 9:47
He knew the * of each of them, so Lk 11:17
your heart and * will also be. Lk 12:34
*, but those of God who sent me. Jn 7:16
forgive your evil *— for I can see Act 8:22
their inmost * and motives; Rom 2:16
And no one can know God's * 1Co 2:11
can't accept these * from God, 1Co 2:14
to know the Lord's *, or to discuss 1Co 2:16
of the very * and mind of Christ. 1Co 2:16
But when I became a man my * grew 1Co 13:11
As he listens, his secret * will 1Co 14:25
results: impure *, eagerness for Gal 5:19
or our evil * might lead us into. Eph 2:3
prayers, desires, *, or hopes. Eph 3:20
Now your attitudes and * must all Eph 4:23
His peace will keep your * and Php 4:7
thing: Fix your * on what is true Php 4:8
him by your evil * and actions, yet Col 1:21
built on men's * and ideas, instead Col 2:8
a person's evil * and desires. Col 2:23
Let heaven fill your *; Col 3:2
examines our hearts' deepest *. 1Th 2:4
your faith, and your clean *. 1Ti 4:12
thinking only pure * about them. 1Ti 5:2
gives you the evil * that young men 2Ti 2:22
into our innermost * and desires Heb 4:12
of man's own evil * and wishes. Jas 1:14
These evil * lead to evil Jas 1:15
own evil, lustful *, and those who 2Pe 2:10
widely in their * about what sin 1Jn 5:17f
to write you some * about the Jud 1:3
in God's *, and she was punished to Rev 16:19

THOUSAND
your 'brother' a * silver pieces as Gen 20:16
there were six hundred * of them, Ex 12:37
about three * men died that day. Ex 32:28
and a hundred of you, ten *! Lev 26:8
And may he multiply you a * Deu 1:11
but I will show kindness to a * Deu 5:9,10
God who for a * generations keeps Deu 7:9
single enemy chase a * of them, Deu 32:30
And two put ten * to flight, Deu 32:30
and forty * strong—led the other Jos 4:12,13
or three * of us to destroy it; Jos 7:3
So approximately three * soldiers Jos 7:4
Joshua sent thirty * of his bravest Jos 8:3,4
sent another five * men to join the Jos 8:11,12,13
thirty * men already hiding there. Jos 8:11,12,13f
Perhaps the additional five * Jos 8:11,12,13f
* in all, was wiped out that day. Jos 8:25
put to flight a * of the enemy, for Jos 23:10
so that ten * of the enemy were Ju 1:4,5,6
killed about ten * of the strongest Ju 3:29
to mobilize ten * men from the Ju 4:6
at Kedesh, ten * men volunteered. Ju 4:10
So Barak led his ten * men down Ju 4:14
Among forty * men of Israel, Ju 5:8
So twenty-two * of them left, and Ju 7:3
left, and only ten * remained who Ju 7:3
fifteen * troops were in Karkor. Ju 8:10
for one hundred twenty * had Ju 8:10
died, about a * men and women. Ju 9:49
So forty-two * people of Ephraim Ju 12:6
So three * men of Judah went down Ju 15:11
killed a * Philistines with it. Ju 15:15
I've killed a * men, Ju 15:16,17
"Each of us will give you a * Ju 16:5
as three * people in the balconies Ju 16:27
his mother, "That * dollars you Ju 17:2
Instead, twenty-six * of them Ju 20:14,15
twenty-two * Israelis that day. Ju 20:21
* men, all experienced swordsmen. Ju 20:25
and the ten * men in ambush west of Ju 20:33
Eighteen * of the Benjamin Ju 20:44
Rimmon, but five * were killed Ju 20:45
way, and two * more near Gidom. Ju 20:45
lost twenty-five * brave warriors Ju 20:46,47
So they sent twelve * of their Ju 21:10,11,12
Israel, killing four * of them. 1Sa 4:2
Thirty * men of Israel died that 1Sa 4:10
were three hundred * of them in 1Sa 11:8
addition to thirty * from Judah. 1Sa 11:8
he selected three * special troops 1Sa 13:2
and took two * of them with him to 1Sa 13:2
while the other * remained with 1Sa 13:2
army of three * chariots, six 1Sa 13:5
chariots, six * horsemen, and so 1Sa 13:5
There were two hundred * troops 1Sa 15:4
addition to ten * men from Judah. 1Sa 15:4
so he took three * special 1Sa 24:2
He had three * sheep and a 1Sa 25:2
sheep and a * goats, and was at his 1Sa 25:2
corps of three * troops and went to 1Sa 26:2
THEN DAVID MOBILIZED thirty * 2Sa 6:1
cavalry and twenty * infantry; 2Sa 8:4
He also slaughtered twenty-two * 2Sa 8:5
he destroyed eighteen * Edomites 2Sa 8:13
they hired twenty * Syrian 2Sa 10:6
and Zobah, one * from the king of 2Sa 10:6
and ten * from the land of Tob. 2Sa 10:6
field, also forty * cavalrymen, 2Sa 10:18
"give me twelve * men to start out 2Sa 17:1
You are worth ten * of us, and it 2Sa 18:3
and twenty * men laid down their 2Sa 18:7
King David. A * men from the tribe 2Sa 19:17
and seventy * men died throughout 2Sa 24:15
sacrificed one * burnt offerings! 1Ki 3:4
Solomon owned forty * chariot 1Ki 4:26
and employed twelve * charioteers. 1Ki 4:26
Then Solomon drafted thirty * 1Ki 5:13
to Lebanon, ten * a month, so that 1Ki 5:14
Solomon also had seventy * 1Ki 5:15
laborers, eighty * stonecutters in 1Ki 5:15
it had a twelve * gallon capacity. 1Ki 7:26
ten chariots, and ten * infantry; 2Ki 13:7
Once Amaziah killed ten * 2Ki 14:7
If you have two * men left who 2Ki 18:23
King Nebuchadnezzar took ten * 2Ki 24:14
He also took seven * of the best 2Ki 24:16
troops and one * craftsmen and 2Ki 24:16
and the greatest was worth a *! 1Ch 12:14
To a * generations: 1Ch 16:15
David captured a * of his 1Ch 18:4
chariots, seven * cavalry, and 1Ch 18:4
cavalry, and twenty * troops. 1Ch 18:4
David killed twenty-two * of them; 1Ch 18:5
* Edomites in the Valley of Salt. 1Ch 18:12
Literally, "a * talents of 1Ch 19:6f
He hired thirty-two * chariots, 1Ch 19:7
he killed seven * charioteers and 1Ch 19:17,18
and forty * of their troops. 1Ch 19:17,18
Literally, "a hundred * talents 1Ch 22:14f
"Twenty-four * of them will 1Ch 23:4,5
instructed, "six * are to be 1Ch 23:4,5
and judges, four * will be temple 1Ch 23:4,5
guards, and four * will praise the 1Ch 23:4,5
The next day they brought a * 1Ch 29:21
young bulls, a * rams, and a 1Ch 29:21
rams, and a * lambs as burnt 1Ch 29:21
chariots, sixty * cavalrymen and an 2Ch 12:3
oxen and seven * sheep—it was part 2Ch 15:11
Three hundred * Judean troops 2Ch 17:14,15
than the sand of a * seashores. Job 6:3
even one question of a * he asks? Job 9:3
And now, although ten * enemies Ps 3:6
The cattle on a * hills! Ps 50:10,11
is better than a * anywhere else! Ps 84:10
back to dust. A * years are but as Ps 90:4
Though a * fall at my side, Ps 91:7
side, though ten * are dying around Ps 91:7
Though a * generations pass he Ps 105:8,9
Though a man lives a * years Ecc 6:6
jeweled with a * heroes' shields. Sol 4:4
better than ten * others! Sol 5:10
one * pieces of silver from each. Sol 8:11
shall have my * pieces of silver Sol 8:12
One of them will chase a * of Is 30:17
BELSHAZZAR THE KING invited a * Dan 5:1
Even if I gave her ten * laws, Hos 8:12
city that sends a * men to battle, Amo 5:3
he asked the next man. 'A * Lk 16:7
I have seven * others besides you Rom 11:4
For although you may have ten * 1Co 4:15
by, than ten * words while 1Co 14:19
that a day or a * years from now is 2Pe 3:8
until the * years were finished. Rev 20:3
reigned with Christ for a * years. Rev 20:4
life until the * years had ended. Rev 20:5
shall reign with him a * years. Rev 20:6
When the * years end, Satan will Rev 20:7

THOUSANDS
into countless * and millions, like Gen 22:17
* hundreds, fifties, and tens. Ex 18:25
but I lavish my love upon * of Ex 20:6
to many * by forgiving their sins; Ex 34:7
and out of the many * of Israel, Num 31:4,5
in charge of *, hundreds, fifties, Deu 1:15
Surrounded by ten * of holy Deu 33:2
And the * of Manasseh." Deu 33:17
been defeated and * of the Israeli 1Sa 4:17
*, and David his ten thousands!" 1Sa 18:7
thousands, and David his ten *!" 1Sa 18:7
"They credit David with ten * 1Sa 18:8
ten thousands and me with only *. 1Sa 18:8
* and David his ten thousands'?" 1Sa 21:11
thousands and David his ten *'?" 1Sa 21:11
* and David his ten thousands!' 1Sa 29:5
thousands and David his ten *!' 1Sa 29:5
entire army fled. * of men are dead 2Sa 1:4
Sheep by the * out in our fields. Ps 144:12-15
You are loving and kind to *, Jer 32:18
he will have many * of his enemies Dan 11:12
For if you offered him * of rams Mic 6:7
of rams and ten * of rivers of Mic 6:7
ask my Father for * of angels to Mt 26:53
the man was filled with * Lk 8:30
THE CROWDS grew until * Lk 12:1
thousands upon * were milling about Lk 12:1
brother, how many * of Jews have Act 21:20

THREAD
much as a single * from you, lest Gen 14:23
tied a scarlet * around the wrist Gen 38:28
with the scarlet * on his wrist was Gen 38:30
and scarlet * and cloth, and Ex 35:25
woven from fine-twined linen *. Ex 38:9
with blue, purple, and scarlet *. Ex 38:18
woven from fine-twined linen *. Ex 39:2
*, just as God had directed Moses. Ex 39:4,5
his sons from fine-twined linen *. Ex 39:27
scarlet *, and the hyssop branch. Lev 14:6
scarlet *, and hyssop branches. Lev 14:49
and scarlet *, as well as the Lev 14:51,52
and scarlet *, and throw them into Num 19:6
*: for instance, wool and linen. Deu 22:11
like * and fell from his wrists! Ju 15:14
the bowstrings like cotton *, Ju 16:9
of fine linen and purple *." Est 1:6f
Your lips are like a * of Sol 4:3
short day my life hangs by a *. Is 38:12
come; the * of your life is cut. Jer 51:13

THREADBARE
and dressed in * clothes, and you Jas 2:2

THREADS
scarlet * of fine-twined linen. Ex 28:5,6
the same material—* of gold, blue, Ex 28:8
and scarlet * of fine-twined linen Ex 28:15
scarlet * into fine linen cloth. Ex 38:23
cut it into wire *, to work into Ex 39:3
and scarlet *, just as Jehovah had Ex 39:28,29

THREAT
terrified by this *, brought their Ex 9:20
be a constant * in your family from 2Sa 12:10
you are no * to even the least 2Ki 18:24

THREATEN
My enemies shout against me and * Ps 55:3
They scoff at God and * his Ps 73:8
lies about me and * me with death. Ps 109:20
They do not listen when you *; Is 26:11
with you and they * you with death Jer 38:25
will know that what I *, I do. Eze 5:13
What I * always happens. Eze 12:25
and * those who will not pay! Mic 3:5
be afraid of those who * you. Mt 10:26
when he suffered he did not * to 1Pe 2:23

THREATENED
that his life was being * by Esau. Gen 27:42
to Moses and * to kill him. Ex 4:24
I have continually * him and his 1Sa 3:13
replied. "He * to kill me if I 1Sa 19:17
life have been *, and I said to 2Sa 14:15,16
all the evil I have ever *. Jer 35:17
do to this city everything I *; Jer 39:16
that all I have * will happen to Jer 44:29
as he had *, but now it will be a Dan 11:29
that * to send them to the bottom. Jon 1:4
A fierce storm developed that * Lk 8:23
The Council then * them further, Act 4:21
The jailer was * with death if Act 16:23
* with death, has God deserted us? Rom 8:35

THREATENING
and Tobiah sent many * letters to Neh 6:19
of my mouth, * you with death. Hos 6:5
BUT PAUL, * with every breath and Act 9:1
Don't keep * them; Eph 6:9

THREATENS
save me from the pit that * me. Ps 69:15

THREATS
letters shouted * in the Jewish 2Ch 32:18
But I am deaf to all their *; Ps 38:13,14
For we are facing death * Ps 44:22
carry out my * of punishment." Jer 1:12
If these * of yours are really Jer 17:15
their whispered *, and am afraid. Jer 20:10
even though their * are sharp and Eze 2:6
you take it by fraud and * and Mic 2:2
No! His * are for your good, to Mic 2:7
extort money by * and violence; Lk 3:14
And now, O Lord, hear their *, Act 4:29

THREE
* sons, Shem, Ham, and Japheth. Gen 5:32
And he had * sons—Shem, Ham, and Gen 6:9,10
and make * decks inside the Gen 6:16
of Ararat. * months later, Gen 8:5
The names of Noah's * sons were Gen 9:18
From these * sons of Noah came Gen 9:19
who were the * sons of Noah; Gen 10:1
* sons, Abram, Nahor, and Haran. Gen 11:26

(THREE Con't)

noticed * men coming toward him.	Gen 18:2
make enough for the * of them!"	Gen 18:6
He saw in the distance * flocks	Gen 29:2
since I have given him * sons!"	Gen 29:34
sons to take them * days' distance,	Gen 30:35,36
learn of their flight for * days.	Gen 31:22
circumcised. But * days later,	Gen 34:25
Esau married * local girls from	Gen 36:2,3
They lived at Chezib and had *	Gen 38:3,4,5
About * months later word	Gen 38:24
saw a vine with * branches that	Gen 40:9,10
"The * branches mean three days!	Gen 40:12
"The three branches mean * days!	Gen 40:12
Within * days Pharaoh is going	Gen 40:13
* baskets of pastries on my head.	Gen 40:16
"The * baskets mean three	Gen 40:18,19
"The three baskets mean *	Gen 40:18,19
Joseph told him. "* days from now	Gen 40:18,19
Pharaoh's birthday came * days	Gen 40:20
them all into jail for * days.	Gen 42:17
and * hundred pieces of silver!	Gen 45:22
she hid him at home for * months.	Ex 2:1
us to go * days' journey into the	Ex 3:18
"We must take a * days' trip	Ex 5:3
over all the land for * days.	Ex 10:22
to Egypt after * days, but to keep	Ex 14:5
were there * days without water.	Ex 15:22
for his household—about * quarts	Ex 16:16
for everyone—* quarts apiece;	Ex 16:18
as usual, six quarts instead of *;	Ex 16:22
they were to take * quarts of it to	Ex 16:32
container and put * quarts of manna	Ex 16:33
the manna—held about * quarts;	Ex 16:36
Sinai peninsula * months after the	Ex 19:1
If he fails in any of these *	Ex 21:11
"There are * annual religious	Ex 23:14
At these * times each year,	Ex 23:17
of acacia wood * feet long, 1½ feet	Ex 25:23
It will have * branches going	Ex 25:32,33
decorated with * almond flowers.	Ex 25:32,33
7½ feet wide, and * feet high.	Ex 27:1
* posts imbedded in three sockets.	Ex 27:14,15
three posts imbedded in * sockets.	Ex 27:14,15
With one of them offer * quarts	Ex 29:40
inches square and * feet high, with	Ex 30:2
So they did, and about *	Ex 32:28
to celebrate these * annual	Ex 34:22
On each of these * occasions all	Ex 34:23
your God those * times each year.	Ex 34:24
using acacia wood, * feet long, 1½	Ex 37:10
six branches, * from each side.	Ex 37:18
inches square and * feet high, with	Ex 37:25
each with * posts and three bases.	Ex 38:14,15
each with three posts and * bases.	Ex 38:14,15
and only * quarts of fine white	Lev 14:21
not eat the first * crops, for they	Lev 19:23
a great evil. All * shall be burned	Lev 20:14
consisting of * pints of wine.	Lev 23:13
These * tribes led the way	Num 2:3-31
These * tribes were next in line	Num 2:3-31
of gold was about * pounds).	Num 7:84,85,86
They traveled for * days after	Num 10:33
* or four feet above the ground.	Num 11:31
covered with them, * feet thick!"	Num 11:31f
here, you *," he commanded.	Num 12:3,4
sacrificed, use * quarts of fine	Num 15:3,4
flour mixed with * pints of oil,	Num 15:3,4
accompanied by * pints of wine for	Num 15:5
flour mixed with * quarts of oil,	Num 15:8,9
of oil, plus * quarts of wine for	Num 15:10
of Peleth), all * from the tribe of	Num 16:1
as the Lord commanded him. The *	Num 20:27
your beating me these * times?"	Num 22:28
beat your donkey those * times?"	Num 22:32
for destruction. * times the	Num 22:33
you have blessed them * times.	Num 24:10
grain offering of * quarts of	Num 28:5
flour mixed with * pints of oil.	Num 28:5
consisting of * pints of strong	Num 28:7
and for each lamb, * quarts of	Num 28:13
for a ram, and * pints for a lamb.	Num 28:14
shall be * quarts of fine flour.	Num 28:20,21
with the ram, and * quarts with	Num 28:28,29
with the ram, and * quarts with	Num 29:3,4
six with the ram; and * with each	Num 29:9,10
the two rams; and * quarts for	Num 29:15
Red Sea and on for * days into the	Num 33:8
his guilt. * of these six Cities	Num 35:13,14
of Canaan, and * on the east side	Num 35:13,14
to set apart * cities east of the	Deu 4:41
the Lord your God * times a year at	Deu 16:16
there must be at least two or *.	Deu 17:6
you must set apart * Cities of	Deu 19:2,3
Divide the country into *	Deu 19:2,3
* additional Cities of Refuge.	Deu 19:9
There must be at least two, and *	Deu 19:15
Jordan River. "In * days we will	Jos 1:10,11
"Hide there for * days until the	Jos 2:16
and stayed there * days, until the	Jos 2:22
or * thousand of us to destroy it;	Jos 7:3

So approximately * thousand	Jos 7:4
* days later the facts came	Jos 9:16
reached their cities in * days.	Jos 9:17
descendants of the * sons of Anak:	Jos 15:14
there are the * cliffs), with their	Jos 17:11
Select * men from each tribe and	Jos 18:4
The Lord also instructed that *	Jos 20:8
they were descendants of the *	Ju 1:20
Only * hundred of the men drank	Ju 7:5,6
Midianites with these * hundred!"	Ju 7:7
only * hundred men with him.	Ju 7:8,9
He divided the * hundred men into	Ju 7:16
hundred men into * groups and gave	Ju 7:16
River with his * hundred men.	Ju 8:4
Abimelech. * years later God	Ju 9:22,23
* groups hiding in the fields.	Ju 9:43
But now after * hundred years	Ju 11:26
from the strong!" * days later	Ju 14:14
So he went out and caught *	Ju 15:4
So * thousand men of Judah went	Ju 15:11
"You've made fun of me * times	Ju 16:15
* thousand people in the balconies	Ju 16:27
so he stayed * days, and they all	Ju 19:4
And the Lord gave Hannah * sons	1Sa 2:21
in each of those * cities from all	1Sa 7:16
that were lost * days ago, for they	1Sa 9:20
Tabor you will see * men coming	1Sa 10:3
one will be carrying * young	1Sa 10:3
another will have * loaves of	1Sa 10:3
that there were * hundred thousand	1Sa 11:8
his army into * detachments, and	1Sa 11:11
he selected * thousand special	1Sa 13:2
a mighty army of * thousand	1Sa 13:5
at Michmash. * companies of	1Sa 13:17
Saul had * sons, Jonathan, Ishvi,	1Sa 14:49
brothers. The * oldest—Eliab,	1Sa 17:13
I will come out and shoot *	1Sa 20:20
bowed himself * times and they	1Sa 20:41f
so he took * thousand special	1Sa 24:2
He had * thousand sheep and a	1Sa 25:2
his elite corps of * thousand	1Sa 26:2
* DAYS LATER, when David and his	1Sa 30:1
eat or drink for * days and nights,	1Sa 30:11,12
"My master left me behind * days	1Sa 30:13
So Saul, his armor bearer, his *	1Sa 31:6
and his * sons on Mount Gilboa.	1Sa 31:8
the Amalekites. * days later a man	2Sa 1:1
to Asahel. But * hundred and sixty	2Sa 2:31
It remained there for * months,	2Sa 6:11
Ammihud) and stayed there *	2Sa 13:37,38,39
because it weighed * pounds and was	2Sa 14:26
He had * sons and one daughter,	2Sa 14:27
Then he took * daggers and	2Sa 18:14
of Judah within * days and to	2Sa 20:4
than the * days he had been given.	2Sa 20:5
after year for * years, and David	2Sa 21:1
These are the names of the Top *	2Sa 23:8
He was one of the * men who, with	2Sa 23:9
valley of Rephaim, * of The	2Sa 23:13
So the * men broke through the	2Sa 23:16
Of those * men, Abishai, the	2Sa 23:18,19
Once he took on * hundred of the	2Sa 23:18,19
equal to The *, though he was not	2Sa 23:18,19
as much renown as the Top *.	2Sa 23:22
was not actually one of the Top *.	2Sa 23:23
The Thirty, plus the Top *, plus	2Sa 23:24-39f
that I will give him * choices."	2Sa 24:12
or to flee for * months before your	2Sa 24:13
or to submit to * days of plague?	2Sa 24:13
morning, and it lasted for * days;	2Sa 24:15
But * years later two of	1Ki 2:39
When it was * days old, this	1Ki 3:17,18
These rooms were * stories high,	1Ki 6:6
The wall of the inner court had *	1Ki 6:36
the hall, set in * tiers, one tier	1Ki 7:3,4
facing each other from * walls.	1Ki 7:3,4
The Great Court had * courses of	1Ki 7:12
oxen standing tail to tail, *	1Ki 7:25
facing north, * west, three south,	1Ki 7:25
west, * south, and three east.	1Ki 7:25
west, three south, and * east.	1Ki 7:25
peace offerings * times a year on	1Ki 9:25
each piece) and * hundred shields	1Ki 10:16,17
and once every * years a great load	1Ki 10:22
He had seven hundred wives and *	1Ki 11:3
"Give me * days to think this	1Ki 12:5
people returned * days later, the	1Ki 12:12
upon the child * times, and cried	1Ki 17:21
IT WAS * years later that the Lord	1Ki 18:1
Then he dug a trench about * feet	1Ki 18:32
FOR * YEARS there was no war	1Ki 22:1
Then fifty men searched for *	2Ki 2:17
heard about the * armies marching	2Ki 3:21
"The * armies have attacked and	2Ki 3:23
of dove's dung brought * dollars!	2Ki 6:25
And two or * eunuchs looked out	2Ki 9:32
up and struck the floor * times.	2Ki 13:18
now you will be victorious only *	2Ki 13:19
was successful on * occasions in	2Ki 13:25
troops for * years besieging	2Ki 17:5
city of Samaria. * years later	2Ki 18:10

I will heal him, and * days from	2Ki 20
Temple again * days from now."	2Ki 20
for * years, but then rebelled.	2Ki 24
Zephaniah, and the * Temple guards	2Ki 25:1
Judah had * sons by Bath-shua, a	1Ch 2
Neariah had * sons:	1Ch 3:2
Azel's brother Eshek had * sons:	1Ch 8:3
with Saul and his * sons, Jonathan,	1Ch 10
So Saul and his * sons died	1Ch 10
body and the bodies of his * sons.	1Ch 10:1
leader of The Top *—the three	1Ch 11:1
The Top Three—the * greatest heroes	1Ch 11:1
The second of The Top * was	1Ch 11:1
Another time, * of The Thirty	1Ch 11:1
to his men, these * broke through	1Ch 11:18,1
but he was not as great as The *.	1Ch 11:2
He was nearly as great as The *,	1Ch 11:24,2
with David for * days, for	1Ch 12:3
of Obed-edom for * months, and the	1Ch 13:1
Lord has offered you * choices.	1Ch 21:10,1
You may have * years of famine,	1Ch 21:1
of famine, or * months of	1Ch 21:1
of Israel, or * days of deadly	1Ch 21:1
Then David divided them into *	1Ch 23:
fourteen sons and * daughters.	1Ch 25:4,
tail to tail, * facing north, three	2Ch 4:
facing north, * west, three south,	2Ch 4:
west, * south, and three east.	2Ch 4:
west, three south, and * east.	2Ch 4:
and at the * annual festivals—the	2Ch 8:1
Every * years the king sent his	2Ch 9:2
Rehoboam told them to return in *	2Ch 10:
people returned in * days to hear	2Ch 10:1
for * years without difficulty;	2Ch 11:1
brother Eliab. * sons were born	2Ch 11:1
He lasted * years.	2Ch 13:
his capital. * hundred thousand	2Ch 17:14,1
them * days to cart it all away!	2Ch 20:2
Each of the * leaders led a third	2Ch 23:
that for the next * years he	2Ch 27:
Literally, "males from * years	2Ch 31:16
reign, but lasted only * months.	2Ch 36:
But he lasted only * months and	2Ch 36:
* subclans of priests—Habaiah,	Ez 2:6
There will be * layers of huge	Ez 6:
camped there for * days while I	Ez 8:1
Jerusalem within * days and that	Ez 10:7,
Within * days, on the fifth day	Ez 10:
* days after my arrival at	Neh 2:11,1
to them for two or * hours, and for	Neh 9:
Two or * weeks later,	Est 3:1
do not eat or drink for * days,	Est 4:16
* DAYS LATER Esther put on her	Est 5:
of seven sons and * daughters, and	Job 1:2,
rushed in: "* bands of Chaldeans	Job 1:17
When * of Job's friends heard of	Job 2:11
THE * MEN refused to reply further	Job 32:1
angry with Job's * friends because	Job 32:3
more sons and * more daughters.	Job 42:13,14
craving more: no, * things!	Pro 30:15,16
There are * things too wonderful	Pro 30:18,19
There are * things that make the	Pro 30:21,22,23
There are * stately monarchs in	Pro 30:29,30,31
and conquer; * is even better, for	Ecc 4:12
says that within * years, without	Is 16:13,14
is ended, two or * in the highest	Is 17:6
be their ally; the * will be	Is 19:24
for the last * years, is a symbol	Is 20:3
reads, "within * years, according	Is 21:16f
reigned for * brief months in the	Jer 22:11f
finished reading * or four columns,	Jer 36:23
his assistant, the * chief Temple	Jer 52:24,25
weigh the hair into * equal parts.	Eze 5:1
even if these * men were here, the	Eze 14:16
Those * only would be saved, but	Eze 14:16
even if these * men were in the	Eze 14:18
These were * cities of ancient	Eze 27:10f
were * guardrooms on each side;	Eze 40:7-12
Here too there were * guardrooms	Eze 40:21
There were hooks, * or four	Eze 40:43
These rooms were in * tiers, one	Eze 41:6
and all * had recessed windows.	Eze 41:15,16
The rooms were in * tiers,	Eze 42:3
east and west for * miles alongside	Eze 48:18
there will be * gates, one named	Eze 48:30,31
* YEARS AFTER King Jehoiakim began	Dan 1:1
Daniel and his * friends looked	Dan 1:15
we throw * men into the furnace?"	Dan 3:24
accountable to * presidents (Daniel	Dan 6:2
and prayed * times a day, just as	Dan 6:10
He is asking favors of his God *	Dan 6:13
It held * ribs between its teeth,	Dan 7:5
among them, and * of the first ones	Dan 7:8
As for the other * animals,	Dan 7:12
and destroyed * of the others—the	Dan 7:20
ten, and will destroy * of them.	Dan 7:24
his hands for * and a half years.	Dan 7:25
the following * and a half years as	Dan 9:25f
been in mourning for * full weeks.	Dan 10:2
the future holds. * more Persian	Dan 11:2
not end until * and a half years	Dan 12:7

HREE Con't)
* and a half years (verse 7) plus Dan 12:11f
or * at the most, he will set us Hos 6:2
* Israelite kings were Hos 7:7f
rain * months before the harvest. Amo 4:7
People from two or * cities Amo 4:8
Eliphaz, the wisest of Job's * Ob 1:8f
And Jonah was inside the fish * Jon 1:17
the fish three days and * nights. Jon 1:17
take * days to walk around it. Jon 3:3
and so thick that * chariots could Zep 2:15f
These * who have come from so Zec 6:15
And I got rid of their * evil Zec 11:8
the great fish for * days and three Mt 12:39,40
and * nights, so I, the Messiah, Mt 12:39,40
the earth * days and three nights. Mt 12:39,40
the earth three days and * nights. Mt 12:39,40
here with me for * days now, and Mt 15:32
killed, and that * days later he Mt 16:21
If you want me to, I'll make * Mt 17:4
Literally, "* tabernacles" or Mt 17:4f
For where two or * gather Mt 18:20
At noon and again around * Mt 20:5
dawn, you will deny me * times!" Mt 26:34
Then he returned to the * Mt 26:40
of God and rebuild it in * days.' Mt 26:60,61
crows, you will deny me * times." Mt 26:75
build it again in * days, can you? Mt 27:40
was covered with darkness for * Mt 27:45
hours, from noon until * o'clock. Mt 27:45
About * o'clock, Jesus shouted, Mt 27:46
once said, 'After * days I will Mt 27:63
and mother and his * disciples, he Mk 5:40
About * o'clock in the morning he Mk 6:48
have been here * days, and have Mk 8:1
rise again * days afterwards. Mk 8:31
"We will make * shelters here, Mk 9:5
and killed and * days later I will Mk 9:30,31
but after * days I will come back Mk 10:34
you will deny me * times." Mk 14:30
Then he returned to the * Mk 14:37
human hands and in * days I will Mk 14:58
twice, you will deny me * times." Mk 14:72
Temple and rebuild it in * days! Mk 15:29,30
lasting until * o'clock that Mk 15:33
Elizabeth about * months and then Lk 1:56
* days later they finally Lk 2:46,47
been no rain for * and one-half Lk 4:25,26
be killed; and * days later I will Lk 9:22
We'll put up * shelters—one for Lk 9:33
"Now which of these * would you Lk 10:36
to borrow * loaves of bread. Lk 11:5,6
be split apart, * in favor of me, Lk 12:52
'I've waited * years and there Lk 13:7
you will deny me * times, declaring Lk 22:34
you will deny me * times." Lk 22:61
There all * were Lk 23:32,33
for * hours, until three o'clock. Lk 23:44
for three hours, until * o'clock. Lk 23:44
happened * days ago— some women Lk 24:21
in * days I will raise it up!" Jn 2:19
and you can do it in * days?" Jn 2:20
They were * or four miles out Jn 6:18,19
"Die for me? No—* times before the Jn 13:38
* o'clock daily prayer meeting. Act 3:1
About * hours later his wife came Act 5:7
His parents hid him at home for * Act 7:20
and was there * days, blind, going Act 9:8,9
was about * o'clock—and in this Act 10:3
The same vision was repeated * Act 10:16
him, "* men have come to see you. Act 10:19
back to life again * days later and Act 10:40,41
"This happened * times before Act 11:10
Just then * men who had come to Act 11:11
to preach, and for * Sabbaths in a Act 17:2
for * months, telling what Act 19:8
He was in Greece * months and Act 20:3
fell * stories to his death below. Act 20:9
Remember the * years I was with Act 20:31
* DAYS AFTER Festus arrived in Act 25:1
courteously and fed us for * days. Act 28:7
It was * months after the Act 28:11
Syracuse, where we stayed * days. Act 28:12
Others joined us at The * Taverns Act 28:15
by a soldier. * days after his Act 28:17
There are * things that 1Co 13:13
No more than two or * should 1Co 14:27
Two or * may prophesy, one at a 1Co 14:29,30
buried, and that * days afterwards 1Co 15:4
* times I was beaten with rods. 2Co 11:25
Once I was stoned. * times I was 2Co 11:25
prick my pride. * different times 2Co 12:8
us that if two or * have seen a 2Co 13:1
It was not until * years later Gal 1:18
two or * witnesses to accuse him. 1Ti 5:19
Think over these * 2Ti 2:7
two or * witnesses to his sin. Heb 10:28
for * months, and were not afraid. Heb 11:23
for the next * and one half years! Jas 5:17
So we have these * witnesses: the 1Jn 5:6,7,8
lived with him for * years, and Rev 1:13f
$20, or * pounds of barley flour, Rev 6:6
a denarius, and * choenix of barley Rev 6:6f
happen when the * remaining angels Rev 8:13
fall during the * and a half years Rev 11:6
When they complete the * and a Rev 11:7
and for * and a half days their Rev 11:8,9
But after * and a half days, the Rev 11:11
Dragon, for * and a half years. Rev 12:14
And I saw * evil spirits Rev 16:13
split into * sections, and cities Rev 16:19
There were * gates on each Rev 21:13

THREE-DAY
We must take a * trip into the Ex 8:27

THREE-INCH
hollow, with * walls. Jer 52:21

THREE-MONTH
A * inter-regnum by his son Jer 36:30f

THREE-PRONGED
would put a * fleshhook into the 1Sa 2:13,14

THREE-QUART
And when they poured it into a * Ex 16:18

THREE-YEAR
ABIJAM BEGAN HIS * reign as king 1Ki 15:1
during their * training period, Dan 1:5
When the * training period was Dan 1:18,19

THREE-YEAR-OLD
told him to take a * heifer, a Gen 15:9
heifer, a * female goat, a Gen 15:9
female goat, a * ram, a turtle-dove Gen 15:9
along with a * bull for the 1Sa 1:24

THRESH
He doesn't * all grains the Is 28:27
Rise, *, O daughter of Zion; Mic 4:13

THRESHED
after the grain is * and the grapes Deu 16:13
O my people, * and winnowed, I Is 21:10
For they have * my people in Amo 1:3
as grain is * with iron rods. Amo 1:3

THRESHING
(meaning "* Place of Gen 50:10
offering from your * floor, and Num 15:19,20,21
your own * floor and wine press. Num 18:30
Joash's son, Gideon, had been * Ju 6:11
some wool on the * floor tonight, Ju 6:37
at Keilah robbing the * floors. 1Sa 23:1
But when they arrived at the * 2Sa 6:6
He was by the * floor of Araunah 2Sa 24:16
* floor of Araunah the Jebusite." 2Sa 24:18
And David replied, "To buy your * 2Sa 24:21
you can use the * instruments and 2Sa 24:22
for the * floor and the oxen. 2Sa 24:24
on the * floor near the city gate. 1Ki 22:10
who was * wheat at the time. 1Ch 21:19,20
use the * instruments for wood 1Ch 21:23
from his great * floor that reaches Is 27:12
with a stick. A * wheel is never Is 28:27
and sharp-toothed * instrument to Is 41:15
is like the wheat upon a * floor; Jer 51:33
to other gods on every * floor. Hos 9:1
of spring. The * floors will pile Joe 2:24
* floor, helpless before Israel. Mic 4:12
Those who do the plowing and * 1Co 9:10

THRESHING-FLOOR
barley tonight out on the *. Ru 3:2
go on down to the *, but don't let Ru 3:3
So she went down to the * that Ru 3:6,7
that a woman was here at the *." Ru 3:14
But as they arrived at the * of 1Ch 13:9
by the * of Ornan the Jebusite. 1Ch 21:15
at the * of Ornan the Jebusite. 1Ch 21:18
So he left the * and bowed to the 1Ch 21:21
this * from you at its full price; 1Ch 21:22
here at Ornan's * is the place 1Ch 22:1
* of Ornan the Jebusite had been. 2Ch 3:1
to bring in the grain from the *? Job 39:12

THRESHOLD
with her hands digging into the *. Ju 19:27
will walk on the * of the temple of 1Sa 5:5
Literally, "above the * of Eze 9:3f

THRESHOLDS
beams, doors, and * throughout the 2Ch 3:7

THREW
Then Abraham * himself down in Gen 17:17
robe, and * him into an empty Gen 37:24
was furious. He * Joseph into Gen 39:20
So he * them all into jail for Gen 42:17
JOSEPH * HIMSELF upon his father's Gen 50:1
So he * it down—and it became a Ex 4:3
son's penis, and * it against Ex 4:25,26
them—Aaron * down his rod before Ex 7:10
Then Moses * the blood from the Ex 24:8
terrible anger he * the tablets to Ex 32:19
I * them into the fire, and . Ex 32:24
Literally, "Moses * the blood Lev 8:24f
fine dust, and * it into the stream Deu 9:21
of their land and * them away into Deu 29:28
* it in front of the city gate. Jos 8:29
Then the Lord * them into a Jos 10:10
Then the Lord * the enemy into a Ju 4:15
on the roof * down a millstone. Ju 9:53
marriage, Samson * a party for Ju 14:10,11
so he * her across the donkey's Ju 19:28
who * down a millstone on him?' 2Sa 11:19,20,21
Saul's family. He * stones at the 2Sa 16:6
They * Absalom's body into a 2Sa 18:17
a field and * a garment over him. 2Sa 20:12
Sheba's head and * it out to Joab. 2Sa 20:22
Elijah went over to him and * his 1Ki 19:19
the city well and * the salt in and 2Ki 2:21
They destroyed the cities, * 2Ki 3:25
Elisha said. He * it into the 2Ki 4:41
a stick and * it into the water; 2Ki 6:6
So they * her out the window, and 2Ki 9:33
so they hastily * his body into the 2Ki 13:20,21
it to dust and * the dust on the 2Ki 23:6
this that he * him into jail. 2Ch 16:10
and * them into Kidron Brook. 2Ch 30:14
against you. They * away your law, Neh 9:26
was very upset and * out all of his Neh 13:8
To celebrate the occasion, he * Est 2:18
their robes and * dust into the air Job 2:12
to the wind. I * them away like Ps 18:42
and * their bodies into a cistern. Jer 41:7
They * me in a well and capped Lam 3:53
of her fall, for I * her down to Eze 31:16
with ropes and * them into the Dan 3:21
the soldiers as they * them in! Dan 3:22
And then they * him in. Dan 6:16
gods for help and * the cargo Jon 1:5
Then they picked up Jonah and * Jon 1:15
You * me into the ocean depths; Jon 2:3
So I took the thirty coins and * Zec 11:13
mother were, they * themselves down Mt 2:11
and * their garments over the colt Mt 21:7
And some in the crowd * down Mt 21:8
Then he * the money onto the Mt 27:5
the soldiers * dice to divide up Mt 27:35
And the robbers also * the same Mt 27:44
and the disciples * their cloaks Mk 11:7
him, while others * down leafy Mk 11:8
* his body out of the vineyard. Mk 12:8
'The Rock the builders * away Mk 12:10
him—and * dice for his clothes. Mk 15:24
The demon * the man to the Lk 4:35
* him into a violent convulsion. Lk 9:42
colt to Jesus and * some of their Lk 19:35
And they * all sorts of other Lk 22:65
And they * him out. Jn 9:34
Literally, "cast lots," or, "* Act 1:26f
They yelled and * their coats Act 22:23
The following day they * out the Act 27:19
the coast, they * out four anchors Act 27:29
who sinned, but * them into hell, 2Pe 2:4
and * it down upon the earth; Rev 8:5
thrones before God * themselves Rev 11:16
a millstone and * it into the ocean Rev 18:21
1,000 years, and * him into the Rev 20:3

THRICE
brandish it twice, *, to symbolize Eze 21:14

THRILL
Yes, my heart will * to your Pro 23:15,16
your hearts will *, for merchants Is 60:5

THRIVE
made room for us and we shall *." Gen 26:22
For your lands will * with Is 32:13
They shall * like watered grass, Is 44:4
* like a plant in the field!' Eze 16:6,7
the vine began so well, will it *? Eze 17:10
will * as generations pass. Joe 3:20

THRIVING
and raised a * crop of sins. Hos 10:13

THROAT
exhausted; my * is dry and hoarse; Ps 69:3
and grabbed him by the * and Mt 18:28
Literally, "Their * is an open Rom 3:13f

THRONE
a new king came to the * of Egypt Ex 1:8
heir to his *, to the oldest child Ex 11:5
and sits upon his * as king, then Deu 17:18
will then follow him upon the *. Deu 17:20
sons upon your * and I will make 2Sa 7:12
you stole his * and now the Lord 2Sa 16:7,8
king and would sit upon your *? 1Ki 1:13
king and would sit upon your *. 1Ki 1:17
have selected to sit upon your *? 1Ki 1:24
shall sit upon my *, just as I 1Ki 1:30
him upon my * as the new king; 1Ki 1:35
Solomon is sitting on the *, and 1Ki 1:46,47
to sit upon my * while I am still 1Ki 1:48
The king stood up from his * as 1Ki 2:19
He ordered that a * for his 1Ki 2:19
has given me the * of my father 1Ki 2:23,24
always sit upon this *." 1Ki 2:45
your *, shall build me a Temple.' 1Ki 5:5
There was also the * Room or 1Ki 7:7
always sit upon the * of Israel. 1Ki 8:25
always be upon the * of Israel.' 1Ki 9:5
and set you on the * of Israel. 1Ki 10:9
He also made a huge ivory * and 1Ki 10:18
There was no other * in all the 1Ki 10:20
And I will place you on the * of 1Ki 11:37
he died, his son Nadab took the *. 1Ki 14:20

(THRONE Con't)
and he was on the * seventeen years 1Ki 14:21
and his son Abijam took the *. 1Ki 14:31
had been on the * thirty-one years 1Ki 16:23
had been on the * thirty-eight 1Ki 16:29
I saw the Lord sitting on his *, 1Ki 22:19
he ascended the *, and he reigned 1Ki 22:42
and his son Jehoram took the *. 1Ki 22:50
and prepare to fight for his *. 2Ki 10:2,3
And he sat upon the king's *. 2Ki 11:19
He came to the * in the 2Ki 13:9,10
assassinated him and took the *. 2Ki 15:14
and he took the * for himself. 2Ki 15:30
on your * high above the angels, 2Ki 19:15
Amon's son Josiah upon the *. 2Ki 21:24
city of Masrekah came to the *. 1Ch 1:47
one of your sons upon your *; 1Ch 17:11
down from the * and appointed his 1Ch 23:1
on the * of his Kingdom of Israel. 1Ch 28:5
to take the * of his father David; 1Ch 29:23
He also made a huge ivory * 2Ch 9:17
No other * in all the world could 2Ch 9:19
"I saw him upon his * surrounded 2Ch 18:18
one of his descendants upon the *. 2Ch 21:7
and seated the king upon his *. 2Ch 23:20
years old when he ascended the *. 2Ch 36:9
until King Darius took the *. Ez 4:4,5
king was sitting upon his royal *. Est 5:1
to his * and talk with him there. Job 23:3
He shrouds his * with his Job 26:9
heavens and knock God from his *? Job 35:6
from your * that it is good. Ps 9:4
Literally, "You sit on the *, Ps 9:4f
he sits upon his * to judge Ps 9:7,8
You welcomed him to the * with Ps 21:3
of our fathers surrounded your *; Ps 22:3,4
Your *, O God, endures forever. Ps 45:6
nations, sitting on his holy *. Ps 47:8
pick on me at a time when my * Ps 62:3,4
to try to force me from the *. Ps 62:3,4
his *, from now until eternity!" Ps 89:3,4
Your * is founded on two strong Ps 89:14,15
have an heir; his * will be as Ps 89:29
forever, and his * will continue to Ps 89:35,36
Literally, "his * as the sun Ps 89:35,36f
his splendor and overturned his *. Ps 89:44
The world is his *. Ps 93:1
your * is established." Ps 93:1f
are the foundation of his *. Ps 97:2
Lord has made the heavens his *; Ps 103:19
Jehovah has established your * Ps 110:2
would sit on my * and succeed me. Ps 132:11
Literally, "for the * is Pro 16:12f
even to help him usurp the *. Ecc 4:15
stands up from his * to shake up Is 2:19
He was sitting on a lofty *, and Is 6:1
from the * of his father David. Is 9:7
I will take the highest *. Is 14:13
from ever sitting on his *. Is 14:22
establish David's * forever, and on Is 16:4,5
and on that * he will place a just Is 16:4,5
will mount his * in Zion and rule Is 24:23
HEAVEN IS MY * and the earth is my Is 66:1
be known as the * of the Lord, and Jer 3:17
sitting on David's *, and the Jer 13:13
yourself and the * of your glory by Jer 14:21
But our refuge is your *, Jer 17:12
on the * here in Jerusalem; Jer 17:25
of Judah, sitting on David's *; Jer 22:2
to sit on David's *, and there Jer 22:4
Josiah on the *: His family will Jer 22:18
"The Lord will establish my *!" Jer 22:24,25f
the * of David or rule in Judah. Jer 22:30
Branch upon King David's *. Jer 23:5,6
sits on David's *—and make them Jer 29:16,17
I will bring to the * the true Son Jer 33:15
heir sitting on the * of Israel. Jer 33:17
have a son to reign upon his *; Jer 33:20,21
"sitting on the *" under the Jer 36:30f
upon the * of David. Jer 36:30
I will set his * upon these Jer 43:10
And I will set my * in Elam, Jer 49:38
the same! Your * continues from Lam 5:19
what looked like a * made of Eze 1:26
SUDDENLY A * of beautiful blue Eze 10:1
sitting on the * of a god on your Eze 28:2,3
is the place of my *, and my Eze 43:7
him from his royal * and took away Dan 5:20
He sat upon a fiery * brought in Dan 7:9
beside the * and asked him the Dan 7:16
the Egyptian * and declared war Dan 11:7f
down from his * and laid aside his Jon 3:6
He leaves his * in heaven and Mic 1:3
sons will never sit upon your *. Nah 1:14
God, for the heavens are God's *. Mt 5:34
shall sit upon my glorious * in Mt 19:28
the * of God and by God himself. Mt 23:22
I shall sit upon my * of glory. Mt 25:31
him the * of his ancestor David. Lk 1:32
sit on David's *. Act 2:30
"And now he sits on the * of Act 2:33
'The heaven is my *,' says the Act 7:48,49
his * and made a speech to them. Act 12:21
boldly to the very * of God and Heb 4:16
place of honor by the * of God. Heb 12:2
before his *; Rev 1:4
city where Satan's * is, at the Rev 2:13
beside me on my *, just as I took Rev 3:21
on his * when I had conquered. Rev 3:21
it!—a * and someone sitting on it! Rev 4:2
like an emerald encircled his *. Rev 4:3
issued from the *, and there were Rev 4:5
Directly in front of his * were Rev 4:5
one sitting on the *, who lives Rev 4:9
crowns before the *, singing, "O Rev 4:10
was sitting on the *, a scroll with Rev 5:1
in front of the * and the Living Rev 5:6
of the one sitting upon the *. Rev 5:7
surrounding the * and the Living Rev 5:11
one sitting on the *, and to the Rev 5:13
one sitting on the *, and from the Rev 6:16
in front of the * and before the Rev 7:9
upon the *, and from the Lamb." Rev 7:10
around the * and around the Elders Rev 7:11
before the * and worshiping God. Rev 7:11
here before the * of God, serving Rev 7:15
The one sitting on the * will Rev 7:15
"in the center of the *"; Rev 7:17f
be, "at the heart of the *." Rev 7:17f
the * will feed them and be their Rev 7:17
the golden altar before the *. Rev 8:3
stands before the * of God, saying Rev 9:13
was caught up to God and to his *. Rev 12:5
power and * and great authority. Rev 13:2
in front of the * of God and before Rev 14:3
* of the Creature from the sea, Rev 16:10
came from the * of the temple in Rev 16:17
She boasts, 'I am queen upon my * Rev 18:7
upon the *, and said, "Amen! Rev 19:4
And out of the * came a voice Rev 19:5
And I saw a great white * and the Rev 20:11
I heard a loud shout from the * Rev 21:3
And the one sitting on the * Rev 21:5
flowing from the * of God and the Rev 22:1
for the * of God and of the Lamb Rev 22:3

THRONE'S
eyes, stood at the * four sides. Rev 4:6

THRONES
were sitting on * placed on the 1Ki 22:10
The two kings were sitting on * 2Ch 18:9
them upon eternal, kingly *. Job 36:7
They shall sit on * around the Ps 45:16
and set their * at the gates of the Jer 1:15
Come down from your * and sit in Jer 13:18
down from their * and lay aside Eze 26:16
kings and sets others on their *. Dan 2:21
I watched as * were put in place Dan 7:9
and to overthrow * and destroy the Hag 2:22
sit on twelve * judging the twelve Mt 19:28
you let my two sons sit on two * Mt 20:21
right to say who will sit on the * Mt 20:23
"We want to sit on the * next to Mk 10:37
to place you on * next to mine. Mk 10:40
He has torn princes from their * Lk 1:52
and you will sit on * judging the Lk 22:30
on your *, leaving us far behind! 1Co 4:8
already on your *, for when that 1Co 4:8
Twenty-four smaller * surrounded Rev 4:4
sitting on their * before God threw Rev 11:16
Then I saw *, and sitting on them Rev 20:4

THRONGED
JERUSALEM'S STREETS, ONCE * Lam 1:1
Then the men * to Daniel's house Dan 6:11
with him, and the crowd * behind. Mk 5:24

THRONGS
surrounded by vast * of angels. 2Ch 18:18
up, and all her drunken *. Is 5:14
filled with joyous * who come to Lam 1:4
as a result, such * soon Mk 1:45

THROUGHOUT
plants * the earth, and all the Gen 1:29
and construct decks and stalls * Gen 6:14
So also * the remainder of the Gen 11:12,13f
* all the land of Egypt; Gen 41:29
What you say goes, * all the land Gen 41:40
So Joseph became famous * the Gen 41:45
the crops grown * Egypt, storing Gen 41:48
the terrible famine * the land. Gen 43:1
His sobs could be heard * the Gen 45:2
So Joseph made it a law * the Gen 47:26
their descendants * Israel. Gen 49:7
to be used * all generations. Ex 3:15
and there was blood * the land of Ex 7:21
a terrible stench * the land. Ex 8:14
lice, * all the land of Egypt." Ex 8:16
will send swarms of flies * Egypt. Ex 8:21
and animals alike, * the land." Ex 9:9
men and animals alike * all Egypt. Ex 9:10
the hail to fall * all Egypt, upon Ex 9:22
a plant * all the land of Egypt. Ex 10:15
The wail of death will resound * Ex 11:6
and there was bitter crying * all Ex 12:30
firstborn males * the land of Ex 13:
nor barrenness * your land, and you Ex 23:2
So Moses sent a message * the Ex 36:4
which was used * the Tabernacle. Ex 38:2
This continued * all their Ex 40:3
This is a permanent law * your Lev 3:
it is their right forever * all Lev 7:3
This is a permanent law * your Lev 23:1
blow loud and long * the land. Lev 25
proclaim liberty * the land to all Lev 25:1
"* that time he must never cut Num 6:
to the Lord * the entire period. Num 6:
and stayed that way * the night. Num 9:1
What sorrow there was * the camp Num 14:3
men * Israel was 601,730. Num 26:5
offering each month * the year. Num 28:1
The girls * the tribes of Israel Num 36:
I will make people * the whole Deu 2:2
their children * all generations! Deu 5:2
upon it, day after day * the year! Deu 11:1
in any village * your land violates Deu 17:2,
Israel obeyed the Lord * the Jos 24:3
true to the Lord * Joshua's Ju 2:7-
from their enemies * his lifetime, Ju 2:1
He also sent messengers * Ju 6:3
Gideon also sent messengers * Ju 7:2
sent the pieces * the land of Ju 20:
There was deep sadness * all Ju 21:
He judges * the earth. 1Sa 2:1
a great cry arose * the city. 1Sa 4:1
was against them * the remainder of 1Sa 7:1
to carry them * all Israel. 1Sa 11:
What joy there was * the city 1Sa 11:
The news spread quickly * the 1Sa 13:3,
sounded the call to arms * Israel. 1Sa 13:3,
Suddenly panic broke out * the 1Sa 14:1
the Philistines * Saul's lifetime. 1Sa 14:52
became very famous * the land. 1Sa 18:3
and you will never do wrong * 1Sa 25:28
and to the people * their land. 1Sa 31:9
that it be sung * Israel. 2Sa 1:17,18
So Michal was childless * her 2Sa 6:23
placed garrisons * Edom, so that 2Sa 8:14
There was deep sadness * the city 2Sa 15:23
as the news spread * the city that 2Sa 19:8,9,10
and seventy thousand men died * 2Sa 24:15
spread quickly * the entire nation, 1Ki 3:28
to serve him * his lifetime. 1Ki 4:21
And there was peace * the land. 1Ki 4:24
* the lifetime of Solomon, all of 1Ki 4:25
Narrow windows were used *. 1Ki 6:4
sixty feet long. * the Temple the 1Ki 6:18
and elsewhere * the land. 1Ki 9:19
And there was mourning for him * 1Ki 14:18
There was homosexuality * the 1Ki 14:24
He sent messengers * all Israel 2Ki 10:20,21
altars to other gods * the land. 2Ki 17:9
* Judah and even in Jerusalem. 2Ki 23:5
both in Jerusalem and * the land. 2Ki 23:24
of Bashan) and * the entire pasture 1Ch 5:16
then they displayed them * the 1Ch 10:9
for joy had spread * the land. 1Ch 12:40
to our brothers * the land of 1Ch 13:2
His authority is seen * the earth. 1Ch 16:14
"Take a complete census * the 1Ch 21:2
famous and glorious * the world; 1Ch 22:5
treasuries * the cities, villages, 1Ch 27:25
and thresholds * the Temple were 2Ch 3:7
Lebanon and * the entire realm. 2Ch 8:6
fortified cities * the land of 2Ch 11:23
to build walled cities * Judah. 2Ch 14:6
And he gave them peace * the 2Ch 15:15
perfect before God * his lifetime. 2Ch 15:17
other places * the country, and in 2Ch 17:2
and supply cities * Judah. 2Ch 17:12
the fortified cities * the nation. 2Ch 17:19
of the shame-idols * the land, and 2Ch 19:3
He appointed judges * the nation 2Ch 19:5
of Judah and * Jerusalem telling 2Ch 24:9
by the trumpets. * the entire 2Ch 29:28
KING HEZEKIAH NOW sent letters * 2Ch 30:1
proclamation * Israel, from Dan to 2Ch 30:5
from city to city * Ephraim and 2Ch 30:10
the distribution * all Judah, doing 2Ch 31:20
And now there was peace at last * 2Ch 32:22
He did this everywhere * the 2Ch 34:7
their God. And * the remainder of 2Ch 34:33
this proclamation * his kingdom, 2Ch 36:22,23
this proclamation * his empire (he Ez 1:1
All Jews * the kingdom may now Ez 1:3
Samaria, and * the neighboring Ez 4:10
in Samaria and * the area west of Ez 4:17
There was great joy * the land Ez 6:21,22
Then a proclamation was made * Ez 10:7,8
houses were scattered * the city. Neh 7:4
own towns and villages * Judah. Neh 7:73
should be made * the cities of the Neh 8:15
all the Levites * the land came to Neh 12:27
of us officials * your empire will Est 1:18
contempt and anger * your realm. Est 1:18
When this decree is published * Est 1:20

HROUGHOUT Con't)
* the whole kingdom of Ahasuerus. Est 3:5,6
and officials * the empire, to each Est 3:12
clothes. And * all the provinces Est 4:3
the Jews * the king's provinces. Est 8:5
The day chosen for this * all Est 8:12
in their cities * all the king's Est 9:1
his fame was known * all the Est 9:4
Meanwhile, the other Jews * the Est 9:16
take their goods. * the provinces Est 9:17
unwalled villages * Israel to this Est 9:19
Jews near and far, * all the king's Est 9:20
All the Jews * the realm Est 9:27
by every family * the countryside Est 9:28
to all the Jews * the 127 provinces Est 9:29-31
is always in trouble * his life. Job 15:20
for he looks * the whole earth, Job 28:23,24
with prosperity * their lives. Job 36:11
whatever he commands * the earth. Job 37:12
limbs, and * his enormous frame. Job 41:12
vileness is praised * the land. Ps 12:8
causes wars to end * the earth, Ps 46:9
Your name is known * the earth, Ps 48:10
you have scattered * the world. Ps 48:10
I will thank you publicly * the Ps 57:9
May your glory shine * the earth. Ps 57:11
Israel and will reign * the world. Ps 59:12,13
of all mankind * the world and far Ps 65:5
How everyone * the earth will Ps 67:3
Bless us with abundant crops * Ps 72:16
helping me everywhere * the land. Ps 74:12
Publish his glorious acts * the Ps 96:3
He gives justice * Israel. Ps 99:4
his praises were sung * the city; Ps 102:21,22
and many rulers * the earth came Ps 102:21,22
is seen everywhere * the land. Ps 105:7
He does whatever pleases him * Ps 135:6
He makes mists rise * the earth Ps 135:7
all that goes on * her household, Pro 31:27
most men have * their lives. Ecc 2:3
Moreover, I notice that * the Ecc 3:16
and sadness * the earth—the tears Ecc 4:1
the evil and crime * the earth. Ecc 4:3
* the land, don't be surprised! Ecc 5:8
Again I looked * the earth and Ecc 9:11
of smoke and cloud * the day, and Is 4:5
its gates are battered down. * Is 24:13
Or possibly, "* the nations of Is 24:13f
prevail * the earth, nor until even Is 42:4
* the skies and made the earth. Is 51:13
respected and admired * the earth. Is 62:6,7
to sound the alarm * the land. Jer 4:5
they are doing * the cities of Jer 7:17
from city to city * the land and Jer 11:6
windows, paneled * with fragrant Jer 22:14
to prevail everywhere * the earth. Jer 23:5,6
Or, "* the land." Jer 23:5,6f
to Babylon. But * the land of Jer 39:10
and * southern Egypt as well: Jer 44:1
exiled to countries * the world. Jer 49:36
and so also eighty-seven times * Eze 2:1f
I will make a clean sweep * the Eze 21:4
I will scatter you * the world Eze 22:15
your population * all Israel, and Eze 36:10
ruined by my people * the world. Eze 36:21
and so also * this passage. Dan 11:6f
strongholds * his dominions, but Dan 11:24
my fruit to you * the year. Hos 14:8
* the generations of the world! Joe 2:2
and publish it * all Israel," says Amo 3:13
sent this message * the city: "Let Jon 3:7
each in his own land * the world. Zep 2:11
everywhere * the land." Zec 5:6
of idol worship * the land, so that Zec 13:2
spread quickly * the city, and soon Mt 14:35
will be preached * the whole world, Mt 24:14
done will be told * the whole Mt 26:13
So he traveled * the province of Mk 1:39
at once, and ran * the whole area Mk 6:55
News is preached * the world, this Mk 14:9
should be taken * the nation. Lk 2:1
Soon he became well known * all Lk 4:14
like wildfire * the whole region. Lk 4:37
preaching in synagogues * Judea. Lk 4:44
in Jerusalem, * Judea, in Samaria, Act 1:8
Meanwhile, the church had peace * Act 9:31
of all he did * Israel and in Act 10:39
And there was great joy * the Act 15:31
he saw everywhere * the city. Act 17:16
but * the entire province! Act 19:26
worshiped not only * this part of Act 19:27
inciting the Jews * the entire Act 24:5
His sin spread death * all the Rom 5:12
there in Corinth and * Greece. 2Co 1:1
Or, "* Achaia." 2Co 1:1f
brothers * your whole nation. 1Th 4:10
and scattered * Pontus, Galatia, 1Pe 1:1
there was silence * all heaven for Rev 8:1
and language groups * the world. Rev 13:7
with her, and businessmen * the Rev 18:3

THROW
"we'll shed no blood—let's * him Gen 37:21,22
of his people to * the newborn Ex 1:22
"* it down on the ground," the Ex 4:3
when he does, Aaron is to * down Ex 7:9
* you out of the country. Ex 11:1
him a tree to * into the water, and Ex 15:25
the feathers and * them on the east Lev 1:15,16,17
Then Aaron's sons shall * the Lev 3:2
the priests shall * the blood Lev 3:7,8
The priest shall * its blood Lev 3:13
and will * them out of the land. Lev 18:25
things or I will * you out of the Lev 18:28
of the land, just as I will * out Lev 18:28
not * you out of your new land. Lev 20:22
they will * their light forward." Num 8:2
and * them into the burning pile. Num 19:6
You will also be able to * out Deu 6:19
The witnesses shall * the first Deu 17:7
and then I will * the sacred dice Jos 18:5,6
by the * of the sacred dice. Jos 18:8
for everyone to * in the gold Ju 8:25
he demanded. "* away your 1Sa 1:14
and demanded, "* this woman out 2Sa 13:17,18
* his head over the wall to you." 2Sa 20:21
his assistant, "* him into the 2Ki 9:25
and his sons.' So * him out on 2Ki 9:26
"* her down!" 2Ki 9:33
he will permanently * you aside. 1Ch 28:9
For they have come to * us out of 2Ch 20:11
determined by a * of the dice; Est 9:24,25
for money, and * your gold away, Job 22:24
and effect. You * me into the Job 30:22
are ready to * me to the ground. Ps 17:11
the scum you skim off and * away; Ps 119:119
with a net to * over and hold me Ps 140:5
their heads, or * them into the Ps 140:10
Come on, * in your lot with us; Pro 1:14
* out the mocker, and you will be Pro 22:10
Judah and * her people into panic. Is 7:6
one of you will * away his golden Is 31:7
Tremble, O women of ease; * off Is 32:11
you and will not * you away. Is 41:9
will say, "Don't * them all Is 65:8
Therefore I will * you out of Jer 16:13
beams and * them on the fire. Jer 22:7
I will * you and your mother out Jer 22:26
the section and * it into the fire, Jer 36:23
a rock to it and * it into the Jer 51:63
in sackcloth; they * dust upon Lam 2:10
then take a few hairs out and * Eze 5:4
"* away your money! Eze 7:19
I will * my net over him and he Eze 17:20
and * them into the fire. Dan 3:20
we * three men into the furnace?" Dan 3:24
Daniel, and * them into the den Dan 6:24
But as she flies, I * my net Hos 7:12
"* me out into the sea," he Jon 1:12
you will * them into the depths Mic 7:19
on the anvil and * them away." Zec 1:21
offer me, and * you out like dung. Mal 2:3
lust, gouge it out and * it away. Mt 5:29
to sin, cut it off and * it away. Mt 5:30
who are evil, and * them into the Mt 13:42
and * it to the dogs," he said. Mt 15:26
to the shore and * in a line, and Mt 17:26,27
to sin, cut it off and * it away. Mt 18:8
sin, gouge it out and * it away. Mt 18:9
hand and foot and * him out into Mt 22:13
from him. And * the useless Mt 25:30
food and * it to the dogs." Mk 7:27
Only those who * away their lives Mk 8:35
perhaps a stone's *, and knelt down Lk 22:41,42
never sinned may * the first!" Jn 8:7
"Let's * dice to see who gets Jn 19:23,24
Then he said, "* out your net on Jn 21:6
we'll really * the book at them." Act 4:17
and * out all of Moses' laws." Act 6:14
and another to * garbage into? Rom 9:21
Now are you going to just * it Gal 3:4
himself, then * off your old evil Eph 4:22
to cast off and * away all these Col 3:8
Put these abilities to work; * 1Ti 4:15
devil will soon * some of you into Rev 2:10
to each other and * parties to Rev 11:10
And they will * dust on their Rev 18:19

THROWING
out of hatred by * something at Num 35:20
was decided by * dice before the Jos 14:1
gods again, * themselves to the Ju 2:19
as he went and * stones at David 2Sa 16:13
in * off the yoke of Judah. 2Ch 21:10
action was determined by * dice. Est 3:7
"* dice" in Persian is "pur." Est 9:26
written a letter * her full support Est 9:29-31
new shirt and * away the old one! Ps 102:26
is like a madman * around Pro 26:18,19
A time for * away; Ecc 3:6
Probably by * dice or something Lk 1:8,9f
in sackcloth and * ashes on their Lk 10:13
clothing, * dice for each piece. Lk 23:34
crew began * the cargo overboard. Act 27:18
by * all the wheat overboard. Act 27:38

THROWN
loss of the rights he had * away. Gen 25:34
He has * both horse and rider into Ex 15:1
material must be * into a defiled Lev 14:40
which something is * Num 35:22,23
which a stone is * without anger, Num 35:22,23
be taken down and * into the cave Jos 10:27
Now the Lord has * us away and Ju 6:13
and they were * into confusion, and 1Sa 7:10
that Nabal had * a big party. 1Sa 25:36
his troops will be * into a panic 2Sa 17:2,3
are as thorns to be * away, 2Sa 23:6
the Jordan River—* away by the 2Ki 7:15
had done that were * out of the 2Ki 21:1
For the people of Judah have * 2Ki 22:17
top of a cliff and * over, so that 2Ch 25:12
nations that were * out of the land 2Ch 28:3
all the utensils * away by King 2Ch 29:19
God has * me into the mud. Job 30:19
They are * down and will not rise Ps 36:12
O Jehovah, why have you * my Ps 88:14
For you have * his crown in the Ps 89:39
For you have rejected me and * me Ps 102:9,10
Lord, have you * us away? Ps 108:11
for they have * away the laws of Is 5:24
be * as refuse in the streets. Is 5:25
is * out like a broken branch; Is 14:19
and * their gods into the fire; Is 37:19
Whenever you have * away your Is 43:12
bodies shall be * out into the Jer 14:16
of Jerusalem and * on the garbage Jer 22:19
His dead body shall be * out to Jer 36:30
Let her be * out like filthy Lam 1:17
in fury and * down to the ground. Eze 19:12
mountains shall be * down; Eze 38:20
be * into a flaming furnace." Dan 3:6
will be * into a flaming furnace. Dan 3:11
But if you refuse, you will be * Dan 3:15
If we are * into the flaming Dan 3:17
Majesty—shall be * to the lions. Dan 6:7
And anyone disobeying will be * Dan 6:12
ground when * or allowed to fall. Hos 4:12f
Israel has * away her chance with Hos 8:3
And you yourselves will be * out Mt 5:13
court and you are * into a debtor's Mt 5:25
chopped down and * on the fire. Mt 7:19
your neck and be * into the sea. Mt 18:6
authority he had * out the Mt 21:23
neck and he were * into the sea. Mk 9:42
one hand than be * into the Mk 9:43,44
down and * into the fire." Lk 3:9
It is worthless and must be * Lk 14:35
If he were * into the sea with a Lk 17:2,3
from me, he is * away like a Jn 15:6
and afterwards they were * into Act 16:23
I've * them all away so that I can Php 3:7
And he saved me from being * to 2Ti 4:17
You suffered with those * into Heb 10:34
blood were * down upon the earth. Rev 8:7
mountain was * into the sea, Rev 8:8,9
whole world—was * down onto the Rev 12:9
brothers has been * down from Rev 12:10
temple in heaven was * wide open! Rev 15:5
city, shall be * away as I have Rev 18:21
away as I have * away this stone, Rev 18:21
False Prophet—were * alive into the Rev 19:20
be * into the Lake of Fire Rev 20:10
And Death and Hell were * into Rev 20:14
he was * into the Lake of Fire. Rev 20:15

THROWS
into crates and * the others away. Mt 13:47,48
and it * him into convulsions so Lk 9:39

THRUST
taken the girl. He * the spear all Num 25:8
for the Lord will * you away. Deu 28:37
by the hair and * his sword into 2Sa 2:16
You have * me down to the darkest Ps 88:6
And they will be * out into the Is 8:22

THRUSTS
He * out your enemies before you; Deu 33:27

THUMB
right ear and the * of his right Lev 8:23
and upon the * of his right hand, Lev 14:14
right ear and the * of his right Lev 14:17
upon the * of his right hand and on Lev 14:25
ear, and upon the * of his right Lev 14:28

THUMBING
into idolatry, * their noses at me Eze 8:17

THUMBNAIL
A * sketch of King Jehoshaphat: 2Ch 20:31

THUMBS
upon their right * and the big toes Ex 29:19,20
upon their right *, and upon the Lev 8:24
and cut off his * and big toes. Ju 1:4,5,6
Our princes are hanged by their *. Lam 5:12

THUMMIM
of the chestpiece the Urim and *, Ex 28:30,31
and deposited the Urim and the * Lev 8:8
Your Urim and your *. Deu 33:8
The Urim and * were holy 1Sa 28:5,6f
until the Urim and * could be Ez 2:62,63

(THUMMIM Con't)
until the Urim and * had been Neh 7:64,65

THUNDER
sent * and hail and lightning. Ex 9:23
Beg God to end this terrifying * Ex 9:28
and the * and hail will stop. Ex 9:29
the Lord, and the * and hail Ex 9:33
was a terrific * and lightning Ex 19:16
and heard the * and the long, Ex 20:18
a mighty voice of * from heaven, 1Sa 7:10
the Lord to send * and rain today, 1Sa 12:17
and the Lord sent * and rain; 1Sa 12:18
Who then can withstand his *?" Job 26:14
We feel his presence in the *. Job 36:33
Listen, listen to the * of his Job 37:2
the roaring of the *—the tremendous Job 37:4
His voice is glorious in the *. Job 37:5
He comes with the noise of *, Ps 50:3
* rolled and crackled in the sky. Ps 77:17
There was * in the whirlwind; Ps 77:18
"in the hiding place of *." Ps 81:7f
where the * hides. Ps 81:7
The mighty oceans * your praise. Ps 93:3
*, earthquake, whirlwind and fire. Is 29:6
in the * of the storm clouds. Jer 10:13
When he speaks there is * in the Jer 51:16
Jesus called them "Sons of *"), Mk 3:16-19
thought it was *, while others Jn 12:29
Lightning and * issued from the Rev 4:5
and there were voices in the *. Rev 4:5
sounded like *, said, "Come!" Rev 6:1
the earth; and * crashed and Rev 8:5
Lightning flashed and * crashed Rev 11:19
or the rolling of mighty *. Rev 14:2
Then the * crashed and rolled, Rev 16:18
of great *, "Praise the Lord. Rev 19:6

THUNDERED
Moses spoke and God * his reply. Ex 19:19
The Lord * from heaven; 2Sa 22:14
The Lord * in the heavens; Ps 18:13
THEN HE *, "Call those to whom I Eze 9:1
and his voice * like the waves Rev 1:15

THUNDERING
pour upon me like a * cataract. Ps 42:7
Look, see the armies * toward Is 17:12

THUNDERS
He * against them from heaven. 1Sa 2:10
of the clouds, and the * within? Job 36:29
The God of glory * through the Ps 29:3
The voice of the Lord * through Ps 29:7
whose mighty voice * from the sky. Ps 68:33
the seven * crashed their reply. Rev 10:3
I was about to write what the * Rev 10:4

THWARTED
and slink away, their hopes *. Ps 112:10

THWARTS
own traps; he * their schemes. Job 5:13

THY
into the house of Jehovah * God." Ex 23:19f

THYATIRA
*, a merchant of purple cloth. Act 16:14
those in Pergamos, *, Sardis, Rev 1:11
of the church in *: Rev 2:18
"As for the rest of you in * who Rev 2:24,25

TIARA
and a lovely * for your head. Eze 16:12

TIBERIAS
also known as the Sea of *. Jn 6:1
Several small boats from * were Jn 6:22,23

TIBERIUS
reign of Emperor * Caesar, a Lk 3:1

TIBHATH
Hadadezer's cities of * and Cun. 1Ch 18:8

TIBNI
followed *, the son of Ginath. 1Ki 16:21
But General Omri won and * was 1Ki 16:22

TICKET
He bought a *, went on board, and Jon 1:3

TIDAL
*, king of Goiim Gen 14:1

TIDE
Judah to turn the * of battle 2Ch 13:15,16
Though the * of battle runs Ps 55:18
for help, the * of battle turns. Ps 56:9
these rules to * them over until Heb 9:10

TIDES
We glide along the * of time as Ps 90:5,6
for her and restrained their *. Eze 31:15
by the roaring seas and strange *. Lk 21:25

TIDINGS
I rewarded him for his 'glad *.' 2Sa 4:10
and bring glad * of good things." Rom 10:15

TIE
acacia wood to * the frames Ex 36:31,32
in the morning. * them on your Deu 6:8
carefully in mind. * them to your Deu 11:18
to obey them, and * them to your Deu 11:18
Can you * him with a rope Job 41:2
and your mother. * their Pro 6:21
the scroll, * a rock to it and Jer 51:63
the hair and * it up in your robe; Eze 5:3
say, "Never * up the mouth of an 1Ti 5:18

TIED
the fire, and then * Isaac and laid Gen 22:9
His brothers were fit to be * Gen 37:11
born, the midwife * a scarlet Gen 38:28
the top, and was * down by an Ex 39:4,5
It was * to the turban with a Ex 39:31
hundred foxes and * their tails Ju 15:4
So they * him with two new ropes Ju 15:12,13
with which he was * snapped like Ju 15:14
"if I were * with seven Ju 16:7
she * him with them. Ju 16:8
as she had * him up she exclaimed, Ju 16:9
"Well," he said, "if I am * Ju 16:11
Delilah took new ropes and * him Ju 16:12
Then he * up a bushel and a half Ru 3:15-18
Your feet were not *— 2Sa 3:33,34
expensive robes, * up the money in 2Ki 5:23
* to silver rings imbedded in Est 1:6
like a stone * to a slingshot! Pro 26:8
you to have a rock * to your neck Mt 18:6
* there, with its colt beside it. Mt 21:2
just as a strong man must be * Mk 3:27
millstone were * around his neck Mk 9:42
* up that has never been ridden. Mk 11:2
in the street, * outside a house. Mk 11:4,5
with a huge rock * to his neck, he Lk 17:2,3
for a donkey * beside the road. Lk 19:30
arrested Jesus and * him. Jn 18:12
As they * Paul down to lash him, Act 22:25
you are no longer * to the law Rom 6:14
They tried to get us all * up in Gal 2:4
and don't get all * up again in the Gal 5:1
yourself become * up in worldly 2Ti 2:4

TIER
three tiers, one * above the other, 1Ki 7:3,4
other, five to a *, facing each 1Ki 7:3,4
with thirty rooms in each *. Eze 41:6
Each * was wider than the one Eze 41:7

TIERS
hall, set in three *, one tier 1Ki 7:3,4
These rooms were in three *, one Eze 41:6
Two doors opened from the * of Eze 41:11
The rooms were in three *, Eze 42:3
building and the * of rooms, Eze 42:4
The upper two * of rooms were Eze 42:5
* had wider walkways beside them. Eze 42:5
The north *, next to the outer Eze 42:7,8
of two units of * was on the south Eze 42:9,10
north and south * of rooms facing Eze 42:13

TIES
my yoke and broke away from my *. Jer 2:20
together by strong * of love, and Col 2:2

TIGHT
The doors have been shut *, the 2Ch 29:7
pride, making a * seal, so no air Job 41:15-17
drawn their arrows * against the Ps 11:2
their belts are *, their Is 5:27
locked up * to keep out looters. Is 24:10
So they bound them * with ropes Dan 3:21

TIGHTEN
Hadadezer went to * his grip along 1Ch 18:3

TIGHTLY
holding * to the "rod of God"! Ex 4:20
THE GATES OF Jericho were kept * Jos 6:1
The sinews of his thighs are * Job 40:17
Hold these virtues *. Pro 3:3
hold on too * and lose everything. Pro 11:24,25
price, and hold on * to all the Pro 23:23
Then let your lips be * closed Ecc 12:4
will be * rationed in Jerusalem. Eze 4:16
was holding * to Peter and John! Act 3:11
Cling * to your faith in Christ 1Ti 1:19
Fight on for God. Hold * to the 1Ti 6:12
Hold * to the pattern of truth I 2Ti 1:13
* around our feet and trip us up; Heb 12:1
only hold * to what you have Rev 2:24,25
Hold * to the little strength you Rev 3:11

TIGLATH-PILESER
was during his reign that King * 2Ki 15:29
messenger to King * of Assyria, 2Ki 16:7
to meet with King *, and while he 2Ki 16:10
money" to * II (2 Kings 16:7, 8). Eze 23:12f

TIGRIS
The third branch is the *, which Gen 2:14
beside the great * River, I looked Dan 10:4

TIKVAH
of Shallum—son of *, son of 2Ki 22:14
Jahzeiah (son of *), Meshullam, and Ez 10:15

TILES
him, took off some * and lowered Lk 5:18,19

TILGATH-PILNESER
captivity by King * of Assyria. 1Ch 5:6
(also known as * III) to invade the 1Ch 5:26
But when *, king of Assyria, 2Ch 28:20

TILL
I did not stop * all were gone. 2Sa 22:38
busy from morning * night offering 2Ch 35:14
How can I be patient * I die? Job 6:11
morning,' and then I toss * dawn. Job 7:4
Will your jealousy burn * every Ps 79:5
bouts that last * late at night—woe Is 5:
young donkeys that * the ground Is 30:
the Gentiles from morning * night. Mal 1:
along beside him * they came to an Lk 10:
eat nor drink * he is dead. Act 23:

TILLAGE
Literally, "the * of the Pro 21:

TILLED
You cleared the ground and * the Ps 80

TILLS
Literally, "He who * his ground Pro 12:1

TILON
Amnon, Rinnah, Ben-hanan, *. 1Ch 4:2

TILT
Who can * the water jars of Job 38:37,3

TIM
but not to teach men (1 *. 1Co 14:3

TIMAEUS
(the son of *) was sitting beside Mk 10:4

TIMBER
imbedded in the * of the wall. 1Sa 19:9,1
to cut cedar * for me, and I will 1Ki 5:
can cut * like you Sidonians!" 1Ki 5
you have asked concerning the *. 1Ki 5
apart and deliver the * to you. 1Ki 5:
cedar and cypress * as he desired, 1Ki 5:1
in cutting the * and making the 1Ki 5:1
quarrymen, * dealers, and stone 2Ki 12:11,1
I have also gathered * and stone 1Ch 22:1
blocks, *, lumber, and beams. 2Ch 34:10,1
* is being laid in the city walls. Ez 5:
topped with a layer of new *. Ez 6:
him to give me * for the beams and Neh 2:
* and even your dust into the sea. Eze 26:1
and bring down *, and rebuild my Hag 1:

TIMBERS
its stones, *, and mortar shall be Lev 14:4
to the Temple walls by cedar *. 1Ki 6:1
and haul away its stones and *. 1Ki 15:2
stones and * and used them to build 2Ch 16:

TIMBREL
a * and led the women in dances. Ex 15:2
a psaltery, a *, a flute, and a 1Sa 10:
the harp and * are heard no more; Is 24:

TIMBRELS
girls playing the * in between. Ps 68:2
and dance merrily with the *. Jer 31:4

TIME
one day (or, 'period of *')." Gen 1:4,5
second day (or, 'period of *')." Gen 1:7,8
a third day (or, 'period of *')." Gen 1:13
fourth day (or, 'period of *')." Gen 1:19
a fifth day (or, 'period of *')." Gen 1:23
a sixth day (or, 'period of *')." Gen 1:31f
The * came when the Lord God Gen 2:7
At harvest * Cain brought the Gen 4:3
It was at this * that beings from Gen 6:1
man living on the earth at that *. Gen 6:9,10
Apparently lighting from * to time Gen 8:7f
Apparently lighting from time to * Gen 8:7f
again, and this *, towards Gen 8:11
and this * she didn't come back. Gen 8:12
of *, to you and to all the earth. Gen 9:13
AT THAT * all mankind spoke a Gen 11:1
By the * Terah was seventy years Gen 11:26
seventy-five years old at that *. Gen 12:4
inhabited by Canaanites at that *. Gen 12:6
There was at that * a terrible Gen 12:10
eighty-six years old at this *. Gen 16:16
Sarah next year at about this *." Gen 17:21
that *, and Ishmael was thirteen. Gen 17:24-27
the * when she could have a baby. Gen 18:11
(From that * on that village Gen 19:22
old age, at the * God had said; Gen 21:1
was 100 years old at that *. Gen 21:4,5
* went by and the child grew and Gen 21:8
About this * King Abimelech, and Gen 21:22
So from that * on the well was Gen 21:31
Philistine country for a long *. Gen 21:34
in Abraham's *, and so Isaac moved Gen 26:1
For a * you will serve your Gen 27:39,40
Finally the * came for him to Gen 29:21
you, and all that * I cared for Gen 31:38
and lost no * in acting upon this Gen 34:18,19
This * he told his father as Gen 37:10
Some * later, Reuben (who was Gen 37:29
ABOUT THIS *, Judah left home and Gen 38:1
again at that *, but to return to Gen 38:11
In the process of * Judah's wife Gen 38:12
After the * of mourning was over, Gen 38:12
In due season the * of her Gen 38:27
One day at about this * Gen 39:7
was around at the *— she came and Gen 39:11
SOME * LATER it so happened that Gen 40:1
for quite some *, and Potiphar Gen 40:4
second dream. This * he saw seven Gen 41:5
"Some * ago when you were angry Gen 41:10
dream. This * there were seven Gen 41:22
major priest-politician of the *. Gen 41:45f
During this * before the arrival Gen 41:50
this * if you had let him come." Gen 43:10

ME Con't)
'hey had a wonderful * bantering Gen 43:34
'ears old at the * of his death. Gen 47:28
As the * drew near for him to Gen 47:29
hat we can't get there in *! Ex 1:19
THERE WERE AT this * a Hebrew Ex 2:1
he * had come for their rescue. Ex 2:25
t this * of their confrontation Ex 7:7
vill die at the * you specify, Ex 8:9
arts, but this * they failed. Ex 8:18
This * I am going to send a Ex 9:14
Well, tomorrow about this * I Ex 9:18
During all that * the people Ex 10:23
his rule at any * during the seven Ex 12:15
during that * anyone who eats Ex 12:19
and didn't have * to wait for bread Ex 12:39
this memorial at the same *. Ex 12:47
saw how much * this was taking, he Ex 18:14
be freed with him at the same *. Ex 21:3
the loss of his * until he is Ex 21:19
not there at the *, then the man Ex 22:14
at the regular * in March, the Ex 23:15
bring me a sacrifice at that *. Ex 23:15
out a little at a *, until your Ex 23:30
that * he neither ate nor drank. Ex 34:28
At that * God Ex 34:28
*, but not as burnt offerings. Lev 2:12
only this * it is a sin offering Lev 4:21
days, after which * their Lev 8:33
during which * she will be under Lev 12:5
At the end of that *, on the Lev 13:5
If during that * the spot Lev 13:22
If after that * the spot has not Lev 13:55
but also for a * after it heals. Lev 15:3
and during that * anyone touching Lev 15:19
on during that * shall be defiled. Lev 15:20
her during this * is ceremonially Lev 15:24
after the normal *, or at some Lev 15:25
at some irregular * during the Lev 15:25
upon during that * is defiled, just Lev 15:26
be offered to the Lord at any *. Lev 22:24
be announced as a * of sacred Lev 23:21
is a solemn * for all the people Lev 23:23,24
it is a * of remembrance, and is Lev 23:23,24
with remorse; this * for atonement Lev 23:32
people, at which * there will again Lev 23:36
harvesting, is the * to celebrate Lev 23:39
shall be holy, a * to proclaim Lev 25:10
debtors, and a * for the canceling Lev 25:10
redeemed at any * by the seller. Lev 25:24
right of redemption during that *. Lev 25:29
redeemable at any *, and are always Lev 25:31
be redeemed at any *, and must be Lev 25:32
At that * he can leave with his Lev 25:41
redeemed by the * the Year of Lev 25:54
children shall be freed at that *. Lev 25:54
fruit long after the normal *! Lev 26:4,5
when sowing * comes again. Lev 26:4,5
on the Sinai peninsula at the *. Num 1:1
AT THE * when the Lord spoke to Num 3:1
"Throughout that * he must never Num 6:5
he promised at the * he took his Num 6:21
Lord at the * he had appointed. Num 9:6,7
at Passover * because of touching a Num 9:10
the lamb at that *, with unleavened Num 9:11
at the regular *, shall be Num 9:13
to Jehovah at the proper *; Num 9:13
If it stayed a long *, then they Num 9:19
time, then they stayed a long *. Num 9:19
location by the * they arrived. Num 10:21
them, they prophesied for some *. Num 11:25
the wilderness of Paran at the *. Num 13:3-15
It was at this * that Moses Num 13:16
were being harvested at that *. Num 13:20
"Eshcol" at that * (meaning Num 13:24
them all the * from when we left Num 14:19
to Moses at this *, "Instruct the Num 15:17,18
is ceremonially impure at the *. Num 18:11
are ceremonially defiled at the *. Num 18:13
*, shall be defiled seven days. Num 19:14
of Edom, "The * has come for Num 20:24
Balak tried again. This * he Num 22:15
Forty years earlier, at the * of Num 26:64,65f
All who at that * were older than Num 26:64,65f
will be even fiercer this * Num 32:14
of Israel from the * Moses and Num 33:1
stayed there for quite a long *. Num 33:9
At the * of this address, King Deu 1:1
"At that * I told the people, 'I Deu 1:9
instructions at that *, also. Deu 1:18
there at Kadesh for a long *. Deu 1:46
lacked nothing in all that *.' Deu 2:7
"At that * I gave the conquered Deu 3:12
"At that * I reminded the tribes Deu 3:18
"At that * I made this plea to Deu 3:23,24,25
Yes, it was at that * that the Deu 4:14
in the land a long *, and you have Deu 4:25
going back to the * when God Deu 4:32
he gave you at that *, Deu 5:22
cast them out a little at a *; Deu 7:22
"But that is the * to be Deu 8:11
that is the * to watch out that Deu 8:14
For all this * you have Deu 9:7
I was on the mountain at the *, Deu 9:9
and all that * I ate nothing. Deu 9:9
But that *, too, he listened to Deu 9:19
"AT THAT * the Lord told me to Deu 10:1
nights the second *, just as I had Deu 10:10
It is * to go in and possess it.' Deu 10:11
Lord cared for you * and again Deu 11:5
defiled at the *, may eat it, just Deu 15:22
was no * for the bread to rise. Deu 16:3
At that * bring to him a Deu 16:10
It is a * to rejoice before the Deu 16:11
This will be a happy * of Deu 16:14
It is a * of deep thanksgiving to Deu 16:15
it shall be a * of great joy. Deu 16:15
at the * will make the decision. Deu 17:9
the court's judgment a second *. Deu 17:13
and of the fleece at shearing *. Deu 18:4
sanctuary at any * and minister in Deu 18:6,7
on duty before the Lord at the *. Deu 19:17
* will rejoice in destroying you; Deu 28:63
If at that * you want to return Deu 30:2
* has come when you must die. Deu 31:14
(It was the second * in Israel's Jos 5:2,3
since that * had been circumcised. Jos 5:4,5
So from that * on they lived on Jos 5:11,12
again, but this * they went around Jos 6:15
The seventh *, as the priests Jos 6:16
but this * you may keep the loot Jos 8:2
in force at the * of this writing. Jos 9:27
* tomorrow they will all be dead! Jos 11:6
(Hazor had at one * been the Jos 11:10
Literally, "a long *." Jos 11:18f
at that * across from Jericho. Jos 13:32
"I was forty years old at the * Jos 14:7
"Now, as you see, from that * Jos 14:10
(Before that * Hebron had been Jos 14:15
office at the * of the accident. Jos 20:6
has lasted for such a long *. Jos 22:2,3
care of you for such a long *." Jos 24:20
conquer part of Israel at that *. Ju 3:12
But when, after a long *, he Ju 3:25
Israel's leader at that *, the Ju 4:4
Barak, "Now is the * for action! Ju 4:14
And from that * on Israel became Ju 4:24
And it takes *. Ju 5:30
harass them. This * it was by the Ju 6:1
more test: this * let the fleece Ju 6:39
By this * King Zebah and King Ju 8:10
Once upon a * the trees decided Ju 9:8
At that * Gaal (the son of Ebed) Ju 9:26
at Arumah at this *, and Zebul Ju 9:41
Has there ever been a * when you Ju 10:12
in Gilead at that *, preparing to Ju 10:17
It was about this * that the Ju 11:4
here for all that *, spread across Ju 11:26
At that * the Spirit of the Lord Ju 11:29
"You failed to help us in our * Ju 12:2
of Ephraim died there at that *. Ju 12:6
of God from the * of his birth; Ju 13:5
that * were the rulers of Israel. Ju 14:4
So that *, as he slept, Ju 16:12
* he has told me everything." Ju 16:18
me one more *, so that I may pay Ju 16:28
was no king in Israel at that *. Ju 18:1
AT THIS * before Israel had a Ju 19:1
they all had a very pleasant *. Ju 19:4
as they were having such a good *. Ju 19:6
But this * the man was adamant, Ju 19:10
For at that * it was agreed by Ju 21:5
(What a sad * it was in Israel Ju 21:15
During the * of their residence Ru 1:3
At lunch * Boaz called to her, Ru 2:14
dear, isn't it * that I try to find Ru 3:1
(The priests on duty at that * 1Sa 1:3
in the process of *, a baby boy 1Sa 1:19,20
here that * praying to the Lord! 1Sa 1:26
member will die before his *. 1Sa 2:31
called the third *, and once more 1Sa 3:8
AT THAT * Israel was at war with 1Sa 4:1
Lord again. This * his head and 1Sa 5:4
and during that * all Israel was in 1Sa 7:2
At that * Samuel said to them, 1Sa 7:3
again at that *, because the Lord 1Sa 7:13
leaving about the * you get there; 1Sa 9:12,13
"About this * tomorrow I will 1Sa 9:16
up; it's * you were on your way!" 1Sa 9:26,27
"At that * the Spirit of the 1Sa 10:6
From that * on your decisions 1Sa 10:7
AT THIS * Nahash led the army of 1Sa 11:1
service from the * he was a lad. 1Sa 12:2
not rain at this * of the year, 1Sa 12:17
BY THIS * Saul had reigned for one 1Sa 13:1
arrived by the * you said you 1Sa 13:11
the people of Israel at that *. 1Sa 14:18
So from that * on King Saul kept 1Sa 18:9
This happened another *, too, for 1Sa 18:11,12
But when the * arrived for the 1Sa 18:19
So, before the * limit expired, 1Sa 18:26
Have you forgotten about the * 1Sa 19:5
The same thing happened a third * 1Sa 19:21
that about this * tomorrow, or the 1Sa 20:12
to it again, this * by his love for 1Sa 20:17
* for ceremonial purification. 1Sa 21:7
He was in Gibe-ah at the *, 1Sa 22:6
* I had consulted God for him! 1Sa 22:15
Ever since that * the place where 1Sa 23:28
"Now's your *!" 1Sa 24:4
Should he spend his * chasing one 1Sa 24:14
at this * for the sheep shearing. 1Sa 25:2
whole * they have been in Carmel. 1Sa 25:7
have come at a happy * of holiday. 1Sa 25:8
us the whole * they were with us. 1Sa 25:15,16
By that * he was sober, and when 1Sa 25:37,38
Then David wasted no * in sending 1Sa 25:39
your power this * for sure," 1Sa 26:8
not need to strike a second *!" 1Sa 26:8
He and his men spent their * 1Sa 27:8
ABOUT THAT * the Philistines 1Sa 28:1
was forty years old at the *. 2Sa 2:10,11
that for a long * they had wanted 2Sa 3:17
"Now is the *!" 2Sa 3:18
He was five years old at the * 2Sa 4:4
At that * David and his troops 2Sa 5:21
* I brought Israel out of Egypt. 2Sa 7:6
And from that * on, Mephibosheth 2Sa 9:10,11
SOME * AFTER this the Ammonite 2Sa 10:1
the Israelis, this * leaving seven 2Sa 10:18
year, at the * when wars begin, 2Sa 11:1
Fight harder next *, and conquer 2Sa 11:25
family from this * on, because you 2Sa 12:10
in deep sorrow for a long *." 2Sa 14:2,3
were weary by the * they reached 2Sa 16:14
replied, "this * I think 2Sa 17:7
be my messenger some other *." 2Sa 18:20
days and to report back at that *. 2Sa 20:4
spent much * in prayer about it. 2Sa 21:1
At the same * he sent a request 2Sa 21:12,13,14
At still another * and at the 2Sa 21:19
Philistines that * when the rest of 2Sa 23:9
it was * to collect the loot! 2Sa 23:10
One * when David was living in 2Sa 23:13
down at harvest * to visit him. 2Sa 23:13
stronghold at the *, for Philistine 2Sa 23:14
Another * he went down into a pit 2Sa 23:20
Another *, armed only with a 2Sa 23:21
of Araunah the Jebusite at the *. 2Sa 24:16
At about that *, David's son 1Ki 1:5
him at any *—not so much as by a 1Ki 1:6
AS THE * of King David's death 1Ki 2:1
but it was done in a * of peace. 1Ki 2:5
lived in Jerusalem for a long *. 1Ki 2:38
At that * the people of Israel 1Ki 3:2
contented nation at this *. 1Ki 4:20
sheep, and, from * to time, deer, 1Ki 4:23
and, from time to *, deer, 1Ki 4:23
occurred at the * of the Tabernacle 1Ki 8:2
in the Ark at that * except the two 1Ki 8:9
Mount Horeb at the * the Lord made 1Ki 8:9
fathers, at the * that he brought 1Ki 8:21
to him the second * (the first time 1Ki 9:2,3
time (the first * had been at 1Ki 9:2,3
completely at the * of the invasion 1Ki 9:20,21
him the right answers every *. 1Ki 10:3
was a very small child at the *). 1Ki 11:16,17,18
but all that * he continually 1Ki 15:34
at this * by the prophet Jehu: 1Ki 16:1
until the * when the Lord sends 1Ki 17:14
And each * when he was told 1Ki 18:10
Has no one told you about the * 1Ki 18:13
until the * of the evening 1Ki 18:29
At the customary * for offering 1Ki 18:36
Finally, the seventh *, his 1Ki 18:44
you by this * tomorrow night." 1Ki 19:2
but about this * tomorrow I will 1Ki 20:5,6
for the first *, but your men may 1Ki 20:9
Only this * replace the kings 1Ki 20:24
Israel again, this * at Aphek. 1Ki 20:26
in Edom at that *, only a deputy. 1Ki 22:47
men, but this * the captain fell to 2Ki 1:13
NOW THE * came for the Lord to 2Ki 2:1
was the king of Judah at this *. 2Ki 3:1f
day at about the * when the morning 2Ki 3:20
from * to time is a holy prophet. 2Ki 4:9
from time to * is a holy prophet. 2Ki 4:9
"Next year at about this * you 2Ki 4:15,16
the child. This * the little boy 2Ki 4:35
Is this the * to receive money 2Ki 5:26
says that by this * tomorrow two 2Ki 7:1
the king about the * when Elisha 2Ki 8:5
Libnah also rebelled at that *. 2Ki 8:22
at about this * tomorrow." 2Ki 10:6
At about that * the Lord began to 2Ki 10:32,33
About this *, King Hazael of 2Ki 12:17
years old at the *, and he reigned 2Ki 14:2
Reigning in Israel at this *: King 2Ki 15:1
Reigning in Judah at that *: King 2Ki 15:8
Reigning in Judah at that *: King 2Ki 15:13
Reigning in Judah at that *: King 2Ki 15:32,33
Reigning in Israel at this *: King 2Ki 16:1
However, at that * King Rezin of 2Ki 16:6

(TIME Con't)

Reigning in Judah at this *: King	2Ki 17:1
At the same * he refused to pay	2Ki 17:4
Reigning in Israel at this *: King	2Ki 18:1
It was at that * that the king	2Ki 18:11
At that * Merodach-baladan (the	2Ki 20:12
of the Lord: The * will come when	2Ki 20:17
and no king since the * of Josiah	2Ki 23:25
At the * of Hadad's death, the	1Ch 1:51-54
a hard * at his birth (Jabez means	1Ch 4:9
control until the * of David.	1Ch 4:31
genealogy at the * of King Jotham	1Ch 5:17
Hagrites until the * of the exile.	1Ch 5:22
At the * of King David, the total	1Ch 7:2
Their descendants, at the * of	1Ch 7:4
At the * of David there were	1Ch 7:9
warriors at the * of King David.	1Ch 7:11
for them a long *, and his brothers	1Ch 7:22
At that * Zechariah, the son of	1Ch 9:21
to them from * to time, for seven	1Ch 9:25
to *, for seven days at a time.	1Ch 9:25
to time, for seven days at a *.	1Ch 9:25
Another *, three of The Thirty	1Ch 11:15
was in the stronghold at the *;	1Ch 11:16
300 men at one * with his spear.	1Ch 11:20
At that * David began the custom	1Ch 16:7
palace for some * he said to Nathan	1Ch 17:1
* I brought Israel out of Egypt.	1Ch 17:5
In all that * I never suggested	1Ch 17:6
" 'When your * here on earth is	1Ch 17:11
as Hamath) at the * Hadadezer went	1Ch 18:3
standing at the * by the	1Ch 21:15
who was threshing wheat at the *.	1Ch 21:19,20
David didn't have * to go there to	1Ch 21:30
BY THIS * David was an old, old	1Ch 23:1
At this * a census was taken of	1Ch 23:3
At that * Egyptian chariots sold	2Ch 1:17
SOLOMON NOW DECIDED that the *	2Ch 2:1
The Ark is still there at the * of	2Ch 5:9
It was at this *, too, that	2Ch 8:3
centers at this *, and constructed	2Ch 8:6
He was in Egypt at the *, where	2Ch 10:2,3
"Now is the * to do it, while	2Ch 14:7
For a long * now, over in	2Ch 15:3
About that * the prophet Hanani	2Ch 16:7
all the people at that *.	2Ch 16:10
"He does it every *.	2Ch 18:17
without food for a *, in penitence	2Ch 20:3
that in a * like this—whenever we	2Ch 20:9
At that * the king of Edom	2Ch 21:8
In the process of *, at the end	2Ch 21:19
"At last the * has come for the	2Ch 23:2,3
But the Levites took their *.	2Ch 24:5
years old at the * he became king,	2Ch 27:1
About that * King Ahaz of Judah	2Ch 28:16
In this * of deep trial, King	2Ch 28:22
in May this *, rather than at the	2Ch 30:2,3
than at the normal * in April,	2Ch 30:2,3
enough * to get notices out.	2Ch 30:2,3
tribe of Israel for a long *;	2Ch 30:5f
And at this * another large group	2Ch 30:24
because their * and energies were	2Ch 31:17,18
SOME * LATER, after this good work	2Ch 32:1
Name just one * when anyone,	2Ch 32:14
But about that * Hezekiah became	2Ch 32:24
spend your * ministering to the	2Ch 35:3
Never since the * of Samuel the	2Ch 35:18
to Babylon at that *, and King	2Ch 36:10
Jerusalem at this * from the	Ez 2:59
and Judah at that *—Haggai, and	Ez 5:1
For by that * many of the	Ez 6:20
men (they arrived at a later *);	Ez 8:2-14
* of the evening burnt offering.	Ez 9:4
at the scheduled * with the elders	Ez 10:14
* in prayer to the God of heaven.	Neh 1:4
And I set a * for my departure!	Neh 2:5,6
ABOUT THIS * there was a great	Neh 5:1
officials to spend * on the wall.	Neh 5:16
were already having a difficult *.	Neh 5:18
and each * I gave the same reply.	Neh 6:4
The fifth *, Sanballat's servant	Neh 6:5,6
who returned at that * were:	Neh 7:7
Jerusalem at that * from the	Neh 7:61
who returned to Judah at that *;	Neh 7:66
your God— it is a * to celebrate	Neh 8:10
it was a * of great and joyful	Neh 8:12
observance; this * they fasted and	Neh 9:1
they lacked nothing in all that *	Neh 9:21
But in their * of trouble they	Neh 9:27
Every * you punished us you were	Neh 9:33
the Holy City, at this *;	Neh 11:1
Jerusalem at this * were	Neh 11:2
chiefs of the Levites at that *:	Neh 12:24
were active in the * of Joiakim	Neh 12:26
I was not in Jerusalem at the *,	Neh 13:6
And that was the last * they	Neh 13:21
About the same * I realized that	Neh 13:23
women of the palace at the same *.	Est 1:9
By that * Mordecai had become a	Est 2:19
The most propitious * for this	Est 3:7
If you keep quiet at a * like	Est 4:14
for just such a * as this?"	Est 4:14
a reminder of the * when Haman (son	Est 9:24,25
them at the * determined by a throw	Est 9:24,25
days at the appointed * each year.	Est 9:27
remembrance of the * of their	Est 9:29-31
"At such a * as this should not	Job 4:6
power of the sword in * of war.	Job 5:20
not be harvested until it's *!	Job 5:26
spend your * persecuting him?	Job 7:17
" 'Yet all the * your real	Job 10:13,14
Can't you see how little * I	Job 10:20,21
You will take your *, and rest in	Job 11:18
down for the last *, and does not	Job 14:11,12
spend their * singing and dancing.	Job 21:12,13
wicked get away with it every *.	Job 21:17
spend all their * just getting	Job 24:5
"I have waited all this *,	Job 32:11,12
He must have spent much * with	Job 34:7,8
waste * trying to please God?'	Job 34:9
Man's work stops at such a *, so	Job 37:7
For I have reserved it for the *	Job 38:22,23
earth, listen while there is *.	Ps 2:10
joys at harvest * as they gaze at	Ps 4:7
Oh, that the * of their rescue	Ps 14:7
was written at a * when the Lord	Ps 18:1
There was a * when I wouldn't	Ps 32:3
while there is * to be forgiven.	Ps 32:6
and spend your * in doing good.	Ps 34:14
town and spend their * cursing me.	Ps 35:16
how brief my * on earth will be.	Ps 39:4
O Lord my God, many and many a *	Ps 40:5
There isn't * to tell of all your	Ps 40:5
but all the * they hate me and	Ps 41:6
And yet for a *, O Lord, you	Ps 44:9
your * with evil and immoral men.	Ps 50:18
care—but now your * of punishment	Ps 50:21
Written by David at the * the men	Ps 54:1
Written by David at the * King	Ps 59:1
Written by David at the * he was	Ps 60:1
They pick on me at a * when my	Ps 62:3,4
O my people, trust him all the *	Ps 62:8
For now is the *—you are bending	Ps 69:13
Give me * to tell this new	Ps 71:18
of peace to the end of *.	Ps 72:7
and all the * their riches	Ps 73:12
Have I been wasting my *?	Ps 73:13
Many and many a * he held back	Ps 78:38
will continue to the end of *.	Ps 89:35,36
his * and publicly disgraced him.	Ps 89:45
We glide along the tides of * as	Ps 90:5,6
Don't turn away from me in this *	Ps 102:2
now is the * to pity her—the time	Ps 102:13
pity her—the * you promised help.	Ps 102:13
until God's * finally came—how God	Ps 105:19
Lord, it is * for you to act.	Ps 119:126
LORD, DO YOU remember that * when	Ps 132:1
find the right decision every *.	Pro 2:9
Don't say "some other *," if	Pro 3:27,28
And he spends his * thinking of	Pro 6:14
it to them in their * of need.	Pro 11:26
only a fool idles away his *.	Pro 12:11
Truth stands the test of *;	Pro 12:19
the right thing at the right *!	Pro 15:23
is born to help in * of need.	Pro 17:17
be ignored in his own * of need.	Pro 21:13
Why waste your *?	Pro 23:4,5
the Lord all the *, for surely you	Pro 23:17,18
times, will each * rise again?	Pro 24:15,16
summertime or rain with harvest *!	Pro 26:1
for help in your * of need.	Pro 27:10
do not spend your * with women—the	Pro 31:3
is silly to be laughing all the *;	Ecc 2:1
THERE IS A right * for everything:	Ecc 3:1
A * to be born, a time to die;	Ecc 3:2
A time to be born, a * to die;	Ecc 3:2
born, a time to die;A * to plant;	Ecc 3:2
A time to plant;A * to harvest;	Ecc 3:2
A time to harvest; A * to kill;	Ecc 3:3
A time to kill;A * to heal;	Ecc 3:3
A time to heal;A * to destroy;	Ecc 3:3
A time to destroy;A * to rebuild;	Ecc 3:3
A time to rebuild; A * to cry;	Ecc 3:4
A time to cry;A * to laugh;	Ecc 3:4
A time to laugh;A * to grieve;	Ecc 3:4
A time to grieve;A * to dance;	Ecc 3:4
A time to dance; A * for	Ecc 3:5
A time for scattering stones;A *	Ecc 3:5
A time for gathering stones;A * to	Ecc 3:5
A time to hug;A * not to hug;	Ecc 3:5
A time not to hug; A * to find;	Ecc 3:6
A time to find;A * to lose;	Ecc 3:6
A time to lose;A * for keeping;	Ecc 3:6
A time for keeping;A * for	Ecc 3:6
A time for throwing away; A * to	Ecc 3:7
A time to tear;A * to repair;	Ecc 3:7
A time to repair;A * to be quiet;	Ecc 3:7
A time to be quiet;A * to speak	Ecc 3:7
A time to speak up; A * for	Ecc 3:8
A time for loving;A * for hating;	Ecc 3:8
A time for hating;A * for war;	Ecc 3:8
A time for war;A * for peace.	Ecc 3:8
is appropriate in its own *.	Ecc 3:
It is better to spend your * at	Ecc 7
about it while there is still *.	Ecc 7
only of having a good * now.	Ecc 7
Why should you die before your *?	Ecc 7:15-
The wise man will find a * and a	Ecc 8
Yes, there is a * and a way for	Ecc 8:6
Then I decided to spend my *	Ecc 8:
at the right place at the right *.	Ecc 9:
For there will come a * when	Ecc 12
up and the * of the singing of	Sol 2:
when the harvest * is over—or when	Is 1
AT THAT * so few men will be left	Is 4
Messiah in Jerusalem at that *.	Is 4:2,3,
By the * this child is weaned	Is 7:15,
At that * the Lord will whistle	Is 7:1
At that * the lush vineyards	Is 7:2
NEVERTHELESS, THAT * of darkness	Is 9
when the harvest * has come, and	Is 9
will be left to return at that *;	Is 10:2
slaughter like the * when Gideon	Is 10:2
of Oreb or the * God drowned the	Is 10:2
At that * the Lord will bring	Is 11:1
for the second *, returning them to	Is 11:1
for the Lord's * has come, the time	Is 13
* for the Almighty to crush you.	Is 13
her * of doom will soon be here.	Is 13:2
autumn morning during harvest *.	Is 18:
But the * will come when that	Is 18:
At that * five of the cities of	Is 19:1
How much * is left?"	Is 21:1
Yet [the distant * will come	Is 23:1
At that * he will remove the	Is 25:
protection. The * will come when	Is 27:
Yet the * will come when the	Is 27:1
at a * and in such simple words!"	Is 28:1
until the end of *, forever and	Is 30:
rain at planting * and with	Is 30:2
In a short *—in just a little more	Is 32:1
our salvation in the * of trouble.	Is 33:
think back to this * of terror when	Is 33:1
At that * the heavens above will	Is 34:
international diplomacy at this *.	Is 36:11
it is a serious *, as when a	Is 37:
Merodach-baladan was at this *	Is 39:1
"The * is coming when everything	Is 39:
God of Israel. * and again I told	Is 48:
told you ahead of * what I was	Is 48:
say, "We knew that all the *!"	Is 48:
request has come at a favorable *.	Is 49:8,
ones? The * will come when God's	Is 51:1
Just as in the * of Noah I swore	Is 54:
the godly die before their * and	Is 57:
you spend your * plotting evil	Is 59:
You spend your * and energy in	Is 59:
bring it all to pass when it is *.	Is 60:2
who mourn that the * of God's favor	Is 61:
For the * has come for me to	Is 63:
Lord at harvest *, carried in	Is 66:2
and wasted their * on nonsense.	Jer 2:
sniffing the wind at mating *.	Jer 2:24
Yet in * of trouble they cry to	Jer 2:26,27
At that * the people of Judah	Jer 3:18
At that * he will send a burning	Jer 4:11,12
your hearts while there is *.	Jer 4:14
in Jeremiah's * (around 626 B.C.	Jer 5:15
to be done. The * is coming, says	Jer 7:32
The stork knows the * of her	Jer 8:7
at God's appointed * each year;	Jer 8:7
A * is coming, says the Lord,	Jer 9:25,26
For I told them at the * I	Jer 11:4
their * of anguish and despair.	Jer 11:12
Their * has come.	Jer 11:23
to me again. This * he said, Take	Jer 13:3
Then, a long * afterwards, the	Jer 13:6
at noon * I will bring death to	Jer 15:8
Yet you have failed me in my * of	Jer 15:17,18
no longer to the * I brought you	Jer 16:14,15
For the * is coming, says the	Jer 23:5,6
At that * Judah will be saved and	Jer 23:5,6
to it, when their * has come, that	Jer 23:12
Each * the message was this:	Jer 25:5
stones, for their * has come to be	Jer 25:34
at the same * as Jeremiah was.	Jer 26:20
grandson until his * is up, and	Jer 27:7
from them for a long * to come."	Jer 29:28
For the * is coming when I will	Jer 30:3
there ever been a * of terror such	Jer 30:7
It is a * of trouble for my	Jer 30:7
AT THAT *, says the Lord, all the	Jer 31:1
The Lord says: The * will come	Jer 31:27
At that * it will no longer be	Jer 31:34
For the * is coming, says the	Jer 31:38,39
At this * Jeremiah was	Jer 32:2
jar to preserve them for a long *.	Jer 32:14
From the * this city was built	Jer 32:31
Nevertheless the * will come when	Jer 33:6
At that * I will bring to the	Jer 33:15
At this * the Babylonian army	Jer 34:7
By the * he finished they were	Jer 36:16
the palace at the *, sitting in	Jer 36:22

ME Con't)

his * the Lord added a lot more!	Jer 36:32
This message, in point of *,	Jer 45:1f
lood *, overflowing all the land?	Jer 46:7
Egypt, a * of great punishment.	Jer 46:20,21
hildren, for the * has come when	Jer 47:4
ut of exile! The * is coming	Jer 48:12
he * of your judgment has come.	Jer 48:44
t the * of Jeremiah and Ezekiel.	Jer 49:8f
For the * has come for Babylon to	Jer 50:27
And the * is coming when God will	Jer 51:18
Then there will be a * of civil	Jer 51:46
For the * is surely coming when	Jer 51:47
But the * is coming for the	Jer 51:52
And yet, O Lord, the * will	Lam 1:21
And every * they stopped, there	Eze 1:25
ounces at a *, one meal a day.	Eze 4:10
From the * I was a child until	Eze 4:14
damnation dawns; the * has come;	Eze 7:7
"Yes, the * has come;	Eze 7:12
For the * has come for the	Eze 7:25
the people, 'It is * to rebuild	Eze 11:3
to you for the * that you are	Eze 11:16
one instead: 'The * has come for	Eze 12:23
come true for a long, long *.'	Eze 12:27
in a very short * you far	Eze 16:47
woman during the * of her	Eze 18:6
your sins while there is yet *.	Eze 18:30
And now the * of punishment has	Eze 21:24
in their * of menstruation."	Eze 22:10f
And when that * comes, then you	Eze 24:24
* when wrong was found in you.	Eze 28:15
At that * I will send swift	Eze 30:9
them at that * of Egypt's doom.	Eze 30:9
again by the * the man arrived.	Eze 33:22
streets at * of sacrifice.	Eze 36:37,38
"A long * from now you will be	Eze 38:8
For at that * an evil thought	Eze 38:10
"And from that * onward, the	Eze 39:22
Their * of treachery and shame	Eze 39:26
At that * the Zadok family of	Eze 43:19
This shall be done at the * of	Eze 45:17
* the water was up to my knees.	Eze 47:4
and science of the *, and God gave	Dan 1:17
You're trying to stall for *	Dan 2:8,9
"Give me a little *," he said,	Dan 2:16
who was out of town at the *	Dan 5:7f
allowed to live a short * longer.	Dan 7:12
Literally, "for a season and a *	Dan 7:12f
This * I was at Susa, the capital	Dan 8:2
capitals of the empire at this *.	Dan 8:2f
days of the coming * of terror—for	Dan 8:19
happen for a long *, so don't tell	Dan 8:26
to me at the * of the evening	Dan 9:21
for at the * of Messiah's death.	Dan 9:25f
from the * the command is given	Dan 9:25
from that * to the very end.	Dan 9:26
after half that *, he will break	Dan 9:27
But in God's * and plan, his	Dan 9:27
sorrows, and this * he understood	Dan 10:1
All that * I tasted neither wine	Dan 10:3
All this * I was looking down,	Dan 10:15
until God's appointed * has come.	Dan 11:27
Then, at the predestined *, he	Dan 11:29
trials, at God's appointed *.	Dan 11:35
and prospering—until his * is up.	Dan 11:36
"Then at the * of the end,	Dan 11:40
he is there his * will suddenly run	Dan 11:45
"AT THAT * Michael, the mighty	Dan 12:1
and there will be a * of	Dan 12:1
Literally, "a *, times, and half	Dan 12:7f
time, times, and half a *	Dan 12:7f
understood until the * of the end.	Dan 12:9
"From the * the daily sacrifice	Dan 12:11
and this * gave birth to a son.	Hos 1:8
"Yet the * will come when Israel	Hos 1:10
at the * of the grape harvest.	Hos 1:9
At that * I will make a treaty	Hos 1:18
At that * I will sow a crop of	Hos 1:23
will be a long * without a king or	Hos 3:4
The * of Israel's punishment has	Hos 9:7
for now is the * to seek the Lord,	Hos 10:12
This is the last * I will destroy	Hos 11:9
to me now, while there is *.	Joe 2:12
"AT THAT *, when I restore the	Joe 3:1
mine forever; the * will come when	Joe 3:17
This vision came to him at the *	Amo 1:2
holiness that the * will come when	Amo 4:2
At that * I will make the sun go	Amo 8:9
be that day. The * is surely	Amo 8:11
"Then, at that *, I will rebuild	Amo 9:11
"The * will come when there will	Amo 9:13
that the harvest * will scarcely	Amo 9:13
For you deserted Israel in his *	Ob 1:11
not have mocked in his * of need.	Ob 1:12
that terrible * of his distress.	Ob 1:14
And all this * Jonah was sound	Jon 1:5
"sleeping at a * like this?	Jon 1:6
The * will come, O Israel, when I	Mic 2:12
my plan, for the * will come when	Mic 4:12
* of Israel's spiritual rebirth;	Mic 5:3
At that same *, says the Lord, I	Mic 5:10
* of punishment is almost here;	Mic 7:4
Slowly, steadily, surely, the *	Hab 2:3
satisfied. The * is coming when	Hab 2:6
("The * will come when all the	Hab 2:14
In this * of our deep need, begin	Hab 3:2
there still is *—before judgment	Zep 2:2
wolves at evening *, who by dawn	Zep 3:3
"Be patient; the * is coming soon	Zep 3:8
"At that * I will change the	Zep 3:9
"At that *, I will gather you	Zep 3:20
* for rebuilding my Temple?"	Hag 1:2
it then the right * for you to live	Hag 1:3,4
'At that * many nations will be	Zec 2:11,12
Babylon had, by the * of	Zec 5:11f
them out of slavery the first *.	Zec 10:11f
a shepherd; this * I was to act the	Zec 11:15
Jerusalem at that * will be even	Zec 12:11
"AT THAT * a Fountain will be	Zec 13:1
evening * it will still be light.	Zec 14:7
Lord of Hosts, to celebrate a *	Zec 14:16
"Every * you say, 'Don't bother	Mal 1:7
At that * my punishments will be	Mal 3:5
laws from earliest *, yet you may	Mal 3:7
at the * of the exile to Babylon).	Mt 1:11
and fourteen from King David's *	Mt 1:17
At about that * some astrologers	Mt 2:1
* when they first saw the star.	Mt 2:7
Live one day at a *.	Mt 6:34
here to torment us before the *?"	Mt 8:29f
"But the * is coming when I	Mt 9:15
will be taken from them. * enough	Mt 9:15
the right words at the right *.	Mt 10:19
For the * is coming when the	Mt 10:26
And from the * John the Baptist	Mt 11:12
come [at the * the Kingdom begins	Mt 11:14
ABOUT THAT *, Jesus was walking	Mt 12:1
hidden since the beginning of *."	Mt 13:34,35
is already past * for supper, and	Mt 14:15
ABOUT THAT * the disciples came to	Mt 18:1
begged him to give him a little *.	Mt 18:29
"At the * of the grape harvest	Mt 21:34
everyone that it was * to come.	Mt 22:3
were used as porches at that *.	Mt 24:17f
it was in Noah's * before the	Mt 24:37,38
"After a long * their master	Mt 25:19
From that * on, Judas watched	Mt 26:16
Master says, my * has come, and I	Mt 26:18
*, saying the same things again.	Mt 26:44
but no! The * has come!	Mt 26:45
Who struck you that *?"	Mt 26:68
Again Peter denied it, this *	Mt 26:72
About that * Judas, who betrayed	Mt 27:3
"At last the * has come!"	Mk 1:15
Another *, on a Sabbath day as	Mk 2:23
hear about the * King David and his	Mk 2:25,26
he couldn't even find * to eat.	Mk 3:20
that they scarcely had * to eat.	Mk 6:31
ONE DAY ABOUT this * as another	Mk 8:1
to spend more * with his disciples,	Mk 9:30,31
By this * they had arrived in	Mk 11:27,28
gave to the people at that *:	Mk 12:1
At grape-picking * he sent one	Mk 12:2
things he taught them at this *:	Mk 12:38
be some warning ahead of *?"	Mk 13:3,4
Lord shortens that * of calamity,	Mk 13:20
my body ahead of * for burial.	Mk 14:8
right * and place to betray Jesus.	Mk 14:11
crows a second * tomorrow morning	Mk 14:30
The third * when he returned to	Mk 14:41
But no! The * for sleep has	Mk 14:41
"Who hit you that *, you	Mk 14:65
the rooster crowed the second *.	Mk 14:72
year at Passover *—any prisoner the	Mk 15:6
One of the prisoners at that *	Mk 15:7
come true at the proper *."	Lk 1:20
was over, for the * had come for	Lk 1:57
ABOUT THIS * Caesar Augustus, the	Lk 2:1
was obviously pregnant by this *.	Lk 2:5
And while they were there, the *	Lk 2:6
When the * came for Mary's	Lk 2:22
At that * Jesus' parents also	Lk 2:24
was governor over Judea at that *;	Lk 3:1
He ate nothing all that *, and	Lk 4:1
of the world in a moment of *;	Lk 4:5
And this * their nets were so	Lk 5:6
not to spend my * with those who	Lk 5:32
But the * will come when the	Lk 5:35
who weep, for the * will come when	Lk 6:21
* of awful hunger is before them.	Lk 6:25
Just at that * the highly prized	Lk 7:2
again from the * I first came in.	Lk 7:45
[Another * he asked,	Lk 8:16
One day about that *, as he and	Lk 8:22
been demon-possessed for a long *.	Lk 8:27
As the * drew near for his return	Lk 9:51
Another *, when he invited a man	Lk 9:59
And don't waste * along the way.	Lk 10:4
difference the next * I am here.'	Lk 10:35
I just can't help you this *.'	Lk 11:7
and from that * on they plied him	Lk 11:53,54
So be ready all the *.	Lk 12:40
be back for a long *,' and begins	Lk 12:45
and to spend his * at drinking	Lk 12:45
ABOUT THIS * he was informed that	Lk 13:1
that it was * for them to arrive.	Lk 14:17
About the * his money was gone a	Lk 15:14
and in all that * you never gave	Lk 15:29
Your brothers can read them any *	Lk 16:29
a day and each * turns again and	Lk 17:4
"The * is coming when you will	Lk 17:22
When harvest * came, he sent one	Lk 20:10
and David's God at the same *?"	Lk 20:44
But Jesus said, "The * is coming	Lk 21:6
there be any warning ahead of *?"	Lk 21:7
and saying, 'The * has come.'	Lk 21:8
there will be a * of special	Lk 21:12
* of its destruction has arrived.	Lk 21:20
triumph ends in God's good *.	Lk 21:24
and at the proper * all sat down	Lk 22:14
For the * has come for this	Lk 22:37
But this is your moment—the *	Lk 22:53
"Who hit you that *, prophet?"	Lk 22:63,64
But the * is soon coming when I,	Lk 22:69
to be in Jerusalem at the *.	Lk 23:7
Once more, for the third *, he	Lk 23:22
but by the * they were finished	Lk 23:56
before entering his * of glory?"	Lk 24:26
By this * they were nearing	Lk 24:28
"but at the * God sent me to	Jn 1:33
"It isn't yet my * for	Jn 2:4
Then it was * for the annual	Jn 2:13
At this * John the Baptist was	Jn 3:23,24
He was alone at the * as his	Jn 4:8
Jesus replied, "The * is coming,	Jn 4:21-24
the Lord came from * to time and	Jn 5:4
came from time to * and disturbed	Jn 5:4
declare that the * is coming, in	Jn 5:25
Indeed the * is coming when all	Jn 5:28
But soon it was * for the	Jn 7:2
not the right * for me to go now.	Jn 7:6
when it is the right *."	Jn 7:8
for if the correct * for	Jn 7:21,22,23
him, for God's * had not yet come.	Jn 7:30
for his * had not yet run out.	Jn 8:20
there is little * left before the	Jn 9:4
So for the second * they called	Jn 9:24
* of the Dedication Celebration.	Jn 10:22,23
So from that * on the Jewish	Jn 11:53
realize at the * that this was a	Jn 12:16
Jesus replied that the * had come	Jn 12:23,24
not mine. The * of judgment for	Jn 12:31
has come—and the * when Satan,	Jn 12:31
the Light while there is still *;	Jn 12:36
out in the custom of that *.	Jn 13:26f
room, Jesus said, "My * has come;	Jn 13:31
all this * I have been with you?	Jn 14:9
"I don't have much more * to	Jn 14:30
and indeed the * is coming when	Jn 16:2
At that * you won't need to ask	Jn 16:23
guardedly, but the * will come when	Jn 16:25
"But the * is coming—in fact,	Jn 16:32
said, "Father, the * has come.	Jn 17:1
During my * here I have kept	Jn 17:12
went on home, and by that * Mary	Jn 20:11
there at the * with the others.	Jn 20:24
and this * Thomas was with them.	Jn 20:26
This was the third * Jesus had	Jn 21:14
asked the question this third *.	Jn 21:17
at supper that * to ask Jesus,	Jn 21:20
the apostles from * to time,	Act 1:3
from time to *, actually alive, and	Act 1:3
And another * when he appeared to	Act 1:6
During this *, on a day when	Act 1:15
the Lord—from the * he was baptized	Act 1:21,22
Some * ago there was that fellow	Act 5:36
"After him, at the * of the	Act 5:37
"We should spend our * preaching,	Act 6:2
Then we can spend our * in	Act 6:4
at that *, as evidence of the	Act 7:8
The second * they went, Joseph	Act 7:13
"As the * drew near when God	Act 7:17,18
"About that * Moses was born—a	Act 7:20
used until the * of King David.	Act 7:45
without food and water all that *.	Act 9:8,9
About this * she became ill and	Act 9:37
And Peter stayed a long * in	Act 9:43
as usual at this * of the	Act 10:30
During this * some prophets came	Act 11:27
ABOUT THAT * King Herod moved	Act 12:1
safety all the * he was in prison.	Act 12:5
But all the * he thought it was a	Act 12:9
true in our own *, in that God	Act 13:32,33
there a long *, preaching boldly,	Act 14:3
Peter has told you about the *	Act 15:14
Literally, "spent some *."	Act 15:33f
province of Ausia at that *.	Act 16:6
* discussing the latest new ideas!	Act 17:21
spent his full * preaching and	Act 18:5
he felt that he had no * to lose.	Act 18:20
After spending some * there, he	Act 18:23
* of John, and all that it meant!	Act 18:25,26

(TIME Con't)
But about that *, a big blowup Act 19:23
at Ephesus this *, as he was Act 20:16
*, I'll call for you again." Act 24:25
* to time and talked with him. Act 24:26
time to * and talked with him. Act 24:26
It came at about the * of the Act 27:9f
No one had eaten for a long *, Act 27:21
but when they had waited a long * Act 28:6
and when the * came to sail, Act 28:10
again, and this * it was in The Act 28:11
So a * was set and on that day Act 28:23
waiting all this * without Rom 2:4
give you * to turn from your sin? Rom 2:4
forward to the * when Christ would Rom 3:25
God more each * we use it until Rom 5:4
at just the right * and died for us Rom 5:6
sinning from the * of Adam until Rom 5:13
been patient with for all this *? Rom 9:22
Yes, for even back in the * of Rom 10:19
At that * I will take away their Rom 11:27
how late it is; * is running out. Rom 13:11
Don't spend your * in wild Rom 13:12,13
expectantly to the * when God will Rom 15:4
and after we have had a good * Rom 15:24
secret from the beginning of *. Rom 16:25,26,27
yours during this * of waiting for 1Co 1:7
There is going to come a * of 1Co 3:13
At that * God will give to each 1Co 4:5
for when that * comes you can be 1Co 4:8
There was a * when some of you 1Co 6:11
for a limited *, so that they can 1Co 7:5
don't rush into it at this *. 1Co 7:27
that our remaining * is very short, 1Co 7:29
An unmarried man can spend his * 1Co 7:32
the * he still feels it is wrong. 1Co 8:10
Olympic races of Paul's *. 1Co 9:25f
For every * you eat this bread 1Co 11:26
speak one at a *, and someone must 1Co 14:27
prophesy, one at a *, if they have 1Co 14:29,30
brothers at one *, most of whom are 1Co 15:6
ourselves a good *: let us eat, 1Co 15:32
This * I don't want to make just 1Co 16:7
to me happy with his * among you; 1Co 16:11
hard * we went through in Asia. 2Co 1:8
Now it is * to forgive him and 2Co 2:7
Yet this short * of distress will 2Co 4:17
earthly bodies is * spent away from 2Co 5:6
me at a favorable *, when the doors 2Co 6:2
* we have the joy of the Lord. 2Co 6:10
the wonderful * he had with you. 2Co 7:7
very sorry for a *, realizing how 2Co 7:8
have an easy * of it at your 2Co 8:13
then at some other * they can 2Co 8:14
turn out that this * I was wrong in 2Co 9:3
This * my personal presence is 2Co 10:11
Each * he said, "No. 2Co 12:9
coming to you again, the third *; 2Co 12:14
THIS IS THE third * I am coming to 2Co 13:1
then, that this * I come ready to 2Co 13:2
* was James, our Lord's brother. Gal 1:19
again, this * with Barnabas; Gal 2:1
forward to this * when God would Gal 3:8,9
who at any * breaks a single one of Gal 3:10
But when the right * came, the Gal 4:4
time came, the * God decided on, he Gal 4:4
for the * when you will finally be Gal 4:19
that next * it might be one of you Gal 6:1
that when the * is ripe he will Eph 1:10
gladness all the *, as though Eph 6:6,7
Pray all the *. Eph 6:18
* you first heard it until now. Php 1:5
and at the same * keep on growing Php 1:9
while all the * you are learning to Col 1:10
don't spend your * worrying about Col 3:2
but now is the * to cast off and Col 3:8
are watching you but all the *; Col 3:22
you ahead of * that suffering would 1Th 3:4
Night is the * for sleep and the 1Th 5:7
and the * when people get drunk. 1Th 5:7
or alive at the * of his return. 1Th 5:10
while at the same * he is 2Th 1:6
there will be a * of great 2Th 2:3
for he can come only when his * 2Th 2:6
and during the * we were with you. 2Th 2:15
and wasting your * in gossiping. 2Th 3:11
* arguing and talking foolishness. 1Ti 1:6
I didn't know Christ at that *. 1Ti 1:13
spending our * in godly living and 1Ti 2:2
proper * God gave to the world. 1Ti 2:6
Don't waste * arguing over 1Ti 4:7
Spend your * and energy in the 1Ti 4:7
and spending much * in prayer; 1Ti 5:5
are spending their * running around 1Ti 5:6
and spend their * gossiping around 1Ti 5:13
and hurt for a long * to come. 2Ti 2:17
right, and all the * be feeding 2Ti 4:2
For there is going to come a * 2Ti 4:3
longer. My * has almost run out. 2Ti 4:6
And now the * has come for me to 2Ti 4:7
The first * I was brought before 2Ti 4:16
And now in his own good * he has Tit 1:3
spending their * in their own Tit 2:5
to that wonderful * we've been Tit 2:13
But when the * came for the Tit 3:4
good deeds all the *, for this is Tit 3:8
Another * he said, "I am his Heb 1:5,6
And still another *—when his Heb 1:5,6
At another * he said, "I will Heb 2:13
And at still another *, "See, Heb 2:13
there is still *, so that none of Heb 3:13
But now is the *. Heb 3:15
those who lived in the * of Moses. Heb 4:2
But he has set another * for Heb 4:7
for coming in, and that * is now. Heb 4:7
"today" being the * to get in. Heb 4:8
And another * God said to him, Heb 5:6
You have been Christians a long * Heb 5:12,13
This * he will come bringing Heb 9:28
sacrifice for all *, and then sat Heb 10:12
and wasting no *, he built the ark Heb 11:7
earth, but, "Next *," he says, Heb 12:26
men, now is the * to cry and groan Jas 5:1
Then he prayed again, this * Jas 5:18
of any sin at any *, that he might 1Pe 3:18
For the * has come for judgment, 1Pe 4:17
in his good * he will lift you up. 1Pe 5:6
At that * God completely 2Pe 2:5
But at the same * the Lord 2Pe 2:7,8
more * for sinners to repent. 2Pe 3:9
He is giving us * to get his 2Pe 3:15,16
I am warning you ahead of *, dear 2Pe 3:17
of God's will at any * in any way. 1Jn 3:5
together and have a joyous *. 2Jn 1:12
without any fruit at picking * Jud 1:12
For the * is near when these Rev 1:3
I gave her * to change her mind Rev 2:21
the * of Great Tribulation and Rev 3:10
This * a red horse rode out. Rev 6:4
It is * to judge the dead, and Rev 11:18
knowing that he has little *." Rev 12:12
Literally, "a * and times and Rev 12:14f
"a time and times and half a *." Rev 12:14f
All that * he blasphemed God's Rev 13:6
For the * has come when he will Rev 14:7
the * has come for his martyrs Rev 14:13
the * has come for you to reap; Rev 14:15
for the * has come for the Rev 19:7
for the * of fulfillment is near. Rev 22:10
And when that * comes, all doing Rev 22:11

TIMELY
* advice is as lovely as golden Pro 25:11

TIMES
I will give seven * your punishment Gen 4:15
be punished seven *, anyone taking Gen 4:24
be punished seventy-seven *!" Gen 4:24
* the grain he sowed. Gen 26:12
you have reduced my wages ten *! Gen 31:41
he bowed low seven * before him. Gen 33:3
* as much as to any of the others! Gen 43:34
the people with justice at all *. Ex 18:22
At these three * each year, Ex 23:17
and harvest *, work only six days, Ex 34:21
your God those three * each year. Ex 34:24
sprinkle it seven * before the Lord Lev 4:6
sprinkle it seven * before the Lev 4:17
sprinkled it seven *, and also Lev 8:11
the blood seven * upon the man Lev 14:7
finger seven * before the Lord. Lev 14:16
of it seven * before the Lord. Lev 14:27
shall sprinkle the house seven *. Lev 14:51,52
and then seven * in front of it. Lev 16:14
the altar seven * with his finger, Lev 16:19
of the Lord—* when all Israel will Lev 23:1
in every home, * for assembling to Lev 23:3
* more severely for your sins. Lev 26:18
send you seven * more plagues Lev 26:21
smite you seven * for your sin. Lev 26:24
and send you seven * greater Lev 26:28
Use the trumpets in * of Num 10:10
*) was founded about 1720 B.C. Num 13:22f
wilderness—and ten * refused to Num 14:22
sprinkle it seven * towards the Num 19:4
your beating me these three *?" Num 22:28
beat your donkey those three *?" Num 22:32
Three * the donkey saw me and Num 22:33
you have blessed them three *. Num 24:10
compulsory at the * of your annual Num 29:39
you a thousand * more, and bless Deu 1:11
fair at all *, even to foreigners! Deu 1:16
you in the latter *, you will Deu 4:30
your God three * a year at the Deu 16:16
the city seven *, with the priests Jos 6:3,4
the city not once, but seven *. Jos 6:15
"You've made fun of me three * Ju 16:15
bowed himself three * and they 1Sa 20:41f
to Egypt ever since ancient *. 1Sa 27:8
"so we have ten * as much right in 2Sa 19:43
will be a hundred * as many people 2Sa 24:3
offerings three * a year on the 1Ki 9:25
the child three *, and cried out to 1Ki 17:21
and again, and again, seven *!" 1Ki 18:43
"How many * must I tell you to 1Ki 22:1
and forth in the house a few *; 2Ki 4:3
seven * and opened his eyes! 2Ki 4:3
Jordan River seven * and he would 2Ki 5:1
*, as the prophet had told him to. 2Ki 5:1
This happened several *. 2Ki 6:1
Stay with the king at all *." 2Ki 11:6,7
was the custom at * of coronation, 2Ki 11:13,1
up and struck the floor three *. 2Ki 13:1
floor five or six *," he 2Ki 13:1
will be victorious only three *." 2Ki 13:1
to obey him at all * and to do 2Ki 23:
of this division in ancient *. 1Ch 9:2
the temper of the * and knew the 1Ch 12:24-3
*, would they not all be yours? 1Ch 21:
blessings in his name at all *. 1Ch 23:1
many groups to serve at various *. 1Ch 24:
In their * of rebellion against 2Ch 15:
"how many * must I tell you to 2Ch 18:1
just as in the * of King Ahab, and 2Ch 21:1
Jerusalem has in * past been a Ez 4:1
our weapons with us at all *. Neh 4:2
Four * they sent the same Neh 6:
on duty at regular *, and that each Neh 7:
to determine when—at regular * Neh 10:3
at the proper * and cared for the Neh 13:3
the temper of the * as well as Est 1:13-1
your words? Ten * now you have Job 19:
to God except in * of crisis. Job 27:1
He opens their ears in * like Job 33:1
for them in their * of trouble. Ps 9:
like silver seven * refined. Ps 12:
Many * you have miraculously Ps 18:5
my God; my * are in your hands. Ps 31:14,1
from death even in * of famine! Ps 33:18,1
He cares for them when * are Ps 37:1
Do you remember those * (but how Ps 42:4,
a tested help in * of trouble. Ps 46:
need to fear when * of trouble Ps 49:
I want you to trust me in your * Ps 50:14,1
I cannot count the * when you Ps 71:1
chose in ancient * from slavery and Ps 74:
For God has given us these * of Ps 81:
*, from the everlasting past. Ps 93:
I will praise you seven * a day Ps 119:16
I can't even count how many * a Ps 139:17,1
But even so, he is fined seven * Pro 6:3
try once you must try a dozen *! Pro 19:1
*, will each time rise again? Pro 24:15,1
in those former *, and in the Ecc 1:8-1
can, and when hard * strike, Ecc 7:1
man sins a hundred * and still Ecc 8:1
think of all those * you sacrificed Is 1:2
you all this power from ancient *? Is 37:2
do as I have done since ancient *. Is 44:
I send good * and bad. Is 45:
And don't forget the many * I Is 46:
at various other * until July of Jer 1:3
sends the harvest *, yet they have Jer 5:23,2
our Savior in * of trouble, why are Jer 14:8
good * pass him by forever. Jer 17:6
do a mighty miracle as in olden * Jer 21:1
more now than you did the other *. Jer 42:2
and so also eighty-seven * Eze 2:1
the * of their fathers until now. Eze 20:4
only of the * the people rebelled. Eze 21:2
for Israel, good * will return. Eze 36:8
in a mighty battle of the end *. Eze 38:2,3
necessarily mean "the end *." Eze 38:15,16
men's advice ten * better than that Dan 1:20
be heated up seven * hotter than Dan 3:19
and prayed three * a day, just as Dan 6:10
favors of his God three * a day." Dan 6:13
Literally, "change the * and the Dan 7:25
take place until the end * come." Dan 8:17
be rebuilt despite the perilous *. Dan 9:25
in the future: * of great Dan 10:1
Jews, at the end *—for the Dan 10:14
until the end *, when travel and Dan 12:4
Literally, "a time, *, and half a Dan 12:7f
idol and for the * when she put on Hos 1:13
to his blessings, in the end *. Hos 3:5
your parties into * of mourning, Amo 8:10
garments worn at * of mourning. Jon 3:4,5
Lord for his help in * of trouble! Mic 3:4
this inscription on it seven *: Zec 3:9
"The traditional fasts and * of Zec 8:19
* as much as he had planted. Mt 13:8
a crop many * greater than the Mt 13:23f
or even a hundred * as much." Mt 13:23f
read the obvious signs of the *! Mt 16:2,3
Seven *?" Mt 18:21
Jesus replied, "seventy * Mt 18:22
receive a hundred * as much in Mt 19:29
equivalent to $20 in modern *, or Mt 20:2f
dawn, you will deny me three *!" Mt 26:34
crows, you will deny me three *." Mt 26:75
and yielded thirty * as much as he Mk 4:8
even sixty or a hundred * as much! Mk 4:8
or even a hundred * as much as was Mk 4:20
back, a hundred * over, homes, Mk 10:30

MES Con't)
ou will deny me three *." Mk 14:30
wice, you will deny me three *." Mk 14:72
as large as he had planted." Lk 8:8
and so the poor fellow is seven * Lk 11:26
re evil *, with evil people. Lk 11:29,30
even if he wrongs you seven * a Lk 17:4
e repaid many * over now, as well Lk 18:30
iving him back four * as much!" Lk 19:8
as much as the original amount! Lk 19:16
ain—five * the original amount. Lk 19:18
vill deny me three *, declaring Lk 22:34
ou will deny me three *." Lk 22:61
No—three * before the cock crows Jn 13:38
here many * with his disciples. Jn 18:2
end you wonderful * of refreshment Act 3:19
in, as prophesied from ancient *. Act 3:21,22
ame vision was repeated three *. Act 10:16
This happened three * before Act 11:10
And he was seen many * during Act 13:31
o come many * before (but was Rom 1:13
Since earliest * men have seen Rom 1:20
hose who sinned in former *. Rom 3:25
who are going through such hard *. Rom 15:26
This plan was hidden in former *, 1Co 2:7
at present. In * like these I think 1Co 7:26
and if a girl gets married in * 1Co 7:28
trouble and hard *, they have mixed 2Co 8:2
been whipped * without number, and 2Co 11:23
Five different * the Jews gave 2Co 11:24
Three * I was beaten with rods. 2Co 11:25
Three * I was shipwrecked. 2Co 11:25
Three different * I begged God 2Co 12:8
at all *, not to hope for evil. 2Co 13:8
what is best for us at all *. Eph 1:8
In olden * God did not share Eph 3:5
the truth at all *—speaking truly, Eph 4:15,16
live and at other * I don't, for I Php 1:23
that in the last * some in the 1Ti 4:1
day, and many * during the long 2Ti 1:3
prefer good * to worshiping God. 2Ti 3:4
urgently at all *, whenever you get 2Ti 4:2
grace to help us in our * of need. Heb 4:16
desire to obey God at all *. Heb 5:7
to do only God's will at all *. 1Pe 2:16
lived in ancient * before the flood 2Pe 2:5
that in the last * there would Jud 1:18
Think about those * of your Rev 2:5
Literally, "a time and * and half Rev 12:14f

IMID
men who are * and frightened." Ju 7:3
I have not been * about it, as Ps 40:9
I came to you in weakness—* and 1Co 2:3

IMNA
(born to *, Eliphaz' concubine). Gen 36:10,11,12
(Lotan had a sister, *. Gen 36:22
clan of *,The clan of Alvah,The Gen 36:40-43
Gatam, Kenaz, *, and Amalek. 1Ch 1:36
and Esau's daughter was named *. 1Ch 1:38,39
Chief *, Chief Aliah, Chief 1Ch 1:51-54

IMNAH
went to * to supervise the shearing Gen 38:12
sheep-shearing at *, and realizing Gen 38:13
Enaim, which is on the way to *. Gen 38:14
past the south of * to the shoulder Jos 15:10,11
Kain, Gibe-ah, *, Halhul, Beth-zur, Jos 15:48-62
Ithlah, Elon, *, Ekron, Eltekeh, Jos 19:41-46
ONE DAY WHEN Samson was in *, he Ju 14:1
were going to *, a young lion Ju 14:5
Upon arriving at * he talked Ju 14:7
Gederoth, Soco, *, and Gimzo with 2Ch 28:17,18

TIMNATH-HERES
of his property in *, in the hill Ju 2:7-9

TIMNATH-SERAH
He chose * in the hill country of Jos 19:50
his own estate at *, in the hill Jos 24:30

TIMON
Prochorus, Nicanor, * Act 6:5

TIMOTHY
where they met *, a believer whose Act 16:1
father a Greek. * was well thought Act 16:2
he circumcised * before they left, Act 16:3
while Silas and * remained behind. Act 17:14
Silas and * to hurry and join him. Act 17:15
of Silas and * from Macedonia, Paul Act 18:5
He sent his two assistants, * Act 19:22
Gaius, from Derbe; and *; Act 20:4
* my fellow-worker, and Lucius Rom 16:21
am sending *—to help you do this. 1Co 4:17
If * comes make him feel at home, 1Co 16:10
Implied in 1 * 4:12. 1Co 16:11f
and from our dear brother *. 2Co 1:1
* and Silvanus and I have been 2Co 1:19
FROM: PAUL AND *, slaves of Jesus Php 1:1
I will send * to see you soon. Php 2:19
There is no one like * for Php 2:20
But you know *. Php 2:22
messenger, and from Brother *. Col 1:1
FROM: PAUL, SILAS and *. 1Th 1:1
Athens and send *, our brother and 1Th 3:2,3
no longer I sent * to find out 1Th 3:5
And now * has just returned and 1Th 3:6
FROM: PAUL, SILAS and *. 2Th 1:1
To: *. 1Ti 1:2
*, you are like a son to me in the 1Ti 1:2
Now, *, my son, here is my 1Ti 1:18
Teach these truths, *, and 1Ti 6:2
Oh, *, you are God's man. 1Ti 6:11
Oh, *, don't fail to do these 1Ti 6:20
To: *, my dear son. 2Ti 1:2
How I thank God for you, *. 2Ti 1:3
OH, *, MY son, be strong with the 2Ti 2:1
YOU MAY AS well know this too, *, 2Ti 3:1
Jesus Christ, and from Brother *. Phm 1:1
that Brother * is now out of jail; Heb 13:23

TIN
bronze, iron, *, or lead— shall be Num 31:22
Armed with his * shield, he Job 15:25,26
the *, the iron and the lead. Eze 22:18,19,20
markets—silver, iron, * and lead. Eze 27:12

TINGLE
hear about it will * with horror. 2Ki 21:12

TINKLE
the bells will * as he goes in Ex 28:35
No longer shall they * with Is 3:18

TINKLING
noses in the air, * bracelets on Is 3:16

TINY
morning it left * flakes of Ex 16:14
He also brought a * Num 7:14
you even a * piece of their land. Deu 2:5
except for a * remnant that managed Jos 10:20
but a * remnant of their forces. Ju 20:35-39
down to the * hyssop which grows in 1Ki 4:33
It was a great triumph for the * 2Ch 24:24
With that * army, how can you Is 36:8,9
* group shall be a mighty nation. Is 60:22
* remnant of what we were before. Jer 42:2
(it will be but a * remnant) shall Jer 44:28
little children and * babies are Lam 2:11
care and sip their * portions of Eze 12:19
They look like * horses, and Joe 2:4
yourselves on your own * power! Amo 6:13
* mustard seed planted in a field. Mt 13:31,32
even as small as a * mustard seed Mt 17:20
It is like a * mustard seed! Mk 4:31,32
"Oh, what * faith you have; Mk 9:19
It is like a * mustard seed Lk 13:19
days, and those with * babies. Lk 21:23
And a * rudder makes a huge ship Jas 3:4
can be set on fire by one * spark. Jas 3:5
clay that is broken into * pieces. Rev 2:27

TIP
of it upon the * of the right ear Ex 29:19,20
of it upon the * of the right ear Lev 14:14
priest upon the * of the man's Lev 14:17
its blood upon the * of the man's Lev 14:25
his hand upon the * of the man's Lev 14:28
the southernmost * of the Sea of Num 34:10,11
feet from wing * to wing tip. 1Ki 6:23-28
feet from wing tip to wing *. 1Ki 6:23-28
A nine-inch rim surrounded the * 1Ki 7:35
approached and touched its *. Est 5:2
at the southern * of the Sea of Eze 47:18
to your southern *, all the way Amo 6:14
if only to dip the * of his finger Lk 16:24

TIPHSAH
Euphrates River, from * to Gaza. 1Ki 4:24

TIPPED
inches thick, * with a 1Sa 17:4-7

TIPPING
of boiling water, * southward, Jer 1:13

TIPS
or five out on the * of the limbs. Is 17:6

TIRAS
Madai,Javan, Tubal,Meshech, *. Gen 10:2
Javan, Tubal, Meshech, and *. 1Ch 1:5-9

TIRATHITES
*, Shime-athites, and Sucathites. 1Ch 2:55

TIRED
sick and * of these local girls. Gen 27:46
Moses' arms finally became too * Ex 17:12
They were very *, but still Ju 8:4
we were * and hungry," he said. Ju 8:15
"You must be very * and hungry and 2Sa 17:28,29
hand was too * to hold his sword; 2Sa 23:10
that the workmen were becoming *; Neh 4:10
and Kedar. I am * of being here Ps 120:5,6
He is too * even to lift his Pro 26:15
I am * out, O God, and ready to Pro 30:2
He gives power to the * and worn Is 40:29
you have grown * of me! Is 43:22
destroy you. I am * of always Jer 15:6
sleeping, for they were very *. Mk 14:40
When they finally * of their Mk 15:20
Jesus was * from the long walk in Jn 4:5,6
And let us not get * of doing Gal 6:9
I never get * of telling you this Php 3:1
never be * of doing right. 2Th 3:13
So take a new grip with your * Heb 12:12

TIRESOME
is unutterably weary and *. Ecc 1:8-11

TIRHAKAH
the king that King * of Ethiopia 2Ki 19:9
received word that *, crown prince Is 37:8,9

TIRHANAH
bore him Sheber, *, Shaaph (the 1Ch 2:48,49

TIRI-A
sons were:Ziph, Ziphah, *, Asarel. 1Ch 4:16

TIRZAH
These girls, Mahlah, *, Hoglah, Num 36:11,12
The king of *. Jos 12:8-24
Noah, Hoglah, Milcah, and *. Jos 17:3
So Jeroboam's wife returned to *; 1Ki 14:17
city of Ramah and returned to *. 1Ki 15:21
king of Israel in *, during the 1Ki 15:28
palace, in the capital city of *. 1Ki 16:9
to besiege *, Israel's capital. 1Ki 16:17
twelve years, six of them in *. 1Ki 16:23
to Samaria from * and assassinated 2Ki 15:14
the lovely land of *, yes, Sol 6:4

TISHBE
from * in Gilead, told King Ahab, 1Ki 17:1

TISHBITE
Literally, "Elijah the *." 2Ki 1:3f

TITHE
in giving me the * of your crops Ex 22:29
he has spoiled, or the * omitted, Lev 5:16
they receive—a * of the tithe, to Num 18:25,26
tithe of the *, to be presented to Num 18:25,26
This * of the tithe shall be Num 18:28,29
This tithe of the * shall be Num 18:28,29
Neither the * of your grain and Deu 12:17
"You must * all of your crops Deu 14:22
Bring this * to eat before the Deu 14:23
you may sell the * portion of your Deu 14:25
to use your entire * for local Deu 14:28
I have not touched the * while I Deu 26:14
everything else—a * of all they 2Ch 31:5,6
and brought a * of the dedicated 2Ch 31:5,6
For you * down to the last mint Mt 23:23
Yes, you should *, but you Mt 23:23
For though you are careful to * Lk 11:42
You should *, yes, but you should Lk 11:42

TITHES
* from the entire land of Israel. Num 18:21
for the people's *, offered to the Num 18:24
a tenth of the * they receive—a Num 18:25,26
part of the * you receive as the Num 18:28,29
the Lord's * if you then give the Num 18:32
sacrifices—your *, your offerings Deu 12:6
this applies to your * of grain, Deu 14:23
to carry your * to that place, Deu 14:24
to give all your * to the Levites, Deu 26:12
given all of my * to the Levites, Deu 26:13
to bring their * to the priests and 2Ch 31:4
brought in the * of their cattle 2Ch 31:5,6
The first of these * arrived in 2Ch 31:7,8
of Zadok replied, "These are *! 2Ch 31:10
the * in all our rural towns. Neh 10:37
received these *, and a tenth of Neh 10:38
was collected as * was delivered to Neh 10:38
offerings, the *, and Neh 12:44
bowls, and * of grain, new wine, Neh 13:5
bringing their * of grain, new Neh 13:12
and bring your * twice a week! Amo 4:4
"You have robbed me of the * and Mal 3:8
Bring all the * into the Mal 3:10
though mortal, received *; Heb 7:8
of all who receive *), paid tithes Heb 7:9
* to Melchizedek through Abraham. Heb 7:9
Abraham paid the * to Melchizedek. Heb 7:10

TITHING
The purpose of * is to teach you Deu 14:23
third year is a year of special *. Deu 26:12

TITLE
He shall have your uniform and * Is 22:21
(And that * belongs to you alone! Jer 10:7
To him belongs the royal *. Zec 6:13
and * is this on the coin?" Mk 12:16
and his * was "The Word of God." Rev 19:13
was written this *: "King of Kings Rev 19:16

TITLES
These will be his royal *: Is 9:6
the names and * of the angels. Heb 1:4

TITUS
70 by * and the subsequent Dan 9:25f
After that he stayed with * Act 18:7
the Gospel. But *, my dear 2Co 2:13
refreshed us by the arrival of *. 2Co 7:6
happier still by *' joy when you 2Co 7:13
to * has also proved true! 2Co 7:14
that we have urged *, who 2Co 8:6
that he has given * the same real 2Co 8:16
If anyone asks who * is, say that 2Co 8:23
When I urged * to visit you, and 2Co 12:18
Barnabas; and * came along too. Gal 2:1
they did not even demand that *, Gal 2:3
Crescens has gone to Galatia, * 2Ti 4:10
To: *, who is truly my son in the Tit 1:4

TIZA
Joha (his brother) from *; 1Ch 11:26-47

TOAH
Jeroham, Eliel, *, Zuph, Elkanah 1Ch 6:33-38

TOASTS
concubines drank * from them to Dan 5:2,3,4
TOB
home and lived in the land of *. Ju 11:3
ten thousand from the land of *. 2Sa 10:6
from Zobah, Rehob, *, and Maacah 2Sa 10:7,8
TOBADONIJAH
Adonijah, Tobijah, and *; 2Ch 17:7,8,9
TOBIAH
*, and Nekoda—a total of 652. Ez 2:60
(the Horonite) and * (an Ammonite Neh 2:10
But when Sanballat and * and Neh 2:19
*, who was standing beside him, Neh 4:3
But when Sanballat and * and the Neh 4:7
WHEN SANBALLAT, *, Geshem the Neh 6:1
spoken to him, but * and Sanballat Neh 6:12,13
all the evil of *, Sanballat, Neh 6:14
and forth between * and the wealthy Neh 6:17
a wonderful man * was, and then Neh 6:19
I had said; and * sent many Neh 6:19
*, and Nekoda—a total of 642. Neh 7:62
a good friend of *, had converted Neh 13:4
into a beautiful guest room for *. Neh 13:5
in the Temple for *— I was very Neh 13:7
TOBIJAH
Adonijah, *, and Tobadonijah; 2Ch 17:7,8,9
"Heldai, *, and Jedaiah will Zec 6:10,11
*, Jedaiah, and also Josiah. Zec 6:14
TOCHEN
Etam, Ain, Rimmon, *, and Ashan; 1Ch 4:32,33
TODAY
One week from * I will begin Gen 7:4
Let me go out among your flocks * Gen 30:31,32
"* I remember my sin!" Gen 41:9
position I have * so that I could Gen 50:20
the flocks watered so quickly *?" Ex 2:18
quotas either yesterday or *?" Ex 5:14
always to remember * as the day Ex 12:17
way the Lord will rescue you *. Ex 14:13
So cook as much as you want to *, Ex 16:23
is your food for *, for today is Ex 16:25
for today, for * is the Sabbath to Ex 16:25
will be no food on the ground *. Ex 16:25
Sanctify them * and tomorrow, and Ex 19:10
Then Moses told the Levites, "* Ex 32:29
olive oil. For *," Moses said, Lev 9:4
"'* Israel shall cross the Deu 2:18
Beginning * I will make people Deu 2:25
Villages') as it is still known *. Deu 3:14
Lord your God are still alive *. Deu 4:4
fair as these I am giving you *? Deu 4:8
this is what you are *. Deu 4:20
as an inheritance, as it is *. Deu 4:38
I will tell you *, so that all will Deu 4:40
but with you who are here alive *. Deu 5:2,3
me and pleaded, '* the Lord our Deu 5:24
commandments I am giving you *. Deu 6:6
commandments I am giving you *. Deu 7:11
all the commandments I give you *. Deu 8:1
"O ISRAEL, LISTEN! * you are to Deu 9:1
bless his name, just as is done *. Deu 10:8
I am giving you *, and to love him, Deu 10:12,13
other nation, as is evident *. Deu 10:15
going to give you *, so that you Deu 11:8
going to give you *, and if you Deu 11:13
"I am giving you the choice * Deu 11:26
I am giving you *, and a curse if Deu 11:27
all the laws I am giving you *. Deu 11:32
I am giving you *, and if you have Deu 13:18
your God that I am giving you *. Deu 15:4,5
I am giving you *—loving the Lord Deu 19:9
afraid as you go out to fight *! Deu 20:3
the Lord your God is giving you *. Deu 26:16
You have declared * that he is Deu 26:17
And the Lord has declared * that Deu 26:18
commandments I enjoin on you *." Deu 27:1f
Israel, listen! * you have become Deu 27:9
Lord your God, so * you must begin Deu 27:10
declaring to you *, God will Deu 28:1
I am giving you *, he will make you Deu 28:13
I am giving you *, then all of Deu 28:15-19
standing * before the Lord your Deu 29:10
contract he is making with you *. Deu 29:12
He wants to confirm you * as his Deu 29:13
stand before him *, but with all Deu 29:14,15
land, where they still live *!' Deu 29:28
I have given you *, then the Lord Deu 30:2
that I command you *, the Lord your Deu 30:7,8
"Look, * I have set before you Deu 30:15
I have commanded you * to love Deu 30:16
against you that * I have set Deu 30:19
"If even *, while I am still Deu 31:27
I have given you *, and pass them Deu 32:46
"*," the Lord told Joshua, "I Jos 3:7
God has said. * you are going to Jos 3:10
And the Lord said to Joshua, "* Jos 5:8,9
and is still called that *. Jos 5:8,9
this day, and even * that place is Jos 7:26
mound of refuse, as it still is *. Jos 8:28
(The pile is still there *. Jos 10:27
and * I am eighty-five years old. Jos 14:10
For you know that if you rebel * Jos 22:17,18
Phinehas replied to them, "* we Jos 22:31
then decide * whom you will obey. Jos 24:15
*, mingled with the Israelis. Ju 1:21
Luz, too, as it is still known *. Ju 1:26
deliverance through me *! Ju 15:18
and the spring is still there *. Ju 15:19
"Stay just * and leave sometime Ju 19:8
in the world did you glean *? Ru 2:19
He'll settle it *." Ru 3:15-18
have seen that * I have bought all Ru 4:9
battle—I was there *," he told 1Sa 4:16
"No one will be executed *; 1Sa 11:13
* the Lord has rescued Israel!" 1Sa 11:13
thunder and rain *, so that you 1Sa 12:17
find out what sin was committed *. 1Sa 14:38
who saved Israel *, shall die? 1Sa 14:45
of God to do a mighty miracle *." 1Sa 14:45
of Israel from you * and has given 1Sa 15:28
you have defied. * the Lord will 1Sa 17:46
dinner either yesterday or *?" 1Sa 20:27
to him. "* is the day the Lord was 1Sa 24:4
kind to me *, for when the Lord 1Sa 24:18
the kindness you have shown me *. 1Sa 24:19
who has sent you to meet me *! 1Sa 25:32
for you saved my life *. 1Sa 26:21
even as I have saved yours *. 1Sa 26:24
"Where did you make your raid * 1Sa 27:10
great man has fallen * in Israel; 2Sa 3:38
tried to kill you. * the Lord has 2Sa 4:8
the king of Israel looked *! 2Sa 6:20
We must really act like men * if 2Sa 10:12
arrived, and now * should I force 2Sa 15:19,20
get to be king! * I will get back 2Sa 16:3
as it is still known *. 2Sa 18:18
my lord the king. * Jehovah has 2Sa 18:31
saved your life * and the lives of 2Sa 19:5
That is why I have come here *, 2Sa 19:20
I am eighty years old *, and 2Sa 19:35
upon your throne? * he celebrated 1Ki 1:25
"who has done * what he promised 1Ki 8:15
to do your will. * you have 1Ki 8:24
just as you are doing *." 1Ki 8:61
known as "The Wasteland" *. 1Ki 9:13
they continue as slaves even *. 1Ki 9:20,21
I will present myself to Ahab *." 1Ki 18:15
and Israel, prove * that you are 1Ki 18:36
I will deliver them all to you *. 1Ki 20:13
to take Elijah away from you *?" 2Ki 2:3
to take away your master *?" 2Ki 2:5
"Why *?" 2Ki 4:23
"How are you *, you murderer! 2Ki 9:31
toilet, which it still is *. 2Ki 10:27
on among them *—they follow their 2Ki 17:34
And it is still called that *. 1Ch 13:11
as is evident *. 2Ch 6:15
*, and how they praised the Lord! 2Ch 20:26
and contempt, as you see us *. 2Ch 29:8
and disgraced, just as we are *. Ez 9:7
a day as this! For * is a sacred Neh 8:9
I have prepared for you *." Est 5:4
as they have done *, and let Est 9:13
"My complaint * is still a Job 23:2
* I am giving you your glory.' Ps 2:7
him calling you * and come to him! Ps 95:7
are you leading your flock *? Sol 1:7
Iraq, still lies in utter ruin *. Is 13:20f
living, can praise you as I do *. Is 38:19
many eastern lands *) only harlots Is 47:2f
Are you not the same *, the Is 51:10
in your mouth! * your work begins, Jer 1:10
For see, * I have made you Jer 1:18
with milk and honey," as it is *. Jer 11:5
is the sad news from the Lord *?" Jer 23:33
and cursed, just as they are *. Jer 25:18
your name very great, as it is *. Jer 32:20
the warning I have given you *. Jer 42:19
And * I have told you exactly Jer 42:21
without an inhabitant, as it is *. Jer 44:22
a sacrifice * in the north country Jer 46:10
and Job were here *, they alone Eze 14:14
as you do even *, shall I listen to Eze 20:31
this date, for * the king of Eze 24:2
"But now note this: From *, this Hag 2:18,19
Give us our food again *, as Mt 6:11
that are here * and gone tomorrow, Mt 6:30
it would still be here *. Mt 11:23
'Why haven't you been working *?' Mt 20:6
go out and work on the farm *.' Mt 21:28
"These Scriptures came true *!" Lk 4:21
"We have seen strange things *." Lk 5:26
seen the hand of God at work *." Lk 7:16
and heard here *: how those who Lk 7:20,21,22
that are here * and gone tomorrow, Lk 12:28
you say, '* will be a scorcher.' Lk 12:55
of healing * and tomorrow; Lk 13:32
Yes, *, tomorrow, and the next Lk 13:33
to be a guest in your home *!" Lk 19:5
salvation has come to this home *. Lk 19:9,10
And Jesus replied, "* you will Lk 23:43
you are seeing and hearing *. Act 2:33
spoken about what is going on *. Act 3
is happening here in this city *! Act 4
'* I have honored you as my son.' Act 13:32
just as you have tried to do *. Act 2
And I am being tried here * Act 2
I am still alive * to tell these Act 26
I asked you to come here * so we Act 28
Our fears for *, our worries Rom 8
It is the same *. Rom 1
Yes, even * when they read 2Co 3
you. * he is ready to save you. 2Co 6
are my Son, and * I have given you Heb 1
to hear his voice * and not let our Heb 3
Never forget the warning, "* if Heb 3
already quoted, "* when you hear Heb 4
"*" being the time to get in. Heb 4
God said to him, "My Son, * I Heb 5
has an important lesson for us *. Heb 9
same yesterday, *, and forever. Heb 13
people who say, "* or tomorrow we Jas 4
TODAY'S
Similarity with * world is Gen 11
Note: The actual value by * Lev 27
who joke about "* sad news from Jer 23
But if you ask him about "* Jer 23:38,
government for * riot, since there Act 19
TOE
upon the big * of his right foot. Lev 8
upon the big * of his right foot. Lev 14
hand and the big * of his right Lev 14
on the big * of his right foot. Lev 14
and upon the big * of his right Lev 14
bare his bones from head to *. Hab 3:1
TOES
and the big * of their right feet; Ex 29:19,2
the big * of their right feet. Lev 8:2
extra fingers or *, or has a Lev 21:1
and cut off his thumbs and big *. Ju 1:4,5
each hand and six * on each foot 2Sa 21:20,2
each hand and six * on each foot 1Ch 20:6,
The feet and * you saw—part iron Dan 2:41,4
TOGARMAH
of Gomer:Ashkenaz, Riphath, *. Gen 10
Ashkenaz, Diphath, and *. 1Ch 1:5-
and bronze dishes, while from * Eze 27:1
and the armies of * from the Eze 38
TOGETHER
* they formed the first day. Gen 1:4,
So they strung fig leaves * to Gen 3
And while they were * there, Gen 4
"This will weld us *," they Gen 11:3,
he called * the men born into his Gen 14:1
So the two of them went on *. Gen 22
ate * beside the pile of rocks. Gen 31:4
THEN JACOB CALLED * all his sons Gen 49
"Call * all the elders of Ex 3:1
each lamb, eat it * in one house, Ex 12:4
So Aaron called them * and Ex 16:1
meal * before the Lord. Ex 18:1
and called * the leaders of the Ex 19
and they had a meal * before the Ex 24:1
two long pieces * side by side. Ex 26:4,
fasten the loops *, so that the Ex 26
them * with fifty bronze clasps. Ex 26:10,1
two long sheets * to form the Ex 36:1
of these draperies * to make one Ex 36:1
to tie the frames * along the Ex 36:31,32
The ephod was held * by shoulder Ex 39:4,
to Moses, "Put * the Tabernacle Ex 40:2
year, the Tabernacle was put *. Ex 40:17
of the Tabernacle, * with their Lev 8:1
the people to meet * for worship; Lev 23:23,24
All the people are to come * Lev 23:26,27
he himself gets * enough money, Lev 25:26
each tribe stayed * under its own Num 2:3-31
used in tying the Tabernacle *. Num 3:25-30
is to be gathered *, you shall blow Num 10:5,6,7f
of them went up * into Mount Hor Num 20:27
Striking his hands * in anger and Num 24:10
* with your family and servants. Deu 16:14
an ox and a donkey harnessed *. Deu 22:10
they will march out * against you Deu 28:7
"Call them all *," the Lord Deu 31:12
JOSHUA NOW CALLED * the troops Jos 22:1
the two tribes lived * after that. Ju 1:16
pressed the fleece * and wrung out Ju 6:38
have a long and happy life *. Ju 9:19
His thirty sons rode around * on Ju 10:4
tied their tails * in pairs, with a Ju 15:4
a pleasant evening * and tomorrow Ju 19:9
and afterward they had supper *. Ju 19:21
And again they cried *, and Orpah Ru 1:14
So they sat down *. Ru 4:1
hill ahead of me and we'll eat *; 1Sa 9:19
the tribal leaders * before the 1Sa 10:20
that no two of them were left *. 1Sa 11:11
were talking *, he spoke well of 1Sa 19:4
And they went out there *. 1Sa 20:11
his troops died * that same day. 1Sa 31:6
They were * in life and in death. 2Sa 1:23
So all seven of them died * at 2Sa 21:9

(TOGETHER Con't)
instance) counted * as one tribe. 1Ki 12:20f
So they went back *, and the 1Ki 13:19
citizens * for fasting and prayer. 1Ki 21:9
So they went on * to Bethel. 2Ki 2:1
So they went on * to Jericho. 2Ki 2:4
So they went on * and stood beside 2Ki 2:6,7
Then Elijah folded his cloak * 2Ki 2:8
all the rivers of Israel put *? 2Ki 5:12
He called * his officers and 2Ki 6:11
the city manager, * with the city 2Ki 10:5
and call * all his worshipers. 2Ki 10:18,19
All of these families lived * near 1Ch 8:30,31,32
So Saul and his three sons died *; 1Ch 10:6
the way, so he called * his army. 1Ch 14:8
Then the people of Judah, * with 2Ch 30:25
weeping mingled * in a loud Ez 3:13
I called * the leaders and the Neh 4:14
Then the Lord told me to call * Neh 7:5
So we agreed * not to neglect the Neh 10:39,40
"Go and gather * all the Jews of Est 4:16
home and gathered * his friends and Est 5:10
Shushan gathered * the next day Est 9:15
had gathered * and stood for their Est 9:16
man, no mediator to bring us *. Job 9:32,33
flesh and knit * bones and sinews. Job 10:11
You bundle them all * as Job 14:17
We shall rest * in the dust!" Job 17:16
enough to keep soul and body *. Job 24:5
* for shelter beneath the nettles. Job 30:7
morning stars sang * and all the Job 38:6,7
of his thighs are tightly knit *. Job 40:17
Both proud and humble *, all who Ps 22:29
Let us praise the Lord *, and Ps 34:3
they come * in meetings filled Ps 35:15
They whisper * about what they Ps 41:7
how often we ate *. Ps 41:9
arrived * to inspect the city. Ps 48:4
shouts, "Gather * my own people Ps 50:5
as we walked * to the Temple of the Ps 55:14
They meet * to perfect their Ps 56:6
Mercy and truth have met *. Ps 85:10
You bound the world * so that it Ps 104:5
knit them * in my mother's womb. Ps 139:13
They will talk * about the glory Ps 145:11
children— all praise the Lord *. Ps 148:13
Wisdom and good judgment live *, Pro 8:12
no leader, they stay * in swarms. Pro 30:24-28
lamb will lie down *, and the Is 11:6
cubs and calves will lie down *, Is 11:7
other any more. * they will fly Is 11:14
the three will be *, and Israel Is 19:24
will gather them * one by one like Is 27:12
until not two of you are left *. Is 30:17
All will fail *. Is 31:3
will be seen by all mankind *." Is 40:5
Carefully they join the parts * Is 41:7
Gather the nations *! Is 43:9
god. * they will stand in terror. Is 44:11
sprout up * from the earth. Is 45:8
Gather * and come, you nations Is 45:20
Consult *, argue your case and Is 45:21
The wolf and lamb shall feed *, Is 65:25
so I will gather * all nations and Is 66:18
Israel will return * from their Jer 3:18
and friends shall collapse *. Jer 6:21
And I will gather * the remnant Jer 23:3
me, I will gather * all the armies Jer 25:8,9
gather them back * again and watch Jer 31:10
live * in peace and happiness. Jer 31:24
"Call * the men of Judah and, as Jer 43:9
across each other and fall *. Jer 46:12
Judah shall join *, weeping and Jer 50:4
Kings and priests * fall before Lam 2:6
Mix the various kinds of flour * Eze 4:9
do: I will gather * all your Eze 16:37
You sat * on a beautifully Eze 23:41
of each body came * and attached to Eze 37:7
Now hold them * in your hand as Eze 37:17
* for a mighty sacrificial feast. Eze 39:17
as the first. * they measure 8 Eze 48:13
his knees knocked * and his legs Dan 5:6
they will return from exile *; Hos 1:11
shall sing * that "God sows!" Hos 1:21,22
the people * for a solemn meeting. Joe 2:15
Gather * and come, all nations Joe 3:11
princes will go into exile *." Amo 1:15
For how can we walk * with your Amo 3:3
Call * the Assyrian and Egyptian Amo 3:9
left—and bring you * again like Mic 2:12
have gathered * against you, Mic 4:11
Lord will gather * the enemies of Mic 4:12
officials crowd * like grasshoppers Nah 3:17
GATHER * AND pray, you shameless Zep 2:1
For it is my decision to gather * Zep 3:8
that all can worship the Lord *. Zep 3:9
* those who were chased away. Zep 3:19
I will gather you * and bring you Zep 3:20
* the nations to fight Jerusalem; Zec 14:1
Let both grow * until the Mt 13:30
For where two or three gather * Mt 18:20
divorce what God has joined *." Mt 19:5,6
But Jesus called them * and said, Mt 20:25
Then the Pharisees met * to try Mt 22:15
your children * as a hen gathers Mt 23:37
"Two men will be working * in Mt 24:40
who called * his servants and Mt 25:14
twelve disciples * and sent them Mk 6:7
joined * permanently in marriage; Mk 10:6,7
separate what God has joined *." Mk 10:9
than all those rich men put *! Mk 12:43,44
angels to gather * my chosen ones Mk 13:27
disciples as they were eating *. Mk 16:14
At daybreak he called * his Lk 6:13
down, shaken * to make room for Lk 6:38
ONE DAY JESUS called * his twelve Lk 9:1
your children * even as a hen Lk 13:34
you would call * your friends and Lk 15:6
Two women will be working * at Lk 17:35,36
Before he left he called * ten Lk 19:13
time all sat down * at the table; Lk 22:14
Then Pilate called * the chief Lk 23:13
the sower and the reaper, both *! Jn 4:36
had come over * and that the Jn 6:22,23
it, and they went * to ask Jesus. Jn 12:22
myrrh and aloes. * they wrapped Jn 19:40
the disciples were * again, and Jn 20:26
As the believers met * that day, Act 2:1
And all the believers met * Act 2:44
They worshiped * regularly at Act 2:46
this—conspiring * to test the Act 5:9
and had called * his relatives and Act 10:24
So he got up and they talked * Act 10:27
and walked along * for a block, and Act 12:10
and Barnabas went * to the Act 14:1
Upon arrival they called * the Act 14:27
of his men, * with others employed Act 19:25
and ate the Lord's Supper *; Act 20:10,11,12
there and we sailed * to Mitylene; Act 20:14
of the Jews got * and bound Act 23:12,13
called the crew * and said, "Men, Act 27:21
arrival, he called * the local Act 28:17
groaning in travail * until now." Rom 8:22f
Work happily *. Rom 12:16
praise the Lord * with one voice, Rom 15:6
had a good time * for a little Rom 15:24
that all of you * are the house of 1Co 3:16
Christ are joined * as one person. 1Co 6:17
Afterwards, they should come * 1Co 7:5
* the blessing of Christ's blood? 1Co 10:16
loaf to eat there *, this shows 1Co 10:16
* in the benefits of his body. 1Co 10:16
idols are united * in sacrificing 1Co 10:20
* for your communion services. 1Co 11:17
When you come * to eat, it isn't 1Co 11:20
upon himself when you meet *. 1Co 11:34
one body when they are all put *. 1Co 12:12
has fitted us all * into one body. 1Co 12:13
So God has put the body * in such 1Co 12:24
to say: All of you * are the one 1Co 12:27
Those who can get others to work * 1Co 12:28
When you meet * some will sing, 1Co 14:26
along too, then we can travel *. 1Co 16:4
By traveling * we will guard 2Co 8:20
happy spirit that we felt * then? Gal 4:15
will gather us all * from wherever Eph 1:10
thus he fused us * to become one Eph 2:15
carefully joined * with Christ as Eph 2:21
seen to be joined * in his church, Eph 3:10
Try always to be led along * by Eph 4:3
body is fitted * perfectly, and Eph 4:15,16
We have shared * the blessings of Php 1:7
We are in this fight *. Php 1:30
other, working * with one heart and Php 2:2
his power that holds everything *. Col 1:17
and knit * by strong ties of love, Col 2:2
for we are joined * by his strong Col 2:19
will stay * in perfect harmony. Col 3:14
joy as we stand * before our Lord 1Th 2:19
our being gathered * to meet him? 2Th 2:1
them to bring them *, by giving 1Ti 2:5
and * we will sing his praises." Heb 2:12
things * and have a joyous time. 2Jn 1:12
we will have much to talk about *. 3Jn 1:14
Literally, "* with all those who Rev 2:22f
strength to him. * they will wage Rev 17:14
Gather * for the supper of the Rev 19:17
and gather them *, with Gog and Rev 20:8

TOHU
His great-grandfather was *, 1Sa 1:1

TOI
When King * of Hamath heard about 2Sa 8:9
for Hadadezer and * were enemies. 2Sa 8:10

TOIL
you, even if you * on it forever! Gen 4:12
forcing them to * long and hard in Ex 1:13,14
saw our hardship, *, and Deu 26:6,7
down here for all your earthly *. Ecc 9:9
They don't * and spin, and yet Lk 12:27

TOILED
Night and day we * and sweated to 1Th 2:9

TOILET
* area shall be outside the camp. Deu 23:12

out sitting on the *, or maybe he 1Ki 18:27
public *, which it still is today. 2Ki 10:27

TOILS
rest from all their * and trials; Rev 14:13

TOKEN
finger as a * of his authority, and Gen 41:41,42
have brought you a * of the first Deu 26:10
send lambs as a * of alliance with Is 16:1
me a present as a * of surrender; Is 36:16
harm and give you as a * and Is 49:8,9
"This wine is the * of God's new Lk 22:20

TOKENS
For the rains he sends are * of Joe 2:23

TOKHATH
Shallum (son of *, son of Hasrah). 2Ch 34:22

TOLA
Issachar and his sons: *, Puvah, Gen 46:8-14
named after their ancestor *. Num 26:23-25
of Israel was * (son of Puah and Ju 10:1
*, Puah, Jashub, Shimron. 1Ch 7:1
The sons of *, each of whom was 1Ch 7:2

TOLAD
Bilhah, Ezem, *, Bethuel, Hormah, 1Ch 4:29

TOLAITES
The *, named after their ancestor Num 26:23-25

TOLD
the oceans," he * them, and to the Gen 1:21,22
And God blessed them and * them, Gen 1:28
we may eat it," the woman * him. Gen 3:2,3
"Who * you you were naked?" Gen 3:11
the fruit when I * you not to, I Gen 3:17
of whom so many legends are *. Gen 6:4
Then God * Noah, "You may all Gen 8:15,16
and his sons and * them to have Gen 9:1
be afraid of you," God * him; Gen 9:2,3
Then God * Noah and his sons, Gen 9:8
outside and * his two brothers. Gen 9:22
father, God * him, "Leave your own Gen 12:1
"You are very beautiful," he * Gen 12:11,12,13
escaped came and * Abram the Gen 14:13
The king of Sodom * him, "Just Gen 14:21
this is what he * him: "Don't be Gen 15:1
Then Jehovah * him, "No, no one Gen 15:4
nighttime sky and * him, "Look up Gen 15:5
And he * him, "I am Jehovah who Gen 15:7
Then Jehovah * him to take a Gen 15:9
Then Jehovah * Abram, "Your Gen 15:13
and * him, "I am the Almighty; Gen 17:1
"What's more," God * him, "I Gen 17:5
God * him, "is to obey its terms. Gen 17:9,10
just as God had * him to. Gen 17:23
a fat calf and * a servant to hurry Gen 18:7
Next year, just as I * you, I Gen 18:14
So the Lord * Abraham, "I have Gen 18:20
your lives," the angels * him. Gen 19:17
him in a dream and * him, "You are Gen 20:3
innocent man? He * me, 'She is my Gen 20:5
and * them what had happened. Gen 20:8
childhood home, I * her, 'Have the Gen 20:13
want to live," the king * him. Gen 20:15
But God * Abraham, "Don't be Gen 21:12
place where God had * him to go. Gen 22:3
donkey," Abraham * the young men, Gen 22:5
where God had * Abraham to go, he Gen 22:9
For the Lord God of heaven * me Gen 24:7
I have * you why I am here." Gen 24:33
'She will,' he * me—'for my Gen 24:40
I could drink, and * me, Gen 24:46
And she * me, 'Nahor's. Gen 24:47
So they * her good-bye, sending Gen 24:59
Then the servant * Isaac the Gen 24:66
And he * her, "The sons in your Gen 25:23
and * him, "Don't go to Egypt. Gen 26:2
if he * them she was his wife; Gen 26:7
her son Jacob and * him what his Gen 27:6,7
I've done as you * me to. Gen 27:19
She sent for Jacob and * him that Gen 27:42
She quickly ran and * her father, Gen 29:12,13
Then Jacob * him his story. Gen 29:12,13
So he * her father, "I'll work Gen 29:18
Then Rachel * him, "Sleep with Gen 30:3
* me that the many blessings I've Gen 30:27
Jehovah now spoke to Jacob and * Gen 31:3
against me," he * them, "and now Gen 31:5
* me that I should mate the white Gen 31:12
do whatever God has * you to." Gen 31:16
what you say to Jacob," he was *. Gen 31:24
me last night and * me, 'Be careful Gen 31:29
a monument, and * his men to Gen 31:46
Jehovah who * me to return to the Gen 32:9
between. He * the men driving the Gen 32:17
the Man * him. Gen 32:28
"No, you mustn't ask," the Man * Gen 32:29
Hamor * Jacob, "My son Shechem Gen 34:8
to Bethel," he * them, "and I Gen 35:3
and someone * Israel about it. Gen 35:22
Then he had another dream and * Gen 37:9
This time he * his father as Gen 37:10
for Joseph, and * him, "Your Gen 37:13,14
"Yes," the man * him, "they Gen 37:17
this in the field," they * him. Gen 37:32

(TOLD Con't)
Then Judah * Tamar, his Gen 38:11
When someone * Tamar that her Gen 38:13
So he returned to Judah and * Gen 38:22
the men of the place had * him. Gen 38:23
"Look," he * her, "my master Gen 39:8
that night, she * him her story. Gen 39:17
The wine taster * his dream Gen 40:9,10
he * his dream to Joseph, too. Gen 40:16
mean three days," Joseph * him. Gen 40:18,19
sages of Egypt and * them about it, Gen 41:8
one night. We * the dreams to a Gen 41:12
and he * us what our dreams meant. Gen 41:12
night," Pharaoh * him, "and none Gen 41:15
So Pharaoh * him the dream. Gen 41:17
up the fat ones! I * all this to my Gen 41:24
same thing," Joseph * Pharaoh. Gen 41:25
that what I have * you is certainly Gen 41:32
and * him all that had happened. Gen 42:29
* him, "and took us for spies. Gen 42:30
Then the man * us, 'This is the Gen 42:33
But Judah * him, "The man wasn't Gen 43:3,4,5
us about our family," they * him. Gen 43:7
had another brother, so we * him. Gen 43:7
So the man did as he was * and Gen 43:17
the household manager * them; Gen 43:23
* that they would be eating there. Gen 43:25
brother, the one you * me about? Gen 43:29
eat with them. He * each of them Gen 43:33
He was also * to put Joseph's Gen 44:2
household manager did as he was *. Gen 44:2
But you * us, 'Don't come back Gen 44:23
and * him what you had said. Gen 44:24
care of the lad. I * him, 'If I Gen 44:32
"Yes," Joseph * him, "these Gen 48:9
Then he * them, "Soon I will Gen 49:29,30
But Joseph * them, "Don't be Gen 50:19
"Soon I will die," Joseph * his Gen 50:24
He * his people, "These Israelis Ex 1:9
"Sir," they * him, "the Hebrew Ex 1:19
the shepherds," they * him; Ex 2:19
"Don't come any closer," God * Ex 3:5
Then the Lord * him, "I have Ex 3:7
Then God * him, "I will Ex 3:12
on the ground," the Lord * him. Ex 4:3
Then the Lord * him, "Grab it by Ex 4:4
the Lord * him. Ex 4:5
Jehovah * him, "When you arrive Ex 4:21
Moses * Aaron what God had said Ex 4:28
were to say, and * him about the Ex 4:28
Aaron * them what Jehovah had Ex 4:30
see Pharaoh. They * him, "We bring Ex 5:1
"We are given no straw and * to Ex 5:16
do to Pharaoh," the Lord * Moses. Ex 6:1
So Moses * the people what God had Ex 6:8,9
to Moses again and * him, "Go Ex 6:10
Next the Lord * Moses, "Get up Ex 8:20
with Pharaoh and * him: "Jehovah, Ex 10:3
The Lord had * Moses, "Pharaoh Ex 11:9
So they camped where they were *. Ex 14:4
Isn't this what we * you, while Ex 14:12
But Moses * the people, "Don't Ex 14:13
of Israel and * them, "This Ex 16:6
And Moses * them, "It is the food Ex 16:15
And Moses * them, "Don't leave Ex 16:19
And he * them, "Because the Lord Ex 16:23
Moses * Aaron to get a container Ex 16:33
Moses did as he was *, and the Ex 17:5,6
"Tomorrow," Moses * him, "I Ex 17:9
you," Moses was *, "and he has Ex 18:5,6
God's decisions," Moses * him. Ex 18:15,16
and * them what the Lord had said. Ex 19:7
He * them, "Get ready for God's Ex 19:15
But the Lord * Moses, "Go back Ex 19:21
"You * them not to! Ex 19:23
"You told them not to! You * me Ex 19:23
and * them what God had said. Ex 19:25
"Don't be afraid," Moses * Ex 20:20
And the Lord * Moses to be his Ex 20:22
He * the elders, "Stay here and Ex 24:14
We are not * what they looked Ex 25:18f
Then the Lord * Moses to collect Ex 30:22,23
Then the Lord * Moses, "Quick! Ex 32:7
Well, I * them, 'Bring me your Ex 32:24
He * them, "Jehovah the God of Ex 32:27
Then Moses * the Levites, "Today Ex 32:29
to the place I * you about, and I Ex 32:34
For the Lord had * Moses to tell Ex 33:5
* me whom you will send with me. Ex 33:12
THE LORD * Moses, "Prepare two Ex 34:1
as the Lord had * him to, taking Ex 34:4
all the people and * them, "These Ex 35:1
And Moses * them, "Jehovah has Ex 35:30,31
So Moses * Bezalel and Oholiab Ex 36:1
with Moses and * him, "We have Ex 36:4-7
Next he * them not to leave the Lev 8:33
"If you leave," he * them, Lev 8:35
of Israel, and * Aaron to take a Lev 9:2
Moses * them, "When you have Lev 9:6
Moses then * Aaron to proceed to Lev 9:7
of Uzziel, and * them, "Go and get Lev 10:4
coats as Moses had * them to. Lev 10:5
THE LORD * Moses to give these Lev 12:1
THE LORD * Moses and Aaron to give Lev 15:1
That is why I * the people of Lev 17:14
THE LORD THEN * Moses to tell the Lev 18:1
THE LORD ALSO * Moses to tell the Lev 19:1
THE LORD * Moses, "Instruct Aaron Lev 22:1
be * how much to pay instead. Lev 27:11,12
gifts," the Lord * Moses, "and Num 7:4,5
stopped where he * them to, then Num 9:18
and whatever the Lord * Moses Num 9:23
Some young men ran and * Moses Num 11:27
They have * this to the Num 14:14
THE LORD * Moses to give these Num 15:1
"Quick!" he * the people, Num 16:26
Aaron did as Moses had * him to, Num 16:47
The Lord * Moses to place Num 17:10
and pomegranates you * us about? Num 20:5
Then the Lord * him, "Make a Num 21:8
where the Lord * Moses, "Summon Num 21:16
The Lord * Moses not to Num 21:34
God * him. Num 22:12
The next morning Balaam * the Num 22:13
That night God * Balaam, "Get up Num 22:20
But the angel * him, "Go with Num 22:35
Balaam * the Lord, "I have Num 23:3,4
'Come,' he * me, 'curse Jacob for Num 23:7-10
demanded King Balak. "I * you Num 23:11
Then Balak * him, "Come with me Num 23:13
And the Lord met Balaam and * Num 23:16
Balaam again * the king to build Num 23:29
Then the Lord * Moses to divide Num 26:52,53
of the tribes and * them, "The Num 30:1
that the Lord * Moses to tell the Num 33:50,51
THE LORD * Moses to tell the Num 34:1
Jehovah our God * us, 'You have Deu 1:6
"At that time I * the people, 'I Deu 1:9
your decisions,' I * them, 'never Deu 1:17
Go and possess it as he * us to. Deu 1:19,20,21
as the Lord our God has * us to.' Deu 1:41
"I * them, but they wouldn't Deu 1:43
But the Lord * me not to be Deu 3:1
land are yours,' the Lord * me. Deu 3:1
and children,' I * them, 'may live Deu 3:19
Horeb, and he * me, 'Summon the Deu 4:10
So Moses * the people, "You must Deu 5:32
"THE LORD YOUR God * me to give Deu 6:1
watched below. He * me to go down Deu 9:12
the Lord * me, 'and I will blot Deu 9:13,14
when the Lord * you to enter the Deu 9:23
"AT THAT TIME the Lord * me to Deu 10:1
for as the Lord * them, he Deu 10:9
for the Lord has * you, 'Never Deu 17:16
all Israel before him and * them, Deu 29:2,3
"And they will be *, 'Because Deu 29:25
* them, "I am now 120 years old! Deu 31:2
for the Lord has * me that I Deu 31:2
stubborn you are," Moses * them. Deu 31:27
and Zoar," the Lord * him. Deu 34:3
Promised Land," the Lord * Moses. Deu 34:4
God has given us!" he * them. Jos 1:10,11
River," Moses had * them, "so Jos 1:12,13
But she had hidden them, so she * Jos 2:4
my country to you," she * them. Jos 2:9
to the mountains," she * them. Jos 2:16
Then Joshua * the people to Jos 3:5
"Today," the Lord * Joshua, "I Jos 3:7
all the people and * them, "Come Jos 3:9
twelve men, and * them, "Go out Jos 4:5
So the men did as Joshua * them. Jos 4:8
Lord now * him to command them. Jos 4:15,16
The Lord then * Joshua to set Jos 5:2,3
the Commander * him, "for this is Jos 5:15
(He had * them previously, "Kill Jos 6:17
Upon their return they * Joshua, Jos 7:3
(The Lord had * Joshua they Jos 8:27
at Gilgal, they * Joshua and the Jos 9:6
And they * him, "We are from a Jos 9:9
it because we were * that Jehovah Jos 9:24
yet * them where to build it). Jos 9:27
Joshua * the captains of his Jos 10:24
did as he had been *: he carefully Jos 11:15
my God, Moses * me, 'The section Jos 14:9
"The Lord * Moses that we were to Jos 17:4
The men did as they were * and Jos 18:9
blessed them and * them to share Jos 22:7,8
of Israel and * them what had Jos 22:32
in this land; I * you to destroy Ju 2:2
message for you," he * him. Ju 3:17,18,19
"Follow me," he * them, "for Ju 3:28
Barak * her. Ju 4:8
When General Sisera was * that Ju 4:12
of the tent," he * her, "and if Ju 4:20
their land. He * you that he is Ju 6:10
our ancestors have * us about—such Ju 6:13
That night the Lord * Gideon to Ju 6:25
But the Lord * Gideon, "There Ju 7:4
There the Lord * him, "Divide Ju 7:5,6
the Lord * Gideon. Ju 7:7
he * them, "do just as I do. Ju 7:17
and Manasseh and * them to come and Ju 7:23
to do whatever he * them to. Ju 9:4
However, someone had * Abimelech Ju 9:42
"Do as I have done," he * his Ju 9:47,48
The woman ran and * her husband, Ju 13:6
his name, but he * me, 'You are Ju 13:7
And he * me not to drink any Ju 13:7
her husband and * him, "The same Ju 13:10
appeared to us and * us this Ju 13:23
he got home he * his father and Ju 14:2
But Samson * his father, "She is Ju 14:3
you hate me, for you have * a Ju 14:16
and haven't * me the answer!" Ju 14:16
"I haven't even * it to my father Ju 14:16
At last, on the seventh day, he * Ju 14:17
* him the answer to his riddle. Ju 14:19
the men of Judah * him. Ju 15:12,13
making fun of me! You * me a lie! Ju 16:10
"You have mocked me again, and * Ju 16:13
* me what makes you so strong!" Ju 16:15
and finally * her his secret. Ju 16:16,17
he had finally * her the truth, so Ju 16:18
time he has * me everything." Ju 16:18
He * them about his contract Ju 18:4
the five spies * the others. Ju 18:14
They * the men of Benjamin who Ju 21:20
did as they were * and kidnapped Ju 21:23
But she * them, "Don't call me Ru 1:20
work again, Boaz * his young men to Ru 2:15
So Ruth * her mother-in-law all Ru 2:19
"Well," Ruth * her, "he said Ru 2:21
"Bring your shawl," he * her. Ru 3:15-18
arrived home. She * Naomi Ru 3:15-18
Then Boaz * him, "Your purchase Ru 4:5
Hannah, for she * her husband, 1Sa 1:21,22
you are doing," Eli * his sons. 1Sa 2:23,24,25
So Samuel * him what the Lord had 1Sa 3:18
When they were * it was because 1Sa 4:6
arrived and * what had happened, a 1Sa 4:13
Eli and * him what had happened. 1Sa 4:14
there today," he * Eli, "and 1Sa 4:16
were attending her * her that 1Sa 4:20
back with a gift," they were *. 1Sa 6:3
And they were *, "Send five gold 1Sa 6:4,5
Kiriath-jearim and * them that the 1Sa 6:21
Then Samuel * them, "Come to 1Sa 7:5
They * him that since his 1Sa 8:5
So Samuel * the people what the 1Sa 8:10
So Samuel * the Lord what the 1Sa 8:21
The Lord had * Samuel the 1Sa 9:15
"That's the man I * you about! 1Sa 9:17
city walls Samuel * Saul to send 1Sa 9:26,27
Then he * him, "I have received 1Sa 9:26,27
Then Samuel * the people again 1Sa 10:25
home town, and * the people about 1Sa 11:4
So they * him about the message 1Sa 11:5
The men of Jabesh then * their 1Sa 11:10
Samuel had * Saul earlier to 1Sa 13:8
what we'll do," Jonathan * him. 1Sa 14:8
Then someone * him that his 1Sa 14:28
of Israel because God * me to. 1Sa 15:1
Listen to what the Lord * me last 1Sa 15:16
And Samuel * him, "When you 1Sa 15:17
on an errand and * you, 'Go and 1Sa 15:18
"I did what he * me to; 1Sa 15:20
So Samuel did as the Lord had * 1Sa 16:4
Then Jesse * his son Abinadab to 1Sa 16:8
any of them," Samuel * Jesse. 1Sa 16:10,11
meant, someone * King Saul, and the 1Sa 17:31
about a thing," David * him. 1Sa 17:32
the king * him. 1Sa 17:56
back to him, he * them, "Tell 1Sa 18:25
with David, * him what his father 1Sa 19:2
David and * him what had happened. 1Sa 19:7
she * them he was sick and 1Sa 19:14
to see Samuel, and * him all that 1Sa 19:18
Someone * him they were at Naioth. 1Sa 19:22
Then Jonathan * David, "I 1Sa 20:12
there, so I * him to go ahead." 1Sa 20:28,29
"Start running," he * the boy, 1Sa 20:36
to the boy and * him to take them 1Sa 20:40
David lied. "He * me not to tell 1Sa 21:2
I have * my men where to meet me 1Sa 21:2
One day the prophet Gad * David 1Sa 22:5
For not one of you has ever * me 1Sa 22:8
When he * him what Saul had done, 1Sa 22:21
and save Keilah," the Lord * him. 1Sa 23:2
of Saul's plan and * Abiathar the 1Sa 23:9
he was * that David had gone into 1Sa 24:1
and some of my men * me to kill 1Sa 24:9,10
I am * that you are shearing 1Sa 25:7
and * him what Nabal had said. 1Sa 25:12
men went and * Abigail, "David 1Sa 25:14
her gifts and * her to return home 1Sa 25:35
and when his wife * him what had 1Sa 25:37,38
at Carmel and * her why they had 1Sa 25:40
for life," Achish * him. 1Sa 28:2
the king * her. 1Sa 28:13
And King Achish * them, "This is 1Sa 29:3
"I swear by the Lord," he * 1Sa 29:6
And the Lord * him, "Yes, go 1Sa 30:8
they * David. 1Sa 30:20

TOLD Con't)
Then Abner * him, "Go on home 2Sa 3:16
"Now is the time!" he * them. 2Sa 3:18
When Joab was * that Abner had 2Sa 3:23
that when someone * me, 'Saul is 2Sa 4:10
never come in here," they * him. 2Sa 5:6
reached David, he * his troops, 2Sa 5:8
but David was * that they were 2Sa 5:17
back to David and * him everything 2Sa 7:17
"In Lo-debar," Ziba * him. 2Sa 9:4
But Hanun's officers * him, 2Sa 10:3
had happened he * them to stay at 2Sa 10:5
she was and was * that she was 2Sa 11:3
Then he * him to go home and 2Sa 11:8
tonight," David * him, "and 2Sa 11:12
was going, he * his messenger, 2Sa 11:19,20,21
understand you," they * him. 2Sa 12:21
So Amnon * him, "I am in love 2Sa 13:4
"Everyone get out of here," he * 2Sa 13:9
Absalom * his men, "Wait until 2Sa 13:28
Jonadab * the king. 2Sa 13:35
great wisdom and * her to ask for 2Sa 14:2,3
king. He * her what to say to him. 2Sa 14:2,3
"Leave it with me," the king * 2Sa 14:8
Yes, Joab sent me and * me what 2Sa 14:19
So the king sent for Joab and * 2Sa 14:21
So Joab * the king what Absalom 2Sa 14:33
"All right," the king * him, 2Sa 15:9
Then the king * Zadok, "Look, 2Sa 15:27
When someone * David that 2Sa 15:31
But David * him, "If you go with 2Sa 15:33,34
"In that case," the king * 2Sa 16:4
"If the Lord has * him to curse 2Sa 16:10
doubt the Lord has * him to do it. 2Sa 16:11
Ahithophel * him, "Go and sleep 2Sa 16:21
* him to, just as David had; 2Sa 16:23
When Hushai arrived, Absalom * 2Sa 17:6
"Quick!" he * them. 2Sa 17:16
David, and he * Absalom about it. 2Sa 17:18
they * him, "cross the Jordan 2Sa 17:21
And they * him how Ahithophel 2Sa 17:21
One of David's men saw him and * 2Sa 18:10
"No," Joab * him, "it wouldn't 2Sa 18:20
"When Joab * me to come, there 2Sa 18:29
"Wait here," the king * him. 2Sa 18:30
And he * them to tell Amasa, 2Sa 19:13
deceived me. I * him, 'Saddle my 2Sa 19:26
So she * him, "There used to be 2Sa 20:18
was happening and * him to stop. 2Sa 24:16
you like," Araunah * the king. 2Sa 24:22
this," his aides * him, "is to 1Ki 1:2
the king's aides * him, "Nathan 1Ki 1:22,23
for Shime-i and * him, "Build a 1Ki 2:36,37
that night and * him to ask for 1Ki 3:5
For the Lord * him, 'Your son, 1Ki 5:5
I will do what I * your father 1Ki 6:11,12
but the Lord * him not to. 1Ki 8:18
land of Egypt, you * your servant 1Ki 8:53
David when I * him, 'One of your 1Ki 9:5
and she * him all her problems. 1Ki 10:2
The half had not been * me! 1Ki 10:7
a hard master," they * Rehoboam. 1Ki 12:2,3,4
made and * the people, "It's too 1Ki 12:28
sons went home and * him what the 1Ki 13:11
So they * him. 1Ki 13:12
and he also * me not to return 1Ki 13:16,17
in the place he * you not to, 1Ki 13:21,22
For the Lord * him to shout 1Ki 13:32
Jeroboam * his wife, "Disguise 1Ki 14:2
who * me that I would become king. 1Ki 14:2
But the Lord * him that the 1Ki 14:5
And the Lord * him what to tell 1Ki 14:5
Then he * her, "I have sad 1Ki 14:6
from Tishbe in Gilead, * King 1Ki 17:1
So he did as the Lord had * him 1Ki 17:5
a prophet," she * him afterward, 1Ki 17:24
And each time when he was * 1Ki 18:10
Has no one * you about the time 1Ki 18:13
who is left," he * them, "but 1Ki 18:22
Then Elijah * them to grab the 1Ki 18:40
* him, "I didn't see anything." 1Ki 18:43
Then Elijah * him, "Go again, and 1Ki 18:43
time, his servant * him, "I saw a 1Ki 18:44
WHEN AHAB * Queen Jezebel what 1Ki 19:1
"I've had enough," he * the 1Ki 19:4
him and * him to get up and eat! 1Ki 19:5
on the mountain," the Lord * him. 1Ki 19:11
Then the Lord * him, "Go back by 1Ki 19:15
I have already * him he could have 1Ki 20:7
So he * the messengers from 1Ki 20:9
him," the king of Israel * them. 1Ki 20:33
Ben-hadad * him, "I will restore 1Ki 20:34
Then the prophet * him, "Because 1Ki 20:36
Then the prophet * him, "The 1Ki 20:42
Ahab * her. 1Ki 21:6
The Lord has also * me that the 1Ki 21:23
to get Micaiah * him what the other 1Ki 22:13
But Micaiah * him, "This I vow, 1Ki 22:14
Micaiah * him. 1Ki 22:15
Then Micaiah * him, "I saw all 1Ki 22:17
But an angel of the Lord * Elijah 2Ki 1:3
When Elijah * the messengers this, 2Ki 1:4,5
they said, "and * us to go back to 2Ki 1:6
Lord has * me to go to Bethel." 2Ki 2:1
"We have a problem," they * 2Ki 2:19
they * her. 2Ki 4:6
When she * the prophet what had 2Ki 4:7
"Call her back again," Elisha * 2Ki 4:15,16
"Yes," she * Gehazi, 2Ki 4:26
the Lord hasn't * me what it is." 2Ki 4:27
He returned to meet Elisha and * 2Ki 4:31
Elisha * Gehazi to use it to feed 2Ki 4:42
Naaman * the king what the little 2Ki 5:4
the prophet," the king * him. 2Ki 5:5
the prophet had * you to do some 2Ki 5:13
as the prophet had * him to. 2Ki 5:14
came to Elisha and * him, "As you 2Ki 6:1
"All right," he * them, "go 2Ki 6:1
Elisha * him. 2Ki 6:16
Then Elisha went out and * them, 2Ki 6:19
Elisha * him. 2Ki 6:22
to the city and * the watchmen what 2Ki 7:10
The king got out of bed and * his 2Ki 7:12
The scouts returned and * the 2Ki 7:15
the prophet had * the king that 2Ki 7:18
ELISHA HAD * the woman whose son 2Ki 8:1
And she * him that it was. 2Ki 8:6
Someone * the king that the 2Ki 8:7
And Hazael replied, "He * me that 2Ki 8:14
go to Ramoth-gilead," he * him. 2Ki 9:1
the young prophet did as he was *. 2Ki 9:4
So he * them what the man had said 2Ki 9:12
to be king," Jehu * the men who 2Ki 9:15
When they returned and * him, he 2Ki 9:36
would happen. He * Elijah the 2Ki 9:36
When a messenger * Jehu that the 2Ki 10:8
"You aren't to blame," he * 2Ki 10:9,10
of his men and * them, "If you let 2Ki 10:24
Jehu went out and * his officers 2Ki 10:25
Elisha * him, "Get a bow and 2Ki 13:15
Then he * the king to put his hand 2Ki 13:16,17
The Lord sent us and * us, 'Go 2Ki 18:25
clothes torn and * him what the 2Ki 18:37
Then he * Eliakim, Shebnah, and 2Ki 19:2
prepare to die," Isaiah * him. 2Ki 20:1
give you a proof," Isaiah * him. 2Ki 20:9
And the men of the city * him, 2Ki 23:17
* him, "We are your relatives, 1Ch 11:1
And the Lord your God has * you, 1Ch 11:2
just as the Lord had * Samuel. 1Ch 11:3
clans of the Levites," he * them. 1Ch 15:12
So Nathan * King David everything 1Ch 17:15
and help me," Joab * his brother; 1Ch 19:12
and bring me the totals," he * 1Ch 21:2
and Joab did as he was *; 1Ch 21:4
Then the angel of the Lord * Gad 1Ch 21:18
it myself," David * him, "but 1Ch 22:7
many men in great wars,' he * me. 1Ch 22:8
But I will give you a son,' he * 1Ch 22:9
as you do what he * you to do and 1Ch 22:11
but God has * me, 'You are not to 1Ch 28:3
He has * me, 'Your son Solomon 1Ch 28:6
blueprint," David * Solomon, "was 1Ch 28:19
to Solomon and * him, "Ask me for 2Ch 1:7
Lord my God," Solomon * Hiram. 2Ch 2:4
For he * him, 'I have never 2Ch 6:4
desire, the Lord * him, but he was 2Ch 6:8
to Solomon and * him, "I have 2Ch 7:12
Rehoboam * them to return in 2Ch 10:5
give you heavier!" he * them. 2Ch 10:14
But the Lord * Shemaiah the 2Ch 11:2
for safety), and * them, "The Lord 2Ch 12:5
to him," he * his people. 2Ch 14:7
to King Asa and * him, "Because 2Ch 16:7
"Well," Ahab * him, "there is 2Ch 18:6,7
The man who went to get Micaiah * 2Ch 18:12
Then Micaiah * him, "In my 2Ch 18:16
has * me," Micaiah continued. 2Ch 18:18
God, where God had * David and his 2Ch 33:7
the king * them. 2Ch 34:21
When they * her of the king's 2Ch 34:22
God has * me to hurry! 2Ch 35:21
After all, we had * the king that Ez 8:22
these treasures well!" I * them; Ez 8:29
corruption. You * us not to let Ez 9:12
Oh, please remember what you * Neh 1:8
for I hadn't * a soul about the Neh 2:11,12
But now I * them, "You know full Neh 2:17
Then I * them about the desire Neh 2:18
on guard. I * everyone living Neh 4:22
They all * me what a wonderful Neh 6:19
they * him everything I had said; Neh 6:19
Then the Lord * me to call Neh 7:5
that Jehovah had * Moses that the Neh 8:14
the prophets who * them to return Neh 9:26
from wine, he * the seven eunuchs Est 1:10
Esther hadn't * anyone that she Est 2:10
Esther still hadn't * anyone she Est 2:20
Queen Esther, who * the king, Est 2:22
eunuchs came and * her about Est 4:4
her attendant, and * him to go out Est 4:5
all Jews, and * him to show it to Est 4:8
Esther * Hathach to go back and Est 4:10
So Mordecai did as Esther * him Est 4:17
When Haman * Zeresh his wife and Est 6:13
for Esther had * the king that he Est 8:1
you have * many a troubled soul Job 4:3,4
men who have been * this same thing Job 15:17-19
their spirits. I * them what they Job 29:25
Have you ever * the daylight to Job 38:13
we are *. Ps 11:3
and know that I have * the truth. Ps 17:3
I have * everyone the Good News Ps 40:9
Our forefathers have * us how you Ps 44:1
their arrogance! I * the wicked to Ps 75:4
what wondrous tales are * of you! Ps 87:3
land as God had * them to, but Ps 106:34
Let lies be * about him, and Ps 109:6
Revive me by your Word. I * you Ps 119:26
He * me never to forget his words. Pro 4:4
a simpleton believes what he is *! Pro 14:15
For the Lord has * me this: Let Is 18:4
it, the Lord * Isaiah, the son of Is 20:2
And Isaiah did as he was *. Is 20:2
the Lord had * me, "Put a Is 21:6,7
winnowed, I have * you all that the Is 21:10
of heaven has * me this: Go and say Is 22:15,16
kind and good. He * them that, but Is 28:12
Hosts has plainly * me that he is Is 28:22
say, "you never * us that!" Is 30:9
But the Lord has * me this: When Is 31:4,5
The Assyrian ambassador * them Is 36:4
* them to say nothing in reply. Is 36:21
and * him all that had happened. Is 36:22
(For Isaiah had * Hezekiah's Is 38:21
Who but I have * you this would Is 41:26
Not one of your idols * you Is 41:28
What idol ever * you they would Is 45:21
times I clearly * you what was Is 46:9
Time and again I * you what was Is 48:3
That is why I * you ahead of Is 48:5
which one has ever * you this: Is 48:14
I have always * you plainly what Is 48:16
what they had not been * before. Is 52:14,15
But what I * them was: Obey me Jer 7:23
Baal, as their fathers * them to. Jer 9:14
For I * them at the time I Jer 11:4
Then the Lord * me all about Jer 11:18
I hid it as the Lord had * me to. Jer 13:5
The Lord * me again: Don't ask me Jer 14:11
I did as he * me, and found the Jer 18:3
the Lord had * him to, the priests Jer 26:7,8
of Judah, he * the people that God Jer 26:18
all the people and * them: "The Jer 27:16
Jeremiah had * him again and Jer 32:5
done one thing you * them to. Jer 32:23
in Egypt. I * them that every Jer 34:14
He also * us not to build houses Jer 35:7
their father * them not to. Jer 35:14
Baruch did as Jeremiah * him to, Jer 36:8
When Micaiah * them about the Jer 36:13
prophets now who * you that the Jer 37:19
don't tell anyone you * me this! Jer 38:24
So he said what the king had * Jer 38:27
* Nebuzaradan to find Jeremiah. Jer 39:11,12
And today I have * you exactly Jer 42:21
The Lord our God hasn't * you to Jer 43:2,3
against us and * you to say this so Jer 43:2,3
(Events * about in chapter 39. Jer 52:1
cry and * me not to fear. Lam 3:57
detail of what I have * you to do. Eze 4:3
Then he * me, "Son of dust, Eze 4:16
fooling when I * them that all this Eze 6:10
the city and did as they were *. Eze 9:7
When the Lord * the man in linen Eze 10:6
came upon me and * me to say: "The Eze 11:5
And I * the exiles everything Eze 11:25
So I did as I was *. Eze 12:7
have never * them anything at all. Eze 13:2,3
prophets have * you lies of safety Eze 21:29
I did all the Lord had * me to. Eze 24:18
And I answered, "The Lord * me Eze 24:20,21
Then he * me to speak to the Eze 37:4
from God, just as he * me to; Eze 37:7
Then he * me to call to the wind Eze 37:9
Then he * me what the vision Eze 37:11
10½ feet long. He * me, "This wall Eze 40:5
"This," he * me, "is the Most Eze 41:4
"This," he * me, "is the Table Eze 41:22
Then he * me: "These north and Eze 42:13
where, my guide * me, the priests Eze 46:19,20
the stream and * me to go across. Eze 47:3
feet and * me to cross again. Eze 47:4
He * me to keep in mind what I Eze 47:6
He * me: "This river flows east Eze 47:8
Then Ari-och * him all that had Dan 2:15
Then he went home and * Hananiah, Dan 2:17
And that night in a vision God * Dan 2:19
and he has * you in your dream what Dan 2:28
he has * you this secret." Dan 2:47
and wizards—and I * them the dream, Dan 4:7
holy gods, and I * him the dream. Dan 4:8
I am * that you can solve all Dan 5:16

(TOLD Con't)
Then they * the king, "That — Dan 6:13
"This fourth animal," he * me, — Dan 7:23
but I * no one what I had seen. — Dan 7:28
which has been * is true." — Dan 8:26f
One day, in a vision, God * him — Amo 1:2
"I won't do it," he * me. — Amo 7:3
for the flocks and * me, 'Go and — Amo 7:15
Then he * them he was running — Jon 1:9,10
doom, as I * you to before!" — Jon 3:1
and you first * me to come here. — Jon 4:2
nothing that I * them happens — Jon 4:3
No, he has * you what he wants, — Mic 6:8
Then the Lord * them (again — Hag 1:13
Then he * me, "They represent — Zec 4:14
"This scroll," he * me, — Zec 5:3
the flock as I had been * to do. — Zec 11:7
So I * them, "I won't be your — Zec 11:9
And the Lord * me, 'Toss it into — Zec 11:13
Then the Lord * me to go again — Zec 11:15
Then he * them, "Go to — Mt 2:7
astrologers had * him the star — Mt 2:16
in Egypt, and * him, "Get up and — Mt 2:19
Isaiah the prophet had * about — Mt 3:3
But Jesus * him, "No! — Mt 4:4
out of here, Satan," Jesus * him. — Mt 4:10
fortunate!" he * them, "for the — Mt 5:3
'Lord, Lord, we * others about you — Mt 7:22
But Jesus * him, "Follow me — Mt 8:22
"All right," Jesus * them. — Mt 8:32
"Yes, Lord," they * him, "we — Mt 9:28
are so few," he * his disciples. — Mt 9:37
Jesus * them, "Go back to John — Mt 11:4
When someone * him they were — Mt 12:46,47
be given," he * them, "and he — Mt 13:12,13
of the story I * about the farmer — Mt 13:18
"The farmer's men came and * — Mt 13:27
Then Jesus * them, "A prophet is — Mt 13:57
because John had * him it was — Mt 14:4
Then he * the people to sit down — Mt 14:19
Immediately after this, Jesus * — Mt 14:22
Then the disciples came and * — Mt 15:12
"Woman," Jesus * her, "your — Mt 15:28
Then Jesus * all of the people to — Mt 15:35
* them, "O men of little faith! — Mt 16:8
your little faith," Jesus * them. — Mt 17:20
in Galilee, Jesus * them, "I am — Mt 17:22,23
king and * him what had happened. — Mt 18:31
Jesus * him, "If you want to be — Mt 19:21
others in my fields,' he * them. — Mt 20:7
"That evening he * the paymaster — Mt 20:8
But Jesus * her, "You don't know — Mt 20:22
indeed drink from it," he * them. — Mt 20:23
The crowd * them to be quiet, but — Mt 20:31
Then Jesus * them, "Truly, if — Mt 21:21
A man with two sons * the older — Mt 21:28
Then the father * the youngest, — Mt 21:30
For John the Baptist * you to — Mt 21:32
JESUS * SEVERAL other stories to — Mt 22:1
But he * them, "All these — Mt 24:2
Jesus * them, "Don't let anyone — Mt 24:4
(* about by Daniel — Mt 24:15
small amount,' he * him, 'so now I — Mt 25:21
with his disciples, he * them, — Mt 26:1
has done will be * throughout the — Mt 26:13
So the disciples did as he * — Mt 26:19
And Jesus had * him, "Yes." — Mt 26:25
Jesus * him, "The truth is that — Mt 26:34
Gethsemane, and * them to sit down — Mt 26:36
Then he * them, "My soul is — Mt 26:38
Judas had * them to arrest the — Mt 26:48
"Put away your sword," Jesus * — Mt 26:52
to Pilate, and * him, "Sir, that — Mt 27:63
Temple police," Pilate * them. — Mt 27:65
and * them what had happened. — Mt 28:11
and said what they were * to. — Mt 28:15
He * his disciples, "I have been — Mt 28:18
They * Jesus about her right away. — Mk 1:29,30
to find him, and * him, "Everyone — Mk 1:36,37
Jesus then * him sternly, "Go — Mk 1:43,44
"Come with me," Jesus * him. — Mk 2:14
were saying, he * them, "Sick — Mk 2:17
He * them this because they were — Mk 3:30
and want to see you," he was *. — Mk 3:31,32
"Go home to your friends," he * — Mk 5:19
feet and * him what she had done. — Mk 5:33
derision, but he * them all to — Mk 5:40
had happened, and * them to give — Mk 5:43
Then Jesus * them, "A prophet is — Mk 6:4
out demons. He * them to take — Mk 6:8,9
her mother, who * her, "Ask for — Mk 6:24
to the king and * him, "I want the — Mk 6:25
their tour and * him all they had — Mk 6:30
Then Jesus * the crowd to sit — Mk 6:39,40
Jesus * her, "First I should — Mk 7:27
Jesus * the crowd not to spread — Mk 7:36
So he * the crowd to sit down on — Mk 8:6
and * the disciples to serve them. — Mk 8:7
things like that," he * Jesus. — Mk 8:32
my follower," he * them, "you — Mk 8:34
mountainside he * them never to — Mk 9:9
One of his disciples, John, * him — Mk 9:38
but we * him not to, for he isn't — Mk 9:38
He * them, "When a man divorces — Mk 10:11
"You lack only one thing," he * — Mk 10:21
"When we get there," he * them, — Mk 10:33
over there," he * them, "and just — Mk 11:2
So they said what Jesus had * — Mk 11:6
He * them, "It is written in the — Mk 11:17
he was gone, and * the gatekeeper — Mk 13:34
"As you are walking along," he * — Mk 14:13
desert me," Jesus * them, "for — Mk 14:27
Judas had * them, "You will know — Mk 14:44
* Joseph he could have the body. — Mk 15:45
just as he * you before he died!' — Mk 16:7
And then he * them, "You are to — Mk 16:15
Mary," the angel * her, "for God — Lk 1:30
which the Lord has * us about." — Lk 2:15
The shepherds * everyone what — Lk 2:17
just as the angel had * them. — Lk 2:20
and the devil * him, "I will — Lk 4:6,7
"Be silent!" he * the demon. — Lk 4:35
them and * them to be silent. — Lk 4:41
help the man. They * him what a — Lk 7:4
When they * John about it, he — Lk 7:18
Then Jesus * him this story: "A — Lk 7:41
had seen it happen * how the — Lk 8:36
"Go back to your family," he * — Lk 8:39
But Jesus * him, "No, it was — Lk 8:46
before him and * why she had — Lk 8:47
"She's gone," he * her father; — Lk 8:49
"John the Baptist," they * him, — Lk 9:19
And we * him not to. — Lk 9:49
But Jesus * him, "Anyone who — Lk 9:62
"Yes," he * them, "I saw Satan — Lk 10:18
Jesus * him. — Lk 10:28
and * him to take care of the — Lk 10:35
Finally he * his gardener to cut — Lk 13:7
His master was angry and * him to — Lk 14:21
the point, he * them this story: — Lk 15:10
When the younger * his father, — Lk 15:12
is back,' he was *, 'and your — Lk 15:27
to do a single thing you * me to; — Lk 15:29
JESUS NOW * this story to his — Lk 16:1
you signed,' the accountant * him. — Lk 16:5,6
ONE DAY JESUS * his disciples a — Lk 18:1
Then he * this story to some who — Lk 18:9
But the disciples * them to go — Lk 18:15
around him he * them, "As you — Lk 18:31
He was * that Jesus from — Lk 18:37
Jesus * him, "This shows — Lk 19:9,10
Jerusalem, he * a story to correct — Lk 19:11
people again and * them this story: — Lk 20:9
this story he had *, they wanted — Lk 20:19
being * that summer is near. — Lk 21:30
Jesus * them, "In this world the — Lk 22:25
There he * them, "Pray God that — Lk 22:40
When they * him yes, Pilate said — Lk 23:7
Don't you remember what he * you — Lk 24:6,7
there who * them Jesus is alive! — Lk 24:22,23
Then the two from Emmaus * their — Lk 24:35
Father and has * us all about him. — Jn 1:18
John * them, "I merely baptize — Jn 1:26
Then John * about seeing the Holy — Jn 1:32
me to baptize he * me, 'When you — Jn 1:33
brother Peter and * him, "We have — Jn 1:41
He found Philip and * him, "Come — Jn 1:43
for Nathanael and * him, "We have — Jn 1:45
Moses and the prophets * about! — Jn 1:45
just because I * you I had seen you — Jn 1:50
But his mother * the servants, — Jn 2:5
Then Jesus * the servants to — Jn 2:7,8
selling doves, he * them, "Get — Jn 2:16
I * you that I am not the Messiah. — Jn 3:28
get your husband," Jesus * her. — Jn 4:16
Then Jesus * her, "I am the — Jn 4:26
to the village and * everyone, — Jn 4:28,29
who * me everything I ever did! — Jn 4:28,29
"He * me everything I ever did!" — Jn 4:39
not just because of what you * us. — Jn 4:42
Then Jesus * him, "Go back home. — Jn 4:50
had * him, "Your son is healed." — Jn 4:53
Jesus * him, "Stand up, roll up — Jn 5:8
"The man who healed me * me — Jn 5:11
and * him, "Now you are well; — Jn 5:14
Jewish leaders and * them it was — Jn 5:15
I judge as I am *. — Jn 5:30
scraps," Jesus * his disciples, — Jn 6:12
them and * them not to be afraid. — Jn 6:20
Jesus * them, "This is the will — Jn 6:29
But the trouble is, as I have * — Jn 6:36
But now I have * you how to get — Jn 6:63
So Jesus * them, "I'm not — Jn 7:16
But Jesus * them, "[Not yet! — Jn 7:33
Jesus * them, "These claims are — Jn 8:14
I am * to by the one who sent me; — Jn 8:26
* you the truth I heard from God. — Jn 8:40
Jesus * them, "If that were so, — Jn 8:42
Then Jesus * them this: "If I — Jn 8:54
man's eyes, and * him, "Go and — Jn 9:7
And he * them, "A man they call — Jn 9:11
over my eyes and * me to go to the — Jn 9:11
So he * them how Jesus had — Jn 9:15
had been blind and * him, "Give — Jn 9:24
the man exclaimed. "I * you — Jn 9:27
Then Jesus * him, "I have come — Jn 9:39
"I have already * you, — Jn 10:25
Then he * them plainly, "Lazarus — Jn 11:14
Bethany, they were * that Lazarus — Jn 11:17
Jesus * her, "Your brother will — Jn 11:23
Jesus * her, "I am the one who — Jn 11:25
"Yes, Master," she * him. — Jn 11:27
from the mourners, * her, "He is — Jn 11:28
They * him, "Come and see." — Jn 11:34
"Roll the stone aside," Jesus * — Jn 11:39
Jesus * them, "Unwrap him and — Jn 11:44
Philip * Andrew about it, and — Jn 12:22
Then Jesus * them, "The voice — Jn 12:30
ideas, but I have * you what the — Jn 12:49
He * me, "It is the one I honor — Jn 13:26
Then Jesus * him, "Hurry—do it — Jn 13:27
me—just as I * the Jewish leaders. — Jn 13:33
Jesus * him, "I am the Way—yes, — Jn 14:6
of everything I myself have * you. — Jn 14:26
Remember what I * you—I am going — Jn 14:28
I have * you these things before — Jn 14:29
I have * you this so that you — Jn 15:11
fact that I have * you everything — Jn 15:15
you everything the Father * me. — Jn 15:15
Do you remember what I * you? — Jn 15:20
"I HAVE * you these things so — Jn 16:1
I have * you all this so that — Jn 16:33
by doing everything you * me to. — Jn 17:4
"I have * these men all about — Jn 17:6
I have * them many things while I — Jn 17:13
"I * you I am he," Jesus said; — Jn 18:8
Caiaphas was the one who * the — Jn 18:14
by your own laws," Pilate * them. — Jn 18:31
to the people and * them, "He is — Jn 18:38
the Jewish leaders * him, "If you — Jn 19:12
and Pilate * him to go ahead. — Jn 19:38
* them, "I have seen the Lord!" — Jn 20:18
Then he breathed on them and * — Jn 20:22
Then Jesus * him, "You believe — Jn 20:29
besides the ones * about in this — Jn 20:30,31
"Then feed my lambs," Jesus * — Jn 21:15
Then Jesus * him, "Follow me." — Jn 21:19
I * you about Jesus' life and — Act 1:1
In one of these meetings he * — Act 1:4
them back in, and * them never — Act 4:18
* them what the Council had said. — Act 4:23
Then he * them, "Go over to the — Act 5:19
beaten, and then * them never again — Act 5:40
and * him to leave his native — Act 7:3
But God also * him that these — Act 7:6
them,' God * him, 'and afterwards — Act 7:7
"But the man in the wrong * — Act 7:27
"Moses himself * the people of — Act 7:37
They * Aaron, 'Make idols for — Act 7:40
And he * them, "Look, I see the — Act 7:56
* the people there about Christ. — Act 8:5
But Paul was * about their — Act 9:24
the apostles and * them how Paul — Act 9:27
bodyguard, and * them what had — Act 10:8
Then they * him about Cornelius — Act 10:22
Peter * them, "You know it is — Act 10:28
radiant robe! He * me, 'Cornelius, — Act 10:31
what he has * you to tell us!" — Act 10:33
Then Peter * them the whole — Act 11:4
The Holy Spirit * me to go with — Act 11:12
messengers. He * us how an angel — Act 11:13
to him and * him to send messengers — Act 11:13
the angel had * him. — Act 11:14
Then the angel * him, "Get — Act 12:8
to quiet down and * them what had — Act 12:17
Barnabas and Paul * about the — Act 15:12
Peter has * you about the time — Act 15:14
Holy Spirit had * them not to go — Act 16:6
Then they * him and all his — Act 16:32
So the jailer * Paul they were — Act 16:36
Their reaction, when he * them — Act 17:18
and * him, "Don't be afraid! — Act 18:9
Egypt, someone had * him about — Act 18:25,26
When they arrived he * them, — Act 20:18
Holy Spirit has * me in city after — Act 20:23
have been * that you are against — Act 21:21
"And the Lord * me, 'Get up and — Act 22:10
there you will be * what awaits you — Act 22:10
"Then he * me, 'The God of our — Act 22:14
just as you have * the people — Act 23:11
and * them what they had done. — Act 23:14
and came to the armory and * Paul. — Act 23:16
"Tomorrow," he * him, "the — Act 23:20
"Don't let a soul know you * me — Act 23:22
the governor * him, and ordered him — Act 23:35
* the Jews to wait for the — Act 24:22
listened as he * them about faith — Act 24:24
here," he * him, "whose case was — Act 25:14
wanted to spare Paul, so he * — Act 27:43
to his house. He * them about the — Act 28:23
Scriptures * about it long ago). — Rom 3:21,22
So, when God * Abraham that he — Rom 4:18
* them what he wanted them to do. — Rom 5:13

(TOLD Con't)
cloud of glory and * you how very Rom 9:4
twin children, God * her that Esau, Rom 9:10-13
For God * him he had given him Rom 9:17
has believed me when I * them?" Rom 10:16
the Good News has been * to the Rom 10:18
says, and just as I have * you. Rom 16:25,26,27
what I * you Christ could do for 1Co 1:6
Chloe's house have * me of your 1Co 1:11
of Psalms, we are * that the Lord 1Co 3:20
Don't you realize that God * 1Co 9:13
who * you, and of his conscience. 1Co 10:28
For I am * that everyone hastily 1Co 11:21
We are * in the ancient 1Co 14:21
what had been * to me, that Christ 1Co 15:3
and we have * everyone how 2Co 1:20
I have * you all my feelings; 2Co 6:11
When he * me how much you were 2Co 7:7
mind at ease. I * him how it would 2Co 7:14
I told him how it would be—* him 2Co 7:14
I have always * you the truth and 2Co 7:14
because I have * him all about your 2Co 8:22
are ready, as I * them you would 2Co 9:3
ready after all I have * them! 2Co 9:4
saved than the one we * you about; Gal 1:8
himself, who * me what to say. Gal 1:12
their faith. God * Abraham about Gal 3:8,9
But the Scriptures say that God * Gal 4:30
God has * us his secret reason Eph 1:9
someone has * us something Eph 4:14
as I have * them to treat you. Eph 6:9
For I have * you often before, Php 3:18
And he is the one who has * us Col 1:8
do all the Lord has * you to." Col 4:17
What we * you produced a powerful 1Th 1:5
as we have solemnly * you before. 1Th 4:6
own work, just as we * you before. 1Th 4:11
believed what we * you about him. 2Th 1:10
Don't you remember that I * you 2Th 2:5
Through us he * you the Good 2Th 2:14
just as the Lord * us through his 1Ti 1:18
fulfill all he has * you to do, so 1Ti 6:14
These things I have * you are Tit 3:8
but we are * that Melchizedek Heb 7:8
God, and when God * him to leave Heb 11:8
a lamb as God had * them to and Heb 11:28
to do whatever God * him to; Jas 2:22
about, for he * them to write down 1Pe 1:11
They were finally * that these 1Pe 1:12
sinned, never * a lie, never 1Pe 2:22
What I have * you here should 1Pe 5:12
And he has * us from the very 2Jn 1:6
They have * the church here of 3Jn 1:6
Lord Jesus Christ * you, that in Jud 1:17
and they were * to rest a little Rev 6:11
They were * not to hurt the Rev 9:4
Then he * me, "You must prophesy Rev 10:11
stick and * to go and measure the Rev 11:1
court," I was *, "for it has been Rev 11:2

TOLERABLE
world's seasoning, to make it *. Mt 5:13

TOLERATE
and cannot * the slightest sin. Ps 5:4
I will not * anyone who secretly Ps 101:5
I know you don't * sin among your Rev 2:2
against you. You * some among you Rev 2:14

TOLERATED
from stone. God * man's past Act 17:30

TOLL
vast tribute, custom, and *. Ez 4:20

TOMB
beside Rachel's * at Zelzah, in the 1Sa 10:2
buried it in Abner's * in Hebron. 2Sa 4:12
his body into the * of Elisha. 2Ki 13:20,21
own new rock-hewn *, and rolled a Mt 27:60
you sealing the * until the third Mt 27:64
the other Mary went out to the *. Mt 28:1
The women ran from the *, badly Mt 28:8
been guarding the * went to the Mt 28:11
for his body and buried it in a *. Mk 6:29
it in a rock-hewn *, and rolled a Mk 15:46
they carried them out to the *. Mk 16:1
So they entered the *—and there Mk 16:5
The women fled from the *, Mk 16:8
in a new, unused * hewn into the Lk 23:53
and saw it carried into the *. Lk 23:55
ointments to the *— and found that Lk 24:1
in a * for someone who is alive? Lk 24:5
Literally, "returned from the * Lk 24:9f
(The women who went to the * Lk 24:10
However, Peter ran to the * to Lk 24:12
were at his * early this morning Lk 24:22,23
been in his * for four days. Jn 11:17
was going to Lazarus' * to weep; Jn 11:31
Then they came to the *. Jn 11:37,38
where there was a new *, never Jn 19:41
and because the * was close at Jn 19:42
came to the * and found that the Jn 20:1
body out of the *, and I don't know Jn 20:2
ran to the * to see; Jn 20:3,4
time Mary had returned to the * Jn 20:11
and his * is still here among us. Act 2:29
and buried in the * Abraham bought Act 7:16
from the cross and placed in a *. Act 13:29

TOMBS
rocks, and even in * and cisterns. 1Sa 13:6
not in the royal *, and his son 2Ch 28:27
For they desecrated the * of the Amo 2:1
rocks broke, and * opened, and Mt 27:52
wander among the * and in the wild Mk 5:5
lived in a cemetery among the *. Lk 8:27

TOMORROW
"Do it *," Pharaoh said. Ex 8:10
All this will happen *." Ex 8:23
Well, * about this time I will Ex 9:18
If you refuse, * I will cover Ex 10:4,5
Lord has appointed * as a day of Ex 16:23
"*," Moses told him, "I will Ex 17:9
Sanctify them today and *, and Ex 19:10
Then, the day after *, I will Ex 19:11
and announced, "* there will be a Ex 32:5
for * they shall have meat to eat. Num 11:18
in the valleys, * you must turn Num 14:25
you, take censers * and light them, Num 16:6,7
Korah, "Come here * before the Num 16:16
"For *," he said, "the Lord Jos 3:5
in preparation for *, for the Lord Jos 7:13
this time * they will all be dead! Jos 11:6
will be angry with all of us *. Jos 22:17,18
together and * you can get up early Ju 19:9
And the Lord said, "Go, for * I Ju 20:27,28
"About this time * I will send 1Sa 9:16
will rescue you before * noon!" 1Sa 11:9
"We surrender. * we will come out 1Sa 11:10
was planning. "* morning," he 1Sa 19:2
And David replied, "* is the 1Sa 20:5
this occasion, but * I'll hide in 1Sa 20:5
about this time *, or the next day 1Sa 20:12
they will miss you * when your 1Sa 20:18
By the day after *, everyone 1Sa 20:19
men remains alive by * morning!" 1Sa 25:22
men would be alive * morning." 1Sa 25:34
by the Philistines *, and you and 1Sa 28:19
all have gone home * morning." 2Sa 2:27
* you may return to the army." 2Sa 11:12
kill you by this time * night." 1Ki 19:2
about this time * I will send my 1Ki 20:5,6
that by this time * two gallons of 2Ki 7:1
at Jezreel at about this time *." 2Ki 10:6
*, go down and attack them! 2Ch 20:16
Go out there *, for the Lord is 2Ch 20:17
again with Haman * to the banquet I Est 5:7,8
for you. And * I will explain what Est 5:7,8
us; and * we are invited again! Est 5:12
Shushan do again * as they have Est 9:13
DON'T BRAG ABOUT your plans for * Pro 27:1
the difference, for * we die." Is 22:13
let it go on and on, and * will Is 56:12
today and gone *, won't he more Mt 6:30
"So don't be anxious about *. Mt 6:34
God will take care of your * too. Mt 6:34
sky tonight means fair weather *; Mt 16:2,3
a second time * morning you will Mk 14:30
today and gone *, don't you suppose Lk 12:28
miracles of healing today and *; Lk 13:32
Yes, today, *, and the next day! Lk 13:33
Between now and * morning when Lk 22:34
the rooster crows * morning, you Lk 22:61
the cock crows * morning, you will Jn 13:38
"*," he told him, "the Jews Act 23:20
And Festus replied, "You shall * Act 25:22
our worries about *, or where we Rom 8:38
What's the difference? For * we 1Co 15:32
say, "Today or * we are going to Jas 4:13
know what is going to happen *? Jas 4:14
from now is like * to the Lord. 2Pe 3:8

TON
You have advisors by the *—your Is 47:13

TONGS
flowers, lamps, *, cups, snuffers, 1Ki 7:49
decorations, *, lamp snuffers, 2Ch 4:21
of * picked out a burning coal. Is 6:6

TONGUE
dog shall move his * against any of Ex 11:7
And his word was on my *. 2Sa 23:2
no evil, my * shall speak no lies. Job 27:4
Or put a noose around his *? Job 41:1
sun-baked clay; my * sticks to my Ps 22:15
Then watch your *! Ps 34:13
do harm, O man with the lying *. Ps 52:4
help, with praises ready on my *. Ps 66:17
land of foreign *, then the lands Ps 114:1
O lying *, what shall be your Ps 120:3
deeds shall be on every *; Ps 145:6
A wise man holds his *. Pro 10:14
a man with good sense holds his * Pro 11:12
means controlling the *! Pro 13:3
for a soft * can break hard bones. Pro 25:15
are under your *, and the scent of Sol 4:11
to me, and every * shall swear Is 45:23
and I will make your * stick to Eze 3:26
I will loosen your * and let you Eze 3:27
the man's * with the spittle. Mk 7:33
water and cool my *, for I am in Lk 16:24
joy and my * shouts his praises! Act 2:26
me and every * confess to God." Rom 14:11
earth, and every * shall confess Php 2:11
control his sharp * is just fooling Jas 1:26
If anyone can control his *, it Jas 3:1
So also the * is a small thing, Jas 3:5
And the * is a flame of fire. Jas 3:6
And the * is set on fire by hell Jas 3:6
but no human being can tame the *. Jas 3:8
control of your *, and guard your 1Pe 3:10

TONGUES
who finally found their *! Gen 45:15
Their * are filled with Ps 5:9
Their * are like swords. Ps 57:4
They cut me down with sharpened *; Ps 64:3
is none and their * are parched Is 41:17
faces and sticking out your *? Is 57:4
"They bend their * like bows to Jer 9:3
With practiced * they fool and Jer 9:5
For their * aim lies like Jer 9:8
The children's * stick to the Lam 4:3,4
tribes with strange, difficult *. Eze 3:6
that their * can't tell the truth! Mic 6:12
* will decay in their mouths. Zec 14:12
"they will speak in new *." Mk 16:17f
like flames or * of fire appeared Act 2:3
Literally, "in other *." Act 2:4f
for they heard them speaking in * Act 10:46,47
Their * are loaded with lies. Rom 3:13
able to "speak in *," that is, to 1Co 14:2
So a person "speaking in *" 1Co 14:4
of "speaking in *" but, even 1Co 14:5
in unknown *, he should pray also 1Co 14:13
I will pray in unknown * and also 1Co 14:15
I will sing in unknown * and also 1Co 14:15
I thank God that I "speak in *" 1Co 14:18
in *" in an unknown language. 1Co 14:19
able to "speak in *" is not a 1Co 14:22
say it is wrong to "speak in *"; 1Co 14:39
And his subjects gnawed their * Rev 16:10

TONIC
and is a * for all you do. 1Ti 4:8

TONIGHT
Let's fill him with wine again *, Gen 19:34
you * because of the mandrakes." Gen 30:15
"You must sleep with me *!" Gen 30:16
the land of Egypt * and kill all Ex 12:12
However, stay here * so that I Num 22:19
at the place where you camp *." Jos 4:2,3
threshing floor *, and if, in the Ju 6:37
Stay just *, and we will have a Ju 19:9
let's stay here *." Ju 19:11
I became pregnant *, and bore sons, Ru 1:12
* out on the threshing-floor. Ru 3:2
Stay here *, and in the morning Ru 3:13
"If you don't get away *," 1Sa 19:11
"Well, stay here *," David told 2Sa 11:12
men to start out after David *. 2Sa 17:1
at the ford of the Jordan River *. 2Sa 17:16
told him, "cross the Jordan *!" 2Sa 17:21
they are coming * to kill you." Neh 6:10
sky * means fair weather tomorrow; Mt 16:2,3
Then Jesus said to them, "* you Mt 26:31
Lord—has been born * in Bethlehem! Lk 2:11
"But God said to him, 'Fool! * Lk 12:20
for Caesarea at nine o'clock *! Act 23:23,24

TONS
$30,000,000 in silver; 800 * of 1Ch 29:6,7
and 4,600 * of iron. 1Ch 29:6,7

TOOK
a deep sleep, and * one of his ribs Gen 2:21
he disappeared, for God * him! Gen 5:21-24
NOW A POPULATION explosion * Gen 6:1
earth women and * any they desired Gen 6:1
Then Shem and Japheth * a robe Gen 9:23
Then Terah * his son Abram, his Gen 11:31
at that time. He * his wife Sarai, Gen 12:5
Lot * a long look at the fertile Gen 13:10
So Sarai * her maid, an Egyptian Gen 16:1
(This * place ten years after Gen 16:2,3
Then, that very day, Abraham * Gen 17:23
for that woman you * is married." Gen 20:3
Then King Abimelech * sheep and Gen 20:14
But when he * seven ewe lambs and Gen 21:28,29
his donkey, and * with him his son Gen 22:3
And Abraham * the knife and Gen 22:10
So he * the ram and sacrificed Gen 22:13
instructions. He * with him ten of Gen 24:10
were up, they each * solemn oaths Gen 26:31
Then she * Esau's best Gen 27:15
For he * my birthright, and now Gen 27:36
it was dark, Laban * Leah to Jacob, Gen 29:23
Then Jacob * fresh shoots from Gen 30:37
at Paddan-aram—and * everything Gen 31:17-20
household gods and * them with her) Gen 31:21
a curse upon anyone who * them. Gen 31:32
No, I * the loss. Gen 31:39
So Jacob * a stone and set it up Gen 31:45
So Jacob * oath before the mighty Gen 31:53

(TOOK Con't)
children, and * them across the Gen 32:22,23,24
saw her, he * her and raped her. Gen 34:2
Simeon and Levi, * their swords, Gen 34:25
the fields, and * all the women Gen 34:29
Then Esau * his wives, children, Gen 36:6,7,8
One day Joseph's brothers * their Gen 37:12
and they * him along to Egypt. Gen 37:28
coat, and * the coat to their Gen 37:32
that, for Joseph * care of Gen 39:23
in my hand, so I * the grapes and Gen 40:11
told him, "and * us for spies. Gen 42:30
So they * the gifts and double Gen 43:15
and * them to Joseph's palace. Gen 43:17
They quickly * down their sacks Gen 44:11
He * five of his brothers with Gen 47:2
Soon afterwards Jacob * to his Gen 47:31
Joseph * the boys by the hand, Gen 48:12,13
that land which I * from the Gen 48:22
So she * him home and nursed Ex 2:9
And when he did, and * it out Ex 4:6
And when he did, and * it out Ex 4:7
So Moses * his wife and sons and Ex 4:20
Then Zipporah his wife * a flint Ex 4:25,26
So they * ashes from the kiln and Ex 9:10
The Israelis * with them their Ex 12:34
Moses * the bones of Joseph with Ex 13:19
sister of Aaron, * a timbrel and Ex 15:20
Then Jethro * Moses' wife, Ex 18:2
Moses * half of the blood of Ex 24:6
the mountain. He * the calf and Ex 32:20
So Moses * two tablets of stone Ex 34:4
restore what he *, adding a twenty Lev 6:4,5
Then he * Aaron and his sons and Lev 8:6
Then Moses * the anointing oil Lev 8:10
Then he * the young bull for the Lev 8:14
for it. He * all the fat covering Lev 8:15,16
Moses killed it and * some of Lev 8:23
Then he * the fat, the tail, the Lev 8:25
Moses then * it all back from Lev 8:28
Now Moses * the breast and Lev 8:29
Next he * some of the anointing Lev 8:30
"(The man who * the goat out Lev 16:26
So they * the youth out of the Lev 24:23
the Egyptians, I * for myself all Num 3:13
So Moses * a census of the eldest Num 3:42
the other leaders * a census of the Num 4:34
it to the person he * it from. Num 5:7
* his vow to become a Nazirite." Num 6:21
and the Lord * of the Spirit that Num 11:25
so large that it * two of them to Num 13:23
They also * some samples of the Num 13:23
So they * him outside the camp Num 15:36
So Eleazar the priest * the 250 Num 16:39
So Moses did as instructed. He * Num 20:9
The next morning Balak * Balaam Num 22:41
So King Balak * Balaam into the Num 23:14
So King Balak * Balaam to the Num 23:28
* Joshua to Eleazar the priest. Num 27:22
Then the Israeli army * as Num 31:9,10,11
"They agreed to this; I * the Deu 1:15
"So it * us thirty-eight years Deu 2:14,15
cattle, which we * as our reward, Deu 2:35,36
Of course we also * all of the Deu 3:5
tribe of Manasseh, * over the whole Deu 3:14
spared him. I * your sin—the calf Deu 9:21
the first two, and * the tablets up Deu 10:3
them, and * their land and gave it Deu 29:8
told them. They * twelve stones Jos 4:8
circumcision rite * place was named Jos 5:2,3
tribe of Judah) * some loot for Jos 7:1
I wanted them so much that I * Jos 7:21
all the Israelites * Achan, the Jos 7:24
was going down, he * down the body Jos 8:29
* the enemy armies by surprise. Jos 10:9
territories. It * seven years Jos 11:18
So Joshua * the entire land just Jos 11:23
But I * your father Abraham from Jos 24:3
laws of God, and * a huge stone as Jos 24:26
and * possession of the land. Ju 2:6
The young men of Israel * their Ju 3:6
The Spirit of the Lord * control Ju 3:10
the Israelis and * possession of Ju 3:13
Then Jael * a sharp tent peg and Ju 4:21
Then she * a tent pin and a Ju 5:26
that the Israelis * to the Ju 6:2
broth in a pot, he * it out to the Ju 6:19
So Gideon * ten of his servants Ju 6:27
So he * Purah and crept down Ju 7:11
and the Israelis * the heads of Ju 7:25
Then he * the leaders of the city Ju 8:16
So Gideon killed them and * the Ju 8:21
told them to. He * them to his Ju 9:5
was happening and * refuge in the Ju 9:46
These attacks * place east of the Ju 10:7,8
people, so Israel * over all of Ju 11:21,22
God of Israel who * away the land Ju 11:23
Then Manoah * a young goat and a Ju 13:19
some honey! He * some of the honey Ju 14:9
killed thirty men, * their Ju 14:19
harvest, Samson * a young goat as a Ju 15:1
Delilah * new ropes and tied him Ju 16:12
out his eyes and * him to Gaza, Ju 16:21
So his mother * a fifth of it to Ju 17:4,5
accent, they * him aside and asked Ju 18:3
the shrine and * the idols, the Ju 18:17
with them, and he * along the Ju 18:20
So he * them home with him. Ju 19:21
the donkey's back and * her home. Ju 19:28
When he got there he * a knife Ju 19:29
So the men of Israel * courage Ju 20:22,23,24
the girls who * part in the Ju 21:23
Naomi * care of the baby, and the Ru 4:16,17
so small, they * him to the 1Sa 1:24
After the sacrifice they * the 1Sa 1:25
THE PHILISTINES * the captured Ark 1Sa 5:1
came and * the Ark to the hillside 1Sa 7:1
So Samuel * a suckling lamb and 1Sa 7:9
Samuel then * a stone and placed 1Sa 7:12
Then Samuel * Saul and his 1Sa 9:22
the city, Samuel * Saul up to the 1Sa 9:25
THEN SAMUEL * a flask of olive oil 1Sa 10:1
him presents, but he * no notice. 1Sa 10:27
very angry. He * two oxen and cut 1Sa 11:7
special troops and * two thousand 1Sa 13:2
When they arrived, Samuel * one 1Sa 16:6
brothers, Samuel * the olive oil he 1Sa 16:13
shepherd and * off early the next 1Sa 17:20
sword over it, and * a step or two 1Sa 17:38,39
he exclaimed, and * them off 1Sa 17:38,39
shepherd's bag, * out a stone, 1Sa 17:48,49
(Later David * Goliath's head to 1Sa 17:54
Then he * David to Saul and 1Sa 19:7
Then she * an idol 1Sa 19:13
So Samuel * David with him to 1Sa 19:18
into the field and * a young boy 1Sa 20:35
so he * three thousand special 1Sa 24:2
Then Abigail hurriedly * two 1Sa 25:18
who * the law into his own hands! 1Sa 25:30,31
Quickly getting ready, she * 1Sa 25:42
So Saul * his elite corps of 1Sa 26:2
So David * the spear and jug of 1Sa 26:12
So David * his six hundred men 1Sa 27:2,3
they hit, and * for themselves the 1Sa 27:9
But Saul * a solemn oath that he 1Sa 28:10
But David * strength from the 1Sa 30:6
afraid to, so Saul * his own sword 1Sa 31:3,4
to Beth-shan and * down the bodies 1Sa 31:12
Then I * his crown and one of his 2Sa 1:10
Joab and his men * Asahel's body 2Sa 2:32
of Saul. He * advantage of his 2Sa 3:7
So Ish-bosheth * her away from 2Sa 3:15
at Hebron, Joab * him aside at the 2Sa 3:27
And they * Ish-bosheth's head and 2Sa 4:12
* it from Saul, your predecessor. 2Sa 7:15
So Hanun * David's men and shaved 2Sa 10:4
command, and * them out to fight 2Sa 10:9
the traveler, he * the poor man's 2Sa 12:4
and David * the king of Rabbah's 2Sa 12:29,30
So Tamar * it to him. 2Sa 13:10
Literally, "* hold of him and 2Sa 15:5f
He * two hundred men from 2Sa 15:11
and the Levites * the Ark of the 2Sa 15:24
* the Ark back into the city. 2Sa 15:25,26
Then he * three daggers and 2Sa 18:14
Then Ahima-az * a short cut 2Sa 18:23
the troops, but it * him longer 2Sa 20:5
Joab said, and * him by the beard 2Sa 20:8,9,10
Once he * on three hundred of the 2Sa 23:18,19
on the ground, * on a lion that was 2Sa 23:20
brother. He * General Joab and 1Ki 1:7
David's bodyguard * Solomon to 1Ki 1:38
At Gihon, Zadok * a flask of 1Ki 1:39
the king, for they * care of me 1Ki 2:7
he * them back to Jerusalem. 1Ki 2:40
* Shime-i outside and killed him. 1Ki 2:46
in the night and * my son from 1Ki 3:20
and * mine to sleep beside her. 1Ki 3:20
So it * seven years to build. 1Ki 6:38
* thirteen years to construct. 1Ki 7:1
finished, Solomon * into the 1Ki 7:51
Then the priests * the Ark into 1Ki 8:6
country. It * six months to 1Ki 11:16,17,18
officials who * him to Egypt (he 1Ki 11:16,17,18
the donkey and * it back to the 1Ki 13:29
died, his son Nadab * the throne. 1Ki 14:20
him and then * the shields back to 1Ki 14:28
and his son Abijam * the throne. 1Ki 14:31
Then Asa * all the silver and 1Ki 15:18
And he * the boy's body from her 1Ki 17:19
Then Elijah * him downstairs and 1Ki 17:23
torn down. He * twelve stones, one 1Ki 18:31
all, and Elijah * them to Kishon 1Ki 18:40
cities my father * from your 1Ki 20:34
and his son Jehoram * the throne. 1Ki 22:50
Then he * his oldest son, who 2Ki 3:27
So he * him home, and his mother 2Ki 4:20
Gehazi * the bags from the 2Ki 5:24
So the woman * her family and 2Ki 8:2
So Hazael * forty camel-loads of 2Ki 8:8,9
But the next day Hazael * a 2Ki 8:15
His officials * him by chariot 2Ki 9:28
And he * them out to the cistern 2Ki 10:14
King Joash * all the sacred 2Ki 12:18
King Joash * many hostages and 2Ki 14:14
at Ibleam and * the crown himself. 2Ki 15:10
assassinated him and * the throne. 2Ki 15:14
and he * the people away to 2Ki 15:29
and he * the throne for himself. 2Ki 15:30
Ahaz * the silver and gold from 2Ki 16:8
of Syria. They * away the 2Ki 16:9
So the Assyrians * over Samaria 2Ki 17:24
Hezekiah * the letter from the 2Ki 19:14
So they * the message to the king. 2Ki 22:20
the Temple and * it outside 2Ki 23:6
His officers * his body back in 2Ki 23:30
Then he * King Jehoahaz to Egypt, 2Ki 23:34
King Nebuchadnezzar * ten 2Ki 24:14
Nebuchadnezzar * King 2Ki 24:15
He also * seven thousand of the 2Ki 24:16
the city * out after him and 2Ki 25:4,5
They also * all the pots, 2Ki 25:14,15
The general * Seraiah, the chief 2Ki 25:18
from him and also * Kenath and its 1Ch 2:23
* possession of it for themselves. 1Ch 4:40,41
of Manasseh. They * them to Halah, 1Ch 5:26
to do it, so Saul * his own sword 1Ch 10:4
So the leaders of Israel * the 1Ch 15:28
says to you, I * you from being a 1Ch 17:7
silver and gold he * from the 1Ch 18:11
David also * great amounts of 1Ch 20:2
And they * care of the 1Ch 23:32
When David * his census he didn't 1Ch 27:23
his sons, the Lord * pleasure in me 1Ch 28:4
Solomon now * a census of all 2Ch 2:17
This celebration * place in 2Ch 5:3
they all * part in the ceremonies 2Ch 5:11,12
Jerusalem and * away all the 2Ch 12:9
from God, he * courage and 2Ch 15:8
and Jehoram. They * copies of The 2Ch 17:7,8,9
much that it * them three days to 2Ch 20:25
up his courage and * some of the 2Ch 23:1
But the Levites * their time. 2Ch 24:5
the money, and * the chest back to 2Ch 24:11
Then he * a census and found that 2Ch 25:5,6
Then Amaziah * courage and led 2Ch 25:11
King Amaziah of Judah now * the 2Ch 25:17
* him as a prisoner to Jerusalem. 2Ch 25:23
and he * hostages, including 2Ch 25:24
of booty which they * to Samaria. 2Ch 28:8
on donkeys, and * them back to 2Ch 28:15
The king * the gold bowls from 2Ch 28:24
outer court, which * eight days to 2Ch 29:17
and the priests * the blood and 2Ch 29:22
from the hills and * his idol from 2Ch 33:15
and Shaphan * it to the king, along 2Ch 34:15,16
Everyone present in Jerusalem * 2Ch 35:17
Jerusalem, and * away the king in 2Ch 36:6
Nebuchadnezzar also * some of 2Ch 36:7
He also * home with him all the 2Ch 36:18
* with him all the royal princes. 2Ch 36:18
the Gileadite and * her family Ez 2:61
They * with them 736 horses, 245 Ez 2:66,67
until King Darius * the throne. Ez 4:4,5
from Judah. I * the opportunity to Neh 1:2
with me—ever * off our clothes. Neh 4:23
the Gileadite and * her family Neh 7:63
They * with them 736 horses, 245 Neh 7:68,69
more hours they * turns confessing Neh 9:3
they completely * over the land Neh 9:22
fertile land; they * over houses Neh 9:25
they * that day into Jerusalem. Neh 13:15
So Haman * the robes and put them Est 6:11
The king * off his ring—which he Est 8:2
though again they * no property. Est 9:15
Then Job * a broken piece of Job 2:8
gone by when God * care of me, Job 29:2
the city gate and * my place among Job 29:7
He reached down from heaven and * Ps 18:16
You * me safely from my mother's Ps 22:9,10,11
into joy! He * away my clothes of Ps 30:11
and we * root and filled the land. Ps 80:9
Anything I wanted, I *, and did Ecc 2:10
He plowed it and * out all the Is 5:2
So they * the king's message to Is 37:5
Hezekiah appreciated this and * Is 39:2
and perfumes. He * them into his Is 39:2
the nations that * their lands. Is 54:3
they * back to Egypt with them. Jer 22:13f
So I * the cup of fury from the Jer 25:17
They * him prisoner and brought Jer 26:23
the false prophet, * the yoke off Jer 28:10
Zephaniah * the letter over to Jer 29:29
fathers when I * them by the hand Jer 31:32
Then I * the sealed deed Jer 32:11
Then Jeremiah * another scroll Jer 36:32
The Babylonians * Coniah to Jer 37:1f
But Irijah wouldn't listen; he * Jer 37:14
They * Jeremiah from his cell and Jer 38:6
So Ebedmelech * thirty men and Jer 38:11
garments which he * to the cistern Jer 38:11
all the officials * steps to do as Jer 39:13
OF the guard, * Jeremiah to Ramah Jer 40:1

'OOK Con't)
Soon after he * them with him Jer 41:10
had done, they * all their men and Jer 41:12
Then he * to Babylon, as Jer 52:15
And he * along all the bronze Jer 52:18
He also * the firepans and the Jer 52:19
The captain of the guard * along Jer 52:24,25
found hiding. He * them to the Jer 52:26
Then, eleven years later, he * Jer 52:29
of the guard, and * 745—a total of Jer 52:30
So I * the scroll. Eze 3:2
The Spirit lifted me up and * me Eze 3:14,15
to be a hand and * me by the hair. Eze 8:3
human hands) and * some live coals Eze 10:7,8
clothes, who * them and went out. Eze 10:7,8
it before! You * the very jewels Eze 16:17
And you * my sons and daughters Eze 16:20
a willow tree. It * root and grew Eze 17:6
came to Jerusalem and * away Eze 17:12,13
of loyalty. He * a seedling and Eze 17:12,13
him were gone, she * another of her Eze 19:5
But I * a solemn oath against Eze 20:23,24
and killed her and * away her Eze 23:10
from Senir. They * a cedar from Eze 27:5
and in a vision he * me to the land Eze 40:2
Then he * me over to the Eze 40:6
Then he * me around to the south Eze 40:24
Then he * me over to the inner Eze 40:28
Then he * me along the court to Eze 40:32
Then he * me around to the north Eze 40:35
Then the Spirit * me up and Eze 43:5
Measuring as he went, he * me Eze 47:3
When he returned to Babylon, he * Dan 1:1
royal throne and * away his glory, Dan 5:20
with the Romans and * over. Dan 11:21f
the Lord and he * away our king. Hos 10:3
other Savior. I * care of you in Hos 13:5
in my anger, and I * them away Hos 13:11
* them far from their own land. Joe 3:6
But the Lord * me from caring Amo 7:15
* him far away to foreign lands; Ob 1:12
And they * the bushel basket and Zec 5:9
So I * two shepherd's staffs, Zec 11:7
And I * my staff called "Grace" Zec 11:10
So I * the thirty coins and threw Zec 11:13
Then Satan * him to Jerusalem to Mt 4:5
Next Satan * him to the peak of a Mt 4:8
of Isaiah, "He * our sicknesses Mt 8:17
girl was lying and * her by the Mt 9:25
the girl, who * it to her mother. Mt 14:11
and he * the five loaves and two Mt 14:19
ground, and he * the seven loaves Mt 15:36
But Peter * him aside to Mt 16:22
SIX DAYS LATER Jesus * Peter, Mt 17:1
to Jerusalem, he * the twelve Mt 20:17
arrived and * them all away. Mt 24:39
who * their lamps and went to Mt 25:1
As they were eating, Jesus * a Mt 26:26
And he * a cup of wine and gave Mt 26:27
ahead to pray. He * Peter with him Mt 26:37
Literally, "* counsel against Mt 27:1f
"They * the thirty pieces of Mt 27:9
But first they * him into the Mt 27:27
After the mockery, they * off the Mt 27:31
and * him out to crucify him. Mt 27:31
Joseph * the body and wrapped it Mt 27:59
bedside, and as he * her by the Mk 1:31
The man jumped up, * the Mk 2:12
So they * him just as he was Mk 4:36
girl and she * it to her mother. Mk 6:28
He * the five loaves and two fish Mk 6:41
Then he * the seven loaves, Mk 8:6
Jesus * the blind man by the Mk 8:23
Peter * him aside and chided him. Mk 8:32
Six days later Jesus * Peter, Mk 9:2
But Jesus * him by the hand Mk 9:27
Then he * the children into his Mk 10:16
As they were eating, Jesus * Mk 14:22
Then he * a cup of wine and gave Mk 14:23
He * Peter, James and John with Mk 14:33
Then the Roman soldiers * him Mk 15:16,17
their sport, they * off the purple Mk 15:20
when the crucifixion * place. Mk 15:25
For he * notice of his lowly Lk 1:48
of Nazareth. He * with him Mary, Lk 2:5
child, his parents * him to Lk 2:22
was there and * the child in his Lk 2:28
Then Satan * him up and revealed Lk 4:5
Then Satan * him to Jerusalem to Lk 4:9,10,11
mobbed him and * him to the edge of Lk 4:29
roof above him, * off some tiles Lk 5:18,19
He went into the Temple and * Lk 6:4
food and never * a drop of liquor Lk 7:33
* his twelve disciples with him. Lk 8:1
Then he * her by the hand and Lk 8:54
Jesus * the five loaves and two Lk 9:16
Eight days later he * Peter, Lk 9:28
Literally, "* care of him." Lk 10:34f
to answer, Jesus * the sick man by Lk 14:4
his belongings and * a trip to a Lk 15:13
climbed down and * Jesus to his Lk 19:6
Then he * a glass of wine, and Lk 22:17
Then he * a loaf of bread; Lk 22:19
THEN THE ENTIRE Council * Jesus Lk 23:1
So he * down Jesus' body and Lk 23:53
morning they * the ointments to the Lk 24:1
the food and then * a small loaf of Lk 24:30
This incident * place at Bethany, Jn 1:28
they exclaimed. "It * Jn 2:20
Then Jesus * the loaves and gave Jn 6:11
Then they * the man to the Jn 9:13
Then Mary * a jar of costly Jn 12:3
Passover visitors * palm branches Jn 12:13
the supper table, * off his robe, Jn 13:4
First they * him to Annas, the Jn 18:13
than ever. He * Jesus back into Jn 19:9
And from then on I * her into Jn 19:27
So he came and * it away. Jn 19:38
Then Peter * the lame man by the Act 3:7,8
and * him out and buried him. Act 5:6
executioners—* off their coats and Act 7:58
his danger, they * him to Caesarea Act 9:30
as soon as he arrived, they * him Act 9:39
When they had finished, James * Act 15:13
This is the letter they * along Act 15:23
Barnabas * Mark with him and Act 15:39
so he * no chances, but put them Act 16:24
* them before the Council instead. Act 17:6
Paul went down and * him into Act 20:10,11,12
and visited us. He * Paul's belt, Act 21:11
The second day Paul * us with him Act 21:18
and * 4,000 members of the Act 21:37,38
The commander * the boy by the Act 23:19
Then I * him to their Council to Act 23:28
the soldiers * Paul to Antipatris. Act 23:31
garrison, came and * him violently Act 24:7
Then he * some hardtack and gave Act 27:35
he thanked God and * courage. Act 28:15
God, they * wood and stone and made Rom 1:23
because Jesus * away their sins. Rom 3:26
in Jesus who * away their sins. Rom 3:26
sight—before the ceremony * place. Rom 4:11
listen to him. He * you as his own Rom 9:4
the Lord Jesus * bread, and when 1Co 11:23
In the same way, he * the cup 1Co 11:25
For God * the sinless Christ and 2Co 5:21
No, you * me in and cared for me Gal 4:14
towards us that he * away all our Eph 1:7
Then he * the two groups that had Eph 2:15
had not obeyed. He * this list of Col 2:14
In this way God * away Satan's Col 2:15
to Abraham: God * an oath in his Heb 6:13
then Abraham * a tenth of all he Heb 7:2
of the spoils he * from the kings Heb 7:4
God * an oath that Christ would Heb 7:20
on by others who * their places. Heb 7:23
on the day when I * them by the Heb 8:9
and once for all * blood into that Heb 9:12
No, he * his own blood, and with Heb 9:12
of God's laws, he * the blood of Heb 9:19
which forever * those sins away. Heb 10:4f
that is why God * him away to Heb 11:5
he was gone because God * him. Heb 11:5
He is the one who * God's wrath 1Jn 2:2
throne, just as I * my place with Rev 3:21
He stepped forward and * the Rev 5:7
And as he * the scroll, the Rev 5:8
So I * it from his hand, and Rev 10:10
So the angel * me in spirit into Rev 17:3
And the world leaders, who * part Rev 18:9
In a vision he * me to a towering Rev 21:10

TOOL
the stones with a *, for that would Ex 20:25
for it is a * by which its owner Deu 24:6
any other * at the building site. 1Ki 6:7
come as Satan's *, full of satanic 2Th 2:9

TOOLED
and * it into the form of a calf. Ex 32:4

TOOLS
bring out its * to dismantle you. Jer 22:7
your bodies become * of wickedness, Rom 6:13
and you want to be * in the hands Rom 6:13

TOOTH
if her * is knocked out, knock Ex 21:24
out his slave's *, he shall let him Ex 21:27
let him go free to pay for the *. Ex 21:27
eye for eye, * for tooth. Lev 24:20
eye for eye, tooth for *. Lev 24:20
Life for life, eye for eye, * for Deu 19:21
*, hand for hand, foot for foot; Deu 19:21
with a sore *, or trying to run on Pro 25:19
his own eye. If a * gets knocked Mt 5:38
out the * of the one who did it.' Mt 5:38
for an eye and a * for a tooth." Mt 5:38f
for an eye and a tooth for a *." Mt 5:38f

TOP
At the * of the stairs stood the Gen 28:13
he was camped at the * of a ridge; Gen 31:25
God there at the * of the mountain, Gen 31:54
In the * basket were all kinds Gen 40:17
payment at the * of his sack! Gen 42:25
there at the * of each was the Gen 42:35
silver cup at the * of Benjamin's Gen 44:2
the panel at the * of the door and Ex 12:23
will stand at the * of the hill, Ex 17:9
went to the * of the hill. Ex 17:10
So the Lord came down upon the * Ex 19:20
Moses up to the * of the mountain, Ex 19:20
into the cloud at the *. Ex 24:15
* looked like a raging fire. Ex 24:17
mountain *, and was there for forty Ex 24:18
the edge of the *, and a gold ridge Ex 25:25
of the four legs, close to the *; Ex 25:26,27
flower above the * set of branches Ex 25:34,35
at the front. On * of these Ex 26:14
over them a * layer of goatskins. Ex 26:14
at the bottom and * with clasps. Ex 26:24
"Attach the * of the chestpiece Ex 28:22,23,24
outer * edge of the chestpiece. Ex 28:22,23,24
Overlay the *, sides, and horns Ex 30:3
to me on the * of the mountain. Ex 34:2
The * layer of the roof was made Ex 36:19
at both * and bottom by rings. Ex 36:29
and above the * pair, four in all. Ex 37:20,21
it was 7½ feet square at the *, Ex 38:1
straps at the *, and was tied down Ex 39:4,5
a gold ring was placed at the * Ex 39:15-18
the * corners of the chestpiece. Ex 39:15-18
and put on the * layers, just as Ex 40:19
on * of the wood on the altar. Lev 1:12
and placed on * of these one Lev 8:26
leather on * of the scarlet cloth. Num 4:8
and Aaron died on the * of the Num 20:28
and attach it to the * of a pole; Num 21:8
the * leaders of Moab and Midian. Num 22:7
took Balaam to the * of Mount Num 22:41
of Zophim at the * of Mount Pisgah, Num 23:14
Balaam to the * of Mount Peor, Num 23:28
'but go to the * of Mount Pisgah Deu 3:27
you will see from the mountain *.' Deu 3:28
fire at the * of the mountain, all Deu 5:23
Then, since her house was on * Jos 2:15
then west to the * of the mountain Jos 15:8
extended from the * of the mountain Jos 15:9
he stood at the * of Mount Gerizim Ju 9:7
trail at the * of the mountain. Ju 9:25
to the * of the roof to watch. Ju 9:51
them to the * of the mountain Ju 16:3
"Isn't he the * leader of 1Sa 21:11
there at the * of the hill, and 2Sa 2:25
the spot at the * of the Mount of 2Sa 15:32
DAVID WAS JUST past the * of the 2Sa 16:1
a cloth over the * of the well with 2Sa 17:19
to his post at the * of the wall, 2Sa 18:24
a mound to the * of the city wall 2Sa 20:15
These are the names of the * 2Sa 23:8
as much renown as the * Three. 2Sa 23:22
not actually one of the * Three. 2Sa 23:23
The Thirty, plus the * Three, plus 2Sa 23:24-39f
on each side. The * of each stand 1Ki 7:31
A capital at the * of each pillar; 1Ki 7:41-46
But Elijah climbed to the * of 1Ki 18:42
They found him sitting on * of a 2Ki 1:9
and idols at the * of every hill 2Ki 17:10
the leader of The * Three—the three 1Ch 11:11
The second of The * Three was 1Ch 11:12
The * political officers of the 1Ch 27:16-22
Jerusalem at the * of Mount Moriah, 2Ch 3:1
and placed them on * of the 2Ch 3:16
He sent out * government 2Ch 17:7,8,9
taken alive to the * of a cliff and 2Ch 25:12
Some of the * leaders of Ephraim 2Ch 28:12
walked along the * of their wall, Neh 4:3
I led the Judean leaders to the * Neh 12:31,32
along the * of the wall, giving Neh 12:31,32
come out on *, above the godless; Job 17:8
She lays her eggs on * of the Job 39:14
He leads me safely along the * of Ps 18:33
from the * of Mount Hermon, Sol 4:8
builder and * trader of the world? Is 23:8
the least of them right to the *! Jer 6:13
shall grow at the * where the great Jer 26:18
one of the king's * officials, Jer 41:1
walls. The * 7½ feet of each Jer 52:22
the shoot at the * of the tallest Eze 17:3,4
and he exiled the * men of Israel's Eze 17:12,13
twig from the * of the highest Eze 17:22,23
* of Israel's highest mountain. Eze 17:22,23
against the walls to reach the *. Eze 21:22
Every mountain * is filled with Eze 22:9
across the * of the guardrooms. Eze 40:21
The entire * of the hill where Eze 43:12
and this is the * of the altar, Eze 43:15
This * platform of the altar is Eze 43:16
* twenty-one inches on all sides. Eze 43:17
corners of the * platform and in Eze 43:20
Then Michael, one of the * Dan 10:13
the rocks at the * of Carmel, I Amo 9:3
reaches the very * of the hill Zep 1:10
lamps, and at the * there is a Zec 4:2
John to the * of a high and lonely Mt 17:1
*, you must serve like a slave. Mt 20:27
one stone left on * of another!" Mt 24:2

(TOP Con't)
was split apart from * to bottom; Mt 27:51
and John to the * of a mountain. Mk 9:2
was split apart from * to bottom. Mk 15:38
will be left on * of another; Lk 21:6
and all the * religious authorities Lk 22:66
sorrow on * of everything else. Php 2:27
leaning on the * of his cane. Heb 11:21

TOP-RANKING
of The Thirty—the * officers of the 2Sa 23:13
of The Thirty—the * officers of the 2Sa 23:18,19

TOPAZ
stones: A ruby, a *, and an emerald Ex 28:17
a sardius, a *, and a carbuncle; Ex 39:10
its price is far above rubies. * Job 28:19
are round bars of gold set with *; Sol 5:14
stone—ruby, *, diamond, chrysolite, Eze 28:13
The ninth with *; Rev 21:18,19,20

TOPHEL
*, Laban, Hazeroth, and Dizahab. Deu 1:1

TOPHETH
the altar of * in the Valley of the 2Ki 23:10
the altar called * in the Valley of Jer 7:31
be changed from "*," or the Jer 7:32
longer be called "*" or Jer 19:6
As Jeremiah returned from * where Jer 19:14

TOPIC
was the great * everywhere. 2Sa 19:8,9,10
when the whole * of conversation Jer 16:14,15

TOPMOST
and princes [her * buds and shoots Eze 17:12,13

TOPPED
and were * with cedar beams. 1Ki 7:11
in its walls, * with cedar beams, 1Ki 7:12
52½ feet high, * by a 7½-foot 2Ch 3:15
* with a layer of new timber. Ez 6:4

TOPPLE
your famous, huge pillars will *. Eze 26:11

TOPPLES
Lord spins and * the mighty oaks. Ps 29:9
a nation, its government * easily; Pro 28:2

TOPS
were silver; the * of the posts Ex 38:17
* of the posts were also silver. Ex 38:19
*, and for the rods and hooks. Ex 38:28
I see them from the cliff *, Num 23:7-10
the * of the balsam trees, attack! 2Sa 5:24
At the * of the pillars he made 1Ki 7:16-22
capitals at the * of the pillars. 2Ki 25:17
marching in the * of the mulberry 1Ch 14:15
The two flared capitals on the * 2Ch 4:12-16
blankets the * of the mountains. Job 36:30
rocks at the * of the cliffs to try Is 2:21
their idols at the * of the hills, Is 16:12
hills and mountain * and become Is 17:9
trees on the distant mountain *. Is 30:17
to Jerusalem from the mountain *! Is 40:9
too, dwellers in the mountain *. Is 42:11
adultery on the * of the mountains, Is 57:7,8
ravines to the * of the mountains. Eze 32:6
They sacrifice to idols on the * Hos 4:13
Look at them leaping along the * Joe 2:5
"Smash the * of the pillars and Amo 9:1
Literally, "roof *" which, being Mt 24:17f

TOPSAILS
so they lowered the * and were Act 27:17

TOPSY-TURVY
But he turns * the plans of the Ps 146:9

TORCH
and a flaming * that passed between Gen 15:17
entire city to the *, as a burnt Deu 13:16
and a clay jar with a * in it. Ju 7:16
pairs, with a * between each pair. Ju 15:4
you and put this city to the *!" Jer 37:10

TORCHES
their * blazed into the night. Ju 7:19,20
the flaming * in their left hands, Ju 7:19,20
Then he lit the * and let the Ju 15:5
fire or brilliant *, and it was Eze 1:13
like lightning, gleaming like *. Nah 2:4
Now with blazing *, lanterns, and Jn 18:3

TORE
Then Israel * his garments and Gen 37:34
with me." He * himself away, but Gen 39:12
elders of Israel * their clothing Jos 7:6
When he saw her he * his clothes Ju 11:35
to hold him back, and * his robe. 1Sa 15:27
to prophesy! He * off his clothes 1Sa 19:24
David and his men * their clothes 2Sa 1:11
Now she * the robe and put ashes 2Sa 13:19
His aides also * their clothes in 2Sa 13:31
the field, Ahijah * his new robe 1Ki 11:30
prophecies, he * his clothing, put 1Ki 21:27
from sight he * his robe. 2Ki 2:12
for he at least * down the pillar 2Ki 3:2
Israel read it, he * his clothes 2Ki 5:7
When the king heard this he * his 2Ki 6:26-30
through the rip he * in them that 2Ki 6:26-30
temple of Baal and * it down, 2Ki 11:18
their report he * his clothes and 2Ki 19:1
in it, he * his clothes in terror. 2Ki 22:11
He also * down the houses of 2Ki 23:7
of Judah, and * down all the 2Ki 23:8
to Molech. He * down the statues 2Ki 23:11
Then he * down the altars which 2Ki 23:12
He also * down the altar and 2Ki 23:15
and Manasseh and * down the idol 2Ch 31:1
the Temple and * down the altars he 2Ch 33:15
When I heard this, I * my Ez 9:3
had been done, he * his clothes and Est 4:1
Then Job stood up and * his robe Job 1:20
Literally, "* his robe and shaved Job 1:20f
Wailing loudly in despair, they * Job 2:12
The watchman on the wall * off my Sol 5:7
of the meeting, he * his robes and Is 37:1
and * down the walls of the city. Jer 39:8
people in the city * a hole in the Jer 52:7
upon them and * them apart before Dan 6:24
brass claws that * men apart and Dan 7:19
Then the High Priest * at his own Mt 26:65,66
Then the High Priest * at his Mk 14:63,64

TORMENT
into the place of weeping and *." Mt 8:12
You have no right to * us yet." Mt 8:29
here to * us before the time?" Mt 8:29f
Please, I beg you, oh, don't * Lk 8:28
There, in *, he saw Lazarus in Lk 16:23
this place of * lest they come here Lk 16:28

TORMENTED
But, * by thirst, they cried out, Ex 17:3
the plague that * us—so little that Jos 22:17,18
Amnon became so * by his love 2Sa 13:2
hands of those who * you and Is 51:23
prophets who had * them so much! Rev 11:10
And they will be * with fire and Rev 14:10
* day and night forever and ever. Rev 20:10

TORMENTING
and the Ammonites to begin * them. Ju 10:7,8
Lord had sent a * spirit that 1Sa 16:14
you whenever the * spirit is 1Sa 16:15,16
And whenever the * spirit from 1Sa 16:23
The very next day, in fact, a * 1Sa 18:10
harp, suddenly the * spirit from 1Sa 19:9,10

TORMENTORS
Yet our captors, our *, demand Ps 137:3,4

TORMENTS
her, and it * her constantly." Mt 15:22
it now with * and with sorrows. Rev 18:7

TORN
Joseph is without doubt * in Gen 37:33
* to pieces by some wild animal; Gen 44:28
he shall bring the * carcass to Ex 22:13
of itself, or is * by wild animals, Lev 17:15
of itself or is * by wild animals, Lev 22:8
clothes * and dirt on his head. 1Sa 4:12
The Lord has * the kingdom of 1Sa 15:28
with his clothes * and with dirt on 2Sa 1:1
for him with * clothing and earth 2Sa 15:32
until every stone is * down." 2Sa 17:13
of the Lord which had been * down. 1Ki 18:30
with you and * down your altars and 1Ki 19:10
the rocks were * loose, but the 1Ki 19:11
and have * down your altars; 1Ki 19:14
with their clothes * and told him 2Ki 18:37
because you have * your clothing 2Ki 22:18,19
earlier kings of Judah had * down. 2Ch 34:10,11
the wall of Jerusalem is still * Neh 1:3
let my arm be * from its socket! Job 31:22
foundations have been * down." Ps 11:3f
you have * it apart. Ps 60:2
it was like being * apart by Is 38:13
all who go out shall be * apart. Jer 5:6
For though you have * down the Jer 33:4
off their beards, * their clothes Jer 41:5
the underbrush and * me with his Lam 3:11
Thebes will be * apart, Memphis Eze 30:16
I'll have you * limb from limb and Dan 2:5
Abednego shall be * limb from limb Dan 3:29
For his empire will be * apart Dan 11:4
it is he who has * us—he will Hos 6:1
his clothes were * off in the Mk 14:51,52
He has * princes from their Lk 1:52
and yet the net hadn't *. Jn 21:11
prophets and * down God's altars; Rom 11:2,3

TORNADOS
your fiery storms, tempests and *. Ps 83:15
flames and * and terrible storms Is 30:30

TORRENT
"Shouldn't someone stem this * Job 11:2
of justice—a * of doing good. Amo 5:24

TORRENTIAL
gushing, and the * rains subsided. Gen 8:2
sword, disease, * floods, great Eze 38:22

TORRENTS
down in mighty * from the sky, and Gen 7:10,11,12
to sand. * tear away the soil. Job 14:18,19
and even the widest * freeze. Job 37:10
Who dug the valleys for the * of Job 38:25-27
Though the rain comes in *, and Mt 7:25

TORTILLA
Probably some sort of *. Gen 18:6f

TORTURE
Philistines capture me and * me." 1Sa 31:3,4
heathen capture and * me." 1Ch 10
the man to the * chamber until he Mt 18:3
For God's sake, don't * me!" Mk 5:7
I used * to try to make Act 26:1
kill them, but to * them for five Rev 9.
The smoke of their * rises Rev 14:1

TORTURED
"Then you will be * and killed Mt 24.

TORTURING
of the nations that were * you. 1Sa 10:18,1

TOSS
"Come on, let's kill him and * Gen 37:19,2
Moses, * it into the sky as Ex 9:
by the * of the sacred dice. Jos 21:
The first * indicated Joseph of 1Ch 25:9-3
morning,' and then I * till dawn. Job 7:
All night long I * and turn, and Job 30:1
themselves by a * of the dice. Ps 22:1
Don't * me aside, banished Ps 51:1
We * the coin, Pro 16:3
A coin * Pro 18:1
like a ball and * you away into a Is 22:1
You shall * them in the air; Is 41:1
though they * and roar, can never Jer 5:2
"Throw away your money! * it out Eze 7:1
* about, and sink again. Amo 8:
And the Lord told me, '* it into Zec 11:1
we beg you not to * aside this 2Co 6:

TOSSED
as he watched, Moses * it toward Ex 9:1
and you will be * to and fro Deu 28:2
Then we * a coin Neh 10:3
Why have you * me aside? Ps 43:
O Lord, you have * us aside in Ps 44:
Their ships are * to the heavens Ps 107:2
You will stagger like a sailor * Pro 23:3
thorns cut down and * in the fire. Is 33:1
therefore she is * away like Lam 1:8
homes and * out through the nearest Amo 4:3
the air and * up handfuls of dust. Act 22:23
that is driven and * by the wind; Jas 1:6

TOSSES
strike again. He * his enemies Nah 1:10

TOSSING
* away the jawbone, he remarked, Ju 15:16,17
at David and * dust into the air. 2Sa 16:13
You have seen me * and turning Ps 56:8
watching the rich * their gifts Lk 21:1

TOTAL
Also in the * of Jacob's Gen 46:19-22
So the * number of those going to Gen 46:26
included, this * of Jacob's Gen 46:27
So the * number who went with him Ex 1:5
side, there were a * of eight Ex 36:30
old or older, a * of 603,550 men. Ex 38:25,26
Grand *: 603,550 Num 1:20-46
* Num 1:20-46
This * does not include the Num 1:47,48,49
So the * of all those on Judah's Num 2:3-31
So the * of the Reuben side of the Num 2:3-31
So the * on the Ephraim side of Num 2:3-31
So the * on Dan's side of the camp Num 2:3-31
and found the * number of eldest Num 3:43
The money collected came to a * Num 3:50
found that the * number was 2,750. Num 4:36
found that the * of all the Levites Num 4:46,47,48
(so the * weight of the silver Num 7:84,85,86
(so the * weight of gold was Num 7:84,85,86
So the * number of the draftable Num 26:51
The * number of Levites in the Num 26:62
included in the * census figure of Num 26:62
commanded. The * booty (besides Num 31:32-35
* value to be more than $300,000. Num 31:51,52
In this way the * area of our Num 36:3
and the * inheritance came to ten Jos 17:5,6
Rehob—an overall * of twenty-two Jos 19:30,31
Implied in verse 22, where the * Jos 21:20,21,22f
So the * number of cities and Jos 21:26
The * number of cities and Jos 21:41,42
and Zarethan. The * weight of 1Ki 7:47
to the Lord—a * of 22,000 oxen and 1Ki 8:62,63
King Solomon, the * value of which 1Ki 9:27,28
At the time of King David, the * 1Ch 7:2
many sons. The * number of men 1Ch 7:5
A * of 956 Benjaminites returned. 1Ch 9:9
to Jerusalem. The * population 1Ch 21:5
or older. The * came to 38,000. 1Ch 23:3
the final * was never put into 1Ch 27:24
and he didn't send * destruction; 2Ch 12:12
Tobiah, and Nekoda—a * of 652. Ez 2:60
So a * of 42,360 persons returned Ez 2:64,65
as he could. The * value of their Ez 2:69
it to * $1,300,000 in silver; Ez 8:26,27
and twenty gold bowls worth a * Ez 8:26,27
Tobiah, and Nekoda—a * of 642. Neh 7:62
There was a * of 42,360 citizens Neh 7:66
The other leaders gave a * of Neh 7:71
Making a * of twenty children, Job 42:13,14f
745—a * of 4,600 captives in all. Jer 52:30
he will plan * war against Greece. Dan 11:2

TOTALED
there in Egypt * seventy. Gen 46:27

TALED Con't)
nies of Israel * 603,550 (not Num 2:32,33
the Gershon division * 2,630. Num 4:38-41
the half given to the army *: Num 31:36-40
from verses 6 and 7 of the Jos 19:2-7f
ar from these families * 22,600. 1Ch 7:2

ALING
tax against Judah * $230,000. 2Ki 23:33

TALLY
hich must be * destroyed" or else Jos 7:12f
else become * God's. Jos 7:12f
d they were not * destroyed. 2Ki 13:23
he Egyptian Pharaoh is * 2Ki 18:20,21
ey were fully armed and * loyal 1Ch 12:24-37
ould possess was * defiled by the Ez 9:11
ould be so * destroyed that its Zep 2:15f

TALS
d bring me the *," he told 1Ch 21:2
his * 483 years, instead of the Dan 9:25f

TEM
poles erected by their kings. Eze 43:7
way their idols and the * poles Eze 43:9

TTER
d kingdoms * into ruin. Ps 46:6

TTERING
*; they plot my death and use Ps 62:3,4

U
When King * of Hamath learned 1Ch 18:9
or Hadadezer and * had been 1Ch 18:10

UCH
or even * it, or we will die." Gen 3:2,3
nd in constant * with God, he Gen 5:21-24
hat is why I didn't let you * Gen 20:6
r even * its boundaries; Ex 19:12
o hand shall * him, but he shall Ex 19:13
hose who are holy may * it." Ex 29:37f
only what is holy may * them." Ex 30:29f
s holy may * them," or "whoever Lev 6:18f
priests—may * this meat; Lev 6:27
neat or even * their dead bodies; Lev 11:8
neat or even * their dead bodies. Lev 11:11
he must not * anything sacred, nor Lev 12:4
but they must not * the holy Num 4:15
men, and don't * anything that Num 16:26
be careful not to * any of the Num 18:2,3
We won't trample your fields or * Num 21:22
'Burn their idols and do not * Deu 7:25
You may not even * the dead Deu 14:8
not so much as * her feet to the Deu 28:56,57
carrying the Ark * the water with Jos 3:13,14
we will not * them, and we won't. Jos 9:19
your wickedness, I'll not * you. 1Sa 24:13
'These are my prophets—* them 1Ch 16:22
"Who would dare * you?" Est 7:5
to save his life. * his body with Job 2:4,5
him, they got in * with each other Job 2:11
again, so that no evil can * you. Job 5:19
* of water, like a new seedling. Job 14:8,9
"Look, everything the wicked * Job 21:16
Judgment will not * him Ps 32:6
around me, the evil will not * me. Ps 91:7
burst into flame at his *. Ps 104:32
king who tried! "* not these Ps 105:15
mountains smoke beneath your *. Ps 144:5
"They can never * us," you say, Is 28:15
like filthy things you hate to *. Is 30:22
no one can * us here!' Jer 21:13
blood, defiling everything they *. Lam 4:14
straight out to * the others' Eze 1:23
but don't * anyone with the mark. Eze 9:6
they may not * any of my holy Eze 44:13
mouths so that they can't * me; Dan 6:22
that it didn't even * the ground. Dan 8:5
But he roused me with a *, and Dan 8:18
not * us,' will die by the sword. Amo 9:10
my mountain shall * Zec 14:5f
if you will only come and * her." Mt 9:18
I only * him, I will be healed." Mt 9:21
bodies—but can't * your souls! Mt 10:28
him to let them * even the tassel Mt 14:36
around him, trying to * him. Mk 3:10
"If I can just * his clothing, I Mk 5:28
* the fringes of his clothes; Mk 6:56
and begged him to * and heal him. Mk 8:22
But they were afraid to * him for Mk 12:12
He must never * wine or hard Lk 1:15
and the * of his hands healed Lk 4:40
Everyone was trying to * him, Lk 6:19
babies to him to * and bless. Lk 18:15
is I, myself ! * me and make Lk 24:39
"Don't * me," he cautioned, Jn 20:17
And the person who won't * such Rom 14:6
don't * their filthy things, and 2Co 6:17
of Death could not * the oldest Heb 11:28

TOUCHED
never * one ram of yours for food. Gen 31:38
And he was crying. This * her Ex 2:6
herds and flocks will even be *!' Ex 9:4
as he realizes that he has * it. Lev 5:3
Any earthen pot * by the defiled Lev 15:12
defiled by having * the dead, so Num 9:6,7
otherwise dead, or has * a grave. Num 19:18
killed anyone or * a dead body. Num 31:19
I have not * the tithe while I Deu 26:14
carrying the Ark * the water at the Jos 3:13,14
where the boundary * the border of Jos 12:5
and Naarah, and * Jericho, and Jos 16:7
the Angel * the meat and bread Ju 6:21
* became his constant companions. 1Sa 10:26
his head will be *, for he has been 1Sa 14:45
their inner wings * each other at 1Ki 6:23-28
sleeping, an angel * him and told 1Ki 19:5
came again and * him and said, 1Ki 19:7
And as soon as the body * 2Ki 13:20,21
him because he had * the Ark. 1Ch 13:10
So Esther approached and * its Est 5:2
the angry hand of God has * me. Job 19:21
burning coal. He * my lips with it Is 6:7
because this coal has * your lips. Is 6:7
Then he * my mouth and said, Jer 1:9
evil fell on anyone who * them. Jer 2:3
beings as they * against each Eze 3:13
the fire hadn't * them—not a hair Dan 3:27
But a hand * me and lifted me, Dan 10:10
looked like a man—* my lips and I Dan 10:16
seemed to be a man * me again, and Dan 10:18
But when Jesus * her hand, the Mt 8:15
up behind him and * a tassel of his Mt 9:20
Then he * their eyes and said, Mt 9:29
Jesus came over and * them. Mt 17:7
pity for them and * their eyes. Mt 20:34
And Jesus, moved with pity, * him Mk 1:41
the crowd and * his clothes. Mk 5:27
as soon as she had * him, the Mk 5:29
and asked, "Who * my clothes?" Mk 5:30
you, and you ask who * you?" Mk 5:31
and as many as * him were healed. Mk 6:56
then spat and * the man's tongue Mk 7:33
Jesus reached out and * the man Lk 5:13
and * it, and the bearers stopped. Lk 7:14
came up behind and * him, for she Lk 8:43,44
But the instant she * the edge of Lk 8:43,44
"Who * me?" Lk 8:45
who deliberately * me, for I felt Lk 8:46
* him and that now she was well. Lk 8:47
He * her, and instantly she Lk 13:13
And he * the place where the Lk 22:51
him arrested, but no one * him. Jn 7:44
* at all by the ravages of death. Act 13:37
the next, we * at Samos; Act 20:15
"You haven't * food for two Act 27:33
animal * the mountain it must die. Heb 12:20
I have * him with my own hands. 1Jn 1:1

TOUCHES
* it shall be set apart for God. Ex 29:37
whatever * them shall become Ex 30:29
Or if he * human discharge of Lev 5:3
* them shall become holy." Lev 6:18f
Anyone who * anything that is Lev 7:21
anything it * must be put into Lev 11:32
* any food, all of it is defiled. Lev 11:34
of such an animal * any clay oven, Lev 11:35
And if the carcass * grain to be Lev 11:37
If the defiled man * anyone Lev 15:11
And any priest who * a dead Lev 22:4
emission, or who * any reptile or Lev 22:5
thing, or who * anyone who is Lev 22:5
"Anyone who * a dead human body Num 19:11
Anyone who * a dead person and Num 19:13
"If someone out in a field * the Num 19:16
way, or if he even * a bone or a Num 19:16
And anything a defiled person * Num 19:22
westward until it * the Num 34:10,11
of tow snaps when it * the fire." Ju 16:9f
see to it that no one * him." 2Sa 14:8
For they tear the hand that * 2Sa 23:6
when the east wind * it, dying in Eze 17:10
The Lord God of Hosts * the land Amo 9:5
"But if someone * a dead person, Hag 2:13
Jesus * the man. Mt 8:3

TOUCHING
that way he'll die without our * Gen 37:21,22
"Anyone * anything ceremonially Lev 5:2
though he wasn't aware of * it. Lev 5:2
"Anyone * their dead bodies Lev 11:24
"You are also defiled by * any Lev 11:26
Anyone * the dead body of such an Lev 11:27
Anyone * their dead bodies shall Lev 11:31
of disease, anyone * the carcass Lev 11:39
Do not defile yourselves by * Lev 11:43
yourselves by * any of these things Lev 11:44
so anyone * the man's bed is Lev 15:5
apply to anyone * him. Lev 15:7
Anyone * or carrying anything Lev 15:10
that time anyone * her shall be Lev 15:19
Anyone * her bed or anything she Lev 15:21,22,23
Anyone * her bed or anything she Lev 15:27
themselves by * a dead person, Lev 21:1
anyone else * it shall be Num 1:51
been defiled by * a dead person. Num 5:1
time because of * a dead body, or Num 9:10
in the tent, or by * a bone, or Num 19:18
a bone, or * someone who has been Num 19:18
and anyone * the water shall be Num 19:21
by * them with this clothing. Eze 44:19
Everything * the water of this Eze 47:9
in this way before * any food. Mk 7:4
I'm not interested and I'm not * Act 18:15
tasting, or even * certain foods? Col 2:21

TOUCHSTONE
Fairness is the * of everything Ps 99:4

TOUCHY
It is not irritable or *. 1Co 13:5

TOUGH
and stubborn too—as * as they are. Eze 3:8
about me and how * I am, then why Lk 19:22
but even if they are * and cruel. 1Pe 2:18

TOUGHER
I am going to be * on you, not 2Ch 10:11

TOUGHS
If young * tell you, "Come and Pro 1:10

TOUR
later they returned from their *. Num 13:25
Note her walls and * her Ps 48:13
from Babylon on a * of the palace, Is 39:2
* of the various Temple buildings. Mt 24:1
Jesus from their * and told him all Mk 6:30
LONG AFTERWARDS he began a * Lk 8:1

TOW
Literally, "like a string of * Ju 16:9f

TOWARD
bent is always * evil from his Gen 8:21
Then they continued northward * Gen 13:3,4
and arrogant * her mistress Sarai. Gen 16:4
noticed three men coming * him. Gen 18:2
their meal and started on * Sodom; Gen 18:16
So the other two went on * Gen 18:22,23
country, as I have been * you." Gen 21:23
Beer-sheba and journeyed * Haran. Gen 28:10
traveled on * Ephrath (Bethlehem). Gen 35:16
to point his rod * the waters of Ex 7:19
to point the rod * all the rivers, Ex 8:5
as he watched, Moses tossed it * Ex 9:10
"Point your hand * heaven and Ex 9:22
the people to turn * Piha-hiroth Ex 14:2
and suddenly, out * the wilderness, Ex 16:10
suddenly, as they looked * the Num 16:42
* me," he frantically explained. Num 22:5,6
and looked out * the camp of Israel Num 24:1
across the desert * the Red Sea.' Deu 1:40
the wilderness * the Red Sea, for Deu 2:1
northward * the Moab desert. Deu 2:8
"NEXT WE TURNED * King Og's land Deu 3:1
be utterly callous * his own Deu 28:54
men and started * Ai, accompanied Jos 8:10
"Point your spear * Ai, for I will Jos 8:18
his spear pointed * Ai until the Jos 8:26
turned northwest * Gilgal, opposite Jos 15:7
and Rimmon and turned * Neah. Jos 19:13
turned east * Beth-dagon, and ran Jos 19:27
Then the boundary turned * Ramah Jos 19:29
were leaping up * the sky, and as Ju 13:20
So they ran * the wilderness, Ju 20:42
the wilderness * the rock of Ju 20:45
along the road * Beth-shemesh, 1Sa 6:12
As they were climbing a hill * 1Sa 9:9,10,11
out * them to go up the hill. 1Sa 9:14
three men coming * you who are on 1Sa 10:3
prophets coming * them, and the 1Sa 10:10
one went * Ophrah in the land of 1Sa 13:17
the third moved * the border above 1Sa 13:18
shameful behavior * David. 1Sa 20:34
* the present city center. 2Sa 5:9
great crowd coming * the city along 2Sa 13:34
in—and as I face * the Temple and 1Ki 8:29
when they pray * this place and 1Ki 8:35,36
their sin and pray * this Temple, 1Ki 8:38
miracles) and pray * this Temple, 1Ki 8:41,42
to you, looking * your chosen city 1Ki 8:44
of Jerusalem and * this Temple 1Ki 8:44
to you and pray * this land which 1Ki 8:48
their fathers, and * this city of 1Ki 8:48
have chosen, and * this Temple, 1Ki 8:48
his hands outstretched * heaven. 1Ki 8:54,55
perfect * Jehovah all his days." 1Ki 15:14f
Obadiah saw Elijah coming * him! 1Ki 18:7
"Go and look out * the sea." 1Ki 18:43
Finally, * evening, he died. 1Ki 22:35
then he moved on * Jerusalem to 2Ki 12:17
And * whom have you felt so cocky? 2Ki 19:22
wall and fled out * the Arabah 2Ki 25:4,5
drawn, pointing * Jerusalem, he and 1Ch 21:16
a good heart * God, so that he will 1Ch 29:19
* heaven, and prayed this prayer: 2Ch 6:12,13
to you as I face * this place. 2Ch 6:20,21
when they pray * this Temple; 2Ch 6:20,21
and then we pray * this Temple and 2Ch 6:26
name, and to pray * this Temple, 2Ch 6:32
and they pray * this city of 2Ch 6:34
again, and face * this land you 2Ch 6:37,38
hearts are perfect * him, so that 2Ch 16:9
of Beth-horon, * Samaria, killing 2Ch 25:13
who do not go should contribute * Ez 1:4

(TOWARD Con't)
to give generously * the rebuilding Ez 2:68
* Israel will last forever." Ez 3:11
the Valley Gate * the Jackal's Well Neh 2:13
and lifted their hands * heaven; Neh 8:6
with their faces * the ground. Neh 8:6
in order to turn them * your laws; Neh 9:29
went to the right * the Dung Gate Neh 12:31,32
You have become cruel * me, and Job 30:21
He is merciful and tender * those Ps 103:8
for his mercy * those who fear and Ps 103:11
Revive my heart * you. Ps 119:37
is the first step * becoming wise! Pro 4:7
they will come racing * Jerusalem. Is 5:26
Look, see the armies thundering * Is 17:12
warrior, full of fury * his foes. Is 42:13
the fields * the Jordan valley. Jer 39:4
* the country of the Ammonites. Jer 41:10
it across the fields, * Arabah. Jer 52:7
great storm coming * me from the Eze 1:4
"Son of dust, look over * the Eze 6:2
"Son of dust, look * the north." Eze 8:5
vine that turned * the eagle and Eze 17:6
and branches out * him instead, Eze 17:7
"Son of dust, look * Jerusalem Eze 20:46
"Son of dust, face * Jerusalem Eze 21:2
They will decide to turn * Eze 21:22
"Son of dust, look * the land of Eze 25:2
"Son of dust, look * the city of Eze 28:21
"Son of dust, face * Egypt and Eze 29:2
"Son of dust, face * Mount Seir Eze 35:2
* the land of Magog, and prophesy Eze 38:2,3
I will turn you and drive you * Eze 39:2
Its entry hall faced * the outer Eze 40:37
One face—that of a man—looked * Eze 41:19,20
* the palm tree on the other side. Eze 41:19,20
* Hethlon, then on through Labweh Eze 47:15
It came hurtling * the statue and Dan 2:34
its windows open * Jerusalem, and Dan 6:10
So Gabriel started * me. Dan 8:17
"* the end of their kingdoms, Dan 8:23
of her people are false * God. Hos 10:2
meet another angel coming * him. Zec 2:3
Then I saw two women flying * us, Zec 5:9
mountain will move * the north and Zec 14:4
the north and half * the south. Zec 14:4
Jerusalem, half * the Dead Sea and Zec 14:8
"Your attitude * me has been Mal 3:13
crowding * the Kingdom of Heaven, Mt 11:12
and walked on the water * Jesus. Mt 14:29
* them, and then ran to greet him. Mk 9:15
If your foot carries you * evil, Mk 9:45,46
Now a mob began to crowd in * Mk 15:8
with them * the city of Bethsaida. Lk 9:10
pressing onward * Jerusalem. Lk 13:22
As they continued onward * Lk 17:11
That's exactly how I'll be * you! Lk 19:22
coming * him and said, "Look! Jn 1:29
out across the lake * Capernaum. Jn 6:17
they saw Jesus walking * the boat! Jn 6:18,19
She turned * him. Jn 20:16
saw an angel of God coming * him. Act 10:3
feel their way * him and find Act 17:27
attitude of Christ * the other. Rom 15:5
about the way we have acted * you. 2Co 1:12
but I keep working * that day when Php 3:12
and faultless * every one of you. 1Th 2:10
else, just as our love does * you. 1Th 3:12
is already strong * all the 1Th 4:10
the first step * all kinds of sin. 1Ti 6:10
then God's mercy * you will win out Jas 2:13
full of sympathy * each other, 1Pe 3:8
out and swept * the woman in an Rev 12:15

TOWARDS
lives were only * evil, he was Gen 6:5
and this time, * evening, the bird Gen 8:11
everyone will feel the same * him. Gen 16:9-12
cooling in Laban's attitude * him. Gen 31:2
of camels coming * them in the Gen 37:25
from the basins * the people and Ex 24:8
Then, with hands spread out * the Lev 9:22
and started * the Promised Land. Num 14:40
* the front of the Tabernacle. Num 19:4
"I'm sure I see people coming * Ju 9:37
Goliath walked out * David with 1Sa 17:41,42
she met David coming * her. 1Sa 25:20
he saw a lone man running * them. 2Sa 18:24
saw another man running * them. 2Sa 18:26
and his men coming * him, he came 2Sa 24:20
hands spread out * heaven and said, 1Ki 8:22,23
a day your thoughts turn * me. Ps 139:17,18
Oh, how blind and deaf you are * Is 42:18
Dead Sea and half * the Zec 14:8
* you carrying a pot of water. Mk 14:13
* Jerusalem with an iron will. Lk 9:51
Jesus went on * Jerusalem, walking Lk 19:28
So overflowing is his kindness * Eph 1:7

TOWED
that was being * behind us, and Act 27:16

TOWEL
wrapped a * around his loins, Jn 13:4
them with the * he had around him. Jn 13:5

TOWER
the city and the * mankind was Gen 11:5
and camped beyond the * of Eder. Gen 35:21
return and break down this *." Ju 8:9
down the city * and killed the Ju 8:17
My refuge and high *. 2Sa 22:3
The watchman on the * of 2Ki 9:17
Literally, "from the * of the 2Ki 18:8f
wall as far as the * of the Hundred Neh 3:1
the Hundred and the * of Hananel; Neh 3:1
the Furnace * in addition to a Neh 3:11
of the upper * of the king's castle Neh 3:25
Water Gate and the Projecting *. Neh 3:26
* and over to the wall of Ophel. Neh 3:27
We walked from the * of Furnaces Neh 12:38
Fish Gate and the * of Hananel, and Neh 12:39
the gate of the * of the Hundred; Neh 12:39
can reach me, and a * of safety. Ps 18:2
in her palaces for a high *." Ps 48:3f
For you have been my high * of Ps 59:16
for you are my high * of safety, Ps 59:17
For you are my refuge, a high * Ps 61:3
he is my fortress, my * of Ps 144:2
as the * of David, jeweled with a Sol 4:4
as an ivory *, your eyes as limpid Sol 7:4
like the * of Lebanon overlooking Sol 7:4
and every high * and wall, and Is 2:15
the Lord, from the * of Hananel at Jer 31:38,39
Gate, and from the * of Hananel to Zec 14:10
juice, and built a watchman's *. Mk 12:1
when the * of Siloam fell on them? Lk 13:4

TOWERED
It * above all the other trees. Eze 31:5

TOWERING
and evil man, * like a cedar of Ps 37:35,36
to the mighty, * Rock of safety. Ps 61:2
There he built his * temple, Ps 78:69
it was very great, * above the Eze 19:11
In a vision he took me to a * Rev 21:10

TOWERS
portable *, and battering rams Deu 20:20
with walls, *, gates, and bars." 2Ch 14:7
He built fortified * in Jerusalem 2Ch 26:9
stones from the * and battlements. 2Ch 26:15
and * on the wooded hills. 2Ch 27:4
Walk around and count her many *! Ps 48:12
the heavens. It * above the earth. Ps 108:5
Literally, "My breasts are its * Sol 8:10f
are counting your * and estimating Is 33:18
I will make your * of sparkling Is 54:12
too, and tear down all her *. Jer 48:18
they will build siege * and make Eze 21:22
walls of Tyre and tear down her *. Eze 26:4
* are manned by men from Gamad. Eze 27:11
and with 1500 *, should be so Zep 2:15f

TOWN
citizens of the *: "Sir," he Gen 23:10
outside the *, beside a spring. Gen 24:11
of the * to go back again." Gen 38:23
orphans, and widows of your *. Deu 16:14
elders of his home * shall send for Deu 19:12
you in whatever * he shall choose, Deu 23:15,16
or a foreigner living in your *. Deu 24:14,15
along to the * of Chesalon on the Jos 15:10,11
and put it in Ophrah, his home *. Ju 8:27
* they would go along with it. Ju 9:3
The people at the nearby * of Ju 9:46
it back to the * where, following Ju 9:49
on the outskirts of the *. Ju 14:5
from the * of Bethlehem, in Ju 17:7,8
So the five men went on to the * Ju 18:7
came out of the * to attack, the Ju 20:31
the * as they chased after Israel. Ju 20:31
them and be drawn away from the *. Ju 20:32
knew whether the seer was in *. 1Sa 9:9,10,11
Saul's home *, and told the people 1Sa 11:4
* he asked, "What's the matter? 1Sa 11:5
was buried in Ramah, his home *. 1Sa 28:3
warriors from that * traveled all 1Sa 31:12
Absalom's home *, its people 2Sa 15:9f
went to his home *, set his affairs 2Sa 17:23
* of Rehoboth became the new king. 1Ch 1:48
Bezer (a desert *), Jahzah, 1Ch 6:78,79
* and spend their time cursing me. Ps 35:16
I am the talk of the * and the Ps 69:12
Justice," and "The Faithful *." Is 1:26
who lived in the * of Anathoth in Jer 1:1
Nehelam was Shemaiah's home *, Jer 29:24f
who was out of * at the time. Dan 5:7f
Gilgal, the * where Baal-worship Hos 9:15f
who lived in the * of Moresheth Mic 1:1
Micah bitterly declaims each *, Mic 1:11f
Micah bitterly declaims each *, Mic 1:11f
Micah bitterly declaims each *, Mic 1:11f
Micah's home *. Mic 1:14f
of saving her. The * of Achzib has Mic 1:14
JESUS WAS BORN in the * of Mt 2:1
'O little * of Bethlehem, you are Mt 2:6
under, both in the * and on the Mt 2:16
the lake to Capernaum, his home *. Mt 9:1
spread his fame all over the *. Mt
until you leave for the next *. Mt 1
his home *, Nazareth in Galilee, Mt 13:5
evening he was in * again and saw Mt
and were near the * of Bethphage on Mt
now arrived at the * of Capernaum Mk
disciples to Nazareth, his home *. Mk
except in his home * and among his Mk
Later, as they left *, a great Mk 1
of Judea to the * where Zacharias Lk 1:3
here in your home * like those you Lk 4
is accepted in his own home *! Lk 4
Later on as Jesus left the * he Lk 5
"If the people of a * won't Lk
"If a * welcomes you, follow Lk 10:
"But if a * refuses you, go out Lk 10
the dust of your * from our feet as Lk 1
must not return to *— remember Lk 17
Andrew and Peter's home *. Jn 1
he arrived at the * of Cana, where Jn 4:46
the believers in the * of Lydda. Act 9
The news raced through the *, and Act 9
There, in the * of Salamis, they Act 1
Afterwards they preached from * Act 13:
from town to * across the entire Act 13:
landing at the port * of Perga. Act 13
Barnabas, and ran them out of *. Act 13
feet against the * and went on to Act 13
them once more before leaving *. Act 16
traveling from * to town casting Act 19
from town to * casting out demons Act 19
in Cilicia which is no small *. Act 21
woman from the * of Cenchreae, will Rom 1
to such and such a *, stay there a Jas 4:

TOWNS
* and driving out the Amorites. Num 21:31,
All of the cities, *, and Num 31:9,10,
many of the * in Gilead, and Num 32:
also took all of the unwalled *. Deu
all the * and villages of Ekron. Jos 15:
Megiddo, with their surrounding *; Ju 1:
Women came out from all the * 1Sa 18
one of the country * instead of 1Sa 27
its surrounding *, on the east by 1Ch 7:
as far as Ayyah and its *. 1Ch 7:
Gath and its surrounding *. 1Ch 18
Then he went to the seaport * of 2Ch 8:17,
and he acquired many *, for God 2Ch 32:28,
from their homes in the other *. Ez 3
* and villages throughout Judah. Neh 7:
the tithes in all our rural *. Neh 10:
other cities and * of Judah and Neh 11
Some of the * where the people of Neh 11:25-
and its *. Neh 11:25-
*, with no one living in them." Jer 9:1
her surrounding * all the evil I Jer 19:1
the neighboring * shall be burned. Jer 49
neighboring *, says the Lord. Jer 49:1
Gomorrah and their neighboring *. Jer 50:4
go on to other * as well, and give Mk 1:3
The herdsmen fled to the nearby * Mk 5:1
man started off to visit the Ten * Mk 5:2
of Galilee by way of the Ten *. Mk 7:3
on the way, coming from other *. Lk 8:
pairs to all the * and villages he Lk 10:
As they came to the * of Lk 19:2
their neighboring *, all full of Jud 1:

TRACE
be no * of yeast in your homes; Ex 12:1
blot out every * of Amalek." Ex 17:1
For seven days no * of yeast Deu 16:
healed of every * of his leprosy! 2Ki 5:1
Thus Jehu destroyed every * of 2Ki 10:2
shadow, gone so soon, without a *. 1Ch 29:1
"Let's wipe out every * of Ps 74:
every * of all this idol worship. Eze 11:1
a map and on it * two routes for Eze 21:19,2
dawn have left no * of their prey. Zep 3:
me of every * of my disease." Lk 5:1
Hate every * of their sin while Jud 1:2

TRACED
his genealogy was * back through: 1Ch 6:33-3
genealogy was * back through: 1Ch 6:39-4
Merari's ancestry was * back 1Ch 6:44-4

TRACHONITIS
brother Philip, over Iturea and *; Lk 3:1

TRACK
"Am I supposed to keep * of him Gen 4:9
that no one kept * of the amount. Gen 41:49
Punish false witnesses. * down Pro 19:5

TRACKED
Gilead is a city of sinners, * Hos 6:8

TRACT
the digestive * and out again? Mt 15:17
his own, not one little * of land. Act 7:5

TRADE
Jacob: "All right, * me your Gen 25:31
here among us and ply their *. Gen 34:21
I will * you food in exchange." Gen 47:16
We will * ourselves for food, Gen 47:19
but if you decide not to *, the Ex 13:13

ADE Con't)
d profits from * with the kings 1Ki 10:15
cut off all * with Jerusalem. 1Ki 15:17
piece of better land in *. 1Ki 21:2
to * it, and he refused!" 1Ki 21:6
addition, there was a * 2Ch 9:13,14
but he too worked on the wall. Neh 3:8
ying the * routes of the world. Ps 107:23
100th flattery is her stock in *. Pro 5:3
orth-south * routes along the Eze 26:2
eir goods to barter for your *. Eze 27:9
rian wool to * for all the rich Eze 27:18
hey bring choice fabrics to * Eze 27:24
e unrighteousness of your *." Eze 28:18f
ey * them for a pair of shoes. Amo 2:6
oon * with Herod's country. Act 12:20
ADED
u might live; I * their lives for Is 43:4
ywhere that has * in its old gods Jer 2:10,11
ver be sold or * or used by Eze 48:14
eir slaves; they * a young lad Joe 3:3
Esau did: he * his rights as the Heb 12:16
ADEMARK
iolence is your *. Is 59:6
ADER
uilder and top * of the world? Is 23:8
ADERS
hmaelite * who were taking gum, Gen 37:25
o when the * Gen 37:28
who was away when the * came by) Gen 37:29
Meanwhile, in Egypt, the * sold Gen 37:36
f the Ishmaelite *, he was Gen 39:1
dom sends her * to buy your Eze 27:16
here will be no more grasping * Zec 14:21
ADES
f Tarshish with whom she * Eze 38:13
, and addressed them as follows: Act 19:25
ADESMEN
The merchants and * camped Neh 13:20
nd the skilled *—the carpenters Jer 24:1
rmy, and the * who were left. Jer 52:15
RADING
ou may establish * posts in 1Ki 20:34
Great * centers in Arabia. Eze 38:13f
RADITION
o inaugurate this * and to pass it Est 9:27
decided upon this * as a Est 9:29-31
nder your feet for the sake of *. Mk 7:9
order to protect your man-made *. Mk 7:12,13
however, this * of circumcision is Jn 7:21,22,23
RADITIONAL
Form yourselves into the * 2Ch 35:4,5
continue their * custom of fasting Zec 7:3
"The * fasts and times of Zec 8:19
go to eat the * Passover supper. Mk 14:12
This is still the * greeting Lk 22:47f
the old, * rules of my religion. Gal 1:14
It is * to suppose that Paul was Gal 4:15f
RADITIONS
disobey the ancient Jewish *?" Mt 15:2
"And why do your * violate the Mt 15:3
as required by their ancient *. Mk 7:3
orders and substitute your own *. Mk 7:8
follow the Jewish * and customs. Act 21:20
RAFFIC
to control the * at the gate, but 2Ki 7:17
RAGEDY
of all the * you see around you. Deu 28:34
prophet Jehu. The * occurred 1Ki 16:13
*") because of what had happened. 1Ch 7:23
know full well the * of our city; Neh 2:17
oldest brother's house, * struck. Job 1:12,13
heard of all the * that had Job 2:11
swiftly away, filled with *. Job 9:25
Tell me, for I fear some * awaits Dan 2:1
RAGIC
after the * consequence of what he Ex 6:8,9
RAIL
Far down the distant *, Num 24:15-19
the * at the top of the mountain. Ju 9:25
As she was riding down the * on 1Sa 25:20
They followed a * of clothing 2Ki 7:15
who led Israel down that evil *. 2Ki 15:24
they hide beside the *, listening Ps 56:6
against the rocks on the *. Ps 91:12
and from stumbling off the *. Pro 3:23
She staggers down a crooked *, Pro 5:6
world, follow the * of my flock to Sol 1:8
behind a * of misery and death. Is 59:7
TRAILED
Great crowds * along behind, and Lk 23:27
TRAILS
dark and treacherous *, and fall. Jer 23:12
TRAIN
with a long * of camels carrying 1Ki 10:2
leading many captives in his *. Ps 68:18
These older women must * the Tit 2:4
Let God * you, for he is doing Heb 12:7
Men have trained, or can *, every Jas 3:7
They * themselves to be greedy; 2Pe 2:14
TRAINED
There were 44,760 armed, *, and 1Ch 5:18
there were 50,000 * warriors; 1Ch 12:24-37
were 40,000 * and ready troops. 1Ch 12:24-37
* in singing praises to the Lord; 1Ch 25:6,7
was Jehozabad, with 180,000 * men. 2Ch 17:18
old and older, all * and highly 2Ch 25:5,6
For a perfectly * army Is 14:31
as a calf must be * for the yoke. Jer 31:18
to idols. I * him from infancy, I Hos 11:3
walls like picked and * commandos. Joe 2:7
Our earthly fathers * us for a Heb 12:10
Men have *, or can train, every Jas 3:7
TRAINING
stop and all military * will end. Is 2:4
their three-year * period, planning Dan 1:5
When the three-year * period was Dan 1:18,19
and * camps will be closed down. Mic 4:3
a thorough Jewish * from my Act 26:4
it roughly, * it to do what it 1Co 9:27
submit to God's * so that we can Heb 12:9
TRAITOR
demanded, "Which of you is the *? 2Ki 6:11
son, and was a * to his master. 2Ch 13:6
have been a * to your people. Ps 73:15
death, but a false witness is a *. Pro 14:25
Don't let people call you a * Is 8:12
own ears what a * he is, for he has Jer 26:11
arrested him as a *, claiming he Jer 37:13
This man is a *." Jer 38:4
king: "Amos is a * to our nation Amo 7:10
replace Judas the *, who has gone Act 1:24,25
TRAITORS
I loathed these * because they Ps 119:158
know so well what * you are, rebels Is 48:8
TRAMP
a fugitive and a * upon the earth, Gen 4:12
and made me a fugitive and a *; Gen 4:14
TRAMPLE
We won't * your fields or touch Num 21:22
And you shall * on their backs!" Deu 33:29
ground, and * my life in the dust. Ps 7:5
Don't let these proud men * me. Ps 36:11
for he will * down our foes. Ps 60:12
30 could be, "* upon those who Ps 68:30f
even * them beneath your feet! Ps 91:13
* them like dirt beneath his feet. Is 10:5,6
tender plants you * down beneath Is 37:27
permitted him to * kings underfoot Is 41:2
yourselves, but * down the rest? Eze 34:18
They * the poor in the dust and Amo 2:7
the truth! You * the poor and Amo 5:11
brass and you will * to pieces many Mic 4:13
You will * the grapes, but get no Mic 6:15
Go into the pits to * the clay, Nah 3:14
They will * the pearls and turn Mt 7:6
They will * the Holy City for Rev 11:2
TRAMPLED
knocked down and * and killed as 2Ki 7:17
And he couldn't, for the people * 2Ki 7:20
and she was * by the horses' 2Ki 9:33
it is * like grass and is Ps 102:3,4
to be * by cattle and sheep. Is 5:5
* and mangled by horses' hoofs. Is 14:19
and * beneath the enemies' feet. Is 28:3
in, you will be * into the ground. Is 28:18
tormented you and * your souls to Is 51:23
In my fury I * my foes. Is 63:3
The Lord has * all my mighty men. Lam 1:15
The Lord has * his beloved city Lam 1:15
But you have * and crushed Lam 3:34,35,36
my flock is what you've * down; Eze 34:19
him down and * him, for there was Dan 8:7
* down like mud in the street. Mic 7:10
* down the nations in your wrath. Hab 3:12
out and * underfoot as worthless. Mt 5:13
fell on a footpath and was * on; Lk 8:5
be conquered and * down by the Lk 21:24
for those who have * underfoot the Heb 10:29
TRAMPLES
He will tread them as a potter * Is 41:25
TRAMPLING
my vineyard, * down the vines, and Jer 12:10
who rob the poor, * on the needy; Amo 8:4
God's laws and * them under your Mk 7:9
TRANCE
being prepared, he fell into a *. Act 10:9,10
I fell into a * and saw a vision of Act 22:17,18
TRANS-JORDAN
and the other to Rabbah in *. Eze 21:19,20
TRANSACTED
legal affairs were usually *. Ru 4:1f
TRANSACTION
not to handle the * in an ordinary Ex 22:25
this publicly validated the *. Ru 4:7
TRANSACTIONS
"In all your * you must use Deu 25:13,14,15
TRANSFER
[When we * the Ark to its new home 1Ch 15:2
TRANSFERRED
had been * to the second harem." Est 2:19f
TRANSFERRING
Israel for a man * a right of Ru 4:7
observe the * of the Ark of the 1Ki 8:1
the ceremony of * the Ark from the 2Ch 5:2
TRANSFIGURATION
from seeing him in glory at the *. Rev 1:13f
TRANSFORM
today, God will * you into the Deu 28:1
to her, and * her Valley of Hos 1:15
will * our lives and hearts. Heb 9:14
TRANSFORMED
can die, must be * into heavenly 1Co 15:53
TRANSGRESSED
Instead, they had * his covenant 2Ki 18:12
me—all your forebears * my law. Is 43:27
TRANSGRESSION
for he will not pardon your *; Ex 23:21
iniquity and * and sin." Ex 34:7f
from destroying him for this *. Dan 8:12
TRANSGRESSIONS
own *, for they rebel against you. Ps 5:10
take away the awful stain of my *. Ps 51:1
TRANSIENT
our days here on earth are as * Job 8:9
TRANSJORDAN
and Northern *, where lies the road Is 9:1
TRANSLATE
There is no "right" way to * Gen 1:2f
Can just anyone understand and * 1Co 12:30
TRANSLATED
* either "Jehovah" or "Lord." Ex 3:15f
The Hebrew word here * "lamb" Ex 12:3,4f
language, and it was * to him. Ez 4:7
The letter you sent has been * Ez 4:18
the decree was * into the Est 8:9,10
Nicolaitans, when * from Greek to Rev 2:6f
TRANSLATION
Either * is permissible, but Eze 34:29f
This * follows the Greek version. Hos 4:18f
The * here follows the Syriac Zec 11:13f
TRANSPARENT
or pimple with * skin, leprosy is Lev 13:1
a woman has white, * areas in the Lev 13:38
The city itself was pure, * gold Rev 21:18,19,20
And the main street was pure, * Rev 21:21
TRANSPLANTED
For they are * into the Lord's Ps 92:13
TRANSPORT
sky and seemed to * me to Eze 8:3
TRANSPORTATION
with the Tabernacle and its *. Num 1:50
for the * of these items. Num 4:26
service and *, was 8,580. Num 4:46,47,48
with clothing, *, supplies for the Ez 1:4
TRANSPORTED
And the king of Assyria * 2Ki 17:24
king of Assyria * the Israelis to 2Ki 18:11
TRANSPORTING
to be in charge of * the silver, Ez 8:25
a gift to the Lord, * them gently Is 66:20
TRAP
in a * and all of them died; Jos 8:22
be a snare and a * to you, a pain Jos 23:13
God was setting a * for the Ju 14:4
them from falling into some *. Job 33:17,18
let him fall into his own *. Ps 7:15
* they set has snapped on them. Ps 9:15
Pull me from the * my enemies Ps 31:4
yet they laid a * for me and dug a Ps 35:7
My enemies have set a * for me. Ps 57:6
I am in a * with no way out. Ps 88:8
For he rescues you from every *, Ps 91:3
These proud men have set a * to Ps 140:5
When a bird sees a * being set, Pro 1:17
not these men; they * themselves! Pro 1:18
They lay a booby * for their own Pro 1:18
If you can get out of this * you Pro 6:5
A prostitute is a dangerous *; Pro 22:14
The man who sets a * for others Pro 26:27
Flattery is a *; Pro 29:5,6
Fear of man is a dangerous *, but Pro 29:25
will step into a *, for destruction Is 24:18
They have set a * to kill me, yet Jer 18:20
"He will * himself," they say, Jer 20:10
He who flees shall fall in a * Jer 48:44
from the * shall run into a snare. Jer 48:44
O Babylon, I have set a * for Jer 50:24
a deep pit to * them at Acacia. Hos 5:2
* them in their own fortresses. Hos 11:6
for its food. A * doesn't snap Amo 3:5
You are a dangerous * to me. Mt 16:23
him, and tried to * him into saying Mt 19:3
of some way to * Jesus into saying Mt 22:15
Of course they were trying to * Mk 10:2
to talk with him and try to * him Mk 12:13
trying to * him into saying Lk 11:53,54
They were trying to * him into Jn 8:6
other blessings * them into Rom 11:9
man's own brilliance to * him; 1Co 3:19
that Satan can't * him with many 1Ti 3:7
from Satan's * of slavery to sin 2Ti 2:26
TRAPPED
Israelites are * now, between the Ex 14:3

(TRAPPED Con't)
has * himself in a walled city!" 1Sa 23:7
I was *, and bound 2Sa 22:6
against me. * and helpless, I Ps 18:5
You may have * yourself by your Pro 6:2
as a stag that is *, waiting to be Pro 7:22
and be broken, * and captured. Is 28:13
imprisoned, *, fair game for all, Is 42:22
is gone, and those * inside begin Jer 19:9
Don't get *! Jer 51:6
we are * and desolate, destroyed. Lam 3:47
their hunters and * him in a pit Eze 19:4
* him in a pit and captured him. Eze 19:8
then we are * because he will ask, Lk 20:5

TRAPS
They are caught in their own *; Job 5:13
He walks into *, and robbers Job 18:8,9
now surrounded by * and sudden Job 22:10,11
This rabble trip me and lay * in Job 30:12
Catch them in their own *; Ps 5:10
catch their victims in their *. Ps 10:9
meet in secret to set their *. Ps 64:5
God * them and destroys them. Ps 94:12,13
The wicked have set their * for Ps 119:110
Keep me out of their *. Ps 141:9
the * my enemies have set for me. Ps 142:3
They set their * for men. Jer 5:26
they have hidden * along my path. Jer 18:22
Fear and * and treachery shall Jer 48:43
Your trusted friends will set * Ob 1:7
you caught in your *—now terror Hab 2:17

TRASH
while the mocker feeds on *. Pro 15:14
and the * cans in the Temple of Zec 14:20

TRAVAIL
with panic like a woman in *! Ps 48:6
*, there I awakened your love." Sol 8:5
us like that of women in *. Jer 6:24
Literally, "until she who is in * Mic 5:3f
in * together until now." Rom 8:22f

TRAVEL
the lad and I will * yonder and Gen 22:5
So they could * either by day or Ex 13:21
my Angel shall * on ahead of you; Ex 32:34
but I will not * among you, for Ex 33:3
along the way you want me to * Ex 33:13
When the * signal is blown, the Num 10:5,6,7
Lord's * instructions to Moses. Num 10:13
"Let us * through your land," Num 21:22
eleven days to * by foot from Mount Deu 1:1
and I can still * and fight as well Jos 14:11
him, "It's getting too late to *; Ju 19:11
enough strength to * forty days and 1Ki 19:8
them to let me * through their Neh 2:7
only the redeemed will * there. Is 35:9
days of long ago. * there, and you Jer 6:16
Don't * the roads! Jer 6:25
no one dares even to * through? Jer 9:12
their business to * through the Jer 14:18
As you * into exile, set up road Jer 31:21
no one will even * through them. Eze 33:28
end times, when * and education Dan 12:4
a road for the Lord to * on! Lk 3:4
So he continued to * around Lk 4:44
along too, then we can * together. 1Co 16:4
by the churches to * with me to 2Co 8:19

TRAVELED
left that place and * southward Gen 12:8
SO THEY LEFT Egypt and * north Gen 13:1
and * home again to Beer-sheba. Gen 22:19
JACOB * ON, finally arriving in Gen 29:1
* on toward Ephrath (Bethlehem). Gen 35:16
So he * to Shechem from his home Gen 37:13,14
So Aaron * to Mount Horeb, the Ex 4:27
Israelites * to a new campsite. Num 2:3-31
in line whenever the Israelis *. Num 2:3-31
up the rear whenever Israel *. Num 2:3-31
So it was that they camped or * Num 9:23
the order in which the tribes *. Num 10:28
They * for three days after Num 10:33
back in before they * again. Num 12:15
from there they * to the valley of Num 21:12
Then Israel * to Beer (meaning Num 21:16
THE PEOPLE OF Israel now * to the Num 22:1
"Then we left Mount Horeb and * Deu 1:19,20,21
For the nation of Israel had * Jos 5:6
Joshua * all night from Gilgal Jos 10:9
of Israel, as we * through the Jos 24:17
wilderness, and * along the eastern Ju 11:18
They * all through the hill 1Sa 9:4
from that town * all night to 1Sa 31:12
the river, and * all the next 2Sa 2:29
then they * all night and reached 2Sa 2:32
Meanwhile Sheba had * across 2Sa 20:14
wealthy clans who * to the east 1Ch 4:34-39
as he was told; he * all through 1Ch 21:4
These men * out across the 2Ch 23:2,3
who * from Babylon to Jerusalem Ez 7:1
and Temple workers * with him. Ez 7:7,8,9
children, and our goods as we *. Ez 8:21
each other and * from their homes Job 2:11
You have * far, even to hell Is 57:9
Canal, and they * straight ahead, Eze 10:22
no one even * through it; Zec 7:14
Jesus * all through Galilee Mt 4:23
Jesus * around through all the Mt 9:35
all over Judea * out into the Mk 1:5
So he * throughout the province Mk 1:39
Leaving that region they * Mk 9:30,31
the way, as he * to Caesarea. Act 8:40
Peter * from place to place to Act 9:32
Stephen's death * as far as Act 11:19
Then they * back through Pisidia Act 14:24
Next they * through Phrygia and Act 16:6
NOW THEY * through the cities of Act 17:1
in Corinth, Paul * through Turkey Act 19:1
I have * many weary miles and 2Co 11:26

TRAVELER
for food for the *, he took the 2Sa 12:4
I am a * passing through the Ps 39:12

TRAVELERS
but also for foreigners and *. Num 35:15
* used the narrow, crooked side Ju 5:6
When he saw the * camped in the Ju 19:17
Your roads lie in ruins; * Is 33:8
no one lives nor even * pass by. Jer 51:43
of the *, east of the Dead Sea. Eze 39:11
It will block the path of the *. Eze 39:11
with friends among the other *. Lk 2:44
beside the road, begging from *. Lk 18:35
the missionary * himself, but tells 3Jn 1:10

TRAVELING
in Canaan. * through Canaan, they Gen 12:6
And when God sent me * far from Gen 20:13
and began * all across the land. Gen 41:46
As Moses and his family were * Ex 4:24
"Eat it with your * clothes on, Ex 12:11
poor and for those * through, for I Lev 19:10
the Levites. When *, each tribe Num 2:3-31
units to wherever the camp is *; Num 4:15
(for they were * the same route as Num 21:1
Ezi-on-geber, and * northward Deu 2:8
Micah's house as he was * through. Ju 17:7,8
But as he was * along, a lion 1Ki 13:24,25
the wilderness, * all day, and sat 1Ki 19:4
among the people, * from Beer-sheba 2Ch 19:4
Lord to act! Keep * steadily along Ps 37:34
evil road you are * and from the Jer 25:5
* past the ruins of your land. Eze 5:14
Something is * through the sky!" Zec 5:5
from Judea and was * in Galilee. Jn 4:46,47
Jews who were * from town to town Act 19:13
Paul's * companions, for trial. Act 19:29
Several men were * with him, Act 20:4
believers and his * Act 21:12
each other. By * together we will 2Co 8:20
Some of the brothers * by have 3Jn 1:3
taking care of the * teachers and 3Jn 1:5
For they are * for the Lord, and 3Jn 1:7

TRAVELS
where no one lives or even *. Jer 2:6
and in his * came to the Act 9:32

TRAVERSED
This desert would be * in Eze 20:35,36f

TRAY
But when she set the serving * 2Sa 13:9
John the Baptist's head on a *. Mt 14:8
was brought on a * and given to the Mt 14:11
the Baptist—right now—on a *!" Mk 6:25
back his head on a *, and gave it Mk 6:28

TRAYS
The snuffers and * are to be Ex 25:38
*, and the reservoir of olive oil. Num 4:9
12 golden * (the trays weighing Num 7:84,85,86
12 golden trays (the * weighing Num 7:84,85,86
1,000 gold *, Ez 1:9,10
1,000 silver *, Ez 1:9,10

TREACHEROUS
Do not spare these evil, * men. Ps 59:5
enemies, these liars, these * men. Ps 144:11
A * man must walk a rocky road. Pro 13:15
The rebel walks a thorny, * road; Pro 22:5
them a rough and * path, but Is 26:7
is less guilty than * Judah! Jer 3:11
they are all adulterous, * men. Jer 9:2
down dark and * trails, and fall. Jer 23:12
by all their wine, for it is *. Hab 2:5

TREACHEROUSLY
Probably Jason, * removed by the Dan 11:22f

TREACHERY
fathers' sins of * against me. Lev 26:40,41
Ahaziah, "There is *, Ahaziah! 2Ki 9:23
power, but this * was discovered. 2Ki 17:4
brings to birth his * and lies; Ps 7:14
all their waking hours planning *. Ps 38:12
the evil man's * is his undoing. Pro 11:6
prevails and * is everywhere. Is 24:15,16
of * against me, says the Lord. Jer 5:11
Fear and traps and * shall be Jer 48:43
Jerusalem won't understand this *; Eze 21:23
they acted in * against their God. Eze 39:23
Their time of * and shame will Eze 39:26
there is *, for the men of Judah Mal
Lord has seen your * in divorcing Mal
received for his * and falling Act

TREAD
causes the good to walk a steady * 2Sa 2
tasting it, and to * out the grape Job 2
with a glance; * down the wicked Job 4
name that we * down our enemies; Ps
He will * them as a potter Is 4
who * the juice from the grapes. Jer 2
ripe and waiting. * the winepress, Joe
You will * our sins beneath your Mic
Then you will * upon the wicked Mal

TREADING
and saw some men * winepresses on Neh 1
"Don't you realize that those * Job 22:1
heard no more; the * out of the Is 1
red, as from * out the grapes?" Is
Ephraim is accustomed to * out Hos 1
* them beneath their feet. Zec
eating when it is * out the wheat. 1Co
an ox when it is * out the 1Ti

TREADS
"Don't muzzle an ox as it * out Deu 2
For he * down our foes. Ps 10
though the paths he * are new. Is 4
no one * the grapes with shouts Jer 48

TREAS
consecrated the * ures—the Ez 8

TREASON
of Zimri and his * are written in 1Ki 16
is treachery, Ahaziah! *!" 2Ki 9
* -Treason she screamed 2Ki 11:13
"Treason! *!" 2Ki 11:13
her clothes and screamed, "*! 2Ch 23
and screamed, "Treason! *!" 2Ch 23
him there for this * against me. Eze 17
They are all guilty of *, for Act 1

TREASURE
crown—a $50,000 * made from solid 2Sa 12:29
Almighty himself shall be your *; Job 22
I would * it like a crown. Job 31
Your laws are my joyous * Ps 119:
laws like one who finds a great *. Ps 119:
money or hidden *, then wisdom will Pro 2:3,
His every word is a * of Pro
There is * in being good, but Pro 1
than great * and trouble with it. Pro 15:
Literally, "There is precious * Pro 21:
with * to pay for Egypt's aid. Is 3
Their * will be divided by the Is 33:
showing them his * house full of Is 3
and every * found and taken. Ob
a * a man discovered in a field. Mt 13:
buy the field—and get the *, too! Mt 13:
his * things both new and old." Mt 13:
and you will have * in heaven; Mt 19:
* in heaven—and come, follow me." Mk 10:
Wherever your * is, there your Lk 12:
will become * for you in heaven—and Lk 18:
But this precious *—this light 2Co 4
be storing up real * for themselves 1Ti 6:

TREASURE-HOUSES
brought the money to Pharaoh's *. Gen 47:

TREASURED
but Mary quietly * these things in Lk 2:

TREASURER
marshal, his chief *, and his chief 2Ki 18:
the city *, to repair the Temple. 2Ch 34
Shaphan the *, and Asaiah, the 2Ch 34:
He instructed Mithredath, the * Ez 1
Judas was their *, Jesus was Jn 13:
the road but the * of Ethiopia, a Act 8:
Erastus, the city *, sends you Rom 16:

TREASURERS
decree to all the * in the Ez 7:
captains, judges, *, counselors, Dan 3

TREASURES
And the * of the sand." Deu 33:
and all the * of the palace, and 1Ki 15:
them all his *—the silver, gold, 2Ki 20:
I showed them all my *." 2Ki 20:
All the * of your ancestors will 2Ki 20:
home all the * from the Temple and 2Ki 24:
* to aid in the construction. 1Ch 29
took away all the * of the Temple 2Ch 12
He carried off all the * and 2Ch 25:2
as well as the * from the palace; 2Ch 25:2
and the palace *, it did no good. 2Ch 28:2
Many * from the Temple were taken 2Ch 36:1
in the Temple, and * from both the 2Ch 36:1
"Guard these * well!" Ez 8:2
whose castles are full of rich *. Job 3:14,1
"His * will be lost in deepest Job 20:2
and gold dust— * that no bird of Job 28:
has ever walked upon those *; Job 28:
filled with your * so that their Ps 17:13,1
Israel has vast * of silver and Is 2:
Where will your * be safe? Is 10:
people and carried off their *. Is 10:1
to them all his *—everything. Is 39:

REASURES Con't)
own, all my priceless *." Is 39:4
you have—all the * stored up by Is 39:6
And I will give you * hidden in Is 45:3
You shall be fed with the * of Is 61:6
me—the most precious of their *. Jer 2:32
and * as spoil to the enemy. Jer 15:12,13
And so I will give all your * to Jer 17:2,3
All the famed * of the city, with Jer 20:5
all the Temple * that Jer 27:18
from Babylon the * of this Temple, Jer 28:6
to bring him their * of wheat, Jer 41:8
women. Her * shall all be robbed; Jer 50:37
* and leave the Temple in ruins. Eze 7:22
they seize * and extort wealth; Eze 22:25
wealth—gold and silver and many *. Eze 28:4
He will capture all the * of Dan 11:43
all my precious * and carried them Joe 3:5
of ungodly * and lying scales. Mic 6:10
There seems to be no end of *. Nah 2:9
Literally, "The *" or "that Hag 2:7f
rendering: "The * of the nations Hag 2:7f
"Don't store up * here on earth Mt 6:19
reveals the rich * within him. Mt 12:35
have double *—from the Old Mt 13:52
Your * there will never disappear; Lk 12:33
we will share his *—for all God Rom 8:17
* available to them in Christ; Eph 3:8
* of wisdom and knowledge. Col 2:3
sights on the rich * and joys of Col 3:1
to own all the * of Egypt, for he Heb 11:26

REASURIES
the gold in the * of the Temple and 2Ki 12:18
and * in the Tabernacle of God. 1Ch 9:26
of the palace *, and Jonathan (son 1Ch 27:25
of the regional * throughout the 1Ch 27:25
surroundings—the *, the upstairs 1Ch 28:11
areas, and the * for the gifts 1Ch 28:12
They were stored in the Temple *. 2Ch 5:1
in charge of the *, the wave Neh 12:44
"Have you visited the * of the Job 38:22,23
and sends the winds from his *. Ps 135:7
I fill their *. Pro 8:21
and from his * he brings the wind. Jer 10:13
the rain and the winds from his *. Jer 51:16

REASURY
you his wonderful * of rain in the Deu 28:12
Sealed as jewels within my *. Deu 32:34
and must be brought into his *." Jos 6:19
were kept for the Lord's *. Jos 6:24
for the Lord's * was disobeyed. Jos 7:1
took into the * of the Temple the 1Ki 7:51
left in the Temple * and all the 1Ki 15:18
and palace *, also the gold cups. 2Ki 14:14
in the Temple and in the palace *. 2Ki 18:15
Lord and placed in the Temple *. 1Ch 26:20,21,22
was the chief officer of the *. 1Ch 26:23,24
at the Temple * with Jehiel (a 1Ch 29:8
and concerning the * personnel. 2Ch 8:15
He had to construct special * 2Ch 32:27
funds from the royal *. Ez 7:20
placed in the * of the Temple." Ez 8:29
and olive oil to the Temple *. Neh 13:12
into the royal * for the expenses Est 3:9
* for the destruction of the Jews. Est 4:7
placed them in the * of his god in Dan 1:1
me, 'Toss it into the Temple * Zec 11:13
of the Temple known as the *. Jn 8:20

TREAT
the Egyptians will * me well Gen 12:11,12,13
"How could you * us this way?" Gen 26:10
"Should he * our sister like a Gen 34:31
"Why did you have to * me like Gen 43:6
"Don't * us like this," they Ex 5:15
he may no longer * her as a Ex 21:9
but must * her as a daughter. Ex 21:9
Lord and you must * it as holy. Ex 30:37
nor * my Tabernacle like an Lev 21:12
You must not * me as common and Lev 22:32,33
you, you must not * him as an Lev 25:39
the foreigner must * him as a hired Lev 25:53
If you are going to * me like Num 11:15
But beware that you do not * the Num 18:32
not sell her or * her as a slave, Deu 21:14
Is this the way you * Jehovah? Deu 32:6
"Is this the way to * your 2Sa 16:17
to * us better than he did." 1Ki 12:2,3,4
reply and * them with kindness." 2Ch 10:7
Don't * me as a common sinner or Ps 26:9,10
"I will * him as my firstborn Ps 89:27
"Good or bad, we'll * them all Pro 1:12
will expect you to * him as a son! Pro 29:21
seems to * some good men as though Ecc 8:14
work for you and * them fairly and Is 58:6
O God, why do you * us as though Is 63:19
I will * them like spoiled figs, Jer 24:8
For others will * you as you Mt 7:2
will treat you as you * them. Mt 7:2
them back. * others as you want Lk 6:31
others as you want them to * you. Lk 6:31
the guards to * him gently and not Act 24:23
That is how husbands should * Eph 5:28
And you slave owners must * your Eph 6:9
just as I have told them to * you. Eph 6:9
loved brothers. * the older women 1Ti 5:2
and if you don't * her as you 1Pe 3:7

TREATED
and it shall be * by you as holy. Ex 30:32
Tanned rams' skins and specially * Ex 35:5-9
red, and specially * goatskins. Ex 35:23
They must be * like any other Lev 19:34
as ordinary slaves, or * harshly; Lev 25:43
of Israel, shall not be * so. Lev 25:46
"I have * seventy kings in this Ju 1:7
Eli's sons. They * all of the 1Sa 2:13,14
for they * the people's offerings 1Sa 2:17
that is the way he * all of the 2Sa 12:31
of Babylon. He * Jehoiachin kindly 2Ki 25:28
children will be * mercifully by 2Ch 30:9
You have * us like sheep in a Ps 44:11
it that you are finally * fairly. Ps 48:11
justice to all who are * unfairly. Ps 103:6
I have not * you as slaves. Is 43:23
worship them. She * it all so Jer 3:9
* them as though I hated them. Jer 12:8
I will see that they are well * Jer 24:6
gold—are * as earthenware pots. Lam 4:2
Even aged men are * with Lam 5:12
her and * her with great contempt. Eze 28:24
nations that * them with such Eze 28:26
his messengers and * them Mt 22:6
would suffer and be * with utter Mk 9:12,13
prophets were * that way too! Lk 6:23
to be mocked and * shamefully and Lk 18:32
the way I * the church of God. 1Co 15:9
You know how badly we had been * 1Th 2:2
All must be * exactly the same. 1Ti 5:21
the Son of God and * his cleansing Heb 10:29
up, refused to be * as the grandson Heb 11:24,25

TREATIES
make any * or show them mercy; Deu 7:2
make no peace * with the people Ju 2:2

TREATING
Why, you would be * godly and Gen 18:25
the Egyptians were * them; Neh 9:10
in our home, * them as our own Job 31:18
I punish my body, * it roughly, 1Co 9:27

TREATMENT
done that deserves * like this, to Gen 20:9,10
they are giving you the same *. 1Sa 8:8
have I done to deserve this *?" 1Sa 29:8
him preferential * over all the 2Ki 25:28
Giving preferred * to rich people Pro 28:21
What have we done to merit such * Jer 16:10
to their * of my people. Jer 25:14
between God's * of good men and Mal 3:18
received the same *, only worse, Mk 12:4

TREATMENTS
are given beauty *, and after Est 2:3
her for the beauty *, gave her Est 2:9
months of beauty * with oil of Est 2:12,13,14

TREATS
Israelite, and * him as a slave or Deu 24:7
And * them as princes 1Sa 2:8
For God * everyone the same. Rom 2:11
manner. God * us all the same; Rom 3:30
I am not one of those who * Gal 2:21

TREATY
We've decided to ask for a * Gen 26:28
preparation for the * ceremonies. Gen 26:30
"No, do not make a peace * of Ex 34:15
to ask for a peace * with you." Jos 9:6
For if you do, we cannot make a * Jos 9:7
went ahead and signed a peace *. Jos 9:14,15
leaders because of the peace *. Jos 9:18
* except the Hivites of Gibeon; Jos 11:19
have violated the * I made with Ju 2:20
Jehoiada made a * between the 2Ki 11:17
signed a * to ally themselves Ps 83:5
This is his never-ending * with Ps 105:10,11
make a seven-year * with the Dan 9:27
to conclude a * of peace between Dan 11:6f
At that time I will make a * Hos 1:18
my * and revolted against my laws. Hos 8:1
For they broke their * with their Amo 1:9
They will all sign a * giving Rev 17:13

TREE
he placed the * of Life, and also Gen 2:9
Life, and also the * of Conscience, Gen 2:9
fruit from the * of Conscience—for Gen 2:16,17
"It's only the fruit from the * Gen 3:2,3
"Have you eaten fruit from the * Gen 3:11
the * of Life and lives forever?" Gen 3:22
the entrance to the * of Life. Gen 3:24
the shade of this * while I get Gen 18:3,4
And Abraham planted a tamarisk * Gen 21:33
beneath the oak * near Shechem. Gen 35:4
oak * in the valley below Bethel. Gen 35:8
"Joseph is a fruitful * beside a Gen 49:22
green thing—not a *, not a plant Ex 10:15
Lord showed him a * to throw into Ex 15:25
of gum from the bark of a *. Num 11:7
then hanged on a *, his body shall Deu 21:22
not remain on the * overnight. Deu 21:23
hanging on a * is cursed of God. Deu 21:23
you spy one in a *, and there are Deu 22:6
king of Ai on a * until evening, Jos 8:29
* that was beside the Tabernacle. Jos 24:26
"Deborah's Palm *," between Ramah Ju 4:5
beneath the oak * at Ophrah, on the Ju 6:11
oak *, and presented it to him. Ju 6:19
First they asked the olive *, Ju 9:8
"Then they said to the fig *, Ju 9:10
"But the fig * also refused. Ju 9:11
This is the family * of Boaz, Ru 4:18-22
the pomegranate * at Migron. 1Sa 14:2
beneath an oak * playing with his 1Sa 22:6
beneath the oak * at Jabesh and 1Sa 31:13
of a great oak *, and his hair 2Sa 18:9
found him sitting under an oak *. 1Ki 13:14
high hill and under every green *. 1Ki 14:23
the mighty cedar *, 'Give your 2Ki 14:9
hill and under every green *; 2Ki 17:10
choicest cypress * and have 2Ki 19:23
THE FAMILY * of every person in 1Ch 9:1
beneath the oak * at Jabesh and 1Ch 10:12
of a cedar *, 'Give your daughter 2Ch 25:18
the hills and under every green *. 2Ch 28:4
Literally, "hanged on a *." Est 2:23f
I am like a fallen, rotten *, Job 13:27,28
"For there is hope for a *—if Job 14:7
off his flower as the olive *." Job 15:33f
are broken like a * in the storm. Job 24:20
But I am like a sheltered olive * Ps 52:8
"with coals of the broom *." Ps 120:4f
Wisdom is a * of life to those Pro 3:18
Trust in God and flourish as a *! Pro 11:28
Godly men are growing a * that Pro 11:30
Literally, "it is a * of life." Pro 13:12f
when a * falls, whether south or Ecc 11:3
lover is an apple *, the finest in Sol 2:3
Literally, "The fig * puts forth Sol 2:13f
other incense *, as well as myrrh Sol 4:13,14
slim like a palm *, and your Sol 7:7
up into the palm * and take hold of Sol 7:8
King Solomon: "Under the apple * Sol 8:5
* or a garden without water. Is 1:30
will be like a * cut down, whose Is 6:13
is chopping down the mighty *! Is 10:33
be cut off, chopped down like a *; Is 11:1
dead branches of a *, broken off Is 27:11
that will find a * free from rot Is 40:20
Part of the * he burns to roast Is 44:16
and forests, yes, and every *; Is 44:23
the shade of every *, and slay your Is 57:5
be like a budding *, or like a Is 61:11
hidden behind a * in the garden, Is 66:17
from the branch of an almond *." Jer 1:11
On every hill and under every * Jer 2:20
every hill, beneath every shady *. Jer 3:6
by worshiping idols under every *; Jer 3:13
They cut down a * and carve an Jer 10:2,3
his green olive *, beautiful to see Jer 11:16
the * has ordered it destroyed. Jer 11:17
idols beneath each *, high in the Jer 17:2,3
He is like a * planted along a Jer 17:8
into the water—a * not bothered by Jer 17:8
under every green * and great oak Eze 6:13
the tallest cedar * and carried it Eze 17:3,4
grow as quickly as a willow *. Eze 17:5
came along, this * sent its roots Eze 17:7
I let this * grow and prosper? Eze 17:9
pull out the *, roots and all! Eze 17:16
* wither and the dry tree grow. Eze 17:24
tree wither and the dry * grow. Eze 17:24
every high hill and under every *! Eze 20:27,28
* will die, green and dry alike. Eze 20:47
This * was taller than any other Eze 31:8
decorated with palm * decorations. Eze 40:16
hall and the palm * decorations Eze 40:22
* decorations along the walls. Eze 40:26
It had palm * decorations on the Eze 40:31
there were palm * decorations on Eze 40:34
and it had palm * decorations on Eze 40:37
toward the palm * on one side, and Eze 41:19,20
the palm * on the other side. Eze 41:19,20
"I saw a very tall * out in a Dan 4:10,11
"He shouted, 'Cut down the *; Dan 4:14
For the * you saw growing so Dan 4:20
that *, Your Majesty, is you. Dan 4:22
'Cut down the * and destroy it, but Dan 4:23
I am like an evergreen *, Hos 14:8
like a *, they will be Mal 4:1
to chop down every unproductive *. Mt 3:10
you can identify a * by its fruit. Mt 7:16
And a * producing an inedible Mt 7:18
Yes, the way to identify a * or Mt 7:20
"A * is identified by its fruit. Mt 12:33
by its fruit. A * from a select Mt 12:33
and grows into a * where birds can Mt 13:31,32
noticed a fig * beside the road. Mt 21:19
the fig * withered up. Mt 21:19
did the fig * wither so quickly?" Mt 21:20

(TREE Con't)
learn a lesson from the fig *. Mt 24:32
they look like * trunks walking Mk 8:24
he noticed a fig * in full leaf, so Mk 11:13
Then Jesus said to the *, "You Mk 11:14
passed the fig * he had cursed, Mk 11:20
had said to the * on the previous Mk 11:21
The fig * you cursed has Mk 11:21
here is a lesson from a fig *. Mk 13:28
Yes, every * that does not Lk 3:9
"A * from good stock doesn't Lk 6:43
choice fruit. A * is identified by Lk 6:44
man planted a fig * in his garden Lk 13:6
that mulberry * over there and send Lk 17:6
into a sycamore * beside the road, Lk 19:4
the fig *, or any other tree. Lk 21:29
the fig tree, or any other *. Lk 21:29
*, what will they do to you?" Lk 23:31
do this when the * is green, what Lk 23:31f
fig * before Philip found you." Jn 1:48
I had seen you under the fig *? Jn 1:50
For if the roots of the * are Rom 11:16
from Abraham's *, some of the Jews, Rom 11:17
a wild olive *, were grafted in. Rom 11:17
of his own special olive *. Rom 11:17
you are now a part of God's *; Rom 11:18
graft them back into the * again. Rom 11:23
of a wild olive *—and graft you Rom 11:24
into his own good *—a very unusual Rom 11:24
who is hanged on a * is cursed" Gal 3:13
Can you pick olives from a fig * Jas 3:12
* of Life in the Paradise of God. Rev 2:7
Literally, "the * of life"—used Rev 22:2f
eat the fruit from the * of Life. Rev 22:14
his share in the * of Life, and in Rev 22:19

TREES
plant, and fruit * with seeds Gen 1:11,12
and all the fruit * for your food. Gen 1:29
sorts of beautiful * there in the Gen 2:9
* producing the choicest of fruit. Gen 2:9
they hid themselves among the *. Gen 3:8
the * beside them as they ate. Gen 18:8
field, and all the * in the field. Gen 23:17,18
almond, and plane *, and peeled Gen 30:37
upon the people, animals, and *." Ex 9:22
killed, and the * were shattered Ex 9:25
twelve springs and seventy palm *; Ex 15:27
all kinds of fruit *, do not eat Lev 19:23
boughs of fruit * laden with fruit, Lev 23:40
boughs of leafy *—such as willows Lev 23:40
crops, and the * will be loaded Lev 26:4,5
its crops, nor your * their fruit. Lev 26:20
and whether there are many *. Num 13:20
As cedar * beside the waters. Num 24:3-9
of water and seventy palm *; Num 33:9
and olive * you didn't plant—and Deu 6:10,11,12
grape vines, fig *, pomegranates, Deu 8:8
up in the hills, or under the *. Deu 12:2
a city, don't destroy the fruit *. Deu 20:19
just don't cut down the *. Deu 20:19
But you may cut down * that Deu 20:20
*, don't go over the boughs twice; Deu 24:20
Olive * will be growing Deu 28:40
For the * will drop their fruit Deu 28:40
The locusts shall destroy your * Deu 28:42
and Jericho, the city of palm *; Deu 34:3
He then hanged them on five * Jos 10:26
"The City of Palm *," and the two Ju 1:16
called "The City of Palm *." Ju 3:13
Once upon a time the * decided Ju 9:8
wave to and fro over the *?' Ju 9:9
my head above all the other *?' Ju 9:11
be mightier than all the other *?' Ju 9:13
"Then all the * finally turned Ju 9:14
grain, and destroying the olive *. Ju 15:5
them and come out by the balsam *. 2Sa 5:23
the tops of the balsam *, attack! 2Sa 5:24
of juniper * and playing every sort 2Sa 6:5
snakes, fish, and *—from the great 1Ki 4:33
Figures of angels, palm *, and 1Ki 6:29
cherubim, palm *, and open flowers, 1Ki 6:32
Angels, palm *, and open flowers 1Ki 6:35
Cherubim, lions, and palm * 1Ki 7:36
great supply of algum * and gems. 1Ki 10:11
the wells, and felled the fruit *; 2Ki 3:25
Jordan, they began cutting down *; 2Ki 6:4
altars in the groves of *. 2Ki 16:4
grain, wine, olive *, and honey. 2Ki 18:31,32
mulberry * and attack from there. 1Ch 14:14
of the mulberry *, that is your 1Ch 14:15
Let the * in the woods sing for 1Ch 16:33
yards and sycamore * in the 1Ch 27:28
Also send me cedar *, fir trees, 2Ch 2:8
Also send me cedar trees, fir *, 2Ch 2:8
trees, and algum * from the Forests 2Ch 2:8
engraved with palm * and chains. 2Ch 3:5
in Jericho, the City of Palm *. 2Ch 28:15
palm, and fig * and to make huts in Neh 8:15
oliveyards and many, many fruit *; Neh 9:25
or from our fruit and olive *. Neh 10:35
They are like * along a river Ps 1:3
It splits the giant * of Lebanon. Ps 29:5,6
we were like the mighty cedar *, Ps 80:10
flourish like palm *, and grow tall Ps 92:12
Let the * of the forest rustle Ps 96:12
sing among the branches of the *. Ps 104:12
there are fruit *, vegetables and Ps 104:14
Their grape vines and fig * were Ps 105:33
all the * lay broken on the Ps 105:33
and healthy as young olive *. Ps 128:3
willow *, for how can we sing? Ps 137:2
hills, the fruit * and cedars, the Ps 148:9
shaded by the cedar * and firs." Sol 1:17
* of a forest shake in a storm. Is 7:2
The sycamore * are cut down, but Is 9:8,9,10
cuts down the forest * in Lebanon. Is 10:34
Even the * of the woods—the fir Is 14:8
the woods—the fir * and cedars of Is 14:8
are left on the * when the harvest Is 17:6
You will be like lonely * on the Is 30:17
leaves, as ripe fruit from the *. Is 34:4
cedars and choicest cypress *. Is 37:24
I will plant *—cedars, myrtle, Is 41:19
myrtle, olive *, the cypress, fir Is 41:19
The mountains and hills, the * of Is 55:12
Where once were thorns, fir * Is 55:13
where briars grew, the myrtle * Is 55:13
box *—to beautify my sanctuary. Is 60:13
live as long as * and will long Is 65:21,22
Cut down her * for battering rams; Jer 6:6
animals, * and plants will be Jer 7:20
their fruit * will die, and all the Jer 8:13
should plant fruit *, for we will Jer 29:28
who clear a forest of its *. Jer 46:22,23
Are they as useful as *? Eze 15:2
cuts down the high * and exalts the Eze 17:24
of water to all the * around. Eze 31:4
It towered above all the other * Eze 31:5
envy of all the other * of Eden. Eze 31:9
caused the * of Lebanon to weep. Eze 31:15
And all the other proud * of Eze 31:16
glorious among the * of Eden—the Eze 31:18
Their fruit * and fields will Eze 34:27
from your fruit * and fields, and Eze 36:30
* alternating with the cherubim. Eze 41:17,18
and palm *, just as on the walls. Eze 41:25
and carved palm * on both sides of Eze 41:26
many * were growing on both sides Eze 47:7
All kinds of fruit * will grow Eze 47:12
and the olive * for moisture and Hos 1:21,22
oaks and poplars and terebinth *. Hos 4:13
beautiful as olive *, fragrant as Hos 14:6
bark from the fig *, leaving trunks Joe 1:7
the fig * are dying; Joe 1:12
the apples shrivel on the *; Joe 1:12
pastures and burned up all the *. Joe 1:19
The * will bear their fruit; Joe 2:22
the fig * and grape vines will Joe 2:22
as cedar *, and strong as oaks! Amo 2:9
locusts ate your figs and olive *. Amo 4:9
mouths of those who shake the *. Nah 3:12
Even though the fig * are all Hab 3:17
among the myrtle * beside a river. Zec 1:8
And I see two olive * carved Zec 4:3
the two olive * on each side of the Zec 4:11
Weep, O cypress *, for all the Zec 11:2
Different kinds of fruit * can Mt 7:17
So the * having the inedible Mt 7:19
* and spread them out before him. Mt 21:8
scrub fruit nor do * from poor Lk 6:43
and entered a grove of olive *. Jn 18:1
crucifixion was near a grove of *, Jn 19:41
They are like fruit * without any Jud 1:12
—like green fruit from fig * Rev 6:13
rustled in the *, and the ocean Rev 7:1
earth nor sea nor *—until we have Rev 7:3
one-third of the * were burned, and Rev 8:7
grass or plants or *, but to attack Rev 9:4
two prophets are the two olive *, Rev 11:4
On each side of the river grew * Rev 22:2

TREMBLE
(Isaac begins to * noticeably. Gen 27:33
The mighty men of Moab *; Ex 15:15
the whole earth * with fear because Deu 2:25
* before him, all the earth! 1Ch 16:30
The pillars of heaven * at his Job 26:11
Make them * in fear; Ps 9:20
let the mountains *! Ps 46:3
You have caused this nation to * Ps 60:2
Let the earth * before him. Ps 96:9
Let the nations *! Ps 99:1
and their rulers * before the Lord, Ps 102:15
*, O earth, at the presence of Ps 114:7
your laws! I * in fear of you; Ps 119:120
earth *—no, four it cannot stand: Pro 30:21,22,23
your limbs will * with age, and Ecc 12:3
The hills will *, and the rotting Is 5:25
the idols of Egypt *; Is 19:1
take place. *, O women of ease; Is 32:11
Remote lands * and mobilize for Is 41:5
The nations would * before you; Is 64:2
who fear him, and * at his words: Is 66:5
and the princes will * in fear; Jer 4
you don't even * in my presence? Jer 5:
The whole earth shall * at his Jer 10:
for my people and will * with awe! Jer 33
The people will * with fear, for Eze 7:26,
"Son of dust, * as you eat your Eze 12:
strong knees will * and become as Eze 21
How the islands * at your fall! Eze 26:
They shall greatly * for their Eze 32:
I decree that everyone shall * Dan 6:25,
to Beth-aven; *, land of Benjamin! Hos 5
The people of Samaria * lest Hos 10
Let everyone * in fear, for the Joe 2
before them and the heavens *. Joe 2:
The Lion has roared—* in fear. Amo 3
The land will * as it awaits its Amo 8
high. I * when I hear all this; Hab 3:1
knew, she began to * and fell to Lk 8:4
rest—we ought to * with fear Heb 4
strongly that they * in terror! Jas 2:1

TREMBLED
heard what happened, and they *. Ex 15:1
and all the people *. Ex 19:1
The earth * Ju 5
for his heart * for the safety of 1Sa 4:1
* with fear at what awaited them. 1Sa 13
Ahimelech * when he saw him. 1Sa 21
Then the earth shook and *; 2Sa 22
Suddenly, fear gripped me; I * Job 4:1
reeled, and mountains shook and *. Ps 18
the earth * and the heavens shook. Ps 68
how it feared! It * to its depths! Ps 77:1
The earth * and shook. Ps 77:1
and his people * with fear as the Is 7
and saw that they * and shook. Jer 4:2
of the world * before him in fear. Dan 5:1
The mountains watched and *. Hab 3:1

TREMBLES
"MY HEART * at this. Job 37:
the earth * and stands silently Ps 76
The earth sees and *. Ps 97:
The earth * at his glance; Ps 104:3
contrite heart, who * at my word. Is 66:
The whole land * at the approach Jer 8:1
Babylon * and writhes in pain, Jer 51:2

TREMBLING
They were filled with terror. * Gen 42:2
Lord will give you * hearts, Deu 28:6
of the city came * to meet him. 1Sa 16:
And come, *, 2Sa 22:4
and they were * because of the Ez 10:
or * before him, he was furious. Est 5:
"The dead stand naked, * before Job 26:5,6
rejoice with *. Ps 2:1
They come * from their Ps 18:43,44,4
Stark fear overpowers me. * and Ps 55:
I lie awake, *. Is 21:4
"There is only fear and *. Jer 30:5
nightmare, and awoke * with fear. Dan 2:1
still *, to my hands and knees. Dan 10:10
So I stood up, still * with Dan 10:11
and they shall come *, submissive Hos 3:5
and my people shall return * Hos 11:10
They will come * out from their Mic 7:17
stand aghast, pale-faced and *. Nah 2:10
while you stand * and helpless. Hab 2:7
Then the frightened woman, * at Mk 5:33
The women fled from the tomb, * Mk 16:8
* with fear, the jailer called Act 16:29
to you in weakness—timid and *. 1Co 2:3
without so much as *, although 2Pe 2:10
They will stand far off, * with Rev 18:10

TREMENDOUS
That year Isaac's crops were * Gen 26:12
It was a * day for Joshua! Jos 4:14
think of all the * things he has 1Sa 12:24
and captured it. * amounts of loot 2Sa 12:29,30
with such * miracles and power. 2Ki 17:35,36
he had a * army—the army of God. 1Ch 12:22
and children, and * amounts of 2Ch 28:8
six months, a * display of the Est 1:4
These * statements you have made Job 13:12
* voice of his majesty. Job 37:4
"I should mention, too, the * Job 41:12
"The * strength in his neck Job 41:22
For you have done such * things Ps 18:1
the laver and twelve bulls was *. Jer 52:20
for a * reward awaits you up in Mt 5:12
Here I forgave you all that * Mt 18:32
"The first man reported a * Lk 19:16
Nazareth by doing * miracles Act 2:22
they have done a * miracle, and Act 4:16
the Lord gave me * opportunities to 2Co 2:12
I had were so *, God was afraid I 2Co 12:7
This * choir—144,000 strong—sang Rev 14:3

TREMENS
and have delirium *, and you will Pro 23:33

TRENCH
Then he dug a * about three feet 1Ki 18:32
off the altar and filled the *. 1Ki 18:35

TRENCHES
* to hold the water he will send. 2Ki 3:16

:END
id that the * and direction of Gen 6:5
nd this * is evident not only Act 19:26

ESPASS
e meat of the * offering and sin Eze 46:19,20

ESPASSED
et out, for you have *, and the 2Ch 26:17,18

ESPASSES
ther of us * across this line Gen 31:47,48
ho is in heaven forgive your *." Mk 11:26,f

ESSES
held captive in your queenly *. Sol 7:5

IAL
ot be brought to * for causing her Num 5:31
fair * establishes his guilt. Num 35:12
*, and not be killed in revenge. Jos 20:9
the king for *, Absalom called 2Sa 15:2
he meeting and put Naboth on *. 1Ki 21:12
n this time of deep *, King Ahaz 2Ch 28:22
hen I called a public * to deal Neh 5:7
t the * I shouted at them, "The Neh 5:8
ven strangers received a fair *. Job 29:16
)on't bring me to *! Ps 143:2
rom prison and * they led him Is 53:8
f Babylon for * and sentencing. Jer 32:4
hen, at the end of this * Dan 1:13
'es, and you must stand * before Mt 10:18
o say at your *, for you will be Mt 10:19
rrested and stand *, don't worry Mk 13:11
And when you are brought to * Lk 12:11
esus' * before Caiaphas ended in Jn 18:28
he apostles to be brought for *. Act 5:21
eaten us without * and jailed Act 16:37
raveling companions, for *. Act 19:29
should return with him for the *. Act 25:5
he following day opened Paul's *. Act 25:6
Jerusalem and stand * before me?" Act 25:9
"When they came here for the *, Act 25:17
* on these charges in Jerusalem. Act 25:20
will surely stand * before Caesar! Act 27:24
The Romans gave me a * and Act 28:18
patiently every * and persecution, Rev 14:12

RIALS
Let our leaders arrange * for Ez 10:14
* the Lord had brought upon him. Job 42:11
me and drew me out of my great *. Ps 18:16
You have been my help in all my * Ps 27:9
their *, at God's appointed time. Dan 11:35
by great * and persecutions. Dan 12:10
you will have many * and sorrows; Jn 16:33
into problems and * for we know Rom 5:3
us in our hardships and *. 2Co 1:3,4
through all these * here, just as I Php 1:20
the * and sorrows it brought you. 1Th 1:6
These * are only to test your 1Pe 1:7
test tube of fiery *, it will bring 1Pe 1:7
through the fiery * ahead, for this 1Pe 4:12
glad—because these * will make you 1Pe 4:13
rest from all their toils and *; Rev 14:13

RIBAL
These were the * leaders elected Num 1:16
with its flagpole and * banner; Num 2:1
and at the center of these * Num 2:1
Here are the * locations: Num 2:3-31
and sent these twelve * leaders: Num 13:3-15
that each of their * chiefs is to Num 17:1
the plains, divided by * areas. Num 24:2
"Execute all the * leaders of Num 25:4
the priest, the * leaders, and Num 27:1
and the other * leaders and said, Num 32:2
Joshua, and the * leaders of Num 32:28
mountain, all your * leaders came Deu 5:23
* leaders supervised the lottery. Jos 14:1
BUT THE * leaders of Ephraim were Ju 8:1
So Samuel called the * leaders 1Sa 10:20
officials, and the * officers and Jer 29:1
same as those of the * sections. Eze 45:7
boundaries as the * units, with the Eze 48:8

TRIBE
land of Seir:The * of Lotan,The Gen 36:20,21
tribe of Lotan,The * of Shobal,The Gen 36:20,21
of Shobal,The * of Zibeon,The tribe Gen 36:20,21
of Zibeon,The * of Anah,The tribe Gen 36:20,21
tribe of Anah,The * of Dishon,The Gen 36:20,21
* of Ezer,The tribe of Dishan. Gen 36:20,21
tribe of Ezer,The * of Dishan. Gen 36:20,21
people like any other * in Israel. Gen 49:16
and girl of the * of Levi who Ex 2:1
The heads of the clans of the * Ex 6:15
the clans of the * of Levi, in the Ex 6:16
the name of that * will be engraved Ex 28:21
of Hur, of the * of Judah), and Ex 31:1
the * of Dan) to be his assistant; Ex 31:6
of Hur of the * of Judah) as Ex 35:30,31
son of Ahisamach, of the * of Dan. Ex 35:34
of Hur, of the * of Judah) was the Ex 38:22
of Ahisamach of the * of Dan); Ex 38:23
a woman of another *, and he shall Lev 21:7
from his own *, for he must not be Lev 21:14,15
outside the *, she may not eat the Lev 22:12
daughter of Dibri of the * of Dan. Lev 24:11
indicating their * and family. Num 1:2-15
assisted by leaders from each *:" Num 1:2-15
* Num 1:2-15
man indicating his * and family, Num 1:17,18,19
* Num 1:20-46
the entire * of Levi from the Num 1:47,48,49
Each * of Israel shall have a Num 1:52
and Aaron: "Each * will have its Num 2:1
*: Judah Num 2:3-31
When traveling, each * stayed Num 2:3-31
their camps, each * under its own Num 2:34
"Summon the * of Levi and present Num 3:6
a census of the * of Levi, Num 3:14,15
Kohath division of the Levite *. Num 4:1
division of the * of Levi, all of Num 4:21,22,23
of the Levite *, all of the men Num 4:29
Amminadab of the * of Judah. Num 7:12
Zuar, chief of the * of Issachar, Num 7:18-23
chief of the * of Zebulun, came Num 7:24-29
Shedeur, chief of the * of Reuben; Num 7:30-35
* of Simeon, with the same gifts. Num 7:36-41
of Deuel, chief of the * of Gad. Num 7:42-47
chief of the * of Ephraim, brought Num 7:48-53
prince of the * of Manasseh, came Num 7:54-59
chief of the * of Benjamin, with Num 7:60-65
He was the chief of the * of Dan Num 7:66-71
chief of the * of Asher, brought Num 7:72-77
* of Naphtali, with his offerings; Num 7:78-83
the march was the * of Judah Num 10:14
Next came the * of Issachar, led Num 10:15
of Zuar, and the * of Zebulun, led Num 10:16
divisions of the * of Levi were Num 10:17
Next was the * of Simeon headed Num 10:19
and the * of Gad led by Num 10:20
Next in line was the * of Num 10:22
and the * of Manasseh led by Num 10:23
and the * of Benjamin, led by Num 10:24
by the flag of the * of Dan under Num 10:25
Ammishaddai; the * of Asher, led Num 10:26
and the * of Naphtali, led by Num 10:27
send one leader from each *. Num 13:2
of Zaccur, from the * of Reuben; Num 13:3-15
Shaphat, son of Hori, from the * Num 13:3-15
of Jephunneh, from the * of Judah; Num 13:3-15
Igal, son of Joseph, from the * of Num 13:3-15
Palti, son of Raphu, from the * of Num 13:3-15
Gaddiel, son of Sodi, from the * Num 13:3-15
Gaddi, son of Susi, from the * of Num 13:3-15
Ammiel, son of Gemalli, from the * Num 13:3-15
Sethur, son of Michael, from the * Num 13:3-15
Nahbi, son of Vophsi, from the * Num 13:3-15
Geuel, son of Machi, from the * of Num 13:3-15
all three from the * of Reuben, to Num 16:1
to be on the rod of the * of Levi. Num 17:1
representing the * of Levi, had Num 17:8
Your kinsmen, the * of Levi, are Num 18:2,3
a member of the * of Levi shall Num 18:4
As for the * of Levi, your Num 18:21
Salu, a leader of the * of Simeon. Num 25:14
how many of each * and clan are Num 26:2
The * of Reuben: 43,730. Num 26:5-11
In this * were the following Num 26:5-11
The * of Simeon: 22,200. Num 26:12-14
In this * were the following Num 26:12-14
The * of Gad: 40,500. Num 26:15-18
In this * were the following clans Num 26:15-18
The * of Judah: 76,500. Num 26:19-22
In this * were the following clans Num 26:19-22
The * of Issachar: 64,300. Num 26:23-25
In this * were the following clans Num 26:23-25
The * of Zebulun: 60,500. Num 26:26,27
In this * were the following clans Num 26:26,27
The * of Joseph: 32,500 in the Num 26:28-37
The * of Benjamin: 45,600. Num 26:38-41
In this * were the following clans Num 26:38-41
The * of Dan: 64,400. Num 26:42,43
In this * was the clan of the Num 26:42,43
of Dan. The * of Asher: 53,400. Num 26:44-47
In this * were the following clans Num 26:44-47
Serah. The * of Naphtali: 45,400. Num 26:48-50
In this * were the following Num 26:48-50
These are the families of the * Num 26:58,59
Conscript 1,000 men from each * Num 31:4,5
Then the clan of Machir of the * Num 32:39
clan of the * of Manasseh, occupied Num 32:41
from each *, as listed below: Num 34:16-28
* Num 34:16-28
of Machir, of the * of Manasseh, Num 36:1
But if they marry into another * Num 36:3
to the * into which they marry. Num 36:3
total area of our * will be Num 36:3
"The men of the * of Joseph have a Num 36:5
long as it is within their own *. Num 36:6
of the land of the other * will shift to Num 36:7
shift to any other *, for the Num 36:7
of every * is to remain permanently Num 36:7
within their own *, so that their Num 36:8
that their land won't leave the *. Num 36:8
shall move from one * to another.' Num 36:9
own * of Manasseh (son of Joseph); Num 36:11,12
inheritance remained in their *. Num 36:11,12
So choose some men from each * Deu 1:13
some from every *, and appointed Deu 1:15
twelve spies, one from each *. Deu 1:23
*, tall as the giants of Anakim; Deu 2:10
They were a large and powerful * Deu 2:21
and destroyed the * of Avvim living Deu 2:23
The clan of Jair, of the * of Deu 3:14
wilderness, for the * of Reuben; Deu 4:43
Ramoth, in Gilead, for the * of Deu 4:43
and Golan, in Bashan, for the * Deu 4:43
set apart the * of Levi to carry Deu 10:8
(That is why the * of Levi does Deu 10:9
of the Levite * will not be given Deu 18:1
God has chosen the * of Levi, of Deu 18:5
woman, family or * of Israel—begins Deu 29:18
And may his * increase!" Deu 33:6
Then Moses said concerning the * Deu 33:8
Concerning the * of Benjamin, Deu 33:12
Concerning the * of Joseph, he Deu 33:13
Of the * of Zebulun, Moses said: Deu 33:18
Concerning the * of Gad, Moses Deu 33:20
Of the * of Dan, Moses said: Deu 33:22
Of the * of Naphtali, Moses said: Deu 33:23
Of the * of Asher: Deu 33:24
from each *, for a special task. Jos 3:12
one from each *, each to take a Jos 4:2,3
river—one for each *, just as the Jos 4:8
of Zerah, of the * of Judah) took Jos 7:1
* to which the guilty man belongs. Jos 7:14
And that * must come by its clans Jos 7:14
and the * of Judah was indicated. Jos 7:16
The other half of the * of Jos 13:8
The Land Given to the * of Levi: Jos 13:14
any land to the * of Levi: instead, Jos 13:14
The Land Given to the * of Jos 13:15
area to the * of Reuben: Their Jos 13:15
boundary of the * of Reuben. Jos 13:23
The Land Given to the * of Gad: Jos 13:24
Moses also assigned land to the * Jos 13:24
no land to the * of Levi for, as he Jos 13:33
The decision as to which * would Jos 14:1
Jordan River. The * of Joseph had Jos 14:3,4
A delegation from the * of Judah, Jos 14:6
THE LAND GIVEN to the * of Judah Jos 15:1
of land to the * of Judah: Jos 15:20
The * of Judah also inherited Jos 15:37-44
The territory of the * of Judah Jos 15:45
But the * of Judah could not Jos 15:63
The Land Given to the * of Jos 16:5,6
property as the men of our *." Jos 17:4
The northern boundary of the * of Jos 17:7
belonged to the * of Ephraim. Jos 17:8
belonged to the * of Ephraim, Jos 17:9
a large, strong * you will surely Jos 17:16,17,18
Select three men from each * and Jos 18:4
will be assigned to each *. Jos 18:5,6
which * should have each section: Jos 18:10
The Land Given to the * of Jos 18:11
families of the * of Benjamin lay Jos 18:11
of the cities of the * of Judah. Jos 18:14
assigned to the * of Benjamin. Jos 18:20
land given to the * of Benjamin: Jos 18:21-28
were given to the * of Benjamin. Jos 18:21-28
THE LAND GIVEN to the * of Jos 19:1
The * of Simeon received the next Jos 19:1
also given to the * of Simeon. Jos 19:8
The Land Given to the * of Jos 19:10
The third * to receive its Jos 19:10
The Land Given to the * of Jos 19:17-23
The fourth * to be assigned its Jos 19:17-23
The Land Given to the * of Asher: Jos 19:24,25,26
The fifth * to be assigned its Jos 19:24,25,26
The Land Given to the * of Jos 19:32
The sixth * to receive its Jos 19:32
assignment was the * of Naphtali. Jos 19:32
The Land Given to the * of Dan: Jos 19:40
The last * to be assigned its land Jos 19:40
to conquer, so the * of Dan Jos 19:47,48
of the land of the * of Reuben; Jos 20:8
in the territory of the * of Gad; Jos 20:8
in the land of the * of Manasseh. Jos 20:8
THEN THE LEADERS of the * of Levi Jos 21:1
* of Levi, descendants of Aaron). Jos 21:4
The * of Benjamin gave them these Jos 21:17,18
from the * of Ephraim: Jos 21:20,21,22
were given by the * of Dan: Jos 21:23,24
The * of Issachar gave four Jos 21:28,29
The * of Asher gave four cities Jos 21:30,31
The * of Naphtali gave: Jos 21:32
four cities by the * of Zebulun: Jos 21:34,35
other half of the * was given land Jos 22:7,8
The leaders of the * of Judah, Ju 1:3
asked help from the * of Simeon. Ju 1:3
When the * of Judah moved into Ju 1:16
of the Kenite *—accompanied them. Ju 1:16
The Lord helped the * of Judah Ju 1:19
The * of Benjamin failed to Ju 1:21
As for the * of Joseph, they Ju 1:22,23
The * of Manasseh failed to drive Ju 1:27
they still live among the * of Ju 1:29
And the * of Zebulun did not Ju 1:30

(TRIBE Con't)
nor did the * of Asher drive out Ju 1:31,32
And the * of Naphtali did not Ju 1:33
As for the * of Dan, the Amorites Ju 1:34
and Sha-albim, the * of Joseph Ju 1:35
(But the * of Reuben didn't go. Ju 5:15
Yes, the * of Reuben has an uneasy Ju 5:16
in the whole * of Manasseh, and I Ju 6:15
He was from the * of Issachar, Ju 10:1
THEN THE * of Ephraim mobilized Ju 12:1
"Are you a member of the * of Ju 12:5
of Manoah, of the * of Dan, who Ju 13:2,3
of the army of the * of Dan, Ju 13:25
at that time. The * of Dan was Ju 18:1
troops of the * of Dan set out from Ju 18:11
priest to a whole * in Israel Ju 18:19
Then the people of the * of Dan Ju 18:28
worshiped by the * of Dan as long Ju 18:31
was a man of the * of Levi living Ju 19:1
a village of the * of Benjamin, so Ju 19:14
one piece to each * of Israel. Ju 19:29
were sent to the * of Benjamin, Ju 20:12
"Which * shall lead us against Ju 20:18
So the * of Benjamin lost Ju 20:46,47
population of the * of Ju 20:48
a man from the * of Benjamin. Ju 21:1
"Was any * of Israel not Ju 21:5
loss of their brother *, Benjamin. Ju 21:6
"gone—an entire * of Israel has Ju 21:6
of the * of Benjamin are dead?" Ju 21:16
so that an entire * of Israel will Ju 21:17
a man of the * of Ephraim who lived 1Sa 1:1
your branch of the * of Levi could 1Sa 2:30
A man from the * of Benjamin ran 1Sa 4:12
Several men of the * of Levi 1Sa 6:15
man from the * of Benjamin. 1Sa 9:1
"I'm from the * of Benjamin, the 1Sa 9:21
of all the families of the *! 1Sa 9:21
the Lord, and the * of Benjamin was 1Sa 10:20
each family of the * of Benjamin 1Sa 10:21
a member of the * of Judah who 1Sa 17:12
Be like the * of Judah who have 2Sa 2:7
Ephraim, the * of Benjamin, and all 2Sa 2:9
Abner's troops from the * of 2Sa 2:25
from the * of Benjamin) were dead. 2Sa 2:31
the leaders of the * of Benjamin; 2Sa 3:19
own *, my own flesh and blood!" 2Sa 19:11,12
A thousand men from the * of 2Sa 19:17
the * of Joseph to greet you." 2Sa 19:20
"The king is one of our own *. 2Sa 19:42
These four were from the * of 2Sa 21:22
Gibe-ah, of the * of Benjamin; 2Sa 23:24-39
man from each *—responsible for 1Ki 4:7
of a widow of the * of Naphtali, 1Ki 7:14
him be king of one *, for David's 1Ki 11:12,13
battalions from the * of Joseph. 1Ki 11:27,28
But I will leave him one * 1Ki 11:32
him except for the * of Judah, who 1Ki 12:16,17
Only the * of Judah 1Ki 12:20
counted together as one *. 1Ki 12:20f
Ahijah, from the * of Issachar) 1Ki 15:27
* of Judah remained in the land. 2Ki 17:18
of half of the Menuhoth *. 1Ch 2:52
* of Simeon went to Mount Seir. 1Ch 4:42
members of the * of Amalek. 1Ch 4:43
and influential * in Israel, and 1Ch 5:2
He was a prince of the * of 1Ch 5:6
the priests by the * of Benjamin. 1Ch 6:60
The * of Ephraim gave these 1Ch 6:66-69
The * of Issachar gave them 1Ch 6:72
The * of Asher gave them Abdon, 1Ch 6:74
The * of Naphtali gave them 1Ch 6:76
The * of Zebulun gave them Rimmono and 1Ch 6:77
Jericho, the * of Reuben gave them 1Ch 6:78,79
The * of Gad gave them Ramoth in 1Ch 6:80
the clans of the * of Issachar 1Ch 7:5
The * of Manasseh, descendants of 1Ch 7:29
were all from the * of Benjamin. 1Ch 8:40
Among the members of the * of 1Ch 9:7,8
Adina (son of Shiza) from the * of 1Ch 11:26-47
leaders of the * of Reuben; 1Ch 11:26-47
were all of the * of Benjamin. 1Ch 12:2
warriors from the * of Gad also 1Ch 12:8-13
From the * of Simeon, 7,100 1Ch 12:24-37
From the * of Benjamin, the same 1Ch 12:24-37
* Saul was from, there were 3,000. 1Ch 12:24-37
(Most of that * retained its 1Ch 12:24-37
From the * of Ephraim, 20,800 1Ch 12:24-37
From the * of Issachar there were 1Ch 12:24-37
200 leaders of the * with their 1Ch 12:24-37
From the * of Zebulun there were 1Ch 12:24-37
From the * of Dan there were 1Ch 12:24-37
From the * of Asher, there were 1Ch 12:24-37
of the men of the * of Levi who 1Ch 23:3
Eliezer were included with the * 1Ch 23:14,15
(This census of the * of Levi was 1Ch 23:27
Anathoth in the * of Benjamin), who 1Ch 27:12
he has chosen the * of Judah, and 1Ch 28:4
Let Rehoboam rule his own * of 2Ch 10:16
The people of the * of Judah, 2Ch 10:17
* of Israel for a long time; 2Ch 30:5f
carcasses for each * to present its 2Ch 35:12
Leaders from the * of Judah: Neh 11:4,5,6
Leaders from the * of Benjamin: Neh 11:7,8,9
The people of the * of Benjamin Neh 11:31-35
to live with the * of Benjamin. Neh 11:36
The little * of Benjamin leads Ps 68:27
and gave each * of Israel its Ps 78:55
family, the * of Ephraim, and Ps 78:67
and chose the * of Judah—and Mount Ps 78:68
the mighty * of Kedar, will end. Is 21:16
An Arab * living in the desert Jer 49:28f
of the Levite *, who are my Eze 43:19
And the men of the * of Levi who Eze 44:10
of Zadok, of the * of Levi, Eze 44:15
giving a portion to each *. Eze 45:8
* of Joseph (Ephraim and Manesseh Eze 47:13
Otherwise, each * will have an Eze 47:14
to the * where they now live. Eze 47:23
the rest of their * of Levi did. Eze 48:11
made to each *, says the Lord God. Eze 48:29
chosen, all from the * of Judah. Dan 1:6
But I will have mercy on the * Hos 1:7
Chaldeans: a * of Semites living Hab 1:6f
There the little remnant of the * Zep 2:7
of the priest * of the Jews, a Lk 1:5
of the Jewish * of Asher, and was Lk 2:36,37
He was of the * of Levi, from the Act 4:36
a man of the * of Benjamin, who Act 13:21
but came from the * of Judah, Heb 7:12,13,14
belonging to the * of Levi, but on Heb 7:16
The Lion of the * of Judah, the Rev 5:5
nation, *, language and people. Rev 14:6

TRIBE'S

So the Simeon * inheritance came Jos 19:9

TRIBES

from the * of Canaanites and Gen 13:7
* at the places indicated: Gen 14:5,6
of twelve * that bore their names. Gen 25:16
become a great nation of many *! Gen 28:2
These are the names of the * that Gen 36:20,21
That is, the * of Simeon and Levi Gen 49:7f
clans of the various * of Israel: Ex 6:14
there were twelve * of Israel. Ex 24:4
them the names of the * of Israel. Ex 28:9
so that all the * are named in the Ex 28:10
one of the * of Israel and the name Ex 28:21
the names of the * of Israel on the Ex 28:29
the names of the * of Israel, just Ex 39:6,7
names of the twelve * of Israel. Ex 39:14
like the other *, but will receive Lev 25:33
These three * led the way Num 2:3-31
These three * were next in line Num 2:3-31
chiefs of the *, the men who had Num 7:2
the chiefs of the * of Israel. Num 7:84,85,86
of the * shall lay their hands Num 8:10
the * of Israel shall come to you. Num 10:4
is blown, the * camped on the east Num 10:5,6,7
at the second signal, the * on Num 10:5,6,7
Last of all were the * headed by Num 10:25
the order in which the * traveled. Num 10:28
The * of the Gileadites: Num 26:28-37
the land among the * in proportion Num 26:52,53
the larger * to be given more Num 26:54
land, the smaller * less land. Num 26:54
of the larger * have a lottery, Num 26:55,56
* draw for the smaller sections." Num 26:55,56
when it was divided among the *. Num 26:62
the leaders of the * and told them, Num 30:1
the leaders of the * are to make a Num 31:26
and Gilead, the * of Reuben and Gad Num 32:1
all the men of the * of Gad and Num 32:29
The * of Gad and Reuben said Num 32:31
and cities—to the * of Gad, Reuben, Num 32:33
proportion to the size of your *. Num 33:54
among the larger *, and the smaller Num 33:54
will be allotted to the smaller *. Num 33:54
nine and one-half *, for the Num 34:13
tribes, for the * of Reuben and Num 34:14,15
of the land among the *." Num 34:29
the larger * with many cities Num 35:8
the smaller * will give fewer." Num 35:8
The girls throughout the * of Num 36:8
land to the * of Reuben, Gad, and Deu 3:12
To the * of Reuben and Gad I gave Deu 3:12
of Machir. The * of Reuben and Gad Deu 3:16
"At that time I reminded the * Deu 3:18
men led the other * across the Deu 3:18
given victory to the other *, too. Deu 3:20
Land, as their brother * do; Deu 10:9
allotted to one of the *. Deu 12:14
given property like the other *. Deu 18:1
Levi, of all the *, to minister to Deu 18:5
Promised Land, the * of Simeon, Deu 27:12
blessing, and the * of Reuben, Deu 27:13
and gave it to the * of Reuben and Deu 29:8
man from all the * of Israel, to Deu 29:21
officers of your * so that I can Deu 31:28
of the leaders of the *! Deu 33:5
the leaders of the * of Reuben, Jos 1:12,13
lead the other * across the Jordan Jos 1:14
all, one for each of the twelve *. Jos 4:5
the other * of the Lord's army Jos 4:12,1
you must come by *, and the Lord Jos 7:1
Joshua brought the * of Israel Jos 7:1
dividing the land among the *. Jos 11:2
the land to the * of Reuben and the Jos 12
Joshua to the other * of Israel. Jos 12
among the nine * and the half-tribe Jos 13:2-
Manasseh, and the * of Reuben and Jos 13
nine and a half * of Israel. Jos 14
the two and a half * on the east Jos 14:3,
two separate *, Manasseh and Jos 14:3
SOUTHERN BOUNDARY of the * of Jos 16:
Then the two * of Joseph came to Jos 17:1
"Fine," said the * of Joseph, Jos 17:16,17,1
seven of the * of Israel had not Jos 18:
And of course the * of Gad and Jos 18:
* by the throw of the sacred dice. Jos 18:
to the * of Judah and Joseph. Jos 18:1
*, with the boundaries indicated; Jos 19:4
the leaders of the * of Israel Jos 19:5
to divide the land among the *. Jos 19:5
and the leaders of the various *. Jos 21:
* of Judah, Simeon, and Benjamin. Jos 21:
These cities were given by the * Jos 21:
the * of Reuben, Gad, and Zebulun. Jos 21:
the Levites. The * of Judah and Jos 21:9-1
troops from the * of Reuben, Gad, Jos 22:
your brother *, even though the Jos 22:2,
go to war against their brother *. Jos 22:1
* of Reuben, Gad, and Manasseh. Jos 22:1
the ten *, and each a clan leader. Jos 22:1
they said to the * of Reuben, Gad, Jos 22:1
this from the * of Reuben, Gad, and Jos 22:3
assigned to the * of Joseph. Jos 24:3
"Which of our * should be the Ju 1:
two * lived together after that. Ju 1:1
of Israel, the * moved into their Ju 2:
the * of Naphtali and Zebulun. Ju 4:
But the * of Zebulun and Naphtali Ju 5:1
for there were no * in the area Ju 18:
now one of our * is missing?" Ju 21:
made a breach in the * of Israel. Ju 21:1
before the Lord by * and clans." 1Sa 10:18,1
REPRESENTATIVES OF all the * 2Sa 5:
"But there are ten * in 2Sa 19:4
heads of the * and clans—to observe 1Ki 8:1
and give ten of the * to you! 1Ki 11:3
Of the twelve *, Judah and 1Ki 11:32
son and give ten of the * to you. 1Ki 11:35
men from the other *, a great mob 1Ki 12:18
represent each of the * of Israel, 1Ki 18:31
Literally, "each of the * of the 1Ki 18:31f
all the cities of the * of Israel. 2Ki 21:7
area from the * of Issachar, Asher, 1Ch 6:62
the * of Reuben, Gad, and Zebulun. 1Ch 6:63
* of Judah, Simeon, and Benjamin. 1Ch 6:64,65
families from the * of Israel, and 1Ch 9:2
Then some families from the * of 1Ch 9:3
River—where the * of Reuben and 1Ch 12:24-37
But he didn't include the * of 1Ch 21:6
affairs of the * of Reuben, Gad, 1Ch 26:31,32
the * of Israel were as follows: 1Ch 27:16-22
the heads of the *, the army 1Ch 29:6,7
heads of the * and clans—for the 2Ch 5:2
from the other * of Israel, the 2Ch 10:18
from the other * now abandoned 2Ch 11:13,14
King Ahaz ruled two * of 2Ch 28:19f
However, some from the * of 2Ch 30:11
from the northern * returned again 2Ch 31:1
from the northern * and the people 2Ch 31:5,6
the leaders of the * of Judah and Ez 1:5
for the twelve * of Israel. Ez 6:17
You gave him to the desert * to Ps 74:13,14
of the nomadic * of the desert; Jer 25:24
Symbolic mother of the northern *, Jer 31:15f
but rather, a group of Arab *. Jer 49:30f
"Attack those wealthy Bedouin * Jer 49:31
* with strange, difficult tongues. Eze 3:6
deserts, peopled by nomadic *. Eze 20:35,36f
And Bedouin * from the desert to Eze 25:9,10
Judah and her allied *.' Eze 37:16
all the other * of Israel.' Eze 37:16
I will take the * of Israel and Eze 37:18,19,20
the land among the * of Israel, you Eze 45:1
land to the twelve * of Israel: The Eze 47:13
boundaries among the * of Israel. Eze 47:21
"HERE IS THE list of the * and Eze 48:1
to the remaining * are as follows: Eze 48:23
honor of one of the * of Israel. Eze 48:30,31
as much as do the * of Israel." Zec 9:1f
judging the twelve * of Israel. Mt 19:28
judging the twelve * of Israel. Lk 22:30
The twelve * of Israel strive Act 26:7
* of Israel, as listed here: Rev 7:4-8
peoples, nations, *, and kings." Rev 10:11
And the names of the twelve * of Rev 21:12

TRIBULATION

times of great *—wars and sorrows, Dan 10:1
"After the * ends, then the sun Mk 13:24
the time of Great * and Rev 3:10
out of the Great *," he said; Rev 7:14

IBULATIONS
e Kingdom of God through many *. Act 14:22
IBUTE
lso levy a two percent * of all Num 31:30
aid him * each year. 2Sa 8:2
nd brought him annual * money. 2Sa 8:6
as forced to pay * to 2Sa 8:14
hey brought him annual * of 1Ki 10:25
pay * to Israel any longer. 2Ki 1:1
hey paid Israel an annual * of 2Ki 3:4
pay the annual * to Assyria. 2Ki 17:4
nd refused to pay * any longer. 2Ki 18:7
will pay whatever * you demand 2Ki 18:14
nd paid him * for three years, but 2Ki 24:1
nds that paid annual * to him. 2Ch 9:13,14
ach brought him annual * of 2Ch 9:24
ut you must pay annual * to 2Ch 12:8
nd annual *, and the Arabs donated 2Ch 17:11
he Ammonites paid annual * to 2Ch 26:8
hem an annual * of $200,000 in 2Ch 27:5
lanning to place them under *. 2Ch 32:1
nnual * from Judah of $250,000. 2Ch 36:3
eceived vast *, custom, and toll. Ez 4:20
ING AHASUERUS NOT only laid * Est 10:1
ho lust after the * of smaller Ps 68:30f
ICK
What sort of * is this?" Gen 29:25
heir kindness is a *; Pro 23:6,7,8
ing retorted, "I can see your *! Dan 2:8,9
icked men who * the innocent, Mal 3:5
o fool with your * questions? Mt 22:18
esus saw their * and said, Mk 12:15
We do not try to * people into 2Co 4:2
ower, and will * everyone with 2Th 2:9
ICKED
The serpent * me," she replied. Gen 3:13
was here and * me and has carried Gen 27:35
o say, 'God * them into coming to Ex 32:12
ICKERY
What do you mean by this *?" Gen 29:25
esorted to * to save themselves. Jos 9:3,4,5
and bribes and * prevail. Hab 1:4
He saw through their * and said, Lk 20:23
of every sort of * and villainy, Act 13:10
ICKS
as a tack in plotting your evil *. Ps 52:2
The smooth * of evil men will be Is 32:7
all strategies and * of Satan. Eph 6:11
ICKY
I do not have fellowship with *, Ps 26:4
IED
at that time. He * always to Gen 6:9,10
her, and * to win her affection. Gen 34:3
His family all * to comfort him, Gen 37:35
Judah exclaimed. "We * our Gen 38:23
she sobbed. "He * to rape me, Gen 39:14,15
had around here * to rape me, and Gen 39:17
Then the magicians * to do the Ex 8:18
The Egyptians * to flee, but the Ex 14:27
* to follow through the sea; Ex 15:19
they shall be * in a court but not Lev 19:20
Balak * again. Num 22:15
because he has * to draw you away Deu 13:10
they even * to hire Balaam, the Deu 23:4
until he has been * by the judges, Jos 20:6
from Ephraim * to cross the river, Ju 12:5
to capture him if he * to leave. Ju 16:2
nerve entirely and * to hide in 1Sa 13:6
to close in, David * his best to 1Sa 23:26
your enemy Saul who * to kill you. 2Sa 4:8
of Israel, they * to capture him; 2Sa 5:17
zeal, had * to wipe them out. 2Sa 21:2
And in the morning when I * to 1Ki 3:21
Solomon * to kill Jeroboam, but 1Ki 11:40
Once when Queen Jezebel had * to 1Ki 18:3,4
But his officers * to reason with 2Ki 5:13
* unsuccessfully to crush the 2Ki 8:21
how I've always * to obey you and 2Ki 20:3
where he was * and sentenced before 2Ki 25:6
and his brothers * to comfort him. 1Ch 7:22
that no one * to keep count! 2Ch 5:6
have * to be faithful to God." 2Ch 19:3
He continually * to follow the 2Ch 20:32
Joash * hard to please the Lord 2Ch 24:2
Then the local residents * to Ez 4:4,5
visit, our enemies * to talk them Neh 4:12
who have * to discourage me." Neh 6:14
because he * to destroy you. Est 8:7
but no one *, for they were Est 9:1
You have * to make me feel Job 20:3
like Adam, I have * to hide my Job 31:33
Lord, for I have * to keep your Ps 26:1
of Ziph * to betray him to Saul. Ps 54:1
For all who * to hurt me have Ps 71:24
My patience was severely * by Ps 95:9
He destroyed many a king who *! Ps 105:14
I have * my best to find Ps 119:10
From my earliest youth I have * Ps 119:52
Evil men have * to drag me into Ps 119:61
For I have * to live according to Ps 119:94
Then I * to find fulfillment by Ecc 2:4,5,6
everything I had *, it was all so Ecc 2:11
I have * my best to be wise. Ecc 7:23
"My beloved * to unlatch the Sol 5:4
If a man * to buy it with Sol 8:7
until they are * and condemned. Is 24:22
how I've always * to obey you in Is 38:3
You have * to get them to be Jer 5:3
have not * to follow in my paths. Jer 14:10
* to defend them from your anger. Jer 18:20
They have not * to hold you back Lam 2:14
astrologers have * to read that Dan 5:15
The Lord says, "A shepherd * to Amo 3:12
They * harder to row the boat Jon 1:13
king of Moab, * to destroy you Mic 6:5
are humble—all who have * to obey. Zep 2:3
For you will be arrested and *, Mt 10:17
interview him, and * to trap him Mt 19:3
and * to keep it a secret that he Mk 7:24
Galilee where he * to avoid all Mk 9:30,31
When the mob * to grab him, he Mk 14:51,52
Confused and disturbed, Mary * to Lk 1:29
sleeping mat. They * to push Lk 5:18,19
And he * to see him. Lk 9:9
The crowds ahead of Jesus * to Lk 18:39
a very rich man), * to get a look Lk 19:3
So they * to get him to say Lk 20:19
have already been * and condemned Jn 3:18
The Jewish leaders * to find him Jn 7:11
a man before he is even *?" Jn 7:51
You haven't * this before, [but Jn 16:24
Then Pilate * to release him, but Jn 19:12
fighting. He * to be a peacemaker. Act 7:26
Upon arrival in Jerusalem he * to Act 9:26
But when they * it on a man Act 19:15
He motioned for silence and * to Act 19:33
just as you have * to do today. Act 22:3
citizen who hasn't even been *?" Act 22:25
And I am being * here today Act 23:6
that he be * by Roman law. Act 24:8
not convict a man before he is *. Act 25:16
this, and * to kill me, but God Act 26:21
out to sea. They * at first to face Act 27:14,15
and no one * to stop him. Act 28:31
They * to misunderstand, Rom 1:31
But the Jews, who * so hard to Rom 9:31
whole country, and * as hard as I Gal 1:14
the very faith he * to wreck." Gal 1:23
laws or not. They * to get us all Gal 2:4
and I * to obey every Jewish rule Php 3:6
left you), we * hard to come back 1Th 2:17
come and I, Paul, * again and 1Th 2:18
though they * his patience sorely; Heb 3:9
them * it, they all were drowned. Heb 11:29
hasn't helped those who have * it! Heb 13:9
strong after being * in the test 1Pe 1:7
which your fathers * to take, and 1Pe 1:18
of them I have * to remind you—if 2Pe 3:1
you aren't strong, but you have * Rev 3:8
TRIES
now he * to tell us what to do! Gen 19:9
"The prophet who * to lead you Deu 13:5
anyone who * to break through. 2Ki 11:6,7,8
But kill anyone who * to come to 2Ki 11:15
Hezekiah when he * to persuade you 2Ki 18:31,32
And kill anyone who * to help 2Ch 23:13,14
a trustworthy man * to quiet them. Pro 11:13
a cool-tempered man * to stop Pro 15:18
The man who * to be good, loving Pro 21:21
* a better life is soon attacked. Is 59:15
For everyone who * to honor Lk 14:11
* to put them out of the church. 3Jn 1:10
TRIFLING
for he is * with the death of 1Co 11:29
TRIM
"You must not * off your hair on Lev 19:27
it with fresh oil and * the wicks. Lev 24:3,4
ocean ships and * harbor craft—all Is 2:16
TRIMMED
or clothes nor * his beard since 2Sa 19:24,25
"All the girls jumped up and * Mt 25:7,8
TRIMS
"Every morning when Aaron * the Ex 30:7
TRIP
after our first * to Egypt to buy Gen 43:20
"We must take a three days' * Ex 5:3
We must take a three-day * into Ex 8:27
rise to take with them on the *. Ex 12:39
nor * up a blind man as he walks. Lev 19:14
is not away on a *, and yet refuses Num 9:13
worn out from our long, hard *." Jos 9:13
or not our * will be successful." Ju 18:5
went on the annual * to the 1Sa 1:21,22
He has just arrived back from a * 1Sa 9:12,13
your strength for the * back." 1Sa 28:22
he is away on a *, or is asleep and 1Ki 18:27
Those who made the * also Ez 2:55,56,57
for the Lord gave them a good *. Ez 7:7,8,9
This rabble * me and lay traps Job 30:12
my husband is away on a long *. Pro 7:19
man, though you * him up seven Pro 24:15,16
Literally, "for a * to the Ecc 10:15f
abilities—and then left on his *. Mt 25:15
returned from his * and called them Mt 25:19
As he was starting out on a *, a Mk 10:17
went on a * to another country. Mk 13:34
"A Jew going on a * from Jerusalem Lk 10:30
and took a * to a distant land, and Lk 15:13
this long * out here every day." Jn 4:15
reported on their *, telling how Act 14:27
like a perfect day for the *; Act 27:13
of things we would need for the *. Act 28:10
that I will have a safe *. Rom 1:10
For I am planning to take a * to Rom 15:24
forward to this *, because I have 2Co 8:22
on this special * just to see how Col 4:8
lawyer and Apollos with their *; Tit 3:13
around our feet and * us up; Heb 12:1
TRIPLE-BRAIDED
three is even better, for a * Ecc 4:12
TRIPPING
your * feet, O queenly maiden. Sol 7:1
TRIPS
*, how much more so on this one!" 1Sa 21:5
So Jehoshaphat made no more * to 2Ch 19:4
her along on these * just as the 1Co 9:5
TRIUMPH
a great shout of * and rushed after 1Sa 17:52
the heathen nations laugh in *. 2Sa 1:20
the Lord will cause you to *!" 1Ki 22:12
And * in your praise.' 1Ch 16:35
war would end in * for the king. 2Ch 18:12
It was a great * for the tiny 2Ch 24:24
Oh, do not let them *. Job 17:3,4
the earth, the * of the wicked has Job 20:5
You refuse to let them * over me. Ps 30:1
haven't let my enemies * over me. Ps 41:11
The godly shall rejoice in the * Ps 58:10
And I will shout in * over the Ps 60:8
Who will bring me in * into Ps 60:9,10
wicked be allowed to * and exult? Ps 94:3
and I will shout in * over the Ps 108:9
will, and I know that I will *. Is 50:7
and sat in * at the middle gate. Jer 39:3
is avenged and God's people *?" Dan 8:13
THIS IS THE prayer of * Hab 3:1
taste victory and shout with *. Zec 9:15
Gentile * ends in God's good time. Lk 21:24
world Christ's * at the cross where Col 2:15
spread rapidly and * wherever it 2Th 3:1
TRIUMPHANT
Shout * praises to the Lord! Ps 47:1
of Israel shall be justified, *. Is 45:25
TRIUMPHANTLY
Then Zebul turned on him *. Ju 9:38
Christ returned * to heaven after Eph 4:8
TRIUMPHED
the Lord, for he has * gloriously; Ex 15:1
Sing to the Lord, for he has * Ex 15:21
of Judah * as the Ethiopians fled. 2Ch 14:12
Assyria first * over us until now. Neh 9:32
my trouble, and * over my enemies. Ps 54:7
time when Gideon * over Midian at Is 10:26
The enemy has *." Lam 1:9
and evil * and prospered. Dan 8:12
has done, he has * over us so that 2Co 2:14
TRIUMPHS
To sing of the * of the Lord. Ju 5:11
TRIVIAL
"With * proofs like these, Act 26:28
my arguments are * or strong, both Act 26:29
TROAS
Mysia province to the city of *. Act 16:8
We went aboard a boat at *, and Act 16:11
and were waiting for us at *. Act 20:5
*, Turkey, where we stayed a week. Act 20:6
far as the city of *, the Lord gave 2Co 2:12
the coat I left at * with Brother 2Ti 4:13
TROD
thistle and * it into the ground! 2Ki 14:9
and he * the winepress of the Rev 19:15
TRODDEN
Or, "Let them be * down and Ps 58:7f
"I have * the winepress alone. Is 63:3
In my wrath I have * my enemies Is 63:3
And the grapes were * in the Rev 14:20
TROOP
so not one enemy * survived the Jos 11:8
can scale any wall, attack any *. Ps 18:29
Literally, "When he sees a *, Is 21:6,7f
TROOPS
commander of his *, came to Abraham Gen 21:22
As a result, Joshua and his * Ex 17:13
and keep your * across the Jordan Num 32:21
here, but your *, fully armed, must Jos 1:14
The * of Reuben, Gad, and the Jos 4:12,13
of his bravest * to hide in ambush Jos 8:3
men to join the * in ambush on the Jos 8:11,12,13
When Joshua and the * who were Jos 8:20,21
Their combined *, along with a Jos 11:4
Joshua and his * arrived Jos 11:7
JOSHUA NOW CALLED together the * Jos 22:1
As Joshua sent away these *, he Jos 22:7,8

(TROOPS Con't)
So the * of Reuben, Gad, and the Jos 22:9
Take your * and attack the Ju 7:8,9
caused the enemy * to begin Ju 7:22
Then Gideon sent for the * of Ju 7:23
Ephraim summoning * who seized the Ju 7:24
fifteen thousand * were in Karkor. Ju 8:10
foes,"—for the * of Midian, being Ju 8:23,24
So six hundred armed * of the Ju 18:11
and 450,000 * to assemble with one Ju 20:1
* died in that day's battle. Ju 20:44
* are dead on the battlefield. 1Sa 4:17
some will be made to lead his * 1Sa 8:12
thousand special * and took two 1Sa 13:2
and warned his * that they stank to 1Sa 13:3,4
vast mass of enemy *, they lost 1Sa 13:6
come, and Saul's * were rapidly 1Sa 13:8
him how many enemy * there are!" 1Sa 14:6
go out among the * and tell them to 1Sa 14:34
But the * retorted, "Jonathan, 1Sa 14:45
There were two hundred thousand * 1Sa 15:4
And it was only when my * 1Sa 15:21
the Philistine * and shout his 1Sa 17:23
commander of his *, an appointment 1Sa 18:5
and David led his * against the 1Sa 19:8
Saul sent * to watch David's 1Sa 19:11
thousand special * and went to 1Sa 24:2
* and went to hunt him down. 1Sa 26:2
leading out their * by battalions 1Sa 29:2
two wives. His * rounded up all 1Sa 30:20
his * died together that same day. 1Sa 31:6
of Ish-bosheth's * to Gibeon from 2Sa 2:12
led David's * out to meet them. 2Sa 2:13
Abner's * from the tribe of 2Sa 2:25
stopped chasing the * of Israel. 2Sa 2:28
some of David's * returned from a 2Sa 3:22
The command of the Israeli * 2Sa 4:2,3
David now led his * to Jerusalem 2Sa 5:6
But David and his * defeated 2Sa 5:7
David, he told his *, "Go up 2Sa 5:8
At that time David and his * 2Sa 5:21
thousand special * and led them to 2Sa 6:1
And when Joab and his * attacked, 2Sa 10:13
additional Syrian * summoned by 2Sa 10:15,16
These * arrived at Helam under 2Sa 10:15,16
did the * go so close to the city? 2Sa 11:19,20,21
city to let his * move past him to 2Sa 15:17,18
Go on back and take your * with 2Sa 15:19,20
and he and his * will be thrown 2Sa 17:2,3
be spending the night among the *; 2Sa 17:8
panic among your * and everyone 2Sa 17:9
you should personally lead the *. 2Sa 17:11
and company commanders over his *. 2Sa 18:1
the city as all the * passed by. 2Sa 18:4
And all the * heard the king 2Sa 18:5
* were beaten back by David's men. 2Sa 18:7
congratulate the *, for I swear by 2Sa 19:7
household and * across, and helped 2Sa 19:18
out to notify the *, but it took 2Sa 20:5
shouted to Amasa's *, "If you are 2Sa 20:11
and called his * back from the 2Sa 20:22
and were killed by David's *. 2Sa 21:22
180,000 special *—to force the rest 1Ki 12:21
chariot *, plotted against him. 1Ki 16:9
'By the * from the provinces.' 1Ki 20:14
So he mustered the * from the 1Ki 20:15
Ahab's * marched out of the city. 1Ki 20:16
to him, "Some * are coming!" 1Ki 20:17
down the cry ran through his *. 1Ki 22:36,37
now joined also by * from Edom, 2Ki 3:9
his * to many glorious victories. 2Ki 5:1
to mobilize their * there!" 2Ki 6:9
is, and we'll send * to seize 2Ki 6:13
there were *, horses, and chariots 2Ki 6:15
to fifty mounted *, ten chariots, 2Ki 13:7
with Assyrian * for three years 2Ki 17:5
185,000 Assyrian *, and dead bodies 2Ki 19:35
of the best * and one thousand 2Ki 24:16
the king and his * made a hole in 2Ki 25:4,5
The Babylonian * surrounding the 2Ki 25:4,5
trained, and brave * in the army of 1Ch 5:18
of King David, numbered 36,000 *; 1Ch 7:4
leaders of 22,034 * (all of whom 1Ch 7:7
the Israeli *, who turned and fled 1Ch 10:1
heard that their * had been routed 1Ch 10:7
a hundred normal *, and the 1Ch 12:14
officer of Manasseh's *. 1Ch 12:20
From Judah, 6,800 * armed with 1Ch 12:24-37
were 3,700 * under the command of 1Ch 12:24-37
and 37,000 * equipped with shields 1Ch 12:24-37
*, all of them prepared for war. 1Ch 12:24-37
were 40,000 trained and ready *. 1Ch 12:24-37
were 120,000 * equipped with every 1Ch 12:24-37
cavalry, and twenty thousand *. 1Ch 18:4
* in Damascus, the Syrian capital. 1Ch 18:6
to enlist mercenary *, chariots, 1Ch 19:6
were joined by the * King Hanun had 1Ch 19:7
So Joab and his * attacked the 1Ch 19:14
by Abishai's *, saw that the 1Ch 19:15
additional * from east of the 1Ch 19:16
and engaged the enemy * in battle. 1Ch 19:17,18
and forty thousand of their *. 1Ch 19:17,18
Then King Hadadezer's * 1Ch 19:19
each with 24,000 *, including 1Ch 27:1
He had charge of 24,000 * who 1Ch 27:2,3
He had charge of 24,000 * who 1Ch 27:4
commanded 24,000 * during the ninth 1Ch 27:12
as many Israeli *—strong, 2Ch 13:3
elite * of Israel that day. 2Ch 13:17
King Jeroboam's *, and captured 2Ch 13:18,19
army of 1,000,000 * from Ethiopia 2Ch 14:9,10
Asa sent his * to meet them there. 2Ch 14:9,10
Three hundred thousand Judean * 2Ch 17:14,15
of unusual piety, with 200,000 *. 2Ch 17:16
These were the * in Jerusalem in 2Ch 17:19
"I'm with you all the way. My * 2Ch 18:3,4,5
at the Israeli *, and it struck the 2Ch 18:33
"Sir, do not hire * from Israel, 2Ch 25:7
If you let them go with your * 2Ch 25:8
of 307,500 men, all elite *. 2Ch 26:13
great numbers of his *. 2Ch 28:5
army officers and * to protect me! Neh 2:9
He sends his * to surround my Job 19:12
all day long the enemy * press Ps 56:1
You sent * to ride across our Ps 66:12
proud *, and strike them down. Is 10:16
worst contingent of my master's *? Is 36:8,9
For I will send these enemy * Jer 8:17
their homes as * of soldiers come Jer 18:22
in Daniel 5. The * of Cyrus the Jer 25:12f
your streets by * on every side. Eze 28:23
I will mobilize your * and Eze 38:4
Your * will be weak and helpless Nah 3:13
a legion consisted of 6,000 *. Lk 8:30f
while the enemy * are still far Lk 14:32
When the mob saw the * coming, Act 21:32

TROPHIES
the armies of the world are his *. Ps 47:9

TROPHIMUS
and Tychicus and *, who were Act 20:4
had seen him with *, a Gentile Act 21:29
and I left * sick at Miletus. 2Ti 4:20

TROPHY
For you are our * and joy. 1Th 2:20

TROUBLE
has noticed my *"), for she said, Gen 29:32
*—now my husband will love me." Gen 29:32
burdens, in deep * because of their Ex 2:23
If the priest sees that the * Lev 13:20
is no further *, it can be put back Lev 13:58
He will not * Israel! Num 23:18-24
Terrible * will come upon them, Deu 31:17
God stirred up * between King Ju 9:22,23
Why come now when you're in *?" Ju 11:7
and that they were in serious *. Ju 20:40,41
one would tell him what the * was. 1Sa 14:39
is well and that there is no * 1Sa 20:21
in any kind of *, such as being in 1Sa 22:2
is going to be * for our master and 1Sa 25:17
All that I get for my * is 1Sa 25:21
"Because I am in deep *," he 1Sa 28:15
said to Amnon, "What's the *? 2Sa 13:4
"What's the *?" 2Sa 14:5,6
You will save those in *, 2Sa 22:28
"Have you come to make *?" 1Ki 2:13
* to go to Jerusalem to worship; 1Ki 12:28
"He is stirring up * despite the 1Ki 20:7
her and ask her what the * is. 2Ki 4:26
a day of *, insult, and dishonor. 2Ki 19:3
the * is— listen to every 2Ch 6:28
plaguing them with all sorts of *. 2Ch 15:6
We are in enough * with God as it 2Ch 28:13
arrived, he caused * for King Ahaz 2Ch 28:20
her of the king's *, she replied, 2Ch 34:22
But in their time of * they cried Neh 9:27
Great * has come upon us and upon Neh 9:32
find out what the * was, and why he Est 4:5
THAT NIGHT THE king had * sleeping Est 6:1
me be born to come to all this *. Job 3:10
I was not fat and lazy, yet * Job 3:26
But now, when * strikes, you Job 4:5
sin and * who harvest the same. Job 4:7,8
rich mock those in * and are quick Job 12:5
No, you will be in serious * Job 13:10
how few his days, how full of *! Job 14:1
"A wicked man is always in * Job 15:20
"How long are you going to * me, Job 19:2
"He shall run into * at the peak Job 20:22
They never have *, and God skips Job 21:17
to his cry when * comes upon him? Job 27:9
did I not weep for those in *? Job 30:25
then he takes the * to point out Job 36:9
for them in their times of *. Ps 9:9
* when they call to him for help. Ps 9:12
You know what * and grief they Ps 10:14
IN YOUR DAY of *, may the Lord be Ps 20:1
Don't leave me now, for * is near Ps 22:9,10,11
even keep me from getting into *! Ps 32:7
But now that I am in * they are Ps 35:15
and their refuge when * comes. Ps 37:39
a tested help in times of *. Ps 46:1
fear when times of * come, even Ps 49:5
in your times of *, so I can rescue Ps 50:14,
God has rescued me from all my *, Ps 54
For when I was in * I promised Ps 66:1
for I am in deep *. Ps 69:1
But I am in deep *. Ps 70
They aren't always in * and Ps 73
Why take the * to be pure? Ps 73:1
All I get out of it is * and Ps 73:1
I am in deep * and I need his Ps 77
his anger, sending sorrow and *. Ps 78:4
cried to me in * and I saved you; Ps 81
and answer me, for I am deep in *. Ps 86
I will call to you whenever * Ps 86
I will be with him in *, and Ps 91:1
A prayer when overwhelmed with *. Ps 102
Moses serious *, for he became Ps 106:3
in their *, and he saves them. Ps 107:2
through oppression, * and sorrow. Ps 107:3
lies have brought me into deep *. Ps 119:85,8
plot and stir up * all day long. Ps 140
Bring me out of all this * Ps 143:1
Some day you'll be in *, and Pro 1:2
his debt, you are in serious *. Pro 6:
that only leads to sorrow and *. Pro 10:1
wise leadership, a nation is in *; Pro 11:1
Lies will get any man into *, but Pro 12:1
is constant * for the wicked. Pro 12:2
God's Word and find yourself in *. Pro 13:1
messenger can cause a lot of *. Pro 13:1
is angry with those who cause *. Pro 14:3
being good, but * dogs the wicked. Pro 15:
than great treasure and * with it. Pro 15:1
A lazy fellow has * all through Pro 15:1
boasting is looking for *. Pro 17:1
and tumbles into constant *. Pro 17:2
closed and you'll stay out of *. Pro 21:2
rejoice when your enemy meets *. Pro 24:1
care is headed for serious *. Pro 28:1
and gets into all kinds of *. Pro 29:2
falls when he is alone, he's in *. Ecc 4:1
man's * lies heavy upon him; Ecc 8:6,
be * and anguish and dark despair. Is 8:2
What's the * in this busy, happy Is 22:
Oh, what a day of crushing *! Is 22:
our salvation in the time of *. Is 33:
All the land of Israel is in *; Is 33:
"This is a day of * and Is 37:
'O God,' I cried, 'I am in *—help Is 38:14
and great *, I will be with you. Is 43:2
it cannot get him out of his *. Is 46:7
Help those in *! Is 58:10
But the * is that your sins have Is 59:2
Yet in time of * they cry to me Jer 2:26,27
It will let you know when * Jer 6:17
Savior in times of *, why are you Jer 14:8
is only * and terror everywhere. Jer 14:19
in the day of *, nations from Jer 16:19
Bring confusion and * on all who Jer 17:18
and in all their * I will turn my Jer 18:17
For my life has been but * and Jer 20:18
It is a time of * for my Jer 30:7
have been in great * and have been Jer 44:18
rise against her in her day of *. Jer 51:2
the day of * nears. Eze 7:7
fair. The * is they aren't fair. Eze 33:17
have * on the way, and disappear. Dan 11:19
for as soon as * comes, they will Hos 5:15
"In my great * I cried to the Jon 2:2
Lord for his help in times of *! Mic 3:4
The Lord is good. When * comes, Nah 1:7
for the day of * to come upon the Hab 3:16
after a while when * comes, or Mt 13:21
the lake the disciples were in *. Mt 14:23,24
and in great *, for he often falls Mt 17:15
them,' and there will be no *." Mt 21:3
"Just as a man can prevent * Mt 24:43
so you can avoid * by always being Mt 24:44
said, "His * is that he's Mk 3:22
were in serious *, rowing hard and Mk 6:48
Jesus replied, "Your * is that Mk 12:24
But the * is, as I have told you Jn 6:36
they went over and stirred up *. Act 17:13
find out what the * was all about. Act 22:30
believe there is * ahead if we go Act 27:10
leave misery and * behind them. Rom 3:16
The law is good, then, and the * Rom 7:14
is plain where the * is: sin still Rom 7:20
When we have * or calamity, when Rom 8:35
Be patient in *, and prayerful Rom 12:12
to go to all that *, for every day Rom 14:5
because he has * controlling his 1Co 7:36
An athlete goes to all this * 1Co 9:25
We are in deep * for bringing 2Co 1:6,7
But in our * God had comforted 2Co 1:6,7
who caused all the *, has not 2Co 2:5,6
and hardship and * of every kind. 2Co 6:4
outside, * was on every hand and 2Co 7:5
going through much * and hard 2Co 8:2
The * with you is that you look 2Co 10:7
Their * is that they are only 2Co 10:12
that I am in * here and have been 2Ti 2:9

ROUBLE Con't)
up it causes deep *, hurting many Heb 12:15
stealing or making * or being a 1Pe 4:15

ROUBLED
spirit from God * Saul, David would 1Sa 16:23
master not to be * by the sneers 2Ki 19:5,6
Problems * the nation on every 2Ch 15:5
you have told many a * soul to Job 4:3,4
no wonder my spirit is so *. Job 21:4
My heart is * and restless. Job 30:27
tempest-tossed and *, I will Is 54:11
Their hearts are * like a wild Jer 49:23
with indignation and deeply *. Jn 11:33
Now my soul is deeply *. Jn 12:27
"LET NOT YOUR heart be *. Jn 14:1
So don't be * or afraid. Jn 14:27
he was deeply * by all the idols he Act 17:16
So that when others are *, 2Co 1:3,4

ROUBLEMAKER
and was such a * for his nation. 1Ch 2:7
For we have found him to be a *, Act 24:5

ROUBLEMAKERS
they will be constant liars and * 2Ti 3:3

ROUBLERS
when he will send * to spill her Jer 48:12

ROUBLES
May he rescue me from all my *." 1Sa 26:24
along with him in all of his *." 1Ki 2:26
You look like a man with deep * Neh 2:1
"You saw the * and sorrows of Neh 9:9
"Oh, that my sadness and * were Job 6:2
thrones. If * come upon them, and Job 36:8
to ransom Israel from all her *. Ps 25:22
There I'll be when * come. Ps 27:5
listened to my * and have seen the Ps 31:7
him and saved him out of his *. Ps 34:6
and saves him out of all his *. Ps 34:17
not escape all *—he has them too. Ps 34:19
enemies rejoice over me in my *. Ps 35:24
who rejoice at my * be themselves Ps 35:26
He helps them out of their *. Ps 41:1
I be tense with fear when * come? Ps 62:2
I be tense with fear when * come? Ps 62:6
full of *, and death draws near. Ps 88:3
in their *, and he rescued them! Ps 107:13
the Lord in their *, and he helped Ps 107:19
They give me strength in all my * Ps 119:49,50
IN MY * I pled with God to help me Ps 120:1
My * pile high among these haters Ps 120:5,6
Though I am surrounded by *, you Ps 138:7
pouring out my * before him. Ps 142:1
of the terrible * I will bring upon Is 20:3
see your * and isn't being fair? Is 40:27
ones—full of * and in a stupor (but Is 51:21
And we thought his * were a Is 53:4
I will send great * upon Is 66:4
this land and pour great * down; Jer 10:18
Don't I have * enough already? Jer 45:3
All my enemies have heard my * Lam 1:21
Valley of * into a Door of Hope. Hos 1:15
At last your * will be over—you Zep 3:15
We are pressed on every side by * 2Co 4:8
These * and sufferings of ours 2Co 4:17
see right now, the * all around us, 2Co 4:18
not yet seen. The * will soon be 2Co 4:18
Share each other's * and Gal 6:2
all the * you were going through. 1Th 3:2,3
you know that such * are a part of 1Th 3:2,3
our own crushing * and suffering 1Th 3:7
all the crushing * and hardships 2Th 1:4
You know how many * I have had 2Ti 3:11
all the terrible * ahead of you. Jas 5:1

TROUBLESOME
This is all very vexing and *! Ecc 8:14

TROUBLING
something is deeply * her and the 2Ki 4:27
wicked cease from *, and there the Job 3:17
"there's no use * the Teacher Lk 8:49
who has been * and confusing you. Gal 5:10

TROUGH
into the watering * and ran down to Gen 24:20

TROUGHS
the watering * so that the flocks Gen 30:38
water * for their father's flocks. Ex 2:16
their kneading * into their spare Ex 12:34

TROUSERS
wear linen turbans and linen *; Eze 44:18

TRUCE
against it, first offer it a *. Deu 20:10
If it accepts the * and opens Deu 20:11
they have come for * or for war." 1Ki 20:18
instead he sent a * delegation of 2Ki 18:18
formed a * team and went out of the Is 36:3
* team to discuss terms of peace. Lk 14:32

TRUE
these reports are * or not. Gen 18:21
being so kind and * to him, and for Gen 24:27
whether your story is * or not. Gen 42:16
And he said, "It must be *! Gen 45:28
see whether it was * that none of Ex 9:7
And he said, "If it is * that I Ex 34:9
whether my word comes * or not!" Num 11:23
that just as it is * that all the Num 14:20,21
Lord, so it is * that not one of Num 14:22
and this shall be * forever from Num 15:15,16
The same is * if he is killed Num 35:18
predictions come * but he says, Deu 13:2
facts to see if the rumor is *. Deu 13:12,13,14
if there is no doubt it is *, Deu 17:4
accusations are *, and she was not Deu 22:20
the Lord had promised them came *. Jos 21:45
to the only * altar of our God. Jos 22:19
promises to you have all come *. Jos 23:14
This was also * of the Ju 1:29
The people had remained * to the Ju 2:7-9
away from the * faith of their Ju 2:17
"If it is really * that you are Ju 6:17
That is the * account of how Ju 8:28
of Jotham, Gideon's son, came *. Ju 9:56,57
"When all this comes * and the Ju 13:17
But there is one problem. It's * Ru 3:12
said will come *, I will cause your 1Sa 2:34
everything he says comes *; 1Sa 9:6
prophecies came * that day. 1Sa 10:9
"Yes, it is *," they replied. 1Sa 12:5
the Lord with * enthusiasm, and 1Sa 12:20
"It's * that the army spared the 1Sa 15:15
"That's not *!" 1Sa 20:2
day you have seen that it isn't *. 1Sa 24:9,10
tell you whether or not this is *. 1Sa 25:8
See 1 Samuel 31:3, 4 for the * 2Sa 1:10f
"Is it * that Amnon raped you? 2Sa 13:20
The word of the Lord is *. 2Sa 22:31
he was honest and * and faithful to 1Ki 3:6
about his great wisdom was *. 1Ki 10:4
things going on here is all *. 1Ki 10:6
yet I have been a * servant of 1Ki 18:12
to light the wood is the * God!" 1Ki 18:24
* that there is no God in Israel? 2Ki 1:3
But it was *; 2Ki 4:17
* prophet of God here in Israel." 2Ki 5:8
So it was * that two gallons of 2Ki 7:16
"Is this *?" 2Ki 8:6
for everything he says comes *. 2Ki 10:9,10
And this is still *. 2Ki 13:23
to Jehu came *, that Jehu's son, 2Ki 15:12
Lord, it is * that the kings of 2Ki 19:17
But they were not * to the God 1Ch 5:25
about you in my own country is *! 2Ch 9:5
worshiped the * God, and have not 2Ch 15:3
not had a * priest to teach them. 2Ch 15:3
shall be our king—will be * again. 2Ch 23:2,3
respond with * thanksgiving and 2Ch 32:25
written in the scroll will come *. 2Ch 34:24
Jeremiah came *, that the land must 2Ch 36:21
for you are always * to your word. Neh 9:8
them good laws and * commandments, Neh 9:13
experience that all of this is *. Job 5:27
They understand. But * wisdom Job 12:13
to fear the Lord is * wisdom; Job 28:28
but has no * motherly love. Job 39:13
hearts and lives are * and right. Ps 7:10
they are the * nobility. Ps 16:3
All his promises prove *. Ps 18:30
What I want from you is your * Ps 50:14,15
But * praise is a worthy Ps 50:23
He will let me see my wish come * Ps 59:10
and will give * justice to their Ps 67:4
with a * heart and skillful hands. Ps 78:71,72
to see your promises come *. Ps 119:82
you are * to your promises. Ps 143:11
faithful and * to your wife. Pro 5:15
he signals his * intentions to Pro 6:12,13
Everything I say is right and *, Pro 8:6,7
will all come *, and so will the Pro 10:24
but when dreams come * at last, Pro 13:12
A * friend is always loyal, and a Pro 17:17
Any story sounds * until someone Pro 18:17
distinguishing the * from false. Pro 20:8
* humility and respect for the Pro 22:4
Every word of God proves *. Pro 30:5
children playing king. * leaders? Is 3:12
a traitor for staying * to God. Is 8:12
He will bring * justice and peace Is 9:7
Yes, it is * that they even rob Is 10:2
you heard in Cyprus are all *. Is 23:1
Spirit will make it all come *. Is 34:16
It is *, O Lord, that the kings Is 37:18
you remember how * I've been to you Is 38:3
Everything I prophesied came *, Is 42:9
you are my witnesses that it is * Is 43:12
concerning Cyrus would come *? Is 45:21
my word, for it is *—that every Is 45:23
one cares about being fair and *. Is 59:4
You don't know what * peace is, Is 59:8
for I have * servants there. Is 65:8
his * servants by another name. Is 65:15
But the Lord is the only * God, Jer 10:10
from God, why don't they come *?" Jer 17:15
dreams and let my * messengers Jer 23:28
but if you are * to me, then I'll Jer 25:6
for it is absolutely * that the Jer 26:15
Another * prophet of the Lord, Jer 26:20
May your prophecies come *! Jer 28:6
Only when his message comes * can Jer 28:9
will bring to the throne the * Son Jer 33:15
Or, "the * vine from the roots of Jer 33:15f
Christ was the * vine, the only Jer 33:15f
vine, the only * expression of Jer 33:15f
"That's not *," Jeremiah said. Jer 37:14
and elders who stayed * to God. Lam 4:16
come * for a long, long time.' Eze 12:27
His prophecy will not come *, and Eze 14:9
When it comes *, the boldest Eze 21:7
This will all come *. Eze 30:9
king said to Daniel, "Is this *? Dan 2:26
"Is it *, O Shadrach, Meshach, Dan 3:14
which has been told is *." Dan 8:26f
in the law of Moses has come *; Dan 9:13
be used in reference to the * God. Hos 1:16f
For the paths of the Lord are * Hos 14:9
remodel your courts into * halls Amo 5:15
yet not one * kernel will be lost. Amo 9:9
*, many nations have gathered Mic 4:11
God, just and * and yet forgiving Zec 8:8
don't swear that something is * Zec 8:17
in promises that don't come *? Zec 10:2
them, and to make them all come *. Mt 5:17
* sons of your Father in heaven. Mt 5:45
She replied, "That's *, sir, but Mk 7:28
you have spoken a * word in saying Mk 12:32
come * at the proper time." Lk 1:20
from God shall surely come *." Lk 1:37
May everything you said come *." Lk 1:38
"These Scriptures came * today!" Lk 4:21
They know the message is *, and Lk 8:13
Therefore, if what you say is *, Lk 11:18
And it is * that the citizens of Lk 16:8
you with the * riches of heaven? Lk 16:11
concerning me will come *. Lk 18:31
'but it is always * that those who Lk 19:26
don't panic. *, wars must come, but Lk 21:9
yet my words remain forever *. Lk 21:33
* to me in these terrible days, Lk 22:28
about me to come *: 'He will be Lk 22:37
me by the prophets will come *." Lk 22:37
in the Psalms must all come *?" Lk 24:44
have seen these prophecies come *. Lk 24:48
that Jesus Christ is the * Light. Jn 1:6,7
Later on, the one who is the * Jn 1:9
an honest man— a * son of Israel." Jn 1:47
refer to him, and had all come *! Jn 2:22
"All too *!" Jn 4:17,18
For it is * that one sows and Jn 4:37
that all he says about me is *! Jn 5:32,33
And now he offers you * Bread Jn 6:32
from heaven. The * Bread is a Jn 6:33
For my flesh is the * food, and Jn 6:55
food, and my blood is the * drink. Jn 6:55
I am the * Bread from heaven; Jn 6:58
how to get this * spiritual life. Jn 6:63
sent him is a good and * person. Jn 7:18
"These claims are * even though I Jn 8:14
* Father is God himself." Jn 8:41
But it is *—I know him and fully Jn 8:55
But the * sheep did not listen to Jn 10:8
concerning this man have come *." Jn 10:41
had come * before their eyes. Jn 12:16
that isn't * of everyone here." Jn 13:10
do well to say it, for it is *. Jn 13:13
done to you. How * it is that a Jn 13:16
me,' and this will soon come *. Jn 13:18
is *—one of you will betray me." Jn 13:21
"I AM THE * Vine, and my Father Jn 15:1
be granted! My * disciples produce Jn 15:8
discuss what is *. Jn 16:30f
you, the only * God, and Jesus Jn 17:3
witness, and his witness is *; Jn 19:35f
and he knows what he says is *, Jn 19:35f
Scriptures to come * concerning Act 1:16
It isn't *! Act 2:15
him, "Are these accusations *?" Act 7:1
How * this proved to be, for in Act 7:38
"It's really *!" Act 12:11
ancestors has come * in our own Act 13:32,33
If this is *, we shouldn't Act 17:29
everything Tertullus said was *. Act 24:9
eyes to their * condition so that Act 26:18
*, some of them were Rom 3:3
will always prove * and right, no Rom 3:4
Yes, it is * that some of the Rom 11:25
Be decent and * in everything you Rom 13:12,13
show that God is * to his promises Rom 15:8
knows that you stand loyal and *. Rom 16:19
are the * followers of Christ. 1Co 1:12
proof that what is preached is *; 1Co 1:22
back from the * wisdom from above. 1Co 3:18
what I am about to say is *. 1Co 10:15
Is this really *? 1Co 11:22
course that isn't * if the dead do 1Co 15:15
that is as * as my pride in your 1Co 15:31
will come *—"Death is swallowed up 1Co 15:54
stand * to the Lord; 1Co 16:13

(TRUE Con't)
And that is even more *, if 2Co 1:12
As surely as God is *, I am not 2Co 1:18
will help us to be * to what we 2Co 3:4
We know these things are * by 2Co 5:7
don't have * and honest hearts. 2Co 5:12
that we are * ministers of God. 2Co 6:4
We stand * to the Lord whether 2Co 6:8
not the sorrow of * repentance and 2Co 7:10
to Titus has also proved *! 2Co 7:14
It is * that I am an ordinary, 2Co 10:3
Some of you are saying, "It's * 2Co 12:16
we are the * descendants of Gal 3:29
Now this * story is an Gal 4:24,25
only what is good and right and *. Eph 5:9
That is the only * Php 3:3
My beloved friends, stay * to the Php 4:1
And I ask you, my * teammate, to Php 4:3
on what is * and good and right. Php 4:8
assurance that what we said was *. 1Th 1:5
and * God only is your Master. 1Th 1:9
you are standing * to the Lord. 1Th 3:7
*, and if it is, then accept it. 1Th 5:21
How * it is, and how I long that 1Ti 1:15
IT IS A * saying that if a man 1Ti 3:1
It is quite * that the way to 1Ti 3:16
the * teaching you have followed. 1Ti 4:6
do and think. Stay * to what is 1Ti 4:16
wrong ideas and believe what is *. 2Ti 2:25
You know they are * for you know 2Ti 3:14
teach us what is * and to make us 2Ti 3:16
it all I have kept * to him. 2Ti 4:7
this is especially * among those Tit 1:10
And this is *. Tit 1:13
goes along with * Christianity. Tit 2:1
things I have told you are all *. Tit 3:8
have always proved * and people Heb 2:2
these messages are * by signs and Heb 2:4
in heaven, the * place of worship Heb 8:2
God himself, with * hearts fully Heb 10:22
TO LOVE each other with * Heb 13:1
and who remains * to the Lord—not Jas 1:27
to make them pure and * to him. Jas 4:8
they stayed * to him then, even Jas 5:11
I have given you a * statement of 1Pe 5:12
what the prophets said came *. 2Pe 1:19
who gave them * messages from God. 2Pe 1:20,21
difference between * and false. 1Jn 2:21
We know this is * because the 1Jn 3:24
know in their hearts that it is *. 1Jn 5:10
us understand and find the * God. 1Jn 5:20
his Son, who is the only * God; 1Jn 5:20
stays clean and *, and that you are 3Jn 1:3
when these things will all come *. Rev 1:3
who is holy and *, and has the key Rev 3:7
the faithful and * Witness [of Rev 3:14
Lord, holy and *, how long will it Rev 6:10
Just and * Rev 15:3,4
your punishments are just and *." Rev 16:7
for his judgments are just and * Rev 19:2
Literally, "These are the * words Rev 19:9f
"Faithful and *"—the one who Rev 19:11
and *: It is finished! Rev 21:5
and *: 'I am coming soon!' Rev 22:6,7

TRUER
There is no * statement than Job 34:12

TRUEST
But the * witness I have is not Jn 5:34

TRULY
He was the only * righteous man Gen 6:9,10
son Shechem is * in love with your Gen 34:8
instead of * worshiping the Lord or 2Ki 17:34
Temple I have built is * yours. 2Ch 6:33
Temple for you, * believing that 2Ch 20:9
to honor a man who * pleases me?" Est 6:6
honors those who * please him!' Est 6:9
Have you ever known a * good and Job 4:7,8
But how can a man be * good in Job 9:2
Oh, that he would make you * see Job 11:6
they can produce nothing * good. Job 15:34
and bless all who * worship God; Ps 7:9
a blameless life and is * sincere. Ps 15:2
Only those who are * good shall Ps 101:6
a * happy land where Jehovah is Ps 144:12-15
If you can find a * good wife, Pro 31:10
Nothing is * new; Ecc 1:8-11
his law and made it * glorious. Is 42:21
*, O God of Israel, Savior, you Is 45:15
O ISRAEL, IF you will * return to Jer 4:1
alone: That they * know me, and Jer 9:24
then they shall * be my people Jer 31:33
their children. *, your mother must Eze 16:45
them, that they are * my people. Eze 20:12
Then they shall * be my people Eze 37:23
And if they are * ashamed of Eze 43:11
"*, O Daniel," the king said, Dan 2:47
Then the Lord God of Hosts will * Amo 5:14
then you will say, "*, the Mal 1:5
can see them. *, that is all the Mt 6:5
sorry for them. *, that is the only Mt 6:16
as you leave. *, the wicked cities Mt 10:15
"*, of all men ever born, none Mt 11:11
and humility. *, Tyre and Sidon Mt 11:22
it would still be here today. *, Mt 11:24
the Sabbath? And *, one is here Mt 12:6
to * forgive your brothers." Mt 18:35
"for God alone is * good. Mt 19:17
Then Jesus told them, "*, if you Mt 21:21
of those who * accept God's message Mk 4:20
"Only God is * good! Mk 10:18
"*, this was the Son of God!" Mk 15:39
hell without * turning to God! Lk 3:7
and you will * be acting as sons of Lk 6:35
"Only God is * good, and no one Lk 18:19
Jesus said to them, "You are * my Jn 8:30,31
"*, anyone welcoming my Jn 13:20
God's paths, or even * wanted to. Rom 3:11
we trust Jesus can we * obey him. Rom 3:31
are only to those who are * Jews. Rom 9:6
into a Jewish family is * a Jew! Rom 9:6
make them * Abraham's children. Rom 9:7
But the person who * loves God 1Co 8:3
We have been kind and * loving 2Co 6:6
you * were my very own children. 2Co 6:13
proof that I was * an apostle, sent 2Co 12:12
test and * belong to the Lord. 2Co 13:6
men of faith who * trust in God. Gal 3:7
*, dealing truly, living truly Eph 4:15,16
truly, dealing *, living truly Eph 4:15,16
truly, dealing truly, living * Eph 4:15,16
Then make me * happy by loving Php 2:2
Do you want to be * rich? 1Ti 6:6
To: Titus, who is * my son in the Tit 1:4
be gentle and * courteous to all. Tit 3:2
Yes indeed, it is good when you * Jas 2:8
them, then you will be * wise! Jas 3:13
So be * glad! 1Pe 1:6
need for living a * good life: he 2Pe 1:3
that Jesus is * the Son of God? 1Jn 5:5
To: Dear Gaius, whom I * love. 3Jn 1:1
fire—only then will you * be rich. Rev 3:18

TRUMPET
As the * blast grew louder and Ex 19:19
and the long, frightening * blast; Ex 20:18
"Different * blasts will be Num 10:5,6,7
a * made from a ram's horn. Jos 6:3,4
blew a long, loud * blast, Joshua Jos 6:16
So when the people heard the * Jos 6:20
Ephraim, he blew a * as a call to Ju 3:27
and he blew a * as a call to arms, Ju 6:34
gave each man a * and a clay jar Ju 7:16
Then he blew his * and his men 2Sa 2:28
Then Joab blew the *, and his 2Sa 18:16
blew a * and yelled, "We want 2Sa 20:1
And he blew the * and called his 2Sa 20:22
a *, shouting, "Jehu is king!" 2Ki 9:13
interspersed with * obbligatos, the 2Ch 5:13,14
The priests formed a * corps. 2Ch 29:25,26
when you hear the * blow you must Neh 4:19
into battle when the * blows. Job 39:24
Sound the *! Ps 81:3
blast of the *, for they shall walk Ps 89:14,15
Praise him with the * and with Ps 150:3
When I blow the *, listen! Is 18:3
In that day the great * will be Is 27:13
SHOUT WITH THE voice of a * blast; Is 58:1
"Listen for the sound of the *! Jer 6:17
Warn with * blasts in Gibeah and Hos 5:8
Let the blast of the warning * be Joe 2:1
Sound the * in Zion! Joe 2:15
* calls and battle cries; Zep 1:16
the Lord God shall sound the * Zec 9:14
sound of a mighty * blast, and they Mt 24:31
an eye, when the last * is blown. 1Co 15:52
For there will be a * blast from 1Co 15:52
For there was an awesome * Heb 12:19
sounded like a * blast, saying, Rev 1:10
like a mighty * blast, spoke to me Rev 4:1
The first angel blew his *, and Rev 8:7
Then the second angel blew his *, Rev 8:8,9
The fourth angel blew his * and Rev 8:12
THEN THE FIFTH angel blew his * Rev 9:1
The sixth angel blew his * and I Rev 9:13
angel blew his *, then God's veiled Rev 10:7
angel blew his *, and there were Rev 11:15

TRUMPET-CALL
archangel and the great * of God. 1Th 4:16

TRUMPET-PLAYING
me were joined by the * priests— Neh 12:40,41

TRUMPETER
their sides. The * stayed with me Neh 4:18

TRUMPETERS
by her bodyguard and many *; 2Ki 11:13,14
priests who were *, while others 2Ch 5:11,12
officers and the * surrounding him, 2Ch 23:12
and *." Rev 18:22f

TRUMPETING
His priests, * as they go, will 2Ch 13:12

TRUMPETS
"The Festival of *: Lev 23:23,24
be announced by loud blowing of *. Lev 23:23,24
let the * blow loud and long Lev 25:9
Moses, "Make two * of beaten Num 1
When both * are blown, the Num 1
are permitted to blow the *. Num 1
you sound the alarm with these *. Num 1
Use the * in times of gladness, Num 10:
THE FESTIVAL OF * shall be Num 2
with * blaring. Num 3
with the priests blowing their *. Jos 6:
blowing continually on their *. Jos 6:
for the *," Joshua commanded. Jos 6:
the clay jars and * they had among Ju 7:
my group blow our *, you blow yours Ju 7:
Suddenly they blew their * and Ju 7:19,
same, blowing the * in their right Ju 7:19,
much shouting and blowing of *. 2Sa 6:
"As soon as you hear the *," 2Sa 15:
Then blow the * and shout, 'Long 1Ki 1:
and the * were blown and all the 1Ki 1:
was rejoicing and blowing *. 2Ki 11:13,
snuffers, bowls, *, or similar 2Ki 12:13,
tambourines, cymbals, and *. 1Ch 13
of horns and *, the crashing of 1Ch 15:
their * regularly before the Ark. 1Ch 16
They used their * and cymbals to 1Ch 16:
Then, when the priests blew the * 2Ch 7
mercy, and the priests blew the *. 2Ch 13:13,
with * blaring and horns sounding. 2Ch 15:
and * and proceeded to the Temple. 2Ch 20:
and blowing *, and the singers 2Ch 23:
of the Lord, accompanied by the *. 2Ch 29:
the singers sang and the * blew. 2Ch 29:
priestly robes and blew their *; Ez 3:
The priests who played the * were Neh 12:35,
a mighty shout, with * blaring. Ps 47
Let the cornets and * shout! Ps 98
* and the enemies' battle cries. Jer 4:1
"The * shout to Israel's army, Eze 7:
as the warriors shout and * blare. Amo 2:
do—blowing * in the synagogues and Mt 6.
God, and they were given seven *. Rev 8:
with the seven * prepared to blow Rev 8
remaining angels blow their *." Rev 8:1
more pianos, saxophones, and *. Rev 18:2

TRUNK
only the * of his body was left 1Sa 5:

TRUNKS
* and branches white and bare. Joe 1:
they look like tree * walking Mk 8:2

TRUST
off. I * in your salvation, Lord. Gen 49:1
Lord by betraying a *, it is sin. Num 5:5,
times refused to * me and obey me— Num 14:2
and so that your * in him would Deu 8:1
walls you will * to protect you. Deu 28:5
But King Sihon didn't * Israel, Ju 11:2
"* the Lord and sincerely 1Sa 12:2
be fooled by that god you * in. 2Ki 19:1
an office of great *, for they were 1Ch 9:2
For we * in you alone to rescue 2Ch 14:1
you have put your * in the king of 2Ch 16:
many a troubled soul to * in God Job 4:3,
* in God still be your confidence? Job 4:
"If God cannot * his own Job 4:18,1
he slay me, yet will I * in him. Job 13:15
Why, God doesn't even * the Job 15:1
"Let him no longer * in foolish Job 15:3
Literally, "* in vanity." Job 15:31
"If I have put my * in money, Job 31:2
he is so strong, will you * him? Job 39:1
of those who put their * in him! Ps 2:12
Put your * in the Lord, and Ps 4:5
rejoice who puts his * in you. Ps 5:1
yet forsaken those who * in you. Ps 9:10
But I will always * in you and in Ps 13:5
LORD, I * in you alone. Ps 31:1
be shamed by what they * in; Ps 31:17
for those who * and reverence you. Ps 31:19
surrounds those who * in the Lord. Ps 32:10
he does is worthy of our *. Ps 33:4
For we are trusting him. We * his Ps 33:21
shower down on all who * in him. Ps 34:8
disappear. * in the Lord instead. Ps 37:3
do to the Lord. * him to help you Ps 37:5
but those who * the Lord shall be Ps 37:9
Because they * in him, he helps Ps 37:40
the Lord, and put their * in him. Ps 40:3
given to those who * the Lord, and Ps 40:4
who are proud, or who * in idols. Ps 40:4
gloomy and discouraged? * in God! Ps 43:5
I do not * my weapons. Ps 44:6
They * in their wealth and boast Ps 49:6
I want you to * me in your times Ps 50:14,15
despise God and * in their wealth, Ps 52:7
Lord himself. I * in the mercy of Ps 52:8
Yes, I will * the promises of Ps 56:3,4
O my people, * him all the time. Ps 62:8
All who * in him exult, while Ps 63:11
in the Lord, and * and praise him. Ps 64:10
block to those who * in you. Ps 69:6
believe in God or * in him to care Ps 78:22
Revive us to * in you. Ps 80:18

RUST Con't)
blessed are those who * in you. Ps 84:12
He gives food to those who * Ps 111:5
For all who fear God and * in him Ps 112:1
O Israel, * the Lord! Ps 115:9
O priests of Aaron, * the Lord! Ps 115:10
All of you, his people, * in Ps 115:11
It is better to * the Lord than Ps 118:8
for me, for I * and revere you. Ps 119:38
taunt me, for I * your promises. Ps 119:40,41,42
All those who fear and * in you Ps 119:74
Let all others join me, who * and Ps 119:79
pointing out how much I * in you. Ps 119:147
THOSE WHO * in the Lord are steady Ps 125:1
* the Lord—on all who obey him! Ps 128:1
to those who reverence and * him. Ps 128:4
* in the Lord—now, and always. Ps 131:3
And so do all who * in them! Ps 135:18
of you who * and reverence him. Ps 135:20
of those who reverence and * him; Ps 145:19
The first step is to * and Pro 1:7,8,9
to reverence and * the Lord, and Pro 1:29
sense, then * the Lord completely; Pro 3:4,5
don't ever * yourself. Pro 3:4,5
Instead, * and reverence the Pro 3:7,8
* in your money and down you go! Pro 11:28
* in God and flourish as a tree! Pro 11:28
happy the man who puts his * in Pro 16:20
it on to others: * in the Lord. Pro 22:17,18,19
O my son, * my advice—stay Pro 23:26,27,28
To * a rebel to convey a message Pro 26:6
A man is a fool to * himself! Pro 28:26
but to * in God means safety. Pro 29:25
Her husband can * her, and she Pro 31:11
Don't ever put your * in him! Is 2:22
and in Judah will * the Lord, the Is 10:20
I will * and not be afraid, for Is 12:2
in whom we *, for whom we waited. Is 25:9
all those who * in him, whose Is 26:3
to the Lord! * in the Lord God Is 26:4
* in Pharaoh for his protection. Is 30:2
I tell you and * instead in frauds Is 30:12
"Don't let this God you * in Is 37:10
who * in God (Isaiah 57:1,2). Is 38:18f
the seas have put their * in him. Is 42:4
But those who * in idols and Is 42:17
of light, let them * the Lord, let Is 50:10
has rejected the ones that you *. Jer 2:37
my name, which you * for help, and Jer 7:13,14
Don't * them, no matter how Jer 12:6
mind and put your * in false gods, Jer 13:24,25
man who puts his * in mortal man Jer 17:5
Pharaoh too, and all who * in him. Jer 46:25
Don't * anyone, not your best Mic 7:5
"Note this: Wicked men * Hab 2:4
What fools you were to * what you Hab 2:18
She does not * the Lord, nor seek Zep 3:2
will * in the name of the Lord. Zep 3:12
"Don't be afraid. Just * me." Mk 5:36
it is for those who * in riches Mk 10:24
"for those who * in riches." Mk 10:24f
* me, and she'll be all right." Lk 8:50
his position of * and assign him to Lk 12:46
wealth, who will * you with the Lk 16:11
All they needed to do was to * Jn 1:11,12
But Jesus didn't * them, for he Jn 2:24,25
those who * him to save them. Jn 3:18
But those who don't * him have Jn 3:18
And all who * him—God's Son—to Jn 3:36
* me, you are really trusting God. Jn 12:44
all who put their * in me will no Jn 12:46
You are trusting God, now * in Jn 14:1
faith and * in Christ to save us. Rom 1:17
guilty"—if we * Jesus Christ to Rom 3:21,22
him if we * in Jesus Christ, who in Rom 3:24
the basis of their * in Jesus who Rom 3:26
In fact, only when we * Jesus can Rom 3:31
rules, but only * in Christ? Rom 4:9
nation who * God as Abraham did. Rom 4:17
for his faith and * grew ever Rom 4:20
in us and helps us * God more each Rom 5:4
to hope and * that he will get it. Rom 8:24
gives to those who * in him Rom 10:4
if you continue to love and * him. Rom 11:22
I don't even * my own judgment on 1Co 4:3
sacred * and I have no choice. 1Co 9:17
You can * God to keep the 1Co 10:13
useless and your * in God is empty, 1Co 15:14
understanding and * that I planned 2Co 1:15,16
of our great * in God through 2Co 3:4
But what if we * Christ to save Gal 2:17
believe in Christ and fully * him. Gal 3:5
men of faith who truly * in God. Gal 3:7
nation who * in me as you do." Gal 3:8,9
And so it is: all who * in Gal 3:8,9
who were the first to * in Christ. Eph 1:12
we come with Christ and * in him. Eph 3:12
living within you as you * in him. Eph 3:17
them to * him as their Savior; Eph 4:11
put my * and hope in Christ alone. Php 3:7
at rest as you * in Christ Jesus. Php 4:7
heard how much you * the Lord, and Col 1:4
to save you, * him, too, for each Col 2:6
Christians will * and respect you, 1Th 4:12
And we * the Lord that you are 2Th 3:4
showed me how to * him and become 1Ti 1:14
souls if they * in him, living 1Ti 2:15
confidence and bold * in the Lord. 1Ti 3:13
good, learning to * him and love 1Ti 6:11
proud and not to * in their money, 1Ti 6:17
their pride and * should be in the 1Ti 6:17
I know how much you * the Lord, 2Ti 1:5
the one in whom I *, and I am sure 2Ti 1:12
* those of us who have taught you. 2Ti 3:14
of your love and * in the Lord Phm 1:5
* in God along with my brothers." Heb 2:13
and our joy and our * in the Lord. Heb 3:6
Because they didn't * him. Heb 3:19
Do not let this happy * in the Heb 10:35
and try to * the Lord as they do. Heb 13:7
continued to * the Lord in sorrow; Jas 5:11
though not seeing him, you * him; 1Pe 1:8
Because of this, your * can be in 1Pe 1:21
disappoint those who * in him." 1Pe 2:6
Quietly * yourself to Christ 1Pe 3:15
what is right and * yourself to the 1Pe 4:19
Stand firm when he attacks. * 1Pe 5:9
assurance and *, and get whatever 1Jn 3:21
them who did not * and obey him. Jud 1:5
to his commands and * in Jesus." Rev 14:12

TRUSTED

the son of Shomer—both * aides. 2Ki 12:21
of bronze. He * very strongly in 2Ki 18:5
and he did, for they * in him. 1Ch 5:20
and the king * their judgment. Est 1:13-15
The wealth he * in shall reject Job 18:14
they * you and you delivered them. Ps 22:3,4
Oh, let it never be said that I * Ps 25:20
and have * you without wavering. Ps 26:1
I * in him, and he helped me. Ps 28:7
against me—a man I completely *; Ps 41:9
hope; I've * you from childhood. Ps 71:5
For you * in your wealth and Jer 48:7
O wicked daughter, you * in your Jer 49:4
me—you * in your beauty instead; Eze 16:15
destruction. Your * friends will Ob 1:7
who * you, who walk in peace. Mic 2:8
believe you! He * God—let God Mt 27:41,42,43
care of the Lord in whom they *. Act 14:23
First of all, God * them with his Rom 3:2
he * God to keep his promise. Rom 4:13
wisdom that can be *, and I will be 1Co 7:25
And so we, too, have * Jesus Gal 2:16
Christ and * him to save you. Gal 3:2
to be saved, and * Christ, were Eph 1:13
And now just as you * Christ to Col 2:6
life because you * the Word of the Col 2:12
God, * by him to tell the truth; 1Th 2:4
been * to do this work for him. Tit 1:3
Enoch * God too, and that is why Heb 11:5
Noah was another who * God. Heb 11:7
Abraham * God, and when God told Heb 11:8
him, Abraham still * in God and his Heb 11:17
child, they * that God would save Heb 11:23
And it was because he * God that Heb 11:27
The people of Israel * God and Heb 11:29
These people all * God and as a Heb 11:33
But others * God and were beaten Heb 11:35
faith, though they * God and won Heb 11:39
say, that Abraham * God, and the Jas 2:23
when you * Christ to save you; 1Pe 1:22
women of old, who * God and fitted 1Pe 3:5

TRUSTING

gods instead of * completely in the 1Ki 11:4
And if you say, "We're * the 2Ki 18:22
Don't let him fool you into * in 2Ki 18:30
A man without God is * in a Job 8:14
safety," when I am * in the Lord? Ps 11:1
Don't fail me, Lord, for I am * Ps 25:2
will ever be disgraced for * him. Ps 25:3
But I was * you, O Lord. Ps 31:14,15
For we are * him. Ps 33:21
of * and fearing the Lord. Ps 34:11
But I am * you to save me. Ps 55:23
And since I am * him, what can Ps 56:3,4
I am * God—oh, praise his Ps 56:10,11
O GOD, HAVE pity, for I am * you! Ps 57:1
for I am serving you and * you. Ps 86:2
he is my God, and I am * him. Ps 91:2
because I too am * in your Word. Ps 119:74
wait expectantly, * God to help, Ps 130:5
me in the morning, for I am * you. Ps 143:8
for the Lord and of * him. Pro 2:3,4,5
he is * you. Pro 3:29
Greed causes fighting; * God Pro 28:25
But in * Pharaoh, you will be Is 30:3
to Egypt for help, * their mighty Is 31:1
But perhaps you say, 'We are * Is 36:7
Don't let him talk you into * in Is 36:15
he is * what can never give him Is 44:20
Only if you return to * me will I Jer 15:19
As a reward for * me, I will Jer 39:18
on you for aid [instead of * me Eze 29:6
to deliver his * servants when they Dan 3:28
Ephraim will be laughed at for * Hos 10:6
the full reward of * in a Hos 10:13
who are as * as little children. Lk 10:21
as * as these little children's. Lk 18:16,17
trust me, you are really * God. Jn 12:44
You are * God, now trust in me. Jn 14:1
to keep him from * the Lord. Act 13:8
life will find it through * God." Rom 1:17
We are saved by *. Rom 8:24
We are saved by trusting. And * Rom 8:24
But if we must keep * God for Rom 8:25
For salvation that comes from * Rom 10:8
foolish to keep on * God to save 1Co 15:17
We boldly say what we believe [* 2Co 4:13
is a result of my * in the Son of Gal 2:20
life will find it through * God." Gal 3:11
I am * the Lord to bring you back Gal 5:10
have been saved through * Christ. Eph 2:8
And even * Eph 2:8
not only of * him but also of Php 1:29
And I am * the Lord that soon I Php 2:24
laws, but by * Christ to save me; Php 3:9
shifting from * him to save you. Col 1:23
Spirit and by your * in the Truth. 2Th 2:13
and I feel sure you are still * 2Ti 1:5
of everlasting life through * him. 2Ti 1:10
salvation by * in Christ Jesus. 2Ti 3:15
to the end, * God just as we did Heb 3:14
therefore let us never stop * Heb 4:14
true hearts fully * him to receive Heb 10:22
by faith, * him in everything. Heb 10:38
lessons from him about * God. Heb 11:4
God and be free—* that they would Heb 11:35
You see, he was * God so much Jas 2:22
receive it, because you are * him. 1Pe 1:5
And your further reward for * 1Pe 1:9
pleasure by * Christ to help him. 1Jn 5:4

TRUSTS

her, "my master * me with Gen 39:8
he * in will be his only reward. Job 15:31
O Lord, the poor man * himself to Ps 10:14
And because the king * in the Ps 21:7
him great because he * in my name. Ps 91:14
and * the Lord and obeys him. Ps 119:63
But he who * in me shall possess Is 57:13
But blessed is the man who * in Jer 17:7
but Judah still * in God and is Hos 11:12
And he knows everyone who * in Nah 1:7
but the righteous man * in me, Hab 2:4
who * in me to lose his faith, Mt 18:6
Everyone who * in him is freed Act 13:39
God and no longer * the Lord, and Jas 5:19

TRUSTWORTHY

while a * man tries to quiet them. Pro 11:13
a beloved and * child in the Lord. 1Co 4:17
be taken there by * messengers you 1Co 16:3
Teach these great truths to * men 2Ti 2:2
show themselves to be entirely *. Tit 2:10
is a strong and * anchor for our Heb 6:19
is * and true: It is finished! Rev 21:5
* and true: 'I am coming soon!' Rev 22:6,7

TRUTH

whether you are telling me the *; Gen 42:20
and rich in steadfast love and *. Ex 34:5,6
offering—to bring out the * Num 5:15
I reported what I felt was the *, Jos 14:7
and serve him in sincerity and *. Jos 24:14
told her the *, so she sent for the Ju 16:18
But the * is that I am only a 1Sa 20:3
indeed God, and your words are *; 2Sa 7:28
And if you live in honesty and * 1Ki 9:4
to swear to the * of his claim. 1Ki 18:10
"Be fearless in your stand for * 2Ch 19:11
There isn't one bit of * to the Neh 6:8
"This * was given me in secret, Job 4:12
"It is wonderful to speak the *, Job 6:25,26
my mind tastes * when I hear it. Job 12:11
are going to twist the * for him? Job 13:8
how they pervert the *! Job 17:12
"The * remains that if you do Job 18:5
"The * is that the wicked live Job 21:7
can tell you the *, that the evil Job 21:29
I will speak the * with all Job 33:3
you the * of what I am saying. Job 36:2
I am telling you the honest *. Job 36:4
establish my honor and * before Ps 7:7,8
all he says is purest *, like Ps 12:6
and know that I have told the *. Ps 17:3
with his lovingkindness and his *. Ps 25:10
and your * as my ideals. Ps 26:3
and * to all the congregation. Ps 40:10
light and your *—let them lead me. Ps 43:3
Defending *, humility, and Ps 45:4
And lying more than *! Ps 52:3
all who love * Ps 60:4,5
be displayed because of the *." Ps 60:4,5f
lovingkindness and * to guard and Ps 61:7
Literally, "in the * of your Ps 69:13f
They will awaken to the * as one Ps 73:20

(TRUTH Con't)
Mercy and * have met together. Ps 85:10
and peace have kissed! * rises Ps 85:11
constant lovingkindness and of *; Ps 86:15
* is as enduring as the heavens. Ps 89:2
Mercy and * walk before you as Ps 89:14,15
the nations fairly and with *! Ps 96:13
are formed from * and goodness, and Ps 111:8
your lovingkindness and your *. Ps 115:1
us very dearly, and his * endures. Ps 117:2
about me, but the * is that I obey Ps 119:69
These proud men who hate your * Ps 119:85,86
Help me, for you love only *. Ps 119:85,86
your commandments are based on *. Ps 119:151
There is utter * in all your Ps 119:160
they swear to the * of what is Ps 144:8
meaning in these nuggets of *." Pro 1:5,6
For wisdom and * will enter the Pro 2:10
for I speak the *—don't turn away. Pro 4:1
he will not listen to the *; Pro 5:23
There is living * in what a good Pro 10:11
Telling the * gives a man great Pro 12:14
* stands the test of time; Pro 12:19
A witness who tells the * saves Pro 14:25
A wise man is hungry for *, while Pro 15:14
is atoned for by mercy and *; Pro 16:6
* from a rebel or lies from a Pro 17:7
a rebel who has no heart for *. Pro 17:16
*—he enjoys his sinning too much. Pro 19:28
are, but are they telling the *? Pro 20:6
He who values grace and * is the Pro 22:11
of God's * on these points! Ecc 9:5f
of God's * on these points! Ecc 9:5f
of God's * on these points! Ecc 9:10f
for they have no light or * in Is 8:20
clothed with fairness and with *. Is 11:5
horror of the * of my warnings will Is 28:19
will believe the *, and complainers Is 29:24
they say, "Don't tell us the *; Is 30:10,11
until * and righteousness prevail Is 42:4
designed to be my messengers of *? Is 42:19
No, for I, Jehovah, speak only * Is 45:19
fairness is unknown. * falls dead Is 59:14
Yes, * is gone, and anyone who Is 59:15
oath shall swear by the God of *; Is 65:16
Lord, you will take naught but *. Jer 5:3
the Lord. The * is this: You will Jer 29:10
"and don't try to hide the *." Jer 38:14
tell you the *, you will kill me. Jer 38:15
finding out the *, for the Jer 38:27
out who tells the *, I or they! Jer 44:28
who could know the * if they wanted Eze 12:2
raised in oath of * to give the Eze 47:14
As a result, * and righteousness Dan 8:12
so * and righteousness perished." Dan 8:12f
"Divine *" comes to them Hos 4:12
hearts would not accept the *. Hos 7:13
you despise people who tell the *! Amo 5:10
their tongues can't tell the *! Mic 6:12
God in * and in righteousness." Zec 8:8f
Here is your part: Tell the *. Zec 8:16
festivals if you love * and peace! Zec 8:19
people all the * he got from me. Mal 2:6
For the time is coming when the * Mt 10:26
you for hiding the * from those who Mt 11:25
* understood the illustrations. Mt 13:12,13f
All who stumble on this rock of * Mt 21:44
and teach the * regardless of the Mt 22:16
Jesus told him, "The * is that Mt 26:34
is the absolute *—you can say to Mk 11:22,23
you tell the * no matter what! Mk 12:14
And I tell you this in solemn *, Mk 14:9
to reassure you of the * of all Lk 1:4
one who knew the *, instead of Lk 4:32
But this is the simple *—some of Lk 9:27
For you hide the * from the Lk 11:52
Work hard to get in, for the * is Lk 13:24,25
You always tell the * and don't Lk 20:21
and *. And some of us have seen Jn 1:14
that God is a fountain of *. Jn 3:33,34
Jesus replied, "The * of the Jn 6:26
to, who learn the * from him, will Jn 6:45
one you don't know, and he is *. Jn 7:28
and he is *." Jn 8:26
you will know the *, and the truth Jn 8:32
and the * will set you free." Jn 8:32
I told you the * I heard from God. Jn 8:40
and a hater of *—there is not an Jn 8:44
is not an iota of * in him. Jn 8:44
And so when I tell the *, you Jn 8:45
And since I am telling you the * Jn 8:46
Jesus: "The absolute * is that I Jn 8:58
Way—yes, and the * and the Life. Jn 14:6
"In solemn * I tell you, anyone Jn 14:12,13
the Spirit who leads into all *. Jn 14:17
Holy Spirit, the source of all *. Jn 15:26
When the Holy Spirit, who is *, Jn 16:13
guide you into all *, for he will Jn 16:13
teaching them your words of *. Jn 17:17
need for growth in * and holiness. Jn 17:19
you hit a man for telling the *?" Jn 18:23
And I came to bring * to the Jn 18:37
All who love the * are my Jn 18:37
"What is *?" Jn 18:38
perish, you despisers [of the * Act 13:41
telling you the *, either publicly Act 20:20
* in order to draw a following. Act 20:30
You can find out the * of our Act 24:8
I speak words of sober *. Act 26:25
men who push away the * from them. Rom 1:18
For the * about God is known to Rom 1:19
they knew was the * about God, they Rom 1:25
fight against the * of God and walk Rom 2:8
are full of all knowledge and *. Rom 2:20
But when I learned the *, I Rom 7:9
I want you to know about this * Rom 11:25
you a full understanding of the *; 1Co 1:5
Or, "interpreting spiritual * in 1Co 2:13f
of honor and sincerity and *. 1Co 5:8
but rejoices whenever * wins out. 1Co 13:6
the absolute *: the reason I 2Co 1:23
*, as all who know us will agree. 2Co 4:2
I have always told you the * and 2Co 7:14
every ounce of * I possess—that I 2Co 11:10
and ever, knows I tell the *. 2Co 11:31
the *, but for the truth." 2Co 13:8f
the truth, but for the *." 2Co 13:8f
change the * concerning Christ. Gal 1:7
following the * of the Gospel, I Gal 2:14
enemy because I tell you the *? Gal 4:16
you back from following the *? Gal 5:7
and made the lie sound like the *. Eph 4:14
follow the * at all times—speaking Eph 4:15,16
tell the *, for we are parts of Eph 4:25
the strong belt of * and the Eph 6:14
* and telling others about Christ. Php 1:7
me here to use me to defend the *. Php 1:16,17
if you fully obey the * you have. Php 3:16
fully believe the *, standing in it Col 1:23
vigorous in the * you were taught. Col 2:7
to you of the * of our message. 1Th 1:5
God, trusted by him to tell the *; 1Th 2:4
they have said "no" to the *; 2Th 2:10
the *, and enjoying their sins. 2Th 2:12
and by your trusting in the *. 2Th 2:13
strong grip on the * that we taught 2Th 2:15
to understand this *: That God is 1Ti 2:4
is the absolute *—as God's minister 1Ti 2:7
to teach this * to the Gentiles, 1Ti 2:7
and holds high the * of God. 1Ti 3:15
This is the * and everyone 1Ti 4:9,10
day will reveal the terrible *. 1Ti 5:24
sin—don't know how to tell the *; 1Ti 6:5
Hold tightly to the pattern of * 2Ti 1:13
I am comforted by this *, that 2Ti 2:11
They have left the path of *, 2Ti 2:18
But God's * stands firm like a 2Ti 2:19
who are mixed up concerning the *. 2Ti 2:25
but they never understand the *. 2Ti 3:7
And these teachers fight * just 2Ti 3:8
listen to the *, but will go around 2Ti 4:3
them to know God's *—the kind of Tit 1:1
truth—the kind of * that changes Tit 1:1
Their belief in the * which they Tit 1:9
it blinds people to the *, and Tit 1:10
have turned their backs on the *. Tit 1:14
and believing the * and doing Tit 2:2
your love of the * and the fact Tit 2:7
after knowing the * of forgiveness, Heb 10:26
lives, through the * of his Word, Jas 1:18
him understand the * again, that Jas 5:19
the wonderful * of the prophets' 2Pe 1:19
can think of, and laugh at the *. 2Pe 3:3
and refusing to accept the *. 1Jn 1:8
come upon you, and you know the *. 1Jn 2:20
need to know the *, but I warn you 1Jn 2:21
and he is the *, and no liar; 1Jn 2:27
Since the * is in our hearts 2Jn 1:2
much peace, and with * and love. 2Jn 1:3
the *, obeying God's command. 2Jn 1:4
Such people are against the * and 2Jn 1:7
But everyone, including * 3Jn 1:12
him, and you know I speak the *. 3Jn 1:12
stoutly defend the * which God Jud 1:3
faithfully reveals all * to us. Rev 1:5
heed the * stated in this Book. Rev 22:9

TRUTHFUL
For they cannot speak one * Ps 5:9
Never forget to be * and kind. Pro 3:3
A * witness never lies; Pro 14:5
when his people are * and fair. Pro 16:13
We have been *, with God's power 2Co 6:7
And the Holy Spirit, forever *, 1Jn 5:6,7,8

TRUTHFULLY
"Which of you can * accuse me of Jn 8:46

TRUTHFULNESS
yes, utter sincerity and *. Ps 51:6
A good man is known by his *; Pro 12:17

TRUTHS
I will reveal these * to you so Ps 78:4
They nail down important *. Ecc 12:11
to know some * about the Kingdom of Mk 4:11,12
Judgment by the * I have spoken. Jn 12
and a half, teaching the * of God. Act 18
and the great * of God's Word—that 1Co 1
the deep * of God) is what the 1Co 14
from him the * concerning himself, Eph 4
Teach these *, Timothy, and 1Ti
Teach these great * to 2Ti
these great * that I am in trouble 2Ti
carefully to the * we have heard, Heb
teaching ('deeper *,' as they call Rev 2:24

TRY
and everyone who sees me will * Gen 4
to * to handle all by yourself. Ex 18
They must not come up here to * Ex 19
the boundaries to * to come up Ex 19
cost: don't * to make a profit! Lev 25
You must not provoke him and * Deu 6
long as you live, * to help the Deu 2
with his army to * to help defend Jos 10
who may * to kill him in revenge. Jos 20
Did he * to recover his land Ju 11
in the area strong enough to * it. Ju 1
her to * to win her back again. Ju 1
it time that I * to find a husband Ru
Saul agreed, "let's * it!" 1Sa 9:9,10
grabbed at him to * to hold him 1Sa 15
and I'll no longer * to harm you; 1Sa 26
to get me. I'll * my luck among the 1Sa 2
his aides to * to find a medium so 1Sa 28:7
your ways and * to do your will as 1Ki 8
his people. Now * with every fiber 1Ch 22
For when you do, everything you * 2Ch 24
any who might * to harm them; Est 9
But they did not * to take Haman's Est 9:7-
Even when I * to forget my Job 7:13,
And who am I that I should * to Job 9
you use lies to * to help him out. Job 13
I would * to take away your Job 16
and * to break me with your words? Job 19
* to see my side of this argument. Job 31
comb to * to find a single fault, Job 33
"Listen now and * to understand. Job 34
out to God as they * to struggle up Job 38
Will he beg you to desist or * Job 41
and you will never * it again! Job 41
No, it's useless to * to capture Job 41
up, let alone * to conquer him. Job 41
How strange that men should * to Ps 2
that, O Lord; I * to walk a Ps 26
joy, all those who * to obey him. Ps 32
* to live in peace with everyone; Ps 34
to * to force me from the throne. Ps 62:3
Protect me from death, for I * to Ps 86
* to realize what this means—the Ps 100
I will * to walk a blameless Ps 101
Don't * to stop me from obeying Ps 119:11
My enemies are so many. They * to Ps 119:15
If I * to hide in the darkness, Ps 139:1
but loves those who * to be good. Pro 15:9,1
If you * once you must try a Pro 19:1
If you try once you must * a Pro 19:1
our steps, why * to understand Pro 20:2
Don't * to disclaim Pro 24:11,1
while wise men * to keep peace. Pro 29
I decided to * the road of drink, Ecc 2
Don't * to defend yourself by Ecc 5:6,
It will be too late then to * to Ecc 12
of the cliffs to * to get away from Is 2:2
Don't * to comfort me—let me cry Is 22
Woe to those who * to hide their Is 29:1
from God, who * to keep him in the Is 29:1
Let them * to tell us what Is 41:2
stargazers, who * to tell you what Is 47:1
They will *, but they will fail. Jer 1:1
listen to them or even * to hear. Jer 7:2
horoscopes and * to read their fate Jer 10:2,
If they were mine, they would * Jer 23:2
"and don't * to hide the truth." Jer 38:1
she does not even * to cover it. Eze 24
off all those who * to escape and Eze 35
kingdoms will * to strengthen Dan 2:4
persecution, and * to change all Dan 7:2
Listen, and * to understand the Dan 9:2
and * to pass the blame to him! Hos 4:4
his God, nor even * to find him. Hos 7:10
Tyre and Sidon, don't you * to Joe 3:4
are wise will not * to interfere Amo 5:13
And though you * and try to save Mic 6:14
And though you try and * to save Mic 6:14
to * to fool the people then. Zec 13:4
Hosts will say, '* to if you like, Mal 1:4
And you claim this isn't evil? * Mal 1:8
"* it! Mal 3:10
is going to * to kill the child." Mt 2:13
Don't * to get by as you are, Mt 3:9
hypocrites do, who * to look wan Mt 6:16
to what I say and * to understand: Mt 15:10
but were afraid to * because of the Mt 21:46
met together to * to think of some Mt 22:15
themselves don't even * to keep. Mt 23:4
corruption. You * to look like Mt 23:28

RY Con't)
and didn't * to prove his points by Mk 1:22
to * to take him home with them. Mk 3:21
Satan comes at once to * to make Mk 4:15
he said, "and * to understand. Mk 7:14
to talk with him and * to trap Mk 12:13
But if you say so, we'll * Lk 5:5
"* to show as much compassion as Lk 6:36
the way to court, * to settle the Lk 12:58
is that many will * to enter but Lk 13:24,25
of oxen and wanted to * them out. Lk 14:19
Let those in Jerusalem * to Lk 21:21
"to * the Spirit of the Lord." Act 5:9f
in before them to * to find out Act 22:30
to * to find out what he had done. Act 23:28
Because of this I * with all my Act 24:16
I used torture to * to make Act 26:11
They finally decided to *. Act 27:40
and the rest to * for it on planks Act 27:44
is this: when we * to gain God's Rom 4:15
and when I * not to do wrong, I Rom 7:19
people jealous and * to wake them Rom 10:19
Don't * to act big. Rom 12:16
Don't * to get into the good Rom 12:16
other any more. * instead to live Rom 14:13
and * to build each other up. Rom 14:19
Now I will * to answer your other 1Co 7:25
to * to keep you from marrying. 1Co 7:35
person is like, I * to find common 1Co 9:22
And don't * the Lord's 1Co 10:9
Don't think only of yourself. * 1Co 10:24
I follow, too. I * to please 1Co 10:33
No, but * your best to have the 1Co 12:31
then * to collect it all at once. 1Co 16:2
I want you to * to accept me and be 2Co 1:13,14
on to Macedonia to * to find him. 2Co 2:13
We do not * to trick people into 2Co 4:2
We never * to get anyone to 2Co 4:2
We * to live in such a way that 2Co 6:3
we do we * to show that we are true 2Co 6:4
and the Jews, who * to follow Gal 4:24,25
* to keep the other Jewish laws; Gal 6:13
of your love. * always to be led Eph 4:3
Don't be fooled by those who * Eph 5:6
Don't act thoughtlessly, but * Eph 5:17
Never once did we * to win you 1Th 2:5
evil, but always * to do good to 1Th 5:15
in Ephesus and * to stop the men 1Ti 1:3,4
sneer at those who * to be good. 2Ti 3:3
Do * to be here before winter. 2Ti 4:21
to * their best to satisfy them. Tit 2:9
arrives, please * to meet me at Tit 3:12
* to stay out of all quarrels and Heb 12:14
* to trust the Lord as they do. Heb 13:7
So let it grow, and don't * to Jas 1:4
evil and do good. * to live in 1Pe 3:11
* hard to live without sinning; 2Pe 3:14
believes this will * to stay pure 1Jn 3:3
to give you. * to help those who Jud 1:22
In those days men will * to kill Rev 9:6

TRYING
"What were you * to do?" Gen 44:15
"Are you * to test God's Ex 17:2
"Why are you * to do all this Ex 18:14
If you see your enemy * to get Ex 23:5
Whom are you * to fool? Num 16:14
"Are you * to discourage the Num 32:7
yourselves by * to make a statue of Deu 4:16,17
"If you see someone * to get an Deu 22:4
were still * to figure it out. Ju 14:14
The tribe of Dan was * to find a Ju 18:1
who say that I am * to harm you? 1Sa 24:9,10
you that I am not * to harm you and 1Sa 24:11
for what you are * to do to me, but 1Sa 24:12
And who is the king of Israel * 1Sa 24:14
"Are you * to get me killed?" 1Sa 28:9
My own son is * to kill me, and 2Sa 16:11
Queen Jezebel was * to kill the 1Ki 18:13
and now they are * to kill me, 1Ki 19:10
and now they are * to kill me, 1Ki 19:14
He is only * to get an excuse to 2Ki 5:7
King Hezekiah is * to persuade 2Ch 32:11
* to frighten and dishearten them. 2Ch 32:18
around us who are * to destroy us? Neh 5:9
You're just * to scare us into Neh 6:9
"Are you still * to be godly when Job 2:9
So what's the use of *? Job 9:29
"Who are you * to fool? Job 18:2
is worthless in * to get it; Job 28:18
'Why waste time * to please God?' Job 34:9
yourself when I am * to find you. Ps 27:9
to you and stopped * to hide them. Ps 32:5
Dishonor those who are * to kill Ps 35:4
Meanwhile my enemies are * to Ps 38:12
these who are * to destroy me. Ps 40:14,15
violent, godless men are * to Ps 86:14
them, they are * to destroy me. Ps 109:4
and know that I am * to help them. Ps 141:6,7
those who are * to harm me; Ps 143:12
he will only hate you for * to Pro 9:7,8
If they stop *, the Lord will Pro 15:9,10
When a man is * to please God, Pro 16:7
if they are * to bribe him! Pro 21:27
for he is * to bribe you, and no Pro 23:1
Don't weary yourself * to get Pro 23:4,5
the taverns, * out new mixtures. Pro 23:29,30
* to cheat him out of his rights. Pro 24:15,16
or * to run on a broken foot. Pro 25:19
* to get rich quick is evil and Pro 28:22
Don't always be * to get out of Ecc 8:2,3
So why are you * to find out Is 8:19
among those they are * to help. Is 31:3
is in heavy labor * to give birth, Is 37:3
own interest, each * to get as much Is 56:11
dreams they are * to get my people Jer 23:27
What are you * to tell us?" Eze 24:19
You're * to stall for time until Dan 2:8,9
He spent the rest of the day * to Dan 6:14
As I was * to understand the Dan 8:15
But sinners * it will fail. Hos 14:9
Are you * to take revenge on me, Joe 3:4
and killed those * to escape; Ob 1:14
* to kill the child are dead." Mt 2:20
"Who are you * to fool with your Mt 22:18
around him, * to touch him. Mk 3:10
message to others, * to plant good Mk 4:14
Of course they were * to trap Mk 10:2
Supreme Court were * to find Mk 14:55
You are * to escape hell without Lk 3:7
Everyone was * to touch him, for Lk 6:19
would never think of * to keep. Lk 11:46
host of questions, * to trap him Lk 11:53,54
to the dinner were * to sit near Lk 14:7
were * to find some way to get Lk 19:47
Jesus' murder, * to find a way to Lk 22:2
They stood there puzzled, * to Lk 24:4
While I am * to get there, Jn 5:7
Who's * to kill you?" Jn 7:20
this the man they are * to kill? Jn 7:25
They were * to trap him into Jn 8:6
And yet some of you are * to Jn 8:37
But instead you are * to kill Jn 8:40
"Are you * to teach us?" Jn 9:34
in Judea were * to kill you. Jn 11:8
were at the house * to console Mary Jn 11:31
and Barnabas said, * to keep him Act 13:8
at the synagogue, * to convince the Act 18:4
Moreover, he was * to defile the Act 24:6
the crew advised * to go further up Act 27:12
good enough" and * to keep his Rom 3:21,22
Because they were * to be saved Rom 9:32
Instead they are * to make Rom 10:3
are * to get by keeping his laws. Rom 10:4
now they were * to kill him too. Rom 11:2,3
the Lord, you are * to honor him; Rom 14:6
that I have been * to start 1Co 1:15
I am * to make you ashamed. 1Co 6:5
What am I * to say? 1Co 10:19
Now here is what I am * to say: 1Co 12:27
for we know what he is * to do. 2Co 2:11
The old way, * to be saved by 2Co 3:6
is freedom [from * to be saved by 2Co 3:17
Are we * to pat ourselves on the 2Co 5:12
It is not as though we were * to 2Co 10:15
You can see that I am not * to Gal 1:10
no, I am * to please God. Gal 1:10
If I were still * to please men I Gal 1:10
a sudden, are you * to make these Gal 2:14
destroying, of * to be saved by Gal 2:18
by *—and failing—to obey the laws. Gal 2:19
by * to keep the Jewish laws? Gal 3:2
For if * to obey the Jewish laws Gal 3:3
do you think that * to obey them Gal 3:3
of your * to obey the Jewish laws? Gal 3:5
win God's favor by * to keep the Gal 3:11
Here's what I am * to say: God's Gal 3:17
religion of * to get to heaven by Gal 4:9
You are * to find favor with God Gal 4:10
What they are * to do is to shut Gal 4:17
of that system of * to please God Gal 4:24,25
God by * to obey the Gal 4:24,25
Anyone * to find favor with God Gal 5:3
of yours who are * to convince you Gal 6:12
of death while * to do for me the Php 2:30
what is right, and * constantly to Col 3:10
become discouraged and quit *. Col 3:21
masters, not only * to please them Col 3:22
both God and man, * to keep us 1Th 2:16
* to find me, and finally did. 2Ti 1:17
Be humble when you are * to 2Ti 2:25
the foolishness of * to be saved by Heb 6:1
There is no use * to bring you Heb 6:4
* to do what he wants us to? 1Jn 2:3
Anyone * to harm them will be Rev 11:5

TRYPHAENA
Say "hello" to * and Tryphosa, Rom 16:12

TRYPHOSA
Say "hello" to Tryphaena and * Rom 16:12

TUBAL
Madai,Javan, *,Meshech, Tiras. Gen 10:2
Javan, *, Meshech, and Tiras. 1Ch 1:5-9
Meshech, Rosh and * were in Asia Is 66:19f
Meshech, Rosh, *, Javan, and to the Is 66:19
Merchants from Javan, * and Eze 27:13
"The princes of Meshech and * Eze 32:26
(Meshech, *, Gomer, Beth-togarmah) Eze 38:2,3f
king of Meshech and *. Eze 38:2,3
you, Gog, leader of Meshech and *. Eze 39:1

TUBAL-CAIN
other wife, Zillah, was born *. Gen 4:22

TUBE
lie straight as a * of brass. Job 40:18
tried in the test * of fiery 1Pe 1:7

TUBERCULOSIS
and with * and burning fever; Lev 26:16
He will send *, fever, Deu 28:22

TUBES
flowing into them through seven *. Zec 4:2
golden bowls through two golden *. Zec 4:12

TUGGING
and the men were * at Paul from Act 23:10

TUITION
It is senseless to pay * to Pro 17:16

TUMBLE
cliffs shall *; Eze 38:20
the mountains * down before his Nah 1:6

TUMBLES
and * into constant trouble. Pro 17:20

TUMBLING
that came * down into our camp. Ju 7:12,13
walls of Jericho * down after the Heb 11:30

TUMOR
gold models of the * caused by the 1Sa 6:4,5

TUMORS
Egyptian boils, *, scurvy, and Deu 28:27
of the rats and *, and let the cows 1Sa 6:8
and * were placed upon the cart. 1Sa 6:11
golden rats and * from the cart and 1Sa 6:15
The five gold models of * which 1Sa 6:17

TUMULT
shouting and the * in the camp of 1Sa 14:19
Don't you hear the * and Ps 83:2
Hear the * on the mountains! Is 13:4
It is the * and the shout of many Is 13:4
Moab shall go down in * as the Amo 2:2

TUNE
For no one will recognize the * 1Co 14:7

TUNELESS
deaf and *, with quavering voice. Ecc 12:4

TUNIC
More literally, "an ornamented * Gen 37:3f
tunic," or "long-sleeved *." Gen 37:3f
Apparently a sort of sleeveless * Ex 28:4f
a robe, a checkered *, a turban, Ex 28:4
"Weave Aaron's * from Ex 28:39
on him, and the *, ephod, Ex 29:5
Peter put on his * (for he was Jn 21:7

TUNNEL
through the water * into the city 2Sa 5:8
Dig a * through the city wall Eze 12:5

TUNNELS
They drill * in the rocks and Job 28:10

TURBAN
a robe, a checkered tunic, a *, Ex 28:4
ribbon to the front of Aaron's *. Ex 28:37,38
make the *, too, of this linen; Ex 28:39
head the * with the golden plate. Ex 29:6
the front of the *, engraved with Ex 39:30
It was tied to the * with a Ex 39:31
and placed on Aaron's head the * Lev 8:9
linen coat, shorts, belt, and *. Lev 16:4
also have a clean * on his head?" Zec 3:5,6

TURBANS
* to give them honor and respect. Ex 28:40
The chestpiece, the beautiful *, Ex 39:28,29
and flowing * on their heads. Eze 23:14,15
They must wear linen * and linen Eze 44:18

TURKEY
Egypt and southern *, where his 1Ki 10:28
They escaped into eastern *—the 2Ki 19:37
Regions of Asia Minor, now in *. Eze 27:13f
Regions of Asia Minor, now in *. Eze 27:14f
Caspian, currently in central *. Eze 38:2,3f
a province of what is now *. Act 2:9f
him left Paphos by ship for *, Act 13:13
return again to *, and visit each Act 15:36
there, he left for * again, going Act 18:23
traveled through * and arrived in Act 19:1
he stayed awhile longer in *. Act 19:22
this part of * but all around the Act 19:27
with him, going as far as *; Act 20:4
to their homes in *, and had gone Act 20:4
Troas, *, where we stayed a week. Act 20:6
day I set foot in * until now I Act 20:18
some Jews from * saw him in the Act 21:26,27
from Ephesus in *, and assumed Act 21:29
But some Jews from * were there Act 24:18
port on the southeast coast of *. Act 27:7,8f
province in what is now called *. Gal 1:1f
To: The seven churches in *. Rev 1:4
letter to the seven churches in *: Rev 1:11

TURKISH
* provinces of Cilicia, and Ausia. Act 6:9

(TURKISH Con't)
* province of Ausia at that time. Act 16:6
everyone in the * province of Act 19:10
several stops along the * coast. Act 27:2

TURMOIL
there silently the * within me grew Ps 39:2,3
unmoved despite the * everywhere. Ps 46:5
When I saw this, what * filled my Ps 73:21
its people live in *, yet its Ps 75:3
my heart is in *, quiet me and give Ps 94:19
heart was so filled with *? Ps 132:1
with internal * and you sinned. Eze 28:16
nations will be in *, perplexed by Lk 21:25

TURN
land, and it will * to blood." Ex 4:9
and the river will * to blood! Ex 7:17
in the homes will * to blood." Ex 7:19
the people to * toward Piha-hiroth Ex 14:2
he in * will have ten judges Ex 18:21
* back from your fierce wrath. Ex 32:12
your fierce wrath. * away from this Ex 32:12
"And I will * my face against Lev 17:10
And I myself will * against that Lev 20:3
who * to other gods than me. Lev 20:5
The next day it was Eliasaph's *, Num 7:42-47
tomorrow you must * back into the Num 14:25
will * away from the people." Num 25:4
If you * away from God like Num 32:15
older generation, * around now and Deu 1:40
here long enough. * northward. Deu 2:3
road and won't * off into the Deu 2:27
* from God to worship other gods. Deu 11:16
Then the Lord will * from his Deu 13:17
indecent lest he * away from you. Deu 23:14
Israel—begins to * away from the Deu 29:18
his curses and * them against your Deu 30:7,8
law, and if you * to the Lord your Deu 30:10
But if your hearts * away and Deu 30:17
I will * away from them because Deu 31:18
* away from God and his commands; Deu 31:29
Now I, in *, will make them Deu 32:21
with fear at this * of events. Jos 7:5
to * up in the ways he wanted. Jos 14:1
Far be it from us to * away Jos 22:29
Each in * fought against you but Jos 24:11
gods, he will * upon you and Jos 24:20
The Philistines in * sent a huge Ju 15:9
Israeli army to * around and attack Ju 20:35-39
* your back on him in any way. 1Sa 12:20
with us—they'll * against us. 1Sa 29:4
But he refused to * away, so 2Sa 2:23
if we have to * and run, and half 2Sa 18:3
* and run away; 2Sa 22:41
everything you do, wherever you *. 1Ki 2:3
please don't * me down." 1Ki 2:16
"I hope you won't * me down." 1Ki 2:20
them if they * to you again and 1Ki 8:33,34
their senses and * to you and cry 1Ki 8:47
or your children * away from me and 1Ki 9:6
did not * away from his evil ways; 1Ki 13:33
* Samaria into handfuls of dust!" 1Ki 20:10
Judah to * from their evil ways; 2Ki 17:13
in your mouth and * you back on the 2Ki 19:28
you, and if they * to you and call 2Ch 6:24
as our God, and * from our sins 2Ch 6:26
land of exile they * to you again, 2Ch 6:37,38
ignore me—do not * your face away 2Ch 6:42
search for me, and * from their 2Ch 7:14
men of Judah to * the tide of 2Ch 13:15,16
fierce anger will * away from us. 2Ch 29:10
They in * summoned their fellow 2Ch 29:15
fierce anger will * away from you. 2Ch 30:8
For if you * to the Lord again, 2Ch 30:9
not continue to * away his face 2Ch 30:9
But Josiah refused to * back. 2Ch 35:22
who built from the * in the wall to Neh 3:20
You punished them in order to * Neh 9:29
to * from their wickedness. Neh 9:35
The Levites, in *, gave a portion Neh 12:47
Then, as each girl's * came for Est 2:12,13,14
* to go to the king, she accepted Est 2:15
one listens; they * to their gods, Job 5:1
Those who * from God may be Job 5:3
The caravans * aside to be Job 6:15-18
you are dashed—you * away from me Job 6:19-21
"Before you * to God and stretch Job 11:13,14
Why do you * away from me? Job 13:24
rest, won't you? * away your angry Job 14:6
And you * against God and say Job 15:13
who can * him from his purposes? Job 23:13
All night long I toss and *, and Job 30:18
and mankind would * again to dust. Job 34:15
to * away from their sin. Job 36:10
for crime. * back from evil, for Job 36:21
will you forever * my glory into Ps 4:2
what to do, which way to *. Ps 5:8
God will * them back in shame. Ps 6:10
has made my darkness * to light. Ps 18:28
* back until all were conquered. Ps 18:37
You made them * and run; Ps 18:40
They will * and flee when they Ps 21:12
best to those who humbly * to him. Ps 25:9
Keep your lips from lying. * Ps 34:14
me. * them back and confuse them. Ps 35:4
Stop your anger! * off your Ps 37:8
Confuse them! * them around and Ps 40:14,15
Blessed be God who didn't * away Ps 66:20
* to ashes and their peace Ps 69:22
and * again and comfort me. Ps 71:21
* could teach their children too. Ps 78:6
* us again to yourself, O God. Ps 80:3
* us again to yourself, O God of Ps 80:7
* us again to yourself, O God of Ps 80:19
Or, "* to us." Ps 85:4f
How long will you delay? * away Ps 90:13
Don't * away from me in this time Ps 102:2
But if you * away from them, then Ps 104:29
they die and * again to dust. Ps 104:29
and begged him to * from his wrath, Ps 106:23
* me away from wanting any other Ps 119:37
your path, but I will not * aside. Ps 119:110
a day your thoughts * towards me. Ps 139:17,18
way I ought to * to miss the traps Ps 142:3
don't * away from me or I shall Ps 143:7
and join us"—* your back on them! Pro 1:10
in crime—men who * from God's Pro 2:11,12,13
the Lord, and * your back on evil; Pro 3:7,8
I speak the truth—don't * away. Pro 4:1
Literally, "Forget not nor * from Pro 4:5f
Avoid their haunts—* away, go Pro 4:15
don't even * your head to look. Pro 4:25
Be sensible and * off the flow! Pro 10:19
A poor man's own brothers * away Pro 19:7
will * to gravel in their mouths. Pro 20:17
they serve will * sour in your Pro 23:6,7,8
be if you * out to be sensible! Pro 27:11
He won't * aside for anyone. Pro 30:29,30,31
investments that * sour, and soon Ecc 5:13,14
or to * to me to heal them." Is 6:10
not repent and * to him, the Lord Is 9:13
To whom will you * then for your Is 10:3
then he will * upon the Assyrians Is 10:12
Do not * us over to our foes. Is 16:3
For the Egyptians will * to the Is 19:22
is dawning now. * again to God, so Is 21:12
as you said! You * mighty cities Is 25:2
thoughts * often to the Lord! Is 26:3
it will people * away from Is 26:9
people, for they * away from God. Is 27:11
yet it will all * out to your Is 30:5
Your own breath will * to fire Is 33:11
will * to cries of fear. Is 43:14
have caused you to * away from me Is 47:10
I can * the rivers into deserts, Is 50:2
I do not rebel nor * away. Is 50:5
for sinners—those who * from Is 52:1
Let them * to the Lord that he Is 55:7
and made us sin and * against you? Is 63:17
Why don't you * from all this Jer 2:25
would never * away from me again. Jer 3:19
they refuse to * from their sins. Jer 5:3
and prophecies and * them into Jer 5:14
we are terrorized at every *. Jer 6:25
fork where he made the wrong *. Jer 8:4,5
"And I will * Jerusalem into Jer 9:11
they refuse to * back to me from Jer 15:7
of Israel, all who * away from you Jer 17:13
was forming didn't * out as he Jer 18:4
instead of good; * back from your Jer 18:11
and in all their trouble I will * Jer 18:17
* my people from their evil ways. Jer 23:22
message was this: * from the evil Jer 25:5
will listen and * from their evil Jer 26:3
* him over to the mob to kill him. Jer 26:24
for I will * their mourning into Jer 31:13
for the yoke. * me again to you and Jer 31:18
to tell you to * back from your Jer 35:15
Perhaps even yet they will * Jer 36:7
will * out well for us." Jer 42:6
* back from their wicked ways; Jer 44:5
here: I will * Pharaoh Hophra, Jer 44:30
calves. They * and run, for it is Jer 46:20,21
and all her people * to flee. Jer 49:24
Let him * the other cheek to Lam 3:30
repent and * again to the Lord. Lam 3:40
us for so long? * us around and Lam 5:21
Afterwards, * over and lie on Eze 4:6
you so that you can't * over from Eze 4:8
I will * my eyes away and show Eze 7:4
they did not * when they changed Eze 10:9-13
will you * away my people from me? Eze 13:19
of those who * from me to idols. Eze 14:5
I will * upon him and make a Eze 14:8
sinful man has, in *, a son who Eze 18:14
I only want him to * from his Eze 18:23
and decided to * from his sins and Eze 18:28
own actions. Oh, * from your sins Eze 18:30
Lord God says. *, turn and live! Eze 18:32
Turn, * and live! Eze 18:32
They will decide to * toward Eze 21:22
And I will * the city of Rabbah Eze 25:5
I desire that the wicked * from Eze 33:11
ways and live. *, turn from your Eze 33
Turn, * from your wickedness, for Eze 33
you a blood bath—your * has come! Eze 3
to have their * of being covered Eze 3
I will * you and drive you Eze 3
Then he shall * around and go Eze 46
The leaves will never * brown and Eze 47
Lord, please * away your furious Dan 9
"After this he will * his Dan 11
He will * homeward again, but Dan 11
he will once again * his armies Dan 11
The prophecy takes a * here. Dan 11:
and those who * many to Dan 1
There your daughters * to Hos 4:
are, Ephraim will * to Assyria, to Hos 5:
strong, yet now they * against me. Hos 7:
them at every * and publicly Hos
when I * away and leave you alone. Hos 9:
That is why the Lord says, "* to Joe 2:
I will * them back into the Joe 2:
the pastures will * green again. Joe 2:
I will * over this city and Amo
If you * against Israel, what Amo
If you * against them, what hope Amo
I will no longer * away from Amo
the Temple will * to weeping then. Amo
"And I will * your parties into Amo 8:
All your allies will * against Ob 1
and let everyone * from his evil Jon 3
that makes you * away from me? Mic 6
up in anger and * on you and take Hab 2
will * to ashes in their hands? Hab 2:
But he will * again and favor Zec 1
to * from all their evil ways. Zec 1
They shall * the land into a Zec 11
And you * up your noses at the Mal 1:
to, I will * on you with curses. Mal 2
His constant theme was, "* from Mt 3
your sins * to God Mt 3
began to preach, "* from sin, and Mt 4:
from sin, and * to God, for the Mt 4:
for you can't * one hair white Mt 5:
on one cheek, * the other too. Mt 5:
who ask, and don't * away from Mt 5:4
the pearls and * and attack you. Mt 7:
and understand and * to God again, Mt 13:
said, "Unless you * to God from Mt 18:
you to repent and * to God, and you Mt 21:3
convert, and then * him into twice Mt 23:1
Then I will * to those on my Mt 25:4
their decision to * their backs on Mk 1:
"God's Kingdom is near! * from Mk 1:1
not understand or * to God, or be Mk 4:11,1
everyone they met to * from sin. Mk 6:1
my name will quickly * against me. Mk 9:3
a Jew to * to the Lord his God. Lk 1:1
Literally, "to * the hearts of Lk 1:17
what this child will * out to be? Lk 1:6
invite sinners to * from their Lk 5:3
*, were surrounded by the crowds. Lk 6:17,1
when you enter it, * around and Lk 9:
leave your evil ways and * to God? Lk 13:
then they will * from their sins.' Lk 16:3
Literally, "It shall * out unto Lk 21:13
of sins for all who * to me. Lk 24:4
Don't * my Father's House into a Jn 2:1
nor * to me to heal them." Jn 12:4
the sun shall * black and the Act 2:2
one of you must * from sin, return Act 2:3
to God and * to him so he can Act 3:19
right before God. * from this Act 8:22
in Israel to * from sin to God. Act 13:24
you are invited to * from the Act 14:15
the Gentiles who * to God must obey Act 15:19
a desire to * from sin to God and Act 19:4
Now it was Paul's *. Act 24:10
* me over to these men to kill me. Act 25:10,1
their sins and * to God—and prove Act 26:20
and * to me to heal you." Act 28:27
give you time to * from your sin? Rom 2:4
in refusing to * from your sin; Rom 2:5
No matter which way I * I can't Rom 7:18
* the Jews from all ungodliness. Rom 11:26
When the Lord comes, he will * on 1Co 4:5
to stop himself or wait his *. 1Co 14:32
Each, however, in his own *: 1Co 15:23
come when he will * the kingdom 1Co 15:24
friends, let us * away from 2Co 7:1
lives to help us * away from sin 2Co 7:10
I don't want it to * out that 2Co 9:3
didn't reject me and * me away. Gal 4:14
is all going to * out for my good. Php 1:19
in the church will * away from 1Ti 4:1
alone and have nowhere else to *. 1Ti 5:16
in *, pass them on to others. 2Ti 2:2
we suffer, and * against Christ, 2Ti 2:12
Christ, then he must * against us. 2Ti 2:12
God's help, to * away from their 2Ti 2:25
God wants us to * from godless Tit 2:12
they made whole armies * and run Heb 11:34
to die rather than * from God and Heb 11:35

URN Con't)
* first this way, and then that. Jas 1:7,8
We can make a large horse * Jas 3:3
makes a huge ship * wherever the Jas 3:4
itself, and can * our whole lives Jas 3:6
* away from evil and do good. 1Pe 3:11
then afterwards * his back on the 2Pe 2:21
those who * again to their sin. 2Pe 2:22
now!) and * back to me again and Rev 2:5
unless they * again to me, Rev 2:22
hold to it firmly and * to me Rev 3:3
you, unless you * from your Rev 3:19
prophesy, and to * rivers and Rev 11:6
is your * to be angry with them. Rev 11:18
and now, in *, you have poured Rev 16:6
But cowards who * back from Rev 21:8

URNED
Then he * to Sarah. Gen 20:16
Isaac, she * upon Abraham and Gen 21:10
Gad (meaning "My luck has *!" Gen 30:11
"Your father has * against me," Gen 31:5
As far as I am concerned, God * Gen 50:20
husband you've * out to be!" Ex 4:25,26
the rod that * into a serpent. Ex 7:15
the rod, and the river * to blood. Ex 7:20
and they, too, * water into blood; Ex 7:22
And they * against Moses, Ex 14:11
Then the people * against Moses. Ex 15:24
Then he * to Aaron. Ex 32:21
the spot has not * white, the Lev 13:4
leprosy, for it has all * white; Lev 13:13
If the spot has indeed * Lev 13:16,17
at the spot has * white, then the Lev 13:20
Moses and Aaron * away and went Num 20:6
country, Israel * back and Num 20:21,22
They next * their attention to Num 21:33
the priest) has * away my anger, Num 25:10,11
"THEN WE * back across the Deu 2:1
"NEXT WE * toward King Og's land Deu 3:1
How quickly you * away from him! Deu 9:16
lest his heart be * away from the Deu 17:17
instead, he * the intended curse Deu 23:5
the city, so they * upon their Jos 8:20,21
Then they * back to Debir, Jos 10:38
then the border * east from the Jos 13:27,28
to Debir, where it * northwest Jos 15:7
Ephron before it * northward to Jos 15:9
From Janoah it * southward to Jos 16:7
There the border * south, Jos 18:14
and Rimmon and * toward Neah. Jos 19:13
Shihor-libnath, * east toward Jos 19:27
Then the boundary * toward Ramah Jos 19:29
How quickly they * away from the Ju 2:17
died, the people * from doing right Ju 2:19
sight, for they * against Jehovah Ju 3:7
people of Israel * once again to Ju 3:12
Then the Lord * to him and said, Ju 6:14
"Then all the trees finally * to Ju 9:14
Then Zebul * on him triumphantly. Ju 9:38
Then the people of Israel * away Ju 10:6
Finally the Israelis * to Ju 10:10
the wedding, he * off the path to Ju 14:8
for him to handle, he * back home. Ju 18:26
Baal-tamar, it * and attacked, and Ju 20:33
when the Lord has * his back on me Ru 1:21
And wherever he *, he was 1Sa 14:47
As Samuel * to go, Saul grabbed 1Sa 15:27
champion was dead, they * and ran. 1Sa 17:50,51
So Doeg * on them and killed them, 1Sa 22:18
gave him victories wherever he *. 2Sa 8:6
Then suddenly his love * to 2Sa 13:15
But suddenly the king * to Ittai, 2Sa 15:19,20
Then Absalom * to Ahithophel and 2Sa 16:20
victory was * into deep sadness. 2Sa 19:2
Judah and Benjamin * around and 2Sa 20:2
But the tables are *, and 1Ki 2:15
Then the king * around and faced 1Ki 8:14
and sure enough, they * his heart 1Ki 11:3
Then Elijah * to the prophets of 1Ki 18:25
And sure enough, as he * to go 1Ki 20:36
Then the prophet * to another man 1Ki 20:37
Then he * to Jehoshaphat and 1Ki 22:4
Then he * to the people 1Ki 22:28
they * back! 1Ki 22:32,33
his bald head. He * around and 2Ki 2:24
So the army of Israel * back in 2Ki 3:27
so he * around and returned home. 2Ki 15:19,20
Hezekiah * his face to the wall. 2Ki 20:2
same idols, and * his back on the 2Ki 21:22
who so completely * to the Lord and 2Ki 23:25
troops, who * and fled and were 1Ch 10:1
But as it * out, the Philistine 1Ch 12:19
and the Syrians * and fled. 1Ch 19:14
Ornan saw the angel as he *, and 1Ch 21:19,20
Then David * to Solomon and said: 1Ch 28:8
THEN KING DAVID * to the entire 1Ch 29:1
Then the king * around to the 2Ch 6:3
He now * his energies to 2Ch 8:2
So the king * down the people's 2Ch 10:15
they * around and deserted him. 2Ch 10:16
Lord's anger was * aside and he 2Ch 12:12
But whenever they have * again 2Ch 15:4
For the Ammonites and Moabites * 2Ch 20:23
job, they * against each other! 2Ch 20:23
Jehoram had * away from the Lord 2Ch 21:10
this * out to be a fatal mistake; 2Ch 22:7
because they had * away from the 2Ch 28:6
So the army officers * over the 2Ch 28:14
Temple and * their backs on it. 2Ch 29:6
* to God and came to Jerusalem. 2Ch 30:11
old scroll which * out to be the 2Ch 34:14
and silver items * over to Ez 1:11
relocated in Judah * from their Ez 6:21,22
our God will be * away from us." Ez 10:14
well, your people * to sin again, Neh 9:28
God * the curse into a blessing. Neh 13:2
The king * to his aides. Est 5:5
them, though it * out quite to the Est 9:1
their sorrow was * to gladness and Est 9:22
have sinned and * away from God Job 1:5
O God, you have * me to skin and Job 16:8
God has blocked my path and * my Job 19:8
Those I loved have * against me. Job 19:19
the wicked touch has * to gold! Job 21:16
I have not * aside. Job 23:11
These sons of theirs have also * Job 30:8
and gladness has * to mourning. Job 30:31
I have never * away even a stranger Job 31:32
For they * aside from following Job 34:27
You have * on my light! Ps 18:28
he has not * and walked away. Ps 22:24
Then, Lord, you * your face Ps 30:6,7
Then he * my sorrow into joy! Ps 30:11
Even my best friend has * against Ps 41:9
If we had * away from worshiping Ps 44:20
But all have * their backs on Ps 53:3
fully armed, * their backs and fled Ps 78:9
how earnestly they * around and Ps 78:34
Again and again they * away and Ps 78:41
— how he * their rivers into Ps 78:44
They * back from entering the Ps 78:57
At that point God * the Ps 105:25
the land, and * the nation's water Ps 105:29
I was headed, and * around and came Ps 119:59,60
No, I haven't * away from what Ps 119:102,103
come and find me for I have not * Ps 119:176
the Lord, and you * your back on Pro 1:30
For you * away from me—to death; Pro 1:32
JUST AS WATER is * into irrigation Pro 21:1
So I * in despair from hard work Ecc 2:20-23
The wise man is * into a fool by Ecc 7:7
upright, each has * away to follow Ecc 7:29
and tenderly have * against me. Is 1:2
Born to be bad, they have * their Is 1:4
Because you have * from the God Is 17:10
The strongest forts are * to Is 25:2
When Hezekiah heard this, he * Is 38:2
they will be * away. Is 42:17
grief. We * our backs on him and Is 53:3
In a moment of anger I * my face Is 54:8
day, no weapon * against you shall Is 54:17
Because of sin he has * his face Is 59:2
He has * away. Is 59:11
in Zion who have * away from sin. Is 59:20
Therefore you have * away from us Is 64:7
from us and * us over to our sins. Is 64:7
find in me that * them away and Jer 2:4,5
and corruption and * my inheritance Jer 2:7
their rulers * against me, and Jer 2:8
of Israel who have * their backs on Jer 3:21
For even your children have * Jer 5:7
they have * against me and gone Jer 5:23,24
own family, have * against you. Jer 12:6
But then they * away. Jer 13:11
You have forsaken me and * your Jer 15:6
For they have deserted me and * Jer 18:15
They have * away from the ancient Jer 18:15
For Israel has forsaken me and * Jer 19:4
who * away to the idols of Baal. Jer 23:27
No, they * from their wickedness Jer 26:19
Lord, my God. I * away from God Jer 31:19
They have * their backs upon me Jer 32:33
Then Jeremiah * to the Rechabites Jer 35:18,19
who seek his life, just as I * Jer 44:30
* them loose in the mountains. Jer 50:6
have * and conquered her. Lam 1:3
pitfall in my path and * me back. Lam 1:13
He has * against me. Lam 3:3
my strength has * to water, for Lam 3:18
our dance has * to death. Lam 5:15
for she has * away from my laws and Eze 5:5,6,7
were nations who * their backs to Eze 16:3f
vine that * toward the eagle and Eze 17:6
But then Oholah * to other gods Eze 23:4,5
bother her. She * to even greater Eze 23:19,20
from which you * away, disgusted. Eze 23:22
forgotten me and * your backs upon Eze 23:35
him, for he has * to the good and Eze 33:16
Therefore I * my face away from Eze 39:23
destroy them. I * my face away and Eze 39:24
we have * away from you and Dan 9:11
though she has * to other gods and Hos 3:1
deserted me and * to other gods. Hos 4:10
"The sun will be * into darkness Joe 2:31
Then the Lord * from this plan Amo 7:6
joy will be * to cries of despair. Amo 8:10
"When I had lost all hope, I * Jon 2:7
false gods have * their backs on Jon 2:8
But now the Lord of Hosts has * Nah 2:13
this message. They * stubbornly Zec 7:11
when they cried to me, I * away. Zec 7:13
* many from their lives of sin. Mal 2:6
* from sin by doing worthy deeds. Mt 3:8
Jesus * around and spoke to her. Mt 9:22
because they hadn't * to God. Mt 11:20
* to God from all their evil ways. Mt 12:41
Jesus * on Peter and said, "Get Mt 16:23
Then he * to James and John and Mt 20:22
have * it into a den of thieves." Mt 21:13
from him, so he * around in the Mk 5:30
Jesus * and looked at his Mk 8:33
Jesus watched him go, then * Mk 10:23
have * it into a den of robbers." Mk 11:17
show that they had * to God and Lk 3:3
Then he * to his disciples and Lk 6:20
Then he * to the woman and said Lk 7:44
But they were * away! Lk 9:53
But Jesus * and rebuked them, Lk 9:55
each other. He * now to his Lk 12:1
Then he * to the crowd and said, Lk 12:54
Then he * to them: "Which of you Lk 14:5
Then he * to his host. Lk 14:12
following him. He * around and Lk 14:25
your reach and you * it down," he Lk 19:42
but you have * it into a den of Lk 19:46
Now he * to the people again and Lk 20:9
listening, he * to his disciples Lk 20:45
So when you have repented and * Lk 22:32
At that moment Jesus * and looked Lk 22:61
Then Pilate * to the chief Lk 23:4
But Jesus * and said to them, Lk 23:28
Then John's two disciples * and Jn 1:37
he had * the water into wine. Jn 4:46,47
disciples * away and deserted him. Jn 6:66
Then Jesus * to the Twelve and Jn 6:67
Then the Pharisees * on the man Jn 9:17
So I * Jn 13:25
shall suddenly be * to wonderful Jn 16:20
Jesus said. She * toward him. Jn 20:16
Peter * around and saw the Jn 21:20
"Then God * away from them and Act 7:42
Lydda and Sharon * to the Lord when Act 9:35
the entire city * out to hear them Act 13:44
and Iconium and * the crowds into a Act 14:19
in great distress, * and spoke to Act 16:18
"Paul and Silas have * the rest Act 17:6
defense, Gallio * to his accusers Act 18:14
and * over to the Romans.' Act 21:11
even their women * against God's Rom 1:26
Every one has * away; Rom 3:12
Not all the Jews have * away from Rom 11:5
over it and * it down, think how Rom 11:12
When God * away from them it Rom 11:15
it meant that he * to the rest of Rom 11:15
but because the pain * you to God 2Co 7:9
us, and how you * away from your 1Th 1:9
them have already * away from the 1Ti 5:15
Some people have even * away from 1Ti 6:10
* against the Christian faith. 2Ti 3:8
been * away from the grace of God. Tit 1:11
have * their backs on the truth. Tit 1:14
and then have * against God. Heb 6:6
But we have never * our backs on Heb 10:39
and the grass * green and the Jas 5:18
Later, he * the cities of Sodom 2Pe 2:6
ago, for they have * against our Jud 1:4
and holy, but * to a life of sin. Jud 1:6
When I * to see who was speaking, Rev 1:12
and a third of the sea * red as Rev 8:8,9
and now they were * loose to kill a Rev 9:15
it has been * over to the nations. Rev 11:2

TURNING
Spirit of God." * to Joseph, Gen 41:39
quickly * away from the laws of Deu 9:12
It will also prevent him from * Deu 17:20
on your not * aside in any way from Deu 28:14
to Beth-shemesh. * northwest again, Jos 15:10,11
and Mount Baalah. * again to the Jos 15:10,11
God of Israel by * away from him Jos 22:16
Then, * to Jether, his oldest Ju 8:20
they had sinned by * away from him 1Sa 12:10
by * against us in the battle? 1Sa 29:4
Then, * to Shime-i, he vowed, 2Sa 19:23
* to Jehoshaphat, Ahab 1Ki 22:18
Then, * to those around them, 2Ch 18:27
of Amaziah's * away from God, and 2Ch 25:27
Gate, and at the * of the wall. 2Ch 26:9
by * back from following him. Ps 18:21
You have seen me tossing and * Ps 56:8
Why are you * your face from me, Ps 88:14
in shallow soil, * sere and yellow Ps 129:6,7
But if you keep on * your backs Is 1:20
The cart is * over! Is 46:1

(TURNING Con't)
the vines, and * all its beauty Jer 12:10
of * them back from their sins. Jer 23:14
name: Look, I am * them over to Jer 29:21
flew straight forward without *. Eze 1:9
going straight forward without *. Eze 1:12
* from our sins and doing right. Dan 9:13
Ephraim's hair is * gray, and he Hos 7:9
They are all murderers, * against Mic 7:1
And * to Joshua he said, "See, Zec 3:4
Jesus stood there amazed! * to Mt 8:10
Then, * to the paralyzed man, Mt 9:5,6
Then, * to the paralyzed man, Mk 2:9,10,11
Then * to his enemies he asked, Mk 3:4
hell without truly * to God! Lk 3:7
Then, * to the paralyzed man, Lk 5:23,24
Jesus was amazed. * to the crowd Lk 7:9
Then, * to the twelve disciples, Lk 10:23
Then * to his disciples he said, Lk 12:22
"Then * to the others standing Lk 19:24
the floor and * over their tables! Jn 2:15
* to Philip he asked, "Philip, Jn 6:2-5
by * you back from your sins." Act 3:26
then he knelt and prayed. * to Act 9:40
the privilege of * to him and Act 11:18
them with fasting, * them over to Act 14:23
necessity of * from sin to God Act 20:21
I am amazed that you are * away Gal 1:6
baptized we are * to God and asking 1Pe 3:21
lies about God, * against even 2Pe 2:1

TURNS
If it * out that you don't have a Gen 42:16
or if he * it into another man's Ex 22:5
If the hair in this spot * white, Lev 13:3
If the hair in the bright spot * Lev 13:25
taking * raping her until morning. Ju 19:25
If it * on me I catch it by the 1Sa 17:35
dish and * it upside down to dry. 2Ki 21:13
from the Armory, where the wall *. Neh 3:19
hours they took * confessing their Neh 9:3
God and * away from all evil. Job 2:3
he has eaten * sour within him. Job 20:14
For the water changes and * to Job 38:30
for help, the tide of battle *. Ps 56:9
You speak, and man * back to Ps 90:3
He dries up rivers, and * the Ps 107:34
Again, he * deserts into Ps 107:35
But he * topsy-turvy the plans of Ps 146:9
A SOFT ANSWER * away wrath, but Pro 15:1
He * them wherever he wants to. Pro 21:1
strong drink * bitter in the Is 24:9
man and * his heart away from God. Jer 17:5
its mind and * to evil and refuses Jer 18:10
when the Lord * against an entire Eze 5:15
But if a wicked person * away Eze 18:21
However, if a righteous person * Eze 18:24
When a good man * away from Eze 18:26
And if a wicked person * away Eze 18:27
will not save him if he * to sin; Eze 33:12
if he repents and * from his sins. Eze 33:12
die and then he * from his sins and Eze 33:14
good man * to evil, he shall die. Eze 33:18
But if the wicked * from his Eze 33:19
Prospering wherever he *, he will Dan 8:24
every thought; he * the morning to Amo 4:13
Orion, who * darkness into morning, Amo 5:8
and if it * out to be a godly Mt 10:13
day and each time * again and asks Lk 17:4
But whenever anyone * to the Lord 2Co 3:16

TURTLE-DOVE
ram, a * and a young pigeon, and Gen 15:9

TURTLE-DOVES
choose either * or young pigeons. Lev 1:14

TURTLEDOVE
pigeon or a * for a sin offering. Lev 12:6
Protect your * from the hawks. Ps 74:19
Literally, "The voice of the * is Sol 2:12f
*, and the crane, and the swallow. Jer 8:7

TURTLEDOVES
he shall bring two * or two young Lev 5:7
"If he is too poor to bring * or Lev 5:11
bring two * or two young pigeons. Lev 12:8
"He shall also bring two * or Lev 14:22
"Then he must offer the two * or Lev 14:30
he shall take two * or two young Lev 15:14
she shall take two * or two young Lev 15:29
he must bring two * or two young Num 6:10
a pair of * or two young pigeons" Lk 2:24

TUTOR
(the son of Hachmoni) was their *. 1Ch 27:32

TWELFTH
On the * day came Ahira, son of Num 7:78-83
became the new king during the * 2Ki 8:24,25
over Judah had begun in the * 2Ki 9:29
*, the group led by Jakim; 1Ch 24:7-18
*, Hashabiah and twelve of his 1Ch 25:9-31
The commander of the * Division 1Ch 27:15
during the * month of each year. 1Ch 27:15
Or, "the * day of the first Ez 8:31f
This was done in April of the * Est 3:7
IN MID-FEBRUARY OF the * year of Eze 32:1
Literally, "In the * year, on the Eze 32:17f
Some manuscripts read, "In the * Eze 33:21f
The * with amethyst. Rev 21:18,19,20

TWELVE
Salt Sea). For * years they had Gen 14:4
a great nation. * princes shall be Gen 17:20
These * sons of his became the Gen 25:16
of * tribes that bore their names. Gen 25:16
Here are the names of the * sons Gen 35:22
"Sir," they said, "there are * Gen 42:13
We are * brothers, sons of one Gen 42:32
father blessed his * sons with. Gen 49:28
* springs and seventy palm trees; Ex 15:27
the mountain, with * pillars around Ex 24:4
there were * tribes of Israel. Ex 24:4
names of the * tribes of Israel. Ex 39:14
Priest shall place * loaves of Lev 24:5-8
and sent these * tribal leaders: Num 13:3-15
and each of the * chiefs (including Num 17:6
shall sacrifice * young bulls, two Num 29:17
where there are * springs of water Num 33:9
* spies, one from each tribe. Deu 1:23
"Now select * men, one from each Jos 3:12
"Tell the * men chosen for a Jos 4:2,3
So Joshua summoned the * men, Jos 4:4
on your shoulder—* stones in all, Jos 4:5
all, one for each of the * tribes. Jos 4:5
They took * stones from the Jos 4:8
monument of * stones in the middle Jos 4:9
and there the * stones from the Jos 4:20
population of Ai, * thousand in Jos 8:25
Altogether there were * of these Jos 19:15,16
The Merari division received * Jos 21:7
Levites was given * cities in all. Jos 21:40
cut her body into * parts and sent Ju 19:29
So I cut her body into * pieces Ju 20:6
So they sent * thousand of their Ju 21:10,11,12
Joab agreed, so * men were chosen 2Sa 2:15
SAID, "give me * thousand men to 2Sa 17:1
weighed more than * pounds and who 2Sa 21:16
There were also * officials of 1Ki 4:7
The names of these * officers 1Ki 4:8-19
employed * thousand charioteers. 1Ki 4:26
The foundation stones were * to 1Ki 7:10
It rested on * bronze 1Ki 7:25
had a * thousand gallon capacity. 1Ki 7:26
One large tank and * oxen 1Ki 7:41-46
two lions on each step—* in all. 1Ki 10:20
his new robe into * parts, and 1Ki 11:30
Of the * tribes, Judah and 1Ki 11:32f
* years, six of them in Tirzah. 1Ki 16:23
He took * stones, one to 1Ki 18:31
and he reigned * years. 2Ki 3:1
received by lot * cities from the 1Ch 6:63
The second, Gedaliah, along with * 1Ch 25:9-31
The third, Zaccur and * of his 1Ch 25:9-31
The fourth, Izri and * of his sons 1Ch 25:9-31
Fifth, Nethaniah and * of his sons 1Ch 25:9-31
Sixth, Bukkiah and * of his sons 1Ch 25:9-31
Seventh, Jesharelah and * of his 1Ch 25:9-31
Eighth, Jeshaiah and * of his 1Ch 25:9-31
Ninth, Mattaniah and * of his sons 1Ch 25:9-31
Tenth, Shime-i and * of his sons 1Ch 25:9-31
Eleventh, Azarel and * of his sons 1Ch 25:9-31
Twelfth, Hashabiah and * of his 1Ch 25:9-31
Thirteenth, Shuba-el and * of his 1Ch 25:9-31
Fourteenth, Mattithiah and * of 1Ch 25:9-31
Fifteenth, Jeremoth and * of his 1Ch 25:9-31
Sixteenth, Hananiah and * of his 1Ch 25:9-31
Seventeenth, Joshbekasha and * of 1Ch 25:9-31
Eighteenth, Hanani and * of his 1Ch 25:9-31
Nineteenth, Mallothi and * of his 1Ch 25:9-31
Twentieth, Eliathah and * of his 1Ch 25:9-31
Twenty-first, Hothir and * of his 1Ch 25:9-31
Twenty-second, Giddalti and * of 1Ch 25:9-31
Twenty-third, Mahazi-oth and * of 1Ch 25:9-31
Twenty-fourth, Romamti-ezer and * 1Ch 25:9-31
was divided into * regiments, each 1Ch 27:1
commanders of the * army divisions, 1Ch 28:1
There were * of these oxen 2Ch 4:4
The huge tank and the * oxen under 2Ch 4:12-16
reign, with * hundred chariots, 2Ch 12:3
MANASSEH WAS ONLY * years old 2Ch 33:1
sacrificed; and * male goats were Ez 6:17
for the * tribes of Israel. Ez 6:17
I appointed * leaders of the Ez 8:24
* oxen for the nation of Israel; Ez 8:35
seventy-seven lambs; and * goats Ez 8:35
for the entire * years that I was Neh 5:14
laver and * bulls was tremendous. Jer 52:20
the land to the * tribes of Israel: Eze 47:13
Nebuchadnezzar. * months after Dan 4:29
had been sick for * years with Mt 9:20
JESUS CALLED HIS * disciples to Mt 10:1
Here are the names of his * Mt 10:2,3,4
to his * disciples, he went off Mt 11:1
there were * basketfuls left over! Mt 14:20
certainly sit on * thrones judging Mt 19:28
judging the * tribes of Israel. Mt 19:28
he took the * disciples aside, and Mt 20:17
Then Judas Iscariot, one of the * Mt 26:14
eating with the *, he said, "One Mt 26:20,
Judas, one of the *, arrived with a Mt 26:
Then he selected * of them to be Mk 3:14,
These are the names of the * he Mk 3:16-
was alone with the * and with his Mk 4:
for * years with a hemorrhage. Mk 5:
(She was * years old. Mk 5:41,
And he called his * disciples Mk
and afterwards * basketfuls of Mk 6:43,
"*," they said. Mk 8:
to Bethany with the * disciples. Mk 11:
He replied, "It is one of you * Mk 14:
When Jesus was * years old he Lk 2:41,
and chose * of them to be the inner Lk 6:
and took his * disciples with him. Lk 8
dying, a little girl * years old. Lk 8:
bleeding for * years, and could Lk 8:43,
together his * apostles and gave Lk 9
Late in the afternoon all * of Lk 9:
still, * basketfuls of scraps Lk 9:
Then, turning to the * disciples, Lk 10:
Gathering the * around him he Lk 18:
who was one of the * disciples, Lk 22
judging the * tribes of Israel. Lk 22:
by Judas, one of his * disciples. Lk 22:
And * baskets were filled with Jn 6:
Then Jesus turned to the * and Jn 6:
Then Jesus said, "I chose the * Jn 6:
of the *, who would betray him. Jn 6:
Jesus replied, "There are * Jn 11
So the * called a meeting of all Act 6
* patriarchs of the Jewish nation. Act 7
The men involved were about * in Act 19
was no more than * days ago that I Act 24:
ancestors. The * tribes of Israel Act 26
later by the rest of "the *." 1Co 15
The name given to Jesus' * 1Co 15:
out of all * tribes of Israel, as Rev 7:4-
a crown of * stars on her head. Rev 12
* gates guarded by twelve angels. Rev 21:
twelve gates guarded by * angels. Rev 21:1
And the names of the * tribes of Rev 21:1
The walls had * foundation Rev 21:1
of the * apostles of the Lamb. Rev 21:1
and was built on * layers of Rev 21:18,19,2
The * gates were made of pearls Rev 21:2
of Life, bearing * crops of Rev 22:

TWENTIETH
All who have reached their * Ex 30:1
on the * day of the second month Num 10:1
Jerusalem, in the * year of the 1Ki 15:
*, the group led by Jehezkel; 1Ch 24:7-1
*, Eliathah and twelve of his sons 1Ch 25:9-3
Literally, "the * day of the Ez 10:9
In December of the * year of the Neh 1:
of Judah—from the * until the Neh 5:1

TWENTY
there are only *?" Gen 18:3
it for the sake of the *." Gen 18:3
whose it is! * years I've been Gen 31:3
Yes, * years—fourteen of them Gen 31:4
him to them for * pieces of silver, Gen 37:2
have as his tax * percent of all Gen 47:2
upright piece. * of these frames Ex 26:18,1
there will also be * of these Ex 26:2
and be held up by * posts, fitting Ex 27:9,1
into * bronze post holders. Ex 27:9,1
held up by * posts fitted into Ex 27:1
[the shekel is * gerahs], half a Ex 30:13
There were * frames on the south Ex 36:2
There were also * frames on the Ex 36:25,2
There were * posts to hold Ex 38:1
feet long, with * bronze posts and Ex 38:1
census who were * years old or Ex 38:25,2
by paying for the loss, plus a * Lev 5:1
he took, adding a * percent fine, Lev 6:4,
has used, with * per cent added; Lev 22:14
from the age of * to sixty shall Lev 27:3
a woman from the age of * to Lev 27:4
a boy from five to * shall pay Lev 27:5
then he shall pay * percent more Lev 27:13
that amount plus * percent, and the Lev 27:14,15
he shall pay * percent in addition Lev 27:19
* gerahs shall be the shekel." Lev 27:25
of its worth, plus * percent; Lev 27:27
"Take a census of all the men * Num 1:2-15
of Israel who were * years old or Num 1:17,18,19
(The shekel is * gerahs. Num 3:47,48f
adding * percent and returning it Num 5:7
or two, or five or ten or even *! Num 11:19,20
Not a single one of you * years Num 14:29
of Israel who are * years old or Num 26:2
had been under * years of age, and Num 26:64,65f
than * years of age were now dead. Num 26:64,65f
Egypt, no one over * years of age Num 32:10,11
for the Israelis for * years. Ju 4:2,3
for one hundred * thousand had Ju 8:10
Minnith, including * cities, and as Ju 11:33
judge for the next * years, but the Ju 15:20
He had judged Israel for * years. Ju 16:31
The Ark remained there for * 1Sa 7:2

WENTY Con't)
and left, about * men in all, and 1Sa 14:14
and Benjamin. * men accompanied 2Sa 3:20
cavalry and * thousand infantry; 2Sa 8:4
Ziba, who had fifteen sons and * 2Sa 9:10,11
so they hired * thousand Syrian 2Sa 10:6
There was a great slaughter and * 2Sa 18:7
fifteen sons and * servants; 2Sa 19:17
task in nine months and * days. 2Sa 24:8
At the end of the * years during 1Ki 9:10
palace, he gave * cities in the 1Ki 9:11,12
and * individual loaves of barley 2Ki 4:42
cavalry, and * thousand troops. 1Ch 18:4
of Levi who were * years old or 1Ch 23:24
IT WAS NOW * years since Solomon 2Ch 8:1
of 300,000 men * years old and 2Ch 25:5,6
AHAZ WAS * years old when he 2Ch 28:1
and the Levites * years old and 2Ch 31:17,18
The Levites who were * years old Ez 3:8
with * of his sons and brothers; Ez 8:19
$3,000,000 in gold; and * gold Ez 8:26,27
Making a total of * children, Job 42:13,14f
it must always be exchanged for * Eze 45:12
The Assyrian invasion came about * Hos 4:19f
olive press, there were only *. Hag 2:16,17
perhaps * to thirty gallons each. Jn 2:6

WENTY-BUSHEL
Before, when you expected a * Hag 2:16,17

WENTY-DOLLAR
handed the innkeeper two * bills Lk 10:35

WENTY-EIGHT
Israel, in Samaria, for * years. 2Ki 10:36
* sons and sixty daughters). 2Ch 11:21

WENTY-FIFTH
no work on the * day of September Lev 16:29,30
Or, "* day of the month Elul." Neh 6:15f
EARLY IN APRIL of the * year of Eze 40:1

WENTY-FIRST
evening of the * day of the month. Ex 12:18
*, the group led by Jachin; 1Ch 24:7-18
*, Hothir and twelve of his sons 1Ch 25:9-31

TWENTY-FIVE
to sixty shall pay * dollars; Lev 27:3
for sowing is valued at * dollars. Lev 27:16
at the age of *, and are to retire Num 8:23,24
also inherited * other cities with Jos 15:37-44
So the tribe of Benjamin lost * Ju 20:46,47
reigned in Jerusalem for * years. 1Ki 22:42
Amaziah was * years old at the 2Ki 14:2
and reigned * years, in Jerusalem. 2Ch 20:31
AMAZIAH WAS * years old when he 2Ch 25:1
JOTHAM WAS * years old at the time 2Ch 27:1
In summary, then, he was * years 2Ch 27:8
HEZEKIAH WAS * years old when he 2Ch 29:1
Jehoiakim was * years old when 2Ch 36:5
altar, were about * men standing Eze 8:16
where I saw * of the most prominent Eze 11:1
conquest of Israel * years later. Hos 1:4,5f
C., and * years later had mastered Hab 1:6f

TWENTY-FIVE-POUND
tipped with a * iron spearhead, and 1Sa 17:4-7

TWENTY-FOUR
stayed there for almost * hours! Jos 10:13
Baasha reigned for * years, but 1Ki 15:32,33
"* thousand of them will 1Ch 23:4,5
his throne. * smaller thrones Rev 4:4
with * Elders sitting on them; Rev 4:4
and ever, the * Elders fell down Rev 4:10
But one of the * Elders said to Rev 5:5
there before the * Elders, in front Rev 5:6
And as he took the scroll, the * Rev 5:8
And the * Elders fell down and Rev 5:14
Then one of the * Elders asked Rev 7:13
And the * Elders sitting on their Rev 11:16
Living Beings and the * Elders; Rev 14:3
Then the * Elders and four Living Rev 19:4

TWENTY-FOURTH
*, the group led by Maaziah. 1Ch 24:7-18
*, Romamti-ezer and twelve of his 1Ch 25:9-31
Literally, "the * day" of the Neh 9:1f

TWENTY-NINE
* days after that, Gen 8:13
Nahor was * years old at the Gen 11:24,25
In all, there were * of these Jos 15:21-32
reigned in Jerusalem for * years. 2Ki 14:2
he reigned * years, in Jerusalem. 2Ch 25:1
he reigned * years, in Jerusalem. 2Ch 29:1

TWENTY-ONE
Zedekiah was * years old when he 2Ch 36:11
ZEDEKIAH WAS * years old when he Jer 52:1
The base is * inches high, with a Eze 43:13
and it extends * inches beyond the Eze 43:13
This platform is * inches Eze 43:14
narrower platform, * inches Eze 43:14
* inches up from the corners. Eze 43:15
of the altar is * feet square. Eze 43:16
the top * inches on all sides. Eze 43:17
and ram; and * gallons of olive Eze 45:24
But for * days the mighty Evil Dan 10:13

TWENTY-SECOND
*, the group led by Gamul; 1Ch 24:7-18
*, Giddalti and twelve of his sons 1Ch 25:9-31

TWENTY-SEVEN
pillars, each * feet high and 1Ki 7:15
The wheels were * inches high, 1Ki 7:32
Each pillar was * feet high, 2Ki 25:17
of that area. * hundred 1Ch 26:31,32
For the pillars were each * Jer 52:21

TWENTY-SEVENTH
(This occurred during the * year 1Ki 16:10
from prison on the * day of the 2Ki 25:27
In the * year of King Eze 29:17

TWENTY-SIX
These * Jos 18:21-28
Instead, * thousand of them Ju 20:14,15
General Hananiah. * hundred brave 2Ch 26:12

TWENTY-SIX-OUNCE
* gold nails were used. 2Ch 3:9

TWENTY-SIXTH
during the * year of the reign of 1Ki 16:8

TWENTY-THIRD
But in the * year of his reign 2Ki 12:6
Israel during the * year of the 2Ki 13:1
*, the group led by Delaiah; 1Ch 24:7-18
*, Mahazi-oth and twelve of his 1Ch 25:9-31

TWENTY-THREE
He was Israel's judge for * Ju 10:2
* cities in the land of Gilead. 1Ch 2:22
He was * years old when he began 2Ch 36:2
For the past * years, Jeremiah Jer 25:2,3
The other replied, "* hundred Dan 8:14
Literally, "* hundred mornings Dan 8:14f
heard about the * hundred days to Dan 8:26

TWENTY-TWO
heaven, standing * feet and more Gen 7:20
overall total of * cities and their Jos 19:30,31
So * thousand of them left, and Ju 7:3
who judged Israel for * years. Ju 10:3
* thousand Israelis that day. Ju 20:21
He also slaughtered * thousand 2Sa 8:5
Jeroboam reigned * years, and 1Ki 14:20
and Ahab reigned for * years. 1Ki 16:29
Ahaziah was * years old when he 2Ki 8:26
(He and * members of his family 1Ch 12:24-37
David killed * thousand of them; 1Ch 18:5
had * sons and sixteen daughters. 2Ch 13:21
Ahaziah was * years old 2Ch 22:2
Amon was * years old when he 2Ch 33:20,21

TWENTY-YEAR-OLDS
didn't include the *, or those 1Ch 27:23

TWICE
Tell them to gather * as much as Ex 16:5
On the sixth day they gathered * Ex 16:22
I am giving them * as much on the Ex 16:28,29
the rock *, and water gushed out; Num 20:11
Moses struck it, not once, but *. Num 20:12f
trees, don't go over the boughs *; Deu 24:20
For forty days, * a day, morning 1Sa 17:16
appeared to him * to warn him 1Ki 11:9,10
"Please grant me * as much 2Ki 2:9
warriors against * as many Israeli 2Ch 13:3
Your army is * as large as mine, 2Ch 13:8
Jerusalem once or *, but I spoke Neh 13:20
In fact, the Lord gave him * as Job 42:10
* as many as he had before. Job 42:13,14f
Two can accomplish more than * as Ecc 4:9
a thousand years * over, but Ecc 6:6
Lord will give her * as many Is 40:2
and brandish it *, thrice, to Eze 21:14
and bring your tithes * a week! Amo 4:4
This has already happened *: Two Zec 13:8f
then turn him into * the son of Mt 23:15
*, you will deny me three times." Mk 14:72
I go without food * a week, and I Lk 18:12
in Thessalonica you sent help *. Php 4:16
for others—give * as much to her. Rev 18:6

TWIG
and most tender * from the top of Eze 17:22,23

TWIGS
city munching on * and branches. Is 27:10
The birds will pluck off her * Eze 31:13

TWILIGHT
waiting for the * 'when no one will Job 24:14,15
sense, walking at * down the Pro 7:8,9

TWIN
Then the other * was born with Gen 25:26
arrived and she had * sons. Gen 38:27
became the parents of * sons, 1Ch 2:4
Your breasts are like * fawns of Sol 4:5
Thomas, nicknamed "The *," said Jn 11:16
Thomas, "The *," was not there at Jn 20:24
Thomas, "The *," Nathanael from Jn 21:2
time it was in The * Brothers of Act 28:11
about to bear him * children, God Rom 9:10-13
a servant to Jacob, his * brother. Rom 9:10-13

TWINED
two strands of * gold attached to Ex 39:15-18

TWINKLING
sun and moon, and all you * stars. Ps 148:3
a moment, in the * of an eye, when 1Co 15:52

TWINS
And sure enough, she had *. Gen 25:24
years old when the * were born. Gen 25:26
are like two fawns, yes, lovely *. Sol 7:3
Literally, "* of a gazelle." Sol 7:3f

TWIST
Never * justice to benefit a Deu 16:19
Does God * justice? Job 8:3
are going to * the truth for him? Job 13:8
to accept a bribe to * justice. Pro 17:23
by those who * and change the truth Gal 1:7

TWISTED
Two chains of pure, * gold shall Ex 28:13,14
means of two * cords of pure gold. Ex 28:22,23,24
They are a stubborn, * generation. Deu 32:5
the people have * the laws of God Is 24:4,5
your teachers have * them up to Jer 8:8
afraid and look on with * faces. Eze 27:35
Justice is * between them. Mic 7:3
minds, warped and *, and have 2Ti 3:8
have * his letters around to mean 2Pe 3:15,16

TWISTING
excuse for * justice against him. Ex 23:6
They are always * what I say. Ps 56:5
* back and forth, getting nowhere. Ecc 1:3-7
You are * my words and inventing Jer 23:36

TWO
For God made * huge lights, the Gen 1:16
way that the * become one person. Gen 2:24
Lamech married * wives—Adah and Gen 4:19
was 600 years, * months, and Gen 7:10,11,12
of every sort. * by two they came, Gen 7:16
Two by * they came, male and Gen 7:16
outside and told his * brothers. Gen 9:22
* sons were born to Eber: Gen 10:25
Arpachshad, born * years after the Gen 11:10,11
So the other * went on toward Gen 18:22,23
THAT EVENING THE * angels came to Gen 19:1
Look—I have * virgin daughters, Gen 19:8
But the * men reached out and Gen 19:10
your wife and your * daughters who Gen 19:15
of his wife and * daughters and Gen 19:16
mountains with his * daughters. Gen 19:30
his son Isaac and * young men who Gen 22:3
So the * of them went on Gen 22:6
and * five-ounce golden bracelets Gen 24:22
Jokshan's * sons were Sheba and Gen 25:3
womb shall become * rival nations. Gen 25:23
and bring me * young goats, and Gen 27:8,9,10
family and married * additional Gen 28:9
Now Laban had * daughters, Gen 29:16
then searched the * tents of the Gen 31:33
them earning your * daughters, and Gen 31:41
Literally, "* encampments." Gen 32:1f
herds and camels, into * groups; Gen 32:7
And now I am * armies! Gen 32:10
his * wives and his two Gen 32:22,23,24
his two wives and his * Gen 32:22,23,24
a column, with his * concubines and Gen 33:2
move they made, * of Dinah's Gen 34:25
just as he had his * brothers. Gen 38:11
ONE NIGHT * years later, Pharaoh Gen 41:1
the famine years, * sons were born Gen 41:50
father, "Kill my * sons if I don't Gen 42:37
that my wife had * sons, and that Gen 44:27
These * years of famine will Gen 45:6
With Joseph's * sons included, Gen 46:27
So, taking with him his * sons, Gen 48:1
And now, as to these * sons of Gen 48:5
Rachel died after only * children Gen 48:7
Israel looked over at the * boys. Gen 48:8
"Simeon and Levi are * of a Gen 49:5
again, he saw * of them fighting. Ex 2:13
Moses' father-in-law goes under * Ex 3:1f
you after these * signs, then take Ex 4:9
be placed on the * side-frames of Ex 12:7
and against the * side panels, so Ex 12:22
* side pieces, he will pass over Ex 12:23
there will be enough for * days? Ex 16:28,29
along with Moses' * sons, Gershom Ex 18:3
your wife and your * sons." Ex 18:5,6
and under each of them will be * Ex 18:21
God's appearance * days from now, Ex 19:15
"If * men are fighting, and one Ex 21:18
"If * men are fighting, and in Ex 21:22
it dies, then the * owners shall Ex 21:35
corners, * rings on each side. Ex 25:12
the * ends of the lid of the Ark. Ex 25:18
* long pieces, one for each side. Ex 26:3
to join these * long pieces Ex 26:4,5
of each of these * wide pieces, to Ex 26:10,11
Thus the * widths become one. Ex 26:10,11
frames to fit into—* bases under Ex 26:18,19
silver bases, * bases for each Ex 26:21
and * frames at each corner. Ex 26:23
frames—* bases under each frame. Ex 26:25
It will consist of * pieces, Ex 28:7
Take * onyx stones, and engrave Ex 28:9
Fasten the * stones upon the Ex 28:12
reminder. * chains of pure, Ex 28:13,14
This chestpiece is to be of * Ex 28:16
of * twisted cords of pure gold. Ex 28:22,23,24
The other ends of the * cords Ex 28:25

(TWO Con't)
front edges of the * settings of Ex 28:25
Then make * more golden rings Ex 28:26
place them on the * lower, inside Ex 28:26
also make * other golden rings Ex 28:27
Possibly they were * stones that Ex 28:30,31f
a young bull and * rams with no Ex 29:1
the young bull and the * rams. Ex 29:3,4
gall bladder and * kidneys, and the Ex 29:13
bladder and the * kidneys and the Ex 29:22
"Each day offer * yearling lambs Ex 29:38
on each of * sides, construct two Ex 30:4
sides, construct * gold rings to Ex 30:4
he gave him the * tablets of stone Ex 31:18
on both sides of * stone tablets. Ex 32:15
THE LORD TOLD Moses, "Prepare * Ex 34:1
So Moses took * tablets of stone Ex 34:4
the * stone tablets in his hands. Ex 34:4
forming * long roof-sheets. Ex 36:10
the edges of these * long sheets, Ex 36:11,12
thus tying the * long sheets Ex 36:13
Each frame had * clasps joining Ex 36:22
connected to its base by * clasps. Ex 36:24
silver bases, * for each frame. Ex 36:25,26
beneath them, * for each frame. Ex 36:30
four feet, * rings at each end. Ex 37:3
He made * cherubim of beaten Ex 37:7
at the * ends of the golden lid. Ex 37:7
around the edge. * gold rings were Ex 37:27
The [* Ex 39:6,7
onyx stones, attached to the [* Ex 39:6,7
these gold rings, * strands of Ex 39:15-18
the chestpiece. * gold rings were Ex 39:19
to the ephod. * other gold rings Ex 39:20
inward parts, the * kidneys and the Lev 3:3,4,5
organs, the * kidneys with the Lev 3:9,10,11
the insides, the * kidneys and the Lev 3:15,16
the entrails, the * kidneys and Lev 4:9
he shall bring * turtledoves or two Lev 5:7
two turtledoves or * young pigeons Lev 5:7
the insides, the * kidneys and the Lev 7:4
sin offering, the * rams, and the Lev 8:1
the liver, and the * kidneys and Lev 8:15,16
gall bladder, the * kidneys with Lev 8:25
shall last * weeks, during which Lev 12:5
she must bring * turtledoves or two Lev 12:8
turtledoves or * young pigeons. Lev 12:8
he shall require * living birds of Lev 14:4
day, he shall take * male lambs Lev 14:10
he cannot afford * lambs, then he Lev 14:21
"He shall also bring * Lev 14:22
two turtledoves or * young Lev 14:22
"Then he must offer the * Lev 14:30
two turtledoves or * young pigeons Lev 14:30
cleansing, using * birds, cedar Lev 14:49
day he shall take * turtledoves or Lev 15:14
two turtledoves or * young pigeons Lev 15:14
she shall take * turtledoves or two Lev 15:29
two turtledoves or * young pigeons Lev 15:29
AFTER AARON'S * sons died before Lev 16:1
then bring him * male goats for Lev 16:5
Then he shall bring the * goats Lev 16:7
You shall not marry * sisters, Lev 18:18
don't sow your field with * kinds Lev 19:19
This shall consist of * loaves Lev 23:17
one young bull, and * rams. Lev 23:18
sin offering, and * male yearling Lev 23:19
loaves of bread in * rows upon the Lev 24:5-8
paid for him * and a half dollars; Lev 27:6
The responsibility of these * Num 3:25-30
The responsibility of these * Num 3:36,37
day, he must bring * turtledoves or Num 6:10
two turtledoves or * young pigeons Num 6:10
each drawn by * oxen—a wagon for Num 7:3
* leaders and an ox for each one; Num 7:3
to the Levites. * wagons and four Num 7:7
platter weighing * pounds and a Num 7:13
and for the peace offerings * Num 7:17
(each weighing about * pounds); Num 7:84,85,86
the spot between the * cherubim. Num 7:89
the Tabernacle * days, a month, or Num 9:22
to Moses, "Make * trumpets of Num 10:1
*, or five or ten or even twenty! Num 11:19,20
But * of the seventy—Eldad and Num 11:26
large that it took * of them to Num 13:23
people of Israel; * of the spies, Num 14:6
against Moses. * hundred and fifty Num 16:2
be a payment of * and a half Num 18:16
of Israel, for the * of you Num 20:24
As Balaam and * servants were Num 22:22,23
went between * vineyard walls. Num 22:24
This Dathan and Abiram were the * Num 26:5-11
without defect. * of them shall be Num 28:3
"On the Sabbath day, sacrifice * Num 28:9,10
to the Lord of * young bulls, one Num 28:11
to the Lord * young bulls, one ram, Num 28:19
It shall consist of * young Num 28:27
young bulls, * rams, and fourteen Num 29:13
six quarts for each of the * Num 29:14
young bulls, * rams, and fourteen Num 29:17
young bulls, * rams, fourteen male Num 29:20

ten young bulls, * rams, and Num 29:23
nine young bulls, * rams, and Num 29:26,27
eight young bulls, * rams, and Num 29:29
seven young bulls, * rams, and Num 29:32
then divide it into * parts. Num 31:27
Also levy a * percent tribute of Num 31:30
* percent of these to the Levites. Num 31:47
the land of the * kings of the Deu 3:8
God has done to those * kings. Deu 3:21
wrote them on * stone tablets. Deu 4:13
Bashan—they were * Amorite kings Deu 4:47
and he wrote them out on * stone Deu 5:22
in my hands the * tablets inscribed Deu 9:15
told me to cut * more stone tablets Deu 10:1
wood and hewed out * stone tablets Deu 10:3
like the first *, and took the Deu 10:3
there must be at least * or Deu 17:6
There must be at least *, and Deu 19:15
"If a man has * wives but loves Deu 21:15
woven from * kinds of thread: for Deu 22:11
"If * men are fighting and the Deu 25:11
And * put ten thousand to flight, Deu 32:30
THEN JOSHUA SENT * spies from the Jos 2:1
of Jericho that * Israelis who were Jos 2:2
Sihon and Og, the * Amorite kings Jos 2:10
Then the * spies came down from Jos 2:23
Then Joshua said to the * spies, Jos 6:22
take more than * or three thousand Jos 7:3
them—divided into * groups, half of Jos 8:33
you did to the * kings of the Jos 9:10
given land to the * and a half Jos 14:3,4
The tribe of Joseph had become * Jos 14:3,4
Then the * tribes of Joseph came Jos 17:14
Levites, received * cities and Jos 21:27
to drive out the * kings of the Jos 24:12
Trees," and the * tribes lived Ju 1:16
Each man receives a girl or *; Ju 5:30
"Divide them into * groups decided Ju 7:5,6
Then the other * hundred of his Ju 7:19,20
Oreb and Zeeb, the * generals of Ju 7:25
raids. The * kings fled, but Ju 8:12
while his other * groups cut them Ju 9:44
girl friends for * months, weeping Ju 11:37
with her friends for * months. Ju 11:38
So they tied him with * new ropes Ju 15:12,13
them, with the * gateposts, right Ju 16:3
the * pillars supporting the roof. Ju 16:25,26
my hands against the * pillars. Ju 16:25,26
and * thousand more near Gidom. Ju 20:45
his * sons, Mahlon and Chilion. Ru 1:1
Naomi was left with her * sons. Ru 1:3
and said to her * daughters-in-law, Ru 1:8
He had * wives, Hannah and 1Sa 1:2
* sons of Eli—Hophni and Phinehas. 1Sa 1:3
Hannah three sons and * daughters. 1Sa 2:21
Little Samuel was growing in * 1Sa 2:26
I will cause your * sons, Hophni 1Sa 2:34
and hitch to it * cows that have 1Sa 6:7
were carried out. * fresh cows were 1Sa 6:10
me, you will see * men beside 1Sa 10:2
you and offer you * of the loaves, 1Sa 10:4
He took * oxen and cut them into 1Sa 11:7
no * of them were left together. 1Sa 11:11
and * years over Israel." 1Sa 13:1f
troops and took * thousand of them 1Sa 13:2
pass between * rocky crags which 1Sa 14:4
and * daughters, Merab and Michal. 1Sa 14:49
There were * hundred thousand 1Sa 15:4
and took a step or * to see what it 1Sa 17:38,39
out and killed * hundred 1Sa 18:27
So the * of them renewed their 1Sa 23:18
off with David and * hundred 1Sa 25:13
Then Abigail hurriedly took * 1Sa 25:18
loaves of bread, * barrels of wine, 1Sa 25:18
dressed sheep, * bushels of roasted 1Sa 25:18
raisin cakes, and * hundred fig 1Sa 25:18
He had his * wives with 1Sa 27:2,3
accompanied by * of his men. 1Sa 28:7,8
(David's * wives, Ahino-am and 1Sa 30:5
When they reached Besor Brook, * 1Sa 30:9,10
of a fig cake, * clusters of 1Sa 30:11,12
and David rescued his * wives. 1Sa 30:18,19
Brook and the * hundred men who had 1Sa 30:21
He reigned in Mahanaim for * 2Sa 2:10,11
The * armies then began to fight 2Sa 2:17
with these * sons of Zeruiah. 2Sa 3:39
then fell to * brothers, Baanah and 2Sa 4:2,3
have to fight on * fronts, he 2Sa 10:9
"There were * men in a certain 2Sa 12:1
Then, * years later, when 2Sa 13:21-24
replied, "and my * sons had a 2Sa 14:5,6
in Jerusalem for * years and had 2Sa 14:28
He took * hundred men from 2Sa 15:11
He was leading * donkeys loaded 2Sa 16:1
loaded with * hundred loaves of 2Sa 16:1
Then the * men crawled out of 2Sa 17:21
But he gave them the * sons of 2Sa 21:8
Then Rizpah, the mother of * of 2Sa 21:10
Was the sea split in *. 2Sa 22:16
Benaiah killed * giants, 2Sa 23:20
You know that Joab murdered my * 1Ki 2:5

of * men who were better than he. 1Ki 2:
But three years later * of 1Ki 2:
Soon afterwards * young 1Ki 3:
house, just the * of us, and 1Ki 3:17,
living child in * and give half to 1Ki 3:2
in Lebanon and * months at home. 1Ki 5:
Solomon placed * statues of angels 1Ki 6:23-2
Literally, "he made * cherubim." 1Ki 6:23-2
to wing tip. The * angels were 1Ki 6:23-2
opening, and its * olive-wood 1Ki 6:3
There were * folding doors of 1Ki 6:3
He cast * hollow bronze pillars, 1Ki 7:1
pillars he made * lily-shaped 1Ki 7:16-2
hundred pomegranates in * rows. 1Ki 7:16-2
of the rim were * rows of ornaments 1Ki 7:2
of ornaments an inch or * apart, 1Ki 7:2
* pillars; 1Ki 7:41-4
Four hundred pomegranates in * 1Ki 7:41-4
cover the bases of the * capitals; 1Ki 7:41-4
time except the * stone tablets 1Ki 8:
gold beaten into * hundred pieces 1Ki 10:16,1
And there were * lions on each 1Ki 10:2
And as the * of them were alone 1Ki 11:2
the king had * gold calf-idols made 1Ki 12:2
He reigned * years, beginning in 1Ki 15:2
but he reigned only * years. 1Ki 16:
kingdom of Israel was split in *; 1Ki 16:2
hundred of them in * caves—fifty in 1Ki 18:3,
hundred of them in * caves and fed 1Ki 18:1
to waver between * opinions?" 1Ki 18:2
Now bring * young bulls. 1Ki 18:2
contain * measures of seed." 1Ki 18:32
army looked like * little flocks of 1Ki 20:2
The * armies camped opposite each 1Ki 20:2
Then summon Naboth, and find * 1Ki 21:1
Then * men who had no conscience 1Ki 21:1
before the * kings, who were 1Ki 22:1
and he reigned * years. 1Ki 22:5
of the Lord; and * female bears 2Ki 2:2
So their * armies, now joined 2Ki 3:
take her * sons as his slaves. 2Ki 4:
eaten a bite or * they cried out, 2Ki 4:4
But please give me * mule-loads 2Ki 5:17
to tell you that * young prophets 2Ki 5:22
and * suits to give to them." 2Ki 5:22
He gave him * expensive robes, 2Ki 5:23
up the money in * bags, and gave 2Ki 5:23
and gave them to * of his servants 2Ki 5:23
this time tomorrow * gallons of 2Ki 7:1
the king sent out * charioteers to 2Ki 7:14
So it was true that * gallons of 2Ki 7:16
And * or three eunuchs looked 2Ki 9:32
to do it. "* kings couldn't stand 2Ki 10:4
to pile them in * heaps at the 2Ki 10:8
made * calves from molten gold. 2Ki 17:16
If you have * thousand men left 2Ki 18:23
in the * courts of the Temple; 2Ki 23:12
the weight of the * pillars and the 2Ki 25:16
Eber had * sons: Peleg (which 1Ch 1:19
Abraham's son Isaac had * sons, 1Ch 1:34
He also had * girls (by the same 1Ch 2:16
Hezron) had * wives, 1Ch 2:18
Shammai's brother Jada had * 1Ch 2:32
had * sons named Peleth and Zaza. 1Ch 2:33
the father of Tekoa, had * wives— 1Ch 4:5
killed the * famous giants 1Ch 11:22
were placed into * divisions named 1Ch 24:1
and Levites. * groups from the 1Ch 24:6
and * to each of the storehouses. 1Ch 26:17
road, and * to the nearby areas. 1Ch 26:18
Solomon placed * sculptured statues 2Ch 3:10
At the front of the Temple were * 2Ch 3:15
the backs of * rows of metal oxen. 2Ch 4:3
The construction of the * 2Ch 4:12-16
The * flared capitals on the tops 2Ch 4:12-16
The * sets of chains on the 2Ch 4:12-16
* sets of chains on the capitals, 2Ch 4:12-16
the Ark except the * stone tablets 2Ch 5:10
also, * hundred fifty of them 2Ch 8:10
The * kings were sitting on 2Ch 18:9
at the end of * years, his 2Ch 21:19
Jehoiada arranged * marriages 2Ch 24:3
Then King Joash ordered * hundred 2Ch 25:23
King Ahaz ruled * tribes of 2Ch 28:19f
but he lasted for only * years. 2Ch 33:20,21
There were also * beautiful Ez 8:26,27
done in a day or *, for there are Ez 10:13
aloud to them for * or three hours, Neh 9:3
divided them into * long lines to Neh 12:31,32
at the palace, * of the king's Est 2:21
An investigation was made, the * Est 2:23
* or three weeks later, Est 3:12
and Teresh, * of the king's Est 6:1
the day the * decrees of the king Est 9:1
to celebrate these * days at the Est 9:27
to confirm these * days annually as Est 9:29-31
"O God, there are * things I beg Job 13:20
you and with your * friends, for Job 42:7
Your throne is founded on * Ps 89:14,15
that made you cut yourself in *? Ps 114:5
Have * goals: wisdom—that is, Pro 3:21

VO Con't)
God, I beg * favors from you Pro 30:7
here are * things never Pro 30:15,16
can accomplish more than twice Ecc 4:9
lso, on a cold night, * under Ecc 4:11
nd defeated, but * can stand Ecc 4:12
bird in the hand is worth * in Ecc 6:9
pon a dance before * armies." Sol 6:13f
our * breasts are like two Sol 7:3
our two breasts are like * Sol 7:3
nd I will give * hundred pieces to Sol 8:12
eraphs. With * of their wings Is 6:2
eir faces; with * others they Is 6:2
eir feet, and with * they flew. Is 6:2
has-beens, Rezin and Pekah. Is 7:4
alk (verse 4) the * invading kings Is 7:14f
nd knows right from wrong, the * Is 7:15,16
have a cow and * sheep left. Is 7:21,22
arvest is ended, * or three in the Is 17:6
ot * of you are left together. Is 30:17
ext year, and * years from now Is 37:30
ames of Marduk and Nabu, the * Is 46:1f
Well, those * things shall Is 47:9
These * things have been your Is 51:19
For my people have done * evil Jer 2:13
rom here and * from there, Jer 3:14
saw * baskets of figs placed Jer 24:2
Within * years I will bring back Jer 28:3
hat within * years he will release Jer 28:11
And sure enough, * months later Jer 28:17
and besieged it. * years later, in Jer 39:2
gate between the * walls back of Jer 39:4
siege to the city for * years. Jer 52:5
gate between the * walls near the Jer 52:7
The Babylonians dismantled the * Jer 52:17
The weight of the * enormous Jer 52:20
four faces and * pairs of wings! Eze 1:6
Each had * pairs of wings Eze 1:11
had * wings covering his body. Eze 1:23
city, including * officers, Eze 11:1
for your nose and * more for your Eze 16:12
Babylon [the first of the * eagles Eze 17:12,13
and on it trace * routes for the Eze 21:19,20
"Son of dust, there were * Eze 23:2,3
reigns of the last * Judean kings, Eze 23:17f
* weeks later, Eze 32:17
they be divided into * nations. Eze 37:22
The distance between the * Eze 40:23
there were * tables where the Eze 40:39
there were * more tables. Eze 40:40
In the inner court, there were * Eze 40:44
side to form * pillars, each of Eze 40:48,49
the inner court. * doors opened Eze 41:11
the Temple, including its * walls. Eze 41:15,16
each with * faces, and of palm Eze 41:17,18
each with * swinging sections. Eze 41:24
The upper * tiers of rooms were Eze 42:5
composed of * units of tiers was on Eze 42:9,10
There was a walk between the * Eze 42:11
"* special sections of land Eze 45:7
shall be given * sections. Eze 47:13
the ground, on * feet, like a man; Dan 7:4
I saw a ram with * long horns Dan 8:3
Then I heard * of the holy angels Dan 8:13
"The * horns of the ram you saw Dan 8:20
of peace between their * lands. Dan 11:6f
from those first * occasions. Dan 11:29
Then I, Daniel, looked and saw * Dan 12:5
Hebrew: "* others," probably Dan 12:5f
Literally, "In * days." Hos 6:2f
* years before the earthquake. Amo 1:2
mouth * legs and a piece of ear. Amo 3:12
People from * or three cities Amo 4:8
And I see * olive trees carved Zec 4:3
Then I asked him about the * Zec 4:11
and about the * olive branches Zec 4:12
bowls through * golden tubes. Zec 4:12
represent the * anointed ones who Zec 4:14
Then I saw * women flying toward Zec 5:9
like * mountains made of brass. Zec 6:1
perfect harmony between the *!' Zec 6:13
* mercies for each of your woes! Zec 9:12
So I took * shepherd's staffs, Zec 11:7
and snapped it in *, showing that I Zec 11:10
This has already happened twice: * Zec 13:8f
you married, the * of you became Mal 2:15
every baby boy * years old and Mt 2:16
appeared to them * years before. Mt 2:16
of Galilee, he saw * Mt 4:18
the beach he saw * other brothers, Mt 4:21
their gear for a mile, carry it *. Mt 5:41
"You cannot serve * masters: God Mt 6:24
* men with demons in them met him. Mt 8:28
As Jesus was leaving her home, * Mt 9:27
(What do they cost? * for a penny? Mt 10:29
and sent them * and two before his Mt 11:1f
sent them two and * before his Mt 11:1f
loaves of bread and * fish!" Mt 14:17
and he took the five loaves and * Mt 14:19
leaders of * different parties. Mt 16:1f
one eye than to be in hell with *. Mt 18:9
But if not, then take one or * Mt 18:16
"I also tell you this—if * of Mt 18:19
For where * or three gather Mt 18:20
to his wife. The * shall become Mt 19:5,6
become one—no longer *, but one! Mt 19:5,6
let my * sons sit on two thrones Mt 20:21
let my two sons sit on * thrones Mt 20:21
* blind men were sitting beside Mt 20:30
* of them into the village ahead. Mt 21:1
The * disciples did as Jesus Mt 21:6
A man with * sons told the older Mt 21:28
Which of the * was obeying his Mt 21:31
stem from these * laws and are Mt 22:40
"* men will be working together Mt 24:40
the other left. * women will be Mt 24:41
begins in * days, and I Mt 26:2
him and Zebedee's * sons James and Mt 26:37
Finally * men were found who Mt 26:60,61
"Which of these * shall I Mt 27:21
* robbers were also crucified Mt 27:38
and sent them out * by two, with Mk 6:7
*, with power to cast out demons. Mk 6:7
five loaves of bread and * fish. Mk 6:38
He took the five loaves and * Mk 6:41
unquenchable fires of hell with *! Mk 9:43,44
* feet that carry you to hell. Mk 9:45,46
blind than have * eyes and see the Mk 9:47
they are no longer *, but one. Mk 10:8
sent * of his disciples on ahead. Mk 11:1
Off went the * men and found the Mk 11:4,5
came and dropped in * pennies. Mk 12:42
PASSOVER OBSERVANCE began * Mk 14:1
He sent * of them into Jerusalem Mk 14:13
So the * disciples went on ahead Mk 14:16
* robbers were also crucified Mk 15:27
And even the * robbers dying with Mk 15:32
his first * words ("Eloi, Eloi") Mk 15:34f
he appeared to * who were walking Mk 16:12
of turtledoves or * young pigeons" Lk 2:24
"If you have * coats," he Lk 3:11
He noticed * empty boats Lk 5:2
about it, he sent * of his Lk 7:19
The * disciples found Jesus while Lk 7:20,21,22
loaned money to * people—$5,000 to Lk 7:41
of bread and * fish among the lot Lk 9:13
Jesus took the five loaves and * Lk 9:16
Then * men appeared and began Lk 9:30
and the * men standing with him. Lk 9:32
you, follow these * rules: Lk 10:8,9
innkeeper * twenty-dollar bills Lk 10:35
Literally, "* denarii," each the Lk 10:35f
favor of me, and * against—or Lk 12:52
this story: "A man had * sons. Lk 15:11
anyone else can serve * masters. Lk 16:13
That night * men will be asleep Lk 17:34
the other left. * women will be Lk 17:35,36
"* men went to the Temple to Lk 18:10
of Olives, he sent * disciples Lk 19:29
dropped in * small copper coins. Lk 21:2
"we have * swords among us." Lk 22:38
* others, criminals, were led out Lk 23:32,33
the * criminals on either side. Lk 23:32,33
Suddenly * men appeared before Lk 24:4
That same day, Sunday, * of Lk 24:13
Then the * from Emmaus told their Lk 24:35
was standing with * of his Jn 1:35
Then John's * disciples turned Jn 1:37
* DAYS LATER Jesus' mother was a Jn 2:1
and he did, for * days, long Jn 4:40,41
At the end of the * days' stay he Jn 4:43,44
Your laws say that if * men Jn 8:17
So the * sisters sent a message Jn 11:3
was for the next * days and made no Jn 11:6
Finally, after the * days, he Jn 11:7
There they crucified him and * Jn 19:18
of the * men crucified with Jesus; Jn 19:32
looked in and saw * white-robed Jn 20:12
and * other disciples. Jn 21:2
glimpse, suddenly * white-robed men Act 1:10
The assembly nominated * men: Act 1:23
So the * disciples were brought Act 4:7
and saw * men of Israel fighting. Act 7:26
where his * sons were born. Act 7:29
Lydda, they sent * men to beg him Act 9:38
Cornelius called * of his household Act 10:7
between * soldiers with others Act 12:6
people of those * cities, but the Act 12:20
the street as the * men urged them Act 13:43
The men chosen were * of the Act 15:22
send to you these * official Act 15:25
This went on for the next * Act 19:10
And he leaped on * of them and Act 19:16
He sent his * assistants, Act 19:22
and kept it up for * hours: "Great Act 19:34
Then the commander called * of Act 23:23,24
him. * years went by in this way; Act 24:27
"You haven't touched food for * Act 27:33
began eating, all * hundred Act 27:37
Literally, "a place where * seas Act 27:41f
Paul lived for the next * years Act 28:30
Obey the laws, then, for * Rom 13:5
too, for these same * reasons. Rom 13:6
his sight the * become one person. 1Co 6:16
No more than * or three should 1Co 14:27
* or three may prophesy, one at a 1Co 14:29,30
say that the other * brothers 2Co 8:23
your help. So, * good things 2Co 9:12
The Scriptures tell us that if * 2Co 13:1
that Abraham had * sons, one from Gal 4:22
of God's * ways of helping people. Gal 4:24,25
These * forces within us are Gal 5:17
Then he took the * groups that Eph 2:15
wife, and the * shall be one." Eph 5:31
plead with those * dear women, Php 4:2
For that day will not come until * 2Th 2:3
Hymenaeus and Alexander are * 1Ti 1:20
unless there are * or three 1Ti 5:19
and his oath, * things we can Heb 6:18
of worship there were * rooms. Heb 9:1
* or three witnesses to his sin. Heb 10:28
to his * sons, Jacob and Esau. Heb 11:20
each of Joseph's * sons as he stood Heb 11:21
and some by being sawed in *; Heb 11:37,38
And yet, of the * strangers, you Jas 2:6
ends, but there are * more coming! Rev 9:12
And I will give power to my * Rev 11:3
These * prophets are the two Rev 11:4
These two prophets are the * Rev 11:4
and * candlesticks standing Rev 11:4
the death of the * prophets who had Rev 11:10
But she was given * wings like Rev 12:14
of the earth, with * little horns Rev 13:11

TWO-FACED
fellowship with tricky, * men; Ps 26:4

TWO-HORNED
rushed furiously at the * ram. Dan 8:6

TWO-HUNDRED-POUND
He wore a bronze helmet, a * coat 1Sa 17:4-7

TWO-THIRDS
by side in rows. * of each row, as 2Sa 8:2
The other * shall stand guard at 2Ki 11:6,7,8
for the lambs. * of all the nation Zec 13:8

TYCHICUS
and Timothy; and * and Trophimus, Act 20:4
*, who is a much loved brother Eph 6:21
*, our much loved brother, will Col 4:7
He and * will give you all the Col 4:9
for I need him. (* is gone too, as 2Ti 4:12
send either Artemas or * to you. Tit 3:12

TYING
the loops, thus * the two long Ex 36:13
of the ephod by * the rings of the Ex 39:21
used in * the Tabernacle together. Num 3:25-30
and old alike, by * magic charms on Eze 13:18

TYPE
The names in bold face * are 1Ch 1:1f
The use of bold * or italic type 1Ch 1:1f
The use of bold type or italic * 1Ch 1:1f
appeared in bold face *. 1Ch 1:5-9f
She was the brash, coarse *, Pro 7:11,12
A very common * of divination by Eze 21:21f
(There were many men of this * Mk 2:15
But Martha was the jittery *, and Lk 10:40

TYPHOON
a heavy wind of * strength (a Act 27:14,15

TYPICAL
A * case of discrimination (cf. Lk 9:53f

TYRANNIZED
mercy of their aides, who * them; Neh 5:15
My people were * without cause Is 52:4

TYRANNUS
of * and preached there daily. Act 19:9

TYRANNY
them from the * of the Syrians; 2Ki 13:5
You were unrestrained in *. Is 14:6

TYRANT
The unjust * will reap disaster Pro 22:8
Who can demand that a * let his Is 49:24
testimony, the * who comes out of Rev 11:7

TYRANT'S
will live to see the * downfall. Pro 29:16

TYRANTS
by instant punishment of the *. Job 35:12
heathen, kings are * and each minor Mt 20:25
Don't be *, but lead them by 1Pe 5:3

TYRE
on the south, to * on the north. Jos 15:47
fortified city of * and came to the Jos 19:29
Then King Hiram of * sent cedar 2Sa 5:11
and then to the stronghold of *, 2Sa 24:7
KING HIRAM OF * had always been a 1Ki 5:1
Hiram to come from *, for he was a 1Ki 7:13
had been a foundry worker from *. 1Ki 7:14
to King Hiram of * as payment for 1Ki 9:11,12
Hiram came from * to see the 1Ki 9:11,12
KING HIRAM OF * sent masons and 1Ch 14:1
The men of * and Sidon brought 1Ch 22:4
to King Hiram at *, requesting 2Ch 2:3
his father is from here in *. 2Ch 2:14
King Hiram of * had given to him, 2Ch 8:2
from the people of * and Sidon, Ez 3:7
There were also some men from * Neh 13:16

(TYRE Con't)
The people of *, the richest Ps 45:12
Ammon, Amalek, Philistia and *; Ps 83:7
Philistia and *, or even distant Ps 87:4
THIS IS GOD'S message to *: Is 23:1
Weep, O ships of *, returning home Is 23:1
* was originally a colony of the Is 23:1f
* was originally a colony of the Is 23:4f
Flee to Tarshish, men of *, Is 23:6
this disaster on *, empire builder Is 23:8
who consign * to the wild beasts. Is 23:13
For seventy years * will be Is 23:15,16
Lord will revive *, but she will be Is 23:17
and all the kings of * and Jer 25:22
Edom, Moab, Ammon, * and Sidon, Jer 27:3
* and Sidon will be destroyed. Jer 47:4
"Son of dust, * has rejoiced Eze 26:2
stand against you, *, and I will Eze 26:3
They will destroy the walls of * Eze 26:4
says the Lord God. * shall become Eze 26:5
the north—against * with a great Eze 26:7
damage done to * by Nebuchadnezzar, Eze 26:14f
I will destroy * to the ground. Eze 26:19
dust, sing this sad dirge for *: Eze 27:2
a wondrous city as *, destroyed in Eze 27:32
to the prince of *: The Lord God Eze 28:2,3
of dust, weep for the king of *. Eze 28:12
to a human king of *, and some seem Eze 28:12f
of Babylon fought hard against *. Eze 29:18
* capitulated to Nebuchadnezzar at Eze 29:18f
what he was "shortchanged" at *. Eze 29:18f
during those thirteen years at *, Eze 29:20
* capitulated to Nebuchadnezzar at Eze 29:20f
what he was "shortchanged" at *. Eze 29:20f
to get drunk. * and Sidon, don't Joe 3:4
The Lord says, "The people of * Amo 1:9
to the walls of *, and it will burn Amo 1:10
near Damascus, and *, and Zidon, Zec 9:2
Though * has armed herself to Zec 9:3
their hopes that * would stop the Zec 9:5
been done in wicked * and Sidon Mt 11:21
Truly, * and Sidon will be Mt 11:22
into the parts of * and Sidon." Mt 15:21f
to * and Sidon. Mt 15:21
from as far away as * and Sidon. Mk 3:7,8
went to the region of * and Sidon, Mk 7:24
From * he went to Sidon, then Mk 7:31
the seacoasts of * and Sidon had Lk 6:17,18
done in the cities of * and Sidon, Lk 10:13
Yes, * and Sidon will receive Lk 10:14
* and Sidon arrived to see him. Act 12:20
at the harbor of *, in Syria, where Act 21:3
The next stop after leaving * was Act 21:7

UCAL
Massa, addressed to Ithiel and *: Pro 30:1

UEL
Ma-adai, Amram, *, Banaiah, Ez 10:34-42

UGH
things you hate to touch. "*!" Is 30:22

ULAI
Elam, standing beside the * River. Dan 8:2

ULAM
and he had sons named * and Rakem. 1Ch 7:16
*, the first, 1Ch 8:39

ULAM'S
* son was Bedan. 1Ch 7:17
* sons were prominent warriors 1Ch 8:40

ULCER
in the spot, and an * developing. Lev 13:9,10

ULLA
The sons of * were: 1Ch 7:39

ULTIMATE
it is the * of honor. Eze 27:10
as in John 1:1—the * method of Rev 19:13f

UMBILICAL
When I first saw you, your * cord Eze 16:4

UMMAH
Mahalab, Achzib, *, Aphek, and Jos 19:30,31

UMPIRE
but there is no * between us, no Job 9:32,33

UNABATED
The terrible storm raged * many Act 27:20

UNABLE
they had been * to answer Job's Job 32:3
duties and be * to give justice to Pro 31:5
away and disappear, * to help. Is 47:15
They flee to Heshbon, * to go Jer 48:45
looking down, un* to speak a word. Dan 10:15
was both blind and * to talk—was Mt 12:22
They just sat there, * to take it Mk 6:51
stricken silent, * to speak until Lk 1:20
and was * to straighten herself. Lk 13:11
made him blind, * to see the 2Co 4:4

UNACCOUNTED
seven years * for at the time of Dan 9:25f

UNAFRAID
You will lie down * and many Job 11:19
goes to war, he is * and does not Job 39:21-23
live in peace and safety, *." Pro 1:33
*, with no one to chase them away. Is 17:2
lie down in peace and safety, *; Hos 1:18
as the young and tender, lived *? Nah 2:11

UNAIDED
So I executed vengeance alone; *, Is 63:5

UNALTERABLE
He laid out an * line of Lam 2:8

UNANIMOUS
There was * consent, for everyone 1Ch 13:4
This was their * decision at Ps 83:5
vote for the death sentence was *. Mk 14:63,64

UNANIMOUSLY
so it was * decided to continue the 2Ch 30:23
and deputies have * decided that Dan 6:7
wise to us, having * agreed on our Act 15:25

UNANNOUNCED
being ready for my * return. Mt 24:44
Lord will arrive * and unexpected, Mt 24:50

UNANOINTED
infected wounds, * and unbound. Is 1:5,6

UNANSWERABLE
in arguing over * questions and Tit 3:9

UNANSWERED
Their hopes remain *. Is 44:9

UNASHAMED
a prostitute, and completely *. Jer 3:3
you, for your sins are open and *. Eze 21:24

UNATTAINABLE
Nothing will be * for them! Gen 11:6

UNAUTHORIZED
Offer no * incense, burnt Ex 30:9
by being eaten by * persons, for Lev 22:15
of Israel that no * person—no one Num 16:40
any * person entering the Temple. 2Ch 23:7
consecrated and all * personnel. 2Ch 23:19

UNAWARE
but he was * of her lying down or Gen 19:33
you * of what you clearly see! Ex 23:8
Perhaps Hezekiah was * of the Is 38:18f

UNAWARES
let my sudden coming catch you *; Lk 21:34,35

UNBEARABLE
and made life * for the Israelis Ju 4:2,3

UNBELIEF
as an indictment of Israel's *. Is 30:8
there, because of their *. Mt 13:58
And because of their * he Mk 6:5
days of * and sin, I, the Messiah, Mk 8:38
He rebuked them for their *—their Mk 16:14
The world's sin is * in me; Jn 16:9
Jews leave their * behind them and Rom 11:23

UNBELIEVABLE
your bed of prostitution. *! Eze 16:16
The Lord says, "This seems * to Zec 8:6
He did * miracles such as making Rev 13:13

UNBELIEVABLY
of Samaria were * evil, for they Jer 23:13

UNBELIEVERS
You yoke yourselves with *, thus Is 30:1
talking about * who live in sexual 1Co 5:10
Christian brother in front of *. 1Co 6:6
and * aren't yet ready for it. 1Co 14:22

UNBELIEVING
This evil, * nation is asking Mt 16:4
Literally, "O * generation." Mk 9:19f
too, are evil and * and are leading Heb 3:12

UNBENDING
Your necks are as * as iron; Is 48:4

UNBIBLICAL
justifies the means, an * idea. Lk 16:9f

UNBIND
He shall * her hair and place Num 5:18

UNBLED
* meat of strangled animals. Act 15:20
from * meat of strangled animals, Act 15:27,28,29
idols, not to eat * meat from Act 21:25

UNBLEMISHED
be six lambs and a ram, all *. Eze 46:4

UNBORN
generations yet * shall hear of Ps 22:31

UNBOUND
infected wounds, unanointed and *. Is 1:5,6
"I see four men, *, walking Dan 3:25

UNBREAKABLE
promised with an * oath that one of Act 2:30

UNBROKEN
forever in * fellowship with God. Rom 6:10

UNBURDEN
God, will * myself of the burden Jer 23:38,39

UNBURIED
Their dead will be left *, and Is 34:3
die in this land, * and unmourned, Jer 16:6

UNCEASING
my people with * blows of rage and Is 14:6

UNCERTAIN
value by today's standards is *. Lev 27:3f
The text is * in the original 2Sa 1:21f
of the Hebrew wording is *. 2Sa 23:20f
The meaning of the term is *. 1Ch 11:22f
The meaning of the term is *. 1Ch 15:20f
The meaning is *. 1Ch 15:21f
that he sawed them to pieces is *. 1Ch 20:3f
It is * whether this phrase was Ps 49:2
Syria, with the outcome still *; Ps 60
meaning of the Hebrew word is *. Is 52:14,1
Your help is as * as a seasonal Jer 15:17,
stands at a fork, * whether to Eze 21:
their identification is *. Eze 27:1
The text here is *. Eze 27:1
The Hebrew text is *. Hos 4:1
text of this verse is very *. Hab 1:1
The Hebrew is *. Zec 14:
then make will be *, as you turn Jas 1:7
your lives is as * as the morning Jas 4:1

UNCERTAINTY
in * will speak out plainly. Is 32

UNCHANGED
his mind remained * and he refused Ex 9
me remains *, and who can turn him Job 23:1
has planned against her stands *. Jer 51:2

UNCHANGING
For his God is the living, * God Dan 6:25,2
his love. His * plan has always Eph 1

UNCIRCUMCISED
but no * person shall ever eat Ex 12:4
sword before these * heathen 1Ch 10:
by letting the * into my Eze 44:

UNCIRCUMCISION
the fruit thereof as their *." Lev 19:2

UNCIVIL
kicked me out in a most * way." Gen 26:2

UNCIVILIZED
to civilized people and * alike; Rom 1:1

UNCLE
"Flee to your * Laban in Haran. Gen 27:4
marry one of your cousins—your * Gen 28:
to visit his * Laban, his mother's Gen 28:
So Esau went to his * Ishmael's Gen 28:
I have been living with * Laban Gen 32:
has taken what belongs to his *; Lev 20:2
his brothers, his *, nephew, or Lev 25:4
Saul's * asked him. 1Sa 10:1
his * asked. 1Sa 10:1
his cousin Abner, his * Ner's son. 1Sa 14:50,5
Jonathan, David's *, a wise 1Ch 27:3
his nurse and by his aunt and *. 2Ch 22:1
*, who had adopted her." Est 2:15
A man's * will be the only one Amo 6:1

UNCLE'S
the sheep were his *, Jacob went Gen 29:1
the stone and watered his * flock. Gen 29:1
has intercourse with his * widow, Lev 20:2
Literally, "his * wife." Lev 20:20
His * daughter. Est 2:7

UNCLEAN
ceremonially *—such as the dead Lev 5:
* shall not be eaten, but burned; Lev 7:1
Any priest who is ceremonially * Lev 7:2
is ceremonially *, whether it is Lev 7:2
Literally, "shall declare him * Lev 13:3
Literally, "pronounce him *." Lev 13:25
Literally, "pronounce him *." Lev 13:27
Literally, "*, unclean." Lev 13:45
Literally, "Unclean, *." Lev 13:45
ceremonially * until evening, and Lev 15:
on is ceremonially * until evening, Lev 15:8
bath and be * until the evening. Lev 15:16
far behind you—it is * to you. Is 52:11
ritually clean and ritually *." Eze 44:23
that makes you *." Mt 15:11
godless and "*" by the Jews. Eph 2:11
too, were still *, even though they Eph 2:11

UNCLEANNESS
whether it is * from man or beast, Lev 7:21
for he has uncovered her *. Lev 20:18
them from all their sins and *." Zec 13:1

UNCLEAR
The Hebrew is *. 2Ki 16:18f
The meaning is *. Is 38:18f
it is * whether this person is of Rev 9:1f
the exact antecedent is *. Rev 19:9f

UNCLEARED
shall be like an * wilderness, or a Eze 22:24

UNCLES
Give them land along with their * Num 27:6,7
then it shall go to his *. Num 27:10
But if he has no *, then it Num 27:11
visited his *—his mother's Ju 9:1
So his * went to the leaders of Ju 9:3

UNCLOUDED
power of the sun in * brilliance. Rev 1:16

UNCOMFORTED
*-For they are dead Mt 2:18

UNCONCERN
throw off your *. Is 32:11

UNCONCERNED
her own, and is * though they die, Job 39:16

UNCONQUERED
them to scout the * territory and Jos 18:4
of the nations yet * as well as the Jos 23:4,5
left * by Joshua when he died. Ju 2:21
O BABYLON, THE *, come sit in the Is 47:1

UNCONSCIOUS
until they fall * to the floor, to Jer 51:39

OOKED
d how tasteless is the * white Job 6:5,6,7
'OUNTED
, sacrificing * sheep and oxen. 1Ki 8:5
r vast, * wealth is stripped Nah 2:9
:OUTH
Caleb, was *, churlish, 1Sa 25:3
:OVER
erally, "* the nakedness of," Lev 18:6f
:OVERED
he has * her uncleanness. Lev 20:18
ttocks *, to the shame of Egypt. Is 20:4
'ty-three cisterns have been * Jer 41:9f
iid, and * a door to a hidden Eze 8:8
d I have left it there, *, to Eze 24:8
:ULTIVATED
lie fallow before the Lord, *. Lev 25:4
:UT
e only * stones and boulders. Ex 20:25
rd your God. Use * boulders, and Deu 27:5,6
nbilical cord was *, and you had Eze 16:4
DECIDED
ate those who are * whether or Ps 119:113
ill they stood there *, filled Lk 24:41
DEFILED
stained by sin, * by sinners, and Heb 7:26
r you, pure and *, beyond the 1Pe 1:4
or they are spiritually *, pure Rev 14:4
DER-SIZED
eighted scales and * measures; Amo 8:5
DERBRUSH
e has dragged me into the * and Lam 3:11
DERCARRIAGES
hey were constructed with * 1Ki 7:27-30
DERCLOTHES
e caps and the * were all made of Ex 39:28,29
DERFOOT
trample kings * and to put Is 41:2
shes *," says the Lord of Hosts. Mal 4:3
ut and trampled * as worthless. Mt 5:13
ho have trampled * the Son of God Heb 10:29
IDERGARMENTS
ut on his linen * and his linen Lev 6:10
IDERGO
Each of you must * purification Jos 7:13
as good for me to * this Is 38:17
hat the more we * sufferings for 2Co 1:5
when you * these same sufferings. 2Co 1:6,7
IDERGOING
ey are *, and to take them to the Ex 3:17
NDERGONE
When the priests had * the 2Ch 5:11,12
hey had not * the purification 2Ch 30:17,18,19
NDERGROUND
nd found a gushing * spring. Gen 26:19
ome of these * leaders and their 2Ki 25:23
NDERLYING
Some fell on thin soil with * Mk 4:5,6
oundation laid upon the * rock. Lk 6:47,48
NDERMINE
That kind of talk will * the Jer 38:4
A heavy rainstorm will * it; Eze 13:11
NDERNEATH
And * are the everlasting arms. Deu 33:27
the earth, while * there is fire. Job 28:5
His words were sweet, but * were Ps 55:21
brick boiling vats, with ovens *. Eze 46:23
down the mountains * his feet: Amo 4:13
saintly men, but * those pious Mt 23:28
saw an altar, and * it all the Rev 6:9
NDERSHORTS
Also make linen * for them, to Ex 28:42
NDERSIDE
On the * of the rim were two 1Ki 7:24
NDERSTAND
they won't * each other's words!" Gen 11:7
so that I will * you and walk Ex 33:13
"*, therefore, that the Lord Deu 7:9
language you don't *— a nation of Deu 28:49
you hearts that * or eyes that see Deu 29:4
Oh, that they could *! Deu 32:29
He, of course, didn't * what 1Sa 20:39
"We don't * you," they told him. 2Sa 12:21
speak in Aramaic, for we * it. 2Ki 18:26
And all who were old enough to * Neh 8:1
they could hear and * God's words. Neh 8:12
were old enough to *, had separated Neh 10:28
are wise. They *. Job 12:12
describe. I * what you are saying. Job 13:1
What do you * that we don't? Job 15:9
to his reply, and * what he wants. Job 23:4,5
"Listen now and try to *. Job 34:16
No one can begin to * eternity. Job 36:26
Can anyone really * the Job 36;29
Do you * the balancing of the Job 37:16,17
about and did not *, things far too Job 42:3
made— I cannot * how you can Ps 8:4
If we had, we could * your Ps 44:19
Can't they * anything? Ps 53:4
Unthinking people do not * them! Ps 92:6
Make me * what you want; Ps 119:27
unfolds, even the simple can * it. Ps 119:130
help me to * them and I shall Ps 119:144
steps, why try to * everything that Pro 20:24
You cannot * the height of Pro 25:2,3
Evil men don't * the importance Pro 28:5
I cannot * man, Pro 30:3
wonderful for me to *—no, four! Pro 30:18,19
HOW WONDERFUL TO be wise, to * Ecc 8:1
repeatedly, you won't * them. Is 6:9
or to hear or to *, or to turn to Is 6:10
the only language they can * is Is 28:11
for God has made him see and *. Is 28:26
you can't *, will disappear. Is 33:19
for we * it quite well. Is 36:11
Don't you yet *? Is 40:28
this miracle and * that it is God Is 41:20
You see and * what is right but Is 42:20
they will not * the reason why—that Is 42:25
me and to * that I alone am God. Is 43:10
so that you could clearly *. Is 48:16
For they shall see and * what Is 52:14,15
at last and really * that I, the Is 60:16
nation whose language you don't * Jer 5:15
How can you say, "We * his Jer 8:8
Who is wise enough to * all this? Jer 9:12
truly know me, and * that I am the Jer 9:24
* at last that I alone am God. Jer 16:21
done something too horrible to *. Jer 18:13
you will * what I am telling you. Jer 30:24
where you can't * the language— Eze 3:5
Israel: Don't you * what this Eze 17:12,13
Jerusalem won't * this Eze 21:23
But if he doesn't, please *, Dan 3:18
all the world may * that the Most Dan 4:17
they came, none of them could * Dan 5:8
As I was trying to * the meaning Dan 8:15
said, "you must * that the events Dan 8:17
by the dream and did not * it. Dan 8:27
am here to help you * God's plans. Dan 9:22
Listen, and try to * the meaning Dan 9:23
said but I didn't * what he meant, Dan 12:8
and none of them will *. Dan 12:10
is sealed, for you refuse to *. Hos 4:14
Whoever is wise, let him * these Hos 14:9
my thoughts nor * my plan, for the Mic 4:12
you are willing to * what I mean, Mt 11:14
were permitted to * about the Mt 13:11
will hear and see but not *. Mt 13:12,13
'They hear, but don't *; Mt 13:14
and * and turn to God again, and Mt 13:16
the Kingdom and doesn't * it; Mt 13:19
Do you *?" Mt 13:51
I say and try to *: You aren't Mt 15:10
"Don't you *?" Mt 15:16
Won't you ever *? Mt 16:9
they will not * or turn to God, or Mk 4:11,12
But if you can't * this simple Mk 4:13
more you will * what I tell you. Mk 4:24
as much as they were ready to *. Mk 4:33
listen," he said, "and try to *. Mk 7:14
"Don't you * either?" Mk 7:18
Can't you *? Mk 8:17
Literally, "Do you not yet *?" Mk 8:21f
But they didn't * and were afraid Mk 9:32
But they didn't * what he Lk 2:50
words and do not *, just as the Lk 8:10
Listen well, if you would * my Lk 14:35
But they didn't * a thing he Lk 18:34
* at last these many Scriptures! Lk 24:45
and yet you don't * these things? Jn 3:10,11
said, "This is very hard to *. Jn 6:60
But they still didn't * that Jn 8:27
Why can't you * what I am Jn 8:43
didn't * what he meant, so he Jn 10:6
* nor turn to me to heal them." Jn 12:40
Jesus replied, "You don't * now Jn 13:7
"Do you * what I was doing? Jn 13:12
tell you, but you can't * it now. Jn 16:12
Now we * that you know Jn 16:30
sent me and will * that you love Jn 17:23
to you now, but * clearly that I Jn 19:4
and asked, "Do you * it?" Act 8:30
"And we * that he came here to Act 9:21
"We * that some believers from Act 15:24
light but didn't * what was said. Act 22:9
and see but not *, for your hearts Act 28:26
* and turn to me to heal you." Act 28:27
it is easy to *: just as you used Rom 6:19
DON'T YOU * yet, dear Jewish Rom 7:1
* what the law really demanded. Rom 7:9
I don't * myself at all, for I Rom 7:15
For they don't * that Christ has Rom 10:3
They don't * that Christ gives Rom 10:4
And did they * [that God would Rom 10:19
that they do not * what we are Rom 11:8
How impossible it is for us to * Rom 11:33
of Christ before will see and *. Rom 15:21
a Christian can't * and can't 1Co 2:14
can * what the Holy Spirit means. 1Co 2:14
the world, who can't * him at all. 1Co 2:15
power to * what he is saying. 1Co 12:10
Can just anyone * and translate 1Co 12:30
we can see and * only a little 1Co 13:12
since they won't be able to * you. 1Co 14:2
don't *, how would that help you? 1Co 14:6
*, how will he know what you mean? 1Co 14:9
for those who * them, but to me 1Co 14:10
a language I don't *, my spirit is 1Co 14:14
I can * the praise I am giving; 1Co 14:15
those who don't * you be praising 1Co 14:16
that people can * and be helped by, 1Co 14:19
in who does not * about these 1Co 14:24
cannot see and * the real meaning 2Co 3:14
upon him, or to * the amazing 2Co 4:4
has made us * that it is the 2Co 4:6
they would all * just what I had Gal 2:2
clearly and really * who Christ is Eph 1:16,17
I pray that you will begin to * Eph 1:19
able to feel and *, as all God's Eph 3:18,19
end of it or fully know or * it. Eph 3:18,19
him, and they cannot * his ways. Eph 4:17,18
I know this is hard to *, but Eph 5:32
than the human mind can *. Php 4:7
you * what he wants you to do; Col 1:9
to be saved and to * this truth: 1Ti 2:4
you to * how they apply to you. 2Ti 2:7
but they never * the truth. 2Ti 3:7
so it's hard to make you *. Heb 5:11
spiritual food and * the deeper Heb 5:14
One could * why Abraham would do Heb 7:5
someone helps him * the Truth Jas 5:19
the prophets did not fully *. 1Pe 1:10
words help us to * many things that 2Pe 1:19
"the things they do not *." 2Pe 2:12f
are not easy to *, and there are 2Pe 3:15,16
don't * that we are his children. 1Jn 3:1
help us * and find the true God. 1Jn 5:20
they do not *, and, like animals, Jud 1:10
of measurement that John could *. Rev 21:17f
UNDERSTANDING
experienced, and *, and I will Deu 1:13
Foolish, without *. Deu 32:28
them, 'Please be * and let them Ju 21:22
Give me an * mind so that I can 1Ki 3:9
great wisdom and *, and a mind with 1Ki 4:29
intelligent, and * son to build 2Ch 2:12
He takes away the * of Job 12:24,25
have kept them back from * this. Job 17:3,4
know where to find wisdom and *. Job 28:12
to forsake evil is real *.' Job 28:28
"Listen to me, you with *. Job 34:10
And he is perfect in his *. Job 36:5
parts, and given * to the mind?" Job 38:36f
give me wisdom and *, no wonder I Ps 119:104
His power is absolute! His * is Ps 147:5
wanted them to be *, just and fair Pro 1:3
is a treasure of knowledge and *. Pro 2:6
the earth; his * established all Pro 3:19
Let me give you *. Pro 8:4,5
where to discover knowledge and *. Pro 8:12
results in every other kind of *. Pro 9:10
than gold, and * than silver! Pro 16:16
the Lord can give them * wives. Pro 19:14
to search for * about everything in Ecc 1:12-15
it destroys his *. Ecc 7:7
or planning, or knowing, or *. Ecc 9:10
Dull their *, close their ears Is 6:10
of wisdom, *, counsel and might; Is 11:2
full of sense and *, and those who Is 32:4
can fathom the depths of his *. Is 40:28
and closed their minds from *. Is 44:18
me and opens my * to his will. Is 50:4
will guide you with wisdom and *. Jer 3:15
retarded children who have no *. Jer 4:22
out the heavens by his *. Jer 51:15
You have used your wisdom and * Eze 28:4
special ability in * the meanings Dan 1:17
profound mysteries beyond man's *. Dan 2:22
and the * of what it means." Dan 2:23
* as though he were himself a god. Dan 5:11
with divine knowledge and *. Dan 5:12
before the Lord and pray for *; Dan 10:12
"Those with spiritual * will Dan 11:33
all my heart and * and strength, Mk 12:33
Realizing this man's *, Jesus Mk 12:34
everyone with his * and answers. Lk 2:46,47
I am of the earth, and my * is Jn 3:31
man of considerable insight and *. Act 13:6,7
your eyes against *, for you don't Act 28:27
given you a full * of the truth; 1Co 1:5
in your * of these things. 1Co 14:20
in * matters of this kind. 1Co 14:20
so sure of your * and trust that I 2Co 1:15,16
and * were veiled and blinded too. 2Co 3:14
lives and by our * of the Gospel 2Co 6:6
with real certainty and clear *. Col 2:2
an ever deeper * of the love of God 2Th 3:5
mature in our *, as strong Heb 6:1
UNDERSTANDS
and * and knows every thought. 1Ch 28:9
knows what we should do; he *. Job 12:13
Literally, "one who * riddles"; Dan 8:23f

(UNDERSTANDS Con't)
to the message and * it and goes Mt 13:23
ordinary language that everyone *. 1Co 14:15
how well he * us and knows what is Eph 1:8
This High Priest of ours * our Heb 4:15
and * their problems very well. Heb 5:1

UNDERSTOOD
know that Joseph * them as he was Gen 42:23
Judah and Israel, * from David's 2Sa 3:37
men who * the temper of the times 1Ch 12:24-37
Have you never heard nor *? Is 40:21
time he * what the vision meant. Dan 10:1
it will not be * until the end Dan 12:4
to be * until the time of the end. Dan 12:9
truth * the illustrations. Mt 13:12,13f
Then at last they * that by Mt 16:12
proverbs they all *), "How can Mk 3:23
asked the crowd. "We * that Jn 12:34
we * some people met for prayer; Act 16:13
men of the world have not * it; 1Co 2:8
you heard it and * about God's Col 1:6
if you have once * the Good News Heb 6:4

UNDERTOOK
he *, for the Lord was with him. 1Sa 18:14

UNDERWENT
So the priests and the Levites * 1Ch 15:14
of spirit as he * in the Garden, Heb 5:7f
SINCE CHRIST SUFFERED and * pain, 1Pe 4:1

UNDERWORLD
That burns to the depths of the *, Deu 32:22
Literally, "Sheol," "the *." Is 28:15f
of those in the * who entered long Eze 26:20
at the terrifying powers of the * 2Pe 2:12
and the earth and the * gave up Rev 20:13

UNDESERVED
An * curse has no effect. Pro 26:2
dead—only by his * favor have we Eph 2:5

UNDESERVING
forgotten to be kind to one so *? Ps 77:9
help me, * as I am, to obey your Ps 119:29,30
been poured out upon us * sinners; Rom 1:5
happiness of an * sinner who is Rom 4:6

UNDILUTED
it is poured out * into God's cup Rev 14:10

UNDISPUTED
was now the * ruler of Israel, for 2Ch 1:1

UNDISTURBED
People now living * will be cut Jer 25:37
lived there * from all invasions. Jer 48:11
shall remain there *, for he will Mic 5:4

UNDO
Don't * the work of God for a Rom 14:20

UNDOING
the evil man's treachery is his * Pro 11:6
His mouth is his *! Pro 18:6,7
in Israel, and this to their *. Lk 2:34,35
for God's House will be my *." Jn 2:17

UNDONE
lived, and now they lie * in hell; Eze 32:24
leave the more important things *. Mt 23:23
not leave these other things *. Lk 11:42
Leave nothing * that you ought to 2Ti 4:5

UNDRAINED
You must not eat meat with * Lev 19:26

UNEASY
Yes, the tribe of Reuben has an * Ju 5:16

UNEDUCATED
were obviously * non-professionals, Act 4:13
yes, to the educated and * alike. Rom 1:14

UNEMPLOYED
who use the nets will all be *. Is 19:8

UNENDING
surely find me. * riches, honor, Pro 8:18
feet; * work is now our lot. Lam 5:5
of life—an *, glorious future. Rev 2:10

UNEQUALED
Praise his * greatness. Ps 150:2

UNEXPECTED
or lies from a king are both *. Pro 17:7
he is like an * flood sweeping away Pro 28:3
unannounced and *, and severely Mt 24:50
you, * as a thief, and punish you. Rev 3:3

UNEXPECTEDLY
That day of the Lord will come * 1Th 5:2
surely coming, as * as a thief, and 2Pe 3:10
Or, "suddenly," "*." Rev 3:11f
"Take note: I will come as * as Rev 16:15
Or, "suddenly," "*." Rev 22:6,7f
Or, "suddenly," "*." Rev 22:12f

UNFAILING
Your goodness and * kindness Ps 23:6
Pour out your * love on those Ps 36:10
give you all the * mercies and love Is 55:3

UNFAIR
God for him! It's * for you to 1Sa 22:15
of the judges and lets them be *. Job 9:24
"If I have been * to my Job 31:13
him to court before an * judge. Ps 109:6
Because the wicked are *, their Pro 21:7
This is not only foolish, but *. Ecc 2:20-23
It seems so *, that one fate Ecc 9:2,3
to those who issue * laws, says the Is 10:1
men who use any excuse to be *. Is 29:21
we are and how * we are, for we Is 59:13
Am I the one who is *, or is it Eze 18:25
keep saying: 'The Lord is *!' Eze 18:29
it is you who are *, not I. Eze 18:29
doesn't it seem * to you that my Lk 10:40
But isn't this * for God to let Rom 3:26
Was God being *? Rom 9:14
For God is not *. Heb 6:10

UNFAIRLY
justice to all who are treated *. Ps 103:6

UNFAIRNESS
justice and love *, and fill Mic 3:9

UNFAITHFUL
or not she has been * to him. Num 5:30
should he be * to his promise. 1Sa 20:16
rebellious, *, refusing to give Ps 78:8
another become * to their wives. Pro 23:26,27,28
For you have been * and worshiped Jer 11:15
But from the man who is *, even Mt 25:29
assign him to the place of the *. Lk 12:46
True, some of them were *, but Rom 3:3
You are like an * wife who loves Jas 4:4
and those who are * to me, and the Rev 21:8

UNFAITHFULNESS
must be punished for their *. Eze 44:10

UNFEELING
Am I *, like stone? Job 6:12

UNFIT
would make them * for my altar. Ex 20:25
* for me to live in, and Lev 20:3
otherwise they will be * to make Lev 21:6
you and make you * for God." Mk 7:23
* and ordered to stand aside. 1Co 9:27

UNFOLDS
As your plan *, even the simple Ps 119:130

UNFORGETTABLE
Tell the world about his * deeds. Ps 9:11

UNFORGIVEN
to forgive them, they are *." Jn 20:23

UNFORTUNATE
this matter; it's * that the king 2Sa 15:3
their traps. The * are overwhelmed Ps 10:10

UNFRUITFUL
Literally, "the land is *." 2Ki 2:19f

UNGODLINESS
and the floods of * mounted a Ps 18:4
he shall turn the Jews from all *. Rom 11:26

UNGODLY
when the * are around me. Ps 39:1
In those days the *, the Is 32:5
the prophets, all *, wicked men. Jer 23:11
subside, and some * men will come, Dan 11:34
of * treasures and lying scales. Mic 6:10
of both the righteous and *. Act 24:15
of darkness which the * do. Eph 5:12
of * men with the vast flood. 2Pe 2:5
for all the * in the future to look 2Pe 2:6
to punish the * until the day of 2Pe 2:9
day, when all * men will perish. 2Pe 3:7

UNGRATEFUL
* to them, and thoroughly bad. 2Ti 3:2

UNHALLOWED
it were common and *, and insulted Heb 10:29

UNHAPPY
better than to be an old, * man. Ecc 6:5
I'll not make them * with another 2Co 2:1

UNHARMED
* and will soon become pregnant. Num 5:28
in Egypt, leaving them * Num 28:16
deadly adders will pull it out *. Is 11:8
And he himself shall leave *. Jer 43:12
his coming home again *.' Lk 15:27
the snake into the fire and was *. Act 28:5

UNHEALTHINESS
None are to have any defects or * Eze 43:25

UNHEARD-OF
But soon * terror will fall on Ps 53:5

UNHEEDED
my voice goes * in their councils. Ps 120:7

UNHOLY
of Aaron, placed * fire in their Lev 10:1
and offered * fire" Lev 10:1f
of Sinai when they used * fire. Num 3:4
offered * fire before the Lord. Num 26:61
made * by eating non-kosher food! Mt 15:11

UNIFORM
Joab was wearing his * with a 2Sa 20:8,9,10
in an ordinary soldier's *. 1Ki 22:30
He shall have your * and title Is 22:21
put on a waiter's * and serve them Lk 12:37

UNIFORMLY
of goats' hair (* forty-five feet Ex 36:14,15

UNIFORMS
around in splendid *, his 1Ki 10:5
their spectacular * and his 2Ch 9:4
no more the blood-stained * of Is 9:5
handsome *—all of them desirable. Eze 23:12
in striking red *, with handsome Eze 23:14,15
See their scarlet *! Nah 2:3

UNIFY
land, to * them into one nation. Eze 37

UNIMPORTANT
she will be an *, minor kingdom. Eze 29
are not just an * Judean village, Mt
education or social position is *; Col 3
Lord not to argue over * things. 2Ti 2

UNIMPRESSED
and he returned to his palace, *. Ex 7

UNINHABITED
you and leave you deserted and *. Jer 2
Her island shall become *, a Eze 2
It will be completely *. Eze 29

UNINJURED
returned home, *, the prophet Jehu 2Ch 1

UNINTENTIONALLY
* breaks any of my commandments. Lev
If a priest sins *, and so Lev
anyone sins by * defiling what is Lev 5:
is thrown *, or in which a stone is Num 35:22,
of killing someone *, he can run to Jos 2

UNINTERRUPTED
These were not in * sequence. Dan 9:2

UNION
and the other "*," and I fed the Zec 1
Then I broke my other staff, "* Zec 11:
Godly children from your *. Mal 2:
And what * can there be between 2Co 6:
been baptized into * with Christ Gal 3:
live in vital * with him. Col 2
God through your * with Christ. Col 2:

UNIQUE
you as his own * people, just as Ex 13
You have made a * nation and have 1Ch 17:
Or, "his * Son." Jn 1:1
Or, "the * Son of God." Jn 3:1
Or, "the * Son of God." Jn 3:1

UNISON
They all responded in *, "We Ex 19
and the people answered in *, Ex 24

UNIT
place of God, becomes a single *. Ex 26
All was cast as one * with the 1Ki 7:
shall be your standard * of Eze 45:1
for liquid. The * of weight shall Eze 45:1
the Roman military * handling the Lk 23:4

UNITE
* with you to become one people. Gen 34:1
And * him with Israel; Deu 33
permission to * in the defense of Est 8:1
May every fiber of my being * in Ps 86:1
Israel will * and have one leader; Hos 1:1
of the earth * in an attempt to Zec 12
The kings of the earth * to fight Act 4:25,2

UNITED
as we are must present a * front! Gen 13
armies for a * attack on Gibeon. Jos 10
nations * in one vast alliance Ju 6:3
So the whole nation * in this Ju 20:1
The band and chorus * as one to 2Ch 5:13,1
say, "let us be * to the Lord with Jer 50
You were * to your wife by the Mal 2:1
and be forever * to his wife. Mt 19:5,
and his wife are * so that they are Mk 10:
that they will be * just as we are, Jn 17:1
Then all the believers * in this Act 4:2
of Israel—are * against Jesus, your Act 4:2
Literally, "* with him in the Rom 6:5
mind, * in thought and purpose. 1Co 1:1
whereas a * family may, in God's 1Co 7:1
the sacrifices, are * by that act. 1Co 10:1
to these idols are * together in 1Co 10:2
enough by your * disapproval. 2Co 2:5,

UNITEDLY
to Jerusalem to plead * with him. 2Ch 20:

UNITING
armies, and * to crush Israel. Jos 11:
and on the west, * forces to Is 11:1

UNITS
come and carry the * to wherever Num 4:1
These * were called up for active 1Ch 27:1
Here is the list of the * and 1Ch 27:1
composed of two * of tiers was on Eze 42:9,1
and doors—they were identical *. Eze 42:1
Smaller * shall be the ephah Eze 45:1
*, with the Temple in the center. Eze 48:8
to me, using standard *). Rev 21:17
The angel used normal * of Rev 21:17

UNITY
and political *, just think of what Gen 11:6
that the bond of * between Judah Zec 11:14
me—the glorious * of being one, as Jn 17:22

UNIVERSAL
There will be * peace, and all Mic 4:3
passages indicate Christ's * rule. Zec 9:10
be bowed down with * Zec 12:12,13,14

UNIVERSE
corners of the *, I will bring you Neh 1:9
Must he change the order of the * Job 34:33
Do you know the laws of the * Job 38:33
established all the * and space. Pro 3:19

(UNIVERSE Con't)
about everything in the *. Ecc 1:12-15
"Hail to the King of the *!" Mk 11:10
He regulates the * by the mighty Heb 1:3

UNJUST
All who cheat with * weights and Deu 25:16
" 'Cursed is he who is * to the Deu 27:19
Don't be so *. Job 6:29
Are you * Job 10:4-7
this: God is never wicked or *. Job 34:12
nobles, 'You are wicked and *'? Job 34:18
Rescue me, O God, from these * Ps 71:4
The * tyrant will reap disaster Pro 22:8
WOE TO * judges and to those who Is 10:1
of God: Have I been * to Israel? Jer 2:31
who gets his wealth by * means. Jer 17:11
rain on the just and on the * too. Mt 5:45

UNJUSTIFIED
held responsible for * bloodshed. Deu 19:10

UNJUSTLY
or * attacking those I dislike. Ps 7:4
Rescue those who are * sentenced Pro 24:11,12

UNKIND
those who say * things about you. 1Pe 3:9

UNKNOWN
* to both you and your ancestors. Deu 8:3
a kind of bread * before) so that Deu 8:16
like me from an * family find 1Sa 18:23
I heard an * voice that said, Ps 81:5
and sinful to rush into the *. Pro 19:2
fairness is *. Is 59:14
literally is, of course, *. Lk 8:30f
inscription on it—'To the * God.' Act 17:23
and speaking in * languages, and 1Co 13:8
than to speak in * 1Co 14:5
rather than in * languages. 1Co 14:7
of speaking in * tongues, he should 1Co 14:13
I will pray in * tongues and also 1Co 14:15
I will sing in * tongues and also 1Co 14:15
in tongues" in an * language. 1Co 14:19
or speak in an * language, or tell 1Co 14:26
is speaking in the * language, but 1Co 14:26
should speak in an * language, and 1Co 14:27
the * language but not publicly. 1Co 14:28

UNLATCH
"My beloved tried to * the door Sol 5:4

UNLEASH
Why hold back your power? * your Ps 74:11

UNLEAVENED
with freshly baked * bread. Gen 19:3
with * bread and bitter herbs. Ex 12:8
"This annual 'Celebration with * Ex 12:17
the Pilgrimage of * Bread, when for Ex 23:15
with oil, and * wafers with oil Ex 29:2
from the basket of * bread that was Ex 29:23
the Feast of * Bread for seven Ex 34:18
of thanksgiving, * short bread Lev 7:12
Literally, "* loaves mingled with Lev 7:12f
along with * wafers spread with Lev 7:12
top of these one * wafer, one wafer Lev 8:26
"The Festival of * Bread: This Lev 23:6
oil; * wafers spread with oil; Num 6:15
with * bread and bitter herbs. Num 9:11
Eat the sacrifice with * bread. Deu 16:3
bread. Eat * bread for seven days Deu 16:3
The Festival of * Bread, Deu 16:16
invaded, and they made * bread. Jos 5:11,12
* bread from a bushel of flour. Ju 6:19
kneaded dough and baked * bread. 1Sa 28:24
* Bread for the next seven days. 2Ch 35:17
Feast of * Bread for seven days. Ez 6:21,22
killed and eaten with the * bread. Lk 22:7

UNLESS
But never eat animals * their Gen 9:4
again * your brother is with you.' Gen 43:3,4,5
We cannot go * you let Benjamin Gen 43:3,4,5
come back here * your youngest Gen 44:23
'We can't, * you let our youngest Gen 44:26
not be held— * the ox was known to Ex 21:29
a dead person, * it is a near Lev 21:2,3
holy sacrifices * he is a priest; Lev 22:10
may eat these * anyone is Num 18:11
Your families may eat these * Num 18:13
drink your water * we pay whatever Num 20:19
must not be killed * a fair trial Num 35:12
* their Rock had abandoned them, Deu 32:30
* the Lord had destroyed them? Deu 32:30
happens to you * this rope is Jos 2:17,18
this window and * all your Jos 2:17,18
you any longer * you completely rid Jos 7:12
negotiate with you * you bring me 2Sa 3:13
"We don't want you as our king * 1Ki 12:2,3,4
Jeroboam thought, "* I'm 1Ki 12:26
Don't slow down for my comfort * 2Ki 4:24
the curse of God * we obeyed God's Neh 10:29
the king again * he had especially Est 2:12,13,14
is doomed to die * the king holds Est 4:11
to needy friends * they gave you Job 22:6
wicked every day. * they repent, Ps 7:12
I would have died * the Lord had Ps 94:17
and perished * your laws had been Ps 119:92
* THE LORD builds a house, the Ps 127:1
work is useless. * the Lord Ps 127:1
They can't rest * they cause Pro 4:16
your secrets to a gossip * you Pro 20:19
* you have the extra cash on Pro 22:26,27
Can a rod strike * a hand is Is 10:15
will burn them up, * these enemies Is 27:4,5
themselves. * you circumcise your Jer 9:25,26
who would dare to come * invited. Jer 30:21
you with death * you tell them what Jer 38:25
They refuse to even offer help * Eze 13:18
of a dead person, * it is his Eze 44:25
to get across * I were to swim. Eze 47:5
means * you tell us what it was?" Dan 2:7
"Would I be roaring as a lion * Amo 3:4
A trap doesn't snap shut * it is Amo 3:5
But none of this will happen * Zec 6:15
"But I warn you—* your goodness Mt 5:20
demon won't leave * you have prayed Mt 17:21
them, and said, "* you turn to Mt 18:3
"In fact, * those days are Mt 24:22
be again. And * the Lord shortens Mk 13:20
also will perish * you leave your Lk 13:3
And you, too, will perish * you Lk 13:5
become my disciple * he first sits Lk 14:33
For * you are honest in small Lk 16:10
I tell you this: * you are born Jn 3:3
is this: * one is born of water Jn 3:5
* I do more and more miracles?" Jn 4:48
For no one can come to me * the Jn 6:44
* you eat the flesh of the Messiah Jn 6:53
* the Father attracts him to me." Jn 6:65
in your sins; for * you believe Jn 8:24
Don't believe me * I do miracles Jn 10:37
of the earth. * I die I will be Jn 12:23,24
* it were given to you from above. Jn 19:11
won't believe it * I see the nail Jn 20:25
the believers that * they adhered Act 15:1
But life is worth nothing * I Act 20:24
all die * everyone stays aboard." Act 27:31
who know what to do, * they do it. Rom 2:12-15
save them * they believe in him? Rom 10:14
And how can they hear about him * Rom 10:14
and tell them * someone sends him? Rom 10:15
* the Holy Spirit is helping him. 1Co 12:3
unknown languages—*, of course, you 1Co 14:5
* each note is sounded clearly. 1Co 14:7
firmly believe it, * of course you 1Co 15:2
Why do it * you believe that the 1Co 15:29
into a plant * it "dies" first. 1Co 15:36
happy either, * I came with joy. 2Co 2:3
against the pastor * there are two 1Ti 5:19
give him life, * he has sinned that 1Jn 5:16
* they turn again to me, Rev 2:22
turn to me again. * you do, I will Rev 3:3
so I must punish you, * you turn Rev 3:19

UNLIKE
father's God—quite * the people 2Ch 17:4
But he was an evil king, * his 2Ch 28:1
be better off, * the wicked, who Ecc 8:13
* what they were used to hearing! Mk 1:22

UNLIMITED
His understanding is *. Ps 147:5
of his glorious, * resources he Eph 3:16

UNLOADED
Tyre, in Syria, where the ship *. Act 21:3

UNLOOSE
shoes I am not worthy to *." Mk 1:7f

UNLOVED
heard that I was *, and so he has Gen 29:33

UNMARKED
and had him buried in an * grave. Jer 26:23

UNMARRIED
son, daughter, brother, or * Lev 21:2,3
child, brother or * sister. Eze 44:25
He had four * Act 21:9
of being able to stay happily *. 1Co 7:7
stay * if you can, just as I am. 1Co 7:8
is best for a person to remain *. 1Co 7:26
from worry. An * man can spend his 1Co 7:32

UNMINDFUL
Don't sit back, * of my tears. Ps 39:12

UNMIXED
until at last the * horror of the Is 28:19

UNMOURNED
Jerusalem eight years, and died *. 2Ch 21:20
land, unburied and *, and their Jer 16:6

UNMOVED
heart had been *, and that he would Ex 7:14
And why did Asher sit * Ju 5:17
The world stands *. 1Ch 16:30
therefore it stands * despite the Ps 46:5
obedience to God, but I stand *. Ps 119:51
Mount Zion, * by any circumstance. Ps 125:1
is worshiped, a city quiet and *. Is 33:20
left, while Jerusalem stands *. Zec 12:6

UNNECESSARY
do no * Jer 17:21,22

UNNI
Jehiel, *, Eliab, Benaiah, 1Ch 15:18
Jehiel, *, Eliab, Ma-aseiah, and 1Ch 15:20

UNNO
Bakbukiah and *, their fellow Neh 12:9

UNNOTICED
charities have not gone * by God! Act 10:4

UNNUMBERED
cavalrymen and an * host of 2Ch 12:3
Surrounded by * chariots, the Ps 68:17
and * virgins available to me; Sol 6:8

UNOFFERED
be left * until the next morning. Ex 23:18

UNOPPOSED
Syrian king will march onward *; Dan 11:16

UNPLEASANT
of God and never anything *?" Job 2:10
doing your duty, even when it's *. Ecc 8:2,3

UNPRECEDENTED
of a magnitude * in human history. Rev 16:18

UNPREPARED
They lived quietly, and were *. Ju 18:7

UNPRODUCTIVE
poised to chop down every * tree. Mt 3:10

UNPROTECTED
is an * land of unwalled villages! Eze 38:11

UNPUNISHED
don't let sin go *, and that you Num 14:17,18
He shall not go * for this sin. Pro 6:29
evil man will not go * forever. Pro 11:21
punish you, yes—you will not go *. Jer 30:11
You shall not go *! Jer 49:12
I will not leave her * any more. Amo 1:3
I will not leave her * any more. Amo 1:6
I will not leave them * any more. Amo 1:9
I will not leave him * any more. Amo 1:11
I will not leave them * any more. Amo 1:13
I will not leave them * any more. Amo 2:1
I will not leave them * any more. Amo 2:4
I will not leave them * any more. Amo 2:6
slain by wicked leaders, who go *. Zec 11:5

UNQUENCHABLE
Therefore, my * wrath is poured 2Ch 34:25
You have given him the * joy of Ps 21:6
by the * fire of my anger. Jer 7:20
into the * fires of hell with two! Mk 9:43,44

UNREALIZED
killed, his kingdom still *. Dan 9:26

UNREASONABLE
for making such * demands." Ex 5:16

UNREASONING
filled with * terror and ran to Dan 10:7

UNRECORDED
This quotation, * in the book Mk 1:3f

UNRELENTING
he was pitiless in * anger. Amo 1:11

UNRELIABLE
The Egyptian Pharaoh is totally * 2Ki 18:20,21
My brother, you have proved as * Job 6:15-18
An * messenger can cause a lot of Pro 13:17
Putting confidence in an * man is Pro 25:19

UNRESPONSIVE
nature as dead and * to sin, and Rom 6:11

UNRESTRAINED
You were * in tyranny. Is 14:6
Weeping *; Mt 2:18
with * weeping and wailing. Mk 5:38

UNRIGHTEOUSNESS
Literally, "in the * of your Eze 28:18f
by means of the mammon of *; Lk 16:9f

UNROLL
on this scroll, and to * it?" Rev 5:2
seal and began to * the scroll. Rev 6:1

UNROLLED
on both sides. He * it, and I saw Eze 2:9,10
Then he * the scroll to the Rev 6:3
"Go and get the * scroll from the Rev 10:8

UNRUFFLED
the older men to be serious and *; Tit 2:2

UNRULY
But you are * as the wild waves Gen 49:4
are a stubborn, * people, and I Ex 33:3
"You are an *, stubborn people. Ex 33:5
yes, it is an *, stubborn people, Ex 34:9

UNSAVED
his power, but is a sign to the *. 1Co 14:22
Even so, if an * person, or 1Co 14:23
and an * person or a new 1Co 14:24
the saved and the * all around us. 2Co 2:15
no longer as the * do, for they are Eph 4:17,18
pleasure of the * world, you cannot Jas 4:4
you behave among your * neighbors; 1Pe 2:12

UNSCATHED
that will walk in almost *. Is 43:14

UNSCORCHED
their coats were *, and they Dan 3:27

UNSCRUPULOUS
been completely * and has broken Gen 31:7

UNSEALED
for my lips will be *—oh, how I Ps 51:14,15
and also the * copy, and publicly, Jer 32:11

UNSEEN
dough, which works * until it has Lk 13:20,21
seeking for the * Rom 2:7

(UNSEEN Con't)
evil rulers of the * world, those Eph 6:12
the exact likeness of the * God. Col 1:15
He is the King of the ages, the * 1Ti 1:17
Or, "the glories of the * 2Pe 2:10f

UNSELFISH
Let everyone see that you are * Php 4:5

UNSETTLED
mind will be as * as a wave of the Jas 1:6

UNSHAKABLE
For God's plans are *. Dan 11:36
It is as strong and * as heaven Lk 16:17
that only * things will be left. Heb 12:27

UNSHEATH
I will * my sword and destroy Eze 21:3

UNSHRUNK
patch an old garment with * cloth? Mt 9:16
an old garment with * cloth! Mk 2:21

UNSKILLED
superintended the * laborers who 2Ch 34:13

UNSOWN
over wasteland, *, without crops, Deu 29:23

UNSPARINGLY
For God shall hurl at him *. Job 27:22

UNSPEAKABLE
days you held Sodom in * contempt. Eze 16:56

UNSPIRITUAL
Such things are earthly, *, Jas 3:15

UNSPOKEN
May my spoken words and * Ps 19:14

UNSTABLE
is that Saul's * mental condition 1Sa 17:55f
They make a game of luring * 2Pe 2:14
they are as * as clouds driven by 2Pe 2:17

UNSTAINED
for he is holy and blameless, * Heb 7:26

UNSTOP
blind, and * the ears of the deaf. Is 35:5

UNSUCCESSFULLY
Admah, Zeboiim, and Bela (Zoar), * Gen 14:8,9
tried * to crush the rebellion: 2Ki 8:21

UNSUSPECTING
I had been as * as a lamb or ox Jer 11:19

UNTAMED
wild one—free and * as a wild ass! Gen 16:9-12

UNTAPPED
all the mighty, * treasures of Col 2:3

UNTHANKFUL
he is kind to the * and to those Lk 6:35

UNTHINKING
* people do not understand them! Ps 92:6

UNTIE
it. * them and bring them here. Mt 21:2
ridden. * him and bring him here. Mk 11:2
Don't you * your cattle from Lk 13:15
"* him," Jesus said, "and bring Lk 19:30

UNTIRINGLY
And seek his face *. 1Ch 16:11

UNTRAINED
work from an * apprentice than from Pro 26:10

UNTRUE
"DO NOT PASS along * reports. Ex 23:1
people have been * to me, Hos 1:2
which cannot be *, speaks of those Jn 10:34,35,36

UNTRUSTING
heart is evil and * finds evil in Tit 1:15

UNTRUSTWORTHY
And if you are * about worldly Lk 16:11

UNTRUTH
bows to shoot their arrows of *. Jer 9:3

UNTYING
As they were * it, some who were Mk 11:4,5
are you doing, * that colt?" Mk 11:4,5
as they were * it, the owners Lk 19:33
"Why are you * our colt?" Lk 19:33

UNUSED
stand there, silent and *. Nah 2:13
laid it in a new, * tomb hewn into Lk 23:53

UNUSUAL
God has filled them both with * Ex 35:35
* beauty taking her evening bath. 2Sa 11:2
an * altar in a heathen temple. 2Ki 16:10
man of * courage, and Jehoiada. 1Ch 12:24-37
son Zechariah, a man of * wisdom; 1Ch 26:14,15
of * piety, with 200,000 troops. 2Ch 17:16
in this * way as a king of Israel. 2Ch 28:19f
* thing—to destroy his own people! Is 28:21
God also gave Joseph * wisdom, so Act 7:10
the power to do * miracles, so Act 19:11
good tree—a very * thing to Rom 11:24
There was nothing * about the Gal 4:23
had given them an * child, they Heb 11:23
is no strange, * thing that is 1Pe 4:12
always demand some * 2Pe 3:15,16

UNUSUALLY
The men of this area were * Gen 13:13
saw that he was an * beautiful Ex 2:1
things that are small but * wise: Pro 30:24-28
Stephen (a man * full of faith and Act 6:5

UNUTTERABLY
the * vile god of the Ammonites. 1Ki 11:7

everything is * weary and Ecc 1:8-11

UNVEIL
Now he continues to * his power. Ps 29:10

UNVEILS
THIS BOOK * some of the future Rev 1:1

UNWALLED
we also took all of the * towns. Deu 3:5
the Jews in the * villages Est 9:19
an unprotected land of * villages! Eze 38:11

UNWANTED
Moab like an old, * bottle. Jer 48:38
into a field and left to die, *. Eze 16:5

UNWILLING
Egyptians will be * to drink it." Ex 7:18
But if you are * to obey the Jos 24:15
However, the Lord was * to end 2Ch 21:7

UNWORTHILY
from the cup *, not thinking about 1Co 11:29

UNWORTHY
shown yourselves * of eternal Act 13:46
of the Lord in an * manner, he is 1Co 11:27

UNWRAP
Jesus told them, "* him and let Jn 11:44

UNYIELDING
you will be as * as bronze, and the Deu 28:23

UPHAZ
and gold from *, and give them to Jer 10:9

UPHILL
men the path is not * and rough! Is 26:7

UPHOLD
Lord is of them that * my soul." Ps 54:4f
I will * you with my victorious Is 41:10
whom I *; Is 42:1

UPHOLSTERS
She also * with finest tapestry; Pro 31:22

UPPER
* deck—and put a door in the side. Gen 6:16
and cover his * lip and call out as Lev 13:45
you shall always have the * hand. Deu 28:13
Then he gave her the * and Jos 15:18,19
From there it ran to * Jos 16:5,6
So Caleb gave her the * and lower Ju 1:15
and the * floor 10½ feet wide. 1Ki 6:6
reign that the * gate of the Temple 2Ki 15:34,35
near the conduit of the * pool. 2Ki 18:17
She built Lower and * Beth-horon 1Ch 7:24
the * road, to Shuppim and Hosah. 1Ch 26:16
gate, four to the * road, and two 1Ch 26:18
were used. The * rooms were also 2Ch 3:9
He fortified the cities of * 2Ch 8:5
their way from the * Gate to the 2Ch 23:20
He built the * Gate of the 2Ch 27:3
He dammed up the * Spring of 2Ch 32:30
foundations of the * tower of the Neh 3:25
then to the * room at the corner. Neh 3:31
shall my enemy have the * hand? Ps 13:2
Spring to the * reservoir, near the Is 7:3
whistle for the army of * Egypt, Is 7:18
Egypt" refers to * Egypt where the Is 7:18f
from Assyria, * and Lower Egypt, Is 11:11
AH, LAND BEYOND the * reaches of Is 18:1
nation whose land the * Nile Is 18:2
the outlet of the * pool, along the Is 36:2
(This room was just off the * Jer 36:10
coming from the * north gate, each Eze 9:2
of Pathros [along the * Nile Eze 30:14
facing north. The * two tiers of Eze 42:5
one, because the * tiers had wider Eze 42:5
court were, the * stories were set Eze 42:6
sinks again. The * stories of his Amo 9:6
Jordan River, and * Galilee where Mt 4:15,16
Don't let evil get the * hand Rom 12:21

UPRAISED
mighty power and * fist to strike Ps 136:11,12
in fear beneath the * fist of God. Is 19:16
they will not look to see your * Is 26:11
in the * arms of the cavalry! Nah 3:3

UPRIGHT
his stone headrest * as a memorial Gen 28:18
wide, standing *, with grooves on Ex 26:15,16
to mortise into the next * piece. Ex 26:17
Literally, "and made you go *." Lev 26:13f
you are such fine, * people that Deu 9:5
Literally, "*." Job 1:1f
Literally, "the * in heart." Ps 7:10f
Literally, "with the * you show Ps 18:25f
the upright you show yourself *." Ps 18:25f
Literally, "all who are * in Ps 32:11f
"knows the days of the *." Ps 37:18f
blameless, the *, the man of Ps 37:37
just and all the * will rejoice. Ps 94:15
but his blessing is on the *. Pro 3:33
God protects the * but destroys Pro 10:29
The * speak what is helpful; Pro 10:32
The * are directed by their Pro 11:5
The Lord preserves the * but Pro 22:12
O evil man, leave the * man Pro 24:15,16
But men who encourage the * to do Pro 28:10
God has made men *, each has turned Ecc 7:29

UPRIGHTLY
Literally, "walk *." Ps 84:11f

UPROAR
"Why is the city in such an *?" 1Ki 1:41
The whole city is in terrible *. Is 22:2
that all Jerusalem was in an *. Act 21:31
in all the * and confusion, he Act 21:34

UPROOT
he will * the people of Israel 1Ki 14:15
be large enough to * that mulberry Lk 17:6

UPROOTED
But the vine was * in fury and Eze 19:12

UPSET
This * Abraham very much, for Gen 21:11
"Don't be * over the boy or your Gen 21:12
But Joseph was * and displeased Gen 48:17
"Don't get so *," Aaron Ex 32:22
Samuel was terribly * and went to 1Sa 8:6
Please don't * them, but go back 1Sa 29:7
Don't be so *, since it's all in 2Sa 13:20
are probably as * as a mother bear 2Sa 17:8
What has made you so * and 1Ki 21:5
to him: "Why are you so *? 2Ki 5:8
I was very * and threw out all of Neh 13:8
sick, and I am * and disturbed. Ps 6:3
Don't be *. Ps 42:11
A fool is so * by a little work Ecc 10:15
For I will * the battle plans Jer 19:7
you are so * over all these Lk 10:41
from here have * you and questioned Act 15:24
things to be disorderly and *. 1Co 14:33
for all of you and * because you Php 2:26
Please don't be * and excited, 2Th 2:1
only * people and make them angry. 2Ti 2:23

UPSETTING
divisions and are * people's faith, Rom 16:17

UPSIDE
a dish and turns it * down to dry. 2Ki 21:13
rest of the world * down, and now Act 17:6

UPSTAIRS
sitting in a cool * room and said Ju 3:20
him and escaped across an * porch. Ju 3:22,23
her and carried it * to the guest 1Ki 17:19
had fallen off the * porch of his 2Ki 1:2
returning *, he stretched himself 2Ki 4:35
treasuries, the * rooms, the inside 1Ch 28:11
as usual in his * bedroom, with its Dan 6:10
He will take you * to a large Mk 14:15
He will take you * to a large Lk 22:12
he left the * room and went as Lk 22:39
meeting in an * room of the house Act 1:13
burial and laid her in an * room. Act 9:37
they took him * where Dorcas lay. Act 9:39
midnight! The * room where we met Act 20:8
They all went back * and ate the Act 20:10,11,12

UPWARD
all the males a month old and *. Num 26:62
Rock, and continues * from there. Ju 1:36
from three years old and *." 2Ch 31:16f
The road of the godly leads *, Pro 15:24
spirit of man goes * and the spirit Ecc 3:21
Weeping, they climb the * road to Is 15:5
gazed steadily * into heaven and Act 7:55

UPWARDS
as flames shoot * from a fire. Job 5:7
When they flew *, the wheels went Eze 1:19,20,21

UR
he was born (in * of the Gen 11:28
Sarai, and left * of the Chaldeans Gen 11:31
out of the city of * of the Gen 15:7
Eliphal (son of *); 1Ch 11:26-47
brought him from * of the Chaldeans Neh 9:7

URBANUS
own children, and *, our fellow Rom 16:9

URES
the treas *—the equipment and money Ez 8:28

URGE
"Find David and * him not to 2Sa 17:16
For I have come to * sinners, not Mt 9:13
the hedges and * anyone you find to Lk 14:23
AND SO I solemnly * you before God 2Ti 4:1
In the same way, * the young men Tit 2:6
* slaves to obey their masters Tit 2:9

URGED
the Lord and * the people to go on Num 32:12
Gibeon," he * them, "for they Jos 10:4
with him, she * him to ask her Jos 15:18,19
she * him to ask her father for Ju 1:14
Her father * him to stay awhile, Ju 19:4
SAUL NOW * his aides and his son 1Sa 19:1
his friends. They * him to attend, 1Ki 12:2,3,4
and * him to say the same thing. 1Ki 22:13
Naaman * him to take them, but he 2Ki 5:16
Then his disciples * him to send Mt 15:23
Immediately the Holy Spirit * Mk 1:12,13
being * by the Spirit out into the Lk 4:1
disciples came and * him to send Lk 9:12
Jesus' brothers * him to go to Jn 7:3
interfered and * the governor to Act 13:8
as the two men * them to accept the Act 13:43
And she * us until we did. Act 16:15
it that we have * Titus, who 2Co 8:6
When I * Titus to visit you, and 2Co 12:18

URGENT
But he was very *, until at last Gen 19:3
next morning the angels became *. Gen 19:15
Then Pharaoh sent an * call for Ex 10:16
And the Egyptians were * upon Ex 12:33
"yes" or "no" on * matters. Ex 28:30,31f
* messages to the following kings: Jos 11:1
Hear my * cry. Ps 86:6

URGENTLY
money in hand, and * explained to Num 22:7
the Word of God * at all times, 2Ti 4:2
And now I want to * remind you, 2Jn 1:5

URGES
and the spirit within me * me on. Job 32:18
"Come home with me," she * Pro 9:16
matter; she * them to practice Rev 2:20

URGING
* him until finally he gave in. Ju 19:7
otherwise, she stopped * her. Ru 1:18
Absalom kept on * the matter 2Sa 13:27
But they kept * until he was 2Ki 2:17
forever * them on to evil deeds. Ps 36:1
to sin by * them to drink your Amo 2:12
Consequently, at her mother's *, Mt 14:8
Meanwhile, the disciples were * Jn 4:31
Jesus and strongly * all his Act 2:40
the privilege of * everyone to come 2Co 5:18
else instead, * you to stoutly Jud 1:3

URI
Bezalel (son of *, and grandson of Ex 31:1
(the son of * and grandson of Hur Ex 35:30,31
Bezalel (son of * and grandson Ex 38:22
Geber (son of *), whose area was 1Ki 4:8-19
*, and Uri's son was Bezalel. 1Ch 2:20
by Bezalel (son of *, son of Hur) 2Ch 1:5,6
Shallum, Telem, and *. Ez 10:24

URI'S
Uri, and * son was Bezalel. 1Ch 2:20

URIAH
of Eliam and the wife of *. 2Sa 11:3
Joab: "Send me * the Hittite." 2Sa 11:6
his home. But * didn't go there. 2Sa 11:9
When David heard what * had done, 2Sa 11:10
* replied, "The Ark and the 2Sa 11:11
So * stayed around the palace. 2Sa 11:12
Joab and gave it to * to deliver. 2Sa 11:14
Joab to put * at the front of the 2Sa 11:15
So Joab assigned * to a spot 2Sa 11:16
fighting; and * was killed along 2Sa 11:17
—then tell him, '* was killed, 2Sa 11:19,20,21
and * the Hittite is dead too." 2Sa 11:24
For you have murdered * and 2Sa 12:9
* the Hittite—thirty-seven 2Sa 23:24-39
affair concerning * the Hittite. 1Ki 15:5
sent it back to * the priest with a 2Ki 16:10
description. * built one just like 2Ki 16:11,12
He instructed * the priest to 2Ki 16:15
* the priest did as King Ahaz 2Ki 16:16
* the Hittite; 1Ch 11:26-47
(the son of * the priest), Eleazar Ez 8:33
Meremoth (son of *, son of Neh 3:4
Meremoth (son of *, son of Neh 3:21
Anaiah, *, Hilkiah, and Ma-aseiah. Neh 8:1
and his murder of *, her husband. Ps 51:1
I asked * the priest and Is 8:2
of the Lord, * (son of Shemaiah) Jer 26:20
sent to kill him. * heard about it Jer 26:21
several other men to capture *. Jer 26:22
(his mother was the widow of *); Mt 1:6

URIAH'S
have insulted me by taking * wife. 2Sa 12:10

URIEL
Assir, Tahath, *, Uzziah, Shaul. 1Ch 6:22,23,24
of Kohath; with * as their leader; 1Ch 15:4-10
Levite leaders: *, Asaiah, Joel, 1Ch 15:11
Micaiah (daughter of * of Gibeah). 2Ch 13:1

URIM
the chestpiece the * and Thummim, Ex 28:30,31
deposited the * and the Thummim Lev 8:8
the use of the *, and Eleazar will Num 27:21
Your * and your Thummim. Deu 33:8
him, either by dreams, or by *, 1Sa 28:5,6
The * and Thummim were holy 1Sa 28:5,6f
until the * and Thummim could be Ez 2:62,63
until the * and Thummim had been Neh 7:64,65

URINE
excrement and drink their own *!" 2Ki 18:27
own dung and drink his own *." Is 36:12

USAGE
Or, by Hebrew *, "When his son, Gen 5:3,4,5f
Or, by Hebrew *, "After this Gen 5:3,4,5f
Or, by Hebrew *, "there was born Gen 11:12,13f
The subsequent * of the word 1Ch 1:24-27f
not, in Hebrew *, necessarily mean Eze 38:15,16f

USE
they are yours to * for food, in Gen 9:2,3
collected bitumen to * as mortar. Gen 11:3,4
wrong * of the knowledge gained. Gen 11:6f
* your best flour, and make Gen 18:6
to comfort him, but it was no *. Gen 37:35
Israel that I will * my mighty Ex 6:6
above the door. * the blood of the Ex 12:7
this event you are to * no yeast; Ex 13:3
Forward, march! * your rod—hold Ex 14:16
"You shall not * the name of Ex 20:7
Or, "* the name of the Lord your Ex 20:7f
nor * it to swear to a falsehood. Ex 20:7
* only uncut stones and boulders. Ex 20:25
for each side. * loops at the Ex 26:4,5
wide section; and * the other six Ex 26:9
the sacred tent.) * fifty loops Ex 26:10,11
pure olive oil to * in the lamps of Ex 27:20
When engraving these names, * Ex 28:11
as God's oracle; * the same gold, Ex 28:15
for yourselves. * this money for Ex 30:16
"* this," he said, "to anoint Ex 30:26,27
* it to anoint Aaron and his Ex 30:30
the incense: "* sweet Ex 30:34
"You must not * leavened bread Ex 34:25
priests could * it for washing. Ex 40:30
to the Lord, * animals from your Lev 1:2,3
a burnt offering, * only a bull Lev 1:2,3
"If anyone wishes to * a bird as Lev 1:14
for their own *, but it is all Lev 2:10
"* no yeast with your offerings Lev 2:11
the Lord, he may * either a bull or Lev 3:1
to the Lord's * Aaron and his sons Lev 8:30
able to afford—and * one of the Lev 14:22
* fortune telling or witchcraft. Lev 19:26
in judgment. * accurate Lev 19:35,36
the equipment needed for their *; Num 3:36,37
connected with their * and repair. Num 4:32
told Moses, "and * these wagons Num 7:4,5
division for their *, and four Num 7:7
these trumpets. * the trumpets in Num 10:10
If a lamb is being sacrificed, * Num 15:3,4
"If the sacrifice is a ram, * Num 15:6
I will * these rods to identify Num 17:5
through the * of the Urim, and Num 27:21
by fire, you shall * yearling male Num 28:3
for whatever food or water you *. Deu 2:6
" 'You must never * my name to Deu 5:11
serve him and to * his name alone Deu 6:13
Well, the Lord your God will * Deu 7:19
When you arrive, * the money to Deu 14:26
"Every third year you are to * Deu 14:28
Do not * the firstborn of your Deu 15:19
Instead, * it for food for your Deu 15:22
valuable for food. * them for the Deu 20:20
of it, but don't * a sickle. Deu 23:25
so that he can * it through the Deu 24:12,13
you must * accurate scales and Deu 25:13,14,15
the Lord your God. * uncut Deu 27:5,6
We will * them to build a Jos 4:6
Instead, I will * these nations Ju 2:22
really going to * me to save Israel Ju 6:36
For the Lord is going to * you to Ju 7:15
the Tabernacle for the Lord to *. 1Sa 1:28
youth and will * your animals for 1Sa 8:16
But Samuel replied, "It's no *! 1Sa 15:26
had a spear or sword he could *. 1Sa 21:8
best to escape, but it was no *. 1Sa 23:26
If he sins, I will * other 2Sa 7:14
"* anything you like," Araunah 2Sa 24:22
and you can * the threshing 2Sa 24:22
foreign wives to * for burning 1Ki 11:8
on you, but I'll * scorpions!' 1Ki 12:11
Elisha told Gehazi to * it to 2Ki 4:42
some special gift, * it to pay for 2Ki 12:4,5
Now don't * any more money for 2Ki 12:7
to the priests for their own *. 2Ki 12:16
the priest to * the new altar for 2Ki 16:15
be only for my personal *." 2Ki 16:15
Don't * Hebrew, for the people 2Ki 18:26
* it as seed for next year's crop; 2Ki 19:29
could ever again * it to burn his 2Ki 23:10
or verses. The * of bold type or 1Ch 1:1f
and they could * their left hands 1Ch 12:2
that he kept for his own *. 1Ch 18:4
"Take it, my lord, and * it as 1Ch 21:23
burnt offerings; * the threshing 1Ch 21:23
for the fire and * the wheat for 1Ch 21:23
lamps, each according to its *. 1Ch 28:15
and basins for * in connection with 2Ch 4:11
of the Temple for * that day as a 2Ch 7:7
on you, but I'll * scorpions!' 2Ch 10:11
I will not * Shishak to pour out 2Ch 12:7
And may God * you to defend the 2Ch 19:11
it was agreed to * it for making 2Ch 24:14
in the * of spear and sword. 2Ch 25:5,6
and Jerusalem to * only the one 2Ch 32:12
"And you, Ezra, are to * the Ez 7:25
containers for * by the ministering Neh 10:39,40
So what's the * of trying? Job 9:29
you * lies to try to help him out. Job 13:10
Can you * a wild ox to plow Job 39:10
beloved people. * your strong right Ps 60:4,5
they plot my death and * lies and Ps 62:3,4
You will * it as an ornament! Ps 76:10
* your mighty power to rescue us. Ps 80:2
receive every blessing you can *! Ps 81:10
own * these pasturelands of God!" Ps 83:12
Of what * are your miracles when Ps 88:10
smell, nor * their hands or feet! Ps 115:7
good * of everything he finds. Pro 12:27
they want to * you as their pawn. Pro 23:6,7,8
They won't die if you * a stick Pro 23:13,14
a rebel, don't * foolish arguments Pro 26:4,5
But those who * God's wisdom are Pro 28:26
There's no * arguing with a fool. Pro 29:9
and there is no * thinking of Ecc 1:12-15
contentment—well, what's the *? Ecc 6:6
So there's no * arguing with God Ecc 6:10
for sashes they'll * ropes; Is 3:24
Its immediate * here refers to Is 7:14f
—and * it on you to shave off Is 7:20
to give you. * capital letters! Is 8:1
* the nets will all be unemployed. Is 19:8
to the poor and needy for their *. Is 26:6
men who * any excuse to be unfair. Is 29:21
large enough to * for carrying Is 30:14
all the lies they * to oppress the Is 32:7
He will * him to put an end to Is 48:14
There is no * now in burning Jer 6:20
like spoiled figs, too bad to *. Jer 24:8
to him all your cattle for his *. Jer 27:6
assigned for the * of the sons of Jer 35:4
to Jeremiah, "* these rags under Jer 38:12
I will * you, says the Lord, to Jer 51:20
And * one quart of water a day; Eze 4:11
don't * more than that. Eze 4:11
right, you may * cow dung instead Eze 4:15
a sharp sword and * it as a Eze 5:1
head and beard; * balances to weigh Eze 5:1
I gave you gold to * in Eze 7:20
"Why do people * this proverb Eze 18:2
God, you will not * this proverb Eze 18:3
He will call his magicians to * Eze 21:21
most tender cuts. * only the best Eze 24:5
and spears, to * for fuel—enough to Eze 39:9
They will * the possessions of Eze 39:10
"Son of dust, notice carefully; * Eze 44:5
"You must * honest scales, Eze 45:10
always * the opposite passageway. Eze 46:9
is for public *—homes, pasture and Eze 48:15
to the city, for public *. Eze 48:18
by the * of puns their failures. Mic 1:11f
by the * of puns their failures. Mic 1:11f
by the * of puns their failures. Mic 1:11f
Quick! * your swiftest chariots Mic 1:13
gold will be of no * to you in that Zep 1:18
all who come to worship may * any Zec 14:21
And who would * old wineskins Mt 9:17
people * when they cast them out? Mt 12:27
always * these hard-to-understand Mt 13:10
That is why I * these Mt 13:12,13
said that he would * so many, he Mt 13:34,35
to *, and I have doubled it.' Mt 25:22
"* your own Temple police," Mt 27:65
What story shall I * to Mk 4:30
"And those who believe shall * Mk 16:17
Whatever measure you * to Lk 6:38
has listening ears, * them now!" Lk 8:8
"there's no * troubling the Lk 8:49
obey us when we * your name." Lk 10:17
"And besides, what's the * of Lk 12:25
* of worrying over bigger things? Lk 12:26
It's taking up space we can * for Lk 13:7
this to mean: "* your money for Lk 16:9f
they could * against him, but Jesus Jn 8:6
Those who heard Jesus * this Jn 10:6
dipped into them for his own *! Jn 12:6
Make * of the Light while there Jn 12:36
you ask for because you * my name. Jn 16:23
" 'King' as you * the word or as Jn 18:34
the word or as the Jews * it?" Jn 18:34
plan, let you * the Roman Act 2:23
nothing unless I * it for doing the Act 20:24
THEN WHAT'S THE * of being a Jew? Rom 3:1
more each time we * it until Rom 5:4
us sinners who had no * for him. Rom 5:6
he have a right to * the same lump Rom 9:21
chosen to * ideas the world 1Co 1:27
to you I didn't * lofty words and 1Co 2:1
So we * the Holy Spirit's words 1Co 2:13
Some * gold and silver and jewels; 1Co 3:12
the whole world to *, and life and 1Co 3:22
a great price. So * every part of 1Co 6:20
should make good * of their 1Co 7:31
But be careful not to * your 1Co 8:9
week, and * it for this offering. 1Co 16:2
You can * this on those preachers 2Co 5:12
being, but I don't * human plans 2Co 10:3
win my battles. I * God's mighty 2Co 10:4
I will * these weapons against 2Co 10:6
to * such weakness for his glory. 2Co 12:5
power to * in dealing with you. 2Co 13:4
for I want to * the Lord's 2Co 13:10
Don't * bad language. Eph 4:29
So * every piece of God's armor Eph 6:13
here to * me to defend the Truth. Php 1:16,17
* to conquer all else everywhere. Php 3:21
by Christ for his own * and glory. Col 1:16

(USE Con't)
Christ Jesus could * me as an 1Ti 1:16
Be sure to * the abilities God 1Ti 4:14
you and * you to help others. 1Ti 4:16
Tell them to * their money to do 1Ti 6:18
* you for his highest purposes. 2Ti 2:21
been of much * to you in the past, Phm 1:11
to be of real * to both of us. Phm 1:11
There is no * trying to bring you Heb 6:4
it represents were still in *. Heb 9:8
alive no one can * it to get any of Heb 9:17
Dear brothers, what's the * of Jas 2:14
for God's * in building his house. 1Pe 2:5
be sure to * them to help each 1Pe 4:10
there is no * praying for him. 1Jn 5:16
to him, "Begin to * the sickle, Rev 14:15
with the sickle, "* your sickle Rev 14:18

USED
Literally, "sons of God" * here Gen 6:1f
that it will be * to pronounce Gen 12:2f
yourselves to be * for next year's Gen 47:24
be * throughout all generations. Ex 3:15
magicians of Egypt * their secret Ex 7:22
charioteers—was * in the chase; Ex 14:9
The omer—the container * to Ex 16:36
that will be * to carry the table. Ex 25:26,27
"All utensils * in the work of Ex 27:19
to be * as God's oracle; Ex 28:15
in some way and * by the High Ex 28:30,31f
ram * in the ordination Ex 29:31
eat those items * in their Ex 29:33
day to be * to worship Jehovah; Ex 35:2
Onyx stones and stones to be * for Ex 35:5-9
the priests, to be * when Ex 35:10-19
Some other women gladly * their Ex 35:26
onyx stones to be * for the ephod Ex 35:27
the Tabernacle he * frames of Ex 36:20
utensils to be * with the altar—the Ex 38:3
All the nails * in constructing Ex 38:20
was * throughout the Tabernacle. Ex 38:24
The amount of silver * was 9,575 Ex 38:25,26
The silver left over was * for Ex 38:28
bronze, which was * for casting the Ex 38:29
for all the nails * in the Ex 38:29
to be * while ministering in the Ex 39:1
This same cloth was * for Aaron's Ex 39:1
All the utensils * there in the Ex 39:33-40
"If the animal * as a burnt Lev 1:10
oil may also be * as an offering. Lev 2:4
It was * symbolically for Lev 2:13f
"If a goat or sheep is * as a Lev 3:6
The fat shall be * just as in Lev 4:35
or if a bronze kettle is *, it Lev 6:28
animals, may be * for other Lev 7:24
Apparently a kind of sacred lot * Lev 8:8f
which may be * for food include any Lev 11:2,3
After that it may be * again. Lev 11:32
If the water * to cleanse the Lev 11:34
branches, to be * for the Lev 14:4
be * to anoint the man's head. Lev 14:18
*, and the house replastered. Lev 14:42
bull and the goat * for the sin Lev 16:27
has *, with twenty per cent added; Lev 22:14
of Sinai when they * unholy fire. Num 3:4
and all the ropes * in tying the Num 3:25-30
various utensils * in the Num 3:31-35
silver to be * for summoning the Num 10:1
you * to do in serving other gods. Num 15:39
they were * before the Lord; Num 16:38
"The Lord has * Israel to destroy Num 32:3,4
"(The Emim * to live in that Deu 2:10
"(That area, too, * to be Deu 2:20
he * to bring you out of Egypt? Deu 7:19
Tabernacle may be * for that." Jos 22:29
So that day the Lord * Israel to Ju 4:23
Travelers * the narrow, crooked Ju 5:6
The same name is * here as in Ju 6:16f
charges," or, * mockingly, "Let Ju 6:32f
which he * to hire some worthless Ju 9:4
have never been *, I will be as Ju 16:11
that it could be * for roasting. 1Sa 2:15
for he has been * of God to do a 1Sa 14:45
May the Lord be with you as he * 1Sa 20:13
which were * as lots in determining 1Sa 28:5,6f
King Hadadezer's officers had *. 2Sa 8:7
So she told him, "There * to be 2Sa 20:18
Narrow windows were * 1Ki 6:4
The stones * in the construction 1Ki 6:7
All the utensils and furniture * 1Ki 7:48
crews. They * to run back and forth 1Ki 9:27,28
Solomon * the algum wood to make 1Ki 10:12
(Silver wasn't * because it 1Ki 10:21
My father * whips on you, but 1Ki 12:11
the palace guards * these instead. 1Ki 14:27
And King Asa * these materials to 1Ki 15:22
For no matter how much they *, 1Ki 17:16
and * the stones to rebuild the 1Ki 18:32
killed them, and * wood from the 1Ki 19:21
out the pillar * for the worship of 2Ki 10:26
It was not * to buy silver cups, 2Ki 12:13,14
* to invade the land each spring. 2Ki 13:20,21
he * King Jeroboam II to save her. 2Ki 14:27
So the old altar was * only for 2Ki 16:15
and * magic and sold themselves to 2Ki 17:17
King Hezekiah * all the silver 2Ki 18:15
He practiced black magic and * 2Ki 21:6
all the equipment * in the worship 2Ki 23:4
instruments * for the sacrifices. 2Ki 25:14,15
* in the sacrifices and worship; 1Ch 9:28
(or Jebus, as it * to be called) 1Ch 11:4
from him and * it to kill him. 1Ch 11:23
He exulted, "God has * me to 1Ch 14:11
They * their trumpets and 1Ch 16:42
bronze and * it for the Temple. 1Ch 18:8
the instruments * in offering 1Ch 18:8
to be * for worship and sacrifice. 1Ch 28:13
solid gold hooks * in handling the 1Ch 28:17
silver to be * for overlaying the 1Ch 29:4,5
This will be * for the articles 1Ch 29:4,5
And expensive cedar lumber was * 2Ch 1:15
gold nails were *. 2Ch 3:9
The priests * the tank, and not 2Ch 4:6
Great quantities of bronze were * 2Ch 4:17,18
But in the Temple only gold was * 2Ch 4:19
made and had * to praise the Lord. 2Ch 7:6
citizens, but * them as soldiers, 2Ch 8:9
The king * the sandalwood to 2Ch 9:11
his merchants. He * some of the 2Ch 9:15
And cedar was * as though it were 2Ch 9:27
My father * whips on you, but 2Ch 10:11
And as they shouted, God * King 2Ch 13:15,16
and timbers and * them to build 2Ch 16:6
He also * the Levites for this 2Ch 17:7,8,9
spoons and bowls * for incense, and 2Ch 24:14
* in the sacrifices and offerings. 2Ch 24:14
and then * by the Levites to pay 2Ch 34:10,11
The Lord * the king of Babylon to 2Ch 36:17
great and small, * in the Temple, 2Ch 36:18
site, and it was * immediately to Ez 3:3
These funds are to be * Ez 7:17
left over may be * in whatever way Ez 7:18
cut branches and * them to build Neh 8:16
(They * the original musical Neh 12:35,36
The room had previously been * Neh 13:5
* in the king's service. Est 8:9,10
Lord, where is the love you * to Ps 89:49
the kind you * to do, and let the Ps 90:16
For your laws are my guide. I * Ps 119:67
laws, for you have * them to Ps 119:93
like those you * to have. Is 1:26
The term * here, "branch of the Is 4:2,3,4f
Here it is * differently to Is 4:2,3,4f
punning often * by the prophets: Is 5:7f
The controversial Hebrew word * Is 7:14f
We have therefore properly * this Is 7:14f
After the Lord has * the king of Is 10:12
They will not be hoarded but * Is 23:18
and * to burn beneath the pots. Is 27:11
A sledge is never * on dill, but Is 28:27
flesh as though * for slaying lambs Is 34:6
Aramaic was the language * in Is 36:11f
in coarse cloth * for making sacks, Is 37:1
I've burned it for heat and * it Is 44:19
as the term is * here, is the Is 52:13f
where is the love for us you * to Is 63:15
godly paths you * to walk in, in Jer 6:16
The Lord * to call you his green Jer 11:16
Nor can you who are so * to doing Jer 13:23
evil and their power is * wrongly. Jer 23:10
roofs have been * to offer incense Jer 32:29
next to the one * by the palace Jer 35:4
in the Hebrew expression * here. Jer 36:30f
where * clothing was kept. Jer 38:11
Though you have * many medicines, Jer 46:11
Cyrus was * of God to conquer Jer 51:20f
even your stones shall never be * Jer 51:26
and ash shovels * at the altar, and Jer 52:18
the other items * in the Temple. Jer 52:18
His strength is * against them to Lam 2:4
* to do on days of holy feasts! Lam 2:7
Those who * to eat fastidiously Lam 4:5
Give us back the joys we * to Lam 5:21
expression is * for the Messiah as Eze 2:1f
you * it instead to make idols! Eze 7:20
No, for vines can't be * even Eze 15:3
the asking. You * the lovely Eze 16:16
against me. You * the beautifully Eze 16:18
your idols! And * my oil and Eze 16:18
I gave you; you * it as a lovely Eze 16:19
You have * your wisdom and Eze 28:4
to each other as they * to be. Eze 37:7
it will be * by the priests, who Eze 45:4
sold or traded or * by others, for Eze 48:14
she * in worshiping Baal, her god! Hos 1:8
be * in reference to the true God. Hos 1:16f
ancient practice * by sorcerers, Hos 4:12f
* for sacrifices to your idols. Hos 12:11
IT * TO be when Israel spoke, the Hos 13:1
your citizens are so * to lying Mic 6:12
* to say to those they cursed! Zec 8:13
about you and * your name to cast Mt 7:22
Only new wineskins are * to store Mt 9:17
on the beach. He * many Mt 13:2,3
illustration Jesus *: "The Kingdom Mt 13:24
He also * this example: Mt 13:33
Jesus constantly * these Mt 13:34,35
were * as porches at that time. Mt 24:17f
* among men in Eastern lands. Mt 26:49f
where the clay was * by potters, Mt 27:7
what they were * to hearing! Mk 1:22
The light couldn't be seen or *. Mk 4:21
He * many such illustrations to Mk 4:33
He * many such warnings as he Lk 3:18
Elijah the prophet * a miracle to Lk 4:25,26
Then Jesus * this illustration: Lk 5:36
or small—will be * to measure what Lk 6:38
Jesus * in his sermons: "What good Lk 6:39
For John the Baptist * to go Lk 7:33
he * this illustration: "Suppose Lk 11:5,6
Then he * this illustration: "A Lk 13:6
So Jesus * this illustration: Lk 15:3,4
bread made without yeast was *. Lk 22:1
they were * for Jewish ceremonial Jn 2:6
Jesus * to say, "A prophet is Jn 4:43,44
was a new tomb, never * before. Jn 19:41
* until the time of King David. Act 7:45
Scripture and then * many others to Act 8:35
he was greatly * of God to Act 18:27
"I * to believe that I ought to Act 26:9
against them. I * torture to try Act 26:11
against us. He * Christ's blood and Rom 3:25
wickedness, to be * for sinning; Rom 6:13
to be * for his good purposes. Rom 6:13
just as you * to be slaves to all Rom 6:19
those things you * to do, for all Rom 6:21
Your "husband," your master, * Rom 7:4
But sin * this law against Rom 7:8
that it is, that * what was good to Rom 7:13
beautiful, to be * for holding Rom 9:21
effectively he has * others, but I Rom 15:18
* me to win the Gentiles to God. Rom 15:18
at all, and * it to bring down to 1Co 1:28
gifts we have even * the very words 1Co 2:13
be * to build on that foundation. 1Co 3:12
of material each builder has *. 1Co 3:13
I have * Apollos and myself as 1Co 4:6
All their lives they have been * 1Co 8:7
Yet we have never * this right, 1Co 9:12
or not it has been * as a sacrifice 1Co 10:27
and still * after Judas was gone 1Co 15:5f
died to the old life we * to live. 2Co 5:13,14
after I have first * them on you 2Co 10:6
greatly God had * me in winning the Gal 2:7,8,9
For you * to see the meaning of Gal 3:1
from these chains as you * to be. Gal 4:12
All of us * to be just as they Eph 2:3
that * to separate us. Eph 2:14
jealous of the way God has * me. Php 1:15
was made to be eaten and * up. Col 2:22
such things. You * to do them when Col 3:7
Those laws are good when * as 1Ti 1:8
* to scoff at the name of Christ. 1Ti 1:13
The expensive dishes are * for 2Ti 2:20
the cheap ones are * in the kitchen 2Ti 2:20
forget the way you * to show your Heb 6:10
instruments were * for worship. Heb 9:21
command, and had * the waters to 2Pe 3:5,6
people * to be members of our 1Jn 2:19
rose to die again. As * here the Rev 1:5f
the word * symbolically through the Rev 19:2f
The angel * normal units of Rev 21:17f
Literally, "the tree of life"—* Rev 22:2f
the leaves were * for medicine to Rev 22:2

USEFUL
Are they as * as trees? Eze 15:2
on a stand to shine and be *. Mk 4:21
a greater and more * power than to 1Co 14:5
is done must be * to all, and build 1Co 14:26
from God and is * to teach us what 2Ti 3:16
Onesimus (whose name means * Phm 1:11
and * to our Lord Jesus Christ. 2Pe 1:8

USEFULNESS
strength and * by means of the Jn 15:3

USELESS
Will you chase dry, * straws? Job 13:25
yet you are saying all these * Job 27:12
but they are *, stupid fools. Job 30:2
No, it's * to try to capture Job 41:9
Make their weapons * in their Ps 58:7
our enemies, for man's help is *. Ps 60:11
our enemies, for men are * allies. Ps 108:12
a house, the builders' work is *. Ps 127:1
becomes as * as a paralyzed leg. Pro 26:7
it was all so *, a chasing of the Ecc 2:11
on broken masts with * tackle. Is 33:23
But they are as * as dried grass Is 47:14
They give * medicine for my Jer 8:11
It was utterly *! Jer 13:7
all your weapons * against the king Jer 21:3,4
Jerusalem's gates are *. Lam 2:9
of yours are as * as foxes for Eze 13:4
So they are * both before and Eze 15:5,6
of the forest—* before being burned Eze 15:5,6

ELESS Con't)
urned and certainly * afterwards! Eze 15:5,6
' Pharaoh fall * to his sides. Eze 30:25
is arm will become * and his Zec 11:17
nd throw the * servant out into Mt 25:30
rown away like a * branch, Jn 15:6
eir wisdom to be * nonsense. 1Co 1:20
ur preaching is * and your trust 1Co 15:14
oor, weak, * religion of trying to Gal 4:9
'hrist is * to you if you are Gal 5:4
am the most * Christian there is, Eph 3:8
nd that all our work had been *. 1Th 3:5
onfusing and *, and even harmful. 2Ti 2:14
t was weak and * for saving Heb 7:18
o faith at all—it is dead and *. Jas 2:17
believing" is * without doing Jas 2:20
'hese men are as * as dried-up 2Pe 2:17

ELESSNESS
ife of * and frustration? Job 3:23

ES
which he * for fortune telling? Gen 44:5
Whoever * it will prosper! Pro 17:8
ower than the man who * it? Is 10:15
he axe and * it to make an idol. Is 44:13
And after his care, he * part of Is 44:15
For the man who * well what he Mt 25:29
Usually a host * the best wine Jn 2:10
For it * God's good laws for its Rom 7:13
book of Job, God * man's own 1Co 3:19
wherever we go he * us to tell 2Co 2:14
For God sometimes * sorrow in 2Co 7:10
to sin which he * to catch them 2Ti 2:26
And the Holy Spirit * all this to Heb 9:8

SHERED
God isn't * in with visible signs. Lk 17:20

SING
"* acacia wood, make an Ark 3¾ Ex 25:10
* beaten gold, and place them at Ex 25:18
"* ACACIA WOOD, make a square Ex 27:1
by silver rods, * silver hooks, the Ex 27:17
of the workmen, * blue, purple, and Ex 28:5,6
"Then, * the most careful Ex 28:15
linen, * a checkerboard pattern; Ex 28:39
amounts of each, * the usual Ex 30:35
Then he made a table, * acacia Ex 37:10
Next, * pure gold, he made the Ex 37:15,16
again * pure, beaten gold. Ex 37:17
the pure incense, * the techniques Ex 37:29
Literally, "* the standard of the Lev 5:15f
on a griddle, * olive oil, and Lev 6:21
of cleansing, * two birds, cedar Lev 14:49
* a fifth of a bushel for each. Lev 24:5-8
by making a loaf, * coarse flour Num 15:19,20,21
perhaps he was * the bathroom. Ju 3:24
to the Lord, * the wooden idol as Ju 6:26
the custom of * choirs in the 1Ch 16:7
God himself ! * every resource 1Ch 29:2
King Solomon, * polished bronze. 2Ch 4:12-16
Is Forever," * the musical 2Ch 7:6
ships to Tarshish, * sailors 2Ch 9:21
* cymbals, psalteries, and harps. 2Ch 29:25,26
out of the rubbish and * again!" Neh 4:1
You say God is * a fine-toothed Job 33:10
"Why are you * your ignorance to Job 38:2
But stop * this term, "God's Jer 23:36
it over a fire, * dried human dung Eze 4:12
God, must I be defiled by * dung? Eze 4:14
in it, * foreigners to do it. Eze 30:12
After that, * the door through Eze 46:19,20
far richer than the others. * his Dan 11:2
cheating again—* your weighted Amo 8:5
how skilled they are in * them! Mic 7:3
"Those * swords will get killed. Mt 26:52
and asked them (* proverbs they all Mk 3:23
* your name to cast out demons; Mk 9:38
then and there for * this Mk 12:12
And even the bailiffs were * Mk 14:65
been written * as their source Lk 1:1,2
* your name to cast out demons. Lk 9:49
You can ask him for anything, * Jn 14:12,13
Yes, ask anything, * my name, Jn 14:14
* my name, he will give it to you. Jn 15:16
Ask, * my name, and you will Jn 16:24
But the Jews were * the word Jn 18:34f
by * the name of the Lord Jesus. Act 19:13
I speak this way, * the Rom 6:19
* them to make me guilty of death. Rom 7:11
God is * us to speak to you: we 2Co 5:20
they sent me, and * it up while I 2Co 11:8,9
stop it and begin * those hands of Eph 4:28
like his own, * the same mighty Php 3:21
things, for he is * your sufferings 2Th 1:5
all the people, * branches of Heb 9:19
conquests, and, * lust as their 2Pe 2:18
what insulting language he is *. 3Jn 1:10
to me, * standard units). Rev 21:17

USUAL
wearing her widow's clothing as *. Gen 38:19
people of Israel had light as *. Ex 10:23
* on the sixth day of each week." Ex 16:5
as *, six quarts instead of three; Ex 16:22
The next day Moses sat as * to Ex 18:13
with her, he must pay the * dowry Ex 22:16
each, using the * techniques of Ex 30:35
along with the * grain offering and Num 15:23,24
oil, and the * drink offering. Num 28:9,10
to the * daily sacrifices. Num 28:23
accompanied by the * grain Num 29:14
accompanied by the * grain Num 29:18
defect— and the * grain offering Num 29:21
(along with the * grain and drink Num 29:25
by the * grain offerings and drink Num 29:26,27
male goat with the * grain and Num 29:28
to the * daily sacrifices. Num 29:28
their * grain and drink offerings. Num 29:30
In addition to the * daily Num 29:31
male goat and the * grain and drink Num 29:31
goat, with the * grain and drink Num 29:34
male goat with the * grain and Num 29:38
down again as * and overflowed the Jos 4:18
in their * battle formation. Ju 20:30
of the Temple as *, for he was 1Sa 3:15
at his * place against the wall. 1Sa 20:24,25
offerings, and the * drink offering 2Ch 29:35
country and farm the land as *." Jer 27:11
come on their * schedule, only then Jer 33:20,21
times hotter than *, and called Dan 3:19
and knelt down as * in his upstairs Dan 6:10
He refused his * entertainment Dan 6:18
again today, as *, and forgive us Mt 6:11
from there. His * method of Mk 4:2
So the * vast crowd was there as Mk 6:34
* Jewish rituals before eating. Mk 7:2
For as * the news of his arrival Mk 7:24
and as * he taught them. Mk 10:1
That evening as * they left the Mk 11:19
Literally, "kiss"—the * oriental Mk 14:44f
him to release a prisoner as *. Mk 15:8
home, he went as * to the synagogue Lk 4:16
collector—with the * reputation for Lk 5:27
the * great crowd at his heels. Lk 7:11
You neglected the * courtesy of Lk 7:46
just as * right up to the day when Lk 17:27
Yes, it will be 'business as *' Lk 17:30
went as * to the Mount of Olives. Lk 22:39
December 25 was the * date for Jn 10:22,23f
I was praying as * at this time of Act 10:30
After the * readings from the Act 13:15
and Silas to Beroea, and, as *, Act 17:10

USUALLY
An ephod was * a linen pouch worn Ju 8:27f
legal affairs were * transacted. Ru 4:1f
season when wars * began) Joab led 1Ch 20:1
the evil man is * spared in the day Job 21:30-32
* believed to be a revived Roman Dan 7:23f
"You're different from most. * a Jn 2:10
for anything—* they wouldn't even Jn 4:9
it is good. But * it is best to be 1Co 7:2
* a person should keep on with 1Co 7:20
Don't you realize that it is * Jas 2:6
* no one will hurt you for 1Pe 3:13

USURIOUS
Or, "at * interest." Eze 18:13f
Or, "at * interest." Eze 18:17f

USURP
even to help him * the throne. Ecc 4:15

USURPER
"The *, the son of Remaliah" is Is 7:1f

USURY
stop this business of *. Neh 5:10
Or, "without any *." Eze 18:8f
by all your taxes, fines, and *; Amo 5:11

UTENSIL
wooden * must be rinsed in water. Lev 15:12

UTENSILS
"All * used in the work of the Ex 27:19
for hanging the * on the walls, Ex 27:19
and all its *, the incense altar, Ex 30:26,27
carrying poles, and all of its *; Ex 35:10-19
and its carrying poles and *; Ex 35:10-19
Then he made bronze * to be used Ex 38:3
grating, the altar *, the bases for Ex 38:29
The table and all its *; Ex 39:33-40
lampstand with its lamps, *, and Ex 39:33-40
The poles and the *; Ex 39:33-40
All the * used there in the work Ex 39:33-40
and place the * on it, and bring in Ex 40:4
upon all of its * and parts, and Ex 40:9
and its *, sanctifying it; Ex 40:10
also sprinkled the * of the altar Lev 8:11
the various * used in the Num 3:31-35
All of the remaining * of the Num 4:12
All of the altar * are to be Num 4:14
and all the *, the clan of Kohath Num 4:15
the altar and its *, on the day he Num 7:1
and gold and the * of bronze and Jos 6:19
bronze and iron * were kept for the Jos 6:24
All the * and furniture used in 1Ki 7:48
that all of the *, the altar, and 2Ch 4:19
sanctified all the * thrown away by 2Ch 29:19
all the valuable Temple *. 2Ch 36:19
$200,000 in silver *; Ez 8:26,27

UTHAI
One family was that of * (the son 1Ch 9:4
From the clan of Bigvai—*, Zaccur, Ez 8:2-14

UTMOST
* bounds of the everlasting hills. Gen 49:26
I prayed for them with * Ps 35:13
their food with * care and sip Eze 12:19

UTTER
Otherwise you will come to * Gen 45:11,12
would be an * disaster to you." Ex 23:33
Literally, "You must not * the Deu 5:11f
your enemies in * confusion; Deu 28:25
scoffers with their * failure! Ps 40:14,15
yes, * sincerity and truthfulness. Ps 51:6
to God, and sings for * joy! Ps 98:4
There is * truth in all your Ps 119:160
He remembered our * weakness, for Ps 136:23
I was being formed in * seclusion! Ps 139:15
adultery is an * fool, for he Pro 6:32
how pleasant, O love, for * Sol 7:6
will be in * ruin because the Jews Is 3:8
country is an * wasteland, and Is 6:11
Babylon, in Iraq, still lies in * Is 13:20f
warriors of Moab cry in * terror. Is 15:4
The earth has broken down in * Is 24:19
the land, until it lies in * ruin; Jer 4:20
spare them from * destruction. Jer 13:14
I myself will expose you to * Jer 13:26
in amazement at its * desolation. Jer 18:16
always my soul will live in * Lam 3:20
of Sodom, where * disaster struck Lam 4:6
for they are * rebels). Eze 2:7
of water in * despair because of Eze 12:19
with relish, in * contempt for me, Eze 36:5
people in * spiritual darkness, Jon 4:11
"Nineveh lies in * ruin." Nah 3:7
become a place of * ruins, a place Zep 2:15
were overcome with * amazement. Mk 7:37
and be treated with * contempt. Mk 9:12,13
God, they became * fools instead. Rom 1:22
we can say with * honesty that in 2Co 1:12

UTTERED
Then Jesus * another loud cry, Mk 15:37

UTTERLY
and Gomorrah are * evil, and that Gen 18:20
and Gomorrah, and * destroyed Gen 19:25
Joshua that I will * blot out every Ex 17:14
But if her father * refuses to Ex 22:17
Literally, "shall be * Ex 22:20f
you must * conquer them and break Ex 23:24
your enemies shall live in it, * Lev 26:32
done, I will not * destroy them and Lev 26:44
However, anything * devoted to Lev 27:28
Literally, "that soul shall be * Num 15:31f
Hormah (meaning "* Destroyed"). Num 21:3
his cities, and * destroyed Deu 2:33,34
towns. We * destroyed the kingdom Deu 3:6
your God has * forbidden this. Deu 4:23
you will then be * destroyed. Deu 4:26
show them mercy; * wipe them out. Deu 7:2
doom is sealed. * detest it, for it Deu 7:26
that city and * destroy all of its Deu 13:15
destroy every living thing. * Deu 20:17
Land, you are * to destroy the name Deu 25:19
among you will be * callous toward Deu 28:54
my death you will * defile Deu 31:29
and beard and sat down * baffled. Ez 9:3
Haman hurried home * humiliated. Est 6:12
For I am * helpless, without any Job 6:13
And even if I am * innocent, I Job 9:21
lye to make them * clean, even so Job 9:30
and tornados. * disgrace them Ps 83:16
Literally, "Oh, forsake me not * Ps 119:8f
"* worthless!" Pro 20:14
It is all * ridiculous. Ecc 2:20-23
says the Preacher; * futile. Ecc 12:8
your 'apples'—for I am * lovesick. Sol 2:5
as the sun, so * captivating?' Sol 6:10
(But all sinners shall * perish, Is 1:28
And all idols will be * Is 2:18
will be as * destroyed as Sodom and Is 13:19
of Egypt is * stupid and wrong. Is 19:11
those from Memphis are * deluded. Is 19:13
He will * destroy them and Is 34:2
He will * rout the armies of the Is 48:14
and Tahpanhes to * destroy Israel's Jer 2:16
But they too had * rejected their Jer 5:5
lie upon lie, and * refuse to come Jer 9:6
until I have * destroyed them. Jer 9:16
It was * useless! Jer 13:7
to the palaces and * destroy them, Jer 17:27
you, and I will * destroy you and Jer 25:8,9
Even if I * destroy the nations Jer 30:11
Memphis shall be * destroyed, and Jer 46:19
her god Marduk will be * Jer 50:2
heaps of ruins and * destroy her; Jer 50:26
Or have you * rejected us? Lam 5:22
and * consume them in the desert. Eze 20:13
and you will be * wiped out, your Eze 21:32
Cherithites and * destroy those Eze 25:16
river and I will * destroy the land Eze 29:10

(UTTERLY Con't)
with my fist and * destroy you. Eze 35:3
I will * wipe out the people of Eze 35:7
O my people Israel, be * ashamed Eze 36:32
* defile the sanctuary of God. Dan 9:27
you are * defiled. Hos 5:3
other gods, Israel * defiled. Hos 6:10
That is why you are not already * Mal 3:6
The disciples were * amazed and Mt 21:20
"Without God, it is * impossible. Mk 10:27
so the baby born to you will be * Lk 1:35
to him shall be * destroyed.' Act 3:23
with him, I am * worthless.' Act 13:25
When we were * helpless with no Rom 5:6
I would be * miserable. 1Co 9:16
everything else will be * supreme. 1Co 15:28
were living * apart from Christ; Eph 2:12
and stand * guilty before him. Jas 2:11
she shall be * consumed by fire; Rev 18:8

UZ
were:*, Hul, Gether, Mash. Gen 10:23
Their names were:*, the Gen 22:20-23
The children of Dishan:*, Aran. Gen 36:28,29,30
Arpachshad, Lud, Aram, *, Hul, 1Ch 1:17
Dishan's sons were * and Aran. 1Ch 1:42
THERE LIVED IN the land of * a Job 1:1
of the land of * and the kings of Jer 25:19,20
people of Edom, in the land of *? Lam 4:21

UZAI
Palal (son of *) carried on the Neh 3:25

UZAL
Jerah, Hadoram, *, Diklah, Obal, Gen 10:26-30
Jerah, Hadoram, *, Diklah, Ebal, 1Ch 1:20-23
wine from * for your wares." Eze 27:19f

UZZA
of his palace at *, and his son 2Ki 21:18
in the garden of *, and his son 2Ki 21:26
the father of * and Ahihud. 1Ch 8:6,7
cart. * and Ahio drove the oxen. 1Ch 13:7
oxen stumbled and * reached out his 1Ch 13:9
blazed out against *, and killed 1Ch 13:10
he had done to *, and he named the 1Ch 13:11
place "The Outbreak Against *." 1Ch 13:11
Nekoda, Gazzam, *, Paseah, Besai, Ez 2:43-54
Gazzam, *, Paseah, Besai, Neh 7:46-56

UZZAH
by Abinadab's sons, * and Ahio. 2Sa 6:3
oxen stumbled and * put out his 2Sa 6:6
flared out against * and he killed 2Sa 6:7
of Wrath upon *" (which it is 2Sa 6:8
Mahli, Libni, Shime-i, *, Shime-a, 1Ch 6:29,30

UZZEN-SHEERAH
Lower and Upper Beth-horon and *. 1Ch 7:24

UZZI
*, the father of 1Ch 6:4-15
Bukki, *, Zerahiah, 1Ch 6:50-53
*, Rephaiah, Jeri-el, Jahmai, 1Ch 7:2
Ezbon, *, Uzziel, Jerimoth, Iri. 1Ch 7:7
Elah (the son of *, the son of 1Ch 9:7,8
Zerahiah was the son of *; Ez 7:1
* was the son of Bukki; Ez 7:1
at the Temple was * (son of Bani, Neh 11:22,23
*, leader of the Jedaiah clan; Neh 12:12-21
*, Jehohanan, Malchijah, Neh 12:42

UZZI'S
* son was Izrahiah among whose 1Ch 7:3

UZZIA
* from Ashterath; 1Ch 11:26-47

UZZIAH
Also known as "*." 2Ki 14:21f
Also called *. 2Ki 15:1f
at that time: King *, who had been 2Ki 15:13
Concurrent with: Jotham (son of *) 2Ki 15:30
Father's name: King * 2Ki 15:32,33
Like his father *, 2Ki 15:34,35
Or, "*." 1Ch 3:10-14f
Assir, Tahath, Uriel, *, Shaul. 1Ch 6:22,23,24
Jonathan (son of *) was chief of 1Ch 27:25
* as their new king. 2Ch 26:1
While Zechariah was alive * was 2Ch 26:5
all elite troops. * issued to them 2Ch 26:14
"It is not for you, *, to burn 2Ch 26:17,18
* was furious, and refused to set 2Ch 26:19
So King * was a leper until the 2Ch 26:21
When * died, he was buried in 2Ch 26:23
of his father *—who had, however, 2Ch 27:2
Jehiel, *. Ez 10:21
Athaiah (son of *, son of Neh 11:4,5,6
the reigns of King *, King Jotham, Is 1:1
THE YEAR KING * died I saw the Is 6:1
and grandson of *), Jerusalem was Is 7:1
*, Jotham, Ahaz, and Hos 1:1
to him at the time * was king of Amo 1:2
in the days of *, king of Judah, Zec 14:5
Joram was the father of *; Mt 1:8
* was the father of Jotham; Mt 1:9

UZZIAH'S
The other details of * reign from 2Ch 26:22

UZZIEL
of Kohath:Amram, Izhar,Hebron, *. Ex 6:18
The sons of *:Misha-el, Elzaphan, Ex 6:22
the sons of *, and told them, "Go Lev 10:4
grandsons Izhar Hebron * Num 3:25-30
Elizaphan (son of *) Num 3:25-30
Rephaiah, and *—all sons of Ishi. 1Ch 4:42
Amram, Izhar, Hebron, *. 1Ch 6:2
were:Amram, Izhar, Hebron, *. 1Ch 6:18
Ezbon, Uzzi, *, Jerimoth, Iri. 1Ch 7:7
112 from the subclan of *; 1Ch 15:4-10
Izhar, Hebron, and *. 1Ch 23:12
The sons of * were led by Micah, 1Ch 23:20
The * group was led by his son 1Ch 24:24,25
Mattaniah, *, Shebuel, Jerimoth, 1Ch 25:4,5
after Amram, Izhar, Hebron, and *. 1Ch 26:23,24
Jeduthun clan, Shemaiah and *. 2Ch 29:12,13,14
of the province. * (son of Neh 3:8

V
Shalmaneser * of Assyria. Is 14:29f

VACILLATE
How long will you *, O wayward Jer 31:22

VAGABOND
wandering like a * among the flocks Sol 1:7

VAIN
you will sow your crops in *, for Lev 26:16
Your strength shall be spent in *; Lev 26:20
They looked in * for help; 2Sa 22:42
"But I search in *. Job 23:8
must the godly wait for him in *? Job 24:1
Literally, "meditate a * thing." Ps 2:1f
be said that I trusted you in *! Ps 25:20
You will look for them in *. Ps 37:10
I have pleaded, but all in *. Pro 1:24
hopes of evil men are all in *. Pro 10:28
to seek him, but I searched in *. Sol 3:2
You will look for them in *—they Is 41:12
my work for them seems all in *; Is 49:4
have worked in *—their work shall Jer 51:58
and save us, but we look in *. Lam 4:17
"I looked in * for anyone who Eze 22:30
I shout to you in *; Hab 1:2
They work so hard, but all in *! Hab 2:13
The earlier prophets pled in * Zec 1:4
But their efforts were in *. Mk 14:55

VAINLY
The people of Maroth * hope for Mic 1:12

VAIZATHA
Aridai, and *. Est 9:7-10

VALET
He shouted for his * and 2Sa 13:17,18

VALIANT
and * warriors, says the Lord God. Eze 39:20
Perhaps the * Maccabees and their Dan 11:32f

VALID
of honor to accept * criticism. Pro 25:12

VALIDATED
this publicly * the transaction. Ru 4:7

VALIDITY
See context for * of the Ps 116:15f

VALLEY
Jordan * to the east of them. Gen 13:11
armies in Siddim * (that is, the Gen 14:3
(that is, the * of the Salt Sea). Gen 14:3
Sea * (four kings against five). Gen 14:8,9
As it happened, the * was full Gen 14:10
other kings at the * of Shaveh Gen 14:17
called King's *), the king of Sodom Gen 14:17
So Isaac moved to Gerar * and Gen 26:17
new well in Gerar *, and found a Gen 26:19
oak tree in the * below Bethel. Gen 35:8
Shechem from his home at Hebron *. Gen 37:13,14
now known as the * of Eshcol where Num 13:23
The Israelis named the * Num 13:24
River * are the Canaanites." Num 13:29
traveled to the * of the brook Num 21:12
is stated that the * of the Arnon Num 21:14
then to the * in the plateau of Num 21:20
returned from the * of Eshcol, they Num 32:9
were camped in the * of the Arabah Deu 1:1
the Amorites, the * of the Arabah, Deu 1:7
and came to the * of Eshcol, and Deu 1:24,25
of the Arnon River *, and including Deu 2:35,36
including all the cities in the *. Deu 2:35,36
* of the Arnon to Mount Hermon. Deu 3:8
of the * of the Arnon River. Deu 3:16
"So we remained in the * near Deu 3:29
of the Arnon River * to Mount Deu 4:48
and lead it to a * where there is Deu 21:4
is running water—a * neither plowed Deu 21:4
and the Jordan *; Deu 34:3
The Lord buried him in a * near Deu 34:6
brought them to the * of Achor. Jos 7:24
is called "The * of Calamity." Jos 7:26
the edge of a * north of the city. Jos 8:11,12,13
himself spent the night in the *. Jos 8:11,12,13
across the *, went out early the Jos 8:14
its place over the * of Aijalon!" Jos 10:12
and eastward into the * of Mizpah; Jos 11:8
to Baal-gad in the * of Lebanon, at Jos 11:17
the way from the * of the Arnon Jos 12:1
edge of the Arnon *, and from the Jos 12:2
the middle of the * of the Arnon Jos 12:2
the Jordan River * as far north as Jos 12:3
Baal-gad in the * of Lebanon and Jos
on the edge of the * of the Arnon Jos
the city in the *, and crossed the Jos
on the edge of the * of the Arnon Jos 1
the middle of the *, to beyond the Jos 1
mountain above the *, Beth-peor, Jos 1
In the * were Beth-haram, and Jos 13:2
went through the * of Achor to Jos
on the south side of the *. Jos
passed through the * of Hinnom, Jos
mountain above the * of Hinnom and Jos
northern end of the * of Rephaim. Jos
Beth-shean and the * of Jezreel Jos 17:16,1
beside the * of Hinnom, north of Jos 1
Hinnom, north of the * of Rephaim. Jos 1
across the * of Hinnom, crossed Jos 1
and ended at the * of Iphtahel. Jos 1
as Zebulun in the * of Iphtahel, Jos 1
of the *, who had iron chariots. Ju
let them come down into the *; Ju
Down into the * Ju
command they rushed into the *. Ju
and camped in the * of Jezreel. Ju
in the * beside the hill of Moreh. Ju
camped in the * just below, the Ju 7
crowded across the * like Ju 7:1
Delilah over in the * of Sorek. Ju
This happened in the * next to Ju 1
wheat in the *, and when they saw 1Sa
the * of Zeboim near the desert. 1Sa 1
let's cross the * to the garrison 1Sa
were camped in the * below them. 1Sa
a buildup of forces at Elah *. 1Sa
hills, with the * between them. 1Sa
army were camped at the * of Elah. 1Sa 17
you killed in the * of Elah. 1Sa 2
other side of the * and beyond the 1Sa 3
across the Jordan *, crossed the 2Sa 2
out across the * of Rephaim. 2Sa 5
out across the * of Rephaim. 2Sa 5
at the * of Salt, and then 2Sa 8
into the nearest * until every 2Sa 17
in the King's *, for he said, "I 2Sa 18
were at the * of Rephaim, three of 2Sa 23
of the * of Gad, near Jazer; 2Sa 2
Olives, across the * from 1Ki 1
to fill this dry * with trenches to 2Ki 3
nor rain, but this * will be filled 2Ki 3
Aroer River in the * of the Arnon 2Ki 10:32
ten thousand Edomites in Salt *; 2Ki 1
of the Kidron * outside Jerusalem, 2Ki 2
of Topheth in the * of the Sons of 2Ki 23
scattered the pieces in Kidron *. 2Ki 23
of Craftsman * (called that because 1Ch 4
east side of Gedor * in search of 1Ch 4:34
When the Israelis in the * below 1Ch 1
were camped in the * of Rephaim, 1Ch 11
were raiding the * of Rephaim, and 1Ch 1
raided the * again, and again 1Ch 14
Edomites in the * of Salt. 1Ch 18
* between Succoth and Zeredah. 2Ch 4:17,
Mareshah, in the * of Zephathah, 2Ch 14:9,
at the end of the * that opens into 2Ch 20:
gathered in the * of Blessing, as 2Ch 20:
his army to the * of Salt, and 2Ch 25:
Gate, and the * Gate, and at the 2Ch 26
He even went out to the * of 2Ch 28
offerings in the * of Hinnom. 2Ch 33
in the Kidron *, and then to the 2Ch 33:
the battle at the * of Megiddo. 2Ch 35:
out through the * Gate toward the Neh 2:
and entered again at the * Gate. Neh 2:14,
Hanun, built the * Gate, hung the Neh 3:
Beer-sheba to the * of Hinnom. Neh 11:25-
Lod, Ono (the * of the Craftsmen). Neh 11:31-
* and to prosper you there. Job 36:
through the dark * of death I will Ps 23
men of Edom in the * of Salt. Ps 60
When they walk through the * of Ps 84
of Shechem, and also Succoth *. Ps 108
of Sharon, the lily of the *." Sol 2
and out to the * to see the Sol 6:1
grain fields in the * of Rephaim. Is 17
Literally, "The * of Vision." Is 22:
by her rich *—Samaria, the pride Is 28
by a fertile * will suddenly be Is 28
flocks, and the * of Achor shall be Is 65:1
Go and look in any * in the land! Jer 2:2
Topheth in the * of Ben-Hinnom, and Jer 7:3
or the "* of Ben-Hinnom," to the Jer 7:3
to the "* of Slaughter"; Jer 7:3
will dump the bodies in that *. Jer 7:3
it out into the * of Ben-Hinnom by Jer 19:
me and turned this * into a place Jer 19:
Lord, when this * shall no longer Jer 19:
or "Ben-Hinnom *," but "The Jer 19:
but "The * of Slaughter." Jer 19:
bodies shall be heaped in this *. Jer 19:1
And as it will be in this *, so Jer 19:1
ash dump in the * shall be holy to Jer 31:4
altars to Baal in the * of Hinnom. Jer 32:3

(VALLEY Con't)
the fields toward the Jordan *. Jer 39:4
"Go out into the * and I will talk Eze 3:22
as I had seen it before in the *. Eze 8:4
of the Lord to a * full of old, dry Eze 37:1
all across the *, and the bones of Eze 37:7
his armies in the * of the Eze 39:11
place to "The * of Gog's Army." Eze 39:11
the * of Gog's Army to bury them. Eze 39:15,16
and the Jordan * to the Dead Sea, Eze 47:8
for in the * of Jezreel I am about Hos 1:4,5
the nation in the * of Jezreel." Hos 1:4,5
* of Troubles into a Door of Hope. Hos 1:15
the "* Where Jehovah Judges" Joe 3:2
Or, "* of Jehoshaphat." Joe 3:2f
bring them to the * of Joe 3:12
* for the verdict of their doom! Joe 3:14
is near, in the * of Judgment. Joe 3:14
of the Lord to water Acacia *. Joe 3:18
glorious Jordan * lies in ruins. Zec 11:3
in the * of Megiddo." Zec 12:11f
who was killed in the * of Zec 12:11
making a very wide * running from Zec 14:4
You will escape through that *, Zec 14:5
Literally, "for the * of my Zec 14:5f
over the Jordan *, and, in fact, Mt 3:5
Olives across the * from Jerusalem, Mk 13:3,4
the * on the Mount of Olives. Lk 24:50f

VALLEY'S
Lord, when that * name will be Jer 7:32

VALLEYS
living in the *, tomorrow you must Num 14:25
them spread before me as green *, Num 24:3-9
gushing springs, *, and hills; Deu 8:7
It is a land of hills and * with Deu 11:11
from the *, too, even though they Jos 17:16,17,18
had charge of those in the *. 1Ch 27:29
out in the * and on the plains. 2Ch 26:10
hillsides and in the fertile *. 2Ch 26:10
Who dug the * for the torrents Job 38:25-27
and the * are carpeted with grain. Ps 65:13
* sank to the levels you decreed. Ps 104:7,8
He placed springs in the *, and Ps 104:10
deserts into fertile, watered *. Ps 107:35
into the desolate * and caves and Is 7:19
They fill your choicest * and Is 22:6,7
Fill the *; Is 40:4
them fountains of water in the *! Is 41:18
shall be raised above the *. Is 49:11
in the *, under overhanging rocks. Is 57:5
are the smooth stones in the *. Is 57:6
Like cattle grazing in the *, so Is 63:14
The fertile * were wilderness and Jer 4:26
plateaus or in the *, shall be Jer 48:8
You are proud of your fertile *, Jer 49:4
you and against the rivers and *. Eze 6:3
and * and rivers of the land. Eze 31:12
and fill the * with your bones. Eze 32:5
hills, your * and your rivers will Eze 35:8
dales and *, and to the ruined Eze 36:4
dales and * of Israel: The Lord God Eze 36:6
and flow into the * like wax in Mic 1:4
their stones into the * below. Mic 1:6
Fill up the *! Lk 3:5

VALOR
God we shall do mighty acts of *. Ps 108:13

VALUABLE
and he gave many * presents to Gen 24:53
down trees that aren't * for food. Deu 20:20
given each of them * gifts of money 2Ch 21:3,4
* presents for King Hezekiah, too. 2Ch 32:23
all the * Temple utensils. 2Ch 36:19
bowls and other * items which King Ez 1:7
Wisdom is far more * than gold Job 28:17
They are more * to me than Ps 119:71,72
For such wisdom is far more * Pro 3:13,14,15
My instruction is far more * Pro 8:10
Good sense is far more * than Pro 20:15
A GOOD REPUTATION is more * than Ecc 7:1
the future these papers will be *. Jer 32:15
Are they even as * as a single Eze 15:2
anything very * to offer to God!' Mal 1:7
And you are far more * to him Mt 6:26
You are more * to him than many Mt 10:31
And how much more * is a person Mt 12:12
of every kind, * and worthless. Mt 13:47,48
Never fear, you are far more * to Lk 12:7
And you are far more * to him Lk 12:24
ten * silver coins and loses one. Lk 15:8
clothes and with * gold rings on Jas 2:2

VALUABLES
man to whom the * were entrusted Ex 22:8
gold, and other * were weighed in Ez 8:33

VALUATION
to the priest's *, and the field Lev 27:19

VALUATIONS
All the * shall be stated in Lev 27:25

VALUE
his birthright to be of no *." Gen 25:34f
he shall pay double * as his fine. Ex 22:4
of a * determined by Moses. Lev 5:17,18
be worth whatever * you demand. Lev 6:6
it will have no * as a sacrifice, Lev 7:17,18
Note: The actual * by today's Lev 27:3f
to the priest to * it, and he shall Lev 27:11,12
more than the * set by the priest. Lev 27:13
will decide its * and the man shall Lev 27:14,15
field to the Lord, * it in Lev 27:16
Jubilee, then the * shall be in Lev 27:18
shall estimate the * until the Year Lev 27:23
that estimated * to the Lord, and Lev 27:23
he must add a fifth to its *. Lev 27:31
total * to be more than $300,000. Num 31:51,52
The exact * cannot be Deu 22:19f
Their * was estimated at Ju 8:26
of knowing the * of the silver. 2Sa 18:11f
Solomon, the total * of which was 1Ki 9:27,28
wasn't considered to be of much *! 1Ki 10:21
* than the common sycamore! 1Ki 10:27
to her, plus the * of any crops 2Ki 8:6
pounds sterling at current *. 1Ch 19:6f
gifts of the same * as she had 2Ch 9:12
away everything of * in the king's 2Ch 21:17
The total * of their gifts Ez 2:69
have about as much * as ashes. Job 13:12
Even the wisest is of * only to Job 22:2
kings about their *, and they will Ps 119:44,45,46
For the * of wisdom is far above Pro 8:11
I did— that wisdom is of more * Ecc 2:13,14
So of what * is all my wisdom? Ecc 2:15
greater * than the gold of Ophir. Is 13:12
crop of greatest *, and though it Is 17:10
my people and determine their *. Jer 6:27
have no * in that day of wrath. Eze 7:19
—this magnificent sum they * you Zec 11:13
*, and are safe from thieves. Mt 6:20
pearl of great *—and sold Mt 13:46
What can be compared with the * Mt 16:26
(Someone estimated the * of the Act 19:18,19
Is there any * in the Jewish Rom 3:1
measuring your * by how much faith Rom 12:3
not it keeps its *, and what was 1Co 3:13
these sacrifices are of some *? 1Co 10:19
it would be of no * whatever. 1Co 13:3
And if being a Christian is of * 1Co 15:19
And what * was there in fighting 1Co 15:32
of lasting * by ourselves. 2Co 3:5
rags. The * of your gold and Jas 5:3

VALUED
is * at twenty-five dollars. Lev 27:16
gold to Solomon * at $3,500,000! 1Ki 9:14
the horses were * at $150 each. 1Ki 10:29
the finest gold, * at $18,000,000. 2Ch 3:8
Everyone listened to me and * my Job 29:21
You * us at nothing at all. Ps 44:12
five shekels shall be * at five Eze 45:12
at which he was * by the people of Mt 27:9

VALUELESS
Prayers to their gods are *. Deu 32:31

VALUES
the man who * his soul will stay Pro 22:5
He who * grace and truth is the Pro 22:11
a person has a wrong sense of *. Tit 3:11
the numerical * of the letters in Rev 13:18

VANIAH
Bedeiah, Cheluhi, *, Meremoth, Ez 10:34-42

VANISH
and * as quickly as a dream. Ps 90:5,6
Jerusalem will * like a dream! Is 29:7
Bullies will * and scoffers will Is 29:20
and earth, shall * from the earth, Jer 10:11
the Lord declares, "it will *. Nah 1:12
idols that he worships—all will *. Zep 1:3

VANISHED
* as a cloud before a strong wind. Job 30:15
and fertility had * with him. Eze 8:14f
how you have * from the seas! Eze 26:17
And islands *, and mountains Rev 16:20

VANISHES
As a cloud disperses and *, so Job 7:9
All the strength of Israel * Lam 2:3
For your love * like morning Hos 6:4

VANITY
Literally, "trust in *." Job 15:31f
Literally, "from beholding *." Ps 119:37f
Or, "*." Hos 12:11f

VANQUISH
had hoped to * them, though it Est 9:1

VANQUISHED
Yes, the Lord has * Israel like Lam 2:5

VAPOR
the * above from the water below. Gen 1:7,8
He draws up the water * and then Job 36:27
lightning across the * droplets. Job 41:18
He calls for the * to rise from Amo 9:6

VAPORS
of God brooding over the dark *. Gen 1:2
And God said, "Let the * Gen 1:6
Praise him, * high above the Ps 148:4
the * to rise around the world; Jer 51:16

VARIETIES
locusts of all *—ordinary Lev 11:21,22
produces good fruit; poor * don't. Mt 12:33

VARIETY
The falcon (any *), Deu 14:11-18
The raven (any *), Deu 14:11-18
The sea gull, the hawk (any *), Deu 14:11-18
The stork, the heron (any *), Deu 14:11-18
O Lord, what a * you have made! Ps 104:24
all the rich * of goods you make. Eze 27:18
their fruit. A * that produces Mt 7:18
A tree from a select * produces Mt 12:33

VARIOUS
With him were all the * kinds of Gen 7:8,9
nations in * lands, each with a Gen 10:5
living in the * nations that Gen 10:32
clans of the * tribes of Israel: Ex 6:14
People of * sorts Ex 12:38
over them. (The * kinds of bread Ex 29:2
This summarizes the * steps in Ex 38:21
concerning the * places where Lev 14:54
the altars, the * utensils used in Num 3:31-35
can assist with * light duties in Num 8:25,26
these are the * regulations: Num 19:14
they camped at * places along the Num 33:49
These cities shall be in * parts Num 35:8
and the leaders of the * tribes. Jos 21:1
had been living in * places as far Ju 4:11
gates, discussing * issues with the Ju 9:35
"* suggestions were made, until 1Ki 22:20
They had been built by the * 2Ki 23:19
* other tasks in the Tabernacle. 1Ch 6:48
to care for the * vessels used in 1Ch 9:28
many groups to serve at * times. 1Ch 24:3
All tasks were assigned to the * 1Ch 24:5
of Levi in their * clans. 1Ch 24:30
guard duty at the * gates without 1Ch 26:13
* groups of priests and Levites; 1Ch 28:13
to make these * items, as well as 1Ch 28:14
And these * groups of priests 1Ch 28:21
of Judah, in * other places 2Ch 17:2
2,410 silver bowls (of * designs), Ez 1:9,10
divided into their * service corps, Ez 6:18
homes in the * cities of Judah). Neh 11:3
with all the * kinds of work God Ecc 3:10
of Judah, and at * other times Jer 1:3
Mix the * kinds of flour together Eze 4:9
besides all the * idols worshiped Eze 8:10
and measured the * sections of its Eze 40:24
He will invade * lands on the Dan 11:41
a tour of the * Temple buildings. Mt 24:1
people of their * diseases—healing Lk 7:20,21,22
But there are * kinds of 1Co 3:12
doing good and obeying * rules Col 2:20
and wonders and * miracles and by Heb 2:4
satisfied with the * sacrifices and Heb 10:8
But see Isaiah 11:2, where * Rev 1:4f

VASE
of God is as fragile as a clay *! Job 13:12

VASHTI
Queen * gave a party for the Est 1:9
to bring Queen * to him with the Est 1:11
to Queen *, she refused to come. Est 1:12
others, "Queen * has wronged not Est 1:16
they learn what Queen * has done. Est 1:17
that Queen * be forever banished Est 1:19
over the loss of *, realizing that Est 2:1
shall be the queen instead of *." Est 2:4
declared her queen instead of *. Est 2:17

VAST
If you refuse, I will send * Ex 8:2
and herds—a * exodus of cattle. Ex 12:38
That evening * numbers of quail Ex 16:13
"A * horde of people has arrived Num 22:5,6
"The king says that a * horde Num 22:11
and see before you * numbers of Deu 20:1
along with a * array of horses and Jos 11:4
And the Lord gave all that * Jos 11:8
in one * alliance against Israel. Ju 6:33
enemy camp. The * armies of Ju 7:12,13
all the * armies of Midian!" Ju 7:15
as the whole * enemy army began Ju 7:21
When the men of Israel saw the * 1Sa 13:6
strange sight—the * army of the 1Sa 14:16
When Saul saw the * army of the 1Sa 28:5,6
joy because of the * amount of loot 1Sa 30:16
of horses with a * number of 1Ki 10:26
comparison to the * Syrian forces 1Ki 20:27
you defeat this * army, and you 1Ki 20:28
mules, and oxen. * supplies of 1Ch 12:40
Let the * seas roar, 1Ch 16:32
your name we attack this * horde. 2Ch 14:11
off * quantities of plunder. 2Ch 14:13
As a result, additional * 2Ch 14:14
Libyans and their * army, with all 2Ch 16:8
surrounded by * throngs of angels. 2Ch 18:18
that "a * army is marching against 2Ch 20:2
who gave me my * empire, has now Ez 1:2
* tribute, custom, and toll. Ez 4:20
emperor of * Media-Persia, with its Est 1:1
them into his * reservoirs. Ps 33:7
Your kindness and love are as * Ps 57:10
and how he sent * swarms of flies Ps 78:45

(VAST Con't)
collected into its * ocean beds, Ps 104:7,8
insects swarmed in * clouds from Ps 105:31
His glory is far more * than the Ps 108:5
of multitudes—a * host of men have Pro 7:26
Israel has * treasures of silver Is 2:7
They will come in * hordes, Is 7:19
All the land will be one * Is 7:24
he destroyed the * host of the Is 9:4
too, and send a * cloud of smoke Is 9:18
Assyria's * army is like a Is 10:18
He is destroying all of that * Is 10:33
it a * wasteland of destruction. Is 24:1
all the * myriads of stars. Is 45:12
of many lands. * droves of camels Is 60:6
For I the Lord am bringing * Jer 4:6
* multitudes fall in heaps. Jer 46:16
the sea on the day of your * ruin. Eze 27:27
You and all your allies—a * and Eze 38:9
capture * booty and many slaves. Eze 38:12
north with your * host of cavalry Eze 38:15,16
You and all your * armies will Eze 39:4
"And I will make a * graveyard Eze 39:11
of a * multitude of people. Dan 10:5,6
who will rule a * kingdom and Dan 11:3
* forces of Syria and defeat them. Dan 11:10,11
a whirlwind; his * army and navy Dan 11:40
wine is gone! A * army of locusts Joe 1:6
He was preparing a * swarm of Amo 7:1
of treasures. Her *, uncounted Nah 2:9
your city with * wealth, but your Nah 3:16
This is the fate of that *, Zep 2:15
the capital of so * an empire, a Zep 2:15f
will become one * plain, but Zec 14:10
the wilderness, a * crowd was Mt 14:14
And a * crowd brought him their Mt 15:30
the Jordan River. * crowds Mt 19:2
a * crowd surged along behind. Mt 20:29
far and wide and * numbers came to Mk 3:7,8
of the lake, a * crowd gathered Mk 5:21
So the usual * crowd was there Mk 6:34
was joined by a * host of Lk 2:13
even faster and * crowds came to Lk 5:15
all will become one * heap of Lk 21:6
Look around you! * fields of Jn 4:35
he was bringing * multitudes of Heb 2:10
of ungodly men with the * flood. 2Pe 2:5
and there was a * earthquake; Rev 6:12
After this I saw a * crowd, too Rev 7:9
And from the Serpent's mouth a * Rev 12:15
a * crowd in heaven, "Hallelujah! Rev 19:1

VASTLY
education shall be * increased!" Dan 12:4
increased * in Jerusalem; Act 6:7

VASTNESS
let the * of the roaring seas Ps 96:11
Let the sea in all its * roar Ps 98:7

VAT
the stands. Each * was six feet 1Ki 7:38

VATS
Then he made ten brass *, and 1Ki 7:38
Five of these * were arranged on 1Ki 7:39
Ten movable stands holding ten *; 1Ki 7:41-46
and the water * they supported, and 2Ki 16:17
He also constructed ten * for 2Ch 4:6
not the *, for their own washing. 2Ch 4:6
The bases for the *, and the vats 2Ch 4:12-16
The bases for the vats, and the * 2Ch 4:12-16
your wine * with the finest wines. Pro 3:9,10
boiling *, with ovens underneath. Eze 46:23

VAULT
buried in his own * that he had 2Ch 16:13,14
walking on the * of heaven.' Job 22:14

VAULTS
and from the royal * and sent it as 2Ki 16:8

VEAL
milk and the roast *, he set it Gen 18:8

VEDAN
* and Javan bring Arabian yarn, Eze 27:19

VEGETABLE
like pancakes fried in * oil. Num 11:8

VEGETABLES
food, in addition to grain and *. Gen 9:2,3
field to gather * and came back 2Ki 4:39
are fruit trees, * and grain for Ps 104:14
ten-day diet of only * and water; Dan 1:12
fed them only * and water, without Dan 1:16
at all and eat * rather than eat Rom 14:2

VEGETATION
and they ate every bit of * the Ex 10:15
without a shred of *—just like Deu 29:23

VEIL
she covered her face with her *. Gen 24:65
herself with a * to disguise Gen 38:14
make a * from blue, purple, and Ex 26:31
other on the outer side of the *. Ex 26:35
just outside the *, near the place Ex 30:6
them, he put a * over his face; Ex 34:33
the * until he came out again; Ex 34:34
Afterwards he would put the * on Ex 34:35
The * to enclose the Holy Place; Ex 35:10-19
* was made from woven linen, with Ex 36:35
into it. The * was then attached Ex 36:36
supporting the * required 9,500 Ex 38:27
and install the * to enclose the Ex 40:3
and set up the * to screen it, just Ex 40:21
room outside the *, and set the Ex 40:22
next to the *, and burned upon it Ex 40:26
in front of the * that bars the way Lev 4:6
the Lord, in front of the *. Lev 4:17
Place behind the *, where the Ark Lev 16:1
powder, and bring it inside the *. Lev 16:12
blood within the *, and sprinkle it Lev 16:15
he went behind the *, and leave Lev 16:23
go in behind the *, nor come near Lev 21:23
stands outside the * that secludes Lev 24:3,4
Tabernacle, the *, and any repairs Num 3:31-35
the * and cover the Ark with it. Num 4:5
Then they will cover the * with Num 4:6
that is within the *, for the Num 18:7
room he placed a * of blue and 2Ch 3:14
Instantly the death * was placed Est 7:8
Literally, "behind your *." Sol 4:3f
on the wall tore off my *. Sol 5:7
remove your *; Is 47:2
out, and I will * the heavens and Eze 32:7
A heavy * hung in front of the Mk 15:38f
for himself; the * separated him Mk 15:38f
Now this * was split from above, Mk 15:38f
the thick * hanging in the Temple Lk 23:45
did, who put a * over his face so 2Co 3:13
covered by a thick *, because they 2Co 3:14
For this * of misunderstanding 2Co 3:14
sins, then the * is taken away. 2Co 3:16
But we Christians have no * over 2Co 3:18

VEILED
prostitute, since her face was *. Gen 38:15
You have * yourself as with a Lam 3:44
Not only Moses' face was *, but 2Co 3:14
were * and blinded too. 2Co 3:14
then God's * plan—mysterious Rev 10:7

VEILING
with darkness, * his approach with Ps 18:11

VEILS
and * of shimmering gauze. Is 3:19
lingerie, beautiful dresses and *. Is 3:23
were permitted to go without *. Is 47:2f
* and selling them indulgences. Eze 13:18
I will tear off the magic * and Eze 13:21
Or, "He * his power." Hab 3:4f

VENGEANCE
Don't seek *. Lev 19:18
to Moses, "Take * on the Num 31:1
* is mine, Deu 32:35
Taking * on his enemies, Deu 32:40,41
"Now my * will strike again!" Ju 15:7
* on my enemies is all I want." 1Sa 18:25
and taking * into your own hands, I 1Sa 25:26
carrying out * with my own hands. 1Sa 25:33
Literally, "when he sees the *." Ps 58:10f
O Lord, take sevenfold * on Ps 79:12
LORD GOD, TO whom * belongs, let Ps 94:1
of * from the wronged husband. Pro 5:9f
no mercy on you in his day of *. Pro 6:34
will take awesome * on these Is 29:14
For it is the day of *, the year Is 34:8
I will take * upon you and will Is 47:3
with robes of * and of godly fury. Is 59:17
So I executed * alone; Is 63:5
Lord taking * upon his enemies. Is 66:6
Shall I not send my * on such a Jer 5:9
minds, let me see your * on them. Jer 20:12
a day of * upon his enemies. Jer 46:10
The Lord has taken *. Jer 50:15
his * on all of Babylon's sins. Jer 51:6
This is his * on those who Jer 51:11
her and arouse my wrath and *. Eze 24:8
They will carry out my furious *. Eze 25:14
I will execute terrible * upon Eze 25:17
The Lord's * will soon fall upon Ob 1:15
And I will pour out my * upon the Mic 5:15
that is why he takes * on those Nah 1:2
Literally, "days of *." Lk 21:22f
for * as the blood of Abel did. Heb 12:24

VENGEFUL
and cursed by my * enemies. Ps 44:15,16

VENISON
because of the * he brought home, Gen 25:28
and get me some *, and prepare it Gen 27:2,3,4
to hunt for the *, she called her Gen 27:5
Here is the delicious * you Gen 27:19
Isaac: "Then bring me the *, and Gen 27:25
"Here I am, father, with the *. Gen 27:31
was just here with *, and I have Gen 27:33

VENOM
They drink the wine of serpent *. Deu 32:33
with *, and his speech reveals it. Mt 12:35

VENOMOUS
lions and swift * snakes live—and Is 30:6

VENT
I am like a wine cask without a *! Job 32:19
Give * to your anger. Job 40:11
But now he will give full * to Is 42:

VENTURE
of its inhabitants to * outside; Mic 1:1
of its inhabitants to * outside; Mic 1:1
of its inhabitants to * outside; Mic 1:1

VENTURED
a favorable reading," the man *. 2Ch 18:

VERB
Zaanan sounds like a * meaning Mic 1:1
Zaanan sounds like a * meaning Mic 1:1
Zaanan sounds like a * meaning Mic 1:1

VERDICT
who refused God's *, and they will Deu 17:
valley for the * of their doom! Joe 3:1
if the church's * favors you, but Mt 18:
What is your *?" Mt 26:65,6
What is your *?" Mk 14:63,6
the people, and announced his *: Lk 23:1

VERGE
I find myself upon the * of sin; Ps 38:1
with fish and on the * of sinking. Lk 5:
you may be on the * of failing to Heb 4:

VERIFY
standing there to * the report. 1Sa 17:2

VERITABLE
* population explosion among them. Gen 47:2
there was a * population Ex 1:

VERSE
longer godly in character (* 3). Gen 6:
* 14 is a repetition of the names Gen 36:13,14
of the names listed in * 5. Gen 36:13,14
See * 18. Ex 6:20
Literally, * 30 reads: "But if a Ex 21:30
Implied in remainder of the *. Lev 5:16
* 1 applied to ordinary priests. Lev 21:1
More literally, * 7 reads: "But Num 10:5,6,7
See * 16. Num 13:3-15
Implied. See * 17. Num 19:12
expected from Bethel (* 17). Jos 8:11,12,13
Implied in * 16, where a sub-total Jos 21:9-16
Implied in * 22, where the total Jos 21:20,21,22
Implied in chapter 2, * 22; Ju 3:1
and chapter 3, * 4. Ju 3:1
Implied in chapter 2, * 22; Ju 3:1
and chapter 3, * 4. Ju 3:1
Gideon's mind: see * 13) will now Ju 6:16
Implied in * 14. Ju 16:8
Implied in * 31. 1Ki 7:27-30
Implied in * 21. 2Ki 2:19f
Chapter 1, * 17, says King Jehoram 2Ki 3:1f
See * 10. 2Ki 15:15f
Also called Pul, in * 19 above. 2Ki 15:29f
to in the following * or verses. 1Ch 1:1f
a different Sheshan than in * 31. 1Ch 2:34,35f
See * 12. 1Ch 7:15f
not the same Shime-i as in * 7. 1Ch 23:8,9f
King Jehoram's daughter, * 11. 2Ch 22:11f
See * 11. Job 26:13f
Implied in * 7. Job 29:12f
This * was quoted by Christ as Ps 40:7f
Implied in * 8. Ps 61:5f
An alternate rendering of * 30 Ps 68:30f
The Hebrew of this * is not clear. Pro 18:19f
Implied in * 5. Sol 1:6f
enough to talk (* 4) the two Is 7:14f
"virgin," in * 14, as otherwise Is 7:14f
Implied in * 9. Is 21:1f
Implied in previous *. Is 42:22f
Some believe this * as well as Is 65:1f
Some believe this * as well as Is 65:1f
(almond) in * 11 and shoqedh Jer 1:12f
(watching) in * 12: "For I am Jer 1:12f
Implied. See * 18. Jer 22:13f
This * probably refers to the Jer 30:21f
see note on chapter 7, * 18. Jer 44:17f
In contrast, see * 11. Eze 20:25f
* 30, omitted in the Septuagint Eze 40:29,30f
Implied in * 22. Dan 7:26f
told is true." * 14 is the basis Dan 8:26f
years mentioned in * 24, leaving Dan 9:25f
see * 27 and the Revelation. Dan 9:25f
Compare * 18. Dan 11:13f
Three and a half years (* 7) plus Dan 12:11f
in the preceding chapter and *. Hos 1:11f
Micah's home town. See * 1 of Mic 1:14f
Implied in * 1 and 3:18. Nah 1:11f
Implied in * 1 and 3:18. Nah 1:13f
The Hebrew text of this * is very Hab 1:11f
Implied in remainder of *. Mt 1:20f
meaning of this * of Scripture, Mt 9:13
of this Scripture *, 'I want you to Mt 12:7
This * is omitted in many of the Mt 17:21f
This * is omitted in many Mt 18:11f
* 16 is omitted in many of the Mk 7:15,16f
are identical with * 48) are Mk 9:43,44f
are identical with * 48) are Mk 9:45,46f
Many ancient authorities add * 26, Mk 11:26,f
reading this * in the Scriptures? Mk 12:10
* 28 is omitted in some of the Mk 15:28f
From * 3. Literally, "most Lk 1:1f
women," as in * 42 which appears Lk 1:28f

VERSE Con't)
Implied in * 33. Lk 14:28f
Some ancient authorities add * 17, Lk 23:17,f
paraphrase relates this to * 47. Lk 24:49f
witness of his Father. See * 37. Jn 5:32,33f
A paraphrase of this *—that goes Jn 18:34f
Literally this * reads, "Are you Jn 18:34f
see footnote chapter 1, * 1. Act 1:1f
Implied in * 31. Act 2:29f
Implied in * 31. Act 2:30f
Implied in * 31. Act 2:34f
See * 5. Act 6:8f
Many ancient manuscripts omit * 37 Act 8:37f
See chapter 15, * 38. Act 13:13f
Other interpretations of this * 1Jn 5:6,7,8f
faith of Jesus." * 12 implies Rev 14:13f
Implied in * 18. Rev 17:9f

VERSED
Ezra was well * in Jehovah's laws Ez 7:6

VERSES
So also in * 6, 9, 12, 15, 18, Gen 5:3,4,5f
Implied in * 20 and 26. Gen 25:21f
* 29 and 30 repeat the names Gen 36:28,29,30f
the names listed in * 20, 21. Gen 36:28,29,30f
That is, the preceding laws in * Ex 34:27f
See * 8–11. Lev 9:15f
offerings recorded in * 13 to 17. Num 7:18-23f
offerings recorded in * 13 to 17. Num 7:24-29f
offerings recorded in * 13 to 17. Num 7:30-35f
offerings recorded in * 13 to 17. Num 7:36-41f
offerings recorded in * 13 to 17. Num 7:42-47f
offerings recorded in * 13 to 17. Num 7:48-53f
offerings recorded in * 13 to 17. Num 7:54-59f
offerings recorded in * 13 to 17. Num 7:60-65f
offerings recorded in * 13 to 17. Num 7:66-71f
offerings recorded in * 13 to 17. Num 7:72-77f
offerings recorded in * 13 to 17. Num 7:78-83f
Implied. See * 1–4. Deu 27:8f
are explained in chapter 4, * 2–7. Jos 3:12f
Implied. See * 41 and 44. Jos 15:37-44f
Implied in * 51, 54, 57, 59, 60, Jos 15:48-62f
Implied in * 24 and 28, where the Jos 18:21-28f
Totaled from * 6 and 7 of the Jos 19:2-7f
to in the following verse or *. 1Ch 1:1f
Implied in * 2–4 and 6. Ps 82:1f
the pagan customs of * 18 and 26. Eze 20:25f
Certain aspects of * 12 and 14 Eze 26:14f
In this passage (* 11–19) some Eze 28:12f
to apply these * with discernment. Eze 28:12f
for the future; see * 17, 19, 23. Dan 8:9f
sequence. See * 25–27. Dan 9:24f
See chapter 1, * 6, 9, and 10. Hos 1:23f
is frequent word play in * 10–14. Mic 1:11f
is frequent word play in * 10–14. Mic 1:11f
is frequent word play in * 10–14. Mic 1:11f
boxes with Scripture * inside, Mt 23:5
* 44 and 46 (which are identical Mk 9:43,44f
* 44 and 46 (which are identical Mk 9:45,46f
* 9 through 20 are not found in Mk 16:9f
Later manuscripts add to * 55 and Lk 9:55f
expressly prohibited in * 8 and 9. 1Co 6:12f
Implied in * 7, 10. 1Co 11:5f
Implied. See * 19 and 28. 1Co 14:18f
of these * could read: "If you 1Pe 2:2,3f
See chapter 13, * 11–16. Rev 19:20f

VERSION
translation follows the Greek *. Hos 4:18f
here follows the Syriac *. Zec 11:13f

VERSIONS
This clause appears in some *, not Gen 27:38f
as it is spelled in many modern *. Ex 3:15f
enemies," in some ancient *. Is 9:11,12f
Some * read "Zedekiah." Jer 27:1f
Some * read, "a covenant they Jer 31:32f
Some * read, "190 days." Eze 4:4,5f
Some ancient * add, "Blessed are Lk 1:28f

VERTEBRAE
* lie straight as a tube of brass. Job 40:18

VESSEL
Your mighty * flounders in the Eze 27:26

VESSELS
Literally, "with the * of the Num 31:6f
gold, and all the * dedicated for 1Ki 7:51
all the sacred * which had 1Ki 8:3,4
along with the silver and gold * 1Ki 15:15
for the various * used in the 1Ch 9:28
along with all the other sacred *. 2Ch 5:4,5
who carry home the * of the Lord. Is 52:11
in * consecrated to the Lord. Is 66:20

VESTIBULE
* 22¾ feet wide and 17½ feet long. Eze 40:7-12

VESTIBULES
"There were * round about, and Eze 40:29,30f

VESTIGE
get rid of every * of idol worship Zec 13:2

VETERANS
will perish, young boys and * too. Is 34:7

VEXATION
You shall cry in sorrow and * Is 65:14

VEXING
This is all very * and Ecc 8:14

VIA
Obviously this does not mean * Ju 1:24f

VIAL
Now take a * of olive oil and go 1Sa 16:1
"Take this * of oil with you, 2Ki 9:1

VIALS
a harp and golden * filled with Rev 5:8

VICE-REGENT
His son Jotham became *, in 2Ch 26:21

VICINITY
of Judah in the * of Beth-horon, 2Ch 25:13
Benjamin, in the * of Jerusalem and Jer 33:13

VICIOUS
all mankind was * and depraved, he Gen 6:12,13
a * king, says the Lord of Hosts. Is 19:4
and spreading * rumors! Is 58:9
It was far more brutal and * than Dan 7:7
power from this * king, to consume Dan 7:26
teachers, like * wolves, will Act 20:29
the * circle of sin and death. Rom 8:2

VICIOUSLY
men who * persecute the poor. Ps 10:2
I have and how * they hate me! Ps 25:19

VICTIM
possession of his * or has already Ex 21:16
Land, a murder * is found lying in Deu 21:1
girl is as innocent as a murder *; Deu 22:25,26,27
The * of a wicked plot." 2Sa 3:33,34
Its intended * will be no more Pro 26:2
a neighbor to the bandits' *?" Lk 10:36
looking for some * to tear apart. 1Pe 5:8

VICTIMS
May each of his children be * of 2Sa 3:29
He divided his * by making them 2Sa 8:2
other with the bodies of his *. 2Ki 21:16
and made them drop their *. Job 29:17
Like hunters they catch their * Ps 10:9
vast host of men have been her *. Pro 7:26
she waits for her * as one after Pro 23:26,27,28
with the blood of your innocent *. Is 1:15
They growl over their * like the Is 5:30
* like a hunter hiding in a blind. Jer 5:26
of Jerusalem, * of famine and war; Jer 14:16
they will no longer be your *, Eze 13:21
tear apart their *, and they Eze 22:27
she despised, all * of the sword. Eze 32:21
It devoured some of its * by Dan 7:7
stand against it or help its *. Dan 8:4
lying in ambush for their *; Hos 6:9
hunting for their *—out for Zep 3:3
demons to come out of their *. Mk 1:34
didn't want the * hanging there the Jn 19:31
as they left their *, and many who Act 8:7

VICTOR
The * became both proud and Dan 8:8
He is the Righteous One, the *! Zec 9:9

VICTOR'S
at the end of a * parade, to be 1Co 4:9

VICTORIES
So the Lord gave him * wherever 2Sa 8:6
led his troops to many glorious *. 2Ki 5:1
highest heaven and sends great *. Ps 20:6
*—it is strong but it cannot save. Ps 33:16,17
Decree * for your people. Ps 44:4

VICTORIOUS
For they were * over the Gen 14:5,6
And sure enough, Israel was * Num 21:35
out to meet the * army, but Moses Num 31:13
happened when the * Israeli army 1Sa 18:6
Lord made him * wherever he went. 2Sa 8:14
make you * over the army of Moab! 2Ki 3:18
now you will be * only three 2Ki 13:19
* conquest, but all to no avail. Is 29:8
I will uphold you with my * right Is 41:10
It is he who makes us * through 1Co 15:57
To everyone who is *, I will give Rev 2:7
He who is * shall not be hurt by Rev 2:11
Every one who is * shall eat of the Rev 2:17
those who had been * over the Evil Rev 15:2

VICTORS
Then the * plundered Gen 14:11
We bow our necks beneath the *' Lam 5:5

VICTORY
cry of * or defeat, but singing." Ex 32:18
given * to the other tribes, too. Deu 3:20
and he will give you the *!' Deu 20:4
swords or bows that brought you *! Jos 24:12
And I will give them a great *." Ju 1:2
this song about the wonderful *: Ju 5:1
But did not win the *. Ju 5:19
and the Lord gave him the *. Ju 11:32
given you a great * over your Ju 11:36
a great * to Israel as a result? 1Sa 19:5
about David's * over the army of 2Sa 8:9
credit for the * instead of me." 2Sa 12:28
* was turned into deep sadness. 2Sa 19:2
and the Lord gave him a great *. 2Sa 23:10
and God gave him a great *. 2Sa 23:11,12
"You will have a great *, for 1Ki 22:15
arrow, full of * over Syria; 2Ki 13:16,17
Lord saved them with a great *. 1Ch 11:14
them, will you give me the *?" 1Ch 14:10
And the Lord gave David * 1Ch 18:6
Lord gave David * after victory. 1Ch 18:13
Lord gave David victory after *. 1Ch 18:13
power and glory and * and majesty. 1Ch 29:11
for God will give you a great *!" 2Ch 18:3,4,5
It will be a glorious *!" 2Ch 18:14
* with feasting and gladness. Est 9:17
You gave me * in every battle. Ps 18:43,44,45
the news of your *, flags flying Ps 20:5
Give * to our king, O Lord; Ps 20:9
Don't give them * over me. Ps 25:2
and gives * to his anointed king. Ps 28:8
You surround me with songs of *. Ps 32:7
Don't give * to those who fight Ps 35:19
Only you can give us the * over Ps 44:7
Go on to *, Ps 45:4
their idols to flaunt their *. Ps 74:4
For he has won a mighty * by his Ps 98:1
He has announced this * and Ps 98:2,3
and now he has given me the *. Ps 118:14
For you grant * to kings! Ps 144:10
but * comes from God. Pro 21:31
gods ever gained * over the armies Is 36:18
whom * meets at every step? Is 41:2
God has given him * over many Is 41:2
give him * over kings and princes. Is 41:25
send you out to * even though you Is 45:5
shortly after Nebuchadnezzar's * Jer 36:1f
skies their mighty shouts of *. Jer 51:14
will be a glorious * for Israel on Eze 39:13
Lord gave him * over Jehoiakim. Dan 1:1
after this great *, he will have Dan 11:12
He will give you *. Zep 3:17,18
They will taste * and shout with Zec 9:15
The Lord will give * to the rest Zec 12:7
end all conflict with his final *, Mt 12:20
this, overwhelming * is ours Rom 8:37
has given him the * over everything 1Co 15:28
is swallowed up in *." 1Co 15:54
O death, where then your *? 1Co 15:55,56
since future * is sure, be strong 1Co 15:58
resurrection and * over Satan, he Eph 4:8

VIE
of Israel could * with King Josiah 2Ch 35:18

VIEW
go to bed with them in public *. 2Sa 12:11
expose yourself to public *. Is 47:2
rocks in open * for all to see; Eze 24:7
Antiochus IV fades from * and the Dan 11:40f
point of *, and not from God's." Mt 16:23
point of * and not from God's." Mk 8:33
So from God's point of *, all men Lk 20:37,38
But from God's point of * Abraham Rom 4:1
of *, but keep it to yourself; Rom 14:22
Father's point of *, is the one who Jas 1:27
into public *, in these last days, 1Pe 1:20
incredible, in * of a world Rev 9:16f

VIGOR
and served his masters with *. Gen 49:15
"His * is depleted by hunger; Job 18:12
But my enemies persecute with *, Ps 38:19

VIGOROUS
son, the child of my * youth. Gen 49:3
dinner table as * and healthy as Ps 128:3
Sons * and tall as growing plants. Ps 144:12-15
when compared with * young men! Is 59:10
rejoice; * health will be yours. Is 66:14
* in the truth you were taught. Col 2:7

VIGOROUSLY
Clap your hands *, then take a Eze 21:14

VILE
Whatever made you think of this * Gen 20:9,10
* god of the Ammonites. 1Ki 11:7
Again, he may prevent a * man Job 34:29,30
You curse and lie, and * Ps 50:19
the land with your * prostitution. Jer 3:2
for she is * through and through. Jer 6:6
You have heard the * names they Lam 3:61
the world how really * you are." Nah 3:6
All these * things come from Mk 7:23
'You * and wicked slave,' the Lk 19:22
wanted to—yes, * and sinful things Rom 1:24
more; the * will become more vile; Rev 22:11
the vile will become more *; Rev 22:11

VILENESS
* is praised throughout the land. Ps 12:8
proportion to the * of their sins. Eze 39:24

VILLAGE
to that little * over there instead Gen 19:18,19,20
See, the * is close by and it is Gen 19:18,19,20
(From that time on that * was Gen 19:22
was rising as Lot reached the *. Gen 19:23
journeyed to Iraq, to Nahor's *. Gen 24:10
the * were coming to draw water. Gen 24:11
* are coming out to draw water. Gen 24:13
the previous name of the nearest * Gen 28:19
entrance to the * of Enaim, which Gen 38:14
road at the entrance of the *?" Gen 38:21
of Jubilee. But * houses—a village Lev 25:31
But village houses—a * is a Lev 25:31

(VILLAGE Con't)
or woman, in any * throughout your Deu 17:2,3
and ending at the * of Kiriath-baal Jos 18:14
The * musicians Ju 5:11
Gather at the * well Ju 5:11
*, as was the custom of the day. Ju 14:10,11
came to Gibe-ah, a * of the tribe Ju 19:14
in, they camped in the * square. Ju 19:15
a * in Benjamin," he began. Ju 20:4
we have punished the * of Gibe-ah. Ju 20:8,9,10
But the men defending the * Ju 20:21
all around the *, and went out Ju 20:29
rushed into the * and slaughtered Ju 20:35-39
city and * in the entire land. Ju 20:48
* was stirred by their arrival. Ru 1:19
chief men of the *, and asked them Ru 4:2
ranch there, near the * of Carmel. 1Sa 25:2
came out of the * cursing them. 2Sa 16:5
and live in the * of Zarephath, 1Ki 17:8,9
men went to the * of Geruth Jer 41:16,17
The present * on this site is so Eze 47:15f
herdsman living in the * of Tekoa. Amo 1:1
but a small Judean *, yet you will Mic 5:2
unimportant Judean *, for a Mt 2:6
Whenever you enter a city or *, Mt 10:11
sent two of them into the * ahead. Mt 21:1
"Stay at one home in each * Mk 6:10
"And whenever a * won't accept Mk 6:11
led him out of the *, and spat upon Mk 8:23
"Don't even go back to the * Mk 8:26
"Go into that * over there," he Mk 11:2
to Nazareth, a * in Galilee, to a Lk 1:26
from the Galilean * of Nazareth. Lk 2:4
was no room for them in the * inn. Lk 2:7
*, guarding their flocks of sheep. Lk 2:8
They ran to the * and found their Lk 2:16
When he came to the * of Lk 4:16
One day in a certain * he was Lk 5:12
up from every * in all Galilee and Lk 5:17
disciples to the * of Nain, with Lk 7:11
out as he approached the * gate. Lk 7:12
mourners from the * were with her. Lk 7:12
guest in only one home at each *. Lk 9:4
rooms for them in a Samaritan *. Lk 9:52
The people of the * refused to Lk 9:53
and they went on to another *. Lk 9:56
"When you enter a *, don't shift Lk 10:7
they came to a * where a woman Lk 10:38
He went from city to city and * Lk 13:22
and village to *, teaching as he Lk 13:22
as they entered a * there, ten Lk 17:12
to go to the next *, and as they Lk 19:30
walking to the * of Emmaus, seven Lk 24:13
at Bethany, a * on the other side Jn 1:28
a wedding in the * of Cana in Jn 2:1
he approached the * of Sychar, he Jn 4:5,6
gone into the * to buy some food. Jn 4:8
went back to the * and told Jn 4:28,29
streaming from the * to see him. Jn 4:30
Many from the Samaritan * Jn 4:39
begged him to stay at their *; Jn 4:40,41
going from * to village, for he Jn 7:1
from village to *, for he wanted to Jn 7:1
the * where David was born." Jn 7:41,42
stayed outside the *, at the place Jn 11:30
the desert, to the * of Ephraim, Jn 11:54

VILLAGERS
evening, all the * who had any sick Lk 4:40

VILLAGES
other cities and * of the plain, Gen 19:25
they are * or are fortified; Num 13:19
All of the cities, towns, and * Num 31:9,10,11
to Kenath and its surrounding *, Num 32:42
of Avvim living in * scattered Deu 2:23
*) as it is still known today. Deu 3:14
of its surrounding *, slaughtering Jos 10:37
with all of its outlying *. Jos 10:39
cities with their surrounding *. Jos 15:21-32
cities with their surrounding *. Jos 15:33-36
other cities with their *: Jos 15:37-44
all the towns and * of Ekron. Jos 15:45
of Ashdod with their nearby *; Jos 15:46
of Ashdod with its *, and Gaza with Jos 15:47
* as far as the Brook of Egypt; Jos 15:47
country with their surrounding *: Jos 15:48-62
cliffs), with their respective *. Jos 17:11
their surrounding * were given to Jos 18:21-28
cities with their respective *: Jos 19:2-7
and each of their surrounding *. Jos 19:15,16
all, each with its surrounding *. Jos 19:17-23
cities and their surrounding *. Jos 19:30,31
cities with their surrounding *. Jos 19:35-39
the surrounding * were given to Jos 21:9-16
Ekron, with their surrounding *. Ju 1:18
or no contact with the nearby *. Ju 18:7
nearby * with a plague of boils. 1Sa 5:6
capital cities and * alike. 1Sa 6:4,5
* controlled by the five capitals. 1Sa 6:18
alive in the * they hit, and took 1Sa 27:9
including the * of Jair (the son of 1Ki 4:8-19
and its sixty surrounding *. 1Ch 2:23
by Gezer and its *, and finally by 1Ch 7:28
* as far as Ayyah and its towns. 1Ch 7:28
and Lod and their surrounding *). 1Ch 8:12
They were chosen from their * on 1Ch 9:22
And their relatives in the * 1Ch 9:25
and * of the people of Ammon. 1Ch 20:1
*, and fortresses of Israel. 1Ch 27:25
*, and were living there. 2Ch 28:17,18
in Jerusalem and its nearby *; Ez 2:70
one of the * in the Plain of Ono. Neh 6:2
own towns and * throughout Judah. Neh 7:73
(and their surrounding *), Neh 11:25-30
surrounding *), Ziklag, Neh 11:25-30
Meconah and its *, Neh 11:25-30
surrounding *), Lachish Neh 11:25-30
Bethel (and its surrounding *), Neh 11:31-35
the surrounding * and from the Neh 12:28
from the * of the Netophathites; Neh 12:28
own * as suburbs of Jerusalem. Neh 12:29
in the unwalled * throughout Israel Est 9:19
into the fields and stay in the *. Sol 7:11
in the mountain * and in the cities Jer 33:13
All the * and cities, whether Jer 48:8
And the mountain * of Israel Eze 33:28
an unprotected land of unwalled *! Eze 38:11
conquer the Negeb's outlying *. Ob 1:20
all the cities and * of that area, Mt 9:35
and followed by land from many *. Mt 14:13
go to the * and buy some food." Mt 14:15
Then he went out among the *, Mk 6:6
away to the nearby * and farms and Mk 6:35,36
Wherever he went—in * and Mk 6:56
out to the * of Caesarea Philippi. Mk 8:27
of the cities and * of Galilee Lk 8:1
circuit of the *, preaching the Lk 9:6
away to the nearby * and farms, to Lk 9:12
and * he planned to visit later. Lk 10:1
several Samaritan * along the way Act 8:25

VILLAINY
of trickery and *, enemy of all Act 13:10

VINDICATE
Rise up, O Lord my God; * me. Ps 35:23
He will * you with the blazing Ps 37:6
For Jehovah will * his people, Ps 135:14
Through them I will * my holiness Eze 39:27

VINDICATED
you have * me; Ps 9:4
The Lord has * us. Jer 51:10
holiness will be * in your terrible Eze 38:15,16
his court and * his people, giving Dan 7:22

VINE
he said, "I saw a * with three Gen 40:9,10
*, and washed his clothes in wine. Gen 49:11
we were a tender * and drove away Ps 80:8
plight and care for this your *! Ps 80:14
Strip the branches from each *, Jer 5:10
checks each * to pick what he has Jer 6:9
Or, "the true * from the roots of Jer 33:15f
Christ was the true *, the only Jer 33:15f
low but spreading * that turned Eze 17:6
*, producing leaves and fruit. Eze 17:8
Though the * began so well, will Eze 17:10
"Your mother was like a * beside Eze 19:10
But the * was uprooted in fury Eze 19:12
Now the * is planted in the Eze 19:13
"And I will raise up a notable * Eze 34:29
grapes will blight upon the *. Hos 9:2
luxuriant * all filled with fruit! Hos 10:1
arranged for a * to grow up quickly Jon 4:6
"I AM THE true *, and my Father Jn 15:1
fruit when severed from the *. Jn 15:4
"Yes, I am the *; Jn 15:5
fig tree, or figs from a grape *? Jas 3:12

VINEDRESSERS
for the crops as * and plowmen. Jer 52:16
well may you * weep. Joe 1:11

VINEGAR
my awful thirst they offered me *. Ps 69:21
or * that sets the teeth on edge. Pro 10:26
Literally, "like * upon soda." Pro 25:20f

VINES
of fruit from the *, and don't pick Lev 19:10
*, not even the seeds or skins! Num 6:3,4
crops—the figs, *, and pomegranates Num 20:5
barley, of grape *, fig trees, Deu 8:8
don't glean the * after they are Deu 24:21
for worms will destroy the *. Deu 28:39
shall destroy your trees and *. Deu 28:42
Their grape * and fig trees were Ps 105:33
and the grape * are in blossom. Sol 2:13
whether the grape * were budding or Sol 6:11
see whether the * have budded and Sol 7:12
his vineyard with the choicest *. Is 5:2
cut down the best of the grape *; Is 16:8
Lord, will tend the fruitful *; Is 27:3
those fruitful * of other years. Is 32:12
the fields and *, so Jerusalem will Is 33:4
trampling down the *, and turning Jer 12:10
"Son of dust, what good are * Eze 15:2
No, for * can't be used even for Eze 15:3
are like the * of the Eze 15:5,6
They have ruined my * and Joe
the fig trees and grape * will Joe 2:
of grapes from the * of the earth, Rev 14:

VINEYARD
and planted a *, and he made wine. Gen 9:20,
and it gets into another man's *; Ex 22
of the field or * an equal amount Ex 22
the road went between two * walls. Num 22:
Has anyone just planted a * but Deu 20
other crops in the rows of your *. Deu 22
from another man's *, but do not Deu 23:
the same for the grapes in your *; Deu 24:
eat the fruit of the * you plant. Deu 28:
and as far away as * Meadow. Ju 11:
Jezreel, had a * on the outskirts 1Ki 21
"I asked Naboth to sell me his * 1Ki 21
I'll get you Naboth's *!" 1Ki 21
the * Naboth wouldn't sell you? 1Ki 21:
So Ahab went down to the * to 1Ki 21:
He will be at Naboth's *, taking 1Ki 21:
with her own hands she plants a * Pro 31:
Solomon had a * at Baal-hamon Sol 8:1
But as for my own *, you, O Sol 8:1
NOW I WILL sing a song about his * Is 5:
My Beloved has a * on a very Is 5:
his * with the choicest vines. Is 5:
Why did my * give me wild grapes Is 5:
fences and let my * go to pasture Is 5:
They are the * that I spoke Is 5:
An acre of * will not produce Is 5:1
is my *; Is 27:
have ravaged my *, trampling down Jer 12:1
crying in every *, for I will pass Amo 5:1
planted a * with a hedge around it, Mt 21:3
then leased the * to some farmers Mt 21:3
him out of the * and killed him. Mt 21:3
and lease the * to others who will Mt 21:4
"A man planted a * and built a Mk 12:
and threw his body out of the *. Mk 12:
all, and lease the * to others. Mk 12:
"A man planted a * and rented it Lk 20:
him out of the * and killed him. Lk 20:1
them and rent the * to others." Lk 20:1

VINEYARDS
The same rule applies to your * Ex 23:1
and prune your * and harvest your Lev 25:
your * during that entire year. Lev 25:4
nor given us fields and *. Num 16:14
fields, nor through your *; Num 20:17
your * or drink your water." Num 21:22
didn't dig, and * and olive trees Deu 6:10,11,12
You will plant * and care for Deu 28:39
I gave you * and olive groves for Jos 24:13
* on the outskirts of the town. Ju 14:5
and hide in the *, and when the Ju 21:20
of your fields and * and olive 1Sa 8:14
and * and commissions in his army? 1Sa 22:7
* and sheep and oxen and servants? 2Ki 5:26
had the oversight of the king's *; 1Ch 27:27
had many farms and *, both on the 2Ch 26:10
*, and homes to these rich men; Neh 5:2,3,4
Restore their fields, *, Neh 5:11
with cisterns and * and oliveyards Neh 9:25
even glean the * of the wicked. Job 24:6
*, and reap their bumper crops! Ps 107:37
program: homes, *, gardens, parks Ecc 2:4,5,6
to tend the *, but see what it Sol 1:6
Literally, "but my own * are Sol 1:6f
little foxes are ruining the *. Sol 2:15
and go out to the * and see whether Sol 7:12
At that time the lush * will Is 7:23
of Heshbon and the * at Sibmah. Is 16:8
for Jazer and the * of Sibmah. Is 16:9
The happy singing in the * will Is 16:10
plow your fields and tend your *. Is 61:5
My people will plant * and eat Is 65:21,22
Go down the rows of the * and Jer 5:10
plant *, for you will be there Jer 29:5
Again you will plant your * upon Jer 31:5
selling houses and * and fields." Jer 32:15
or plant crops or * and not to own Jer 35:7
poor, and gave them fields and *. Jer 39:10
O men of Sibmah, rich in *, I Jer 48:32
their homes and plant their *. Eze 28:26
I will destroy her * and her Hos 1:12
There I will give back her * to Hos 1:15
mildew on your farms and your *; Amo 4:9
from the lush * you are planting. Amo 5:11
they shall plant * and gardens and Amo 9:14
Or if your * were robbed of all Ob 1:5
from the * they have planted." Zep 1:13

VIOLATE
"Do not * your daughter's Lev 19:29
She has seen foreign nations * Lam 1:10
* the direct commandments of God? Mt 15:3

VIOLATED
for he has * my contract." Gen 17:14
rights have been *—you shall take Deu 17:8
man because he has * the virginity Deu 22:23,24
I have not * or forgotten any of Deu 26:13
he has, for he has * the covenant Jos 7:15

'IOLATED Con't)
these people have * the treaty I Ju 2:20
We have not * your covenant. Ps 44:17
For these evil men have * your Ps 119:126
Lord their God and * his agreement Jer 22:9
my wishes, and * my Sabbaths—their Eze 20:16
scorned them and * my Sabbaths and Eze 20:23,24
Your priests have * my laws and Eze 22:26
of the law but often * its intent. Mt 3:7f
* the customs of our ancestors. Act 28:17

IOLATES
Anyone who * this law is guilty Lev 22:16
your land * your covenant with God Deu 17:2,3

IOLATING
a prostitute, thus * her father's Lev 21:9
guilty and die for * these rules. Lev 22:9
people of Israel for * this law. Num 18:5
For they worshiped other gods, * Deu 29:26
* the covenant of our fathers! Mal 2:10

IOLATION
involving * of sacred affairs; 2Ch 19:11

'IOLATIONS
cases or other * of the laws and 2Ch 19:10

'IOLENCE
They are men of * and injustice. Gen 49:5
You deliver me from *. 2Sa 22:49
May the * he plans for others Ps 7:16
he hates those loving *. Ps 11:5
them with their own * and strife. Ps 55:9
Literally, "for I have seen * and Ps 55:9f
Literally, "you deal out the * of Ps 58:1f
and from *, for their lives are Ps 72:14
Preserve me from their *, for Ps 140:4
of all who live by * and murder. Pro 1:19
eat and drink wickedness and *! Pro 4:17
mouth of the wicked conceals *." Pro 10:6f
* boomerangs and destroys them. Pro 21:7
days plotting * and cheating. Pro 24:2
At whom did you direct your * and Is 37:23
with sin; * is your trademark. Is 59:6
your taskmasters! * will disappear Is 60:18
streets echo with the sounds of *; Jer 6:7
Jerusalem is filled with *, so I Eze 7:23
There is * everywhere, with one Hos 4:2
because of their * against the Joe 3:19
With blinding speed and * he Amo 5:9
evil ways, from his * and robbing. Jon 3:8
it by fraud and threats and *. Mic 2:2
wealthy through extortion and *; Mic 6:12
and * in cities everywhere. Hab 2:17
with evil gain of * and fraud. Zep 1:9
Jerusalem, city of * and crime. Zep 3:1
But I say: Don't resist *! Mt 5:39
of Heaven suffers * and men of Mt 11:12f
and men of * take it by force." Mt 11:12f
extort money by threats and *; Lk 3:14
them (without *, for they were Act 5:26,27
was exposed to the * of the waves Act 27:41

VIOLENT
shook with a * earthquake. Ex 19:18
Oh, listen to my prayer. For * Ps 54:3
men defy me; *, godless men are Ps 86:14
Preserve me from the *, who plot Ps 140:1
They will die a * death. Pro 1:19
Don't envy * men. Pro 3:31
be killed— the * man who fights at Is 29:21
These fierce, * people, with a Is 33:19
a cruel and * nation who will Hab 1:6
party advocating * overthrow of the Mk 3:16-19
and threw him into a * convulsion. Lk 9:42
reacted with * jealousy and Act 5:17
the mob grew so * that the soldiers Act 21:35

VIOLENTLY
* away from Abraham's servants. Gen 21:25
Ephraim were * angry with Gideon. Ju 8:1
a robber, and * like a bandit. Pro 24:34
He has * broken down his Temple Lam 2:6
convulsed the man * and left him. Mk 1:26
came and took him * away from us, Act 24:7
I was so * opposed to them that I Act 26:11

VIPERS
Sons of *! Mt 23:33

VIRGIN
Look—I have two * daughters, and Gen 19:8
Literally, "a *." Gen 24:15,16f
Literally, "a *." Ex 22:16f
Literally, "a *." Lev 21:2,3f
He must marry a *. Lev 21:13
She must be a * from his own Lev 21:14,15
'She was not a * when I married Deu 22:13,14
she was not a * when she married; Deu 22:17,18
has falsely accused a * of Israel. Deu 22:19
and she was not a *, the judges Deu 22:20
Here, take my * daughter and Ju 19:24
Literally, "for she was a *, and 2Sa 13:2f
days for * daughters of the king. 2Sa 13:17,18
* to be your concubine and nurse. 1Ki 1:2
Sennacherib: The * daughter of Zion 2Ki 19:21
sign—a child shall be born to a *! Is 7:14
"*" and sometimes "young woman." Is 7:14f
This, of course, was not a * Is 7:14f
in that a * (Mary) conceived and Is 7:14f
higher meaning, "*," in verse 14, Is 7:14f
O dishonored *, daughter of Sidon, Is 23:12
helpless * daughter of Zion—laughs Is 37:22
of a young man who marries a *; Is 62:5
I will rebuild your nation, O * Jer 31:4
For you shall return again, O * Jer 31:21
medicine, O * daughter of Egypt! Jer 46:11
Weep with sorrow, as a * weeps Joe 1:8
But while she was still a * she Mt 1:18
'Listen! The * shall conceive a Mt 1:23
a * until her Son was born; Mt 1:25
in Galilee, to a *, Mary, engaged Lk 1:27
I am a *." Lk 1:34

VIRGINITY
proof of her * to the city judges. Deu 22:15
the * of another man's fiancée. Deu 22:23,24
consecrating her to perpetual *. Ju 11:39f
upon her and robbed her of her *. Eze 23:8
gave your * to those from Egypt. Eze 23:21

VIRGINS
* of marriageable age were saved. Ju 21:10,11,12
and unnumbered * available to me; Sol 6:8
her * have been dragged away. Lam 1:4
and despair. The * of Jerusalem Lam 2:10
Literally, "*." Mt 25:1f
Literally, "*." Act 21:9f
spiritually undefiled, pure as *, Rev 14:4
with women, for they are *." Rev 14:4f

VIRILE
At dawn he seems so strong and * Job 8:16

VIRTUAL
So they remained in * widowhood 2Sa 20:3

VIRTUE
your own power or * but because I, Is 55:5
their * and scorned everyone else: Lk 18:9

VIRTUES
Hold these * tightly. Pro 3:3
of the comparative * of wisdom and Ecc 2:12

VISIBLE
God isn't ushered in with * signs. Lk 17:20

VISION
to Abram in a *, and this is what Gen 15:1
upon Abram, and a * of terrible Gen 15:12
the night God spoke to him in a *. Gen 46:2
Then Micaiah told him, "In my * 2Ch 18:16
It came in a nighttime * as Job 4:13
In a * you spoke to your prophet Ps 89:19
THIS IS THE * God showed Isaiah Is 13:1
I see an awesome *: oh, the Is 21:2
Meanwhile (in my *) Is 21:6,7
Literally, "The Valley of *." Is 22:1f
Lord gave me this *. Jer 24:1
or prophetic * to guide them. Lam 2:9
I saw, in this *, a great storm Eze 1:4
Lord there, just as in my first *! Eze 3:23
And so ended the * of my visit to Eze 11:24
Then he told me what the * meant: Eze 37:11
upon me, and in a * he took me to Eze 40:2
And that night in a * God told Dan 2:19
and now, even this * of the king's Dan 2:23
meaning of this *, suddenly a man Dan 8:15
have seen in your * will not take Dan 8:17
"And then in your * you heard Dan 8:26
Literally, "The * of the evenings Dan 8:26f
in the earlier *, flew swiftly to Dan 9:21
the meaning of the * that you saw! Dan 9:23
Belteshazzar) had another *. Dan 10:1
he understood what the * meant. Dan 10:1
When this * came to me (Daniel Dan 10:2
I, Daniel, alone saw this great * Dan 10:7
When I saw this frightening * my Dan 10:8
"in order to fulfill the *." Dan 11:14f
In my * I have seen the sons of Hos 9:13
a * and many a parable and dream. Hos 12:10
One day, in a *, God told him Amo 1:2
Israel. This * came to him at the Amo 1:2
God showed me in a *: He was Amo 7:1
and did not fulfill the *. Amo 7:3
a *, a basket full of ripe fruit. Amo 8:1
In a * the Lord God showed Obadiah Ob 1:1
THIS IS THE * God gave to Nahum, Nah 1:1
prophet Habakkuk in a * from God: Hab 1:1
when the * will be fulfilled. Hab 2:3
the prophet), in a * in the night: Zec 1:7
THE ANGEL showed me (in my *) Zec 3:1
must have seen a * in the Temple. Lk 1:22
seen a * of the Messiah's glory. Jn 12:41
The Lord spoke to him in a *, Act 9:10
I have shown him a * of a man named Act 9:12
afternoon he had a *—it was about Act 10:3
in this * he saw an angel of God Act 10:3
The same * was repeated three Act 10:16
What could the * mean? Act 10:17
puzzling over the *, the Holy Act 10:19
But God has shown me in a * that Act 10:28
praying, I saw a *—a huge sheet, Act 11:5
it was a dream or *, and didn't Act 12:9
Paul had a *: Act 16:9
* and told him, "Don't be afraid! Act 18:9
a * of God saying to me, 'Hurry! Act 22:17,18
disobedient to that * from heaven! Act 26:19
They have seen a *, they say, and Col 2:18
things to his servant John in a *; Rev 1:1
Then in my * I heard the singing Rev 5:11
spread out before me in my *; Rev 9:17,18
AND NOW, IN my *, I saw a strange Rev 13:1
And this woman you saw in your * Rev 17:18
In a * he took me to a towering Rev 21:10

VISION'S
heaven to explain the * meaning. Rev 1:1

VISIONS
would communicate by * and dreams; Num 12:6
and also in the * of Iddo the seer 2Ch 9:29
in dreams, in * of the night when Job 33:15
of Amoz, in the * he saw during the Is 1:1
They prophesy of * and Jer 14:14
opened to me and I saw * from God. Eze 1:1
Israel say, 'His * won't come true Eze 12:27
their own * and claiming to have Eze 13:2,3
claimed to see '*' you never saw, Eze 13:7
you for these '*' and lies. Eze 13:8
talk of seeing '*' that you never Eze 13:23
Your 'prophets' describe false * Eze 22:28
it in the other *, first by the Eze 43:3
the meanings of dreams and *. Dan 1:17
dreams, and your young men see *. Joe 2:28
Don't bother us here with your * Amo 7:13
came to Micah in the form of *. Mic 1:1
about you and cut off all your *; Mic 3:6
*, and your old men dream dreams. Act 2:17
Let me tell about the * I've had, 2Co 12:1
If you hear of people having * 2Th 2:1
*, dreams, and even face to face Heb 1:1

VISIT
there to commemorate Jehovah's *. Gen 12:7
"This is obviously no friendly * Gen 26:27
to Paddan-aram to * his Uncle Gen 28:5
went out to * some of the Gen 34:1
and Ephraim, he went to * him. Gen 48:1
he went out to * his fellow Hebrews Ex 2:11
During his * he saw an Egyptian Ex 2:11
back to Egypt and * my relatives. Ex 4:18
has come to * you," Moses was Ex 18:5,6
the people are ready for my *. Ex 19:10
however, when I come to * these Ex 32:34
went down to * Egypt and stayed Num 20:15
down at harvest time to * him. 2Sa 23:13
and went to Gath to * the king. 1Ki 2:40
he went out to * his father, who 2Ki 4:18
"Go and * the prophet," the 2Ki 5:5
(son of Jehoram) came to * him. 2Ki 8:29
too, for he had gone to * him. 2Ki 9:16
We are going to Samaria to * the 2Ki 10:13
Isaiah the prophet went to * him. 2Ki 20:1
nation came to * him, and to hear 2Ch 9:23
down to Samaria to * King Ahab, and 2Ch 18:2
Ahaziah went to * him, but this 2Ch 22:6
It was during this * that Ahaziah 2Ch 22:7
Hanani came to * me with some men Neh 1:2
went home for a *, our enemies Neh 4:12
Why should I stop to come and * Neh 6:3
A few days later I went to * Neh 6:10
they come to * me while I am sick; Ps 41:6
Don't * your neighbor too often, Pro 25:17
Oh, what will you do when I * you Is 10:3
son) went to * him and gave him Is 38:1
I will * them with death. Jer 8:12
And so ended the vision of my * Eze 11:24
of lustful men who * prostitutes. Eze 23:44
another, "let us * the mountain of Mic 4:2
For the Lord God will * his Zep 2:7
you sick or in prison, and * you?' Mt 25:39
in prison, and you didn't * me.' Mt 25:43
So the man started off to * the Mk 5:20
Or, "to * Decapolis." Mk 5:20f
Zacharias lived, to * Elizabeth. Lk 1:39,40
the mother of my Lord should * me! Lk 1:43
for he has come to * his people and Lk 1:68
God for the * of the angels, and Lk 2:20
villages he planned to * later. Lk 10:1
just arrived for a * and I've Lk 11:5,6
the Passover paid a * to Philip, Jn 12:21
into his mind to * his brothers, Act 7:23
During this * he saw an Egyptian Act 7:24
from place to place to * them, Act 9:32
and ask him to come and * you." Act 10:5,6
and Paul to * him, for he wanted to Act 13:6,7
and Samaria to * the believers, Act 15:3
to Turkey, and * each city where Act 15:36
Literally, "return now and * Act 15:36f
for a * with Festus. Act 25:13
him go ashore to * with friends and Act 27:3
For I long to * you so that I Rom 1:11,12
been so long in coming to * you. Rom 15:22
I am coming to * you after I have 1Co 16:5
a passing * and then go right on; 1Co 16:7
I begged Apollos to * you along 1Co 16:12
have arrived here for a * 1Co 16:17
I haven't come to * you yet is that 2Co 1:23
unhappy with another painful *." 2Co 2:1
forward to my *, and how sorry you 2Co 7:7

(VISIT Con't)
first place, to * you and encourage 2Co 8:6
suggestion that he * you again—but 2Co 8:17
for a *. 2Co 12:2,3
When I urged Titus to * you, and 2Co 12:18
when I come to * you I won't like 2Co 12:20
third time I am coming to * you. 2Co 13:1
warning, as I come now for this *. 2Co 13:1
to Jerusalem for a * with Peter, Gal 1:18
Then after this * I went to Gal 1:21
when I return to * you again. Php 1:26
how worthwhile that * was. 1Th 2:1
God's minister, to * you to 1Th 3:2,3
you remember our * with joy and 1Th 3:6

VISITED
to you, 'I have * my people, and Ex 3:16
that Jehovah had * them and had Ex 4:31
ONE DAY GIDEON'S son Abimelech * Ju 9:1
him whenever he * the parade Ju 13:25
officials of Jericho * Elisha. 2Ki 2:19
Joash * him and wept over him. 2Ki 13:14
"Have you * the treasuries of Job 38:22,23
of Ashdod, and I * the nations of Jer 25:21
he would, and * me in the prison. Jer 32:8
elders of Israel * me, to ask me Eze 14:1
sick and in prison, and you * Mt 25:36
had said to the people they *. Mk 6:30
"The next day he * them again Act 7:26
Barnabas and Paul now * Jerusalem Act 12:25
the time God first * the Gentiles Act 15:14
he * the church [at Jerusalem Act 18:22
arrived from Judea and * us. Act 21:11
and welcomed all who * him, Act 28:30
he * me and encouraged me often. 2Ti 1:16
the spirit that he * the spirits in 1Pe 3:19

VISITING
One day, when * the city of Gen 20:1
The next day as he was out * Ex 2:13
A hired servant or a * foreigner Ex 12:45
no one * the priest, for Lev 22:10
just been there * the king and had 2Sa 3:23
of Judah was * King Ahab of Israel, 1Ki 22:2
Let her hold you back from * a Pro 7:5
village he was *, there was a man Lk 5:12
and Phrygia * all the believers, Act 18:23
his friends from * him or bringing Act 24:23
to me while I was * in Antioch, 2Ti 3:11
were just strangers * down here. Heb 11:13

VISITOR
"Here I am, a * in a foreign Gen 23:4
tents like a mere *, as did Isaac Heb 11:9

VISITORS
One day Isaac had * from Gerar. Gen 26:26
your household—your slaves and *. Ex 23:12
residents, and the * from Israel, 2Ch 30:25
besides * from other countries! Neh 5:17
few, and were only * in Canaan. Ps 105:12
immigrants and * are forced to Eze 22:7
was so packed with * that there Mk 2:2
it was so full of * that he Mk 3:20
crowd of Passover * took palm Jn 12:12
areas of Libya, * from Rome—both Act 2:10
all of you, * and residents of Act 2:14
Dear brothers, you are only * 1Pe 2:11

VISITS
true that his * didn't seem to cost 2Co 12:16
me often. His * revived me like a 2Ti 1:16

VITAL
produce fruit and be * and green. Ps 92:14
and betray some * information. Pro 5:2
live in * union with him. Col 2:6

VITALITY
be given renewed health and *. Pro 3:7,8

VOICE
Isaac: (to himself) "The * is Gen 27:22
"I am God," the * replied, Gen 46:3,4
will listen to the * of the Lord Ex 15:26
God, he heard the * speaking to him Num 7:89
nation heard the * of God speaking Deu 4:33
He let you hear his * Deu 4:36
But when you heard the loud * Deu 5:23
we have even heard his * from the Deu 5:24
as we have, the * of the living God Deu 5:26,27
to the terrifying * of God again, Deu 18:16
with a mighty * of thunder from 1Sa 7:10
Saul recognized David's * and 1Sa 26:17,18
was no reply, no *, no answer. 1Ki 18:29
And a * said, "Why are you here, 1Ki 19:13
not obeyed the * of the Lord, a 1Ki 20:36
the dreadful silence came this *: Job 4:16
He takes away the * of orators, Job 12:20
My bones burn with fever. The * Job 30:31
listen to the thunder of his *. Job 37:2
tremendous * of his majesty. Job 37:4
His * is glorious in the thunder. Job 37:5
The * of the Lord echoes from the Ps 29:3
So powerful is his *; Ps 29:4
young calves! The * of the Lord Ps 29:7
of Kadesh. The * of the Lord spins Ps 29:9
Raise your * in song to him who Ps 68:4
mighty * thunders from the sky. Ps 68:33
I heard an unknown * that said, Ps 81:5
* goes unheeded in their councils. Ps 120:7
for all of them shall hear your *. Ps 138:4
CAN'T YOU HEAR the * of wisdom? Pro 8:1
and tuneless, with quavering *. Ecc 12:4
Literally, "The * of the Sol 2:12f
* and see your handsome face. Sol 2:14
I heard the * of my beloved; Sol 5:2
companions may listen to your *; Sol 8:13
With one * they all cry out, Is 14:10
Then I heard a * shout out, Is 21:8,9
Your * will whisper like a ghost Is 29:4
you will hear a * behind you say, Is 30:21
cause his majestic * to be heard Is 30:30
hailstones. The * of the Lord Is 30:31
his people will listen to his *. Is 32:3
enemy runs at the sound of your *. Is 33:3
I hear the * of someone shouting, Is 40:3
The * says, "Shout!" Is 40:6
SHOUT WITH THE * of a trumpet Is 58:1
and the * of weeping and crying Is 65:19
It is the * of the Lord taking Is 66:6
It is his * that echoes in the Jer 10:13
her mighty * is stilled as the Jer 51:55
shore, or like the * of God, or Eze 1:24
came a * from the crystal sky Eze 1:25
the * of someone speaking to me: Eze 1:27,28
was as the * of Almighty God when Eze 10:5
so that his * could never again be Eze 19:9
his arrival, your * will suddenly Eze 24:27
* or plays well on an instrument. Eze 33:32
these words, a * called down from Dan 4:31
Then he heard a *! Dan 6:21
heard a * saying to it, "Get up! Dan 7:5
I heard a man's * calling from Dan 8:16
and haven't listened to your *. Dan 9:11
brass, and his * was like the Dan 10:5,6
And I heard his *—"O Daniel, Dan 10:11
The Lord's * calls out to all Mic 6:9
won't listen even to the * of God. Zep 3:2
And a * from heaven said, "This Mt 3:17
He does not raise his *! Mt 12:19
over them, and a * from the cloud Mt 17:5
on him, and a * from heaven said, Mk 1:11
out the sun, and a * from the cloud Mk 9:7
over and spoke to him in a low *. Mk 10:35
*, "Eli, Eli, lama sabachthani?" Mk 15:34
*, my baby moved in me for joy! Lk 1:44
John was "a * shouting from the Lk 3:4
upon him, and a * from heaven said, Lk 3:22
And a * from the cloud said, Lk 9:35
Then, as the * died away, Jesus Lk 9:36
speak, his * returned to him. Lk 11:14
crowd as with one * they shouted, Lk 23:18
He replied, "I am a * from the Jn 1:23
dead shall hear my *—the voice of Jn 5:25
hear my voice—the * of the Son of Jn 5:25
shall hear the * of God's Son, and Jn 5:28
sheep hear his * and come to him; Jn 10:3
him, for they recognize his *. Jn 10:4
for they don't recognize his *." Jn 10:5
also, and they will heed my *; Jn 10:16
My sheep recognize my *, and I Jn 10:27
Then a * spoke from heaven saying, Jn 12:28
When the crowd heard the *, Jn 12:29
Then Jesus told them, "The * was Jn 12:30
he ran to see, the * of the Lord Act 7:31
drowning out his * with their Act 7:57
heard a * saying to him, "Paul! Act 9:4
And the * replied, "I am Jesus, Act 9:5
of someone's * but saw no one! Act 9:7
Then a * said to him, "Go kill Act 10:13
The * spoke again, "Don't Act 10:15
And I heard a * say, 'Kill and Act 11:7
"But the * came again, 'Don't Act 11:9
When she recognized Peter's *, Act 12:14
the * of a god and not of a man!" Act 12:22
ground and heard a * saying to me, Act 22:7
then with one * they shouted, Act 22:22
"except it be for this one *." Act 24:21f
and I heard a * speaking to me in Act 26:14
together with one *, giving glory Rom 15:6
will be afraid to raise his *!" 2Co 10:1
If you have really heard his * Eph 4:21
to hear his * today and not let our Heb 3:7,8
if you hear God's * speaking to Heb 3:15
who heard God's * speaking to them Heb 3:16
blast, and a * with a message so Heb 12:19
Mount Sinai his * shook the earth, Heb 12:26
I heard that glorious, majestic * 2Pe 1:17,18
*, scolding and rebuking him. 2Pe 2:16
God said so with a * from heaven 1Jn 5:6,7,8
witnesses: the * of the Holy Spirit 1Jn 5:6,7,8
in our hearts, the * from heaven at 1Jn 5:6,7,8
baptism, and the * before he died. 1Jn 5:6,7,8
I heard a loud * behind me, a voice Rev 1:10
voice behind me, a * that sounded Rev 1:10
bronze, and his * thundered like Rev 1:15
and the same * I had heard before, Rev 4:1
A mighty angel with a loud * was Rev 5:2
Beings, with a * that sounded like Rev 6:1
And a * from among the four Rev 6:6
and I heard a * speaking from the Rev 9:1[illegible]
said when a * from heaven called to Rev 10:[illegible]
Then the * from heaven spoke to Rev 10:8
Then a loud * will shout from Rev 11:12
Then I heard a loud * shouting Rev 12:10
a fearsome * like the Dragon's. Rev 13:11
And I heard a * in the heavens Rev 14:13
AND I HEARD a mighty * shouting Rev 16:1
Then I heard another * calling Rev 18:4
And out of the throne came a * Rev 19:5

VOICES
Their * rose in a great chorus Num 14:2
I hear * high upon the windswept Jer 3:21
* of the bridegrooms and brides. Jer 7:34
that the happy * of bridegrooms and Jer 33:10,11
death, and their * prevailed. Lk 23:23
and there were * in the thunder. Rev 4:5
there were loud * shouting down Rev 11:15
bells and happy * of the Rev 18:23
Again and again their * rang, Rev 19:3

VOID
Or, "shapeless and *." Gen 1:2f
*, and Jehovah will forgive her. Num 30:8
is * and Jehovah will forgive her. Num 30:12

VOLCANO
from a *, will set it all on fire. Is 30:33

VOLUME
an ever-increasing * of wrath upon Job 10:17
As a result, our sales * is going Act 19:26

VOLUMES
weights, and *—and give full Lev 19:35,36

VOLUNTARILY
my consent—I lay down my life *. Jn 10:18

VOLUNTARY
vow or is simply a * offering to Lev 7:16
a vow or as a * offering, must Lev 22:21
of the Lord. * offerings of the Ez 3:5
Moreover, you are to collect * Ez 7:16

VOLUNTEER
any * crop that may come up; Ex 23:11
for yourself the * crops that come Lev 25:5
food shall be the * crops that grow Lev 25:12
will eat the * wheat, and use it as 2Ki 19:29
of every kind will *, and the army 1Ch 28:21
you will have only * grain this Is 37:30
Though they * for exile, I will Amo 9:4

VOLUNTEERED
Kenaz, * to lead the attack; Ju 1:13
at Kedesh, ten thousand men *. Ju 4:10
already * for Saul's army to fight 1Sa 17:13
I found that not one Levite had *! Ez 8:15
Johanan * to kill Ishmael Jer 40:15
Darius' reign, and * their help. Hag 1:14,15
Many false witnesses *, but they Mk 14:56

VOLUNTEERING
If I were * my services of my own 1Co 9:17

VOLUNTEERS
"Whoever * shall be our king!" Ju 10:18
"Any * to go down there with 1Sa 26:5,6,7
*, and they were highly honored. Neh 11:2

VOMIT
Literally, "that the land * not Lev 18:28f
you will not * you out again." Lev 20:22f
until you * it from your noses; Num 11:19,20
He will * the plunder he gorged. Job 20:15
and you will * it, and have to take Pro 23:6,7,8
As a dog returns to his *, so a Pro 26:11
Their tables are covered with *; Is 28:8
you are drunk and * and fall and Jer 25:27
Moab shall wallow in her *, Jer 48:26
it with sin and it will * you out. Mic 2:10

VOMITED
as it * out " Lev 18:28f
to what he has *, and a pig is 2Pe 2:22

VOMITS
Literally, "the land * out her Lev 18:25f

VOPHSI
Nahbi, son of *, from the tribe of Num 13:3-15

VOTE
And the * for the death Mk 14:63,64
death, I cast my * against them. Act 26:10

VOTED
of Jerusalem had * to celebrate the 2Ch 30:2,3
whole congregation * to send Act 15:22

VOUCH
well before you * for his credit! Pro 11:15

VOW
Jacob: "Well then, * to God that Gen 25:33
And Jacob vowed this * to God: Gen 28:20
pillar and made a * to serve me. Gen 31:13
the sons of Israel * before God Ex 13:19
"If anyone makes a rash *, Lev 5:4
vow, whether the * is good or bad, Lev 5:4
* he has taken, he is guilty. Lev 5:4
sin, and need not fulfill the *. Lev 5:6
is because of a * or is simply a Lev 7:16
to fulfill a * or as a voluntary Lev 22:21
will offering, but not for a *. Lev 22:23
makes a special * to give himself Lev 27:1
given. The * may not be changed; Lev 27:10

'OW Con't)
takes the special * of a Nazirite, Num 6:1
period of his *, even if it is the Num 6:6,7
for his * of consecration remains Num 6:6,7
The days of his * that were Num 6:12
again with a new *, and must bring Num 6:12
the period of his * of separation Num 6:13
sign of his * of separation. Num 6:18
wine, for he is freed from his *. Num 6:20
took his * to become a Nazirite." Num 6:21
But I * by my own name that just Num 14:20,21
to fulfill a *, or a free-will Num 15:3,4
something, that * must not be Num 30:1
person making the * must do exactly Num 30:1
she has made a * with penalties, Num 30:4
nothing, then her * shall stand. Num 30:4
let her make the *, or feels that Num 30:5
"If she takes a * or makes a Num 30:6
learns of her * and says nothing on Num 30:7
he hears of it, her * shall stand. Num 30:7
to accept her * or foolish pledge, Num 30:8
divorced, she must fulfill her *. Num 30:9
when she makes the *, and her Num 30:10
does nothing, the * shall stand; Num 30:11
hears of it, her * is void and Num 30:12
or nullify her *, but if he says Num 30:13
to permit the *, whatever penalties Num 30:15
make a * you don't intend to keep. Deu 5:11
"When you make a * to the Lord, Deu 23:21
Once you make the *, you must Deu 23:23
And * by my existence, Deu 32:40,41
because of the * which the leaders Jos 9:18
For I have made a * to the Lord Ju 11:35
or satisfied his * by consecrating Ju 11:39f
And she made this *: "O Lord of 1Sa 1:11
today. I * by the name of the God 1Sa 14:39
Far from it! We * by the life of 1Sa 14:45
he declared, "I * by the Lord that 2Sa 3:28
a sacred * by being kind to him." 2Sa 9:3
of my * to your father Jonathan. 2Sa 9:7
Uriah's wife. I * that because of 2Sa 12:11
"I * by God," he replied, "that 2Sa 14:11
fulfillment of a * I made to him 2Sa 15:7,8
him, "go and fulfill your *." 2Sa 15:9
But Ittai replied, "I * by God 2Sa 15:21
out manure. I * that those of your 1Ki 14:11
But Micaiah told him, "This I *, 1Ki 22:14
But Micaiah replied, "I * by God 2Ch 18:13
* to carry out their promises. Neh 5:12
"I * by the living God, who has Job 27:2
until I die I will * my Job 27:5
my * of praising you each day. Ps 61:8
praise, and thus fulfill our *. Ps 65:1
not rescind his *, that you are a Ps 110:4
So when you talk to God and * to Ecc 5:4
was all a mistake [to make the * Ecc 5:6,7
has taken this *, and sworn to it Jer 51:14
to legally declare my marriage *. Eze 16:8
is a sacred * to God, for the Mt 5:34
it is a sacred *, for the earth Mt 5:35
a * shows that something is wrong. Mt 5:37
custom, for he had taken a *. Act 18:18
Probably a * to offer a sacrifice Act 18:18f
Probably a * to offer a sacrifice Act 18:22f
his * to offer a sacrifice seven Act 21:26,27
their * to Christ and marry again. 1Ti 5:11

VOWED
So the servant * Gen 24:9
And Esau *, thereby selling all Gen 25:33
And Jacob * this vow to God: "If Gen 28:20
an animal that is * to be given to Lev 27:9
Then the people of Israel * to Num 21:2
was very angry. He * that not one Deu 1:34,35
because of you; he * that I could Deu 4:21,22
anything you have * to give the Deu 12:17
you have * to the Lord your God. Deu 23:23
the Lord, and he * that he wouldn't Jos 5:6
in fact had * that he would do it. Ju 2:15
Meanwhile Jephthah had * to the Ju 11:30,31
her father, who did as he had *. Ju 11:39
Samson *. Ju 15:7
THE LEADERS OF Israel had * at Ju 21:1
So I have * that the sins of Eli 1Sa 3:14
Finally Saul agreed, and *, "As 1Sa 19:6
But David * that he would eat 2Sa 3:35,36
living God," he *, "any man who 2Sa 12:5
Then, turning to Shime-i, he *, 2Sa 19:23
She replied, "My lord, you * to 1Ki 1:17
And the king *, "As the Lord 1Ki 1:29
this very day," the king *. 2Ki 6:31
Gedaliah * that if they would 2Ki 25:24
wives (they * to divorce their Ez 10:16-19
to this oath and * to accept the Neh 10:29
and they * before God that they Neh 13:25
He has * it by his holiness! Ps 60:6,7
him the sacrifice I * I would. Ps 116:14
pay everything I * to the Lord. Ps 116:18,19
Then I * that I would do it; Ps 132:2-5
Obey the king as you have * to Ecc 8:2,3
Look and see, for the Lord has * Is 49:18
to him and * to serve him. Jon 1:16
only the Lord, as you have *. Nah 1:15
* to give her anything she wanted. Mt 14:7
like," the king *, "even half of Mk 6:22,23
And all the others * the same. Mk 14:31

VOWING
not a sin if you refrain from *! Deu 23:22

VOWS
a witness of our * that I will not Gen 31:51,52
and normal fulfillment of your *. Lev 23:38
And he must renew his * that day Num 6:11
Tell them, 'The Lord * to do to Num 14:28
in connection with *, or as Num 29:39
to fulfill your *, your free-will Deu 12:6
promised in your *, and your burnt Deu 12:26,27
that you promptly fulfill your *; Deu 23:21
and * of the priests and Levites. Neh 13:29
I will publicly fulfill my * in Ps 22:25
For you have heard my *, O God, Ps 61:5
with burnt-offerings to pay my *. Ps 66:13
Fulfill all your * that you have Ps 76:11
this day have I paid my *." Pro 7:14f
its halves to solemnize your *. Jer 34:18,19
out your promises and * to her! Jer 44:25
You lightly broke your solemn * Eze 16:59,60
not break your * to God, but must Mt 5:33
But I say: Don't make any *! Mt 5:34
shave their heads and take some *. Act 21:23
Honor your marriage and its *, Heb 13:4

VOYAGES
dangerous for long * by then, Act 27:9

VULGAR
Help me to refuse the low and * Ps 101:3

VULTURE
The *, the stork, Lev 11:13-19
The eagle, the *, Deu 14:11-18
The *, the cormorant, Deu 14:11-18
I am like a * in a far-off Ps 102:6
A * circles ominously above the Jer 48:40
fly as swift as a * and will spread Jer 49:22
Like a *, the enemy descends upon Hos 8:1

VULTURES
And when the * came down upon Gen 15:11
to prevent the * from tearing at 2Sa 21:10
the country shall be eaten by *." 1Ki 21:24
out by ravens and eaten by *. Pro 30:17
to eat; the * will tear bodies all Is 18:6
them swarms of * and wild animals Jer 12:9
to tear, and the * and wild animals Jer 15:3
apart by * and wild animals. Jer 16:4
* and wild animals to feed upon. Jer 19:7
bodies to the * and wild animals. Jer 34:20
I will give you to the * and wild Eze 39:4
burrow there; the * and the owls Zep 2:14
is, there the * will gather. Mt 24:28
the body is, the * gather!" Lk 17:37
and their bodies left to the *. Lk 17:37f

WAD
He will * you up in his hands Is 22:18

WADI
(* el-Arish) to the Mediterranean. Eze 47:19
(* el-Arish) to the Mediterranean. Eze 48:27,28

WADI-EL-ARISH
to your descendants from the * Gen 15:18
the boundary will follow the * Num 34:5

WAFER
bread, and one * from the basket of Ex 29:23
one unleavened *, one wafer spread Lev 8:26
wafer, one * spread with olive oil, Lev 8:26

WAFERS
* with oil poured over them. Ex 29:2
but without yeast. * made without Lev 2:4
with unleavened * spread with olive Lev 7:12
unleavened * spread with oil; Num 6:15
and one of the * (also made without Num 6:19
offerings, and the * made without 1Ch 23:29

WAFT
upon my garden and * its lovely Sol 4:16

WAFTING
and as incense * up to you. Ps 141:2

WAGE
and has broken his * contract with Gen 31:7
to * Jehovah's war against Midian. Num 31:3
Pay him his * each day before Deu 24:14,15
"200 denarii," a year's *. Mk 6:37f
equivalent of a modern day's *. Lk 10:35f
a denarius being a full day's *. Jn 6:7f
Together they will * war against Rev 17:14

WAGES
(meaning "*"), for she said, Gen 30:18
"What * do you want?" Gen 30:31,32
Give them to me as my *. Gen 30:31,32
And you have reduced my * ten Gen 31:41
pay your men whatever * you ask; 1Ki 5:6
to the end of the week and his *. Job 7:2
By not paying * you are building Jer 22:13
They will receive the * of Zep 2:10
were no jobs, no *, no security; Zec 8:10
as my *. Zec 11:12
the workman is worthy of his *! Lk 10:7
The reapers will be paid good * Jn 4:36
For the * of sin is death, but Rom 6:23

WAGGED
by, and * their heads in mockery. Mk 15:29,30

WAGON
by two oxen—a * for every two Num 7:3
you groan as a * groans that is Amo 2:13

WAGONS
brothers to take * from Egypt to Gen 45:19
So Joseph gave them *, as Pharaoh Gen 45:21
when he saw the * filled with food Gen 45:27
* Pharaoh had provided for them. Gen 46:5
They brought six covered *, each Num 7:3
* for the work of the Tabernacle. Num 7:4,5
So Moses presented the * and the Num 7:6
the Levites. Two * and four oxen Num 7:7
use, and four * and eight oxen Num 7:8
None of the * or teams was given Num 7:9
with chariots and * and a great Eze 23:24

WAHEB
and the city of *, lie between the Num 21:14

WAIL
Yes, the * of the people of Ex 3:9
the animals. The * of death will Ex 11:6
crying with a loud and bitter *. Est 4:1
So I * and lament for Jazer and Is 16:9
a heap of ruins. *, you ships that Is 23:14
the words of God, O women who *. Jer 9:20
Teach your daughters to * and Jer 9:20
weep and *. Jer 48:20
Yes, I * for Moab, my heart is Jer 48:31
weep and *, hiding in the hedges, Jer 49:3
And they shall * for you, Eze 26:17
mourners to * and lament. Amo 5:16
I will * and lament, howling as a Mic 1:8
"* in sorrow, you people of Zep 1:11

WAILED
they *. Ex 17:2
in Egypt," they *, "or even here Num 14:2

WAILING
recognize him. * loudly in despair, Job 2:12
Let there be no * at her grave; Eze 24:17
Listen to the * of Israel's Zec 11:3
with unrestrained weeping and *. Mk 5:38
the Jewish leaders * with her, he Jn 11:33

WAILS
Hear the *! Jer 48:39

WAIST
a goblet filled with wine. Your * Sol 7:2
From his * up, he seemed to be Eze 1:27,28
and from his * down he seemed to Eze 1:27,28
from his * down, he was made of Eze 8:2
from his * up, he was all Eze 8:2
feet after that it was up to my *. Eze 47:5
his *, and glowing, lustrous skin! Dan 10:5,6
stripped to the *) and jumped into Jn 21:7

WAIT
"* until the bridal week is Gen 29:27
assigned Joseph to * on them. Gen 40:4
have time to * for bread to rise to Ex 12:39
and * for us until we come back; Ex 24:14
are you going to * before clearing Jos 18:3
of the city lay in * all night at Ju 16:2
would you * for them to grow up? Ru 1:13
her husband, "* until the baby is 1Sa 1:21,22
Go to Gilgal and * there seven 1Sa 10:8
Saul earlier to * seven days for 1Sa 13:8
then we will stop and * for 1Sa 14:9
Hurry, hurry, don't *." 1Sa 20:38
Absalom told his men, "* until 2Sa 13:28
* there for a message from you. 2Sa 15:28
"* here," the king told him. 2Sa 18:30
Even if we * until morning, some 2Ki 7:9
just * and see what I'll be like!' 2Ch 10:10
Why must the godly * for him in Job 24:1
Shall I then continue to * when Job 32:16
is no need to * for some great Job 34:23
at last, if you will only *. Job 35:14,15
dens, or lie in * in the jungle? Job 38:39,40
Don't be impatient. * for the Ps 27:14
Yes, * and he will help you. Ps 27:14
Rest in the Lord; * patiently for Ps 37:7
And I will * for your mercies—for Ps 52:9
O GOD IN Zion, we * before you in Ps 65:1
They wouldn't * for him to act, Ps 106:13
How long must I * before you Ps 119:84
No wonder I * expectantly for Ps 119:131
That is why I * expectantly, Ps 130:5
in the air; they * in ambush with a Ps 140:5
Don't repay evil for evil. * for Pro 20:22
It is better to * for an Pro 25:6,7
tomorrow—* and see what happens. Pro 27:1
If you * for perfect conditions, Ecc 11:4
I will * for the Lord to help us, Is 8:17
Blessed are all those who * for Is 30:18
But they that * upon the Lord Is 40:31
watch in fear and * for word of Is 41:5
Those who * for me shall never be Is 49:23
they shall * for me and long for Is 51:5
who works for those who * for him! Is 64:4
"Why should we * here to die? Jer 8:14
Therefore we will * for you to Jer 14:22
good to those who * for him, to Lam 3:25

(WAIT Con't)
It is good both to hope and * Lam 3:26
But afterward he must * seven Eze 44:26
And blessed are those who * and Dan 12:12
and I will * for you." Hos 3:3
his help; I * for God to save me; Mic 7:7
now, and * to see what answer God Hab 2:1
I will quietly * for the day of Hab 3:16
"But his creditor wouldn't *. Mt 18:30
* while he went on ahead to pray. Mt 26:36
do we need? Why * for witnesses? Mk 14:63,64
to * until his father's death. Lk 9:59
Literally, "but * here in the Lk 24:49f
down to the shore to * for him. Jn 6:16
told the Jews to * for the Act 24:22
But * a minute! Rom 2:1
We, too, * anxiously for that day Rom 8:23
us to * patiently and confidently. Rom 8:25
service—* for each other; 1Co 11:33
to stop himself or * his turn. 1Co 14:32
Don't * until I get there and 1Co 16:2
for God wanted them to * and Heb 11:40
and bless you. * patiently for the Jud 1:21
to injure earth and sea, "*! Rev 7:3

WAITED
and the people * until she was Num 12:15
and * as all the people passed by. Jos 3:17
were locked, they *, thinking that Ju 3:24
to Nabal and * for his reply. 1Sa 25:9
they stopped and * so that he could 2Sa 6:13
The prophet * for the king beside 1Ki 20:38
They * eagerly with open mouths. Job 29:23
Evil came instead. I * for the Job 30:26
Elihu had * until now to speak Job 32:4
"I have * all this time, Job 32:11,12
I * PATIENTLY for God to help me; Ps 40:1
Then he * for the harvest, but Is 5:2
in whom we trust, for whom we *. Is 25:9
merciful, for we have * for you. Is 33:2
Long have we * for this hour and Lam 2:16
to shade him as he * there to see Jon 4:5
the soldiers, and * to see what was Mt 26:58
'I've * three years and there Lk 13:7
The people * for him to begin Act 28:6
but when they had * a long time Act 28:6
Then Abraham * patiently until Heb 6:15
to God, though he * patiently for 1Pe 3:20

WAITER'S
them and put on a * uniform and Lk 12:37

WAITING
Sin is * to attack you, longing Gen 4:7
in an open field, * to be watered. Gen 29:2
When they met Moses and Aaron * Ex 5:20
again and, without * to see if any Lev 13:36
(While they were * for him to Ju 9:25
Eli was * beside the road to 1Sa 4:13
without * for you to arrive." 1Sa 13:12
Hushai the Archite * for him with 2Sa 15:32
all Israel is * for your decision 1Ki 1:20
* for the Lord to give him peace. 1Ki 5:2,3
children who were * to be slain, 2Ki 11:2,3
and adulterers, * for the twilight Job 24:14,15
* to pounce upon the poor. Ps 10:9
lions hiding and * their chance. Ps 17:12
I am surrounded by * enemies. Ps 27:11
Evil men spy on the godly, * for Ps 37:32
For I am * for you, O Lord my Ps 38:15
for my steps, * to kill me. Ps 56:6
Strong men are out there *. Ps 59:3
the Lord, * for him to rescue me. Ps 62:1
the Lord, * for him to rescue me. Ps 62:5
with weeping, * for my God to act. Ps 69:3
in the smoke, exhausted with *. Ps 119:83
that is trapped, * to be killed Pro 7:23
me and * for me will you be saved; Is 30:15
beside the road * for a client! Jer 3:2
watching me, * for a fatal slip. Jer 20:10
the good I have * for my people, Jer 29:32
bear, like a lion, * to attack me. Lam 3:10
they are * for us there. Lam 4:19
your final doom is *. Eze 7:5,6
stood before him, * to be judged. Dan 7:10
of punishment *—and I wanted so Hos 6:11
Fear grips the * people; Joe 2:6
the harvest is ripe and *. Joe 3:13
Multitudes, multitudes * in the Joe 3:14
mercies * for them from the Lord! Jon 2:8
the one we are * for, or shall we Mt 11:3
a vast crowd was * for him and he Mt 14:14
hill, a huge crowd was * for them. Mt 17:14
standing around * for jobs, so he Mt 20:3
outside were * for Zacharias to Lk 1:21
By now Elizabeth's * was over, Lk 1:57
arms, for they had been * for him. Lk 8:40
are ready and * for his return. Lk 12:37
now, instead of * until you die!' Lk 15:12
so that it will be * to befriend Lk 16:9f
on the platforms (* for a certain Jn 5:3
on the shore [* to see Jesus Jn 6:22,23
and Cornelius was * for him, and Act 10:24
Now here we are, * before the Act 10:33
While Paul was * for them in Act 17:16
ahead and were * for us at Troas. Act 20:5
Can't you see that he has been * Rom 2:4
For all creation is * patiently Rom 8:19
Literally, "* for the revelation Rom 8:19f
after all these long years of *. Rom 15:23
this time of * for the return of 1Co 1:7
he can without * to share with the 1Co 11:21
you promised is on hand and *. 2Co 9:5
pains of a mother * for her child Gal 4:19
In heaven a crown is * for me 2Ti 4:8
* for them since the world began. Heb 4:3
We know he is ready and * because Heb 4:4
still * for the people of God. Heb 4:9
eagerly and patiently * for him. Heb 9:28
God's right hand, * for his Heb 10:13
we hope for is * for us, even Heb 11:1
he was confidently * for God to Heb 11:10
brothers who are * for the Lord's Jas 5:7
But he is *, for the good reason 2Pe 3:9
Dear friends, while you are * for 2Pe 3:14
And remember why he is *. 2Pe 3:15,16
darkness, * for the judgment day. Jud 1:6
He stood * on an ocean beach. Rev 12:17

WAITS
If he * more than a day and then Num 30:15
a princess, * within her chamber, Ps 45:13
or * for me outside my home! Pro 8:34
Like a robber, she * for her Pro 23:26,27,28
In the evening Israel * in Is 17:14
a hat, the man who * in hiding to Is 29:21
Yet the Lord still * for you to Is 30:18
the dough and * for it to rise—so Hos 7:4
like a farmer who * until the Jas 5:7

WAKE
Abner and Saul, "* up, Abner!" 1Sa 26:14
He leaves a shining * of froth Job 41:31,32
* up, O harp and lyre! Ps 108:2
When will you * up? Pro 6:9
when you * up in the morning, let Pro 6:22
* up, wake up, Jerusalem! Is 51:17
Wake up, * up, Jerusalem! Is 51:17
* UP, WAKE up, Jerusalem, and Is 52:1
WAKE UP, * up, Jerusalem, and Is 52:1
They shall sleep and not * up Jer 51:57
* up and weep, you drunkards, for Joe 1:5
jealous and try to * them up by Rom 10:19
time is running out. * up, for Rom 13:11
but you are dead. Now * up! Rev 3:2

WAKEN
*! Rouse yourself! Ps 44:23
Lord, *! Ps 59:4
And when I * in the morning, you Ps 139:17,18
And you will * at dawn with the Ecc 12:4
never to * again, says the Lord. Jer 51:39
but now I will go and * him!" Jn 11:11

WAKENED
during the night he got up and * Gen 32:22,23,24
a man inside had * from a nightmare Ju 7:12,13
Suddenly, around midnight, he * Ru 3:8
or is asleep and needs to be *!" 1Ki 18:27
when the living * the next Is 37:36
(Then Jeremiah *. Jer 31:26
The disciples went to him and * Mt 8:25
Frantically they * him, shouting, Mk 4:38
The jailer * to see the prison Act 16:27

WAKENS
Morning by morning he * me and Is 50:4

WAKES
"He goes to bed rich, but * up Job 27:19
thirst when he * up, so your Is 29:8

WAKING
them or even * up, because the Lord 1Sa 26:12
their * hours planning treachery. Ps 38:12

WALK
One evening as he was taking a * Gen 24:63
shall * through on dry ground! Ex 14:16
able to * again, even with a limp, Ex 21:19
you and * acceptably before you. Ex 33:13
I will * among you and be your Lev 26:12
and will make you * with dignity. Lev 26:13
you continue to * against my Lev 26:23
then I will * against your wishes, Lev 26:24
As far as one could * in a day in Num 11:31
you are at home or out for a *; Deu 6:7
God. * in his ways and fear him. Deu 8:6
You must * blamelessly before Deu 18:13
the widow shall * over to him in Deu 25:9
only obey him and * in his ways. Deu 28:9
I * in my own stubborn way!' Deu 29:19
Your entire army is to * around Jos 6:3,4
On the seventh day you are to * Jos 6:3,4
And those who are poor and must *. Ju 5:10
worshipers will * on the threshold 1Sa 5:5
forward and * in front of Samuel. 1Sa 16:8
He causes the good to * a steady 2Sa 22:34
which they should *, and send rain 1Ki 8:35,36
I tell you and * in my path and do 1Ki 11:38
Strength and gladness * beside 1Ch 16:27
* where you tell them to go. 2Ch 6:31
"Should you not * in the fear of Neh 5:9
two long lines to * in opposite Neh 12:31,3
you, can you * steadily forward to Job 11:15
the heavens, and * with his nose in Job 20:6
out the right road for me to *. Ps 25:4
I try to * a straight and narrow Ps 26:1
Go, inspect the city! * around Ps 48:12
Those who * my paths will receive Ps 50:23
so that I can * before the Lord in Ps 56:13
they shall * the blood-stained Ps 58:10
* in the strength of the Lord God. Ps 71:16
help his son to * in godliness. Ps 72:1
* through the awful ruins of the Ps 74:3
When they * through the Valley Ps 84:6
from those who * along his paths. Ps 84:11
Literally, "* uprightly." Ps 84:11f
Mercy and Truth * before you as Ps 89:14,15
* in the light of your presence. Ps 89:14,15
I will try to * a blameless path, Ps 101:2
Make me * along the right paths Ps 119:35
I have refused to * the paths of Ps 119:101
Show me where to *, for my prayer Ps 143:8
from God's ways to * down dark Pro 2:11,12,13
Can he * on hot coals and not Pro 6:28
A treacherous man must * a rocky Pro 13:15
while princes * like servants! Ecc 10:7
they are! They * bent-backed Is 1:4
O Israel, come, let us * in the Is 2:5
with self-assurance as they *. Is 3:18
The people who * in darkness Is 9:2
Can a cane * by itself?" Is 10:15
to * around naked and barefoot. Is 20:2
making them * naked and barefoot, Is 20:4
"No, this is the way; * here." Is 30:21
No evil-hearted men may * upon Is 35:8
God will * there with you; Is 35:8
they shall * and not faint. Is 40:31
When you * through the fire of Is 43:2
that will * in almost unscathed. Is 43:14
If such men * in darkness, Is 50:10
to * in, in the days of long ago. Jer 6:16
must be carried, for it cannot *. Jer 10:5
and if I * in the streets, there Jer 14:18
and * the muddy paths of sin. Jer 18:15
They shall * beside the quiet Jer 31:9
and said to him, "* through the Eze 9:4
and * away into the night; Eze 12:6
My people will * upon you once Eze 36:12
A 17½-foot * ran between the Eze 42:4
There was a * between the two Eze 42:11
to take those who * proudly and Dan 4:37
him to *, I held him in my arms. Hos 11:3
For the people shall * after the Hos 11:10
right, and good men * along them. Hos 14:9
For how can we * together with Amo 3:3
take three days to * around it. Jon 3:3
I will * naked and barefoot in Mic 1:8
who trusted you, who * in peace. Mic 2:8
and to * humbly with your God. Mic 6:8
* humbly and do what is right; Zep 2:3
and I will let you * in and out Zec 3:7
nor carry the lame that cannot *; Zec 11:16
out the path where he will *.' Mt 3:3
as they * through the markets. Mk 12:38
the Enemy, and to * among serpents Lk 10:19
as you * through the markets! Lk 11:43
people as they * along the street. Lk 20:46
during the * down the road. Lk 24:32
Jesus was tired from the long * Jn 4:5,6
"ANYONE REFUSING TO * through Jn 10:1
man can * safely and not stumble. Jn 11:9
while longer. * in it while you Jn 12:35
of Jesus Christ of Nazareth, *!" Act 3:6
and godliness had made this man *? Act 3:12
and * along beside the chariot." Act 8:29
The believers learned how to * in Act 9:31
truth of God and * in evil Rom 2:8
see, and let them * bent-backed Rom 11:10
live in them and * among them, and 2Co 6:16
Holy Spirit, and * in each other's 2Co 12:18
there are many who * along the Php 3:18
now we may * right into the very Heb 10:19
they shall * with me in white, Rev 3:4
neither see nor hear nor *! Rev 9:20
not need to * naked and ashamed." Rev 16:15

WALKED
presence I have *, will send his Gen 24:40
So the people of Israel * Ex 14:22
The people of Israel had * Ex 14:29
While the people of Israel * Ex 15:19
Whenever they * past the altar Ex 40:32
some of the land he had * over. Deu 1:36
Ehud * over to him as he was Ju 3:20
* ahead of him with a huge shield. 1Sa 17:4-7
And he * over to some others and 1Sa 17:30
Goliath * out towards David with 1Sa 17:41,42
They * into the kitchen as 2Sa 4:6,7
David * up the road that led to 2Sa 15:30
He * upon dark clouds. 2Sa 22:10
the Lord from Judah * up to him. 1Ki 13:1
and the child died just as she * 1Ki 14:17
but you have * in the evil paths 1Ki 16:2

ALKED Con't)
mri simply * in and struck him 1Ki 16:10
crifice, Elijah * up to the altar 1Ki 18:36
s shoulders and * away again. 1Ki 19:19
on of Chenaanah) * over and 1Ki 22:24
hen the prophet went down and * 2Ki 4:35
nd Gehazi * from the room a 2Ki 5:27
e mother of the boy * in! 2Ki 8:5
ey too * in the same evil paths 2Ki 17:19
iterally, "they * in the way of 2Ch 11:17f
on of Chenaanah) * up to Micaiah 2Ch 18:23
orever" as they * along praising 2Ch 20:21
e, too, * in the evil ways of 2Ch 22:3
f even a fox * along the top of Neh 4:3
meet them. We * from the Tower Neh 12:38
o wild animal has ever * upon Job 28:8
* safely through the darkness; Job 29:3
in the sources of their depths? Job 38:16
e has not turned and * away. Ps 22:24
ath and steadied me as I * along. Ps 40:2
iscussions as we * together to the Ps 55:14
em, they * awhile behind him; Ps 78:34
* by the field of a certain Pro 24:30,31
e dust and * upon your backs." Is 51:23
t that point Jeremiah * out. Jer 28:11
e calf when you * between its Jer 34:18,19
ou * among the stones of fire. Eze 28:14
e east, if one * through the Eze 40:23
nd here again, if one * through Eze 40:27
e did not lie or cheat; he * Mal 2:6
nd * on the water toward Jesus. Mt 14:29
e country and * the fifty miles Mt 15:21
hen Jesus * out on them. Mt 16:4
mashed the shackles and * away. Mk 5:3,4
nd she jumped up and * around! Mk 5:41,42
e * out to them on the water. Mk 6:48
s they arrived he * up to Jesus. Mk 14:45
e said, and * over to the edge Mk 14:68
t him as they * by, and wagged Mk 15:29,30
ut he * away through the crowd Lk 4:30
hen he * over to the coffin and Lk 7:14
over and looked at him lying Lk 10:32
n his donkey and * along beside Lk 10:34
nd sing as they * along, praising Lk 19:36,37
He * away, perhaps a stone's Lk 22:41,42
udas * over to Jesus and kissed Lk 22:47
And Peter * out of the Lk 22:62
As they * along they were Lk 24:14
wo of his disciples, Jesus * by. Jn 1:36
* past them and left the Temple. Jn 8:59
But he * away and left them, and Jn 10:39
so now they * the half mile back to Act 1:12
So they passed through and * Act 12:10
way from birth, so he had never *. Act 14:8
wives and children * down to the Act 21:5
of Israel had * around them seven Heb 11:30
that is why only those who have * 1Jn 4:6

ALKING
of the Lord God * in the garden; Gen 3:8
shoulders and, * backwards into the Gen 9:23
"Who is that man * through the Gen 24:65
I owned nothing except a * stick! Gen 32:10
and your * stick," she replied. Gen 38:18
* stick is the father of my child. Gen 38:25
and her maids were * along the Ex 2:5
wearing your * shoes and carrying Ex 12:11
your * sticks in your hands; Ex 12:11
when you are out *, at bedtime, and Deu 11:19
the Lord your God, * in all his Deu 11:22
Lord your God and * his paths), Deu 19:9
by seven priests * ahead of the Jos 6:3,4
Ahio was * in front, and was 2Sa 6:4
As they were * along, talking, 2Ki 2:11
As he was * along the road, some 2Ki 2:23
king of Israel was * along the wall 2Ki 6:26-30
strength of Egypt just by * by!" 2Ki 19:24
He is way up there, * on the Job 22:14
skies, or the moon * down her Job 31:26
Even when * through the dark Ps 23:4
would follow me, * in my paths! Ps 81:13
evil, and * only in his paths. Ps 119:3
common sense, * at twilight down Pro 7:8,9
who has been * naked and barefoot Is 20:3
No wonder you are * in the gloom. Is 59:9
But as he was * through the Jer 37:13
* on through the passageway I saw Eze 40:7-12
"I see four men, unbound, * Dan 3:25
to earth, * on the mountaintops. Mic 1:3
They will become like * corpses, Zec 14:12
One day as he was * along the Mt 4:18
and shoes, or even a * stick; Mt 10:10
lame people now * without help, and Mt 11:5
ABOUT THAT TIME, Jesus was * one Mt 12:1
came to them, * on the water! Mt 14:25
over to you, * on the water." Mt 14:28
the crippled were * and jumping Mt 15:31
One day as Jesus was * along the Mk 1:16
As he was * up the beach he saw Mk 2:14
his disciples were * through the Mk 2:23
them except their * sticks—no food, Mk 6:8,9
they saw something * along beside Mk 6:49
they look like tree trunks * Mk 8:24
As they were * along he asked Mk 8:27
and Jesus was * along ahead; Mk 10:32
and as he was * through the Temple Mk 11:27,28
"As you are * along," he told Mk 14:13
he appeared to two who were * Mk 16:12
his disciples were * through some Lk 6:1
The lame are * without a limp. Lk 7:20,21,22
"Don't even take along a * Lk 9:3
As they were * along someone said Lk 9:57
* along ahead of his disciples. Lk 19:28
you will see a man * along Lk 22:10
followers were * to the village of Lk 24:13
them and began * beside them. Lk 24:15
them as they were * along the road Lk 24:35
He rolled up the mat and began *! Jn 5:9
they saw Jesus * toward the boat! Jn 6:18,19
AS HE WAS * along, he saw a man Jn 9:1
He was at the Temple, * through Jn 10:22,23
stood there a moment and began *! Act 3:7,8
Then, *, leaping, and praising Act 3:7,8
When the people inside saw him * Act 3:9
when they saw Aeneas * around. Act 9:35
leaped to his feet and started *! Act 14:10
for as I was out * I saw your many Act 17:23
Anyone who says he is * in the 1Jn 2:9
fellow man is "* in the light" 1Jn 2:10

WALKS
Literally, "if he * abroad with Ex 21:19f
Any animal that * on paws is Lev 11:27
nor trip up a blind man as he *. Lev 19:14
holy, for the Lord * among you to Deu 23:14
strength. He * into traps, and Job 18:8,9
But the good man * along in the Pro 4:18
stay away from where she *, lest Pro 7:25
The rebel * a thorny, treacherous Pro 22:5
by the way he * down the street! Ecc 10:3
from her lovers, * the streets to Is 23:15,16
he has stolen and * along the paths Eze 33:15
them out. He * ahead of them; Jn 10:4
as soon as he * away, he can't Jas 1:24
from him who * among the churches Rev 2:1
* among the golden candlesticks." Rev 2:1f

WALKWAYS
tiers had wider * beside them. Eze 42:5

WALL
His branches shade the *. Gen 49:22
The south * was 150 feet long; Ex 38:9
The north * was also 150 feet Ex 38:11
the surface of the *, he shall Lev 14:37
If the spots have spread in the * Lev 14:39
spotted section of *, and the Lev 14:40
Tabernacle as a * between the Num 1:53
against the *, crushing Balaam's Num 22:25
on top of the city *, she let them Jos 2:15
though against an invisible *!" Jos 3:13,14
entrance passage through the *. Ju 1:24
of its weight, hung upon a *. Ju 8:27f
intending to pin him to the *. 1Sa 18:11,12
imbedded in the timber of the *. 1Sa 19:9,10
at his usual place against the *. 1Sa 20:24,25
they were like a * of protection to 1Sa 25:15,16
fastened to the * of Beth-shan. 1Sa 31:10
his sons from the * and brought 1Sa 31:12
the men on the * attacked us; 2Sa 11:24
on the Jerusalem * saw a great 2Sa 13:34
at the top of the *, he saw a lone 2Sa 18:24
* and began battering it down. 2Sa 20:15
his head over the * to you." 2Sa 20:21
By your strength I leap over a *. 2Sa 22:30
Temple and the * around the city. 1Ki 3:1
which grows in cracks in the *. 1Ki 4:33
built out from the *—so the beams 1Ki 6:6
wings reached from * to wall, while 1Ki 6:23-28
from wall to *, while their inner 1Ki 6:23-28
The * of the inner court had 1Ki 6:36
Fort Millo, the * of Jerusalem, and 1Ki 9:15
of Aphek, but the * fell on them 1Ki 20:30
to bed with his face to the *! 1Ki 21:4
as a burnt offering upon the *. 2Ki 3:27
walking along the * of the city, a 2Ki 6:26-30
against the * and on the horses; 2Ki 9:33
and broke down its * from the Gate 2Ki 14:13
the people on the *, "Listen to 2Ki 18:28
But the people on the * remained 2Ki 18:36
a ramp against its *, nor even 2Ki 19:32
Hezekiah turned his face to the * 2Ki 20:2
hole in the inner * and fled out 2Ki 25:4,5
head to the * of Dagon's temple. 1Ch 10:10
across the room, from * to wall. 2Ch 3:11,12,13
across the room, from wall to *. 2Ch 3:11,12,13
the Temple, five against each *; 2Ch 4:7
each * on the right and left. 2Ch 4:8
Gate, and at the turning of the *. 2Ch 26:9
by repairing the * wherever it was 2Ch 32:5
a second * outside it. 2Ch 32:5
rebuilt the outer * of the City of 2Ch 33:14
of David and the * from west of the 2Ch 33:14
are not good; the * of Jerusalem is Neh 1:3
inspecting the *, and entered again Neh 2:14,15
Let us rebuild the * of Jerusalem Neh 2:17
Let's rebuild the *!" Neh 2:18
his servants, will rebuild this *; Neh 2:20
rebuilt the * as far as the Tower Neh 3:1
next section of *, and beyond him Neh 3:4
trade, but he too worked on the *. Neh 3:8
needed from there to the Broad *. Neh 3:8
was next down the * from them. Neh 3:9
repaired the * beside his own Neh 3:10
in addition to a section of the *. Neh 3:11
1,500 feet of * to the Dung Gate. Neh 3:13
Then he repaired the * from the Neh 3:15
of the * in his own district. Neh 3:17
on the section of * across from the Neh 3:19
the Armory, where the * turns. Neh 3:19
the turn in the * to the home of Neh 3:20
a section of the * extending from a Neh 3:21
the portion of the * from Azariah's Neh 3:24
Ophel repaired the * as far as the Neh 3:26
Tower and over to the * of Ophel. Neh 3:27
The priests repaired the * Neh 3:28
also rebuilt the * next to his own Neh 3:29
completed the * from that corner to Neh 3:32
that we were rebuilding the *. Neh 4:1
they can build the * in a day if Neh 4:1
of their *, it would collapse!" Neh 4:3
us who are building your *." Neh 4:5
At last the * was completed to Neh 4:6
the breaks in the * were being Neh 4:7
all returned to our work on the *; Neh 4:15
I stayed at work on the * and Neh 5:16
officials to spend time on the *. Neh 5:16
rebuilding of the *—though we had Neh 6:1
is why you are building the *. Neh 6:5,6
The * was finally finished in Neh 6:15
AFTER THE * was finished and we Neh 7:1
who lived near the * must guard the Neh 7:3
section of * next to his own home. Neh 7:3
the new Jerusalem *, all the Neh 12:27
the people, the gates, and the *. Neh 12:30
to the top of the * and divided Neh 12:31,32
the *, giving thanks as they went. Neh 12:31,32
to the Broad *, then from the Neh 12:38
out here, camping around the *? Neh 13:21
can scale any *, attack any troop. Ps 18:29
like the pillars of a palace *. Ps 144:12-15
defense, a high * of safety. Pro 18:11
Demolish an old *—and be bitten Ecc 10:8,9
Look, there he is behind the *, Sol 2:9
The watchman on the * tore off my Sol 5:7
Literally, "if she be a *." Sol 8:9f
Literally, "I am as a *." Sol 8:10f
high tower and *, and all the Is 2:15
city * to shout out what he sees. Is 21:6,7
So I put the watchman on the *, Is 21:8,9
to be so firmly fastened to the *! Is 22:25
rain that melts down an earthen *. Is 25:4
check the foundation * you built; Is 28:17
a bulging * that bursts and falls; Is 30:13
the people on the * will hear." Is 36:11
listening on the *, "Hear the Is 36:13
his face to the * and prayed: Is 38:2
army against a high city *. Jer 15:20
they breached the *, and the city Jer 39:2
him; the * of Babylon has fallen. Jer 51:44
a hole in the city * and all the Jer 52:7
broken every fortress, every *. Lam 2:2
and the city, like a * of iron. Eze 4:3
I made out an opening in the *. Eze 8:7
"Now dig into the *," he said. Eze 8:8
Dig a tunnel through the city * Eze 12:5
I dug through the * with my hands. Eze 12:7
a hole in the *, taking only what Eze 12:12
My people build a flimsy * and Eze 13:10
builders that their * will fall. Eze 13:11
And when the * falls, the people Eze 13:12
your whitewashed *, and it will Eze 13:14
against the * will be completed; Eze 13:15
* and its builders will be gone. Eze 13:15
build again the * of righteousness Eze 22:30
pictures she saw painted on a *! Eze 23:14,15
building a siege * and raising a Eze 26:8
The man began to measure the * Eze 40:5
He told me, "This * is 10½ feet Eze 40:5
that goes through the eastern *. Eze 40:6
8¾ feet along the * between them. Eze 40:7-12
Then he measured across to the * Eze 40:19
the northern * and measured it. Eze 40:20
came to an inner * and a passageway Eze 40:23
came to the inner * and a Eze 40:27
inner * and its south passageway. Eze 40:28
as the passageways of the outer *. Eze 40:28
of the inner *, and measured it. Eze 40:32
gate of the inner *, and the Eze 40:35
Then he measured the * of the Eze 41:5
to the Temple * for support. Eze 41:6
of the Temple * as it rose higher. Eze 41:7
The outer * of these rooms was Eze 41:9
around the inner * of the Temple. Eze 41:19,20
were the inner * of the court. Eze 42:3
But a * extended from the end of Eze 42:7,8
each side, with a * all around it Eze 42:16-20

(WALL Con't)
the outer * leading to the east. Eze 43:1
mine, with only a * between, and Eze 43:8
to the inner * at the other end Eze 46:2
door through the * at the side of Eze 46:19,20
Then he brought me outside the * Eze 47:2
with its 1½-mile *, there will be Eze 48:30,31
with its 1½-mile *, the gates will Eze 48:32
The south *, also the same Eze 48:33
of the * opposite the lampstand. Dan 5:5
writing on the *, and tells me what Dan 5:7
writing on the *, and tell me what Dan 5:15
the nearest breach in the *. Amo 4:3
a *—and puts his hand on a snake. Amo 5:19
standing beside a * built with a Amo 7:7
The Lord will tear down her * and Mic 1:6
For the Lord himself will be a * Zec 2:5
and built a * around it and dug a Mk 12:1
the *, must surely be a thief! Jn 10:1
through an opening in the city *! Act 9:25
Literally, "you whitewashed *." Act 23:3f
escaping through a * of flames. 1Co 3:15
God and every * that can be built 2Co 10:5
in the city *, and so I got away! 2Co 11:33
breaking down the * of contempt Eph 2:14
like glass! The * was made of Rev 21:18,19,20

WALL'S
back to the outer * eastern Eze 44:1
"THE LORD GOD says, the inner * Eze 46:1

WALLED
been * up on either side of them. Ex 14:29
Literally, "in a * city." Lev 25:29f
even though in * cities, may be Lev 25:32
But first we will need to build * Num 32:17
They live in high * cities. Deu 9:1
there in great, * cities, but if Jos 14:12
has trapped himself in a * city!" 1Sa 23:7
sixty * cities with bronze gates; 1Ki 4:8-19
build * cities throughout Judah. 2Ch 14:6
us Jerusalem as a * city in Judah. Ez 9:9
again. Her * cities will be silent Is 27:10
fight against the * cities of Judah Is 36:1
crush * cities into ruined heaps. Is 37:26
and they shall sack your * cities Jer 5:17
Come, let us go to the * cities Jer 8:14
* cities of Judah still standing. Jer 34:7
He has * me in; Lam 3:7
Literally, "He has * up my ways Lam 3:9f
and * and filled with people!' Eze 36:35
down go the * cities and Zep 1:16

WALLET
He has taken a * full of money Pro 7:20

WALLOW
Moab shall * in her vomit, Jer 48:26
back and * in the mud again." 2Pe 2:22

WALLOWING
upon their heads and * in ashes. Eze 27:30

WALLS
sea, with * of water on each side; Ex 14:21
them between the * of water along Ex 14:23
They stood as solid * to hold the Ex 15:8
But the Lord let down the * of Ex 15:19
wide, with curtain * 7½ feet high, Ex 27:18
on the *, will be made of bronze. Ex 27:19
The drapes for the * of the court; Ex 35:10-19
feet wide; the * were made from Ex 38:12
All the drapes making up the * Ex 38:16
composing the * of the court. Ex 38:18
of the sanctuary * and for the Ex 38:27
The drapes for the * of the court Ex 39:33-40
streaks in the * of the house which Lev 14:37
Then he shall order the inside * Lev 14:41
without fortifying * around it—are Lev 25:31
road went between two vineyard *. Num 22:24
* for 1500 feet in each direction. Num 35:4
and that the * of their cities rise Deu 1:28
with high * and barred gates. Deu 3:5
seduced within the * of a city, Deu 22:23,24
down your highest *—the walls you Deu 28:52
* you will trust to protect you. Deu 28:52
the * of the city will fall down; Jos 6:5
And suddenly the * of Jericho Jos 6:20
the * of the fort and set on fire. Ju 9:49
When they reached the city * 1Sa 9:26,27
would be shooting from the *? 2Sa 11:19,20,21
ropes and drag the * of the city 2Sa 17:13
of the Temple against the outer *. 1Ki 6:5
The rooms were connected to the * 1Ki 6:6
inserted into the * themselves. 1Ki 6:6
to the Temple * by cedar timbers. 1Ki 6:10
over the stone * was carved with 1Ki 6:18
feet high. Its * and ceiling were 1Ki 6:20
carved on all the * of both rooms 1Ki 6:29
facing each other from three *. 1Ki 7:3,4
The huge stones in the * were 1Ki 7:11
hewn stone in its *, topped with 1Ki 7:12
around, with four-inch-thick *. 1Ki 7:15
repairing the * of this city his 1Ki 11:27,28
The rest fled behind the * of 1Ki 20:30
standing on the * will hear you." 2Ki 18:26
me to the people on the * too? 2Ki 18:27
double * near the king's garden. 2Ki 25:4,5
tearing down the * of Jerusalem. 2Ki 25:10
They fastened his armor to the * 1Ch 10:10
timber and stone for the *. 1Ch 22:14
overlaying the * of the buildings. 1Ch 29:4,5
with the inner * and ceiling 2Ch 3:4
into the * to add to the beauty; 2Ch 3:6
All the *, beams, doors, and 2Ch 3:7
with angels engraved on the *. 2Ch 3:7
three east. The * of the tank were 2Ch 4:5
* and installing barred gates. 2Ch 8:5
* and gates to protect himself: 2Ch 11:5-10
with *, towers, gates, and bars." 2Ch 14:7
yards of the * of Jerusalem 2Ch 25:23
and broke down its *, also those of 2Ch 26:6
rebuilding of the * on the hill 2Ch 27:3
gathered on the * of the city, 2Ch 32:18
and broke down the * of Jerusalem 2Ch 36:19
they have already rebuilt its * Ez 4:12
is rebuilt and the * finished, you Ez 4:16
this Temple and finish these *?" Ez 5:3
is being laid in the city *. Ez 5:8
*, and for a house for myself." Neh 2:8
see the broken * and burned gates. Neh 2:13
the cleared spaces behind the *. Neh 4:13
living outside the * to move into Neh 4:22
protects me like the * of a fort! Ps 31:21
Note her * and tour her palaces, Ps 48:13
build the * of Jerusalem." Ps 51:18f
Though they patrol their * night Ps 55:10
*, leaving us without protection. Ps 80:12
You have broken down the * Ps 89:40
every stone in her * and feel Ps 102:14
* and prosperity in your palaces. Ps 122:7
No enemy attacking the *, but Ps 144:12-15
and its * were broken down. Pro 24:30,31
as a city with broken-down *. Pro 25:28
we broke down the * and destroyed Is 10:13
will find a refuge within her *. Is 14:32
armies! The * of Jerusalem are Is 22:5
You inspect the * of Jerusalem Is 22:9,10,11
some down for stone for fixing *. Is 22:9,10,11
Between the city *, you build a Is 22:9,10,11
The high * of Moab will be Is 25:12
We are surrounded by the * of his Is 26:1
dust; its * come crashing down. Is 26:5
outside your * are counting your Is 33:18
up an earthen bank against its *. Is 37:33
picture of Jerusalem's * in ruins. Is 49:16
and make the * of your houses from Is 54:11
your gates and * of shining gems. Is 54:12
house, within my * —a name far Is 56:5
Who Rebuild Their * and Cities." Is 58:12
war will end. Your * will be Is 60:18
on your * who shall cry to God Is 62:6,7
and along all its *, and in all the Jer 1:15
smash down the * of Jerusalem. Jer 6:6
injustice into its * and oppression Jer 22:13
against the city *, and the Jer 32:24
outside the * shall come in and set Jer 32:29
to strengthen the * against the Jer 33:4
between the two * back of the Jer 39:4
and tore down the * of the city. Jer 39:8
they need neither * nor gates. Jer 49:31
She surrenders! Her * have Jer 50:15
knock down her * and houses into Jer 50:26
Set many watchmen on your *; Jer 51:12
For the wide * of Babylon shall Jer 51:58
between the two * near the king's Jer 52:7
tearing down the * of the city. Jer 52:14
hollow, with three-inch *. Jer 52:21
Therefore the ramparts and * fell Lam 2:8
before the Lord. O * of Jerusalem, Lam 2:18
me into a place of high, smooth * Lam 3:9
Temple * are scattered in the Lam 4:1
battering rams surrounding the *. Eze 4:1
If you go outside the *, there Eze 7:15
So I went in. The * were covered Eze 8:10
as foxes for rebuilding your *! Eze 13:4
to strengthen the * of Israel Eze 13:5
against the * to reach the top. Eze 21:22
within your * is bent on murder. Eze 22:6
Thus they repair the * with Eze 22:28
They will destroy the * of Tyre Eze 26:4
rams against your * and with sledge Eze 26:9
dust, and your * will shake as the Eze 26:10
merchandise and break down your *. Eze 26:12
of Bashan. The * of your cabin are Eze 27:6
their shields hang upon your *; Eze 27:10
are the sentinels upon your *; Eze 27:11
upon the *, perfecting your glory. Eze 27:11
cliffs shall tumble; * shall Eze 38:20
inward through the * along both Eze 40:16
and along the guardroom *. Eze 40:16
the inside of the *, and thirty Eze 40:17
the *, opening onto this pavement. Eze 40:17
It extended out from the * into Eze 40:18
It had windows along the * as Eze 40:25
palm tree decorations along the *. Eze 40:26
the windows along its * and entry. Eze 40:29,30
along the * and in the entry hall; Eze 40:33
decorations on the * of each side Eze 40:
fastened along the * of the entry Eze 40:
inner court. Its * extended up on Eze 40:48,
was 24½ feet wide with 5¼-foot *. Eze 40:48,
long. Its * were 8¾ feet thick. Eze 41:
the Temple, including its two *. Eze 41:15,
The inner * of the Temple were Eze 41:15,
also paneled. The * were decorated Eze 41:17,
and palm trees, just as on the *. Eze 41:
* at the entry of the inner court. Eze 45:
by 52½ feet wide, enclosed by *. Eze 46:21,
Around the inside of these * Eze 46:
Jerusalem's streets and * will be Dan 9:
they scale the * like picked and Joe 2
they run upon the *; Joe 2
So I will set fire to the * of Amo 1
So I will set fire to the * of Amo 1:
"So I will set fire to the * of Amo 1:
city proper—the * of which were Jon 3:
show themselves outside their *. Mic 1:
and tear down your * and demolish Mic 5:
to the * to set up their defenses. Nah 2
many bricks for repairing your *! Nah 3:
against their * and capture them! Hab 1:
The very stones in the * of your Hab 2:
miles around with * 100 feet high Zep 2:1
Many will live outside the city * Zec 2
decorated stonework on the *." Mk 13
earth against your * and encircle Lk 19:4
the memorial decorations on the *. Lk 21:
It was faith that brought the * Heb 11:3
beyond the city * [that is, outside Heb 13:1
like jasper. Its * were broad and Rev 21:
and west. The * had twelve Rev 21:1
the city and its gates and *. Rev 21:1
thickness of the * and found them Rev 21:1

WAN
who try to look * and disheveled so Mt 6:1

WANDER
You must * in the desert like Num 14:3
days, you must * in the wilderness Num 14:34,3
"The Lord made us * back and Num 32:1
you to * with us, who knows where? 2Sa 15:19,2
causes princes to * among ruins; Ps 107:4
me * off from your instructions. Ps 119:1
I used to * off until you Ps 119:6
Those who plot evil shall * away Pro 14:2
You have loved to * far from me and Jer 14:1
and * there among the foreigners; Lam 4:1
Men will * everywhere from sea Amo 8:1
led astray and * like lost sheep; Zec 10:
the night he would * among the Mk 5:
will no longer * in the darkness. Jn 12:4
For if you * beyond the teaching 2Jn 1:
wild waves. They * around looking Jud 1:1

WANDERED
For many years we * around in the Deu 2:
* around in this great wilderness; Deu 2:
When they * from country to 1Ch 16:2
I have * away like a lost sheep; Ps 119:17
their backs on God and * far away. Jer 3:2
who have * away and are lost. Eze 34:
My sheep * through the mountains Eze 34:
Like sheep you * away from God, 1Pe 2:25

WANDERING
earth, * from place to place." Gen 4:12
of Beer-sheba, * aimlessly. Gen 21:14
A man noticed him * in the Gen 37:15
"I have been * in a foreign Ex 18:3
the years you were * in the Deu 11:5
ox or sheep * away, don't pretend Deu 22:1
and leaves them *, lost and Job 12:24,25
They were * homeless in the Ps 107:4
there instead of * like a vagabond Sol 1:7
chased by dogs, * like sheep Is 13:14
She is a lonely, * wild ass. Hos 8:9
They will be * Jews, homeless Hos 9:17
him, and he began * around begging Act 13:11
of * around in the wilderness. Act 13:18
sheep and goats, * over deserts and Heb 11:37,38
will have saved a * soul from Jas 5:20
his brother is * in spiritual 1Jn 2:11

WANDERS
He * around begging for food. Job 15:23,24
like a bird that * from its nest. Pro 27:8
sheep, and one * away and is lost, Mt 18:12

WANT
and didn't * you to see me naked. Gen 3:10
land you *, and we will separate. Gen 13:9
If you * that part over there to Gen 13:9
Or, if you * the west, then I'll Gen 13:9
'They will * my wife and will Gen 20:11,12
* to live," the king told him. Gen 20:15
"I don't * to watch him die," Gen 21:16
But the old man said, "I don't * Gen 24:33
"But we * Rebekah here at least Gen 24:55
I * to report back to my master." Gen 24:56
Isaac: "Come over here. I * to Gen 27:21
How much do you *?" Gen 29:15
to Laban, "I * to go back home. Gen 30:25
"What wages do you *?" Gen 30:31,32

ANT Con't)
e demanded. "I * to marry her." Gen 34:4
So you * to be our king, do Gen 37:8
Well, what do you *?" Gen 38:18
ow you * to take Benjamin too! Gen 42:36
ell me when you * them to go," Ex 8:9
But just who is it you * to Ex 10:8
with you and * to observe the Ex 12:48
o cook as much as you * to Ex 16:23
ouse, or * to sleep with his wife, Ex 20:17
with his wife, or * to own his Ex 20:17
For I * the people of Israel to Ex 25:8
Do you * the Egyptians to say, Ex 32:12
along the way you * me to travel Ex 33:13
and mercy to anyone I * to. Ex 33:19
Obey my laws if you * to live Lev 25:17,18
them, and they * to please the Num 15:3,4
among you who * to please the Num 15:13,14
you * to make yourself our king? Num 16:13
We only * to pass through, and Num 20:19
home if you don't * me to go on." Num 22:34
"You mean you * to sit here Num 32:6
We don't * land on the other Num 32:19
who * to avenge his death; Num 35:12
all we * is permission to pass Deu 2:28
Lebanon. I * to see the result of Deu 3:23,24,25
obey them if you * to live and Deu 4:1
slave doesn't * to leave—if he says Deu 15:16
beautiful girl you * as your wife, Deu 21:11
and the Lord does not * to see Deu 23:14
naked, and in * of everything. Deu 28:47,48
no one will even * to buy you." Deu 28:68
If at that time you * to return Deu 30:2
the enemy kings * to fight the Jos 11:20
them whether they * to be ruled by Ju 9:2
* God's blessing, listen to me! Ju 9:7
'If you really * me, come and Ju 9:15
will certainly * to tell everyone Ju 13:17
his father, "She is the one I *. Ju 14:3
I * to rest against them." Ju 16:25,26
"What do you *, chasing after us Ju 18:23
"What do you mean, 'What do I * Ju 18:24
"No," they said. "We * to go Ru 1:10
leave you, for I * to go wherever Ru 1:16
be my God; I * to die where you Ru 1:17
"I * to talk to you a minute." Ru 4:1
If you * it, Ru 4:4
Literally, "if you * to redeem Ru 4:4f
as much as you *, but the fat must 1Sa 2:16
What do you *?" 1Sa 3:4,5
the cows go wherever they * to. 1Sa 6:8
* me to be their king any longer. 1Sa 8:7
"Even so, we still * a king," 1Sa 8:19
said, "for we * to be like the 1Sa 8:20
tell you what you * to know and 1Sa 9:19
have said, 'We * a king instead!' 1Sa 10:18,19
you just * to see the battle!" 1Sa 17:28
on my enemies is all I *." 1Sa 18:25
that you * this son of a nobody 1Sa 20:30
Take that if you * it, for there 1Sa 21:9
we certainly don't * to go to 1Sa 23:3
"Please listen to what I * to 1Sa 25:24
Israel, you won't * the conscience 1Sa 25:30,31
whom do you * me to bring up?" 1Sa 28:11
promised to and because you * to! 2Sa 7:21
If so, I * to fulfill a sacred 2Sa 9:3
my son. I * no more bloodshed." 2Sa 14:11
"I * to know one thing," the 2Sa 14:18
good things you * to give him." 2Sa 19:37
"We * nothing to do with David. 2Sa 20:1
a saying, 'If you * to settle an 2Sa 20:18
All I * is a man named Sheba 2Sa 20:21
"and we don't * to see Israelites 2Sa 21:4
I will buy it, for I don't * to 2Sa 24:24
If you * to save your own life 1Ki 1:12
"What do you *?" 1Ki 1:16
'I am glad you * to do it,' he 1Ki 8:18
"We don't * you as our king 1Ki 12:2,3,4
the people will * a descendant of 1Ki 12:26
"I * it for a garden," the king 1Ki 21:2
"He's just the man we *." 2Ki 3:12
"I * no part of you," Elisha 2Ki 3:13
the woman I * to speak to her." 2Ki 4:11,12
Does she * me to put in a good 2Ki 4:13
servant Naaman; I * you to heal him 2Ki 5:6
"What did that crazy fellow *? 2Ki 9:11
"Since you * me to be king," 2Ki 9:15
"Do you * the shadow on the 2Ki 20:9
asked him, "What did these men *? 2Ki 20:14
just because you * to be kind to 1Ch 17:19
Make your people always * to obey 1Ch 29:18
so that he will * to obey you in 1Ch 29:19
me the kingdom— this is all I *! 2Ch 1:9
where I * you to sacrifice to me. 2Ch 7:12
"If you * to be their king," 2Ch 10:7
If you * to read about the sons 2Ch 24:27
"But now I * to make a covenant 2Ch 29:10
message: "I don't * a fight with 2Ch 35:21
and we do not * to see you taken Ez 4:14
who made the king * to beautify the Ez 7:27
Your Majesty, I * you and Haman to Est 5:4

me what you really *, and I will Est 5:6
he * to honor more than me?" Est 6:6
them whatever you * to in the Est 8:8
But now, what more do you *? Est 9:12
All I * is a reasonable Job 6:24
to the Almighty. I * to talk this Job 13:3
Does God * your help if you are Job 13:8
Speak some sense if you * us to Job 18:2
and live in caves for * of a home. Job 24:8
point, go ahead. I * to hear it, Job 33:32
We can choose the sounds we * to Job 34:3
we can choose the taste we * in Job 34:3
and * no drivers shouting at them! Job 39:7
"Do you still * to argue with Job 40:2
who are wise, who * to please God. Ps 14:2
but yours." I * the company of Ps 16:3
The one thing I * from God, the Ps 27:4
Do you * a long, good life? Ps 34:12
So if you * an eternal home, Ps 37:27
you really * from your people. Ps 40:6
goats that I really * from you. Ps 50:9
What I * from you is your true Ps 50:14,15
I * your promises fulfilled. Ps 50:14,15
fulfilled. I * you to trust me in Ps 50:14,15
You don't * penance; Ps 51:16
It is a broken spirit you * Ps 51:17
Israel doesn't * me around. Ps 81:11
in the Lord, who * above all else Ps 84:5
Tell me where you * me to go and Ps 86:11
HALLELUJAH! I * to express Ps 111:1
I * to follow them consistently. Ps 119:5
Make me understand what you *; Ps 119:27
If you will only help me to * Ps 119:32
With all my heart I * your Ps 119:58
don't let me * to be with Ps 141:4
they did. "I * to make the Pro 1:4
he said. "I * to warn young Pro 1:4
they will face. I * those already Pro 1:5,6
Yes, if you * better insight and Pro 2:3,4,5
from evil men who * you to be their Pro 2:11,12,13
If you * a long and satisfying Pro 3:1
If you * favor with both God and Pro 3:4,5
you; * attacks you in full armor. Pro 6:11
If you * to find the road to Pro 7:27
TO LEARN, YOU must * to be taught. Pro 12:1
Lazy people * much but get Pro 13:4
you * them broadcast to the world. Pro 20:19
Their kindness is a trick; they * Pro 23:6,7,8
Do you * justice? Pro 29:26
everything they *, but he doesn't Ecc 6:2
Do all you * to; Ecc 11:9
I don't * your fat rams; Is 1:11
I don't * to see the blood from Is 1:11
I * nothing more to do with them. Is 1:12,13
"We * to see what you can do!" Is 5:19
I don't * them to see or to hear Is 6:10
If you * me to protect you, you Is 7:9
to do what I don't * you to do. Is 30:1
* any more of your reports!" Is 30:10,11
at all, nothing to make us * him. Is 53:2
It shall accomplish all I * it Is 55:11
Is this what I *—this doing of Is 58:5
No, the kind of fast I * is that Is 58:6
what they earn. I * you to share Is 58:7
and they shall * the good and hate Is 59:21
they don't * it at all. Jer 6:10
"No, that is not the road we *!" Jer 6:16
if you obeyed. I * to give you a Jer 11:5
Lord, I don't * the people Jer 17:16
I don't * them doomed! Jer 17:16
We will continue to live as we * Jer 18:12
live the way they * to, "The Lord Jer 23:17
things of mine to anyone I * to. Jer 27:5
"If you * to live, submit to the Jer 27:12
so that they shall * to honor me; Jer 31:33
"I * to ask you something," the Jer 38:14
If you * to come with me to Jer 40:4
But if you don't * to come, Jer 40:4
all those I * killed, and capturing Jer 43:11
capturing those I * captured, and Jer 43:11
We will do whatever we * to. Jer 44:17
hands of those who * them Jer 46:26
"Mamma, Mamma, we * food," they Lam 2:12
the wicked when I * you to tell Eze 3:18
wanted to, but they don't * to; Eze 12:2
righteous, when I didn't * it so. Eze 13:22
who say they * my words—all will be Eze 14:10
I only * him to turn from his Eze 18:23
wherever you will, wherever you *. Eze 21:16
land, for I don't * my people Eze 46:18
I * you all to know about the Dan 4:2
I don't * your sacrifices—I want Hos 6:6
I don't want your sacrifices—I * Hos 6:6
I don't * your offerings—I want Hos 6:6
I don't want your offerings—I * Hos 6:6
you will have all the food you *. Joe 2:26
"I * to see a mighty flood of Amo 5:24
because you can, you do. You * a Mic 2:2
he said. "I * to see whether it is Zec 2:2
but only if you * to." Zec 11:12
And what does he *? Mal 2:15

didn't * to publicly disgrace her. Mt 1:19
John didn't * to do it. Mt 3:14
away from those who * to borrow. Mt 5:42
"Do for others what you * them Mt 7:12
"if you * to, you can heal me." Mt 8:2
Jesus touches the man. "I * Mt 8:3
do you * with us, O Son of God? Mt 8:29
I *—I want you to be merciful.' Mt 9:13
I want—I * you to be merciful.' Mt 9:13
verse, 'I * you to be merciful more Mt 12:7
more than I * your offerings,' you Mt 12:7
because he didn't * to back down in Mt 14:9
I don't * to send them away Mt 15:32
If you * me to, I'll make three Mt 17:4
However, we don't * to offend Mt 17:26,27
Jesus told him, "If you * to be Mt 19:21
to give away my money if I * to? Mt 20:15
And if you * to be right at the Mt 20:27
do you * me to do for you?" Mt 20:32,33
"Sir," they said, "we * to Mt 20:32,33
But I * your will, not mine." Mt 26:39
"If you * to, you can make me Mk 1:40
touched him and said, "I * to! Mk 1:41
and * to see you," he was told. Mk 3:31,32
and told him, "I * the head of Mk 6:25
For they didn't * to believe! Mk 6:52
"Master," they said, "we * you Mk 10:35
"We * to sit on the thrones next Mk 10:37
"What do you * me to do for Mk 10:51
blind man said, "I * to see!" Mk 10:51
"What we * to know is this: Mk 12:23
can aid them whenever you * to; Mk 14:7
Yet I * your will, not mine." Mk 14:36
"Is he the one you * released?" Mk 15:9
That is why you * to be baptized! Lk 3:7
"What do you * us to do?" Lk 3:10
"Go away! We * nothing to do with Lk 4:34
then they won't * to eat." Lk 5:35
seems to * the fresh and the new. Lk 5:39
Treat others as you * them to Lk 6:31
"What do you * with me, Jesus, Son Lk 8:28
you everything you *—just because Lk 11:8
of these who * to murder you. Lk 12:4
out of here if you * to live, for Lk 13:31
his father, 'I * my share of your Lk 15:12
can read them any time they * to.' Lk 16:29
asked the man, "What do you *?" Lk 18:41
"Lord," he pleaded, "I * to Lk 18:41
"Where do you * us to go?" Lk 22:9
But I * your will, not mine." Lk 22:41,42
"What do you *?" Jn 1:38
matter is that you * to be with me Jn 6:26
miracles if you * us to believe you Jn 6:30,31
Why do you * to hear it again? Jn 9:27
Do you * to become his disciples Jn 9:27
"Who is he, sir, for I * to." Jn 9:36
lay it down when I * to and also Jn 10:18
said, "Sir, we * to meet Jesus." Jn 12:21
* to be my disciples, tell them Jn 12:26
and go where you * to go before the Jn 12:35
"Oh, there is so much more I * Jn 16:12
Father, I * them with me—these Jn 17:24
"But we * him crucified," they Jn 18:31
So if you * me to, I'll release Jn 18:39
The Jewish leaders didn't * the Jn 19:31
you where you don't * to go." Jn 21:18
Jesus replied, "If I * him to Jn 21:22
He only said, "If I * him to Jn 21:23
You didn't * him freed—this Act 3:14
"What do you *, sir?" Act 10:4
"Now what is it you *?" Act 10:21
Now tell me what you *." Act 10:29
So now they * us to leave Act 16:37
things and we * to hear more." Act 17:20
* to hear more about this later." Act 17:32
"Pretend you * to ask a few more Act 23:15
is it you * to tell me, lad?" Act 23:19
* to get some more information. Act 23:20
But we * to hear what you Act 28:22
for you don't * to see and hear and Act 28:27
So I * you to realize that this Act 28:28,29
your help, for I * not only to Rom 1:11,12
I * you to know, dear brothers, Rom 1:13
from death and you * to be tools in Rom 6:13
you, making you * to do whatever Rom 7:5
all, for I really * to do what is Rom 7:15
I do what I don't * to—what I Rom 7:15
do right. I * to but I can't. Rom 7:18
When I * to do good, I don't; Rom 7:19
Now if I am doing what I don't * Rom 7:20
life that when I * to do what is Rom 7:21
In my mind I * to be God's Rom 7:23,24,25
I * to be kind to someone, I will. Rom 9:15
will take pity on anyone I * to." Rom 9:15
* God's salvation for themselves. Rom 11:11
I can make them * what you Gentiles Rom 11:14
I * you to know about this truth Rom 11:25
So if you don't * to be afraid, Rom 13:3
you will not * to harm or cheat Rom 13:9
with his wife or * what is his, or Rom 13:9
but only * gain for themselves. Rom 16:18

(WANT Con't)
This makes me very happy. I * you Rom 16:19
Jews because they * a sign from 1Co 1:22
I can do anything I * to if 1Co 6:12
I can't easily stop when I * to. 1Co 6:12
Here I * to add some suggestions 1Co 7:12
In all you do, I * you to be free 1Co 7:32
from marrying. I * you to do 1Co 7:35
I don't * to do this to him. 1Co 8:13
agree, because I * to help them. 1Co 9:20
And I don't * any of you to be 1Co 10:20
food offered to idols if you * to; 1Co 10:23
Take any meat you * that is sold 1Co 10:25
accept the invitation if you * 1Co 10:27
But there is one matter I * to 1Co 11:3
Do you * me to praise you? 1Co 11:22
AND NOW, BROTHERS, I * to write 1Co 12:1
* any misunderstanding about them. 1Co 12:1
This time I don't * to make just 1Co 16:7
go right on; I * to come and stay 1Co 16:7
you will), I * you to try to accept 2Co 1:13,14
is that I don't * to sadden you 2Co 1:23
strong already, I * to be able to 2Co 1:24
I * to make you happy, not sad. 2Co 1:24
I didn't * to hurt you, but I had 2Co 2:4
I don't * to be harder on him 2Co 2:5,6
bodies at all. We * to slip into 2Co 5:4
NOW I * to tell you what God in 2Co 8:1
Now I * you to be leaders also in 2Co 8:7
I * to suggest that you finish 2Co 8:10
God knows we are honest, but I * 2Co 8:21
I don't * it to turn out that 2Co 9:3
and waiting. I * it to be a real 2Co 9:5
I don't * to carry out my present 2Co 10:2
it, but I don't * anyone to think 2Co 12:6
for I don't * your money. 2Co 12:14
I don't want your money. I * you! 2Co 12:14
* that Christ speaks through me. 2Co 13:3
no, for we * you to do right even 2Co 13:7
for I * to use the Lord's 2Co 13:10
for we did not * to confuse you Gal 2:5
can it be that you * to go back Gal 4:9
now by those who * us to keep the Gal 4:29
I only wish these teachers who * Gal 5:12
and the good things we * to do Gal 5:17
but they * you to be circumcised Gal 6:13
you to share. I * you to realize Eph 1:18
Last of all I * to remind you Eph 6:10
insight, for I * you always to see Php 1:10
And I * you to know this, dear Php 1:12
has used me. They * reputations as Php 1:15
Sometimes I * to live and at Php 1:23
Do you love me enough to * to Php 2:1
you, helping you * to obey him, and Php 2:13
And now I * to plead with those Php 4:2
stomach or hunger, plenty or *; Php 4:12
Christians here * to be remembered Php 4:22
as we know how. We * to be able to Col 1:28
and because you * to please him. Col 3:22
visit with joy and * to see us just 1Th 3:6
just as much as we * to see you. 1Th 3:6
And now, dear brothers, I * you 1Th 4:13
They * to become famous as 1Ti 1:7
So I * men everywhere to pray 1Ti 2:8
Do you * to be truly rich? 1Ti 6:6
This being so, I * to remind you 2Ti 1:6
gift, does not * you to be afraid 2Ti 1:7
that makes you * to do right. 2Ti 2:22
and the way I live and what I *. 2Ti 3:10
them just what they * to hear. 2Ti 4:3
will make people * to believe in Tit 2:10
Now I * to ask a favor of you. Phm 1:8,9
* to do it without your consent. Phm 1:14
I didn't * you to be kind because Phm 1:14
for heaven—I * you to think now Heb 3:1
will know what I * them to do Heb 8:10
so that they will * to obey them, Heb 8:10
us * to serve the living God. Heb 9:14
that they will * to obey them." Heb 10:16
God's will if you * him to do for Heb 10:36
something we * is going to happen. Heb 11:1
But they didn't * to. Heb 11:16
If you * to keep from becoming Heb 12:3
and we * to keep it that way. Heb 13:18
is a short one. I * you to know Heb 13:23
If you * to know what God wants Jas 1:5
and go wherever we * by means of a Jas 3:3
within you? You * what you don't Jas 4:2
have what you * is that you don't Jas 4:2
aim is wrong—you * only what will Jas 4:3
If you * a happy, good life, keep 1Pe 3:10
Do you * more and more of God's 2Pe 1:2
First, I * to remind you that in 2Pe 3:3
And now I * to urgently remind 2Jn 1:5
more, but I don't * to say it in 2Jn 1:12
I have much to say but I don't * 3Jn 1:13
'I am rich, with everything I *; Rev 3:17

WANTED
is the delicious venison you *. Gen 27:19
except to decide what he * to eat! Gen 39:6
told him. "He * to know whether Gen 43:7
who * to kill you are dead." Ex 4:19
I didn't, for I * to demonstrate my Ex 9:16
they gave them whatever they *. Ex 12:36
and everyone who * to consult with Ex 33:7
man and woman who * to assist in Ex 35:29
explained to him what Balak *. Num 22:7
refused to do what he * them to. Num 32:10,11
gold worth $500. I * them so much Jos 7:21
them to turn up in the ways he *. Jos 14:1
that he could have any city he *. Jos 19:50
For God * to give opportunity to Ju 3:1
and mother that he * to marry her. Ju 14:2
*, so the arrangements were made. Ju 14:7
did whatever he * to—whatever Ju 17:6
you * a king to reign over you. 1Sa 12:12
for himself—just because he * to! 1Sa 12:22
* to know more about his family! 1Sa 17:55f
they had * David as their king. 2Sa 3:17
was because God * to pour out his 2Sa 5:12
living, for he * to be kind to 2Sa 9:1
"Because I * you to ask the king 2Sa 14:32
for that is the way the Lord * 1Ki 2:15
*, and it would be given to him! 1Ki 3:5
Temple of the Lord he * to build. 1Ki 5:2,3
father, David. He * to build a 1Ki 8:17
he had always *, the Lord appeared 1Ki 9:1
Anyone who * to could be a 1Ki 13:33
me and to do whatever I * him to. 1Ki 14:8
was and what he *," Jehu replied. 2Ki 9:11
God or to do what he * them to do. 2Ki 18:12
For Josiah * to follow all the 2Ki 23:24
David * a drink from the 1Ch 11:17
"I * to build it myself," David 1Ch 22:7
"My father David * to build this 2Ch 6:7
and wills, and * him above 2Ch 15:15
take more than he *, but those who Est 1:8
and * no part of him and his ways. Job 21:14
anything they *, and let the Job 22:17
"How he * to lure you away from Job 36:16
"for I have always * it this way. Ps 132:14
for he * them to be understanding, Pro 1:3
Anything I *, I took, and did Ecc 2:10
homesickness and * to be back among Sol 6:12
your God when he * to lead you and Jer 2:17
and sacrifices I * from your Jer 7:22
whatever they * to, following their Jer 7:24
that they * above all to disobey. Jer 31:33f
no one has * to return to me, or Jer 44:10
they * to, but they don't want to; Eze 12:2
had to pay them, for no one * you. Eze 16:33,34
And now, because I * to cleanse Eze 24:13
I * so much to bless you! Hos 6:11
I * TO forgive Israel, but her Hos 7:1
against me. I * to redeem them but Hos 7:13
never loved him and never * to." Zep 1:6
vowed to give her anything she *. Mt 14:7
his story— they * to get rid of Mt 21:46
How often I have * to gather your Mt 23:37
came along and * to take him on a Mt 24:1
celebration—anyone they *. Mt 27:15
Herodias * John killed in Mk 6:19
The Jewish leaders * to arrest Mk 12:12
asked him where he * to go to eat Mk 14:12
outside and * to see him, he Lk 8:20
As they went a woman who * to be Lk 8:43,44
the man agreed—but * to wait until Lk 9:59
for that is the way you * it. Lk 10:21
The man * to justify (his lack of Lk 10:29
How often I have * to gather your Lk 13:34
bought a field and * to inspect it, Lk 14:18
of oxen and * to try them out. Lk 14:19
you *, and Lazarus had nothing. Lk 16:25
he had told, they * him arrested Lk 20:19
them, for he * to release Jesus. Lk 23:20
they * to sin in the darkness. Jn 3:20
to village, for he * to stay out of Jn 7:1
And some * him arrested, but no Jn 7:44
They * to see Jesus, and as they Jn 11:56
Jesus realized they * to ask him Jn 16:19
liked and go wherever you * to; Jn 21:18
Moses and * to return to Egypt. Act 7:39
and tell him what God * him to do. Act 10:22
* to hear their message from God. Act 13:6,7
and as many as * Act 13:48
Barnabas agreed, and * to take Act 15:37
Paul * to go in, but the Act 19:30
his crime. He * to find out why the Act 22:24
And because Felix * to gain favor Act 24:27
* to spare Paul, so he told them Act 27:43
* to, though guarded by a soldier. Act 28:16
The Romans gave me a trial and * Act 28:18
was like and what he * them to do. Rom 1:21
do whatever they * to—yes, vile and Rom 1:24
God's paths, or even truly * to. Rom 3:11
told them what he * them to do. Rom 5:13
how very much he * to bless you. Rom 9:4
would know what he * you to do. Rom 9:4
because of what God * and chose. Rom 9:10-13
I did this because I * your 1Co 2:5
keep from preaching it if I * to. 1Co 9:16
it because they * to, and not 2Co 8:3
And he did this because he * to! Eph 1
for God * all of himself to be Col 1:
you once more. We * very much to 1Th 2:
to feed us, but we * to show you, 2Th 3
I really * to keep him here with Phm 1:1
you had to but because you * to. Phm 1:
the paths I * them to follow." Heb 3:
they * to, doing their work. Heb 9.
If they had * to, they could have Heb 11:1
for God * them to wait and share Heb 11:4
And afterwards, when he * those Heb 12:1

WANTING
longer * her after marrying her. Ex 21:
and without * to harm an Num 35:22,2
for me, * to obey my commandments. Deu 5:2
serious about * to return to the 1Sa 7:
Turn me away from * any other Ps 119:3
it is God, * them to repent. Is 42:2
Any jack * you need not search, Jer 2:2
were outside, * to talk with him. Mt 12:46,4
Anyone * to be a leader among you Mt 20:2
murder, adultery, * what belongs Mk 7:2
and said, "Anyone * to be the Mk 9:3
Literally, "* to justify Lk 10:29
* to borrow three loaves of bread. Lk 11:5,
us, and anyone * to come to you Lk 16:2
are still babies, * your own way? 1Co 3:
will hurt you for * to do good. 1Pe 3:1
and you know that no one * to 1Jn 3:1

WANTON
their ankles, with * eyes that rove Is 3:1
Like a * wife who gives herself Jer 3:

WANTS
they said. "He * to pretend we Gen 43:1
that everyone who * to may bring me Ex 25:
"WHEN ANYONE * to give an Lev 3:
but the man * to redeem it, then Lev 27:13
If anyone * to buy back this Lev 27:31
among you and * to celebrate the Num 9:14
his border, and he * me to go at Num 22:11
you today. He * to confirm you Deu 29:13
for the Lord * a man who will 1Sa 13:14
the man he * and has already 1Sa 13:14
If he is angry and * you killed, 1Sa 20:13
to the woman who * him to live, for 1Ki 3:27
be sure of what he * us to do." 1Ki 22:5
him, 'The Lord * to know why you 2Ki 1:6
"The king * to know whether you 2Ki 9:18
is what the Lord *, it is good." 2Ki 20:19
For God * Israel always to 2Ch 2:4
king like you! He * them to be a 2Ch 9:8
to them, "God * to know why you 2Ch 24:20
loves me, and * to grant my Est 5:7,8
reply, and understand what he *. Job 23:4,5
Whatever he * to do, he does. Job 23:13
everything God * them to, and day Ps 1:2
for God * his loved ones to get Ps 127:2
the evil-minded only * to fight. Pro 13:2
All he * to do is yell. Pro 18:2
He turns them wherever he * to. Pro 21:1
The man who * to do right will Pro 28:20
But the man who * to get rich Pro 28:20
offerings. Who * your sacrifices Is 1:12,13
* to make a little bet with you! Is 36:8,9
But he replied, "My master * Is 36:12
not just you. He * them to know Is 36:12
whenever anyone * to curse someone Jer 29:22
"Jerusalem, the Place Nobody *." Jer 30:17
well and give him anything he *." Jer 39:11,12
anyone listen who * to, and let Eze 3:27
who * to, for they are rebels. Eze 3:27
"The Lord God * to know whether Eze 20:30
will tell him what he * to know." Dan 2:24
* to, even the lowliest of men!' Dan 4:17
No, he has told you what he *, Mic 6:8
says, 'If anyone * to be rid of his Mt 5:31
your life and live as he * you to. Mt 6:33
"If anyone * to be a follower of Mt 16:24
"If any of you * to be my Mk 8:34
Whoever * to be great among you Mk 10:43
And whoever * to be greatest of Mk 10:44
I am willing to do whatever he *. Lk 1:38
all, "Anyone who * to follow me Lk 9:23
"Anyone who * to be my follower Lk 14:26
are doing what God * them to. Jn 3:21
The Father * this kind of worship Jn 4:21-24
he * to, just as the Father does. Jn 5:21
myself great, God * this for me and Jn 8:50
"He is here and * to see you." Jn 11:28
* us to obey you instead of him! Act 4:19
Yes, you know what he *; Rom 2:18
marry someone else if she * to. Rom 7:3
God takes pity on those he * to. Rom 9:16
just because he * to be, and he Rom 9:18
to any brother who * to join you, Rom 14:1
* to do is wrong shouldn't do it. Rom 14:23
* to fill our bodies with himself. 1Co 6:13
Christian, but she * to stay with 1Co 7:12
Christian, and he * her to stay 1Co 7:13
stay, for God * his children to 1Co 7:15
what it should, not what it * to. 1Co 9:27

[W]ANTS Con't)
But if anyone * to argue about 1Co 11:16
put each part just where he * it. 1Co 12:18
the kind he * it to have; 1Co 15:38
kind of sorrow God * his people to 2Co 7:9
have to give. God * you to give 2Co 8:12
than he really * to, for cheerful 2Co 9:7
things your evil nature * you to. Gal 5:16
he * us to have out of his rich Eph 4:7
and do whatever the Lord * you to. Eph 5:17
and then helping you do what he *. Php 2:13
saved me for and * me to be. Php 3:12
understand what he * you to do; Col 1:9
For God * you to be holy and 1Th 4:3,4
of children he * to have—will make 2Th 1:11
that if a man * to be a pastor 1Ti 3:1
A widow who * to become one of 1Ti 5:9
that anyone who * to argue will be Tit 2:8
that God * us to turn from godless Tit 2:12
message that God * to save us—has Heb 4:2
priest just because he * to be. Heb 5:4
Anyone who * to come to God must Heb 11:6
If you want to know what God * Jas 1:5
And remember, when someone * to Jas 1:13
him, for God never * to do wrong Jas 1:13
are doing what Christ * you to. Jas 2:12
without doing what God * you to? Jas 2:20
wherever the pilot * it to go, even Jas 3:4
is, "If the Lord * us to, we shall Jas 4:15
Remember, if God * you to 1Pe 3:17
and discover what he * you to do. 2Pe 1:5
trying to do what he * us to? 1Jn 2:3
thirsty one come—anyone who * to; Rev 22:17

[W]AR
NOW * FILLED the land— Gen 14:1
And they were constantly at * Gen 25:18
If we don't, and * breaks out, Ex 1:10
"For the Lord will be at * with Ex 17:15,16
as if they are preparing for *!" Ex 32:17
by bringing * against you. Lev 26:25
destroying you with * as you go. Lev 26:33
as prisoners of *, and slaves. Lev 26:36
are able to go to *, indicating Num 1:2-15
Land and go to * against your Num 10:9
and clan are able to go to *." Num 26:2
wage Jehovah's * against Midian. Num 31:3
other spoils of * were brought to Num 31:12
for Jehovah's *, and keep your Num 32:20
king of Heshbon. * against him and Deu 2:24
"King Sihon then declared * on Deu 2:32
mighty miracles, *, and terror? Deu 4:34
fail declare * against that city Deu 13:15
"WHEN YOU GO to * and see before Deu 20:1
"When you go to * and the Lord Deu 21:10
"When you are at *, the men in Deu 23:9,10
fever, infections, plague, and *. Deu 28:22
of * to accomplish all of this. Jos 11:18
land finally rested from its *. Jos 11:23
to * against their brother tribes. Jos 22:12
more of * against Reuben and Gad. Jos 22:33
of Moab started a * against Israel, Jos 24:9
go to * against the Canaanites?" Ju 1:1
might know *" Ju 3:1f
began their * against Israel. Ju 11:4
me by coming to * against me; Ju 11:27
AT THAT TIME Israel was at * with 1Sa 4:1
had been before. * broke out 1Sa 19:8
armies for another * with Israel. 1Sa 28:1
"The Philistines are at * with 1Sa 28:15
THAT WAS THE beginning of a long * 2Sa 3:1
As the * went on, Abner became a 2Sa 3:6
was no longer at * with the 2Sa 7:1
and how the * was prospering. 2Sa 11:7
were at * with Israel, and David 2Sa 21:15
Later, during a * with the 2Sa 21:18
He gives me skill in * 2Sa 22:35
it was an act of *, but it was done 1Ki 2:5
There was constant * between 1Ki 14:30
* between Israel and Judah. 1Ki 15:6
There was lifelong * between King 1Ki 15:16
have come for truce or for *." 1Ki 20:18
FOR THREE YEARS there was no * 1Ki 22:1
of Syria was at * with Israel, he 2Ki 6:8
"Do we kill prisoners of *? 2Ki 6:22
of Ahab) in his * against Hazael, 2Ki 8:28
to * against Gath and captured it; 2Ki 12:17
of Joash and his * with King 2Ki 14:15
* on Ahaz and besieged Jerusalem; 2Ki 16:5
of whom were strong and fit for *. 2Ki 24:16
the Hagrites in * and moved into 1Ch 5:10
They declared * on the Hagrites, 1Ch 5:19
number of men of * from these. 1Ch 7:2
numbered 36,000 men of *. 1Ch 7:40
in * and exiled to Manahath. 1Ch 8:6,7
all of them prepared for *. 1Ch 12:24-37
The next * was against the 1Ch 20:4
During another * with the 1Ch 20:5
For these men dedicated their * 1Ch 26:27
and declared * against the rest of 2Ch 11:1
Early in his reign * broke out 2Ch 13:1
So there was no more * until the 2Ch 15:19
* on him and built the fortress 2Ch 16:1
mobilized for * against Israel. 2Ch 17:1
declared * on King Jehoshaphat. 2Ch 17:10
to * with Ramoth-gilead or not?" 2Ch 18:3,4,5
saying—that the * would end in 2Ch 18:12
* against Ramoth-gilead or not?" 2Ch 18:14
Meunites declared * on Jehoshaphat 2Ch 20:1
calamity such as *, disease, or 2Ch 20:9
Ahab), who was at * with King 2Ch 22:5
and declared * on King Joash of 2Ch 25:17
He declared * on the Philistines 2Ch 26:6
And he produced engines of * 2Ch 26:15
His * against the Ammonites was 2Ch 27:5
his * against the armies of Edom. 2Ch 28:16
been killed in *, and our sons and 2Ch 29:9
for a council of *, and it was 2Ch 32:3
and Josiah declared * on him. 2Ch 35:20
power with which I am at *." 2Ch 35:21f
power of the sword in time of *. Job 5:20
"You shall laugh at * and Job 5:22
will die in *, or starve to death. Job 27:14
the time when I will need it in *. Job 38:22,23
when he goes to *, he is unafraid Job 39:21-23
to save anyone. A * horse is a poor Ps 33:16,17
declare * on them for their Ps 35:1
smooth, but in his heart was *. Ps 55:21
the time he was at * with Syria, Ps 60:1
Scatter all who delight in *. Ps 68:30
reminders of his * against Egypt Ps 81:5
but they are for *, and my voice Ps 120:7
don't go to * until they agree. Pro 20:18
Don't go to * without wise Pro 24:6
A time for *; Ecc 3:8
than weapons of *, but one rotten Ecc 9:18
of * into implements of peace. Is 2:4
for * against us—and perish! Is 8:9,10
Call your councils of *, develop Is 8:9,10
the blood-stained uniforms of *; Is 9:5
sharp arrows and the terrors of *! Is 21:15
lands tremble and mobilize for *. Is 41:5
out of your land—all * will end. Is 60:18
How long must I see * and death Jer 4:21
will be neither famine nor *! Jer 5:12
assurances of peace when all is *. Jer 6:14
fully armed, mounted for *. Jer 6:23
goddess of love and *, was called. Jer 7:18f
The noise of * resounds from the Jer 8:16
snorting of their * horses can be Jer 8:16f
is * and famine and disease. Jer 14:12
no * or famine will come. Jer 14:13
say no * shall come nor famine. Jer 14:15
nor famine. By * and famine they Jer 14:15
victims of famine and *; Jer 14:16
They shall die from * and famine, Jer 16:4
of Babylon, has declared * on us! Jer 21:1
I will call for * against all the Jer 25:29
I will send *, famine and disease Jer 27:8
Why should you choose * and Jer 27:13
warning of *, famine and plague. Jer 28:8
them, I will send *, famine and Jer 29:16,17
won't be killed in * and carnage, Jer 34:4
death by * and famine and disease. Jer 34:17
will be free from * and hunger and Jer 42:13,14
to Egypt, the * and famine you Jer 42:16
be destroyed by * and famine until Jer 44:27
recover from the ravages of *. Jer 46:26
are heroes, mighty men of *"? Jer 48:14
warriors! * shall devour her Jer 50:37
to mobilize for * on Babylon. Jer 51:27
be a time of civil * as the Jer 51:46
disease and * will stalk your Eze 5:17
I, even I the Lord, will bring * Eze 6:3
from * and famine and disease. Eze 6:11
those in exile; * will destroy Eze 6:12
I will expose you to the * you Eze 11:8
death by * and famine and disease. Eze 12:16
"Or when I bring * against that Eze 14:17
destroy all life: *, famine, Eze 14:21
with them shall perish in that *. Eze 30:5
They shall * against Egypt and Eze 30:11
with a flood, and * and its Dan 9:26
will plan total * against Greece. Dan 11:2
and declared * against the Dan 11:7f
Therefore the terrors of * shall Hos 10:14
* will swirl through their Hos 11:6
far and wide: Get ready for *! Joe 3:9
I killed your lads in * and drove Amo 4:10
each other, for all * will end. Mic 4:3
*, to fight against those nations. Zec 14:3
will proclaim * against each other, Mk 13:8
filled with civil * is doomed; Lk 11:17
dream of going to * without first Lk 14:31
nature, that is at * with my mind Rom 7:23,24,25
in many battles and win the *. Rev 6:2
to the earth; * and killing broke Rev 6:4
to kill with * and famine and Rev 6:8
will declare * against them and Rev 11:7
Then there was * in heaven; Rev 12:7
Together they will wage * Rev 17:14
who justly punishes and makes *. Rev 19:11

WAR-LORDS
The enemy * have cut down the Is 16:8

WARD
this would * off further Num 17:10
tailor, living in the second *. 2Ch 34:22

WARDROBE
This is the * they shall make: a Ex 28:4

WAREHOUSE
your island * is filled to the Eze 27:25

WARES
and all sorts of * and selling them Neh 13:16
her traders to buy your many *. Eze 27:16
wine from Uzal for your *." Eze 27:19f
and Chilmad all send their *. Eze 27:23
Your riches and *, your sailors Eze 27:27

WARFARE
There was continuous * between 1Ki 15:32,33
of Babylon through *, famine and Jer 32:36

WARM
Just as they were beginning to * Ju 19:22
lie in your arms and keep you *." 1Ki 1:2
lay in his arms to * him (but he 1Ki 1:3,4
body began to grow * again! 2Ki 4:34
sheep to keep him *, or if I have Job 31:19,20
Do you know why you become * Job 37:16,17
the earth, to * them in the dust. Job 39:14
made * clothes for all of them. Pro 31:21
other, but how can one be * alone? Ecc 4:11
to make a fire to * himself and Is 44:15
and to keep him * and fed and well Is 44:16
fire to sit beside to make you *! Is 47:14
own light, and * yourselves from Is 50:11
not enough clothes to keep you *. Hag 1:6
had felt strangely * as he talked Lk 24:32
Jesus, and there was * fellowship Act 4:33
and * us in the rain and cold. Act 28:1
and we feel this * love everywhere Rom 5:5
GIVE A * welcome to any brother Rom 14:1
giving her a * Christian welcome. Rom 16:1
even enough clothes to keep us *. 1Co 4:11
your loyalty and * love for me, 2Co 7:7
enough clothing to keep me *. 2Co 11:27
bless you; stay * and eat hearty," Jas 2:16

WARMER
But then he calls for * weather, Ps 147:18

WARMING
Peter * himself at the fire. Mk 14:66,67
stood there with them, * himself. Jn 18:18

WARMLY
him * and brought him home. Gen 29:12,13
and they greeted each other *. Ex 4:27
father-in-law and greeted him *; Ex 18:7
She thanked him *. Ru 2:10,11
Mahanaim, he was * greeted by Shobi 2Sa 17:27
So, * welcome each other into the Rom 15:7
just as Christ has * welcomed you; Rom 15:7
Shake hands * with each other. Rom 16:16
Greet each other * in the Lord. 2Co 13:12
other *, with all your hearts. 1Pe 1:22

WARMS
the sun comes up and * the earth. Nah 3:17

WARMTH
For it is probably his only *; Ex 22:27
same blanket gain * from each Ecc 4:11
*, and Peter joined them there. Lk 22:55

WARN
"Go back down and * the people not Ex 19:21
said to Moses, "* your brother Lev 16:1
I am Jehovah. * the priests to Lev 22:9
Do as they ask, but * them about 1Sa 8:9
to him twice to * him specifically 1Ki 11:9,10
sent prophets to * both Israel and 2Ki 17:13
again and again to * them, for he 2Ch 36:15
You sent your prophets to * them Neh 9:30
proven guilty? I * you, you Job 19:29
Literally, "(even) the cattle (* Job 36:33f
For they * us away from harm and Ps 19:11
"I want to * young men about Pro 1:4
of your mind to * you of danger and Pro 6:23
Today your work begins, to * the Jer 1:10
been announced. * the other Jer 4:16
at Beth-haccherem; * everyone that Jer 6:1
But who will listen when I * Jer 6:10
evil path, even though I * them. Jer 8:4,5
Therefore go and * all Judah and Jer 18:11
again and again to * you, but you Jer 26:5
came to Mizpah to * Gedaliah that Jer 40:13,14
If you refuse to * the wicked Eze 3:18
But if you * them and they keep Eze 3:19
and you refuse to * him of the Eze 3:20
But if you * him and he repents, Eze 3:21
"Therefore * them that the Lord Eze 14:6,7
blows the alarm to * them, then Eze 33:3
the alarm and * the people, he is Eze 33:6
to what I say and * them for me. Eze 33:7
But if you * him to repent and Eze 33:9
Sound the alarm! * with trumpet Hos 5:8
I sent my prophets to * you of Hos 6:5
I sent my prophets to * you with Hos 12:10
"But always, first of all, I * Amo 3:7
he said, "and * them of their Jon 3:1
"But I * you—unless your Mt 5:20
five brothers—to * them about this Lk 16:28

(WARN Con't)
ashamed, but to * and counsel you 1Co 4:14
lessons to us—to * us against doing 1Co 10:11
now I * them again, and all 2Co 13:2
* you against all that is wrong. 1Th 5:12
Dear brothers, * those who are 1Th 5:14
but encourage and * each other, Heb 10:25
the truth, but I * you as those who 1Jn 2:21

WARNED
from the tree I * you about?" Gen 3:11
Abraham *. Gen 24:6
they had strictly * him against Gen 28:6,7,8
And again he * Aaron and his Lev 8:35
these things I have * you against; Lev 20:23
"Stay out!" he *, and, Num 20:20
"Then the Lord * us, 'Don't Deu 2:9
He had * them about this, and in Ju 2:15
Then Gideon * them, "When the Ju 8:7
But someone * Abimelech about Ju 9:25
I have * the young men not to Ru 2:8,9
the dreadful things I * Eli about. 1Sa 3:12
garrison and * his troops that they 1Sa 13:3,4
"Tomorrow morning," he * him, 1Sa 19:2
tonight," Michal * him, "you'll 1Sa 19:11
Abner *. 2Sa 2:21
The Lord strictly * me against 1Ki 13:16,17
Immediately Elisha * the king of 2Ki 6:9
he had * them to obey his 2Ki 17:13
his prophets had * would happen. 2Ki 17:23
as the Lord had * through his 2Ki 24:2
Hanun's counselors * him, "Don't 1Ch 19:2,3
The prophets * us that the land Ez 9:11
in any way. You * us that only if Ez 9:12
May all sinners be *. Job 36:33
I * the proud to cease their Ps 75:4
ones of mine," he *, "and do not Ps 105:15
But, my son, be *: there is no Ecc 12:12
they will claim I never * them. Is 30:9
I set watchmen over you who * Jer 6:17
When you were prosperous I * Jer 22:21
God," when I have * you not to Jer 23:38,39
Lord who did it, just as he had *. Lam 2:17
exactly as you * us you would do, Dan 9:12
"He has done just what he * us Zec 1:5,6
the prophets * them that this Zec 7:7
Herod, for God had * them in a Mt 2:12
Then, in another dream, he was * Mt 2:22
"You sons of snakes!" he *. Mt 3:7
Jesus sternly * them not to tell Mt 9:30
Jesus * them; Mt 16:6
Then he * the disciples against Mt 16:20
See, I have * you. Mt 24:25
But he strictly * them not to Mk 3:12
But Jesus * them not to tell Mk 8:30
I have * you! Mk 13:23
his disciples and * them, "More Lk 12:1
have * them again and again. Lk 16:29
happen you will remember I * you. Jn 16:4
These disciples * Paul—the Holy Act 21:4
commander * the boy as he left. Act 23:22
stone. God * them of this in the Rom 9:33
From this lesson we are * that we 1Co 10:6
I have already * those who had 2Co 13:2
still with you we * you ahead of 1Th 3:4
to a brother who needs to be *. 2Th 3:15
tabernacle, God * him to follow Heb 8:5

WARNING
gave the man this *: "You may eat Gen 2:16,17
on Cain as a * not to kill him. Gen 4:15
But I am * you that you must Ex 8:29
day, as a * to the entire nation. Num 26:5-11
descendants as a *: You will Deu 28:46
people of Israel as my * to them. Deu 31:19
solemn * to the people of Israel. Deu 31:26
rebuild Jericho, * that when the Jos 6:26
but I'm * you now that the honor Ju 4:9
refused to listen to Samuel's *. 1Sa 8:19
the Lord fulfilled his * by 1Ki 13:26
Despite the prophet's *, Jeroboam 1Ki 13:33
with this parting *: "I know that 2Ch 25:16
from pride, and * them of the Job 33:17,18
* you—his wrath will soon begin. Ps 2:12
Shout out a * to Laish, for the Is 10:30
and give no * when danger comes. Is 56:10
This is your last *, O Jerusalem. Jer 6:8
The Lord says: Take * and live; Jer 17:21,22
attention to this *, I swear by my Jer 22:5
This is my * to my people, says Jer 23:16
* of war, famine and plague. Jer 28:8
the * I have given you today. Jer 42:19
whenever I send my people a *, Eze 3:17
For it is a * to the people of Eze 4:3
For he heard the * and wouldn't Eze 33:5
If he had heeded the *, he would Eze 33:5
Without * he will destroy them. Dan 8:25
the land without * and do something Dan 11:24
Suddenly, without *, my judgment Hos 6:5
Let the blast of the * trumpet be Joe 2:1
LISTEN, YOU PRIESTS, to this * Mal 2:1
who sent you this * to return to Mal 2:4
Will there be some * ahead of Mk 13:3,4
children's souls. I am * you! Lk 17:2,3
And will there be any * ahead of Lk 21:7
each of you God's *: Be honest in Rom 12:3
that"—let this be a * to you. 1Co 10:12
[Well, this is my third *, as I 2Co 13:1
who will listen, * them and Col 1:28
be given a first and second *. Tit 3:10
Never forget the *, "Today if Heb 3:15
When he heard God's * about the Heb 11:7
I am * you ahead of time, dear 2Pe 3:17
continue to be a * to us that there Jud 1:7

WARNINGS
when he hears the * of this curse, Deu 29:19
Lord's specific and repeated *. 2Ki 17:12
ancestors, and despised all his *. 2Ki 17:15
idols despite the Lord's stern *. 2Ki 17:15
the book and its * that this land 2Ki 22:18,19
entered the land. * from the Lord 2Ch 33:10
your laws or listen to your *. Neh 9:34
people, while I give you stern *. Ps 81:8
of my * will finally dawn on you. Is 28:19
Cry out your *, but don't expect Jer 7:27
they wouldn't listen to my *." Jer 36:31
it was full of * and sorrows and Eze 2:9,10
they will heed my *, so that I'll Zep 3:7
Moses and the * of the prophets. Mt 5:17
He used many such * as he Lk 3:18
to notice the * all around you Lk 12:56
in the skies—*, evil omens and Lk 21:25

WARNS
But if someone * you that this 1Co 10:28
the Holy Spirit * us to listen to Heb 3:7,8

WARPED
Anyone who talks like that is * Ps 14:1
a man with a * mind is despised. Pro 12:8
These arguers—their minds * by 1Ti 6:5
They have dirty minds, * and 2Ti 3:8

WARRANTS
And we hear that he has arrest * Act 9:14

WARRED
and * against the land of Israel. Dan 8:9

WARRING
been laid waste by * armies—because Jer 25:38
For I had seen this horn * Dan 7:21

WARRIOR
The Lord is a *— Ex 15:3
NOW JEPHTHAH WAS a great * from Ju 11:1
* who was armed with a spear; 2Sa 23:21
reputation as a * and leader. 1Ch 5:24
was a mighty * from Kabzeel, killed 1Ch 11:22
Ishmaiah from Gibeon (a brave * 1Ch 12:3-7
are a * and have shed much blood.' 1Ch 28:3
Then Zichri, a great * from 2Ch 28:7
The Lord will be a mighty *, full Is 42:13
me like a great *, and before him, Jer 20:11

WARRIORS
But now the * of Amalek came to Ex 17:8
land is full of *, the people are Num 13:32
belonging to the *—amounted Num 31:42-46
and all its mighty * are already Jos 6:2
for they were great *. Jos 17:1
thousand brave * that day, leaving Ju 20:46,47
had done, * from that town 1Sa 31:12
the mighty * who surrounded them! 2Sa 16:6
they are mighty * and are 2Sa 17:8
stouthearted *, all included in the 1Ch 7:5
These five mighty * were chiefs of 1Ch 7:7
mighty * among their descendants; 1Ch 7:9
* at the time of King David. 1Ch 7:11
and were all skilled * and chiefs. 1Ch 7:40
Ulam's sons were prominent * who 1Ch 8:40
* went out to the battlefield 1Ch 10:12
bravest of David's * (who also 1Ch 11:10
Other famous * among David's men 1Ch 11:26-47
of the famous * who joined David at 1Ch 12:1
Great and brave * from the tribe 1Ch 12:8-13
They were brave and able *, and 1Ch 12:21
of Simeon, 7,100 outstanding *. 1Ch 12:24-37
20,800 mighty *, each famous in his 1Ch 12:24-37
there were 50,000 trained *; 1Ch 12:24-37
and the mightiest * of Israel. 1Ch 19:8
400,000 seasoned * against twice as 2Ch 13:3
kings, and Ephraim great *. Ps 60:6,7
The bravest * of Moab cry in Is 15:4
escape, nor the mightiest of *. Jer 46:6
The hearts of her mightiest * Jer 48:41
of the mightiest * will disappear Jer 49:22
Go up, O my *, against the land Jer 50:21
and die; her * will all be killed. Jer 50:30
Panic shall seize her mightiest * Jer 50:36
her * in their coats of mail. Jer 51:3
wise men, rulers, captains, *. Jer 51:57
The mighty * in the nether world Eze 32:21
and valiant *, says the Lord God. Eze 39:20
And now, O Lord, bring down your * Joe 3:11
as the * shout and trumpets blare. Amo 2:2
Your swiftest * will stumble in Amo 2:14
They will be mighty * for God, Zec 10:5
They shall be like mighty *. Zec 10:7
* Rev 9:16

WARS
in The Book of the * of Jehovah, Num 21:14
not experienced the * of Canaan. Ju
There will be no more * against 2Sa 7:10,
at the time when * begin, David 2Sa 1
of the numerous * going on, and he 1Ki 5:
activities—his * and the other 1Ki 14:
and his * are described in The 1Ki 22:
including his * against King 2Ki 13:
power, and his *, and how he 2Ki 14:
had been many * between them. 1Ch 18:
the season when * usually began) 1Ch 20
many men in great *,' he told me. 1Ch 22
There were continual * between 2Ch 12:
There were external *, and 2Ch 15
From now on you shall have *." 2Ch 16
not only with his * against the 2Ch 26
and in his * with the Meunites. 2Ch 26
including his * and other 2Ch 27
world, and causes * to end Ps 46
and who delight in aggressive *." Ps 68:3
Then at the last all * will stop Is 2
power and wisdom have won these *. Is 10:
am sending terrible * upon you." Jer 25:
great tribulation—* and sorrows, Dan 10
* between Egypt and Syria. Dan 11:
all weapons, and all * will end. Hos 1:
For in their * in Gilead to Amo 1:
forever in their heartless *? Hab 1:
Roman *, six million under Hitler. Zec 13:
When you hear of * beginning, Mt 24
many astray. And * will break out Mk 13
And when you hear of * and Lk 21
True, * must come, but the end Lk 21

WARSHIPS
For God destroys the mightiest * Ps 48:
For Roman * Dan 11:30,3

WARY
Be as * as serpents and harmless Mt 10:1

WASH
the camel drivers to * their feet. Gen 24:3
with them, and to * themselves and Gen 35:
and have them * their clothes. Ex 19:1
Cut up the ram and * off the Ex 29:1
Aaron and his sons shall * their Ex 30:1
They must always * before doing Ex 30:2
Tabernacle and * them with water; Ex 40:1
must * his clothes immediately. Lev 11:2
the carcass shall * his clothes and Lev 11:2
its carcass shall * his clothes and Lev 11:4
the man need only * his clothes and Lev 13:
who is cured shall * his clothes, Lev 14:
and eyebrows, and * his clothes and Lev 14:
in the house shall * his clothing. Lev 14:4
* his clothes and bathe himself. Lev 15:
* his clothes and bathe himself. Lev 15:
* his clothes and bathe himself. Lev 15:
* his clothes and bathe himself. Lev 15:1
that person must * his clothes and Lev 15:1
sits upon shall * his clothes and Lev 15:21,22,2
defiled, and shall * his clothes Lev 15:2
shall afterwards * his clothes Lev 16:2
the burning shall * his clothes and Lev 16:2
wild animals, must * his clothes Lev 17:1
But if he does not * his clothes Lev 17:1
* them off into the bitter water. Num 5:2
* their clothing and themselves. Num 8:
"Then he must * his clothes, and Num 19:
the animal must * his clothes, and Num 19:8
of the heifer must * his clothes Num 19:1
then the defiled person must * Num 19:1
must afterwards * his clothes; Num 19:2
On the seventh day you must * Num 31:24
and shall * their hands over the Deu 21:6
tell him to go and * in the Jordan 2Ki 5:1
If it's rivers I need, I'll * at 2Ki 5:12
simply to go and * and be cured!" 2Ki 5:1
vats for water to * the offerings, 2Ch 4:6
Even if I were to * myself with Job 9:30
to enter them. I * my hands to Ps 26:6
* me, cleanse me from this guilt. Ps 51:2
and I shall be clean again. * me Ps 51:7
Oh, * yourselves! Is 1:16
* it—don't put it in water at all. Jer 13:1
Literally, "to * with the fist." Mk 7:3f
offer me water to * the dust from Lk 7:44
"You Pharisees * the outside, but Lk 11:39
told him, "Go and * in the Pool of Jn 9:7
Pool of Siloam and * off the mud. Jn 9:11
and began to * the disciples' feet Jn 13:5
"you shall never * my feet!" Jn 13:8
Simon Peter exclaimed, "Then * Jn 13:9
you ought to * each other's feet. Jn 13:14
draw close to you. * your hands, Jas 4:8
Christ died to * away our sins. 1Jn 1:9

WASHBASIN
and the * and its pedestal. Ex 30:28
The bronze * and its bronze Ex 38:8
The * and its base; Ex 39:33-40
Set the * between the Ex 40:7
Then anoint the * and its Ex 40:11
Next he placed the * between the Ex 40:30
the altar and the * and its Lev 8:11

'ASHBASIN Con't)
.iterally, "Moab is my *; Ps 108:9f

ASHED
Then he * his face and came out, Gen 43:31
/ine, and * his clothes in wine. Gen 49:11
lead, * up on the seashore. Ex 14:30
hem and they * their clothing. Ex 19:14
sons * their hands and feet there. Ex 40:31
they stopped and *, just as the Ex 40:32
the legs are to be *, then the Lev 1:9
egs shall first be * with water. Lev 1:13
t must be * in a holy place. Lev 6:27
and his sons and * them with water, Lev 8:6
He then * the insides and the Lev 8:21
Then he * the insides and the Lev 9:14
article to be *, then isolated for Lev 13:54
spills on must be * and remain Lev 15:17
themselves and * their clothes, and Num 8:21
up off the ground, * himself, 2Sa 12:20
He had not * his feet or clothes 2Sa 19:24,25
and armor were * beside the pool of 1Ki 22:38
of their lives * out forever? Job 22:15,16
sheep's wool, newly shorn and *; Sol 4:2
I have * my feet, and should I Sol 5:3
white as freshly * ewes, perfectly Sol 6:6
Jerusalem will be * and rinsed of Is 4:2,3,4
guilt that cannot ever be * away. Jer 2:22
had been neither * nor rubbed with Eze 16:4
be * away, your idol worship gone. Eze 36:25
* before being taken to the altar; Eze 40:38
I neither * nor shaved nor combed Dan 10:3
bowl of water and * his hands Mt 27:24
while the fishermen * their nets. Lk 5:2
feet, but she has * them with her Lk 7:44
sent and * and came back seeing! Jn 9:7
when it was * away, he could see! Jn 9:15
his feet * to be entirely clean. Jn 13:10
and Teacher, have * your feet, you Jn 13:14
That same hour he * their Act 16:33
now your sins are * away, and you 1Co 6:11
her holy and clean, * by baptism Eph 5:26
have been * with pure water. Heb 10:22
where his blood * our sins away. Heb 13:12
not because our bodies are * 1Pe 3:21
and a pig is * only to come back 2Pe 2:22
"they * their robes and whitened Rev 7:14

VASHING
the priests could use it for *. Ex 40:30
after * his clothes, he is free. Lev 13:34
faded after the *, then he shall Lev 13:56
But if after * it there is no Lev 13:58
into service after another *." Lev 13:58
ceremony by * his clothes and Lev 15:13
and not the vats, for their own *. 2Ch 4:6
first performing the * ceremony." Mk 7:5
* required by Jewish custom. Lk 11:37,38
be * our feet like this!" Jn 13:6
After * their feet he put on his Jn 13:12
it by * of water with the word." Eph 5:26f
and pity—by * away our sins and Tit 3:5
drink, rules for * themselves, and Heb 9:10
are all who are * their robes, to Rev 22:14

WASTE
I will * them with hunger, Deu 32:24
'Why * time trying to please God?' Job 34:9
to get rich. Why * your time? Pro 23:4,5
Don't * your breath on a rebel. Pro 23:9
But you say, "Don't * your Jer 2:25
But they replied, "Don't * your Jer 18:12
land of Chaldea an everlasting *. Jer 25:12
their land has been laid * by Jer 25:38
* away beneath their punishment. Eze 4:17
Ammonites into a * land where Eze 25:5
Because she has been laid *, I Eze 26:2
and cause her to * away and die of Hos 1:3
them * to their farthest borders; Zep 3:6
"What a * of good money," they Mt 26:8,9
this "*," as they called it. Mk 14:4,5
And don't * time along the way. Lk 10:4
Don't * time arguing over foolish 1Ti 4:7

WASTED
and bodies * from sorrow and fear. Deu 28:65
Then David * no time in sending 1Sa 25:39
Baal and * their time on nonsense. Jer 2:8
otherwise the good seed will be * Jer 4:3
land, and there * all his money on Lk 15:13
"so that nothing is *." Jn 6:12
the Lord is ever * as it would be 1Co 15:58

WASTELAND
hot springs in the * while he was Gen 36:24
the Arabah (or, *), bounded by the Deu 3:17
live, in the * near Gilgal, where Deu 11:30
a burned over *, unsown, without Deu 29:23
"These cities are a *!" 1Ki 9:13
still known as "The *" today. 1Ki 9:13
is an utter *, and they are all Is 6:11
making it a vast * of destruction. Is 24:1
made a * of this entire country. Jer 10:25
land shall become a desolate *; Jer 25:11
become deserted *, and all who pass Jer 50:13
become a desolate *, and the Eze 29:9
a desolate * like a wilderness. Zep 2:13

WASTELANDS
and the *, desolate and gloomy. Job 30:3
will lie as * for forty years. Eze 29:12
the parched * where they will die; Joe 2:20
into the Judean * to see and hear Mk 1:5
had to stay out in the barren *. Mk 1:45
into the barren * of Judea, where Lk 4:1

WASTES
body, as when a sick man * away. Is 10:18
and her cities shall be eternal * Jer 49:13

WASTING
Have I been * my time? Ps 73:13
and * your time in gossiping. 2Th 3:11
of a flood, and * no time, he built Heb 11:7

WATCH
But if you refuse to obey, * out. Gen 4:7
"I don't want to * him die," Gen 21:16
"* out what you say to Jacob," Gen 31:24
Just stand where you are and *, Ex 14:13
Sinai as all the people *. Ex 19:11
Tabernacle as all the people *. Num 8:9
and they all assembled to *. Num 16:19
As they *, speak to that rock Num 20:8
I * them from the hills. Num 23:7-10
as all the people *, charge him Num 27:19
"But * out! Deu 4:9
is the time to * out that you don't Deu 8:14
driven away as you *, and will Deu 28:31
You will * as your sons and Deu 28:32
He will * their power ebb away, Deu 32:36
to the top of the roof to *. Ju 9:51
"Now * as the Lord does great 1Sa 12:16
Saul kept a jealous * on David. 1Sa 18:9
Saul sent troops to * David's 1Sa 19:11
sent out spies to * his movements. 1Sa 26:3,4
to Joab, "Let's * some sword play 2Sa 2:14
he could * her mix some dough; 2Sa 13:8
For you * their every move. 2Sa 22:28
their descendants * their step and 1Ki 2:4
request: Please * over this Temple 1Ki 8:29
I will constantly * over it and 1Ki 9:2,3
that he would * over and guide his 2Ki 8:19
He was forced to * as his sons 2Ki 25:7
"* your step—I have not appointed 2Ch 19:6
He went out personally to * as 2Ch 34:4
And an honor guard keeps * at his Job 21:30-32
grievances against others. * out! Job 36:18
I kept close * on all his laws; Ps 18:22
I will advise you and * your Ps 32:8
Then * your tongue! Ps 34:13
They will * in awe. Ps 52:6
truth to guard and * over me, and Ps 61:7
Literally, "as a * in the Ps 90:4f
your head to look. * your step. Pro 4:26
listen! * yourself, lest you be Pro 5:2
My son, * your step before the Pro 24:21,22
family forever—so * your business Pro 27:23,24
perhaps to * it as it runs through Ecc 5:11
while you *, foreigners are Is 1:7
Though you * and watch as I Is 6:9
Though you watch and * as I Is 6:9
as honest men, to * me as I wrote Is 8:2
God will * quietly from his Is 18:4
as I * them being destroyed. Is 22:4
I'll * to keep all enemies away. Is 27:3
the heavens, then *, for it will Is 34:5
The lands beyond the sea * in Is 41:5
Look high in the skies and * the Is 51:6
saying and * what they are doing. Jer 6:27
No wonder my anger is great! * Jer 7:18
And now, Jeremiah, as these men * Jer 19:10
together again and * over them as a Jer 31:10
made Zedekiah * as they killed his Jer 39:6
Judah and, as they * you, bury Jer 43:9
For I will * over you, but not Jer 44:27
beside the road to *, and shout to Jer 48:19
Don't stand and *—flee while you Jer 51:50
He made Zedekiah * while his Jer 52:10
publicly while all the nations *. Eze 5:8
during the daylight so they can *. Eze 12:4
As they *, lift your pack to Eze 12:6
at your fall! They * dismayed.' Eze 26:18
come to land and * upon the Eze 27:29
the coastlands *, incredulous. Eze 27:35
He said to me: "Son of dust, * Eze 40:4
seven shepherds to * over us, eight Mic 5:5
* for the enemy attack to begin! Nah 2:1
you * the thickest forests felled. Zec 11:2
them, for I will * over the people Zec 12:4
*, FOR THE day of the Lord is Zec 14:1
as the dross is burned away. Mal 3:3
"* NOW," THE Lord of Hosts Mal 4:1
"* out!" Mt 16:6
thieves by keeping * for them, so Mt 24:43
gathered outside the door to *. Mk 1:32,33
things begin to happen, * out! Mk 13:9
Be on the * [for my return Mk 13:33
gatekeeper to * for his return. Mk 13:34
Don't let me find you sleeping. * Mk 13:35,36,37
stay here and * with me." Mk 14:34
Couldn't you * with me even one Mk 14:37
me even one hour? * with me and Mk 14:38
into darkness. So * out that the Lk 11:35
beside the road, to * from there. Lk 19:4
"* out! Lk 21:34,35
Keep a constant *. Lk 21:36
he went, to * him heal the sick. Jn 6:2-5
order to draw a following. * out! Act 20:31
* out! Rom 11:20
always critical and catty, * out! Gal 5:15
* out for those wicked Php 3:2
keep at it; * for God's answers Col 4:2
* for his return and stay sober. 1Th 5:6
Keep a close * on all you do and 1Ti 4:16
best blessings. * out that no Heb 12:15
spiritual lives. * out that no one Heb 12:16
For their work is to * over your Heb 13:17
* what you do and what you think; Jas 2:12
Be careful—* out for attacks from 1Pe 5:8
so that you can * out and not be 2Pe 3:17
* out for the false leaders—and 2Jn 1:7
in a cloud as their enemies *. Rev 11:12
first Creature was there to * him. Rev 13:14
crying as they * the smoke ascend, Rev 18:18

WATCHCARE
you—my constant * over you night Act 20:31

WATCHED
The servant said no more, but * Gen 24:21
Moreover, he * for the stronger Gen 30:41
The baby's sister * from a Ex 2:4
performed the miracles as they *. Ex 4:30
of his officials *, Aaron hit the Ex 7:20
as he *, Moses tossed it toward Ex 9:10
as all the nations * in wonder. Lev 26:45
Mount Hor as all the people *. Num 20:27
As the people *, Moses laid his Num 27:22
The Lord your God has * over you Deu 2:7
while the people had * below. Deu 9:10,11
the mountain as you all * below. Deu 10:4
their belongings, as all Israel *! Deu 11:6
him, as all Israel *, "Be strong! Deu 31:7
over, the people * the priests Jos 4:11
And as the people of Israel *, Jos 8:32
The mother of Sisera * through Ju 5:28
Then they just stood and * as the Ju 7:21
*, the Angel ascended in the fire! Ju 13:20
mayors had * for awhile, they 1Sa 6:16
Saul's daughter, * from a window 2Sa 6:16
Then, as all the people *, 1Ki 8:22,23
young prophets * from a distance. 2Ki 2:6,7
for David as she * from the window 1Ch 15:29
and I have * your people offer 1Ch 29:17
As the leaders of Israel *, the 2Ch 5:4,5
Now, as all the people *, he 2Ch 6:12,13
* to snuff out any sign of life. Job 16:9
"For forty years I * them in Ps 95:10
on me as I have * human affairs: Ecc 9:13
seen as I have * the world go by, a Ecc 10:5
the prison guards *, I handed the Jer 32:12
He did so while I *. Eze 10:2
And as I *, the cherubim flew Eze 10:19
worshiped many idols as I *. Eze 16:50
Then, as I *, the muscles and Eze 37:8
But as you *, a Rock was cut Dan 2:34
And as I *, its wings were pulled Dan 7:4
Then, as I * in my dream, a Dan 7:7
I * as thrones were put in place Dan 7:9
As I *, the brutal fourth animal Dan 7:11
and as I *, one of these horns Dan 8:3
The mountains * and trembled. Hab 3:10
hill, and as they *, his Mt 17:2
From that time on, Judas * for Mt 26:16
Then they sat around and * him Mt 27:36
Jesus' enemies * him closely. Mk 3:2
The crowd * Jesus in awe as he Mk 9:15
Jesus * him go, then turned Mk 10:23
Temple and sat and * as the crowds Mk 12:41
floor as the crowd *, and then left Lk 4:35
And immediately, as everyone *, Lk 5:25
and the Pharisees * closely to see Lk 6:7
Jesus * him go and then said to Lk 18:24
The crowd *. Lk 23:35
fish, and he ate it as they *! Lk 24:43
and sometimes you * and sympathized Heb 10:33
I have * your hard work and your Rev 2:2
AS I *, the Lamb broke the first Rev 6:1
I * as he broke the sixth seal, Rev 6:12
As I *, I saw a solitary eagle Rev 8:13
and from there I * that wondrous Rev 21:10

WATCHER
"Has my sin harmed you, O God, * Job 7:20
Literally, "a *, a holy one." Dan 4:13f
Literally, "a holy *." Dan 4:23f

WATCHERS
the *, demanded by the Holy Ones. Dan 4:17

WATCHES
toss it into the sky as Pharaoh *. Ex 9:8
someone shall kill her as he *. Num 19:1
*—her hide, meat, blood, and dung. Num 19:5
say, 'and * every move I make.' Job 33:11
"For God carefully * the goings Job 34:21

(WATCHES Con't)
their place. He * what they do and Job 34:25
For the Lord * over all the plans Ps 1:6
He closely * everything that Ps 11:4
This he knows, for he * my every Ps 18:24
and closely * everything they do. Ps 33:13,14,15
* every movement of the nations. Ps 66:7
or a slave girl * her mistress for Ps 123:2
be with me that he * for me daily Pro 8:34
A sensible man * for problems Pro 27:12
hard worker, and * for bargains. Pro 31:18
she says. She * carefully all that Pro 31:27
* over us with tender jealousy? Jas 4:5

WATCHING
be sure no one was *, then killed Ex 2:12
* until he reached its entrance. Ex 33:8
who were * Samson and making fun Ju 16:27
"But he's out in the fields * 1Sa 16:10,11
As Saul was * David go out to 1Sa 17:55
(The people * noticed through the 2Ki 6:26-30
All the people had been * and 2Ch 7:3
for the Lord was * over me. Ps 3:5
"God isn't *," they say to Ps 10:11
But the eyes of the Lord are * Ps 33:18,19
Lord are intently * all who live Ps 34:15
For he is always *, never Ps 121:3,4
For God is closely * you, and he Pro 5:21
The Lord is * everywhere and Pro 15:3
The godly learn by * ruin Pro 21:12
*, and no one would laugh at me. Sol 8:1
11 and shoqedh (*) in verse 12: Jer 1:12f
am * over my word to perform it." Jer 1:12f
For I am closely * you and I see Jer 16:17
* me, waiting for a fatal slip. Jer 20:10
While all the people are *, bake Eze 4:12
in the sight of all those * you. Eze 28:18
But suddenly, as he was *, Dan 3:24
to recognize that I am * them. Hos 7:2
on the hillsides * the sheep, Amo 1:1
"The eyes of the Lord God are * Amo 9:8
the Lord is closely * all mankind, Zec 9:1
I am closely * their movements Zec 9:8
sheep, who were *, realized that Zec 11:11
for him were * from a distance. Mt 27:55
other Mary were sitting nearby *. Mt 27:61
Some women were there * from a Mk 15:40
were * as Jesus was laid away. Mk 15:47
the Pharisees were * him like hawks Lk 14:1
* their opportunity, they sent Lk 20:20
the Temple, he was * the rich Lk 21:1
Galilee, stood in the distance *. Lk 23:49
spoke to the girl * at the gate, Jn 18:16
that they were * the gates of the Act 9:24
of *, and gone without food. 2Co 6:5
your master is * and then shirk Eph 6:6,7
they are * you but all the time; Col 3:22
in heaven who is closely * you. Col 4:1
But you know from * me that I am 2Ti 3:10
of men of faith * us from the Heb 12:1
For the Lord is * his children, 1Pe 3:12
* everything that concerns you. 1Pe 5:7
the skies while everyone was *. Rev 13:13

WATCHMAN
Now the * on the Jerusalem wall 2Sa 13:34
When the * climbed the stairs to 2Sa 18:24
came closer, the * saw another man 2Sa 18:26
the son of Zadok," the * said. 2Sa 18:27
The * on the Tower of Jezreel 2Ki 9:17
The * called out to the king that 2Ki 9:18
the * exclaimed. 2Ki 9:20
the * to the fortified cities." 2Ki 18:8f
* on the wall tore off my veil. Sol 5:7
the Lord had told me, "Put a * Is 21:6,7
So I put the * on the wall, and Is 21:8,9
to me: "*, what of the night? Is 21:11
the night? *, what of the night? Is 21:11
The * replies, "Your judgment Is 21:12
appointed you as a * for Israel; Eze 3:17
that land choose a *, and when he Eze 33:2
But if the * sees the enemy Eze 33:6
charge the * with their deaths. Eze 33:6
I have appointed you as a * for Eze 33:7
a platform for the *, then leased Mt 21:33

WATCHMAN'S
abandoned like a * shanty in the Is 1:8
grape juice, and built a * tower. Mk 12:1

WATCHMEN
city and told the * what had 2Ki 7:10
Then the * shouted the news to 2Ki 7:11
king's eunuchs, * at the palace Est 6:1
as * in the Temple every night. Ps 134:1
reigns. The * shout and sing with Is 52:8
people—the Lord's *, his Is 56:10
Literally, "*." Is 62:6,7f
I set * over you who warned Jer 6:17
The day shall come when * on the Jer 31:6
Set many * on your walls; Jer 51:12

WATCHTOWER
So it was also called "The *" Gen 31:49
arrived at the * that looks out 2Ch 20:24
He built a * and cut a winepress Is 5:2
O Jerusalem—the * of God's Mic 4:8
I WILL CLIMB my * now, and wait to Hab 2:1

WATCHTOWERS
where the * are, until at last the Is 32:14

WATER
the vapor above from the * below. Gen 1:7,8
Then God said, "Let the * Gen 1:9,10
"earth," and the * "seas." Gen 1:9,10
(However, * welled up from the Gen 2:6
flowed through the garden to * it; Gen 2:10
As the * rose higher and higher Gen 7:18
until finally the * covered all Gen 7:19
And the * covered the earth 150 Gen 7:24
the subterranean * sources ceased Gen 8:2
of dead animals floating on the *. Gen 8:7f
a good indication of the * level. Gen 8:7f
for the * was still too high. Gen 8:9
So Noah knew that the * was Gen 8:11
door to look, and the * was gone. Gen 8:13
tree while I get * to refresh your Gen 18:3,4
a canteen of * to Hagar's shoulders Gen 21:14
When the * was gone she left the Gen 21:15
the village were coming to draw *. Gen 24:11
village are coming out to draw *. Gen 24:13
and I will * your camels too!' Gen 24:14
named Rebekah arrived with a * Gen 24:15,16
Then she said, "I'll draw * for Gen 24:19
and kept carrying * to the camels Gen 24:20
feed for them, and * for the camel Gen 24:32
comes out to draw *, "Please give Gen 24:43
"Please give me a drink of *!" Gen 24:43
And I'll * your camels too!" Gen 24:44
with her * jug upon her shoulder; Gen 24:45
and drew * and filled the jug. Gen 24:45
and I will * your camels too!' Gen 24:46
"We have found *" —in the well Gen 26:32
"Why don't you * the flocks so Gen 29:7
empty well—there was no * in it. Gen 37:24
and given * to refresh their feet; Gen 43:24
she had drawn him out of the *. Ex 2:10
came to draw * and fill the water Ex 2:16
water and fill the * troughs for Ex 2:16
"he drew * for us and watered Ex 2:19
signs, then take * from the Nile Ex 4:9
Moses to hit the * of the Nile with Ex 7:17
and even the * stored in bowls and Ex 7:19
The fish died and the * became Ex 7:21
they, too, turned * into blood; Ex 7:22
to get drinking *, for they Ex 7:24
it out over the *, and the sea will Ex 14:16
sea, with walls of * on each side; Ex 14:21
the walls of * along the bottom of Ex 14:23
in the sea. The * covered the path Ex 14:28
The * covers them. Ex 15:5
let down the walls of * on them Ex 15:19
were there three days without *. Ex 15:22
couldn't drink the * because it was Ex 15:23
the *, and the water became sweet. Ex 15:25
the water, and the * became sweet. Ex 15:25
But upon arrival, there was no *! Ex 17:1
"Give us *!" Ex 17:2
the Nile with—and * will come Ex 17:5,6
he was told, and the * gushed out! Ex 17:5,6
with food and with *, and I will Ex 23:25
and the altar, and fill it with *. Ex 30:17,18
* and made the people drink it. Ex 32:20
and the altar, and fill it with *. Ex 40:7
Tabernacle and wash them with *; Ex 40:12
and filled it with * so that the Ex 40:30
legs shall first be washed with *. Lev 1:13
washed them with *, and he clothed Lev 8:6
and the legs with *, and burned Lev 8:21
but all other * creatures are Lev 11:10
I'll repeat it again—any * Lev 11:12
*, and is defiled until evening. Lev 11:32
If the * used to cleanse the Lev 11:34
is *, that water is not defiled; Lev 11:36
is water, that * is not defiled; Lev 11:36
the * or crawls upon the ground. Lev 11:46
pot held above running *. Lev 14:5
birds over fresh * in an Lev 14:50
over the fresh *, and shall Lev 14:51,52
utensil must be rinsed in *. Lev 15:12
clothes and bathing in running *. Lev 15:13
and take holy * in a clay jar and Num 5:17
of bitter * that brings a curse. Num 5:18
bitter * that causes the curse. Num 5:19
wash them off into the bitter *. Num 5:23
woman to drink the *, it becomes Num 5:24
require the woman to drink the *. Num 5:26
her husband, the * will become Num 5:27
Do this by sprinkling * of Num 8:7
as a source of * for the Num 19:9
seventh days with * [run through Num 19:12
The cleansing * was not sprinkled Num 19:13
are to be added to spring * in a Num 19:17
dip them into the * and sprinkle Num 19:18
and sprinkle the * upon the tent Num 19:18
the Lord, and the * to cleanse him Num 19:20
The man who sprinkles the * must Num 19:21
and anyone touching the * shall Num 19:21
There was not enough * to drink Num 2
Why, there isn't even * enough to Num 2
and tell it to pour out its *! Num 2
You will give them * from a rock, Num 2
Must we bring you * from this Num 20
the rock twice, and * gushed out; Num 20
we won't even drink * from your Num 20
even drink your * unless we pay Num 20
concerning the * at Meribah. Num 20
people, and I will give them *." Num 21
Sing of the *! Num 21:17
your vineyards or drink your *." Num 21
be blessed with an abundance of *, Num 24:
order * to come out of the rock." Num 27
purified with the purification *. Num 31
shall be purified by the * alone.' Num 31
of * and seventy palm trees; Num 3
was no * for the people to drink). Num 33
Pay them for whatever food or * Deu
He gave you * from the rock! Deu 8
I didn't even take a drink of *. Deu
bread nor drinking *, for you had Deu 9
Jotbathah, a land of brooks and *. Deu 1
it out on the ground, like *. Deu 12
it out upon the ground like *. Deu 15
there is running *—a valley neither Deu 2
and * when you came out of Egypt; Deu 2
chop your wood and carry your *. Deu 29:
the Ark touch the * with their Jos 3:13,
Ark touched the * at the river's Jos 3:13,
near Zarethan, the * began piling Jos 3:15
And the * below that point flowed Jos 3:15
came out, the * poured down again Jos 4:
their wood and carrying their *. Jos 9:
* for the service of our God." Jos 9:
please give us springs of * too." Ju 1:
"Please give me some *," he Ju 4:
He asked for * Ju 5:
wrung out a whole bowlful of *! Ju 6:
So Gideon assembled them at the * Ju 7:
men who cup the * in their hands to Ju 7:
So the Lord caused * to gush Ju 15:
go and help yourself to the *." Ru 2:
ceremony, drew * from the well and 1Sa 7
going out to draw * and asked them 1Sa 9:9,10,
Should I take my bread and my * 1Sa 25:
of * and then get out of here!" 1Sa 26:
spear and jug of *, and they got 1Sa 26:
jug of * that was beside his head? 1Sa 26:
*, and his strength soon returned. 1Sa 30:11,
up through the * tunnel into the 2Sa 5
our lives are like * that is 2Sa 14:
of that good * in the city well!" 2Sa 23:
ranks and drew * from the well and 2Sa 23:
and contained 240 gallons of *. 1Ki 7:
nor would I eat or drink even * 1Ki 13
or drink any * while I'm here, and 1Ki 13
or to drink any * at Bethel. 1Ki 13:16,
with me and give you food and *." 1Ki 13:
some * at the old man's home. 1Ki 13:
eaten and drunk * in the place he 1Ki 13:21,
and he asked her for a cup of *. 1Ki 17:
had fed them with bread and *. 1Ki 18:3
and fed them with bread and *? 1Ki 18:
"Fill four barrels with *," he 1Ki 18:3
* over the carcass and the wood." 1Ki 18:3
and the * ran off the altar and 1Ki 18:3
evaporated all the * in the ditch! 1Ki 18:3
on hot stones, and a jar of *! 1Ki 19
him with bread and *—and only 1Ki 22:2
together and struck the * with it; 2Ki 2
River, and struck the * with it. 2Ki 2:13,
And the * parted and Elisha went 2Ki 2:13,1
but the * is bad, and causes our 2Ki 2:1
And sure enough! The * was 2Ki 2:2
but there was no * for the men or 2Ki 3:
to hold the * he will send. 2Ki 3:1
be filled with *, and you will have 2Ki 3:1
sacrifice was offered—look! *! 2Ki 3:2
and soon there was * everywhere. 2Ki 3:2
red as it shone across the *! 2Ki 3:2
a stick and threw it into the *; 2Ki 6:
and dipped it in * and held it over 2Ki 8:1
and the * vats they supported, and 2Ki 16:1
and how he brought * into the 2Ki 20:2
camp, drew some * from the well, 1Ch 11:18,1
like * bursting through a dam!" 1Ch 14:1
It held 3,000 barrels of *. 2Ch 4:
ten vats for * to wash the 2Ch 4:
him with bread and * until I return 2Ch 18:2
and made many * reservoirs, for he 2Ch 26:1
king of Assyria come and find *?" 2Ch 32:
and brought the * down through an 2Ch 32:3
cemetery, the * reservoir, and the Neh 3:1
* Gate and the Projecting Tower. Neh 3:2
in front of the * Gate and Neh 8:
in front of the * Gate, and read Neh 8:
plaza beside the * Gate, or at the Neh 8:1
were hungry and * from the rock Neh 9:1
from heaven or * for their thirst. Neh 9:2
then they went to the * Gate on Neh 12:37

WATER Con't)
my groans pour out like *. Job 3:24
upon the earth to * the fields, Job 5:10
* there, their hopes are dashed. Job 6:19-21
or grass without * to keep it Job 8:11-13
myself with purest * and cleanse my Job 9:30
touch of *, like a new seedling. Job 14:8,9
his spirit go? As * evaporates Job 14:11,12
* grinds the stones to sand. Job 14:18,19
in sin as a sponge soaks up *! Job 15:16
You must have refused * to the Job 22:7
They dam up streams of * and pan Job 28:11
He draws up the * vapor and then Job 36:27
*, and tender grass springs up? Job 38:25-27
For the * changes and turns to Job 38:30
Who can tilt the * jars of Job 38:37,38
"He makes the * boil with his Job 41:31,32
drained away like *, and all my Ps 22:14
My strength evaporated like * on Ps 32:4
wisdom as the oceans are with *. Ps 36:6
AS THE DEER pants for *, so I long Ps 42:1
Let them disappear like * into Ps 58:7
weary land where there is no *. Ps 63:1
showers that * the earth! Ps 72:6
burst forth to give your people *; Ps 74:15
them through! The * stood banked up Ps 78:13
them plenty of *, as though gushing Ps 78:15
us decent food as well as *?" Ps 78:19,20
blood has flowed like *. Ps 79:3
you complained there was no *. Ps 81:7
of your shout the * collected into Ps 104:7,8
They give * for all the animals Ps 104:11
* into blood, poisoning the fish. Ps 105:29
He opened up a rock, and * Ps 105:41
Then the * returned and covered Ps 106:11
or as the * he drinks, or the rich Ps 109:18
Praise him who planted the * Ps 136:6
Literally, "*." Pro 9:17f
like * from a mountain spring. Pro 13:14
"as when one lets out *." Pro 17:14f
JUST AS * is turned into Pro 21:1
is like cold * to the thirsty. Pro 25:25
full, and the * returns again to Ecc 1:3-7
it is * over the dam; Ecc 1:12-15
the * to irrigate my plantations. Ecc 2:4,5,6
a well of living *, refreshing as Sol 4:15
the * brooks, deep and quiet. Sol 5:12
tree or a garden without *. Is 1:30
* supplies and kill her leaders; Is 3:1
and * to these weary fugitives! Is 21:14
for * from the lower pool! Is 22:9,10,11
pushes down the * with his hands. Is 25:11
every day I'll * them, and day Is 27:3
or a little * from the well. Is 30:14
of adversity and * of affliction, Is 30:20
you streams of * flowing down each Is 30:25
will have all the * they need. Is 33:16
springs of * in the thirsty land. Is 35:7
and garden and *, until I can Is 36:16
When the poor and needy seek * Is 41:17
I will give them fountains of * Is 41:18
In the deserts will be pools of * Is 41:18
for giving them * in the Is 43:20
For I will give you abundant * Is 44:3
he divided the rock, and * gushed Is 48:21
upon the ground to * the earth, and Is 55:10
a pot of boiling *, tipping Jer 1:13
me, the Fountain of Life-giving *; Jer 2:13
broken cisterns that can't hold *! Jer 2:13
wash it—don't put it in * at all. Jer 13:1
The nobles send servants for * Jer 14:3
deep into the *—a tree not bothered Jer 17:8
There was no * in it, but there Jer 38:6
even her * supply will fail. Jer 50:38
I will dry up her river, her * Jer 51:36
Pour out your hearts like * to Lam 2:19
my strength has turned to *, for Lam 3:18
rock. The * flowed above my head. Lam 3:54
for there is not a drop of * left. Lam 4:3,4
We must even pay for * to drink; Lam 5:4
And use one quart of * a day; Eze 4:11
And the * will be portioned out Eze 4:16
both bread and *, and to look at Eze 4:17
and all knees as weak as *. Eze 7:17
ration out your * as though it Eze 12:18
tiny portions of * in utter despair Eze 12:19
with plenty of * to become a Eze 17:8
foliage because of all the *. Eze 19:10
tremble and become as weak as *. Eze 21:7
a pot of * on the fire to boil. Eze 24:3
of * to all the trees around. Eze 31:4
because of all the * at its roots. Eze 31:5
for its roots went deep to *. Eze 31:7
went deep into the *, are comforted Eze 31:16
That you take the best * for Eze 34:18
all they have to drink is * that Eze 34:19
sprinkled clean * on you, for you Eze 36:25
At that point the * was up to my Eze 47:3
This time the * was up to my Eze 47:4
Everything touching the * of Eze 47:9
Wherever this * flows, everything Eze 47:9
diet of only vegetables and *; Dan 1:12
vegetables and *, without the rich Dan 1:16
*, each different from the other. Dan 7:3
to pour down * on the earth in Hos 1:21,22
help, for there is no * for them. Joe 1:20
flow with milk. * will fill the dry Joe 3:18
of the Lord to * Acacia Valley. Joe 3:18
for a drink of * to a city that had Amo 4:8
calls forth the * from the ocean Amo 5:8
famine of bread or *, but of Amo 8:11
at all, nor even drink any *. Jon 3:7
fire, like * pouring down a hill. Mic 1:4
Nineveh is like a leaking * Nah 2:8
Store up *! Nah 3:14
Onward swept the raging *. Hab 3:10
Or, "in *." Mt 3:11f
* I baptize those who repent of Mt 3:11
came up out of the *, the heavens Mt 3:16
cliff and drowned in the * below. Mt 8:32
even a cup of cold * to a little Mt 10:42
a net into the * and gathers in Mt 13:47,48
came to them, walking on the *! Mt 14:25
over to you, walking on the *." Mt 14:28
and walked on the * toward Jesus. Mt 14:29
falls into the fire or into the *; Mt 17:15
I was thirsty and you gave me *; Mt 25:35
sent for a bowl of * and washed his Mt 27:24
* but he will baptize you with Mk 1:8
came up out of the *, he saw the Mk 1:10
full of * and about to sink. Mk 4:37
far out on the *, the man had seen Mk 5:6
he walked out to them on the *. Mk 6:48
the fire or into * to kill him. Mk 9:22
gives you a cup of * because you Mk 9:41
towards you carrying a pot of *. Mk 14:13
saying, "I baptize only with *; Lk 3:16
a little into the *, so that he Lk 5:3
bother to offer me * to wash the Lk 7:44
Sabbath and lead them out for *? Lk 13:15
of his finger in * and cool my Lk 16:24
along carrying a pitcher of *. Lk 22:10
*, but right here in the crowd is Jn 1:26
* in order to point him out to Jn 1:31
to fill them to the brim with *. Jn 2:7,8
tasted the * that was now wine, not Jn 2:9
is this: Unless one is born of * Jn 3:5
"born of *" as meaning the normal Jn 3:5f
Some think this means * baptism. Jn 3:5f
there was plenty of * there. Jn 3:23,24
woman came to draw *, and Jesus Jn 4:7
would ask me for some living *!" Jn 4:10
Where would you get this living * Jn 4:11
How can you offer better * than Jn 4:12
again after drinking this *. Jn 4:13
"But the * I give them," he Jn 4:14
said, "give me some of that *! Jn 4:15
he had turned the * into wine. Jn 4:46,47
movement of the *, for an angel of Jn 5:3
and disturbed the *, and the first Jn 5:4
the pool at the movement of the *. Jn 5:7
rivers of living * shall flow from Jn 7:38
poured * into a basin, and began Jn 13:5
spear, and blood and * flowed out. Jn 19:34
jumped into the * [and swam ashore Jn 21:7
*," he reminded them, "but you Act 1:5
of *, and the eunuch said, "Look! Act 8:36
and the eunuch said, "Look! *! Act 8:36
the * and Philip baptized him. Act 8:38
came up out of the *, the Spirit of Act 8:39
without food and * all that time. Act 9:8,9
*, but you shall be baptized with Act 11:16
found 120 feet of * below them. Act 27:28
work was to * it, but it was God, 1Co 3:6
God sent them food to eat and * 1Co 10:3,4
they drank the * that Christ gave 1Co 10:3,4
by washing of * with the word." Eph 5:26f
goats, along with *, and sprinkled Heb 9:19
have been washed with pure *. Heb 10:22
Does a spring of * bubble out Jas 3:11
* and then with bitter water? Jas 3:11
water and then with bitter *? Jas 3:11
No, and you can't draw fresh * Jas 3:12
clean by the *, but because in 1Pe 3:21
springs of *, promising much and 2Pe 2:17
is he who came by * and blood." 1Jn 5:6,7,8f
Literally, "not by * only, but by 1Jn 5:6,7,8f
water only, but by * and blood." 1Jn 5:6,7,8f
Literally, "the Spirit, and the * 1Jn 5:6,7,8f
to the springs of the * of Life. Rev 7:17
a third of all the * on the earth Rev 8:11
a vast flood of * gushed out and Rev 12:15
of the * of Life—as a gift! Rev 21:6
me a river of pure * of Life, clear Rev 22:1
let him come and drink the * of Rev 22:17

WATER-CARRIERS
wood-choppers and * for the people Jos 9:27

WATER'S
standing at the * edge while the Lk 5:2

WATERED
Jordan River, well * everywhere Gen 13:10
in an open field, waiting to be *. Gen 29:2
the stone and * his uncle's flock. Gen 29:10
the shepherds and * their flocks. Ex 2:17
the flocks * so quickly today?" Ex 2:18
"he drew water for us and * the Ex 2:19
night upon my fields and * them. Job 29:19
deserts into fertile, * valleys. Ps 107:35
They shall thrive like * grass, Is 44:4
Their life shall be like a * Jer 31:12
For they are * by the river Eze 47:12
They will be a * garden and Hos 14:7

WATERED-DOWN
pure, but now diluted like * wine! Is 1:22

WATERFALL
upon them like a *, and Ephraim Hos 5:10
roaring of a great * or the rolling Rev 14:2

WATERFALLS
to deep at the noise of your *." Ps 42:7f

WATERING
So she emptied the jug into the * Gen 24:20
After * them, the stone was Gen 29:3
and begin the * until all the Gen 29:8
rods beside the * troughs so that Gen 30:38
By * others, he waters himself. Pro 11:24,25
within them, * them forever with Jn 4:14
the planting or * isn't very 1Co 3:7

WATERLESS
from death in a * pit because of Zec 9:11
Literally, "passes through * Mt 12:43,44,45f

WATERPOT
Then the woman left her * beside Jn 4:28,29

WATERPOTS
Six stone * were standing there; Jn 2:6

WATERPROOFED
papyrus reeds, * it with tar, put Ex 2:3

WATERS
the darkness and *," or even, Gen 1:2f
there be a dome to divide the *." Gen 1:6f
Then God said, "Let the * teem Gen 1:20
the subterranean * burst forth upon Gen 7:10,11,12
to blow across the *, and the Gen 8:1
as the * continued to go down, Gen 8:5
his rod toward the * of Egypt: all Ex 7:19
sea, so that the * will come back Ex 14:26
dry land, and the * had been walled Ex 14:29
The * divided! Ex 15:8
They sank as lead in the mighty *. Ex 15:10
(meaning "Rebel *"), because it Num 20:13
As cedar trees beside the *. Num 24:3-9
incident at the * of Meribah Num 27:14
"I have taken the City of *." 2Sa 12:26,27f
He drew me out from the *; 2Sa 22:17
"The Lord has healed these *. 2Ki 2:21
like stones beneath the mighty *. Neh 9:11
with dense clouds dark as murky *. Ps 18:11
He rescued me from deep *. Ps 18:16
Literally, "When the great * Ps 32:6f
He * the earth to make it fertile. Ps 65:9
* the furrows with abundant rain. Ps 65:10
in the mire; the * rise around me. Ps 69:1
me, and from these deep * I am in. Ps 69:14
of * covering up the mountains. Ps 104:6
happened, Jordan River, to your *? Ps 114:5
deliver me from deep *, from the Ps 144:7
forth their * onto the earth; Pro 8:24
By watering others, he * himself. Pro 11:24,25
life; its * keep a man from death. Pro 14:27
Many * cannot quench the flame Sol 8:7
Literally, "have refused the * of Is 8:6f
for as the * fill the sea, so shall Is 11:9
And the * of the Nile will fail Is 19:5
When you go through deep * and Is 43:2
a way through the *, making a path Is 43:16
will lead them beside the cool *. Is 49:10
again permit the * of a flood to Is 54:9
Lord, the Fountain of living *. Jer 17:13
Literally, "the great * were held Eze 31:15f
will disturb those * any more. Eze 32:13
Therefore the * of Egypt will be Eze 32:14
roar of rushing * and the whole Eze 43:2
* and make them fresh and pure. Eze 47:8
Sea, for its * will be healed. Eze 47:9
it had burned up the * and was Amo 7:4
I sank down into the floods of * Jon 2:3
very near. The * closed above me; Jon 2:5
is filled, as the * fill the sea, Hab 2:14
the mighty * piled high. Hab 3:15
Life-giving * will flow out from Zec 14:8
through the * of the Red Sea. 1Co 10:1
and had used the * to form the 2Pe 3:5,6
And I heard this angel of the * Rev 16:5
sits upon the many * of the world. Rev 17:1

WATERY
like the * blood of a dead man; Rev 16:3

WAVE
the land of Egypt, * after wave of Ex 12:51
* of them crossing the border. Ex 12:51
and his sons, to * them in a Ex 29:24
ordination ram and * it before the Ex 29:26
pint of oil, and * them before the Lev 14:24
He shall * it before the Lord in Lev 23:9,10,11
"The priests shall * these Lev 23:20

(WAVE Con't)
woman's hand and * it before Num 5:25
The priest shall then * it all Num 6:20
you all of these '* offerings' Num 18:19
and man, just to * to and fro over Ju 9:9
I expected him to * his hand over 2Ki 5:11
treasuries, the * offerings, the Neh 12:44
* offerings were for the priests. Neh 13:5
For a crime * has engulfed Job 24:2
Your wrath lies heavy on me; * Ps 88:7
wave after * engulfs me. Ps 88:7
and * his hand over the Is 11:15
Shout to them, O Israel, and * Is 13:2
battle cries. * upon wave of Jer 4:20
Wave upon * of destruction rolls Jer 4:20
a chip of wood upon an ocean *. Hos 10:7
part of a great * of immigrants to Zep 2:5f
* of fear had swept over them). Lk 8:37
And a great * of persecution of Act 8:1
What a * of awesome joy swept Act 20:10,11,12
as unsettled as a * of the sea that Jas 1:6

WAVED
but he * the breasts and right Lev 9:21
your homes to be * before the Lord Lev 23:17
that were * before the Lord. Num 6:20
This loaf must be * back and Num 15:19,20,21
So Paul stood, * a greeting to Act 13:16
as though I had * a placard before Gal 3:1

WAVER
"How long are you going to * 1Ki 18:21

WAVERING
and have trusted you without *. Ps 26:1

WAVES
But you are unruly as the wild * Gen 49:4
captains are dead beneath the *. Ex 15:4
The * of death surrounded me; 2Sa 22:5
and darkness and * of horror. Job 22:10,11
* of affliction have come upon me. Job 30:27
and here shall your proud * stop!' Job 38:11
All your * and billows have gone Ps 42:7
You rule the oceans when their * Ps 89:9
Let the * clap their hands in Ps 98:8,9
the storm winds; the * rise high. Ps 107:25
calms the storm and stills the *. Ps 107:29
to lie beneath the *, dead, their Is 43:17
and great * of righteousness. Is 48:18
the sea, between the roaring *. Is 51:15
make the roaring *—his name is Lord Jer 31:35
she is covered by its *. Jer 51:42
stilled as the * roar in upon her. Jer 51:55
wings roared like * against the Eze 1:24
nations against you like ocean *. Eze 26:3
the terrible * of enemy attack. Eze 26:19
covered by your wild and stormy *. Jon 2:3
"I sank beneath the *, and death Jon 2:5
for the * will be held back. Zec 10:11
up, with * higher than the boat. Mt 8:24
the wind and *, and the storm Mt 8:26
around at the high *, he was Mt 14:30
storm arose. High * began to break Mk 4:37
struggling against the wind and *. Mk 6:48
and * subsided and all was calm! Lk 8:24
even the winds and * obey him?" Lk 8:25
of the * and began to break apart. Act 27:41
along the beach by the wild *. Jud 1:13
like the * against the shore. Rev 1:15
crowd, or like the * of a hundred Rev 19:6

WAVING
by a gesture of * it before the Lev 7:14
the Lord by * it before the altar. Lev 7:30
of * them before the altar. Lev 8:27
the Lord by * it before the altar; Lev 8:29
by the gesture of * it before him, Lev 10:14
the Lord by the gesture of * them. Lev 10:15
of * them before the altar. Lev 14:12
by * it before the altar; Lev 14:21
by the gesture of * them before the Num 18:8
by the gesture of * them before the Num 18:11
the gesture of * before the altar. Num 18:18
by the gesture of * before the Num 18:24
the gesture of * before the altar. Num 18:25,26
the gesture of * before the altar. Num 31:29
by the gesture of * before the Deu 12:6
Lord by * them before his altar. Deu 12:17
who were joyously * branches of 2Sa 6:5
See the flags * as their enemy Is 13:2

WAVY
gold, and he has *, raven hair. Sol 5:11

WAX
My heart melts like *; Ps 22:14
melt them like * in fire! Ps 68:2
The mountains melt like * before Ps 97:5
the valleys like * in fire, like Mic 1:4

WAY
There is no "right" * to Gen 1:2f
and it was excellent in every *. Gen 1:31
* that the two become one person. Gen 2:24
image of his father in every *. Gen 5:3,4,5
Construct a skylight all the * Gen 6:16
as they looked the other *. Gen 9:23
the * to Gerar, in the Gaza strip; Gen 10:15-19
lived all the * from Mesha to the Gen 10:26-30
So, in that *, God scattered them Gen 11:8
on their homeward *, taking with Gen 14:11
This is the * it happened: One Gen 18:1
went with them part of the *. Gen 18:16
And the Lord went on his * when Gen 18:33
you like and be on your * again." Gen 19:2
don't hurt the lad in any *," Gen 22:12
and God blessed him in every *. Gen 24:1
guide me in this *: Here I am, Gen 24:42
whether to move this * or that." Gen 24:49
(which is a little * to the Gen 25:18
"How could you treat us this * Gen 26:10
me out in a most uncivil *." Gen 26:27
it just the * I like it—savory and Gen 27:2,3,4
in his father's favorite *. Gen 27:14
shall hew your * with your sword. Gen 27:39,40
shapely, and in every * a beauty. Gen 29:17
In this * God has made me Gen 31:9
This is a strange * to act. Gen 31:28
Esau was on the * to meet Gen 32:6
stay with you and lead the *." Gen 33:12
will take her and be on our *." Gen 34:17
they were still a long * away. Gen 35:16
well here; that * he'll die Gen 37:21,22
which is on the * to Timnah. Gen 38:14
with Joseph in a very special *. Gen 39:3
Joseph, by the *, was a very Gen 39:6
out of her * as much as possible. Gen 39:10
This is the * I will test your Gen 42:15
In this * I will know whether you Gen 42:20
us, 'This is the * I will find out Gen 42:33
with me and we will be on our *; Gen 43:8
their * with their loaded donkeys. Gen 44:3
"Don't quarrel along the *!" Gen 45:24
they were on the *, and would soon Gen 46:28
Let's figure out a * to put an Ex 1:10
Moses looked this * and that to Ex 2:12
whether to share in this * Ex 12:3,4
to fight their * through, even Ex 13:17,18
* the Lord will rescue you today. Ex 14:13
had been along the *, and how the Ex 18:8
themselves. That * it will be Ex 18:22
an image or worship it in any *; Ex 20:5
has come in this * to show you his Ex 20:20
not oppress a stranger in any *; Ex 22:21
if you do so in any *, and they Ex 22:23
in an ordinary *, with interest. Ex 22:25
to them in any *, and you must not Ex 23:24
runs all the * from end to end of Ex 26:28
In this * Aaron shall carry the Ex 28:29
marked in some * and used by the Ex 28:30,31f
In this * Aaron will be wearing Ex 28:37,38
"This, then, is the * you shall Ex 29:35
to destroy you along the *." Ex 33:3
along the * you want me to travel Ex 33:13
gold all the * around the sides. Ex 37:2
bars the * to the Holy of Holies. Lev 4:6
in this * the priest shall make Lev 4:20
In this * the priest shall make Lev 5:13
in just the same * as he had the Lev 9:15
"If a man is burned in some *, Lev 13:24
In this * the house shall be Lev 14:51,52
In this * you will know whether Lev 14:57
In this * you shall cleanse the Lev 15:31
for in this * the priest will be Lev 17:6
do it in the right *, eating the Lev 22:29,30
exactly the same *: fracture for Lev 24:19
These three tribes led the * Num 2:3-31
Lord in a special *, he must not Num 6:1
In this * you will dedicate the Num 8:14
them in this *, they shall go in Num 8:15
that * throughout the night. Num 9:15
In this * they journeyed at the Num 9:18
are on our * to the Promised Land. Num 10:29
the land all the * from the Num 13:21
(By the *, Hebron was very Num 13:22
In this * you will pay for your Num 14:33
of Levi shall assist you in any *. Num 18:4
died in any other *, or if he even Num 19:16
Balaam was on the *, he left the Num 22:36
He thrust the spear all the * Num 25:8
In this * the Lord will continue Num 27:21
In this * the land will not be Num 35:33
In this * the total area of our Num 36:3
In this * none of the land of Num 36:7
In this * no inheritance shall Num 36:9
going by * of Mount Seir! Deu 1:1
and assist them in every *. Deu 1:15
led them all the *, and had Deu 1:33
every step of the * for all these Deu 2:7
We are on our * across the Jordan Deu 2:29
any *, for I am the Lord your God. Deu 5:9,10
whole * he has laid out for you; Deu 5:32
longer go your own * as you do now, Deu 12:8
(By the *, be very careful not Deu 12:19
"That is the only * you will be Deu 16:20
In this * you will purge all evil Deu 17:7
this is the * to know: If the Deu 18:22
In this * you will be able to Deu 19:10
In this * you will purge out evil Deu 19:19
In this * you will put away the Deu 21
In this * you shall put away this Deu 21:
don't look the other *. Deu 22
in this * evil will be cleansed Deu 22:
In this * you will reduce crime Deu 22:25,26,
or the Moabites in any *. Deu 23
* from the laws I have given you; Deu 28:
I walk in my own stubborn *!' Deu 29:
Is this the * you treat Jehovah? Deu 32
Israel— all the * from Negeb Jos 1
the best * to attack us." Jos 2
men went all the * to the Jordan Jos 2
This is only fair after the * I Jos 2:12,1
then go on your *." Jos 2:
will no longer bind us in any *." Jos 2:2
the others all the * to Beth-horon Jos 10:
killing them along the *. Jos 10:
continued all the * to Azekah; Jos 10:1
On the * back, Joshua captured Jos 11:
extended all the * from Mount Jos 11:1
stretched all the * from the valley Jos 12:
So in this * the Lord gave to Jos 21:4
"Soon I will be going the * of Jos 23:
Literally, "the * into the Ju 1:24
(who, by the *, was very fat! Ju 3:17,18,1
it to me in this *: I'll put some Ju 6:3
And it happened just that *! Ju 6:3
decided by the * they drink. Ju 7:5,
Later, Gideon returned by * of Ju 8:1
everyone else who passed that *. Ju 9:2
all the * to the city gate. Ju 9:4
Punish us in any * you think Ju 10:1
slaughter all the * from Aroer to Ju 11:3
They started on their * again, Ju 18:2
get up early and be on your *." Ju 19:
man came by on his * home from his Ju 19:1
"We're on the * home from Ju 19:1
door to be on his *, he found her Ju 19:2
killed along the *, and two Ju 20:4
"There must be some * to get Ju 21:1
me in a * that injures you." Ru 1:1
Israelites in this * when they came 1Sa 2:13,14
did not reply or respond in any *. 1Sa 4:2
(By the *, that large rock at 1Sa 6:18
killing them all along the *. 1Sa 7:11
to know and send you on your *. 1Sa 9:19
it's time you were on your *!" 1Sa 9:26,27
who are on their * to worship God 1Sa 10:3
us in any * and you have never 1Sa 12:4
turn your back on him in any *. 1Sa 12:20
all the * to Shur, east of Egypt. 1Sa 15:7
I don't make decisions the * you 1Sa 16:7
In the same * all seven of his 1Sa 16:9
towns along the * to celebrate and 1Sa 18:6
helped you in any * he could. 1Sa 19:4
But David dodged out of the * and 1Sa 19:9,10
In that * David got away and went 1Sa 19:18
But on the * to Naioth the 1Sa 19:23
Saul was on the * to Ziph to search 1Sa 23:14,15
Saul was on his * to Ziph, he and 1Sa 23:24,25
God's chosen king in any *." 1Sa 24:6
and gone on his *, David came out 1Sa 24:7,8
Is there any better * for him to 1Sa 29:4
Along the * they found an 1Sa 30:11,12
We were on our * back from 1Sa 30:14
from you, all the * from Dan to 2Sa 3:9,10
* responsible for Abner's death. 2Sa 3:37
* for you and will destroy them." 2Sa 5:24
all the * from Geba to Gezer. 2Sa 5:25
example of the * the Lord made him 2Sa 8:14
that is the * he treated all of 2Sa 12:31
He had no * of talking to her, 2Sa 13:2
said nothing one * or the other 2Sa 13:21-24
As they were on the * back to 2Sa 13:29,30
if you will find a * to bring your 2Sa 14:14
So in this * Absalom stole the 2Sa 15:6
him to lead the *—six hundred 2Sa 15:17,18
"Is this the * to treat your 2Sa 16:17
There is no * of knowing the 2Sa 18:11f
helped them in every * they could. 2Sa 19:18
With the body out of the *, 2Sa 20:13
As for God, his * is perfect; 2Sa 22:31
noisy celebration all along the *. 1Ki 1:40
for that is the * the Lord wanted 1Ki 2:15
who doesn't know his * around. 1Ki 3:7
In this * they will always learn 1Ki 8:40
So he went back another *. 1Ki 13:10
"Which * did he go?" 1Ki 13:12
was on the * to see King Ahab, 1Ki 18:5
You go one * and I'll go the 1Ki 18:5
that *, he stopped for dinner. 2Ki 4:8
Don't talk to anyone along the *. 2Ki 4:29
them, "You've come the wrong *! 2Ki 6:19
equipment all the * to the Jordan 2Ki 7:15
had been close to him in any *. 2Ki 10:11
at a shepherd's inn along the *. 2Ki 10:12
comparison to the * I am going to! 2Ki 10:17
it is simply a * of easier 1Ch 1:1f
killed himself in the same *. 1Ch 10:5
*, so he called together his army. 1Ch 14:8
all the * from Gibeon to Gezer. 1Ch 14:16

'AY Con't)
n whatever * they were needed. 1Ch 23:32
an be interpreted either *. 1Ch 28:12f
he gold, by the *, was of the 2Ch 3:6
Solomon did not deviate in any * 2Ch 8:15
Literally, "they walked in the * 2Ch 11:17f
'I'm with you all the *. 2Ch 18:3,4,5
We have no * to protect ourselves 2Ch 20:12
On the * Jehoshaphat stopped and 2Ch 20:20
wending their * from the Upper Gate 2Ch 23:20
In that * God executed judgment 2Ch 24:24
unusual * as a king of Israel. 2Ch 28:19f
been doing it in the proper *." 2Ch 30:5f
In this * King Hezekiah handled 2Ch 31:20
His prayer, and the * God 2Ch 33:19
dishonored in this *, we have Ez 4:14
message in any * shall have the Ez 6:11
used in whatever * you and your Ez 7:18
us from the enemies along the *. Ez 8:22
enemies and bandits along the *. Ez 8:31
to help those nations in any *. Ez 9:12
their countries on my * to Judah; Neh 2:7
obeyed God and did not act that *. Neh 5:15
* you can save yourself!" Neh 6:7
so that they could find their *. Neh 9:12
them the * through the night. Neh 9:19
around the other * to meet them. Neh 12:38
to be desecrated in this *." Neh 13:18
husbands the same *, and there will Est 1:18
* with the king to the banquet." Est 5:14
him, 'This is the * the king honors Est 6:9
"This is the * the king honors Est 6:11
But the wicked shall find no * Job 11:20
I would speak in such a * that it Job 16:5
He is * up there, walking on the Job 22:14
they must get out of the *. Job 24:4
he lighted the * before me and I Job 29:3
not go out of my * to help others— Job 31:34
sinned by speaking of God that *. Job 33:12
* you have talked about God. Job 34:36
what to do, which * to turn. Ps 5:8
The Lord is famous for the * he Ps 9:16
down—somehow they'll find a *! Ps 10:6
the other * when I am in need? Ps 13:1
How perfect in every *! Ps 18:30
me, guarding, guiding all the *. Ps 23:4
and look the other * when I go by. Ps 31:11
See for yourself the * his Ps 34:8
Why do you look the other *? Ps 44:24
forgiveness does not come that *. Ps 49:7
tribe of Benjamin leads the *. Ps 68:27
and does not look the other *. Ps 69:33
In this * each generation has Ps 78:7
blind and stubborn *, living Ps 81:12
Or, "set us in the * of his Ps 85:13f
I am in a trap with no * out. Ps 88:8
from me, and looking the other *? Ps 88:14
from springs along the *. Ps 110:7
The only * to begin is by Ps 111:10
Those gates are the * into the Ps 118:20
hide along the * to kill me, I will Ps 119:95
I hate every other *. Ps 119:128
is your * with those who love you. Ps 119:132
because of the * my enemies have Ps 119:139
I have always wanted it this *. Ps 132:14
alone know which * I ought to turn Ps 142:3
for crime is their * of life, and Pro 1:16
of having your own *, and Pro 1:31
the dawn gives * to morning Pro 4:18
only I had not demanded my own *! Pro 5:12
let embarrassment stand in the *. Pro 6:3
of conduct by demanding his own *. Pro 18:1
be known by the * he acts—whether Pro 20:11
that happens along the *? Pro 20:24
wine and luxury are not the * to Pro 21:17
they are on their * to poverty. Pro 23:19,20,21
How a ship finds its * across the Pro 30:18,19
Literally "the * of a man with a Pro 30:18,19f
justice is giving * to crime and Ecc 3:16
go on its sinful * so that he can Ecc 3:18
See the * God does things and Ecc 7:13
a time and a * to do what he says. Ecc 8:5
Yes, there is a time and a * for Ecc 8:6,7
by the * he walks down the street! Ecc 10:3
sweet, lovable in every *. Sol 5:16
Look the other *, for your eyes Sol 6:5
punishment is on the *." Is 3:11
Then we'll fight our * into Is 7:6
the child was even on the *). Is 8:2
anybody—no one can show her the *. Is 19:15
reaches all the * from the Is 27:12
you say, "No, this is the *; Is 30:21
the most stupid cannot miss the *. Is 35:8
the * you have raged against me. Is 37:28
Help is on the *!" Is 41:27
I am the Lord, who opens a * Is 43:16
your salvation is on the *. Is 51:5
the other * when he went by. Is 53:3
This is the * I will punish my Jer 1:16
to lead you and show you the *! Jer 2:17
army is on the * from the north, Jer 6:1
all the * from Dan in the north." Jer 8:16f
and that I love to be this *. Jer 9:24
lamb or ox on the * to slaughter. Jer 11:19
illustrates the * that I will rot Jer 13:8,9
been that *—you just won't listen! Jer 22:21
and to those who live the * they Jer 23:17
me in the same * as their fathers Jer 23:27
the evil that has come your *. Jer 25:7
no place to hide, no * to escape. Jer 25:35
her destroyer is on the *; Jer 48:15
They shall ask the * to Zion and Jer 50:5
They lost their * and didn't Jer 50:6
They had no * of estimating it. Jer 52:20
That was the * the glory of the Eze 1:27,28
all the * to the borders of Israel, Eze 11:10
God says: Your doom is on the *; Eze 21:7
"Prophesy to them in this *: Eze 21:14
ahead in the same *, and sinned Eze 23:11
I saw the * she was going, Eze 23:13
"Because of the * your might Eze 29:6
that *, neither men nor animals. Eze 29:11
In this * they will know that I, Eze 34:30
them for the evil * they lived. Eze 36:19
assist the people in a general *. Eze 44:14
the passageway and out the same *; Eze 46:8
They must never go out the same * Eze 46:9
the * from En-gedi to En-eglaim. Eze 47:10
also extending all the * across. Eze 48:26
and his legs gave * beneath him. Dan 5:6
some fault in the * Daniel was Dan 6:4
to think of some * to get Daniel Dan 6:14
out of its * and no one could stand Dan 8:4
blocked my *. Dan 10:13
* back, past the prince of Persia; Dan 10:20,21
trouble on the *, and disappear. Dan 11:19
lands on the *, including Israel, Dan 11:41
This will illustrate the * my Hos 1:2
make her lose her *, so that when Hos 1:6
is on the *. Joe 1:15
tip, all the * from Hamath to the Amo 6:14
"Who can ever reach us * up Ob 1:3
become a refuge, a * of escape. Ob 1:17
surely will not come our *." Mic 2:6
He will look the other *! Mic 3:4
My legs give * beneath me and I Hab 3:16
Everyone passing that * will Zep 2:15
not pass to other things that *." Hag 2:12
This will illustrate the * my Zec 11:5
the area all the * from the Gate of Zec 14:10
before me to prepare the *. Mal 3:1
in a dream to go home another *. Mt 2:12
But on the * he was frightened Mt 2:22
In that * you will be acting as Mt 5:45
other, or else the other * around. Mt 6:24
Literally, "the * that leads to Mt 7:13f
multitudes who choose its easy *. Mt 7:13
You can detect them by the * Mt 7:16
Yes, the * to identify a tree or Mt 7:20
wine. That * both are preserved." Mt 9:17
Literally, "prepare your * before Mt 11:10f
pleased you to do it this *! Mt 11:26
That is the * it will be at the Mt 13:49
As Jesus was on the * to Mt 20:17
was coming that *, they began Mt 20:30
to think of some * to trap Jesus Mt 22:15
were Moses, the * they keep making Mt 23:2
As they were on the * to the Mt 27:32
As the women were on the * into Mt 28:11
Literally, "make ready the * of Mk 1:3f
to speak to anyone along the *. Mk 1:43,44
But as the man went on his * he Mk 1:45
* through the stunned onlookers! Mk 2:12
part of the old * of doing things. Mk 2:21
this * before touching any food. Mk 7:4
of Galilee by * of the Ten Towns. Mk 7:31
and prepare the *—and that he had, Mk 9:12,13
"How long has he been this *?" Mk 9:21
But it certainly isn't God's *. Mk 10:6,7
Now they were on the * to Mk 10:32
Literally, "Go your *." Mk 10:52f
A little * off he noticed a fig Mk 11:13
On the * they were discussing Mk 16:3
upon him in some special *." Lk 1:66
prepare the * for the Messiah. Lk 1:76
found their * to Mary and Joseph. Lk 2:16
First go and prove by the * you Lk 3:8
prophets were treated that * too! Lk 6:23
you, to prepare the * before you.' Lk 7:27
on the *, coming from other towns. Lk 8:4
On the * across he lay down for Lk 8:23
And don't waste time along the *. Lk 10:4
"Salute no one in the *." Lk 10:4f
for that is the * you wanted it. Lk 10:21
continued on their * to Jerusalem Lk 10:38
Pharisees and the * they pretend to Lk 12:1
perhaps the other * around. Lk 12:52
A father will decide one * about Lk 12:53
accuser on the * to court, try to Lk 12:58
"Well, in the same * heaven will Lk 15:7
In the same * there is joy in Lk 15:10
you to act that *, to buy Lk 16:9
or else the other * around—you will Lk 16:13
were trying to find some * to get Lk 19:47
In the same *, when you see the Lk 21:31
trying to find a * to kill him Lk 22:2
best * to betray Jesus to them. Lk 22:4
they were on their * back to Lk 24:33,34
My work is to prepare the * for Jn 3:28
I am here to prepare the * for Jn 3:28
Samaria on the *, and around noon Jn 4:4
While he was on his *, some of Jn 4:51
Father doing, and in the same *. Jn 5:19
pilgrims on their * to Jerusalem Jn 6:2-5
who sent me, not to have my own *. Jn 6:38
and in the same * those who partake Jn 6:57
real father when you act that *." Jn 8:41
Those who come in by * of the Jn 10:9
Jesus was on the * to Jerusalem Jn 12:12
too late for you to find your *. Jn 12:35
going, so how can we know the *?" Jn 14:5
Jesus told him, "I am the *—yes, Jn 14:6
And this is the * to have Jn 17:3
"Is that the * to answer the Jn 18:22
Peter was grieved at the * Jesus Jn 21:17
villages along the * to preach the Act 8:25
but went on his * rejoicing. Act 8:39
the *, as he traveled to Caesarea. Act 8:40
the Lord on the * to Damascus, what Act 9:27
on them—and sent them on their *. Act 13:3
who had been that * from birth, so Act 14:8
stopping along the * in the cities Act 15:3
are saved the same *, by the free Act 15:11
we went a little * outside the city Act 16:13
perhaps feel their * toward him and Act 17:27
the * of God more accurately." Act 18:25,26f
along the *, in all the cities he Act 20:2
to pay my own * and even to supply Act 20:34
* to talk to God's High Priest?" Act 23:4
pulling him this * and that. Act 23:10
We will kill him on the *." Act 23:15
I believe in the * of salvation, Act 24:14
Two years went by in this *; Act 24:27
start us on our * to Rome by ship; Act 27:1
As the darkness gave * to the Act 27:33
on the Appian *. Act 28:15
to come to God in this same *. Rom 1:16
You are so sure of the * to God Rom 2:19
(That is the * some people Rom 3:5
shown us a different * to heaven Rom 3:21,22
laws, but by a new * (though not Rom 3:21,22
saved in this same *, by coming to Rom 3:21,22
In this * he was being entirely Rom 3:25
in this same *, because Jesus took Rom 3:26
God save only the Jews in this *? Rom 3:29
The only * we can keep from Rom 4:15
us in the same * he accepted Rom 4:24
helpless with no * of escape, Rom 5:6
I speak this *, using the Rom 6:19
not in the old *, mechanically Rom 7:6
but in the new *, [with all of your Rom 7:6
to show me the * of life resulted Rom 7:10
No matter which * I turn I can't Rom 7:18
And in the same *—by our faith Rom 8:26
that is not God's * of salvation. Rom 10:3
and in that * save some of them. Rom 11:14
Do things in such a * that Rom 12:17
Either * we are his. Rom 14:8
Try instead to live in such a * Rom 14:13
In this * aim for harmony in the Rom 14:19
and by the good * I have lived Rom 15:19
In this * I have preached the Rom 15:19
Gospel of Christ all the * from Rom 15:19
you can send me on my * again. Rom 15:24
come to see you on my * to Spain. Rom 15:28
Help her in every * you can, for Rom 16:1
still babies, wanting your own *? 1Co 3:3
and in the same * the husband no 1Co 7:4
In the same * the Lord has given 1Co 9:14
churches feel the same * about it. 1Co 11:16
In the same *, he took the cup 1Co 11:25
But that isn't the * God has made 1Co 12:18
together in such a * that extra 1Co 12:24
Love does not demand its own *. 1Co 13:5
In the same *, we can see and 1Co 13:12
In the same *, if you talk to a 1Co 14:9
In this * all who have the gift 1Co 14:31
properly in a good and orderly *. 1Co 14:40
the * I treated the church of God. 1Co 15:9
In the same *, our earthly bodies 1Co 15:42
(and, by the *, these are the 1Co 16:1
the * we have acted toward you. 2Co 1:12
and see you on my * to Macedonia, 2Co 1:15,16
could send me on my * to Judea. 2Co 1:15,16
The old *, trying to be saved by 2Co 3:6
in the new *, the Holy Spirit 2Co 3:6
Commandments is the * to be saved. 2Co 3:15
of Christ that *, merely as a human 2Co 5:16
We try to live in such a * that 2Co 6:3
the Lord by the * we act, so that 2Co 6:3
he remembers the * you listened to 2Co 7:15
This is one * to prove that your 2Co 8:8
In this * each will have as much 2Co 8:14

(WAY Con't)
* we are handling this large gift. 2Co 8:20
that in some * you will be led away 2Co 11:3
you a different * to be saved. 2Co 11:4
work in just the same * we are. 2Co 11:12
food—it's the other * around; 2Co 12:14
have made money from us some *." 2Co 12:16
steps, doing things the same *. 2Co 12:18
like the * I will have to act. 2Co 12:20
a different "* to heaven," which Gal 1:6
For there is no other * than the Gal 1:7
preaches any other * to be saved Gal 1:8
swear that the * to heaven which I Gal 1:11
(By the *, their being great Gal 2:6
said that the only * we can be Gal 3:11
How different from this * of Gal 3:12
of faith is the * of law which says Gal 3:12
be a different * of gaining God's Gal 3:18
than Abraham's *, for he simply Gal 3:18
us a different * to get out of the Gal 3:21,22
The only * out is through faith Gal 3:21,22
Jesus Christ; the * of escape is Gal 3:21,22
Let me put it another *. Gal 3:24
And that is the * it was with us Gal 4:3
us, for that is the * God planned. Gal 4:7
people. One * was by giving them Gal 4:24,25
Mount Sinai, by the *, is called Gal 4:24,25
the Spirit has his * with us are Gal 5:17
For Christ himself is our * of Eph 2:14
in just the * he had always Eph 3:11
live and act in a * worthy of those Eph 4:1
and more in every * like Christ who Eph 4:15,16
in its own special * helps the Eph 4:15,16
But that isn't the * Christ Eph 4:20
Spirit sorrow by the * you live. Eph 4:30
the same * you submit to the Lord. Eph 5:22
wife in the same * Christ is in Eph 5:23
of the * we are parts of the body Eph 5:32
jealous of the * God has used me. Php 1:15
for God's * of making us right Php 3:9
it to be the only * to really know Php 3:10
then went on my *, leaving Php 4:15
and asking that the * you live Col 1:10
In this * God took away Satan's Col 2:15
will pay you in a * that you won't Col 3:25
if he comes your *. Col 4:10
By the *, after you have read Col 4:16
really wonderful * your faith has 2Th 1:3
of the fair, just * God does 2Th 1:5
him back steps out of the *. 2Th 2:7
who are on their * to hell because 2Th 2:10
harming them in every * I could. 1Ti 1:13
Pray in this * for kings and all 1Ti 2:2
should be the same *, quiet and 1Ti 2:9,10
good, not for the * they fix their 1Ti 2:9,10
It is quite true that the * to 1Ti 3:16
let them follow the * you teach 1Ti 4:12
(By the *, this doesn't mean you 1Ti 5:23
In the same *, everyone knows 1Ti 5:25
and showed us the * of everlasting 2Ti 1:10
You know what I believe and the * 2Ti 3:10
It is God's * of making us well 2Ti 3:17
Very soon now I will be on my * 2Ti 4:6
* they act, one knows they don't. Tit 1:16
In the same *, urge the young men Tit 2:6
In this * they will make people Tit 2:10
think of it this *: that he ran Phm 1:15
If he has harmed you in any * or Phm 1:18
Only in that * could he deliver Heb 2:15
once gave * to them and sinned. Heb 4:15
in the same * God chose Aaron. Heb 5:4
him, or forget the * you used to Heb 6:10
came with God's new and better *. Heb 9:10
And in the same * he sprinkled Heb 9:21
by Moses in this *, by being Heb 9:23
new, life-giving * which Christ has Heb 10:20
there is no * to get rid of it. Heb 10:26
there is no * to count them. Heb 11:12
which, by the *, hasn't helped Heb 13:9
and we want to keep it that *. Heb 13:18
Then be happy, for when the * is Jas 1:3
turn first this *, and then that. Jas 1:7,8
"You say the * to God is by faith Jas 2:18
I have faith by the * I act." Jas 2:18
over himself in every other *. Jas 3:1
it in a gentle and respectful *. 1Pe 3:15
(That, by the *, is what baptism 1Pe 3:21
they will be punished for the * 1Pe 4:5
statement of the * God blesses. 1Pe 5:12
letting God have his * with you. 2Pe 1:6
The more you go on in this *, 2Pe 1:8
and his * will be scoffed at. 2Pe 2:2
and their destruction is on the *. 2Pe 2:3
That is the * it is with those 2Pe 2:22
though it sometimes seems that *. 2Pe 3:9
I am on my * to heaven; 1Jn 2:4
That is the * to know whether or 1Jn 2:5
and can see his * without stumbling 1Jn 2:10
blind so that he cannot see the *. 1Jn 2:11
God's will at any time in any *. 1Jn 3:5
around, and the * to find out if 1Jn 4:2
That is another * to know whether 1Jn 4:6
sinning in a * that does not end in 1Jn 5:16
a Christian ever sin in such a *? 1Jn 5:17f
Don't encourage him in any *. 2Jn 1:10
on their * with a generous gift. 3Jn 1:6
have wormed their * in among you, Jud 1:4
in every evil * imaginable. Jud 1:18
will stand a long * off, crying as Rev 18:17
dimensions—1,500 miles each *. Rev 21:16

WAYLAY
(Their plan was to * and kill Act 25:3

WAYS
him 120 years to mend his *." Gen 6:3
and instructing them in God's *. Ex 18:15,16
Or, "show me your *," or, "show Ex 33:13f
soon be following their evil *. Ex 34:12
in any of these *, for these are Lev 18:24
"for you know the * of the Num 10:31
and going your own *, as you used Num 15:39
Walk in his * and fear him. Deu 8:6
and follow evil *, you shall Deu 8:19
walking in all his *, and clinging Deu 11:22
harvest and in so many other *; Deu 16:15
only obey him and walk in his *. Deu 28:9
take care of them in other *. Jos 13:33
to turn up in the * he wanted. Jos 14:1
to their sinful *, so God helped Ju 3:12
was growing in two *—he was getting 1Sa 2:26
laws of God and follow all his *; 1Ki 2:3
follow your * and try to do your 1Ki 8:25
to follow the good * in which they 1Ki 8:35,36
did not turn away from his evil *; 1Ki 13:33
following the evil * of Jeroboam; 2Ki 13:6
Judah to turn from their evil *; 2Ki 17:13
for their evil * when the people of 2Ki 21:9
from their wicked *, I will hear 2Ch 7:14
in the good * of your father 2Ch 21:12
nor the good * of King Asa, but 2Ch 21:12
He, too, walked in the evil * of 2Ch 22:3
They sinned in so many *, but Neh 9:18
integrity of your *, your hope." Job 4:6f
wanted no part of him and his *. Job 21:14
and helps them in many *. Job 24:22,23
* to follow him more closely. Ps 1:2
love in wonderful *, O Savior of Ps 17:7
he will teach the * that are Ps 25:9
low-down * and live good lives. Ps 37:27
Then I will teach your * to Ps 51:13
to leave their guilty, stubborn *. Ps 68:21
the wonderful * he rescues me. Ps 73:28
O God, your * are holy. Ps 77:13
They refused to follow his *. Ps 78:10
learned their evil *, sacrificing Ps 106:35
ill because of their sinful *. Ps 107:17
*, for his glory is very great. Ps 138:5
turn from God's * to walk down Pro 2:11,12,13
Literally, "never return to the * Pro 2:19f
Don't copy their *. Pro 3:31
Learn from their * and be wise! Pro 6:6
God's * are as mysterious as the Ecc 11:5
quit your evil *. Is 1:16
all her evil * around the world. Is 23:17
you work in strange, mysterious *. Is 45:15
earth, so are my * higher than Is 55:9
do good, who follow godly *. Is 64:5
But those who choose their own *, Is 66:3
Your * have brought this down Jer 4:18
They don't know the * of God. Jer 5:4
for they know the * of the Lord and Jer 5:5
they continue in their wicked *. Jer 6:29
you quit your evil * I will let you Jer 7:3
Their * are futile and foolish. Jer 10:2,3
learn my people's * and claim me as Jer 12:16
back to me from all their evil *. Jer 15:7
renounces its evil *, I will not Jer 18:8
turn my people from their evil *. Jer 23:22
from their evil *, and then I can Jer 26:3
open to all the * of men, and you Jer 32:19
from your wicked * and to stop Jer 35:15
from their evil * and ask the Lord Jer 36:7
turn back from their wicked *; Jer 44:5
Literally, "He has walled up my * Lam 3:9f
of the four * their faces looked. Eze 10:9-13
turn from his wicked * and live. Eze 18:23
turn from his evil * and live. Eze 33:11
heathen, picking up their evil *; Hos 7:8
punish her for all her evil *. Hos 7:12
will be justly punished for his *. Hos 12:2
*, from his violence and robbing. Jon 3:8
stop to their evil *, he abandoned Jon 3:10
gods and foreign *, and their Zep 1:8f
all their evil * from dawn to dusk Zep 3:7
to turn from all their evil *. Zec 1:4
"If you don't change your * and Mal 2:1
to God from all their evil *. Mt 12:41
to discuss * of capturing Jesus Mt 26:4
but sincerely teach the * of God. Mk 12:14
'The old * are best,' they say." Lk 5:39
leave your evil * and turn to God? Lk 13:3
think, but teach the * of God. Lk 20:21
to them in many * that it was Act
to go their own *, but he never Act 14
to worship God in * that are Act 18
thinking of new * of sinning and Rom 1
and walk in evil *—God's anger will Rom
how his * will really satisfy you. Rom 1
and who are sinning in these *. 1Co 5
There are many * in which God 1Co 1
leaders in so many *—you have so 2Co
of God's two * of helping people. Gal 4:24,
and teaching them in the * of God. Eph 4:
and they cannot understand his *. Eph 4:17,
given themselves over to impure *. Eph 4:
in your evil *—rotten through and Eph 4:
their ignorance of God and his *. 1Th 4
in many different * to our fathers Heb
don't slip back into your old * 1Pe 1:
from the wicked * of the world by 2Pe 2:
Are your *, Rev 15:
"Now go your * and empty out the Rev 16

WAYSIDE
and live in some * shack in the Jer 9

WAYWARD
law concerning a * wife—or a Num 5:
"Put away from you a * mouth." Pro 4:2
of this * girl, a prostitute. Pro 7:8
How long will you vacillate, O * Jer 31:

WE'D
"We tried our best. * be the Gen 38:
it; * rather be killed by a man!" Ju 8:
One of his officers replied, "* 2Ki 7:

WE'RE
"* on the way home from Ju 19:1
"* defeating them again!" Ju 20:
But David's men said, "* afraid 1Sa 23
Ramoth-gilead? And * sitting here 1Ki 22
"That's the man * after." 1Ki 22:32,3
And if you say, "* trusting the 2Ki 18:2
on us. * perfectly safe!" Jer 12
From now on, as far as * Mal 3:14,1
"Lord, save us! * sinking!" Mt 8:2
of a quarrel? Why, * just God's 1Co 3

WE'VE
is blessing you. * decided to ask Gen 26:2
If you find a single thing * Gen 31:3
"But * never had a public Gen 38:2
* got to do something about it." Ju 19:3
he exclaimed. "* got him now! 1Sa 23
Forget all this gloom; * heard Is 30:10,1
With our own eyes * seen her Lam 2:1
make up to you for what * done?" Mic 6:
Then how they praised God. "* Mk 2:1
had left behind. "* given up Mk 10:2
they mumbled. "* never heard Jn 7:4
said to each other, "* lost. Jn 12:1
in languages * never learned? 1Co 12:3
wonderful time * been expecting, Tit 2:1

WEAK
"You have come to see how * we Gen 42:1
to Moses, "When did I become *? Num 11:2
they are strong or *, many or few; Num 13:1
become as * as anyone else." Ju 16:
I will be as * as other men." Ju 16:1
become as * as anyone else." Ju 16:16,17
Those who were * are now strong. 1Sa 2:4
David became * and exhausted. 2Sa 21:1
those who are * or falling, or lie Job 4:3,4
Pity me, O Lord, for I am *. Ps 6:2
Who else protects the * and Ps 35:10
He feels pity for the * and Ps 72:13
My knees are * from fasting and Ps 109:24
legs will become *, and your teeth Ecc 12:3
you are sick and * and faint, Is 1:5,6
fools your rulers are? * as women! Is 3:12
"Now you are as * as we are!" Is 14:10
will be as * as women, cowering in Is 19:16
it looks so fine, but it is so * Is 28:17
worn out, and strength to the *. Is 40:29
He grows hungry and thirsty, * Is 44:12
Was I too * to save you? Is 50:2
They are so * that the wind can Is 57:13
oppressing the *, and to stop Is 58:9
THE Lord isn't too * to save you. Is 59:1
armies and we are * with fright. Jer 6:24
I will make her * among the Jer 49:15
lands shall become as * as women. Jer 50:37
game too * to keep on running from Lam 1:6
and all knees as * as water. Eze 7:17
tremble and become as * as water. Eze 21:7
You haven't taken care of the * Eze 34:4
as iron, and some as * as clay. Dan 2:41,42
and I grew pale and * with fright. Dan 10:8
even realize how * and old he is. Hos 7:9
How * and helpless he must be!' Joe 2:17
Let the * be strong. Joe 3:10
The strong will all be *, and the Amo 2:14
Your troops will be * and Nah 3:13
I will save the * and helpless Zep 3:19
Spirit, though you are few and *.' Zec 4:6
He does not crush the *, Mt 12:20
willing, but how * the body is!" Mt 26:41

EAK Con't)
illing enough, the body is *." Mk 14:38
Did you find him * as grass, Lk 7:24
ou, even though his faith is *. Rom 14:1
iterally, "Receive him that is * Rom 14:1f
/e are *, but not you! 1Co 4:10
hat is why many of you are * 1Co 11:30
'es, they are *, dying bodies 1Co 15:43
hat is, in our * bodies. 2Co 4:7
am an ordinary, * human being, 2Co 10:3
: me and I seem * and powerless, 2Co 10:7
he things that show how * I am. 2Co 11:30
nly about how * I am and how great 2Co 12:5
Iy power shows up best in * 2Co 12:9
m glad to boast about how * I am; 2Co 12:9
or when I am *, then I am 2Co 12:10
Christ is not * in his dealings 2Co 13:3
within you. His *, human body died 2Co 13:4
Ve, too, are * in our bodies, as 2Co 13:4
Ve are glad to be * and despised 2Co 13:9
o another poor, *, useless Gal 4:9
ender care of those who are *; 1Th 5:14
Even when we are too * to have 2Ti 2:13
was frail and * like ours (except Heb 5:7f
: was * and useless for saving Heb 7:18
igh priests were * and sinful men Heb 7:28
fter they had been * or sick. Heb 11:34
ollow you, though * and lame, will Heb 12:13

EAKENED
and they have * the faith of some 2Ti 2:18

EAKENS
ipon princes, and * the strong. Job 12:21

EAKER
dynasty became * and weaker. 2Sa 3:1
dynasty became weaker and *. 2Sa 3:1
divided into four * nations, not Dan 11:4
Or, "is growing * day by day." Mk 9:18f
out the faith of others is *; Rom 14:2
is * than yours. 1Co 8:9
and honoring them as the * sex. 1Pe 3:7

EAKEST
army officers; the * was worth a 1Ch 12:14
On the day when I was *, they Ps 18:18
of Jerusalem; the * among them will Zec 12:8
And some of the parts that seem * 1Co 12:22

EAKNESS
He remembered our utter *, for Ps 136:23
and God in his *—Christ dying on 1Co 1:25
I came to you in *—timid and 1Co 2:3
is to use such * for his glory. 2Co 12:5

EAKNESSES
understands our *, since he had the Heb 4:15

'EALTH
Lot, and all his *—the cattle and Gen 12:5
off all their * and food, and went Gen 14:11
will inherit all my *." Gen 15:2,3
they will come away with great *. Gen 15:14
He was soon a man of great *, Gen 26:13
your * has increased enormously; Gen 30:30
All his * is at our father's Gen 31:1
father's * will come to us anyway! Gen 31:14
and children, and * of every kind. Gen 34:29
and flocks—all the * he had gained Gen 36:6,7,8
Showing * and extravagance. Gen 49:11f
much of the * of Egypt with them. Ex 14:8
share their great * with their Jos 22:7,8
And anyway, you own all the * of 1Sa 9:20
* and honor than his father. 1Ch 29:25
asked for personal * and honor, and 2Ch 1:11
you such riches, *, and honor as no 2Ch 1:12
for God had given him great *. 2Ch 32:28,29
of the * and glory of his empire. Est 1:4
to them about his *, and his many Est 5:11
But just take away his *, and Job 1:11
you like with his *, but don't harm Job 1:12,13
stolen and their * slakes the Job 5:5
Death shall devour him. The * he Job 18:14
rewarded; * will give him no joy. Job 20:18
against him. His * will disappear Job 20:28
up to find that all his * is gone. Job 27:19
depends on *, or if I have looked Job 31:25
Lord restored his * and happiness! Job 42:10
is not in * but in seeing you and Ps 17:15
godly than to own an evil man's *; Ps 37:16
They trust in their * and boast Ps 49:6
to be ransomed by mere earthly *. Ps 49:8,9
You must leave your * to others. Ps 49:10
For the power of their * Ps 49:14
and trust in their *, and become Ps 52:7
us into * and great abundance. Ps 66:12
lest strangers obtain your *, Pro 5:10
The rich man's * is his only Pro 10:15
Lord's blessing is our greatest *. Pro 10:22
and some poor people have great *! Pro 13:7
* from gambling quickly Pro 13:11
* from hard work grows. Pro 13:11
but when a sinner dies, his * is Pro 13:22
great * gotten by dishonest means. Pro 16:8
The rich man thinks of his * as Pro 18:11
God takes the * away from him and Ecc 2:24-26
thinking that * brings happiness! Ecc 5:10
the advantage of *—except perhaps Ecc 5:11
a man has received * from the Lord, Ecc 5:19,20
men very great * and honor, so that Ecc 6:2
your * and make a god from it! Is 46:6
bringing you the * of many lands. Is 60:5
away, bringing their * with them. Is 60:9
to receive the * of many lands. Is 60:11
will deliver your * and treasures Jer 15:12,13
who gets his * by unjust means. Jer 17:11
For you trusted in your * and Jer 48:7
for all their * has disappeared. Jer 48:36
trusted in your * and thought no Jer 49:4
they seize treasures and extort * Eze 22:25
to get great *—gold and silver and Eze 28:4
Your great * filled you with Eze 28:16
carrry off her *, plundering Eze 29:19
the ground. Her * is taken away, Eze 30:4
Using his * for political Dan 11:2
the property and * of the rich and Dan 11:24
Suddenly they and all their * Hos 5:7
But the more * I give her, the Hos 10:1
carried off his * and divided Ob 1:11
will give their * as offerings to Mic 4:13
Her vast, uncounted * is stripped Nah 2:9
city with vast *, but your enemies Nah 3:16
shepherds—for their * is gone. Zec 11:3
Jerusalem. The * of all the Zec 14:14
the delights of *, and the search Mk 4:19
to divide his * between his sons. Lk 15:12
about worldly *, who will trust you Lk 16:11
will give half my * to the poor, Lk 19:8
Her masters' hopes of * were now Act 16:19
have big names or power or *. 1Co 1:26
happiness or sadness or * should 1Co 7:30
and leaves great * for his little Gal 4:1
and now we can share in the * of Tit 3:7
as they see the * of good things in Phm 1:6
a man by his * shows that you are Jas 2:4
Your * is even now rotting away, Jas 5:2
that comes from * and 1Jn 2:16
In one moment, all the * of the Rev 18:17
made us all rich from her great *. Rev 18:19

WEALTHY
Lot too was very *, with sheep Gen 13:5
and he became very *, with many Gen 30:43
In this way God has made me * at Gen 31:9
power and might that made you *. Deu 8:17
was Phoenician, and they were *. Ju 18:7
in Bethlehem who was a very * man. Ru 2:1
of Paran. A * man from Maon owned 1Sa 25:2
old now, about eighty, and very *. 2Sa 19:31,32
Israel and Judah were a *, 1Ki 4:20
of the princes of * clans who 1Ch 4:34-39
He died at an old age, * and 1Ch 29:28
* as well as being very popular. 2Ch 17:5
So Hezekiah became very * and was 2Ch 32:27
and the * politicians of Judah. Neh 6:17
daughters, and was immensely *, Job 1:2,3
their pomp, and * princes whose Job 3:14,15
They are * and need deny Job 21:12,13
healthy, *, fat, and prosperous; Job 21:23,24
the * live wherever they chose. Job 22:8
He himself shall be *, and his Ps 112:3
love and follow me are indeed *. Pro 8:21
A * man has many "friends"; Pro 19:4
but if a sinner becomes *, God Ecc 2:24-26
not be heroes! * cheaters will not Is 32:5
"Attack those * Bedouin tribes Jer 49:31
Babylon. O * port, great center of Jer 51:13
laid waste, I shall become *!' Eze 26:2
"The Arabians, and Kedar's * Eze 27:21
homes of the *—their winter Amo 3:15
Your rich men are * through Mic 6:12
In a * home there are dishes made 2Ti 2:20
who have become * by selling her Rev 18:15

WEANED
by and the child grew and was *; Gen 21:8
until the baby is *, and then I 1Sa 1:21,22
stayed home until the baby was *. 1Sa 1:23
a child who is * from the breast. Ps 131:2
By the time this child is * Is 7:15,16
After Gomer had * Lo-ruhamah, she Hos 1:8

WEAPON
if he is killed with a wooden *. Num 35:18
Not a * could be found! Ju 5:8
since he had no *, he ripped the Ju 14:6
that I came away without a *!" 1Sa 21:8
equipped with every kind of *. 1Ch 12:24-37
breaking and burning every *. Ps 46:9
his military strength is my * Is 10:5,6
But in that coming day, no * Is 54:17
Each is right in place. No * can Joe 2:8

WEAPONRY
of armies and of *, but our boast Ps 20:7
too with all their *, and so shall Eze 38:5

WEAPONS
him, but their * were shattered by Gen 49:24
So they strapped on their * and Deu 1:41
and make his * and chariot 1Sa 8:12
does not depend on * to fulfill his 1Sa 17:47
Stripped of their *, and dead. 2Sa 1:27
surround the king, * in hand, and 2Ki 11:6,7,8
The guards, with * ready, stood 2Ki 11:11
for the king, * in hand, and kill 2Ch 23:7
large numbers of * and shields. 2Ch 32:5
worked with * within easy reach Neh 4:17
And we carried our * with us at Neh 4:23
and all their * will be broken. Ps 37:15
I do not trust my *. Ps 44:6
Make their * useless in their Ps 58:7
There he breaks the * of our Ps 76:3
Wisdom is better than * of war, Ecc 9:18
* of war into implements of peace. Is 2:4
They are his * against you, O Is 13:5
You run to the armory for your *! Is 22:8
and makes the * of destruction. Is 54:16
Their * are deadly; Jer 5:16
will make all your * useless Jer 21:3,4
and brought out * to explode his Jer 50:25
all her * break in her hands, for Jer 51:56
Tell them to bring their * with Eze 9:1
honor with their * beside them, Eze 32:27
I will knock your * from your Eze 39:3
* will give them all they need. Eze 39:10
help from her armies or her *." Hos 1:7
and I will destroy all *, and all Hos 1:18
will drop their * and run for their Amo 2:16
destroy all the * you depend on, Mic 5:10
He destroys your *. Nah 2:13
You destroyed with their own * Hab 3:14
* and carries off his belongings. Lk 11:22
killed by enemy *, or sent away as Lk 21:24
* they arrived at the olive grove. Jn 18:3
All of the godly man's arsenal—* 2Co 6:7
and * of attack—have been ours. 2Co 6:7
I use God's mighty *, not those 2Co 10:4
These * can break down every 2Co 10:5
With these * I can capture rebels 2Co 10:5
I will use these * against every 2Co 10:6

WEAR
over them to * them down under Ex 1:11
"You're going to * yourself Ex 18:18
Aaron shall * the ephod whenever Ex 28:35
after Aaron shall * these clothes Ex 29:30
of pure gold to * on the front of Ex 39:30
don't * clothes made of half wool Lev 19:19
Tie them on your finger, * them Deu 6:8
"A woman must not * men's Deu 22:5
a man must not * women's clothing. Deu 22:5
"Don't * clothing woven from two Deu 22:11
incense, and to * a priestly robe 1Sa 2:28
Literally, "* an ephod." 1Sa 2:28f
instructed her. "* mourning 2Sa 14:2,3
Let us * sackcloth and put ropes 1Ki 20:31
Ahab said to Jehoshaphat, "You * 1Ki 22:30
robes, but I'll not * mine!" 1Ki 22:30
Their clothes didn't * out and Neh 9:21
"Mountains * away and disappear. Job 14:18,19
the innocent shall * that clothing, Job 27:17
How they talk about me when I * Ps 69:11
to God! * fine clothes—with a dash Ecc 9:8
they'll * sacks instead of robes. Is 3:24
They * sackcloth through the Is 15:3
your sins, and to * clothes made of Is 22:12
Strip off your pretty clothes—* Is 32:11
the earth shall * out like a Is 51:6
each other; they * themselves out Jer 9:5
loincloth and * it, but don't wash Jer 13:1
You eat the best food and * the Eze 34:3
"They must * only linen clothing Eze 44:17
for they must * no wool while on Eze 44:17
They must * linen turbans and Eze 44:18
they must not * anything that Eze 44:18
the clothes they * while Eze 44:19
Most High God, and * down the Dan 7:25
You will * funeral clothes and Amo 8:10
Everyone must * sackcloth and Jon 3:8
No one will * prophet's clothes Zec 13:4
important than what to eat and *. Mt 6:25
a heavy yoke. * my yoke—for it Mt 11:29,30
For they love to * the robes of Mk 12:38
food to eat or clothes to *. Lk 12:22
Then he said to them, "You * a Lk 16:15
Yes, if she refuses to * a head 1Co 11:6
then she should * a covering. 1Co 11:6
But a man should not * anything 1Co 11:7
So a woman should * a covering 1Co 11:10
a woman should * a covering when 1Co 11:16
God's approval. * shoes that are Eph 6:15
She is permitted to * the Rev 19:8

WEARIED
and * me with all your faults. Is 43:24
—has * you, how will you race Jer 12:5
You have * the Lord with your Mal 2:17
"* him?" Mal 2:17
"How have we * him?" Mal 2:17

WEARILY
hot sun and sat * beside the well. Jn 4:5,6
We have worked * with our hands 1Co 4:12

WEARINESS
for he was fast asleep from *. Ju 4:21
O God, to refresh it in its *! Ps 68:9,10

(WEARINESS Con't)
I have lived with * and pain and 2Co 11:27

WEARING
would think he was * a fur coat! Gen 25:25
Afterwards she resumed * her Gen 38:19
a long journey, * your walking Ex 12:11
In this way Aaron will be * it Ex 28:37,38
anointing oil and * the special Lev 21:10
that which she was * when she was Deu 21:13
They sent ambassadors to Joshua * Jos 9:3,4,5
all, all * their priestly robes. 1Sa 22:18
Saul disguised himself by * 1Sa 28:7,8
and was * priests' clothing. 2Sa 6:14
She was * a long robe with 2Sa 13:17,18
Joab was * his uniform with a 2Sa 20:8,9,10
them that he was * an inner robe 2Ki 6:26-30
you is the queen, * jewelry of Ps 45:9
and all others * heathen clothing. Zep 1:8
a man who wasn't * the wedding robe Mt 22:11
by * on their arms little prayer Mt 23:5
Literally, "* only a linen Mk 14:51,52f
for she is * me out with her Lk 18:4,5
Then Jesus came out * the crown Jn 19:5
and love, and * as our helmet the 1Th 5:8
* a long robe circled with a Rev 1:13

WEARS
* one of the special robes." 2Ki 10:22

WEARY
who were faint and * and lagging Deu 25:18
"We are * from chasing after Ju 8:5
was * and faint as a result. 1Sa 14:28
were with him were * by the time 2Sa 16:14
him while he is * and discouraged, 2Sa 17:2,3
and there the * are at rest. Job 3:17
these long and * nights. Job 7:3
"I AM * of living. Job 10:1
Depression haunts my days. My * Job 30:17
* land where there is no water. Ps 63:1
Don't * yourself trying to get Pro 23:4,5
everything is unutterably * and Ecc 1:8-11
They never *, never stumble, Is 5:27
captive, stumbling, * and hungry. Is 8:21
and water to these * fugitives! Is 21:14
rock within a hot and * land. Is 32:2
my eyes grew * of looking up for Is 38:14
the earth, never grows faint or *? Is 40:28
they shall run and not be *; Is 40:31
I should say to all these * ones. Is 50:4
You grew * in your search, but Is 57:10
this * running after other gods? Jer 2:25
We are * of worshiping idols on Jer 3:23
them. I am * of holding it in. Jer 6:11
For I have given rest to the * Jer 31:25
added more! I am * of my own Jer 45:3
Our hearts are faint and *; Lam 5:17
would make their * journey for a Amo 4:8
*, thirsting for the Word of God. Amo 8:13
* we grow of our present bodies. 2Co 5:2
I have traveled many * miles and 2Co 11:26
Don't be * in prayer; Col 4:2
my * heart will praise the Lord. Phm 1:20
fainthearted and *, think about his Heb 12:3

WEATHER
snow, but in hot *, disappears. Job 6:15-18
But then he calls for warmer *, Ps 147:18
snow, rain, wind and *, all obey. Ps 148:8
*, or rubbing salt in his wounds. Pro 25:20
will lie open to the wind and *. Zep 2:14
at reading the * signs of the Mt 16:2,3
sky tonight means fair * tomorrow; Mt 16:2,3
morning means foul * all day—but Mt 16:2,3
several days. The * was becoming Act 27:9
But shortly afterwards, the * Act 27:14,15

WEATHERWORN
patched shoes, * saddlebags on Jos 9:3,4,5

WEAVE
"* Aaron's tunic from Ex 28:39
"Well," he said, "if you * my Ju 16:13

WEAVER
it is cut short as when a * stops Is 38:12

WEAVER'S
was as huge as a * beam! 2Sa 21:19
spear was as thick as a * beam. 1Ch 11:23
of his spear was like a * beam! 1Ch 20:5

WEAVERS
and as *—they excel in all the Ex 35:35
The skilled * first made ten Ex 36:8,9
and send me * to make purple, 2Ch 2:7
unemployed. The * will have no Is 19:9

WEAVING
at engraving, *, and at Ex 38:23
about stonework, carpentry, and *; 2Ch 2:14

WEB
God is trusting in a spider's *. Job 8:14
as a spider *, as full of cracks as Job 27:18

WEDDED
Stay away from her, for she is * Hos 4:17

WEDDING
additional field as a * present. Jos 15:18,19
When he returned for the *, he Ju 14:8
had been best man at Samson's *. Ju 14:20
arrived for the *, Saul married her 1Sa 18:19
as a bridegroom going to his *, Ps 19:5
old enough to sing their * songs. Ps 78:63
his * day, his day of gladness." Sol 3:11
I am like a bridegroom in his * Is 61:10
will seek to hide her * dress? Jer 2:32
your gladness and your * feasts; Jer 25:10
'We played * and you weren't Mt 11:17
a great * dinner for his son. Mt 22:1
his servants, 'The * feast is Mt 22:8
the * robe [provided for him Mt 22:11
you are here without a * robe?' Mt 22:12
refuse to eat at the * feast? Mk 2:19
happy men fast? Do * guests go Lk 5:34
it if we play "*" and you don't Lk 7:32
Lord's return from the * feast. Lk 12:36
are invited to a * feast, don't Lk 14:8
was a guest at a * in the village Jn 2:1
After the * he left for Capernaum Jn 2:12
No more joyous * bells and happy Rev 18:23
for the time has come for the * Rev 19:7
to the * feast of the Lamb." Rev 19:9
beautiful as a bride at her *. Rev 21:2

WEDDINGS
—banquets and parties and *—just Mt 24:37,38

WEDGE
the robe, the * of gold, his sons, Jos 7:24

WEDLOCK
breaking * living with other men. Eze 16:38
not born out of *—our true Father Jn 8:41

WEEDS
wheat, and * instead of barley." Job 31:40
flourish like *, there is only Ps 92:7
with thorns, and covered with *; Pro 24:30,31
* in the furrows of the field. Hos 10:4

WEEK
has ended. One * from today I will Gen 7:4
One * later, when Noah was 600 Gen 7:10,11,12
almost gone. A * later he released Gen 8:12
"Wait until the bridal * is Gen 29:27
The following *(continued in next Ex 7:25
This annual memorial * will Ex 13:9
on the sixth day of each *." Ex 16:5
Six days a * are for your daily Ex 20:9
—the seventh day of every *—which Lev 23:3
from the normal business of the *. Lev 23:3
to the end of the * and his wages. Job 7:2
from * to week and month to month. Is 66:23
from week to * and month to month. Is 66:23
and bring your tithes twice a *! Amo 4:4
*—the honor fell to him by lot Lk 1:8,9
"There are six days of the * to Lk 13:14
food twice a *, and I give to God a Lk 18:12
that happened there last *." Lk 24:18
"on the first day of the *." Jn 20:1f
speak to them again the next *. Act 13:42
The following * almost the Act 13:44
Turkey, where we stayed a *. Act 20:6
first day of the *," by Jewish Act 20:7f
and stayed with them a *. Act 21:4
At the end of the * when we Act 21:5
*, and use it for this offering. 1Co 16:2

WEEK'S
of those whose * work was done and 2Ch 23:8

WEEKLY
your regular * days of holy rest. Lev 23:38
as well as for the * Sabbath and 2Ch 31:3
on Saturday, the * Jewish holy Jn 9:14f

WEEKS
Eight more * went by. Gen 8:14
in deepest mourning for many *. Gen 37:34
the Festival of *, the Festival of Ex 34:22
shall last two *, during which time Lev 12:5
the Festival of *, or Pentecost), Num 28:26
"Seven * after the harvest Deu 16:9
your God called the Festival of *. Deu 16:10
The Festival of *, Deu 16:16
the Festival of *, and the Festival 2Ch 8:13
of food for many *, but all this is 2Ch 31:10
Two or three * later, Est 3:12
Two * later, Eze 32:17
Literally, "seventy *" or Dan 9:24f
been in mourning for three full *. Dan 10:2
SEVEN * HAD gone by since Jesus' Act 2:1
touched food for two *," he said. Act 27:33

WEEP
found a place where he could *. Gen 42:24
For they * to me saying, 'Give us Num 11:13
until David could * no more. 1Sa 20:41
wept until they could * no more. 1Sa 30:4
But now, O women of Israel, * for 2Sa 1:24
How I * for you, my brother 2Sa 1:26
Don't *! Neh 8:11
"And did I not * for those in Job 30:25
caused widows to *, or refused Job 31:16
Day and night I * for his help, Ps 42:3
For I groan and * beneath my Ps 55:2
I * with grief; Ps 119:28
* because your laws are disobeyed. Ps 119:136
and the sword. *, Philistine Is 14:31
* for the fate of Nebo and Medeba; Is 15:2
I will *, weep, weep, for Moab; Is 16:1
I will weep, *, weep, for Moab; Is 16:1
I will weep, weep, *, for Moab; Is 16:1
The fishermen will * for lack of Is 19
Let me alone to *. Is 22
you to repent, to * and mourn and Is 22:1
*, O ships of Tyre, returning home Is 23
* for your harbor, for it is Is 23
you shall * no more, for he will Is 30:1
But now your ambassadors * in Is 33
Put on clothes of mourning and * Jer 4
and * bitterly as for an only son. Jer 6:2
Neither * for them nor pray nor Jer 7:1
and * alone upon the mountains; Jer 7:2
I * for the hurt of my people; Jer 8:2
I would * forever; Jer 9
neither * nor plead for them; Jer 11:1
Who will * for you? Jer 15
Do not mourn or * for them, for Jer 16
Don't * for the dead! Jer 22:1
Instead * for the captives led Jer 22:1
will not * for him when he dies. Jer 22:1
*, for your allies are gone. Jer 22:2
* and moan, O evil shepherds; Jer 25:3
They will * for you and say, Jer 34
in terror and all the land will *. Jer 47
O friends of Moab, * for her and Jer 48:1
"Moab lies in ruins; * and wail. Jer 48:2
in vineyards, I * for you even more Jer 48:3
destroyed! *, daughter of Rabbah! Jer 49
Put on garments of mourning; * Jer 49
Babylon too has fallen. * for her; Jer 51
For all these things I *; Lam 1:1
of the men who * and sigh because Eze 9
Do not *; Eze 24:1
you shall not mourn or *. Eze 24:2
on sackcloth and * for you with Eze 27:3
"Son of dust, * for the king of Eze 28:1
The Lord God says, *, for the Eze 30:2,
caused the trees of Lebanon to *. Eze 31:1
Let all the nations * for her and Eze 32:1
"Son of dust, * for the people Eze 32:1
Wake up and *, you drunkards, for Joe 1
* with sorrow, as a virgin weeps Joe 1
well may you vinedressers *. Joe 1:1
well may you vinedressers weep. * Joe 1:1
your God, and * before him there. Joe 1:1
Call for the farmers to * with Amo 5:1
Woe to the city of Gath. *, men Mic 1:1
*, weep for your little ones. Mic 1:1
Weep, * for your little ones. Mic 1:1
when strong men will * bitterly. Zep 1:1
your forests. *, O cypress trees, Zec 11
All of Israel will * in profound Zec 12:12,13,1
is for you who *, for the time will Lk 6:2
we sang a dirge and you didn't * Lk 7:32
Jerusalem, don't * for me, but for Lk 23:2
was going to Lazarus' tomb to *; Jn 11:3
to happen to me, and you will *. Jn 16:2
And the nations will * in sorrow Rev 1
The merchants of the earth will * Rev 18:1

WEEPING
it was called "The Oak of *." Gen 35
Then, * with joy, he embraced Gen 45:1
Benjamin and Benjamin began * too. Gen 45:1
and * bitterly before the Lord. Ex 2:2
their tent doors *, and the anger Num 11:1
THEN ALL THE people began * Num 14
* at the door of the Tabernacle. Num 25
* because I'll never marry." Ju 11:3
God until evening, * bitterly. Ju 21
and there was * everywhere. 1Sa 5:1
as far as Behurim, * as he went. 2Sa 3:1
They soon arrived, * and sobbing, 2Sa 13:3
the Mount of Olives, * as he went. 2Sa 15:3
was * and mourning for Absalom. 2Sa 19
and kept on *, "O my son Absalom! 2Sa 19
So the shouting and the * Ez 3:1
of the Temple, * and praying and Ez 10
the Jews, fasting, *, and despair Est 4
My eyes are red with * and on my Job 16:1
My eyes are dim with * and I am Job 17
has heard my * and my pleading. Ps 6
Day and night I keep on *, Ps 22
his favor lasts for life! * may Ps 30
My eyes are red from *; Ps 31:9,1
my eyes are swollen with *, Ps 69
the Valley of * it will become a Ps 84
My eyes grow dim with *. Ps 88
Yes, they go out *, carrying Ps 126
*, WE SAT beside the rivers of Ps 137
every home comes the sound of *. Is 15
Zoar and Eglath. *, they climb the Is 15
of *, from one end to the other. Is 15
Flee to Tarshish, men of Tyre, * Is 23
and there will be * and sorrow. Is 29
and the voice of * and crying Is 65:1
Listen to the * of my people all Jer 8:1
Sobbing and *, I point to their Jer 9:1
Hear Jerusalem * in despair. Jer 9:1
In Ramah there is bitter *, Rachel Jer 31:1

WEEPING Con't)

is * for her children and she	Jer 31:15
hills of Luhith, * bitterly, while	Jer 48:5
* and seeking the Lord their God.	Jer 50:4
give yourselves no rest from *	Lam 2:18
you heard my *!	Lam 3:56
mountains, each * for his sins.	Eze 7:16
will stand helpless, * in despair.	Eze 7:26,27
and there sat women * for Tammuz,	Eze 8:14
mainland shore, * bitterly and	Eze 27:30
lie all night before the altar, *.	Joe 1:13
Come with fasting, *, mourning.	Joe 2:12
the people and the altar, *;	Joe 2:17
in the Temple will turn to * then.	Amo 8:3
with all her maidens * after her;	Nah 2:7
princes are *, for their glorious	Zec 11:3
* unrestrained;	Mt 2:18
Rachel * for her children,	Mt 2:18
into the place of * and torment."	Mt 8:12
There shall be * and gnashing of	Mt 13:42
there shall be * and gnashing of	Mt 13:50
there is * and gnashing of teeth.'	Mt 22:13
there will be * and gnashing of	Mt 24:51
shall be * and gnashing of teeth.'	Mt 25:30
with unrestrained * and wailing.	Mk 5:38
"Why all this * and commotion?"	Mk 5:39
him at his feet, *, with her tears	Lk 7:38
people, but he said, "Stop the *!	Lk 8:52
"And there will be great * and	Lk 13:28
When Jesus saw her * and the	Jn 11:33
But your * shall suddenly be	Jn 16:20
The room was filled with * widows	Act 9:39
But he said, "Why all this *?	Act 21:13
to themselves, * and crying,	Rev 18:15

WEEPS

as Esau *.	Gen 27:38
My heart * for Moab!	Is 15:5
Therefore all Moab *.	Is 16:7
and * over their wicked deeds!	Jer 12:4
Bitterly she *.	Lam 1:4
Weep with sorrow, as a virgin *	Joe 1:8

WEIGH

because they were too heavy to *!	1Ki 7:47
bronze that it was too much to *.	1Ch 22:3
bronze were used, too heavy to *.	2Ch 4:17,18
They * less than air on scales.	Ps 62:9
use balances to * the hair into	Eze 5:1

WEIGHED

The entire lampstand * 107	Ex 37:23,24
gold box of incense which * only	Num 7:14
only because it * three pounds and	2Sa 14:26
whose speartip * more than twelve	2Sa 21:16
gems and * seventy-five pounds!	1Ch 20:2
bronze that I haven't even * it;	1Ch 22:14
David * out enough gold and	1Ch 28:14
He also * out enough silver for	1Ch 28:15
to its use. He * out the gold for	1Ch 28:16
tables, and he * the silver for the	1Ch 28:16
Then he * out the gold for the	1Ch 28:17
Finally, he * out the refined	1Ch 28:18
Temple of God. I * the money as I	Ez 8:26,27
valuables were * in the Temple by	Ez 8:33
my sadness and troubles were *.	Job 6:2
bore, our sorrows that * him down.	Is 53:4
and * out the silver and paid him.	Jer 32:10
It will be * out with great care	Eze 4:16
"Tekel means '*'—you have been	Dan 5:27
have been * in God's balances and	Dan 5:27

WEIGHING

pure frankincense, * out the same	Ex 30:34
a silver platter * two pounds and a	Num 7:13
12 silver platters (each * about	Num 7:84,85,86
12 silver bowls (each * about one	Num 7:84,85,86
12 golden trays (the trays * about	Num 7:84,85,86
hailstones * a hundred pounds	Rev 16:21

WEIGHS

he * carefully everything you do.	Pro 5:21
A king sitting as judge * all the	Pro 20:8
and * the mountains and the hills?	Is 40:12

WEIGHT

The exact * is not known.	Ex 25:39f
The exact * cannot be	Ex 30:22,23f
The exact * cannot be	Ex 38:27f
(so the total * of the silver was	Num 7:84,85,86
(so the total * of gold was about	Num 7:84,85,86
of its *, hung upon a wall.	Ju 8:27f
The total * of these pieces was	1Ki 7:47
your * and pierces your hand.	2Ki 18:20,21
to estimate the * of the two	2Ki 25:16
hundred shekels of gold by *."	1Ch 21:25f
each item, and the * of the gold	Ez 8:34
the clouds are not split by the *.	Job 26:8
let them fall beneath the * of	Ps 5:10
Who else knows the * of all the	Is 40:12
as though they had no * at all.	Is 40:15
The * of the two enormous pillars	Jer 52:20
The unit of * shall be the	Eze 45:12
* of the fish, there were so many!	Jn 21:6

WEIGHTED

its branches were * down with	Dan 4:12
and fathers are * down with shame	Dan 9:8
for the nation is * with sin, and	Hos 9:7
* scales and under-sized measures;	Amo 8:5
the grapevines will be * down	Zec 8:12

WEIGHTS

*, and volumes—and give full	Lev 19:35,36
All who cheat with unjust * and	Deu 25:16
they also checked all the * and	1Ch 23:29
all the * in the bag are his	Pro 16:11f
Literally, "diverse * and diverse	Pro 20:10f
Literally, "diverse *	Pro 20:23f
their bags of false, deceitful *?	Mic 6:11

WELCOME

yet even so, you shall * your	Gen 3:16
nations did not * you with food and	Deu 23:4
the men of Judah to * King David.	2Sa 19:16
me, you would * and comfort me.	Ps 27:10
always *, safe from all attacks.	Ps 71:3
and swallows are * to come and nest	Ps 84:3
trust in you will * me because I	Ps 119:74
often, or you will outwear your *!	Pro 25:17
you because you * foreigners from	Is 2:6
wait for him! You * those who	Is 64:5
* them all day long—have rebelled;	Is 65:2
nether world will * her as she	Eze 32:21
gentle dew or the * showers of	Mic 5:7
Any city or home that doesn't *	Mt 10:14
"Those who * you are welcoming	Mt 10:40
And when they * me they are	Mt 10:40
If you * a prophet because he is	Mt 10:41
And if you * good and godly men	Mt 10:41
* the one sent to you from God."	Mt 23:39
Come out and * him!'	Mt 25:5,6
who * you are welcoming me.	Lk 10:16
me until you say, '* to him who	Lk 13:35
Only a few would * and receive	Jn 1:11,12
and you refuse to * me, though you	Jn 5:43
And to * me is to welcome the	Jn 13:20
And to welcome me is to * the	Jn 13:20
there, telling them to * him.	Act 18:27
on the beach to * and warm us in	Act 28:1
In other words, how * are those	Rom 10:15
GIVE A WARM * to any brother who	Rom 14:1
but Paul says to * them anyway.	Rom 14:1f
So, warmly * each other into the	Rom 15:7
giving her a warm Christian *.	Rom 16:1
the doors of * were wide open.	2Co 6:2
Right now God is ready to *	2Co 6:2
things, and I will * you, and be a	2Co 6:17
a fine * and set his mind at ease.	2Co 7:13
of his glad * when we come with	Eph 3:12
all my cares. * him in the Lord	Php 2:29
said before, give Mark a hearty *	Col 4:10
the wonderful * you gave us, and	1Th 1:9
and brings the * news that your	1Th 3:6
give him the same * you would give	Phm 1:17
gave a friendly * to the spies.	Heb 11:31
He not only refuses to * the	3Jn 1:10

WELCOMED

and ran to meet them and * them.	Gen 18:2
stood up to meet them, and * them.	Gen 19:1
Hezekiah * them and showed them	2Ki 20:13
inner court, he * her, holding out	Est 5:2
You * him to the throne with	Ps 21:3
You have * me as your guest;	Ps 23:5
and they have come and been *!	Eze 23:40
And he * them, teaching them	Lk 9:11
named Martha * them into her home.	Lk 10:38
But the Galileans * him with	Jn 4:45
at Jerusalem * us cordially.	Act 21:17
of the island. He * us courteously	Act 28:7
and * all who visited him,	Act 28:30
the Good News has * it, for Isaiah	Rom 10:16
just as Christ has warmly * you;	Rom 15:7
to you before. You * it then and	1Co 15:1
*, let God's curse fall upon him.	Gal 1:9

WELCOMES

And any of you who * a little	Mt 18:5
"Anyone who * a little child like	Mk 9:37
me, and anyone who * me is	Mk 9:37
"If a town * you, follow these	Lk 10:8,9

WELCOMING

"Those who welcome you are * me.	Mt 10:40
me they are * God who sent me.	Mt 10:40
mine, is * me and caring for me.	Mt 18:5
this in my name is * me, and anyone	Mk 9:37
me is * my Father who sent me!"	Mk 9:37
"Those who welcome you are * me.	Lk 10:16
"Truly, anyone * my messenger is	Jn 13:20
welcoming my messenger is * me.	Jn 13:20

WELD

"This will * us together," they	Gen 11:3,4

WELFARE

tithe for local * programs: Give	Deu 14:28
A good man is concerned for the *	Pro 12:10

WELL

God knows very * that the	Gen 3:5
will treat me * because of you,	Gen 12:11,12,13
the Jordan River, * watered	Gen 13:10
Later that * was named "The Well	Gen 16:14
Later that well was named "The *	Gen 16:14
between me and your children as *.	Gen 17:7,8
slave as * as to everyone born in	Gen 17:12
"*," Abraham said, "I figured	Gen 20:11,12
opened her eyes and she saw a *;	Gen 21:19
the king about a * the king's	Gen 21:25
that this * is mine."	Gen 21:30
So from that time on the * was	Gen 21:31
Beer-sheba ("* of the Oath"),	Gen 21:31
tree beside the *, and prayed there	Gen 21:33
"*, the land is worth 400 pieces	Gen 23:14,15
"*, this afternoon when I came	Gen 24:42
"*, while I was still speaking	Gen 24:45
"*," they said, "we'll call	Gen 24:57
Jacob: "* then, vow to God that	Gen 25:33
His shepherds also dug a new *	Gen 26:19
"This is our land and our *,"	Gen 26:20
So he named the *, "The Well of	Gen 26:20
So he named the well, "The * of	Gen 26:20
Isaac's men then dug another *,	Gen 26:21
So he called it, "The * of	Gen 26:21
So he called it, "The * of Room	Gen 26:22
there, and his servants dug a *.	Gen 26:25
"*," they said, "we can	Gen 26:28
—in the * they had been digging.	Gen 26:32
So he named the *, "The Well of	Gen 26:33
So he named the well, "The * of	Gen 26:33
lying beside a * in an open field,	Gen 29:2
stone covered the mouth of the *.	Gen 29:2
over the mouth of the * again.	Gen 29:3
"He's * and prosperous.	Gen 29:6
went over to the * and rolled away	Gen 29:10
*, Jacob was in love with Rachel.	Gen 29:18
"*, let's be going," Esau said.	Gen 33:12
"*," Esau said, "at least let	Gen 33:15
his father as * as his brothers;	Gen 37:10
toss him into a * and tell father	Gen 37:19,20
throw him alive into this * here;	Gen 37:21,22
empty *—there was no water in it.	Gen 37:24
Joseph out of the * and sold him to	Gen 37:28
to get Joseph out of the *.	Gen 37:29
"*, what do you want?"	Gen 38:18
*, when her husband heard his	Gen 39:19
everything ran smoothly and *.	Gen 39:23
every kernel * formed and plump.	Gen 41:5
Joseph's suggestions were *	Gen 41:37
"He is alive and *."	Gen 43:28
"* then," Joseph replied,	Gen 47:16
of the land, as * as all of	Gen 50:8
*, this is what happened: A	Ex 2:5
mother, "and I will pay you *!"	Ex 2:9
there beside a *, seven girls who	Ex 2:15
"*, where is he?"	Ex 2:20
help you to speak *, and I will	Ex 4:12
*, and I will tell you what to do.	Ex 4:15
let my people go? *, tomorrow	Ex 9:18
"Very *," Moses replied.	Ex 10:29
"*, because the people come to	Ex 18:15,16
"If a man digs a * and doesn't	Ex 21:33
the owner of the * shall pay full	Ex 21:34
donkeys a rest, as * as the people	Ex 23:12
us out of Egypt.' *, I told them,	Ex 32:24
into the fire, and *	Ex 32:24
oil, and should be * cooked, then	Lev 6:21
as * as those that have legs.	Lev 11:41,42
shall declare that all is *.	Lev 13:23
pronounce him *, and after washing	Lev 13:34
scarlet thread, as * as the living	Lev 14:51,52
the woman as * as the man must	Lev 15:18
holiness as * as her own, shall be	Lev 21:9
among you as * as those made by	Lev 22:25
the foreigner as * as to the	Lev 24:15,16
we are * able to conquer it!"	Num 13:30
"They know full * the power you	Num 14:13
this land, who are * aware that you	Num 14:14
of the land. *, instead I will	Num 14:31
to Beer (meaning "A *").	Num 21:16
the people sang:Spring up, O *!	Num 21:17,18
This is a *The leaders dug.	Num 21:17,18
"*, the Lord heard their	Deu 1:34,35
that all will be * with you and	Deu 4:40
Then all would go * with them in	Deu 5:29
that all will go * with you, and so	Deu 6:3
If you obey him, all will go *	Deu 6:18
For it always goes * with us	Deu 6:25
of Egypt you remember so *;	Deu 7:15
you out of Egypt? *, the Lord your	Deu 7:19
If you do, all will be * with you	Deu 12:24,25
God, all will go * with you and	Deu 12:28
and gets along * with you— then	Deu 15:16
Only then will all go * with you.	Deu 19:13
*, go home and get married!	Deu 20:7
so that they will be * fed.	Deu 26:12
future generations of Israel as *.	Deu 29:14,15
"I know perfectly * that your	Jos 2:9
kept me alive and * for all these	Jos 14:10
and fight as * as I could then!	Jos 14:11
in Israel as * as for the Israelis	Jos 20:9
yet unconquered as * as the land of	Jos 23:4,5
"You know very * that God's	Jos 23:14
as * as on the coastal plains.	Ju 1:9
Gather at the village *	Ju 5:11
he said. "*, here they are!"	Ju 8:15

(WELL Con't)
"*," Samson replied, "if I Ju 16:7
"*," he said, "if I am tied Ju 16:11
"*," he said, "if you weave my Ju 16:13
were there as * as three thousand Ju 16:27
cursing about—*, I stole it!" Ju 17:2
"*, stay here with me," Micah Ju 17:10,11
"*, then," they said, "ask God Ju 18:5
the priest replied, "all is *. Ju 18:6
"*, come on," he said. Ju 19:28
us as * as to your dead husband!" Ru 2:20
"*," Ruth told her, "he said Ru 2:21
"*, what happened, dear?" Ru 3:15-18
"*, whatever you think best," 1Sa 1:23
Those who were * are now 1Sa 2:5
water from the * and poured it out 1Sa 7:6
"*," the servant said, "I have 1Sa 9:8
Lord your God, then all will be *. 1Sa 12:14
"*," Saul replied, "when I saw 1Sa 13:11
"Hello there," he said. "*, I 1Sa 15:13
But he replied, "All is *. 1Sa 16:5
"*, there is the youngest," 1Sa 16:10,11
you and you'll soon be * again." 1Sa 16:15,16
"*, find out!" 1Sa 17:56
together, he spoke * of David and 1Sa 19:4
arrived at the great * in Secu. 1Sa 19:22
"Your father knows perfectly * 1Sa 20:3
then I'll know that all is *. 1Sa 20:7
is * and that there is no trouble. 1Sa 20:21
"*," the priest replied, "I 1Sa 21:9
to you, as my father is * aware." 1Sa 23:17
"*, praise the Lord!" 1Sa 23:21
May the Lord reward you * for the 1Sa 24:19
"*, Abner, you're a great 1Sa 26:15
Finally the woman said, "*, whom 1Sa 28:11
You know perfectly * that he came 2Sa 3:24,25
They found him at the * of Sirah 2Sa 3:26
"*, stay here tonight," David 2Sa 11:12
"*, tell Joab not to be 2Sa 11:25
"The sword kills one as * as 2Sa 11:25
tell him he is doing *." 2Sa 11:25
"*," Jonadab said, "I'll tell 2Sa 13:5
"*, then," Absalom said, "if 2Sa 13:26
I might as * have stayed there. 2Sa 14:32
But if he is through with me, *, 2Sa 15:25,26
"*," Hushai replied, "this 2Sa 17:7
them inside a * in his backyard. 2Sa 17:18
the top of the * with grain on it 2Sa 17:19
* and hurried on to King David. 2Sa 17:21
"*, whatever you think best," 2Sa 18:4
out to the king, "All is *!" 2Sa 18:28
for I know very * how much I 2Sa 19:20
"*, money won't do it," the 2Sa 21:4
"*, then," they replied, "give 2Sa 21:5,6
that good water in the city *!" 2Sa 23:15
(The * was near the city gate. 2Sa 23:15
the * and brought it to David. 2Sa 23:16
"Everything was going * for 1Ki 2:15
You replied, 'Very *, I will do 1Ki 2:42
govern your people * and know the 1Ki 3:9
fire to the Lord—*, there was no 1Ki 10:5
and serve them *, you can be their 1Ki 12:7
hard on you, *, I'll be harder! 1Ki 12:10
is sick and all those who are *. 1Ki 14:10
and it might as * be now." 1Ki 19:4
"*, it's your own fault," the 1Ki 20:40
sell you? *, you can have it now! 1Ki 21:15
"*, there's one," King Ahab 1Ki 22:8
ask whether the king will get *? 2Ki 1:3
"*," he said, "bring me a new 2Ki 2:20
Then he went out to the city * 2Ki 2:21
all right and if the child is *." 2Ki 4:26
"*," Naaman said, "all right. 2Ki 5:17
so we might as * go out and 2Ki 7:4
Lord whether I will get * again." 2Ki 8:8,9
"You know very * who he was and 2Ki 9:11
in Jezreel, as * as all of his 2Ki 10:11
"You have done * in following my 2Ki 10:30
Jordan River, as * as all of 2Ki 10:32,33
You know perfectly * what the 2Ki 19:11
from the Bethlehem * beside the 1Ch 11:17
*, and brought it back to David. 1Ch 11:18,19
to Jerusalem, as * as a great 1Ch 18:8
chariots, as * as the support of 1Ch 19:7
* qualified for their work. 1Ch 26:8
various items, as * as the 1Ch 28:15
as * as all the political and 2Ch 1:2,3
as * as all the public prayers. 2Ch 6:29
the Temple as * as his own palace. 2Ch 7:11
chariot cities, as * as in 2Ch 9:25
as * as being very popular. 2Ch 17:5
"*," Ahab told him, "there is 2Ch 18:6,7
When he was * established as the 2Ch 25:3
no matter how * you fight; 2Ch 25:8
the Temple, as * as the treasures 2Ch 25:24
offerings, as * as for the weekly 2Ch 31:3
* as from the people of Jerusalem. 2Ch 34:9
as * as gifts for the Temple. Ez 1:6
you might as * forget about this Ez 4:16
leader, Ezra was * versed in Ez 7:6
Many ordinary people as * as Ez 7:7,8,9
*, praise the Lord God of our Ez 7:27
"Guard these treasures *!" Ez 8:29
"*," they replied, "things are Neh 1:3
"*, what should be done?" Neh 2:4
the Jackal's * and over to the Dung Neh 2:13
full * the tragedy of our city; Neh 2:17
duty as * as work during the day. Neh 4:22
gates until * after sunrise, and to Neh 7:3
But when all was going *, your Neh 9:28
the Presence, as * as grain Neh 10:33
of the times as * as Persian law Est 1:13-15
friends as * as being the chief Est 1:13-15
of his reign. *, the king loved Est 2:17
"*," suggested Zeresh his wife Est 5:14
he, when you pay him so *?" Job 1:9
"*, have you noticed my servant Job 2:3
know full * I've not committed? Job 10:4-7
All wisdom will die with you! *, Job 12:3
you can fool God as * as men? Job 13:9
" '*,' you say, 'at least God Job 21:19
All who saw me spoke * of me. Job 29:11
* that I have no one to help me. Job 30:13
[But I might as * save my breath, Job 30:28,29
I know full * that Almighty God Job 31:2,3
Mark this *, O Job. Job 33:31
to approach him? *, does a man wish Job 37:19,20
Mark this *: The Lord has set Ps 4:3
Come, O Lord, and make me *. Ps 6:4
and knowing all is * between us. Ps 17:15
me, I might as * give up and die. Ps 28:1
LET ALL THE joys of the godly * up Ps 33:1
asking him to make them *; Ps 35:13
great joy to all who wish me *. Ps 35:27
about it, as you * know, O Lord. Ps 40:9
Be gracious, Lord, and make me * Ps 41:10
O splendid many-peaked ranges! * Ps 68:15,16
O God, you know so * how stupid I Ps 69:5
us decent food as * as water?" Ps 78:19,20
he says, "and Manasseh as *; Ps 108:8
and all goes * for the generous Ps 112:5
Now teach me good judgment as * Ps 119:66
listen to me and make me * again. Ps 119:149
as * as with human joys. Ps 128:5
is marvelous—and how * I know it. Ps 139:14
Drink from your own *, my son—be Pro 5:15
Rulers rule * with my help. Pro 8:16
Be sure you know a person * Pro 11:15
Her husband is * known, for he Pro 31:23
The man who works hard sleeps * Ecc 5:12
*, one thing, at least, is good: Ecc 5:18
for a man to eat *, drink a good Ecc 5:18
contentment—*, what's the use? Ecc 6:6
God gives one as * as the other—so Ecc 7:14
lives, I know very * that those who Ecc 8:12
Whatever you do, do *, for in Ecc 9:10
Dig a *—and fall into it! Ecc 10:8,9
incense tree, as * as myrrh and Sol 4:13,14
You are a garden fountain, a * Sol 4:15
doors, the new as * as old, for I Sol 7:13
But all is * for the godly man. Is 3:10
you exhaust the Lord's as *! Is 7:13
as * as to all your fertile acres. Is 7:19
for their lives. * may you scream Is 10:30
though it grows so * that it will Is 17:11
or a little water from the *. Is 30:14
for we understand it quite *. Is 36:11
But I know you *—your comings Is 37:28
When King Hezekiah was * again, Is 38:9
boil, and he will get * again." Is 38:21
very sick and now was * again. Is 39:1
warm and fed and * content, and Is 44:16
distant future, as * as to Cyrus. Is 45:13f
I'll never lose my children." * Is 47:9
new, for I know so * what traitors Is 48:8
Some believe this verse as * as Is 65:1f
Some believe this verse as * as Is 65:1f
I see full * what they are Is 66:18
and rich, and * fed and well Jer 5:28
and well fed and * groomed, and Jer 5:28
do as I say and all shall be *! Jer 7:23
is * when that isn't so at all! Jer 8:11
*—that no war or famine will come. Jer 14:13
that all was *, speaking of things Jer 14:18
all curse me. *, let them curse! Jer 15:11
me, yet I spoke * of them to you Jer 18:20
the needy and all went * for him. Jer 22:16
All is *"; Jer 23:17
asks you, "*, Jeremiah, what is Jer 23:33
I will see that they are * Jer 24:6
were priests as * as kings) as well Jer 30:21f
well as kings) as * as to the final Jer 30:21f
Mark your pathway *. Jer 31:21
was there, as * as Delaiah (son of Jer 36:12
spared and all will go * for you. Jer 38:20
"Look after him * and give him Jer 39:11,12
I will see that you are * cared Jer 40:4
said, "and all will go * for you. Jer 40:9
for as you know so *, we are only a Jer 42:2
will turn out * for us." Jer 42:6
throughout southern Egypt as *: Jer 44:1
eat and we were * off and happy! Jer 44:17
They lied and said that all was * Lam 2:1
They threw me in a * and capped Lam 3:5
within the *, and you heard me! Lam 3:5
O Lord, repay them * for all the Lam 3:6
Though the vine began so *, will Eze 17:1
soil where it had grown so *." Eze 17:1
don't bring your gifts to me as *! Eze 20:3
Boil the meat *, until the flesh Eze 24:
Cook the meat * and then empty Eze 24:1
refuses to heed it—*, if he dies Eze 33:
voice or plays * on an instrument. Eze 33:3
north, as * as many others. Eze 38:
many fields, are * informed, alert Dan 1:3,
to the test. *, at the end of the Dan 1:1
* as chief over all his wise men. Dan 2:4
worship the statue, all will be *. Dan 3:1
"*, look!" Dan 3:2
of heaven, as * as here among the Dan 4:3
"I might as * return to my Hos 1:
broad daylight as * as in the Hos 4:
Israel will know it all too *. Hos 9:
O Israel, how * I remember those Hos 9:1
* may you farmers stand so Joe 1:1
* may you vinedressers weep. Joe 1:1
come, as * as those of spring. Joe 2:2
your punishment is * deserved. Amo 3:
I know them all so *. Amo 5:1
is *—the Lord is here among us. Mic 3:1
old and feeble, as * as the young Nah 2:1
assistance, as * as Put and Libya. Nah 3:
as * as Israel. Zec 9:
knows perfectly * that you need Mt 6:31,32
healed,' my servant will get *! Mt 8:8,9
"Because people who are * don't Mt 9:12
"Daughter," he said, "all is * Mt 9:22
And the woman was * from that Mt 9:22
and it fell into a * on the Mt 12:11
Testament as * as from the New!" Mt 13:52
You hypocrites! * did Isaiah Mt 15:7
"*," they replied, "some say Mt 16:14
from that moment the boy was *. Mt 17:18
"*, then," Jesus said, "the Mt 17:26,27
"*, then," he said, "give it to Mt 22:21
man's property. *, we had among us Mt 22:25
For the man who uses * what he Mt 25:29
said to Jesus, "*, what about it? Mt 26:62
For he knew very * that the Mt 27:18
days, can you? *, then, come on Mt 27:40
to other towns as *, and give my Mk 1:38
can make me * again," he pled. Mk 1:40
have proof that you are * again." Mk 1:43,44
stopped and she knew she was *! Mk 5:29
your faith has made you *; Mk 5:34
described you very * when he said, Mk 7:6,7
he said, "You have answered * Mk 7:29
answered well—so * that I have Mk 7:29
brother's name. *, there were Mk 12:20,21,22
that Jesus had answered *. Mk 12:28
that it would be * to recheck all Lk 1:3
laws in spirit as * as in letter. Lk 1:6
wife is also * along in years." Lk 1:18
stone deaf as * as speechless, and Lk 1:62f
Soon he became * known throughout Lk 4:14
All who were there spoke * of him Lk 4:22
to everyone that you are *." Lk 5:14
and Judea, as * as from Jerusalem. Lk 5:17
How * he knew their thoughts! Lk 6:8
* enough to deal with his speck! Lk 6:42
and my servant will be * Lk 7:6,7,8
him and that now she was *. Lk 8:47
Didn't God make the inside as * Lk 11:40
was not robed as * as they are. Lk 12:27
in drunkenness— *, his master will Lk 12:46
You interpret the sky * enough, Lk 12:56
standing around, "*, is it within Lk 14:3
" '*, then,' said his master, Lk 14:23
Listen *, if you would understand Lk 14:35
"*, in the same way heaven will Lk 15:7
your faith has made you *." Lk 17:19
times over now, as * as receiving Lk 18:30
"* said, sir!" Lk 20:39
us loving forgiveness as *. Jn 1:17
"* then, who are you?" Jn 1:21
he came to Jacob's *, located on Jn 4:5,6
sun and sat wearily beside the *. Jn 4:5,6
said, "and this is a very deep *! Jn 4:11
The woman said, "*, at least I Jn 4:25
beside the * and went back to the Jn 4:28,29
to see him at the *, they begged Jn 4:40,41
all was *—his son had recovered. Jn 4:51
him, "Would you like to get *?" Jn 5:6
and told him, "Now you are *; Jn 5:14
for as I know so *, you don't have Jn 5:41,42
a man completely * on the Sabbath? Jn 7:21,22,23
accepted as fact. *, I am one Jn 8:18
about him! *, God doesn't listen Jn 9:31
*, her brother Lazarus, who lived Jn 11:1
and head as *—not just my feet!" Jn 13:9
do * to say it, for it is true. Jn 13:13
I know so * each one of you I Jn 13:18
teach you much, as * as remind you Jn 14:26

LL Con't)
ough him, as you * know. Act 2:22
: I know all will be * with me Act 2:26
the Romans—as * as the people Act 4:27
o are * thought of by everyone; Act 6:3
er all Egypt, as * as putting him Act 7:10
* as to the people of Israel. Act 9:15
is *, I have sent them." Act 10:20
d godly man, * thought of by the Act 10:22
u have done * to come so soon. Act 10:33
, I began telling them the Act 11:15
we will offer it to Gentiles. Act 13:46
mothy was * thought of by the Act 16:2
lp us." *, that settled it. Act 16:10
e people of the city, as * as Act 17:8,9
e Athenians as * as the Act 17:21
you know so * from what Act 19:26
know full * that after I leave Act 20:29
e law, and * thought of by all Act 22:12
u know very * I am not guilty. Act 25:10,11
d then replied, "Very *! Act 25:12
s the Jews are * aware, I was Act 26:4
," YOU MAY be saying, "what Rom 2:1
u Jews think all is * between Rom 2:17
then, are we Jews better than Rom 3:9
ey have faith. * then, if we are Rom 3:31
Christ? *, what about Abraham? Rom 4:9
able to do anything he promised. Rom 4:21
ow that all is *, for we know how Rom 5:5
THEN, SHALL we keep on sinning Rom 6:1
then, am I suggesting that Rom 7:7
know perfectly * that what I Rom 7:16
then, has God failed to fulfill Rom 9:6
fuse to listen. * then, why does Rom 9:19
then, what shall we say about Rom 9:30
* between themselves and God. Rom 11:9
*," you may be saying, "those Rom 11:19
bility to do certain things *. Rom 12:6
serving others, serve them *. Rom 12:7
e laws and you will get along *. Rom 13:3
ese things so * that you are able Rom 15:14
know very * how foolish it 1Co 1:18
ord knows full * how the human 1Co 3:20
ave I been a good servant? *, I 1Co 4:3
ou are * thought of, while we 1Co 4:10
married man can't do that so *; 1Co 7:33
o the person who marries does * 1Co 7:38
idols? *, we all know that an 1Co 8:4
am wrong? *, I'll tell you why. 1Co 10:31
Do you want me to praise you? *, 1Co 11:22
You might as * be talking to an 1Co 14:9
aying. *, then, what shall I do? 1Co 14:15
, my brothers, let's add up what 1Co 14:26
Corinthians? *, you are mistaken! 1Co 14:36
ut if anyone still disagrees—*, 1Co 14:38
hen we might as * go and have 1Co 15:32
o help them as * as all others 1Co 16:16
on't know me very * (I hope 2Co 1:13,14
o Macedonia, as * as afterwards 2Co 1:15,16
, when I got as far as the city 2Co 2:12
who brag about how * they look and 2Co 5:12
are * intentioned and honest. 2Co 5:12
or me, *, I overflowed with joy! 2Co 7:7
am sure all is * between us again. 2Co 7:16
himself and how * he has done, it 2Co 10:18
are Hebrews, do they? *, so am I. 2Co 11:22
of Abraham? *, I am too. 2Co 11:22
the Jews, as * as from the hands of 2Co 11:26
I begged God to make me * again. 2Co 12:8
must be punished. [*, this is my 2Co 13:1
know very * that we cannot become Gal 2:16
* then, why were the laws given? Gal 3:19
* then, are God's laws and God's Gal 3:21,22
You were getting along so *. Gal 5:7
plan of salvation. *, if I preached Gal 5:11
of work * done, and won't need to Gal 6:4
his grace—for how * he understands Eph 1:8
and special ability to do it *. Eph 3:7
gift of being able to preach *; Eph 4:11
and dying—*, that's better yet! Php 1:21
struggle now, as you know so *. Php 1:30
me in my need; *, he and I have Php 2:25
As you * know, when I first Php 4:15
sacrifice that pleases God *. Php 4:18
teaching them as * as we know how. Col 1:28
getting along so *, happy because Col 2:5
be gracious as * as sensible, for Col 4:6
as you very * know, and God knows 1Th 2:5
perfectly * that no one knows. 1Th 5:2
saying, "All is *, everything is 1Th 5:3
For you * know that you ought to 2Th 3:7
to you: Fight * in the Lord's 1Ti 1:18
Also, he must be * spoken of by 1Ti 3:7
and if they do *, then they may be 1Ti 3:10
Those who do * as deacons will 1Ti 3:13
as deacons will be * rewarded both 1Ti 3:13
make sure everyone learns them *. 1Ti 4:11
She must be * thought of by 1Ti 5:10
Has she brought up her children * 1Ti 5:10
as * as to other Christians? 1Ti 5:10
Pastors who do their work * 1Ti 5:17
should be paid * and should be 1Ti 5:17
So we should be * satisfied 1Ti 6:8
Christian life down here as *. 1Ti 6:19
Guard * the splendid, God-given 2Ti 1:14
paid * if he raises a large crop. 2Ti 2:6
so God can say to you, "* done." 2Ti 2:15
* as some made from wood and clay. 2Ti 2:20
YOU MAY AS * know this too, 2Ti 3:1
Some day their deceit will be * 2Ti 3:9
It is God's way of making us * 2Ti 3:17
The men you choose must be * Tit 1:6
*, Moses did a fine job working Heb 3:5
understands their problems very *. Heb 5:1
*, when all was ready the priests Heb 9:6
*, how much more do I need to Heb 11:32
ruled their people *, and received Heb 11:33
judge them on how * they do this. Heb 13:17
sit on the floor"—*, judging a Jas 2:3
"*, good-bye and God bless you; Jas 2:16
But someone may * argue, "You Jas 2:18
plus nothing; *, I say that good Jas 2:18
Believing in one God? *, remember Jas 2:19
does, as * as by what he believes. Jas 2:24
him, for the Lord will make him *; Jas 5:15
or silver, as you very * know. 1Pe 1:18
and to those who reject him, * 1Pe 2:7
the blows, God is * pleased. 1Pe 2:20
are really getting along quite *! 2Pe 1:12
Son; I am * pleased with him." 2Pe 1:17,18
You will do * to pay close 2Pe 1:19
say, "so you might as * be bad. 2Pe 2:19
sure that all is *, and will not 1Jn 2:28
and he knew very * that his 1Jn 3:12
enough to live *, and sees a 1Jn 3:17
*, I would like to say much more, 2Jn 1:12
that all is * with you and that 3Jn 1:2
"I know you *; Rev 3:8
"I know you *—you are neither Rev 3:15
in their tails as *, for their Rev 9:19
prophets are, as * as all those who Rev 22:9

WELL-ADVISED
of how shrewd or * he is, can stand Pro 21:30

WELL-AGED
clear, * wine and choice beef. Is 25:6

WELL-BEHAVED
He must have a * family, with 1Ti 3:4

WELL-EARNED
Your * punishment is on the way." Is 3:11
me happiest is the * reward you Php 4:17

WELL-FED
They are *, lusty stallions, Jer 5:8

WELL-FORMED
up the seven plump, * heads! Gen 41:7
the seven fat, * heads of grain) Gen 41:26

WELL-FORTIFIED
These were * cities with high Deu 3:5

WELL-KNOWN
I am sending another * brother 2Co 8:18

WELL-ROUNDED
for I am a man of * knowledge. Job 36:4

WELL-SET
their * hair will all fall out; Is 3:24

WELL-TAUGHT
these things to * Christians to 1Ti 4:3

WELL-TRAINED
Both armies were composed of *, 2Ch 14:8

WELL-WATERED
and you will be like a * garden, Is 58:11

WELLED
(However, water * up from the Gen 2:6

WELLS
So they filled up his * with Gen 26:15
And Isaac redug the * of his Gen 26:18
Then the Egyptians dug * along Ex 7:24
water from your *, but will stay on Num 20:17
you didn't build, * you didn't dig, Deu 6:10,11,12
the *, and felled the fruit trees; 2Ki 3:25
at many conquered *, and I 2Ki 19:24
"You boast of * you've dug in Is 37:25
from the *, but the wells are dry. Jer 14:3
from the wells, but the * are dry. Jer 14:3

WELTS
with bruises and * and infected Is 1:5,6

WENDING
from the Temple, * their way from 2Ch 23:20

WEPT
there Abraham mourned and * for Gen 23:1
I go now?" he * to his brothers. Gen 37:30
Going into his bedroom, he * Gen 43:30
Then he * aloud. Gen 45:2
other's arms and * a long while. Gen 46:29
and * over him and kissed him. Gen 50:1
*, "Oh, for a few bites of meat! Num 11:4,5
you, and you have * for Egypt.' Num 11:19,20
Then they returned and * before Deu 1:45
"the place where people *"). Ju 2:5
Then the Israeli army * before Ju 20:22,23,24
up to Bethel and * before the Lord Ju 20:26
and * until David exceeded." 1Sa 20:41f
* until they could weep no more. 1Sa 30:4
They mourned and * and fasted 2Sa 1:12
And the king and all the people * 2Sa 3:32
And all the people * again for 2Sa 3:33,34
living, you * and refused to eat; 2Sa 12:21
David replied, "I fasted and * 2Sa 12:22
and his officials * with them. 2Sa 13:36
* as they climbed the mountain. 2Sa 15:30
Joash visited him and * over him. 2Ki 13:14
your clothing and * before me in 2Ki 22:18,19
in despair and * before me—I have 2Ch 34:27
beautiful Temple—* aloud, while Ez 3:12
I have * until I am exhausted; Ps 69:3
I have * before you day and night. Ps 88:1
Then the people * before the Lam 2:18
The women * for Tammuz, the god of Eze 8:14f
and prevailed. He * and pleaded for Hos 12:4
he *, "and now it is too late. Lk 19:42
And as she *, she stooped and Jn 20:11
them, and they * aloud as they Act 20:37
he * bitter tears of repentance. Heb 12:17
Then I * with disappointment Rev 5:4

WEREN'T
They * there to see the miracles Deu 11:3
They * there when Dathan and Deu 11:6
Why * we content with what we had? Jos 7:7
There * even any guards, so they Ju 18:27
But Achish's officers * happy 1Sa 21:11
and Solomon and I * invited. 1Ki 1:26
But they * gods at all; 2Ki 19:18
The gods of those nations * able 2Ch 32:13
as though they * her own, and is Job 39:16
They * impressed by the wonder Ps 106:7
for they * gods at all, but Is 37:19
us as though we * your people, as Is 63:19
there, you still * satisfied, so Eze 16:28
Babylon—and you still * satisfied. Eze 16:29
she'd say they * for her—that they Hos 8:12
wedding and you * happy, so we Mt 11:17
we played funeral but you * sad.' Mt 11:17
them * sure it really was Jesus! Mt 28:17
quietly when the crowds * around. Lk 22:6
If this * so, I would tell you Jn 14:2,3
arrested him if he * a criminal!" Jn 18:30
You * lying to us, but to God." Act 5:4
the jail, the men * there, so they Act 5:22
made against him * at all what I Act 25:18
people who * even looking for him. Rom 10:20
and that they * being honest about Gal 2:14
believed, and * following the truth Gal 2:14

WEST
on the * and Ai on the east. Gen 12:8
Or, if you want the *, then I'll Gen 13:9
east to * and from north to south; Gen 28:14
Located just * of the Jordan Gen 50:10f
sent a very strong * wind that blew Ex 10:19
On the * side there will be six Ex 26:22
and rods. The * side of the court Ex 27:12
each frame. The * side of the Ex 36:27
So, on the * side, there were a Ex 36:30
* side was seventy-five feet wide; Ex 38:12
Location: * side of Num 2:3-31
* side of Tabernacle Num 3:16-24
River on the *, from Chinnereth to Deu 3:17
Ebal are mountains * of the Jordan Deu 11:30
Sea in the * to the Euphrates River Jos 1:4
WHEN THE NATIONS * of the Jordan Jos 5:1
Bethel and the * side of Ai; Jos 8:9
ambush on the * side of the city. Jos 8:11,12,13
of the nations * of the Jordan Jos 9:1
mountain areas of Dor, on the *; Jos 11:1
kings of Canaan, both east and *; Jos 11:1
east, and on the *, extending to Jos 12:5
on the * side of the Jordan. Jos 12:7
and Mount Halak, * of Mount Seir, Jos 12:7
is located), then * to the top of Jos 15:8
Then the border circled * of Jos 15:10,11
the Archites; and * to the border Jos 16:1
So now, land on the * side of Jos 17:2
brook and as far * as the Jos 17:10
of Jericho, then * through the hill Jos 18:12
From there it circled to the *, Jos 19:11
The boundary on the * side went Jos 19:24,25,26
of Asher on the *, and with the Jos 19:34
land on the * side of the Jordan. Jos 22:7,8
They camped first at a place * Ju 18:12
men in ambush * of Geba jumped up Ju 20:33
all the kingdoms * of the Euphrates 1Ki 4:24
*, three south, and three east. 1Ki 7:25
by Naaran, on the * by Gezer and 1Ch 7:28
sides: east, *, north, and south. 1Ch 9:24
on both the east and * banks. 1Ch 12:15
of the * gate and the 1Ch 26:16
each day to the * gate, four to the 1Ch 26:18
of Israel * of the Jordan River; 1Ch 26:30
*, three south, and three east. 2Ch 4:4
an aqueduct to the * side of the 2Ch 32:30
and the wall from * of the Spring 2Ch 33:14
lands * of the Euphrates River. Ez 4:10
subjects * of the Euphrates River. Ez 4:11
the area * of the Euphrates River: Ez 4:17
of the lands * of the Euphrates, Ez 5:3
officials * of the Euphrates: Ez 6:6

(WEST Con't)
in the provinces * of the Euphrates Ez 7:21
people * of the Euphrates River; Ez 7:25
all the provinces * of the Ez 8:36
to the governors * of the Euphrates Neh 2:7
When I arrived in the provinces * Neh 2:9
all mankind from east to *! Ps 50:1
from us as the east is from the *. Ps 103:12
east and the Philistines on the *. Is 9:11,12
east and on the *, uniting forces Is 11:14
those in the * will praise the Is 24:14
army against the nations of the *. Is 37:24
in Hezekiah's activities in the *. Is 39:1f
I will gather you from east and * Is 43:5
* will know there is no other God. Is 45:6
from north and * and south." Is 49:12
the name of God from * to east. Is 59:19
Send to the * to the island of Jer 2:10,11
from the lowlands * of Judah, the Jer 17:26
you look—east, *, north or Eze 7:2
A large building stood on the *, Eze 41:12
was the building * of the Temple, Eze 41:15,16
There, at the extreme * end of Eze 46:19,20
"The southern border will go * Eze 47:19
"On the * side, the Eze 47:20
the same east and * boundaries. Eze 48:2
lines on the east and the *. Eze 48:3
boundaries on the east and the *. Eze 48:5,6,7
east and * for three miles Eze 48:18
on east and *, while its south Eze 48:27,28
on the 1½ miles of the * side, Eze 48:34
appeared from the *, so swiftly Dan 8:5
shall return trembling from the *. Hos 11:10
Or, "will go *." Zec 6:6f
*, wherever they are scattered. Zec 8:7
from east to *, for half the Zec 14:4
sky from east to *, so shall my Mt 24:27
*, you say, 'Here comes a shower.' Lk 12:54
side—north, south, east, and *. Rev 21:13

WESTERN
I'll stay here in the * section. Gen 13:9
"Your * boundary will be the Num 34:6
* shores of the Lake of Galilee; Jos 12:3
The Jordan River was the * Jos 13:23
The Jordan River was the * Jos 13:27,28
The * border was the shoreline of Jos 15:12
[The * half of the northern Jos 16:8
This was the * boundary. Jos 18:14
Jordan River. The * boundary began Jos 19:34
sank into the * skies, he died. 2Ch 18:34
Let the * coastlands glorify the Is 42:12
its eastern and * boundaries are Eze 45:7
Those are the eastern and * Eze 48:1
same eastern and * boundary lines. Eze 48:4
It has the same eastern and * Eze 48:8
to the eastern and * boundaries of Eze 48:21,22
clear across to the * border. Eze 48:23
these same eastern and * borders. Eze 48:24

WESTWARD
rear of the building, facing *. Ex 26:26,27
south and then * until it touches Num 34:10,11
where it will bend * to the Jordan Eze 47:18
their armies * without hindrance. Rev 16:12

WET
around the camp was * with dew; Ex 16:13
but if the seeds are * and the Lev 11:38
the fleece is * and the ground is Ju 6:37
while the ground around it is *!" Ju 6:39
the ground is * from my wounds. Job 16:13
They are * with the showers of Job 24:8
every night my pillow is * with Ps 6:6
Let him be * with the dew of Dan 4:23
your back * with dew from heaven. Dan 4:25
cows, and his body was * with dew; Dan 4:33
and his body was * with the dew of Dan 5:21
impure salt; when *, the salt Lk 14:34f

WET-EYED
She found the disciples * with Mk 16:10,11

WHALE
And over there, the * you made to Ps 104:26

WHATEVER
call them; and * he called them, Gen 2:19,20
like this to me? * made you think Gen 20:9,10
full price for it, * is publicly Gen 23:9
to stay? * it is, I'll pay it." Gen 30:28
So go ahead and do * God has told Gen 31:16
"I will give * you require. Gen 34:11
to Joseph. "Do * he tells you Gen 41:55
that they gave them * they wanted. Ex 12:36
her shall be fined * amount the Ex 21:22
of his life * is laid upon him." Ex 21:30f
donkey or sheep or * it is, he Ex 22:4
holy, so that * touches it shall be Ex 29:37
* touches them shall become holy. Ex 30:29
on to the people * instructions God Ex 34:34
a ram without defect, worth * fine Lev 5:15
be forgiven for * it is he has done Lev 5:17,18
must be worth * value you demand. Lev 6:6
shall be given * remains of the Lev 7:9
"As to fish, you may eat * has Lev 11:9
birds, and * swims in the water or Lev 11:46
or leather goods or * it is in. Lev 13:56
tooth for tooth. * anyone does to Lev 24:20
Year of Jubilee—* it would cost to Lev 25:50
Give them to the Levites for * Num 7:4,5
of the Lord; and * the Lord told Num 9:23
unless we pay * you demand for it. Num 20:19
* the Lord directs me to say." Num 22:8
must say * Jehovah tells me to?" Num 23:26
to permit the vow, * penalties to Num 30:15
Pay them for * food or water you Deu 2:6
doing * he thinks is right; Deu 12:8
let him live among you in * town Deu 23:15,16
be prompt in doing * it is you Deu 23:21
agreed to do * he told them to. Ju 9:4
You keep * your god Chemosh Ju 11:24
keep * Jehovah our God gives us! Ju 11:24
you must do * you promised the Ju 11:36
"You can't blame me for * Ju 15:3
so everyone did * he wanted Ju 17:6
to—* seemed right in his own eyes. Ju 17:6
out and you can do * you like to Ju 19:24
man did * he thought was right. Ju 21:25
I'll do * you say." Ru 3:5
you your petition, * it is!" 1Sa 1:17
"Well, * you think best," 1Sa 1:23
and demand that * it brought up be 1Sa 2:13,14
me and do * I tell him to do. 1Sa 2:35
should be based on * seems best 1Sa 10:7
Tell me and I will make right * I 1Sa 12:3
I'm with you heart and soul, * 1Sa 14:7
Please give us a present of * is 1Sa 25:8
(Absalom did * Ahithophel told 2Sa 16:23
"Well, * you think best," the 2Sa 18:4
Let him go with you and receive * 2Sa 19:37
him * I would have done for you." 2Sa 19:38
Shime-i replied, "* you say." 1Ki 2:38
will pay your men * wages you ask; 1Ki 5:6
or plague—or * the problem is— 1Ki 8:37
in my path and do * I consider 1Ki 11:38
me and to do * I wanted him to. 1Ki 14:8
"and that * you say is from the 1Ki 17:24
they will take away * they like!" 1Ki 20:5,6
to pay for * repairs are needed." 2Ki 12:4,5
I will pay * tribute you demand 2Ki 18:14
doing each day * needed to be 1Ch 16:37
priests in * way they were needed. 1Ch 23:32
our cities—* the trouble is— 2Ch 6:28
and give each one * he deserves, 2Ch 6:30
* God says is what I will say." 2Ch 18:13
Persia gave them * assistance they Ez 1:6
may be used in * way you and your Ez 7:18
are to give Ezra * he requests of Ez 7:21
any amount of salt; and * else Ez 7:23
everywhere, * their rank, will be Est 1:20
these people—* you think best." Est 3:11
What do you wish? * it is, I will Est 7:2
Jews, telling them * you want to in Est 8:8
permission for * other decree Est 8:8f
to him. * you wish will happen! Job 22:28
* he wants to do, he does. Job 23:13
his hand, and do * he commands Job 37:12
He loves * is just and good; Ps 33:5
"It's fatal, * it is," they Ps 41:8
Every law of God is right, * it Ps 119:128
He does * pleases him throughout Ps 135:6
but the foolish man spends * he Pro 21:20
And I know this, that * God does Ecc 3:14
* is, has been long ago; Ecc 3:15
* is going to be has been before; Ecc 3:15
and enjoy his work * his job may Ecc 5:18
* they did in their Ecc 9:6
earthly toil. * you do, do well, Ecc 9:10
my people; * he says will be done; Is 22:22
"* the Lord says is good. Is 39:8
come to pass, for I do * I wish. Is 46:10
you and speak * I tell you to. Jer 1:7
and tell them * I tell you to say. Jer 1:17
they kept on doing * they wanted Jer 7:24
Instead they have done * they Jer 9:14
obey me and do * I commanded them, Jer 11:4
We have no intention * of doing Jer 18:12
speak to them * words I give you. Jer 19:1
"I have no intention * of doing Jer 37:14
to obey * he says we should do! Jer 42:5
We will do * we want to. Jer 44:17
will be like. Pack * you can carry Eze 12:3
Wherever you go, * you do, all is Eze 21:24
chunk by chunk in * order it Eze 24:6
obey my laws and do * I command. Eze 36:27
guilt offerings. * anyone gives to Eze 44:29
with the ram, and * amount he is Eze 46:5
With the lamb, he is to bring * Eze 46:7
began to play, everyone—* his Dan 3:7
he does * he thinks best among Dan 4:35
You have made no progress *. Hos 10:9
give me my pay, * I am worth; Zec 11:12
away as Syria. And * their illness Mt 4:24
Kingdom of Heaven; * doors you lock Mt 16:19
in heaven; and * doors you open on Mt 16:19
And I tell you this—* you bind Mt 18:18
in heaven, and * you free on earth Mt 18:18
* was right at the end of the day. Mt 2
and I am willing to do * he wants. Lk 1
and running over. * measure you use Lk 6
hidden wickedness. * is in the Lk 6
question * is set before you. Lk 1
(1) Eat * is set before you. Lk 10:
evident as yeast in dough. * they Lk 1
will have to take * seat is left at Lk 1
"Do * he tells you to." Jn
so * he tells me to say, I say!" Jn 12
"* is he saying?" Jn 16:17
say, 'Kill and eat * you wish.' Act 1
close to the Lord, * the cost. Act 11
and argued against * Paul said. Act 13
of sex sin, and do * they wanted Rom 1
He will give each one * his Rom
you want to do * God said not to, Rom
no obligations * to your old sinful Rom 8:
Pay everyone * he ought to have: Rom 1
one * praise is coming to him. 1Co
* situation God has put you into. 1Co 7
So, dear brothers, * situation a 1Co 7:
I want you to do * will help you 1Co 7:
me help them. Yes, * a person is 1Co 9:
you want to. Eat * is on the table 1Co 10:
others, it would be of no value *. 1Co 1
The local language, * it is. 1Co 14
But * I am now it is all because 1Co 15:
seed of wheat, or * it is you are 1Co 15:
be strong; and * you do, do it 1Co 16:
I do too. And * I have forgiven (to 2Co 2:
Each of us will receive * he 2Co 5:
for your benefit. * we do, it is 2Co 5:13,
and to us, for * directions God 2Co 8
as gladly, giving * you can out of 2Co 8:
you can out of * you have. 2Co 8:
you believe * anyone tells you even 2Co 1
like that! But * they can boast 2Co 11:
he reaches * age his father set. Gal 4
special abilities—* he wants us to Eph 4
and do * the Lord wants you to. Eph 5:
here in jail! But * their motive Php 1:
But * happens to me, remember Php 1:
* HAPPENS, DEAR friends, be glad Php 3
die with him. So, * it takes, I Php 3:
hearts. And * you do or say, let Col 3:
with others * God has given them. 1Ti 6:
that you could do * was needed to Tit 1
For * God says to us is full of Heb 4:
sacred tent and on * instruments Heb 9:
But * is good and perfect comes Jas 1:
willing to do * God told him to; Jas 2:
[Let him do * criticizing must be Jas 5
masters and do * they tell you—not 1Pe 2:
They do * they feel like; 2Pe 2:
For a man is a slave to * 2Pe 2:
trust, and get * we ask for 1Jn 3:2
we can believe * God declares. 1Jn 5:
If we love God, we will do * he 2Jn 1
animals, they do * they feel like, Jud 1:
doing * evil they feel like; Jud 1:1
I will give to each of you * you Rev 2:2

WHATSOEVER
we assume no responsibility *; Jos 2:

WHEAT
One day during the * harvest, Gen 30:1
bloom), but the * and the emmer Ex 9:3
made with finely ground * flour. Ex 29.
First *, and the Harvest Festival. Ex 34:2
stray grains of * from the ground. Lev 19:
it is a land of * and barley, of Deu 8:
And the finest of the *; Deu 32:1
had been threshing * by hand in the Ju 6:1
LATER ON, DURING the * harvest, Ju 15:
and then the * harvest, too. Ru 2:2
were reaping * in the valley, and 1Sa 6:1
of the year, during the * harvest; 1Sa 12:1
to get a sack of *, but then 2Sa 4:6,
serving bowls, * and barley flour, 2Sa 17:28,2
125,000 bushels of * for his 1Ki 5:1
eat the volunteer *, and use it as 2Ki 19:2
who was threshing * at the time. 1Ch 21:19,2
use the * for the grain offering. 1Ch 21:2
sacks of crushed *, 20,000 barrels 2Ch 2:1
So send along the *, barley, 2Ch 2:1
of *, and 10,000 sacks of barley. 2Ch 27:
and give them *, wine, salt, and Ez 6:
1,225 bushels of *; Ez 7:2
*, and weeds instead of barley." Job 31:4
barns with plenty of the finest *. Ps 147:1
your barns with * and barley and Pro 3:9,1
is like a heap of * set about Sol 7:2
My people have sown * but reaped Jer 12:1
a difference between chaff and *! Jer 23:28
good crops, the * and the wine and Jer 31:12
their treasures of *, barley, oil Jer 41:8
like the * upon a threshing floor; Jer 51:33
flour mixed from *, barley, beans, Eze 4:9
with * from Minnith and Pannag, Eze 27:17
Or, "with *, minnith and Eze 27:17f
a bushel of * or barley for every Eze 45:13

EAT Con't)
eep for the * and the barley Joe 1:11
h again with *, and the presses Joe 2:24
em your moldy *— the Lord, the Amo 8:6
ads of * and eating the grain. Mt 12:1
d sowed thistles among the *. Mt 13:25
ou'll hurt the * if you do. Mt 13:29
em, and put the * in the barn.' Mt 13:30
the thistles and the *. Mt 13:36
stles among the * is the devil; Mt 13:39
ads of * and eating the grain. Mk 2:23
the heads of *, rubbing off the Lk 6:1
thousand bushels of *,' was Lk 16:7
sift you like *, but I have Lk 22:31
e a kernel of * that falls into Jn 12:23,24
oduce many new * kernels—a Jn 12:23,24
throwing all the * overboard. Act 27:38
hen it is treading out the *. 1Co 9:9
y little seed of *, or whatever 1Co 15:37
terally, "A choenix of * for a Rev 6:6f
d fine flour; *, cattle, sheep, Rev 18:13

EAT-HEADS
d later the * formed and finally Mk 4:28

EEDLING
r *, until he yielded to her. Pro 7:21

EEL
e * is broken at the cistern; Ecc 12:6
threshing * is never rolled on Is 28:27
und the potter working at his *. Jer 18:3
em, one * belonging to each. Eze 1:15
nber and each * was constructed Eze 1:16
ith a second * crosswise inside. Eze 1:16
terally, "a * within a wheel," Eze 1:16f
terally, "a wheel within a *," Eze 1:16f
ach of the four cherubim had a * Eze 10:9-13
e had a second * crosswise Eze 10:9-13
hat is, the * was a living part Eze 10:17f

EELED
they * around to attack him. 1Ki 22:32,33
hen the king dismantled the * 2Ki 16:17

EELS
heir chariot * began coming Ex 14:25
on't we hear the sound of the *?' Ju 5:28
ad four bronze * and bronze axles, 1Ki 7:27-30
he stands rode on four * which 1Ki 7:32
f the stands. The * were 1Ki 7:32
nd were similar to chariot *. 1Ki 7:33
oofs, and the * of their chariots Is 5:28
as the chariots go rushing by; Jer 47:3
his, I saw four * on the ground Eze 1:15
each. The * looked as if they Eze 1:16
he four * had rims and spokes, Eze 1:18
he * moved forward with them. Eze 1:19,20,21
When they flew upwards, the * Eze 1:19,20,21
eings stopped, the * stopped. Eze 1:19,20,21
our living beings was in the *; Eze 1:19,20,21
pirit went, the * and the living Eze 1:19,20,21
he sound of their * beside them. Eze 3:13
he whirling * beneath the cherubim Eze 10:2
rom between the *, the man went in Eze 10:6
eside one of the *, and one of Eze 10:6
f the construction of these *, Eze 10:9-13
Each of the four * was covered Eze 10:9-13
nto the air the * rose with them, Eze 10:15,16
o did the *, for the spirit Eze 10:17
f the cherubim was in the *. Eze 10:17
lew with their * beside them to Eze 10:19
he air with their * beside them, Eze 11:22
n on flaming *, and a river of Dan 7:9
against her, * rumbling, horses' Nah 3:2

HENEVER
* he went in to sleep with her, Gen 38:9
was winning; but * he rested his Ex 17:11
Aaron shall wear the ephod * he Ex 28:35
These are to be worn * Aaron and Ex 28:43
And Jehovah said to Moses, "* Ex 30:11,12
* Moses went to the Tabernacle, Ex 33:8
but * he went into the Ex 34:34
and feet there. * they walked past Ex 40:32
the Tabernacle. * the cloud lifted Ex 40:36
"* a man's semen goes out from Lev 15:16
"* a woman menstruates, she Lev 15:19
of mercy are, just * he chooses. Lev 16:1
Tabernacle, and * the Tabernacle Num 1:51
These three tribes led the way * Num 2:3-31
in line * the Israelis traveled. Num 2:3-31
They brought up the rear * Israel Num 2:3-31
is to remind you, * you notice the Num 15:39
So Moses made the replica, and * Num 21:9
against him. * anyone is judged Num 35:31
here among us * we call upon him? Deu 4:7
of Ephraim, and * a fugitive from Ju 12:5
to excite him * he visited the Ju 13:25
So she cried * she was with him Ju 14:17
send out a servant * anyone was 1Sa 2:13,14
the Hebrews. So * the Israelites 1Sa 13:20
lifetime. And * Saul saw any brave, 1Sa 14:52
to play for you * the tormenting 1Sa 16:15,16
And * the tormenting spirit from 1Sa 16:23
harp, as he did * this happened. 1Sa 18:10
passing day. * the Philistine army 1Sa 18:30
* they face this place to pray; 1Ki 8:30
O Lord, hear and answer them * 1Ki 8:52
these instead. * the king went to 1Ki 14:28
and afterwards, * he passed that 2Ki 4:8
a place to stay * he comes by." 2Ki 4:10
needs repairing. * anyone brings a 2Ki 12:4,5
into it. * the chest became full, 2Ki 12:10
"* someone commits a crime, and 2Ch 6:22
of his bodyguard. * the king went 2Ch 12:11
you stay with him! * you look for 2Ch 15:2
God's laws. But * they have turned 2Ch 15:4
honest hearts. * a case is 2Ch 19:10
a time like this—* we are faced 2Ch 20:9
our work. And * the workers who Neh 4:12
conquer them. Yet * your people Neh 9:28
in deep reverence * he passed by, Est 3:2
of wisdom. But * she jumps up to Job 39:18
I will call to you * trouble Ps 86:7
Enjoy prosperity * you can, and Ecc 7:14
and over in simple words * he can; Is 28:13
no other Savior. * you have thrown Is 43:12
you in my hand. * I announce that Jer 18:7
all evil, so that * anyone wants to Jer 29:22
and cold. And * Jehudi finished Jer 36:23
for Israel; * I send my people a Eze 3:17
for they are rebels. But * I Eze 3:27
help from Egypt. * she thinks of Eze 29:16
will be cleansed. * anyone sees Eze 39:15,16
with each bushel. * the prince Eze 46:12
and care for you. * you enter a Mt 10:11
And * those possessed by demons Mk 3:11
such strength that * he was put Mk 5:3,4
"And * a village won't accept Mk 6:11
Herod was disturbed * he talked Mk 6:20
by a demon. And * the demon is in Mk 9:18
you can aid them * you want to; Mk 14:7
"* you enter a home, give it Lk 10:5
at midnight. But * he comes there Lk 12:38
the Sabbath, too, * you obey Moses' Jn 7:21,22,23
then prophesy * you can—as often as Rom 12:6
Do this in remembrance of me * 1Co 11:25
but rejoices * truth wins out. 1Co 13:6
But * anyone turns to the Lord 2Co 3:16
That's why * we can we should Gal 6:10
resist the enemy * he attacks, and Eph 6:13
his great peace. * we pray for you Col 1:3
uses to catch them * he likes, and 2Ti 2:26
at all times, * you get the chance, 2Ti 4:2
of the first room * they wanted to, Heb 9:6
will listen to us * we ask him for 1Jn 5:14
marvelous things * the first Rev 13:14

WHEREAS
to know the Lord; * a united family 1Co 7:14

WHEREIN
visit every city * we proclaimed Act 15:36f
Literally, "* righteousness 2Pe 3:13f

WHEREUPON
to receive it, * Ehud reached Ju 3:21
* the Lord said to him, "But I, Ju 6:16

WHEREVER
to keep track of him * he goes?" Gen 4:9
to mention, * we come, that you are Gen 20:13
will protect you * you go, and will Gen 28:15
And you shall live among us * you Gen 34:9,10
and * he went the shout arose, Gen 41:43
Go and find it * you can; Ex 5:10,11
from head to foot * he looks, then Lev 13:12
units to * the camp is traveling; Num 4:15
to * it stopped, and camped there. Num 9:17
be. * you go, the land is yours. Deu 11:24
* you go, just as he has promised. Deu 11:25
the heathen altars * you find Deu 12:2
I said to Moses: "* you go will be Jos 1:3
your God is with you * you go." Jos 1:9
altar of the Lord—* it would be Jos 9:27
for I want to go * you go, and to Ru 1:16
you go, and to live * you live; Ru 1:16
let the cows go * they want to. 1Sa 6:8
* he turned, he was successful. 1Sa 14:47
I have been with you * you have 2Sa 7:9
So the Lord gave him victories * 2Sa 8:6
made him victorious * he went. 2Sa 8:14
your own life that * you go, I will 2Sa 15:21
in everything you do, * you turn. 1Ki 2:3
the coast to * you need them; 1Ki 5:9
of the band * there was room. 1Ki 7:36
have done * they have gone; 2Ki 19:11
repairing the wall * it was broken 2Ch 32:5
and people lived * their family Neh 11:20
let the wealthy live * they chose. Job 22:8
for she goes * the slain are." Job 39:30
his neck strikes terror * he goes. Job 41:22
strength and protects me * I go. Ps 18:32
in the markets and * you look. Ps 55:11
Hear my prayer! For * I am, Ps 61:2
angels to protect you * you go. Ps 91:11
He turns them * he wants to. Pro 21:1
and their God. * they look there Is 8:22
bless his people. * they plant, Is 32:20
what has happened * the kings of Is 37:11
of sinning, and * you go you leave Is 59:7
"for you will go * I send you and Jer 1:7
from there, * you are scattered. Jer 3:14
crags. * you run to escape my Jer 16:16
the kings of Judah—* incense has Jer 19:13
of my flock from * I have sent Jer 23:3
and cursed * I compel them to go. Jer 24:9
you * you go, as your reward. Jer 45:5
covered his body. * their spirit Eze 1:12
in the wheels; so * their spirit Eze 1:19,20,21
"Tell Israel, * you look—east, Eze 7:2
* you will, wherever you want. Eze 21:16
wherever you will, * you want. Eze 21:16
and unashamed. * you go, whatever Eze 21:24
will be healed. * this water flows, Eze 47:9
Prospering * he turns, he will Dan 8:24
near and far * you have driven us Dan 9:7
* I look there is oppression and Hab 1:3
and west, * they are scattered. Zec 8:7
They will go * they wish, and Zec 10:12
they wish, and * they go, they will Zec 10:12
Enormous crowds followed him * Mt 4:25
the Kingdom. And * he went he Mt 9:35
return. And * the carcass is, Mt 24:28
* the Good News is preached." Mt 26:13
and stretchers. * he went—in Mk 6:56
solemn truth, that * the Good News Mk 14:9
no moth can destroy them. * your Lk 12:34
were following him * he went, to Jn 6:2-5
you liked and go * you wanted to; Jn 21:18
following Philip * he went, and was Act 8:13
permitted to live * he wanted to, Act 28:16
Let me say first of all that * I Rom 1:8
He will punish sin * it is found. Rom 2:12-15
* they go they leave misery and Rom 3:16
Yes, for it has gone * they are; Rom 10:18
teach in all the churches * I go. 1Co 4:17
and * there is sin, death results. 1Co 15:22
us so that now * we go he uses us 2Co 2:14
all together from * we are—in Eph 1:10
boundaries, for * we go we find 1Th 1:8
and triumph * it goes, winning 2Th 3:1
turn around and go * we want by Jas 3:3
a huge ship turn * the pilot wants Jas 3:4
by the devil. For * there is Jas 3:16
following the Lamb * he goes. Rev 14:4

WHET
That I will * the lightning of my Deu 32:40,41

WHETS
My son, honey * the appetite, and Pro 24:13,14

WHICHEVER
the sin sacrifice * bird is handed Lev 5:8
two young pigeons—* he is able to Lev 14:22
(* pair he is able to afford). Lev 14:30
and punish * one of us is guilty. 1Sa 24:15
The prophets of Baal may choose * 1Ki 18:23

WHIM
At his * they rose or fell. Dan 5:19
you should obey their every *! Mt 23:3
on some mere human * or dream. Gal 1:11
your every *, and now your fat Jas 5:5

WHIMS
of the universe to suit your *? Job 34:33

WHINED
are as good as dead," they *. Num 17:12,13
they *. Num 21:5
she *. Ju 16:15
Amaziah *. 2Ch 25:9

WHINING
And they turned against Moses, *, Ex 14:11

WHIP
Guide a horse with a *, a donkey Pro 26:3
Why will you force me to * you Is 1:5,6
his people and the * that scourges Is 9:4
Assyria is the * of my anger; Is 10:5,6
I give my back to the *, and my Is 50:6
And I replied, "I see a * made Jer 1:11
and severely * you and send you Mt 24:51
with a leaded *, and handed him Mk 15:15
and begins to * the men and women Lk 12:45
Jesus made a * from some ropes Jn 2:15
back with a leaded *, and the Jn 19:1
legal for you to * a Roman citizen Act 22:25

WHIPPED
Then they * the Israeli Ex 5:14
the man to be *, and fine him one Deu 22:17,18
like a reed * about in a stream; 1Ki 14:15
and had him * and put in the stocks Jer 20:2
tried, and * in the synagogues. Mt 10:17
And after he had * Jesus, he gave Mt 27:26
the chief priests * up the mob to Mk 15:11
he had ordered him bound and *. Act 22:29
jail oftener, been * times without 2Co 11:23

WHIPPINGS
the scars of the * and wounds from Gal 6:17

WHIPS
My father used * on you, but I'll 1Ki 12:11
My father used * on you, but I'll 2Ch 10:11
"My father punished you with *, 2Ch 10:14
with their *, the Lord is good. Ps 129:3,4
Hear the crack of the * as the Nah 3:2
of others with * in your Mt 23:34

(WHIPS Con't)
flog me with their * and kill me; Mk 10:34
stripped and beaten with wooden *. Act 16:22
* to make him confess his crime. Act 22:24
cut open with *, and others were Heb 11:36
When he * you it proves you are Heb 12:6

WHIRL
They * and sway beneath the blast. Ps 29:9

WHIRL-WHEELS
beside him—"The *," as I heard Eze 10:9-13

WHIRLED
cyclone and the wicked are * away. Pro 10:25

WHIRLING
wind, like * dust before a storm. Is 17:13
in between the * wheels beneath the Eze 10:2

WHIRLWIND
Elijah to heaven—by means of a *! 2Ki 2:1
was carried by a * into heaven. 2Ki 2:11
You throw me into the * and Job 30:22
THE LORD answered Job from the *: Job 38:1
spoke to Job again from the *: Job 40:6
There was thunder in the *; Ps 77:18
like a * sweeping from the Negeb. Is 21:1
thunder, earthquake, * and fire. Is 29:6
his chariots are like a *; Jer 4:13
* to sweep away these wicked men. Jer 23:19
to nation—a great * of wrath shall Jer 25:32
Suddenly the devastating * of the Jer 30:23
with the strength and fury of a *; Dan 11:40
the wind and they will reap the *. Hos 8:7
shepherding a *—a dangerous game! Hos 12:1
battle like a * in a mighty storm. Amo 1:14
came out like a *, thinking Israel Hab 3:14
I scattered them as with a * Zec 7:14
a * off the desert from the south. Zec 9:14

WHIRLWINDS
all away; * shall scatter them. Is 41:16

WHISKEY
O Lemuel, to drink wine and *. Pro 31:4

WHISPER
there was the sound of a gentle *. 1Ki 19:12
he does, merely a * of his power. Job 26:14
They * together about what they Ps 41:7
Your voice will * like a ghost Is 29:4
I do not * obscurities in some Is 45:19
their houses and * about you at the Eze 33:30
What I * in your ears, proclaim Mt 10:27
Jesus' chest," to * his inquiry. Jn 13:25f

WHISPERED
David's men * to him. 1Sa 24:4
for sure," Abishai * to David. 1Sa 26:8
in secret, as though * in my ear. Job 4:12
bend low and hear my * Ps 31:2
they poured forth a * prayer. Is 26:16
Yet on every side I hear their * Jer 20:10
say about me and their * plans. Lam 3:62
and what you have * in the inner Lk 12:3

WHISPERING
But when David saw them *, he 2Sa 12:19
My enemies are *, "God has Ps 71:10
of the city, * to men going by, Pro 9:15
"Son of dust, your people are * Eze 33:30
each other and * behind each 2Co 12:20

WHISPERINGS
Don't listen to their * and Is 8:19

WHISPERS
or beloved wife * to you to come Deu 13:6,7

WHISTLE
be amazed and will * with 1Ki 9:8
At that time the Lord will * for Is 7:18
When I * to them, they'll come Zec 10:8

WHISTLING
nations far away, * to those at the Is 5:26

WHIT
idol that can help him not one *! Is 44:10
You didn't care a * about my Is 47:7

WHITE
Then if you ever find any * Gen 30:33
spotted with any * patches, and all Gen 30:35,36
trees, and peeled * streaks in Gen 30:37
told me that I should mate the * Gen 31:12
out again, it was * with leprosy! Ex 4:6
it was *, like coriander seed, Ex 16:31
If the hair in this spot turns *, Lev 13:3
"But if the * spot in the skin Lev 13:4
has not turned *, the priest shall Lev 13:4
see if there is a * swelling in the Lev 13:9,10
in the skin with * hairs in the Lev 13:9,10
leprosy, for it has all turned *; Lev 13:13
later changes to *, the leper will Lev 13:16,17
turned completely *, then the Lev 13:16,17
but which leaves a * swelling or a Lev 13:19
sort of reddish *, the man must go Lev 13:19
spot has turned *, then the priest Lev 13:20
that there are no * hairs in this Lev 13:21
reddish-white or *, then the Lev 13:24
bright spot turns *, and the Lev 13:25
that there are no * hairs in the Lev 13:26
"If a man or a woman has *, Lev 13:38
there is a reddish * spot, it may Lev 13:42
there is a reddish * lump that Lev 13:43
and only three quarts of fine * Lev 14:21
suddenly became * with leprosy. Num 12:10
Those who ride on * donkeys Ju 5:10
a leper, his skin as * as snow. 2Ki 5:27
The decorations were green, *, Est 1:6
black, red, *, and yellow marble. Est 1:6
robes of blue and * and the great Est 8:15
is the uncooked * of an egg—my Job 6:5,6,7
We will clothe the priests in *, Ps 132:9
* hair is a crown of glory and is Pro 16:31
Your teeth are * as sheep's Sol 4:2
Your teeth are * as freshly Sol 6:6
crimson, I can make you * as wool! Is 1:18
that black is * and white is Is 5:20
that black is white and * is Is 5:20
even when your hair is * with age. Is 46:4
from Helbon, and * Syrian wool to Eze 27:18
His clothing was as * as snow, Dan 7:9
trunks and branches * and bare. Joe 1:7
bay and *, each with its rider. Zec 1:8
the third by * horses and the Zec 6:3
by * horses will follow it there, Zec 6:6
for you can't turn one hair * or Mt 5:36
his clothing became dazzling *. Mt 17:2
his clothing was a brilliant *. Mt 28:3
became dazzling *, far more Mk 9:3
sat a young man clothed in *. Mk 16:5
and his clothes became dazzling * Lk 9:29
head—the hair—was * like wool." Rev 1:14f
was * as wool or snow, and his Rev 1:14
and I will give to each a * Rev 2:17
they shall walk with me in *, for Rev 3:4
will be clothed in *, and I will Rev 3:5
And to purchase from me * Rev 3:18
all were clothed in *, with Rev 4:4
in front of me was a * horse. Rev 6:2
on the earth?" * robes were given Rev 6:11
Lamb, clothed in *, with palm Rev 7:9
in *, and where they come from?" Rev 7:13
and I saw a * cloud, and someone Rev 14:14
in spotlessly * linen, with golden Rev 15:6
Then I saw heaven opened and a * Rev 19:11
in finest linen, * and clean, Rev 19:14
clean, followed him on * horses. Rev 19:14
the one riding the * horse, and all Rev 19:21
And I saw a great * throne and Rev 20:11

WHITE-HAIRED
and of falling—a *, withered old Ecc 12:5

WHITE-ROBED
in and saw two * angels sitting at Jn 20:12
suddenly two * men were standing Act 1:10

WHITE-STREAKED
So the flocks mated before the * Gen 30:39,40

WHITENED
"they washed their robes and * Rev 7:14

WHITENESS
in all its lovely *, and scatters Ps 147:16

WHITER
and his teeth are * than milk. Gen 49:12
Wash me and I shall be * than Ps 51:7
purer than snow, * than milk, more Lam 4:7f

WHITEST
as snow, his hair like * wool. Dan 7:9
and * and finest of linens." Rev 19:8

WHITEWASH
them for it—and cover it with *! Eze 13:10
Why did you * it and cover up its Eze 13:12
Thus they repair the walls with * Eze 22:28

WHITEWASHED
I will break down your * wall, Eze 13:14
shall slap you, you * pigpen. Act 23:3
Literally, "you * wall." Act 23:3f

WHITHER
you is asking me * I am going." Jn 16:5f

WHITTLE
to * down the size of Israel. 2Ki 10:32,33

WHO'S
"Hey, * that girl over there?" Ru 2:4,5
your mind! * trying to kill you?" Jn 7:20

WHOLE
of the * earth—to be cursed. Gen 3:14
under the * heaven, standing Gen 7:19
and Gomorrah); the * section was Gen 13:10
servant told Isaac the * story. Gen 24:66
a furnace, and the * mountain shook Ex 19:18
Lord appeared to the * assembly. Lev 9:23
then the * estimate shall stand; Lev 27:17
cattle of the * nation." Num 3:41
For one * month you will have Num 11:19,20
promise them meat for a * month! Num 11:21
population of this * Num 32:3,4
be easy to conquer the * area. Deu 1:41
throughout the * earth tremble with Deu 2:25
took over the * Argob region Deu 3:14
the * way he has laid out for you; Deu 5:32
* earth to be his own chosen ones. Deu 7:6
They will see that the * land is Deu 29:23
song to the * assembly of Israel: Deu 31:30
who is Lord of the * earth, will Jos 3:11
army conquered the * country—the Jos 10:40
"The * congregation of the Lord Jos 22:16
My family is the poorest in the * Ju 6
But Joash retorted to the * mob, Ju 6
wrung out a * bowlful of water! Ju 6
and watched as the * vast enemy Ju 7
from Egypt; the * territory from Ju 1
be a priest to a * tribe in Israel Ju 18
So the * nation united in this Ju 20
gleaned, it came to a * bushel! Ru 2
girls right through the * harvest; Ru 2
have ravaged the * land—the capital 1Sa 6
to the Lord as a * burnt offering 1Sa
you need a * army to settle this? 1Sa 1
a wife, and his * family will be 1Sa 17
animals, and the * world will know 1Sa 17
to fight the * Philistine army!" 1Sa 2
* time they have been in Carmel. 1Sa 2
us the * time they were with us. 1Sa 25:15
our master and his * family—he's 1Sa 25
Thus the * nation, both Judah 2Sa 3
returned, and the * city is 1Ki 1:44
King Solomon ruled the * area 1Ki 4
(For the Lord had made the * 2Ki
in and kill the * bunch of them. 2Ki 10
presence of the * assembly, David 1Ch 29
Then a * gang of worthless 2Ch 1
forth across the * earth, looking 2Ch 1
of Ahab, and his * life was one 2Ch 2
throughout the * land of Israel 2Ch 3
Our * history has been one of sin; Ez
they did the * thing—cut the Neh
one bit of truth to the * story. Neh
You subdued * nations before Neh 9
the * kingdom of Ahasuerus. Est 3:
and heard the * story from him; Est
the innocent. The * earth is in Job 9:
are misinterpreting the * thing. Job 1
when your * premise is so wrong?" Job 21:
* earth, under all the heavens. Job 28:23,
joy. The * earth shall see it and Ps 22:
and my * body is diseased. Ps 38
* lifetime is but a moment to you. Ps 39:
Let the * earth be filled with Ps 72:
to Israel. The * earth has seen Ps 98:2
Let the * earth shake. Ps 99
The * city celebrates a good Pro 11:
man cannot see the * scope of God's Ecc 3:
that youth, with a * life before Ecc 11:
Lord of Hosts; the * earth is Is 6
left—and the * country is an utter Is 6:
across the * land, even into the Is 7:
* nation will be a pastureland; Is 7:21,
be a pastureland; * flocks and Is 7:21,
them and will destroy your * land. Is 13
But at last the * earth is at Is 14
This is my plan for the * Is 14:
of Willows. The * land of Moab is Is 15
What are they looking at? The * Is 22
In that day the * land of Judah Is 26
fill the * earth with her fruit! Is 27
Let's see if the * collection of Is 57:
among you, and the * city of Jer 3:
The * land trembles at the Jer 8:
King. The * earth shall tremble at Jer 10:
I hear its mournful cry. The * Jer 12:
travel through the * country, Jer 14:
the Lord, when the * topic of Jer 16:14,1
this * city will be destroyed. Jer 27:
until the * scroll was destroyed. Jer 36:2
Because the * land is full of Jer 50:3
oh, the terror. The * earth Jer 50:4
against that * land of the Jer 51:
made the * earth drink and go mad. Jer 51:
and desolate the * day through. Lam 1:1
For the * lot of them are hard, Eze 3:
sins, leading the * nation into Eze 8:1
So says the Lord. The * country Eze 26:1
and sell the * land to wicked men. Eze 30:1
animals of the * earth will devour Eze 32:
got possession of the * country! Eze 33:2
"The * world will rejoice when I Eze 35:1
the * earth revolves around them!' Eze 38:1
in each tier. The * structure was Eze 41:
waters and the * landscape lighted Eze 43:
Then the * statue collapsed into Dan 2:3
mountain that covered the * earth. Dan 2:3
be ruler over the * province of Dan 2:4
it will devour the * world, Dan 7:2
for dew—and the * grand chorus Hos 1:21,2
For in those days the * world Mic 4:
Ethiopia and the * land of Egypt Nah 3:
For the * land will be devoured Zep 1:18
have patrolled the * earth, and Zec 1:1
sorrow. The * nation will be Zec 12:12,13,14
your * nation has been robbing me. Mal 3:
for the * wide world belongs to Mt 5:
the pigs, and the * herd rushed Mt 8:32
the * world—and lose eternal life? Mt 16:26
and then the * cup will be clean. Mt 23:26
throughout the * world, so that all Mt 24:14
throughout the * world, wherever Mt 26:13
That afternoon, the * earth Mt 27:45

HOLE Con't)
ın throughout the * area to spread Mk 6:55
ınd the * crowd ate until they Mk 8:8,9
he gains the * world and loses Mk 8:36
riests and the * Jewish Supreme Mk 14:55
Vonder fell upon the * Lk 1:65
vildfire throughout the * region. Lk 4:37
nmediately the * herd rushed down Lk 8:33
ınd the * crowd was badly Lk 8:35
nd buy enough for this * mob?" Lk 9:13
ı gaining the * world when it Lk 9:25
o him than a * flock of sparrows. Lk 12:7
nd be rejected by this * nation. Lk 17:25
f Olives, the * procession began Lk 19:36,37
larkness fell across the * land Lk 23:44
Or, "the * world." Lk 23:44f
But the * group was terribly Lk 24:37
f we let him alone the * nation Jn 11:48
hould the * nation perish?" Jn 11:50
Look—the * world has gone after Jn 12:19
vere written, the * world could Jn 21:25
praising God. The * city was Act 2:47
This sounded reasonable to the * Act 6:5
eventually the * country would Act 7:5
Then the * population of Lydda Act 9:35
Then Peter told them the * story. Act 11:4
and elders and the * congregation Act 15:22
This indicates how deeply the * Act 19:20
The * population of the city was Act 21:30
to give the * earth to Abraham and Rom 4:13
Literally, "The * creation has Rom 8:22f
Now if the * world became rich Rom 11:12
he has enriched your * life. 1Co 1:5
He has given you the * world to 1Co 3:22
Suppose the * body were an 1Co 12:17
Or if your * body were just one 1Co 12:17
be of real help to the * church. 1Co 14:12
sea all night and the * next day. 2Co 11:25
my own age in the * country, and Gal 1:14
For the * Law can be summed up Gal 5:14
that * system of Jewish laws. Eph 2:15
Under his direction the * body is Eph 4:15,16
parts, so that the * body is Eph 4:15,16
displayed to the * world Christ's Col 2:15
life, for then the * church will Col 3:14
brothers throughout your * nation. 1Th 4:10
have missed this * idea and spend 1Ti 1:6
how can he help the * church? 1Ti 3:5
in front of the * church so that no 1Ti 5:20
in Christ Jesus. The * Bible 2Ti 3:16
to boldly preach a * sermon for all 2Ti 4:17
Already * families have been Tit 1:11
And so a * nation came from Heb 11:12
Abraham a * nation of descendants! Heb 11:18
they made * armies turn and run Heb 11:34
and can turn our * lives into a Jas 3:6
Isn't it because there is a * Jas 4:1
it because your * aim is wrong—you Jas 4:3
destroyed the * world of ungodly 2Pe 2:5
the Lord saved a * nation of people Jud 1:5
scoffers whose * purpose in life is Jud 1:18
one deceiving the * world—was Rev 12:9

WHOLEHEARTED
and give them your * love because 1Th 5:13
They must be earnest, * 1Ti 3:9
It is * and straightforward and Jas 3:17

WHOLEHEARTEDLY
of Nun)—for they * followed the Num 32:12
"You must * obey all of these Deu 26:16
have begun * to obey all of the Deu 30:2
As long as I live I'll * obey. Ps 119:33,34
other and agreeing * with each Php 2:2

WHOLESALE
slaughtered * on Mount Gilboa. 1Sa 31:1
agents purchased them at * prices. 1Ki 10:28
purchase entire herds at * prices. 2Ch 1:16
to commit adultery * and to gang up Jer 5:7

WHOLESOME
the food was * and good, without Ex 16:24
My advice is * and good. Pro 8:8
a sweet, * fragrance in our lives. 2Co 2:15
we claim by our * lives and by our 2Co 6:6
living in the * fear of God, giving 2Co 7:1
are the sound, * teachings of the 1Ti 6:3

WHOLLY
disgraced in man, * evil as he is. Gen 6:3
because he had * followed the Lord, Deu 1:36
those who were * dedicated to God. 1Sa 1:11f
omit verse 37 * or in part. Act 8:37f
law itself was * right and good. Rom 7:12

WHOMSOEVER
and appoint over them * I please. Jer 50:44

WHORE
"You son of a *!" Ju 11:1

WHORES
and off they go to find some *. Hos 4:18

WICKED
even though he does such * things. Gen 8:21
were unusually *, and sinned Gen 13:13
and that everything they do is *. Gen 18:20
to kill the godly with the *! Gen 18:25
godly and * exactly the same! Gen 18:25
begged, "don't do such a * thing. Gen 19:7
But Er was a * man, and so the Gen 38:7
How can I do such a * thing as Gen 39:9
What a * thing you have done!' Gen 44:5
May I never be a party to their * Gen 49:6
"I will not acquit the *." Ex 23:7f
and what a * bunch they are. Ex 32:22
these * people complain about me? Num 14:26,27
the tents of these * men, and don't Num 16:26
not—you are a *, stubborn people. Deu 9:6
But the * shall be silenced in 1Sa 2:9
As that old proverb says, '* is 1Sa 24:13
'Wicked is as * does,' but despite 1Sa 24:13
The victim of a * plot." 2Sa 3:33,34
May the Lord repay * men for 2Sa 3:39
wicked men for their * deeds." 2Sa 3:39
more shall I do to * men who kill a 2Sa 4:11
And what about all the * things 1Ki 2:44
But he was even more * than his 1Ki 16:30
man, but not as * as his father and 2Ki 3:2
But he was as * as Ahab and the 2Ki 8:18
he followed the * paths of 2Ki 13:2
he was as * as the kings of 2Ki 16:3
and is even more * than the 2Ki 21:11
But the oldest son, Er, was so * 1Ch 2:3
again; the * nations won't conquer 1Ch 17:9
turn from their * ways, I will hear 2Ch 7:14
"Should you be helping the *, and 2Ch 19:2
of Israel, who was a very * man. 2Ch 20:35
But he was as * as the kings who 2Ch 21:6
Yes, as * as Ahab, for Jehoram 2Ch 21:6
(The followers of * Athaliah had 2Ch 24:7,8
Esther replied, "This * Haman is Est 7:6
For there in death the * cease Job 3:17
and the fangs of the * are broken. Job 5:16
with shame, and the * destroyed." Job 8:22
perfect, God would prove me *. Job 9:20
earth is in the hands of the *. Job 9:24
send joy and prosperity to the *? Job 10:3
But the * shall find no way to Job 11:20
"A * man is always in trouble Job 15:20
"This * man is fat and rich, and Job 15:27,28
sinners, into the hands of the *. Job 16:11
prosper, it is because you are *. Job 18:5
"The confident stride of the * Job 18:7
the triumph of the * has been Job 20:5
all the * shall destroy him. Job 20:22
This is what awaits the * man, Job 20:29
"The truth is that the * live on Job 21:7
"Look, everything the * touch Job 21:16
Yet the * get away with it every Job 21:17
me of rich and * men who came to Job 21:28
the innocent shall laugh the * to Job 22:19
even glean the vineyards of the *. Job 24:6
"The * snatch fatherless Job 24:9
"The * rebel against the light Job 24:13
him any more. For * men are broken Job 24:20
otherwise are my * enemies. Job 27:7
"This is the fate awaiting the * Job 27:13
Every house built by the * is as Job 27:18
this: God is never * or unjust. Job 34:12
nobles, 'You are * and unjust'? Job 34:18
openly strikes them down as * men. Job 34:26
* way you have talked about God. Job 34:36
He does not reward the * with Job 36:6
the haunts of * men and stopped the Job 38:15
tread down the * where they Job 40:12
flatteries to gain their * ends. Ps 5:9
he is angry with the * every day. Ps 7:11
The * man conceives an evil plot, Ps 7:14
and destroyed the *, blotting out Ps 9:5
the * in their own snares! Ps 9:16
The * shall be sent away to hell; Ps 9:17
these proud and * men who viciously Ps 10:2
These * men, so proud and Ps 10:4
Why do you let the * get away Ps 10:13
Break the arms of these * men. Ps 10:15
For the * have strung their bows, Ps 11:2
He puts the righteous and the * Ps 11:5
brimstone on the * and scorch them Ps 11:6
Don't punish me with all the * Ps 28:3
But let the * be shamed by what Ps 31:17
Many sorrows come to the *, but Ps 32:10
will surely overtake the *; Ps 34:21
the hearts of the *, forever urging Ps 36:1
Don't let their * hands push me Ps 36:11
NEVER ENVY THE *! Ps 37:1
For the * shall be destroyed, Ps 37:9
Only a little while and the * Ps 37:10
and you will see the * destroyed. Ps 37:34
Because of his * heart, his dark Ps 53:1
put an end to these * men, O God. Ps 54:5
fields of slaughtered, * men. Ps 58:10
* men, these gangs of criminals. Ps 64:1
So let the * perish at the Ps 68:2
the prosperity of the proud and *. Ps 73:3
I am ready, I will punish the *! Ps 75:2
I told the * to lower their Ps 75:4
out upon the * of the earth. Ps 75:8
shower special favors on the *? Ps 82:2
nor shall the * overpower him. Ps 89:22
I will see how the * are Ps 91:8
that although the * flourish like Ps 92:7
Lord, how long shall the * be Ps 94:3
Who will protect me from the *? Ps 94:16
and rescues them from the *. Ps 97:10
heaven to consume these * men. Ps 106:18
of the * into deserts of salt. Ps 107:34
* slander me and tell their lies. Ps 109:2
Though the * hide along the way Ps 119:95
to your laws. The * have set their Ps 119:110
themselves. The * are the scum you Ps 119:119
promised. The * are far from Ps 119:155
For the * shall not rule the Ps 125:3
Surely you will slay the *, Lord! Ps 139:19
Don't let these * men succeed; Ps 140:6,7,8
against the * and their deeds. Ps 141:5
who love him, but destroys the *. Ps 145:20
topsy-turvy the plans of the *. Ps 146:9
but brings the * into the dust. Ps 147:6
* men, for the Lord is with you; Pro 3:24,25,26
The curse of God is on the *, but Pro 3:33
Don't do as the * do. Pro 4:14
The * man is doomed by his own Pro 5:22
for you a worthless and a * man; Pro 6:12,13
* man's riches continue forever. Pro 10:3
of the * conceals violence." Pro 10:6f
names of * men stink after them. Pro 10:7
The * man's fears will all come Pro 10:24
and the * are whirled away. Pro 10:25
so how can the * expect a long, Pro 10:27
the upright but destroys the *. Pro 10:29
but the * shall lose everything. Pro 10:30
is helpful; the * speak rebellion. Pro 10:32
their honesty; the * shall fall Pro 11:5
while letting the * fall into it. Pro 11:8
decay of the * drives it downhill. Pro 11:11
while the * can expect only wrath. Pro 11:23
how much more the *! Pro 11:31
good men and condemns the *. Pro 12:2
The * accuse; the godly defend. Pro 12:6
The * shall perish; Pro 12:7
is constant trouble for the *. Pro 12:21
the * plunge ahead—and fall. Pro 12:26
A good man hates lies; * men lie Pro 13:5
Literally, "but the * never get Pro 13:25f
The work of the * will perish; Pro 14:11
the * are crushed by their sins. Pro 14:32
good, but trouble dogs the *. Pro 15:6
The Lord hates the gifts of the * Pro 15:8
the deeds of the *, but loves those Pro 15:9,10
the thoughts of the * but delights Pro 15:26
The Lord is far from the *, but Pro 15:29
the *, for punishment. Pro 16:4
The * man stares into space with Pro 16:30
* sons and share their estate. Pro 17:2
The * enjoy fellowship with Pro 17:4
fellowship with others who are *; Pro 17:4
The * live for rebellion; Pro 17:11
the * and condemn the innocent. Pro 18:5
Literally, "the tillage of the * Pro 21:4f
Because the * are unfair, their Pro 21:7
by watching ruin overtake the *. Pro 21:12
The * will finally lose; Pro 21:18
Literally, "the * is a ransom for Pro 21:18f
Or, "The * man is brazen; Pro 21:29f
of the *. Pro 22:12
Don't envy the *. Pro 24:19,20
He who says to the *, "You are Pro 24:24
with the *, it is like polluting a Pro 25:26
Pretty words may hide a * heart, Pro 26:23
THE * FLEE when no one is chasing Pro 28:1
When the * succeed, everyone is Pro 28:12
A * ruler is as dangerous to the Pro 28:15
When the * prosper, good men go Pro 28:28
when the * meet disaster, good Pro 28:28
but with the * in power, they Pro 29:2
A * ruler will have wicked aides Pro 29:12
A wicked ruler will have * aides Pro 29:12
When rulers are *, their people Pro 29:16
good hate the badness of the *. Pro 29:27
* hate the goodness of the good. Pro 29:27
and some of the * live on and on. Ecc 7:15-17
On the other hand, don't be too * Ecc 7:15-17
I have seen * men buried and as Ecc 8:9,10
off, unlike the *, who will not Ecc 8:13
though they were *, and some wicked Ecc 8:14
* men as though they were good. Ecc 8:14
see you doing all these * things; Is 1:16
But say to the *, "Your doom Is 3:11
letting the * go free and putting Is 5:23
are all filthy-mouthed, * liars. Is 9:17
He will rule against the * who Is 11:4
for its evil, the * for their sin; Is 13:11
For the Lord has crushed your * Is 14:5
Your kindness to the * doesn't Is 26:10
* rebels, come, return to God. Is 31:6
peace, says the Lord, for the *. Is 48:22
Let men cast off their * deeds; Is 55:7
Literally, "the *." Is 57:20f
Among my people are * men who Jer 5:26

(WICKED Con't)
is no limit to their * deeds. Jer 5:28
they continue in their * ways. Jer 6:29
If you stop your * thoughts and Jer 7:5
Why are the * so prosperous? Jer 12:1
and weeps over their * deeds! Jer 12:4
Because of the * things that Jer 15:4
you from these * men and rescue you Jer 15:21
thing there is, and desperately *. Jer 17:9
the prophets, all ungodly, * men. Jer 23:11
to sweep away these * men. Jer 23:19
He will slaughter all the *. Jer 25:31
burst upon the heads of the *. Jer 30:23
back from your * ways and to stop Jer 35:15
turn back from their * ways; Jer 44:5
soon be ruined. O * daughter, you Jer 49:4
But he was a * king, just as Jer 52:2
If you refuse to warn the * when Eze 3:18
has been even more * than the Eze 5:5,6,7
and * men of pride shall live. Eze 7:10,11
foreigners and to * men as booty. Eze 7:21
for all of the * counsel being Eze 11:1
* that the Lord has deported them. Eze 11:15
to the nations how * they have Eze 12:16
And you have encouraged the * by Eze 13:22
your own eyes how * they are, and Eze 14:22
as * as you and your daughters. Eze 16:48
the * person for his wickedness. Eze 18:20
But if a * person turns away Eze 18:21
you think I like to see the * die? Eze 18:23
to turn from his * ways and live. Eze 18:23
And if a * person turns away Eze 18:27
with all the other *, for when the Eze 21:29
and sell the whole land to * men. Eze 30:12
When I say to the *, 'O wicked Eze 33:8
When I say to the wicked, 'O * Eze 33:8
not repent—that * person will die Eze 33:8
no pleasure in the death of the *; Eze 33:11
I desire that the * turn from his Eze 33:11
And when I tell the * he will Eze 33:14
But if the * turns from his Eze 33:19
But the * shall continue in their Dan 12:10
priests are *, the people are too. Hos 4:9
and people for all their * deeds. Hos 4:9
The homes of the * are full of Mic 6:10
courts, for the * far outnumber the Hab 1:4
We are *, but they far more! Hab 1:13
Should you be silent while the * Hab 1:13
"Note this: * men trust Hab 2:4
You crushed the head of the * and Hab 3:13
no one heeds—the * know no shame. Zep 3:5
by * leaders, who go unpunished. Zec 11:5
of their own * leaders, and they Zec 11:6
part of a worthless, * shepherd. Zec 11:15
I will move swiftly against * men Mal 3:5
The proud and * will be burned up Mal 4:1
Then you will tread upon the * Mal 4:3
Truly, the * cities of Sodom and Mt 10:15
had been done in * Tyre and Sidon Mt 11:21
and separate the * people from the Mt 13:49
casting the * into the fire; Mt 13:50
"He will put the * men to a Mt 21:41
of being the sons of * men. Mt 23:31
"But his master replied, '* man! Mt 25:26
were the * farmers in his story. Mk 12:12
am betrayed into the hands of * Mk 14:41
Even the most * will lend to Lk 6:34
and to those who are very *. Lk 6:35
preach—even the most * of them Lk 7:29
Even * Sodom will be better off Lk 10:12
'You vile and * slave,' the Lk 19:22
They were the * tenants in his Lk 20:19
When you say they are * and Rom 2:1
Remove this evil cancer—this * 1Co 5:7
punishment their * deeds deserve. 2Co 11:15
big, and saying * things about each 2Co 12:20
care about the *, impure things you 2Co 12:21
us, doing every * thing that our Eph 2:3
and against huge numbers of * Eph 6:12
Watch out for those * Php 3:2
Then this * one will appear, 2Th 2:8
many evil pleasures and * desires. Tit 3:3
any more in the * things they do, 1Pe 4:4
just escaped from such * living. 2Pe 2:18
escaped from the * ways of the 2Pe 2:20
mistakes of these * men, lest you 2Pe 3:17
any evil teacher in this * world. 1Jn 4:4
only Son into this * world to bring 1Jn 4:9
is doing and what * things he is 3Jn 1:10

WICKEDNESS
extent of human *, and that the Gen 6:5
for the * of the Amorite nations Gen 15:16
and to do so is horrible *. Lev 18:17
land become full of enormous *. Lev 19:29
to wipe out * from among you. Lev 20:14
No, it is because of the * of Deu 9:4
because of the * of the other Deu 9:5
Oh, please overlook the awful * Deu 9:27
fear such * as this among you. Deu 13:11
of your * in asking for a king!" 1Sa 12:17
your *, I'll not touch you. 1Sa 24:13
Please forgive this foolish * of 2Sa 24:10
because of our * (and we have been Ez 9:13
stand here before you in our *?" Ez 9:15
they refused to turn from their *. Neh 9:35
Just the slightest *, and I am Job 10:15
hearts give birth only to *." Job 15:35
in every home where there is *. Job 18:6
"He enjoyed the taste of his *, Job 20:12
It is because of your *! Job 22:5
the earth, to end the night's *? Job 38:13
I know you get no pleasure from * Ps 5:4
are filled to the brim with *. Ps 5:9
End all *, O Lord, and bless all Ps 7:9
to them in proportion to their *; Ps 28:4
but all who love * shall perish. Ps 37:28
How you love *—far more than Ps 52:3
ever more bold in their *." Ps 52:7
"strengthened himself in his *." Ps 52:7f
is internal—* and dishonesty are Ps 55:10
of *. For Jehovah God is our Ps 84:10
They eat and drink * and Pro 4:17
* never brings real success; Pro 12:3
are being destroyed by their *. Pro 13:6
* loves company—and leads others Pro 16:29
about the law is to praise *. Pro 28:4
to myself the * of folly, and that Ecc 7:25
Certainly a man's * is not going Ecc 8:8
He will burn up all this *, Is 9:18
away from * and do what is right. Is 26:9
You felt secure in all your *. Is 47:10
Your own * will punish you. Jer 2:19
of all the * of my people Israel. Jer 7:12
It is because of the * of Israel Jer 11:17
O Lord, we confess our *, and Jer 14:20
full of stubbornness and *!" Jer 18:12
into a place of shame and *. Jer 19:4
will see your * and be ashamed. Jer 22:22
For it is because of them that * Jer 23:15
No, they turned from their * and Jer 26:19
of all their *, and I will not pity Jer 33:5
Because of all their * they lie Jer 44:2,3
loathe themselves for all this *. Eze 6:9
the morning dawns, for your * and Eze 7:10,11
see the * going on in there!" Eze 8:9
to all your other *—woe, woe upon Eze 16:23
But now your greater * has been Eze 16:57
all his father's *, so that he Eze 18:14
and the wicked person for his *. Eze 18:20
away from his * and obeys the law, Eze 18:27
you despite your *, then, O Israel, Eze 20:44
and burn out the * within you. Eze 22:15
is pitted with rust and with *. Eze 24:6
For her * is evident to all—she Eze 24:7
to destroy her as her * deserves. Eze 31:11
Turn, turn from your *, for why Eze 33:11
turns from his * and does what's Eze 33:19
*, I consumed them in my anger. Eze 43:8
and are full of *, yet because of Dan 9:15
continue in their *, and none of Dan 12:10
The king is glad about their *; Hos 7:3
All their * began at Gilgal; Hos 9:15
But you have cultivated * and Hos 10:13
Israel, because of your great *. Hos 10:15
with the * of these men. Joe 3:13
you, for your * rises before me; Jon 1:2
lie awake at night, plotting *; Mic 2:1
for the great * of her people. Mic 7:13
He said, "She represents *," Zec 5:8
center of world idolatry and *. Zec 5:11f
named 'The Land of *' and their Mal 1:4
destroyed by God for their *. Mt 11:21f
destroyed by God for their *. Mt 11:23f
belongs to others, *, deceit, Mk 7:22
concession to your hardhearted *. Mk 10:5
evil deeds from his hidden *. Lk 6:45
by God in judgment for their *. Lk 10:13f
still dirty—full of greed and *! Lk 11:39
Turn from this great * and pray. Act 8:22
and who can express the * of the Act 8:33
of every kind of * and sin, of Rom 1:29
of *, to be used for sinning; Rom 6:13
life with all its hatreds and *. 1Co 5:8
its * that did that sort of thing; Col 3:9
It is full of *, and poisons Jas 3:6
of the terrible * he saw everywhere 2Pe 2:7,8
be a partner with him in his *. 2Jn 1:11

WICKS
it with fresh oil and trim the *. Lev 24:3,4

WIDE
Make it 450 feet long, 75 feet * Gen 6:15
long, 2¼ feet *, and 2¼ feet high. Ex 25:10
gold, 3¾ feet long and 2¼ feet *. Ex 25:17
long, 1½ feet *, and 2¼ feet high. Ex 25:23
Put a molding four inches * Ex 25:25
long and six feet *, dyed blue, Ex 26:1
feet across and six feet *. Ex 26:7,8
tarpaulins into one * section; Ex 26:9
other six for another * section. Ex 26:9
each of these two * pieces, to join Ex 26:10,11
high and 2¼ feet *, standing Ex 26:15,16
7½ feet *, and three feet high. Ex 27:1
*, with ten posts and ten sockets. Ex 2
long, and 75 feet *, with curtain Ex 2
feet long and six feet *). Ex 36:1
long, 2¼ feet *, and 2¼ feet high. Ex
it was 3¾ feet long and 2¼ feet * Ex
long, 1½ feet * and 2¼ feet high. Ex 3
west side was seventy-five feet *; Ex 3
side was also seventy-five feet *. Ex 3
were 22½ feet *, each with three Ex 38:1
long and 7½ feet *, just the same Ex 3
a half feet long by six feet *. Deu
the city gates were left * open. Jos
You have made * steps for my 2Sa 2
feet *, and forty-five feet high. 1Ki
being 7½ feet *, the second floor 9 1Ki
floor 9 feet *, and the upper floor 1Ki
and the upper floor 10½ feet *. 1Ki
feet *, and thirty feet high. 1Ki
long, 75 feet *, and 45 feet high. 1Ki
forty-five feet *, with a porch in 1Ki
each 7½ feet high, and 6 feet *. 1Ki 7:1
At the same moment a * crack 1Ki
he dug a trench about three feet * 1Ki 1
"with a * leather belt." 2Ki
feet long and thirty feet *. 2Ch
feet *, and fifteen feet high. 2Ch
"Yes, O my God, be * awake and 2Ch
I will listen, * awake, to every 2Ch
from danger into a * and pleasant Job 3
You have made * steps beneath my Ps 1
Yes, open * the gates and let Ps
Open your mouth * and see if I Ps 8
You open * your hand to feed them Ps 104
he created—his * world and all his Pro 8
Before every man there lies a * Pro 14
Before every man there lies a * Pro 16
feared far and *, a conquering, Is 1
eyes of Israel will open * to God; Is 3
will be to us as a * river of Is 33
Come to me with your ears * open. Is-5
Your gates will stay * open Is 60
For the * walls of Babylon shall Jer 51
is 10½ feet high and 10½ feet *." Eze 4
it was 10½ feet *. Eze 4
inches high and eighteen inches *. Eze 40:7
22¾ feet * and 17½ feet long. Eze 40:7
was 87½ feet long and 43¾ feet *. Eze 40
was 87½ feet long by 43¾ feet *. Eze 40:29,
was 87½ feet long by 43¾ feet *. Eze 40
The entrance was 24½ feet * with Eze 40:48,
Thus the entry hall was 35 feet * Eze 40:48
The entrance hall was 17½ feet * Eze 4
its doorway was 10½ feet *, with Eze 4
Each room was seven feet *. Eze 4
terrace yard, which was 8¾ feet *; Eze 41:
122½ feet * by 157½ feet long. Eze 41:
was also 175 feet *, and so was Eze 41:
was 175 feet long by 87½ feet *. Eze 4
rooms were not as * as the lower Eze 4
miles *. Eze 4
miles *. Eze 4
miles *, shall be the residence Eze 4
by 52½ feet *, enclosed by walls. Eze 46:21,
miles *. Eze 48
miles *, north to south, Eze 48:
miles *, south of the Temple Eze 48:
high and nine feet * and set it up Dan 3
will have a * ministry of teaching Dan 11:
Announce this far and *: Get Joe 3
will be opened * to the enemy and Nah 3:
feet long and fifteen feet *!" Zec 5
making a very * valley running from Zec 14
for the whole * world belongs to Mt 5
is broad, and its gate is * Mt 7:
had spread far and * and vast Mk 3:7
While * awake one afternoon he Act 10
the prison doors * open, and Act 16:2
for there is a * open door for me 1Co 16
the doors of welcome were * open. 2Co 6
how long, how *, how deep, and how Eph 3:18,
Everything about us is bare and * Heb 4:
And God will open * the gates of 2Pe 1:1
in heaven was thrown * open! Rev 15
was a square as * as it was long; Rev 21:1

WIDELY
languages, thus * scattering them Gen 11
are separated so * from each other, Neh 4:1
"those who have read * in many Dan 1:3,
Their story spread * among the Mt 28:1
will be * known and honored. Lk 21:1
"What I teach is * known, for I Jn 18:2
Commentators differ * in their 1Jn 5:17

WIDEN
on! * the pathway before him! Lk 3:

WIDENED
He has * the boundaries of our Is 26:1

WIDER
than the earth and * than the sea. Job 11:
Each tier was * than the one Eze 41:
tiers had * walkways beside them. Eze 42:

WIDEST
and even the * torrents freeze. Job 37:1

WIDOW
and to remain a * there until his Gen 38:11
intercourse with his uncle's *, Lev 20:20
If a man marries his brother's *, Lev 20:21
He may not marry a *, nor a Lev 21:14,15
But if she is a * or divorced Lev 22:13
"But if the woman is a * or is Num 30:9
not sleep with his father's * Deu 22:30
without a son, his * must not marry Deu 25:5
to marry the *, then she shall go Deu 25:7
refuses, the * shall walk over to Deu 25:9
foreigner, the orphan, and the *.' Deu 27:19
the Moabitess, the * of Mahlon, to Ru 4:10
and Abigail of Carmel, Nabal's *. 1Sa 27:2,3
and Abigail the * of Nabal from 2Sa 2:2
Abigail, the * of Nabal of Carmel. 2Sa 3:3
"I am a *," she replied, "and 2Sa 14:5,6
being the son of a * of the tribe 1Ki 7:14
his mother was Zeruah, a *. 1Ki 11:26
There is a * there who will feed 1Ki 17:8,9
city he saw a * gathering sticks; 1Ki 17:10
this * with whom I am staying?" 1Ki 17:20
Then Er's *, Tamar, and her 1Ch 2:4
his father's *, and she gave birth 1Ch 2:24
fatherless and his wife a *; Ps 109:9,10
I'll never be a *; Is 47:8
Like a * broken with grief, she Lam 1:1
maiden, or the * of a priest; Eze 44:22
(his mother was the * of Uriah); Mt 1:6
should marry the * and their Mt 22:24
children, so his * became the Mt 22:25
should marry his * and have Mk 12:19
married the *, but soon he died Mk 12:20,21,22
Then a poor * came and dropped Mk 12:42
"That poor * has given more than Mk 12:43,44
for she had been a * for Lk 2:36,37
to help the * of Zarephath—a Lk 4:25,26
for everyone. A * of that city Lk 18:3
shall marry the * and their Lk 20:28
His brother married the * and Lk 20:30
Then a poor * came by and Lk 21:2
"this poor * has given more than Lk 21:3
A * who wants to become one of 1Ti 5:9
Literally, "enrolled as a *." 1Ti 5:9f
I am no helpless *. Rev 18:7

WIDOW'S
she laid aside her * clothing and Gen 38:14
wearing her * clothing as usual. Gen 38:19
a * garment in pledge of her debt. Deu 24:17
Let me remind you again that a * 1Ti 5:16

WIDOWED
has sexual intercourse with his * Deu 27:23
Parents kept a * daughter-in-law Ru 1:11f
fathers dead, our mothers *. Lam 5:3
only son of his * mother, and many Lk 7:12

WIDOWHOOD
So they remained in virtual * 2Sa 20:3
in one day: * and the loss of your Is 47:9
and the sorrows of * will be Is 54:4

WIDOWS
"You must not exploit * or Ex 22:22
be * and your children fatherless. Ex 22:24
justice to the fatherless and *. Deu 10:18
foreigners, or to * and orphans Deu 14:29
foreigners, *, and orphans. Deu 16:11
orphans, and * of your town. Deu 16:14
for the migrants, orphans, and *; Deu 24:19
for the migrants, orphans, and *. Deu 24:20
*, so that they will be well fed. Deu 26:12
the *, just as you commanded me; Deu 26:13
You sent * away without helping Job 22:9
are taken. Poor * must surrender Job 24:3
They refuse to help the needy *. Job 24:21
And I caused the *' hearts to Job 29:13
the poor or caused * to weep, or Job 31:16
he gives justice to the *, for he Ps 68:5
and their * died before they could Ps 78:64
They murder *, immigrants, and Ps 94:6,7
and cares for the orphans and *. Ps 146:9
of the proud but cares for *. Pro 15:25
the poor, the fatherless, and *. Is 1:17
won't defend the * and orphans. Is 1:23
upon even the * and orphans, for Is 9:17
for the poor, the * and orphans. Is 10:2
rob the * and fatherless children. Is 10:2
orphans, * and foreigners. Jer 7:6
There shall be countless *; Jer 15:8
Let their wives be * and be Jer 18:21
and immigrants, orphans and *; Jer 22:3
and let your * depend upon me. Jer 49:11
orphans and * are wronged and Eze 22:7
they multiply the * in the land. Eze 22:25
You have driven out the * from Mic 2:9
Tell them to stop oppressing * Zec 7:10
hands, or oppress * and orphans, or Mal 3:5
are evicting * from their homes. Mt 23:13,14
shamelessly cheat * out of their Mk 12:40
There were many Jewish * needing Lk 4:25,26
to cheat * out of their property. Lk 20:47
that their * were being Act 6:1
as the * who spoke Hebrew. Act 6:1
with weeping * who were showing one Act 9:39
and *, presenting her to them. Act 9:41
married, and to *—better to stay 1Co 7:8
The church should care for * who 1Ti 5:5
The younger * should not become 1Ti 5:11
for these younger * to marry again 1Ti 5:14
for the care of * who are all alone 1Ti 5:16
of orphans and *, and who remains Jas 1:27

WIDTH
fifteen feet and the * 2¼ feet. Ex 36:21
entire thirty-foot * of the house, 2Ch 3:4
and the * will be ninety feet. Ez 6:3
the entire outside * of the Eze 40:13
of 87½ feet and a * of 43¾ feet. Eze 40:36
same length and * and the same Eze 42:11

WIDTHS
Thus the two * become one. Ex 26:10,11

WIELDS
"This message is from him who * Rev 2:12

WIFE
is joined to his * in such a way Gen 2:24
Now although the man and his * Gen 2:25
listened to your * and ate the Gen 3:17
The man named his * Eve (meaning Gen 3:20
Adam and his * with garments made Gen 3:21
with Eve his *, and she conceived Gen 4:1
Then Cain's * conceived and Gen 4:17
To Lamech's other *, Zillah, was Gen 4:22
* and your sons and their wives. Gen 6:18
He boarded the boat with his * Gen 7:7
very day with his * and his sons, Gen 7:13
Noah, his *, and his sons and Gen 8:18,19
He took his * Sarai, his nephew Gen 12:5
he asked Sarai his * to tell Gen 12:11,12,13
you they will say, 'This is his *. Gen 12:11,12,13
didn't you tell me she was your *? Gen 12:18
escort—Abram, his *, and all his Gen 12:20
with his *, and Lot, and all that Gen 13:1
her to Abram to be his second *. Gen 16:2,3
her the privilege of being your *. Gen 16:5
Sarai your *—her name is no longer Gen 17:15
"Where is Sarah, your *?" Gen 18:9
Lot, "take your * and your two Gen 19:15
the hands of his * and two Gen 19:16
But Lot's * looked back as she Gen 19:26
'They will want my * and will Gen 20:11,12
and returned Sarah his * to him. Gen 20:14
Abimelech for taking Abraham's *. Gen 20:18
over the boy or your slave-girl *; Gen 21:12
that Milcah, the * of Abraham's Gen 22:20-23
land, with no place to bury my *. Gen 23:4
and find a * for him there." Gen 24:4
girl from there to be my son's *. Gen 24:7
you have appointed as Isaac's *. Gen 24:14
and his * Milcah. Gen 24:15,16
the * of Nahor," she replied. Gen 24:24
"Now when Sarah, my master's *, Gen 24:36
to be the * of my master's son.' Gen 24:44
son of Nahor and his * Milcah.' Gen 24:47
Yes, let her be the * of your Gen 24:51
tent, and she became his *. Gen 24:67
Keturah was his new *, and she Gen 25:1
Sarah, Abraham's * was buried. Gen 25:9,10
if he told them she was his *; Gen 26:7
and exclaimed, "She is your *! Gen 26:9
this man or his * shall die." Gen 26:11
blessing, to get a * from there, Gen 28:6,7,8
you'll give me Rachel as my *." Gen 29:18
"Now give me my *, so that I can Gen 29:21
Bilhah to be his *, and he slept Gen 30:4
Jacob, to be his *, and soon Gen 30:9
and longs for her to be his *. Gen 34:8
me have her as my *," he begged. Gen 34:11
give me the girl as my *." Gen 34:12
Descended from his * Adah, born Gen 36:10,11,12
grandchildren from his * Basemath. Gen 36:13,14
to Esau and his * Basemath while Gen 36:17
of Esau and his * Oholibamah Gen 36:18,19
King Hadad's * was Mehetabel, Gen 36:31-39
In the process of time Judah's * Gen 38:12
time Potiphar's * began making eyes Gen 39:7
yourself because you are his *. Gen 39:9
And he gave him a *, a girl named Gen 41:45
'You know that my * had two sons, Gen 44:27
buried Abraham and Sarah his *; Gen 49:31
buried Isaac and Rebekah his *; Gen 49:31
of the girls, Zipporah, as his *. Ex 2:21
Egyptian master's * and neighbors. Ex 3:22
So Moses took his * and sons and Ex 4:20
Then Zipporah his * took a flint Ex 4:25,26
Then Jethro took Moses' *, Ex 18:2
your * and your two sons." Ex 18:5,6
to sleep with his *, or want to own Ex 20:17
a slave, then his * shall be freed Ex 21:3
But if his master gave him a * Ex 21:4
or daughters, the * and children Ex 21:4
my master, my *, and my children, Ex 21:5
then takes another *, he may not Ex 21:10
fail to sleep with her as his *. Ex 21:10
and accept her as his *. Ex 22:16
nor your aunt—the * of your Lev 18:14
your daughter-in-law—your son's *; Lev 18:15
nor your brother's *, for she is Lev 18:16
in which case his * was left to a Lev 18:16f
However, if your * dies, then it Lev 18:18
nor with anyone else's *, to Lev 18:20
with another man's *, both the man Lev 20:10
with his father's *, he has defiled Lev 20:11
Literally, "his uncle's *." Lev 20:20f
Literally, "his brother's *." Lev 20:21f
that if a man's * commits adultery, Num 5:11,12
shall bring his * to the priest Num 5:15
a wayward *—or a husband's Num 5:29
against his *— to determine Num 5:29
Moses because his * was a Cushite Num 12:1
referring to his * Zipporah, the Num 12:1f
is to a second * of Moses. Num 12:1f
the * of Amram, son of Kohath. Num 26:58,59
a man and his * and between a Num 30:16
for another man's *, nor envy him Deu 5:21
or beloved * whispers to you to Deu 13:6,7
your *, take her home with you. Deu 21:11
oldest son is the * he doesn't Deu 21:15
son, the son of the * he loves. Deu 21:16
of the * his father doesn't love. Deu 21:17
this man to be his *, and now he Deu 22:16
She shall remain his * and he may Deu 22:19
the other man's * must be killed; Deu 22:22
Literally, "his father's *." Deu 22:30f
about his *, he may write a letter Deu 24:1
to be at home, happy with his *. Deu 24:5
fighting and the * of one Deu 25:11
and his beloved * and his children Deu 28:54
Achsah to be the * of anyone who Jos 15:16
it, so Achsah became Othni-el's *. Jos 15:17
my daughter Achsah as his *!" Ju 1:12
a prophetess, the * of Lappidoth. Ju 4:4
tent of Jael, the * of Heber the Ju 4:17
The * of Heber the Kenite— Ju 5:24
by his legitimate *, and when these Ju 11:1
appeared to the * of Manoah, of the Ju 13:2,3
* as she was sitting in the field. Ju 13:9
Manoah ran back with his * and Ju 13:11
talked to my * the other day?" Ju 13:11
sure that your * follows the Ju 13:13,14
as Manoah and his * watched, the Ju 13:20
Manoah and his * fell face Ju 13:20
his *, "for we have seen God!" Ju 13:22
But his * said, "If the Lord Ju 13:23
"Why must you go and get a * Ju 14:3
said to his new *, "Get the answer Ju 14:15
So Samson's * broke down in tears Ju 14:16
and abandoned his * and went back Ju 14:19
So his * was married instead to Ju 14:20
*, intending to sleep with her; Ju 15:1
That afternoon as he and his * Ju 19:9
virgin daughter and this man's *. Ju 19:24
raped my * until she was dead. Ju 20:5
With him were his *, Naomi, and Ru 1:1
"Make me your * according to Ru 3:9
Mahlon, to be my *, so that she can Ru 4:10
Phinehas's *, who was pregnant, 1Sa 4:19
Saul's * was Ahino-am, the 1Sa 14:50,51
daughters for a *, and his whole 1Sa 17:25
oldest daughter Merab as your *. 1Sa 18:17
His name was Nabal and his *, a 1Sa 25:3
and when his * told him what had 1Sa 25:37,38
to ask her to become his *. 1Sa 25:39
So she became his *. 1Sa 25:42
had forced David's * Michal, Saul's 1Sa 25:44
was Amnon, born to his * Ahino-am. 2Sa 3:2
me my * Michal, Saul's daughter." 2Sa 3:13
"Give me back my * Michal, for I 2Sa 3:14
of Eliam and the * of Uriah. 2Sa 11:3
Why didn't you go home to your * 2Sa 11:10
wine and dine and sleep with my *? 2Sa 11:11
murdered Uriah and stolen his *. 2Sa 12:9
insulted me by taking Uriah's *. 2Sa 12:10
The man's * put a cloth over the 2Sa 17:19
grandsons of Saul by his * Aiah. 2Sa 21:8
daughter Merab, the * of Adri-el. 2Sa 21:8
the Shunammite, as my *." 1Ki 2:17
a *—the sister of Queen Tahpenes. 1Ki 11:19
Jeroboam told his *, "Disguise 1Ki 14:2
So his * went to Ahijah's home at 1Ki 14:4
out, "Come in, * of Jeroboam! 1Ki 14:6
Then Ahijah said to Jeroboam's *, 1Ki 14:12
So Jeroboam's * returned to 1Ki 14:17
his *, Jezebel, asked him. 1Ki 21:5
apart the body of your *, Jezebel. 1Ki 21:23
as Ahab, for his * Jezebel 1Ki 21:25
ONE DAY THE * of one of the 2Ki 4:1
given to Naaman's * as a maid. 2Ki 5:2
Dogs shall eat Ahab's * Jezebel 2Ki 9:10
the * of Jehoiada the High Priest. 2Ki 11:2,3f
daughter to be a * for my son.' 2Ki 14:9
(She was the * of Shallum—son of 2Ki 22:14
city of Pai (his * was Mehetabel, 1Ch 1:50
two girls (by the same *) named 1Ch 2:16
Jerahmeel's second * Atarah was 1Ch 2:26
The sons of Abishur and his * 1Ch 2:29
* of Jarha, his Egyptian servant. 1Ch 2:34,35

(WIFE Con't)
to his *, Ahino-am of Jezreel. 1Ch 3:1
the son of his * Maacah, who was 1Ch 3:2
Ithream, the son of his * Eglah. 1Ch 3:3
While he was in Jerusalem, his * 1Ch 3:5
Eshtemoa's * was a Jewess; 1Ch 4:18
Hodiah's * was the sister of 1Ch 4:19
Naphtali (descendants of Jacob's * 1Ch 7:13
Machir's *, also named Maacah, 1Ch 7:16
Afterwards, his * conceived and 1Ch 7:23
land of Moab by Hodesh, his new *: 1Ch 8:8,9,10
His * Hushim had borne him Abitub 1Ch 8:11
Jeiel (whose * was Maacah) lived 1Ch 9:35,36,37
Jerusalem, David's * Michal, the 1Ch 15:29
Solomon now moved his * (she was 2Ch 8:11
and the * of Jehoiada the priest. 2Ch 22:11
prophetess, the * of Shallum (son 2Ch 34:22
Everyone who has a heathen * will Ez 10:14
day is out, the * of every one of Est 1:18
and Zeresh his *, and boasted to Est 5:10
"Well," suggested Zeresh his * Est 5:14
When Haman told Zeresh his * and Est 6:13
His * said to him, "Are you Job 2:9
My own * and brothers refuse to Job 19:17
for another man's *, then may I Job 31:9
I die, and may my * be in another Job 31:10
fatherless and his * a widow; Ps 109:9,10
to the childless *, so that she Ps 113:9
Your * shall be contented in Ps 128:3
faithful and true to your *. Pro 5:15
rejoice in the * of your youth. Pro 5:18
commits adultery with another's *. Pro 6:29
A worthy * is her husband's joy Pro 12:4
The man who finds a * finds a Pro 18:22
* annoys like constant dripping. Pro 19:13
If you can find a truly good *, Pro 31:10
of life, for the * God gives you is Ecc 9:9
Jerusalem, once my faithful *! Is 1:21
to Isaiah's young * and her newborn Is 7:14f
with my * and she conceived, and Is 8:3
young * abandoned by her husband. Is 54:6
Like a wanton * who gives herself Jer 3:6
you have been like a faithless * Jer 3:20
them as a husband does his *." Jer 31:32f
Yes, you are an adulterous * who Eze 16:32
Adultery with a neighbor's *, a Eze 22:11
going to take away your lovely *. Eze 24:16
and in the evening my * died. Eze 24:18
II's former * Laodice, was the Dan 11:7f
*—I am no longer her husband. Hos 1:2
"Go, and get your * again and Hos 3:1
and earned a * by tending sheep. Hos 12:12
interference, your * will become a Amo 7:17
your best friend—not even your *! Mic 7:5
as a husband for his captive *. Zec 1:14
You were united to your * by the Mal 2:15
Keep faith with the * of your Mal 2:15
hesitate to take Mary as your *! Mt 1:20
home to be his *, but she remained Mt 1:24
to be rid of his *, he can divorce Mt 5:31
who divorces his *, except for Mt 5:32
his * Herodias, his brother Mt 14:3
the debt, also his * and children Mt 18:25
and be forever united to his *. Mt 19:5,6
may divorce his * by merely writing Mt 19:7
who divorces his *, except for Mt 19:9
sisters, father, mother, *, Mt 19:29
became the second brother's *. Mt 22:25
children, and the * was passed to Mt 22:26
had been the * of each of them. Mt 22:26
So whose * will she be in the Mt 22:28
For she was the * of all seven of Mt 22:28
court, Pilate's * sent him this Mt 27:19
Herodias, his brother Philip's *. Mk 6:17,18
his * a letter of dismissal." Mk 10:4
and he and his * are united so Mk 10:8
a man divorces his * to marry Mk 10:11
And if a * divorces her husband Mk 10:12
In the resurrection, whose * will Mk 12:23
had been the * of each of them?" Mk 12:23
corps. (His * Elizabeth was, like Lk 1:5
* Elizabeth will bear you a son! Lk 1:13
I'm an old man now, and my * is Lk 1:18
Soon afterwards Elizabeth his * Lk 1:24
had not heard what his * had said. Lk 1:62f
his brother's *, and for many other Lk 3:19,20
Joanna, Chuza's * (Chuza was King Lk 8:3
he does his own father, mother, * Lk 14:26
"So anyone who divorces his * Lk 16:18
remember what happened to Lot's *! Lk 17:32
leaving home, *, brothers, parents, Lk 18:29
* will she be in the resurrection? Lk 20:33
* of Cleopas, and Mary Magdalene. Jn 19:25
Ananias (with his * Sapphira) who Act 5:1
* had agreed to this deception. Act 5:2
About three hours later his * Act 5:7
from Italy with his *, Priscilla. Act 18:2,3
Literally, "his own *." Act 24:24f
*, a Jewess. Act 24:24
and that Sarah his *, at ninety, Rom 4:19
and Rebecca his * was about to bear Rom 9:10-13
And you won't sin with his * or Rom 13:9
living in sin with his father's *. 1Co 5:1
man having his own *, and each 1Co 7:2
The man should give his * all 1Co 7:3
woman, and the * should do the same 1Co 7:3
for it belongs also to his *. 1Co 7:4
both husband and * to refrain from 1Co 7:5
of a husband or *, and others he 1Co 7:7
A * must not leave her husband. 1Co 7:10
husband must not divorce his *. 1Co 7:11
a Christian has a * who is not a 1Co 7:12
with the help of his Christian *. 1Co 7:14
And the * who isn't a Christian 1Co 7:14
But if the husband or * who isn't 1Co 7:15
husband or * should not insist that 1Co 7:15
and how to please his *. 1Co 7:33
The * is part of her husband as 1Co 7:39
about a * that is a believer?" 1Co 9:5f
I had a *, and if 1Co 9:5
about a * that is a believer?" 1Co 9:5f
you about: that a * is responsible 1Co 11:3
and one from his freeborn *. Gal 4:22
But the baby of the freeborn * Gal 4:23
in charge of his * in the same way Eph 5:23
For since a man and his * are now Eph 5:28
himself when he loves his *! Eph 5:28
(That the husband and * are one Eph 5:31
his *, and the two shall be one." Eph 5:31
love his * as a part of himself; Eph 5:33
and the * must see to it that she Eph 5:33
another man's *, because the Lord 1Th 4:6
He must have only one *, and he 1Ti 3:2
Deacons should have only one * 1Ti 3:12
they must have only one * and Tit 1:6
You are like an unfaithful * who Jas 4:4
Remember that you and your * are 1Pe 3:7
many to be Peter's * to whom 1Pe 5:13f
you the bride, the Lamb's *." Rev 21:9

WIFE'S
heard his * story, he was furious. Gen 39:19
father's * daughter; Lev 18:11
"because his * father gave her to Ju 15:6
and his * name was Maacah. 1Ch 8:29

WILD
God made all sorts of * animals Gen 1:25
the domestic and * animals of the Gen 3:14
and *—and reptiles and birds of Gen 7:14,15
domestic and * animals, and Gen 7:21
"All * animals and birds and Gen 9:2,3
and cattle and * animals—that I Gen 9:9,10,11
This son of yours will be a * Gen 16:9-12
one—free and untamed as a * ass! Gen 16:9-12
and killed by * animals, did I show Gen 31:39
that a * animal has eaten him. Gen 37:19,20
coat. A * animal has eaten him. Gen 37:33
torn to pieces by some * animal; Gen 44:28
But you are unruly as the * Gen 49:4
If it was attacked by some * Ex 22:13
attacked and killed by a * animal. Ex 22:31
and the * animals would become too Ex 23:29
and drink at a * party, followed by Ex 32:6
for food, * or domesticated, or the Lev 5:2
and killed by * animals, may be Lev 7:24
his hair grow in * disarray, and Lev 13:45
or is torn by * animals, must wash Lev 17:15
or is torn by * animals, for this Lev 22:8
Cattle and * animals alike shall Lev 25:6,7
crops that grow * in the fields. Lev 25:12
I will send * animals to kill Lev 26:22
Israel has the strength of a * ox. Num 23:18-24
Israel has the strength of a * ox, Num 24:3-9
men began going to * parties with Num 25:1
for if he did, the * animals would Deu 7:22
The * goat, the ibex, Deu 14:3,4,5
to the birds and * animals, and no Deu 28:26
I will set * beasts upon them, Deu 32:24
With the strong horns of a * ox Deu 33:17
with * thorns and briars. Ju 8:16
saw the Ark they went * with joy! 1Sa 6:13
and * animals," Goliath yelled. 1Sa 17:44
to the birds and * animals, and the 1Sa 17:46
"I never let my men run * when 1Sa 21:5
rocks and * goats of the desert. 1Sa 24:2
the day and the * animals from 2Sa 21:10
and came back with some * gourds. 2Ki 4:39
But just then a * animal passed 2Ki 14:9
Just then a * animal came by and 2Ch 25:18
* animals will leave you alone. Job 5:22
When * donkeys bray, it is Job 6:5,6,7
to be wise as a * donkey's colt is Job 11:12
Like the * donkeys in the Job 24:5
find that grows *, and must even Job 24:6
the mines. No * animal has ever Job 28:8
his power. The * animals hide in Job 37:8
"Who makes the * donkeys wild? Job 39:5
"Who makes the wild donkeys *? Job 39:5
"Will the * ox be your happy Job 39:9
Can you use a * ox to plow with? Job 39:10
or the * animals destroy them. Job 39:15
other * animals on which he preys. Job 40:20
and oxen, and * animals too, the Ps 8:7
from the horns of these * oxen. Ps 2
Literally, "the * beasts." Ps 74
us, and the * animals feed on us. Ps 8
made me as strong as a * bull. Ps 9
There the * donkeys quench their Ps 10
pastures for the * goats, and Ps 10
He feeds the * animals and the Ps 1
and cedars, the * animals and Ps 14
of God, the people run *; Pro 2
that grew were * and sour and not Is
Why did my vineyard give me * Is
will live on curds and * honey. Is 7:2
overnight. The * animals of the Is 1
birds and * animals to eat; Is
summer, and the * animals will gnaw Is
who consign Tyre to the * beasts. Is 2
cities empty. * herds of donkeys Is 3
ostriches. The * animals of the Is 3
the desert! The * animals in the Is 4
as * goats caught in a net. Is 5
Come, * animals of the field; Is
come, * animals of the forest, Is
You are a * donkey, sniffing the Jer
moving in on some * animal! Jer 4
So I will send upon them the * Jer
gone the birds and * animals. Jer 9
wicked deeds! The * animals and Jer 1
of vultures and * animals to pick Jer 1
is no grass. The * donkeys stand Jer 1
the vultures and * animals to Jer 1
apart by vultures and * animals. Jer 1
and * animals to feed upon. Jer 1
to the vultures and * animals. Jer 34
like a * sea in a raging storm. Jer 49
Hazor shall be a home for * Jer 49
it shall be a home for the * Jer 50
* animals lurking in the ruins. Lam 5
will come, but * animals will Eze 5
of dangerous * animals into the Eze 14
food to the * animals and birds. Eze 2
her twigs and the * animals will Eze 31
upon you and the * animals of the Eze 3
shall be eaten by * animals, and Eze 33
conquer them nor * animals attack. Eze 34
and * animals to devour you. Eze 3
everyone to eat. * animals rested Dan 4
him eat grass with the * animals! Dan 4
all to eat, the * animals living in Dan 4
and he lived among the * donkeys; Dan 5
* animals will eat their fruit. Hos 1
you and the * animals, birds, and Hos 1
She is a lonely, wandering * Hos
Even the * animals cry to you Joe 1
there will be * shouts of battle Amo 1
by your * and stormy waves. Jon
You terrified the * animals you Hab 2
All sorts of * animals will have Zep 2
his food was locusts and * honey. Mt
locusts and * honey were his Mk
tombs and in the * hills, screaming Mk
of Jesus were * with rage, and Lk 6:
Paul was like a * man, going Act
a * olive tree, were grafted in. Rom 11:
part of a * olive tree—and graft Rom 11:
Don't spend your time in * Rom 13:12,
there in fighting * beasts—those 1Co 15:
drunkenness, * parties, and all Gal 5:
leading up to God—* ideas that stir 1Ti 1:3
* or disobedient to their parents. Tit 1
getting drunk, * parties, drinking 1Pe 4
along the beach by the * waves. Jud 1:
famine and disease and * animals. Rev 6

WILDERNESS
She hiked out into the * of Gen 21:
he grew up in the * of Paran, and Gen 21:20,
"Go into the * to meet Moses." Ex 4:
out into the *, for a religious Ex 5
trip into the * and sacrifice there Ex 5
* and sacrificing to their God. Ex 5:7
people go to worship him in the *. Ex 7:
Don't go out into the *." Ex 8:
trip into the * and sacrifice there Ex 8:
a route through the Red Sea *. Ex 13:17,
in Etham at the edge of the *. Ex 13:2
Egyptians than dead in the *." Ex 14:1
moved out into the * of Shur and Ex 15:2
the Sihn *, between Elim and Mt. Ex 16
* to kill us with starvation." Ex 16
out toward the *, from within the Ex 16:1
them with in the *, when he brought Ex 16:3
would become a *, and the wild Ex 23:2
man shall let it loose in the *. Lev 16:2
numbered them in the * of Sinai." Num 1:17,18,1
the Lord in the * of Sinai when Num 3
left the Sinai *, and followed the Num 10:1
it stopped in the * of Paran. Num 10:1
* and will be a great help to us. Num 10:3
to encamp in the *, and you will Num 10:31
and camped in the * of Paran. Num 12:1
in the * of Paran at the time. Num 13:3-1
the * of Zin to Rehob near Hamath. Num 13:2

(WILDERNESS Con't)
of Israel in the * of Paran at Num 13:26
even here in the *, rather than be Num 14:2
to take care of them in the *. Num 14:16
Egypt and in the *—and ten times Num 14:22
turn back into the * in the Num 14:25
You will all die here in this *! Num 14:29
dead bodies shall fall in this *. Num 14:32
must wander in the * for forty Num 14:34,35
me shall die here in this *.' Num 14:34,35
Lord's orders to return to the *. Num 14:41
Israel were in the *, one of them Num 15:32
in this terrible *, and that now Num 16:13
arrived in the * of Zin in April Num 20:1
us into this * to get rid of us, Num 20:4
of Egypt to die here in the *?" Num 21:5
Iye-abarim, in the *, a short Num 21:11
in the *, battling them at Jahaz. Num 21:23
census taken in the * of Sinai! Num 26:64,65
them, "They shall die in the *." Num 26:64,65
"Our father died in the *," Num 27:3,4
my instructions in the * of Zin. Num 27:14
in Kadesh, in the * of Zin. Num 27:14
and forth in the * for forty years Num 32:13
even longer in the *, and you will Num 32:15
the edge of the *), and Pihahiroth Num 33:5,6
the Etham *, camping at Marah. Num 33:8
Sea, and then in the * of Sihn. Num 33:11
From Rephidim they went to the * Num 33:15-37
from the * of Sinai to Num 33:15-37
to Kadesh (in the * of Zin); Num 33:15-37
* of Zin, along the edge of Edom. Num 34:3
the Arabah in the * of Moab, east Deu 1:1
again here in the *, just as a Deu 1:31
they said would die in the *. Deu 1:39
"THEN WE TURNED back across the * Deu 2:1
wandered around in this great *; Deu 2:7
"Then from the * of Kedemoth I Deu 2:26
in the *, for the tribe of Reuben; Deu 4:43
you through the * for all those Deu 8:2
great and terrible * with the Deu 8:15
He fed you with manna in the * Deu 8:16
God out in the *, from the day you Deu 9:7
them into the * to slay them." Deu 9:28
in the *, until your arrival here. Deu 11:5
you through the *, yet your clothes Deu 29:5
protected them in the howling * Deu 32:10
Meribath-kadesh, in the * of Zin. Deu 32:51
the people of Israel in the *. Deu 34:11,12
the years in the *, and none of the Jos 5:4,5
forth across the * for forty years Jos 5:6
fled across the * as though badly Jos 8:15
crisscrossing the *, and today I am Jos 14:10
Edom, crossed the * of Zin, and Jos 15:1
on into the * of Zin to Hezron Jos 15:2,3,4
* and the hill country to Bethel. Jos 16:1
country and the * of Beth-aven. Jos 18:12
They were Bezer, in the * of the Jos 20:8
Then Israel lived in the * for Jos 24:7
through the *, and preserved us Jos 24:17
land in the Negeb * south of Arad, Ju 1:16
the thorns and briars of the *." Ju 8:7
Moab through the *, and traveled Ju 11:18
from the * to the Jordan River. Ju 11:21,22
So they ran toward the *, but Ju 20:42
army fled into the * toward the Ju 20:45
plagues when Israel was in the *. 1Sa 4:8
David now lived in the * caves 1Sa 23:14,15
in the southern part of the *. 1Sa 23:19
further into the * of Maon in the 1Sa 23:24,25
had gone into the * of Engedi; 1Sa 24:1
Meanwhile David went down to the * 1Sa 25:1
sent men from the * to talk to our 1Sa 25:14
We protected his flocks in the * 1Sa 25:21
* and was hiding on Hachilah Hill. 1Sa 26:1
at the edge of the * where David 1Sa 26:3,4
before I disappear into the *." 2Sa 15:28
the * for any who become faint." 2Sa 16:2
across at once into the * beyond; 2Sa 17:16
your long march through the *." 2Sa 17:28,29
Then he went on alone into the * 1Ki 19:4
will search the * for your master; 2Ki 2:16
"We'll attack from the * of 2Ki 3:6,7,8
through the * for seven days; 2Ki 3:9
Gad also went to David in the *. 1Ch 12:8-13
by Moses in the * were on the hill 1Ch 21:29
assistant, while he was in the *. 2Ch 1:2,3
that opens into the * of Jeruel. 2Ch 20:16
went out into the * of Tekoa. 2Ch 20:20
looks out over the *, as far as 2Ch 20:24
abandon them to die in the *! Neh 9:19
years you sustained them in the *; Neh 9:21
I have placed them in the * and Job 39:6
and shakes the * of Kadesh. Ps 29:8
us in the barren * and sending us Ps 44:19
he was hiding in the * of Judea. Ps 63:1
green, lush pastures in the *; Ps 65:11,12
people through the *, the earth Ps 68:7
He split open the rocks in the * Ps 78:15
guiding them safely through the *. Ps 78:52
your hearts as Israel did in the * Ps 95:8
in a far-off *, or like an owl Ps 102:6
kill them in the * and send their Ps 106:26
people through the *, for his Ps 136:16
be very long—the * of Lebanon will Is 29:17
Sharon has become a *; Is 33:9
EVEN THE * and desert will rejoice Is 35:1
Springs will burst forth in the * Is 35:6
a road for the Lord through the *; Is 40:3
I will make a road through the * Is 43:19
them water in the *, yes, springs Is 43:20
her barren * will become as Is 51:3
Jerusalem is a desolate *. Is 64:10
through the barren *, a land of Jer 2:6
The fertile valleys were * and Jer 4:26
Why is the land a * so that no Jer 9:12
all its beauty into barren *. Jer 12:10
plains in the barren *; Jer 17:6
*, when Israel sought for rest. Jer 31:2
hide in the *! Jer 48:6
*, a dry and desert land. Jer 50:12
ruins—she is a dry * where no one Jer 51:43
If we hide in the *, they are Lam 4:19
We went into the * to hunt for Lam 5:9
desolate from the * in the south to Eze 6:14
Now the vine is planted in the * Eze 19:13
eyes, and led them into the *. Eze 20:9,10
There in the * they refused my Eze 20:13
But I swore to them in the * Eze 20:15
I didn't finish them off in the * Eze 20:17
out my fury upon you in the *. Eze 20:21
they were in the * that I would Eze 20:23,24
Literally, "the * of the Eze 20:35,36f
as I did in the * after I brought Eze 20:35,36
*, or a desert without rain. Eze 22:24
drunkards from the *, who put Eze 23:42
of exile lay empty as a barren *; Eze 36:34
and planted lush crops in the *. Eze 36:36
bring her into the *, and speak to Hos 1:14
days when I led you through the *! Hos 9:10
I took care of you in the *, in Hos 13:5
a desolate wasteland like a *. Zep 2:13
They shall turn the land into a * Zec 11:6
preaching out in the Judean *. Mt 3:1
a shout from the *, 'Prepare a Mt 3:3
went out to the * to hear him Mt 3:5
THEN JESUS WAS led out into the * Mt 4:1
into the barren * to see John, what Mt 11:7
So when Jesus came out of the *, Mt 14:14
live out in the barren *," Isaiah Mk 1:3
He lived in the * and taught that Mk 1:4
went out alone into the * to pray. Mk 1:35
out in the lonely * until he began Lk 1:80
from the barren *, 'Prepare a road Lk 3:4
But he often withdrew to the * Lk 5:16
out into the Judean * to see?" Lk 7:24
in palaces, not out in the *. Lk 7:25
was lost in the *, wouldn't you Lk 15:3,4
from the barren *, shouting as Jn 1:23
And as Moses in the * lifted up Jn 3:14
they journeyed through the *! Jn 6:30,31
When your fathers in the * ate Jn 6:48-51
through the * for forty years. Act 7:36
to be, for in the *, Moses was the Act 7:38
or Tabernacle, through the *. Act 7:44
of wandering around in the *. Act 13:18
to our people in the * long ago. 1Co 10:1
and he destroyed them in the *. 1Co 10:5
and as a result died in the *. Heb 3:17
The woman fled into the *, where Rev 12:6
to fly into the * to the place Rev 12:14
took me in spirit into the *. Rev 17:3

WILDEST
safely camp in the * places and Eze 34:25

WILDFIRE
* throughout the whole region. Lk 4:37

WILDLIFE
reptiles and * of every kind." Gen 1:24
a hunting ground overrun by *. Is 7:24

WILDLY
and burst into tears, sobbing *. Gen 21:16
My heart beats *, my strength Ps 38:10
they bump * through the streets! Nah 3:2

WILDS
a lion from the * of Jordan Jer 49:19

WILES
are destroying you with their *. Num 25:18

WILLFUL
who are proud and *, daring even to 2Pe 2:10

WILLING
Why were you * to let me marry Gen 12:19
"Are you * to go with this Gen 24:58
But Onan was not * to have a Gen 38:9
remained who were * to fight. Ju 7:3
So I am * to act like a fool in 2Sa 6:21
Yes, and I am * to look even 2Sa 6:22
clean heart and a * mind, for the 1Ch 28:9
The king's officials made * 2Ch 35:8
I am * to face the consequences. Job 13:13
and make me * to obey you. Ps 51:12
Anyone * to be corrected is on Pro 10:17
will be * to be taught! Is 29:24
he is * for, to go with each lamb. Eze 46:5
he is to bring whatever he is * Eze 46:7
as much as the prince is * to Eze 46:11
and were * to die rather than serve Dan 3:28
Only those who are * to learn Dan 12:10
and if you are * to understand Mt 11:14
If ever you were * to listen, Mt 11:15
For the spirit indeed is *, but Mt 26:41
For though the spirit is * Mk 14:38
I am * to do whatever he wants. Lk 1:38
if you are *, please take away this Lk 22:41,42
Then they were * to let him in, Jn 6:21
him, "Are you * to go to Jerusalem Act 25:9
he would be * to stand trial on Act 25:20
for is the opportunity, God *, Rom 1:10
In my mind I want to be God's * Rom 7:23,24,25
that I would be * to be forever Rom 9:1
For if God was * to take you who Rom 11:24
there will be * to accept the money Rom 15:31
the result is that they are * to 1Co 9:22
If the Lord is *, I will send Php 2:19
I am more than * to suffer if 2Ti 2:10
The Lord *, we will go on now to Heb 6:3
He was * to die a shameful death Heb 12:2
this world, being * to be despised Heb 13:13
and be * to do what they say. Heb 13:17
did, when he was * to obey God, Jas 2:21
* to do whatever God told him to; Jas 2:22
It allows discussion and is * to Jas 3:17
that he is not * that any should 2Pe 3:9

WILLING-HEARTED
and women came, all who were *. Ex 35:22

WILLINGLY
the land, he * bent his shoulder to Gen 49:15
Who offered themselves so *! Ju 5:9
offer their gifts * and joyously. 1Ch 29:17
*, dressed in holy altar robes. Ps 110:3
listened to him so * and received 2Co 7:15
So you wives must * obey your Eph 5:24
obey them * because of your love Col 3:22
Spirit, Christ * gave himself to Heb 9:14
care for it *, not grudgingly; 1Pe 5:2

WILLOW
the * trees, for how can we sing? Ps 137:2
would grow as quickly as a * tree. Eze 17:5

WILLOWS
trees—such as * that grow by the Lev 23:40
the * there beside the stream. Job 40:22
and flee across the Brook of *. Is 15:7
grass, like * on a river bank. Is 44:4

WILLPOWER
But if a man has the * not to 1Co 7:37

WILLS
their hearts and *, and wanted him 2Ch 15:15

WILT
the green forests of Lebanon *. Nah 1:4
as persecution begins, they *. Mk 4:17

WILTED
enough, but soon * beneath the hot Mk 4:5,6

WIN
that he couldn't * the match, he Gen 32:25
her, and tried to * her affection. Gen 34:3
But did not * the victory. Ju 5:19
her to try to * her back again. Ju 19:3
and all who * souls are wise. Pro 11:30
It is harder to * back the Pro 18:19
the righteous will finally *. Pro 21:18
Be patient and you will finally * Pro 25:15
does not always * the race, nor the Ecc 9:11
even the lame will * their share. Is 33:23
He won't *." Is 41:6
How you plot and scheme to * your Jer 2:33
You can't *! Jer 32:5
and * them over to his side. Dan 11:32
stand firm, you will * your souls. Lk 21:19
used me to * the Gentiles to God. Rom 15:18
so that I can * them to Christ. 1Co 9:19
Gospel and I can * them to Christ. 1Co 9:20
And so, by agreeing, I can * 1Co 9:21
So run your race to *. 1Co 9:24
So run your race to win. To * 1Co 9:25
* a blue ribbon or a silver cup, 1Co 9:25
I fight to *. 1Co 9:26
that we work so hard to * others. 2Co 5:11
plans and methods to * my battles. 2Co 10:3
no one can ever * God's favor by Gal 3:11
are so anxious to * your favor are Gal 4:17
each other to * control over us, Gal 5:17
opportunities to * people to Php 1:22
Never once did we try to * you 1Th 2:5
toward you will * out over his Jas 2:13
possibly fight and * this battle 1Jn 5:5
See to it that you * your full 2Jn 1:8
in many battles and * the war. Rev 6:2

WIND
He sent a * to blow across the Gen 8:1
But someone got * of what he Gen 27:42
and withered by the east *. Gen 41:6
* to blow all that day and night; Ex 10:13
east * had brought the locusts. Ex 10:13
a very strong west * that blew the Ex 10:19

(WIND Con't)
and a strong east * blew all that Ex 14:21
But God blew with his *, and the Ex 15:10
leaf driven in the * will send them Lev 26:36
The Lord sent a * that brought Num 11:31
On the wings of the *. 2Sa 22:11
* brought a terrific rainstorm. 1Ki 18:45
but the Lord was not in the *. 1Ki 19:11
After the *, there was an 1Ki 19:11
You won't see * nor rain, but 2Ki 3:17
suddenly a mighty * swept in from Job 1:19
Job, blowing words around like *? Job 8:2
leaf that is blown about by the *? Job 13:25
Are they driven before the * Job 21:18
The east * carries him away, and Job 27:21
as a cloud before a strong *. Job 30:15
when the south * is blowing and Job 37:16,17
Where is the home of the east *? Job 38:24
blow away like chaff before the *. Ps 1:4
scorch them with his burning *. Ps 11:6
swiftly to my aid with wings of *. Ps 18:10
as dust and cast them to the *. Ps 18:42
like chaff in the *—wind sent by Ps 35:5
* sent by the Angel of the Lord. Ps 35:5
warships with a breath of *. Ps 48:7
them off like smoke before the *; Ps 68:2
And he led forth the east * and Ps 78:26
the south * by his mighty power. Ps 78:26
in a moment like a breath of *. Ps 78:39
like chaff before the *— as a Ps 83:13
blown by the * and gone forever. Ps 103:16
He rides upon the wings of the *. Ps 104:3
Let fire and hail, snow, rain, * Ps 148:8
As surely as a * from the north Pro 25:23
you can stop the * or hold onto Pro 27:16
Who else holds the * in his Pro 30:4
to rise again. The * blows south Ecc 1:3-7
is all foolishness, chasing the *. Ecc 1:12-15
even this was like chasing the *. Ecc 1:16-18
a chasing of the *, and there was Ecc 2:11
all is foolishness, chasing the * Ecc 2:17
of foolishly chasing the *. Ecc 2:24-26
is foolishness, chasing the *. Ecc 4:4
is all foolishness, chasing the *. Ecc 4:16
he has been working for the *. Ecc 5:16
it's chasing the *. Ecc 6:9
that observeth the * shall not sow Ecc 11:4f
the pathway of the *, and as the Ecc 11:5
The Girl: "Come, north *, Sol 4:16
come, south *, blow upon my Sol 4:16
of their chariots spin like the *. Is 5:28
sending a mighty * to divide it Is 11:15
like chaff by the *, like whirling Is 17:13
away like chaff before the *. Is 29:5
its chaff blown away by the *. Is 30:24
Israel from the storm and *. Is 32:2
the * carries them off like straw. Is 40:24
the * shall blow them all away; Is 41:16
idols are all as empty as the *. Is 41:29
They are so weak that the * can Is 57:13
like reeds in the * and putting on Is 58:5
And our sins, like the *, sweep Is 64:6
sniffing the * at mating time. Jer 2:24
send a burning * from the desert Jer 4:11,12
roll down upon us like a storm *; Jer 4:13
his treasuries he brings the *. Jer 10:13
as the east * scatters dust; Jer 18:17
have disappeared with a puff of *; Jer 22:22
Scatter the last third to the *, Eze 5:2
when the east * touches it, dying Eze 17:10
by a strong * from the east; Eze 19:12
Then he told me to call to the * Eze 37:9
and the * blew them all away. Dan 2:35
Therefore, a mighty * Hos 4:19
They have sown the * and they Hos 8:7
ISRAEL IS CHASING the *, yes, Hos 12:1
by the *, like a cloud of smoke. Hos 13:3
but the east *—a wind of the Lord Hos 13:15
the east wind—a * of the Lord from Hos 13:15
flung a terrific * over the sea, Jon 1:4
a scorching east * to blow on Jon 4:8
They sweep past like * and are Hab 1:11
lie open to the * and weather. Zep 2:14
up and rebuked the * and waves, and Mt 8:26
Grass blowing in the *? Mt 11:7
For the * had risen and they were Mt 14:23,24
back into the boat, the * stopped. Mt 14:32
Then he rebuked the * and said to Mk 4:39
And the * fell, and there was a Mk 4:39
against the * and waves. Mk 6:48
into the boat and the * stopped! Mk 6:51
grass, moved by every breath of *? Lk 7:24
was sleeping the * began to rise. Lk 8:23
he said, and the * and waves Lk 8:24
"When the south * blows you say, Lk 12:55
Just as you can hear the * but Jn 3:8
But Paul's nephew got * of their Act 23:16
Beating into the * with great Act 27:7,8
Just then a light * began blowing Act 27:13
and a heavy * of typhoon strength Act 27:14,15
and were thus driven before the *. Act 27:17
a day later a south * began Act 28:13
swift as the * and as servants made Heb 1:7
is driven and tossed by the *; Jas 1:6

WINDBAG
You are nothing but a *. Job 15:2

WINDBAGS
they say, "are * full of words Jer 5:13

WINDING
and there were * stairs going up to 1Ki 6:8

WINDOW
looked out of a * and saw Isaac Gen 26:8
let them down by a rope from a *. Jos 2:15
hanging from this * and unless all Jos 2:17,18
scarlet rope hanging from the *. Jos 2:21
of Sisera watched through the * Ju 5:28
down to the ground through a *. 1Sa 19:12
watched from a * and saw King David 2Sa 6:16
and fixed her hair and sat at a *. 2Ki 9:30
He looked up and saw her at the * 2Ki 9:32
So they threw her out the *, and 2Ki 9:33
"Open that eastern *," he 2Ki 13:16,17
watched from the * and saw him 1Ch 15:29
I was looking out the * of my Pro 7:6
sitting on the * sill, went fast Act 20:9
not even a lamp in a * will ever Rev 18:23

WINDOWS
Narrow * were used throughout. 1Ki 6:4
There were forty-five * in the 1Ki 7:3,4
Each of the doorways and * had a 1Ki 7:5
if the Lord made * in the sky!" 2Ki 7:2
the Lord opened the * of heaven!" 2Ki 7:19
open—he opened the * of heaven— Ps 78:23
the wall, now looking in at the *. Sol 2:9
in through your * into your homes. Jer 9:21
rooms and many *, paneled Jer 22:14
There were * that narrowed Eze 40:16
walls. The * were also in the exit Eze 40:16
There were *, an entry hall and Eze 40:22
It had * along the walls as the Eze 40:25
the * along its walls and entry. Eze 40:29,30
and there were * along the walls Eze 40:33
and all three had recessed *. Eze 41:15,16
with wood above and below the *. Eze 41:15,16
There were recessed * and carved Eze 41:26
bedroom, with its * open toward Dan 6:10
coming like thieves through the *. Joe 2:9
hooting from the gaping *; Zep 2:14
if you do, I will open up the * Mal 3:10

WINDS
the Pishon; it * across the entire Gen 2:11,12
He makes the * blow and sets the Job 28:25
when the * have cleared away the Job 37:21
He calls to the storm *; Ps 107:25
and sends the * from his Ps 135:7
If I ride the morning * to the Ps 139:9
and the spring * blow and all the Ps 147:18
* will not reach them any more. Is 49:10
by the fierce * off the desert. Jer 13:24,25
to the *. Jer 49:32
the people of Elam to the four *; Jer 49:36
and the * from his treasuries. Jer 51:16
scatter to the *, sending the sword Eze 5:12
* and send the sword after them. Eze 12:14
great hailstones and mighty * Eze 13:11
will be scattered to the four *. Eze 17:21
Come from the four *, O Spirit, and Eze 37:9
So I spoke to the * as he Eze 37:10
* blowing from every direction. Dan 7:2
*, and knows your every thought; Amo 4:13
'I scattered you to the * but I Zec 2:6,7
rise and the storm * beat against Mt 7:25
come, and storm * beat against his Mt 7:27
even the * and the sea obey him?" Mt 8:27
"From the four *, from one end of Mt 24:31f
even the * and seas obey him?" Mk 4:41
but when the hot * of persecution Lk 8:13
even the * and waves obey him?" Lk 8:25
but the * had become too strong, Act 27:7,8
go, even though the * are strong. Jas 3:4
as clouds driven by the storm *. 2Pe 2:17
fig trees buffeted by mighty *. Rev 6:13
back the four * from blowing, so Rev 7:1

WINDSTORM
and a mighty * hit the mountain; 1Ki 19:11
of a mighty * in the skies above Act 2:2

WINDSWEPT
I hear voices high upon the * Jer 3:21

WINE
planted a vineyard, and he made *. Gen 9:20,21
Heaven, brought him bread and *. Gen 14:18
Come, let's fill him with * and Gen 19:32
Let's fill him with * again Gen 19:34
he also drinks the * Jacob brings Gen 27:25
good harvest of grain, and new *. Gen 27:27,28,29
*—what is there left to give?" Gen 27:37
and he poured * over it as an Gen 35:13,14
baker and his * taster, so he Gen 40:1
The * taster told his dream Gen 40:9,10
I was holding Pharaoh's * cup in Gen 40:11
you back your job as his * taster. Gen 40:13
He sent for his * taster and Gen 40:20
Then he restored the * taster to Gen 40:2
Pharaoh's * taster, however, Gen 40:2
Then the king's * taster spoke Gen 41
to my position of * taster, and the Gen 41:1
forth, and the * flowed freely! Gen 43:3
vine, and washed his clothes in *. Gen 49:1
His eyes are darker than * and Gen 49:1
crops and your *, and the Ex 22:2
also 2½ pints of *, as a Ex 29:4
with flour and the * libation as in Ex 29:4
"Never drink * or strong drink Lev 10:8,
consisting of three pints of *. Lev 23:1
Along with the bread and the *, Lev 23:1
strong drink or * or even fresh Num 6:3,
wine or even fresh *, grape juice, Num 6:3,
*, for he is freed from his vow. Num 6:2
pints of * for a drink offering. Num 15:
pints of * for a drink offering. Num 15:
of * for the drink offering. Num 15:1
*, grain, and every other crop. Num 18:1
him of grain and *, as though it Num 18:2
own threshing floor and * press. Num 18:3
pints of strong * with each lamb, Num 28:
pints of * with each bull, four Num 28:1
grapes for your *, and olive oil. Deu 11:1
your grain and new * and olive oil, Deu 12:1
of grain, new *, olive oil, and the Deu 14:2
ox, a sheep, some *, or some strong Deu 14:2
olive press, and your * press. Deu 15:1
the grain, the new *, the olive Deu 18:4
or drink the *, for worms will Deu 28:3
Your grain, new *, olive oil, Deu 28:5
or grapes for * and strong drink, Deu 29:6
They drank the sparkling *. Deu 32:14
They drink the * of serpent Deu 32:33
they sacrificed their fat and *? Deu 32:38
Prospering in a land of corn and * Deu 33:28
pressed to make *—for he was hiding Ju 6:11
quit producing the * that cheers Ju 9:13
the local god, the * flowed freely Ju 9:27
Don't drink any * or beer, and Ju 13:4
not to drink any * or beer, and not Ju 13:7
or drink any * or beer, or eat Ju 13:13,14
of food and * for ourselves." Ju 19:19
her morsels of food in the *." Ru 2:14f
and a bushel of flour and some *. 1Sa 1:24
the third will have a bottle of *. 1Sa 10:3
carrying a load of food and *. 1Sa 16:20
two barrels of *, five dressed 1Sa 25:18
some *, and a cake of raisins. 2Sa 6:19
* and dine and sleep with my wife? 2Sa 11:11
grapes, and a small barrel of *. 2Sa 16:1
men to eat; the * is to be taken 2Sa 16:2
Food and * are no longer tasty, 2Sa 19:35
"I have neither food nor * to 2Ki 6:26-30
eating, drinking *, and carrying 2Ki 7:8
grain, *, olive trees, and honey. 2Ki 18:31,32
flour, *, incense, and spices. 1Ch 9:29
cakes, raisins, *, oil, cattle, and 1Ch 12:40
some *, and a cake of raisins. 1Ch 16:3
for his * production and storage. 1Ch 27:27
20,000 barrels of *, and 20,000 2Ch 2:10
olive oil, and * you mentioned, 2Ch 2:15
them with food, olive oil, and *. 2Ch 11:11
shoes, food, and *, and put those 2Ch 28:15
and grain, new *, olive oil, money, 2Ch 31:5,6
for his grain, new *, and olive 2Ch 32:28,29
them with food, *, and olive oil. Ez 3:7
and give them wheat, *, salt, and Ez 6:9
990 gallons of *; Ez 7:22
his * he asked me, "Why so sad? Neh 2:1
demanded food and * and $100 a day Neh 5:15
first of the new * and olive oil. Neh 10:37
of grain, new *, and olive oil to Neh 10:39,40
of grain, new *, and olive oil. Neh 13:5
of grain, new *, and olive oil to Neh 13:12
their donkeys with *, grapes, figs, Neh 13:15
abundance of royal *, for the king Est 1:7
half drunk from *, he told the Est 1:10
During the * course the king said Est 5:6
Again, during the * course, the Est 7:2
I am like a * cask without a Job 32:19
is a cup of pale and sparkling *. Ps 75:8
man aroused by *, he routed his Ps 78:65
to cultivate, and * to make him Ps 104:15
I will bring him an offering of * Ps 116:13
the thank-offering of * for Ps 116:13f
your * vats with the finest wines. Pro 3:9,10
* GIVES FALSE courage; Pro 20:1
becomes poor; * and luxury are not Pro 21:17
taste of strong * deceive you. Pro 23:31
O Lemuel, to drink * and whiskey. Pro 31:4
* for those in deep depression. Pro 31:6,7
a good glass of *, accept his Ecc 5:18
A party gives laughter, and * Ecc 10:19
for your love is sweeter than *. Sol 1:2
Your love is better than *. Sol 1:4
How much better it is than mere * Sol 4:10
I drink my * with my milk." Sol 5:1
lovely as a goblet filled with *. Sol 7:2
as the best of *, smooth and Sol 7:9

(WINE Con't)
I would give you spiced * to Sol 8:2
to drink, sweet pomegranate *. Sol 8:2
now diluted like watered-down *! Is 1:22
the * presses has ceased forever. Is 16:10
will fail, the * will be gone, the Is 24:7
No more are the joys of * and Is 24:9
form in the streets, crying for *; Is 24:11
well-aged * and choice beef. Is 25:6
Stagger, and not from *! Is 29:9
Come, take your choice of * and Is 55:1
"We'll get some * and have a Is 56:12
and take away your grain and *. Is 62:8
shall drink the * you pressed. Is 62:9
All your jugs will be full of *. Jer 13:12
bottle shall be filled with *." Jer 13:12f
send them a cup of * expressing Jer 16:7
drunkard does from *, because of Jer 23:9
from my hand this * cup filled to Jer 25:15
the wheat and the * and the oil, Jer 31:12
rooms and offer them a drink of *. Jer 35:2
I set cups and jugs of * before Jer 35:5
We have never had a drink of * Jer 35:8
of * grapes and other crops. Jer 40:12
She is like * that has not been Jer 48:11
The presses yield no *; Jer 48:33
with all their *, I will prepare a Jer 51:39
* from Uzal for your wares." Eze 27:19f
No priest may drink * before Eze 44:21
best of food and * from his own Dan 1:5
and * given to them by the king. Dan 1:8
feast where the * flowed freely. Dan 5:1
have been drinking * from them Dan 5:23
All that time I tasted neither * Dan 10:3
But now I will take back the * Hos 1:9
in its season, or * at the time of Hos 1:9
*, women, and song have robbed my Hos 4:11
pour out * for sacrifice to God. Hos 9:4
are ruined and all your * is gone! Joe 1:5
of grain and * to bring to the Joe 1:9
offerings of grain and * for you. Joe 1:13
grain and * to the Lord as before! Joe 2:14
you much corn and * and oil, to Joe 2:19
overflow with olive oil and *. Joe 2:24
girl for * enough to get drunk. Joe 3:3
"Sweet * will drip from the Joe 3:18
sacrifices of * they purchased with Amo 2:8
them to drink your *, and you Amo 2:12
nor drink the * from the lush Amo 5:11
You drink * by the bucketful and Amo 6:6
hills of Israel will drip sweet *! Amo 9:13
eat their crops and drink their *. Amo 9:14
to you the joys of * and Mic 2:11
but get no juice to make your *. Mic 6:15
their *, for it is treacherous. Hab 2:5
They will never drink * from the Zep 1:13
some bread or * or meat, will it Hag 2:12
The abundance of grain and * will Zec 9:16,17
They shall be happy as with *. Zec 10:7
Hananel to the king's * presses. Zec 14:10
were leather bags for storing *. Mt 9:17f
to store new *? Mt 9:17
pressure, and the * would be Mt 9:17
wineskins are used to store new *. Mt 9:17
doesn't even drink * and often goes Mt 11:18
And he took a cup of * and gave Mt 26:27
not drink this * again until the Mt 26:29
gave him drugged * to drink; Mt 27:34
a sponge with sour * and put it on Mt 27:48
to put new * into old wineskins. Mk 2:22
They would burst. The * would be Mk 2:22
New * needs fresh wineskins." Mk 2:22
Then he took a cup of * and gave Mk 14:23
never again taste * until the day I Mk 14:25
(Golgotha means skull.) * Mk 15:23
it with sour * and held it up to Mk 15:36
He must never touch * or hard Lk 1:15
And no one puts new * into old Lk 5:37
for the new * bursts the old skins, Lk 5:37
the skins and spilling the *. Lk 5:37
* must be put into new wineskins. Lk 5:38
drinking the old * seems to want Lk 5:39
But I eat my food and drink my * Lk 7:34
Now take it easy! *, women, and Lk 12:19
Then he took a glass of *, and Lk 22:17
For I will not drink * again Lk 22:18
another glass of *, saying, "This Lk 22:20
saying, "This * is the token of Lk 22:20
by offering him a drink—of sour *. Lk 23:36
invited too. The * supply ran out Jn 2:3
water that was now *, not knowing Jn 2:9
Usually a host uses the best * Jn 2:10
he had turned the water into *. Jn 4:46,47
A jar of sour * was sitting Jn 19:29
meat or drinking * or doing Rom 14:21
from the cup of * at the Lord's 1Co 10:16
he took the cup of * after supper, 1Co 11:25
Don't drink too much *, for many Eph 5:18
completely give up drinking *. 1Ti 5:23
but there is no olive oil or *." Rev 6:6
"do not damage the oil and *." Rev 6:6f
them share the * of her intense Rev 14:8
drink the * of the anger of God; Rev 14:10
* of the fierceness of his wrath. Rev 16:19
by the * of her immorality." Rev 17:2
fatal * of her intense immorality. Rev 18:3
*, olive oil, and fine flour; Rev 18:13

WINEPRESS
* of Zeeb, as it is now called; Ju 7:25
He built a watchtower and cut a * Is 5:2
"I have trodden the * alone. Is 63:3
his beloved city as grapes in a *. Lam 1:15
Tread the *, for it is full to Joe 3:13
into the great * of God's wrath. Rev 14:19
trodden in the * outside the city, Rev 14:20
and he trod the * of the Rev 19:15

WINEPRESSES
some men treading * on the Sabbath, Neh 13:15

WINES
of all kinds of * every ten days. Neh 5:18
your wine vats with the finest *. Pro 3:9,10
and mixed the *, and sent out her Pro 9:2
and drink the * that I have mixed. Pro 9:5
She brings * from Helbon, and Eze 27:18
without the rich foods and *! Dan 1:16
as fragrant as the * of Lebanon. Hos 14:7

WINESKIN
I am shriveled like a * in the Ps 119:83

WINESKINS
patched * and dry, moldy bread. Jos 9:3,4,5
these * were new, but now they Jos 9:13
And who would use old * Mt 9:17
Only new * are used to store new Mt 9:17
than to put new wine into old *. Mk 2:22
be spilled out and the * ruined. Mk 2:22
New wine needs fresh *." Mk 2:22
new wine into old *, for the new Lk 5:37
New wine must be put into new *. Lk 5:38

WING
of the room; each * was 7½ feet 1Ki 6:23-28
feet from * tip to wing tip. 1Ki 6:23-28
feet from wing tip to * tip. 1Ki 6:23-28
Literally, "one * of a cherub, 2Ch 3:11,12,13f
beings were joined * to wing, and Eze 1:9
joined wing to *, and they flew Eze 1:9
long as the inner * that faced the Eze 42:7,8
*, parallel to the longer wing. Eze 42:7,8
wing, parallel to the longer *. Eze 42:7,8

WINGED
* insects are a defilement to you Deu 14:19,20
where * sailboats glide along the Is 18:1

WINGS
to myself as though on eagle's *. Ex 19:4
* spread out above the gold lid. Ex 25:20
with outstretched * that Ex 37:9
Then, grasping it by the *, he Lev 1:15,16,17
He spreads his * over them, Deu 32:11
She carries them upon her *— Deu 32:11
under whose * you have come to take Ru 2:12
On the * of the wind. 2Sa 22:11
their outspread * reached from wall 1Ki 6:23-28
while their inner * touched each 1Ki 6:23-28
it under the * of the angels. 1Ki 8:6
manner that their * spread out over 1Ki 8:7
so now their * overshadowed the 1Ki 8:7
gold angels whose * were stretched 1Ch 28:18
outer room, with * stretched 2Ch 3:11,12,13
placed it beneath the angels' *; 2Ch 5:7,8
their * spread over the Ark and 2Ch 5:7,8
"The ostrich flaps her * Job 39:13
and spreads her * to the south? Job 39:26
hide me in the shadow of your * Ps 17:8
he sped swiftly to my aid with * Ps 18:10
refuge in the shadow of your *. Ps 36:7
Oh, for * like a dove, to fly Ps 55:6
your * until this storm is past. Ps 57:1
beneath the shelter of your *! Ps 61:4
the protecting shadow of your *. Ps 63:7
covered all over as * cover doves! Ps 68:11,12,13
He will shield you with his *! Ps 91:4
He rides upon the * of the wind. Ps 104:3
though they had the * of a bird! Pro 23:4,5
With two of their * they covered Is 6:2
them beneath her *, and the kites Is 34:15
They shall mount up with * like Is 40:31
Oh, for * for Moab that she Jer 48:9
will spread his * against Bozrah. Jer 49:22
had four faces and two pairs of *! Eze 1:6
And beneath each of their * I Eze 1:8
Each had two pairs of * Eze 1:11
to attach to the * of the living Eze 1:11
Each being's * stretched straight Eze 1:23
touch the others' *, and each had Eze 1:23
each had two * covering his body. Eze 1:23
And as they flew, their * roared Eze 1:24
stopped they let down their *. Eze 1:24
It was the noise of the * of the Eze 3:13
And the sound of the * of the Eze 10:5
had, beneath his *, what looked Eze 10:7,8
faces and four *, with what looked Eze 10:21
like human hands under their *. Eze 10:21
Then the cherubim lifted their * Eze 11:22
"A great eagle with broad * full Eze 17:3,4
between the two * of the building, Eze 42:11
like a lion, but it had eagle's *! Dan 7:4
And as I watched, its * were Dan 7:4
on its back it had * like those of Dan 7:6
us, with * like those of a stork. Zec 5:9
will rise with healing in his *. Mal 4:2
her *, but you wouldn't let me. Mt 23:37
her *, but you wouldn't let me. Lk 13:34
glory—with their * stretched out Heb 9:5
* spread out as though in flight. Rev 4:7
Beings had six *, and the central Rev 4:8
of their * were covered with eyes. Rev 4:8
of iron, and their * roared like an Rev 9:9
But she was given two * like Rev 12:14

WINGTIP
wings stretched * to wingtip across 2Ch 3:11,12,13
wingtip to * across the room, from 2Ch 3:11,12,13

WINING
Why are yours * and dining?" Lk 5:33

WINK
Literally, "* with the eye." Ps 35:19f

WINKING
* at sin leads to sorrow; Pro 10:10

WINNERS
given to the * of the original 1Co 9:25f

WINNING
with my sister and I am *!" Gen 30:8
rod in his hands, Israel was *; Ex 17:11
the soldiers of Amalek were *. Ex 17:11
A war horse is a poor risk for * Ps 33:16,17
God's people and *, until the Dan 7:21
God had used me in * the Gentiles, Gal 2:7,8,9
some have special ability in * Eph 4:11
wherever it goes, * converts 2Th 3:1
home after * a great battle against Heb 7:1

WINNOW
Winnowers shall come and * her Jer 51:2

WINNOWED
O my people, threshed and *, I Is 21:10

WINNOWERS
and destroy it. * shall come and Jer 51:2

WINNOWING
that he will be * barley tonight Ru 3:2

WINS
life and * approval from the Lord. Pro 8:35
Or, "He that is wise * souls." Pro 11:30f
The good man * his case by Pro 13:2
the Bow that * the battle, the Zec 10:4
with my mind and * the fight and Rom 7:23,24,25
but rejoices whenever truth * out. 1Co 13:6
or is disqualified and * no prize. 2Ti 2:5

WINTER
* and summer, day and night." Gen 8:22
you make the summer and the * Ps 74:17
summer, gathering food for the *. Pro 6:8
but store up food for the *. Pro 30:24-28
She has no fear of * for her Pro 31:21
For the * is past, the rain is Sol 2:11
animals will gnaw bones all *. Is 18:6
the wealthy—their * mansions and Amo 3:15
both in * and in summer. Zec 14:8
not be in *, or on the Sabbath. Mt 24:20
that your flight will not be in *. Mk 13:18
It was *, Jn 10:22,23
place to spend the *—most of the Act 27:12
to Phoenix, in order to * there; Act 27:12
you, perhaps all *, and then you 1Co 16:6
Do try to be here before *. 2Ti 4:21
decided to stay there for the *. Tit 3:12

WINTERED
a ship that had * at the island. Act 28:11

WINTERIZED
The king was in a * part of the Jer 36:22

WIPE
* out wickedness from among you. Lev 20:14
* you off the face of the earth. Deu 6:15
utterly * them out. Deu 7:2
us and attack us and * us out. Jos 7:9
he will completely * you out from Jos 23:15,16
zeal, had tried to * them out. 2Sa 21:2
not been able to * them out 1Ki 9:20,21
and I will * Jerusalem as a man 2Ki 21:13
He had decided to * Judah out of 2Ki 24:3,4
up his mind to * out even the Ps 34:16
Angrily destroy them. * them out. Ps 59:12,13
"Let's * out every trace of Ps 74:8
Come, they say, and let us * out Ps 83:4
But as for you—I will * you out Is 14:30
The Lord God will * away all Is 25:8
back my anger and not * you out. Is 48:9
And I will * Jerusalem off the Jer 19:8
I will * out what I established. Jer 45:4
cause her enemies to * her out. Jer 49:37
fierce pursuit and * them off the Lam 3:66
* out everyone left in Israel?" Eze 9:8
with my fist and * out her people, Eze 25:13
and I will * out the Cherithites Eze 25:16
And when I destroy Egypt and * Eze 32:15
I will utterly * out the people Eze 35:7
plan in all of this to * us out? Hab 1:12

(WIPE Con't)
and say, 'We * the dust of your Lk 10:11
feet and to * them with the towel Jn 13:5
And God will * their tears Rev 7:17
He will * away all tears from Rev 21:4

WIPED
will be forgotten and * out; Gen 41:30
in all, was * out that day. Jos 8:25
the slaughter and * out the five Jos 10:20
* out—every male, no matter who. 2Ki 9:8
the entire family was * out in 1Ch 10:6
at Baal-perazim and * them out. 1Ch 14:11
Israelis had not completely * out. 2Ch 8:7,8
Ethiopian army was * out so that 2Ch 14:13
* out as Sodom and Gomorrah were. Is 1:9
You shall be completely * out. Jer 51:26
will be utterly * out, your memory Eze 21:32
You will be * out, O people of Eze 35:15
that the men of Gibeah were * out? Hos 10:9
all her enemies will be * out. Mic 5:9
have been * out and we are safe!" Nah 1:15
will be * out, and if anyone Zec 13:2
and she * them off with her hair Lk 7:38
tears and * them with her hair. Lk 7:44
feet and * them with her hair? Jn 11:1
with it and * them with her hair. Jn 12:3

WIPES
Jerusalem as a man * a dish and 2Ki 21:13

WIPING
flank of Moab, * out her frontier Eze 25:9,10

WIRE
and cut it into * threads, to work Ex 39:3

WISDOM
giving him great *, ability, and Ex 31:3
reputation for * and intelligence. Deu 4:6
of the spirit of *, for Moses had Deu 34:9
for great * and told her to ask for 2Sa 14:2,3
glad that Solomon had asked for *. 1Ki 3:10
you have asked for * in governing 1Ki 3:11
the great * God had given him. 1Ki 3:28
God gave Solomon great * and 1Ki 4:29
In fact, his * excelled that of 1Ki 4:30
So the Lord gave great * to 1Ki 5:12
Lord had blessed Solomon with *, 1Ki 10:1
heard about his great * was true. 1Ki 10:4
country about your * and about the 1Ki 10:6
been told me! Your * and prosperity 1Ki 10:7
day after day listening to your *! 1Ki 10:8
him and listen to his God-given *. 1Ki 10:24
son Zechariah, a man of unusual *; 1Ch 26:14,15
Now give me * and knowledge to 2Ch 1:10
long life, but for * and knowledge 2Ch 1:11
the * and knowledge you asked for! 2Ch 1:12
Solomon's fabled *, she came to 2Ch 9:1
my own eyes. Your * is far greater 2Ch 9:6
the * God had put into his heart. 2Ch 9:23
"And you, Ezra, are to use the * Ez 7:25
They were men of * who knew the Est 1:13-15
But the * of the past will teach Job 8:10
All * will die with you! Job 12:2
But true * and power are God's. Job 12:13
Yes, with him is strength and *. Job 12:16
That would be your highest *. Job 13:5
Do you have a monopoly on *? Job 15:7,8
they have passed this * to us: Job 15:17-19
where to find * and understanding. Job 28:12
or sapphires. * is far more Job 28:17
He knows where * is and declares Job 28:27
'Look, to fear the Lord is true *; Job 28:28
and gives them * and instruction, Job 33:16
silence and I will teach you *!" Job 33:33
With your *, would we then dare Job 37:19,20
Or, "Who has put * in the inward Job 38:36f
for God has deprived her of *. Job 39:17
he gives me * in the night. Ps 16:7
Your decisions are as full of * Ps 36:6
will be quoted as having great *. Ps 49:13
Oh, give me this *. Ps 51:6
my life with your * and counsel; Ps 73:24
And in * you have made them all! Ps 104:24
For growth in * comes from Ps 111:10
rules can give me * and Ps 119:104
* shouts in the streets for a Pro 1:20
How long will you scoff at * and Pro 1:22
I'll pour out the spirit of * Pro 1:23
will be given * and good sense. Pro 2:1
treasure, then * will be given you, Pro 2:3,4,5
For the Lord grants * Pro 2:6
every time. For * and truth will Pro 2:10
Only * from the Lord can save a Pro 2:16,17
be conceited, sure of your own *. Pro 3:7,8
Literally, "the man that finds * Pro 3:13,14,15f
For such * is far more valuable Pro 3:13,14,15
Nothing else compares with it. * Pro 3:16,17
* is a tree of life to those who Pro 3:18
The Lord's * founded the earth; Pro 3:19
Have two goals: *—that is, Pro 3:21
Cling to *—she will protect you. Pro 4:6
And with your *, develop common Pro 4:7
If you exalt *, she will exalt Pro 4:8,9
Love * like a sweetheart; Pro 7:4
CAN'T YOU HEAR the voice of *? Pro 8:1
For the value of * is far above Pro 8:11
compared with it. * and good Pro 8:12
live together, for * knows where to Pro 8:12
hate evil. For * hates pride, Pro 8:13
"I, *, give good advice and Pro 8:14,15
* HAS BUILT a palace supported on Pro 9:1
fear of God are basic to all *. Pro 9:10
"I, *, will make the hours of Pro 9:11
more fruitful." * is its own Pro 9:12
A mocker never finds the * he Pro 14:6
Wise men are praised for their *; Pro 14:24
* is enshrined in the hearts of Pro 14:33
How much better is * than gold, Pro 16:16
* is a fountain of life to those Pro 16:22
* is the main pursuit of sensible Pro 17:24
He who loves * loves his own best Pro 19:8
man. * is mightier than strength. Pro 24:5
* is too much for a rebel. Pro 24:7
whets the appetite, and so does *! Pro 24:13,14
But those who use God's * are Pro 28:26
Literally, "I have not learned * Pro 30:3f
I have greater * and knowledge." Ecc 1:16-18
For the more my *, the more my Ecc 1:16-18
to my course of seeking *. Ecc 2:3
virtues of * and folly, and anyone Ecc 2:12
I did— that * is of more value Ecc 2:13,14
So of what value is all my *? Ecc 2:15
Then I realized that even * is Ecc 2:15
life searching for *, knowledge, Ecc 2:20-23
please him *, knowledge, and joy; Ecc 2:24-26
You can get anything by either * Ecc 7:12
it didn't work. * is far away, and Ecc 7:24
determined to find * and the reason Ecc 7:25
interpret them. * lights up a man's Ecc 8:1
In my search for * I observed all Ecc 8:16,17
Then I realized that though * is Ecc 9:16
a king of fools. * is better than Ecc 9:18
can outweigh much * and honor. Ecc 10:1
power and * have won these wars. Is 10:13
him, the Spirit of *, Is 11:2
they plead with their idols for * Is 19:3
Will they still boast of their *? Is 19:11
Where has their * gone? Is 19:12
teacher and gives the farmer *. Is 28:29
In his *, he will send great Is 31:2
place, along with * and knowledge Is 33:6
Your "*" and "knowledge" have Is 47:10
me his words of * so that I may Is 50:4
you with * and understanding. Jer 3:15
man bask in his *, nor the mighty Jer 9:23
by his power and *, and by his Jer 10:12
shall rule with * and justice and Jer 23:5,6
You have all * and do great and Jer 32:19
made the earth by his power and *. Jer 51:15
They have no *—none at all! Jer 51:17
You have used your * and Eze 28:4
Yes, your * has made you very Eze 28:5
* and defile your splendor! Eze 28:7
the perfection of * and beauty. Eze 28:12
you corrupted your * for the sake Eze 28:17
with great * by asking, "Why is Dan 2:14
he alone has all * and all power. Dan 2:20
He gives wise men their *, and Dan 2:21
you have given me * and glowing Dan 2:23
to be as full of * and Dan 5:11
filled with enlightenment and *. Dan 5:14
Literally, "* is justified by her Mt 11:19f
land to hear the * of Solomon; Mt 12:42
with his * and his miracles. Mt 13:53,54
astonished at his * and his Mk 6:2,3
minds to the * of faith." Lk 1:17
to the * of the just." Lk 1:17f
was known for * beyond his years; Lk 2:40
Literally, "but * is justified of Lk 7:35f
to listen to the * of Solomon; Lk 11:31
Christ, the * and power of God and Jn 1:1f
Christ, the * and power of God and Jn 1:14f
against Stephen's * and spirit. Act 6:10
God also gave Joseph unusual *, Act 7:10
taught him all the * of the Act 7:22
How great are his * and knowledge Rom 11:33
their * to be useless nonsense. 1Co 1:20
For God in his * saw to it that 1Co 1:21
oratory and human *, but the Holy 1Co 2:4
words of great *, but not the kind 1Co 2:6
back from the true * from above. 1Co 3:18
For the * of this world is 1Co 3:19
he stumbles over his own "*" 1Co 3:19
has given me * that can be trusted, 1Co 7:25
to give you * to see clearly and Eph 1:16,17
When I think of the * and scope Eph 3:14,15
treasures of * and knowledge. Col 2:3
he alone is God, and full of *. 1Ti 1:17
supply of * to all who ask him; Jas 1:5
are not God's kind of *. Jas 3:15
But the * that comes from heaven Jas 3:17
riches, and the *, and the Rev 5:12
"Blessing, and glory, and *, and Rev 7:12

WISDOM'S
come to * banquet and drink the Pro 9:5

WISE
And it would make her so *! Gen 3:6
each tribe who are *, experienced, Deu 1:13
is as * and prudent as Israel!' Deu 4:6
Oh, that they were *! Deu 32:29
But you are as * as an angel of 2Sa 14:20
spoke was as * as though it had 2Sa 16:23
But a * woman in the city called 2Sa 20:16
For we always give * counsel. 2Sa 20:18
people with her * advice, and they 2Sa 20:22
You are a * man and will know 1Ki 2:6
You are a * man, and you will 1Ki 2:9
that of any of the * men of the 1Ki 4:30
"Praise God for giving David a * 1Ki 5:7
a * counselor and an educated man. 1Ch 27:32
to David such a *, intelligent, and 2Ch 2:12
When she discovered how * he 2Ch 9:3
and Elnathan, who were very * men. Ez 8:16
For God is so * and so mighty. Job 9:4
"Mere man is as likely to be * Job 11:12
are *. They understand. Job 12:12
"You are supposed to be a * man, Job 15:2
the experience of * men who have Job 15:17-19
for I do not find a * man among Job 17:10
What * things you have said! Job 26:3
is not mere age that makes men *. Job 32:8,9
"Listen to me, you * men. Job 34:2
Who is * enough to number all Job 38:37,38
who are *, who want to please God. Ps 14:2
They protect us, make us *, and Ps 19:7,8
they are no longer * and good. Ps 36:3
are * and filled with insight. Ps 49:3
Proud man! * man! Ps 49:10
Listen, if you are *, to what I Ps 107:43
How can men be *? Ps 111:10
to make the simple-minded *!" Pro 1:4
I want those already * to become Pro 1:5,6
How does a man become *? Pro 1:7,8,9
wisdom upon you, and make you *. Pro 1:23
the humble. The * are promoted to Pro 3:35
Listen, and grow *, for I speak Pro 4:1
Learn to be *," he said, "and Pro 4:5
Determination to be * is the Pro 4:7
the first step toward becoming *! Pro 4:7
Learn from their ways and be *! Pro 6:6
don't refuse it—and be *. Pro 8:33
learn how to be *." Pro 9:6
But a * man, when rebuked, will Pro 9:7,8
Teach a * man, and he will be Pro 9:9
A * youth makes hay while the sun Pro 10:5
The * man is glad to be Pro 10:8
A * man holds his tongue. Pro 10:14
A fool's fun is being bad; a * Pro 10:23
a wise man's fun is being *! Pro 10:23
The good man gives * advice, but Pro 10:31
in shame, but the meek become *. Pro 11:2
Without * leadership, a nation is Pro 11:14
and all who win souls are *. Pro 11:30
Or, "He that is * wins souls." Pro 11:30f
but a * man listens to others. Pro 12:15
A fool is quick-tempered; a * man Pro 12:16
words of the * soothe and heal. Pro 12:18
A * man doesn't display his Pro 12:23
A * YOUTH accepts his father's Pro 13:1
humble, take advice and become *. Pro 13:10
The advice of a * man refreshes Pro 13:14
A * man thinks ahead; Pro 13:16
Be with * men and become wise. Pro 13:20
Be with wise men and become *. Pro 13:20
A * WOMAN builds her house, while Pro 14:1
But the * man's speech is Pro 14:3
The * man looks ahead. Pro 14:8
A * man is cautious and avoids Pro 14:16
* man is crowned with knowledge. Pro 14:18
* men are praised for their Pro 14:24
A * man controls his temper. Pro 14:29
A * teacher makes learning a joy; Pro 15:2
a * son considers each suggestion. Pro 15:5
A mocker stays away from * men Pro 15:12
A * man is hungry for truth, Pro 15:14
to the * men's hall of fame. Pro 15:31,32
will make you both * and honored. Pro 15:33
death and a * man will appease it. Pro 16:14
The * man is known by his common Pro 16:21
From a * mind comes careful and Pro 16:23
A * slave will rule his master's Pro 17:2
few words and settled mind is *; Pro 17:27,28
thought to be * when he is silent. Pro 17:27,28
A * man's words express deep Pro 18:4
Ability to give * advice Pro 18:20
A * man restrains his anger and Pro 19:11
and be * the rest of your life. Pro 19:20
Reprove a * man and he will be Pro 19:25
heart, the * man will draw it out. Pro 20:5
A * king stamps out crime by Pro 20:26
The * man learns by listening; Pro 21:11
The * man saves for the future, Pro 21:20
oil in the dwelling of the *." Pro 21:20f
The * man conquers the strong man Pro 21:22
Listen to this * advice; Pro 22:17,18,19
to your thoughtful, * words. Pro 23:15,16

WISE Con't)
O my son, be * and stay in God's Pro 23:19,20,21
for joy—what pleasure a * son is! Pro 23:24,25
Any enterprise is built by * Pro 24:3,4
A * man is mightier than a strong Pro 24:5
Don't go to war without * Pro 24:6
When you enjoy becoming *, there Pro 24:13,14
he is smarter than seven * men. Pro 26:16
Young men who are * obey the law; Pro 28:7
A * son makes his father happy, Pro 29:3
while * men try to keep peace. Pro 29:8
A rebel shouts in anger; a * man Pro 29:11
that are small but unusually *: Pro 30:24-28
These are the * sayings of King Pro 31:1
When she speaks, her words are * Pro 31:26
So I worked hard to be * Ecc 1:16-18
for the * man sees, while the Ecc 2:13,14
that happened to * and foolish Ecc 2:13,14
For the * and fool both die, and Ecc 2:16
my son will be a * man or a fool? Ecc 2:19
It is better to be a poor but * Ecc 4:13
* men and fools alike spend their Ecc 6:7,8
who is * lives a far better life. Ecc 6:7,8
Yes, a * man thinks much of Ecc 7:4
be criticized by a * man than to be Ecc 7:5
The * man is turned into a fool Ecc 7:7
To be * is as good as being rich; Ecc 7:11
but being * has many advantages. Ecc 7:12
So don't be too good or too *! Ecc 7:15-17
A * man is stronger than the Ecc 7:19
I have tried my best to be *. Ecc 7:23
I declared, "I will be *," but Ecc 7:23
said to be *, but not one woman! Ecc 7:27,28
HOW WONDERFUL TO be *, to Ecc 8:1
be punished. The * man will find a Ecc 8:5
godly and * men are in God's will; Ecc 9:1
battle, and that * men are often Ecc 9:11
There was in the city a * man, Ecc 9:15
if the * man is poor, he will be Ecc 9:16
quiet words of a * man are better Ecc 9:17
and honor. A * man's heart leads Ecc 10:2
be * and sharpen the blade. Ecc 10:10
It is pleasant to listen to * Ecc 10:12,13
the Preacher was *, he went on Ecc 12:9
only a * man, but a good teacher; Ecc 12:10
manner. The * man's words are like Ecc 12:11
Students are * who master what Ecc 12:11
good judges and * counselors like Is 1:26
Woe to those who are * and shrewd Is 5:21
We are great and *. Is 10:13
province. Her * counselors are all Is 19:3
line of * men they have come from? Is 19:11
What has happened to your "* Is 19:12
If they are *, let them tell you Is 19:12
The "* men" from Zoan are also Is 19:13
I make * men give opposite advice Is 44:25
These * teachers of yours will Jer 8:9
Are they then so *? Jer 8:9
Who is * enough to understand all Jer 9:12
The Lord says: Let not the * man Jer 9:23
Among all the * men of the earth Jer 10:7
We have our own priests and * men Jer 18:18
Then some of the * old men stood Jer 26:17
all your * men of days gone by? Jer 49:7
Babylon—her princes and * men too. Jer 50:35
All her * counselors shall Jer 50:36
I will make drunk her princes, * Jer 51:57
men from Zemer. * old craftsmen Eze 27:9
that you are as * as God, an enemy Eze 28:6
and * astrologers in his realm. Dan 1:20
execute all the * men of Babylon. Dan 2:12
He gives * men their wisdom, and Dan 2:21
to execute the * men of Babylon, Dan 2:24
Daniel replied, "No * man, Dan 2:27
well as chief over all his * men. Dan 2:48
I called in all the * men of Dan 4:6
and wisdom. My * men and Dan 5:15
"And those who are *—the people Dan 12:3
Whoever is *, let him understand Hos 14:9
Therefore those who are * will Amo 5:13
In that day not one * man Ob 1:8
Edom was noted for her * men; Ob 1:8f
For I will fill the * men of Edom Ob 1:8
Where are your * men? Mic 4:9
to the Lord if you are *! Mic 6:9
In God's * plan, when you Mal 2:15
follow them are *, like a man who Mt 7:24
themselves so *, and for revealing Mt 11:25
"I will send you prophets, and * Mt 23:34
"Are you a * and faithful Mt 24:45
But only five of them were * Mt 25:2,3,4
So Jesus grew both tall and *, Lk 2:52
and worldly * and for revealing Lk 10:21
in your * power will let them do. Act 4:28
select seven men, * and full of the Act 6:3
So it seemed * to us, having Act 15:25
Claiming themselves to be * Rom 1:22
I know that you are * and good, Rom 15:14
To God, who alone is *, be the Rom 16:25,26,27
no matter how * they seem to be, 1Co 1:19
So what about these * men, these 1Co 1:20
philosophy and seems * to them. 1Co 1:22
God's * plan for their salvation. 1Co 1:24
by the world as * and great. 1Co 1:27
Our words are * because they are 1Co 2:7
telling of God's * plan to bring us 1Co 2:7
following the * men of this world. 1Co 3:21
such * and sensible Christians! 1Co 4:10
the church who is * enough to 1Co 6:5
won't, he has made a * decision. 1Co 7:37
the ability to give * advice; 1Co 12:8
And if it seems * for me to go 1Co 16:4
think you are so *—yet you listen 2Co 11:19,20
how perfectly * he is when all of Eph 3:10
Don't be fools; be *: make the Eph 5:15,16
asking him to make you * about Col 1:9
enrich your lives and make you *; Col 3:16
* in all your contacts with them. Col 4:5
people, but to be * and strong, and 2Ti 1:7
and it is these that make you * 2Ti 3:15
If you are *, live a life of Jas 3:13
them, then you will be truly *! Jas 3:13
brag about being * and good if you Jas 3:14
out to others. Our * and beloved 2Pe 3:15,16

WISELY
He very * scattered his other 2Ch 11:23

WISER
I will give you a * mind than 1Ki 3:12
He was * than Ethan the Ezrahite 1Ki 4:31
So King Solomon was richer and * 1Ki 10:23
So King Solomon was richer and * 2Ch 9:22
who are older are said to be *; Job 32:7
* than the animals and birds?' Job 35:11
They make me * than my enemies, Ps 119:98
Yes, * than my teachers, for I Ps 119:99
They make me even * than the Ps 119:100
wise to become the * and become Pro 1:5,6
a wise man, and he will be the *; Pro 9:9
He shall be the servant of a * Pro 11:29
a wise man and he will be the *. Pro 19:25
You are * than Daniel, for no Eze 28:2,3
not because I am * than any living Dan 2:30
plan of God is far * than the 1Co 1:25

WISEST
that you find the * man in Egypt Gen 41:33
you are the * man in the country! Gen 41:39
the * and corrupt their decisions. Deu 16:19
"Are you the * man alive? Job 15:7,8
Even the * is of value only to Job 22:2
impressed by the world's * men!" Job 37:24
right is the * life there is. Pro 4:11
He will despise the * advice. Pro 23:9
and even the * man who says he Ecc 8:16,17
their * counselors as fools." Is 29:14
The * of men who worship idols Jer 10:8
all the * men of my kingdom have Dan 4:18
Eliphaz, the * of Job's three Ob 1:8f
far wiser than the * plan of the 1Co 1:25
wisest plan of the * man, and God 1Co 1:25

WISH
them to you to do with as you *. Gen 19:8
us wherever you * and carry on your Gen 34:9,10
possessions. They * to settle in Gen 47:1
accept a fine instead, if they *. Ex 21:30
All of you who * to, all those Ex 35:5-9
I only * that all of the Lord's Num 11:29
"We * we had died in Egypt," Num 14:2
or anywhere they *, for it is their Num 18:31
Balaam shouted. "I * I had a Num 22:29
Eat as much of this meat as you * Deu 12:15
Eat all the fruit you *; Deu 20:19
you may do with us as you *." Jos 9:25
"What do you *?" Ju 1:14
you can do with them as you *!" Ju 9:33
However, if you * to bring Ju 13:16
can buy it if you *, with these Ru 4:4
and you can do to us as you *." 1Sa 11:10
fondest * will be fulfilled!" 1Sa 23:20
power, to do with as you *'!" 1Sa 24:4
I surely * I were the judge; 2Sa 15:4
Rehoboam is according to my *." 1Ki 12:23,24
whichever one they * and cut it 1Ki 18:23
to Elisha, "What * shall I grant 2Ki 2:9
her mistress, "I * my master would 2Ki 5:3
as you *," Ornan said to David. 1Ch 21:23
But we * you to know that if Ez 4:13
to control it. We * to declare Ez 4:16
"We * to inform you that we went Ez 5:8
"What do you *, Queen Esther? Est 5:3
my deepest *, is that if Your Est 5:7,8
What do you *? Est 7:2
Whatever you * will happen! Job 22:28
Well, does a man * to be Job 37:19,20
Our dearest * against him will Ps 35:25
But give great joy to all who * Ps 35:27
He will let me see my * come true Ps 59:10
How I * I could go into your Ps 63:2
their hearts could ever * for! Ps 73:7
Help me to love your every *; Ps 119:80
to pass, for I do whatever I *. Is 46:10
you will no longer * for "the good Jer 3:16
Settle in any city you * and live Jer 40:10
at you, to do with you as they *. Eze 23:24
They will go wherever they *, and Zec 10:12
give to anyone I *—if you will only Lk 4:6,7
And though I have no * to make Jn 8:50
kill and eat any of them you *." Act 10:13
'Kill and eat whatever you *.' Act 11:7
and now I * to tell you about him. Act 17:23
us far behind! I * you really were 1Co 4:8
but you certainly may if you *. 1Co 7:6
if you wish. I * everyone could 1Co 7:7
problems that I * you didn't have 1Co 7:28
I * you all had the gift of 1Co 14:5
but, even more, I * you were all 1Co 14:5
Our greatest * and prayer is that 2Co 13:9
How I * I could be there with Gal 4:20
I only * these teachers who want Gal 5:12
I * YOU could know how much I have Col 2:1
those who do not * to know God, and 2Th 1:8
you as good as you * you could be! 2Th 1:11
I * you were one or the other! Rev 3:15
upon the earth as often as they *. Rev 11:6

WISHED
* to, brought burnt offerings too. 2Ch 29:31
but those who * could have as much Est 1:8
she *, to enhance her beauty. Est 2:12,13,14
turn out as he *, so he kneaded it Jer 18:4
until he grew faint and * to die. Jon 4:8
yours to sell or not, as you *. Act 5:4

WISHES
"If anyone * to use a bird as Lev 1:14
"ANYONE WHO * to sacrifice a Lev 2:1
to walk against my *, then I will Lev 26:23
walk against your *, and I, even I, Lev 26:24
the Lord and then * to redeem it, Lev 27:14,15
extend congratulations and good *. 1Ki 5:1
in the heavens, and does as he *. Ps 115:3
Hezekiah a present and his best *, Is 39:1
laws, ignored my *, and violated my Eze 20:16
shall obey my laws and all my *. Eze 37:24
relatives, send you their good *. Rom 16:21
over us, and our * are never free Gal 5:17
in line with the Holy Spirit's *. Eph 6:18
of man's own evil thoughts and *. Jas 1:14

WISHING
"Look, I am the one you were * Job 33:6
Don't always be * for what you Lk 12:15

WIT'S
drunkards and are at their * end. Ps 107:27

WITCHCRAFT
nor use fortune telling or *. Lev 19:26
bad as the sin of *, and 1Sa 15:23
despite all your * and magic. Is 47:9
I will put an end to all *—there Mic 5:12
and *, their immorality and theft. Rev 9:21

WITCHES
by consulting * and mediums? Is 8:19
"Check these *' words against Is 8:20
and * to show them what to do. Is 19:3
But you—come here, you *' sons, Is 57:3

WITHDRAW
If God were to * his Spirit, Job 34:14
and you can't * what you said. Pro 25:8,9,10
and force Nebuchadnezzar to * his Jer 21:1
will scare him off, and he will * Dan 11:30,31
and the stars * their light. Joe 3:15

WITHDRAWN
He has * his protection as the Lam 2:3
He has * from them and they are Hos 5:6
gifts and his call can never be *; Rom 11:29

WITHDREW
Babylonian army * from Jerusalem to Jer 37:5
"Nevertheless, again I * my Eze 20:22
Nebuchadnezzar * from the siege Eze 30:21f
Literally, "* into the parts of Mt 15:21f
and his disciples * to the beach, Mk 3:7,8
But he often * to the wilderness Lk 5:16

WITHER
Suddenly it begins to *, even Job 8:11-13
Their leaves shall never *, and Ps 1:3
These enemies of God will * like Ps 37:20
trodden down and * like grass." Ps 58:7f
and their flowers *, for they have Is 5:24
river bank will * and blow away. Is 19:7
The earth languishes, the crops * Is 24:4,5
* like the grass and disappear? Is 51:12
Like autumn leaves we fade, * and Is 64:6
and let its leaves * and die. Eze 17:9
No, it will * away completely Eze 17:10
tree * and the dry tree grow. Eze 17:24
the pomegranates *; Joe 1:12
a drought to * the grain and Hag 1:11
did the fig tree * so quickly?" Mt 21:20

WITHERED
shriveled and * by the east wind. Gen 41:6
stalk, came seven *, thin heads. Gen 41:23
the seven thin and * heads of Gen 41:27
fall to the ground like a * grape. Job 15:33
* before the evening shadows fall. Ps 90:5,6
is trampled like grass and is *. Ps 102:3,4
white-haired, * old man, dragging Ecc 12:5
You will perish like a * tree or Is 1:30

(WITHERED Con't)
it is dry and hard and *. Lam 4:8
Its branches were broken and * by Eze 19:12
barren, *, sickly, with no grain; Hos 8:7
all joy has * with them. Joe 1:12
For the heat has * the pastures Joe 1:19
of Mount Carmel * and dried, and Amo 1:2
one field, another was dry and *. Amo 4:7
of the shelter * in the heat, the Jon 4:6
plant, so that it * away and died. Jon 4:7
them and they * and died, for they Mt 13:6
the fig tree * up. Mt 21:19
saw that it was * from the roots! Mk 11:20
The fig tree you cursed has *!" Mk 11:21
* and died for lack of moisture. Lk 8:6
and fades away, *—killed by the Jas 1:10,11

WITHERING
shadows. I am * like grass, while Ps 102:11

WITHERS
for a moment like a flower—and *; Job 14:2
The grass *, the flower fades Is 40:7
The grass *, the flowers fade, Is 40:8
and their work * and the wind Is 40:24
a useless branch, *, and is Jn 15:6

WITHHELD
* even your beloved son from me." Gen 22:12
me and have not * even your beloved Gen 22:16

WITHHOLD
No good thing will he * from Ps 84:11
Don't * repayment of your debts. Pro 3:27,28
and then I can * all the punishment Jer 26:3

WITHHOLDING
Cursed be those * their swords Jer 48:10

WITHHOLDS
is no escape. He * the rain, and Job 12:15

WITHSTAND
Who then can * his thunder?" Job 26:14
no one can * it or question it. Ecc 8:4
Jews couldn't * his proofs that Act 9:22

WITLESS
They are a foolish nation, a *, Is 27:11
Ephraim is a silly, * dove, Hos 7:11
to me anyway—a * man, a fool—while 2Co 11:16

WITNESS
the Eternal God [to * the covenant Gen 21:33
They named it "The * Gen 31:47,48
will stand as a * against us [if Gen 31:47,48
between us as a * of our vows that Gen 31:51,52
affirming on the * stand something Ex 23:1
When on the * stand, don't be Ex 23:2,3
there being no *, and he is Num 5:13
only if there is more than one *; Num 35:30
on the testimony of only one *; Deu 17:6
anyone on the testimony of one *. Deu 19:15
If anyone gives false *, Deu 19:16
and if the * is lying, his penalty Deu 19:18
to tell lies on the * stand. Deu 19:20
shall not show pity to a false *. Deu 19:21
"I call heaven and earth to * Deu 30:19
and earth to * against them. Deu 31:28
"The Altar of *," for they said, Jos 22:34
said, "It is a * between us and Jos 22:34
so it will be a * to testify Jos 24:27
Again and again you * against me Job 10:17
"Yet even now the * to my Job 16:19
moon, my faithful * in the sky!" Ps 89:37
*Sowing discord among brothers Pro 6:16-19
A truthful * never lies; Pro 14:5
a false * always lies. Pro 14:5
A * who tells the truth saves Pro 14:25
death, but a false * is a traitor. Pro 14:25
A false * shall be punished and a Pro 19:9
A worthless * cares nothing for Pro 19:28
A false * must be punished; Pro 21:28
an honest * is safe. Pro 21:28
of Samaria to * the scandalous Amo 3:9
be called to * your complaint. Mic 6:1
about me, yes, to * to the world. Mt 10:18
God sent John the Baptist as a * Jn 1:6,7
he was only a * to identify it. Jn 1:8
is to the * of his Father. Jn 5:32,33f
But the truest * I have is not Jn 5:34
you about John's * so that you will Jn 5:34
but I have a greater * than John. Jn 5:36
their * is accepted as fact. Jn 8:17
Well, I am one *, and my Father Jn 8:18
borne *, and his witness is true; Jn 19:35f
borne witness, and his * is true; Jn 19:35f
testified to this in public *. Act 13:31
he never left himself without a *; Act 14:17
And when your * Stephen was Act 22:20
you as my servant and my *. Act 26:16
I call upon this God to * against 2Co 1:23
We believe men who * in our 1Jn 5:9
my faithful *, was martyred among Rev 2:13
the faithful and true * [of all Rev 3:14

WITNESSED
who had personally * the amazing Jos 24:31
to each other, for he has * them. 1Sa 20:23
and sealed and *—in the country of Jer 32:44

WITNESSES
(you men are * of my promise, and Gen 45:11,12
"You are * to the fact that I Ex 20:22
and earth are * that you shall be Deu 4:26
two or three. The * shall throw Deu 17:7
"Yes," they replied, "we are * Jos 24:22
and asked them to sit as *. Ru 4:2
with these respected men as *. Ru 4:4
Then Boaz said to the * and to Ru 4:9
the * replied, "We are witnesses. Ru 4:11
the witnesses replied, "We are *. Ru 4:11
king are my *," Samuel declared, 1Sa 12:5
Punish false *. Pro 19:5
*—they have no respect for anyone. Is 33:8
Where are the * of anything they Is 43:9
If there are no *, then they must Is 43:9
But I have *, O Israel, says the Is 43:10
You are my * and my servants, Is 43:10
you are my * that it is true. Is 43:12
You are my * —is there any other Is 44:8
They themselves are * that this Is 44:9
of purchase before *, and weighed Jer 32:10
Hanamel and the * who had signed Jer 32:12
it before these *—even though the Jer 32:25
everything you say by these *. Mt 18:16
and looked for * who would lie Mt 26:59
agreed to be false *, these always Mt 26:60,61
What need have we for other *? Mt 26:65,66
Many false * volunteered, but Mk 14:56
Why wait for *? Mk 14:63,64
need do we have for other *?" Lk 22:71
us as * of Jesus' resurrection. Act 1:21,22
* that Jesus rose from the dead. Act 2:32
And John and I are * of this Act 3:15
And we are * of these things, Act 5:32
The lying * testified again that Act 6:13
The official *—the Act 7:58
"And we apostles are * of all he Act 10:39
him to certain * God had selected Act 10:40,41
You yourselves are our *—as is 1Th 2:10
are two or three * to accuse him. 1Ti 5:19
ringing confession before many *. 1Ti 6:12
were two or three * to his sin. Heb 10:28
So we have these three *: the 1Jn 5:6,7,8
to my two * to prophesy 1,260 days Rev 11:3

WITNESSING
and for being faithful in their *. Rev 6:9

WITS
their *' ends to know what to do; Is 19:3
have lost my * to talk like this; 2Co 11:16

WIVES
Lamech married two *—Adah and Gen 4:19
and Zillah, "Listen to me, my *. Gen 4:23
any they desired to be their *. Gen 6:1
wife and your sons and their *. Gen 6:18
and their *, to escape the flood. Gen 7:7
Ham, and Japheth, and their *. Gen 7:13
his sons and their * all Gen 8:18,19
two additional * from there, Gen 28:9
besides the * he already had. Gen 28:9
One of these new * was Mahalath, Gen 28:9
Let me take my * and Gen 30:26
Jacob set his * and sons on camels, Gen 31:17-20
or take other *, I won't know, but Gen 31:50
his two * and his two concubines Gen 32:22,23,24
daughters as * for your young men. Gen 34:9,10
Then Esau took his *, children, Gen 36:6,7,8
of his father's * Bilhah and Gen 37:2
to carry their * and little ones, Gen 45:19
ones and their *, in the wagons Gen 46:5
* of Jacob's sons, was sixty-six. Gen 46:26
of my * and thus dishonored me. Gen 49:4
sexual intercourse with your *." Ex 19:15
so that your * will be widows and Ex 22:24
other gods, as * for your sons—and Ex 34:16
me by worshiping their *' gods. Ex 34:16
of his father's *, nor his sister Lev 18:8
us there, and our * and little ones Num 14:3
their * and sons and little ones. Num 16:27
"Our children, *, flocks, and Num 32:26
" 'But your * and children,' I Deu 3:19
He must not have too many *, Deu 17:17
"If a man has two * but loves Deu 21:15
* while their husband was living. Deu 22:30f
*, for she belongs to his father.' Deu 27:20
ones and your * and the foreigners Deu 29:11
them, "so your * and children and Jos 1:14
their girls as *, and the Israeli Ju 3:6
sons, for he married many *. Ju 8:30
Of all of Gideon's *, only Ju 9:2f
And how shall we get * for the Ju 21:7
given to them as *, and they Ju 21:14
"What shall we do for * for the Ju 21:16
be some way to get * for them, so Ju 21:17
who still needed *, "Go and hide Ju 21:20
them home with you to be your *! Ju 21:21
find enough * for them when we Ju 21:22
He had two *, Hannah and 1Sa 1:2
He had his two * with 1Sa 27:2,3
(David's two *, Ahino-am and 1Sa 30:5
and David rescued his two *. 1Sa 30:18,19
Give them their * and their 1Sa 30:22
So David and his *—Ahino-am from 2Sa 2:2
married additional * and 2Sa 5:13
and she became one of his *; 2Sa 11:27
I gave you his palace and his * 2Sa 12:8
I will give your * to another 2Sa 12:11
* to keep the palace in order. 2Sa 15:16
with your father's *, for he has 2Sa 16:21
tent to lie with his father's *. 2Sa 16:22
daughters, your * and concubines; 2Sa 19:5
that his ten * he had left to keep 2Sa 20:3
longer sleep with them as his *. 2Sa 20:3
Pharaoh's daughter—one of his *. 1Ki 7:8
dowry—she was one of Solomon's *. 1Ki 9:16
He had seven hundred * and three 1Ki 11:3
for these foreign * to use for 1Ki 11:8
* and the best of your children!" 1Ki 20:2,3
your silver, gold, *, and children, 1Ki 20:5,6
he could have my * and children and 1Ki 20:7
Jehoiachin, his * and officials, 2Ki 24:15
Hezron) had two *, 1Ch 2:18
the father of Tekoa, had two *— 1Ch 4:5
of his father's *, his birthright 1Ch 5:1
them had several * and many sons. 1Ch 7:4
It was Machir who found * for 1Ch 7:15
Shaharaim divorced his * 1Ch 8:8,9,10
married additional * and became the 1Ch 14:3
any of his other * and concubines 2Ch 11:21
(he had eighteen * and sixty 2Ch 11:21
for them to have several * apiece. 2Ch 11:23
He married fourteen * and had 2Ch 13:21
their little ones, *, and children, 2Ch 20:13
You, your children, your *, and 2Ch 21:14
including his sons and his *; 2Ch 21:17
and daughters and * are in 2Ch 29:9
taken them as * for their sons. Ez 9:2
our heathen * and to send them away Ez 10:3
married heathen * (they vowed to Ez 10:16-19
to divorce their * and acknowledged Ez 10:16-19
Each of these men had heathen *, Ez 10:44
and many had children by these *. Ez 10:44
who, with their * and sons and Neh 10:28
will be respected by their *!" Est 1:20
harem where the king's * lived. Est 2:12,13,14
to mourn them, not even their *. Job 27:15
can give them understanding *. Pro 19:14
become unfaithful to their *. Pro 23:26,27,28
I have sixty other *, all Sol 6:8
* raped by the attacking hordes. Is 13:16
husbands and * and grandparents. Jer 6:11
homes and take their fields and *. Jer 6:12
I will give their * and their Jer 8:10
Husbands, *, sons and Jer 14:16
Let their * be widows and be Jer 18:21
* and have lied in my name. Jer 29:23
* or our sons or daughters either. Jer 35:8
All your * and children will be Jer 38:23
of your * in Judah and Jerusalem? Jer 44:9
knew that their * had burned Jer 44:15
Both you and your * have said that Jer 44:25
with their fathers' * and lie Eze 22:10
and joys—their * and their sons and Eze 24:25
and his princes, *, and concubines Dan 5:2,3,4
and you and your officers and * Dan 5:23
their children and *, and the lions Dan 6:24
children and your *, and filled Nah 2:12
husbands and * apart, to face Zec 12:12,13,14
in divorcing your * who have been Mal 2:14
there be no divorcing of your *. Mal 2:16
of the * of the leading men." Act 17:4f
including * and children walked Act 21:5
assurance to you * that your 1Co 7:16
to you husbands concerning your *. 1Co 7:16
For that reason those who have * 1Co 7:29
* may be as though they didn't." 1Co 7:29f
with other men's *, and 23,000 fell 1Co 10:8
and the taking of other men's *. 2Co 12:21
each other. You * must submit to Eph 5:22
So you * must willingly obey Eph 5:24
of love to your * as Christ showed Eph 5:25
should treat their *, loving them Eph 5:28
You *, submit yourselves to your Col 3:18
and kind to your * and not bitter Col 3:19
Their * must be thoughtful, not 1Ti 3:11
*, FIT IN with your husbands' 1Pe 3:1
be careful of your *, being 1Pe 3:7

WIZARD
"A medium or a *—whether man or Lev 20:27
medium, or *, or call forth the Deu 18:11
magician, or * can tell the king Dan 2:27

WIZARDS
and *, for I am Jehovah your God. Lev 19:31
mediums and * instead of me and I Lev 20:6
and * from the land of Israel. 1Sa 28:3
and patronized mediums and *. 2Ki 21:6
the mediums and *, and every kind 2Ki 23:24
call upon mediums, * and witches Is 19:3
and *—and I told them the dream, Dan 4:7

WOE
* to Moab! Num 21:27-30
they cried out. "* upon us, 1Sa 4:7
and weep beneath my burden of *. Ps 55:2
and *—every day and all day long! Ps 73:14

WOE Con't)
* to the land whose king is a Ecc 10:16,17
* to you who get up early in the Is 5:11
at night—* to you drunken bums. Is 5:11
* to those who drag their sins Is 5:18
* to those who are wise and Is 5:21
their own eyes! * to those who are Is 5:22
* TO UNJUST judges and to those Is 10:1
* TO THE city of Samaria, Is 28:1
of Israel! * to her fading beauty, Is 28:1
* TO JERUSALEM, Is 29:1
* to those who try to hide their Is 29:15
* TO MY rebellious children, says Is 30:1
* TO THOSE who run to Egypt for Is 31:1
* TO YOU, Assyrians, Is 33:1
* to the man who fights with his Is 45:9
can you be!"? * to the baby just Is 45:10
*, woe upon us, for we are doomed. Jer 4:13
Woe, * upon us, for we are doomed. Jer 4:13
hills. * upon you, O Jerusalem! Jer 13:27
And * to you, King Jehoiakim, Jer 22:13
You have said, * is me! Jer 45:3
* to the city of Nebo, for it Jer 48:1
* to you, O Moab; Jer 48:46
Not even her cattle—* to them, Jer 50:27
our head. * upon us for our sins. Lam 5:16
will befall you; * upon woe, Eze 7:26,27
woe upon *, disaster upon Eze 7:26,27
them anything at all. * upon them! Eze 13:2,3
Tell them the Lord God says: * Eze 13:18
other wickedness—*, woe upon you, Eze 16:23
wickedness—woe, * upon you, says Eze 16:23
they mocked my people in their *. Eze 21:28
world will mock you for your *. Eze 23:32
"For the Lord God says: * to Eze 24:6
"* to Jerusalem, City of Eze 24:9
God says to you: * to the shepherds Eze 34:2
* to my people for deserting me; Hos 7:13
* TO THOSE lounging in luxury at Amo 6:1
her. * to the city of Gath. Mic 1:10
* TO YOU who lie awake at night, Mic 2:1
* IS ME! Mic 7:1
* TO NINEVEH, City of Blood, full Nah 3:1
"* to you for getting rich by Hab 2:9
"* to you who build cities with Hab 2:12
"* to you for making your Hab 2:15
had made. * to those who command Hab 2:19
And * to you Philistines Zep 2:5
* TO FILTHY, sinful Jerusalem, Zep 3:1
off their feet. * to this Zec 11:17
"* to you, Chorazin, and woe to Mt 11:21
"Woe to you, Chorazin, and * to Mt 11:21
"* upon the world for all its Mt 18:7
is inevitable, but * to the man who Mt 18:7
"* to you, Pharisees, and you Mt 23:13,14
Yes, * upon you hypocrites. Mt 23:15
Blind guides! * upon you! Mt 23:16
"Yes, * upon you, Pharisees, and Mt 23:23
"* to you, Pharisees, and you Mt 23:25
"* to you, Pharisees, and you Mt 23:27
"Yes, * to you, Pharisees, and Mt 23:29,30
"And * to pregnant women and to Mt 24:19
just as was prophesied, but * to Mt 26:24
"* to pregnant women in those Mk 13:17
"But * to you Pharisees! Lk 11:42
"* to you Pharisees! Lk 11:43
of trying to keep. * to you! Lk 11:47
"* to you experts in religion! Lk 11:52
disciples, "but * to the man who Lk 17:1
fulfilled. * to expectant mothers Lk 21:23
I would be utterly miserable. * 1Co 9:16
* upon them! Jud 1:11
crying loudly, "*, woe, woe to the Rev 8:13
loudly, "Woe, *, woe to the people Rev 8:13
"Woe, woe, * to the people of the Rev 8:13
The second * is past, but the Rev 11:14
Be glad! But * to you people of Rev 12:12
She brewed many a cup of * for Rev 18:6

WOES
because God has heard your *. Gen 16:9-12
them of the reason for their *. Deu 31:21
two mercies for each of your *! Zec 9:12

WOKE
Then Jacob * up. Gen 28:16,17
At which point, Pharaoh * up! Gen 41:4
Then Pharaoh * up again and Gen 41:7
Then I * up. Gen 41:21
And he * up and yanked his hair Ju 16:14
And he * up and thought, "I Ju 16:20
Then Solomon * up and realized it 1Ki 3:15
slept in peace and * up safely, for Ps 3:5
* me, as though I had been asleep. Zec 4:1
They rushed over and * him up. Lk 8:24
Now they * up and saw Jesus Lk 9:32

WOLF
"Benjamin is a * that prowls. Gen 49:27
In that day the * and the lamb Is 11:6
prayers! The * and lamb shall feed Is 65:25
run when he sees a * coming and Jn 10:12
And so the * leaps on them and Jn 10:12

WOLVES
mingle there with * and hyenas. Is 34:14
the "desert *" shall pounce Jer 5:6
Your leaders are like *, who Eze 22:27
more fierce than * at dusk. Hab 1:8
Her judges are like ravenous * at Zep 3:3
but are * and will tear you apart. Mt 7:15
sending you out as sheep among *. Mt 10:16
sending you out as lambs among *. Lk 10:3
like vicious *, will appear among Act 20:29

WOMAN
a *, and brought her to the man. Gen 2:22
Her name is '*' because she was Gen 2:23
So the serpent came to the *. Gen 3:1
we may eat it," the * told him. Gen 3:2,3
The * was convinced. Gen 3:6
"but it was the * you gave me who Gen 3:12
Then the Lord God asked the *, Gen 3:13
From now on you and the * will Gen 3:15
of you into the *, and between your Gen 3:15
Then God said to the *, "You Gen 3:16
God created man and * and Gen 5:2
So Sarah laughed silently. "A * Gen 18:12
Why did she say 'Can an old * Gen 18:13
for that * you took is married." Gen 20:3
sending along the * who had been Gen 24:59
Every * will ask for jewels, Ex 3:22
hurt a pregnant * so that she has a Ex 21:22
But if any harm comes to the * Ex 21:23
whether man or *, and the eye is Ex 21:26
"If an ox gores a man or * to Ex 21:28
man and * who wanted to assist in Ex 35:29
"If a man or * has a sore on the Lev 13:29,30
"If a man or a * has white, Lev 13:38
After sexual intercourse, the * Lev 15:18
"Whenever a * menstruates, she Lev 15:19
You may not marry both a * and Lev 18:17
with a * who is menstruating; Lev 18:19
and a * must never give herself Lev 18:23
man and * shall be put to death. Lev 20:10
both the man and the * must die, Lev 20:11
intercourse with a * and with her Lev 20:14
If a * has sexual intercourse Lev 20:16
animal, kill the * and the animal, Lev 20:16
intercourse with a * during her Lev 20:18
*—shall surely be stoned to death. Lev 20:27
prostitute, nor a * of another Lev 21:7
*, for he is a holy man of God. Lev 21:7
a widow, nor a * who is divorced, Lev 21:14,15
a * from the age of twenty to Lev 27:4
a half dollars; a *, five dollars. Lev 27:7
anyone, man or *, betrays the Lord Num 5:5,6
And the * shall be required to Num 5:21,22
(When he requires the * to drink Num 5:24
require the * to drink the water. Num 5:26
either a man or a * takes the Num 6:1
of the Cushite * he had married." Num 12:1f
*, and they said, "Has the Lord Num 12:1
"If a * promises the Lord to do Num 30:3
"But if the * is a widow or is Num 30:9
whether of a man, *, animal, bird, Deu 4:16,17
whether a man or *, you must free Deu 15:12
"If anyone, whether man or *, in Deu 17:2,3
then that man or * shall be taken Deu 17:5
"A * must not wear men's Deu 22:5
The most tender and delicate * Deu 28:56,57
The day that any of you—man or * Deu 29:18
inn operated by a * named Rahab, Jos 2:1
go to a * instead of to you!" Ju 4:9
to burn it, a * on the roof threw Ju 9:53
"Never let it be said that a * Ju 9:54
The * ran and told her husband, Ju 13:6
There was a * lying at his feet! Ru 3:8
it be known that a * was here at Ru 3:14
May the Lord make this *, who has Ru 4:11
from this young * be as numerous Ru 4:12
"I am the * who stood here that 1Sa 1:26
The barren * now has seven 1Sa 2:5
of a perverse, rebellious *." 1Sa 20:30f
intelligent *, was named Abigail. 1Sa 25:3
the * demanded. 1Sa 28:9
Finally the * said, "Well, whom 1Sa 28:11
When the * saw Samuel, she 1Sa 28:12
When the * saw how distraught he 1Sa 28:21
to that of the * until he finally 1Sa 28:23
on the bed. The * had been 1Sa 28:24
find fault with me about some *? 2Sa 3:8
city, he noticed a * of unusual 2Sa 11:2
at Thebez by a * who threw down 2Sa 11:19,20,21
"Throw this * out and lock the 2Sa 13:17,18
So Tamar lived as a desolate * in 2Sa 13:20
he sent for a * of Tekoa who had a 2Sa 14:2,3
When the * approached the king, 2Sa 14:4
And the * replied, "How can I 2Sa 14:19
But a wise * in the city called 2Sa 20:16
As he approached, the * asked, 2Sa 20:17
"All right," the * replied, "we 2Sa 20:21
Then the * went to the people 2Sa 20:22
Then the other * interrupted, 1Ki 3:22
"No," the first * said, "the 1Ki 3:22
Then the * who really was the 1Ki 3:26
But the other * said, "All right, 1Ki 3:26
the baby to the * who wants him to 1Ki 3:27
mother was Naamah, an Ammonite *. 1Ki 14:21
A prominent * of the city invited 2Ki 4:8
the * I want to speak to her." 2Ki 4:11,12
But it was true; the * soon 2Ki 4:17
that * from Shunem is coming. 2Ki 4:25
of the city, a * called to him, 2Ki 6:26-30
She replied, "This * proposed 2Ki 6:26-30
ELISHA HAD TOLD the * whose son 2Ki 8:1
So the * took her family and 2Ki 8:2
"Here is the * now, and this is 2Ki 8:5
bury this cursed *, for she is the 2Ki 9:34
of a Jewish * from Dan in Israel; 2Ch 2:14
old or young, man or *. 2Ch 15:13
was Shime-ath, a * from Ammon; 2Ch 24:26
was Shimrith, a * from Moab. 2Ch 24:26
she was a very beautiful *. Est 1:11
whether man or *, who goes into the Est 4:11
"You talk like some heathen *. Job 2:10
with panic like a * in travail! Ps 48:6
A beautiful * lacking discretion Pro 11:22
A WISE * builds her house, while a Pro 14:1
while a foolish * tears hers down Pro 14:1
with a crabby * in a lovely home. Pro 21:9
with a quarrelsome, complaining *. Pro 21:19
home with a cranky, quarrelsome *. Pro 25:24
day and a cranky * are much alike! Pro 27:15
A bitter * when she finally Pro 30:21,22,23
She is a * of strength and Pro 31:25
last, but a * who fears and Pro 31:30
Literally, "the * whose heart is Ecc 7:26f
be said to be wise, but not one *! Ecc 7:27,28
Live happily with the * you love Ecc 9:9
O most beautiful * in all the Sol 1:8
of Jerusalem: "O * of rare Sol 5:9
and sometimes "young *." Is 7:14f
pangs, like those of a * in labor. Is 13:8
of a * giving birth to a child. Is 21:3
We suffered as a * giving birth, Is 26:17
it is a serious time, as when a * Is 37:3
he will groan and cry like a * Is 42:14
SING, O CHILDLESS *! Is 54:1
that if a man divorces a * who Jer 3:1
* giving birth to her first child; Jer 4:31
You will writhe in pain like a * Jer 13:21
as of a * in labor. Jer 22:23
Literally, "a * shall court a Jer 31:22f
or, "a * shall encompass a man." Jer 31:22f
live—not a man, * or child among Jer 44:7
like the pangs of a * in labor. Jer 50:43
punished and as a * breaking Eze 16:38
nor lie with any * during the time Eze 18:6
* your mother was—like a lioness! Eze 19:2
Her name was known to every * in Eze 23:10
he may not marry a divorced *. Eze 44:22
Pain has gripped you like a * in Mic 4:9
see a * sitting inside the basket! Zec 5:7
even looks at a * with lust in his Mt 5:28
rabbi's home, a * who had been Mt 9:20
And the * was well from that Mt 9:22
be compared to a * making bread. Mt 13:33
A * from Canaan who was living Mt 15:22
Then he said to the *, "I was Mt 15:24
"*," Jesus told her, "your Mt 15:28
created man and *, and that a man Mt 19:4
a divorced * commits adultery." Mt 19:9f
While he was eating, a * came in Mt 26:7
In the crowd was a * who had Mk 5:25
Then the frightened *, trembling Mk 5:33
Right away a * came to him whose Mk 7:25
he made man and * to be joined Mk 10:6,7
and last of all, the * died too. Mk 12:20,21,22
brothers and the * rise from the Mk 12:25
during supper a * came in with a Mk 14:3
Mary Magdalene—the * from whom he Mk 16:9
As they sat down to eat, a * of Lk 7:37
and who the * was, he said to Lk 7:39
know what kind of * this one is!" Lk 7:39
Then he turned to the * and said Lk 7:44
See this * kneeling here! Lk 7:44
And Jesus said to the *, "Your Lk 7:50
As they went a * who wanted to be Lk 8:43,44
When the * realized that Jesus Lk 8:47
they came to a village where a * Lk 10:38
As he was speaking, a * in the Lk 11:27
handicapped * who had been bent Lk 13:11
him Jesus said, "*, you are healed Lk 13:12
free this Jewish * from the bondage Lk 13:16
illustration: A * has ten valuable Lk 15:8
a divorced * commits adultery." Lk 16:18
himself, 'but this * bothers me. Lk 18:4,5
Finally the * died also. Lk 20:32
Peter denied it. "*," he said, Lk 22:57
Literally, "*, what have I to do Jn 2:4f
Soon a Samaritan * came to draw Jn 4:7
some food. The * was surprised Jn 4:9
"Please, sir," the * said, Jn 4:15
"But I'm not married," the * Jn 4:17,18
"Sir," the * said, "you must Jn 4:19
The * said, "Well, at least I Jn 4:25
him talking to a *, but none of Jn 4:27
Then the * left her waterpot Jn 4:28,29

(WOMAN Con't)
Then they said to the *, "Now Jn 4:42
brought a * caught in adultery and Jn 8:3
to Jesus, "this * was caught in Jn 8:4
in front of the crowd with the *. Jn 8:9
joy as that of a * in labor when Jn 16:21
every man and * in all the earth. Jn 17:2
Joppa there was a * named Dorcas Act 9:36
and a * named Damaris, and others. Act 17:34
Let me illustrate: when a * Rom 7:2
PHOEBE, A DEAR Christian * from Rom 16:1
own wife, and each * having her own 1Co 7:2
right as a married *, and the wife 1Co 7:3
And if a Christian * has a 1Co 7:13
But a married * must consider 1Co 7:34
And that is why a * who publicly 1Co 11:5
And if it is shameful for a * to 1Co 11:6
image, and man's glory is the *. 1Co 11:7
The first man didn't come from * 1Co 11:8
but the first * came out of man. 1Co 11:8
So a * should wear a covering on 1Co 11:10
* to have power on (her) head." 1Co 11:10f
For although the first * came 1Co 11:12
Is it right for a * to pray in 1Co 11:13
than this—that a * should wear a 1Co 11:16
his Son, born of a *, born as a Gal 4:4
you can rejoice, O childless * Gal 4:27
of the free *, acceptable to God Gal 4:31
must not marry a * who already has Jas 2:11
honest men. No * can escape their 2Pe 2:14
To: That dear * Cyria, one of 2Jn 1:1
permitting that * Jezebel, who Rev 2:20
I saw a * clothed with the sun, Rev 12:1
He stood before the * as she was Rev 12:4
his throne. The * fled into the Rev 12:6
he persecuted the * who had given Rev 12:13
* in an effort to get rid of her; Rev 12:15
There I saw a * sitting on a Rev 17:3
against God. The * wore purple and Rev 17:4
built on seven hills where this * Rev 17:9
rivers that the * is sitting on Rev 17:15
him—all hate the *, and will attack Rev 17:16
And this * you saw in your Rev 17:18
beautiful—like a * clothed in Rev 18:16

WOMAN'S
amount the * husband shall demand, Ex 21:22
and for a * menstrual period; Lev 15:33
Literally, "the Israelite * Lev 24:11f
offering from the * hand and wave Num 5:25
for the murdered * husband and Ju 20:3
He went to the * home at night, 1Sa 28:7,8
old, this * baby was born too. 1Ki 3:17,18
But one day the * son became sick 1Ki 17:17
his lot, for the * husband will be Pro 6:34
as a menstruating * rags." Is 64:6f
the world, this * deed will be Mk 14:9
had said, "If a * first child is a Lk 2:23
because of the * report: "He told Jn 4:39
lands along with the free * son. Gal 4:30
as suddenly as a * birth pains 1Th 5:3

WOMB
* shall become two rival nations. Gen 25:23
breasts and of the *, blessings of Gen 49:25
Literally, "all that opens the * Ex 34:19f
for the Lord had sealed her *; 1Sa 1:5
from my mother's *," he said, Job 1:21
shut my mother's *, for letting me Job 3:10
directly from the * to the grave. Job 10:19
from my mother's * and brought me Ps 22:9,10,11
them together in my mother's *. Ps 139:13
The barren * Pro 30:15,16
while it is yet in its mother's *. Ecc 11:5
From within the * he called me by Is 49:1
from my mother's * to serve him who Is 49:5
formed within your mother's *; Jer 1:5
*, that it had been my grave! Jer 20:17
the *, or never even be conceived. Hos 9:11
resisting in the *—how stubborn! Hos 13:13
your mother—the * from which you Lk 11:27
mother's * and be born again?" Jn 3:4

WOMBS
The curse of barren *; Deu 28:15-19
I will ask for * that don't give Hos 9:14

WOMEN
looked upon the beautiful earth * Gen 6:1
with human *, their children became Gen 6:4
men and * slaves, and camels. Gen 12:16
the * and other captives. Gen 14:16
men and *—and gave them to Gen 20:14
and the other * of the household, Gen 20:17
for God had stricken all the * Gen 20:18
It was evening, and the * of the Gen 24:11
The other * will think me blessed Gen 30:13
A leafy plant eaten by peasant * Gen 30:14f
our rights to those of foreign *; Gen 31:15
Literally, "The manner of * is Gen 31:35f
Laban replied, "These * are my Gen 31:43
and many servants, both men and *. Gen 32:5
Then Esau looked at the * and Gen 33:5
and took all the * and children, Gen 34:29
him, "the Hebrew * have their Ex 1:19
not slow like the Egyptian *!" Ex 1:19
* to nurse the baby for you?" Ex 2:7
Tell all the men and * of Israel Ex 11:2
the * and children, going on foot. Ex 12:37
a timbrel and led the * in dances. Ex 15:20
men or *—or your cattle or your Ex 20:10
So they all did—men and *, boys Ex 32:2,3
Both men and * came, all who Ex 35:22
The * skilled in sewing and Ex 35:25
Some other * gladly used their Ex 35:26
donated by the * who assembled at Ex 38:8
This applies to men and * alike. Num 5:3
[besides all the * and children Num 11:21
And the men and * Num 21:27-30
These * were of the half-tribe of Num 27:1
captives all the * and children, Num 31:9,10,11
"Why have you let all the * Num 31:15
* who have had sexual intercourse. Num 31:17
including the * and babies. Deu 2:33,34
*, and children alike. Deu 3:6
Do the same with your * slaves. Deu 15:17
*, children, cattle, and booty. Deu 20:14
in Israel, either men or *; Deu 23:17,18
"—men, *, children, and foreigners Deu 31:12
in it—men and *, young and old; Jos 6:21
including the * and children and Jos 8:35
These * came to Eleazar the Jos 17:4
Moses, these five * were given an Jos 17:5,6
Above all * who live in tents. Ju 5:24
died, about a thousand men and *. Ju 9:49
of Benjamin—men, *, children, and Ju 20:48
All the men, married *, and Ju 21:10,11,12
since all the * of the tribe of Ju 21:16
the * asked. Ru 1:19
Stay right behind my * workers; Ru 2:8,9
And the * of the city said to Ru 4:14
and the neighbor * said, "Now at Ru 4:16,17
seducing the young * who assisted 1Sa 2:22
Just before she died, the * who 1Sa 4:20
Amalek nation—men, *, babies, 1Sa 15:3
killed Goliath. * came out from all 1Sa 18:6
not slept with any * for awhile." 1Sa 21:4
families—men, *, children, and 1Sa 22:19
This is the same man the * of 1Sa 29:5
off all the * and children. 1Sa 30:2
But now, O * of Israel, weep for 2Sa 1:24
Than the love of *! 2Sa 1:26
everyone—men and * alike—of a loaf 2Sa 6:19
give half to each of these *!" 1Ki 3:25
because the * they married would 1Ki 11:2
our * to have miscarriages." 2Ki 2:19
the bellies of the pregnant *!" 2Ki 8:12
and ripped open the pregnant *. 2Ki 15:16
* wove robes for the Asherah-idol. 2Ki 23:7
(men and * alike) a loaf of 1Ch 16:3
200,000 Judean * and children, and 2Ch 28:8
of clothing to the * and children 2Ch 28:15
200 choir members, both men and *. Ez 2:64,65
crowd of men, *, and children Ez 10:1
we have married these heathen *. Ez 10:2
for you have married heathen *; Ez 10:10
about you and from these *." Ez 10:11
245 choir members, both men and *. Neh 7:67
for great joy. The * and children Neh 12:43
Jews had married * from Ashdod, Neh 13:23
led into idolatry by foreign *. Neh 13:26
* of the palace at the same time. Est 1:9
your empire. For * everywhere will Est 1:17
and old, * and children—must all be Est 3:13
the godly men and * in the land; Ps 16:3
all the world—men, * and Ps 33:8
Literally, "honorable *." Ps 45:9f
The enemy flees. The * at home Ps 68:11,12,13
Now all the * of Israel are Ps 68:11,12,13
children with * of the street? Pro 5:16
Honor goes to kind and gracious * Pro 11:16
your time with *—the royal pathway Pro 31:3
are many fine * in the world, but Pro 31:29
both men and *, and others were Ecc 2:7,8
I adjure you, O * of Jerusalem, Sol 3:5
The Young * of Jerusalem: "Who Sol 3:5
King Solomon, O young * of Zion; Sol 3:11
The Young * of Jerusalem: "Oh, Sol 5:1
I adjure you, O * of Jerusalem, Sol 5:8
The Young * of Jerusalem: "O Sol 5:8
Such, O * of Jerusalem, is my Sol 5:16
THE YOUNG * of Jerusalem: "O Sol 6:1
*, where has your loved one gone? Sol 6:1
an equal! The * of Jerusalem were Sol 6:9
The Young * of Jerusalem: Sol 6:12
I adjure you, O * of Jerusalem, Sol 8:4
The Young * of Jerusalem: "Who Sol 8:4
Weak as *! Is 3:12
the haughty Jewish *, who mince Is 3:16
die in battle; the *, ravaged, Is 3:25,26
alive that seven * will fight over Is 4:1
of Judah. The * of Moab are left Is 16:2
will be as weak as *, cowering in Is 19:16
Listen, you * who loll around in Is 32:9
Tremble, O * of ease; Is 32:11
us like that of * in travail. Jer 6:24
fires, and the * knead dough and Jer 7:18
to the words of God, O * who wail. Jer 9:20
they shall fall like fragile *. Jer 25:34
their sides like * in labor?" Jer 30:6
his Hebrew slaves, both men and *. Jer 34:9
said that all the * left in your Jer 38:21,22
and these * will taunt you with Jer 38:21,22
rescued—soldiers, *, children and Jer 41:16,17
In the crowd were men, * and Jer 43:6
Then all the * present and all Jer 44:15
"And," the * added, "do you Jer 44:19
of them, men and * alike, who had Jer 44:20
all, including the *: "Listen to Jer 44:24
* in the pains of giving birth. Jer 48:41
disappear like that of * in labor. Jer 49:22
gripped her as they do * in labor. Jer 49:24
lands shall become as weak as *. Jer 50:37
they have become as *. Jer 51:30
Tender-hearted * have cooked and Lam 4:10
They rape the * of Jerusalem and Lam 5:11
there sat * weeping for Tammuz, Eze 8:14
The * wept for Tammuz, the god of Eze 8:14f
girls, * and little children; Eze 9:6
out against the * prophets too who Eze 13:17
says: Woe to these * who are Eze 13:18
you before the eyes of many *. Eze 16:40,41
* in their time of menstruation." Eze 22:10f
wives and lie with menstruous *. Eze 22:10
* will be taken away as slaves. Eze 30:17
nor for the god beloved of *, Dan 11:37
Wine, *, and song have robbed my Hos 4:11
* ripped open with a sword. Hos 13:16
slaves, men and * alike, and put Joe 2:29
open pregnant * with their swords. Amo 1:13
in Samaria—you * who encourage your Amo 4:1
will be weak and helpless as *. Nah 3:13
Then I saw two * flying toward Zec 5:9
be aged men and * hobbling through Zec 8:4
the loot divided, the * raped; Zec 14:1
heathen * who worship idols. Mal 2:11
besides all the * and children. Mt 14:21
men besides the * and children! Mt 15:37,38
"And woe to pregnant * and to Mt 24:19
other left. Two * will be going Mt 24:41
many godly men and * who had died Mt 27:52
And many * who had come down from Mt 27:55
Then the angel spoke to the *. Mt 28:5
The * ran from the tomb, badly Mt 28:8
As the * were on the way into the Mt 28:11
"Woe to pregnant * in those Mk 13:17
Some * were there watching from a Mk 15:40
They and many other Galilean * Mk 15:41
in white. The * were startled, but Mk 16:5
The * fled from the tomb, Mk 16:8
are you among *," as in verse 42 Lk 1:28f
above all other *, and your child Lk 1:42
Some * went along, from whom he Lk 8:2
Wine, *, and song for you!" Lk 12:19
whip the men and * he is supposed Lk 12:45
other left. Two * will be working Lk 17:35,36
behind, and many grief-stricken *. Lk 23:27
coming when the * who have no Lk 23:29
including the * who had followed Lk 23:49
As the body was taken away, the * Lk 23:55
were dazzled. The * were terrified Lk 24:5
(The * who went to the tomb were Lk 24:10
days ago— some * from our group of Lk 24:22,23
gone, just as the * had said." Lk 24:24
Several *, including Jesus' Act 1:14
* alike, and they shall prophesy. Act 2:18
Lord, crowds both of men and *. Act 5:14
men and * alike and jailing them. Act 8:3
and many men and * were baptized. Act 8:12
both men and *, so that he could Act 9:2
up both the godly * and the civic Act 13:50
the Scriptures to some * who came. Act 16:13
also many important * of the city. Act 17:4
Greek * and many men also. Act 17:12
both men and * to prison. Act 22:4
so that even their * turned against Rom 1:26
relationship with *, burned with Rom 1:27
plan men and * need each other. 1Co 11:11
been born from * ever since, and 1Co 11:12
and * come from God their Creator. 1Co 11:12
be covered? For * are proud of 1Co 11:14,15
* should be silent during the 1Co 14:34
it is improper for * to express 1Co 14:35
even merely men or *, but we are Gal 3:28
two dear *, Euodias and Syntyche. Php 4:2
to help these *, for they worked Php 4:3
And the * should be the same 1Ti 2:9,10
Christian * should be noticed for 1Ti 2:9,10
or fancy clothes. * should listen 1Ti 2:11
I never let * teach men or lord 1Ti 2:12
and suffering to * when their 1Ti 2:15
Treat the older * as mothers, 1Ti 5:2
loving care of * whose husbands 1Ti 5:3
to tell men and * everywhere about 2Ti 1:1
sin-burdened * and teach them their 2Ti 3:6
new doctrines. * of that kind are 2Ti 3:7
Teach the older * to be quiet and Tit 2:3

MEN Con't)
ese older * must train the Tit 2:4
in the younger * to live Tit 2:4
d some *, through faith, Heb 11:35
the saintly * of old, who 1Pe 3:5
ke a game of luring unstable *. 2Pe 2:14
h *, for they are virgins." Rev 14:4f

MEN'S
nan must not wear * clothing. Deu 22:5
n's and * choirs and orchestras. Ecc 2:7,8
that * heads should be covered? 1Co 11:14,15
eir hair was long like *, and Rev 9:8

N
d he conquered the city and * Ju 1:13
t General Omri * and Tibni was 1Ki 16:22
at is why they *. 1Ki 20:23
t the king * the argument, and 1Ch 21:4
I have * your favor, O king, Est 7:3
r he has * a mighty victory by Ps 98:1
the plunder they have *. Is 9:3
d wisdom have * these wars. Is 10:13
you have * back a brother. Mt 18:15
ave * them by my message and Rom 15:19
r he is one of those I * to 1Co 4:17
ve been * to Christ through me. 1Co 9:2
hen Christ has finally * the 1Co 15:28
nd the more of you who are * to 2Co 4:15
nesimus, whom I * to the Lord Phm 1:10
all he had * in the battle and Heb 7:2
d as a result * battles, Heb 11:33
usted God and * his approval, Heb 11:39
ord, they will be * by your 1Pe 3:1
u have * your battle with Satan. 1Jn 2:13
arts, and have * your struggle 1Jn 2:14
d have already * your fight with 1Jn 4:4

N'T
ne Lord replied, "They * kill Gen 4:15
understand each other's words!" Gen 11:7
nd God replied, "I * destroy it Gen 18:29
nd God replied, "I * do it if Gen 18:30
nd God said, "Then I * destroy Gen 18:31
ke of the ten, I * destroy it." Gen 18:32
nd * destroy that little city. Gen 19:21
ith my son. I * have it." Gen 21:10
ame that you * defraud me or my Gen 21:23
they * send anyone, then you Gen 24:41
Will you or * you be kind to my Gen 24:49
acob: "But mother! He * be Gen 27:11,12
* know, but God will see it. Gen 31:50
nd the land * be abandoned." Gen 47:19
UT MOSES SAID, "They * believe Ex 4:1
ne! They * do what I tell them to. Ex 4:1
even listen to me any more; Ex 6:12
et even then Pharaoh * listen Ex 7:4
ut Moses replied, "That * do! Ex 8:26
o that you * even be able to see Ex 10:4,5
Moses, "Pharaoh * listen, and this Ex 11:9
nd you * need to lift a finger!" Ex 14:14
our great power they * attack us! Ex 15:16
But the people * come up into Ex 19:23
f crops that you * know what to do Lev 26:10
And if you still * listen to me Lev 26:27
locks and herds it * be enough! Num 11:22
your vineyards; we * even drink Num 20:17
your borders. We * trample your Num 21:22
The Lord * let me do it." Num 22:13
But anything that * stand heat Num 31:23
that their land * leave the tribe. Num 36:8
the main road and * turn off into Deu 2:27
But if it refuses and * make Deu 20:12
and rebellious and * obey; Deu 21:20
the Lord your God * bless you when Deu 23:20
"If you * listen to the Lord Deu 28:15-19
Lord your God and * obey these Deu 28:15-19
* get a single bite of the meat. Deu 28:31
for them, but you * eat the grapes Deu 28:39
but there * be enough olive oil to Deu 28:40
turn away and you * listen—if you Deu 30:17
"If you * betray us, we'll see Jos 2:14
small city and it * take more than Jos 7:3
we will not touch them, and we *. Jos 9:19
the Levites * receive any land; Jos 18:7
of Manasseh * receive any more, for Jos 18:7
So go away; I * save you any Ju 10:13
that you * kill me yourselves." Ju 15:12,13
"No," they replied, "we * do Ju 15:12,13
but if he *, then I will, I swear Ru 3:13
happens, for Boaz * rest until he Ru 3:15-18
of Israel, you * want the 1Sa 25:30,31
and * reply by prophets or dreams; 1Sa 28:15
heathen nations * bother them as 2Sa 7:10,11
you, and you * die for this sin. 2Sa 12:13
that you * let anyone harm my son. 2Sa 14:11
"Well, money * do it," the 2Sa 21:4
"I hope you * turn me down." 1Ki 2:20
"You know I * refuse you." 1Ki 2:20
be killed, too, but I * do it now. 1Ki 2:26
father David, I * do this while you 1Ki 11:12,13
and serve—there * be any dew or 1Ki 17:1
swear to God that I * leave you!" 2Ki 2:1
swear to God that I * leave you." 2Ki 2:4
swear to God that I * leave you." 2Ki 2:6,7
But if not, then you *." 2Ki 2:10
he will send. You * see wind nor 2Ki 3:17
that I * go home without you." 2Ki 4:30
you * be able to buy any of it!" 2Ki 7:2
to the animals it * be any greater 2Ki 7:13
you * be able to buy any of it!" 2Ki 7:19
says that I * conquer Jerusalem. 2Ki 19:10
"The Lord says you * recover." 2Ki 20:1
the wicked nations * conquer them 1Ch 17:9
O our God, * you stop them? 2Ch 20:12
to you by Moses—I * ever again 2Ch 33:8
No, I * do it!" Neh 6:11
who long for death, and it * come; Job 3:20,21
of the day? Why * you let me Job 7:19
his home for security, it * last. Job 8:15
The sun * rise, the stars won't Job 9:7
The sun won't rise, the stars * Job 9:7
So give him a little rest, * Job 14:6
all of you are. * you ever stop Job 16:3
but my spirit * let me stop. Job 20:3
God * let him keep it down. Job 20:15
They despise me and * come near Job 30:10
If they * listen to him, they Job 36:12
your behalf, and * destroy you as I Job 42:8
mouth wide and see if I * fill it. Ps 81:10
But no, my people * listen. Ps 81:11
He punishes the nations—* he Ps 94:10
me if they like—I * mind that if Ps 109:28
you so often but still you * come. Pro 1:24
your finger so you * forget. Pro 6:21
of vengeance. You * be able to buy Pro 6:35
and * return for several days." Pro 7:20
Your riches * help you on Pro 11:4
the charges * stick because Pro 11:9f
A lazy man * even dress the game Pro 12:27
to fool himself and * face facts. Pro 14:8
Some men are so lazy they * even Pro 19:24
If you * plow in the cold, you Pro 20:4
cold, you * eat at the harvest. Pro 20:4
discipline * hurt them! Pro 23:13,14
* die if you use a stick on them! Pro 23:13,14
The lazy man * go out and work. Pro 26:13
Then you * need to go to a Pro 27:10
He * turn aside for anyone. Pro 30:29,30,31
The fool * work and almost Ecc 4:5,6
out to heaven, I * look or listen. Is 1:15
all of them take bribes and * Is 1:23
we * be mocked as old maids." Is 4:1
and sheep. I * prune it or hoe it, Is 5:6
repeatedly, you * understand them. Is 6:9
still you * know what they mean.' Is 6:9
The shepherds * let their sheep Is 13:20
But they * listen; Is 28:11
shame—he * help one little bit! Is 30:5
and lies and * repent, therefore Is 30:12
Mere words * substitute for Is 36:5
you the Lord * let you be conquered Is 36:15
Surely God * let him get away Is 37:4
says, "Don't worry. He * win." Is 41:6
thing in place so it * fall over! Is 41:7
been wronged. He * be satisfied Is 42:4
are towards God! Why * you listen? Is 42:18
Why won't you listen? Why * you Is 42:18
is right but * heed nor do it; Is 42:20
you hear but you * listen. Is 42:20
to protect them. * even one of you Is 42:23
But O my people, you * ask my Is 43:22
you * know where it comes from. Is 47:11
* experience any peace, either. Is 59:8
free from God; we * have anything Jer 2:31
surely you * be angry about such Jer 3:4,5
punished them, but they * change! Jer 5:3
They have lied and said, "He * Jer 5:12
But you said, "No! We * pay Jer 6:17
to bury that there * be room enough Jer 7:32
nails, so that it * fall over, and Jer 10:4
Yet the people say, "God * bring Jer 12:4
great that there * be room enough Jer 19:11
been that way—you just * listen! Jer 22:21
But you * listen; Jer 25:7
and Judah. It * be like the one I Jer 31:32
God says you * be killed in war and Jer 34:4
and Jerusalem, * you learn a lesson Jer 35:13
again and you * listen or obey. Jer 35:14
And you * listen to me anyway." Jer 38:15
Jeremiah replied, "You * get Jer 38:20
they listen or not (but they *, Eze 2:7
Israel, and they * listen to you Eze 3:7
good deeds * help him—he shall die Eze 3:20
You will sue for peace, but you * Eze 7:25
but they *, for they are rebels. Eze 12:2
face, for he * be able to see. Eze 12:12
say, 'His visions * come true for a Eze 12:27
easily enough—it * take a big crew Eze 17:9
Jerusalem * understand this Eze 21:23
to die, and you * be buried, for I Eze 29:5
their fires. They * cut wood from Eze 39:10
And if you * tell me what it was Dan 2:5
Your deeds * let you come to God Hos 5:4
with anxiety, but * ask my help. Hos 7:14
because they * return to me. Hos 11:5
swiftest runners * be fast enough Amo 2:15
And still you * return to me," Amo 4:11
vision. "I * do it," he told me. Amo 7:3
and said, "I * do that either." Amo 7:6
sworn: "I * forget your deeds! Amo 8:7
you priests and prophets who * Mic 3:11
blow; he * need to strike again. Nah 1:9
But these things I plan * happen Hab 2:3
In her pride she * listen even Zep 3:2
she * have room enough for all! Zec 2:4
punish them, and I * change this Zec 8:14,15
And I * spare them either," Zec 11:6
So I told them, "I * be your Zec 11:9
line of David * be filled with Zec 12:7
Or by saying that God * punish Mal 2:17
* have room enough to take it in! Mal 3:10
Your grapes * shrivel away before Mal 3:11
tell us that bread * feed men's Mt 4:4
simple 'Yes, I will' or 'No, I *.' Mt 5:37
and gone tomorrow, * he more surely Mt 6:30
"DON'T CRITICIZE, AND then you * Mt 7:1
to your children, * your Father in Mt 7:11
'Lord,' but still * get to heaven. Mt 7:21
his house, it * collapse, for it is Mt 7:25
For it * be you doing the Mt 10:20
so they * see and hear Mt 13:16
no food? * you ever understand? Mt 16:9
But this kind of demon * leave Mt 17:21
what will he do? * he leave the Mt 18:12
favors you, but he * accept it, Mt 18:17
And Jesus said, "Then I * answer Mt 21:27
farm today.' 'I *,' he answered, Mt 21:29
For you * let others enter the Mt 23:13,14
of Heaven, and * go in yourselves. Mt 23:13,14
yourself, 'My Lord * be coming for Mt 24:48
you, but you * always have me. Mt 26:11
everyone else deserts you, I *." Mt 26:33
"And whenever a village * Mk 6:11
what you eat * harm your soul? Mk 7:18
solemnly—he * lose his reward. Mk 9:41
Good News, who * be given back, a Mk 10:30
To which Jesus replied, "Then I * Mk 11:33
the dead, they * be married—they Mk 12:25
but I * be here much longer. Mk 14:7
poisonous, it * hurt them; Mk 16:18
then they * want to eat." Lk 5:35
about the fact that they * repay. Lk 6:35
call me 'Lord' when you * obey me? Lk 6:46
"If the people of a town * Lk 9:5
Mary has discovered it—and I * Lk 10:42
you this—though he * do it as a Lk 11:8
is here [but this nation * listen Lk 11:32
the people. You * accept it for Lk 11:52
to think, 'My Lord * be back for a Lk 12:45
for if that happens you * be Lk 12:59
and loses one. * she light a lamp Lk 15:8
And then * she call in her Lk 15:9
matters, you * be in large ones. Lk 16:10
If you cheat even a little, you * Lk 16:10
they * bother to read them. Lk 16:30
"But Abraham said, 'If they * Lk 16:31
the prophets, they * listen even Lk 16:31
signs. You * be able to say, 'It Lk 17:21
day, but I * be here," he said. Lk 17:22
And Jesus responded, "Then I * Lk 20:8
come, but the end * follow Lk 21:9
For I tell you now that I * eat Lk 22:16
I tell you, you * believe me or let Lk 22:67,68
seen—and yet you * believe me. Jn 3:10,11
thirsty again and * have to make Jn 4:15
Jesus asked, "* any of you Jn 4:48
Yet you * come to me so that I Jn 5:40
And you * be able to come where I Jn 7:34
* be able to come where I am'?" Jn 7:36
So if you follow me, you * be Jn 8:12
you much, but I *, for I say only Jn 8:26
They * follow a stranger but Jn 10:5
but I * be with you very long." Jn 12:8
things so that you * be staggered Jn 16:1
if I don't, the Comforter * come. Jn 16:7
At that time you * need to ask Jn 16:23
And I * need to ask the Father to Jn 16:26
"You * talk to me?" Jn 19:10
he replied, "I * believe it unless Jn 20:25
They * stop at anything that you Act 4:28
terrible things * happen to me." Act 8:24
that you * believe when you hear it Act 13:41
I * know what to say." Act 19:40
the people here * believe you when Act 22:17,18
But no, you * listen; Rom 2:5
obey God's laws, * God give them Rom 2:26
him up for us all, * he also surely Rom 8:32
The angels *, and all the powers Rom 8:38
place, he * spare you either. Rom 11:21
And you * sin with his wife or Rom 13:9
must not look down on those who *. Rom 14:3
And if you are one of those who * Rom 14:3
And the person who * touch such Rom 14:6
there * be splits in the church. 1Co 1:10
so that Satan * be able to tempt 1Co 7:5

(WON'T Con't)
*, he has made a wise decision. 1Co 7:37
Then you * know whether or not it 1Co 10:27
to idols, and you * risk having a 1Co 10:27
at home so that he * bring 1Co 11:34
they * be able to understand you. 1Co 14:2
other people present * be helped. 1Co 14:17
"NO," I SAID to myself, "I * do 2Co 2:1
that he * be able to recover. 2Co 2:7
quite small and * last very long. 2Co 4:17
I hope I * need to show you when 2Co 10:2
to visit you I * like what I find, 2Co 12:20
* like the way I will have to act. 2Co 12:20
in the hope that I * need to scold 2Co 13:10
do, and then you * always be doing Gal 5:16
Then we * need to look for Gal 5:26
well done, and * need to compare Gal 6:4
in a way that you * like—for he has Col 3:25
things, and you * be surprised as 1Th 5:4
consciences * even bother them. 1Ti 4:2
But anyone who * care for his own 1Ti 5:8
yes, but they * really believe 2Ti 3:5
But they * get away with all this 2Ti 3:9
a time when people * listen to the 2Ti 4:3
They * listen to what the Bible 2Ti 4:4
I say this because I * be around 2Ti 4:6
because there * be anything to Tit 2:8
I * mention how much you owe me! Phm 1:19
ahead for you, you * become bored Heb 6:12
power, and you * be spending the 1Pe 4:2
to him, we * be sinning either; 1Jn 3:6
in need, and * help him—how can 1Jn 3:17
Others *. 1Jn 4:6
for if it is, the world * listen 1Jn 4:6
so you * be naked and ashamed; Rev 3:18
* be able to—death will not come. Rev 9:6

WONDER
Esau: (bitterly) "No * they call Gen 27:36
as all the nations watched in *. Lev 26:45
If you *, 'How shall we know Deu 18:21
No * we are afraid of you! Jos 2:11
No * I give thanks to you, O 2Sa 22:50
If they have done that here, I * Est 9:12
he is! No * he 'worships' you! Job 1:10
Those who knew him will * where Job 20:7
not man; no * my spirit is so Job 21:4
"No * I am so terrified in his Job 23:15
us. No * men everywhere fear him! Job 37:24
No * we are happy in the Lord! Ps 33:21
No * I can sing your praises! Ps 57:7
it by his holiness! No * I exult! Ps 60:6,7
How great your power! No * your Ps 66:3
them. No * they will be so glad! Ps 69:32
* I am always praising you! Ps 71:6
No * you are greatly feared! Ps 76:7
see them all. No * the years are Ps 90:9
for me, O Lord. No * I am glad! Ps 92:4
They weren't impressed by the * Ps 106:7
sacred promises; no * I exult! Ps 108:7
no * I hate every false teaching. Ps 119:104
no * I love to obey your laws! Ps 119:119
Your laws are wonderful; no * I Ps 119:129
understand it. No * I wait Ps 119:131
I will sing about their *, for Ps 119:172
Yes, glorious things! What *! Ps 126:3
No * all the young girls love you! Sol 1:3
* all the young girls love you!" Sol 1:4
see nor know. No * those who Is 44:9
and no one seems to care or * why. Is 57:1
who injure you. No * you are in Is 59:9
No * you are walking in the gloom. Is 59:9
in the gloom. No * you grope like Is 59:10
darkest night! No * you are like Is 59:10
No * my anger is great! Jer 7:18
destruction. No * they scoff and Jer 20:8
them justice. No * the Lord has Lam 3:34,35,36
"No * I stand against you," Nah 3:5
So the people were saying, "No * Mk 6:14
* fell upon the whole Lk 1:65
and asked, "I * what this child Lk 1:66
said, "No * he can cast them out. Lk 11:15
No * you can't believe! Jn 5:44
* you don't believe me either." Jn 5:47
'No * my heart is filled with joy Act 2:26
breaking them. No * the Scriptures Rom 2:24
so is it no * his servants can do 2Co 11:15
and never need to * whether he Heb 6:17

WONDER-WORKING
A * God? Ex 15:11

WONDERED
thought and * what it all meant. Gen 37:11
you, and * that no one intervened. Is 59:16
about it, and * what he meant by Mk 9:10
and * why he was taking so long. Lk 1:21
Then the disciples * among Lk 22:23
Moses saw it and * what it was, Act 7:31
with a beach and * whether they Act 27:39
They * what the Spirit of Christ 1Pe 1:11
And they * when and to whom all 1Pe 1:11

WONDERFUL
exclaimed, "*—another boy!" Gen 35:17
They had a * time bantering back Gen 43:34
you will see the * way the Lord Ex 14:13
about all the * things God had done Ex 18:1
for the Lord has given * promises Num 10:29
in Egypt, and the * cucumbers and Num 11:4,5
people, "It is a * country ahead, Num 14:7
us into the * country you promised, Num 16:14
Where is the fertile land of * Num 20:5
what * sheep country it was. Num 32:1
And it is all * sheep country, Num 32:3,4
This is your * thought for the Deu 4:39
descendants—a * land 'flowing with Deu 11:9
that will produce * crops of grain, Deu 11:14
He will open to you his * Deu 28:12
and has done such * things for you Deu 28:63
and much cattle and * crops; Deu 30:9
That is their * heritage. Jos 18:7
this song about the * victory: Ju 5:1
and the Angel did a strange and * Ju 13:19
* thing and done these miracles." Ju 13:23
a * deliverance through me today! Ju 15:18
fertile, * place—a real paradise. Ju 18:9,10
"This is *!" Ru 2:22
knows what a * person you are. Ru 3:11
all Israel is there anyone as *? 1Sa 26:15
armor and sent the * news of Saul's 1Sa 31:9
How much they were loved, how * 2Sa 1:23
joy of that day's * victory was 2Sa 19:2
He gives * deliverance to his 2Sa 22:51
to whom God gave such * success; 2Sa 23:1
failed of all the * promises 1Ki 8:56
when she saw the * foods on his 1Ki 10:5
and about the * things going on 1Ki 10:6
"Everything is *," he replied, 1Ki 11:22
This is * news, and we aren't 2Ki 7:9
the * news before their idols. 1Ch 10:9
given me these * promises just 1Ch 17:19
It is going to be a * temple 2Ch 2:5
palace, and how * the food at his 2Ch 9:4
They all told me what a * man Neh 6:19
in your * mercy delivered them! Neh 9:28
you despite the * things you did Neh 9:35
For he does * miracles, marvels Job 5:9
"It is * to speak the truth, but Job 6:25,26
"What * helpers you all are! Job 26:2
consider the * miracles of God. Job 37:14
with * perfection and skill? Job 37:16,17
things far too * for me. Job 42:3
What a * inheritance! Ps 16:6
Show me your strong love in * Ps 17:7
of the * things you have done. Ps 22:22
blessing, and shall have * peace. Ps 37:11
has a * future ahead of him. Ps 37:37
time to tell of all your * deeds. Ps 40:5
What fellowship we had, what * Ps 55:14
Tell the world how * he is. Ps 66:2
for your lovingkindness is *; Ps 69:16
exclaim, "What a * God he is!" Ps 70:4
to others of the * things you do. Ps 71:17
You have done such * things. Ps 71:19
of Israel, who only does * things! Ps 72:18
about the * ways he rescues me. Ps 73:28
Those * deeds are constantly in Ps 77:12
And they forgot about the * Ps 78:11,12
day long in your * reputation and Ps 89:16
and for all of his * deeds! Ps 107:8
and for all of his * deeds! Ps 107:15
and for all of his * deeds! Ps 107:21
and for all of his * deeds! Ps 107:31
For the Lord has done this * Ps 116:7
Open my eyes to see * things in Ps 119:18
I will obey these * laws of yours. Ps 119:106
your * promise to rescue me. Ps 119:123
Your laws are *; Ps 119:129
a day because of your * laws. Ps 119:164
HOW * IT is, how pleasant, when Ps 133:1
sing to his * name. Ps 135:3
This is too glorious, too * to Ps 139:6
advice, and how * it is to be able Pro 15:23
he pays * interest on your loan! Pro 19:17
It is a * heritage to have an Pro 20:7
you have a * future ahead of you. Pro 23:17,18
but what a * thing it is for a Pro 29:18
There are three things too * for Pro 30:18,19
HOW * TO be wise, to understand Ecc 8:1
It is a * thing to be alive! Ecc 11:7
Young man, it's * to be young! Ecc 11:9
THIS SONG OF songs, more * than Sol 1:1
the gardens, how * that your Sol 8:13
royal titles: "*," "Counselor," Is 9:6
In that * day you will say, Is 12:4
Lord, for he has done * things. Is 12:5
In that * day when the Lord gives Is 14:3
though you plant a *, rare crop of Is 17:10
you do such * things! Is 25:1
The Lord of Hosts is a * teacher Is 28:29
time and with * harvests and with Is 30:23
Now he has a * idol that can't so Is 44:13
and a new earth—so * that no one Is 65:17
And I thought how * it would be Jer 3:19
can do for you the * things I swore Jer 11:5
And the * heritage I reserved Jer
fathers long ago—a * land that Jer 3
But I will give you many * gifts Dan
free of the burden of her * king! Hos
What a * God he is! Hab
How * and beautiful all shall be! Zec 9:1
because you are my followers—*! Mt
The report of this * miracle Mt
Peter blurted out, "Sir, it's * Mt
leaders saw these * miracles, and Mt 2
and will do * miracles, so that if Mt 2
HERE BEGINS THE * story of Jesus Mk
* things God has done for you; Mk
She had heard all about the * Mk
said, "Everything he does is *; Mk
"Teacher, this is *!" Mk
who will do * miracles that would Mk 1
If you're so *, save yourself and Mk 15:2
has given you this * blessing." Lk
Let's see this * thing that has Lk 2
who do you good—is that so *? Lk 6
They told him what a * person the Lk
a * thing God has done for you." Lk 8
blurted out, "Master, this is *! Lk 9
over all the * things he was doing, Lk 9
rejoiced at the * things he did. Lk 13
all the * miracles Jesus had done. Lk 19:36
"This is * stuff!" Jn 2
only knew what a * gift God has for Jn 4
Some said, "He's a * man," Jn 7
"He says such * things!" Jn 7
you will see a * miracle from God Jn 11
to * joy [when you see me again Jn 16
And how * was their joy as they Jn 20
give me * joy in your presence.' Act 2
by the * thing that had happened. Act 3
sins and send you * times of Act 3
telling about the * things we saw Act 4
God for this * miracle— the Act 4
When he arrived and saw the * Act 11
you the * thing I promised David.' Act 13
named Apollos, a * Bible teacher Act 18
care and to his * words which are Act 20
Now this * statement—that he was Rom 4
Now we rejoice in our * new Rom 5
given his * new life to enjoy. Rom
What can we ever say to such * Rom 8
And how * it will be when they Rom 11
and now it is even more * when Rom 11
Oh, what a * God we have! Rom 11
And since they received this * Rom 15
God for all the * gifts he has 1Co
you into this * friendship with his 1Co
even imagined what * things God has 1Co 2
tell us about the * free gifts of 1Co 2:
built upon this * message; 1Co 1
this strange and * secret: we shall 1Co 15:
and have been a * encouragement to 1Co 16:
What a * God we have—he is the 2Co 1:3
you who see his * answers to your 2Co 1:
has given us this * work [of 2Co 4
will have * new bodies in heaven, 2Co 5
This is the * message he has 2Co 5:
of the * time he had with you. 2Co 7
have mixed their * joy with their 2Co 8
* grace of God shown through you. 2Co 9:1
his Son—his Gift too * for words. 2Co 9:1
say that I am as * as these other 2Co 10:1
telling you how * they are, so here 2Co 11:1
Now all praise to God for his * Eph 1
God has given me the * privilege Eph 3
for such * blessings as these. Eph 4
of all your * help in making known Php 1
which is far more * than the human Php 4
to share all the * things that Col 1:1
This is the * news that came to Col 1:2
us about the * welcome you gave us, 1Th 1
of the really * way your faith has 2Th 1
Don't ever forget the * fact that 2Ti 2
forward to that * time we've been Tit 2:1
out upon us with * fullness—and all Tit 3
For this * news—the message that Heb 4
God contains far more * promises. Heb 8
Don't ever forget those * days Heb 10:3
brought us his * new agreement; Heb 12:2
be glad for the * message we have Jas 1:2
man has great power and * results. Jas 5:1
There is * joy ahead, even though 1Pe 1
and it is all so strange and * 1Pe 1:1
of the darkness into his * light. 1Pe 2:
you will have the * joy of sharing 1Pe 4:1
and being called by his * name! 1Pe 4:1
rich and * blessings he promised; 2Pe 1:
But when you consider the * truth 2Pe 1:1
does, then we have * fellowship and 1Jn 1:
strong—sang a * new song in front Rev 14:

WONDERFULLY
all my life, * bless these boys. Gen 48:1
You have guided them * Ex 15:1
Yes, you have been * kind to me 1Sa 24:1
Solomon replied, "You were * 1Ki 3:

ONDERFULLY Con't)
Sheba heard how * the Lord had 1Ki 10:1
bless me and help me in my work; 1Ch 4:10
m * until he was very powerful. 2Ch 26:15
ank you for making me so * Ps 139:14
by keeping abreast of the facts. Pro 24:3,4
e Lord is * good to those who Lam 3:25
d I am * pleased with him." Mt 3:17
d if God cares so * for Mt 6:30
n, and I am * pleased with him. Mt 17:5
od has decided to * bless you! Lk 1:30
d the one who so * comforts and 2Co 1:3,4
d he is * able to help us. Heb 2:18

NDERING
NE DAY DAVID began * if any of 2Sa 9:1
hile I was * what this could Dan 8:5
me again, * what had happened. Lk 24:12
ch other, * whom he could mean. Jn 13:22
ey were frantic, * what would Act 5:24
couldn't rest, * where he was and 2Co 2:13

NDERS
hat * God has done for them!' Num 23:18-24
iracles and *, and the power and Deu 7:19
e did great and terrifying * Deu 34:11,12
om us about the * of the Lord; Ps 22:30
heaven who does such * for me. Ps 57:2
ou are the God of miracles and *! Ps 77:14
ho can forget the * he Ps 111:4
word of encouragement does *! Pro 12:25
bribe does *; Pro 18:16
urpose of my going; none * why. Jn 16:5
ay miracles and * be done by the Act 4:30
atiently did many * and signs and 2Co 12:12
ue by signs and * and various Heb 2:4
l the * God has promised them. Heb 9:15

NDROUS
gain praise him for his * help; Ps 43:5
city of God, what * tales are Ps 87:3
ell the world about his * love. Is 12:4
will spread a * feast for everyone Is 25:6
he Lord has done this * thing. Is 44:23
nd so I have taken away these * Jer 5:25
here ever such a * city as Tyre, Eze 27:32
watched that * city, the holy Rev 21:10

OOD
Make a boat from resinous *, Gen 6:14
p early, chopped * for a fire upon Gen 22:3
braham placed the * for the Gen 22:6
we have the * and the flint to Gen 22:7
nd placed the * in order, ready Gen 22:9
aid him on the altar over the *. Gen 22:9
goat-skins, acacia *, olive oil for Ex 25:1
'Using acacia *, make an Ark 3¾ Ex 25:10
Make poles from acacia * Ex 25:13,14
'Then make a table of acacia * Ex 25:23
Make the poles from acacia * Ex 25:28
made from acacia *, each Ex 26:15,16
"Make bars of acacia * to run Ex 26:26,27
on five acacia * posts, overlaid Ex 26:37
"USING ACACIA *, make a square Ex 27:1
acacia * overlaid with bronze. Ex 27:6
It shall be made from acacia *. Ex 30:1
carved from the * of the altar—they Ex 30:2
of acacia * overlaid with gold. Ex 30:5
as a jeweler and in carving *. Ex 31:5
Acacia *; Ex 35:5-9
and some brought the acacia * Ex 35:24
of acacia * standing on end. Ex 36:20
bars from acacia * to tie the Ex 36:31,32
posts of acacia *, overlaid with Ex 36:36
This was constructed of acacia * Ex 37:1
Then he made poles from acacia * Ex 37:4
using acacia *, three feet long, 1½ Ex 37:10
altar was made of acacia *. Ex 37:25
poles were gold-plated acacia *. Ex 37:28
was also constructed of acacia *; Ex 38:1
of acacia *, overlaid with bronze. Ex 38:6
and quarter it, and build a * Lev 1:6,7
and its head and fat upon the *. Lev 1:8
fat, on top of the * on the altar. Lev 1:12
burned there on a * fire. Lev 4:11,12
The priest shall put on fresh * Lev 6:12
article of *, or of clothing, a Lev 11:32
take some cedar *, a scarlet Lev 14:4
with the cedar *, the scarlet Lev 14:6
two birds, cedar *, scarlet thread, Lev 14:49
and dip the cedar *, hyssop Lev 14:51,52
gathering * on the Sabbath day. Num 15:32
Eleazar shall take cedar * and Num 19:6
of leather, goat's hair, or *." Num 31:20
idols made from * and stone, idols Deu 4:28
So I made an Ark of acacia * and Deu 10:3
neighbor to chop *, and the axe Deu 19:5
whether carved of * or made from Deu 27:15
shall worship gods of * and stone! Deu 28:36
known, gods made of * and stone! Deu 28:64
chop your * and carry your water. Deu 29:11
of *, stone, silver, and gold. Deu 29:17
their * and carrying their water. Jos 9:21
servants to chop * and carry water Jos 9:23
as * for the fire on the altar." Ju 6:26
So the people broke up the * of 1Sa 6:14
* to build a fire on the altar. 2Sa 24:22
made from olive *, each fifteen 1Ki 6:23-28
* for the entrance to the Temple. 1Ki 6:33
doors of cypress *, and each door 1Ki 6:34
Solomon used the algum * to make 1Ki 10:12
been such a supply of beautiful *. 1Ki 10:12
and lay it on the * of their altar, 1Ki 18:23
putting any fire under the *; 1Ki 18:23
and lay it on the * on the Lord's 1Ki 18:23
to light the * is the true God!" 1Ki 18:24
don't put any fire under the *." 1Ki 18:25
He piled * upon the altar and 1Ki 18:33
and laid the pieces on the *. 1Ki 18:33
over the carcass and the *." 1Ki 18:33
young bull, the *, the stones, the 1Ki 18:38
them, and used * from the plow to 1Ki 19:21
that men had made of * and stone. 2Ki 19:18
instruments for * for the fire and 1Ch 21:23
bronze, iron, *, and great 1Ch 29:2
will begin cutting * from the 2Ch 2:16
with cypress *, plated with pure 2Ch 3:5
should supply the * for the burnt Neh 10:34
They supplied * for the altar at Neh 13:31
to him, and brass is rotten *. Job 41:27,28
embers to coals and * to fire." Pro 26:21f
a chariot from the * of Lebanon. Sol 3:9
it is piled high with *. Is 30:33
carved by men from * and stone. Is 37:19
* and carves the figure of a man. Is 44:13
uses part of the * to make a fire Is 44:15
"Why, it's just a block of *! Is 44:19
I fall down before a chunk of *?" Is 44:19
* for brass, your stones for iron. Is 60:17
worship idols made of * and stone. Jer 3:9
up these people like kindling *. Jer 5:14
Watch how the children gather * Jer 7:18
you, serving gods of * and stone. Eze 20:32
Heap on the *; Eze 24:10
They won't cut * from the fields Eze 39:10
* above and below the windows. Eze 41:15,16
be an altar, but it was made of *. Eze 41:21
base and sides were all of *. Eze 41:22
brass and iron, * and stone. Dan 5:2,3,4
gold, brass, iron, *, and Dan 5:23
For they are asking a piece of * Hos 4:12
a chip of * upon an ocean wave. Hos 10:7
God, they took * and stone and made Rom 1:23
well as some made from * and clay. 2Ti 2:20
brass, stone, and *—which neither Rev 9:20
and every kind of perfumed *, and Rev 18:12

WOOD-CHOPPERS
but they became * and Jos 9:27

WOODCARVER
Then the * takes the axe and Is 44:13

WOODED
and towers on the * hills. 2Ch 27:4
as the distant * hills and mountain Is 17:9

WOODEN
* utensil must be rinsed in water. Lev 15:12
is to bring you a * rod with his Num 17:1
if he is killed with a * weapon. Num 35:18
and to make a * Ark to keep them Deu 10:1
to cut down the * idol of the Ju 6:25
Lord, using the * idol as wood for Ju 6:26
He stood on a * stand made Neh 8:1
carry around the * idols and pray Is 45:20
They call a carved-up * post Jer 2:26,27
You have broken a * yoke but these Jer 28:13
And there was a * canopy over the Eze 41:25
their lifeless * idols to arise and Hab 2:19
stripped and beaten with * whips. Act 16:22
[as Jesus was hung upon a * cross Gal 3:13
and Aaron's * cane that budded. Heb 9:4
and most expensive * carvings, and Rev 18:12

WOODS
* and killed forty-two of them. 2Ki 2:24
Let the trees in the * sing for 1Ch 16:33
Even the trees of the *—the fir Is 14:8
places and sleep safely in the *. Eze 34:25

WOODSMAN'S
the enemy as a * axe cuts down the Is 10:34

WOODSMEN
Send your * to the mountains of 1Ki 5:6
* who clear a forest of its trees. Jer 46:22,23

WOOL
don't wear clothes made of half * Lev 19:19
thread: for instance, * and linen. Deu 22:11
way: I'll put some * on the Ju 6:37
lambs and the * of 100,000 rams; 2Ki 3:4
then there will be lamb's * Pro 27:25,26,27
She finds * and flax and busily Pro 31:13
sheep's *, newly shorn and washed; Sol 4:2
I can make you white as *! Is 1:18
the worm shall eat them like *; Is 51:8
and white Syrian * to trade for all Eze 27:18
they must wear no * while on duty Eze 44:17
as snow, his hair like whitest * Dan 7:9
will destroy her as a moth does *; Hos 5:12
and scarlet * to sprinkle with. Heb 9:19
head—the hair—was white like *." Rev 1:14f
was white as * or snow, and his Rev 1:14

WOOLEN
"If leprosy is suspected in a * Lev 13:47,48
fabric, linen or * covering, or Lev 13:52

WORD
the Hebrew * for Eve sounds similar Gen 3:20f
* that means "life-giving." Gen 3:20f
like the Hebrew * for "hair." Gen 25:25f
a Hebrew * sounding like the name. Gen 30:6f
* soon reached Jacob of what had Gen 34:5
they couldn't say a kind * to Gen 37:4
with the flocks, and bring me *." Gen 37:13,14
About three months later * Gen 38:24
The Hebrew * is not specific. Gen 39:12f
let me say just this one * to you. Gen 44:18
couldn't say a *, they were so Gen 45:3
ONE DAY NOT long after this, * Gen 48:1
Hebrew * meaning "to draw out." Ex 2:10f
no regard for the * of Jehovah left Ex 9:21
The Hebrew * here translated Ex 12:3,4f
When * reached the king of Egypt Ex 14:5
* SOON REACHED Jethro, Moses' Ex 18:1
let me give you a * of advice, and Ex 18:19,20
must accept his *, and no Ex 22:11
Near East, the * "salt" is a Lev 2:13f
is a homonym of the * "good." Lev 2:13f
Now you shall see whether my * Num 11:23
'I have listened to the * of God, Num 24:3-9
and could not say a * of my own? Num 24:13
everyone is terrified if the * Jos 2:9
"Not a single * from any of you Jos 6:10
you if you go back on your *." Jos 24:27
a prostitute. * soon spread that Ju 16:2
land of Gilead. (* of the Ju 20:3
This was a play on words. The * 1Sa 1:19,20f
sounds like the * "to ask." 1Sa 1:19,20f
have rejected the * of Jehovah, he 1Sa 15:23
the countryside. * soon reached 1Sa 23:13
Nabal's widow. * soon reached Saul 1Sa 27:4
Literally, "Jehovah sent * by 2Sa 12:25f
David agreed, and sent * to 2Sa 13:7
for every * Ahithophel spoke was 2Sa 16:23
* SOON REACHED Joab that the king 2Sa 19:1
They sent * to the king, "Return 2Sa 19:14
The * of the Lord is true. 2Sa 22:31
And his * was on my tongue. 2Sa 23:2
The next morning the * of the 2Sa 24:11
For you haven't said a * as to 1Ki 1:27
When * reached Solomon that 1Ki 1:51
* of the king's decision spread 1Ki 3:28
not one * has failed of all the 1Ki 8:56
When Baasha received * of the 1Ki 15:21
several years until I say the *!" 1Ki 17:1
The city officials then sent * 1Ki 21:14
to this further * from the Lord. 1Ki 22:19
"just say the * and fifty of our 2Ki 2:16
Literally, "the * of the Lord is 2Ki 3:12f
to put in a good * for her to the 2Ki 4:13
* that he had left Lachish). 2Ki 19:8
"Listen to the * of the Lord: The 2Ki 20:16
The subsequent usage of the * 1Ch 1:24-27f
the Hebrew * meaning "distress." 1Ch 4:9f
The * in the Hebrew for 1Ch 28:12f
sent * to him of Solomon's death. 2Ch 10:2,3
was his final * to them. 2Ch 19:11
people of Judah. * reached 2Ch 20:2
to the king this * from the Lord. 2Ch 34:28
Thus the * of the Lord spoken 2Ch 36:21
for you are always true to your *. Neh 9:8
because the * for "throwing dice" Est 9:26
and nights, no one speaking a *; Job 2:13
"Will you let me say a *? Job 4:2
I were sinless I wouldn't say a *. Job 9:15
they cannot speak one truthful *. Ps 5:9
He speaks no careless *; Ps 12:6
Without a sound or *, silent in Ps 19:3,4
mouth to speak one * of complaint, Ps 39:9
You have made the * "Jew" a Ps 44:14
even know the meaning of the *! Ps 58:1
I will not take back one * of Ps 89:34
By reading your * and following Ps 119:9
to see wonderful things in your *. Ps 119:18
Revive me by your *. Ps 119:25
you; your * has been my comfort. Ps 119:52
I too am trusting in your *. Ps 119:74
Forever, O Lord, your * stands Ps 119:89
I will remain obedient to your *. Ps 119:101
your * above all your name." Ps 138:2f
How swiftly his * flies. Ps 147:15
His every * is a treasure of Pro 2:6
a * of encouragement does wonders! Pro 12:25
Despise God's * and find yourself Pro 13:13
Take my * for it—proud men shall Pro 16:5
Every * of God proves true. Pro 30:5
the * of the Holy One of Israel. Is 5:24
The controversial Hebrew * used Is 7:14f
words against the * of God!" Is 8:20
Therefore hear the * of the Lord, Is 28:14
Now go and write down this * of Is 30:8
and answered not a *, for Hezekiah Is 36:21
king received * that Tirhakah, Is 37:8,9

(WORD Con't)
fade, but the * of our God shall Is 40:8
for * of Cyrus' new campaigns. Is 41:5
None other said one *! Is 41:26
With one * I have saved you. Is 43:12
go back on my *, for it is Is 45:23
without meaning a * of it, when you Is 48:1
The meaning of the Hebrew * is Is 52:14,15f
afflicted, yet he never said a *. Is 53:7
and had never spoken an evil *. Is 53:9
for the hungry, so also is my *. Is 55:11
Your name shall be a curse * Is 65:15
heart, who trembles at my *. Is 66:2
There is * play here between Jer 1:12f
over my * to perform it." Jer 1:12f
The * of God has angered them; Jer 6:10
have rejected the * of the Lord. Jer 8:9
HEAR THE * of the Lord, O Israel: Jer 10:1
I have proclaimed your * to them. Jer 15:15
"What is this * of the Lord you Jer 17:15
people: Hear the * of the Lord, Jer 17:20
saying: Hear the * of the Lord. Jer 18:11
Listen to the * of the Lord, kings Jer 19:3
me speak a * of kindness to them; Jer 20:8
his name—then his * in my heart is Jer 20:9
Hear the * of the Lord! Jer 22:29
faithfully proclaim my every *. Jer 23:28
Does not my * burn like fire? Jer 23:29
don't leave out one * of all I Jer 26:2
* in every nation of the earth. Jer 26:6
He gave me every * of all that I Jer 26:12
* that you have heard from me." Jer 26:15
Therefore listen to the * of God, Jer 29:20
them to him * by word, and he had Jer 36:18
to him word by *, and he had Jer 36:18
"Send this * to Ebed-melech the Jer 39:16
"Listen to the * of the Lord, all Jer 44:24
But listen to the * of the Lord, Jer 44:26
"O prostitute, hear the * of the Eze 16:35
and say: Hear the * of the Lord. Eze 20:47
spoken one * to them at all. Eze 22:28
* is that comes from the Lord!" Eze 33:30f
shepherds, hear the * of the Lord: Eze 34:7
but the * for "plant" is in the Eze 34:29f
heard each evil * you spoke against Eze 35:12
hear the * of the Lord God. Eze 36:4
Then this further * came to me Eze 36:16
who speaks a * against the God of Dan 3:29
Aramaic * for "father" can also Dan 5:11f
looking down, unable to speak a *. Dan 10:15
this was a tainted * because Hos 1:16f
HEAR THE * of the Lord, O people Hos 4:1
sea, seeking the * of the Lord, Amo 8:12
weary, thirsting for the * of God. Amo 8:13
In the Hebrew, there is frequent * Mic 1:11f
Shaphir sounds like the Hebrew * Mic 1:11f
Beth-ezel sounds like a * for Mic 1:11f
In the Hebrew, there is frequent * Mic 1:11f
Shaphir sounds like the Hebrew * Mic 1:11f
Beth-ezel sounds like a * for Mic 1:11f
In the Hebrew, there is frequent * Mic 1:11f
Shaphir sounds like the Hebrew * Mic 1:11f
Beth-ezel sounds like a * for Mic 1:11f
you, with never a * from God. Mic 3:6
learned, that God's * endures! Zec 1:5,6
For now 'Judah' is a * of Zec 8:13
every * of God is what we need." Mt 4:4
Your * is enough. Mt 5:37
and when he spoke a single *, all Mt 8:16
Day for every idle * you speak. Mt 12:36
choke out God's *, and he does less Mt 13:22
gave her no reply—not even a *. Mt 15:23
been able to say a * before were Mt 15:31
The Greek * is not clear on Mk 1:8f
The Greek * is not clear on Mk 1:8f
And he preached the * to them. Mk 2:2
and they sent * for him to come out Mk 3:31,32
have spoken a true * in saying that Mk 12:32
it was a boy. The * spread quickly Lk 1:58
on him to listen to the * of God. Lk 5:1
Just speak a * from where you Lk 7:6,7,8
When * came back of what had Lk 9:54
all who hear the * of God and put Lk 11:28
hung on every * he said. Lk 19:48
Literally, "the *," meaning Jn 1:1f
Literally, "the *," meaning Jn 1:14f
The * "yet" is included in Jn 7:8f
(the * "Siloam" means "Sent"). Jn 9:7
When Martha got * that Jesus was Jn 11:20
" 'King' as you use the * or as Jn 18:34
But the Jews were using the * Jn 18:34f
God—the Living *—on Mount Sinai. Act 7:38
if you have any * of instruction Act 13:15
to hear them preach the * of God. Act 13:44
we proclaimed the * of the Lord." Act 15:36f
As they were killing him, * Act 21:31
"May I have a * with you?" Act 21:37,38
Paul came to that *, then with one Act 22:22
with this final * from Paul ringing Act 28:25
Have they heard God's *? Rom 10:18
of which could speak a single *. 1Co 12:2
Prophets—those who preach God's *, 1Co 12:28
of God's *—that is what you need; 1Co 14:6
preaching God's *, [even though 1Co 14:24
Those who are taught the * of God Gal 6:6
by washing of water with the *." Eph 5:26f
and God's *; Eph 5:26
And now a * to you parents. Eph 6:4
the Spirit—which is the * of God. Eph 6:17
speak a * of blame against you. Php 2:15
holding out to them the * of Life. Php 2:16
you trusted the * of the mighty God Col 2:12
And now the * of the Lord has 1Th 1:8
said as the very * of God—which, of 1Th 2:13
good by the * of God and prayer. 1Ti 4:5
preach God's *. 1Ti 4:13
But the * of God is not chained, 2Ti 2:9
Know what his * says and means. 2Ti 2:15
to preach the * of God urgently at 2Ti 4:2
them patiently with God's *. 2Ti 4:2
very first principles in God's *. Heb 5:12,13
things of God's * until you become Heb 5:14
know how good the * of God is, and Heb 6:5
who have taught you the * of God. Heb 13:7
the truth of his *, and we became, Jas 1:18
but the * of the Lord will last 1Pe 1:25
Eat God's *—read it, think about 1Pe 2:2,3f
listen to God's *, nor obey it, and 1Pe 2:8
And now this * to all of you: You 1Pe 3:8
AND NOW, A * to you elders of the 1Pe 5:1
the heavens by the * of his 2Pe 3:5,6
strong, with God's * in your 1Jn 2:14
for preaching the * of God, and for Rev 1:9
Literally, "you have kept my *." Rev 3:8f
for preaching the * of God and for Rev 6:9
Literally, "fornication," the * Rev 19:2f
his title was "The * of God." Rev 19:13
proclaiming the * of God, and who Rev 20:4

WORDING

The meaning of the Hebrew * is 2Sa 23:20f

WORDS

way to translate these *. Gen 1:2f
won't understand each other's *!" Gen 11:7
speaking these *, Rebekah was Gen 24:45
Moses reported the * of the Ex 19:8
heard these stern *, they went into Ex 33:4
the *, "Consecrated to Jehovah." Ex 39:30
Jehovah's * to the people; Num 11:24
reported God's * to the people! Num 14:39
speaking the * when the ground Num 16:31
not go beyond the * of Jehovah, and Num 24:13
He hears the * of God Num 24:15-19
you heard his * but didn't see Deu 4:12
you even heard his * from the Deu 4:36
to us, but these * which he has Deu 29:29
"Now write down the * of this Deu 31:19
wrote down the * of the song and Deu 31:22
My * shall fall upon you Deu 32:2
recited all the * of this song to Deu 32:44,45
These laws are not mere *—they Deu 32:47
This was a play on *. 1Sa 1:19,20f
These * of David persuaded his 1Sa 24:7,8
with fright because of Samuel's *. 1Sa 28:20
indeed God, and your * are truth; 2Sa 7:28
THESE ARE THE last * of David: 2Sa 23:1
And may these * of my prayer be 1Ki 8:59
of Israel even the * you speak in 2Ki 6:12
allies will give you more than *? 2Ki 18:20,21
A play on *. 1Ch 4:9f
The * he commanded 1Ch 16:15
Zechariah's last * as he died 2Ch 24:22
when you heard my * against this 2Ch 34:27
and despised their *, scoffing at 2Ch 36:16
could hear and understand God's *. Neh 8:12
his suffering was too great for *. Job 2:13
not denied the * of the holy God. Job 6:10
Job, blowing * around like wind? Job 8:2
someone stem this torrent of *? Job 11:2
What good do such * do? Job 15:3
what to say! Your * are based on Job 15:4,5
ever stop your flow of foolish *? Job 16:3
and try to break me with your *? Job 19:2
Job's * are ended. Job 31:40
For I am pent up and full of *, Job 32:18
vent! My * are ready to burst out! Job 32:19
The meanings of these * are not Ps 9:16f
May my spoken * and unspoken Ps 19:14
For all God's * are right, and Ps 33:4
I am as full of * as the speediest Ps 45:1
Your * are filled with grace; Ps 45:2
all gods, is awesome beyond *; Ps 47:2
world—listen to my *, for they are Ps 49:1
He broke his promises. His * Ps 55:21
heart was war. His * were sweet, Ps 55:21
lying from their earliest *! Ps 58:3
they aim their bitter * like Ps 64:3
their * strut through the earth. Ps 73:9
But it was only with their * Ps 78:36
Jesus applies these * to himself. Ps 110:1f
with these same *: "His Ps 118:2
I have thought much about your * Ps 119:11
and cheer me with your *. Ps 119:28
May I never forget your *; Ps 11
Nothing is perfect except your *. Ps 11
me; your * are sweeter than honey. Ps 119:102,
Your * are a flashlight to light Ps 119:
but I stand in awe of only your *. Ps 119:
Their * sting like poisonous Ps 1
He told me never to forget his * Pro
nor turn from the * of my mouth." Pro
Guard my * as your most precious Pro
of evil in it. My * are plain and Pro
the * of fools are a dime a dozen. Pro 1
Evil * destroy. Pro
the * of the wise soothe and heal. Pro 12
wrath, but harsh * cause quarrels. Pro
Gentle * cause life and health; Pro 1
Literally, "but kind * are Pro 15.
in kind *. Pro 15
the evil man pours out his evil * Pro 15
Kind * are like honey—enjoyable Pro 16
The man of few * and settled mind Pro 17:27
A wise man's * express deep Pro 1
His mouth is his undoing! His * Pro 18
Literally, "the *." Pro 22:
to take back your * of appreciation Pro 23:6,
thrill to your thoughtful, wise *. Pro 23:15
Pretty * may hide a wicked heart, Pro 26
mere * are not enough—discipline Pro 29
For the * may not be heeded. Pro 29
Do not add to his *, lest he Pro 3
When she speaks, her * are wise, Pro 31
He praises her with these *: Pro 31
Literally, "the * of the Ecc 1
on earth, so let your * be few. Ecc
is ruin in a flood of empty *; Ecc 5:
The more * you speak, the less Ecc 6.
But even so, the quiet * of a Ecc 9:
to listen to wise *, but a fool's Ecc 10:12
The wise man's * are like goads Ecc 12
inlaid with these *: 'With love Sol 3:
the Hebrew * for "justice" and Is 5
you hear my * repeatedly, you won't Is
"Check these witches' * against Is 8:
at a time and in such simple *!" Is 28:
over in simple * whenever he can; Is 28:
amounts to mere * learned by rote, Is 29:
deaf will hear the * of a book, and Is 29:
fury; his * consume like fire. Is 30:
and everything in it hear my *. Is 34
worth? Mere * won't substitute for Is 36
wall, "Hear the * of the great Is 36:
God will rebuke him for those *. Is 37
Are you so deaf to the * of Is 40:
* he gave before the worlds began? Is 40:
in the future. My * were scarcely Is 48
God will make my * of judgment Is 49
The Lord God has given me his * Is 50
And I have put my * in your Is 51:
Hear the * of God, all you who Is 66
and tremble at his *: Your brethren Is 66
I have put my * in your mouth! Jer 1
In accord with my * spoken Jer 1:
O my people, listen to the * of Jer 2:
of * with no divine authority. Jer 5:
I'll take your * and prophecies and Jer 5:
Listen to the * of God, O Jer 9:
Your * are what sustain me; Jer 15:
to them whatever * I give you. Jer 19
for God has decreed holy * of Jer 23
yet they say their * are mine. Jer 23:
You are twisting my * and Jer 23:
But listen now to the solemn * I Jer 28
Babylon—all the * written above— Jer 51:6
dust, let all my * sink deep into Eze 3:
say they want my *—all will be Eze 14:
I, the Lord, have spoken these *. Eze 17:2
then at last her * will be Eze 29:2
boasted great * against the Lord. Eze 35:
listen to the * of God, for the Eze 37
So I spoke these * from God, just Eze 37:
carve on it these *: 'This stick Eze 37:
and carve these * on it: 'This Eze 37:1
speaking these *, a voice called Dan 4:3
could read the * but could not Dan 5:
meaning of those *, I will clothe Dan 5:
Suddenly, as he spoke these *, I Dan 10:1
I have slain you with the * of my Hos 6:
but of hearing the * of the Lord. Amo 8:1
* of comfort and assurance. Zec 1:1
"represents the * of God's curse Zec 5:
afraid to hear the * that God, the Zec 7:1
have wearied the Lord with your *. Mal 2:1
the right * at the right time. Mt 10:1
Your * now reflect your fate Mt 12:3
But evil * come from an evil Mt 15:1
but my * remain forever. Mt 24:3
Mark my *—I will not drink this Mt 26:2
to fulfill the * of the prophets as Mt 26:5
speaking these *, a cloud covered Mk 9:
do not contain the *, "for those Mk 10:24
but my * stand sure forever. Mk 13:31
Suddenly Jesus' * flashed through Mk 14:72

ORDS Con't)
s first two * ("Eloi, Eloi") Mk 15:34f
or my * will certainly come true Lk 1:20
the * of Isaiah the prophet, Lk 3:4
that fell from his lips. Lk 4:22
that even demons obey him?" Lk 4:36
ut these crowds hear the * and Lk 8:10
ose who hear the * of God, but Lk 8:12
nd steals the * away and prevents Lk 8:12
nd believe God's * but whose faith Lk 8:14
hey listen to God's * and cling Lk 8:15
e ashamed of me and of my * now. Lk 9:26
ve you the right * even as you Lk 12:12
ve you the right * and such logic Lk 21:15
nd the * of the ancient Lk 21:22
et my * remain forever true. Lk 21:33
nd as he said the *, a rooster Lk 22:60
im with these *: "This is the Lk 23:38
ou," and with those * he died. Lk 23:46
"The Lord has really risen! Lk 24:33,34
od—speaks God's *, for God's Jn 3:33,34
ou alone have the * that give Jn 6:68
stens gladly to the * of God. Jn 8:47
in me? The * I say are not my Jn 14:10
eaching them your * of truth. Jn 17:17
t these * Pilate brought Jesus Jn 19:13
e spoke these * I have quoted, Act 2:29
these * of his I have quoted Act 2:34
hese * of Peter's moved them Act 2:37
s soon as Ananias heard these *, Act 5:5
concerning the Kingdom of God; Act 8:12
hen I thought of the Lord's * Act 11:16
rophets' * read every Sabbath. Act 13:27
on't let the prophets' * apply Act 13:40
o his wonderful * which are able Act 20:32
or I remembered the * of the Act 20:35
speak * of sober truth. Act 26:25
e had said these *, the Jews Act 28:28,29f
That God's * will always prove Rom 3:4
hat it cannot be expressed in *. Rom 8:26
n the * of the Scripture, "I Rom 9:10-13
n other *, how welcome are those Rom 10:15
n other *, he will feel Rom 12:20
with profound * and high sounding 1Co 1:17
didn't use lofty * and brilliant 1Co 2:1
power was in my *, proving to those 1Co 2:4
do speak with * of great wisdom, 1Co 2:6
o fall. Our * are wise because 1Co 2:7
even used the very * given to us by 1Co 2:13
not * that we as men might choose. 1Co 2:13
So we use the Holy Spirit's * to 1Co 2:13
rather speak five * that people can 1Co 14:19
than ten thousand * while 1Co 14:19
I will write these final * of 1Co 16:21
real, that it goes beyond mere *. 2Co 8:8
Son—his Gift too wonderful for *. 2Co 9:15
think my deeds and * are merely 2Co 10:2
describe or put in * (and anyway I 2Co 12:4
close my letter with these last *: 2Co 13:11
I will write these closing * in Gal 6:11
Quarreling, harsh *, and dislike Eph 4:31
give me the right * as I boldly Eph 6:19
taught and let his * enrich your Col 3:16
think of the * we spoke as being 1Th 2:13
of Christ's * and stirring up 1Ti 6:4
stone with these * written on it: 2Ti 2:19
saying in the * already quoted, Heb 4:7
* God spoke to you, his child? Heb 12:5
speak to them better than any *. 1Pe 3:1
corners, their * help us to 2Pe 1:19
of the prophets' *, then the light 2Pe 1:19
you the * of our Lord and Savior. 2Pe 3:1
John wrote it all down—the * of Rev 1:2
him a new song with these *: Rev 5:9
Their * are not to be revealed." Rev 10:4
the * of God will be fulfilled. Rev 17:17
Literally, "These are the true * Rev 19:9f
to me, "These * are trustworthy Rev 22:6,7

WORE
So, after that, they * no Ex 33:6
linen garments he * when he went Lev 16:23
all * golden earrings. Ju 8:23,24
Lord's helper and * a little linen 1Sa 2:18
Literally, "* a linen ephod." 1Sa 2:18f
nine feet tall! He * a bronze 1Sa 17:4-7
intense as the day * on, and King 1Ki 22:35
David also * a linen ephod. 1Ch 15:27
One of them * linen clothing and Eze 9:2
As I prayed, I fasted, and * rough Dan 9:3
hair and he * a leather belt; Mt 3:4
hair and he * a leather belt; Mk 1:6
They * breastplates that seemed Rev 9:9
their riders * fiery-red Rev 9:17,18
The woman * purple and scarlet Rev 17:4

WORK
ceased from this * he had been Gen 2:2
when he ceased this * of creation. Gen 2:3
from the hard * of farming this Gen 5:28-31
for you to * for me without pay. Gen 29:15
So he told her father, "I'll * Gen 29:18
to * for me another seven years!" Gen 29:27
So Jacob agreed to * seven more Gen 29:28
thing, I'll go back to * for you. Gen 30:31,32
and my hard *, and that is why he Gen 31:42
going about his *—as it happened, Gen 39:11
the people from their *? Ex 5:4,5
Load them with * and make them Ex 5:9
don't have enough *, or else you Ex 5:17
Get back to *. Ex 5:18
and no * of any kind may be done on Ex 12:16
and your regular *, but the Ex 20:9
On that day you are to do no * of Ex 20:10
"* six days only, and rest the Ex 23:12
"All utensils used in the * of Ex 27:19
that will lend dignity to his *. Ex 28:2
anyone who does any * on that day Ex 31:14,15
shall be killed. * six days only, Ex 31:16
and harvest times, * only six days, Ex 34:21
"* six days only; Ex 35:2
to assist in the * given to them by Ex 35:29
we will be needing in the *. Ex 35:35
who felt called to the * to begin. Ex 36:1
wire threads, to * into the blue, Ex 39:3
beautiful piece of *, just like the Ex 39:8
there in the * of the Tabernacle. Ex 39:33-40
And Moses inspected all their * Ex 39:43
So at last Moses finished the *. Ex 40:33
thus setting him apart for his *. Lev 8:12
You must do no * on the Lev 16:29,30
and all ordinary * shall cease. Lev 23:7
"you shall do no hard *." Lev 23:7f
don't do any * that day. Lev 23:21
Don't do any * on the day of the Lev 23:25
Don't do any * that day, for it Lev 23:28
who does any kind of * that day. Lev 23:30,31
don't do any hard * that day. Lev 23:35
and no heavy * is permitted. Lev 23:36
assigned for the * connected with Num 1:50
are able to * in the Tabernacle. Num 4:3
This, then, is the sacred * of Num 4:15
the sacred * of the Tabernacle. Num 4:21,22,23
for the * of the Tabernacle. Num 7:4,5
of the Tabernacle to do their *. Num 8:15
to himself as you * in the Num 16:8,9
impropriety in your priestly *. Num 18:1
for the * of the Tabernacle. Num 18:6
Only the Levites shall do the * Num 18:23
hard * shall be done on that day. Num 28:18
that day you may do no hard *. Num 28:25
there is to be no hard * by Num 28:26
day, and no hard * may be done. Num 29:1
and no * of any kind may be done. Num 29:7
that day no hard * shall be done; Num 29:12
you must do no hard * that day. Num 29:35
This is my command. * the other Deu 5:13
Lord your God; no * shall be done Deu 5:14
Lord and to do his * and to bless Deu 10:8
God will bless you and your *. Deu 14:29
of your herds to * your fields, and Deu 15:19
Don't do any * that day. Deu 16:8
Levites who * there regularly. Deu 18:6,7
He is the Rock. His * is perfect. Deu 32:4
And shall * before you at the Deu 33:10
And accept the * they do for you. Deu 33:11
the Canaanites to * as slaves. Jos 17:13
the Canaanites to * as slaves, but Ju 1:28
way home from his * in the fields. Ju 19:16
And when she went back to * Ru 2:15
and axes and * in the brick kilns; 2Sa 12:31
"Because I * for the man who is 2Sa 16:18
these officials and their *. 1Ki 4:8-19
send my men to * beside them, and I 1Ki 5:6
a skilled craftsman in bronze *. 1Ki 7:13
So he came to * for King Solomon. 1Ki 7:14
last completed the * in the Temple 1Ki 7:40
Israelis for this *, although they 1Ki 9:22
bless me and help me in my *; 1Ch 4:10
choirs carried on their * there. 1Ch 6:32
* with saws, iron picks, and axes, 1Ch 20:3
"By hard * I have collected 1Ch 22:14
So get to *, and may the Lord be 1Ch 22:16
will supervise the * at the 1Ch 23:4,5
The * of the Levites was to 1Ch 23:28
they also did the custodial * and 1Ch 23:28
The * was assigned (by coin-toss) 1Ch 24:7-18
a list of their names and their *: 1Ch 25:1
well qualified for their *. 1Ch 26:8
concerning the * of the various 1Ch 28:13
and courageous and get to *. 1Ch 28:20
the * ahead of him is enormous; 1Ch 29:1
and skilled engravers to * beside 2Ch 2:7
does exquisite * with brass and 2Ch 2:14
He will * with your craftsmen and 2Ch 2:14
So at last he completed the * 2Ch 4:11
could not continue their *. 2Ch 5:13,14
Levites to their * of praise and of 2Ch 8:14
alone may help them in their *. 2Ch 13:10
keep up the good * and don't get 2Ch 15:7
"'It will *,' the Lord said; 2Ch 18:21
the Lord has destroyed your *." 2Ch 20:37
those whose week's * was done and 2Ch 23:8
So the * went forward, and 2Ch 24:13
"That is the * of the priests 2Ch 26:17,18
who are consecrated to this *. 2Ch 26:17,18
them until the * was finished—and 2Ch 29:34
had reported to *—for the Levites 2Ch 29:34
They set to * and destroyed the 2Ch 30:14
under the names of their * corps. 2Ch 31:17,18
SOME TIME LATER, after this good * 2Ch 32:1
They organized a huge * crew to 2Ch 32:4
music while the * progressed. 2Ch 34:12
begin their * at the Temple again. 2Ch 35:2
at Jerusalem. The * force was made Ez 3:8
"Let us * with you, for we are Ez 4:2
you may have no part in this *. Ez 4:3
So the * ended until the second Ez 4:24
city walls. The * is going forward Ez 5:8
and the other leaders in their *. Ez 6:7
continued in their *, and they were Ez 6:14
corps, to do the * of God as Ez 6:18
we began our * on December 15, Ez 10:16-19
to those who would be doing the *. Neh 2:16
And so the * began. Neh 2:18
them was the * crew led by Zaccur Neh 3:2
carried on the * from the corner to Neh 3:25
heard that the * was going right Neh 4:7
us and kill us, thus ending our *. Neh 4:11
Now we all returned to our * on Neh 4:15
"The * is so spread out," I Neh 4:19
duty as well as * during the day. Neh 4:22
I stayed at * on the wall and Neh 5:16
"I am doing a great *! Neh 6:3
to scare us into stopping our *." Neh 6:9
realized that the * had been done Neh 6:16
leaders gave gifts for the *. Neh 7:70
And we agreed not to do any * Neh 10:31
necessary for the * of the Temple Neh 10:33
priests doing the * at the Temple Neh 11:10-14
of the * outside the Temple; Neh 11:15,16,17
They also appreciated the * of Neh 12:45
certain that each knew his *. Neh 13:30
Man's * stops at such a time, so Job 37:7
you let him decide where to *? Job 39:11
skies and see the * of your Ps 8:3
you have endorsed my *, declaring Ps 9:4
peace with everyone; * hard at it. Ps 34:14
Literally, "embroidered *." Ps 45:14f
according to the * we do for him. Ps 62:12
My zeal for God and his * Ps 69:9
shall see their God at * for them. Ps 69:32
and men go off to * until the Ps 104:23
How he must rejoice in all his *! Ps 104:31
house, the builders' * is useless. Ps 127:1
It is senseless for you to * so Ps 127:2
The Lord will * out his plans Ps 138:8
king to make them *, yet they Pro 6:7
All our * adds nothing to it! Pro 10:22
than to be too proud to *—and Pro 12:9
Hard * means prosperity; Pro 12:11
* returns many blessings to him. Pro 12:14
* hard and become a leader; Pro 12:24
wealth from hard * grows. Pro 13:11
The * of the wicked will perish; Pro 14:11
the * of the godly will flourish. Pro 14:11
* brings profit; Pro 14:23
Commit your * to the Lord, then Pro 16:3
weights in the bag are his *." Pro 16:11f
Hunger is good—if it makes you * Pro 16:26
Stay awake, * hard, and there Pro 20:13
things but his hands refuse to *. Pro 21:25,26
"I can't go to *!" Pro 22:13
The master may get better * from Pro 26:10
The lazy man won't go out and *. Pro 26:13
Hard * brings prosperity; Pro 28:19
the day's * for her servant girls. Pro 31:15
does a man get for all his hard *? Ecc 1:3-7
found great pleasure in hard *. Ecc 2:10
fruits of all my hard * to others. Ecc 2:18
despair from hard * as the answer Ecc 2:20-23
hasn't done a day's * in his life; Ecc 2:20-23
does a man get for all his hard *? Ecc 2:20-23
does one really get from hard *? Ecc 3:9
of * God has given to mankind. Ecc 3:10
of God's * from beginning to end. Ecc 3:11
be happy in their *, for that is Ecc 3:22
The fool won't * and almost Ecc 4:5,6
get by, than to * hard when, in the Ecc 4:5,6
his hard * has been for nothing; Ecc 5:16
and enjoy his * whatever his job Ecc 5:18
To enjoy your * and to accept Ecc 5:19,20
will be wise," but it didn't *. Ecc 7:23
in all the hard * which God gives Ecc 8:15
A fool is so upset by a little * Ecc 10:15
and whose leaders * hard before Ecc 10:16,17
few to do their *, and there will Ecc 12:3
like jewels, the * of the most Sol 7:1
to do this *, to satisfy my anger. Is 13:3
live when I have finished up my *. Is 13:12
fishermen will weep for lack of *; Is 19:8
the * of my hands, in his midst." Is 29:23f
has finished its * in the heavens, Is 34:5
on them and their * withers and the Is 40:24
why have I named you for this *? Is 45:4

(WORK Con't)
me concerning the * of my hands? Is 45:11
you * in strange, mysterious ways. Is 45:15
I replied, "But my * for them Is 49:4
not what you would * out, neither Is 55:8
man who refuses to * during my Is 56:2
those who * for you and treat them Is 58:6
Today your * begins, to warn the Jer 1:10
* on the Sabbath day but make it Jer 17:21,22
and refuse to * on the Sabbath day Jer 17:24
Don't dwindle away! And * for Jer 29:7
Literally, "for your * shall be Jer 31:16f
do the * that God has given them! Jer 48:10
* of the Lord, the God of Hosts. Jer 50:25
* shall be destroyed by fire! Jer 51:58
Chaldean army to * tearing down the Jer 52:14
unending * is now our lot. Lam 5:5
let it finish its * of punishing Eze 7:8,9
the * you gave me to do." Eze 9:11
again until its * is finished. Eze 21:5
not pay the army for all this *. Eze 29:18
to do maintenance * and to assist Eze 44:14
The first day he returns to * Eze 44:27
the Levites who * at the Temple. Eze 45:5
during the six * days but open on Eze 46:1
she can * for him from within. Dan 11:17
Now let the sickle do its *; Joe 3:13
What is your *? Jon 1:8
though you did no * to put it Jon 4:10
They * so hard, but all in vain! Hab 2:13
take courage and *, for 'I am Hag 2:4
rejoice to see the * begin, to see Zec 4:10
they are going out to do his *. Zec 6:5
Before the * began there were no Zec 8:10
their * for God with pure hearts. Mal 3:3
At once they stopped their * Mt 4:22
* so hard beneath a heavy yoke. Mt 11:28
the Temple may * on the Sabbath? Mt 12:5
asked Jesus, "Is it legal to * Mt 12:10
would you * to rescue it that day? Mt 12:11
and sent them out to *. Mt 20:2
Didn't you agree to * all day for Mt 20:13
go out and * on the farm today.' Mt 21:28
find you faithfully doing your *. Mt 24:46
*, too, and earned another $2,000. Mt 25:17
master praised him for good *. Mt 25:21
" 'Good *,' his master said. Mt 25:23
It's against our laws to * by Mk 2:24
He laid out his employees' * for Mk 13:34
going about his * in the Temple—for Lk 1:8,9
Jewish law to * on the Sabbath." Lk 6:2
seen the hand of God at * today." Lk 7:16
from the * I plan for him is not Lk 9:62
sits here while I do all the *? Lk 10:40
to *," he shouted to the crowd. Lk 13:14
hypocrite! You * on the Sabbath! Lk 13:15
heaven is narrow. * hard to get in, Lk 13:24,25
of you doesn't * on the Sabbath?" Lk 14:5
in heaven appoints each man's *. Jn 3:27
man's work. My * is to prepare the Jn 3:28
sent me, and from finishing his *. Jn 4:34
Do you think the * of harvesting Jn 4:35
others did the *, and you Jn 4:38
"You can't * on the Sabbath! Jn 5:10
works even until now, and I *." Jn 5:17f
But you * on the Sabbath, too, Jn 7:21,22,23
falls and all * comes to an end. Jn 9:4
holy day when all * was forbidden. Jn 9:14f
for any good *, but for blasphemy; Jn 10:33
And he does his * through me. Jn 14:10
And again, 'Let his * be given to Act 1:20
As John was finishing his * he Act 13:25
to God for the * now completed. Act 14:26
done the Lord's * humbly—yes, and Act 20:19
it for doing the * assigned me by Act 20:24
the Lord Jesus—the * of telling Act 20:24
among the Gentiles through his *. Act 21:19
so that I could * among you and see Rom 1:13
It is given to those who do not * Rom 4:4,5
desires were at * within you, Rom 7:5
we each have different * to do. Rom 12:4,5
in charge of the * of others, take Rom 12:8
Never be lazy in your * but Rom 12:11
their sorrow. * happily together. Rom 12:16
on doing God's *, serving you. Rom 13:6
Don't undo the * of God for a Rom 14:20
am through with my * here, and I am Rom 15:23
Spirit—pray much with me for my *. Rom 15:30
you believed. My * was to plant 1Co 3:6
and Apollos' * was to water it, but 1Co 3:6
be rewarded for his own hard *. 1Co 3:8
Everyone's * will be put through 1Co 3:13
* still stands, will get his pay. 1Co 3:14
we have been doing the Lord's *. 1Co 4:5
keep on with the * he was doing 1Co 7:20
for doing the Lord's * 1Co 7:29
keep anyone from doing God's *. 1Co 7:30
* and thinking how to please him. 1Co 7:32
the result of my hard * for him. 1Co 9:1
And those who * at the altar of 1Co 9:13
God who does the * in and through 1Co 12:6
Those who can get others to * 1Co 12:28
in the Lord's *, for you know that 1Co 15:58
doing the Lord's * just as I am. 1Co 16:10
like them who * hard at your side 1Co 16:16
the * of such men as these. 1Co 16:18
we have done a good * among you. 2Co 3:2
us this wonderful * [of telling his 2Co 4:1
that we * so hard to win others. 2Co 5:11
You went right to * on the 2Co 7:11
* someone else has done among you. 2Co 10:15
set for us, our * among you will be 2Co 10:15
* in just the same way we are. 2Co 11:12
continued their * with the Jews. Gal 2:7,8,9
Holy Spirit and * miracles among Gal 3:5
I am afraid that all my hard * Gal 4:11
satisfaction of * well done, and Gal 6:4
the air, who is at * right now in Eph 2:2
me this special * of showing God's Eph 3:2,3
mighty power at * within us is able Eph 3:20
to do better * for him, building up Eph 4:12
of his for honest * so he can give Eph 4:28
Don't * hard only when your Eph 6:6,7
he isn't looking; * hard and with Eph 6:6,7
in the Lord's *, will tell you all Eph 6:21
who began the good * within you Php 1:6
For God is at * within you, Php 2:13
my * among you was so worthwhile. Php 2:16
his life for the * of Christ and Php 2:30
are my joy and my reward for my *. Php 4:1
those who * in Caesar's palace. Php 4:22
But part of my * is to suffer for Col 1:24
This is my *, and I can do it Col 1:29
mighty energy is at * within me. Col 1:29
to please him. * hard and Col 3:23
that all our * had been useless. 1Th 3:5
own *, just as we told you before. 1Th 4:11
of your church who * hard among you 1Th 5:12
As for the * this man of 2Th 2:7
of lawlessness is already at *." 2Th 2:7f
cleansing you by the * of the 2Th 2:13
ideal of hard * we set up for you. 2Th 3:6
how you should * for your living. 2Th 3:9
who does not * shall not eat." 2Th 3:10
refusing to *, and wasting your 2Th 3:11
to *, and earn their own living. 2Th 3:12
accept it. We * hard and suffer 1Ti 4:9,10
Put these abilities to *; 1Ti 4:15
Pastors who do their * well 1Ti 5:17
those who * hard at both preaching 1Ti 5:17
"Those who * deserve their pay!" 1Ti 5:18
CHRISTIAN SLAVES SHOULD * hard 1Ti 6:1
rather they should * all the 1Ti 6:2
evil things and * instead at what 1Ti 6:11
us for his holy *, not because we 2Ti 1:9
for doing his *, just as an athlete 2Ti 2:5
wins no prize. * hard, like a 2Ti 2:6
and even harmful. * hard so God 2Ti 2:15
ashamed when God examines your *. 2Ti 2:15
been trusted to do this * for him. Tit 1:3
and ready for any honest *. Tit 3:1
heavens are the * of your hands. Heb 1:10
and his * was mostly to Heb 3:5
He is resting from his *, just as Heb 4:10
* in the same way God chose Aaron. Heb 5:4
* at the cross could be performed. Heb 5:7f
How can he forget your hard * for Heb 6:10
Moses had never given them that * Heb 7:12,13,14
was canceled because it didn't *. Heb 7:18
Their * is connected with a Heb 8:5
far more important * than those who Heb 8:6
The old agreement didn't even *. Heb 8:7
they wanted to, doing their *. Heb 9:6
For their * is to watch over your Heb 13:17
And the Holy Spirit has been at * 1Pe 1:2
part of the * God has given you. 1Pe 2:21
you must also * hard to be good, 2Pe 1:5
So, dear brothers, * hard to 2Pe 1:10
are doing a good * for God in 3Jn 1:5
with them in the Lord's *. 3Jn 1:8
I have watched your hard * and Rev 2:2
and turn back to me again and * Rev 2:5

WORK-CREW
Then they whipped the Israeli * Ex 5:14

WORKED
Jacob raged at Laban. "I * for Gen 29:25
and * the additional seven years. Gen 29:30
You know how hard I've * for Gen 31:6
I * for you through the Gen 31:40
you will have * so hard to grow. Deu 28:33
I gave you land you had not * Jos 24:13
So she * there all day, and in Ru 2:17
They all * hard ferrying the 2Sa 19:18
He replied, "I have * very hard 1Ki 19:10
workers who * at Beth-ashbea, 1Ch 4:21-22
they all * for the king: 1Ch 4:23
They sang with joy as they *. 2Ch 23:18
Lord his God. He * very hard to 2Ch 31:21
Men from the city of Jericho * Neh 3:2
trade, but he too * on the wall. Neh 3:8
they also * on the section of Neh 3:19
city—for the workers * hard. Neh 4:6
but from then on, only half * Neh 4
And the masons and laborers * Neh 4
We * early and late, from sunrise Neh 4:20
So I * hard to be wise instead Ecc 1:16
they have * hard but it does them Jer 12
many lands have * in vain—their Jer 51
you have * so hard to get." Hag 1
'Those fellows * only one hour, and Mt 20:1
* all day in the scorching heat.' Mt 20:1
One of the maids who * for the Mk 14:66
"Sir," Simon replied, "we * Lk
these years I've * hard for you and Lk 15
Jesus replied, "I * on the Jn 7:21,22
Paul lived and * with them, for Act 18
hands of mine * to pay my own way Act 20
She has * hard in the church Rom 1
too, who has * so hard to help us. Rom 1
who has * so hard for the Lord. Rom 16
We have * wearily with our hands 1Co 4
for I have * harder than all the 1Co 15
It makes no difference who * the 1Co 15
faced angry mobs, * to exhaustion, 2Co
I have * harder, been put in 2Co 11
women, for they * side by side with Php
and they * with Clement, too, and Php
I can assure you that he has * Col 4
brothers, how hard we * among you? 1Th
buying it; we * hard day and night 2Th

WORKER
had been a foundry * from Tyre. 1Ki 7
or other * in the Temple shall be Ez 7
She is energetic, a hard *, and Pro 31
our fellow *, and beloved Stachys. Rom 1
Epaphras, our much-loved fellow * Col
He is a hard * and serves the Col
brother and fellow *, God's 1Th 3
much loved fellow *, and to the Phm

WORKERS
all metal * in bronze and iron." Gen 4:2
shall pay your hired * promptly. Lev 19
Stay right behind my women *; Ru 2:8
and I'm not even one of your *!" Ru 2
The families of the linen * who 1Ch 4:21-
smiths and bronze and iron *. 1Ch 22
silversmiths, brass and iron *; 2Ch
the Temple *, and the rest of the Ez 2
and Temple * traveled with him. Ez 7:7,8
Next to them the * were led by Neh 3
entire city—for the * worked hard. Neh 4
And whenever the * who lived in Neh 4
However, the Temple * (whose Neh 11
Lazy men are soon poor; hard * Pro 10
keep right on oppressing your *. Is 58
so great, and the * are so few," Mt 9
more * for his harvest fields." Mt 9
to hire * for his harvest field. Mt 20
is so plentiful and the * so few. Lk 10
For government * need to be paid Rom 13
They have been my fellow * in Rom 16
the Lord's *, and to dear Persis, Rom 16
us that Christian * should be paid 1Co 9
rest of my fellow * whose names are Php 4
become one of the special church * 1Ti 5
that Christ's people are poor *. 1Ti 6
Demas and Luke, my fellow *. Phm 1:2
Hear the cries of the field * Jas 5

WORKING
seven years * to pay for Rachel. Gen 29:2
anyone * on that day must die. Ex 35
have a genuine priest * for me!" Ju 17:1
He replied again, "I have been * 1Ki 19:1
who was * with the reapers. 2Ki 4:1
experienced crews * alongside 2Ch 8:17,1
the men who were * on the Temple. Ez 5
and the people have been * on it Ez 5:1
Next was a group of Levites * Neh 3:1
he has been * for the wind. Ecc 5:1
going, there is no * or planning, Ecc 9:1
by a snake! When * in a quarry, Ecc 10:8,
a weaver stops his * at the loom. Is 38:1
found the potter * at his wheel. Jer 18
because he was * for me during Eze 29:2
It is open to anyone * in the Eze 48:1
'Why haven't you been * today?' Mt 20
"Two men will be * together in Mt 24:4
the older son was in the fields *; Lk 15:2
Two women will be * together at Lk 17:35,3
and so it will be with men * side Lk 17:35,3
because he is * on the Sabbath." Jn 9:1
happens to us is * for our good if Rom 8:2
* at the house of Aristobulus. Rom 16:1
Such teachers are not * for our Rom 16:1
Apollos and I are * as a team, 1Co 3
and I alone keep * for our living, 1Co 9
God told those * in his temple to 1Co 9:1
it, but God * in me, to bless me. 1Co 15:1
includes our * there with you. 2Co 10:1
you, where no one else is *; 2Co 10:1
for all we need is faith * Gal 5
time, as though * for Christ, doing Eph 6:6,
with each other, * together with Php 2:

ORKING Con't)
and battling side by side. Php 2:25
et, but I keep * toward that day Php 3:12
though you were * for the Lord Col 3:23
e is the one you are really * Col 3:24
ewish Christians * with me here, Col 4:11
e must be hard * and thoughtful, 1Ti 3:2
Vell, Moses did a fine job * in Heb 3:5
nd I have been * so hard to get. 2Jn 1:8

ORKMAN
r, "like a master *." Pro 8:30f
* may eat from the orchard he Pro 27:18
r the * is worthy of his wages! Lk 10:7
hen every * who has built on 1Co 3:14
e a good *, one who does not 2Ti 2:15

ORKMAN'S
hen she took a tent pin and a * Ju 5:26

ORKMANSHIP
Then, using the most careful *, Ex 28:15
from gold, silver, and bronze; Ex 35:32
iece of * when finished. Ex 39:3
hink about. Your * is Ps 139:14

ORKMEN
killed of the *, using blue, Ex 28:5,6
ut finally the * all left their Ex 36:4-7
he * were energetic under the 2Ch 34:12
arried in the materials to the *. 2Ch 34:13
nd *," he said to the king. 2Ch 34:17
were appointed to supervise the *. Ez 3:8
hat the * were becoming tired; Neh 4:10

ORKS
* without regard to human means! 1Sa 17:47
was superintendent of public *. 1Ki 4:1
And tell of his marvelous *. 1Ch 16:9
His public * program was also 2Ch 17:13
the Jew, who * at the Chancellery. Est 6:10
* for which he is so famous. Job 36:24
Praise him for his mighty *. Ps 150:2
A bribe * like magic. Pro 17:8
She * far into the night! Pro 31:18
and let her * praise her in the Pro 31:31f
a great public * program: homes, Ecc 2:4,5,6
or brother, yet he * hard to keep Ecc 4:8
The man who * hard sleeps well Ecc 5:12
their pride and all their evil *. Is 25:11
*"—none of which will save you. Is 57:12
who * for those who wait for him! Is 64:4
For the good * of a righteous Eze 33:12
But if he * hard, he may learn as Lk 6:40
into dough, which * unseen until it Lk 13:20,21
Literally, "My Father * even Jn 5:17f
have them or * hard to get them. Rom 9:16
ways in which God * in our lives, 1Co 12:6
And as the Spirit of the Lord * 2Co 3:18
and signs and mighty * among you. 2Co 12:12
They should be rich in good * and 1Ti 6:18
itself by good * is no faith at Jas 2:17
well, I say that good * are Jas 2:18
for without good * you can't prove Jas 2:18
your good * when Christ returns. 1Pe 2:12
Yet it is always new, and * for 1Jn 2:8
to destroy these * of the devil. 1Jn 3:8

WORKSHOP
I seek him in his * in the Job 23:9
Idle hands are the devil's *; Pro 16:27

WORLD
time that beings from the spirit * Gen 6:1
from the spirit * were sexually Gen 6:4
God, the * was rotten to the core. Gen 6:11
the people of the * were separated Gen 10:25
from scattering all over the *." Gen 11:3,4
Similarity with today's * is Gen 11:6f
and the entire * will be blessed Gen 12:3
He hadn't a worry in the * with Gen 39:6
"What in the * is the matter?" Gen 40:7
all over the *, Joseph opened up Gen 41:56,57
"What in the * are you talking Gen 44:7
"What in the * did the people do Ex 32:21
into the greatest nation in the *. Deu 28:1
All the nations in the * shall Deu 28:10
When God divided up the * among Deu 32:8
foolish Gentile nations of the *. Deu 32:21
"Where in the * did you glean Ru 2:19
And he has set the * in order. 1Sa 2:8
"Where in the * did you go?" 1Sa 10:14
and the whole * will know that 1Sa 17:46
Who else in all the * would let 1Sa 24:19
of the most famous men in the *! 2Sa 7:9
Setting fire to the *. 2Sa 22:9
And no one in all the * will be 1Ki 3:13
all the * so splendid as that one. 1Ki 10:20
"What in the * is the matter?" 1Ki 21:5
God in all the * except in Israel; 2Ki 5:15
"Tell the peoples of the * 1Ch 16:8
The * stands unmoved. 1Ch 16:30
and glorious throughout the *; 1Ch 22:5
be so great a king in all the *!" 2Ch 1:12
No other throne in all the * 2Ch 9:19
"All the * knows that anyone, Est 4:11
darkness, and chased out of the *. Job 18:18
and dispenses justice for the *. Job 34:13
give you all the nations of the *. Ps 2:8
judge justly the nations of the *. Ps 9:7,8
Tell the * about his Ps 9:11
Where in all the * can dependable Ps 12:1
these men of the * whose only Ps 17:13,14
message reaches out to all the *. Ps 19:3,4
Everything in all the * is his! Ps 24:1
the * about your faithfulness? Ps 30:9
Let everyone in all the *—men, Ps 33:8
For when he but spoke, the * Ps 33:9
shall sit on thrones around the *! Ps 45:16
fear even if the * blows up, and Ps 46:2
ruin upon the *, and causes wars Ps 46:8
by every nation in the *!" Ps 46:10
The Gentile rulers of the * have Ps 47:9
armies of the * are his trophies. Ps 47:9
have scattered throughout the *. Ps 48:10
all around the *—listen to my Ps 49:1
his life—and the * loudly applauds Ps 49:18
* is mine, and everything in it. Ps 50:12
and will reign throughout the *. Ps 59:12,13
the * and far away upon the sea. Ps 65:5
All the * shouts with joy, and Ps 65:13
Tell the * how wonderful he is. Ps 66:2
Send us around the * with the Ps 67:2
Praise God, O *! Ps 67:5
the lightning lighted up the *! Ps 77:18
The heavens are yours, the *, Ps 89:11
and strength. The * is his throne. Ps 93:1
Literally, "The * is established Ps 93:1f
on the seashores of the *! Ps 93:4
Sing it everywhere around the *! Ps 96:1
O nations of the *, confess that Ps 96:7
He rules the *. Ps 96:10
flashes out across the *. Ps 97:4
judge the * with perfect justice. Ps 98:8,9
You bound the * together so that Ps 104:5
your power to all the *. Ps 106:8
plying the trade routes of the *. Ps 107:23
around the *, in every nation. Ps 108:3
Though all the nations of the * Ps 118:10
He sends his orders to the *. Ps 147:15
* and all his family of mankind! Pro 8:31
you want them broadcast to the *. Pro 20:19
Who but God has created the *? Pro 30:4
fine women in the *, but you are Pro 31:29
God is letting the * go on its Ecc 3:18
on here in the *, where people have Ecc 8:9,10
I have watched the * go by, a sad Ecc 10:5
woman in all the *, follow the Sol 1:8
For in those days the * will be Is 2:3
peace to all the nations of the *. Is 9:7
part of his plan to conquer the *. Is 10:7
banner of salvation to all the *. Is 11:10
Tell the * about his wondrous Is 12:4
known his praise around the *. Is 12:5
And I will punish the * for its Is 13:11
The nations of the * will help Is 14:2
All the * begins to sing! Is 14:7
their domain. * leaders and earth's Is 14:9
were against the nations of the *. Is 14:12
earth and the kingdoms of the *? Is 14:16
who destroyed the * and made it Is 14:17
nor rebuild the cities of the *. Is 14:21
reaches everywhere around the *. Is 14:26
let all the * take notice! Is 18:3
the merchandise mart of the *. Is 23:2,3
builder and top trader of the *? Is 23:8
to all her evil ways around the *. Is 23:17
the nations of the *." Is 24:13f
still your lot, O men of the *. Is 24:17
you; the * is shaken beneath you. Is 24:18
The * staggers like a drunkard; Is 24:20
around the *—a delicious feast of Is 25:6
let the * and everything in it Is 34:1
will I see my friends in this *. Is 38:11
No, for all the peoples of the * Is 40:15
He dooms the great men of the * Is 40:23
justice to the nations of the *. Is 42:1
in all the *, he is the one who Is 42:5
Who in all the * is as blind as Is 42:19
show the * that he is righteous. Is 42:21
to all the * the glory of his law; Is 42:22
wilderness of the * for my people Is 43:19
some day honor me before the *. Is 43:21
me, and all the * from east to Is 45:6
and he made the * to be lived in, Is 45:18
Let all the * look to me for Is 45:22
knee in all the * shall bow to me, Is 45:23
never end, Queen Kingdom of the *. Is 47:7
greatest in the *—listen to the Is 47:8
seashores of the *, too many to Is 48:19
the nations of the * to bring my Is 49:6
All the * shall know that I, the Is 49:26
the * around you—will rejoice. Is 55:12
from around the * will flow to you, Is 60:5
known around the *, has glorified Is 60:9
The kings of the * will cater to Is 60:11
of the *, for I will make you so. Is 60:15
the nations of the * his justice; Is 61:11
For since the * began no one has Is 64:4
All the * will see the good hand Is 66:14
For the Lord will punish the * Is 66:16
you as my spokesman to the *." Jer 1:5
nations and the kingdoms of the *. Jer 1:10
land, the finest in the *. Jer 3:19
the nations of the * and they will Jer 4:2
I set the shorelines of the * by Jer 5:22
I will scatter them around the * Jer 9:16
the * there isn't anyone like you. Jer 10:7
at his anger; the * shall hide Jer 10:10
will horrify the peoples of the *. Jer 15:4
from around the * will come to you Jer 16:19
all the * will be shocked at the Jer 25:11
and all the kingdoms of the *. Jer 25:26
I will scatter them around the *. Jer 29:18
you nations of the *, and publish Jer 31:10
in Israel and all around the *. Jer 32:20
The people of the * will see the Jer 33:9
you over all the * as exiles. Jer 34:17
* is before you—go where you like. Jer 40:4
before the outside * knew what had Jer 41:4
a care in the *, boasting that they Jer 49:31
to countries throughout the *. Jer 49:36
Tell all the * that Babylon will Jer 50:2
shall be heard around the *. Jer 50:46
the vapors to rise around the *; Jer 51:16
all the earth! The * can scarcely Jer 51:41
In all the * has there ever been Lam 2:13
*,' and 'Joy of All the Earth'?" Lam 2:15
the lowly of the *, and deprived Lam 3:34,35,36
one in all the *—would have Lam 4:12
will be scattered into all the *. Eze 5:10
to the * and an awesome example to Eze 5:15
among the nations of the *. Eze 6:8
countries of the *, yet I will be a Eze 11:16
exposed to all the *, and you are Eze 16:57
and they will scorch the *. Eze 20:47
And all the * will see that I, Eze 20:48
All the * shall know that it is Eze 21:5
to all the nations of the *. Eze 22:4
you throughout the * and burn out Eze 22:15
shall be exposed to all the *. Eze 23:29
And all the * will mock you for Eze 23:32
long ago the nether * of the dead. Eze 26:20
of the *, the Lord God speaks. Eze 27:3
most beautiful city in all the *.' Eze 27:3
'Where in all the * was there ever Eze 27:32
the * my holiness among my people. Eze 28:25
All the great nations of the * Eze 31:6
with all the proud men of the *. Eze 31:14
her to the nether *—those nations Eze 31:17
of Eden—the nations of the *. Eze 31:18
Send them down to the nether * Eze 32:18
in the nether * will welcome her as Eze 32:21
"The whole * will rejoice when I Eze 35:14
by my people throughout the *. Eze 36:21
of the * shall know I am the Lord. Eze 36:23
from around the * to their own Eze 37:21
the nations of the * will hear what Eze 38:23
the * who would ask such a thing! Dan 2:10
* events are under his control. Dan 2:21
come to an end, another * power Dan 2:39
statue—will rise to rule the *. Dan 2:39
language in every nation of the *: Dan 4:1
be seen by everyone in all the *. Dan 4:10,11
and all the * was fed from it. Dan 4:12
is that all the * may understand Dan 4:17
kingdoms of the *, and gives them Dan 4:17
for all the * to see, with its Dan 4:20
the * trembled before him in fear. Dan 5:19
the nations of the *, so that all Dan 7:14
of the * forever and forever." Dan 7:18
told me, "is the fourth * power Dan 7:23
it will devour the whole *, Dan 7:23
the generations of the *! Joe 2:2
the armies of the * into the Joe 3:2
up and scatter her across the *. Amo 9:8
Let all the peoples of the * Mic 1:2
of the *, praised by all nations; Mic 4:1
people from all over the * will Mic 4:1
For in those days the whole * Mic 4:2
greatly honored all around the *. Mic 5:4
will refresh the * like a gentle Mic 5:7
you the laughingstock of the *; Mic 6:16
All the * will stand amazed at Mic 7:16
the * how really vile you are." Nah 3:6
on the * scene, the Chaldeans, Hab 1:6
march across the * and conquer it. Hab 1:6
in his own land throughout the *. Zep 2:11
"In all the * there is no city as Zep 2:15
represent the four * powers that Zec 1:19
see everywhere around the *." Zec 4:10
of * idolatry and wickedness. Zec 5:11f
People from around the * will Zec 8:20,21
be a heavy stone burdening the *. Zec 12:3
in all the * that refuses to come Zec 14:17
God is doing all around the *; Mal 1:5
All around the * they will offer Mal 1:11
of the * and all their glory. Mt 4:8
for the whole wide * belongs to Mt 5:5
flavor, what will happen to the *? Mt 5:13

(WORLD Con't)
shall come from all over the * Mt 8:11
me, yes, to witness to the *. Mt 10:18
Of all the *." Mt 12:21
in this * or in the world to come. Mt 12:31,32
in this world or in the * to come. Mt 12:31,32
The field is the *, and the seed Mt 13:38
the harvest is the end of the *, Mt 13:39
shall it be at the end of the *: Mt 13:40
way it will be at the end of the * Mt 13:49
the whole *—and lose eternal life? Mt 16:26
"Woe upon the * for all its Mt 18:7
"Then who in the * can be Mt 19:25
return, and the end of the *?" Mt 24:3
hated all over the * because you Mt 24:9
the whole *, so that all nations Mt 24:14
such as the * has never before seen Mt 24:21
And the nations of the * will see Mt 24:30
"The * will be at ease Mt 24:37,38
you from the founding of the *. Mt 25:34
the whole *, wherever the Good News Mt 26:13
even to the end of the *." Mt 28:20
to prepare the * for his coming. Mk 1:2
of this * and the delights of Mk 4:19
he gains the whole * and loses his Mk 8:36
"Then who in the * can be saved, Mk 10:26
earth, and in the * to come he Mk 10:30
from all over the *—from the Mk 13:27
throughout the *, this woman's deed Mk 14:9
Or, "over the entire *." Mk 15:33f
to go into all the * and preach the Mk 16:15
Savior you have given to the *. Lk 2:29,30,31
of the * in a moment of time; Lk 4:5
gaining the whole * when it means Lk 9:25
the Kingdom of God to all the *." Lk 9:60
founding of the *— from the murder Lk 11:50
the * to take their places there. Lk 13:29
* are more clever [in dishonesty! Lk 16:8
the * will be [as indifferent to Lk 17:26
"And the * will be as it was in Lk 17:28
eternal life in the * to come." Lk 18:30
to all the nations of the *; Lk 21:24
life, like all the rest of the *. Lk 21:34,35
Jesus told them, "In this * the Lk 22:25
Out in the * the master sits at Lk 22:27
Or, "the whole *." Lk 23:44f
on everyone coming into the *. Jn 1:9
But although he made the *, the Jn 1:10
the world, the * didn't recognize Jn 1:10
For God loved the * so much that Jn 3:16
* to condemn it, but to save it. Jn 3:17
came into the *, but they loved the Jn 3:19
comes to the * through the Jews." Jn 4:21-24
He is indeed the Savior of the *. Jn 4:42
and he gives life to the *." Jn 6:33
so great, prove it to the *!" Jn 7:4
for the * can't hate you; Jn 7:7
people, "I am the Light of the *. Jn 8:12
You are of this *; Jn 8:23
in the *, I give it my light." Jn 9:5
Then they asked him how in the * Jn 9:10
Since the * began there has Jn 9:32
have come into the * to give sight Jn 9:39
and sent into the * by the Father Jn 10:34,35,36
of God scattered around the *. Jn 11:52
Look—the whole * has gone after Jn 12:19
The time of judgment for the * Jn 12:31
Literally, "prince of this *." Jn 12:31f
the prince of this *, shall be Jn 12:31
shine in this dark *, so that all Jn 12:46
to save the * and not to judge it. Jn 12:47
the * that you are my disciples." Jn 13:35
all truth. The * at large cannot Jn 14:17
be gone from the *, but I will Jn 14:19
and not to the * at large?" Jn 14:22
like the peace the * gives. Jn 14:27
evil prince of this * approaches. Jn 14:30
of me so that the * will know that Jn 14:31
you get enough hate from the *! Jn 15:18
it hated you. The * would love you Jn 15:19
out of the *, and so it hates you. Jn 15:19
The people of the * will Jn 15:21
will convince the * of its sin, and Jn 16:8
Literally, "he will convict the * Jn 16:8f
of this * has already been judged. Jn 16:11
what I mean? The * will greatly Jn 16:20
Father into the * and will leave Jn 16:28
the * and return to the Father." Jn 16:28
up, for I have overcome the *." Jn 16:33
we shared before the * began. Jn 17:5
They were in the *, but then you Jn 17:6
"My plea is not for the * but Jn 17:9
Now I am leaving the *, and Jn 17:11
And the * hates them because they Jn 17:14
them out of the *, but to keep them Jn 17:15
They are not part of this * any Jn 17:16
As you sent me into the *, I am Jn 17:18
them into the *, and I consecrate Jn 17:18
the * will believe you sent me. Jn 17:21
one—so that the * will know you Jn 17:23
you loved me before the * began! Jn 17:24
"O righteous Father, the * Jn 17:25
But my Kingdom is not of the *." Jn 18:36
I came to bring truth to the *. Jn 18:37
* could hardly contain the books! Jn 21:25
bless the entire * through the Act 3:25
the rest of the * upside down, and Act 17:6
"He made the * and everything in Act 17:24
of the * from one man, Adam, Act 17:26
justly judging the * by the man he Act 17:31
around the *—will be forgotten!" Act 19:27
the entire * to riots and Act 24:5
You are to tell the * about this Act 26:16
us out around the * to tell all Rom 1:5
is becoming known around the *. Rom 1:8
be the just Judge of all the *. Rom 2:5
say that the * speaks evil of God Rom 2:24
Though everyone else in the * is Rom 3:4
one in all the * is innocent." Rom 3:10
in fact, all the * stands hushed Rom 3:19
throughout all the *, so everything Rom 5:12
the *, and death through sin." Rom 5:12f
—the things that overcame the * Rom 8:20,21
disappear, and the * around us will Rom 8:20,21
so that all the * would hear about Rom 9:17
Now if the whole * became rich Rom 11:12
a blessing the * will share in Rom 11:12
of the * to offer his salvation; Rom 11:15
customs of this *, but be a new and Rom 12:2
all around the * will have faith in Rom 16:25,26,27
saw to it that the * would never 1Co 1:21
the * calls foolish and silly. 1Co 1:21
to use ideas the * considers 1Co 1:27
by the * as wise and great. 1Co 1:27
despised by the *, counted as 1Co 1:28
nothing those the * considers 1Co 1:28
of this *, who are doomed to fall. 1Co 2:6
our benefit before the * began. 1Co 2:7
But the great men of the * have 1Co 2:8
the man of the *, who can't 1Co 2:15
For the wisdom of this * is 1Co 3:19
following the wise men of this *. 1Co 3:21
He has given you the whole * to 1Co 3:22
For you can't live in this * 1Co 5:10
going to judge and govern the *? 1Co 6:2
things the * offers should make 1Co 7:31
for the * in its present form 1Co 7:31
last days as the * nears its end. 1Co 10:11
condemned with the rest of the *. 1Co 11:32
languages in the *, and all are 1Co 14:10
Death came into the * because of 1Co 15:21
Or am I like a man of the * who 2Co 1:17
god of this evil *, has made him 2Co 4:4
by what the * thinks about them or 2Co 5:16
restoring the * to himself, no 2Co 5:19
The * ignores us, but we are 2Co 6:9
from this evil * in which we live. Gal 1:4
things of the * was killed long Gal 6:14
before he made the *, God chose us Eph 1:4
in this * or in the world to come. Eph 1:21
in this world or in the * to come. Eph 1:21
of the unseen *, those mighty Eph 6:12
of darkness who rule this *; Eph 6:12
of wicked spirits in the spirit *. Eph 6:12
of God in a dark * full of people Php 2:15
out all over the * and changing Col 1:6
the spirit * with its kings and Col 1:16
is now spreading all over the *. Col 1:23
to the whole * Christ's triumph at Col 2:15
"by the rudiments of the *." Col 2:20f
for this * as a dead person does. Col 3:3
life was still part of this *; Col 3:7
came into the * to save sinners—and 1Ti 1:15
the proper time God gave to the *. 1Ti 2:6
and alone in the *, if they are 1Ti 5:5
we came into the *, and we can't 1Ti 6:7
long before the * began—to show his 2Ti 1:9
sermon for all the * to hear. 2Ti 4:17
the * began—and he cannot lie. Tit 1:1
the * and everything there is. Heb 1:2
And the future * we are talking Heb 2:5
death for everyone in all the *. Heb 2:9
for them since the * began. Heb 4:3
powers of the * to come, and then Heb 6:5
nor part of this *, and once for Heb 9:11
and again, ever since the * began. Heb 9:26
he came into the *, "O God, the Heb 10:5
know that the * and the stars—in Heb 11:3
of the rest of the *—which refused Heb 11:7
back to the good things of this *. Heb 11:15
ill-treated—too good for this *. Heb 11:37,38
*, being willing to be despised Heb 13:13
For this * is not our home; Heb 13:14
to much in this * should be glad, Jas 1:9
by his contacts with the *. Jas 1:27
this *—makes you an enemy of God? Jas 4:4
of the unsaved *, you cannot also Jas 4:4
long before the * began, but only 1Pe 1:20
from the evil pleasures of this *; 1Pe 2:11
The end of the * is coming soon. 1Pe 4:7
all around the * are going through 1Pe 5:9
the whole * of ungodly men with the 2Pe 2:5
Or, "the glories of the unseen * 2Pe
wicked ways of the * by learning 2Pe
did destroy the * with a mighty 2Pe
CHRIST WAS ALIVE when the * began, 1Jn
loving this evil * and all that it 1Jn
They are from this evil * itself. 1Jn
And this * is fading away, and 1Jn
that the end of the * is near. 1Jn
dear friends, if the * hates you. 1Jn
Christ is already abroad in the *. 1Jn
any evil teacher in this wicked *. 1Jn
These men belong to this *, so, 1Jn
and the * pays attention to them. 1Jn
for if it is, the * won't listen 1Jn
into this wicked * to bring to us 1Jn
now tell all the * that God sent 1Jn
the rest of the * around us is 1Jn
the people of the * before him in Jud
love the evil things of the *; Jud
upon the * to test everyone alive. Rev
sent out into every part of the *. Rev
The kings of the earth, and * Rev
in view of a * population of Rev 9
kingdom of this * now belongs to Rev 1
the * from this day to eternity." Rev 11
hailstorm and the * was shaken by a Rev 1
the whole *—was thrown down onto Rev
But woe to you people of the *, Rev 12
All the * marveled at this Rev
language groups throughout the *. Rev
the founding of the * in the slain Rev
before the founding of the *." Rev 1
he required all the * to worship. Rev 13
the people of the * to make a great Rev 13
the nations of the * and made them Rev
power to destroy the * with fire, Rev 14
the rulers of the * to gather them Rev 16
the armies of the * near a place Rev 16
the * fell in heaps of rubble; Rev 16
upon the many waters of the *. Rev
The kings of the * have had Rev
Worship Everywhere around the *." Rev 1
of Life before the * began, will be Rev 1
throughout the * have grown rich Rev 1
And the * leaders, who took part Rev 1
"Where in all the * is there Rev 18
known around the * and she deceived Rev 18
the nations of the * and gather Rev 2
the rulers of the * will come and Rev 21

WORLD'S
For he is not impressed by the * Job 37
oceans and all the * clamor. Ps 6
The * poorest credit risk is the Pro 27
become the * greatest attraction, Is
"You are the * seasoning, to Mt 5
You are the * light—a city on a Mt 5
of God who takes away the * sin! Jn 1
The * sin is unbelief in me; Jn 1
debaters of this * great affairs? 1Co 1
Spirit (not the * spirit) to tell 1Co 2
as judged by this * standards, you 1Co 3
long ago, and the * interest in me Gal 6
from following the * ideas of how Col 2
and not only ours but all the *. 1Jn 2
Dear children, this * last hour 1Jn 2
their garments with the * filth; Rev

WORLDLY
concerning * Saul becoming 1Sa 10:
intellectuals and * wise and for Lk 10:
about * wealth, who will trust you Lk 16:
become tied up in * affairs, for 2Ti 2
for all these * things, these 1Jn 2:
concerned about * affairs and the 1Jn 4

WORLDS
words he gave before the * began? Is 40:

WORLDWIDE
them * powers of government. Dan 7:
And there will be a * Rev 11:

WORM
and the * my mother and my sister. Job 17:13,
who is but a * in his sight?" Job 25
But I am a *, not a man, scorned Ps 22
the * shall eat them like wool; Is 51
me, for their * shall never die; Is 66:
But God also prepared a *! Jon 4
The next morning the * ate Jon 4
hell, where the * never dies, and Mk 9:4

WORMED
teachers have * their way in among Jud 1

WORMS
for * will destroy the vines. Deu 28:3
"My skin is filled with * and Job 7
dust, both eaten by the same *. Job 21:2
him. * shall feed sweetly on him. Job 24:2
now maggots are your sheet, * Is 14:1
as * crawling from their holes. Mic 7:1

WORMWOOD
in the end she is bitter as *." Pro 5:4
Literally, "*." Rev 8:11

WORN
It shall always be * when he goes Ex 28:37,3

(WORN Con't)
for them, to be * beneath their Ex 28:42
These are to be * whenever Aaron Ex 28:43
This robe was * when Aaron Ex 39:25,26
garments to be * while ministering Ex 39:41
his sons, to be * when on duty. Ex 39:41
old, and your shoes haven't * out! Deu 29:5
* out from our long, hard trip." Jos 9:13
* by priests on their chests. Ju 8:27f
he had never * such things before. 1Sa 17:38,39
The belt was probably that * by a 2Sa 18:11f
king himself has *, and the king's Est 6:7,8
So every hope of man is * away. Job 14:18,19
I am * out with pain; Ps 6:6
* out, and strength to the weak. Is 40:29
garments * at times of mourning. Jon 3:4,5
evil judge can be * down like that, Lk 18:6
They will become * out like old Heb 1:11

WORN-OUT
to Joshua wearing * clothing, as Jos 9:3,4,5
They will grow old, like * Ps 102:26

WORRIED
by now my father will be more * 1Sa 9:5
your father is * about you and is 1Sa 10:2
was especially *, for he was the 1Sa 17:11f
David was seriously *, for in 1Sa 30:6
nor * by long months of drought. Jer 17:8
* about what will happen to us. Dan 3:16
Why are you so * about having no Mt 16:8
"And yet you think I'm * that we Mk 8:21
he was * and puzzled, for some Lk 9:7

WORRIES
The chief jailer had no more * Gen 39:23
and soothes their pains and *. Ps 41:3
for ransom never * the poor man! Pro 13:8
Will all your * add a single Mt 6:27
Our fears for today, our * about Rom 8:38
Let him have all your * and 1Pe 5:7

WORRY
He hadn't a * in the world with Gen 39:6
"Don't * about it," the Gen 43:23
Don't * about your property, for Gen 45:20
"Don't *," the old man said, Ju 19:20
Now don't * about a thing, my Ru 3:11
And don't * about those donkeys 1Sa 9:20
"Don't * about a thing," David 1Sa 17:32
It's not anything to * about!" 2Sa 13:20
"Don't * about that!" 2Sa 14:10
"Get up and eat and don't * 1Ki 21:7
"You need not * about your home Job 5:24
Don't fret and *—it only leads to Ps 37:8
rich must * and suffer insomnia. Ecc 5:12
his neighbor and says, "Don't *. Is 41:6
whom you came. You * at being so Is 51:1
rebels who despise me, "Don't *! Jer 23:17
"So my counsel is: Don't * about Mt 6:25
They don't * about what to Mt 6:26
"And why * about your clothes? Mt 6:28
They don't * about theirs. Mt 6:28
"So don't * at all about having Mt 6:31,32
And why * about a speck in the Mt 7:3
"When you are arrested, don't * Mt 10:19
So don't *! Mt 10:31
stand trial, don't * about what to Mk 13:11
don't * about getting them back. Lk 6:30
is choked out by * and riches and Lk 8:14
he said, "Don't * about whether Lk 12:22
And if * can't even do such Lk 12:26
And don't * about food—what to Lk 12:29
don't * at all that God will Lk 12:29
to * about their being Gentiles! Act 11:12
"Don't *," he said, "he's all Act 20:10,11,12
Paul and said, "Don't *, Paul; Act 23:11
strong, he didn't * about the fact Rom 4:19
ahead and sin and not * about it? Rom 6:15
But now you need no longer * Rom 7:6
Well, I don't * over what you 1Co 4:3
a Christian shouldn't * about it; 1Co 7:18
Don't let that * you—but of 1Co 7:21
do, I want you to be free from *. 1Co 7:32
Oh, don't *, I wouldn't dare say 2Co 10:12
have the constant * of how the 2Co 11:28
life don't need to * about whether Gal 5:6
Don't * about anything; Php 4:6
Don't * about making a good Col 3:12
His sacrifice frees us from the * Heb 9:14

WORRYING
Tell him to quit *," the Lord Is 7:4
type, and was * over the big dinner Lk 10:40
besides, what's the use of *? Lk 12:25
the use of * over bigger things? Lk 12:26
everyone else seems to be * Php 2:21
don't spend your time * about Col 3:2

WORSE
We'll deal with you far * than Gen 19:9
The famine became * and worse, Gen 47:13
The famine became worse and *, Gen 47:13
even * than their ancestors had. Ju 2:19
Peninnah made matters * by 1Sa 1:6
then you will be * off than you 2Sa 19:7
* than that of their ancestors. 1Ki 14:22
But Omri was * than any of the 1Ki 16:25
he was * than any other king of 1Ki 16:30
my problems go from bad to *. Ps 25:17
There is one thing * than a fool, Pro 26:12
* even than their fathers were. Jer 7:26
for right and go from bad to *; Jer 9:3
been * than your fathers were! Jer 16:12
prophets of Jerusalem are even *! Jer 23:14
You have been * than a Eze 16:31
And to make matters *, he Dan 2:1
For it was getting * and worse. Jon 1:11
For it was getting worse and *. Jon 1:11
tear away and make the hole *. Mt 9:16
And so he is * off than before." Mt 12:43,44,45
If that happens we'll be * off Mt 27:64
and leaves the hole * than before. Mk 2:21
was no better but, in fact, was *. Mk 5:26
treatment, only *, for his head was Mk 12:4
look * with a new patch on it! Lk 5:36
* off than he was before." Lk 11:26
"Do you think they were * Lk 13:2
or something even * may happen to Jn 5:14
* we are, the better God likes it! Rom 3:8
We are no * off if we don't eat 1Co 8:8
have never heard a * preacher!" 2Co 10:10
Such a person is * than the 1Ti 5:8
will become * and worse, deceiving 2Ti 3:13
become worse and *, deceiving many, 2Ti 3:13
he is * off than he was before. 2Pe 2:20

WORSHIP
himself down in * before the Lord, Gen 17:17
and *, and then come right back." Gen 22:5
pillar shall become a place for *; Gen 28:22
build an altar to * the God who Gen 35:1
* God here upon this mountain!" Ex 3:12
him go away and * me, but you have Ex 4:23
a religious feast, to * me there.' Ex 5:1
go to * him in the wilderness. Ex 7:16
says, "Let my people go and * me. Ex 8:1
says, "Let my people go and * me. Ex 8:20
says, "Let my people go to * me. Ex 9:13
Let my people go so they can * Ex 10:3
and said, "Go and * Jehovah—but Ex 10:24
"You may * no other god than me. Ex 20:3
to an image or * it in any way; Ex 20:5
Remember, you must not make or * Ex 20:23
"You must not * the gods of Ex 23:24
All of you except Moses are to * Ex 24:1
the obelisks they *, and cut down Ex 34:13
For you must * no other gods, Ex 34:14
* his idol, you are apt to do it. Ex 34:15
daughters, who * other gods, as Ex 34:16
holy day to be used to * Jehovah; Ex 35:2
Do not make or * idols, for I am Lev 19:3,4
all Israel will assemble and * me. Lev 23:1
for assembling to *, and for Lev 23:3
the people for *, and all ordinary Lev 23:7
the people to meet together for *; Lev 23:23,24
you must never * carved images, Lev 26:1
hills where you * your idols, and I Lev 26:30
your places of *, and will not Lev 26:31
in the * of Baal, the god of Moab; Num 25:3
They are causing you to * Baal, Num 25:18
of Israel to * idols on Mount Peor, Num 31:16
hills where they * their idols. Num 33:52
sky to * the sun, moon, or stars. Deu 4:19
There, far away, you will * Deu 4:28
" 'Never * any god but me. Deu 5:7
don't * images, whether of birds, Deu 5:8
to any images nor * them in any Deu 5:9,10
"You must not * the gods of the Deu 6:14
beginning to * their gods. Deu 7:4
Have no pity, and do not * their Deu 7:16
into your home and * it, for then Deu 7:26
Lord your God and * other gods Deu 8:19
love him, and to * him with all Deu 10:12,13
Lord your God and * him and cling Deu 10:20
souls, and will * him, then he Deu 11:13
not turn from God to * other gods. Deu 11:16
* the gods of these other nations. Deu 11:28
do these nations * their gods?' Deu 12:30
and then go and * as they do! Deu 12:30
'Come, let us * the gods of the Deu 13:2
You must never * any God but Deu 13:4
to you to come and * these foreign Deu 13:6,7
that they * foreign gods, first Deu 13:12,13,14
heathen do when they * their idols Deu 14:1
you into idol * and into Deu 20:18
the Lord your God, and * him. Deu 26:10
and you must never * other gods. Deu 28:14
and while in exile you shall * Deu 28:36
There you will * heathen gods Deu 28:64
God and desires to * these gods of Deu 29:18
are drawn away to * other gods— Deu 30:17
prosperous, and * other gods and Deu 31:20
all of you will * him forever." Jos 4:24
have to * the Lord God of Israel? Jos 22:24,25
that we, too, may * the Lord with Jos 22:26,27
much less swear by them or * them. Jos 23:7
For if you * other gods he will Jos 23:15,16
and in Egypt. * the Lord alone. Jos 24:14
forsake the Lord and * other gods! Jos 24:16
"You can't * the Lord God, for he Jos 24:19
If you forsake him and * other Jos 24:20
will * and obey the Lord alone." Jos 24:24
and the next generation did not * Ju 2:10
to the ground in humble *. Ju 2:19
once again to * other gods, and Ju 6:1
that you must not * the gods of the Ju 6:10
* the idols Baal and Baal-berith. Ju 8:33
to abandon me and to * other gods. Ju 10:13
at Shiloh to * the Lord of the 1Sa 1:3
to * the Lord once more. 1Sa 1:19,20
way when they came to Shiloh to *. 1Sa 2:13,14
to * God at the altar at Bethel; 1Sa 10:3
And they pleaded, 'We will * you 1Sa 12:10
"Now if you will fear and * the 1Sa 12:14
sure now that you * the Lord with 1Sa 12:20
"Trust the Lord and sincerely * 1Sa 12:24
and go with me to * the Lord." 1Sa 15:25
with me to * the Lord your God." 1Sa 15:30
sent me away to * heathen gods. 1Sa 26:19
distant lands to * you (for they 1Ki 8:41,42
away from me and * other gods and 1Ki 9:6
They encouraged him to * their 1Ki 11:4
trouble to go to Jerusalem to *; 1Ki 12:28
God whom I * and serve—there won't 1Ki 17:1
of Israel into the * of idols. 2Ki 3:3
could * Jehovah on Israel's soil. 2Ki 5:17f
the god Rimmon to * there and leans 2Ki 5:18
only those who * Baal are here; 2Ki 10:23
for the * of Baal, and burned it. 2Ki 10:26
he continued to * Jeroboam's gold 2Ki 10:31
and they continued to * the 2Ki 13:6
to * idols and led them into sin. 2Ki 13:11
colonists did not * the Lord when 2Ki 17:25
from Babylon how to * the Lord. 2Ki 17:27,28
they were never to * or make 2Ki 17:35,36
They were to * only the Lord who 2Ki 17:35,36
God's laws and never * other gods. 2Ki 17:37
never * other gods. 2Ki 17:38
You must * only the Lord; 2Ki 17:39
people continued to * other gods. 2Ki 17:40
to * it by burning incense to it; 2Ki 18:4
For you require everyone to * at 2Ki 18:22
Temple when the people come to *. 2Ki 22:3,4
used in the * of Baal, Asherah, and 2Ki 23:4
every kind of idol *, both in 2Ki 23:24
used in the sacrifices and *; 1Ch 9:28
* the Lord when clothed with 1Ch 16:29
* into the Temple of the Lord!" 1Ch 22:19
of your fathers. * and serve him 1Ch 28:9
to be used for * and sacrifice. 1Ch 28:13
But it will be a place to * 2Ch 2:6
distant lands to * your great name, 2Ch 6:32
given you, and * idols, then I 2Ch 7:19
the people to * idols instead of 2Ch 11:15
they could freely * the Lord God of 2Ch 11:16
into a contract to * only the Lord 2Ch 15:12
early years, and did not * idols. 2Ch 17:3
to * the God of their ancestors. 2Ch 19:4
he compelled his people to * them. 2Ch 21:11
and Judah * idols just as in the 2Ch 21:13
dedicated to the * of God had been 2Ch 24:7,8
and to * shame-idols instead! 2Ch 24:17,18
that no one could * there, and made 2Ch 28:24
bowed low before the Lord in *. 2Ch 29:29
forever, and * the Lord your God so 2Ch 30:8
campaign against idol * was begun. 2Ch 31:1
and other heathen centers of *. 2Ch 31:1
offerings, and to * and give thanks 2Ch 31:2
his people to * the idols of the 2Ch 33:2
of Judah * the Lord God of Israel. 2Ch 33:16
of them to * Jehovah their God. 2Ch 34:33
and all the angels of heaven * Neh 9:6
They did not * you despite the Neh 9:35
be permitted to * at the Temple. Neh 13:1
to conduct the * services had Neh 13:10
I will * you with deepest awe. Ps 5:7
and bless all who truly * God; Ps 7:9
Or, "The rules governing the * of Ps 19:9f
of every nation shall * him. Ps 22:27
mortal—born to die—shall * him. Ps 22:29
the Lord and * the God of Jacob. Ps 24:6
keeps his promises. I * only you; Ps 31:5,6
how you hate all those who * Ps 31:5,6
All the earth shall * you and Ps 66:4
from remotest lands will * him. Ps 67:6,7
But those refusing to * God will Ps 73:27
You must never * any other god, Ps 81:9
O Lord, for I * only you. Ps 86:4
* only him among the gods! Ps 96:4
Bring your offering and come to * Ps 96:8
* the Lord with the beauty of Ps 96:9
Let those who * idols be Ps 97:7
Exalt the Lord our God, and * at Ps 99:9
the earth came to * him. Ps 102:21,22
And those who make and * them Ps 115:8
I will * you and offer you a Ps 116:17
come to * as the law requires, to Ps 122:4
That is where we will go to * Ps 132:7
we will * at his footstool." Ps 132:7f

(WORSHIP Con't)
The heathen * idols of gold and Ps 135:15
I face your Temple as I *, Ps 138:2
and ceremonies of * to Israel— Ps 147:19
will flow there to * the Lord. Is 2:2
They are man-made, and yet you * Is 2:8
their Lord and will not * him; Is 3:8
they * what their hands have made! Is 17:8
and they shall * the same God. Is 19:23
but now we * you alone. Is 26:13
* the Lord in his holy mountain. Is 27:13
and since their * amounts to mere Is 29:13
everyone in Judah * only at the Is 36:7
No wonder those who * them are so Is 44:9
All that * these will stand Is 44:11
himself a god—a god for men to *! Is 44:15
All who * idols shall be Is 45:16
Then they fall down and * it! Is 46:6
and liars! You * your idols with Is 57:5
the valleys. You * them and they, Is 57:6
you * idols there, deserting me. Is 57:7,8
up and * someone other than me. Is 57:7,8
How anxious they are to * Is 58:2
and caves to * evil spirits, and Is 65:4
and his Temple and * gods of Is 65:11
Those who * idols that are Is 66:17
All mankind shall come to * me Is 66:23
them into fools who * idols? Jer 2:4,5
has gone to other gods to * them. Jer 3:8
* idols made of wood and stone. Jer 3:9
* gods that are not gods at all. Jer 5:7
Listen to it, all of you who * Jer 7:2
adultery, lie, and * Baal and all Jer 7:9
continued to * her (chapter 44). Jer 7:18f
Are they ashamed because they * Jer 8:12
The wisest of men who * idols are Jer 10:8
Say this to those who * other Jer 10:11
my people to *), then they shall be Jer 12:16
* in the fields and on the hills. Jer 13:27
can go ahead and * your idols all Jer 16:13
to * from many parts of Judah. Jer 26:2
heart and mind to * me forever, for Jer 32:39
their hearts to * me, and they Jer 32:40
have descendants who will * me." Jer 35:18,19
to * at the Temple of the Lord. Jer 41:5
Why then have you, who * Milcom, Jer 49:1
shall no longer come and * him; Jer 51:44
the false "*" of his people; Lam 2:7
every trace of all this idol *. Eze 11:18
"Son of dust, these men * idols Eze 14:3
they * idols," says the Lord God. Eze 15:8
And used my oil and incense to * Eze 16:18
of Israel and * them, and does not Eze 18:6
the idols and * them, and does not Eze 18:15
the Lord, all Israel shall * me. Eze 20:40
actually came into my Temple to *! Eze 23:39
blood; you * idols, and murder. Eze 33:25
to me their * was as foul as Eze 36:17
be washed away, your idol * gone. Eze 36:25
the adulterous * of other gods or Eze 43:7
the people to * other gods, causing Eze 44:12
for public *—sin offerings, burnt Eze 45:17
He shall * inside the passageway Eze 46:2
The people shall * the Lord in Eze 46:3
on the ground to * King Dan 3:5
some of the Jews of refusing to *! Dan 3:8
* the golden statue when the band Dan 3:10
* the golden statue you set up." Dan 3:12
to * the golden statue I set up? Dan 3:14
* the statue, all will be well. Dan 3:15
serve your gods or * the golden Dan 3:18
or * any god except their own. Dan 3:28
you * continually, deliver you." Dan 6:16
your God, whom you * continually, Dan 6:20
the rights of * are restored. Dan 8:26
Instead of these he will * the Dan 11:38
* me at Gilgal and at Bethel. Hos 4:15
Their * is mere pretense. Hos 4:15
Instead, they * heathen gods, Hos 7:14
you * was made by human hands! Hos 8:6
altars, but they are not to * me! Hos 8:11
who * idols. Jacob fled to Syria Hos 12:11
And those who * the idols of Amo 8:14
I * Jehovah, the God of heaven, Jon 1:9,10
(Those who * false gods have Jon 2:8
"I will never * anyone but you! Jon 2:9
Israel in her sin of idol *. Mic 1:13
all the nations around us * idols! Mic 4:5
Never again will you * what you Mic 5:13
thanksgiving, and * only the Lord, Nah 1:15
them all to * her false gods, Nah 3:4
Then they will * their nets and Hab 1:16
your report, and I * you in awe for Hab 3:2
every remnant of those who * Baal; Zep 1:4
They 'follow the Lord,' but * Zep 1:5
and everyone shall * him, each in Zep 2:11
so that all can * the Lord Zep 3:9
they began to * him in earnest. Hag 1:12
Everyone left will * God and be Zec 9:7
vestige of idol * throughout the Zec 13:2
each year to * the King, the Lord Zec 14:16
to Jerusalem to * the King, the Zec 14:17
all who come to * may use any of Zec 14:21
heathen women who * idols. Mal 2:11
is foolish to * God and obey him. Mal 3:14,15
lands, and have come to * him." Mt 2:2
so that I can go and * him too!" Mt 2:8
you will only kneel and * me." Mt 4:9
"The Scriptures say, '* only the Mt 4:10
*, and his disciples were hungry; Mt 12:1
Their * is worthless, for they Mt 15:9
*—the synagogue—where he preached. Mk 1:21
Their * is a farce, for they Mk 7:6,7
down on their knees to "*" him. Mk 15:19
get down on your knees and * me." Lk 4:6,7
Jesus replied, "We must * God, Lk 4:8
the only place of *, while we Jn 4:20
* the Father here or in Jerusalem. Jn 4:21-24
For it's not where we * that Jn 4:21-24
counts, but how we * —is our Jn 4:21-24
—is our * spiritual and real? Jn 4:21-24
have his help to * as we should. Jn 4:21-24
The Father wants this kind of * Jn 4:21-24
those who * him and do his will. Jn 9:31
land of Israel and * me here.' Act 7:7
He had gone to Jerusalem to * at Act 8:27
fell to the floor before him in *. Act 10:25
he has those who * him and do good Act 10:35
the people's * instead of giving Act 12:23
to turn from the * of these foolish Act 14:15
to put away idols and * only him. Act 17:30
men to * God in ways that are Act 18:13
in Jerusalem to * at the Temple, Act 24:11
admit it or * him or even thank him Rom 1:21
He let you * him, and gave you Rom 9:4
as special days to * God, but Rom 14:5
those who meet to * in their home. Rom 16:5
did, nor * idols as they did. 1Co 10:7
dance" in * of the golden calf. 1Co 10:7
But in public * I would much 1Co 14:19
on his knees and * God, declaring 1Co 14:25
to * angels, as they say you must. Col 2:18
don't * the good things of life, Col 3:5
other object of adoration and *. 2Th 2:4
all the angels of God * him." Heb 1:5,6
the true place of * built by the Heb 8:2
were rules for * and there was a Heb 9:1
Inside this place of * there were Heb 9:1
instruments were used for *. Heb 9:21
earthly place of * that he did Heb 9:24
bouts, and the * of idols, and 1Pe 4:3
is, at the center of satanic *; Rev 2:13
plagues still refused to * God! Rev 9:20
altar, and them that * therein." Rev 11:1f
themselves down in *, saying, "We Rev 11:16
he required all the world to *. Rev 13:12
anyone refusing to * it must die! Rev 13:15
will sit as Judge. * him who made Rev 14:7
And * before you, Rev 15:3,4
* Everywhere around the World." Rev 17:5
prophets for the * of false gods. Rev 19:2f
Then I fell down at his feet to * Rev 19:10
and his servants will * him. Rev 22:3
* the angel who showed them to me; Rev 22:8
in this Book. * God alone." Rev 22:9

WORSHIPED
And there he again * the Lord. Gen 13:3,4
Then I bowed my head and * and Gen 24:48
built an altar and * Jehovah; Gen 26:25
and bowed their heads and *. Ex 4:31
people bowed their heads and *. Ex 12:27
a calf, and * it, and sacrificed to Ex 32:8
because they had * Aaron's calf. Ex 32:35
Then all the people * from their Ex 33:10
fell down before the Lord and *. Ex 34:8
to execute all who had * Baal. Num 25:5
For they * other gods, violating Deu 29:26
To new gods never before * Deu 32:17
before him and * him and said, Jos 5:14
and they * other gods. Jos 24:2
your ancestors * when they lived Jos 24:14
the God loved and * by their Ju 2:12-14
and * Baal and the Asheroth idols. Ju 3:7
Lord again, and * the heathen gods Ju 10:6
they no longer * Jehovah at all. Ju 10:6
have * idols," they confessed. Ju 10:10
foreign gods and * only the Lord; Ju 10:16
So Micah's idols were * by the Ju 18:31
and Ashtaroth and * only the Lord. 1Sa 7:4
the Tabernacle and * the Lord. 2Sa 12:20
where people * God, David found 2Sa 15:32
Egypt; they * other gods instead. 1Ki 9:9
from nations where idols were * 1Ki 11:1
Solomon * Ashtoreth, the goddess 1Ki 11:5
great sin, for the people * them. 1Ki 12:30
like his father, he * many idols 1Ki 15:26
he had * idols and had led the 1Ki 16:19
before him; he * idols as Jeroboam 1Ki 16:26
the Lord, and have * Baal instead. 1Ki 18:18
guilty because he * idols just as 1Ki 21:26
"Ahab hardly * Baal at all in 2Ki 10:17
Israel summoning those who * Baal; 2Ki 10:20,21
an evil king. He * idols, as King 2Ki 15:1
because the people * other gods, 2Ki 17:
Yes, they * idols, despite the 2Ki 17:1
In their foolishness they * 2Ki 17:1
shameful idols and * Baal and the 2Ki 17:1
us because we have not * him." 2Ki 17:2
But these foreigners also * their 2Ki 17:2
Those from Babylon * idols of 2Ki 17:3
those from Cuth * their god 2Ki 17:30
and the men of Hamath * Ashima. 2Ki 17:30
and Tartak were * by the Avvites, 2Ki 17:31
They also * the Lord, and they 2Ki 17:32
These colonists from Babylon * 2Ki 17:41
yes—but they also * their idols. 2Ki 17:41
had done: he * the same idols, and 2Ki 21:21
me aside and have * other gods and 2Ki 22:17
instead they * the idols of the 1Ch 5:25
because the people * idols. 1Ch 9:1
and * and thanked the Lord. 2Ch 7:3
and they * other gods instead. 2Ch 7:22
the people haven't * the true God, 2Ch 15:3
"Why have you * gods who couldn't 2Ch 25:15
because you have * these idols, and 2Ch 25:16
in Israel and * the idols of Baal. 2Ch 28:2
ceremony everyone * the Lord as the 2Ch 29:28
did, and bowed their heads and *. 2Ch 29:30
me and have * heathen gods, and I 2Ch 34:25
the High Priests, * the heathen 2Ch 36:14
all those who * him, and that Ez 8:22
then they bowed and * the Lord Neh 8:6
And everyone * the Lord their Neh 9:3
and I have * them by kissing my Job 31:27
assembly places where we * you. Ps 74:8
O Lord our God, once we * other Is 26:13
They will never be * again. Is 27:9
is *, a city quiet and unmoved. Is 33:20
hordes you've * all these years. Is 47:12
and their prophets * Baal and Jer 2:8
so, that you haven't * idols? Jer 2:23
so Israel has * other gods on every Jer 3:6
such a God to be feared and *? Jer 5:22
people ashamed when they * idols? Jer 6:15
—whom they have loved and *. Jer 8:2
they pleased and * the idols of Jer 9:14
been unfaithful and * other gods. Jer 11:15
They * other gods and served them; Jer 16:11
for they have * worthless idols! Jer 16:19
of Judah have * before—and they Jer 19:4
with them, for they * idols." Jer 22:9
wickedness and * the Lord and Jer 26:19
you have made and * here in Egypt, Jer 44:8
idols * by the people of Israel. Eze 8:10
statues of men and * them, which is Eze 16:17
satisfied, so you * the gods of Eze 16:29
She insolently * many idols as I Eze 16:50
You have * idols far more than Eze 16:51
they have * idols and murdered my Eze 23:37
a wall between, and * their idols. Eze 43:8
before Daniel and * him, and Dan 2:46
—fell to the ground and * the Dan 3:7
and I praised and * the Most High Dan 4:34
to be *, there will be 1,290 days. Dan 12:11
but he * Baal and sealed his Hos 13:1
those who formerly * the Lord, but Zep 1:6
one Lord—his name alone will be *. Zec 14:9
local synagogue came and * him. Mt 9:18
But she came and * him and pled Mt 15:25
There they met him and * him—but Mt 28:17
And they * him, and returned to Lk 24:52
where our ancestors *?" Jn 4:20
And he * Jesus. Jn 9:38
They * together regularly at the Act 2:46
godly Gentiles who * at the Act 13:43
who * God and lived next door to Act 18:7
goddess * not only throughout this Act 19:27
before him and * him, the Eternal Rev 4:10
Elders fell down and * him. Rev 5:14
They * the Dragon for giving him Rev 13:4
and they * the strange Creature. Rev 13:4
Lamb's Book of Life—* the evil Rev 13:8
for they have * the Creature and Rev 14:11
fell down and * God, who was Rev 19:4
mark, and who * his statue. Rev 19:20
and who had not * the Creature or Rev 20:4
the Lamb are * in it everywhere. Rev 21:22

WORSHIPER
sure that every * wears one of the 2Ki 10:22
She was already a * of God and, Act 16:14
is really an idol *—he loves and Eph 5:5

WORSHIPERS
of Dagon nor his * will walk on the 1Sa 5:5
Baal, and call together all his *. 2Ki 10:18,19
them comes, for we * of Baal are 2Ki 10:18,19
Any of Baal's * who don't come 2Ki 10:18,19
Glory in the Lord; O * of God, Ps 105:3
Then our fathers joined the * of Ps 106:28
can they save their * from Cyrus? Is 46:1
the bones of their * will lie Eze 6:4-7
gifts of *, will all be burned. Mic 1:7
cheats and thieves and idol *. 1Co 5:10
who are idol *, adulterers or 1Co 6:9,10

WORSHIPERS Con't)
been enough; the * would have been Heb 10:2
and to count the number of *. Rev 11:1
demons, and idol * and all Rev 21:8

WORSHIPING
moment with head bowed, * Jehovah. Gen 24:26
with their sin of * false gods, and Ex 23:33
play the harlot * their gods." Ex 34:15f
against me by * their wives' gods. Ex 34:16
also bowing down and * the idols. Num 25:2
destroyed many people for * idols. Deu 4:3
their example in * their gods. Deu 12:30
with God by * other gods, the sun, Deu 17:2,3
people will begin * foreign gods in Deu 31:16
of their sins in * other gods. Deu 31:18
may make our children stop * him. Jos 22:24,25
including the * of heathen gods. Ju 2:11
Instead, they were * and bowing Ju 2:12-14
* Baal and the Ashtaroth idols. Ju 2:12-14
Jehovah by * other gods instead. Ju 2:17
And soon Israel was * their gods. Ju 3:6
do was just stand there * God! Ju 7:15
But all Israel soon began * it, Ju 8:27
ONCE AGAIN ISRAEL sinned by * Ju 13:1
* the Baal and Ashtaroth idols. 1Sa 12:10
stubbornness is as bad as * idols. 1Sa 15:23
get them started * their gods. 1Ki 11:2
specifically against * other gods. 1Ki 11:9,10
angered the Lord by * idol-gods. 1Ki 14:15
of Israel into the sin of * idols. 1Ki 15:34
for they had led Israel into * 1Ki 16:13
Sidonians, and then began * Baal. 1Ki 16:31
Israel into the sin of * idols. 1Ki 22:52,53
Israel into the sin of * idols. 2Ki 14:24
Israel in the sin of * idols. 2Ki 15:9
of Israel into the sin of * idols. 2Ki 15:28
instead of truly * the Lord or 2Ki 17:34
and as he was * in the temple of 2Ki 19:37
did the same, * the Lord. 2Ch 20:18
people of Jerusalem in * idols; 2Ch 21:11
him for * the gods of Edom. 2Ch 25:20
of the Lord, for * the sun, moon 2Ch 33:4,5
the Israelis in * the Lord God. Ez 6:21,22
assisted them in * God and Neh 12:45
into shame by * these silly idols, Ps 4:2
If we had turned away from * our Ps 44:20
* idols, would God not know it? Ps 44:20
And one day while he was * in Is 37:38
me to my face by * idols in many Is 65:3
me and for * other gods—yes, idols Jer 1:16
* these other gods? Jer 3:2
him by * idols under every tree; Jer 3:13
We are weary of * idols on the Jer 3:23
And stop * idols as you do now to Jer 7:6
to listen to me and * idols. Jer 11:10
not forget to sin, * idols beneath Jer 17:2,3
Don't anger me by * idols; Jer 25:6
by * their abominable idols there. Jer 32:34
ways and to stop * other gods and Jer 35:15
against them for * other Jer 44:2,3
and stopped * her we have been in Jer 44:18
that we were * the 'Queen of Jer 44:19
a stop to Moab's * false gods and Jer 48:35
anger on you for your * of idols. Eze 7:3
(son of Shaphan) * the pictures. Eze 8:11
the Lord, facing east, * the sun! Eze 8:16
and stop * them in your hearts. Eze 14:6,7
them your allies and * their gods Eze 16:28
your lovers—your * of idols—and the Eze 16:36
fathers did, and keep on * idols? Eze 20:30
If you insist on * your idols, go Eze 20:39
* their idols, defiling herself. Eze 23:7
upon yourself by * the gods of Eze 23:30
your harlotry, your * of idols. Eze 23:49
filthy lewdness, of * your idols. Eze 24:13
and with the * of idols, so I Eze 36:18
other gods or by * the totem poles Eze 43:7
and * idols inside the Temple. Dan 11:30,31
against me by * other gods." Hos 1:2
that she used in * Baal, her god! Hos 1:8
* foreign gods has sapped their Hos 7:9
from my help by * the idols that Hos 8:4
"What profit was there in * all Hab 2:18
themselves down before him, *. Mt 2:11
He kneels before him, *. Mt 8:2
him, holding his feet and * him. Mt 28:9
night and day, * God by praying and Lk 2:36,37
little about him, * blindly, while Jn 4:21-24
One day as these men were * and Act 13:2
You have been * him without Act 17:23
And then, instead of * the Rom 1:23
If you have special days for * Rom 14:6
on his head [when *, for his hat is 1Co 11:7
it is * him with our spirits. Php 3:3
and prefer good times to * God. 2Ti 3:4
Day and I was *, when suddenly I Rev 1:10
down before the throne and * God. Rev 7:11
* the Creature from the sea Rev 14:9
the Creature and was * his statue. Rev 16:2

WORSHIPS
who makes and * an idol, even in Deu 27:15
forsaken me and * Ashtoreth, the 1Ki 11:33
don't let anyone in who * the 2Ki 10:23
No wonder he '*' you! Job 1:10
He falls down before it and * it Is 44:17
its own evil desires and * idols; Jer 13:10
in Israel who * idols and then Eze 14:4
laws of God, but * idols on the Eze 18:11
loves idols and * them, and loans Eze 18:12
idols that he *—all will vanish. Zep 1:3
is a swindler, or * idols, or is a 1Co 5:11
loves and * the good things of this Eph 5:5

WORST
it was the * locust plague in all Ex 10:14
"Surely the * is over and I have 1Sa 15:32
were some of the * offenders. Ez 9:2
* enemies to be at peace with him. Pro 16:7
And the * sort of anarchy will Is 3:5
Do your *, O Syria and Israel, Is 8:9,10
the smallest and * contingent of my Is 36:8,9
Are they not the * of rebels, Jer 6:28
to Jerusalem the * of the nations Eze 7:24
a man's * enemies will be right in Mt 10:36
with the * sort of sinners!' Mt 11:19
Were they the * sinners in Lk 13:4
is with even the * sinners, so that 1Ti 1:16
that is the * sort of lie. Jas 3:14

WORTH
"Well, the land is * 400 pieces Gen 23:14,15
without defect, * whatever fine Lev 5:15
be * whatever value you demand. Lev 6:6
of its *, plus twenty percent; Lev 27:27
and some silver * $200, and a bar Jos 7:21
$200, and a bar of gold * $500. Jos 7:21
You are * ten thousand of us, and 2Sa 18:3
Each year Solomon received gold * 1Ki 10:14
of armor (gold * $6,000 went into 1Ki 10:16,17
($1,800 * of gold in each). 1Ki 10:16,17
and all the other houses of any *. 2Ki 25:9
the weakest was * a hundred 1Ch 12:14
and the greatest was * a thousand! 1Ch 12:14
$3,000,000,000 * of gold bullion, 1Ch 22:14
bullion, $2,000,000 * of silver, 1Ch 22:14
of $85,000,000 * of gold from Ophir 1Ch 29:4,5
and $20,000,000 * of purest silver 1Ch 29:4,5
back $13,000,000 * of gold to him! 2Ch 8:17,18
a billion dollars * of gold each 2Ch 9:13,14
shields, each * $280,000, and 300 2Ch 9:15
smaller shields, each * $140,000. 2Ch 9:16
and twenty gold bowls * a total Ez 8:26,27
"Is mere man of any * to God? Job 22:2
When a good man speaks, he is * Pro 10:20
she is * more than precious gems! Pro 31:10
A bird in the hand is * two in Ecc 6:9
What are the Pharaoh's promises *? Is 36:5
give me my pay, whatever I am *; Zec 11:12
For is anything * more than his Mk 8:37
There is really only one thing * Lk 10:42
"That perfume was * a fortune. Jn 12:5
But life is * nothing unless I Act 20:24
Being a Jew is * something if you Rom 2:25
and of little * in order to shame 1Co 1:27
be * nothing at all without love. 1Co 13:2
Moses' face is * nothing at all in 2Co 3:10
That experience is something * 2Co 12:5
I am really * nothing at all. 2Co 12:11
hard work for you was * nothing. Gal 4:11
else, counting it * less than Php 3:8
and his religion isn't * much. Jas 1:26

WORTHLESS
Israel that some * rabble have led Deu 13:12,13,14
he is a * drunkard.' Deu 21:20
used to hire some * loafers who Ju 9:4
They destroyed only what was * or 1Sa 15:9
is as * as a dead dog or a flea? 1Sa 24:14
Then a whole gang of * rebels 2Ch 13:7
Coral or crystal is * in trying Job 28:18
For they gather with the * Ps 35:16
brag about their * gods—for every Ps 97:7
I am * and despised, but I don't Ps 119:141
Let me describe for you a * and a Pro 6:12,13
Literally, "A * man devises Pro 16:27f
A * witness cares nothing for Pro 19:28
"Utterly *!" Pro 20:14
now mixed with * alloy! Is 1:22
For Egypt's promises are *! Is 30:7
See, they are all foolish, * Is 41:29
You are *, with nothing good in Is 48:10
All are *, silly; Jer 10:15
for they have worshiped * idols! Jer 16:19
Toss it out like * rubbish, for Eze 7:19
customs and laws which were *. Eze 20:25
of Israel are the * slag left when Eze 22:18,19,20
Because you are * dross, I will Eze 22:18,19,20
His promises will be *. Dan 11:23
return she gets their * promises. Hos 12:1
the part of a *, wicked shepherd. Zec 11:15
Woe to this * shepherd who Zec 11:17
out and trampled underfoot as *. Mt 5:13
of every kind, valuable and *. Mt 13:47,48
Their worship is *, for they Mt 15:9
"Good salt is * if it loses its Mk 9:50
It is * and must be thrown out. Lk 14:35
with him, I am utterly *.' Act 13:25
and incited some * fellows from the Act 17:5
in God is empty, *, hopeless; 1Co 15:14
Take no part in the * pleasures Eph 5:11
Yes, everything else is * when Php 3:8
and disobedient, * so far as doing Tit 1:16

WORTHLESSNESS
Then when you realize your * Jas 4:10

WORTHWHILE
will finally have nothing * left. Pro 11:29
do good shall be given a * reward. Pro 28:10
In my opinion, nothing is *; Ecc 1:2
was nothing really * anywhere. Ecc 2:11
that my work among you was so *. Php 2:16
once thought very *—now I've thrown Php 3:7
brothers, how * that visit was. 1Th 2:1
for this kind of thing isn't *; Tit 3:9

WORTHY
me good— I am not * of the least Gen 32:10
committed a crime * of death, and Deu 21:22
every man * of death shall be Deu 24:16
Who is * to be praised; 2Sa 22:4
to be a strong and * successor. 1Ki 2:2
But who can ever build him a * 2Ch 2:6
another queen more * than she. Est 1:19
he does is * of our trust. Ps 33:4
But true praise is a * sacrifice; Ps 50:23
For he alone is *. Ps 148:13
A * wife is her husband's joy and Pro 12:4
land and find it * of destruction. Is 34:11
nobles and find them * of death. Is 34:11
isn't * to be counted as a nation. Jer 33:24
turned from sin by doing * deeds. Mt 3:8
I am not * to carry his shoes! Mt 3:11
I am not * to have you in my home; Mt 8:8,9
me, you are not * of being mine; Mt 10:37
me, you are not * of being mine. Mt 10:37
me, you are not * of being mine. Mt 10:38
I invited aren't * of the honor. Mt 22:8
I am not even * to be his slave. Mk 1:7
shoes I am not * to unloose." Mk 1:7f
in fact, I am not even * of being Lk 3:16
home, for I am not * of any such Lk 7:6,7,8
If it is * of the blessing, the Lk 10:6
for the workman is * of his wages! Lk 10:7
longer * of being called your son. Lk 15:19
not * of being called your son—' Lk 15:21
consider yourselves * of praise. Lk 17:10
who are counted * of being raised Lk 20:34,35
* to suffer dishonor for his name. Act 5:41
* of imprisonment or death. Act 23:29
If I have done something * of Act 25:10,11
he has done nothing * of death. Act 25:25
* of death or imprisonment." Act 26:31
For I am the least * of all the 1Co 15:9
and act in a way * of those who Eph 4:1
your duty as a * pastor who is fed 1Ti 4:6
with me in white, for they are *. Rev 3:4
"O Lord, you are * to receive the Rev 4:11
question: "Who is * to break the Rev 5:2
because no one anywhere was *; Rev 5:4
and proved himself * to open the Rev 5:5
words: "You are * to take the Rev 5:9
Lamb is *" (loudly they sang Rev 5:12
He is * to receive the power, and Rev 5:12

WOUND
burn, * for wound, lash for lash. Ex 21:25
burn, wound for *, lash for lash. Ex 21:25
I * and heal— Deu 32:39
the blood from his * running down 1Ki 22:35
taunts pierce me like a fatal *; Ps 42:10
tore his robes and * himself in Is 37:1
You can't heal a * by saying Jer 6:14
Desperate is my *. Jer 10:19
an incurable bruise, a terrible *. Jer 30:12
* and no medicine does any good. Jer 30:13
For your * is deep as the sea. Lam 2:13
for my people's * is far too Mic 1:9
Therefore I will * you! Mic 6:13
There is no healing for your * Nah 3:19
from the cross, * it in the cloth Mk 15:46
the fatal * was healed! Rev 13:3

WOUNDED
a youth who attacked and * me. Gen 4:23
* all the way to the city gate. Ju 9:40
The bodies of the dead and * 1Sa 17:52
overtook Saul and * him badly. 1Sa 31:3,4
Thousands of men are dead and * 2Sa 1:4
for I am badly *," he groaned to 1Ki 22:34
King Joram was * in the battle, 2Ki 8:28
King Joram, who was lying there *. 2Ki 9:16
Philistine archers shot and * him. 1Ch 10:3
his chariot, "for I am badly *." 2Ch 18:33
King Jehoram of Israel was *, 2Ch 22:5
Joash severely *—his own officials 2Ch 24:25
their arrows and fatally * him. 2Ch 35:23
from the city; the * cry for help; Job 24:12
* by iceballs from heaven. Ps 78:48
found me and struck and * me. Sol 5:7
But he was * and bruised for our Is 53:5

(WOUNDED Con't)
and lie mortally * on the ground. Jer 14:17
for I have * you cruelly, as Jer 30:14
and they lay * in their tents, yet Jer 37:10
will be heard the groans of the *. Jer 51:52
Their lives ebb away like those * Lam 2:12
has come you will be * unto death. Eze 21:29
your fall; the * will scream as the Eze 26:15
to destroy; the * shall be slain in Eze 28:23
as one who has been * unto death. Eze 30:24
He has *—he will bind us up. Hos 6:1
"I have gathered your * and taken Zep 3:17,18
He, too, was * and chased away. Lk 20:12
and fatally *, so that your Rom 6:6
his heads seemed * beyond Rev 13:3
* and then came back to life. Rev 13:14

WOUNDING
And he did, * him. 1Ki 20:37
with an axe, or * him with a sword, Pro 25:18

WOUNDS
later, when their * were sore and Gen 34:25
flesh of their * had been healed. Jos 5:8,9
to rest and recover from his *. 2Ki 8:29
to Jezreel to recover from his *. 2Ki 9:15
For though he *, he binds and Job 5:18
multiplies my * without a cause. Job 9:17
that the ground is wet from my *. Job 16:13
* are festering and full of pus. Ps 38:5,6
brokenhearted, binding up their *. Ps 147:3
his own soul. * and constant Pro 6:33
with bloodshot eyes and many *? Pro 23:29,30
weather, or rubbing salt in his *. Pro 25:20
is a form of hatred and * cruelly. Pro 26:28
* from a friend are better than Pro 27:6
*, unanointed and unbound. Is 1:5,6
and to cure the * he gave them. Is 30:26
her sickness and * are ever Jer 6:7
people's grievous *, for they Jer 8:11
he will heal us and bind our *. Jer 14:19
your health again and heal your *. Jer 30:17
Yet there is no cure for your *. Jer 46:11
shall mock at her for all her *. Jer 50:13
pierced with many *, there on your Eze 28:8
Literally, "(These are) * I Zec 13:6f
* with medicine and bandaged them. Lk 10:34
and showed them [the * in Lk 24:40
I see the nail * in his hands—and Jn 20:25
the whippings and * from Jesus' Gal 6:17
For his * have healed ours! 1Pe 2:24
* that once had caused his death. Rev 5:6
that struck and bit with fatal *. Rev 9:19

WOVE
* robes for the Asherah-idol. 2Ki 23:7
He * my sins into ropes to hitch Lam 1:14

WOVEN
It shall have a * band around Ex 28:32
robes, with their * sashes, and Ex 29:9
veil was made from * linen, with Ex 36:35
it was * from finespun linen, Ex 36:37
it consisted of drapes * from Ex 38:9
court were * of fine-twined linen. Ex 38:16
* from fine-twined linen thread. Ex 39:2
one-piece * sash made of the same Ex 39:4,5
joined its beautifully * sash. Ex 39:20
the beautifully * sash of the ephod Ex 39:21
The main part of the ephod was *, Ex 39:22
with its beautifully * belt. Lev 8:7
"Don't wear clothing * from two Deu 22:11
in beautiful clothing * with gold. Ps 45:13
their clothing is * of cruelty! Ps 73:6
John's clothing was * from Mt 3:4
His clothes were * from camel's Mk 1:6

WRAP
those sins that * themselves so Heb 12:1

WRAPPED
are to be * in a blue cloth, Num 4:12
It is * in a cloth in the clothes 1Sa 21:9
"He is an old man * in a robe." 1Sa 28:14
When Elijah heard it, he * his 1Ki 19:13
and I * my cloak around you to Eze 16:8
the seaweed * itself around my Jon 2:5
Joseph took the body and * it in Mt 27:59
a son. She * him in a blanket Lk 2:7
You will find a baby * in a Lk 2:12
Jesus' body and * it in a long Lk 23:53
robe, * a towel around his loins, Jn 13:4
Together they * Jesus' body in a Jn 19:40
All ten are * up in this one, to Rom 13:9

WRAPPINGS
in and saw the empty linen *; Lk 24:12

WRAPS
upon nothing. He * the rain in his Job 26:8
and * up the oceans in his cloak? Pro 30:4

WRATH
Turn back from your fierce *. Ex 32:12
dead too, and his * will come upon Lev 10:6
Israel and God's *—to protect them Num 1:53
instructions the * of God will Num 18:5
* of Jehovah will be upon us." Jos 9:20
"The Place of * upon Uzzah" 2Sa 6:8
Because of his *. 2Sa 22:8
have done, God's * is upon you. 2Ch 19:2
justly, lest the * of God come down 2Ch 19:10
So the * of God came down upon 2Ch 24:17,18
Therefore the * of the Lord has 2Ch 29:8
themselves, so the * of the Lord 2Ch 32:26
Therefore, my unquenchable * is 2Ch 34:25
for why should we risk God's * Ez 7:23
up and the fierce * of our God will Ez 10:14
And now you are bringing more * Neh 13:18
So they did, and the king's * was Est 7:10
volume of * upon me and bring fresh Job 10:17
God will rain down * upon him. Job 20:23
disappear beneath the * of God. Job 20:28
I am warning you—his * will soon Ps 2:12
Turn off your *. Ps 37:8
Man's futile * will bring you Ps 76:10
the fire of his * burned against Ps 78:21
When God saw their deeds, his * Ps 78:59
Pour out your * upon the godless Ps 79:6
so that all your *, your blazing Ps 85:3
Your * lies heavy on me; Ps 88:7
Your fierce * has overwhelmed Ps 88:16
How long will your * burn like Ps 89:46
we are overwhelmed by your *. Ps 90:7
and heavy here beneath your *. Ps 90:9
Therefore in mighty * I swore Ps 95:11
against me, because of your *. Ps 102:9,10
from his *, and not destroy them. Ps 106:23
the wicked can expect only *. Pro 11:23
A SOFT ANSWER turns away *, but Pro 15:1
First to feel his * will be the Is 3:14
* of the Lord of heaven's armies. Is 9:19,20
day of his * and fierce anger. Is 13:9
the heavens in my * and fierce Is 13:13
* against your enemies has passed. Is 26:20
afar, aflame with *, surrounded by Is 30:27
like fire. His * pours out like Is 30:28
he will give full vent to his *; Is 42:14
out such fury and * on his people Is 42:25
you forever, nor always show my *; Is 57:16
the day of his * to their enemies. Is 61:2
In my * I have trodden my enemies Is 63:3
Therefore your * is heavy on us. Is 64:5
and his * upon his enemies. Is 66:14
For all this I am full of the * Jer 6:11
and forsaken this people of his *. Jer 7:29
at last you shall feel my *. Jer 10:18
where you are hiding from my *. Jer 16:16
drank from this cup of God's *. Jer 25:26
this cup of my * until you are Jer 25:27
great whirlwind of * shall rise Jer 25:32
fierceness of his * until it has Jer 30:24
escape from my * except those who Jer 44:14
shall escape my *, but all who Jer 44:28
to explode his * upon his enemies. Jer 50:25
to me in the day of his fierce *. Lam 1:12
In his * he has broken every Lam 2:2
of Israel vanishes beneath his *. Lam 2:3
together fall before his *. Lam 2:6
that come from the rod of God's *. Lam 3:1
for the * of God is on the land. Eze 7:12
but no one listens, for my * is Eze 7:14
have no value in that day of *. Eze 7:19
of anger and with hailstones of *. Eze 13:13
Then at last my * against the Eze 13:15
the fire of my * until it becomes a Eze 21:31
smelt you with the heat of my *. Eze 22:18,19,20
I will blow the fire of my * Eze 22:21
Lord, have poured my * upon you." Eze 22:22
consume you with the fire of my *. Eze 22:31
her and arouse my * and vengeance. Eze 24:8
For in my jealousy and blazing * Eze 38:19
in my *. Hos 13:11
In your *, remember mercy. Hab 3:2
Was your * against their sin that Hab 3:8,9f
down the nations in your *. Hab 3:12
It is a day of the * of God Zep 1:15
you in that day of the Lord's *. Zep 1:18
the terrible day of his * begins. Zep 2:2
from his * in that day of doom. Zep 2:3
my fiercest anger and * upon them. Zep 3:8
That is why such great * came Zec 7:12
could escape the coming * of God? Mt 3:7
and * upon this people. Lk 21:23
the * of God remains upon them." Jn 3:36
to come a day of * when God will be Rom 2:5
the means of saving us from his *. Rom 3:25
Christ to save them from God's *. Rom 4:4,5
us from all of God's * to come. Rom 5:9
for the terrible * of God is upon Eph 5:6
He is the one who took God's * 1Jn 2:2
out undiluted into God's cup of *. Rev 14:10
the great winepress of God's *. Rev 14:19
with the terrible * of the Living Rev 15:7
of the * of God upon the earth." Rev 16:1
wine of the fierceness of his *. Rev 16:19
of the * of Almighty God. Rev 19:15

WREATH
lions and oxen were * decorations. 1Ki 7:27-30
Literally, "a * that quickly 1Co 9:25f

WREATHS
and decorated with * on each side. 1Ki 7:27-30
decorated on the outside with *. 1Ki 7:31
surrounded by * were engraved on 1Ki 7:36

WRECK
the very faith he tried to *." Gal 1:23

WRECKED
for they were * at Ezion-geber. 1Ki 22:48
They * the temple and converted 2Ki 10:27
and you are * in the heart of the Eze 27:26

WRECKING
I will call for a * crew to Jer 22:7

WRENCHED
with a spear; he * the spear from 2Sa 23:21
Let my shoulder be * out of Job 31:22
her hand and * her shoulder out of Eze 29:7

WRESTED
But Geshur and Aram * these 1Ch 2:23

WRESTLED
and a Man * with him until dawn. Gen 32:22,23,24
Yes, he * with the Angel and Hos 12:4

WRESTLING
(meaning "*"), for she said, "I Gen 30:8

WRETCH
and said, 'You evil-hearted *! Mt 18:32

WRETCHED
They replied, "Are you a * Jn 7:52
you are * and miserable and poor Rev 3:17

WRETCHEDNESS
Open your eyes and see our *, how Dan 9:18

WRING
to the altar and * off its head, Lev 1:15,16,17

WRINGING
to him first, * its neck, but not Lev 5:8

WRINKLE
a single spot or * or any other Eph 5:27

WRINKLED
You make him old and *, then send Job 14:20,21

WRIST
thread around the * of the child Gen 38:28
thread on his * was born, and he Gen 38:30

WRISTS
golden bracelets for her *. Gen 24:22
on his sister's *, and heard her Gen 24:29,30
like thread and fell from his *! Ju 15:14
charms on their * and furnishing Eze 13:18
bracelets on your * and beautiful Eze 23:42
handcuffs from his * and smashed Mk 5:3,4
And the chains fell off his *! Act 12:7

WRITE
Moses, "* this into a permanent Ex 17:14
ones and I will * upon them the Ex 34:1
And the Lord said to Moses, "* Ex 34:27
Then the priest shall * these Num 5:23
forehead, and * them on the Deu 6:9
before breakfast! * them upon the Deu 11:20
Every creditor shall * "Paid in Deu 15:2
his wife, he may * a letter stating Deu 24:1
and then * the laws of God in the Deu 27:2,3,4
Lord your God. * all of these laws Deu 27:8
"Now * down the words of this Deu 31:19
demanded that he * down the names Ju 8:14
"You * bitter things against me Job 13:26
Oh, that I could * my plea with Job 19:23,24
We will * songs to celebrate your Ps 21:13
I will * a lovely poem to the Ps 45:1
Hold these virtues tightly. * Pro 3:3
precious possession. * them down, Pro 7:3
"Make a large signboard and * on Is 8:1
endangered them! * down all these Is 8:16
Now go and * down this word of Is 30:8
For if you don't * it, they will Is 30:9
The Lord God of Israel says, * Jer 30:2
And * this also concerning Israel Jer 30:4
"Get a scroll and * down all my Jer 36:2
and * down every one of them. Jer 36:2
Get another scroll and * Jer 36:28
"Son of dust," he said, "* Eze 24:2
about it. * out all the directions Eze 43:11
those fingers to * this message: Dan 5:24,25
* off Moresheth Mic 1:14
And the Lord said to me, "* my Hab 2:2
People will * their friends in Zec 8:20,21
a man has to do is * his wife a Mk 10:4
'Tear it up and * another one for Lk 16:5,6
that we should * to them to refrain Act 15:20
But what shall I * the Emperor? Act 25:26
him and then tell me what to *. Act 25:26
Next on my list of items to * you 1Co 11:17
AND NOW, BROTHERS, I want to * 1Co 12:1
I will * these final words of 1Co 16:21
Oh, how I hated to * that letter! 2Co 2:4
and not making me * about myself. 2Co 12:11
I will * these closing words in Gal 6:11
the Lord: I will * my laws in their Heb 8:10
agreement: I will * my laws into Heb 10:16
he told them to * down the events 1Pe 1:11
I don't want to * it, for I hope 3Jn 1:13
been planning to * you some Jud 1:3
now I find I must * of something Jud 1:3
And then I heard him say, "* Rev 1:11
be afraid! * down what you have Rev 1:19
"* a letter to the leader Rev 2:1

WRITE Con't)
"I * to inform you of a message Rev 2:1
of the church in Smyrna * this Rev 2:8
"* this letter to the leader Rev 2:12
"* this letter to the leader Rev 2:18
of the church in Sardis * this Rev 3:1
"* this letter to the leader Rev 3:7
and I will * my God's Name on Rev 3:12
"* this letter to the leader Rev 3:14
I was about to * what the Rev 10:4
above me saying, "* this down: At Rev 14:13
And then he said to me, "* Rev 21:5

WRITER
speediest * pouring out his story. Ps 45:1
to be John, the * of this book. Jn 13:23f
Luke, the * of this book, now Act 16:10f
just as the Psalm * did when he 2Co 4:13

WRITER'S
a * case strapped to his side. Eze 9:2
the man with the * case, and said Eze 9:3
carrying the * case, reported back Eze 9:11

WRITERS
families of the * living at 1Ch 2:55
himself, and the * of the New Is 52:13f
men, and inspired *, and you will Mt 23:34

WRITHE
My heart, my heart—I * in pain; Jer 4:19
You will * in pain like a woman Jer 13:21
a woman in labor. * and groan in Mic 4:10

WRITHED
We too have * in agony, but all Is 26:18

WRITHES
birth, who cries and * in pain. Is 26:17
Babylon trembles and * in pain, Jer 51:29

WRITHING
* serpent, the dragon of the sea. Is 27:1
ground * and foaming at the mouth. Mk 9:20

WRITING
When Moses had finished * down Deu 31:24
in force at the time of this *. Jos 9:27
in * from the hand of the Lord." 1Ch 28:19
still there at the time of this *. 2Ch 5:9
his kingdom, putting it into *: 2Ch 36:22,23
of Judah see in * all the terrible Jer 36:3
me a scroll, with * on both sides. Eze 2:9,10
of a man's hand * on the plaster of Dan 5:5
Whoever reads that * on the wall, Dan 5:7
Since the * was in familiar Dan 5:8f
the * or tell him what it meant. Dan 5:8
He will tell you what the * Dan 5:12
tried to read that * on the wall, Dan 5:15
* her a letter of dismissal?" Mt 19:7
I, Tertius, the one who is * Rom 16:22
I am not * about these things to 1Co 4:14
And I am not * this to hint that 1Co 9:15
We are * to all of you Christians 2Co 1:1
people ought to be * about me and 2Co 12:11
I am * this to you now in the 2Co 13:10
Lord: This is Paul * to you, chosen Eph 1:1
which I am * with my own hand, as I 2Th 3:17
I am * these things to you now, 1Ti 3:14
guarantee this by * it here with my Phm 1:19
Dear brothers, I am not * out a 1Jn 2:7
I am * these things to all of 1Jn 2:12
And I am * to you younger boys 1Jn 2:13
So I am not * to you as to those 1Jn 2:21
sake, who is * this letter to you. Rev 1:9
a scroll with * on the inside and Rev 5:1

WRITINGS
the * of Moses himself prove this. Lk 20:37,38
passage from the * of the prophets, Lk 24:27
they read Moses' * their hearts are 2Co 3:15

WRITTEN
the Book he had *—the Book of the Ex 24:7
I have * on tablets of stone, so Ex 24:12
were * with the finger of God. Ex 31:18
Ten Commandments * on both sides of Ex 32:15
(God himself had * the Ex 32:16
me out of the book you have *." Ex 32:32
Moses had * down their movements Num 33:2
on which he had * the Deu 9:10,11
obey all the laws * in this book, Deu 28:58,59
And all the curses * in this book Deu 29:20
the commandments * in this book of Deu 30:10
had * in the book of God's laws. Jos 8:34
the instructions * in the book of Jos 23:6
keep each of his commands * in 1Ki 2:3
* in the book The Acts of Solomon. 1Ki 11:41
reign are * in The Annals of the 1Ki 14:29
and conquests—are * in The Annals 1Ki 16:4-7
of Elah's reign is * in The Annals 1Ki 16:14
his treason are * in The Annals of 1Ki 16:20
cities he built—is * in The Annals 1Ki 22:39
of King Joram is * in The Annals of 2Ki 8:23
of Judah, are * in The Annals of 2Ki 13:12
of King Menahem is * in The Annals 2Ki 15:21
history is * in The Annals of the 2Ki 15:36
Temple, with God's laws * on it!" 2Ki 22:8
When the king heard what was * 2Ki 22:11
laws which were * in the book that 2Ki 23:24
of Josiah is * in The Annals of the 2Ki 23:28
David have been * in the history of 1Ch 29:29
the history * by Nathan the 1Ch 29:29
the history * by the prophet Gad. 1Ch 29:29
biography is * in the history of 2Ch 9:29
in the histories * by Shemaiah the 2Ch 12:15
of Asa is * in The Annals of the 2Ch 16:11
first to last are * in the history 2Ch 20:34
of the Lord * in the law of Moses, 2Ch 25:4
of King Amaziah is * in The Annals 2Ch 25:26
activities, is * in The Annals of 2Ch 27:7
things he did are * in The Book of 2Ch 32:32
is all * in The Annals of the Kings 2Ch 33:18
these laws that are * here." 2Ch 34:21
All the curses * in the scroll 2Ch 34:24
to do what was * in the scroll. 2Ch 34:31
as it is * in the law of Moses. 2Ch 35:12
the Lord, all are * in The Annals 2Ch 35:27
evil he did, are * in The Annals of 2Ch 36:8
and this is what was * in it: Neh 7:5
the Jew) had * a letter throwing Est 9:29-31
by the king, are * in The Book of Est 10:2
This song of David was * at a time Ps 18:1
for your law is * upon my heart!" Ps 40:8
* after Nathan the prophet had Ps 51:1
* by David to protest against his Ps 52:1
* by David at the time the men of Ps 54:1
* by David at the time King Saul Ps 59:1
* by David at the time he was at Ps 60:1
Those whose names are * down to Is 4:2,3,4
testify that I had * it (before the Is 8:2
This was * many years before Cyrus Is 44:28f
See, here is my decree all * out Is 65:6
says: You have * a letter to Jer 29:25
For he has * to us here in Jer 29:28
word, and he had * them down in ink Jer 36:18
Baruch all he had * before, only Jer 36:32
after Baruch had * down all God's Jer 45:1
the words * above— and gave the Jer 51:60
read what I have * and say, 'Lord, Jer 51:61,62
us—the curse * in the law of Moses Dan 9:11
Every curse against us * in the Dan 9:13
I am here to tell you what is * Dan 10:20,21
are * in the Book will endure it. Dan 12:1
horses will have * on them, "These Zec 14:20
He had *, Mt 3:3
"In them it is * that at the Mt 19:4
For it is * in the Scriptures Mt 26:31
In the book * by the prophet Mk 1:2
He told them, "It is * in the Mk 11:17
have already been * using as their Lk 1:1,2
But Jesus replied, "It is * in Lk 4:4
So it is * in the Scriptures." Lk 4:8
ancient Scriptures * by the Lk 21:22
Yes, everything * about me by Lk 22:37
They stopped short, sadness * Lk 24:17
that everything * about me by Moses Lk 24:44
And he said, "Yes, it was * Lk 24:46
As it is * in the Scriptures, Jn 6:45
and the signboard was * in Jn 19:20
Pilate replied, "What I have *, Jn 19:22
"What I have written, I have *." Jn 19:22
Jesus' life were *, the whole world Jn 21:25
the Ten Commandments * on them. Act 7:44
And all the prophets have * Act 10:43
the prophets had * about, though Act 13:27
* in the books of prophecy; Act 24:14
never had God's * laws, for down in Rom 2:12-15
God's laws are * within them; Rom 2:12-15
his * laws but don't obey them. Rom 2:12-15
For it is *, "As I live," says Rom 14:11
These things that were * in Rom 15:4
they were * down so that we could 1Co 10:11
nothing is * between the lines! 2Co 1:13,14
are a letter from Christ, * by us. 2Co 3:3
It is not a letter * with pen and 2Co 3:3
are * in God's Book of the Law." Gal 3:10
For it is * in the Scripture, Gal 3:13
another, if it is * down and Gal 3:15
For it is * that Abraham had two Gal 4:22
names are * in the Book of Life. Php 4:3
with these words * on it: "The 2Ti 2:19
I've * you this letter because I Phm 1:21
because it is * that God rested on Heb 4:4
Ten Commandments * on them, and a Heb 9:4
they have *, for, like lights 2Pe 1:19
I have * this to you who believe 1Jn 5:13
The fate of such people was * Jud 1:4
its horns. And * on each head were Rev 13:1
names were not * down before the Rev 13:8
Or "those whose names were not * Rev 13:8f
Name * on their foreheads. Rev 14:1
* all over with blasphemies Rev 17:3
A mysterious caption was * on her Rev 17:5
have not been * in the Book of Life Rev 17:8
A name was * on his forehead, Rev 19:12
On his robe and thigh was * this Rev 19:16
to the things * in The Books, each Rev 20:12
of Israel were * on the gates. Rev 21:12
and on them were * the names of the Rev 21:14
are * in the Lamb's Book of Life. Rev 21:27
and his name shall be * on their Rev 22:4
it and all else * in the scroll." Rev 22:6,7
up what you have *, for the time of Rev 22:10
to what is * here, God shall add to Rev 22:18

WRONG
of right and *, good and bad. Gen 2:16,17
the bud because of * motives and Gen 11:6f
and * use of the knowledge gained. Gen 11:6f
intention of doing anything *." Gen 20:5
from the sky, "Hagar, what's *? Gen 21:17
it was very * of him [to deny a Gen 38:10
got your right hand on the * head! Gen 48:18
he said to the one in the *. Ex 2:13
my people have been * all along. Ex 9:27
right and who is *, and instructing Ex 18:15,16
do not * them. Lev 19:33
Literally, "for his *." Num 5:7f
anything else is * with it, you Deu 15:21
seen someone do * when he hasn't, Deu 19:16
You must have the * man!" 1Sa 9:21
right whatever I have done *." 1Sa 12:3
"You have certainly done *, but 1Sa 12:20
"That is very *," Saul said. 1Sa 14:33
to the leaders, "Something's *! 1Sa 14:38
What is *? 1Sa 14:41
"What is *?" 1Sa 16:4
and you will never do * 1Sa 25:28
Saul confessed, "I have done *. 1Sa 26:21
been a fool, and very, very *." 1Sa 26:21
as though we had done something *. 2Sa 19:5
the Lord, "What I did was very *. 2Sa 24:10
what is right and what is *. 1Ki 3:9
of doing something * and then, 1Ki 8:31
'We have sinned, we have done *'; 1Ki 8:47
what was clearly * and refused to 1Ki 11:6
in Israel, did * and angered the 1Ki 14:22
did not realize that these were *. 1Ki 15:14
them, "You've come the * way! 2Ki 6:19
things that were *, and they had 2Ki 17:9
at Lachish: "I have done *. 2Ki 18:14
now how * I was to do this." 1Ch 21:8
mother encouraged him in doing *. 2Ch 22:3
So in all this Job said nothing *. Job 2:10
Tell me, what have I done *? Job 6:24
difference between right and *? Job 6:30
If you could prove me * I would Job 13:19
Tell me, what have I done *? Job 13:23
And if indeed I was *, you have Job 19:4
when your whole premise is so *?" Job 21:34
will only admit that you were *. Job 22:21
put right all the * in your home, Job 22:23
me a liar and claim that I am *?" Job 24:25
the Almighty show me that I am *; Job 31:35
have done that is *, or how they Job 36:9
Prove them *, Ps 4:6
holding myself back from doing *. Ps 18:23
For though I did them no *, yet Ps 35:7
that they have seen me doing *! Ps 35:21
planning how to keep away from *. Ps 36:4
and fair and knows right from *. Ps 37:30,31
And hate what is *. Ps 45:7
O Lord, because I've done them *. Ps 59:3
permitting * to defeat right? Ps 94:20
punished them when they went *. Ps 99:8
suffered no man to do them *." Ps 105:14f
What's *, Red Sea, that made you Ps 114:5
Keep me far from every *; Ps 119:29,30
I thought about the * direction Ps 119:59,60
lest the godly be forced to do *. Ps 125:3
right from *, how to find the right Pro 2:9
and exult in doing *, for they Pro 2:14
they do is crooked and *. Pro 2:15
The man who knows right from * Pro 3:13,14,15
to do *A false witnessSowing Pro 6:16-19
judges who is right and who is *. Pro 8:14,15
give them up even when they are *. Pro 13:19
gloomy, everything seems to go *; Pro 15:15
man enjoys folly, something is *! Pro 15:21
Plans go * with too few Pro 15:22
It is * to accept a bribe to Pro 17:23
It is * for a judge to favor the Pro 18:5
Men have died for saying the * Pro 18:21
To plan evil is as * as doing it. Pro 24:8
It is * to sentence the poor, and Pro 24:23
and says, "What's * with that?" Pro 28:24
then say, "What's * with that?" Pro 30:20
What is * cannot be righted; Ecc 1:12-15
people feel it is safe to do *. Ecc 8:11
is *, and what is wrong is right; Is 5:20
is wrong, and what is * is right; Is 5:20
and knows right from *, the two Is 7:15,16
of Egypt is utterly stupid and *. Is 19:11
that all their suggestions are *; Is 19:14
they keep on doing * and take no Is 26:10
eyes to all enticement to do *. Is 33:15
"Stop, you're doing it *!" Is 45:9
the right from * and cherish my Is 51:7
but he had done no *, and had Is 53:9
minds the very thought of doing *! Is 55:7
who checks himself from doing *. Is 56:2
you continually do * and those Is 59:8
good and hate the *—they and their Is 59:21

(WRONG Con't)
I hate robbery and *. Is 61:8
Instead, they did * before my Is 66:4
They are smart enough at doing *, Jer 4:22
when he is on the * road and Jer 8:4,5
the fork where he made the * turn. Jer 8:4,5
You're getting the * impression. Jer 13:13
but * since their earliest days; Jer 32:30
them right from *, but they would Jer 32:33
Because of all the * she did to Lam 1:3
You have seen the * they did to Lam 3:59
he is cruel and robs and does *. Eze 18:18
between right and *, and they Eze 22:26
that time when * was found in you. Eze 28:15
what is right and what is *. Eze 44:23
right to * and wrong to right." Dan 7:25f
right to wrong and * to right." Dan 7:25f
to know right from *, yet you are Mic 3:1
within the city, and he does no *. Zep 3:5
And so everything you did went * Hag 2:15
a vow shows that something is *. Mt 5:37
him it was * for him to marry her. Mt 14:4
he meant the * teaching of the Mt 16:12
Temptation to do * is inevitable, Mt 18:7
one of them, 'I did you no *! Mt 20:13
"What has he done *?" Mt 27:23
kept saying it was * for the king Mk 6:17,18
"If your hand does *, cut it Mk 9:43,44
"What has he done *?" Mk 15:14
* will be punished only lightly. Lk 12:48
And is it * for me, just because Lk 13:16
man hasn't done one thing *." Lk 23:40,41
a * step, because of the dark." Jn 11:10
It is *!' Act 7:26
"But the man in the * told Moses Act 7:27
"We see nothing * with him," Act 23:9
hearts they know right from *. Rom 2:12-15
you know right from * and favor Rom 2:18
You say it is * to commit Rom 2:22
all have gone *. Rom 3:12
That would be * while he was Rom 7:3
such desires are * and arousing all Rom 7:8
what I am doing is *, and my bad Rom 7:16
and when I try not to do *, I do Rom 7:19
right, I inevitably do what is *. Rom 7:21
Hate what is *. Rom 12:9
But if you are doing something *, Rom 13:4
the Ten Commandments say is *. Rom 13:9
Love does no * to anyone. Rom 13:10
yours about what is right and *. Rom 14:1
they think it is *, and will go Rom 14:2
them whether they are right or *. Rom 14:4
others say it is * and foolish to Rom 14:5
doing something he thinks is *. Rom 14:13
is nothing really * with eating Rom 14:14
But if someone believes it is *, Rom 14:14
do it because for him it is *. Rom 14:14
Remember, there is nothing * with Rom 14:20
meat, but it is * to eat it if it Rom 14:20
there is nothing * with what you Rom 14:22
wants to do is * shouldn't do it. Rom 14:23
is *, and so for him it is wrong. Rom 14:23
is wrong, and so for him it is *. Rom 14:23
those who feel these things are *. Rom 15:1
and to stay innocent of any *. Rom 16:19
the ones who do *, cheating others, 1Co 6:8
who thinks it is * to eat this food 1Co 8:10
the time he still feels it is *. 1Co 8:10
to do something he thinks is *. 1Co 8:12
But remember this—the * desires 1Co 10:13
just because he thinks I am *? 1Co 10:30
even notice when others do it *. 1Co 13:5
and never say it is * to "speak 1Co 14:39
from everything *, whether of body 2Co 7:1
of you has suffered any * from us. 2Co 7:2
to whom he did the *. 2Co 7:12
I was * in my boasting about you. 2Co 9:3
Did I do * and cheapen myself and 2Co 11:7
Please forgive me for this *! 2Co 12:13
seen a *, it must be punished. 2Co 13:1
he was doing for it was very *. Gal 2:11
find that we are *, and that we Gal 2:17
But it takes only one * person Gal 5:9
not freedom to do *, but freedom to Gal 5:13
be doing the * things your evil Gal 5:16
But when you follow your own * Gal 5:19
everyone else is * except those in Gal 5:20
there will be * doctrine, envy, Gal 5:20
be one of you who is in the *. Gal 6:1
If he sows to please his own * Gal 6:8
about right and * and have given Eph 4:19
when they see how * they really Eph 5:13
between right and *, and to be Php 1:10
their * and shallow answers built Col 2:8
warn you against all that is *. 1Th 5:12
who are teaching such * doctrine. 1Ti 1:3,4
done what they knew was *. 1Ti 1:19
They will say it is * to be 1Ti 4:3
to be married and * to eat meat, 1Ti 4:3
to do all kinds of * things to get 1Ti 6:9
not be doing things that are *." 2Ti 2:19
teachers of those who are *. 2Ti 2:24
* ideas and believe what is true. 2Ti 2:25
us realize what is * in our lives; 2Ti 3:16
with them where they are *. Tit 1:9
a person has a * sense of values. Tit 3:11
You love right and hate *; Heb 1:9
difference between right and *. Heb 5:12,13
from * by practicing doing right. Heb 5:14
keep from doing *, but later God Heb 7:28
has to show you where you are *. Heb 12:5
give in and do * when he is Jas 1:12
wants to do * it is never God who Jas 1:13
never wants to do * and never Jas 1:13
So get rid of all that is * in Jas 1:21
that you are guided by * motives. Jas 2:4
know better, do *, our punishment Jas 3:1
your whole aim is *—you want only Jas 4:3
Let there be tears for the * Jas 4:9
one another, declaring it is *. Jas 4:11
law is right or *, but to obey it. Jas 4:11
punish all who do *, and to honor 1Pe 2:14
doesn't mean you are free to do *. 1Pe 2:16
if you are beaten for doing *; 1Pe 2:20
for doing good than for doing *! 1Pe 3:17
is nothing * with sexual sin. 2Pe 2:2
money he could make by doing *; 2Pe 2:15
who will do every * they can think 2Pe 3:3
us and to cleanse us from every *. 1Jn 1:9
Because Cain had been doing * and 1Jn 3:12
that we have done *, the Lord will 1Jn 3:20
Every * is a sin, of course. 1Jn 5:17
"Yet there is one thing *; Rev 2:4
doing * will do it more and more; Rev 22:11

WRONGDOING
Ask these men right here what * Act 24:20
the curse for our * upon himself. Gal 3:13

WRONGDOINGS
to them in their *, and I will Heb 8:12

WRONGED
since he has * her by no longer Ex 21:8
But if the person he * is dead, Num 5:8
rather, you have * me by coming Ju 11:27
that I am being * and will bless me 2Sa 16:12
"Queen Vashti has * not only the Est 1:16
of vengeance from the * husband. Pro 5:9f
given to all who have been *. Is 42:3
of Israel and Judah have been *. Jer 50:33
on those who * his people and Jer 51:11
orphans and widows are * and Eze 22:7
God, nor, sir, have I * you." Dan 6:22

WRONGLY
do evil and their power is used *. Jer 23:10

WRONGS
beneath their * and groan beneath Job 35:9,10
And keep me from deliberate *; Ps 19:13
and for many other * he had done, Lk 3:19,20
Even if he * you seven times a Lk 17:4

WROTE
Moses * down the laws; Ex 24:4
* out the Covenant—the Ten Ex 34:28
* them on two stone tablets. Deu 4:13
and he * them out on two stone Deu 5:22
He again * the Ten Commandments Deu 10:4
Then Moses * out the laws he had Deu 31:9
So, on that very day, Moses * Deu 31:22
of a king were; he * them in a book 1Sa 10:25
Then Saul * to Jesse, "Please 1Sa 16:22
the Lord's enemies," he * them. 1Sa 30:26
Finally the next morning David * 2Sa 11:14
3,000 proverbs and * 1,005 songs. 1Ki 4:32
So she * letters in Ahab's name, 1Ki 21:8
THEN JEHU * a letter to the city 2Ki 10:1
secretary and * down the names and 1Ch 24:6
Then Elijah the prophet * him 2Ch 21:12
Hezekiah will fail, too," he *. 2Ch 32:17
to reign, they * him a letter of Ez 4:6
their associates * a letter to him Ez 4:7
of July—and they * as Mordecai Est 8:9,10
Mordecai * in the name of King Est 8:9,10
Mordecai * a history of all these Est 9:20
He * them to teach his people how Pro 1:2
to watch me as I * so they could Is 8:2
* this poem about his experience: Is 38:9
Jeremiah * them a letter from Jer 29:1
Baruch * down all the prophecies. Jer 36:4
Jeremiah * on a scroll all the Jer 51:60
himself saw the fingers as they *. Dan 5:5
Afterward King Darius * this Dan 6:25,26
had a dream and he * it down. Dan 7:1
I had seen (Daniel * in his Dan 7:15
*: O little town of Mt 2:5
The Matthew who * this book. Mt 9:9f
surprise *, "His name is John!" Lk 1:63
For David himself * in the book Lk 20:42,43
the prophets * in the Scriptures! Lk 24:25
believe Moses. He * about me, but Jn 5:46
believe what he *, no wonder you Jn 5:47
and * in the dust with his finger. Jn 8:6
Then he stooped down again and * Jn 8:8
him in this. They * to their Act 18:27
for the ones we * to them about: Act 21:25
Then he * this letter to the Act 23:2
For Moses * that if a person Rom 10:5
meant when he *: "I will praise Rom 15:9
When I * to you before I said not 1Co 5:9
That is why I * as I did in my 2Co 2:3
Remember that the man I * about, 2Co 2:5,6
I * to you as I did so that I 2Co 2:9
rid of the sin that I * you about. 2Co 7:11
I * as I did so the Lord could 2Co 7:12
faith—and God * this promise down Gal 3:17
And read the letter I * to them. Col 4:16
the person who * the will is dead. Heb 9:16
the death of the person who * it. Heb 9:17
Though they * about it, they had 1Pe 1:10
John * it all down—the words of Rev 1:2

WROUGHT
* iron, cassia and calamus, Eze 27:19

WRUNG
* out a whole bowlful of water! Ju 6:38

XERXES
Perhaps * (486–465) who launched Dan 11:2f

YAHWEH
be pronounced "*," as it is Ex 3:15f
In this paraphrase "*" is Ex 3:15f

YANK
me, a noose to * me up and leave me Ps 140:5
I will * her idolatry out of her Zec 9:7

YANKED
And he woke up and * his hair Ju 16:14
Then the prophet * off the 1Ki 20:41
first ones were * out, roots and Dan 7:8
Bartimaeus * off his old coat Mk 10:50

YANKING
* a dog's ears is no more foolish Pro 26:17

YARD
king's castle beside the prison *. Neh 3:25
an empty cistern in the prison *. Jer 38:6
to the prison * until the day that Jer 38:28
terrace *, which was 8¾ feet wide; Eze 41:11
facing the Temple *, measuring 122½ Eze 41:12
Temple *, and to another building. Eze 42:1
facing the Temple * are holy; Eze 42:13

YARDS
sat down a hundred * or so away. Gen 21:16
the king's olive * and sycamore 1Ch 27:28
two hundred * of the walls of 2Ch 25:23
and its immediately surrounding *. Eze 41:13

YARDSTICK
a man carrying a * in his hand. Zec 2:1

YARN
Vedan and Javan bring Arabian *, Eze 27:19

YAWNING
me from the * jaws of death! Jon 2:6

YEA
Then they saluted, yelling, "*! Mk 15:18

YEAR
Literally, "in the 601st *, in Gen 8:13f
occurred in the * of Abraham's Gen 11:32f
the thirteenth *, they rebelled. Gen 14:4
One * later, Ched-or-laomer and Gen 14:5,6
Sarah next * at about this time." Gen 17:21
Then the Lord said, "Next * Gen 18:10
hard for God? Next *, just as I Gen 18:14
That * Isaac's crops were Gen 26:12
The next * they came again and Gen 47:18
this event each * (this is a Ex 12:14
day of the 430th * that all of Ex 12:40,41
each *, when Jehovah brings you Ex 13:4,5
days each * you must explain to Ex 13:8
Literally, "in its season from * Ex 13:10f
"in its season from year to *." Ex 13:10f
in the seventh *, and need pay Ex 21:2
during the seventh *, and let the Ex 23:11
At these three times each *, Ex 23:17
I will not do it all in one *, Ex 23:29
"Once a * Aaron must sanctify Ex 30:10
dates appointed each * in March; Ex 34:18
your God those three times each *. Ex 34:24
in the second *, the Tabernacle was Ex 40:17
each *, because of their sins." Lev 16:34
And the fourth * the entire crop Lev 19:24
Finally, in the fifth *, the Lev 19:25
which are to be observed each *: Lev 23:4
before the Lord every seventh *. Lev 25:1
during the seventh * the land is to Lev 25:4
vineyards during that entire *. Lev 25:4
for it is a * of rest for the Lev 25:5
Any crops that do grow that * Lev 25:6,7
"Every fiftieth *, on the Day Lev 25:8
For the fiftieth * shall be Lev 25:10
It shall be a * when all the Lev 25:10
"What a happy * it will be! Lev 25:11
for it is a holy * of Jubilee Lev 25:12
for you. That * your food shall be Lev 25:12
Yes, during the * of Jubilee Lev 25:13
we eat the seventh *, since we are Lev 25:20
to plant or harvest crops that *?' Lev 25:20
crops the sixth * that will last Lev 25:21,22
of the eighth * are harvested!' Lev 25:21,22
new owner until the * of Jubilee; Lev 25:28
but at the Jubilee * it must be Lev 25:28

YEAR Con't)
he has up to one * to redeem it, Lev 25:29
within the *, then it will belong Lev 25:30
owner in the * of Jubilee. Lev 25:30
owner in the * of Jubilee. Lev 25:31
owners in the * of Jubilee; Lev 25:33
you only until the * of Jubilee. Lev 25:40
left before the * of Lev 25:50
by the time the * of Jubilee Lev 25:54
seventh * when you lived upon it. Lev 26:34,35
his field in the * of Jubilee, then Lev 27:17
but if it is after the * of Lev 27:18
until the next * of Jubilee. Lev 27:18
rights to it at the * of Jubilee Lev 27:20
When it is freed in the * of Lev 27:21
value until the * of Jubilee, and Lev 27:23
Lord, and in the * of Jubilee the Lev 27:24
of the second * after the Num 1:1
lamb a * old for a guilt offering. Num 6:12
60 male lambs a * old. Num 7:88
the second * after leaving Egypt: Num 9:1
a month, or a *, that is how long Num 9:22
of the second * of Israel's Num 10:11
for forty years—a * for each day, Num 14:34,35
first grain that is cut each *. Num 15:19,20,21
each month throughout the *. Num 28:14
month of each *, you shall Num 28:16
each *; there shall be a solemn Num 29:1
the fortieth * after the people of Num 33:38,39
be returned at the * of Jubilee." Num 36:4
day after day throughout the *! Deu 11:12
tithe all of your crops every *. Deu 14:22
"Every third * you are to use Deu 14:28
"AT THE END of every seventh * Deu 15:1
Don't refuse a loan because the * Deu 15:9
end of the sixth * you have owned Deu 15:12
your God each * at his sanctuary. Deu 15:20
God three times a * at the Deu 16:16
for a * he shall be free to be at Deu 24:5
"Every third * is a year of Deu 26:12
"Every third year is a * of Deu 26:12
tithing. That * you are to give all Deu 26:12
of every seventh *—the Year of Deu 31:10,11
seventh year—the * of Release—at Deu 31:10,11
at Shechem that *, held in the Ju 9:27
for four days each * to lament the Ju 11:40
I will give you ten dollars a * Ju 17:10,11
Each * Elkanah and his families 1Sa 1:3
Every * it was the same—Peninnah 1Sa 1:7
The next * Elkanah and Peninnah 1Sa 1:21,22
Each * his mother made a little 1Sa 2:19
the *, during the wheat harvest; 1Sa 12:17
TIME Saul had reigned for one *. 1Sa 13:1
In the second * of his reign, he 1Sa 13:1
for a * and four months. 1Sa 27:7
paid him tribute each *. 2Sa 8:2
IN THE SPRING of the following *, 2Sa 11:1
He cut his hair only once a * 2Sa 14:26
reign that lasted * after year for 2Sa 21:1
lasted year after * for three 2Sa 21:1
provisions for one month of the *. 1Ki 4:7
of the fourth * of Solomon's reign 1Ki 6:1
May in the fourth * of Solomon's 1Ki 6:37
of the eleventh * of his reign. 1Ki 6:38
a * on the altar he had built. 1Ki 9:25
Each * Solomon received gold 1Ki 10:14
In the fifth * of Rehoboam's 1Ki 14:25
* of Jeroboam's reign in Israel. 1Ki 15:1
in the twentieth * of the reign of 1Ki 15:9
in the second * of the reign of 1Ki 15:25
during the third * of the reign of 1Ki 15:28
the twenty-sixth * of the reign of 1Ki 16:8
the twenty-seventh * of the reign 1Ki 16:10
The following * he called up the 1Ki 20:26
But during the third *, while 1Ki 22:2
during the fourth * of the reign of 1Ki 22:41
It was during the seventeenth * 1Ki 22:51
This occurred in the second * of 2Ki 1:17
* of the reign of King Jehoshaphat 2Ki 3:1
"Next * at about this time you 2Ki 4:15,16
*, just as Elisha had predicted. 2Ki 4:17
during the fifth * of the reign of 2Ki 8:16
during the twelfth * of the reign 2Ki 8:24,25
reigned only one *, in Jerusalem. 2Ki 8:26
* of the reign of King Joram of 2Ki 9:29
In the seventh * of Queen 2Ki 11:4
But in the twenty-third * of his 2Ki 12:6
the twenty-third * of the reign of 2Ki 13:1
the thirty-seventh * of the reign 2Ki 13:9,10
DURING THE SECOND * of the reign 2Ki 14:1
the fifteenth * of the reign of 2Ki 14:23
Finally, in the ninth * of King 2Ki 17:6
It was during the fourth * of his 2Ki 18:9
was the seventh * of the reign of 2Ki 18:9
(during the sixth * of the reign of 2Ki 18:10
and the ninth * of the reign of 2Ki 18:10
Later, during the fourteenth * of 2Ki 18:13
promised: This * my people will eat 2Ki 19:29
and in the third * they will have 2Ki 19:29
In the eighteenth * of his reign, 2Ki 22:3,4
in the eighteenth * of the reign of 2Ki 23:23
* of Nebuchadnezzar's reign. 2Ki 24:12
25 of the ninth * of the reign of 2Ki 25:1
into the eleventh * of his reign. 2Ki 25:2
of the nineteenth * of the reign of 2Ki 25:8
thirty-seventh * of his captivity. 2Ki 25:27
This occurred during the first * 2Ki 25:27
him a large sum of money every *. 1Ch 18:2
large amounts of money every *. 1Ch 18:6
fortieth * of King David's reign. 1Ch 26:31,32
for active duty one month each *. 1Ch 27:1
on duty the first month of each *. 1Ch 27:2,3
duty the second month of each *. 1Ch 27:4
on duty the third month of each *. 1Ch 27:5,6
duty the fourth month of each *. 1Ch 27:7
on duty the fifth month of each *. 1Ch 27:8
on duty the sixth month of each *. 1Ch 27:9
duty the seventh month of each *. 1Ch 27:10
duty the eighth month of each *. 1Ch 27:11
during the ninth month of each *. 1Ch 27:12
on duty the tenth month of each *. 1Ch 27:13
the eleventh month of each *. 1Ch 27:14
the twelfth month of each *. 1Ch 27:15
fourth * of King Solomon's reign. 2Ch 3:2
worth of gold each * from the kings 2Ch 9:13,14
in the fifth * of King Rehoboam's 2Ch 12:2
in the eighteenth * of the reign of 2Ch 13:1
of the fifteenth * of King Asa's 2Ch 15:10
* of King Asa's reign. 2Ch 15:19
IN THE THIRTY-SIXTH * of King 2Ch 16:1
In the thirty-ninth * of his 2Ch 16:12
So he died in the forty-first * 2Ch 16:13,14
In the third * of his reign he 2Ch 17:7,8,9
he reigned one *, in Jerusalem. 2Ch 22:2
IN THE SEVENTH * of the reign of 2Ch 23:1
month of the first * of his reign, 2Ch 29:3
old, in the eighth * of his reign, 2Ch 34:3
During the eighteenth * of his 2Ch 34:8
* of the reign of Josiah. 2Ch 35:19
But in the first * of King Cyrus 2Ch 36:22,23
DURING THE FIRST * of the reign of Ez 1:1
* of their arrival at Jerusalem. Ez 3:8
until the second * of the reign of Ez 4:24
during the first * of his reign, Ez 5:13
"In this first * of the reign of Ez 6:3
in the sixth * of the reign of Ez 6:15
in the seventh * of the reign of Ez 7:7,8,9
In December of the twentieth * of Neh 1:1
the thirty-second * of the reign of Neh 5:14
work every seventh * and to forgive Neh 10:31
regular times each *—the families Neh 10:34
the thirty-second * of the reign of Neh 13:6
IT WAS THE third * of the reign of Est 1:1
This was the * of the great Est 1:1
of the seventh * of his reign. Est 2:16
of the twelfth * of the reign of Est 3:7
* was the date indicated. Est 3:7
of the following *, and their Est 3:13
days at the appointed time each *. Est 9:27
Every * when each of Job's sons Job 1:4
the days of the month of that *. Job 3:6
THE * KING Uzziah died I saw the Is 6:1
came to me the * King Ahaz died: Is 14:28
IN THE * when Sargon, king of Is 20:1
"But a long * from now, Is 21:16
the * of a hireling," like 16:14. Is 21:16f
the city of David. * after year Is 29:1
Year after * you make your many Is 29:1
little more than a *—suddenly Is 32:10
of vengeance, the * of recompense Is 34:8
SO IN THE fourteenth * of King Is 36:1
from the king of Assyria: This * Is 37:30
next *, and two years from now Is 37:30
in the thirteenth * of the reign of Jer 1:1
of the eleventh * of the reign of Jer 1:3
them rain each * in spring and fall Jer 5:23,24
at God's appointed time each *; Jer 8:7
brief months in the * 609 B.C. Jer 22:11f
during the fourth * of the reign of Jer 25:1
This was the * Nebuchadnezzar, Jer 25:1
the thirteenth * of the reign of Jer 25:2,3
during the first * of the reign of Jer 26:1
ON A DECEMBER day in that same * Jer 28:1
year—the fourth * of the reign of Jer 28:1
This very * your life will end Jer 28:16
Lord in the tenth * of the reign of Jer 32:1
* of Nebuchadnezzar's reign). Jer 32:1
day after day, * after year, I Jer 32:33
day after day, year after *, I Jer 32:33
IN THE FOURTH * Jer 36:1
of the fifth * of the reign of King Jer 36:9
IT WAS IN January of the ninth * Jer 39:1
in the fourth * of the reign of Jer 45:1
in the fourth * of the reign of Jer 46:2
C., the * King Josiah died. Jer 47:1f
For rumors will keep coming * by Jer 51:46
rumors will keep coming year by *. Jer 51:46
During the fourth * of Zedekiah's Jer 51:59
In the ninth * of Zedekiah's Jer 52:4
month during the nineteenth * Jer 52:12
in the seventh * of Jer 52:28
On February 25, of the 37th * of Jer 52:31
of Babylon that *, was kind to King Jer 52:31
Literally, "in the thirtieth *." Eze 1:1f
* of punishment ahead for Israel. Eze 4:4,5
Each day will represent one *. Eze 4:6
* of King Jehoiachin's captivity, Eze 8:1
Literally, "in the seventh * of Eze 20:1f
of the ninth * (of King Eze 24:1
in the eleventh * (after King Eze 26:1
LATE IN DECEMBER of the tenth * Eze 29:1
In the twenty-seventh * of King Eze 29:17
A * later, Eze 30:20
C., the * Jerusalem fell to Eze 30:20f
of the eleventh * of King Eze 30:20
IN MID-MAY OF the eleventh * of Eze 31:1
It was the * 587 B.C. Eze 31:1f
C., the * Jerusalem fell. Eze 31:1f
IN MID-FEBRUARY OF the twelfth * Eze 32:1
Literally, "In the twelfth *, on Eze 32:17f
read, "In the twelfth *." Eze 33:21f
* of our exile, late in December, Eze 33:21
the twenty-fifth * of our exile—the Eze 40:1
fourteenth * after Jerusalem was Eze 40:1
the first month of the Hebrew *. Eze 45:18f
it only until the * of Release Eze 46:17
seventh *) when he is set free; Eze 46:17
* of the reign of King Cyrus. Dan 1:21
ONE NIGHT IN the second * of his Dan 2:1
ONE NIGHT DURING the first * of Dan 7:1
IN THE THIRD * of the reign of Dan 8:1
IT WAS NOW the first * of the Dan 9:1
In that first * of his reign, Dan 9:2
IN THE THIRD * of the reign of Dan 10:1
Mede in the first * of his reign. Dan 11:1
do each * at the Tabernacle Feast. Hos 12:9
my fruit to you throughout the *. Hos 14:8
the events of the * 612 B.C. Nah 2:1f
* of the reign of King Darius I. Hag 1:1
of the second * of King Darius' Hag 1:14,15
IN EARLY OCTOBER of the same *, Hag 2:1
in the second * of the reign of Hag 2:10
* of the reign of King Darius. Zec 1:1
in the second * of the reign of Zec 1:7
* of the reign of King Darius. Zec 7:1
*, as they had been doing so long. Zec 7:3
to Jerusalem each * to worship the Zec 14:16
prisoner each * during the Passover Mt 27:15
This * there was a particularly Mt 27:16
prisoner each * at Passover Mk 15:6
which they attended each *. Lk 2:41,42
IN THE FIFTEENTH * of the reign of Lk 3:1
the acceptable * of the Lord." Lk 4:18,19f
'Leave it another *, and I'll Lk 13:8
If we get figs next *, fine; Lk 13:9
High Priest that *, said, "You Jn 11:49
Caiaphas, the High Priest that *. Jn 18:13
from prison each * at Passover. Jn 18:39
*, teaching the many new converts. Act 11:26
there the next * and a half, Act 18:11
because it was late in the *, Act 27:9
For God had promised, "Next * I Rom 9:9
started to do a * ago, for you were 2Co 8:10
ready to send an offering a * ago. 2Co 9:2
then only once a *, all alone, and Heb 9:7
in the Holy of Holies each *. Heb 9:25
again and again, * after year, but Heb 10:1
again, year after *, but even so Heb 10:1
town, stay there a *, and open up a Jas 4:13
readiness for that * and month and Rev 9:15

YEAR-OLD
This animal shall be a * male, Ex 12:5
the Lord, a * lamb without defect. Num 6:14
of his children, except for his * 2Ki 11:2,3

YEAR'S
be used for next * seed, and as Gen 47:24
the first of each * crop to the Ex 34:26
a sample of each * new crops by Num 15:19,20,21
use it as seed for next * crop; 2Ki 19:29
Lord God says: On each New * Day Eze 45:18
Literally, "200 denarii," a * Mk 6:37f

YEARLING
"Each day offer two * lambs upon Ex 29:38
offering, also a * calf and a Lev 9:3
calf and a * lamb, all without Lev 9:3
she must bring a * lamb as a burnt Lev 12:6
defect, one * ewe-lamb without Lev 14:10
to the Lord a male * lamb without Lev 23:12
to the Lord seven * lambs without Lev 23:18
male * lambs for a peace offering. Lev 23:19
a * ewe lamb without defect; Num 6:14
a male * lamb as burnt offerings; Num 7:15
male goats, and five male * lambs. Num 7:17
12 * male goats (with the grain Num 7:87
* male lambs—each without defect. Num 28:3
day, sacrifice two * male Num 28:9,10
male * lambs—all without defect. Num 28:11
* male lambs—all without defect. Num 28:19
one ram, and seven * male lambs. Num 28:27
* male lambs—all without defect. Num 29:2
one ram, seven * male lambs—each Num 29:8
and fourteen male * lambs —each Num 29:13
and fourteen male * lambs—each Num 29:17

(YEARLING Con't)
fourteen male * lambs—each without Num 29:20
and fourteen male * lambs—each Num 29:23
and fourteen male * lambs—each Num 29:26,27
and fourteen male * lambs—each Num 29:29
and fourteen male * lambs—each Num 29:32
ram, seven male * lambs—each Num 29:36
"Each morning a * lamb must be Eze 46:13
Lord with offerings of * calves?" Mic 6:6

YEARLY
happened: those * sacrifices Heb 10:3

YEARNS
because my heart * for Jerusalem, I Is 62:1

YEARS
earth, and mark the days and *." Gen 1:14,15
Adam: Adam was 130 * old when his Gen 5:3,4,5
Adam lived another 800 *, Gen 5:3,4,5
Seth: Seth was 105 * old when his Gen 5:6,7,8
Afterwards he lived another 807 * Gen 5:6,7,8
Enosh: Enosh was ninety * old Gen 5:9,10,11
Afterwards he lived another 815 * Gen 5:9,10,11
Kenan: Kenan was seventy * old Gen 5:12,13,14
Afterwards he lived another 840 * Gen 5:12,13,14
* old when his son Jared was born. Gen 5:15,16,17
Afterwards he lived 830 *, Gen 5:15,16,17
Jared: Jared was 162 * old when Gen 5:18,19,20
Afterwards he lived another 800 * Gen 5:18,19,20
Enoch: Enoch was sixty-five * old Gen 5:21-24
Afterwards he lived another 300 * Gen 5:21-24
Methuselah: Methuselah was 187 * Gen 5:25,26,27
afterwards he lived another 782 * Gen 5:25,26,27
Lamech: Lamech was 182 * old when Gen 5:28-31
Afterwards Lamech lived 595 *, Gen 5:28-31
Noah: Noah was 500 * old and had Gen 5:32
I will give him 120 * to mend his Gen 6:3
He was 600 * old when the flood Gen 7:6
when Noah was 600 *, two months, Gen 7:10,11,12
Noah lived another 350 * after Gen 9:28
and was 950 * old at his death. Gen 9:29
born two * after the flood when Gen 11:10,11
the flood when Shem was 100 * old; Gen 11:10,11
after that he lived another 500 * Gen 11:10,11
When Arpachshad was thirty-five * Gen 11:12,13
lived another 403 *, and had many Gen 11:12,13
Shelah was thirty * old when his Gen 11:14,15
born, living 403 * after that, and Gen 11:14,15
Eber was thirty-four * old when Gen 11:16,17
He lived another 430 * Gen 11:16,17
Peleg was thirty * old when his Gen 11:18,19
He lived another 209 * Gen 11:18,19
Reu was thirty-two * old when Gen 11:20,21
He lived 207 * after that, with Gen 11:20,21
Serug was thirty * old when his Gen 11:22,23
He lived 200 * afterwards, with Gen 11:22,23
Nahor was twenty-nine * old at Gen 11:24,25
He lived 119 * afterwards, and Gen 11:24,25
By the time Terah was seventy * Gen 11:26
when he was 145 * old, so that his Gen 11:32f
Abram was seventy-five * old at Gen 12:4
For twelve * they had all been Gen 14:4
in a foreign land for 400 *. Gen 15:13
(This took place ten * after Gen 16:2,3
(Abram was eighty-six * old at Gen 16:16
WHEN ABRAM WAS ninety-nine * old, Gen 17:1
"Me—100 * old? Gen 17:17
Abraham was ninety-nine * old at Gen 17:24-27
(Abraham was 100 * old at that Gen 21:4,5
WHEN SARAH WAS 127 * old, she Gen 23:1
Isaac was forty * old when he Gen 25:20
for even after many * of marriage Gen 25:21
Isaac was sixty * old when the Gen 25:26
work for you seven * if you'll give Gen 29:18
So Jacob spent the next seven * Gen 29:20
"I worked for seven * for Gen 29:25
to work for me another seven *!" Gen 29:27
Jacob agreed to work seven more *. Gen 29:28
and worked the additional seven *. Gen 29:30
through these many *, and how your Gen 30:29
Twenty * I've been with you, and Gen 31:38
Yes, twenty *—fourteen of them Gen 31:41
and six * to get the flock! Gen 31:41
Joseph was now seventeen * old. Gen 37:2
ONE NIGHT TWO * later, Pharaoh Gen 41:1
are seven * of prosperity ahead. Gen 41:26
will be seven * of famine following Gen 41:27
the seven * of prosperity. Gen 41:27
The next seven * will be a period Gen 41:29
will be seven * of famine so great Gen 41:30
of the good * will be erased. Gen 41:31
of the next seven *, so that there Gen 41:34,35
when the seven * of famine come. Gen 41:36
He was thirty * old as he Gen 41:46
for the next seven * there were Gen 41:47
During those *, Joseph Gen 41:48
After seven * of this, the Gen 41:49
of the famine *, two sons were born Gen 41:50
So at last the seven * of plenty Gen 41:53
Then the seven * of famine Gen 41:54
These two * of famine will grow Gen 45:6
five * of famine ahead of us. Gen 45:11,12
130 long, hard *, and I am not Gen 47:9
Jacob lived seventeen * after Gen 47:28
* old at the time of his death. Gen 47:28
Joseph was 110 * old when he Gen 50:22
hundred * after Joseph's death. Ex 1:8f
One day, many * later Ex 2:11
Several * later the king of Egypt Ex 2:23
(Levi lived 137 *. Ex 6:16
(Kohath lived 133 *. Ex 6:18
Moses was eighty * old and Aaron Ex 7:7
lived in Egypt 430 *, and it was on Ex 12:40,41
the manna forty * until they Ex 16:35
serve only six * and be freed in Ex 21:2
the end of six * as the men are. Ex 21:7
your crops for six *, but let the Ex 23:10
who were twenty * old or older, a Ex 38:25,26
For six * you may sow your field Lev 25:3
forty-nine *, a fair price shall be Lev 25:14,15,16
the number of * until the Jubilee. Lev 25:14,15,16
If the Jubilee is many * away, Lev 25:14,15,16
if few *, the price will be low; Lev 25:14,15,16
to the number of * left before the Lev 25:50
a servant for that number of *. Lev 25:50
If there are still many * until Lev 25:51
if the * have passed and only a Lev 25:52
* you refused to let it lie idle; Lev 26:34,35
desolate all the * that you are Lev 26:34,35
A boy one month to five * old Lev 27:6
to the number of * remaining until Lev 27:18
all the men twenty * old and older Num 1:2-15
who were twenty * old or older to Num 1:17,18,19
thirty to fifty * of age who were Num 4:35
thirty to fifty * old and who were Num 4:46,47,48
been founded seven * before Tanis Num 13:22
Not a single one of you twenty * Num 14:29
desert like nomads for forty * Num 14:33
for forty *—a year for each day, Num 14:34,35
given you over the * through Moses, Num 15:22
who are twenty * old or older, to Num 26:2
Forty * earlier, at the time of Num 26:64,65f
* of age, and so were not counted. Num 26:64,65f
twenty * of age were now dead. Num 26:64,65f
no one over twenty * of age would Num 32:10,11
for forty * until all that evil Num 32:13
when he was 123 * old. Num 33:38,39
forty * after the people of Deu 1:1
"It was forty * ago, at Mount Deu 1:6
For many * we wandered around in Deu 2:1
all these forty * as you have Deu 2:7
"So it took us thirty-eight * to Deu 2:14,15
who thirty-eight * earlier were old Deu 2:14,15
long, prosperous * ahead of you. Deu 6:2
"In the * to come when your son Deu 6:20
all those forty *, humbling you and Deu 8:2
For all these forty * your Deu 8:4
through all the * you were Deu 11:5
that for six * he has cost you less Deu 15:18
For forty * God has led you Deu 29:5
told them, "I am now 120 * old! Deu 31:2
Moses was 120 * old when he died, Deu 34:7
thing the Lord did forty * ago Jos 4:23
died during the * in the Jos 5:4,5
for forty * until all the men who Jos 5:6
It took seven * Jos 11:18
"I was forty * old at the time, Jos 14:7
these forty-five * since Jos 14:10
and today I am eighty-five * old. Jos 14:10
in the wilderness for many *. Jos 24:7
In later * when the Israelis Ju 1:28
were under his rule for eight *. Ju 3:8
Then, for forty * under Othni-el, Ju 3:11
For the next eighteen * the Ju 3:14
at peace for the next eighty *. Ju 3:30
for the Israelis for twenty *. Ju 4:2,3
was peace in the land for forty *. Ju 5:31
the people of Midian, for seven *. Ju 6:1
*—all during Gideon's lifetime. Ju 8:28
Three * later God stirred up Ju 9:22,23
Israel's judge for twenty-three *. Ju 10:2
judged Israel for twenty-two *. Ju 10:3
This went on for eighteen *. Ju 10:9
But now after three hundred * Ju 11:26
was Israel's judge for six *. Ju 12:7
He judged Israel for seven * Ju 12:9,10
He judged Israel for ten * and Ju 12:11,12
He was Israel's judge for eight * Ju 12:14
them in subjection for forty *. Ju 13:1
the next twenty *, but the Ju 15:20
He had judged Israel for twenty * Ju 16:31
(Eli was ninety-eight * old and 1Sa 4:15
He had judged Israel for forty *. 1Sa 4:18
there for twenty *, and during that 1Sa 7:2
"Saul was * old when he 1Sa 13:1f
and two * over Israel." 1Sa 13:1f
He's been with me for *, and I've 1Sa 29:3
Ish-bosheth was forty * old at 2Sa 2:10,11
He reigned in Mahanaim for two *; 2Sa 2:10,11
for seven and one-half *. 2Sa 2:10,11
He was five * old at the time 2Sa 4:4
seven *, since the age of thirty. 2Sa 5:4,5
He then ruled thirty-three * in 2Sa 5:4,5
so he reigned for forty * 2Sa 5:4,5
Then, two * later, when Absalom's 2Sa 13:21-24
and stayed there three *. 2Sa 13:37,38,39
Jerusalem for two * and had not yet 2Sa 14:28
After four *, Absalom said to the 2Sa 15:7,8
I am eighty * old today, and 2Sa 19:35
year for three *, and David spent 2Sa 21:1
you choose seven * of famine across 2Sa 24:13
Israel for forty *, seven of them 1Ki 2:11
But three * later two of 1Ki 2:39
(This was 480 * after the people 1Ki 6:1
So it took seven * to build. 1Ki 6:38
took thirteen * to construct. 1Ki 7:1
At the end of the twenty * during 1Ki 9:10
once every three * a great load of 1Ki 10:22
family of Edom. * before, when 1Ki 11:15
for forty *, and then died and was 1Ki 11:42
Jeroboam reigned twenty-two *, 1Ki 14:20
He was forty-one * old when he 1Ki 14:21
throne seventeen * in Jerusalem, 1Ki 14:21
Israel, and reigned forty-one *. 1Ki 15:10
He reigned two *, beginning in 1Ki 15:25
Baasha reigned for twenty-four *, 1Ki 15:32,33
Judah, but he reigned only two *. 1Ki 16:8
throne thirty-one * when Omri began 1Ki 16:23
twelve *, six of them in Tirzah. 1Ki 16:23
thirty-eight * when Ahab became the 1Ki 16:29
and Ahab reigned for twenty-two * 1Ki 16:29
several * until I say the word!" 1Ki 17:1
IT WAS THREE * later that the Lord 1Ki 18:1
FOR THREE * there was no war 1Ki 22:1
Jehoshaphat was thirty-five * 1Ki 22:42
in Jerusalem for twenty-five *. 1Ki 22:42
and he reigned two *. 1Ki 22:51
and he reigned twelve *. 2Ki 3:1
that will last for seven *." 2Ki 8:1
of the Philistines for seven *. 2Ki 8:2
Jehoram was thirty-two * old 2Ki 8:17
reigned in Jerusalem for eight *. 2Ki 8:17
Ahaziah was twenty-two * old 2Ki 8:26
in Samaria, for twenty-eight *. 2Ki 10:36
They lived there for six * while 2Ki 11:2,3
Joash was seven * old when he 2Ki 11:21
IT WAS SEVEN * after Jehu had 2Ki 12:1
reigned in Jerusalem for forty *. 2Ki 12:1
reigned in Samaria for sixteen *. 2Ki 13:9,10
Amaziah was twenty-five * old at 2Ki 14:2
in Jerusalem for twenty-nine *. 2Ki 14:2
Amaziah lived fifteen * longer 2Ki 14:17
reign lasted forty-one *. 2Ki 14:23
Length of his reign: 52 *, in 2Ki 15:1
beginning of his reign: 16 * old 2Ki 15:1
had been the king there for 27 *. 2Ki 15:1
had been the king there for 38 * 2Ki 15:8
had been the king there for 39 * 2Ki 15:13
Length of reign: 10 *, in Samaria 2Ki 15:17
had been the king there for 39 * 2Ki 15:17
Length of reign: 3 *, in Samaria 2Ki 15:23
had been the king there for 50 * 2Ki 15:23
Length of reign: 20 *, in Samaria 2Ki 15:27
had been the king there for 52 * 2Ki 15:27
had been the king there for 20 * 2Ki 15:30
His age when he became king: 25 * 2Ki 15:32,33
Duration of his reign: 16 *, in 2Ki 15:32,33
had been the king there for 2 * 2Ki 15:32,33
Age: 20 * old 2Ki 16:1
Duration of reign: 16 *, in 2Ki 16:1
had been the king there for 17 * 2Ki 16:1
Length of his reign: 9 *, in 2Ki 17:1
had been the king there for 12 * 2Ki 17:1
troops for three * besieging 2Ki 17:5
Length of his reign: 29 *, in 2Ki 18:1
beginning of his reign: 25 * old 2Ki 18:1
had been the king there for 3 * 2Ki 18:1
Three * later (during the sixth 2Ki 18:10
I will add fifteen * to his life 2Ki 20:6
age at beginning of his reign:12 * 2Ki 21:1
Length of his reign: 55 *, in 2Ki 21:1
beginning of his reign: 22 * old 2Ki 21:19,20
Length of his reign: 2 *, in 2Ki 21:19,20
beginning of his reign: 8 * old 2Ki 22:1
Duration of his reign: 31 * in 2Ki 22:1
like it in all the * of the kings 2Ki 23:22
His age when he became king: 23 * 2Ki 23:31,32
His age when he became king: 25 * 2Ki 23:36,37
Length of his reign: 11 *, in 2Ki 23:36,37
for three *, but then rebelled. 2Ki 24:1
beginning of his reign: 18 * old 2Ki 24:8,9
His age when he became king: 21 * 2Ki 24:18,19
Length of his reign: 11 *, in 2Ki 24:18,19
he reigned seven and one-half *. 1Ch 3:4
he reigned another thirty-three *. 1Ch 3:4
* that he was under house arrest: 1Ch 3:17,18
You may have three * of famine, 1Ch 21:12
Levi who were thirty * or older. 1Ch 23:3
who were twenty * old or older were 1Ch 23:24
of the land of Israel for forty *; 1Ch 29:26,27
the Tabernacle 500 * before the 2Ch 1:2,3f
IT WAS NOW twenty * since Solomon 2Ch 8:1
Every three * the king sent his 2Ch 9:21
over all of Israel for forty *. 2Ch 9:30
for three * without difficulty; 2Ch 11:17

RS Con't)
luring those * there was an 2Ch 11:17
; Rehoboam reigned seventeen * 2Ch 12:13
asted three *. 2Ch 13:1
he first ten * of his reign, 2Ch 14:1
nd did not worship idols. 2Ch 17:3
w * later he went down to 2Ch 18:2
vas thirty-five * old, and 2Ch 20:31
nty-five *, in Jerusalem. 2Ch 20:31
was thirty-two * old when he 2Ch 21:5
eigned eight *, in Jerusalem. 2Ch 21:5
ne end of two *, his intestines 2Ch 21:19
was thirty-two * old when he 2Ch 21:20
t *, and died unmourned. 2Ch 21:20
ziah was twenty-two * old 2Ch 22:2
rally, "forty-two * old"; 2Ch 22:2f
hile Athaliah reigned as queen. 2Ch 22:12
ASH WAS SEVEN * old when he 2Ch 24:1
eigned forty *, in Jerusalem. 2Ch 24:1
AZIAH WAS TWENTY-FIVE * old 2Ch 25:1
nty-nine *, in Jerusalem. 2Ch 25:1
,000 men twenty * old and older, 2Ch 25:5,6
or fifteen * after the death of 2Ch 25:25
ll, he reigned fifty-two *, 2Ch 26:3
THAM WAS TWENTY-FIVE * old at 2Ch 27:1
ned sixteen *, in Jerusalem. 2Ch 27:1
the next three * he received 2Ch 27:5
was twenty-five * old when he 2Ch 27:8
ned sixteen *, in Jerusalem. 2Ch 27:8
AZ WAS TWENTY * old when he 2Ch 28:1
ned sixteen *, in Jerusalem. 2Ch 28:1
ZEKIAH WAS TWENTY-FIVE * old 2Ch 29:1
nty-nine *, in Jerusalem. 2Ch 29:1
rally, "males from three * 2Ch 31:16f
Levites twenty * old and older 2Ch 31:17,18
NASSEH WAS ONLY twelve * old 2Ch 33:1
-five *, in Jerusalem. 2Ch 33:1
on was twenty-two * old when he 2Ch 33:20,21
he lasted for only two *. 2Ch 33:20,21
y * of his father Manasseh; 2Ch 33:22
SIAH WAS ONLY eight * old when 2Ch 34:1
reigned thirty-one *, in 2Ch 34:1
when he was sixteen * old, 2Ch 34:3
four * later he began to 2Ch 34:3
was twenty-three * old when 2Ch 36:2
oiakim was twenty-five * old 2Ch 36:5
reigned eleven *, in Jerusalem; 2Ch 36:5
oiachin was eight * old when 2Ch 36:9
lekiah was twenty-one * old 2Ch 36:11
reigned eleven *, in Jerusalem. 2Ch 36:11
for seventy * to make up for 2Ch 36:21
make up for the * when the 2Ch 36:21
the Babylonians for seventy *. Ez 1:1f
Levites who were twenty * old Ez 3:8
entire twelve * that I was Neh 5:14
forty * you sustained them Neh 9:21
re patient with them for many *. Neh 9:30
h tragedy. My * disappear like Job 9:26
h, for the * gone by when God Job 29:2
, in my early *, when the Job 29:4
lived 140 * after that, Job 42:16
through the * of infancy. Ps 22:9,10,11
m pining away with grief; my * Ps 31:9,10
d in all my * I have never seen Ps 37:25
led * of life, as rich and full Ps 61:6
m * of terror and disaster. Ps 78:33
sert * and grieved his heart. Ps 78:40
thousand * are but as Ps 90:4
wonder the * are long and Ps 90:9
venty * are given us! Ps 90:10
t even the best of these * are Ps 90:10
place the evil * with good. Ps 90:15
or forty * I watched them in Ps 95:10
me die half through my *! Ps 102:24
u are forever, and your * never Ps 102:27
the * that followed, the Ps 105:24
t his * be few and brief; Ps 109:8
se * of my earthly pilgrimage. Ps 119:54
of your life more fruitful." Pro 9:11
early * while there is hope. Pro 19:18
ezekiah lived 200 * after Pro 25:1f
ough a man lives a thousand * Ecc 6:6
fore the evil * come—when you'll Ecc 12:1
nd within sixty-five * Ephraim, Is 7:8
irteen * after this Is 7:8f
thin a couple of *, before this Is 8:4
at within three *, without fail, Is 16:13,14
the last three *, is a symbol Is 20:3
vithin three *, according to the Is 21:16f
r seventy * Tyre will be Is 23:15,16
es, after seventy *, the Lord Is 23:17
ose fruitful vines of other * Is 32:12
ext year, and two * from now Is 37:30
ill let you live fifteen more *. Is 38:5
am robbed of my normal *, and Is 38:10
hat occurred in * gone by, or what Is 41:22
his was written many * before Is 44:28f
u've worshiped all these *. Is 47:12
rried them through all the *. Is 63:9
ildren in the * to come! Jer 2:9
et for * on end my people have Jer 2:32
For the past twenty-three *, Jer 25:2,3
down through the *, God has sent Jer 25:4
the king of Babylon for seventy *. Jer 25:11
Then, after these * Jer 25:12
Literally, "the seventy *." Jer 25:12f
Within two * I will bring back Jer 28:3
that within two * he will release Jer 28:11
for you will be there many *. Jer 29:5
Literally, "for seventy *." Jer 29:10f
plan to stay many *, that we should Jer 29:28
there for many * until you die. Jer 32:5
must be freed after serving six *. Jer 34:14
besieged it. Two * later, in the Jer 39:2
This event occurred six * after Jer 51:59f
ZEDEKIAH WAS TWENTY-ONE * old Jer 52:1
he reigned eleven * in Jerusalem. Jer 52:1
laid siege to the city for two *. Jer 52:5
Then, eleven * later, he took Jer 52:29
five * after that he sent Jer 52:30
I can never forget these awful *; Lam 3:20
in June, when I was thirty * old, Eze 1:1
for 390 * by captivity and doom. Eze 4:4,5
the * of Judah's punishment. Eze 4:6
"And in all these * of adultery Eze 16:22
* after King Jeconiah was Eze 20:1
have reached the limit of your *. Eze 22:4
For forty * not a soul will pass Eze 29:11
lie as wastelands for forty *. Eze 29:12
end of the forty * he will bring Eze 29:13
during those thirteen * at Tyre, Eze 29:20
that through the * of exile lay Eze 36:34
In distant * you will swoop down Eze 38:8
future—in the latter * of history. Eze 38:15,16
that after many * had passed, I Eze 38:17
fuel—enough to last them seven *. Eze 39:9
For seven * they will need Eze 39:10
THREE * AFTER King Jehoiakim began Dan 1:1
For seven * let him have the Dan 4:16
For seven * let him eat grass Dan 4:23
For seven * this will be your Dan 4:25
the cows for seven * until you Dan 4:32
"At the end of seven * Dan 4:34
his hands for three and a half *. Dan 7:25
must lie desolate for seventy *. Dan 9:2
down through the *, with your Dan 9:6
"The Lord has commanded 490 * Dan 9:24
or "seventy sevens" (of *). Dan 9:24f
It will be forty-nine * plus 434 Dan 9:25
be forty-nine years plus 434 *. Dan 9:25
This totals 483 *, instead of the Dan 9:25f
instead of the 490 * mentioned in Dan 9:25f
24, leaving seven * unaccounted for Dan 9:25f
three and a half * as at least a Dan 9:25f
"After this period of 434 *, the Dan 9:26
of this prophecy is many * away." Dan 10:14
"Several * later an alliance Dan 11:6
fulfilled many * later in the Dan 11:6f
and for many * afterward he will Dan 11:8
"A few * later the Syrian king Dan 11:13
not end until three and a half * Dan 12:7
Three and a half * (verse 7) plus Dan 12:11f
of Israel twenty-five * later. Hos 1:4,5f
came about twenty * later and the Hos 4:19f
*: Zechariah, Shallum, Pekahiah. Hos 13:11f
to tell you? In * to come, tell Joe 1:3
* before the earthquake. Amo 1:2
the desert forty *, to possess the Amo 2:10
to me for forty * while you were Amo 5:25,26,27
fifty-one * before this prophecy. Nah 3:8f
and twenty-five * later had Hab 1:6f
help us, as you did in * gone by. Hab 3:2
followed about ten * after this Zep 1:1f
and then, a dozen * later, the Zep 1:1f
Christ who, 500 * later, came often Hag 2:8,9f
Hosts, for seventy * your anger has Zec 1:12
those seventy * of exile when you Zec 7:5
Long * ago, when Jerusalem was Zec 7:7
to you through the *, the Mal 2:14
every baby boy two * old and under, Mt 2:16
appeared to them two * before. Mt 2:16
sick for twelve * with internal Mt 9:20
for twelve * with a hemorrhage. Mk 5:25
through the * and had become poor Mk 5:26
(She was twelve * old. Mk 5:41,42
though dead for hundreds of *, Mk 12:27
my wife is also well along in *." Lk 1:18
for eighty-four * following seven Lk 2:36,37
following seven * of marriage. Lk 2:36,37
was known for wisdom beyond his *; Lk 2:40
When Jesus was twelve * old he Lk 2:41,42
Jesus was about thirty * old when Lk 3:23-38
*, and hunger stalked the land; Lk 4:25,26
dying, a little girl twelve * old. Lk 8:42
for twelve *, and could find no Lk 8:43,44
enough stored away for * to come. Lk 12:19
'I've waited three * and there Lk 13:7
for eighteen * and was unable to Lk 13:11
has held her for eighteen *?" Lk 13:16
'All these * I've worked hard for Lk 15:29
land to live for several *. Lk 20:9
"It took forty-six * to build Jn 2:20
had been sick for thirty-eight *. Jn 5:5
* old—sure, you've seen Abraham!" Jn 8:57
man who had been lame for forty *. Act 4:22
and there become slaves for 400 *. Act 7:6
"Forty * later, in the desert Act 7:30
the wilderness for forty *. Act 7:36
forty * in the desert, Israel? Act 7:42
by the Angel. * later, when Joshua Act 7:45
been a sorcerer there for many *; Act 8:9,10,11
and bedridden for eight *. Act 9:33
them through forty * of wandering Act 13:18
Judges ruled for about 450 *, and Act 13:19,20
Benjamin, who reigned for forty *. Act 13:21
This went on for the next two *, Act 19:10
Remember the three * I was with Act 20:31
who led a rebellion a few * ago Act 21:37,38
what awaits you in the * ahead.' Act 22:10
affairs for many *, and this gives Act 24:10
"After several * away, I Act 24:17
him. Two * went by in this way; Act 24:27
Paul lived for the next two * in Act 28:30
And * later, when this son, Rom 9:10-13
after all these long * of waiting. Rom 15:23
Fourteen * ago I 2Co 12:2,3
It was not until three * later Gal 1:18
THEN FOURTEEN * later I went back Gal 2:1
hundred and thirty * later when God Gal 3:17
days or months or seasons or *. Gal 4:10
should be at least sixty * old 1Ti 5:9
and your * will never end." Heb 1:12
with them forty *, though they Heb 3:9
God angry for all those forty *? Heb 3:17
King David long * after man's first Heb 4:7
for hundreds of * until Jesus Heb 10:4f
us for a few brief *, doing the Heb 12:10
You have spent your * here on Jas 5:5
for the next three and one half *! Jas 5:17
but long * later, during yours. 1Pe 1:12
day or a thousand * from now is 2Pe 3:8
keep without change through the *. Jud 1:3
with him for three *, and from Rev 1:13f
3½ *, as in Daniel 12:7. Rev 11:2f
3½ *, as in Daniel 12:7. Rev 11:3f
three and a half * they prophesy, Rev 11:6
three and a half * of their solemn Rev 11:7
Dragon, for three and a half *. Rev 12:14
chains for 1,000 *, and threw him Rev 20:2
the thousand * were finished. Rev 20:3
with Christ for a thousand *. Rev 20:4
until the thousand * had ended. Rev 20:5
shall reign with him a thousand *. Rev 20:6
When the thousand * end, Satan Rev 20:7

YEAST
to eat only bread made without *. Ex 12:15
Only bread without * may be Ex 12:18
be no trace of * in your homes; Ex 12:19
anything that has * in it shall be Ex 12:19
must not eat anything made with *; Ex 12:20
dough without *, and bound their Ex 12:34
of this event you are to use no *; Ex 13:3
only bread without *, and there Ex 13:6,7
there must be no * in your homes, Ex 13:6,7
*, just as I commanded you before. Ex 23:15
bread made without *, and thin Ex 29:2
with olive oil but without *. Lev 2:4
Wafers made without * and spread Lev 2:4
*, and mingled with olive oil. Lev 2:5
"Use no * with your offerings of Lev 2:11
for no * or honey is permitted in Lev 2:11
You may offer * bread and honey Lev 2:12
it shall be eaten without * in Lev 6:16
it is baked it must be without *. Lev 6:17
basket of bread made without *; Lev 8:1
bushel of fine flour containing *. Lev 23:17
a basket of bread made without * Num 6:15
basket of bread made without *. Num 6:17
(made without *), and one of the Num 6:19
(also made without *), and put them Num 6:19
For seven days no trace of * Deu 16:4
shall eat no bread made with *. Deu 16:8
made without * (either fried or 1Ch 23:29
Only bread without * shall be Eze 45:21
and mixes in the * until it Mt 13:33
"beware of the * of the Mt 16:6
But again I say, 'Beware of the * Mt 16:11
that by "*" he meant the wrong Mt 16:12
bread made with * was purged from Mt 26:17
"Beware of the * of King Herod and Mk 8:15
no bread made with * was eaten. Mk 14:1
It will become as evident as * Lk 12:2
It is like * kneaded into dough, Lk 13:20,21
bread made without * was used. Lk 22:1

YEASTLESS
serve only * bread." Ex 12:20
* dough they had brought along. Ex 12:39
It was * because the people were Ex 12:39

YELL
All he wants to do is *. Pro 18:2

YELLED
"Stand back," they *. Gen 19:9
out of here," the Egyptians *. Ex 14:25

(YELLED Con't)
Joshua * to the people, "Shout! Jos 6:16
and wild animals," Goliath *. 1Sa 17:44
he * at him. "Do you think I 1Sa 20:30
blew a trumpet and *, "We want 2Sa 20:1
"Throw her down!" he *. 2Ki 9:33
"You liar!" he *. 2Ch 18:23
they *. Ps 137:7
they *. Jer 26:9
furnace and *: "Shadrach, Meshach, Dan 3:26
quiet, but they only * the louder. Mt 20:31
And the mob * back, "His blood Mt 27:25
King of the Jews," they *. Mt 27:29
some of the people * at him. Mk 10:48
they * at him. Mk 15:29,30
they * at him. Mk 15:32
man, but he only * the louder, Lk 18:39
"Away with him," they *. Jn 19:15
But Paul * to him, "Don't do it! Act 16:28
They * and threw their coats Act 22:23

YELLING
left hands, all *, "For the Lord Ju 7:19,20
after them, * at them to stop. Ju 18:23
at the door and * at the old man to Ju 19:22
Then they saluted, *, "Yea! Mk 15:18
officials began *, "Crucify! Jn 19:6
They grabbed him, *, "Men of Act 21:28

YELLOW
below the skin and * hair is found Lev 13:29,30
not spread and no * hair has Lev 13:32
to see if any * hair develops, Lev 13:36
black, red, white, and * marble. Est 1:6
turning sere and * when half grown, Ps 129:6,7
the housetops, burnt * by the sun. Is 37:27
some were sky-blue and others *. Rev 9:17,18

YES
"*," Adam admitted, "but it Gen 3:12
that I created. *, and the animals Gen 6:7
because of man. *, I will destroy Gen 6:12,13
made like God. *, have many Gen 9:7
a great nation. *, you are pregnant Gen 16:9-12
a son from her! *, I will bless her Gen 17:16
And Abraham said to God, "*, do Gen 17:18
men of the city—*, Sodomites, young Gen 19:4
said, '*, he is my brother.' Gen 20:5
"*, I know," the Lord replied. Gen 20:6
"*, Lord?" Gen 22:1
"Take with you your only son—*, Gen 22:2
"*, Lord!" Gen 22:11
and she says, '*, certainly, and I Gen 24:14
she replied. "*, we have plenty Gen 24:25
successful. *, find a girl from Gen 24:40
So tell me, * or no. Gen 24:49
Take her and go! *, let her be Gen 24:51
And she replied, "*, I will go." Gen 24:58
Esau: "*, father?" Gen 27:1
Isaac: "*? Gen 27:18
Jacob: "*, of course." Gen 27:24
sleepless nights. *, twenty Gen 31:41
a great nation, *, many nations; Gen 35:11
Abraham and Isaac. *, I will give Gen 35:12
"*," the man told him, "they Gen 37:17
"*," he sobbed, "it is my son's Gen 37:33
"*, you are," he insisted. Gen 42:12
"*," they replied. Gen 43:28
and we said, '*, we have a father, Gen 44:20
a great nation. *, it was God who Gen 45:8
* -Jacob answered Gen 46:2
"*," Joseph told him, "these Gen 48:9
"*, do!" Ex 2:8
Jebusites live. *, the wail of the Ex 3:9
sent me!' *, tell them, 'Jehovah, Ex 3:15
"*," Moses said, "I will ask Ex 8:29
*, Jehovah is his name. Ex 15:3
"*" or "no" on urgent matters. Ex 28:30,31f
by my glory. *, I will sanctify Ex 29:44
makes you holy. *, rest on the Ex 31:14,15
to Moses, "*, I will do what you Ex 33:17
the Promised Land; *, it is an Ex 34:9
"*" or "No" alternatives. Lev 8:8f
"*, all these abominations have Lev 18:27
in the fields. *, during the Year Lev 25:13
*, I will desolate your land; Lev 26:32
in enemy lands. *, then the land Lev 26:34,35
is pursuing them. *, though none Lev 26:37
*, the Levites shall be mine; Num 3:45
to say, '*, let it be so.' Num 5:21,22
Egyptians. *, I have accepted the Num 8:18
*, one law for all!" Num 15:15,16
*, I am the Lord, your God." Num 15:41
before the altar. *, I have given Num 18:19
Jehovah says! *, I shall return Num 24:14
"*, you are strongly situated, Num 24:21,22
arms, had died. *, the hand of the Deu 2:14,15
stone tablets. *, it was at that Deu 4:14
really obey him? *, he humbled you Deu 8:3
you refused to obey him. *, you Deu 9:24
*, fat and bloated; Deu 32:15
succeed. *, be bold and strong! Jos 1:9
here in the land. *, we choose the Jos 24:18
"*," they replied, "we are Jos 24:22
The people replied to Joshua, "* Jos 24:24
*, bless the Lord! Ju 5:2
*, even Mount Sinai quaked Ju 5:5
*, the tribe of Reuben has an Ju 5:16
*, may she be blessed Ju 5:24
like locusts—*, like the sand upon Ju 7:12,13
"*," he said. Ju 11:38
"*," he replied, "I am." Ju 13:11
"*," the priest replied, "all Ju 18:6
And the Lord said, "*." Ju 20:22,23,24
"*, I know," Boaz replied, "and Ru 2:10,11
*, from a pile of ashes— 1Sa 2:8
"*?" 1Sa 3:4,5
* -he asked 1Sa 3:6
* -he asked 1Sa 3:8
say, '*, Lord, I'm listening.' 1Sa 3:9
And Samuel replied, "*, I'm 1Sa 3:10
"*, send it back with a gift," 1Sa 6:3
"*," they replied, "stay right 1Sa 9:12,13
"*, it is true," they replied. 1Sa 12:5
"*, let's go across to those 1Sa 14:6
"*, Jonathan," Saul said, "you 1Sa 14:44
admitted. "*, I have disobeyed 1Sa 15:24
Then Jonathan said, "*, they 1Sa 20:18
impure. *, surely that must be it! 1Sa 20:26
"*, go and save Keilah," the 1Sa 23:2
And the Lord replied, "*, they 1Sa 23:12
me good for evil. *, you have been 1Sa 24:18
And David replied, "*, sir, it 1Sa 26:17,18
And the Lord told him, "*, go 1Sa 30:8
And the Lord replied, "*." 2Sa 2:1
"*," he called back, "it is." 2Sa 2:20
And the Lord replied, "*, go 2Sa 5:19
joy in the Lord. *, and I am 2Sa 6:22
"*, sir, I am," he replied. 2Sa 9:2
"*," Ziba replied, "Jonathan's 2Sa 9:3
Then Nathan replied, "*, but the 2Sa 12:13
"*," they replied, "he is." 2Sa 12:19
in Israel. *, the king will give 2Sa 14:17
"*, my lord?" 2Sa 14:18
can I deny it? *, Joab sent me and 2Sa 14:19
"*, but let me go anyway," he 2Sa 18:23
*, you hold me safe above their 2Sa 22:49
*, God has made 2Sa 23:5
of your enemies— *, I'll give you 1Ki 3:12
throne of Israel. *, O God of 1Ki 8:26
place to pray; *, hear in heaven 1Ki 8:30
I'll be harder! *, my father was 1Ki 12:11
"*," he replied, "I am." 1Ki 13:14
"*, it is," Elijah replied. 1Ki 18:8
"*," the prophet answered. 1Ki 20:14
"*, your brother Ben-hadad!" 1Ki 20:33
"*," Elijah answered, "I have 1Ki 21:20
And they all said, "*, go ahead, 1Ki 22:6
"*," she told Gehazi, 2Ki 4:26
"*," he said, "but my master 2Ki 5:22
Elisha replied, "Tell him, '*.' 2Ki 8:10
"*," Jehonadab replied. 2Ki 10:15
was very angry. *, they worshiped 2Ki 17:12
the Lord, *—but they also worshiped 2Ki 17:41
*, the peaks of Lebanon. 2Ki 19:23
And the Lord replied, "*, I 1Ch 14:10
Sing to him; *, sing his praises 1Ch 16:9
Seek the Lord; *, seek his 1Ch 16:11
*, ascribe to the Lord 1Ch 16:29
guide my people— *, I am giving 2Ch 1:12
as you have.' *, Lord God of 2Ch 6:17
this Temple; *, hear us from 2Ch 6:20,21
"*, O my God, be wide awake and 2Ch 6:40
And all the others agreed. "*," 2Ch 18:11
over in Israel. *, as wicked as 2Ch 21:6
in doing wrong. *, he was as evil 2Ch 22:4
room for Israel. *, he sacrificed 2Ch 28:4
" *, the Lord will destroy this 2Ch 34:24
against you; *, I and my people Neh 1:6,7
punch line: "*, and Esther the Est 5:12
eternal darkness. *, let the Job 3:5
"*, I realize you know Job 12:2
to my neighbors. *, I, a righteous Job 12:4
the ground. *, with him is Job 12:16
the consequences. *, I will take Job 13:14
by his fate. *, that is what Job 18:21
Then he will be on my side! *, I Job 19:27
penalty himself. *, let him be Job 21:20
as a pledge—*, you must have Job 22:6
lift you up again. *, he will save Job 22:29
for the ocean, *, and a boundary Job 26:10
full of clothing— *, he may order Job 27:17
the darkness; *, in my early Job 29:4
out to be fools, *, children of no Job 30:8
it in my hearing, *, you've said it Job 33:8
"*, God often does these things Job 33:29
attention of God. *, he hears the Job 34:28
by dry rushes. *, his breath would Job 41:21
down upon us. *, the gladness you Ps 4:7
I will be glad, *, filled with Ps 9:2
me, O God! *, listen as I pray. Ps 17:6
these wild oxen. *, God will answer Ps 22:21
*, I will stand and praise you Ps 22:25
in battle. *, open wide the gates Ps 24:9
stumble and fall! *, though a Ps 27:3
*, wait and he will help you. Ps 27:
from my foes. *, you are my Rock Ps 3
We trust his holy name. *, Lord, Ps 33:
from the earth. *, the Lord hears Ps 34:
cloth; *, man is frail as breath. Ps 39:
I shall yet praise him again. *, Ps 42:4
God not know it? *, he knows the Ps 44:
our God, our King. *, sing your Ps 47:6
But I was born a sinner, *, from Ps 51
from the heart; *, utter sincerity Ps 51
confidence in you. *, I will trust Ps 56:3
do to me! *, praise his promises. Ps 56:10,
*, be exalted, O God, above the Ps 57:
us to our foes! *, Lord, help us Ps 60:
from him alone. *, he alone is my Ps 62
from him alone. *, he alone is my Ps 62
from childhood. *, you have been Ps 71
continue in the skies! *, forever! Ps 72
gifts. *, kings from everywhere! Ps 72:1
proud and wicked. *, all through Ps 73
"*," the Lord replies, "and Ps 75
I long, *, faint with longing to Ps 84
of your people—*, covered over each Ps 85
*, the Lord pours down his Ps 85:1
on your favor! *, our protection Ps 89:1
poisonous snakes, *, even trample Ps 91:1
all my heart. *, I will bless the Ps 103
of his commands. *, bless the Ps 103:2
bottom. *, as dry as any desert! Ps 106
They were envious of Moses; *, Ps 106:1
beyond expression. *, happy is the Ps 112
your children. *, Jehovah who made Ps 115:1
I shall live! *, in his Ps 116
*, they surround and attack me; Ps 118:1
your promise—*, Lord, to save Ps 119:40,41,4
constant guide. *, wiser than my Ps 119:9
your commands. *, rescue me and Ps 119:15
*, I have searched for them. Ps 119:16
*, glorious things! Ps 126:
shall reap joy. *, they go out Ps 126
*, my begging has been stilled. Ps 131:
HALLELUJAH! *, LET his people Ps 135:
continues forever; *, a Ps 136:2
hear your voice. *, they shall Ps 138:
with them? *, I hate them, for Ps 139:2
*, happy are those whose God is Ps 144:12-1
PRAISE THE LORD! *, really praise Ps 146:
*, even with my dying breath. Ps 146:
HALLELUJAH! *, PRAISE the Lord! Ps 147:
Hallelujah! *, praise the Lord! Ps 147:2
Hallelujah! *, praise the Lord! Ps 148:1
HALLELUJAH! *, PRAISE the Lord! Ps 149:
HALLELUJAH! *, PRAISE the Lord! Ps 150:
Praise him with the cymbals, *, Ps 150:
and good sense. *, if you want Pro 2:3,4,
hills were made. *, I was born Pro 8:2
retort; *, he will snarl at you. Pro 9:7,8
*, the liberal man shall be rich! Pro 11:24,2
What a shame—*, how stupid! Pro 18:1
of common sense. *, my heart will Pro 23:15,1
help themselves. *, speak up for Pro 31:9
*, BUT THERE is a very serious Ecc 6:1
influence on us. *, a wise man Ecc 7:4
do what he says. *, there is a Ecc 8:6,7
perfume to stink! *, a small Ecc 10:1
to seven, *, even to eight." Ecc 11:2
*, remember your Creator now Ecc 12:6
King Solomon: "*, a lily among Sol 2:2
birds has come. *, spring is here. Sol 2:12
are made of honey. *, honey and Sol 4:11
eat and drink! *, drink deeply!" Sol 5:1
land of Tirzah, *, beautiful as Sol 6:4
like two fawns, *, lovely twins. Sol 7:3
And he said, "*, go. Is 6:9
Rezin and Pekah. *, the kings of Is 7:5
for war against us—and perish! *! Is 8:9,10
and orphans. *, it is true that Is 10:2
we did Damascus. *, we have Is 10:10
his people. *, it has already been Is 10:23
—*, a new Branch Is 11:1
That rod is broken, *; Is 14:29
Therefore all Moab weeps. *, Is 16:7
Lord of Hosts. *, the glory of Is 17:4
to the Egyptians. *, they will know Is 19:21
"*, I will drive you out of Is 22:19
is remembered. *, after seventy Is 23:17
will be ashamed! *, let them be Is 26:11
The proud city of Samaria—*, the Is 28:3
with flowers. *, there will be an Is 35:2
"*, now I see it all—it was good Is 38:17
become slaves, *, eunuchs, in the Is 39:7
God is coming!" *, the Lord God Is 40:10
the future holds. *, that's it! Is 41:23
in the wilderness, *, springs in Is 43:20
I, *, I alone am he who blots Is 43:25
of Israel, says—*, it is Israel's Is 44:6
and forests, *, and every tree; Is 44:23
all your lifetime, *, even when Is 46:4
*, I'll tell you things entirely Is 48:8
Yet for my own sake—*, for my Is 48:11
you were cut! *, think about your Is 51:1

Con't)
amine and the sword. Is 51:19
I, *, I, who speaks to them. Is 52:6
en they see him—*, even far-off Is 52:14,15
answer. "*, I am here," he Is 58:9
broad daylight, *, even at Is 59:10
we know what sinners we are. Is 59:12
ruth is gone, and anyone who Is 59:15
ill repay. *, I will repay Is 65:6
" he said, "for terror from Jer 1:14
er gods—*, idols they themselves Jer 1:16
p on pleading; *, even with your Jer 2:9
d they reply, *, we will come, Jer 3:22
and your grapes and figs; Jer 5:17
even my prophets and priests! Jer 6:13
hear or answer. *, I will Jer 7:13,14
ır out my anger, *, my fury on Jer 7:20
*, even you people of Judah. Jer 9:25,26
s the Lord. *, I will certainly Jer 15:21
y more. *, I will bring you back Jer 16:14,15
give me peace. *, bring double Jer 17:18
says the Lord, I will be found Jer 29:14
vill punish you, *—you will not Jer 30:11
hard for me? *, I will give Jer 32:28
ve disappeared. *, fields shall Jer 32:44
ies of Judah. *, the day will Jer 33:14
ır vows. *, I will butcher you, Jer 34:18,19
," said Jeremiah, "there is! Jer 37:17
live in Egypt. *, you will die Jer 42:17
backward glance. *, terror shall Jer 46:5
til it is sated, *, drunk with Jer 46:10
distant land. *, Israel shall Jer 46:27
great. *, I wail for Moab, my Jer 48:31
ere is shouting, *, but not the Jer 48:33
prepare to fight with Babylon, Jer 50:14
march against Babylon, the Jer 50:21
e God of Hosts. *, come against Jer 50:26
e charioteer— *, and the Jer 51:22
says the Lord. Jer 51:52
the Lord has vanquished Israel Lam 2:5
u heard my weeping! *, you Lam 3:57
their snares. *, even our mighty Lam 4:20
, the time has come; Eze 7:12
u are saying? *, I know it is, Eze 11:5
ults?' *, it will surely fall. Eze 13:13
r your love! *, you are an Eze 16:32
, your sisters, Sodom and Eze 16:55
stroyed her. *, the terrors that Eze 23:32
any treasures. *, your wisdom has Eze 28:5
r his army. *, I have given him Eze 29:20
eople of Thebes. *, I will set Eze 30:16
his sides. *, when I place my Eze 30:25
u her light. *, darkness will be Eze 32:8
ave never seen. *, terror shall Eze 32:10
cry for the sorrows of Egypt. Eze 32:16
l their people. *, they Eze 32:25
rtile and good. *, I will give Eze 34:14
will feed them, *—feed them Eze 34:15,16
ome among them. *, I will be their Eze 37:27
built is holy. *, this is the Eze 43:12
*," they said, "we did indeed, Dan 3:24
*," the king replied, "it is Dan 6:12
s you see us now; *, all of us—the Dan 9:7
e strong—*, strong!" Dan 10:19
ind of sin. *, I have seen a Hos 6:10
The inspired men are mad." *, Hos 9:7
ll are doomed. *, it will be a Hos 9:12
SRAEL IS CHASING the wind, *, Hos 12:1
ought with God. *, he wrestled Hos 12:4
n all your lifetime, *, in all Joe 1:2
and on a snake. *, that will be a Amo 5:20
drink it, too; *, drink and stagger Ob 1:16
*," Jonah said, "it is; Jon 4:9
er mother-in-law. *, a man's Mic 7:6
*," replies the Lord, "I will Mic 7:15
, I will punish those who Zep 1:9
, and in the highlands, too; Hag 1:11
And the priests answered, "*." Hag 2:13
Satan; *, I, the Lord, for I have Zec 3:2
greatly concerned—*, furiously Zec 8:2
Let's go now!' *, many people, Zec 8:22
'I will strengthen Judah, *, and Zec 10:6
*, you will escape as your people Zec 14:5
altar of the Lord—*, even the sick Mal 1:8
you great joy. *, he is surely Mal 3:1
'*, in Bethlehem," they said, Mt 2:5
Say just a simple '*, I will' or Mt 5:37
on the fire. *, the way to Mt 7:20
"*," Jesus said, "I will come Mt 8:7
"*, Lord," they told him, "we Mt 9:28
the synagogues. *, and you must Mt 10:18
me, *, to witness to the world. Mt 10:18
Or a prophet of God? *, and he Mt 11:9
little children. *, Father, for it Mt 11:26
say "*," so they could arrest Mt 12:10
than a sheep! *, it is right to do Mt 12:12
"*," they said, "we do." Mt 13:51
"*, it is!" Mt 15:27
"*," they replied, "we are Mt 20:22
"*," Jesus replied. Mt 21:16
and he said, '*, sir, I will.' Mt 21:30
Hypocrites! *, woe upon you Mt 23:15
"*, woe upon you, Pharisees, and Mt 23:23
mercy and faith. *, you should Mt 23:23
"*, woe to you, Pharisees, and Mt 23:29,30
the sanctuary. *, all the Mt 23:36
And Jesus had told him, "*." Mt 26:25
"*," Jesus said, "I am. Mt 26:64
"*," Jesus replied. Mt 27:11
The man looked around. "*!" Mk 8:24
"Oh, *," they said, "we are!" Mk 10:39
Jesus replied, "*, look! Mk 13:2
"*, these are the events that Mk 13:30
"*," Jesus replied, "it is as Mk 15:2
to our ancestors, *, to Abraham Lk 1:72,73
The Savior—*, the Messiah, the Lk 2:11
and cut you down. *, every tree Lk 3:9
much loved Son, *, my delight." Lk 3:22
When that happens, rejoice! *, Lk 6:23
But did you find a prophet? *! Lk 7:26
Another said, "*, Lord, I will Lk 9:61
their remorse. *, Tyre and Sidon Lk 10:14
"*," he told them, "I saw Lk 10:18
*, thank you, Father, for that is Lk 10:21
Then Jesus said, "*, now go and Lk 10:37
He replied, "*, but even more Lk 11:28
You should tithe, *, but you Lk 11:42
the markets! *, awesome judgment Lk 11:44
"*," said Jesus, "the same Lk 11:46
and the sanctuary. *, it will Lk 11:51
"*, every man is a fool who gets Lk 12:21
my destination. *, today, Lk 13:33
or sisters—*, more than his own Lk 14:26
the man replied. '*, here is the Lk 16:5,6
them all. *, it will be 'business Lk 17:30
plead with him day and night? *! Lk 18:8
"*," Jesus replied, "and Lk 18:29
" '*,' the king replied, 'but it Lk 19:26
as a criminal!' *, everything Lk 22:37
And he replied, "*, I am." Lk 22:70
"*," Jesus replied, "it is as Lk 23:3
When they told him *, Pilate said Lk 23:7
And he said, "*, it was written Lk 24:46
someone else, *, John the Baptist, Jn 5:32,33
life! *, I am the Bread of Life! Jn 6:48-51
called out, "*, you know me and Jn 7:28
These stupid crowds do, *; Jn 7:49
indeed be free— (*, I realize that Jn 8:37
Some said *, and some said no. Jn 9:9
"*, Lord," the man said, "I Jn 9:38
listen to them. *, I am the Gate. Jn 10:9
"*," Martha said, "when Jn 11:24
"*, Master," she told him. Jn 11:27
and exclaimed, "*, it is true—one Jn 13:21
Jesus told him, "I am the Way—*, Jn 14:6
will do for you. *, ask anything, Jn 14:14
"*, I am the Vine; Jn 15:5
*, your cup of joy will overflow! Jn 15:11
the Father or me. *, I'm telling Jn 16:4
from the Father. *, I came from Jn 16:28
"*," Jesus said. Jn 18:37
"*," Peter replied, "You know I Jn 21:15
"*, Lord," Peter said, "you Jn 21:16
men dream dreams. *, the Holy Act 2:18
"*," she replied, "we did." Act 5:8
and murdered. *, and you Act 7:53
"*, Lord!" Act 9:10
he said, '*, John baptized with Act 11:16
praising God! "*," they said, Act 11:18
Lord's work humbly—*, and with Act 20:19
"*, I certainly am." Act 22:27
and the Gentiles. *, I am going to Act 26:17
God's very own—*, his holy people. Rom 1:6,7
uncivilized alike; *, to the Rom 1:14
*, they knew about him all right, Rom 1:21
they wanted to—*, vile and sinful Rom 1:24
*, you know what he wants; Rom 2:18
*, you teach others—then why Rom 2:21
ceremony? *, being a Jew has many Rom 3:2
been like. *, all have sinned; Rom 3:23
put out of sight. *, what joy Rom 4:8
Jesus Christ. *, Adam's sin Rom 5:18
Have they heard God's Word? *, Rom 10:18
? *, for even back in the time of Rom 10:19
start bragging. *, it is true that Rom 11:25
confess to God." *, each of us Rom 14:12
Oh, *, and I baptized the 1Co 1:16
let me help them. *, whatever a 1Co 9:22
*, if she refuses to wear a 1Co 11:6
*, the body has many parts, not 1Co 12:14
most necessary. *, we are 1Co 12:23
to life again. *, they are weak, 1Co 15:43
a terrible death; *, and we expect 2Co 1:10
"*" when he really means "no"? 2Co 1:17
of person. My "*" means "yes." 2Co 1:18
My "yes" means "*." 2Co 1:18
He isn't one to say "*" when he 2Co 1:19
in Christ. *, even today when they 2Co 3:15
*, we live under constant danger 2Co 4:11
*, God will give you much so that 2Co 9:11
I PLEAD WITH you—*, I, Paul—and I 2Co 10:1
and disunity. *, I am afraid that 2Co 12:21
we told you about; *, if an angel Gal 1:8
*, and those who depend on the Gal 3:10
or leader. *, his honor is far more Eph 1:21
in the Lord—*, to the point of Eph 4:13
for the better. *, you must be a Eph 4:24
May God bless you all. *, I pray Php 1:2
*, I am still needed down here Php 1:25
And sincere? *, so much so that Php 3:6
in Christ alone. *, everything Php 3:8
It is you! *, you will bring us 1Th 2:19
Now we beg you—*, we demand of 1Th 4:1
and murder. *, these laws are made 1Ti 1:10,11
*, but they won't really believe 2Ti 3:5
delivered me. *, and those who 2Ti 3:12
*, and the Lord will always 2Ti 4:18
your very soul! *, dear brother, Phm 1:20
those who believe; *, God has Heb 2:4
death for us. *, because of God's Heb 2:9
but as a human being—*, a Jew. Heb 2:16
*, the old system of priesthood Heb 7:18
of sacrifice; *, to slay even Heb 11:18
* indeed, it is good when you Jas 2:8
harvest to ripen. *, be patient. Jas 5:8
just say a simple * or no, so Jas 5:12
Message to men. *, our natural 1Pe 1:24
*, he is very precious to you who 1Pe 2:7
are his children. *, dear friends, 1Jn 3:2
—*, not only at his baptism but 1Jn 5:6,7,8
Christ our Lord; *, splendor and Jud 1:24,25
and every eye shall see him—*, Rev 1:7
and in terror when he comes. *! Rev 1:7
to idol feasts. *, you have some Rev 2:15
* take it and eat it," he said. Rev 10:9
their full reward. *, says the Rev 14:13
say, "*, Lord God Almighty, your Rev 16:7
*, God himself will be among them. Rev 21:3

YESTERDAY
me as you did that Egyptian *?" Ex 2:14
your quotas either * or today?" Ex 5:14
for dinner either * or today?" 1Sa 20:27
It seems but * that you arrived, 2Sa 15:19,20
born but * and know so little; Job 8:9
A thousand years are but as * to Ps 90:4
they replied, "* afternoon at Jn 4:52
me as you killed that Egyptian *?' Act 7:28
Jesus Christ is the same *, Heb 13:8

YET
and suffering; * even so, you shall Gen 3:16
slept with her *, so he said, Gen 20:4
ever have a baby? * I have given Gen 21:7
face, and * my life is spared." Gen 32:30
land of Egypt. * even then Pharaoh Ex 7:4
cattle were dead, * when he found Ex 9:7
even * you will not obey him." Ex 9:30
they were not * out of the ground. Ex 9:32
officials sinned * more by their Ex 9:34
Don't you know even * that all Ex 10:7
*, even though the elders saw Ex 24:11
gods of gold. * now if you will Ex 32:32
is not defiled; * anyone who pulls Lev 11:36
Literally, "not * redeemed, nor Lev 19:20f
on a trip, and * refuses to Num 9:13
and * you promise them meat for Num 11:21
will take you to * another place. Num 23:27
there shall be * another assembly Num 29:12
to harm an enemy—* the man dies, Num 35:22,23
war, and terror? * that is what the Deu 4:34
I say it * again: Jehovah your Deu 9:6
and * again at Kibroth-hattaavah. Deu 9:22
your God. And * he rejoiced in Deu 10:15
new house, but not * dedicated it? Deu 20:5
but not * eaten any of its fruit? Deu 20:6
she married; * here is the proof.' Deu 22:17,18
But even * the Lord hasn't given Deu 29:4
the wilderness, * your clothes Deu 29:5
old when he died, * his eyesight Deu 34:7
* told them where to build it). Jos 9:27
of Israel had not * entered and Jos 18:1
we have not even * been cleansed Jos 22:17,18
of the nations * unconquered as Jos 23:4,5
their enemies. * even then Israel Ju 2:17
"You haven't caught them *! Ju 8:6
the Midianites, * you have Ju 9:18
rescued you? * you continue to Ju 10:13
(Manoah didn't * realize that Ju 13:16
for they had not * driven out the Ju 18:1
Literally, "did not * know 1Sa 3:7f
your name greater *, so that you 2Sa 7:9
years and had not * seen the king, 2Sa 14:28
concubines; and * you act like 2Sa 19:5
are holding out. * you are my own 2Sa 19:11,12
of the Lord hadn't * been built. 1Ki 3:2
I have built! And *, O Lord my 1Ki 8:28
gods. * Solomon did it anyway. 1Ki 11:2
he will kill me; * I have been a 1Ki 18:12
instructed him. * even so he 2Ki 12:3
to deliver it. * perhaps the Lord 2Ki 19:4
the birthright, * Judah was a 1Ch 5:2
You know that I am but a dog, * 1Ch 17:18
had the people as * really decided 2Ch 20:33
me have never * failed to conquer a 2Ch 32:13

(YET Con't)

nation has ever * been able to	2Ch 32:15
though it is not * completed.	Ez 5:16
or why, for as * I had said nothing	Neh 2:16
protested. "* we must sell our	Neh 5:5
every ten days. * I refused to make	Neh 5:18
we had not * hung all the doors of	Neh 6:1
conquer them. * whenever your	Neh 9:28
again! But *," he added, "all	Est 5:13
I was not fat and lazy, *	Job 3:26
He will * fill your mouth with	Job 8:21
" 'You have made me, and * you	Job 10:8
" '* all the time your real	Job 10:13,14
Or, "Though he slay me, * will I	Job 13:15f
be a wise man, and * you give us	Job 15:2
"* I am innocent, and my prayer	Job 16:17
"* even now the Witness to my	Job 16:19
"*, finally, the innocent shall	Job 17:8
was wrong, you have * to prove it.	Job 19:4
nose in the air, * he shall perish	Job 20:7
people like that. * the wicked get	Job 21:17
thing like that.) * they forgot	Job 22:18
the wounded cry for help; * God	Job 24:12
"* sometimes	Job 24:22,23
very great now, * in a moment they	Job 24:24
about him as I do; * you are saying	Job 27:12
arguments and * had condemned him.	Job 32:3
being oppressed. * when he chooses	Job 34:29,30
power of the rich; * none of them	Job 35:9,10
"God is almighty and * does not	Job 36:5
the Almighty, and * he is so just	Job 37:23
to him! And * you have made him	Ps 8:5
For you have never * forsaken	Ps 9:10
looking for him! * there is	Ps 10:5
generations * unborn shall hear	Ps 22:31
did them no wrong, * they laid a	Ps 35:7
I am poor and needy, * the Lord	Ps 40:17
I shall * praise him again.	Ps 42:4,5
* I am standing here depressed	Ps 42:6
* day by day the Lord also pours	Ps 42:8
you enough! And * for a time, O	Ps 44:9
rich they are, * not one of them,	Ps 49:7
applauds success— * in the end he	Ps 49:19
fighting me, * he will rescue me.	Ps 55:18
wrong. * they prepare to kill me.	Ps 59:4
Suddenly the deed is done, * they	Ps 64:4
to your people. * it is so hard to	Ps 73:16
my spirits droop, * God remains!	Ps 73:26
live in turmoil, * its pillars are	Ps 75:3
like a river! * they kept on with	Ps 78:17
and the meat was * in their mouths,	Ps 78:30
young men. * even so the people	Ps 78:32
their promises. * he was merciful	Ps 78:38
* though he did all this for	Ps 78:56
And *—blessed be the Lord	Ps 89:52
their sins, * punished them when	Ps 99:8
* how quickly they forgot again!	Ps 106:13
by their sin. *, even so, he	Ps 106:44
to hate and fight me, * they do!	Ps 109:3
a roaring flame. * beneath his flag	Ps 118:12
finished me off, * I refused to	Ps 119:87
how can we sing? * our captors, our	Ps 137:3,4
is very great. * though he is so	Ps 138:6
make them work, * they labor hard	Pro 6:8
he is looking for, * it comes	Pro 14:6
There is hope for you *!	Pro 23:17,18
to his mouth! * in his own opinion	Pro 26:16
to catch and kill, * are found even	Pro 30:24-28
fool is blind. And * I noticed that	Ecc 2:13,14
man or a fool? And * all I have	Ecc 2:19
a son or brother, * he works hard	Ecc 4:8
Literally, "and there are *	Ecc 5:8f
its existence, * that is better	Ecc 6:5
Both have the same problem, * the	Ecc 6:7,8
it is * in its mother's womb.	Ecc 11:5
pomegranates were blossoming *.	Sol 6:11
They are man-made, and * you	Is 2:8
* a tenth—a remnant—will survive;	Is 6:13
and destroyed, * Israel will be	Is 6:13
and judgment, * in the future these	Is 9:1
That is why his anger is not *	Is 9:17
against Judah. * even after all of	Is 9:21
God's anger is not * satisfied.	Is 9:21
forest, * it will be destroyed.	Is 10:18
along the shore, * only a few of	Is 10:22
but I am not through with Dibon *!	Is 15:9
that you plant it, * you will never	Is 17:11
* [the distant time will come when	Is 23:18
all our efforts. * we have this	Is 26:19
them his mercy. * the time will	Is 27:12
whenever he can; * over this	Is 28:13
Zoan and Hanes, * it will all turn	Is 30:5
mountain tops. * the Lord still	Is 30:18
of affliction, * he will be with	Is 30:20
for strength, * you rely on him for	Is 36:5
But do you not * know that it	Is 37:26
Don't you * understand?	Is 40:28
them in battle. *, though set on	Is 42:25
with sacrifices. * my requests for	Is 43:23
any help at all. * he cannot bring	Is 44:20
and through. * for my own sake and	Is 48:9

in you at all. * for my own	Is 48:11
* even now, be free from your	Is 48:20
without response. * I leave it all	Is 49:4
* they say, "My Lord deserted	Is 49:14
for her own son? * even if that	Is 49:15
disappear? And * you have no fear	Is 51:13
he shall be highly exalted. *	Is 52:14,15
* it was our grief he bore, our	Is 53:4
to follow our own. * God laid on	Is 53:6
afflicted, * he never said a word.	Is 53:7
* it was the Lord's good plan to	Is 53:10
and tomorrow will be better *!"	Is 56:12
tell my people of their sins! *	Is 58:2
sweep us away. * no one calls upon	Is 64:7
And *, O Lord, you are our	Is 64:8
forbidden foods. * they say to one	Is 65:5
And *, the days will come	Is 65:16
and they are mine. * I will look	Is 66:2
thing as this. And * my people have	Jer 2:10,11
out from stone. * in time of	Jer 2:26,27
her wedding dress? * for years on	Jer 2:32
a cause. And * you say, "I	Jer 2:35
many lovers, * I have invited you	Jer 3:1
unashamed. And * you say to me,	Jer 3:4,5
of Israel. * she paid no	Jer 3:8
of the Lord has not stopped *.	Jer 4:8
on Jerusalem. * the sword is even	Jer 4:10
You can * be saved by casting out	Jer 4:14
"*," he says, "there will be a	Jer 4:27
the harvest times, * they have no	Jer 5:23,24
it's not there! * the priests and	Jer 6:14
* the Lord pleads with you still:	Jer 6:16
Israel says: Even *, if you quit	Jer 7:3
the land deserted. * the people	Jer 12:4
you grievously, * help us for the	Jer 14:7
and disease. And * the prophets and	Jer 14:18
is gone down while it is * day.	Jer 15:9
to pay—* they all curse me.	Jer 15:10
at their sins. * you have failed me	Jer 15:17,18
ON * ANOTHER occasion God spoke to	Jer 16:1
a trap to kill me, * I spoke well	Jer 18:20
it in any longer. * on every side	Jer 20:10
*, cursed be the day that I was	Jer 20:14
I have not sent these prophets, *	Jer 23:21
I gave them no message, * they	Jer 23:21
Judah, will all * be carried away	Jer 27:22
before. * God will rescue them!	Jer 30:7
kind to thousands, * children	Jer 32:18
it should! And * you say to buy	Jer 32:25
of the enemy, * the Babylonians	Jer 33:5
Perhaps even * they will turn	Jer 36:7
been imprisoned *, so he could go	Jer 37:4
in their tents, * they would	Jer 37:10
daughter of Egypt! * there is no	Jer 46:11
like stallions, * your mother	Jer 50:12
perhaps she can * be healed.	Jer 51:8
we rebelled. And *, O people	Lam 1:18
you have done. And *, O Lord, the	Lam 1:21
* there is one ray of hope: his	Lam 3:21
Although God gives him grief, *	Lam 3:32
gates! * God permitted it because	Lam 4:13
of the world, * I will be a	Eze 11:16
for perhaps even * they will	Eze 12:3
God did not send you. And * you	Eze 13:6
hair had grown; * you were naked.	Eze 16:6,7
solemn vows to me, * I will keep	Eze 16:59,60
"* you say: 'The Lord isn't	Eze 18:25
"And * the people of Israel keep	Eze 18:29
your sins while there is * time.	Eze 18:30
hags? * that is what they did.	Eze 23:44
Suddenly, she will die. * you	Eze 24:16
O Egypt? * your doom is the pit;	Eze 32:19
"And * your people are saying	Eze 33:17
he shall live. * you are saying	Eze 33:20
only one man and * he got	Eze 33:24
has fallen, * a third great power	Dan 2:39
Perhaps even * God will spare	Dan 4:27
this, * you have not been humble.	Dan 5:22
don't tell anyone about them *."	Dan 8:26
of wickedness, * because of all	Dan 9:16
history. And * every one of your	Dan 12:1
"* the time will come when	Hos 1:10
condemned him; * he doesn't return	Hos 7:10
* now they turn against me.	Hos 7:15
Perhaps even * he will decide to	Joe 2:14
"* think of all I did for them!	Amo 2:9
ever enough. * you wouldn't return	Amo 4:8
smell. And * you refused to come.	Amo 4:10
Perhaps even * the Lord God of	Amo 5:15
across the world. * I have promised	Amo 9:8
sifted in a sieve, * not one true	Amo 9:9
Perhaps even * God will decide to	Jon 3:9
* to this very hour my people	Mic 2:8
right from wrong, * you are the	Mic 3:2
you're paid. (And * you fawn upon	Mic 3:11
Judean village, * you will be the	Mic 5:2
in utter ruin." * no one anywhere	Nah 3:7
as Put and Libya. * Thebes fell	Nah 3:10
* I will rejoice in the Lord;	Hab 3:18
perhaps even * the Lord will	Zep 2:3
mildew and hail. *, even so, you	Hag 2:16,17

cattle—and * they will be safe.	Zec
and * forgiving them their sins!"	Zec
in the streets, * the Lord will	Zec
One, the Victor! * he is lowly,	Zec
prisoners, for there is * hope!	Zec 9:
a * future disaster foretold here?	Zec 13
* there will be continuous day!	Zec 1
I am your Father and Master, *	Mal
the same God. And * we are	Mal 2:
* you cover the altar with your	Mal 2:
earliest time, * you may still	Mal
Surely not! And * you have robbed	Mal
They don't worry about theirs. *	Mt 6:
You have no right to torment us *	Mt 8:
the Baptist. And *, even the lesser	Mt 11:
only one hour, and * you've paid	Mt 20:11,
must come, but the end is not *.	Mt 24
smallest of seeds, * it grows to	Mk 4:31,
Don't you even * have confidence	Mk 4:
"And * you think I'm worried	Mk 8:
Literally, "Do you not *	Mk 8:2
Take away this cup from me. * I	Mk 14:
* Elijah was not sent to them.	Lk 4:25,
than John. And * the least citizen	Lk 7:
Not much more than that. * God	Lk 12
(* those who speak against me	Lk 12:
their food, and * they get along	Lk 12:
They don't toil and spin, and *	Lk 12:
with my friends. * when this son	Lk 15:
It would be a colt, not * broken	Lk 19:
* my words remain forever true.	Lk 21:
*—stay here in the city until the	Lk 24:
"It isn't * my time for	Jn 2
teacher, and * you don't understand	Jn 3:10,
seen—and * you won't believe me.	Jn 3:10,
the Baptist was not * in prison.	Jn 3:23,
point to me! * you won't come to	Jn 5:4
"* it is not I who will accuse	Jn 5:4
Literally, "I go not up (*) unto	Jn 7:
The word "*" is included in	Jn 7:
for God's time had not * come.	Jn 7:3
But Jesus told them, "[Not *!	Jn 7:3
but the Spirit had not * been	Jn 7:3
* returned to his glory in heaven.	Jn 7:3
for his time had not * run out.	Jn 8:2
of Abraham!) And * some of you are	Jn 8:3
prophets died, and * you say that	Jn 8:5
"He can heal blind men, and *	Jn 9:3
Jesus replied, "Don't you even *	Jn 14:
these miracles and * they hated	Jn 15:2
leaving me alone. * I will not be	Jn 16:3
haven't * ascended to the Father.	Jn 20:1
fish; and * the net hadn't torn.	Jn 21:1
from Galilee, and * we hear them	Act 2:
as * he had no children!	Act 7:
Spirit, for as * he had not come	Act 8:1
Perhaps God will * forgive your	Act 8:2
'For I have never * eaten	Act 11:
* only a few days later, some	Act 14:1
do nothing rash. * you have	Act 19:3
against my life. * I never shrank	Act 20:2
same hope I have! *, O King, for me	Act 26:
for these crimes, * they went right	Rom 1:3
things is just. * some claim that	Rom 3:
glorious ideal; * now God declares	Rom 3:2
he had not * given his laws to	Rom 5:1
Adam and Christ who was * to come!	Rom 5:1
DON'T YOU UNDERSTAND *, dear	Rom 7:
at all.) *, even though Christ	Rom 8:1
* what we suffer now is nothing	Rom 8:1
something we don't * have—for a man	Rom 8:24
hasn't happened *, it teaches us to	Rom 8:2
* faith comes from listening to	Rom 10:17
to you Gentiles. * the Jews are	Rom 11:28
And * again, "Praise the Lord, O	Rom 15:1
Christ has never * been heard,	Rom 15:20
* when I am among mature	1Co 2:6
said about us. * right up to the	1Co 4:13
your purity, and * you let this	1Co 5:6
Haven't you * learned that your	1Co 6:19
What about girls who are not *	1Co 7:25
right to them? * we have never used	1Co 9:12
who accept it. * I have never	1Co 9:15
he pays my salary; * I have freely	1Co 9:19
refreshment. * after all this most	1Co 10:5
and punished. *, when we are	1Co 11:32
unbelievers aren't * ready for it.	1Co 14:22
other apostles, * actually I wasn't	1Co 15:10
Hadn't I really made up my mind *	2Co 1:17
come to visit you * is that I don't	2Co 1:23
* that old system of law that led	2Co 3:7
last very long. * this short time	2Co 4:17
heaven which we have not * seen.	2Co 4:18
We own nothing, and * we enjoy	2Co 6:10
was so very rich, * to help you he	2Co 8:9
himself would do. * some of you are	2Co 10:1
the surface. * if anyone can claim	2Co 10:7
* I don't feel that these	2Co 11:5
I have never * asked you for one	2Co 11:8,9
apostles. * I am not surprised!	2Co 11:14
a brainless fool. * those other	2Co 11:18

ET Con't)

'ou are so wise—* you listen gladly 2Co 11:19,20
inners, and * we Jewish Gal 2:16
here is, * I was the one chosen Eph 3:8
and dying—well, that's better *! Php 1:21
* it was because of this that God Php 2:9
* if anyone ever had reason to Php 3:4
all I should even *, but I keep Php 3:12
and actions, * now he has brought Col 1:21
desires were not * cut away. Col 2:13
we suffered there. * God gave us 1Th 2:2
there may * be in your faith. 1Th 3:10
* we hear that some of you are 2Th 3:11
We have not * seen all of this Heb 2:8
enter my rest." * the promise Heb 4:6
* while Christ was here on earth Heb 5:7
relative, and * Abraham paid him. Heb 7:6
For although Levi wasn't born *, Heb 7:10
After all, you have never * Heb 12:4
who love him. And *, of the two Jas 2:6
from them. And * the reason you Jas 4:2
is dropping fast, * it will stand Jas 5:3
as we are, and * when he prayed Jas 5:17
building the ark. * only eight 1Pe 3:20
the world began, * I myself have 1Jn 1:1
You have heard it all before. * 1Jn 2:8
For though we have never * seen 1Jn 4:12
* these false teachers carelessly Jud 1:8
Glorious Ones. * Michael, one of Jud 1:9
"* there is one thing wrong; Rev 2:4
worship; and * you have remained Rev 2:13
"And * I have a few things Rev 2:14
"* I have this against you: You Rev 2:20
"* even there in Sardis some Rev 3:4
Don't do anything *—hurt neither Rev 7:3
but isn't now. And *, soon he will Rev 17:8
and the seventh is * to come, but Rev 17:10
who have not * risen to power; Rev 17:12

IELD

No longer will it * crops for Gen 4:12
When you obey, the land will * Lev 25:19
and the land will * bumper crops, Lev 26:4,5
for your land shall not * its Lev 26:20
as they were, but * yourselves to 2Ch 30:8
The lush * of this land passes Neh 9:37
Or will you *? Job 40:2
to * and disobey your laws. Ps 119:87
He expected them to * a crop of Is 5:7
Ten bushels of seed will * but a Is 5:10
pastureland will * plenty of milk, Is 7:21,22
from then would * a bumper crop. Is 37:30f
The presses * no wine; Jer 48:33
and fields will * bumper crops, and Eze 34:27
and is willing to * to others; Jas 3:17

IELDED

and the Lord again * to my pleas Deu 10:10
* and got up and sat on the bed. 1Sa 28:23
For the earth has * abundant Ps 67:6,7
her wheedling, until he * to her. Pro 7:21
into good soil and * thirty times Mk 4:8
Literally, "* up the spirit." Lk 23:46f

YIELDING

I am like an evergreen tree, * my Hos 14:8

YIELDS

land and it * its bountiful crops. Ps 85:12
As the churning of cream * Pro 30:33

YIRON

Edre-i, Enhazor, *, Migdal-el, Jos 19:35-39

YOKE

of everything. A * of iron shall be Deu 28:47,48
in throwing off the * of Judah. 2Ch 21:10
you to do. You * yourselves with Is 30:1
Long ago you shook off my * and Jer 2:20
Make a * and fasten it on your Jer 27:2
you would strap a * on a plow-ox. Jer 27:2
your neck under Babylon's *! Jer 27:8
I have removed the * of the king of Jer 28:2
I will surely remove the * put on Jer 28:4
prophet, took the * off Jeremiah's Jer 28:10
broken a wooden * but these people Jer 28:13
says: I have put a * of iron on the Jer 28:14
I will break the * from their necks Jer 30:8
a calf must be trained for the *. Jer 31:18
to hitch me to a * of slavery. Lam 1:14
put her under a heavy * before; Hos 10:11
you from the * of slavery to this Nah 1:13
work so hard beneath a heavy *. Mt 11:28
Wear my *—for it fits Mt 11:29,30
Gentiles with a * that neither we Act 15:10

YOKED

defect, one that has never been *. Num 19:1
has never been *, and lead it to a Deu 21:3
before have been *—and shut their 1Sa 6:7

YOKES

instruments and ox * for wood to 2Sa 24:22
have * of iron on their necks. Jer 28:13

YONDER

and I will travel * and worship, Gen 22:5

YOU'D

Naturally * prefer a younger man, Ru 3:10
were with us. * better think fast, 1Sa 25:17
what I thought * do, Lord, when I Jon 4:2

YOU'LL

the serpent hissed. "* not Gen 3:4
if * give me Rachel as my wife." Gen 29:18
Make me your king and * soon Ju 9:29
they said. "* not get any of Ju 11:1
you and * soon be well again." 1Sa 16:15,16
him, "* be dead by morning." 1Sa 19:11
fellow is alive, * never be king. 1Sa 20:31
to eat so * regain your strength 1Sa 28:22
"* never come in here," they 2Sa 5:6
Tell him * feel better if she 2Sa 13:5
"* have to shout louder than 1Ki 18:27
king replied. "* have to pay." 1Ki 20:40
* pay for it with your own life." 2Ki 10:24
"* find out soon enough," 2Ch 18:24
his wealth, and * see him curse you Job 1:11
like standing grain, * not be Job 5:26
long. Soon * look upon me dead. Job 7:8
Some day * be in trouble, and Pro 1:26
If you live that kind of life, * Pro 4:12
Keep your mouth closed and * stay Pro 21:23
It is far better not to say * do Ecc 5:5
* no longer enjoy living. Ecc 12:1
strength; but * have none of this. Is 30:15
"Ugh!" * say to them. Is 30:22
* care, O careless ones. Is 32:10
For * get no help from Egypt. Is 36:8,9
* get no help from them at all. Is 47:14
come too close, * defile me! Is 65:5
" 'No,' he replied. '* hurt the Mt 13:29
From now on * be fishing for the Lk 5:10
boat, and * get plenty of them!" Jn 21:6

YOU'RE

exclaimed. "* going to wear Ex 18:18
Zebul said. "* just seeing Ju 9:36
Why come now when * in trouble?" Ju 11:7
"What about the sheep * supposed 1Sa 17:28
side. * not even sorry for me. 1Sa 22:8
"Well, Abner, * a great fellow, 1Sa 26:15
* as perfect as an angel of God. 1Sa 29:9
"* talking about yourself," 1Ki 18:18
you to the man * looking for." 2Ki 6:19
the whole story. * just trying to Neh 6:9
"Sure, I know all that. * not Job 9:2
"Stop, * doing it wrong!" Is 45:9
Then tell them: * getting the Jer 13:13
see your trick! * trying to stall Dan 2:8,9
preach and prophesy until * paid. Mic 3:11
"I don't know what * talking Mk 14:68
in three days! If * so wonderful, Mk 15:29,30
"So * the Messiah, are you? Lk 23:39
us, too, while * at it!" Lk 23:39
he said. "* different from Jn 2:10
to the man * living with now." Jn 4:17,18
hide like this! If * so great, Jn 7:4
The crowd replied, "* out of Jn 7:20
"I'm the man * looking for," he Act 10:21
They didn't believe her. "* out Act 12:15

YOU'VE

begged, "since * been so kind to Gen 19:18,19,20
saved my life, and * granted me Gen 19:18,19,20
"What is this * done to us?" Gen 20:9,10
"That Hebrew slave * had around Gen 39:17
"No, father," he said. "* got Gen 48:18
husband * turned out to be!" Ex 4:25,26
she whined. "* made fun of me Ju 16:15
Micah retorted. "* taken away Ju 18:24
"Tell me what * done," Saul 1Sa 14:43
she screamed, "* deceived me! 1Sa 28:12
king, as * so long desired." 2Sa 3:21
and confirm everything * said." 1Ki 1:14
told them, "* come the wrong way! 2Ki 6:19
whose hilltop altars * destroyed. 2Ki 18:22
been with you everywhere * gone; 1Ch 17:8
for he knows everything * done. Job 11:6
know these things * been saying? Job 12:3
my hearing, yes, * said it again Job 33:8
bird will tell them what * said. Ecc 10:20
"You boast of wells * dug in Is 37:25
Call out the demon hordes * Is 47:12
tree * bowed low before idols. Jer 2:20
my flock is what * trampled down; Eze 34:19
to drink is water that * fouled. Eze 34:19
with all of you for what * done. Hos 5:2
about the miracles * seen me do— Mt 11:4
one hour, and yet * paid them just Mt 20:11,12
years old—sure, * seen Abraham!" Jn 8:57
them with me—these * given me—so Jn 17:24
"Bring some of the fish * just Jn 21:10
As you know so well from what * Act 19:26

YOUNG

But Haran died *, in the land Gen 11:28
All I'll accept is what these * Gen 14:24
turtle-dove and a * pigeon, and to Gen 15:9
Sodomites, * and old from all over Gen 19:4
But the * men looked at him as Gen 19:14
son Isaac and two * men who were Gen 22:3
Abraham told the * men, "and the Gen 22:5
So they returned to his * men, Gen 22:19
about this, a beautiful * girl Gen 24:15,16
and bring me two * goats, and I'll Gen 27:8,9,10
hairy skin of the * goats, and Gen 27:16
herds have their *, and if they are Gen 33:13
daughters as wives for your * men. Gen 34:9,10
"I'll send you a * goat from my Gen 38:17
to take the * goat back to her, and Gen 38:20
way, was a very handsome * man. Gen 39:6
We told the dreams to a * Hebrew Gen 41:12
Judah is a * lion that has Gen 49:9
foreskin of her * son's penis, and Ex 4:25,26
"Do not boil a * goat in its Ex 23:19
Then he sent some of the * men Ex 24:5
as priests: get a * bull and two Ex 29:1
with the * bull and the two rams. Ex 29:3,4
"Then bring the * bull to the Ex 29:10
shall sacrifice a * bull as a sin Ex 29:36
the camp, but the * man who Ex 33:11
You must not cook a * goat in its Ex 34:26
either turtle-doves or * pigeons. Lev 1:14
he must offer a * bull without Lev 4:3
But the remainder of the * Lev 4:11,12
they shall offer a * bull for a sin Lev 4:14
The priest shall then cart the * Lev 4:21
* pigeons as his guilt offering; Lev 5:7
turtledoves or * pigeons as his sin Lev 5:11
anointing oil, the * bull for the Lev 8:1
Then he took the * bull for the Lev 8:14
The carcass of the * bull, with Lev 8:17
offering, and a * pigeon or a Lev 12:6
two turtledoves or two * pigeons. Lev 12:8
turtledoves or two * pigeons Lev 14:22
turtledoves or two * pigeons Lev 14:30
turtledoves or two * pigeons and Lev 15:14
turtledoves or two * pigeons and Lev 15:29
He must bring a * bull for a sin Lev 16:3
to the Lord the * bull as a sin Lev 16:6
has sacrificed the * bull as a sin Lev 16:11
the blood of the * bull and Lev 16:14
did with the blood of the * bull. Lev 16:15
He must smear the blood of the * Lev 16:18
And the * bull and the goat Lev 16:27
it must be a * bull or a sheep or Lev 22:19
If the * bull or lamb presented Lev 22:23
defects, one * bull, and two rams. Lev 23:18
Out in the camp one day, a * man Lev 24:10
turtledoves or two * pigeons to the Num 6:10
He brought a * bull, a ram, and Num 7:15
24 * bulls, Num 7:88
Have them bring a * bull and a Num 8:8
another * bull for a sin offering. Num 8:8
the heads of the * bulls and offer Num 8:12
Some * men ran and told Moses Num 11:27
"If the sacrifice is a * bull, Num 15:8,9
bull, ram, lamb, or * goat. Num 15:11,12
one * bull for a burnt offering. Num 15:23,24
and prepare seven * bulls and seven Num 23:1
and a * bull and a ram were Num 23:2
a * bull and a ram on each." Num 23:3,4
and he offered up a * bull and a Num 23:14
to prepare seven * bulls and seven Num 23:29
a * bull and ram on every altar. Num 23:30
some of the * men began going to Num 25:1
to the Lord of two * bulls, one Num 28:11
to the Lord two * bulls, one ram, Num 28:19
It shall consist of two * bulls, Num 28:27
consisting of one * bull, one ram, Num 29:2
to him—of one * bull, one ram, Num 29:8
shall be thirteen * bulls, two Num 29:13
for each of the thirteen * bulls; Num 29:14
sacrifice twelve * bulls, two rams, Num 29:17
offer eleven * bulls, two rams, Num 29:20
to sacrifice ten * bulls, two rams, Num 29:23
sacrifice nine * bulls, two rams, Num 29:26,27
sacrifice eight * bulls, two rams, Num 29:29
sacrifice seven * bulls, two rams, Num 29:32
to the Lord—of one * bull, one ram, Num 29:36
and 32,000 * girls. Num 31:32-35
result in your * people's beginning Deu 7:4
"You must not boil a * goat in Deu 14:21
you, and all the * men of Israel Deu 21:21
and there are * ones or eggs in it Deu 22:6
don't take the mother with the *. Deu 22:6
Let her go, and take only the *. Deu 22:7
will have no mercy upon * or old. Deu 28:50
Even as an eagle overspreads her * Deu 32:11
Shall terrorize * men and girls Deu 32:25
He is a * bull in strength and Deu 33:17
and he was as strong as a * man. Deu 34:7
in it—men and women, * and old; Jos 6:21
The * men found her and rescued Jos 6:23
with them. The * men of Israel took Ju 3:6
home and roasted a * goat, and Ju 6:19
There he captured a * fellow Ju 8:14
So the * man pierced him with his Ju 9:54
Israel, that the * girls went away Ju 11:40
Then Manoah took a * goat and a Ju 13:19
going to Timnah, a * lion attacked Ju 14:5
easily as though it were a * goat! Ju 14:6
a party for thirty * men of the Ju 14:10,11
gave the answer to the * men. Ju 14:17

(YOUNG Con't)
and gave it to the * men who had Ju 14:19
Samson took a * goat as a present Ju 15:1
One day a * priest Ju 17:7,8
The * man agreed to this, and Ju 17:10,11
Noticing the * Levite's accent, Ju 18:3
they talked to the * priest, and Ju 18:15,16
the * priest demanded when he Ju 18:18
The * priest was then quite happy Ju 18:20
slain, but the * virgins of Ju 21:10,11,12
These * men, Mahlon and Chilion, Ru 1:4,5
I have warned the * men not to Ru 2:8,9
Boaz told his * men to let her Ru 2:15
give you from this * woman be as Ru 4:12
So the sin of these * men was 1Sa 2:17
were seducing the * women who 1Sa 2:22
its people, * and old, with the 1Sa 5:9
they saw some * girls going out to 1Sa 9:9,10,11
one will be carrying three * 1Sa 10:3
said to his * bodyguard, "Come on, 1Sa 14:1
any brave, strong * man, he 1Sa 14:52
One of them said he knew a * 1Sa 16:18
only David but a * goat and a 1Sa 16:20
does this * fellow come from?" 1Sa 17:55
field and took a * boy with him to 1Sa 20:35
have if only your * men have not 1Sa 21:4
he sent ten of his * men to Carmel 1Sa 25:5
Ask your * men and they will 1Sa 25:8
The * men gave David's message to 1Sa 25:9
her * men, "and I will follow." 1Sa 25:19
brought to you and your * men. 1Sa 25:27
"Let one of your * men come over 1Sa 26:22
The * man replied, "If you swear 1Sa 30:15
hundred * men who fled on camels. 1Sa 30:17
Then David said to the * man who 2Sa 1:13
Then he said to one of his * men, 2Sa 1:15
sword play between our * men!" 2Sa 2:14
So David ordered his * men to 2Sa 4:12
Mephibosheth had a * son, Mica. 2Sa 9:12
* men were kept strictly apart. 2Sa 13:2
except ten of his * wives to keep 2Sa 15:16
fruit are for the * men to eat; 2Sa 16:2
deal gently with * Absalom." 2Sa 18:5
please don't harm * Absalom.' 2Sa 18:12
Ten of Joab's * armor bearers 2Sa 18:15
"What of * Absalom?" 2Sa 18:29
"What about * Absalom? 2Sa 18:32
enemies be as that * man is!" 2Sa 18:32
One of Joab's * officers shouted 2Sa 20:11
and when Joab's * officers saw that 2Sa 20:12
"is to find a * virgin to be your 1Ki 1:2
* goats at the Serpent's Stone. 1Ki 1:9
Soon afterwards two * prostitutes 1Ki 3:16
* men with whom he had grown up. 1Ki 12:8
And the * men replied, "Tell 1Ki 12:10
and followed that of the * men; 1Ki 12:13,14
Now bring two * bulls. 1Ki 18:23
and I will prepare the other * 1Ki 18:23
So they prepared one of the * 1Ki 18:26
altar and cut the * bull into 1Ki 18:33
and burned up the * bull, the wood, 1Ki 18:38
There the * prophets of Bethel 2Ki 2:3
as fifty of the * prophets watched 2Ki 2:6,7
When the * prophets of Jericho 2Ki 2:15
the road, some * boys from the city 2Ki 2:23
fight, old and *, and stationed 2Ki 3:21
One day as he was teaching the * 2Ki 4:38
One of the * men went out into 2Ki 4:39
to use it to feed the * prophets. 2Ki 4:42
tell you that two * prophets from 2Ki 5:22
And the Lord opened the * man's 2Ki 6:17
forts, kill the * men, dash their 2Ki 8:12
summoned one of the * prophets. 2Ki 9:1
So the * prophet did as he was 2Ki 9:4
the house, and the * man poured the 2Ki 9:6
Then Jehoiada brought out the * 2Ki 11:12
of Zadok, a * man of unusual 1Ch 12:24-37
"Solomon my son is * and 1Ch 22:5
Israel, is still * and 1Ch 29:1
brought a thousand * bulls, a 1Ch 29:21
* men who had grown up with him. 2Ch 10:8,9
for he was * and frightened and 2Ch 13:7
comes along with a * bullock and 2Ch 13:9
old or *, man or woman. 2Ch 15:13
allegiance to the * king, who was 2Ch 23:2,3
taking seven * bulls, seven rams, 2Ch 29:21
So they killed the * bulls, and 2Ch 29:22
In all, there were 70 * bulls 2Ch 29:32,33
the people 1,000 * bulls for 2Ch 30:24
and the princes donated 1,000 * 2Ch 30:24
dividing it to * and old alike. 2Ch 31:14,15
30,000 lambs and * goats for the 2Ch 35:7
offerings, and 3,000 * bulls. 2Ch 35:7
and killed their * men, even going 2Ch 36:17
killing even * girls and old men. 2Ch 36:17
Give the priests in Jerusalem * Ez 6:9
celebration 100 * bulls, 200 rams, Ez 6:17
* lovelies for the royal harem. Est 2:3
a beautiful and lovely * cousin, Est 2:7
along with many other * girls. Est 2:8
that the Jews—* and old, women and Est 3:13
camels, mules, and * dromedaries Est 8:9,10
Though they are fierce as * Job 4:10
Old and * alike will be Job 18:20
Even * children despise me. Job 19:18
Though still a * man, his bones Job 20:11
elders. The * saw me and stepped Job 29:8
than I deride me—* men whose Job 30:1
These * men, having humbled me, Job 30:11
and said, "I am * and you are Job 32:6
They die * after lives of Job 36:14
to satisfy the * lions' appetites Job 38:39,40
ravens when their * cry out to God Job 38:41
seen them giving birth to their *? Job 39:1
birth to their *, and carry their Job 39:2,3
Their * grow up in the open Job 39:4
She ignores her * as though they Job 39:16
Now take seven * bulls and seven Job 42:8
me apart, like * lions hiding and Ps 17:12
and skip before him like * calves! Ps 29:5,6
Even strong * lions sometimes go Ps 34:10
these * lions are out to get it. Ps 35:17
I have been * and now I am old. Ps 37:25
Tear out the teeth of these * Ps 58:6
will sweep away both old and *. Ps 58:9
the finest of Israel's * men. Ps 78:31
Their * men were killed by fire Ps 78:63
there have their *, O Lord of Ps 84:3
of the Lord! * and old shall hear Ps 89:1
chosen a splendid * man from the Ps 89:19
Then the * lions roar for their Ps 104:21
How can a * man stay pure? Ps 119:9
Children born to a * man are Ps 127:4
and healthy as * olive trees. Ps 128:3
the * ravens cry to him for food. Ps 147:9
and their judges, * men and Ps 148:12
"I want to warn * men about some Pro 1:4
If * toughs tell you, "Come and Pro 1:10
EVERY * MAN who listens to me and Pro 2:1
* man, do not resent it when God Pro 3:11,12
* MEN, LISTEN to me as you would Pro 4:1
* men, listen to me, and never Pro 5:7
* man, obey your father and your Pro 6:20
lad, a * man lacking common sense, Pro 7:7
Listen to me, * men, and not only Pro 7:24
And so, * men, listen to me, for Pro 8:32
rebuke; a * mocker doesn't. Pro 13:1
The glory of * men is their Pro 20:29
* men who are wise obey the law; Pro 28:7
of the good die * and some of the Ecc 7:15-17
* man, it's wonderful to be Ecc 11:9
Young man, it's wonderful to be * Ecc 11:9
of being * cause you to forget Ecc 12:1
now while you are *, before the Ecc 12:6
No wonder all the * girls love Sol 1:3
No wonder all the * girls love Sol 1:4
is like a gazelle or * deer. Sol 2:9
a gazelle or a * stag on the Sol 2:17
The * Women of Jerusalem: "Who Sol 3:5
King Solomon, O * women of Zion; Sol 3:11
The * Women of Jerusalem: "Oh, Sol 5:1
The * Women of Jerusalem: "O Sol 5:8
THE * WOMEN of Jerusalem: "O Sol 6:1
The * Women of Jerusalem: Sol 6:12
The * Women of Jerusalem: "Who Sol 8:4
a little sister too * for breasts. Sol 8:8
like a gazelle or * deer upon the Sol 8:14
and sometimes "* woman." Is 7:14f
refers to Isaiah's * wife and her Is 7:14f
no joy in their * men, and no mercy Is 9:17
no mercy on the * people of Babylon Is 13:18
and barefoot, both * and old, their Is 20:4
The oxen and * donkeys that till Is 30:24
a lion, even a * one, kills a Is 31:4,5
and the strong * Assyrians will be Is 31:8
The strongest will perish, * Is 34:7
eggs and hatch her * and nestle Is 34:15
and gently lead the ewes with *. Is 40:11
and the * men will all give up. Is 40:30
* wife abandoned by her husband. Is 54:6
when compared with vigorous * men! Is 59:10
* plants springing up everywhere. Is 61:11
of a * man who marries a virgin; Is 62:5
Only sinners will die that *! Is 65:20
I'm far too *! Jer 1:6
to please me as a * bride long ago Jer 2:2
the gatherings of * men, and on Jer 6:11
the streets; the * men gather no Jer 9:21
And so their * men shall die in Jer 11:21,22
* men and sorrow to their mothers. Jer 15:8
her nest with * she has not hatched Jer 17:11
blind and lame, * mothers with Jer 31:8
be gone. The * girls will dance Jer 31:13
men folk—old and *—will take their Jer 31:13
Your * men lie dead in the Jer 49:26
of Israel. Her * men will fall in Jer 50:30
No one shall be spared; both * Jer 51:3
too, both old and *, young men and Jer 51:22
old and young, * men and maidens, Jer 51:22
her many sins; her * children are Lam 1:5
streets—old and *, boys and girls, Lam 2:21
It is good for a * man to be Lam 3:27
to the * girls of Jerusalem. Lam
Even the jackals feed their *, Lam
They take away the * men to Lam
the * no longer dance and sing. Lam
them all—old and *, girls, women Ez
my people, of both * and old alike, Eze
I made to you when you were *. Eze 16:
grew into a strong * lion, and Eze
two sisters who as * girls became Eze 2
all attractive * men, captains and Eze
those handsome * men on fine Eze 2
days when as a * girl you gave your Eze 2
with them—handsome * men of high Eze 2
daily terror. The * men of Eze 3
flocks and herds gave birth to *. Eze
as a strong * lion among the Eze
* bulls of Bashan for my feast! Eze 3
face—that of a * lion—looked toward Eze 41:1
"The second day, sacrifice a * Eze 4
sacrifice a * bull with no Eze 4
shall provide a * bull for a sin Eze 4
consist of seven * bulls and seven Eze 4
without blemish. A * goat will also Eze 4
one * bull, in perfect condition; Eze
With the * bull, he must bring a Eze
be one bushel with the * bull; Eze 4
back as captives—* men of the royal Dan
were four of the * men chosen, all Dan
brought all the * men to the king Dan 1:1
king found these * men's advice ten Dan
and your * men see visions. Joe
they traded a * lad for a Joe
Even a * lion, when it growls, Amo
"Beautiful girls and fine * men Amo
the * and tender, lived unafraid? Nah
the enemy will consume you like * Nah
"Go tell this * man," said the Zec
make the * men and girls flourish; Zec 9:1
Hear the * lions roaring—the Zec
nor look after the *, nor heal the Zec 1
But when the * man heard this, Mt 1
up and crowded the * plants so that Mk
joy, but, like * plants in such Mk
There was, however, a * man Mk 14:5
sat a * man clothed in white. Mk
turtledoves or two * pigeons" was Lk
patches, and the * grain stalks Lk
gave me even one * goat for a feast Lk 1
Jesus rode along on a * donkey, Jn 1
When you were *, you were able Jn 2
prophesy, and your * men shall see Act 2
Just outside that door are the * Act
dead, and the * men came in and, Act 5
at the feet of a * man named Paul. Act 7
and as Paul spoke on and on, a * Act 2
me to bring this * man to you to Act 23
or ignore him [because he is * 1Co 16
little of you because you are *. 1Ti 4
evil thoughts that * men often 2Ti 2
In the same way, urge the * men Tit
and the ashes of * cows could Heb 9
And you * men, I am talking to 1Jn 2
God, and to you * men who are 1Jn 2
Dear * friends, you belong to God 1Jn

YOUNGER
and what Ham, his * son, had done, Gen 9:24
she said to her * sister, "I slept Gen 19
night, and the * girl went in and Gen 19
The name of the * girl's baby Gen 19
shall be a servant of the *!" Gen 25
rights to his * brother. Gen 25
older, and her * sister, Rachel. Gen 29
to marry off a * daughter ahead of Gen 29
let Joseph's * brother Benjamin go Gen 4
you don't have a * brother, then Gen 42
of Ephraim, the * boy, and his left Gen 48
nation, but his * brother shall Gen 48
inheritance to his * son, the son Deu 21:
son of his * brother Kenaz, Ju 1:
Caleb's * brother) to save them. Ju
Do I have * sons who could grow Ru 1:
a * brother of her former husband. Ru 1:1
Naturally you'd prefer a * man, Ru 3:
man, and was Absalom's * brother. 1Ki
or those *, for the Lord had 1Ch 27:
the counsel of the * ones. 2Ch 10:
"BUT NOW THOSE * than I deride Job 3
But, then, the * generation grows Ecc 4:
ashamed of all I did in * days." Jer 31:
north of you; your * sister is Eze 16:
of James the * and of Joses), Mk 15:
When the * told his father, 'I Lk 15:
"A few days later this * son Lk 15:
and the * men covered him with a Act 5
Talk to the * men as you would to 1Ti 5
The * widows should not become 1Ti 5:
better for these * widows to marry 1Ti 5:
must train the * women to live Tit 2
You * men, follow the leadership 1Pe 5
And I am writing to you * boys 1Jn 2:1

YOUNGEST
there until his * son Shelah was Gen 38:

OUNGEST Con't)
of Canaan. Our * brother is there Gen 42:13
until this * brother comes here. Gen 42:15
but bring your * brother back to Gen 42:20
one is dead, and the * is with Gen 42:32
bring your * brother back to me. Gen 42:34
"Is this your * brother, the one Gen 43:29
to the *, much to their amazement! Gen 43:33
going on down the line to the *. Gen 44:12
your * brother is with you.' Gen 44:23
you let our * brother go with us. Gen 44:26
were set up, his * son would die. Jos 6:26
*, Jotham, who escaped and hid. Ju 9:5
"Well, there is the *," Jesse 1Sa 16:10,11
David was the * son, and was on 1Sa 17:14,15
I will give you my * daughter." 1Sa 18:21
the gates, his * son, Segub, died. 1Ki 16:34
only his * son, Jehoahaz, 2Ch 21:17
his * son, as their new king (for 2Ch 22:1
Then the father told the *, 'You Mt 21:30

OUNGSTER
"There's a * here with five Jn 6:8,9

OUNGSTER'S
A * heart is filled with Pro 22:15

OUTH
I have killed a * who attacked Gen 4:23
for killing that * should be Gen 4:24
from his earliest *, and even Gen 8:21
the anguish of his *, and for the Gen 41:51
shepherds from our *, as our Gen 46:34
son, the child of my vigorous *. Gen 49:3
So they took the * out of the Lev 24:23
the * of Israel to exercise faith Ju 3:1
May he restore your * and take Ru 4:15
the finest of your * and will use 1Sa 8:16
the * replied. 1Sa 14:7
found an Egyptian * in a field and 1Sa 30:11,12
the prophet asked. The * showed 2Ki 6:6
bring up all the follies of my *. Job 13:26
snatched away in *, and the Job 22:15,16
From my * I have been sickly and Ps 88:15
Satisfy us in our earliest * Ps 90:14
My * is renewed like the eagle's! Ps 103:5
From my earliest * I have tried Ps 119:52
PERSECUTED FROM MY earliest * Ps 129:1
rejoice in the wife of your *. Pro 5:18
A wise * makes hay while the sun Pro 10:5
A WISE * accepts his father's Pro 13:1
be a poor but wise * than to be an Ecc 4:13
Everyone is eager to help a * Ecc 4:15
but remember that *, with a whole Ecc 11:10
Honor him in your * before the Ecc 12:1
The shame of your * and the Is 54:4
I'm only a *!" Jer 1:6
killed off the flower of your *. Jer 9:21
her choicest * are doomed to Jer 48:15
command to crush the noblest *. Lam 1:15
them to kill their finest *. Lam 2:4
The cream of our *—the finest of Lam 4:2
remembered your *, but have angered Eze 16:43
as lewd as in her *, when the Eze 23:8
from her * when she was a Eze 23:19,20
long ago in her *, after I had Hos 1:15
Your finest * lie dead. Nah 2:13
my livelihood from my earliest *.' Zec 13:5
faith with the wife of your *. Mal 2:15
one of them," the * replied. Mt 19:20
Literally, "from my *." Mk 10:20f
taught his laws from earliest *. Rom 2:18

YOUTHFUL
he groaned to his * armor Ju 9:54
as a child's, firm and * again. Job 33:25
Overlook my * sins, O Lord! Ps 25:6,7

YOUTHS
compared with any of the other *. Sol 2:3
neighbors, * revolting against Is 3:5
Even the * shall be exhausted, Is 40:30
Their * do not forget to sin, Jer 17:2,3
and their * die in battle! Jer 18:21
to select some of the Jewish * Dan 1:3,4
with the other * your age," he Dan 1:10
nourished than the * who had been Dan 1:15
God gave these four * great Dan 1:17

Z
"I am the A and the *," Rev 1:8
am A and *, the First and Last!" Rev 1:11
I am the A and the *—the Rev 21:6
I am the A and the *, the Rev 22:13

ZA-ANANNIM
away as the Oak of *, near Kedesh. Ju 4:11

ZAANAN
with their shame; * sounds like a Mic 1:11f
The people of * Mic 1:11
with their shame; * sounds like a Mic 1:11f
with their shame; * sounds like a Mic 1:11f

ZAANANNIM
at the oak in *, and extended Jos 19:33

ZAAVAN
The children of Ezer:Bilhan, *, Gen 36:27
The sons of Ezer: Bilhan, *, and 1Ch 1:42

ZABAD
Nathan's son was *; 1Ch 2:36
Eleadah, Tahath, *, Shuthelah, 1Ch 7:20,21
* (son of Ahlai); 1Ch 11:26-47
The conspirators were *, whose 2Ch 24:26
Mattaniah, Jeremoth, *, Aziza. Ez 10:27
Mattenai, Matattah, *, Eliphelet, Ez 10:33
Je-iel, Mattithiah, *, Zebina, Ez 10:43

ZABAD'S
Nathan's son was Zabad; * son 1Ch 2:37

ZABBAI
*, Athlai. Ez 10:28
Next to him was Baruch (son of * Neh 3:20

ZABDI
Carmi, grandson of *, and Jos 7:1
and the family of * was indicated. Jos 7:17
Jakim, Zichri, *, Eli-enai, 1Ch 8:19,20,21
vineyards; and * from Shiphma was 1Ch 27:27
Mattaniah (son of Mica, son of *, Neh 11:15,16,17

ZABDI'S
was indicated. * family was Jos 7:18

ZABDIEL
who was assisted by * (son of Neh 11:10-14

ZABUD
* (son of Nathan) was the king's 1Ki 4:1

ZACCAI
From the subclan of *, 760; Ez 2:3-35
From the subclan of *, 760; Neh 7:8-38

ZACCHAEUS
a man named *, one of the most Lk 19:1
up at * and called him by name! Lk 19:5
and called him by name! "*!" Lk 19:5
* hurriedly climbed down and took Lk 19:6
Meanwhile, * stood before the Lk 19:8

ZACCUR
Shammu-a, son of *, from the tribe Num 13:3-15
father of * and grandfather of 1Ch 4:26
his brothers Shoham, *, and Ibri. 1Ch 24:26,27
were his sons *, Joseph, Nethaniah, 1Ch 25:2
The third, * and twelve of his 1Ch 25:9-31
From the clan of Bigvai—Uthai, *, Ez 8:2-14
work crew led by * (son of Imri). Neh 3:2
Hashabiah, *, Sherebiah, Neh 10:9-13
Micaiah, son of *, son of Asaph), Neh 12:35,36
and I appointed Hanan (son of *, Neh 13:13

ZACHARIAS
a Jewish priest, *, who lived when Lk 1:5
was king of Judea. * was a member Lk 1:5
of Aaron.) * and Elizabeth were Lk 1:6
One day as * was going about his Lk 1:8,9
* was in the sanctuary when Lk 1:11,12
* was startled and terrified. Lk 1:11,12
angel said, "Don't be afraid, *! Lk 1:13
* said to the angel, "But this Lk 1:18
were waiting for * to appear and Lk 1:21
where * lived, to visit Elizabeth. Lk 1:39,40
name would be *, after his father. Lk 1:59
* was apparently stone deaf as Lk 1:62f
Instantly * could speak again, Lk 1:64
Then his father * was filled with Lk 1:67
John (the son of *), as he was Lk 3:1

ZADOK
(son of Ahilud). * (son of Ahitub) 2Sa 8:17
Abiathar and * and the Levites 2Sa 15:24
* took the Ark back into the city. 2Sa 15:25,26
Then the king told *, "Look, 2Sa 15:27
So * and Abiathar carried the Ark 2Sa 15:29
advice. * and Abiathar, the 2Sa 15:35,36
Then Hushai reported to * and 2Sa 17:15
the son of *," the watchman said. 2Sa 18:27
Then David sent * and Abiathar 2Sa 19:11,12
Sheva was the secretary, and * 2Sa 20:25
were the priests * and Benaiah, the 1Ki 1:8
But * the priest and Benaiah 1Ki 1:26
"Call * the priest," the king 1Ki 1:32
mule, and * the priest and Nathan 1Ki 1:34
So * the priest, Nathan the 1Ki 1:38
At Gihon, * took a flask of 1Ki 1:39
him to Gihon with * the priest and 1Ki 1:44,45
own mule. And * and Nathan have 1Ki 1:44,45
* as priest instead of Abiathar. 1Ki 2:35
Azariah (son of *) was the High 1Ki 4:1
* and Abiathar were priests; 1Ki 4:1
name: Jerusha (daughter of *) 2Ki 15:32,33
*, the father of 1Ch 6:4-15
*, the father of 1Ch 6:4-15
*, Ahima-az. 1Ch 6:50-53
Meshullam, son of *, son of 1Ch 9:10,11
the command of *, a young man of 1Ch 12:24-37
Then David called for * and 1Ch 15:11
David left * the priest and his 1Ch 16:39
the historian; * (son of Ahitub) 1Ch 18:16
David consulted with *, who 1Ch 24:3
of these leaders: * the priest, 1Ch 24:6
of King David, *, Ahimelech, and 1Ch 24:31
Over the descendants of Aaron, *; 1Ch 27:16-22
they anointed * as their priest. 1Ch 29:22
was Jerushah, daughter of *. 2Ch 27:1
of * replied, "These are tithes! 2Ch 31:10
Shallum was the son of *; Ez 7:1
* was the son of Ahitub; Ez 7:1
Meshezabel) and * (son of Baana). Neh 3:4
* (son of Immer) also rebuilt the Neh 3:29
*, Jaddu-a, Pelatiah, Neh 10:14-27
Meshullam, son of *, son of Neh 11:10-14
I put Shelemiah the priest, * the Neh 13:13
descendants of *—for they alone of Eze 40:46
At that time the * family of the Eze 43:19
"However, the sons of *, of the Eze 44:15
is, the sons of * who obeyed me and Eze 48:11
Azor was the father of *; Mt 1:14
Azor was the father of Zadok; * Mt 1:14

ZADOK'S
Then * son Ahima-az said, "Let 2Sa 18:19

ZAHAM
marriage—Jeush, Shemariah, and *. 2Ch 11:19

ZAIR
the city of *, but was quickly 2Ki 8:21

ZALAPH
Hanun (the sixth son of *); Neh 3:30

ZALMON
forces to Mount * where he began Ju 9:47,48
* from Ahoh; 2Sa 23:24-39
melting in the forests of *. Ps 68:14

ZALMONAH
Hor and camped in *, then at Num 33:41

ZALMUNNA
*, the kings of Midian," he said. Ju 8:5
Literally, "are Zebah and * Ju 8:6f
Zebah and King * with a remnant of Ju 8:10
Zebah and King *, and you refused Ju 8:15
Zebah and King *, "The men you Ju 8:18
Then Zebah and * said to Gideon, Ju 8:21
and *, Ps 83:11

ZAMZUMMIM
called '*' by the Ammonites. Deu 2:20

ZANOAH
Eshtaol, Zorah, Ashnah, *, Jos 15:33-36
Jezreel, Jokde-am, *, Kain, Jos 15:48-62
The people from *, led by Hanun, Neh 3:13
*, Adullam (and their Neh 11:25-30

ZANOAHITES
of the Gedorites, Socoites, and *. 1Ch 4:18

ZAPHON
Succoth, *, and the rest of the Jos 13:27,28
its army at * and sent this message Ju 12:1

ZARED
of the brook * and set up camp. Num 21:12

ZAREPHATH
of *, near the city of Sidon. 1Ki 17:8,9
So he went to *. 1Ki 17:10
coastal strip as far north as *. Ob 1:20
help the widow of *—a foreigner Lk 4:25,26

ZARETHAN
city of Adam, near *, the water Jos 3:15,16
of Beth-shean near * below Jezreel, 1Ki 4:8-19
River between Succoth and *. 1Ki 7:41-46

ZATTU
From the subclan of *, 945; Ez 2:3-35
From the clan of *: Ez 10:27
From the subclan of *, 845; Neh 7:8-38
Parosh, Pahath-moab, Elam, *, Neh 10:14-27

ZAZA
had two sons named Peleth and *. 1Ch 2:33

ZEAL
of his * for his God, and because Num 25:12,13
but Saul, in his nationalistic *, 2Sa 21:2
Apparently Jehu in his * exceeded 2Ki 10:11f
me! My * for God and his work Ps 69:9
idols with great * beneath the Is 57:5
of God, but it is misdirected *. Rom 10:2

ZEALOT
Simon (also called "The *"), Act 1:14

ZEALOTS
Simon (a member of "The *," a Mt 10:2,3,4
Simon (a member of the *, a Lk 6:14,15,16

ZEALOUS
Literally, "they are all * for Act 21:20f

ZEBADIAH
*, Arad, Eder, Michael, Ishpah, 1Ch 8:15,16
*, Meshullam, Hizki, Heber, 1Ch 8:17,18
Jo-elah and * (sons of Jeroham 1Ch 12:3-7
* (the third), 1Ch 26:2,3
was later replaced by his son *. 1Ch 27:7
Nethaniah, *, Asahel, Shemiramoth, 2Ch 17:7,8,9
affairs; and * (son of Ishmael), a 2Ch 19:11
From the clan of Shephatiah—* (son Ez 8:2-14
Hanani, *. Ez 10:20

ZEBAH
from chasing after * and Zalmunna, Ju 8:5
Literally, "are * and Zalmunna Ju 8:6f
By this time King * and King Ju 8:10
never catch King * and King Ju 8:15
Then Gideon asked King * and King Ju 8:18
Then * and Zalmunna said to Ju 8:21
let all their princes die like * Ps 83:11

ZEBEDEE
father *, mending their nets; Mt 4:21
John, the sons of *, brought them Mt 20:20
of James and John (the sons of *). Mt 27:56
left their father * in the boat Mk 1:20
James and John (the sons of *, but Mk 3:16-19
John, the sons of *, came over and Mk 10:35
too—James and John, the sons of *. Lk 5:10

(ZEBEDEE Con't)
Literally, "the sons of *." Jn 21:2f
ZEBEDEE'S
James (* son), Mt 10:2,3,4
He took Peter with him and * two Mt 26:37
the beach, he saw * sons, James and Mk 1:19
ZEBIDAH
His mother's name: * (daughter of 2Ki 23:36,37
ZEBINA
Je-iel, Mattithiah, Zabad, *, Ez 10:43
ZEBOIIM
Admah, and *, near Lasha. Gen 10:15-19
Shemeber, king of *, and Gen 14:2
Gomorrah, Admah, *, and Bela) Gen 14:3
*, and Bela (Zoar), unsuccessfully Gen 14:8,9
and Admah and *, destroyed by the Deu 29:23
I forsake you like Admah and *? Hos 11:8
ZEBOIM
the valley of * near the desert. 1Sa 13:18
Hazor, Ramah, Gittaim, Hadid, *, Neh 11:31-35
ZEBUL
He and his friend * should be our Ju 9:28
But when *, the mayor of the Ju 9:30
*, "Look over at that mountain! Ju 9:36
"No!" * said. Ju 9:36
Then * turned on him Ju 9:38
at this time, and * drove Gaal and Ju 9:41
ZEBULUH
* 57,400 Num 1:20-46
ZEBULUN
She named him * (meaning Gen 30:20
Simeon, Levi, Judah, Issachar, *. Gen 35:23
* and his sons: Sered, Elon, Gen 46:8-14
"* shall dwell on the shores of Gen 49:13
Issachar, *,Benjamin, Dan, Ex 1:1
* -Eliab (son of Helon) Num 1:2-15
Issachar * Eliab (son of Num 2:3-31
of the tribe of *, came with his Num 7:24-29
*, led by Eliab, the son of Helon. Num 10:16
son of Sodi, from the tribe of *; Num 13:3-15
The tribe of *: 60,500. Num 26:26,27
clans named after the sons of *: Num 26:26,27
* Elizaphan (son of Num 34:16-28
Gad, Asher, *, Dan, and Naphtali Deu 27:13
Of the tribe of *, Moses said: Deu 33:18
"Rejoice, O *, you outdoorsmen, Deu 33:18
The Land Given to the Tribe of *: Jos 19:10
its assignment of land was *. Jos 19:10
The northern boundary of * Jos 19:14
and ran as far as * in the Valley Jos 19:27
coincided with the * boundary in Jos 19:34
the tribes of Reuben, Gad, and *. Jos 21:7
four cities by the tribe of *: Jos 21:34,35
And the tribe of * did not Ju 1:30
from the tribes of Naphtali and *. Ju 4:6
When Barak summoned the men of * Ju 4:10
From Machir and from *. Ju 5:13,14
But the tribes of * and Naphtali Ju 5:18
Manasseh, Asher, *, and Naphtali, Ju 6:35
The next judge was Elon from *. Ju 12:11,12
and was buried at Aijalon in *. Ju 12:11,12
Judah, Issachar, *, Dan, Joseph, 1Ch 2:1
the tribes of Reuben, Gad, and *. 1Ch 6:63
The tribe of * gave Rimmono and 1Ch 6:77
From the tribe of * there were 1Ch 12:24-37
away as Issachar, *, and Naphtali 1Ch 12:40
Over *, Ishmaiah (son of Obadiah); 1Ch 27:16-22
and Manasseh and as far as *. 2Ch 30:10
Manasseh, and * turned to God and 2Ch 30:11
Issachar, and * were ceremonially 2Ch 30:17,18,19
* and Naphtali are right behind. Ps 68:27
Though soon the land of * and Is 9:1
Then comes *, also extending all Eze 48:26
gates of Simeon, Issachar and *; Eze 48:33
Galilee, close to * and Naphtali. Mt 4:12,13
"The land of * and the land of Mt 4:15,16
* Zebulum Rev 7:4-8
ZECHARIAH
* became the new king of Israel. 2Ki 14:29
New king of Israel: * 2Ki 15:8
But * was an evil king in the 2Ki 15:9
mother's name: Abi (daughter of *) 2Ki 18:1
Je-iel, *, 1Ch 5:7,8
At that time *, the son of 1Ch 9:21
Ner, Nadab, Gedor, Ahio, *, 1Ch 9:35,36,37
*, Ja-aziel, Shemiramoth, Jehiel, 1Ch 15:18
cymbals; and *, Azi-el, 1Ch 15:20
Nethanel, Amasai, *, Benaiah, and 1Ch 15:24
His associates were *, Je-iel, 1Ch 16:5
Isshiah, and by Isshiah's son *. 1Ch 24:24,25
* (the oldest), 1Ch 26:2,3
*, the fourth. 1Ch 26:11
of the north gate to his son *, a 1Ch 26:14,15
in Gilead, Iddo (son of *); 1Ch 27:16-22
Obadiah, *, Nethanel, and Micaiah. 2Ch 17:7,8,9
(son of *, son of Benaiah, son of 2Ch 20:14
Azariah, Jehiel, *, Azariah, 2Ch 21:2
God came upon *, Jehoiada's son. 2Ch 24:20
plotted to kill *, and finally King 2Ch 24:21
While * was alive Uzziah was 2Ch 26:5
to please God. * was a man who had 2Ch 26:5
was Abijah, the daughter of *. 2Ch 29:1
From the Asaph clan, * and 2Ch 29:12,13,14
subclan of Merari. * and Meshullam, 2Ch 34:12
Hilkiah, *, and Jehiel, the 2Ch 35:8
time—Haggai, and * (the son of Ez 5:1
Haggai and * (son of Iddo). Ez 6:14
From the clan of Parosh—*, and 150 Ez 8:2-14
From the clan of Bebai—* (son of Ez 8:2-14
Elnathan, Nathan, *, and Meshullam, Ez 8:16
Mattaniah, *, Jehiel, Ez 10:26
Hash-baddenah, *, and Meshullam. Neh 8:1
Athaiah (son of Uzziah, son of *, Neh 11:4,5,6
son of *, son of the Shilonite). Neh 11:4,5,6
of Amzi, son of *, son of Pashhur, Neh 11:10-14
*, leader of the Iddo clan; Neh 12:12-21
the trumpets were * (son of Neh 12:35,36
Micaiah, Eli-o-enai, *, Neh 12:40,41
Messiah (Jeremiah 23:5, * 3:8). Is 4:2,3,4f
I asked Uriah the priest and * Is 8:2
Ezra, Haggai, and *, nor with the Dan 5:31f
lifetime—*, Shallum, and Pekahiah. Hos 7:7f
years: *, Shallum, Pekahiah. Hos 13:11f
Lord were given to * (son of Zec 1:1
the Lord came to * (son of Zec 1:7
Babylon had, by the time of *, Zec 5:11f
message from the Lord came to *. Zec 7:8,9
righteous Abel to * (son of Mt 23:35
* 13:7. Mt 26:31f
to the murder of * who perished Lk 11:51
are described, and * 4:2–6, giving Rev 1:4f
But see * 4:2–6, where the Rev 4:5f
but see * 4:2–6, 10, where the Rev 5:6f
* 4:3, 4, 11. Rev 11:4f
ZECHARIAH'S
The rest of the history of * 2Ki 15:11
killing his son. * last words as he 2Ch 24:22
ZECHER
Gedor, Ahio, *, Mikloth who was 1Ch 8:30,31,32
ZEDAD
* and Ziphron to Hazar-enan. Num 34:7,8,9
to *; then to Berothah and Eze 47:15
ZEDEKIAH
One of the prophets, * (son of 1Ki 22:11
Then * (son of Chenaanah) walked 1Ki 22:24
and he changed his name to *. 2Ki 24:17
New king of Judah: * 2Ki 24:18,19
But now King * rebelled against 2Ki 24:20
of the reign of King * of Judah. 2Ki 25:1
Jehoiakim, *, Shallum. 1Ch 3:15
Jeconiah, *. 1Ch 3:16
One of them, * (son of 2Ch 18:10
Then * (son of Chenaanah) walked 2Ch 18:23
brother * as the new king of Judah 2Ch 36:10
* was twenty-one years old when 2Ch 36:11
oath of loyalty. * was a hard and 2Ch 36:13
*, Seraiah, Azariah, Neh 10:1
of Josiah's son *, king of Judah, Jer 1:3
THEN KING * sent Pashhur (son of Jer 21:1
King * doubtless had in mind God's Jer 21:1f
"Go back to King * and tell him Jer 21:3,4
will deliver King * himself and all Jer 21:7
"But the rotten figs represent * Jer 24:8
Some versions read "*." Jer 27:1f
prophecies to *, king of Judah. Jer 27:12
of the reign of *, king of Jer 28:1
of Kolaiah) and * (son of Jer 29:21
Lord make you like * and Ahab whom Jer 29:22
of the reign of *, king of Judah Jer 32:1
King * had put him there for Jer 32:3
and that King * would be caught Jer 32:4
Go tell *, king of Judah, that Jer 34:2
But listen to this, O *, king of Jer 34:4
delivered the message to King *. Jer 34:6
Lord after King * of Judah had Jer 34:8
(for King * had ordered everyone Jer 34:9
And I will surrender *, king of Jer 34:21
(son of Shaphan), * (son of Jer 36:12
Instead he chose * (son of Jer 37:1
But neither King * nor his Jer 37:2
Nevertheless, King * sent Jer 37:3
eventually King * sent for him to Jer 37:17
Then King * commanded that Jer 37:21
So King * agreed. Jer 38:5
One day King * sent for Jeremiah Jer 38:14
So King * swore before Almighty Jer 38:16
Then Jeremiah said to *, "The Jer 38:17
Then * said to Jeremiah, "On Jer 38:24
the reign of King * of Judah, that Jer 39:1
When King * and his soldiers Jer 39:4
The king of Babylon made * watch Jer 39:6
just as I turned *, king of Judah, Jer 44:30
of the reign of *, king of Judah: Jer 49:34
and exile to Babylon along with * Jer 51:59
* WAS TWENTY-ONE years old when Jer 52:1
saw to it that * rebelled against Jer 52:3
and caught King * in some fields Jer 52:8
He made * watch while his sons Jer 52:10
who had deserted * and had come Jer 52:15
God says it is a message to King * Eze 12:10
"Even King * shall go out at Eze 12:12
a member of the royal family [* Eze 17:12,13
"Nevertheless, * rebelled Eze 1
out the tree, roots and all!) * Eze 1
O King *, Eze 2
two Judean kings, Jehoiakim and *. Eze 2
ZEDEKIAH'S
36–37). But * hopes were dashed. Jer
* ambassadors to Nebuchadnezzar. Jer
Then he gouged out * eyes and Jer
During the fourth year of * Jer 5
(Seraiah was quartermaster of * Jer 5
In the ninth year of * reign, on Jer
ZEEB
Oreb and *, the two generals of Ju
by his name, and * at the winepress Ju
of *, as it is now called; Ju
and * across the Jordan to Gideon. Ju
capture Oreb and *, the generals of Ju 8
and *; Ps 8
ZELA
Irpeel, Taralah, *, Ha-eleph, Jebus Jos 18:2
ZELEK
* from Ammon; 2Sa 23:2
* from Ammon; 1Ch 11:2
ZELOPHEHAD
(Hepher's son, *, had no sons. Num 26:2
ONE DAY THE daughters of * came Num
and his son * was their father. Num
"The daughters of * are correct. Num 27
of our brother * to his daughters. Num
the daughters of *: 'Let them be Num
The daughters of * did as the Num 3
However, Hepher's son * (grandson Jos
Another descendant was *, who had 1Ch
ZELZAH
at *, in the land of Benjamin; 1Sa
ZEMARAIM
arrived at Mount *, in the hill 2Ch
ZEMARITES
Sinites,Arvadites, *, Hamathites. Gen 10:15
Arvadites, *, and Hamathites. 1Ch 1:13
ZEMER
helmsmen are skilled men from *. Eze 2
ZEMIRAH
*, Joash, Eliezer, Eli-o-enai, 1Ch
ZENAN
*, Hadashah, Migdal-gad, Dilean, Jos 15:37
ZENAS
Do everything you can to help * Tit 3
ZENITH
But at the * of his power, his Dan 1
ZEPHANIAH
his assistant *, and the three 2Ki 25
I, Joel, Azariah, *, Tahath, Assir, 1Ch 6:33
of Malchiah) and * the priest (son Jer 2
a letter to * (son of Ma-aseiah) Jer 29
you have said to *, "The Lord has Jer 29
* took the letter over to Jer 29
of Shelemiah) and * the priest (son Jer 3
chief priest, and * his assistant, Jer 52:24
from the Lord. To: * (son of Cushi, Zep
(son of *), where they will stay. Zec 6:10
ZEPHATH
of * and massacred all its people. Ju 1:
ZEPHATHAH
in the valley of *, and King Asa 2Ch 14:9,
ZEPHI
Teman, Omar, *, Gatam, Kenaz, 1Ch 1:
ZEPHO
Teman, Omar, *, Gatam, Kenaz, Gen 36:10,11,
Omar,The clan of *,The clan of Gen 36:15,
ZEPHON
named after their ancestor *. Num 26:15-
ZEPHONITES
The *, named after their ancestor Num 26:15-
ZER
Ziddim, *, Hammath, Rakkath, Jos 19:35-
ZERAH
were:Nahath, *, Shammah, Mizzah. Gen 36:13,
Nahath,The clan of *,The clan of Gen 36:
by: King Jobab (son of *), from Gen 36:31-
was born, and he was named *. Gen 38:
Shelah, Perez, * (however, Er and Gen 46:8-
named after their ancestor *. Num 26:12-
named after their ancestor *. Num 26:19-
great-grandson of *, of the tribe Jos 7
and the clan of * was singled out. Jos 7:
Achan, the son of *, sinned against Jos 22:
Nahath, *, Shammah, and Mizzah. 1Ch 1:
* from Bozrah became the new king. 1Ch 1:4
*. So Judah had five sons. 1Ch 2
The sons of * were: 1Ch 2
*, Shaul. 1Ch 4:
Zimmah, Joah, Iddo, *, Jeatherai. 1Ch 6:19,20,2
Malchijah, Ethni, *, Adaiah, Ethan, 1Ch 6:39-4
there were also the sons of *, 1Ch 9
subclan from *, who had 24,000 men 1Ch 27:
from Netophah in *, with 24,000 men 1Ch 27:
under the leadership of General *. 2Ch 14:9,
a descendant of *, a son of Judah) Neh 11:2
and * (Tamar was their mother); Mt 1
ZERAHIAH
*, the father of 1Ch 6:4-1

(ZERAHIAH Con't)
Bukki, Uzzi, *, 1Ch 6:50-53
Meraioth was the son of *; Ez 7:1
* was the son of Uzzi; Ez 7:1
(son of *), and 200 other men; Ez 8:2-14

ZERAHITES
The *, named after their ancestor Num 26:12-14
The *, named after their ancestor Num 26:19-22

ZERED
" 'Now cross * Brook,' the Lord Deu 2:13
get across * Brook from Kadesh! Deu 2:14,15

ZEREDAH
from the city of * in Ephraim; 1Ki 11:26
valley between Succoth and *. 2Ch 4:17,18

ZERERAH
Beth-shittah near *, and to the Ju 7:22

ZERESH
his friends and * his wife, and Est 5:10
"Well," suggested * his wife Est 5:14
When Haman told * his wife and Est 6:13

ZERETH
and Helah bore him *, Izhar, and 1Ch 4:7

ZERETH-SHAHAR
Sibmah, * on the mountain above the Jos 13:19

ZERI
sons: Gedaliah, *, Jeshaiah, 1Ch 25:3

ZEROR
Abiel, grandson of *, 1Sa 9:1

ZERUAH
his mother was *, a widow. 1Ki 11:26

ZERUBBABEL
* and Shime-i. 1Ch 3:19,20
*, Jeshua, Nehemiah, Seraiah, Ez 2:2
priests, and * (son of She-alti-el) Ez 3:1
the direction of * (son of Ez 3:8
they approached * and the other Ez 4:2
But * and Jeshua and the other Ez 4:3
God of Israel to * (son of Ez 5:1
"Their leaders were:*, Neh 7:7
* (son of She-altiel) and Jeshua: Neh 12:1
So now, in the days of * and Neh 12:47
This man Coniah's grandson, *, was Jer 22:30f
delivered it to * (son of Hag 1:1
Then * (son of She-alti-el), the Hag 1:12
But take courage, O * and Joshua Hag 2:4
Tell *, the governor of Judah, Hag 2:21
I will take you, O * my servant, Hag 2:23
"This is God's message to *: Zec 4:6
however high, can stand before *! Zec 4:7
* will finish building this Temple Zec 4:7
"* laid the foundation of this Zec 4:9
the plumbline in the hand of *. Zec 4:10
Shealtiel was the father of *; Mt 1:12
* was the father of Abiud; Mt 1:13
Rhesa's father was *; Lk 3:23-38

ZERUBBABEL'S
* children were: 1Ch 3:19,20
Rhesa's father was Zerubbabel;* Lk 3:23-38

ZERUIAH
(Joab's brother and the son of *). 1Sa 26:5,6,7
Joab (the son of *) led David's 2Sa 2:13
nothing with these two sons of *. 2Sa 3:39
was Joab (son of *), and his 2Sa 8:16
was the sister of Joab's mother *. 2Sa 17:25
brother, Abishai (the son of *); 2Sa 18:2
But Abishai the son of * came to 2Sa 21:17
Joab (son of *), was the greatest. 2Sa 23:18,19
armor bearer of Joab (son of *); 2Sa 23:24-39
* and 1Ch 2:16
Joab, the son of *, was the 1Ch 11:5,6
Abishai (son of *) then destroyed 1Ch 18:12
Joab (son of *) was 1Ch 18:15
*, and anyone else of distinction 1Ch 26:28

ZERUIAH'S
* sons were Abishai, Joab, and 1Ch 2:16

ZEST
all the * of lustful men who visit Eze 23:44

ZETHAM
Ladan: Jehiel the leader, *, Joel; 1Ch 23:8,9
* and Joel, the sons of Jehieli. 1Ch 26:20,21,22

ZETHAN
Chenaanah, *, Tarshish, Ahishahar. 1Ch 7:10

ZETHAR
Bigtha, Abagtha, *, and Carkas— to Est 1:10

ZIA
Sheba, Jorai, Jacan, *, and Eber. 1Ch 5:13

ZIBA
He heard about a man named * who 2Sa 9:2
"Are you *?" 2Sa 9:2
"Yes," * replied, "Jonathan's 2Sa 9:3
"In Lo-debar," * told him. 2Sa 9:4
king summoned Saul's servant *. 2Sa 9:9
*, who had fifteen sons and twenty 2Sa 9:10,11
All the household of * became 2Sa 9:12
of the hill when *, the manager of 2Sa 16:1
the king asked *. 2Sa 16:2
And * replied, "The donkeys are 2Sa 16:2
"He stayed at Jerusalem," * 2Sa 16:3
"In that case," the king told * 2Sa 16:4
"Thank you, thank you, sir," * 2Sa 16:4
him, including *, the servant of 2Sa 19:17
O king, my servant * deceived me. 2Sa 19:26
I am lame. But * has slandered me 2Sa 19:27
"My decision is that you and * 2Sa 19:29

ZIBA'S
of Saul, and * fifteen sons and 2Sa 19:17

ZIBEON
granddaughter of * the Hivite), Gen 36:2,3
tribe of *,The tribe of Anah,The Gen 36:20,21
The children of *: Gen 36:24
Lotan, Shobal, *, Anah, Dishon, 1Ch 1:38,39

ZIBEON'S
* sons were Aiah and 1Ch 1:40

ZIBIA
Jobab, *, Mesha, Malcam, 1Ch 8:8,9,10

ZIBIAH
(His mother was *, from 2Ki 12:1
His mother's name was *, from 2Ch 24:1

ZICHRI
sons of Izhar:Korah, Nepheg, *. Ex 6:21
Jakim, *, Zabdi, Eli-enai, 1Ch 8:19,20,21
Ishpan, Eber, Eliel, Abdon, *, 1Ch 8:22-25
Athaliah, Jaareshiah, Elijah, *. 1Ch 8:26,27
of *, who was the son of Asaph). 1Ch 9:15,16
Joram, *, and Shelomoth. 1Ch 26:25
Over Reuben, Eliezer (son of *); 1Ch 27:16-22
Next was Amasiah (son of *), a 2Ch 17:16
and Elishaphat (son of *). 2Ch 23:1
Then *, a great warrior from 2Ch 28:7
Their chief was Joel, son of *, Neh 11:7,8,9
*, leader of the Abijah clan; Neh 12:12-21

ZIDDIM
*, Zer, Hammath, Rakkath, Jos 19:35-39

ZIDON
and *, too, shrewd though they be. Zec 9:2

ZIHA
*, Hasupha, Tabbaoth, Keros, Ez 2:43-54
*, Hasupha, Tabbaoth, Keros, Neh 7:46-56
* and Gishpa) all lived in Ophel. Neh 11:21

ZIKLAG
Chesil, Hormah, *, Madmannah, Jos 15:21-32
Bethul, Hormah, *, Beth-marcaboth, Jos 19:2-7
So Achish gave him * (which still 1Sa 27:6
at their city of *, they found that 1Sa 30:1
land of Caleb, and had burned *." 1Sa 30:14
When he arrived at *, he sent 1Sa 30:26
had returned to * after 2Sa 1:1
Bethuel, Hormah, *, 1Ch 4:30
joined David at * while he was 1Ch 12:1
to David as he was en route to *: 1Ch 12:20
against the Amalek raiders at *. 1Ch 12:21
surrounding villages), *, Neh 11:25-30

ZILLAH
married two wives—Adah and *. Gen 4:19
To Lamech's other wife, *, was Gen 4:22
One day Lamech said to Adah and * Gen 4:23

ZILLE-THAI
Jakim, Zichri, Zabdi, Eli-enai, *, 1Ch 8:19,20,21

ZILLETHAI
Michael, Jozabad, Elihu, *. 1Ch 12:20

ZILPAH
a servant girl, *, to be her maid. Gen 29:24
her servant-girl * to Jacob, to be Gen 30:9
soon * presented him with a son. Gen 30:10
Then * produced a second son, Gen 30:12
The sons of *, Leah's Gen 35:26
wives Bilhah and *, was to shepherd Gen 37:2
sons of Jacob and *, the slave-girl Gen 46:18

ZIMARAIM
Beth-arabah, *, Bethel, Avvim, Jos 18:21-28

ZIMMAH
Libni, Jahath, *, Joah, Iddo, 1Ch 6:19,20,21
*, Shime-i, Jahath, Gershom, Levi. 1Ch 6:39-43
(son of *) and Eden (son of Joah). 2Ch 29:12,13,14

ZIMRAM
*, Jokshan, Medan, Midian 1Ch 1:32

ZIMRAN
several children:*, Jokshan, Gen 25:1

ZIMRI
Midianite girl was *, son of Salu, Num 25:14
Then General *, who had charge 1Ki 16:9
city of Tirzah. * simply walked in 1Ki 16:10
Then * declared himself to be 1Ki 16:10
But * lasted only seven days; 1Ki 16:15,16
heard that * had assassinated the 1Ki 16:15,16
When * saw that the city had 1Ki 16:18
The rest of the story of * and 1Ki 16:20
You son of a * who murdered his 2Ki 9:31
*, Ethan, Heman, 1Ch 2:6
Alemeth, Azmaveth, *. 1Ch 8:36
of Alemeth, Azmaveth, and *; 1Ch 9:42
* was the father of Moza. 1Ch 9:42
and all the kings of *, Elam and Jer 25:25

ZIMRI'S
* son was Moza. 1Ch 8:36

ZIN
of * to Rehob near Hamath. Num 13:21
in the wilderness of * in April Num 20:1
in the wilderness of *. Num 27:14
in Kadesh, in the wilderness of *. Num 27:14
Kadesh (in the wilderness of *); Num 33:15-37
of *, along the edge of Edom. Num 34:3
in the direction of *. Num 34:4
in the wilderness of *. Deu 32:51
the Wilderness of *, and ended at Jos 15:1
the Wilderness of * to Hezron Jos 15:2,3,4

ZINA
Or "*." 1Ch 23:10,11f

ZION
*, now called the City of David. 2Sa 5:7
So David made the stronghold of * 2Sa 5:9
the Tabernacle in *, the City of 1Ki 8:1
daughter of * isn't afraid of you! 2Ki 19:21
the fortress of *, later called the 1Ch 11:5,6
City of David, also known as *, 2Ch 5:2
Literally, "Upon *, my holy Ps 2:6f
Literally, "in *." Ps 9:11f
the gates of the daughter of *." Ps 9:14f
from * now to save his people. Ps 14:7
you aid from his sanctuary in *. Ps 20:2
Temple on your holy mountain, *. Ps 43:3
He lives upon Mount * in Ps 48:1
See Mount * rising north of the Ps 48:2
all to see—Mount *, joy of all the Ps 48:2
Literally, "Mount *." Ps 48:11f
Literally, "Out of *, the Ps 50:2f
on Mount *. Ps 50:2
good in your good pleasure unto *; Ps 51:18f
Oh, that God would come from * Ps 53:6
O GOD IN *, we wait before you in Ps 65:1
with envy at Mount *, the mount Ps 68:15,16
his holy temple high upon Mount *. Ps 68:17
Literally, "*." Ps 69:35f
Literally, "Mount *." Ps 74:2f
He lives upon Mount *. Ps 76:2
Judah—and Mount * which he loved. Ps 78:68
to meet with the Lord in *. Ps 84:7
Literally, "*." Ps 87:1f
Jehovah sits in majesty in *, Ps 99:2
rod of your strength out of *." Ps 110:2f
Literally, "from *." Ps 110:2f
*, unmoved by any circumstance. Ps 125:1
Literally, "from *." Ps 128:5f
Literally, "*." Ps 132:13f
Literally, "*." Ps 133:3f
The Lord bless you from *—the Ps 134:3
"the Lord be blessed from *." Ps 135:21f
for them the happy songs of *! Ps 137:3,4
Literally, "*." Ps 146:10f
Praise your God, O *! Ps 147:12
King Solomon, O young women of *; Sol 3:11
his fist at Jerusalem on Mount *. Is 10:32
his throne in * and rule gloriously Is 24:23
Here on Mount * in Jerusalem, Is 25:6
Stone in *—a firm, tested, precious Is 28:16
will come and fight upon Mount *. Is 31:4,5
along that road to *, singing the Is 35:10
virgin daughter of *—laughs at you Is 37:22
beautiful clothes, O *, Holy City; Is 52:1
neck, O captive daughter of *. Is 52:2
* who have turned away from sin. Is 59:20
BECAUSE I LOVE *, because my heart Is 62:1
go up to * to the Lord our God." Jer 31:6
upon the hills of *, and shall be Jer 31:12
They shall ask the way to * and Jer 50:5
The roads to * mourn, no longer Lam 1:4
Sound the trumpet in *! Joe 2:15
your God in *, my holy mountain. Joe 3:17
Literally, "*." Joe 3:21f
lair—from his Temple on Mount *. Amo 1:2
BUT IN THE last days Mount * will Mic 4:1
their King from Mount * forever. Mic 4:7
pain, O people of *, for you must Mic 4:10
Rise, thresh, O daughter of *; Mic 4:13
Sing, O daughter of *; Zep 3:14
Escape, escape to * now!' Zec 2:6,7
"There shall come out of * a Rom 11:26
up into Mount *, to the city of the Heb 12:22
standing on Mount * in Jerusalem, Rev 14:1

ZIOR
(or, Hebron), *, Maon, Carmel, Jos 15:48-62

ZIPH
Hazor, Ithnan, *, Telem, Be-aloth, Jos 15:21-32
Maon, Carmel, *, Juttah, Jezreel, Jos 15:48-62
caves in the hill country of *. 1Sa 23:14,15
* to search for him and kill him. 1Sa 23:14,15
But now the men of * went to Saul 1Sa 23:19
So the men of * returned home. 1Sa 23:24,25
was on his way to *, he and his men 1Sa 23:24,25
NOW THE MEN from * came back to 1Sa 26:1
he was the father of *, who was 1Ch 2:42
Jehallelel's sons were:*, Ziphah, 1Ch 4:16
Gath, Mareshah, *, 2Ch 11:5-10
of * tried to betray him to Saul. Ps 54:1

ZIPHAH
Jehallelel's sons were:Ziph, *, 1Ch 4:16

ZIPHION
Gad and his sons: *, Haggi, Shuni, Gen 46:16,17

ZIPHRON
through Zedad and * to Hazar-enan. Num 34:7,8,9

ZIPPOR
Moab (the son of *) realized how Num 22:2,3
Listen to me, you son of *. Num 23:18-24

ZIPPORAH
one of the girls, *, as his wife. Ex 2:21
Then * his wife took a flint Ex 4:25,26
Then Jethro took Moses' wife, *, Ex 18:2
to his wife *, the Midianite Num 12:1f
ZITHER
accompanied by the *), were his six 1Ch 25:3
ZITHERS
by singing and by *, harps, 1Ch 13:8
Literally, "were to lead with * 1Ch 15:21f
loud playing on the harps and *. 1Ch 15:28
they played the harps and *. 1Ch 16:5
of *, harps, and cymbals. 1Ch 25:1
playing of cymbals, harps, and *; 1Ch 25:6,7
ZIZ
up the slopes of * at the end of 2Ch 20:16
ZIZA
Benaiah, * (the son of Shiphi, son 1Ch 4:34-39
Abijah, Attai, *, and Shelomith. 2Ch 11:20
ZIZAH
four sons: Jahath was greatest, * 1Ch 23:10,11
ZOAN
Tanis (or *, as it was pronounced Num 13:22f
Literally, "the plains of *." Ps 78:43f
What fools the counselors of * Is 19:11
The "wise men" from * are also Is 19:13
power extends to * and Hanes, yet Is 30:4
and * and Thebes shall lie in Eze 30:14
ZOAR
countryside around * in Egypt. Gen 13:10
The king of Bela (later called *). Gen 14:2
and Bela (*), unsuccessfully Gen 14:8,9
named *, meaning "Little City." Gen 19:22
Afterwards Lot left *, fearful of Gen 19:30
trees; and *," the Lord told him. Deu 34:3
His people flee to * and Eglath. Is 15:5
will be heard as far away as *. Jer 48:2,3,4
and to Jahaz; from * to Horonaim Jer 48:34
ZOBAH
kings of *, and the Philistines. 1Sa 14:47
(son of Rehob) of * in a battle at 2Sa 8:3
lands of Rehob and *, one thousand 2Sa 10:6
the Syrians from *, Rehob, Tob, and 2Sa 10:7,8
Igal (son of Nathan) from *; 2Sa 23:24-39
King Hadad-ezer of * who had 1Ki 11:23
king) when David destroyed *. 1Ki 11:24
King Hadadezer of * (as far as 1Ch 18:3
Mesopotamia, Aram-maacah, and *. 1Ch 19:6
ZOBEBAH
Koz was the father of Anub and *; 1Ch 4:8
ZODIAC
constellations of the southern *. Job 9:9
ZOHAR
Ephron the son of *, the Hethite, Gen 25:9,10
Ohad, Jachin, *, and Shaul (Shaul's Gen 46:8-14
Jachin, *, Ex 6:15
ZOHAR'S
as to ask Ephron, * son, to sell Gen 23:8
ZOHETH
The sons of Ishi:*, Ben-zoheth. 1Ch 4:20
ZOPHAH
*, Imna, Shelesh, Amal. 1Ch 7:35
The sons of * were: 1Ch 7:36,37
ZOPHAI
Amasai, Ahimoth, Elkanah, *, 1Ch 6:25,26,27
ZOPHAR
the Shuhite, and * the Naamathite. Job 2:11
* THE NAAMATHITE replies to Job: Job 11:1
THE SPEECH OF * the Naamathite: Job 20:1
the Shuhite, and * the Naamathite Job 42:9
ZOPHIM
into the fields of * at the top of Num 23:14
ZORAH
Eshtaol, *, Ashnah, Zanoah, Jos 15:33-36
*, Eshta-ol, Ir-shemesh, Jos 19:41-46
Dan, who lived in the city of *. Ju 13:2,3
the cities of * and Eshta-ol. Ju 13:25
buried him between * and Eshta-ol, Ju 16:31
from the cities of * and Eshta-ol Ju 18:2
to their people in * and Eshta-ol. Ju 18:8
Dan set out from * and Eshta-ol. Ju 18:11
*, Aijalon, and Hebron. 2Ch 11:5-10
En-rimmon, *, Jarmuth, Neh 11:25-30
ZORATHITE
These were known as the * clans. 1Ch 4:2
ZORATHITES
descended the * and Eshtaolites). 1Ch 2:53
ZORITES
half the Manahathites, and the *; 1Ch 2:54
ZUAR
Nethanel (son of *) Num 1:2-15
son of * Num 2:3-31
the son of *, chief of the tribe of Num 7:18-23
the son of *, and the tribe of Num 10:15
ZUPH
His great-great-grandfather was *. 1Sa 1:1
in the land of *, Saul said to the 1Sa 9:5
Eliel, Toah, *, Elkanah II, Mahath, 1Ch 6:33-38
ZUR
of *, a Midianite prince. Num 25:15
Rekem, *, Hur, and Reba. Num 31:8
Rekem, *, Hur, and Reba. Jos 13:21
*, Kish, Baal, Nadab, Gedor, Ahio, 1Ch 8:30,31,32
Gibeon, Abdon (the oldest), *, 1Ch 9:35,36,37
ZURI-SHADDAI
Shelumi-el (son of *) Num 1:2-15
the son of *, chief of the tribe of Num 7:36-41
by Shelumi-el, the son of *; Num 10:19
ZURIEL
* (son of Abihail) Num 3:31-35
ZURISHADDI
(son of *) Num 2:3-31
ZUZIM
The * in Ham; Gen 14:5,6

A

°**Gen1**:2:6f:7,8f:13f:19f:23f:26:31f/2:4:7:7f[2]:7:8:
10:18[2]:21:22:23:24[2]/3:4:13:17[2]:20f:24/4:1[2]:2[2]:3:
12[2]:14[2]:15:17[2]:20:23:26/5:1/6:8:14:16[3]:17:
19,20[4]/7:2/8:1:6:7:7f:8:12/9:5,6:13:20,21[2]:23:
24,25/10:5:9:9f:9:9f:22/11:1:2:3,4[3]:27:29/12:2[2]:
6:10:17/13:8[2]:10:12/14:18:19,20:23:24/15:1:2,3
:4:9[5]:12[2]:13:15:17[2]/16:7:9-12[4]:15/17:2,3,4[3]:7,8:
12:16:17[2]:19:20/18:5:7[2]:10:11:12[3]:13:14:18[2]:19:
22,23:25/19:3:7:18,19,20:26:28:30:31/20:3[2]:7:8:
9,10:11,12[2]:16/21:1:7[2]:8:13:14:15:16:18:19[2]:
20,21[2]:25:30:33:34/22:2:3:6:13[3]:18:20-23/23:4[3]
:5,6:9:19,20/24:1:4:5:7:11:14:15,16:15,16f:15,16
:17:22:25:26:28f:31[2]:35[2]:38:39:40:42:43:45:48:
63:67/25:12-15:18:21:23:25:25f:27[2]:30:32/26:1:
4:8:11:13:19[2]:21:24:25:27:28:30:31:34/27:11,12:
16[2]:39,40/28:2:6,7,8[2]:11[2]:12:18:22[2]/29:2[2]:5:9:
14:17:20:22:24:26:29:31:32:34:35/30:2:5:6f[2]:6:7
:8:10:12:14f:14:19:21:22:23,24:27:28:35,36:43/
31:2:10:13:24:25:26:27[2]:28:32[2]:36,37:42:44:45[2]:
46:47,48:51,52:54[2]/32:10:13,14,15:16:18:
22,23,24/33:2:10:17/34:14[2]:31/35:11:13,14:16:
17:20/36:1:2,3:4[2]:13,14f:22:24/37:3[2]:4:5:11:
13,14:15:19,20[2]:25:26,27:31:33/38:1:2:6:7:8:9[2]:
10:11:14:15:17:18:21:24:28/39:1[2]:3:4:6[2]:9[2]/40:5
:9,10:16:18,19:20:23/41:5:7:10:11:12[2]:13:14:15:
22:29:33:34,35f:38:41,42:45[3]:45f[2]:48/42:16:18:
19:24/43:2:16:30:32:34/44:5:7:10:15:18:19[2]:20[3]
:25:33/45:3:7:8:26/46:2:3,4:8-14:16,17:29/47:
24:26:27/48:4:7:16:19/49:5:6[2]:9[2]:13:14:17:19:
21:22[2]:27:29,30/50:3:7:9:10[2]:11:26/**Ex1**:7[2]:8:10
:20/2:1[3]:3:4:5:6:11[2]:15:22[3]/3:2[2]:8[3]:11:17/4:2:3:
4:10[2]:11:14:20:25,26[2]:29/5:1[3]:3:7,8:19/6:4:15/7
:4:9[2]:10:15/8:14:23:27/9:3:14:18:24/10:4,5:6:15[2]
:19:21:26/11:3:7[2]/12:3,4:3,4f:3,4:5[3]:11:14:17:21
:22[2]:24:30:32:38f:38:45[2]/13:3:4,5:6,7:8:13[2]:16:
17,18:21[2]/14:14:16:20:21[2]/15:3:5:11:20:25/16:
6:18[2]:20:23[2]:26:28,29:32:33[2]:36[2]/17:9:10f:12:13
:14/18:3:12f:18:19,20:21/19:6[2]:9:13:16[4]:18[2]/20:
7:8:9:10:12:18:25/21:2:3[2]:4[2]:6:7[2]:9[3]:12:13:14:16[2]
:18:19:20:21:22[2]:26:27:28:30:30f:31[2]:32:33[3]:35:
36/22:1[2]:2[2]:3[2]:4:9:10[2]:14[2]:16[2]:16f[2]:18:21:25:26:
31/23:2,3:5:6:8[2]:9:12:15:19:29:30[2]/24:1:10:11:
17/25:8:9[3]:11:17:23:24:25[2]:31:39f/26:6:9:12:13:
14[2]:31:36:37/27:1:4[2]:9,10:16:21/28:4:4f:4[4]:11:
12:15:16:17[2]:18[2]:20[2]:21:32[2]:36[2]:37,38:39:43/29:
1:3,4:14:18:24:25:26:31:36[2]:40:41:42/30:1:3:10[2]
:11,12[2]:13:13f[2]:17,18[2]:25:33:35/31:5:12,13:16[2]/
32:1:4:5:6:8:9:10:18:21:22:23:29:30:31:35/33:3[2]:
5:11:15/34:5,6:7:14:15:20[3]:26:33/35:1:2[2]:33/36
:4-7:14,15:30:37/37:2:6:8:10:11:12[2]:20,21[2]:26/
38:4[2]:17:23:25,26:27f/39:3:6,7:8:9[2]:10[3]:11[2]:12:
13[2]:14:15-18:21:23[2]:31/40:13:29[2]/**Lev1**:2,3[2]:6,7
:9f:10[4]:14:15,16,17:15,16,17f/2:1:2:3:6:7:9:10:
12f:13f:13:14:15:16/3:1[2]:6[3]:7,8:9,10,11:12:14:17
/4:3[3]:10[2]:11,12[3]:14[2]:20:21[2]:23:26:28:32[2]:33:35/
5:1:4[2]:6:7:10:11[3]:12[2]:15:16:17,18[3]:19/6:2:3:4,5:
6:11:15[2]:19,20[3]:21:22,23:27:28/7:5:6[2]:8:12:14:
15:16[3]:17,18:19:29/8:1:8f:21:26:27/9:2[4]:3[3]:4[3]:8:
14:17:21/10:6:13:19/11:32[2]:33:36/12:2:5[2]:6[6]:8[3]
/13:1[2]:3:6:8:9,10:14,15:18[2]:19[2]:22:24:25:27:28:
29,30[3]:36:37:38[2]:40[2]:41:42:43:44:45[2]:47,48[2]:49[2]
:51:59/14:1:4[2]:10:12:13[2]:21[3]:22[2]:24:31[2]:40:41:
45:55[2]:56[3]/15:1:3:6:13:15[2]:16[2]:19[2]:24:26:30[2]:32[2]
:33/16:3[4]:5:6:9:10:11:12:13:21:22:22f:24:29,30[2]:
31[2]/17:5:6:7:8,9[3]:10:13[2]/18:6:7[2]:10:11:13:16f:
17:19:23[4]/19:5:12:14:15:18:19:20[3]:21:29/20:1[2]:
10:11:12:14[3]:15:16:17[2]:18[2]:19:20:21:21f:24[2]:25:
27[2]/21:1:2,3[2]:2,3f:4:7[5]:9:13:14,15[4]:18[2]:19:20[3]:
21/22:3:4[4]:10[2]:11:12:13:17,18[3]:19[4]:20:21[3]:22:23[2]
:26,27[2]:28[2]:29,30/23:9,10,11:12[2]:13[4]:14:15,16:
17[3]:18f:19[2]:21[2]:23,24[2]:25:28:30,31:32:35:36:41/
24:5-8[3]:9[2]:10[2]:21/25:5:10[3]:11:12:14,15,16:24:27
:29[2]:29f:31[2]:35:37:39:40[2]:47:49:50:52[2]:53[3]/26:8[2]
:10:25:36[3]/27:1[2]:3:4:5[2]:6[4]:7[3]:9:11,12[2]:13[2]:16[2]:
17:21:22[2]:29:30:31/**Num1**:2-15:52:53/2:3-31/3:
14,15:38:39:40[2]:42:43:50/4:1:6:7:8[2]:9:10:11[2]:12:
13:14:20:21,22,23:29:34:38-41/5:1:5,6:8:9,10:
11,12:15[3]:17:18:21,22:23:26:27:29[2]/6:1[4]:11[2]:12[4]
:14[6]:15:17:20[2]:21[2]/7:3:11:13[2]:14:15[3]:16[2]:88/8:8[3]
:11[2]:12[2]:19:21/9:6,7:10[2]:12:13:14:19[4]:22[2]/10:8:
31:33/11:4,5:7:11:15:19,20:21:31[2]:33/12:1:1f[3]:6
:11/13:23[2]:27[2]/14:2:4:7:8:12[2]:24[2]:29:34,35/15:
3,4[7]:5:6:7[3]:8,9:10:19,20,21[3]:23,24[3]:27[3]:30[2]:
37,38[2]/16:1:2:8,9:13:15:17:29:30:32:38[3]:39:40[2]:
42:46/17:1:6:10/18:4:6:10:16[2]:17:19:19f:23:
25,26[2]/19:1:9:10:11:13:14[2]:15:16[3]:17:18[3]:21:22
/20:2:3:8:20/21:8:8f:8:11:16:17,18:27-30:35/22:
5,6:11:15:18:22,23[2]:24:26:27:29[2]/23:2[2]:3,4[3]:5:7-
7-10:13:14[2]:18-24[4]:30/24:3-9[3]:13[2]:15-19/25:6:7
:14:15/26:2:5-11:28-37[2]:44-47:55,56:58,59:62/
27:1[2]:3,4:8[2]:16:17[2]/28:1:3:5:6:8:9,10:12[2]:13:14[3]:
15:17:18:20,21:22[2]:25:26[2]:27/29:1:2:3,4:5[2]:7:8:
11:12:16[2]:19[2]:22[2]:25[2]:28[2]:31[2]:36:38/30:1:3[2]:4:6[2]
:9:14:15:16[2]/31:9,10,11:19:26:28:30:50:54/32:
14:42/33:9/34:10,11/35:6:12:16:17:18:21:22,23[2]
:32[3]/36:1:5/**Deu1**:9:11:17:23:24,25:31:33[2]:46/2:
5[2]:10:21:26/3:11[2]/4:6:9:16,17[2]:18[2]:24[2]:25:34:37
/5:2,3:9,10[3]:11:15:16[2]:24:29/6:3[2]:7:15/7:2:6:7:9
:13:16:21:22[2]:25:26/8:3:5:7:8:9[2]:16/9:3:6:9:
13,14/10:1:7:9/11[2]:11:12:28:29[2]/12:4,5[2]:14/13:
1:6,7:12,13,14:16[2]:17/14:19,20:21[3]:26/15:1:2:9[2]
:12[2]:14:18[2]:22/16:2:3[2]:8:10:11:12:14:15[3]:16[2]:19
/17:1:6:8:13:14:15:16:20/18:10[2]:11:15[2]:18:20/
19:5:14:21/20:2:5:6:10[2]:19/21:1[2]:3:4[2]:11:13:14:
15:16:17:18[2]:20:22[3]:23/22:5[2]:6[2]:8:10:13,14[3]:
17,18:19f:19:20:21:22:23,24[2]:25,26,27:28,29[3]:30
/23:1:2:5:9,10:13[2]:15,16:17,18[2]:19:20[2]:21[2]:22:
24:25[2]/24:1[2]:5[2]:6[3]:7[2]:14,15[4]:17:19/25:1[3]:5[2]:9:
13,14,15/26:2,3:5:8:10:12:15:19/27:2,3,4[3]:12:13
:18:22[2]:25/28:9:20:27:31:33:36[2]:37[2]:46:47,48:49[2]
:50:55:68/29:12[2]:18:23[2]/30:16:18/31:15:20:26/
32:5:8:20:22:28:30/33:5:17[2]:20[2]:21:22:24:28/34
:6:7/**Jos1**:6:12,13/2:1[2]:3:10:15[2]/3:1:2,3,4[2]:5:12:
13,14:15,16[2]/4:2,3[3]:5:6:7:8:14:20:22/5:2,3:6:13[2]
/6:3,4[3]:5:6-9:10:16:26/7:3:21[2]:26/8:11,12,13:17
:22:28:29[2]/9:3,4,5:6[2]:7:9:11:14,15[2]:22:23/10:2:5
:8:10:11:14:16:18[2]:20:21:27/11:4:8:18f:19/12:5:
7/13:2-7/14:1:3,4:6:13,14:15/15:18,19[2]/17:
16,17,18/18:4:17/19:49/20:3:4:5:9/21:9-16:9-
9-16f:9-16:20,21,22:27:32:38,39/22:2,3:10:13:
14:24,25:26,27:28:34/23:10:13[5]/24:9:20:25[2]:26[2]
:27/**Ju1**:2:24:26:36/2:3/3:1:4:15[2]:16:17,18,19[2]:
20[2]:25[2]:27[2]/4:4:5:9:15:17:18:21[2]/5:7:8[2]:23:25:
26[2]:30/6:11[2]:18:19[4]:26:28[2]:31[2]:32:34[2]:38/7:
12,13[2]:16[3]:21/8:10:14:20:21:21f:25:27f[2]:31[2]/9:3
:6:8[2]:19:47,48:49[2]:51:53[2]:54/10:3:12/11:1[3]:3:10
:11:17:30,31:33:34:35:36:39/12:5[2]/13:2,3:5[2]:6:7[2]
:18:19[4]/14:1:3[2]:4:5:6:8:10,11:12:16:18/15:1[2]:4:8
:9:15[2]:16,17[3]:18:19/16:1:4:5:9f:10:16,17:19:
23,24/17:1:3:4,5[2]:7,8:7,8f:7,8:9:9f:9:10,11[2]:13:
13f[2]/18:1:7:9,10[2]:12:14:19[3]:22:30/19:1[3]:3:4:6:9:
14:22:23:24:29:30/20:4:6:8,9,10[2]:16[2]:35-39[2]/21
:1:13:15[2]:18/**Ru1**:1[2]:11f[2]:12:13/2:1:7:10,11:17:
20:20f/3:1:2:6,7[2]:8:10[2]:11[2]:12:14:15-18[4]/4:1:7[2]:
10:11:13:16,17/**1Sa1**:1:8:11:19,20:19,20f:24[2]/2:
8:13,14[3]:18[2]:18f:19:26:27:28:35:36/3:7:11:20/4:
12:12f:13:20/5:6:8:9/6:3[2]:7:8:9:14[4]:17/7:6[2]:9[2]:
10:12/8:5:9:11:15:17:19:22/9:1:3:6:7:8:9,10,11:
12,13[2]:16:26,27/10:1:3:5[5]:6:9:11:12[2]:17:18,19:
25[3]:26/11:2:4:11:15/12:1:2:3:12:17:19:22/13:5:
14:20:21[3]:22:23/14:1:4:6:15:16:24,25:27[2]:28[2]:29
:33:43[3]:45/15:6:12:28:29/16:1[2]:2[2]:7[2]:12:14:
15,16[2]:17:18[3]:20[3]/17:2:4-7[8]:8:10:12:14,15:16:18
:22:25:26:28:29:32:33[4]:34[3]:35:38,39[3]:40:43[2]:45[2]
:46:48,49:50,51[2]:52/18:9:10[2]:17:19:22:23[2]/19:2:
5[2]:12:13:21:24/20:3:16[2]:20:21:28,29:30:30f:30:
35/21:2:8[3]:9:14,15[2]/22:13:14/23:7:23:26:27/24
:3:6:14[2]:17/25:2[3]:3[2]:8[3]:11:15,16:17:21:25[2]:27:29
:30,31:36:37,38:44/26:5,6,7:8:13:15:19:20:21:25
/27:7/28:2:7,8[2]:10:13:14:24/30:11,12[2]:25:26/
2Sa1:1[2]:17,18/2:5:18/3:1:6:7:8:12:17:20:21:22:
27:33,34[2]:35,36:38[2]/4:4:5:6,7:11/5:3:11:20:23:
24/6:3:12:13:14f:16:19[3]:20:21/7:2:5f:6[2]:7:8:
10,11:13:27/8:2:3:8/9:2:3:8:12/11:2[2]:5:6:8:14:
16:18:19,20,21[2]/12:1:3[2]:4[2]:5:10:24:29,30/13:1:2
f:3:4:6:12:16:17,18:20:21-24[2]:25:28:34/14:2,3[3]:
5,6[2]:11:14[2]:20:25:26[2]:27/15:1:2:4:7,8:13[2]:19,20[2]
:28:30:33,34/16:1:5[2]:13:22/17:2,3:7:8:9:10:11:
17:18[3]:19:27/18:2[2]:7:9:11:11f[2]:12:17[2]:18:21:23:
24:27:29/19:7:17:22:35/20:1[3]:6:8,9,10:12[3]:15:
16:18:21/21:1:10:12,13,14:16[2]:18:19:20,21/22:
14:30:32f:34:35/23:4:10:11,12[3]:18,19:20[3]:21[2]/
24:1:2:3:14:15:22:24/**1Ki1**:2:6[2]:27:39:40:42/2:2:
5:6:8:9[2]:14[2]:16:19:23,24:25:36,37:38:40/3:5:6:7:
8:9:11:12:14:15[2]:17,18:24[2]/4:1:8-19:20:29:33/5:
1:2,3:5[2]:7:12:14[2]:17/6:3:20:31/7:3,4:5:6[2]:8:13[2]:
14[2]:23:24f:26[2]:31:35:41-46[2]/8:1:7:10:12,13[2]:16[2]
:17:21:31:37:62,63:64:65/9:7:8:13:17,18:25:26[2]/
10:2:9:10[2]:11:12:18:19[2]:22:26[2]/11:7:14:16,17,18[2]
:19:20:24:26:29/12:2,3,4:7:18:26:30:32,33f:
32,33/13:1:2:5:7:18[2]:20:24,25:33:34/14:3[2]:10:
13:14:15[2]/15:3:19:22:26/16:1:11:24:32:34/17:3:
8,9:10[2]:11:12[4]:13:24/18:3,4:12:13:27:32:40:41[2]:
42:44[2]:45[2]/19:3:4:6:7:9:11[2]:12[2]:13:19:21[2]/20:13
:20[2]:21:23:25[2]:28[2]:36[2]:38:39[2]/21:1[2]:2[2]:21/22:3:
7:15:17:22:23:47:52,53/**2Ki1**:6:8[2]:9:10:12:17/2:
1:6,7:10:11[2]:19[2]:20/3:1f:2:9:11:26:27/4:1:2:8:9:
10[6]:13:14:15,16:17:19:22[2]:23:28:35:38:39:40:42[2]
/5:1[2]:2[2]:5:7:8:10:12:14:17f:27/6:1:6:10:14:23:25[5]
:26-30:32[3]/7:1:6[2]:10:15/8:1:5:8,9:13:15/9:2:5:
13:16:17:18:19:22:30:31:34/10:1:2,3:8:12:17:
18,19:25:27/11:2,3[3]:5:12:17[2]/12:4,5[2]:8:9[2]/13:1:
15:20,21/14:2:3[2]:5:8:9[2]:13:19/15:3:5:19,20[2]:
34,35/16:3:7:8:10[3]:13[3]/17:21:26:35,36/18:4:9:
14:17:18:20,21:23/19:3[2]:28[2]:29:30:31:32[2]/20:7:
8:9:12/21:3,4,5:6[2]:7:13[2]:24:26/22:8/23:3:10:22:
30:33/24:8,9/25:4,5[2]:19:25:30/**1Ch1**:1f:10:43/2
:3:7:10:17:19:21:31:34,35f:34,35:46:48,49/3:9:
19,20/4:9:9f:18:21-22/5:2[2]:6:9:22:24[2]/6:44-47:
54:78,79/7:2:16:22:23[2]/9:9:14:25:31/10:13/11:
3:5,6:11:12:13:14:17:22[3]:23[2]:26-47/12:3-7:14[2]:
18:20[2]:22:24-37/13:7/14:2:11:15/15:1:24:27:29[2]
/16:3[2]:15/17:1[2]:6:7:9:12:18:21[2]:27/18:2:4[2]:6:8:
14/19:2,3:5:6f/20:4:5:6,7[2]/21:1:2:3:13:14[2]:24/
22:5:6:9[2]:14f[2]:14/23:3:10,11/24:6/25:1:6,7/26:
4,5:14,15/27:4:16-22:23:32:32f/28:2[2]:2f:3:4:9[2]/
29:8:15[3]:16:19:21[3]/**2Ch1**:1:4:9:10:11:12:14/2:1[2]
:2:4[2]:5[2]:6[3]:6f:12[2]:13[2]:14[2]:17/3:4:11,12,13f:14:15
/4:1:2:5:9/5:10:13,14/6:1:5,6[2]:12,13:22:28/7:7:
9:20:21/8:17,18/9:1:7:8[2]:9[2]:13,14[2]:17:18[2]/10:4:
7:19/11:12/12:2/13:6[2]:7:8:9[2]/14:14/15:3[2]:12/
16:9:13,14[2]/17:7,8,9:13:16:17/18:1:2[2]:3,4,5:12:
14:16:19,20:21:22/19:10:11/20:2:3:9:21:24:28:
31:32:35/21:7:14/22:7:9[2]:11[2]/23:2,3:4:5,6:7:8[2]:
10:11[2]:12:15,16,17/24:7,8:9:15:20[2]:23:24:26[2]/
25:1:5,6:7:12:15:18[3]:23:27/26:4:5:10:21:23/28:6
:7:9:19f/29:2:6:10:21:24:25,26/30:5:5f[2]:12:13:
15:26/31:1:3:5,6[2]:17,18/32:3:4:5:8:13[2]:19:24/
33:19[2]/34:2:9:31/35:14:18:21/36:4:13:22,23/
Ez1:2:4:5/2:2:60:64,65/3:11:13/4:6:7:8,9:15:19[2]
/5:4:11:13:14:17/6:1:3:4:11[2]:17/7:6:7,8,9:10:14[2]
:21/8:2-14:18[2]:20:21[2]:26,27:29:34:35/9:8[3]:9:12:
15/10:1:7,8:13:14/**Neh1**:11/2:1:4:5,6:8[2]:10:
11,12[2]/3:8[2]:11:17:21[2]/4:1[2]:3:4:12/5:1:7[3]:15[2]:18[4]
/6:2:3:10[2]:11:19/7:2:4:6:57,58,59:62:66:71/8:1:
9[2]:10[2]:11:12[2]:15:18/9:8:10:12[2]:16:17[2]:18:23:29f
:31:35/10:32:34:34f:35:37:38[3]/11:1:3:4,5,6:
22,23:22,23f:24[2]/12:1:22:38:47[2]/13:1:2:4:5[2]:7:
15:25:28/**Est1**:4:5:9:11:13-15:19[2]/2:5[2]:7:8:9:10:
19[2]:20:23f/3:3,4:8:9:14:15/4:1:8:11:14[2]/5:4:9:
14/6:6:13/7:9/8:5:8:9,10:13:17[2]/9:4:20:24,25[3]:
29-31[2]/10:3/**Job1**:1[2]:2,3:4[2]:5:8:14,15:19/2:3:4,5
:7:8:13/3:4f:5:23[2]/4:1:2:3,4:6:7,8:13:15:20/5:7:
26/6:3:5,6,7:14:15-18:22:24:27[2]/7:1[2]:7:9:20/8:6
:14[2]:16:20/9:2:3[2]:12:15:17/10:3:16:20,21:22[2]/
11:2:12[2]/12:3:4[2]:14:15:23:24,25/13:12:25:27,28[2]
/14:2[3]:5:6[2]:7:8,9:10:11,12[3]:14/15:2[2]:7,8:16:20:
23,24:33/16:5:8:14:21/17:6:7:10/18:15/19:3:15[2]
:27[3]/20:3:5:8:11:26/21:7:33/22:6:18/23:2:16,17
/24:2:3[2]:8:9[2]:20:24:25/25:6/26:10[2]:14/27:6:14:
18[2]/28:3,4:26/29:16[2]:18:25/30:9:15[2]:28,29[2]/31
:1[2]:11[2]:12:32:36/32:8,9:11,12:19[2]/33:10[2]:20:
23,24[3]:25/34:6:19:20:23:24:25:29,30[2]:34,35/35:
11:16/36:4:16:21:22:25/37:7:19,20/38:28:39,40
/39:10:19:20:26:29/40:7[2]:12:15:17:18:19:24/41:
1[2]:2[2]:5[2]:7:15-17:20:24:30:31,32/42:8:11[2]:13,14f:
17/**Ps1**:3:4/2:1f:2/3:1/6:5f/7:2:11/8:5:5f:5/9:9
/10:6/11:1f/14:1[2]/15:2:4:5/16:6/18:1:2[4]:4:10f:
12:19:22:30[2]:31:33:34f/19:1:3,4:5f:5[2]:10/21:3:4
/22:6[2]:16:18/26:7:9,10:11/27:3:5/28:9/30:5:6,7
/31:2:12[2]:21/32:3[2]:4:9[2]/33:10:16,17[3]:20/34:12/
35:7[2]:11/37:10:25:26:30,31:35,36[2]:37[3]/38:3,4[2]:
11:13,14/39:4:5,6[2]:11[2]:12/40:2:3:5/41:9/42:4,5
:7:10/44:9:11:12:14:18/45:1[2]:13:15/46:1:4/47:5
/48:2:3f:6:7/49:8,9:18/50:3:5f:10,11:18:23/51:5
:10:16f:17[3]/52:1:2:8:9/53:1:2/54:4/55:6:13/57:
6[2]/58:9:11/59:16/60:4,5/61:3/62:3,4:7/63:1/
64:6/66:10/68:5:19/69:6:13:31/70:4/71:3/73:6:
12[2]:15:18:20[2]/74:5,6:11:15/75:8/76:5/77:19[2]:
20/78:14[2]:15:16:38:39[2]:49:52:57:65:71,72/79:1
/80:8/83:4:5:14[2]/84:6:10[3]/85:13/86:8:17/87:5:
6/88:4:8/89:3,4:19:19f:19:35,36:49/90:1:4[2]:4f:
5,6[2]/91:7:13:16/92:1:10/94:20[2]/95:1:3:10/96:1
/98[2]:6/101:2/102:1:6[2]:7:12:18:26[2]/103:9:13/
104:9:24/105:8,9:14:16:17:24:39[2]:41[2]/106:9:15f
:19,20:29/107:7:30/109:9,10:12,13:18:22,23[2]:25
/110:4/111:9[2]/112:2:6[2]/113:9/114:3/116:17/
118:12/119:6:9:19[2]:31:56:83:105:162:164:176/
122:9/123:2[2]/124:7[2]/126:1/127[2]:3:4/131:2/
132:2-5[3]:11:17:17f:18/136:13:21:22/139:17,18/
140:5[3]/141/142:4[2]/144:2:4[2]:9[2]:12-15[2]/146:4/
147:10[2]/149:1:6,7/**Pro1**:7,8,9:7,8,9f:17[2]:18:19:
20:27/2:6:16,17/3:1:4,5:11,12[2]:16,17:18:22/4:3:
4:8,9:10:11:24:24f/5:3:4[2]:6:10:18:19f[2]/6:1:5[3]:6:
10[2]:11:12,13[3]:16-19:23[2]:26[2]:27:30/7:4[2]:5:7[2]:8,9:
13:19:20:22:23[2]:26/8:9:30:30f/9:1:2:7,8[3]:9[2]:13/
10:1[2]:3:5[3]:8:9[2]:11:14[2]:18[2]:20[3]:21[2]:23[2]:25[2]:26[2]:
27/11:3:9f:10:11:12[2]:13[2]:14:15:22[3]:28:29:30/12
:4:5:8[3]:10:11:14:15[2]:16[2]:17[2]:23[2]:24:25:27/13:1[2]:
3:5:6:12f:14[2]:15[3]:16[2]:17:22[2]:23/14:1[2]:3:5[2]:6:9f:

(A Con't)
13:15^2:16^2:17^2:25^3:26^2:27^2:28^3:29:30^2:32:34^2:35
/15:1:2^3:5^2:12:13^4:14:15:16:18^2:19:20^2:21:28^2/
16:7:8:11f:12^2:14^2:18:21:22^2:23:25:27f^2:31/17:1:
2:6:7^2:8:8f:10^4:11f:12^2:13:14:16:17^2:21:22^2:23:
24:25^3:27,28/18:2:4:5:6,7:9:10:11^2:13:14:16:18:
19:20:22^3:24^2/19:1f:3:4:6:7:8:9^2:10^2:11:12:13^3:
14:15:19^2:22:25^2:26^2:28/20:2:3^2:5:7:8:11:19:21^2:
25:26:27:28/21:8^3:9^2:10:14:15^2:17:18f:19:28:29
/22:1:3:4:5:6:13:14^2:15:26,27:29/23:1:1f:4,5:
6,7,8:9:13,14:15,16:17,18:19,20,21:24,25^2:
26,27,28^3:32:34^2/24:5^2:7^2:10:13,14:26:30,31:
32,33^3:34^2/25:11:12:13^2:14^2:15:18^2:19^2:20:23^2:
24^3:26^3:28^2/26:2:3^6:4,5:4,5f:6^2:7^3:8^3:9^3:10:11^2:
12^2:13:14:17:18,19^2:21^2:22:23^3:24,25,26:27^2:28/
27:3:6:7:8^2:10^2:11:12:13:14^3:15^3:17:18:19^2:20f:
21^2:22/28:2:3:6:7^4:10^2:13:15^2:16^3:17:20:21^2:24^2:
26^2:27/29:3^2:4:5,6:9:11^2:12:14^2:15:18^2:19f:20^2:
21^2:22:23:24^2:25/30:2:6:8:10:15,16^2:17:18,19^5:
18,19f^3:20:21,22,23^5:29,30,31:32:33/31:10:16^2:
17:22:25:30/**Ecc1**:3-7:12-15/2:3:4,5,6:11:12:19^2
:20-23^2:24-26^2/3:1:2^4:3^4:4^4:5^4:6^4:7^4:8^4:12/4:8^2:
10:11:12:13:14:15/5:1^3:6,7^2:9:16:17:18^2:19,20^2/
6:1:2^2:3^3:4:6^2:7,8:9/7:1:2:3:4^2:5^2:6:7^2:9:15-17:19
:20:26/8:1:5^2:6,7^2:8:12^2:14:15/9:4^2:5f^2:8:10f:12^5
:13:14^3:15:17^2:18/10:1^2:2^2:3:4:5:8,9^3:10:11f:
12,13^2:14:15^2:15f:16,17^2:19:20/11:2f:3:5^2:7:8:10
/12:3:5:10^2/**Sol1**:7:9:13:14:16/2:2:9:17^2/3:4:6:9
/4:3:3f:4:5:9:12^3:13,14:15^2/5:2/6:5:7f:13:13f/7:
2^2:3f:7/8:8:9f:9^2:10f:11:14/**Is1**:4:8:9:12,13:21^2:
25:30^2/3:6:9:10:17/4:2,3,4f:5/5:1^3:2^2:7:9:10^2:18^2
:26:30/6:1:3:5^3:6^2:8:11:13^3/7:2^2:11:14^2:14f^4:17:
21,22^3:24/8:1^2:3:4:12:18/9:2^2:6^2:18/10:3:8^2:10:
14^2:15^3:16:17:18^2:19^2:21:22:25:26:27f:30^2:34/
11:1^3:6:8^2:10^2:11:12:15^2:16/13:8/14:17:19^2:23:
29^2:31:32/15:8/16:1:4,5/17:1^2:6^3:10:11:13^2/18:
2:4^2:7/19:1:4^2:14^2:19:20^2:23:24/20:3/21:1:3^2:5:
6,7:6,7f:8,9:16:16f:17/22:5^2:9,10,11:18^2:21:
23,24/23:1f:4f:7:13:15,16/24:1:13:18^2:20^3:22/
25:4^4:5:6^2:9:11/26:7:16:17:20/27:7,8^2:11^3/28:1:
2^2:4:6:10^2:15:16^2:17^2:21:23,24:27^4:29/29:4:7:8^2:
10:11:16:17^2:18:21/30:2f:13:14^3:17:21:29^3:33/
31:4,5^3/32:1:2^3:10^3/33:6:9:19:20^2:21/34:4:6^2:13
:16/35:6:7:8/36:2:3:4:6^2:8,9:16^2:17^3:21:22/37:1:
3^3:7:25:29^2:30:30f:32/38:12^3:14^2/39:1:1f:2/40:3^2
:11:15:16:19:20^4:22:26/41:7:15:25/42:6:10:13^2:
14:16:22/43:9:16^2:19^2/44:4:5:10:11:13^3:15^3:17:
19^3:20/45:13:21^2/46:1:6^2/47:7:8/48:1:18/49:2:
3:6:8,9^2:15:16:22:24^2/51:1:6:10:15:20:21/52:3:
14,15/53:2^2:3:4:7^3:9^2:10:12/54:6:7:8^2:9:11:14/
56:5:7:12/57:11:13:14/58:1:8:11/59:7:15:19:20
/60:8:15:22^2/61:7:9:10^2:11^2/62:2:3:5^3/63:14:19
/64:4:6f:10/65:8:9:10:12:15:16:17:18^2:20:21,22^2
/66:2^2:3^3:7,8^2:11:12:13:17:19:20:22:24/**Jer1**:6:
11:13:17:18/2:2:3:6:7^2:10,11:12:14:23^2:24:26,27^2
:30:31:32:33:34:35/3:1^3:2^4:3:4,5:6:20^2:23/4:2:4:
6:7^2:11,12^2:13^2:16:18:20:27:31/5:6:9:10:15^2:15f:
22:26^2:27:29:30/6:1:2^2:5f:7:9:14:22:23^2/7:11:18f^2:
28:31/8:4,5:6^2:8:14/9:1:7:9:10:12:25,26^2/10:2,3^2
:5^3:14:25/11:1:5:9:19:23/12:1:6:8:13/13:1:4:6:
11^2:21^2:23/14:2^2:8:17/15:10^2:12,13:14:17,18^3:
20^2/16:7^2:8^2:13:14,15/17:4:6:8^3:11^2:21,22/18:4:
7:9:13:20:22/19:1:4:5/20:8^2:10:11^2:15/21:1:6:
12:14/22:5:7:8:11:12:14^2:15^2:16:19:22:23^2:24,25
f:26:28/23:5,6^2:9:19:23:28:29:38,39f/25:8,9:11:
31:32:38/26:6:11:18:23/27:2^3:16/28:1^2:9:13:14
/29:1:10:11^2:23:25:26:28/30:7^2:12:19:21^2/31:8:
9:10:12:18:22f^4:31:32:32f^2/32:4:6,7:14^2:22:40/
33:9:20,21:24/34:13:21:22/35:2:5:8:13/36:2:5:
19:22^2:22f^2:26:26f:30f:32/37:1f:10:13^2:15,16:21
/38:4:6^2:9:11^2/39:7:10:18/40:8:11:12:15/41:1:7
/42:2:22/43:12/44:2,3:7:8^2:15:28/46:5:8:10^2:19
:20,21^4:22,23^2:24:27/47:2:3/48:2,3,4^2:9:26:35:
39:40:42:44^2:45/49:2:8f:9,10:14^2:19:20:22:23^2:
27:30f^2:31:33/50:3:12^2:21:22:24:29:32:39:41:43:
44/51:1:7^2:14:17:25:27^2:29:33^2:34,35:37^3:39:43:
46:60:61,62:63/52:2:7^2:22:23:30:34/**Lam1**:1^2:3:
11:13:14:15^2:16/2:1:3:6^2:9^2:18/3:9:10^2:15:27:44
:52:53^2/4:3,4,6:11:12/**Eze1**:1:4^3:10^2:16:16f^3:24:
25:26^2:27,28^2/2:3:4:5:8:9,10^2/3:12:12f:17^2:20:
27/4:1^3:3^2:4,5:9:10^2:11:12:14/5:1^2:2^2:3:4^2:14:15
/6:1:8/7:7:13:26,27/8:2:3:8^2:11^2/9:2:4/10:1:2:
9-13^3:14^2:17f/11:14:16:19/12:1:3:5:6:10:11:12:
12f:13f:16:21:27/13:10:11:13^2:18:19^2/14:1:6,7:8
:9^2/15:2/16:1:3:5:6,7^2:8:12^2:13:15:19:20:24:30^2:
31:38^2:45:47:54/17:3,4^2:5^2:6:8:9^2:12,13^4:15:
22,23/18:4:5:7:10^2:14:21:24:26:27:28:31^2/19:2^2:
3^2:4:6^2:8:9:10:11:12:14f/20:5,6^2:12^2:15:20:21:
23,24:29f:37/21:4:9,10,11:14:15:19,20^2:21:21f:
22:27:31/22:4^2:5:11^3:13:24/23:10:14,15:19,20:
21:24:27:33:41^2:48/24:3:6:15:26^2:27/25:5^2:7/26
:4:5:7:8^2:14:14f:14:21/27:5^3:10:11f:26:32/28:2,3^3
:9:12f:14f:16/29:7:9:11:18f:20f/30:2,3^2:4:18^2:20
:21^2/31:2,3^2:11:12/32:2^2:3:7:25:27^2:30/33:1:2^2:
7:12:32:33/34:5^2:12:18:23:24:25:26:29:29f/35:1
:6/36:12:13:15:17f:20:26^2:34/37:1:7:10:11:15:
16:26/38:2,3f^2:4:8:9^3:15,16:19/39:11:13:15,16^2:
17/40:2^3:3^3:7-12^5:17:23:26:27:36^2:38^2/41:3:5:7:
8:9:12:19,20^2:25/42:3:4:7,8,9,10:11:12:16-20^2/
43:8:13:14^2:15:17:19^2:22^3:23:24:25^4/44:14:22^3:
24:25^2:27:31/45:1:2:6^2:8:11^3:13:18:21:22^2:23^2/
46:4:5:7^2:13^2:14,15^3:16:17:19,20:21,22:23/47:1:
5:12/48:10:15:17^2/**Dan1**:3,4f:9:12/2:1^2:10^3:16:
19:28:31^2:34:35^2:37:39:44/3:1:4:6:10:11:13:15:
22:25:25f:27:29^2/4:3:5:10,11^2:13f^2:15:16:23f:23:
25:31/5:1^2:5:7:11^2:13:16:18:29/6:1:7^2:8:10:12^2:
13:17:21:23:24/7:1:2^2:4^3:5^2:6:7:8^2:9:10:12:12f^2:
13:23f:25/8:3:5:9f:12:15^2:16:18:23f:25:26/9:1:4:
12:15:23:25f^2:26^2:27^2/10:5,6^3:9:10:15:16:17:18/
11:2:3^3:6:6f:7f:10,11^2:13^2:14:15:17:18:20^2:21:22:
23:24:25^2:29:30,31:32f:33:34:37f:38:40f:40/12:1
:4:5:7:7f^2:11f/**Hos1**:2^2:3:4,5f:6:8:10^2:11:3:5:12:
15:16f:18:23/3:2:3:4^2/4:1:5:10:12:15^2:16:19/5:2
:3:9:10f:10:12:14/6:2:8:10:11/7:1:4:5:6:8:11:12:
16/8:1:8:9:10/9:10f:11:12/10:1:6:7:11:12:13^3/
11:1^2:4:10:11^2/12:1^2:2:3:4:10^2:11:12:13/13:1:3:
7^2:8^2:13:15:16/14:7/**Joe1**:2:6:6f:6:8:14^2/2:2^2:5^2:
11:14:15^2:19:20:27/3:3^3:8:18/**Amo1**:1:2^2:14^2/2:
6:7:13/3:4^3:5:12^5/4:4:8^2/5:3^3:7:18:19^7:20:24^2/6:
10:12:14/7:1^2:4:7^3:8^2:10^2:14^2:17^2/8:1^2:2:6^2:11^2/
9:9/**Ob1**:1:1f:1:11:17^2:18/**Jon**:3^2:4^2:6:9,10:9,10f
:14:17/3:3:3f:4,5:10/4:2:5:6:7:8:11/**Mic1**:4:6:8:
11f^6:15/2:2:12^4/3:6:12^2/4:7:9/5:1:2:7:8/6:2/7:1^2
:4:6/**Nah1**:10:15/2:1:7:8/3:11/**Hab1**:1:6:6f:6:8^2
/2:2^3:3:18/3:1f:3:6:14:19^2/**Zep1**:1:1f:7:7f:10:13:
14:15^3:17^2:18/2:5f:6^2:9:13^2:14:15^2:15f/3:6:9f:
17,18^2:20^2/**Hag1**:1:7:11^3:14,15/2:6:12:13:14:
16,17:23/**Zec1**:7:8^3:14:15/2:1^2:5/3:2f:2:5,6:9:10
/4:2^2/5:1:2:6:7:9:11f/6:10,11/7:2:14/8:6:13^2/9:
7:8:9:11:13:14:16,17^2/10:1:2:3/11:4^2:6:8:12f:15^3
:16/12:2:3:6^2/13:1^2:5^2:6^2:6f^2:8f:8/14:4:5f:12:16
/**Mal1**:6^2:7:14^3/2:5:6:8/3:2:3:8:10:12:16:17/4:1^2
/**Mt1**:1:18:19:19f:20:21:23^2:25/2:4:6:7:12:13:19
:23/3:3^2:4:16:17/4:7:8:15,16:18^2:21^2/5:12:14^2:
23^2:25:28:31:32:34:35:37^2:38^2:38f^2:41:43/6:2^2:3
:16:25:27:34/7:3^3:9^3:10:12:14:16:18^2:20^2:24:26:
27/8:2:4:5,6:14:15:16:19f:23:24:28:30:32/9:1:2^2:
8^2:9^2:12:20^2:32^2:36/10:2,3,4^2:10^2:11^2:13:24^2:29:
34:35^3:36:41^4:42^2/11:8^3:9^2:10:18f:19^2:28/12:10^2
:11:12^2:14:22:25^2:33^3:34:35:38:41:42^2:43,44,45^3
:46,47/13:2,3^2:4:8^2:17:19:20:21:22:23^2:23f^2:24:
31,32^3:33^2:44^3:45:46^2:47,48^2:55:57:58/14:5^2:6^2:
8:11:13^2:14:26/15:11f^2:13,14:22^2:23:29:30:31^2:
34/16:18:23^2:24/17:1:5^2:14^2:20:25:26,27^2/18:2:
5:6:10:12^2:15^2:21:23:28:29/19:5,6:7^2:9f:23:24^3:
29/20:2:2f^2:3^2:20:26:27:28:29/21:2:5:13^2:19:26:
28:33^3:36:41:43:46/22:1^2:11:12:16f:19^2:24:25:
31:34,35^2:41/23:11:24^2:37/24:1:15:23:26:31:32:
43:45:48/25:14:18:19:23:24,25:32:35:38:43:44/
26:5:7^2:8,9^2:10:26:27:30:36:39:47:51:59^2:69:73/
27:7^2:10:16:19:24^2:28:29^3:32:37:48^2:54f:55:57:
59:60:66f/28:2:3:4:12,13/**Mk1**:2:4:4f:6:7:10:11:
19^2:23^2:29,30:32,33:40:43,44:45^2/2:2:3^2:23/3:1^2
:4^2:6f^2:7,8,9:10:16-19^2:24:25:27/4:1:3:4:8:20^2:21^4
:26:28:31,32:37:38:39/5:1^2:7,8:11:15:21:25^2/6:
2,3^3:4:5:8,9:11^2:15:20:21:25:28:29:31:32:34:37:
37f:39,40:49/7:6,7:11:17:24:25^2:26:32^2/8:3:7:10
:11:12f:22:33:36/9:2:7^2:14:17:26:36:37:38:41:42
/10:4^2:5:6,7:11:12:15:17^2:20:25^3:26:30:35^2:45:
46^2/11:2:4,5:13^2:17^2:25:32^2/12:1^5:12:15:18:19^2:
26:27:32:35:42:43,44/13:20:28^2:34^2:35,36,37/
14:2:3^2:4,5:6:11:13^2:15:19:23:25:26:30:35:43:45:
47:51,52^2:51,52f:54:68:70/15:8^2:10:15^2:16,17^2:
19:22:26:34:36^2:38f^2:40:46^3/16:4:5/**Lk1**:5^4:8,9f:
10:13:16:17:22:26:27^3:31:34^2:39,40:42:57:63:69
/2:1:4:7^3:12^3:13:22:23^2:24:25^3:34,35:36,37^2:40/
3:1:4^2:7:22^2/4:3:5:9,10,11:12:13:25,26^2:27:31:33^2
:38:39/5:3:4:5:7:8:12^2:18,19^2:27^2:29:31:36^4/6:6:
9:14,15,16^2:17,18:23:25:39:40:41:43:44:45^2:
47,48^3:49^4/7:2:4:5:6,7,8:9:12:16^2:20,21,22:26^2:
32:32f:33:33f:34:34f:37^2:39:41/8:1:4:5^2:8:10:16:
22:23^2:27^4:30f:32:33:35:37:39:41^3:42:43,44:49/
9:3^2:4:5:5f:34:35:37:38:39:42:47:48:52:53f:58:59
/10:4:5:7:8,9:10:11:12:13f:18:24:25:30^2:31:32:
33:33f:35f:36:38^2/11:1:5,6^3:8:11^2:12:14^2:16f:17:
24^2:27:29,30:31:33^2:34^2:36:37,38:44:52:53,54/
12:6^2:7:14:16^2:21:25:37:39:42,43,44^2:45:50:53:
54:55/13:6^2:7:10:11:19^3:23:31:33:34/14:1^2:3:5:8
:10:12:15^2:16^2:18:28:32:34f/15:3,4:8^2:11:13^3:14:
15:19:20:22:23:27:29^2/16:1^2:7:10:15:18:19:20:
26/17:2,3,4:6:7,8,9:12^2:16:22/18:1:2^2:3^2:4,5:10^2
:11:12^2:13^2:18:21:25^3:34:35:36/19:1^2:3:4:5:7:11:
12^2:16:17:18:21:30^2:38:46^2:48/20:3:6:9^3:12:16:
19:24:28:29:37,38:41^2/21:2:4:12:13:13f:18:27:
36/22:2^3:5:8:10^2:12:17:19:21:23:29:36^2:37:41,4
:44:47:48:52:54:55:56:58:60/23:2:4:6:8^2:11:14:
18:32,33:36:38:43:50,51,52^3:53^2/24:5:11:17:19^2
30:37:39:42:50f/**Jn1**:6,7:8:11,12:13:14:23:28:3
32:42:47/2:1^2:10:12:15:16:18/3:1^2:10,11:14^3:22
29:33,34/4:7^2:9^2:10:11^3:14:19:27,28,29:43,44:
46,47^2/5:3:12:16:34:35:36/6:2-5^2:7:7f^2:8,9^2:14:
18,19:33:70/7:12^2:18:21,22,23^2:28:33:35:48:49:
51:52/8:2:3:37:40:44^2:48:52^2:55/9:1:2:8:11:14:
16:17/10:1^2:2:5:12^2:20^2:21^3:32:33/11:3:8:9:10:
12,13:18:37,38^3:40:44:47:52:55/12:2:3:5:12:14:
15:16:21:21f:23,24^3:28:35:40f:41:46/13:4:5:16:
34/14:19:27/15:4:5^2:6^2:13:15:20/16:2:4:16^2:21,
17:7:8/18:1:3:9:10:18:23:26:27:28f^2:30:32f:34f^2
35:37:39:40/19:1:2:12^2:13f:19:29^3:31:34:38:39:
40:41:41f:41/20:7/21:2:4:9/**Act1**:4:5:9:13:15:18
/2:2^2:9f:30:40:43/3:2:5:7,8^2:14:21,22/4:1f:4:11:
16:21:22:37/5:1:4:6:8:9:30:31:34/6:2^2:5^3/7:2f:3:
6:9:11:17,18:20:22:24:26:27:30^2:35:37:41:44:46:
58/8:1:3:9,10,11^3:27:32^2:36/9:2:3:4:10^2:11:12^2:
19:23:25:33:36^2:43/10:1^2:2^2:3:5,6:7:9,10:11:13:
22:26:27:28^2:30^2:32:39/11:5^2:7:24^2:26:28/12:7:
9:10:12^2:13:19:20:21:22^3:23/13:2:6,7^3:14:16^2:21
:22^2:29:36:37:47:50/14:3:5,6^2:8:17:19^2:28/15:6:
10:14:30/16:1^3:3:9^2:11:12:13^2:14^3:16^2:22:26:34/
17:1:2:4:5^2:12:15:18:31:32:34^3/18:2,3^2:7:9:11:14
:15:18:18f^2:19:20:22f^2:24^2:25,26/19:4:9:13:14:
15^2:17:18,19:23:24:25:26:29:31:34:38/20:1:3:6:7
:9:10,11,12:15:17:30:35/21:2:4:10:26,27^2:29:30:
37,38^3:39:40/22:3^2:6:7:12^2:17,18^2:22:25:26:27:
28:29/23:6:9^2:12,13:15:21:22:23,24:27:30/24:4:
5^3:10:12:14:15:16:17:24^2:25/25:10,11^2:13^2:14:
16:20:27/26:4:7:8:12:13:14:26:28/27:1:2:2f:2:
7,8f:12^3:13^2:14,15^2:16:21:28:34:35:39^2:41:41f/
28:1:3:4:6^2:10:11:13^2:16:18:23/**Rom1**:1:3:10:
11,12:14:27^2/2:1:5:19:25:29/3:1:2:4:5:7:21,22:
21,22f:21,22:25f/4:4,5^2:10:11:16:18^3:19^2/5:14:
15/6:2,3:5:6/7:1:2:4:6:9:21:23,24,25^2/8:3^3:9:23:
24/9:4:5:6^2:9:10-13:21^3:22:23,24:27:33/10:5:10
/11:1^3:5^2:7:10:12^3:13:17:18^3:24^2:26:28:33/12:1:
2^2:6:7^2:8:14:17/14:1:6:13:20/15:15,16^2:17:20:24
:25:27:29:32/16:1^2:5:10:13:22:23/**1Co1**:5:12:15:
22:28/2:4:14:16/3:5:8:13:15^3:18/4:2:3:5:9:17/5:
1:3,4^2:6:11^4/6:1:7:11:12:15:16^4:20/7:3:4:5:7:10^4
:12^3:13^3:14^5:15:18^2:19^2:20:21^2:22^2:24^2:26:28:33:
34^3:36:37^2:39/8:1:4:5:10:11^2:12/9:4:5f^2:5:5f^2:5:
7^2:9:13:17:19^2:21:22:24:25^2:25f:25/10:1:3,4:3,4f
:3,4:12:27^3:32/11:3:4:5^3:6^3:7^2:10^4:13:14,15:16^2:
28/12:2:7:13:15^3:16:19^2:24:27:28:29/13:2:11^3:
12^2/14:2:4:5:9:11^3:14:22^2:24^2:27:29,30^2:32^2:37:
40/15:19:31:32:36^3:37:38^2:45:45f:48^2:49^2:52^2/
16:3:5:7:9:17:18:20/**2Co1**:3,4:10:15,16:17:23/2:
11:14:15:16^3:17/3:1:2:3:13:14/4:7/5:5:16:17^3/
6:2^2:3:15^2:18/7:7:8^2:9:10:13/8:10:18/9:2:5:6^3:
12/10:10/11:1:2:4^2:6:16^3:17:21:29:33/12:2,3f:
2,3:4:7^3:9:11^2:13^2:16/13:1:3:7/**Gal1**:1f:1:6:12:18
/2:3:5:14^2:20/3:1^2:5:10:12:13^2:15:18:21,22/4:1^2
:4^2:15f:18:19:26:27/6:1:3:7:8:9^2/**Eph1**:4:9/2:8:9
:11:20:21/3:1/4^2:11^2:12:22:24:27:29/5:1:2:5:23:
27^3:28^3:31:33^2/6:2:3:4:21/**Php1**:7:11:12:13:25:
28^2:30/2:3:7:8^2:9:15^2:17:20:22/3:5^4/4:10:12:18
/**Col1**:20:22/2:9:11^2:12:13:18^2:23/3:3:10:11:12:
17:25/4:1:7:9:10^3:11:12/**1Th1**:5/2:6:7:9:11:17/
3:2,3/4:11:12:13:16/5:2:3^2:4/**2Th2**:3:15/3:6:8:
15/**1Ti1**:1:2/3:1^4:2^3:3:4:5:6^2:10:16^2/4:6:8^2:12:
16/5:8^2:9:9f:16:21:22^2:23/6:2^2:3:5:7:10:12:13:19
/**2Ti1**:14:16:18/2:3:6^2:8:9:15:17:19^4:20/3:1:5f:
11:15/4:3:8:17/**Tit1**:6:12:15^2/3:10:11^2/**Phm1**:1:
8,9:15:16^3:22/**Heb2**:7:9:10:14:16^2:17/3:3^2:5^2:17
/4:9/5:1^2:4:6:7f^3:10:12,13^3/6:7:12:14^2:15:16:18:
19/7:1^2:2:3:4^2:5:6^2:7:11:12,13,14:16^2:17:19:20:
21:24/8:4:5:6^2:8/9:1^2:3^2:4^2:7:14:16^2:24/10:1:5:9
:28:31/11:6:7:9:11:12^2:16:18:28:31:33^2:34:35/
12:1:2:7:10:11:12:13:14:16:18:19^2:28:29/13:9^2:
11:22/**Jas1**:1:3:5:6^2:9:10,11^2:18:22:23^3:26/2:2:3
:4:11^2:15:24:25/3:3^2:4^2:5^2:6^2:11:12^3:13:18/4:1:2
:4:13^3/5:7:11:12:14:16:20/**1Pe1**:6:12:18:20:23:
24/2:2,3f:2,3:22:24/3:4:10:15/4:9^2:14:15:16/5:1
:4:8:10:12^2/**2Pe1**:1:3:9/2:1:7,8:13^2:14:16:19^2:20
:22^2/3:5,6:7:8^2:10^2:13/**1Jn1**:10/2:4^2:5:6:7:22:23
/3:2:5:9:10^2:14:15:17^2/4:1:2:6:8:13:19:20/5:1:
6,7,8:10:16^2:17:17f^2:18/**2Jn1**:7^2:11:12/**3Jn**:5:6:
9:15/**Jud**:1^2:5:6:7^2:12/**Rev**:1:3:8:9:10^3:11:13f:13^2
:16/2:1^2:14:17^2:18:20^2:22:27^2/3:1:3:8:12^2:17/4:
1^2:2:3^3:6:7^2/5:1^2:2^2:6:8:9:10/6:1:2^3:4^2:5^2:6^2:6f^3:
8:11:12:14/7:1:9:10/8:3^2:5:8,9^4:10^2:11:12^3:13/9
:1f:13:15:16f^2/10:1^2:2:3^2:4:10/11:1:6:7:8,9:10:
11:12^2:13^2:19^2/12:1^3:3:4:5^2:6:10:14^2:14f^2:15/13:
1:2^2:11^2:14:16:17:18/14:1:2^3:3:4:9:13:14:14f:14^2

A Con't)
0:20/15:7/16:1:3:15:16:17:18^2:21/17:3^2:4:5:9:
3:17^2/18:2^3:6:8:15:16:17:19:21^3:23^2/19:1:5:6^2:
0:11:12:15/20:1:3:4:6:8:11/21:1^2:2^2:3:6^2:10^2:
1:15:16^2:17f^2:21/22:1:2f:2:9:13

9100

BOUT

Gen1:14,15/3:11/8:1/11:3,4/17:21/21:6:22:25/
4:15,16/25:22:34/26:7:35/29:12,13:14/30:22:
0/34:4/35:22/38:1:24/39:7:11/40:23/41:8^2:28
1,42/43:7:23:27:29/44:7/45:13:20/46:33/48:
1/Ex1:8f/2:15/3:13:16/4:28/5:7,8/9:18/10:2/
1:4/12:26/13:14/16:16:36/18:1:7:9^2/25:39/32
:28:34/38:4/Lev5:1/6:3/8:24f/10:16/11:
9,30/27:10/Num7:13:14:84,85,86^5/9:8/11:1:7:
8/13:22f/14:13:26,27/17:10/20:5/22:22,23/
4:25f/30:5/Deu4:9:10/6:6:7/8:19/11:8:10:19/
2:19/13:11:12,13,14/15:10/17:13/19:20/21:
1/24:1/28:21/30:16/31/32:7/Jos1:8^2/2:5/3:
,3,4/7:5:9:10,11/14:6/15:18,19/22:11/Ju1:14/
:10:15/3:29/4:5f/5:1:3/6:13/7:12,13/9:7:25:
2:49/11:4/12:3/13:8:12/14:6:19/17:2/18:4:8/
9:2:30/20:12:31:35-39/Ru2:10,11:19/3:11/4:4
1Sa2:23,24,25/3:12/4:6:14/6:2/7:3:7/8:9/9:5^2
12,13:16:17:20/10:2:11/11:4:5/12:9/13:15/14:
4^2/16:2/17:25:28:32:55f:58/18:20/19:3:5^2/20:
^{3}:12^3:19:26/21:11/22:2/23:13/24:4/25:36:
37,38/28:1/29:5/2Sa3:8:26:28/4:1/8:9/9:2/10:
,8/12:18/13:13:20:21-24:26/14:10/17:5:18/18
32/19:8,9,10:31,32/21:1:16/1Ki1:5:11:18/2:28:
44/5:2,3/10:4:6^2:14/11:9,10/12:2,3,4/14:5:15/
6:13/18:18:27:32:44/20:5,6:16/21:2:7:27/22:3
/2Ki1:16/3:20:21/4:15,16:19/5:8/6:11/8:3:5/9:
18:19/10:6:32,33/12:7:17/14:10:13/15:15/19:
27^2/21:7:12/22:9,10/1Ch16:8:24/2Ch2:4:14/9:
5/16:7/19:3/23:2,3/24:27^2/25:9:19/28:10:16/
32:19:24:31/34:26/35:24,25/Ez4:4,5:16/10:11/
Neh1:2/2:11,12:16:18/4:8/5:1:7/6:16/9:14:30/
13:23/Est1:13-15/2:11:22/3:3,4:8/4:4:7/5:7,8:
11/7:5/Job5:24/13:12:17:25/20:23/21:4/22:14
/23:4,5/24:10/27:11:12/28:22/30:18/31:14/32:
13/34:36/35:14,15/38:17,18:19/41:9/42:3^2:5:7
/Ps1:2/9:1:11/19:2/22:30/26:7/30:9/31:13/35:
11:14:22/40:9:17/41:7/45:10,11/49:6/50:3:8/
52:1/59:16/69:11:19/71:18:24/73:17:28/77:12/
78:4:11,12/88:12/89:1^2:51/96:3/97:7/98:1/101
/104:34/105:2/107:22:43/109:6:15:20/115:12/
119:11:44,45,46:59,60:69:97:148:172/138:5/
139:1:14:17,18/145:5:7^2:11:12^2/Pro1:4/5:7/7:
25/13:16/17:9/18:2/20:14/24:11,12:28,29/25:
18:27/27:1/28:4:5/30:32/Ecc1:12-15:16-18f/2:
18/3:10/6/7:2/8:9,10/9:15/10:14/12:1/Sol5:9
/7:2/Is5:1:7:22/6:2/8:6/12:4/19:11/27:13/30:
10,11/32:6/36:19/38:9/43:26/44:8/47:7^2/48:1
/51/59:4/61:10/65:1:17:24/Jer2:36/3:4,5:16/5
:15f/7:13,14/11:18/14/17:15/22:11/23:34:
38,39/26:21/29:27/30:14/33:3/36:13/37:7/40:
16/49:28/50:14/52:1:23/Lam3:62/4:20/Eze8:
16/11:15/16:2/18/23:6/33:30^2:31/34:6/36:21/
39:25/40:14:29,30f:42/43:11/44:5/45:11f:12/
Dan3:16/4:2/6:4:10:12/7:19:20/8:26^2/Hos1:
4,5/4:19f/7:3^2/Joe1:3/Amo4:5/8:8/Ob1:16/
Jon3:3f^3/4:2:4/Mic3:6/Hab1:5/Zep:1f/Hag2:
11:21/Zec1:14/4:11:12/5:2/7:3:5/8:9/13:6f/
Mal3:16/Mt2:1/3:3/4:23/5:11:12/6:2:5:16:25:
26:28^2:31,32^2:34/7:3:22/9:30:35/10:18:19/11:1
f:2:4:5:7:16/12:1:16:24/13:11:18:19/14:1:21:25
/15:31/16:8:11:21/17:25/18:1/20:18:22/21:28:
45/22:5:42/24:14:15:41/26:59:62:70/27:3:46/
28:14/Mk1:29,30/2:25,26/3:7,8/4:11,12:13:14:
37:38/5:16:20:27/6:14^2:43,44:48/7:6,7:24f:25/8
:1:8,9:16:19:27:31:32/9:10:11:12,13:16:34/10:3
/11:18:30/12:26/13:11/14:4,5:49:57:68:71/15:
3,4:9:25:31:33/Lk1:8,9:56:66:78/2:1:15:17:19:
33/3:14:23-38/5:30/6:35:41/7:3:18:24:31/8:10:
22:39/9:2:9:11:14^2/10:15:26:42/11:5,6:19:25f:
42:49/12:1:11:17:22:29:53:56/13:1:4:14:18/15:
14/16:2:11:13:28/17:22:28/19:22:27/20:19^2/21
:5:14/22:37^2:49:59:60/23:8/24:17^2:18:27:36:44
/Jn1:15:18:30:32:39:45/3:12:25f/4:1:9:21-24^3:
32:52/5:31:32,33:34:37:44:46/6:27:43:52/7:12:
36:43:49/8:5:14:27:54^2/9:15:29:30/10:19/11:4/
12:17:18:22:34/15:26:27/16:13:17,18:25/17:6/
18:19:34f/19:14/20:30,31/21:8:21/Act1:1:3:8^2:
15/2:6:11:40:41/3:12:24/4:4:16:18:20:33/5:7:
20:21:28:36/6:11/7:20/8:4:5:34:35/9:13:20:24:
27:30:37/10:3:22:36,37:43:46,47/11:12:20/12:1
/13:19,20:22:27:32,33/14:2:4/15:2:12:14/17:3:
18:19:23:30:32/18:25,26^2:27/19:7:23:27:39/20:
24:25/21:37,38/22:6:30/23:11:29/24:24:25/25:
2:19^2/26:13:16^2:26/27:9f:9:27/28:15f^2:22:23^2:
31^2/Rom1:3:8:9:16:19:21:25/2:1^2:27/3:4:18:
21,22:27/4:1:9:19/6:15:21/7:6:13/8:38/9:10-13
:17:30/10:14^2:15:17:18/11:2,3^2:8:13:18:25:26/
14:1:1f:2/15:14:27/16:17:19/1Co1:20:23/2:10:
12:13/3:4/4:2:3^2:7:13:14:15/5:1:3,4:6:10/7:1:18
:25:33/8:1:4/9:5f^2:9:10:22/10:11:15:27:29/11:3:
13:16^2:17:18^2:22:23:29:34/12:1^2:31/13:2^2:6:12/
14:24/16:1/2Co1:8:12:19:24/2:4:5,6:14/3:1^2:4:
6/4:4:5^2/5:12^2:13,14:16/7:7^2:11^2/8:6:10:15:22/
9:1:3/10:8:10^2:16:17^2:18/11:4:6:10:21^2:30/12:1:
5^2:6:9:10^2:11^2:20:21/Gal1:8:16/2:2:14:17/3:2:
8,9/4:12:23/5:6:10/6:14:17/Eph1:13/3:4:6:7/4:
8:13^2:14:19/5/6:21/Php1:5:7^2:14:18/2:4:18:19:
21/3:19/4:6^2:8^3/Col1:6:8:9^2:28/3:2:12/1Th1:3:
8^2:9/5:1:4/2Th1:4:10/2:1^2/1Ti:2/5:22:24/2Ti1:
1:8/2:2/3:11/Tit1:12/2:7/3:9/Phm1:1/Heb1:
5,6/2:5:6:12/3:1:13/4:8^2:13^2/5:12,13/6:1^3:2:16
/9:10/10:8:32/11:4:7:19:37,38/12:3:16/13:3:9:
17/Jas3:13:14/4:11:16/5:9:13:20/1Pe1:10:11:
12/2:1:2,3f/3:1:3:9/5:7/2Pe2:1:12:18:20:21/3:1
:9:15,16/1Jn1:3/2:18:26/3:7/4:3:5/5:10:17:17f
/3Jn1:4:9:10:14/Jud:3:9:14^2/Rev:9/2:5:6:9:10/
3:19/9:21/10:4:11/12:4/19:10/20:4

1136

ABOVE

Gen1:6:7,8/7:17:18:20/10:32/22:17/36:15,16/
49:25/Ex6:19/12:7:22/25:20:22:34,35/30:6/36:
14,15/37:20,21/39:21/Lev8:15,16/14:5/15:25/
16:1:13/27:3f/Num5:30/7:89/9:22/11:31/12:
10/14:14/Deu7:14/9:17/10:15/11:21/28:23/33
:24/Jos13:19/15:8/Ju5:24/9:11/1Sa4:4/9:22/
10:23/13:18/2Sa6:1:21/22:14:17:49/1Ki7:3,4:
27-30/11:32/2Ki15:29f/19:15/23:12/1Ch13:6:
6f/16:25/2Ch4:2/15:15/33:7/34:4/Neh10:1/
Job17:8/28:18/31:2,3/35:5/Ps7:7,8:17/9:2/18:
13/21:7/46:4/47:2:8/48:2/50:21/57:5^2:11/78:
17:35:56/80:1/83:18/84:5/87/91:1:9/92:1/95:3
f/99:2/103:11/105:39/107:11/108:5/113:4/
118:11/119:117/138:2f/148:4^2/Pro4:23/8:11/
Is5:16/13:10/34:4/37:16,17/40:22/48:13/49:
11/Jer31:33f/35:4/48:40/51:60/Lam3:54/Eze
1:22:25f:25:26/8:11/9:3:3f/10:1:4:18:19/11:22:
23/19:11/29:15/31:5:10/32:8/41:6:15,16:17,18
/Dan12:6/Jon2:5/Mt10:24/23:3/27:37/Mk2:4
/5:11/15:26:38f/Lk1:42/5:18,19/9:34/23:38/
Jn8:23/16:26f/19:11/Act2:2:6/27:4f/Rom8:39
/1Co3:18^2/15:47/Eph1:21/Php2:9/Heb9:5/
Jas5:9/1Pe2:4/Rev14:13

167

ACROSS

Gen2:5:6:11,12/6:11/8:1/9:23/11:9/19:28/25:
18/31:47,48/32:22,23,24/41:46/Ex8:2/9:18/14
:9/19:24/26:7,8:9:26,27:35/39:10/Num4:26/24
:2/26:63/27:12/31/32:6:7:21/33:50,51/36:13/
Deu1:40/2:1:14,15:23:29/3:18:20:28/32:47:49^2
/34:1^2:2/Jos1:2:10,11:14/3:6:11/4:1:7:10:12,13
:23/5:6/8:14:15/13:32/17:5,6/18:16/19:33/20:
8/22:10/24:3/Ju3:22,23/5:4:17/7:12,13:24:25/
9:7/11:26:29/16:3/19:28/20:1/1Sa5:11/14:6/
17:8:40/30:16/2Sa2:29/4:6,7/5:18:22/17:16:22
:24/18:8:23/19:8,9,10:15:16:18:31,32:33:36:41/
20:14/24:13/1Ki7:10/11:7/19:19/2Ki2:8:13,14
/3:22/11:11/19:35/1Ch5:11/6:78,79/13:5/2Ch
2:16/3:11,12,13:14/4:2/16:9/17:4/18:23/20:4/
21:17/23:2,3/Neh3:19/Est6:1/Job8:16/37:3/
38:32/41:18:30/Ps19:5/65:10/66:6:12/74:15/
83:14/97:4/106:9/141:6,7/147:14/Pro30:18,19
/Ecc8:16,17/Sol4:1^2/6:5/Is7:19/15:7/23:2,3/
30:6/41:18/50:3/Jer8:19/9:22/25/31:38,39/39
:4/46:12/48:34/52:7/Lam2:3/Eze5:2/31:12/32
:8/37:1:7/40:13:19:21:23:27/42:11/47:3:5/48:1:
23^2:26/Dan8:16/11:10,11/Joe2:5/Amo7:10/9:
8/Jon3:3f/Mic1:8/5:5/Nah3:18/Hab1:6/3:3:
12:15/Zec6:7/14:5/Mt4:25/8:23/9:1/13:4/16:
5/19:1/24:27/27:32:60:66f/Mk4:3/5:21/6:45/
11:7/13:3,4/15:33/Lk7:17/8:23:26/17:24/19:
35/23:44/24:17:50f/Jn6:17:22,23:24/11:37,38/
Act5:15/13:6,7/16:11:23/17:26/19:21/27:7,8:
17/Rev1:13/12:10/15:6/20:9/21:17

232

AFTER

Gen4:17/5:3,4,5f:3,4,5:3,4,5f/7:3/8:3,4:6:13/9:
28/10:1:32/11:10,11^2:12,13f:12,13:14,15:20,21/
12:1/13:14/14/15:16/16:2,3/17:7,8:12/19:3/21
:4,5:11/22:20-23/24:67/25:11:21/26:18/27:
8,9,10/29:3:14/30:25/31:36,37/35:8^2:17/36:
18,19:40-43/37:26,27/38:12:29/39:10:23/41:14
:49/43:20/44:4/47:28/48:1:7/Ex1:8f/4:9:10/5:
1/6:8,9/11:1/12:17:51/14:4:5:10:17:28/15:9/16
:1/17:15,16/19:1:2,3:11/21:6:8/22:30/29:37/30
:13f/33:6/Lev6:16:18/7:9:15/8:33/10:12/11:32
/12:7^2/13:34:55:56:58^2/14:48/15:3:18:25:28/
16:1:11:17/17:15/18:14f/22:6/23:9,10,11:43/
25:46/26:4,5:9:26/27:18/Num1:1/3:47,48f:50f/
6:18:19:20/8:15:22:25,26/9:1/10:13:33/11:3:6/
12:14/14:10,11/16:11,12/19:12/25:8:9/26:1:5-
5-11^5:12-14^5:15-18^7:19-22^6:23-25^5:26,27^4:28-37^{13}
:38-41^9:42,43:44-47^7:48-50^5:57^3/27:13/32:42/
33:3,4:5,6:38,39:41/35:28/Deu1:1/3:14:20/11:
12/15:17/16:9:13/21:14/22:13,14/23:3:13/24:
19:21/31:1:16:27:29/32:50/Jos1:1/2:11:12,13:
22/5:8,9/6:11/7:2/8:16/10:21:36/14:15/15:13/
18:1/19:47,48/22:28/23:1/24:6:29/Ju1:1:16/3:
17,18,19:25:31/4:1/5:31/7:8,9:19,20/8:5/10:1/
11:16:25:26:39/13:12/18:22:23:29/20:31:42/Ru
1:8/2:4,5/3:6,7/1Sa1:9:25/3:2,3/4:3/6:16/9:5:
25/10:5/14:37/17:35:52:57/18:1:6:21/19:8/20:
15:19/23:13:14,15/24:1:7,8^2/26:9/30:8:9,10/
2Sa1:1/2:19:21:24/3:8:22/5:13/6/8:1:13/10:1:
19/11:4:10/13:4:37,38,39/14:28/15:7,8/17:1:
28,29/19:39/20:6:7:8,9,10/21:1:12,13,14:17/22
:1/23:4:5:11,12/24:10/1Ki6:1:9/8:35,36/9:25/
10:8/13:14:23/17:7/18:33/19:11:12^2:20/20:23/
22:32,33/2Ki1:1/3:5/4:40/5:20/6:23:25/7:8/8:
3/9:27/10:15/11:20/12:1/14:22/15:14/18:5/22
:20/24:7/25:4,5/1Ch1:11,12/2:19:24/4:8/6:31/
12:19/13:1/14:3:12/17:1/18:13/19:16/20:1/23:
6:7:8,9:10,11:12/24:1/26:12:23,24/2Ch12:12:13
/18:31/19:4/20:21/21:11:17,18/22:4/24:11:17,18/25:
25:27/26:2:17,18/30:21/32:1/33:14/34:8:28/36
:17/Ez8:22:33/9:10:13/Neh2:11,12/3:14/5:7/6
:15/7:1:3:6:63/Est2:1:4/3:3,4:15/Job7:6/15:
27,28/19:26/20:17/29:18:22/30:5^2/36:14/42:7:
16:17/Ps10:15/49:11:13/51:1:8/68:30f/70:2,3/
84:6/88:7/102:8:28/110:4f/119:7/145:13/Pro
10:7/19/23:26,27,28/25:1f/27:25,26,27/Ecc2:3
:12f/6:12/7:27,28/Is1:21/7:8f:10/9:13:21/10:
12/13:20/21:8,9^2/23:17/29:1/44:15/56:11/64:
12/Jer2:25/3:15/7:18f:25/9:22/14:19/24:1/25:
12:26/29:1/30:21f/32:16:33^2/33:15f/34:8:14/
35:15/36:1f:27/38:16/39:11,12/41:10/45:1/51:
59f/52:30/Lam3:66/Eze5:2:12/7:5,6/12:14/15:
5,6/16:28/17:15:18/20:1:35,36/26:1/37:25/38:
8:17/40:1/44:31/46:19,20/47:5/Dan1:1:11:16/
2:39^2/4:8:29/9:26:27/10:20,21/11:12:18:20/12:
7/Hos1:7f:8:5:7:15/4:2:12/7:7/11:10/14:8/Joe
1:4^2/2:28/Amo7:1/9:3/Jon1:6/Mic2:3/Nah:2:7
/Zep1:1f/Zec3:10/11:16/Mt1:12/2:9:13/3:16/
13:21/14:22/17:9/19:1/22:18:23:46/24:29:34f/
25:19/26:32:48:73/27:26:31:35:53:62f:63/Mk1:
14/6:45:52/8:8,9,10/9:9/10:1f:34/12/13:24/14:
28/16:12f/Lk1:3:48:59/2:22:43/3:19,20:21/4:
38/5:39/7:24:42/9:10:49/13:31/15:30/19:28:47
/20:31/22:20:58/23:9/24:27/Jn2:12:22/3:1/4:
13:40,41:54/6:1/7:10:26:31/11:7/12:16:19:36/
13:12/14:9/16:16/18:1:8/20:19/21:15/Act1:1:3
:9/2:1f/3:15/4:31/5:4:30:37/8:25/9:23:28/10:
40,41/11:19/12:4:12/13:3:15:22:36/14:21/15:3
:7/16:18/17:8,9:27/18:5:7:18:23/19:21/20:23:
29/21:1:7:19/22:17,18/24:17/25:1:23/27:38/28
:11:17:25/Rom1:21/2:12-15/4:11/7:3/8:4:5:6^2:
11/14:17/15:23:24/1Co7:16/9:27/10:5/11:25:
34/14:31/15:5f:6:8:9:24:32/16:5/2Co4:17/9:4/
10:6:16/Gal1:13:21/3:2:19/4:23/6:9/Eph4:8/
Php3:17/Col4:16/1Th2:15:17/1Ti1:19/5:11/6:
7/Tit1:11/2:12/3:10/Heb4:1:7:10/5:9/7:1/9:17
:19:27/10:1:8:11:26/11:30:34/12:4:15/1Pe1:7/
3:11/4:2/5:10/2Pe1:9:15/2:7,8:13/3:5,6/Jud1:
4:14/Rev4:8^2/6/7:9/9:20/11:11/14:17/17:8:11
/18:1/19

759

AGAIN

Gen1:4,5/7:3/8:10:12:21^2/9:9,10,11:15/13:3,4/
18:1:27/19:2:33:34:35/21:32/22:15:19/23:12/
24:20/25:1/26:21:22:31/29:3:33:34:35/30:7:17:
19:31,32/31:7^3/32:1:10^2:22,23,24/34:26/35:5:9
/37:1/38:11:23/41:5:7/43:2:3,4,5:21:28/44:13:
25/45:4/46:3,4:30/47:10:15:18/48:11:21/Ex2:
13/4:4:6:7^2:6:10:11/8:1:29:31,32/10:1:14:28:29
/11:6/12:16:20/13:16/14:4:5:13:26/21:8:19/24:
7/34:34:35/37:17/Lev8:34:35/9:23/11:12:32/
12:7:8/13:5:6^2:7:8:16,17:27:32:34:36:51:53/14:9
:19:39:43:44:48/16:17:23:24/20:22f/22:7:13/23
:36/25:13:28/26:4,5:42/27:14,15:19:20/Num1:
51/3:14,15/6:11:12:20/12:14:15/16:8,9:41/17:
10/18:5:6/19:17/20:2/22:15:25:27/23:29/28:25
/32:31/Deu1:31^2:43/4:29/5:25/9:5:6:22^3/10:4:
10/11:5/17:16/18/24:4/28:31:68/30:4:5:6:9/33
:11/Jos4:18:21/5:11,12/6:11:12,13,14^2:15/8:6/
15:10,11^2/22:17,18/Ju2:19:20/3:12:17,18,19/4:
1:19/5:11^2/6:1^2:16f/9:42/10:6:10:15/13:1:8:9^2:
10/15:7/16:12:13:22:28/18:21/19:3:8^2/20:

(AGAIN Con't)
27,28:30:32/21:8,9/Ru1:6,7:14/2:15/3:1/4:
16,17/1Sa1:18/3:6^2:9^2/4:10/5:3:4:11/7:13/8:
22^2/10:25^2/12:1:10/13:3,4/15:11:30:35/16:
15,16/17:38,39/20:17/23:4^2:22:27/27:1:11^2/
2Sa2:22/3:33,34/5:22/10:18/11:13/12:21:23/
13:10/14:14:17:29^2/15:25,26/19:8,9,10:30:37:
43/20:8,9,10/21:17/22:39/24:1/1Ki1:31/8:
33,34^2/13:4:6^2:24,25/17:14:22/18:1:22:34:43^3/
19:6:7:14:19/20:5,6:26/2Ki1:12/2:4/4:15,16:34:
35/5:7:17:19/6:22/8:8,9/13:5/17:13^2/19:30/20
:4:8/21/23:10/1Ch9:2/11/14:13:14/17:9/19:5:
17,18:19/20:4/21:28/29:22/2Ch1:12/6:37,38/7
:6/15:4/19/23:2,3/24:11:17,18/25:10/29:35/30
:9/31:1/32:15/33:8/35:2/36:15^2/Ez5:1/9:10:14
/Neh2:14,15/4:1/5:8/9:28:30:38/13:6:11:21/
Est2:1:12,13,14/5:7,8:12/7:2/8:4/9:13:15/Job2
:1/3:6/5:18:19^2/7:10/10:9:17^2/14:7:8,9:11,12:
13:14/16^2/20:9/21:21/22:29/27:6^2/33:8^2:14^2:
25/34:15:29,30/35:6^2/40/41:8/Ps4:1/27:13^2/
28:5/30:2/31:16/36:12/37:35,36/39:13/41:10/
42:4,5^2:10^2:11/43:5^2/48/51:2:7:8:12/53:6/60:1
/71:20:21/77:7/78:41^2/80:3:7:18:19/85:4:6/90:
16/94:15/104:9:23:29/106:13:43^2/107:12:26:35
/119:8:106^2:107:149:154:156/137:5,6/Pro2:19/
24:15,16/Ecc1:3-7^3/2:3/3:15/4:16/9:11/Sol1:2^2
/5:3/6:13/Is1:5,6^2:26/6:13^3/8:1:5/9:3/13:20^2/
14:1/21:12^2/23:15,16^2:17/24:20/26:14:19^2/27:
9/28:10:13:16:19^2/29:17/32:15/37:30:31/38:9:
11^2:21/39:1/42:9/43:25/44:26/47:1:5:12/48:3/
49:8,9/51:3:11/52:3:5:8/53:10/54:9^2/60/62:4:8^2
/63/65:10/Jer2:1:31/3:1^2:7:12:14:19:22/6:9^2/7
:10:13,14^2/8:2:4,5^2/10:20/11:1:7:9:15/12:17/13
:3:6/14:11/16:14,15/18:4:18/20:9/22:10:12:27/
23:4/24:6/25:4^2/26:5^2/27:16^2:22/28:11/29:10:
14:19^2/30:3:10:17:18:21/31:4:5:10:15:16:17:18:
21:23:40/32:5^2:15:37:40:43:44/33:10,11:13:23/
34:11:16:22/35:14^2/36:28:32/39:1/42:18/43:8/
44:4:14/46:16/47:6/49:2:33/50:3:5^2:8:19:34:39:
40/51:26:39:57/Lam3:40/5:21/Eze:9/6:1/11:
14:17:24/12:1:21/13:9/16:1:8:53:55:63/17:14:
17/18:1/19:9/20:14:22/21:5:8:24^2/22:23:30/23
:1/24:15/25:1/26:20/28:25/29:13:15^2/30:21/
33:1:18:22/34:15,16:29/35:1:9/36:8:11:12^2:22:
24:30:33:34/37:3:5:9:12:14:15/38:12/39:26:29/
40:27/43:1/44:26/46:21,22/47:4/Dan2:7/4:26/
6:15/8:13:27/9:6^2:15:17/10:16:18:20,21/11:8:9:
19:29:30,31:40/12:13/Hos1:6:8:11:14/3:1/5:4:
15/6:2/11:11/12:9/14:3/Joe2:2:22:24:26^2:27:
28/3:7/Amo1:3^2:6^2:9^2:11^2:13^2/2:1^2:4^2:6^2/8:2:5:
8:14/9:5:13:14:15/Jon1:12/2:4/3:1/Mic1:16/2:
3:7:12/4:7:8/5:13/6:5^2/7:8:19/Nah1:9:15^2/2:2:
13^2/3:3/Hab:2/Zep2:7/3:10:20/Hag1:13/Zec:
3:12:17^3/2:1:6,7/5:1:8/6:1/8:4:8/9/10^2:9^2/11:
15/13:3/14:11/Mal1:4/Mt2:9^2/5:32:33/6:7,8^2:
11/9:18:25/13:16:45:47,48/14:2/15:17:25/16:
11:21:25/17:22,23/18:16/19:24/20:5:6:19/21/
23:39/24:21/25:14/26:29:32:42:43:44:72/27:1:
21:31:40:50:52:63/28:6/Mk1:40:43,44/2:13/3:
1:20/4:1/5:10^2/6:14:15/7:37^2/8:1:25:28:31/9:
26:30,31/10:10:24:34:48^2/11:14:27,28/13:19/
14:25:28:39:40:70/15:20/Lk1:64/2:15:20/5:5:
26/6:10/7:6,7,8:14:20,21,22:45^2/9:7:11:22/12:
59/13:6^2:18:35/14:6/15:27/16:29^2/17:4:22/18:
33/20:9:36/22:16:18:32:45/24:6,7^2:12:46/Jn1:
33/2:22/3:3:4^2:7:13/4:15/5:29/6:35:44:53:62/8
:2:7:8:10:21/9:27/10:17:18:19:31:39/11:8:22:23
:25^2:37,38/12:9:28/13:12/14:19:20:28/16:16:20
:22/18:7:25:27:38/19:4:9:13/20:9:21:26/21:1/
Act1:20/2:24/3:15:20:26/4:10:17:18/5:28:30:40
/6:13/7:26/8:39/9:12/10:15:16:40,41/11:9/13:
30:32,33:34:42/14:21:25/15:36/16:7:23^2/17:31
/18:21:23/19:9:34/20:25:38/23:15:20/24:21:25
/26:8/27:28/28:11/Rom4:17:25/6:4:9:14f:14/7:
4/8:11:23:34/10:7/11:23:24/14:9/15:11:24/
1Co3:20/7:5:39:40/11:26/15:12:15:20:22:23:29^2
:32:35:42:43^2/2Co1:10^2:13,14/4:9:14/5:12:15/7
:2:16^2/8:17/11:6^2:16:21:23^3/12:8:14/13:2/Gal1
:9/2:1/3:5/4:9:19/5:1:3:21/Eph2:5/5:33/Php1:
26:27/2:26:28/3:1^2:10:18/4:2:4:10/Col3:1:4/
1Th2:18^2:19/3:10:11/4:14/5:23/2Th2:1/1Ti3:
16/5:11:14:16/2Ti1:4/2:8:23/4:8/Heb5:12,13/
6:1^2:4:6^2:14^2/9:25^2:26^2:28^2/10:1^2:17:25/11:19^2:
34:35/12:17/13:20,21/Jas4:4/5:18^2:19/1Pe1:3^2
/2Pe:16/2:20:22^2/1Jn1:3/3:9/5:6,7,8/Rev1:5f:
8/2:5:22/3:3/7:16/10:8/18:14:22^2:23/19:3^2:6/
20:3:4:10/22:9
1146

AGAINST
Gen4:24/10:9f^2/13:13/14:2:8,9:17/16:9-12/20:
6:16/28:6,7,8/30:23,24/31:5:47,48/34:6,7/39:9
/42:36/Ex1:10/2:19/4:25,26/10:16^2/11:7/12:
22^2/14:11:25:31/15:7:24/16:2:7,8,9^2/17:7:8/18:
13/20:20/22:24/23:6:21/24:6/32:10:11:12:33/
34:15:16/Lev3:2:7,8:13/5:15/6:2/17:10/19:16f
/20:3:5:6:23/26:17:23:24:25:40,41^3/Num1:53/5
:27:29/10:9/11:1:33/12:9/13:31/14:2:9:29:
34,35:36,37,38/16:2:11,12:19:41/17:5/20:2:13:
24/21:5^2:7^2/22:25/23:18-24/25:3/26:5-11/27:
3,4:14/31:3/32:10,11:14:23/35:30/Deu1:26:43:
44/2:14,15:24/3:3/6:15:16:22/7:4:19:23:24/9:1:
7:16:24/11:3:4:17:25/13:5:15/15:2:7:9/20:4:10:
18/22:30f/24:14,15^2/28:7:47,48:49/29:7:20:27/
30:7,8^2:19/31:17:27:28/33:7:17/Jos1:17,18/3:
13,14:15,16/7:20/9:1/10:18/15:15/21:44/22:12
:16^2:19:20:22,23:29:31:33/23:1:3:15,16/24:8:9:
11^2:27/Ju1:1:10:12/2:12-14:15:20/3:7:8:10:16:
21/4:1:24/5:13,14:23/6:33/9:18:31:33:49/10:
10:18/11:4:6:8:27^2:32/12:1/16:25,26^2:29/19:30
/20:14,15:18:22,23,24:27,28:34/1Sa2:10^2:
23,24,25/7:13/11:1:11/12:14:15:23/13:12/14:
33:34:47/17:21/18:17:30/19:4:8/20:16:24,25/
22:8:13^2:15/24:11/26:19/27:10/29:4^2/31:1/
2Sa1:6/3:28/5:6:19/6:7:10/7:10,11/10:11/11:
23/12:11:13/15:10:13/18:28:31/20:21/22:40/
24:1:17/1Ki2:23,24/6:5/8:44:46/11:9,10/12:19:
23,24/13:16,17:32^2/15:20:27/16:9/20:25:26/
2Ki3:5:6,7,8:21/8:12:28/9:14^2:33/10:4:9,10/12:
17:20/13:12:18/14:19/15:10:25:29:30/17:4:7/
18:7:20,21/19:5,6:26:28:32/21:23/23:26:33/24:
2:20/1Ch5:22/10:4/11:13/12:19:21/13:10:11/
19:11/20:1:4/2Ch4:7:8/6:24:36:39/8:3/11:1:4^2
/13:3:12^2:15,16/14:11/15:5:6/17:1/18:2:14:17:
19,20/20:2:6:12:23^2:29:37/21:17/25:27/26:7:16
/27:5/28:10:16/30:7/31:1/34:27/35:20/36:13:
17/Ez4:6:15:19/7:23/10:2/Neh1:6,7/2:19/4:8/
5:1:7:11:18/9:10:26/Est3:5,6/6:13/8:3/9:1/Job
6:4/8/9:27/10:17^2/13:26/14:17:20,21/15:13^2:
25,26/16:4:10/19:11:19/20:27/24:13/31:35/33:
13/35:14,15/36:17:19/39:21-23/40:11/Ps2:1:2
/3:1/4:4/5:10/7:6/11:2/15:4:5/17:7:13,14/18:4
:5/21:11/26:1:9,10/27:3/31:13/35:15:20:25:26/
37:12,13/38:19/41:9/44:10/50:7:21/51:1:4^2/52
:1^2/54:3/55:10:18/56:1/60:11/64:8/73:9/74:1:
22^2/76:5/78:17:19,20:21:31:40:49:56/81:5/83:3
:5/85:4/89:42/91:12/102:9,10/105:25/106:7:40
:43/107:11/108:12/118/119:23/137:9/138:7/
139:20/140:4/141:5/147:13/Pro3:29/6:27/15:
9,10/17:11f/18:1/21:30:31f/24:28,29/Sol3:8/
Is1:2/2:12/3:5:8:13/5:25/7:2:5/8:7,8:9,10:
14,15:20/9:8,9,10:11,12^2:19,20:21^3/10:14:25^2/
11:4:14/13:2:5:16:17/14:12:22:31/18:4/19:1:2^5:
17:20/20:1/22:6,7/23:11/25:8/26:14:20/27:4,5
/28:2:11:15/29:3/30:2f/31:2:3/34:2^2/36:1:5:8,9
/37:21:23^2:24:28:29:33/39:1f/41:25/42:24/43:
14:27/45:1/50:8/54:17^2/57:16/59:12:15/63:10^2
:17/66:18:19:24/Jer1:18/2:8:15f:16:17:19/3:13^2
:25/4:16:17:28/5:6:11:15:23,24/6:11:18,19:22:
28/11:9/12:5^2:6/13:14:19/14:7/15:6:12,13:20^2/
16:10^2/18:11:18:23/21:3,4,5:10:13/22:18/23:9:
20:30,31/25:8,9^2:13:29:30^3:31:32/26:11:12:13:
19/28:8:16/29:32/30:6/32:24/33:4:8/34:1:3:22
/36:2/37:18/39:1/40:2,3/41:9/43:2,3/44:23/46
:2:18/48:1:2,3,4^2:26:42/49:14:19:22:30:34/50:1:
7:9:14:15:21^3:24:26:31:42^2:44:45/51:1^2:2:5:25^2:
28:29:46:48:60/52:3:4/Lam2:4^2/3:3:5:37:42:46:
60/4:20/Eze1:24/2:3^2/3:13/4:1:7/5:8:15/6:2:3^2
/7:13/8:17/9:8/11:4/13:2,3:5:9:15:17/14:9:13
:17/15:7/16:17:42^2/17:15^2:20/18:14/20:8^2:13:
21:22:23,24:38:46/21:2^2:2f:3:22^2:24:28/22:25/
23:22:24:25:46:48/24:8/25:2:15/26:3^2:7:8:9/28:
7:21/29:2:8:10:18/30:11:22/32:20/33:2:16/34:
2:9,10/35:2:3:12:13/36:5/38:2,3^2:11:15,16:17:
21^2/39:1^2:23/40:17/Dan3:29/7:11:21/8:4:9:10:
12f/9:5:9:13/11:2f:2:5:7f:7^2:10,11:14:25^2:27:32f
:39/12:1/Hos1:2/4:1:7/5:5/7:13:15/8:1:5/10:
10^2/12:2/13:16^2/Joe2:25/3:19/Amo:1^2/5:19/6:
14/7:2:5:16/Ob1:1:7/Jon:13/Mic:2:12/2:8/4:
11/6:1:2/7:1:8:9/Nah1:11/2:13/3:2:5:10/Hab1
:6f:10/2:11/3:8,9f^2/Zep1:17/2:5/3:11/Hag2:12
:13/Zec1:12/2:8/7:10/9:13:14/10:3/12:4:9/13:
7/14:3:13:14f/Mal3:5^3/Mt5:23/6:12:14,15/7:
25:27/10:21:35^3/11:20/12:16:25:31,32^2:41:42/
16:18:20/17:25^2:26,27/18:15:21/20:15/24:7/26
:59/27:1f:6:12/Mk2:24:25,26/3:24:26:28:29/6:
48/7:10/9:39:40/10:11/11:25/13:8/14:55/15:
3,4/Lk6:2:7:47,48:49/8:45/9:5:5f:50/11:4:18:23
:51/12:10^2:52/14:31/15:18:21/18:3/19:43/21:
10^2:14/23:5:14:19/Jn6:41/8:6/13:25f/18:29/19
:12/Act4:25,26^4:27/5:39/6:1:10:12:13^2/7:19:45
/10:28/12:1/13:45:50:51/14:2/15:21/16:20,21:
22/18:12/19:9:38/20:3:16:19/21:21^2:26,27:28^2
/23:7/24:1:2^2:4:5:19/25:8:18:26:27/26:10:14f/
28:19:21:27/Rom1:18:26/2:8/3:25/4:8/5:14/7:
8/8:7:20,21:31/9:17:22/10:5/11:25:30/14:16/
15:3/1Co6:1:18/8:12^2/10:10:11:13^2:23/11:27/
15:28/2Co1:23/5:19/8:20/10:2:5:6:12/11:29/
13:8f/Gal2:11/3:21,22/Eph2:2:16/4:17,18/6:11
:12^3/Php2:15/Col1:22/2:14/3:19/1Th1:10/2:
15/5:12/2Th2:3/1Ti3:2/5:14:19/2Ti2:12^2/3:8^2
/4:15/Tit2:5:14/Heb3:7,8^3:11:13:15^2:16/4:7/6:
6/7:1/12:4/Jas2:13/3:9/4:6^2:11/5:3:6/1Pe2:11
:12/3:16/5:5/2Pe2:1:11/1Jn:2:14:18/3:4^2/4:3^2:
4:10/5:17f/2Jn1:7^2/Jud:4:15^2:22/Rev:15/2:14:
16:20/6:10/11:7/13:4:5:7:7f/14:5/16:14/17:3:
14/18:20/19:19
1116

AHEAD
Gen23:14,15/24:7/29:26/31:16/32:21/33:3:14/
41:26/45:5:11,12/46:28/Ex4:12/8:25:28/23:31
/32:34/Num10:34/14:3:7:42:44/32:17:24/Deu6
:2/11:25/28:53/Jos6:3,4/9:14,15/24:12/Ru2:2
/1Sa9:19:24:26,27/12:2/17:4-7:37:41,42/20:22:
28,29:37/25:19/30:20/2Sa5:19/7:3/14:12/15:1
/18:23^2/19:17/1Ki17:13/18:46/19:7:19/22:6:
12:15:22/2Ki2:17/4:31:41:43/6:1/1Ch29:1/
2Ch14:7/18:3,4,5:14/Neh4:7/12:37/Est3:11/8:
8/9:5/Job12:6/22:28/23:14/33:32/Ps37:37/41
:13/92:7/119:105/139:3/Pro4:25/12:26/13:14:
16/14:8:16/20:18/21:31/22:3/23:17,18/24:
13,14/27:12/Ecc9:2,3:7/10:16,17/11:2/Is1:1/
29:9/41:23/42:16:23/43:9/44:7/48:5/52:12/57:
1/65:24/Jer16:8:13/25:7/44:25/Eze4:4,5/10:
22/19:14/20:39/23:11/Dan10:19/Joe2:3/Amo
4:4/Zec11:9/Mt21:1:8:9/26:36:50/Mk6:33/10:
32/11:1:9/13:3,4:8/14:16:21/16:7/Lk6:26/7:27
:40/9:52/10:1/12:50:56/18:39/19:4:28:29:
36,37:41/21:7/22:8:12/Jn5:7/7:21,22,23/10:4/
12:27/16:1/19:38/Act:22/20:5:13:23/22:10/26:
1/27:10/Rom1:24:32/6:15/14/15:1/1Co7:9:28
/10:1:23:27/2Co9:5/Php3:13/1Th:4/4:15/Heb
6:12:20/11:1:13/Jas5:1/1Pe1:6/4:12/2Pe3:17/
Jud1:13
188

ALL
Gen1:7,8:13:19:21,22:25:26:28:29:30:31/2:1:9/3
:1:14:15:17:19:20/4:21f:22f/6:7:12,13^2:16:17:21
/7:1^2:4:8,9:19:21^2:23^2/8:1:15,16:17:18,19^3:21/9
:2,3:9,10,11:13:15:19/10:15-19:26-30:32/11:1:
3,4:6:8/12:5:20/13:1:6:7:15:17/14:4:11:12:14:
16:19,20:24/15:2,3^2/16:5/17:7,8:9,10:12:13:20:
24-27/18:5:18:19:25/19:4:21:25/20:7:8:18/21:6
:11:24/22:18^2/23:10:13:17,18/24:31:33:60/25:4
f:31:33/26:3:4^2:15/27:19:25:27,28,29^3:37/28:14
:15/29:3:8:22/30:27:31,32^2:34:35,36^2/31:1:8^2:
12f:12:21:32:35f:36,37:38:43^2/32:10/33:8/34:
6,7:23:24^2:27:28:29:30^3/35:2:4:5:26/36:5:6,7,8^2:
40-43/37:7:11:19,20:26,27:35/39:4:5:22/40:17:
20:23/41:3:7:8:19:22:24:29:30:34,35f:34,35:40:
41,42:44:46:48:51:54:56,57/42:2:6:11:17:21:29/
43:8^2:23/44:9:16/45:1:8:9:10^2:11,12:13:18:20:
23:26/46:1:6^2:7:15:31/47:1:13:14:17:20^2:21:26/
48:15:16/49:1:10/50:7:8:14:15/Ex1:15,16:22/3:
15:16:20/4:14:19:31/5:23/6:25:26/7:19:20/8:5:
10:11:16:22:23:25:28/9:6:9:10:14^2:15:16:22:24:
25:26:27:29:31/10:6:7:8:9:13:14:15:19:22:23^2/
11:2:5:8^2/12:3,4:6:10:12^3:21:22:26:27:29^2:30^2:
31:37:40,41:46:47:48:50:51f/13:1:1f:12:14:15^3/
14:4:5:7:16:17:18:21:23:26:28/15:7:15/16:6:13/
18:1:8^3:12:14^2:18:22:25/19:5^2:8:11:16:18/20/22
:5/23:13:21:22:27:29/24:1:2:3^2/25:11:25:36/26:
25:28/27:3:17:19^2/28:10:20/29:13:18/30:14:25:
26,27^2:28/31:6^2:7/32:2,3:8:10:13:17:26^2/33:8:
10/34^3:11:19f:20:23:28:32/35:1:4:5-9^2:10-19^2:
20:22:35/36:1^2:4-7:34/37:2:8:11:17:20,21:22:
23,24^2:25:26/38:2:16:17:20:21:24:25,26:29/39:
6,7:13:21:22:25,26:28,29:32:33-40^2:42:43^2/40:9^2
:15:16:25:38^2/Lev1:5:13/2:3:9:10:16/3:15,16/4:
8:13:18:19:26:31:34/6:9:17/7:3:4:10^2:35:36/8:1:
4:15,16^2:26:27:28:34:36/9:3:5:24/10:3:6:8,9:11/
11:10:13-19^4:21,22:23:34:41,42:47/13:12:13:23:
33/14:8:9:45/16:17:21^2:22:29,30:35/17:1/18:18
:26:27/19:23:37/20:3:5:8:14:22:23:26/21:24/22
:17,18:31/23:1:7:18:21:22:23,24:26,27:35:36:37:
42/24:13,14^2:15,16:17/25:6,7:10^3/26:3:8:26:
34,35:44:45/27:25:25f/Num1:2-15:17,18,19:54/
2:3-31/3:3:7,8,9^3:11,12:13^3:25-30:36,37:39:40:
49/4:3:12:14:15:21,22,23:26:29:35:37:46,47,48/
5:1^2:26/6:12:19:20^2/8:9:11:16^2:17^2:18:20/9:2,3:
12:14^2/10:25:32/11:1:10:13:18:21:22:29^2:31:32^3
/13:21:22:26/14:1^2:7:10,11:15:19:20,21^2:26,27:
29:36,37,38/15:15,16^3:22:25:26:33f:35/16:1:2:3^2
:6,7,8,9:16:17:19^2:22^2:27:28:34:41/17:12,13/18:

ALL Con't)
8^2:9:11^2:19:20/**19**:18/**20**:8^2:27/**21**:2:25,26:
1,32/**22**:26/**23**:6/**24**:15-19/**25**:3:4:5:6:8:10,11/
6:2:62:64,65f:64,65/**27**:16:19:20/**28**:11:18:19:
5:26/**29**:1:2:7:12:40/**31**:8:9,10,11^2:13:15:17^2:
9:20:26:28:30:41:48,49/**32**:3,4:6:10,11:13:16:
8:20:24:27:29:33:34,35,36/**33**:3,4^2:52^2/**35**:7:29
0/**Deu1**:1:7:8^2:9:12:16:33/**2**:5:7^2:14,15^2:28:
3,34:35,36^2/**3**:1:3:4:5:8^2:10^2:13:21:23,24,25^2/**4**
:29:32:40:48:49/**5**:1:23:26,27:29^2:31:32/**6**:1:2:
:5:18:19:22^2:24:25/**7**:1:6:7:11:14:15^2:16:18:22/
1:2:4/**9**:5:7:9/**10**:4:12,13^2/**11**:3:5:6^2:13^2:22^2:
3:32/**12**:2:7:10:11:18:24,25:28^2:31:32/**13**:3:9:
1:15^2:16/**14**:10:22/**15**:1:4,5:18:19/**16**:3:18/**17**:
^{2}:19/**18**:1:5:14:17/**19**:8:9:13^2/**20**:3:11:14:19/
1:21/**23**:9,10/**24**:19/**25**:13,14,15:16:19/**26**:11:
2:13:16:17:18/**27**:1f:8:9:10:14:15:16:17:18:19:
0:21:22:23:24:25:26/**28**:1:10:15-19:22:25:34:37
5^2:47,48:51:58,59:60:61:62:64/**29**:2,3:10:14,15
0:21^2:27/**30**:1:2:3:6:7,8:10/**31**:1:7:10,11^2:12:
4:28/**32**:7:21:22:35:40,41:44,45:46/**33**:16:23/
os1:4^2:6:8/**2**:7:9:12,13:17,18:23:24/**3**:1:7:9:10:
3,14:15,16:17/**4**:1:5:10:14^2:23:24^2/**5**:4,5:6/**6**:2:
:19/**7**:3:15:23:24/**8**:1:6:16:22:24:25:33^2:34/**9**:9:
4/**10**:6:9:10:11:14:25:37:39:42/**11**:1:4:6:8:9:10:
2^2:14^2:15:17^2:18:19:21^2:22/**12**:1:8-24/**13**:2-7^6:
0:11:12:25:30:33/**14**:3,4:10/**15**:21-32:33-36:45
17:16,17,18/**18**:1:21-28/**19**:17-23:49/**21**:19:40:
3:44/**22**:5:17,18:22,23:33/**23**:3:4,5^2:6:14^2/**24**:1
11:23^2:27/**Ju1**:17/**2**:10:12-14/**3**:17,18,19/**4**:7:9:
6:24/**5**:10:24:31/**6**:3,4:9:13^2:18:23:35/**7**:2:5,6^2:
:8,9:14:15^2:18:19,20/**8**:9:10:14:22:23,24^2:27:28
34:35/**9**:2f:5:11:13:14:16:40:45:49/**10**:6/**11**:11:
1,22^2:26^2:33/**13**:17/**14**:3:13:16/**15**:5:12,13:
6,17^2/**16**:2:29:30/**18**:6:15,16:19:24:27/**19**:4:25
20:16:25:29/**21**:6:10,11,12:14:16/**Ru1**:9/**2**:2:
0,11:17:19/**3**:5:11/**4**:4:9:11^2/**1Sa2**:8:13,14:28:
9:36/**3**:12:20/**4**:6:14:20/**5**:7/**6**:1:3:9/**7**:2:5:6:11:
6/**8**:5/**9**:4:6:9,10,11:20:21/**10**:9:17:18,19^2:24^3/
11:2^2:7:11:14:15/**12**:7:13:14:18:19:24/**13**:19/**14**:
:14:16:24,25:26:31:36:37:40:48/**15**:7:11:14:18:
2/**16**:5:9:10,11:17/**17**:37:52/**18**:6:15,16:21:22:
5:28:30/**19**:5:18:24^2/**20**:7:15:21:34/**22**:11,12^2:
4:18^2:19:22/**23**:13:23/**24**:19/**25**:1:21:24:26:
0,31/**26**:15:16:24/**27**:5/**28**:3^2:9:18:20/**30**:2:17:
8,19:20^2:25/**31**:12/**2Sa1**:12/**2**:3:9:16:27:29:31:
2/**3**:8:9,10:13:18:21:31:32:33,34/**5**:1:25/**6**:11:
4:19/**7**:21:23/**8**:4:11,12/**9**:7:10,11:12/**10**:15,16
/**12**:12:16:31/**13**:9:20:21-24:25:27:29,30:32,33^2
/**14**:13:14:21/**15**:6:9:13:22/**16**:6:14:21^2:21f/**17**:
2,3:4:10:14:22^2/**18**:4:5:8:12:23:28:29:31:32^2/**19**:
5:8,9,10:11,12:14^2:18:20:28^2:29:30:36:39/**20**:2:
20:21^2/**21**:5,6:9/**22**:1:3:4:9:14:31:38:40:41/**23**:
11,12:18,19:24-39/**24**:2:7:23/**1Ki1**:3,4:9^2:19:20:
39:40^2:44,45:46,47/**2**:3:18:26:38:44/**3**:3:13:15:
21:24:26:28/**4**:8-19^3:24:25:31/**5**:13/**6**:3:9:11,12:
23-28:29:32/**7**:33:35:37:41-46:48:51/**8**:1:3,4:5:
22,23:39:43^2:50:53:54,55:56:58:59:60^2:62,63:66
/**9**:1:11,12^2/**10**:2:3:6:20^2:21:23:26/**11**:16,17,18:
32/**12**:1:16,17^2:20:21:23,24/**13**:34/**14**:9:10^2:13:
16:21:26/**15**:12:14f:17:18^2:20^2:22:26:29:34/**16**:
4-7^2/**18**:3,4:12:19^2:20:24:26:29:30:36:38:40/**19**:
4:20:21/**20**:4^2:13^2/**21**:22/**22**:6:10:12:17:22:23:
36,37:43:46/**2Ki1**:10/**2**:17/**3**:19/**4**:2:26:41:43/**5**:
12:15:17:19:21/**6**:1/**7**:10:15/**8**:27/**9**:7:11:22/**10**:
1:7:11^2:14:17^3:18,19^2:20,21^2:25:29:31:32,33:36/
11:1:6,7,8:13,14:19/**12**:2:7:9:18^2/**14**:14:28/**15**:
29/**17**:9f:15:16:20:23:37:39/**18**:6:12:13:15:16:
31,32/**19**:12:15:17:18:19:25:27:35/**20**:6:9:13:15:
17:19/**21**:7:21:24/**23**:1:3:4^2:8:19:22:24:25/**24**:7:
12:13^2:14:16/**25**:4,5:9:11:13:14,15^2:16:19:26:28
/**1Ch2**:55/**4**:10^2:21-22:23:27:42/**5**:17:20/**6**:48:
49^2:54/**7**:3:4:5^2:7:40/**8**:8,9,10:30,31,32:40/**9**:6:9
:13:17,18:26:33,34^2/**10**:2:3/**12**:2^2:3-7:18:23:24-
24-37^2:38^2/**13**:1:5:6:8/**14**:16:17/**15**:3:12:24:27/
16:10:25:28:30:31:36/**17**:6:10:16:17:21/**18**:4:14
/**19**:2,3:17,18/**20**:3^2/**21**:4:23/**22**:2:12:17/**23**:2:
13:24^2:29:31/**24**:5/**25**:6,7^3/**26**:4,5:6,7:8^2:11:13:
30:31,32/**28**:1^2:4^2:12/**29**:3:4,5:12:16^2:17:19:20:
21:23:24:25:30/**2Ch1**:2,3^2:9:12/**2**:14:17/**3**:7/**4**:
12-16:19:22/**5**:2:4,5:11,12^2:13,14/**6**:12,13:14^2:
29:30:33:37,38:40/**7**:3:4,5:6:8:13:21:22/**8**:10/**9**:
2:11:19:20^2:22:26:30/**10**:1/**11**:16/**12**:9^2:13/**13**:9
/**14**:13:14/**15**:6:8:9:10:15^2/**16**:4:8^2:10/**17**:2:5:
7,8,9^2:10/**18**:3,4,5:9:11:12:16:21:34/**19**:5:11/**20**:
3:4:6^2:15:18:20:25/**21**:3,4:9:14/**23**:8:9:12^2:
15,16,17:19:20:21/**24**:2:5:9:10:14:20:23/**25**:5,6:
19:24/**26**:3:13:17,18/**28**:9:23/**29**:4,5:16:17:19:
24:32,33:36/**30**:1:2,3:14/**31**:5,6:9:10:12,13:
17,18:19^2:20/**32**:8:12:17:21:32:33/**33**:7:8:14:18:
22:25/**34**:21:24:29:30:31:32:33^2/**35**:6:16:18:19:
24,25:27/**36**:8:14:18^2:19^2:22,23^2/**Ez1**:3:6:11/**3**:
8:9:11/**5**:4/**6**:12:16/**7**:17:21:25:28/**8**:20:22^2:33:
36/**9**:10/**10**:5^2:6:9:12/**Neh4**:15:23/**5**:8:13:17:18:
19/**6**:1:14^2:19/**7**:5:43,44,45:60/**8**:1^2:6:9/**9**:1:6^2:
14:21:25:26:28:32:36:38/**10**:1:28:29:36:37:38/
11:10-14:18:21:24/**12**:22:27/**13**:3:8:11:12:14:15:
16:24:26/**Est1**:1:5:11:21:22^2/**2**:15:18:23/**3**:2:5,6^2
:8:13^2:14/**4**:3:8:11:13:16/**5**:7,8:13:14/**6**:13/**8**:
9,10^3:11:12:13/**9**:1:3:4:16:20^2:24,25:27^2:29-31/
10:3^2/**Job1**:8:10:14,15:16:19:22/**2**:3^2:9:10:11/**3**:
10:14,15/**4**:10:11/**5**:27/**6**:4:10:24/**7**:21^2/**8**:19/**9**:
2:22/**10**:13,14/**11**:2:11^2:13,14:16/**12**:2:5:10/**13**:
26/**14**:5:14:15:17/**15**:2:13:14:30:32^2:34/**16**:2^2:
15:22/**17**:10/**18**:4:16:17/**19**:10:14/**20**:17:20:22:
26/**21**:14:18/**22**:5:6:23:27/**23**:4,5:14:16,17/**24**:5
:7:24/**25**:3:4/**26**:2:4/**27**:12:19/**28**:12:16:21:
23,24:27:28/**29**:11^2:14:19/**30**:2:11:14:18/**31**:7,8:
12:32/**32**:11,12/**33**:3:12:20/**34**:4:15:19:21^2/**35**:4
/**36**:33/**37**:7:15/**38**:6,7:21^2:37,38/**40**:10:19/**41**:
34^2/**42**:11^3:15/**Ps1**:3:6/**2**:3:4:8/**3**/**5**:6:11/**6**:7:9:
10/**7**:7,8^2:9^3:17/**8**:1:7:8/**9**:1:2:9:10:14:17/**10**:2:3:
18/**12**:1:6/**14**:1:2:3^2/**16**:4:5/**17**:7:15/**18**:3^2:13:14
:22:23:30:37:38:40/**19**:3,4/**20**:1:4:5^2/**21**:7:8:13/
22:6:14:20:22:23f:23:25^2:26:29:31/**23**:4:6/**24**:1:
10/**25**:3:8:17:22/**26**:1/**27**:4:6:9:12/**28**:3:4/**29**:9:
10/**30**:5:9/**31**:5,6:11:20:23^2/**32**:4^2:5^2:11^2:11f/**33**
:1:4:6:8:10/**34**:2^2:4:7:8:14:15:17:19/**35**:10:22:27:
28/**36**:5:7/**37**:4:11:15:25:28/**38**:12:13,14/**39**:5,6
:12/**40**:5:7:10:12:14,15/**41**:3f:6/**42**:3:7:11/**44**:1:
12:13:14:17/**45**:2:17/**46**:4/**47**:2^2:6,7:9/**48**:2^2/**49**:
1:8,9:10:12:14:18:20/**50**:1:6:10,11^2:12:21:22/**51**:
4/**53**:2:3/**54**:7/**55**:8/**56**:1:5:8/**58**:1/**59**:14,15/**60**:
4,5/**61**:6/**62**:8/**63**:11/**64**:6:8/**65**:1:3:4:5:7:11,12:
13/**66**:1:4:16/**67**:2:5/**68**:1:11,12,13^2:22:26:30/
69:4:5:18:19:32:34^2:36/**71**:3:8^2:18:22:24^2/**72**:7:
10:11^2:15:17^2/**73**:4:10:12:14^2:19:24/**74**:9,10:17:
22/**75**:3/**76**:11/**77**:2/**78**:17:25:35:38:45:51f:56^2/
79:4/**81**:3/**82**:5:6:7:8^2/**83**:11:18^2/**84**:5/**85**:3:8/
86:2:5:9:12/**87**:5:7/**88**:17:18/**89**:5:6:11:16:27:48
:50/**90**:1:8:9/**91**:1:9/**92**:1:2:9/**93**:4/**94**:15/**95**:3:4
/**96**:10/**97**:1:3:5:7:8,9:12/**98**:7^2/**99**:2/**101**:3:4/
102:5:18/**103**:1:3:6:10/**104**:11:20:24:28:29:30:
31:34^2:35^2/**105**:1:14:21:33:35/**106**:5:8:29:48/
107:8:11:15:21:31/**108**:7/**109**:11:16:25:27:28/
111:1:7^2/**112**:1:5:6:10/**115**:11:13:16/**116**:10,11f:
12:18,19/**117**:1^2/**118**:10:17/**119**:1:2:49,50:54:58
:67:69:74:78:79:97:117:118:135:151:160:163/
121:7/**122**:4:5:6:8/**124**:1/**128**^{2}:3/**129**:5/**131**:1/
132:9/**135**:6:9:18:20:21/**138**:1:2^2:2f:4^2/**139**:13/
140:2/**142**:7/**143**:4:11:12/**144**:3/**145**:10:15:18:
20:21/**146**:4/**147**:13:16:18/**148**:2^2:3:8:11:13^2/
149:1/**Pro1**:12:13:19:19f:21:24:33/**3**:9,10:19/**4**:
23/**6**:8:9:14:21:22:24/**8**:17:31:32/**9**:3:7,8:10/**10**:
7:22:24:28/**11**:7:30/**13**:6/**15**:11:19:27/**16**:11f/
18:2/**19**:20/**20**:8:23/**21**:4/**22**:2/**23**:1:12:17,18:
23/**24**:9:11,12:21,22:28,29/**25**:2,3:27/**26**:
24,25,26/**27**:25,26,27/**29**:22/**30**:5/**31**:12:21:27:
29/**Ecc1**:3-7:8-11:12-15/**2**:1:9^2:10:11:15:17^2:18:
19:20-23^4/**3**:10:20/**4**:1:3^2:5,6:8^2:13:16/**5**:6,7:9:
16^2:17/**6**:2:10:11/**7**:20/**8**:9,10^2:14:15^2:16,17/**9**:1
:2,3:9:11/**10**:14/**11**:6:9/**12**:8:9/**Sol1**:3:4:8/**2**:15/
3:8/**4**:10/**6**:8:9/**Is1**:1:12,13:14:16:23:28:29/**2**:4^3:
9:13^2:14:16^2:17:18/**3**:10:17:24^3/**4**:1:2,3,4:5^2/**5**:2^2
:14:16:30/**6**:7:12^2/**7**:14:19:24/**8**:7,8^2:9,10:16/**9**:
2:5:7:13:17^2:18:21/**10**:16:19:28,29:31:33/**11**:6:9:
10:11:16/**12**:6/**13**:9/**14**:7:10:11:31/**15**:5/**16**:6:7:
10:13,14^2/**18**:3:6^2:7/**19**:3:7^2:8:10:14/**21**:2^2:4:8,9
:10/**22**:3:9,10,11:21:22/**23**:1:7^2:9:17/**24**:1:7:14:
23^2/**25**:8^2:11/**26**:2:3:9:12:18^2/**27**:3:9:12/**28**:27/
29:7:8:11:20/**30**:5:10,11^2:18:22:28^2:33/**31**:3/**32**:
6^2:7:8:14:16/**33**:9:11:15^2:16:19/**34**:12:16^2/**35**:3:
10^2/**36**:18:20:22/**37**:2:16,17:18:19:20:25:26^3:28:
29:32:36/**38**:1:10:13:15:17^2/**39**:2:4:6:8/**40**:5:6:
12:15^2:16^2:17:23:26:30/**41**:11:12:15:16:24:29^2/
42:3:5:6f:10^2:19:22^2/**43**:7:9:17:18:24:27/**44**:11^2:
12:20:24:25/**45**:6:10:12:13:14^2:16:17:22:23:24^2:
25/**46**:3:4:5:10/**47**:9:10:12:14:15/**48**:7:10:14^2/
49:1:4^2:17:18:21:23:25:26/**50**:4:9/**51**:1:11^2:12:
13:16/**52**:10:11^2/**53**:2:11^2/**54**:5:13/**55**:1:3:11:12
/**56**:1:7:10:12/**57**:6:16:19/**58**:9:11/**59**:9:15/**60**:1:
2:3:9:15^2:18:20:21:22/**61**:3:9:11/**62**:3:6,7^3:8/**63**:
7:9^2/**64**:5:6:8:9:11:12/**65**:2:3:6:8^3:16:25/**66**:4:5:
6:10:14:17:18:20:23:24/**Jer1**:14:15^2:18/**2**:3:25:
26,27:29:36/**3**:2:4,5:9^2:17:23/**4**:4:5:22:23^2:26:27
:29^3/**5**:1:6:7:16:22:25/**6**:4:10:11:14:15:18,19:29/
7:2:9:10:11:12:13,14:19:23:32/**8**:6:7:10:11^2:13:
14:16f:19/**9**:2:4:5:10:12:25,26^2/**10**:2,3:7^2:15:16/
11:1:4:6:8:18:19:20/**12**:4:5:10:15/**13**:1:12:13:19:
22/**14**:2:10:13:16:18/**15**:7^2:9^2:10:12,13:17,18/
16:9:10:13:18^2:20/**17**:2,3^2:8:10:13:18:20^3:26/**18**:
11:16:17:21:23/**19**:8:9:13:14:15/**20**:3:4:5:6^2:7:16
/**21**:3,4:7:12/**22**:4^2:7:15:16:17:20:22^2/**23**:4:11:
12:17:24:32/**24**:8/**25**:1:7:8,9^2:10:11:13^2:15:17:
19,20^2:22:24:25:26^2:29:30:31^3/**26**:2^2:3:7,8:12:13
:17/**27**:5:6^2:7:10:12:15:16^2:19,20,21^2:22^2/**28**:1:3
:4:5:6:7:11:14^2/**29**:1:4:10:20:22:25:31/**30**:2:7:14:
16^2:24/**31**:1:7:12:13^2:18:19:25:33f:38,39:40/**32**:
13:19^2:20:23:27:29:30:37:39:42^2/**33**:5:8:9:13^2:14
/**34**:1^2:8:9:10:17/**35**:3^2:8:17/**36**:2:3:4:5:6:8:9:12:
21:31^2:32/**38**:4:5:9:20:21,22:23:27/**39**:1:3:6:9:13
/**40**:1:9:11:12/**41**:3:7^2:12:16,17/**42**:1:4:8:10/**43**:
1:2,3:4^2:5^2:6:11/**44**:1:2,3^2:8:12:15^3:20:21:22:23:
24^2:26:27:28:29/**45**:1:5/**46**:7:9:14:16:25^2:28/**47**:
2:4/**48**:2,3,4^2:8:11:18:21^2:24:26:29:34:36:45/**49**:
1:5:7^2:9,10:15:17:24:29^2:32^2/**50**:2:3:7:13^2:14:16:
23:27:30:36:37/**51**:6:10:12:17^3:18:24^2:28:29:31:
32:34,35^2:39:41:47:52:56^2:60^2/**52**:4:7:8:10:13:18^2
:27:30:32/**Lam1**:2^2:3:5:6:7^2:8:11:12^2:15:16:19:
21/**2**:2:3:9:13:14:15^3:16:22/**3**:2:14:17^2:18:46:62:
64/**4**:5:12^2:17/**5**:1:18/**Eze1**:15:27,28^2/**3**:3:10:19
/**4**:8:12:14:15/**5**:4:8:10:11:13:14:15/**6**:4-7:9:10:
11/**7**:8,9:10,11:13^2:14:17^2:20:26,27/**8**:2:10^2/**9**:2:
4:6:9:10/**11**:1:3:10:12:13:18/**12**:6:7:9:10:19:23:
24:28/**13**:2,3:7:10:20/**14**:10:21:23/**15**:4/**16**:3f:
14:22:23:37:43^3:55:57^3:58:61:63^2/**17**:9:15:16:17:
21/**18**:4:14:21:22:24/**19**:5:10/**20**:4:5,6:32:38:40:
43:48/**21**:5:7:12^2:13:24:27:29/**22**:4:8:14:28:31/
23:6:12:17:23^2:29^2:30^2:32:35:36:44:48:49/**24**:4:7^2
:12^2:13:18:19:23/**25**:4:5:17/**26**:12:16/**27**:3:9:12:
18:22:23:27:29:32:34^2:35/**28**:13:15:17:18:19:22:
26/**29**:2:5:6:15:18/**30**:5:6:9/**31**:2,3:4:5^2:6:9:12:
14^2:16^2:17:18^2/**32**:4:10:12^2:13:16:21^2:22:23:25:
26^3:27:30^3:31:32/**33**:33/**34**:8:12:19^2:23/**35**:4,5:7^2
:11:13:15/**36**:4:10:31:32:34:36^2/**37**:7:11^2:16:22:
23:24:25/**38**:4:5:6:9:12:15,16^2:20:23/**39**:4:6:10:
11:17:21:26:27/**40**:4:21:29,30:41:46/**41**:15,16:
19,20:22/**42**:16-20/**43**:10:11:13:14^2:17/**44**:5:7:9
:13:20:24:25:30/**45**:1:2:4:8:15:16:17:22/**46**:4:6/
47:10:12:22:23/**48**:5,6,7:12:26/**Dan1**:6:17:18,19
:20^2/**2**:1:10:12:15:20^2:22:35:44:45:48:49/**3**:2^2:3:
4:15/**4**:2:6:10,11:12:17:18:20:21:28:35:37/**5**:11:
16:19:22:23/**6**:3:18/**7**:6:8:14^2:15:16:25:26:27^3/**8**
:24/**9**:6:7^2:8:10:11:12:13^2:16:27^2/**10**:3:15/**11**:17:
22:35:37:43/**12**:6:8/**Hos1**:8^2:10:11:13^2:18^2:
21,22/**4**:3:6:9/**5**:1^2:2:7:14/**7**:2:4:12:16/**9**:4:7:12:
15^2/**10**:1:14/**12**:8/**13**:10:15^2/**Joe1**:2^2:5^2:12:13:
14:16:19/**2**:3:12:15:26:28/**3**:5:7^2:9:11:12/**Amo1**:
1:2:7:8:10:12/**2**:2:3:5:9:14/**3**:2^2:7:9:12:13/**4**:5:12
/**5**:9:11:12:16:18:25,26,27/**6**:3:6:12:14/**7**:1:10/**9**
:1:5:10:12^2/**Ob1**:5:7^2:8:10:15:21/**Jon**:5/**2**:7:8:9/
3:7/**4**:11/**Mic1**:1:2:7^2:13/**2**:2:12/**3**:6:11/**4**:1^3:3^2:
5:9:13/**5**:4:9:10:12:13/**6**:5:8:9:11:13:16/**7**:1:9:16^2
/**Nah1**:8/**2**:7/**3**:4^2:5:7:8:10:12:17:19/**Hab1**:3:9:
12/**2**:5:6:7:8:13:14:17:18:19:20/**3**:8,9:16:17^2/
Zep1:2:3^2:8:11^3:18/**2**:3^2:11:14^2:15/**3**:2:7:8:9:11:
14:19:20/**Hag1**:9:11^2:14,15/**2**:4:7^2:15:16,17/
Zec1:4^2:9:16/**2**:2:4^2:5:6,7:11,12:13/**3**:7:8:10/**4**:7
:14/**5**:3/**6**:5/**7**^{2}/**8**:2:11:12:17/**9**:1:5:10:12:16,17/
10:2:4^2:6:9:10/**11**:2:3/**12**:2:3^2:4:6:9:10:12,13,14
/**13**:1:2:8/**14**:5:9:10^2:12:14^2:15:17:19:21/**Mal1**:
5:8:9:11/**2**:6:9:10/**3**:5:10:12/**4**:1:4/**Mt1**:17f/**2**:3:
3f/**3**:5:15:15f/**4**:8:9:23:24:25/**5**:14:15,16^2:17:18:
18f:20:29:33/**6**:2^2:4:5:6:27:29:31,32^2/**7**:13:21:24
/**8**:10:11:16^2:26:32/**9**:22:24:25:31:31f:33:35/**10**:
22:23:30/**11**:2:11:13:28/**12**:15:20:21:31,32:41:
43,44,45/**13**:31,32:37:41:56/**14**:5:21:29:36/**15**:
23:30:33:35/**16**:2,3:9:10:18/**18**:7:26:32/**20**:
11,12:13:14/**21**:26:44/**22**:3:10:24:28:37:40^3/**23**:
3:8:13,14:15:35:36:37/**24**:2:8:9:14:21:22:30:33:
34f:39/**25**:7,8:31:32/**26**:31:35:42:56^2:57:65,66/
27:54/**28**:9f:12,13^2:14:18:19:20/**Mk1**:4:5:32,33/
2:12/**3**:4:7,8:23/**4**:13:19:22:38/**5**:5:27:31:38:39:
40/**6**:22,23:30:37:50^2/**7**:6,7:11:14:22:23/**8**:17:18
/**9**:6:16:26:27:30,31:35:49/**10**:4^2:21:28:30:32:44^2
:52/**11**:9:17:22,23:26,f:31:32/**12**:9:17:20,21,22^2:
28:30:33^2:43,44/**13**:3,4:13:20:26:27/**14**:15:23:27
:31:50:53/**15**:3,4:42,43/**16**:15/**Lk1**:3:4:6:28f:42:
50:59^2:61:71:78/**2**:14:18:39:51/**3**:6:19,20/**4**:1:5:
6,7:13:14:18,19:22:40/**5**:5:17/**6**:12:17,18:27:37:
47,48/**7**:9:18:20,21,22:28:29:30:33:35f:40/**8**:17:
21:24:39:50:53/**9**:1^2:8:12:23:26:33:43:49:58:60/
10:1:19:27^4:33f:40:41/**11**:7:10:25:26:28:33/**12**:3
:20:24:27:29:30:31:35:40:42,43,44:56/**13**:3:5:17:
28:29/**14**:7:10:17:18:33/**15**:13^2:29^2/**16**:14/**17**:
24:27:29/**18**:22:31:42:43/**19**:19:36,37:38/**20**:14:
25^2:33:37,38/**21**:3:6^2:12:24:28:33:34,35/**22**:12:
14:65:66:70/**23**:5:32,33:56/**24**:21:25:26:44:47^2/
Jn1:1f:4:11,12^2:13:14f:16:18:50/**2**:15:19:22/**3**:1:
3:28:36/**4**:17,18:21-24:35:51/**5**:18:22:27:28:
32,33/**6**:2-5:8,9:10:39:44:45:48-51:53/**7**:26:31/**8**
:7:40:48:51/**9**:4^2:14:14f:15/**10**:8:10:41/**11**:42:52
/**12**:17:37:46:48/**13**:10:11:18:23f:31/**14**:9:17/**15**

(ALL Con't)
:26:26/16:1:13:15:25:33/17:1:2:6:10:11:12:21:
23/18:4,5:6:14:20:37/19:11:35/21:3^2:17f:23:24:
25/Act1:19:24,25/2:6:7:8:11:13:14:17:18:26:32:
40:41:43:44:47/3:11:13:18:21,22:24:26/4:5:10:
12:24:27:31:32:33f:33:34,35/5:11:13:24:28:32/6
:2:14/7:10^3:14^2:15:16:22:43/8:37/9:8,9:21^2:26:
27:40/10:12:14:20:36,37^2:38:39:42:43:44/11:6:
10:14:18/12:5:9/13:10:16:26^2:29:37:39:49/14:2:
22/15:4:5^2:7:11:17:20:38/16:14:15:26:28:32:33:
34/17:7:16:17:21^2:26:27/18:2,3:8:21:23:25,26^2:
28/19:17:26:27:32/20:1:2:10,11,12^2:27:32:38/
21:12:13:17:20:20f:25:31:34/22:12:30/23:1:6:8:
9/24:16/25:18:24:26/26:14:18:20:26:30/27:20:
21:24:31:35:37:38:43/28:9:10:30:31/Rom1:5^2:
6,7:8:9:16:18:20:21^2:26/2:4:5:10:10f:12-15:16:
17:20:26/3:2:9^2:10:12:19^2:21,22:23^2:25:27:30^2/
4:1:4,5:16:17/5:2:5:9^2:11:12^2:17^2:18:20:21/6:7:
10:17:19^2:21/7:3:6:8:15/8:9:14:17:19:20,21:27:
28:29:32:37:38/9:5:8:17:17f:22:29^2/10:4:5:12^2/
11:1:2,3:5:9:25:26^2:32:32f:32/12:2:4,5^2:12:16/
13:7:8^3:9:10:12,13/14:2:3:5:17/15:6:14:15,16:17
:19^2:20:23:33/16:4:5:15:16:24:25,26,27/1Co1:2:
3:4:8:19:20:21:23:28/2:10:15/3:3:13:16:18:22^3/
4:7:8:10:17/5:6:8/6:5:7:12f/7:3:7:16:17:19:23:
28:32:34:36/8:2:4:6:6f:7:10:11/9:4:19:22:25/10:
1:3,4f:5:11:16:17^2:18:19/11:6:10:12:16^2:21/12:4
:6:11:12:13^2:26^2:27:29:30/13:1:2^2:8:12/14:2:5^2:
10:23:24:26:29,30:31:33/15:7:8:9^2:10^2:14:15:18:
22^2:23:24:25:27:28:34:37:39:48:51^2:52^2:55,56:
57/16:2:6:12:16:19:20:24^2/2Co1:1:12:20:22/2:
5,6^2:15/3:1:10/4:2^2:5:10:17:18/5:4:10:13,14:15^2
:18/6:7^2:11^2/7:4:5:16/8:5:18:22:24/9:3:4/10:10
/11:4:13:19,20:25:28/12:1:9:10:11:13:15:19^2/13
:2:3:4:5:8:13:14/Gal1:1:5^2:6:13:14:16:23/2:2:4:6
:13:14^2:17/3:4:7:8,9:14:16^2:21,22^2:26:28:29/4:
11/5:1:6:9:21/6:14:16:18/Eph1:6:7:8:10:11:13^2:
14:16,17:22/2:2:3:6:7:14:18/3:6^2:9:10^2:14,15:
18,19/4:4^2:6^3:10:10f:13^2:15,16:23/5:6/6:6,7^2:10
:11^2:13:18^2:21:24/Php1:1:2:3:5:13:19:20/2:1:12
:19:26:28^2/3:7^2:8:12^2:13^2:15:19:21/4:5:8:9:18:
19:21:22/Col1:6:10:12:14:15:15f:16:17:18:19:20^2
:23:28/2:3:7:9:13:15:19/3:4:8:9:11:14:22:23:24/
4:1:5:9:17/1Th1:7/3:2,3:5:7:13:13f/4:3,4:10:14/
5:1:3^2:5:12:24:26:27/2Th1:4:10:12/2:11:12:15:
17/3:16:17:18/1Ti1:5:10,11^2:15/2:1:2:4:5:6/4:8^2
:9,10:16/5:21:22/6:2^2:7:9:10:11:13:14:17/2Ti1:
10:12:15:16/3:9:11/4:2^2:7:8:17:18:21/Tit1:8:10:
12:15/3:2:6:7:8^2:14:15^2/Heb1:3^2:5,6:13/2:8:9:
15:16/3:14:17:18/4:1^2:4:12:13/5:1:7f:7:9:12,13/
6:12:16:18/7:2:4:9^2:11:12,13,14:25:27^2/9:4:6:7^2:
8:12:15^2:19^2:23^2:26:28/10:2:10:12:14:24:27:34:
36/11:3^2:13^2:26:29:31:32:33:39/12:4:8:9:14:23^2
/13:4:7:20,21^2:24,25^2/Jas1:5:10,11:17:21/2:5:7:
17/3:1:14:17/4:6/5:1:12/1Pe1:2:3:5:10:11:12^2:
22:24^2/2:2,3:4:9:14:16:21:25/3:8:18:22/4:5:8:11
/5:5:7:9:11^2:14/2Pe1:1:4^2/2:6:12:21/3:7:18/
1Jn1:5/2:1:2:7:12:15:16:18:19:27:28:29/4:14:18
/5:1:3:6,7,8:10:19/3Jn1:2/Jud:3:7:12:13:15:
24,25^2/Rev:2:3:5^3:8^2/2:9:19^2:22:22f:23:29/3:6:
13:14/4:4:11/5:3/6:9:15/7:4-8:9:11/8:1:7:8,9:
11/9:15:17,18:21/10:6/11:4:18/12:5:9:17/13:3:
6^2:7:8:12^2/14:7:13/15:2^2:3,4/16:3:8:11:14:15:16
:19/17:3:13:14:16/18:1:3^2:6:14:17^2:18:19^2:23:24
/19:5:10^2:18:20:21/21:4^2:5:7:8:25:26/22:6,7:8:9
:11:14:15:16

5310

ALMOST
Gen8:11/27:30/43:2/Ex17:4/Lev25:51/Jos10:
13/Ju13:6/1Sa3:2,3/4:5/20:37/2Sa23:22/1Ki3
:8/1Ch12:22/2Ch21:9/Neh6:1/Ps73:2/119:87/
Ecc4:5,6/Is43:14/Jer38:9/Eze16:51/30:2,3/
Dan9:2f/Hos:7/Joe1:15/Mic7:4/Mt19:23/24:
32/Mk10:23/Act13:44/21:26,27/1Co15:8/2Co
2:4/Php:27/4:12/2Ti:6/Heb9:22/Jas5:9

38

ALONG
Gen2:11,12f/3:14/8:18,19/16:7/17:24-27/19:2:
25:26/20:7/22:17/24:45:48:59/32:7:12/33:15/
37:2:13,14:28/41:18/42:5/43:22:27/44:2:6/45:
11,12:24/46:5/Ex2:3:5/4:17:24/7/9:27/12:39/
13:17,18/14:2:23:25/18:3:8/23:1/25:25/26:
10,11/29:3,4:41/33:3:13/36:11,12:17:31,32:33/
37:12/39:25,26/Lev7:12/8:28:31/10:15/11:
41,42/14:6:20:31/20:5/23:18:20/24:5-8/Num5:
8/6:17^2/8:8/10:34/11:12:17/13:29/15:23,24/
16:32/20:4/21/22:22,23/27:3,4:6,7/28:7:14/29:
25:30/33:3,4:49/34:3:12/Deu2:35,36/4:18/15:
16/29:11/Jos2:12,13:22/5:1/6:23/7:15/9:1/10:
10/11:4/13:21/15:2,3,4^2:5:8:10,11:21-32:46/16:
8/17:5,6/18:18/24:1/Ju7:10/9:3:25^2:37/11:18:
26/15:5/18:15,16:20/19:3/20:31:45/21:19/1Sa
1:24/5:7/6:12/7:11/13:5/17:18:52/18:6/22:16/
25:42/26:3,4/27:8/30:11,12/2Sa2:24/3:16/6:
20/8:11,12/11:7:17/13:34/15:22/22:43/1Ki1:
40/2:26/5:9/6:3:5/7:24/8:3,4/9:17,18/10:10:11
/13:24,25/14:16/15:15/2Ki1:9/2:11:23/3:9:21/
4:29/6:26-30/9:25:27/10:12:16^2/12:18/17:6/18
:11:17/1Ch6:78,79/18:3/25:9-31/2Ch2:15/3:4/
5:4,5/13:9/20:21/34:15,16/Ez3:7/8:18:22:31/
Neh1:2/2:9/4:3/7:5/12:31,32/Est2:6:8/Job3:
14,15/9:8:11/42:15/Ps1:3/17:4/18:33/32:8/37:
34/40:2/72:10/77:20/78:13:27/84:11/89:41/90
:5,6/110:7/119:35:95:110/135:8/139:24/Pro1:
21/2:18/4/17:1/20:24/Ecc7:18/12:5^2/Sol3:6/
Is3:16/8:11/10:4:22/15:5/18:1/19:7/23:2,3/33
:6/35:9:10/36:2/41:7/42:16/44:11/46:4/48:17:
19/59:10/Jer1:15/8:4,5/11:13/17:8/18:22/24:
1/25:19,20/26:22/27:19,20,21/40:1/47:7/49:3/
51:59/52:15:18:24,25/Eze8:11/16:15^2/17:7/21:
29/23:13/25:16/26:2^2/27:35/30:14/31/32:2/
33:15/34:5/40:7-12:16^2:25:26:29,30:32:33:43/
41:5/47:2:3:6:10:12:18/Dan1:1/6:24/11:8/Hos
1:10/6:9/13:7/14:9/Joe2:5/Jon1:4/Nah2:4/
Zec7:7/Mt4:18:19/6:9/9:27/14:29/15:32/20:
29/21:8:9/22:16/24:1/Mk1:16:18:43,44^2/2:14/
4:17/5:18/6:33:49/8:3:27/10:32/11:8/14:13:
51,52/15:7/Lk1:18/2:38/8:2/9:3:57/10:4:31:33
:34/12:24/19:28:36,37^2:40/20:46/22:10:35:49/
23:13:27/24:14:15:35:50/Jn8:48/9:1/12:14/18:
15^2/Act3:2/7:44/8:25:29:36:40/12:10/15:3:23:
25:36:37/16:7:15:17/19:29/20:2/23:21/26:18/
27:2:5:7,8:13:29/Rom8:29/9:4/13:3/15:10/1Co
7:7/9:5/10:1:20/14:16/16:4:11:12/2Co4:14/11:
28/Gal2:1/4:30/5:7/Eph2:2:6/4:3/5:10:18/6:
21/Php2:19/3:18/4:11/Col2:5/4:7/2Th1:7/1Ti
5:18/Tit2:1:12/Heb:13/5:11:12,13/6:9/9:19/
2Pe1:12/2/3/Jud1:13:23/Rev2:22/12:4/20:8

433

ALREADY
Gen27:33/28:9/Ex1:5/21:16/Lev27:26/Num10
:21/16:46:47/21:34/25:9/30:14/34:14,15/Deu1
:1/31:9/Jos6:2/8:11,12,13f/10:8/13/14:3,4/17:
1/18:7/19:15,16/23:4,5/Ju4:14/8:6f:10/18:1/
Ru4:6f/1Sa2:23,24,25/5:11/12:12/13:14/17:13
/21:14,15/2Sa5:4,5/17:9/1Ki6:10/10:13/20:7/
1Ch17:17/29:3:14/2Ch20:2/28:15:17,18/Ez4:
12/Neh5:2,3,4:5:18/Job10:10/40:5/Ps14:7/
Pro1:5,6/Ecc10:16,17/Is:23/43:19/Jer33:5/45:
3/Eze17:8/19:14/Nah2:1/Zec13:8f/Mal2:1/3:
6/Mt5:28/6:25:31,32/14:15/17:12/Mk9:12,13
/10:40/15:44/16:4/Lk1:1,2/5:32/8:29/19:25/
Jn3:18/5:24/6:6:47/10:25/11:17/12:28/13:1/
15:3/16:11/19:33/Act4:3/16:14/27:9f/Rom3:9
/4:11^2:17/8:10f:24/10:8/15:20/1Co3:11:21/4:8^2
/5:3,4/7:18:27/2Co1:13,14:24/3:7/13:2/Gal1:6
/Eph:14/3:2,3:14,15/1Th4:1:10/5:11/2Th2:1:6:
7:7f/1Ti5:15/6:6/2Ti2:18/Tit1:11/Heb4:7:10/
8:11/12:23/Jas2:11/2Pe1:12/3:1/1Jn2:18/3:2/
4:3:4/Jud1:5/Rev17:10

138

ALSO
Gen1:16/2:9:11,12/5:3,4,5f/10:15-19/11:12,13f
:32f/14:7/17:20/21:13/22:24/26:19:26:34/27:
25:31/30:23,24/31:49/35:6:19/36:1:13,14/41:
26:27:43/42:25^2/44:2:29/46:16,17:19-22:
23,24,25/Ex12:3,4f:29/20:25/21:29:35/25:
34,35/26:20:26,27:29/27:13/28:4:27:42/29:13:
15,16:22:32:40/31:1/36:25,26/37:20,21/38:1:
11:13:19:23/39:19:41/Lev2:4/7:8/8:11/9:3:14/
11:25:26:34:40/14:22:49/15:3/16:25/18:14f:28f
/19:1/23:13/24:17/25:49/Num4:26^2:33/6:14:
19/7:10:14/8:23,24/11:17/12:1f/13:18:23/15:
17,18/16:10:17:36,37/18:12:25,26/22:5,6/25:2^2
/26:19-22:44-47/28:11:15:22:26:30/29:6:11:16:
19:25:28:34:38/31:8:20:30:53/35:15/Deu1:18/3
:5:17^2/4:29:48/6:19/17:20/24:3/27:7/31:9/Jos
4:9/12:3:5/13:10:21:22:24:26/15:13:33-36:37-
37-44:45:47^2:48-62^2/16:9/17:11/18:13/19:8^2:
29:41-46/20:7:8/21:9-16/24:33/Ju1:18:29/6:35
/7:24/8:9:17:31/9:11/10:9/17:4,5/19:10/Ru2:
10,11/1Sa7:6/10:5/19:20:24f/20:15/22:19/25:
43/28:20/31:5/2Sa2:18/3:19/5:9/8:2:3:5:8/10:
18/13:31/15:9f/21:8/23:20:24-39/1Ki1:25/3:
13/4:7:28/5:15/6:16/7:7:11:40/9:19:25/10:4:11
:18/12:31:32,33/13:16,17/21:23/22:44:46/2Ki3
:9/8:22/10:32,33/11:17/13:23/14:7:14:21f/15:
1f:25:29f:34,35f/16:4:15:18/17:9:29:32:41/18:8
/19:27/22:9,10/23:5:7:8:12:15:24/24:16/25:
14,15:30/1Ch1:13-16:24-27f:32:38,39/2:16:21:
23:48,49:55/3:6-8:9:16f/4:8:32,33/5:12:22:26/6
:64,65/7:16/8:6,7:14:17,18/9:2:6/11:10:22/12:
8-13/15:1:16:27/16:41/18:2/19:17,18/20:2:6,7
/22:3:14/23:28:29/24:1/26:4,5:6,7:28/28:12:13:
15/29:8:21/2Ch1:12/2:8:14/3:9/4:1:6:8:9:11:20
/5:2/8:6:10:14/9:10:17:18:19:29/11:11/12:9/14
:5/17:7,8,9^2:13/20:2/21:3,4/22:1f/25:5,6/26:6:
7:10/27:3/28:5:8:12/29:18/31:3:5,6/32:5:17:
28,29/33:15/34:26/35:2/36:7:18:22,23/Ez1:1:4
/2:55,56,57:61/3:5^2/5:4/7:15:24/8:16:19:26,27
/10:23/Neh2:8/3:19:29/5:16/6:7/7:3:63:67/8:
15/10:30:32:33:35/11:10-14:19:22,23/12:28:29:
45/13:4:10:16/Est2:7/4:8/8:14/9:7-10:12:15:18
/10:2/Job7:3/21:25/30:8/32:3/42:13,14/Ps:8/
68:19/94:10^2/102:18/108:7/132:12/Pro7:3/11:
10:21:24,25/25:27/31:22/Ecc2:7,8/4:7:11/11:8
/Is19:13/42:6/45:13f/55:5:11/56:7/65/Jer9:
25,26/14:9/26:20/28:4f/30:4/32:11/35:7/36:
30f/49:20/51:20f/52:19/Lam1:22/Eze2:1f/16:
21/21:28/23:16f/36:11/38:2,3f/39:1/40:16:42/
41:14:17,18/45:20:23/48:24:26:33/Dan2:43/5:
11f/10:1/11:6f:16/Hos6:11/12:2/Amo3:14/Jon
4:7/Zec3:5,6/6:14/Mt4:7:18/10:2,3,4/13:33/
17:12/18:19:25/20:4/22:26:27/27:38:41,42,43:
44/28:8/Mk8:7/15:27:31/Lk1:18/2:24:36,37:
38/4:12/6:14,15,16/8:15/12:34/13:3/16:22/19:
18/20:32/Jn3:5f/5:37/6:1/7:47/10:16:18/12:9:
39/15:23:27/17:20/19:35:35f/20:3,4f:6/Act1:
14^2:23/2:38/5:37/7:6:8:10:58f/11:1:20/13:1:26
/14:23/15:7:20:22/17:4:12:18/19:27:31/21:10:
13:20/23:11/24:26/26:20/Rom1:15/3:26/4:9^3:
12:19/8:17:23:32/15:9:27f:31/16:13/1Co7:4/9:
10:23/14:1:13:15^2:34/15:28:39:44/2Co4:14/5:
13,14/7:7:14/8:7:15:23/11:16/Gal3:8,9/6:14/
Eph2:22/Php1:29/Col4:9:11:13/1Th:6:14/1Ti3
:7:13/2Ti4:13/Phm1:16:23/Heb:10/3:2/6:17/7
:1:2/9:28/10:30/Jas2:11:17/3:5/4:4/1Pe2:8/3:
18/2Pe1:5/2:9/1Jn:23/3:16/5:6,7,8/Rev1:3:4f/
2:19/14:17/17:3f:10

594

ALWAYS
Gen6:9,10/8:21/27:27,28,29/Ex12:17/13:15/
19:9/25:30/28:30,31:37,38/29:28/30:20:31/33:
7/Lev7:34/19:15^2/23:3/25:27:31/Num9:16/
Deu4:10/5:29/6:25/8:18/11:12/14:23/15:11/
16:1/24:18/28:13:33/Jos9:23/1Sa2:30/12:12/
18:5/19:4/20:2:5/2Sa10:2/20:18/1Ki1:1/2:4:
45/5:1/8:25:40:61/9:1:4:5/14:8/17:14:16/22:8:
18/2Ki20:3:10/1Ch17:14:23:24^2/23:25:31/29:
18/2Ch2:4/6:16:20,21/7:3:16:18/13:5/19:9/21:
7/26:5/Neh2:1/4:20,21/9:8:17/10:35/Job1:10/
3:25/14:20,21/15:20/20/31:18/Ps1:2/4:1/9:18
/10:7/13:5/16:8/17:2/22:9,10,11/31:1/38:17/
56:5/71:3:6/73:5/85/89:28:29/100:5^2/106:3/
107:1/111:9/119:2:144/121:3,4:8/131:3/132:
14/144:2/Pro7:1/8:30/14:5/16:2/17:17/18:15/
23:29,30/Ecc7:20/8:2,3/9:11/Is26:4/28:23,24/
38:3/48:16/55:11/57:16:20/66:22/Jer2:22/3:
4,5/12:1/15:6/17:25^2/20:8/28/33:18/35:7:
18,19/44:17/Lam3:20/Eze12:25/36:32/45:9:12^2
/46:9/47:12/Dan6:10/9:4:7/Hos7:16/12:6/
Amo3:7/5:25,26,27/Hab3:6/Mt13:10/18:10f/
19:20/24:44/26:11^2:13:60,61/28:20/Mk7:4/10:
1/14:7/Lk1:10/6:26/7:35/9:39:57/12:15:31/13
:6:22/14:8/17:1/19:26/20:21/Jn1:1/5:7/8:25:
29/11:42/12:8/14:2,3/15:16/17:6/Act2:25/9:
36/14:17/23:1/24:16/26:5/Rom1:30/3:4/4:15^2
/12:12/13:3/16:19/1Co1:9/9:21/11:19/13:7^3/
15:58/2Co1:19/5:9/7:14/Gal2:10/5:3:15:16/6:
7:10/Eph1:5/2:7/3:11/4:3/5:20/Php1:10:11:20^2
:27/2:12/4:4:10/Col1:3:10^2:11:12/3:15^2:20:22/
4:1:12/1Th1:2/5:15:16:17:18/2Th3:4/1Ti1:19/
5:10/6:17:18/2Ti2:13/4:18/Tit3:1/Phm1:4/
Heb1:8/2:2^2:4/3:10/6:1/7:7:20:25/9:7/10:16/
12:10/Jas1:5/3:8/1Pe2:23/5:7/2Pe3:15,16/
1Jn2:7:8:24:29/4:1/Jud1:21/Rev:5

285

AMONG
Gen3:8:14/7:1/13:12/14:13/17:6:9,10:16:20/19
:9/23:5,6:10/24:5:35:40/30:31,32/34:9,10^3:21:
23:30/35:11/40:15/42:21:24/47:27/49:14/Ex2:
3:5:13/12:19:48:49/15:11/19:5/23:11:25:33/25
:8/29:45:46/30:11,12/33:3:5/Lev6:29/7:6/10:3
/11:13-19:47/15:31/16:16:29,30/17:8,9:10:12:
13/18:26/20:1:14/21:4:14,15f/22:17,18:25/23:
22/25:6,7:45:47/26:11:12:25:30:33:38^2/Num1:
16/5:3:21,22:27/8:14:16:17:19/9:14/11:3:19,20
/14:10,11/15:13,14:26:29:30/16:3:8,9:46^2:47/
18:23/19:10/21:6/26:52,53:62/27:8/31/32:30/
33:54/34:13^2:29/36:1/Deu1:19,20,21/4:7^2:27/5
:14/6:15/7:21/9:1/13:5:11:12,13,14/14:21:29/
15:7:11/17:7/18:18/19:19/21:9:11:21/22:
25,26,27/23:7:14:15,16/24:7/26:11/28:21:25:

ONG Con't)
:56,57:64:65/29:11/30:1/31:12:17/32:8:
3:16/Jos3:10/6:25/7:1:10,11/8:33:35/9:22
3/13:2-7:13/15:63/16:10/19:49:51/20:4/
:31/Ju1:29:31,32:33/3:5/5:8:16/7:8,9/14:
12:16/21:5/Ru2:10,11:15/1Sa:28:36/4:3/
/13:6/14:3:15:18:30:34:41/15:6/16:13/19
22:14/24:2/25:7/27:1:7:11/30:5:17:22/
:6/17:8:9/19:28/22:50/1Ki1:8/3/4:31/6:
:53/11:20/14:21:31/22:40/2Ki5:2/11:2,3/
/17:6:25:26:32:34/21:7/1Ch1:13-16/7:3:9/
:14/11:11:20:24,25:26-47^2/16:35/24:4:29/
0/28:4^3:5/2Ch7:13/19:4:7/20:5:22/24:16/
3:33/35:24,25/36:22,23/Neh1:8/5:9/8:7,8/
:36/11:10-14/Est4:3/10/Job2:8/3:6/8:17/
:10/27:17/28:13/29:7/30:6:7:9/34:4/40:19:
s1:5/16:10/18:49/22:18/44:11:14/45:9/
:11/53:2/55:9/57/65:4/68:11,12,13f:18/78
0/80:6/82:1f/83:8f/84:3/86:8/87:4/96/
12:18/105:13:37/106:35/107:40/113:8/
5,6^2/Pro6:16-19/16:31/30:24-28/Ecc11:2/
/Sol1:7/2:2:16/4:5/6:3:9:12/Is1:31/2:21/3
5:17/8:14,15/10:4:16/11:6:7:8:12/12:4f:6/
5^2/21:11/27:13/31:3/32:4/33:14/48/50:
1/53:8/61:9/63:11/65:4:8:15/Jer3:17:19/4
:26/6:15/7:18f/8:12:17/10:7/11:9/12:16/
/17:25/18:13/22:23/24:10/29:8:15:23/34:5
14/40:11/44:7/49:15:16/50:23/Lam1:2/3:
:15/Eze1:13/2:5/3:14,15/6:4-7:8:9:13/12:
/13:9/14:6,7:9/16:6,7:14/19:6/20:22:38/22
26/25:4:9,10/26:13/28:14:25/30:26/31:2,3:
8^2/32:2:9f:9:18:25:28^2:29:32/33:24:33/34:
4/36:20:22:23/37:1:21:26:27:28/39:7:21:28
7:9/44:24/45:1/47:21:22/Dan4:35^2/5:21/7
1:14:24/Hos8:5:8/9:6:17/10:4:14/11:9/Joe
:27/3:2/Amo6:1/9:3/Ob1:2:4:11/Mic3:11/
5:14/7:18/Zep2:14/3:11:15:17,18:20/Hag1
2:3:5/Zec1:8/2:10:11,12/7:14/8:12/9:10/
/12:6:8/Mal1:10:11:14/Mt10:16/12:15:28
7:25:39:57/18:2:20/20:25:26^2/21:25:38/22:
26:11:49f/27:35:56/28:15/Mk2:15/4:7:41/
4:5/6:2,3:4:5:6/9:36/10:43^2/11:31/14:4,5:7:
15:28/Lk1:1,2:3f:28f/2:9:44^2:46,47/5:21/7:
6/8:2:14:27/9:13:46/10:3:19/12:9/13:19/17:
/19:39:47f/20:5/22:17:21:23:24:26:38:47f/
36/Jn1:11,12:14:27/3:12/6:43/7:12:25:31:
9:16/15:24/19:23,24/20:19:26/21:23/Act1:
19/2:29/3:21,22:23f/4:15:33/5:12:17/6:3:8/
7/13:1/14:2:14/15:7:12/17:34/19:33/20:25:
21:19:32/28:25:28,29f/Rom1:6,7:13^2:13f/10
11:34/15:9/1Co1:10:26/2:6/3:16/5:1:7/6:2/
18/12:25/14/15:5f/16:11/2Co3:2/6:16/10:
/12:12/Gal3:5/5:9:15/Eph:3/Php2:15:16/
h2:7:9^2/4/5:12:13/2Th1:10/2:13f/1Ti3:16/
1:10/3/Heb11:28/12:15/Jas2:19/4:1:12/5:
1Pe2:12/4:17/2Pe1:10/2:1:13/Jud1:4:12/
v1:13/2:1:1f:2:5:13:14:15/5:3/6:6/14:4/21:3
661

N

en4:15/8:11:20/11:6f/12:7:8/13:18/16:1/18:
/19:32/20:4/21:20,21/22:9/23:5,6/26:25/27:
,4/29:2/30:6f/32:6/33:20/34:6,7/35:1:3:7:
,14/37:3f:24:36/41:53/42:18:23/44:18:20/48
16/50:25/Ex1:10/2:1:11:19/5:21/10:13:16/
16f/17:15,16/20:5/21:6:9:13:28:33/22:1:5:9:
:14:19:25/23:1:4:7:13f:15:20:22:33/24:4/25:1
/28:4:17:18:19^3:20:32:39/30:10f:13f:15:32/
:4:17/32:5/33:2:5/34:9/38:23/39:4,5:11:12^2:
/Lev1:2,3:9:13/2:2f:4^2/3:1/4:21/5:2/6:21/7:
:24:25/9:4/11:27:35:39/13:9,10:11:39/14:5:
:53/15:1f:32f/16:34/17:3,4:8,9:10:11:13^2:15/
:22/20:1:15:16/21:4:12/22:17,18:21:22:24/
:8:15,16:17:36^2/24:1:3,4:10^2:18:21/25:39:47/
:9:27/Num5:15:15f/7:3/15:3,4^2:19,20,21:25/
:16:18/21:31,32/22:4:22,23/23:7-10/24:3-9/
:6:8:11/29:34/32:42/35:22,23^2:24/Deu4:
,17:33:38/5:5/7:26/9:12/10:3/14:26/15:17/
:2:22/17:15/18:12:15:18/19:4/20:1/21:8/22:
10/23:20^2/25:4/27:5,6:15:21:25/28:11:37:49/
:11/Jos2:1:11/3:13,14/8:2:14:30:31/13:1/15:
3,19/17:5,6/19:30,31/22:10:12:16/23:2/Ju1:
:3:22,23:27:31/5:11:16/6:24:26:31/7:1/8:27:
7f:27:32/9:25:29:32/11:20:26/13:16/17:3:4,5/
8:7:14/19:3:16/20:29/21:4:6:17/Ru2:1/3:10/4
/1Sa1:11f/2:1:23,24,25:28f:31/7:17/10:12f/
2:2/13:21^2/14:14:35/15:18/18:1:5:23/19:5:
,10:13:16/20:6:36/21:5/22:6/28:14/29:9/30:
1,12:13^2/2Sa1:8:13/6/7:18:19/14:2,3:20:32/
7:8:25:27/19/20:7:18:19/22:30/23:5:21/24:18
1:25/1Ki1:15:41/2:5/3:1:9:16/5:11/6:5:10/7:
4/8:37:39/9:7/10:29/12:20/13:11:14:18/14:4:
21/15:13:17/16:32/19:5:11/22:25:30:34/2Ki1:3
:9/3:4/4:14/5:7/6:26-30/8:24,25f:27/10:2,3/13
:2:11/15:9:18:24:28:29/16:10:11,12/18:24/19:
32/21:6/25:17/1Ch4:17^2/7:28/9:26/11:16:
18,19:23/15:16:20/16:17:29/17:27/18:10/21:
15:18:22:26/23:1/27:32/29:28/2Ch2:3:9:14^3/7:
13/11:1:17/12:3:14/14:9,10/15:16/17:14,15/18
:9:24:33/21:15/22:5/23:12/25:5,6/27:5/28:1/
29:25,26:35/32:6:21:30/33:2:7:22/34:14/36:3:5
:9:13/Ez7:15/8:18/9:12/Neh2:10/4:8/6:5,6/13
:13^2/Est1:7/2:23/8:15/9:19:21:28/Job6:5,6,7/
10:17/11:10/14:3/18:4/19:11:23,24/21:30-32/
29:12/31:21:29/34:29,30/36:19/40:15/42:17/
Ps2:9/7:14/9:12/18:34/19:5/37:16:27:32/38:
16/54:5/55:12/68:30f/69:31/73:19^2:22/74:18/
76:7:10/81:5:9/89:3,4:29:47/102:6/105:18/106
:19,20/109:6/116:13/119:40,41,42/130:3,4^2/
135:12/Pro3:22f:32/4:3/6:26:32/7:22:23/10:6/
11:7/12:5/13:17:22/14:4^2/16:28:29f:32/17:6:20
/18:11:19/20:3:7/21:8^2:9:10:14:28:29/23:22:32
/24:26:28,29/25:6,7^2:18:19:24/26:2:9:10:17/27:
6/28:3/30:18,19/Ecc2:24-26/3:19/4:13/6:5/10
:8,9/12:10/Sol2:3:14/4:13,14f/6:4f:9:10f/7:4/
Is1:10/5:7f:10/6:11/14:19:24:29/19:19/21:2/
22:23,24/25:4/28/29:2:6/30:8/32:6/33/35:2/
37:8,9:33/38:21/40:19^2/43:14/44:10:12:13:15/
45:18/46:6/48:14/53:9:10/55:3:13/56:5/58:11/
61:8/65:16/66:3^3:11:17/Jer1:11:18/2:7:19:
26,27/3:18/5:15/6:21:26:27/10:2,3/13:11/17:1
/22:4:24,25f/23:7/25:12/26:2:15:18:23/29:31/
30:12:14/31:3:33f/32:35:40/33:9:17/35:1f/38:6
:7/44:22^2/47:7/48:38/49:28f/50:5:9:44/51:12/
Lam2:4:5:8/4:12/Eze1:10^2/4:3^2/5:15^2/8:7/10:
14^2/11:3:7:11/12:23/14:15:19/16:3:25:32:45:
59,60/17:12,13/19:10/20:33:41/22:24/23:46/
24:24/28:7:10:19:23^2/29:8:14/30:21f/33:2:12:
28:32/37:26/38:2,3f:10:11:15,16f/40:7-12f:22:
23^2:25:47/41:21/42:9,10/45:2:12/46/47:14:22/
Dan2:11:39/4:16:19:25/5:21/8:23:23f/11:2f:6:7
:17:21/12:7f/Hos1:4,5^2:11/3:4/8:13/10:7:11/
13:11f/14:8/Joe2:11/Amo3:11/Ob1:1/Mic:6:7f
:8/5:12/6:16/7:1/Nah1:6:8:14/2:10/Hab:14/3/
Zep1:4/2:15f/Zec1:9/12:3:10^2/14/Mal3:17/
Mt1:20/2:6:13:19/5:22:38f^2/7:18^2/8:12/9:16/
12:35:39,40/13:2,3:28/15:18/20:1/21:42/23:18
/26:16:72/27:4:33:58:64/28:2/Mk1:22/2:21/3:
29/4:1/6:8,9/12:11/13:5/14:1^2:32/15:7:42,43/
16:9f/Lk1:3f:11,12:18:43/2:9/5:12:36/6:45/7:
37/9:3:46:51/10:4:25:30:34/11:12:45/12:16:53
/16:1:9:9f:15/18:6/19:33/20:21^2/22:6:20:43:59
/23:19/24:22,23/Jn1:22:47/3:1:4:25/5:4/8:7:
16:44/9:4:16:24/12:29/13:15/18:36/19:35/Act
1:6:13:17:24,25:26/2:30/5:19:31:34/6:9:15/7:
24:30/8:26/9:25:37/10:1:3:22/11:13/12:7:21:
23/13:19,20/17:18:29/19:36:40/20:22f/21:31/
22:25/25:16/26:3/27:1:6:12:23:26/28:3:7/Rom
3:13:13f/4:6/9:17/14:12/15:26/1Co3:10/6:13/
7:32/8:4/9:1:2:9:12:25:27/11/12:16^3:17:29/13:
8:10/14:9:19:23:24:26:27/15:9:50:52/2Co2:15/
8:2:8:13:22/9:2:9/10:2:3/11:14/12:12/Gal1:8/3
:1/4:14:24,25/Eph5:10f:32/Php1:20/1Th:7/
2Th3:5:15/1Ti1:3,4^2:16/3:6:16/5:1:18/2Ti2:5/
Tit2:7/Phm1:8,9/Heb:13/2:16/3:11:18/5:7f/6:
13:16:17/7:20/8:3/9:7:9:28/11:4:23/12:19:20/
13:10:20,21/Jas4:4^2/5:11/1Pe2:2,3f/5:1/2Pe2:
6:22/1Jn:7/Rev1:1:20f/2:10/4:3:7^2/6:9/7:17f/
8:1/9:9:16:16f:16/12:15:17/14:15/15:2/16:17f^2:
21/19:15:17/20:1/21:17f
968

AND

Gen1:1:2f^2:3:4,5^4:4,5f^2:6^2:7,8f:9,10^3:11,12^6:13f^2:
14,15^5:16^2:17:18^4:19f^2:20^2:21,22^6:23f^2:24^4:25^3:
26^2:27:28^6:29^2:30^3:31:31f^2/2:1:3^2:4:6:7^2:8:9^2:
11,12:14:15:16,17^2:18:19,20^3:21^2:22^2:23:24^2:25/
3:6^4:7^2:8:10^2:12:14:15^5:16^2:17^2:18^2:19:21^2:22:23
:24/4:1^2:4^3:5^2:8^2:12:14^4:16:17:19:20:21f:21:22f:
22:23^2:25:26/5:2^3:3,4,5^2:6,7,8^2:9,10,11^2:
12,13,14^2:15,16,17^2:18,19,20^2:21-24^3:25,26,27^2:
28-31^2:32^2/6:1f:1:4:5^2:7^4:9,10^2:11:12,13^2:14^2:15
:16^3:17:18^2:19,20^3:21:22/7:2:3:3f:4^4:7^2:8,9^5:
10,11,12^3:13^3:14,15^3:16^2:17:18:20:21^4:22:23^4:24
/8:1^2:2:7^2:7f:9^2:11:12:13:17^2:18,19^4:20^2:21:21f^2:
21^2:22^4/9:1^3:2,3^4:5,6^2:7^2:8:9,10,11^4:12:13:15^3:
16,17:18:20,21^3:22^2:23^2:24,25^3:26,27:26,27f:
26,27^2:29/10:1:9:10:11,12^2:13,14:15-19^3:20:24:
25^2:31/11:2^2:2f:3,4^2:5:6:6f^2:7:8:10,11^2:12,13f:
12,13^3:14,15^2:16,17^2:18,19^2:20,21:22,23:24,25^2:
26:27:28:29:31^3:32:32f/12:1^2:2^2:3^2:4:5^3:6:7^2:8^4:
10:11,12,13^3:14:15:16^2:18:19:20^3/13:1^4:3,4^2:5^2:
6^2:7^2:9:10:11^3:13:15:16:17:18/14:1:2:3:5,6^2:7^2:
8,9^2:10^3:11^4:12:13^2:14:15:16^3:17:18^2:19,20^2:22:
24/15:1^2:5^2:6:7:9:10^3:11:12^2:14:17^2:19,20,21/16
:1,2,3^3:4^3:5f:6:8:9-12^5:13:14:15/17:1^2:7,8^6:9,10:
11:12:16^3:17:18:19^3:20:21:22:23^2:24-27^2/18:2^2:
3,4:5:6^2:7^3:8^3:10:11^2:12:16^2:18:19^3:20^2:22,23^2:
24:25:26:27^2:28:29:30:31:32:33^2/19:1^2:2:3:4:5:8:
9^3:10^2:11:13:15^2:16^3:17:18,19,20^4:21:24^2:25^3:26
:27:28^3:29:30:31:32:33^2:34^2:35^3:36/20:1^2:2:3:5:7^2
:8^3:9,10:11,12^3:13:14^5:15:16:17^2/21:1^2:3:6:8^3:9:
10^2:13:14^2:16^3:17:18^2:19^2:20,21^4:22^2:26:27:
28,29:30:32:33^2:34/22:1:2^2:3^3:5^4:6:7:8:9^3:10^2:13
:14:16:17^3:18:19/23:1:7:9:10:11^2:13^2:14,15:
17,18^2:19,20/24:1:3:4:7^4:9f:10:11:12:13:14^2:
15,16^2:18:20^2:22:25^2:27^2:29,30^4:31^2:32^3:35^7:36:
37:38:40:41:44^2:45^3:46^2:47^3:48^2:49:50:51:53^4:54^2
:55:56:57:58:60:61^2:63:64:65:67^3/25:1:3^2:4:6:
9,10^2:12-15:17:17f:18:21f:22:23^2:24:28:33:34^3/
26:1:2:3^4:4^3:5:7:8:9:10:13^2:14^3:16^2:17:18^2:19:20^3
:22^2:24^2:25^3:26:29^2:30^2:33^2:34:35/27:2,3,4^7:6,7:
8,9,10^3:11,12^2:13:15:16^2:17:19:21:23:25^3:26^3:
27,28,29^4:30:31^2:33^2:34:35^2:36:37^3:39,40^2:41:42^2
:45:46/28:1^2:2^2:4:5:6,7,8^5:9^2:10:11:12^3:13^2:14^3:
15^2:18^2:20^4:21:22^2/29:4:6:8^2:10^4:11:12,13^5:14:
16:17:23:24:27:29:30^3:32:33^3:34^2:35^3/30:3:4:5^2:
6^2:7:8:10:13:14:15:17^3:21:22:23,24^2:26^2:29^2:30:
31,32^2:35,36^7:37^2:38:39,40^5:41:42:43^2/31:3^3:4:5^2
:7^3:8^2:10^3:12:12f:12:13^2:14:15:16^2:17-20^4:21^4:23
:24:27^2:28:29:30:33:34:36,37^3:38^3:39^2:40^2:41^2:
42^2:43^4:44^3:45:46^4:47,48:50:51,52:53^2:54^2:55^4/
32:1^2:5^3:7^2:9^2:10^2:11^2:12:13,14,15:17:21:
22,23,24^6:25^2:29:30:31/33:2^4:4^4:5^2:6:7^4:8^3:11^2:
12^2:13^3:14^2:15:17^2:18:20^2/34:2:3:6,7:8:9,10^5:11^2
:13:16^2:17:18,19^4:20^2:21^2:23:24:25^3:26^2:27:28^3:
29^3:30^4/35:1^2:2^2:3^2:4^2:5:7^2:8^2:9:10:11^3:12^3:
13,14^2:16:18:19:20^2:21:22:28,29^2/36:2,3:4^2:5^2:
6,7,8^2:15,16:17:18,19^2:22:28,29,30f:31-39/37:2:
4:5:7^3:8^2:9^2:10^3:11:13,14^4:16:17:19,20^2:21,22:24
:25:26,27^2:28^2:29:30:31:32^2:34^2:35^2/38:1^2:2:
3,4,5^2:7:9:11^2:12:14^3:15:16:18^4:20:22^2:24:25:26:
27:29^2:30/39:1:3:4:5:7^2:10:12^2:13:14,15^2:16:17:18,19^3:
21:23^2/40:1:4:6:8:9,10^2:11^3:13:14^3:15:17:18,19^3:
20^4/41:2:3^2:5^2:6:7^2:8^2:10^2:11:12:13^3:14^2:15^2:18:
19:20:21:22^2:24:26:27^2:30:32:33:34,35:37:41,42^3
:43:44:45^2:46:47:49:51:55:56,57^2/42:2:6^2:11:13^2
:16:18:19:20:21^2:22:24^2:26:27:29:30:32:33^2:34:
36:38/43:2:7:8^3:10:11:13^2:14^2:15^3:16:17:18:20:
21^2:23:24^2:27:28:30^2:31:32^3:33:34^2/44:1:3:4^2:6:
9:10:11:12:13:14^2:16^2:18:20^5:21:24:25^2:28^2:29^2:
30^2:31:33/45:1:2:4:7:8^2:9:10^2:11,12:13^2:14:15:
16:17:18^3:19^3:21:22^2:23^2:25:26:27:28^2/46:1^2:3,4^2
:5^2:6^3:7^2:8-14^{10}:15:16,17^5:18:19-22^5:23,24,25^5:
28:29^3:30:31^4:32^3:33:34/47:1^3:2:3:5,6^2:7:9:11:12
:13^2:14^2:17:18^4:19^3:20:22:23^2:24^4:26:27^2:29:30^2:
31/48:1:2:3^2:4:3^2:5^4:6^2:7:9^2:10^2:11:12,13^2:14:15:
16^3:17:20:21:22^2/49:1^2:3:4^2:5^2:6:7:7f:11:11f:12:
13:15:19:23:25^2:26:27:31^3:33/50:1^2:4:5:6:7^2:8^3:9
:10:12,13^2:14:16,17:18^2:19:21^2:22^2:23:24^4:26^2/
Ex1:6:7:10^3:11^2:12:13,14^4:15,16:17:18^2:20^2:21/
2:1^3:3:5^3:6:7^2:8:9^3:10:11^2:12^2:14^3:15^2:16:17^2:19:
21:23:24^2/3:1f:2:6:7:8^3:9:12:13:15:16^3:17^4:18^2:
20:21:22^3/4:2:3^2:4:5^2:6^2:7^2:9^3:10:10f:12^2:14^2:15^2
:16:17:18^2:20^3:21:23^3:24^3:25,26^2:27^2:28^2:29^2:30:
31^5/5:1:2^3:3^2:6:7,8:9^2:10,11^2:15:16^2:17:18:20:21^2
:23^2/6:2,3:4^2:5^2:6^2:7^3:8,9:8,9f:10:11:13^2:17:20^3:
23:25^2:26^2:27:28,29^2/7:1:2:3:4:5:6:7:8:9:10^4:11:
13^2:14:15:17^2:18:19^3:20^3:21^2:22^4:23/8:1^2:3,4^4:5:
6:7:8^4:9:12^2:13^2:15:16:17^3:19^2:20^3:21:23:24^2:25^3
:26:27:28:29:30:31,32^3/9:1:3:4:6:7:8:9^2:10^3:11:
13^2:14^3:16:17^2:19:20:22^2:23^3:25^3:27^3:28^2:29^2:30
:31^3:32:33^3:34/10:1^2:2^2:3^2:4,5:6^2:7^2:8^2:9^2:11^2:12
:13^3:14^2:15^2:16^3:17:18:19:20:21:22:24^3:25^2:26:
27:28/11:1^2:2^2:3^3:5^2:6:7:8^2:9:10/12:1:2:7^2:8:9:
11:12^3:13^2:16^2:21^4:22^3:23^2:23f:23^2:24^2:25^2:26:
27^3:28:29:30^3:31^4:32^3:33:34^2:35^4:36^2:37^2:38^2:39
:40,41^2:43:46^2:48^3:49:50/13:1:3:4,5^2:6,7:11:12^2:
14:15:21:22/14:2^2:3:4^3:5:7:9^2:10^2:11:13^2:14:15:
16^2:17^4:18:20^3:21^2:23:24:25:26^2:27:28^3:29:30:31^3
/15:1^2:2^2:4:7:9:10:12:14:16:17:18:19:20:21^2:22^2:
25^2:26^2:27^3/16:1^2:3:4^2:6^2:7,8,9^2:10:11,12^3:13^2:
14:15:17:18^2:19:20^4:21^2:22:23^3:24^2:25:26:28,29:
31^3:33^2:34/17:2:3:5,6^3:7^3:10^2:11:12^2:13:14:
15,16/18:1^2:4^2:5,6^3:7^2:8^4:9:10^2:11:12f:12^3:15,16^2
:18:19,20^3:21^3:23^3:24:25^2/19:2,3^3:4:5:6:7^2:9:10^3:
12:14^2:15:16^4:17:18:19^2:20^2:21:23:24^3:25/20:5^2:
6:9:11^4:12:18^4:19:22:24^4:25:26^2/21:2f^2:2^2:4^3:5^2:
6^2:9^2:10:13^2:14:18^2:19:22^2:23:24:26:27:28:29^3:
32:33^2:34:35^3:36^2/22:1:2:3:5:6^2:7:9^2:10^2:11^2:13:
14^2:15:16^2:23:24^3:27^2:28:29^2:30:31^2/23:2,3:10:
11^3:12^3:13:16:21:23^3:24^2:25^2:26:27:28^2:29:31^4:
33/24:1:2:3^2:4:5:6:7^3:8^2:9:10:11:12^3:13:14^2:15:
16^2:18^3/25:1^2:9:10:11:12:13,14:17^2:18:20:21:22^3
:23:24:25:26,27:29^2:30:31^2:34,35:36^2:37:38:39/

(AND Con't)

26:1:7,8:9:13:14:15,16:23:24:29[2]:31:33:35[2]:36:
37/27:1:2:3:5:9,10:11:12:16[2]:18:19:21[2]/28:1[2]:4:
5,6:7:8[2]:9:11:13,14:15:17:18:19:20:21:26:30,31:
30,31f:33,34:35:36:37,38[2]:39:40[2]:41[2]:43[3]/29:1[2]:
2[3]:3,4[3]:5[2]:6:7:9[2]:10[2]:11:12:13[3]:14[2]:15,16[2]:17[3]:18[2]
:19,20[6]:21[6]:22[5]:23[2]:24:25:26:27:28:30:31:32:33:
35:37:39:41:42:43[2]:44[3]:45[2]:46/30:2:3[2]:8[2]:11,12:
15:16:17,18[3]:19[2]:21:22,23:24:26,27[2]:28[2]:30:31:
32[2]:34:35[2]:36:37/31:1:3[3]:4:5:6:8:9:10:11:12,13:
16:17[4]/32:2,3[2]:4:5:6[3]:8[4]:10[3]:11:13[3]:14:19[3]:20[4]:
22:24[2]:25:26[3]:27[4]:28:29:31[2]:32:33:34[2]:35/33:1:2
:3[2]:4[2]:5:7:8:9:12[2]:13:14[2]:16[2]:17[2]:19[2]:20:22[2]:23/
34:1:2:3:4[2]:5,6[6]:7f[2]:7[3]:8:9[3]:10:11:13:13f:14:15[2]:
16[2]:19:20:21[2]:22[2]:23:24[2]:25:26:27[2]:28[2]:30:31[3]:
32:35/35:1:5-9[6]:10-19[13]:21:22[2]:23[3]:24[2]:25[5]:27:
28[4]:29:30,31[2]:32:33[2]:34[2]:35[2]/36:1[4]:3:4-7:8,9:
14,15:16:18:19:21:29:34[2]:35:36:37:38[2]/37:1[2]:2[2]:
4:5:6:7:10:13:15,16:17:20,21:22:23,24:25:26:29/
38:1:3:8:10[2]:11[3]:12[3]:14,15:17[3]:18[2]:19[2]:20:21:22:
23[3]:27:28[3]:29[3]/39:1:3[3]:4,5[2]:6,7:8:10:11:12:13:
15-18:23:24:25,26:27:28,29[4]:32:33-40[9]:41[2]:43[2]/
40:3:4[3]:6:7[2]:8:9[6]:10:11:12[2]:13[2]:14:15[2]:18:19:20[2]:
21:23:24:26:27:29[3]:30[2]:31[3]:32:33[2]:34:35:36:38/
Lev1:2,3[2]:4:5:6,7[2]:8[3]:9[2]:10:11[2]:12[2]:13:15,16,17[6]
/2:1[2]:2:3:4:5:6:8:12:14:15:16/3:2:3,4,5[4]:6:7,8:
9,10,11[2]:13:14:15,16[2]/4:3:4[2]:6[2]:9[2]:10:11,12[2]:13:
15:17[2]:18:19:20:21:22:24[2]:25[2]:26:27:29[2]:30[2]:31[3]
:33[2]:34[2]:35[2]/5:6[4]:7:9:10:12[2]:13:14:16[3]:17,18/6:
1:3:4,5[2]:6:7[2]:9:10[3]:11:12[2]:15[3]:16:17:19,20[4]:21:
25[2]:28/7:2[2]:4[2]:6:7:12:15[3]:17,18[3]:19:21:24:28:30:
31:34[2]:35[2]:37[3]/8:1[3]:5:6[2]:7[2]:8[2]:9:10[2]:11[3]:13:14[2]:
15,16[5]:17:18:19[3]:20[2]:21[2]:22:23[4]:24[2]:25:26[2]:27:
28[2]:29:30[7]:31[2]:32:35[3]:36/9:1[2]:2[3]:3[2]:4[2]:5[2]:7[3]:8:9[3]
:10:11:12[3]:13:14[2]:15:17:18[4]:19[4]:20:21:22:23[3]:24[4]
/10:1[2]:1f:2:3[2]:4[4]:5[2]:6[6]:7:8,9[2]:10[2]:11:12[3]:13:14[3]:
15[3]:16[2]:17[2]:19:20/11:1:9:21,22:23:25:28:32[2]:33:
35:37:38:40:44:46:47[3]/12:2:6:7[2]:8/13:1:3[2]:4:5[2]:
6[4]:8[2]:9,10:11:12:20:21[2]:23[2]:24:25[2]:26[2]:27:28[2]:
29,30:31:32[3]:33:34[3]:36:37[3]:43:44:45[3]:46:49[2]:51:
52[2]:55[2]:57/14:1:4[2]:6:7[2]:8[2]:9[4]:10:11:12[2]:13:14[3]:
15:16[2]:17[2]:19[2]:20:21[2]:22[2]:24[2]:25[3]:27:28[2]:31[2]:
33,34[2]:35:39:40:41:42:44[3]:45:48:49:51,52[3]:53/
15:1:4:5[2]:6[2]:8[2]:10[2]:11[2]:12:13:14[2]:15:16:17:18:19
:21,22,23[2]:24:26:27[3]:29:30[3]:33[2]/16:1:3:4[2]:5:6:8[2]
:10[2]:11:12[2]:14[3]:15[4]:16[2]:17[3]:18[2]:19[2]:20[2]:21:22:
23[2]:24[4]:26[2]:27[4]:28[2]:29,30:31:33[2]:35/17:1[2]:3,4:5[3]
:6[2]:10:11:13[2]:14:15[3]:16/18:4,5:16f[2]:17[2]:23:24:
25:26[3]:27:29,30/19:1[2]:7:8:9:10[2]:13:19:22:23:24[2]
:30:31:32:35,36[2]:37/20:3[3]:4[2]:5[2]:6[2]:7:9:10:11:12:
14:15:16:17:19:20:21:22:24[2]:25[3]:26/21:4:6[2]:7:10
:14,15:16,17:22:24[2]/22:1:3:4:6:7:9:11:13[2]:16:
17,18[3]:26,27:28:32,33[3]/23:1:3:7:9,10,11[2]:18[2]:19[2]
:20:22:23,24:26,27:29:30,31:32[3]:36:38:39:40[3]:43
/24:3,4[2]:9[2]:10:11:13,14[2]:15,16:21:23/25:3[2]:4:5:
6,7[2]:9:10[2]:17,18:19:23[2]:25:26:27[2]:31:33[2]:34:36[2]:
37:38:39:40:41[2]:42:45:47[2]:52:54/26:2:4,5[4]:6:8:9[2]
:11[2]:12[2]:13:13f:16[4]:17:18:19[2]:21[2]:22[2]:23:24:25[2]:
26:27:28:29:30[3]:31[2]:33:34,35[2]:36[2]:38:40,41[3]:42[3]
:43:44:46/27:6[2]:7:8[2]:10:11,12:14,15[3]:19:20:21:
23:24:25f:30:32[3]:33[3]/Num1:2-15[3]:17,18,19[4]:
47,48,49:50:51[2]:53/2:1[3]:3-31/3:2f:3:4[3]:6:7,8,9[2]:
10:11,12:13:25-30:31-35:36,37[3]:38[2]:39[2]:40[2]:41:
43[2]:45:47,48:51[2]/4:1:5[3]:6:7[2]:8:9:10:11:12:13:14[2]
:15[3]:16[2]:17,18,19[3]:20:21,22,23[2]:25:26[3]:32[2]:34[2]:
36:42-45:46,47,48[4]/5:1:3:7[2]:8:11,12:14[2]:17[2]:18:
19:21,22[2]:23:25[2]:26[2]:27[3]:28[2]:30/6:5:6,7:8:11[4]:
12:14:15[2]:16:17:19[2]:20[2]:21:22,23:24,25,26[2]:27[2]/
7:1[2]:3[2]:4,5:6:7:8[2]:13:15:17[2]:18-23:30-35:42-47:
66-71:72-77/8:4:7[2]:8:11:12[2]:13:14:15[2]:16:17:19[3]
:20[2]:21[2]:22:23,24/9:1:6,7[4]:9:10:11:12[2]:13[2]:14[2]:
15[2]:17:18:20,21[2]:23/10:1:5,6,7[2]:9[2]:10[3]:12:14:16:
17[2]:20:23:24:27:29:30:31:31f:35:36/11:1:2:4,5[4]:
6:7:8[2]:10:17[3]:18[2]:19,20:21[2]:22:24[3]:25[5]:26[2]:27:
28:29:31[2]:32[3]:33:34:35/12:1:1f:2:3,4:5[3]:6[2]:7,8:9:
13:14[2]:15:16/13:3-15:18:19[3]:20[2]:22[2]:23:26[2]:27[2]:
28[3]:29[2]:30:33/14:1:2:3[3]:5:6:7:8[3]:9[2]:10,11:12[3]:14[5]
:17,18[3]:22[4]:24:25:26,27:29:30:31:36,37,38:40:43[2]
:45[3]/15:3,4[2]:7:13,14:15,16:19,20,21[2]:23,24[3]:25[4]:
26:28[2]:30:31[2]:33[3]:36:37,38:39[2]/16:1[3]:2:3[4]:5[3]:6,7[4]
:8,9:10:11,12[2]:13:14:15[2]:16:17:18[4]:19[2]:20[2]:22:
23,24[2]:25:26[2]:27[6]:28:30[4]:32[4]:33[2]:35:36,37:38:39
:40:41:42:43,44[3]:45:46[4]:47[3]:48[3]:50/17:5:6:8[3]:10
/18:1[3]:2,3[2]:5:7[2]:8:9:10:11[2]:13:14,15:16:17:18:19[3]
:22[2]:23:24:27:28,29:30:31[2]/19:1[3]:4:5:6[3]:7[3]:8[3]:9:
10[3]:12[2]:13[2]:14:18[5]:19[3]:20[2]:21:22/20:1[2]:2:3:4:5[2]:
6[3]:7:8[3]:10[3]:11[4]:12[2]:13:15[2]:16[2]:17:19[2]:20:21,22:
23:25[2]:26[2]:28[3]:29/21:1:2:3[3]:4:5[3]:6[2]:7[2]:8:9:10:12[2]
:13:14:15:16:17,18[2]:19:23:24:25,26:27-30[5]:31,32
:35[4]/22:1:2,3[2]:5,6[5]:7[2]:8:9:11[2]:14:16,17:18:20:21:
22,23:26:31[2]:33[2]:36:38:40[3]/23:1[2]:2[2]:3,4[5]:7-10:
11:14[3]:16[2]:17:18-24[5]:29[2]:30[2]/24:1:3-9[7]:10[2]:13[2]:
15-19[5]:20:21,22:23,24[2]:25/25:2[2]:3:6:7:8[2]:10,11:
12,13[2]:18/26:1:2:3,4:5-11[6]:19-22:28-37:55,56:
58,59[2]:60:61:62:63:64,65f:64,65/27:1[2]:3,4:6,7:8:
9:10:12:17:18:19[2]:21[2]:22:23/28:1[2]:8:9,10:11:12:
13[2]:14:15:18:19:20,21:25[2]:27:28,29:31[2]/29:1:2[2]:
3,4:6[2]:7:9,10[2]:11[2]:12:13:15:16:17:18:19:21[2]:22[2]:
23:24:25:26,27[2]:28:29:30:31[2]:32:33:34:37[2]:38:
39[2]/30:1:3:4:5:6:7[2]:8:10:11[2]:12:15:16[3]/31:1:4,5:
7:8:9,10,11[5]:12[3]:13[2]:14:16[2]:17:19[2]:20:24[2]:25:26[3]
:27:28:30:31:32-35:42-46:48,49[3]:50:51,52[4]:54/
32:1[2]:2[3]:3,4[2]:6:9:10,11[3]:12[2]:13:15[2]:16:20:21:22[2]:
23:24[3]:25:26:28:29:31:33[3]:37,38:39[2]:40:41:42[3]/
33:1:5,6:8:9:11:13:38,39:41:46:47:48:52[2]:53:54:
55:56/34:4[2]:7,8,9[3]:10,11:12:13:14,15[2]:16-28[2]/
35:2:3[2]:6[2]:9,10:13,14:15:16[2]:17:21:22,23:24:25:
27[2]:28:33/36:1[2]:4:11,12:13/Deu1:1[2]:7[4]:8[3]:11[2]:
12:13[2]:15[3]:17[2]:18:19,20,21[4]:22:24,25[2]:26:27[2]:28[2]
:30:31[2]:33[3]:34,35:37[2]:40:41[2]:43:44[2]:45/2:5:7[2]:8[2]
:11:12:13:21[2]:23:24:25:27:28:29:32:33,34[3]:35,36
:37[2]/3:1[2]:3[2]:5:6:7:10[3]:11[2]:12[2]:13:14:16:17:18[2]:
19:23,24,25[2]:26:27:28/4:1[4]:6[2]:8:9[2]:10[3]:11[2]:12:
13:19:25[4]:26[2]:27:28:29[2]:30:33:34:35:36:37:38:
39[2]:40[2]:43:44,45,46[3]:47:49/5:1[2]:5[3]:9,10[3]:15:16:
22:22f:22[2]:23:24[3]:26,27[5]:28[3]:29:30:31[4]:33[2]/6:2:
3[3]:5:6:7[2]:9:10,11,12[5]:13[2]:15[2]:16:18[3]:21:22[3]:24[2]/
7:1:3[2]:4:5[3]:7:8[2]:9[2]:10:13[8]:15[2]:16:18:19[4]:21[2]:22:
23[2]:24:25:26/8:1[2]:2[2]:3[3]:4:6:7:8[2]:9[2]:11:12,13[6]:14:
15[3]:16[2]:17:18:19[2]/9:1[2]:3:5[2]:9[2]:10,11:12:13,14[3]:
17:18:20:21[3]:22[2]:23:25:26:27[3]:29[2]/10:1[2]:2:3[2]:4:
5:6:7[2]:8[3]:10[3]:11[2]:12,13[5]:14:15[2]:16:17[3]:18[3]:20[3]:
21/11:1:2:3:4[3]:5:6[5]:8:9[3]:10:11:13[4]:14[2]:15[2]:17[3]:
18:19:20:21:22:23:24:25:28[2]:29:30:31/12:3:6[3]:7[2]
:10[3]:11:12[3]:14:15[2]:17[3]:18:20-23[4]:24,25:26,27[3]:
28:30[2]:31/13:2:3:4:6,7:8:11:15[2]:16[2]:17[3]:18[2]/14:
2:3,4,5:6:9:19,20:23[2]:25[2]:26:29[4]/15:9:10:13:14:
15:16[2]:17[2]:18:19[3]:20/16:4:7:11[3]:13:14[3]:15:18:19[2]
:22/17:5:7:9[2]:10:13:14[2]:18[2]:20/18:1[3]:3:4:6,7:8:
12[2]:15:18:19:20/19:1[2]:2,3:5[3]:6,7:8:9:10:11[3]:12[2]:
15:17:18/20:1[2]:2:4:5:6:7[2]:8:11:12:14:17:18:20/
21:1:2:4[2]:5[3]:6:7:8:10:11:12:13[2]:15[3]:17:19:20[3]:21[2]
:22[2]/22:2[2]:4:5:6:7:8[2]:9:10:11:15:16:17,18[2]:19[2]:
20:21:22:23,24[3]:25,26,27:28,29[2]:30f/23:4:7[2]:11[2]
:13:14[2]:15,16:23/24:1:3:7:8:12,13[3]:14,15:17[2]:18:
19[2]:20/25:1[3]:5:7:8[2]:9:10:11:13,14,15:16:18[3]/26:
1[2]:2,3[2]:4:6,7[3]:8[3]:9[3]:10[2]:11[2]:12:13:14:15[3]:16:17[4]:
18[2]:19[2]/27:1:2,3,4[4]:5,6[2]:7:9:12:13[2]:15[2]:16:17[2]:
18:19[2]:20:21:22:23:24:25:26/28:2-6[2]:8[2]:9:10:11:
12:13[3]:14:15-19[3]:20:21:22:23:24:25[2]:26[2]:27:28:
29[2]:31[2]:32:33:36[3]:37:39:41:42:43[2]:44:45:46:
47,48[2]:50:51[3]:52:53:54[2]:56,57[4]:58,59[2]:60:61[2]:63[3]
:64:65[2]:66[2]:67:68/29:2,3[3]:5:6:7:8[4]:10:11[3]:13[2]:16
:17[2]:18[2]:20[3]:22[3]:23[4]:25:28:29/30:1:2[2]:3[2]:4[2]:5[2]:6[4]
:7,8[3]:9[3]:10[2]:11:12[2]:14:15:16[5]:17:19[2]:20[4]/31:2f:3[2]
:4:5:7:8:9:12[3]:13:14[3]:16[3]:17[2]:19:20[6]:21:22:23[2]:
27:28[3]:29[3]/32:1:2:4:6:7:12:13:14[3]:15:16:19[2]:22[2]:
23:24[2]:25[2]:30:32:35:36[2]:38[2]:39[2]:40,41[5]:44,45:46
:49:50[2]/33:2[2]:6:7[2]:8[2]:9[2]:10[2]:11:12[2]:13:15:16[2]:17[2]
:18:19:20[2]:23:25[2]:27:28:29[2]/34:1:2[3]:3[3]:4:7:9:
11,12[4]/Jos1:1:4:6[2]:7[2]:8[2]:9[2]:10,11[2]:12,13[2]:14[2]:16
:17,18[2]/2:1:5:6:7:10[4]:12,13[3]:14:17,18[2]:21:22:23[2]
/3:1[2]:2,3,4:6[2]:9[2]:10[2]:13,14[3]:15,16:17[2]/4:2,3[2]:5:8
:9:11:12,13[2]:14[2]:18[2]:19:20:21:23:24/5:1[2]:4,5:6[3]:
8,9[2]:11,12[3]:13:14[2]:15/6:2[2]:5:6-9:11:12,13,14:17:
19[4]:20[4]:21[2]:22[2]:23[2]:24[4]:25[2]:26:27/7:1[2]:3:4:5:6[2]:
9[4]:10,11[4]:13:14[5]:15[2]:16:17[2]:18:19:21[3]:22:23:24[3]
:25[2]:26[3]/8:1[2]:2[2]:5:7:9[3]:10:11,12,13:14:15:16:17:
19[3]:20,21[3]:22[2]:23:24:27:29:31:32:33[2]:34:35[2]/9:1[2]
:3,4,5[2]:6:9[2]:10[2]:11[3]:12:13[2]:14,15[3]:17[2]:19:21:22:
23:24:27[2]/10:1[4]:2[2]:4[2]:6[2]:7[2]:9:10[3]:11:12[2]:13[3]:14[2]
:15:16:18:19:20[2]:21:22,23[2]:25:27[2]:28[2]:30:31:32:
33:34,35:37[2]:39:40[3]:41:43/11:1:4[2]:6:7[2]:8[3]:9[2]:10:
11:12:14:15:16[2]:17:21[2]:22:23/12:2:3[2]:4:5[2]:6[3]:7[2]:
8-24[3]/13:1:2-7[2]:8[2]:9:10:11:12[3]:17:20:21[3]:25:26[2]:
27,28[2]:30:31[2]/14:1[3]:3,4[4]:6:7:8:9:10[2]:11[2]:13,14:
15/15:1:2,3,4[3]:7:8:9:10,11[3]:14:16:18,19[2]:21-32:
33-36:37-44f:37-44:45:46:47:48-62f:48-62/16:1[4]
:5,6:7[3]:8/17:1:2:3[2]:4[3]:5,6[2]:10[4]:11:14:15[2]:
16,17,18[6]/18:1:4[3]:5,6:7[3]:8:9[2]:11:12:13:14:16[2]:17
:19:21-28f:21-28[2]/19:2-7f:2-7:11:12[2]:13[2]:14:
15,16:17-23:24,25,26:27[2]:28:29[2]:30,31[2]:33[2]:34[4]:
35-39:41-46:47,48[2]:49:50:51/20:2f:3:4[3]:6[2]:7:8:9
/21:1[2]:2:4:5:6:7:8[2]:9-16[3]:17,18[2]:20,21,22[2]:23,24[2]
:25:26:27[2]:28,29:30,31[2]:32:34,35:36,37:38,39:
41,42:43[3]:44[2]/22:1:2,3[2]:4[2]:5[2]:6:7,8[2]:9[2]:12:13[2]:
14:15:16:19:21:22,23:24,25[3]:26,27[4]:30[2]:32[2]:33[4]:
34[2]/23:1:2[2]:3[2]:4,5[2]:9:12:13[3]:15,16/24:1[2]:2[2]:3[2]:4[2]
:5[2]:6:7[3]:8[2]:9:10:11[3]:12[2]:13[2]:14[3]:15:16[2]:17:18:19[2]
:20[2]:23:24:25[2]:26[2]:31/Ju1:2:3:4,5,6[4]:7[2]:8:9:10:
13[2]:15[2]:16:17[2]:18:22,23:24:25[2]:26:30:33:34:35[2]:
36/2:1[2]:3[3]:6:7-9[2]:10[2]:12-14[4]:15:19:23/3:1f:1:1f:
5:6[2]:7[2]:8:10[2]:13[2]:16:17,18,19:20:21:22,23[2]:24
25[2]:27:29[2]:30/4:2,3:5[2]:6[2]:7:10[2]:11:12:13:15[3]:
:17:18[2]:19:20:21[4]:22[3]:24[3]/5:1:3:4:6:10[4]:11:12
13,14[2]:15:17[2]:18:25:26[2]:27:29:30[3]/6:1:2:3,4[5]:
9[4]:10:11:12:13[2]:14[2]:15:16f:16:18:19[4]:20[2]:21[4]:
:25[2]:27[2]:28:30:31:33[2]:34[2]:35[2]:37[2]:38[2]/7:1[2]:3[2]
:5,6:8,9[2]:11[3]:12,13[5]:14:15[2]:16[2]:18[3]:19,20[5]:21[2]
22[3]:23[4]:25[4]/8:2,3:5:6[2]:6f:7[2]:8:9[2]:10:11:12:14[2]
15[3]:16[2]:17[2]:18:20:21[2]:22[2]:25:26:27f:27[2]:28:30
32:33/9:2[3]:3[2]:5[2]:6[2]:7:9[2]:11:13:15[3]:16:17[2]:18[2]:
:20[2]:21:22,23[2]:24:26:27:28[2]:29[3]:31[2]:32:33[2]:34
35:37:38[3]:39:40:41[3]:43[3]:45:46:47,48:49[3]:50:5
54:55:56,57/10:1:3:4:6[4]:7,8:9[2]:10[3]:12:13:14:1
16[2]/11:1:3:6:7:11[2]:13:18[2]:19:20:21,22[2]:23:24:
:26:29[3]:32:33:34:35:36:37:38:39/12:1:3[2]:4[2]:5:
9,10[3]:11,12:14:15/13:2,3:4:5:6[3]:7[2]:8:9:10[2]:11:
13,14:17:19[4]:20[3]:21:23[3]:24:25[2]/14:2[2]:3:4:5:6[2]
8[2]:9[2]:12:14:16[2]:17[2]:18:19[5]/15:4[2]:5[3]:6[3]:8:9:10[2]
12,13[2]:14[3]:15:18[3]:19[2]/16:1:2[2]:3[2]:5[3]:8:9:12:13:
:15:16,17[2]:19[2]:20[2]:21[3]:23,24:25,26:27:28:30[2]:
/17:2:3:4,5[3]:9[2]:10,11[4]/18:2[2]:3:4:7[4]:8:9,10[2]:11
14:15,16[2]:17[2]:19:20[2]:21:22:24[2]:25:27[3]:28[2]:30[3]
19:2[3]:3[2]:4:8[2]:9[5]:17:19[2]:21:22[2]:24[2]:25:26:28:29
20:1[4]:3:5:6:7:8,9,10[2]:13:18:21:22,23,24[3]:25:26
27,28[3]:30[2]:31[3]:32:33[2]:34:35-39[4]:40,41[2]:42[2]:43
45:48[4]/21:2[2]:4[3]:5:6:7:8,9:10,11,12[2]:14:19:20:2
:22[4]:23[3]:25/Ru1:1[3]:3:4,5[2]:8[3]:9[3]:12[3]:14[3]:15:16
17:18[2]:19:21[2]:22/2:2f:2:3:6:7:8,9[2]:10,11[5]:13:1
:14f:15:16[3]:17:18:19:21:23[2]/3:1:2:3[3]:4[3]:5:6,7[4]:
13[2]:14:15-18[4]/4:1:2:4:5:7:9[2]:10:11[4]:12[3]:13:14:
15[2]:16,17[3]/1Sa1:2:3[3]:4:7:10:11[5]:12,13:15,16:1
:19,20[2]:21,22[4]:24[2]:27:28/2:3[2]:7[2]:8[2]:10:11:13,1
:15:18:19:20[2]:21[2]:26[2]:27:28[4]:29:30:32[2]:33[2]:34
35[2]:36/3:2,3:4,5:6[2]:8[2]:9[2]:10[3]:13[2]:14[2]:16,17:19
20:21,4:1/4:2:3[2]:4:10[2]:11[3]:12[2]:13:14[2]:15:17[4]:1
:19[2]:20:21,22[2]/5:4[2]:6:9[2]:11[2]:12/6:2[2]:4,5[5]:6[2]:7[2]
:9[2]:10:11[2]:12[2]:13:14[3]:15[5]:17:18:19:21[2]/7:1[2]:2:
4[2]:5:6[2]:7:9[3]:10[2]:11:12[3]:13:14[3]:16[2]:17[2]/8:1:2:3:
8[2]:11:12[3]:13[3]:14[3]:15:16[2]:17:20:22[3]/9:1:2[2]:3:4:
:7:8:9,10,11[3]:12,13:14:16:18:19[2]:20[2]:21:22[2]:24
25:26,27/10:1[3]:2[2]:3[2]:4:5[2]:6[3]:8[2]:9[2]:10[3]:12:14:1
18,19[5]:20:21[2]:22:23[3]:24:25[2]:27[3]/11:1:3:4:5:6:7
8:10:11[2]:12:14:15[3]/12:2:3[2]:4:5:6:7:8[2]:9[2]:10[5]:1
12:13:14[5]:15:17:18[4]:20:23[2]:24:25/13:1f[2]:2[2]:3,4
5[2]:6[3]:7[3]:8:9:10:11[2]:12:13:14[2]:15:16[2]:18:19:22/
14:2:3:4:5:7:9:10:12:13[4]:14:15[2]:17[2]:19[2]:20[3]:21
23:27:28[2]:31[2]:32[3]:34[5]:35:36:40[3]:41[4]:42[2]:46:47
48[2]:49[3]:50,51[2]:52/15:3[2]:6:9[3]:12:14:15[2]:17:18[3]:
19:20:21[3]:22:23[2]:24[2]:25:27:28[2]:29:30:31:32:33
34:35/16:1[2]:2:3:5[4]:6:7:8:9:12[2]:13[3]:14[2]:15,16:1
:20[2]:21[2]:23[3]/17:1[2]:3:4-7[2]:8[3]:11f:11[2]:13:14,15[2]:
16:17:18[2]:19:20[2]:21:22:23:25[3]:26:27:30[3]:31:33
34[2]:35[2]:36[2]:37[3]:38,39[3]:40[3]:43:44[2]:45[2]:46[5]:47:
48,49[3]:50,51[5]:52[3]:53:58[2]/18:1:4[3]:5[2]:6[4]:7:8:10:
11,12[3]:13:15,16:17:20:22[3]:27[3]:28:29/19:1:3:4[2]:
:6:7[2]:8[3]:9,10[2]:11:13[2]:14[2]:17:18[2]:20[3]:22[2]:23:24[2]
20:1:2:3:5[2]:11:12:13[2]:14[2]:16[2]:20:21:23:24,25:3
31:34:35:36:38:39:40[2]:41:41f[2]:42[2]/21:5:8:10:1
12:13/22:1[2]:3:5:7[2]:8:9,10[2]:11,12[2]:13[5]:14:15:17
18:19[4]:20:23/23:2[2]:4:5[3]:8[2]:9[2]:10:11[2]:12[2]:13[2]:
14,15:16:17:18:19:20[2]:22[2]:23[3]:24,25:26[2]:28/24
2[2]:3:4:7,8[3]:9,10:11:14:15[3]:17:20[2]:21:22[2]/25:1[2]:
:3[3]:6[2]:7:8:9:11[3]:12:13:14[2]:15,16[4]:17:18[2]:19:23:
26[2]:27[2]:28:30,31[2]:33:35:37,38[2]:37,38f:39:40:42
26:1:2:3,4:5,6,7[5]:8:11[2]:12[2]:14:16[2]:17,18[2]:19:21
22:23[2]:25[3]/27:1:2,3[2]:7[2]:8[2]:9[2]:10[3]:11[2]:12[2]/28:1
3[2]:4[2]:5,6:5,6f:7,8:9:14:15[2]:16:17[2]:19[3]:22:23[2]:24
:25[2]/29:1:2[2]:3[2]:5:6[2]:10/30:1[2]:2:3[2]:5:8:9,10:
11,12[4]:13:14[3]:16[3]:17[3]:18,19[2]:20[2]:21:22[2]:23:24[2]
25:27-31/31:1[2]:2[2]:3,4[4]:5:6:7[4]:8:9[3]:10:12[3]:13/
2Sa1:1[2]:4[4]:6:9:10f:10:11:12[5]:13:15:17,18[2]:19:20
22[2]:23[2]:24:26:27/2:1[2]:2[2]:3[2]:4:5:6[2]:7[2]:9:10,11:1
16:17[3]:18:19:20:21:23[3]:24:26:28:29[2]:30[2]:31:32[3]
3:1[3]:4:8:9,10:12:17:18:19[2]:20:21:22:23:24,25[2]:
26[2]:27:28:29:30:31[2]:32[2]:33,34:35,36:37:38[2]:39/
4:1:2,3:4[4]:5:6,7[3]:8:11[2]:12[5]/5:1:2[2]:3:4,5:6:7[2]:8[3]:
10:11:12:13[3]:17:18:19[2]:20[2]:21:22:23:24:25/6:1:
:5[4]:6:7:8:9:11[2]:13[2]:14[2]:15:16[3]:17[2]:19[4]:20:21[2]:22
/7:1:7:8:9[2]:10,11:12:13:14:15:17:18[2]:19:21:22:
23:24:25[2]:26[2]:28[2]:29[2]/8:1:2:4:6[2]:8:10[2]:11,12[2]:1
:15:16:17[2]:18f:18/9:2:5,6[2]:7:9:10,11[4]/10:1:2:4[3]:
6[2]:7,8[2]:9:11[3]:12:13[2]:14:19[2]/11:1:2:3[2]:4:7[2]:8[2]:10
11[6]:12:13:14:15[2]:17:19,20,21:22:23:24[2]:25f:25:
27[3]/12:1:3[3]:4[2]:6:7:8[4]:9[2]:11:13:14:15:16[2]:17:20[3]:
21[2]:22[2]:24[4]:25[2]:26,27[2]:28:29,30[3]:31[3]:31f[2]:31/1
:1:2:2f:5[2]:6[2]:7[2]:8:10:11:13:14:15:17,18[2]:19[2]:21-
21-24:27:28[2]:29,30[2]:31[2]:32,33:36[3]:37,38,39/14:
2,3[2]:4:5,6[2]:7:9:15,16[3]:17:19[2]:20:21[2]:22[2]:23:25:
26[2]:27:28:30[2]:31:32:33[3]/15:1[2]:2[3]:4:5:5f:9:9f:12:
14:16:17,18[2]:19,20[4]:21:22[2]:23[2]:24[3]:25,26:27:28:
29[2]:30[3]:32:33,34[2]:35,36[4]/16:1:2[3]:3:5:6[2]:7,8[2]:9:

D Con't)
2:13[4]:14[2]:15:18:19[2]:20:21[2]:22/**17**:2,3[7]:4:8[4]:
:11[2]:13[3]:14:15[2]:16[2]:17[2]:18:20[4]:21[3]:22[2]:23[2]:
5:26:27[2]:28,29[5]/**18**:1:2:3[4]:5[3]:7[2]:8:9[2]:10:11[2]:
2[2]:13[2]:14:15:16:17[2]:21:23[2]:25:26:27:28:31:
3/**19**:1:3:4:5[4]:6[2]:7:8,9,10[5]:11,12[3]:13:14[2]:15[2]
18[2]:19[2]:26:28:29:31,32[2]:33:35:35f:35[2]:37[2]:
9[2]:40[2]:41:43[3]/**20**:1:2[3]:4:6:7[2]:8,9,10[5]:11:12[2]:
17:20:22[5]:23:23f:24:25[2]/**21**:1[2]:3:4[2]:7:8:10[2]:
3,14[2]:15[3]:16[2]:17:19:20,21[4]:22/**22**:1:2:3[3]:6[2]:
:10:12:15:18:20:22:23:24:35:38:40:41:43:45
9:50:51[2]/**23**:2:5[2]:5f:9:10:11,12[3]:13:16[2]:
9[2]:20[2]:21:23:24-39f/**24**:1:4:5:6[2]:7[4]:8:9[2]:10:
15[2]:16:17:18[2]:20[2]:21[2]:22[2]:23:24:25[5]/**1Ki1**:2 [2]
5[2]:6:7[2]:8[3]:9[2]:11[2]:12:13[2]:14[2]:15:17:18:19[4]:20
22,23:24:25[7]:26[3]:28:29:30:31:32[2]:33:34[3]:35
37:38:39[3]:40:41[2]:42:44,45[7]:46,47[2]:49,50[3]:51
/**2**:2:3:4[2]:5:6:8:9:10:11:12[2]:15[2]:17:19:22[2]:
4:25:26:28:30:31[2]:32:33[3]:34[2]:35:36,37[3]:40[2]:
42:43:44:45:46/**3**:1[3]:3[2]:4[2]:5[2]:6[4]:8:9[2]:10:11:
14[2]:15[4]:17,18:19:20[3]:21:22[4]:23:25:26:28/**4**:1[4]
9[9]:20:21[2]:23[2]:24:25[4]:26:27:28:29[2]:31[3]:32:33:
5:1:2,3:6[2]:8[2]:9[2]:10:11[2]:12[2]:14[2]:16:17:18[3]/**6**:2
8:9:11,12[2]:13:15:18:20[3]:21,22:23-28:29:30:
34:35[2]:36:38/**7**:2:5:6:11:12:14:15:16-22[3]:16-
2f:23:25:26:27-30[7]:33[2]:34:36:37:38[2]:39:40[2]:
6[3]:48:49:50:51/**8**:1:5[2]:6:7:8[2]:14[2]:20[2]:21:
3[3]:25[2]:27:28[2]:29[4]:30:31:32:33,34[4]:35,36[6]:38
:41,42[4]:43[4]:44[2]:45:46[3]:47[3]:48[3]:49[2]:50:52[2]:
5:56:58[2]:59[3]:60:61[2]:62,63[3]:64:65:66[2]/**9**:1[2]:
:4[2]:6[2]:7[4]:8[3]:9:10:11,12[3]:13:15[2]:16:17,18:19[4]:
21[3]:22:23:25[2]:27,28/**10**:2[2]:5[3]:6:7[2]:8:9[2]:10:11[2]
:13:15[2]:16,17[2]:18:19[2]:20:21:22[2]:23:24:25[2]:
27:28:29[2]/**11**:1:3[2]:5:6:7:8:11[3]:12,13[2]:14:
7,18[5]:19:21:23:25:27,28:29[2]:31[2]:32f:32:33[5]:
37[2]:38[3]:40:41:43[3]/**12**:1:2,3,4:7[3]:8:10:12:
4:16,17[4]:18:19:20:20f:21:23,24[3]:25:27:28:29
:32,33[2]/**13**:2[2]:3:4:5:6:7[3]:9:11[3]:13:14:15:
7:18[3]:19[2]:21,22[4]:24,25[5]:27:28[2]:29[2]:32:34[2]/
2:3[2]:4:5:7:8[2]:9[2]:10[2]:10f:11:12:13:14:15:16:17:
19:20:21:22:23[3]:24:25:26[2]:27:28:30:31/**15**:3:
6f:8:10:12:13:15:16:18[3]:19:20[3]:21:22[4]:23[2]:24
27:30:32,33/**16**:2:3:4-7[3]:10[2]:11:13[2]:18[2]:19:
21:22:24:26:28:29:31[2]:32:33:34/**17**:1:3:4:5:6[3]
:10:12[4]:13[3]:14[2]:15[4]:17:19[3]:20:21[2]:22[3]:23:24/
1:3,4[2]:5[4]:7:8:10[2]:11[2]:12[2]:13[3]:14:16:18[2]:19:20:
:24[3]:25[2]:26[2]:27:28[2]:30:32:33[4]:34[2]:35[2]:36[3]:37
:39:40[2]:41:42:43[5]:44[2]:45[2]:46/**19**:1:2:3:4[3]:5[3]:
7[3]:8[4]:10[4]:11[3]:12[2]:13[3]:14[2]:15:16:17:18:19[3]:20[5]
/**20**:1[3]:2,3[2]:5,6[3]:7[3]:9:12:13:14:16:20[3]:21[2]:22:
:26:27:28[2]:29[2]:30[2]:31[2]:32:33[3]:34:36[2]:37[2]:39[2]
:42:43/**21**:4[2]:5:6:7[2]:8:9:10[3]:12:13[3]:21:22[2]:24:
22:1:3:4[4]:6f:6[2]:10:11:12[2]:13:17:19:20:21:22[2]:
:25:26:27[3]:28:29:34:35[2]:36,37[2]:38[2]:39:40:42:
45[2]:49:50:51:52,53[2]/**2Ki1**:1:2:3[2]:6[2]:10[3]:12[3]:
:17/**2**:3:5:6,7:8[3]:9:11[2]:12[2]:13,14[4]:15[2]:16:17:
21[2]:22:23:24[3]:25/**3**:1:2:4[2]:6,7,8[2]:12:13:15:17[2]
:20[2]:21[2]:23[2]:24[2]:25:25f:27[2]/**4**:1:3[2]:4[2]:5[2]:6:7[4]:
0[2]:14:17:19:20:21:22[2]:24:25:26[3]:27[2]:28:31[2]:
:34[3]:35[3]:36:37[2]:39[2]:41[3]:42:43:44/**5**:2:5[2]:7[2]:8:
10[2]:11[4]:12[2]:13[3]:14[3]:15[2]:18:20:21:22[2]:23:24:
:27[3]/**6**:1:6[4]:7:10:11:13[3]:14:15[2]:17[3]:18:19[3]:20 [3]
:23[2]:24:25[2]:26-30[2]:32/**7**:4[2]:6[3]:7[2]:8[4]:9[2]:10[4]:
:13:14:15[2]:16[3]:17[2]:18[2]:19:20/**8**:1:2:3[2]:4:5[2]:6:
:10:11:12:14:15[3]:17:18:19:20:21[2]:24,25:29/**9**
3:6[3]:7:9:10[2]:11[2]:12:13:16:17[3]:19:21:22:23:24[3]:
26:30[2]:32[3]:33[3]:34:35:36[2]/**10**:1:2,3[4]:5[3]:6:7[2]:8:
0[2]:11:12:13[2]:14[2]:15:16:17[2]:18,19[2]:20,21[2]:23:
:25[4]:26:27:29:30:32,33[2]:35/**11**:2,3[2]:4[2]:6,7,8:9
:11:12[4]:13,14[5]:16:17[2]:18[4]:19[5]:20/**12**:3:7[2]:9:
:11,12[3]:15:16:17:18[4]:20:21[2]/**13**:2:3[2]:4:5:6:7:
10[2]:11:13[2]:14:14f:15[2]:16,17[2]:18[2]:20,21[3]:23[4]:
/**14**:2:4:7:8[3]:9[2]:10[3]:12[2]:13[2]:14[3]:15:16:18:19[2]:
:22:25:27:28[4]:29/**15**:3:4:5:7:10[2]:12:14[2]:15:16[2]
3:19,20:24:25[2]:28:29[2]:30[2]:34,35:37/**16**:4[2]:5[2]:6:
7f[2]:8[3]:9:10[3]:11,12:13[2]:14[2]:15[3]:17[3]:18:20/**17**:3:
3:9:10[2]:11[2]:12:13[2]:14:15[2]:16[4]:17[3]:21:22:24[4]:
:27,28[2]:30:31[3]:32:34:35,36:37:40:41/**18**:4:6:7[2]
:9:10:11[3]:12:13:14:15:16[2]:17[2]:18:20,21:22:24 [2]
5[3]:26:27[2]:31,32:34:37[3]/**19**:1[2]:2[2]:3:4:7[2]:12:13[2]:
:15:16[2]:18[2]:21[2]:22[2]:23[2]:24:26:27[2]:28[3]:29[3]:30
2:34[2]:35:37[3]/**20**:1[2]:3[2]:5[4]:6[4]:7[3]:8:11:11f:12:13:
:15:18:19:20[3]/**21**:3,4,5[3]:6[4]:7[2]:9:11[2]:12:13[2]:14:
:16[2]:18:22:23:24:26/**22**:5,6[3]:8:12,13[4]:14[4]:
,16:17[3]:18,19[6]/**23**:1[6]:3[3]:4[5]:5[3]:6[3]:8[2]:11:12:13[3]:
:15[2]:16:17[2]:19:20:22[2]:23:24[3]:25[2]:27[2]:29:30[2]:
3:34/**24**:1:2[2]:3,4:12[3]:13[2]:14[3]:15[2]:16[3]:17f:17:20
25:1:4,5[5]:6:7[2]:9:11:13[3]:14,15[3]:16[2]:18:19:21:22:
3[3]:24[2]:25[3]:26:28:29/**1Ch1**:1:1f:5-9[6]:11,12:13-
3-16[2]:17:18:19:20-23:28-31[2]:32[2]:33:34:35:36:
7:38,39[3]:40[2]:41:42[2]:46:50[2]/**2**:3:4[2]:5:6:7:9:10:11

:12:15:16[2]:18[2]:20:21:23[3]:24:25:27:28[2]:29[2]:30:31
:32:33:34,35:43:46:47:48,49[2]:50:51:52:53[2]:54:55
/**3**:4:5:6-8:19,20:21,22[2]/**4**:2:5:6:7[2]:8:10[4]:11,12:
13[2]:17:18[2]:19:23:25:26:27:31:32,33:40,41[5]:42:
43/**5**:2[2]:4:5:6:7,8[4]:9[2]:10:12[2]:13:15:16[2]:17:18[2]:19
:20[2]:21:23:24:26[3]/**6**:4-15:31:33-38:49[3]:54:
55,56,57[2]:58,59:60:61:62:63:64,65[3]:70:71:73[2]:
75:76:77:78,79[2]:81/**7**:3:4:7:9:11:12:14:15:16[2]:17
:18:19:20,21:22:23:24[2]:28[5]:29[2]:40[2]/**8**:6,7[2]:8,9,10
:11:12[2]:13:29:33:40[2]/**9**:2[3]:3:5:6:17,18:19[4]:20:22[2]
:23:24:25:26:27:28[2]:29[2]:30:31[2]:33,34[2]:39:41:42:
43/**10**:1[3]:2[3]:3:4[3]:6:7[5]:8[2]:9[2]:10:12[4]:13:14[2]/**11**:1:1
f:2[3]:3:4:5,6:7:9[3]:13:14[3]:16:17:18,19[2]:21:23[3]:
24,25:26-47[2]/**12**:2[2]:3-7[2]:8-13[3]:14:15[2]:16:17[2]:18[3]
:19[3]:21[2]:24-37[10]:39:40[4]/**13**:2[3]:3:6:7:8[3]:9:10[2]:11[2]
:12:14[2]/**14**:1[2]:2:3[2]:10[3]:11:14[2]:15:16:17/**15**:1:2:
4-10:11[3]:14:16[3]:17:18:19:20[2]:21:23:24[3]:25[2]:26[2]:
27:28[3]:29/**16**:1[2]:3[2]:4[2]:5[2]:6:8:9:11:12,13[2]:16:17:
19:25:27[2]:28:29:32:34:35:36[3]:37:38:39:40:41[2]:
42[2]:43[2]/**17**:2:4:7:8[2]:9[2]:10:11[2]:12:13[2]:14[2]:16[3]:21[3]
:22:23[2]:24[3]/**18**:1[2]:2:4:6:8[3]:10[5]:11[2]:13:14:16:17[2]/
19:2,3:4:6[2]:7:8:9:10[2]:12[3]:13[3]:14[3]:17,18[3]:19[2]/**20**:
1[2]:2[2]:3[3]:4:6,7[2]:8[2]/**21**:2[2]:4[2]:5:6:7[2]:10,11:12:14:15
:16[3]:17[2]:19,20[2]:21:22:23[2]:24:26[4]:28:29/**22**:1:3[2]:
4:5[3]:9[2]:10[4]:11[2]:12:13[3]:14f:14[3]:15[3]:16[4]:18:19[2]/
23:1:2:4,5[2]:6:7:8,9[2]:10,11[2]:12:13:13f:13[2]:14,15:
17:19:20:21[2]:22:23:24[2]:25:26:28:29[2]:30[2]:31:32[3]/
24:1[4]:3:4:5:6[7]:20:22:24,25[3]:26,27[2]:29:30:31[2]/**25**:
1[4]:2:3[2]:4,5[2]:6,7[3]:9-31[45]/**26**:6,7[2]:8:9:11:14,15[2]:16 [2]
:17:18:19:20,21,22[2]:23,24[2]:25:26[3]:28[2]:29[2]:30[2]:
31,32[3]/**27**:1[2]:5,6:25[2]:27[3]:28:29:30:32:33:34/**28**:
1[2]:2[3]:3:4[3]:5:6:7[2]:8[3]:9[4]:10:11[2]:12:12f:13[3]:14:15[2]:
16[2]:17[3]:18:20[2]:21[4]/**29**:1[3]:2[2]:3:4,5[4]:6,7[2]:9[2]:10:11 [5]
:12[5]:13:14[2]:17[2]:18[2]:19:20[2]:21[2]:22[2]:22f:22:23[2]:24
:25[3]:26,27:28[2]:29:30[4]/**2Ch1**:2,3[2]:5,6[2]:7[2]:8[2]:9:10:
11[5]:12[4]:13:14:15[2]:17[2]/**2**:1:2:4[7]:6:7[6]:8[2]:9:10:12[4]:
14[10]:15:16[3]:17:18/**3**:1:3:4:5[2]:7:10:14:16f:16:17[3]/
4:1:2:3:4:6[2]:7:8[3]:9:11:12-16[3]:17,18:19:20:22[2]/**5**:
2:4,5:6[2]:7,8[2]:11,12[5]:13,14[5]/**6**:3:4:5,6[2]:10[2]:11[3]:
12,13[2]:14[2]:15:16:18:20,21[4]:22:23:24[3]:25[2]:26[4]:27 [3]
:30[2]:31:32[3]:33[3]:34[2]:35:36[4]:37,38[5]:39[2]:40:41[3]:42
/**7**:1[2]:3[4]:4,5[2]:6[2]:10[3]:12[2]:14[5]:16[2]:18:19:20[2]:21:22 [2]
/**8**:1[2]:2:3:4:5[2]:6[5]:7,8:9:11:13[2]:14[2]:15:17,18[2]/**9**:1[2]
:2:3:4[6]:6:7:9[2]:10[2]:11[3]:12:13,14:16:18:21:22:23:
24[2]:25[2]:26[2]:27:28:29[2]:31[2]/**10**:2,3[2]:4:7:8,9:10:12:
14:16[2]:18:19/**11**:1[2]:3[3]:4:5-10[3]:11[4]:12[2]:13,14[3]:15 [2]
:16:17:17f:18:19:20:21[3]:22:23[3]/**12**:1[2]:3[2]:4:5[3]:6[2]:
7:9[2]:10:11:12:13:15[3]:16/**13**:1:4:6:7[2]:9[4]:10[2]:11[3]:
13,14[2]:15,16[3]:17:18,19[3]:20[2]:21[2]:22/**14**:1:3[2]:4:5:
7[2]:8[2]:9,10:11:12[2]:13[2]:14:15[2]/**15**:2[2]:3:4:6:7:8[4]:9[3]:
11[2]:13:14:15[4]:16[2]:17:18[2]/**16**:1:2[3]:3[2]:4[2]:5:6[5]:7:8[4]:
9:10:11:13,14[3]/**17**:1:2:3:6:7,8,9[3]:11[3]:12[2]:13:17/
18:2[3]:3,4,5[2]:8:9:10:11[2]:12[2]:14:16:19,20[3]:21:23[2]:
25[2]:26[2]:28:31[2]:33[2]:34[2]/**19**:2:3:6[3]:8[3]:10[3]:11[3]/**20**:
1[2]:3[2]:5:7:8:9[4]:10[3]:13:15[2]:16:17[2]:18[2]:19[2]:20[4]:21[2]:
22[4]:23[3]:25[3]:26:28[2]:29:31:37/**21**:1:2:3,4[2]:5:6:9[2]:
11:13[3]:14:15:16:17[2]:19[2]:20[2]/**22**:2:4:6:8[3]:9[2]:11[2]:
12[2]/**23**:1[2]:2,3[2]:4:5,6[2]:7:8[2]:9[2]:10:11[4]:12[8]:13,14[2]:
15,16,17[8]:18:19:20[2]:21[2]/**24**:1:3[2]:4:5[3]:6[3]:7,8[2]:9:.
10[4]:11[3]:12[4]:13:14[6]:16:17,18[3]:20:21:22[2]:23[3]:25:
26:27[2]/**25**:1:5,6[5]:9:10:11[2]:12:13:14[3]:15:16:17:18
:19[2]:22[2]:23:24[3]:26:27[3]:28[2]/**26**:2:4:5:6[4]:7:8:9[2]:10 [5]
:11:14:15[3]:16[2]:17,18[2]:19:20:21[3]:23/**27**:1:3:4[3]:5:7[2]
:8:9/**28**:1:2:3:4[2]:5:7[2]:8[2]:9[3]:10[2]:11:12:13:14:15[6]:
16:17,18[4]:19f[2]:19:21:23:24[3]:25:26[2]:27/**29**:1:3:
4,5[3]:6[2]:7[2]:8[2]:9[3]:11:12,13,14[7]:15[3]:16[2]:17:18[4]:19:
21[2]:22[5]:23:24[2]:25,26[3]:27:28:29:30[3]:31[3]:32,33[2]:
34:35[3]:36[2]/**30**:1:2,3[2]:4:6:7[2]:8[2]:9[4]:10[3]:11[2]:12:13:
14[3]:15[2]:16:17,18,19[2]:20[2]:21[2]:22[2]:24[5]:25:27[3]/**31**:
1[3]:2[5]:3[3]:4:5,6[7]:7,8[4]:9:10:12,13[2]:14,15[2]:16:16f:
17,18[3]:19[2]:20:21[2]/**32**:1:3[2]:4[2]:5[4]:6[3]:7:9:11:12[3]:13
:16:17:18:20:21[3]:22[2]:23:24[2]:25[4]:26:27[4]:28,29[4]:
30:31:32[3]:33[2]/**33**:1:3[3]:4,5:6[4]:7[2]:8[2]:9:10:11[3]:12:
13[3]:14[4]:15[4]:16[3]:18[2]:19[5]:20,21:23:25/**34**:3[3]:4[2]:5:
6[2]:7:8[3]:9:10,11[4]:12[2]:13:15,16:17[3]:18:20[2]:21[2]:24:
25[2]:27[4]:28[2]:29:30[4]:31[2]:32[3]:33[2]/**35**:2:3[3]:4,5:6[2]:7[2]
:8[4]:9[5]:10[2]:11:13[3]:14:15[2]:17:18[3]:20:23:24,25[4]:26[2]
:27/**36**:5:6:7:8[2]:9[2]:10[2]:11:13:15[2]:16[2]:17[3]:18[4]:19[3]
:20:22,23[2]/**Ez1**:1f:3:4[2]:5[3]:6:7[2]:11/**2**:1:3-35[5]:
40,41,42[2]:58:59[2]:60:61[2]:62,63:64,65[2]:66,67:69[2]:
70[5]/**3**:1[3]:3[2]:4:5:7[5]:8[3]:9[2]:10[2]:11[3]:12[2]:13/**4**:1[2]:2[2]:3[2]
:4,5[2]:6[2]:7[4]:8,9[2]:10[4]:12[2]:14[2]:15:16:17[3]:18:19[2]:20[2]
:23[2]/**5**:1[4]:3[4]:5:6:8[2]:10:11[2]:12[3]:14[3]:15:16[2]:17/**6**:3 [2]
:5[3]:6:7[2]:9[3]:10[2]:11[2]:12[2]:13:14[4]:16:17[2]:18:20:
21,22[4]/**7**:6:7,8,9[2]:10[2]:13:14[3]:15:16[2]:17:18:19[2]:
21:23[2]:25[3]:26:28[4]/**8**:1:2-14[12]:15[3]:16[2]:17[2]:18[4]:19 [2]
:20:21[3]:22[3]:23[2]:24:25[4]:26,27[2]:28[3]:29[2]:30:31[4]:33 [2]
:34[2]:35:36[2]/**9**:1[3]:2[2]:3[3]:4:5:6[2]:7[3]:8:9[2]:10[2]:12[3]:13[3]:
14/**10**:1[4]:3[2]:4[2]:5[4]:6[2]:7,8[4]:9[4]:10:11[2]:12:13:14[3]:15:
16-19[3]:24:44/**Neh1**:3:4:5[4]:6,7[3]:9:11/**2**:3:4:5,6:8[4]
:9:10:11,12:13[3]:14,15[3]:17[2]:18[3]:19[3]:20/**3**:1[3]:2:3[2]:

4[2]:5:6[3]:7[2]:10:11:12:13[2]:14[3]:15[3]:16:23:26:27:29:
30:31:32/**4**:1[7]:4:7[4]:8:9[2]:10:11:12:14[4]:15[2]:17[2]:19[2]
:20,21[2]:23/**5**:2,3,4[2]:5[2]:8:10:11[2]:12[3]:13[5]:14:15[4]:
16:18[2]:19/**6**:1:3:4:5,6[2]:7:10:11:12,13[3]:14:16[3]:17[2]
:18:19[2]/**7**:1[3]:2:3[4]:4:5:8-38[6]:60:61[2]:62:63[2]:64,65:
67[2]:68,69:70:71:72[2]:73[2]/**8**:1[5]:6[3]:7,8[2]:9[2]:10[2]:11:
12[3]:13[2]:15[2]:16[2]:17:18/**9**:1[3]:3[3]:4:5[2]:6[4]:7[2]:8[3]:9[2]:10
:11:12:13[3]:14:15[2]:16[2]:17[5]:18:19:20:21:22[3]:23:24
:25[6]:26[2]:27[2]:28[3]:29[2]:31:32[8]:34:35:37[3]:38[4]/**10**:28 [3]
:29:30:31[3]:33[3]:34:35:36[2]:37[4]:38[2]:39,40[4]/**11**:1[2]:2:
3:7,8,9:10-14:15,16,17[2]:19:20:21:22,23:25-30[6]:
31-35/**12**:1:9:12-21:22[2]:24[2]:26[3]:27[2]:28:29[2]:30[2]:
31,32:34:35,36:37:39[3]:40,41:42[3]:43[2]:44[5]:45[3]:46[2]
:47[2]/**13**:1:4:5[3]:7:8:9[2]:10:11[2]:12[2]:13[3]:14:15[3]:16[2]:
18[3]:19[2]:20:21[2]:22:23:24[2]:25[5]:26[2]:29[3]:30[2]:31[2]/
Est1:1:4:5[2]:6:6f:6[2]:7:10:13-15[3]:16:18[4]:19[2]:21:22 [2]
/**2**:2[2]:4[2]:6[2]:7[4]:9[2]:11:12,13,14[4]:15:17:18[2]:19f:21[2]:
22:23/**3**:5,6:7:8[2]:9:10:11:12[4]:13[3]:14:15[2]/**4**:1[4]:3[4]:
4[3]:5[3]:6:7[2]:8[3]:10:11:14:16[6]/**5**:1:2[2]:4[2]:5:6:7,8[2]:10[3]:
11[4]:12[3]:14[4]/**6**:1[3]:6:7,8[2]:9[2]:10[3]:11[3]:13/**7**:1:3[3]:4[2]:
6:7:10/**8**:1:2[2]:3[2]:4[2]:5[2]:6:7[2]:8[2]:8f[2]:9,10[7]:11[2]:13:14
:15[4]:16[3]:17[5]/**9**:3[2]:4[2]:5:7-10:12[2]:13[2]:14[2]:15:16[2]:
17[2]:18[2]:19[2]:20[2]:22[2]:23:24,25[3]:27[2]:28:29-31[4]:32/
10:2[3]:3[2]/**Job1**:1:2,3[3]:4[2]:5[4]:7:8:10[2]:11:12,13[3]:
14,15:16[3]:17[2]:18:19[3]:20:20f:20:21[2]/**2**:1:3[2]:4,5:7:
8:9:10:11[3]:12[2]:13/**3**:1:2,3:5:7:13:14,15[2]:17:19[2]:
20,21[3]:23:26/**4**:3,4:5:7,8[3]:10:11:14:21/**5**:5:7:8:8f
:11[3]:15:16[2]:18:19:20:22/**6**:2:5,6,7:8,9:15-18[2]:19-
19-21[3]:30/**7**:1:2:3[2]:4:5:7:9:10:15:18:20:21[3]/**8**:4:
5:6[3]:7:8:9:16:19:21:22/**9**:4:8:9[2]:13:14:16:17:19:
21:24:27:30:31[2]:32,33:35/**10**:1:3[3]:8:10:11[3]:12[3]:
13,14:15[2]:16:17[3]:20,21:22/**11**:5:7:9:10[2]:11:13,14[2]
:17:18:19/**12**:3:4:5:6:10:12:13:14:15[2]:16[2]:17:18:
20:21:23[2]:24,25[3]/**13**:6:13[2]:14:19:21:22:26:27,28
/**14**:2:3:6:7:8,9[2]:10:11,12:13:15[2]:16:18,19:20,21[3]
:22/**15**:2:13[2]:14:16:17-19[2]:21:23,24:27,28[2]:33:
35/**16**:4[2]:7:8:9[2]:11:12:14:15:16:17/**17**:1:7:9[2]:12:
13,14[3]/**18**:3:4:5:8,9:14:16:18:20/**19**:2:4:6:7:8:9:
10:13:17:20[2]:25:26/**20**:5:6:16:17:19:24:25:27/**21**
:2,3:5:6:7[2]:8:9:12,13[2]:14[2]:17[2]:23,24:25:28:29:30-
30-32[2]:33/**22**:7:8:9:10,11[3]:15,16:19:21:22:23:24:
26:27[2]:28:29:30/**23**:2:3:4,5[2]:7[2]:8:10:13:14:14f/
24:1:3[2]:5:6:8:9:10:11:13[2]:14,15[2]:16:19:22,23[3]:25
/**25**:2:3:4:5/**26**:2:7:8:10[2]:12/**27**:6:8:15:17:20:21:
23/**28**:1:2:3,4[3]:6:9:10:11:12:14:17:22:23,24:25:
26:27[2]:28/**29**:3:5:6:7:8[3]:9:12:13[2]:14:15:16:17:19:
20[2]:21[2]:22:24[2]:25[2]/**30**:3[3]:4:6[2]:9:10[2]:12:13:15:18 [2]
:19:20:21[2]:22:23:25:27:28,29[2]:30:31/**31**:4:5:7,8:
10[2]:12:15:19,20:27[2]:34[2]:35:37:40/**32**:2:3:6[3]:10:
13:18[2]:21,22/**33**:4:6[3]:7:8:10:11[2]:14:16[2]:17,18[3]:
19:20[2]:21:22:23,24:23,24f:25:26[4]:27:31:33/**34**:4:
13:15:16:18[2]:19:20[2]:24:25:29,30:32:37/**35**:4:6[2]:
9,10:11[2]:14,15/**36**:2:5[2]:8[2]:11:12:14:16[2]:19:27:29
:30/**37**:3:6:10:11:12:14:15:16,17[2]:23[2]/**38**:3:5:6,7 [2]
:8,9:10:11[3]:12:15[2]:19:21:22,23:25-27[2]:29:30:33:
34:35:36:36f:37,38/**39**:2,3:4:6:7:15:16:21-23[4]:24
:25:26/**40**:7[2]:8:9:10:16:24/**41**:1:8:10:12:15-17:
23[2]:27,28:29/**42**:2:3:4:6[3]:7:8[6]:9[3]:10:11[5]:12:13,14
:15[2]:16/**Ps1**:2[3]:3:6/**2**:2:3:5[2]:6:8:10:12[2]/**3**:3:4:5[2]:
6:7[2]/**4**:3:4:5:8/**5**:3:4:6:7:9/**6**:3[3]:4:5f:7:9:10/**7**:2[2]:
5:7,8:9[3]:10[2]:11:12[2]:13:14[2]:17/**8**:1[2]:2:3[2]:5[3]:7[2]:8[2]:
9/**9**:1:3:5[2]:13:14:19[2]/**10**:1:2[2]:3:4:5:7[2]:8:10:14:16
:17:18/**11**:2:3:5:6[2]:7:7f/**12**:2[2]:5:8/**13**:5[2]/**14**:1[2]:4:
6/**15**:1[2]:2:5/**16**:3:5:6:8:9:11/**17**:1[2]:3[3]:4[2]:10:11:
12:13,14[4]:15[2]/**18**:2[3]:3:4:5:6:7[3]:9:12:14:16[2]:20:21
:24[2]:25:27:32:34:37:39:40:42:43,44,45[2]:47:48:50[2]
/**19**:2:5:6:7,8[2]:9f:11:13[2]:14[2]/**20**:3:4:6:7:8[2]/**21**:3:
4[2]:5[2]:7:9,10:12/**22**:2:3,4:5:6[2]:7[2]:9,10,11[2]:14:16:
17:21[2]:22:23:24[2]:25:26[2]:27:28:29/**23**:2,3:4f:6[2]/
24:3:4[2]:6:7:8:9/**25**:6,7[2]:8:9:10[2]:13:16:19:21:22/
26:1:2[2]:3:4:5:6:7:9,10:11:12/**27**:1:2:4:6:7:8[2]:10[2]:
11:12:14[4]/**28**:1:2:7:8:9[2]/**29**:1:5,6[2]:8:9[2]/**30**:2:3:
6,7[2]:9:10:11[2]/**31**:2:3:7:9,10:11[3]:12:19:22/**32**:1:3:
4:5[2]:8[2]:11/**33**:2:4:5:6[2]:8[2]:10:13,14,15/**34**:1:3:4:6 [2]
:7:8:11[4]:14:15:17:19/**35**:2:4:6:7:8:10[4]:14:16:17[2]:
18:20:25:26:28[2]/**36**:2:3[2]:6:8:12/**37**:2:3[2]:5:8:10:
11:15:16:18:20:21:25[2]:26[2]:27:28:29:30,31[2]:32:
34[2]:35,36:38:39:40/**38**:5,6[2]:7:8:10:11:12:15:19:
20/**39**:2,3:5,6:7:13/**40**:1:2[3]:3[2]:4:5[2]:6:8:10:11:12:
13:14,15:16:17[2]/**41**:2[2]:3[2]:4:5:6[3]:10:13[2]/**42**:2:3[2]:
4,5:6[3]:7[2]:8[2]:10/**43**:3:4:5/**44**:1:3[3]:4:5:9[2]:10[2]:11:
13:14:15,16:17:19[2]:20:24:26[2]/**45**:4[2]:7:8:12/**46**:1:
2[2]:3:6[2]:9[2]/**47**:1:4/**48**:5:8:9:12:13:14/**49**:1[2]:3:6:
11:14:16:18:19/**50**:3f:4:9:10,11[2]:12:13:14,15:16:
18[3]:19[2]:21:22/**51**:1[3]:3:4[3]:6:7[2]:8:10:12:13[2]:17[2]:18[2]
:19[2]/**52**:1:3:5[2]:6:7[2]:8:9[2]/**53**:1[2]:2:3[2]:4:6/**54**:1:5:7/
55:2:3[3]:5:6:7:9:9f:10[2]:11[3]:12:13:15[2]:16:17[3]:23/
56:3,4:8[2]:12:13/**57**:3:4:7:8:10/**58**:1:7f:8:9:11/**59**:
1:3:5[2]:7:8:10[2]:11:12,13[2]:14,15[2]:16/**60**:1[2]:3:6,7:8 [2]
/**61**:2:5:6:7[3]:8/**62**:2:3,4[2]:6:7:10,11[2]:12[2]/**63**:1:2:3
:7/**64**:6:6f[2]:9:10[3]/**65**:1[2]:4:5[2]:7:8:9:10:13[2]/**66**:4:6:

(AND Con't)
9:11:12[2]:15:16[2]:20[2]/**67**:2:4:6,7/**68**:1:3:6[2]:8:
11,12,13:17:22:27[3]:30f:35/**69**:1:3:5:7[2]:9[2]:10[2]:11:
12:13[2]:14:16:17:18:19[2]:22:23:25:26:27:29:33:34[2]
:35/**70**:2,3:5/**71**:2[2]:4:6:8:9:13:14:15:16:17:18[3]:
19:21[2]:23:24[2]/**72**:1:3:4[2]:5[2]:6:8:10[3]:12:13[2]:14:15[3]
:17:19/**73**:2:3:4:5:6:8:9:10[3]:12:14[2]:17:18:22:24[2]:
25:28/**74**:2:3:4:5,6[3]:7[2]:8:9,10:11:15:16[2]:17:20:21
:22:23/**75**:2:3:5[2]:6,7[2]:8:10/**76**:1:6:8:9:11:12/**77**:
1:2:3:6:10:14:15:17:18:20/**78**:4:5:7[2]:9:11,12[2]:13:
14:18:21:24:26[2]:30:31:32:33[2]:34:38[3]:40:41[3]:42[2]:
45[2]:47:49:50[2]:51:53:55:56:57:58:59:61:63:64:65:
66[2]:68[2]:69[2]:71,72[3]/**79**:1:2:6:9:11:13/**80**:1[2]:2[2]:3:
4:5:6:7:8[2]:9[3]:13:14[3]:16:18:19/**81**:2:3:7:10:12/**82**:
1f:4:5:6:8/**83**:1:2:3:4:6[3]:7:8:8f:9:10:11[2]:15:16:17
/**84**:2:3[4]:6:7:9:11[2]/**85**:2:5:7[2]:10[2]:11:12/**86**:1[2]:2:5
:7:9[4]:10:11:14:15[2]:16[2]:17/**87**:4[2]:7/**88**:1:3:8:13:
14:15/**89**:1[2]:2:7:9:12[2]:14,15[2]:16:18:19:21:23:24[2]
:26[2]:27:28:30,31,32:35,36[2]:40:42:43:44:45:52[2]/
90:3:5,6[2]:8:9:10[3]:12:13:17[2]/**91**:2:3:15[2]:16/**92**:2:
3[2]:5:11:12:13:14[2]:15/**93**:1/**94**:3:6,7[2]:9[2]:11:12,13[2]
:15:18[2]:19[2]/**95**:4:5:7[2]:8:10/**96**:4:6[2]:7:8:13/**97**:2[2]:
3:4:8,9[3]:10:11:12/**98**:1:2,3:4:6:7:8,9/**99**:3:6[2]:7:8:
9/**100**:4:5[3]/**101**:1:3:4:5:6:7:8/**102**:2:3,4[3]:5[2]:8:
9,10:13[2]:14:15:18:20[2]:21,22[2]:24:25:26[2]:27/**103**:
2:4:7[2]:8[3]:11:13:15[2]:16:17,18:22/**104**:1[2]:3:7,8[3]:9:
10:12[2]:13:14[2]:15[3]:16:18[2]:19:20:23:24:25:26[2]:28[2]
:29[2]:30/**105**:2:4[2]:5,6:8,9:10,11:12:13:15:18:20:
22:23:25:26:28:29:31:32:33:34:35:36:37[3]:39:40[2]:
41[2]:45/**106**:3[2]:4:5[2]:6:7:8:11[2]:16:17[2]:18:21,22:23[3]
:25[2]:27:28:29:30:33:35:36:37,38:40:41,42:43[2]:44
:45:46:47[2]/**107**:1:5[2]:6:7:8:9:10:12:13:14[2]:15:16:
18:19[2]:20:21:22:23:26:27[2]:28:29:31:32:34:36:37[2]
:38:39:40:41[2]:42/**108**:1:2:6:7:8:9[2]/**109**:1:2:3:5:6:
8:9,10:11:14:15:16[2]:19:20:24[2]:26:28:31/**110**:1:3:
4:6/**111**:3:4:7[2]:8[2]/**112**:1:3:4:5:9:10/**113**:2:6:7[2]:8
/**114**:2[2]:3/**115**:1:3:4:5:8[2]:12[2]:13[2]:14:15/**116**:1:2:
3:6[2]:13:15:16:17/**117**:2/**118**:3:5[2]:10:11:14[2]:19:
20:21:23:24:27,28[2]/**119**:2:3:8:9:11:14:15:16:19[2]:
23:24:26:28:31:33,34:38:39:40,41,42:44,45,46[3]:
48:49,50:54:55:57:59,60[2]:63[2]:68:70:71,72:74:
75,76,77[2]:79[2]:83:85,86:87:92:93:104[2]:105:106[2]:
108:114[2]:119:124:132:135:137:138:139:140:141
:143:144:145:147:149[2]:153:154:159:165[2]:166:
167:174:176/**120**:1:4:5,6:7/**121**:2:6:7:8[2]/**122**:4:7
:8:9/**123**:2:3,4[2]/**124**:4,5:7:8/**125**:2[2]:5[2]/**126**:2[2]:6/
128:1:2:3[2]:4:6/**129**:2:6,7:8/**130**:7[2]/**131**:1:3/**132**:
8:11[2]:15/**133**:2[2]:3/**134**:2:3/**135**:6[2]:7[2]:9:11[2]:12:
14:15:16:17:18:20/**136**:9[2]:11,12:14:18:20:24/
137:9:9f/**138**:2:3/**139**:1:3[2]:5[2]:12:13:14:16:17,18:
20:23:24/**140**:2:5[2]:6,7,8[3]/**141**:2:3:5:6,7:6,7f:6,7/
142:3[2]/**143**:1f:3:7:12[3]/**144**:1:2[2]:5:6:7:12-15/**145**
:1[3]:5:7:8:9:10:11:12[2]:14:16:17:19[2]:21[2]/**146**:4:6[2]:
7[3]:8:9[2]/**147**:1:2:4:8:9:11:13:14:16:17:18[2]:19/**148**
:3[2]:5:6:7:8[2]:9[2]:10[2]:11[2]:12[2]:13/**149**:3:6,7:8:9/**150**
:1:3[2]:4[2]/**Pro1**:3:5,6:7,8,9[2]:7,8,9f:10:11[2]:13:16:19
:21[2]:22:23[2]:25:26:27[2]:29[2]:30:31:33/**2**:1[2]:3,4,5[4]:6
:7,8:10:11,12,13:14:15:16,17:18:20:22/**3**:1:3:4,5[3]
:6[2]:7,8[3]:9,10[3]:11,12:13,14,15[2]:19:20:21[2]:22:23[2]/
4:1:3:4:5[2]:7[2]:8,9:10[2]:16:17[2]:19:22:26/**5**:2:3:5:6:7
:9[3]:10:11:12:15:19f:19:21:22/**6**:3:6:11[2]:12,13[3]:
14[2]:20:22[2]:23:26:27:28:33:34/**7**:1:2:3:7:10[2]:
11,12:13[2]:15:16,17:20:21:24:25/**8**:1[2]:4,5:6,7[2]:8:9
:12[2]:13[2]:14,15[2]:18:20:21:25:26[2]:27,28,29[3]:30:31[2]
:32:33:35/**9**:2[2]:3:5:6:9[2]:10:11:12:13[3]:15/**10**:9:14:
19:22f:24:25/**11**:1:10:16:21:22:24,25[2]:28[2]:29:30
/**12**:2:4[2]:9[2]:14:17:18:22:24[2]:26/**13**:5:7:8:9:10:12:
13[2]:16:18:20[2]/**14**:8:12:16:22[2]:26/**15**:3[2]:4:16:23:
30[2]:31,32:33[2]/**16**:6:11f:13:14:16:18:19[2]:21:23:
24:25:27f:29:29f:31/**17**:1:2:3:15:17:20:25:26:
27,28/**18**:5:10:17:18:23/**19**:1[2]:2:3:8:9:11:13:14:
15:16:17:20:22:23:25[2]:29/**20**:10f:11:12:13:23:25
:28/**21**:3:4:7:17:20f:21[2]:22:23:24:31/**22**:1:2:3[2]:4[2]
:6:8:10[2]:11:13:17,18,19:20,21:22,23:24,25:29/**23**
:1[2]:6,7,8[3]:19,20,21[3]:22:23:26,27,28:29,30[3]:31:33[2]
:35[2]/**24**:2:3,4:9:11,12[3]:13,14:15,16:18:21,22[3]:23:
30,31[3]:34/**25**:1:2,3[2]:4,5:8,9,10[3]:15:21,22/**26**:3:6:
12:13:18,19[2]:20:21f:27[2]:28/**27**:1:3:4:12[2]:15:20:
21:23,24[2]:25,26,27[3]/**28**:6[2]:13:16:22:24/**29**:1:5,6:
9[2]:11:13:15:17[2]:18:21:22/**30**:1:2:4[3]:6:9[2]:11,12[2]:
17[2]:18,19:20:24-28:33/**31**:4[2]:5:6,7[2]:9[2]:11:13[2]:15
:16:18:19,20:25[2]:26:27:28:30[2]:31:31f/**Ecc1**:3-7[8]:
8-11[2]:12-15[2]:16-18:16-18f/**2**:3:4,5,6[2]:7,8[8]:9:10:
11:12[2]:13,14[2]:16[2]:18:19[2]:20-23[3]:24-26[4]/**3**:12:13[3]
:14:15[2]:16:17:18[2]:19[2]:20:21:22/**4**:1[2]:3[3]:4:5,6[2]:8[3]:
12[3]:13:14:16[2]/**5**:1[2]:4:5:6,7[2]:8[3]:8f:9:12:13,14:17:
18:19,20[3]/**6**:2[4]:3[2]:4:7,8[2]/**7**:2:6:13:14:15-17[2]:18:
20[2]:24:25[3]:26f:29/**8**:1:4:5:6,7:8:9,10:12:14[2]:15:
16,17[2]/**9**:1:5f[2]:6:7:10f:11[3]:14[2]:15[2]:16/**10**:1:2:5:6
:8,9[3]:10:14:16,17[4]:18:19[2]/**11**:4f:5:8:10/**12**:2[4]:3[3]:
4[2]:5[2]:6[3]:7[2]:9[2]:12:13/**Sol1**:1f:2:3:6:7:8[2]:11:17/**2**:3
:4:5:6:7:8:10:11:12:13[2]:14[2]:16:17[2]/**3**:2:3:4[2]:5:6[2]:
8:10:11/**4**:2:3:6[2]:8f:8:11[3]:13,14[5]:16[2]/**5**:1[3]:2:3:4:5
:7[2]:10:11:12/**6**:2:3:4:6:8[2]:9[2]:11:12/**7**:7[2]:8[2]:9[2]:10:
11:12[5]:13/**8**:1:2:3:6:9:10[2]:12:14/**Is1**:1[2]:2[3]:3[2]:4:
5,6[6]:7:8[2]:9:10:12,13[2]:17[2]:18:20:21:23[2]:25:26[3]:27
:29:31/**2**:1:2[2]:3:4f:4:5:6:7[3]:8[2]:9:10:12[2]:13:14[2]:15[2]
:16[2]:17:18[2]:19:20[2]:21[2]/**3**:1[2]:2:3:5:6:8:9[2]:14:18:
19[2]:20[2]:21:22[5]:23:24/**4**:1[2]:2,3,4[4]:5[3]:6[2]/**5**:2[5]:3:5[2]:
6:7:7f[2]:13[2]:14[2]:16:17[2]:19[2]:20[3]:21:22:23:24[3]:25:
26:28:29[2]:30[2]/**6**:1:2:4:5:6:7:8:9[2]:10:11[2]:12[2]:13[3]/
7:1[2]:2:3:4:5:6[2]:8[3]:9:14f[3]:14:15,16f[3]:15,16[2]:17[3]:
18[3]:19[2]:20:21,22[5]:25/**8**:1:1f:2:3[3]:4[2]:5:6[3]:7,8[2]:
9,10[3]:11:12:14,15[4]:16:18[2]:19[2]:21[5]:22[3]/**9**:1[4]:3:4:6
:7[2]:11,12[2]:13:14,15:17[2]:18[3]:21[2]/**10**:1:2[2]:4:5,6[3]:9[2]
:10:11:12[2]:13[4]:14[2]:16:17[3]:17f:18:20:25:27:28,29:
31:33[2]/**11**:2[3]:4:5:6[5]:7[2]:8:11[2]:13:14[4]:15/**12**:2[2]:6/
13:2[2]:4:5:8:9[2]:11[2]:13[2]:16:17:19[2]:20:21:22/**14**:1[3]:
2:3[2]:4:5:6:7:8:9:11:13:14:16[2]:17[3]:19:20:21:22[2]:
23:24:25:30:32/**15**:1:2[2]:3:4:5[2]:6:7:9/**16**:3:4,5[2]:6:
8[3]:9[4]:11:13,14/**17**:2:3[2]:6:7:8:9[2]:11[2]:14/**18**:2[3]:5:6[2]
:7[2]/**19**:3[2]:5[3]:7:8:10[2]:11:13:18:19[2]:20:21[3]:22[3]:23[5]
:24[2]:25/**20**:1:2[3]:3[2]:4[3]:5,6[2]/**21**:2[3]:3:5:6,7:6,7f[2]:8,9[3]
:10:12:14:15[2]/**22**:2:5[2]:6,7:9,10,11:12[3]:13[5]:15,16[2]
:18:19:20:21[4]:23,24[2]:25[2]/**23**:2,3:8:9:13:15,16:18
/**24**:1[2]:2[6]:3:4,5:7:8:9:10:14:15,16[2]:17:18:19:20:
21:22[2]:23[2]/**25**:1[2]:2:3:6:8[3]:10[2]:11:12/**26**:5:6:7[2]:9:
10:12:14[3]:17:19:20/**27**:1:3[2]:4,5[3]:6[3]:9[2]:10[2]:11:12:
13[3]/**28**:1:2:3[2]:4:6:7[3]:10[2]:12:13[4]:15[2]:17[3]:18:19[2]:
21[2]:23,24[2]:26:29/**29**:2[2]:3[2]:6:7:8:9[3]:10:13[2]:14:17[2]
:18[2]:19:20[2]:21:23[4]:24/**30**:1:2:3:4:6[3]:8[2]:10,11:12[3]
:13:15[2]:20:21[2]:22[3]:23[2]:24:25:26[2]:28[2]:30[6]:32[2]/**31**
:1[2]:2[2]:3:4,5[5]:7:8[3]:9/**32**:2[3]:4[2]:6[2]:8:9:12:13[2]:14[2]:17[2]
:19:20[3]/**33**:1:2:4:5[3]:6[2]:8:9:10[2]:11:12:13:15:16:17
:18:20:21:22[2]:24[2]/**34**:1[2]:2:3[2]:4[2]:5:6[2]:7[2]:9:11[5]:12:
13[3]:14[2]:15[4]:16[2]:17[2]/**35**:1:2[3]:5[2]:6[3]:7:8:10[2]/**36**:1:3[3]
:4:5:7[2]:8,9:10:11[2]:12[2]:16[4]:17:19[3]:20:21:22[3]/**37**:1[3]
:2[2]:3[3]:6:7:8,9[2]:13[3]:14:15:16,17:19[2]:20:22[2]:23[2]:24[2]
:25:27:28[3]:29[3]:30[2]:31[3]:34:35:36:38[3]/**38**:1[2]:2:3:5[3]
:6:7:10[2]:14:16[3]:18:21[2]:22/**39**:1[2]:2[3]:3:4:7/**40**:2[2]:4
:6:7:11:12[3]:14:17:19:20[2]:22:23:24[2]:26[2]:27:29[2]:
30:31[2]/**41**:1:2[2]:3:4:5[2]:6:7[2]:8:9[2]:11:13:15:16:17[3]:
18:19:20:21:24:25[4]/**42**:4:5[6]:6:7[2]:8:9:11[2]:12:13:
14:15[3]:16[2]:17:18:20:21:23:24:25[3]/**43**:2:3[2]:4[2]:5:6[2]
:8[2]:10[4]:11:15:17:19:20:21:23:24:25:28/**44**:3[3]:5:6:
7:12[2]:13[3]:14:15[5]:16[3]:17[3]:18[2]:19[2]:21:23[3]:24:25:
26:27:28[2]/**45**:1:2[3]:3[2]:4:5:6[2]:7[2]:8:10:12[2]:13[3]:14[4]:
16:18[4]:19[2]:20[2]:21[2]:23[2]:24[3]/**46**:1:1f:3:4[2]:5:6[3]:7[2]:
9[2]:11[3]:13[2]/**47**:1[2]:2:2f:3[2]:5:6:9[2]:10[2]:11:13:15[2]/**48**
:1:3:4:6:8:9[2]:11:13:14:15:16[3]:17:18:19:21/**49**:3:5[2]
:7[2]:8,9[4]:10:11:12[2]:13:15:16:17:18[2]:19:20:21:22[2]:
23[2]:25[2]:26[2]/**50**:1[2]:2[2]:4:5:6:7:10:11[2]/**51**:1[2]:3[4]:5[2]:
6[2]:7:8[2]:9:11[2]:12[2]:13[3]:14:16[3]:17:19[3]:20[2]:21:23[2]/
52:1:3:4[2]:5[3]:6:7:8:11[2]:12:13f[2]:14,15[3]/**53**:2:3[3]:4:5[2]
:6:7[2]:8:9:10[2]:11[2]:12[3]/**54**:1:3[2]:4:9:10:11[2]:12[2]:13[2]:
14:16[2]:17/**55**:1[2]:2:3:5:7:9:10[5]:11[2]:12[2]:13[2]/**56**:1[2]:
2:3[2]:4[2]:5:6[6]:7[2]:10:11:12[3]/**57**:1:3:4[2]:5:6:7,8:9:10:
12[2]:13:14:15[4]:17:18[2]:19:20/**58**:2:3[2]:4:5[3]:6[2]:7[3]:8[2]
:9[2]:10:11[4]:12[2]:13[4]:14[2]/**59**:1:2:3[3]:4[2]:5:6:7[3]:8[2]:10:
12:13:14:15[2]:16[2]:17[2]:19:21[4]/**60**:4[2]:6[3]:7[2]:8:10[2]:
13[2]:14[2]:15[2]:16[4]:17:18:19/**61**:1[2]:2:3:4:5[2]:6:7[2]:8[2]:
9:10/**62**:1:2:4[2]:5:6,7[4]:8[2]:11[2]:12[4]/**63**:5:6[2]:7:8:9[4]:
10[2]:11:12:15[2]:16:17[3]:18/**64**:1:2:3:5:6[3]:7:8[2]:9:11:
12/**65**:2:3:4[3]:5:7:8:9:10:11[3]:12:13:14[2]:15:16[2]:17:
18:19[4]:21,22[2]:23:24:25[3]/**66**:1:2[3]:4[2]:5[2]:9:12:14:
15[2]:16[2]:17[2]:18:19:19f[3]:19:20[5]:21[2]:22:23:24[3]/**Jer**
1:3[2]:5:7:8[2]:9:10[6]:11:12[2]:12f:13:15[3]:16:17[3]:18[4]/**2**
:1:2[3]:3:4,5:6[3]:7[4]:8[3]:9:10,11[2]:12[2]:13:14:15[2]:16[2]:
17[2]:18:20[2]:23:25:26,27[2]:28:30:31:33:34:35:37/**3**:
1:3:4,5[2]:7[2]:8:9[3]:12:13:14[2]:15[2]:16:17[3]:18:19[2]:20:
21:22[2]:23[2]:24[4]:25[2]/**4**:1:2[4]:3:4[2]:5:6f:7:8:9[3]:11,12:
15:16[2]:19:21:23[2]:24[2]:25[2]:26[2]:28:29:30[3]/**5**:1[5]:4:5[2]
:6:7[3]:10:11:12:14[3]:15f[2]:17[7]:19[2]:20:21:22[2]:23,24[3]
:25:27[2]:28[4]:29:31/**6**:2[2]:3:5:6:7:10:11[3]:12[2]:13[2]:14
:16:21[2]:24[2]:26[2]:27[2]:28:30/**7**:2:4:5[2]:6[4]:7:9[2]:10[3]:
12:13,14[5]:15:17:18[3]:18f:18:20:21:22:23[3]:26[2]:28:
29[2]:31[2]:32:33[2]:34[4]/**8**:1[4]:2[5]:3:4,5:6:7[2]:10[3]:13[2]:14[2]
:16[3]:17:19:20/**9**:1:2[2]:3:4:5:6:7:10[3]:11:13:14:15:
16:19:20:22:24[3]:25,26[2]/**10**:2,3[4]:4[4]:5[2]:6:7[2]:8:9[2]:
11:12[3]:13[2]:16:18:20:21:23:25/**11**:1[3]:4[3]:5[2]:6[2]:7[2]:8
:9[2]:10[2]:11:12[2]:13:15[4]:16[3]:17:18:19:20:21,22[3]/**12**
:2[2]:3:4[2]:5[2]:9:10:11:14:15[2]:16[2]:17/**13**:1[2]:2:4:6:7[2]:
8,9:10[2]:11:12:13[2]:14[2]:15:16:18:18f:18:19f:19:22[2]
:24,25:27[2]/**14**:2:3[2]:4:9:10[2]:12[3]:14:15:16[3]:17[2]:18[4]
:19[3]:20:21/**15**:1:2[2]:3[2]:6:7[2]:8[2]:9:12,13:14:15:16:
19:20:21/**16**:1:2:3[2]:4[4]:5[2]:6[3]:8:9:10[2]:11:12[2]:13[4]:
16:17:18[2]:19:21[3]/**17**:2,3:4[2]:5:7[2]:8:9:10:11[3]:12:13[2]
:14:15:18:19[2]:20[3]:21,22:23:24[3]:25[3]:26[7]:27[2]/**18**:2[2]
:3:4:7:9[2]:10[3]:11[3]:12:15[2]:16:17[2]:18[2]:20:21[3]:22/**19**
:1[3]:3[2]:4[3]:5:7[4]:8:9[2]:10:11[3]:12:13[2]:14:15/**20**:2[2]:4[4]:
5[3]:6[5]:8[4]:9[2]:10[2]:11[3]:12[2]:13:18[2]/**21**:1[4]:3,4[2]:5:6[3]:7[2]
:9[4]:10[2]:11:14/**22**:1[2]:2[2]:3[2]:4[2]:6[3]:7:8:9[2]:11:12:13[3]:
14[2]:15:16[3]:17[2]:19:22[2]:23:24,25:24,25f:24,25[2]
:28/**23**:1:2[2]:3[4]:4[2]:5,6[4]:9:10[2]:11:12[4]:13:14[3]:15:
23:24:25:28[2]:32:34[4]:36[2]:38,39[2]:40[2]/**24**:1[4]:2:3
7:8:9[3]:10[4]/**25**:4:5[2]:7:8,9[6]:10[2]:11:12f:12:14:15
:17:18[4]:19,20[5]:21[2]:22[3]:23[3]:24[2]:25[2]:26[4]:27[3]:28
30:34[2]:35:36/**26**:2:3[2]:4:5[2]:6:7,8[2]:9:10:11[2]:12:1
14:15[3]:16[2]:17[2]:18[2]:19[4]:20:21[3]:23[2]:24/**27**:2:3:5
6:7[5]:8[2]:9:10[3]:11:13[3]:15[2]:16[3]:17:18[2]:19,20,21[4]
/**28**:1:4[2]:5:6:8[2]:10:11:13:14[2]:15:17/**29**:1[7]:3[2]:5
:7[2]:8:10[2]:11[2]:14[4]:15:16,17[3]:18[4]:19:21:22:23:24
25[2]:26[4]:28[2]:29:31[2]:32/**30**:3[3]:4[2]:5:8[2]:9:10[3]:11:1
14:16[2]:17[2]:18:19[4]:20:21[2]:22[2]/**31**:4:5:6[2]:7:8[2]:9
10[2]:12[7]:13[4]:15:16:17:18:20[2]:22:23:24[4]:25:27:2
:31:33:34[3]:35[3]:37:38,39:40[4]/**32**:4[3]:5[2]:8:10[3]:11
12[3]:13:14[2]:15[4]:17:18[2]:19[4]:20[2]:21[2]:22:23[2]:24[2]
:28:29[4]:30:32[2]:33:35[2]:36:37[2]:38[2]:39[3]:40[2]:41:4
43[2]:44[6]/**33**:2:3:4:5[2]:6[2]:7[2]:8[2]:9[4]:10,11[4]:12[3]:13[2]
14:15:16[2]:18[3]:20,21[3]:22[2]:23:24[3]:25,26[4]/**34**:1[3]
3[3]:4:5[2]:7:9:10[2]:11:11f:15:16[2]:17[4]:20[2]:21[2]:22[5]/
:1f:2[2]:3[3]:5[2]:7[2]:8:10:11:13[2]:14[2]:15[3]:17:18,19/**36**
2[3]:3:4:7:8:12:14,15[2]:18:19:20:21:22:23[3]:24,25[2]
26[3]:28:29[2]:30:30f:30:31[5]:32/**37**:3:4:7:8:10[3]:
15,16[2]:21/**38**:1[3]:3:4[2]:6[2]:10:11[3]:13:14:15:17[2]:1
19:20:21,22[3]:23[3]:25[2]:27[3]:28/**39**:1[2]:2:3[6]:4[2]:5[2]:6
:8:9[2]:10[2]:11,12:13[3]:14[2]:18/**40**:1:2,3:4:5[3]:6:7:8[2]
:10[5]:11[5]:12[3]:13,14:15[2]/**41**:1:2[2]:3[2]:5[4]:6:7[2]:8:10:
11:12:13,14[2]:16,17[2]:18/**42**:1[3]:2:3:4:8[3]:9[2]:10:11
12:13,14[4]:16[2]:17:18[4]:20[2]:21:22/**43**:2,3[4]:4[3]:5:6
:8:9:10:11[3]:12[4]:13[2]/**44**:1[2]:2,3[2]:4[2]:5:6[5]:7:8[4]:9[5]
:11:12[4]:13:14:15:17[7]:18[3]:19[4]:20:21[5]:23[2]:25[5]:26
27[2]:29[2]:30f/**45**:3[2]/**46**:2:3:4:6:9[5]:12[2]:14:16:17:1
20,21:25[2]:26:27[3]/**47**:2[2]:3:4[2]:5[3]:6:7/**48**:1[2]:2,3,4
:8:11[2]:12:17:18[2]:19:20[2]:21[2]:22[3]:23[3]:24[4]:26:27[2]
28:29:32[2]:33:34[3]:35:36:37[3]:38[3]:39:43[2]:44:45:4
/**49**:1:2[2]:3[2]:4:5:8f[2]:9,10[3]:11:13[2]:14:15:16:17:18
19[2]:20:22:23:24[2]:27[2]:28:29[3]:30f:30:32[2]:36:37:3
/**50**:1:3:4[2]:5:6[2]:7:9[2]:10:11[2]:12:13[2]:18:19[4]:21:23
24:25:26[2]:30:31:32[2]:33[2]:34:35:37[2]:38[2]:39:40[3]:4
:44:46/**51**:1:2[2]:3[2]:5:7:9:11[2]:14[2]:15:16[2]:18[3]:19:2
:21[2]:22[3]:23[3]:24:25[2]:26f:27:28[2]:29:30:32:34,35[4]
36:37:39[2]:40:44[3]:47:48:50[2]:56[2]:57:58:59:61,62
63:64/**52**:1:3[3]:4:5:7[2]:8:9:10:11[3]:13[3]:14:15[3]:16:1
:18[5]:19[4]:20[2]:21:23:24,25[3]:30:31:32[2]:33[2]:34/**La**
1:2f:3:5:6:7[2]:8[2]:9:11[2]:12:13[2]:14:18[5]:19:20[2]:21[3]
22[2]/**2**:5[2]:6[3]:8:9[2]:10:11[2]:12:14:15[3]:16[3]:17[2]:19:2
21[2]/**3**:3:4:5[2]:8[2]:11[3]:12:13:15:16[2]:17:19:26:30:3
34,35,36[3]:38:39:40[2]:41:42:43:45:47:48,49:50:5
56:57:62[2]:63:65:66/**4**:7:8[2]:10:13:15:16:17/**5**:6:
11:13:14:17:18:21/**Eze1**:1:4:6:7:8:9:10[2]:11:13[2]
14:16:18[2]:19,20,21:23:24:25:26:27,28[4]/**2**:1:1f:1
2[2]:3:5:6[2]:8:9,10[4]/**3**:1[2]:3:7[2]:8:11:12:13:14,15[3]:18
19[2]:20[4]:21[2]:22[2]:23[3]:24[2]:25:26:27[3]/**4**:1[5]:3[2]:4,5:6
7:8:9:11:12[2]:14:16[3]:17[3]/**5**:1[2]:2:3:4[2]:5,6,7:8:10[2]
11:12[2]:13:14:15:16:17[5]/**6**:2:3[2]:4-7[2]:9:10:11:11f
11[3]:12[2]:13[4]:14/**7**:4[2]:8,9[2]:10,11[4]:13:15:17:18[3]:2
21:22:24:26,27[4]/**8**:3[3]:5:6[2]:8:9:10:13:14:14f:16[2]:
17:18/**9**:2[2]:3[3]:4[3]:5:6[4]:7[3]:8:9[3]:10[2]:11/**10**:2[3]:3:4[2]
:6[2]:7,8[4]:9-13:14:15,16[2]:18:19[2]:21:22/**11**:1[2]:3:3f:
4:5:6:7:7f:9[2]:10:11:12:13[2]:17[2]:18:19[2]:20[2]:22[2]:23
24:25/**12**:3:5:6[2]:7:10:11:13[2]:14[2]:15:16[3]:19[3]:20[2]
23:24/**13**:2,3:6:7:8:9[3]:10[2]:11:12[2]:13[2]:14[3]:15[2]:18
:18f:19[2]:20[2]:21[2]:22:23/**14**:2:4:5:6,7[4]:8[2]:9[3]:10:11
:13[3]:14[2]:17[2]:19[3]:20:21:22[2]/**15**:3:4:5,6[2]:7[2]:8/**16**
:3f:4:5:6,7[7]:8[3]:9,10[2]:11:12[2]:13[7]:15:16:17[4]:18[2]:19
:20[4]:22[3]:23:24:25:26:27[2]:28:29:36:37[2]:38:39[6]:
40,41[2]:42[2]:45[5]:46:48[2]:49[3]:53[2]:55[3]:57[3]:61[4]:62:63
/**17**:3,4[2]:6[4]:7:8:9[4]:12,13[7]:14[2]:15:16[3]:17[2]:20[3]:21[2]
22,23[3]:24[4]/**18**:2f:4[2]:5[2]:6[3]:7[3]:8[4]:9[2]:10:11:12[5]:13[2]
14:15[3]:16[3]:17[3]:18[2]:19:20:21[4]:22:23:24[2]:26[2]:27[3]:
28[2]:29:30:31[2]:32/**19**:3[2]:4[2]:5:6[2]:7:8[2]:9:11[2]:12[2]:13
:14f:14/**20**:1:5,6[4]:8[2]:9,10:12[2]:13[2]:15:16:18:21:
23,24[2]:25:25f:26:27,28[5]:29:30:31:32:33[2]:34:
35,36[2]:37:38[3]:40[2]:41:43:44:46[2]:47[4]:48/**21**:2[2]:3[2]
5:6[2]:7[2]:9,10,11:12:13:14:16:17[2]:19,20[3]:21:22:23
:24[3]:26:27:28[2]:29[2]:31[2]:32/**22**:3[2]:4[2]:5:7[4]:9:10f:10
:12[2]:13[2]:14[2]:15:16:18,19,20:22[2]:25:26[4]:27:28:29
:30:31/**23**:4,5[4]:6:7:8:9:10[2]:11:14,15:17[3]:17f:18[2]:
21:22:23[4]:24[3]:25[5]:26:27[3]:29[3]:32[3]:33:34:35:36:37
:38:40[3]:41[2]:42[2]:44:45:46[2]:47[3]:48:49/**24**:3:4[2]:5:6
8[3]:10[3]:11:13[3]:14:17:18:20,21[3]:22:23[2]:24:25[4]:27[3]
/**25**:2:3[2]:4:5[2]:6[2]:8:9,10[3]:11:12:13[2]:15[2]:16[2]:17/**26**
:2[2]:3:4[2]:6:7[2]:8:9:10:11:12[5]:14f[2]:16[3]:17/**27**:7:8:10
:11:12:13[2]:14:15[2]:16[2]:17[2]:17f:17[2]:18:19[2]:21[3]:22[2]
:23[2]:24[2]:26:27[5]:29:30[2]:31[3]:32:34:35/**28**:2,3:4[3]:5:
7:8:12f:12:13:16:16f:17:18:21:22[2]:23:24[4]:25:26[2]
/**29**:2[2]:4:5[4]:7[2]:8[2]:9:10[2]:12:14[2]:18[3]:19:21[3]/**30**:2,3
:5[4]:6:7:8[2]:11[2]:12[2]:13[3]:14[2]:15[2]:17[2]:18:19[2]:20f:21:
22[3]:23:24[3]:25/**31**:2,3[3]:4:5:6[2]:7:10:12[5]:13:14:15[2]:
16[2]:17:18[3]/**32**:2[2]:4[4]:5[2]:6:7[3]:9:10:12:13[2]:14:15[2]:
16:18:24:26:27[2]:28:29:30:32[2]/**33**:2:3[2]:4:5:6[2]:7:8:
9[2]:11:12[2]:14[4]:15[2]:16:17:19[2]:22:24:25:27[2]:28[3]:30

ND Con't)
'**34**:2:3:4[2]:6[3]:8[3]:9,10[2]:11:12[2]:13[5]:14:15,16[5]:
18:20:21[3]:22[4]:23[2]:24[2]:25[2]:26[2]:27[3]:28:29:30:
35:2:3[2]:4,5[2]:7:8:10:11[2]:12:13:15[2]/**36**:2:3[3]:4[5]:
:9[3]:10[2]:11:12[2]:14:18:19:20:23:26[4]:27[2]:28[3]:
30[2]:31:33:35[2]:36[2]:37,38[3]/**37**:1:3:4:5:6[4]:7[3]:8[2]:
0[2]:12[2]:13:14[2]:16[3]:18,19,20[2]:21:23[2]:24[3]:25[3]:
:27[2]:28/**38**:2,3:2,3f:2,3:4[3]:5:6[3]:9[3]:11:12[3]:13[6]:
16[2]:19:21:22:23[3]/**39**:1:2[2]:3:4[2]:6[3]:7:9[4]:11[4]:14:
16[2]:17[5]:18[2]:20:21:22:23[2]:24:25[2]:26[2]:27:28:29
.2[2]:3:4[3]:5f:5:6:7-12[2]:16[2]:17[2]:19:20[2]:21[2]:22[2]:
:24[2]:25[3]:26:27[4]:28[2]:28f:29,30f[3]:29,30[5]:32:33[4]
35:36[2]:37[2]:39:41[2]:42[2]:43:44:45:47[2]:48,49/**41**
:3[2]:5:6:8:11:13:15,16[5]:17,18:19,20[2]:21:22[2]:
25[2]:26[2]/**42**:1:3:4:6:9,10[2]:11[3]:12:13[3]:16-20f/
2[2]:3[2]:4:5[2]:6:7[3]:8:9[2]:10:11[4]:12:13[2]:14:15:18[2]:
:21:23:24:25:26:27[3]/**44**:2[2]:3:4[2]:5[4]:6:7:9:10:11[2]
:14:15:16:18:19:23[2]:23f:24[3]:26:27[2]:29[2]:30/**45**
:4:5:7[3]:8:9[3]:11[2]:12:14:15:17[2]:19[3]:20:22:23:24[3]
/**46**:1:2[3]:3:4:5[2]:6:8:10:11[2]:12[3]:14,15[2]:18[2]:
20[2]:21,22/**47**:1:2:3:4:5:7:8[3]:11:12[3]:13:14:16[3]:
18:19:22[2]/**48**:1[4]:2[2]:3:4:5,6,7[3]:8:9:11[2]:13:15:
20:21,22[3]:24:27,28[2]:30,31:32:33:34:35/**Dan1**
3,4[3]:3,4f[2]:3,4[2]:5:6:8:9:10[2]:11:12[2]:13:15[2]:16[2]:
:18,19[2]:20[3]/**2**:1[5]:4:5[3]:6[2]:10:11:12:13[2]:16[2]:17[2]
:20[2]:21[2]:22:23[4]:24[2]:25:26:28:31[2]:32[2]:33:34[2]:
:37:38[2]:39:40:41,42[3]:43:45[4]:46[3]:48:49/**3**:1[2]:2
:5f:7f:7:8:10:10f:11:12:13:14:15[2]:16:17:19[2]:
:21:22[2]:23:24:25[2]:26[2]:27[3]:28[2]:29[2]:30/**4**:3[2]:4:
8:9:10,11:12[4]:14[2]:15[3]:17:19[2]:22[2]:23[4]:24:25[2]:
30[2]:32[2]:33[3]:34[4]:36[4]:37[4]/**5**:2,3,4[8]:6[2]:7[3]:9[2]:10[2]:
:12[2]:14[2]:15[2]:16:18[3]:19:20[2]:21[5]:22:23[7]:24,25:
27:28[2]:29[2]:31:31f:31/**6**:3[2]:4[4]:6:7:8:10[2]:11:12[3]
:15[2]:16[2]:17[3]:18[2]:20:23[2]:24[4]:25,26[2]:27:28/**7**:1:
5:6[2]:7[4]:8[3]:9[2]:10[2]:11[2]:12f:13:14:15:16[2]:18:19[3]:
:21:22[2]:24:25[3]:25f[2]:25:26[3]:27[3]:28/**8**:3:4[2]:7[4]:8[2]
:9[3]:10f:10:10f:11:12[3]:12f[2]:13:14f:16:17:18:20
:22:23:23f:24[2]:26[2]:26f:27[4]/**9**:3[3]:4[4]:5:6[3]:7[2]:8[3]:
1[2]:12[2]:13:14:15:17:18[2]:19[2]:20[3]:22:23:24[3]:25f[3]
:26[4]:27[3]/**10**:1[2]:3:5,6[5]:7:8[3]:9:10[2]:11[2]:12[2]:16[3]:
:18:19[2]:20,21/**11**:1:3:4[2]:5[2]:6f[2]:6[4]:7f:7[2]:8[2]:
11:14:15[4]:16[2]:18[2]:19:20f:21f:21:24[4]:25[2]:26:
f:28:30,31[4]:32:32f:32:33[2]:34:35[4]:36:38:39:40f:
:41[2]:42:43[2]:44[2]:45[3]/**12**:1[3]:2[4]:3[2]:4:5:6:7[2]:7f:
:11:11f:12[2]:13[2]/**Hos1**:1[2]:2:3[2]:4,5:4,5f:6:7f:8:
:10:11[2]:11f:11:3[3]:4:5[3]:6:8:9[2]:10:11:12[2]:13[4]:14[2]
5:17:18[5]:19[4]:20[2]:21,22[3]:23:23f:23[2]/**3**:1[4]:2:3[2]:4
/**4**:2[4]:3[3]:4:5[2]:6:8:9[2]:10[2]:11:13[3]:14:15:18:19f/**5**
:2:4:5:6[2]:7:8[2]:11[2]:13:14[2]:15[3]/**6**:3:4[2]:9:11/**7**:1:
5:6:7f:7:9[2]:12:14:15:16/**8**:1:2:3:4[2]:7:13:14/**9**:1:
:6[2]:7[2]:8:10:12[2]:15f:16/**10**:1:2[2]:3:5:8[5]:9f:11:12[2]
3[2]:14[2]/**11**:1:2:4:5:6:7[2]:8:8f:9[2]:10:11:12[2]/**12**:1[2]:
:6[2]:9:10[2]:11:12:13/**13**:1:2[2]:4:5:6[2]:8:11:12:15[3]/
:2[3]:4[2]:5:7[3]:8[2]:9[2]/**Joe1**:4:5[2]:7[3]:9:10:11[2]:13:14[2]:
:17:19:20/**2**:2[3]:3:4:5:7:10[3]:11:13[3]:14[2]:15:16[2]:
:18:19[2]:20[3]:21:22[2]:24[2]:25:27[3]:28[2]:29[2]:30[4]:31[2]
:1:2[2]:3:4[2]:5[3]:6:7:8[2]:9:10:11[2]:13:15[2]:16[3]:18[2]:19
)/**Amo1**:2[5]:3[2]:5[2]:5f:6[2]:7:8[2]:9[4]:10[2]:11[2]:12:12f:
2:14[2]:15[2]/**2**:1[2]:2[2]:3[2]:4[3]:5[2]:6[3]:7[3]:8:9[2]:10[2]:11[2]:
:14:15:16/**3**:1:6:9:10:11[2]:12[2]:13:14:15[3]/**4**:1:2:
4[3]:5[2]:7:9[4]:10[2]:11[2]:13[3]/**5**:2[2]:4:5:6[3]:7[2]:8[3]:9:11[2]:
:14:15:16[2]:17[2]:18[2]:19[2]:20:21[2]:22:25,26,27[2]/**6**:
:2[3]:4:5:6:8[3]:9:10[3]:11:12[3]:13[2]/**7**:3:4:6:8[2]:9[2]:10:
[2]:12:14:15[2]:17[4]/**8**:5[3]:8[2]:9:10[3]:12:13[2]:14[3]/**9**:1[2]:
3[2]:4:5[3]:6:7:8[2]:11:12[2]:13:14[6]/**Ob1**:1:2:4:6[4]:7[2]:9:
)[2]:11:13:14[2]:16[3]:19[3]:20[2]:21[2]/**Jon**:2:3[2]:5[2]:6[3]:7[2]:
10[2]:11:12:14:15[2]:16[2]:17[2]/**2**:2[2]:3[2]:4:5:6:7:10[2]/**3**
:3:3f:4,5[3]:6[3]:7[2]:8[3]:9:10[2]/**4**:2[2]:5[2]:6[3]:7:8[2]:9:10:11[2]
Mic1:1[3]:3:4:5[4]:6[3]:8[3]:10:11:13:16/**2**:2[2]:3:4[3]:9:10[2]
1:12:13/**3**:2[2]:3:4:5:6[2]:7:9:10[2]:11[4]:12/**4**:2[3]:3[4]:4:
:6[2]:7[2]:8:10[3]:13[3]/**5**:4[3]:5[2]:6:8:11[2]:13:14[2]:15/**6**:1[2]:
.4[2]:5[3]:7:8[4]:10:12:14[4]:15:16/**7**:1:3[3]:4:9[2]:10:11:
2[4]:14[3]:16/**Nah1**:3[2]:4[2]:5[2]:7:11f:13:13f:14[4]:15[2]/
1f:1:2[2]:4:7[2]:10:11[3]:12[4]:13/**3**:2:3[2]:4:5[2]:6:9[3]:10:
1:13[3]:14:16:17[3]/**Hab1**:3[4]:4[3]:5:6f[2]:6[2]:7:10[3]:11:
2:14:15:16/**2**:1:2[3]:4[2]:5:6:7[3]:8:10:11:12:15[3]:16:
7:19[2]/**3**:2:3[2]:6:7:8,9f:8,9:10:10f:11[2]:12:13:16:
7[4]:19[2]/**Zep1**:1:1f[2]:3[3]:4[2]:5[2]:6[3]:7:7f:8[2]:8f[2]:9[3]:10:
2:15[2]:16[2]:17:18/**2**:1:2[2]:3:4:5[2]:6:7:8[2]:9[6]:11:13[2]:
4[2]:15f[3]/**3**:1:5:6:7:8[3]:11[2]:12[2]:13[3]:14:15[2]:17,18[2]:
9[4]:20[3]/**Hag1**:1:6:7:8[4]:9[2]:10:11[6]:12[2]:14,15[2]/**2**:2[2]
3[3]:6[3]:7:7f:7:8,9[2]:12:13[3]:14[2]:15:16,17[2]:18,19[6]:21
22[4]:23/**Zec1**:1:3:5,6[2]:7:8[2]:9:11[2]:12:13[2]:14:16:
7[3]:18:19:21[2]/**2**:4:5:9:10:11,12[2]/**3**:1:2[2]:4[2]:5,6:7[3]
8:9:9f:10[3]/**4**:2:3:6:7:9:12/**5**:1:2:3[2]:4[3]:5:7:8[2]:9[2]:
1f:11/**6**:1:3:4:6:7:8[2]:10,11[4]:12:13:14:15/**7**:2:3[3]:
[4]:6[3]:7:8,9[4]:10[3]:11:14/**8**:3[4]:4[2]:5[2]:7:8[4]:8f:9:12:13:
4,15[3]:19[2]:19f:19:20,21[3]:22:23/**9**:1:2[2]:3[2]:4[3]:5[3]:7[2]
8[2]:10:14:15[2]:16,17[4]/**10**:1[2]:2[2]:3[2]:6:7:9:10[3]:11:12
11:2:4:5:6[3]:7[2]:8[2]:9:10[3]:11:12:12f:13[2]:14:15:16:
7[2]/**12**:1[2]:2:3:4:5:6:7:8:10[4]:11:12,13,14[2]/**13**:1[2]:2[2]
:3[2]:6[2]:7[4]:8:9[5]/**14**:1:4[2]:5[3]:6[2]:7:8[2]:9:10:11[2]:12[2]:13:
14[2]:15:17:19[2]:20:21/**Mal1**:2,3[3]:4[2]:6:8[3]:10[2]:11:
12:13[3]:14[2]/**2**:1[2]:3[2]:5[2]:6[2]:7:8:10:11[2]:13:14:15:16/
3:1:2:3:4:5[4]:7:8[2]:9:10:11:12:13:14,15[4]:16[3]:17[2]:18[2]
/**4**:1[2]:2/**Mt1**:1:2:3:11:17[2]:20:21[2]:23:24:25/**2**:2:3:
3f:8[4]:9:9f:11[3]:13[3]:14:15:16[2]:19:20[2]:21:23/**3**:4[2]:5[2]
:6:7:10[2]:11f:11:12:16:17[2]/**4**:2[2]:6:8[2]:9:11[2]:12,13[2]:
15,16[4]:17:18:19:20[2]:21[2]:22:23[2]:24[2]:25[4]/**5**:1[2]:5:6:
7:11[2]:12:13[2]:17[2]:19[3]:20:22[2]:23:24[5]:25[2]:29:30[2]:
32:34:35[2]:38f:40:42:43:45[3]/**6**:2:4:5[2]:6[3]:7,8[2]:12:
13f[2]:16[2]:18:20:23[2]:24[2]:25[4]:26:28:30[2]:31,32[2]:33[2]
/**7**:1:3:6[2]:7[3]:11:12f:13:14[2]:15:18:19:22[2]:24:25[2]:
26:27[2]:29:29f/**8**:3:4:5,6[3]:7:8,9[11]:11[3]:12[2]:13:15[2]:
16[2]:17:20:21f:23:25:26[4]:27:28:32[4]:34[3]/**9**:1:4:5,6:
7[2]:9[3]:10:13[2]:14[2]:15:16[2]:17[3]:18[2]:19:20:22[2]:23[2]:
24:25[3]:28:29:30:33:35[3]:36[2]:37:38/**10**:1[3]:7:8:10[2]:
11:13:15:16:17[2]:18[2]:21[3]:25:28:30:35[2]:37:38:40:
41[2]:42/**11**:1f[4]:4:5[5]:9:10:11:12[2]:12f:13:14:17:18[2]:
19[5]:21[3]:22:23:25[3]:27[2]:28:29,30[3]/**12**:1[2]:2:3:4:5:6:
10:11:12:13:14:15:18:21:22[3]:25:26[2]:27:34:35:36:
39,40[3]:41[4]:42[3]:43,44,45[4]:46,47:49:50/**13**:1:2,3:4[2]
:5:6[2]:7:8[2]:10:11:12,13[2]:15[3]:16[5]:17[2]:19[2]:20:21[3]:
22[3]:23[3]:25:27:30[3]:31,32[2]:33:36:38:39:40:41[2]:42[3]
:44:46:47,48[5]:49:50:52f:53,54[3]:55[3]:56:57[2]:58/**14**
:1f:3:9:11[2]:12[2]:13:14[2]:15[3]:17:19[4]:20[2]:21:22:
23,24[2]:29:30:31:32:35:36/**15**:1:3:4:5,6[2]:10[2]:11:
12:13,14:17:18:19:21:21f:21:22:25[2]:26:28[2]:29[2]:
30[5]:31[5]:32[2]:33:34[2]:36[5]:37,38[3]:39[2]/**16**:1:6:8:9:10:
11:12:18[2]:19[2]:21:21f[2]:21:23[2]:24[2]:25:26:27:28/
17:1[2]:2[2]:3[2]:4[2]:5[2]:7:8:11:12[3]:14[2]:15:18[2]:20:21:
22,23[3]:24:26,27[3]/**18**:2:3[2]:5[2]:6:8[2]:9[2]:11:12[3]:13:15[2]
:16:17:17f:18[2]:21:25[2]:26[2]:27[2]:28[2]:29[2]:30:31:32[2]
/**19**:1:2:3:4:5,6[4]:8:9[2]:9f:12[2]:13:14:15[2]:18:19[2]:21[4]
:26:28:29[2]:30/**20**:2:3:5:6[2]:7:8:11,12:14:16[2]:18[3]:
19[4]:20[2]:22[2]:24:25[2]:27:28:29:30:32,33:34[3]/**21**:1[2]:
2:3:7[2]:8[3]:9:11:12[2]:14[3]:15[4]:19[2]:20:21[3]:23[3]:26:27:
28:29:30:31:32[5]:33[2]:35:38:39:41:43:45/**22**:3:4:5:
6:7[2]:8[2]:9:10[3]:12:13[3]:16:19:20:21:22[2]:23:24:25:
26[2]:27:29:32:32f:37:38,39:40[3]:46/**23**:1:2:3:5:6[2]:
7[2]:8:9:10:12[2]:13,14[3]:15:18:20:21[2]:22[2]:23[3]:24:25[2]
:26:27[3]:28:29,30[3]:32:34[5]:35:37:38/**24**:1:3:5:7[3]:9[2]
:10[3]:11[2]:12:14[2]:19[2]:20:21:23:24[2]:26[2]:28:29[3]:30[4]:
31[3]:32:35:36:37,38[2]:39:40:45:46:48:49[2]:50:51[3]/
25:1:2,3,4:5,6:7,8:9:10[2]:13:14:15[2]:16[2]:17:18:19:
22:23:24,25[2]:24,25f[2]:24,25:28:29:30[2]:31:32[2]:33[2]
:35[3]:36[3]:37[2]:38[2]:39:40:41[2]:42[2]:43[4]:44:45:46/**26**:
2[2]:3:4:7:8,9:10:13:15[2]:17:18[3]:19:22:25:26[5]:27[4]:
30:31:32:35:36[2]:37[4]:38:39[2]:40:41:42:43:45[2]:47:
49[2]:50:51:53:55[2]:56:58[4]:59[2]:60,61:62:64[2]:67[2]:69
:71:73:74[2]:75/**27**:1:3[3]:5[2]:7[2]:10:12:17:20[2]:22:24[2]:
25[2]:26[2]:27:28:29[4]:30[3]:31[2]:32:36:37:39[2]:40:
41,42,43[3]:44:47:48[3]:49:50:51[3]:52[3]:53[2]:54[2]:55:56[4]
:58[2]:59:60[2]:61:62:63:64[2]:66/**28**:1:2[2]:3:4:6:7[3]:8:9[3]
:11:12,13[2]:14:15[2]:17:18:19[3]:20[2]/**Mk1**:2:3:4:5[3]:6[2]
:9:10:11:12,13[2]:15:16:17:18:19:20[2]:21[2]:22:23:25
:26[2]:27:29,30[2]:31[4]:32,33[2]:34:35:36,37[2]:38:39:40[2]
:41[2]:43,44:45/**2**:1:2:4:8:9,10,11:12:13:14[2]:15[2]:18[2]
:20:21:22:23[2]:25,26[3]:27:28/**3**:1:3:5:6:7,8[5]:9:10:
11:13[3]:14,15[2]:16-19:20:23:25:26:27:31,32[5]:34:
35[2]/**4**:1[2]:4[3]:5,6:7:8:10:11,12:17:18:19[4]:20:21:24:
27[3]:28[2]:29[2]:31,32:36:37:39[3]:40:41[3]/**5**:3,4[4]:5[3]:6[2]:
7,8:9:10:13[4]:14:15[2]:17[2]:19[2]:20[2]:22:23[2]:24:26[2]:
27[2]:29[2]:30:31:33[2]:34:35:36:37[3]:38:39[2]:40[3]:41,42[2]
:43/**6**:1:2,3[7]:4[2]:5[2]:6:7[2]:11:13[2]:17,18:20[3]:21[2]:
22,23[3]:24:25:27:28[3]:29:30[2]:31[2]:33[2]:34[2]:35,36[4]:
38[2]:39,40:41[3]:42:43,44:45[3]:47:48[2]:51:54:55[3]:56[5]
/**7**:2:4[3]:8:9:10[2]:12,13[2]:14[2]:15,16:17:20:22:23:24[3]
:25[2]:26:27:30[2]:32[2]:33[2]:34:35:37[2]/**8**:1:3:6[2]:7:8,9[3]:
10:12:13[2]:14:15:17:18:20:21:22[2]:23[3]:25[2]:27[2]:28:
31[5]:32:33[3]:34[4]:35:36[2]:38[3]/**9**:2:3:4[2]:6:7:8[3]:10:
12,13[4]:15:17:18[4]:20[2]:21:22[2]:25[2]:26[4]:27[3]:29f:
30,31[2]:32:33:35[2]:36:37:42:43,44f:45,46f:45,46:
47[2]:48/**10**:1f[2]:1[4]:2:5:6,7[2]:8[2]:9:12[2]:14:16[2]:17[2]:19:
21[4]:22:23:28:29[2]:30[2]:31:32[3]:33[3]:34[3]:35[2]:37:39[2]:
41:42[2]:44:45:46:48:49:50[2]:52[3]/**11**:1[2]:2[2]:3[2]:4,5:6:
7:9[2]:11[4]:14:15[4]:16:18:21:22,23[3]:24:27,28[2]:27,28
f/**12**:1[4]:3:5:7:8[2]:9[2]:11:12[2]:13:13f:13:14:15[2]:16:
17:19:20,21,22[8]:24:25:26[3]:29:30[4]:32:33[4]:34:36:
37:38[2]:39:40:41[2]:42:43,44/**13**:3,4[3]:6:7[2]:8[3]:9[3]:10:
11:12:13:17:18:20:21:22:24:25:26:27[2]:28:29:31:
33:34:35,36,37/**14**:1[2]:4,5:7[2]:8:9[2]:11[3]:16[2]:18:19:
22[4]:23[3]:24[2]:26:27:28:31:32[3]:33[3]:34[2]:35[2]:37:38:
39[2]:40[2]:43[3]:44:45:46:47:53:54[2]:55:57:58:60:62[2]:
63,64[2]:65[3]:66,67:68:69:71:72[2]/**15**:1:3,4:15[3]:
16,17[2]:19[3]:20[2]:21:22:24[2]:28:29,30[3]:31:32[2]:34f[2]:
36[4]:37:38:40[2]:41[2]:42,43[2]:44:45:46[3]:47/**16**:1[3]:4[2]:
5:7:8:9:10,11[2]:15[2]:16:17[2]:18[3]:19:20[3]/**Lk1**:1,2:3:
6:7:8,9:11,12:13[2]:14[2]:15:16:17[3]:17f:18:20:21:22:
23:24:28:29:31[2]:32[2]:33:35:38[2]:41:42[2]:44:48:51:
52:53:54:55:56:57:58[2]:59:62f:63:64:65:66[2]:67:68
:74:75[2]:76:78:79[2]:80/**2**:4:6:7[2]:9:10:14:16[3]:17:19:
20[2]:25:27[2]:28:32:33:34,35[2]:36,37[3]:38[3]:40[2]:44:45
:46,47[2]:48:51[2]:52[3]/**3**:1[3]:3:6:8[2]:9[2]:12:14[3]:15[2]:17[2]:
19,20:21:22[2]/**4**:1:5:6,7[3]:8:9,10,11[2]:13:16:17:
18,19[3]:20[2]:22:25,26[2]:29[2]:30:31:35:39[3]:40:41[2]:42
/**5**:3:4[2]:5:6:7[2]:8:10[2]:11[2]:13[3]:14:15[2]:17[3]:18,19:21:
22:23,24:25[2]:26[3]:27:28:29:30:33[3]:37[2]:39/**6**:1[2]:2:
3:4[3]:5:6:7:8:9:10[2]:11:12:13:17,18[4]:19:20:22[3]:23:
25:26:30:33:34:35[3]:37f:38[2]:39:41:42:45:47,48[3]:
49/**7**:2:3:4:5:6,7,8[8]:10:12:14[2]:15[2]:16[2]:17:
20,21,22[5]:23:26:28:29[2]:30[2]:32:32f[2]:33[2]:34[4]:34f:
36:37:38[3]:39:40:41:44[2]:45:47:48:50/**8**:1[2]:3[4]:5[3]:6:
7:8:10:12[3]:13[3]:14[5]:15[2]:16:17:18:19:20:21[2]:22:23[2]
:24[4]:25[4]:27:28:29:32[2]:33[3]:35[3]:37[3]:39:41[3]:43,44[2]:
45:47[3]:50:51[2]:53:54:55[2]/**9**:1[2]:2:5:6:7:8:9:10:11[3]:
12[3]:13[2]:16[3]:17[2]:18:22[4]:23[3]:25:26[3]:28:29[3]:30[2]:31
:32[5]:33[4]:34:35:38:39[3]:42[3]:44:45:48[2]:49[2]:54:55:
55f[2]:56:58:59:59f[2]:60/**10**:1[2]:2:3:4:7[2]:8,9:10:13[3]:
14:15:16[2]:19[4]:21[4]:22[3]:24[3]:27[4]:28:30[3]:31[2]:32:33f:
33:34[2]:35:37:38:40[3]:42/**11**:1:2:4[2]:5,6:7:8:9[4]:10:
13[2]:14:17:19:21:22[4]:25[2]:26[3]:27:28:31[3]:32[2]:33:34
:39:42:43:49[3]:50:51:52:53,54[2]/**12**:1[3]:3:5:7:8:11[2]:
15:18[2]:19[3]:19f:23:24[2]:25:26:27[2]:28[2]:29[2]:33[2]:34:
35:36[2]:37[4]:42,43,44[2]:45[4]:46[2]:49:50:51:52:53[2]:54[2]
:55/**13**:3[2]:4:5:6[2]:7:8[2]:11:13[2]:15:16:17:19:20,21:
22:23:24,25:26:27:28[4]:30[2]:32[3]:33:35[2]/**14**:3:4[3]:9[2]
:10[2]:11:12:13:16:18[2]:19:20:21[5]:23[2]:25:26f[2]:27[2]:
28:29:30:31:33[2]:34f:35/**15**:1:2:3,4[3]:5:6:8[4]:9[2]:13[3]
:14:16:17[2]:18[2]:19:20[5]:21[2]:22[3]:23:24[2]:26:27[2]:28[2]:
29[2]:31[2]:32[3]/**16**:2:3[3]:4:5,6[2]:7[2]:8:9f:11:12:13[3]:16[2]:
17[2]:18[2]:19[2]:21:22[2]:23:24:25[2]:26[3]:29:31/**17**:2,3:4[2]
:6:7,8,9[3]:11:12:14[3]:19[2]:23:25:27[4]:28[4]:29[2]:33:34:
35,36:37f/**18**:1:7:8:9:10:12:13:15:16,17[2]:19:20:
22[2]:24:28[2]:29:31:32[2]:33[3]:42:43[3]/**19**:1:4:5:6[2]:8[2]:
9,10[2]:11:13:14[2]:15:17:21:22[2]:24:26:27[2]:29:30[2]:
31:33:34:35:36,37[2]:41:42[2]:43[2]:44[2]:45:47[2]/**20**:1[3]:
8:9[3]:10:11[2]:12[2]:14:15:16[2]:17:18[2]:19:21:23:24:25
:26:28:29:30:31[2]:36[2]:37,38:40:44:45:46[3]/**21**:2:5:
6:7:8:9[2]:10:11[4]:12[4]:13:15:16[3]:17[2]:21:22:23[2]:24[3]:
25[4]:27:28:33[2]:34,35[2]:36:37,38[2]/**22**:1:2:4[2]:5:7:8:
10:11:12:13[2]:14[2]:15:17[2]:19[2]:24:25[2]:25f:27:29[2]:
30[2]:32[2]:33:34:35:36[3]:39:41,42[2]:43:44:45:47:50[2]:
51[2]:52[3]:54[2]:55[2]:56:58:60:61:62:63,64[2]:65:66:
67,68:70/**23**:2:4[2]:7:8:10:11[3]:12:13:14[2]:15:16:18:
19:22:23[2]:25[2]:27:28[2]:30[2]:32,33:34:35[2]:37:39:43:
44:45:46:47:48:50,51,52[3]:53[2]:55:56[2]/**24**:2:5:6,7[2]
:9[2]:10[3]:12[2]:15[2]:18:19[2]:20[3]:21[2]:22,23[2]:24:27[2]:28:
30[3]:31:32:33,34:35:36[2]:39:40:41:43:44[2]:46[3]:47:
49[2]:50:51[2]:52[2]:53/**Jn1**:1f[2]:1:4:5:11,12[2]:14:14f[2]:
14[4]:17:18:19:27:29:32:33:34:36:37:38:39[2]:41:42[2]
:43:44:45[2]:46:48:51[2]/**2**:2[2]:3:6:7,8:10[2]:11:12:13:
14[2]:15[4]:19:20:22[2]/**3**:4:5:10,11[3]:13:14:18:20:22[3]:
26[2]:29:30[3]:31[2]:32:35:36[2]/**4**:1:3:5,6[2]:7:9:10:11:12[3]
:15:16:17,18:21-24[2]:25:28,29[3]:34:35:36[2]:37:38:
40,41:45:46,47[3]:48:50[2]:52:53[2]/**5**:4[2]:6:8:9:13:14:
15:17f:17:19:20[2]:22:24[2]:25[2]:26:27:29[2]:30[3]:32,33
:34:35[2]:36:37:39:43:47/**6**:2-5[2]:8,9:10:11[3]:13:15:
17[2]:18,19:20:21:21f:22,23[2]:24:25:32:33:37:39:40
:42:44:53:54[2]:55:56[2]:57:58[2]:61:64:65:66:67:69[2]:
70/**7**:3:6:7:8:11:14:18:21,22,23[2]:24:26:27:28[3]:29
:32:34:35:36[2]:37:44:45:52:53/**8**:2[2]:3[2]:6:7:8:9:10:
11[2]:13:14:18:21[3]:26[2]:28:29:32[2]:33:35:37:40:44[2]:
45:46:49:50[2]:50f:52[2]:53:54:55:56:59[2]/**9**:4:6[2]:7[4]:
8:9[2]:11[5]:15:17:19:20:24:25:28:30:31:34:35:37:38
:39/**10**:3[4]:4:8:9[3]:10:12[4]:13:14[2]:15[2]:16[2]:18[3]:22,23
:24:25:27[2]:28:29:30:34,35,36:38:39:40:41:42/**11**:
1[2]:5:6:9[2]:11:15:16:19[3]:22:25:26:28[3]:33[2]:34:
37,38:41:44[2]:45[2]:46:47:48[3]:49:54[2]:55:56:57/**12**:
2:3[3]:5:6:9:11:12:13:17:21:22:23,24[2]:26[2]:28[2]:31:
31f[2]:32:34:35:36:40:47[2]:48:50/**13**:1[3]:5[2]:9:12[2]:13[2]
:14[2]:18:20:21:25:26f:26:29:31:32[2]:33:34:36/**14**:
2,3[2]:4[2]:6[2]:7:8:10[2]:11:12,13[2]:14:15,16[3]:17[2]:19:20[2]
:21[3]:22:23[3]:24:26:27[2]/**15**:1:2:3:4:5:6[2]:7[2]:10:13:
14:16:19:20:22:24[2]:26:27/**16**:2:5:8[3]:8f[2]:10:14:16[2]
:20:21:22[2]:23[2]:24[2]:25:26:27:28[2]:29:30:30f:33[2]/
17:1:2:3[2]:5:6[2]:8[3]:10[3]:11[2]:13:14:17:19[2]:21[4]:23[2]:
25:26[3]/**18**:1:3[3]:6:7:8:10:12[2]:16:18[2]:19:20[2]:27:28:
29:31[2]:33:35:37:38/**19**:2[3]:3:4:5[2]:6:9:13:14:17:18:
19:20[2]:23,24:25:27[2]:28:29[2]:30[2]:31:32:34[2]:35:35f[3]
:36,37:38[2]:39:42[2]/**20**:1:2[4]:3,4f:3,4:5[3]:6:7:8[2]:11[4]:
12[2]:13:14:15[2]:17[3]:18:20[2]:21:22:25[2]:26[2]:28:29:
30,31/**21**:2[2]:6[2]:7[2]:8:9[2]:11[2]:12[2]:13:18[3]:20:21f:24[2]
:25/**Act1**:1[2]:3[2]:6[2]:7:8[2]:9:11[2]:13:14:15:18:19:20:
21,22:23:26[2]/**2**:1[2]:2:3:4[2]:6[2]:8:10:11[2]:12:14[2]:17[4]:
18[2]:19[4]:20:21:23:24:26:28:29[2]:30[2]:31[3]:32:33[3]:34
:37[2]:38[2]:39[2]:40:41:42[2]:43:44[2]:45:46[2]:47/**3**:1:2:3:
4:7,8[6]:9:10:11:12[3]:13:15[3]:16:17:19[3]:20:24:25:26
/**4**:1:2:3:6[2]:8:9:10[2]:13[3]:14:15:16:18:19:20:21:23[2]
:24[3]:25,26[2]:27[2]:29[2]:30[3]:31[2]:32[2]:33[2]:34,35[2]:37/**5**:
2:4:6[3]:8:9[3]:10[3]:11:12:14[3]:15:16[3]:17[2]:18[2]:19:20:
21[4]:22:23:24[2]:26,27[2]:28[2]:29:31[2]:32[2]:33:34[2]:36:
37:38[2]:40[2]:42[3]/**6**:3[3]:4:5[2]:6:7[2]:8:8f:9[3]:10:11:12:

(AND Con't)
12:13:14/7:3[2]:4:5:6[2]:7[2]:8[3]:9:10[2]:11[2]:13:14:15:16
:21[3]:22[3]:26[2]:27:29:31[2]:32[2]:33:34:35[3]:36[4]:38:39:
41[2]:42[3]:43[2]:45:46:48,49:50:51:52:53:54:55[2]:56[2]:
57:58[2]:59:60[2]/8:1[3]:2f:2:3[3]:5:7:12[3]:13[3]:14:17[2]:22
:23:25[2]:27:28:29:30[2]:31[2]:32:33:35:36:37:38[2]:39[2]
:40/9:1:2:4:5:6[2]:8,9[2]:11[3]:12:14:15[2]:16:17[4]:18:19:
20:21[2]:22[2]:24:27[2]:28:29:30:31[4]:32:33:34[2]:35:37[2]
:39:40[3]:41[3]:42:43/10:2:3:4[2]:5,6[2]:7:8[2]:9,10:11:12:
13:17:20[2]:22[3]:23:24[3]:27[2]:31:32:33:35[2]:38[4]:39[2]:
40,41[2]:42[3]:43:46,47/11:1:3:6:7[2]:10:12[2]:13:14:17
:18[2]:19:20:21:23[3]:24:26:28:30/12:2:4:7[3]:8[3]:9:10[5]
:11[2]:13:16:17[4]:19[2]:20[2]:21[2]:22:23:24:25[2]/13:1[3]:2[2]
:3[2]:4:5:6,7[2]:8[2]:9:10:11[5]:12:13[2]:14:15[2]:16[2]:17:18:
19,20[2]:21:22:23:25:26:27:29:31:32,33[2]:36[2]:39:
41:42:43[3]:45[2]:46[3]:48[2]:50[4]:51:52[2]/14:1[3]:2:3:4:5,6[4]
:7:9[2]:10[2]:12:13:14[2]:15[4]:17[3]:18:19[3]:20:21[2]:22:23[2]
:25:26:27:28/15:1[2]:2[4]:3:4[3]:5[3]:6:7:9:10:12[2]:15:16:
19:20:22[4]:23[2]:24:25:26:27,28,29[2]:27,28,29f:
27,28,29:30:31:32:33[3]:34,35[2]:36:36f:37:39:40,41[2]
/16:1[2]:2:3:4:5:6:9:10f:11[2]:12[2]:13:14[2]:15[3]:16:17:
18[2]:19[2]:22[3]:23[2]:24:25[3]:26:27:29[3]:30:31[2]:32:33[2]:
34[2]:37[3]:38:39[3]:40[2]/17:1[2]:2:3[2]:4[2]:5[3]:6[4]:7:8,9:10[2]:
11[2]:12:13:14:15[3]:17[2]:18[2]:19:20:23[2]:24[3]:25[3]:26[3]:
27[2]:28[2]:30:31:34[3]/18:1:2,3:4:5[3]:6[2]:7:8[2]:9:10:11:
12:14:15[3]:16:17:18[3]:18f:21:22f:22:23[2]:24:25,26[7]:
27[2]/19:1:3:4:6[2]:8[3]:9[2]:10:11:12:15:16[3]:17[3]:18,19[3]
:21:22:25:26[2]:27[2]:28:29[2]:32:33[2]:34:36:37:38[2]:39
:40:41/20:1:3:4[4]:5[2]:6:7:9[3]:10,11,12[3]:13:14:15:19[2]
:21:22:23:24:25:28[2]:31[2]:32[4]:34:35:36:37/21:1:3:
4:5[2]:6:8:11[4]:12:14:15:16:17:18:20[2]:21:23:24[4]:25:
26,27[2]:28[2]:29:30[2]:32[2]:33[2]:34[2]:36:37,38:40[2]/22:1
:3:4[3]:7[2]:8:10[4]:11:12:13[2]:14[2]:15:16[3]:17,18:19:20:
23[2]:24:26:27:28:29[2]:30/23:6[2]:10[4]:11:12,13:14[2]:
16[2]:17:18:19:21:23,24[3]:27:30:33:34:35/24:1:2[2]:3
:5:7:10[2]:12:13:14:15[2]:16:17:18[2]:22:23:25[4]:26:27
/25:2[2]:3:4:6:9:12[2]:15[2]:17:19:20:22:23[2]:24[2]:25:26[2]
/26:3:4[2]:5:7:10:12:13:14:15:16[2]:17[2]:18[2]:19:20[4]:
21:22[2]:23[2]:26:29[2]:30[2]:32/27:1:3[2]:4:5[2]:6:7,8[2]:9:
10:11:12[2]:13[2]:14,15[3]:17[2]:19:21[3]:23:24[2]:27:28[2]:
29[2]:30:31:32:35[3]:36:39[2]:40[2]:41[2]:42:43:44[2]/28:1[2]
:4:5:6[2]:7:8[3]:9:10:11:15[2]:17[2]:18:20:23[4]:24:25:26:
27[5]:28,29f:28,29:30:31[2]/Rom1:1:4:5[3]:6,7[3]:8:9[2]:
10[2]:13:14[3]:17:20[4]:21[3]:23[6]:24[2]:26[2]:27[2]:28:29[3]:30
:31:32[2]/2:1:2:3[2]:5:7[2]:8:9[2]:10[2]:12-15:16:17:18:20[2]
:22:26[2]:27:29/3:2:4:7:13[2]:14:16:17:19:21,22[3]:25[3]
:26[2]:27:28:29/4:3[2]:7[2]:11[4]:12:13:14:15:17[2]:18:19[2]
:20[2]:22[2]:23:25/5:2[2]:3:4[4]:5[2]:6:9:10[2]:12:12f:14:15[2]
:16:17:19:21[2]/6:1[2]:2,3:4:5[3]:6:7:8:9:11[2]:13:14:15[2]
:16[2]:18[2]:19[2]:21:22[3]/7:4[4]:5:6[3]:8:9:11:12:13[2]:14:
16:18:19:23,24,25[2]/8:2[2]:3[2]:4:6:7:9:11:13[2]:15[2]:16
:17:19:20,21[3]:22[2]:23[3]:24[2]:25:26[2]:27:28[2]:29:30[3]:
33:34[2]:35:38[2]/9:1[3]:4[3]:5:6:7:9:10-13[5]:15:16:18:
21:22:23,24[2]:25:26:29[2]:32:33/10:1:3:5[3]:6[2]:8:9:
10:12:14[2]:15[3]:19[2]:20:21/11:1[2]:2,3[2]:4[2]:6:8[2]:9[3]:10
:11[2]:12:13:14:15[2]:16[2]:17[2]:20[3]:22[2]:23:24:25:26[2]:
28:29:31:33[3]:34:35:36/12:1:2[3]:4,5[2]:8[2]:10:12:13:
16:20/13:2:3:5:7[3]:9:12,13[4]:14/14:1:2[2]:3:4:5:6[2]:9[2]
:11:15[2]:17[2]:18:19:23/15:1[4]:4[2]:5:6:8:9[3]:10:11:12[2]
:13:14[2]:15,16[2]:19[2]:21:23:24[2]:26:27:28:29:30:32:
33/16:3:4:7[2]:9[2]:10:12[2]:13:14[2]:15[3]:17[2]:18:19[2]:21[3]
:23[2]:25,26,27[4]/1Co1:1:2[3]:3[3]:5:7[2]:8[2]:9:10:11:12[2]:
13:14:16:17[2]:19:20:21[3]:22[2]:23:24:25:27[2]:28:30[2]/
2:1:2:3:4[2]:6:10[2]:11:12[2]:14:15[2]:16/3:2[2]:3:4:5[2]:6:8
:10:11:12[4]:13:14:16:17[3]:18:19:20[3]:22[5]:23[2]/4:1:4:
6:7[2]:8:9:10:11:14:16:17:19[2]:21[2]/5:2[3]:3,4[3]:5[2]:6:8[4]
:10[2]:12[2]:13/6:1:2:3:6:7:11[3]:12f:13[3]:14:15[2]:16[2]:
17:19/7:2:3:4:5:7:8:9:10:11:13[2]:14:15:16:17[2]:18:
19:22[3]:23[2]:25:28[2]:29:32:33:34:34f:34[2]:37[2]:38:40
/8:4[2]:5:6[3]:7[2]:8:12/9:1:5[3]:6[2]:7[4]:8:10:11:12:13:15:
17[2]:19[3]:20[2]:21[2]:22[2]:23:27/10:1:2:3,4:3,4f:3,4:
3,4f:5:7[2]:8:9[2]:10[2]:11:13[3]:15:16:18:19[2]:20:21[2]:23[2]
:24:26[2]:27[2]:28:29:30:31/11:1:2:3:5:6:7:9:10:11:
12[2]:16:18[2]:19:21[2]:22[3]:23:24[4]:25[2]:26:27[2]:28:29[3]:
30[2]:31:32/12:1:3[2]:6:8[2]:9:10[3]:11[2]:13[2]:16[2]:18:22[2]:
23:24:26:27[2]:30/13:1[2]:2[2]:3:4:5:7:8[3]:9:10[2]:11[3]:12[2]
:13[2]/14:1:3:4:5:6[3]:8:10:11:15[2]:16:18f:19:22:23:
24[2]:25[2]:26:27[2]:28:31[3]:33[2]:34f:36[2]:39:40/15:1:2:
4[2]:5:5f:7:9:10[2]:11:14[2]:15[2]:17[2]:19:20:21:22:26:27
:30:32[4]:34[2]:37:39[3]:40f:40[3]:41[3]:42:43:46:50:51:
52[2]:55,56:58/16:1:2[2]:4:6:7[2]:9:14[2]:15[3]:16:17:18:
19[2]:20:23/2Co1:1[2]:2[2]:3,4[6]:5:6,7[2]:8[2]:9:10[4]:11:12[3]
:13,14[3]:15,16[3]:19[2]:20[2]:21[2]:22[2]/2:2:4[2]:7[2]:10[2]:13[3]
:14:15:16:17/3:1[2]:3:5[2]:13:14[4]:15:17:18[2]/4:1:2:7[2]
:8[2]:9:13:14:15[2]:17[3]/5:1[2]:4[2]:5:8:9:10:11:12[3]:
13,14:15:18[2]:21/6:3:4[2]:5:6[4]:7:10:12[2]:15[2]:16[6]:17:
18[3]/7:1:3[2]:4:5[2]:7[3]:10[2]:11[5]:13:14[2]:15[2]/8:2[2]:3[2]:5:
6:9:14:15:19:22:23[2]:24/9:2:4:5[2]:8:10[5]:11[2]:12:13:
14[2]/10:1:2[2]:3:5[3]:6:7[3]:10:12:13:15:17:18/11:1:3:
6:7[2]:8,9[4]:15:19,20[4]:21:22[2]:23[3]:25:26[6]:27[4]:29:31:
33[2]/12:1:4[2]:5:6[2]:7[2]:9:10[3]:11:12[2]:13:14[4]:15:16:18[2]
:19:20[7]:21[5]/13:2[2]:4[2]:5[2]:6:9[2]:10:11[3]:14/Gal1:1[2]:
3[2]:4:6:7:8:10:13:14:15[2]:16[2]:17:18:19:21:22:24/2:
1:2:3:4:5:6:7,8,9[3]:10:12:13[2]:14[2]:15:16[3]:17[3]:19:20[3]
/3:1:2:5[2]:8,9:10:14:15:16[3]:17[3]:19:21,22:24:25:27
:29[2]/4:1:2:3[2]:6:7:9[2]:14[2]:15:16:18:20:22:24,25[2]:
26:28:29:30[2]/5:1[2]:2:5:6:10:11:12:12f:13:15:16[2]:
17[2]:20[4]:21:23[2]:24:26[2]/6:1:2[2]:4:5:7:8[2]:9[2]:10:12:
13:14:15:16[2]:17/Eph1:2[2]:5:6:8[2]:10:11:12:13[2]:14[2]
:15:16,17[2]:20:22[2]:23/2:2:3:5:6:7:8:10[2]:11[3]:12:13
:14:15[3]:16:17[2]:19[2]:20[2]:22[3]/3:5:6[3]:7[2]:8:9:10[2]:12:
13[2]:14,15[3]:17[2]:18,19[5]:21/4:1:2:3:4:6[4]:8:11:12:13[2]
:14:15,16[5]:17,18[2]:19[3]:21:22[2]:23:24[2]:25:28:29[2]:
31[2]/5:2[2]:4[2]:5[2]:8:9[2]:11[2]:13[2]:14[2]:17:18:19[2]:20:23:
25:26[2]:27:28[2]:31[3]:33[2]/6:2:3[2]:4[4]:6,7[2]:9[2]:11:12[3]:
13:14:17[2]:18:19[2]:21:22:23[2]:24/Php1:1[3]:2[3]:6:7[2]:
8:9[3]:10[2]:11:12:14[3]:16,17:18:19:20[2]:21:23[2]:25[2]:
26:28:30[2]/2:1:2[3]:4:6:7[2]:8:9:10[2]:11:12:13:14:15:
17[2]:18:19:21:24:25[2]:26:27[2]:28[2]:29:30/3:1[2]:3:5:6[3]
:7:9:10[3]:12:13:14:15:17:18:19:20:21/4:1[2]:2[2]:3[3]:5
:6:7[2]:8[6]:9[2]:10:13:15[2]:19:20:22/Col1:1:2:4:5[2]:6[2]:
8:9:10[3]:12:13[2]:14:15:16[5]:17:18:20:21[3]:22[2]:23[4]:
24:25:26,27[5]:28:29/2:1[2]:2[3]:3:6:7[4]:8[3]:10:12[2]:13:
14[2]:15:16:18:19[2]:20[2]:22:23[3]/3:1[2]:3:4[2]:5:8[2]:9:10[3]
:11:12[4]:13:15[3]:16[5]:17[2]:19[3]:20:21:22:23[2]:25/4:1:
2:4[2]:7:8[2]:9[2]:10[2]:11:12[2]:13[2]:14:15[2]:16:17/1Th1:1[4]
:2:3[3]:5[2]:6[2]:8:9[2]:10[2]/2:2:3:5:7:9[2]:10[2]:11:13[2]:14:
15[3]:16:17:18[2]:19[3]:20/3:2,3[4]:4:5:6[5]:7:9[2]:10[2]:11:
12[3]:13/4:1:3,4[3]:5:6:7[2]:10:11:12[2]:13:14:16[3]:17[2]:
18/5:3[2]:4:5[3]:6:7:8[2]:12:13[2]:14:15:21:23[5]:28/2Th
1:1[2]:2[3]:3:4[2]:6:7:8:10[2]:11:12[2]/2:1[4]:3[2]:4[3]:6:7:8:9[2]:
10[2]:12[2]:13:15[2]:16[3]:17[2]/3:1:3:4[2]:5:6:8:11:12:13:
14/1Ti1:1:2[4]:3,4[4]:5[2]:6[2]:9[3]:10,11[2]:12:14:15[2]:17[3]:
19[2]:20/2:2[3]:3:4:5[2]:7[3]:8[2]:9,10[4]:11[2]:13:14[2]:15[2]/3:
2[4]:3[2]:4:6:7:8:10[2]:12:13[2]:15:16[2]/4:1:2:3[2]:4:5[2]:6:7[3]
:8[2]:9,10[3]:11:12[2]:13:15:16[3]/5:2:5[2]:6:7:9:10:11:12:
13:14[2]:15:16[2]:17[2]:18:21[2]:22:24/6:1:2:3:4[4]:6:7:8:
9[2]:10:11[5]:12:13:15[2]:16[3]:17[2]:18:19:20/2Ti1:1:2[2]:
3[3]:5[2]:6[2]:7[3]:9[2]:10[2]:11[2]:12[2]:13:13f:15:16[3]:17:18/2
:2:4:5:7:8:9:10:11:12[3]:13[2]:14[3]:15:17[2]:18:19[2]:20[3]:
22[3]:23:25[2]:26[2]/3:2[3]:3[5]:4:6[2]:8[4]:9:10[4]:11:12:13[2]:
15:16[3]/4:1[3]:2[4]:5:7[4]:8:10:13:17[2]:18[3]:19[2]:20:21[2]/
Tit1:1[3]:3[2]:4[2]:5:6[2]:8[3]:9[2]:11:13:14[2]:15[4]:16/2:2[4]:3[2]
:4:5[3]:7[2]:8:9:10:12[3]:13:14[2]:15/3:1[3]:2:3[5]:4:5[2]:6:7[2]:
9[2]:10:11:13/Phm1:1[4]:3[2]:5[2]:6:7:8,9:12:13:20:21:
22:24/Heb:1:2[2]:3[4]:4:5,6[3]:7:8[2]:9:10:12[3]:13:14/2:
2:3:4[3]:5:6:7:8:9:10[2]:12:13[2]:14[3]:17[3]:18[3]/3:1:4:5[2]:
6[3]:7,8[3]:10:12[2]:16:17[2]:18:19/4:3:4:6[2]:7:12[2]:13:15
:16[2]/5:1[5]:6:7:7f[5]:7:8:12,13[4]:14[2]/6:1[2]:2[3]:4[2]:5[2]:6[2]:
7:8[3]:10:11:12[2]:14[3]:17:18:19:20/7:1[2]:2[2]:3[2]:4:6:7:
11:12,13,14:17:18:19:21:22:24:26[2]:27[2]:28/8:1:2:
3[2]:8:10[3]:11[2]:12[2]:13/9:1[3]:3:4[3]:6:7[5]:8[2]:9:10[4]:12[4]:
13[3]:14[2]:15:16:19[4]:20:21[2]:22:23:25:26:27[2]:28[2]/
10:1:2:3:4:4f:5:6:8:10[2]:12:15:16:17[2]:18:19:21:22:
23:24[2]:25:29[4]:33[3]:34:38:39/11:3[2]:4[3]:5:6:7[4]:8[2]:9[2]
:10:11:12[2]:13:14:16:17[3]:19:20:21[2]:22[2]:23[2]:27[2]:
28[2]:29:31:32[6]:33[2]:34[2]:35[3]:36[2]:37,38[6]:39[2]:40/12:
1[3]:2[2]:3:4:5:10:11:13[3]:14[2]:17[2]:18:19:22:23[3]:24[2]:
28[2]/13:4[2]:6:7:8:11:12:16:17[3]:18:20,21[3]:24,25/
Jas1:1:2:4[2]:5:6:7,8[2]:10,11[2]:12:13[2]:14:15:17[2]:18[2]:
19:21[2]:22:23:25:26:27[4]/2:1:2[3]:3[3]:5:6[2]:7:8[2]:9:10:
11:12:14:15:16[4]:17:23[3]:25/3:1:3:4:6[5]:7[2]:9:10[2]:11
:12:13:14[4]:15:16:17[6]:18[2]/4:1:2[2]:3:6[2]:7:8[3]:9[2]:10:
11:13[2]:15:16:17/5:1:2:3[2]:5:6:8:11:12:13:14[2]:15[2]:
16[2]:17[2]:18[3]:19[2]/1Pe1:1[2]:2[5]:3:4[3]:5:7[5]:8:9:11[3]:12[3]
:13:17:18:21[2]:22:24[2]:25/2:1[2]:2,3f[3]:2,3:5[2]:6:7[2]:8[3]:
9:12:14[2]:17:18[3]:20[2]:24/3:4:5:6[2]:7[3]:8[2]:9:10:11[2]:
15[3]:19[2]:21[2]:22[3]/4:1:2:3[2]:4[2]:5:11[3]:13:14:15:16:17[2]
:19/5:1[3]:4[2]:5:7[2]:9:10[3]:11:13f[2]/2Pe1:1[4]:2[3]:3:4[4]:5[2]
:6:7[2]:8[2]:9:10[2]:11[2]:12:13,14:16[2]:19[3]/2:1:2[2]:3:4:5[2]
:6[3]:9[2]:10[2]:11[2]:12[3]:13:14[3]:15:16:17:18[2]:19:20[4]:21
:22[2]/3:1[3]:3:5,6[2]:7[2]:9:10[4]:11:12[3]:13:14[2]:15,16[5]:
17:18[4]/1Jn1:1:2[2]:3[3]:4[2]:5:6:7[2]:8:9[2]:10/2:1:2[3]:3:5:
8[3]:10[2]:11:13[3]:14[3]:15:16[2]:17[2]:18:20:21:22[2]:24:25
:26:27[4]:28[3]:29/3:1:2:3:5[2]:9:10[2]:12[2]:14:15:16:17[2]
:18:19:20:21:22[2]:23[2]:24/4:2:3:4:5:6:7[3]:8:12:13[2]:
14[2]:15[2]:16[3]:17[5]:18:21/5:1[2]:2[2]:3:4:5:6,7,8[2]:6,7,8f[2]
:6,7,8[2]:6,7,8f[2]:6,7,8:9[2]:11[2]:14:15[2]:16[2]:17f[2]:18:19[2]
:20[4]/2Jn1:1:3[4]:4:5:6:7[2]:8[2]:9:10:12[2]/3Jn:2:3[2]:5:6
:7:9:10[3]:11:12:14:15/Jud:1[2]:2[2]:4:5[2]:6[2]:6f:7[4]:8:10[2]
:11[3]:12[3]:13[2]:14:15:16:20:21:23:24,25[8]/Rev:1:2[3]:
3:4[4]:4f:5[2]:6:7[2]:7f:7[2]:8:8f[2]:8[3]:9[2]:10:11[6]:13:13f:14:
15:16[2]:17,18[3]:19:20[2]/2:1:1f:1:2[2]:5[3]:6f:8[2]:9:10:12
:13[2]:14[2]:16[2]:17[2]:19[4]:20:21:23[3]:28/3:1[2]:3[3]:5[2]:7[3]:
8:9:10:12[4]:14:17[5]:18[5]:19[2]:20[4]/4:1[3]:2[3]:3:5[2]:6:7:8[4]
:9[4]:10[2]:11[3]/5:1[3]:2:3:5[2]:6[4]:6f:7:8[2]:9[3]:10[2]:11[2]:12[6]:
13[9]:14[3]/6:1:2[3]:3[2]:4[3]:5:6:6f[2]:7:8[6]:9[3]:10[2]:11[2]:12[3]:
14[5]:15[7]:16[3]:17/7:1:2[3]:9[3]:10[2]:11[5]:12[7]:13:14:15:
16:17[3]/8:2[2]:3[2]:4:5[4]:7[3]:8,9[3]:10[2]:11:12[5]/9:1[2]:2[2]:3[2]
:7:8:9:10:11[2]:13:15[4]:16f:17,18[4]:19:20[2]:21[3]/10:1:
2[2]:3[2]:5:6[7]:8[2]:9[2]:10[2]:11/11:1[3]:1f[3]:3:4:6[4]:7[3]:8,9[3]:
10[3]:11[3]:12:15[4]:15f:16:17[2]:18[4]:19[5]/12:1:2:3[2]:5[2]:7[2]
:8[2]:10[4]:11:13:14[2]:14f[2]:15[2]:16:17/13:1[5]:2[4]:3:4
6[2]:7[3]:8:8f:10[2]:14[2]:15:16[3]:17/14:1[2]:2:3[3]:4:6[2]:7
:9[2]:10[3]:11[4]:12[2]:13[2]:14[3]:15:16:17:19:20[3]/15:1
:3,4[6]:5:7[2]:8[2]/16:1[2]:2[3]:3[2]:4[2]:5[2]:6[3]:7[2]:9[2]:10[2]:11
12:13[2]:13f:15[2]:16:17:18[3]:19[3]:20[2]:21[2]/17:1[2]:2
3f[2]:4[5]:5:7:8[3]:8f[2]:9:10:13:14[5]:15[2]:16[4]:18/18:1:
f:3:5:6:7[2]:8[3]:9[2]:10:11:12[8]:13[7]:14:15[2]:16[3]:17[3]:
19[3]:20[3]:21[3]:22:22f:22:23[3]:24[2]/19:1:2[2]:3[2]:4[3]:5
:8[2]:9[2]:10[2]:11[4]:12[2]:13:14:15:16[2]:18[7]:19[2]:20[4]:2
20:1:2:3[2]:4[4]:6[3]:8[2]:9[3]:10[4]:11[3]:12[3]:13[2]:14[2]:15/2
1[2]:2:3[2]:3f:4:5[3]:6[2]:7[2]:8[8]:9[2]:10:11[2]:12[2]:13:14:15
17:18,19,20:21:22:23[2]:24[2]:25:26[2]/22:1[2]:3[2]:4[2]
6,7[2]:8[2]:9:11[2]:12:13[3]:14:15[6]:16:17[2]:18:19

31.

ANOTHER

[2]Gen4:25[2]/5:3,4,5:6,7,8:9,10,11:12,13,14:
18,19,20:21-24:25,26,27/8:6/9:9,10,11:28/11
10,11:12,13:16,17:18,19/24:55/25:18/26:21/
:27:33[2]/30:23,24[2]/35:17/37:9/41:22/42:1/43
7:32/Ex2:10f/10:3:14/12:3,4/21:10:14:35/22
:6/26:9:36/36:16:28/Lev13:33:58/16:17/20:
21:7/23:36/24:20/Num8:8/19:1/23:13:27/29
:12:35/32:41/35:20/36:3:9/Deu2:23/4:34/5:
/9:18/16:10:13/22:13,14:23,24/23:24/24:10/
:24/29:28/34:10/Jos4:9/8:11,12,13/10:14/1
:18,19/20:9/21:27/22:19/Ju15:6/19:8/20:25
Ru1:9/1Sa2:7/10:3/13:18/17:20/18:11,12:21
28:1/2Sa8:14/11:25:25f/12:11/18:26[2]/21:18
19/23:20:21/1Ki4:8-19/6:8/7:6/11:7:23:26/1
10/20:5,6:22:25:30:35:37/21:28/2Ki1:11/4:5
7:8/18:31,32/23:22:34/1Ch1:10/2:48,49/3:4
19/7:15/9:5:12[2]/11:15/16:20/17/18:13/20:5
6,7/29:1/2Ch23:5,6/25:12/30:23:24/Ez2:59/
Neh3:19/5:7/7:61/9:1/Est1:19/2:12,13,14:18
Job1:16:17:18/22:1/31:9:10/35:8/Ps71:19/7
6,7/87:4/105:13/Pro23:26,27,28:35/28:13/2
1/30:20/Ecc4:7/5:13,14/9:13/10:5/Sol6:12f/
2:1/13:8/23:15,16/29:12/38:4/65:5:15/Jer2:
10,11:36/9:4/15:6/16:1/18/22:8/26:20/29:24
30:1/31:34/34:9/36:24,25:28:32/Lam3:38/Ez
14,15/4:17/5:2/7:5,6/15:7/17/19:5/22:1/24:
/26:1/28:20/30:1/32:17/37:16/38:1/41:10/4
1/43:23/47:4:5/Dan2:39/7:8:24/8:1/10/Hos
6:2/4/7:7/Amo4:7[2]/9:13/Mic4:2/7:18/Hag2:
20/Zec1:7/2:3/4:8/6:9/7:1/8:18/Mal4:5/Mt
12:22/8:8,9:21/13:24:31,32/19:9/20:1/21:33:
35/22:5/24:2/25:14:15:16:17/26:71/Mk2:23/
26/8:1/12:4/13:2:34/14:58/15:37/Lk6:6:39/8
16:25/9:56:59:61/13:8/14:19:20/15:8/16:5,6/
19:44/20:11/21:6/22:20/Jn10:16:41/11:15/1
15,16/18:15/Act1:6:10/9:39/13:35:37/17:7/1
32/20:10,11,12/21:34/Rom9:21:29/13:11/14:
20/15:10/1Co3:3/4:6/6:1:6/10:8/11:21/12:2:
10/14:16:26/15:41/2Co2:1/8:18:22/11:4:8,9/
Gal3:15:24/4:9/Eph:3:32/1Th:6:9/1Ti5:18/
Heb1:5,6[2]/2:13[2]/4:7/5:4:6/8:7/11:8/Jas2:2:2
/4:11/5:16/1Pe3:8/1Jn2:8/3:11:23/4:6/2Jn1:
:13/Rev6:8/7:2/8:3/10:1/13:11/14:6:8:17/15:
/18:4:18

36

ANY

Gen2:5:16,17/3:1/6/9:5,6/13:9/18:3,4/20:16[2]
22:12/23:11/24:6:23/27:2,3,4/30:33:35,36/31:
7:39/37:3/43:34/44:9:29/47:5,6/48:6/49:16/
Ex3:5/5:7,8/6:8,9:12/11:7[2]/12:5:10:15:16:44:
46/13:3/16:27/17:12/18:11/20:4[2]:5[2]:10/21:11
:19:23/22:10:20:21:23:31/23:11:13:24/24:14/
28:37,38/29:34/30:32:33[2]/31:14,15/33:16/34:
15/Lev1:10/4:2:23:27:35/5:3:5:11:12:13/6:4,5:
18[2]:27:30/7:16:17,18:19:20/10:14/11:2,3:12:26
:27:32:34[2]:35:44/13:36/14:56/15:1:4:9:12:17/
17:3,4:10:12/18:8:21:23:24:26:29,30[2]/19:6:7:34
/20:25/21:9:11:16,17[2]:18/22:4:5[2]:8:11:22:24/
23:14:21:25:28:30,31:35/25:6,7[2]:24:31:32/27:1
:26:33/Num3:31-35[2]/4:27/6:6,7:21/8:13/9:10:
12/11:31/15:3,4[2]/17:10/18:1[2]:2,3:4:5:16:20/19
10:15:16/22:16,17/29:7/36/Deu1:17:32/2:9:19
/4:16,17:23/5:7:9,10[2]:14/7:2:7:15/13:4/14:2:
3,4,5:6:11-18[5]/15:2:7:21/16:8:21/17:2,3/18:6,7
:10:20[2]/20:6/23:2:6:9,10:17,18:24/24:5/26:11:
13:14:19/28:14/29:18/Jos2:11:20/3:2,3,4/6:10
18/7:12/11:13/13:14/18:7[2]/19:50/20:4/Ju7:3
8:35/9:41/10:13:15/11:1/13:4[2]:7:12:13,14/16:
16,17/18:27/21:5/Ru2:8,9:16:22/1Sa:2/4:20/5
7/8/12:4:20/14:52/16:10,11/18:4/19/20:2/21:
4[2]/22:2:15:23/24:6/25:15,16:25/26:5,6,7/29:4/
30:22/2Sa7:19:22/9:1/12:5/16:2/1Ki1:6/4:30/
6:7/9:22/13:9:16,17/16:25:30:33/17:1/18:23:
25:26/2Ki1:1/4:6/5:17[2]/6:33/7:2:13:19/8:6/10
:11:18,19/12:7/17:35,36/18:7:33:35/19:11/25:
9/1Ch4:9/17:6/23:22/2Ch2:5/8:9:15/9:22/11:

NY Con't)
20:9/23:7/29:11/32:14:15/36:16/Ez6:11:12[2]
13:20:22:24/9:12/Neh5:10:13/9:17/10:31[3]/
t2:17/3:8/9:1/Job2:3/6:13/8:11-13/11:17/
9/17:15/18:19/22:2:3[2]/24:9:20/27:10/31:
:22:31/34:19/Ps8:4/14:2:4/18:29[2]/34:10/35
/49:12:20/58:1/73:4f/77:13/81:9/82:7/87:1
9:8/91:5:10/106:9/119:37/125:1/135:5/147:
/Pro12:13/14:34/18:17/23:23/24:3,4/25:14/
:1:17/30:4/Ecc1:16-18/2:7,8:9:10/7/9:6:15/
11:1/2:2:3/3:8/5:9/Is1:11/3:7/5:6/8:11/11:
/29:21/30:10,11/35:9/36:18/37:11/41:28/44
20/45:1/49:10/54:15/55:2/59:8/65:19/Jer2:
:24/6:17/10:5/11:15/12:17/14:11[2]:12:14/16:
4,15/18:12/20:9/27:8:11/29:26/30:13:14/31
/36:24,25/37:14:17:21/40:10:16/42:11:21/
:2,3:26/48:2,3,4/Lam1:12/4:3,4:20/Eze1:17/
7/4:14[2]/6:12/7:16/9:10/10:9-13/14:11/18:3:
3f:24/20:31/22:26/24:6/25:7:8/29:16/31:8/
:13/33:32/36:14/38:2,3f/39:14/43:7:22:25[2]/
:13:24:28:31/46:6/Dan2:30/3:18:28:29[2]/5:19[2]
:7:12/7:7:23/11:37/12:1/Hos1:7:18/8:7/Joe
17/Amo1:3:6:9:11:13/2:1:4:6/6:10/9:7/Ob1:
/Jon3:7/Nah:8/Hab1:13/Zec11:9/14:17:21/
al1:9/Mt5:34/7:29f/10:9:14/12:31,32/16:5:
/18:5:6/21:19/22:46/25:7,8/Mk3:28/6:5/7:4
5,16f/8:34/9:3/11:13/12:34/13:21/15:6/Lk4:
/7:6,7,8/10:4/11:17:31/12:24:42,43,44/13:6:
16:29/20/21:7:29/22:51/Jn4:48/7:17/8:33/
:33/12:26f/14:5/15:7/17:16/18:31f:38/20:27
1:5/Act3:6/8:16/9:2/10:13/13:15/17:27/19:
/22:5[2]/23/24:12[2]:23/25:27/27:42/Rom3:1[2]:
/4:15/6:9:12:13/14:1:2:13/16:19/1Co1:13:14
5/3:11/7:19/8:13/9:4:12:16:19/10:20:25:27/
:1:15:16:31/14:18:35:37/2Co5:17/6:12[2]/7:2/
20/11:5/12:17:18/Gal1:1:8[2]:9/3:10:25/6:15/
ph1:21/2:9/5:3:27/Php2:1/1Th:3/3:10/2Th:6
/1Ti6:7/2Ti2:13/Tit3:1/Phm1:18/Heb:5,6/4:
/7:3/9:17/10:23/12:7/13:6/Jas1:7,8/1Pe3:1:
3[2]/4:4/2Pe2:5/3:9/1Jn:5[2]/4:4/2Jn1:10/Jud:
2/Rev:5/13:17/18:22/20:3:11f/22:19
663

NYONE
en2:5/4:15:24[2]/17:14/19:12:35/24:41/26:11/
1:32/Ex12:15:19/21:12:15:17/22:7:16:19:20/
3:7/30:33:38/31:14,15[2]/33:19/35:2/Lev1:14/
:1/3:12/4:2/5:1:2:4:15:17,18/6:2/7:21:25:
6,27:29/11:24:27:28:31:36:39:40/13:1:9,10:45
14:46:47/15:5:6:7:8:10:11:19:21,22,23:27:33/
7:8,9:10:13:14:15/18:20/19:13:17/20:1:6:9/22
5:16:21/23:29:30,31/24:15,16:18:19:20/25:25:
9/27:31/Num1:51/3:10:38/5:5,6/9:13[2]/11:32
15:30/16:3[2]/18:7:11/19:13:18:20:21/21:8:9/
8:26/30:1/31:19/35:11:20:22,23:31/36:6/Deu
:42/15:22[2]/17:2,3/18:12:19/19:2,3:6,7:11:15:
6/20:5:6:7:8/21:23/22:8/24:7/27:15:16:26/
os1:17,18/2/6:17:26/15:16/20:9/Ju3:28/4:20
16:6:7:16,17/18:28/21:5:8,9:18/1Sa2:13,14/9:
/10:23/11:7/14:24,25:28/17:25/22:14/26:12:
5/30:24/2Sa9:3/14:10:11/15:2:3:4:5/1Ki3:12
13:33/19:17/2Ki4:29/7:9/9:15/10:23:24/11:
,7,8:15/12:4,5/1Ch16:21/26:28/2Ch13:9/15:
3/23:13,14/32:14/Ez6:11/7:26/10:7,8/Neh2:
0:16/Est:10:20/4:11/Job:20/17:15/21:29/24:
2,23:25/31:19,20:30/32:21,22/34:34,35/35:12
36:5:29/Ps5:1/10:12/14:1/15:2:3/33:16,17/45
7/88:12/101:5/119:63/Pro8:9:13/10:17[2]/14:
1/25:8,9,10/27:18/30:29,30,31/Ecc2:12/Is33:
/41:11:24/42:8/55:1/56:3/59:15/Jer2:3:10,11
8:6[2]/10:7/23:24/27:5/29:22/30:20/32:6,7/38:
2:24:27/Eze3:27[2]/9:6/14:4/20:11/22:30/33:4/
39:15,16/44:29/45:20/48:19/Dan3:6:11/4:17:
25:32/5:21/6:7:12/8:26/Jon2:9/Mic7:5/Hab2:
2/Zec13:3/Mt5:19:28:31:47/7:8/8:4/9:30/10:
32:33/12:30:50/15:4/16:24:25[2]/17:9/18:4/19:9
:12:29/20:26/21:3/23:8:9/24:4:23/27:15/Mk1:
43,44/3:35/4:14/5:37/7:10/8:30:38/9:35:37[2]:
40:41/10:15/11:3:25/13:5:21/Lk3:14/4:6,7/5:
14/6:30/7:4/8:8:14:51:56/9:21:23:36:48:50:62/
11:23/12:48/14:23:26:26f/16:13:18[2]:26/18:
16,17:26/19:8:31/21:8/Jn3:15:16:31/5:21:24/6
:46:47:48-51:54:58/7:11:18[2]:37:38/8:47/9:
22,23:32/10:1:29/11:25[2]:57/12:42:47/13:20/14
:9:12,13:24/15:6:23/16:30:30f/19:12/Act2:21/
3:23/10:28:46,47/25:10,11/Rom2:2:29/3:6:15/
4:8/5:7/8:9/9:15/10:13:15/12:18/13:10/14:23/
1Co1:16:31/2:11/3:17/4:3/5:11/6:5/7:30:36/8:
2/9:18:19/10:32/11:16:27:34/12:30/14:38/16:
11:22/2Co2:10/3:16/4:2[2]:3/7:2/8:23/9:7/10:17
/11:4/12:6/Gal1:8:9:16/2:17/3:13/5:3:11:21/6:
3/Eph1:21/4:28/5:5/Php3:4/Col2:16:18/1Th:6
:9/4:8/2Th3:8:14/1Ti4:12/5:3:8/6:4/Tit2:8:15/
3:2:10/Heb1:9/5:1/7:19/10:26/11:6/Jas1:13:
25:26/2:14:18/3:1/5:13:14:19/2Pe1:9/3:4/1Jn
2:6:9:27/3:7:15/4:16:20/5:10/2Jn1:10/Rev2:7/
3:20/11:5/13:4:9:10f[2]:15/14:9/22:17:18:19
490

ANYWHERE
Gen19:31/38:22/47:5,6/Ex13:6,7/34:3:10/Lev
13:14,15/17:3,4:8,9/Num18:31/Deu12:4,5:13:
15/1Sa9:4/1Ki17:7/2Ki5:25/2Ch6:5,6/32:14/
Job17:3,4/41:33/Ps84:10/Ecc2:11/5:8/Sol3:3/
5:6/Is58:4/Jer2:10,11/19:11/Lam1:21/Eze20:
5,6/Nah3:7/Zec14:17/Mt27:24/Mk1:45/Rom
3:12/13:1/1Co1:29/1Th5:3/Rev:4
39

ARE
Gen1:28/2:11,12/3:2,3:9:9f:14:20f:22/4:6:11/6:
4/9:2,3/10:1/11:6/12:11,12,13[2]/13:8/15:2,3/
16:8:9-12[2]/17:19/18:20:21:28:29[2]:30[2]:31:32/19
:8:9:15:22/20:3:7:13/21:28,29:30/23:5,6/24:8[2]:
13:23:41[2]:42:47:58/27:22:24:27,28,29[2]/28:4:13
/29:8:15/30:27:31,32/31:12f:26:43[3]:49:50/32:
17[3]:18/33:5:8:13[2]/34:14:21:22:30/35:3:22/36:9
:18,19:20,21:31-39:40-43[2]/37:13,14[2]:15:17/39:9
/40:14/41:26:39/42:1:7:8,9:11[2]:12[2]:13:14f:14:
15:16:19:19f:20[2]:22:31:32:33:34/43:29/44:4:7[2]/
45:11,12[2]/46:8-14:30:31:32/47:1:3:5,6:8:18/48:
8:9/49:3[2]:4:5[2]:12[2]:28/50:18/Ex1:9[2]:19/2:13:14 [2]
/3:5:13:17/4:18:19:21:22/5:4,5:16[2]/6:14:16:19:
24:25:26/7:17/8:26/9:17/10:7:11/12:15:19:25:
33:43:48/13:1:3:8:11:15/14:3:13[2]/15:4:15/16:
7,8,9/17:2:4/18:14/19:10/20:9:10:22/21:1:7:18:
22/22:6:25:31/23:14:15:22/24:1:2:14/25:15:18f
:26,27:36:38/26:4,5:7,8:32/27:3:17/28:10:25:43
/29:33:37f:44/30:2[2]:5:21/31:6:11/32:9:12:17:22
:26/33:3:5:12:16:17/34:12:15[2]/35:1:10-19/36:1
/39:6,7/Lev1:9/2:8:9:14/4:2:11,12:13:24:29:33/
6:14:19,20:25[2]:27/7:1:2:10:11/9:4/10:7:15/11:8
:10:13-19:23:26:29,30:38:39:46:47/12:6[2]:7/13:
21:26:37:39:59/14:13:32[3]:54:57/15:18/16:1:3:
29,30[2]/18:17:24[2]:26:29,30/19:8:23/20:19/23:1:
3[2]:4[2]:18:20:26,27:36:37[2]:38[2]:39:42[2]/24:9[2]:13,14
/25:14,15,16:20:21,22:23:31[2]:34[2]:35:42:51:55/
26:34,35:36:40,41/27:3f:28:34/Num1:2-15[2]:50[2]:
51/2:3-31/3:2f:7,8,9[2]:11,12:13:40:41/4:3:4:12:
13:14[2]:21,22,23:26[2]:29:30,31/5:1:18/6:20:21:
22,23/8:13:16:17:23,24[2]/9:10[2]:11/10:3[2]:8:29:31
f/11:12:15:21:29/13:18[2]:19[3]:20:28[2]:29[2]:30:31:
32/14:9:12:14[2]:25:30:40[2]:41:43/15:11,12:15,16:
15,16f:29:39/16:3:5:6,7:10:11,12[3]:14:36,37:38/
17:12,13/18:1:2,3:5:6[2]:8:9[2]:10:11:12:13:17f:18:
19:24/19:14[2]:17/20:14:16/21:27-30[2]/22:5,6[2]:9:
12:32/23:7-10[2]/24:3-9:14:15-19:21,22/25:18[3]/
26:2[2]:3,4:28-37:57:58,59:63/27:6,7/28:1[4]:9,10:
26:31[2]/29:2:6[2]:9,10:11:19:23:36:39[2]/30:5:16/31[2]
:26:30/32:7:14[2]:27:29/33:9/34:13:16-28:29/35:
3:13,14:15:29:34/36:8:13/Deu1:9:13:17:28[2]/2:
11:29/3:1/4:2:4:5[2]:20:25:26:44,45,46/5:2,3:33/
6:1:7:13/7:1:6:17[2]:25/9:1[4]:4:5:6[3]:13,14:26:29/
10:5/11:8:10:12:19[2]:30[2]:31/12:1:13:15[2]:16:20-
20-23/14:1:3,4,5[2]:10:19,20:21:28/15:7[2]:11/16:
17:21/18:1/19/20:8:15f:16/22:6:20/23:1:7:9,10
:17,18[2]/24:12,13:21/25:11:16:19/26:1:12:18/27
:15/28:2-6:20:21[2]:32:45:47,48:51:54:61/29:10:
11:12:21:27:29[2]/30:1:4:12:13:14:16:17:18/31:16
:21:24:27[2]/32:5[2]:20:21:29:31:32:37:38:40,41:47[3]
/33:3:4:11:23[2]:27:29/Jos1:2:7/2:3:9:11:16:
17,18:24/3:2,3,4:8:10:12f:13,14/4:2,3:21:22[2]/5:
13/6:2:3,4:5/7:7:12[3]:21:26/8:6/9:8:9:13:25/10:
6:8/13:1[2]/17:11:15:16,17,18[3]/18:3:7/19:2-7f/
22:16/24:13:15:22/Ju4:22/5:10/6:13:17:31:36:
37/7:2:3:4:10:11/8:2,3f:5:6f:15/9:19:31:33:37:
38/10:4/11:25[2]/12:1:5/13:7:8:11/15[2]/16:6:9:10
:20/17:9/18:3:18/19:12,13/21:16/Ru2:8,9:13/3
:9[2]:10:11/4/1Sa2:4[2]:5[2]:23,24,25:29[2]:30:33/3:13
/4:8:17/5:10/7:3/8:7:8:18/9:6:16/10:3:4/11:12
/12:5:23/13:12/14:6:9:11:41:44/15:15:18:28/
16:10,11[2]/17:18:28[2]:33/19:22/20/21:1:5/22:8:
17/23/24:12:17:20/25:7:10:28:29[2]/26:17,18/28
:2:9[2]:12:15/29:3:6:9/30:13:20/2Sa1:4:5:8:13/3:
28:29/4:2,3/5:1:14,15,16/7:21:22:28[2]/9:2:10,11
/10:11:12/11:11/12:7:21:26,27/13:5:35[2]/14:2,3
:9:14:17:20/15:3:15:19,20[2]:35,36[2]/16:2[3]:21f/17:
2,3:8[2]:9:10/18:3/19:11,12[3]:13:14:27:35:37:43/
20:11:17:19/21:17/22:26:27[2]:29/23:1:6:8/24:2:
3:22/1Ki1:14:21:25:34:42:46,47/2:4:6:9:15:22/
3:8/8:10:22,23:33,34:35,36:37:51:61/9:13[2]/10:7
:8[2]/11:12,13/13:14:18/14:6:10:19:29/15:31/16:
4-7:20/17:24/18:9:19:21:25:36:37/19:9:10:13:
14:18/20:2,3[2]:17:31/21:7/22:3:4[3]:11:45/2Ki1:3:
6[2]/3:6,7,8[2]:19/4:4/5:8/6:1:9/7:12/8:13/9:7:18:
22:31/10:5:6[2]:13[3]:15:18,19:23:34/11:5[2]/12:4,5/
13:12:14/14:10:15/15/18:24:27/19:4:15:19:27/
20:14:20/21:14/1Ch1:1:1f/2:18:25:55/3:10-14:
17,18/4:1:32,33:34-39/6:1:33-38/9:17,18/11:1:
10/12:1:17:18[2]/14:4-7/15:2:12/16:4:22:26/17:4
:10:17[2]/19:2,3:12[2]/21:3:13/22:8:16/23:4,5/28:3[2]
:21/29:12[2]:14:15[2]:17/2Ch2:8/6:14[2]:24:26:28:31
f/13:8:10:11:22/14:11/16:9/18:3,4,5:22:24/19:
3:9:10/20:6:9[2]:10:12:34/23:5,6/24:20:22/25:19
/26:17,18:22/28:10:13:26/29:9:19/31:10/32:8:
32/34:15,16:21:27/35/36:8:22,23/Ez2:36-39:
40,41,42/4:2[2]:12:14:19/5:11[2]/6:3:8/7:15:16:17:
19:21:25[3]/8:1:29/9:6:7:15/10:10:13/Neh1:2:3[2]:
9:10/2:1:3:17:19/4:1[2]:4:5:19/5:5[4]:7:8[2]:9[2]:10/6:
5,6[2]:8:10/7:39-42:43,44,45/9:6:7:8:17:31:36:37/
13:17:18:21/Est2:3/3:3,4:8/4:13/5:12/7:4:5/9:
13/10:2/Job1:19/2:9/3:8:14,15:17:18:19/4:3,4[2]
:5:6:10:18,19:20[2]/5:4:5:13:16:24/6:3:4:19-21[2]:
25,26[2]/8:9:11-13:17/9:12:32,33/10:2:4-7/11:4:
7:8/12:3:5:12:13:16:19/13:1:4[3]:7:8:9:20/14:
11,12:20,21[2]/15:2[2]:4,5[2]:7,8[2]:10:12:21:34/16:2:
16/17:7:8:11[2]/18:2:5/19:2:29/20:25/21:9:10:
12,13[2]:18[2]:23,24:26:27/22:3:4:5:10,11:15,16:29
/23:14f/24:2[2]:3:4:5:8:10[2]:11:13:14,15[2]:16:20:24
/25:5/26:2:8:13:13f:14/27:5:7[2]:12/28:8:11f/30:
1:2:3:17/31:40/32:6:7[2]:16:19/34:17:18[2]:34,35/
35:7/36:8:17/37:12:19,20/38:2:21/39:8:30/40:
8[2]:9:17:18/41:14:15-17:25:27,28/Ps1:2:3:5/2:1:
7/3:1:3/5:9[3]:11/6:7/7:10/9:6:9:16f:20/10:1:7[2]:
10:14[2]:18/11:3/12:1:3,4/14:2[2]:3:6/16:2:3:6f:9/
17:2:10:11:12:13,14/18:25[2]/19:1[2]:7,8:9:9f:10[2]:
12/22:3,4:14:29/23:4/24:6[2]/25:5:9:11:15/26:4/
27:12/28:1/29:9/31:1:3:4:4f:9,10[2]:9,10f:14,15[2]:
16:18:23[2]:24/32:1:7:11:11f/33:4:11:18,19:21[2]:
22/34:2:15:18[2]:21/35:3:4:15:17:20:24:28/36:3:6[3]
:9:12/37:14:19:23:26[2]:33/38:1:2:3,4[2]:5,6[2]:12/39
:1/40:4[2]:5:12:14,15:17[2]/41:1:3:6:11/43:2/44:4:
22[2]:23/45:2[2]:5:8:9/47/48:6:10:11/49:3:6:14[2]/
50:7,10,11/52:2:9/53:3:5/54:3/55:10:15:18/56:
1:5[2]/57:3:4[2]:10/58:1:3:4,5/59:3:9:12,13:14,15:
17/60:6,7/61:3/62:3,4:9/63:3:10/64:4/65:5:13[2]
/66:3/67:4/68:11,12,13:22:27:29/69:3:4:13[2]/70
:2,3/71:1:2:5:7:10:15:16/72:14:16/73:1:10:18:
23/74:2:9,10[2]/75:3/76:5:7/77:12:13:14:15/79:8
/80:16/81:4/82:5[3]:7:8/83:2:3:18/84:3:4:5[2]:12/
86:5:8:10[2]:13:14:15/87:3/88:5:10:14:18/89:2:10
:11:14,15:17:26:50/90:2:4[2]:5,6:7:9[2]:10[3]:12/91:4:
7:8/92:5:13[2]/93:4/94:10:11:14/95:4:5:7/96:5:6
/97:2:8,9[2]:12/100:3/101:6/102:12:27/103:6:14:
15:17,18/104:1[2]:3:4:14:16:18:21:28/106:1:3[2]:4/
107:10:23:26:27:41:42:43/108:9:12/109:4:21:24
:26:28/110:4/111:1:7:8:9/112:1/113:6/115:4:8[2]
/116:10,11:10,11f:15/118:15,16:20:27,28/119:1
:2:19:24:35:38:39:43:49,50:66:68:70:71,72:
75,76,77:82:98:102,103:105:111:113:114[2]:118:
119:129:136:137[2]:138:142:144:149:151[2]:155:
157:159:160/120:7/122:2,3,5/124:7/125:1:4[2]/
127:3[2]:4/138:2/139:8[2]:12:17,18:17,18f:17,18:22
/140:4:13/141:6,7[2]:6,7f:8/142:5:6/143:1:10:11:
12[2]/144:4:8:10:12-15/145:7/Pro1:1:19f:27/2:
3,4,5:19/3:22:32:35[2]/5:3:22/6:1:16-19:33/7:15/
8:4,5:9:18:19:20:21:32/9:10:17:18/10:1:4:13[2]:20
:25:28/11:5:7:17[2]:20:30[2]/12:12:19:20[2]:25/13:4:
6:7:18:19/14:7:21:24[2]:32:35/15:11:26f/16:2:11f [2]
:13:15:24:27[2]/17:3:4:6:7:24/18:8[2]:10:24/19:7:
17:24/20:1:6[2]/21:3:4:7:17:24:27/22:2:14/23:
19,20,21/24:9:10:11,12:21,22:24/27:3:6:9:15:20
:25,26,27/28:1:5:7:11:12:26/29:5,6:13:16[2]:19/
30:1:11,12:13,14:15,16:18,19:21,22,23:24-28[4]:
29,30,31/31:1:5:26:29[2]/Ecc1:8-11[2]/3:13:16:18:
22/4:3/5:1:8f:13,14/6:10/7:2/9:1:2,3:5f[2]:10:10f:
11[2]:17/10:16,17/11:3:5/12:2:4:6:11[2]/Sol1:1f[2]:6
f:7:9:10:15[2]:16/2:12:13[2]:15[2]/3:8:10/4:1[2]:2:3[2]:5:
7:11[2]:13,14:13,14f:15/5:12:13[2]:14:15/6:4:4f:6:7:
9/7:1:3:6:7[2]:9:12:13/8:10f/Is1:1:4:5,6:7[2]:12,13:
15[2]:18:23:27:31/2:8/3:9:10:12/4:2,3,4/5:7[2]:8:
12:21:22:27:28[2]:30/6:7[2]:11[2]:12/7:5/8:6[2]:12:19:
20:21/9:8,9,10:17:19,20/10:12:13:28,29[5]:31/13:
5:8:22/14:1:9:10[2]:11[3]:12[2]:25:31/15:4:6[2]/16:2:6
/17:2:6:14/18:5/19:3:11:12:13[3]:14/21:3:5[2]:5f/
22:1[2]:3:5:6,7,15,16/23:1:4/24:6:8[2]:9:12:14:17:
20:22/25:1:2:4[2]/26:1:12:14[2]/27:11[2]/28:5:6:8:9:
15:20/29:9[2]:11:13/30:7:9:16:17:18:27:29/31:3[3]:
6/32:14/33:9:13:15:18:24/35:4/36:5:7:17:19/
37:4:16,17:20:31/38:1/39:3/40:2[2]:15[2]:16:17[2]:21[2]
:26/41:3:8[2]:14:17:23:24:29[2]/42:18:19:22[2]/43:1:
4:8:9[2]:10:12/44:8:9[3]:17:21:22:25/45:11:20/46:1 [3]
:3/47:1:10:14/48:4[3]:8:10/49:3/50:8/51:5:10:14:
16/52:5:7:11/53:6/55:8:9[2]/56:3:6:10[2]:11[2]/57:6[2]
:7,8:13:20/58:2[2]:3[2]:7[2]/59:3[2]:4:7:9[2]:10:12:13[2]/
60:4:8/61:9/63:2:8:15:16/64:5[2]:6[2]:8[4]:9:10:11/

(ARE Con't)
65:1:8^2:23:24/66:2:3:17:18^2/Jer1:1:18/2:10,11:
12:22:24:26,27:28:29:31/3:3:14:22:23/4:13^3:22^2
:29/5:3:6:7:8:10:11:13:16^2:17:26:27^2:31/6:2:7:
10:13:23:24:25:27^2:28^2/7:5:10:17:19:26/8:3:6:9:
12:20/9:2:10:19:25,26/10:2,3:6:8:14^2:15:21/11:
13^2:14:20/12:1^2:2/13:18^2:19f^2:23/14:3:4:8:9^4:13
:14/15:2:5:9:15:16^2:19/16:16:20/17:13:14:15:17
/18:2:6:19/20:7:10:12/21:13/22:4:6:13^2:17:20^2:
22:24,25/23:10:11:14^4:16:21:23:26^2:27:32:33:36
:38,39/24:6:10/25:5^2:6:12:18:27/27:10:14:15:16
:18/28:15/29:8:11:21/30:14:16:17/31:11:15:18:
29f:30/32:18^2:19/33:5:24^2/34:18,19:22/35:11/
36:19/37:9:19/40:4:8:16/42:2/44:7:8:24:26:27/
45:5/46:1/48:14:15:25^2:30:33:34:41^2:46^2/49:1^2:
4:7:23^2:25:28:29:31/50:7:11:17:24:34:38:42^2/51
:17:18^2:20f:32^2:51/Lam1:1:2:4:5:6^2:16:18:21:22
/2:5:9^3:11:20^2/3:39:47^2:58/4:1:2:3,4:5:8:9:14:15
:18^2:19^2/5:2:3:12^2:17:18:22/Eze2:4:5:6^2:7/3:8:9
:18:19:26:27/4:10:12/6:9:11/7:13:24/8:6^2:12/9:
9/11:1^2:5:7f:13:15:16:17/12:3^2:5/13:2,3:4:15:18
/14:22^2:23/15:2^3:4:5,6^2/16:3:20:27:30:32:33,34:
43:45:52:57/18:2:2f:4:29/20:8:12:20:30:34:38/
21:24:26:32/22:4:7^3:8^2:9:10:12:18,19,20^3:26:27:
28/23:45/24:6:19/27:5:6:7:8:11^2:15:25:26:35/
28:2,3^4:6:19^3/30:11/31:2,3:14:16:17:18/32:2:4:
23^2:26:27^2:28:30:32/33:10^2:17:20:24:25:30:31^2:
32/34:4:30:31^2/35:12^2/36:3:7:20:35/37:
18,19,20/38:7:12^2:13:14:17/39:18:19^2/40:4/42:
13^2:14/43:11:13:17:18:19^2:25/44:14:20^2/45:7:
15/46:17/47:12:13:16:22^2:23/48:1:23:29/Dan1:
3,4/2:11:21:37:38^2/3:5:12:14:16:17/4:31:35/5:
13:14:26/7:24/8:20:26/9:4:7^2:8:15:18:26/11:35:
36/12:1:3:10:12/Hos1:1:10^2:11:4:23^4/4:6:9^2:12:
14/5:1:3:6:13/6:9/7:4^2:16/8:1:2:9:11^2/9:4^2:6:7^2:
9:12:13:15:16/10:2^2:11/11:7/12:11/13:10:12/
14:9/Joe1:5:9^2:10^3:11:12^2:13:17:20^2/2:2:10^2:23
/3:4/Amo:10:12/4:2:4:11:13/5:7:11^2:12^2:13:23/
6:9:10:13^2/9:6:7^2:8/Ob1:1:3/Jon:8^2/Mic:1:11:
16/2:4:5:7:12/3:1:2/4:9^2/5:2/6:9^2:10^2:12^2:16/7:
1^2:3:4:17/Nah1:3:5:9:15/2:1^2:6/3:3:6:8:18/Hab
1:7:8^2:11:12:13^2:14^2:16/2:5^2:19/3:2:17^2/Zep1:
13/2:3:9/3:3^2:4:12/Zec1:5,6:9:19/2:2/3:8/4:6:9
/5:10/6:4:5^2/8:6:7:19/9:13^2/10:2:8/11:2:3:9/13
:3:6:6f:9^2/14:20/Mal1:4:8/2:1:7:10^2/3:1:6:12:
14,15/Mt1:1:17:17f:18/2:6:18:20/3:9^3/4:3:6/5:
3:4:5:6:7:8^2:9:10^3:11^2:13:14:22^4:23:25:34:39:40:
47^2:48/6:7,8:18:20:21:23:25:26^2:30:31,32/7:15:
19:21:23:24:26/8:4:22:26/9:4:5,6:12:17^2:37/10:
2,3,4:19:23:30:31:37^2:38:40^2/11:3^2:6:14:16/12:2^2
:48:49/13:15^2:16:38:39:40:41:52/14:33/15:5,6:8
:13,14:15:20:27/16:2,3:8:13:18:23^2/17:11:26,27
/18:5:20/19:12^2:17:30^2/20:22^3:23:25/21:3:15/
22:12:14^2:16:18:40^2/23:8:11:13,14:15:20:21:22:
25:27:28:31:32:39/24:9:22:45:48/25:23/26:10:
69:70:73/27:11:13:40:41,42,43^2/28:5/Mk1:11^2:
24^2:43,44/2:5:9,10,11/3:11:16-19:27:31,32:33:
34/4:11,12^2:38/5:7,8:9/6:2,3:10/7:9:12,13:23:
28/8:4:17:18:27:28^2:29:33/9:1:41:43,44f^2:45,46f^2
:49/10:8^2:31:38^2:39/11:3:4,5:25^2/12:1:31:34:38:
40/13:1:11:13:15,16^2:30/14:13:49:61:70^2:71/15
:2/16:9f:15:16/Lk1:13:20:28f:31:42/3:7:8^2:11:
22/4:3:4:6,7:9,10,11:34:41/5:14^2:20:23,24:33^2:
39/6:2:14,15,16:20:21^2:22:25:30:35:39:47,48:49
/7:6,7,8:19:20,21,22^3:25:32:47^2:48/8:14:16:21:
24:45/9:13:18:26:27:55f:60f/10:16^3:20:21:23:41
/11:7:11:19^2:28:29,30:36:39:42:44^2:47/12:7:11:
12:15^2:24:27:28:37:38:41:54/13:12:14^2:27:30^2/
14:8:9:31:32/15:31/16:2:8^2:10:11:12:16:25/17:
14:17/18:8:19:31/19:17:21:31:33^2/20:5:6:21:
34,35:36^3:37,38:47^2/21:6:17^2/22:25f:41,42:46:
59:60:70/23:3:3f:29:31:34:37:39:40,41/24:5:17:
25:38/Jn1:13:21^3:22:33:42:49/3:1:3:21/4:12:35^2
/5:14:23:38/6:30,31:67:69/7:25:52/8:10:13:14:
23^2:25:29:30,31:33:34:37^2:38:40:41:43:44:52:53^2
/9:28^2:34:39^2:40^2:41/10:24^2:26:30:32:34,35,36/
11:8:9:27:47/12:34^2:44:45:49/13:10:11:33:35:36
/14:1:2,3:5:9:10^2:22/15:5:10:14:15/16:2:6:19:29
/17:10^2:11:16:21^2:22/18:4,5:7:8:21:29:33:34f:37^2
/19:9:12/20:13:15^2:23^2:29:30,31/21:17:18/Act1
:6:7:11/2:7:9:15^2:32:33/3:15:25^2/4:27/5:9:32:
35/6:3/7:1:26:28:33/9:4:5/10:14:31:33:34:35:
39/11:6/13:32,33/14:11:15^3/15:10:11/16:17:
20,21^3:28:37/17:6:7:20:22:28^2/18:13/19:15:38:
39:40/20:32^2/21:13:20:20f:21:23:24/22:7:8:15:
26:27/23:3:20:21^2/24:3/25:9/26:3:4:14^2:15^2:16:
18^2:24:26:29/28:22:27/Rom1:6,7^2/2:1^3:5:10:12-
12-15:17:19^2:20:23:25:28/3:1:5^2:8:9^2:13:14:15:
19:20:21,22:26:28:30:31/4:7^2:8:11^2:14^3:16^2/5:3:
4:5:10:17/6:7^2:13:14^2:18:21:22^2/7:4^4:6f:7^2:8/8:3
:8:9^2:13:14^2:16:17^2:24:28:35^2:36:39/9:6^2:8:16^2:
20:22:23,24:25:26/10:3:4:12:15^3:18/11:4:5:7:8:
16^2:18^3:20:28^2:31:33/12:4,5^2:7:8^2:13:14:15^2:17/
13:2:3:4:9/14:3:4^3:6^2:7:8:15/15:1:4:14^2:26:31/
16:4:7^2:14:15:17^2:18^3/1Co1:4:7:12^3:18:18f:18:
18f:23/2:6:7^2/3:1^2:3^4:4:4f:8:9^3:12:16:17:20:22^2/
4:7^2:8:10^4:13:19/5:2:3,4:6:10:11:12^2/6:2:4:4f:8:
9,10:11^2:12f:15:17/7:7:10:12:17:21:22^3:25:26:27
:29:34/8:5:6f:8/9:1:22^2/10:6:12:15:16^2:17^2:18:
19^3:20:22^2:23:32/11:14,15:19:20:22:26:30:32/
12:3^3:5^2:6^2:10^2:12:13^4:22:23:24:26:27:29:30/13:
12:13/14:7:8:10^2:12:16:21:23:27:32f:34^2:34f^2:36
/15:6:12:15:17^2:18:19:20f:22^2:29:34:34f:37:39^3:
40f:42:43:44^3:50:52/16:1^3:9:11:15/2Co1:1:3,4:
6,7:12:13,14:20/2:2:16^2:17^3/3:1:3:14:15/4:2:5:8^2
:9:10:15^3:16:17/5:7:8^2:9:11:12^2:13,14^2:18:20/6:
4:8:9^2:10:16/7:3:6/8:7:8:12:20^2:21:23/9:2:3:7:
12:13/10:1^2:2:11:12^2:14:16/11:5:12^2:13^2:18:
19,20:22^3:26:28/12:4:14:16/13:4^2:5^2:7:9^2/Gal1:
6^2:7/2:6:14^2:15:17:18/3:4:7:10^2:19:21,22^2:26:27
:28^4:29^2/4:6:7^2:10:17^3:18:19:24,25:28:29^2:31/5:
2:4^2:5:6:11:15:17^4:18:25/6:1:6:12^2:13:16/Eph1:
7:10:18/2:2:3:10:19^2:21:22^2/3:1:2,3:6:10:13/4:4
:17,18^3:25^2:26:27:29/5:4:13:15,16:28:29,30:31:
32/6:8:9:12:15:22/Php1:3:11:15^2:27:30/2:1^2:4:
15^2:19/3:3:4:11:15:18^2:19:20/4:1:3:5:8:10:18/
Col1:5:10:11:22:26,27/2:5:10:19^4:22:23/3:10:22
:24/4:8:11/1Th1:10/2:15:20/3:2,3:6:7^2/4:12:13:
15^2:16:17/5:3:4:5:10:11:13:14^3/2Th1:4^2:6:7/2:1
:10/3:4:11/1Ti1:2:3,4:8:9:10,11^2:20/2:1:2^2:15/3
:10/4:4:12/5:4:5^2:6:10:11:13:16:19:23/6:1:3^2:6^2:
11:17/2Ti1:5:15/2:12:13^2:14:17:19^2:20^3:24:25^3/
3:6:7:14/4:8/Tit1:7:9:10:11:12^2:16/2:7/3:8:13/
Heb1:5,6:8:10:14^2/2:3:4:5:6:14:18/3:1:6:12^2:14
/4:12/5:1^2:12,13/6:9:11/7:8:17:21/8:1/9:15:23:
28/12:5:6/13:3:4:14:16:24,25/Jas2:4:7:9:12:14:
18:19/3:4:9:13:14:15^2:18/4:4:13/5:2:5:7:9:11:17
/1Pe1:3:5:7:8:14/2:5^2:9^4:10:11^2:12:16^3:18^2:19:
20^2/3:7:9:14:21^2/4:11^2:14:17:18:19/5:2:5^3:9:14
/2Pe1:10:12:13,14/2:10:11:12:13:14:17^3:19/3:
13:14:15,16^3/1Jn1:3:6^2:7:8:10/2:3:5:14:16^2:20:
26:29/3:1^2:2:4:7^2:12:19:21:22:24/4:1:4:5:6:7^3:13
:18^2/5:1:6,7,8f:14:19:20^2/2Jn1:4:7^2:9/3Jn:3:5^2:
7^2:11^2/Jud:7:12^4:16^2:24,25^2/Rev:4f:8f:20^2/2:2^2:
9:10:18:20/3:1:2:4:9f^2:9^2:15:16:17/4:5f:11/5:6f:
9/7:13^2:14:15/9:12/10:4/11/12:10/13:18/14:4:
4f:5:12:13:18/15:3,4^3/16:5:7:15^2/17:3f:7:12:14/
18:5:14^2/19:2:9^2:9f:10^2/20:6:10/21:8:22:22f:27/
22:6,7^2:9^2:11:14^2:15

4282

AREN'T

Ex16:7,8,9/33:15/Num23:25/Deu20:19:20/Jos
2:14/Ju18:9,10/1Sa1:8/26:15/29:4/2Sa10:3/
13:32,33/16:17/19:8,9,10/1Ki21:5/2Ki4:6/5:12
/7:9/10:9,10/Neh2:1/Job19:3:22/Ps51:16/73:
5/Pro30:24-28/Is7:13/50:1/58:3/59:9/Jer37:9
/49:1/Eze33:17/Dan3:25/Hos5:7/Mt12:7/15:
11/22:8/Mk7:15,16/12:14/16:6/Lk12:1/Jn1:
24,25/4:17,18/5:31:43/8:47:57/10:12/18:17:25
/Act19:26/21:25:37,38/Rom3:20/8:3/1Co5:2/
6:12/7:8:27/10:13/14:22/16:17/2Co9:4/13:5/
Gal4:18/1Ti3:7/5:25/Heb12:8/Jas2:14/2Pe:19
/Jud1:23/Rev2:2:9/3:8:9

75

AROUND

Gen3:7/6:16/13:10/14:7/27:16/37:7/38:21:28/
39:11:14,15:17/42:1/49/Ex14:19/16:13/19:23/
24:4/25:11:24:25^2/27:17/28:32/30:3/37:2:11:
12:26/39:23:25,26/40:8/Lev13:33/25:31:44/
Num1:53/3:36,37/11:10:24:31:32/21:4/Deu1:
40/2:1:7/17:14/22:8/28:34:47,48/Jos6:3,4^2:11:
12,13,14:15/11:4/15:9/17:16,17,18/23:12/24:4
/Ju2:19/6:10:39/7:21/8:11:26/9:34/10:4/11:18
/19:22/20:29:35-39/Ru3:8/4:9/1Sa2:22/8:20/
14:2/17:28/21:14,15/24:7,8/26:5,6,7/2Sa3:8/
11:12/13:28/14:26/20:2:12/22/24:6/1Ki3:1:7/
7:15/8:14/10:5/18:26:30:32/19:6:21/22:11:19:
32,33/2Ki2:24/4:20/7:10/9:5:22:23/10:9,10/15
:19,20/16:3/23:7:16/1Ch5:16/10:3/11:8/14:14
/2Ch4:2/6:3/10:16/13:13,14/18:6,7:27/20:10/
23:10/33:14/Ez10:1/Neh4:6/5:9/12:38/13:21:
25/Job8:2/15:23,24/21:8:29/23:16,17/29:5/36:
30/41:1/Ps1:1/36:11/39:1/40:14,15/45:16/48:
12/49:1/59:6/67:2/69:1/78:34/79:4/80:13/81:
11/88:17/91:7/96:1/108:3/118:12/119:59,60/
128:3/139:11/Pro6:21/7:13/11/25:20/26:
18,19/28:19/29:3/Ecc1:3-7/4:7:16/Is12:5/14:
26/20:2/23:17/25:6/29:3/32:9/33:1/40:19/45:
20/46:7/55:12/58:10/60:5:9:11/Jer2:10,11/5:6
:15f/6:3/9:16/16:19/17:26/26:17/29:18/32:20/
46:14/49:29/50:32:46/51:16/52:4/Lam5:21/
Eze1:17:18:27,28/4:1/9:4/11:12/12:6/16:8/20:
32/29:17/30:20/31:4/34:26/36:4:36/37:1:21
38:12/40:5:17:24:28f:35/41:19,20/42:16-20/
13:17:20/45:2/46:12:23/47:2/Dan1:3,4/3:25
27/5:7:16:29/8:3:27/10:5,6/Hos:14f/Jon2:5,
3:4,5/Mic4:5/5:4/7:16/Hab1:3:6f/Zep2:5f:1
Zec1:15/2:1/4:10/8:20,21/Mal1:5:11/Mt6:2
9:22:35/11:19/14:30:35/15:31/20:3:5:6/21:3
24:30/26:71/27:36/Mk2:13/3:5:9:10:34/4:1,
11:21:30:31:32:41,42/6:10:54/8:24^2:25/9:8:3
42/10:23/11:11/12:1/14:18:70/15:31/Lk4:4
5:8/6:10/7:15:49/9:5/10:7/12:52:56/14:3:17:
/16:1:13/18:31/22:6:25:55/Jn1:38/4:5,6:35^2,
2-5/11:52/13:4:5:23f/18:18/21:13:20^2/Act6:
8:26/9:35/10:38/13:11:18/14:20/16:25/19:2
22:6/24:18:22/25:7/28:13/Rom1:5:8/8:20,21
16:25,26,27/1Co4:11/9:26/12:2/2Co2:15/4:5
18/7:5/12:14/Php1:13/1Ti5:6:13/2Ti4:3:6/T
2:3/Heb11:30/12:1/Jas3:3/1Pe5:8:9/2Pe1:4
:7,8/3:11:15,16/1Jn2:10/4:1/5:19/2Jn1:7/Ju
13/Rev7:11^2/11:8,9/16:19/17:5/18:23

3

AS

Gen2:15/3:7:14^2:15:22/4:1:15:21f:25/6:3:11:
12,13:22/7:8,9:16:18/8:5:22^2/9:13:18f:20,21:2
/10:9/11:2:3,4/12:4:11,12,13/13:8:14^2/14:5,6
8,9:10^2:14^2:17:23/15:12:13:17/16:6:9-12^2:13/
17:1:2,3,4:7,8:12^2:13:20^2:23:24-27/18:1:5:8:12
14/19:1:2^3:4:8:14:23:26:28:35/20:16/21:1:4,5:
12:17:23:27:30/22:2:13/23:8:10:13:16:19,20/2
:14:15,16:51:60:63/25:22:27/26:1:3^2:4^2:29:31^2
27:8,9,10:19:30^2:37:38/28:14^2:18:21/29:9:12,
:18/30:16:31,32:34:43/31:25:32:36,37:45:47,4
51,52/32:10:12:31/33:3:8:10^2:10f^2:13:15:17^2/
:6,7:9,10:11:12:22/35:13,14/36:15,16/37:3:10
38:8:9:10:11:15:18:19:24:25:28/39:1:9:10^2:11^2
12^2/40:13:22/41:8^2:13:21^2:38:41,42:46:54/42:
5^2:14f:23:34^2:35^2/43:11:12:17:18:19:21:34^2/44
1^2:2:7:15:18:33/45:16:21/46:34/47:9^2:11:24:2
29/48:5^3:7:14:20^2:22/49:4:7f:9/50:6:8^2:12,13:2
/Ex1:15,16^2/2:5:13:14:15:21/3:1:2:15f/4:7:12:
16:24:30/5:10,11^2:13:16^2:20/6:7/7:1:6:10:13:1
:20^2:22/8:9:10:13:15:17:19:20:24:27:31,32/9:8
10:12:18:29^2:30:35/10:23/12:17:19^2:25:28:31:
32:33^4:35:42:48^2/13:9^2:16^3:19/14:9:10:20/15:
8:10/16:4^2:5^2:14^2:16^2:22^2:23^3:28,29^2:31:32:34/
17:5,6:7:11^2:13/18:21/19:4:11:16:18:19/20:8:2
/21:3:7^2:9^2:10:16:22/22:3:4:16:26:30/23:12^2:1
19:31^2/24:10^2/26:36/27:8/28:3:11:12^2:15^2:32:
35:36:41/29:1:14:15,16:19,20:25:28:36:40:41/
30:22,23:24:30:32:37/31:4:5:6:10:18/32:13:17/
33:9:11/34:4:9:10:16:18:29/35:24:30,31:35^2/3
25/38:18/39:4,5:6,7:23:25,26:28,29:31:43/40:
13:15^2:16:19:21:23:27:29:32/Lev1:2,3:4:10:13:
14/2:3^2:4^2:10:12^2:16/3:6:9,10,11:12:14/4:3:10
20:21:23^3:26:28^3:31:32:33:35^2/5:2:3^2:7:8:10:11
12^2:13:15:17,18:19/6:15:17:21:22,23/7:5:11:15
17,18:19:34:35/8:9:13:15,16:17:29:31/9:5:7:8:
10:14:15:21^2/10:5:6:7:18:19/11:9:25:27:41,42^2,
12:2:5:6/13:45:46^2/14:12:13:17:24:28:51,52^2/
15:18^2:25:26/16:6:9:10:11:15/17:5:6:11/18:28:
28f/19:14:18:23f:27:34/20:1/21:4:9^2/22:21:23:
25^2:26,27:32,33/23:9,10,11:12:17f:18:20:21:40/
24:15,16^2:22:23/25:35:39:40^2:42:53^3/26:19^2:33
36^2:37:39:43:45/27:8:9:11,12:13:16:21:32/Num
1:17,18,19:53/2:3-31/3:3:6:7,8,9:39:41^2:42:51/
:15:30/6:20/7:15:18-23:24-29:30-35:48-53:60-
60-65:66-71:72-77:84,85,86/8:9:11:13:16:19^2:2
/9:4,5:6,7:18^2:22^2/10:31f:34:35/11:3:31^2:33/12
1f^2:10:12/13:3-15:16f:22f:23:27:30:31^2/14:19:
20,21^2:24:32/15:10:15,16f:36:39/16:3:5:8,9:15:
38:40:42:47/17:10:11:12,13^2/18:12:17:19:21:27
:28,29:30:32/19:1:5:9/20:8:9:27^2/21:1^2:24^2:27-
27-30^2:34/22:22,23/23:7-10^4:18-24:30/24:1:3-9
/25:6:10,11^3:18/26:5-11:52,53:63:64,65/27:13:
17:19:22^2:23/28:1:3:6:12^2:19:22:26/29:5:6:25:
28:31:39/30:1/31:9,10,11:22:31:41:54/32:5:23:
27:31/33:2:49^2:55:56/34:1:16-28/35:2/36:6:7:
10/Deu1:11:13:15:19,20,21:30:31:36:38:40:41/
2:5:7:10:11:12:21^3:23^2:28:30:35,36/3:1:6:10^2:14
/4:6^2:7:8^2:15:21,22:33:38^2:44,45,46:48/5:5:14:
26,27/6:2^2:3:16:19:24/7:1/8:5:9^2:20/9:3/10:4:5
8:9^2:10^2:15:22^2/11:4:6:21^2:25/12:4,5^2:8:11:15^5:
20-23:30/13:11:16:17/14:1:23:27/15:6:8^2:9:14:
21:22/16:3^2:6^2:10:17^2/17:15:18/18:8:10:17/19:
8/20:3:10/21:11:14/22:25,26,27^2/23:6^2:13:23/
24:6:7:9:12,13^2:14,15/25:4:6:10:17/26:13:15:18:
19/27:9/28:11:23^3:24^2:29:31:32^2:41:46:56,57:62
:63:68/29:8:13^2:14,15^2:16/30:1:9/31:3:4:5:7:13^2
:19:26/32:10:11^2:34:50/34:1^3:5:7^2/Jos1:5^3:16:
17,18^2/2:5/3:7:13,14^4:15,16:17/4:2,3:8^2:12,13:
14^2:18^4:20/5:13/6:16:20^2/7:5^2:22/8:2:5:6:8:15:

(AS Con't)
29:31:32/**9**:1^2:3,4,5:12:25/**10**:1:2^3:11:12:27:30:
32:34,35:39:40/**11**:4^2:8^2:9:12:15:20:23^2/**12**:3^4/
13:2-7:10^2:25^2:27,28^2:33/**14**:1:10:11^4:12:13,14:
15/**15**:1:18,19^2:47^2:48-62/**16**:1^2:10/**17**:4^2:5,6:10^2
:13/**18**:9/**19**:8^3:27^2/**20**:2:7^2:9^2/**21**:9-16:44/**22**:
2,3^2:4:7,8:24,25:26,27:31/**23**:4,5^3:8:10:15,16^3/
24:2:5:15:17:26/**Ju1**:9^2:12:13:14:20:22,23^2:26:
28:33:34/**2**:4:7-9^2:10:18^2:22/**3**:6:20:22,23:27/**4**:
11^2:16^2:21/**5**:31^2/**6**:3,4^2:13:16f:26^2:27:28:34:36:
40/**7**:1^2:12,13:17:18^2:21:22^2:25/**8**:21f:33^2:34/**9**:
33^3:35:47,48:52/**10**:10/**11**:3^2:30,31:33^2:39/**13**:9:
19:20^2:24/**14**:5:6^2:9:10,11^2/**15**:1:10:14:19/**16**:7^2
:9^2:11^2:12^2:16,17^2:20:23,24:27^2/**17**:3:4,5:7,8:
10,11:12:13f/**18**:1:2:13:30^2:31^2/**19**:6:9:10^2:14:
15:22/**20**:1^2:8,9,10^2:31^2:35-39/**21**:14:23/**Ru2**:3:
20^2:22/**3**:15-18/**4**:2:4:8:11^2:12^2/**1Sa1**:7:10:
12,13:19,20:28^2/**2**:2^2:8:16^3:28:31/**3**:10:15:19/**4**:
9^2:13/**6**:6:12^3:14:17/**7**:6:9:10:15/**8**:1:7:9:22/**9**:
9,10,11^2:14:16/**10**:5^3:9:16:24/**11**:2:7:10:14/**12**:1
:3:7:15^2:16:23/**13**:3,4^2:5^2:10:14:21/**14**:7:13:28:
31:36:41:42:47/**15**:22^2:23^4:27:33/**16**:1:4:13/**17**:
20:23:24^2:27:48,49:52^2:55/**18**:10:15,16:17/**19**:4:
5:6:7:9,10/**20**:8:13:17^2:20:31^2:35:36:41^2/**21**:
14,15/**22**:2:14^2/**23**:11:17:26/**24**:3:4:13^2:14^2:15/
25:13:20:26^2:29:37,38f:42/**26**:15:24/**28**:5,6f:17/
29:2:9^4:10^2/**30**:3:20/**2Sa1**:1/**2**:7:8:10,11:16:24/
3:6:9,10:16^3:17:21^3:27:35,36/**4**:2,3,4:5:6,7/**5**:4,5
:25/**6**:16:21/**7**:10,11:15:18:23:25:26:29/**8**:2/**9**:1:
10,11/**11**:2:23:25^2/**13**:11:17,18:20:29,30:35/**14**:
2,3:13^2:20^2:25:32/**15**:10^2:11:12:15:23:30^3:32:
33,34:37/**16**:5:13:23^3/**17**:8^2:11^2:17:25/**18**:4:9:14
:18:25:32:33/**19**:2:3:5:8,9,10:13:14:15:18:26:27:
43^2/**20**:3:8,9,10^3:17/**21**:19^2/**22**:31:44/**23**:4^2:6:8:
22^2/**24**:3^2:7^2:16:24/**1Ki1**:5:6:12:20:21^3:27:29:30
:34:35:37:41:43:44,45/**2**:1:8:14:17:19:27:31:35^2:
42/**3**:7:13^2:14:15:28/**5**:5:6:8:10^2:12/**6**:10:11,12/
7:32:35/**8**:10:14:20:22,23:25:29:40:43:46:54,55:
57:61:64/**9**:4:5:11,12:13:16:20,21/**10**:9:20:27^2/
11:4:6:29^2:33:38/**12**:2,3,4:16,17:20f^2:21:23,24:
26/**13**:1:5:11:18:24,25/**14**:2:8:10:17:18:24^2:27/
15:1:3^3:13:19:28:29/**16**:3:4-7^2:15,16:24:26:31:34
/**17**:1^2:5:10:11:15^3:16/**18**:12^2:28:30:32f^2/**19**:4:5:
11:16:21/**20**:2,3:7:12:16:17:25:34:36^3:39:41/**21**:
19:22:25:26/**22**:17:22:27f:35:36,37:38:43/**2Ki1**:
14:17/**2**:1:6,7^2:9^2:11:12:19:22:23/**3**:2^2:15:22:24:
27/**4**:1:4:15,16:17:25:38:44/**5**:2:14^3:27^2/**6**:1^2:5:
18:20^2:25:26-30/**7**:4:16:17/**8**:4:8,9:18^2:27/**9**:4:9:
22^3:26:27^2/**10**:11^2:15^3:17:24:25^2:32,33^4:36/**11**:
2,3:12:13,14/**13**:5:7:20,21^2/**14**:3^2:5^2:7:21f:24^2:
25/**15**:3:16:18:29/**16**:2:3^3:6:8:9:16/**17**:1^2:14^2:17f
:19:21:23/**18**:4:5^2:8^2:24^2/**19**:3:12:29^2:37/**21**:
3,4,5:6:13/**22**:15,16/**23**:8^3:10:16^2:19:21:27:30/
24:2/**25**:7:11:18:22:23:28:29^2/**1Ch1**:24-27/**3**:16f
/**4**:2:32,33^2/**5**:1:7,8^2:11^2:24:26/**6**:4-15:16:77/**7**:
28^2/**9**:19:29/**11**:3^2:4:10:18,19,21^2:23^2:24,25^2/**12**
:2^2:3-7-8-13:19^2:20:23:40^2/**13**:2:9/**14**:11:16/**15**:
4-10^6:15:18:29^2/**16**:18:38:40:42/**17**:5:8^2:9:10:13
:17:24/**18**:3^2:8^2:11/**19**:7^2/**20**:3/**21**:4:12:14:19,20
:23/**22**:10:11/**23**:1:8,9f:14,15:31^2/**24**:6:19:31/**25**
:6,7/**26**:4,5:10:26/**27**:5,6:16-22/**28**:2:6:7:10:15^2/
29:2^2:11:15:21:22f:22^3/**2Ch1**:2,3^2:5,6:9^2:10:12:
15^2/**2**:3:8:10:16^2:17:18^3/**3**:1/**4**:3/**5**:2:4,5:10:
11,12:13,14^2/**6**:5,6^3:12,13^2:15:16:20,21:26:27:29^2
:31f^2:33:36/**7**:1:7:8^2:11^2:12:17^2/**8**:4:7,8,9/**9**:12:
20:25^2:26^2:27^3/**11**:12:17/**12**:2:13/**13**:3:8^2:9:10:
12:15,16/**14**:12:13^2:14/**15**:2^3/**16**:5^2/**17**^{3}:7,8,9/
18:16:32^2:34/**19**:1:11^2/**20**:5:9:13:21:24^2:26:29:
32:33/**21**:3,4:6^4:13^3/**22**:1:4^2:9^2:12/**23**:4:5,6:11:
18^3/**24**:22:25/**25**:3:14:23:24^2/**26**:1:4:5^2:20^2/**28**:
13:16:19f/**29**:2:8:15:24:27:28:32,33/**30**:5:8:10^2:
12:16/**31**:3^3:4:5,6/**32**:19/**33**:6:22:23/**34**:2:4:9^2:
13:14:31/**35**:4,5:8:10:11:12:13:16:24,25/**36**:1:4^2:
9^2:10:12:13:20/**Ez1**:6^2/**2**:62,63:69^2/**3**:1:4/**4**:2^2:3
:14:16/**5**:14:15/**6**:5:14:17:18/**7**:6:7,8,9^2:15:28f/**8**
:21:26,27^3:28:35/**9**:2:6^2:7:9:12:15/**10**:1:5:16-19^2
/**Neh1**:11/**2**:1:16/**3**:1^2:16^2:26^2:31^2/**4**:14:22^2/**5**:7
:8:13/**7**:64,65/**8**:1^2:7,8:9^2:14:18/**9**:32/**10**:29:33^2:
34:36:38^2/**12**:24:29:31,32:44:45/**13**:1:4:13:19/
Est1:8^2:13-15^4/**2**:7:8:9:12,13,14:20:21/**3**:1:11:
14:15/**4**:5:14:17/**5**:9/**6**:4:10/**7**:4:7:8/**8**:9,10:12f:
13:17/**9**:13:24,25:29-31^2:32/**Job1**:6:18/**2**:6/**3**:
20,21/**4**:6:10:12:13:15:18,19^2/**5**:7^2:25^2/**6**:15-18^2
/**7**:9/**8**^{2}/**9**:32,33/**10**:22^3/**11**:8^2:12^2:17^2/**12**:11:12
:19/**13**:1:2^2:9^2:12^4/**14**:2:11,12^2:17/**15**:14^2:16:
23,24:33f/**16**:4:8:12:21/**17**:10/**19**:11:15:22:25:
27^2:28/**20**:6:23/**21**:33/**22**:6/**23**:10^2/**24**:3:9:11:
19:22,23/**25**:5/**27**:3^2:6^2:12^2:18^4/**29**:12:15:16:23:
25^3/**30**:5:15:17:19:24:28,29/**31**:18:37/**33**:10:15:
23,24:25^2/**34**:7,8^2:26:29,30/**37**:13:18:21/**38**:6,7:
30^2:35:39,40:41/**39**:16/**40**:9^4:15:17^2:18/**41**:24:
27,28^2:30^2/**42**:7:8:9:10^2:13,14f^2:15^2/**Ps4**:1:7/**5**:
8/**7**:2/**10**:14/**11**:1f/**12**:5/**16**:6/**17**:8^2:15/**18**:11:
31:35:42/**19**:5^4/**22**:12/**23**:5/**24**/**25**:21/**26**:3:9,10
/**28**:1/**30**:6,7/**33**:12/**34**:22/**35**:14/**36**:5^2:6^4/**37**/
38:13,14/**39**:2,3:5,6:11^3:12/**40**:2:7f:7:9/**42**:1/**45**^{2}
:15/**49**:7:11:13:15/**52**:2/**54**:5/**55**:14/**57**:4:10^2/
58:4,5:8^2/**59**:16/**61**:6^2/**63**:4^2/**67**:1/**68**:11,12,13/
69:9:13/**72**:1:5^2:6^2:16^2:17/**73**:2:20:25^2:28^3/**74**:2
/**75**:9/**76**:10/**77**:13^2:20/**78**:8:15:19,20^2:27^2:55:
57:65:69:71,72/**80**:1:8/**81**:5/**82**:7/**83**:4:9^2:10:11:
14/**84**:9/**89**:2^2:3,4:7^2:12:14,15:19f:27:29^2:35,36f
:37:38:51/**90**:4:4f:5,6^4:11:12/**92**:10^2:12/**95**:8/
101:2/**102**:7:11/**103**:10:11^2:12^2/**104**:15:33^2/**105**
:10,11:17:26/**106**:9^2:16:27:34/**107**:22:30/**108**:4:
8/**109**:7:18^3:21^3:22,23^2/**110**:1/**115**:3:8^2/**116**:2^2/
119:7:29,30:31^2:33,34^2:58:65:66^2:75,76,77:107:
130:132:154:170/**121**:8/**122**:4:9/**123**:2/**124**:7/
125:1:2/**126**:4/**128**:3^2:5^2/**129**:6,7/**131**:2/**132**:13
/**133**:2^2:3^2/**134**:1/**135**:4:12/**136**:21/**137**:8/**138**:2
/**139**:12^2/**140**:6,7,8/**141**:2^2:6,7f/**143**:2:6/**144**:2:
12-15/**145**:15/**146**:2^2:5/**149**:4,5/**Pro2**:3,4,5/**3**:
11,12/**4**:1:3:10:12:14/**5**:3^2:4f:4:19f/**6**:11:31^2/**7**:2
:22^2:23/**10**:13^2/**11**:28/**17**:14f/**18**:11/**19**:12^4/**20**:
8:14/**21**:1/**22**:7/**23**:4,5:6,7,8:26,27,28/**24**:7:8^2:
32,33/**25**:6,7:11^2:13^2:18^2:20^2:23^2:27:28^2/**26**:4,5^3
:4,5f:6^2:7^2:11:21^2:23/**27**:9^2:14:17^2/**28**:1:15^2/**29**:
21/**30**:13,14^2:29,30,31:33/**Ecc2**:7,8:11:13,14:15:
20-23/**3**:12^2/**4**:9^2/**5**:1^2:11:16/**6**:3/**7**:6^2:11^2:14^2/
8:2,3:9,10:13^2:14^2/**9**:13/**10**:5/**11**^{3}/**12**:7/**Sol1**:5^2:
15/**2**:2:3/**4**:2:4:13,14^2:15/**5**:2:5:15/**6**:4^3:4f:5:6:
10^3:10f:13f/**7**:2:4^2:5:9^2:13^2/**8**:6^3:10f:12/**Is1**:9:10
:18^5/**2**:2f:6:22/**3**:12^2:18/**4**:1:2,3,4f/**5**:7f:25/**6**:8:9
:12/**7**:2:6:11:11f^2:13:14f:17:19^2/**8**:2^2:12/**9**:4/**10**:
7:9^3:14:18:22^2:24:27:34/**11**:9:16/**13**:2^2:4:8:12^2:
19^2/**14**:9:10^2:19:20:30/**16**:1:8^2/**17**:3:5^2:6:9^2/**18**:
4:5/**19**:16^2/**20**:2:4/**21**:5f/**22**:4/**23**:6:15,16/**25**:1:
5:10:11/**26**:17/**27**:7,8^3/**28**:4:21:23,24/**29**:2:8^2:
14/**30**:8:13:18:26^2:29/**31**:4,5:8/**32**:2^2:5:7/**33**:4:
16:21/**34**:4^2:6/**35**:2^4/**36**:16:22/**37**:1:3:4:14^2:
16,17^2:18:26:27^4:33/**38**:8:12:19/**40**:2^2:10:14:15:
17:26/**41**:4:8:21:25:29^2/**42**:1f:6:19^2:19f:19/**43**:3:
7:8:23/**44**:7:13:28/**45**:13f^2:14/**47**:8:14^2/**48**:4^4:19^2
:20/**49**:2:8,9:18^2/**51**:3^2:9:20/**52**:13f/**53**:7^2:12/**54**
:9^2/**55**:8:9:10/**56**:3^2:6:11^4/**57**:5:9/**58**:2^2:10^2:12:
13/**59**:10:17:20:21/**60**:2^2/**62**:4:5/**63**:2:11:19^2/
64:4:5:6f/**65**:1f^4:8:10:18:21,22^3:25/**66**:1^2:3^3:7,8^3
:11:13:19:20:22^2/**Jer1**:3:5/**2**:2:10,11:28^2:30:36/
3:17:18/**4**:23^2/**5**:3:9:15f^2:29^2/**6**:2:9:26:28^2/**7**:6:
13,14:15:23:31/**8**:6^2:7/**9**:9^2:14/**10**:2,3/**11**:5:13^2:
19^2/**12**:3:8:14:16/**13**:5:10:11:17:19:21:24,25/**14**:
8^2:9:10:22/**15**:12,13:14:17,18^4:19/**16**:6^2:8:14,15
/**17**:1^2:2,3,4:27/**18**:3:4:6^2:8:10:12:17:22/**19**:10:
11^2:12:14/**20**:4:6/**21**:1/**22**:6^2:11:22:23:24,25:30
/**23**:7:8:9:14^2:27:34/**25**:8,9:14:18:30/**26**:6:14^2:
20/**27**:2:11/**28**:4f/**29**:3:26/**30**:7^2:14^2:18:20:21f^4/
31:1:2:10:15f:18:21:32f:33f^2:36^2/**32**:4:8:12:13:
20:24^2:35:42/**33**:5^2:22:24/**34**:5:15:17:18,19/**36**:
4:8:12^2:21:28:30f/**37**:1f^2:4:13^2:21^2/**38**:5/**39**:6:7:
13:18/**40**:2,3:5:7:10/**41**:6/**42**:2:18/**43**:2,3:9:12^2/
44:1:6:13:17^3:22:30/**45**:1:5/**46**:18^3:20,21:22,23:
24^2/**47**:3/**48**:2,3,4^2:13:46/**49**:5:18^2:20:21^2:22^2:
24/**50**:11:15:16:18:21:29:34:37^2:40:45/**51**:7:30:
46:49:53^2:55/**52**:2:3:15:16:24,25:33^2/**Lam1**:5:15
:18:21:22/**2**:3:4:6:7:11:13:17:19/**3**:24:39:44:45:
52/**4**:2:8^2/**Eze1**:14:15:16:16f:22:24/**2**:1f:2/**3**:3:8^2
:9^2:13:17:23/**4**:12^2/**5**:1/**7**:16:17^2:21/**8**:1:4/**9**:7/
10:5:9-13:15,16:19:22/**11**:21/**12**:4:6:7:18^2:22/
13:4^2/**14**:22/**15**:2^4/**16**:15:19:30:36:38^2:47:48^3:
50/**17**:5^2:16:19/**18**:3/**20**:5,6:12:26:27,28:30:31^2:
35,36:39:41/**21**:7^2/**22**:2/**23**:2,3:8^2:10^2:18:21:24:
25:33:37/**24**:22:24/**25**:9,10/**26**:10:14f:15/**27**:11f
:28:32/**28**:6^2:8:9/**29**:5:10^2:12/**30**:17:18:24/**31**:
2,3:11/**32**:2:14^3:19^2:21:24:27:29/**33**:7:11:27:31:
33/**34**:8:17/**35**:6:11/**36**:2:3:9:17^2:17f:25:34/**37**:7^2
:8:10:17/**38**:2,3f:6^2/**39**:8/**40**:18:20:21:22:23:24:
25:28:31:32:33:36/**41**:7:25/**42**:5^2:6:7,8^2:9,10:11
/**43**:3:22:24:25/**44**:13:15:24:28/**45**:1:7/**46**:11^2:
12:13/**47**:3:10:22/**48**:8:13:23/**Dan1**:3,4:7:9:
18,19^3:21/**2**:1:34:35^2:38:40:41,42^4:45^2:48^2:49^2/
3:22:24:26^2/**4**:13:30^2:33^2:35^2:36/**5**:5^2:11^2:12:13
/**6**:3:10^2/**7**:4:7:8:9^3:11:12/**8**:3^2:4:12:15:17:22^2:
25/**9**:3:7^2:12:17:24:25f:26:27/**10**:4:17:19/**11**:6:7:
20:29:36:39:44/**12**:3^2/**Hos1**:4,5:3^3:4:7:15:20/**4**:
5^3:6:10:16/**5**:3:10f:12:14:15^2/**6**:3^2:5^2/**7**:4:8^2:12/
8:8/**9**:1:4:6:9^2:10^2/**10**:6:7:14/**11**:1:4:9^2:10/**12**:9:
14/**14**:5:6^3:7^2/**Joe1**:2:6^2:8/**2**:3:4:14:23^2:26:32/**3**:
3:20/**Amo1**:3:5^2:5f^2:5:6/**2**:2:4:9^3:13/**3**:4/**4**:11/**5**:
8:14:19/**6**:5^2:7:9^2:13/**7**:1/**8**:8;10^2/**9**:6:7:9/**Ob1**:4^2
:11:15:20^2/**Jon**:4/**3**:1/**4**:5/**Mic1**:8^2:11:12:16/**3**:8
/**4**:13/**5**:8^2/**7**:1^2:4:7:14:17:20^2/**Nah1**:15/**2**:11^2/**3**
:2^2:9^2:10^2:13:16/**Hab1**:7/**2**:4:14/**3**:2:6/**Zep1**:17^2
/**2**:9:15^2/**Hag1**:6:7/**2**:3:14:18,19/**Zec1**:14^2/**2**:8f
/**3**:3/**4**:1/**6**:13^2/**7**:3:7:14/**8**:6:13^4/**9**:1f^2:1^2:7^2:14:
16,17^2/**10**:5:6:7/**11**:1:2:4:7:12:15/**12**:1:8^3:10^2/
13:6f:9/**14**:1:5:20^2/**Mal1**:13^2/**2**:1/**3**:3:4:14,15^2:
17/**4**:3/**Mt1**:19:20^2:24/**3**:9:16^2/**4**:18:24^2/**5**:1:13:
45:48/**6**:2:7,8:10:11:12:16:29^2:33/**7**:2:15:16:21:
29^2:29f/**8**:1/**9**:8:9:10^2:14^2:18:19:27/**10**:8^2:14:16^4
:32^2:42/**11**:8/**12**:13:27:39,40:46,47/**13**:2,3:4:8^2:
23f:25:40:43:52^2/**14**:13^2/**17**:2:5:9:20^2/**18**:3:4:17
f:33/**19**:19:29/**20**:11,12^2:17:28:29/**21**:1:2:6:10:
18:44:46/**22**:30:31:38,39^2/**23**:8:9:29,30:37/**24**:1:
3:17f:21:27:37,38:43/**25**:32/**26**:2:19:20,21:24:26
:56:69/**27**:10:17:19:29:32:33:36:60/**28**:1:6:9:11/
Mk1:4:16:22:22f:31:38:45^2/**2**:6:14:18:23/**3**:7,8^2:
10:27/**4**:1:3:8^3:17^2:20^2:27:33^2:33f:35:36/**5**:1:3,4:
11:14:15:29^2/**6**:11:33:34:47:52f:56^2/**7**:3:4:24/**8**:
1:15:25:27/**9**:9:12,13:14:15:41/**10**:1^2:14:15^3:17:
19:21:32:42:45:46^2/**11**:1:2:4,5:12:19:20:27,28/
12:26:31^2:33:35:38:41/**13**:1:2:3,4:19/**14**:4,5:13:
16:18:21:22:45^2:65/**15**:2:8:29,30:47/**16**:7:14/**Lk**
1:1,2:6^2:8,9:10:28f:62f^2:70/**2**:20:22:29,30,31:38/
3:1:18:21:23-38/**4**:16:32^2:33:35:40/**5**:1:9:11^2:17^2
:25:27:29/**6**:1:4:10:13:17,18^2:31:35:36^2:40/**7**:12:
24:36/**8**:5^2:8^3:10:22:27:28^2:34:43,44/**9**:5f:5:18:
29:33:34^2:36:37:42:43^2:46:51:57/**10**:3:8,9:11:18:
20:21^2:27^2:38:39/**11**:1^2:5,6f:8:13:27:29,30:36:
37,38:40^2:43/**12**:2^2:8:12:14:26:27^2:37:39/**13**:1:
10:22:27:28:34/**14**:1:25/**15**:19/**16**:17^2:21/**17**:11:
12:14:16f:24^2:26^2:27:28:30/**18**:13:16,17^2:20:29:
30^2:31:35/**19**:1:8:9,10:14:16^2:17:29:30:32:33:
36,37^2:41/**20**:19:37,38^2:46/**21**:1:4:8:13:24:31/
22:10^2:13:21:24:37:39:44:47:60/**23**:3:14f:18:24:
25:26:31:55:56/**24**:14:24:29:30:31:32:35^2:36:39:
40:43:49/**Jn1**:6,7:17:23:35:47/**3**:5f:8:12:14/**4**:
5,6:8:21-24/**5**:12:14:16:18:21:23:30:41,42/**6**:1:
17:18,19:30,31:36:45:58/**7**:21,22,23:35/**8**:3,17:
20:30,31:54:55^2/**9**:1:8:14:29/**10**:15:22,23:
34,35,36/**11**:51:56/**12**:11:38:39:46/**13**:4f:9:15:
27^2:31^2:33:34^2/**14**:18:26^2/**15**:9:10:12^2:24/**16**:21
/**17**:5:11:12:14:18:21^2:22:23^2/**18**:6:15:25:34^2:34
f/**19**:17:22:40/**20**:11:20:21:26/**21**:18/**Act1**:6:10:
11:15:17:21,22:24,25/**2**:1:22:25:33/**3**:2^2:3:7,8:12
:21,22:26^2/**4**:23^2:27^2/**5**:4:5^2:12:15:35:37/**6**:1^2:15^2
/**7**:2f:5:8:10^2:17,18:21:23:28:31:42:53f:58f:59/**8**:
7:9,10,11:15^2:16:26:32^2:36:40/**9**:3:8,9:15^2:18:39^2
/**10**:2:7^2:9,10:19:25:28:29^2:30:44:46,47/**11**:15^2:
19^2:24:29^2/**12**:25^2/**13**:2:5:19,20:22:25:32,33:42:
43:47:48^2/**14**:9:17:20/**15**:7:8:9:12:31/**16**:4:14:16
:25/**17**:2:8,9^2:10:12:21^2:22:23:28:29/**18**:2,3^2:8:
14:24/**19**:5^2:25:26^2/**20**:4^2:6^2:9:16:28:37/**21**:25:
31:35:37,38:40/**22**:1:3:6:12^2:20:25/**23**:6:11:22:
31/**24**:4:5:10:14:15:18^2:24:25/**25**:20/**26**:4:10:16:
29:31/**27**:4f:18:25:27:30:33/**28**:3:8:10:17:20f/
Rom1:3:13:17:27/**2**:1:2:19/**3**:7:10:25/**4**:16:17^3/
5:9:14/**6**:5:11:19/**7**:2^2:4:9:10^2:14:18:22/**8**:3:22:
23^2:26:27:31/**9**:4:5:23,24:27f:29/**10**:8^2/**11**:5:12:
13^4:27/**12**:3:4,5:6^2:18^2/**13**:9^3:12,13:14/**14**:4:5:7:
11:14:17/**15**:3:7:13:15,16:19:28^2/**16**:1:8:22:
25,26,27^4/**1Co1**:18:22:27:28:31/**2**:13:16/**3**:1^2:8:
18:19:22/**4**:1:5:6:7^2:14:15:16/**5**:3,4^2/**6**:7:12f:13:
14:17:18/**7**:3:7:8:17:29^2:29f:34:35^2:39^2/**8**:7:13^2/
9:5^3:8:13:20:21^3:22/**10**:2^2:3,4:6:7:10:11^3:27/**11**:
1:10:17/**12**:7/**13**:11:12^3/**14**:9:25:34/**15**:3:4:8:31^2
:32:39:44:48:49:58/**16**:10:16^2:18^2/**2Co1**:13,14^2:
15,16^2:18^2:22^2/**2**:3:5,6^2:9:12^2:15^2:16/**3**:7:10:13:
14:18/**4**:2^2:5:8:10:13/**5**:4:5:16:20/**6**:1:13/**7**:1:3:
12/**8**:11:14^2:18:22/**9**:3:5:7:9:12:13^2/**10**:1:11^2:12^2
:15:17/**11**:1:2:3:5:6:16:26^2/**12**:16^2:19/**13**:1:2:4^2/
Gal1:4:14^2/**2**:4:7,8,9^2:21/**3**:1^2:5:8,9:11:13:14:16:
20/**4**:4:5:6:12^3:14:28:29/**5**:10:14:21/**6**:14:17/
Eph1:11^2:13/**2**:3:7^2:11:16:21/**3**:2,3:9:17:18,19/**4**
:1:11^3:17,18:32/**5**:1:2:10:24:25:27:28:29,30:33/**6**
:5:6,7:9:15:16:19^2:20/**Php1**:7:15:19^2:20:27:28:
30/**2**:1:3:6:8:15:17:23^2/**4**:7:8:15/**Col1**:6:21:22:
28^2/**2**:6:18:19:20^2/**3**:3^2:15:17:23/**4**:4:6^2:10^2/
1Th1:3/**2**:4:5:6^2:7^2:9:10:11:13^2:14:19/**3**:5:6^4:8^2:
12/**4**:5:6:11:12:13/**5**:3^2:4:8:11:24/**2Th1**:11^2/**2**:4:
7:9/**3**:1^2:15^2:17/**1Ti1**:3,4:7:8:10,11:12:16:18/**2**:7
/**3**:8:10^2:13:15:16/**4**:6/**5**:1^2:2^2:9f:10^2:18:22:23/**6**
:10:19/**2Ti1**:4:5^3:14:15/**2**:3^2:4:5:8:20^2/**3**:1:8:9:
11/**4**:9^2:12/**Tit1**:13^2:16/**2**:1:15/**3**:12^4/**Phm1**:6^2/
Heb1:3:4:7^3:13/**2**:14:15:16^2/**3**:2:3:7,8:14:15:17/
4:2:10:11/**5**:6:7f:10/**6**:1:11^2:15:20/**7**:7:11:
12,13,14:27/**8**:5:6:13/**9**:7:8^2:11:18:24:25:27:28/
10:5^2:6:7:12:25:29/**11**:9:19^2:21:22:24,25:27:28^2:
29:30:33/**12**:3:8:15:16^2:18:24/**13**:3:7:9:11/**Jas1**:
6^2:7,8:12:18:20:21:24^2/**2**:8^2:10^2:23:24^2:26/**4**:6:
14^2/**5**:3:7:17^2/**1Pe1**:7:10:15:18:20:24/**2**:2,3f:2,3:
6:13:16/**3**:6:7^2:15/**4**:6:11/**2Pe1**:3:13,14^2/**2**:1:10:
13:17^4:18:19/**3**:3^4:10^2:15,16/**1Jn1**:4:7/**2**:6:8^2:21^2
:27/**3**:2^2:6:7/**4**:11^2:13:17:19/**5**:6,7,8^2/**2Jn1**:1:4:7

(AS Con't)
/3Jn:2:9/Jud:4:13^2:23^3/Rev:5f:14:17,18/2:1f:4:5:6:14:24,25^2:27/3:1:3:10f:12:21/4:1:3:7/5:8:9/6:1:12:14/7:1^2:4-8/8:8,9:13/9:1f:2:19/10:10/11:2f:3f:6^2:8,9:12/12:4^3/13^2:8f:13/14:4^2:7:20^2/16:13:15^2/17:11/18:5^2:6^2:9:18^2:21/19:10^2:13f/20:8/21:2:6:16^3/22:1:2f:9

ASK 5046

^{4}Gen23:8/24:14:41:57/26:28/31:39/32:29/40:14/44:4:5/50/Ex3:13:22/6:27/8:29/11:2/12:26/13:14/18:15,16/Lev25:20/Num9:8/22:16,17/Deu12:30/29:24/32:7:37/Jos4:6:21/9:6:11:14,15/15:18,19/Ju1:14/9:2/13:6:18/18:5/20:18/1Sa1:19,20f/2:20/8:9/9:9,10,11^2/10:14/14:36/19:3/22/23:9/25:8^2:39/27:10/28:7,8:15:16/2Sa2:7/13:5/14:2,3:12:29:32/17:5/19:8,9,10/20:18/21:3/1Ki1:13/2:14:16:17:18:19/3:5:13/5:6/12:27/14:3:5/22:7/2Ki1:2:3^2:16^2/4:13:26/8:8,9^2/22:12,13/1Ch10:14/2Ch1:7/7:21/18:6,7/34:26/Ez8:17:22/Neh1:11/Est2:11/5:14/6:4/Job9:12/12:7,8,9^2/21:29/40:7/42:3/Ps2:8/73:11/86:5/122:8/Pro29:26/Sol6:10/Is7:11^2/8:19/14:16/17:8/21:12/22:9,10,11/30:1/43:22/44:20/45:19/Jer5:19/6:16/8:19/10:21/13:22/14:11/15:5/16:10/21:1/23:35:37:38,39/32:6,7/33:3/36:7:14,15/37:3:7/38:14/42:4/50:5/Eze14:1:3:4:6,7/17:12,13/18:19/20:1:3:31/21:7/36:37,38/38:13/Dan2:10/9:18/Hos7:14/9^2/Amo5:18/6:10:12/Mic:6/Hag2:2:11/Zec8:20,21:22/10:1:2/Mal2:17/Mt5:42/6:7,8:10/7:7^2:11/9:38/10:12/11:2/12:39,40/18:1:19/21:22:25/22:16:34,35:46/26:53/27:20/Mk5:31/6:22,23:24/9:32/12:34/Lk7:3:19/9:45:61/11:7:13:19/20:3:5:40/Jn1:19/4:9:10/9:21/11:22/12/13:24/14:12,13:14:15,16/15:7:16/16:19:23^3:24:26f:26:30f/18:21/21:12:20/Act9:11/10:5,6/23:15^2:20/24/Rom10:12:14/11:1/12/13:14/1Co6:1/9:11/10:16:25:27:29/14:1:12:35^2/15/2Co11:8,9/12:2,3:13/Gal3:2:5/Eph:20/6:18:19/Php4:3/2Th3:1:9/1Ti4:5/Phm1:8,9^2:21/Jas:5^2:6:7,8/4:2:3/1Jn3:22/4:2/5:14:16/Rev2:24,25

ASKED 277

Gen3:1:11:13/4:6:9/12:11,12,13/17:20/18:9:17/19:12/22:7/24:5:17:23:39:47:58:65/25:22/26:7:16:27/29:4:7/30:31,32/32:17:27:29/33:5:8/37:10:15:32/38:16:17:20:21/40:7/42:14:22/43:7^2:27:29/44:19/47:3:8/48/Ex2:7:18/3:3,4:13/4:2:11/8:30:31,32/10:7:11/12:35/14:5/16:15:22:28,29/18:7/33:17:18/Num22:9:28:30:37/Jos14:6/15:18,19/17:14/18:3/24:9/Ju1:3:14/5:25/6:40/8:5:8:18/9:8:9:11/10:18/11:17:19/12:5/13:11:12:17/14:3:12:18/15:10/17:9/18:3:8:15,16/19:17/20:3:18:22,23,24:27,28/21:16/Ru1:19/2:7:10,11/3:15-18/4:2/1Sa1:19,20^2:26:27/3:4,5:6:8/4:6:14/6:2:4,5/9:9,10,11:18/10:14:15:22/11:1:5/12:1:13/13:12/14:37/15:16/16:2:4/17:26:30:55/20:6:10:27:28,29/21:1:8:11/23:2:4/25:10/26:5,6,7/28:5,6:15/30:8:13:15/2Sa1:3:8/2:1/5:19:23/6:9/7:7/9:2:3:4:7/11:10/12:19/13:6:20:26/14:5,6:13:18/16:2:3:17:20/17:6:20/19:21:24,25/20:17/21:3:4/24:13:21/1Ki1:11:16:24/2:13:14:16:20:22/3:10:11^2:12/5:8/7:13/9/10/11:21:22/12:6:9:20/13:12:14/17:10/18:7:21/20:9:14^2:32/21:5:6/22:4:6:7:15:22/2Ki1:4,5/2:3:5:10/3:11/4:2:14:23/5:21:25:26/6:6/7:3/8:6:12:13:14/9:5:11/10:13/12:7/20:11:14:15/23:17/1Ch13:12/14:10:14/2Ch1:11:13^2:12/9/10:6:8,9^2/18:2:3,4,5:6,7:14:19,20/19:2/24:6/25:16/28/31:9/32:4/Ez5:4:9/7:6/Neh1:2/2:1:4/13:17/Est1:13-13-15/5:3/6/7:2/Job1:7:8/2:2:3/6:22:23/31:30/Ps21:4/78:29/105:40/Is8:2/38:22/39:4/40:6/41:28/52:3/Jer1:13/37:17:18/38:27/40:15/Eze8:15:17/12:9/Dan1:8:8f/2:18/3:14/5:13/7:16:19:20/12:6/Hos13:10/Amo8:2/Jon1:8/Hag2:13/Zec1:9:19:21/2:2/4:4:5:11:13/5:2:6:10/6:4/Mt2:4/8:27/9:4:14:15:28/12:10/13:28:36/14:8:19/15:15:16:34/16:13:15/17:10:19:24:25/18:21:32/19:3:7:18:25/20:6:20:21:22:24/21:10:15:20:42/22:12:20:23:41:43/24:3/26:15:17:22:25:55/27:11:17:21:22:58/Mk1:27/2:18/3:3:4:23/4:10:21:30:40/5:9:30:39/6:37:38/7:5:17:18/8:5:16:23:27:29/9:12,13:16:21:23:28:33/10:2:3:5:17:18:26:36:41:51/12:16:28:35/13:3,4/14:12:19:22:48:60:61/15:2:3,4:9:12:42,43:44/Lk1:34:62:66/2:49/3:12:14/4:22:36/5:3:34/7:20,21,22:24:31:36/8:9:16:25:30:45/9:18:20/10:29/11:16:37,38/12:41/13:2:18:23/14:5:18/15:26/16:5,6,7/17:17:20:37/18:18:19:36:41/19:33/20:13:41/22:9:31:35:52:63,64/23:3:6:9:50,51,52/24:5:19:30:38:41/Jn1:21:24,25:38:50/3:9/4:7:27:33:48:52/5:6/6:2-5:52:67/7:15:35:51/8:19:22/9:2:8:10:12:15:19:26:40/10:24/11:34:40:47:56/12:34/13:12:25:37/16:5f:17,18:31/18:4,5:7:17:25:26:29:33:34/19:9:15:31:38/20:13:15/21:17^2:21/Act1:6/2:12/3:3/4:16/5:8/7:1:27:46/8:30:34/9:5:21:40/10:4:46,47/12:20/13:25:28:42/16:3:15/18:20/19:2:3/21:33:37,38/22:5:8:26:27/23:18:19:34/25:9:15:20/26:15/28:20/1Co7:1/9:15/16:20/2Co9:5/11:8,9/Col2:2/1Th:6/1Ti3:10/Tit1:5/Rev7:13/10:9/17:7

ASKING 601

Gen20:17/Jos11:20/14:12/Ju11:17/20:12/1Sa10:2/12:17:19/16/17:25:29/20:19/2Sa21:12,13,14/1Ki9:8/15:22/2Ki1:6/17:4/1Ch16:4/21:3/Neh6:2/Job35:9,10/Ps:13/Is6:8/8:6/Eze16:15/29:16/Dan2:14/6:11:13/Hos4:12/7:14/Zep3:10/Mt2:1:7/12:38/16:1:4/20:22/Mk1:36,37/9:11/10:38/15:8/Lk10:25/11:9:29,30/Jn7:11/14:9/16:5f:19/17:15/18:19:21:34f:39/Act20:17/21:25/2Co1:17/Eph:16,17/Col:9^2:10/4:12/1Th3:10/1Pe:21

ASKS 64

Gen46:33/Ex10:3/19:8/22:10/Deu6:20/1Sa20:6/2Sa11:19,20,21/2Ch32:10/Job9:3/Ps4:2/21/Pro12:26/Sol8:8/Is40:25/50:1/52:5/66:9/Jer5:22:29/7:19/9:9/23:29:33/44:7/Eze17:9/18:23/21:13/Dan6:7/Amo2:11/Hag1:2/Zec13:6/Mal1:13^2/Mt7:8:9:10/21:3/Mk11:3/Lk6:30/11:10:11^2:12/17:4/19:31/Act2:21/7:42:48,49/1Co10:27/2Co8:23/Php4:13/1Pe3:15

AT 52

Gen1:2:21,22/2:1:5:6:9/3:2,3:15:24/4:3/5:3,4,5:6,7,8,9,10,11:12,13,14:15,16,17:18,19,20:25,26,27:28-31/6:1:9,10/8:14/9:29/11:1:2f:24,25:31:32/12:4:6^2:10/13:12/14:5,6^2:17/15:14:15:18f/16:16/17:17:21:24-27/18:1/19:3:9:14:15/20:2:11,12/21:1:4,5/22:9:11/23:9:17,18^3/24:15,16:22:52:55/25:7,8:17:18:21:27/26:22^3:34/28:2:11:13/29:4:22:25/31:1:9:10:13:17-20:23:25:36,37:54/32:11:22,23,24:25/33:2:5:14^2:15:18/35:6:7^2:9:13,14:26:27^2:28,29/36:31-39f/37:13,14:29:33/38:3,4,5:11:13:14:21/39:5:7^2:11/41:4:14:53/42:1:25:35/43:11:19:25:29:32^2/44:2:3/46:3,4/47:28/48:3:8:12,13^2/49:23/50:4:10:23:26/Ex2:1^2/3:6:20/5:21:23/7:7/8:9/9:28/10/11:8/12:15:23:23f:29:47/13:4,5:17,18:20:21/14:13/15:8:23:25/17:1:5,6:8:9:11:15,16/18:4,5,6:22/19:2,3:13:17/20:18/21:3:7/22:14:26:27/23:15^2:16:17:30/24:1:2:4:15:17/25:13,14:18:19:26,27/26:4,5:13:23:24/27:4:7/28:22,23,24:27/29:3,4:11:12:32:42/32:6:19:25:26/33:9/34:18:28/36:4-4-7:28:29^2/37:3:5:7:23,24/38:1:2:7:8:14,15:23^2:29/39:4,5:15-18:19:23:32:33-40/40:5:8:22:28:33^2:38/Lev1:5:15,16,17/2:12/3:2:7,8:13/4:7^2:18^2:24:25:30:34/5:9^2/6:25/7:2/8:9:15,16:31:35/9:9/12:7/13:5:20:51/14:11:13^2:23:39/15:14:25:29/16:7/17:3,4:5:6:8,9/19:6:21/22:24/23:5:36:39/25:14,15,16:24:27:28:31:32:37:41:54/26:32:34,35:40,41^2:43/27:16:20/Num1:1^2/2/3:3:7,8,9:14,15:25-30:39/4:20/6:10:13:18:21^2/8:23,24^2/9:6,7^2:10:11:13^2:16:18:23/10:3:5,6,7:10^2:14:29:33/11:1/12:5:7,8:12/13:3-15:16:20:22:24:26:30/15:3,4:17,18/16:18:27:34:38:43,44:50/17:5/18:11:13/19:14/20:1:2:3:10:14:16:23:24/21:8:9:23:33:34/22:11^2:24:26:36^2/23:13:14:25/24:1:20:21,22/25:1:6/26:64,65f^2/27:14/28:6/29:39/30:3:16/32/33:5,6:7:8:15-37:38,39:42:43:44:49/34:3:7,8,9:10,11:12/35:20/36:4/Deu1:1f:1^3:6:9:16:18:19,20,21:33:46/2:2:16,17:18:22:29^2:32/3:1^2:6:11:12^2:18:23,24,25/4:3:10:11:14:15:48/5:2,3:4:22:23/6:7^2:16/7:22^2/9:5:8:9:10,11:22^3:23/10:1/11:19^2/12:4,5:17/14:23/15:1:9:12:20:22^2/16:2:6:10:11:13:15^2:16/17:6:9/18:4:6,7:16^2/19:15:17/22:21/23:9,10:11/24:5:12,13/26:2,3/27:2,3,4/28:20:56,57:63/29:1/30:2:4:14/31:10,11^3:15/32:21:25:51/33:2^2:8^2:10/34:11,12/Jos2:1^3:5/3:1:8:13,14:15,16^2/4:2,3:9:15,16:19:23/5:10/6:12,13,14:15/7:5/8:9:11,12,13:14:30:33^2/9:6^2:17:27/10:1:6:10:16:21:27:30:32:34,35:39:43/11:5:7:10:17/12:4/13:2-7:32/14:3,4:6:7/15:1^2:2,3,4,5:7:10,11/16:1:5,6^2:7/18:1:9:10^2:12:14:19/19:14:17-23:29:33^3:34:51^2/20:6/22:9:12:17,18:28/24:1:6:25:29:30:33/Ju1:4,5,6:17:36/2:1:7-9^2/3:12:17,18,19:20:28:30/4:4:5:10:12/5:5:11:15:16:17:27/6:6,7:11:27/7:5,6:17:24:25^2/8:2,3^2:11:18:26:28/9:5:6:7:25:26:27:35:36:41^2:46/10:6:17^2/11:11:16:18^2:20:29/12:1:4:6:7:9,10:11,12/13:6/14:4:6:7:8:16:17:20/15:11:14/16:2:16,17:25,26:28:30/17:7,8/18:1:2:12:21:23:27:31/19:1:3:7:22^2:25:26/20:1:3:4:22,23,24/21:1:2:5^2:10,11,12,13/Ru1:22/2:7:14/3:8:14^2/4:16,17/1Sa1:3^2:7:9^2:2?/2:22/3:21,4:1/4:1^3:12/5:1:9/6:18:21/7:3:6:7:13:16:17/9:8:22:26,27/10:2:3^2:6:10:17:26/11:1,12:17/13:3,4^2:5:7^2:11:16:19:23/14:2^2:18/15:4:27:30:33/16:4:6:7:10,11/17:2:19:20:41,42:43^2/18:4:11,12/19:5:9,10^2:18:19:22^2/20:12^2:18:19:20:24,25:30:33^2:42/21:7:11/22:6:9,10,11,12^2/23:1:7:16:18:21:23/24:3:9,10/25:1:2^2:8^2:14:40/26:1:3,4:13:16/27:2,3/28:4^2:7,8^2:15:21/29:1^2:2,/30:1:3:26/31:13/2Sa2:10,11:13:24:25:29:32/3:2?:26:27^2:30:32/4:1:4^2:5:8/5:1:3:9:14,15,16:20:21/6:6:8/7:1/8:3:13/9:4:7:13/10:4:5:15,16/11:1:8:9:13:15:19,20,21:22/12:4/13:15:21-24:28:34/14:22:33/15:7,8:14:16:17,18:28:32/16:3:6:7,8^2:13:15/17:13:16^2:17:24:27/18:4:24^2/19:8,9,10:15:28/20:3:4:8,9,10:12:14:18:20:22/21:9:10^2:12,13,14^3:15:18:19^2:20,21/23:11,12:13^2:14/24:5:16/1Ki1:5:6:9:13:39/2:8:19:27:46/3:2:4:21/4:20/5:14/6:7^2:14:16:23-28/7:16-22^2:27-30:34:40:41-46^2/8:1:2:9^3:21:60/9:2,3:10:11,12:14:20,21/10:22:26:28:29/11:16,17,18/12:1:2,3,4:27:32,33/13:2:4:5:16,17:19:20:21,22/14:2:4:6/15:13/16:1:9/17:3:10/18:5:7:36^2/19:13:19/20:13:26/21:18/22:4:6f:20:34:47:48/2Ki1:2^2/2:5:18/3:1f:2:13:20:24/4:2:15,16:27:37/5:9:11:12:15:24/6:4:8:13:32/7:8:9:17:20/8:5:11:22:28/9:10:14:21:27:30:31:32^2/10:6^2:7:8:12:17:29:32,33/11:6,7,8^2:13,14:18/12:9:20/13:6:16,17/14:2:11:21/15:1^2:8:10:13:25:32,33/16:1:4^2:6:10f/17:1:4:10/18:1^2:11:14:22/19:8:18:21:24/20:5:12:19/21:1:18:19,20/22:1:3,4:9,10/23:1:3:8:9:15:16:17^2:19:29^2:33/24:3,4:8,9:13/25:8:17:20:23:29/1Ch1:51-54/2:21:55/4:9:21-22:28/5:17/6:4-15:32/7:2:4:9:11:20,21/8:6,7:28:29/9:21:25:33,34^2/10:12/11:1:13:16:20/12:1:21:23/13:9:11/14/15:24/16:2:7:37:43/18:3/19:4:5:6f:7:9/20:4:6,7/21:6:15:18:19,20:22/22:1:14/23:3:4,5:13:24:28:31/24:3/26:12:13:31,32/28:21/29:2:8:12:28/2Ch1:14:16:17?/2:3:4/3:1:8^2:15:17/4:11:17,18/5:3:9:10:11,12:13,14/6:34/7:6:8^2/8:3:6:13/9:4:19/10:2,3^2/11:1/12:4:13/13:4:9/14:14/15:16/16:2:10:13,14/17:13/18:3,4,5:9:33^2/19:4/20:2:5:16:22:24:35:37/21:8:19^2/22:5^2/23:2,3^2:4:5,6:12:13,14:15,16,17:19/24:5:15/25:21/26:9^2:16/27:1/28:4/29:4,5:25,26/30:1:2,3^2:13:16:21:24/31:1:14,15:16/32:12:21:22:23:33/33:12:13:24/34:8:9:14^2/35:2:20:21f:22/36:10:16/Ez1:5:7/2:59/3:8/5:1:16/6:2:3:13/7:7,8,9:19/8:2-14:15:17^2:21:29:31^2:32^2/10:7,8:14/Neh1:1^2/2:11,12:14,15:18/3:31/4:1^2:6:23/5:8^2:15:16:17/6:7/7:3:7:61:66/8:1:16/9:12:37/10:34^2/11:1:2:10-14:22,23:31-35/12:24:25:37:39/13:1:6:24:31/Est1:1:9/2:5:8:21^3/4:3:14/5:9/6:1:10/7:3/8:14/9:13:14:15:18:24,25:27/10:3/Job1:12,13/3:1:8:11:12:13^2:17:18:19:22/4:6/5:14:16:22:23/6:5,6,7^2:10:28/8:16/10:18/12:4/13:16/14:8,9/16:4:9:20/19:25/20:21:22/21:5:18:19:30-32/22:5:21/24:14,15:16/26:11:12/27:22:23/29:8/30:14:17/31:26:29/33:32/34:20:32/35:14,15/36:18^3:32/37:1:7:21:22/39:7:25^2:27/40:15/41:29^2/42:12^2:17/Ps1:1/4:7^2/9:13:14:20/11:2/14:1/18:15^2:39/21:12/22:13/25:6,7/29:10/31:18/33:9/34:5:14/35:19:25:26/36:4/37:12,13/38:11/39:2,3/42:7f/43:2/44:12^2:13/48:5/51:9/54:1/55:20/58:8:11/59:1^2:6:8^2:14,15/60:1^2/61:2/62:3,4/63:5:6/64:3:4:8:9/67:1/68:2:11,12,13:15,16/69:26:32/71:7/73:8:12/74:15:18/78:14:34:60/80:16/81:3:7/83:5:9:10/91:6f:7/95:8/99:9/102:8/104:7,8:14:22:32^2/105:22:25:39/106:7:12:21,22:28:32/107:27/114:7/118:15,16/119:55:62:107/121:5f/127:2/128:3/132:7f/136:9/141:6,7f/144:3/Pro1:22/3:34/7:8,9:11,12:14f/8:1^3:30:34/9:7,8:14^2/10:10/13:12/14:9f/15:23/16:7/17:5:24/20:4/21:2/23:23:34/31:1:6,7/Ecc2:11/5:18/6:3:11/7:2^2/9:5:11^2/12:4:5:6^2/Sol1:7/2:9/5:2/7:13/8:1:11/Is2:4:20:21/3:5/4:1:2,3,4f:5/5:2:11:12:26/7:3:18:23/8:21/10:20:22:26:28,29^4:32^2/11:6:11:13/13:8/14:4^2:7^2:8:16/16:1:2:8:12/17:7/19:3:18:19/21:4:8,9^3/22:1/25:7:9/28:5:10:19:21/29/30:19:23/32:3:6:15:18/33:3:20/34:4:14/36:7:11f/37:4:7^2:8,9:16,17:19:22^2:23/38:12/39:1f:8/40:15/41:2:7:24/44:12:20:22/45:10/47:8:14/48:10/49:7:8,9/51:1:22/52:6/53:2/54:3/55/59:10:19/60:16/65:4:20/66:2:5:11:12:20:24/Jer1:3:15/2:12:24:31/3:6:9:18/4:11,12:22^2:24:29/5:7^2:22/6:1:4:10:15:25/7:18f/8:7:11:16/10:10:18/11:4/12:8/13:1/14:19/15:7:8:10:17,18/16:20:21/17:11:15:19^2/18:3:16/19:8/20:2:17/22:20^2:22/23:5,6:32/25:11/26:6:9:

(AT Con't)
18:20/27:1/28:11/30:21/31:1:14:34:38,39^3/32:2/33:15/34:7/36:1f:8:9:22:24,25/37:5/38:6:14/39:3:5/40:8:10:12/41:5:9f:12/42:20/43:7:8:9/46:2:7:27/47:3:6/48:13^2:27/49:8f:17:27/50:13:14:43:46/51:17^2:41/52:3:17:18:26/Lam1:15:19:20/2:1:16/3:12:14:29:57/4:5:11:15:17:22/5:4/Eze1:10:15/2:5/3:16:17/4:10^2:17/5:2^2:11:13/6:4-7:9:12/8:16:17/9:2:6/10:3:22/12:4:12/13:2,3:7:10:15/16:42/17:3,4/18:13:13f:17:17f/20:9,10:16:21:40:43/21:15:19,20:21/22:28/23:24/24:17/25:3:6/26:16:18/27:28:29:33/28:9:10:19:24/29:13:18f^2:20:20f^2:21/30:9^2:13/31:5:16/32:23/33:30/34:8:27/35:15^2/36:2:30:37,38/37:13/38:10:20/39:7:14:20/40:7-12:23^2/41:3^2:7:14:21/42:12/43:3:19:21/44:24/45:5:12^2:17:19/46:2:6:8:11:19,20^2/47:3:18:19/48:1:27,28/Dan1:13:15/2:49/3:19/4:8:19:34:34f/5:7f:19:21:23:29:31/6:16/7:8/8:2:2f:6:8:9:15:23f/9:12:16:21:24:25f^2/10:14/11:4:13f:27:29:35:40/12:1:13f/Hos1:9:18:23/4:4^2:15^2/5:1:2:6/6:2/7:16/8:10/9:8:11:15/10:5:6:8:14/11:10/12:4:9/Joe2:5:13/3:1:17/Amo1:2/2:8/3:14/4:4/5:22/6:1:2:6/8:8:9^2/9:3^2:11/Ob1:5^2:13:14/Jon:6/3:4,5:7/4:10/Mic1:8:9/2:1^2/3:7/5:3:10/6:5^2:14/7:3:16^2/Nah1:4/Hab:5:8:10/2:2:6:19/3:6:8,9/Zep1:10/2/3:3:9:15:20/Hag1:5:9/Zec:4:5,6:15/2:11,12/3:1/4:2/6:7:10,11/7:2:5/8:16:23/11:13/12:7:11/13:1:6/14:7:11:14/Mal1:9:13/2:4/3:5/Mt1:11/2:1:7/3:2f/4:17f:20:22/5:20:28/6:26:28:31,32:34/7:22:28/8:14:29/9:9:10:23:24/10:7f:15:19^2/11:14:24/12:18:41/13:34,35:40:49/14:3:6:8:30:34/16:2,3:9:12:21/17:6:12:14/18:13/19:4:26/20:4:5:6:9:27/21:34/22:44/23:6^2/24:17f:23:26:30:33:34:37,38/25:27:33^2:34/26:3^2:18:34:47:56:64:65,66/27:9:39:54:62:64:66f/28:10/Mk1:15:18:21:22:26/2:8:14:19/3:5:6:31,32:34/4:15:17:29:38/5:1:23:30:33^2:40/6:2,3:10:50:53:54:56/7:6,7:25/8:17:18:22:33^2/9:14:18:20:33/10:21:27:32:37^2:48/11:11/12:1:2:12:17:36:38:39^2/13:1:29:35,36,37^2/14:3:4,5:14:47:62:63,64:65:66,67^2/15:6:7:11:29,30^3:31:32/16:1:12:19/Lk1:14:20:23:41/2:21:22:24:33:49/3:1/4:20:32:33:39:41:42/5:2:14:27/6:10:11:13/7:2:6,7,8:11:16:38:49/8:26:35:41:51:55/9:4:31:39:58:61:61f/10:32/11:5,6f:5,6:13:31^2:32/12:24:27:29:38^3:45/13:1:3:5:17/14:5:9:10:14:15/15:17/16:14:20:26/17:12:14:35,36/18:13:40/19:3:5:23/20:17:26:42,43:44:46/22:14^2:21:27:30:50:54:56:58:61^2:65:66/23:2:7:8:17,f:25:32,33:35:39:53/24:22,23:31:39^2:45/Jn1:28:33:36:42/2:1:11:23/3:7:23,24^2:29/4:8:20:25:40,41^2:43,44:45:46,47^2:52/5:7/6:2-5f:21f:39:40:44:54:66/7:11:31/8:2:7:59/10:22,23^2:32/11:10:17:20:29:30:31:32:45/12:2:16:48/13:22:23f^2:23:28:30/14:17:22/16:23:29/18:3:16:39/19:6:11:13^2:17:31:39:42/20:7:12:24/21:4:7:17:20:23/Act1:11:12:14/2:42^2:46/3:4:5:10:12/4:17:28/5:12:15:19:21^2:22:33:37/6:15/7:8:20:21:29:55:56:58:59/8:25:27:40/9:20:38/10:4:17:30:33/11:11:12:15:22:26/12:13:18:22/13:1:9:12:13:37:43/14:1:8:13:14:28/15:1:2:7:23:30:34,35:38/16:6:11:15:19/17:8,9:14:19:22/18:4:6:18:18f:19:21:22^2:22f/19:3:9:18,19^2:26:28:35:38:39/20:5:6:15^2:16:17^2:26/21:3:5:8:13:16:17:21:25/22:3/23:1:10:23,24:35/24:11/25:3:4:18:23/26:4/27:3:5:7,8:9f:14,15:20:29/28:11:13:15^2:30f/Rom1:10:20/2:16/3:9:27/4:1:19^2/5:6/7:5:15:23,24,25/8:9:20,21:34:36/11:1:27/12:18/14:2/15:23/16:10:11/1Co1:11:28/2:15/3:3:13/4:5:9^3:10/6:7^2/7:19:26:27/8:10/9:4:13/10:16:19:21^4:25/11:22:34/12:8/13:2:12/14:27:29,30:35/15:6:9:34:44:54/16:2:8:10:12:16/2Co3:2:7:10/4:18/5:4:8:12/6:2:10/7:13/8:11:13:14/10:7/11:6:13:19,20:32/12:11:19/13:5:8/Gal1:6:16:19/3:10/4:20/Eph1:1:8:20/2:2:15:16^2/3:13:17:18,19:20/4:3:15,16:19/6:16/Php1:9:13:23/2:1:10:13:30/4:7:18/Col1:15:26,27:29/2:1:2:15/3:23/4:2:15:16/1Th1:1/2:2:16/5:10:20/2Th1:6/2:7f/3:17/1Ti1:13^2/2:6/5:4:9:17/6:1:11/2Ti1:18^2/3:2:3:12:17/4:2:13:19:20^2/Tit3:12/Heb2:13^2/5:7f^3:7/8:1/9:26/10:12:33/11:3:36/12:8:18:21/Jas1:23/2:2:7:17/5:10/1Pe1:2:12/2:16/3:9:18/4:4/5:13f/2Pe1:9/2:2:5:7,8:10:12:21/3:3:7:14/1Jn1:5/2:19:26/3:5:8:15/4:17/5:3:6,7,8^2:17f/Jud1:8^2:9:10:12^2/Rev:13f:17,18/2:1:4:13/3:2:3:9:20/4:6/7:1:17f/8:3/9:14/10:9/11:8,9/12:10/13:3/14:13/15:1/17:6:8:8f/18:15:20/19:10/21:2

2791

BE

Gen1:3:6f:9,10:14,15:20:26/2:16,17:18/3:5^2:14:15:16/4:7:12:24^2/6:1:3/7:1:3/8:22/9:2,3:5,6:14:24,25f:24,25:26,27:26,27f^2:26,27/11:6/12:2:2f:3:19/13:16/14:19,20^2/15:1:4:5:8:13:16/16:2,3^2:9-12^3/17:2,3,4:5:6:7,8^3:9,10:11^2:12:13^2:14:16:17:20:21/18:10f:18:25^3:30:32/19:2:15:18,19,20:31/20:11,12/21:12^2:17:23/22:18/23:5,6:8/24:6:7:14:44^2:49^2:51/25:23^2:34f/26:3:4:9:10/27:11,12:13:21:27,28,29^2:39,40^2:41:45/28:14:15/29:2:7:24:29/30:3:4:6f:9:26:34/31:3:8:29^2/32:5:20/33:12:15/34:8:11:14:15:17:22:23:30/35:10:11^2/37:8:11:26,27/38:8:9^2:14:17:23:29/39:9/40:22/41:27:29:30^2:31^2:36:38:40/42:33:34:37/43:8:11:14:25:29/44:9:10:16:17:18:31/45:2:5:6:10:28/46:3,4/47:5,6:19^2:24:25/48:6:16:21/49:4:6:7:13:17:26/50:19:21/Ex2:6:12/3:14f^2:15f:15/4:14:16^2:17:19:25,26/5:7,8:17:18/6:1:7:13/7:1:2:15:18/8:3,4^2:5:9:10:11:21^2:22^2/9:4/10:4,5:6:14:26/11:1:3:6/12:2:5:6:7:9:11:13:15:16^2:18:19^2:22:32:48^2/13:6,7^2:13^2/14:12^2:13:14f/16:11,12:25:26:28,29:32/17:14:15,16/18:19,20:21:22^3:23^2/19:5:6:13/20:17:20^2:22:24/21:2:3^2:6:7:8:12:15:16:17:18:19:20:21:22:23:28^2:29^2:32^2:36^2/22:1^2:3^3:8:11:13:18:19:20:20f:24:27:29/23:2,3:7:9:13:15:18^2:19:22:26:33/24:10/25:1:9:15^2:19:20:26,27:31:34,35^2:36:38:40/26:4,5:7,8:12:15,16:20:22:24:25:35/27:3:8:9,10^2:11:12:13:14,15:16:17:18:19/28:1:5,6:8:10:13,14:15:16:17:18:19:20:21:29:30,31^3:33,34:37,38^4:42:43^2/29:2:9:15,16:21:29:34:37^2:42:43:45/30:1:2^2:5:10:11,12:13:22,23f:29f:31:32^2:33:35:38/31:6:14,15/32:5:30:33/33:3:19f^2/34:2:3:7:12^2:18:20^3:25/35:2:5-9:10-19:27:32:35/37:15,16/38:3:27f/39:1:6,7f:41^2/40:15^2/Lev1:2,3:4:9^2:9f:10:13:15,16,17:15,16,17f/2:2:3:4^2:5:7:9:13/3:1^2:6/4:7:11,12:18:19:20:25:26^2:31^2:32:34:35^2/5:6:7:9:10:12:13:16:17,18^2:19/6:6^2:7:9:12:13:15:16:17:18:19,20:21^2:22,23^3:25:27:28^2:30^2/7:2^2:4:6:7:8:9:12:13:14^2:15^2:16:17,18^4:19^3:20:21:24:25:26,27:30:32,33:34:35:38/8:32:33/10:3:10:14:15/11:2,3:4-7:20:21,22:24:27:28:31:32^3:35:37:39:40:41,42^2:44:45^2:47^2/12:2:3:5:7:8^2/13:1^2:3^2:4:6:7:11:14,15:16,17:20:21:25:26:29,30:31^2:32:34^2:42:49^2:52:54:55:55f^2:58/14:4:6:9:13:17:18:20:21:29:31:35:36^2:37:40:42:45:46:51,52/15:10:11:12^2:16:17:19^2:20:21,22,23:24:26:27^2/16:8:9:10^3:17:27:32^2:34/17:3,4:6:7:8,9^2:14:15^2/18:18:19:29,30^2/19:1:5:6:7:8:15^2:17:20^2:21:22:24^2:34:35,36/20:1:7:9:10:12:14:15:16f:17:18:21:26^2:27/21:6^2:9:11:14,15^2:22/22:1:3:6:7:9:15:19^2:20^2:21:22:23:24:26,27:32,33/23:4:5:6:9,10,11:13^2:17:20:21^2:23,24:29:32:33,34:35:36:37:38/24:3,4:5-5-8^3:9:17:19:20/25:6,7^2:10^3:11:12:13:14,15,16^3:24^2:28:32:33^2:38:42:46^2:48:50:54/26:4,5^2:12^2:13:16:20:22:25:26^2:33:36:38:45/27:8:9^2:10:11,12:13:14,15:18:19:20:21:25:25f^2:27:28:29:29f^2:33^3/Num1:51:53/2:1/3:10:31-35:38:41:43:45/4:3:10^2:12:13^2:14^3:16^2:24:28/5:8^2:19:21,22^2:27:28:31/6:9:18^2:24,25,26/8:13:14:19^2/9:2,3:10:13/10:1:5,6,7:5,6,7f:8:10:31/11:15:22/12:12:14^2/13:20/14:3:9:20,21:42/15:3,4^2:7:10:15,16:15,16f:19,20,21^2:23,24^2:25:26:28:30:31:31f^2:40/16:6,7f:8,9:16:17^2:22:26^2:38:40/17:1/18:2,3:10:14,15:16^2:17^4:18:21:22:23:25,26:28,29^2:30:32/19:7:8:9:10:11:12^2:13:14:16:17:19:20:21:22/20:13:17/22:20/23:7-10:18-24^3/24:3-9^2:21,22:23,24/25:12,13/26:54/27:3,4:8:17:21/28:3:4:5:6:7:9,10:11:13:14^2:17:18^2:20,21^3:23:24^2:25:26^2:27:28,29/29:1^3:3,4:5:6:7^3:8:9,10:12^2:13:16/30:1:15/31:23^4:24:27:29:51,52/32:14:15:22:23:32/33:54^3:55/34:3:4:6:10,11:13/35:5:6:7:8:11:12^2:13,14:16^3:21:25:30:31:32:33^2:34/36:3:4:6/Deu1:16:17:19,20,21:27:29:41:42/2:4^3:20/3:1:22/4:9:20:26^3:27:40/5:1:14/6:1:3:13:18^2:19/7:2:4:6:10:14^2:16:18:21:24:25/8:11:20/10:15/11:17^2:23:25:27:29/12:15:17^2:18^2:19:20-23:24,25:26,27^3:28/13:5:9:16:17:18/14:2:3,4,5:6:7:8:9:19,20:29/15:1:9:11:17/16:2:4^2:5:6:8:10:12:13:14:15^3:20/17:5^2:6:10:11:12:13:15^2:16:17^2:19/18:1^2:3:8:9^2:10^3:11:18/19:5:6,7^3:10^2:15:17:18:19:20/20:1:3:5:19/21:21/22:9:9f:16:17,18:19f:19:21:22^2:23,24:25,26,27/23:12:14:21:23/24:5^3:8:14,15:16^2:17/25:1^3:6^2:10:12/26:19/27:15:22:23f/28:20:23^2:25^2:26^2:27:29:31^4:32:33:40^2:41:44^2:47,48^2:54:56,57:62/29:18:20:25/30:20/31:6^4:7^2:8^2:10,11:17:23^2:27/32:37:40,41/33:13:14:16:25/Jos1:3:5^2:6^2:7^2:8:9:17,18/2:19/3:2,3,4/4:7/6:10:18:19^2/7:10,11:12f:15:18/8:1:29/9:8:11:20:23:27/10:8^2:18^2:25^2:27/11:6^2/13:1:2-7/15:16/17:16,17,18/18:5,6/19:17-23:24,25,26:40/20:3:5:8:9/22:5:17,18:22,23:26,27:29^2/23:4,5:6:7:11:13:14/24:15:27/Ju1:1/2:3^2/4:2,3:18^2/5:8:24^2:30/6:16f:16:23:32f:39/7:5,6^2:11^2/8:21:22^2:23,24/9:2:10:13:14:18:28^3:38:54/10:18/11:8:30,31/13:1:5^2:6:7^2:13,14/14:7/16:10:11:13/17:10,11/18:5:19^3:25/19:1:9:20:27/20:8,9,10:32/21:17^2:18:21:22/Ru1:11:16^2:17:18/2:10,11:22/3:2:14:15-18/4:10:11:12:14/1Sa1:11^2:23/2:7^2:9:10:13,14:15:16:28:30:31:32:35/3:14:20/4:3^2/6:6:18/7:1/8:7:9:12^3:17:20/9:5:12,13/10:1:3:7:8/11:1:7:12:13/12:9:14:15:20:23:25/14:10:39:45/15:1:33/16:1:15,16/17:9^2:25:28:33:37/18:1:8:17:18:21:25/19:4:6:11/20:13^2:16:19^2:26:28,29:30:31:32/21:13:14,15/22:23/23:17^3:20:22/24:20^2/25:17:26:34/26:11:19^2:25/27:1/28:2^2:13:19^2/30:22/2Sa1:17,18:21/2:6^2:7^2:26/3:8:29^4/5:2/6:22/7:8:9:10,11^2:14^2:24:26/9:1:7^2/10:12/11:11:19,20,21:25/12:5:10:22/13:6:12:12f:13:20:25:28/14:7^2:11:14:14f:17/15:14^2:19,20:33,34/16:2:3:21f/17:2,3:8:9:10:17:21:28,29/18:3:13:20^2:28:32/19:6:7:8,9,10:35:43/20:3^2:18/21:12,13,14/22:4:47:48/23:4:6:7^2/24:3:17/1Ki1:2:13:17:21:24:27:30:37:48:52/2:2:4:7:15:19:22:26:33:36,37/3:5:13:26/5:7/8:8:15:16:52:53:56:57:59/9:5^2:8:9/10:8:9:21/11:12,13:36^2/12:7^2:10:11:16,17:27:28:32,33/13:2^2:21,22:32:33/14:5:6:11^2/15:19/16:4-7^2:10/17:1:13^2:14/18:27:31f:44/19:4:15:16:17^2/21:18:24^2/22:5/2Ki1:15/2:5/3:13:17/4:7:43^2/5:10:13:27/6:16/7:1:2:12:13:19/8:13/9:3:8:15:20:22:36/10:2,3:5:18,19:22:23:30/11:2,3:17/12:7:8/13:19/14:6:9:10/15:12/16:15^2/18:20,21:29/19:3:5,6:10:11:30/20:5:6:8:17^3:18:19/22:12,13:17:18,19/24:17/25:24^2/1Ch1:24-27f/2:34,35/4:10/11:2^2:4:5,6/12:18/13:2:5/16:25^2:31:36:37:39/17:9:10:13^2:14:19:21:24/19:13/21:3/22:5:9^2:10^2:11:13:16:19/23:4,5^2/24:5/28:6:10^2:12f:13:16:20^2/29:1:4,5^2:14/2Ch1:12/2:4:5:6^3:9^2:12/4:19/5:9/6:4:5,6:40:41/7:16^2:18:20:21:22/9:8^2:19/10:4^2:7:8,9:10:11:16:19/13:5:9/15:7/18:14:19,20:21/19:2:3:7^2:11^2/20:15^2:17:20:21/21:14:15/22:7/23:2,3^2:5,6:15,16,17/24:6^2:7,8:24/25:8:16/28:13^2:16/29:8:24:27/30:7:8:9^2/31:5,6/32:7^3/33:4,5:7^2:25/34:14/35:1/36:16:22,23/Ez2:62,63/3:13/4:3:12:13:16/5:13:15/6:1:3^4:4^2:5:6:10:11^2:12:21,22/7:6:17^2:18:24:26/8:25:29/9:9/10:7,8:13:14^3/Neh1:11/2:3:4:5,6:16/4:10:14/6:5,6:7:12,13/7:3^2/8:10:14:15/10:31:32:35:38/12:44/13:1:9:18:19^3/Est1:8:18:19^2:20/2:4:12,13,14/3:9:13:14^2/6:13/7:4^2/8:2:8:8f:13^3:17/9:1:12:13:28/Job1:21/2:9/3:2,3:4^2:6^2:7:10:13:20,21:23/4:6:10:11/5:3:21:23:24:25:26/6:8,9:11:14:15-18:27:29/7:10:11:18:21/8:22/9:2:24:27:31^2/10:18/11:12^2:16:17^2/12:14/13:5^2:9:10:13:16^2:20/14:3:11,12/15:2:14^2:15:21:22:29:31/18:5:6:7:14:16:18:20/19:27/20:6:17:18:24:26/21:20:21/22:3:23:25^2/23:7/24:24/25:4/27:15/28:3,4:13:15:17:20:23,24/30:8:24/31:7,8:10:11:22^2:28/32:7:21,22^2/33:6:7/34:19:33:36/36:11:19:33/37:19,20/39:9/41:7/Ps4:4f/6:10/7:3:5/9:2:17:18^2/10:16:18/12:1/13:2/14:1/16:4/17:15/18:2:50/19:9f:13:14/20:1:5/21:9,10/22:26/23:4:6/25:3^2:20/27:5:7:14^2/28:5/31:2:17/32:6:9/34:1f:22/35:8:25:26/37:3:4:6:7:9^2:11:15^2:16:17:26:28:29:33:34:38^2/39:4:13/40:5:16/41:4:5:10/42:4,5^2:11^2/43:5/45:16:17/46:10/48:14/49:8,9:11:13:14:14f:16/51:2:7^2:14,15/53:4:6/57:5:11/58:7f:8/60:4,5f/61:4/62:2:6:10,11/63:5:11/65:4/66:20/67:4/68:3:30f:35/69:4:6^2:23:25:28:28f:30:32:35/71:3/72:6:15^2:16^2:17^2:18:19^2/73:13/74:21/76:11/77:2:7:9/78:8:61:62/79:5:10/80:3:4:7:19/81:9f:14/83:17/84:2:10/85:5:9/86:3/87:5^2/88:10/89:6:12:19:24:28:29:37:38:52/91:5:15/92:9:14/93:5/94:3:15:16/96:4:10:11/97:1:7:12/98:2,3/101:6:8/102:18:28/104:34/105:14/106:31:48/107:42/109:6:7:8:9,10:12,13^2/110:3:7/111:10/112:2:3^2:6:9:10/113:5/118:6:24/119:6:58:78:80:116:133/120:3:4/122:7:9/124:6/125:3/126:4/128:2:3/129:5:6,7:8/132:7:18/135:21f/137:8:9f/139:7:20:21/140:6,7,8:9/141:4:5/145:6/147:11/148:6/Pro1:3:7,8,9:26:28/2:1:3,4,5:11,12,13^2:19:22f:22/3:3:7,8^2:22f:24,25,26/4:5:7:26/5:2:15:18:23/6:6:15:27:30:34:35/7:11,12:23/8:11:33:34/9:6:9/10:8:17:18^2:19/11:15:21^2:24,25:29:31/12:1:9:24/13:10:20^2:24/14:22^2/15:9,10:12:23:31,32/16:5:7:10:32/17:8f:11:11f:21:27,28/18:24/19:1:8:9^2:20:22:25:29/20:11:13:21/21:13:21:28/22:1:10:13:24,25:29/23:1:19,20,21/24:7:17:18:19,20:24:25/25:4,5:6,7:8,9,10:15/26:2:9:13:24,25,26/27:11^3:18:21:25,26,27/28:6:10:13:18^2:27/29:1:19/30:6:18,19f/31:5:30^2/Ecc1:12-15:16-18/2:1^2:16:19^2/3:2:7:12:14:15:22^2/4:5,6:9:11:12:13^2:16/5:1^2:8:18/6:3^2:4:5:10:12/7:5^2:6:9:11:15-17^3:23^2:27,28^2/8:1^2:2,3:5:12:15/9:2,3:4:7:11:16^2/10:8,9:10/11:7:8:9/12:2:3^2:4^2:5:12^2/Sol1:4:7/2:17/3:6/6:12/7:8/8:3:9f:14/Is1:4:16:17:20:26:27:31/2:2f:3:5:

(BE Con't)
11:16:17:18/**3**:4:6:7:8:14:20:24^2/**4**:1^3:2,3,4^2/**5**:3:
5:6:8:14:15^2:25/**6**:11:13/**7**:4:8:11f:14:14f:15,16:
15,16f:17:21,22^3:24/**8**:1^2:9,10:14,15:18:21:22^2/
9:1^2:3:5^2:6^2:11,12^2/**10**:3:4^2:8:17:18:19:22^2:24/
11:1:3:5:6^2:9:10^2:15/**12**:2/**13**:9:10:12:15:16^2:19:
20:21:22/**14**:1:2:14:15:16:17:20:25:29^2/**15**:1:5/
16:10:11:13,14^2/**17**:3:4:5:6^2:9:11/**18**:6/**19**:5:8:
10:15:16:18:19:20:23:24^3:25^3/**20**:5,6/**22**:13:14:
17:21:22^2:23,24:25/**23**:4:5:12:13:15,16:17:18/**24**
:2:3:6:7:22:23/**25**:2:10:12/**26**:11^2:21/**27**:2:9:10:
13^2/**28**:3:4:5:13:17:18:22/**29**:2:3:5:9:16:17^2:19:
20:21:22:24^2/**30**:3:14:15:17:19:20:22:26^2:30/**31**:
4,5:8^2/**32**:4:5^2:6:7:8^2:12:13:14:19/**33**:1:2^2:12:16^2
:19:21:23/**34**:3:7:9^2:12^2:16/**35**:2:4:7:8:9:10^2/**36**:
12:15:20/**37**:6:10:11:30/**38**:18/**39**:6^2:8/**40**:5^2:9:
13:30:31/**41**:10:12:13:15:18/**42**:2:4:4f:6f:6:13:17^2
:19:24/**43**:1:2^2:5:10:20/**44**:2^2:8:14:19:26^2:27^2:28
/**45**:1:9:14^2:16:17^2:18^2:24:25/**46**:4^2/**47**:1:3:5:8:
11/**48**:20/**49**:8,9:11:15:18^2:19^2:23:25:26/**50**:7:9
/**51**:3:7:13:14/**52**:13:14,15/**53**:11^2/**54**:3:4:5:10:
13^2:15^2/**55**:13/**56**:1:3:7:12/**58**:8:10:11:12:14/**59**
:8/**60**:7:12^2:13^2:15:17:18:19^2:20:21:22/**61**:5:6^2:9
:11/**62**:2:4^2:12^2/**63**:8:11:16/**64**:5:9/**65**:10^2:12:13^2
:15:18^2:19:20:21,22:23^4:25f:25/**66**:5^2:7,8:10:12:
14:16:20:21:22:24^2/**Jer1**:8^2:17:18^2/**2**:21:22:37/
3:4,5:7:12:16^2:17^2:19^2/**4**:2:3:4:9:14:19:27:28/**5**:3
:6:12:19:22^2/**6**:6:9^2:18,19:21:26/**7**:4^2:20:23^3:28:
31:32^3:33^2/**8**:2^2:9:13:16f/**9**:9:11:16:22:24/**10**:2,3
:5^2:15:24/**11**:4^2:5:19:21,22/**12**:14:16:17/**13**:12^2:
12f:17:19:27/**14**:6:16^3:19/**15**:8:12,13/**16**:4:14,15^2
/**17**:13:23:25^2:27/**18**:7:15:21^2:22/**19**:6:11^4:12^2/
20:5:6:11:14:15:16/**21**:1:10^2/**22**:3:4:9:19:22:28/
23:3:4^2:5,6^2:12^2:40/**24**:7^2:9/**25**:11:34:37/**26**:15:
18/**27**:8:11:16:17:18:22/**28**:9/**29**:5:10:14:18:24f:
26:28^2/**30**:8:10^2:16^4:18^2:19:20:21^2:22^2/**31**:4:8:
12^3:13:15:16f:18:32:33^2:34:37:38,39:40^2/**32**:3:4:
15^2:31:38^2:43:44/**33**:9^2:10,11:16:18:20,21:22^2:
24/**34**:3^2:4:9:14/**36**:6:30/**37**:1:17:21^3/**38**:3:17:
18:20:21,22:23^3/**39**:17/**40**:9:15/**42**:5:12:13,14:
18^3:20/**43**:2,3/**44**:12:27:28/**46**:19:27^3/**47**:4:5:6^2:
7^2/**48**:2,3,4:7:8^2:9:10:13:15:38:42:43/**49**:2:3:4:
9,10^2:13:17^2:19:20^2:26:28:29^3:32:33^2:36/**50**:2^2:3
:5^2:9:10:12:13:19:20:22:25:26:27:30:37:39^2:45:
46/**51**:3^2:6:8:14:26^3:29:34,35^2:36:46:49:52:53:58^3
:61,62/**Lam1**:17^2/**3**:27:59/**Eze1**:26:27,28^2/**2**:6^3:
8/**3**:9/**4**:4,5:14:16^3/**5**:10:12:13/**6**:4-7^2:8/**7**:10,11
:12:13^2:16:17/**8**:2:3/**10**:5:17f/**11**:7:7f:10:11:16:
20^2/**12**:3:11:12:20:23:25/**13**:9^2:15:21/**14**:10:11^2:
14:16^2:18:20/**15**:3/**16**:20:42^2:52:54^2:55:61:63/
17:14^2:20:21^2/**18**:20^2:22:24^2/**19**:5:9/**20**:31:32^2:
35,36f:41:47:48/**21**:7:29:32^2/**22**:14:16:24/**23**:25^3
:29:46:48:49/**24**:16:17:20,21:23:27/**25**:9,10:14/
26:13:14:20^2:21/**28**:2,3:9:12f:14:23/**29**:5:11:13:
14:15^2:21/**30**:7^2:13:16^3:17:18^2/**31**:12:14:18^2/**32**:
8^2:9:10:14:19:20:31/**33**:9:13:16:24:27:28/**34**:8:
12:15,16:22:23:24^2:26:29/**35**:8:9^2:10:15/**36**:8^2:
10:11:12:15:23:25^3:28^2:30:32:34:37,38/**37**:7:22^2:
23:24:25:27^2/**38**:2,3f^3:7:8^2:15,16:20/**39**:7:11:13:
14:15,16:26^2:27/**40**:2:14:39:43:47/**41**:3:21/**42**:
14/**43**:10:18:19:22:25/**44**:2:5^2:10:11^2:12:15:24:
29^2:30/**45**:1^2:2^2:3:4^2:5:6:7:8:9:11^2:12^3:17^2:20:21^2
:23/**46**:1:2:4:11:12^3:13:14,15^2:18/**47**:5:9:10:11^2:
12^3:13:17:20:22:23/**48**:9:13:14:16:29:30,31^2:32:
34:35/**Dan2**:13:20:39:40:41,42^2:44:48:49/**3**:6:11
:13:15^2:19:28:29/**4**:10,11:19:23:25:27:32/**5**:2,3,4
:7:10:11:28:31f/**6**:7:8^3:12^2:15:23:25,26/**7**:10:11:
13:23f:23:25:27/**8**:13:24^3:25^3/**9**:24^2:25^2:26^2:27/
10:12:18:19^2:20,21/**11**:2:4^2:6^3:12:16:17:20:21:22
:23^2:26:27:29:32:33:36:42:43:45/**12**:1:4^2:6:9:10:
11^2/**Hos1**:2:10:11:10:16f:17/**3**:3:4/**4**:10:16/**5**:6:
11/**8**:5:6:10/**9**:2:3:11:12:17/**10**:2:5:6^3:15^2/**12**:2:
6/**13**:1:16/**14**:2:4:7^2/**Joe1**:16/**2**:1:17^2:18:20:21:
27:31:32/**3**:10:15:16:17:19/**Amo1**:7:12f:14/**2**:11
:14:15/**3**:4:12:14/**4**:3/**5**:5:14^2:16:17:18^2:19:20/**6**
:5:7^2:10^2:11:12/**7**:9:11^2:17/**8**:3^2:5:10^2/**9**:1:8:9^2:
13:15/**Ob1**:5^2:6:8:9:10^2:15:18^2:21/**Jon3**:4,5/**4**:3:
4:9^2/**Mic1**:7^2:15/**2**:3/**3**:12^2/**4**:1:2:3^2:4:7:10/**5**:2:
4:5:8^2:9:12/**6**:1:7:8:10:11/**7**:4:6:8:9:10:11:13f:16:
18/**Nah1**:15/**2**:9/**3**:12:13^2:19/**Hab1**:5^2:13:14:15
/**2**:3^3:16:17:20/**3**:14:18:19/**Zep1**:13^2:17:18^2/**2**:4
:7:9:12:15f/**3**:8^2:10:11^3:12:13:14:15:16^2/**Hag1**:8
/**2**:5:8,9/**Zec1**:4:12:16/**2**:4^2:5^2:9:11,12^3:13/**3**:2:9
/**5**:2/**6**:7/**7**:8,9^2/**8**:3:4:5:7:8^2:8f:12^3:13^3:16:19:
20,21:23/**9**:2:4:5^4:7:13:16,17^2/**10**:5:6:7^3:10:11:
12/**11**:1:9/**12**:3^2:7:8^2:11:12,13,14/**13**:1:2^2:4:8^2/
14:1^3:7^3:9^3:10:11^2:13:14^2:19:20:21^2/**Mal1**:9:11^2:
14/**2**:5:16/**3**:5:10:11:12:17/**4**:1^2/**Mt1**:18:23:24/
2:4:23/**3**:7:10:13:14/**4**:1:24/**5**:4:6^2:7:12^2:13:18
f:19^2:24:29^2:31:45:48/**6**:1:5:10:19:21:22:23:
31,32:34/**7**:1:7^2:9:10:13:17/**8**:3:4:8,9:12/**9**:9:13:
15:17:21/**10**:12:13:15:16:17:19:20^2:22:26^2:28:36
:41^2:42/**11**:7:11:22:23:24/**12**:7:21:29:31,32^2:37^2:
39,40^2/**13**:12,13^2:33:40:42:47,48:49:50:56/**14**:2:
13:27:35/**15**:13,14/**16**:4:19^2:21^2:24:26/**17**:4:7:
20:22,23^2/**18**:1:6^2:8:9:17f:18:20:23:26:29:30/**19**:
5,6:21:25:30^2/**20**:15:16:18:19:26^2:27:28^2:31/**21**:
3:26:43:44^2/**22**:1:28:45/**23**:3:7:9:10:11^2:12^2:
13,14:18:26/**24**:2:5:7:8:9:12:13:14:20:21:22:24:
27:29^2:29f:30:36:37,38:39:40^2:41^2:42:48:51/**25**:
1:13:14:29^2:30:32/**26**:2:5:13^2:31:37:39:42:46:48:
54:58:60,61:63/**27**:25:64/**28**:5:10:14:20/**Mk1**:3:
4:7:40:41:43,44/**2**:14:15:19:20:22:24/**3**:14,15:27^3
:28:29/**4**:11,12:21^2:24:25^2:31,32/**5**:28:36/**6**:50/
8:16:31^2:34:38/**9**:6:12,13:19^2:30,31:35^2:39f:42:
43,44:45,46:49f/**10**:6,7:15:26:30^2:31^3:33^2:38^2:39
:43^2:44^2:45:49f/**11**:17:22,23/**12**:7:13:17:23:25^2:
26:35:37:40^2/**13**:2:3,4:6:8:9^2:10:11:12:13:18:19^2:
22:29:33:34/**14**:2:7:9:33:55/**15**:15:20/**16**:6:9f:16^2
:18^2/**Lk1**:3:8,9f:13:15^2:17:20:27:30:32^2:35:54:55
:57:59:60:66:76:78/**2**:1:6:10:23:32:34,35^3:49/**3**:3^2
:7:9:12:14/**4**:18,19^2:22:35:41/**5**:10^2:12:13:14:15:
27:35:36:38/**6**:13:17,18:21:23:35^3:37f:38/**7**:
6,7,8^3:33/**8**:16:17:18^3:43,44:50^2/**9**:4:22^2:26:31:
44:46:59:62/**10**:12:15^2/**11**:2:4:9:36:50:51/**12**:1^2:
3^2:4:10^2:11:15:19f:32:34:35:36:37:38:39^2:40:
42,43,44:45:47:48:52:53:55:59/**13**:23:24,25:28:
30^2:33/**14**:10:11^2:15:18:23:26^2:27:35/**15**:7/**16**:2:
9f:10^2:12:13:22/**17**:1:2,3:6:21:22^2:24:25:26:28:
30:34^2:35,36^3:37:37f/**18**:6:13:14^2:26:30:32^2:34/
19:5:7:12:17:19:22:30/**20**:14:18^2:19^2:20:33:
37,38f:41:44:46/**21**:6^2:7:11:12^2:13:14:15:16:22^2:
23:24^2:25^2:26:31/**22**:26:37:40:58:67,68:69/**23**:7:
29:32,33:43/**24**:6,7^2:17:18:20:47/**Jn1**:19:27:42/
2:17/**3**:4:5f:7^2:14:20^2/**4**:1:15:19:21-24:28,29:36^2
/**5**:24:28:34/**6**:20:26:27:35:41:45^2/**7**:4:21,22,23:
26:27:33:34:36:39:41,42^2/**8**:12:16:25:30,31:36:
55/**9**:9:17:22,23:41/**10**:1:9:16:33:34,35,36/**11**:
32:39:52/**12**:8:15:23,24:26^2:31:35:42:48/**13**:1:6:
8:10:23f/**14**:1:2,3:8:12,13:17:19^2:27:28:31/**15**:4:
7:11:22:24/**16**:1:2:4:13^2:16:20:21:25:32^2/**17**:11:
13:21^2:26/**18**:28:33:34f^2/**19**:16:31:36,37/**20**:27/
Act1:5:17:20:24,25/**2**:7:21:26:30:31:36:38/**3**:17:
23/**4**:30/**5**:21:31^2:34:36:38:39/**7**:9:26^2:35:38/**8**:
20:27:33f:36/**9**:8,9:17/**10**:42:45:46,47/**11**:14:16
/**12**:6:15/**13**:11:40:46/**14**:9/**15**:1:5/**16**:15:30:31/
17:17/**18**:6:9:14:21/**19**:27:36:39/**20**:26:28/**21**:
11:13:14^2:22:24:34:37,38:40/**22**:5:10:11:16^2/**24**:
5:8:15:19:21f/**25**:18:20/**26**:2:23:32/**27**:17f:24:25
:26:29:39/**Rom1**:4:6,7^2:11,12^2:22/**2**:1^2:5:8:9:
10:27/**3**:6:20:21,22:25f/**4**:4,5^2:7:19/**5**:2:3:7:17:
19^2/**6**:6:11:13^3:14f:14:16^2:17:19^2/**7**:3:4:8:13^2:21:
23,24,25:23,24,25f/**8**:5:15:23^2:26:29:31:36:39/**9**
:1^2:10-13:15:17f:18:21:23,24:26:27^2:29:30:32:33
/**10**:1:5^2:9:11:13:20/**11**:6:10:11:15^2:16^2:18:19^2:
20^2:22:24:26:29:34:36/**12**:1:2:3:8:11:12^2:13:15:
18:20/**13**:3:4:6:8:12,13^2/**14**:3:9:18^2:22/**15**:7:9:
10:12^2:17:27f:30:31^2:32:33/**16**:1:13:20:24:
25,26,27/**1Co1**:1:2:8:10^3:19:20/**3**:2:5:8:10^2:12:
13:15:18:21/**4**:1:5:6:8^2:9^2/**5**:3,4^2:5:6:11/**6**:3:4f:7^2
/**7**:2:5^2:16^2:17:21:23:25^3:29f:31:32:40/**8**:6:9:11/
9:10:12:14:16:27/**10**:2:12^2:20:22:23^2:29:32:33/
11:14,15^2:31:32/**12**:8:10:19:23:24/**13**:1:2:3:7/**14**
:1:2^4:9:11^2:12:16:17^2:19:20^3:24:25:26:27:31:33:
34:37:39:40/**15**:9:13:25:26:28:30:32:33:35:43^2:
44:51:52:53:55,56^2:58^2/**16**:3:5:6:8:12:13/**2Co1**:1
:5:13,14^2:15,16:17:24/**2**:3^2:5,6:7:14/**3**:1:4:6:14:
15:17:18/**4**:6:7:18/**5**:1:3:4:8:10:16:18:20/**6**:3:6:
14:15^2:16^3:18^2/**7**:8:14/**8**:7:11:22/**9**:3^2:4:5:8:9:13
/**10**:1:2:5:8:11:15:16^2/**11**:1:2^3:3:4:26:31/**12**:6:7:
9:11:21/**13**:1:5:7:9:11^2:14^2/**Gal1**:1:3:8^2:10:15/**2**:
3:5:16^2:17:18:21/**3**:11:15:17:18:21,22/**4**:9:12:19^2
:20:21/**5**:11:14:16:20/**6**:1:4:7:8:10:12^2:13:16:18/
Eph1:1:2:4:10:11:13:18/**2**:3/**3**:10:17:18,19^2:20:
21/**4**:2^2:3^2:12:14:23:24:30^2:32/**5**:2:3^2:4:5:6:10f:
12:15,16^3:18:23:31^2/**6**:3:5:11:13:22:24/**Php1**:10
:11:20^3:23:24:25:28/**2**:3^2:4:5:12:16:17^2:18:21:28
/**3**:1:2^2:4^2:10:11:12^2:13:19/**4**:2:4:8:9:12:20:22:23
/**Col1**:1:10:11:19:28/**2**:18:20:22/**3**:10:12:13:15^2
:17:19/**4**:1:2^2:4:5:6:17/**1Th1**:1/**2**:5:9:16/**3**:10/**4**:
3,4:7^2:9:11:13:16:17/**5**:3^2:4:6:14:16:18:21:23:28
/**2Th1**:9:10:11:12^2/**2**:1:3^2:12:13f/**3**:2:8:13:14:15:
16:18/**1Ti1**:5^2:12/**2**:4:9,10^2:12/**3**:1:2^4:3^3:6^2:7:8^3:
9:10^3:11:13:14/**4**:3^2:6:12^2:14/**5**:7:9:10:13:14:17^2
:20:21:22^2/**6**:1^2:6:8:9:11:15:16:17^3:18:19^2:21/
2Ti1:4:7^2:8^2:11/**2**:1:15^2:17:19:21:24^2:25/**3**:1^2:2:
3^4:4:5:9/**4**:2:5:6^2:13:15:16:18:21:22/**Tit1**:6:7^3:8^2
:9^2:11/**2**:2^2:3^3:5^2:7:8^3:10:13/**3**:1:2:5:8:10:14:15/
Phm1:11:14:15:25/**Heb2**:5:17^3/**3**:7,8/**4**:1:13/**5**:
4^3:6:7f^3:10:12,13:14/**6**:1^2:12:17/**7**:3f:12,13,14:
20:23^2:24:25/**8**:4^2:9:10^3:12/**9**:16:23/**10**:2:13:27:
29:34:37/**11**:3:16:24,25:35/**12**:2:5^2:17:27/**13**:2:4
:5:9:10:13:17:20,21:24,25/**Jas1**:2:4:6^2:7,8:9:
10,11^2:16:20:21/**2**:5:12:13/**3**:1^3:5:13:16/**4**:4:8:9^3
:11:16/**5**:7:8:9:12:13^2:16/**1Pe1**:5:6:9:15^2:16:21/
2:1^2:2,3f:6:12:24/**3**:1:3:4:6:7:8:9:14:15/**4**:1:2^2:4:
5:7:10:11^2:12:13^2:14:17/**5**:3:4:8:11:13f:14/**2Pe1**:
5:19/**2**:1^2:2:12^2:12f:14:19^2:21/**3**:4:7:10:11:13:14^2
:17:18/**1Jn1**:4:9/**2**:3:19:24:28^2/**3**:1:2^2:6:12:13:
17^2:19:20f/**4**:14:17/**5**:15/**2Jn1**:11/**Jud**:2:7:12:
22:23:24,25/**Rev**:3:7:17,18^2:19/**2**:10:11:17:27/**3**
:5:9:12^2:14:18^2/**6**:10:13/**7**:12:16^2:17f:17/**8**:8,9/**9**
:6:9/**10**:4:6:7/**11**:5:8,9^2:10:13:18:19/**12**:12/**13**:
10^2:10f^2:10:16/**14**:5:10/**15**:1:2/**17**:8:8f:10:12:17
/**18**:4:8:14:21:22^2:23^2/**19**:7/**20**:3:6:7:10^2/**21**:3^2:
3f:4:7^2:17:22:26:27/**22**:3^2:4:5^2:11

5530

BECAUSE

Gen2:3:23/**3**:17/**5**:28-31/**6**:12,13/**11**:6f:9/**12**:3:
3f:11,12,13:16/**14**:23/**16**:9-12/**21**:13:31/**22**:16:
18/**24**:48/**25**:28/**26**:5:9:24/**27**:20:41/**29**:10^2:15:
31/**30**:6f:15:27/**31**:31/**32**:28:31/**34**:13:27/**35**:7:
15/**36**:6,7,8/**37**:3/**38**:26/**39**:9/**42**:21:22/**43**:18/
47:20/**Ex1**:9:21/**2**:10:23/**6**:8,9:8,9f/**9**:11/**12**:39/
14:11/**15**:16:23/**16**/**18**:11:15,16:22/**19**:18:23/
21:26/**22**:15/**23**:2,3/**24**:4/**32**:35/**34**:30/**39**:43/
40:35/**Lev2**:13/**5**:11/**7**:16/**10**:6/**11**:4-7^3/**15**:15:
31/**16**:16:34/**17**:11/**18**:12:13:24/**19**:1:20/**20**:3/
21:21:23/**22**:16/**25**:14,15,16/**26**:21:39:40,41/**27**
:27/**Num3**:49/**6**:24,25,26/**9**:10/**11**:1:3:34/**12**:1:
1f^3/**13**:24/**14**:16:19/**16**:38/**20**:12:13:21,22/**22**:
22,23f:29:32/**25**:12,13^3/**27**:3,4/**30**:5/**Deu1**:17:
36:37/**2**:25:30/**3**:26/**4**:21,22:25:37/**5**:15/**7**:7:8^2:
12/**9**:4^2:5^3:6:12:20:28^2/**12**:15/**13**:10/**14**:8/**15**:
4,5:9:10:18/**18**:12/**22**:23,24^2/**23**:5:9,10/**28**:20:
34:45:47,48:55:67/**29**:25/**31**:18/**33**:21^2/**Jos6**:1:
25/**7**:1/**9**:18^2:24^2/**10**:14/**14**:13,14/**22**:19:24,25^2:
31/**Ju2**:20/**5**:23/**6**:6,7/**8**:27f/**9**:18/**11**:8:37/**15**:6
/**17**:13/**19**:30/**21**:15/**Ru1**:1/**1Sa**:6:19,20/**3**:13/**4**
:6:21,22^2/**6**:19^2/**7**:2:13/**8**:18/**9**:6:12,13/**10**:1/**12**:
22/**15**:1:23/**18**:11,12/**19**:1/**20**:10/**26**:12/**28**:15:
18:20/**30**:13:16/**2Sa1**:6/**2**/**3**:30/**5**:12/**7**:21^2/**9**:7
/**10**:2/**12**:10:11:25:25f/**13**:21-24/**14**:13:15,16:26
:32/**16**:12:18/**19**:41/**21**:1:7/**22**:8/**1Ki3**:6:11/**5**:
2,3/**7**:47/**8**:11:35,36/**10**:21/**11**:2:39/**13**:7:21,22/
14:16/**15**:13:30/**16**:4-7:13/**20**:28:36:42/**21**:2:19:
20:20f:26:29/**2Ki1**:4,5,6:16^2/**2**:23/**5**:27/**8**:19/**10**
:30/**11**:2,3f/**12**:2/**15**:5/**17**:7:26/**18**:4/**19**:18:28/
21:11^2/**22**:18,19^2/**24**:3,4/**25**:16/**1Ch4**:9:14/**7**:23
/**9**:1:22:27/**10**:13/**13**:10/**15**:13:26/**17**:19^2/**19**:
2,3/**21**:6/**23**:10,11/**29**:3/**2Ch1**:11/**2**:5:11/**6**:24:
26^2/**7**:10:22/**12**:7/**14**/**15**:16/**16**:7/**17**:3/**19**:2/**20**
:37/**21**:3,4:10:12:13/**22**:9/**23**:21/**24**:16:24/**25**:
16/**26**:20/**27**:6/**28**/**29**:9:36/**30**:2,3:17,18,19/**31**:
17,18/**34**:27/**Ez3**:11/**4**:15/**5**:5/**6**:21,22/**7**:10:28
/**9**:4:13/**10**:6:9^2/**Neh6**:18^2/**8**:12/**9**:10:37:38/**Est**
3:3,4/**8**:7/**9**:26/**10**:3/**Job6**:5,6,7:25,26/**10**:4-7/
11:18/**18**:4:5/**20**:21/**21**:28/**22**:4:5/**31**:21:38,39/
32:1:2:3:4/**33**:13/**35**:12f:14,15/**36**:12/**39**:11/**42**:
8:11/**Ps5**:11/**6**:7/**7**:17/**9**:2/**13**:6/**16**:1:8/**17**:6/**21**
:7/**23**:1/**27**:11/**31**:1:7:9,10:16/**37**:30,31:40/**38**:
3,4,5,6:8f/**41**:11:12/**44**:3:13:22/**51**:1/**52**:9f/**53**:1
/**57**:3/**59**/**60**:4,5f/**65**:1/**66**:7/**67**:4/**69**:9/**71**:7/**72**
:3/**78**:10:22:62/**82**:5/**86**:17/**89**:24/**91**:14^2/**102**:5
:9,10^2/**106**:17:45/**107**:17/**109**:21:26/**116**:1:2/
119:74:98:136:139:149:158:159:164:168:173/
135:3/**143**:1:11:12/**Pro5**:23/**8**:14,15/**11**:9f/**15**:
12/**21**:7/**Ecc2**:17/**8**:11:13:15/**12**:9/**Sol1**:6/**6**:13
/**Is2**:6:19/**3**:8/**5**:13/**6**:7/**8**:20:21/**9**:7/**10**:16:27f/
17:10/**19**:25/**30**:12/**37**:29/**38**:15/**43**:4/**49**:7/**50**:
1:7/**53**:11:12/**54**:15f/**55**:5^2/**57**:11/**58**:3/**59**:2:9/
61:1/**62**^{2}/**65**:11/**Jer2**:35/**4**:4:19:28/**5**:14/**6**:
18,19/**7**:8:12:13,14/**8**:12:14/**9**:13/**11**:8:17/**13**^{2}:
22:24,25/**14**:5/**15**:4:7:12,13:15/**16**:11:18/**19**:15
/**20**:7:17/**21**:12/**22**:9:15/**23**:9:15/**25**:8,9:38/**26**:3
/**28**:16/**29**:15:31/**30**:15/**33**:5/**34**:17:18,19/**35**:14
:17:18,19/**36**:29:31/**44**:2,3:22:23/**46**:15/**50**:13:
38/**51**:51:64/**Lam1**:3:12/**3**:48,49/**4**:13/**Eze5**:9:
11/**8**:14f/**9**:4/**10**:9-13/**11**:15/**12**:19/**13**:20/**14**/
15:8/**16**:14:36:43/**18**:17:18:22/**19**:10/**20**:14:16:
23,24:43/**21**:7/**22**:18,19,20/**23**:18:35/**24**:13/**25**:
3:6:8:12:15/**26**:2/**28**:6:17/**29**:6:10:20/**31**:5:9:10/
32:10/**33**:29/**35**:4,5/**36**:6:20:22/**42**:5/**43**:8/**44**:3:
12/**Dan2**:30:47/**3**:22/**6**:23/**7**:11/**9**:7:8:16^2:18^2:
19/**Hos1**:16f/**4**:6:9:19/**5**:11/**8**:1/**9**:15:17/**10**:15/
11:5/**Joe3**:19/**Amo7**:17/**Ob1**:3:10/**Jon**:12/**4**:9/
Mic1:5/**2**:1/**3**:12/**7**:13f/**Nah3**:4/**Hab2**:17/**Zep1**
:17/**Hag**:9/**2**:15/**Zec4**:6/**8**:2/**9**:11/**10**:6/**Mal2**:1:
13:14/**Mt5**:10:11/**7**:4/**8**:8,9/**9**:12:29:32:36/**10**:
22:41^2/**11**:20/**12**:24/**13**:21:34,35:58/**14**:4:9^2/**16**
:7/**17**:20/**18**:5:7f:20:32/**20**:7:15/**21**:46/**24**:9/**27**:
18/**Mk1**:22:34/**3**:30/**4**:5,6/**6**:2,3:5:17,18:34/**9**:
17:41/**11**:18/**12**:40/**13**:13/**15**:10/**16**:12/**Lk1**:20:

(BECAUSE Con't)
4/2:7:20/3:8/4:41/6:22/7:6,7,8/8:19/9:53/11:8
:20/13:14:16/15:2:6/19:11:21/20:5/21:17:26/
22:28:29/Jn1:50/2:23/3:20:23,24:35/4:39:42^2/
5:18:27:43/6:26^2:41:57/7:7:29:39/8:37:40:43/9:
16:41/10:13:17:26/11:10:42/12:11:18:42/13:31
/14:11:12,13^2:21:23/15:21:27/16:3:4:10:11:23:
27/17:9:14:20:24/19:7:42^2/20:13:29/21:6/Act4
:21/8:6:9,10,11/12:23/14:12/16:6:34/20:38/22:
29/23:6/24:16:27/26:6/27:9:9f/28:20/Rom2:5:
12-15:17:18:24:28^2/3:3:26:27/4:1:9:11:13^2:19:
22/5:1:2:5:11:13^2:17:19^2/6/7:6:14:17/8:3:7:10:
10f:35/9:1:10-13^2:16^2:18:32/11:18:20^2:28/12:
14/13:5/14:14/15:27:30/1Co1:22^2/2:5:7:10:14/
3:2:7/6:11:13:20/7:2:5:27:36/8:11:13/9:19:20/
10:30:31/11:10f/12:15:16/15:10:15:21^2:22/16:
11/2Co1:15,16/3:4:5:14/4:5:8:11:12/5:11:13,14
/6:12^2/7:9^2/8:3^2:22/9:13:14/11:7:11/12:7:21/
13:7/Gal1:24/2:12:16^2/3:6:11/4:6:16:31/6:14/
Eph1:3:5:6:11:13:18/2:6:8:13:18/3:1:21/4:2:14:
17,18:32/5:9/6:1/Php1:5:13:14:15:16,17/2:9:26
:30/3:14/4:17:19/Col1:28:29/2:4:5^2:12/3:22^2/
1Th4:6/5:13/2Th1:3^2:10^2:12/2:10:13:13f/1Ti1:
13/2:9,10:13/3:6/4:8:12/5:10:11:12:23/6:1:2:10
/2Ti1:9^2:16/2:9/4:6/Tit1:7/2:8/3:5^2:6:7/Phm1:
5:7:8,9:14^2:16:21/Heb2:9^2/3:19/4:1:2:4/5:1:4:7
/6:12/7:2:5:18:22/8:4:6:11/10:19:22^2/11:5:7:10
:11:27:28:31/12:2/Jas2:21:25/4:1:3/5:1:11/1Pe
1:3:5:14^2:21:22/2:5:8/3:21^2/4:13/5:2/2Pe2:2:
7,8/1Jn1:9/2:12:13^3/3:3:6:7:9:12:22:24/4:1:4:
16^2:17/5:6,7,8:10:20/Jud1:4/Rev3:10/5:4/6:17
/8:11:13/14:8/16:21
1058

BEEN
Gen2:2/3:23/9:4/14:14:16/19:18,19,20/20:16/
21:23/24:59/26:32/29:14/30:27/31:7:35f:38/
32:4:28/33:11/34:27/42:23:36/43:27/44:4:6/46
:34^2/49:23/Ex4:10/5:23/7:14/9:18:24:27/10:6/
11:6/12:44^2:48/14:29/15:21/16:22/18:3:8^2/21:
29/22:12:31/28:30,31f/32:25/33:12/34:10/Lev
5:10/7:15:35/8:5:26:30:34/10:12:14:16/14:42/
18:27/22:15/25:45:54/26:26/Num3:49/5:1:27:
30/6:19/13:22/14:26,27/16:3/19:1:16:18^2:20/
21:9:25,26/26:64,65:64,65f:64,65/27:6,7/34:
14,15/Deu1:1^2/2:12:30/3:23,24,25/4:25/8:4/9:
24/13:18^2/16:13/17:8:18/21:3/24:4/29:6/33:
29/34:10:11,12/Jos2:3/3:2,3,4/4:10^2/5:4,5^3:6:
8,9/8:20,21:31/10:14^2:17:27/11:10:15/14/15:
13/17:1/19:9^2/20:6/21:4/22:17,18/23:9/24:33
/Ju1:15/4:11/6:22:28/8:10:19/9:20/10:12/11:
13:26/13:2,3:21/14:20/15:16,17/16:2:11:16,17^2
/18:1:29/19:30/21:6/Ru2:7/3:2/4:15/1Sa1:
12,13/2:15:23,24,25^2/4:9:17^2:19:21,22/5:4/6:7:
17/7:14/8:5/9:20:23/10:2:16^2/12:2:12/13:23/
14:4:21:30:45:48/15:32/17:33/19:7/20:5:27:41
/21:6/23:28/24:11:18/25:7:21/26/27:11/28:24
/29:3/30:5:21:27-31/2Sa1:4/2:16:17/3:23^2/5:
4,5:17:21/7:6:9:27/9:2/10:19/12:8/13:32,33^2/
14:2,3:15,16:28/15:10/17:8:17^2/19:3:7/20:5/
1Ki1:27:37/3:2:15/5:1:2,3^2/7:14:32:40/8:3,4:7:
20:54,55/9:2,3;20,21/10:7:12/11:15/12:19/13:
5:21,22/16:18:23:29/18:12:30/19:14/21:3/2Ki3
:2:26:27/5:2:25^2/6:11/8:6/9:12:14/10:6:11:31/
14:28/15:1:8:13:17:23:27:30:32,33/16:1/17/18:
35/19:24/22:12,13/23:1:5:11:19:22/1Ch9:21/
10:3:7/12:39/13:3/14:11/17:1:8/18:10^2/29:29/
2Ch1:8/3:1/6:41/7:3:10/9:11/16:9/18:16/21:
10:13/24:7,8/25:13/28:19/29:2:7^3:8:9/30:5f^2/
31:10/32:15/34:17^2:21/35:14:18/36:22,23/Ez2
:1/3:11/4:10:15:18:19:20/5:16/6:3:14:21,22/8:
28/9:7:8:13/Neh2:1:3:16/6/7:64,65^2/8:17/13:2
:4:5:10:11/Est2:6^2:19f/4:1:5/7:4/8:7:8f/Job3:
16/7:3/10:19/12:3/15:17-19/20:5/21:29/22:20
/30:3:5/31:13:27/32:3:14/38:17,18/42:7/Ps2:2
/11:3f/17:1/18:50/22:9,10,11/27:9/32:1/37:25
/40:9/59:16/60:3/71:6:24/73:13:15/74:12/78:7
/79:1/88:15/90:1/119:52:54:56:92:121/124:1^2:
2,3/129:2/131/Pro7:26^2/22:20,21/30:32/Ecc1:
8-11:12-15/3:15^2:15f/4:3/5:16^2/Sol:2/Is1:9/7:
17/10:23/16:13,14/20:3/21:8,9/24:11/30:31:33
/33:9/38:3/39:1/42:3:14/43:23/48:19/51/52:
14,15/53:10/57:11/64:5/65:2/Jer2:31^2/3:2:4,5:
20/4:10:15/10:20/11:15:19/13:22/14:17/15:9:
14/16:12:13:19/19:13/20:17:18/22:21/25:2,3:
18:38/29:1/30:7/32:24:29/33:10,11/36:7/37:4:
15,16/38:1:27/40:5/41:9f:10:18/44:10:18^2/48:
2,3,4:11:21/49:16/50:6:33/51:7:51/52:2:20/
Lam1:4/2:13/4:11/Eze:14/5:5,6,7/8:14f/12:16
/16:3:4:16:31:45:48:57/23:40/26:2^2/30:4:21:24
/33:22:33/40:4/42:14/43:6/44:9/Dan1:15:
18,19/2:1:24/4:17/5:22:23:27/8:26f/9:12/10:2:
12/11:6f/12:7/Hos1:2/10:9/13:4:8/14:1/Joe2:
2/Amo5:25,26,27/Mic1:11f^3/Nah:15/Zec4:1^2/
5:3/6:15/7:3/8:9^2/10:2/11:5:7/13:5/Mal2:14/
3:9:13/Mt1:20/4:12,13/7:23/9:20/10:25/11:12
:21:23:27/13:34,35/15:31^2:32/20:6/21:42/22:
26/25:21:23/26:24:32:73/27:3/28:11:12,13:18/
Mk3:10/5:18:19:25/8:1/9:12,13^2:21:34/10:40/
11:2/12:23/13:19/14:21/Lk1:1,2:58:72,73/2:11
:36,37:38:48/3:21/4:25,26/6:26/8:27:35:36:38:
40:43,44/9:32:45/10:13/11:1/13:7:11/14:20/19
:17/20:37,38f/22:51/23:2:8:50,51,52/24:2/Jn1:
1/3:18/4:27:45/5:5:6:36/6:14/7:15:39:45:47/8:
28:33/9:17:18:24:32/11:17:21:32:39/12:5:38f/
14:9/15:27/16:5f:11/18:19:20/19:38/20:12/Act
1:21,22/2:39/4:22/8:9,10,11:16:32/10:31/14:8:
26/15:4:5:21/17:23:32/18:2,3:27/19:18,19/20:
33/21:21/22:25/24:10/26:5/Rom1:5/2:1:4:18/
3:21,22f:21,22/4:12/5:1/7:23,24,25/8:22f/9:22:
23,24:30/10:18/11:7:17:28/14:2:6:14/15:15,16^2
:20^3:21:22/16:3:13:17/1Co1:15/2:16/3:1/4:3:5:
6:11:12:13/5:3,4:7/6:12f/7:18:23/8:1:4:7/9:2/
10:20:27:28/11:2:12:25/12:13^2/13:10/15:3:8:27
/16:5:17:18/2Co1:12:13,14:19/2:5,6:10/6:5:6:7^2
:9/8:2^2/11:23^2:26:27/12:7/13:2/Gal2:2:7,8,9:18
:20/3:27/5:6:10:13/6:15^2/Eph1:5:13:18^2/2:5:8:
13:15:16/4:1:4:11/Php1:12:29/2:22:25:26/3:5/
4:10/Col1:5/3:12/4:11/1Th2:2:10:17/3:5/1Ti2:
7/5:9:10:15/2Ti2:9/3:13:14/Tit1:1:3:9:11/2:13
/Phm1:11:13/Heb2:2:11:15:18/4:2:3/5:6:12,13
/7:4:5:11:12,13,14:26/8:6:7:13/9:26/10:2^2:10:
18:22^2/11:34/Jas2:13/1Pe1:2:12:22/2:2,3:9:10
/3:21/2Pe1:16/1Jn:2/2:12:13:24/3:9^3:11:12:14
/2Jn1:8/Jud:3:12/Rev2:20/3/6:9:11/7:2/9:15/
11:2/12:10/13:12/14:3:4:11/15:2:3,4/16:6/17:2
:8/20:4
885

BEFORE
^{2}Gen12:18/13:3,4:10/17:17/18:5:8/19:3:27:35/
21:26/23:7:10/24:52/26:1:18/27:2,3,4:8,9,10:
27,28,29:30/30:39,40:41/31:17-20:32:36,37:53/
32:20/33:3:6/34:20/36:31-39/37:7:9:10/41:14:
21:50/42:2:6:24/43:14:15:26:28/44:14/45:28/
46:8-14/47:10/48:5:20/49:8/50:16,17:18/Ex1:
18/2:23/4:7:19:28/5:10,11:13:16:21/6:8,9/7:10:
16/8:26/9:11:13/11:6:10/13:19/14:16/15:25/
16:7,8,9/18:12:19,20/20:10/21:3^2:6/22:8:9/23:
15:17:20:23^2:27:28/24:11/25:30/27:21/28:12:
30,31^2/29:11:23:26:30:42/30:8:20^2/32:5/33:2:
12:13:19:19f/34:8:10:11:20:23:24^2/40:23:25/
Lev1:5^2:11/2:16/3:3,4,5/4:4:6:7:15:17:18/5:19/
6:7:14:22,23:25:30/7:14:30/8:21:26:27:29/9:2:5
:21:24/10:1:3:4:14:15:17:19/12:7/14:11:12:16:
18:21:23:24:27:29:31:36/15:14:15:30/16:1:7:10:
13:18/20:23/23:9,10,11:17:20:26,27:28:33,34:
39:40/24:3,4:5-8/25:1:4:14,15,16:50/26:17:37/
Num3:4/5:16:18:25:30/6:12:16:20^2/7:10/8:12/
10:35/11:16/12:3,4:15/13:22:30:33/14:5:
36,37,38/15:15,16:15,16f:19,20,21:23,24:25:28:
33/16:6,7:8,9:16:22:38:40:45:49/17:7/18:8:11:
18:24:25,26/20:6:9:13/22:19:30:31:41/24:3-9:
25f/25:3:4:6/26:61/27:5:14:16/28:7/29:12/31:
29:50:54/32:22/33:3,4/35:32/Deu1:42:45/2:22
/4:10^2:34/8:16/9:3:5:17:18:25/10:8:10^2/11:19/
12:6:7:12:17:18^2:31/14:23:26/15:20/16:8:10:11:
16/18:13/19:17^2/20:1:2^2:8/21:5:19/22:17,18/
23:14/24:14,15/26:4:5:8:10:13/27:7/28^2:25:31:
40:62/29:2,3:10:14,15/30:15:19/31:8:10,11:14:
21/32:17:52/33:1:10:27:29/34:11,12^2/Jos2:8:
17,18/3:1:2,3,4/4:18:23/5:14/6:20/7:6:16:17/8:
3,4:5:6:33:35/9:18:19/10:14/11:12/13:2-7/14:1
:15/15:9/18:3/22:10/23:9/24:1:17/Ju2:12-14/
3:16/6:9/9:45/11:11:26/12:9,10/14:16:18/16:
12:16,17:20:22/19:1:10/20:1:18:22,23,24:26/21
:2:5/Ru3:10:14/1Sa2:15^2:20:31:36/3:7:10/4:7:9
:20/5:3:4/6:7:20/7:6/8:11/9:24^2/10:18,19:20:
21:25/11:9:15/12:3^2:7/14:24,25^2/15:30^2:33/17:
16:27:38,39/18:26/19:7/20:5:19/21:6:7f/24:7,8
/25:23/27:9/28:14/31:3,4/2Sa1:1/2:26/5:3/6:5
:14:16:21/7:18:26:29/9:5,6:8/10:3/12:16/13:9:
11/14:20:22:33/15:14:28/17:22/19:18/20:6/21:
5,6:9/22/23:16/24:13/1Ki1:5:16:22,23:28:30:
31:53/3:15:22/8:5:14:22,23:31:54,55:59:61/10:
12/11:15/12:20/14:9:28/16:25:33/18:7/19:11/
20:11/21:29/22:10/2Ki1:13/2:6,7:9/4:27/5:15/
6:32/15:18/17:8/18:5:20,21/19:9:14:25:26:32/
20:4/22:18,19^2/25:6:7/1Ch1:43/4:21-22/10:4:9
/11:3/13:8:10/14:15/15:13/16:1:4:6:27:29:30:
33:37f/17:9:16:21/21:16:21:30/22:5:8/23:27:30
/24:1/28:2:8/29:15:20:22^2/2Ch1:2,3f:5,6:12/2:
4:6f/5:6/6:5,6^2:12,13:22:24/9:11/13:13,14/14:
15/15:17/18:9:14:19,20/19:6/20:3:9^2:13:29/23:
15,16,17/24:13:20/25:14:16/29:6:23:29:30/32:
6:13/33:19/34:7:27^2:31/Ez3:6/5:15/6:5/7:28^2/
8:21/9:5:15/10:3:9:10/Neh7:5/8:9/9:24/13:4:
25/Est1:18/2:12,13,14/3:2/5:9/6/7:6:8/8:1:3:4
/9:24,25/Job1:6:17:20/2:1/4:15/8:11-13/9:13/
10:20,21/11:13,14/13:15f/14:6/15:7,8:32/16:2
/21:18/24:9/25:4/26:5,6/29:3/30:11:15:20/34:
23^2/35:2,3/38:21/39:2,3/41:10^2/42:5:10:13,14f
/Ps1:4/2:12^2/4:4/5:3/6:5/7:7,8^2/9:14/10:5/18:
38:39:43,44,45^2:47/22:9,10,11:22:25/24:3:6/26
/27:9/29:2:5,6/35:6:13:18^2/37:11:33/38:13,14/
39:9:13/40:3/42:2/44:10/45:5/47:3/50:22/51:
16/56:13/59:14,15/61:7/62:1:5:8/65:1/66:15/
68:2:8:35/69:10/71:21/72:9:11/76:5:7:8/78:13:
63:64/81:15/83:13/85/86:9/88:1:15/89:14,15:
23:35,36f:45/90:2^2:5,6:8/95:2:6:9/96/97:3:5/98
:6:8,9/99:5/100:1:2/102:15^2/104:25/107:32^2/
108:1/109:6/110:1/111/114:3/116:18,19/119:
84:147/131:2/135:9/136:13/138:1:1f^2/139:4:16^2
/142:1/144:2/147:17/Pro8:22:23:24^2:25:26/11:
15/14:12:19:33/15:28/16:18^2:25/18:13:16/20:
25/22:2:29/24:21,22:27/25:8,9,10/30:7/31:15/
Ecc1:8-11:16-18/2:7,8:9/3:15/7:15-17/10:11f:
16,17/11:10/12:1:6/Sol2:17/6:12:13f/Is1:4/2:9
:16/6:11/7:14f:15,16f/8:2:4/9:8,9,10/10:9/13:
16/16:13,14/17:13/18:5/23:17/25:3/26:7:14/
28:6/29:5/37:14:36/38:1/40:2:21/41:1/42:9:16^2
/43:21/44:11:15:17:19:28f/45:2:14/48:6/49:1:
16:23/52:8:10:14,15/53:2f:7^2:11/57:1/58:3:8/
59:12/60:14/63:12/64:2:3/65:1^2:6:12:24/66:4:
7,8/Jer1:5^2/2:20:22:36/4:26:31/6:7:20/7:10:30
/8:2/10:10:14/11:12/12:1/13:16^2:27/15:1:14/
16:9:13/18:17:23/19:4/20:11/21:1f:12/27:18:
19,20,21/30:7:18:20/32:4:6,7:10:25/33:9:10,11
/34:3/35:5/36:7:28:32/37:1f:14/38:10:16:27/
39:15:16/40:4/41/42:2/44:10:17/46:15:24/47:1
/51:24/52:10/Lam1:7/2:6:8:18:22/5:7/Eze1:4/
4:1:14/5:9:14^2/8:4/12:12f:13f/15:5,6^2/16:16:19
:37:40,41/18:6:15/19:9/20:1:9,10/21:6:30/23:
18:41/28:17/29:16/30:22:24/32:10/33:31/36:6:
11:23/38:15,16/39:27/40:38/41:22f/42:14^2/43:
3:24/44:3:15:21:26/Dan2:1:46^2/3:3:13/4:36/5:
2,3,4:19/6:22:24:25,26/7:10^2:23/8:26/10:5,6:12
/11:22:24/Hos1:6:20/8:5/10:11/Joe1:13:14:16
/2:2:3:10:14:31/Amo1:2/2:9/4:7/9:13/Jon1:2:
16/3:1/Mic2:13/4:8:13/5:8/6:6/7:11/Nah1:6^2/
3:8f:15/Hab1:2:9:16/2:20/3:1:5/Zep2:2^2/3:20/
Hag2:3:16,17:18,19^3/Zec:13/3:1:3:9f/4:7^2/6:5/
8:10/12:7:8/Mal3:1:4:11/Mt2:9f:11:16/3:3:8/5
:22:23:25/6:7,8/8:2:29f/9:8/10:18:23:32:33/11:
1f:10f/12:43,44,45/14:19/15:2:30:31/17:10:14:
25/18:26:29:32/19:15/21:8:23:31/24:17:21:
37,38/25:32/26:34:55:75/27:11:17:24:29/28:9/
Mk1:35/2:12:21/3:11:27^2/5:6:22/6:22,23:41:52
/7:2:4/8:6:14/9:11/10:33/11:8/13:9^2:10/14:30:
60:72/15:42,43/16:7/Lk1:8,9:15/2:21/3:4/5:8:
12/6:4:25/7:6,7,8:27/8:28:47/9:16/10:7:8,9/11:
26/12:9:11:58/14:29:30/17:7,8,9/19:8:13:27/
20:3:26/21:12^2/22:15:61:66/23:12:47/24:4:5:26
:44/Jn1:1:15:30:48/4:49/5:14/6:36/7:40:51/8:
58/9:4/10:8/11:55/12:1:16:35/13:1:33:38/14:
29/15:18/16:5f:24/17:5:24/18:28/19:14:41:42/
20:26/Act2:20/3:13:16/4:7/5:26,27/6:12/7:2:
10/8:21:32/9:15/10:25:30:33/11:10/12:6^2/13:
24/14:13/15:5:36/16:3^2:19:29:34:40/17:6:22/
18:12:18f:22f/19:21/21:37,38f/22:30/23:1:20:
30/24:16:21/25:9:10,11:16:26/26:2/27:14,15:
17:24:35/28:11/Rom1:13:20/3:19/4:10^2:11:12:
20/5:21/9:10-13^2:25/14:10/15:19:21:25/16:7:
17/1Co2:7/4:5/5:9/7:18/10:13/11:23:28:31/12
:2/15:1/2Co2:3/5:10^2/7:3:14/12:21/Gal1:15:17
/3:1/4:3:8:27/5:21/Eph1:4^2/3:2,3/Php:18/Col
1:15:17:22/4:10/1Th2:2:19/3:13/4:6:11/1Ti3:6:
10/6:12:13^2/2Ti1:9/4:1^2:16:21/Tit1:1/Heb2:17
/5:7f^2/9:18:24/10:6:11/11:5/12:1/Jas2:11:4:10
/1Pe1:20/3:22/2Pe2:5:20/1Jn:1:7/3:19/5:6,7,8
/Jud1:15/Rev:4/2:5/3/4:1:6:10^2/5:6:8/6:10/7:
9:11:15/8:2:3/9:13:17,18/11:4:16/12:4:10/13:8:
8f/14:3/15:2:3,4/17:8:11/20:12
1339

BENEATH
Gen1:9,10/15:5/18:8/21:15/35:4:8/49:25/Ex2:
23/9:19/14:27/15:4/18:21/20:26/23:5/28:42/
30:4/36:30/37:20,21:27/Lev14:37/15:10/26:7/
Num16:31/Deu22:4/28:23/Jos2:6/7:21:22/13:
2-7/24:26/Ju3:21:22,23/6:11:19/9:15/1Sa22:6
/31:13/2Sa18:9/22:39/1Ki19:5/2Ki13:7/18:
20,21/19:26/1Ch10:12/2Ch5:7,8/33:20,21/
Neh9:11/Job4:9/6:8,9/18:15/20:28/30:7/35:
9,10^2/Ps5:10/10/18:9:36/29:9/31:20/38:3,4/
39:10/55:2/57:1/58:9/60:3/61:4/63:7/90:9/91:

(BENEATH Con't)
12/124:4,5/144:5/145:14/146:8/Pro11:5/Is1:4/8:14,15/10:5,6/19:16/24:18/25:10/27:11/28:3/34:15/37:27/40:7/43:17/49:7/51:6/54:16/57:5/Jer3:6/6:15/15:17,18/17:2,3/32:2/Lam2:3/3:28:34,35,36:66/5:5:13/Eze1:8:15/4:17/10:2:7,8:20/21:9,10,11/23:33/24:5:9/26:19/27:7:34/29:7/31:6:12:17/32:27/43:17/47:1/Dan4:12/5:6/7:7/Hos14:7/Jon2:5/Mic1:4/7:19/Nah1:3/Hab2:15/3:16/Zec9:15/10:5/Mt11:28/15:27/20:25/22:20:44/23:37/Mk4:5,6/Lk8:6/11:46/20:42,43/2Co10:7/Heb1:13/1Pe2:20/Rev5:13/12:1

150

BUT

Gen2:16,17:19,20/3:12/4:5:7^2:9:10/6:1f:8:18/7:13/8:9/9:4/11:5:28:30:31/12:11,12,13^2:17/13:6/14:4:8,9:22:24/15:2,3:8:10:14:15/16:1:9-12/17:2,3,4:5:15:17:21/18:15:22,23:27:32/19:3:8:10:14:22:26:33/20:3:4:7/21:9:12:23:28,29/22:7/23:14,15/24:5:8^2:21:33:38:39:54:55:56/26:8:21:35/27:5:11,12:22:39,40^2:42/29:2:17:20^2:25:31/30:6f:15:30:42/31:1:7^2:29:30:32:33:35f:42:50/32:12:22,23,24:26/33:10:13/34:2:5:22:23:25/35:10:16:18/37:2:10:11:18:21,22:35/38:7:9:11^2:20:21:25:26:29/39:10:12:14,15:21/40:8:17:22/41:3:6:8:15:16:19:24:30:54/42:7:8,9:20:21:22:25:27:34:38/43:1:3,4,5:7:8/44:4:22:23/45:3:5:22:26:27/46:3,4/47:15:18:30/48:6:11:14:17:19^2:21/49:4:19:24/50:8:15:19:24/Ex1:12:15,16:17:22/2:15:17/3:11:13:19/4:1:10:13:21:23/5:3:10,11:17/6:1:8,9:12/7:3:12:22/8:7:15:18:19:22:25:26:28:29:31,32/9:4:6:12:16:21:30:32/10:1:8:20:23:24/11:7/12:9:23:44:48/13:13/14:5:13:20:24:27/15:10:13:19/16:3:20:26:27^2/17:1:3:8:11/18:22:26/19:13:21:23:24/20:6:10:19:25/21:3:4:5:8:9:13:18:22:23:28:30:30f:32:36^2/22:3:8:12:15:17/23:5:11:22:30/25:15/32:11:18^2:30/33:3:11:12:20:23/34:9:14:20:31:34/36:4-7/40:37/Lev1:13:15,16,17/2:3:4:9:10:12:12f/3:1/4:11,12:28/5:8/6:18:29/7:16:17,18:19:20:24:31/9:11:21/10:1:6:7:14:19^2/11:4-7:10:38/12:8/13:4:7:12:14,15:16,17:19:21:23:26:28:31:33:35:37:39^2:41:53:56:58/14:32:43:48/15:3/16:29,30/17:16/18:14f/19:18:20/21:23/22:13^2:23:26,27/23:25/25:4:20:28^2:30:31:33:40:46/26:14:15:23:40,41:43:44/27:8:9:11,12:13:18:20:22:27/Num3:4:38/4:15:28/5:8:13:20:28/8:25,26/9:6,7:10:13:19:20,21:22/10:4:5,6,7f^2:30/11:6:21:26:29:33/12:1f:2:7,8:14/13:28:30/14:9:10,11:13:20,21:24:25:32:40:41:44/15:30/16:11,12:22:30:41:45:49/17:12,13/18:2,3:7:32/19:12:20/20:12:12f:16:17:18:19:20/21:23:24^2:33/22:18:20:22,23^2:35^2:38/23:7-10:12:26/24:11:14:20:21,22:25f/25:2:6:9/26:5-11:19-19-22:61:62/27:3,4:11/28:17/30:4:5:8:9:12:14/31:14:23:28/32:9:14:17^2:23:27:30:32/33:55/35:15:16:22,23:28:30/36:3/Deu1:12:22:26:29:32:40:42:43:44:45/2:11:12:19:21:28:30:33,34/3:1:7:19:26:27^2/4:4:9:12:15:19:21,22:26:27:29/5:2,3:7:9,10:14:23:25/7:10:18/8:11:19/9:3:19:20:27/10:11:22/11:7:16:32/12:10:17/13:2:4/14:7^2:21/15:6^2:7:16:18:23/18:14:20/19:11/20:5:6:12:14:20/21:15/22:20:25,26,27^2/23:5:7:20:22:24:25/24:21/25:1:7/26:5:19/28:7:12:14:25:31:32:38:39:40:65:68/29:4:7:14,15:29/30:10:14:17/31:3/32:5:9:15:27:31:34:52/34:4:6/Jos1:14/2:2:4^2:6:17,18:19/3:13,14/6:2:15^2:19/7:1:10,11/8:2:9:14:29/9:3,4,5:8:12:13:14,15:18:19:25:27/10:14:33/11:6:14/13:33/14:8^2:12/15:63/17:8:12/19:47,48/20:6/22:11:19:28/23:6:8:15,16/24:3:6:8:10:11:15^2:19:21/Ju1:4,5,6:15:28:30:35/2:10:15:17:19/3:6:9:11:15:17,18,19:25/4:2,3:8:9/5:15:18:19:23:29:31/6:10:11:15:16:18:27:31:39:40/7:4:10/8:1:2,3:4:6:8:12:20:23,24:27:33/9:9:11:13:20:25:30:40:52/10:1:6:11:15/11:1:7:17:18:20:21,22:26:27:28:37/12:2:6/13:2,3:7:9:16:23/14:3:6:9:13:19/15:1:2:11:12,13:14:18:20/16:12:19:20:22/18:29/19:2:5:7:10:15:16:18:24:25:28/20:13:21:32:33:35-39^2:42:45/21:10,11,12:14:18/Ru1:4,5:8:11:14:16:17:20/3:3:10:12^2:13/1Sa1:2:5:15,16/2:9:16:22:23,24,25^2:32/3:2,3:16,17/4:20/5:3:4:9:10/6:9:19/7:10/8:3:9:18:19/9:4:6:7/10:14:16:18,19:21:27/11:1:2:11:13/12:9:12^2:15:20:25/13:8:10:11:14:16/14:1:10:19:31:36:37:39:43:45/15:8:15:20^2:26:30:33:35/16:2:5:7^2:8:9:10,11:14:18:20/17:9:28:34:45:54/18:6:10:11,12:13:15,16:17:19:21:23:25/19:1:9,10^2:16:20:21:23/20:3:5:7:8:15:17:22:24,25:27:32/21:4:11/22:14:17^2/23:3:9:14,15:19:24,25^2:26:27/24:3:5:9,10:11:12:13:22/25:3:14:15,16:19:21:25^2:29/26:3,4:11^2:19/27:1/28:5,6:10:16:23/29:3:4:6:7:9^2/30:6:9,10:22:23/31:3,4:11/2Sa1:9:24/2:8:19:21:23:31/3:7:13:22:26:27:35,36/4:4:6,7:9/5:7:17:22/6:6:10:16:20:22/7:4:15/9:7:10,11:13/10:3:18/11:1:9:13^2:27/12:3:4:12:13:14:17:19:21:23^2/13:3:9:11:14:16:21-24:25:32,33/14:7:14:14f:15,16:20:24:29^2/15:5:10:11:19,20^2:21:25,26:33,34/17:5:18/18:2:22:23:29/19:8,9,10:22:27^2:28:37:41:43/20:2:3:5:12:16/21:2^2:8:17/22:7:19:27:28:42/23:6:16:18,19:23/24:3^2:3f:4:10:14:16:24/1Ki1:1:3,4:8:10:18:19:26:52/2:5:7:8:9:15:16:26:39:45/3:7:19:21:26/5:4/8:8:12,13:16:18:19:27/9:11,12/10:7:8/11:9,10:16,17,18:22:32:35:39:40/12:8:11^2:15:18:22/13:8:18^2:24,25/14:5:8:9:13/15:4:26:34/16:2:8:15,16:21:22:25:30/17:7:12:13^2:17/18:12:15:21:22:23:25:26:29:42:43/19:5:9:10:11^2:12:14/20:5,6:9:20:23:27:30:35:40/21:3:17/22:2:5:7:8:14:23:30:32,33:43:48:49:52,53/2Ki1:3:10:13/2:1:4:6,7:10:17^2:19/3:2:5:9:11:13:17:18:22:24:25:26/4:1:17:20:23:27^2:30:31:38:40:43/5:1:8:11:13:16^2:17:20:22:24:26/6:5:26-30:32/7:2^2:4:5:10:17:19/8:10:13:15:18:21^2:26/9:15:18:27:35/10:4:9,10:18,19:31/11:15/12:6:13,14:20/13:2:4:6:11:19:23/14:3:6:9^2:10:11:19:24/15:4:9:15:18,19,20:24:34,35/16:2:5/17:1:4:14:19:25:29:33:40:41/18:18:20,21:27:36/19:3:18/20:19/21:9:23/22:18,19/23:19:26:29/24:1:20/25:12:25/1Ch2:3:23:31:33/4:27:40,41/5:1:25/6:49/7:20,21/8:8,9,10/10:4:11/11:5,6:14:18,19:21:23/12:17:19/13:9/14:8:12/15:29/16:26/17:3:18/19:2,3:17,18/20:4:6,7/21:3:4:6:8:13:15:17^2:30/22:8:9/24:1/27:24/28:3:9/29:14:15/2Ch1:11/2:6^2/4:19/5:9/6:1:5,6:8:9:18/7:19/8:9/10:8,9:11:14^2/11:2/12:1:8:14/13:8:10:11/14:9,10:15/15:2:4:7:17/16:8:12^2/18:1:6,7^3:13:17:19,20:29:30:31:33:34/19:3:4/20:12:15:17:35/21:3,4:6:10:13:20/22:2f:7/24:5:17,18:19:24:25/25:2:4:7:9:19:20:27/26:7:16:19/27:2/28:1:9^2:20:23:27/29:10:34/30:8:10:12:17,18,19/31:4:10/32:8:24:26/33:2:9:17:20,21:23:25/34:26/35:21:22/36:2:5:9:16:22,23/Ez2:62,63/3:12/4:3:13/5:1:3:5^2:12:13/9:1:8:9/10:2:13/Neh1:9/2:3:10:14,15:17:19:20^2/3:5:8/4:7:9:16/5:8:15/6:2:11:12,13/7:4:61:73/9:16:17:19:26:27:28:29:30:31:35/11:1/13:21:26/Est1:8:12:13-15:16/2:1/3:2:3,4,5,6^2:11/4:4:14^2/5:9:13/6:12/9:1:5:7-10:12:16:18/10:1/Job1:11:12,13/2:10/3:9/4:5:16:20/5:1^2:3/6:14:15-18^2:22:25,26/7:7:8/8:9:10:18:20/9:2:11:18:20:29:32,33/11:8:20/12:13/14:10:13:16:20,21/15:2:6:29/16:4:5:6:20/17:3,4:7/19:16:25:27/20:3:5:14/21:16:19:22:29/22:8:13/23:8:9:10:12/24:18:24/25:6/27:8:12:17:19/28:12:13:22/30:1:2:20:28,29^2/31:6:18:30:32/32:3:5:8,9:11,12/33:23,24:27:32:33/34:4:5:31/35:2,3:12:13:14,15/36:6:7:13:17/38:21/39:13:18/41:27,28/42:5^2/Ps1:2:4:6/2:4:12/3:3/5:1:7:11/7:6:7,8/9:20/11:3:4/12:3,4/13:5/14:3/16:2/17:15^2/18:18:26:27:31:41^2/19:12/20:7/21:11/22:2:6/25:3:11/29:9/30:5/31:8:14,15:17:23/32:3:10/33:9:11:16,17:18,19/34:10:16:19:22/35:9:12:13:15:17:20:27/37:9:11:15:17:20:21:22:28:33:35,36^2:37:38/38:13,14:19/39:2,3:4:5,6/40:6:10:16/41:5:6/42:4,5:6:11/44:3:22/46:6/49:12:15:20f/50:9:16:21:23/51:5/52:8/53:3:5/54:4/55:13:16:21^2:23/56:3,4/57:6/59:11:16/60:4,5/62:3,4:5/63:9:11/64:7/66:12:19/68:3:6:21/69:13:29/70:4:5/71:20/73:2:23:25:27:28/75:6,7:9/78:30:36:50:52:53:67/80:12/81:11:13:16/82:5:7/86:15/87:5/89:33/90:4:5,6:10/91:8/92:10:12:15/96:5/101:2:7/102:24:26:27:28/103:14:17,18/104:21:29:35/105:12:14:26/106:14:15:15f:23:35:43/107:39:41/108:9:10:13/109:4:21:30/110:7/112:8/115:16:18/116:12/118:11:13:17:18/119:19:23:51:61:69:70:78:81:83:109:110:113:118:141:151:157:161:163/120:7/125:5/129:2/130:3,4/132:7:18/136:15/138:6/140:12/141:5/144:4:12-15/145:20/146:5:9/147:6:11:18/Pro1:18:24^2:33/3:32:33:34:35/4:18/5:4:4f/6:9:15:31:32/7:24/8:36/9:7,8:18/10:5:6:6f:7:8:9:11:12:20:21:25:29:30:31/11:2:11:14:18:20:26/12:8:10:13:15:18:21:23:25:27/13:4:12:22:23:25f/14:3:4:12:22:25:32:33:34/15:1:6:8:9,10:25:26:26f:27:29:31,32/16:1:2:22:25:33/17:3:8f:22:24/18:14:24/19:7:12:14:21/20:6:14:17:21/21:2:15:20:25,26:29:31/22:12:15/23:17,18/24:15,16:25/26:24,25,26/27:7:19:21/28:1:2:5:10:11:13:14:16:18:20:26:27/29:1:2:3:4:5,6:16:18:24:25:26/30:4^2:24-28^2/31:12:29:30/Ecc1:3-7:3-7f:3-7:16-18/2:1:11:20-23:24-26/3:11/4:4:5,6:10:11:12:13:16/5:12/6:1:2:3:6/7:12:23:26:27,28/8:12/9:2,3^2:5:11:15:17:18/10:12,13:14/11:8:9:10/12:4:9:10^2:12/Sol1:5^2:6:6f/3:1:2/5:3:6^3/6:9/8:12/Is1:3:20:21:22:28/3:10:11/5:2:6:7^2:9:10:12:16:25/6:9/7:1:7:12:17:21,22/8:9,10:14,15/9:8,9,10:17:19,20/10:4:7:13:22:32/11:1:4/12:1/13:20/14:1:7:15:19:29:30/15:9/16:12^2:13,14/17:13:14/18:5:7/19:13/21:16/22:3:9,10,11:13:25/23:17:18/24:14:15,16/25:4/26:7^2:13:18/27:7,8/28:7:11:12:16:17:27^2/29:2:5:8^3:13/30:1:3:15:16:29/31:4,5:8/32:8:19/33:1:2:7:10:19/36:7:12:21/37:4:8,9:19:26:28/38:10:15/40:8:15:31/41:2:7:8:9:24:25:26/42:1f:14:17:20^2:22/43:1:10:18:22/44:10:26/45:17:21^2/46:1:13/47:6:14/48:6:10:15:22/49:4:25/50:11/51:1^2:6:8:21^2:23/53:1:2:5:8:9:10/54:7:8:10:17/55:5/56:2/57:3:10:13:17:18:20^2/58:13/59:2:11/60:2/63:5:10/64:5:6/65:1f^2:2:7:8:11:13^2/66:3:5/Jer1:19/2:7:9:25:30:36/3:1:7:8:10:20/4:10:11,12:22:28/5:3^2:4:5:10:18:23,24:31/6:10:16:17:29/7:4:11:13,14:23:24:26:27^2/8:2:4,5:7:15^2/9:25,26/10:10:12:14:16:19:24/11:8:12:16/12:2:3:13^2:15:17/13:1:7:11/14:3:6:10:19:22/15:2:20/16:4:14,15/17:7:12:18:21,22:23:24:27/18:4:10:12:15:23/19:6/20:7:11:18/21:1f/22:5:6:15:17:21:23:30f/23:8:14:18:36:38,39/24:2:8/25:2,3:4:6:7/26:5:13:15:19:21:24/27:11/28:7:13/29:10:15/30:16:18/31:16:18:19:20:28:33/32:23:30:31:33:37:40/33:25,26/34:4:5:10:14:16/35:6:7:11:14:15:16/36:17:24,25:26/37:2:13:14:17:21/38:1:2:6:19:21,22/39:5:10:17/40:1:4:5:13,14^2:16/41:1:7:11/42:12:13,14:21/44:5:18:26:27:28^2/45:4/46:5:17:20,21:26:27:28^2/47:7/48:11:15:30:33:45:47/49:4:5:6:9,10:11:16:30f:39/50:8:28:34/51:5:8:9:19:46:52/52:2:8:16/Lam1:17/2/3:34,35,36:55/4:3,4^2:8:11:15:17:21:22/5:7:18/Eze1:7/2:4:7/3:8:14,15f:14,15:18:19^2:20:21:27/5:17/6:8/7:14:25:26,27/8:6:15/9:6:9/10:9-13/11:7:7f:12:16:21/12:2^2:13:16/13:23/14:11:16/15:4/16:6,7:15:33,34^2:43^2:53:57/17:6:7:14:15/18:5:7:10:11:14:16:18:21/19:12/20:8:9,10:13:14:15:21:23,24^2:38:39/21:23/22:13:30/23:4,5:8:11:17:19,20:45/24:12:17:23/27:26/28:2,3:9/29:7:13:14/30:24/31:10/32:2:25/33:6^2:8:9:13:19:20:25:31^2:32:33/34:3:18:26:29f/36:8:11:14:20:22:32^2:35:37,38/37:8:12/38:2,3f:13:18/39:25/40:34:38/41:21/42:7,8/44:1:3:12:26/45:8/46:1:9^2:17/47:11/Dan1:8:10/2:5:6:8,9:14:28:30:34:35:39:43:44/3:8:12:15:18:24/4:7:15:18:23:26:28/5:8:8f:10:15:17:20:23/6:4:10/7:4:6:12:18:26:28/8:8:12:17:18:24:24f:25:26:27/9:1:5:7:9:13:14:18:27^2/10:7:10:13/11:2:4:5:6^2:7:9:12:14:17:18:19:20:21:24:25:27:29:32:32f:33:35:42:44:45/12:4:8:9:10:13/Hos1:7:6:7:9:14:16f/4:14:15/5:2:6:13/6:7/7:1:9:12:13:14/8:3:4:10:11:13:14/9:4:8:10/10:1:3:11:13/11:2:3:5:12/12:2:7:8:11:14/13:1:4:6:13:15/14:9/Joe2:3/3:7:16:20/Amo2:9:12/3:7:12/4:6:7:8/5:18^2:25,26,27/6:2:3:12/7:10:14:15/8:11:12/9:10/Ob1:17/Jon:3:4:13/2:6:9/3:4,5/4:7/Mic1:12/2:3/3:8/4:1:9:10:12/5:2/6:5:14:15^2/7:4:13:13f/Nah1:3:8:12/2:2:6:8:13/3:15:16:17/Hab1:2:11:13:14^2/2:3:4:5:13:19:20/Zep1:5:6/2:15/3:5^2:7:8/Hag1:6:9/2:4:7f:13:14:15:18,19:23/Zec1:3:4,5,6:15/2:6,7/4:6/5:5/6:15/7:6:13/8:6:11:13/9:10f/11:8:12/12:4/13:7:8/14:10:18/Mal1:2,3:4:6:9:11:12/2:8:9/3:2:7:13/4:2/Mt1:18:19:25/2:12:22/3:7:7f:11:15/4:4:12,13/5:19:20:22:22f:28:32:33:34:39:44:48/6:3:6:13:14,15:17:23:31,32/7:14:15:21:23:26/8:15:20^2:22:24:26/9:5,6:15:18:31:34/10:6:17:22:26:28:33:39/11:17:19/12:2:3:7:15:16:24:28:39,40:43,44,45^2/13:6:8:12,13^2:14^2:16:17:21:22:25:31,32/14:5:6:9:13:16:27:30/15:5,6:8:18:20:23:25/16:2,3:4:11:22/17:5:12:16:21:25/18:6:7:16:17:26:28:30/19:5,6:8:13:14:17:22:26:29f:30/20:10:22:23:25:26:28:31/21:13:15:19:28:29:30:35:36:38:44:46/22:3:5:11:14:18:23:29:31:32:34,35/23:3:12:16:18:23^2:25:28:37/24:2:6:8:13:22:35:36:48/25:2,3,4:9:10:12:18:26:29:31:46/26:5:11:24:32:39:41:45:54:56:60,61:63:70:73/27:12:14:23:27:34:41,42,43:49/28:6:8:17/Mk1:8:34:38:45^2/2:6:9,10,11:16:17:20:25,26:27/3:4:12:16-19:22:29/4:5,6:8:13:17:19:20:34:37/5:15:19:26:32:36:40/6:19:20:26:33:37:49:50/7:4:6,7:11:15,16:19:24:26:28:36/8:14:24:30/9:7:10:18:20:27:29f:32:34:38:42/10:6,7:8:14:19:27:31:34:38:40:43:45:48/11:13:17:25:26,f:32/12:3:7:12:13:14:17:20,21,22:26:40/13:7:9:11^2:13:20:31/14:2:6:7:21:28:41:47:49:55:56:59/15:5:11:12:14:23:31/16:4:6:9f:10,11:12:13:16/Lk1:7:13:18:34:60/2:10:19:34,35^2:36,37:43:44:49:50/3:16:19,20/4:4:24:30:41:42:43/5:5:16:18,19:21:23,24:30:35:36:39/6:2:8:24:25:40:47,48:49/7:6,7,8:26:34:35:35f:42:44:45:46:47/8:6:10:12:13^2:14:15:38:43,44:46:50:52:56/9:11:13:24:27:34:40:42:45:47:50:53:55:55f:58^2:59:59f:61:62/10:7:10:20:32:33:40:41/11:8:15:20:24:25f:28:29,30:31:32:39:42^2

(BUT Con't)
12:5:9:14:20:21:30:38:45:48:56/13:6:14:15:
4,25:26:34/14:18:22:28/15:2:22:29:32/16:1:9:
f:15^2:16:17:25:29:30:31/17:1:7,8,9:22:25/18:
,5^2:8:13^2:14:15:20:23:34:39/19:3:7:14:20:25:26
39:41:46:47:48/20:6:10:11:14:16:19:21:34,35:
7,38:47/21:4:6:8:9:12:13:18:20/22:21:22:25:26
27:32:34:36:41,42:47:48:51:53:60:67,68:69/23:
:9:18:21:23:25:28^2:40,41^2:56/24:1:3:11:16:20:
9:37:49f/Jn1:10:11,12:13:18:26:31:33:42/2:5:
0:21:24,25/3:6:8:12:16:17:18:19:21:32:36/4:1:
1:14:17,18:20:21-24^2:27:45/5:9:14:17:23:24:30
32,33:34:36:38:43:44:46/6:8,9:17:18,19:20:27:
6:37:39:43:48-51:54:63:64/7:2:6:7:10:13:16:18:
1,22,23:26:27:28:30:33:34:39:41,42:44:49/8:2:
:7:14:16:20:26:27:28:33:35:38:40:42:54:55^2:59/
:3:5:9:16:21:25:26:28:29:31:41/10:5:8:26:33:38
39:41/11:4^2:8:11:12,13:20:37,38:39:40:42:46:51
52/12:4:6:8:16:23,24:27:37:39:42:48:49/13:8:
0:36:37/14:10:17:19:22:26:28:31/15:7:18:19:
2:24:26/16:5:5f:7:12:13:16:20:22:24:25:32:33/
17:6:9:15:20:25/18:11:26:31:34f:36:37:39:40^2/
19:4:9:12:13f:15:23,24:33/20:5:14:17:26:29:
30,31/21:3:4:18:23/Act1:5:8/2:13:21:23:30/3:6 ^{2}
15:18/4:4:10:17:19/5:1:3:4:13:19:22:23:29:34:
36:37:39/6:1:9:10/7:5:6:7:9:11:17,18:25:27:39:
47:51:55/8:2:4:12:20:26:27:39/9:1:7:13:15:24:
26:29:38:40/10:9,10:26:28:40,41^2:46,47/11:2:9:
15:16:19/12:5:9:20/13:8:14:22:24:25:28:30:45:
46:51/14:2:4:14:17:18:20/15:5:24:38/16:1:7:24:
28:37/17:5:11:13:19:30:32:34/18:6:12:14:15:17:
20:21:25,26/19:9:15^2:23:26:27^2:30:34/20:17:24
/21:7:13^2:20/22:3:9:19:21:28/23:8:16:21:30/24:
4:7:14:18:20:23/25:4:10,11^2:18:19:21:25^2:26/26
6:8:22:25:27/27:7,8:11:14,15^2:21:22:26:31:39:
41:43/28:5:6:19:20f:22:25:26/Rom1:11,12:13:
16:18:21:25/2:1:5:8:10:12-15^2:23:25:27:29/3:3:
5:8:21,22^2:26/4:1:4,5^2:9^2:13:15:20/5:8:15:17:18:
20:21/6:10:13:14:15:22:23/7:2:3:4:6^2:7:8:9:12:
13:14:15:17:18:23,24,25^3/8:3:5:6:9:10:10f^2:13:
15:17:25:26:32:37/9:4:8:10-13^2:31/10:2:3:6:14:
16:18:21/11:7:17:18:22^2:25:28:30:31/12:2:11:16
:21/13:3:4:14/14:1f:2:5:14:17:20:22:23/15:
15,16:18:20:23:25/16:18:19:25,26,27/1Co1:10:
13:17:18:24/2:4:6:8:10:14:15:16/3:1:6:7:10:12:
15^2/4:4:10^2:14:19/5:10:11:12:13/6:6:8:11:12:13 ^{3}
:17/7:2:6:7:9:11:12^2:15:17:19:21:25:27:28:33:34:
36:37:39:40/8:1:3:6:9/9:12^2:17:24:25/10:13:23^2
:28:29:33/11:3:7:8:9:11:16:19:21:31/12:3:4:5:6:
12:13:18:20:31/13:1:2:3:6:8:10:11:12^2/14:2^3:3:4
:5:6:11:14:17:19:20:21:22:24:26:28^2:29,30:34f:
38/15:10^2:12:20:22:35:40f:43^2:44:45:47:48:51^2:
53/16:5:9:11:12/2Co1:6,7:9:11/2:4:13:14:16/3:
3^2:6:14:16:18/4:5:7:8^2:9^2:11:12:18^2/5:4:8:12:
13,14:15:19/6:8:9^3:10^2:12/7:7:8:9:10:11/8:3:8:
10:14:17:21/9:3:6^2:8:13/10:1:3:7:8:10:13:18/11:
3:12:16:21:23:26:30:33/12:1:2,3:5:6:9:16:17/13:
3:4^2:8f:10/Gal1:15/2:5:11:12:16:17:20/3:13:16:
19:20:25:28/4:1:4:7:14:23:26:30:31/5:5:9:13:15:
19:22/6:8:13/Eph2:4:11:13:19/3:5/4:20/5:11:
13:17:29,30:32/6:12:14:20/Php1:15:18:20:22:
24:27:28:29/2:4:7:22:27/3:7:9:12:13:20/4:10:14
:17/Col1:24:26,27/2:11:19:23/3:8:12:22/1Th2:
7:8:12:13:16:17:18/3:2,3/4:7:8:9/5:4:8:9:15:21/
2Th1:3/2:7:13/3:3:9:15/1Ti1:6:9:13:16/2:14:15
/3:3:11:16/4:1:8^2/5:1:4:6:8:24:25/6:3:9:17/2Ti1
:7:9/2:12:19:22/3:5:7:9:10:11:14/4:3:4:8:13:15:
17/Tit1:10:15:16/2:1:3:10/3:2:4:5:8/Phm1:8,9:
11:14^2:16^2:19/Heb:2:5,6:8:11:12/2:9:16/3:3:4:5
:6:9:10:15:16/4:2:6:7:14/5:1:7f^2:11:12,13/6:8:12
/7:3:6:8:12,13,14:16:19:24:28/8:4:6:8:10/9:5:7:
9:12:23:26:28/10:1:3:12:25:27:39/11:13^2:16:19:
24,25:29:35/12:10:11:13:22:26^2/Jas1:6:10,11:
17:25^2:26/2:9:10:11:13:18^2/3:5:8:17/4:6^2:11^2/5
:12/1Pe1:12:15:19:20:25/2:9:16:18:20:25/3:12:
14:18:21/4:2:5:16/5:2:3:5:13f/2Pe1:5:9:13,14:
19/2:1^2:3:4:7,8:12:16:19/3:8:9:13:18/1Jn1:6:7:9
/2:1:2:4:5:9:10:17:19:20:21:23:27/3:1:2:4:6:8^2:
14:17:20:21/4:3:6:8:10:17:20:21/5:5:6,7,8:6,7,8f
:16:17f/2Jn1:12/3Jn:9:10:12:13/Jud:3:6:9:10:
12^2:13:20:23/Rev:4f:17,18/2:2:6:9^2:21/3:1:5:8:9
f:9:16/4:5f/5:3:5:6f/6:6/9:4:5:6^2:12:19:20/10:7:
9:10/11:2:11:14:18/12:11:12:14:16/13:2:3:10:
11/16/17:8:10/18:20/19:10/20:9:11/21:8:27/
22:9

4416

BY

Gen5:3,4,5f^2/6:11/7:16/8:14:20f/11:9:12,13f:26
:28/12:6/19:18,19,20/21:8:23:28,29/22:13:14:
16/23:17,18:19,20/24:3/26:15/27:42/29:25/30:
14f:22:27f/31:26:31:39:39f^2:44/32:16^2/36:31-
31-39f:31-39^7/37:28:29/38:3,4,5^2:14:15/39:1:6:
12:18:21/41:6:16:37:50/42:15/43:10:32/44:5:
28/46:18:23,24,25/47:26/48:12,13:20/49:23:24
/50:11/Ex3:17:21/4:4/5:3:7,8/8:26:29/9:15:20:
29:34/11:3/12:42/13:17,18:21^3/14:7^2/15:16/16
:21/17:1:3:7/18:18/21:4:8/22:5:13:31/23:1:2,3:
5/26:4,5/27:9,10:11:14,15:17/28:5,6:22,23,24:
28:30,31f:37,38:41/29:36:43/30:32/32:6:13/33:
12f:17f:22/34:7:15:16:20/35:21:29/36:3:14,15:
24:29:38/38:8:12:19:21^2:23/39:4,5^2:21^2/40:18/
Lev1:4:15,16,17/2:2f:9/4:35/5:12:15:16:17,18/
6:2^4:3:15:18^2:22,23:30/7:14:19:24:25:30:38/8:5:
8f:27:28:29:34/9:13/10:12:13:14:15/11:26:43:
44/13:14,15:52/14:12:17:21/15:12:13:32^2/16:9:
16^2:21:27:32/17:15/18:4,5f:27/19:29:31/20:1:
12:25/21:1:6/22:1:3:4:8:15^3:25^2:26,27/23:8:
9,10,11:13:23,24:25:26,27^2:36^2:37:40/24:5-8:9^2:
13,14/25:14,15,16:24:48:54/26:25^2:36/27:3f:13:
16:29:32/Num1:2-15/2:32,33:34/3:39:47,48f/4:
32/5:1:5,6/6:9/7:3:30-35:60-65:78-83:84,85,86/
8:7/9:6,7/10:14:15:16:19:20:21:22:23:24:25:26:
27/11:14:32f:34/12:6/13:22/14:17,18:20,21:
36,37,38:42/15:3,4^2:5:10:13,14:19,20,21:22:25^2:
27/16:25:28/18:8^3:9:10:11:18:19:24:25,26/19:
18^2/21:24:27-30/22:25:26:33/23:3,4:15/24:1:2:
3-9^2:10:23,24/25:12,13:18/26:5-11:12-14:15-18
:52,53:63/27:14/28:3:6:8:9,10:13:26:28,29/29:6
:14:18:26,27/31:4,5:6:23:28:29/32:17:28/33:3,4 ^{2}
:38,39:54/34:13/35:16:20:21:33/36:1/Deu1:1^2:
9:27:33/2:12^2:20^2:30/3:11:17/4:1:11:16,17:25:
34:38:44,45,46^2/5:14^2:22/6:2/8:1:3^2/9:26:29/
10:20/12:6:17:19/13:1:5/16:1:10/17:1:2,3:12:
18:19/18:1^2:9/19:14/21:9/22:21/24:6/25:11/
27:15/28:25:56,57/29:22:23:25/31:7/32:21:27:
40,41/33:2:5:13:14:29/Jos2:1:3:12,13:15/3:
13,14:17/4:10/6:3,4:6-9^2:25/7:5:14^4:18/8:10:33
/9:22/10:9:11/11:4:6:14/12:1:7^2/13:21/14:1:1f:
6/15:1/18:8:10/20:6/21^2:8:23,24:34,35/22:4:13
:16:19:22,23:29/23:7/Ju2:12-14:17:18:21/3:
17,18,19:30/4:2,3:20:22/5:19/6:1:11/7:2:5,6:24
:25/8:10:11:13:21:27f:28/9:2^2:16:19:32/10:3:16
/11:1:27:33:39f/13:1^2/16:25,26^2:27/18:30:31/
19:16/20:8,9,10/21:5:7/Ru1:6,7:11f:19/2:7/3:
10:13/1Sa1:4:6/2:9:16:33/3:1:2,3:14/4:18/6:
4,5:9:15:17:18^2/7:14/9:5:6/10:18,19:20/12:9^2:
10:19:23/13:1:11:23/14:33:34:39:41:45/15:30/
16:7^2:20/17:35:43/18:4:5:10:17:21/19:5:11/20:
3^2:12:17:19^2:34/22:6/24:21/25:22:26^2:29:34:
37,38/26:5,6,7:16:19/27:12/28:5,6^3:7,8^2:15^2:19
/29:2:4:6/30:15/2Sa2:16:17^2:27/3:7:8:18:24,25:
28:29/4:9/5:21:23/6:3:5:22/8:1:2^2/9:3/10:
15,16^2/11:1:19,20,21/12:5:10:25f/13:2/14:11^2/
15:21^2:23/16:14:15:18^2/17:27/18:4:7:11f:13/19
:7:27/20:8,9,10/21:8:22/22:6:9f:16:30^2/23:2:
18,19/24:1:16/1Ki1:6:17:19:25:30:44,45/2:
23,24/3:6:9/6:6:10/7:6^2:36:40:51/8:21:29^2:37^2:
56:62,63/9:8/10:5/12:18/13:9:16,17:24,25:26/
14:11^2:15/15:30/16:1:4-7^3:34^2/17:3:12:18/18:
10:15:19:24:44/19:2^2:11:15:17^2/20:14:19:22:33:
39/21:24^2/22:6f/2Ki2:1:11^2/3:9:13:14/4:10/5:
16/6:33/7:1:15/8:21:27/9:7:28:33/10:11f/11:
2,3:13,14/14:9:28/15:5:24/16:3:11,12/17:4:20:
31/18:4:12/19:5,6:10:24^2:28:33/22:9,10/23:5:
11:14:19:21:26:30/24:7/25:16:20/1Ch1:32:33/2
:3:16/5:1:6:12/6:28:29,30:49:54:60:62:63:64,65:
70:71/7:9:20,21:28^4/8:8,9,10:30,31,32/9:22:
33,34/11:20/12:19/13:8^2/14:12:14/15:20/16:4^2
:41/17:24/19:4:7:15:16/20:6,7:8/21:12:15:17:
25f:26:29:30/22:14/23:1:16:18:19:20/24:5:5f:7-
7-18^{25}:19:21:24,25^2:26,27^2:31/25:3:8/26:13:
20,21,22:26:28/27:7:34^2/28:12:20/29:29^2/2Ch1
:2,3:4:5,6:10/2:7:14/3:6:15/4:11/5:1:11,12/6:1/
7:4,5:21/8:14:17,18/9:18:21/10:15:19/12:15^2/
13:3^2:8/14:9,10/17:5:19/18:13:18/19:10/20:3:
15:28/21:9/22:11:12^2/23:5,6:12^2/24:6:22:24/
25:18/26:11:15:16:22/27:2/28:3/29:17:19:27/
30:5f:9:12:16/31:5,6:12,13^2:17,18/32:5^2:11^2/33:
2:8:10:13/34:9^2:10,11:33/35:4,5^2:13:15^2:17/36:
3:10:22,23/Ez1:1/2:2/3:10/4:3:4,5:10/5:11/6:4
:5:14^3:16:20/7:26:28/8:20^2:33/9:2:7:11/10:16-
16-19^2:44/Neh1:10/3:2:3:6:8:13:14:18:19/4:10/
6:3:7:12,13/7:6/8:18/9:12:19:29f/10:29:39,40^2/
11:1:7,8,9:10-14:19:22,23/12:24:40,41:42:44:45
/13:18:26/Est1:20/2:6:12,13,14^2:19/3:2:7:10:
13:15/8:8f:9,10:12f:14^2/9:24,25:28:29-31^3/10:2:
3/Job4:20/5:2/7:6/9:11/10:12/11:2/13:25/15:
12:17-19:21/16:12/17:2/18:12:13:20/19/21:18:
26/22:10,11:30/23:7/24:22,23/26:8:12:13/27:2
:15:17:18/28:3,4/29:2/31:23:27:28:35/33:12/
34:20/35:12/36:7:15:31/37:12:24/38:10/40:21:
22:23/41:7:20/Ps2:4/4:2:6/5:7/6:5/10:10:17/
18:8f:21/22:6^2:12:18/24:5/27:11/31:3:11^3:17^2/
35:2:5:8:26/37:18^2:22^2:23/39:8/40:7f/42:8/44:
3^2:5:14:15,16:18:26/46:10/49:4:5:8,9/50:3:5:5f/
52:1:8/54:1/57:4/59:1/60:6,7/62:10,11/63:8:10
/64:8/65:6/68:17/77:15:19/78:14^2:26:46:48^2:
58:63:65/79:1:11/80:16/81:2/83:1/88:13/89:7:
10:12/90:7/91:1/92:3:10/94:12,13:23/95:9/98:
1:2,3:5/102:28/103:16/104:34/106:7:16:41,42^2:
43/107:10/110:3/111:6:10/112:6/118:22:26/
119:7:9:25:40,41,42:90,91:133/124:2,3^2/125:1/
126:4/129:6,7^2:8^2/135:15/138:2:3:7/140:9/144
:12-15/147:4:7/149:3/Pro1:5,6:19:27/3:9,10:20
/4:3/5:22/6:2/9:15/10:21/11:3^2:5:24,25/12:17^2
/13:2:6/14:1:32/16:6^2:8:12f:21/17:3/18:1/19:3
/20:11:26/21:8:11^2:12:14/22:16^2/23:10,11/24:
3,4^2:11,12:24:30,31/25:1/26:2^2/27:19:21/30:17 ^{2}
:24-28:32/31:14/Ecc2:4,5,6/4:5,6/5:6,7:8/6:10
/7:5^2:6:7:12:27,28/8:4/9:11^2/10:3:5:8,9:15/Sol
1:1:12:17/2:7/3:5/4:9^2/7:4/Is1:20/4:1:2,3,4:
2,3,4f/5:5:7f/7:1:4:15,16:24/8:19/9:4:19,20^2/10
:13:15:23/11:3/13:14^2:16:21/14:19:26/17:13:14
/19:15:23/21:4:6,7f/22:2^2/24:4,5:6/25:5/26:1:
11/27:12/28:1:4:7:11/29:13/30:24:27/31:8/33:
11:15:23/36:15^2:18/37:6:10^2:19:27:29:34/38:12
:13:20/39:6/40:5:26:28/41:4:13:18:22/43:1/44:
14:24^2:25/45:3:4:17:23/47:6:13/49:1:7^2/50:4:9/
52:4:5:13f/53:3:11/54:6:13:15/55:4/59:19/60:
15/62:2/64:8/65:3:15:16:21,22:23/66:13:16^2/
Jer2:17:18/3:2:13/4:2:10:14:26/5:22:31/6:5:14
/7:4:13,14:18f^2:20/8:9/9:25,26/10:2,3:12^2/13:
22:24,25/14:15:21/15:2/16:4/17:6:8^2:11:16/18
/19:1:8/20:4:7/21:9^2:10/22:5:8:13f:13/23:27/
25:6:13:16:37:38/27:5:19,20,21/28:4/29:1:14/
31:15f:32/32:3:6,7:17:24:34:43/34:16:17/35:4/
36:16:18:21:30f/37:17/38:2:3:6:18:23:27:28/39:
17/40:5/41:1:8:9:9f:10:18/42:12:22/43:2,3/44:
12:13:14:18:25:26:27:30f/46:2:6:18/47:1:3/48:
20:26/49:2:7:13:15:16:17:28/50:1:13:39^2:41^2/
51:15^2:17:26f:37:41:42:43:46:51:58/52:7^2/Lam1
:12/2:14:15:21/3:43/4:9:13/5:12:18/Eze2:6/3:
12:14,15f/4:4,5:14/5:12/6/7:24/8:3:10/9:6/12:
16/13:5:10:18:19:22:23/14:14:19/16:6,7:8:25:
26:28:43:52:57^2:61/17:14:21/18:7:12/19^2/20:
11:25f:35,36f:44/21:21:21f/23:30/24:6:17:20,21
:22^2/25:12:14/26:6:8:14f^2/27:11/28:23/29:12/
30:6:7^2:14:17:21f/31:18/32:20:22:23:25^2:26:28:
32/33:22:27^2/34:13:29/35:11/36:4:17:21:23:34
/37:1/40:28f:29,30:33/41:2:6:12/42:2/43:3:7^2:8
:9:22/44:7:19:25:29:31/45:4:6/46:9:18:21,22^2/
47:12/48:10:13:14:15/Dan1:8:10:11:15/2:14:18
:34:39f:39:43/3:25/4:10,11:15:17^2:23:30:35/7:7:
15/8:9f:11^2:14:23f:25^2:27/9:13:15:25f/10:16/11
:2:4:7f:13f:21:22f:30,31:30,31f:33/12:7:10/Hos1
:2:7f/4:12f/5:11/7:16/8:4:6/12:8:12:13/13:2:3:
16/14:1/Joe2:17/Amo:6:12/3:1/4:2:7/5:11:19^2
/6:3:6:8/7:9/9:10/Ob1:11/Jon2:3/Mic1:11f^3/2
:2/4:1:2/6:10/Nah2:1:3^2/3:8f:8/Hab1:13/2:4f:5
:9:10:16/3:1f:2:11:19/Zep1:13:18/2:12/3:3:4:5/
Hag2:14/Zec4:6^3:7/5:4:11f/6:2^2:3^2:6^2/7:2:12/
11:1:5/12:1/13:6f:9/Mal1:2,3:11/2:5:10:11:15:
17^2/3:4/Mt1:18:20/2:3/3:8:9:13:14/4:1^2:3:24/
5:31:34:35^2:36/6:5:6:7,8/7:16^2:17:20/8:4/9:5,6:
25:34/11:12f:19f:21f:23f^2:27^3/12:10:27:28:33:
37:43,44,45/13:47,48/14:13^2/15:5,6:11:12:
13,14:15/16:1:12/17/18:16:28/19:7:12/21:23:
23f:42/22:1:29:33:41/23:5^2:16^2:18^2:20^2:21^3:22^3:
29,30:34:35/24:15:43:44:45/25:1:5,6:14/26:24:
47:71:73/27:7:9:39:41,42,43:54:66f/28:15/Mk1
:2:9:14:22:23:31:32,33:43,44^2/2:9,10,11:24/3:5:
7,8:11:22:30^2/4:27:34/5:18:20:21:41,42/6:4:7:
32/7:3:15,16^2:17:19:25:31/8:23:31/9:10:17:18f:
27/10:46/11:27,28:30/12:14:40/14:19:21:34:43
/15:10^2:29,30:38f/16:20/Lk1:8,9:8,9f:42:57:61:
62:72,73:74:75/2:5:13:21:22:34,35:36,37:52/3:8
:13:14:16/4:1:4f:22:33:41/5:9:14:23,24/6:10:
17,18^2:26:44/7:6,7,8:24:29/8:14:54/9:5:22/10:
13f:25:30:31^2:33f/11:3:18:19^2:37,38:41:44/12:
53f:53/14:4/15:30/16:9f:22/17:16f:25:35,36/18
:37/19:5^2:8:24/20:1:2:4:17:19:46/21:2:17:20:22:
24^2:25/22:27:37:39:40:47/23:2^2:36:39:44:56^2/
24:19:26:28:44/Jn1:15:24,25:36/2:21/3:33,34/
5:19:36/6:15:33:57/7:21,22,23:35/8:9:26:48:52
/9:4/10:3:9:21:34,35,36/11:39:51/12:48/13:26/
14:6:24:26/15:3^2:15/16:1:14/17:3:4/18:20:25:
28f:31:32f:36/19:7:26f/20:11/21/Act1:16^2:
21,22/2:1:6:15:16:22:39/3:3:7,8:11:12:13:26/4:
7^2:10:11:25,26:30/5:15:16:30:32/6:3:9/7:35:36:
44:48,49:53f:54/8:13/10:4:5,6:11:14:17:22:23:
31:32:38^2/11:5:8:28/13:4:13:17:19,20:27:31:37/
14:3:26/15:2:8:10:11/16:2:4/17:11:16:29:31^2/
18:21:28/19:13^2:15:20:21:31:33:40/20:3:7f:13^2:

(BY Con't)
22f:24/21:11:28:30/22:11^2:12:28/23:3:10:12,13:
19:27/24:8^2:27^2/25:14:23:24^2/26:10:18:20/27:1
:9:9f:38/28:3:16:17:18/Rom1:2:4:6,7:11,12:17/
2:23/3:7:20:21,22^3:28^2:31/4:1:4,5^2:6:8:9:11:12:
15:16/5:1:8:9:10/6:4/7:8:11:23,24,25/8:3^2:5:9:
11:14:24:26:39/9:30:31:32^2/10:3:4:10:19:20/11:
6^2:36/12:3:21/13:4^2/14:13:15:22^2/15:15,16^2:19 ^{4}
:20:30:32/16:7:18/1Co1:1:2:2f:2:27:28/2:9:13:
16/3:3:18/4:1:9:20/6:14/7:23/8:12/9:10:13:14:
21/10:1:3,4:18:29/11:25:32/12:3^2:13/14:2:19:
24/15:5^2:6^2:27:30:33/16:1:3/2Co1:1:11/2:3:5,6:
10:11:17/3:2:3^2:5:6:14^2:17/4:8/5:1^2:4:7^2:16^2/6:
3:6^3/7:13^2/8:9:11:19:20/9:8/10:4/11:3:6:8,9:33
/12:7:12/13:4/Gal1:1:7:10/2:5^2:6:14:15:16^4:18:
19^2:21/3:2:11^2:12:13:15:20:21,22:23:27/4:9:10:
15f:24,25^4:29^2/5:3:4:5:12:18:25/6:1:6:16/Eph1:
1:5:7:13/2:5^2:11:14:14f:15^2:22/3:5:6:20/4:3:19:
26:30/5:6:18:21:26:26f:31/6:16:22/Php1:24:27
/2:2:5:19:25/3:4:9^3/4:3/Col1:1:3:16:20:21/2:2:
11^2:14:19:20:20f:20/3:12/4:16/1Th2:2:4/3:13/
4:6:8/5:4:8/2Th2:1:8:13^3/3:6/1Ti1:1^2:3,4/2:6:
14/3:7:13^2:16^2/4:5:6^2/5:10:15:23/6:2:5:15:19/
2Ti1:1:10/2:8:11/3:5:12:13:15:16/Tit1:3/2:5/3:
3:5/Phm1:19/Heb:1:3:4/2:3^2:4^2:5:9:11:14/3:13
/5:4:5:14/6:1:6:10:13/7:5:16:23:26^2:28/8:2^2:4:9
/9:11:12:14:22:23^2:26/10:10:14:20:26^2:28:38/
11:3^2:4^2:20:21:22:24,25:31:34:37,38^2/12:2:27:28
/13:9^2:10:15:20,21/Jas1:6:10,11:27/2:4^2:11:14:
17:18^2:22^2:24^2:25/3:3:5:6:14:15/5:12:15/1Pe2:
7:9:10/3:1:21^3/4:6:16/5:3:12:13f/2Pe1:4:17,18:
20,21/2:13:15:17:19:20/3:5,6:17/1Jn2:3/3:18:
19/4:9/5:2:4:5:6,7,8f^3/3Jn1:3^3/Jud:1:7:13:23^2/
Rev1:5:7:20f/2:6f:11:13:14/3:1:7:18/4:11/6:13/
7:14/8:12/9:2/10:1:6:7/11:5:19/12:11^2:16/13:
14/14:2/16:9/17:2:16/18:8:15/19:8/21:12:17f

2645

CAN

Gen4:7^2:13/12:11,12,13/13:14/15:5:8/18:13:19
/19:2:5:15:22/23:5:15:22/24:50:55/26:28/27:31/29:
7:21:27/32:8/33:13/34:21/38:17/39:9/41:15^2/
42:34/43:12/44:10:16^2:17:18:21/45:10/Ex4:11:
17/5:10,11:22/6:12/10:1:2:3:10:24/12:3,4f/16:
4/18:22^2/19:9/21:13/22:27/24:12/25:8/30:30/
31:6:10/35:33^2/Lev13:58/21:4/25:19:24:41:49/
Num5:8/8:25,26/12:14/16:45/22:5,6:11:19/23:
7-10^2:12:18-24/24:23,24/35:6:33/Deu1:12/3:
23,24,25:27/4:10:32/5:26,27/6:10,11,12:24/7:
17/9:1/14:29/24:12,13/28:56,57/30:13:14/31:
28/Jos2:5/4:7/8:29/14:11/15:18,19/17:
16,17,18/18:4/20:3/22:28/Ju6:15/7:14/9:33/
13:12:15/16:10:13:15:25,26/17:10,11/19:9:24/
20:13/Ru2:2:10,11/3:10/4:4:5:10/1Sa2:30/4:8/
6:18:20/9:6:8:18/10:27/11:3:10/12:5/16:2/17:
33:38,39/18:21:23/19:3/20:4:13:31:36/21:3:4/
25:17/26:9/28:2/30:15/2Sa3:9,10:39/6:9/7:20
/9:7/12:23/14:10:17:19/15:3:33,34/17:12:13/
18:20/19:26:28:35f/20:16/21:3:4/22:30:39/24:
21:22/1Ki3:9/5:6:8:9/12:7/18:5/20:23/21:15/
2Ki2:19/3:11/4:10:13:14:22/5:7/6:1^2:26-30^2/9:
22/10:4/18:19:23:31,32:35/22:5,6/1Ch17:18/
19:2,3/28:12f/2Ch2:4:6:16/13:8:9/14:11/16:9/
18:19,20^2/20:6:9/24:5:6/32:10:14/Ez9:10:15/
10:13/Neh4:1/5:8/6:7^2/9:5/Est1:19/4:14/5/8:
6:8:8f/Job3:8f/5:19/6:11/8:19/9:2:3:12/10:4-7
/11:8:15:16/12:11/13:9:11:19/14:4/15:14:34:
35/17:15/21:22:29:34/22:13:17/23:9:13/24:25^2
/25:4^2/26:14/28:3,4:7:12:20^2/30:13/32/33:5/
34:3^2:29,30^2/36:18:23:26:29/37:18:22/38:20:31 ^{2}
:32:34:35:37,38:39,40/39:10:12/40:8:9:14^2:24/
41:1:2:5:10^2:13:15-17^2:26/42:2^2:4/Ps3:3/8:4/9:
14/10:6/11:3/12:1:3,4/18:2^3:29/19:6:12:13/22:
9,10,11:17/25:15/30:6,7:9^2/33:10:20/35:18/36:
2/40:5^2/41:10/42:2/44:7:8/48:13/49:7/50:
14,15^2:22/51:14,15/53:4:6/56:3,4:10,11:13/57:
7/58:9/60:4,5/61:3/62:7:8/70:5/71:11/73:28/
74:9,10/76:5:7/77:2/78:4/81:10/84:4/85:6/88:
10:11^2:12^2/89:6:35,36:48^2/90:11^2/91:10:13/92:
6/94:21,22/96:10/106:2^2:47/108:10^2/111:4:10/
112:8/113:5/115:6:18/116:7:12/118:6^2/119:9:
17:20:31:88:104:117:130:134/130:3,4/137/139:
7^2:20/142:5:7/147:17/Pro2:16,17/3:24,25,26:
27,28/6:3:5:14:27:28/8:11/10:27/11:21^2:23^2/
13:3:17/14:10^2/15:7/16:1:2/18:14/19^2:20/20:9:
11:21/21:2:11:30/22:17,18,19/23:4,5:12:23/24:
28,29/25:15/27:16^2:21:23,24/28:13/30:20/31:
10:11:30/Ecc1:8-11/2:12f:19:24-26/3:12:14:18:
21:22/4:9^2:11:12^2:16/5:9/6:2:12^3/7:14:18/8:4:
6,7:8:16,17/9:18/10:1:3:14/11:10/12:12/Sol2:4
/3:6/4:12/5:15/8:7/Is1:18^2/5:8:19:22/8:19/10:
14:15^2/11/14:16:17:27^2/15:7/17:10^2/19:13:15/
20:5,6/21:12/28:11:13:15/29:11:16/30:18/33:
14:15:21/36:8,9:14:17:20/38:15:19/40:13:18^2:
27:28/41:7:21^2:24/43:9^2:13:20/44:7^2:10:19:20/
45:9:19/46:1^2:5:10/49:15:24^2/50:2^2/52:3/55:6/
56:3:11/57:13^3/59:1/64:5/66:1/Jer2:10,11:22:
23:24:28:32^2/3:4,5:23/4:14/5:1:4^2:7:22^2/6:29/7
:9/8:8:16f/9:7/10:5/11:15/13:19f:23^2/14:22^2/
15:2:12,13/16:13:20/17:9:10:14^2/18:15/19:11/
21:12:13/23:18:24:35/25:5/26:3/28:9/31:37/33
:20,21/36:3/47:7/49:19:20/50:29:44^2/51:8:9:41
:50/Lam2:6:13^3/3:20:37/4:3,4:8/Eze11:20/12:
3^2:4:12/13:7/16:28/24:27/25:5/33:10/34:25/
37:3:18,19,20/38:2,3f/40:4/Dan2:4:7:8,9:10:11:
26:27/3:15:29/4:18^2:35/5:11f:12:16^2/6:15/10:
17^2:19/11:17:27/Hos1:21,22/5:13/7:1/9:4/10:
13/11:8^3/13:9/14:3/Joe2:8:11:14/Amo:11:14/3
:3/5:6/6:12^2/8:5/Ob1:3/Jon2:9/3/Mic2:1:3/3:
11/6:6/Nah1:6/3:19/Hab1:7/2:2:19/Zep3:2:3:
9/Hag2:3/Zec3:10/4:7/8/Mal3:2^3/Mt2:8/3:9/
5:31/6:5:19:23/7:5:13:16^2:17/8:2/9:18:28:34/
10:28^2:29/11:19/12:24:29:31,32/13:33:47,48:56
/14:2:15/16:26/17:4/18:23/19:11:12:17:25/21:
21^2:22/22:1:45/23:16:18/24:33:43:44/25:1:14/
26:73/27:40^2:65/Mk1:40/2:7:16:28/3:23:26:27:
28:29/4:30:31,32/5:28/6:14/8:23/9:22:23/10:
26/11:22,23:24/12:37/13:14:29:34/14:7:44/15:
29,30/Lk1:34/2:29,30,31/3:8/4:22/5:12:21/6:8
:34:40:42^2/7:20,21,22^2:31:35/8:16/11:15:18/12
:4:33^2/13:7:18/14:27:33/16:13:26:29/18:6:26:
27/19:19/20:44/21:31/22:11:48/24:39/Jn1:5:
22:46/2:20/3:3:4:6:8:12/4:28,29/5:19:32,33:40/
6:2-5:27:44:52:60:65/7:3:6:15:26/8:46/9:11:19:
30/10:18:21:29/11:9/12:8:35:40/14:2,3:5:6:
12,13:28/15:4/16:22:23/17:1:24/19:35/Act2:7:
12/3:17:19/4:17/6:4/8:20:21:23:31:33:33f:37/9
:12/10:46,47/11:14/18:10/19:38:39/20:26/21:
22/22:5/24:8:11/26:8/Rom1:11,12/2:20/3:
21,22:26:27:31/4:12:15/5:1:3:18/6:1:15:16^2/7:3
:4:6:13^3/8:4:8:31^2:35:38/9:23,24/10:14^2/11:13:
14:29:34/12:1:6:17/13:6:12,13/14:9/15:6:24:27
:32/16:1/1Co1:4:15:29/2:11^2:14:16f/3:11:12:13
/4:5:8/5:7/6:12/7:5:8:25:32/9:19:20:21^2/10:13^2
:30/11:16:18:21:22/12:3^3:21:28^2:30^2/13:12/14:
5^2:13:15:16^2:19:28:31:39/15:53/16:4:6:16/2Co1
:3,4:5:9:12/2:2/3:3:5:12:14:18/4:7:18/5:12^2/6:3
:14:15^2:16/7/8:3:11:14^2:23/9:10:11/10:2:5^3:7^2/
11:14:15:21^2/12:2,3:6/13:8f/Gal1:10/2:5/3:4:7:
11^2:14^2/4:6:9:27^2/5:14/6:10:12^2:13/Eph1:18/2:
7:9/3:12/4:28/5:5:31/Php1:24/2:15:19/3:7:8/4
:7:8:13/Col1:11:16:29/3:25/4:13/1Th2:3/3:8:9
/4:14:15/5:10/2Th2:6/1Ti1:16/2:2/3:5/5:16:24
/6:14:16^2/2Ti1:18/2:15:19:21:26/3:14/4:9/Tit1
:1/3:7:12:13/Phm1:15/Heb2:3/3:4/4:3:13/5:1:
4:7f:12,13/6:10:18^3/7:3f:15:22/9:17:22/10:23^2/
11:4:6/12:9:11:28/13:6^2:10:19/Jas2:1:3:18/3:1:
3:5^2:6:7:8:12/4/5:11/1Pe1:13:21^2:22/2:15:24/
2Pe1:9/2:14/3:3:4:17/1Jn1:9/2:3:10:21/3:10:
17:21/4:17:20/5:2:4:9:15:17f/2Jn1:12/3Jn:12/
Jud1:4:21/Rev2:11:17:19:29/3:6:7^2:8:13:22/6:
17/13:9/14:5

1197

CAN'T

Gen13:8:16/24:5:39/25:22/41:16/43:11/44:26/
Ex1:19/6:30/22:3/Num11:14/Deu30:12/Jos24
:19/Ju7:2/14:13/15:3/19:12,13/21:18/Ru4:6/
1Sa5:7/9:12,13/12:21/26:19/29:8/30:22/2Sa
13:26/14:14/20:6/1Ki13:16,17/18:12/2Ki22:17
/Ez10:13/Job:20,21/12:14/15:15/22:13/Ps53:
4/78:19,20/115:5/139:17,18/140:10/Pro4:16/
8:1/15:7/19:19/22:13/24:10/25:8,9,10^2/27:22/
Ecc6:3/Is1:14/3:12/29:11:12:15/30:3/33:19/
44:13/45:10/48:7/Jer1:6/2:13:25/6:14/15:
12,13/18:6/20:9^2/32:5/38/Lam4:18/Eze3:5:25
:26/4:8/15:3/Dan2:1:5:8,9/5:15/6:22/Hos12:8
/Amo2:6:15/Mic6:12/Mt5:20:36/7:4:18/10:28
/16:2,3/27:6:41,42,43/Mk4:13/7:11:18/8:17:
24/9:17:50/11:33/14:2/15:31/Lk6:42/11:7/12:
26/13:27/14:14/18:27/Jn2:4/3:8/5:7:10:44/7:4
:7:41,42/8:43/9:9/13:8:36:37/15:4:5/16:12/Act
4:16/8:36/17:25/Rom2:4/7:15:17:18^2/8:3:38^2/
1Co2:14^3:15/5:10/6:2:12/7:9:33/9:4/10:13/11:
22/12:21/2Co1:24/Gal6:7/Col1:16/1Ti3:5:7/6
/Tit2:5/Heb11:3/Jas1:24/2:18/3:12/4:2/1Jn2:
23/3:2:9

166

CANNOT

Gen43:3,4,5/44:22:34/Ex30:22,23f/38:27f/Lev
14:21/27:27/Num9:10/23:18-24/Deu22:19f/
Jos2:17,18/7:13/9:7/Ju11:35/2Sa23:17/1Ki8:
27/20:9f/1Ch21:24/2Ch6:18/Job3:24/4:18,19/
9:32,33/22:14/23:8:9/28:15:17:19:21/36:26/37
:5:21:23/41:27,28/Ps5:4:9/6:5/8:4/14:1/21:11/
33:16,17^2/37:21/38:13,14/49:14/69:4/71:15/
76:4/77:12/93:5/115:17/135^2/139:12/Pro4:5/
14:13/25:2,3/30:3:21,22,23/31:8/Ecc1:12-15/3
:11/Sol8:7/Is3:7/19:15/35:8/38:18:18f:18/40:
20/44:18:20/45/46:1:7^2/47:14/Jer1:18^2/2:22/
4:19/6:20/8:17/10:5^2/11:12/13:19/14:17/16/
19:11/20/23:23/25:28/31:15/32:35/33:22/
Lam3:7/Dan6:8^2:12:15/Hos5:4/9:14/14:3/
Amo5:2/Mic1:14/7:18/Nah2:8/Hab1:13/Zep:
18/Zec11:16/Mt6:24/12:25:29/26:42/Lk12:1/
14:26/16:13/Jn3:5/6:53/8:21:22/10:34,35,36/
13:33/14:17/Act4:20/24:13/Rom8:26:38/11:10
/15:1/1Co3:1/10:21^2/11:17/15:50:53/2Co3:14
/Gal2:16:17/3:15^2/5:2/Eph4:17,18/1Ti3:2/2Ti
2:4:13/Tit1:1/Heb6:6/7:16/10:5/11:1/Jas4:4/
1Jn2:11/5:18

156

COULD

Gen3:13/8:8/13:6/18:11/20:17/24:46/26:10/
31:8:29:39:43/34:18,19:28/41:8:24:38/42:24/
43:7:10/44:1/45:2/48:10/50:20/Ex1:22/2:3/9:
15/13:21/16:32/29:46/32:12/38:21/40:30:38/
Num11:31/15:34/22:18:41/23:7-10/24:13^2/
Deu2:14,15:30/3:18/4:21,22:42/6:23/8:16/9/
32:29:30/Jos5:1/6:20/8:27/11:4/14:11/15:63/
17:12/18:7:8/19:50/20:9/21:44/Ju3:17,18,19/5
:8/7:15/14:3/16:6:19/19:22/20:16/Ru1:11:18/
2:7:14/1Sa1:5/2:15:30/14/19:4:15/20:28,29:41
/21:8/28:7,8/30:4/2Sa2:18:22/5:6:8/6:13/13:8:
13/15:4/16:22/17:14/18:33/19:18:28/1Ki3:1/8
:8/10:3f:8/13:33/14:4/20:7/2Ki3:21/5:17f/6:
17/9:36/23:1:10/1Ch1:24-27f/12:2/13:5/17:21
/28:2/29/2Ch5:9:13,14/9:2:4:6:19/11:16/20:24
/28/31:4/35:18/36:16/Ez1:6/2:59:62,63:69/3:
13/5:10/8:22/9:12/Neh4:10:22/7:61/8:1:12/9:
11:12/13:19:26/Est1:8:11/3:3,4/7:4^2/8:8f/Job
2:12/4:2/9:16:32,33:35/13:19/19:23,24/23:3:7/
31:14^2:21/34:17/40:4/Ps37:35,36/42:4,5/44:6:
19/49:11^2/55:12^2/63:2/68:30f/73:7/78:6:25:44
:64/105:22/107:12/119:71,72/137:9f/Ecc2:3:9
/4:14/7:27,28/Sol8:1/Is5:4/8:2/10:19/28:12/
35:6/37:19/48:5:16/Jer2:21^2:33/4:23/9:2/37:4
/44:22/48:9/49:4/51:9/Lam1:16:19^2/4:12:20/
Eze1:8:17/3:19/10:5:9-13^2:17f/12:2^2:7/16:15/
17:14/19:9/20:11:25:25f/21:21f:23/22:30/29:
18/33:22/Dan1:13/3:26/4:10,11/5:8:8f^2/6:2:4:
17/7:4/8:5:25/10:16/Hos11:4/Jon4:2/Mic6:11
/Nah3:9/Hab2:18/Zep:15f/Zec3:5,6/5:7/Mt3:
7/8:28/9:5,6:30:33/12:10:22:34/16:11/17:20/
20:34/22:10:15/25:27/26:8,9:53:55/Mk1:4/2:8
:9,10,11:15/6:6:42/7:11:35/9:3:11:12,13/10:52/
11:13/12/14:4,5:8/15:45/16:3/Lk1:29:64/5:3:
23,24/7:42/8:32:43,44/9:59f/11:53,54/13:6:13
/18:43/19:23:48/20:19/24:4/Jn1:48/7:27/8:6:
26/9:10:15:16:32/11:55:57/13:22/19:31/21:25/
Act2:24/4:13:14/5:4:9/7:21:48,49/8:9,10,11/9:
2:18/10:17:46,47/11:29/13:39/14:18/15:1:7/16
:10/22:12:13/25:21/26:32/27:19:39:43/28:20^2/
Rom1:13:28/2:19/3:2:6:7/4:4,5/5:20/10:5^2/11:
32:35/1Co1:6/2:16/7:7/10:11/12:2:17/13:1:2/
16:6/2Co1:9:15,16^2/2:9/3:7:13/7:11:12/8:3:4:9
/11:8,9/Gal1:10:14:16/2:19:21/3:17:18:21,22:
23/4:3:5:20:30/Eph5:27/Php3:4^3/4:10/Col1:22
/2:1/1Th3:1:5/2Th1:11/1Ti:13:16:20/Tit:5/2:
14/3:7/Phm1:8,9:15/Heb2:14:15:17/3:18/5:7f^3
/7:5:23:28/9:8:13:18/10:1:2:11/11:15:27:28/
1Pe1:10/2:2,3f/4:6/2Pe2:15/1Jn3:5/5/3Jn1:4
/Rev5:4/11:19/13:14:17/14:3/15:8/16:12/17:6
/19:20/20:3/21:17f:22

450

COULDN'T

Gen19:11/32:25/34:14/37:4/38:20:22/45:3:26/
Ex7:21:24/9:11/14:20/15:23/Num9:6,7/22:26/
Ju12:6/16:16,17/21:22/1Sa1:7/9:4/10:14/19/
2Sa1:10/11:2/1Ki13:4/2Ki7:2:19:20/10:4/2Ch
7:1/13:7/25:15/Neh2:14,15/5:2,3,4/13:24/Job
4:16/Ps132:2-5^2/Pro7:21/Sol3:1/5:6/8:7/Eze
20:9,10:14/36:20/Dan2:1/4:7/6:4/Jon1:13/Mt
9:32/13:17/15:30/17:16:19/18:25/21:32/26:40
/Mk1:45/2:4/3:20/4:21/5:41,42/6:5/7:24/9:18
:28/14:37/15:44/Lk1:22/2:45/5:18,19/8:19/9:
40/11:14/12:17/14:20/Jn9:33/11:37,38/12:39
/21:4:6/Act9:22/18:17/21:34/25:7/27:14,15/
Rom4:18/1Co3:2/9:5:16/2Co2:13/Php:30/Heb
3:19

93

DID

Gen1:27^2/6:22/7:5/18:13^2/20:16/21:1/24:46/
25:34f/26:9/30:16/31:36,37-39/34:5/38:26:29/
39:2:12/40:15/42:21:35/43:6^2:17/44:2/45:5^2:

D Con't)
17:31/48:14/50:12,13:15:16,17/Ex1:8f/2:14
20/4:4:6:7/5:22/6:2,3/7:6:20/8:6:7:13:17:24
32^2/9:6/10:20:22/11:10/12:27:28:35/13:8:
8/14:11:27/16:34/17:3^2:5,6/19:4/24:11/28
32:2,3:21:28/40:15/Lev8:36/10:7/14:17:28
15/Num3:16-24/8:3/9:23/11/12:5/13:3-15
22/16:18:47/17:11/20:5:9:12:12f:12:27/22:
:37/23:30/25:12,13/27:13:14:22/31:31/32:
5:10/Deu1:32/2:13:29/3:1/4:3:9:33:34:35/5
:16/7:18:22/8:3:17/11:3:4/23/24:9/25:17/
/30:5:9/32:27/34:11,12/Jos2:10/4:8:23:24
5/8:2:5:6:18/9:9:10:14,15:24/11:9:13:15/18
2:22,23/24:7:11:13^2:17/Ju1:28:30:31,32:33
0^2:11:22:23/5:16:17^3:19:23:31/6:27^3:29:40/
,20/8:27:35/11:14,15:25:38:39/13:19/14:6
:11/16:14/17:6/18:3:8/20:12/21:23:25/Ru2
9:23/1Sa3:4,5:7f:16,17/4:20/10:14:15/14:
8/15:19:20:24/16:4/18:10/22:13^2/25:21/
0/28:18/2Sa1:14:22/3:35,36/4:12/5:20:25
0,11/11:19,20,21/12:12/13:6:8:16/14:19:
0:31/15:12:33,34/16:23/18:13/19:19/20:6:
10/21:5,6/22:38/23:10/24/1Ki1:31f/2:44/3
8:25:32/9:4/11:2:6^2:33:38:41/12:2,3,4/13:
7:33/14:8:22/15:4:14/16:3:33/17:5:15/18:
^{2}:43/20:25:34:37/21:22:26/22:24:43^2/2Ki1
4:16:17/2:3/4:5/6:6:7:18:20/8:14:19/9:4:11
2/13:15:16,17/14:28/16:2:5:16/17:25/18:7:
20:14/21:1:9:21/23:9:26/1Ch5:20/10:14/14
17:9:13:21/18:11/19:2,3:19/21:4/23:27:28/
/29:20/2Ch4:17,18/7:17/8:15/10:16/12:14
3/18:23:29/20:18:33/25:2:5,6/27:3/28:21:
29:22:30/30:20/31:9/32:26:30:32/33:23/34:
32/35:12:24,25/36:8/Ez4:7/5:1:5/8:23/9:9
h2:16/3:3/4:1/5:13:15/9:17:20:26:31:35^2/
8/Est1:13-15:18/2:9/4:17/6:3/7:10/9:7-10
/10:3/Job1:22/3:12^2/10:18/26:4/29:14:19/
25/32:6/33:28/38:5/42:3:9/Ps18:22:23:37/
31/27:12/34:5/35:7:13/40:3/44:1:3/51:4:16
/77:11/78:4:8:37:50:56/83:9^2:10:11/95:8/
:5,6/106:34/107:6/114/118:13/119:
76,77/120:1/135:9/137:7/143:5/Pro1:3:29/
2:10:12/9:6/Is5:4/9/10:9^3:24/11:16/20:2/
9/36:19^2/37:12:23^2/39:3/40:14/41:20/42:24
3:5/50:1/57:16/64:3/65:16/66:4/Jer2:4,5^2:
36/7:12:13,14:15/11:8/13:5:7/14:15/15:4/
11/18:3/20:17/22:8^2:15/23:27:32/25:19,20/
19/31:2:19/34:5/36:8:14,15:17:28:30f/37:1/
21/44:2,3/51:34,35/Lam1:3/2:17/3:59/Eze:
8/9:7/10:2:9-13:17:22/12:7:11/13:6:12/16:
61/20:23,24:30:35,36/23:8:33:44/24:18/28:
36:11:31/40:18:25/48:11/Dan3:24/4:2:36/8
7/Hos1:5/9:9/11/Amo2:4:9/4:6:11/7:3/Ob
0/Jon:9,10/2:10/4/Mic7:14/Hab3:2/Hag2:
15/Zec8:14,15/9:7/11:11/14:5/Mal1:6/2/3:
/Mt1:24/2:4/5:38/7:29f/11:7:21:23/12:3:13
:58/14:31:36/15:7/19:8/20:5:13:28/21:6:20:
22:10/23:29,30/25:37:39:40:44/26:19:54:62
1f/Mk3:2:5:13:30/5:27/8:19/10:3:5/Lk1:
2:49/4:23/6:3:8:10:19/7:17:24:25:26/9:15/
13/11:48/13:17/22:35/24:19/Jn1:15/2:9:22
/3:17/4:1:28,29:38:39:40,41/5:14/6:11:25:
58/9:11:21:26^2/10:8/12:7/18:9:15:34f/19:25
,37/21:3:6/Act2:43/3:7,8:17/5:8^2:12/6:8/7:
/8:6:13:27/9:39/10:46,47:48/11:30/12:8/14:
15:9/16:15/19:2:3/22/23:18/Rom1:32/3:25
4,5:10:17/5:9:13:6/5:7:4:9/8:7:32/9:10-13/
19/11:21/16:7/1Co1:13/2:5/9:12/10:5:6:7:9
/15:20:21/2Co1:10:17/2:3:9/3:13/4:10:13/5
/7:11:12^2/8:3/11:7/12:12:17:18/13:2/Gal2:
5^2:10/3:2:20/4:8:12:24,25/Eph1:5:13/2:6/3:
/Php2:6/3:14/4:15/Col1:20/3:9/1Th2:5:14/
/2Th:1/2Ti1:17/Tit3:6/Heb1:13/2:16/3:5:
:14:15/4:10:11/5:5/7:11:12,13,14:16:27/8:9/
4/11:4:9:10:28:31/12:3:16:18:24:25/Jas2:21:
:25/1Pe1:10/2:23/4:1/2Pe2:4:5/3:4:5,6/1Jn
:8/3:12/Jud1:5:9/Rev2:5:14/9:4:21/12:11/
:13/16:9/20:5

771

IDN'T

n3:10/8:1:12/12:18/18:15/19:35/20:6/21:26
0:42/31:22:27:28:32:33:34/38:11/42:7:22:23:
/44:8:15/47:22^2/Ex1:17/3:2/9:16/12:39/32:
34:29/Lev26:34,35/Num22:34:37/23:26/24:
2/Deu4:12:15/6:10,11,12^3/7:7/9:9/10:10/
:4:5/22:1:23,24/Jos2:4/7:7/8:14/10:13/Ju3:
/5:15/8:1/10:11/11:20/12:1/13:6^2:16/14:4:6
/16:20/20:34/21:22/1Sa1:2/2:12:27:28^2/3:
5:6/5:12/6:3/7:13/10:16/13:8/14:1/15:17:19
7:55f/19:17/20:26:39/22:17/23:13:14,15/24:
:18/25:19:25:36/27:9/30:22/2Sa11:9:10:13:
19,20,21/14:32/18:11:29/19:24,25:43/20:
8,9,10/1Ki1:10:13:19/2:42/3:13/8:16:31/9:22/
10:7/18:43/22:18/2Ki2:17:18/4:1:41/10:9,10:
29:31/12:3/14:4:6/15:4:34,35/17:40/23:18/
1Ch15:26/16:21/21:6:30/27:23/2Ch8:9/9:6/12
:12/16/18:17/20:7^2:10/23:8/25:4/32:25/33:23
/35:15/Neh3:5/9:17^2:19:21^2:34/Job3:11/10:18
/Ps18:43,44,45/35:15/50:21/66:20^2/69:4/78:
10:22:38/Pro23:35/24:11,12/Ecc1:8-11/7:23/
Is29:16/45:4:19^2/47:7/53:3/65:12/Jer3:7/6:15
/11:8:19/14:14/17:23/18:4/23:36/29:31/44:21
/49:1/50:6/Eze13:12:22/20:8:9,10:17/23:19,20
/34:8/48:11/Dan3:24:27/6:18/8:5/12:8/Jon3:
10/Mal1:2,3/Mt:19/2:12/3:14/9:36/14:9/20:
13/21:16:25:30:42/25:24,25f^2:43/26:55:62/27:
41,42,43/Mk1:22/2:18:25,26/6:52^2/9:6:32/11:
31:32/14:40:49:59/16:10,11:12/Lk2:43:44:48:
49:50/3:14/5:5/7:32f^2:44/9:36:45/11:40/17:17
/18:34/19:23/20:5/21:4/22:53/24:11:16/Jn1:3:
10:31:33/2:24,25/4:1:38/5:13/6:32:64/7:5:45/8
:10:27:48/9:27/10:6:41/11:40:51/12:16/15/16:
4/18:26/19:31:33/20:5:14/Act2:4/3:14/4:21/5:
13:28/7:25:50:52/12:9:15/13:27/15:38/19:32/
20:27/22:9/23:5/24:22/27:39/28:24/Rom4:4,5:
19/6:20/7:13/11:20/15:3/1Co1:14:17/2:1/7:28
:29f/11:8/13:1:2:3/2Co2:4/7:14/11:8,9/12:13^2:
16/Gal1:16:17:22/4:14/Php:10/1Th2:13/2Th3:
9/1Ti1:13^2/6:7/Phm1:14^2/Heb3:19/4:2^3:5/7:
18/8:7/11:16

344

DO

Gen3:13/4:7/8:21/11:6/12:2/13:9/17:18/18:5^2:
19:20:25^2:30/19:7:8:9^2:12:22/20:9,10/21:12:22
/24:6:49/26:3^2:5/27:8,9,10:13:43/29:5^2:15:25/
30:28:30:31,32^2/31:7:16:26/32:9:12:32/33:15/
34:15:23/37:8/38:11:18:25/39:9/41:16:25:28:
38:55/42:22/43:11/44:5:7:15:34/47:29:31/Ex2:
8:14/4:1:2:5:12:15:21:28^2/5:4,5:7,8:22/6:1:30/7
:11/8:10:18:25:26^2/9:17:34/10:1:26:28/15:26/
17:4/18:14:18/19:8:12:15/20:7:10:25/22:23:31
/23:1^2:2,3:9:19:21:29:32/32:11:12:21/33:5:17/
34:3:10:12:15^2:17/35:33/40:16/Lev4:13/8:5:31
/10:6^4/11:43:44/16:29,30/18:17:24^3:26:28^2:
29,30^2/19:3,4:19:23:27:29:31:33^2/20:4:23/22:
29,30/23:7f:8:21:25:28:35/24:12/25:6,7/26:10:
16/Num1:47,48,49/4:17,18,19/8:7:15/9:23/10:
29/12:11^2/14:9^2:28/15:39/16:3:6,7:15:28/18:
16:23:32/19:12/22:13:18/23:18-24/24:14/28:
25/29:35/30:1^2:3^2:5/32:6:10,11:20:23:24:31/
Deu1:12:30:42/2:19/3:1:21:23,24,25/4:2:16,17:
19/5:14:16/6:2:19/7:2:3:16^2:19:21:22:23:25^2:26
/8:1:2:16/9:5/10:8:9/11:16:17/12:8:14:15:18:
20-23:24,25:28:30^3:32/13:8^2/14:1:7:27/15:10:
17:18:19^2/16:8/18:12:14^2:17/19:16/21:8/22:9^2
/23:15,16:23:24/24:19/25:7/26:17:19/28:8:9:
12:20:29:62/29:9/30:5:9/31:6:13:29/33:11/Jos
1:7/3:5/7:8/8:2/9:7^2:8:25/10/15:18,19/17:15/
22:19:24,25/23:6:7^2/Ju1:14/2:15/6:16f:17/7:15
:17^2/8:21/9:4:33:47,48/11:7:9:25:36/15:10:
12,13/16:20/18:14:23:24^2/19:23:24^2:30/21:16/
Ru1:11:15:17/2:22/3:3:4:5:13/4:6/1Sa1:26/2:
35^2/3:4,5:6:8:11:12:18/6:2/8:7:9:22/11:10/14:6
:7:8:10:36:45/15:19/16:2:7/17:8:36/20:2:4:8:30
/21:12/22:3:9,10:18/23:9/24:4:9,10:12/25:28/
26:25/28:5,6:7,8:11:13:15:22/30:13:24/2Sa1:3:
5/3:9,10:24,25:39/4:11/5:23/7:5:25:29/9:10,11
/12:5:12:18/13:2f:5:12:12f:28/14:7:13^2/15:15:
25,26/16:11:20/18:3:12/19:13:27:38:43/20:1/
21:3:4^3:5,6/23:17/24:19/1Ki1:11:12:16/2:3:4:6:
8:17:26:31:42/5:5:8/6:11,12^3/8:18:22,23^2:25:31
:32:43:58/9:6/11:12,13:22:38/12:6^2:9^2:15/14:8/
18:14:34^2/20:9f:10^2:13:14/21:25:29^2/22:3:5:21:
22/2Ki2:5/3:10:11/4:2^2:13:14/5:13/6:15:22:26-
26-30/8:12:13/9:18^2:19:22/10:4^2:5/16:6/17:41
/18:12^2:24:25/19:29/20:3:8:9:11/21:9/22:12,13
/23:3/25:26/1Ch4:10/10:4/14:14/17:17:24/19:
13/21:3:6:8:17/22:8:11^2/28:10/2Ch6:14:33^2:42 ^{2}
/7:11/10:8,9^2:15/11:4/13:8:12/14:7/15:13:18:
19,20:21/19:10/20:12/23:13,14/24:20/25:7:9/
28:13:14/30:7:8/32:7:10:13:14/33:9/34:31/Ez1
:4^2/4:14:22/5:9/6:6:18/9:14/10:5:11:12/Neh4:
1:5^2/5:2,3,4:12/6:11/7:2/9:32/10:31/13:14:21:
27/Est1:13-15/3:11:14/4:13:16^2/5:3/6:6:10/7:
2/8:17/9:12^2:13/Job1:8:12,13/2:6/5:17/6:5,6,7
/11:7/12:13/13:2:9:11:20:24/14:15/15:3^2:7,8:9^3
/16:18/17:3,4:10/18:5/21:15/22:17/23:13:14/
27:12/28/29:25/30:13/31:2,3:4:34/33:23,24/34
:25/35:2,3:14,15/36:13:19:20/37:12:15:16,17^2/
38:5:17,18:19:33/39:1:2,3:26/40:2^2:14/41:6:29/
42:2/Ps1:1^2:3/2:1f/4:4/5:8/9:1/10:5^2:13/11:3/
12:5/16:4:7/18:3:25/22:1/23:2,3/24:4/26/27:9 ^{2}
:11/33:13,14,15/34:12/35:21/36:10/37:5^2:14/
40:5:8/41:7/42:4,5:11/44:6:24^2/49:16/51:18f:
19/52:1:4/54:5/56:3,4:10,11:12/59:5/60:12/62
/64:5/69:4:27:28/71:17/74:11/79:8/83:9:17/86
:10/90:16/92:5:6/94:21,22/105:14f:15/108:13/
109:3:27:29/118:6/119:2:29,30:33,34^2:68:125:
155:165:168/125:3:4/127:1/132:2-5:10/135:18
/137:7/141:4/143:10/Pro1:15/2/3:6:7,8:11,12/
4:10:14^2/5:21/6:4^2:9:14:16-19/14:2/16:12/18:2
/19:19/22:17,18,19:28:29/24:17/25:16/27:2/28
:10:20/29:26/30:6/31:3/Ecc1:8-11/2:1:12f:24-
24-26/5:4:5^2/8:2,3:5:11/9:5f^2:10^2:10f:15/10:2^2/
11:9^2/12:3:14/Sol2:7/8:8/Is1:3:12,13:17/2:6/5
:7f:19/8:9,10:11:16/9:7/10:3/13/14:21:24:26/
16:3:12/19:3^2:12/21:2/22:15,16/25:1:8/26:9:11
/27:9/28:21:26/29:13:15/30:1^2/32:8/33:15/34:
16/36:8,9:10:14:20/37:11:26:28/38:19/40:16/
41:10:21:23:24/42:20/43:12:13:18:19/44:7:26:
28/45:10:11:19/46:1:5:10:11^2/47:7/48:5/49:6/
50:5:6:7/51:18/55:2/56:1/57:18/58:8:9:13/59:6
:7:8/63:19/64:5/65:12/Jer1:6:11:13/2:31^2/4:30^2
/5:21^2/7:6:9:13,14:23:27/8:6:17:22/9:7/10:5:24
/11:4:5:6:8:15/12:5/13:17/14:19:21^2:22/16:5/
17:2,3:21,22/18:6:11:19/21:1/22:3:8/23:10:14:
16/24:3/25:30/26:9^2:14:19/27:9:13/28:6/29:10
:23/30:6^2:15/31:7:36/32:19:20:40:41:42/33:9:
14/34:15/36:3/38:5:19/39:13:16/40/41:18/42:
3:5:10:19:20/44:4:17:19:21:26/45:5/48:10:14:
44/49:20:24/50:9:15:29/51:12/Lam1:21/2:7/3:
44/4:21/5:20^2/Eze4:3/5:9:13/7:26,27/8:6^2/9:
11/12:4:25:28/14:16/16:30:37:43:45:47/17:9:
24/18:2:21:23:32/20:7:9,10:31/21:13:24/22:14
/23:24/24:14:16:22:24/27:9/30:12/32:10/33:25^2
/35:10:11/36:27:32:36/39:27/43:26/44:14/45:
20/46:19,20/47:10/Dan1:18,19/3:29/4:27:35/6
:15/9:12:15/10:20,21/11:3:24:32:36/Hos3:3/4:
10:12:15/6:4/9:1:5:9/12/Joe3:13/Amo:10/6:12
/7:3:5:6:8:12:14/8:2/Jon1:6:9,10:11/4:2/Mic2:
1:7/3:4/4:2^2:12/7:8:15:16/Hab1:5^2:7/2:3:4:19/
3:2/Zep1:6/2:3:11/Hag:8,9/Zec1:21/3:7/4:2:
10/5:2/6:5/8:14,15/9:1f/11:7/Mal1:13/3:3:5:6:
8:10:13:14,15^2/Mt1:19/3:14:15^2/5:46:47/6:1:2:
3^2:7,8:16^2/7:12^2:22/8:8,9:29/9:12:14^2:28^2:36/
10:29/11:4:26/12:2:12:27/13:10:29:51^2/14:2/
15:2:3:34/16:15/17:10:25^2/18:7:10f:12:19:35/
19:3:16:20/20:32,33^2/21:15:21:23f^2:28:31:40^2/
23:3^3:5/24:24/25:13/26:50/27:22/Mk2:18:19:
28/3:4/4:13:24/5:7,8/6:5:14:38/8:5:11:12:21f:
27:29/9:18:22:24/10:2:4:17:18:24f:35:40:51^2/11
:26,f/12:9^2:35/13:22:34f:34:35,36,37/14:2:29:
60^2:63,64/15:12/Lk1:38:45/3:10^2:14/4:12:23:
34/5:33:34^2/6:9^2:27:32^2:33^3:35:37:43:46/7:
6,7,8:42/8:10:28/9:20:53/10:25:28:37:40/11:8:
11^2:12:13:19/12:25:26:47:51:57/13:2:24,25:33/
14:10/15:29/16:5,6:7:8f/17:7,8,9/18:18:19:27:
41/20:13:15^2:16:34,35/22:9:23:48:71/23:25:31:
31f/24:38:39:41/Jn1:11,12:22:24,25:38^2:48:50/
2:4f:5:19:20/3:4:8:9/4:21-24:35:48/5:19:20:36/
6:6:7:28:38/7:17:21,22,23:31^2:49^2/8:11:29:33:
40:44:53:55^2/9:16:17:26:27^2:31:33:35/10:25:
34,35,36:37:38:41/11:1:26:47:56/12:28/13:12:
13:15:17:24:27/14:11:12,13^3:14:17:29:31/15:5:
20/16:7:31/17:25/18:34f/20:30,31/21:15:16:18
/Act1:20/2:37/4:16:17:20:25,26:28/5:4:35:38/7
:51/8:9,10,11:30/9:15/10:4:17:22:35/12:11/13:
25:34:39/14:3/15:27,28,29/16:20,21:28:30/19:
11:36/21:37,38/22:3:10/23:21/24:14:15/26:9:
27^2/Rom1:21:24:26:32/2:1:3^2:7:7f:10f:12-15^3:
21:22^2:22f/3:2:4:20:28/4:4,5:9:11:21/5:9:13/6:
12^2:13:21/7:5:15^2:17:18:19^3:21^2:22:23,24,25/8:
12^2/9:4:19/11:2,3:4:8:20^2:23:24:26/12:2:4,5:6:7
:8:17/13:9:12,13/14:1f:3:4:14:16^2:21:22:23^2/15:
1^3:24:27^2/1Co1:6:9:17/2:6:16/4:7:16^2:17:21/5:
1:3,4/6:8:12^2:13/7:1:3:5:7:18:25:32:33:35/8:8:
10:11:12:13/9:5^2:9:10:21:23:25:27/10:13:23:25:
31:33/11:13:22^3:24:25:26/12:10:24:25:28:29/13
:2:5/14:15^2:36/15:1:15:29:58/16:14^2:15:16:19/
2Co1:3,4:10:24^2/2:1:2:3:8:10:11/3:1:5:6/4:2:8:
18/5:9:13,14/6:4:7:14^2/7:12/8:8:10:15:24/9:2/
10:1:13/11:1:7:11:12:15:16^2:17:22:29/12:5:13^2/
13:5^2:7:8f/Gal3:3:8,9:15/4:2:10^2:12:17:20/5:10:
13:16:17^3/Eph1:4/3:7:20/4:12^2:17,18/5:1:6:9:
12:17/6:1:8:9:14/Php1:7:20:28/2:1:12:13:14:30 ^{2}
/4:5:7:13/Col1:9:29/2:20/3:5:6:7:17:23:25/4:12
:17/1Th:5/5:15:19:20:24/2Th1:3:8/2:7:9:17/3/
1Ti1:10,11/2:1/3:10:11:13/4:2:8:16/5:7:16:17:
21:24:25/6:6:9:14:18:20/2Ti1:5/2:3:4:22/3:16:
17/4:2:5:21^2/Tit1:3:5/2:3:7:15^2/3:8:10:13/Phm
1:8,9:14:21:24/Heb2:9/3:15/4:2:7:11:15/6:10:
16^2/7:5/8:10/10:1:7:23:25:35:36/11:11:32/13:6
:7:9:16:17^2/Jas1:5:12:13^3:25/2:12:16:17:22/3:1:

(DO Con't)
3/4:11:12:14:15:17/5:9:12/1Pe1:15:17:22/2:14^2
:15:16^2:18:20/3:6:11:12:13:15^2:16/4:2:4:11/2Pe
1:2:5:19/2:12:12f:19/3:3:15,16/1Jn1:4:9/2:3:4:
5:15:24:29/3:2:20:23:24/4:18^2/5:3/2Jn1:6:11/
3Jn1:10:11/Jud:4:10^2:11:19/Rev:3/2:6:14/3:3/
6:6f/7:3:13/10:4/11:2/13:10:14/18:4:6/19:20/
22:9:10:11:15

1823

DOES

Gen4:15/8:21/31:53/38:21/42:14/Ex7:9/12:26
/19:12/21:8:21/31:14,15^2/Lev4:13:28/7:26,27/
11:4-7^4:12:26/13:4:21:23:28^2:32:40/17:16/18:
29,30/23:29:30,31/24:20/25:30/27:10:27/Num
1:47,48,49/10:32/16:8,9:30/19:12:13/24:23,24
/30:11/Deu8:18/10:9:12,13/15:3/19:9/23:14/
27:26/32:4:11/Ju1:24f/6:31/21:18/1Sa12:16:
17/14:19/17:47:55/24:13/25:10/28:14/2Sa14:
14f/24:3f/1Ki1:52/2:23,24/2Ki4:13/1Ch1:1f/3:
9/2Ch2:14/18:17/Neh4:1/Est1:13-15/Job:10/
5:9/6:11/8:3/9:10:13/10:3/12:7,8,9/13:8/14:10
:11,12/15:6/16/19:22/21:9/23:13/24:12/26:14
/27:10/33:13^2:29/35:6:12:14,15^2/36:5:6:7:23/
37:18:19,20:23/38:19^2:28/39:21-23/Ps9:12/15:
3:5/20:6/31:1/32:6/33:4/34:9:19/46:8/49:7/50
:3f/53:1:2/57/64:9/69:33/72:18/73:11/76:12/
96:3/99:4/103:2/105:1/111:7/112/115:3/116:
15/135:6/136:4/145:9:17/Pro1:7,8,9/5:6/10:2/
12:4:25/17:20f:22/18:16/20:11/24:13,14/26:
4,5/29:24/31:28:31/Ecc1:3-7/2:1:20-23/3:9:14:
17/5:19,20/7:13/8:11/9/Is26:7/28:9:23,24:25/
29:16/37:3/40:26/44:15/45:7:9^2/57:6/65:25/
Jer3:6/8:7/11:1/12:13/22:15/23:9:29/26:16/
30:13/31:10:32f/51:26f/Lam3:33/Eze18:5:6:15
:17:18:19:27/24:7:19/33:8:14:19/38:15,16f/44:
9/Dan3:29/4:35/6:27/9:14/Hos5:12/9:9/Joe2:
26/Nah1:3/Zep3:2:5/Hag2:12:13/Zec4:4/Mal
1:4/2:15/3:14,15/Mt8:8,9/9:11/12:19^2:20/13:
22/17:25/18:7/22:12:43/24:6/Mk2:7:8/3:35/4:
10:21/7:37/8:12f:16:36/9:43,44/Lk3:9/5:21/6:
36/7:6,7,8:23:49/8:18/10:25:26/12:6:25/14:26f
:26:27/17:1:18/20:17/Jn4:25/5:17:19:21/6:54:
61/7:7:36/8:22:37:44/11:24:47/14:10/Act25:16
/26:8/Rom2:2/3:3:26:29:31/6:15^2/9:19:22/11:
11/13:3:10/14:22:23/16/1Co1:9/3:7/4:2/6:18:
19/7:34:38^2/9:5/12:6:15:29:30/13:5^2:11/14:24/
15:27/16:22/2Co1:3,4:19/6:12/7:10/Gal3:5/
Eph4:11/Php2:1/Col3:3/4:10:14/1Th3:12/2Th
1:5/3:6:10/2Ti1:7/2:15/Tit3:9/Heb1:3:13/3:3/
4:8/12:7/Jas1:25/2:16:20:24/3:11/1Pe1:24/5:
13f:13/1Jn1:7/2:22:29/3:9/4:2/5:12^2:16/2Jn1:
1/3Jn:9

354

DOESN'T

Ex21:18:33/Lev4:27/6:3/Num19:20/23:18-24/
Deu14:7/15:16/17:1:16/18:22/21:15:17/24:1/
Ju9:36/1Sa3:13/6:3/24:11/2Sa15:3/1Ki1:11/2
:9/3:7/8:46/2Ki4:14/6:26-30/1Ch5:1/Job10:15
/12:3:7,8,9/13:9:11/15:15/19:16/24:1/33:20/
34:10:19^2/35:13:14,15/Ps81:11/94:6,7:10/Pro5
:6/12:23/13:1:16/18:2/19:10/25:14/26:1/27:
23,24/28:9:14/31:30/Ecc5:1/6:2:6/8:6,7:16,17/
Is26:10/28:27:28/29:15/40:27/59:9:11/Jer8:22^2
/Eze:12/9:9/18:15:16:19/33:6:9/Dan3:18/Hos
1:3:8/7:9:10/11:3/Amo3:5/Hag1:9/Zec11:17/
Mal2:13:17/Mt10:14/11:18/13:19:21/15:26/
17:24/Mk7:19/Lk6:43/8:13/10:40/14:5/16:17
/17:7,8,9/18:16,17/Jn2:10/8:54/9:31/10:21/12
:47/14:17:24^2/15:2:15/17:25/Act7:48,49/17:24
/25:27/Rom8:9:24:35/9:7:21/1Co3:3:4/6:13/7:
19:37:38:40/8:8/9:7/10:16:23/11:14,15:21/14:
8:9:23/15:36/2Co4:2/6:15/10:18/Gal1:6/3:16/
5:11/6:15/1Ti5:23/Heb:12,13/12:8/Jas1:9:12:
20:23:26/2:17/1Pe:16/1Jn:4:11:23/3:10:14/4:8
:20/5:10^2/2Jn1:10

164

DOING

Gen2:2/16:5/20/21:28,29/37:2/48:19/Ex2:13/
10:2/11:9/16:23/30:20/Lev16:28/25:14,15,16/
Num23:18-24/30:1/32:14/Deu4:9/6:18/9:4/12
:8/13:18/18:12/23:21/32:19/Ju2:19/15:11/18:
3:18/1Sa2:23,24,25:30/10:1/17:28/18:17/25:
19:39/26:23/29:3/2Sa6:7/21/11:25/15:19,20
/1Ki8:31:61/19:9/20:7:40/22:3/2Ki17:22/1Ch
16:37/2Ch12:6/20:10/21:6/22:3/24:22/30:5f/
31:20/Neh2:16:19/3:28/4:1/5:7:8:9/6:3/11:10-
10-14/13:21/Job9:12/10:2/13:4:9/15:12/22:13
/Ps1:2/7:3/10:14/18:20:23/19:13/26:11/34:14
/35:17:20:21/83:2/94:10/112:1/118:23/141:4/
Pro2:14/3:21/4:11/14:35/24:8/Ecc5:4:6,7/8:
2,3/Is1:16/8:12/26:10/45:3:9/49:5/55:7/56:2/
57:17/58:5/59:4/66:18/Jer3:4,5/4:22^2/5:19/6:
27/7:17:24/13:23/18:12/21^2/22:4/23:14:23/25
:5/34:15/37:14/44:22/49:1/Lam2:20/Eze7:8,9
/8:6^2:12/33:15:31/36:22/37:18,19,20/Dan4:35
/8:25/9:13/Hos4:14/Amo5:24/Zec7:3/Mal1:5
/Mt3:8/6:3/10:20/11:2/21:3/24:46/25:40/Mk
2:21:24/3:4/9:39/11:3:4,5/12:11/14:6/Lk7:18/
9:43/12:48/13:32/17:7,8,9/19:31:33/23:34/Jn
3:21^2/4:34/5:19:20/8:43/9:41/13:7:12/16:2/17
:4/18:29/Act2:22/3:13/5:9/9:36/10:38/11:23/
13:41/14:15/15:4/19:14/20:24/22:26/24:13/26
:20/Rom1:27:28/2:3/3:12:19:20:27/7:16:17:20/
8:5/9:10-13/12:21/13:3^2:4:6/14^2:13:21:22/1Co
1:7/4:5/6:9,10/7:20:29:30:32/9:25/10:11:33/11
:2/12:10/15/16/2Co8:10/11:12/12:6:18/Gal1:
13/2:11/4:17:18/5:16/6:4:9:12/Eph1:12/2:3/3:
13/5:15,16:28/6:6,7/Php1:11:18/2:4/4:9/Col1:
10/2:20/1Th4:11/5/2Th3:13/1Ti1:13:19/4:6/6
:19/2Ti2:5:19:26/Tit1:16/2:2:14/Heb:10/3:9/5
:14/7:28/9:6/10:24:36/12:7:10/13:20,21/Jas2:
12:20/4:17/1Pe1:14/2:19:20/3:6:17^2/4:19/2Pe
2:15/1Jn:17/3:7:12:22/5:3/3Jn1:5:10/Jud:16/
Rev2:2:26/13:14/22:11

298

DON'T

Gen15:1/18:3,4:30/19:7:17^2:18,19,20/20:7/21:
12:16:17/22:12/24:6:8:33:56/26:2/28:1/29:7:8/
30:27/31:24^2/42:16:37/43:3,4,5:9:23/44:32/45:
5:20:24/46:3,4/50:19:21/Ex1:10/3:5/4:8:9:18:
19/5:2:3:7,8^3:15:17/8:25:28/10:7:28/12:10/13:
3/14:13/16:19:28,29^2/19:24/20:19:20:25:26/22
:27/23:2,3^2:33/32:22/33:13:15:16/35:3/Lev18:
3/19:9^2:10^2:13:16^2:17^2:18^2:19^2/23:21:25:28:35/
25:4^2:5^2:36:37/Num4:17,18,19/12:12/13:20/14
:9:17,18:42:43/16:26/22:12:34/23:25/32:19:23
/Deu1:17:19,20,21^2:29/2:5:9/3:22/5:8:11/6:13
/7:2:18/8:11:14:15:20/9:4:7:8:26:27/12:9:30/13
:3:8/14:21^2:27/15:9:10:13:23/16:8:11:14/18:2/
19:13/20:1:3:19^2/21:14:23/22:1:2:4:6:10:11/23:
7:19:21:25/24:19:20:21/25:4/28:49/31:8/32:39
/33:11/Jos2:5/3:2,3,4/6:18/8:1/9:7/10:8:19:25
/11:6/22:20/23:12/Ju4:18/5:28/6:23:39/13:4^2:
18/14:3:16/15:11/16:6:15/19:20:23:24/Ru1:8:
16:20/2:8,9/3:3:11:14/4:4/1Sa1:15,16/6:6:9/8:
7/9^2:20/12^2/16:7^2/17:32:33:55/19:11/20:3:8:
13:30:38/21:4/23:3:17/25:25/26:9/28:13/29:7/
2Sa1:20/3:9,10/5:23/9:7/12:21/13:12^2:20:28/
14:10:13/18:12:22/19:6:7:22/21:4/24:24/1Ki1:
18:21/2:6:16:36,37/3:26/12:2,3,4/17:13/18:25:
40/20:8:10:11/21:7/22:8:23/2Ki1:14:15/2:16/4
:15,16:24:29/5:26/6:9:16:31/9:12:15/10:18,19:
23:25/11:15/12:7/17:26/18:29:30:31,32^2/19:10^2
/23:18/1Ch16:22/19:2,3/28:20/2Ch7:19/13:5/
14:11/15:7/16:8/18:6,7/20:12:15^2:17/23:13,14
/24:5/25:19/29:11/32:12:13:15^2/35:3:21^2/Ez6:
7/Neh4:14/5:9/6:14/8:9:11/Job1:12,13/6:29:
30/9:11/10:2/13:4:21^2/15:9/20:4/22:15,16/27:
12/28:13/30:10:20^2/32:13:21,22^2/33:5/34:31/
36:18^2/Ps6:1/7:2/9:19/10:12/13:4^2/14/22:
9,10,11:19/25:2^3/26:9,10/27:9^2:12^2:14/28:3/31
:1:17/32:9/35:19^2:20:22^2:24:25/36:11^2/37:7:8:
34/38:1:21^2/39:10:12/40:11:17/41:10/42:11^2/
44:23/50:13/51:9:11^2:14,15:16:18/55:1/56:7/
58:1/59:11/62:10,11^2/69:6^2:8:14:15:17/70:2,3:
5/71:1:9^2:12:18/74:21:23/83:1:2^2/89:30,31,32/
91:5/95:8/102:2:24/103:8/109:1:14:17/119:8:
10:22:31:115:121:122:141/131:1^2/138:8/140:
6,7,8^2:11/141:4:5:8/143:2:7/146:3/Pro1:15/3:
4,5:7,8:21:27,28^2:29:30:31^2/4:1:13:14:16:25:27/
5:8/6:3:4^2:25^2/7^3/8:33/9:7,8:18/10:19/12:22/
13:24/17:14/19:18/20^2:19:22/22:22,23:26,27/
23:1:4,5:6,7,8^2:9:10,11:12:13,14:17,18:19,20,21:
22:31/24:1^2:6:11,12^2:15,16:19,20^2:21,22:28,29^2
/25:6,7,8,9,10^2:16:17/26:4,5:24,25,26/27:1:2/
28:5:17/29:7:26/30:32/Ecc1:8-11/5:1:4:6,7:8/7
:9:10^2:13:15-17^3:21,22:26/8:2,3:13/9:5/10:4/12
:1/Sol1:6:8/Is:3:11^3/2:22/3:7/6:10/7:9/8:12^2:
13:19/10:24/13:15/14:29/22:4/29:9/30:1:9:
10,11^2/36:8,9:11:12:14:15:16:18:19:20/37:6:10:
13/38:3/40:9:28^2/41:6:13/43:1:5:19/44:2^2:8^2/
45:5/46:8:9/51:7/55:2^2/56:3:6/58:2:3^2:7/59:8/
65:5:8/Jer1:7:8:17/2:25^2:28:29/4:6/5:4:15:22/6
:8:10:25^2/7:4:8:17:27^2/8:7:12/10:2,3^2:5:24:25/
12:6^2/13:1^2:12/14:9:11^2/15:15/16:8^2/17:15:16^2
:17/18:12:18:23^2/22:10:21/23:16:17/25:6/26:2
/27:14:16:17/29:6:8^2/30:10^2:14/31:16/33:
20,21/35:6:14/36:19/37:9:20/38:14:24/40:4^2/
42:11/45:3:5/46:27^2/49:9,10/51:6:46:50/Eze2:
6^3:8/3:9/4:11/9:6/12:2:6/16:52:61/17:12,13/
20:18^2:39/24:17^2/33:8:32/46:18/Dan2:8,9:24:
43/4:19/5:10/8:26/9:18:19/10:12:19/Hos4:4:6:
16/6:6^2/7:9/9:14/10:3:4/13:10/Joe2:17^2/3:
Amo5:5/6:10/7:2:5:13:16/Ob1:3/Jon:14^2/4
/Mic2:6^2/6:5/7/Zep3:16/Hag1:9/2:5/Zec1
14/3:8/4:5^2:13/7:6/8:13:14,15:17^2/10:2/11:
Mal1:6:7/2:1/3:18/Mt1:20/3:9/5:15,16:17:
35:36:39:42/6:1:2:3:5:7,8:13:16:19:25:26^2:28
31,32:34/7:1:6^2/8:4/9:12:14/10:5:9:10:19:26
:31:34/11:6/12:33/13:14^2:21/14:27/15:16:1
32/16:9:10/17:7:26,27/18:10/19:4:13:14:18
20:22/21:21:27/22:31^2/23:3^2:4:8:9:10/24:4:
26^2:42/26:53:70:72:74/27:13/28:5:10/Mk1:
43,44/4:17:38:40/5:7,8:36/6:10:50/7:5:18/8
26/9:39:50/10:14:19^5:38/11:33/12:10:24^2:2
13:5:11:15,16^2:21:33:35,36,37/14:68:71/15:3
16:6/Lk1:13:30/2:10/3:8:14^2/4:23/5:10/6:3
35:49/7:6,7,8:13:32^2/8:28:50/9:3:55f:58/10:
7^2/11:4:7:13/12:4:11:15^2:22:24:27:28:29^2:32
:3:15:27/14:5:8:12:28/17:23/18:7:11:20^4/20:
21/21:8^2:9:14:34,35^2/22:34:36:51:57:60/23:
34:40,41/24:6,7:39:44:49/Jn2:16/3:7:10,11:
18:36/4:11:32/5:14:28:41,42:44:47^2/6:43:64,
28/8:14:19^2:35:45:46:47/9:12:21:25:29:30/1
25:26:37:38/12:15/13:7:8/14:5:9:10:27:30/1
19:21/16:7:17,18:30/17:14^2/19:10/20:2:13:1
27/21:18/Act2:15/3:6/7:40:60/10:15/11:9/
40/15:11/16:28:37/18:9^2/19:2/20:10,11,12/
11:21:22/25:10,11/27:24/28:27^2/Rom2:4^2:1
12-15^2:21:22:25:27/6:2,3:16/7:1:15^2:19:20/8
24:26/9:20/10:3:4:6:7/11:22:24/12:2:9:14:16
18:19:21/13:3:12,13:14/14:1:2:3:13:15:16:20
/1Co1:16/3:3:16:21/4:3^2/5:1:6:11/6:2:3:9,10
13:15:16/7:21:27^2/8:7:8:13/9:4:13:16:20^2:22
10:9:10:20:24:25:27:28:32/12:1:21^2/14:6:14^2
:20/15:16:33/16:2:7:11/2Co1:13,14:23/2:5,6
1/4:5:8^2/5:12/6:14:17/8:13/9:1:3:7/10:2:3:7
:12/11:5:11:16:19,20/12:2,3^2:6:11:14^2:21/Ga
12/3:25/4:10:20:21/5:1:6/6:7:9:13:17/Eph3:
/4:19:26^2:29:30/5:6:7:15,16:17:18/6:4:6,7:9/
Php1:22:23/2:3^2:4/3:12/4:6^2/Col2:8:16:18/3
5:9:12:21:25/4:2:3/1Th1:8/2:9:11/4:9/5:1/2
2:1^2:3:5:16/3:15/1Ti:15/4:7:12/5:3:19/6:1:5:
21/2Ti2:8:23/3:5/4/Tit1:16/2:15/3:9/Heb4:
5:11/6:1:2:9/10:32/12:5^2:8/13:2:3:16/Jas1:4
7,8^2:16:19:22/2:6:16:21/3:1:13:14/4:2^3:3:4:1
5:9/1Pe1:14/2:1/3:3:7:9^2/4:4:12:15/5:3/2Pe
8/1Jn2:27/3:1^2:7:13/4:1/2Jn1:7:10^2:12/3Jn
:13/Jud:7/Rev:17,18^2/2:2:4/3:17^2/7:3/10:4/
:10/22:9

13

DONE

Gen1:25/4:10/9:24,25/12:18/20:9,10^2:16/26
29/27:19:41:45/31:12/34:13/42:28/44:5/Ex
16/14:5:31/18:1:8:9/34:10/38:21/39:6,7/Lev
17,18/8:34/18:27/20:4/23:14/24:20/26:32:4
Num4:37/6:18/8:22/14:10,11/16:11,12:28^2/
2,3:28:30/23:11:18-24^2/25:12,13/28:18/29:1
12/31:4,5/Deu2:30/3:21:23,24,25/5:14/9:4:1
10:8:21/12:7:31/26:14/28:63/29:24/Jos5:2,3
8,9/7:19/8:33/9:24/10:1/19:51/22:2,3:11:24,
/23:3/24:31/Ju2:7-9:10/8:2,3:35/9:16^2:19:
47,48/13:23/15:10/20:12:31/1Sa1:23/2:3/10
18,19/12:1:3:7:20:24/13:11/14:43/17:29:36/
:4:18/20:1:32/22:21/24:6/25:30,31^2/26:17,18
21/28:17/29:8/31:11/2Sa2:6/3:8:24,25/6:8/
23/10:12/11:10:27/12:9:11/13:12f:21-24/19:
38/21:11/22:25/24:17/1Ki1:27/2:5/8:15:20:4
/9:8/11:4:33/13:11/14:9/15:30/17:18/18:9:3
36/19:1/21:19:29/22:43/2Ki1:4,5:6:16/5:13:
/8:4/9:15/10:9,10:16:30/12:7/15:18/17:9:11/
18:14/19:11/20:6/21:1:3,4,5:9:11:15:21/23:17
19/1Ch10:11/13/16:37/17:17/21/24:31/26:1
/29:17/2Ch2:17/6:10/7:21:22/11:17/19:2/23
/24:16/Ez10:13/Neh2:4/4:10/5:19/6:16/9:8/
13:14/Est1:17/3:7/4:1/5:14/9:12:13:17/Job2
/6:24/10:15/11:6/13:23/19:10/21:30-32/31:2
:28:37/34:32/36:9/Ps17:1/18:24/20:5/22:22/
28:5/37:18/38:19/39:9f/40:5/52:9f/59:3/64:4
66:5/68:28/71:8:19/74:3/78:11,12/92:4/102:
/105:14:45/106:21,22/109:15:27/116:7:12/11
:15,16/119:121/126:2/147:20/Pro4:16/Ecc1:
8-11^2/2:20-23/11:4/Sol1:6/Is5:4:13/12:5/22:
22/23:9/31:2/33:13/34:8/38:10/40/41:4/44:
23:26/53:9/58:3/63:7/Jer2:13:23:35/7:13,14:
31/8:6/9:14/14:10/16/18:6:13/19:8/23:2/24:
4,5/29:23:27/32:20:23:30:31/34:14/36:24,25/
37:18^2/38:9/41:11/44:17/50:15:29/51:10:24/
Lam1:12:21^2/3:64/Eze:19/5:9/6:11/7:26,27/
10/13:5/14:23/16:61:63^2/18:26/20:32:43/24:
22:23:24/25:14:17/26:14f/29:9/32:15/36:32/
37:14/38:23/39:21/43:11/45:17/Dan9:12/11:
24/Hos5:2/Joe2:20:21/3:7/Amo:7/9/Ob1:12:

ONE Con't)
Jon:8/2:9/Mic6:3:6/7:9/Zec1:5,6/4:7/8:2/
1:7/2:12/Mt6:10/11:20:21:23/13:28/21:4:
23:5/26:10:13:42:58/27:3:23:66f/Mk1:28/5
20:32:33/6:30/10:52/11:18/14:8/15:14/Lk
/2:48/3:19,20/4:37/8:39/9:10:50/10:13/11
12:42,43,44/17:10:16/18:29/19:15:36,37/
5:31:40,41:54/Jn2:7,8/5:9:29/7:31/10:32/
8:37/13:15/14:12,13/15:24/18:35/Act3:17
:9:10:13:16:30/9:13/10:33/14:11/15:12/20:
21:14:22:33/23:14:28/25:10,11:25/26:26:31
m1:5/3:27/5:1:11/7:23,24,25:23,24,25f/9:
13:19/12:1:20/14:23/15:17:19/1Co1:31/6:
11:17/14:26:40/15:21/2Co2:14/3:2/4:5/5:
7:11/8:1/10:15:17:18/12:21/Gal5:8/6:4/
1:11:16,17/2:7:9:13:18/3:6/Php:3/4:14:19/
1:22:28/2:7/2Th1:10/1Ti:19/5:10/2Ti2:15/
1/4:14/Heb:13/10:24/13:2/Jas4:9/5/1Pe2:
:16/1Jn:4:20/5:16/Jud1:15/Rev6:10/18:6/
8/20:12/22
496

OWN
1:16/7:10,11,12/8:5/11:7/12:10/15:11:12:
17/18:21/19:9:17:24:33/21:16/22:12/23:9/
11:20:32:45:46/28:11:12/37:25:35/41:43/42
:38/44:11:12:31/45:9/46:3,4^2/49:9/50:
17:18/Ex1:11/2:5:25/3:21/4:3^2/7:9:10:15/9:
33/14:24/15:5:19/16:4/19:10:11:14:16:20:
24:25/23:24/24:4/25:20/26:9:12/27:5/32:1:
:15/33:9/34:8:13^2:27:29/37:9/39:4,5/Lev9:
13:20/14:47/22:7/26:30/Num1:51/3:14,15/
/6:27/10:17:36/11:17:25/13:23:29/14:45/16
:33/20:15/22:26:27/23:18-24/24:15-19/25:2
:18/33:2/34:5/35:17/Deu1:42/3:18/4:39/5:
0/7:5/9:12:15:25/10:5:22/12:3/16:6/20:19:
23:7/25:1:18/26:15/28:49:52/29:6/30:12/
19:22:24/32:23/Jos1:15/2:23/4:18/6:5/8:29^2
:11:19:27^2/15:10,11/18:13:16^2:17:18/Ju1:
/4:14/5:4:13,14^2:15/6:25^2:30/7:1:4:10:11^2:
13/8:2,3:9:14:17/9:15:28:36:44:53/12:1/14:
:16/15:11/16:30:31/19:26:27/20:48/Ru1:9/3
4^2:6,7^2:13/4:1^2/1Sa1:11/2:7/3:9/5:4/9:16/
5/16:10,11/19:12/20:24,25/41/21:13/23:4:
20/25:1:20/26:2:5,6,7:10:14/31:12/2Sa2:24:
/8:2/11:19,20,21/15:24/17:13/18:7:25:26/19
:18/20:15/22:10:28/23:7:13:20/1Ki1:5:53/2:
6:20/4:21:33/12:16,17/15:13/16:10/18:30:
:42:44/19:4:5:6:10:14/21:16/22:35:36,37/
i1:10:11:12/3:2/4:24:35/5:14:21:26/6:1:4/7:
/8:1/9:24:33/10:32,33/11:18/14:13/15:24/
:10/18:4^2/19:23/20:3:11f/21:13/23:7:8:11:12
:15/25:9:10:14,15/1Ch4:40,41/14:16/21:26/
:1/24:6/2Ch1:13/6:12,13:20,21/7:1/10:15/
:3^2/15:16/17:6/18:2/19:10/20:16/21:9f:14:
/22:8/23:15,16,17^2/24:17,18/26:6:19/30:14/
:1/32:5:30/33:15/34:4:7^2:10,11/36:19/Ez3:7
:3/Neh1:3:4:6,7/2:3/3:9:18/4:11/9:13/12:23
st3:15/8:3/Job1:20/3:26/6:4/7:21/8:17/11:
/14:7:11,12/16:7:22/17:16/18:14/19:10/20:
:23:24/22:29/25:3/27:15/30:14/31:26/34/36
8/39:30/40:12:21:23/Ps2:12/3:5/4:6:8/10:6/
:3f:6:7f/13:4/14:2/18:9:16/29:5,6/31:4,15/
:13,14,15/34:8/35:12/36/37:6/38:16/44:5/
:5/53:2/55:15/57:3/58:7f/60:12/63:9/64:3:7
7:1/68:34/69:13/71:1:2:20/73:18/74:8/76:12
7:17/78:2,3:6:24:27/80:1:3:7:12:14:19/85:11:
/86:1:16/88:6/89:23:40:43/90:5,6/102:2:
10:19:23/105:27:32/107:16/108:13/109:
,23/110:5/116:2/119:78:135:153/133:2/135:
/139:8/140:10/144:5:7:12-15/146:8/147/148:
/Pro2:11,12,13/3:20/5:5:6/7:3:8,9/11:28/12:4
4:1/19:5/20:1/24:21,22:30,31/25:8,9,10/26:
7/Ecc9:9/10:3/11:8/12:11/Sol1:6:10/4:8/6:2:
11/Is3:12/4:2,3,4/5:5:15/6:13/7:3:18/8:16^2/
8,9,10:16/10:9:13:16:33:34^2/11:1:6:7/14:12:
5^2:30:31/15:9/16:8^2/18:2/21:1/22:9,10,11:19/
4:12:19/25:4:11^2/26:5/28:17/30:2:6:8:13:25:
0/32:15/33:12/36:7/37:24:27/38:3:8/44:14:15
7:19/45:2:14/46:6:7/53:4/55:10/57:5/60:20/
3:15/64:1:2:3:11/Jer1:10/4:13:18:23:26/5:1:
0/6:6^2/8/10:2,3:18/11:11/12:10/13:13:18/15:
/16:16/17:2,3/18:2/23:12/25:4:37/26:10/30:2
31:9/32:29/33:4/36:2^2:4:12:18/38:6:12/39:8/
3:13^2/45:1/46:15:22,23/48:18^2/49:16/50:3:26
51:3:4:25:30/52:14/Lam1:2:7:16/2:6:8:18/3:
0/4:11/Eze1:13:24:27,28/6:12/7:24/8:2/13:
1:14/16:39/17:24/19:12/24:2/25:11/26:4:12:
6/28:17/31:11:12:16:17:18/32:20:29:30/34:14
5,16:18:19/38:8:9:20/39:6/40:2/41:10/43:3/
7:18/Dan2:35/3:10:15:23/4:12:13:14:23^2:31/6
0/7:1:9:25/8:7:17/9:6:8:18/10:15/11/Hos1:
18:21,22/5:10/7:12/8:14/10:2/Joe1:3/3:11/
Amo1:10:12:14/2:2:5/4:13/6:2/8:9/9:1:2^3:6/
Ob1:2:4/Jon:3^2:5:6/2:3:6/3:4,5:6/4:8/Mic1:4:6
/3/4:3/5:11/7:10/Nah1:6:15/3/Hab1:8/2:16:
17^2/3:12/Zep1:16/2:7/3:13/Hag1:8/Zec5:8/7:
12/8/12:12,13,14/13:7/Mt2:11/3:10:16/5:1/7:
19/8:1:11/9:9/11:23/13:1:47,48/14:9:19/15:35
/17:9:26,27/18:2:10:19:26:29/21:8/23:23/24:2/
25:5,6/26:36/27:40:41,42,43:55/28:2/Mk2:4/3
:11/4:1:39/5:6:13:22/6:39,40/8:6/9:35/10:17:
52/11:8/15:19:29,30:32:36:46/16:19/Lk3:9^2/4:
6,7:20:40/5:4:18,19/6:17,18:24:38:39:49/7:36:
38/8:23:24:33:41/9:14:54/10:15/11:7:37,38/12
:18/13:7:9/14:31:33/17:7,8,9:29/18:6/19:5:6:
36,37:42/21:6:24:25/22:14:41,42/23:49:53/24:
30:32/Jn5:4/6:2-5:10^2:16:18,19:42:48-51/8:2:6:
8/10:11:15:17:18^2/11:32/12:13:25^2/13:12/15:
13/17:8/19:13:31:38/Act7:34/8:14:27:38/9:3:
25/10:5,6:20:21:32/11:5:27/12:17/13:43/16:16
:23:29/17:6/19:26:35^2/20:10,11,12:17:38/21:5:
29:32/22:25/23:7/26:13:14/27:22/Rom2:12-15
/8:35/10:6/11:2,3:4:12/14:3:10/15:25/1Co1:28
/4:5/6:3/10:7:11/14:25/15:24:32/2Co4:9^2/5:1/
10:4:5/11:7:33/Gal1:13/3:15:17/Eph1:8/2:14/
3:14,15^2:17/4:9^2:10:26/Php1:25/3:6/Col2:7/3:
2/1Th4:16/2Th2:4/3:12/1Ti1:13/6:2:19/Heb1:
3/8:4/9:1:23^2:25/10:7:12/11:13:30/12:1/Jas2:1
/5:18/1Pe1:6:11/2Pe:17,18/1Jn3:16/Rev1:2:
11:19/3:12/4:10/5:8:14/7:11/8:5:7/10:1/11:15:
16/12:9:10:11:12:13/13:8:13/14/15:1/18/19:4:
10:15/20:1:9/21:2:5/22:2:8
964

EITHER
Gen31:47,48:53/Ex3:15f/5:14/12:5/13:21/14:
29/38:14,15/Lev1:14/3:1:6/18:10/Num6:1/30:
13/Deu2:9:27/15:10/16:2/23:17,18/1Sa16:8/
20:27/28:5,6/2Ki9:20/1Ch23:29/28:12f/Pro27:
10/Ecc7:12:15-17/10:20/Is29:9/59:8/Jer15:
12,13/23:38,39f/35:8/Eze34:29f/40:48,49/
Amo7:6/Zec9:10f/11:6/Mt12:31,32:37/21:27/
27:38/Mk7:18/11:33/12:5/15:27/Lk2:24/20:8
/23:32,33/Jn5:47/19:18/Act20:20/Rom9:10-
10-13/11:21/14:8/1Co12:10/2Co2:3/3:1/Eph1
:21/2Ti2:5/Tit3:12/Jas5:12/1Jn2:23/3:6/Rev
13:17
67

ELSE
Gen15:4/19:12/26:16/39:11/42:5/Ex4:13/5:
7,8:17/15:11/20:17:23/22:9^2:14/34:7/Lev15:10
/25:26:34:49/27:20:27/Num1:51/3:10/4:32/16
:3^2/18:7/20:19/Deu4:34:35/5:21/15/20:5:6:7/
22:3/23:19/28:30^3/33:29/Jos2:17,18/7:12f/Ju
9:25/16:7:16,17/Ru3:12/1Sa9:2/10:23/15:6:8:
15:20/20:8/21:3:9/24:19/2Sa2:21/3:35,36/7:
19/14:25/1Ki3:12/11:11/14:5:6/20:40^2/21:25/
2Ki7:7/1Ch17:18/26:28/2Ch6:23/9:12/10:16/
14:11/15:15/18:18/23:5,6/31/Ez7:23/Job24:
22,23/31:7,8:10:23/34:7,8/41:33/Ps10:12/22:
9,10,11/35:10/39:5,6/40:5^2/45:7/49:19/72:12/
73:5/84:10/108/Pro3:13,14,15/4:15:23^2/8:22/
14:10/25:8,9,10/30:4^2/Ecc2:12/Sol4:12/Is3:5/
8:13/40:12^2/41:26^2/42:8/44:7:25/45:6/Jer1:17
/4:4/9:7/32:6,7/Eze12:3/39:10/Dan4:18/5:17/
Hos4:4/Amo5:6/Hag2:14/Mt3:11/5:47/6:24/
19:20/23:3/26:33/Mk9:2:6/10:11/13:35,36,37/
Lk8:14/12:1/13:7/16:13^2:18/18:9:11:19/22:58:
59/24:9/Jn1:1/3:31/4:37/5:7:32,33/10:20:29/
11:24:25/14:11/17:10/18:34f/Act1:20:21,22/3:
6/4:12/8:34/25:10,11/26:6/27:19/Rom1:14/3:
4/6:16/7:3:23,24,25/8:32/13:9/14:21/15:20/
1Co1:16/2:11/4:3/7:11/10:29/11:16:17/12:8:9:
10:31/14:26:29,30/15:28/2Co8:21/10:15:16/12
:13/Gal1:12:16/3:15/5:20/6:4/Eph1:21/2:3/
Php2:21:27/3:8^2:10:17:21/Col1:17/1Th2:6/3:
12/5:15/1Ti:3:16:20/Heb1:9/3:10/5:1/7:24/
Jas1:13/2:3/5:12/1Jn2:19/2Jn1:1/Jud:3/Rev2
:5:16:17/22:6,7
235

ENTIRE
Gen2:11,12:13/12:3/18:26/19:31/39:8:22/41:
40/45:8/Ex8:17/10:4,5/11:6/12:15:16/14:9/25
:31/27:18/30:3/37:23,24/39:33-40/Lev2:2/4:
13:21/6:17^2/8:21/16:20/18:25/19:24/25:4/26:
26/Num1:47,48,49/4:10:16/6:3,4:6,7:8/8:7:11/
15:26/16:19/18:21/22:30/26:3,4:5-11:64,65/32
:15/34:1/Deu1:7:34,35/3:4:6/4:33/13:16/14:28
/31:30/34:11,12/Jos2:24/4:19/5:2,3:4,5:8,9/6:
3,4:18/7:1/8:25:35/9:24/10:28:32:33:37/11:16:
23/15:47/18:9/22:20/Ju1:25/4:13/6:15/8:2,3f:
12:17/9:51/16:30/19/20:1:19,20:26:48^2/21:6:
17/Ru1:19/2:21/1Sa1:11:19,20/3:13/5:11/9:4/
13:3,4:22/14:15/15:3/17:25/19:8/22:4:16/23:8:
23/25:28/28:19/30:17/2Sa1:4/3:9,10/4:8/8:14
/10:7,8/17:11:12:13:16:24/19:3:7/21:10/24:8/
1Ki3:28/6:7:15:38/8:11/10:21/11:15:25/14:13/
15:5/16:11/18:5/20:19:20/2Ki5:15/6:24/9:8/
13:22/15:16/23:1/24:7/25:1/1Ch5:16/10:6/19:
7/28:21/29:1/2Ch1:16/3:4/8:6/14:4:13/29:17:
24:28/30:12/35:16/Ez3:9/4:4,5:20/5:5/6:21,22
/Neh4:6/5:14/10:28/Job1:2,3/34:29,30/Ps35:
18/74:8/79:3/80:11/97:8,9/109:11/Ecc12:13/
Is6:4/36:8,9/41:2/Jer10:25/25:11/26:2/31:40/
37:10/49:26/Eze5:15/40:13/42:4:15/43:12:17/
48:20:23:35/Dan6:3/Amo1:12f/3:1/7:4/Mic1:6
/Zec5:3/Mt8:34/9:26/21:10/26:59/27:27/Mk
1:28/5:13/15:1:16,17:33:33f/Lk23:1/Jn4:53/
11:51/Act3:25/5:11:21/10:2/13:6,7:44/15:3/16
:31/18:21f/19:26/21:5/24/Rom5:12/1Co12:7/
14:4/Heb9:8/Rev19:21
237

EVEN
Gen1:2f/2:11,12/3:2,3:16/4:12/6:4/8:21^2/22:
12:16/25:21/27:36/31:42/37:5/39:10/41:31/43
:23/48:19/Ex4:10:18/6:12/7:4:19/8:3,4/9:4:6:7
:30/10:4,5:7:24/11:5/13:3:17,18/16:27/19:12:
22/21:14:19/24:11/32:27:29/33:5/34:7:21/35:3
/Lev5:2/11:8:11/13:40:55/19:13/21:11/25:5:32
:45/26:17:21:23:24/Num4:20/6:3,4^2:6,7/11:
19,20/12:6/14:2:10,11:17,18:23/17:12,13/19:
12:16/20:5:17:19/22:15/24:1:13/32:14:15/Deu
1:16:19,20,21:28:37/2:5/4:36/5:9,10:14:24/6:3/
7:14/9:9/12:3:20-23:31/13:6,7:15/14:8/15:22/
19:6,7:15/21:17:18/23:3:4/27:15/28:33:53:61:
68/29:4:19/30:5/31:21:27/32:11:26/33:9/Jos2:
9/7:26/17:16,17,18/22:2,3:17,18/23:7/24:20/
Ju2:17:19/5:5/7:12,13/13:2,3:18/14:16/18:
9,10:27/19:16:19/Ru1:12/2:13/3:10^2/1Sa2:15/
8:19/9:7:24/12:4/13:6:12/14:15:22:24,25/18:
15,16:29/20:2/21:5/22:8/23:3:24,25/24:11/25:
17:22:29/26:12:23:24/2Sa2:27/3:39/4:2,3/5:2:
6:8/6:22/11:13/17:10/1Ki1:11:18:37:46,47^2/8:
27/9:20,21/11:2:7:12,13:22/12:11:31/13:8^2/14:
22/16:11:30/18:38/2Ki3:19:25/4:43/5:17f/6:
12:25/7:9:19/8:18/12:3/16/17:17:19:31/18:4:
16:24^2/19:32/21:3,4,5:7:9^2:11:14/23:5:8:9/1Ch
11:2/16:21/17:20/22:14/29:25/2Ch2:6/4:22/6:
18/7:20/12:12/15:16/17:6:11/22:9/25:15/26:8:
23/27:2/28:3^2:21/30:17,18,19^2/33:4,5:9/34:6/
35:24,25/36:13:17^2/Ez2:62,63/9:1:9:13^2:14/10:
10/Neh1:9/2:16/4:3/5:2,3,4/7:64,65/9:18:24:
29/13:26/Est5:3:6/7:2:4:8/8:8f/9:6/10:1/Job3:
4:18/4:18,19/7:13,14:19/8:11-13:18/9:3:14:15:
16:20:21:28:30:31^2/10:18/12:22/15:15^2/16:19/
19:15:16:18:26f/21:6:16/22:2:30/24:3:6:20/25:
5/27:2:15/28:19:21/29:6:8:16/31:32/33:19:20/
34:6^2:33:34,35/35:6:14,15/36:13:33f/37:10/40:
23/41:9/Ps9:6/15:4/16/17:3/18:43,44,45/19:
14/22:1/23:4/31:9,10f:11/32:7/33:18,19/34:10
:16:20/35:11:15/37:19/38:11/39:8/41:9/46:2/
49:5/55:19/58:1/67:6,7/68:18/69:4:8:9:20^2/72:
2:16/73:23/77:4/78:19,20:23:32:64/79:3/84/87
:4/90:10^2/91:13/92:14/105:30/106:8:28:37,38:
44:46/109:4/119:23:32:55:100:130/133:3/135:
17/139:4:10:12:17,18/144:3/146:2/Pro4:25/5:
6/6:30:31/11/12:10:27/13:16:19/14:20/16:4:7/
17:27,28/19:24/20:11/22:26,27/23:35/24:1/26:
15/27:7/28:3/30:2:24-28/31:31/Ecc1:16-18/2:
10:15:24-26/3:11:16/4:12:14:15/5:1/6:3^2:4:5/8:
2,3:16,17/9:5:17/10:1:7:20/11:2f/Sol6:9/Is1:3:
12,13:15:18/3:9/5:19:25/7:19/8:2:4/9:11,12:17:
19,20:21/10:2:4/13:20/14:8/15:4:6/16:8/17:10
/23:12/28:22/31:4,5:9/32:4/33:23/35:1:8/36:
8,9/40:20:30/42:4:23/45:5/46:1:4/47:6:14/48:
20/49:15:19:25/51:12/52:14,15/55:1/57:9:11/
58:3^2/59:10/63:16/65:17:24/66:7,8:11/Jer2:2:6
:8:9:10,11/3:3:8:16/4:10/5:2:7:22/6:9:11:13:15/
7:3:26^2:31/8:4,5:12/9:16:25,26/11:8/12:4:6/13:
11/14:19/15:1^2:5/16:8/18:13/19:5/20:10/22:
18:24,25/23:14:18^2/28:14/30:11/31:32f/32:25:
34/36:7^2/37:10/43:6/44:7:10/46:20,21/48:32/
49:9,10:20/50:27:38:45/51:26:43/Lam1:10/2:1
/4:3,4:20/5:4:12/Eze2:6/3:9/5:5,6,7:8/6:3/7:13
/11:11/12:3^2:12/13:18/14:16:18/15:2:3:4/16:
27:31:51/17:8/20:13:31/21:4:27/22:12:29/23:
11:19,20:39:40/24:7/26:12/32:8/33:28/34:23/
36:11/Dan2:23:38/3:18:25:27/4:17:27:36/6:24
/8:5:11:25/9:9:13:20/10:17/11:4:36/Hos3:1:4/
4:3/7:1:9:10/8:12/9:8:11:16/10:14/11:3/12/
Joe1:20/2:14:16:29:32/Amo:15/3:4/5:15/6:9:
12/Jon3:7^2:9/Mic4:5/7:1:4:5/Nah2:11/Hab3:
17^2/Zep1:3:4/2:3/3:2/Hag2:16,17:18,19/Zec3:
2f/7:6:14/8:22/11:16/12:11/13:2/Mal1:2,3:8/3

(EVEN Con't)
:10/**Mt4**:25/**5**:22:28:29:30:34:36:46:47:48/**6**:7,8
/**7**:4:11/**8**:27/**10**:10^2:42/**11**:11:18/**12**:8:31,32/
13:8:12,13:23:23f/**14**:36/**15**:5,6:23:27/**16**:11/**17**
:5:20/**18**:14/**21**:15:16:21:32/**22**:6/**23**:4:10/**24**:
17:24:33:36^2/**25**:29/**26**:40:60,61:70:72:74/**28**:20
/**Mk1**:7:27/**2**:2:28/**3**:7,8:20:28/**4**:8:20:25:38:40:
41/**6**:8,9:20:22,23:52/**7**:28:37/**8**:26/**10**:45/**13**:
15,16^2:22:32/**14**:31:37:44f:59:65:71/**15**:32/**16**:
18/**Lk1**:15/**2**:21/**3**:12:16/**4**:36/**5**:15/**6**:5:32:33:
34/**7**:5:6,7,8:17:29:29f/**8**:18:25:29/**9**:3^2:33:34:58
/**10**:4:12:17/**11**:13:28:42/**12**:12:26:38/**13**:34/**14**
:22:24:35/**15**:2:16:17:29/**16**:10:17:31:31f/**17**:4:
7,8,9:22/**18**:6:13/**19**:21:26/**20**:37,38:47/**21**:16/
22:33:34:47:57/**23**:40,41/**Jn1**:11,12:27:51/**3**:12:
14/**4**:9:17,18/**5**:14:17f:21/**6**:36:39:60/**7**:5:35:51
/**8**:10:14:52:55:57/**10**:38/**11**:22:25/**12**:42/**13**:38
/**14**:9^2:12,13/**15**:2:9/**20**:21/**21**:17/**Act2**:39/**5**:9:
39/**6**:11/**7**:52/**8**:3/**10**:44/**11**:3/**14**:18/**19**:12:32/
20:34/**21**:28/**22**:2:25/**23**:8/**26**:11/**27**:22/**28**:17/
Rom1:21:26:28/**2**:12-15:20:29/**3**:11:25/**4**:18:20
/**5**:7/**6**:21/**8**:10:22:23:26:32/**9**:10-13:30/**10**:19:
20/**11**:15/**14**:1:16:22/**15**:1:15,16/**1Co1**:9:17:19/
2:1:9:13/**3**:2:12:22/**4**:3:4:11/**5**:1:6:11/**6**:2:4:4f:8:
12/**7**:38/**9**:12:20/**10**:31/**11**:14,15:30/**13**:2:5:9/
14:5:6:7:21:23:24/**15**:9:34/**2Co1**:9:12:13,14/**3**:
14:15/**7**:12/**9**:1/**11**:4:16/**12**:11:15:21/**13**:7/**Gal1**
:15:22/**2**:3:4:13/**3**:15:28/**4**:1:8:13:14^2/**5**:11/**6**:13
/**Eph1**:4/**2**:5:8:11/**3**:20/**5**:7:12:13/**6**:20/**Php2**:8:
8f:12:17/**3**:12/**4**:14:16/**Col1**:22/**2**:21/**1Th**:2:11:
15/**3**:4/**4**:10/**2Th3**:10/**1Ti1**:13:16/**3**:14/**4**:2:3/**5**:
24/**6**:10/**2Ti1**:8:15/**2**:9:13:14/**Phm1**:19:21/**Heb**
:1:9/**4**:3:5/**5**:8/**6**:9/**7**:4:9:28/**8**:4^2:7:10/**9**:18/**10**:
1:32/**11**:1:7:8:9:12:18:40/**12**:17:20/**Jas2**:11:21^2:
23/**3**:4/**4**:3/**5**:2:11/**1Pe1**:6:8^2:12/**2**:18:23/**3**:11:
14/**4**:6:17/**2Pe1**:3:5:12/**2**:1:4:10/**3**:9/**1Jn**:2:7:19
:20/**2Jn1**:10/**3Jn**:7/**Jud**:8:9/**Rev2**:10:13/**3**:2:4/
13:15:17/**18**:13:23

1064

FOR

Gen1:4,5:16:29:30/**2**:5:15:16,17:18^2:19,20/**3**:5:
18:19:20f^2:20/**4**:1:12:14:15:24:25^2/**5**:21-24/**6**:7:
12,13/**7**:1:2^2:8,9:10,11,12:17/**8**:2:9:20/**9**:2,3^2:
5,6:16,17/**10**:1:25/**11**:6/**13**:1:6:12:15/**14**:4:5,6:
21/**15**:1:2,3:4:13:16^2/**16**:5^2:9-12:13^2/**17**:5:7,8:14
:20/**18**:6:14:15:18^2:19:24:26:28:31:32/**19**:2:4:8:
13:14:16:17:18,19,20:22:31/**20**:2:3:7^2:9,10:16^2:
18^2/**21**:7:11:12:14:17:18:20,21:34/**22**:3:6^2:7:9:
12/**23**:1:4:5,6:9^2/**24**:4:7:14:17:18:19:22:23:25:27^2
:31^2:32^2:40:53/**25**:21:25f:31/**26**:7^3:9:12:16^2:22^3:
24:28:30^2/**27**:1:2,3,4:5^2:27,28,29:36^2:38:39,40:
42:45^2/**28**:1:4:6,7,8:11:14:22/**29**:9:15^2:18:20:21:
25^2:27:32:33:34^2:35/**30**:2:6:8:13:16:18^2:20^3:
23,24^2:26^3:27:30^2:31,32:35,36^2:38:41/**31**:4:6:8:
12:14:15:21:22:30:32^2:36,37:38^2:39:40:42:49/**32**
:8:10:11:13,14,15^2:18:26:30/**33**:10:11:17:19/**34**:
4:6,7:8:9,10:14^2:18,19^2:21/**35**:3:18/**36**:6,7,8/**37**:
8^2:13,14:15:16:25:26,27^2:28:34^2:35/**38**:3,4,5:6:
11^2:13/**39**:5:23/**40**:4:15:17:20^2/**41**:8:14:15:32:
38^2:47:48:51^2:52:55/**42**:2:4:5:17:19:23:25:26:27:
30:33:35:37:38/**43**:10:21^2:23:25^2:30^2:32/**44**:5:16
:18^2:22:31:34/**45**:5:11,12:20:21/**46**:3,4:5:30:33:
34^2/**47**:4^2:5,6:14:15^2:17:19:20:22:23:24^4:29^2/**48**:
4:7/**49**:4:6^2:7:13:20:29,30/**50**:10:11:15:16,17:20^2
/**Ex1**:5/**2**:1:7:9:16:19:20:22:25/**3**:5:6:7:11:22/**4**:
10:12:14:19:24/**5**:1^2:7,8^2:16^2:20:21^2/**6**:1/**7**:17:
24/**8**:23:28/**9**:11:16:19:21:27:30:31:32/**10**:9:11^2:
15:16:22:24:25:26^2/**11**:2:3/**12**:11:12^2:15:16:19:
21^2:23:24:27:30:33:35^2:37:39/**13**:3:6,7:8:13:19/
14:3:8:11:14:25:31/**15**:1:17:21:26/**16**:3:4:7,8,9^2:
16^3:18:25^2:26^2:28,29^2/**17**:4:5,6:7:12:15,16/**18**:1^2
:2:3:4:9:10:12f:15,16:18:21^2:22/**19**:5:10:15:21:
23/**20**:5^2:9:11^2:20:24:25^2:26/**21**:19:21^2:24^2:25^3:
27:30f:36/**22**:1^3:3:5:7:9:10:11:12:14:23:27^3:29:
30:31/**23**:6:7:8:10:11:15:20:21:23:29:33/**24**:14:
18/**25**:1^3:8:12:17:22:26,27:37:39/**26**:3^2:9:18,19:
21:25:26,27:36:37/**27**:2:6:9,10^2:19:21/**28**:2:4:12:
27:32:40:42:43/**29**:1:22^2:26:29^2:30:33:34:35:36^2:
37^3:41/**30**:1:10f:10^2:11,12:13f:15^2:16^2:29f:32:37^3
:38/**31**:10^2:11:12,13:14,15:16^2:17/**32**:1:7:13:17:
23:29^2:30:34/**33**:1:3:5^2:7:13:15:17:20/**34**:12:14^2:
15:16:18:24:27:28/**35**:5-9^4:10-19^7:21^2:27:28^2/**36**
:20:25,26:30:31,32:37/**37**:29/**38**:5:27^3:28^2:29^5/
39:1^2:6,7f:23:27:33-40^2:41^3/**40**:5:6:10:29:30/
Lev1:2,3:4:4f:13/**2**:10:11:12f:13f:15/**4**:7:14:20^2:
21^2:26:28:29:31^2:35/**5**:2:6:10:13^2:16^3:17,18^2:19/
6:7:15:16:29/**7**:1:4:6:7:14:16:17,18^3:19:20:21:24:
34:36/**8**:1:12:14:15,16:18:21:33^2:34:35/**9**:2^2:3^2:4
:7^2:8:9:15/**10**:4:7:10:13:14:15:16:17/**11**:2,3:8:28:
41,42:44:45^2/**12**:2:4:5:6:7:8^3/**13**:3:4:11^2:13:19:
20:21:26:31:33:50:52:54:55/**14**:4^2:8:13:18:19:20:
21^2:22^2:23:24:25:29:31^3:32:38:53^2/**15**:3:15^3:19:
24:30^4:32:33^2/**16**:1^2:3^3:5^2:6^2:8f^2:10f^2:11:16^2:17^2:
18:20:21:24^3:25:26f^2:27:29,30:31:33:34^2/**17**:1^2:6
:7:11^2:13:14^2/**18**:4,5:6:10:10f:16:17:18:21:22:24:
29,30/**19**:1:3,4:7:8:10^3:12:16:18:22:23:30:31:34:
35,36:37/**20**:1:3:7:8:9:11:13:16:18:19:21:23:26/
21:2,3:4:7:8:12:14,15:18:23/**22**:1:3:5:7:8:9:10:15^2
:16:20:22:23:25^2:26,27:29,30:31:32,33/**23**:3^2:7:
14:19^2:22^2:23,24^2:28^2:29:32^2:33,34:40/**24**:1:5-8:
9^2:11:18f:19:20^3:22^3/**25**:1:3:5^4:6,7:10^2:12^2:
14,15,16:17,18:33:34:38:42:46:50:55/**26**:1:2:6:
13:16:18:20:24:26:28:34,35^3:36:40,41:43^3:44:45^2
/**27**:6:10^2:16:26:28:32:33:34/**Num1**:47,48,49:50^2
/**3**:7,8,9:11,12:13^2:31-35:36,37^2:38^2:41^2:47,48:
49/**4**:16^2:20:21,22,23:25:26:29:32:35:46,47,48/**5**
:7:7f:8:15^2:15f:21,22:31^2/**6**:1:5:6,7:11^3:12:17:20^2
/**7**:3^2:4,5^2:7:9:11:16:17:87^2:88/**8**:8:12^3:17^2:19/**9**:
13:14:19/**10**:1^2:10:29:31:31f:32:33^2/**11**:2^2:4,5^2:
13^2:18:19,20^4:21:25:29:34^2/**12**:1f:11:14:15/**13**:
30/**14**:9^2:26,27:32:33^2:34,35^3:42/**15**:5:7:10:
11,12:15,16^3:23,24^2:25^2:26:27:28:31:37,38:41/
16:17:28:36,37:38^2:46^2:47^2/**17**:5/**18**:1^2:5:6:7:9:
11^2:16^2:19:20:21^2:24^2:31^2:32/**19**:9^3:10:11:20/**20**
:8:19:24^3:29^2/**21**:1:7^2:24f:27-30/**22**:5,6^2:12:
16,17:29:32:40/**23**:1:5:7-10:18-24^3:29/**25**:10,11:
12,13^2:18/**26**:55,56^2:62:64,65/**27**:14:16:17/**28**:1
:12:13^2:14^2:15:22:30/**29**:5:6:11:14^2:15:16:19:22:
38/**30**:14/**31**:1:18:19:27:30:32-35:48,49:50:53/
32:3,4:10,11:12:13:15:16^2:17:20:24^2:27:29/**33**:8:
9:14:56/**34**:14,15/**35**:3^2:4:11:12:15^2:28:29:31:33^2
:34/**36**:7/**Deu1**:8:9:10:17^2:30:31^2:33:40:41:42:
46/**2**:1^2:5:6:7:9:14,15:19:22:35,36^2/**3**:7:19:22^2:
23,24,25^2:28/**4**:2:3:5:6:7:9:23:29^2:31:34:39:42:
43^3/**5**:5:9,10:21^2:29:32/**6**:7:15:18:25/**7**:6:7:9:16:
21:22:25:26^2/**8**:2:4:7:10:12,13/**9**:4:6:7:9:18^2:19^2:
25:28/**10**:9^2:10:12,13:19/**11**:5:10:12:14:15:17:25
:31/**12**:4,5:7:9:12:20-23/**13**:3:5/**14**:1:21:24:27:
28/**15**:2:4,5^2:10:18^2:19:22^2/**16**:1:3^2:3f:4:8:13:15:
16:18:19:22/**17**:8^2:12:16^3/**18**:2:3:5:10^2:15:16/**19**
:10:12:21^5/**20**:4^2:5:7:14:16:20^2/**21**:5:13^2:14:23/
22:2:3:7:11:19:23,24:25,26,27/**23**:2:4:5:14:17,18
:20:21:23/**24**:4:5:6:8:12,13:14,15:16^3:19:20:21^2/
26:5:14/**27**:15:20/**28**:24:27:32:37:38:39^2:40:
47,48:63:64/**29**:5:6^3:20:26:29/**30**:9:12:20/**31**:2:6
:7^2:8:21^2:23:27:29/**32**:9^2:20:22:40,41:51/**33**:7:11
:21^3/**34**:8^2:9:10/**Jos1**:5:6:7:8:9/**2**:7:8:10^2:11:
12,13:16^2:17,18:24/**3**:1:5^2:10:12/**4**:2,3:5:6:8^2:14:
15,16/**5**:2,3:4,5:6^2:15/**6**:2:3,4:10:12,13,14:17:18:
23:24:26f/**7**:1^3:9:12:13^2:15:21:22/**8**:1:2:3,4^2:6:7:
18:23:26:27^2/**9**:1:6:7:11^2:20:23:24:27^3/**10**:2:4:5:
6:8:13:14:19:20:25:42^2/**11**:5:6:9:13:14:15:20^2/
13:8:12:33/**14**:3,4:10/**15**:9:18,19^3/**17**:1:15:
16,17,18^2/**18**:4:7/**19**:9^2:50/**20**:5:8:9^3/**21**:2^2/**22**:
2,3:5:10:17,18:28:29^2:34/**23**:2:3^2:4,5:10^2:13:
15,16/**24**:7:13^2:15:17:18:19:20:31:32/**Ju1**:14^2:
22,23:25:34/**2**:7-9:10:12-14:17:18/**3**:1:7:8:11:14:
17,18,19:28:30/**4**:2,3^3:4:14:17:19:20:21:22^2/**5**:3:
25:28:30:31/**6**:1:6,7:11:18:22:26^2:27^3:30^2:31/**7**:2
:8,9:15:18^2:19,20^2:22:23/**8**:1:5:8:10:21f:22:23,24
:25:28:30:35/**9**:5:17^2:21:24:25^3:56,57/**10**:2:3:9^2/
11:5:17:26:34:35:36:37:38:40/**12**:1:3:7:9,10:
11,12:14/**13**:1:5:6:7:17:18:20:22/**14**:3:4^2:8:10,11^2
:16:17/**15**:3:11:20/**16**:5:16,17:18^2:28:31/**17**:2:3^2
:6:7,8:9:13/**18**:1:7^2:9,10^2:19:26:28^2/**19**:15:18:19^2
:20:23:28/**20**:3:6:8,9,10:27,28:35-39^2:46,47/**21**:
5:6:7:14:16^2:17:21:22^2/**Ru1**:6,7:8:11:12:13^2:16:
20/**2**:7:12:16:19:20/**3**:1:9:10^2:11:14:15-18^2/**4**:2:
4:6:6f:7:8:15/**1Sa1**:5:11:11f:19,20:21,22:24:28^2/
2:1^2:8:11:15:17:19^2:22:23,24,25:29^2:36/**3**:15/**4**:4
:7:13^2:18^2:21,22/**5**:11/**6**:1:2:14:16:18/**7**:2:5:6:10
:12:14:15:17/**8**:3^2:5:6:7:13:16:20/**9**:3:16:20:23:
24^2:26,27/**10**:7:8^2:14:18,19:21/**11**:1:13/**12**:7^2:12
:13:17^2:19^3:22^2:23^2:24/**13**:1:8:11:12^2:14^2:19^3:21^5
:22/**14**:6^2:9:10:12:18:26:44:45/**15**:2:6:11:19:23:
24:29:32:35/**16**:1^3:7:10,11^2:12:15,16:22/**17**:1:11
f:13:16:20:25:26:31:36:38,39/**18**:6^2:11,12:14:
15,16:17:19:21/**19**:5/**20**:2:5:6:8:17^2:23:26:27:34:
42/**21**:4:7:9:10/**22**:3^2:8^2:13:15^3:17/**23**:4:6:7:
14,15:20:22/**24**:2:9,10:11:12:17^2:18:19/**25**:1:2:8^2
:9:11:17^2:21^2:28^3:30,31:33^2:34:35:37,38^2:39/**26**:
8:9:16:19:21:23^2/**27**:1:4:7:9/**28**:1:2:3:15:20:22/
29:3:4/**30**:6^2:11,12:25:26/**31**:13/**2Sa1**:7:9:10:10
f^2:12^3:16:17,18:21:24:26^2/**2**:5:10,11^2:19/**3**:8^2:11:
12:14:17:18:27:31:33,34:37:39/**4**:10/**5**:4,5^2:6:10:
11:19^2:24^2/**6**:7:11:16:17/**7**:3:6:10,11^2:12:20:23:
27:28:29/**8**:3:4:10/**9**:1:5,6:10,11^2/**10**:2:5:11:
15,16/**11**:2:4:10:26:27/**12**:4^2:6^2:9:13:22:28/**13**:2^2
:2f:5:6^2:7:8:13:17,18^2:37,38,39/**14**:2,3^4:7:9:13^2:
15,16:21:22:28:29^3/**15**:2:12^2:19,20:28:32/**16**:2^4:
7,8:11:18:21:23/**17**:10:14:17:20:28,29/**18**:3^2:5:
12^2:18:31:33/**19**:1:2:7:8,9,10:11,12:20:21:22^2:26
:34:38^2/**20**:3:11:18/**21**:1^2:3:4:8:12,13,14/**22**:
18:20:21^2:25^2:28:31:37:40^2:42/**23**:6:14:15/**24**
:14:15:16:22^2:24^2/**1Ki1**:2:15:20:27:35:42:49,
51/**2**:7:9:11:15^2:17:19:22:23,24:26:28:30:32^2:
36,37:38:42/**3**:2:5:9:10:11^3:12:13^2:27/**4**:7^3:8-
22:27:28:34/**5**:2,3:5^2:6^2:7:9:10:11:17:18/**6**:20
/**7**:8:13^2:14:37:51/**8**:12,13:16^2:17:20^2:21:22,2
39:41,42:44:48:50:51:53:64^2:65:66/**9**:7:11,12
14:19^3:20,21:22:24/**10**:3^2:7:8:9:12^3:13^2/**11**:7^2
:9,10:12,13^3:14:15:21:25:29:31:32^2:33:34^2:36
/**12**:1:5:16,17:23,24:30:32,33/**13**:4:5:9:13:16,
28:32/**14**:5:6:13^2:15:18:22:24/**15**:4f:5^2:14:32,
34/**16**:4-7:13:15,16:19:24:29:32:34/**17**:1:4:7:1
13:14:16:24/**18**:10:18:25:36:41:45/**19**:3:7:10:
/**20**:9:18^2:22:23:29:38/**21**:2:3:9:22:25:26/**22**:1
8:12:15:31:34:42:48^2:52,53/**2Ki1**:17/**2**:1^2:4:6,
16:17/**3**:2:9^2:13:14:17^2:18/**4**:7:8:10:13^2:14:24
:43^2/**5**:1^2:5:17/**6**:9:16:19:23:25:32/**7**:1:6:16:1
20/**8**:1^2:2:8,9:17:27/**9**:3:5^3:16:20:25:26:34^2/**1**
2,3^2:9,10:11f^2:12:16:17:18,19:24:26:29:31:36/
:2,3^3/**12**:1:4,5:7^2:8:13,14:15:16^2/**13**:4^2:7:9,10:
:16,17:19:23/**14**:2:6^4:9:10:26/**15**:1:8:13:16:17:
:27:30^2:32,33/**16**:1:6:11,12:15^3/**17**:1:4:5:21:
35,36:38/**18**:1:6:12:14:22:26^2:27:36/**19**:4:7:8:
30:34^3/**20**:6^2:12/**21**:1:3,4,5:6:9:15/**22**:1:7:12,1
:17/**23**:1:5:7:13^3:21:24:27/**24**:1:3,4:7:16/**25**:
14,15:16:26:29:30/**1Ch1**:19/**2**:7/**4**:23^2:34-39:
40,41/**5**:9:20:22/**6**:49/**7**:4:5:15:22/**9**:17,18:21:
25:26^2:28:29:31/**10**:12:13:14/**11**:9/**12**:18:19:2
24-37^3:38:39^3:40/**13**:3:4:11:14/**14**:2:15/**15**:1:2
11^2:12:14:22:23:29/**16**:1:4:25:33^2:34:37:40:41,
17:1:2:6:17^3:21:25:27/**18**:4:8:10/**19**:2,3^2:12^2/**2**
1:7:8:13:23^4:24:30/**22**:1:2:3^2:5:6:9:13:14:18^2/**2**
2:13:14,15:17:25:29:31/**24**:4:5/**25**:4,5/**26**:8:13
26:27:28:30/**27**:1:23^2:24:27:28/**28**:2^2:3:6:9:10:
11:12^3:12f:13^2:15^2:16^3:17^2:18^2:20/**29**:1^2:2:4,5^3
:10:15^2:16:17:18:19:26,27/**2Ch1**:1:4:7:9:10:11
12:17^2/**2**:1^2:4^2:6:8:9:12/**3**:1/**4**:6^2:9:11:12-16^2:1
/**5**:2:11,12/**6**:1:4:5,6:9:10^2:30:34:42/**7**:4,5:7^3:8
14:16:17:20/**8**:11^3/**9**:7:11^2:12:20:30/**10**:1:5:13
11:4:12:13,14:17^2:23/**12**:5:14/**13**:7:8:9:10:11:1
13,14/**14**:1:2:6:11:13/**15**:2:3:4:6:7:9:15^2/**16**:9^2
10:13,14^2/**17**:1:7,8,9/**18**:1:2^2:3,4,5:6,7:10:11:1
31:32:33/**19**:7:10:11/**20**:3^2:8:9:11:15:17^2:23:30
21:6:7/**22**:1:3:4:7^2:9^2:10:12^2/**23**:2,3:5,6^2:7:8^2:
15,16,17/**24**:3:5:6:14^3:16^3:20:22:24:25/**25**:4^3:7
:20^2:25/**26**:5:8:10:15:17,18^3/**27**:5/**28**:2:3^2:11:1
19^2:20:23/**29**:6:11:15:21^3:23:24^3:32,33:34/**30**:
5f:9^2:10:13:15:17,18,19^3:21:22:23:24:26/**31**:1:3
:10^2:17,18:21/**32**:3:7:8:23^2:25:27^2:28,29^4/**33**:2:
4,5:12:20,21:22/**34**:3^2:9^3:21^3:25^2/**35**:7:9:12:14
15:17:21:24,25^2/**36**:12:13:15:21^2:22,23/**Ez1**:1f
4^2:6/**2**:69/**3**:3:4:5:7^2:12/**4**:2:13:16:22/**5**:4/**6**:9:
:17:20:21,22/**7**:6:7,8,9:17:19:20^2:21:23^2:28/**8**:1
:16^2:17:22^2:34:35/**9**:2:6:8:9:10/**10**:2^2:3:6:10:13:
14/**Neh1**:4^2:6,7:9:11/**2**:1:3:5,6:8^6:11,12^2:16/**4**:
5:6:12:14:19/**5**:2,3,4^2:5:7:14:18^2:19^2/**6**:7^2:10^2:1
/**7**:4:5^2:70^2:72/**8**:1:9:10:11:15:17/**9**:1:3^2:5:8:10:
11:17:20:21:28:30:35/**10**:28:29:32:33^4:34:37:
39,40/**12**:29:43^2:44:47/**13**:2:5^3:6:7:14:29:31^2/
Est1:1:5^2:7:8^2:9:11:13-15^2:16:17/**2**:2:3:9^3:10:
12,13,14^2:18:20/**3**:2:7:9:15/**4**:2:5:7:8:11:14:16^2
5:4:7,8:12/**6**:3/**7**:4:7^2/**8**:1:6:8f:12:12f:17/**9**:1:3:4
:12:16:26/**10**:3^2/**Job1**:2,3:4:5^2/**2**:4,5:13^3/**3**:5:9:
10^2:13:17:20,21^3:24/**4**:2:6:18,19/**5**:1:3:6:7:9:18:
27/**6**:3:4:8,9:13:19-21:22^2:29/**7**:2:8:16:21^2/**8**:5:
:15/**9**:4:15:17:22:28:32,33/**10**:4-7:15:20,21/**11**:
:11:19/**12**:4:6:10/**13**:4:6:7:8:15/**14**:2:7^2:11,12:2
/**15**:4,5:11:23,24:31:32:34/**16**:7:22/**17**:10^2/**18**:
11/**19**:7:10:21:25:29/**20**:2^2:3:5:19:29^2/**21**:20:21
30-32/**22**:6:14:17^2:24/**24**:1:2:5^2:8:12:14,15:18:
20:21/**26**:10^3/**27**:6:10:12:22/**28**:8:15:16:17:21:
23,24:26/**29**:2:12:13:14:15^2:19:22:23^2/**30**:7:11:
23:24:25^2:26^2:28,29^2/**31**:7,8:9:11:15:18:23:28:3
:38,39/**32**:2:7:18/**33**:4:6:12:14:20^2:23,24^2:29:32
/**34**:5:9:13:19:21:23:27:36:37/**35**:2,3/**36**:2:4:20:
21:24^2/**37**:6:19,20:21^2:24/**38**:3:6,7:21:22,23^2:
25-27^2:30:41/**39**:7:8:10:17:30/**40**:7/**41**:4:14/**42**:
3:7:8^2:10:11:12/**Ps1**:4:6/**2**:2:6:7/**3**:5:8/**4**:1:2:3:8
/**5**:1:5:6:7:9:10:11:12/**6**:2^2:5:5f:8/**7**:4:5:6:9:16/**9**
9:10^2:12^2:15:16:18/**10**:2:3:4:13^2/**11**:1:2:7/**12**:5/
14:5/**16**:1:10/**17**:1^2:2:15^2/**18**:1^2:6:7:19:20:21:24
:30:31:34:39^2:41:49/**19**:11/**20**:5^2/**21**:2^2:4:7:11:
13/**22**:2:3,4:5:9,10,11:15:24:28:30:31/**23**:4:5/**25**
:2:3:4:5:11:14:15^2:16:21/**26**:1:3:12/**27**:10:12:14/
28:1:4:5:6/**29**:2/**30**:1:5/**31**:2:4^2:4f:7:13:17:19^2:
21:22:23/**32**:1^2:8:11/**33**:1:4:9:11:16,17^2:21:22/
34:4:5:7:8:9:15:17:18:22/**35**:1:3:7^2:13:16:17:24/
36:6:9/**37**:7:9:10:12,13:17:19:24:28:32:34:37^2/
38:9:15^2:18:20^3/**39**:4:5,6:8:9:9f:11^2:12/**40**:1:3:5:
8:12^2/**41**:4/**42**:1^2:2:3:4,5:4,5f:11^2/**43**:2:5^2/**44**:4:

FOR Con't)
:12:22/**45**:1:8:10,11/**47**:1:2:4^2:9/**48**:2:3f:7:8:10:
1:14/**49**:3:7:8,9^2:14:14f:15^2:17:20/**50**:6:7:8:
0,11:12:17:22/**51**:3:14,15:18/**52**:9^3/**53**:2:4:5/
4:3^2:6/**55**:2:6:9f:15:18:19/**56**:6:9^2:12:13/**57**:1:2
5/**58**:1/**59**:3:7:9:10:11:14,15:16^2:17/**60**:2:11:12
61:2^2:3:5^2/**62**:1^2:5^2:8:12/**63**:1^2:3/**64**:6/**65**:8:9/
6:6:9:14:16:17^2/**67**:2:4:6,7/**68**:5:6:9,10:18:21:
8^2/**69**:3:4:7:9:9f:11:13:16:17:21^2:26:32^2:33:35/
0:5/**71**:2:3:8^2:23:24/**72**:12:13:14:15f:15/**73**:2:3:
:27:28/**74**:15:20:21/**75**:3:6,7:9/**76**:12/**77**:2:3:
1/**78**:2,3:5:11,12^2:13:22:24:29:39:54:56:71,72/
9:2:7:8^2:9/**80**:14:15:16:17f/**81**:4:10:16/**82**:7:8/
3:12/**84**:11/**85**:8:13/**86**:1:2^2:3:4:5:10:13/**87**:5/
8:3:9:13/**89**:5:6:11:14,15:35,36:39:49/**91**:3:9:
1:14/**92**:1f:2:4^2:13/**94**:6,7:14/**95**:3:7:9:10:11/
6:4:5:12^2:13/**97**:7:11^2/**98**:1:4:8,9/**99**:6:9/**100**:5
102:3,4:9,10:14^2:16:17:18/**103**:2:10:11:14:20/
04:9:11:14:15:18:21:34/**105**:1:4^2:5,6:16:20:38:
0:42/**106**:1:13:19,20:24^2:31:33:39/**107**:1^2:8^2:9:
5^2:16:21^2:31^2:40/**108**:4:12:13/**109**:4:5^2:7:16:21
28:31/**111**:1:3:8:9:10^2/**112**:1:2:5:7/**113**:4/**114**:3
/**115**:3/**116**:7^2:12^2:13f:13:15f/**117**:2/**118**:1:6:
1:27,28:29^2/**119**:2:6:20:22:23:27:29,30:35:38^2:
9^2:40,41,42^3:43:48:49,50:51:54:62:66:71,72:
5,76,77:78:81^2:85,86^2:90,91:93:94:99:101:110:
21:123:125:126^2:131:142:146:153:155^2:158:
66:167:168:171:172:174:176/**120**:7^2/**121**:1:3,4:
/**122**:1:6:8/**123**:2^2:3,4/**125**:3/**126**:2^2:6/**127**:2^2/
29:3,4/**130**:1:5:6^2:7/**132**:2-5^2:9:10:11:14:16:17 ^{2}
133:2/**135**:4:14:21/**136**:1:2:3:4:5:6:7:8:9:10:
1,12:13:14:15:16:17:18:19:20:21:22:23:24:25:
6/**137**:3,4^2/**138**:2^2:4:5:8^3/**139**:12:14:22/**140**:4:
:13/**141**:1^2:4:8/**142**:3^2:6^3:7/**143**:2:6^3:7:8^2:10^2:
2/**144**:4:10/**145**:13:15:19/**146**:3:4^2:8:9/**147**:13:
8/**148**:5:13/**149**:4,5^2/**150**:2/**Pro1**:3:16:18:20:
5:28^2:29:32^2/**2**:3,4,5^3:6:10:14:21/**3**:4,5:11,12:
3,14,15:22:24,25,26:32/**4**:1:3:13:16^2:22^2:23/**5**:
:6:14:21/**6**:1:7:8:12,13:16-19:23:25:26:29:30:32
34/**7**:11,12:15:19:20:26:27/**8**:6,7^3:11:12:13:17:
7,28,29:32:34^2:35/**9**:7,8:10/**10**:27/**11**:7:15:18:
6:27^2/**12**:10:20^2:21/**13**:8:22:24/**14**:6:7:24^2:26:
7/15:14:16:25:33/**16**:4^2:5:6^2:12:12f/**17**:11:13:
6:18:19:26^2/**18**:5:15:21/**19**:10^2:23:28/**20**:3:22^2
21:18f:20:25,26:31/**22**:1:3:4:17,18,19:22,23/**23**
:4,5:6,7,8^2:10,11:17,18^2:19,20,21:24,25:
6,27,28^2:32/**24**:2:7:11,12,13,14:18:19,20,21,22:
8,29/**25**:4,5:6,7:15:27/**26**:20:24,25,26^2:27/**27**:1
0:12:25,26,27^3/**28**:14:21/**29**:5,6:10:13:18:19f:
9:20^2:24:26/**30**:5:9:10:18,19:24-28:29,30,31/
1:4:5:6,7^2:9:15^2:18:19,20:21^3:23:26:31/**Ecc1**:3-
-7^2:12-15:16-18/**2**:1:4,5,6:10:12f:13,14:16:20-
0-23^4:24-26^3/**3**:1:5^2:6^2:8^4:12:13:19:21:22^3/**4**:4:
:12/**5**:1:4:8:9:16^3:18^2:19,20/**6**:4:7,8:12^2/**7**:2:3:6
0^2:21,22:25/**8**:2,3:6,7^2:8:16,17/**9**:2,3:4:5:7:9^2:
0/**10**:6:15:15f:16,17:20/**11**:1:2:3:4:6:9/**12**:3:10:
3:14^2/**Sol1**:2:7/**2**:5:11:15/**3**:1:9/**5**:2:4:6/**6**:5/**7**:
:13^2/**8**:6:8:12^2/**Is1**:2:3^2:12,13^2:15:28/**2**:3:9:11/
:10:14:17:18:24/**4**:2,3,4/**5**:2:7f^2:12:13:16:24:27 ^{2}
6:5/**7**:8:11:15,16f:18:25/**8**:9,10^2:12:16:17:18:20
9:3:4:6:13:16:17:19,20/**10**:2:3:12:28,29:30:32/
1:5:9:10:11:12:16^2/**12**:2:5:6/**13**:3:6^2:9:11^2:13:
7/**14**:5:13:20:24:26:30:31/**15**:2:5/**16**:3:4,5:7:8:
^{3}:11^2/**17**:3:6:7:8^2/**18**:4:6/**19**:3:8:9:17:20^2:22:25
20:3:4/**21**:5:6,7f:12/**22**:4:8:9,10,11^5:12:13:
5,16:17:25/**23**:1^2:4:9:10:14:15,16^2:18^2/**24**:4,5:
1:14:15,16:18:20/**25**:1:6:9:10/**26**:2:4:6:7:9^3:11:
2:16:19^2:20:21/**27**:4,5:7,8:9f:11/**28**:2:6:13:15^2:
2:26/**29**:2:10:11:23/**30**:2^2:3:4:6:7:9^2:14:15^2:16:
8^3:19:23:33/**31**:1:2:3:9/**32**:6:8:10:11:12^2:13/**33**
:2^2:6^2:7^2:8^2:22^2:24/**34**:2:5:6^3:8^2:11:13:16/**35**:2:
:10/**36**:5^2:6:8,9^2:11^2:16:21/**37**:1:4^2:7:11:16,17:
9:27:30:32:33:35/**38**:1:14:15:17^2:18:18f:21/**39**:
/**40**:3:15/**41**:1:5^2:8^2:9:10:12:14:18/**42**:6:22^2:24
43:1:3^2:4:5:7^2:14:19^3:20:21:23^2:25:26^2/**44**:3^3:9^2
15:19:21:22:23^2:28/**45**:4^2:13:18:19^2:21:22^2:23/
6:3:4:7^2:9:10:13/**47**:1:6/**48**:8:9^2:11^2:17:19:21:
2/**49**:4^3:5:10:11:13^2:15:18:21^2:23^2:25/**50**:1^2:2:9
51:1:4:5^2:6:8:10:15^2:20:22/**52**:1:3:8:9:12^2:14,15
53:4:5:8:10:11:12/**54**:1:3:5:6:7:10^2:15/**55**:2:3^2:
f:7:9:10^2/**56**:1:3^2:4:5:6:7^2:8:10:11/**57**:2:7,8^2:14:
6:19:21/**58**:6/**59**:3:11:12:13:18^2:19:21/**60**:1^2:4:
:7:9:10:12:15^2:17^4:19:20:21/**61**:3^3:8^2:10/**62**:1^2:
^{2}:4:5:6,7,10/**63**:4^2:7:15:17:17f/**64**:2:3:4^3:7/**65**:1
5:7^3:8^2:10:12:14:15:16:17:21:22:23/**66**:1:4:5:7,8
10:12:15:16:24/**Jer1**:7:8:12f:14:16^2:18:19/**2**:8:9
10,11^2:13^2:21:23:24:26,27:28:32:36:37/**3**:1:2:3:
:12:14:16:17:19:22:25/**4**:5:6:7:8:10:13:17:22^2:
1^2/**5**:3:5:6:7:8:9:10:11:22:23,24:26^2/**6**:1:3:4:6^3:
:11:12:16:17:20:23:25:26^2:29/**7**:11:13,14:16^3:
9:30:32^2:33:34/**8**:6:9^2:10:11^2:13:14:15:16:17:21

/9:1:2:3^2:8:9:10:17,18:21:25,26/**10**:2,3:5^2:6:14:
18:24:25/**11**:4:5:7:11:14^4:15:20^2:21,22:23/**12**:3^2:
6:13/**13**:10:15:16:18:19:24,25/**14**:3:4:6:7:8:11:
16^2:17:21:22/**15**:1:2^2:5^2:9^2:10:14:15:20/**16**:3:4:5 ^{2}
:7:9:14,15:16^2:17:18:19/**17**:2,3:4^2:6:13^3:14/**18**:
15:20:22^2/**19**:4:7^2:11:12/**20**:4:6:9:10:12:13:18/
21:5:10:14/**22**:4:6:7:9:10^3:11:11f:13:16:18:20^3:
24,25:24,25f:30/**23**:1^2:2:4^2:5,6:9^2:10^2:12^2:13:15:
16:21:32:33:34^2:36/**24**:4,5:7/**25**:1:2,3:11:12:14:
15:27:29:31:33:34:36/**26**:2:3:5:11:14:15:16:18:
19^2/**27**:6:10:14:17:19,20,21:22/**28**:14/**29**:5:6:7^3:
9:10:10f:10:11^4:13:19:23^2:28^3:32^2/**30**:2:3:7^2:8:9:
9f:9:10:11:12:14^2:21/**31**:2^2:3:7^3:8:9:11:13^3:15^2:
16:16f:17:18^2:19:20:21:22:25:29:30^2:32f:34:37:
38,39^2/**32**:3:4:5:6,7:8^2:14:15:17:18:19:25:27:30:
39^2:44/**33**:4^2:5^2:9:10,11^2:14:17/**34**:5^2:9^2:18,19:
21/**35**:4:6/**36**:4:6:22:31/**37**:3:9:15,16:17:20/**38**:
9:11:14:19:20:26:27^2/**39**:18/**40**:2,3^2:4:9:10^2:16/
41:13,14:16,17:18^2/**42**:2^2:6^2:8^2:10^2:11:18:19:20^2
:22/**43**:5:7:10/**44**:2,3^2:7:8:17:19:27^2/**45**:5^2/**46**:
10^2:11^3:14^2:19^2:20,21^2:27:28/**47**:4^2:7/**48**:1:2,3,4 ^{2}
:6:7:8:9^3:17:18:21:26:27:29:31^2:32^3:35:36^2:38:39
:42:44/**49**:2:3^2:5:8:9,10:13:19:23:28:30^2:33/**50**:3
:7:9:12:13:14:20:24^2:27^2:29^2:31:32:34^3:39:42^2:
44:45/**51**:5:8:9:11:12:17^2:19:24:25:26:27:29:33:
34,35^2:39:46:47:48:52:55:56:58/**52**:5:7^2:8:11:16:
21/**Lam1**:3:5^2:6:8^2:11^2:16:17^2:18^2:19^2:20:21:22/
2:5:7:9:13:16:19:22/**3**:17:18:20:25^2:26:27:28:29:
31:33:37:39:42:47:58:64/**4**:1:3,4^3:5^2:6:16:17:19:
22/**5**:4:6:9:16:20/**Eze1**:19,20,21:26/**2**:1f:4:5:6:7
/**3**:10:14,15:17:18:20:26:27/**4**:3:4,5^3:6:13:14/**5**:2
:4:5,6,7:11:15/**6**:9^3:11^2/**7**:3^2:8,9,10,11:12:13:14:
16:19^3:23^2:25^3:26,27^2/**8**:12:14:14f:18/**9**:9:10/**10**
:7,8:9-13:17:21/**11**:1:3^2:5:11:16:19:21^3/**12**:3^2:11
:12:23:24:25:27/**13**:4:8:10^2:16:19:23/**14**:1:5:6,7^2
:10:22/**15**:3^2:4/**16**:5:8:12^3:14:15:16:24:31^2:33,34^2
:40,41:43^2:45^2:52:54:58:59,60^2:61^2/**17**:15:16:18:
19:20/**18**:2:4^2:18:19^2:20^4:24:26:28:31/**19**:1:5/**20**
:5,6:7:9,10:14:19:20:23,24:27,28:31:40/**21**:3:
9,10,11^2:12:15^2:19,20:21:22:23:24:28:29:32^2/**22**:
7:14:27:30:31/**23**:6:8:14,15:17f:23:24:27:28:32:
34:37:39^2:40^3:45:47:48:49^2/**24**:2:6^2:7^2:12:23^2:27
/**25**:5:6:7:17/**26**:5^2:7:14^2:17:19/**27**:5:8:19f:
20:31:36/**28**:2,3:10:12:17:18:25/**29**:3^2:5:6:11:12:
15:16:18^2:18f:19:20^2:20f/**30**:2,3^2:5:6:10:18:22/
31:7:14^2:15:16/**32**:2:10:11:16^3:18^2:20:32/**33**:5:6:
7^2:8:11:12:13:16:18:25/**34**:4:6:8^2:9,10^2:11:12:17:
18^2:19:21:26:29f/**35**:4,5:10:11:12/**36**:5^3:8^2:9:11:
12:15:19:24:25:30:31:32^2:36:37,38/**37**:5:21:23:
25:28/**38**:10:12:19/**39**:5:9:10^3:11:12:13^2:14:17:
18:19:23^2:25:28^2:29/**40**:4:21:39^2:45:46^2/**41**:6/
42:13:14/**43**:11:18:19:20:21:22:25:26^2/**44**:2:7:8:
10:11:13^2:15:17:27:28:30/**45**:2:4^2:5:6:7:9:11^3:12:
13:15:17^2:20:22^2:23:24^2:25/**46**:5^2:7:12:14,15:18
/**47**:9:12^3:13:22^2/**48**:1:8:11:14:15:17^2:18^2:30,31^3
:32:34/**Dan1**:8:9^2:10:18,19/**2**:1:8,9:20:22:23:30^2
:36:37:43/**3**:20:28:29/**4**:3:9:12:16:17:18^2:19:20^2:
21:22:23:25:31:32:37/**5**:11:11f:12^2:23/**6**:3:4:7:
12:14:16:22:25,26/**7**:12:12f:21:25/**8**:7:9f:12:19:
25:26f:26:27^2/**9**:2:7:12:16^2:17:18:19:20:23:25f^2/
10:2:11^2:13:14:17:19/**11**:2:4:8:19:21:24:25:
27:30,31:36:37^3/**12**:1^2:9:13/**Hos1**:4,5:6:9:11:2:4
:5^2:7^2:10:13^4:21,22^4:23/**3**:1:2:3^2/**4**:5:6:7:8:9:10:
12^2:14^2:17:18^2/**5**:1:2:4:7:15^3/**6**:4:9:11/**7**:4:7:12:
13^2:14^2:16/**8**:2:10:12:13:14/**9**:1:4^2:7^2:10:11:14^3:
15/**10**:6:7:10^2:12/**11**:7:9:10/**12**:1:2:4:8:11:14/**13**
:1:4:10^2:12:14^2:16/**14**:1:3:4:8:9/**Joe1**:5:11^2:13^2:
18^2:19:20^3/**2**:1:13:15:17:18:20:21^2:23:26:32/**3**:2 ^{2}
:3^2:4:7:9:12:13:14^2:19:21^2/**Amo1**:3:5f:6:9:11:13/
2:1^2:4:6^2:9:16/**3**:2:3:4:6:14/**4**:8:13/**5**:1:3:5:7:12:
16^2:17:18^3:20:25,26,27/**6**:11/**7**:2:5:15/**8**:2:5:6:
13/**9**:4:6:7:9:12/**Ob1**:5^3:7:8f:8:10:11:18:21/**Jon**:
2:3:5^2:11:12:14^4:17/**2**:8:9^3/**3**:6/**4**:2^2:6:8:9^2:10:11
/**Mic1**:2:6:9:11f^6:12:13:14:16^2/**2**:7:8:10/**3**:3:4:8 ^{2}
/**4**:2:3:4:9:10:11:12/**5**:4/**6**:2:4:6:7:10:13/**7**:1:6:7^3
:8:9^2:10^2:13:15:16:18/**Nah1**:14:15/**2**:1:2:5/**3**:9:
14^2:19^3/**Hab1**:2:4:5:7:11:12/**2**:3:5:6:9:15:19/**3**:2
:6:16/**Zep1**:7:8f^2:17:18/**2**:5:6:7:10:14:15/**3**:2:3^2:
8:11:15,17,18/**Hag1**:1:2:3,4:9:11/**2**:4:5:6:8,9:14:
23/**Zec1**:9:10:12:14:15/**2**:2:4:5:8:10:11,12:13/**3**:
2:7/**4**:2:6f:7^2:10^2/**5**:5/**8**:6:9:10:12:13:22:23/**9**:1:
1f:5:9:12^2:16,17/**10**:1:2^2:3:5:6:8:10:11/**11**:2:3^2:4:
6:16:17/**12**:4:9:10^4:11/**13**:3:6f:7/**14**:1:3:4:5:5f/
Mal1:2,3:4:11:14/**2**:5:7:8:9:11:14:16/**3**:1:2:3:6^2:
9:10:11:12:14,15^2/**4**:2/**Mt1**:20:21/**2**:2:5:6:8:12:
13:14:16:18^2:20/**3**:2:3:9:15/**4**:2:4:6:11:17:18:19/
5:3:4:5:6:7:8:9:10:12:14:15,16^2:26:29^2:32:34:35^2:
36:38f^2:41:44:45/**6**:1:13f:16^2:24:25:26:30^2:31,32
/**7**:2:7:8:9:10:11:12^2:13:21:23:25:27:29/**8**:4:8,9:
12:15:22/**9**:2:5,6:8:13:15:16:17f:17:20:21:24:36^2
:38/**10**:10^2:11^2:17:18:19:20:26:29:39/**11**:3:10:13

:18:21:21f:23:23f:25^2:26:29,30^4/**12**:8:34:36:
39,40^3:41:42:43,44,45^2/**13**:6:12,13:15:16^2:22^2:
34,35:45/**14**:3:4:5:6:8:12:14:15:23,24:26/**15**:2:4:
5,6:9:19:22:23:27:32:33:36/**16**:4:17:25^3:27/**17**:4 ^{3}
:14:15^2:20:26,27/**18**:5:6:7:10:12:19^2:20:25:27/
19:9:12:13:14:17:22:23:24^2/**20**:1:2f:3:13:23:24:
28^2:32,33:34/**21**:7:16:22:26:32:33:36:38:46/**22**:1^2
:11:14:15:28:30:43/**23**:3:5:8:9:10:13,14:15:16:19
:23:29,30:39/**24**:5:18:21:22:24:27:42:43:44:48/
25:7,8:9:11:13:14:18:19:21:29:34:35:41:42/**26**:5:
8,9:10:12:13:16:24^2:26:27:28:31:41:43:48:50:53:
59:65,66:69:73/**27**:4:6:7:18:19:20^2:24:45:47:55:
58/**28**:2:5:6:10:14:16/**Mk1**:2:3:4f:12,13^3:16:17:
31:32,33:36,37:38:43,44/**2**:2:7:9,10,11/**3**:4:5:6:
7,8^2:10:31,32/**4**:11,12:19:20:28/**5**:7,8:9:14:19:20
:25:28/**6**:14:17,18^2:21:22,23:24:29:31^2:32:35,36:
37:41:43,44:50:52^2:52f/**7**:3:4^2:5:6,7^2:8:9:10:11^2:
19:21:23:24:29:37/**8**:1:3:4:6:11:35^2:37/**9**:5:6:17:
34:38:39:40:42:49f/**10**:6,7:14:19:21:22:23:24:24f
:25^2:29:45^2:51/**11**:7:9:10:11:13^2:17:24:32/**12**:1:4
:12^3:13:23:25:27^2:36:38:43,44/**13**:2:6:8:9:15,16:
19:20:22:33:34^2:35,36,37^2/**14**:1:4,5:6:8:11:14:21
:23:24:27:36:38:40:41:60:63,64^2:66,67:70/**15**:7:
10:24:34f:35:38f^2:42,43:44/**16**:6:14/**Lk1**:7:8,9:
13:15:17:20:21:23:24:30:37:42:44:48:49:55:57^2:
59:63:66:68:76^2/**2**:3:6:7:10:14:20:22:23:24:26:
29,30,31:34,35,36,37^2:38f:40:41,42,44^2:45:48/**3**:
3f:4:7:12:19,20^2/**4**:1:6,7:9,10,11:13:15:25,26^3:32
:39:42:43/**5**:7:8:9:10:14:16:23,24:27:36:37/**6**:7:9
:17,18:19:20^2:21^4:23^2:24:26^2:28:30:32:34:35:37:
38^2:39:47,48/**7**:5:6,7,8:19:30:32f:33:36:39:47/**8**:
6:10:13:18:23:27:29:30:35:37:39:40^2:42:43,44^2:
46:53/**9**:7:12^2:13:14:16:22:24:33^3:45:48^4:50^2:51:
52:53:55f:60f:62^2/**10**:2:7:13^2:13f^2:21^3:24:29/**11**:
2:4:5,6:7:11^2:12:13:16:19:21:23:24:29,30:31:32:
37,38:42:43:44:46:47:50:52^2:53,54/**12**:3:12:15^2:
19^2:23:24:28^2:29:30:32:36:37^2:38:39^2:40:45:47:
48:57:59/**13**:7:11:14:15:16^2:24,25^2:29:31:33^2/**14**
:8^2:10:11:12:14:17:20:24^2:28:33:35^2/**15**:3,4:22:
24:29^2:32/**16**:2:5,6:7:8:8f:9f:10:13:21:24:28/**17**:
2,3:7,8,9:10:16:21:22:22f:22:23:24/**18**:1:2:3:4,5^2
:11:14:16,17:22:23:24:25^2:29/**19**:5:9,10:21:30^2:
35:36,37:39:44:48/**20**:6:9:13:19^2:33:34,35:36:
37,38:40:42,43:46/**21**:4:8:10:12:13f:15:19:22:23:
26:28:36f/**22**:6^2:11:12:16:17:18:19^2:20f:27:32:37^2
:44:55:59:71^2/**23**:7:8:15:17,f^2:19^2:20:22:23:25:
28^3:29:31:31f:34^3:40,41:44:50,51,52:54/**24**:5:16:
39:40:47/**Jn1**:15:17:18:22:23:33:42:45:46/**2**:4:6:
10:12^2:13:14:17:19:24,25/**3**:17:16:18:19:20:22:
28^2:33,34^2/**4**:7:9:10^2:17,18:21-24^3:35:37:40,41^2:
45/**5**:1:3:4:5:7:20:24:30:32,33:35:38:39:41,42:44
:46/**6**:2-5^2:6:16:22,23,24:27^2:38:40:44:46:55:64/
7:1:2:3:5:6:7:10:13^2:18^2:19^2:21,22,23^3:27:30:34:
36:38:41,42:52/**8**:12:14:16:20:21:24:26^2:29:39:
42:44^2:49:50/**9**:4:21:24^2:29:36/**10**:2:3:4:5:7:11:
12:13:15:18^2:22,23f:29:32:33^2/**11**:4:6:15^2:17:22:
26:39:41:47:50:51:52^2:56/**12**:6^2:7:11:15:23,24:
25:26:30:31:35^3:39:41:43:45:47:49/**13**:11:13:26f
:29:33:35:37^2:38/**14**:2,3:12,13^3:17^3:19:28^2:30/
15:2:3:4:5:13:15:16:18:19:21:22/**16**:2:4:7^3:13:23 ^{3}
:27:32:33/**17**:2:8:9^2:19:20^2:21:26/**18**:2:4,5:7:14:
18:20:23:28:31f:33:37/**19**:23,24^3:31:38^2:42/**20**:9
:15:17/**21**:7:12/**Act1**:7:10:15:16^2:18:24,25/**2**:4:5
:7:15:21:24:26:29:34:38:39:46/**3**:3:6:13:15:21,22 ^{2}
/**4**:11:12:13:21^2:22:27:34,35:36:37/**5**:8:13:21^2:
26,27:28:31^2:41/**6**:6/**7**:3:6:11:14:17,18:20:33:36:
38:40^2:46^2/**8**:5:9,10,11:15:16^2:20:21:23:24:26:33
/**9**:7:11^2:15:16:19:33:36^2:37:39/**10**:12:12f:14:21:
22:24:27:28:29:33:36,37:38:46,47:48/**11**:8:25:26
/**12**:4:5:10:12:17^2:19^2:20^2/**13**:2^2:4:6,7:11:13:14:
15:19,20:21^2:22:24:26:27:34^2:36:38:40:41:47/**14**
:5,6:20:22:23:26:28/**15**:9:15:21^2:26:27,28,29:39:
40,41/**16**:3:7:10:13:16:29:38/**17**:2:5:7:15:16:17:
20:23:25:28:31^2/**18**:2,3:10:12:18^2:18f:19:20:21:
22f:23:28/**19**:8:10:29:33:34:40^3/**20**:1^2:3:5:7:16:
21:24:27:28:31:32:33:35/**21**:2:13^2:15:20f:22:24^2:
25^2:26,27:29/**22**:5^2:12:17,18:21:25/**23**:5:8:23,24
:27/**24**:3:4:5:10^2:21f:21:22:24:25^2:26/**25**:1:5:13:
14:17:26:27/**26**:3:7:14f:16:18:21:22:29/**27**:6:9^2:
13:21:23:24:25:29:33:34^2:37:43:44/**28**:6:7:8:10:
17:18^2:22:27^2:30/**Rom1**:5:8^3:9:10:11,12^2:14:16:
17:19:20f:21:23:26:27:32/**2**:1:3:5^2:7:9:10:11:12-
12-15^2:17f:20:28:29^3/**3**:1:5^2:7:9:19:20:21,22:25^3:
26^2/**4**:1:3:4,5^3:4,5f:8:10:12:15:16:20^2:23:24:25:
25f/**5**:1:2^2:3^2:5:6^2:7:8^2:9^2:10:11:12:13:14:15/**6**:
2,3:5:7:10:13^3:14:15:21:23/**7**:4:13^2:15/**8**:2:3:10:
10f:13:14:16:17:19^2:19f:20,21:22:23:24:25:26^3:
27:28:29:32^2:33:34^4:36^2:37:38^2:39/**9**:1:4:6:7:9:
15:17^2:19:21:22^2:23,24:25:28:29/**10**:2:3:5:8:9:10
:11:12:16:18:19:20/**11**:6:7:11:16:19:21:24:28:29:
32:33:34:36^2/**12**:1:4,5:12^2:13^2:17:19:20/**13**:1:3:4^2

(FOR Con't)
:6:6:8[2]:11[2]/**14**:1:1f:2:3:5[2]:6[2]:9:11:14[2]:15:17[2]:19:
20:23[2]/**15**:1[2]:3:9:13:15,16[2]:17:24[2]:26[2]:27:27f:29
:30[3]/**16**:1:4:10:12:13:18[2]:22:23:25,26,27/**1Co1**:4
:5:6:7[2]:9[2]:11:12[2]:13:15:17[3]:19:21:24:30/**2**:2:7:9:
16/**3**:3:8:17:19:21/**4**:8:15[2]:17/**5**:5f:7:10/**6**:4f:7:
11[2]:12f:12:13[4]:16:20/**7**:3:4[3]:5:10[2]:14:15:16:17:
18:19:23:24:25:26:29[3]:31/**8**:10:11[2]/**9**:1:2:6:9:11:
12:13:15:16:17:23:25:27/**10**:1:3,4f:8:10:12:13:15
:24:26:28:30:31:33[2]/**11**:5:6:7:9[2]:10f:10:12:13:
14,15:17[2]:21:23:24[2]:26[2]:29[2]:33[2]/**12**:1:10:18:25[3]
/**13**:3:10/**14**:1:5:7[3]:10:12[2]:13:14:16:22:24:34:35[2]
/**15**:1[2]:3:8:9:10:13:17:25:27:29:31:32[2]:34:37:42:
43:44:45:52:53:55,56:57:58[2]/**16**:2:4:5:9[2]:10:12:
13:17[2]:19:20:24/**2Co1**:5:6,7:9[2]:11[3]:12:24/**2**:2:10
:11[2]:14:16/**3**:6:7:11[2]:14/**4**:5:6:12:13:15[2]/**5**:1[2]:3:
5:8:10[2]:13,14[3]:15[3]:19:21/**6**:2:14:16/**7**:2:3:5:7:8[2]:
10:11[2]:12/**8**:1:5[2]:7:8:10:16:17:20:24[2]/**9**:2:7:8:10:
11:13:14:15[2]/**10**:13:14:15[2]:18/**11**:2[4]:6:8,9[3]:17:
32/**12**:2,3[2]:5:10[2]:11:12:13[2]:14[3]:15:18:20/**13**:1:7:
8:8f[2]:10/**Gal1**:4:7:12:15:18[2]:20/**2**:4:5[2]:6:7,8,9:10
:11:12[2]:16:19:19f:20:21[2]/**3**:1:2:3:4:6:10:13[2]:18:
21,22:26/**4**:1:3:5:7:11[2]:12:14:15:17:19[3]:20:22:27
:30/**5**:2:6:8:11:13:14:17:19:20:26/**6**:4:5:9:12:14:
17/**Eph1**:4:5:6:8[2]:9:11:12[2]:14:15:16,17[3]/**2**:1:7:9[2]
:11:13:14:15:16:18:21/**3**:1:6:8:13:18,19:21/**4**:1[2]:
2:5:8:11[2]:12:17,18[2]:23:25:27:28/**5**:2[3]:4:5:6:8:
15,16:18:20:23:25:28:29,30[2]/**6**:6,7:8:12:18[2]:19[2]:
20[2]:22/**Php1**:3:4:7:8:9[2]:10:11:13:16,17:18:19[3]:
20[2]:21[2]:23[2]:26:28:29[2]:30/**2**:13:17:18[3]:20:26[2]:28:
30[3]/**3**:1:2:3[2]:5:9:12:14[2]:18:19/**4**:1[2]:3:6:8:10:11:
13:19:21/**Col1**:3:4:8:10:13:16:19:20[3]:22:23:24[3]:
26,27[3]:28/**2**:1[3]:2[2]:5:6:7:9:12:13:16[2]:17:19:22:23
/**3**:3:5:12:14:15:18[2]:20:22:23[2]:24:25[2]/**4**:2:3[2]:6[2]:
12:13[2]/**1Th1**:2[2]:5[2]:6:8:9/**2**:4[2]:6[2]:7:13:16:19[2]:20/
3:2,3:9[3]:10[2]/**4**:1:3,4:6:7:9:12:14:16/**5**:2:5:6:7:9:
10:15:18[2]:24:25:26/**2Th1**:3[2]:5[2]:6:10:11:12/**2**:3:6
:7:12:13/**3**:1:2:6:7:8:9:17/**1Ti1**:3,4:5:9[2]:12:13:14
:19/**2**:1[4]:2:4[2]:6:9,10[2]/**3**:2:5:8:15[2]/**4**:3:4[2]:5:8:9,10[3]
:12/**5**:4:5[2]:8:14:15:16:18:23/**6**:1:2:3:10[2]:12:15:
17:19[2]/**2Ti1**:3[2]:4:7:8[3]:9:12/**2**:2:4:5:11:12:13:17:
20:21:25/**3**:2:10:14/**4**:3[2]:5:7[2]:8:10:11:15:16:17:
19/**Tit1**:3:6[2]:7:10:15/**2**:1[2]:11:14[2]/**3**:1:4:8:9:11:
12[2]:14/**Phm1**:1:4:8,9[2]:13:15:18:22[2]:23/**Heb**:5,6:
14[2]/**2**:2[2]:6:7[2]:9[3]:10[3]:12:14:17:18/**3**:1[2]:2:9:10:14:
17/**4**:2:3[2]:5:6:7:9:12[2]/**5**:1[2]:4:7f[2]:10:12,13/**6**:4:8:
10[3]:12:13:18[2]:19:20/**7**:5:10:12,13,14:15:18:19:
25:26:27[2]/**8**:5:7:8:13/**9**:1:9[2]:10[2]:12:14[2]:15:19:21
:24[2]:26[2]:28[2]/**10**:1:2:4[2]:4f:5:6:10[2]:12[2]:13:14:15:
20:23[2]:24:29:30:36/**11**:1[2]:2:6:10:11:13:16[3]:19:23
:26[2]:31:37,38:40[2]/**12**:6:7[2]:10[3]:13:14:15:16:19:24
:25:29/**13**:2:3:4:5:11:14:16:17[3]:18[2]:20,21:22/**Jas**
1:3:4[2]:5:6:9:10,11:12:13:18:20:21[2]:23:25/**2**:5:11:
13:18/**3**:1[2]:15:16/**4**:2[2]:9:14/**5**:3:4:5:7[3]:8:9:10:11[2]
:12:14:15:16:17/**1Pe1**:3:4[2]:5:6:9:11:16:17:19:20:
22:23[3]/**2**:2,3f[2]:2,3[2]:5:9:11[2]:12[2]:13:14:15:17:19:
20[3]:21:24/**3**:1:6:9[5]:12:13:14[2]:16:17[2]:18:20:21/**4**:
1:5:8[3]:9:12:14[2]:15:16[2]:17[2]:19/**5**:2[2]:5:7:8[2]:12:13f
/**2Pe1**:3[2]:4:5:7:9:11:16:19:20,21/**2**:4:5:6:13[2]:19/
3:7:9[2]:14[2]:15,16/**1Jn1**:9[2]:10/**2**:1:2:7[2]:8[2]:11[2]:15:
16[2]:20:22:23:27/**3**:1:4:6:9:11:14[2]:16[2]:19:20:22/**4**
:1:6:7:8:10[2]:12:18[2]:19:20/**5**:4:14:16:18/**2Jn1**:7:9
:12/**3Jn**:5:7[2]:12:14:15/**Jud**:3:4:6:7:11[2]:12[2]:13:16
:21:23/**Rev**:3:5:9[3]:13f/**2**:3:9[2]:10[2]:24,25/**3**:2:4:12
/**4**:11/**5**:5:9[2]/**6**:6:6f[2]:9[2]:10/**7**:17/**8**:1/**9**:5:7:10:15
:19/**11**:2[2]:8,9:15:17/**12**:6[2]:10:11[2]:12:14[3]/**13**:4:5:
10[4]:18/**14**:4:4f:7:11:12:13:13f:13[2]:15[2]:18[2]/**15**:
3,4[2]/**16**:6:11:14/**17**:12:14:17/**18**:3:5[2]:6[2]:8:9:11[2]:
12:19:20[2]:24/**19**:2:2f:6:7[2]:10:17/**20**:2:3:4[3]:6[2]:8:
11f/**21**:1:5:16:22:23/**22**:2:3:5[2]:10/**Act8**:33f
9173

FROM
Gen1:4,5:7,8:11,12:18/**2**:2:6:7:7f[3]:10:16,17:
19,20:21/**3**:2,3:5:11:14:15:17:19[2]:21:22:23[2]/**4**:4:
10:11:12[2]:14[2]:16/**5**:1:2:28-31/**6**:1:4:7:12,13:14/
7:4:10,11,12/**8**:7f:21/**9**:19:24,25/**10**:11,12:13,14
:15-19[2]:21:26-30:32/**11**:3,4:32f/**13**:7/**14**:17:21:
23/**15**:18/**16**:8[2]/**17**:14:16:23/**18**:10:16:17/**19**:4:
22:24:28[2]:29:36/**20**:6:13/**21**:17:18:20,21:25:31/
22:11:12:15:16:24/**23**:13/**24**:5:7:8:28f:38:40[2]:41
:46:47:48/**25**:6:9,10:18:20:29:30/**26**:9:26/**27**:
8,9,10:16:30:39,40/**28**:6,7,8:9:12:14[2]/**29**:26f/**30**:
16:26:30:33:37:39,40[3]/**31**:16:31:32:39/**32**:4:11/
33:19/**34**:6,7:26/**35**:1:7:9/**36**:2,3:6,7,8:10,11,12:
13,14:20,21:31-39[6]/**37**:13,14:25/**38**:8:9:17:29/
39:1:9:12/**40**:15:18,19:20/**41**:3:14:19:46:56,57[2]/
42:5:7[2]:24/**43**:1:2:33:34/**44**:8:11:29/**45**:19/**46**:8-
8-14:31:34/**47**:1:22/**48**:5:6:7[2]:16:22/**49**:6:10:26:
29,30:32/**Ex2**:3:4:17:23/**3**:7:8:17:22/**4**:3:9/**5**:1:
4,5:20/**6**:6:7:27/**7**:24/**8**:2:12:30/**9**:8:10:19:20/**10**
:11:14:18/**11**:5:8:8f/**12**:2:15:18:19:21:29:39:42:
51:51f/**13**:10f:13:14:17,18/**14**:9:24:30/**15**:22/**16**
:4:10:23:28,29:32[2]:33/**18**:4:8:10[2]:11:13:25/**19**:1:
2,3:5:7:13:15:16:17:18/**20**:2:18:20:22:25/**21**:14:
36/**22**:14:16f/**23**:7:25:28:31[2]/**24**:8:12:16/**25**:1:
13,14:15:22:28:32,33/**26**:1:12:15,16:28:31:33:35
:36/**27**:6:8:9,10:18/**28**:3:4f:28[2]:39:42/**29**:21:23:
25:29:40/**30**:1:2:8:10:21/**32**:1:7:11:12[3]:27/**33**:1:
10:15:16/**34**:11:24:29/**35**:22:23:32/**36**:4-7:8,9:
27:31,32:33:35:37:38/**37**:4:6:18:29/**38**:8:9:12:
25,26[2]/**39**:2[2]:4,5:8:15-18:27/**40**:15:27/**Lev1**:1:
2,3/**2**:4:5:14[2]/**4**:11,12/**5**:6:8/**7**:12:20:21[2]:23:25[2]:
26,27:34:35/**8**:26:28/**9**:2:10:19:22:24/**10**:2:4:8,9
:13/**11**:9[2]/**12**:4/**13**:12:20:23:25:28:41:56/**14**:9:
14:19:28:56/**15**:16:31/**16**:12:19:29,30/**17**:3,4:5:
7:10/**18**:16f:24:29,30/**19**:8:9:10:35,36/**20**:3:6:14
:17:26/**21**:14,15:16,17:22[2]/**22**:3[2]:21:26,27:32,33
/**23**:3:17[2]:21:29:30,31:41:43/**24**:3,4:5-8/**25**:
14,15,16:42:44:55/**27**:3:4:5:24/**Num1**:2-15:16:
47,48,49:53/**2**:3-31/**3**:13/**4**:3:13:29/**5**:1[2]:7:17:19
:25/**6**:3,4:9:20/**7**:84,85,86:89/**8**:5,6:11:14:16/**9**:
6,7:13/**10**:8:9:11:21/**11**:3:7:8[2]:19,20:31:35/**12**:1f[3]
:10:15/**13**:2:3-15[12]:21:22:25/**14**:9:19/**15**:3,4[2]:
15,16:19,20,21[3]:30:37,38/**16**:1:8,9:15:21:23,24:
26:27:29:35:36,37:38:45:46/**17**:8/**18**:6:21:22:27:
28,29:30/**19**:13:17:19/**20**:8:9:10:14f[2]:17:21,22:
26:28/**21**:4:12:24/**22**:5,6:10:11:33:41/**23**:7-10[5]:
27/**24**:3-9:11:15-19[2]:21,22:23,24/**25**:4/**26**:5-11:
63/**27**:21/**31**:4,5:12:42-46:50:51,52/**32**:7:8:9[2]:
10,11:15:17:22/**33**:1:8:15-37[23]:41:45:49/**34**:4:5:
10,11[2]:16-28/**35**:4:12:25:29:32/**36**:5:9:13/**Deu1**:
1:7:13:15:23:27:44/**2**:14,15:26:35,36[3]:37[2]/**3**:8:
16:17:28/**4**:2[2]:5:12:15:20:26:28:32:33:34:36[2]:37:
48/**5**:4:6:22:23:24:26,27/**7**:6:20:24/**8**:15/**9**:5:7:
10,11:12[2]:13,14:15:16:24:26:29/**10**:4:6:7/**11**:10:
16:17:24[2]:29[2]/**12**:10:20-23:32/**13**:5:8:10[2]:17/**15**
:2:14:19/**16**:3/**17**:7:12:17:18:19:20[3]/**18**:5:18:19:
20[2]:21:22/**19**:13:19/**20**:18/**21**:2:9:21/**22**:8:11:21
:22/**23**:4:8:9,10:14:15,16:17,18:20[3]:22:24/**24**:7:9
:19:20/**25**:9:17:19[2]/**26**:2,3:4:10:15/**27**:2,3,4:15/
28:12:14:21:35:41:56,57:63:64:65/**29**:18:20:21:
22/**30**:3/**31**:17:18:21:29/**32**:13[2]:13f:39:49/**33**:2[2]
:3:12:22:26:28/**34**:1[2]/**Jos1**:4[2]/**2**:1:15:17,18:21:
23/**3**:12/**4**:2,3[2]:8:15,16:20/**5**:11,12[2]/**6**:3,4:5:10:
20/**7**:8:12:13:21/**8**:7:11,12,13f:20,21:22/**9**:3,4,5:
6:8:9:12:13:23/**10**:9:11:19:22,23:31:41[2]/**11**:17:
23/**12**:1:2[2]:5/**13**:2-7[4]:9:16:26[2]:27,28:30:32/**14**:6:
7:8:10:15/**15**:7[2]:9[3]:46:47/**16**:1[2]:5,6:7:8/**17**:7[2]:9:
16,17,18/**18**:4:13:15:16:17/**19**:2-7f:9:11:12:
24,25,26/**20**:3:8/**21**:5:7:20,21,22:27/**22**:1:14:16:
17,18:29[2]:30:31/**23**:4,5:6:9:13[2]:15,16/**24**:3:10:
17[2]:32/**Ju1**:3:14:36/**2**:1:12-14:16:17:18:19/**3**:1:
20:28:31/**4**:6:11:13:15:21:24/**5**:4:13,14[4]/**6**:3,4:9[3]
:11:14:16f[2]:19:21:32/**7**:5,6:12,13:22:24/**8**:5:14:
21:22:23,24:27:34/**9**:2f:4:15:17:43:44/**10**:1:3:6:
11:15/**11**:1:3:13[3]:16:21,22[2]:23:26:33/**12**:5:11,12
:13/**13**:5[2]:6[2]:7:8:20/**14**:3:14:15/**15**:14:19/**16**:3:5
:12:25,26/**17**:2:4,5:7,8:9[2]/**18**:2:7:11:22:28/**19**:1:
16[2]:17:18/**20**:1[2]:13:18:31:32:33:35-39:42/**21**:1:
8,9:19/**Ru1**:1:1f:22/**2**:4,5:6/**3**:15-18/**4**:3:5:9:11:
12/**1Sa2**:8[2]:10:23,24,25:27:28:29/**3**:1:7:16,17:
20/**4**:3[2]:8:12[2]:13:16:18/**5**:1/**6**:7:15:17:20/**7**:3:6:
10:11:14:16/**8**:8:13/**9**:1:12,13:16[2]:21:26,27/**10**:7
:18,19[4]/**11**:5:8/**12**:2:10[2]:23/**13**:1f:11/**14**:30:31:
45:48/**15**:2:4:6:7:23:26:28/**16**:13:21:23/**17**:4-7:
18:23:25:34:35:37[2]:40:48,49:50,51:55/**18**:6:9:10:
13:19:23/**19**:9,10/**20**:1:2:3:41/**22**:17/**23**:6/**24**:1:
15/**25**:2:7:8:10:11:11f:14:15,16[2]:26:29:33:34:39:
43:44/**26**:1:20:24/**28**:3:17/**30**:6:8:13:14:16[2]:25:
26/**31**:1:12[2]/**2Sa1**:1:3[2]:13:17,18:20:22/**2**:2[2]:12:
15:22:25:26:31/**3**:9,10[2]:15:18[2]:22:37/**4**:2,3[2]:9/**5**:
8:13:25/**6**:3:10:16/**7**:8:10,11:15/**8**:5:8:10:11,12/
9:3:10,11/**10**:6[3]:7,8:15,16:18/**11**:2f:19,20,21/**12**:
3[2]:4:7:10:29,30/**14**:7:14:15,16:17:32/**15**:11:
17,18:28/**16**:23/**17**:11/**18**:14:16:19:21:23:31[2]/
19:8,9,10:16:17:24,25:28:31,32:41/**20**:2:7:8,9,10
:21:22/**21**:10f:10[2]:12,13,14:22/**22**:1[2]:3:4:7:9[2]:14:
17[2]:18[3]:22:24:37:44:46:49[2]/**23**:8:11,12:16:20:21:
24-39[27]/**24**:2/**1Ki1**:3,4[2]:29:39:49,50:53/**2**:7:8:19
:31[2]/**3**:20/**4**:7[2]:8-19:21:23[2]:24:33:34/**5**:7:9:13:18
/**6**:6:8[2]:15:16:23-28[3]/**7**:3,4:7:9:13:14:23:33:37/**8**
:1:8[2]:10:16:33,34:35,36:39:41,42:43:49:51:53:
54,55:65/**9**:6:7[2]:11,12:20,21:24:27,28/**10**:3f:11:
13:15:24:28/**11**:1[2]:3:7:11:12,13:26:27,28:29:31:
34:35/**12**:2,3,4[2]:15:18:20:28[2]:31[2]/**13**:1:2:3:11:14
:18:20:21,22:33[2]/**14**:7[2]:8:15/**15**:27:29/**16**:1:24:
34/**17**:1:4:6:15:19:24/**18**:10:38:44/**19**:17:21/**20**:
9:13:14:15:28:34:41/**21**:1:19/**22**:35:46/**2Ki1**:10:
12[2]/**2**:3:6,7:10:12:23[2]/**3**:6,7,8:9:20/**4**:3:4:9:25:
42[2]/**5**:17:20:21:22:24:26:27/**6**:10:23:33/**8**:20:29
/**9**:2:15/**10**:20,21:28:32,33/**11**:2,3:10:19/**12**:1:7:
15/**13**:5/**14**:13:14:25/**15**:14:19,20:25/**16**:8[2]:
11,12:14:15:17/**17**:8:13:16:18:21[2]:24:27,28[2]:30[2]:
31:32:33:39:41/**18**:8f:16[2]:17:19:29:33:35/**19**:7:
14:19/**20**:5:6:8:14[2]/**21**:7:8:15:16/**22**:15,16/**23**:6:
17:18:30/**24**:7:13:14/**25**:8:21:27/**1Ch1**:44:45:46:
47:48:50/**2**:3:17:23:53:55/**3**:1/**4**:10:21-22:42/**5**:
2:11:23/**6**:33-38:44-47:62:63:64,65/**7**:2:5/**8**:40/
9:2:3:22:25:33,34/**10**:8/**11**:11:17:18,19:22[2]:23:
26-47[33]/**12**:1:3-7[6]:8-13:16:19:20:24-37[14]:40[2]/**13**
:5:5f:5:7/**14**:14:16/**15**:4-10[6]:17:29/**16**:20[2]:35/**17**
:5[2]:7:13[2]:21[2]/**18**:5:8:11/**19**:6:7:16:17,18/**20**:2[2]:3
:4/**21**:2f:22:26/**23**:1:26/**24**:6[2]/**25**:1/**26**:19:
20,21,22:25:29:30/**27**:8:9:10:11:12:13:14:15:27[2]:
28:29:30[2]/**28**:4[3]:5:19/**29**:4,5:12:14:16/**2Ch1**:4/**2**
:8:14[2]:16[2]/**3**:6:11,12,13/**4**:2:12-16/**5**:2:9[2]/**6**:5,6:
20,21:23:25:26:27:30:32:33:35:39:42/**7**:1:8[2]:14[2]:
20/**8**:11:13:15/**9**:2:10:13,14[2]:23:26:28/**10**:2,3:18
/**11**:13,14:16:19/**12**:5/**14**[2]:9,10:14[2]/**15**:2:8:9[2]:16
/**16**:2[2]:7:9/**18**:26/**19**:4/**20**:2[2]:3:4:13:23:25:27:34
:37/**21**:10/**23**:12:20[2]/**24**:1:6[2]:26[2]/**25**:5,6[2]:7[2]:11:
14[2]:15:23:24[2]:27/**26**:3:5:15:21[2]:22/**27**:5/**28**:6:7:
8:10:24/**29**:4,5:10:12,13,14[7]:25,26:31/**30**:5:6:8:9
:10:11:16:17,18,19:25:27/**31**:1:5,6:9:10[2]:16f:16/
32:11:15:17:23:31/**33**:8:10:14:15[2]/**34**:5:9[2]:28:33
/**35**:14:18[3]:22/**36**:3:7:10:12:18/**Ez1**:7/**2**:1:3-35
:36-39[4]:40,41,42[3]:59:62,63[2]:70/**3**:1:7[2]:13/**4**:10[2]:
11:12:23/**5**:1:14/**6**:5:8:11:21,22/**7**:1:12:16:20/**8**:
1:2-14[15]:22:31/**9**:2:3:8:11/**10**:7,8:11[2]:14:25:26:
27:28:29:30:31,32:33:34-42:43/**Neh1**:2[2]/**3**:5:7[3]:
8:9:13:15[2]:19:20:21:22:24:25:32/**4**:13:16:19:
20,21/**5**:1:8:14[2]:17/**6**:10:11/**7**:8-38[31]:39-42[4]:
43,44,45[3]:61:64,65[2]/**8**:1:7,8:15:18/**9**:1:5:7:9:13:
15[2]:20:27[2]:28:32:35/**10**:28:35/**11**:1:4,5,6:7,8,9:
10-14:22,23f:25-30/**12**:28[2]:29:38:39:44/**13**:3:8:
16:19:23/**Est1**:1[2]:10:19/**2**:9/**3**:8:10/**4**:7:14/**6**:1:
4/**7**:8:9/**8**:2:9,10:15/**9**:22:28[2]/**Job1**:1:5:7[2]:10:16
:19:21/**2**:2[2]:3:7[2]:10:11/**3**:17:19/**4**:1:2:20/**5**:3:7:
15:20[2]:21:24:27/**6**:8,9:19-21[3]/**7**:10/**8**:19/**10**:4-7:
10:19/**13**:16:24/**14**:3:11,12[2]/**15**:17-19[2]/**16**:13:
22/**17**:3,4/**18**:16:17:18/**19**:9/**20**:10:25[2]/**21**:9/**22**
:1/**23**:13/**24**:9:11:12:18/**27**:3:13:22/**28**:2[2]:5:19:
21/**30**:5:14:28,29/**31**:19,20:22/**33**:17,18[2]:23,24:
30/**34**:22:27:29,30[2]/**35**:6/**36**:10:16:21[2]:25/**37**:9[2]
:15:22/**38**:1:3:8,9:16:19[2]:28:41/**39**:12:29[2]/**40**:6/
41:3:19:20[2]:21/**Ps2**:3/**3**:1:4:4f:8/**5**:4/**7**:1:13/**9**:4:
13/**10**:16/**11**:2:4/**12**:7/**14**:2:7/**17**:5:13,14/**18**:1:3
:6:8[2]:15:16[2]:17[2]:21:23:25:42:43,44,45:48[2]/**19**:5f:
6[2]:10:11:12·13/**20**:1:2:6/**22**:9,10,11:12:20[2]:20f[2]:
21[2]:25f:30/**24**:5/**25**:17[2]:20[2]:22/**26**:12/**27**:4/**28**:7
/**29**:3/**30**:1:3[2]:6,7:9/**31**:2:4:9,10[2]:14,15:20/**32**:7[2]
/**33**:13,14,15:18,19/**34**:4:13:14:16:20/**35**:3:10[3]/
36:4:8[2]:9/**37**:6:30,31:40/**39**:8:9/**40**:2:6:11/**41**:13
/**42**:9/**43**:1/**44**[2]:20/**45**:9/**49**:7:15/**50**:1:2:9:14,15
:19:23/**51**:2:5:6:9:11[2]/**52**:5[2]/**53**:2:6/**54**:7/**55**:8:
19/**56**:13[2]/**57**:3[2]/**58**/**59**:1[2]:2/**62**:1:3,4:5:7/**64**:1:
4/**65**:5/**67**:6,7/**68**:6:17:20:22f:33/**69**:14[2]:15:17:
18:28:29/**71**:2:3:4:5:6:15:17:20/**72**:8[2]:10[2]:11:14[2]
/**73**:20/**74**:2:12:19[2]/**75**:6,7[2]/**76**:8/**78**:2,3[2]:6:15:
16:24:41:42:48:57:65:70:71,72/**79**:13/**80**:8[2]:11:
13:14/**81**:6:7/**82**:4/**83**:7/**84**:11/**85**[2]/**86**:2:13/**88**:
5:14:15/**89**:3,4:18:19:25:33:46:48/**90**:13/**91**:3[2]:
12/**92**:3/**93**:1[2]/**94**:12,13:16/**95**:10/**97**/**98**:5/**99**:
7/**101**:4:8/**102**:2:19/**103**:4:12[2]:17,18:19/**104**:10:
29/**105**:13:14:17:31:37:39:40/**106**:10:18:23:36:
43:47:48/**107**:2:3:14:20/**109**:9,10:15:22,23[2]:24:
31/**110**:2f:7/**111**:8:10/**113**:3:7[2]/**114**:1[2]:8/**116**[3]:
16/**118**:26/**119**:10:11:29,30:37:37f:52:102,103:
105:115:134:152:155:157:176/**120**:2/**121**:7/**124**
:8/**127**:2:3/**128**:5f/**129**:1/**130**:8/**131**:2/**134**:3/
135:7:21f/**136**:6f:17:24/**139**:7:12/**140**:1[2]:4:10/
142:6/**143**:7:9/**144**:7[3]:10:11/**146**:8/**148**:1/**Pro1**:
7,8,9:15:32/**2**:9:11,12,13[2]:16,17[2]:22f/**3**:13,14,15
:23[2]/**4**:5f:24f:24:27/**5**:8:9f:15/**6**:5[2]:6[2]:22:24/**7**:5[2]
:14f[2]:16,17:25/**8**:23:35/**9**:3/**10**:6/**11**:8/**12**:26/**13**
:11[2]:14/**14**:4:7:25:27/**15**:12:29:31,32/**16**:17:23/
17:7[2]/**18**:22/**19**:6:7:23:25/**20**:8:21:30/**21**:16:31/
22:24,25/**23**:26,27,28/**25**:4,5[2]:23:25/**26**:10[2]:15/
27:6[2]:8[2]:18:22/**28**:8:18/**29**:21/**30**:1:7/**31**:14:31/
Ecc2:7,8:10:20-23:24-26[3]/**3**:9:11:13:14:20/**4**:11:
14/**5**:6,7:8:9:19,20[2]/**7**:26/**8**:8[2]:9,10/**Sol3**:1:6:9:
10/**4**:8[3]:8f[2]:13,14:15/**8**:5:11/**Is1**:4:5,6:11:15/**2**:1
:2:3:6:10:19:21/**3**:14/**4**:6[2]/**5**:28/**7**:3:15,16/**8**:7,8:
19/**9**:7:18/**10**:3:19/**11**:1[2]:11:12:16[2]/**12**:3/**13**:5:
10:13:19/**14**:3[2]:12:22:29:31/**15**:3:4:8/**16**:4,5/**17**:
10/**18**:4/**19**:11:13[2]/**21**:1[2]:11:13:15:16/**22**:5[2]:
9,10,11[2]:19/**23**:1:2,3[3]:15,16/**24**:11:15,16:18[2]/**25**
:4[3]/**26**:9:12:18:21/**27**:7,8[2]:11:12[2]/**29**:4:8:9[2]:15:
19/**30**:1:14[2]:16:27:33/**32**:2:15/**33**:18/**34**:4:10:17
/**36**:2:8,9:18:20[2]/**37**:3:6:7:8,9:16,17:19:26:30[2]:
30f:32/**38**:1[2]:6:17:20/**39**:2:3[2]:5/**40**:9:19:20:22/
41:2:9:17:25/**42**:23/**43**:5:6[2]:13:27/**44**:8:13:18/
45:6:8:20/**46**:1[2]:6:11[2]/**47**:4:10:11:14/**48**:8:11:20

(OM Con't)
:5:8,9:12^2:23:24/50:6:11^2/51:1^3:7:8:17:21:22
:1^2:2^3:3:12/53:2:4:8/54:6:11/55:7:10/56:2:5:
57:1:14/58:7:8:10/59:2^2:19:20/60:1:2:4:5:6:
3:1^2:2:4:15^2:16/64:1:7/66:6:19f:20:23/Jer1:
4/2:16:20:25:26,27:31:33:36/3:6:14^2:18:19:
24:25/4:6^2:6f:7:11,12:15^2:16/5:3:4:6:10:15f:
6:1^2:13:20:22/7:2:18f:22:32/8:4,5:16:16f/9:3
18/10:9^2:11:13:18:22/11:6:12/12:9:12:14^2/
3:14:18^2:20/14:1:2:3:10:18/15:7^2:15:21^2/16
5:14,15^2:16^2:17:19/17:5:13:15:26^4/18:1:11:
14:15:20:22/19:11:14/20:3:13/21:1f/22:2:8:
/23:3:7:8:9:14:22:24:25:30,31^2:33:34:36:
39/24:10/25:1:2,3:5^2:15^2:16:17^2:18:19,20:26:
30^2:32:33/26:1:2:3:10:15:19:20/27:1:15:16^2:
28:1:2:6:9/29:1:4:28/30:8:10^2:18/31:2:5:8^2:
11:16:19:38,39^2:40/32:1:6,7:8:31:33:37/33:
:17:19/34:1^2:8:13:21/35:13:15/36:6:7:9:11:
37:5:11:17/38:6:12/40/41:5:6/42:4:11:
14:17^2/43:1:5:12/44:5:7:12:14^2:16:30f/46:9:
20,21:24:26:27^2/47:2:4^2/48:2,3,4:5:10:11^3:12
:19:28:33:34^3:44:45^2/49:1:2:5:14:19:32/50:1:
:9:15:26:37:41^2:44/51:2:6:7:9:16:25:31:44:45^2
:58/52:3:7:8:33/Lam1:6:13/2:1^2:14:18/3:1:
50:55/5:6:9:10:16:19/Eze1:1:4:5:11:13:25:25
7,28^2/4:8:9:12:14/5:4:5,6,7:12/6:1:11:14/7:1:
/8:2^2:6/9:2:3/10:4:6:7,8:17f:18/11:3:7f:9:14:
:19:23/12:1:8:16:17:21/13:2,3:6:7:9:18:19:20:
/14:1:5:9:16/15:1:2:7/16:1:33,34/17:1:11:
23/18:8:16:21:23:26:27:28:30/19:8:11:12:14
0:1:4:9,10:34:35,36f:38:41:45/21:1:4:8:19,20:
:21f:28:29/22:1:18,19,20:28:29:30/23:16f:
20:21:22:23:24:27:32:42^2:48/24:1:5:15:25:26
5:4:7:9,10:13/26:1:7:16:17/27:1:5^2:6^2:7:8^2:9^2:
:11^2:11f:11:12:13:14:15:17:18:19f/28:1:2,3:11
:16:16f:18:18f:20:25/29:1:10:13:16:17:18^2/
:1:6:21f/31:1:12/32:1:17/33:1:11^2:12:14:19:
:30f/34:1:9,10:12:13:17^2:25:27/35:1/36:16:20
3:30:33/37:7^2:9:15:21^2:23/38:1:2,3f:6:8^2:12:
,16/39:2:3:10:17:22:23:27:29/40:13:15:18:21:
,48,49/41:7:10:11/42:6:7,8:9,10^2:12:16-20/
:2:6:14:15^2:17:23:25/44:5:10:31/45:9:15/46:9
8/47:1:10:12:15:17:18^2:19:20/48:1:19:23:
,28/Dan1:1:5:6/2:5:34:45/3:29/4:12:13:14^2:
:25^2:31:33/5:2,3,4^2:5:13:20:23^2/6:7:17:20:23:
^{2}/7:2:3:10:12:13:26/8:5:12:16/9:2:11:13:15:
:24:25:26:27/10:5,6:16/11:7f:17:23:29:30,31f:
0f^2:44/12:11/Hos1:1:2:7^2:11:8:10:15/3:2/4:15
7/5:6/7:12/8:4^2:10/9:4:12:15/11:3:10:11^3/12:
6:7:9/13:4:14^2:15/14:5:7:8/Joe1:1:3:7:15/2:
^{2}:20/3:6:7:8:16:18^2/Amo1:1:2^2:5f/2:8:10/3:1:
:12^2/4:3:8:11/5:8:11:18/6:10:14^2/7:6:8:14:15
6:17/8:12/9:6:7/Ob1:1f:1:8f:16/Jon:2:3^2:8:
10/2:1:2:6^2:8:9/3:4,5^2:6:8^2:9/4:11f/Mic1:1:11
/2:9/3:1:6:7/4:1:2^2:7:10/5:2:6:14/6:3:15/7:1:9
2^4:17^2/Nah1:13:15/2:13/3:19/Hab1:1:8:11:
4/2:12/3:3:3f^2:4:8,9f:11:13/Zep1:1:13/2:3:14^2
3:7:11/Hag1:1:1f:10:12/2:10:16,17:18,19^3:20/
ec1:1^2:4:5,6,7:14/2:6,7^2:13^2/4:8:9/6:1:10,11^3:
2:15^3/7:1:8,9:11:12/8:7:18:20,21^2:23/9:7:8:10^2
0f:11:14/10:4:8:10:12/11:6/13:1:5:6f/14:4:5:8
0^3:13/Mal1:11:14/2:1:6^2:12:13:15/3:7:11:
4,15/Mt1:17f:17^3:21/2:1:6:7:15:18/3:2:3:4:5^3:
:12:13:17/4:6^2:17^2:24:25^3/5:40:42:47/6:1:13:
3f:20/8:11/9:15:22/10:14:27/11:12:25/12:33:
1:42:43,44,45/13:2,3:12,13:19:49:52^2/14:13/
5:1:9:18:19:20:22:26/16:17:21:23^3/17:5:9:18/
8:3/19:1:17f/20:22^2:23/21:8:11:25^2:43/22:40/
3:13,14:34:35:39/24:27:29f:29:31:31f^2:32:43/
5:19:28:29^2:32:34/26:16:17:27:39:69:71/27:10:
9:32:40:41,42,43:45:51:55^2:57:64^2:66/28:2:7:8
Mk1:5^2:6:9:11:15:32,33:39:45/2:20/3:7,8^3:22/
:1:19:25/5:1^2:3,4:26^2:30:35/6:10:11:12:16:30:
1:34/7:1:4:10:17:21:23:26:28:31:33/8^2/9:7:9:
0/10:1f:6,7:20f:38^2:39:47/11:8:16:20/12:25:34
13:3,4:27^2:28/14:23:35f:36:70/15:21:28f:29,30
32:38f^2:38:40:42,43:46/16:3:8:9:12:14/Lk1:1f:
,2,3:15:22:37:50:52:69:71^2:74/2:4/3:1:3^2:4:6:8:
17:22/4:9,10,11:18,19:22:25,26:34/5:3:10:17^2:
32:35f/6:17,18^3:19:30:35:43^2:45^2/7:6,7,8:12:17:
23f:44:45/8:2^2:3:4:12:16:18:26:27:46:49/9:5:8:
19:35:37:54:62/10:7:11:18:21:30:42/11:7:14:15:
15f:16f:20:27:43:50:51:52^2:53,54/12:3:13:31:36:
46:48:52/13:1:2:15:16:22:29/14:1/15:2:25/16:2
.15:21:26:30^2:31/17:7,8,9:29:31/18:35:37/19:4:
8:24:36,37:45/20:2:5:6:34,35:36:37,38/22:41,42
:43:45:59/23:5:18:26:45:49:50,51,52:55/24:9f:
16:19:22,23:27:35:46:47:49/Jn1:13^2:16:19:23:
32:39:44:45:46/2:9:10:15:17:18:22/3:6:8^2:19:20:
31/4:5,6:21-24:30:34^2:35:39:46,47:54/5:4:21:34
:43:44/6:22,23:30,31:32:33:38:41:42:44:45:48-
48-51^2:58^2:64/7:1:13:17:27:38:41,42:52/8:14:23^2
:40:42:43:44:52:59/9:1:6:16:17:33/10:5:28:29/
11:4:18:28:37,38:40:51:53/12:3:21:27:28:36:42/
13:1:4/14:7:10:19/15:4^2:5:6:16:18:26:27/16:2:8:
11:27:28:30^2/17:7:8:15/18:11:39/19:9:11:21:27:
39/20:1/21:2:14/Act1:1:3:6:21,22^3/2:5:7:9:10:
21:24:32:38:40/3:2:16:19:21,22^2:23f:26/4:2:10:
17:36/5:16/6:9^2/7:16:17,18:37:42:53/8:22:26:
28:32:33/9:3:14:18:32/10:23:40,41/11:5:19:20:
27/12:5:11^2:20/13:1:6,7^2:8:13f:15^2:24:29:31:39:
46:47/14:3:8:15:18:19/15:1:7:14:15:18:20^3:23:
24^2:27,28,29^2:27,28,29f:27,28,29/16:4:14:32/17
:5:26:27:29^2/18:2,3^3:5:6^2:22:24/19:4:13:26:35:
37/20:4^2:7f:18:19:20:21:27/21:1:10:16^2:25:
26,27:29:39/22:6:16:30/23:10^2:26:34/24:7:18:
23:26/25:7/26:4:13:17:19:23/27:2:4:4f:6:13:29:
30:44/28:13:15f^2:21^3:23^2:25:28,29/Rom1:1:4:
6,7^2:17:17f:18^2/2:4:5:10:12-15:18^2:29^2/3:1:13:
25/4:1:4,5:12:15:17:24/5:9:13/6:7:9:13:18:22/7
:4:6f:23,24,25/8:2:3:11:20,21:23:29:35:38:39/9:
7:10-13:25/10:8:9:17/11:2,3:5:15:17^2:24:25:26:
36/12:2:6/13:5:9/14:1:17:22:23/15:15,16^2:19^2:
27^2:31/16:1:17:20:25,26,27/1Co1:1^2:8:22:30:30
f/2:4:6:7:14/3:18^2/4:7/5:2:5:7/6:14:18/7:5:10:
11:12:22:23:25:30:32:35^2:40/9:9:12:15:16:18:25
/10:6:9:11:13:16^2:17:21/11:8:12^2:27:28:29/12:2
:3:8:23/13:8/14:4:12:21:29,30:32:37^2/15:3:4:5f:
12:15:20:21:37:38:40^2:41:42:47^2:48:52/16:2/
2Co1:1^2:6,7:10:11/2/3:1:3:5:6:10:16:17/4:3:7:
14/5:6:9:15:16/6:3:9:17/7:1:2:10:11/8:22/9:10/
10:5/11:3:5:8,9:12:26^7:33/12:1:6:7:16/Gal1:1^4:3^2
:4:6:8:12/2:2/3:7:12:13/4:12:14:17:22^2/5:4:7:12
:17^2/6^2/Eph1:2:10:11:20/2:5:6:8:10:12:13:17/3:
9/4:10:17,18:21:30/5:8:14/6:10:20:23/Php1:1:5
:10:28/2:12^2:14/3:11:20/4:9:19/Col1:1^2:18:18f:
21^2:23/2:5:7:11:12:19:20/3:1:15/4:12/1Th1:1^3:
6:8:9:10^2/2:4:6^2:14^2:16:17/3:2,3/4:1:15:16/5:22
:28/2Th1:1:7:9/2:1^2:6:13/3:3:5:6:8:14:17/1Ti1:
1:5/2:8/3:13/4:1/5:13:15:22/6:5:10:11:14:15/
2Ti1:1:14:15/2:8:20:21:22:25:26/3:10:16/4:17:
18/Tit1:1:11:12:14:16/2:12:14/Phm1:1^2:6:7:15:
18/Heb:4/2:1:2:4/3:12/4:10:13/5:7:7f^3:8:14/6:
18:20/7:4:10:12,13,14:16:28/8:6/9:13:14:15:23
/10:34/11:3:4:12:23:33:35^2/12:1:3:25:26/13:5:7
:9^2:20,21:24,25/Jas1:1:15:17:27/3:12^3:17/4:2:7
/5:11:19:20/1Pe1:1:2:3:8:17:18:21:22:23^2/2:11:
16:24:25^2/3:10:11:20:21^2/5:8/2Pe1:1:4:9:17,18:
20,21/2:9:16:18:19:20/3:1^2:8:15,16/1Jn1:2:7:9/
2:1:7:13:16^3:24:27:28/3:11:14:16/4:1:2^2:3^2:6:7/
5:6,7,8^2:21/2Jn1:1:5:6:8:13/3Jn:1:7:11:15/Jud:
1:16:23:24,25^2/Rev:1f:1:3:4^3:5^2:5f:5:13f^2:16f:20f
/2:1:1f:5:6f:7:8:12:17:18/3:2:5:10:10f^2:12^2:14:14
f:18^3:19/4:3^3:5/5:3:7:9:13/6:6:13:16^2/7:1:2:9:10^2
:13:16/8:4:5:10/9:1f:1:2:3:13:17,18/10:1:4:8^2:10
/11:5:8,9:11:12:15:15f/12:8:10:14:15/13:13/14:
2:3:4:9:13f:13:15:17:18/15:6:8/16:1:10:12:13:17
:21^2/17:3f/18:1:3:4^2:9:19/19:1:3/20:1:9:11/21:
2:3:4:8:10^2:21/22:1:14:15

4901

GET

Gen18:3,4/19:2:12:14:15/20:11,12/21:10:18/26
:7:9/27:2,3,4:13/28:6,7,8/29:7/30:28/31:41/33:
15/34:4/37:21,22:29/42:16:27/47:24/50/Ex1:
19/2:18/5:4,5:18/7:24/8:20:30/9:13/10:26:28/
11:1/12:3,4:21:33/14:5:15:17:25/16:33/18:14/
19:15/21:13/23:5/29:1/32:22:27/Lev10:4/19:
17/25:14,15,16/Num11:12:13/14:3/16:21:
23,24:26:45/20:4:8:8f/22:20:26/24:11/27:18:21
/Deu2:14,15/4:19/19/20:7/22:4/24:10/28:31/
Jos1:10,11/3:2,3,4/7:10,11:13/10:19/Ju1:25/5:
30/6:18/7:5,6:8,9:15/9:29/11:1:19/13:15/14:3^2
:15/15:11/16:31/18:25/19:9:28/21:7:17/Ru3:1
/1Sa6:21/7:3/9:12,13:26,27/10:3/11/15:6/17:
26/19:11:12:14/20:31/23:6/24:19/25:13:21/26:
11:22/27:1/28:9/29:10/2Sa2:22/3:21:24,25/4:
6,7/11:2/12:17:28/13:9:15/15:14/16:3^2:7,8/20:
1/1Ki3:23/11:2/17:11/18:44^2/19:5:7/20:22:33
/21:7^2/22:9:13/2Ki1:3/2:10/5:7:12:20^2/7:12/8:
8,9/9:1:18:19:21/11:15/13/23:35/1Ch11:18,19
/13:12/22:16/28:9:20/2Ch10:16/15:7/18:8:12:
19,20:33/24:5/25:19/26:17,18^2:20^2/30:2,3/Ez4
:22/Neh2:14,15/4:10/5:5/8:15/13:27/Est3:3,4
/5:14/Job10:16/11:13,14/19:7/21:17/24:3:4/
28:13:18:20/31:21:38,39/38:3:19/41:15-17/Ps5
:4/10:13/27:12/35:17/36:2/41:8/56:7/71:11/
73:14:28/74:9,10/103:8/127:2/130:3,4/139:7/
145:8/Pro1:13/3:30/6:3:5/7:25/9:7,8/10:4/12:
9:13/13:4:25f/19:20/21:25,26/23:4,5:12:23^2/26
:10:27/28:20^2:22/31:9/Ecc1:3-7/2:20-23/3:9/4:
5,6/6:2:7,8/7:12/8:2,3/11:4/Sol5:3^2/7:12/Is2:
21/3:7:10:11/5/30:16/33:18/36:8,9/37:4/38:21
/40:24/46:7/47:14/55:2/56:11:12^2/58:4:14/Jer
1:17/5:3/8:10/10:17/13:6/15:1/18:18/20:10/
23:27:30,31/36:2:21:28/38:20/46:16:19/48:44/
50:6/51:61,62/Lam4:15/Eze7:25/13:18/16:15:
52/20:7:8:35,36/23:34/28:4/33:24/47:5/48:1/
Dan4:14:26/6:14/7:5/Hos3:1/7:5/12:1/Joe3:3:
9/Amo7:12/8:5/Jon1:6/4:2/Mic2:7/6:15^2/Nah
3:10:14/Hab1:17/2:6/Zep3:3/Hag1:9:11/Zec8
:9:13/11:15/13:2/Mal3:14,15/Mt2:13:20/3:9/
4:3:10/5:20/6:2:5:16/7:4:5:21/8:8,9:18/9:24/13
:44^2/14:22^2/15:23:33/16:23/17:7/18:3/19:17:
23:27/20:10/21:22:31:38:46/22:24/26:15:52/
Mk2:4/4:17/5:41,42^2/6:31:45^2/7:17/8:33/10:
17:23:33/11:18/14:41:42:59/Lk4:6,7/6:38:42^2/
8:19:54/11:7:8/12:17:20:24/13:9:24,25:31/14:5
:15:24/16:2:9f/17:5/18:16,17:18:31/19:3:23:26:
47/20:19:34,35/22:35:46:52/Jn1:23/2:16/3:3/
4:11:16/5:6:7/6:25:63/14:2,3:4:6/15:18/20:15/
21:6/Act2:15/9:6:17:34:40/12:7:8/18:25,26/20:
16/22:10/23:20:23,24^2/25:21/27:39/28:20/
Rom2:29/4:16/8:24/9:16:31/10:4/12:13:16:21/
13:3/1Co3:14/6:12/7:7:21:28/9:13:15:18:23/11
:21/12:28/14:5/15:34:50/16:2/2Co2:3/4:2:9^2/7
:11/9:6^2/11:15/12:19/Gal1:13/2:4/3:21,22/4:9
/5:1:20/6:7:9^2:12/Eph4:26/Php2:28/3:1/4:11/
Col2:19/3:25/1Th5:3:7/2Th3:12/1Ti4:13/6:9/
2Ti2:23/3:9/4:2/Tit3:9/Heb4:1:3:5:6:8:11/6/9:
17/10:18:26/Jas1:12:21/4:2:3/1Pe1:5:17/2:1:
20:23/3:7/5:2/2Pe2:3/3:15,16/1Jn:22/5:18/
2Jn1:8/Jud:16/Rev3:18/10:8/12:15/13:17

539

GETS

Ex22:5:6:10/Lev25:26/Num31:28/Deu15:16/
2Sa13:28/20:6/1Ki:39/Pro11:18/12:27/14:14/
18:6,7/21:20/28:13/29:22/31:15/Jer17:11/
Hos12:1/Mt5:38/10:41/Lk8:13/11:15:26/12:
21/18:4,5/Jn5:7/19:23,24/1Co7:28/9:24/11:21
/2Co10:1:10/2Ti2:6/Heb3:3/9:16/2Pe2:20

37

GO

Gen4:8/7:1/8:5:15,16/11:7:31/12:1/13:9/18:
3,4:27/19:18,19,20:34/21:18/22:2:3:9/23:11:
14,15/24:4:38f:41:51:55:58^2/26:2:16/27:8,9,10:
13/28:2:15/30:25:31,32^2/31:16:30/32:26^2/33:
14/37:13,14:30/38:23/42:2:4:16:19:33:38/43:2:
3,4,5^2:13:30/44:10:17:25:26:30/45:28/46:3,4^2:
31/47:23/50:5:6/Ex2:7/3:13:18^2:19:20:21/4:12
:18^2:21^2:23:27/5:1:2^2:10,11:17/6:1^2:11^2:28,29/7
:5:14:15:16/8:1^2:8:9:15:20:25^2:28^2:29:31,32/9:1^2
:7:13:17:28/10:1:3:7:8^2:9:11:17:20:24:27/11:1:8
/12:21:22:31^2:32/13:15:17,18/14:17/16:4:28,29
/19:10:12:21:24/21:4:5:26:27/23:5:23/28:43/
29:35/30:8:20/32:7:27:34/33:14:16/34:9:15:24
/39:23/Lev6:12:13/10:4:8,9/13:19/14:3/16:15:
18:23:24/21:23/26:6:13f:33/Num1:2-15/4:
17,18,19/5:9,10/6:6,7:13/8:15/10:5,6,7:9/13:17
:30/14:17,18:40:42/16:30/20:17/21:4/22:11:13
:20:34^2:35/23:15/24:1:11:13/26:2/27:10:11:12:
18/32:6:12:17:24:27:29/33:38,39/34:4/36:3/
Deu1:7:8:19,20,21:26:40:41:42/2:28:29/3:27/4:
21,22/5:5:26,27:29:30/6:3:18^2/8:1:3/9:12/10:
11/11:8:24:25/12:8:9:28:30/19:13/20:1:3:5:6:7:
8/21:10:14/22:4:7/24:19:20/25:7/26:11/27:
2,3,4/28:2-6:15-19:34/30:4/31:2f:8/32:49/Jos1
:3:9:10,11/2:16:19/4:5/6:1:22/8:1:20,21/9:11/
10:19/15:16/22:4:12/24:27/Ju1:1/4:8^2:9^2/5:15
/6:14:18/7:4:10/9:2:3:38/10:13:14/11:37:38/14
:3/18:2:9,10:20/19:12,13:25/20:18:19,20:27,28^2
/21:20/Ru1:10:16^2/2:2^2:8,9/3:3:4:15-18/1Sa:
4,5:6:9/6:6:8:9/9:5:6:9,10,11^2:14:19:24/10:8:9:
14/11/14:4:6:34:37/15:3:18:25:27/16:1:23/17:
35:37:55/19:3/20:6:22:28,29^2:31/23:2^2:3:4:13:
22:23/24:3/25:19/26:5,6,7^2:8/29:6:7/30:8:21:
22:24/2Sa2:1:21/3:16:31/5:8:19^2:23/7:3:8/11:9
:10:11:13:19,20,21/12:11:23/13:5:7:13/14:12:
21:24:30/15:7,8:9:19,20^2:21:33,34/16:9:21/17:
16:18/18:21:22:23^2/19:7:26:36:37:38/24:18/
1Ki1:13:53/2:2:26:36,37/8:11/11:22/12:16,17:
23,24:27:28/13:8:12/14:2:12/17:3:8,9:13/18:1:
5^2:8:11:14:41:43^2/19:11:15:20^3/20:31:33:36/21:
18/22:6:9:12:15:20:22^2:49/2Ki1:3:6:15/2:1:17:
18/3:13:23/4:4:7:23:30:41:43/5:3:5:10:13/6:1:9
:13/7:4^2:9/9:1:27:34/10:25/12:8/18:14:25/19:2
/20:5:8:9:10/23:1/1Ch12:19/14:10:14:15/16:34
/17:4/21:10,11:30/2Ch6:31:34/10:16/11:3:4/
13:12/16/18:3,4,5^2:8:11:14^2:19,20:21/20:3:16:
17/23:5,6:8/24:5:6/25:8/34:21/Ez1:4/Neh:11/
4:22/6:11/8:13:15/9:11:15/12:37/13:6/Est2:2:
15/3:11/4:5:8:10:16^2/5:14/8:8/Job5:8/7:4:9:15
/8:2/9:11/12:6/13:7/14:10/15:22/16/17:5:10:
13,14:16/18:4/19:28/22:17/23:3/24:10/26:5,6/

(GO Con't)
33:27/33:28:32/36:2/38:20/42:8/Ps6:8/10:15/
15:1/18:32/25:4:8:17/30:5/31:11/34:10/37:25/
38:21/43:4/45^2/48:12/63:2:9/81:12/86:11^2/89:
35,36:46/91:11/100:4/102:26/104:23/109:28/
118:19/121:8/126:6/132:7:7f:11/139:8^2/Pro1:
22/4:15/5:8/6:3:29/7:25/11:21:28/15:15:22/20
:18^2/21:31/22:13^2/23:35/24:6:21,22:23/25:
8,9,10/26:1:13/27:10/28:28/Ecc1:3-7/3:18:20/
9:7/10:5/12:12/Sol3:4:11/4:6/7:11:12/Is2:3/5:
5:11:23/6:8^2:9/7:3:25/8:6f:11/9:1/10:9:31/13:
20/15:2/22:15,16/23:6/24:7/26:20/29:9/30:6:8
:21/35:8:10/36:4:10/37:32/38:5/42:24/43:2^2:
19/45:2:23/47:2f/48:20/49:24/52:11:12/56/59
:7/60:20/62:10^2/65:4:24/66/Jer1:7:17/2:2:23:
28/3:12/4:21/5:5:6:10/6:25/7:2:10:12/8:14/9:2
:3/11:6/13:1:6/14:18/15:2:10/16:13/17:19/18:
2:11/21:3,4:9/22:1/24:9/25:29:32/28:13/30:11
/31:6/34:2/35:13/37:4:12/38:20/40:4^2:5^2:9/41:
8/42:3:19:20/43:2,3:6/44:25:28/45:5/46:11/47:
3:6/48:45/49:12:17:30:31/50:9:21:33/51:7:9:50
/Lam3:66/4:18/Eze1:17/3:1:11:22:24/7:15/8:9
/9:7/10:2:6:9-13^2/12:3^2:12/18:15/20:29:39/21:
22:24/31:12/32:30/33/34:29/38:12/39:9/44:3:
30/45:24/46:5^2:8:9^3:12/47:3:19/48:11/Dan6:6/
8:14/10:19:20,21/11:15/12:9:13/Hos1:2/3:1:3/
4:13:18/10:6/11:8/Amo1:5f^2:15/2:2/4:4:5/6:2^2
/7:15/8:9/Jon1:2:3/3:1/Mic1:11:11f^3/2:13/3:6
/7:3/Nah1:7/3:14/Zep1:5:16/2:15f/Hag1:8/
Zec2:4/6:6:6f:6:7/8:20,21^2/9:14/10:12^2/11:4:5:
9:15/12:12,13,14/14:3:16/Mal4:2/Mt2:8^2:12^2:
22/5:24/6:6/7:23/8:4:8,9^3:13:19:21f:28:34/9:
5,6:13:15:36/10:5:7/11:1:4:23/14:15/17:20:
26,27/18:12:15:16/19:21:24/20:7:14/21:28:30/
22:9/23:13,14:15/24:17:26/25:9:12:46/26:18:
32:42:50/28:7:10:19/Mk1:38:43,44/2:9,10,11/
3:14,15/4:17/5:18:19:34:37/6:35,36:38/7:29/8:
26/10:21:23:25:52f/11:2/13:15,16/14:12:28:32:
42:44/16:7:15/Lk2:4:15:27/3:8/4:34/5:4:14:
23,24:34/6:37/7:6,7,8^2:20,21,22:33:40:50/8:37:
38:39:46:48/9:5:13:57:59f/10:3:10:37/11:44/13
:27:32/14:21:23/15:3,4:18:28/16:3/17:14:19:23
/18:12:15:24:25/19:30/22:9:12:33/23:22/Jn1:
43/3:4:8:28:29^2/4:4:16:50/5:8/6:68/7:3^2:6^2:8:8f
:21,22,23:35/8:11/9:7:11/10:9/11:6:7:11:15:16:
44:55/12:35^2/13:29:33:36/14:28/15:16/16:7:10
:23/18:8:28/19:38/20:5:15:17/21:18^2/Act4:21/
5:20:40/8:26:29/9:6:11:15/10:13:20^2/11:12/14:
16/16:6:10:35:39/17:8,9/19:4:21^2:30:38/20:3/
21:4:12:24/22:10:16/24:22:25/25:9:12/26:1/27
:3:10:12:22/Rom1:8:24:26/3:16:26/4:14/6:15/
10:7:15/11:29/14:2:5:15/15:1:20:25/1Co4:17/5
:6^2/6:1:4/7:9:11:28/10:23:27/15:32/16:4:7:12/
2Co1:11/2:9:14/3:12/4:5/11:18/12:1/Gal1:6:
16^2:17/4:9/5:12f:16/Eph3:17/4:26/5:10/Php1:
23/Col:28/2:7/1Th1:8/2Th2:4/2Ti3:5/4:3/Tit2
:3/Heb3:18:19/4:11/6:1:3/9:8:18/10:22/11:8/
13:13/Jas3:3:4/1Pe4:12/2Pe1:8:9/1Jn:6/2:17/
Jud1:8/Rev2:14/3:3:12/10:8/11:1/16/17:8:8f:
11:11f/20:8:9

1167

GOES

Gen4:9/22:14/27:22:26/41:40/Ex3:1f/7:15/22:
6/27:21/28:29:30,31^2:35^2:37,38/33:22/Lev13:
45/15:16/17:13/23:32/Deu2:8/6:25/16:6/19:5
/Ju21:19/2Ki5:18/Neh6:5,6/Est4:11/Job27:19
/39:21-23:30/41:22/Ps85:13/97:3/100:5/112/
120:7/Pro11:13:16/16:18/19:15/20:21/22:3/
25:2,3/26:20/30:4/31:16:27/Ecc3:21^2/8:9,10/
Is31:4,5/41:3/Jer8:4,5/17:8:19/Eze26:15/40:6
/Dan11:44/Joe2:3/Amo6:10/Zec12:8/Mal1:5/
Mt8:8,9/11:18/12:43,44,45/13:23/26:24f/Mk9
:48/Lk1:50/11:24:26/23:5/Jn18:34f/1Co9:25/
11:18:21/13:8/2Co8:8/2Th3:1/1Ti5:18/Tit2:1/
Heb1:5,6/9:17/Rev14:4

85

GOING

Gen6:17/12:7/13:15:16/15:12/16:8/18:21/19:
14/21:10/28:12/29:9/32:17/33:12/35:3/37:17/
38:14/39:11/40:13/41:25:32^2/42:15:18:19:22/
43:7:30/44:12/46:26/49:1/Ex3:10/5:7,8:22/7:
17/9:14/10:7/12:37/14:5/16:4/17:1:7/18:18/
19:9/25:32,33/33:15/34:10:12/Lev8:5/18:3:24^2
:29,30/25:1/Num11:15:18/13:22/15:1:17,18:39
/23:25/24:14/25:1/32:7:9/34:10,11/35:34/Deu
1:1/4:32/5/11:8:13/20:4/30:18/32:47/Jos2:9/
3:2,3,4:10/7:3:7/8:29/10:25:27/15:2,3,4/18:3/
19:11/23:14^2/Ju6:17:36:37/7:14:15:24/12:1/13
:7^2:8:23/14:5/17:3/18:26/19:17:28/Ru2:8,9/
1Sa2:22/3:11:12:20/4:6/9:9,10,11/15:15:30/20
:2:42/22:3/23:17/24:20/25:17/27:1/29:4/30:
9,10/2Sa2:24/10:2:12/11:18/15:35,36/17:8/19
:8,9,10/20:6/21:17/1Ki1:41/2:2:8:15/5:2,3/6:8
/10:6/17:11/18:6:21/19:2/20:10/21:21:22/22:
36,37/2Ki1:3/2:5/8:13/10:6:13:17:18,19/11:9/
17:34/19:27:28/22:15,16/1Ch12:19/19:2,3/
2Ch2:5:9/10:11/23:8:12/26:17,18/28:10/36:17
/Ez5:8/Neh1:2/4:7/6/9:28/Job3:23/6:25,26/
11:10/13:8:15/18:4/19:2/21:27/34:17:18/35:
14,15/38:3/40:8/Ps19:5:5f/38:10/39:1/73:11/
122:1/139:4/Pro7:22/9:15/14/23:1/Ecc3:15/7:
2/8:6,7:8:16,17/9:10:12/10:14/Is1:1/3:10/8:1:
16/9:7/19:12/21:2/22:1/29:15/30:16/36:2/38:
1/43:18:19/44:7/46:9:10/48:3:5/Jer2:36/5:29/
7:11/11/19:8/26:10/33:3/37:7/39:4/40/42:
13,14:15:17:22/49:28/52:7/Eze1:12:13/6:11/8:
9/11:13/12:11/16:37/20:30/23:13/24:16/36:7/
37:5/40:3:34:40/42:14/Dan8:19/Joe1:2/Amo:2
/8:12/Jon1:2/Hab:5/3:2/Zec2:2/5:3/6:5/8:3:
20,21/Mt2:13/9:9:19/15:20:23/16:21:22/17:9:
22,23/24:39:41/25:7,8:14/26:46:58/28:7:16/
Mk2:21/4:13/5:7,8/6:31/9:30,31/10:32:46/11:
27,28/13:3,4/16:7/Lk1:8,9/5:33/6:21/7:38:49/
9:11:44/10:30/14:31/15:26/17:14/18:4,5:31:36
:37/19:5/24:27/Jn2:16/3:12:26/6:6:21:67/7:1:
35/8:14:21^2:22/10:24/11:8:31:47/12:33/13:30:
36/14:2,3:4:5:12,13:22:28:31/16:4:5^2:5f:17,18:
20/18:4,5/19:4/21:3/Act1:6/3:24/5:9/7:28/8:3
/9:8,9/12:5/14:5,6/15:10/16:7:16/18:23:27/19:
26/20:4:13:22/23:20/26:17/27:30/Rom2:5/15:
26/1Co1:31/3:13/6:2:14/8:13/13:2:12/14:6/
2Co1:22/2:2/4:9/8:2/10:11:14:17/12:5^2:14/Gal
3:4/4:27/Eph2:11/Php1:19^2:20/2:8:23/Col1:6:
11/3:24/1Th:2,3/5:1/2Th1:4/2:7/1Ti:1/2Ti:12
/3:1/4:3/Phm1:11/Heb6:1/11:8:27/13:3/Jas4:
13:14/1Pe1:6/4:12/5:9/2Pe3:11/1Jn2:11/3:2/
4:3/Jud1:21/Rev17:1

423

GONE

Gen7:13/8:11:13/12:19/13:14/21:15/27:41/30:
26/37:30/42:36/43:2:10/47:15:18/Ex8:15/12:
32/24:14/Lev13:40:41/14:3:48/Num11:6/16:
46/Deu28:51/31:16/Ju6:21:28/21:6^3/Ru1:15/
1Sa3:2,3/4:21,22/9:7/14:3:17/15:12^2/20:41/24
:1:7,8/30:22/2Sa2:8:27/6:13:19/7:9/17:20/22:
38/24:8/1Ki2:41/2Ki7:10:14/9:16/19:11/1Ch
17:5:8/29:15/2Ch10:2,3/Neh2:5,6/9:32/Job4:
20/5:24/6:5,6,7^2/7:10:21/10:19/15:21/20:7/24
:24/27:19:21/29:2/31:31/Ps17:4/30:6,7/32:5/
37:35,36/42:7/49:14/73:2/74:9,10/77:8/78:39/
79:5/88:8:18/90:10/103:16/105:38/107:18/
Pro10:7/19/Ecc6:12/7:6/9/12:4/Sol2:11/5:6/
6:1:2/Is3:20:24/5:9/14:11/15:6/16:10^2/17:1/
19:12/21:4/23:1:10/24:7/26:14/27:4,5/28:4/30
:2:22/32:12:13/33:19/34:12/35:10/37:11/38:8/
40:2/41:12:22/44/50:1/51:22/59:15/Jer3:8:20
/4:25/5:23,24/8:13/9:10^2/10:20/14:16/15:9/
19:9/22:20/25:7/31:12:15/37:9/38/48:33/49:7
/50:3/51:30/52:6/Lam1:6/3:17:18/5:16/Eze:
16/7:13/8:12/9:9/13:15/16:20/18:6/19:5:14f/
32:29/34:4/36:25/37:11/Dan2:5/10:17/Hos:11
/14:4/Joe1:5:9:10:11/Mic:16/4:9/Hab1:11/3:2
/Zec11:3/Mal3:7/Mt2:13/6:30/11:7/17:21/25
:10:14/Mk1:42/5:21:30/7/9:8/13:34/Lk8:49/
12:28/15:14/19:7:13/23:45/24:3:24:28/Jn4:8/
5:32,33/6:22,23/11:11/12:19/14/16:16/18:2/
Act1:11:24,25/2:1/7:11/8:27/10:4:7/20:5/27:9f
:20/Rom2:28/3:12/10:18/13:12,13/1Co4:11/7:
18:19:31/15:5f:29:55,56/2Co6:5/11:8,9:23:27/
Gal3:3/Col:9/1Ti6:17/2Ti1:15/4:10:12/Heb:14
/6:20/10:2/11:5:15/Jas1:10,11/4:14/2Pe1:15/
2:15/Rev18:14^2:17/21:4

261

GOT

Gen13:8/19:33:35/21:14/22:3/27:42/28:18/31:
36,37/32:22,23,24/37:23/43:22:25/48:18/Ex12
:30/Lev10:5/24:10/Jos15:18,19/Ju3:25/6:38/7
:1/8:8/14:2/15:6/19:29:30/1Sa9:26,27/10:12f/
19:18/23:7/26:12/28:7,8:23/30:18,19/2Sa11:
13/12:20/13:34/15:2/18:23/1Ki3:20/18:42/19:
4:8/2Ki6:15/7:12/2Ch9:6/19:3/23:1/Job2:11/
Sol3:1/Jer36:17/Eze20:29/33:24/Zec11:8/13:
6/Mal2:6/Mt8:15:23/13:2,3/15:39/Mk1:31/4:
1/5:18/8:10:13/13:3,4/15:36/Lk4:39/18:4,5/
Jn6:17:24/11:20/13:4/20:3,4/21:9/Act10:27/
14:20/23:12,13:16/25:2/1Co10:7/2Co2:12/11:
33

82

HAD

Gen1:25:31/2:2:8:21/3:1:23/4:1:26/5:32/6:6:
9,10/7:13:16/8:20/9:24,25^2/11:10,11:12,13:
14,15:16,17:18,19:24,25:26:27:29:30/12:4:5/13:
3,4^2/14:4:14:16/16:1:2,3/17:23/18:33/19:14:
:33/20:2:8:18/21:1^2:25/22:3:9:20-23:24/23:1
24:20:22:28f:48:54:59:62/25:9,10:11:21:24:34
26:1:14:18^4:26:32/27:6,7:41/28:6,7,8^4:9/29:1
16:17:32:33:34:35/30:30/31:10:17-20:32:34^2/
34:5:13:27/35:2:13,14:15:27/36:4^2:5:6,7,8:13,
:22:31-39/37:1:5:9/38:3,4,5:11:13:20:21:22:27
39:13^2:14,15^2:17:23/40:5:8:16:22/41:5:11:15:
:22:51:54/42:4:23:24:29/43:2:6:7:10:21:27:30:
34/44:1:6:19:24:27/45:21:27^2/46:5/47:11/48:
17/49:33/50:12,13:14/Ex2:1:10:11:22:25/4:2
28:30:31^4/5:6/6:8,9^2/7:10:13:14:22/8:12:15:1
24/9:12:21:24:34:35/10:13:15:23/11:9/12:28:
39:40,41:48/13:9:17,18:19/14:8:29^2:31/16:3^2:
18^3:20:22:32:34/18:1^2:2:8^4:9/19:7:25/21:29/2
3:7:11/32:16:25:35/33:5:15:17/34:4:32:33:34/
36:22/37:2:18/38:17/39:4,5:25,26:28,29:31:4
40:16:19:21:23:27:29:32/Lev8:9:13:17:26:29:3
34^2:36/9:5:7:10:15:16:21/10:1:5:16:19/20:21f,
24:23/Num1:17,18,19:47,48,49/3:4:38:42:49:
/7:2:18-23/8:4:22/9:4,5:6,7^2:19/11:4,5^2:34/12
1f:10:14/13:3-15:26/14:2:16:36,37,38/15:36/
:3:19:31:47^2:49^2/17:8^2/20:3:12f/21:9:24f:25,2
27-30/22:2,3:29/24:1:11/25:5:8:9:10,11/26:1:
28-37:44-47:64,65:64,65f:64,65^3/27:3,4^2:6,7:2
/31:17:41:42-46:53/32:1:10,11^2:37,38/33:2^2:3
:38,39:56/Deu1:1^3:19,20,21:24,25:33^3:34,35:3
/2:1:12:14,15^2:22:35,36:37/3:6:10:18/6:23/9:9
10,11^3:12^3:16:18:21:23/10:2:4:5:10/19:6,7/22:
13,14/25:10/29:1/31:9:24/32:18^2:26:30^2:44,4
/34:5:9^2/Jos1:12,13/2:2:4:6:17,18:22:23/4:8:1
:12,13:14/5:1:4,5^4:6^4:7:8,9/6:17/7:7:22:24/8:
20,21^2:24:27:31^2:34:35/9:1:3,4,5:18/10:1^4:13:1
:17:27:39:40/11:1:9:10:12:15^3:20:23/12:6/13:8
:12^2:13:15:21:29:33^2/14:3,4^2:7:8:13,14:15/15:1
/17:1:3^2:5,6/18:1^2/19:9^2:50/21:4:43:44:45/22:
7,8:11:20:32/23:1/24:13:31^2:32^2:33/Ju1:8:19:
20/2:7-9^3:10:11:12-14^2:15^2:19/3:1:4:26/4:2,3:
11^2:17/6:11:20:22:27:28/7:8,9^2:12,13^2/8:10:25
30:31:34:35/9:42:43/11:1:3:13:30,31:39/12:
9,10:14/13:2,3:21/14:6:9:19:20/16:2:9:18:20:3
:31/17:4,5:6/18:1:7:28^2:29/19:1:4:8:21/20:3:31
32:35-39:42/21:1:8,9:15/Ru1:6,7^2:8:18/2:1:17^2
/3:6,7:14/4:1:6f/1Sa1:2^2:5^2:12,13/2:15:20/3:
2,3:7^2:8:15:18/4:3:6:7:13:14:18^2:19:21,22/5:3:4
:11/6:6:7:16:17:19:21/7:2:14/8:10:21/9:15:23:
25/10:13:16^2:21:26/12:10/13:1:3,4:8:20:23/14:
3:4^2:6:17:21:24,25:27^2:28:30:48:49/15:12^2:35/
16:4:13:14^2:18/17:12:13:38,39:50,51:57/18:1:6
:11,12:20:25/19:7^2:9,10:17:18:21/20:26:37:41/
21:6:8/22:15:21/23:13:21/24:1:7,8:19/25:2:12:
21:34:36:37,38^2:40:44/26:1:12/27:2,3:4:8:11/2
:3^3:9:20:24/30:1:3:5:11,12^2:14^2:16:18,19:21:27-
27-31/31:1:7:11/2Sa1:1:10f:12:13/2:4:8:17/3:
23^2:35,36/5:4,5:12:13:17:21:25/6:8:10:13:17:19
/7:17/8:3:7:11,12/9:1:2:10,11:12/10:5:6:19/11:
4:5:10:27/12:3:8:19/13:1:2:3:15:21-24^2/14:2,3:
5,6:27:28^2:33/15:17,18:24/16:23^2/17:6:14:15^2:
17^2:20^2:21:24:25/18:13:18:29f/19:3:5:6^2:15:
24,25:31,32:39:41/20:3:5:14/21:2^2:11:12,13,14^3
/22:1/23:14/24:10:19/1Ki1:3,4:6/2:11:28:40:4
/3:10:12:15:17,18:28/4:25/5:1:2,3^2:12:15/6:36/
7:5:12:14:26:27-30:32:40/8:3,4:7:9:53:54,55:66/
9:1^2:2,3:11,12:14:15:16:20,21:24:25:26/10:1:4^2:
7:10:13:16,17:19/11:2:3:4:9,10:15^3:16,17,18:23:
24:27,28:29/12:2,3,4:6:8:23,24:28:32,33f/13:5^2:
11^2:13:26:28/14:18:21:26/15:5:12:13:15^2:25:29:
30/16:4-7^2:9:12:13:15,16:18:19^3:23:26:29/17:5:
16/18:2:3,4^3:16:30:31f:33/19:1^2:4:21/20:19/21:
1:9f:13:26/22:31:38:41:43:49^2:52,53/2Ki1:2:17/
2:9:15:22/3:2^2:3:26/4:1^2:7:17^2:40:44/5:1^2:2^2:4:
13:14/6:10/7:6:10^2:14:16:17^2:18:19^2/8:1^2:6^2:7:
19/9:1:12^2:14:15:16:18:27:29:30/10:6:8:9,10:11:
15:17:25:31/11:10/12:1:18^2/13:2:5:7:22:25/14:
5^2:6:23:24:25:26:27:28/15:1:3:8:13:17:18:23:27:
30:32,33/16:1:2:11,12:14:18/17:1:3:7:8^2:9^2:10:
11^3:13^3:15:19:23:35,36^2:38/18:1:4^2:12^2:16:36:37
/19:8:18:26/20:4:8:12/21:1:3,4,5^3:7:9^2:21/23:1:
4:5^3:8:11:12^2:13:15:16:19^3:22:24:27:30:31,32:35
/24:2:3,4^2:13/25:11:23/1Ch1:19:32:34/2:3:4:16
:17:18:22f:31:32:33:34,35^3:46:48,49/3:6-8:9:
21,22:23:24/4:5:9:27^3/5:24:25/6:31/7:4:15:16:
23/8:8,9,10:11:38:39:40/9:19:21:35,36,37:44/
10:3:7:11:13/11:3:10:13:16:20/12:22:23:39:40/
13:1:10:11/14:2^2/15:15/16:1:40/17:1:15/18:9:
10^2/19:5^2:7/20:1/21:6:28/23:10,11:17/24:1:28/
25:4,5/26:6,7:31,32/27:2,3:4:7:9:11:23:23f:27:
28:29:30^2/28:12:12f/2Ch1:1:2,3f:5,6:12/2:1:3:
17/3:1^3/5:10:11,12/7:3:6^2:10:11/8:1:2:7,8:11:
12:13/9:4:11:12:18:23:25/10:2,3:6:8,9/11:13,14
:15:17:21/12:5:13^2/13:13,14:21/15:3:8:9:11:15:

(HAD Con't)
3,14/17:2:13/18:30/20:23:24:27:29[2]:30:33/21:
3,4[2]:6:7:10/22:1:7[2]/23:9:18/24:3:7,8[2]:9:16:24/
25:3:5,6:13/26:5:10[2]:20/27:2/28:6:17,18[2]:19[2]:
21:23[2]/29:2:15:17:24[2]:25,26:34:36/30:2,3,5:5f[2]:
17,18,19/31:1:5,6:17,18/32:25:27:28,29/33:3:
4,5:7:15:22/34:4:8:10,11:18/35:10:14:16:18/36:
13:15:17/Ez1:1f:7[2]/2:1:59:62,63:70/3:1:7:8:11/
4:1:10/5:14[2]/6:20:21,22[2]/7:6:10/8:15[2]:22[2]:25:
28/9:1:2[2]/10:5:7,8,9:16-19:44[2]/Neh1:2/2:1:9:
11,12:16[2]:18[2]/4:15/5:2,3,4[2]:8:13:15[2]/6:1[2]:12,13[2]
15:16:18:19/7:1[2]:5[2]:61:64,65[2]/8:1:14:15:17/9:
15:23/10:28/12:25:29:43/13:2[2]:4[2]:5[3]:6:7:10[2]:13
19:23/Est1:8/2:1:6[2]:7[2]:10:12,13,14:15f:19f:19:
20/3:2:3,4/4:1:5:7/5:11[2]/6:1[3]:4:13:14/8:1:1f:2:
8f:16:17/9:1:4:16:24,25:28:29-31[2]/Job1:2,3:4:
21/2:11/3:13/6:30/9:16/22:18/29:12/31:28/32
2[2]:3[2]:4:5:14/35:2,3/42:5:7:11:12:13,14f/Ps18:1
/44:19:20/51:1/55:14/66:18/73:15/78:11,12:30
:34:42:45:57:60/94:17/95:9/106:21,22:30:34/
119:87:92/123:3,4/124:1[2]/129:3,4/Pro2:22/5:
12[2]/7:14f/23:4,5/Ecc2:11/8:9,10/Sol3:4/8:11/
Is1:5,6:9/8:2:3/14:17/21:6,7/30:31/36:21:22/
37:8,9:14:27/38:8:21:22/39:1[2]/40:15/42:21/48:
18[2]/52:14,15/53:9[2]/55:3/Jer3:24/4:25/5:5:15f[2]
/11:19/13:5:7/15:10/16:14,15/18:8:10/19:14/
20:2:17[2]/21:1f/23:8:25/24:1/25:17/26:7,8[2]:19:
23/28:11/29:1/30:15/31:3:20/32:3:5:8[2]:12:16/
34:8:9[2]:10:15/35:8/36:18[2]:24,25:27:32/37:1f:4:
12:15,16[2]/38:1:27[3]/39:9:11,12:13/40:7[2]:11:12:
13,14:15/41:4:5:8[2]:10:11:16,17:18[2]/42:10/43:1:
5[2]:6/44:15:17:20:30f/45:1/51:60/52:2:15[2]:20[2]:
22/Lam1:7:10/2:17/3:34,35,36/4:20/Eze1:6:10
:11:18:23/2:5/8:3:4:14f[2]/9:3/10:7,8:9-13[2]:14:
15,16:20:21:22/11:25/16:4:5:6,7:9,10:20:33,34/
17:10/20:5,6:15:22/23:10:11:39/24:18/28:14/
31:8[2]:17/33:5:22[2]/35:4,5/36:25/37:8/38:17/40:
25:26:28:31[2]:32:37/41:15,16:23/42:5:15/43:3:6
/47:5:6/Dan1:9:15:18,19[2]/2:1[3]:15:19:24/3:3:22
/4:5/6:3:10:24/7:1:4:6[2]:7:8:15:21:28/8:1:5/9:2f:
21/10:1:2/11:29/Hos1:6:8:15/13:6/Amo1:5f/3:
4/4:8/7:4[2]/8:10/Ob1:5/Jon:7:17/2:7/3:10/
Mic1:11f[3]/Hab:6f/2:18/Hag1:1f/Zec4:1[2]/5:11
f/7:2:3:12/10:6/11:7:10/Mal3:16/Mt2:12:16[2]/
3:3[2]/4:12,13/7:29/8:33/9:20/11:1:7:20:21:23/
12:7:11/13:6:8:34,35:53,54/14:3:4:12:23,24:32/
15:31[2]/16:5:7/17:9[2]:20:25/18:30:31:32:33:34/
19:1:8/20:24/21:23[2]/22:5:12:25:26:34,35:46/25
:20:22/26:1:24:25[2]:30:48:55:73:75/27:3[2]:18:19:
26:34:52:55/28:11[2]:12,13:16/Mk1:27:28:45/3:
7,8:10:22/4:5,6:8/5:3,4:6[2]:18:20:21:25:26[2]:27:
29:30:32:33[2]:43/6:17,18:29:30[2]:31:34/7:17:25/
8:14[2]/9:9[2]:12,13[3]:34/10:28:41/11:6:18:20:21:
27,28/12:23:28/14:11:16:21:44:50/15:38f:41[2]/
16:9:10,11:12:14:19/Lk1:7:57:58:62f[2]:65/2:4:15
:17[2]:20[2]:23:26[2]:27:36,37:38[2]:39/3:3:19,20[2]:21/4
:13:25,26:37:40/5:4:8:14/6:17,18/7:1:12:39:43/
8:2[3]:8:27:29:35[2]:36[2]:37:38:40:43,44[3]:47:50:56/9
:10:32[2]:36:45:54/10:13/11:1:29,30/12:16/13:1:
11:14/14:6:18:19:20:21:24/15:3,4:11/16:8:25[2]/
17:16/18:2:3/19:14:15[2]:20:36,37/20:2:19:31:
37,38f/22:13:17:19:51:61/23:8[2]:47:49:50,51,52[2]
/24:2:9:12:21[2]:22,23:24:32:35[2]/Jn1:50/2:9:22[2]/
4:1:4:8:17,18:27:45[2]:46,47[2]:51:52:53/5:5:6:13:
15:18/6:14:22,23[2]:30,31/7:10:11:13:30:39[2]:45/
8:20/9:10:15:17:18:22,23:24:35/11:12,13:17:19:
21:30:32:57/12:1:9:11:16:17:18:20:23,24:29:37:
38:41/13:1[3]:5:26:27/14:7/15:20:22/16:5f/17:1/
18:2:3:9:18:19:26/19:17:23,24:30:30f:38:39/20:
7:8:11:12/21:14:20/Act1:4/2:1[2]:30/3:10:11:12:
26/4:2:13:14:22:23/5:2:7:11:13:25:30:40:41/6:5
:11/7:5:17,18:21:25:35:41/8:4:6:9,10,11:14:16[2]:
27:32/9:8,9:27[2]:29:31:39/10:3:8:17:22:24:40,41
/11:11:12:13:14:22/12:11:17[2]:18:19:25/13:6,7:
27:29:31:34:36/14:8[2]:9:11:26[2]:27/15:3:4:5:12:
13:24:33:36:38/16:6:9:27/17:8,9:18:23:32/18:
2,3[2]:18[2]:20:24:25,26[4]:27/19:18,19/20:5:16:21:
36/21:9[2]:10:19:29[2]:33/22:11:24:29:30/23:12,13
:14:28/24:18/25:23/27:7,8[2]:21:37/28:6:11:15:
17:21:25:28,29f/Rom2:12-15/4:1:11[3]/5:2:6:13:
14[2]/7:7:9/9:7:9:10:13:27/10:19/11:
2,3/15:24/1Co2:8/3:2:18/9:5/11:24/12:19/13:
1:2[2]/14:5/15:3:8/2Co1:6,7/2:4:13/7:7[2]:11/8:15[2]
/12:1:7/13:2/Gal1:15/2:2:6:7,8,9[2]:11:17/3:1:6:
21,22/4:1:22:23:27/Eph1:13/2:12:15/3:9:11/4:
9/Php2:27/3:4/Col2:14/1Th:2:6:15:17/3:5[2]/
1Ti1:13:16:20/2Ti3:11/4:16/Phm1:14/Heb2:
14/3:18/4:4:6:15/5:7f:8:9/6:7:15/7:2:3:4:5:11[2]:
12,13,14[2]:23/8:7:9/9:10:15:19:23:26[2]/11:5:11:
13:15:18:23[2]:28:30[2]:33:34:39/12:18/Jas5:6/
1Pe1:10/3:20/4:3/2Pe2:21/3:5,6[2]/1Jn2:7:11/3
:12/Jud1:3/Rev3:21/4:1:7:8/5:6[2]/6:5:9:11/7:2/
8:1:4/9:7:10:15/10:10/11/12:6:13/13:1:2:12/14
:1:3:17/15:2:8/16:2/17:1:2:3:6/19:20/20:4[4]:5:
10:12/21:1:9:14

2393

HAS

Gen3:22/4:25/5:28-31/7:3/9:4/13:8/14:19,20/
16:2,3:9-12/17:14/18/19:13[2]/20:16/21:6:17/24
:35[2]:36:50:51:56/26:22/27:8,9,10:27,28,29:30:
31:35:36/28:4/29:32[2]:33/30:6:11:16:18:20:
23,24:30[2]/31:5[2]:7[3]:9:12:15[2]:16[2]:42/32:28/33:11
/37:19,20:33/39:9[2]/41:28:32:39:45:52/42:8,9:
21:28:36/44:4/45:7:8:9:11,12/48:9:11:15:16/49
:9[2]:11:23/Ex3:9:13:14:15:18/4:5/5:3:10,11:23/
6:7/7:9:16/9:18/10:6:12/11:6/12:19:44[2]/13:3/
15:1[2]:4:14:21/16:7,8,9:15:16:23:28,29/18:5,6[2]:
10[2]/20:17:20/21:8[2]:16:22:36/22:8:9:11:12:31/
23:4:30/24:8/28:30,31f/32:1:23:33/35:4:10-19:
30,31:33:34:35/Lev4:13/5:3:4:16:17,18/6:4,5/7
:15:20:21/8:5:35/10:6:11:12:15:17/11:4-7:9/13:
4:5[2]:7:8:12:13:16,17:18:20[2]:25:29,30:32[2]:34:37:
38:39:41:51:53:55[2]:56/15:1:6:32f:33/16:11:17:
20/19:22/20:3:4:9:11:12:14:15:16:17:18[2]:20[2]:21
:24/21:2,3[2]:18:19:20[4]/22:4:6:13[2]:14:16:20:21:22
:23:24/25:13:29:54/26:26/27:20[2]:22/Num5:7:
19:27:28:30/6:19/10:29/11:18/12:2/14:9:22:24
:29:34,35:40/15:22:31/16:3:5:6,7:8,9:10:11,12:
28:29:46[2]/19:1:13:16[2]:18[3]:20[2]/20:24/21:27-30[2]
/22:5,6:11/23:7-10[3]:17:18-24[6]/24:3-9[2]:11:15-19[2]
/25:10,11:12,13[2]/27:8:9:10:11:18/30:1[2]:4:5:14/
31:21/32:3,4:7:21:31/35:6:11/36:6/Deu1:10:
19,20,21:31:41/2:7:29:30/3:19:20[2]:21/4:5:7:8:
20:21,22:23[2]:31/5:1:22:24:32/6:10,11,12[2]:20:24[2]
/7:6/8:10:20/9:4[2]/10:21:22/11:4:17:21:25/12:1
:7:15/13:5:10:12,13,14/14:2:6:21/15:2:6:14:18:
21/16:17/17:16:18/18:5:6,7:22[2]/19:1:16/20:5:6
:7:13/21:1:3:5:15:18:22:23/22:4:17,18:19:21:
23,24/24:1:4/25:19/26:2,3:9:11:18/27:21:22:23
/28:9:47,48:56,57:63[3]/29:5:6:24:29[2]/31:2:3:14/
32:5:6[2]:22/33:29/34:10/Jos1:10,11:12,13/2:11
/3:9/6:16/7:8:10,11[2]:13:15[4]/8:8/10:14/14:10/
17:14/18:3/20:6/22:2,3:4:24,25/23:3[3]:4,5:9[2]:10[2]
:13:15,16[2]/24:20:27/Ju1:7/3:28/4:6:14/5:16/6:
13[3]/8:7/10:12/11:26:36/15:10:16,17/16:18:
23,24/18:1:9,10/19:18/21:3:6/Ru1:13:15:20:21[2]
/2:7:20:22/3:2:3:15-18/4:11:14:15:16,17/1Sa1:
27/2:1[2]:5[2]:8:23,24,25/4:7:17[2]/7:12/9:12,13/10:
1:24/11:13/12:2:7:12:13:24/13:14[2]/14:45/15:
11:22:23:26:28[2]:33/16:6:10,11/17:25[2]:33:36/18
:7/19:4/20:3:15:23:32/21:2:11/22:7:8/23:7[2]:21:
22:28/25:21:26:30,31[3]:32:34:39[2]/26:8:11:19/28
:9:15:16[2]:17[2]:18/29:5/30:23/2Sa1:21/2:16/3:
18:38/4:8/5:2:24/7:6:23/10:3/12:13/13:29,30:
32,33/14:14f/15:10:13/16:7,8:10:11:21/17:7:8:
9:13/18:19:25:28:31/19:27:35/20:21/22:25:33:
36/23:5[2]/24:17/1Ki1:19[2]:25:27:29:37:43:46,47:
48/2:23,24/3:12/5:4/8:12,13:15:20[2]:56[2]:58/9:8:
9/10:12/11:33[4]/12:19:23,24/13:9/18:10:13:22/
21:3:5:20:23:29[2]/22:8:23[2]:28/2Ki1:4,5:9/2:1:4:
6,7:16:21/3:6,7,8:10:13/5:22/6:11:32:33/7:6:12
/8:1:4:8,9:10:13:22/9:3/10:9,10/17:26/18:27:35
/19:3:4/20:5/21:11[2]/23:25/1Ch1:5-9f/11:2/13
/14:11[2]/15:2/17:26/19:2,3/21:8:10,11:24/22:
18/23:25/28:3:4[3]:5[2]:6:7:10/29:1:4,5:14/2Ch1:
12/2:11:12/6:1:4:10:36:41/7:21:22/10:19/15:4/
16:7/18:6,7:16:18:22[2]:27/19:6/20:37/21:10/23:
2,3/24:20/25:8:16/29:7:8[2]:11/30:8/31:10/32:8:
15/34:17:21/35/36:22,23/Ez1:2/4:3:15:18:19/
5:9/6:3:12/7:25/9:7/10:14/Neh9:32/13:11/Est
1:16:17/4:11:14/6:7,8/7:9/8:7/9:12/Job1:16/2:
3:9/3:25/6:4[2]/7:20/9:4:8/13:7/15:27,28:30/16:
7:9:11:12/17:6/18:11/19:6:8:9:10[2]:13:21:26/20:
5:14:19:20:26/21:16:29:30-32/23:10:14:16,17[2]/
24:2/27[2]:8:14/28:8[2]/30:11:15:19:31/31:7,8:27/
32:11,12[2]/33:4/34:5:13/36:25/38:17,18:28:36f/
39:13:17/42:3/Ps2:2:7/4:3/6:8/7:12/9:15/13:6
/14:7/18:13:24:28:35/20:5/22:14:15:24[2]/24:2f/
27:8/28:5[2]:6/30:6,7[2]/31:21:22/32:1[2]:9/33:12:
13,14,15/34:9:16:19/37:17:37/40:3/41:9/44:17
/45:7/46:11/47:5/48:3f:8/50:1:4:21/53:5/54:7/
58:1/60:6,7[2]/66:5/67:6,7/68:15,16/69:19:20/
71:11/74:3:18/77:7:8:9[2]:10f/78:7/79:1:3[2]/81:4
/83:8/88:16/89:18:41/94:23/98:1:2,3[2]/102:18:
23/103:10:12:19/107:2[2]/108:7[2]/109:11:15/110
:2:4/111:6:9/115:16/116:7:8:12/118:14:15,16:
18:22:24/119:52:56/124:6/126:2/127:5/129:
3,4/130:5/131:2/133:3/135:4/146:5/147:13:19:
20/148:5:14/Pro3:13,14,15/5:23/7:20:26/8:36
/9:1:2:13/10:9:17:25/15:19/16:4/17:16/19:4[2]/
23:24,25/24:19,20/26:2/30:4/31:21[2]:25/Ecc1:
8-11:12-15/3:10:11:15[2]:15f:19/5:4:16[2]:19,20/6:
2:3/7:12:29[2]/8:8/9:13/10:15/Sol1:4:6[2]/2:12/3:
8/5:11/6:1:2/8:9/Is2:6:7/5:1:9:25/6:7/7:17/8:
11:14,15:18/9:3:7:8,9,10:17/10:12:22:23/12:2:5
/13:4:6/14:5:11:24:27:32/16:9:10:13,14/17:1/
18:4:7/19:12[2]:14:17/20:3/21:10:17/22:8:14:
15,16:25/23:8:9:11/24:3:11[2]:19/25:8/26:12:15[2]
:18:20/27:7,8[4]/28:22:26/29:10[2]/30:33/31:4,5/
33:7:9[2]/34:5:8:16:17/36:6:20/37:11[2]:16,17/38:
15[2]/40:5:10:12:14/41:2[2]:4/42:14[2]:21/43:9/44:
13:18:23/45:1:21/48:14:20/49:2:5:7:8,9:13:14:
18:21/50:4:5/51:20/52:9[2]:10/53:11:12/54:1:6:
10/58:14/59:2:11/60:9/61:1[2]:2[2]:3:9:10[2]/62:8:
11:12/63:4:7[2]/64:4/65:23/66:2[2]:7,8/Jer2:10,11[2]
:14:37/3:1:6:8[2]/4:15/5:25:30/6:4:6:9[2]:10:12/7:
29/8:14:19/9:21[2]/11:16:17:23/12:5/13:15/14:2
:18:19/16:10/17:7:10:11/18:6:13/19:4:13/20:3:
13:18/21:1/23:9:12:17:18:20[2]:33:37/25:2,3:4:7:
31:33:34:36:38[2]/26:11:13:16/27:8:13/28:9[2]:11:
15/29:4:7:15:26:28:31[2]:32/30:7:9f:24[2]/31:7/32:
24:31/33:10,11/34:21/38:21,22/40:2,3:5/41:6/
42:19/43:2,3/44:7:10[2]/45:3/46:15/47:4:7/48:8:
10:11[2]:12:19:21:26:30:32[2]:36:42:44/49:14:24:30
/50:14:15[2]:25:27:28:29[2]:31:40/51:5:7:8:10[2]:11:
12:13:14:29:34,35[2]:42:44[2]:51/Lam1:5:9:10:12:
13[3]:15[3]:17/2:1[2]:2[3]:3:5[2]:6:7[2]:9:11:13:17[2]/3:1:2:3:
4[2]:5:7[2]:9:9f:9:11:12:15:16[2]:18[2]:34,35,36:42/4:1:
11:16/5:1:15[2]/Eze:5,6,7[2]/7:5,6:7:10,11:12:13:
25/8:12/9:9/11:15[2]/12:23:28/13:17/16:16:51:
57/18:6:10:14:26:28/19:14/21:7:23:24:27:29/
24:2:6f:13:24:26/26:2[3]/28:5/29:19/30:4:21:24/
31:10[2]/32:15:22:29/33:15:16:21:33/34:9,10/35:
6:8/36:35/44:9/45:20/48:2:8/Dan2:20:28:37:
39[2]:45:47/4:17:24/5:11:26/6:22/8:26f/9:11[2]:12
:13:24/10:11:12/11:27/12:7/Hos1:2:5:8[2]:21,22
/3:1/4:12/5:6/6:1[2]/7:9:10/8:3:4:7:9:11:14[2]/9:7
/10:9/12:1:14/Joe1:12:17:19/2:20:21:32[2]/Amo
1:5:6:8:11:15/2:3:16/3:6:8[2]/4:2:3/5:25,26,27/6:
8/8:3:7/9:12/Ob1:1[2]:18/Jon:12/Mic:2:14/2:2:
4/4:9/5:3f/6:2:8/Nah2:6:13/3:19/Hab2:6:13/
Zep1:7[3]:7f/2:15/3:17,18/Hag1:7/Zec:5,6:10:12
:14/2:8:13/3:2f/7:7/9:3/10/13:5:8f/Mal1:13/2:
8:12:14[2]/3:9:13/Mt1:20/3:2f/4:17f/5:23:28/8:
13/9:18:22/10:7f/11:18f:27/12:28/13:12,13[3]:17
:28/15:22/16:17[2]/17:12/18/19:5,6/21:42[2]/24:
21:23[2]:26/25:29/26:10:12:13:18:45/27:23/28:6:
7/Mk1:15/4:25[3]/5:19[2]:34/6:16/7:15,16f:29/9:
21/10:4:9:29:52/11:2:21/12:43,44/13:28/14:8[2]:
27:41/15:14/16:6/Lk1:13:30:45:49:52:53:54[2]:
68[2]:72,73/2:11:15[2]/3:16/4:18,19[2]/7:16:33f:34:
44:45:46:50/8:8:10:18[2]:39:48/9:55f/10:24:42/
11:5,6:20:29,30/12:5:42,43,44/13:16:20,21:
24,25/14:28:34/15:8:24:27[2]:32/16:17/17:19:21
/18:29:42/19:7:9,10:25:38/21:3:4[2]:8:20:32/22:
16:18:29:31:37/23:2:15:22/24:6,7:33,34/Jn1:1:
18[3]/3:1:31:32:35/4:10/5:24[2]:26[2]:36:37/6:27:29:
37:39:47:54/8:17:29:35/9:29:31:32/10:13:18:20
:29/11:11:39/12:19:31:38f:40/13:10:31/14:9[2]:
30/15:3:9:25/16:8:11:13/17:1/18:11/19:35f[2]/
20:21/Act1:8:11:21,22:24,25/2:36:39/3:13:16[2]/
5:3/7:40/9:13:14:17:34/10:28:33:35:36,37/11:
18/12:11/13:32,33/15:14/17:7:25:31[3]/19:26/
20:23/22:14/23:17/25:10,11:25/26:24/27/28:
20/Rom1:5[2]:19/2:4:29/3:2:11:12[2]:13:19:21,22:
21,22f:27/5:1:2[2]:5:9:11/6:9:17/7:4:20:23,24,25[2]
/8:2:10:10f:22f:23:24:33[2]:35/9:4:6:22:23,24:30/
10:3:9:16[2]:18[2]/11:1:2,3:7:8:11:13:17:23:28[2]:32/
12:1:3:6[2]:8[2]:19:20/13:1[2]/14:2:3:6:14/15:7:17:18[2]
:20[3]/16:1[2]:6:12:13/1Co1:4:5[3]:6:20:24:27:28:31/
2:9[2]:10:12[2]:15:16/3:10[2]:13:14:15:21:22[3]/4:9:10
/5:1:7/6:11:12:13:20/7:4[3]:10:12:13:17:18:19:22[2]
:25:33:36:37[2]/8:1:4/9:1:7:14:17:19/10:13:20:27:
28/11:21:23:25:26/12:13:14:18[3]:20:24:28/14:6:
13:26:32[2]/15:1:20:21:25:27:28[2]:41:48:49/16:2:
12/2Co1:3,4:21:22/2:5,6[2]:10:14[2]/3:6/4:1:4:5:6:
12/5:5[2]:10:17:18:19/6:16:17/7:2:14/8:1:2:16/
10:15:17:18/12:7/13:10/Gal1:12/3:1:11:13:25/
4:2:6:7:9:27/5:1:6:7:8[2]:10:17/Eph1:3:5:6:8:9:11:
14:16,17:18[2]:22/2:7:10:13:14:16:17:18/3:2,3:5:6
:7[2]/4:11:14[2]:32/6:1:9/Php1:12[2]:14:15:16,17:28:
29/2:22:26/3:3/4:19/Col1:8[2]:12:13:20:21:22[2]:
25:26,27[2]:28/2:7:8:20/3:11:12:18:25/4:13:17/
1Th1:4:8/2:16/3:6/4:7/5:9/2Th1:3:10:12/2:1:
16/1Ti1:9/3:1/4:14/5:8:10[4]:20/6:12:14:16:18/
2Ti1:1:10:11/2:4:10:18/4:6:7:10[2]:14/Tit1:1:3:
12/2:15/3:11/Phm1:7:18/Heb:2[2]:9/2:4[2]:11:18/
3:1:3/4:2:3[2]:7:10:14/5:4:10/6:7[2]:12:16:18[2]:20/7
:7:21:25:26/8:6:13/9:9:15:17:24:25/10:15:20:23
:24:36:38/11:7:16/12:1:5:24/13:5:7/Jas1:3:
10,11:12/2:5[2]:10:11/3:1/4:5/5:16:19/1Pe1:2:3:
4:12:16:17/2:2,3,4:7:14:21/4:10:17/2Pe1:4:9:10
:13,14/2:20:22/3:4:7:15,16/1Jn1:2:5/2:13:18:

(HAS Con't)
23:23:25:27/3:8:9^3:11:15:17:24/4:13:15:20:21/5
:10:11^2:12^2:16^2:18:20/2Jn1:6/Jud:3:6:13/Rev:6
:17,18/2:20/3:1:7/5:5:9/6:17/11:2/12:10^2:12^2/
14:7:13:15:18:18f/16:17f^2/17:9/18:2:6:7:20/19:
2^2:7^2:9/21:4:23/22:6,7:12

2204

HAVE

Gen1:29/3:11:17/4:1^2:10:11:14:23/6:12,13/7:2:
4/9:1:2,3:7:13/11:6/12:11,12,13:18/14:22:24/
15:2,3:4:18/16:6:8/17:5:9,10:17:20/18:5:11:12:
13:19^3:20:27:31/19:8:12/20:9,10:11,12:13:17/
21:7^3:10:23:26/22:7:12:16^3:18/23:5,6/24:14:19:
23:25:31:33:40:44/26:10:16:27:29^3:32/27:33:37^3
:45/28:14:15/29:21:27:31:34/30:20:23,24:26:27
f:29:33:34/31:8:12:26:27:30:35f:36,37^2:41:42:43
/32:4:5:28:30/33:9^2:10f:11:13/34:11:23:30/37:
16:26,27/38:9/39/40:14/41:15^2:32:41,42:44/42
:2:7:8,9:10:12:16:36/43:6:10:21:22:23/44:5:16:
20:28/45:10:16/46:30:31:32:34^2/47:4:9:23:25:
26/48:22/50:20/Ex1:18:19/3:7^2:8:9^2:12:16^2/4:
2:10^3:17:21:23^2/5:7,8:17:23/6:5:28,29/7:1:17/8
:10/9:15:27:29/10:1:26/12:13:39/13:3/14:4:5:
11/15:13^2:16:21/16:3:11,12^2/18:3:21^2/19:4:10:
15/20:12:22/21:4/22:26/23:20:32/24:12/25:20:
32,33/28:3:32/30:14/31:1:3:6^3/32:1:7:8^2:9:13:
29:30:31^2:32/33:12:12f:12:16:17^2:22/34:9:10:17
:27/36:4-7/Lev1:15,16,17/3:6/5:10/6:3:17/7:
17,18:34:35/9:6/10:14:18:19/11:4-7^3:12:23:
41,42/13:6^2:28:45/14:33,34:39:42:44:48/17:11/
18:6f:23:27/19:23/20:12:13:23:24:25^2:26:27/21:
16,17/22:15/23:22/24/25:45:52/26:1:10:13:32:
44/27:6/Num1:52/2:1/3:11,12/4:15/5:1^2:20/7:
4,5/8:8:15:16^2:18:25,26/11:6:12:17:18:19,20^3:
22/13:27/14:10,11:14:15:17,18:19:20,21:24:
26,27^2:31:34,35:40:43/15:25/16:3^2:15^2:28^2:30:
38:41/17:5/18:8:19:20:24/20:4:12:17:24/21:5:7^2
:22:27-30/22:10:12:28:29:30:32:33:34:38^2/23:
3,4^2:11^2:18-24^3/24:3-9^2:10/25:10,11:18/26:
55,56/27:6,7:12:13/28:1/31:15:17:19:48,49:50/
32:5:17:18:19:20:22:23^2:24:27/33:53/34:14,15:
16-28:29/35:28/36:5/Deu1:6:28^2:41/2:3:5:7^2:9:
19:31/3:21:23,24,25^2/4:3:9^2:25^2:30/5:16:24:
26,27:28^2:29/6:2:3:10,11,12/7:13:16/8:10:12,13^4
/9:7:24/10:9:21/11:2:7:8:9:10:15/12:12:17:
26,27:31^2/13:8:12,13,14:17:18^2/14:3,4,5:7^2:8:27
:29/15:12:18/16:13/17:2,3:8:14^2:17/18:16:17:
22/19:6,7/20:9/21:7^2:8:14:15/22:8/23:13:23^2/
24:8:18/25:13,14,15/26:1:10^2:13^2:14^4:15:17^2/
27:9:10/28:13:14:33^2:50:64:66/29:2,3:17:22/30:
1^3:2^2:3^2:15:16:18:19/31:5:13:16:20^2/32:21:36:
46/33:3:4/34:11,12/Jos2:3:10:12,13:16/3:2,3,4
/5:8,9/6:2/7:7:10,11^3:12f:19:20:25/8:1:6:8:31/9
:6:9:13:19:22:24/10:4:8/13:2-7/17:14:16,17,18^3
/18:7:10/19:50/22:2,3^4:17,18:22,23^2:24,25^3:
26,27:28:31^2/23:3:4,5^2:8:14/24:22^2/Ju1:7^2:12:
15/2:2:3:20/3:17,18,19^2/5:8/6:10:13:22/8:2,3:
19:22:23,24/9:16^2:18^2:19^2:20:31:47,48/10:10^3:
14:15/11:7:26:27^2:35^2/13:2,3^2:7:22:23^2/14:16:
18/15:10:12,13:18/16:11:12:13:14:25,26/17:3:
13/18:9,10:24/19:9:19/20:6:8,9,10/21:7:18:22^2
/Ru1:11:12/2:8,9:10,11^2:12/3:10/4:4:5:9^2:10^2/
1Sa2:1:3:23,24,25:29^2:34:36/3:13:14/4:7:9^2:16/
6:4,5:7^2/8:5:8:9/9:7^2:8:16^2:20:21:26,27/10:2:3^2:
18,19^3/12:1^2:2:3^5:4^2:13^2:19:20/13:1f:11:13:14/
14:24,25:29:30/15:2:13:15:20:23:24^2:26:30:32/
16:1^3:2:4:5/17:25^2:29:36:45/19:5:17/20:1:8:42/
21:2:4^3:9:14,15/22:13:22/23:10:11:23/24:6:9,10
:11^3:17:18:19/25:7^3:8^2:27/26:17,18:19^2:21^2:24/
27:12/28:15^2/29:8:9/30:22/2Sa1:4:19:25:27/2:
6:7:22:27/3:8:24,25:33,34/7:3:6:7^2:9^3:10,11^2:18:
22:23^2:25:26^2:27^2:28:29^2/9:9:10,11/10:9/12:8:9^2
:10:11:13:14:21:26,27f/13:32,33/14:2,3:7:13^3:
15,16^2:22:32^2/15:3/16:21/17:10:11:13/18:3:11:
18:21:26:31:33/19:7:20:28:30:38:42:43/22:22:
32:36:37:38:39^2:40^2:41^2:44^2/23:17/24:3:17:21:
24^2/1Ki1:20:24^2:27:35:42:44,45^2/2:13:14:16:20:
43/3:6:7:11:12:16/5:4:8^2/8:11:12,13:20:21:24:
27:28:29:33,34:35,36^2:39:40:44:47^2:48^3/9:2,3^4:7^2
/10/11:11^2:22:32:36^2/13:7:21,22^3/14:6:8:9^4:15/
16:2^2/17:4:8,9:12:18^2:20/18:9:12:18^2:27:36:37/
19:10^2:14^4:18/20:4:7^2:18:28:31:36:40:42/21:15:
19:20^2:20f^2:22^2/22:15:25/2Ki1:4,5:6:14:16:17/2
:9:10:19^2/3:17:23:27/4:2:10:14:15,16:28/5:13:
20:22:25:27/6:26-30/7:4:12^2/9:5:15/10:2,3:5:16
:18,19:30/13:19^2/14:10/17:26/18:14:23:25:33/
19:5,6:11^3:12:17:18:20:22^2:23^4:24:27:29^2:30/20:
15/21:7:15^2/22:8:12,13^2:17^3:18,19/23:17:27/
1Ch4:43/12:17^2/13:3/15:12/17:8^2:16:17^2:18:19
:20:21^2:22^2:25^2/21:12:17:30/22:8^2:14^2:15:18/23
:4,5/28:2:3:6/29:2:3:14:16:17^2:19:29/2Ch1:8^2:9^2
/6:1:5,6^3:8:10^2:15:16:18:20,21:24:26:27:33:34^2:
37,38:39/7:12^2:16:19:20^2/9:6/10:7/11:23/12:5^2
:7/13:8:9^2:10:11/15:3^2:4/16:7:9^2/18:27/19:2:3:
6/20:11^2:12:20:37/21:7:12:13^3:14/24:20/25:15:
16^4/26:17,18/28:9/29:6:7^2:9:18:19/30:6/31:10/
32:8:13/33:7/34:15,16:17:21:25^2:27^3/35:21/36:
22,23/Ez4:2:3:12^2:14:19^2:20^3:21/5:16/6:11:12/
9:8^3:9:10:13^2:14:15/10:2:10^2:12/Neh1:6,7^2:9/2:
3:20/4:5/5:8:9/6:7:14/9:6:8:10:29:32:33:37^2/13
:14:22:29/Est1:8/5:4/6:10^2/7:3:4/8:7/9:12^2:13:
19/Job1:5:5f:7:8^2:10^2:16:17^2:21/2:2:3/3:16^2/4:
3,4^2:7,8/5:16:27/6:5,6,7:10:14:15-18:22^2:23:24/
7:3:20/8:11-13/10:3:4-7f:8:10:19^2:20,21^2/11:18^2
/12:4/13:1:12^2:23/14:5:6:8,9/15:4,5:7,8^2:17-19^2
/16:2:3:8:10:15/17:3,4:11/18:3:19/19:3:4:14^2:
19:20/20:2:3/21:11:17:25/22:6^2:7:20:21/23:11^2
:12^2/24:3:21^2/26:2:3^2/27/30:2:3:8:9:13:19:21:
27/31:5:7,8^4:9:12:13:16:18:19,20:21:22:24:26:27
:29:30:31:32^2:33:37:38,39/32:11,12/33:1:2:8:9:
12:23,24:32/34:6:7,8:31:32:36:37/35:6:16/36:2:
9^2/37:21/38:12:13:14:16:22,23^2/39:1:2,3:6:19:
20/40:2:5/42:7^2/Ps2:6:7f/3:1/4^3:7/8:2:3:5:6/9:
4^2:5:10:13:14:15/10:14^2/11:2:3:3f/12:5/13:2:4/
14:3/16:1:2:11/17:1^2:3^3:4^2:5:13,14/18:1:21^2:24:
28:35:36:39:43,44,45:50^2/20:3/21:2:4:5^2:6^2/22:
1:9,10,11^3:15:16:22/23:1:5:5f/25:3:5:19/26:1^2:3
:4/27:9/30:1:10/31:4:5,6:7^2:8^2:9,10^2:19/32:1:9/
35:11:17:21:25/36:1:12/37:11:16:19:25^3:35,36/
38:2:13,14:18:19/39:9f/40:4:5:6:6f:7:9^2:10^2:12/
41:4:12^2/42:7:9:11/43:2/44:1^2:9^2:10^2:11:13:14:
17:18^2/47:9/48:4:6:8:10/49/50:5:8:17:22/51:1^2:
8/52:9f/53:3/54/55:9f:12^2/56:1:8^3:12:13/57:1:
6^3/59:1:16/60:1^2:2^2:3:4,5/61:5^2/63:7/65:4/66:
10:13:18/68:11,12,13:28/69:1:3:26^2/71:3:6^2:8:
15:17^2:19:20:24/72:12/73:4f:7:12:13:15:25:28/
74:1:12:22/75:3/76:11/77:10:15/79:7/80:5:6:
12:15^2/81:9/82:6/84:3:9^2/85:1^2:10^2/86:13/88:1
:5:6:8^2:14:15:16/89:3,4^2:10:19:20:29:35,36:39^2:
40:42:43:44:45:47:49/90:1/92:4:10:11/93:1/94:
17/97:8,9/101:3/102:3,4:9,10:13/104:24^2/106:
6/108:11^2/109:3:27/112:2:9/116:16/119:4:6:7:
7f:10:11:13:29,30:40,41,42:52:54:61:69:70:71,72
:78:80:81:85,86^2:92:93:94:101:110:118:121:126:
132:139:140:152:154:157:161^2:165:166:167:168
:173:174:176^2/122:4/123:3,4^3/124:2,3:4,5:7/
125:5/127/129:2/132:13:14:17/135:14/137:2:8
/138:2f/139:1/140:5:9/141:1/142:3/143/147:
20/Pro1:24^2:25:31/2:16,17:22/3:21/4:4:10:11/
6:2:3:5:7:34/7:14f:26/8:6,7/9:5/10:7/11:29/12:
3:11f/13:7:23/14:20:26:32/16/18:21/20:7:9:12
/22:26,27/23:6,7,8:17,18:33:35/25:4,5/28:16/
29:1:12:14/30:3f:17:24-28:32/31:2/Ecc1:8-11:
12-15:16-18/2:3:19/3:10/4:3^2/5:10:11:13,14/6:
1:2:7,8/7:15-17:23/8:2,3:9,10^3/9:2,3:5:6:13/10:
5^2:6:7/Sol3:3/4:8:9:12/5:2:3^2/6:5:8/7:12^2:13/8:
8:10:12/Is1:2:4^3:9:12,13:20:26/3:6:7:8:9:14^2/5:
3:4:7:8:12:13:24/6:5/7:11:14f:20^2:21,22/8:6f:
14,15:18:20^2/9:3:16:19,20/10:10:11:13:14/13:3^2
:12:18/14:1:4:8:20:22:25/16:8:10/17:7:8^2:10/18
:5/19:9:11:13:25/20:5,6/21:8,9:10:15/22:21/24:
4,5/25:1/26:12:18:19/27:11/28:12:15:20/30:2^2:
15:29/31:2:7/33:1^2:2:8^2:13:16/34:5/36:8,9:10:
16:18/37:7:11^2:18:24:26:28:29:30/38:17^2/39:4:
6/40:21/41:9^2:24:25:26/42:1:3:4:6^2:16/43:1^2:7:
10:12^4:19:21:22:23^4:24^2:28/44:7:11:22:28/45:4:
10:11:12^2:13:13f:23/46:3:11/47:6:10:13/48:6:11^2
:15^2:16^2:18:19^2/49:4:13:15:16/50:2:5:7/51:12:
13^2:16:17^2:19:20/53:5:10/54:8:9:16^2:17^2/55:1:5
:7/56:6:12/57:7,8:9^2:11:16:18/58:3^2/59:2:13:20
/60:9:10/61:4:7/62:6,7/63:3^2:17:18/64:5:7/65:
2^2:8:10:11/66:19:24/Jer1:9:16:18/2:10,11:13^3:
15f:17:18:21:23:26,27:28^2:30^2:31^3:32/3:1^2:2:3:
4,5:6:20^3:21:24:25^2/4:10:17:18:19:22^2:28:29:31/
5:3^3:7:12:22:23,24^3:25/6:20:24^2:27:30/7:13,14:
25:30^2:31/8:2:6:8:9:10:19/9:10:11:13:14:16/10:
11:20:21:25/11:7:9:10:13:15^2:20/12:4:6^2:7^2:8^2:9
:10:11:13^2:15/13:19:22:24,25^2/14:7:10^3:14:15:
17:18:19/15:6:9:11^2:14^2:15:17,18^3/16:2:5:10:12:
13:18:19^2/17:4:13/18:12:13:15^2:18:20:22^2/19:4^2
:5:8:15^2/20:7:8:11:12/21:10/22:21:22/23:1:2^2:3
:11:17:21:32:38,39/24:4,5/25:2,3:4:7^2:8,9^2:13:
18:29/26:2^2:4:9:11:12:15:19/27:5:6^2:15/28:2:13^2
:14^2:16/29:6^2:9:10:11:23^4:25:26:32/30:2:7:10:14^2
:15:21/31:3^2:16:18^2:20:25/32:6,7:17:19:20^3:23^2:
24:29:30^2:33:34:35^2:42^2:43/33:4:5^2:17:20,21:24:
25,26/34:5:16^2:18,19^2/35:5:8^2:10^2:14:15:16^2:17:
18,19^2/36:7:30/37:14:18^3/38:4:9:19:21,22^2/40:
2,3:15/41:9f/42:10:19:21/43:10/44:2,3:5:8:9:17
:18^2:23^2:25^2:26:29/45:3^2/46:6:11:12:20,21:28/
48:2,3,4:11:29:35:38/49:1:13:14:16:23:24/50:6:
7:15:21:24^2:33/51:17:24:30^2:58:61,62^2:63/Lam
1:3:4:8:10:11^2:16:20:21^4:22/2:11:14^2:16^2:21^2:22
/3:17^3:19:22:34,35,36:42^2:43:44:45:46:52:58:59:
60^2:61^2:64/4:10:12/5:7:8:21:22/Eze2:3:5/3:8:9:
17:19:21/4:3:8:14^3/5:9^2:11:15:17/6:11/7:10,11:
19:26,27/8:12:15:17/9:1:10^2:11/11:6:8:12^2:16/
12:9:16/13:2,3^2:5:6:7^2:16:19^2:22^2/16:3:22:27^2:
28:30:31^2:37:43^2:45:47:48:51^2:61:63^2/17:21:24/
18:2f:12/20:25f:31:32:42:43:44:48/21:9,10,11:
13:17:29^2:32/22:4:14^2:22:25:26^2:31/23:34:35:37^2
:39:40:43/24:8:14:22:23/25:8:12:15:17/26:2:5:
14:16:17/27:4^2:10:34:36/28:4:10:17:25/29:3^2:5:
9:20/30:8:12:21/32:9:15:25:29:32/33:5:7:11:13:
25:29:30:31/34:4^2:5:19:24:27/35:12:13/36:2:7^2:
32:36/37:11:14:28/38:10:11:12:23/39:5:8:19:21
:25/40:4^2/42:14/43:10:11:23:25/44:6:7^2:8^2:12:
13/47:14:22^2/48:33/Dan1:3,4f:3,4^2/2:5:10:23/
3:12^2:18/4:16:18:22:26:30/5:14^2:15:22:23^3:27^2/
6:7:22/8:17:19:23/9:5^2:6:7:9:10^2:11:12:13:15:24
/10:11:16:19:20,21/11:6f:12:19:30,31:33:37:39/
12:9:13/Hos1:2:6:7:11^2:20/4:6:10^2:11:12/5:1:3^2
:7:10/6:5:10/7:13:15/8:1:4:5:7:14/9:1:8:13/10:9
:11^2:13^2/11:4:7/12:8/13:4^2:8/14:1:3/Joe1:2:7/
2:2:26:28/3:5:6:7^2/Amo1:3^2:9:13/2:1:4^3:6^2/3:2:
7:10:12/4:1:12/5:14:15:18/9:7:8:9:15/Ob1:12^4:
15/Jon:6:8:14/2:4:6:8:9/Mic1:16/2:9:10/4:11/
5:13/6:3:5:14/7:1:9^2:19/Nah1:12:14:15^2/Hab:5
:12:14/2:5:7:8^2:10/3:2/Zep1:13^3:17/2:3:8:10:14
/3:3:6^2:17,18:19/Hag1:6:7:11^2/2:8,9:15:18,19^3:
23/Zec1:5,6:11:16:19:21^2/2:4:10/3:2^2:4:5,6:9f/
5:3/6:8:15^2/8:2:4:9^2:19/9:11/10:2^2:8:9/11:5^3/
12:5/14:17:20/Mal1:2,3:7:9:10/2:1:8^2:9^2:11:14:
17^2/3:7^2:8^2:10:13:14,15/Mt1:21/2:2^2:15/3:8/4:
15,16/5:17:18:22:26/6:2:12^2:25/7:3:23/8:8,9^3:
13:20^3:29:29f/9:2:5,6:13:27:33/10:8:23:25:35/
11:12:21/12:7/13:9:12,13:15:17^2:21:52/14:5:17
/15:22:32:34/17:15:21/18:6:10:15:33/19:16:21^2
:29/20:23:30/21:13:21/22:32f/23:29,30:37/24:
25:45/25:21^2:22:23:27^2:29/26:8,9:11^2:32:50:
65,66^2/27:1f:4^2:46/28:18:20/Mk1:24:43,44/2:
9,10,11:28/3:9/4:23:40/6:11:38/7:3:4:6,7:11^2:
29^2/8:1^2:3:5:21/9:12,13:19:22:23:24^2:45,46:47/
10:21^2:30:40^2:47:48/11:17:22,23^2:24/12:19:26:
27^2:32:38/13:19:23/14:4,5:7:14:31:60:63,64/15:
34:45/Lk1:1,2:13:14:22:31:34/2:29,30,31^3:48^2/
3:8:11^2:12/4:34/5:8:23,24:26/6:9:23:24:26:30/7
:6,7,8:9:16:20,21,22:40/8:18/9:13:27:50:53:58^3:
59f/10:13:19:23:24/11:4:45:48:53,54/12:3^2:4:15
:18:19:22:24:33^2:49:51/13:34/14:9:10/15:17:18:
21:23:30:31/16:4:24:28:29/17:10:13:23/18:8:
16,17^2:22:28:29:38:39/19:8:9,10:17:26^2:44:46/
21:4:16/22:15:24:25:28:28f:31:32^2:36^2:38:52:71^2
/23:14:16:22:29/24:4:26:28:39:41:48/Jn1:14:16
:22:24,25:26:41:45/2:4f:10:18^2/3:10,11:13:15:
16:18:36/4:11:15:17,18:21-24^2:32:42/5:7:26:29^2
:32,33:34^2:36^2:41,42:43:46/6:14:36^2:38^2:40:46:
53:63:68/7:26:47/8:16:25:28:28f:28^2:33:35:42:
49:50:51/9:37:39/10:16:17:18:25:32:33:41/11:
21:27/12:5:28:46:47:48:49/13:10:14:15^2/14:7^2:
9:11:12,13:26:29:30/15:9:11:15:22:27/16:1:3:22
:25:33^4/17:2^2:3:6^2:7:8:9:10:11:12:12f:13:14:22:
26^2/18:9:20^3:21:30:35:36:39/19:10:11^2:15:22^2:
35/20:2^2:13^2:15^2:18:25:29:30,31/21:12:24/Act1
:24,25/2:21:29:34/3:6:24/4:7:16/5:28:31/6:14/
7:34^3:40/8:19:21/9:12:13/10:4:14:19:20:31:33:
36,37:43^2:46,47/11:8/12:15/13:2:15:28:31:
32,33:32,33f:46:47/14:15/15:21:24:26^2/16:17^2:
37/17:6:23/18:17/19:37^3:38/20:19^2:21:33/21:
20:21:22:23:24:37,38/22:3:15/23:1:11:21/24:2^2:
5:6:10:12:19:25/25:8:10,11:12:15:25:26/26:5:7:
16/27:21^2/28^2:27/Rom1:10:13:20^3:20f/2:1:12-
12-15:18:27:28/3:9:12:17:21,22:23:30/4:1:4,5:9:
12:14:15:16:18:19/5:1^2:10/6:2,3:5:17:18/7:7^2/8
:9^2:12:23:24:35/9:16:20:21:22:23,24:32:33/10:2:
12:14:18/11:4^2:5:7^3:14:17:25^2:32:33/12:4,5/13:
4:7/14:1f:6:10/15:15,16^2:19^3:19f:21^2:22:24:26:
27f:28/16:3:17:25,26,27^2/1Co1:7:11:13:15:26:
30/2:8^2:13:14:16/3:1:2^2:4:10:11:15/4:3:5:6^3:7^3:
8:11^2:12^3:13^2:15^2:18:19/5:1:3,4^2/6:1:7:9,10^2:11:
12f/7:10:23:25:28:29:29f/8:7^2/9:2:4^2:5f^2:7^2:11:
12^3:15:17:19/10:13/11:2:6:10f:12:23:30/12:11:
12:13^2:23:25:28^2:29:30:31/13:3:10:11/14:12:23:
29,30:31:35:37/15:6:10:15:18:32:34:35:38:40:41
:42:43:46:48:49:52^2:53/16:2:5:17^2:18^2:20/2Co1:
3,4:12^2:13,14:19:20/2:5,6:10/3:2:18/4/5:1:2:10:
12:13,14/6:5:6^2:7^2:9:10:11:14/7:2:3:4^3:9:11:14:
16/8:2^2:6:7:11:12^2:13:14^2:16:17:21:22:24/9:2:4:
5/10:6:10:13/11:6:8,9:13:16:19,20:23^3:26^3:27^4:
28/12:6:10:11^3:15:16:18:19:20:21^2/13:1:2:4:6:
11/Gal2:4:14:16^2:18:20^2/3:3:4:14:21,22:27/4:9:
15^2:16:20:21/5:6:13:21:24/6:4:11:15^2/Eph1:11:
15:16,17:18/2:5:8:9:13:16/3:6/4:1:4^2:6:7:11^3:

(HAVE Con't)
9:21:31/5:15,16/6:9^2/Php1:7^2:14^2:15:20:30/2:
5:27/3:8^2:10^2:16:18/4:10^2:11^2:12:14:17:18/Col
:4:5:9:23/2:1^2:2^2:10^2:18^2:23/3:3:5:12/4:1:6:8:
1:16/1Th2:6:10:15/3:9/4:6:13:14/2Th1:10:11/
:1:10^2/3:9/1Ti1:6:9:16:19^2/2:7/3:2:4:12^2/4:6:
,10/5:3^2:4:9:14:15:16/6:8:10^2:12:21/2Ti1:12:
5/2:2:9^2:13:18^2:22^3/3:8^2:10:11:14^2/4:7^2/Tit1:1^2
3:6^2:9:11:14/3:8:10:12/Phm1:7:13/Heb:5,6:5,6
/2:1:2^2:7:8^2:11^2:15/4:3:8:13/5:5:6:12,13^2/6:4:6^2
7:19/8:1:7/9:11:15:26/10:2^3:5:7:9:10:18:22^2:
29:38:39/11:12:13:15/12:1:4:5:18:22:28/13:2^2:5
7:9:10:16:22/Jas1:21/2:6:11^3:13^2:14:15:17^2:18^2
3:7/4:2^3:9:12/5:3:4^2:5:6:13:20/1Pe1:8:11:22^2:
23/2:2,3f:4:5:9:10:24:25/3:16:21/4:1:3:5:13:17:
18/5:7:10:12^3/2Pe1:1:6:15:16^2:19^2/2:13:14:15:
18/3:1:15,16/1Jn1:1^2:2:3^2:7:8:10^2/2:7^2:12:13^2:
14:18^2:19:23:24:27:28/3:6:14^2:20^2/4:3:4:6:12:14
16:18/5:6,7,8:12^2:13^2/2Jn1:8:9^2:12/3Jn:3:4:6:7
13:14/Jud:4^2:11:12:15^2:19/Rev:4:9:19/2:2^3:3:9
13:14:15:20:24,25^2/3:8:8f:8^2:10:11:12:20/4:11/
5:10/7:3/9:4/11:6:17^2:18/14:4f:4:11^3/15:3,4/
16:6^2/17:2^2:8:10:12/18:3^2:3f:3:15:21/19:10/22:
14:15:16

4039

HAVEN'T

Gen27:36/Ex5:14/33:12/Lev10:17/Num16:14/
Deu8:4^2/29:5^2/Ju8:6/10:12/14:16^2/16:15/1Sa
13:12/14:41/26:15/2Sa7:7/1Ki1:27/3:11/17:
12/2Ki5:25/12:7/19:25/1Ch22:14/2Ch1:11^3/
15:3/24:6/Job35:2,3/Ps41:11/119:102,103/
Pro22:20,21/Is1:5,6/44:8/48:6^2/Jer2:23:35^2/3:
2/25:2,3/29:27/35:9/Eze34:4/Dan6:12/9:11/
Mal2:1/Mt8:10/12:3:5/20:6/25:9/Mk2:17/Lk
1:20/6:3/15:7/16:3/Jn6:36/14:5/16:24/20:17:
29/Act27:33/Rom9:19/1Co6:19/14:2/2Co1:23
/8:12/Php3:12/1Ti1:7/Rev3:4

73

HAVING

Gen2:2/19:31/29:35/38:9/Ex13:17,18/22:19/
35:10-19/Lev13:9,10/15:24/Num5:27/6:9/8:7/
9:6,7/10:13/13:22/Deu17:20/22:13,14/Jos10:
21/Ju19:5:6/1Sa1:8^3/8:11/11/2Sa12:6/24:8/
1Ki20:38/Neh5:18/12:46/Job30:5:11/Ps49:13
/Pro1:31/Ecc7:4/8:9,10:15/Is56:5/58:13/Jer3:
23/13:21/Eze1:17/32:31/42:3/46:18/Dan11:
30,31/Mt6:31,32/7:19/16:8/Lk1:25/11:52/21:
36/Jn11:12,13/Act2:5/15:25/24:22f/28:28,29f
/Rom1:27/8:30/14:1/1Co7:2^2/10:27/15:24/
2Co5:4:15/7:1/8:11/Eph5:26f/Php2:18:20/3:5
/2Th2:1/1Ti3:2/2Ti:5f:13/Tit1:8/Heb4:4/6:8:
20f/9:14/Jas5:5/1Pe2:15/Rev1:13f/17:11

85

HE

Gen1:4,5^2:11,12:16:21,22^2:25:27:31/2:2:3:8:9:
19,20^2:21/3:1:6:15:16:20:22:23/4:9:17:20:21f:
22:22f:26/5:6,7,8:9,10,11:12,13,14:15,16,17:
18,19,20:21-24^3:25,26,27:28-31^2/6:3:6^2:7:9,10^3:
12,13/7:6:7/8:1:8:12:21/9:20,21^2:24,25^2:26,27/
10:9:11,12^2:15-19/11:6:10,11:12,13:16,17:18,19
:20,21:22,23:24,25:26:28:32f/12:5^2:8:9:11,12,13^3
:18/13:3,4^3:8:11^2/14:12:14:15/15:1:7/16:4:9-12^2
:13/17:14:17^2/18:1^2:2^2:3,4:7:8:18:33/19:1^2:2:3^2:
7:9:14:27:28:33:35:37:38/20:2:4:5^2:7^2:9,10:16^2/
21:1:4,5:10:13:17:20,21:28,29/22:1:6:9:11:13:24
/23:3:10:11:16:17,18/24:7^2:10:11:12:15,16:21:
22:23:27:29,30:34:35:36:40:48:53^2:54:56:63^2:65:
67/25:5:6:20:23:25:28:34^2/26:7^4:12:13:14:16:20
:21:22^3:23:24:25:33:34/27:1^2:8,9,10^2:11,12:22:
23:25:31:36^2:41^2:42:45/28:5:9:11^2:12:13:16,17:
18:19/29:2:6:12,13^4:18:20:23:30:33/30:2^2:4:15:
16:20:35,36:39,40^2:41:43/31:1^2:4:5:7:8^2:13:15^3:
17-20^3:21:23:24:25:33:34:36,37:42/32:1^3:7:8:11:
13,14,15:16:17^2:18:20:22,23,24:25^2:29:30:31^2/
33:3^2:17:19^2:20/34:2:3:4^2:5:11:18,19^2:31/35:3:4
:7:13,14:16:22/36:6,7,8:24/37:6:9^2:10^2:13,14:15
:21,22:26,27:29:30:33:35/38:2:9^3:10:11^2:14:15:
16:17:18^2:20:21:22^2:26:29^2:30/39:1:2:4:6^3:7:8:9^2
:10:11:12^3:13:14,15^2:18:19:20/40:1:7:9,10:16^2:
20^2:21:22/41:1:5^2:8^3:9:12:13:14:17:25:28:38:43:
45:45f:45:46^2:51:52:55^3/42:1:7^2:8,9:12:17:23^2:
24^3:25:28:38/43:3,4,5:7^3:14:16:17:18:23:27^2:28:
29:30^2:31^2:33:34/44:1:2^2:5:6^2:12:16:17:20:25:31
/45:1^2:2:3:4^2:5:8:14:15:22^2:23:24:26^2:27:28/46:
2:34/47:1:2:10:14:22:28:29/48:1:2:8:10^2:14^2:15:
16:17^2:18:19:20/49:9:10f:11:15^2:17:19:23:27:
29,30:33/50:2:5:6:16,17^2:20:21:22:23:24/Ex1:9:
21:22/2:1:6^2:10^2:11^2:13^3:14:15^2:18:19:20:22:23:
25/3:3,4:6:10:16:20^2/4:2:3:4:6:7:11:14^3:16:21/5
:1:6:22:23/6:1^2:8,9:11/7:2:9:13:14:15:22:23/8:
12:15:19:20:24:27/9:7^2:10:12:27:34/10:8:19:20:
26:27/11:1^3:8f:10/12:23^2:23f:25:27^3:44/13:4,5:
9:11:17,18:19/14:4:8/15:1^2:2^2:4:21/16:4:7,8,9:
23:32/17:5,6:10f:11/18:2:3:5,6:10:11:14:21:25/
19:8:9:13:15/20:11:17/21:2f:2:3^6:4^2:6:8^3:9^2:10^2:
11:12:13:16:18:19:19f:19^2:23:27:30f/22:1:3^3:4^2:
5^2:7:8:9:11:13:15^2:16:17:27^2/23:2,3:21^3/24:4:5:
6:7^2:11:14:16/28:3:29:30,31^2:35^3:37,38/30:7:8^2:
26,27/31:4:5:18/32:5:11:12:17:19:20^2:21^2:26:27
:29/33:7:8:9/34:5,6:9:14:28:29:32:33:34^4:35^2/
35:32:33^2/36:17:20:31,32:37/37:4:6:7:10:13:
15,16:17:23,24:26:29/38:3:4:9:23/40:19:20:21:
22:24:25:28:30:33/Lev1:6,7f:14:15,16,17/2:2:8/
3:1:13/4:3:4:8:18:20:23:24:26:27:28^2:29:31:32:
33/5:1:2:3^4:4^3:5:6:7^2:9:10^2:11^3:12:13:15:16^4:
17,18^2:19/6:3:4,5^5:6:7:11/7:20:21:30:36/8:6:7:8
:11^2:12:14:15,16^3:18:20:21:24^2:25:30:33:34:35^2/
9:9:10:11:12^2:13:14:15^3:16:17:18^2:19:21/10:3:16
:17:19:20/11:25/13:1:7^2:11^2:12:13:28:31:33:34^2:
34f:37:40:41:44:45:46:52:53:56:57/14:4:8:9:10:
13:17:21^3:22^2:23:25:27:28^2:30^2:36^2:37:38:41:44:
45:48:49:50:53/15:4^2:8:9:13:14:16:24/16:1:3:4:6
:7:12:13^2:14:15^2:16:17:18^2:20^2:21:23^2:24:25:32/
17:15:16^2/19:14/20:3:9:11:15:17:18:20:21/21:
2,3:4:7^2:8:12:13:14,15^2:14,15f:21^2:22:23/22:3:6:
7:8:10:14^2:16/23:9,10,11/24:12:15,16^2:23/25:
13:26:27:29:37:40:41:48:49^2:51^3:52^3:53:54^2/27:
1:8^2:10:11,12:13:19:20^2:22:23:29:31/Num1:1:
17,18,19f/5:7^3:8:14:18:19^2:21,22:24:26:30/6:3,4^2
:5^3:6,7:8:9^3:10:11:12:13:14:20:21^3:24,25,26/7:1:
14:15:42-47:66-71:89/8:2^2:21/9:1:6,7:8:13:14:
18/10:36/11:2:18:24:33/12:1f:2:3,4^2:5:7,8^2:9:11
/13:30/14:8:9:16^4:24^2:43/15:27:28:30:31^2:33/
16:3:4:5^2:10:26:31:36,37:38:47:48/17:7:8^2:10/
18:1:16/19:1^2:5:7:8:12^3:16^2:19:20^2/20:7:9:10:13
:14^2:16:20^2:24/21:1:2:8:9:23:27-30:31,32/22:2,3^2
:5,6^2:7:10:11^2:15:16,17:18:19:21:22,23f:22,23:25
:30:31^2:36:37:41/23:3,4^2:7-10:14:17:18-24^8/24:
1^3:3-9^2:10:15-19^4:21,22:23,24/25:4:7:8^2:10,11:
12,13^4/26:64,65/27:3,4^3:6,7:9:10:11:14:21/30:1
:5:7:12^2:14^2:15^2/31/32:10,11^4:15:42/33:38,39^2/
35:11:18:19:21^2:25:31/Deu1:11^2:17:19,20,21:30
:31:34,35^2:36^2:38:45/2:22:30/3:1:26:28/4:3:5:9:
10:13:15:21,22^3:24:30:31^2:35:36^2:37^2:38:
44,45,46/5:4:5^2:16:21:22:22f:22:25:32/6:
10,11,12^2:17:23^3:24^3/7:1^2:4:6:7:8^3:10:12:13^3:15:
19:21:22^3:23:24/8:3^2:10:15:16^2:17:18/9:4:5:8:
10,11^2:12:19:23^2:28^4/10:2^2:4^2:9:11:12,13:15^2:17
:18^2:21^2/11:3:4:14:15:17:25/12:4,5:7:8:11:14:18
:29:31/13:2:5:10:17/14:2:23/15:2:4,5:6^2:10:16^2:
17:18/17:1:11:15:16:17^2:18^2:19^2:20/18:2:6,7:8^2:
15:18:22^2/19:5:6,7^2:8^2:9:16^2:19/20:4^2/21:15:16^2
:17^2:20/22:16:19^2:22:23,24:28,29^2/23:1:5:11:13:
14:15,16/24:1^2:5:12,13:14,15^3/25:7:8/26:2,3:
6,7:8:11:17^2:18:19^2/27:17:18:19:20:21:22:23:24:
25/28:9^2:11:12^2:13:21:22^2:27:28:36:47,48:55^3:
60/29:2,3:6:12:13^3:19:24:25:29/30:3^2:4:5^2:6:9:
10:20/31:2:4:6:8:9:15:23:25/32:3:4^3:6^2:8:9:11:
14:16:20:36:40,41/33:2:3:9:12:13:14:16:17:20:
21^3:24:26:27^2:29^2/34:7^2:11,12^2/Jos1:10,11:
12,13:17,18^2/2:3^2/3:5:10/4:21:24/5:6^3:14/6:17
/7:15^2:17:24/8:5:11,12,13:14:29^2/9:9/10:1:2:4:
18:26/11:1:12:15^2:21:23/12:5/13:12:33^3/14:1^2:
13,14/15:13:15:16:18,19^2/17:3/19:50^4/20:3:4:6^2
/21:43:44/22:4^2:7,8:22,23/23:2:3:4,5:9:10:15,16^3
/24:9:17:18:19^2:20^2:23:29:30:33/Ju1:7:13:14:24
:25/2:10:12-14:15^2:18:20:21/3:8:9:10^2:15:16^2:
17,18,19^4:20:24:25:27^2:28:31/4:2,3:13:14:18:19:
20:21^3:22:24/5:23:25:27:30/6:8:10^2:11:19:22:27^2
:30:34:35:38^2:40/7:8,9:11:12,13:15^2:16:17^2/8:5^2
:8:9:14^2:15^2:16:16f:17:20:25:29:30:31:34:35/9:2:
4^2:5:7:18:26:28^2:30:31:33:36:38^2:43^2:47,48^3:54^2:
55/10:1:2^3:5:7,8:16/11:3:13^3:20:25:29:30,31:33:
35^3:36:38:39:39f/12:5^2:6^2:7:9,10^4:11,12:14^2:15/
13:5^2:6^4:7^3:11:12:16:17:23:24:25/14:1:2^3:6^3:7^2:8^3
:9^4:12:16:17:18:19^2/15:2:3:4:5:8^2:10:14:15:16,17
:18^2:19^2/16:2^2:3:4:8:9:11:12^2:13:14^2:16,17^2:18^2:
20^2:21:25,26:30^3:31/17:2:3:4,5^2:6:7,8^2:9/18:4^2:
15,16:18:20:26/19:3:4:6:7:9:16:17^2:21^2:23^2:27:
28^2:29^2/20:4/21:25/Ru1:9/2:4,5:8,9:14:21:22/3
:2^2:3:4^2:6,7:8:9:10:13^2:14:15-18^3/4:1^2:6f:8:13:14
:15^2:16,17/1Sa1:2:4:5^2:14:24:27:28/2:1:3:7^2:8^2:
9:10^3:11:15:22^2:26^3:28/3:2,3:4,5^3:6:8:9^2:13:15:
16,17:18:21,4:1/4:3:16:18^3/6:4,5/7:3:12:16:17^3
/8:11:13:14:15:16:17:20/9:1:2:3:6^3:12,13^3:16:17
:26,27/10:10:12f:13:15:16^3:21^2:22^3:23:25:27/11
:5^2:6:7^2:8:9/12:1:2:6:7:8:9:12:22^2:24/13:1f^2:2:
3,4^2:8:9:10:13:14^2:15/14:1^2:10:27^3:39:45:47^3:48:
52/15:6:8:11^3:12^2:13:18:20:22:23:26:29^3:32:35^2
/16:2:4:5^2:10,11:12:13:18^2:19:21/17:4-7^2:8:11f:
14,15:20:23^2:25:26^2:27:28^2:30:33^2:34:36:37:
38,39^2:40:43^2:47^2:50,51^2:55:55f/18:5^2:8:10^2:14:
15,16^2:20:21:22:25:27:28:29/19:2:4^3:5:6:7:9,10:
11:14:15:17:20:21:22:23:24/20:1:2^2:3:7^3:12:13^2:
16:17^2:23:26:28,29^3:30:32^2:33:34:36:39:41^2/21:
1^2:2:8^2:10:11^2:13^2/22:6:7:9,10:14:17^2:19:21:22/
23:7^2:9:11:13:14,15:16:19^2:22^2:23:24,25:26/24:1
:2:4:6:9,10^2:12:14:15^3:17:19/25:2:5:10^2:13:14:21
:25^2:30,31:35:36:37,38^2:37,38f:39^2/26:10:11:19:
24/27:2,3:4:8:11^2:12/28:3:5,6^2:7,8^3:10:14^2:15:
17^3:18:20^2:21:23^2/29:3:6/30:7:11,12:13:16:26^3/
31:3,4:5^2/2Sa1:1:3:7^2:8:9:10:10f^2:13:15^3:21:24/
2:5:10,11:19^2:20^2:23^3:28:30^2/3:2:7:8:11:16^3:18:
19:21:24,25^3:26:27:28:35,36^2:37/4:1:4^2:5:10/5:
4,5^3:8:9:20^3:23/6:7^2:10:12:13:17:18:20/7:13:14^2
/8:2^2:3:4:5:6:8:10^2:11,12:13:14/9:1^2:2^2:4:8:9:
10,11^2/10:5:7,8:9^2:10:17/11:2^3:3:4:5:7:8^2:9:10:
13^2:16:19,20,21:23:25/12:3^3:4:5:6^2:11:17:18^2:19^3
:20:23^2:24:31^2/13:2^2:8:9^2:10:11:13:14^3:15^3:16:
17,18^2:21-24^3:25^2/14:2,3^2:5,6:10:11:12:14f:20:
24^2:26:27:29^2:32^3:33/15:2:3:7,8:10^2:11:12^2:14:
16:25,26^2:30/16:1:3^2:4:6:7,8:13:16^2:21/17:2,3^2:
5:9^2:14:15:16^3:18:21:23:27/18:4:9:14^2:18^2:23:24
:25^3:26^2:27:28:29:32:33/19:8,9,10^2:13:15:21:23:
24,25:26:31,32:34:39:42/20:3^4:5:6:8,9,10^4:17^2:
22/21:7:8^2:12,13,14^2/22:1:3:4:7:10^2:11:15:17^2:
18:20:25:31:33:34:35:42:51/23:4:5^2:5f:8:9:10:
11,12:16^2:17:18,19^4:20:21^2:23/24:10^2:16:17:20:
21/1Ki1:1:3,4:5:6:7:9^2:10:15:16:19^2:24:25^2:33:
37:42:44,45:46,47:48:52^4:53^2/2:1:4:5:8^2:11:13:
15:17^2:19:20:22^3:23,24:25:28:29:30:31:32:34:38:
40^3:42/3:1^2:3:5:6:11:15^4:25/4:31^2:32:33/5:1^2:
2,3^2:5:7:8:10:12/6:1:11,12:21,22^2:23-28f:33/7:8^2
:13:14^2:15:16-22:27-30:38:41-46/8:12,13:15^2:16
:17:18:20:21:25:31:32:54,55^2:57^2:58^2:59/9:1:
11,12^3:13:16:19:20,21:24^2:25^2:26/10:3f:4:5:9:13
:16,17:18/11:3:7:9,10:16,17,18:19:21:22:24^2:
27,28^2:33^2:40:42/12:2,3,4^3:6:8:9:13,14:15:16,17:
20^2:21:25:31:32,33^3/13:2:3:4^2:6:10:11:12:14^3:
16,17^2:21,22^2:24,25:26^2:27:28:30:31:33/14:4:5:6^2
:13:15:16:20:21^3:26:31/15:3:8^2:11:12:13^2:15^2:19
:20:21:23:24^2:25:26^2:27:29^2:34^3/16:4-7^2:8:11^2:
18:19^2:26:28:30^2:31:32:33:34^2/17:5:6:10^4:11:19^2
:21:22:23/18:7:10:12:17:21:22:25:27^3:30:31:32:
33^3:40:43:46/19:1:3:4^3:5^2:6^2:8:9:10:13:14:19:21^2
/20:2,3:7^4:9:14:15:26:31:32^2:33:36:37:39/21:2:4
:6:13:18:21:22^2:26^2:27:29/22:4:5^2:8^2:15:18:22:
24:28:34:35:39:42^2:43^2:44:46:50:51:52,53^2/2Ki1
:2^2:4,5^4:7:8:9/2:5:12:13,14^2:17:18:20:21:23^2:24:
25/3:1:2^2:3:11^2:16:26^2:27/4:1^5:3:7:8^2:10^2:11,12^2
:13:14^2:15,16:18:19:20^2:23:29:31:33:34:35:36^2:
38^2:39:41/5:1^3:3:7^2:8^2:10:11^2:12:13:14:15:16:17
f:21^2:22^2:23:24:25^2/6:1:3:5:7:8:10:11:13:15:17:
18:19:21:26-30^4:32/7:17:20/8:1:6:8,9^2:10:11:14^2
:15:17^2:18^2:19^2:21^2:24,25:26^2:27^2:28:29^2/9:1:4^2:
5^3:10:11^2:12^2:15:16:17:18:19:20^2:21:24:27:32:33
:34:36^2/10:8:9,10^4:11f:12:13^3:14:15^3:17^2:20,21:
22:25:29:31:32,33:35/11:4:5:10:17:19^2:21/12:1:
3:17:18:21/13:2^2:3:9,10:11^2:14:15:16,17^3:19:23/
14:2:3^2:4:5^2:6:7:8:14:16:19:20:22:24:27^3:28^2:29/
15:3:4:5:7:9:16:18^2:19,20:22:24:28:29^2:30:32,33:
34,35^2:38/16:2:3^2:4:6:10^2:10f:10:14:15^2:18^2:20/
17:4:13^2:15:18:20:21:26:34:39/18:4:5^2:6:7^2:8:12:
16^2:18:22:27:29:31,32/19:1:2:7^2:8^2:9:10:15:32^2:
33^2:37/20:3^2:5:7:11:12:19:20^2:21/21:1:3,4,5^2:6^2:
7:11:16:18^2:21^2:22:26/22:1:8:9,10:11:12,13/23:
3^2:4:5:6^2:7:8^2:11:12^3:13:14^2:15^3:16^2:17:19^2:20^3:
29:30:31,32:33:34^3:36,37/24:2:3,4^2:6:16:17:
18,19/25:6^2:7^2:9:10:28:29^2/1Ch2:16:34,35^2:42/
3:4^3:5:17,18/4:8:10:21-22/5:1:6:9:20/6:31/7:16:
23/8:8,9,10/9:10,11:19:35,36,37/10:4:13/11:
5,6:8:11:13:14:15:17:18,19^2:20:21^2:22:23:24,25^2
:26-47^2/12:1:18:19:20:21:22:24-37/13:2:10^2:11^2
:13/14:1:2:3:8:11^2:16/15:1:12/16:3:4:14:15:17:
22:23:25:33:34/17:1:12:13/18:2:3:4^2:6^2:7:8:10:
11^2:13/19:4:5:6:7:8:10:17,18^3/20:1:2:3:3f^3:6,7/
21:1:2:4^2:5:6^2:15^2:16:19,20:21:26:28:30/22:6:8:9
:10^2:11:12:13:18^2/23:1:2:13:17:25/24:3/26:10:
23,24/27:2,3:4:5,6:7:9:23:23f:24/28:2:4:5:6:7^2:9:
10:12:12f:13:15:16^2:17:18:20^3/29:1:4,5:19:23:25
:28/2Ch1:2,3^3:4:5,6^2:14/2:3:5:11:13:14^4:18/3:
14:16:17^2/4:1:2:6:7:8^2:9:11/5:13,14/6:1:4^3:9:10:
12,13^2:23:30/7:3^2:10:11^2:22/8:2^2:4:5:6^2:7,8:9:11^2
:12:14^3:17,18/9:2:3:4:8^2:15:17:26:27:31/10:2,3^3:
4:6^2:8,9^2:13^2:14:18/11:11:15^2:20:21^2:22:23/12:1
:4:7:12:13:14^2:16/13:1:7:8:12:20:21/14:3:5:7:
9,10:11/15:2^4:4:8^3:9:15:16:18^2/16:3:5:8:9:10:12:
13,14^3/17:2:3:4:5:6:7,8,9^3:13/18:2^2:6,7^3:8:14:17^2
:21:22:23:27:31:32:33:34/19:2:4:5:6:11/20:3:15:
20:21:31^2:32^2:33/21:1:3,4^3:5^3:6:7:11:19:20^4/22:
2^2:3:4:8:9^2:12/23:15,16,17:18/24:1^2:3:5:15:16^2:
20^3:22:25/25:1^2:2:3^2:4:5,6^3:14:15:24^2:27/26:2:3:
4:5:6^2:8:9:10^3:11:15^3:16^2:17,18:19:20:23^2/27:1^2:

(HE Con't)
3:4:5:6:8[3]:9[2]/28:1[3]:2:3[2]:4:9[2]:19:20:23[3]:25:27/29
:1[2]:3:4,5:8:19:21:25,26/30:6:8:17,18,19/31:3:4:
21/32:5:6:7:8:11:17:19:21:24:25:27:28,29[3]:30[3]:
31:32:33/33:1[2]:2:3:4,5[2]:6:7:12:14[2]:15[2]:16:19:
20,21[3]:23[2]/34:1[2]:2:3[3]:4:5:6:7[2]:8[2]:10,11:14:17:18[2]
:19:31:32/35:2:3:21[2]:22[2]:23:24,25[2]:26/36:2[2]:3:5[2]
:8:9[2]:10:11[2]:12:13[3]:15:18:22,23/Ez1:1:8/2:61:
69/3:11/5:12/6:11/7:6:21[2]/8:18[2]:21:23/10:11/
Neh2:1:18/3:8:12:14:15[2]:16/4:1[3]/6:5,6[3]:7:10[3]/
7:63/8:1[5]:15/9:5:8:18/11:22,23/13:7:26/Est1:8
:10:13-15[2]:21/2:1[2]:4:6:7:9:11:12,13,14:17[2]:18/3
:1:2:3,4[2]:8/4:1:2:4:5/5:2[2]:5:9[3]:10:11:12:13:14/6:
1[2]:4:6:7,8:11/7:7[2]:8[2]/8:1:2:7[2]/9:4:12[2]:24,25[2]/10
:3[2]/Job1:2,3[3]:4:8:9:10[3]:18:21/2:3[2]:4,5:10/3:2,3/
5:9:10:12:13:18[2]:19:20/6:4/7:2[2]/8:4:6:14:15:16:
18[2]:19:21/9:3:5:6:7:8:9:10:11[2]:12:12f:16:17:18:
19:22:23:24:28/11:5:6[2]:8:10:11[2]/12:6:7,8,9:13[2]:
14[2]:15[2]:17:18:19:20:21:22:23[2]:24,25/13:7:9:15f
/14:2[2]:5:6:11,12:14:20,21[3]/15:21:22[2]:23,24[2]:
25,26:29:30:31:32[2]/16:9:12[2]:14:21/17:6/18:7:
8,9:10:11:14[2]:16:18:19/19:9:10[2]:11:12:13:16:25:
27/20:7[2]:8:12:14:15[2]:17[2]:19[2]:20[3]:21:22:23:24:26
/21:17:21[2]:23,24:29:30-32/22:4:13[2]:14[2]:18:25:
27:29/23:4,5:6[2]:9:10[3]:13[2]:14[2]:16,17/25:2:4/26:
8:9:10:12:13:14/27:10:14:17:19:20:21:22/28:11f
:23,24:25:26:27[2]:28/29:3/31:4:14:15:37/32:1:2:
3:4:5[2]:11,12[2]/33:11:13[2]:16:21:26:27:28:30/34:
7,8:9:11:13:17:19[2]:21:25[2]:28:29,30[3]:33/35:12:13
:14,15[3]/36:5:6:7:9:10:13:15:16:19:23:24:27:30:
31:32[2]/37:6:11:12:13:18:23[2]:24/39:9:10:11:21-
21-23[3]:24:25[3]/40:9:15:19:20:21:23/41:3:4:18:22
:25:29:30:31,32[3]:34[2]/42:7:12:13,14f:17/Ps2:4:5
/3:1:4:7:8/4:3/6:9/7:10[2]:11:12[2]:16:17/9:7,8:9:
12[2]:16/11:4[2]:5[2]:6:7/12:3,4:6[2]/13/14/16:5[2]:6:7[2]:
8/18:2[4]:6:7:9:10:11:14:16[2]:17:19[2]:24[2]:30[2]:31:32:
33[2]:34:41:47:48[2]/20:2:3:4:5[2]:6[2]/21:1:2:4:7[2]/22:
24[3]:31/23:2,3[3]/24:2:2f:3/25:9:10:13:14:15/27:5[2]
:14[2]/28:5[2]:6:7[2]/29:10:11[2]/30:6,7:11[2]/31:21/32:
6[2]/33:4:5:6:7:9:10:12:13,14,15[2]:18,19:20[2]/34:4[2]
:5:8:9:15:17:18:19:22/35:9/37:4:5:6:12,13:17:19
:21:23:28:30,31:34:35,36:37:39:40/39:5,6:11[2]/
40:1:2:3[2]/41:1:2[2]:3:5/42:11[3]/43:5:5f:5/44:21/
45:10,11/46:5:7:8:11/47:2:3:4:8:9/48:1:14/49:
8,9f:15:19/50:3:4[2]:6/53:1/54:4:5/55:16:17:18:
20:22[2]:23/57:3[2]/58:9:10f/59:10[2]/60:1:6,7[2]:9,10[2]
:12/62:2:6:7:8:12/63:1/64:5:9/65:6:7:9[2]:10:
11,12/66:2:6:7[3]:9[2]:16:18:19[3]/68:3:5[3]:6:18[2]:19:
20[2]:21/69:35/70:4/72:12:13:14:15:15f/73:26[2]:
27:28/75:6,7/76:2:3:11:12/77:1:2:7:9[2]:11/78:4:
5:13:14:15:19,20:23[2]:24:25:26:27:28:29:33:34:
38[2]:39:42:43:44:45:46:47:49[2]:50:51[2]:52:53:54[2]:
55:56:59:60[2]:61:62:66:67:68:69:70:71,72/81:5:7:
16[2]/82:1:1f/84:11[2]/85:8/87:1:4:6[2]/89:7:18:20:
24:25:26:29/90:11/91:2[2]:3:4:11:14[2]:15/92/93:1
/94:6,7:9:10[4]:12,13:18:23/95:4:5:7[2]/96:2:3:8:10[2]
:13/97:10/98:1:2,3:8,9/99:1:4[2]:6:7:9/100:3:5/
102:16:17[2]:18:23/103:2:3[2]:4[2]:5:6:7:8[2]:9:10:12:
13:14:19/104:3:10:13:19:20:31:34[2]/105:1:5,6[2]:7
:8,9:12:14:14f:14:15:16:17:21:22:28:32:34:36:39:
40:41:42:43:44/106:15:23:26[2]:33:40:41,42:43:
44:45/107:2:3:6:7:9:12:13:14:16:19:20:25:28:29:
30:33:35:36:38:41/108:7:8:13/109:11:15:16:17[2]:
18[2]:31/110:5:6[2]:7/111:4:5[2]:6:7:9/112:3:4:7[2]:8:9[2]
/113:4:6:9/114:8/115:3[2]:9[2]:10[2]:11[2]:12[2]:16/116:
1:2:5[2]:6:8:12:15/117:2/118:5:6:7:14[2]:29/120:1/
121:3,4[2]:5:6:7:8/127:5/129:3,4/130:5:7:8/132:
18/135:3:5:6:7:8:9:10:21/136:1:11,12:23:25/
137:9f/138:6[2]/140:12/144:1:2[4]/145:4:9[2]:17:18:
19[2]:20/146:4:6:7:8:9[2]/147:2:3:4:5:8:9:13:14:15:
16:18:19:20/148:5[2]:6:13:14/149:4,5:9/150:1/
Pro1:2:3:4/2:7,8[2]:9/3:6:9,10:11,12:24,25,26:29:
32/4:4[2]:5/5:21:23[3]/6:12,13[2]:14[2]:15:28:29:30[2]:
31[2]:32:34/7:20:21[2]:22:23/8:13:22:27,28,29[3]:31:
34/9:7,8[2]:9[2]/10:3:14:20:22f/11:24,25:29:30f/12
:4:11f:15:27[2]/13:22/14:6[2]:15[2]:17:29:35/15:12:
15:28:29/16:11:17:25/17:5:27,28/18:2:15/19:7:
8:17:25:28/20:11[2]:14[2]/21:1[2]:13:20:25,26:30/22:
6[2]:11:13:16:22,23:29/23:1:9:10,11/24:11,12[2]:17
:24/25:8,9,10:14:21,22/26:4,5[2]:13:14:15:16:
24,25,26[2]/27:7:14:18:19[2]/28:3:13[2]:16/29:9:15:
17:21:24/30:5:6:10:29,30,31[2]/31:23:28/Ecc2:
20-23/3:12:13:18/4:8[3]:10:14:16/5:1:6,7:9:10:12:
15:16:17/6:2:3:12/7:1/8:5:6,7[2]:16,17/9:1:12[2]:
15:16[2]/10:3:12,13:15/11:4f[2]/12:9[3]:10[2]/Sol2:4[2]:
6:8:9:16/5:2[2]:6:11/6:2:3/7:10/8:4:7[2]:11/Is1:1:
10/2:3:21/3:2:7:13:16:17/5:2[4]:7[2]:16:25:26/6:1:
7:9:11/7:4:12/8:14,15:17:20/9:4[2]:7[2]:18/10:5,6:
7[2]:8:9:12:17:27:32:33:34/11:3:4:5:10[2]:12[2]:16[2]/
12:1[2]:2:4:5/14:1:24/16:4,5/18:5[2]:7/19:20[2]:22:
25/20:2/21:6,7[2]:6,7f:8,9/22:9,10,11:18:21[2]:22:
23,24/23:11[2]:12/24:1/25:7:8[2]:9:11/26:3:5:6:15[2]
/27:7,8[3]:11/28:2:6:9:10:12:13:16:22:23,24:25:26
:27:28/29:8:10:11:12:15:16[3]:23f/30:3:5:10,11:
14:18[3]:19[2]:20[2]:25:26:28/31:2[2]:4,5[5]/32:2[2]:6/33:
5:22/34:2:11:16[2]:17/35:4:5[2]/36:2[2]:7:8,9:12[3]:13:
14/37:1:2:4:7[2]:8,9:14:16,17:30:34[2]:38/38:2:3:6:
9:15:21:22/39:1f:1:2/40:10[2]:11[2]:14[2]:15:21:22:
23:24:29/41:3[2]:4:6:8:25[2]:26/42:1:2[2]:3[3]:4:4f:5:13
:14[4]:15[2]:16[3]:21[2]:24/43:25/44:12:13[2]:14[3]:15[3]:16:
17[3]:20[2]:28[2]/45:1[2]:7:13:18[2]/46:11/48:14[2]:21[2]/
49:1:2:3:7:14/50:4:8/51:1:12/52:9:12:13:14,15:
14,15f/53:2:3[2]:4:5[3]:7[5]:8[2]:9[2]:10[2]:10f:11[4]:12[4]/54:
5/55:4:6:7[2]/56:11/57:13/58:8:9/59:1[2]:2:9:11[2]:
16[2]:17[2]:18:19:20/60:19/61:1:2:3:10/62:3:6,7/
63:7[2]:8[2]:9[3]:10:12:14/65:21,22/66:3/Jer1:7:9:14
/2:17:35/3:1/4:7:11,12[2]:27/5:12/6:9/8:4,5[4]:22/
9:21/10:12:13[3]:16:17/11:16/13:3:15:16/14:1:19
/16:14,15/17:6[2]:8:10[3]:11/18:3:4[3]:18/19:14[2]/20:
2:3[2]:4:10:13:17/21:1f:10/22:8:12:13f[2]:15:16:18[2]
:19:28/23:5,6:8:18:20:35:37/25:30:31:38/26:11[2]
:12[2]:13[2]:16:18:19:21/27:8:12:19,20,21/28:1:4f:9
:11/29:3:4:22:28:32/30:21[2]:24/31:11:26/32:5:
6,7:8[2]:28/33:10,11:15:20,21/34:1:2:3:9:21/35:7:
18,19/36:12:16:18:24,25[2]:30:32/37:1:4[2]:12:13[2]:
14:18:21/38:5:8:9[2]:10:11[2]:13:16:27/39:5:7:10:
11,12[3]:15/40:2,3[2]:5:9/41:6[3]:9[2]:10[2]:18/42:4:5:8:
12:21/43:10[2]:11[2]:12[3]:13/44:22[2]/48:12:32:44[2]/
49:14/50:34:40[2]/51:5:7:12[2]:15:16[3]:17[3]:19:34,35
:44/52:1[2]:2:3:10:11:15:16:18:19:26:29:30:33:34/
Lam1:13[3]:14[2]:16/2:1:2[2]:3:4[2]:5:6:7[2]:8:9:17[4]/3:2:
3:4:5:6:7[2]:8:9:9f:9:10:11:12:15:16[2]:32:33:42/4:
11:16/Eze1:27,28[2]/2:1:1f:2:3:9,10/3:1:3:4:10:
20:21[2]:22:24/4:16/8:2[2]:3:5:6:7:8:9:12:13:14:14f:
15:16:17/9:1:7:9[2]/10:2:5/12:2:12[2]:12f[2]:13:13f[2]:
13/16:2/17:5:12,13[2]:16:18:19:20/18:4:9:13:14:
17[2]:18:19:21:22:24[2]:26[2]:27:28[3]/19:6[2]:7:9/20:11:
21:49/21:21:23/22:1:28/23:22/24:2:24/25:1/26
:8[2]:9/27:1/29:13:18f:19:20:20f/30:11:24:25/32:
17:31[2]/33:1:3:4:5[3]:6:8:9[2]:12[2]:13:14[2]:15[4]:16:18:
19:22:24/34:23/35:1/36:4:20/37:1:3:4:7:9:10:
11[2]/38:2,3f/39:15,16/40:2:4:5:6[2]:13:14:19:20:
23:24:27:28[2]:32:35:45:47:48,49/41:1:3:4:5:13:22
/42:1:13:15[2]:16-20/43:1:3:18/44:2:3[2]:4:9:22[2]:23
:26[2]:27[2]/45:23:25/46:2:5[3]:6:7[5]:12[2]:17[2]:18:19,20
:21,22:24/47:1:2:3[2]:4:6:8/48:19/Dan1:1[2]:3,4[2]:8f
:8:8f:10[2]:18,19/2:1[3]:16:17:20:21[2]:22[3]:24:28:29:
47:48/3:2:14:17:18:19:24:26:28/4:1:3:14:17:25:
29:31:32:35[2]:37/5:2,3,4[2]:7:9:11[2]:12[2]:19[3]:21[6]:29
/6:3:4:10[2]:13:14:16:18:19:21:22:23:27[3]/7:1[2]:9:
13[2]:14:16:17:23:25/8:7[3]:10:11:15:17[2]:18:19:24[3]:
25[4]/9:13:14[3]:27/10:1:9:11:12:16:19[2]:20,21/11:2
:3:7:8[3]:12:13:16:17:18:19:20:21:23:24[3]:25:29[2]:
30,31[3]:32:36:37[3]:38:39[2]:41:43:44[2]:45[2]/12:7:8[2]:9
/Hos1:4,5f:4,5:7f:21,22/5:6:13/6:1[4]:2:3/7:4:5:9[2]
:10/9:9/10:3:12/11:2:3:4/12:3[4]:4[3]/13:1[2]:13:15[2]
/Joe2:13[3]:14[2]:17:19:21:23:32/3:16/Amo1:1:2:
11[2]/3:12/4:2:13/5:6:9:14/6:10[4]/7:1:3:4:7:8:10:
11/8:2/9:6/Ob1:1/Jon:3[3]:6[2]:9,10[3]:12/2:2/3:1:6
:10/4:2:5[2]:8[2]/Mic1:3[2]/2:2:13f/3:4/4:2[2]:3:6:9/5:
4[2]:5[2]:6/6:2[2]:7[2]:8[2]/7:7:9/Nah1:2[3]:3[3]:7[2]:8[2]:9[2]:10:
12:14:15[2]/2:13/Hab3:3:4f:6[3]:19/Zep1:3:7:7f:
12:18/2:11:13/3:5:17,18[4]/Hag2:14/Zec1:3:5,6[3]
:9:10:19/2:2:5:8:13/3:3:4:5,6,9/4:2:6:7f:9:13:14
/5:2:3:5:6:8[2]:11/6:5:12:12f:13/7:12/9:9[2]:10:15/
10:1/11:16[2]/13:5:6/Mal1:8:9:13[2]/2:6[4]:15:16:17
/3:1:2[3]:3[2]:4:16[2]/Mt1:19:20[2]:21:23:24/2:4[2]:7[2]:
14:16[2]:21:22[2]:23/3:3[2]:4:6:7[3]:11:12:14:16/4:2:3:
6:9:12,13[2]:18[2]:21[2]:23:24:25/5:1:3:19:25:31:32:
38:45/6:14,15:18:30:33[2]/7:9:10[2]:29/8:1:2:3:8,9[3]
:10:16:17:18:23:26/9:2:3:5,6:9:13:15:18[2]:22:24:
28:29:34[2]:35[2]:36:37/10:41/11:1:1f:2:9:11:14:18f
:20[2]/12:3:4:9:10:13[2]:15[2]:16:18[2]:19[2]:20[2]:22[2]:24[2]:
26:29f:43,44,45:48:49[2]:50/13:2,3[2]:4:8:11:12,13[3]
:21[2]:22:25:28:29:33:34,35[2]:36:37:44[2]:46[2]:47,48[2]
:52:53,54:56:58/14:1f:2[2]:5:7:9[2]:13[2]:14:18:19[2]:22
:23,24:26:27:30[3]/15:3:15[2]:24:26:30:36/16:2,3:7:
12:13:15:20[2]:21[3]:22/17:5:7:9:12[2]:13:15[2]:25[3]/18:
12[2]:13[2]:15:17[2]:25[2]:28:29:30:32:34/19:1:2:4:15[2]:
22[2]/20:2:3:4[2]:5:6:7:8:13:17:21:22:23:32,33/21:2
:9f:10:13:14:17[2]:18[2]:19[2]:23[2]:25:26:29[2]:30[2]:34:36
:40:41/22:1:3:4:5:8:11:12:18:20:21:31:34,35:41:
42:45/24:2:3:26:33f/25:12:14:15:20:21:29[3]/26:1
:7:18:19:20,21[2]:23:23f:24:27:36:37:38:39:40[2]:42:
43:44:45:47:48:53:55:70:72:74:75/27:3[2]:4:5:9:17
:18:19:23:24[2]:26[2]:34[2]:36:41,42,43[4]:47:60:64/28:
5:6[4]:7[2]:9:18/Mk1:2:4:5:6:8:10:12,13:15:16:19:
20:21:22:28:29,30:31[2]:34[2]:35:38:39:40:45[3]/2:1:2[2]
:5:7[2]:9,10,11:14[2]:16:17:19:20:25,26/3:2[2]:4:5[3]:9[2]:
12:13[2]:14,15:16-19[2]:20[3]:26[2]:30[2]:31,32[2]:33:34/4:
1[2]:3:8:10:11,12:21[2]:25:33:34[3]:36:39:40/5:3,4[3]:5:
18:19[2]:23:30:32:34:35:39[2]:40[2]:41,42/6:1:2,3[2]:5:
6[2]:7:8,9:10:14:15:16:17,18:20[4]:21:26:27:34[3]:38:
41[2]:45[2]:46:47:48[3]:50[2]:51:52:56/7:6,7:10:14:17[3]:
18:19:20:24[2]:29:31:34:36:37[2]/8:1:5:6[2]:8,9:10:12
:13:16[2]:24:25:26:27:29:31[4]:32[2]:34[2]:36/9:6[2]:7:9[2]:
10:12,13[2]:15:16:17[2]:20[2]:21[3]:25[2]:26:27:30,31[2]:32
:33:35:36[2]:38:41:42/10:1:1f[2]:1:4[2]:5:6,7:8:10:11[2]:
14:16[2]:17:21[2]:22[2]:28[2]:30:33:36:47:48:49/11:2:9:
11[2]:12:13[3]:15:17:18:20:27,28:30:31/12:1:2:5:6:7
:9[2]:12:13:16:17:20,21,22:27:28:35:36:37:38:41:
43,44/13:1:3,4:5:14f:20:34[2]/14:11[2]:12:13[2]:14:
15:20:21:23:24:32:33:34:35:36:37[2]:39:40:41[2]:43:
45[2]:51,52[2]:68:69:71[2]:72/15:9:10:14:15:23:28:31:
34f[2]:35:36:39[2]:41:44:45/16:6[2]:7[2]:9:10,11:12[2]:13
:14[2]:15:19/Lk1:15[3]:16:17[3]:19:21:22[3]:23:32:33:
38:45[2]:48:49:51:52:53:54[2]:55:60:63:64:68:69:70:
72,73:80[3]/2:4:5:10:21[2]:23:25:26[2]:29,30,31:32[2]:
34,35:41,42:44[2]:46,47:49:50:51/3:1:11:13:14:15:
16:17:18[2]:19,20:21:23-38/4:1:13:14:16[2]:17:
18,19[2]:20:21:23:30:31:32[2]:33:35:37:38[2]:39:41[2]:
42:43:44/5:1:2:3:4[2]:8:9:12[4]:14:16:17:21:22:
23,24:27/6:3:4:6:7:8[3]:10[2]:12:13:14,15,16:17,18:
20:35:39:40[2]/7:1:3:4:5:6,7,8:9:12:13:14[2]:17:19:
20,21,22:23f:24:27:28:33:33f:34:37:39[2]:40:42:44
:48:49/8:1:2[2]:4:5:8[3]:10:16:18[2]:19:21:22[2]:23[2]:24[2]
:25:27[2]:28[2]:29:37:39[2]:48:49[2]:50:52:54:55/9:2:3:
7:9:10:11[2]:16:18[2]:20:21:22:23:28:29:33:34:39:43
:45:47:49:51:52:59:59f/10:1:16:18:21:23:27:29:
31[2]:33[2]:34[2]:35[2]:39/11:1:2:5,6:7:8[2]:11:12:15[2]:17[2]
:23[2]:26:27:28,29,30:33:37,38[2]/12:1:7:16:17[2]:22:
28:31:36:37:38[2]:39:42,43,44[2]:45:47[3]:48:54:58/
13:1:2:6[3]:7[2]:10:11:13:14:17:18[2]:22[2]:23:24,25:27
/14:1[2]:5[2]:7[2]:10:11:12[2]:17:18:19:25:26[2]:28:29:30:
32:33/15:2:10:14:15:16:17[2]:20[2]:24:25[2]:26:27:29:
32[3]/16:5,6[2]:7:15:21:23:24:25:31f/17:2,3[4]:4:7,8,9[5]
:14:16[2]:22[2]/18:2:4,5:8:9:13:23[2]:27:31:34[2]:36[2]:37
:38:39:40[2]:41/19:3:4:5[2]:7:11:13[3]:15[2]:20[2]:24:25:
29:40:41[2]:42:45:47:48[2]/20:1[2]:2:3:4:5:6:9:10:11[2]:
12:16:18:19[2]:23:25:30:37,38[2]:37,38f:41[2]:45/21:
1[2]:3:8:29:37,38/22:4:5:6:10[2]:11:12:15:17[3]:19[3]:
20:36:37:38:39:40:41,42:44[3]:45:46:47:51:52:57:
60:61:67,68[2]:70/23:2:5[2]:6:8:9:20:22[2]:25[2]:35[2]:42:
46:47:50,51,52:53/24:6,7[4]:12[2]:17:19:21[2]:29:30:
31:32:33,34:35:38:40[2]:41:43:44:45:46:50/Jn1:1:
3[2]:8:10[2]:11,12[2]:15:16:18:19:20[2]:21:23:30:31:33[4]
:34:38:39[2]:42:43/2:4:5:7,8:9:10[2]:11:12:14:16:21:
22[2]:23[2]:24,25/3:1:5:8:16:23,24:26:30:31:32[3]:35/
4:3:4:5,6[2]:8:10:12:14:25[2]:32:39[2]:40,41:42:43,44:
46,47[3]:51:52/5:6[2]:9:18:19[2]:20:21[2]:23:27:32,33:
46:47/6:2-5[3]:6[3]:11:14:15:20:22,23:29:32:33:39:
41:42[3]:52:59:60:65:71/7:1:9:10:15:26[2]:27[3]:28:29
:35[2]:36:39:41,42[2]:46:48:50:51[2]/8:2[2]:3:7[2]:8:20:21
:22[2]:23:25:26:27:28:29[2]:39:42:44[4]:56/9:1:6[2]:7:9:
10:11:12[2]:15[2]:16:17[2]:18:19[2]:20:21:25:26[2]:30:31:
33:35:36:37:38/10:3:4:6:7[2]:12[2]:13:19:20:22,23:
29:34,35,36:39:42/11:4:6[2]:7:11:12,13:14:25:26:
28:33:34[2]:36:37,38:39:43:51:54:56/12:1:6[2]:15:
21f:33[2]:34:37[2]:40f:41[2]:50/13:1[2]:4:5:6:11[2]:12:22:
26:26f:26[2]:37/14:10:15,16[2]:17[2]:21:26:30/15:2[2]:
3:6:16:26/16:7:8[2]:8f:13[4]:14:15:17,18[2]:19:23/17:
1[2]:2/18:4,5[2]:6:7:8:9[2]:17:19:22:25[2]:28:30:33:34f:
38[2]/19:7[2]:8:9:11f:17:21:26f:26[2]:27:30:33:35f[3]:
38/20:6:8:9:15[2]:17:20:21:22:25:27:30,31/21:4:5:
6:7:12:17[2]:19:21:23/Act1:1:3[3]:4[2]:5:6:7:9:11[2]:18[3]
:20:21,22[2]/2:25:29[2]:30:32:33:34[2]/3:3:7,8[3]:10:11
:12:16:19:21,22[2]:26/4:9:32:36:37[2]/5:5:15:19:34:
35:36:37[2]/7:2:4:5:8:12:15:22:23:24:26[3]:27:31:36
:56:60[2]/8:6[2]:9,10,11[2]:13[2]:16:18:19:27[2]:30:31:32[3]
:38:40[2]/9:2[3]:3:4:8,9[3]:10:11:12:14:16:19[2]:20:21:
26[2]:28:29:33:34:39[2]:40[2]:41/10:2[2]:3[2]:4:9,10[2]:11:
15:17:21:23:27:31:33:35:38:39[2]:40,41:42:48/11:
5:13:14:15:16:17:23[2]:26[2]:29/12:3:5:6[2]:8:9:11:12:
13:17[2]:19[3]:20[2]:21:23[2]/13:6,7[2]:11:12:16:18:19,20
:22:24:25[2]:27:29:31:35:36:47/14:8:9[2]:12:16:17[2]:
20[2]/15:8[2]:9[3]:13/16:3:9:18:24:27:30:33[2]:34[2]/17:
2[2]:16[2]:17:18[2]:23:24[3]:25[2]:26[3]:27:30:31[2]/18:2,3[2]:
7:16:18:19[2]:20[2]:21[2]:22:23:25,26[4]:27:28/19:1:2:3
:8:9[2]:16:21:22[2]:25:33:34:35:41/20:2:3[3]:7[2]:
10,11,12[3]:14:16:17:18:36[2]:38[2]/21:9:11:13:14:28:
32:33[3]:34[2]:37,38:40/22:3:8:14:22:24:29:30/23:5
:6:17:20:21:22:25:27:28:34[2]/24:2:5:6[2]:8:22:23:
24:25[2]:26[2]:27/25:1:4:6:8:14:16[2]:20:24:25[2]/26:2:
32[2]/27:10:25:33:35:43[2]/28:4:6:7:15:16:17:20f:
23[2]:25:28,29f/Rom1:4:5:6,7:21/2:4[2]:6:7[2]:8:12-
12-15[2]:17:18:26:29/3:6[2]:7:18:21,22:25[4]:26[2]/4:1:
4,5[2]:7:9[2]:10[2]:11:12:13:18:19[2]:20[2]:21[2]:23:24:25/
5:2:9[4]:10[2]:13[2]:19[2]/6:4:5[2]:10[2]:16/7:2[2]:3[2]:
23,24,25/8:3:9:10f:11:18:23:24:27:29:30[2]:32[2]:33
:34:35:39/9:4[5]:5:8:13:16:17:18[2]:19:21:22:
23,24:25:33/10:4:5:10:19:21/11:2,3[2]:9:10:15:21[2]
:22:23:24:26:29:32/12:1[2]:19[2]:20[4]/13:4[2]:7/14:6[3]:
9:13:14:22:23[5]/15:3:9[2]:12:18[2]/16:5/1Co1:4:5[2]:8[2]

(HE Con't)
9^2:21:28:30^3:30f/2:11:16^2/3:7:10:15^3:19:22^3/4:
2:5:17^2/6:11:12f:14:16:19:20/7:7:12:13:18^3:19:
20:22:24:33:36^2:37^2:39/8:2^2:10^2:12/9:9^2:10^3:19:
22/10:1:3,4:5:13^3:22:30/11:4:21:24^2:25:26^2:27:
29^3:34^2/12:9:10^4:18^2:20:28/14:9^2:13^3:23:24^2:25 ^{2}
33^2:38f/15:3:4^2:5:6:14:24:25:28:38:45:57/16:10
11:12^3/2Co1:3,4^2:5:6,7:9:10:17:19^4:20^2:22^2/2:
5,6:7^2:11:13:14^2/3:4:6:7:17/4:13/5:5:10^2:15:17^2
19:20:21:21f/6:2/7:7^3:12:14:15^2/8:9^3:14:15^2:16
17^4:22^2:23/9:6^2:7^2/10:1^3:10^2:18/11:4/12:6^2:9:
16^3/13:4^3:10/Gal1:4:6:23/2:3:11:12^4/3:6:8,9:14
:15:18:20/4:1^2:2^2:4:5:7:23:24,25^2:27/5:8:10:16:
22/6:3^3:4^2:7:8^5/Eph1:4^2:5^2:6:7:8^2:9:10:11^2:14^3:
16,17:18/2:4:5:5f:5:7:10:12:14:15^4:17/3:5:6:7:9:
10:11:16:21/4:7:8^2:9^2:10:10f:11:12:28^2:30/5:5:
23:25:27:28:31^2/6:6,7:9:13/Php1:28^2/2:6:8:13:
19^2:22:25:26^2:27^2:30/3:4:21^3/4:19/Col1:7:8:9:
13:15:15f:17:18^3:18f:18:21:22^2:26,27/2:7:10:11:
13^2:14/3:1:11:24^2:25^2/4:7:9:10:12:13/1Th1:10/
2:19/4:8:13/5:10:24/2Th1:5:6:10^2:11/2:4^3:6:7^2:
8:10:14^2/3:3:10:14^2/1Ti1:14:16:17^2/2:1:4:13:15
/3:1:2^3:3^2:4:5:6:7/5:1:8:18:20^2/6:4:14/2Ti1:1:3:
8:9:10:12:16^2:17^2:18/2:6:8^2:12:13^3:26^2/4:1:10:
15:17/Tit1:1:3:15/2:14^2/3:5:6:7^2:10:11^2/Phm1:
11:15^2:16^2:18/Heb:2^3:3^2:4:5,6^2:8:10:13/2:9:10:
11:12:13:14^2:15:16:17:18^3/3:5:6:7,8:9:11:18^3/4:
3^2:4^2:7^2:8^2:10:13:15^2/5:1^5:4^2:5:7:7f^5:8:9:12,13^2/
6:10:14:15:16^3:17^2:18^3/7:2^3:3^2:4^2:7:10:17:21^2:25^4
:26^2:27^3/8:2:4^3:6:8/9:7:11^2:12^2:14:16:17^2:19:20:
21:24:25:26^2:28^2/10:4f:5:9^2:14^2:15:17:23^2:24:36
/11:5^2:6:7^3:8^3:9^2:10:11:16:17:19^2:21^2:22^3:24,25:
26^2:27^3:28^3/12:2^3:5^2:6^3:7:16:17^2:21:26^2:27^2/13:
20,21:23/Jas1:5^3:9:10,11:12^2:17:18f:18:23:24^3:
25^3:26/2:21^2:22^3:23:24^2/3:1/4:6:7:10:12^2/5:9:
11:13:14:17:18/1Pe1:11:16:17^2:18:19:20/2:4:7:
8:14:22:23^3:24^2/3:18^3:19:20/4:1:19/5:1:6:7:8:9:
10/2Pe1:1:3^2:4^2:5:9:17,18/2:5:6:7,8^2:10:15:20^2:
21:22/3:4^2:5,6:9^4:14^2:15,16^3/1Jn1:1:2:9:9f:10/2
:2^2:3:4^2:6:9:11^3:22:23:25:27^4:28/3:1:2^2:5^2:7:8:9^2:
10:12^2:20:24^2/4:8:9:10:13^2:15:16^2:17:18^3:20^4/5:
1:3:6,7,8^2:6,7,8f:6,7,8^2:10^2:11:14:15^2:16^2:20/
2Jn1:6^2:10/3Jn:10^5/Jud:9:15:24,25/Rev:2:5^2:6^2
:7^2:16:17,18/2:1:11:14:23/3:5:12^3:20/5:6:7:8:12
/6:2:3:5:9:12/7:2:14/9:2/10^2:9:10:11/11:15/12:
4^2:5:10:12:13:17/13:4:6:10f^2:12^2:13:14^3:15:16/
14:4:7^2:17/17:1:8^2:11:14/18:2/19^2:9f:9:10:12:13
:15^3/20:2:3^3:8:12:15/21:3:4:5:7:10:16^2:17/22:1:
9:10:12

9139

HER

Gen2:22:23/3:6^2/4:2/8:11/12:11,12,13^2:14:15^2:
16:17:19^2/16:1:2,3^2:4:5:6:7:13/17:15:16^4/19:31:
33^2:34/20:2^2:4:6:7^3:11,12^2:13/21:10:14:19/23:1
:3:5,6/24:14:15,16^2:17^2:21:22:28:28f:29,30^2:45^3:
46:47^2:51^2:53:55:57:58:59^2:60:61:65^2:67/25:22:
23/26:7:9:10/27:6,7/29:9:12,13^4:16:18:19:21^2:
23:24:26:29:30:31/30:1:3:4:9:14:17^2:21:22^2/31:
21^2:34:35f/33:2:7/34:2^3:3^2:4:8^2:11:13:14:17/35:
20/36:10,11,12:13,14:31-39/38:8:9^3:11^4:13:14:
15^2:16:18^2:19:20^3:22:23:24^2:25^3:26^2:27/39:7:8:
10^2:16:17:19/46:18:23,24,25/48:7/Ex2:5^2:6:7:8:
10/3:22/4:25,26/18:2/21:8^6:9^2:10^3:22:24^2/22:
16^2:17^2/Lev12:2:3:4:5:5f:6:7^2:8/15:19:21,22,23:
24:26:27:30^2:33^2/18:7:14f:16f:17:18:20:25f/19:
20f:29/20:14:18^2/21:9^2/22:13^3:28/Num5:15:16:
18^4:19^2:24:27^5:30:31^2/12:1f:12:13:14^3/14/19:1^3
:4:5/22:22,23:25:27:33/25:8/30:3:4^2:5^7:7^3:8^3:9:
10:11:12^2:13^2/Deu21:12^3:13^3:14^6/22:7:13,14^3:
15:16^2:17,18:19:21^3:23,24:25,26,27:28,29f:28,29^2
:30f/24:1^3:3:4:17/25:5^3:11:12/28:56,57^2/32:11^2
:35/Jos2:15:17,18/6:17:22:23^4:25^2/7:8/8:2/15:
18,19^3/Ju1:14^2:15/4:5:5f:8:18:20:22/5:27:29/
11:35:38^2:39:39f^2/13:2,3:6:9:10:13,14:24/14:2:3
:7:17/15:1^2:2^4:6^2/16:5:6:8:16,17:18:19/17:3/19:
2:3^5:4:25^4:27^3:28^2:29/20:6:13/Ru1:3:4,5:6,7:8^2:
11f^2:14^2:15^3:18^2/2:8,9^2:14^2:14f:15^2:16:18^2:19:21
/3:6,7:14:15-18^6/4:5:6:10:13^2/1Sa1:4:5^2:6:7^2:
12,13:18:19,20^2:21,22^2/2:19/4^2:20^2:21,22^2/18:
19/25^2:20^2:35^3:36:39:40:42^2/28:7,8:10:13/2Sa3
:14:15^2:16/6:23/11:2:4^2:5:26:27^2/12:24/13:1^2:2 ^{2}
:2f:8:11:14^2:15^3:16:17,18^2:19^3:20^3/14:2,3^3:8/17:
20/20:22/1Ki1:3,4^2:11:16/2:19:22/3:1:19^2:20^2:
22:26/8:37/9:24/10:2:3:3f:5:13^2/14:5^2:6^2:17/17
:8,9:10:11:13:15^2:19/21:6:9/2Ki4:1^2:5^2:6^2:7:9:
11,12:13^5:14^2:15,16^2:18:20:22:25:26^3:27^3:30:36:
37/5:3/6:26-30/8:2:3:5:6^3/9:10:30^2:32:33^3:35^4:
36^2/11:1:13,14^2:15^3:16^2/14:26:27/18:20,21/
1Ch2:4/4:19/2Ch8:11/9:1:2^2:12/22:10/23:12:
13,14^3:15,16,17^2/34:22/Ez2:61/Neh7:63/Est1:
11^2/2:1:9^7:11:12,13,14^5:15f:15:17^3/4:4:5:8^2/5:1:
2^2:3/7:2/8:1/9:29-31/Job3:12/31:10:26/38:32/
39:13:14:16^2:17:26:27:28^2:29:30/Ps25:22/45:13
:14/48:3f:12:13^2/51:1/68:31/81:14^2/83:4/87:6/
102:13:14^2/123:2/130:8/132:15:16^2/137:5,6:7/
Pro3:18/4:6:8,9:24/5:3:8^2:9:19^2/7:4:5^2:11,12:13
:14f:21^5:22:25^2:26:27/9:3:12:14:18/12:4/14:1^2/
17:12/23:26,27,28/27:16/30:21,22,23:21,22,23f
/31:11^2:12:15^2:16:21:22:23:26:27:28^4:31^2:31f^4/
Ecc7:26^2/Sol8:5^2:8:9^2/Is3:2^2/5:14^2/7:6:14f/10:
11/13:22/14:2:32/17:6:14/19:3:15:22/23:15,16
:17:18/27:4,5:6:7,8^4:9^4:10/28:1^2:4:7/29:2/30:7/
32:2/34:15^4/36:6/37:22/40:2^5/42:14/43:28/49:
15^2/50:1^2/51:3^2:18^2/53:7/54:6/61:10/62:1^2:6,7
/63:18/65/66:10^3:11:12^5/Jer2:15^2:16:32^2/3:1:7
:9:10:20:23^2/4:31/6:5:6:7^2/7:12:18f/8:7/14:5/
15:9^3/17:11^2/19:8:15/25:11/29:7/30:18/31:15:
23/33:6/44:17:18:19^3:25/46:20,21^2:27/48:2,3,4 ^{4}
:5:9:11:12:13^2:15^2:17:18:25^2:26^2:27^2:30^3:39:41^3/
49:2^2:9,10^3:13:14:15:24^2:37^2:38/50:2:3^2:9:13^2:
14:15^3:19:26^4:27:29:30^2:35:36^2:37^3:38:44:46/51:
2^4:3:4:8^2:9^5:11:28:29:30:36^2:43:47^2:53:55^2:56^4:
57:58:64/Lam1:1:2^5:3^2:4^2:5^3:6^3:7^3:8^4:9:10^3:11:
17^4/2:5:9:16^2:17^2/4:13:22/Eze:7^2/5:5,6,7/7:23
/13:5/16:2:3:26:32:45^2:46^2:48:49:50:57/17:
12,13^2:14^2:15/18:6/19:2:3:5^2/20:5,6^3/22:2/23:
4,5^3:8^5:9:10^4:11^2:12:13:16:17^2:18^2:19,20^2:27:31:
32/24:7:8:9:17/25:3:9,10^2:13^3/26:4^3:5:6/27:16/
28:24^2/29:2^2:7^3:12:14:16:19:21/30:4^2:6:7:8:18^2/
31:11^4:12^6:13^2:15:16^4:17^4/32:7:12:16^2:21^2:22:29^2
/33:28^2/36:13/37:16/38:11/Dan11:6^4:7/Hos1:
2:6^2:7^4:9:10:11:2^3:3^2:4:6^4:7:8^2:9^3:10^3:11^2:12^4:13^4
:14^3:15^5/3:1^2:2^2:3/4:16:17/5:3:5^2:12/6:9/7:1:2:
12^4/8:3^3:10^2:12^2:13:14/9:16/10:1^3:2:7:11^4/13:
11f:16^5/14:6:7/Joe2:16/3:17/Amo1:3:5:6:7/3:
14/5:2:6/6:8/9^2/Ob1:1f:1:8f/Mic:6^3:7^2:9:13:14
/3:8/5:9^2/7:6^2:13/Nah2:7^2:8^2:9:10/3:2:4^2:4f:9:
10^4/Zep2:14^4/3:2^2:3^2:4^2/Zec1:17^2/5:8:10/7:7/
8:2:4/9:3:4^2:5:7^4/12:3:4^2/14:18/Mt1:19:19f:19:
20:25/2:18/5:28:31^2:32^2/8:15^2/9:18^2:22:25:27/
10:35^2/11:19f/14:4:7:8:11/15:22^2:23^4:28^2/19:7
/20:22/21:5^2/23:37^3/24:32/26:10/Mk1:29,30:
31^3/5:23^2:33:34:35:41,42^3:43/6:24^2:28/7:26:27:
29:30/10:11:12/12:20,21,22:43,44/14:6^2/16:
10,11/Lk1:28:30:36^2:41:56:58^2/2:6:7:19:51/4:
38:39^2/7:12:13:35f:38^2:44^2:47:48/8:2:47:48:49^2:
54:55^2:56/10:38:39:40:41:42/11:31/12:53/13:
12:13:14:16:34^3/15:9^2/18:3:4,5^2/20:31:33/Jn4:
7:16:26:28,29/8:3:5:7:10/11:1^3:23:25:28^2:31^2:33^2
:40/12:3:7/16:21^2/19:26:27/20:13:14^2:15/Act5:
8:10^3/7:21/9:37^3:40f:40:41^3/12:15/16:14:15^2:
16:18^3:19/19:37^2/Rom7:2^3/9:10-13/16:1^3/1Co
6:16/7:2:3^2:4^2:10:11:12^2:13:14:34:39^2/9:5/11:3^2
:5^4:6^2:10:10f:13/2Co:2^2/Gal4:19:24,25:30/Eph
5:25:26:27:33/1Th2:7/5:3/1Ti:10:16/Heb11:11 ^{2}
:31/Jas4:4/1Pe3:6^2:7/5:13/2Jn1:1/Rev2:21^2:
22^2:22f:22:23/12:1^2:2^2:4:6^2:14:15:16:17/14:8/
17:2^2:4:5:6:9:16^2/18:3:3f:3^2:4^3:5^3:6^3:8^2:9^4:10:11:
15:19:20^2:23^3/19:2:3/21:2

1626

HERS

Gen3:15^2/Pro14:1/31:31/Is10:11/Jer12:14

6

HIM

Gen2:18/3:2,3:5:23^2:24/4:6:9:15:17:25:26/5:21-
21-24:28-31/6:3:22/7:5:8,9:23/8:11/9:2,3:26,27
/11:12,13f/12:1:4:8:11,12,13:18^2/14:17:18:21:
23/15:1:4:5:6:7:9/16:9-12^2:15/17:1^2:2,3,4:5:
9,10:19^2:20^2:23/18:2:9:10:19^2:22,23/19:3:6:14:
17:26:29:32^2:33:34^2:35^2/20:2:3^2:7:14:15/21:3:
4,5:16:18:20,21:22/22:2:3^2:9:10:11:20-23/23:
19,20/24:1:4:9f:10:18:27:29,30:32:35:36:39:54:
61:64:67/25:1:9,10:25:26/26:2^2:7^2:12:14:22:24:
32/27:6,7:11,12:16:17:22:25^2:26:31:33:36:37^3:
39,40:41:42:44/28:1^2:6,7,8/29:12,13^4:15:20:21:
28:33:34^2:35/30:3:4:5:6:8:10:11:13:16:18:20^2:
23,24/31:2:3:7:17-20:23:24^2:25:32/32:1:20:
22,23,24:28:29^3/33:3:4^3:6/34:8/35:7:9^2:10:11:
13,14:15:18^2:26:28,29/36:9/37:3^2:4:8:10:13,14:
15:17:18^3:19,20^3:21,22^5:24:26,27:28^2:32^2:33:35/
38:6:7:10^2:11:16:18:22^2/39:4:12:17:21^2:22:23/
40:11:14:18,19:20:23/41:15:17:33:39:41,42:45^2:
51/42:4:6^2:22:24:29:30:37:38/43:3,4,5:6:7^2:9:10
:20:23:26^2:28/44:14:20:21^2:24:28:29:32^2:34/45:
9:13:26:27^2:28/46:2:5:8-14:16,17:32:34^2/47:2:8:
20:29^2/48:1^2:2:3:9:10:12,13:18/49:9:23^2/50:1^2:
5^2:14:15:16,17:18:26/Ex1:1:5:18:19/2:1:3:4:9^3:
10^3:19:20^2:21/3:2:3,4:5:7:12:16:18^2:20/4:2:3:4:5
:11:15:16^2:19:21^2:22:23:24:25,26:28/5:1:2:3:15/
6:10:11/7:9:15:16^2/8:1:8:20:29/9:1^2:13:30/10:1
:3:7/13:12/14:31/15:2^2:11:25^2/16:7,8,9/17:7:9:
12/18:2:7:15,16:19,20:21^2/19:2,3:13/20:20/21:
3:4:6:14^3:16:18:19:27:30f^2:34/22:2:3:7:10:17:26:
27/23:5:6:21^2:21f:22/24:3/28:39/29:5:18:25:29
/31:3^2:18/32:1:29/33:11:12/34:4:5,6^2:15:30:31^2
:32^2:34/35:29:34/36:4-7/39:43/40:13^2:16:19:29
/Lev1:2,3:4f/5:6:8:10:13:15:16:17,18/6:2:7:21/
7:15/8:8:12:13:29/9:9:13:18:21/10:14/13:3:3f:4
:5^2:6^2:8:11:13:16,17:20:21:22:25:25f:26:27^2:27f:
29,30^2:33:34:36^2:37:40:43:44/14:3:7:11:18:29/
15:7:10:16/16:5/17:10/19:17:22:24/20:3:4:5/
21:12/22:8/23:13/24:12:13,14^3:15,16:20:23/25:
1:27:35^2:36^2:37:39:53/27:6:8:20:21/Num3:7,8,9
:14,15/5:30/6:9/7:89/12:7,8^2/14:24/15:28:31f:
34^2:35:36^2/16:5:11,12:40:47/17:6:11/18:27/19:
13:20^2/20:26:27:29/21:7:8:34/22:5,6:7:9:12:14:
22,23:25:31:35:36:41/23:3,4:13:16:18-24/24:2:
3-9^2:15-19^2/26:58,59/27:18:19^2:20^2:23^2/29:8/
30:15/33:2:41/35:19:20^2:21:27^2:30:31:32/Deu1
:1:30:38/2:24:30:33,34/3:1^2:28/4:7:12:29^2:35:
39/5:5:21/6:5:13^2:16^2:17:18:21:24/7:9:10/8:2:6
:11:16/9:7:8:16:18:20^2:23:25:26/10:12,13^2:20^2/
11:13:22/12:4,5/13:3^2:4:5:9^3:10:18/14:21/15:
10:12^2:13:14^2:18/16:10/17:16:20^3/18:1:18:19:
22^2/19:11:12^4:13/21:5:15:18:19:21:23/22:2:19/
23:15,16^3:21/24:7^2:8:12,13:14,15/25:1:6:8^2:9/
26:2,3:10/28:9:20/29:2,3:14,15:20:21/30:20^2/
31:7:14:23:29/32:19/33:7^2:12^3/34:1:3:6:8:9^2:10
/Jos1:1:17,18/2:11/4:14^3:15,16:24/5:13:14^2:15
/7:13:23/8:20,21/9:9/10:33/13:1/14:13,14^2/15
:18,19^2/20:3:4^2:5/22^2:16:24,25:29/23:11:15,16/
24:1:3^2:4:10^3:14:20/Ju1:4,5,6:14f:14/3:10^2:13:
17,18,19^2:20^2:22,23/4:6:9:18^2:19^2:21:22/5:25/6
:10:12:14:16:19:20:31:34/7:5,6:8,9:19,20/8:20:
31/9:4:18:24:25:31:33:38:54/10:10:15/11:6:25:
30,31:32:34/12:5/13:10:12:17:21:24^2:25/14:6:9:
16:17:18:19^2/15:1:10:11:12,13^3/16:2^3:5^3:8:9:10:
12:16,17:19^3:20:21^2:23,24^2:25,26^2:27:31^2/17:9:
12/18:3^2:15,16:26/19:2:3^3:4:6:7:11:21:22^2:25/
20:3:22,23,24/Ru1:1/2:10,11/3:3:13^2/4:1:5:
16,17/1Sa1:3:11:19,20^2:21,22^2:24:26:27:28^2/2:
19^2:22:27:35:36/3:13:15:16,17:18^2:19:21,4:1/4:
14:21,22/5:3/7:9:16/8:5:13/9:6:7^2:8:16:25:
26,27^3/10:1:9:10:14^2:16:21:23^2:27^2/11:5:7:15/
12:2:10:13^2:15:20:24/13:2:7:10:14^2:15/14:6:8:
28:39:52/15:1:13^2:17:22^2:27^2:28:31:33:35/16:1:
4^2:10,11:12^2:13^2:14:18:21:22/17:4-7:9:24:25^2:31
:32:33:41,42:48,49:50,51:56:57/18:4^2:5:8:10:
11,12^3:13^2:14:15,16^2:17^2:21:22^2:24:27:29^2/19:2^2
:3:4:5:7:9,10^2:11^2:12:14:15^2:16:17:18^3:20:22/20:
3:6:8:17^2:21:22:24,25:28,29:30:31^2:33:35:36:40/
21:1:6:12/22:1:3:9,10:11,12:13^3:15:21/23:2:6:7^2
:11:14,15^5:16^2:17:19:20:22:23/24:2:4:5:7,8^2:9,10
:19/25:1:5:12:17:23:36:37,38:37,38f:37,38/26:1:
2:5,6,7:8^2:9:10:15:19/27:2,3:4:6:12/28:2:3:5,6:
14:23/29:3:4/30:6:8:11,12^2:13/31:3,4^2:5/2Sa1:
6:7:10:10f:15^2/2:4:5:20^2:22:23:30:32/3:12:16:20
:24,25:26^2:27^3:31:33,34:35,36/4:4^2:6,7:10^2/5:1:
3:6:10:12:17:25/6:7:16:20/7:14:15:17/8:2:6^2:10:
14/9:2:3^2:4:5,6:10,11/10:1:2:3:11:17/11:5:7:8^2:
10^2:12:13^2:15:19,20,21^2:25:26/12:14:16:17:18^2:
21:23^2:24/13:4:5^2:6^3:7:8:9:10:11:21-24:25:28/
14:2,3:4:8:10:21:22:24:29^3:32:33/15:1:2:3:4:5^2:5
f^2:7,8^2:9:9f:11:17,18^2:19,20:25,26^2:30:32:33,34/
16:1:3:10:11^2:14:17^2:20:21^2:23/17:2,3^2:6^2:12:16 ^{2}
:21^2:22:28,29^2/18:9:10:11^2:15:19:20:30/19:5:
8,9,10^2:15^2:17:18:24,25:26:30:37^2:38:40^2:41:42:
43/20:2:5:6^2:8,9,10^4:12^3:18:21/21:12,13,14^2:16:
20,21/22:1:9:12^2:31:47/23:10:11,12^3:13:21:23/
24:10:12:13:16:18:19:20:24:24f/1Ki1:1:2:3,4:5:6
:7:13:14:15:16:22,23:25:31:34:35^3:40:42:44,45^2:
53^3/2:6:8:9:13:17:18:22^2:25^2:26:29:31^2:32:36,37
:42:46/3:5^3:6^3:26^2:27:28/4:21:34/5:2,3:5:11/7:
40/8:14:16:18:25:32:59/9:2,3^2:5/10:1:2:3^2:6:13:
24:25:28/11:4:9,10^2:11:12,13:16,17,18:19:20:22:
24:27,28:29^3:32:34/12:2,3,4:16,17:18:21:27/13:
1:4:5:11:12:13:14^2:18:24,25:26:32/14:3^2:5^2:8:13 ^{2}
:16:18:28/15:27^2/16:9:10^2:18:19:25:33/17:5:6:
8,9:19:21:23^2:24/18:2:7^3:11:16:17:21^2:30:43^2:44 ^{2}
/19:5^2:7:8:9:11:15:18:19^2:20/20:7:8:13:17:23:31
:33^2:34:36^2:37:39:41:42/21:2^2:5:10^3:13:19^2:22:
25/22:4:7:8:13^2:14:15^2:17:19:26:27^2:32,33/2Ki1
:6:9^3:13:15:17/2:5:15^2:16:17:19:20:23/3:6,7,8:
12f:27^2/4:1:8:10:15,16:19:20^2:21:27:31:33/5:3:5
:6:8:10:11:13^2:14:15:16:20^2:21^3:23:25:26/6:1:6:7
:10:13:16:17:22:26-30^4:32^3:33/7:17:20/8:6:8,9^2:
10:12:13:14:21:29/9:1:2:3^2:11:15:16:21:25:26^2:
27^3:28^2:31:32:36/10:5:9,10:11:15^3:16:18,19/11:
2,3^2:12^2/12:2:20^2/13:4:14^2:15:19/14:8:19/15:5:
10^2:14:16:19,20:25^2:30/16:3:7^2:16/17:4^2:26/18:
5:7:30:37/19:4:9:37/20:1^2:4:5^2:6:9:14/21:23^2/
23:1:3:17:29^2:30:31,32:33:36,37/24:1:12/25:4,5 ^{2}
:23:28:30/1Ch2:3:19:21:23:46:48,49/3:4/4:6:7:9

(HIM Con't)
:20/7:16:22/8:11/9:20/10:3[2]:14/11:1:3:9:23[3]:
24,25/12:18/13:4:10:14/14:1:2:4-7:8:16:17/15:
2:29/16:8:9:27[2]:29:30:35/17:13:14/18:2:6:10/
19:2,3:10/21:6:28/22:7:9/23:30/25:4,5/26/27:
5,6/28:6:9[4]/29:1:22f:22:23:25:30/2Ch1:1:7/2:6:
6f:6/4:11/6:4[2]:8:16:23[2]:42/7:12/8:2:17,18[2]/9:1:
2:12:13,14:23:24:28/10:2,3:8,9:15:16:18/11:12:
16:20:22/12:1:8[2]/13:7:10:11:20/14:6:7/15:2[4]:4:
15[2]/16:1:7:9:10:13,14/17:11/18:2[2]:6,7[3]:12:14:
16:18:19,20:23:25:26:31[3]:32/19:2[2]/20:4:30:37/
21:9[2]:12:18/22:3:4:6:9[4]/23:11[3]:12/24:3:6:17,18:
21:25[3]/25:14:20:23:27[3]:28[2]/26:4:5:7:8:15:17,18:
20[3]/28:5:20:21:23[2]/29:4,5:11/30:9/32:15:21:25
:28,29:31[2]:33/33:11[3]:13:24:25/34:26:30/35:20:
22:23:24,25[4]/36:12:13:18[2]:22,23/Ez1:2/4:6:7[2]/
5:15/7:6:7,8,9/8:17:22[2]/Neh1:5/2:1:5,6:8/3:4:8
:10:16:20:29/4:3/6:12,13[2]:18:19/8:1/9:7[2]:8[2]/13
:26[3]:28/Est1:11/2:21/3:2:10/4:4:5:7:8:11:17/5:
9:11/6:1:5:6:9[3]:11[2]:13[2]:14/8:2:3:4/10:2/Job1:5:
9:10:11:12,13/2:3:6:9[2]:11[2]:12:13/3:23/5:8/7:17
:18/8:4:19/9:3:4:11:12[2]:13:14:22:34:35[2]/11:10:
13,14/12:4:16/13:8:10[2]:15[2]:15f[2]/14:5:6[2]:20,21[3]:
22/15:4,5:13:15:23,24:25,26:30[2]:31[2]:32/18:8,9:
11:12:13:14:17/19:16:27/20:7:9:14:15:16:17:18:
22:23:25:27:29/21:14:15:19:20[2]:30-32[2]:33[2]/22:
3:14:21:27[2]/23:3:4,5:7:8[3]:9[3]:13:14f/24:1:9:20[3]/
25:5/26:13f/27:8:9:12:20:21[2]:22:23/31:19,20[2]:
35:37/32:2:3:8,9/33:13:23,24[5]:26[2]/34:27/35:6:
7:8:12:14,15/36:11:12:13:15:22:24:26:30/37:
19,20:24/39:11[2]:12:20:21-23/40:15:19:20:23:24[2]
/41:2:4:5[2]:6:8:9:10[3]:26:27,28[2]:29:31,32/42:10:
11[5]:13,14/Ps1:2/2:6:12/3:7/4:3:4:5/5:12/7:15:
16/8:4:5:6/9:9:12[2]/10:4/13/14:5/15:4:5/16:2/
18:1:3:21:30:46/20:3/21:2:3:5[2]:6[2]/22:8[2]:23:24:
26:27:29:30/23:2,3/24:5/25:3:9:10:12:14/27:6/
28:7[2]/29:2[2]:5,6/30:4/31:23[2]/32:6:6f:11[2]/33:1:3
:8:10:18,19:21/34:4:6[2]:7:8:9:15:17[2]:19:20:22/35
:10:13:21:25[2]/37:5:7:22:25:35,36:37[2]:40/40:3:
16/42:2[2]:4,5[2]:11/43:4:5/45:10,11/47:9/48:1/50
:3:18/51:1/53:3/54:1/55:19:20/56:3,4/59:1/62[2]
:5[2]:8[2]:12/63:11/64:10/66:17/67:6,7/68:4:33:35
/69:31:34[2]/71:11[3]/72:2:4:8:9:11[2]:12:14:15:15f:
15[2]:17[2]/73:28[2]/74:13,14/76:11/77:1/78:22:34[2]
:36:40:58:70/81:15/85:9:13/89:6:7[2]:20:21[2]:22[2]:
23[2]:24[2]:27[2]:28[3]:39:40[2]:41:42:43:45[2]/91:2:14[2]:15[3]
:16[2]/92:2:15/95:2[2]:7[2]/96:4:6:8[2]:9:12/97:2:3:7:
12/99:6/100:2[2]:4/102:21,22[2]:24/103:11:13:
17,18[2]:21:22/104:15[2]:34:35[2]/105:4:20[2]:26/106:
2:12:13:23:29:43/107:11:22:32/109:6[3]:7:8:12,13
:17[2]:18:19:30/111:5/112:1:4:6:7/113:3:6/115:
11:13:18/116:13:14:15/117:1/118:2:9:19:27,28
/119:63/127:4/128:1:4/130:6/132:7:17/134:1/
135:1:6:20/136:4:5:6:7:16:17/142:1/144:3:3f/
145:3:18:19:20/146:1:2/147:7:9:10:11[2]:12/148:
1:2:3:4[2]:5:7:14/149:1:6,7:9/150:1:2:3:4[2]:5:6/
Pro2:3,4,5/3:9,10:11,12/5:22/6:26:35/7:10:13[2]:
14f:20:21/9:7,8[2]/11:6/12:14/13:6:23:24[3]/14:2/
16:7:20:29f/17:11f:27,28/18:6,7:10:22/19:7:7f:
19/20:19f/21:3:14:27/22:15/24:15,16[2]:18:28,29[2]
/25:8,9,10:18[3]:21,22[3]/26:24,25,26/27:22/28:17[2]
/29:3:15:21/30:5/31:1:12[2]/Ecc1:12-15/2:19:
24-26[4]/4:10:15:16[2]/5:4[2]:18:19,20/6:3/8:5:6,7:8:
15/9/10:2[2]:12,13/11:8[2]/12:1:2/Sol2:7:8/3:1[2]:2:
3:4[4]:5:11/4:16/5:4:6[3]:8:15/6:1/8:4/Is1:1/2:22/
3:8:10/5:9/6:2/7:3:4[2]:14/8:3:13:17/9:13/10:7/
11:2:10/14:22:27/19:21/21:6,7:12/22:22[2]:23,24[2]
/26:3/28:11:12[2]:26/29:15:16:21:23/30:18[2]/31:
1/32:6/36:3:5:11:15:22/37:3:4[2]:7:8,9:22:38/38:
1[2]/39:5/40:3:10:13:15:16:17:18:22/41:2[2]:25/42
:1:4/44:10:16:20/45:1[2]:9:13f:24[2]/46:7/48:14:15[2]
/49:5[2]/51:1[2]:13/52:14,15/53:2f:2:3[2]:4:6:7:8:10[2]
:12/55:6[2]/56:4:6/61:11/63:7:10/64:4/66:3[2]:5/
Jer1:1/2:15f:19:24:31/3:13:17:25/5:4:19/11:6:
19/17:6/18:18/20:2:3[2]:10:11:13:16/21:3,4/22:
15:16:18/23:38,39/24:1/25:8,9/26:7,8[4]:19:21:
23[4]:24[2]/27:6:7[2]:8[2]/28:9[2]:14/29:26:29:31:32/30:
21/31:20[4]:22/32:3:5:10:13/33:1/35:3:8/36:18:
31/37:13:15,16:17[2]/38:6:10:13[2]:14:16:27[3]/39:5[3]
:7[2]:9:11,12[2]:14[2]/40:1:5:13,14:15/41:2:8:10:12[2]/
42:4:6:12/44:20:23/45:1/46:15:17:25/49:28/50
:43/51:17:31:44:61,62/52:8:9[2]:24,25:31:32[2]:33[2]
/Lam2:8:19/3:24:25[2]:28:29:30[2]:31:32:41/Eze1:
27,28/3:20[3]:21/8:14f/9:4:5/10:9-13/12:12:13[2]/
13:6/14:8[3]:9[2]/17:7:12,13:16:19:20[3]/18:7:12:16:
23/19:4[2]:5[2]:7:8[3]:9[2]/21:27/24/28:12/29:18f:20:
20f/32:2/33:8:9:12[2]:13[2]:16:30/38:2,3/39:1/40:
46/43:3/45:15/46:12[2]:16/Dan1:1:8f:18,19/2:1[2]
:15:22:24:46[2]:48[2]/3:9:13/4:8:15[2]:16:19:23[2]:34:
35[3]/5:6[2]:8:11:12:13:19[3]:20/6:3:4:11:12:16[2]:23/
7:10[3]:13:14:16/8:7[3]:11:12:24:25/9:9/10:19:
20,21/11:5:6:7[2]:8:14:16:17[2]:18[2]:22:25:30,31:38:
39:40[2]:44:45/12:7/Hos1:3:9:7/4:4/5:6/6:3/7:5[2]
:10[2]/9:4/11:1[2]:2:3[4]:4/12[2]:6:14/13:10:13:14[2]:15
/14:9[2]/Joe1:14/Amo:2[2]:9[2]:11/2:3:4/5:8/6:10/
Ob1:11:12:13/Jon:6:14:15:16[2]/3:4,5[2]/4:5:6[2]/
Mic3:4/6:5:7[3]/7:9:17/Nah1:7:12/Hab2:20/3:5
/Zep1:6/2:3:11/Hag1:12/Zec:3:8:9:10/2/3:3:
5,6/4:7:11/6:12:13/12:1:10[3]/13:3[2]/14:5/Mal1:
8/2:5:13:17[2]/3:4:14,15:16[3]:18/Mt1:20:21:25/2:
2:3f:7:8[2]:11[2]:16[2]:19/3:5:15:16:17/4:3:4:5:8[2]:10[2]:
20:22:25/5:22:24/6:7,8:26:33/7:11/8:2:4:5,6:7:
19:22:25[2]:27:28:29:34/9:2:9[2]:14:18:20:21:24:28:
32:38/10:1:2,3,4:25f:31:32:33/11:4:5:6:7[2]:27/12
:10:15:17:18:22:35:38:41:42:43,44,45:46,47[2]/13:
10:12,13[2]:27:36:57/14:3:4[2]:6:14:15:28:31:36/15
:12:16:22:23:25:30:32/16:1:21:22[2]:24/17:3:5:5f:
5:16[2]:17:18:24:25/18:2:15[2]:16:17:17f:21:24:25:
27[2]:28[2]:29[3]:31:32/19:2:3[3]:10:13:21:27/20:18:25
:34/21:7[2]:8[2]:9:14:15:16:23:26:36:37:38:39[2]:41:
46/22:11:13[2]:15:16:19:23:34,35:43:45:46/23:15
/24:1:3/25:5,6:10:14:19:20:21[2]:29/26:4:15:18:
25[2]:34:37:49:50:52:56:57:59:63:65,66:67[2]:69:71:
73/27:1f:2:3:11:12:19[2]:22:26:27:28[2]:29:30[2]:31[3]:
32:34:36:38:39:41,42,43[2]:48:49[2]:55:58:63/28:4:
9[2]:16:17[2]/Mk1:10:12,13:18:20:26:32,33:36,37[2]:
40:41:43,44:45/2:13:14:15:16/3:2[2]:4:7,8:9:10[2]:
11[2]:12:13:16-19[2]:21:22:31,32:34/4:1:10:25[2]:36:
38:41/5:3,4:6[3]:10:18:19:20:21:22:23:24:27:29:30
:31:33:37:40/6:6:20[2]:25:27:30:35:36:44:50:55:56[2]
/7:1:5:6,7:15,16f:17:25:26:32[2]:33/8:11:11f:22[3]:
23[2]:25:26:32[2]:32f:38/9:7:11:15:18[3]:22[2]:25:26:27[2]
:28:32:35:38[2]:39/10:2[2]:13:17:21[2]:23:32:35:35f:
42:48:49[2]:52/11:2[2]:3[2]:7:8:9:14:18:27,28:31[2]:32/
12:3:6[2]:7[2]:8[2]:12[3]:13[2]:16:17:30:33:34[2]:36:37[2]:
43,44/13:3,4[2]/14:1:11:12:13:19:29:33:35:35f:44[2]
:45:46:51,52:55:57:58:61:65[4]:66,67:69/15:2:3,4[2]
:8:13:14:15:16,17[2]:19[3]:20[2]:23:24:29,30[2]:32[3]:36[2]:
38f:41[2]:44/16:7:9:12:14/Lk1:8,9:13:31:32:50:62
:66:72,73/2:5:7[2]:12:14:21:22[2]:26[2]:27:29,30,31:
40:43:44:45[2]:46,47:48/3:4:22/4:1:5[2]:6,7:8:
9,10,11:15:17:18,19:20:22:29[3]:35[3]:36:42[3]/5:1:9:
11:12:13:14:15:17:18,19[2]:27:28/6:7:14,15,16[2]:
17,18:19[2]:29[2]:39:42/7:3:4:15[2]:19[2]:20,21,22[2]:23:
24:25:29:38:39:41:42[2]:43/8:1:4:9:18[2]:19:20:24:
25[2]:27:28:29:31:32:39:40[2]:41[2]:42:43,44:46:47[2]/
9:9:12:19:23:28:30:32:35:37:38:39[5]:41:42[3]:45:47
:49[2]:59:62[2]/10:17:22:25:28:30[3]:31:32:33:34[3]:34f
:35:37/11:1:5,6[2]:11[2]:12:13:14:16f:22[2]:29,30[2]:
37,38:39:53,54[3]/12:7:20:24:36:39:42,43,44[2]:46[2]
/13:12:23:31:35/14:1:4[2]:9:21:25:31/15:15:16[2]:
20[3]:21:22:28:31/16:2:5,6[2]:7:25:27/17:2,3:4:
7,8,9:14:16/18:3:7:15:16,17:18:19:24:26:31/19:
5:8:9,10:14[3]:24:30[2]:31:34:36,37:47/20:5:10[2]:13:
14:15[2]:19[4]:26:37,38/21/22:2:5:10:43:47:47f:54[2]
:56[2]:58:63,64[3]:65:71/23:2:3:7[2]:8[2]:11[2]:14[3]:15:16[2]
:17,f:18:21[2]:22[3]:32,33:35:36[2]:37:38:39:49:56/24
:16:20[3]:29:31:35:42:52/Jn1:4:10:11,12[3]:15:18:
24,25:29:31:36:39[2]:41:43:45:50/2:3:11f:22:
24,25/3:16:18[2]:28[2]:29:33,34[2]:35:36[2]/4:1:21-24[2]
:27[2]:30:33:40,41[4]:42:45:46,47[2]:50:51:53/5:6[2]:8:
14[2]:15:18:20:38:43:46/6:2-5[4]:15[2]:16:21:22,23:
24:25:40[2]:41:44:45:46:54:56:64:65:66:71/7:3:5:
11[2]:12:13:15:18:26:29[2]:30[2]:31:36[2]:37:39:40:43:
44[2]:45[2]:50/8:6[2]:19:29:30,31[2]:44:54:55[3]:59/9:2:7
:8:9:10:15:21[2]:24:28:29:30:31:34:37:39/10:3[2]:4:
5:19:24:31:39:41:42f/11:3:11:15:16:20:22:27:28:
29:30:34:36:44[2]:45:48[2]:57[2]/12:2:4:9:11:13:18:19
:23,24:29:42/13:1:5:6:11:16:23f:24:25:26f:27[2]:
29/14:6:7[2]:9:12,13:17[3]:21[2]:22/15:5/16:7:19:23/
17:2[2]/18:3:4,5:12:13:29:30:31[3]:33[2]/19:2:3:4[2]:6[3]:
9:12[2]:15[3]:17:18[2]:19:33:36,37:38:42/20:2:13:14:
15[3]:16:25:29:30,31[2]/21:12:15:17:19[2]:21:22:23/
Act1:6:9:16/2:22:23[2]:24[2]:33:34:37:39/3:4:7,8:9[2]
:13:14:15[3]:19:23:26/4:19:20:25,26/5:6[3]:30[2]:31:
32:36:37/6:9:11:12[2]:14/7:1:3[2]:4:5[2]:6:7:9[2]:10[4]:20
:21[4]:22:25:30:31:33:57:58[2]:59/8:9,10,11:26:31:
33:35:38:39/9:3:4:10:12[2]:14[2]:16:17:21:23:24:25:
26:27[2]:28:29:30[2]:34:38:39/10:3:4:5,6:13:19:22[4]:
24:25:35[2]:38:40,41[3]:43[2]:48/11:2:13[2]:14:18:26[2]/
12:4[2]:7[2]:8:10:15:17:19:20:22/13:6,7:8:11[2]:13:22[2]
:25:27:28[2]:30:31:34:39/14:3:9:10:19:20/15:8:39
/16:3:9:10f:28:32/17:15[2]:19:23[2]:27[2]:28:30:31[2]:
34/18:6:9:12:17:18:20:25,26[4]:25,26f:27[2]/19:30:
31[2]/20:4:10,11,12:17:37:38/21:18:26,27[3]:29[2]:30
:31:33[2]:35:36[2]:37,38[2]/22:3:13:14:20:22:24[3]:25:29[2]
:30/23:2:3:4:9[2]:10[4]:15:17:19:20:21[2]:23,24:27[2]:
28:30[2]:32[2]:35[2]/24:5:6[2]:7:8:10:23[3]:26[3]/25:2[2]:3[2]:
5:9:14:15:18:20:21[2]:25:26[3]:27/26:26:28/27:3/
28:4:6[2]:8[3]:30:31/Rom1:5:21[3]:28/2:10:23/3:5[2]:7:
24:27:29:31/4:1:3:8:11[3]:18:22/5:1:6/6:4[2]:5[2]:5f:6
:9:11/7:1:2/8:9:15:29:30:32/9:4[2]:10-13:17[3]:33[2]/
10:4:6:9:12:14[5]:15:20/11:2,3:22:24:35:36/12:14
:20/13:3:9[3]/14:1:1f:2:4[2]:6:10:13:14:21:23/15:1:
11:12:13[2]:15,16/16:10:23:25,26,27/1Co1:2:5:31
/2:14:15:16:16f/3:17:19/4:2:5/5:8:13/6:15:16/
7:11[2]:12:13[2]:20:23:24[2]:32:35:36/8:12:13/9:1:13:
22[3]/10:2:24/11:5:23/12:3/13:7[4]:12/14:11:12:
24:26:38/15:7:8:27:28/16:10:11[3]:12/2Co1:10:
22/2:5,6:7[2]:8[2]:13[2]/3:18/4:4[2]:14:15/5:9[2]:10:15:
18:21:21f[2]/7:1:13:14[2]:15[2]/8:18:22/9:9/10:5:10:
17:18/11:23:29[2]/12:10:18/Gal1:1:8:9:18/2:11/
3:2:5:6:21,22:25:27:29/4:2/6:1:8/Eph1:4:10:12:
18:19:20:22/2:6:13:17:22/3:12:17/4:11:12:
17,18:21/5:2:18:33/6:18[2]:20:22/Php1:28:29[2]:
30/2:9[2]:12:13:23:25:26:27:28[2]:29/3:3:9:10[2]/4:6
/Col1:9:10:20:21[2]:22:23:26,27[3]/2:3:6[2]:7[2]:12[3]:23
/3:4:17[2]:22:25/4:8:10f/1Th2:4:12/3:8:13[2]/4:14:
15:17/5:10/2Th1:10[2]:12/2:1:6:7/3:14:15[2]/1Ti1:
12:14/2:15/3:7[2]/5:1:18:19/6:11:16[3]/2Ti1:3:5:
10:12:18/2:11:12[3]/3/4:7:11:12:14:15/Tit1:3/3:
10/Phm1:12[2]:13[2]:17/Heb:3:4:5,6:10/2:3:6:7[2]:8
/3:2:7,8[3]:15[2]:16:18:19/4:7[2]:13:14/5:1:5:6:7:7f[2]:
9:10/6:6[2]:10[2]:14[2]:15:16[2]:18/7:1[2]:6:19:25:26/8:5
/9:28/10:22:30:36:38:39/11:4:5[2]:6[2]:7:8[2]:10:17[2]:
19:23[2]:26:27/12:3:25:28/13:13[2]:20,21[2]:23/Jas1
:5[2]:6[2]:12:13:18:25/2:3:5:11:16[2]:22:23/4:8/5:9:
11:14[3]:15[3]:19:20/1Pe1:2:5:8[4]:9:17:20:21[2]/2:4[2]:
5[3]:6:7/3:6:15:21:22[2]/4:11/5:7:11/2Pe1:2:3:9:
17,18[2]/2:7,8:16[2]:19:21[2]/3:14:18/1Jn1:1[3]:2:5:9/
2:3:4:11:27:28/3:2[2]:5:6[3]:9[3]:12:17[2]:22[2]/4:7:13:15
:16[2]:17[2]:19:20/5:4[2]:14:15:16[3]:18[2]/2Jn1:10[2]:11/
3Jn1:9:12/Jud:1:5:9:15[2]:24,25/Rev:1:5:6:7[2]:11:
13f[3]:17,18/2:1[2]:1f:8:12/3[3]:20[2]/4:3:10[2]/5:9:14/6
:8/7:15/8:3/9:1/10:6:9[2]/12:4:11[2]/13:2:4[2]:5:7:
14/14:1:7:8:15/16:9/17:12:13:16/19:1:5:7:10:
14:20/20:2:3:6/22:3:17:18

5022

HIMSELF

Gen8:21/17:17/22:6/27:22:41/33:17/39:9:12/
43:31:32/44:18/50:1/Ex21:3:4:10/22:8/30:38/
32:16/Lev9:7:15/11:25/14:8/15:5:6[2]:8:10:11:
21,22,23/16:4:6[2]:11:17:24:26:28/17:15/18:23/
21:4/25:26:39:47:49:51:52:53/27:1/Num6:1/16
:8,9/19:12:13:19:20/20:13/24:3-9/Deu10:9/12:
4,5/17:16/18:22/23:11/28:9:20/31:3/33:21/
Jos7:1/8:11,12,13/Ju3:16/6:31:32/1Sa12:22/
13:9/15:12/18:8:17:21/19:22/20:3:16:17:24,25:
41f/23:7/25:21/27:1/28:7,8/29:4/2Sa6:20/12:
18:20/17:15:23/18:2:18/21:7/1Ki1:5:52/3:9/12
:32,33[2]/15:15/16:10/17:21/20:38/21:29/22:31:
32,33/2Ki4:35/5:14:20/9:16/12:18/15:5:10:30/
24:11/1Ch10:5/15:1/17:26/29:1:4,5/2Ch1:10/
2:1:12/7:6/11:5-10/12:12/16:13,14/20:29/24:
21/26:20/32:31/Ez1:7/Est:8/3:1/5:10:11:12/6:
6:7,8/10:3/Job2:8/13:3/15:31/21:19/22:2:25/
23:9/27:10/Ps4:3/7:16/10:14/14:1/16:5/18:11
/24:5/40:7f/45:2/46:5/48:3:3f/49:18/52:7f:8/
53:1:6/55:19/64:7/68:30f/78:19,20/89:18/106:
19,20/110:1f:7/112:3/121:5/130:8/146:4/Pro2
:3,4,5/5:23/8:36/11:24,25/14:8:14/23:10,11/25
:21,22/26:27/28:26/29:15:24/Ecc3:12/12:5/
Sol3:9/Is7:14/9:7/19:21/28:5/37:1/38:15/42:
14/44:15[2]:20/52:13f/56:2:11/59:16:17/63:14/
Jer3:17/20:10/21:7/25:26/36:17/41:9/43:12/
51:26f/Lam4:16/Eze44:25:27/45:22/Dan1:8f[2]/
5:5:11/6:3:14:23/8:25/11:21f/Hos7:5/Mic4:4:7
/7:8/Zep3:15:17,18/Zec2:5/6:12/Mt9:34/11:1
f/12:26/14:13/16:24:25/18:4/23:22/27:3f:5:
41,42,43/Mk3:26/5:5/6:45/12:36/14:66,67/15:
31:38f/Lk1:5:72,73/3:21/7:39/9:62/10:29f/11:
18/12:37/14:11[2]/15:17/16:3/18:4,5/20:13:
37,38:42,43/23:35/24:15:27:36/Jn1:1f:1:8:14f/
4:1/5:18:19:26[2]:37/6:61/7:18/8:41/9:21/11:51
/16:27/18:18/19:7:12/Act1:3/2:29:34/7:37/8:
13:34:40/9:8,9/12:11/13:6,7/14:17/16:27/17:
25/20:32/25:4:10,11:16/Rom1:4/4:17/8:3:30:
33/9:5:25/12:20/14:5:12/15:3/1Co1:24:30/2:
11/3:15/4:4/6:13:16/7:10/11:23:28:29:34/14:4:
32:37/15:27:28/2Co4:1/5:18:19:20/10:1:17:18/
11:2:14/12:12/Gal1:1:12/2:20/3:13:20/4:14/6:
3:4/Eph1:14:23/2:10:14:15:20/3:2,3:8:16/4:10
:21/5:2:27:28[2]:33/6:4/Php2:8/3:4:9/Col1:16:19
/2:2:17/1Th3:11/4:1:9:16/5:23/2Th2:4:7:16/3:
14:16/1Ti2:5/2Ti:13:19:21/Tit:8/Heb:3:18/3:1
:11/5:5:9/6:16:17:19/7:9:27/8:1:8/9:12:14:25/
10:12:22:30/12:21:24/Jas1:24:26/3:1/4:6/1Pe1
:16/2:9/3:18/4:11/5:5/2Pe1:20,21/1Jn2:2:25/
4:21/3Jn1:9:10/Rev:13/5:5/12:13/19:9:13f/21:
3

439

HIS

Gen1:27/2:2:18:21:24[2]:25/3:15:20:21/4:1:2:3:4:

(HIS Con't)
8:8:17:21:26/**5**:1:3,4,5:3,4,5f:3,4,5:3,4,5f^2:6,7,8:
9,10,11:12,13,14:15,16,17:18,19,20:21-24:
25,26,27:28-31/**6**:1f:3:6:9,10/**7**:7:13^2/**8**:9:18,19^2
:21/**9**:1:8:20,21:22^2:23:24,25^2:26,27^2:29/**10**:9:10
:11,12:25/**11**:12,13:14,15:16,17:18,19:22,23:
24,25:28:29^2:31^4:32f/**12**:5^3:11,12,13^3:15:20^2/**13**
:1:11:18/**14**:5,6:8,9:14:16:17/**15**:6/**16**:2,3:9-12/
17:11:14:19:20:23^2/**18**:1:29:33^3/**19**:14^2:16^2:30/
20:2^2:14/**21**:1:7:11:18:20,21:22:32/**22**:3^3:10:13:
19:24/**23**:9:17,18/**24**:2^2:7:9f^2:10:15,16:29,30^2:
35:38^3:40:47:52:67^3/**25**:1:6:9,10:16:17:17f:26:30
:32:33^2:34:34f/**26**:7^2:11:15^2:18^3:19:24:25:26^2:35
/**27**:1:6,7^2:8,9,10:13:14^2:16:18:22:23:26:30:31:
37^2:42/**28**:5^2:6,7,8^3:9:16,17:18/**29**:6:10^4:12,13/
30:4:9:14:39,40^2/**31**:1:7:17-20^3:21:31:46:53:54:
55/**32**:1:3:7:13,14,15:16:18:22,23,24^2:31/**33**:1:2^2
:3:17^2/**34**:4:5:8/**35**:2:16:18:22:27:28,29/**36**:2,3:
6,7,8^2:10,11,12:13,14:17:18,19:24:31-39f:31-39/
37:1:2^5:3^2:4:5:8^2:9:10^3:11^2:13,14:19,20:21,22:23:
26,27^2:28:29:30:34^2:35/**38**:3,4,5:6:9^2:10:11^3:12^2:
16:20:24:26:29:30/**39**:1:2:4:5^3:9:11:12:13:14,15:
18:19/**40**:1^2:9,10:13:14:16:20^2:21/**41**:8:37:41,42^3
:43:45f:51^3/**42**:1:4:6:21^2:25^2:27^2:28:37:38^2/**43**:8:
9:16:29:29f^2:30^2:31:32:34/**44**:1^2:4:9:14:20^4:22^2:
29:31:33/**45**:1^2:2:3^2:15:16:23^2:24^2:27/**46**:1^2:5:6:
7:8-14^7:16,17^2:23,24,25^2:26:29^2:31/**47**:2:7:11:26
:28^2:29:31/**48**:1^2:2:12,13:14^4:17^2:19^2/**49**:1:11^2:
12^2:13:15^2:16:22:26:27:28:31^2:33^3/**50**:1:2:4:5^3:8:
12,13^2:14^2:18:22:23^2:24:25^2:26/**Ex1**:6:9:22/**2**:11^3
:12:14:21:24/**3**:1:6^2/**4**:4:18:20:24:25,26/**5**:21/**6**:
1:20:25/**7**:9:10^2:11:16:17:19:20:23/**8**:15:16:
31,32/**9**:1:7:12:23:33:34/**10**:1:13/**11**:1:5^2:7:10/
12:30:42/**13**:9^2:16:19/**14**:4:5:6:17:21:31/**15**:3:10
:19^2/**16**:7,8,9^2:16^2/**17**:10:11^3:12:13/**18**:1:4:7:8^2:
9:11:17:19,20:24:27^2/**19**:19/**20**:17^2:20:22/**21**:2:
3:4:6^2:7:9:10:15:16:17:18:19f:19:20:21:24^2:26^2:
27:30f:36/**22**:3:4:5^2:8:10:11:16:26^2:27/**23**:5:21/
24:10:13/**27**:21/**28**:1:2^2:29:30,31:37,38:41:43^2/
29:1:3,4:6:7:8:9:10:15,16:19,20^2:21:22:24:28:29^2
:32:35:44/**30**:11,12:13:19:21:30/**31**:6:10/**32**:14:
15:30/**33**:11:19f/**34**:4:5,6:15:29:30:33:35/**35**:10-
10-19/**39**:27:41^2/**40**:12:14/**Lev1**:4^3:14/**2**:3/**3**:2:
7,8:12:13/**4**:4:6:17:23^2:24^2:25:26:28^2:29:30:32:
33:34:35/**5**:5:6^2:7^3:10:11:12:15:17,18/**6**:2:4,5:6:
9:10^2:11:16:19,20:25/**7**:7:17,18:20:21:25:26,27:
29:31:34:35/**8**:1:6:12:14:15,16:18:22:23^2:27:30^3:
31:35:36/**9**:6:8:9^2:12/**10**:6^2:12/**11**:25:28:40/**13**:
1^2:6:12:18:34:41:45^3/**14**:7:8^3:9^3:11:14^2:15:16^2:
17^3:18:19:23:25^2:26:27:28^3:29:47/**15**:1f:5:6:8:10
:11^2:13:15:21,22,23:27/**16**:3:6:11:12:14:17:19:24^2
:26:28:32/**17**:3,4:10:15:16/**18**:7:8:9^3:14f:16f:21/
19:21/**20**:1^2:3^2:5:6:9^2:11^2:12:17^4:19^3:20:20f:20:
21:21f:21/**21**:4:6:10^2:11:12:14,15:14,15f^2:16,17:
20:21:24/**22**:1:7:11^2:17,18/**23**:29/**24**:5-8:9:11:
13,14:15,16:18/**25**:13^2:25^2:41^2:48:49:50:54/**27**:
10:14,15^2:16:17:19:20:22:26/**Num1**:17,18,19:53
/**3**:2:6:7,8,9:10:38:47,48:51/**4**:5:15:16:17,18,19:
27/**5**:7:7f:15:29/**6**:3,4:5^2:6,7^3:9:11^3:12^2:13:18^2:
20:21^3:22,23:24,25,26^2:27/**7**:11:12:18-23:24-29:
30-35:48-53:60-65:66-71^2:72-77:78-83/**8**:13:19:
22/**9**:13/**10**:10:18:29:30/**11**:1:29/**12**:1:1f/**14**:9:
24/**15**:30:31:31f:31:39/**16**:5^2:17:40/**17**:1:5:9/**18**:
31/**19**:4:7:8:10:19:21/**20**:14f:20:25:26:28/**21**:1:2
:23:27-30^2:33:35^2/**22**:2,3:5,6:11:14:21:27:36/**23**:
2:18-24/**24**:10:15-19:23,24/**25**:3:4:8:12,13^3/**26**:
28-37/**27**:1^2:8^2:9:10:23^2/**30**:5:8:16^2/**31**:28/**32**:
15:21:28:42/**33**:38,39:40/**35**:12^2:19:21:28:32/**36**
:1/**Deu1**:30:31:36/**2**:24:32:33,34/**3**:1^3:3:4:11/**4**:
9:12:20^2:36^3:44,45,46:47/**5**:5:21:24^2:32/**6**:2:13:
15:16:22/**7**:6:7:8:9^2:12^2/**8**:5:6:18/**9**:5/**10**:6:8^2:20
/**11**:1:2^2:3:12:13:22/**12**:4,5:11^2:17/**13**:2:4:8:11:
17:18/**14**:2:23:24/**15**:2:4,5:17:20/**16**:2:6:10/**17**:
16:17:18:19^4:20^3/**18**:6,7:8^2:10:19:20/**19**:5:9:11:
12:19/**21**:5:15:16:17^3:18:19:23/**22**:16:19:30:30f^2
:30/**23**:1:2:13:15,16/**24**:1:5:6:10^2:12,13:14,15:16
/**25**:1:5:6:7^2:9^4:10^2/**26**:2,3:17:18^2/**27**:16:17^2:20^2
:22:23/**28**:9:12:20:54^3:55/**29**:2,3:13:20^2:23:24:
26:27/**30**:7,8:16^2/**31**:12^2:14:29/**32**:4:5:10:11^2:16
:19:36:40,41^5/**33**:1:2:3^3:6:7:9:12:13:16:24^2/**34**:7:
9:11,12/**Jos2**:7/**4**:14/**6**:19:26:27/**7**:2:18:24^4/**8**:1
:3,4:10:19:26:31/**9**:24/**10**:22,23:24:25:26:33^2:40:
42:43/**11**:7:9:15/**12**:2:5/**15**:16/**20**:6/**22**:5:19/**23**:
15,16/**24**:3:4:30:33/**Ju1**:1:4,5,6:12:13^2:24^2:25/**2**
:7-9^2:18^2/**3**:8:16^2:17,18,19:21^3:27/**4**:2,3:7:11:12:
13:14:15:16:21:22:24/**5**:10:17^2:22:23:26^2:28^2/**6**:
21:25:27^2:31/**7**:1^2:12,13:15:17:19,20:25/**8**:4:20:
21f:27^2:32/**9**:1^2:3^2:5^2:16:17:18^2:19:21:26:28^2:31:
34:35:41:43^2:44:47,48^3:53:54^2:55/**10**:4:7,8/**11**:1^3
:3^2:13:17:19:25:29:30,31:32:34^2:35:39f/**12**:4:7:
9,10^3/**13**:5:6:7^2:9^2:11:17:20^2:22:23/**14**:2:3:4:5:6:
9:10,11:14:15:19^3:20/**15**:1:6:14^2/**16**:3:6:9:12:14:
16,17:19^3:21:22:29:30^2:31^3/**17**:2^2:4,5^3:6:12/**18**:4^2
:19:22:30/**19**:1:7:9^2:11:12,13:16^2:27/**Ru1**:1^2:6,7:
21/**2**:1:2:4,5:14:15:20:21:22/**3**:3:4:6,7:8:13:14:
15-18/**4**:3:6f:7:8:18-22/**1Sa1**:1^4:3:4:9:11^2/**2**:9:
10^2:19:22:23,24,25:28:31:32:35^2/**3**:13^2:14:19/**4**:
12^2:13:18^2/**5**:3:4^2:5/**7**:1:15:16:17/**8**:1^3:2:5^2:11:
12^3:14:15:16:17/**9**:2:22/**10**:1:11:12:15:24:26^2/
11:11/**12**:3:5:14:15:22^2/**13**:1:3,4:8:10:14/**14**:1^2:
2:3:6:12:17:20:27:28:35:36:45:50,51^3:52/**15**:2:4:
9:27:29/**16**:1:3:5:8:9:13:19:21/**17**:4-7:14,15:22^2:
23:25^2:26:38,39:40^2:41,42:43:47:48,49^3:50,51:
54^2:55:55f:57:58/**18**:1^2:4:5^2:7^2:10:13:22^2:27/**19**:
1^3:2:4:5:8:9,10^2:13:15:24/**20**:16^2:17:24,25:27:
28,29:33^2:34:35:38:40/**21**:11^3:13^2:14,15/**22**:1:3:
6^3:7:11,12:17/**23**:6:8^2:13:16:23:24,25^2:26^2/**24**:1:
3:5:6:7,8^2:14:19^2:22/**25**:1^2:2:3^2:4:5:9:13:17:21:
22:25:28:29:30,31:37,38:37,38f:39^3:41:42/**26**:2:
3,4:5,6,7^2:11^2:16:23/**27**:2,3^2:8/**28**:1:3:7,8^4:25/
29:2:4:5^2:6/**30**:1:3:6:9,10:11,12:17:18,19:20:27-
27-31/**31**:2:3,4^3:5^2:6^3:7:8:9:10^2:12/**2Sa1**:1^2:4:6:
10f:10^2:11:12:15^2/**2**:2:3:6:9:16^2:23^3:28^2:29:30:
32^2/**3**:2:3:7:19:27:29^2:30:35,36:38/**4**:1:6,7^3:8:10:
11^2:12/**5**:2:6:7:8:9:12^3:14,15,16:21/**6**:6:11:14:20
:21/**7**:12:13:14/**8**:2:3:10:13:16^2:18^2/**9**:9:10,11^2/
10:1:2^2:9^2:10:13:19/**11**:2f:8:11:19,20,21:27^2/**12**:
3^4:4:8^2:9:15:20^2:21:29,30^2/**13**:2:3:6:8:9:15:17,18
:21-24^3:25:27:28:31^2:36:37,38,39f^2:37,38,39/**14**:
7:14:24:26:30/**15**:2:5:10:11:14:15:16^2:17,18:22:
23:30^2:31:32/**16**:5:7,8^2:9:13:15:22/**17**:2,3:8:10:
12:16:18:23^5:25^2/**18**:1:2:9^3:13:16:19:20:24:28:33
/**19**:2:4^2:24,25^2:31,32:41/**20**:3^3:8,9,10^6:12:14:21
:22/**21**:1:2:5,6:8:15:17/**22**:1:7^2:8:9^2:13:15^2:16:20
:23:31:51^3/**23**:2:5:10^2:11,12:23/**24**:2:14:20^2:25/
1Ki1:1^2:2:3,4:5^2:6:7:9^2:10:19:25:41:49,50/**2**:1:3^2
:12^2:19^4:26:27:31:33^2:34:40/**3**:1^2:3:7:10:15/**4**:21
:24:27:30:34/**5**:2,3:11/**6**:38/**7**:1:8^2:14:51/**8**:9:
22,23:25:54,55:56^3:58:61:66^2/**9**:15:16:19^2:20,21
/**10**:4:5^2:12:16,17:21:24:28/**11**:2:3:4^2:6:23:25:26
:27,28^3:30:33:34:35:36:43^3/**12**:2,3,4:6:15:16,17^2:
21:25:28/**13**:3:4^2:11:21,22:24,25:26:27:30:31^2:
32:33:34/**14**:2:4:8:19^2:20:22:24:31^3/**15**:1:3^2:5:8^2
:10:11:12:13:14f:15:15f:18:20:23^3:24:26/**16**:4-7^3
:13:20:23:28^2:30:34^3/**17**:19:23/**18**:10:42^3:43:44^2
/**19**:3^2:13^2:19^2:21^2/**20**:1:7:12:15:31:33:38:41:42^2
/**21**:4:5:6:8:25:27:29^3/**22**:3:6:8:9:19:22:31:32,33:
34^2:35^2:36,37^2:38:40^2:42:43:45^2:46:49:50^3:52,53
/**2Ki1**:2:13:17/**2**:8:12:23/**3**:1^2:2^2:4:26:27/**4**:1:
11,12:18:19^2:20:27:34^3:35:37:42/**5**:1^2:3:6:7:9:10:
11^2:13:14:15:20:21:23:24:25:26:27/**6**:5:8:11:17:
24:26-30^2:32^2/**7**:12:13:17/**8**:6:16:19^2:21:24,25:
26:28:29/**9**:2:3:6:11:15:17:24^4:25^2:26:27:28:31/
10:2,3:9,10^2:11:11f:14:18,19:24:25:31:35/**11**:1:
2,3^3:12/**12**:1:2:6:18:20^2:21f:21/**13**:3:7:9,10:12:
14:16,17^2:20,21^2:23:24^2:25/**14**:1:2:3^2:5:6:8:11:
15:16:18:19^2:20:21:22:28^2:29/**15**:1^5:3:4:5^2:7^2:8:9
:15:22:25:29:32,33^2:34,35:38/**16**:1:2:3:11,12:20/
17:1^2:4:13:15^2:18:23/**18**:1^6:9:12:17^3:18^3/**19**:1:8:
19:37^3/**20**:2:5^3:6:12:13:20:21/**21**:1^5:3,4,5^2:6:16:
18^2:19,20^5:21:22^2:23:26/**22**:1^6:3,4^2:11/**23**:10:16:
18^2:21:25:26:30^3:31,32^4:33:34:36,37^4/**24**:2:3,4:6
:8,9^4:10:12:15:17:18,19^4:20/**25**:1:2:4,5^2:7^3:18:25
:27:29:30/**1Ch1**:13-16:19:32:33:50/**2**:7:13^2:14^2:
15^2:24^2:29:34,35^2:54/**3**:1:2:3:5^2:9/**4**:3-4:9^3:10:
25^2:27/**5**:1^4:4^3:5^2:7,8:9/**6**:25,26,27:29,30:33-38:
39-43:44-47:49/**7**:14:16:22:23:34:35/**8**:8,9,10^2:
11:13:29:30,31,32/**9**:5:6:19:38^2/**10**:2:4^3:5:6:7:8:
9:10^2:12^2:13/**11**:5,6:11:14:17:20^2:23:24,25:26-
26-47/**12**:3-7:18:19^2:24-37^2/**13**:1:2:9:14/**14**:2:8/
15:22/**16**:4^2:5:8:9^2:10:11^2:12,13^4:14:15:16^2:17:
24^2:28:29:34^2:37:39:41:43/**17**:1:11:12:13:14/**18**:
3:4^2:6:10^2:17/**19**:1:2,3^2:5:6:7^2:10:11:12:14:19/
20:2:3^2:5:6,7:8/**21**:3:6:15:16:19,20:27:28/**22**:5:6:
9^3:10^3:12:17:18/**23**:1:7:10,11:12:13^2:14,15:17:22
:27/**24**:20:21:22:23^3:24,25^2:26,27^3/**25**:2:3:4,5:9-
9-31^{23}/**26**:2,3^2:10:11:14,15^4:26:28:29:30/**27**:4:
5,6^2:7:23^2:27:33/**28**:1^3:4:5:6:7:10:12/**29**:10:23:
24:25:26,27:28^2:30^2/**2Ch1**:1/**2**:3:11:14:17/**5**:1:
13,14/**6**:3:9:11:12,13:14:22:29/**7**:6:10:11:22/**8**:1
:2:6^2:11:14/**9**:3:4^3:13,14:16:21:23:31/**10**:5:6:15:
16^2:18/**11**:21:22:23/**12**:1:10:13^2:16/**13**:1^2:6:12:
13,14:18,19:20:22/**14**:1^2:2:5:7:8:9,10:13/**15**:16:
17:18/**16**:4:5:9:12^2:13,14^4/**17**:1:2:3:4:5:7,8,9:13^2
:18/**18**:1:2:3,4,5:6,7:8:18:30:31:33:34/**19**:9:11/
20:18:20:21:25:30:31:32:35/**21**:1:2:3,4:6:7:8:9^2:
10:11:17^3:19^2/**22**:1^2:2:3:4^2:5:7:9^2:11:12^2/**23**:1^2:
2,3:11^2:12:15,16,17:20/**24**:1:17,18:20:22^2:25:27
/**25**:1:3:4:11:17:27/**26**:2:3:4:7^3:8:11^2:16:19:21^3:
23/**27**:1:2^2:5:6:7^2:9/**28**:1:3:5^2:6:16^2:23^2:25:26:27
/**29**:1:2^2:3:6:10:23:29/**30**:2,3:4:8^2:9:12:17,18,19:
27/**31**:7,8^2:10:12,13:14,15:20/**32**:3:5:7:15:21^3:
22:27^2:28,29^2:31:33^2/**33**:2:3:6:7:10:12:13^2:14:15
:18:19^3:20,21^2:22^2:23:24^2:25/**34**:2^2:3^2:8:15,16:
19:31^2:33/**35**:3:4,5:9:20:22^2:23:24,25^3:26/**36**:5:7
:8:12:15^3:19:20:22,23/**Ez1**:1:3:7/**3**:1^2:7:11/**4**:4,5
/**5**:5:13/**6**:11^2/**7**:6^2:23^2:28^2/**8**:17:18:19:25:36/**9**:
4/**10**:14/**Neh1**:5:11/**2**:1:20/**3**:10:12:17:18:28:29
:30/**4**:1/**6**:5,6:18^2/**7**:3/**8**:1^2/**9**:5:8:10/**10**:29/**11**:
15,16,17/**12**:45/**13**:6:8:30/**Est1**:1:4:8:10:13-15^3:
21:22^3/**2**:2^2:7f:7^2:9:15:16:18:20/**3**:3,4:10^3:12/**4**:
1:11^2/**5**:1:5:10^2:11^2:12:14^2/**6**:1:3:12:13^2/**7**:7^2/**8**:
2:3/**9**:4:24,25:29-31/**10**:2:3^3/**Job1**:4^2:5:10^2:11:
12,13:20:20f^2:21/**2**:3:4,5^2:6:9:13/**3**:1:19/**4**:17:
18,19/**6**:4^2:5,6,7:8,9^2/**7**:2:18/**8**:15:16:17/**9**:5:13:
34/**11**:8:9/**12**:14:16/**13**:7:11:16/**14**:1:10:11,12:
20,21/**15**:7,8:11:20:23,24^2:25,26^2:29:31:33f:33/
16:9:12:13:21/**18**:7:11:12:13:15:16:17:20/**19**:6:
11:12/**20**:6:7:9^2:10^2:11:12^2:18:21:22:23:25^2:26^2:
27:28/**21**:14:17:19:20:21:30-32/**22**:21:22/**23**:3:
4,5:6:9:11:12:13^2:15/**24**:22,23/**25**:3^2:6/**26**:8:9^2:
11:12:13:14^2/**27**:8:9:17^2:19:23/**28**:8/**29**:25/**30**:
24^2/**32**:1:13/**33**:6:10:25:26:27:30/**34**:14:22:33/
35:6/**36**:5:6:10:13:24:31:32:33/**37**:2:3:4:5^2:7:11:
12:13/**39**:19:20:21-23/**40**:16^2:17^2:18^2:24/**41**:1:2
:7^2:12^2:13^2:14:15-17^2:18:19:20:21^2:22:23:24:30:
31,32/**42**:8:10^2:11^3:12:13,14:15:16/**Ps1**:2/**2**:2f:3
:7:12^4/**3**:1:4:4f:8/**5**:11/**7**:12^2:14:15/**8**:5:6/**9**:7,8:
11/**10**:16/**11**:4:6:7:7f/**14**:7/**15**:3:5/**18**:1:6:6f:6:8^2
:9:11:12:14:21:22:24:30/**19**:1:5:5f/**20**:2/**21**:3:4^2/
22:8:23^2:26/**24**:1/**25**:10^2:13:14/**27**:4^3:6:13/**28**:8^2
/**29**:1^3:2^2:4:9:10^2:11/**30**:4^2:5^2:6,7/**31**:5,6:21:23/
32:6:11/**33**:5:7:9:11^2:12:18,19:21/**34**:1:1f:2:3:6:8
:16:17/**35**:10:27/**37**:24:28:34/**39**:5,6:11/**40**:16/
41:3f^2/**42**:3:4,5:4,5f:8^2/**43**:5/**45**:1/**46**:5/**47**:4^2:8:
9/**49**:7:12:18:20/**50**:4/**51**:1^2/**52**:7f/**53**:1^3/**55**:19:
20:21^3/**56**:10,11^2/**57**:3^2/**59**:1:10/**60**:1:6,7/**62**:9/
64:7/**65**:6:9/**66**:2:5:7:8:9:20/**68**:4^2:5f:17:18:21:
22:23:34^2:35/**69**:9:30:33:35:36/**72**:1:3:7:9:15:17:
19^2/**73**:8/**75**/**76**:2/**77**:3:8^2:9/**78**:5:6:7^2:10^2:21:26
:38:40:41:42:49:50:52:54:56:59^2:60:61^2:62^2:66:
69:70:71,72/**81**:5/**84**:11/**85**:8^2:9^2:12:13:13f/**87**:
1/**89**:3,4^2:22:23:29:30,31,32:35,36^2:35,36f:39:41
:42:43:44^2:45:48/**91**:4^2:11/**92**:2:3:9:13:15/**93**:1/
94:12,13:14^2/**95**:4:5:7/**96**:2^2:3:6:8f:10:11:12/**97**:
2:3:4:6^2:10:12f/**98**:1^2:2,3^2/**99**:5:6:7:9/**100**:3^2:4^3:
5/**101**/**102**:15:16:19:20:21,22/**103**:7:11:17,18^2:
19:20^3:21/**104**:3:4^2:14:15:31:32^2/**105**:2^2:4:5,6:7:
7f:8,9^2:10,11:14:17:18^2:19:22:23:26:28:37:42^2:
43:45/**106**:12^2:16:17:23^2:24:25:40:45^2/**107**:8^2:
15^2:21^2:22:31^2/**108**:5/**109**:7^2:8:9,10^2:11:12,13^2:
14:15:18:19^2:22,23/**110**:4:5/**111**:1^2:3^2:5:6^2:7:9:
10^2/**112**:1:2:3:3f:5:7:8:9:9f/**113**:1:2:4/**115**:11/
116:9:13:15:15f/**117**:2/**118**:1:2:3:4:10:11:12:17:
29/**119**:2:3/**121**:8/**123**:2^3/**125**/**126**:1/**127**:2:3:5^2
/**130**:3,4/**132**:7f^2:18/**133**:2^2/**135**:1^2:3:4:7:9:12:
14^2:19:20/**136**:1:2:3:4:5:6:7:8:9:10:11,12:13:14:
15:16^2:17^2:18:20:21:22^2:23:24:25:26/**138**:5:8/
142:1/**144**:4/**145**:3:9:21/**146**:4:5^2/**147**:1:5^2:10:
11:15^2:17:19:20/**148**:2:5:6:13:14^2/**149**:1^2:3:4,5^2:
6,7^2:9/**150**:1:1f:2^2/**Pro1**:2/**2**:6:7,8/**3**:11,12^2:19:
20:32:33/**4**:4/**5**:22/**6**:1:12,13^2:14^2:26:27:28:31:
32:33:34^2/**8**:27,28,29:30^3:31^2/**10**:5:6:8:14:15^2:
16:17:26/**11**:3^2:6:7:9f^2:12:15:26:27:29/**12**:4:10:
11f^2:11:17:23^2/**13**:1:2:22^2/**14**:3:10:20:26:28:29/
15:3:5:8:20^2:20f:28/**16**:4:7:11f:12^2:13:20:21:22:
27:27f:29f:30/**17**:2:6^2:12:18:25^2:27,28/**18**:1:2f:
6,7^3:11:14:19/**19**:3^2:6:7:8:11^2:12:13:14:18^2:19:
25:26:28/**20**:2:14:20:27:28/**21**:8:10:13^2:22:25,26
/**22**:5:8/**23**:1/**24**:11,12:15,16:19,20^2:28,29/**25**:
4,5:20^2/**26**:3:4,5f:4,5:11^2:14:15^3:16:18,19:
24,25,26^3/**27**:21:22:23,24/**28**:7:13:16:24/**29**:3:4:
11:12:15:18/**30**:4^4:6:10:17^3:29,30,31/**31**:1:11/
Ecc1:3-7/**2**:20-23^2:24-26^2/**3**:13/**5**:9:16:17:18^3:
19,20/**6**:3^2:4/**7**:7:18:29/**8**:8^2/**9**:14/**10**:4:12,13/
12:5:13/**Sol1**:4:12/**2**:3^2:6^2:16/**3**:7:8^3:11^3/**4**:16/**5**
:11:12:13^3:14^2:15:16/**6**:2^3:3:12f/**8**:3^2/**Is1**:3/**2**:5:
10:19^3:21:22/**3**:6:8:13^2:14/**5**:1:2:7^2:25^5/**6**:1:3/**7**:
2:17/**8**:1:7,8:14,15:18^2/**9**:4:6^2:7^2:11,12:16:17^2:
19,20^2:21/**10**:5,6^2:7:8:12:14:22:26:27:32/**11**:3:8:
11:15/**12**:4^2:4f:5:6/**13**:5^2:9/**14**:1:3:17:22^3:24:27^2
:29^2:32/**15**:5/**16**:6/**18**:4:7/**19**:17/**20**:1:2^2/**22**:8:
18:23,24/**23**:9:11/**24**:4,5:23^2/**25**:8:10:11/**26**:1/
27:1:11:12:13/**28**:5:15:21:25^2/**29**:23f^2/**30**:2:3:4:
18^2:26:27^2:28:29:30^3:31:32/**31**:2^3:3:7/**32**:3^2:20/
33:17/**34**:2:16/**35**:2/**36**:7:12^2/**37**:1:2^2:6:7:8,9:30
:33:34:37:38^3/**38**:2:9:12:18f/**39**:1:2^3/**40**:6:10:11^2
:12^2:13:17:20:22:26:28/**41**:6:24/**42**:5:10:12:13:
14:21:22^2:24:25/**44**:10:12^2:15^2:16:17:28f/**45**:1:9
:10:13/**46**:7/**47**:4/**48**:16:20/**49**:2^2:5:10:13:24/**50**
:4^2:7:10/**51**:20:22/**52**:8:9:10:14,15/**53**:1:4^2:8:10:
10f:10:11:12/**54**:5/**56**:4^2:6^3:10/**58**:8/**59**:2:16:17:
18^2/**61**:2:3:10:11^2/**62**:1^2:3:4:5:6,7:8:11/**63**:1^2:7^2:

(HIS Con't)
9:10:11^3:12^2/65:11:15/66:3:5:6:14^3:15^2:16/Jer2
:3f/4:7:13^2:26/5:8:14/7:29/8:4,5,8/9:23^3/10:10^2
:12^2:13^2:16^2:21:23^2/11:8^2:16:19^2/12:5^2:14:15/
13:18f:23^2/16:14,15/17:5^2:7:10^2:11^3:26/18:3:6:
18/20:9^2/21:1/22:9:11:12:15:18^3:24,25f^2:24,25:
28:30^2/23:5,6/24:8/25:1:2,3:4:12:19,20^2:30^2:38
/26:7,8:12/27:6:7^3:8/28:9/29:31:32^2/30:24/31:
7:10^2:30:32f:35/32:19/33:2:10,11:20,21:25,26/
34:1:9:21/35:3/36:21:23:30f:30:31^2/37:1f:2:18/
38:6:16^2/39:1:4:6:9:14^2/40:8/41:7:13,14:15:
16,17/42:7:8:9:11/43:10^2:12^2/44:30f^2:30/46:2:
10:26/48:7/49:3:22/50:18:25^3:28:34:43^2/51:6:
11^3:14:15^2:16:19^2:21:34,35:44/52:1:3:4:8:10^2:11^2
:24,25^2:30:34^2/Lam1:12:15^2/2:1^3:2:3^2:4^2:5:6^2:7^2
/3:3:11:12:13:22:23^2:32/4:11:20/Eze1:10^3:11^2:
23:27,28^2/3:20^3/7:13:16/8:2^2/9^3/10:7,8^2/12:12
f^2:13f^2:14:27/13:17/14:9/16:15/17:16:17:18/18
:10:12:13^2:14:17:18^2:19:20^4:21:22^2:23:24^2:26:27^2
:28/19:9/20:1/21:5^2:21/24:27/26:10/29:19:20/
30:11:22^2:24:25/31:2,3:18/32:31:32/33:4:5^2:8^2:
9:11:12:13^3:14:16:19:20/34:12/35/38:6/39:11^2
/40:3:5/43:2^2/44:25:26/45:1:8/46:2:7f:12:16:17^2
:18^2/Dan1:1^2:3,4:3,4f:5^2:8:9:15:18,19:20/2:1^4:
13:17:18:21:46:48/3:2^2:7:19:20:22:24:28^2:29/4:
3:33^4:34/5:1:2,3,4:6^3:7:7f:9^2:12:19:20^3:21^3:22:
23:29/6:3:4:5:10^2:11:12:13:17^2:18^2:22:23:25,26^2
:27/7:1:9^2:14^2:15:22^2:24^2:25:26/8:7:8^2:11:16:24:
24f:24:25/9:2:20:26:27^3/10:5,6^5:11/11:1:2:4^4:5:
6f:7f:9:12^2:15:17:18:20:21f:23^2:24:25:26^3:29:32:
36:37:38:39:40:43:45^2/Hos1:11/3:5/5:7/6:2/7:
10^2/11:4^2/12:2:3:5:13:14/13:1:14:15^3/Joe2:11^2:
14:16:18^2/3:16^2/Amo1:2^4:10:11:15/2:7/3:12/4:
2:13^2/5:8:15:19/6:8:10/9:6^2/Ob1:11^3:12^2:13^2:
14/Jon:14/2:1/3:6^2:7:8^2:9:10/4:8/Mic1:2:3:4/2
:7/3:4:5/4:2^2:4:6:12/5:3:4^3/6:1:2/7:6^2:7:9:18/
Nah1:3^3:4:5:6^2:8:10:12/2:5/Hab:4f:20/3:3^3:4:4f
:4:6:13/Zep1:7^2:7f:18/2:2:3:7:11:12:15/3:5:15/
Hag1:3,4:13:14,15/2:12:14/Zec1:14/2:1:6,7:8:
13/3:2:4:5,6/5:4/6:5:12f/7:2:12/8:22/9:10:14^3:
15:16,17^3/10:3/11:17^4/13:3:4:6f/14:4:5:5f:9/
Mal1:2,3:4:6^2:14/2:5:12:15/3:1:2:14,15/4:2/Mt
1:2:5^2:6:11:18:21:22:24/2:2:11:13:20:21/3:1:4:
11:16/4:6:24/5:1:28^2:31:32:35:38:45/6:29/7:9:
24:25:26:27/8:5,6^2:8,9:18:21:23/9:1:1f:10:20:31:
37:38/10:1:2,3,4:11:24^2:25^2:32:35:36/11:1:1f:2:
20^2/12:1^2:3:11:13:16:19:20:21:26:29:29f:34:35:
46,47:49/13:2,3^2:10:19:21^3:22:24:25:31,32:36:
44:52f:53,54^3:55^2:56:57^2/14:1f:2:3^2:9^2:11:12:22:
31:36/15:4:23:32/16:13:21:24:25^2:27/17:1:2^3:
10/18:6:15:23:24:25:26:27:30/19:5,6^2:7:9:13:15:
23:29/20:1:4/21:29:31^2:34^2:35:36:37:43:45/22:
1:5^2:6:7:8:13:21:22:24:25:33:34,35:45/23:1/24/
25:14:15:19^2:21:23:26:41/26:1:7:23f:65,66:67:
73/27:3:18:24:25:29^2:31:32:35:37:41,42,43:44:
50:60:64^2/28:3^2:6:7:9:12,13:18/Mk1:2^2:3:3f:6^2:
7^2:16:21:22^2:27:29,30:45/2:1:4^2:12:14^2:15^3:16:
18:23:25,26/3:4:5:7,8^2:9:14,15:21^2:22:27^3:30:
31,32/4:2:3:10:26:27:29:34^3:35:38/5:3,4:20:23:
27:28:31:33:35:40/6:1^2:2,3^3:4^3:5:7:14:17,18:20:
21:26^2:27:28:29:35,36:45:55:56/7:2:10:11:17:24:
25:32:33/8:1:4:6:10:11:23^2:25^2:26:27:33:34:36:
37/9:1:2:3:18:19:27:28:30,31:36:38:41:42/10:1f^2
:4:6,7:8:10:11:14:15:16^2:23:30:50/11:1/12:2^2:4^2:
6:7:8:12:17^2:19^2:37^2:43,44/13:1:20:34^2/14:3:10:
12:32:39:43:47:50:51,52:63,64^2:65/15:16,17:20:
24:26^2:27:34f:37:39^2:41:42,43/16:6:7:12/Lk1:5:
8,9^2:14:15:16:17:22:23:24:32:33:48:50:51:54^2:55
:59:62f:63:67:68:69:70:72,73:75:77:80/2:3:5:22:
28:40^2:41,42:43:46,47:48^2:51/3:1:9:16:16f:19,20^2
:23-38/4:9,10,11:15:16:22:24:32:40:41/5:8:10:
15:18,19:25^2:29:30/6:1:3:11:13^3:17,18:20:39:40:
41:42:45/7:1:3:10:11^2:12:13:15:19:20,21,22:23:
33:36:38^2:40/8:1:3^2:5:9:19:22:42:43,44/9:1:16:
18:23^2:24^2:29:29f:29:31:36:41:42:43:49:51:59^2:
59f/10:2:7:29:30:34^2:35/11:1^2:7:14:15:16:18^2:
21:22^2:37,38/12:1:17^2:22:27:37:38:39:42,43,44^2:
45:46^2:47:53/13:6:7:17/14:12:17:21^2:23:26f:26^2
:27:31^2:33/15:12^4:13^2:14:15:17:20^2:21:22^2:27:28
:31/16:1^2:2:5,6:18:20:21:23:24/17:1:2,3:7,8,9^3:
22:33^2/18:1:4,5:7:13^2:24/19:6:8:9,10:12:14:15:
19:28/20:4:5:10^2:14^2:16:19:25^2:26:28:30:45/21:
5/22:11:27:47:50/23:11:14:26:34/24:9:22,23^3:
26:40^2:50/Jn1:5:11,12^2:11,12f:14:14f:18:27^2:35:
41:45/2:2:5:11^2:11f:12:17:21:22/3:4:16:17:22:
29:35/4:1^2:5,6:8:12:21-24:27:34:43,44:45:46,47^2
:51^3:52:53/5:11:17:18:22:24:26:32,33f:32,33/6:
2-5:12:16:22,23:24:40:52:53:60:61:66/7:1:5:10:
18:39/8:6:12:20:39:47/9:2^3:8:15:18:20:27:28:31
/10:3^2:4:5:11:12:41/11:4:7:8:16:17:32:44:51:54^2
/12:4:6:9:16^2:23,24:47:50/13:1^4:4^2:10:12:16:23f:
23:25f:32/14:10:22/15:10:13^2:15:20/16:13:
17,18:29:32/18:1:2:19:22:25:28:32:32f/19:2:17:
23,24^2:25:26^2:29:30^2:33:34:35f:36,37/20:18:20:
25^2/21:7:11:14/Act1:1:3:18^2:19:20^2:24,25/2:23:
26:29:31:34:40/3:2:7,8:12:13:26/4:10:32/5:1:2:
7:17:21:26,27:35:36:37:40:41/7:3^2:4:5^2:6:10:12:
13^2:14^2:15:17,18^2:20:23^3:25:27:29:35:48,49:56:
57:60/8:12:28:32:33^2:33f^2:33:39/9:12:17:18:22^2
:25:27:30^2:32:41/10:2:7^2:9,10:24:25:43/12:5:7:
11:15:21^2/13:8:11^2:25:29:35:36^2/14:10:17/15:
14:18/16:1:3:9:10f:27:32:33:34^2/17:3:7:18:25:
27/18:2,3:5:6:8:14^2:18:27/19:4:6:9:12^2:16:22:25
:31/20:3:9:10,11,12:28^2:32^2/21:11:12:19:26,27:
32/22:14:15:24:30/23:10:23,24:26:30/24:23^2:24
:24f/25:1:12:13f:16:25/26:1f:1/28:3:8:17:20f^2:
23:30:30f/Rom1:3:6,7:9:18:20:21/2:4:6:12-15:
17^2:18:20:27^2:29^2/3:2^2:3:7:20:21,22:24:25/4:1^2:
3:4,5^2:9:11^2:12:13^2:15^2:19^2:20:22:23/5:1:5:8:9:
10^3:12:13^2:15/6:2,3:4:5f:5:8:13:16:22/8:3:15:16:
17^5:19:23:28:29^2:30:32:33:36:38/9:4^2:5:6:10-13^2
:22:23,24^2:25:28^2:31/10:4:5:10^4:12:19^3:21/11:1:
2,3:11^3:15:17^2:24:28^2:29^2:30:33^3:34:36^2/12:2:20
/13:8:9^2:12,13/14:1:3:8/15:1:8:9:10/16:13^2:15:
23^3/1Co1:2:3:7:9:21^2:25/2:2:10^2:12/3:8:10:14:
16:19/4:2/5:1:1f:5/6:6:9,10:14:16/7:2:3:4^3:11:
14:15:25:32:33^2:34:36/8:1:2:6/9:7^2:13/10:10^2:
16:28:29/11:4:7^3:23:24/12:6:8:28^2/13:12^2/14:
21:22:24:25^2:32:38:38f/15:22:23^2:25:27:28^2:48/
16:11:15/2Co1:5:11:12:20:22^3/3:6:7:13:14:16/4
:1^2:6:15/5:5:10:18/7:7:9:10:12:13/8:1/9:7:9:15^2
/10:1:10/11:15:29/12:5:16/13:3:4/Gal1:6:15:16
/2:7,8,9/3:11:16^4:19:20:21,22/4:1^2:2^2:4:5:6^2:7:
22^2:24,25/5:17:24/6:4:5:8:17/Eph1:2:4^3:5^2:6^3:7^2
:8:9:10:11:14:19:21:22:23/2:5:7:8:13:15/3:2,3^2:5^2
:6:7^2:10^3:12:14,15:16^2:18,19:20:21/4:7:8:11:
15,16^2:17,18:21:28/5:1:23^3:28^2:29,30^2:31^2:33/6:
19:22/Php1:2^2:6^2/2:7:21:30/3:20:21/4:6:7:19/
Col1:2:4:11:13:14:16:17:18^2:19:20^2:21^2:22:24:25^2
:26,27/2:14:19^2/3:4:12:15:16/4:10:11:12^2:13:14
:15/1Th2:4:11:12^2/3:13f/4:5:8/5:6:9:10:24/2Th
1:5:7:8:9:10^2:11/2:6:8^2/3:6^2:16/1Ti1:2:12:13:18
/2:6/3:2:5:7:16^2/4:9,10:14/5:5:8^2:20:22/6:1/
2Ti1:2:9^3:11:12:16^2/2:4:5:13:15:19:21/4:1:8^2:18
/Tit1:3:4^2:15/2:13:14/3:5:7/Phm1:3^2:5:23/Heb
:1:2:3:4^2:5,6^2:7:8:13:14/2:10^2:11:12:17/3:3:5:7,8^2
:9^2:11:18/4:1^2:3:10:16/5:1:7f^2:7^2/6:10:13:17:18^2
:20/7:2:3f:3^2:12,13,14:21:25:28^2/8:11/9:1:7:12:
14/10:4f:13^2:20:25:27:28:29^2:37/11:4:7^2:11:17^2:
20:21:22^2:28:31:39/12:2:3:5:6:7:8:10:16:18:24:
26/13:12:13:15:20,21^2/Jas1:10,11:12:18f:18^2:
23:26^2:27/2:2:4:13:21:22^3/3:1:3/5:7:11:15:20/
1Pe1:2:3:4:5:7:11^2:14:15:25/2:2,3:5^2:9:21:23:24^2
/3:12:18^2/4:13^2:16/5:1^2:4:6:10:12/2Pe1:3^3:4:6:
16^3:17,18/2:2:5:16^2:21/3:5,6:9:15,16^4/1Jn1:3:6:
7/2:1:9:10^2:11:22:24:29/3:1^2:6:10:12^3:15:23/4:3
:9^2:10^2:12:13:14:16:18:19:20^2:21/5:1:6,7,8:9:10:
11:12:14:18:20/2Jn1:3:11/Jud:3:11^2:14:21:
24,25^4/Rev:1:4:5:6^2:7f:9:13:14:14f:14:15^2:16^2:
16f:16:17,18^2/2:1f:1/3:5^2:21/4:3:4:5/5:6/6:2:5/
7:3:15/8:7:8,9:12/9:1:13/10:1^3:2^3:5:7^2:10/11:15^2
:15f:19/12:3:4:5:7^2:9:10/13:2:3:6:17:18/14:1^2:7:
9^2:11^2:12^2:13:14^2:16:19/15:2^2:8/16:2^2:3:4:8:10^3:
12:13:17:19/17:8:9:10:11^2:12:14:16:17/18:1/19:
2^2:5:7:10:12^3:13:15:16:19:20^2/20:1:4^2:7:13/21:3
:7:15/22:3:4^2:6,7^2:16:19

6722

HOW

Gen3:6:13/4:9/6:12,13/15:8/19:18,19,20/24:14
/26:10/27:11,12^2:20/29:6:15/30:26:28:29^2/31:
6:43/37:13,14^2/38:16/39:9/42:8,9:12/43:7:22:
27^2:29/44:16^2:34/45:13/47:8/49:15^2/Ex2:18/5
:22/6:12/10:2:3/16:28,29/18:1:8:14/19:4/22:27
/32:5/Lev7:38/27:11,12/Num6:27/9:22/10:31f
/12:7,8/14:10,11:26,27/20:15/22:2,3/23:7-10^2/
26:2/Deu1:31/4:8/7:17/8:2^2/9:7:8:16:19/11:4^2:
5:8:23/12:30/18:21/29:16^2/31:13:27^2/32:3:30/
33:3/Jos2:10^2/4:23/9:7/10:1^2/13:32/18:3/Ju1:
25/2:17/5:9:11/6:15/8:28/13:12/16:5:10:13:15
/18:7:15,16:25/21:7/Ru1:13/2:10,11^2/1Sa:1^3:
23,24,25/5:8/10:2:27/14:6:12:29:30/16:2/17:
18:33/18:23:28^2/19:5/20:10:12/21:5/28:21/
2Sa1:4:5:23^2:26^2/2/4:10:11/5:8/6:9:20/7:22/
10:6/11:7^2:18/13:26/14:1:19/17:10:21/19:20:
28/23:15/24:2/1Ki1:1/2:9/10:1:8:9/11:22:
27,28/17:16/18:21/20:14/21:29/22:16:22/2Ki4
:2/9:14:22:31/10:16/13:4/14:28/17:27,28/20:3:
20/1Ch13:12/18:13/21:8/2Ch5:11,12/6:18:19/
7:3/9^2:4^2:8/12/18:15:19,20/20:11:26/23:4/24:
22/25:8:27^2/31:7,8/32:15:22/34:18/35:26/Ez
10:4/Neh1:2^2/2:5,6/5:7:8/9:10/Est5:11/6:1/8:
1f:6/Job1:10/3:8f/4:18,19/5:17/6:5,6,7:11/7:1:
2^2/8/9/10:20,21/12:14/13:3:11:22/14:1^3:4/15:
16:33/16:6/17:12/19:2:28/21:34/22:13/24:18/
25:4:6/26:2:3:4/28:1:3,4:5:6:9^2:13/31:14/34:19
/36:9:16:30/37:15:19,20/38:5:19:33/39:1:2,3:
26/40:4:19/Ps2:1/5:5:6/7:17/8:4/9:13/11:1/13^2
:2^2/18:1:7:14:25:30/19:12/21:1^2/22:9,10,11/25:
11:12:19^2/30:8:9^2/31:5,6:19/34:8/35:17:28/36:
4:7/38:9:17/39:4/40:16/41:9/42:4,5/44:1/46:8
/48:1^2/49:6/51:14,15:16/52:3/53:4/56:1:5/63:
1^3:2:3:7^2/65:4/66:2:3^2/67:4/69:5:10:11:19^2/71:
15/73:1:8/74:9,10:18/75:1/77:16/78:34:40:42:
44:45^2/79:5/80:4/81:14^2/82:2^2/84:1:4/88:10/
89:46^2:47:50/90:12:13/91:8:10/92:5:10/94:3:4:
11/101:2/103:22/104:1:31/105:5,6:19/106:1:
13/107:38/109:6/111:10/116:5^2/118:6/119:5:9
:19:35:39:47^2:49,50:84:97:147:156:159:163^2/
126:2/132:2-5/133:1^2/137:3,4/139:14:17,18^2:
17,18f:20/142:1^2/145:7/147:1^3:5:10:15/Pro1:2^2
:7,8,9:22^2/2:9^2/8:4,5:31:32/9:6/10:27/11:31/15
:11:23/16:16/17:26/18:13/19:7/21:30/23:15,16
/27:11/30:18,19^3:20/Ecc1:8-11^3/2:19/4:11/6:
12/7:21,22/8:1:6,7:9,10/Sol1:3^2:4:10^2:15^2/2:4:
13/4:1^2:3:10^2/6:4/7:1:6^2/8:13/Is1:18/3:15/6:
11/12:4/14:12^2/17:6/20:5,6/21:11/24:1/26:11:
17/29:16/33:18/36:8,9/38:3^2/39:4/40:18:27/
42:18/44:19/45:9/46:1/48:4/52:7/53:1/57:11/
58:2^2/59:13/61:10/63:18/64:1:3:5/Jer2:2^2:21^2:
23:32:33/3:19/4:21^2/5:4:7:22/6:29/7:18/8:8:12
/12:3:4:5:6/13:12:21:27/15:5:11^2:16/17:9:10/
22:16/23:26/31:22/32:24/36:17/47:5:7/48:17:
39/49:12:25/50:6:28/51:41/Lam1:11/2:13/3:
63/4:1/Eze:3/12:16/13:19/14:22/20:3:29/21:
23/22:14/23:39/26:17:18/33:10/36:19/Dan1:
13/2:7/8:13^2/9:18/10:17/12:6:8/Hos4:12f/5:
13/7:9/8:5/9:10^3/10:1/11:8^4/13:13^2/Joe2:2^2:
17/Amo3:3/4:5/5:10^2:18,25/6:13/Jon2:4:9/4:2
/Mic6:5^2:6:11/7:3/Nah1:14/3:6/Hab1:2/Zep2:
15/Hag1:7/2:3/Zec1:12/4:7f/8:17/9:16,17/10:
2/11:16/14:7/Mal1:8/2:17/Mt4:19/5:47/6:23/
7:11/8:18/9:8:24:33/10:25/12:5:12:34/13:55:
56/15:34/16:11/17:17/18:21/19:10/21:20:42/
22:12:45/23:6:7:33:37/26:15:41:54/27:1/Mk2:
5:12:16/3:23:26/4:30/5:19/6:38/7:6,7/8:5:12:
19:20:36/9:19^2:21/10:15:24/11:18/12:37/15:9:
39/16:3/Lk1:25:34:46:47:51^2:54:58:77/2:12/3/
4:22:25,26/6:8:40:42/7:20,21,22/8:18:36/9:41/
10:11:23/11:18:43/12:15:50/13:18:34/14:29
/16:5,6:7/17:5/18:8:24:26/19:22^2/20:37,38:44:
46/21:14/22:35:48/24:32:35^2/Jn1:48/2:24,25/
3:4:12:28:32/4:12:21-24/5:6/6:25:47:52:63/7:
15:27/9:10:15:16:19:26/10:24/11:36/12:16:33/
13:1:16:33/14:4:5/15:13/20:20/21:1/Act1:1/2:
7/3:16/4:9:21/5:4^2:9/7:38/8:31/9:16:27:31/10:
22/11:13:14/12:3:17/14:27/15:36/16:17:34/19:
20/21/25/Rom1:8:9/2:4/3:5^2:6/5:5:9/7:13^3:
23,24,25/8:26/9:1:4:23,24/10:14^3:15^3/11:2,3:4:
12:15:22:33^2/12:2:3/13:11/15:18/1Co1:18:19/
2:16/3:4:10:20^2/6:1/7:32:33/10:13:17/12:3:17^2
/14:6:8:9:16^2/15:35:57/16:2/2Co1:6,7:9:20^2/2:
2:4^2:9/5:2:12:16/6:14:15/7:7^2:8:11:12:14:16/8:
9:12/9:2:7/10:2:12:18/11:28:30/12:5^2:9:17/Gal
1:13/2:7,8,9/3:12:19/4:9:19:20/6:11/Eph1:3:8:
13:19/2:7/3:4:10:18,19^4/5:13:15,16:28/6:21:22
/Php1:7:8:23/2:16:19:28/4:10^2:11:12/Col1:4^2:
28/2:1:12:20/4:7:8/1Th1:5:9:10/2:1:2^2:9/3/4:1
/2Th3:9/1Ti1:12:14^2:15^2:16/3:5/5:25/6:5/2Ti1
:3:4^2:5:18/2:7/3:10:11:15/Phm1:19/Heb6:5:10
/7:4/9:14/10:29:32/11:5:32/12:10:25/13:17/
Jas2:1/4:14/5:11^2/1Pe2:2,3:9:12/2Pe1:1^2/1Jn
2:3/3:1:17/4:9:16:20/5:2^2/2Jn1:4/Rev2:2^2:5:9:
14/6:10/7:4-8/9:16

993

I

Gen1:29/2:18/3:10^2:11:12:15:17^2/4:1^2:9^2:13:15:
23/6:3:7^4:12,13^2:17:18/7:1:2:4^2/8:21^2/9:2,3:
9,10,11^2:12:13:14:15:16,17/12:1:2^2:2f:3:7/13:15
:16:17/14:22:23^2/15:1^2:2,3:7:8:14:18:19,20,21/
16:5:8:9-12:13/17:1:2,3,4:5^2:6:7,8^4:16^2:19^2:20^2/
18:3,4:10:14^2:15:17:19^3:20:21^2:26^2:27^2:28^2:29:
30:31^2:32^2/19:8:18,19,20:21:22:34/20:5:6^3:9,10:
11,12^3:13:16^2/21:7^2:10:13:16:18:23:24:26/22:5:
12:16:17/23:4:9:11^2:13/24:5^2:13:14^3:33^3:34:39^2:
40:42^2:43^2:45^2:46^2:47^2:48:56:58/25:22:30/26:3^4
:4^2:5:9^3:24^2/27:2,3,4^4:8,9,10:13:21:25:31:33:37^2:
41:45^2/28:13^2:15^4:21:22/29:21^2:25:33:34:35/30
:2:8^2:16:20:23,24:25:26^2:27:27f:30^3:33/31:3:8:
10:12^2:13:29:31^3:32:36,37:38^2:39^3:40:43:44:50:
51,52:53/32:4:5^2:10^4:11:26:30/33:8^2:9:10:10f:
11:12:15/34:4:11:12/35:3:11^2:12^3/37:10:17:30^2:
35/38:17:26^2/39:9^2:14,15:18/40:9,10:11^2:12:15^3
/41:9:11:13:15^3:16:17:21:22:24:32:40^2:41,42:44

on't)
14f:15[2]:18:20[2]:22:33:34[2]:37:38/43:9[2]:14/44
18:21:28:29:30:32[5]:34[2]/45:3:4:11,12:28[2]/46:
:30:32/47:9[2]:16:23:30/48:4[2]:5[2]:7[2]:9:11[2]:19:
2[2]/49:1:4:6:7:18:29,30:31/50:5:19:20[3]:21:
Ex2:7:9:14:22/3:6:7:8:9:10:12[2]:13[2]:14f[4]:14:
7:19:20[2]:21/4:1:10[2]:11:12[3]:15[3]:17:18[2]:21[2]:
/5:2[3]:23/6:1:2,3[2]:4[2]:5[2]:6:7[2]:8,9[2]:12:28,29[2]:
7:1:2:3[2]:4:5[2]:17[2]/8:2:8:9:21:22:23:29[2]/9:14:
6[2]:18:27[2]:28:29[2]:30/10:1[2]:2[4]:4,5:10[2]:16:17:
11:1:4:8/12:12[2]:13[4]:17:20/13:16/14:4[3]:17[2]:
15:1:2[2]:9[2]:26[3]/16:4:11,12[2]:28,29/17:4:5,6:9:
18:3:11:15,16[2]/19:4[2]:9[2]:11:24/20:2:5[3]:6:22:
/21:5[2]:13/22:23:24:27[2]/23:7:7f:15:20[2]:22:23
:28:29:30:31[2]:33/24:12[2]:14/25:8[2]:9:16:16f:
2[2]:40/26:30/28:3/29:42:43:44:45:46[4]/30:6:
31:1:6[3]:11:12,13/32:9:10:13[3]:24[2]:30[2]:34[4]/33
2:3[2]:5[3]:12:13:14:16:17:17f:19[2]:19f[3]:19[2]:22[2]:
34:1:5,6:7[2]:9:10[3]:11:18:24:27/**Lev6**:17/7:34
:31/10:3[2]:13:18:19/11:44[2]:45[2]/13[2]/14:
34[2]/16:1/17:8,9:10[2]:11:14/18:1:3:4,5[2]:6:21:
25:27:28[2]:29,30/19:1[2]:3,4:10:12:14:16:18:26:
30:31:32:34:35,36:37/20:3:5:6[2]:7:8:22:22f:23 [3]
:25[2]:26[2]/21:8:12/22:1:3:8:9:16:29,30:31:
33[2]/23:9,10,11:22:30,31:43[2]/24:22/25:1:
18:21,22:38:42:55[2]/26:1:2:4,5:6[2]:9:11:12:13[2]:
:17:18:19:21:22:24[3]:25[2]:26:28:30[3]:31:32[2]:33:
40,41[2]:42[2]:44[2]:45[3]/**Num3**:11,12:13[3]:41:45/5:
:27/8:16[2]:17[2]:18:19/10:10:30/11:12:13:14:
:23:29/12:6:7,8[2]:13/13:2/14:10,11:12[2]:19:
21[2]:22:23:24:26,27:31:34,35[2]/15:1:17,18:41[2]
:15:21:28[2]:45/17:4:5[2]/18:2,3:6:8:16:19:20/
12:18:24/21:16/22:5,6[3]:12:18:19:20:28:29[3]:
32:33:34[3]:35:37[2]:38[3]/23:3,4[3]:7-10[5]:11:12:15:
24[2]:26[2]:27/24:3-9[4]:10:11:12:13[3]:14:15-19/
10,11[3]:12,13/27:12:16/28:1/32:8/33:53:56[2]
:1:16-28:29/35:34/**Deu1**:8:9[2]:13:15:16:17[2]:
19,20,21:23:29:32:39:42:43/2:5[2]:9[2]:19[2]:25:26
/3:12[2]:15:18:19:21:23,24,25[2]/4:1:8:10:21,22[2]
/5:5[2]:6:9,10[4]:11:28[2]:31[2]/6:6/7:11/8:1/9:5:6:
12:13,14[3]:15:16:17[2]:18:19:20:21:24:25:26/10:
3:5[2]:10[3]:11:12,13/11:2:8:13:22:26:27:32/12/
18/14:3,4,5/15:4,5:15/17:2,3/18:17:18[2]:19/
9/22:13,14:16/24:8:18:22/26:10:13[2]:14[5]/27:
10/28:1:13:14:15-19:68/29:19[2]/30:1:2:7,8:15
:18:19[2]/31:2[2]:2f:2:5:14:16:17:18:20[2]:21:23:
2:28:29/32:1:3:20:21:23:24[3]:26:27:35:39[3]:
41[2]:46:49:52/33:4/34[2]/**Jos1**:3[2]:5[3]:6/2:4:5:9:
13[2]:21/3:7[3]/5:8,9:14/6:2:10/7:8:10,11:12:20
[3]/8:1:18/10:8/13:2-7[2]/14:7[3]:8:10:11[4]:12/15:
19/18:4[2]:5,6/20:2/22:2,3/23:2:4,5:14[2]/24:3:
5[2]:7[3]:8[2]:10[3]:11:12:13[2]/**Ju1**:2:7/2:1[4]:2:3:20:21
/3:17,18,19/4:7:19:22/5:3:9/6:14[2]:15[2]:16:16
8:22:37/7:2:8,9:12,13:17:18/8:2,3:7:9:15:19[2]:
24[2]/9:9:11:13:37:47,48/10:11:12/11:13:27:
/12:2:3/13:6[2]:11:13,14/14:3:16[2]/15:2[2]:11:
/16:6:7[2]:11[2]:16,17:20:25,26:28/17:2:3:9[2]:
11:13[2]/18:24[2]/19:18/20:6:27,28/**Ru1**:11:12[2]
3:16:17[2]:21/2:2:8,9:10,11[3]/3:1:2:3:9:12[2]:13[2]/
:4[4]:6:9:10/**1Sa1**:11:15,16[3]:19,20:21,22:26:27:
/2:1[3]:23,24,25:27:28[2]:30[4]:31:32:34[2]:35[3]:36/3:
5[2]:6:11:12[2]:13:14/4:16[2]/7:5/8:7:8/9:16[2]:17:
:24[2]:26,27/10:1:2:8[3]:18,19[2]/11:2/12:1[2]:2[2]:3[7]
17:23[2]/13:11:12[3]/14:24,25:29[2]:39:40:41:43[2]/
:1:2:11[2]:13:14:20[3]:21:24[3]:30:32/16:1[2]:2:3:5:7[2]
2/17:8:9:10:28:29[2]:34:35[2]:36:38,39:43:45:46[2]:
/18:17:18[2]:21:25[2]/19:3:17[2]/20:1:2:3[4]:4:6[2]:8:9[2]
0:12[2]:13:20[2]:22:28,29,30:31:36/21:2[2]:4:5:8[2]:9
2:9,10[2]:15:22[4]/23:2:4:10[2]:11:17:22:23/24:4:6:
10[4]:11[5]:12:17:20/25:7:8:11:19:21:24[2]:25:26:27
4/26:11:16:17,18:19:20:21[2]:23:24/27:1/28:13:
2:21:22/29:6[2]:8[2]/30[2]:13[2]:15/**2Sa1**:6:8:9:10[3]:
:26[2]/2:1[2]:6:7:22[2]:27/3:8[2]:9,10[2]:13:14:18:21[2]:
2:39[2]/4:9:10[2]:11[2]/5:8:19[2]/6:9:21[2]:22[2]/7:2:6[2]:
:8:9[2]:10,11:12[2]:13:14[2]:15:18:20[2]:27[2]/9:2:3:7[2]:
10,11/10:2:11[2]/11[3]/12:5:7:8[2]:11[3]:12:13:22[2]:
3:26,27f/13:4:13:35/14:5,6:7[3]:10:11[2]:15,16[2]:
7:18:19:22:24:32[3]/15:3:4[3]:7,8[3]:19,20:21[2]:28[2]:
3,34[2]/16:3:4:10:12:18:19[3]:20/17:2,3[2]:7:11[2]/18
2:13:18:29:31:33/19:7:13:19:20[3]:22:26[3]:27[2]:28[2]
0:33:34:35:35f:35:36:38[2]/20:16:17:21/21:3:4[2]:
6/22:3:4:6:7:20:22:23[2]:24:25:30[2]:38[2]:39:41:43 [2]
0/23:15:17/24:2:10:12:17:21:23:24[3]/**1Ki1**:12:
1:26:30[2]:35:48/2:2[2]:7:8[3]:13:14:16:17:20[3]:22[2]:
3,24:26:42[2]:45/3:7:8:9:12:13:14:17,18:20:21[2]/
4:5[3]:6[2]:8[3]/6:11,12[4]:13/8:12,13:16[3]:18:20:21:
7:29:44:48/9:2,3[3]:5[3]:7[5]/10:6:7[3]/11:11:12,13[3]:
1:32[2]:33:34[2]:35:36:37:38[4]:39/12:6:9/13:8[2]:9:
4:16,17[3]:18[2]:31/14:2:6:7:8[2]:10[2]:11/15:19/16:2 [2]
2/17:1[2]:4:8,9:12[5]:20:24/18:1:8:9:10:12[2]:13:14:
5[3]:22:23:24:36[2]:41:43:44/19:2[2]:4f:10[2]:14/20:4:
5,6:7:9:9f:10[2]:13[2]:28[2]:34:39:40:42/21:2:6:20:20f
:29[3]/22:4:6:8:14[2]:16:17:18:19:22:27:34/**2Ki1**:10
:12/2:1[2]:3:4[2]:5:6,7[2]:9[2]:10:18/3:6,7,8:13:14[2]/4:2:
11,12:13:12:23:24:26:28:30[2]/5:3:5:6:7[2]:11[2]:12:15:
16[2]:17:18:20:25:26/6:3:19:21[2]:26-30[3]:31:33/7:
12/8:8,9:12:13[2]/9:5:6:9[2]:25:26/10:9,10[2]:15:16:
17:30/14:24/15:9:18:24:28/16:7f/17:21:38/18:
14[2]:31,32/19:10:20:23:24[2]:25[2]:27[3]:28:29[2]:34/20
:3:5:6:8:15/21:7[2]:8[2]:12:13[2]:14[2]:15/22:8:15,16[2]:
18,19:20/23:15:27[4]/**1Ch4**:10/6:33-38/11:18,19
/12:17/13:2:12/14:10[2]/15:12/16:18/17:5:6[2]:7:8[3]
:9:10[3]:11[2]:12:13[3]:14:16:17:18[2]:23[2]:25/19:2,3/21
:8[3]:17:22:23:24[3]/22:5:7:9[3]:10[2]:14[3]:18/23:4,5/28
:2:6[2]:7:8/29:2[2]:3[2]:14:17[3]:19/**2Ch1**:7:9:12[2]/2:4[2]:
6:8:9:10:13/6:1:5,6[3]:10[2]:18:19[2]:20,21[2]:33:34:
37,38/7:12[2]:13[3]:14:15:16:18:19:20[4]/9:5:6[3]/10:
8,9[2]:11:14[2]/11:4/12:5:7[2]/18:6,7:12:13[2]:15:16:
17:18:19,20,21:26:27:33/19:6/25:9:16[3]/29:10/
32:13:15/33:7[2]:8[2]/34:15,16:25:27:28/35:21[2]:21f
/**Ez4**:19:20:21[2]/6:8:12/7:13:14:21:24:28[2]/8:15[2]
:16[2]:17:21:22:24:26,27[2]:28[2]:29/9:3[2]:5[2]:6[2]/10:1:5:
6[2]:10:16-19/**Neh1**:1:2[2]:4[4]:5:6,7[3]:8:9[2]:11[2]/2:1[4]:3 [2]
:4:5,6[2]:7:9,11[2]:13[2]:14,15:16[2]:17:18:20/4:4:13:14[2]
:19[2]:22:23/5:6[2]:7[3]:8:9[2]:10:12:13:13f:13:14[3]:15:
16[2]:17:18/6:2:3[3]:4:7[2]:10:11[5]:12,13:14:19/7:2:3[2]:
5/8:9/10:1/12:26:31,32:38/13:6[3]:7:8:9[2]:10:11[2]:
13[2]:14:15[2]:17:19[2]:21[2]:22:23:25:26:28:30/**Est3**:9
/4:16[4]/5:3:4[2]:6:7,8[2]:13/6:6/7:2:3:4[2]/8:6:7/9:12 [2]
/**Job1**:14,15:16:17:19:21[4]/3:2,3:11:13[2]:24:25:26
/4:14:16/5:8f[2]:27/6:3:5,6,7[2]:8,9:10:11[2]:12:13:22[2]
:23:24[3]:25,26:28:29:30[3]/7:4[3]:12:13,14:15:16:21/
9:2:11:14[2]:15[3]:16:20[3]:21[4]:27:28:30:32,33[2]:34:35 [2]
/10:1[2]:2:12:13,14:15[2]:16:19[2]:20,21[3]/11:3/12:2:
3[2]:4[2]:11/13:1[2]:2:3[2]:6:13[2]:14[2]:15[2]:15f[2]:16:17:18[2]
:19:20[2]:22:23:27,28/14:14:15[2]:16/15:6:17-19/
16:2:3:4[3]:5[2]:6[2]:12:15:17:20:22[2]/17:1:2[2]:7:10:
13,14[2]/19:3:4:7[2]:10:15:16[2]:18:19:20:23,24:25:26
:26f:27:28:29/20:2[2]/21:4:6[3]:16:19:27:29/22:13:
18/23:3[2]:4,5:8[3]:9[2]:11[2]:12:15[2]/24:25/27:2:3[2]:5[3]:
6[3]:11:12[2]/29:3:7:11:12:13[2]:14:15:16:17:18[2]:19:
21:22:24:25/30:1:9[2]:13:14:15:18:19:20[2]:23:24:
25[2]:26[2]:28,29[4]/31:1:2,3,4[2]:5:6:7,8[4]:9:10:12:13:
14[2]:16:19,20:21[3]:22:23:24:26:27:28[2]:29:30:32:
33:34:35[2]:36:37[2]:38,39[2]/32:6[3]:11,12:14:16:17:
18:19:20:21,22[2]/33:1:2:3:6:7[2]:9[3]:11:23,24:27:28:
32[2]:33/34:5:6[4]/35:2,3[2]:4/36:2[3]:3:4[2]/38:3:4:
22,23[2]/39:6/40:4[3]:5:15[2]/41:11:12/42:2:3[2]:4:5[3]:
6:7:8[2]/**Ps2**:6:7:7f:7:8:12/3:1:4:5:6:7/4:1:3:8[2]/5:
1:3:4:7[2]/6:2:3:5[2]:6/7:1:3:4[2]:17[2]/8:3:4/9:1:2[2]:13:
14/10:1/11/12:5[2]/13:1:2:3:4:5:6/16:1:2[2]:3:4:6:7
:8[2]/17:1[2]:3[2]:4:6[3]:15[3]/18:1:2[2]:3[2]:5:6:17:18:21:22 [2]
:23:24[2]:29:32:36:37[2]:38[2]:40:42[2]:43,44,45:49/19:
12:13/20:6/22:2:6:9,10,11:12:17:22[2]:23:24:25[2]/
23:1[2]:4:6/25:1:2:4:5:16:19:20:21/26:1:3:4:5:6:8:
11[2]:12/27:1:3:4[2]:6:7:8:9:11:12:13[2]/28:1[2]:2:7[2]/
30:1:2:3:6,7[2]:8[2]:9:12[2]/31:1:2:5,6[2]:7:9,10[2]:11[2]:12
:13[3]:14,15[2]:17:22[2]/32:3[2]:3f:5[3]:6:8[2]/34:1[2]:2:4/35
:7:9:11:12[2]:13[3]:14:15[2]:17:18[2]:28[2]/37:25[4]:35,36[3]
/38:5,6:8[2]:9:10:13,14[3]:15:16:17:17f:18[3]:19/39:1:
2,3[3]:4:9[2]:10:12[2]/40:1:2:7[2]:8:9[2]:10:12[2]:17/41:4[2]:
6[2]:7:9:10:11:12/42:1:2[2]:3:4,5[2]:6[2]:8:9[2]:11[2]/43:2:
4:5/44:6:8:15,16/45:1[2]:10,11:17/46:10[2]/49:4/
50:7:8:9:12[2]:13:14,15[4]:21[3]:22/51:3:4:5:7[2]:13:
14,15[2]:16:19[2]/52:8[2]:9[2]/54:6[2]/55:1:2:7:8:9f:12[2]:
16:17:20:23/56:3,4[2]:5:9[2]:10,11[2]:12[2]:13/57:1[2]:2:
4:7:9[2]/59:7:9:16:17/60:6:7,8/61:2[2]:4:7:8/62:1:2:
5:6/63:1[3]:2[2]:3:4[2]:5[2]:6:7:8:11/66:13:14[2]:15:16:17
:18:20/68:22f/69:1:3[2]:4[4]:5:7:9:10:11:12:13:14:
17:30/70:5/71:3:6:14[2]:15[2]:16[2]:17:18:22:23:24/
73:2[2]:3:13:14:15[2]:17:21:22[2]:25[2]:28[4]/75:2[2]:3:4[2]:9
:10/77:1[2]:2[3]:3:4[2]:5:6:10:11:12/78:1:2,3,4/80:1/
81:5:6[2]:7[3]:8:10[2]:12:14/82:6/84:2:10/85:8/86:1:
2[2]:3:4:7:11:12[2]/87:4/88:1:8:9[2]:10[2]:13:15[2]/89:1:
3,4[2]:19:20:21:23:24:27:28:30,31,32:33:34[3]:35,36
/91:2[2]:8[2]:9:14[2]:15[2]:16/92:4[2]:10:11/94:17:18:
21,22/95:10:11[2]/101:1[2]:2[4]:4:5[2]:6:7/102:3,4:5:6:
7:9,10,11:13:18:24/103:1:2:22/104:1:33[3]:35/
105:10,11/107:43/108:1:3:7:9f:9/109:4[2]:22,23[2]:
24:25:28[2]:30/110:1/111/116:2[2]:3:4:6:7:9:10,11[2]
:10,11f:12:13:14[3]:16:17:18,19[2]/118:5:6:10:11:12
:17:19:27,28[2]/119:5:6[2]:7f:7[2]:8:10:11:13:15:16:
17f:17:19[2]:20[2]:23:25[2]:26:27:28:29,30[2]:31[2]:32:
33,34[2]:35:38:39:40,41,42[3]:43:44,45,46[2]:47[2]:48[2]:
51:52:53:55:57:58:59,60[2]:61:62:65:67[2]:69:70:74:
75,76,77[2]:78:80:81[2]:83[2]:84:87:88:92:93:94[2]:95:
97[2]:99:101[2]:102,103:104:106:107:109:110:112[2]:
113[2]:117:119:120[2]:121:125[2]:127:128:129:131:
133:134:136:139:140[2]:141[2]:144:145[2]:146[2]:147[2]:
148:152:153:157:158:159:161:162:163[2]:164:166 [2]
:167[2]:168[2]:171:172:173[3]:174:175:176[2]/120:1:5,6
:7/121:1/122:8/123:1/130:5:6/131:1[3]:2/132:2-
2-5[6]:14[2]:15:16:17/135:5/137:5,6[2]/138:1[2]:2[2]:3[2]:
7/139:2:3:4[2]:7[2]:8[2]:9:11:14:15:16[2]:17,18[2]:21[2]:22
/140:6,7,8/141:1[2]:5:6,7:8:10/142:1[2]:3[2]:5[2]:6:7/
143:4[2]:5:6[2]:7:8:9:12/144:9/145:1:5:6:21/146:2[2]
/**Pro1**:4[2]:5,6:24[2]:28/4:1:3:5:10:11:20/5:1[2]:12[2]:
13[2]:14/7:6:14f:15/8:6,7[3]:14,15[2]:17:21:23[2]:24:26
:27,28,29[3]:30[2]:31/9:5:11/20:9[2]/22:13[3]:20,21[2]/
23:15,16:35/24:28,29,30,31:32,33[2]/26:18,19/27
:11/30:2[2]:3:3f:7[2]:9[4]/31:2/**Ecc1**:12-15[3]:16-18[4]:
16-18f:16-18/2:1[2]:3[3]:4,5,6,7,8[4]:9[3]:10[3]:11[2]:12[2]:
13,14:15[2]:17:18[2]:19:20-23[3]:24-26[2]/3:10:12:14:
16:17:18:22/4:1:2:4:7/5:13,14:16/6:1:3/7:15-17
:23[3]:25:27,28[2]:29/8:9,10[2]:12:15[2]:16,17/9:1:11:
13:16/10:5[2]:6:7/**Sol1**:5:7[2]:9f/2:1:3:5:7:8:16/3:1:
2[2]:3[2]:4[2]:5/4:6:9/5:1[3]:2[3]:3[5]:5[2]:6[3]:8[2]/6:3:8:11:12[2]
/7:8[2]:10[2]:12:13/8:1:2[2]:4:5:10:10f:10:12/**Is1**:2:3:
10:11[3]:12,13:14[2]:15[2]:18[2]:19:20:24:25:26/3:7[2]/5:
1[2]:4:5:6[2]:7[2]:9:13[2]/6:1:5[3]:8[3]:9:10:11/7:9:11[2]/8:1:
2[3]:3:7,8:16:17:18:20/10:3[2]:4:7/12:2/13:3[2]:11[2]:
12:13:17/14:13[3]:13f:14:22:23[2]:25:26:30[2]/15:9/
16:9:10:11/18:3[2]/19:2:4:25/20:3/21:2[2]:3[3]:4[2]:
8,9[3]:10:12/22:4:19:20:22:23,24/25:1/26:9[2]/27:
3:4,5[2]/28:16:17:18:23,24/29:2:3[2]:6:11:12:14/30
:1:7:9:12/31:7/32:9/33:10:13:15/34:5/36:10:16:
17:19/37:7:16,17[2]:24[3]:26[4]:28:29[2]:30:35/38:6:8:
10[3]:11[2]:13:14[3]:15:17:19:20/39:4[2]/40:3:6[2]/41:4[2]
:9[2]:10[5]:13[4]:14[3]:17[2]:18[2]:19:25[2]:26:27:28/42:1[3]:6[3]
:8[3]:9[3]/43:1[2]:2:3[2]:4[2]:5[2]:6:7[2]:8:10[2]:11:12[2]:13[2]:14:
15:16:17:19[2]:21:23:25[2]:28/44:3[2]:5[2]:6:7:8[3]:19:21 [2]
:22:24[2]:25[2]:26:27:28[3]/45:2:3[3]:4[2]:5[2]:6[2]:7[3]:8:11:
12[2]:13:13f:13:18:19[6]:22:23[2]/46:3:4[4]:5:9[3]:10[3]:11 [4]
:13[3]/47:3:6:8/48:3[3]:4:5[2]:6[2]:8:9:10:11[2]:12[3]:13:15 [4]
:16:17/49:2:4[3]:6:8,9[4]:11:15:16:22:23:25[2]:26[2]/50
:1[2]:2[5]:3:4[2]:5[2]:6[2]:7[4]/51:1[2]:4:5:12[2]:15:16[3]:22:23/
52:3[3]:4:6[3]/53:12/54:7[2]:8[2]:9[5]:11:12:15:16[2]:17/
55:3[2]:5:11[3]/56:1:3:4:5[2]:7[2]:8/57:6:14:15[2]:16[3]:17:
18[3]:19/58:5:6:7:9:14[2]/60:7:9:10[2]:15:16:17:21:22
/61:8[3]:10/62:1[2]:6,7:8:11/63:1[2]:3[3]:5[4]:6:7[3]/65:2:5
:6[3]:7:8[3]:9[2]:12[4]:16:17:18:19:24[2]/66:2:4[4]:9:12:13:
18[3]:19[2]:21/**Jer1**:5[2]:6[2]:7[2]:8:9:10:11[2]:12:12f:13[2]:
15:16:17[2]:18:19[2]/2:2:6:7:9[2]:15:16:21[2]:22:25:30:
31[2]:35[3]/3:1:7:8:12[2]:14[2]:15:18:19[3]:21:22/4:6:10:
19[3]:21:23[2]:24:25:28[2]:31/5:4:5:6:7[2]:9[2]:15:18:22:
23,24:25:29[2]/6:8:10:11[3]:12:17:18,19:20:21:27:
30[2]/7:3:7[2]:11:12[2]:13,14[5]:15[2]:16[2]:19:20:22[2]:23[3]:
25:27:34/8:3:4,5:6[3]:8:10:12[2]:13:17:21[2]/9:1[2]:2:7[3]
:9:10:11:15:16[2]:24[2]:25,26/10:19:20:23:24/11:1:
4[4]:5[5]:7[2]:8:9:10:11[2]:14:19[2]:20:23/12:1:3:7[2]:8[2]:9:
11:14:15/13:2:5[2]:7[3]:8,9:11:13:14[2]:20:21:24,25[2]:
26:27/14:10[2]:12[3]:13:14:15[2]:16:17:18[2]/15:1:3:4:
6[2]:7[2]:8[2]:10[4]:11[2]:12,13:14:15[2]:16:17,18[3]:19:20:
21/16:5:9:13[2]:14,15[3]:16[3]:17[2]:18:21:21f:21/17:
2,3:4[2]:16[2]:21,22:27/18:2:3:6:7:8[2]:9[2]:10[3]:11:17[2]:
20/19:1:3:5:7[2]:8[2]:9:11:12:13:15[2]/20:4:5:7[4]:9[3]:10
:12:13:14:17:18/21:3,4[2]:5[2]:6:7:10[2]:12:13:14[2]/22
:4:5:6:7:14:21:24,25:26/23:1:2:3[2]:4:5,6:9:11:12:
13:15:20:21[2]:23:24:25:30,31:32:34:36:38,39[4]:40
/24:2:3:4,5:6[4]:7[2]:8:9[2]:10[2]/25:2,3:8,9[4]:10:12[2]:13[2]
:14:15:16:17:18:19,20:21:27:29[2]/26:2:3[2]:4:5:6[3]:
12:14/27:5[3]:6[2]:8[2]:10:15[2]:16:22[2]/28:2:3:4[2]:6:7:
14[2]/29:9:10[2]:11[2]:12:14[3]:16,17:18[2]:19:21:23[2]:31:
32[2]/30:2:3[3]:8:9:10:11[6]:14[3]:15:17:18:19:20:21:22
:24/31:2[3]:3[2]:4:7:8:9[2]:13[2]:14[2]:16:18[2]:19[5]:20[3]:23:
25:27:28[2]:31:32[2]:32f:33[3]:34:36[2]:37/32:8[2]:9:10:
11:12:13:16[2]:27:28:31:33:35:37[3]:38:39:40[2]:41:
42[3]:44/33:3:5[3]:6:7:8:9:10,11:14[2]:15:25,26[4]/34:2
:5:13[2]:14:15:17[2]:18,19[2]:20[2]:21:22[2]/35:3:5:14:15 [3]
:17[3]/36:3[2]:5:31[3]/37:14:18[3]:20/38:5:14:15:19:25
/39:16[3]:17:18/40:4[2]:10:16/42:4[3]:10[3]:11:12:17:
19:21/43:10[3]:11[2]/44:2,3:4[2]:10:11:12[2]:13[2]:26:27 [2]
:28:29[3]:30[2]/45:3[3]:4[4]:5[2]/46:18:25[2]:26:27:28[5]/48:
30:31:32:35:38:44:47/49:2:5:6:8[2]:9,10:11:13:14:
15:16:19[2]:27:32[2]:35:36:37:38[2]:39/50:9[2]:18[2]:19:
20[2]:21[2]:24:31:44[3]/51:1:20:21:24:25[2]:36[4]:39:40:
44:47:57:61,62:64/**Lam1**:14:16:19:20/2:11[2]:13[2]
/3:1:7:8:17:20:24:52[2]:54:55/**Eze1**:1[2]:4:8:15[2]:
27,28[2]/2:1:3:4:8[2]:9,10[2]/3:1:2:3:4:5:6:7:8:9:12f:
14,15:14,15f:14,15:17[2]:18[3]:20:22[2]:23[3]:25:26:27[2]
/4:3:8:8f:13:14[7]:17/5:2:8[2]:9[2]:11[2]:12:13[2]:14:15:
16:17/6:3[2]:4-7:8:9[2]:10[3]:12:13:14[2]/7:3:4[3]:5,6:8,9 [3]
:20[2]:21:22[2]:23:24:26,27[2]/8:1:2:4:5:6:7:8:10:13:
15:18[3]/9:1:5:8[2]:10[2]:11/10:2:9-13,15,16:19:20[2]:
22/11:1:5[2]:8:9:10:11:12:13[2]:16[2]:17:19[2]:20:21:25
/12:7[6]:13:14:15[2]:16[3]:20:23:25[3]:28/13:2,3:7:8:9[2]:
13:14[2]:15:20[2]:21[2]:22:23[2]/14:3:4:5,6,7,8[2]:9:11:13
:14:15:17:19/15:5,6:7[2]:8/16:4:6,7[2]:8[3]:9,10:11:14
:16:17:18:19:27[2]:36:37[3]:38:39:40,41:42:43:48:50[2]
:53:59,60[4]:61:62[2]:63[2]/17:9[3]:12,13:16:19[2]:20[2]:21
22,23[2]:24[5]/18:3:23[2]:25:29:30:32/20:3[2]:5,6[4]:7[2]:
8[2]:9,10[3]:11:12[2]:13[2]:14[3]:15[3]:17[2]:18:19:20:21[2]:22:
23,24[2]:25:26[3]:27,28[2]:29:31[3]:33:34:35,36[3]:37:38[3]

(I Con't)
:41:42[3]:44[2]:47:48:49/21:3[2]:4[2]:5:17:27[2]:30[3]:31[2]:
32/22:4:13:14[3]:15:16:18,19,20:21:22:30[2]:31[3]/23
:4,5[2]:9:13:18[2]:24:25:27:28:31:34:48:49/24:8:9:
13:14[2]:16:18[2]:20,21[2]:22:24:25:27/25:4:5[2]:7[4]:
9,10:11[2]:13:16[2]:17[2]/26:2[2]:3[2]:4:5:6:7:13:14[2]:19:
20:21/27:3/28:10:14:16[2]:17:18:18f:22[4]:23[2]:25[4]:
26[2]/29:3[2]:4:5[2]:6:8:9:10[3]:12[2]:14:16:19:20:21[2]/30
:8[2]:9:12[3]:13:15[2]:16:18:19[2]:21:22[3]:23:24[2]:25[3]:26[2]
/31:9:11[2]:15[2]:16[2]/32:3[2]:5:6:7[3]:9:9f:10[2]:12:13:15[2]
:32/33:2:6:7[2]:8[3]:11[3]:13[2]:14:18:20:22:27:28:29[2]:
31/34:8:9,10[4]:11:12[2]:13[2]:14:15,16[5]:17:20:22[2]:23
:24[2]:25:26[2]:27[2]:29:29f:30:31/35:3[2]:4,5[3]:6[2]:7:8:9:
11[5]:12:13:14:15[2]/36:6:7:9[2]:10:11[3]:18:19[2]:21:22[2]
:23[3]:24:25:26[3]:27[2]:28[2]:29[2]:30:32:33[2]:35:36[3]:
37,38[3]/37:1:3:5:6[3]:7:8:10:12:13:14[3]:18,19,20:21:
23[2]:25:26[2]:27[2]:28/38:2,3:4[2]:11:12[2]:15,16[2]:17[2]:
19:21:22:23[3]/39:1:2[2]:3:4:5:6[2]:7[3]:8:11:13:19:21[2]:
22:23:24:25[2]:27[3]:28[2]:29[2]/40:2:3:4[2]:7-12:20/41:
8/43:3[2]:6:7:8:9:10:27/44:4[2]:5:8:12:28/46:18:
19,20:21,22/47:1:2:5[2]:6:14/Dan2:1[2]:5[2]:6:8,9:16:
23:24:30[2]/3:14:25:29/4:2:3:4:5:6:7:8[2]:9[2]:10,11:
13[2]:30:34[2]:36:37/5:14:16[2]:17/6:22[2]:25,26/7:2:4
:5:7:8:9:11:13:15[2]:16:19:20:21:28[4]/8:1:2:3[3]:5:8f:
13:15:16:17:18:19:27[3]/9:2:3[3]:4:17:20:21:22:23/
10:2:3[3]:4:5,6:7:8[3]:9:11[3]:12:13:14:15:16[3]:17[2]:18:
19:20,21[4]/11:1:2/12:5:8[3]:9/Hos1:4,5[2]:6:7[2]:9:10:
2:3:4[2]:6:7[3]:8:9[4]:10:11:12:13:14:15[2]:17:18[2]:19:20:
21,22:23[3]/3:2:3[2]/4:4:5:6[2]:9:14/5:2:3:10:12[2]:14[2]:
15/6:4:5[2]:6[4]:10:11/7:1:2[2]:12[2]:13:15/8:5:10:12:
13:14/9:8:10[2]:12[2]:13:14[2]:15[3]:16/10:1[2]:10[2]:11[3]/
11:1:2:3[4]:4[3]:7:8[4]:9[5]:10:11/12:8[2]:9[2]:10/13:4[2]:5:7:
8[2]:9:11[2]:14[3]/14:4:5:8[3]/Joe1:2/2:19[2]:20[2]:25[2]:27[2]
:28[2]:29/3:1:2:4:7[2]:8:12:17:21[2]/Amo1:3[2]:4:5:6[2]:7
:8:9[2]:10:11[2]:12:13[2]:14/2:1[2]:2:3:4[2]:5:6[2]:9[3]:10:11:
13/3:1:2[2]:4[3]:6:7[2]:8:14[2]:15/4:6:7[2]:9:10[2]:11[2]:12[2]/
5:1:12:17:21:22[2]:23:24:25,26,27/6:8[2]:14/7:2:3:5
:6:8[3]:9:14[3]/8:2[2]:7:9:10:11/9:1:2[2]:3[2]:4[2]:7[2]:8[2]:9:
11:14:15[2]/Ob1:2:4:8/Jon:2:9,10[2]:12/2:2[2]:3:4[2]:5
:6[2]:7[2]:9[3]/3:1/4:2[5]:3:11/Mic1:8[2]/2:3[2]:12/3:8/4:
10:13/5:10:12:14:15/6:3:4[2]:5[3]:11:13[2]:16[3]/7:1:7[2]
:8[3]:9[3]:10:15[2]:16/Nah1:12:13:14[3]/3:5:6/Hab1:2[3]
:3[2]:5[2]:6/2:1:3/3:2[2]:3:7:16[4]:18[2]/Zep1:2[2]:3:4[2]:5:6
:8:9:12:17/2:8:9:15/3:6[2]:7[2]:8:9:9f:11:17,18[2]:19[3]:
20[2]/Hag1:1:8:9:10:11:13[2]/2:4:5:6:7:7f:7:8,9[2]:
16,17:18,19[3]:21:22:23[2]/Zec1:8:9:14[2]:15[2]:16:18:
19:21/2:1[2]:2[2]:6,7[2]:9:10:11,12/3:2[5]:4[2]:5,6:7[4]:8:9:
9f[2]:9/4:1:2[2]:3:4:5[2]:8:11:13/5:1:2:4:6:7:9:10/6:1:
4/7:13[2]:14/8:2:3[2]:7:8[2]:8f:12:14,15[7]:17:23/9:7:8[3]
:10:11[2]:12[2]/10:3[2]:6[5]:8[2]:9:10:12/11:5:6[3]:7[3]:8[2]:9[3]:
10[2]:11:12[2]:13:14:15:16/12:2:4[2]:6:10/13:2:5[2]:6:6
f:7:9[3]/Mal1:2,3[4]:4:6:10[2]:13:14/2:1[4]:3[2]:4[2]:9/3:1:
5:6[2]:7:10:11:17[2]/4:4:5/Mt2:8:13:15/3:3:11[3]:14:
15:17/4:19/5:17[2]:18[2]:20:22:22f:28:32:34:37[2]:39
:44/6:2/7:23:23f/8:3:7:8,9[6]:10:11:19:20:21/9:2:
5,6:13[3]:15:21[2]:28/10:16:23:25:27[2]:32:33:34:35/
11:14:16:19[2]:21:23:28:29,30[2]/12:7[2]:8:18:27:28:
36:39,40:43,44,45[2]/13:12,13:18:30:34,35[2]:37:41
/15:10:24:32[2]/16:9:10:11[2]:13:15:18:19:27/17:5:
12:16:17:22,23[2]/18:10:11:18:19:20:21:26:29:32:
33/19:9:16:20:24:28/20:13:15[2]:18:19[2]:22:23:28
/21:27:29:30:43/22:8:32:32f:44/23:34:37:39/24
:25:27:31:45:46:47[2]/25:12f:21[2]:22:23:24,25[3]:
24,25f:24,25:26:27:31[2]:32:34:35[3]:40:41:42:45/
26:2:18:22:23:24[2]:25:29[2]:32[2]:33:35:39:42:45:53:
54:55[2]:60,61:63:64:70:72:74/27:4[2]:17:19:21:22:
24:41,42,43:63/28:5:18:20[2]/Mk1:7[2]:7f:8:17:24:
38:41/2:9,10,11:17:28/3/4:13:14:24:30[2]/5:28[2]/
6:16:22,23:25:50/7:11[3]:27:29/8:1:3:19:20:24[2]:
27:29:38[2]/9:17:18:19[2]:23:24:25:30,31[2]:41/10:15[2]
:17:33:34:38[2]:40:45:51/11:33/12:26[3]:27:33:36/
13:23:27:29:32:35,36,37/14:7:9:18:19:21[2]:25[3]:
27:28[2]:29:31:32:36:41:44:48:49:58[2]:62:68:71/15
:12[2]/Lk1:13:19[2]:34[2]:38[2]:44:46:47:66/2:10:
29,30,31[4]:48:49/3:16[2]/4:6,7[2]:24:34:43[2]/5:13:
23,24/6:5:9/7:6,7,8[5]:9:27:31[2]:34:35:40:43:44:45
/8:28:46/9:9[2]:18:20:22[2]:26[2]:40:41:44[2]:57:58[2]:61
:62/10:3:13:15:18:19:21:22:35:40:42/11:7:19:20
:29,30[2]:49/12:8[2]:9:18:40:49:50:51/13:18:24,25:
27[2]:32[2]:34/14:24[2]/15:12:17:18[2]:21:31[2]/16:2:3:4[2]
:9:24:28/17:2,3:17:22:23[2]:24:25:26:30f/18:4,5:8[2]
:11[3]:12[3]:14:18:21:32:33:41/19:5:8[4]:9,10:17:21:
22[2]:23/20:3:8:13[2]:42,43/21:15:32/22:15:16[2]:18:
20:22:27:29:32:33:35:41,42:52:53:57:58:59:60:
67,68:69:70/23:14:16:22[2]:46/24:38:39[3]:44:49/
Jn1:15[4]:20:23:26:27:30[3]:31[2]:33:34[2]:48[2]:50[2]/2:4:
4f:19[2]/3:3[2]:5:10,11[2]:12[2]:13:14:28[3]:29[2]:30:31/4:
10:14:25:26:28,29:32:38:39:48/5:7[3]:17f:24:25:
30[3]:31:32,33:34[2]:36[3]:40:41,42:43[2]:45/6:26:27:
35:36:37:38:39[2]:40:44:46:47:48-51[2]:53[2]:54:56:
57:58:63:65[2]:70/7:7:8f:21,22,23[2]:24:28[2]:29[2]:33[2]
:34:36/8:11:12:14[4]:15:16[2]:18:19:21[2]:22:23[2]:24[2]:
25[2]:26[4]:28[2]:29:30,31:37:38[3]:40[2]:42[2]:43:45:46:49[2]
:50:51[2]:54:55[4]:56:58/9:5[2]:9:11[2]:12:17:25[4]:27:36:
38:39/10:7:9:11:14:15[2]:16[2]:17[2]:18[3]:25[2]:27:28:30
:32:34,35,36:37:38[2]/11:4:11:15[2]:22:25:27:40:42
/12:8:23,24[3]:26:27[2]:28[2]:32[2]:46:47[2]:48:49:50[2]/
13:7:8:12:14:15[2]:18[3]:19:23:25:26:26f:33[2]:34[2]:37[2]
/14:2,3[4]:4:6:7:9[2]:10[2]:11:12,13[5]:14:15,16:18[2]:19[3]
:20[3]:21[2]:23:24:25[2]:26[2]:27[2]:28[5]:29:30:31[2]/15:1:3:
5[2]:9:10:11:12[2]:15[2]:16[2]:17:19:20:22:24:26/16:1:4[3]
:5:5f:7[4]:10:12:15[2]:16:19:22:25[2]:26:27:28:32:33[2]/
17:4:5:6:7:8[2]:11:12[2]:13[3]:14[2]:16:18:19:20:21[2]:22:
23:24:25:26[2]/18:4,5:8[3]:9:11:17:20[4]:21:23:26:35:
36[3]:37[2]/19:4[2]:6:10:21:22[2]:27:35/20:2:3,4:5:8:13
:15:17[2]:18:21:25[2]/21:2:7:15:16:17:22[2]:23[2]:24[2]:
25/Act1:1/2:17:19:25:26:29:34:35:36/3:6:13:15
:17/7:7:32:34[3]:43:48,49:50:56/8:19:23:31:36:37
/9:5:12:13:15:16/10:14:20:28:29[2]:30:33:34/11:5[2]
:7:8[2]:11:15[2]:16:17/13:2:25[2]:32,33[2]:32,33f:34[2]:
41:47/15:16/16:15:18:30/17:21:22:23[3]/18:6[2]:
10:14:21/19:13:15[2]:21:27:40/20:18:19:20:21:22:
24:25[2]:27:29[2]:31:32:33:35[2]/21:13:37,38:39[2]/22:
1:3[4]:4:5[2]:6:7:8[2]:10[2]:11:13:17,18[2]:19[2]:20:21:27:
28[2]/23:1:5:6[3]:27[2]:28:29:30[2]:35/24:4[2]:10[2]:11:12:
14[4]:15:16:17:18[2]:21[4]:25/25:8[2]:10,11[6]:15:16:17:
18:20:21[2]:25:26[2]/26:2:3:4[2]:5:6:7:9[2]:10[2]:11[3]:12:
14:15[2]:16[2]:17[2]:19:20:22[2]:25[2]:26[2]:27:29/27:2:10:
23[2]:25/28:17[2]:19:20[4]:28,29/Rom1:8[3]:9[3]:10[2]:10f
:11,12[4]:13[4]:14:15:16/2/3:8/6:19/7:7[2]:9[5]:10:14:
15[6]:16[4]:17[2]:18[6]:19[4]:20[2]:21[2]:22:23,24,25[2]:
23,24,25f/8:38/9:1[4]:9:10-13:15[4]:33/10:2:16/11:
1[2]:4:13[2]:14:19:25:27[2]/12:1:3/14:11:14/15:9:13[2]
:14:15,16[2]:18[2]:19[3]:19f:21:22:23[2]:24[3]:25[2]:28[2]:29[2]
:31[2]:32/16:4:7:8:17:19:22:23:25,26,27[2]/1Co1:4:
6:10[2]:12:13:14[2]:15:16[2]:17:18:19/2:1[2]:2[2]:3:5[2]:6[2]/
3:1[3]:2:4:5:8:10/4:1:3[3]:6[2]:8:9:14:15[2]:16[2]:17[4]:18[2]:
19:21[2]/5:3,4[5]:9[2]:10[2]:11/6:5:12[6]:15:18/7:7[2]:8[2]:
10:12:25[4]:26:28:32:35[2]:40[3]/8:13[2]/9:1[2]:2[2]:4[2]:5[2]:
6:15[5]:16[4]:17[2]:18:19[3]:20[7]:21[4]:22[4]:23[3]:26[2]:27[3]/10
:12:15:19[2]:20[2]:29:30[2]:33[4]/11:1:2[2]:3:16:17:18:19:
21:22[2]:23:34/12:1[2]:15[2]:16[2]:21[2]:27/13:1[2]:2[4]:3[3]:
11[4]:12[2]/14:5[2]:6[3]:10:11:14[4]:15[6]:18[2]:19:26:37/15:
1:3:8[2]:9[3]:10[3]:11:31:32:34:50:51/16:1:2:3[2]:5[3]:6:7[2]
:8:10:11:12:17:18[2]:21/2Co1:8:13,14[3]:15,16[4]:17[3]:
18:19:23[4]:24[4]/2:1[2]:2[2]:3[7]:4[6]:5,6[4]:9[3]:10[2]:12:13[2]/3
:1:2/4:13[2]/5:11:12:16[2]/6:2:11[2]:13:16[2]:17/7:3[2]:4
:7:8[3]:9[3]:11:12[2]:14[2]:16[2]/8:1:3:7:8[2]:10:13:16[2]:17:
18:21:22[2]:24/9:1[2]:2[2]:3[4]:4[2]:5[2]/10:1[3]:2[5]:3[2]:4:5:6[2]:
7[2]:8[3]:9[3]:12[2]/11:1[2]:2:3:5[2]:6[4]:7[2]:8,9[7]:10[3]:11[2]:12:
14:16[3]:17:18:21:22[3]:23[3]:25[4]:26[2]:27[3]:28:29:30[3]:
31:33[2]/12:2,3[3]:4:5[3]:6[2]:7[4]:8:9[4]:10[6]:11[2]:12[4]:13[3]:
14[3]:15[3]:17:18:19[5]:20[7]:21[3]/13:1[2]:2[6]:3:6[2]:7:10[4]:11[2]
/Gal1:1:6:9:10[4]:11[2]:13[3]:14[2]:15:16[2]:17[3]:18:19:20[3]
:21:22/2:1:2[5]:6:10:11:14[2]:15:18:19[3]:19f[2]:20[3]:21/
3:1:4:5:8,9:17/4:9:11[2]:12[3]:13[2]:14:15:16[2]:18:19:
20[3]:27:28/5:10[2]:11[5]:12:16:21/6:11[2]:14:17/Eph
1:15:16,17[2]:18[2]:19/3:1:2,3:4[2]:8[3]:13:14,15[2]:17/4:
1[2]/5:32:33/6:9:10:19[2]:20[3]:21:22/Php1:2:4:6:7[4]:
10:12:13[2]:18:19[2]:20[8]:22:23[3]:24:25[3]:26:27[2]:30/2:
12[2]:16:17[3]:19:23[2]:24[2]:25[3]:26:28[2]/3:1:2:4[2]:5[4]:6[2]:
7[2]:8[2]:10[2]:11:12[6]:13[3]:14:15[2]:18[2]/4:1:2:3:4:8:10[3]:
11[3]:12[2]:13:15:16:17:18[4]/Col1:23:24[2]:29/2:1[2]:2:
4[2]:5/4:3:4[2]:7:8:9:10:13:16/1Th2:18/3:1[2]:5[4]/4:9:
13:15/5:1:27/2Th1:7/2:5[2]/3:1[2]:13:17[2]/1Ti1:3,4[2]
:5:10,11:12:13[6]:15[2]:20/2:7:8:12/3:14[2]:15/4:13/
5:14:15:21/6:13/2Ti1:3[3]:4[3]:5[2]:6[2]:8[2]:12[6]:13:18/2
:3:9[3]:10:11:23/3:10[5]:11[2]/4:1:6[3]:7[2]:11:12:13:16[2]:
17f:20/Tit1:1:3:5[3]/3:8:12[2]/Phm1:4[2]:5:6:7:8,9[4]:
10:12:13[2]:14[2]:17[2]:19[3]:21[2]:22/Heb:5,6:5,6f:5,6:
13/2:12:13[2]/3:1:10[2]:16/4:3/5:5:11/6:9[4]/8:8:9[3]:
10[4]:12[2]/10:7[3]:9[2]:16[3]:17:30/11:13:32/12:26/13:
5:6:19[2]:22:23[2]/Jas2:18[3]/4:4/1Pe1:16/2:6[2]:11/5
:1[3]:12[5]/2Pe1:1:12:13,14[3]:15:17,18[3]/3:1:3:17/
1Jn1:1[2]:2:3:4/2:1:4[3]:7:12:13[3]:14:21[2]/4:20/5:13:
17/2Jn1:1:4:5:8:12[3]/3Jn:1:2[2]:4:6:9:10[2]:12[2]:13[2]:
14/Jud:3[3]:4:6/Rev:8:8f:9[4]:10[2]:11[2]:12:17,18[3]/2:
1:2[3]:5:6:7:9[3]:10:13:14:16:17:19[3]:20:21:22[2]:23[3]:
24,25[2]:26:28/3:1:3:5[2]:8[2]:9[2]:10:10f:11:12[2]:15[2]:16
:17[3]:19[3]:20[3]:21[3]/4:1[4]:2/5:1:4:6:11:13/6:1:2:3:5[2]
:7:8:9:12/7:1:2:4-8:9:14/8:2:13[2]/9:1:13:16:17,18
/10:1:4:9:10[2]/11:1:2:3/12:1:10/13:1:3:11/14:1:
2:6:13:14/15:1:5/16:1:5:7:7f:13:15/17:1:3:6[2]/18
:1:4:7[3]:21/19:1:6:10[3]:11:17:19/20:1:4[2]:11:12/21
:1:2:3:5[2]:6[2]:7:9:10/22:6,7:8:9:12:13:16[3]:18

8709

I'LL

Gen13:9[3]/14:24/19:8/22:2/24:19:44:49/27:
8,9,10/29:18/30:1:28:31,32/31:32/34:15/38:17
/42:16[2]:37/46:31/Lev11:12/Num22:8/Ju4:8:9/
6:18:37/7:4:7/9:29/11:37/13:16[2]/14:12/16:20/
17:3/19:24/Ru3:5:11:13/4:4/1Sa2:16/17:32:36
:44/18:17/19:3[3]/20:5:7[2]:21/22:23/23[2]/24:13/
26:5,6,7:8[2]:11:21/27:1/2Sa13:5/14:8:9/16:3/
1Ki1:14/2:18:30/3:12/12:10:11[2]/13:7/18:5/1
20/21:7/22:21:30/2Ki5:12/18:23/1Ch19:12/
:1/2Ch10:10:11/18:29/Job7:21/40:14/Ps27:5
39:1/71:8/119:33,34:106/132:18/Pro1:23:26[2]
Is6:8/7:12/27:3[2]/47:8[2]/48/55:2/58:3/Jer5:1:
14/10:18/20:9/25:6/37:20/Eze33:25/Dan2:5
3:15/Hos1:5:6/Mic2:11/6:14/Zep3:7/Zec1:9
Mal2:14/Mt4:9/9:5,6/17:4/21:24/Mk2:
9,10,11/10:5/11:29/12:15/14:31/Lk5:23,24/
:35/11:8/12:5:18[2]:19/13:8:9/16:4/19:22/20:3
13:16/Jn4:15/7:8/18:39/Act3:6/24:25/1Co4:
19/6:12/8:13/10:31/11:34/2Co2:1/Gal5:3/Re
17:7

16

I'M

Gen27:11,12:46/31:35/42:18:19/48/Ex3:11/4
10[2]/6:12:30/16:4/Jos14:12/17:16,17,18/Ju4:
/9:37/Ru2:13/3:2/1Sa1:15,16/3:9:10/9:21/14
7/20:2/29:9/2Sa13:28/20:8,9,10/1Ki12:26/13
9/18:14/2Ki4:9/1Ch17:1/2Ch18:3,4,5/Job10:
:15/13:2/34:5/35:2,3/Ps39:1/94:18/Pro5:7/Is
43:18:19/44:20/Jer1:6[2]/2:35/Lam1:11/Dan:1
/Zec8:20,21/Mk:21/Lk1:18/5:8/12:42,43,44/
16:3[2]/17:15/18:4,5/Jn4:17,18/5:17/7:16/16:4
17:15/19:28/21:3/Act10:21:26:36,37/18:15[2]/
Rom7:17:23,24,25/1Co:6/9:8[2]:26/2Co7:3/11:
21[3]/1Th4:9/1Jn5:17

8

I'VE

Gen1:30/21:26/27:19/28:16,17/30:27:29/31:6
38/41:19/Ju15:16,17/16/1Sa9:6/20:5/25:11/
28:7,8/29:3:6/2Sa9:7/1Ki10:7/19:4[2]/22:28/
2Ki20:3/1Ch17:5/Neh5:19/Job10:4-7/Ps59:3
71:5/119:106:121/Pro3:1/7:14/Is38:3[2]/44:19:
22/57:11/Jer2:25/7:31/17:16/Dan2:1:25/Mt
11:5/19:20/Mk10:20/13:29/Lk11:5,6/13:7/15
29/18:21/19:20/21:31/2Co12:1/Php3:7/Phm
:21

5

IF

Gen2:16,17/3:22/4:7[2]:12:24/8:8/11:6/12:2:
11,12,13/13:9[2]/15:5/18:26:28:29:30/20:7/24:8
21:41:42/26:3:7/27:11,12/28:20/29:7:18:27/30
:31,32:33/31:8:32:39:47,48:50/32:8/33:13/34:
15:23/42:16:19f:20:33:34:37:38/43:7:9:10:11:14
/44:9:19:29:30:32:34/47:5,6/Ex1:10/3:13/4:8:9
/5:3:22/8:2:21:26/9:2/10:4,5/12:3,4:10:44:48/
13:13:16/15:26/18:18:23[2]/19:5/20:7:25/21:2:2
:3[3]:4:5:7:8:9:10:11:13:14:18:19:19f:20:21:22:23:
24[2]:26:27:28:29:30:30f:31:32:33:35:36/22:1:2:3
:4:5[2]:6:7[2]:8:10:12:13:14:15[2]:16:17:23:25:26:27/
23:4:5:22/24:14/29:34/32:17:32[2]/33:5:13:15:16
/34:9:12:15:20/40:37/Lev1:2,3:10:14/2:4:5:7:
14/3:1:6:7,8:12/4:3:13:22:26:27:32/5:3:4:7:11:
15/6:2:17:27:28:30/7:12:16:17,18/8:35/10:6:19
/11:33:34:35:36:37:38:39/12:8/13:1:3[2]:4:5:6:7:8
:9,10:11:12:14,15:16,17[2]:20[2]:21[2]:22:23:24:25:26
:27:28:29,30[2]:31:32[2]:34:35:36:37:38:40:41:42:43
:47,48:51:53:55:56:57:58/14:3:21:36:37:39:43:
44:48/15:11:25/17:16/18:4,5:18/19:8:13:20/20
:4:10:11:12:14:15:16:17:18:20:21:21f/21:18/22:
3:11:12:13:14:17,18:19:23/25:13:14,15,16[3]:
17,18:25:26:28:29:30:35:39:47:49:51:52:53:54/
26:3:14:18:21:23:27/27:8:9:10:11,12:13:14,15:
16:17:18:19:20[2]:22:27[2]:31:33/Num5:8:11,12:19:
20:24:27:28/6:6,7:9/8:19/9:10[2]:14:19[2]:22/10:4:
32/11:15:22/12:1f:14/14:15/15:3,4:6:8,9:22:27
/16:29:30/17:10/18:5:23:32/19:12:16[2]/20:18/
21:2:8/22:18:34/23:3,4:7-10:25/24:13/27:6,7:8:
9:10:11/30:3:5:6:8:9:10:12:14:15/32:20:23:29:
30/33:55/35:11:16:17:18:20:22,23:25:26:30/36:
3/Deu4:1:6:23:32/5:16:25/6:2:3:18/7:16:22/8:1
:19:20/9:28/11:9:13[2]:17:22:27:28/12:20-23:
24,25:28/13:1:2:6,7:12,13,14[3]:18[2]/14:7:24/15:
4,5:7:9:12:16[2]:21[2]:22/17:2,3:4:8:12/18:8:21:22/
19:5:8:11:16:18/20:5:6:8:11:12/21:1:14:15:18:
22/22:1:2:4:6[2]:9:13,14:20:22:23,24:25,26,27:
28,29/23:1:15,16:20:21:22/24:1:2:7:10:12,13:19
/25:1:5:7:8:11/26:19/27:23f/28:1:9:13:15-19:
58,59:62/30:2:7,8:10[2]:17[2]/31:27/Jos1:7:17,18/
2:5:9:14:19:20/6:18/7:7/9:20/14:12/17:15[2]/20:
3:5/22:17,18:19:22,23:28/23:12[2]:15,16[2]/24:15:
20:27/Ju1:24/2:2/4:8:20/6:13:17:27:31:36:37/
7:10[2]/8:6:19/9:7:15[2]:19:20/11:8:30,31/12:5:6/
13:16:23/14:12[2]:13:18/16:2:7:11:13:16,17/Ru1:
12:17/2:7/3:13[2]/4:4[2]:4f:4/1Sa1:11/2:16/3:9:
16,17/4:3/6:4,5:9[2]/7:3/8:11/9:9,10,11/11:3[2]/
12:10:14[2]:15:25/14:9:10:30:44/16:2/17:9[2]:35:
55f/19:11:17/20:6:7[2]:8:9:13[2]:21:22:28,29/21:4:

Con't)
3:23^2/25:22:34/26:19^2/27:5/28:2:16/30:15/
2:22:27/3:9,10:27/7:14/9:1:3/10:11^2:12/11:
0,21/12:8/13:5:25:26/14:7:9:10:14:32^2/15:
14:25,26^2:33,34/16:10/17:6:13:20/18:3^2:13:
3/19:6:7:13:15/20:11:18:21/1Ki1:12:21:52^2
2:22:23,24/3:14/6:11,12/8:22,23:25:31:
4:37^3:46:48/9:4:6/11:38/12:7:10/13:8/18:5
21^2/20:10:31:39/21:2/22:28/2Ki1:10:12/2:
/3:11/4:1:26^2/5:12:13/6:10:26-30:31/7:2:4^4:
2:19/9:17/10:6:24/18:14:20,21:22:23:24/20
21:8/25:24/1Ch12:17^2/14:10/19:12^2/21:3/
3/28:7:9^2/29:17/2Ch6:16:23:24^2:28^2:34:36:
38/7:13^3:14:17:19^2/10:7:10/15:2/18:27/19:
24:27/25:8/28:13:23/30:9^2/33:8/Ez4:13:16
20:25/9:12:15/Neh1:8:9/2:4^2:7/4:1:3/5:13/
/10:31/13:21/Est3:9/4:14:16/5:3:4:6:7,8/6
7:2:3^2:4/8:5^2/9:12:13/Job3:13:23/4:18,19/
/8:4:6:15/9:3:7:15:16:20:21:24:27:30:32,33
:13,14:15:16/11:10/13:8:10:19/14:7:14:
21/15:21/16:4:6/17:5:13,14/18:2:5/19:4/22:
1:23:24:29/27:14/31:5:7,8^3:9:13:16:19,20:
22:23:24:25:26:28:29:31:33:38,39^2/32:14/33:
3,24:23,24f:32:33/34:14:17/35:2,3:6^2:7:
15/36:8:11:12:19/38:4:17,18/40:14/41:8:10
:4/Ps6:5/7:3:4/11:3f/14:2/15:4/27:10/28:1
:24/32:6/34:9/37:24:27/44:19:20/46:2/50:
51:16/53:2/66:18/69:20^2/73:15/81:8:10/85
89:30,31,32/104:29/107:43/109:28^2/119:32:
/124:1^2/130:3,4/132:12/137:5,6^2/139:8^2:9:
141:5/Pro1:10/2:3,4,5/3:1:4,5:27,28/4:4:
12/5^2/6:1:3:5:30/7:14f:27/8:9:13/9:7,8:12/
27^2/13:18^2:24^2/14:7/15:9,10^2:21:31,32/16:
17:13/19:18:19/20:4:12:13:28/21:27/22:1:
22,23/23:13,14:15,16/24:10/25:21,22^2:26/
7:11:14/28:13:16:27/30:4^2:9^2:32/31:5:10/
2:24-26/4:10^2/5:8:19,20/6:3/7:18/9:16/10:
1f/11:4:8/Sol1:8/5/8:1:7:8:9:9f:9/Is1:9:18:
:20/7:9/8:13:20/16:4,5/19:12/20:5,6/23:12
:18/27:4,5/28:12^2/29:9/30:21/36:6:8,9:12/
23/43:9/44:7/46:1/49:15/50:10/54:15/55:1
:13:16/58:8:13/63:16/66:3/Jer2:10,11^2:28/
/4:2/5:1^2/6:8/7:3:5/11:4:5/12^2:16/13:22/14
^{2}/15:1:2:19/17:15:24:27^3/18:8:9/20/22:4:5:
25/23:22:26:38,39/25:6:28/26:4:5:13:15:19/
10:12:15:18/29:7:13/30:11/31:33f/33:20,21
5:7:15/37:10:17/38:15:17:18:20:21,22:25/40:
5/42:6:10:13,14:15:20/49:12/51:6:9/Lam1:
/4:19^2/Eze1:16/3:6:18:19:20:21/7:13:15^2/12
/14:9:14:16:18:22/15:7/18:5:10:14:19:21:24:
/20:11:21:39/27:17f/33:4:5:6:9:12^2:13:15:19/
23:27/43:11/44:9/46:16:17:18/Dan2:5:6:8,9
15^2:17:18/5:16/Hos1:3/8:7:12/9:16/13:9/
no5:18/6:9/7:2:5:7/8:10/Ob1:5^2/Jon:6/4:5/
ic6:7^2:9/Hab2:3/3:17/Hag2:12:13/Zec1:3/3:
8:10:14,15:19/11:9^2:12^2/13:3:6/14:18:19/
al1:4^2/2:1/3:10/Mt4:9:24/5:13:19:21:22^3:23:
:30:31:32:35:38^2:39:40:41:46:47/6:14,15^2:21:
:23:30:33/7:8:9:10:11/8:2:8,9:31/9:18:21/10:
^{2}:32:33:37^2:38:39^2:41^2:42/11:14:15:21:23/12:
1:26:27:28:43,44,45/13:9:29/14:28/15:5,6/
:24:26/17:4:20/18:6:8:9:12:13:15^2:16:17^2:19:
/19:10:17:21/20:15:27/21:3:19:21:22:24:25:
/22:21:24:32f:40/24:23:24:26:46:48/26:24:33
:42:54/27:40:64/28:14/Mk1:40/3:2:26/4:9:
:23/5:28/7:15,16f/8:3:34:35:36/9:22:23^2:41:
^{2}:43,44:45,46:47:50/10:12:26/11:3:13:22,23:
:26,f:29:31:32/12:17/13:14:15,16^2:21:22/14:
:35/15:12:29,30:36/16:18/Lk2:23/3:11^2/4:3:
7:9,10,11/5:5:12/6:29^2:33:34:38:40/7:4:32^2:
/8:8/9:5/10:6^2:8,9:10:13:35/11:8:11^2:12:13:
:19^2:20:23:36/12:8:26:28:31:39^2:42,43,44:45:
:59/13:6:9^2:24,25:31/14:1:5:8^2:26f:28:32:35/
:3,4/16:10:11:12:24:30:31/17:2,3^2:4:6:10:18:
26/19:8:22:31:40/20:5:6:19:28/21:19:36/22^2:
,42:67,68/23:31:31f:35:37/Jn1:24,25/2:18/3:
^{2}/4:10/5:23/6:30,31:62/7:4:11:17:21,22,23:
/8:12:16:17:19:30,31:36:39:42:54:55/9:19:33:
/10:24:34,35,36:38^2/11:21:22:32:40:48/12:25^2
6:26f:26:44:47/13:8/14:2,3:7:15,16:28/15:6:7:
:19:20:22:24/16:7^2/18:23:30:34f:36:39/19:12
0:15:23^2/21:12:22:23:25/Act4:9:17/5:26,27:
:39/8:37/10:15/13/15:27,28,29/16:15:23/17:
:29/18:14:21/19:38:39:40/20:16/24:19/25:
,11^2/26:5:32/27:10/Rom1:10/2:25^2:26:29/3:
8:21,22:24:30:31/4:1:4,5^2:14:16/5:7/7:2:3:7:8:
/8:4:9^2:11:13^2:17:25:28:31:35/9:1:5/10:5:9:
:19/11:6:12:14:16:21:22^2:23:24/12:6:7^2:8^3:13:
:15:20^2/13:3:4:8:9/14:3:6:14:15^2:18:20:23/15
:27f/1Co1:31/2:8/3:15:17:18/4:7:19/5:6/6:12^3
6:17/7:1:6:8:9:11:12:13:14:15:16:18:21:22^2:27^2
:28^2:36:37:39^2:40/8:2:8^2:13/9:2:5^2:12:16^2:17/10
:12:23:27^2:28:30/11:4:6^2:16:17:27:29:31:34/12:
15:16:17:19:26^2/13:1:2^2:3^2:7:12/14:2:6^2:8:9:13:
14:16:23:24:28:29,30^2:35:38:38f/15:2:13:14:15:
16:19:29:32^2:33:58/16:4:7:10:22/2Co1:12:23/2:
2^2/3:9:11/4:3/5:13,14^2/6:13/8:12:23/9:4:5:6^2/
10:7:17/11:4:6:16:30/13:1:7:9/Gal1:8:9:10/2:17
:18:21/3:3:15:16:18:21,22/4:1:15:18/5:2:4:11:
15:25/6:1:3:8^2:9:12/Eph4:21:26:28/6:3/Php1:
22/2:17^2:19/3:4^2:5:15:16/4:7/Col3:25/4:10/
1Th4:8/5:21/2Th2:1/3:14/1Ti2:15/3:1:5:10:15
/4:4:5:6/5:3:4:5:6:20:22/6:2:6:8/2Ti1:8/2:6:10:
12^2:21:25/Tit3:10/Phm1:17^2:18/Heb2:3/3:6:14
:15/4:8/6:4:6:8:16/7:5:11/8:4:7/9:13:16:26/10:
2:26:28:36:38/11:15:19:37,38/12:3:8:20:25^2/13:
23/Jas1:5:7,8:23:25/2:1:2:3:13:14:15:21:26/3:1:
13^2:14/4:4:11:15/5^2:19/1Pe1:7/2:2,3f:12:18^2:
19:20^2/3:1:6:7:10:11:14:15:16:17/4:14:17:18:19
/5:6/2Pe2:21/3:1/1Jn1:4:6:7:8:9:9f:10/2:1:4:24
/3:6:7:8:13:14:17:20:20f:21/4:1:2^2:3:6:8:18:20^2/
5:1:10:15:16^2/2Jn1:6:9^2:10:11/Rev:3/3:20/9:16
f/13:10f^2/20:15/22:18:19
1966

IMPLIED

Gen1:2f:3f/11:29f^2:32f/12:8f/13:5f:7f/14:8,9f:
11f/15:16f/16:13f/17:17f/21:33f/22:1f/24:21f/
25:21f/27:2,3,4f^2:8,9,10f:11,12f/29:26f/31:12f:
35f:47,48f/32:1f:22,23,24f/33:13f/35:8f/36:2,3f
:15,16f:31-39f/37:29f/38:9f:10f/42:3f:4f/44:1f/
48:7f/Ex1:8f/2:11f:24f/11:4f/14:26f/17:5,6f:7f
/22:27f/25:16f/26:31f/29:36f/30:10f/34:7f:28f
/36:35f/38:4f/39:6,7f^2:15-18f:24f:33-40f/Lev5:
6f:16f/14:19f/16:15f/17:11f/19:27f/21:12f/23:
3f:40f/24:18f/25:33f/27:13f:20f/Num2:3-31f/5:
8f:24f/7:14f/8:10f:12f/11:21f/14:17,18f/16:26f
/17:10f/19:12f/20:27f/27:14f:16f/28/29:11f/
32:42f/Deu1:19,20,21f/8:11f/14:1f/18:10f/20:
20f/22:4f/26:2,3f/27:8f:14f:23f/32:25f:34f/33:9
f/Jos1:2f/4:23f/11:18f/13:2-7f^3/15:18,19f:37-
37-44f:48-62f/16:8f/17:1f:2f/18:16f:21-28f/19:
15,16f/21:9-16f:20,21,22f/Ju1:14f/3:1f^2/14:7f/
16:8f:12f/Ru3:10f/1Sa2:16f/6:9f/14:32f:38f/19
:4f:14f:24f/2Sa2:17f/18:9f/19:27f/21:10f/1Ki1:
5f/7:25f:27-30f/11:1f/17:24f/18:5f/19:19f/22:6
f:32,33f/2Ki2:19f/5:24f/6:33f/9:29f/11:2,3f:4f/
13:25f/15:5f/18:4f:24f/24:17f/1Ch1:1f/2:50f/5:
7,8f/6:4-15f:16f:33-38f/7:13f:15f/9:35,36,37f/
10:12f/11:26-47f/12:21f/15:2f/20/26:28f/28:8f
/2Ch1:2,3f/5:2f^2/11:18f/18:1f^2/35:20f:21f/Ez1
:4f:6f/2:1f/6:6f/7:1f/Neh1:1f/3:22f/Est8:2f/
Job1:2,3f:8f:12,13f/4:3,4f/12:12f/21:4f/24:
22,23f/29:12f/30:28,29f/37:13f:19,20f/42:4f:5f
/Ps2:1f:6f:7f:12f/3:3f:7f/4:6f/18:9f/19:5f^2/22:
9,10,11f/30:6,7f:9f/31:2f/38:7f/47:9f^2/49:7f/51
:19f/53:1f/61:5f/62:3,4f^2/66:10f/68:18f:27f/72:
15f/75:10f/81:7f:10f/82:1f/89:3,4f/105:28f:43f
/109:6f/110:1f/115:17f/132:2-5f/136:10f:11,12
f:15f:18f:19f:20f:21f/144:12-15f/Pro4:24f/10:
13f:15f^2/11:16f/12:9f:21f/13:5f/20:12f/21:8f/
22:28f/26:4,5f/27:23,24f/Ecc1:1f:3-7f/3:14f/5:
6,7f^2/Sol1:6f^2/4:4f/7/Is1:10f/2:5f/5:19f/7:1f:
15,16f:17f:20f/8:2f:9,10f/16:3f/17:9f/18:4f/19:
25f/21:1f:6,7f:16f/22:2f^2/23:18f/27:2f:3f:4,5f:
7,8f/32:19f/33:1f/37:8,9f:30f/40:26f/42:5f:22f:
25f/43:3f/44:5f:8f/49:8,9f/52:1f/54/55:4f:13f/
56:9f/65:16f/66:20f/Jer1:13f/2:32f^2:35f/3:2f/
12:3f:5f^2/13:13f:20f/16:8f/17:21,22f/22:13f/23:
9f/26:24f/31:38,39f^4/32:15f/51:5f/Lam4:1f/
Eze1:10f^2/2:7f/4/8:1f/10:9-13f/11:21f/16:28f/
17:12,13f^3:16f/19:3f:5f/21:25f/29:6f:17f/30:14f
/31:1f:10f/36:23f/38:2,3f:13f:15,16f/40:3f:19f:
47f/42:12f/43:3f/44:28f/47:2f:7f:13f/Dan2:34f
/3:7f:29f/7:26f/8:24f/9:3f/12:1f/Hos1:11f:3:2f
/11:4f:10f/12:1f/Jon3:4,5f/4:3f:5f/Nah1:11f:13
f/Hab2:4f/Zep1:18f/Zec:8f/6:7f/11:1f/12:11f/
Mal3:6f/Mt1:20f/2:5f:14f/3:3f/4:12,13f:18f/7:
20f/8:8,9f:11f:19f:22f^2/9:10f/11:13f:14f/12:10f:
11f:41f:42f:46,47f/13:10f:53,54f/15:11f:21f/17:
10f/19:17f/20:21f:23f:28f/21:7f/22:11f/23:5f/
24:37,38f/25:13f/26:73f/27:21f:51f:62f/Mk1:2f
:12,13f:14f/2:4f:9,10,11f:21f:23f/3:27f:30f/9:11f
:19f/10:13f/12:23f:27f/13:10f:33f:35,36,37f/14:
51,52f/15:1f/Lk1:17f/3:13f/6:41f/7:2f/8:1f:16f
:17f:30f/9:34f:41f:46f/10:38f/11:1f:12f:16f:26f:
29,30f:31f:32f/12:53f/14:28f/16:8f:10f/17:16f:
26f^2/18:8f/19:9,10f:21f/22:24f/23:1f:45f:53f/
24:40f^2:49f:50f/Jn3:29f/4:20f/5:14f:17f:32,33f/
6:22,23f:32f:53f/7:33f/8:46f:50f/12:32f/14:27f:
29f/16:1f:20f:24f/20:8f:11f/21:7f:21f/Act1:6f/2
:29f:30f:34f/4:11f/5:21f/8:33f/9:30f:32f/10:11f:
12f:46,47f/11:6f/12:2f:25f/13:16f:37f:41f/15:15
f:16f:36f/16:3f:12f:23f/17:10f:26f/18:7f:17f/19:
8f/21:29f/23:9f/24:18f/27:4f:12f:43f/28:21f/
Rom1:20f/2:7f^2/3:2f:15f:21,22f/5:13f:14f/7:1f:6
f/8:20,21f:26f/9:6f/10:19f/12/1Co7:29f/8:9f/9:
5f^2:21f/10:3,4f/11:5f:7f/14:18f:24f/15:45f:52f/
16:1f:11f/2Co2:3f/3:11f:17f/4:1f:7f:10f:13f/5:
13,14f/7:11f:12f^2/11:8,9f:33f/13:1f/Gal2:12f/3:
13f/Eph2:14f/2Ti1:6f/Heb:1f/5:7f/9:18f/11:5f
/13:13f/Jas5:9f/1Pe2:5f/3:6f/4/2Pe2:12f/1Jn
1:9f/5:6,7,8f/Rev2:10f/3:14f/5:4f/9:11f/14:9f/
16:10f/17:9f/19:12f/20:9f:10f/21:18,19,20f
614

IN

Gen1:1f:14,15:17:26f^2:26^2:31/2:4:7f:8^2:9:15:
16,17:24/3:1:8:14:16:20f/4:16:20:22f/5:1f:3,4,5f
:3,4,5:3,4,5f:21-24^2/6:1f^2:3:4:16:17:18:19,20:21/
7:2:8,9:10,11,12:14,15:16:23/8:1:11:13f^2:17:
18,19/9:2,3^2:13:14:16,17:20,21/10:5:10:15-19:
20:32/11:2:6f:8:28^2:32f/12:5^2:10:14/13:1:7:9:10
:12:14:17/14:3:4:5,6^4:7:8,9:11f:12:14/15:1:13:15
/16:2,3/17:2,3,4^2:12:13:17^3:23/18:1^2:3,4:9/19:
10:12:15:18,19,20:30^2:31:33:34:35/20:3/21:1:7:
9f^2:20,21:22:34/22:4:9:12^2:13:17/23:1^2:4:8:11:
17,18^2:19,20/24:1:35:38:40:42:53:62:63/25:9,10^2
:11:12-15:18:21f:23/26:1:3:6:19:27:29^3:30:31:32
/27:1:14:15:20:30:38f^2:43:45/28:16,17/29:1:2^2:
7:17:18:20:25/30:6f:8:14f^2:14:33:37/31:2:9:11:
17-20:23:24:25:26:36,37:42:47,48^2/32:3^2:21/33:
1:4:18/34:3:5:6,7:8:18,19^2:28/35:2:3:6:8:27/36:
5:6,7,8:9:13,14f:17:24:28,29,30f:31-39:40-43/37
:1:3:7:13,14:15:18:24:25:29:32:33:34:35:36/38:9
:12:26:27/39:1:2:3:4:6:8:11:14,15^2:20:22/40:1^2:
7:9,10:11:14:15:16:17/41:2:10^2:14:19^2:25:33^2:39
:40:41,42^2:48:52:54^3/42:1:2:5^2:6:13:16:19^2:20:
27:28:29:32/43:12:18:33/44:7:8:12:13:16:18:30
/45:10:13:17:18:26/46:2:3,4:5:6:8-14:15^2:19-22^2
:23,24,25:27:28:34^2/47:1^2:4^3:5,6:12:14^2:16:17^2:
27^2:29/48:2:3:5:9/49:1:3^2:6:11:16:17:18:27^2:
29,30^3:33/50:8:12,13^2:22:26^2/Ex1:6:7:13,14:19
/2:3:5:12:13:22:23/3:1f:2:7:9:15f^2:16^2/4:2:4:7:
21/5:19/6:5:16:26:28,29/7:3:10:11:15^2:16:19^2:
25/8:1:3,4^2:5:9:11:20:22:24^3:25/9:12:13:14:19^2:
20:21:24:25^2:26:31/10:2:6:7:9:10:14:19/11:1:3:5^2
/12:3,4^2:7:11:12:19^3:21:27:29^2:30:40,41:46:49/
13:3:6,7:10:10f:13:14:20/14:6:7:9:10:11^2:12:17^2:
24:27:31^2/15:4:6:7:10:11^2:13:16:17^2:20:21/16:3:
4:7,8,9^3:11,12^2:13:14:16:28,29:32:33^2:34^2:35/17
:9:11/18:3:8:15,16:21^2:23/19:1:2,3:8:9:18/20:2:
4^2:5:11^2:12:16f:20:21/21:2:11:16:22:26:29^2:36/
22:2:3:4:9^3:15:21^2:23:25:29/23:2,3^2:9:13f^2:15:17
:19:21f:24:29:31/24:3:8/25:1^2/26:25:30^2:32:34/
27:14,15:16:17:19:20:21/28:3:10:11^2:15:17:20:
29^2:30,31f^2:30,31^2:35^3:37,38:43/29:3,4:8:24^2:26
:30:31^2:32:33^2:39^2:41^2/30:36^2/31:3:5:17/32:15:
19:20:21/33:8:11:22/34:2:4:5,6^3:7:9:10:12:15:18
:20:26:27f:28:29/35:3:10-19:24:25^2:29:33:35^3/
36:1/37:14:20,21/38:4:20:21^2:25,26:29/39:1^2:
6,7^2:10:11:12:13^2:23:33-40^2:41/40:3:4^2:5:6:9:17:
26:38/Lev1:15,16,17/2:4:7:11:13f^2/4:6^2:7:10:17^2
:18:20:31:35^2/5:5:13:16f/6:14:16:19,20^2:26:27:
28:30/7:6:7:8:38/8:10:21:27:31:34/9:4:9:15:16:
17/10:1:1f:5:12:13^2:14:17/11:33:34:37:46/12:5f
/13:1:3:4^2:5:7:9,10^2:18^2:21:24:25:26:27:28:29,30
:31^2:37:38:39:42:43:45:47,48^2:49:55f^2:56:59/14:
5:6:13:17:18:21:29:33,34^2:35:36:37:39:41:47:50:
51,52:55^2:56^2:57/15:12:13:19:26:31:33/16:1:14:
15:17:22:23:24:29,30^3:31:31f:32^2/17:5:6:7:10:11
/18:4,5:4,5f:9:16f:24:26:29,30/19:15:20:24:25:
28:32:33:34:35,36/20:3/21:5:10:11:11f:20:23/
22:11:13:16:23:29,30/23:3^2:9,10,11^2:17:29:32:
38^2:42:43/24:3,4:5-8^2:9:10:12:19/25:11:12:
17,18:19:24:29:29f:30:31:32:33^2:35:45:50/26:
4,5:16:20:32:34,35:36^2:37^2:39:45/27:16:17:18:
19:21:24:25/Num1:1:17,18,19f^2:47,48,49/2:3-
3-31f:3-31^4:32,33:34/3:4:7,8,9:11,12:13^2:25-30:
31-35:40:46:49^2/4:3:6:12:14:16^2:17,18,19:49/5:
17:18:23/6:1:6,7:9:18:20:21/7:3:18-23f:24-29f:
30-35f:36-41f:42-47f:48-53f:54-59f:60-65f:66-71
f:72-77f:78-83f/8:2:11:14:15^2:16:18:19:21:23,24
:25,26/9:2,3:4,5:10:11:18/10:9:10:12:17:21:22:
28:31f:32/11:4,5:8^2:18:22:25:26:31^2/12:5:7,8:14
:15:16/13:3-15:16f:22f:22:26:27:29^3/14:2^3:13:
16:17,18:22^2:24:25^2:29:32:33^3:34,35^3:45/15:1:
17,18:19,20,21:26:31:32:39/16:3:5:8,9:13:17:26:
46:49/17:4^2:7:8:9/18:1:2,3,4:10:23:31^2/19:9:13:
14^2:15:16^3:17:18^2/20:1^2:12/21:4:5:11:14:17,18:
20^2:23:25,26:27-30^2:31,32/22:5,6:7:8:11:22,23^2:
25:26:27^2:30:31/23:18-24/24:3-9^3:10:15-19^2:
21,22:25f/25:3:4/26:3,4:5-11^3:12-14:15-18:19-
19-22^2:23-25:26,27:28-37^4:38-41:42,43:44-47:
48-50:52,53:57:58,59:62^2:63:64,65^4/27:3,4^2:14^3:

(IN Con't)
21:21/28:4[2]:7:8:9,10:15:16:23:31/29:5:6[2]:11[2]:16
:19:22:25:28:31:34:38:39[2]/30:3:10/31:7:21:23:
27:30:47/32:1:13:15:26:30:41/33:5,6:11:15-37:
40[2]:41:49:52:54:55[2]/34:4/35:5:7:8:9,10:13,14:
22,23[2]:25:32:33/36:3:7:9:11,12[2]/**Deu1**:1[3]:8:15[2]:
17:26:27:30:31:34,35:39/2:1:4:7[2]:10:12[2]:21[2]:23:
35,36/3:11:16:19:23,24,25:27[2]:29/4:5:14:16,17:
25[2]:27:30:32:34:39:40:43[3]/5:6:9,10:15:16:29:31:
32:33/6:1:3:7:17:18[2]:19:20:21/7:4:8:12:13:23/8:
1:6:9:11:12,13:14:16[2]:20/9:1:7:15:16:20/10:1:2:
5:9:11:15:19:22/11:3:4:5:8:9:15:18:21:22:23:30:
31/12:1:2[2]:7:9:10:14[2]:18:26,27:28:29:30:31/13:
5:12,13,14:18/14:21:23:27/15:2:4,5:7:10:14:15/
16:3:3f:4:5:10:12:15:16:18:20/17:2,3:7[2]:14:20/
18:4[2]:6,7[2]:8:9/19:1:2,3[2]:10:14:19:21/20:5[2]:6:7:
13:15:16:18/21:1[2]:9:13[2]:21/22:6[3]:9:22:25,26,27 [3]
:28,29/23:6:9,10:15,16:17,18:19:20:21:24/24:7:
8:12,13:14,15:17:18:19:21[2]:22/25:1[3]:7:9[2]:
13,14,15[2]:19/26:1:2,3:5[2]:14:15/27:2,3,4:15/28:
1:2-6[3]:7:8:9:10[2]:11:12:14:15-19[3]:20:25:29[3]:30:
36:47,48:53:55:58,59:61:63:66[2]:67[2]:68/29:2,3:7:
9:16:19:20:21:23:27:28/30:10:12:14:18[2]:20/31:2
f:4:13:15:16:18:24:29/32:10:15:21:24:47:49[2]:50:
51/33:3[2]:5:12:16:17:24:26:28/34:1:5:6[2]:11,12[2]/
Jos1:4[4]:7:10,11[2]/2:2:4:11:20/3:6:10:12f:17/4:
2,3:5:6:9:10:14:19:21/5:2,3:4,5:8,9/6:1:5:17:21:
24:25/7:3:13:14:21:23/8:3,4:9[2]:11,12,13[2]:16:17:
19:20,21:22:25:29:31:33:34/9:9:17:22:24:25:27/
10:6:11:12:13[3]:16:28[2]:34,35:40:42/11:1[6]:17:18f:
21[2]:22[2]/12:2:5[2]:7:8-24[4]/13:2-7[4]:9:10:12:16:21:
24:27,28:29:30:33/14:1:3,4:5:6:9:12/15:15:21-
21-32[2]:33-36[2]:48-62f:48-62:63/16:1:9:10/17:5,6
:9:11:12:16,17,18/18:3:9:13:21-28f:21-28/19:12
:15,16:17-23:27:33:34:35-39:50:51/20:3:4:5:6[2]:7 [3]
:8[3]:9[2]/21:6:9-16f[2]:9-16:19:20,21,22f[2]:27:32:40:
43[2]/22:9:10[2]:14:15:19[2]:20:22,23:24,25[2]:26,27:
29/23:6:7:13[2]/24:7[2]:11:14[2]:15:17:18:26:30:32[3]:
33/**Ju1**:3[2]:7:9[2]:10:15:16[2]:19:21:25:27:28:29/2:2:
3[3]:7-9[2]:15[2]:19:23/3:1:1f[2]:1[2]:7:11:16:20:27/4:2,3 [2]
:5:6[2]:11:18:20/5:6:9:10:19:24:25:28:31/6:2:8:11:
15[2]:16f:19[2]:24[2]:33[2]:37[2]/7:1:5,6[4]:8,9:16:18:19,20[2]
:21:22/8:2,3:6f:10:11:25:27f:27:31:32[3]/9:1:16:
21:24[2]:27:31[2]:32:33:43:44[2]:46/10:1[2]:2:4:5:7,8[2]:9
:14:15:17/11:3:7:11:17:19:29:30,31:35:39/12:1:
2:7:8:9,10:11,12:15[3]/13:1:2,3:9:20/14:1:5:8:15:
16/15:1:4:8[2]:9:11:19/16:2[3]:3:4[2]:5:8f:9:12:15:19[2]
:21:23,24[2]:27/17:1:4,5[2]:6[2]:7,8[2]:9/18:1[2]:2[2]:7[2]:8:
12:14:19[2]:27:28/19:1:2:3:7:12,13:15[2]:16[3]:17:18[2]
:20:27/20:1:4:11:14,15[2]:27,28[2]:30:32:33:35-39[3]:
40,41:44:48/21:15[3]:19:20:22:23[2]:25[2]/**Ru1**:1:1f:
11f:13:22/2:1:7:10,11:14f:17:19:22/3:13:15-18/
4:7[2]:11:14:15/**1Sa1**:1[2]:10:17:19,20:19,20f:24/2:
1:8[2]:9:13,14:17:21:26:27:32:33/3:1:2,3:11:15:
21,4:1/4:6:8:12f:20/5:1:4:5/6:1[2]:7:10:13:18/7:1:
2:6:14:16/8:1[2]:2:3:4:12/9:2[2]:5:6[2]:9,10,11[2]:12,13
:16:19:21:24/10:2:14:22:24:25[2]/11:5:8[2]:15/12:2
:4:8:11:17:20/13:1f:1:2[2]:6[2]:15:16[2]:17:19[2]:22/14:
3:5[2]:14:16[2]:19:22:24,25:47[2]/15:4:5:9:22[4]:33/16:
8:9:10,11:18/17:1[2]:8:12:24:33:40:41,42:45[2]:46:
48,49[2]:54:57:58/18:10:13:14:20[2]:25[2]/19:2:4:
9,10[3]:11:13:15:18:19:22/20:1:5:20:24,25:28,29:
30:34/21:6:8:9[3]/22:2[2]:3:4[2]:6[2]:7:15:18/23:3:7:
14,15[2]:16[2]:19[3]:23:24,25:26:29/24:3:6:9,10:11:19[2]
/25:1:7:15,16:21:24:28:29:39/26:5,6,7:10:15:23
/27:5[2]:9/28:3:5,6f:14:15/29:1:3:4:5:9:10/30:6:
11,12:14:17:27-31/31:2:7:10/**2Sa1**:1:6:9:11:20:
21f:23[2]:25/2:6:10,11[2]:15:18:30/3:12:21:23:27:
32:37:38/4:2,3:2,3f:11:12[3]/5:4,5:6:24/6:4:18:20:
21[2]/7:2[2]:3:5f:6:8:9:19:23[2]/8:2:3:6/9:4:5,6[2]:13/
10:7,8:9[2]/11:1[2]:11/12:1:3:10:11:12:31:31f/13:1:
4:10:12:12f:13[2]:17,18:19:20[2]:21-24:31/14:2,3[2]:4
:5,6:13:15,16:20[2]:25:28/15:2:3[2]:6:7,8:10:12:13[2]:
16:19,20[2]:28/16:4/17:9:18:19:23:26/18:3:6:8:9[2]
:17:18/19:3:7:13:15:18:20:31,32:33:37:43[3]/20:3 [3]
:8,9,10[3]:12[2]:14:16:21:23:24/21:1:2:4:5,6:9:
12,13,14[2]:15:16:22/22:3:7:16:19:24:28:35:42/23
:3:8[2]:9:13:14:15:24-39/24:3[2]:3f:5:6:8:9[2]:20/**1Ki**
1:1:2:3,4[2]:5:22,23:28:41:42[2]:46,47:49,50:51/2:3[2]
:5:6:10:11[2]:13:26[2]:34:36,37:38:42[2]/3:1:2:3:5:11:
13:17,18:19:20[2]:21:25/4:1:8-19[2]:25:28:30[2]:33[3]/
5:6:11:14:15:18[2]/6:1[2]:7:23-28:37[2]:38[2]/7:2:3,4[2]:
6:8:11:12:13:16-22:23:24f:27-30f:39:40:41-46:48
:49/8:1:2:3,4:7:9:12,13:21:22,23:29:30:32:35,36:
37:40[2]:58:59:64/9:2,3:4:11,12:19[2]:20,21:24:26[2]/
10:2:5[2]:6:10[2]:13:16,17[3]:20[2]:21:22:26[2]:27[2]/11:4[2]:
9,10:14:15[3]:20:21:26:27,28:29:36:38:41:42:43[2]/
12:2,3,4[2]:8:15[2]:18:19:20f:21:25:28:29[2]:32,33f/
13:4:5:8:11:21,22[2]:24,25[2]:28:30:31:32[2]:33:34/14
:6:11[2]:13:15:19:21[3]:22:25:29[2]:31/15:1[2]:7:8[2]:9[2]:
15:17:18:20:22:23[2]:24[2]:25[2]:28:31/16:2:4-7[3]:9:10
:12:14:15,16:18:20:21:23:24:27:28[2]:32/17:1:7:
8,9:12[2]:14:16/18:2:3,4[3]:13:15:38/19:9:11[2]:12:13
:18/20:12:21:25:27:30:34[2]:39:42/21:2:3:5:8:9:20
f:24[2]:27[2]/22:10:22:23:25:27[2]:28:30:32,33:35[2]:39
:41:42:43:45:47:50:51:52,53/**2Ki1**:3:6:16:17:18/
2:4:16:19:19f:21:24/3:26:27/4:2:8:9:10:11,12:13
:15,16:19:25:33:35:36:38:40/5:3:5[2]:8:10:12:15[2]:
17f:22:23:24:25:26/6:12:20:25:26-30:32/7:1:2:
10:11:12[2]:15/8:2:4:5:15:17:20:23:24,25[2]:26:28[2]/
9:4:18:19:24:27:28:29:29f/10:6:8:9,10:11[2]:11f[2]:
17[2]:23:25:29:30:31:32,33:34:35:36[2]/11:2,3:4[2]:
6,7,8:10:15:18/12:1:6[2]:9:18:19:20:21[2]/13:5[2]:8:
9,10[3]:12:13:14:20,21:24:25/14:2:3:7:15:16:18:19
:20[2]:23:28/15:1[2]:5:6:7:8:9[2]:11:13:15:17:19,20:21
:23:25[2]:26:27:28:29f:31:32,33[2]:36:37:38[2]/16:1[2]:
4:9:10:17:18:19:20[2]/17:1[2]:4[2]:6[4]:7:9f:11:14:15:18
:19:24:26:29/18:1[2]:5[2]:6:9:11[4]:15[2]:22:24[2]:26:28:
30:31,32[2]/19:2:10:12:28[2]:29:30:31:35:37/20:1:3
:11f[2]:14:15:17:18:20/21:1:3,4,5[2]:6:7[3]:11:16:17:
18:19,20:23:25:26[2]/22:1[2]:3,4:8:11[2]:14:15,16:
18,19/23:1:3:4[2]:5[2]:8:9:10:12[2]:16[2]:19:21:22:23[2]:
24[3]:28:29:30[2]:31,32:33[2]:34:36,37/24:2:5:8,9:12:
13:14:17f:18,19:20/25:3:4,5[2]:10:11:19:22:24:26:
28/**1Ch1**:1f[2]:5-9f:43:46/2:22:34,35f:50f/3:4:5/4
:10[2]:21-22:27:32,33[2]:34-39/5:2:7,8:7,8f:7,8:9:10
:11:14:16[2]:17:18:20:22[2]/6:4-15:16f:19,20,21:
22,23,24:31[2]:48:55,56,57:61:62:66-69:71:76:80/
7:5:7:28:40/8:6,7:8,9,10:13/9:1[2]:2:3:6:13:15,16:
19:20:22:23:25:26[2]:28[2]:29:32:33,34:35,36,37:38
/10:5:6:7[2]:8/11:7:13[2]:14:15f:15[2]:16:22:23:26-47
f/12:8-13[11]:24-37:38[2]/13:6/14:4-7:15/15:1:14:
27:29/16:2:7:10:19[2]:25:32:33:35/17:1[3]:2:6:9:16:
17[2]:20:21[2]/18:6:8:12:13:17/19:2,3:4:9:10:17,18:
19/20:1[2]/21:5[2]:6:16:25:29/22:2:3:8:9:17:18/23:
8,9f:13:19:20:24:25:28:31:32/24:5:6:7-18:30:31/
25:3:6,7[3]/26:11:20,21,22:23,24:30:31,32[2]/27:
5,6:10:12:13:14:15:16-22:25:28:29[2]/28:1[2]:2[2]:4:8
:12f[2]:13:17:19:21/29:3[2]:6,7[3]:10:11[2]:15:19:26,27 [2]
:28:29[2]/**2Ch1**:2,3:4:5,6:12:15/2:2:14[3]:16:17/3:1:
2:16f/4:7:10:11:19/5:1[2]:2[2]:3:6:10:11,12[2]/6:1[2]:
5,6:10:11:12,13[2]:14:24:28[2]:31f:37,38:40:41/7:8:
15/8:4[2]:6:11:12:13:14[2]:15:17,18/9:4[2]:5:9:11:
13,14:16[2]:19:20[2]:22:25[3]:27[2]:29[3]:30:31/10:2,3:5:
12:15/11:1:5-10:12[2]:17f:23/12:1:2:6:12:13:15[2]:
16/13:1[3]:4:10:22/14:1[2]:9,10:11[2]:14/15:3:4:5:8[4]:
9:10:11:17[2]/16:1[2]:4:7[2]:9:11:12[2]:13,14[3]/17:2[3]:3:
4:7,8,9[2]:14,15:18:19[3]/18:1f[2]:9:12:16:21:22:24:
26:31:34[2]/19:3:5:6:8:9:10:11[4]/20:3:6:7:9[2]:20:21:
26:31:34[2]:36/21:1[2]:5:6:10:11[3]:12:13[2]:17:19[2]:20[3]
/22:2:3[2]:9:11[2]:12/23:1:2,3:5,6:7:9:10[2]:12:18/24:
1:5:10:11:13:14:16:21:24:25[3]/25:1:4:5,6:13:18[2]:
21:26:27:28/26:3[2]:4[2]:6[2]:7[2]:9:10[3]:15:17,18:19:20:
21[2]:23/27:1:4:5:7:8[2]:9/28:1:2:3:9:13:15:16:19f:
22:24:25:26:27[2]/29:1:2:3:9[2]:15:17:25,26:29:
32,33[2]/30:2,3[2]:4[2]:5:5f:12:13:14:27/31:3:4[3]:5,6[4]:
7,8:11:12,13:14,15[2]:16:17,18:19[2]:20[2]/32:5:18:20[2]
:21:30[2]:31:32[2]:33/33:1:4,5[2]:6:7[3]:14[2]:15:18:19[2]:
20,21:24/34:1:3:13:15,16[2]:19:22:24:27:30:31:32
/35:1:2:3[2]:4,5:10:12:13:15:16:17[2]:18[2]:19:24,25[2]:
27/36:5:6:7[2]:8:11:14:18:22,23[3]/**Ez1**:1f[2]:2[2]:6:7:
11/2:64,65:70/3:1[2]:4:7:8:10:13/4:2:3:7:10:14:15[2]
:17:19[2]:20/5:1:3:8:14[2]:17[2]/6:1:2[2]:3:4:7:8:9:11:
14:15:18:21,22[3]/7:6:7,8,9[3]:13:16:17:18:21:22:24
:27:28f/8:25:26,27[3]:29:30:33:35:36/9:1:5:8:9[4]:
12:13:15/10:1:2:4:6:9:13[2]/**Neh1**:1:2:4[2]:9:11/2:1
:3:9:10:17:20/3:11:17:20:26/4:1:4:5:7:12:13/5:8 [2]
:9:15:16:19/6:2[2]:5,6:10:15:18/7:1:5:60:70:71[2]:
72[2]/8:1[3]:7,8f:10:13:14:15[2]:16[2]:17/9:1:5:6:9:11:
15:17:18:19[2]:21[2]:22:25:27[2]:28:29:31:36:37/10:
28:31:34:36:37[2]:38:39,40/11:1:3[2]:4,5,6:10-14:
15,16,17:18[2]:21:22,23:24:36/12:8:22:23:26:27[2]:
31,32:44:45:46[2]:47[2]/13:6[2]:7[2]:13:15:16:18:19:22[2]
:24/**Est1**:1:5:6:7:22/2:2:3[2]:9:12,13,14:15:16:18:
20:23/3:1:2:7:8:9:12[3]:14:15/4:2:3:11:13:16/5:2:
11:13:14/6:1:4[2]:5:6:11:13/7:8[2]:9/8:2:8:9,10[4]:11:
17/9:1:4:6:11:12[2]:19:26:29-31/10:2/**Job1**:1:2,3[2]
:5[2]:8:17:18:19[2]:20:22/2:3[2]:10:11:12/3:4:17:
20,21/4:3,4[2]:6:12[2]:13:20/5:2:13:14[2]:20[2]/6:5,6,7
:15-18:19-21[2]:25,26/7:13,14:21/8:11-13:14:17/
9:2:5:24:34/10:1:13,14/11:4:8:10:16:18/12:5[2]:
10:14/13:7:10:14:15:15f:16:27,28/14:4:8,9:
11,12:14/15:16:20:23,24:27,28:31:31f:31/16:5:
15[2]:19/17:6:11:16/18:4:6:10:14/19:6:15:23,24:
29/20:6:11:12:26/21:5:25:26:30-32/22:15,16:20
:22:23:26/23:8:9[3]:11:15/24:1:5:7:8:14,15:16:20:
22,23:24/25:2:4:6/26:2:5,6:8/27:10[2]:14:20/28:
10:13:17:18:21/29:4[2]:8:9:10:11:12f:12:18:23/30
:6[2]:10:11:12:15[2]:22:24:25/31:10:18:24:26/32:
8,9/33:8:11:12:15[2]:16:28:30/34:3:20:23:24:25/
35:9,10:14,15/36:5:12:31[2]:33/37:3:5:8[2]:13:22/
38:12:14:16:22,23:36f:39,40[3]:41/39:4:6[2]:12:14:
21-23:28/40:4:13:24/41:12:22/42:6:7:10:11:
13,14f:15/**Ps1**:2/2:4:5:6:12/3:3:4:5:7/4:1[2]:4[2]:5:
8/5:3:10:11/6:1:4:5f[2]:10/7:5:6:10f/8:6:8/9:3:9:
10:11:11f:12:14f:16:20[2]/10:3:5:8:9:12/11:1:4:7f
/12:1/13:2:3:5[3]/15:1/16:3:6f:7:10/17:3:7:8:9:11
:15[3]/18:2:6:13:17:19:29:30:43,44,45/19:3,4[2]:12
/20:1:2:7/21:1[2]:7:9,10/22:8:15:17:25/23:2,3:5:6
/24:1:5:7:8:9/25:3:5:16:20/26:11/27:4[3]:9:13/28
:4:7[3]:9/29:2:9/30:5:6,7:9:11:12[2]/31:1:7:8:9,10:
14,15:17[2]:20/32:9[2]:10:11:11f/33:1:8[2]:18,19:21:
22/34:1f:8:14[2]:19:22/35:2:3:5:7:8:9:10:13:15[2]:
24/36:1:2:7/37:3[3]:7:10:19:23:25:29:34:40/38:8:
8f:17/39:5,6:7/40:3[2]:4[2]:5:10:11/41:3f/42:4,5/
43:5/44:1:9[2]:11:19:25/45:4:5:8:10,11[2]:13:15:17
/46:1:5:6[2]:10/47:9/48:1:3f:6:9/49:4:6:7f:8,9:14:
19/50:12:14,15/51:10:16:18f:19:19f:19/52:2:6:7[2]
:7f:8/55:4:9f:10:11:15[2]:21/56:1:3,4:7:8[2]:13/57:6
/58:1:1f:7:10/59:3:10:12,13:16/60:1:2:8:9,10/
61:4:5f/62:3,4:9/63:1[2]:4:11[2]/64:5:9:10/65:1[2]:5f:
8:11,12/66:9:10:11:12:14/67:1/68:2:4[2]:5f:9,10:
14:15,16:18:18f:25[2]:29:30:30f:30:31:34:35/69:1:
6:13f:14[2]:17:32:34:35/70:2,3:5/71:9:16:20/72:1:
3:5:7:9:17/73:5:10:25/74:2:5,6/75:3[2]:8:10/76:1 [2]
:2:4:5/77:2:9:12:17:18/78:6:7:11,12:14:15:22[2]:
30:32:39:40:43:48:51:53/80:3:7:18/81:4:7:7f:9:9
f:13/82:1f:5:7:8/83:17:18/84:4:5:7[2]:10[2]:12/85:6
:13f/86:1:3:11:15:16/87:4:7[2]/88:8:10:11:12/89:
6:7:9:13:14,15:16[2]:19:27:37:39:40:43/90:4f:5,6:
14:15/91:6:14:15/92:2:8:14:15/93:1/94:19/95:
1:8:10:11/96:6:9f/97:8,9:12/98:4:7:8,9/99:2[2]:9/
101:2:3:7/102:2:6[2]:14[2]:16:19:20:21,22:23:25/
104:10:17:18[2]:24:26:31/105:3:12[2]:18[2]:21:23:24:
30[2]:31:36/106:5[2]:7:15:21,22:25:26:34:35:39/
107:4:10[2]:13:19:24:26:28/108:3:9/109:12,13:16:
29/110:1f:2:3[2]:3f:5/111:10/112:1[2]:4:7[2]:9:10/
114:5/115:3:11/116:3:9:10,11:10,11f:15f:18,19[2]
/118:5:8:9[2]:14:15,16:19:24:26f/119:3:11:14[2]:16:
18:23:25:40,41,42:49,50:51:59,60:71,72:74[2]:83:
85,86:88:89:109:120:124:135:143:147[2]:160:161:
162/120:1:7/122/123:1/125/126:4/127:5f/128
:3/129:6,7:8/130:3,4:7/131:3/132:6:6f:6:7[2]:9/
133:1/134:2/135:1:6:8:9:18:21/136:15/138:1:4
/139:11:13:15:16:17,18:20:24/140:5[3]:11:13/141
:5/143:1f:3[2]:5:8:10/144:1:12-15[2]/145:17/146:4:
5:6:10/147:8:10:11:16/149:2[2]:4,5/150:1[2]:1f/
Pro1:2:3:5,6:7,8,9:14[2]:20:21[2]:24:26:33/2:
11,12,13:14:21f/3:6:11,12:22/4:18:19:21:23/5:3
:4f:11[2]:18/6:1:3:11:22:31:34[2]/7:1:11,12/8:1:8:
14,15:22:27,28,29:30/9:3:10/10:11:19:26:28/11
:1:2:14:20:22:26:28[2]/12:22/13:13:18/14:12:33:
35/15:6:8:26/16:1:11:11f:20:25:27f:30/17:1:12:
17/18:12[2]:15/19:7:18/20:4:13:17/21:9[2]:13:19:
20f/22:1:13:14:16:17,18,19:20,21/23:6,7,8:
19,20,21:29,30:32/24:6:34/25:2,3:8,9,10:11:13:
19:20[2]:24[2]/26:7:9:16:17:24,25,26[2]:27/27:10:14:
20:21:23,24:25,26,27/28:8:23/29:2[2]:5,6:11[2]:13:
23:25/30:4[2]:24-28[2]:29,30,31:32/31:6,7:23:29:31
f/**Ecc1**:2:8-11[2]:12-15[2]:16-18/2:7,8:9:10:16:20-
20-23[2]/3:10:11[2]:14:15:17:22[2]/4:5,6:10:14/5:1:4 [2]
:6,7[2]:8:18:19,20/6:4:9[2]:12/7:6:11:14:15-17:20:
27,28/8:9,10[2]:15[2]:16,17/9:1:6[2]:10:12[2]:14:15/10
:8,9[2]:11f:14:16,17:20/11:2:5[2]:8[2]:9/12:1:10/**Sol1**
:1f:6f:8:14/2:3[2]:7:9:12f:13:15/3:2:6:8/4:7/5:1:2[2]
:15:16/6:12f/7:4:5:11:12/8:5:6:10:13/**Is1**:1[3]:7:8
:9:12,13:25:29/2:2:3:5:10[2]:17:19:22/3:6:8:15:16:
25,26/4:2,3,4f/5:2:8:11:14:15:17:21:23:25/6:3/
7:2:8f:11:14f[2]:19:20/8:11:17:20/9:1:2[2]:5:8,9,10:
11,12f:14,15:17/10:3:10:13:14:17:20[2]:24:25:26[2]:
30:34/11:6:8:9:10/12:4/13:3:6:8:13[2]:20:20f[2]/14
:1:2:3:6[2]:11:13:13f:18[2]:19[3]:25:30[2]/15:1:2[2]:4[2]/16
:8:10[2]:12[2]/17:5:6[2]:8:14[2]/18:2:4:7/19:16[2]:17:19[2]
:21:23/20:1/21:1f:2:5f:6,7[2]:6,7f:8,9:13/22:2[2]:12:
15,16:18/23:1:15,16/24:9:10:11:12:14:15,16:18:
19:20:21:22:23[3]/25:2:6:9[2]/26:1:2:3[2]:4[2]:9:16:17:
18:19/27:1:2:7,8:13[2]/28:1:10:12:13:14:15:16:18:
21:25/29:6:15:18:19:21:23f:23[2]:24/30:2:3:6:12:
13:15[2]:19:25[2]:29/31:2:4,5:7:9/32:2:4:5:7:9:10[2]:
12:18:20/33:2:5:6:7:8[2]:9:12:14:17/34:1:5:6:13/
35:1:6[2]:7/36:1:2:7[4]:8,9:11:11f:11:12:13:15:21/
37:1:2:3:10:12:22:25:29[2]:30:31[2]:35:38/38:1:3:11 [2]
:12:14:18f:20/39:1f[3]:3:7/40:4:11:12:15[2]:17/41:1
:5:7:12:16[2]:18[2]:22:23/42:1f:1:2:4:5[2]:7:10[2]:11[2]:
17:19:22f:25/43:3:14:19:20[3]/44:7:11[2]:14:20:23:
24:26/45:3:13f:14:15:17:18[2]:19:23:24:25/46:1f:
5:9:13/47:1:2f[2]:3:5:8:9[3]:10:14/48:1:3:10[2]/49:1:2 [2]
:4:8,9:10:13:16:20:22/50:1:6:10:11/51:6:7:9:13:
16[2]:20[2]:21/52:5:6:12:14,15/53:2[3]:9:10/54:4:8:9:
14:17/55:12/56:5/57:2:5:6:10:13:15/58:3:5:10:
13/59:5[2]:9[2]:10:14:16:18:20/60:7:9:10/61:3:6:10
:11/62:1[2]:3:4/63:1[2]:3[2]:6:7[2]:9[2]:14/64:1/65:3:5:7:
14:18:19[2]:21,22[3]:25[2]/66:3:5:6:7,8[2]:11:17:19f[3]:

N Con't)
[2]/Jer1:1[3]:9:10:12f[2]:15:17/2:2:3:4,5:9:10,11:
:15:23[2]:25:26,27[2]:28:36:37/3:2[2]:11:18:19:23:
[2]/4:7:9[2]:11,12[2]:17:19:20[2]:23:29[3]/5:1:15f:19[2]:
:23,24:26:30/6:1:9:11[2]:12:16[2]:18,19:20:24:26:
[2]/7:3:7:10:11[2]:13,14:17:18f:29:30:31:32:34[3]/
0:12:16f:16:22/9:2[2]:7:11:16:19:21[3]:23[3]:24:
,26[2]/10:2,3:4:5:7:9:12:13:14[2]:24/11:4:6:8:13:
:21,22[2]/12:2:5/13:1:4[2]:13:17:18:21:24,25:27/
:3:8:10:12:14:15:18[2]/15:4:17,18[2]/16:3:6:8:9[2]:
,15:16:19:21/17:2,3[2]:4:5:6[2]:7:19:25[2]:26:27/18
:14:16:17:21[2]:22:23/19:5:11:12[2]:13:14/20:1:2
6:9[4]:13/21:1:1f[2]:3,4:7:9:14[2]/22:3:11f:12:15:
:23[3]:26:30/23:5,6:7:11:12:20f:23:24:25:27/24
:8[2]/25:5:10:12f[2]:13:14:19,20:30:36/26:2:6:7,8
:14:15:16:18[2]:23/27:3:11:15:18[4]:19,20,21/28
:5:7:11/29:9:10:12:13:16,17:18:20:21:23:24f:
:26[3]:28:31/30:6:7[2]:10:16:20:24f/31:2:13:15:
:23:24:27:28:33f:35:40/32:1:2:2f[2]:6,7:8[3]:12:15[2]
)[2]:23:29:35:37[2]:41:43:44[6]/33:1:5:10,11:13[6]:16[2]
4:4:5:8:13:15/35:1f:7[2]:8:10:11:15[2]:18,19/36:1
:2:3:6:9:18:20:22[2]:22f:29:30f/37:2:7:10:11:21[3]
8:2:6[2]:7:9[2]:21,22:26/39:1:2:3[2]:5:7:14:15/40:6[2]
10:11[3]/41:1[2]:2:3:10/42:12:17:22/43:4:5:6:7:9
3/44:1[2]:2,3:7:8[2]:9:11:12:13[2]:15:17[3]:18:21[2]:24:
:28:30f/45:1f:1/46:2:5:6:10:14[2]:15:16:22,23:
/47:1f:2[2]:5/48:1:2,3,4[2]:6:7:8:18:19:20:21:26:
[2]:32:37:38:41:44:47/49:1:3:4:7:8f:16[2]:19:22:
:24:26[2]:28f:30f:31[2]:34:38:39/50:3:6:11:19:20[3]
1f[2]:22:23:28:30:32:34[2]:38:39:40[2]:43/51:2:3:4[2]:
10:14[2]:16:17[2]:20:29:30:32:33:34,35[2]:38:43:47:
:56:58/52:1[2]:3[2]:4:6:7[2]:8:9[2]:11[2]:12f:12:18:20:
:24,25[2]:28:30:31:32/Lam1:1:3:7:9[2]:12:13:14:
:19:20/2:1[2]:2[2]:6:7:9:10[4]:11:12:13:15:19[2]:21[2]:
/3:6:7:16:20:24:28:29:41:53:66/4:1:5[3]:6:11:12[2]
7:19:20:21/5:11:14:18/Eze1:1[2]:1f:4[2]:10:16f:17
9,20,21:26/2:1f/3:11:14,15:14,15f:18:19:20:22
3:24/4:3:7:9:13:14:14f:16[2]:17/5:3:15/6:11:12[2]
4[2]/7:4:18:19:20:22:26,27/8:1[2]:4:5:7:9[2]:10:12:
/9:8:11/10:1:2[2]:3:5:6[2]:7,8:9-13[2]:17/11:1:13:
:16:21:24/12:3:7[2]:10f:10:12:13:19:22:25/13:5
2/14:3:4:6,7:18:22/15:5,6/16:5:6,7:15:21:22:
3:25:43:46:47:51:52:55:56[2]:63[2]/17:5:8:10:
2,13:16:19:20:21/18:3:7[2]:12:14:26/19:4[2]:7:8:9:
2:13/20:1:1f:5,6:8:13[2]:14:15:17:21:22:23,24:25
26[2]:32:33:35,36f:35,36:38:40:41:49/21:5:6:14:
9,20[2]:28:30:31:32[2]/22:6:10f:14:18,19,20:22:24:
5:30[2]/23:2,3:6:8:10:11:12:14,15[3]:17:17f:19,20:
9:31:34:39:44/24:1:6:7:18[2]:20,21:22:25:26/25:
9,10/26:1:11:20[3]/27:3:10:11f:13f:14f:15:17:26[2]
0:31:32[2]:33/28:2,3:8:12f:13[2]:15[2]:18f:18:23:25:
6/29:1:3:5:14:16:17/30:5:7:12:13:14:16:21f:24
31:1:6[2]:8[2]:14:15:16/32:1:9:10:17f:21:23:24:25[2]:
7[2]:30[2]:31/33:6:8:9:11:20:21:21f:21:27[3]:30/34:
2:14[2]:15,16:25[2]:26:27:28:29f:29:30/35:11:15/
6:5:17:26f:28:34:36/37:17:18,19,20:25/38:2,3f[4]
[2]:11:13f:14[2]:15,16[2]:15,16f[2]:15,16:19[2]:20:21/
9:2:11:13:23:24:26[3]/40:1:2:3:7-12:7-12f:16[2]:24
29,30f:33:39:41:44:46:47[3]/41:6[2]:10:21/42:3:6:
1:14:16-20/43:3[2]:8:18:20/44:4:7:14:15:17[2]:19:
5[2]/45:4:6:7:15[2]:25/46:3:6:8:9[3]:19,20:21,22/47:
:9:10:14:22/48:8:15:17f:19[2]:30,31/Dan1:1[3]:3,4[2]
f[2]:13:17:20[2]/2:1[2]:4:10:16:19:24:25:28[3]:45:49[2]/
:1:12:13[2]:22[3]:24:25:30/4:1:4:6:8[2]:9:10,11[2]:12:
5:18:19:21:23:25:26:29:32/5:2,3,4[2]:7[2]:8f:11[3]:
1f:13:16[2]:19:20:27:29[2]:31f[2]/6:4:10:15:16:20:23
25,26[2]:27:28[2]/7:2:7:9[2]:15:18:25:26f/8:1:2:8[2]:15
17:19[2]:23f:25[3]:26:26f/9:2:11:12:13:14:15:16:18:
1:24f:24:25f[2]:27/10:1[2]:2:4:5,6:9:12:20,21/11:1:
:5:6f:6:6f[2]:7f:10,11:14:14f:17:18:20f:20[2]:21:
0,31f:30,31:32f:33[2]:35[2]:44/12:1[3]:6:10/Hos1:
,5[3]:10:11:11f:3:6:8:9:10:15[3]:16:16f:18:20:21,22[2]
3:5/4:1:5[2]:8:13:16:19/5:5:8/6:2:2f:2:9:10/7:1:6
10/9:3:8:9:10:11:13/10:4:6:9:13:15/11:3:6:12/
2:1:9[2]:11/13:5[2]:11[2]:13/14:3[2]:5[2]/Joe1:2[2]:3:13:
6:17[2]:18/2:1[2]:3:8:15:23:30:32/3:14[2]:16:17:19:
1/Amo1:1:2:3:6:11:12f[2]:13[2]:14/2:2[3]:7:8[2]:14/3:
:12/4:1:2:3:10:12/5:6:11:13:16:17:19[2]:25,26,27[5]
6:1:2:8:10:13/7:1:2:13:17[3]/8:1:3[2]:9/9:5:6:9:11:
4/Ob1:1:3:8:8f:8:11:12[2]:13:14:19[2]:20/Jon:5:16
2:2:6:7/3:3f:6/4:2:6:11/Mic1:1[2]:2:3:4:5:8:10[3]:
1f[6]:13:16/2:8:12[2]/3:4:7/4:1:2:4[2]:6:7:9[2]:10[3]/5:3
:3:4[2]/6:14/7:3:6:8:10:14:15:16:17/Nah1:1:3[2]:5:
7:11f:13f/2:3:5:6:10/3:3[2]:7[2]:10:11:14:15:17[2]:18
/Hab1:1:2:4:5:12:13:15:17/2:4:5:7:11[2]:13[2]:17[2]:
18:20/3:2[4]:4:7:8,9:12[2]:16:17:18[2]/Zep1:2:3:7[2]:11
12[2]:13:18/2:3:4:5:7[3]:11:14:15[3]/3:2:6:12:13[2]:
17,18[2]/Hag1:1:3,4[2]:8:9:11[2]:12[2]:14,15/2:1:2:3:6:
10[2]:12:18,19f/Zec1:1:4:7[3]:17/2:1:8:11,12/3:1:7[2]
9:10/4/5:9/6:10,11:12f:14/7:1:5[2]:6:11/8:8:8f[2]:
12:19:20,21:22:23/9:3:5:10:11:16,17[3]/10:1:2:3:7
:10[2]/11:2:3:8:10:13/12:3:4:5:6:11:11f[2]:11:
12,13,14/13:2:3:6f:8f:8/14:1:5:8[2]:9:12[2]:13:15:16
:17:20[2]:21[4]/Mal1:10:11/2:8:9:11[3]:14:15[2]:17/3:
10[2]:16:17/4:2/Mt1:20f/2:1[3]:2:5:12:13:16:19[2]:
22:23/3:1:1f:1:5:6:11f[3]:16/4:12,13:15,16[2]:18:21:
23/5:12:14:18:19[2]:22[4]:23:28[2]:30:45[2]:48/6:1:2[2]:5
:9:10:20:21:22:23:29:31,32:33/7:3[2]:4:11:12:21:
22f:25/8:5,6[2]:8,9:10:11:14:28[3]:30:32/9:25:31f:
33:35:38/10:11:17:23:27[2]:28:32:33:36/11:1:1f:2
:7:8:10:11:21[3]:23[2]/12:5[2]:18:25:31,32[2]:39,40[2]:42:
43,44,45:46,47:46,47f:50/13:2,3[2]:5:15:21:24:30:
31,32:33:34,35[2]:40:43:44[2]:47,48:52:53,54[2]:57/
14:3:9:10:13:15:21:23,24:25:26:35/15:5,6:33/16
:1:2,3:4:17:19[2]:27:28/17:4f:11:12:15:18:21f:
22,23:24:26,27/18:1:4:6:8:9:10:11f:18[2]:19:24[2]:
26:30/19:4:8:9f:21:25:28:28f:29f[2]:29/20:2f:5:6:7
:8:11,12:21:32,33/21:8:9f:9:11:14:15:18:22:33:
42:45/22:4:10:11:28:30[2]:32f:36/23:6[2]:9:13,14[2]:
16:21:23:31:32:34:35:39f/24:7:15:16:18:19:20:
21:22:26:30[2]:37,38:40:47/25:10:15:18:21:24,25:
31:36:39:43:44/26:2:7:23f:29:31:49f:49:55:56:58
:59[3]:60,61:63:64:67:69/27:2:6:7:16:29[2]:32:40:44
:51:59:60/28:6:9:18:19/Mk1:2:3:3f[2]:4:5:8f[2]:9[2]:
10:12,13f:19:20:29,30:39:40:45/2:4/3:1:3:9/4:
5,6:17:19:20:34[2]:40/5:5:23:25:26:30:34:35:38:40
/6:4:6:10:19:22,23:26:27:29:35,36[2]:47[2]:48[2]:49:
51:52f:56[2]/7:4:12,13:15,16f:19:30/8:4:8,9:11[2]:
14:17:25:36:38[2]/9:1:12,13:15:17:18:28:29f:
30,31:33:36:37:39:42:43,44f:45,46f:50/10:6,7:10
:21:24:24f:26:30:35:37:49/11:4,5:8:9[2]:11:13[2]:16:
17:22,23[2]:25:26,f[2]:27,28/12:10[2]:12:17:19:23:26:
32:35:39[2]:40:41[3]:42/13:8:9[2]:10:11:14:15,16:17:
18:20:26:32/14:3[2]:9:14:17:22:25:49:51,52[2]:55:
58:62:66,67:68f/15:1:8:16,17:21:25:28f:29,30[2]:
34f:38f[2]:38:41:44:46[3]/16:5:9f:17f/Lk1:6[2]:8,9:10
:11,12:18:19:22:26:28f[2]:36:44[2]:47:61:66:75:79:
80f:80/2:4:7[3]:8:11:11f:12[2]:14:16:19:23:25:27:28:
34,35:36,37:38:39:43:46,47:49:51/3:1[2]:3:4:16:
19,20:22/4:4[2]:5:8:15:20:23[2]:24:25,26:31[2]:33:36:
40:43:44/5:1:3:7:12[2]:17:18,19:29:31/6:1:6:17,18
:23[2]:38:39:41[2]:42[2]:45/7:9:23:25[4]:28:38:45:50/8:
3:7:16:17:22:23:26:27:43,44f:48/9:4:12[2]:14:25:
26[2]:31[2]:38:46:49:52:58/10:1:4f:7:13:13f:13[2]:22:
25/11:5,6f:7:16:27:29,30[2]:43:44:45[2]:52/12:2:3[3]:
8:11[2]:17[2]:21:27:33[3]:36:42,43,44:45:52:54:59/13:
1:4:6:10:14:16:19:24,25:26:27:33:35/14:1:10:28f
/15:3,4:7:8:9:10[2]:22:23:25:28:29/16:2[2]:8:9:10[2]:
15[2]:16:17:19:22:23[2]:24[3]:25/17:2,3:7,8,9:16[2]:20:
21[2]:23:26:28:31:34:35,3[illegible]/18:13:22:30:34/19:1:5
:6:12:15:23:27:38:43:47/20:1:19:21:33:36[2]:37,38
:39:42,43:46[3]/21:1:2:8f:11[2]:21:23:24:25[3]:27:31:
34,35:36:37,38/22:16:19:20f:24:25:27:28:28f:30:
32:44:47:47f:53:55:56:63,64/23:7:19[2]:25:43:45:
48:49:50,51,52:53[2]/24:3:4:5:6,7:12:17:18:18f:25
:40:44:49f:49:53/Jn1:1f[2]:4:11,12:26f:26:31f:31:
32:33f/2:1[2]:11:14:19:20:23/3:12:14:15:16:18:20
:22:23,24:27/4:5,6:21-24:40,41:43,44:45:46,47[3]:
48:54/5:7:14:18:19:24:25:26[2]:28:29:34:46/6:21:
22,23:26:29:35:45:47:48-51:56[2]:57:59[2]/7:5:8f:9:
13:25:26:28[2]:32:35:38:39[2]:41,42:45/8:3[2]:4:6:8:9:
12:16:20:21:24[2]:44:49:58/9:5:7:10:18:22,23:24:
34f:35/10:9[2]:10:16:19:22,23:24:25[2]:34,35,36:38[2]
/11:1:8:15:17:25:26:44[2]:51:55:56/12:1:2:6:7:11:
16:17:23,24:35:46[3]/13:21:26:26f/14:1:10[3]:11[2]:
12,13[2]:17:18:19:20[3]:26f:29/15:4[2]:5[2]:7:10[2]:15/
16:5:5f:9:16:21:26f:29:32/17:2:5:6:11:12f:14:19:
21[3]:23[2]:26[2]/18:16:20[3]:26:28[2]:32f/19:2:13f[2]:17:
20:29:36,37:40/20:5[2]:7:8:11:19:25:30,31[2]/21:2:
6:8:25/Act1:1:3:4[2]:5f[2]:5:8[2]:13:20[2]:26/2:2:4:4f:5:
6:11:13:17:19:26:27:28:29f:30f:31:33:34:34f:34:
36:38:39:41:42:45:46[2]/3:1:6:16:17:21,22:25/4:5[2]
:7:10:11:12:16:18:24[2]:27:28:29:34,35:37/5:7:10:
12:16:18:25:26,27:40[2]:42[2]/6:1:3:4:6:7[2]:9:11:15/
7:2:2f:4[2]:6:9:10:11:12:14:16:17,18:19:27:29:30[3]:
34:38:41:42[2]:43[2]:44[2]:48,49[2]:54/8:1[2]:8:9,10,11:
14:16:21:23:25:28:33:37f:40/9:1:2[3]:10[2]:12:13:14
:19:21[2]:22:25[2]:26:27:29:30:31[3]:32[2]:36:37:40f:41:
42:43/10:1:3:4:12:14:23:24:25:27:28:30:32:35:
36,37:39:43:46,47:48/11:1:2:5:16f[2]:24:28:29:30
/12:5:7:13:14:18:19:20/13:5:8:14:15:17:18:
19,20:24:25:27:29:31:32,33[2]:34:35:38:39:41:48/
14:4:11[2]:14:15:16:22[3]:23[2]:25/15:3:4:21[2]:23:38/
16:2:3:4:5:9f:9[2]:18[2]/17:2:11:13[2]:16:17:21:24[2]:27
:28/18:2,3:8[2]:9:10:12:13:18:18f[2]:20f[2]:21f:22f[2]:
23:24[2]:25,26[2]:27[2]:28/19:1[2]:4:5:6:7:8:10:21f:22:
23:25:26:30:32[2]:38:40/20:2:3:4:6[2]:18:20:21:23:
30:35:37/21:3:11:24[2]:26,27:28:29[2]:31:34:39:40/
22:2:3[4]:5[2]:10:17,18:19:23:30/23:1:6:8:11[2]:33:35
/24:2:9:11:12:14[3]:18:20:24:27[2]/25:1:5:7:15:17:
20:23:24:25/26:4:8:10:11[2]:14:18[3]:20[2]:21:26:29/
27:1:4f:5:9:11:12:21:40/28:1:8:9:11:15:16:17:20f[2]
:23:25:30/Rom1:1:2:6,7:8:9:10f[2]:11,12:15:16:17[2]
:19f:19:26/2:2:5:8:12-15:19:27:29[2]/3:1:4:7:10:
13:19:20:21,22:24[2]:25[2]:26[3]:27:28:29[2]:31/4:4,5[2]:
9[2]:11:17:24/5:1[2]:2:4:11[2]:13:17f:21/6:5f:10:12:
13:20:21/7:1[2]:6[3]:7[2]:10:20:23,24,25[3]/8:3:9[2]:10f:
11:16:20,21:22:22f:26:26f:26[2]:27:34:35:39/9:10-
10-13:17f:29[2]:33[3]/10:4:8:9:10:11:12:14[2]:15:19:
21/11:2,3:5:6:12:14:17[2]:18:21:24:28:31/12:2:3:8[2]
:10:11:12:13:17:20/13:1:9:12,13[4]/14:1f[2]:2:13:15
:18:19[2]:22[2]/15:1:4:5:10:12:13[2]:19:21:22[2]:24:26[2]:
27[2]:27f[2]:31/16:1[4]:3:4:5[2]:7:23:25,26,27[2]/1Co1:2:
2f:10[3]:13[2]:17:21[2]:25:27:29:31/2:3:4:7:13:13f:14
/3:1:3:4:6[2]:10:16:18:19:20:21f/4:5:17[2]/5:1[2]:2:
3,4[2]:5:8:10[2]:11:12/6:3:4f:5:6:9,10[2]:12f[2]:16[2]/7:1:
4:14[2]:15[2]:17[2]:24:25[2]:26:28:31[2]:32:34:34f[2]:40/8:
5:10/9:2:4:7:9:11[2]:12:13:14:15:24:26/10:1:2:3,4:
5:7:8:11:16:20:26:29:33/11:5f:7:10:11:13:16:18:
25[3]:27/12:6[3]:10:24:28[2]:30/13:1[3]:2:7[2]:8:12[3]/14:
2[2]:3:4[2]:5[2]:6:7[2]:9[2]:10:11:13:14:15[4]:16[2]:18:19[3]:20[2]
:21[2]:22:23:24:26[3]:27:28:31:33:34:34f:35:38:39:
40/15:2:10:14:18:19:23:29:31[2]:32[2]:36:40:41:42:
52[2]:54:58/16:1[2]:11f:15:19[2]/2Co1:1:3,4:6,7[2]:8:
12:22/2:3[2]:5,6:9:15:17/3:2:3:4:6[2]:8:10[2]:14/4:1:2[2]
:6[2]:7[2]:12:16:17:18/5:1[2]:6[2]:9[3]:10:11[2]:13,14:19:21
:21f/6:3:4[2]:5:7:12:14:16/7:1:3:4[3]:5:10:13:14:16/
8:1[2]:4[2]:6[2]:7[2]:14:15:18:19:23/9:2[2]:3:12/10:9:16/
11:3[2]:10:12:15:19,20:23:25:26[5]:32:33/12:2,3f:
2,3:4:6[2]:7:9:13:18/13:3:4[2]:7:10:11[2]:12/Gal1:1f:4
:6:14:20:22/2:4[3]:7,8,9[3]:14:16:17:19:20[2]/3:3:5:7:
8,9[3]:10:11:13:15:21,22:23[2]:26:28/4:14:15:24,25
/5:1:8:11:14:20:22:25/6:1:11:13:14[2]/Eph1:3:4:9
:10[2]:11:12[2]:15:20[2]:21[2]/2:2:4:6:7:10:12:19/3:1:
2,3[2]:5:6:8:10[2]:11:12:14,15:17[2]/4:1[2]:6:11[2]:13:
15,16[2]:22:28:30f:31/5:1:11:13:14:19:20:22:23[3]:
24/6:1:12:16:18:20[2]:21/Php1:1:2:5:6:7[2]:9:12:13
:14:16,17:20[2]:25:30[3]/2:1:4[2]:7f:10:14:15:20:22:
25:27:29/3:1:3:7:8:11:18:20/4:3[2]:4:5:7:8:11:12:
14[2]:15:16:19:22/Col1:2:7:12:15:16:18:19:20:23[2]
:26,27/2:1:3:5:6:7[2]:9[2]:12:13[2]:15/3:1:3:4:11:14:
15:16:25/4:1:2:3:5:12:13:15:18[2]/1Th1:6:7:8/2:3
:14/3:1:2,3:7:8:9:10:13/4:1[2]:3,4:5[2]:6:15:17[2]/5:2:
4:8:27/2Th1:1[2]:4[2]:7:9:12/2:4[2]:13:14:15[2]:17/3:6[2]
:8:11[2]:12:14:17/1Ti1:2:3,4:13:18:19[2]/2:2[5]:2f:
9,10:12:15/3:2:10:11:13:16[3]/4:1[2]:7:8[2]:9,10[2]:12/
5:5[2]:8:18:20:21:22:24[2]:25/6:2:4:15:16:17[2]:18[2]:
19:21/2Ti1:1:3:6:8[2]:12[2]:13f:16:17/2:2:4[2]:9[2]:10:
11:14:17:20[3]:21:23/3:1:3:5:10:11:13:15:16/4:2:8
/Tit1:3:4:5:8:9:13:15[2]/2:3:5:6:7:8:10[2]/3:7[2]:9/
Phm1:1[2]:5[2]:6:8,9[2]:10:11:13:16:18/Heb:1[2]:2:3:
10:13/2:6:8:9:10:12:13:14[2]:15:17/3:2:5:6[3]:7,8:
14:15:17:19/4:2:3[2]:5:6:7[2]:8:11:16/5:1:4:7f[2]:9:
12,13[2]/6:1[2]:4:13/7:2:3f:10:26/8:1:2[2]:5:6:9:10[2]:
12/9:1:4[2]:6:8:11:21:22:23[4]:24[2]:25/10:9:12:14:16
:22:24[3]:34:35:38[3]:39/11:2:3:7[2]:9:11:14:17:28:31[2]
:33:34[2]:36:37,38[3]/12:2:8:11:15:16:23[2]/13:3:14:
16:20,21:22/Jas1:4[2]:9[2]:12:18:21:23:25/2:2[3]:3:5:
15:19[2]:20:23:26[2]/3:1:3/5:10:11[2]:15/1Pe1:2:3:4:
5[2]:7:12[2]:15:17:20:21[2]/2:2,3f:5:6:11:21:23:24/3:1
:4:5[2]:6:7:11:15:19[2]:20[2]:21[2]:22[2]/4:3:4[2]:6:13[2]:14f:
16:17/5:4:6:10:12[2]:13:13f[2]:13:14/2Pe1:8:19[2]:
20,21/2:1:3:4:5:6:11[3]:12f:13[2]:15:22/3:1:3:10:12:
15,16:18/1Jn1:4:5:6:7/2:8[3]:9[2]:10[2]:11:12:14:22[2]:
23:24:27[2]:28/3:5[2]:9:10:16:17/4:3:4[2]:10:12:15:16[2]
:20/5:2:6,7,8:9:10:11:13:14:16[3]:17:17f[4]:20[2]:21/
2Jn1:1:2:10:11:12/3Jn:5:8[2]:11/Jud:4:6:7:8:15[2]:
16:18[3]:19:20:21/Rev:1[2]:4:4f:5:7[2]:11:11f:11[3]:13f:
16[3]:20/2:1f[2]:1:7:8:12:13:14:18:19:24,25/3:1:2:4[2]
:5:7:10f[2]:12[2]:14:20/4:1[2]:2[2]:4:5[2]:7[2]/5:1:3:6:11:13[2]
/6:2[2]:5:9:15/7:1:9[3]:13:15:17:17f[2]/9:6:10:11[3]:15:
16f[4]:17,18:19[2]/10:2:6:10/11:2f:3f:3:8,9:12:13:16
:19/12:1:2:7:12:15/13:1:3:6:8:8f[2]:17:18/14:1:3:
10:12[2]:13:13f:14:16:17:20[2]/15:1:5:6/16:3:5:6:10
:13f:15:16:17:18:19[3]/17:3:3f:4:6:8:9f:18/18:4:7:
8:9:10:16:17:18:19[2]:23/19:1:10:13:13f:14:15:17:
21/20:1:2:6:9:12:13[2]:15/21:8:10:15:16[2]:22[2]:27[2]
/22:3:6,7:9:11:14:18:19

9539

INTO

[2]Gen1:9,10/2:7:10:21:22/3:15/4:8/6:19,20/7:1:
8,9:13/8:9/9:23/12:15:15f/13:1/14:10:14/15:5/
16:9-12/17:2,3,4/19:18,19,20/21:14:16/22:10:
17/24:20:38f:67/25:6/27:2,3,4:18/28:16,17/30:
2/31:33[3]:34/32:7/33:2/34:20f/37:19,20:21,22:
24/39:20/40:11/41:34,35[2]:45f/42:17/43:22:24:
30/44:1/45:4/46:3,4:8-14:29[2]/50:12,13:20/Ex1
:22/2:15:24/3:8:18/4:27/5:1:3:7,8/6:4:8,9/7:15:
22/8:3,4[3]:14:25:27/9:8/10:19/12:22[2]:25:34/13:
4,5:11/15:1:5:22:25/16:1:3:18/17:14/18:7/19:
12:18:23/20:21/21:33/22:2:5[2]:6/23:19f:23/24:2
:6:9:12:13:15:18/25:13,14:16f/26:9:17:18,19:31
/27:5:7:9,10:11/28:30,31:37,38:43/30:20:25/32

(INTO Con't)
:10:12:20:24/33:4/34:2:34/35:26/36:24:35:36^2/
37:3:5:13/38:7:23/39:3^3/40:18:21/Lev2:6/4:5:
16/6:15:19,20:22,23:30/7:19/9:23/10:8,9/11:
32:33:36/13:58/14:7:15:16:26:40:51,52:53/16:1
:10:12:21:22:23:26^2:27/18:24/24:10/25:1/26:
40,41/Num1:54/3:38/4:8:11/5:4:17:23/6:19/7:
89/8:22/11:8:31/13:2:17/14:3:8:12:16:24:25:31
:36,37,38:40:44/16:14:30:33:38:39/19:6:18/20:
4:12:27/22:22,23/23:14/25:6:8^2/27:12:17/31:1:
6:24:27:54/32:9:12:32/33:8:38,39:47:50,51/34:
1/35:11/36:3^2/Deu1:24,25:28^2:41:43/2:19:24:
27:29/3:23,24,25/4:1:11:19:21,22/6:10,11,12/7
:1:13:16:24:26/8:7/9:21^2:28/10:22/11:29/12:9/
13:16/15:17/19:2,3:5:11/20:18^2/23:5/24/27:
2,3,4^2:12/28:1:9/29:12:28/31:7:14:20:23/32:29
/Jos1:2/2:19:22/4:5/6:19:20/8:19:33/10:10:26:
27/11:8/15:2,3,4:5/18:5,6:9:18/24:3:4:8/Ju1:16
:24f:34^2:35/2:1:4:6/3:21/4:14^2:15:18^2:21:22/5:
15^2/7:5,6:12,13:16:19,20:22/9:34:39:43:51/11:
18:37/15:9/16:13/18/19:27:29/20:6:35-39^2:45/
Ru2:2:18/4:11/1Sa2:13,14/4:3:4:7/6:9:14:19/7:
10/8:12/9:9,10,11:14:22/11:4:7:11/12:8/14:21:
27:52/17:48,49/19:9,10/20:35:42/23:24,25/24:
1:3:4:18/25:26:30,31/28:25/29:4:11/2Sa2:16:
24/3:31/4:6,7^2/5:8:17/6:10:16/7:13:18/10:14/
12:20/13:8/15:23:25,26:28:29/16:2:13:22/17:
2,3:13^2:16/18:14:17:33/19:2:3/20:6:12/22:43/
23:20/24:14^2/1Ki1:7:15:49,50/2:30/3:15/5:9/6
:6/7:51/8:6/10:16,17^2/11:2:30/13:2:8/14:12/
15:26:30:34/16:13:18:26/18:23:33:44/19:4/20:
2,3:10:27:30:33/21:22/22:30:52,53/2Ki2:11/3:
3:24/4:4^2:39^2:41/5:18/6:5:6/7:4:7:8/9:2:6:16:25
:34/10:7:15:23:25:27/11:13,14:19:20/12:7:9:10:
16/13:11:20,21/14:9:24/15:18:28/17:22/18:30/
19:1:32:37/20:18:20/21:11:16/23:15:19/25:2/
1Ch1:19/5:6:10/6:4-15^2:25,26,27/12:19/15:3:
16/16:1/18:8/19:15/21:13^2:27/22:3:19/23:6:
8,9:10,11:12/24:1:3:4^2/27:1:24/2Ch3:6/5:7,8/8
:2/9:23/10:18/13:12/15:15:18/16:8:10/18:34/
20:16:20:28:35/23:1/26:11/29:12,13,14:16:
25,26/30:14:15/31:2:12,13/34:4:17/35:4,5:10:
22/36:17:22,23/Ez1:1/5:5:14/6:5:11:18/10:6/
Neh1:11/2:11,12:18/4:1:22/5:5:8/6:9:11/9:17:
23:37/12:31,32/13:2:5:15:26/Est2:4:7/3:9:13:
15/4:1:7:11:14/7:7/8:9,10/9:1:22/Job2:12/9:31
/15:7,8:22/16:11/17:13,14/18:8,9:18/20:22/24:
5:16/27:21:23/28:3,4^3/30:3:19:22/33:17,18/35:
5/36:16:18:21:27/39:24/40:13/42:15/Ps4:2/5:
7/7:15/8:3/9:15/27:12/30:11/31:5,6/32:7/33/
37:15/41:13/44:19/46:2:6/57/58:7:8/60:9,10/
61:6/63:2/66:12/73:17:24/78:44:61/92:13/102:
9,10/104:7,8:22:32/105:29:43/106:23/107:30:
34:35/108:10/118:20/119:8:61:85,86/132:7f/
140:10^2/141/147:6/148:5/Pro3:30/5:23/6:22:
23/7/11:8/12:13/16:29:29f:30:33f/17:20/18:
6,7/19:2/21:1/28:17/29:22/31:18/Ecc1:3-7/3:
21/5:13,14/7:7:13/9:12/10:8,9/11:5/Sol1:4:6/
3:2:4^2/4:16/6:11/7:8:11/Is2:4:4f^2:10:19^2:21/5:
13:29/7:6^2:17:19/8:7,8:22/11:15/14:17:23/22:
17:18/24^2/25:2/28:18/36:15/37:19:26:38/39:2
/40:26/44:23:25/47:6:12/48:13/49:11:21/50:2/
51:23/52:3:9/54:1/58:7/60:22/66:20/Jer2:4,5:
7^3/5:14:23,24/7:15/9:11:21/12:10/14:16/16:13
/17:8/18:4/19:1:4/21:3,4:7/22:13^2/23:3:13:32/
26:18/28:14/29:31/31:13:21/32:14:40/35:2:4/
36:23/37:15,16^2/38:6^2:9:20/39:14/41:7:8:15/
44:6/46:26^2/47:6/48:44/49:30/50:26/51:63/
Lam1:14/3:2:9:11/4:18/5:9/Eze2:2/3:10:22:24
/5:1:4:10/8:3:8:16:17/9:2/10:7,8:15,16/11:5:22
/12:6:7^2:11/14:15:19/15:7/16:5:27/17:3,4/19:3
:9/20:9,10:15:27,28:35,36/21:31/23:9:39/25:5^2
/26:12/27:4:26:27/29:4/30:21:25/31:4:11:16/
32:23/37:6:14:22^2/38:4/40:6:7-12f:7-12:18:23:
27:38/41:1:3:17,18:25/42:1/43:4:5/44:7:12/46:
19,20/48:11/Dan2:5:35:44/3:6:11:15:17:20:21:
23:24:29/4:10,11:20:37/5:21/6:1:24/8:7:22/11:
4:10,11:20/Hos1:12:14:15/4:13/13:2/Joe1:14/
2:5:9:20^3:31/3:2:10^2/Amo1:6:9:15/2:6/3/5:8^2:
15:25,26,27/7:11/8:10/9:2/Ob1:13/Jon:3:12:
15/2:3^2/Mic1:4:6^2/4:3^2:10/7:9:19/Nah1:10^2/3:
12:14/Zep1:17/Hag:6:8/2:7f/Zec4:2:12/5:4:8/
8:20,21/9:4:7/10:5/11:6^2:13/12:12,13,14/13:6/
Mal2:8/3:10/Mt1:20/3:9/4:1:3/5:20:25^2:29/6:
13/8:12^2:23:31/9:1:28/11:1f:7/12:4:11:43,44,45
/13:2,3:23:31,32:36:42:47,48^2:50/14:19:22:
23,24:32/15:13,14:21f:36:39/17:15^2:22,23:25/
18:3:6:12/19:3:23/20:4/21:1:12:13:21:31/22:13
:15/23/24:10:16/25:14:27:30:34:35:41:46^2/26:
15:18:45/27:7:27:53/28:4:11:19/Mk1:5:12,13:
21:35/2:22:25,26/3:13/4:1:8:24:37/5:3,4:12:13:
18:40/6:41:45:46:51/7:17:33/8:6:10:13/9:22^2:
42:43,44/10:1:15:16:23/11:2:11:17:22,23/12:13
/13:5:15,16/14:13:16:41/15:16,17:21/16:12:15:
19/Lk1:24/3:9/4:1:42/5:3^2:18,19:37:38/6:4:12:
39:45:49/7:1:24/8:19:29:31:32:33^2:51/9:16:28:
39:42/10:10:38/11:28:34^2:53,54/12:5/13:19:
20,21/14:5:15:21:23/16:9:9f:22f:23:23f/17:2,3:6
:27/19:4:40:46/21:1:12/22:3:10:40f:44/23:26:
42:53:55/24:6,7:51/Jn1:9/2:16/3:3:4:17:19/4:8
:36:43,44:46,47/5:4:7:13:24/6:2-5:15:17:24/8:6
/9:39/10:1:34,35,36/12:6:23,24/13:5:27:30/14:
17/15:6/16:13:28/17:18^2:23/18:15:33/19:9:
23,24:27/20:25^2:27^2/21:7/Act1:9^2:21,22/2:31:
34:35/3:7,8/5:15/7:23:43:45:55/8:1:31:38/9:6:
8,9/10:9,10:28/11:10/13:14/14:19:20:22/16:6:
23:24^2:34/17:7/19:5f/20:10,11,12/21:29:37,38/
22:10:11:17,18:30/27:7,8/28:5:23/Rom1:3:24/5
:2:3:12f/7:14/8:3:15:28/9:6:21:23,24/11:9:23:
24/12:13:16:19/15:7:19/1Co1:9:13/2:7:15/3:3/
5:5/7:2:17:27/10:12:13/12^2/13:12/15:21:36^2:
37:50:53/2Co1:9:21/3:11/4:2/5:4:18:21^2/9:11/
10:5/11:13:14/12:19/Gal1:17/2:5/3:27/4:6/6:
15/Eph1:5/2:3:6/3:12:17/Php:5:21/4:9/Col1:
13:22/2:7:12/3:17/1Th2:12/2Th3:4:5/1Ti1:15/
4:15/5:13/6:7/2Ti1:6^2/2:8:16/3:6/4:18/Tit2:14
/Heb1:11/2:10/3:18/4:3:8:11:12/9:7:8:11:12:
17:18:24/10:5:16:19:20:31:34/12:22/13:11/Jas
1:25/2:2:6/3:9/1Pe1:14:20/2:2,3:9/4:15/2Pe1:
11:19/2:4:6:18/1Jn:2/3:9^2/4:13/2Jn1:10/Jud:
23:24,25/Rev:6/2:7:10:27/4:11/5:6:10/8:8,9/9:
9/12:6:14/14:10:13:19/16:10:17:19/17:3:17/18
:21/19:20/20:3:10:14:15/21:26

1396

IS

Gen1:2f/2:4:13:14^2:23^3:24/3:14/4:6:7:9^2:13/5:1
:1f/6:3:8:12,13:17/8:21/9:5,6^2:18/10:11,12:22/
11:6f^2:9:32f/12:11,12,13:18/13:11/14:3:23:24/
15:1/17:5^2:7,8:9,10:12:15:21/18:1:9:14:20/19:
14:18,19,20^3/20:3:5^2:6^2:7:9,10:11,12/21:9f:10:
12:13:17:22:26^2:30/22:7:12/23:8:9:14,15^2:17,18
/24:14^2:24:35:47:49:65^2:65f/25:12-15:18:19:32^2
:33/26:7:9^2:20:27:28:33/27:11,12^2:18:19:21:22:
27,28,29:32:33:37:43:44/28:13:16,17/29:6:15:
25:27/30:2^2:6f^2:13:28:38/31:1:28:35f:36,37^2:42
/32:11:18:26:27:28:29:30:32/33:10:17^2/34:8:21
/35:20/36:1:13,14f:24/37:10:13,14:26,27:30:32:
33^2/38:14:25:26/39:12f/40:7:8^2:13/41:15:25:28
:32^2:33:38^2:45f/42:2:13^3:14f:15:16:28^2:32^2:33:
36:38^2/43:3,4,5:21:27^2:28:29/44:16:20^2:23:30^2:
31:34/45:3:20:26^2:28/47:3:4^2:15:18^2:23:26/48:
16:18/49:1:7:7f:9:14:21:22:27:32/50:11/Ex1:1/
2:5:20/3:3,4:12^2:15f^2:15:16/4:10f:14^2:22/5:2^2:
16/6:30/7:9/8:10:19/9:14:27:29/10:8:11/12:3,4
:10^2:14:17:24:26:27:38f/13:3:8:14:15:16/14:5:
25/15:2^3:3^2:6:11^3:23:26/16:15^2:16:16f:23:25^2:
26:31:36/17:7:15,16/18:4:11:15,16^2:18:22/19:5:
23/20:10/21:2f:13:16:19^2:20:21:24^2:26:30f^2/22:
2^3:3^2:4^2:6:7^2:8:9:10^2:14^2:15:16:27/23:1:2,3:6:8:
12:15^2:16:21:21f/25:16:17:39f/26:7,8:14/27:8:
21/28:4:16:22,23,24:29:37,38:43/29:1:15,16:18:
19,20:22:30:33:34:35/30:2:6:10:11,12:13f:15:16:
29f:32:33:36:37/31:4:5:12,13:14,15:16^2:17/32:4
:8:11/33:3:13^2/34:9^2:10:11:14:19:27f/35:2:4:34
/Lev1:2,3:4:9:10/2:1^2:2:3^2:4:5:6:7:8:10:11:13f:
13:15/3:1:6:7,8:15,16^2:17/4:21:22:23:24:27:28/
5:1:2:4^2:7:8:9:11^2:15:17,18^2:19/6:4,5:11:17^3:18f:
22,23:25:28^2:29:30/7:6:7:8^2:9^2:12:15:16^5:17,18^2:
19^2:20^2:21^3:24:30:35^2:36/8:31:35/10:1f:3:7:10^4:
12^2:14:17/11:12:27:28:32:33:34^3:35:36^3:37:38:
41,42:47^2/12:2:4:5:6:8/13:1:3:9,10^3:11^3:13:
14,15^2:21:23^2:24:25:26:28^2:29,30:31:34:34f:37^2:
39:40^2:41^2:42:43:44:45:46:47,48:49^2:51:52:55^2:
56:57:58/14:3:4:8:13:21:22:25:27:30:31:36:44^2:
46:53:57^2/15:1:3:4:5:6:8:9:24:26^2:28:31:32^2:33/
16:1:8^2:16:29,30^2:31^2/17:3,4:5:11^3:12:14^3:15/18
:6f:10:10f:12:13:16:17:18:19:22^2:23:25^2:27/19:7:
10:13:15:20^2:25/20:11^2:13:14:17:19:20:21:23:24
/21:2,3:4:7:8^2:12:14,15:18:20:21^2:23/22:3:4^2:5:7^2
:8:10:11:12:13^2:16^2:17,18^2:19:22^2:25:26,27^2:28:
29,30/23:5:6:14^2:17:21:23,24^3:28:30,31:32:
33,34:36^2:39:41:43/24:19/25:4:5:12:14,15,16^4:
21,22:23:26:28:30:31:32:49/26:10:16:17:36/27:
3f:8:9^2:11,12^2:13:16:18:21:22:26:27^2:29f:30^2:33^2
/Num1:17,18,19f:20-46:51/3:47,48f/4:7:15^2:
17,18,19^2:30,31/5:5,6:8^2:13:14:15^2:19:24:28:29:
31/6:5^2:6,7:8:9:20^2:27/8:2:13/9^2:14^2:22/10:4:
5,6,7f:5,6,7:8/11:6:12:14:17:18:19,20/12:1f^3:7,8^2
:12/13:16f^2:18:19:20:23:27^2:32/14:7:8:9:20,21:
22:24:42/15:3,4:6:7:8,9:11,12:15,16:19,20,21^2:
26:27:30^2:37,38:39/16:3:5:10:11,12^2:13:40/17:1^2
/18:4:7^2:11:14,15:16^2:17^2:19:23:31/19:1:9:10:15
:18^2:20:21/20:5/21:8:13:14^2:16:17,18^2/22:38
23:18-24^3/24:3-9^2:15-19:20:21,22/27:8/28:6
15:26/29:11:12/30:3:9^2:10:12:16/31:21:27^2:2
30:48,49:50/32:3,4:8:22:29/33:1/34:13^2/35:
17:18^2:21:22,23^3:25:27:30:31/36:6^2:7/Deu1:
17:30/2:28:29/3:11:13:14/4:6:7:20:24:25:31:
35^2:38:39^3:40:48/5:5:12:14:15:16^2/6:2:4:15:1
20/7:8:9:21^2:25:26^2/8:7:8:9^6:11:14:18/9:4^2:5
25:28/10:8:9^2:11:15:17^2:21^2/11:10^2:11:21:24
/12:8:16:20-23^3:28/13:1:3:12,13,14^4:18/14:2
24/15:1:4,5^2:9:11^2:15:21/16:3:5:11:13:15:18:
/17:4^2:8^3:10^2:11:12:20/18:2^2:8:12^2:16:20:21:
/19:4:14:15:18:21/20:1:4:8:17:18/21:1:4:15:1
20^2:22:23/22:2:5:6:17,18:22:23,24^2:25,26,27:
28,29^2/23:4:19:21^2:22:25/24:4:5:6^2:12,13:14,
18:21:22/25:1^2:9:13,14,15/26:2,3:12:16:17/2
16:17:18:19^2:20:21:22:23:24:25:26/28:8:40:5
61^2/29:6^2:12:13:14,15:23:27/30:11:20/31:3:1
29/32:3:4^4:6^2:27:28:31:34:35^2/33:1:12:17^2:21
22:24:26:27^2:29^2/34:2^2:3:4/Jos1:2:9/2^3:11:
12,13^2:17,18/3:10:11/4:5^2:6:7:9:23:24/5:8,9:
/6:3,4:18/7:12^2:26/8:1:5:28/9:12:24:27/10:1
25:27/12:1:2:7/13:2-7/14:12/15:8:9:18,19^2/
7:15/18:7:17:19/20:3:6/21:9-16f/22:19:28^2:3
34^2/24:17^2:18:19/Ju1:17:26/2:3/3:1:20/4:14
20/5:28:30/6:10:12:13:15:16f^2:17^3:24:31:37^2:
/7:1:14:15:25/8:9:21f^4:23,24:28/9:18:28:33:3
/10:7,8/11:27:39f/12:3/13:7:10:12:17:18/14:
18^2/15:2^2:19/16:2:23,24/18:6^2:9,10:12:14/19
23/21:3:6/Ru1:11:19/2:20:21:22/3:2^2:12^3/4:
15:18-22/1Sa1:1:17:21,22/2:2^2:8:23,24,25:30
:4,5:18/4:4:14:21,22^2/5:5/6:20/9:6^2:7:18:21/
2^2:5:12^2:22^3:24/11:5:7/12:5:13/13:11/14:8:3
34:41^3/15:2:22^2:23^2:28:29^3:32/16:4:5:6:7:8:9:
10,11:12:15,16:18/17:9:26^2:46:55f^2:58/18:18:
/19:5:24:24f^2/20:1:3:5:7^3:10:13:18:21^2:23f:30
31:37/21:1:3:4:9^2/22:8^2:11,12:14^3/23:10:17:1
:22^2:23/24:4:6:9,10:11:13:14^2:15^4/25:8^2:10^2:1
21:25^2:26:27/26:14:15:16:17,18^3:19:22/27:1:5
28:14/29:3:4:5:10/30:25:26/2Sa1:17,18:21f:2
25/2:7:20^2/3:8:18^2/4:2,3f:8:10^2/5:8/6/7:2:3:1
19:22:27/9:3^2:4/11:19,20,21:24:25/12:18:19^2:
21:23:31/13:12:16:20:28:29,30/14:7:14/15:
25,26:27:35,36/16:2:3:7,8:11^2:17:18/17:2,3:6:
10:11:12:13:14/18:3:11f:18:20:22:25:27:28:29:
32^2/19:8,9,10:11,12:20:22:23:29:35:36:37:42/
:6:19:21/21:1/22:2:3^2:4:25:31^2:32:32f:33/23:5
17:20f/24:14^3/1Ki1:2:11:13:18:20^2:22,23:24:3
41:44,45^2:46,47^2:48/2:14:15:16:20:22/3:9^3:22
27/4:1/7:41-46/8:11:19:22,23:27:31:32:35,36:
37^2:43:60^2/9:9:13/10:6/11:22:27,28:41/12:
23,24/13:26:31/14:10:13^2/15:7:23/16:14:27/
:8,9:24/18:7:8:11:14:17:21^2:22:24:27^4:39^2/19:
20:4:7^2:23^2:28:32^2/21:5:20f:21:22/22:8:17:23:
36,37:39/2Ki1:3^3:4,5:6^2:16^2:18/2:3:5:13,14:19
19f/3:11:12f:13:18/4:9:14:25:26^4:27^2:31/5:6:7
:15:21:26/6:1:11:13^2:16/7:9:17/8:5^2:6:23:24,2
/9:11:13:14:17^2:20:23:32:34:36/10:27/12:4,5:
/13:8:16,17:23/14:7:10:18:28/15:6:11:21:26:3
36/16:18f:19/17:34/18:20,21:22/19:3^3:7:17:2
22:25:26:29:31:32/20:19^2/21:11:17:25/23:17^2:
28/24:3,4:5/1Ch1:1f:43/6:54/7:25,26,27/11:7
18,19:22f/12:18:20:23/13:11/14:15/15:20f:21
16:14^2:23:25^2:31:34/17:1:2:11:12:16:20^2:21:24
27/18:13/19/20:3f/21:13:15:24/22:1:5:14:18/
25:1/27/28:2:20^2/29:1^4:3:11^3:12:14/2Ch1:9^2:1
:11/2:5^2:11:13:14^4/5:9:13,14/6:1:11:14:15:22:
23:26:27:28^2:33/7:3^2:6:13:22/8:11/9:5:6:29/10
10/12:6:8:15/13:6:8^2:10:11:12^2/14:5:7^2/16:3:1
/18:6,7^2:13:29/19:2:10/20:2^2:15:17:21:26:34/
23:4/25:7:9:19:26/26:17,18^3/27:7/28:5:9:11:1
19f/29:31/30:9:17,18,19/31:10/32:7^3:11:12:22
33:18:19/34:21:25/35:3:12:21/Ez1:3/2:1:2/3:
11/4:13:16/5:6:8^3:16/6:2:3/7:1:18^2:21:28f/9:6
7:11/10:2:13:16-19:25/Neh1:3:5:9/2:3/4:14:19
/5:7:9/6:5,6^4:7^2/7:5:6:57,58,59/8:9:10^2:11/9:5
18/11:3/12:1/Est1:18:20/2:23f/3:8^2/4:11:16/
:3^2:6:7,8^2:13:14/6:4:5:9:11:13/7:2^3:6/8:8f/9:19
26^3/Job1:8:10/2:3/3:19:23^2/4:7,8:17:21/5:8:2
/6:3:5,6,7^5:12:15-18^2:24:25,26/7:1:5:7^2:17/8:
11-13:14:19/9:4:17:19:22:24:32,33/10:4-7^2:22/
11:2:6:8^3:9:10:12^2:20/12:7,8,9:10:14^2:16/13:12
18:25/14:1:5:7:10:18,19:22/15:11^2:12:16:20:21
27,28:35/16:13:16:17:19^2/17:1:12^2:15/18:4:5:6
10:11:12:13:21/19:6/20:7:16:23:25:29/21:4:7:
15:21:30-32:34/22:2^2:3:4^2:5:10,11:12:13:14:29/
23:2:10:14/24:10:17:18/25:2:3:4:5:6^2/26:12/27
6:13:14:18:19:20:21/28:5:13:14:17:18^2:21:23,24
27:28^3/30:16:23:27:30/31:11:12:23/32:8,9^2:
11,12^2/33:10:12^2:19:23,24^2/34:4^2:7,8:12^2:22:23
/35:2,3:7:9,10:13:14,15^2/36:5^2:9:22^2:23:24:26/

(IS Con't)
37:16,17[2]:23:24/**38**:22,23:24[2]:25-27:29:37,38[2]/
39:11:16:20:21-23:27/**40**:17:19:23/**41**:9:11:20:
23:24:27,28[2]:30:33:34/**42**:3[2]/**Ps2**:4:6:7:10:12/**4**:
2:7/**6**:2:3:6/**7**:10:11[3]:17[2]/**8**:6/**9**:4:9:16:17/**10**:3:4
:4f:5:15:16/**11**:4:7/**12**:2:6[2]:8/**14**:1[3]:3:5:6/**15**:2/
16:5[3]:8/**17**:1:13,14:15[2]/**18**:2[5]:3:24:30[2]:31[2]:46[2]:
47/**19**:5f/**20**:7/**21**/**22**:2:8[2]:9,10,11:28/**23**:1/**24**:2
:8:10/**25**:8:10:12:14/**26**:2:11/**27**:1:4/**28**:7/**29**:4/
30:5:6,7/**31**:1:9,10:19:21/**32**:5:6[2]/**33**:1:4:5[2]:12[2]:
16,17[3]/**34**:8:18/**35**:10:27/**36**:3:5:6:7:9/**37**:12,13[2]
:16:30,31[2]:37:39/**38**:3,4[2]:7/**39**:5,6[2]:7:9:11[3]/**40**:8
:11:16:17/**41**:8/**42**:3:10:11[2]/**43**:5f:5/**44**:8:22/**45**:
1:2:6:7[2]:8:9:10,11:14/**46**:1:4:5:7:11/**47**:2[2]:9/**48**:
1:3:10:10f:14/**49**:5:8,9[2]:13:14[2]:20f/**50**:6:12:
14,15:22:23/**51**:4[2]:17:19/**53**:1[2]:2:3/**54**:4[2]:4f:6/
55:4:10:11:15/**56**:9/**57**:1:7:10/**58**:11[2]/**59**:4:10/
60:2:11/**61**:2/**62**:3,4[2]:6:7:12/**63**:1/**64**:4:6f/**66**:2:
15/**68**:4:5[2]:6:26:34/**69**:3:13:16[2]:20/**70**:4/**71**:7:9:
11:19/**73**:1:4:6:11:12:14:16:20:26[2]/**74**:1:9,10:12:
17:20/**75**:8[2]/**76**:1:2/**77**:8:10:13/**78**:17/**79**:1[2]:3:5:
10/**83**:8/**84**:1:7:10:11/**85**:3:8:9/**86**:8/**87**:7/**88**:3:
4:18/**89**:2:6:7:8[2]:13[3]:14,15[2]:17:18:20:47:49[2]/**90**:
5,6/**91**:1:2[2]:9/**92**:1[2]:7:15[2]/**93**:1[3]:1f[2]:5/**94**:9:11:
19:21,22/**95**:3:7[2]/**96**:4:7:13/**97**:1:11/**98**:4:8,9/
99:1[2]:4[2]:9/**100**:3:5[2]/**102**:3,4[5]:11:13:17/**103**:5:8[2]:
11:12:13:17,18[2]:19/**104**:24:29:30:34/**105**:7[2]:
10,11/**106**:40:41,42/**107**:11:12:30/**108**:1:4:5:8[3]:
9f/**109**:7:18:20/**111**:7:9:10/**112**:1:4:7:8[2]/**113**:2:4[2]
/**115**:2:2f:3:9[2]:10[2]:11[2]:12/**116**:5[2]:15f/**118**:1:2:3:
4:6:7:8:9:14:23[2]:24:26[2]:27,28:29[2]/**119**:28:57:63:
64:69:75,76,77:96:113:121:126:128:132:140:142
:147:156:160:168:172:174/**121**:2:3,4:5[2]/**124**:7:8
/**127**:1:2:5/**128**:4/**129**:1:3,4[2]/**130**:5:7/**131**:2/
132:7:14/**133**:1:2:3/**135**:5:13/**136**:1/**137**:8:9:9f/
138:5:6/**139**:14[2]:17,18/**141**:5/**143**:2:8:10/**144**:1:
2[2]:3:4:8:12-15[3]/**145**:3[2]:8:9[2]:17:18/**146**:4:5[2]:6:10
/**147**:1:2:5[3]:10[2]:11:18/**148**:13[2]/**149**:9/**Pro1**:
7,8,9:16[2]:19:31/**2**:6:7,8:15/**3**:11,12:13,14,15[3]:18[2]
:21:24,25,26:29:33[2]/**4**:7:11[2]/**5**:3:4f:4:9f:21:22/**6**:
9:12,13:14:23:29:30:31:32/**7**:16,17:19:22/**8**:1:
6,7:8[2]:9:10:11:14,15[2]:34[2]/**9**:12:13/**10**:1:6:8:11[2]:
15[2]:17:18[2]:20:21:22:23[2]:26:28:31:32/**11**:3[2]:6:12:
14[2]:17[2]:22:24,25[2]:30f/**12**:1:4:5[2]:8:9:10[2]:13:16:
17:21/**13**:9[2]:12:12f:15:19[2]:22/**14**:2:3:4:6:9:9f:9:
14:15[2]:16:17[2]:18[2]:21:25:27:28[2]:31[2]:33:34:35/**15**:
3:6:14:15[2]:17:19:21:23:29:31,32/**16**:1:2:6[2]:7:8:
12:12f:14:16:17:21[2]:22[2]:25:26:27f:31[2]:32[2]:33/**17**
:1:5:6:8f:10:12:13:14:15[2]:16:17[2]:18:19:20:23:24:
25:27,28[3]/**18**:2:5:6,7:9:10:14:15:19:19f:22:24/
19:2:6[2]:11:12[2]:13:18:22:26:27/**20**:2[2]:3:7:11:15:
16:21:24:25:27:28:29/**21**:1:3:8:9:10:14:15:18f:20
f:25,26:28:29:29f[2]:30:31f/**22**:1:6:7:9:11:13:14:15
:22,23:28/**23**:1[2]:6,7,8:10,11:17,18:24,25:
26,27,28,29,30[4]/**24**:3,4:5[2]:6:7:8:9:13,14:15,16:
23:26/**25**:2,3:6,7:11:12:13:14:18:19:20[2]:21,22[2]:
24:25:26:27[2]:28/**26**:4,5:6:12[3]:15:16:17:18,19[2]:22
:24,25,26:28/**27**:4:5:7[2]:8:13:17:19[2]:20f:20:21:
25,26,27/**28**:1:2[2]:3:4[2]:7[2]:11:12[2]:14[2]:15:21:22:24:
26/**29**:1:5,6:14:18[2]:19:20:25/**30**:4[2]:18,19f:20/**31**
:4:6,7:10:17:22:23:25:26:27/**Ecc1**:2[2]:3-7:8-11[3]:
12-15[5]/**2**:1:13,14[3]:15[2]:17[2]:20-23[2]:24-26/**3**:1:11:
12:14[2]:15[2]:16:18:22[2]/**4**:4[2]:5,6[2]:8[4]:10:12[2]:13:15:
16/**5**:1[2]:5:6,7[3]:8[2]:9[2]:11:13,14[2]:15:16[2]:17:18[2]:
19,20[2]/**6**:1:2:5:7,8:9[2]:12/**7**:1[3]:2[3]:3:5:6[2]:7:8[2]:9:11[2]
:14:19:20[2]:24:25:26:26f:27,28/**8**:4:6,7[2]:8[2]:11:14[2]
/**9**:1:2,3[2]:4[2]:6:9:10:11:12[2]:13:16[2]:18/**10**:4:5:8,9:
11[2]:11f[2]:12,13[2]:14:15:16,17[2]/**11**:3:5[2]:7:8[2]/**12**:2:
6[3]:8:12:13[2]/**Sol1**:2:4:6:13:14/**2**:2:3[2]:6:9[2]:11[2]:12:
12f:14:16[2]/**3**:6:7:10[2]/**4**:4:10[3]:11:12/**5**:9[2]:10:11:
14:16[2]/**6**:3:5:10:12f/**7**:2[2]:4[2]:5[2]/**8**:6[2]:9f:9:9f/**Is1**:
2:8[2]:10:12,13/**2**:1:8:11/**3**:9:10:11[2]:13:24/**4**:2,3,4
f/**5**:7f:14:16[2]:20[8]:25[3]/**6**:3[2]:5:11:13/**7**:1f:2:9:14:
15,16:15,16f[2]/**8**:4:9,10:17[2]:20/**9**:6[2]:7:11,12:17[4]:
19,20:21[2]/**10**:2[2]:5,6[2]:7[2]:15[2]:18:30:33[2]/**11**:10f/
12:2[2]:4:6/**13**:1:4:9/**14**:7[2]:8:19:24:26:28[2]:29[2]:31[2]:
32/**15**:1:6:8/**16**:4,5:6:10/**17**:1[3]:6[2]:14/**18**:2/**19**:1[2]
:11:12/**20**:3/**21**:1[2]:2[2]:3:4:6,7f:6,7:8,9[2]:11[2]:12:13
/**22**:1[3]:2:9,10,11/**23**:1[2]:2,3:7:10:14:15,16/**24**:1[2]:
4,5:6:10:12:13[2]:15,16[2]:18:19/**25**:5:9[2]/**26**:1:4:7:8:
9:21/**27**:3:4,5/**28**:4:7:8:9:11:16:17:20:22:23:24:
27[4]:28:29/**29**:8[2]:15:22/**30**:12:15:16:18:21:33/**32**
:1:15/**33**:5:6:9:20:22/**34**:2[2]:6[2]:8/**35**:4[2]/**36**:2:6[3]:
12:16/**37**:3[3]:7:18:21:23:25:30[3]/**38**:7:10:12[2]:16:
18f[2]/**39**:6:8/**40**:6:7:9:10[2]:14:22[2]:25/**41**:1:4:17:20
:27/**42**:5:8:19[2]:20:21:24:25[2]/**43**:10:11:12:18:28/
44:6[2]:7:8[2]:9:13:20[2]:23:28/**45**:1:5:6[2]:13f:14[2]:18:
21:22:23:24/**46**:1[2]:4:7:9:10:13/**47**:4:11:14/**48**:5:
6:22/**49**:7:16/**50**:1[2]:2[3]:8:9/**51**:5:18:19[2]:22[2]/**52**:5[2]
:6:11:13f[2]:14,15f/**53**:7:11:12/**54**:5[2]:14:17[2]/**55**:1:
3:6:8:11/**56**:2[2]:3:5:12/**57**:1:4:7,8:11[2]:12:20:21/
58:4:5[2]:6:9/**59**:2:6[2]:8:9:14[2]:15[2]:21/**60**:1:22/**61**:1
/**62**/**63**[4]:3:10:11[2]:12:15/**64**:5:10:11/**65**:6/**66**:1[2]:
3[2]:6[3]:7,8:13:19f/**Jer1**:12f:16/**2**:14:19:26,27:34/
3:1[2]:2:3:11:16:21:23/**4**:3:7:10:14:16:18:20:31/**5**:
6:14:19[2]:28:29:31/**6**:1:6[2]:8:14:16[2]:18,19:20:22:
23:25:29[2]/**7**:4:8:11:18:28:32/**8**:4,5:6:11:12:16[2]:
18[2]:19:20[2]:22[2]/**9**:10:12[3]:15:24:25,26[2]/**10**:2,3:6[2]:
10:13:14:16[4]:19[3]:20[2]:23/**11**:1:5:10:17/**12**:11:13/
13:16:19f:20:22[3]:24,25[3]/**14**:4:5:6:8:12:13:19/**15**:
9[2]:10:15:17,18/**16**:6:10:11:14,15/**17**:5:6:7:8:9[3]:
11:12:15:16[2]/**18**:1:6:7:11/**19**:6:9:11/**20**:8:9/**21**:
12/**22**:3:6:15:16:18[2]:20:24,25f:28/**23**:5,6[2]:9:10[4]:
15:16:17:18:19:23:28:29:30,31:33:35[2]:36[2]:37:
38,39f/**25**:12f/**26**:11:15[2]:18/**27**:6:7:16/**28**:4f:9/
29:3:10:26/**30**:1:3:5:7:12:13:14:15[3]/**31**:9:15[2]:17:
20:26:30:33:35:38,39/**32**:6,7:17:20:23:27/**33**:2:3
:10,11:12:16:20,21:25,26/**34**:1:5:8:12/**35**:1:1f[2]/
36:7/**37**[2]:17/**38**:4:9/**40**:2,3,4/**42**:9:15:17/**43**:10/
44:1:6:11:22:23:29/**45**:1:3/**46**:7:8:10[2]:11[2]:12:18[2]
:20,21[2]:24/**47**:1:2:4/**48**:1:2,3,4[3]:11[2]:12:15[2]:16:
17:20:25:29:30:31:33:39[2]/**49**:1:3:7:19:21:28:30/
50:1:10:23:34[3]:38:41:44/**51**:5[2]:9:11:13:16:17[2]:18
:19[4]:20:30:31:32:33:41:42:43:47:52:55[2]:56/**Lam**
1:1:2f:2:3[2]:8:12[2]:16:18:19f:20:21:22/**2**:4[2]:11:13:
15:16:17/**3**:3:17:18:21:22:23:25:26:27:29:38:51[2]:
54/**4**:3,4:6:8:11:17f:18/**5**:4:5:8:16[2]:21/**Eze2**:1f[3]/
3:11/**4**:3[2]/**5**:16/**7**:2:5,6:7:12:14:19:23[2]/**8**:17/**9**:9
/**10**:17f/**11**:3[2]:5[2]:7:7f:15/**12**:6:10:11:22/**13**:6:7:
10:16/**14**:2:9:23/**15**:4:5,6/**16**:17:26:37:38:44:46[2]
:57:58/**17**:24/**18**:4[2]:5[2]:7[2]:8:9:10:13:16:18:19:20:
21:25[2]:29[2]:30/**19**:13[2]:14:14f:14/**20**:12:25f:29[3]/
21:5[3]:7:9,10,11[2]:15:23:24:25:28[2]/**22**:6:9[2]:11:
18,19,20:26/**23**:39:44/**24**:6[2]:7:13:24/**25**:8/**27**:10[2]
:17f:19f:25:27:32:36/**28**:1:2,3/**29**:3:10/**30**:2,3:4:
21f/**31**:18/**32**:19[2]:20:24:29:31/**33**:4:5:6:14:17:30
:30f/**34**:13:18:19[2]:22[2]:29f[3]/**35**:10/**36**:5:13:19:32
/**37**:11/**38**:1:2,3f:11/**39**:15,16:19/**40**:5:45:46/**41**
:4:22:22f/**43**:7:12[4]:13:14[3]:15:16:17:18/**44**:3:5:23[4]
:23f:24:25[2]:26:28/**45**:2:3:7:13/**46**:5:7[4]:11:14,15:
17/**47**:1:15f/**48**:1[2]:5,6,7:8:11[2]:12[2]:14:15:16:18:
19:20:21,22:25:35:35f/**Dan2**:5:11:15[2]:22[2]:26:28:
45[2]:47/**3**:4:14:17/**4**:1:3:8:9[2]:17:18:22:27:31:34:
37[2]/**5**:11:12:26:31f/**6**:5:12:13[2]:15:25,26:27/**7**:1:
14:23:25f/**8**:12f:13[2]:19:21:26:26f[2]/**9**:9:14:18:25/
10:14:17:20,21/**11**:36[2]:37:45/**12**:9:11[2]/**Hos1**:2[2]:
9:11f/**4**:1:2:3[3]:6:9:12f:14:15[2]:17:18:18f/**5**:4:11/**6**
:1:8:11/**7**:3:4:9[2]:11/**8**:3:5:6:8:13/**9**:4[3]:7[2]:16/
10:1:11:12/**11**:9:11:12/**12**:1:2:5:11/**13**:4:10:13[2]/
14:9[2]/**Joe1**:5:6:8:15[2]:18:20/**2**:2:8:11[2]:12[2]:13[3]:17
/**3**:8:13[2]:14:16:21/**Amo1**:2:3/**2**:13/**3**:1[2]:2:4[2]:5[2]:
11[2]:12/**4**:13/**5**:2:8:14:19:23/**6**:13/**7**:1:2[2]:5[2]:10[3]:
13:17/**8**:11/**9**:6:9:11:12/**Jon1**:8[2]:14/**4**:2:4:8:9[3]:
10[2]/**Mic1**:3:5:9:11f[3]:14/**2**:2:4:7:10:11/**3**:5:11[2]:
12/**4**:9[2]/**5**:2:3f/**6**:1:3:5:8[2]:9:10:16/**7**:1[3]:3:4[3]:10[2]:
18/**Nah1**:1:2[2]:3[2]:6:7[2]:11:12:15/**2**:6:7:8:9:10:11/
3:15:18:19[2]/**Hab1**:1:2:3:4[2]:11f:11[2]:12/**2**:5:6:14:
19:20/**3**:1:3[2]:6:17:19[2]/**Zep1**:10:14:15[2]/**2**:2[2]:3:5[2]
:15[2]:15f/**3**:5[2]:8[2]:17,18[3]/**Hag1**:2[3]:3,4[2]:9:10/**2**:3[2]:
7f:12:15:18,19/**Zec1**:11/**2**:2/**3**:2f:9/**4**:2:4:6:7f/**5**:
5:6[2]/**6**:12/**7**/**8**:6:11:13[2]:16:17:18:23/**9**:1[2]:2:3:9[3]:
10f:12/**10**:2:5[2]/**11**:3:13f/**12**:1:9/**13**:6f[4]:7:8f:9/**14**
:1:6f/**Mal1**:1:4:5:8:12:14[2]/**2**:11:14:17/**3**:1:2:3:6:
9:14,15/**4**:1/**Mt1**:23/**2**:2:5:13/**3**:2:2f:9f:10:11:15
:17/**4**:4:17:17f/**5**:3:10:18:20:25:29:34:35[3]:37[2]:40
:43:46:48/**6**:3:5:10:13f:16:22:23:25:34f/**7**:12:12f:
13[2]:14[2]:18:20:21:25/**8**:2:21:27/**9**:3[2]:5,6:15[2]:22:
24:34[2]:37/**10**:7:24[2]:26:41/**11**:9:10:11:14:19f:27/
12:6[2]:10:12[2]:18:23:24:26[2]:30:33:34:35:41:42:
43,44,45[2]:48:50/**13**:12,13:18:24[2]:27:31,32[3]:38:
39[2]:44:45:47,48:49:52f:55:57/**14**:2:15[2]:28/**15**:4:
9:11:20:23:27:28[2]/**16**:4:17:22:26/**17**:4f:5:15:21f
/**18**:4:5:7:11f:12:14:18/**19**:4:9f:10[3]:14:17:23:24:
26/**20**:1:14:15:16:21:26/**21**:5:9:9f:10:13:43/**22**:1
:4[2]:8:13:17:20[2]:21:23:29:30[2]:31:32:36:38,39[2]:42
/**23**:5:8:10:16[2]:17:18:19:25:38/**24**:6:15:26[2]:28:
32[3]:33f:33:42/**25**:5,6:12:24,25:29[2]/**26**:13:23:26:
28[2]:31:34:38:39:41[2]:46:54:56:65,66/**27**:8[2]:17f:
24:33:37:62f/**28**:7[2]:15/**Mk1**:7[3]:8f[2]:15:27:36,37:
38:43,44/**2**:7[2]:9,10,11:18:19:21[2]/**3**:4[3]:22:26:29:
33:35/**4**:14:19:21:22:26[2]:31,32[2]:41/**5**:9:23:27:39
/**6**:4:11:16:35,36[2]:50/**7**:4:6,7:11:12,13:15,16f:19:
20:37/**8**:38/**9**:5:7:17:18:18f:23:26:29f:37[2]:40:47:
50/**10**:4:6,7:18:24:25:27[2]:36:43/**11**:17[2]:22,23[2]:
26,f/**12**:11[2]:14:16:17:18:23:24:28:29:31:32:33/
13:3,4:7:9:21[2]:28:29:35,36,37/**14**:9:18:20:22:24:
24f:34:36:38[2]:42:63,64:68f:69/**15**:2:9:21:28f[2]/**16**
:7/**Lk1**:18[2]:20:25:28:42:43:45:51:61:63:66:69:78[2]
/**2**:10:23:32/**3**:7[2]:9:16/**4**:4:8:18,19[2]:24:36:43/**5**:
4:21[2]:22:23,24:31:32/**6**:9:20[2]:21[2]:22:25:26:33:34
:35:38:39:41:44:45:47,48/**7**:4:19f:23:23f:24:27:
28[2]:30:34:34f:35f:39[2]:47:49/**8**:11[2]:13:14:25[2]:30:
30f:43,44f:52/**9**:7:8:9:12:25:27:33:35:38:39:48[3]:
50[2]:60:62/**10**:2:6:7[2]:8,9[2]:20:21:42/**11**:2:7:9:10:
17[2]:18[2]:21:23[3]:24:25:25f:26:29,30:31:32:36:41:
44:49/**12**:6:21:34:45:48[5]:50[2]:55:57:59/**13**:2:16[2]:
18:19:20,21:24,25[2]:31:35/**14**:3:9:31:32:34:34f:
35[2]/**15**:10:24:27:31:32[3]/**16**:5,6[2]:8:15:17:25:26[2]:
30/**17**:2,3:7,8,9[3]:21:22:37/**18**:4,5:8:19:22:24:25:
26/**19**:42:46/**20**:14:22:24:25[2]:27[2]:33:34,35:
37,38[3]:41[2]/**21**:4:6:28:30:31/**22**:12:19:20:20f:21:
22:27:47f:53:59:69/**23**:2:3:5:6:31f[2]:35:38:43/**24**:
5:22,23:38:39:47/**Jn1**:1:3:4:5:6,7:9:15[3]:18:26:29
:30[2]:33[2]:34:36:45/**2**:10[2]:19:24,25/**3**:5[2]:5f:8:12:
18:19:26[2]:28[2]:29:31[2]:33,34[2]:35[2]/**4**:11:20[3]:21-24[3]
:37:42:43,44:50:53/**5**:20:25[2]:27:28:30[3]:32,33f:
32,33[2]:34:45/**6**:8,9:12:14:26:29:33:36:39:40:42[3]:
45:48-51:55[2]:56:60:63f:65:70/**7**:6:8f:8:17[2]:18[2]:
21,22,23:26[2]:28:35[2]:37:40:41,42:48[2]:49f:51[2]/**8**:
17:18:19[2]:22:24:26:29:35:39:41:43:44[3]:47:50f:54[2]
:55:58/**9**:4:8:12:16[2]:17:19:20:21:24:25:36:37/**10**:
10[2]:13:20:25:29:38/**11**:3:4:10:12,13:14:26:28:34
/**12**:27[2]:36:38:40f/**13**:11:13:16[3]:17:20[2]:21:25:26
:26f/**14**:2,3:7:10:11:17:21:24:28/**15**:1:6[2]:13[2]:23:
24/**16**:2:3:5f:7[2]:9:10:11:12:13:15[2]:17,18[2]:20:21[2]:
26f:30f:32[3]/**17**:3:7:9:21/**18**:20:22:29:31:31f:32f:
36:38[2]/**19**:12:13f:14:22:25:26:27:30:35f[2]:40/**20**:
30,31/**21**:1:7:22:23:24/**Act1**:14/**2**:9f:25[2]:26:29/
3:12:13:24:25/**4**:10:11:12[2]:27[2]/**5**:9:32[2]:38[2]:39:
42/**7**:26:48,49[2]:58f/**8**:2f:9,10,11f[2]:21:23:31:32:
33:37/**9**:5:11:15:20/**10**:5,6:15[2]:20:21:28:32:
36,37[2]:42/**11**:9/**12**:22/**13**:10:22:23[2]:25:26:27:
32,33[2]:34:38:39:47/**15**:16f:18:19:23:27,28,29/
17:3:23:24:25:27[2]:29/**18**:5:15:21f:25,26[2]:28/**19**:
2:25:26[2]:28:34[2]:35:35f:36[2]:40/**20**:24:28:35/**21**:
28:39/**22**:5:8:25:26/**23**:4:8:19:21/**24**:5[2]/**25**:14:
16[2]:19:24[2]:26/**26**:6[2]:7:8:14f/**27**:4f:10:37/**28**:20:
20f:22:28,29/**Rom1**:1:3:5:8:10:11,12f:16[2]:17:17f
:19:19f:20f:26/**2**:4[2]:5:12-15[3]:16:17:22:25:29[4]/**3**:
1:4[2]:5[4]:8[2]:10[2]:12:13:13f[2]:17:27[2]:28/**4**:3:4,5[3]:4,5f
:6:8:9[2]:11:12[2]:13:14:15[2]:16:17[2]/**5**:5:10/**6**:6:19[2]:
23[2]/**7**:2[2]:3:4:7:9:13[2]:14[2]:15:16:17[2]:18:20[2]:21[2]:22
:23,24,25[3]/**8**:1:2[2]:7:9:10f:17:18:19:27:28:31:33:
34[2]:35:37/**9**:1[2]:5:6:18:23,24/**10**:1:2:3:8[3]:9:10:10f
:15/**11**:5:6[3]:7:8[2]:9:15:22[2]:25:33:36/**12**:1:4,5:6:7:
9:12:20[2]/**13**:1[2]:4[2]:7:9[2]:10:11[4]:12,13/**14**:1[2]:1f[2]:2[3]
:3:4:5:6[5]:11:13:14[3]:15:16:17:20[2]:21:22[3]:23[6]/**15**:1
:8:9:15,16:17:22:27/**16**:4:10:17:19:22:25,26,27[4]/
1Co1:9:17:22[3]:24[2]:25[2]:30:31/**2**:9[2]:11[2]/**3**:5:7[2]:13:
17:19:20:23/**4**:2:4[2]:5[3]:7:17[2]:20[2]/**5**:1[2]:2:6[2]:11[3]:12
:13/**6**:1[2]:5:7:12f[2]:13:14:18[2]:19/**7**:1[2]:2:3:9:10[2]:11:
12:15[2]:16:17:19[2]:24[2]:26[2]:28[2]:29[2]:34[4]:36[2]:39/**8**:1[4]
:2:3[2]:4[2]:6:7:9:10[4]:11:12[2]:13/**9**:3:5f[2]:8:9:11:13:17:
18[2]:21:22[2]/**10**:8:10:13:15:20:22:24:25:26:27:29:
31:33[3]/**11**:3[4]:4:5[2]:6:7[3]:10:13:16:17[2]:19:22:23:24[2]
:25:27:28:29[2]:30:32:34/**12**:3[3]:4[2]:5:6:8:10[4]:11:12:
13:20:26:27[2]:28[2]:29[2]:31/**13**:1:2:4:5:6:9:12:13/**14**
:2[2]:3:5:6[3]:7f:7[2]:13:14:22[3]:23:24[2]:25:26[3]:28:29,30[2]
:33:35:37:39:40/**15**:1[3]:2:10:11:13:14[3]:16:19:20:
21[2]:22:29:31[2]:37[3]:40:45:52:54:57:58[2]/**16**:9[2]:10:
11:22/**2Co1**:3,4:12:13,14:18:20:21:22:23:24/**2**:
2:3:7:11[2]:15[3]:16:17/**3**:2:3:6[2]:8:9:10:11[2]:14:15:16
:17[3]/**4**:1:3[3]:4[3]:4f:5:6[2]:7[3]:10[2]:15:16[2]/**5**:1:2:5:6:9:
11[2]:13,14[3]:17:19:20/**6**:2[2]:12[2]:17/**7**:4:10[2]:16/**8**:8[2]
:17[2]:18:21:22:23[2]/**9**:5:8:9/**10**:1:3:5:7:10:11:12:
13:15:16:17/**11**:1:4:15:29:31/**12**:1:5[2]:9:10:14:16
/**13**:1[2]:3[2]:4:7:8:9/**Gal1**:1f:1:7:11:20:23/**2**:20/**3**:5:
8,9:10:11[2]:12[2]:13[3]:15:18:19:21,22[2]/**4**:1:3:7:15:
15f:17:18:22:24,25[2]:26[2]:27/**5**:2:4:6:8:10:20[2]:23/
6:1[2]:3[3]:4:5:9:14:15/**Eph1**:1:7:8:10:14[2]:15:16,17:
19[2]:21:23/**2**:2:4:7:8f:8[2]:9:10:14:20/**3**:6:8:9:10:13
:18,19[2]:20/**4**:5:6:10:12[2]:15,16[3]:28:29:30/**5**:5[2]:6:
8:9:14:23[2]:28[2]:31:32[2]/**6**:1:2:3:6,7,8:13:17:19:21/
Php1:4:6:7:8:9:18:19:22:24:28/**2**:1:9:11:13:17[2]:
19:20:23/**3**:1:3[2]:8:14:19[3]:20[2]/**4**:5:7:8:17:19/**Col**
1:6:7:8:15:15f:16:17:18[3]:18f:18:23[3]:24:26,27[2]:29[2]
/**2**:2[2]:5:9:10/**3**:3:4:5:6:8:9:10[2]:11[3]:15:18:24[3]/**4**:1
:7:10:12:18/**1Th1**:9:10/**2**:19[3]/**4**:6:8:9:10/**5**:1:3[3]:
7:12:18:21[3]/**2Th1**:3[2]:5[2]:6/**2**:4[2]:6[2]:7:7f:7/**3**:3:6:
14:17[3]/**1Ti1**:5:15:16:17[2]:18:19/**2**:1:3:5[2]:6:7/**3**:1:
6:9:16[2]/**4**:3:4:5:6:8[3]:9,10[2]:16/**5**:4:7:8[2]:10:14:18:
21/**6**:2[3]:4[2]:5:10:11:19/**2Ti1**:3[2]:6:9:12[2]:13f/**2**:5:9[2]
:12:19:25/**3**:1:15:16[4]:17/**4**:2[2]:3:8:11:12/**Tit1**:4:8
:10[2]:13:15[2]:16/**2**:11:15/**3**:8:10:11/**Phm1**:1:8,9:
10:11:16:19:23/**Heb**:2:3[2]:4:5,6/**2**:6[2]:8[2]:11[2]:18[2]/
3:1:6:7,8:13:15/**4**:4[2]:7:8:9:10:12[2]:13:14/**5**:1[4]:4:5:
5f:7f[2]:11:12,13[2]/**6**:4:5:8[2]:10:16:18:19/**7**:2[2]:3f:3[2]:
4:7:24:25:26[2]:28/**8**:1[3]:3:4:5:10:13/**9**:16[2]:17:18:
20:22:23:27/**10**:4:5:14:15:16:18:19:20:23[2]:25:26[2]
:31/**11**:1[5]:3f:4:5:6:10:12:16:19/**12**:7:10:11:14:23:
25:29/**13**:6[2]:8:12:13:14:17:18:20,21:22:23/**Jas1**:
2:3:4:5:6:9:10,11:12[2]:13[2]:14:17:19:21[2]:22:23:26[2]
:27[2]/**2**:2:5[2]:6:8:9:10[2]:15:17[2]:18:19:20[2]:24:25:26[4]

(IS Con't)
/**3**:6^3:8:10:14:16:17^5/**4**:1^2:2:3:4:11^3:14^3:15:17^2/**5**:1:2:3^2:8:9^2:11^2:13:14/**1Pe1**:3:4:6^2:7^3:12:15:24:25/**2**:4^2:7:8:11:15:20:21^2/**3**:4:6:12^2:16^2:17:21:22/**4**:6:7:12^2:14f:16:19/**5**:1:7:10:12:13f^4:13/**2Pe1**:1^3:5:7:9:17,18/**2**:2:3:10:13:19:20:22^4/**3**:1:4:8:9^3:10:11:15,16^3/**1Jn1**:1:2^2:5^3:9:9f/**2**:1^4:2^2:4:5:6:7:8:9^2:10:11^2:17:18^3:22^3:27^2:28:29/**3**:2^2:3:4:5:7^3:9:10^3:14:15:16:17:20f:23:24/**4**:1^2:2^3:3^4:4^2:6^4:8:10^2:15^2:16^3:18:20^2/**5**:1^2:5:6,7,8:6,7,8f:6,7,8:9:10^2:11^2:15:16^2:17:17f:19:20^2/**2Jn1**:2/**3Jn**:2^3:10^3:11^2/**Jud**:5:7:13^2:14:16:18:21:24,25^2/**Rev**:3:4^2:5:7:8^3:8f:9^2:17,18:20:20f/**2**:4:6^2:7^2:8^2:11^2:12:13:17^2:18:20:27/**3**:1:2^2:5:6:7^2:10f:13:14^2:18:22/**4**:8^2/**5**:2:12^2/**6**:6/**7**:15/**9**:1f^3:11^2:16f^2/**11**:14:17:18^2/**13**:4^2:8f:10:18/**14**:8^2:10:15/**16**:5:6:17/**17**:1:7^2:8f:10:11:14:15/**18**:2^2:5:8:11:17:18:19/**19**:1:8:9f:10:10f/**20**:5:14/**21**:3:5:6:8^2:25/**22**:3:10:12:18

6914

ISN'T

Gen2:18/**17**:19/**19**:31/**32**:28/**Ex4**:11/**5**:16/**14**:12/**Lev24**:18/**Num20**:5/**Deu8**:3/**14**:24/**Jos6**:18/**Ju13**:4:7:13,14/**14**:3/**18**:19/**Ru3**:1/**1Sa1**:8/**10**:24/**14**:17/**20**:2/**21**:11^2/**24**:9,10/**26**:16/**2Sa17**:8/**20**:20/**1Ki18**:10/**21**:19/**22**:7/**2Ki3**:11/**4**:23/**6**:19/**7**:9/**9**:20/**19**:21/**2Ch18**:6,7/**Ez10**:13/**Neh6**:8/**Job8**:18/**15**:3/**Ps10**:11/**37**:24/**40**:5:6/**50**:9/**94**:6,7/**Pro5**:20/**26**:17/**Is29**:16/**36**:7/**40**:27/**59**:1^2/**Jer2**:23:35/**5**:22/**8**:10:11/**10**:7/**33**:24/**39**:11,12/**Eze9**:5/**11**:7/**18**:25/**33**:17:20/**Dan2**:10^2/**Zec8**:17/**Mal1**:8/**Mt3**:14/**5**:17/**8**:8,9/**9**:13:24/**12**:30/**14**:16/**28**:6/**Mk5**:39/**7**:27/**8**:17/**9**:38:40/**10**:6,7/**16**:6/**Lk3**:8/**4**:22/**8**:52/**9**:49/**11**:23:35/**17**:20/**19**:21/**23**:4/**24**:6,7/**Jn2**:4/**7**:25/**10**:12/**13**:10/**14**:17:27/**15**:20/**21**:23/**Act2**:15/**9**:21/**11**:9/**22**:22/**Rom3**:26/**11**:6/**1Co2**:14/**3**:7/**4**:4/**5**:12/**6**:5/**7**:13:14^2:15/**9**:7:16/**10**:27/**11**:20/**12**:18/**15**:15/**2Co1**:19/**8**:12/**11**:17/**12**:11:19/**Gal5**:8/**Eph4**:20/**6**:6,7/**Php3**:3/**1Ti1**:19/**Tit3**:9/**Heb5**:12,13/**12**:11/**Jas1**:26/**2**:17/**4**:1/**2Pe3**:9/**1Jn4**:8/**5**:3/**Rev17**:8

146

IT

Gen1:4,5^2:9,10:11,12:14,15:24:28:31/**2**:3^2:7:10:11,12:15:18:21:23/**3**:1:2,3^3:5:6^3:7:12^2:17:18:19/**4**:7^2:12^2:17:25:26/**6**:1:6:12,13:14:15/**7**:18/**8**:3,4:8:20:21/**9**:7:23^2/**11**:9/**12**:2f/**13**:8:15/**14**:10/**15**:8:17/**16**:13^2:14/**17**:5^2:7,8^2:12/**18**:1:7:8:14:15:24^2:28:29:30:31:32/**19**:13:14:18,19,20^2:36/**21**:10:22:24:26/**22**:8:10^2:13:14/**23**:5,6:9^2:11:13/**24**:7:11:15,16:65:65f/**25**:22^2:31:33/**26**:20^2:21^2:22/**27**:2,3,4^3:8,9,10^2:18:19:20^2:21:25^2:31^2:32:33^2:42/**28**:4:12:13:18/**29**:23:25/**30**:15:28^2:30:34/**31**:32:36,37:39:45:47,48:49^2:50:51,52/**32**:25:26:28^2:32/**33**:10:20/**34**:4:6,7:12:14/**35**:7^2:8:12:13,14:20:22^2/**36**:31-39:40-43/**37**:3:7^2:9:11^2:13,14:24:32^2:33^2:35/**38**:9f:10:17/**39**:9:11:12/**40**:1:11^2:15/**41**:7:8^2:15:16^2:32^2:38/**42**:4:5^2:6:14f:16:22:35/**43**:11:12:14:18:21^2:23^2/**44**:10:15/**45**:1:5:8:11,12:16:26:28/**46**:3,4/**47**:24:26^2:31/**48**:17^2/**49**:7:10f:32/**50**:11:12,13/**Ex2**:3^3:5:6:15/**3**:2:3,4:15f:21/**4**:3^4:4^2:6^2:7^3:9^2:11:18:25,26/**5**:10,11:16/**6**:8,9:30/**7**:2:9:10:18:21/**8**:10^2:16:22:25/**9**:6:7^2:8:9:10^2:24/**10**:8:13:14^2/**11**:6/**12**:3,4:10:11^2:17:19:27:39:40,41:44:45:46^2/**13**:8:16/**14**:12:16:20^3/**15**:6:7:23:25:26/**16**:6:14:15^3:17:18:19:20^2:27:31^2:32:33^2:34:36/**17**:5,6:7^2:15,16/**18**:22/**19**:18:23^2/**20**:5:7:11:11f:19/**21**:13:29:33^2:35:36/**22**:1:3^2:4:5^2:7:9^2:10^2:11^2:12:13:14^3:15:23:26:27^3:30^2/**23**:4:19:19f:29/**24**:6:16/**25**:11^2:12:13,14:16:24^2:32,33/**27**:5:7:11:21^2/**28**:7:17:21:29:32^2:36:37,38^2/**29**:3,4:7:11:12:14:15,16:18^2:19,20^2:21^2:26^2:34^3:36^3:37^2:37f/**30**:1:2:15:16:17,18^2:30:32^4:33^2:35^2:36^2:37^3:38/**31**:3:7:12,13:14,15:17/**32**:4:5:8^2:11:13:17:20^4:29/**33**:3:7/**34**:9^2:15:20/**36**:22:35:37/**37**:2:5:6:8:9:11:25^2:26/**38**:1:9:18:19/**39**:3^2:9:10:21:31:33-40:43/**40**:3:4:7:9^4:10:11:18:21:27:29:30^2:34:36:37:38/**Lev1**:4^3:5:6,7:9f:10:11^2:12:13:15,16,17^3:15,16,17f/**2**:1:3:4:5:6^3:7:8^3:9:10:13f:15/**3**:1:2:3,4,5:6:7,8^3:13/**4**:4^2:6:13:14^2:15:17:21^3:22:23:24^2:25:26:27:28:29^2:30:31^2:32:33^2:34/**5**:2:3:11^3:12^2:16:17,18^4:19/**6**:3^2:4,5:6:12^2:13:14:15^3:16:17^3:18:21:22,23:26:27:28:29/**7**:6:12:14^2:16:17,18^7:19:20f:21:29:30:35:36/**8**:10^2:11:15,16^3:19:21:23^2:28^2:29^2:30:31:33/**9**:9^2:12:15:17:18:20:21:24/**10**:12^3:13^2:14^3:16:17^2:18:19/**11**:4-7^7:12:28:32^2:33:34:35:37:38:41,42:43/**13**:3:6:11:13:14,15:23:25:28:31:34:37:42:49^2:50:51^2:52:53:55^2:55f:56^2:57^3:58^2:59/**14**:13:14:15:16^2:20:21:27:35:36:39:44:46:53:57/**15**:3:26/**16**:10^2:12:14^2:15^2:16:18:19^2:19f:21^2:22:31/**17**:8,9:11^2:13:14/**18**:18:22:23:28f/**19**:5^2:6^2:7:8:10:13:17:22/**20**:11:12:13:14:17:24^3/**21**:2,3:23^2/**22**:7:11^2:14:17,18:19^3:20:21:22:23:26,27^2:29,30^3/**23**:9,10,11^2:13:17:22:23,24:28:32:36/**24**:3,4^2:18:18f:21/**25**:10:11^2:12:13^2:14,15,16:23:25:26:27:28^3:29:30^3:31:50/**26**:32:34,35^5:43/**27**:8:9^2:10:11,12^3:13:14,15:16^3:18:20^2:21^3:24:26:27^4:33/**Num1**:51^3/**3**/**4**:5:11:16/**5**:5,6:7^2:8:9,10:15^2:17:21,22:24:25^2:26/**6**:6,7:20^2/**7**:1:13:42-47:60-65:84,85,86/**8**:4/**9**:6,7:8:12^2:15:16:17:19^2:20,21:22:23/**10**:12:34/**11**:8^5:15:17:18:19,20:22:25:31/**12**:1f^2/**13**:16:22f:23^2:27:30^2/**14**:7:8^2:13:20,21:22:24:30:34,35/**15**:8:9,19,20,21:23,24:25^2:40/**16**:8,9:10:13:46^3/**17**:1:8:10^2/**18**:6:16:17:27:30^2:31^2/**19**:4:14:15/**20**:8:9:12f:13:17:19/**21**:8^2:14:17,18/**22**:12:13/**23**:18-24^2:27/**24**:11/**26**:62/**27**:3,4:9:10:11:13/**28**:1:7:8:27/**29**:8:12/**30**:5^2:7:8:11:12^2:14/**31**:23:27^2:30:42-46/**32**:1:3,4:19:39/**33**:40:50,51:53/**34**:4:10,11^2:13/**35**:16:17:22,23^2:24:25^2:27/**36**:6:7/**Deu1**:1:6:8^3:19,20,21:24,25:41^2:42/**2**:9:14,15:19:31^2/**3**:9:14^2:26/**4**:14:23:33:37:38:48/**5**:11f:15/**6**:3:22:25/**7**:2:8:16:19:22:23:25^3:26^3/**8**:3:8:9^2:15:16:17^2:18^2/**9**:4^2:5^4:6:7:21^3:28/**10**:8:9:11^2/**11**:12:29/**12**:15^2:16/**13**:12,13,14^3:16/**14**:7:21^4:24:29/**15**:9:10:21^2:22^2:23/**16**:6^2:7:11:15^2/**17**:4:14:19:20/**18**:12:22^2/**19**:20/**20**:5^2:6:10^2:11:12^2:13/**21**:4:7/**22**:1^2:2^4:3:4:6:7:25,26,27/**23**:19:21^2:22:23:25^2/**24**:6^2:11:12,13^4:14,15^2:19^2:21/**25**:4:8/**26**:1:2,3^2:4:14:15/**27**:7/**28**:40/**29**:1:6:8:22/**31**:7^2:19:22/**32**:7:18:27^2:52/**33**:21:27/**34**:4^4/**Jos2**:14/**3**:11:13,14/**4**:7:9:14:15,16:23^2/**5**:2,3:11,12/**6**:18:20:21:24/**7**:3^2:9:10,11^4:23^2/**8**:1:7:19:28:29^2/**9**:12:24^3:27^2/**10**:28:31:32:37/**11**:18:23/**13**:10:11:17:26/**15**:2,3,4:7^2:9:10,11^2:17:18,19/**16**:1:5,6:7/**17**:15:16,17,18/**18**:4:5,6:16:17:18/**19**:11^2:13:27:47,48:50/**21**:9-16:43/**22**:22,23:24,25:28:29:34/**24**:12:15:18:22:26:27/**Ju1**:12:14:26^2/**2**:3:15/**3**:16:20^2:21:22,23/**5**:30/**6**:1:16f:17^3:19^2:20:22:24:25:26:27^2:28^2:29:37:38:39/**7**:5,6^2:12,13^3:16:19,20:25/**8**:21:27^3/**9**:3:9^2:11:33:36:38:45:47,48:49:50:51:52:53:54/**11**:4:10:13:17:23^3:26:35:39f:39/**12**:1/**13**:13:17:18:19:21^2/**14**:6^3:8:9^2:13^2:14:15:16:17:19^2/**15**:15/**16**:9f:16,17/**17**:2^2:3^2:4,5^2/**18**:7:8:9,10^2:19:29/**19**:16:26:30/**20**:27,28:33:35-39^2/**21**:4:5:15/**Ru1**:11:19/**2**:3:7:12:17:18^2:19/**3**:1:14:15-18^3/**4**:4^3:4f:4^3:6^2:7^2:8:10/**1Sa1**:7:17/**2**:13,14^2:15^2:16^2:19:23,24,25:30:31/**3**:4,5:8:18/**4**:3:4:5:6/**5**:3:8:10/**6**:2^2:3^2:7:9:21/**7**:1:6^2:9:12^2/**8**:9:15/**9**:8:9,10,11:24^4/**10**:1:11:25/**12**:5:6:15:17:23/**14**:6:10:43:45/**15**:16:21^2:28/**16**:2:13/**17**:31:35^4:36:38,39^3:48,49:50,51/**18**:11,12:17:20/**19**:5^2:7:9,10:13^2:16:24f/**20**:2:3^2:16:17:22:26^2:33/**21**:6:9^3/**22**:8:11,12:18:22/**23**:26/**24**:3:6^2:9,10:11^2:15/**25**:11:21:39/**26**:8:14:17,18:22/**27**:5/**28**:14:17:24:25/**29**:10/**30**:1:7:25/**31**:3,4/**2Sa1**:17,18^2:20/**2**:23:26/**3**:9,10:18:26:28/**4**:12/**5**:20:24/**6**:3:8:10^2:11:13:17:19/**7**:5:10,11:15:29/**10**:3/**11**:14/**12**:3^4:4^2:12:29,30^2/**13**:2f:10^2:12:13:20:28:32,33^2/**14**:8^2:14:19:20:26/**15**:9f:14:19,20:21:24/**16**:5:7,8:11:22:23/**17**:18:19/**18**:3^4:9:12:13:17:18^2:20/**19**:15:30/**20**:5:8,9,10:15:20:22/**21**:1:4^2:5,6/**22**:9f/**23**:5:10:16^3:17:18,19:20:21/**24**:14:15:23:24^2/**1Ki1**:11:18:39:48/**2**:5^2:14:15:16:20:23,24:26:36,37/**3**:5:15:17,18:19^2:21^3:22:26^2/**5**:2,3/**6**:1:9:38/**7**:2:6:7:25:26:41-46/**8**:6:18:27:31:32/**9**:2,3^2:25/**10**:7^2:8:10:18:19:21/**11**:2:11:16,17,18,19/**12**:6:15:25:32,33/**13**:3:4:8:11:16,17:24,25^3:26:28:29^3/**14**:8:22/**16**:13:18:24^2:34^2/**17**:3:11:15:19/**18**:1:7:8:17:23^4:25:26:34^2:39/**19**:4:11:13/**20**:14/**21**:2:6:7:15:16:18:29/**22**:3:6:21:22:28:34:51/**2Ki1**:3:6:8:16/**2**:3:5:8:12:13,14:20/**3**:13:20:22:25f/**4**:1:17:27:28:41^2:42/**5**:7:13/**6**:5:6^2:7/**7**:2^2:8:9:13:16:19^2/**8**:6^2:15^2/**9**:20:36/**10**:4:11f:18,19:24:26:27^2:29/**11**:18/**12**:1:4,5^2:7:8:9^2:10^2:11,12,13,14:16:17^2:18/**14**:7:9:10:22/**15**:29:34,35/**16**:5:8:10:11,12^3:13^2:14^2:17/**18**:4^3:9:11:16:24:26/**19**:3^2:7:10:14^2:17:22:25:26:29:32^2/**20**:6:7:10:19/**21**:12:13/**22**:8:9,10:11/**23**:4:6^3:10:16:17:18:22:23/**24**:3,4^2/**25**:16/**1Ch1**:1f:19/**4**:40,41/**6**:31:49/**7**:15/**10**:4^2/**11**:14:18,19^6:23/**12**:19/**13**:3:7:11:13^2/**14**:2/**15**:12:13/**16**:1:31:32/**17**:2:21:27/**18**:8^2/**19**:2,3/**20**:1:2^2/**21**:7:12:15:23^3:24^2:26/**22**:3:5:7:8:14/**24**:31/**26**:13/**27**:24/**28**:2:8:20/**29**:1:2:12:16:18/**2Ch1**:4:5,6^2:7/**2**:4:5:6:11:16/**3**:1/**4**:5:12-16/**5**:4,5:7,8/**6**:8:9/**7**:16:18:20^2/**8**:1:3^2:11/**9**:4:6^2:18:19:27/**10**:15/**12**:8/**14**:6:7/**15**:11:15:16/**16**:2/**18**:14:17:19,20:21^2:33/**20**:2:25^2:26/**21**:18/**22**:7/**23**:13,14:15,16,17/**24**:5:10^2:14^2:24/**25**:2:18/**26**:2:17,18:20/**28**:3:13:15:21/**29**:6:16:22:35/**30**:5:5f:13:23/**31**:14,15/**32**:2:3:5^2:12:15/**33**:2:7:14^2:16:22/**34**:15,16:18^2/**35**:3:11:12/**36**:9:22,23/**Ez1**:1/**3**:3:6/**4**:7:13:15^2:16/**5**:8:16^2/**6**:2:3:6:12/**8**:26,27^2:30/**9**:11/**10**:13/**Neh1**:11/**2**:4:5,6:7:17/**3**:1:14:15^2/**4**:3:5:10/**5**:7:12:19/**6**:5,6:7:11:16/**7**:5/**8**:10:12:14/**9**:5:6/**10**:1:31:35/**12**:46/**13**:18/**Est1**:1:5/**2**:15:22/**3**:3,4^2:8:9:10/**4**:4:8:16/**5**:3:4:6^2:14/**6**:4:14/**7**:2^3:3:9^2/**8**:2:5:6:8^2:8f:9,10:13/**9**:1:12^2:13:19:27:28:32/**Job3**:4:5^2:6:8:8f:9^2:10:20,21/**4**:7,8:13:16/**6**:5,6,7^3:15-18:25,26:30/**7**:4:21/**8**:11-13^3:15/**9**:7:21:22:32,33/**10**:2:3:4-7/**11**:16/**12**:6:7,8,9:11:23^3/**14**:7:8,9:20,21^2/**15**:3/**16**:5:6:18/**18**:5/**19**:4/**20**:12:13^2:15:16:29/**21**:15:17/**22**:3^2:4:5/**23**:15/**24**:11:22,23/**27**:6:14:21/**28**:13^2:14:15:17:18:19:20^2:21^2:22:23,24:27^3/**29**:16/**31**:12:14:21:28:36:38,39/**32**:8,9^2/**33**:8^2:32/**34**:24/**35**:2,3:6:13:14,15/**36**:21:27/**37**:3/**38**:17,18:19:21:22,23^2:34:35^2/**39**:27/**40**:11/**41**:8:9^2/**42**:3^2/**Ps7**:3:5:13/**9**:4/**15**^{2}/**18**:8f/**19**:3,4/**22**:8:27/**24**:2f/**25**:20/**27**:11/**28**:4/**29**:5,6^3:8:9/**32**/**33**:1:9:16,17^2/**34**:14/**35**:17:21:22/**37**:5:8:16:21:24:35,36/**38**:19/**39**:9f/**40**:6:9/**41**:8/**44**:1:5:21/**46**:5/**48**:8:11/**49**:8,9^2:14:20f/**50**:9:12^2/**51**:3:4^2:16:17/**52**:6:9f/**53**:1/**54**:6/**55**:12^2:13/**56**:7/**57**:6/**58**:9/**60**:2^3:4,5f:4,5,6,7/**64**:8/**65**:9:11,12/**66**:19/**68**:9,10/**72**:17/**73**:10:14:16^2/**74**:7:9:10,23/**75**:8/**76**:10/**77**:16^2/**78**:36/**81**:10^2/**82**:8/**84**:6/**85**:12/**86**:17/**88**:10/**89**:37:47/**91**:8/**92**:1/**96**/**98**:2,3:7/**102**:3,4/**103**:8/**104**:5:28^2/**105**:14/**107**:42/**108**:5/**109**:6:27^2/**111**:6/**112**/**118**:8:9:23:24/**119**:33,34:71,72:81:90,91:106^2:116:126:128:130/**124**:1/**126**/**127**:2/**131**:1/**132**:2-5:6f:7:14/**133**:1/**139**:4:14^2:17,18/**141**:5^3/**145**:15/**147**:1/**Pro1**:7,8,9:15:17:28/**3**:11,12:13,14,15:18/**5**:6/**6**:3:4^2:29:31^2/**7**:1^2:23/**8**:8:9:11:33/**10**:13:22/**11**:8:11:17:24,25^2:26/**12**:9/**13**:12f:13:14:16:19:24/**14**:6:10:30:33^2/**15**:16:17:23/**16**:3:5:12:14:22:25:26^2:32^2:33/**17**:8:12:14^3:16:18:23:27,28/**18**:5:16:19/**19**:2:3:10:22/**20**:1:3:5:7:16:21:25/**21**:9:15/**22**:6:14:15:17,18,19^3:20,21/**23**:1:6,7,8:29,30:32^2:33^2/**24**:8:11,12:21,22,23:26:30,31/**25**:2,3:6,7:12:16^2:24:26:27^2/**26**:2:27^2/**27**:2:11:14/**28**:5/**29**:4:5,6:11:18:24:26/**30**:4:21,22,23:32/**31**:4:13:16/**Ecc1**:3-7:8-11^2:12-15^2/**2**:1^2:9:11:17:20-23^2:24-26/**3**:14:22/**4**:5,6^2:8^2:13:16/**5**:1:4:5^2:6,7:11^2:16:18:19,20^2/**6**:2^2:10/**7**:2^3:5:6^2:7:11:23:26/**8**:4^2:11/**9**:2,3:4:7:11:14^2:15/**10**:8,9:11:11f:12,13/**11**:3:5:6:7:9:10/**12**:2:7^2/**Sol1**:6/**2**:7f/**3**:4:7^2/**4**:10/**5**:5:9/**6**:5:12/**8**:6:7^3:12:13/**Is1**:18:31/**4**:2,3,4f:6/**5**:2:6^4:22/**6**:4^2:7:11/**7**:1:11f:20/**8**:1:2:7,8:14,15:16^2:20/**9**:7:8,9,10/**10**:2:7:15^2:18:23:25:27/**11**:8:15/**13**:4:9:21/**14**:17:19^2:24:26/**16**:12/**17**:1^2:6:11^4/**20**:1/**21**:2:6,7/**22**:9,10,11:25^3/**23**:1:9:13^3/**24**:1:20^2/**25**:8/**26**:6:9/**27**^{2}/**28**:13^2:17^4:23,24:27^2:28/**29**:3^3:9:11:12:17/**30**:5:8:9:13:26:33^2/**31**:4,5/**34**:1:5:6:8:11:12:13:16^2:17^2/**35**:8^2/**36**:6:10:11/**37**:3:14:18:23^2:26^2:29:30^2:35/**38**:1:8:10:12:13:17^2:20:21/**40**:5:7:20:22/**41**:4:7:20^2:23/**42**:5:9:20:21^2:24:25/**43**:12^2:18:19/**44**:6^2:12:13^2:15:17^3:19^3:24:26:28/**45**:9^2:12:14:23/**46**:6^2:7^6:11/**47**/**48**:1:5^2:6:13:15/**49**:4:5:8,9/**50**:2/**51**:10:22/**52**:6:11^2:14,15/**53**:1:4:8:10/**54**:15^2/**55**:11^5/**56**:5:12/**57**:4:11^2/**58**:3:13:14/**59**:8:9:10/**60**:22^2/**62**:9^2/**63**:1:3/**64**/**65**:9:21,22^3/**66**:3^3:6:12:19f:20/**Jer1**:12:12f/**2**:6:7:19:22:23:30/**3**:4,5,9^2:19:21:23/**4**:18:20:28:30:31/**5**:19:22:31/**6**:4^2:10:11^2:17:18,19^4:29/**7**:2:13,14:22:30:31^2/**8**:12:16/**9**:12/**10**:2,3,4^3:5^4:13:14:19:23:24/**11**:1:5^2:7:8:17^2/**12**:3:11:13/**13**:1^3:2:4:5:7^4:10:16:22/**14**:18/**15**:9:14:15/**16**:18/**17**:8:9:16:21,22,24/**18**:4:8/**19**:1:3:9:12^2/**20**:8:9:17/**21**:10^2/**22**:8:16/**23**:10:12:15:20:29/**24**:4,5/**25**:15:16:17:28/**26**:15^2:21/**27**:2:8:16/**28**:9:10/**29**:1:26:29/**30**:3:7:15:18:23:24/**31**:8:10:18:28:32:34:40/**32**:6,7:8:20:23^2:24:25:28:31^2:36/**33**:9:10,11/**34**:2:15:22^3/**36**:7:21^2:22:23:29^2/**37**:7:8/**38**:6^3:27/**39**:1^2:16/**40**:2,3,9/**42**:6:18:20^2/**44**:15:19:22^2:25:26:27:28/**45**:5/**46**:8^2:10:14^2:20,21/**47**:2:7^2/**48**:1:8:20:29:39:44/**49**:2:20:33/**50**:35:39^3:41/**51**:1:14:61,62:63^2/**52**:3:4:7:17:20:27/**Lam1**:12:21/**2**:6:16:17^2/**3**:12:22:26:27:28:38:42:53/**4**:8:11:13/**Eze1**:4:13:22^2:26:27,28/**2**:9,10^2/**3**:3^3:13:17/**4**:1^3:3:12^3:16^2/**5**:1:2^3:3:15:17/**7**:7:8,9^2:19^3:20^2:21:22:25/**8**:4:17/**9**:3:9/**10**:17f/**11**:3:5:7^3:7f:15/**12**:10:13:18:23:25:28/**13**:10^2:11^2:12^2:13^2:14:15:18:19:22/**14**:9:16^2:22:23/**15**:7/**16**:14:16:19^2:20:28:40,41:54/**17**:3,4:5^2:6:8:9^3:10^4:12,13:22,23:24^2/**18**:4:13:25:28:29/**19**:11:14/**20**:5,6:9,10:12:14:29^2:46:47:48/**21**:5^2:7:9,10,11:13:14:15^2:19,20:27^2:28:31:32/**24**:4:6:6f:7:8:11:12:13:14^3/**26**:5:8:14/**27**:10^2/**28**:18:21^2/**29**:3:9:10:11:16^2/**30**:12^3:18:21^2:25/**31**:1f:4:5^2:7:8^2:9^2:14/**32**:12:15/**33**:4:24:32/**34**:18:24/**36**:5:17:22^2:25:32:36^2/**37**:16^2/**38**:2,3f/**39**:7:8:11:12:13:21:23:27/**40**:6:18:20:23:25^2:26^2:27^2:28:28f:29,30:31^3:32^3:33:37:47:48,49/**41**:3:5:7^2:19,20:21/**42**:16-20^2/**43**:3^2:11:12:13:15:17:18^2:20^2:21:22:26/**44**:1:2^3:5:20:24:25/**45**:1^2:4:5:7:12:19:21/**46**:14,15:16:17:18:19,20/

(IT Con't)

47:5^2:8:14:15f:18/48:8:11:12^2:13:14^2:19/**Dan1**:9:11/2:1:4:5^3:6:7:16:23:26:30:34:40:41,42:44^3:45/3:1:14/4:3:7:10,11:12:14:18:19:23:24/5:7:8:15:26/6:8^3:10:12:15:17:21:27/7:1:4^4:5^2:6^3:7^4:8:14:23^3:26/8:3:4^3:5:13:22:24:27/9:1:15:18:23:25/10:1/11:5:15:16:24:27:28:29/12:1:4^2:6:10/**Hos1**:8:16f/4:3:6:8:9/5:6/6:1/7:4:6:9/8:3:5:6^2:7^2:13/9:4^2:7:12/10:1:9/11:3:11/12:8/13:1/14:9/**Joe1**:3:6/2:2^2:3:11/3:13/**Amo1**:3:6:9:10:11:12:13:14/2:1:2:4:6:8f/3:1:4^2:5:8:10:12^2:13/4:3:5:6/5:8:23/6:8/7:3:4:5:7^2:10/8:8^2:12/9:4:5^2:6:11:12/**Ob1**:5:12:15:16/**Jon**:2:9,10:11:12:13:14/2:10/3:3^2:10/4:2:4:7:9^3:10^2/**Mic1**:11/2:2^2:10^2/3:12/4:2/6:8:14/7:1^2/**Nah1**:12/3:14:16:19/**Hab1**:6/2:2:3:5/3:8,9/**Zep1**:2:14:15^2:18/3:8:17,18/**Hag1**:1^2:2:3,4:6:7:8:9^3/2:3^4:7f:8,9:12:13/**Zec1**:5,6:12:17/2:2:9:11,12/3:7:9/4:4:7:7f^2:9/5:2:3:4:6^2:9/6:6:14/7:7:14/8:6:9:11:17/9:5/10:6/11:10:13:13f/14:5:7/**Mal1**:2,3:4:8:12^2:13/2:4:8:14:17/3:10^3:14,15^2/**Mt1**:19/2:9f/3:14:15/4:3:7:9/5:12:13:15,16:17:25:29^3:30^2:35:38:41/6:2:3:10:16/7:14:25^2:27/8:8,9^3/9:5,6:13:29:30/10:13^2:20^2:29:39^3/11:12f:23:25:26^2:29,30/12:1:2:10:11^2:12:35:42:43,44,45^3/13:2,3:4:19:20:23:28:31,32:33:34,35:40:46:47,48:49/14:4:11:12:15:28/15:11:22:26^2:27:31/16:18:25^2/17:5:18:20:25:26,27/18:6:8^2:9^2:13^2:14:15:17:19:26:29/19:4:8:10^2:23:24^2:27/20:14^2:15:16:23:25:26/21:2:13:19:21:25:33:38:44/22:1:3:12:17:20:21^2/23:3:20^2:21^2/24:14:23:24:26:37,38/25:12:15:16:22:24,25:28:40^2/26:7:8,9^2:23:26^5:27^3:28:29:31:39:42:60,61:62:65,66:70:72/27:1:6:7^2:29:30:34:40:48^2:58:59:60:65:66/28:2:12,13:14:17/**Mk2**:9,10,11:16:21/3:2:4^2:9:20:29:30/4:3:4^3:5,6:8:15:18:21:29:30:31,32^2:37/5:7,8:11:16:32^2:35:41,42/6:11^2:16:17,18:21:22,23:27:28^2:29:35,36:37:49:50:51/7:11:20:24:27^2:36/8:17^2:32:35^2/9:3:10^2:18^2:42:43,44:45,46:47:50^2/10:4:5:6,7:24^2:25:27:36:42:43:46:50/11:4,5:11:13^2:14:17^2:20:24:31/12:1:11:14:16:17^2:33:36/13:33/14:2:3:4,5:20:22^4:23^3:25f:35:47f:68:70/15:2:6:16,17:23:25:26:29,30:36^2:46^2/16:9:18/**Lk1**:3^2:19:57:66/2:10/3:11/4:4:8:17^2:20:39/5:4:17:22:23,24:31:36/6:4^2:7:9^2:10:22:30:37:39:44:47,48^2:49/7:4:6,7,8:14:18:32^2/8:5^3:16^2:21:36:45:46/9:5^2:8:24^2:25:34:39^2/10:5:6:21:26:27:40:42^2/11:8:9:20:21:24^3:26:28:31:33^2:51:52^2/12:2:19:20:25^2:29:32:47:50:55:58/13:6:7^2:8^3:9:14:16^2:18:19^2:20,21^2:24,25:33/14:3:5:15:17:18:30:35/15:3,4:5:8:22:32/16:5,6:7:8:9f^2:15:17/17:5:6^2:21:23:24^2:28:30:33^2:35,36/18:22:24:25:26:43/19:15:20:23:24:26:30:33:42^2:46/20:5:9:14:17:18:22:24:31:41/21:13f/22:16^2:17^2:19^4:22:25:51:55:57:71/23:3:17,f:31f:39^2:44:53^2:55:56/24:4:11:16:25:26:29:30^2:31:36:38:39:43:46/**Jn1**:5:8:20:34/2:4:7,8:9:13:18:19:20^2/3:8^3:17^2/4:20^2:33:37:53/5:2:4:9:15:25:30:45/6:7^2:32:40:45:48-51:53:63f/7:2:4:6^2:7^2:8:21,22,23:26:46:49:51/8:5:16:43:44:45:47:54^2:55/9:2:5:9:11:14:15^2:21:27:33/10:7:17:18^2:22,23:34,35,36^2/11:4:9:37,38:42:45:46:51^2:52/12:3:5:7:11:17:22:25^2:28:29:35^2:42:47/13:1:7:13^2:16:19:21:24:25:26:26f^2:26^2:27^2/14:11^2:12,13:14:17:24/15:7:13:16:18^2:19^2:24/16:7:12:21:32/17:14/18:6:18:23:27:31f:34:34f/19:2:11:14:20:21:22^2:23,24^2:29:30^2:31:38/20:1:14:25/21:1:7:9:12/**Act1**:3:9:16:20/2:2:6:15:21/3:13/4:3:4:5:10^2:16:17/5:2:4^2:38:39/7:23:26:31^2:41:42:44:47^2:48,49:53f/8:2f:30/9:18/10:3:9,10:15:21:28:46,47/11:9^2:10:17:26/12:9^2:13:15:22/13:15:23:32,33:37:41:46^3/15:25:27,28,29^2:31/16:10:18:28/17:23:24:28/18:15^3:24:25,26^2/19:15:24:34:40/20:1:10,11,12:24:35/21:3:11:14:28/22:8:25:28/23:19:21:29:34/24:10:11:21f/25:19:27/26:5^2:6:7:8^2:14f:31/27:4:9:9f:9:13:14,15^2:25:35:39:44/28:4:8:11^2:19:20:28,29/**Rom1**:3:16^2:17^2:21:28/2:12-15^3:19:22^2/3:5:8:13:17:20^2:21,22:26:27:28/4:1:4,5^5:9:10:11:12:13:16:20:24/5:4:13:14/6:15:19/7:3:4^2:7:13^5:17^2:19:20:21:23,24,25^2:23,24,25f/8:7^2:10:12:13^2:24:25:26:35/9:1:10-13:20:26/10:2:8:10:16:18:19/11:5:6^4:8:12^2:13:15^4:23:25:28^2:33/12:4,5^4:8^2:16:19/13:1:7:10^2:11/14:2:3:5:6:11:14^3:15:20^3:22^2:23^3/15:1:17/**1Co1**:18:21:22^2:28:30:31/2:7:8:14:16/3:6^2:10:13:18:19:20/4:4:20/5:1:2:6:12^2/6:1^2:7^2:13:18:20/7:1:2:4^2:9:10:15:18^2:19^2:21:26:27:28^2:34:36^2/8:4:7:8^2:9:10^4:11^2:12:13/9:7:9^2:11:13:14:16:18:22:25:27^4/10:13^2:16^2:23^3:25:26:27^3:28:29:30:31/11:6:13:16:17:18:20:23:24^4:25:29:32/12:3:4:5:6:10:11:12:15:16:18:19:26:27/13:2^2:3:5^3:6/14:2:5:7f:20:22:33:35:39/15:1^3:2^3:10^2:11^2:21:29:31:32:34:36^2:37^2:38^2:52:57:58/16:2^2:4:6:12:14/**2Co1**:8:10:15,16:21:24/2:1:2:4^2:5,6:7:15:17/3:3:10:11:14/4:1:2:3:6:10^2:12/5:4:11^2:13,14^3/6:3/7:8^2:9^3:10:11^2:14/8:3:6:8^3:10:12:13:14:21/9:2^2:3:5^2:8:9:10/10:3:15:18/11:4:6:8,9:10:12:15^2:21/12:5:6:10:14:15:19^2/13:1/**Gal1**:9:16:18/2:2:11:19/3:1:4^2:5:8,9:11^3:13:15:16^2:17:18:20:24/4:3:9:15f:17:18^2:22/5:3:8^2:9/6:1:7:12:15/**Eph1**:19/2:8:9:10/3:5:7:8:11:13:18,19^3/4:9:12^2:26:28/5:8^2:12:13:23:26f:29,30:32:33/6:13/**Php1**:5:7:18:28/2:1:9/3:1^2:3^2:4:8:10^2:11:15:18/4:4:12:19/**Col1**:6^2:17:20:23^2:26,27^2:29/2:14^2:20:23/3:9^2:17:24/4:2:4^2:16/**1Th1**:5:6:8/2:4:6:13^3:19^2/3:1:4/4:13/5:21^3/**2Th1**:3/2:7:10^3/3:1^3:8:9:17/**1Ti1**:15^2:19/2:12:14/3:1:16/4:2:3:4^2:5^2:9,10^2/5:14:18:22:24^2/6:1:10:19:20/**2Ti1**:9^2:12/2:9:11:19^3/3:1:15:16:17/4:2^3:7:16/**Tit1**:3:9:10:11/2:7/3:8:9:11/**Phm1**:6:8,9^2:14:15:18:19^2/**Heb**:5,6/2:10:17:18/3:17/4:2^4:4:12/5:8:9:12,13/6:7^2:8:16^2:18/7:2:12,13,14:18^2:19/8:7^2:9/9:1:4:8:12^3:16:17^2:22:23:24:27/10:4:26:29:31:32/11:1^3:4^2:13:20:22^2:24,25:26:27^2:28:29:30:32/12:6^2:8^2:11^2:15^2:17:20:25/13:2:9:17:18:22/**Jas1**:4:5:10,11:13^2:18^2:19:21^2:22:25^2/2:6:8:9:14:17^3:21:23:26^2/3:1^2:4:5:6:8:9^2:17^4/4:1:2^4:3:4:5:11^2:14^2:17/5:3:11:12:13:18^2/**1Pe1**:3:4:5^2:7^4:10^2:12^3:22:23^2:24/2:2,3f^2:6:8:10:15^2:20/3:9:11^2:14:15:17:19/4:11:13:16:17/5:2^2/**2Pe1**:1:20,21/2:21:22/3:4:5,6:9:10:12/**1Jn1**:9/2:7^2:8^2:15:17:19/3:1:2:7:8^2:14:18:20/4:1^3:2:6^2:8:10:18/5:6,7,8:10:11:17f/**2Jn1**:8:12/**3Jn**:13/**Jud**:16/**Rev**:2:3^2:7f:7:9:10/2:17/3:3/4:2^2:6/5:2:3:4:9:12/6:3:9:10:17/7:4-8/8:5:11/9:1f:2:16f/10:3:4:6^2:7:9^5:10^5/11:2:18^2/12:4:10/13:1:7f:15^2:18/14:2:10:14/15:2/16:6:8:12:17:17f/18:7:21/20:11/21:2:6:11:16^4:22:23^2:24:26:27/22:6,7:11

5342

IT'S

Gen3:2,3/16:5/27:19:32/29:26/43:18/**Ex18**:17/23:9/32:18/**Num14**:41/**Jos7**:3/**Ju6**:23/18:14/19:9:11:20/**Ru2**:6/3:9:12/**1Sa9**:26,27/15:15:26/22:15/**2Sa13**:20^2/15:3/**1Ki12**:28/18:17/20:40/21:2/22:18:36,37/**2Ki4**:23:41/5:12/6/**Job5**:26/14:7/28:14/41:9/**Ps**:8/**Pro17**:21/**Ecc6**:9/8:2,3/11:9/**Is29**:11/41:7/44:19/49:20/55:1/**Jer2**:36/6:14/22:23/40:5/**Dan2**:30/**Mic**:6/**Zec8**:9/**Mal1**:13/**Mt9**:12/17:4/21:11/27:6/**Mk2**:24/6:50/10:23:52/11:24/**Lk6**:2/13:7/**Jn4**:21-24/5:10/11:22/**Act2**:15/12:11/**1Co1**:23/10/13:11/**2Co10**:10/12:14:16/**Heb5**:11

81

ITS

Gen2:15:16,17^2/3:18/17:9,10/22:13/27:17/31:44/36:40-43/37:31/49:9/**Ex6**:4/7:19/12:46/13:10f/16:21/19:12/21:28:36/22:30:31/23:4:5:19/25:31:39/29:10:12:15,16:19,20:31/30:10:26,27^2:28^2/31:8^2:9^2/33:8/34:20^2:26/35:10-19^7:21/36:11,12:24:27/37:3:17:25/38:8/39:20:33-40^3/40:9:10:11:18/**Lev1**:4:8:11:15,16,17/3:2:7,8:13^2/4:4:16:24:33/5:8^3/6:30/7:2:3:15/8:7:8:9:11:14:17:18:22:23/10:18/11:2,3:40^2/13:55/14:25:45/16:15:21/17:14/22:23:26,27/26:20:34,35:42:43/27:14,15:16:27:31/**Num1**:50:52/2:1^2:3-31:34/3:25-30^2/4:25/7:1/10:14:21:22/20:8/24:20/28:15/29:16:19:22:24:33/31:51,52/32:42/34:4/**Deu3**:12:23,24,25/4:34/13:15/14:21/20:6:11^2/21:4/22:1:3:4^2:8/24:6/32:22^2:49/33:16/**Jos3**:13,14/6:2^2/7:14^2/10:1:2:12:13:28:30:37:39/11:10:23/13:11:15^2:15f:24:24f:29:29f/15:47^2/18:4/19:10^2:17-23^3:24,25,26:32:33:40:41-46:47,48/**Ju1**:8:16:17/2:15/5:4/8:27f/9:45/12:1/18:30/**1Sa5**:9:11/6:2/17:35:50,51/19:13/**2Sa7**:23/12:26,27/15:9f/19:35/20:8,9,10/**1Ki4**:25/6:20:32/7:12:26:31^2/8:7/15:22/16:24/20:27/**2Ki1**:1/8:22/13:14f/14:7:13/15:16/16:10/17:21/18:8/19:32/22:15,16:18,19/23:30/25:13:16:21/**1Ch2**:23/6:55,56,57/7:28^4/10:4/12:15:24-37/15:2:15/18:1:2/21:22:27/23:26/28:11:15/**2Ch3**:1/5:2:7,8/7:21/25:22/26:6/29:18^2/32:21/34:24:27:28/35:12/**Ez2**:70/3:3/4:12:15/6:6/**Neh2**:17/3:1:15^2/4:6/11:25-30^4:31-35/**Est1**:1/3:12/5:2/**Job3**:5:10/9:6:26/14:8,9^2/15:27,28/26:12/28:3,4:18/31:22:34:38,39/36:20:32/37:21/38:5:6,7^2:20^2/39:18/**Ps7**:14/19:6/32:9/60:2/68:9,10/75:3^2/77:16/78:7:51:55^2/81:6/85:12/98:7/104:7,8/105:16/106:9/119/137:5,6/140:5/145:4/147:16/**Pro7**:23/9:12/12:13/13:23/14:27/16:33/24:30,31/26:2:9:14/27:8/28:2/30:18,19/**Ecc3**:11:18/6:5/8:1/11:5/**Sol2**:13f/3:10^2/4:16^2/7:7:8/8:10f/**Is4**:2,3,4^2:5/5:14/6:4/7:8:14f^2/8:7,8/13:11:13/14:15:17/16:13,14/19:19/21:17/23:11:13/24:1:4,5:11:12/26:5/28:25/29:16/30:24/34:5:10:11:12:13:15/35:9/37:25:33^2/40:16:19:26/43:17/45:9/49:8,9/54:9/66:13/**Jer1**:15:18/2:7:10,11:30/7:28/12:10:11/13:10/17:8^3/18:10:16/21:10^2:14/22:7:13^2/25:8,9/31:13/34:18,19/35:1f/46:5:22,23/48:1:45/49:1/51:41:42/**Lam2**:2/4:1:11/**Eze3**:1/7:8,9/9:7/13:12:15/17:7:9^2:22,23/19:11:12:14f^2/20:29/21:5^2:9,10,11:28:30/24:13/25:2/31:2,3:4:5:6^3:7:14/36:30/38:8/40:24:28:29,30^2:33:34^2:37:38:48,49/41:1:3:12:13:15,16:22/43:10^2:11^2:13:20/45:7/47:1:9/48:23:27,28:30,31:32/**Dan2**:32^2:33^2:35:36/4:12^4:14^4:15:21^3/6:10/7:4:5^2:6:7^3:10:11^3:19^2/8:4^2:5:8:21/9:26/**Hos1**:9:21,22/5:14/**Joe2**:3/3:13/**Amo**:4/8:8/9:5:11/**Jon4**:6:11:11f:11/**Mic1**:11f^3/7:13f/**Nah1**:5/**Hab3**:8,9f:10:10f/**Zep2**:13:15f/**Zec1**:8/3:9f/**Mt**:7f/5:18/7:13^2:16/12:33/18:7/21:2/24:21:34/**Mk6**:11/9:50/11:7/13:28^2/**Lk5**:3/8:11/9:5/10:10/11:2:25/12:30/13:19/14:34/16:17:26/19:35/21:20/**Jn1**:17/10:10/11:37,38/16:8/**Act2**:24/10:11/11:5/12:10:22/16:26/19:27/**Rom6**:7^2:12/7:1:13:20/8:13:20,21/**1Co3**:13/5:8/7:31/10:11/13:5/**Gal3**:21,22/**Eph4**:15,16/5:23/**Col1**:16^2/3:9/**1Ti5**:16/**Tit1**:5/3:1/**Heb1**:8/13:4/**Jas1**:10,11/3:8/**1Pe2**:15/4:1/**2Pe2**:20/**Rev**:5/5:9/6:2:4:5:8/10:6/12:16/13:1/14:7/16:8/19:12/21:15:16^2:22f:24:25

652

LET

Gen1:3:4,5:6:6f:9,10:11,12:14,15:20^2:21,22:24:26:26f/9:23:26,27^2/11:7/12:19/13:8/16:5f/18:27:30:31:32/19:9:18,19,20^2:31/20:6/23:13^2/24:3:14:37:44:51/27:13/29:31/30:26:31,32:39,40/31:28:32/32:26^2/33:15/34:8:9,10:11/38:18:23/40:14/41:34,35:34,35f:34,35/42:4/43:3,4,5:9:10/44:9:18:26:33^2/46:30:34/48:11/49:21/**Ex1**:15,16:17:18/3:10:19:20/4:21:23:25,26/5:1:2^2:17/6:1^2:11/7:5:14:16/8:1:8:15:20:29:31,32/9:1:7:13:17:28:35/10:3:7:10:17:20:24:27:28/11:1:10/12:3,4:48/13:15:17,18/15:19/18:19,20:22:27/19:24/20:19/21:8:27/22:17:26/23:7:11^2:33/32:10/33:15/34:3/**Lev10**:6/13:45/14:7:53/16:22/19:17/21:10/25:1:9:36/26:28:34,35/**Num4**:17,18,19/5:21,22/6:5:11/7/10:35/11:15:31/12:12:14/13:30/14:17,18/20:17/21:22/22:13/23:7-10:27/24:14/26:55,56^2/30:5^2/31:15/32:5/36:6/**Deu2**:27/3:23,24,25:26/4:36^2/7:3:15/9:13,14/13:2/21:14/22:7/23:15,16/25:7/29:6:19/32:38/33:6:11:16/**Jos2**:12,13:15/5:6/6:10/7:7/8:6/9:20/10:12^2:19/20:4/22:22,23/**Ju1**:34/2:23/3:8/4:2,3/5:8:10/6:1:13:31:32:32f^2:39^2/7:2/8:2,3/9:15:41:54/10:14/11:37/13:1:8/15:1:5/16:30/19:3:25/21:1:22/**Ru2**:15/3:3:13:14/4:4/**1Sa3**:18/4:3/6:6:8/11:14/12:9/15:21/16:22/18:4:17/19/20:12/21:5:13/23:14,15/24:19/26:8:19:22/28/**2Sa1**:21^2/3/12:3:22/13:5:13:27/14:11:12:32^2/15:5:7,8:17,18:25,26:28/16:9:11/17:2,3/18:19:22:23/19:37^2/24:13:17/**1Ki2**:6:21/8:46/11:12,13:34/12:16,17/15:19/17:21/18:40/19:20/20:31^2:32/21:21/**2Ki1**:10:12/3:10/4:27/5:20/6:17:20/7:4:13/9:15/10:23:24:25/18:29:30/**1Ch11**:5,6/12:18:19/13:2:3/16:10:21:31^2:32^2:33/19:13/21:12:13:22/**2Ch6**:36:41^2/10:4:16/14:7:11/16:3/20:10/24:24/25:8/28:9/32:15/**Ez4**:2/5:5:12:15:17/6:6:12/9^2:13/10:14/**Neh2**:3f:7:17/6:10/9:28:32/10:30^2/13:25:27/**Est1**:8/2:2/3:8/5:14/9:13^2/**Job2**:3/3:2,3:4^2:5:7:8:8f:9^2:12/4:2/7:11^2:12:16:19/9:18:34/10:1:18^2:20,21/12:7,8,9/13:13:22/14:6/15:31^2/16:18/17:3,4/20:3:15/21:2,3:19:20^2/22:8/31:7,8^2:22^2:35^2:40/32:10:20:21,22/33:2:27:28:31/36:2:18^2/39:11/40:7:11:19/41:4:10/42:4/**Ps2**:3/5:10/7:2:5:15:16/9:19/10:13/13:4^2/16:11/22:23/24:2:7:9/25:2:20/27:12^2/30:1/31:16:17^2/33:1:8:22/34:2:3:11/35:3:8:19^2:24:25:26:27/36:8:11^2/37:33^2/39:13/41:11/43:3^2/46^2/51:2/55:15/56:7/57:8/58:7:7f:8/59:10:12,13:14,15/62:10,11/66:8/67:1/68:2:26/69:6^2:14:15:22:23:25:28:28f/70:2,3:4/71:1:20/72:8:19/74:9,10:21/76:11/79:8/80:2/83:4:11:12:17/89:33/90:16^2:17/94:1/95:2/96:9:11^2:12/97:1:7/98:6:7^2:8,9/99:1^2:3/102:15:24/103:22/104:35/105:14/106:5:41,42:48/107:22:32/109:6:7:8^2:12,13^2:28/115:2/116:15/118:2:3:4:7/119:8:10:22:31:48:75,76,77:78:79:116^2:122:175^2/121:3,4/124:1:6/125:5/135:1/137:5,6^2/140:6,7,8^2:9^2:10:11/141:4:5^2:8:10/143:8/144:6/145:4/148:5:8:9/149:4,5^2/150:6/**Pro3**:21/4/5:18:19^2:23/6:3:10:12,13:22:25/7:5:25^2/8:4,5^2/10:3^2/17:14/20:1/23:31/24:11,12:17:23/27:2/30:3:18,19f/31:6,7:31f/**Ecc3**:22/5:1:18/11:8^2/12:1:4/**Sol2**:7:14/3:4:5/4:16/7:11:12/8:13/**Is1**:16:19/2:3:5/4:1^2/5:5:6/7:11f/8:12/12:6/13:20/14:21/16:4,5^2/18:2:3:4/19:12/22:4^2:13/26:11/27:2/34:1/36:14:15^2:

(LET Con't)
18/**37**:4:10/**38**:5/**41**:21:22/**42**:12:24/**44**:7[2]/**45**:8[2]:22/**48**:11/**49**:24/**50**:8:10[2]/**52**:9/**55**:7[3]/**56**:3:12/**60**:1/**61**:10/**Jer2**:28/**6**:5:17/**7**:3:4:7:31/**8**:14/**9**:17,18:23:24/**12**:1/**13**:14/**15**:11:15:17,18:19[2]/**18**:21[4]:22:23/**19**:7/**20**:5:8:12:16/**22**:2/**23**:28[2]/**25**:34/**27**:18/**29**:8/**31**:6/**35**:15/**40**:4:5:15/**42**:12/**46**:16/**48**:26/**49**:11/**50**:5:14:16[2]:22:26:33/**51**:9:10/**Lam1**:17[2]/**2**:18/**3**:30:40:41/**4**:15/**Eze1**:24/**3**:10:27[3]/**6**:8/**7**:8,9/**14**:3/**17**:9[2]/**18**:12/**20**:25:26:37/**21**:15/**23**:24/**24**:10:16:17/**25**:4/**28**:18/**31**:14/**32**:16/**33**:25:30f/**34**:3:8/**36**:37,38/**39**:7:23/**43**:9/**44**:20/**Dan1**:13/**4**:15[2]:16:23[2]/**9**:17/**Hos1**:12/**5**:4/**6**:1:3/**7**:13/**11**:8/**13**:10/**14**:9[2]/**Joe2**:1[2]:13:14:17[2]:22/**3**:10:13/**Jon**:7:8:9/**Mic1**:2/**4**/**6**:1/**7**:14/**Hab1**:17/**2**:20/**Zep1**:12/**Zec3**:7/**11**:6/**Mal2**:9:16/**3**:10/**4**:2/**Mt5**:15,16[2]/**7**:4/**8**:21f:22/**11**:29,30/**12**:27/**13**:16:30:43/**14**:36/**16**:24/**18**:17f/**19**:12:14/**20**:21/**23**:8:13,14:37/**24**:4:15f/**26**:39/**27**:41,42,43/**Mk5**:18:37/**6**:56/**7**:15,16f:27f/**10**:14:29/**13**:5:35,36,37/**14**:6/**Lk5**:4/**6**:29:42/**8**:32:51/**9**:60:60f:61/**12**:36/**13**:34/**14**:9/**18**:16,17/**19**:38/**21**:8:21[2]:34,35[2]/**22**:34:67,68/**23**:22/**Jn3**:21/**6**/**7**:37/**11**:44:48:50/**12**:7/**14**:1/**15**:4/**18**:8:16/**21**:19/**Act1**:20[2]:21,22/**2**:23:27/**4**:10:21:28/**5**:40/**7**:42/**8**:19/**9**:25/**11**:5/**13**:16:35:40/**16**:35:37/**17**:7:8,9/**19**:30:38/**20**:26/**22**:5/**23**:22/**27**:3:14,15:32:42/**Rom1**:8:24:26[2]/**3**/**6**:12:13:19/**7**:2/**8**:5/**9**:4/**11**:9[2]:10[2]/**12**:1:21/**14**:4:15:18/**15**:11/**1Co1**:10:31/**3**:18:21f/**4**:19/**5**:6:8[2]/**6**:7/**7**:11:21:24:36/**9**:22[3]/**10**:12:30/**12**:31/**14**:1:35/**15**:1:32/**16**:7:11/**2Co4**:6/**7**:1/**8**:11/**10**:17/**11**:1:33/**12**:1[2]/**Gal1**:8[2]:9/**3**:2:24/**5**:21:25/**6**:4:9/**Eph4**:17,18:26/**5**:3[2]/**6**:22/**Php4**:5:8/**Col2**:7[2]:8:16:18/**3**:2:14:15:16:17/**4**:6/**1Th3**:10/**4**:1/**5**:8/**2Th2**:10/**1Ti**:12[2]/**4**[2]/**5**:16:18/**6**:1[2]/**2Ti1**:8/**2**:4/**Tit**:7:15/**Phm1**:22/**Heb**:5,6/**3**:7,8:11/**4**:14:16/**5**:7f/**6**:1[2]/**10**:20:22:24:25:35/**12**:1[2]:7:28/**13**:13/**Jas1**:4/**4**:8:9[3]/**5**/**1Pe4**:15/**5**:7/**2Pe3**:1/**1Jn**:7:18[2]/**4**:7/**3Jn1**:11/**Rev**:7/**2**:11:17:29/**3**:6:13:21:22/**13**:18/**14**:12/**19**:7/**20**/**22**:17

1071

LITERALLY

[3]**Gen1**:4,5f:6f:7,8f:13f:19f:23f:26f[2]:31f/**2**:24f/**4**:21f:22f/**5**:1f[2]:3,4,5f/**6**:1f/**7**:3f:16f/**8**:5f:13f:20f:21f/**9**:9,10,11f:24,25f/**11**:2f[2]/**12**:15f/**13**:5f:10f/**14**:12f/**15**:18f/**16**:5f/**18**:10f/**24**:9f:15,16f:22f:31f:37f:38f:48f:65f/**25**:17f:34f/**28**:2f[2]:12f:19f/**30**:27f/**31**:12f:35f:39f/**32**:1f:10f/**33**/**34**:20f/**35**:7f/**36**:2,3f:31-39f/**37**:3f:28f/**38**:9f/**42**:14f:19f/**43**:29f/**Ex1**:8f/**2**:25f/**3**:14f/**4**:10f:14f/**6**:8,9f:16f:19f/**11**:8f/**12**:9f:38f/**13**:1f:4,5f:10f/**16**:16f/**18**:5,6f:12f/**19**:22f/**20**:4f/**21**:19f:30f/**22**:16f[2]:20f/**23**:7f:19f:21f/**25**:16f:17f:18f:39f/**30**:10f:13f:22,23f/**33**:12f:17f:19f/**34**:5,6f:7f:13f:15f:19f/**38**:27f/**39**:26f,37f/**Lev1**:4f:6,7f:9f:15,16,17f/**2**:2f:9f:12f/**4**:15f:26f:31f:35f/**5**:15f/**6**:18f/**7**:12f:20f/**8**:24f:28f/**12**:5f/**13**:3f:25f:27f:34f:45f:55f/**15**:1f:32f/**16**:8f:10f:19f:22f:26f:29,30f/**17**:3,4f:7f:14f/**18**:4,5f:6f:10f:25f:28f/**19**:16f:20f:23f/**20**:3f:16f:20f:21f:22f/**21**:2,3f:14,15f/**22**:12f/**23**:5f:7f:17f:18f:23,24f:26,27f:33,34f/**24**:11f[2]:18f/**25**:9f:29f/**26**:4,5f:13f/**27**:25f:29f/**Num1**:1f:17,18,19f/**3**:2f:47,48f:50f/**5**:7f:15f/**6**:27f/**10**:5,6,7f:31f:33f/**11**:3f:8f:34f/**12**:1f/**15**:15,16f:31f:33f/**16**:6,7f:13f/**18**:17f:19f/**19**:17f/**20**:1f:8f:12f/**21**:8f:24f/**22**:22,23f/**29**:1f:6f:7f:12f/**31**:6f:36-40f/**33**:3,4f:38,39f/**34**:4f:5f/**Deu1**:1f/**5**:11f:22f/**11**:6f:21f/**16**:1f:3f/**20**:15f/**22**:9f:19f:28,29f:30f/**27**:1f:2,3,4f/**31**:2f/**32**:15f:32f/**33**:2f/**Jos3**:2,3,4f/**4**:19f/**5**:8,9f[2]/**7**:12f/**8**:32f/**11**:18f/**13**:15f:24f:29f/**14**:1f/**Ju1**:14f:24f/**3**:1f/**6**:16f:32f/**8**:2,3f:6f:16f:21f/**12**:4f/**16**:9f:27f/**17**:7,8f:9f:13f/**Ru1**:1f/**2**:14f:20f/**4**:1f:4f/**1Sa2**:18f:27f:28f/**3**:7f/**17**:18f:55f/**18**:25f/**19**:13f:24f/**20**:23f:30f[2]:41f/**21**:7f:9f/**25**:11f:37,38f/**2Sa6**:14f/**7**:5f/**8**:13f:18f[2]/**11**:2f:25f/**12**:11f:25f[2]/**13**:2f:12f/**15**:5f/**16**:21f/**18**:11f/**19**:35f/**20**:23f/**21**:19f/**22**:9f:32f/**23**:5f/**24**:3f:24f/**1Ki1**:31f/**6**:23-28f/**7**:24f/**10**:1f:3f/**12**:32,33f/**14**:10f/**15**:4f:6f:14f:15f/**18**:31f:32f/**19**:4f/**20**:9f/**21**:20f/**22**:27f/**2Ki1**:3f/**2**:19f/**3**:12f:25f/**4**:42f/**8**:21f/**9**:29f/**10**:13f/**12**:21f/**13**:14f/**16**:7f:10f/**17**:9f:17f:20f/**18**:8f/**19**:15f/**23**:9f/**1Ch2**:22f/**3**:5f/**6**:39-43f/**7**:35f:38f/**9**:32f/**11**:1f:22f/**12**:1f/**13**:5f:6f/**15**:20f:21f/**16**:3f:37f/**18**:16f/**19**:6f/**20**:3f/**21**:2f:25f/**22**:14f/**23**:13f/**24**:5f/**27**:23f:32f/**28**:2f/**2Ch2**:4f:6f/**3**:11,12,13f:16f/**6**:15f/**11**:17f/**16**:1f/**21**:9f/**22**:2f:11f/**31**:16f/**35**:21f/**Ez3**:6f/**6**:11f:15f:19f/**10**:9f/**Neh2**:3f/**3**:16f/**5**:13f/**8**:7,8f/**9**:1f:29f/**10**:34f/**11**:22,23f/**12**:47f/**Est1**:6f/**2**:15f:23f/**3**:10f:12f/**8**:1f/**Job1**:1f:5f:6f:20f/**2**:1f/**3**:4f:8f/**4**:3,4f:6f/**5**:8f/**9**:12f/**10**:4-7f/**15**:31f:33f/**23**:14f/**28**:11f/**36**:33f/**42**:13,14f/**Ps2**:1f[2]:2f:6f:7f/**3**:4f/**4**:1f/**6**:5f/**7**:9f:10f/**9**:2f:4f:11f:14f/**10**:4f/**11**:1f:3f/**16**:6f/**18**:8f:10f:12f:25f:34f/**19**:5f[2]/**22**:20f:23f:25f:26f/**23**:4f:5f/**24**:2f:5f/**28**:2f/**31**:4f:9,10f/**32**:3f:6f:11f[2]/**34**:1f/**35**:19f:24f:27f/**36**:6f:10f/**37**:17f:18f:34f/**38**:17f/**39**:9f/**40**:6f:9f:10f/**41**:3f/**42**:4,5f:7f/**43**:5f/**45**:9f:13f:14f/**47**:4f/**48**:2f:3f:10f:11f/**49**:8,9f:14f:20f/**50**:2f:3f:5f/**51**:7f:14,15f:16f:18f:19f/**52**:1f:7f:9f/**54**:1f:4f/**55**:9f/**58**:1f:10f/**60**:4,5f/**61**:6f/**62**:7f/**63**:11f/**64**:6f/**65**:5f/**66**:12f/**67**:4f/**68**:5f:11,12,13f:22f:30f/**69**:9f:13f:17f:22f:35f/**72**:15f[2]/**74**:2f:19f/**75**:4f/**77**:10f/**78**:43f:51f/**80**:3f:7f:10f:17f[2]/**81**:7f:9f:16f/**82**:1f:5f/**84**:9f:10f:11f/**85**:1f:10f/**87**:1f/**89**:5f:6f:7f:10f:19f:35,36f/**90**:4f:14f/**91**:6f:16f/**92**:1f:10f/**93**:1f/**94**:6,7f/**95**:3f/**96**:8f/**97**:12f/**104**:4f:30f/**105**:7f:14f/**106**:16f/**108**:9f/**110**:2f[2]:3f:4f/**112**:3f:9f/**115**:2f/**116**:10,11f:13f:15f/**118**:19f:22f:26f/**119**:7f:8f:17f:37f/**120**:4f/**121**:5f/**126**:4f/**127**:5f/**128**[2]/**132**:1f:6f:7f:13f:17f/**133**:3f/**135**:21f/**138**:1f:2f/**139**:17,18f/**141**:6,7f/**143**:1f/**144**:3f/**146**:10f/**150**:1f/**Pro1**:7,8,9f:19f/**2**:21f:22f/**3**:13,14,15f:22f/**4**:5f:24f/**5**:4f:11f:19f[2]/**7**:3f:14f[2]/**9**:17f[2]/**10**:6f:27f/**12**:11f/**13**:12f:25f/**15**:20f:26f:27f/**16**:11f:12f:27f:33f/**17**:11f:14f:16f/**18**:2f:10f:14f:18f/**19**:1f:7f/**20**:10f:19f:21f:23f:27f:29f/**21**:4f:18f:20f:31f/**22**:12f/**23**:1f:12f/**25**:13f:20f:23f/**26**:4,5f:21f/**27**:20f/**29**:19f/**30**:3f:18,19f:21,22,23f/**31**:31f/**Ecc1**:1f:3-7f/**2**:12f/**3**:15f/**5**:8f/**7**:26f/**10**:11f:15f/**11**:2f:4f/**Sol1**:6f:9f:10f/**2**:7f:12f:13f/**3**:7f/**4**:3f[2]:8f:13,14f/**6**:4f:7f:10f:12f:13f/**7**:2f:3f/**8**:2f:9f:10f[2]/**Is2**:2f:4f/**7**:11f:15,16f:18f:20f/**8**:1f:6f:9,10f/**10**:27f/**11**:1f:10f:15f[2]/**12**:4f/**14**:13f[2]/**18**:1f:2f/**19**:18f:23f/**20**:5,6f/**21**:5f:6,7f:11f/**22**:1f/**27**:9f/**28**:15f/**29**:1f:23f/**30**:7f/**42**:4f:19f/**45**:13f/**51**:9f/**53**:2f:10f/**54**:1f:15f/**57**:20f/**60**:9f:12f/**62**:6,7f/**63**:17f/**64**:6f/**65**:1f[2]:25f/**Jer2**:3f:15f/**4**:4f/**8**:16f/**13**:12f:19f/**16**:21f/**23**:20f:38,39f/**25**:12f/**29**:10f:24f/**30**/**31**:16f:22f:29f/**32**:2f/**36**:22f/**37**:21f/**49**:32f/**51**:20f/**Lam1**:19f/**2**:1f/**3**:9f/**4**:7f/**5**:15f/**Eze1**:1f:12f:16f:25f/**3**:12f:14,15f:25f/**4**:8f/**6**:11f/**9**:3f/**10**:1f:14f/**11**:3f:7f/**12**:10f:12f:13f/**13**:18f/**17**:5f/**18**:2f/**19**:14f/**20**:1f:25f[2]:29f:35,36f/**21**:2f:19,20f/**24**:6f/**26**:2f/**28**:18f[2]/**31**:15f/**32**:17f:27f/**33**:30f/**34**:29f/**36**:17f:26f/**38**:15,16f/**39**:2f/**41**:22f/**42**:16-20f/**43**:9f/**44**:23f/**46**:7f[3]/**48**:17f:35f/**Dan1**:3,4f:8f[2]/**3**:5f:7f:10f:25f/**4**:13f:19f:23f:34f/**5**:11f/**7**:12f:25f:27f/**8**:9f:10f[2]:14f:23f:24f:26f/**9**:24f/**10**:13f:20,21f/**11**:5f:6f:7f:14f:30,31f:38f/**12**:7f:13f/**Hos1**:11f:16f:21,22f/**3**:5f/**4**:12f/**5**:10f/**6**:3f/**12**/**Joe1**:6f/**3**:21f/**Jon1**:9,10f/**Mic**:7f/**5**:3f/**7**:13f/**Nah3**:4f/**Hab2**:2f/**3**:1f:3f:8,9f:10f/**Zep1**:7f/**2**:5f/**3**:9f/**Hag2**:7f/**Zec3**:2f:9f/**4**:7f/**6**:12f/**8**:8f:19f/**12**:11f/**13**:6f/**14**:5f[2]:16f:20f/**Mal3**:1f/**4**:5f/**Mt1**:17f:19f[2]/**2**:3f:9f/**3**:1f:2f:9f:15f/**5**:18f:20f:22f[3]:29f:38f/**6**:34f/**7**:12f:13f:22f:23f:29f/**8**:4f:15f:19f:20f:29f/**9**:1f:5,6f:15f:31f/**10**:23f/**11**:1f:10f:12f:18f:19f[2]/**12**:8f:10f:23f:24f:29f[2]:31,32f:39,40f:43,44,45f/**13**:19f:23f:37f:41f:52f/**14**:1f:3f/**15**:5,6f:11f:21f/**16**:13f:21f/**17**:4f:5f:10f:12f/**18**:6f:7f:11f:17f:24f/**19**:12f:28f[2]/**20**:2f:18f:28f/**21**:9f:23f:42f:43f:44f/**23**:2f:5f:39f/**24**:3f:15f[2]:17f:22f:24f:27f:29f[2]:30f:33f:36f:39f/**25**:1f:12f:24,25f:31f/**26**:2f:23f:24f:45f:49f:64f:69f/**27**:1f:3f:11f:17f:62f/**28**:9f:19f/**Mk1**:3f:4f:7f:22f/**2**:6f:9,10,11f:16f:25,26f:28f/**4**:33f/**6**:37f:52f/**7**:3f:15,16f:27f/**8**:11f:12f:21f:31f:32f:38f/**9**:9f:12,13f:19f:30,31f:39f:49f/**10**:1f:20f:33f:35f:45f:49f:52f/**11**:27,28f/**12**:13f:43,44f/**13**:14f:22f:26f:30f:32f:34f/**14**:21f[2]:24f:25f:35f:41f:44f:51,52f:62f/**16**:12f:17f/**Lk1**:1f:3f:17f:36f:80f/**2**:7f:11f:12f:14f:25f:38f/**3**:16f/**4**:4f:18,19f:39f/**5**:17f:23,24f:35f/**6**:5f:22f:37f/**7**:19f:23f:29f:32f:33f:34f:35f/**8**:30f/**9**:5f:7f:22f:26f:29f:44f:58f:59f:61f/**10**:4f:21f:29f:32f:33f:34f:35f:41f/**11**:15f:16f:21f:31f/**12**:3f:8f:10f:19f:40f/**14**:26f/**16**:8f:9f:22f:23f/**18**:8f/**19**:9,10f:47f/**21**:8f:13f:22f:23f:27f/**22**:10f:20f:22f:25f:28f:32f:40f:47f:69f/**23**:3f:14f:31f:46f:47f/**24**:6,7f:9f:18f:49f[2]/**Jn1**:1f[3]:11,12f:13f:14f[2]:19f:51f/**2**:4f:11f:18f/**3**:13f:25f/**5**:14f:17f/**6**:2-5f:7f:21f:27f:53f:62f:63f[2]/**7**:8f:49f/**8**:27f:28f:50f/**9**:34f:35f/**10**:42f/**12**:26f:31f:36f:38f:40f/**13**:23f[2]:25f:26f/**14**/**16**:5f:8f:26f:30f/**17**:12f/**18**:31f:34f/**19**:11f:13f:26f:27f:30f:35f:41f/**20**:1f:2f:3,4f[2]:10f/**21**:2f:5f:7f:15f:17f:21f:22f:23f/**Act1**:26f/**2**:4f:9f:23f:42f/**3**:21,22f:23f/**4**:11f:33f/**5**:9f:24f/**6**:8f:12f/**7**:2f[2]:12f:37f:53f:56f/**8**:2f:4f:9,10,11f:23f:33f/**9**:40f/**11**:28f/**13**:13f[2]:16f:32,33f:37f:45f:52f/**15**:16f:24f:27,28,29f:33f:36f/**16**:9f/**18**:21f:25,26f/**19**:8f:21f:35f/**20**:4f:7f/**21**:9f:20f:26,27f:34f:37,38f/**22**:14f/**23**:3f:8f:9f/**24**:1f[2]:21f:22f:24f/**26**:1f:4f:9f:14f:28f/**27**:2f[2]:4f:9f:17f:20f:41f/**28**:10f:20f/**Rom1**:10f:11,12f:13f:17f:19f:23f/**2**:7f:10f:22f:27f/**3**:13f:21,22f:25f:28f/**4**:5f:8f:25f/**5**:12f:17f/**6**:5f:14f/**7**:1f:6f:23,24,25f/**8**:10f:19f:22f:26f/**9**:17f:27f/**10**:10f:21f/**11**:32f/**13**:11f:12,13f/**14**:1f/**15**:27f/**1Co1**:2f/**3**:4f:21f/**5**:5f/**6**:12f/**7**:23f:29f:34f/**8**:6f:9f/**9**:5f[2]:25f/**10**:3,4f[2]/**11**:10f[2]/**14**:32f:34f/**15**:20f:40f:45f[2]/**2Co4**:4f/**5**:21f/**12**:2,3f[2]/**13**:7f:8f/**Gal2**:19f/**Eph**:5f:14f/**4**:10f:30f/**5**:26f/**Php2**:7f:8f/**Col1**:15f:18f/**2**:20f/**4**:10f/**1Th3**:13f/**2Th2**:7f/**1Ti**:2f/**3**:1f/**5**:9f/**2Ti1**:6f:13f/**3**:5f:16f/**4**:17f/**Tit1**:5f:7f/**Heb**:5,6f/**3**:13f/**5**:5f/**6**:2f:20f/**Jas1**:18f/**3**:1f/**1Pe4**:3f/**5**:13f/**2Pe2**:12f[2]/**3**:13f/**1Jn1**:9f[2]/**3**:20f/**5**:6,7,8f[3]/**Rev1**:1f:4f[2]:5f:8f[2]:13f:14f:16f:20f/**2**:1f[2]:8f:12f:15f:18f:22f/**3**:1f[2]:7f:8f:9f:14f[2]/**4**:5f/**5**:6f:9f:11f:12f/**6**:6f[2]:13f:14f/**7**:17f/**8**:8,9f:11f/**9**:1f:14f:16f/**11**:1f/**12**:14f/**13**:7f/**14**:4f:13f:14f:18f/**16**:7f:17f/**17**:8f[2]:11f/**18**:2f:3f:22f/**19**:2f:9f[2]:10f:13f/**20**:11f/**21**:17f:22f/**22**:2f

1461

MAY

Gen2:16,17/**3**:2,3/**8**:15,16/**9**:24,25:26,27:26,27f/**16**:2,3:5/**24**:60[2]/**27**:27,28,29[3]/**28**:2:4[2]/**30**:23,24[2]/**31**:35f:49/**42**:19/**43**:14/**44**:26/**48**:15:16[2]:20/**49**:6:25/**Ex5**:21/**12**:16:18:44:45:48/**13**:13/**19**:12/**20**:3:12:25/**21**:9:10:11:30/**23**:11/**25**:1/**28**:3/**29**:37f/**30**:29f/**33**:20[2]/**34**:25/**35**:5-9/**40**:15/**Lev1**:14/**2**:4:12/**3**:1:6/**6**:18:18f:18:27:29:30/**7**:6:16:19[2]:24/**10**:6:14/**11**:2,3:4-7:8:9:13-19:21,22:32:41,42:47[2]/**13**:42/**14**:35:54/**17**:12/**18**:7:11:15:17/**20**:25/**21**:4:14,15:16,17/**22**:4:7:8:10[2]:11[2]:12:13[2]:23/**25**:3:23:25:27:32:42:44:45:48:49/**27**:10[2]:13:26:27:29:29f:33/**Num3**:10/**4**:27/**6**:3,4:6,7:20:24,25,26[3]/**7**:4,5/**9**:10/**10**:11f/**16**:21:40/**18**:2,3:11:13:16:17:20:31:32/**28**:25/**29**:1:7/**30**:13/**31**:18[2]:24/**32**:22:23/**35**:28:31:32/**Deu1**:11/**3**:19:20/**4**:9:19/**5**:24/**6**:15/**9**:13,14/**11**:8/**12**:14[2]:15[2]:17:20-20-23[2]:26,27/**13**:16/**14**:3,4,5:6:7[2]:8[2]:9:11-18:19,20:21[2]:25/**15**:22[2]/**18**:10/**19**:2,3:5/**20**:14:20/**21**:13:14:16/**22**:19:28,29/**23**:2:3:8:20:24:25/**24**:1:4:14,15/**25**:1/**33**:6:13:14:16:25[2]/**Jos1**:14:15:17,18/**8**:2/**9**:25/**17**:15/**20**:3/**22**:22,23,24,25:26,27:29/**Ju5**:24:31[2]/**9**:19:20[2]/**16**:28/**Ru1**:8:9:17/**2**:12/**4**:11[2]:12:14:15/**1Sa1**:17:23/**3**:16,17/**14**:44/**17**:37/**20**:13[2]:23/**24**:15:19/**25**:6:22/**26**:19:24[2]/**2Sa2**:5:6/**3**:9,10:29:39/**7**:26:29/**10**:12/**11**/**14**:17:24/**15**:19,20/**18**:32/**19**:13/**24**:23/**1Ki1**:31:37[2]:46,47[2]/**2**:23,24:33[2]:44:45[2]/**6**:37/**8**:52:57[2]:58:59:60:61[2]/**18**:23/**20**:9:10:34/**2Ki5**:18[2]/**6**:31/**1Ch12**:17,**15**:2:12/**17**:24:27/**19**:13/**21**:12/**22**:11:12:16/**28**:8/**2Ch6**:20,21/**13**:10/**19**:11/**23**:5,6/**30**:2,3:13:15:17,18,19/**Ez1**:3[2]/**4**/**7**:13:18:20/**Neh2**:20/**4**:4[2]/**5**:13/**Job1**:12,13/**3**:5:6/**5**:3/**10**:20,21/**13**:13:15/**14**:5:8,9:20,21/**27**:16:17/**31**:10[2]/**33**:30/**34**:19:29,30/**35**:8[2]:9,10/**36**:33/**37**:7/**39**:15/**Ps6**:5f/**7**:16/**8**:2/**9**:9/**15**:1/**19**:14/**20**:1[2]:2:3:4:5[2]/**24**:3[2]/**30**:5/**40**:16[2]/**41**:5/**57**:11/**60**:4,5f/**67**:5/**68**:3[2]:15,16/**72**:3:5:6:7:16[2]/**80**/**86**:11/**90**:10/**97**:12/**104**:34/**109**:9,10[2]:11:12,13[2]:19/**112**:7/**115**:14/**119**:17f:43:75,76,77/**122**:6:7:9/**126**:4/**128**:5:6[2]/**129**:5:6,7:8/**132**:9/**Pro6**:2:26:31/**13**:23/**19**:3/**24**:18/**25**:8,9,10/**26**:10:23:24,25,26/**27**:18/**29**:19/**30**:9[2]/**31**:5/**Ecc5**:18[2]/**7**:21,22:26/**11**:2/**Sol6**:13/**7**:8/**8**:13/**Is4**:2,3,4f/**10**:30/**26**:2/**35**:8/**50**:4/**54**:10/**55**:7/**Jer6**:27/**7**:5/**18**:18/**23**:37/**28**:6/**42**:5/**51**:34,35[2]/**Eze4**:15/**12**:12f:13f/**16**:37/**24**:17:22/**37**:9/**40**:46/**44**:3:5:11[2]:13:21:22[2]:31/**46**:17:18/**Dan4**:17/**6**:16/**11**:21f:32f/**Hos4**:15/**9**:3:4[2]/**10**:12/**Joe1**:11[2]/**Zec8**:13[2]/**14**:21/**Mal2**:12/**3**:7/**Mt6**:10:19/**7**:21/**12**:5/**15**:5,6/**19**:7/**23**:3/**Mk10**:9/**16**:9f/**Lk1**:38/**6**:40/**11**:2/**12**:10:38/**16**:9f/**17**:37f/**21**:36/**Jn5**:14/**8**:7/**10**:26/**15**:7/**17**:26/**19**:35f/**Act4**:30/**9**:17/**21**:37,38/**26**:18[2]/**Rom1**:6,7/**2**:1/**3**:29/**11**:19/**14**:2:22/**15**:5:33/**16**:24/**1Co1**:3/**4**:15/**7**:6:14[3]:16:29f:39/**8**:10/**10**:12:23[2]:29:33/**12**:8:24/**14**:29,30/**15**:35:40f/**16**:23/**2Co1**:2:17/**2**:7/**10**:8/**13**:7f:11:14[2]/**Gal1**:3/**6**:16:18/**Eph1**:2/**2**:18/**3**:17:18,19:21/**5**:13/**6**:23:24/**Php1**:2:11:28/**2**:24/**Col1**:2/**2**:4:23/**4**:18/**1Th1**:1/**3**:10:11:12:13/**5**:23[2]:28/**2Th1**:2/**2**:16/**3**:5:14:16:18/**1Ti1**:2/**3**:10/**4**:4:15/**5**:22/**6**:3:21/**2Ti1**:2:16:18/**2**:7/**3**:1/**4**:22/**Tit1**:4/**3**:15/**Phm1**:3/**Heb2**:1/**4**[2]/**5**:7f/**7**:19/**9**:15/**10**:19/**12**:10/**13**:20,21[2]/**Jas2**:18/**5**:16/**1Pe1**:2/**2**:9/**1Jn1**:3/**2**:4:29/**5**:13/**3Jn1**:8/**Jud**:2/**Rev**:4

618

ME

Gen3:10:12[2]:13/**4**:10:14[4]:23[2]:24:25/**12**:11,12,13:18[2]:19/**14**:21/**15**:8/**16**:2,3:5[2]:5f:13:14/**17**:1:7,8:17[2]:20/**18**:13:27:30:31/**19**:18,19,20[4]/**20**:5:6:9,10[2]:11,12:13:16/**21**:6[2]:23[2]:26/**22**:12:16[2]:18/**23**:4:9:11:13[2]/**24**:7[2]:12:27:37:40:42:43:45:46:47:48:49[2]:54/**25**:30:31/**26**:9[2]:24:27/**27**:2,3,4[2]:8,9,10:11,12[3]:13:19[2]:25:26:31:32:34[2]:35:36:38[2]/

ME Con't)
8:20:21:22/29:15:18:21:27:32:33:34/30:1:6^2:13
16:18:20^2:23,24:26:27^2:30:31,32^2/31:5^2:7^2:9:11:
2:13:27:28:29^2:31:35f:36,37:39:42:51,52/32:9^2:
0^2:11^2:12:26^2/33:11:15/34:4:11^2:12:30/35:3:7
37:9:13,14/38:16:17/39:8:9:12:14,15:17/40:8:
4^3/41:10:15:24:52/42:20^2:33:34:36^2/43:6:7:8:9
16:29/44:18^3:29:33:34/45:5^2:7:8^2:9^2:10:11,12:
3^2/46:30:31/47:16:29^2:30^2/48:3^2:4:5:9^2:11:15:
6/49:1:2:4:29,30/50:5:19:20/Ex2:9:14/3:9:13:
4:15/4:1:10:23/5:1:22/6:12:30/7:16/8:1:9:20:
8/9:13/10:3^2:28/11:8:9/12:13:32:32f/13:1/17:
/18:15,16:19,20/19:5:9:23/20:3:5:6:24^2/22:23:
7:29:30/23:15:16:19/24:12/25:1:8:30/28:1:3/
0:30/31:12,13:17/32:2,3:10:23:24^2:26:32:32f:
3/33:12^3:12f:13^2:13f^2:17:20:21/34:2:15:16:20:
5/40:13:15/Lev6:2:17/10:3/14:35/19:7/20:3:5
6:25:26/22:32,33^3/23:1/26:14^2:18:21^2:27^2:
40,41^2/Num3:45^2/11:11^2:12:13:15^3:16/14:
10,11^2:22^2:24:26,27:29:34,35^2/16:28:29/18:11/
20:12:12f:12/22:5,6^2:8:11:13:18:28:29^2:33^2:34:
37:38/23:3,4^2:7-10^3:11:12:13:18-24:26/24:3-9^2:
13:14/27/28:1^2/Deu1:9:17:37^2:42/2:1:16,17:31
/3:1^2:23,24,25:26^2/4:5:10^3:14:21,22/5:5:7:9,10^2
22:23:28:29:31/6:1/9:10,11:12:13,14^2:16:19/10
1:4:5:11/18:15:17:19:20/20:3/25:7/26:2,3:10:
13:14/31:2:16:20/32:21:51/Jos2:12,13^2/5:14/7
19/8:31/10:4/14:6:9:10:12^3/15:18,19^2/24:7:15
/Ju1:7:15/3:28/4:8:19:20/5:30/6:17^2:36:37^2:39^2
/7:2/8:15:23,24/9:2:7:15^2:29:54/10:12:13/11:7^3
:9:27^2:35:37/12:3/13:6^2:7^2/14:3:13:16^3/15:3:11
:12,13^2:18/16:6:10^3:13^3:15^4:16,17:18:28^2:30/17:
10,11:13^2/20:5:7/Ru1:8^2:13:16:17:20^3:21^3/2:7:
10,11:13/3:9:10/4:4/1Sa1:8:11:26:27^2/2:1:16:
28:29^2:30^2:35:36/3:16,17^2/8:7:8/9:18:19:21/10:
2:8:18,19/12:3^2:5:12:23^2/13:11/14:12:42:43:44
/15:1:11:16:20:25:30^2:32/16:2:5:17/17:9:10^2:35
:37^2:43:45:58/18:8:23/19:3:17^2/20:1:2^2:4:7:8^3:
11:13:14:21:28,29/21:2^3:3:9:14,15/22:8^4:11,12:
13^3:15:17^2:23/23:7:11^2:12:21:23/24:9,10:12:15:
17:18^3:19:21/25:22:28:30,31:32:33:34^2:39/26:
5,6,7:8:17,18:19^3:24/27:1^2:12/28:9^2:11^2:12:15^3:
16:19:22/29:3/30:7:13:15^3/31:3,4^3/2Sa1:4:7^2:9:
26/2:7/3:8:9,10:13:14/4:9:10^2/5:19/6:21^2/7:5f:
7:13:19:25:27:28:29/9:8:10,11/10:2:11/11:6/12
:10:22:23:28/13:10^2:11:12:13:16^2/14:4:8:9:10:
11:12:13:15,16:19^2:22^2:32^4/15:4:7,8^2:25,26^2:28:
33,34:35,36^3/16:9:10:11^2:12/17:1/18:13:19:22:
23:29/19:13:19:22:24,25:26:27:28:33:37:38/20:
16:21/21:4/22:3:4:5^2:7:17^2:18^3:19:20^2:21:25:33:
35:36^2:40^3:44^3:45:48:49^3/23:2:3:5/24:13:17:24/
1Ki1:13:17:29/2:4:7:8^2:15^2:16:17:20:23,24^4:31/
3:7:9:14:20:24/5:5:6^2:9/8:29:59/9:4:6/10:7/11:
33/12:5:27/13:7:8:9:15:16,17^2:18^2:31/14:2:8:9^2
/15:19/17:11:13:18:19/18:9:12:37^2/19:10:11:14^2
:20/20:5,6:10:32:35:36:37:39:40/21:6:19:20:23:
29/22:14:18:24:28:34/2Ki2:1:4:6,7:9:10:20/3:
6,7,8^2:15/4:6:13:15,16:27:28:41/5:7:8:11^2:17^2:
18^2:22/6:19:31:32/8:4:8,9:10:13:14/9:15:18:19:
25/10:6^2:15^2:16/16:7f/18:20,21:27^2/19:5,6:27:
28/20:8^2/21:15/22:15,16:17^2:18,19/1Ch4:10^4/
10:4^2/12:17^2/14:10:11/17:6:12:16:17:18:19^2:25:
26/19:2,3:12^2/21:2:8:12^2:13:17:22:24/22:8^2:9/
28:3:4^3:5^2:6:19/2Ch1:7:8:9:10:11/2:7^2:8/6:42^2/
7:12:14:17:19/12:5:8/15:2/16:3/18:17:18:23:27
:29:33/20:15:20/25:19/28:11/29:4,5/32:13:15/
34:21:25:26:27/35:21^3:23/36:22,23^2/Ez1:2^2/4:
18/6:10/7:28^4/8:1/9:4/10:1:2/Neh1:2:6,7:9:11^2
/2:1:4^2:7^2:8^2:9:11,12/4:18:23/5:19/6:2^3:5,6:7:9:
12,13^3:14:19^2/7:5/8:9/12:40,41/13:22:31/Est4:
11:16/5:6:7,8:12:13/6:6^2/8:5/9:12/Job1:14,15:
21/2:3^2/3:10:12^2:25:26/4:2:12:14/6:4^2:10:11:14
:19-21:24:25,26:28/7:3:8^2:11^2:12:16:19:20^2:21/
9:2:18^2:20:28^2:29:31^2:34/10:1:2^2:3:4-7^2:8^2:9:10^2
:11:12^2:13,14^2:16^2:17^3:18^2:20,21/12:12/13:6:13:
15:15f:17:19^2:20:21^2:22^2:23^3:24^2:26:27,28^2/14:
13^3:14:16:17/16:7:8:9^2:10^2:11:12^4:13:14^2:20/17:
1:6:8:16/19:2^2:3:6^2:7:9:10:11^2:14^2:15:17:18:19^2:
21^2:22:25:28/20:3^2/21:2,3^2:5:6:28:34/23:6:10^3:
13:14:15:16,17^3/24:14,15:25/26:2/27:12/29:2:3
:5^2:6:8:11^2:13:20:21:23/30:1:10^2:11^2:12:13:14^2:
15:18:19:20:21^2:22^2:23:27/31:14:15:23:35^3:
38,39/32:10^2:13:14:18^2:20:21,22^3/33:2:4^2:5:7:
27:28:31^2:33/34:2:10:34,35/36:2/38:4:17,18:19
/40:7^2:8/41:10/42:3:4:7/Ps2:7/3:1^2:2:4:5:6:7/4:
1^4:3:7:8/5:1:7:8^4/6:1:2^2:3:4^2:8/7:1:2^4:5^2:6:7,8:10
/9:4:13^3:14^2/11:1/12:5/13:1:3^2:6/16:1:6f:7^3:10:
11/17:2:3:6:7:8^3:9:11^2:12:13,14:15/18:1:2^3:4^2:5:
6:16^3:17^2:18:19^2:20:24:32^2:33^2:34^2:35^3:38:39^2:
40:43,44,45^4:47^2:48^3:50^2/19:12:13^2/20:6/22:1^2:
7:9,10,11^4:13:15:16:20:21^3/23:2,3^3:4:4f:5^2:6/25:
2^2:4^2:5^3:6,7:15:16:17:19:20:21^2/26:1:2:9,10:11:
12/27:2:3^2:5^2:8:9^2:10^2:11:12^3:13^2/28:1^2:3:7/30:
1^2:2:3:6,7^4:9:10^2:11/31:1^2:2:3:4^2:5,6:8^2:9,10:11:
13:14,15^2:16:17:21^2:22^2/32:3:4:5:7^2/34:2:4^2:11/
35:1^2:2:3^2:4:7:9:11:12:15:16:17:18:19:21:22:23:
24:24f:24:26:27/36:11^2/38:1:2:12:15:17:19:20^2:
21:22/39:1:2,3:4^2:8^2:10:13^2/40:1:2^2:3^2:11:12^3:
13^2:14,15:17^2/41:4:6^2:9:10^2:11^2:12^2/42:3:7^2:8^2:
9:10/43:1:2:3^2:5/44:6/49:15^2/50:5f:5:14,15^2:23
/51:1:2^3:3:4:5:6:7:7f:7:8^2:10:11^2:12^2:13:14,15^2/
54:1^2:3:7/55:2^2:3^5:4^2:5:12:16:18^3:20:23/56:1^3:
3,4:5:6:8:9:10,11:13/57:2:3^3:6^2/59:1^3:2:4^2:10^3:
16/60:9,10/61:1:2:3:5:6:7/62:1:3,4^2:5:7/63:3:7:
9/64:3/66:16:20/69:1^2:4^2:6^2:8:9^2:10:11:13:14^4:
15^4:17^2:18^2:19^2:20^2:21^2:29/70:1:2,3^2:5/71:1:2^3:
3^2:4:6^2:8:9^2:14:15:17:18^2:20^2:21^2:23:24/73:2:23:
24^2:24f:28^2/74:12:19/75:9/77:2:7:11/81:7:8:10:
11:13^2/86:1:2^2:4:7:11^2:13^2:14^2:16:17^3/88:5:6:7^2:
8:14:16^2:17/89:24:26:35,36f:38:46:49:50:51/91:
7^2:9:10:14:15/92:4:10/94:16:17:18:19^2/95:9:10
/101:3^2/102:2^2:8^2:9,10^3:23:24/103:2:3:4^2/104:
25/106:4:5/108:6:10^2/109:2:3:4:20^2:21^3:25:26^2:
28^3/111:1/116:3:4:6:7:8:12:13f:13:16/118:5^2:6^2:
7^2:10:11^2:12^2:13^2:14:18^2:21/119:7:8^2:8f:10:11:
12:17:22:23:25:26:27:28:29,30^2:31:32:33,34:35:
36:37:38^2:40,41,42^3:48:49,50^3:51:56:61:64:66:
67:68:69:71,72^4:73:74:75,76,77^3:78:79:80:82:84:
85,86^3:87:94:95:98:100:102,103:104:105^2:107^2:
108:110:115:116^2:117:121:122^2:123:124^2:125:
132:133:134:135^2:143:144:145:146:149^2:150:
153:154^2:156:157:159:161:169:170:171:173:175^2
:176/120:1:2/121:3,4/129:2:3,4/130:2^2/132:11^2
:12/137:5,6/138:3^3:7^2:8^2/139:1:3^2:5:10^2:11:14:
16:17,18^2:17,18f:17,18:23:24^2/140:1^2:4^3:5^4:
6,7,8:9/141:1:3:4:5^3:6,7:8:9/142:3:4^3:5:6^2:7^2/
143:1f:2:3^3:7^2:8^3:9^2:10^2:11^2:12^2/144:1:2^3:7^2:11^2
/Pro1:23:26:28:30:32:33/2:1/4:4:10/5:1:7/6:10
:12,13/7:2:14f:24/8:4,5^2:6,7:17^3:21:22:32:34^3:35
:36^2/9:16/23:35/24:28,29/27:11/30:8^3:18,19/
Ecc1:16-18/2:7,8:9/9:13/Sol1:2:4^2:6^5:7/2:4^2:5:
6:10:14^2:17/3:3/4:8/5:2:7^2/6:5:8/8:1:2:3:6:13/
Is1:2:5,6:11:12,13:16:19:20:28/3:7/5:4/6:8:10/
7:9^2:11/8:1:2:3:5:9,10:18/12:1^2:2/14:28/18:4/
21:2:3:6,7:11/22:4^3:14:15,16/28:22:23,24/29:13
/30:1:2:15^2/31:4,5/32:9/36:5:10^2:16:20/37:
16,17:28/38:14:16^2:17^2:20:22^2/40:25/41:1:9:17
/42:6/43:4:7:8:10:12:20:21:22:23^2:24^4:26:27/44
:1:17:22:24/45:4:5:10:11:19:21:22:23/46:3:5:6:9
:12/47:10^2/48:1:11:12:16/49:1^3:2:3^2:5^4:6:16:21^3
:23/50:4^2:5:7:8^2:9^2/51:1:4:5^2:7/54:13:15/55:3/
57:6:7,8^3:11^3:13:20/58:4/59:21/60/61:1^3:2:10^4/
63:3:4/65:1^4:3:5^3:6:7:9:10:24^2/66:1:23:24/Jer1:
4:11:13:16/2:1:2^3:4,5^2:8^2:9:13:20:22:26,27:29:32
/3:1^2:4,5:6:7:8:10:12:13:19^2:20:22/4:1:2^2:17:19:
21:22/5:6:11:22:23,24^2/6:7:18,19:20^2/7:10:23/
8:19/9:3:6:24:25,26/10:20:24/11:4:5:9^2:10:14:
18^2:19/12:1^2:3:5:8:16:17/13:1:3:5:10:11:22:
24,25:27/14:10:11^2:12/15:1^2:6^2:7:10:12,13:15^3:
16^2:17,18^2:19/16:1:11:12:17/17:14:15:17:18^2:19
:24:27/18:3:10:15:19^2:20:22:23/19:4/20:7^2:8:10
:11^2:12:13:17/22:1:6:21/23:16:17:21:24:27:
38,39/24:1:3:7^2/25:2,3:6^2:7:8,9:15:17/26:4:12^2:
14^2:15^3/28:1:8/29:13^3:19/30:20:21/31:1:3:15:
18^3:32:33:34/32:8:27:30:31:32:33:39:40^2/33:3:8
:9^3:22/34:15:17/35:16:18,19/37:7:18:20/38:15^2
:19^2:24:26/39:18/40:4:10/42:9:20/44:8:10/45:3
/49:1:11:19^2:20/50:44^2/Lam1:12:13^2:14^2:16:20:
21:22/3:2:3^2:4:5^2:6:7^2:9:10:11^3:12:14:15^2:16^2:18
:19:52:53:56:57:59^2:60:61:62/Eze1:1:4:27,28^2/2
:1:2^2:3^2:9,10/3:1:7:12:12f:14,15^3:16:22:24^3/4:16
/6:9/7:1/8:3^3:5:6:7:12:14:16:17/9:9:11/11:1^3:5^2
:12:24:25/12:1:2:8:17:21/13:1:2,3:19/14:1^2:2:3:
5:6,7:11:12:13:22/15:1/16:15:17:20:43:59,60/
17:1:11:20/18:1:25/20:1:2:8:12:13:14:21:27,28:
31:38:39:40^2:41:45:49/21:1:7:8:18/22:12:23/23:
1:4,5^2:35^2:37:39/24:1:8:15:18:20,21/25:1/26/
27:1/28:11:20/29:1:6:17:20/30/31:1/32:17/33:
1:7:21:22^2:23/34:1/36:5:16:17/37:1^2:3:4:7:9:10:
11:15/38:1/40:2^3:4:5:6:24:28:32:35:45:48,49/41
:1:4:22/42:1:13:15/43:1:5^2:6^2:7:18/44:1:2:4:5:7:
10:13:15^2:16:19/46:19,20^2:21,22^2/47:1:2:3^2:4:6^2
:8/48:11/Dan1:10/2:1^2:5:6:8,9^3:16:23:24:26:30
/4:2:5:6:9:18^4:19:27:36^2/5:7:15:16/6:22/7:16:
23/8:15:17:18^2/9:19:21:22/10:2:5,6:7:8:9:10^2:
11:13:18:19:20,21/Hos1:2^2:8:13:15:16:19:20^2/3
:1/4:6^2:7:10:12:15/5:3:15^2/6:6/7:7:13^2:15:16/8:
2:11:13/9:10/11:5:7:8:9:12/13:4:6/Joe2:12^2/3:
4/Amo4:1:6:8:9:11/5:4:21:25,26,27/7:1:3:4:7:8:
15^2/8:1/9:7:12/Jon1:2:12^2/2:2^2:3:4^2:5:6/4:2:3:9
/Mic2:3:8/3:9/5:15/6:1:3^3/7:1:7^3:8:9^4:10^2/Hab
1:3/2:2:4/3:16:19^2/Zep:7:10:11/Hag2:14:16,17
/Zec1:4:9:10:13:20/2:1:3:8:9:11,12/3:1:8/4:1^2:
14/5:3:5/6:8/7:1:5:6:11:13/8:1:6:14,15:18:
20,21/10:9:12/11:4:8:12:13:15:16/Mal1:6:12/2
:1:3:5:6^2:9/3:1:5:7:8^3:9:10:13/Mt2:8/4:9:19/7:4
:21:22/8:2:21f:22/10:18:22:32:33:37^2:38:39:40^3
/11:4:6:10^2:27:28:29,30/12:30^2:31,32/13:16/14
:28:30:31/15:8:22:25:32/16:23^2:24:25:28/17:4:
17:22,23/18:5^2:6:21:26:32/19:14:17^2:21:29/20:
18:19:32,33/22:19/23:37:39/24:30/25:22:24,25
:31:32:35^3:36^2:40:42^2:43^3:45/26:10:11:12:15:
20,21:23f:31:34:38:39:40:46:55^2:64:75/27:10:46
/28:10/Mk1:17:40/2:14/3:28/4:40/5:7,8^2:36/6
:22,23/8:27:33:34:38/9:19:24:37^3:39:39f:42/10:
14:18:21:29^2:33^2:34^4:47:48:51/11:24:30/12:15/
13:13:26:35,36,37/14:18^2:20:27:30:34:36:37:38:
48:49^2:62:72/15:34/Lk1:3:19:20:43:44^2:48:49/2
:29,30,31/4:6,7:18,19^3:23/5:12/6:42:46^2:47,48/
7:23:23f:44:45:47/8:28^2:45:46^2:50/9:23^2:26:44:
48^3:59f:61/10:16^4:40/11:7:18:23^3:29,30/12:8:9:
10:13:14:50:52:53/13:16:34:35/14:26:26f:27:33
/15:19:29^2/16:2:4/17:10:22:23/18:4,5^2:13:
16,17:19:22:31:38:39/19:22:27/20:24/21:27:
34,35/22:19:21:22:28:28f:29:32:34^3:37^2:41,42:
52:53:61:67,68^2/23:14:28:31:42:43/24:39:44:47
/Jn1:30:33^2:43:51/3:10,11:12:15/4:10:15:20:
28,29:34:39:48/5:7^2:11^2:24:30:32,33^2:34:36^2:37:
38:39:40:41,42:43:46^2:47/6:26^2:27:35^2:36:37^2:
38:39:44^3:45:47:56:57^3:62:64:65^2/7:6:7:16:19^2:
28:29:33:34^2:37:38/8:12:14:15:16^2:18:19:21:26:
28:29^3:37:40:42^2:46^2:49^2:50^2:51:54/9:4:11/10:8:
14:15:17:18^2:25:26:27:28:29^2:32:37:38^2/11:15:
25:26:41:42^2/12:26^2:27:32:40:44:45^2:46:47^2:48:
50/13:13:18^2:19:20^3:21:24:26:31^2:32:33^2:36^2:38^2
/14:1:2,3:6:9:10^3:11^2:12,13:15,16^2:20:21^3:23^2:24^3
:26:28^2:29:30:31/15:4^3:5^2:6:7:9:10:14:15:16:18:
20^2:21^2:23:24:25:26:27^2/16:3:5:5f:9:10:14^2:16^2:
20^2:23:27:32^2/17:4:6^2:8^2:9:10:11:12f:12:18:20:
21^2:22:23^3:24^4:25:26/18:11:21^2:34f:39^2/19:10:
11^2:26:27/20:2:15:17:21:29^2/21:15:16:19:22/
Act1:8/2:25^3:26:28^2:34/3:21,22:21,22f/4:10/7:
7:28:37:37f:42/8:19:24^2:31/9:4:11:16:17/10:28^2
:29:30:31/11:11:12^2/12:8:11^2/13:16:22/15:7:13
/18:10/20:22:23:24:25:26:34/22:1:5:6:7^2:8:9:10:
13^2:14:17,18:21:27:28/23:3:11:18^2:19:22/24:4:
10:13:18^2:19:20/25:9:10,11^2:14:15^2:26/26:7:13:
14^2:18:21^2:22:28/27:21:23/28:18^2:27/Rom1:8/
3:7/7:2:7:8^2:10:11^2:14:17^2:20:23,24,25^7/8:2/9:1
:20/10:16/11:4:13:19/14:11/15:15,16:17^2:18:19
:24:29:30^2/16:1:4:6:7:10:11^2:13^2:19/1Co1:11:17
/3:10/4:3:4:15:19/6:12f:12^2/7:10:12:25/9:2:16^2
:17^3:22^2/10:33/11:18:22:24:25/12:31/14:6:11^3/
15:1:3:10^3:12/16:4:6:7:9:11:17:18^2:20/2Co1:1:
13,14^3:15,16:21:23/2:2:3:5,6:9:10:12:13/6:2:12^2
/7:4^2:7^2:11:14^2:16/8:19:24/9:4:5/10:7/11:1^3:7:
8,9^2:16:17:24:27:32/12:1^2:2,3:6:7:8:11^3:13^2:15:
21/13:3:10/Gal1:12^2:15^2:16^2:24/2:6:7,8,9^2:20^3/
3:2:8,9:24/4:12:14^4:15:17:19:21/5:2:21/6:14^2:
17^2/Eph3:2,3^2:7^2:13/4:17,18/6:19^2/Php1:12:15
:16,17^4:19^2:20:21:22:23:26:27:30/2:1^2:2:18:19^2:
22^2:23:25:27^2:28:30/3:9:12^2:15/4:3:8:9^2:10:13^2:
14:17:18:21^2/Col1:25:29/2:1/4:7:10:11:18/1Th:
1/5:26/2Th2:1/3:17/1Ti1:2:12^2:13:14:16^2/5/
2Ti1:8:11:15:16^3:17:18/2:2/3:10:11^2/4:7:8^3:10:
11:14:16:17^3:18^2:19/Tit1:3/3:12/Phm1:13^2:16:
17:18:19^2:20:22^2/Heb:13/2/3:10/4:3/5:7f/8:11
/9:20/10:5:30/13:6:24,25/Jas2:5/1Pe4:15/2Pe
1:13,14/2:9/3:1/3Jn1:3^2:9:10:15/Rev:10:12:
17,18/2:3:4:5:13^2:22:26:27/3:3:4:10:18^3:20^2:21/
4:1/5:5/6:2/7:13:14/9:17,18/10:4:8:9:10:11/14:
13/15:2/16:15/17:1^2:3/19:9/21:5:8^2:9^2:10:17/
22:1:6,7:8:10:12

3981

MINE

Gen14:24/16:2,3:5/18:12/21:30/25:33/30:3:13
/31:8:36,37:43^2/Ex13:1/19:5/25:9/34:19/Lev
20:26/25:23/Num3:11,12:13:41^2:45/8:14:16:17
/Deu32:35/2Sa14:30/24:10/1Ki2:15/3:20:22^2:
26/20:2,3/22:4:30/2Ki23:27/2Ch7:20/13:8/
Job28:1:3,4/41:11/Ps9:6/16:5/50:10,11:12/54:
4/55:20/60:6,7/71:13/72:6/73:26/105:15/108:
8/119:57/Pro4:20/8:18/Sol2:16/6:3/Is8:20/27
:4,5/29:13/30:8/41/43:1/44:2/51:16/55:8/56:3
/66:2/Jer3:7/11:4/15:10:11/17:16/23:21:22/
27:5/Eze16:8/18:4/29:3:10/35:11/36:32/43:8/
Hos1:9^2:11/Joe3:17/Zec8:14,15/Mal3:17/Mt7
:23/10:37^2:38/16:24/18:5:20/20:23/24:9/26:39
/Mk10:40/13:13/14:36/Lk3:16/4:6,7/6:22/11:
5,6/15:24/19:27/21:17/22:41,42/Jn12:30/16:
15/17:10/Act20:34/Rom8:2/2Co2:3/Gal4:15/
Php3:17/2Ti1:3/Heb10:5/1Jn2:26/Rev3:5:9

127

My

Gen4:13:14:23/6:3/9:13^2:15:16,17/12:11,12,13^2
/14:21^2:24/15:2,3^2/16:6:8/17:13:14:19:21/18:
12:17/19:2^2:8:18,19,20^2:34/20:5^2:9,10:11,12^2:
13^2:15/21:10:12:23^3:30/22:8/23:4:9:11:13/24:3
:4^2:7^3:8:12^3:14:24:27^2:35:36^3:37:38f:40^3:42^2:44:
47:48^2:48f:48:49^2:54:56^3:65:65f/26:5:7:24/27:1:
2,3,4:11,12^2:18:20^2:25:26:27,28,29:34:36^2:38:41
/28:21^2/29:14:18:21^2:32^3:34/30:3:6:8:11:15^2:16
:18^2:20:23,24:26^2:30:31,32:33/31:5:11:26:28:30:
35:36,37:41:42^4:43^2:50/32:5:9^3:11^2:12:30/33:5:
8:11:12:15/34:8:11:12/35:3^3:18^2/37:7:9:16:33:
35/38:17:25:26^2/39:8:14,15:18/40:9,10:11:15:
16^2/41:9:13:24:33:52/42:28^2:36:37:38/43:29/
44:5:16:17:27^2:30:32:34/45:3:9:11,12^2:13:28/47
:1^2:5,6:9:29:30/48:5:9:15^2:16^2:19:22^2/49:3^2:4:6:
29,30:32/50:5/Ex1:18/3:7:10:15:16:20/4:10f:18^2
:22/5:1/6:2,3:5:6:7:8,9:12/7:1:3:4:5^2/8:1:20:23/
9:13:16:17^2:27^2:29/10:1:3:16:17/11:9/15:2^5:9/
16:4/17:9:15,16/18:4^3/19:5^2:10/20:6^2:22:25/21
:5^3:14/22:23:24:31/23:21:21f:21:22:23/25:22^2/
28:41/29:43:44/30:31/31:12,13/32:8:10:33:34/
33:12:16:17:19^2:19f:20:22^2:23^3/34:11:27/40:15/
Lev4:2/14:35/15:31/17:10:12/18:4,5:26:29,30/
19:1:19:30^2:37/20:3:3f:3:5:6:8:22/21:12:23/22:1
:31:32,33/25:17,18:23:42:55/26:2^2:3:9:12:15:17:
23:25:28:42:43^2:44:45/Num6:27:27f/9:2,3/10:
30/11:12:23:29/12:7,8^2/14:20,21:22:24/16:28/
19:1/20:18:24/22:5,6:18:30/23:7-10:11/24:3-9:
10:13:14/25:10,11^2/27:14^2/28:1/Deu4:10/5:
9,10:11:12:29:31/9:15:17/10:10/18:18/22:16/
25:7/26:2,3^2:5:13:14/29:19/31:17^2:19:20:27:29
/32:2:21:22:23:27:34^2:39:40,41^7/33:17/Jos1:2^2:
6/2:9:12,13^2/7:10,11:19:21/14:8/23:3/24:5:15/
Ju1:7:12/2:1:22/4:18/5:21/6:15/7:18/8:19:
23,24/9:11:15:17/11:7:35:37/12:3/13:11:18/14
:12:16^2:18^2/15:7/16:13:16,17^4:25,26:28/17:
10,11/18:24^2/19:20:23^2:24/20:5/Ru1:12:13:16^2
/2:8,9^2/3:1:9:11/4:6:6f:10/1Sa1:11^2:15,16:27/2
:1^2:27:28^2:29:30:32:35/3:6:16,17/9:5:16:17:21/
10:2/12:5:23/13:11/14:24,25:39:41/15:2:21:25:
30/16:22/17:34:58/18:17:18:21^2:25/19:3:17/20
:8:9:12:13:14:15/21:2:5:14,15/22:8^2:15:23^2/23:
17^2/24:7,8:9,10^2:11^2:15^2:21^2/25:8:11^4:21:24:28:
33/26:17,18^2:19^2:20:21^2:23:24^2:25/27:1:5/28:2:
21/29:6:9/30:13:15:23/2Sa1:9:10:26/2:7/3:8:
13:14:18:28/4:9/5:20/6:21/7:5:6:7:8:10,11^2:14:
15:16:25:26:29/9:7/11:11/13:4:10:11:13:25:26:
28/14:5,6:7^2:9:11:15,16^3:18:31/15:27/16:3:9:11
/18:5:12:18:20:22:31:33^5/19:4^3:11,12^3:13^2:19:
26^3:28:29:35:37^2/20:6:8,9,10/22:2^3:3^7:4:7^2:19^2:
21^2:22:29^2:33:37:38:39:41:44:45:47^2:49/23:2:5^2:
5f^2:17/24:3f:17:24/1Ki1:13^2:17^2:20:21:24:30:31
:33^2:35:48^2/2:4^2:5^2:15:17^2:20:22:23,24:26:31:32:
43:44/3:6:7^2:11:14:20^2:21^2/5:4:5^2:6:9^2/6:11,12/
8:15:16^3:17:19:20:24:28^2:29:59:61/9:2,3:6:7^2:13
/10:6/11:11:12,13:32:33^2:34^3:36:38^3/12:5:10:11^2
:23,24/13:6:7:27:30:31/14:8^2/16:2^2/17:8,9:12:
18^2:20:21/18:5:7:9:12/19:2:4:4f:16:20/20:4:5,6:
7:9:32:34^2/21:3:20/22:4^2:26/2Ki1:13/2:12^2/3:
6,7,8/4:24:29/5:3:6:12:15:16:18^2:20:22/6:11:15:
26-30^3/9:7^2:21:32/10:6:9,10:30/13:14^2/14:9:10
/16:15/18:19:23:24:27:29:35/19:21:23:29:30:31
:32:34^2/20:5:6^2:15:19/21:7:14/22:17/23:27/
1Ch4:10/11:2/12:17/14:11/16:22^2/17:4^2:5:6:7^2
:9:13^2:14:16:17:23:24:27/21:17^2:23/22:5:8:10^2:
11/28:2^3:3:4^2:5:6^2:7:9:20/29:1:2:3^2:4,5:14:17:19
/2Ch1:8:9:11/2:4:7:8:13:14/6:4:5,6^4:7:10:15:16:
19^3:20,21:40/7:14:16^3:20/9:5:6/10:8,9:10^3:11:
14^2/12:7/16:3/18:3,4,5:16:25/25:16:18:19/29:
11/32:10:15:17/33:8/34:25^2:27/Ez1:2/6:8:10/7
:13:14:28/9:3^2:5^2:6^2/Neh1:2:5:6,7:9:11/2:3:4:
5,6:7^2:10:11,12^3:14,15:16:18^2/4:23/5:13f:14:16:
17:19/6:8:11:14/7:2/13:14:19:22:29:31/Est4:16
/5:7,8^3/6:10/7:2:3^2:4:8/8:6/Job1:5:8:21/2:3/3:
2,3:10:24/4:12:15^2/5:8:8f:27/6:2:4:5,6,7:11:12:
15-18:19-21:29/7:5^2:6:7:11^2:13,14:16:20^2:21/9:
16^2:17:20:25:26:27^2:30:31/10:1:13,14/12:4:11^2/
13:6^2:14^2:15:15f:16:18:23:24:26/14:14/15:17-19
/16:4^2:6:7:8:9:10^2:13:16^2:17:18^2:19^2:20^2/17:3,4:
6:7^2:11^3:13,14^3:15:16/19:5:8^2:9^2:12:13^2:14^2:15^2:
16:17:19:20:21:22:23,24:25:26f:27/20:3/21:4/
23:2^3:4,5:7:12/24:1/26:2:3/27:2^2:4^2:5:6:7/29:4^2:
5:6:7:8:14:18:19:20:21:22/30:1:10:11:12:13^2:15:
16^2:17^2:18:24:27:28,29:30^2/31:1:7,8^2:10:13:15:
19,20:22^2:24:25:27^2:31:32:33:34^2:35^4:37:38,39/
32:10:17:19:20/33:8:11:12/35:9,10/36:3/37:1/
38:2/40:4^2:8/42:7:8^3/Ps2:6^2:6f:7/3:3^4:7/4:1f:1^2:
2/5:1^2:3:8/6:2:3:5:6:7^2:8:9^2:10/7:1^2:5^2:6:7,8:10/
9:1:3:4/13:2^2:3^2:4/14/16:2:5^4:6/17:1:5:9:15/18:
2^3:3:6^2:9:10:14:16:17:23:24:28^3:35:36:37:38:39^2:
48:50/19:12:14^3/22:1^3:6:9,10,11^2:14^3:15^3:16:17:
18:19^2:20:20f^2:22:24:25/23:1:2,3:5:5f^2:6/25:2:
6,7:11:15:17:18^3:20:21/26:2:3:6^2/27:1^2:3:4:6:7:8^3
:9^3:10/28:1:2^2:6:7^3/30:1:2^2:6,7^2:9^2:11^2:12/31:1:
2^2:3^2:4:4f:5,6:7^2:8:9,10^6:9,10f:11^2:13^2:14,15^2:22
/32:3^2:4:5^2:7/34:1f:4/35:3^2:7:10:14:19:23:24^2:
26/37:25/38:3,4^4:5,6^3:7^2:8f:9^2:10^2:11^3:12^2:15:18
:19:22/39:4:5,6^3:7:8:9^2:12^4:13/40:1:2:5:6:6f:8^2:
10:11:12^3:17^3/41:4:5:6:9:11/42:3:4,5:9^2:11^3/43:
2^2:4^3:5:5f:5/44:4^2:6:8:15,16/45:1/49:15/50:5^2:7^2
:8:16^2:17^2:23/51:1:3:5:8:9:14,15^2:18:19/53:4/54
:2:3:4:4f:5:6:7^2/55:1:2:3:4:13^2:23/56:3,4:6:8:9:
13/57:6^2:7:8/59:1^2:3:9^2:10^3:11:16^2:17^4/60:8^2/
61:1:2:3^2:5:8/62:2^2:3,4^3:6^2:7^2:8/63:1:4/64:1^2:3/
66:13:17:18:19/68:24/69:1:3^3:5:8:9:11^2:13:16:
18:20^2:21:29:30^2/70:1:2,3:5/71:1:2^2:5:7^2:9^2:10:
17/73:2:13:21:23:24:26^3/74:12/77:2:6^2:10:12/
78:1^2/81:8:11:13^2:14/83:13/84:3^2:8:10/86:1:6^2:
11:12/87:4:7/88:1:2^2:3:4:8:9^2:13:14:15/89:3,4:
20^2:24:26^3:27:28:30,31,32:33^2:34:37/91:2^3:7:9:
14:16/92:11:15/94:16:19^2:21,22^2/95:9^2:10/101:
2:6^3:7:8/102:1^2:2:3,4^5:5:8:9,10^2:11:23:24/103:1:
3:5^2/104:1:33:34/105:15/108:1:8^2:9f^2/109:1:20:
24:26/110:1^2/111/116:8^2:10,11:10,11f:16/118:
5:7:13:14:19:21:27,28^2/119:10:11:15:18:19:24^2:
26:28:37:40,41,42:43:48:49,50^2:52^2:54^2:55:58:
62:63:66:69:73:75,76,77:78:82:88:92:93:95:98^2:
99:107^2:108:109:111:113:114^3:117:121:123:139:
143:153:154:156:157:159:169:170:174/120:1:
5,6:7/121:2/122:8^2/123:1/129:2:3,4/131:2/132
:1:11^2:12:14/137:5,6^2/138:1:7:8/139:1:2:5:7:13^2
:16:22:23^2/140:6,7,8^3/141:2^2:3^2:4:8/142:1:3:5:6^2
/143:1^2:3:7:8:9:10:12/144:1:2^4:7:12-15/145:1/
146:2/Pro1:25:30/2:1/3^2/4:3^2:5f:10:13/5:1:12:
15/7:1^2:2:6:14f:16,17:19/8:8:9:10:14,15:16:19:
20:32:33:34^2/16:5/20:9/23:15,16^2:19,20,21:
26,27,28^2/24:13,14:21,22/27:11/30:8/31:2/Ecc
1:2:16-18^2/2:3^2:4,5,6:7,8^2:10^2:15:18:19:20-23^3/
7:23:27,28/8:15:16,17/12:12:13/Sol1:6^2:6f:8:9f:
9:12:13^2:14:15/2:2:3:6:7:8:9:10^3:13^2:14:16:17/3:
1^2:4^2:5/4:1:7:8:9^3:10^2:11:12^2:16^2/5:1^9:2^6:3:4^2:5^2
:6^2:7:8:10:16^2/6:3^2:4^2:9^2:12:12f^2/7:10:11:12:13/
8:1:2:2f:3:10f:10:12^2:13:14/Is1:3:4:5,6:12,13:21:
24^2/3:12:15/5:1:4:5:9:29/6:5:7:8:9^3/7:13/8:3:6:
7,8:17:21/10:4^2:5,6^2:7:24:25/11:9/12:2^2/13:3:
12:13/14:6:25^2:26^2:30^2/15:5/16:9:11/18:3/19:
25^2/20:3/21:4^2:6,7:8,9:10/22:4:20:22:23,24/24:
15,16/25:1/26:20/27:3:4,5^2:11/28:19/29:18:22:
23f:23/30:1:10,11:19/31:6/32:18/33:10:13:14/
34:1:5/36:8,9^2:12:18:20/37:21:22:24:35^2/38:7:
10^2:11:12^2:14:15^2:17:20^2/39:4:8/40:1:25/41:8^2:
10:10f:25/42:1^3:6^3:6f:8^3:19:19f:19^2/43:6:7:10^2:
12^2:19:20^2:21:22^2:23:25:26:27/44:1^2:2:3^2:8:17:
19^2:20:21:26:28/45:4^2:11:12:13^3:23^2:24/46:11:
13^2/47:6:7:8^2/48:1:3:5^2:6:9^3:11^4:12^2:13^2:18/49:
1^2:2:3:4^3:5:6:8,9:11:12:14:16:21/50:1:4:6^3:7:8:9/
51:4:5:6^2:7:8^2:16^2:22/52:4:5^2:6^2:13:14,15/53:11
/54:8:9:10^2:11/55:4:8:9^2:11/56:2:3:5^2:7^3:8:9:10/
57:13:14:16:21/58:1:2/59:21^2/60:1:7^2:10^2:13^2:
21/61:8/62:1:10:11/63:3^5:4:6:8/65:2^2:3:6:9:10:
12:13:15:16:18:19:21,22^2:25/66:1^2:2^2:4:5:18:19^3
:20:21:22^2/Jer1:5:9^2:10:12:12f:16/2:3:7:10,11:
13:20^2:21:30:31^2:32/3:4,5:12:15:19:22/4:2:4:17:
19^4:22:27:28^3:31/5:7:9:22:23,24:26:31/6:9:13:
15^2:18,19^4:21:26:27/7:10:11:12^2:13,14:18:20^3:
22:23:25:30^2:33/8:2:7:11:18^2:19:21/9:1^2:9:13^3/
10:18:19^3:20^3:21/11:7:13:15^2/12:3:7^3:8:9:10:13:
16^3/13:11^2:17^2/14:10^2:14:15:17^3/15:1:6:7:10:14
:16^2:17,18:19/16:5^4:11:16^2:18:19^2:21/17:1:4:14:
16:17/18:6:10:13:15:17^2:22/20:8:9^2:10:12:13:15
:17^3:18/21:10:12/22:5:24,25f:24,25/23:1^2:2:3:9:
11:13:16^2:22:25:27:28^2:29:32^2:36:38,39/24:7/25
:8,9:14^2:15^2:27:29/26:5/27:6:15/29:9:19:21:23^2:
32/30:3:7:10:19:21:22/31:1:2:3:9:14^2:18:19:20^2:
33^2:36/32:8:12:29:34:37^2:38/33:5:9:20,21^5:22:
25,26^3/34:15:16/36:2:31/37:20/38:9:25/40:10/
42:18/43:10/44:2,3:4:6:8:11:14:26^2:28/45:3/46:
27:28/48:31:36/49:13:19:37:38/50:6:8:11:21:28
:44/51:24:25:45/Lam1:9:12:13^2:14^3:15:16^3:18^2:
19^2:20^3:21^3:22^2/2:11^3:22/3:4:8:9f:9:13:14:16:18:
20:24^2:48,49^2:50:51:52:54:56^2:57:58^3:59:60:63/
4:3,4:6/Eze2:2:4:7/3:4:10:14,15f:17:23^2:24/4:
14/5:2:5,6,7:11:13/6:8:12/7:3:4:8,9:14:21:23/8:
1:6:17/9:8/11:9:13:20^2:24/12:7^4:13/13:6:9:10^3:
15:18:18f:19^2:20^2:21:23/14:4:6,7:9:10:11:13:19/
16:8^2:18:20:21:26:27:42^2:61^2:62/17:19:20^2/18:4
:9:17:19:21/20:3:8^2:9,10^2:11:12:13^4:14:16^3:19^2:
20:21^3:22^3:23,24^2:27,28:35,36:39:40:44/21:2:3:7
:12:17:28^2:30:31^2/22:8:12:13:14:18,19,20^2:21:22
:24:26^6:30:31^2/23:25:37:38^2:39:41^2:48/24:8:13:
18:20,21/25:3:6:7:11:13:14^2:16/28:22^2:25^2/30:
14:15:24:25/32:3:10:32/34:6:8:9,10^2:11:12:
15,16^2:17^2:19:21:22:23^2:24^2:25:26^2:29:30:31^3/
35:3:4,5^2:11/36:5^2:8:12:18:20:21^2:22:23:27^2:28:
32/37:12:13:14:18,19,20:23:24^3:25^2:26:27^2:28/
38:14:15,16^2:17:18:19:20:23^2/39:7^2:13:18:20:21
23:24:25^2:27^2:28:29^2/43:3:7^3:8^2:19/44:4:7^3:8:9:
12:13:15^2:16^3:23:24^3/45:4:8^2:9/46:18:19,20/47:
3:4:5:7/Dan1:10/2:23:26:45/3:14:15/4:6:8:9:18
:19:30^3:34:36^4/5:15/6:22:25,26/7:2:7:28/8:17:
18:27/9:4^2:18^2:19:20^3/10:3:8:10:13:16:17:18:
20,21/Hos1:2:10^2:4^2:7:10:16^2:16f^2:23^2/4:4:6^3:7:
11/5:5:10:11:15/6:5^3:7^2/7:8:12:13:14/8:1^2:4^2:5/
9:8:9:13:15:17/10:12/11:3:4:5:7:8^2:9:10/12:7:10
/13:11^2/14:4^2:7:8^2/Joe1:7:13/2:1:21:25:26:27^2:
28^2:29/3:2^3:3:5^2:17:21^3/Amo1:3:6/2:7:8:12/3:7:
10/5:23/7:8:15/8:2/9:14/Ob1:16^2:19/Jon2:2:5:
6:7^2:9^2/4:2/Mic1:9/2:8/3:2/4:12^2/5:2:15/6:3:5
/7:8^2:9^2:10^2/Nah1:12/Hab:12^2/2:1^2:2/3:16^2:18
:19/Zep1:4/2:8:9/3:7:8^3:9:11:19/Hag1:2:8^2:9/2
:5:7:23^2/Zec1:15^2:16/2:9:11,12/3:1:7^2:8/4:6^2/5
:4^2/6:8^2:15/8:3:7:8:14,15:23/9:8^2:9:10:13^3/10:3:
11:12^2/11:4:5:10^2:12^2:14/12:9/13:5^2:6f:7^2:9^2/
14:5f:5/Mal1:2,3:6:7:11^3:12:14/2:1/3:5:6:7:10:
17/4:2:4/Mt2:6:15/3:17/5:11:36/6:25/7:21:24:
26/8:8,9^5:20^2:21:21f/9:9:18/10:32^2:33:42/11:5:
10:27:29,30/12:18^5:48^2:49:50^2/13:41:52/15:
13,14:22/16:17:18:27^2:28/17:5:15/18:10:14:19:
35/19:12:28^2/20:7:14:15:21:23:28^2/21:13/22:
44^2/24:6:27:30:31^2:33:35:39:44:45^2:48/25:13:27
:31^2:33^2:34^2:40:41:45/26:12:18^2:26:28:29^2:38:39
:42:50:53/27:46^2/28:7:10/Mk1:11^2:38/2:14/3:
33^2:34:35^3/5:30/6:22,23/7:27/8:34:35:38^2/9:7:
17:37^2:39/10:20f:39^2:45/11:17/12:33:36^2/13:9:
27:29:31:33:34:35,36,37^2/14:8:22:24:24f:34:42/
15:34^2/16:17/Lk1:5:18:20:25:43:44:47:76/2:49
/3:22^2/5:12:20:27:32^2/7:6,7,8^6:27:34^2:44:45:46^2
/8:21^2/9:24:26^2:35^2:38:58:59f/10:22:40/11:23:
29,30:45/12:13^2:18:45:49/13:32/14:26^2:27:33:
35/15:12:18:29/16:5,6:24:27/17:30/19:8:21:46
/20:13:42,43^2/21:8f:12:17:33:34,35:36/22:15:19
:20f:28f:29:30:67,68/23:46/24:39^2:44:49f:49/Jn
2:4:16:17/3:7:28:31/4:34:49/5:17:17f:24:25:30^2:
43/6:32:38:40:43:48-51:54^2:55^2:56^2/7:16:17^2/8:
18:19:28:30,31:37:38:42:49:54:56/9:5:11/10:10:
14:15^2:16:17:18^2:25:26:27^2:29/11:21:22:32/12:7
:23,24:26^2:27:35:48:49/13:8^2:9^2:20:31:35/14:2,3
:7:10^2:12,13:14:20:21:26f/15:1:7:8^2:9:10^2:11:14:
15:16:23:24/16:5:14:15:23:24:26:26f/17:5:9:10:
12:13:21:24/18:36^2:37/19:23,24^2:27/20:13:17^3:
25^2:27^2:28^2/21:2:15:16:17^3:24/Act1:1:8/2:17:
18:26^2:27:28:34/5:38/7:7:34:48,49^2:59/8:19/9:
6:15^2/10:14:46,47/11:15/13:16:22:32,33:47/15:
17:19/16:15/20:19:26:31^2:34/21:13/22:1:11:
17,18^2/23:6/24:10:16:18^3/25:10,11:25/26:2:4:4
f:10:13:16^2:29/Rom1:9:11,12:15/3:7^2/7^2:10:13^2
:14:16:18:22:23,24,25^5/9:1^3:17f:26/10:1^2/15:14:
19:19f:20:23:24:28:30^2/16:3:5^2:7^2:10:11:14:15:
21^2:22/1Co1:13:17^2/2:4^2/3:6/4:3:4:16/7:1:12:
17:40/8:13/9:1^2:3^2:17^2:18^2:19:27/11:1:17:24:25
/13:11^2:12/14:14:26:39/15:31:50:58/16:6:21:24
/2Co1:13,14:15,16^2:17^2:18/2:3:4:5,6:13/6:11^3:
12:13:16:18/7:3:4^2:7:12:14^2/8:3:17:23^2/9:3/10:
2^2:3:8:9:11^2/11:1:16:26:29^2/12:2,3^2:6^2:7^2:9^2:14/
13:1:11/Gal1:1:12:13:14^2/2:3:20/4:11:14:19:
24,25/6:11:14:17/Eph3:2,3:14,15/6:23/Php1:3:
4:7:8:9:14^2:16,17:19:26/2:12:16:17^2:25:28/3:7:8
:13:17:18/4:1^4:3^2:14:15^2/Col1:24:29/2:1:5/4:15
:18^2/2Th3:17^4/1Ti1:18^2/2:1/2Ti1:2:3^3:6:16/2:1
/3:10^3:11/4:6^2:7/Tit1:4/Phm:7:10^3:12:19:20:23
:24/Heb:5,6^2/2:12^2:13^2/4:3:5/5:7f/8:10^3/10:7:
9:16^3/12:5/13:6:24,25/1Pe2:6/5:1^2:12:13f:13/
2Pe1:13,14:16:17,18/3:1/1Jn1:1^2/2:4:12:28/
3Jn1:4:9/Jud:5/Rev:20/2:13:16:20:27/3:5:8f:8:
12^5:16:18:21^3/5:11/9:17,18/10:10/11:3/13:1/
18:4:7/21/22:12:16

3949

NO

Gen1:2f/2:5:19,20/4:12/6:1f/8:9/11:30/15:2,3:
4^2/16:1:2,3/17:5:15:19/19:2:18,19,20/21:26/23
:4:13/24:6:8:21:49/25:21:34f/26:27/27:36:
39,40/29:15/31:39/32:29/33:10:15/34:12:
18,19/35:10/37:17:21,22:24:35/39:9:11:23/40:
8/41:49/42:10^2:31^2/43:1:22/44:17/45:1/47:4/
48:18/49:4/50:21/Ex1:8/2:3:12/3:21/5:10,11:
16:18/6:12:30/8:10:22/9:14:21/10:25/12:16:19
:43:48/13:3:6,7/16:18:25/17:1/19:13/20:3:10/
21:8^2:9/22:8:10:11/23:6:8:18^2:26:32/28:30,31f/
29:1/30:9:11,12/32:18/33:6/34:3^2:14:15:20:24/
36:4-7/Lev1:2,3/2:11^2/3:6/6:30/7:17,18^2/8:8f/
10:12/11:41,42/13:21:23:26^2:32:34:58/15:28/
16:22:29,30/18:16f:19:23/20:21f/21:2,3/22:4:

(O Con't)
:13[2]:21:25/23:7f:22:36/25:26:34:37/26:1:13:
:36:37/27:29:29f:33/Num3:4/5:8:13[2]:19/6:12
:19:25,26/10:30/16:3:40[2]/18:4:20:23:24/22:
:38/23:18-24[2]/26:28-37:62/27:3,4[2]:8:9:10:11
8:17:18:25:26/29:1:7:12:35/32:10,11/33:14/
:30:31:33/36:9/Deu3:26/4:8:35:39/5:14:22f/
10,11,12/7:16:21:24/9:4/10:17[2]/11[2]:23:25/
:8:12/13:8/14:27:29/15:4,5/16:3:4:8/17:4/18
7:10/20:16/21:1/22:25,26,27/23:3:17,18/25:
18/27:23f/28:26:31:50:65:66:68/29:19/30:12:
/31:2:2f:17/32:5:39/34:6/Jos1:5:17,18/2:11[2]
9[2]:20/5:11,12/6:1/7:3/10:21/13:33/14:3,4:15
7:3/21:44/22:24,25:26,27:33/23:9:13/Ju2:2:
:21/4:20/8:34/9:36:37/10:6/11:25:26:27:28/
:2,3/14:6/15:12,13/17:6/18:1:7[2]:28[3]/19:
,13[2]:15:18:23:28/21:8,9:25/Ru1:10:12:13/
a1:5:8:12,13:15,16/2:2[2]:4:5:9:16:31/3:6/4:
,22/10:27/11:11:13/12:4/13:19/14:3:6:24,25
7:39/15:26/16:9/17:50,51/19:5/20:21:41/21:
6/23:26/25:17:39/26:9:21/27:11/29:6/30:4:
:23/2Sa1:21[3]/3:11:37/7:1:10,11:22/10:15,16
2:6/13:2:12f:16[2]:25:32,33[3]/14:5,6:7:8:11:25[2]/
:16:21/16:10[2]:11/17:19/18:3:11f:18:20:22[2]/
:34:35/20:3/22:32:50/23:17/24:3:24/1Ki1:1:
4/2:13:30:32/3:13:22:26/5:4:6/8:22,23:35,36:
/10:5:20:27/11:9,10/13:16,17/14:2:4/17:7:
/18:13:23:26:29[3]/19:4f/21:13:25/22:1:31:47/
Ki1:3:6:16/2:21/3:9:13[2]/4:31/5:15/7:5:10/9:8
0:12:36/10:11/12:15/14:26/18:19:24[2]:25/19:
26/23:10:25[2]/1Ch2:34,35/15:2/17:20[2]/21:24
23:26/24:1:5:28/2Ch1:12/5:6/6:14:26/7:13/9:
9/10:10/14:11/15:5:19/18:29/19:4:7[3]/20:12/
5:4:8/28:21:24/31:17,18/32:15/36:16[2]:17/Ez
3[2]/7:24/Neh2:20/5:14/6:11/13:19:26/Est1:8
4:2/7:4/9:1:15/Job1:10/2:13/3:18/4:21/5:1:4:
4:19:21/6:5,6,7/8:11-13/9:20:32,33[4]:34/10:4-
-7/11:20/12:3:6:14/13:10/14:11,12/15:4,5[2]:30
1[2]/16:5:6/17:3,4:16/18:17/19:7[2]/20:18/21:4:
4:30-32[2]/22:8/23:6:15/24:14,15[2]:18:20:21/27:
:15/28:7[2]:8[2]/29:12:22/30:8:13/32:5:15:17/33
9/34:12:20:22:23/35:2,3/36:26/37:24/38:11/
9:2,3:4:7:13/40:24/41:9:10[2]:11:15-17:26:29/
2:15/Ps5:4/6:1/7:2/10:4f:18/12:2:6/14:1:3/
6:2/18:41/22:2:9,10,11/25:5/26:11/27:3/33:
1/34:1:5/35:7/36:1:3/39:5,6/40:4:5:6/49:5:10
50:8:13:16:22/53:1/57:7/59/60:6,7/62:7/63:1
66:3/69:32/71:6:11/72:12/73:25/76:7/77:2:19
78:44/79:3/81:7:9f:11/84/88:8/89:34:48/90:9
92:4:6/94:21,22/101:3/105:14f:37/108:7/109:
:12,13[2]/119:102,103:104:119:129:131:161/
21:2/127:1/142:4[3]/143:2/144:12-15[2]/Pro6:7:
6-19:34:35/10:2:22f/12:15:21/14:4:10/16/17:
6:16f:21/21:30/23:1:33/24:17:19,20/26:2[2]:9:
7/27:16/28:1:24/29:9/30:15,16[2]:18,19:
1,22,23:24-28:29,30,31/31:21:25/Ecc1:3-7:8-
-11[3]:12-15/3:18:19:22/4:1/5:4/6:10/8:4:8[3]/9:
2,3:6:7:10:15/10:11f:15/12:1:2:12/Sol1:3:4/4:
2/5:6/8:1[2]:9/Is1:3:12,13:16:18:31/3:7[2]:12:18/
:8:12/7:25/8:20/9:5[2]:17[2]/10:2:14/13:10:17:18
/14:8:17:20:25/16:10:12/17:1:2:8[2]/19:9:15/23:
2:17/24:8:9/26:10:18[2]:21/27:7,8/28:22/29:8:
22/30:9:16:19:21/31:4,5/32:6/33:8:21:24/34:
0/35:8:9/36:8,9/37:12:25/40:15[2]:28/41:24:26
/42:22/43:9:10:11:13:24[2]/44:6:8[2]:9/45:5:6[2]:18:
19[2]:21[2]:22/46:7:9/47:6:10:11:14[2]/48:10:19:22/
50:1:2[2]/51:13:22/52:1:3/53:2:9/54:4[2]:17/55:1/
56:10/57:1[2]:11:21/58:6/59:4:9[2]:10[2]:15:16[2]/60:
19/62:6,7[2]/63:3:5/64:4:7/65:17:20[2]:25[2]/66:3:9
/Jer2:6:22:30:36/3:8:16:17/4:4:22[2]:30/5:12:13:
22:23,24:28/6:15:16:17:20[2]:29[2]/7:16:18:33/8:6:
12:15:17:22[2]/9:11:12:21[2]:22/10:6:20:21/11:14/
12:2:6:11:13/13:18/14:5:10:13:15:16:19[2]/16:4:7
:13:14,15/17:6:9:21,22:27/18:12:13:18/19:6/20
:8/21:12:13/23:7:21:32/25:27:29:33:35[2]/26:19/
30:8:10:13[2]/31:29:34/33:25,26/34:9/35:6/36:
24,25:30/37:14/38:6/42:10/44[2]:22:26/45:3/46:
11[2]:17/48:2,3,4:33[2]:42/49:4:9,10:18:33/50:3:14
:20:32:34:40[2]:42/51:3:17:19:30:43:44/52:20/
Lam1:3:4:7:9:16:17:21/2:1:6:11:18/3:34,35,36/
4:3,4:8:12:16:17/5:8:14[2]/Eze3:6/7:3:4:10,11:14:
19/11:7:11/12:25/13:16:21:23[2]/14:16/15:3/16:
4:5[2]:33,34:47/17:9:10:16/18:7:13:19:24/19:14/
21:30/22:26/23:27/24:6f:16[2]:17/25:8:9,10/26:
13:21/28:2,3:9:24/29:16:18/30:13/31:8:14/33:
11:28:31/34:6:8:22:28[2]/36:12:15[2]/37:8:22/39:
26/44:2:7:9:17:21/45:8:12[2]:18/48:19/Dan2:11:
22:27:44/3:29/4:9:18:31:35/6:4:12:13:17/7:4:
28/8:4:7:25/10:16/11:25:27:37:45/Hos1:6[2]:2:9:
10:16f/4:1[3]:10:12f/7:1/8:7/9:1:3:4:15:16/10:9/
11:7:9/12:7/13:4[2]/14/Joel1:13:18:20/2:8:19/3:
17/Amo2:1:14/4:6/5:2:18:23/6:10:12/7:8/Ob1:
16:18/Jon3:3f:7/4:10/Mic1:14/2:7:10/3:11/4:3
/5:12/6:5:6:8:10:15/Nah2:9/3:5:7:15:18:19/
Hab1:2[2]:4:7:14/2:19/3:8,9/Zep1:6:18/2:15/3:2
:3:5[3]:7:11[3]:13:15:17,18/Hag2:12/Zec1:4[2]/4:5:7:
13/7:5:14/8:6:10[4]:13/9:8/10:2/13:4[2]:5/14:6:7:
17:21/Mal1:10/2:13:16/Mt:10/4:4/5:17:37/6:
18/8:4f:19:20[2]:28:29/10:34/13:29/15:20:23/16:
4:8/18:22/19:5,6[2]:26/20:7:13:23/21:3/22:12:23
:30:46[2]/24:36[2]/26:45/Mk1:25/4:5,6:7:19/5:3,4:
19:26:35/6:2,3:8,9[3]:14:16:42/7:6,7/8:17:21/9:2:
25:39/10:8:9:29/11:13:22,23/12:14:18:20,21,22[3]
:31:32:34/13:32/14:1:29:31:41:61/15:5/16:13/
Lk1:7:25:60:61/2:7/3:13/4:24:25,26:40/5:36:37
:39/7:25:28:39/8:16:38:43,44:46:49/9:57:58/10
:4f:15:22[2]/11:15:33:36:44/12:4:33[3]:51/14:6:27:
33/15:16:19/16:10:26:30/18:19/20:27:30:31:40
/22:25:58/23:9:22:29/Jn1:18:21[2]/2:24,25/3:18
/4:21-24:32/5:7:14f:30:44:47/6:27:35:44:65/7:6
:12:13:27:30:44:52/8:11[2]:39:41:46:49[2]:50:51/9:
9/10:13:18:28:29/11:6/12:46/13:8:38/14:5:6:
18:30/15:15:16:22/16:10:16:22/18:17:40/19:9:
11:12:15/21:5/Act1:20/2:16:26:34/4:12[2]:32:
34,35/5:23/7:5[2]:17,18:21:43/8:21:31/9:7/10:38
:46,47/12:16/13:8:25:28:34:37:37f/15:9:12:24:
27,28,29/16:7:24:37/17:25/18:10:20/19:2:36:
40/20:26/21:39[2]/23:8/24:11:18[2]/25:10,11:25:
26/27:21:43/28:4:6:17:18:19:21:31/Rom1:20:
20f[2]/2:5:24:25:29/3:4:9:10[2]:11:12:20:21,22:26:
29:31/4:1:4,5:8/5:5:6[2]/6[2]:9:14/7:1:2[2]:4[2]:6:7:8[2]:
13:17:18/8:1:4:12:33:34:36/9:1:6:20:25/10:11/
11:1:2,3:4:6/13:1:10/14:1f:2:10/15:1/1Co1:15:
19:29/2:9:11[2]/3:21f/6:9,10[2]:12:18/7:4[2]:16:25:
28/8:4:8[2]:10/9:1:5f[2]:17/10:13:17:19/11:22/12:
3[2]:29:31/13:3:7/14:17:27:28/15:11:13:55,56:58
/2Co1:17:19:20/2:1/3:18/5:4:12:15:19:21f/6:3[2]
/7:2:5:8:11/8:20/10:16[2]/11:15/12:6:9:18/13:7/
Gal1:7:10:12[2]:17/2:6:16:20:21/3:5:11:28/4:7:14
/5:11:18:23/Eph2:12:19/3:2,3/4:14:17,18:31/5:
3[2]:11:29,30/6:9/Php1:10:28/2:15:20/3:9:13/4:
2:15/Col1:11/2:23/3:25/1Th1:5/3:1:5/4:13/5:2
:3:13:15:18/2Th2:10/3:16/1Ti5:8:14:20/6:2:14:
16[2]/2Ti2:5/4:16/Phm1:16/Heb:14/2:6/5:4:5/6
:4:8:13/7:3:3f[3]:3:24/8:7:11:12/9:16:17:22:26/10
:18:23[2]:26:35:38:39/11:7[2]:12/12:15:16/Jas2:13[2]
:17:26/3:8:12/5:6:12:17:19/1Pe1:14:17/2:20/3:
13/4:12:16/2Pe1:20,21/2:12:14/1Jn1:5:8/2:27
/3:5[2]:15/4:18/5:16:18/3Jn1:4/Rev:5:5f/2:17/3:
7[2]:8:11:12/5:3:4[2]/6:6/7:14/9:16f/10:6/11:8,9/
13:17/14:3:5:11/15:8/18:7:11:22[3]:23/19:10/20:
6:11:11f/21:1:4:22:23:25:27/22:5[2]:9

1754

NOR

Gen2:5/45:6/Ex11:7/20:10/22:28/23:24:26:32
/34:28/Lev3:17/12:4/17:12/18:7:8:9:12:13:14:
16:20/19:11[2]:13:14:20f:26:28/21:5:7:10:11:12:
14,15[2]:23/22:10/23:14[2]:22/25:11[2]/26:20/27:10
/Num14:44/16:14/18:16:20/20:17/35:32/Deu4
:28[3]:31[2]/5:9,10:21[2]/7:3/9:18/12:17[4]/13:8/14:1
/17:16/21:4/23:2/24:5:16/26:14/28:36:64/30:
13/31:6:8/Jos8:31/Ju1:31,32/2:23/8:23,24:35/
1Sa2:2/5:5/15:29/25:7/2Sa1:21/19:24,25/1Ki
3:26/13:8:28/19:18/2Ki3:17/6:26-30/14:6/19:
32[2]/22:12,13/2Ch20:33/21:12/25:4/Neh4:23[3]/
Job8:20/14:11,12/16:6/18:19[2]/20:9/23/28:14:
16:19/31:30/41:26[3]/Ps10:6/37:25:33/81:9/89:
22:33/91:5:6[2]/103:9/106:34/112:7/115:6[2]:7[2]/
Pro4:5f/10:3/30:8/Ecc9:11/10:20/Sol2:7f/Is5:
13/14:21/35:9/37:33[3]/40:16:21/42:2:3:4:20:24
/43/44:9/49:10/50:5/51:6/57:16/58:13/59:8/
64:9/66:19/Jer5:12/7:16[2]/8:2/9:23[2]/10:5[2]:21/
11:14/13:23/14:14:15/15:10/16:6:13/17:8/18:
18/19:4[2]:5/25:33/33:22/35:6:8/37:2[2]/44:2,3[2]/
46:6/49:31/51:43/Lam1:19/Eze5:11/7:8,9:19:
22/8:18/9:5:10/13:23/16:4[2]/18:6:20/20:8/24:
17/29:11/30:21/32:13/34:4[3]:28:29/44:20/Dan
5:23[2]:31f/6:22/10:3[3]/11:20:37[2]/Hos3:3/5:13/7
:10/14:3/Amo5:11/Jon3:7/Mic4:12/Hab3:17/
Zep3:2/Zec4:6/11:16[4]/Mt12:19/24:36/Mk13:
19:32/Lk6:43/9:3[3]/16:13/18:4,5/Jn6:24/12:40[2]
/13:16/15:4/Act:10/23:8f:12,13:21/25:10,11/
27:20f/28:17/Rom3:18/5:13/8:26/1Co10:7/
2Co7:2/Col3:19/1Ti6:16/Tit2:10/3:2/Heb6:12
/9:11:25/13:5/1Pe2:8/3Jn1:7/Rev3:15/7:3[2]:16
/9:20[3]/20:4/21

292

NOT

[3]Gen3:2,3:4:17/4:5:15/6:3/7:8,9/8:7f/9:18f/13:
6/14:23/15:10:16/17:2,3,4/18:21:24:25:28:32/
19:32/21:9f:10/22:12:16/24:3:37/26:24:29[2]/27:
38:38f/29:3:26/30:6f/31:7:29:35:39:51,52[2]/32:
10:26:32/34:14/35:5/36:6,7,8/37:21,22:26,27:
32/38:9[2]:11:14:16:26/39:12f/41:8:24/42:11:15:
16:22:31:38/43:8/44:30:31:34/45:8/46:15:26/
47:9:29/48:1/49:7f:10/Ex1:8f:19/3:11:19/4:10[2]
:11[3]:21/5:2:23/6:1:2,3/8:31,32[2]/9:6:30:32[2]/10:
10:15[3]:17:19:20:26[2]:27/11:7/12:9:10:13:20:21:
23f:23:27:30[2]:38f:45:46[2]/13:13:17,18/14:5:11:
28/15:26/16:4:16f/17:7/18:17/19:12[2]:15:21[2]:
23/20:4:5:7[2]:13:14:15:16:16f:17:23/21:5:7:8:10:
13:21[2]:28[2]:29:36[2]/22:2:8:11:13:14:15[2]:16:21:22:
25:28:31/23:1[2]:2,3:5:7:7f:9:15:19:21[2]:24[2]:29/24:
11/25:18f:39f/28:32:35/29:33:34/30:2:15[2]:33/
31:14,15/32:11:18:32/33:3:20[2]:23/34:3:15:20:
25:26:33f/39:23/40:35/Lev1:15,16,17/2:12:12f
/4:13/5:6:8:11/6:12/7:16[2]:17,18:19/8:33/10:1f:
6[3]:7:18/11:4-7[5]:8:12:13-19:20:26:36:37:41,42:
43:44:47/12:4/13[2]:5[2]:6:11:21:23:28[2]:32[2]:33:34:
37:39:40:41:53:55[2]:59/14:32:36:48:57/15:3/16:
1:13:17[2]/17:16/18:7:10:11:14f:15:17:18:21:24:
26:28:28f:29,30[2]/19:3,4:7:11:12:13:14:15:19:20f
:20[2]:23:26:27:28:29:31:33[2]/20:4:22:22f:23:25[2]/
21:4:5:6:7[2]:10:11:12:14,15[2]:14,15f:16,17:21:23/
22:1:6:8:12:13:15:20[2]:21:22[2]:23:24:28:32,33/23:
14:22:29/25:11:17,18:20:23:28:30[2]:33:34:39:42:
46:54/26:11:14:20:21:23:31:44/27:10:11,12:20[2]:
22:26:27[2]:28:33[2]/Num1:47,48,49[2]/2:32,33/3:38
/4:15:17,18,19/5:3:15:18:28:30:31/6:3,4[2]:6,7/9:
12[2]:13[2]/10:5,6,7f/11:17:19,20:23/12:7,8[2]:11/13
:19:31/14:9[2]:22:29:42/16:15[2]:28:29:40:49/18:
2,3,4:16:17:22:32[2]/19:9:12:13[2]:18:20/20:2:12:
12f[2]:12[2]:17[2]:19:24/21:22:34:35/22:12/23:7-10[2]:
18-24[4]/24:13[2]:25f/25:2/26:19-22:62:64,65f/27:
3,4:14:17/30:1:3:5/31:48,49/32:16:18/35:12:15
:24[2]:27:33:34/36:4/Deu1:34,35:37:42[2]/2:5:9:
14,15:19[2]:28:35,36/3:1:18:26:27/4:2:16,17:19[2]:
21,22:31/5:2,3:5:9,10:11f:11:17:18:19:20:21:24/
6:14:16/7:3:14[2]:15:16:21:22:25[2]:26/8:1:2/9:5:6[2]
/10:9/11:2:10:16/12:4,5:13:16:19:20-23:30:31:
32/13:3:8[2]/14:3,4,5:7[3]:8[2]:19,20,21/15:3:6:7:18:
19[2]:21/16:5/17:15:17/18:1:8:14:16:19:21:22/19
:6,7[3]:10:21/20:5:6:15:15f/21:7:8:14:15:16:18:23
/22:5[2]:9:13,14:17,18:20:28,29:30/23:1:2:4:14:
15,16[2]:17,18:20:22:24/24:4:5:10:12,13:16/25:5:
6/26:13:14/27:26/28:12:13:14:29:32:33:44:
56,57:61[2]:62/29:14,15:20:29/30:11:12:18/31:2:
6:8:13/32:6[3]:21:27:31:47:52/34:4/Jos1:5/2:11/
5:6:8,9/6:10:15/7:10,11[2]:12/8:17:22:27/9:14,15
:18:19:26/10:8:28:37/11:8:13/13/15:63/17:12:
15/18:1/20:5:9/22:2,3:17,18:19:22,23[2]:26,27:28
:31/23:6:7[2]/24:12:13[3]:19/Ju1:24f:30:33/2:2:10[2]
:17:22:23/3:1:29/4:16/5:8[2]:19:23/6:10[2]:23/7:4/
8:2,3f:23,24:26/9:20/10:6/11:1:14,15:25:27:39f
/12:5/13:7[2]:9:13,14:16/16:9/18:1:5/20:8,9,10:
17/21:5:7:14:17/Ru1:13:18/2:8,9:13:16/1Sa1:
15,16/2:32/3:7f/4:20/6:9/8:3:5:7:18/12:14:17:
22/13:14:22/14:27:34:44:45/15:19:29[2]/16:7:8:9
:10,11[2]:18:20/17:47/19:4:6/20:2[2]:3:9:10:14/21:
2:4/22:8[2]:15/24:7,8:11[2]:13:21/25:8:21:34[2]:35/
26:8/28:18/30:11,12:15/2Sa1:22/3:8:13:33,34[2]
/4:2,3f:11/5:6/7:5:15/11:25/12:8:23/13:12f:20:
29,30:32,33/14:11:14f[2]:28/17:6:12:16:17/19:7:
13:21:22:24,25:35:42/20:1:8,9,10/21:2[2]:17/22:
22:38/23:10:18,19:23/24:24/1Ki1:6:52[2]/2:
23,24:28:43/5:2,3/6:6/7:31:47/8:8:18:32:56/9:6
:20,21/10:3f:7/11:2:11[2]:33[3]:34:39/12:23,24:31/
13:9[2]:16,17[2]:21,22[2]:28:33/14:8/15:3:4:14[2]:26:
29/16:11:31/19:11[2]:12/20:5,6:9:25:28:36/21:3:
7:21:29/22:6:15:28:30:43:52,53/2Ki1:6:16:17/2
:10:18/3:2/4:28/5:16/6:12:22/7:10/8:19/9:18:
19/12:8:13,14:16/13:23/14:3:6:27/16:2:5/17:1:
25:26/19:5,6:32[2]/21:9/22:7:12,13:20[2]/23:9:22:
26/24:3,4/25:24/1Ch1:1f/3:9/5:25/10:14/11:
21/15:13/16:22/17:4:9/21:3:17:24/22:8[2]/23:
8,9f/26:10/28:3:20/29:1/2Ch2:6/4/5:9:13,14/6
:8:9:42[2]/8:7,8:11:15/10:11/11:4/12:7[2]/13:10:12[2]
/14:13:15/15:3:17/17:3/18:3,4,5:14:27:32/19:6
/20:15:17:24:33/21:12:20/23:19/24:25/25:4:7[2]:
16/26:7:17,18[2]/28:3:13:27/29:7/30:2,3:5:5f:7:8:
9:15:17,18,19[2]:20/31:16/32:7:26/34:21:28/35:
18/Ez1:4/2:59:62,63[2]/4:14:22[2]/5:5:16/6:6/7:
25/8:15/9:9:12[3]:14/Neh1:3:6,7/2:16[2]/3:8/4:5[2]
/5:9:15/6:1:11:12,13/7:3:61:64,65[2]/8:10:11:17/
9:20:31:32:35/10:30[2]:31:39,40/13:2:6:10:14:19:
25/Est1:16/2:10/3:5,6:8/4:11:16/5:9/8:8f/9:7-
7-10:16/10:1/Job1:12,13:22/3:26/4:6/5:5:17:
24:26/6:5,6,7:10:25,26:30/7:8:21/8:20/9:2:13:
18:21:24:28:35/10:4-7/13:2:16:20/14:5:11,12[2]:
20,21/15:22:29/16:18/17:3,4:10/18:5/19:27/20
:17[2]:18:21/21:4:9:18:19/22:5/23:11:12/24:13:
16/26:8/27:6:10:15/28:13[2]:14/30:25:28,29/31:
1:19,20:34/32:6:8,9:11,12:14/33:7[2]:9:13:23,24:

(NOT Con't)
33/34:5:6:29,30:32/35:14,15/36:2:5:6:7:13:20/
37:23:24/39:21-23/40:23^2/41/42:3:7/Ps1:1^2:5^2
/3:6/4:4/5:5/9:12:16f:18^2/10:5/12:3,4/14:3^2/
15:3:5/16:4:10^2/17:4:5:15/18:21:22:25:37/22:6:
24^2/23:4/24/26:11/27:9^2/31:8:17/32:6:6f/33:
16,17/34:19/35:13:24/36:2:12/37:33:35,36/39:
9/40:10/44:3:6:9:17:18^2:21:22/45:10,11/46:2:5
/49:7^2:8,9:8,9f:16:17/50:3f:12/51:17/53:3^2/55:
12:22:23/56:10,11/58:1/59:3:5/64:4/65:9/66:
18^2/69:27:28:33:35/75:4f/76:5/78:7:8:36:37:50:
53/79:6^2:8/89:22:34^2/91:7:8/92:6/94:14/101:5^2
:7/103:2:10/105:14:15^2/106:11:23/110:4/112:6
:7/115:1/116:15/118:17:18/119:6:8f:16:109:
110:113:133:155:157:165:176/124:1^2:6/125:3/
129:2/131:1/132:10/137:7/147:20^2/Pro1:18:28
:29/3:11,12:24,25,26/4:5f:12/5:6:12:23/6:27:28
:29/7:23:24/8:27,28,29/10:3/11:21/17:8f:20f/
18:19f/20/21:17/22:28/24:7:17/29:19^2/30:3f:6
/31:3:4:12/Ecc1:8-11:12-15/2:10:20-23/3:5/4:
12/5:5^2:19,20/7:20:27,28/8:5:8:11:13/9:1:2,3:5f^2
:10f:11^2:16/10:6:20/11:4f^2/12:10^2/Sol1:1f/2:7:
7f/3:4:5/6:6/8:4/Is1:3:9:15/2:9/3:8:9/5:2:6:10:
25/6:7:11/7:1:7:8:9:10:12:14f:17/8:9,10:11:19:
20/9:1:11,12:13:17:21/10:4^2:7:25/11:3:13/12:2
/13:20/14:21/15:9/16:3/22:2:9,10,11/23:13:18
/24:20/26:7^2:11^2/27/28:25/29:9^2:13:17/30:14^2:
17/31:2:3^2:4,5:8/32:5^2:10/34:16^2/35:4:6/36:12:
21/37:3:10:26:33:34/38:1/40:16:31^2/41:9:10^2:
14:17:28^2/42:1f:2:3:4f:8^2:16^2:24^2:25/43:2^3:23^3/
44:10:21/45:1:13:18:19:21/46:13/47:3/48:9:11^2
:21/49:10:15^2/50:2:5:6:7:11/51:10:14:18:21/52:
3:12:14,15/54:4:10:14:15/55:5:8/57:6:11:16/58
:13^2/59:2:21/60:12f:20/62:1/63:8/64:5:9/65:6:
7:8^2:19:21,22^2:23^2:25f/66:3:4:9:19f:19:24/Jer1:
18/2:9:20:24:30:37/3:1:12:16^2:25/4:4:8:11,12:
28/5:1:3:7:9^2:10:13:18:21^2/6:14:15:16:18,19:28
/7:16:22/8:2:7:12:20/9:9^2:13:23:25,26/10:7:11:
16:23/11:1:11^2:14:21,22:23/13:14:15/14:10:12^2
:15:21^2/15:17,18:19:20/16:2:5:6:11:20/17:2,3:8:
11:13:16^2:27/18:8:10:15/20:17/21:10/22:13:15:
18^2:20:30f/23:4:16:20:21:24:29^2:32:38,39/24:6^2
/25:8,9:29/26:4:5^2:9:16:24/27:9^2:13:14:15:18/
28:15/29:9:11:16,17/30:11^2:21:24/31:8:9:33f:37
/32:33/33:5:20,21/34:3:14:17/35:1f:7^2:14/36:
24,25^2:30f/37:1:4:14:19:21/38:16:17:18:23:26:
27/39:17/40:7:11/42:6:12:13,14:19:21/43:2,3:7
/44:4:7^3:14:16:19:27/46:6:28^2/48:11:33:44/49:
7:12:30f/50:9:27/51:5:17:26f:57:61,62/Lam1:
19/2:14/3:8:31:33:42:44:57/4:3,4^2:12/Eze2:5:7
/3:5:6:11:14,15f/5:11:17/7:7:8,9:13:22/8:18/9:
5:10/10:9-13:17f/11:7:11:12/12:12f:13:13f/13:
6:10:19^2/14:9:11^2:16:23/16:22:31:33,34:42:43:
47:51:61/17:14:18/18:3:6^2:7:15:17^2:20:21:23:24
:28:29:32/20:7:8:13:15:23,24:25:25f:31:32:38:47
:48/21:4:5:27/22:26:30/23:8/24:7:16:22:23^2/28
:2,3/29:11:18/30:21/32:7:27:31/33:8:9:12^2:15^2/
34:18:26/36:11:14:22:32/38:15,16f/39:7/41:6/
42:5:6/43:7/44:8:9^2:13^2:18:20:22:25:28/46:2/
47:11:22/Dan1:8:8f^2:13/2:11:18:30:43/3:16:27/
4:19/5:8f:22:23:31f/6:23/8:17:24f:24:27/9:14:
24f/11:4:6:14:21/12:4:7:9/Hos1:9^3:10:4^2:7^2:17:
18:23^2/3:3/4:15/5:6/7:13/8:4:6:11/9:4^2:9:17/
10:9/11^3/13:14/Joe2:2:3:13^3:21/3/Amo1:3^2:6^2:
9^2:11^2:13^2/2:1^2:4^2:6^2/3:8/4:6:7/5:13:18^2:22^2:23
/7:3:13:14^2/8:2:11:12/9:1:4:7:8:9:10:15/Ob1:5:
8:12^4/Jon:14/3:7/Mic1:11/2:6/3:5:7/4:12/6:7:
15^2/7:1^3:5^2:8/Nah1:3:12/3:19/Hab1:4:12/2:3^2:
13/Zep:5/3:2:7:13:17,18/Hag1:2:6/2:12:14/
Zec3:2f/4:6:10/7:5:8,9:11/8:13/11:6:16/13:5:6f
/Mal1:4:10:12/2:6:8:9/3:5:6^2:8/Mt2:6:22/3:11
/4:7/5:27:33/6:14,15:29/7:10:21:29:29f^2/8:8,9/
9:13:30/10:13:24^2:29:37^2:38/12:7:19^2:20/13:11:
12,13^2/15:13,14:15:23:24/16:17:18:22:23/17:4f:
9/18:14:16/19:8:10:11/20:28/21:25/22:17:32:
32f:34,35/24:2:6^2:17:18:20:29:36:39f/25:12f:13:
44/26:5:29:39/27:1f/Mk1:7:7f:8f^2:22f/2:2:17:
27/3:12/4:11,12:21:25/5:10:43/6:8,9/7:36/8:12
:21f:30:33/9:29f:38/10:13:24f:26:40:45/11:26,f:
30/12:14:27:34/13:2:7:11:14f:18:20:24:32:34f:
35,36,37/14:31:36/16:9f/Lk1:54:62f/2:26/3:9:
15:16/4:4f:12:25,26:42/5:31:32:36/7:6,7,8:11:
23:25/8:1:10:18:31:43,44f:56/9:3:21:27:33:49:
50:55f:62/10:6:20/11:12:23:42/12:6^2:15:21:25:
27:48/13:3:5:9:14:24,25/14:3:26f:27:35/15:21/
16:12/17:7,8,9:10:31^2/18:11:13:14/19:30:44/20
:6:22:34,35:37,38^2/21:6:18:21/22:18:27:32:32f:
40:40f:41,42:46:58:67,68/23:2:50,51,52/24:39/
Jn1:8:11,12:13:13f:20:27/2:9/3:5f:8:16:17:18:
23,24:28/4:17,18:21-24:35:42/5:23:30:34:37:38:
45/6:20:26:38:39:46:58/7:6:8f:16:30:33:34:36:
39^2/8:15:20^2:23:28:29:37:41:42:44:55/9:16:24:
33/10:8:26:33/11:4:9:22:52/12:6:30:37:47^2:49/
13:9:11:16:18/14:1:10:18:22^2:24/15:22^2:24/16:
5f:13:25:29:30f:32/17:9:12:15:16:20/18:9:11:17:
20:25:31f:36^2:38:40/19:4:6:23,24:36,37/20:24/
Act1:4:7:9/2:24:27:31^2:34/3:23/5:4:7:39/6:1:2/
7:5:32/8:2f:16:21:31:32/10:4:26:34:40,41/11:6:
12/12:22/13:35:36:37/15:1:19/16:6/17:27/18:
15^2/19:26:27^2:31:37/20:22:29/21:4:12:13:25^3/
24:23/25:8^2:10,11:16/26:19:25:26/27:21:22:34/
28:4:26/Rom1:11,12:16:28/2:12-15:21:28:29^2/3
:4^2:7:9:12:19:21,22^3:24:25:27:28/4:3:4,5:6:9:11:
12:13:15:16:22/5:9:13^2:14/6:2,3:12^2:13:15^3:21/
7:5:6:7^4:9:14:19/8:9^2:15:30:32/9:4:6:8:10-13^2:
14:16:19:22:25:26:30:32/10:3:16/11:1:2,3:4^2:5:6
:7:8:11:18^2:20:21:25/13:1:3:9/14:1f:2:3:4^2:7:15:
17:22/15:1:18:31/16:4:18/1Co1:17/2:4:5:6^2:8:
12:13/3:1:2:3:4f:6:9^2:13/4:5^2:6^2:10:14:20/5:3,4:
9:11/6:4:7:12:12f:13:19/7:1:5:6:7:10^3:11:12^3:13:
15:17:19:23f:25:30:34:35:36:37/8:4:8:9:13/9:2:8
:9:15:17:19:26:27/10:5:6:19:20:23^2:25:27:29:33/
11:7:9:22:29:31:32/12:2:10:14:15^3:16^2:23:24:29:
30/13:5^3/14:2:21:22:24:28^2:33:34:34f^2/15:1:10:
15:27:29:34:50:51/16:12:22/2Co1:12:18:23:24/
2:1:3^2:5,6:16:17/3:3^2:5:6:7:8:13^2:14/4:2^2:7:8:18^2
/5:1:3:7:8:13,14:17/6:1:12^2:14/7:2^2:3:7:9^2:10^3/8
:3^2:8^2:10:12/9:5:8:13/10:4:8:9:13^2:14:15:17/11:
14:21:26:29/12:4:5:11:14:18:19/13:2:3:7:7f:8:10
/Gal1:1:10^2:11:18:20/2:3:5^2:15:16:21/3:2:5:17
:21,22^2/4:1:8:12:17:20:26:30:31/5:6^2:13:21/6:9:
15/Eph2:8f:8:9/3:5/5:4/6:12/Php1:27:29/2:6:
21:27/3:13/4:11/Col2:11:13:14:16:19:21/3:19:
22:23/1Th1:5/2:3:4:5:8:9:12/4:5:7:8:12^2:13:15/
5:3:4:5:6:9:19:20/2Th1:3:8/2:3:7/3:2:6:8:10^2/
1Ti1:9:20/2:9,10:14/3:3^2:6:8^2:11^2:16/4:8/5:6:
11:16:21/6:17^2/2Ti1:7:9:12/2:4:9:14:15:19:24/
3:10/4:2:8:16/Tit1:6:7^2/2:3^2:9:15/3:2:5:8/Phm
1:16/Heb2:5:8:11:16/3:7,8:15/4:6:7:8^2:11/5:5:
12,13/6:10/7:6:12,13,14^2:16:28/8:2:9^2/9:8:11:
12:24:28/10:4:6:8:25:26:35:37/11:8:13:16:23:28
:31/12:9:13:14^2:15:18:25:26/13:6:9^2:14:17/Jas1
:5:19:22:25:27/2:11^3:12:18:20^2:26/3:1f:10:15/4:
11:17/5:12^2/1Pe1:7:8:10:12:18:23/2:8:9:11:18:
23/3:6:7:21/5:2^2/2Pe1:5:16/2:4:5:12f/3:9:
15,16:17/1Jn1:10/2:2:5:7:15:16:19:20:21:22^2:
28/3:9:10:12/4:3^2:10:17:18:21/5:6,7,8:6,7,8f:12^2
:16:17/3Jn1:7:9:10^2/Jud:5:9:10:12:19/Rev2:11:
20:24,25/3:5:8:9f:10f/6:6f/7:1:17f/9:4^2:5:6:19:
20/10:4/11:2/12:11/13:8:8f:10/14:4f/15:3,4/
16:9:15/17:8:8f:12/18:4:7:23/20:3:4:5:15/21:17
f/22:10

2989

NOW

Gen2:1:25/3:15:22/4:12/6:1/14:4:8,9/15:16/16
:5/18:11/19:9/20:1:7:16/23:10/24:1:36/25:1:11
/26:1:22/27:2,3,4:8,9,10:36/28:4/29:16:21:32:
34:35/30:15:20:30/31:3:5:13:34:36,37^2:44/32:3:
5:10/33:2/35:1:27/37:2:3:30/38:14/39:1/40:15:
18,19/41:56,57/42:22:24:36/44:30/46/48:5:11/
50:15^2/Ex3:10:17/4:6:7:10:12:23:27/6:1:5^2:10/
7:17/8:28/9:15/10:7/11:4/12:2/13:3:11:15/14:
1:3/16:1:3:7,8,9/17:1:8/18:11:19,20/19:5:10:15
/20:20/23:31/24:1/26:34/28:28/29:19,20/32:
10:29:32:34/35:1/36:4-7/39:27/40:1:12/Lev1:1
/8:5:29/10:8,9/18:28/22:3/Num3:14,15:40:44/
4:29/6:22,23/8:5,6/9:10/10:1/11:6:15:23/12:
3,4/13:1:23/14:15:19:25:40:41:43/16:10:13/18:
1:22/20:16:25/21:21/22:1:24:33/23:11:18-24/
24:1:10:14/25:12,13/26:64,65f/30:1/31:17:19/
Deu1:7:40/2:13:30/3:8:10/4:1:26/5:1:24/6/9:7
/10:12,13:22/11:2/12:8:15:20-23/18:9/20:8/22
:16/26:10/31:2:19:21:28/32:21:38/34:4/Jos1:2
/2:12,13/3:2,3,4:10:12:13,14/4:15,16/5:7/7:8:
25/8:1:8/9:12:13:23:25/10:1:22,23/11:17/13:1:
2-7/14:10^2:11/17:2/20/22:1:4^2/23:2:4,5:8/24:
13:23/Ju1:7:17/2:3:15/4:5:9:14/6:13:16f/7:25^2
/8:4:22/9:16:18:31:38/11:1:7:26^2/15:3:7:18^2/16
:13:15:23,24:25,26/17:13^2/19:16/20:3:7:40,41/
21:2:3/Ru2:1/3:3:10:11/4:16,17/1Sa1:28/2:1:4:
5^2:12:16:22/3:3,8/6:7/7:14/8:8/9:5:9,10,11:
20/10:17/12:2:3:7:14:16:19:20/13:14/14:21:29:
42:43:47/15:1:3:23:25:33/16:1/17:29/18:4:
11,12/19:1:5/20:1:31/21:3/22:22/23:7:13:
14,15:16:19:26/24:20/25:8:27/26:1:24/27:12^2/
28:20:22/29:1:10/2Sa1:24/2:7^2:24/3:1:16:18:
35,36/4:2,3/5:6:7:12/6:9/7:8:19:25/10:6:15,16/
11:25f^2/12:21:28/13:10:15:16:19:34:35:
37,38,39/14:7:25/15:19,20/16:3:7,8:19/17:1:26
/18:1:22/19:7:8,9:10,24,25:31,32/24:3/1Ki1:6:
11:15:20/2:5:16:26:36,37/3:4:7/5:4:6/8:7:12,13
:20^2:25/9:17,18/10:7/11:9,10:11:34/12:25:28/
14:1:4/15:19/16:3:21:24/17/18:8:11:14:19:23:
34/19:2:4:10:14/20:1:19:42/21:15/22:8/2Ki1:6
/2:1:19/3:9:15/4:1:13:38:41/5:15:17/6:15:20/7:
3/8:5/10:16/12:7^2/13:18:19/16:10/17:5/20:1:5
:8/23:19/24:20/1Ch13:12/14:2/15:1:12/17:10:
17:23:25/21:8/22:2:5:6:11:19/23:26/28:1:2:7/
29:3:4,5/2Ch1:1:5,6:8:10/2:1:17/5:2/6:4:5,6:10:
12,13:16:19:41/7:3/8:1:2:11/10:2,3/11:13,14/
12:5/14:7^2:9,10/15:3/16:9/18:6,7:30/20:10:11/
21:14/23:18/24:7,8:20/25:16:17/26:1/28:10:11
/29:10:31^2/30:1/31:2/32:22/34:10,11/35:3/36:
4/Ez1:2:3/2:1/9:8:10:13:14/10:10/Neh1:11/2:
17/4:15/7:73/8:1/9:8:32^2:36/11:1/12:47/13:18
/Est2:5:8/3:2:8/5:6/6:4/8:3:8:8f:9,10/9:12/Job
2:1/3:13/4:5/7:8/12:4/13:6:13/14:16/16:6:19/
19:3/20:20/22:10,11:19/24:24/30:1:6:9:11:15/
31:35/32:4/33:2/34:16:37/38:3/42:5^2:8:12/Ps3
:3:6/4:1/6:8/9:13/10:14/17:18:29:43,44,45/
22:9,10,11/27:9/29:10/30:6,7/32:6/35:15:17:
22/37:25/40:3:17/48:8/50:21/53:6/60:2/66:13
/68:11,12,13/69:13^2/71:9^2:11^2:18/77:6/80:12/
81:6/85:3:4/88:2/89:3,4/91:5/102:13:15/109:
17^2:19/111:9/116:7:12/118:14:22/119:26:
40,41,42:66:67:73:75,76,77:159/122:2,3/131:2:
3/132:7/Pro3:27,28/5:14/6:4/9:18/22:20,21/
24:28,29/Ecc1:16-18/2:1:12:17/3:22/4:8/7:4/
12:6/Sol2:9/7:8/Is1:10:15:21^2:22^2/5:1:3/6:7/8:
17/9:8,9,10/10:22:28,29^2/12:1/14:8:10:11/16:6
:10:13,14/18:4/21:8,9:12:16/23:4/25:1:9/26:13
/28:7/30:8/33:1:7/36:19/37:8,9:30^2/38:10:17:
20/39:1/40:28/41:1:7/42:9:14/43:1/44:13/46/
48:6:16:20/49:5/50:8/51:21/52:3:5:11/54:1:9/
55:6/59:1/63:15:18/65:1/Jer1:13/2:25/3:8/4:6
:10/5:5:19:27/6:20/7:6:13,14:25/9:10/10:17/11
:5:15:16/12:1:14/13:7:23/14:9:10^2:19/15:9/16:
16/17:17/18:11:21/19:10/20:1:3:7/22:22/23:2/
25:2,3:8,9:37/26:18/27:6/28:7:11/29:15/30:17/
31:28/32:5:31:36:43/34:16/36:30/37:19/40:4:7
/42:21/43:5/44:7/45:3/48:11:15:34:39/49:25/
50:8:18:31/51:8:9/Lam1:1^2:2:3:7:8:9/4:5:8:11:
14/5:2:5/Eze4:1:4,5:14/8:8/11:15:21/12:3:28/
16:57/19:13/20:4:21/21:9,10,11^2:24:26/22:1:4:
13/23:22/24:3:11:13/27:13f:14f:26:34/32:23:24
:25:26:28:30/33:22/35:15/36:13/37:17/38:8:12^2
/39:17:25/43:9/47:7:14:23/Dan1:9/2:23:36/4:3
:18:37/8:7/9:1:2f:7:25/10:14:19/11:2:7f:29/12:
6:9:13/Hos1:11^2:7:9:10:23/7:15/8:2:3/10:11:12
/13:2:10/Joe2:12:21/3:11:13/Amo1:5f/2:2/3:7:
9/6:2/7:16/9:11/Ob1:10/Jon:17/3:3:4,5/Mic4:
9^2/6:2/7:4:10/Nah1:13/2:11:13/3:5:18/Hab2:1
:6:8:17^2/3:2/Zep1:6/2:15/3:7/Hag2:3:15:18,19^2
/Zec1:5,6/2:6,7/3:4/4:2/7:6/8:3:11:13:20,21/9:
12/11:5/Mal3:14,15/4:1/Mt3:10/6:5:10:16/8:
22/9:13/10:27/11:2:5:12:15/12:37:41:42/13:18
:52/15:1:29:32/16:28/19:30^2/21:14:33/22:9:17:
31/23:38/24:32/25:21:23/26:6:45:49:54/27:11:
15/28:7/Mk1:21/3:31,32/4:22/5:11:35/6:15:25
:30/7:25/8:23:27/9:1:11/10:31:32:46/11:11/12:
14:26/13:28/14:20:32/15:6:8:10:29,30:38f/16:7
/Lk1:7:18:20:31:48:57/2:29,30,31/5:4:10:15/6:
21:25^2/8:8:41:47:49/9:26:27:32:46/10:1:3:8,9:
36:37/12:1:19:52/13:18:30^2:35^2/15:12/16:1:3:
16:25/18:30/19:8:27:42/20:9:22:33/22:1:7:16:
29:34:36:63,64/23:11:18:44/24:21:49/Jn1:45/2
:4:9/4:17,18:35^2:42:46,47:49/5:14:17f/6:2-5f:12
:32:63/7:6/8:15:52/9:12:14:25/11:11:22:30:39:
54/12:27/13:7:10:17:19:21:27:34:36:37/14:1:7:
17:25:28/15:15:22/16:4:5:12:22:24:30/17:5:7:
11:13/18:3/19:4:14:28/21:12/Act1:6:12:21,22/
2:1:9f:33/3:19/4:4:29/6:3/7:2f/8:12:28/9:6:10:
11/10:5,6:21:29:32:33:46,47/12:8:25/13:11:13:
32,33/14:26/15:10:12:36f/16:10f:19:34:37/17:1
:6:23:30/18:6/20:18:22:25:28:32/21:22/22:16/
23:21/24:10:25/26:3:16/27:9f:34/Rom1:5^2:16/
3:20:21,22^2:24:26/4:9:23/5:1:2:9^2:10:11:21/6:5:
10:14:15:17:18:19:21:22/7:4:6:6f:6:20/8:1:4:17:
18:22f/9:5/11:2,3:12:15:17:18:25:28:31/13:11/
15:23:33/16:17:25,26,27/1Co1:4:7:14:15/3:2/4
/6:11/7:1:10:18:22:23:24:25:28^2/8:4/9:15/10/
12:1:3:4:27/13:9:11:12^3/15:1^2:6:10:19:21:43^2:49
:53/16:1:12/2Co2:7:8:14/3/4:7:18/5:1:6:13,14:
16/6:2:13/7:9:14:16/8:1:7:11:14/11:6/12:9:14/
13:1:2:4^2:10/Gal1:1f:23/2:20/3:3:4:14:16:25:26:
29/4:6:7:9^2:16:20:24,25:27:29/5:1:25/6:15:17/
Eph1:6/2:2:7:13^2:18:19:20/3:5:12:20/4:23/5:8:
28/6:4:20/Php1:5:10:30/2:12:26/3:7:10:18/4:2:
8:20/Col1:21:22:23:26,27/2:2:6/3:1:8:9/1Th1:8
:9/2:15/3:6:7/4:1:13/2Th2:1/3:6:17/1Ti1:18/3:
14/4:8/6:14/2Ti1:10/4:6:7/Tit1:3/2:11/3:7/
Phm1:8,9^2:11:15:16/Heb:2/2:7:9:11:18/3:1:15/
4:7/5:12,13/6:3:18^2/7:19^2/8:13/9:1:11:16:24/

(OW Con't)
.19:23:25/11:16/12:2/13:19:20,21:23/**Jas4**:
/5:1:2:5:7:11/**1Pe1**:3^2:8:12:13:15:17:21:22/2:
:5:10^2:24:25/3:8:21f:22/5:1/**2Pe1**:9/3:8:18/
n2:28/3:2:9:10/4:14/5:20/**2Jn1**:5/**3Jn**:15/
d1:3:6:24,25/**Rev**:17,18/2:5:22/3:2/6:8/7:11
:12:15/11:1:15:15f:17:18/13:1/14:13:18/16:1
'17:8:9:10/18:7:19/20:4/21:3
1457

n15:2,3:8/24:12:42/27:34:38/32:9^2:11/43:20
4:18/49:2:6/**Ex4**:10/15:6:16/32:4:8/34:9/
um10:35:36/12:13/16:22/21:17,18:27-30/24:
9/27:16/**Deu3**:23,24,25/4:1/6:3:4/9:1:26/21:
26:10/27:9/32:1:6:40,41/33:3:7:11:18:23:29/
s7:7:8/**Ju5**:3:12^3:31/6:22/13:8/16:28/21:3/
Sa1:11/4:9/14:41^2/23:10:11/**2Sa1**:19:21:24/7
8:27/14:4/15:31/18:33^2/19:4^2:26/22:3:29:50/
Ki3:7/8:12,13:22,23:25:26:28:52:61/13:2/17:
:20:21/18:26:36:37/**2Ki1**:9:11:13/4:15,16/19
5:16^2:19:30/20:3/**1Ch16**:12,13^2:23:28/17:16:
:19:20/21:17/29:10:11:13:16:18/**2Ch1**:8/6:1:
:16:19:40:41^2:42/13:12/14:11/20:6:7:12:15:
:20/35:21/**Ez9**:6:10:15/**Neh1**:5^2:11/4:4/5:19
:9:14/9:32/13:14:22:29/**Est7**:3/**Job**:12:20/9:
/13:20/16:8:18/17:3,4/30:20/33:31/37:14/
s2:10/3:1:7^2/4:1:6:8/5:1^2:10:12/6:2:4/7:1:9/8:
9/9:1:2:2f:6:13:19/10:12^2:14/12:7/13:3/16:1/
:1:6:7/18:15:35:49/19:14/20:9/21:1:8:13/22:
^{2}/24:7/25:1:4:6,7/26:2:11/27:8:9:11/30:2:8:9
2/31:5,6,9,10:14,15/35:1:23/36:5:7/38:1:15:
/39:12/40:5:9:11:17/41:4/42:1:9:11/43:1:4:5
4:1:9:23:26/45:3:6:10,11/48:10:11^2/50:7/51:
10:14,15:17/52:4:9/54:1:5:6/55:1:9/57:1:7:8:
/58:6/59:1:3:5:9:11:17/60:1/61:5/62:8/63:1/
:1:5/66:3:7:10/67:1:5/68:1:7:9,10:15,16^2:28:
:32/69:1:5:6^2:16:29/70:1:5/71:4:5:8:12:17:22
72:1/73:22/74:1:9,10:18:19:21:22/77:13/78:1/
:1:5:12/80:1^2:3:4:7:14:19/81:8^2/82/83:1:13:
/84:1:3:8:9:12/85:4/86:1:3:4:5:6:14/87:3/88:
9:13:14/89:5:8:46/90:13/92:4:5/93:1/94:5/96
/99:8/100:1/102:24/104:1:24/105:3/106:4:47
108:1:2/109:1:21^2:26/113:1/114:7/115:1:9:10
16:16/118:13:21:25/119:55:64:75,76,77:89:
37:145:151:169:174/120:2:3/122:7/123:1/125
/130:1:7/131:3/132:8:13/135:19:20/137:5,6:
8/138:4/139:1:21:23/140:1:6,7,8/141:8/143:
9/144:3:9/146:10/147:12^2/148:1/149:2^2:6,7/
ro8:4,5/23:19,20,21:26,27,28/24:15,16/30:2:7
31:2:4/**Sol1**:5:7:8/2:7/3:5:11/5:8:9:16/6:1:4:
3/7:1:6/8:4:12:13/**Is1**:2/2:5/3:12/5:19/7:13/8
8:9,10:9,10f/10:16:24:30^2/13:2:5/14:12/18:2
19:12/21:10:13:14/22:17:18/23:1:4:10:12/24:
7/25:1:4/26:8:13:15/30:19/31:6/32:10:11/33:
13/34:1/37:16,17:18:20/38:3:14:16/40:9:27^2/
1:8:14/42:10/43:1:10:22/44:1^2:2^2:23^3/45:8:
5/46:8/47:1^2:5:6:8/49:13^3/51:4:9/52:1:2/54:1:
1/62:5:6,7/63:15:17:19/64:8/**Jer1**:6/2:4,5:23:
1/3:4,5:12:14:22/4:1:14:19/5:3:15:21/6:8:
8,19:26/7:2:29/9:20/10:1:6:7:23/11:13:20/12:
:3^2/13:27/14:7:8:9^2:13:19:20:22/15:16/16:19/
7:13/18:6:19/20:7:12/22:2:29/25:34/30:10^2/
1:3:4:21:22:23^2/32:17/34:4/37:20/42:15:19/
4:26/45:2/46:9:11:27:28/47:5:6/48:17:18:28:
2:43:46/49:3:4:8:25:30/50:11:21:24:31:42/51:
3:25:45/**Lam1**:9:11:18:20:21:22/2:13:18:20/3:
7:55:58:64/4:21/5:1:19/**Eze4**:14/6:3/7:7/9:8/
1:13/12:25/13:4:5/16:35/18:25:29:30:31/20:
9:44:47:49/21:16:25/23:22/26:17/27:3/28:16:
2/29:8/31:18/32:19/33:8:10:11/34:7:17:18/35
15/36:4:11:32/37:4:9:13/44:6/**Dan2**:23:31:47/
4:14:16/4:9:18:27:31/5:22/6:20/9:4:7:8:10:15
17:18:19^4/10:11/**Hos1**:11:17/4:1:15/6:4:11/8:
/9:1:10:14/10:9/13:14^2/14:1:2:3:8/**Joel1**:13^2/2
17:23/3:11/**Amo5**:1:7/6:14/7:2:5/9:7/**Jon1**:14
/2:4:6/**Mic1**:13/2:7:12/4:8:10:13/5:2/6:3:5/7:8
14/**Nah1**:12:15/2:12/3:18/**Hab1**:2:12^2/3:2/
Zep3:14^3/**Hag2**:4:23/**Zec1**:12/3:2f:8/9:9/11:1:
2/13:7/**Mal1**:5:6/**Mt2**:6/6:30/8:26:29/9:27/11:
25/14:31/15:22/16:8/23:37/**Mk9**:19f:25/10:48
51/12:29/**Lk9**:41/10:21/13:34/16:27/**Jn17**:25
/**Act1**:24,25/2:22/4:24:29/26:7:19/**Rom15**:10:
11/**1Co**:55,56/**Gal4**:27/**Eph5**:14/**Heb1**:8/10:5/
Rev4:11/6:10/12:12/15:3,4^2/16:5/18:20
807

OF

^{2}**Gen1**:2:2f:4,5f:7,8f:11,12^2:13f:19f:20:21,22^2:23f
:24^2:25:26:28:31f/2:3:4^2:7:7f^2:7:9^6:10:11,12^3:
11,12f:11,12:13^2:14^2:15:16,17^2:19,20:21:23^2:25/
3:1^3:2,3^2:6:7:8:14:15^2:20:21:22^2:23:24^3/4:3:4:9:
16^3:18f:18:18f:18:18f:18:18f:18:20:21f:21:22f:22
:26f/5:1:1f:1^2:1f:1:3,4,5f:3,4,5:3,4,5f:3,4,5:6,7,8:
9,10,11:12,13,14:15,16,17:18,19,20,25,26,27:28-
28-31^2/6:1f^7:4:5^2:7:8:12,13:17:19,20^3/7:1:2^3:3^3:
4:8,9:14,15^3/8:3,4:5f:7f^2:13f:20/9:2,3:13^2:18^2:18
f:19^2:22:24,25^2:26,27f:26,27/10:1^2:2:3:4:6:7^2:8:8
f:8^2:9^3:10^2:11,12,13,14:15-19^2:20:21:22:25:26-
26-30^3:31:32/11:2:2f^2:3,4:6:6f^4:8:9:10,11:12,13f^2
:24,25:28:29:31^3:32:32f/12:1:2:3:3f:11,12,13^2:14
:15f:16:17:20/13:7^2:9^2:10^2:10f:11:12^3:13:18/14:
1^4:2^5:3^2:5,6^2:8,9^2:10^3:13^2:14:15:16:17^2:18^3:19,20^3
:21:22:23:24^2/15:2,3:2,3f:6:7^3:12:16:17:18f^2/16:
2,3:5^2:7:9-12^2:13:14/17:2,3,4^2:5:6:7,8^2:9,10:11:
12:16:24-27/18:1:3,4:6f:6:16:18^2:20:25:28:31:32
/19:1^2:4:11:12:13:14:15:16:18,19,20:25:26:28:29
:30:33:37^2:38^3/20:1:5:8:9,10^2:17/21:9:10:13^2:14^2
:17:20,21:22:26:31:32/22:2^2:4:6:11:13:15:17:18:
20-23^3/23:1:3:4:5,6^2:9^3:10:11:12:13:14,15:16:
17,18^3:19,20/24:3^2:7^2:9f:10^3:11:12^2:13:14:15,16
:24^2:25:27^2:31f:35^3:37:37f:42:43:44:47:48^2:51:60
:67/25:4f:6:7,8:9,10^2:12-15^4:16^2:17:18^3:19:20^2:
21:23:28:30:32:34:34f/26:1^2:4^2:8^2:13:14^3:15:18:
20:21:22:24^3:29:33:34^3/27:8,9,10,11,12^2:16^3:18:
24:27,28,29^5:32:37^2:39,40:41:42:45^2:46^2/28:1:2^3
:5:9^3:12:13^3:14:19^2:19f:22/29:1:2^2:3:5:10:12,13:
22:25:26/30:1:6f^3:14:15:25:27:28:35,36^2/31:3:5:
11:13:14:15:17-20:21^2:22:25:29:33:35f^2:36,37:
38:39:40:41:42^3:46:47,48^2:49:51,52:53^4:54/32:1:
3:5:6:9^3:10^2:11:16:25:30:31:32/33:4:10:10f:13:
14:15:19^2:20/34:1:2:5:6,7:13:15:18,19:20f:22:25
:27:29:30/35:3:5:7f:8:15:16:18^2:20:21:22^2:23:24:
25:26:28,29/36:1^2:2,3^3:2,3f:2,3^2:5:6,7,8^2:9:13,14
f:15,16^{10}:17^5:18,19^5:20,21^{11}:22^2:23:24:25:26:27:
28,29,30:31-39^{13}:40-43^{16}/37:1:2^2:3:4:11:19,20:
25:28^2:29:36^3/38:2:8:10:12^3:14:16:21^3:22:23:24:
25:27:28/39:1^5:2:4^3:10:23/40:1^3:5:9,10:13:14:16
:17:20/41:1:2:5:8^2:10^3:12^2:13:14:15:17:18:19:22:
23:24:25:26^2:27^3:29^2:30:31:33:34,35f:34,35^2:36:
38:39:40^2:41,42^3:43:44^2:45^3:45f^2:45:46^2:48:49^2:
50^5:51^2:52:53:54^2/42:6^3:7:8,9:13^3:15:16^2:19^2:21:
23:25:27^2:29:32^2:33:35:36:38/43:8:11:12:14:16:
18:23:33^2:34/44:1^2:2:4:7^2:8:9^2:10:11:17:20^2:28:
32:33/45:1:5:6:8^3:9^2:10:11,12^4:15:18^3:20^2:22^3:
23^3:25:26/46:1:3,4:6:8-14^2:15:18:19-22^5:
23,24,25:26^3:27:31:34^2/47:1:2:4:5,6^4:9:11^2:12:
13:15:17:20:21:24:25:26^2:27^2:28:30/48:3:4:5^2:14^2
:15:16:20:21:22^3/49:2:3^2:4^2:5^2:7f:13:14:24^2:25^5:
26^3:29,30^2:32/50:3^2:5:7^2:8^2:9:10f:10^2:11:12,13^3:
14:16,17^2:19:20:21:23^2:24^3:26/**Ex1**:1^2:6:7:8^2:9:
10:11:13,14:15,16:20:21:22/2:1^2:5^2:6:7:10:11:13
:15:16^2:21:23^2:24/3:1^4:2^2:6^2:7:8:9^2:10:12:13:15:
16:18^4:19:22^2/4:5:15:20^2:25,26:27:29^2/5:1:3:6:
16:18/6:1:4:5^2:6:8,9:8,9f:11:13^2:14^5:15^3:16^5:17:
18:19^2:20:21:22:23^2:24^2:25^6:26^3/7:2:3:7:11:16:
17:19:20^2:21:22/8:2:5^2:12:16:19:21:22^2:24:29:30
/9:1:3:4^2:6^2:7:9:11:13:20:21:24:26^2:32:33/10:2:3
:4,5:6^3:10:12:14:15^3:19:21^2:23:28/11:1^2:2:3^2:5^3:
6^2:7^3:8:9/12:2:3,4^3:6^2:7^3:10:12^3:13:14:15:16^3:17^2
:18^4:19^2:21^2:22^2:23:23f:27^3:28:29^3:30^2:31:33^2:35
:36:37^2:38^2:39:40,41^3:42:43:45:46^2:47:50^2:51^3:
51f^3/13:1^2:3^2:4,5^2:4,5f:4,5:6:7:8:9:14:15^2:16^2:
17,18:19^3:20:21^2:22/14:5:7:8^3:9:10:16:17:19^2:20^3
:21:22:23^3:24^2:25:28^2:29^2:30:31/15:1:7:8:14:15^3:
16:19^3:20:22^2:24:26/16:1:5:6^4:7,8,9:10:13:14:15:
17:20^3:22^2:23:27:28,29:32:33:35^2:36/17:1:3:5,6:
7^2:8^2:9^3:10:10f^3:10:11:13:14:15,16/18:2:4^2:5,6f:
8:9:12:15,16:19,20^2:21^4:22/19:1,2,3^2:5^2:6:7:8^2:9:
13:16:17:18:20^2/20:4f:5:6:7:7f:10^2:17:22:23^2:24^2
:26/21:7:11:13:16:19:21:26:30f:32:34^2:35:36^2/
22:1:2:4:5^3:6^2:9:21:26:29:30/23:2,3^2:8^2:9:12:13^2:
15:16^3:19^2:19f:21:23:24^2:26^2:27:31:33/24:1^3:2:4^2
:5:6^2:7^2:9^2:10^2:12:13:16:17^2/25:1:8:9^3:11:12:
13,14:16:17^2:17f:18^3:20:21:22^3:23:24:25:26,27:
30:31:32,33:34:35^2:36:38:39/26:1:3:6:7,8^3:9^2:
10,11^2:12^2:14^3:15,16:18,19^3:20:25,26,27^3:28:34:
35^2:36:37/27:2:3:7:11^2:12:14,15^2:16:19^2:20^2:21/
28:4f:5,6^2:7:8^2:9^2:10:12^2:13,14^2:15:16^2:17:21^3:
22,23,24^5:25^4:26:27:28^3:29^3:30,31^2:32^2:33,34:35^2
:36:37,38^5/29:1:2,3,4:11:12^5:15,16^2:17:
19,20^5:21^2:22^2:23^3:24^2:26^2:27:28^2:29^2:31:32:34:
40^4:42:43:45:46/30:2:3:4:5:6:10:11,12^2:13f:16^2:
22,23^4:24^3:31:32:33:34:35:36^3/31:1^4:3:4^2:6^3:7^2:8
:12,13^2:16^2:17^2:18^2/32:4^2:8:10:11:12:13^2:15:17:
18:19:23:25:26:27^2:29:31:32:32f:33:34/33:4:9:
10:11:16:19:20:22/34:2:4:5,6^4:5,6f:10^2:11^2:13f:
15^2:18:20:22^2:23^2:25^2:26^3:27:29:30^2:31/35:1^2:2:
5-9^3:10-19^8:21:22^2:29:30,31^5:34^4/36:10:11,12:
13^2:14,15:16:17:19^2:20^2:21:25,26:27:30:31,32^2:
33:36/37:1:2:5:6:7^2:8:9:12:13:17^2:19^2:20,21^2:22:
23,24^2:25^2:29/38:1:2:5:6:7:9:10:14,15:16^2:17:18^2
:19:21:22^4:23^3:24^3:25,26^2:27^2:29^2/39:1:3:4,5,6,7^4
:6,7f^2:8:10:14^2:15-18^4:19:20:21^3:22^2:23:24^2:
25,26^2:28,29:30^2:32:33-40^7:42/40:2:3:5^2:6:8:9:
10:12:17:20:22:23:24:28:33:34:35:36:38/**Lev1**:
2,3^2:4^3:5^2:8:11:12:15,16,17^2/2:2:3^2:5:6:7:9^2:11:
13f^3:13:14:16^2/3:1:2^2:7,8^2:13^2/4:2^2:4:6^2:7^4:10^2:
11,12:13:14:15:17:18^3:22^3:25^6:26^2:27:29:30^4:34^4:35
/5:2^3:3:5:7:9^3:11^2:13^2:15f^2:16f:16:17,18^2/6:4,5:9
:10:12:14:15:16^2:17^2:18:19,20^2:22,23^3:26:30/7:7
:9:10^2:12^2:13:14^3:16^2:17,18:23:24^2:26,27:29:30:
34^3:36:38/8:1^2:8f:11:15,16^4:17:22:23^4:24^4:26^2:
27^2:29^2:30^2:31^2:32:35/9:1^2:3:5:9^2:19:20:21:23/
10:1:2:4:6^6:7^2:14^4:15:16^2:17/11:2,3:21,22^2:27:32^2
:34:35:39:44:45^2/12:1:5f:6^2/13:1:5:6:9,10:11:13:
18:19:41:47,48:59/14:3:4^2:5:7:9:10^2:11:12^3:13:
14^5:15:17^5:18:19:21^3:22:23^2:24^2:25^4:26:27:28^5:
29:31:32^2:33,34:35:37^2:40^2:41:45^2:49:50:51,52/
15:1:1f:14:15:19:26:29:31^2:33/16:1^2:5:7:10:12^2:
13^2:14^4:15^3:16^2:17:18^2:19:20:21^3:22:29,30:29,30
f^2:29,30^2:31:32:34^2/17:1:3,4:5^3:6^2:7:8,9:11:12:
13:14^2:15^2/18:1:3^2:6:6f:8:9:10:13:14:16f:21^2:24:
25^2:26^3:27:28:29,30^3/19:1:7:8:9^2:10:12:16:16f:
19^2:21:23:27:29:32:33:34:35,36:37/20:1:4:6:8:17^3
:18:19^3:22^2:23:24/21:7^2:8:9:11:12^2:14,15^2:16,17:
21^2:22:23:24/22:6:7:8:10:12f:13:14:15:17,18:22:
29,30^2:31/23:1^2:3^3:5^2:5f^2:6:7:8^2:9,10,11^3:13^5:14:
15,16^4:17^7:18f:20:21^2:22^2:23,24:23,24f^2:23,24^2:
25:26,27:26,27f^2:30,31^2:32:33,34^2:33,34f^2:33,34:
33,34f:35:36^3:37:38^2:39^4:40^2:42:43^2:44^2/24:1:
3,4^2:5-8^4:9:10^2:11^3:15,16^2:23/25:1:5:9:9f^2:10:12:
13:14,15,16^3:21,22:24:25:27:28:29:30:31:32:33:
34:38^3:40:42:45:46:48:50^4:52:54:55^2/26:2:3:8^3:
10:13^2:21:25:31:36^2:39^2:40,41^2:45:46/27:1:3:4:
16^4:17:18^3:20:21:22:23:24:25f:26:27^3:29f:30^2:32:
33:34/**Num1**:1:1f^2:1^2:2-15^{15}:17,18,19f^2:17,18,19
:17,18,19f:20-46^3:47,48,49:52:53:54/2:1:3-31^{24}:
32,33:34/3:2f:4:6:7,8,9^6:10:11,12^2:13^2:14,15^2:
16-24^2:25-30^6:31-35^8:36,37^4:38^3:39:40:41^2:42^3:
43:45^7:46^2:47,48f:49^3:50:50f/4:1^2:3:6:7:8^2:9:10:
11:12^2:14^2:15^3:16:17,18,19:21,22,23^6:25:26^2:27:
29^3:30,31:34:35^2:38-41:42-45:46,47,48^2/5:1:5,6:
9,10:11,12:15^3:17:18:19:26/6:1^2:3,4:6,7^3:9^2:10:
11:12:13^4:15^2:17:18^3:19^3:20^2:21^2:22,23:24,25,26
:27f:27/7:1:2^2:3:4,5:8:9^2:11^2:12^3:13^3:14:18-23^3:
18-23f:24-29^3:24-29f:30-35^3:30-35f:36-41^3:36-
36-41f:42-47^3:42-47f:48-53^3:48-53f:54-59^3:54-
54-59f:60-65^3:60-65f:66-71^3:66-71f:72-77^3:72-
72-77f:78-83^3:78-83f:84,85,86^4:89/8:4,5,6:7:8:9:
10:11^2:12:14^2:15:16^3:17:18^2:19^2:20:21^2:23,24^2/9
:1^2:2,3^2:2,3f^3:2,3:4,5:6,7:10^3:11:12^2:13:15:16:17:
18:22:23/10:1^2:3:4^2:5,6,7:10^3:11^3:12:14^3:15^2:16^2
:17^4:18^3:19^2:20^2:22^2:23^2:24^2:25^5:26^2:27^2:29:31:
33f:33:34:36/11:1^3:3:4,5^5:7^3:10:11:12:15:16^2:17^2
:25:26:28^2:29:30:33^2:34^2/12:1f^6:5:7,8:9:16/13:2:
3-15^{26}:17:20^2:21:23^4:24^2:26^2:29:32^2:33^3/14:2:3^2
:5:6^3:9^2:10,11^3:14^2:16:17,18:19^2:20,21:22:24:25^3
:29:30^2:31^2:33:34,35^2:36,37,38^2/15:1:3,4^3:5:6^2:7
:8,9^3:10:17,18:19,20,21^2:22:25^2:31:32^2:37,38^2:
39^4:41^2/16:1^6:2:3^4:6,7:8,9^3:11,12:13:15:18:19:22
:23,24:25:26:27^2:34^2:36,37:38^3:39:40^2:42:43,44:
50/17:1^4:4^2:6:7:8:10:12,13/18:1:2,3^2:4^2:5^3:6:7:8:
11^2:12:14,15^3:16^2:17:18^2:19^2:19f:21^2:24:25,26^3:
27:28,29^2:32^2/19:1^2:4^2:9^4:10^3:12:13:16:17f:20/
20:1^2:4:5:6^2:12^2:13:14^2:14f^2:15:16^2:18:20:23^2:24^2
:27:28:29/21:1^2:2^3:3:4^2:5:6:8^3:11:12:13^2:14^4:15:
17,18:20:21:24:24f^4:25,26^2:27-30^4:31,32:33^2/22:
1^3:2,3^3:4:5,6^5:7^2:10:11:15:18:22,23:24:26:27:36:
41^2/23:6:7-10^2:13^2:14^2:17:18-24^5:28/24:1:2:3-9^5
:11:13^2:15-19^6:20^3:21,22^2:23,24/25:1:3^3:4:6^3:7^2:
10,11^2:12,13^3:14^3:15:18/26:1:2^3:3,4^3:5-11^6:12-
12-14:15-18^2:19-22^4:23-25^2:26,27^2:28-37^{12}:38-
38-41^3:42,43^3:44-47^3:48-50^2:51:55,56:57:58,59^5:
62^3:63:64,65f^3:64,65^4/27:1^6:3,4^2:6,7:12:14^6:16^2:
17:18:19:20:21/28:1:3:5^3:7^2:9,10^2:11^2:12^2:13:14:
15:16^3:18^2:20,21^4:24^2:25:26^5:27:28,29^3/29:1^2:1f^2
:1:2:3,4^3:6f:7f^2:7^3:8:9,10^2:11^2:12f^2:12^2:14^3:15:17:
20:23:26,27:29:32:34:36:39:40^2/30:1:7^2:11:12/
31:3:4,5^2:6:6f:7:8^2:9,10,11^3:12^4:13:16^2:19^2:20:26^2
:27^2:28^2:29:30^3:36-40^4:41:42-46^2:47:48,49:54^2/
32:1^3:3,4:5^2:7:8:9:10,11^2:12^2:14^2:17^3:18:19:22^2:
25:26:27:28:29^3:30^2:31:32:33^7:34,35,36:37,38^3:
39^3:41^5/33:1^3:3,4^2:3,4f^2:3,4^2:5,6:7:8:9:11:15-37^5
:38,39^3:38,39f^2:40^3:44:47:48:49:50,51^2:54^2/34:1^2
:3^3:4f:4:5f:6:10,11^3:14,15^3:16-28^{13}:29^2/35:1:2:6:
8:11:12,13:14^4:15:16:19:20:24:25^2:28^2:31:32^2:33
/36:1^{11}:3:4:5^2:6:7^3:8:10,11,12^2:13^2/**Deu1**:1^4:1f^2:
1:1f:1^4:7^4:8^2:15:17:19,20,21:22:24,25^2:28^3:33^2:
36^2:37:38:40/2:1:4:5:7:9^2:10:12^2:14,15:18:19^3:
22:23^2:24^3:25:26^3:30:31:35,36^2:37/3:1^3:4^2:5^2:6:8^4
:10^2:11^4:12^4:13^5:14^4:15:16^3:17:18^2:21:22:
23,24,25^2:26^2:27/4:1:4:11:15:16,17^2:21,22^2:25:
32:33:34:36^2:37:41^2:43^3:44,45,46^3:47^3:48:49^2/5:
1:4:5:8:9,10^4:11f:14^2:15:16:22^2:23:24:26,27^2:32/

(OF Con't)
6:2[2]:3:9:10,11,12[4]:14:15:20:21:23:24:25/7:2:4:6:
7:8:12[2]:13[2]:14[2]:15[2]:18[2]:19[2]:21:24:25/8:3:6:7:8[2]:
14[2]:16/9:4[2]:5[3]:9:10,11:12[2]:13,14:15:21:27[2]/10:3
:4:6[2]:7:8[2]:9[2]:12,13:17[3]:19:22/11:1:4:6[2]:10:11[2]:
13:14:17:20:25:27:28:30[2]/12:1:3:6[3]:9:12:14:15:
17[3]:26,27:28[2]:31/13:2:5[2]:9:10[2]:12,13,14[3]:15[2]:16
:17:18[2]/14:1[2]:2:8:22:23[3]:25/15:1[2]:4,5[2]:9:10:12:
15:18:19[3]/16:1:1f:1:3[2]:4[2]:8[2]:10[2]:13[2]:14[2]:15[2]:16[4]
:18:19:21/17:6:8[2]:12:16:19[3]:20/18:1[2]:3:4[2]:5[2]:6,7[2]
:8:9:11:12:16[3]/19:2,3[2]:4[2]:5:6,7:9:10:11[3]:12:15/
20:1[2]:3:5:6:8:9:15f[2]:16:17:18[2]/21:3:8:15:16:17[3]:
19:20:21[2]:22:23/22:8:9:9f:11:12:13,14:15:17,18:
19f:19:21[2]:23,24[2]:28,29f/23:2:4[2]:8[2]:9,10:13:
17,18:19:24:25/24:8[2]:16[3]:17:22/25:1[2]:6:8:9:10:
11[2]:17:18:19/26:8:10[2]:12:13[2]:14:16:18/27:1:
2,3,4[2]:8:9:10:12:13:15[2]:18:20/28:1[2]:2-6:11:12:
13:14:15-19[3]:20[2]:21:24:25:27:30:31:33:34:36:37:
47,48[3]:50:51:53[2]:55[4]:58,59:60:62:64[2]:67/29:1[2]:
2,3:7[2]:8[2]:9:10:14,15:16[2]:17:18[3]:19:21:22:23:25[4]:
27:28/30:2:3:4:5:6[2]:10:20/31:1:4:6:9[4]:10,11[3]:12:
18:19[2]:21:22:23[2]:26[2]:28:30/32:3:7:8:10:14:15:16
:21[2]:22[2]:26:30:31:32:33:35:40,41[3]:44,45:49[3]:51[3]
:52/33:1[2]:2:5[2]:7[2]:8:10:12[2]:13[3]:14:15[2]:16[2]:17[3]:18[3]
:19[2]:20:21:22[2]:23[3]:24[2]:25[2]:26:28/34:1:3:5[2]:8[2]:9[4]
:11,12/Jos1:1[2]:2:3[2]:4:6:7:8:10,11:12,13,13[5]:15/2:2[2]
:6:9:10:11[2]:12,13:15:24/3:1[2]:2,3,4:2,3,4f[2]:8:11[3]:
13,14:15,16[2]:17/4:2,3:5[3]:7[3]:8:9[2]:10[2]:11:12,13[4]:
14[3]:18:19:19f[2]:19[2]:21:22[2]:24[2]/5:1[2]:2,3[2]:4,5[2]:6:
8,9:8,9f:8,9:10[3]:11,12:13:14/6:1[2]:3,4:5:10:15:18:
19:20[2]:23:26f/7:1[7]:2[3]:3[2]:5[3]:6[2]:9:12[2]:13[2]:14:15[2]:
16[2]:17[4]:19:20:21:23:24[2]:25:26[3]/8:1[2]:3,4:5:9[2]:10:
11,12,13[3]:14[3]:20,21:22[2]:23:24:25:27:28:29[3]:30:
31[2]:32[3]:32f:33[4]:34[3]/9:1[4]:3,4,5:6[2]:9[3]:10[3]:11:
14,15:17:18[4]:19:20:21:23:24:26:27[3]/10:1[2]:3[5]:4:6[2]
:8[2]:10[2]:11:12[2]:13[2]:14[2]:18:19:22,23[2]:24:25:26:27[2]
:28:33:37:39:40[2]:42/11:1[13]:4[2]:5:6:7:8:10[2]:12:13:
14:15:16[2]:17[3]:18[2]:19[3]:20:21[2]:22:23/12:1[4]:2[8]:3[3]:
4[2]:5[6]:6[3]:7[6]:8-24[32]/13:2-7[15]:8[4]:9[3]:10[3]:11[3]:12[3]:13:
14[2]:15[4]:16[4]:20:21[4]:22[2]:23[2]:24[2]:25[3]:27,28[4]:29[2]:
30[3]:31[3]:32:33[2]/14:1[2]:3,4[2]:5:6:7:9:12:13,14:15/
15:1[4]:2,3,4[5]:5:6[3]:7[3]:8[7]:9[3]:10,11[7]:12:13[3]:14[2]:15:
16:17:20[2]:21-32[3]:33-36:37-44:45[3]:46:47[4]:48-62f[2]
:48-62:63[3]/16:1[5]:5,6:8:9[3]:10/17:1[5]:2[2]:3[3]:4:5,6[2]:7[5]
:8[4]:9[6]:10[5]:11:12:14[2]:15:16,17,18[2]/18:1[2]:4:7[5]:8[2]:
11[5]:12[2]:13:14[4]:15[2]:16[7]:17[3]:18:19[2]:20:21-28[3]/19:
1[4]:2-7f:8:10[3]:11:12:13:14[2]:15,16[2]:17-23[2]:
24,25,26:27[3]:29:30,31:32[2]:34:40:47,48[3]:49[2]:50:
51[3]/20:2[2]:3[3]:4:5:6[2]:7[5]:8[10]:9/21:1[3]:3:4[7]:5[3]:6[3]:7:8:
9-16[7]:17,18:19:20,21,22[3]:23,24:25[2]:26[2]:27[4]:
28,29:30,31:32[2]:33:34,35[2]:38,39:40:41,42/22:1[2]:
2,3:4:5:7,8[5]:9[4]:10:11:13[2]:14[2]:15[3]:16[3]:17,18:19[2]:
20:21[3]:22,23[2]:24,25:28[4]:29:30:32:33:34[2]/23:1:2:
4,5[2]:6[2]:7:10[2]:14/24:1:2[3]:3:8[2]:9[2]:11:12[2]:15[2]:17[2]:
20:23:26[2]:28:29:30[3]:31:32[5]:33[2]/Ju1:1[2]:3[5]:4,5,6:
9:10:11:13:14:15:16[5]:17[2]:18[2]:19[3]:20[4]:21:22,23[2]:
24[2]:27:29[2]:30[2]:31,32[3]:33[3]:34:35:36[2]/2:1[3]:5:6[2]:7-
7-9[6]:11:12-14[4]:15:17:18[2]:19:20/3:1[4]:1f:1:4:6[3]:7:
8[2]:9:10[4]:12[3]:13[3]:14:15:17,18,19:22,23:27:28:29[2]
:31/4:1:2,3[2]:4:5:6[4]:9[2]:10:11[3]:14:16:17[4]:20:23/5:
3:4:5[2]:6[2]:8:9:11[5]:12:13,14:15[2]:16:18[2]:19:20:22[3]:
23:24:28[2]/6:1[2]:5:6,7[2]:8[2]:10:11[3]:12:13:15[2]:19:22[2]
:24[2]:25[2]:27[5]:28[2]:29:30:31:32:33[2]:34[2]:35:38/7:1[4]:
2[3]:3[2]:5,6:11:12,13[4]:14[2]:15:17:18,19,20[4]:22[2]:23[2]:
24[2]:25[3]/8:1,2,3[3]:2,3f[2]:5[2]:6:7:10[3]:11:13:14[2]:16:
16f:18:22:23,24:26:27f:28:32[3]:35/9:2:2f[2]:3[2]:4:5:
6[2]:7[2]:15:16:20:21:22,23:24:25[2]:26[2]:27:30:31:37:
38:39:40[2]:41:42:43:44:46[2]:47,48[2]:49[2]:50:51:
56,57[3]/10:1[6]:4[2]:6[2]:7,8[2]:14:17:18/11:1[4]:3[2]:5:7:8:
11:12:13[2]:16:17[3]:18:19:21,22:23:25[2]:26:27:28:
29[3]:30,31:33:40/12:1:2:4[2]:4f:4[2]:5[4]:6[2]:7[2]:13:15/
13:2,3[5]:5[2]:6:7[2]:9:16:21[2]:25[5]/14:3:4:5:6:8[2]:9[2]:
10,11[2]:12:14:17[2]:18:19[2]/15:5[2]:8[2]:10:11[3]:12,13:
14:18[2]:19/16:1:2:3[2]:4:5[2]:9f:10:15:23,24[3]:25,26:
27:28[2]:30/17:1:4,5[2]:7,8[2]:10,11/18:1:2[3]:6:7[2]:11[2]:
12[2]:13[2]:15,16:19[2]:21:22:23:25[2]:26[2]:27[2]:28[2]:30[2]:
31/19:1[4]:8:14[2]:16[2]:18:19:22:26:27:29:30[2]/20:1[2]:
3[4]:5:6:7:8,9,10[4]:12:13[3]:14,15[2]:17[2]:18:19,20:
22,23,24:27,28[5]:31[4]:32[3]:33[2]:34[2]:35-39[10]:43[3]:44:
45[2]:46,47[2]:48[2]/21:1[2]:3[2]:5:6[2]:8,9,10,11,12[4]:13[2]:
14[2]:15:16[3]:17:18:19[3]:20:21:23:24/Ru1:1[2]:3:4,5:
8:11f[2]:13:22/2:2:3:6:8,9,10,11:12:13:14f:16:18:
19:20:20f:23/3:2:6,7:15-18/4:1f:2[2]:5:7:9:10[2]:11:
12[2]:14:15[2]:16,17[3]:18-22/1Sa1:1[4]:3[2]:6:11:17:
19,20[2]:24/2:8[2]:12:13,14[2]:15:17[2]:20:21:22:
23,24,25:26:27f:27:29[2]:30[3]:32:36/3:12:14[2]:15:
20:21,4:1/4:2:3:4[3]:5:6[2]:8:10:11:12:12f:13[3]:17:
21,22/5:1[3]:3:4[2]:5[3]:6[2]:7[2]:8[4]:10[3]/6:2[2]:4,5[3]:8[2]:9:11
:12:13:14[2]:15[3]:17[2]:18:19[3]:21/7:1[3]:3:4:5:6:10:12:
13:15:16[2]/8:3:4:14:15:16:17:18/9:1[5]:4[3]:5:6:16[2]:
19:20:21[3]:22:23[2]:26,27/10:1[2]:2:3[3]:4:5[2]:6:9:10[2]:
12[2]:12f:17:18,19:20:21[4]:24:25:26/11:1[3]:2[2]:3[2]:6:
7[2]:8:10:11[2]/12:2:5:6[2]:7:9[2]:12:17[2]:18[2]:24/13:1:2[3]
:3,4[2]:5[2]:6[2]:7[2]:13[2]:15:16:17[3]:18:19[2]:21:22:23/14:
1:2:3[4]:5[2]:11:14:16:18[2]:19:29:32:36:39:40:41:43[2]:
45[2]:47[2]:50,51[3]/15:1:2:6[3]:7:8:9[3]:14[2]:15:17[2]:21:22
:23[2]:24[2]:26[2]:28[2]:29:32:33:35/16:1[3]:3:4:8:9:10,11
:13:14:15,16:18[2]:20:22/17:2:4-7[5]:10:11f:12[3]:16:
17[2]:19:20:23:25[2]:26:28:32:34:36:37:38,39:41,42:
43:45[4]:46:52[3]:55[2]:55f/18:1:5:8:11,12:13:15,16[2]:
23:25f:29:30/19:1:4:8:9,10[2]:13:14:17:20:23/20:
3:5[3]:9:12:14:15:16:20:22:30:30f:30:30f:37:39:41
/21:1:3:6:9[2]:10[2]:11:12:14,15/22:1:2[2]:3:5[2]:6:7:8[2]:
9,10:11,12:14[2]:15:19:20[2]:22[2]/23:5:9:10:11[2]:12:
13:14,15:17:18[2]:19[3]:22:23:24,25[3]:26:28:29/24:1:
2:4:7,8:9,10:11:14:15[2]:21/25:1:2:3:5:8[2]:10[2]:13:
14:15,16:18[3]:21:22:26:29[2]:30,31[2]:32:34[2]:42:44/
26:2:3,4[2]:5,6,7:10:11[2]:12:16:19[2]:20[2]:22/27:2,3[3]:
5[2]:6:10[2]:12/28:3:4:5,6:5,6f:7,8[2]:9:13:20:21:23/
29:3[2]:5:6:9:11/30:1:6:9,10,11,12[2]:13:14[2]:16[3]:
18,19:20:22[2]:25:26[2]:27-31[2]/31:3,4:7:8:9:10[2]:11:
12/2Sa1:1:4:9:10:12:15:20:21:24:25:26:27/2:2:4[3]
:6[2]:7:9[2]:10,11:12:13[3]:16:17[3]:23:25[2]:28:31[2]/3:1[3]:
3:4:6:7[3]:11:12[3]:14:17:19[3]:21[2]:22:26:27:28:29[3]:30[3]
:33,34:35,36[2]:39/4:2,3[3]:4[5]:6,7:8[2]/5:1[3]:2:3[2]:4,5[3]:
7[2]:8[2]:9[3]:10:11:17:18:22:24/6:1[2]:3:5[3]:6:7:8:9:10[2]:
12:15[2]:18[2]:19[3]:20:21[2]:22/7:2:6:7:8[2]:9:12:19:22:
27[4]/8:2[2]:3[3]:4:8[2]:9[2]:11,12:13:14:16[4]:17[2]:18[2]/9:1:
2:4:7[2]:10,11:12/10:6[4]:7,8:10:12:15,16[4]/11:1[2]:2[2]:
3[2]:9[2]:11:15[2]:18:24:27[2]/12:1[2]:4[2]:7[3]:8:9:11:12:14:
17:25[2]:25f:26,27[2]:26,27f:28[2]:29,30[2]:31[4]/13:2:3:
4:9:13:15:17,18:21-24:25:27:29,30[2]:32,33:34:
37,38,39[2]/14:2,3:4:5,6:7[2]:11:12:13:14:17:20:25:
26:30:32/15:1:2:5f:6[2]:7,8:9f:10:11:12:14[2]:16:
17,18:19,20:24[2]:28:29:30[2]:32[2]/16:1[6]:3:5[3]:7,8[2]:
12:21:21f:22:23/17:4[2]:8:9:10[2]:11:12:13[2]:14[2]:16:
19:21:24:25[3]:26:27[5]/18:2:3[2]:4:6:9[2]:10:11f[3]:14[2]:
15:16:17[2]:23:24[2]:27:29[2]:32/19:2[2]:5:6:7:8,9,10:
11,12:13[2]:14:16[2]:17[3]:20:22:27:30:33:40[2]:41:42[2]:
43[3]/20:1[3]:2:4:11:12:13:14[2]:15:21:23[2]:24/21:1[2]:2[3]
:3:5,6[3]:7:8[4]:9[3]:10[2]:12,13,14[3]:15:16:17[2]:19:19f:
20,21:22/22:5[2]:8[2]:11:15:16[2]:19:31:35:36:44[2]:45:
47/23:1[5]:2:3[2]:4:8:9[4]:10:11,12[3]:13[4]:14:15:17:
18,19[7]:20:20f:20[2]:22:23[4]:24-39[17]:24-39f/24:1:2[4]
:4:5[3]:6:7[2]:9[2]:10:11:13[2]:14[2]:16:18:24f/1Ki1:5:9[3]:
12:27:30:34:35:39:42:48[2]:49,50[2]/2:1:3[3]:4[2]:5[2]:7[3]:
8:11:13:14[2]:16:19:20:23,24:26[2]:27[3]:28[2]:29:31:32[6]
:33:35:36,37:39[2]:42:45/3:1[3]:2[3]:3:4:7:11:13:15[3]:
17,18[2]:23:25:26:28/4:1[3]:7[3]:8-19[18]:21[3]:22[2]:24:
25[2]:30[3]:31:32:33/5:1[3]:2,3[2]:6:7[2]:11[3]:12:14:17[2]/6:
1[4]:3:5[3]:6:7[2]:8[3]:10[2]:11,12:13:15:16:17:18:19[2]:
21,22[2]:23-28[2]:29[3]:30:33:34:36[3]:37[3]:38[2]/7:2[4]:5:6
:8:12[3]:14[3]:16-22[4]:24[2]:26:27-30[3]:31:32:33:34[2]:35
:36:38:39[3]:40:41-46[7]:47:48[3]:49:50[4]:51/8:1[7]:2[2]:6[2]
:9:11:15:17:20[2]:21[2]:22,23[2]:25[3]:26:30[2]:31:35,36:
37:41,42[2]:43:44:48:50:53[3]:54,55[2]:56:59[2]:62,63:
64[2]:65/9:5[3]:7[3]:8:9[3]:10,11,12[3]:13:15[2]:16[2]:20,21[3]:
23[2]:24[2]:26[2]:27,28/10:1:1f[3]:2:5:7:9:10[3]:11:12:13:
15:16,17[5]:21[6]:22:23:25:26[2]:27:29/11:1:4:5[2]:7[3]:
9,10,12,13[3]:14[2]:15:16,17,18:19[2]:23[4]:24[2]:26[2]:
27,28[4]:29:31[4]:32f:32[3]:33[3]:34[2]:35:36:37:39[2]:40[2]:
41[2]:43/12:2,3,4:13,14:16,17[2]:18:19:20[7]:21[2]:
23,24[4]:25[2]:26:28:29:30:31[2]:32,33:32,33f[2]/13:1:2
:21,22:32:34[3]/14:3[3]:6:7[3]:8:10:11:13[4]:14:15[2]:16:
17:19[4]:21[2]:22[2]:24:25[2]:29[2]/15:1[3]:4:7[3]:9[3]:10:14f:
15:15f:16[2]:17:18[2]:19[2]:20[4]:21[2]:22[2]:23[4]:24:25[4]:26:
27[3]:28[4]:29[3]:30[2]:31[3]:32,33[2]:34[3]/16:1:2[3]:3:4-7[5]:8[3]
:9[4]:10[4]:12[2]:13[2]:14[5]:15,16[3]:17:19:20[4]:21[2]:23[2]:24:
25:27[3]:29[2]:30:31[2]:33[3]:34/17:1:3:8,9[2]:10[2]:11:12[4]:
13:14[2]:15:18:20:22/18:3,4[5]:5:10[2]:12[2]:13:15[2]:19[3]
:22:23[2]:25[3]:26[2]:27:29:30:31[2]:31f[3]:32f:36[2]:40:42:
44:46[2]/19:1:3:6:7[2]:8:10[2]:12:13:14[3]:15:16[4]:19[2]/
20:1[2]:2,3[2]:5,6:9:10:11:12:15[3]:16[2]:21[2]:22:23:25[2]:
27:28[3]:30[3]:31:32[2]:33[2]:35:36:41:42:43/21:1:2:7:8
:10:13:18:19:20f:21:22[3]:23[2]:24:25:26[2]/22:2[2]:3:4[2]
:5:6f:7:8:9:11[2]:15:19:22:23[2]:24[2]:26:28:29[2]:31:34[2]
:38:39[4]:40:41[4]:42:44:45[4]:46[2]:50:51[3]:52,53[4]/2Ki
1:1:2[2]:3[2]:6[2]:9[2]:10:11:12:13:13[2]:15:16:17[4]:18[4]/2:1:3[2]
:5:6,7:11[2]:12:13,14[2]:15[2]:16[2]:19[2]:23[2]:24[3]/3:1[2]:1f:
1:3[4]:4[3]:5:6,7,8[4]:10[2]:11[4]:12f:12:13[4]:14[2]:15:18:19:
20:21:24[4]:25:26[3]:27[2]/4:1[3]:2:8:13:15,16:19:21:22
:27:31:39:42[3]/5:1[2]:2[2]:3:5[4]:6[2]:7:8[2]:9:10[2]:11:12[3]:
17:18:22:23/6:1:5:8:9:11[3]:12[3]:14:17[2]:20:21:22[2]:
23:24:25:26-30[3]:32/7:1[3]:2:5:6[4]:8:12[3]:13[3]:15:16[4]:
19[2]/8:2:3:4:5:6[2]:7:8,9[4]:12[2]:13[2]:16[6]:18[2]:21[3]:23[4]:
24,25[2]:24,25f:24,25[4]:26[2]:27:28[3]:29[2]/9:1[2]:2[2]:3:5:
6[2]:7[3]:8:9[5]:11:12:14[4]:16:17:19:21[2]:22:25:26:27:
29[3]:31[2]:34/10:1[3]:2,3[2]:5[4]:6[4]:7:8[2]:11[4]:13[5]:14:15:
17[3]:18,19[4]:20,21:22[2]:23:24[2]:25:26:28:29[2]:30[3]:31[2]
:32,33[6]:34[3]:36/11:1[3]:2,3[4]:2,3f:4[2]:5:10:11:12:
13,14:15[2]:18[4]/12:1[2]:6:9[3]:11,12:17:18[2]:19[4]:21[2]/
13:1[4]:2:3:4:5:6:7:8[4]:9,10[3]:12[6]:13:14:14f:16,17:
20,21[2]:22[2]:23:24:25[2]/14:1[3]:2:6[2]:8[3]:9[2]:11[3]:13[3]:15
:16:18[3]:20[2]:21:23[3]:24[2]:25[3]:26:27:28[3]:29[2]/15:1[6]:
5[2]:6[4]:7:8[3]:9[2]:10:11[4]:12:13[2]:14:15[2]:16:17[4]:18:
19,20[3]:21[4]:23[4]:24:25[2]:26[4]:27[3]:28[4]:29[2]:30[4]:31[4]:
32,33[4]:34,35[2]:36[3]:37[2]:38[3]:39[2]/16:1[4]:3[3]:4:5[3]:6[2]:7[2]:9[3]:
13:14[2]:15[3]:17:18:19[5]:20[2]/17:1[5]:3:4[4]:5[2]:6[5]:7[2]:8:9:
10:11[3]:16:17:18:19:20:20f:21[2]:22:23:24[5]:25:26[3]:
27,28[5]:30[2]:31:33:34[2]:35,36[2]:37[2]/18:1[7]:4[3]:5[2]:6:7:
8f:9[5]:10[5]:11[4]:12:13[4]:14[3]:17[3]:18:19:20,21[2]:23:24:
28:31,32[2]:33[3]:34:37[2]/19:2[2]:3:4:7:9:11:12[3]:13[3]:
15[3]:16:17:18:19:20:21[3]:22:23:24:25:26:28:30[2]:
31:32:34[2]:35:37[2]/20:5[3]:6[3]:7:11:11f[2]:12[3]:16:17:
18[3]:19:20[4]/21:1[7]:3,4,5[3]:6:7[2]:8[2]:9:11:12:13:14:16[3]
:17[4]:18:19,20[7]:22:24:25[3]:26/22:1[8]:3,4[4]:7:9,10:
12,13:14[5]:15,16:17:20/23:1[3]:3:4[4]:5:6[2]:7:8[3]:9f:9:
10[3]:11[4]:12[2]:13[5]:14:15:16:17[2]:18:19[2]:20:21:22[4]:
23[2]:24:25[3]:26:27:28[4]:29[2]:31,32[5]:34:36,37[5]/24:1[2]
:2:3,4[4]:5[5]:7[3]:8,9[6]:10[3]:12[2]:13:14:16[2]:17:18,19[6]:20[2]
/25:1[5]:2:4,5:6:8[4]:9:10:11[2]:12:13:14,15:16:17[2]:19[4]
:20:22[2]:23[6]:25:26[2]:27[6]:30/1Ch1:1:1f[3]:5-9[6]:10[2]:
11,12[2]:13-16:17:19:20-23:24-27f:24-27[9]:28-31:
33[2]:35:36:37:38,39:40:41:42:43[6]:44:45:46[4]:47:
48:49:50[3]:51-54[2]/2:1:4:5:6:7:9:10[3]:11[2]:12[2]:17:
18[2]:21[2]:22[2]:24:25[2]:26:27:29:34,35[2]:42[4]:43:44[3]:
45:47:48:49[4]:50[3]:51[2]:52[2]:53:54:55[3]/3:1[2]:4[3]:5[2]:
9:10-14:15:16:19,20/4:1:2[2]:3-4[6]:5:8[3]:9:10,11,12[5]
:13:14[4]:15[3]:17[2]:18[2]:19[4]:20[2]:21-22[6]:24:26[2]:27:31:
34-39[10]:40,41[7]:42[3]:43[2]/5:1[2]:3:6[3]:7,8[4]:9[2]:10[3]:11[2]
:13:14[2]:15[3]:16[2]:17[3]:18[2]:22[3]:23:24[2]:25[2]:26[3]/6:1[2]:
4-15[24]:16:17:18:19,20,21[2]:25,26,27[2]:28[2]:29,30[2]:
33-38[2]:44-47:49[3]:50-53:54[4]:55,56,57:58,59:60:
61[3]:62[2]:63[2]:64,65:66-69[3]:70[3]:71[3]:72:73:74:76:77[2]
:78,79:80/7:1:2[6]:3:4[2]:5[3]:6:7[4]:8:9:10[2]:11[3]:12[3]:13[2]
:14[2]:17[3]:19:20,21:23:25,26,27[9]:29[3]:30:31[2]:35:
36,37:38:39:40[3]/8:1:3,4,5:6,7[3]:8,9,10[2]:12:13[2]:
15,16:17,18:19,20,21:22-25:26,27:28:29:
30,31,32[2]:33[2]:34[2]:35:36[2]:37:40/9:1[3]:2:3:4[8]:6,7,8[1]
:9[2]:10,11[6]:12[9]:14[4]:15,16[9]:19[2]:20[2]:21[2]:22[2]:23:24:
26[2]:27:28:31:32[3]:39[3]:40[2]:41:42[3]:43/10:1[2]:8[2]:10[3]
:11:12:14/11:1:2:3:4:5,6[5]:7[2]:8:9:10[4]:11[2]:12[4]:14:
15[3]:16:18,19:20:21:22f:24,25:26-47[21]/12:1:1f:2[3]
:3-7[3]:8-13:17:18[3]:20[2]:22:23[2]:24-37[22]:38[3]:40/13:
1:2[2]:3:5:5f[2]:5:6:7:9:10:12[2]:13[3]:14/14:1:3:4-7:9:
11:15:16/15:1:3:4-10[6]:12[4]:14[3]:17[5]:20f:22:24[2]:25[3]
:28[4]:29/16:1[2]:2[2]:3[2]:4[3]:5:7[3]:8:9:12,13[2]:18:28[2]:35:
36:37f[2]:38[2]:39[2]/17:1[2]:2:5:6[2]:7[2]:8:10[2]:11:12:14:
17[2]:19:20:24[2]/18:2:3[2]:4:5:6[2]:7:8[2]:9:10:11:12[2]:13[2]
:14:15[3]:16[2]:17[2]/19:1:2,3[3]:6f:7[2]:8[2]:9[3]:11:13:16:
17,18[2]/20:1[2]:2[4]:4[2]:5[3]:6,7[8]/21:5:6:12[5]:13[2]:15[2]:
16[2]:18[2]:25f:29:30[2]/22:1:2:3[4]:5:6:9:10:11:12:14[2]
:14f[2]:15:17:18:19[3]/23:1:2:3[3]:4,5:6:7:8,9[2]:10,11:
12:13:13f:13:14,15[2]:17:18:19:20:21[2]:22:24[2]:25:
27[3]:28[3]:29:31:32/24:1[2]:4:5:6[7]:20:22:30[2]:31[3]/25:
1[4]:2:4:5,6,7[3]:8:9-31[24]/26:1[3]:4,5:6,7:8[3]:10:11[2]:12
:13:14,15[6]:16:17:19:20,21,22[4]:23,24[4]:25:26[2]:27:
28[5]:29:30[5]:31,32[9]/27:1:2:3[4]:4:5,6[4]:7[3]:8[2]:9[3]:10[2]:
11[3]:12[3]:13[2]:14[2]:15[3]:16-22[17]:23f:24[2]:25[5]:26[2]:27:
28[2]:29[4]:30[3]:31:32:34[2]/28:1[4]:2[2]:4[3]:5[2]:8[4]:9:11[2]:13[2]
:15:16:17:18[3]:19[2]:20:21[2]/29:1[2]:2:3[3]:4,5[5]:6,7[4]:8[2]:
9:10[2]:11:12:16:18:19[2]:21:23:25:26,27[3]:29[2]:30[3]/
2Ch1:1,2,3:2,3f:4:5,6[3]:9[2]:10:14[2]:17[2]/2:2:3:4f:4:7
:8:9:10[4]:12:14[2]:17[2]/3:1[3]:2[2]:4:5:6:8:10[2]:11,12,13f
:14:15:16f:16:17/4:3[2]:4:5[3]:6:9:10[2]:12-16[5]:17,18[2]
:19[3]:22[4]/5:2[5]:3:4,5[2]:7,8[2]:9:10:11,12[3]:13,14[3]/6:4:
5,6[2]:10[2]:12,13[4]:14[2]:16:17:18:20,21:26:27:28:30:
32:33[3]:34:37,38:41[2]/7:1:6:7[2]:8[2]:13:18:20:21:22[3]
/8:1[2]:3:5:7,8[2]:9[2]:10:11[3]:12[2]:13[3]:14[3]:16:17,18[2]
/9:1[4]:3:4:7:9[3]:11:12[3]:13:14[3]:15:16:18:19:20[2]:24:
25:26[2]:29[5]:30/10:1:2,3[3]:8,9:13:14:16:17[2]:18:19/
11:1[2]:3[3]:5-10:11:13,14:15[2]:16:17:17f:18[3]:20:21:
23/12:1:2[2]:3:5:6:9[4]:10[2]:12:13[2]:15/13:1[6]:4[2]:5[2]:6:
7:8[2]:9[4]:10:11[2]:12[2]:13,14[2]:15,16[4]:17:18,19[2]:20:
21:22/14:1[2]:4[2]:5:7:8[2]:9,10[4]:12:13[2]:14:15/15:1[2]:
2:4:5:6[2]:7:8[4]:9[2]:10[2]:11:12:14:17:19/16:1[3]:2:3:4[2]:
5:6:7[4]:8:9:11[4]:12:13,14[2]/17:2[3]:3:4[2]:5[2]:6:7,8,9[6]:
10[2]:11:14,15:16[2]:17/18:1[3]:2,3,4,5[2]:6,7[2]:8[3]:10[2]:
17:18:21[2]:22[3]:23[2]:25:27:28[2]:29:30[2]:31:32:33[4]/
19:1:2[2]:3:4[2]:7:9:10[3]:11[4]/20:1[4]:3:5:6[3]:7:10:11:13:
14[8]:15:16[3]:17:18[2]:19[3]:20[3]:21:22:23:24[2]:26:27:28
:29[2]:31[3]:33:34[5]:35[3]:37/21:1[2]:2,3,4[7]:6[3]:7[2]:8[2]:9:10[2]
:11[2]:12[3]:13[2]:17:19[2]/22:1[2]:2:3:5[4]:7[2]:8[2]:9[3]:10:11[2]
/23:1[8]:2,3:4:5,6:8[3]:10:11[2]:12[2]:15,16,17[2]:18[2]:21/
24:2:5:6[2]:7,8[3]:9[2]:11:12:14:16:17,18[4]:20[2]:21:23[3]:
24[2]:25[3]:27[3]/25:1:4[2]:5,6[2]:11:12:13[5]:14[2]:17[5]:18:
19:20:23[5]:25[3]:26[3]:27/26:1:2:4[2]:5:6[3]:7:9:10:11:13
:14:15:16:17,18[2]:21[5]:22[2]/27:1:2:3[2]:4:5[3]:6:7[3]/28:
2[2]:3[2]:5[3]:6[3]:8:9[2]:10:11[2]:12[6]:15[2]:16[3]:18:19f[2]:19:
20[2]:22:23[4]:24[2]:25[2]:26[3]/29:1[2]:3[3]:4,5[3]:8[2]:9:10:
12,13,14[6]:16:17:18[6]:19:21[2]:25,26:27[2]:30[3]:31:35:
36/30:1,2,3,5f:6[3]:7:9:11:13:15[2]:16[2]:17,18,19[2]:21
:22[2]:24:25:26/31:1[2]:3[2]:4:5,6[5]:7,8:10[2]:14,15[3]:

Con't)
8^3:19^3:20/**32**:1^2:3:4:5^2:7^2:9^3:10^2:11:13^2:15:
18:19^2:20:21^2:22:25:26^2:28,29:30^3:31:32^7/
^{2}:3^3:4,5^2:6^2:7^3:9:14^6:16^3:18^3:19^4:22:25/**34**:2:
:5^4:6:7:8^4:9^3:10,11:12^5:14:15,16^2:17:19:20^2:
2^4:23:26^2:29:30:32:33^3/**35**:1:4,5^3:6^2:8:12:13:
5^2:16:17:18^5:19^2:20:21^2:22:23:24,25^2:26^2:27^2
3^2:4^3:6:7:8^4:10:12:13^2:14^3:15:16^2:17^2:19:20:
2,23^7/**Ez1**:1^4:2^4:3^3:4:5^2:7:8^2:9,10^2/**2**:1^2:2:3-
^{35}:36-39^6:40,41,42^6:43-54:55,56,57:58:59:
61^3:62,63^2:64,65:68^2:69^3:70^3/**3**:1^7:3:4^3:5^2:6:
:7^2:8^7:9^2:10^2:11^2:12/**4**:1:2:3^2:6^2:7:8,9:10:11^2
14:15^2:16:17:19^2:22:24^3/**5**:1^4:3^2:4^2:8^3:11^3:12
:14^3:15:16:17/**6**:2:3^3:4^2:5:6^2:7:9:10:11:12:13:
15f^2:15^2:17:18^2:19:19f^2:20:21,22^4/**7**:1^{18}:6:
^{4}:10^2:11:12^4:14^3:15:16^3:17^3:18:19:20^2:21^5:
23:24:25^2:26^3:27^2:28f:28^4/**8**:1^2:2-14^{26}:15:17^2
:19^2:20:23:24:25^3:26,27^2:28:29^2:30:31:31f^2:
34:35^2:36^5/**9**:1^3:2^3:4^4:7:8^3:9^2:10:11:13^2:15/
^{2}:2^4:3^2:5^2:6^3:9:9f^2:9^4:11:13:14^2:15^3:16-19^2:
1:22:24^2:25^2:26:27:28:29:30:31,32:33:34-42:
4/**Neh1**:1^6:2:3:4:6,7:9:11^2/**2**:4^2:7:8^2:9:10:17^3
19:20/**3**:1^2:2^2:3:4^6:6^2:7:8^2:9^3:10^2:11^3:12^3:13:
15^5:16^2:16f:17^5:18^3:19^4:20^2:21^5:23^2:24^2:25^4:
9^3:30^3:31/**4**:1^2:3:10:12:15:23/**5**:1^2:2,3,4:5:8:
^{2}:13^2:13f:14^4:15:18^3/**6**:1^3:2^2:8:10^2:14:15f:16
18^3/**7**:2^2:3^2:5^3:6^3:8-38^{35}:39-42^6:43,44,45^8:
6:57,58,59^2:60:61:62^2:63^3:64,65^2:66:70^2:71:
3^2/**8**:1^4:7,8:9:10:11^2:12:14^2:15^2:16^2:17^2:18^3
f:3^2:4^2:5:6:7:8:9:10:11:12^2:17^2:18:19^2:22^4:24
27:29f:32^2:36:37^3:38/**10**:9-13^2:28^2:29:31:32:
34f:34:35:36^2:37^5:38^2:39,40^2/**11**:1^2:3^5:4,5,6^{15}
,9^{11}:10-14^{20}:15,16,17^{11}:19:22,23^8:24^4:25-30^3
35^3:36^2/**12**:1^2:8:10,11^5:12-21^{21}:22^7:23^3:24^4:
26^4:27:28:29^2:31,32^5:35,36^7:37:38^2:39^3:42:43^2
:45^2:46^3:47^4:47f/**13**:1:2:4^2:5^2:6^2:7^2:8:12^2:13^4
16^2:17:18^2:19^2:22:23:24^3:25:28^5:29:31/**Est1**:
^{2}:5^2:6f:6:7^2:9:13-15^4:16:18^2:19:22/**2**:1:4:5^3:6
1:12,13,14^6:15f:15^2:16^3:17^2:18^2:19:21:23^2/**3**:
4:5,6^3:7^4:8^3:10f:12f:12:13^3:14:15/**4**:2:5:7:8:
5:1:6:13/**6**:1^3:4:7,8:9:11/**7**:2:3:4:9/**8**:1:2:7:8f^2
0^6:11:12^2:12f:13:15^4:17^2/**9**:1^2:3^2:7-10^2:11^2:
14:16:17:20:21:22:24,25^4:28^2:29-31^8:32/**10**:1
3^3/**Job1**:1:2,3^2:4:5:6f:16:17:21:22/**2**:1f:7^2:8:
11^2/**3**:1:2,3:4f:6^2:9:14,15:23/**4**:6f:9:16:18,19:
5:5:6:12:15:16:17:20^2:27/**6**:3:5,6,7^2:10:12:14
1:2:3:5:11^2:15:18:20/**8**:10^2:21/**9**:2:3:9:13:13f:
24^2:29:34/**10**:1:4-7f:9:17:20,21^3:22^2/**11**:2:4:7
:13,14:15/**12**:7,8,9:10^3:17:20^2:22:24,25/**13**:
26/**14**:1:2:5:6:8,9:13:16:18,19/**15**:1:4,5:7,8:
19:30:33/**16**:2:3:8:9:11:16/**17**:7:10/**18**:1:7:14
:17:18^2/**19**:1:6:9:20:21:29/**20**:1:3:5^2:12:20^2:
25:28/**21**:14:20^2:28^2:30-32/**22**:2^2:5:8:9:10,11
:15,16^2:20:28^2/**23**:1:4,5:10:15/**24**:2:3:4:6:8^2:
17:18:21:24/**25**:1:3/**26**:4:11:13f^2:14^2/**27**:10:
14:16:18:20/**28**:5:7:9:11:16:21:22:25:26/**29**:2
:10:11:17/**30**:8^3:9:27:31/**31**:7,8:21:22^2:23:28
:34:35:40^2/**32**:2^3:8,9:11,12:13:14:18/**33**:4^2:7^3
:13:15:17,18^2:28:30/**34**:4:21:24^2:28^3:33/**35**:
0^2:12:12f/**36**:2:3^2:4:6:12^2:14:21:29:30:33f/**37**
^{2}:5:14:16,17:18:19,20:22:23/**38**:4:8,9:13:15:
:17,18^3:21:22,23:24^2:25-27:29:32^2:33:37,38/
2,3:7:8:14:17:25^3/**40**:10:16:17:18:19/**41**:5:13:
32^2:34^2/**42**:8:11^4:12^2:13,14f:13,14:15/**Ps1**:1^2
/**2**:2:6:7:8:10:12/**3**:1/**4**:1f:2:6/**5**:9^2:10:12/**6**:1:
/**7**:6:9:13:17/**8**:1:3:5:6:9/**9**:2:6^2:7,8:9:12:13^2:
f^2:16f:17:18^2/**10**:3:4:7^2:8:14:15^2:17/**11**:2/**12**:7
4:4:6:7/**15**:4/**16**:3:4:8:11^2/**17**:7:8^2:13,14/**18**:1:
4:6f:10:12:12f:12:14:15:16:19:24:33^2:34f:46:
/**19**:1^2:9f:13^2/**20**:1^2:5^2:7^2/**21**:3:4:6:7:9,10/**22**:
:9,10,11:14:15:16^2:17:18:20f:21:22:23^2:23f:24
:27:30:31/**23**:4:5:6/**24**:3:6:7:8:9:10^3/**25**:6,7^2:
:13:14/**26**:7:8:11/**27**:4^3:6^2:9:12:13/**28**:1:2f:7/
1:2:3^2:4:5,6:7:8:9:10/**30**:3:4:6,7:11:12/**31**:2:3:
,10:13:18^2:20:21:23/**32**:6:7^2/**33**:1:2:3:4:6:8:
:18,19^2/**34**:1:2:5:6:7:10:11:15:16:17/**35**:5:6:10^2
:15:16:20^2:26/**36**:1^2:4:6:7:8:9/**37**:6:7:17^2:18f:
:23:25:35,36:37^2:40/**38**:3,4:5,6^2:8f:17^2/**39**:9:
/**40**:2^2:3^2:5:6:16/**41**:1:2:6:8:13/**42**:3:4,5f:7:7f:
:11/**43**:1:2^2:4:5f/**44**:1^3:13:14:21:22/**45**:1:2:8:9
2^2:14:17/**46**:1:4^3:7^3:11^2/**47**:2:4f:6,7:9^4/**48**:2:2f:
:3:4:6:7:8^4:11/**49**:4:5:7^2:8,9^2:13:14^3:15:20f/**50**:
^{2}:3:10,11:13:14,15:21:22/**51**:1^4:12:14,15:18f:
f/**52**:1:1f:5:6:8/**53**:1:5/**54**:1:4:4f:5/**55**:2:10:14:
:18:20:23/**56**:3,4:9:10,11:13/**57**:1:2:3/**58**:1^2:1f
5:6:9:10^2/**59**:5^2:9:16^3:17^2/**60**:1^3:4,5f/**61**:2^2:4:
:6^2:8/**62**:9:12/**63**:1^2:6:7^2:9:10/**64**:1^2:6:6f:9^2/**65**
:8^2:9^2:13/**66**:2:4:7^2:15:16/**67**:2:5/**68**:2:8:
,12,13^2:14:24:26:27^3:29:30f^3:31:32:35/**69**:6^3:
^{2}:13:13f:14:24:26:28f^2:28^2:33:35/**70**:4/**71**:13:
:16:17:20:22^2/**72**:3:6^2:7^2:8:10:12:15:16^3:18:20^2
/**73**:2:3^2:6:12^2:14:16:17:18:19:20:24:26/**74**:1:2:3
:8:20:23^2/**75**:8^2:9^2:10^2/**76**:3:5^2:6:9:12/**77**:3:5^2:
10:10f:14:15^2:20/**78**:4:9^2:13:14:15:21:23:27:31^2:
33:39:41:43f:45^2:49^2:51:54^3:55:57:67:68/**79**:1:2:
3:9^2:10:11^2:13/**80**:1:4:6:7:10f:14^3:17f:17:17f:19^2
/**81**:4^2:5:6:7f:10^2:16f/**82**:4:5:5f:6:8/**83**:2:3:4:7:8:
12:18/**84**:1^2:3:6^3:7:8^2:10^3:12^2/**85**:1:2:13f/**86**:5:
11:15^2:17/**87**:1:3^2:4^2:5:6/**88**:1:3:10:12^2/**89**:1:5:5
f:6:6f:7:7f:7:8:14,15^2:18:24:26:29:34:35,36:47:48
/**90**:1^2:5,6:10:11^2:14/**91**:1:2:5^2:6/**92**:7:11:12/**93**:
4:5/**94**:4:6,7f:11^2:21,22:23/**95**:1^2:2:3:4^2:9:11/**96**:
5:7:9:11:12/**97**:2:5:8,9^2:10/**98**:2,3:8,9/**99**:2:4:7/
100:3/**101**:6:8/**102**:2:5:9,10^3:14:17:20^2:25/**103**:
1:7:8:11:17,18^2:20^2:21/**104**:1:3^2:4:6:7,8:12:16:24
:25:27:30:34/**105**:3:5,6^3:10,11^2:15:16:21:24:27^2:
31:32:34:38:39:44/**106**:2:7^2:8:16:16f:17:19,20^2:
28:37,38:39^2:45:48/**107**:3:8:10:14:15:16:17:20:
21:23:24:31:32:34^2:43/**108**:6:7:8:13^2/**109**:1:9,10
:14:15:18:25/**110**:2f^2:3:4f:5/**111**:4^2:6^2/**112**:7^2/
113:1/**114**:2^2:7^2/**115**:4^2:10:11:12^2/**116**:5:13:13f^2
:15f^3:17:18,19/**117**:1/**118**:2:3:10:14:15,16^4:17:
19:19f:20:22:22f:26f/**119**:1:31:44,45,46:54^3:64:
80:99:101:105:106:107:114:117:120:121:128:
131:134:139:161:164:165:172/**120**:4f:5,6^3/**122**:
1^2:6:8:9/**123**:3,4^3/**124**:4,5/**127**:5/**128**:5f/**130**:1:
7/**132**:2-5^2:6f:6:8:9:12^2/**133**:2:3/**135**:5:6:8:11^3:
15:19:20:21/**136**:2:3:10:17:19:20:21:26/**137**:1^2:2
:3,4:7/**138**:1:2:4/**139**:3:5:8:13:16:17,18:24/**140**:
4:12/**141**:6,7f:9/**142**:5:7/**143**:5:11/**144**:2:3f^2:7:8:
12-15^4/**145**:8:11^2:12:15:16:17:19/**146**:5:8:9/**147**
:10^2:14:19/**148**:2:7:13:14/**149**:2:9/**150**:1f/**Pro1**:
1^2:5,6^2:13:16:19:19f:23:27:31^2/**2**:3,4,5^3:6:10:
16,17^2:19:19f:20/**3**:7,8:9,10:11,12:18:20:
24,25,26^2:27,28:33/**4**:3:5f:11:12:18:20:24/**5**:3:9:
9f:10:16:18/**6**:3:5:14^2:15:21:23^3:34/**7**:4:6:8,9:14f^2
:16,17:18:20:25:26^2/**8**:1^2:6,7:8:11:13:14,15:20:
27,28,29^2:31/**9**:10^2:11^2:13:14^2:18/**10**:1^2:5:6f:7^2:
11:16:20:21:28^2/**11**:5:11^2:21:26:29/**12**:10^2:11f:
12:18:19:25:27:28/**13**:9:12f:14^2:17:23/**14**:9^2:11^2
:26:27:33^2/**15**:8^2:9,10:11^2:21:24:25:26:29:31,32/
16:14^2:17:22:28:31/**17**:9:10^2:12:17:20:24^2:27,28
/**18**:1:4:10f:11^2:16:19:19f/**19**:20/**20**:2:3:10:11:
18:20:29^2/**21**:4f:9:10:13^2:20f:23:27:30:31f/**22**:8:
10:12:13:14:15/**23**:1:4,5:6,7,8:10,11:13,14:15,16
:17,18:24,25:31/**24**:3,4:9:10:15,16:24:30,31:
32,33/**25**:1^3:2,3^2:6,7:8,9,10:12:16:21,22:24/**26**:7
:9:17:20:28/**27**:10:19:21:23,24/**28**:5:7:8:9:21^2/
29:17:18:20:22:25:27^2/**30**:1^2:5:18,19:18,19f:
29,30,31:33/**31**:1^2:1f:6,7:21^2:22:25^2:29:31^2:31f^2
/**Ecc1**:1f^3:1:12-15^3:16-18^2/**2**:3^4:7,8:9:11:12^2:
13,14:15:18:20-23^3:24-26^2/**3**:10:11^2:13:21^2/**4**:1^2
:3:4:7:8:16^2/**5**:6,7^2:8:10:11^2:17:18:19,20/**6**:9:12/
7:4^2:13:15-17^2:19:25:27,28^2/**8**:2,3:8:9,10:16,17/
9:5f^2:8:9:10f:17^3:18/**10**:1:6:8,9/**11**:5^2:8:9/**12**:1:4:
5^2:6:12:13/**Sol1**:14:1:5^3:7^2:8:10:12:13:14^2/**2**:1^2:
3:7:12^2:12f:14:17/**3**:2:5^3:6^2:7^3:9:10:11^2/**4**:1^3:3:3f
:4:5:6^2:7:8^2:8f^2:9^2:10:11^4:12:13,14f:13,14:15/**5**:1
:2:8^2:9:13:14:15^3:16/**6**:1^2:4:5^2:7f:9:11:12f:12:13/
7:1^2:2:3f:4^2:7:8^2:9^2/**8**:4^2:6:7:9:11:12:14/**Is1**:1^3:4^2
:5,6:9^2:10^2:11^2:12,13:14:15^2:18:21^2:23^2:24^2:26:
29^2/**2**:2:2f:3^3:4^2:5:7^2:8:12:13^2:17^2:19^2:21^3/**3**:1:5:
6:7:9:15^2:16:17:19:24^3/**4**:1:2,3,4^2:2,3,4f^3:5^2/**5**:3:
4:7^3:7f:8:9:10^3:13:14:16:18f:19:24^3:25^2:26:28:30^2
/**6**:2:3:5^2:6^2:12/**7**:1^6:1f:2^2:3:4:5:6:8:8f:9:13:14f^3:
15,16:15,16f:17^2:18:18f^2:18:21,22:23/**8**:1:2:4^2:6:
6f:7,8^2:9,10^3:11:12^2:13^2:14,15:16:18^2:20/**9**:1^2:2^2
:3^2:4:5^3:6:7^3:13:14,15:16^2:18:19,20^2:21/**10**:5,6:7^2
:8:12:14:16^3:17^2:20^2:21:22:23:24^2:26^2:27:27f:
28,29^5:30:31^2:32:33^3/**11**:1:2^5:8:9^2:10:10f^2:10:11^2
:12:14:15f:16/**12**:3^2:6^2/**13**:1:2:4^2:8^2:9^2:11^2:12^2:
14:17:18:19^2:21:22/**14**:1:2:4:6:8^2:9:12^2:13f:13:
13f^3:15:16:18:19:21^2:22:23^5:27:29f:30:31f:32/**15**
:1:2:3:4^2:7:8^2/**16**:1^2:2^2:8^2:9:10^2:12^2:13,14^2/**17**:1^2
:2:3^4:4:5:6^4:7^2:8:9:10:11:14^2/**18**:1:1f^2:4:7/**19**:1^2:
4:5:8:11^4:14:16:17^2:18^3:18f:18^2:19:20^2:25/**20**:1^3:
2:3:4^2:5,6f/**21**:2^2:3^2:5f:8,9:10^2:11^2:13:14:15:16f:
16^2:17^2/**22**:1f:5^5:6,7:9,10,11:12^2:14:15,16^2:19:
20:21:23,24/**23**:1:1f:2,3^2:4f:4:6:7^2:8:9^3:10:11:12:
13:15,16:18/**24**:1^3:4,5^2:6:7:8:9:13f:14:15,16:17^2:
20:21:23^4/**25**:2:5:6^2:7^2:9:12/**26**:1^2:10:15:19:21/
27:1:2:4,5:9:11/**28**:1^5:3^3:5^2:14:15:17^2:18:19^2:22:
25^2:29/**29**:1:6:8^3:10^2:11:17:18^2:19:21:23f:23^2/
30:2f:8^3:10,11^2:12^2:15^2:16:17^4:19:20^2:25:29^5:31^2
:33/**31**:1^2:4,5:7:8^2:9^2/**32**:2:3:4:5:6:7:8:10:11:12^2:
14:17/**33**:2:3:4:5:6:8:9:14^2:16^2:17:18:21:23:24/
34:1:3:6:8^2:9:11^2:12:13:14:16/**35**:2^2:5^2:7:10^2/**36**:
1^3:2:3^2:4^2:6:8,9^3:13^2:15:16^2:17^2:18^3:20^3:22^3/**37**:
1^2:2:3:4^2:6^2:8,9:10:11:12^2:13^4:16,17^4:18:19:20:
21^2:22:23:24:25:29:30:32^2:33:35:36^2:37:38^2/**38**:
5:6:10^2:11:14:15:18f^2:20^3:21/**39**:1^2:2^2:5:7^3/**40**:3:
5:7:8:9^2:12:13:15:16:21:22:23:28^3/**41**:2f:4^2:5:9:
10f:14:15:16^2:18^2:21:28/**42**:1:6:7:13:19^2:22:23/
43:2^2:3:6:9^2:14^3:17:19:22:25:26^2/**44**:2:5^2:6^2:13^2:
15^2:16:19^3:26:28/**45**:1^2:2:3:4:11^2:12:15:25/**46**:1:
1f:5:7:11/**47**:1^2:4^2:5:7^2:8:9:15/**48**:1^3:5:9:10:13^2:
14^3:17:18:19:20/**49**:1:2^2:3:6:7^3:8,9^2:16:19:21:24:
25:26^2/**50**:4:10/**51**:3:6:7:9^2:13^2:15:17^3:18:21:22:
23/**52**:2:7^3:9:10^3:11^2:12^2:13f^3:14,15f/**53**:3:6^2:8:
10:11^2:12^2/**54**:4^2:5^3:8:9^2:10:11^2:12^2:15f:16:17^2/
55:1:3:3f:5:7:8:12:13/**56**:2:6:7^4:8:9^2:10/**57**:3:4:5:
7,8^2:11^3:12:13/**58**:1^2:2^2:4:5:6:8:12:13:14/**59**:2:3:
7^2:9:17^3:19/**60**:1:2^2:3:5:6^2:7^2:9:9f:9^3:11^2:13^2:14^4:
15:16^2:18:20/**61**:1^2:2^2:3^2:6^3:7^2:10^2:11^2/**62**:3:4:5:
6,7:10:12/**63**:1^3:4:7^2:9f^2:11^2:13:14/**64**:2:4:6:11:
12/**65**:3:7:8:9^2:10^2:11^2:16:18:19:23/**66**:3^3:5:6:9:
11:12:14:15^3:16:19f^3:20:21:24/**Jer1**:1^7:3^6:8:10:
11:12:13:14:15^4:17^3:18^2/**2**:3:3f:6^3:7^2:10,11^2:13:
14:16^2:19:21:22:26,27:31^3:32:34/**3**:6:7:9:14:16^2:
17^2:18^2:19:20:21:23^2/**4**:2:3^2:4f:4:7:8^2:16:18:19:
20:25:26:27^2:28:29:31^2/**5**:4:5^2:6:10:11^2:13^2:14^2:
15f^2:17^2:22:25^2:27^2:28/**6**:1:6^2:7:9^2:10:11^4:12:13:
14:16:17:18,19:21^2:23:24^2:26:27:28^2/**7**:2^3:3^2:4:9^2
:11:12^2:13,14:15:17^2:18:18f^3:19:20:21^2:22^2:24:
29:30:31^2:32^2:33:34^3/**8**:1^3:2:3^2:6:7^2:9^2:10:14^2:16
:16f:16:19:21/**9**:1^2:3:4^3:7^2:10:11^2:14:15^2:16:
17,18:20:21:24^2:25,26/**10**:1:2,3:5:6:7^3:8:9:13:14:
16^3:21:22^3:23:25/**11**:1^2:4:7:9:10:12:13:16^2:17^3:
20^2:21,22^3:23^2/**12**:4^2:5:8:9:12^2:13^2:15:16/**13**:7:
8,9:12^3:17:19^2:20:22^2:23:24,25:27/**14**:4:7:8^2:14^2:
16^2:18^2:20:21^2/**15**:1:3:4^4:6:7:9:11:12,13^2:17,18^2
/**16**:6:7:8:9^4:13:14,15^2:19/**17**:1:4^2:8:11:13^2:15^2:
19^2:20^4:25:26^2:27^2/**18**:11^2:12^2:13:14:15^2:18:20:
21:22/**19**:1^5:3^6:4^3:5:6:7:11^2:13^2:14^2:15^2/**20**:1^3:4^2
:5^2:7:8:12^2:16/**21**:1^3:1f^4:3,4^3:7^2:8:10:11:12:13/
22:1:2:3^2:6:7:8:17:18:19:20:22:23^2:24,25^4:26:27:
29:30^2/**23**:1^2:2:3:4:7^2:8:9^3:10^2:13:14^3:15^2:16:18^2
:20:24:26:27:33^2:38,39:38,39f^2:38,39/**24**:1^4:2^2:8^2
:9:10/**25**:1^6:2,3^4:8,9^4:11:12^2:12f:12:14:17:18^2:
19,20^4:21:22^2:24^3:25:26^4:27^3:28:29:31^2:32^3:34:
36:37^2:38^2/**26**:1^4:2^4:3:6:10^2:12:16:17:18^4:19:20^2:
22:24/**27**:1^4:3:4^2:5:6:9:10^2:11^2:12^2:14:17:18^3:
19,20,21^6/**28**:1^4:2^4:4^3:5:6:7:8:9:11:13:14^5/**29**:3^2:
4^2:7:8^2:14:20:21^4:22^2:24f^2:25^3:27:32/**30**:1:2:3:7^2
:8:19:21f:23^2:24/**31**:1:4:5:6:7^2:9:10:12^3:14:15f:
16:19:23^3:27:31:32^2:33f:35:36:37:38,39^2:40^2/**32**:
1^4:2f:3:4:6,7:8:9:10:12^3:14^2:15^2:18:19:20:21:27:
28:31:32^3:35:36^2:39:44^2/**33**:2:4^2:5^2:7:9^3:10,11^3:
13^5:15f^2:15:16:17:22^2:25,26^3/**34**:1^2:2^2:3:4:7:8:9:
13:17:18,19:21^3:22/**35**:1^2:2^3:3^2:4^5:5:6^2:8:11:13^3:
16:17^2:18,19^2/**36**:1f:1^4:2^2:3:4:6:7:9^5:10^4:11^2:12^4:
14,15^3:20:22^2:24,25^2:26:26f:26^2:29:30:30f:30:31^2
/**37**:1^2:1f:1:3^2:5^4:7^2:10:12:13^2:14:15,16:17:18:19
:21:21f/**38**:1^4:3^2:4^3:6^2:8:9:14:17^2:21,22:23:24/**39**
:1^4:2:3:4:5^3:6^2:8:9^2:10:13^2:14^4:16^2/**40**:1^2:5^2:7^3:8^6
:9:11:12:13,14^3/**41**:1^4:5:7:8:9^2:9f:10^4:11^2:15^2:
16,17:18/**42**:2:5:8:9:11:12:15^3:17^2:18^3:19:20/**43**:
2,3^3:5:6:7:9^2:10^4:11^2:12^3:13^3/**44**:1^2:2,3^5:6^2:7^3:8^2:
9^4:11^3:12:14^2:15:17:17f:17^2:18:19^2:20:21^2:24^2:
25^3:26^2:27:30:30f:30^2/**45**:1f:1^3:2:3/**46**:2^8:5:6:9^2:
10^4:11:12^2:13^2:14^2:16:17:18:19^2:20,21^2:22,23:25^4
:26^4/**47**:1:2:5^2:6:7/**48**:1^5:2,3,4^2:5^2:11:13^2:14^2:15:
17:18:20:21:24^2:25:28^2:29^2:31:32:33^2:34^2:37:39^3
:40:41^2:44:46/**49**:1:2:3^2:4:5:6:7^3:8^2:8f:9,10:12:13
:16^2:17:19^2:20:21^2:22^2:23^2:25:26:27^2:28f:28^2:29:
30:30f^3:30:32f:33:34^3:35^2:36/**50**:4:7^2:8:9:11:12:
13^2:17^2:18^4:19:21^3:22^2:25^2:26:29:31:32^2:33^2:34^2
:35^2:38:39^2:43^3:44:45^2:46/**51**:1:2:3^3:4:5^3:6:11^2:
13^2:14^2:17:19^2:20f:25:26f^3:27^2:28^3:33^2:34,35^2:37
:38:39:44^2:45:46^3:48:49:51:52^3:54^2:57:58:59^5:64
/**52**:1^2:3^2:4^3:6^2:9^3:10:11:12^5:14:15^2:16:17:20^3:22^2
:24,25^8:26:28^2:30^2:31^6:34/**Lam1**:1:3:7^2:12^2:14/**2**
:1^5:3^2:6:7^2:8:10^2:15:17^2:18:20:22/**3**:1:9:15:21:26:
32:34,35,36^2:48,49^3:51:66/**4**:2^2:3,4^3:6^3:7:9:11:13^2
:20:21^3/**5**:4:7:11:15:18/**Eze1**:1:4:5:6:7:8:10^5:11^3:
13:15:16:17:19,20,21:22:24^2:26:27,28^2/**2**:1:1f^4:3^2
:4:6^2:8:9,10^2/**3**:1^2:4^2:7^2:9:10:12^2:12f:13^3:14,15:
14,15f:14,15:16:17:18:20:22:23:26/**4**:1^4:3^3:4,5:6:
7^2:8:9^2:10:11:14^3:15:16/**5**:1:2^3:3:9:12^2:14^2:16^2:
17/**6**:2^2:3^2:4-7:8^2:9:12/**7**:3:7^5:8,9:10,11^3:12:13^2:
19^2:23:24^2:25/**8**:1^4:2:3:4^2:5^2:6^2:7:10^3:11^5:12^2:14:
14f:16^2:17/**9**:2:3^2:3f:4^3:7:9^3/**10**:1^2:2:3^2:4^6:5^3:6:
7,8^2:9-13^6:14^2:17f^2:17:18^2:19^3:20:22/**11**:1^7:4:5^2:
10:11:13:15:16:17:18:19^2:22^2:23:24^2/**12**:2:6^2:9^2:
10:11^2:13:16:18:19^3:22^2:24^2:25:27^2/**13**:2,3^2:4:5:
9:13^3:17:18^2:18f:19^3:23^2/**14**:1^2:3:5:6,7:8:9:11:12
:13^2:14:15:17:19:20/**15**:2:5,6^2/**16**:2:3:3f:6,7:9,10^2
:14:16:17:21:22^2:25:27^2:29^2:32:35:36^2:37:40,41:
43:44:46:53^2:58/**17**:2^2:3,4^2:5f:8:9:12,13^7:16:17:
18:21:22,23^4/**18**:2:6^2:10:11:14:17:22:23:24:25:
29^2:30/**19**:1:3:5^2:7:8:9^2:10:14f^2:14/**20**:1f:1^2:3^2:4^4
:5,6^2:7:8^2:9,10^2:12:14^2:15:20:22:23,24:25:25f:
27,28:29^2:32:35,36f:35,36^2:38:39:40:41:43:46^2:

(OF Con't)
49/**21**:2:6:7:9,10,11:12:19,20[2]:19,20f:21:21f:21:
23[2]:24:25[2]:28:29[3]:31[2]/**22**:2[2]:3[2]:4[4]:5:8:10f:12:14:
18,19,20[3]:21:23:24[3]:26:30:31/**23**:2,3:4,5[2]:7:8[2]:9:
12:14,15:16f:17:17f:19,20f:23:26:27:29[2]:30:33:
34:35:36[2]:39:42:44:49/**24**:1[2]:2[2]:3:6:9:13[2]:16:
20,21[2]:25[2]:27/**25**:2[2]:4:5[3]:6:9,10[2]:12[2]:14:15:16/
26:1:2[3]:2f:4:5:7[2]:8:10:13[2]:14f[2]:19:20[5]/**27**:2:3:5:6[4]
:7:10f:10:12:13f:14f:16:17:18:22[2]:25:26:26f:26:
27:31:32[2]:33[2]:36/**28**:2,3[4]:7:8[2]:10:12[2]:12f:12:13[2]:
14[2]:14f:16[4]:16f[2]:17[3]:18f[2]:18:19:21[2]:23:25[2]/**29**:1[3]
:2:3[2]:6[3]:7:9:10[2]:13:14[2]:15:16:17[2]:18[5]:18f[2]:19[2]:20
:20f[2]:21/**30**:2,3[4]:4:6:9:10[2]:11:13:14:15[2]:17:18:20[3]
:21[3]:22:24[5]:25[6]/**31**:1[2]:2,3[4]:4:5:6:8:9[3]:11:12[2]:14:
15:16[3]:18[4]/**32**:1[2]:2[4]:4[2]:6:10[2]:11[2]:12[2]:14:16:17f:
18[3]:20:21:22[2]:23[2]:24[2]:25:26[4]:30/**33**:2[2]:7[2]:10:11:
12[2]:13:15:16:20:21[2]:22:24[3]:27:28:29:30:31/**34**:2[3]
:4:6:7:13[2]:14:15,16:18:26:27:29f:30:31/**35**:2:7:
10:11[2]:15/**36**:1:4[2]:6[2]:7:8:11:15:17[2]:18:20:22:23:
24:26[2]:26f[2]:32:34[2]:37,38/**37**:1[3]:3:4:7:11[2]:12[2]:16:
18,19,20:21:22:25:26/**38**:2,3[2]:2,3f[2]:2,3:6:8[2]:11:
13[2]:15,16[2]:17[2]:18:19:21:22/**39**:1[2]:2:2f:2:7:8:9[2]:
10:11[5]:12:14:15,16:17[2]:18[3]:21:22:24:25:26:27:
28/**40**:1[3]:2:4[2]:5:6:7-12[3]:7-12f:7-12:13[2]:14:15:16:
17:19[2]:21:24:26:28:29,30f:31:32:33:34:35:36[3]:37[2]
:38:39[2]:40:43[2]:46[3]:47[2]:48,49[2]/**41**:1:3:5[2]:7[2]:8:9[3]:
10[2]:11:14:15,16[4]:17,18[3]:19,20[3]:21[4]:22[2]:23:26/
42:1[2]:2:3[3]:4[2]:5:7,8,9:11:13[2]:14[2]:16-20/**43**:2[4]
:4:5:7[4]:10[3]:11[2]:12[2]:13:14:15:16:18[4]:19:20[3]:25:27
/**44**:2:3:4[3]:5[3]:6:8:9:10[2]:13:15[4]:22:25:30[3]/**45**:1[2]:2
:7[3]:8:9:11[3]:12:13:14:16:17[2]:18f:19[6]:20:21:22[2]:23[3]
:24[2]:25[2]/**46**:1:2:3[2]:5[4]:7[3]:8:11:14,15[2]:16[2]:17[3]:
19,20[6]:21,22[2]:23[2]/**47**:1[2]:2:7:9:10[2]:12:13[2]:14:16:
18[2]:19[2]:21/**48**:1[2]:2:3:4:8:10:11[4]:12[3]:13:14:15[2]:17:
21,22[3]:23:24[2]:27,28:30,31[3]:33:34:35[3]/**Dan1**:1[4]:
3,4[4]:3,4f:5:6[2]:12:13:15:17[2]:18,19[3]:20:21[2]/**2**:1:5:
12:18:19:20:23[3]:24:25:29:30:31:32[4]:33:34:35:37:
38:39:41,42:43[2]:44[2]:45[3]:47[3]:48:49[3]/**3**:1[2]:2[3]:4:5f:
7f:8[2]:10f:12:15:17:20[2]:25f:26[3]:27[2]:28:29[3]:30/**4**:1[3]
:6[2]:8:9:13:15[2]:16[2]:17[3]:18[2]:19:21:22:23[3]:25:29:30
:31:32[2]:34:34f:35[3]:36:37[2]/**5**:1:2,3,4[2]:5[2]:7:7f:8:11[6]
:14:16[2]:19:21[4]:23[3]:26:31/**6**:2:3:7:8:11:12:13[2]:14[3]
:16:17[2]:20:24:25,26[2]:27:28[2]/**7**:1[2]:3:6[2]:7[3]:8:9:10[4]:
11[2]:13[2]:14[2]:16[2]:18[2]:20:22[2]:23:24:24f:24:26[2]:27:
27f[2]:28/**8**:1[2]:2f[2]:2:3:4:8:8f[5]:9[2]:9f:10:10f:10:10f:
11[2]:12:13[3]:15[2]:16:17:19[2]:20[2]:21[2]:22:23:23f:25[3]:
26:26f:26/**9**:1[4]:2[2]:4[2]:7[4]:8:11[2]:13:15[2]:16:20:21:23
:24f:24[2]:25f[5]:26:27/**10**:1[4]:3:5,6[4]:11:13:13f:13[3]:
14:20,21[3]/**11**:1:4:5[2]:6:6f:6[5]:6f[3]:6[3]:7f:7[2]:9:10,11[3]:
12:15[2]:16:20f:22:23:24[2]:26:32:33[2]:34:35[2]:36:37[2]
:38:38f:39:40:40f[2]:40[2]:41[2]:43/**12**:1[2]:2:3:5:6:7f[2]:7
:9:10:13[2]:13f/**Hos1**:1[6]:2:3:4,5:4,5f:4,5[2]:4,5f[2]:7:7f
:10[2]:11[2]:11f:3:9[2]:15[2]:16:19:21,22[2]:23/**3**:2[2]/**4**:1[3]:
7[2]:8:11:12:13[2]:18/**5**:1[2]:2:4:5[2]:7:8:9[2]:10[2]:12/**6**:2:
3[2]:5[2]:8[2]:9[3]:11/**7**:5:16/**8**:1:9:10[2]:11:13[2]/**9**:3[2]:4:5:
7[2]:8:10:10f[2]:11:13:15f:15:16:17/**10**:1:2:4:5[2]:7:8:
9:10:11:12[3]:13[2]:14:14f:15[3]/**11**:1:4:8f:11/**12**:5:6:
11[3]:13/**13**:2:3:5:10:11f:15[3]/**14**:2:4:6:7:9/**Joe1**:1:
2[2]:6[2]:9[4]:10:13[2]:14:15:15f:16/**2**:1[2]:2[4]:3:5[3]:11[2]:13:
14:17[3]:18:23[3]:28:30:31:32/**3**:1:2:2f:4:6:8:12:13:
14[3]:18[2]:19:21[2]/**Amo1**:1:2[6]:3:4:5[3]:7:8[2]:9:10:12:
12f:13:14[2]/**2**:1[3]:4[2]:6[2]:8f:8:9[2]:10:15:16/**3**:2[2]:7:9[2]:
10:12:13:14:15/**4**:1:2:8:10[2]:11:12:13/**5**:1:4:5[3]:6:
12:13:14:15[2]:16:18[2]:21:22:23:24[2]:25,26,27[4]/**6**:1:
3[2]:4:5:8[2]:9:10:12:14[2]/**7**:1:9[2]:10:12[2]:14[2]:17[2]/**8**:1:
2:3[2]:6[4]:7:10[4]:11[3]:12:13:14/**9**:1:3[2]:5:6:7[3]:8:11:12[2]
:13[3]:14/**Ob1**:1[2]:1f[2]:5:7:8f[2]:8[2]:9:10:11[2]:12[2]:13[2]:
14:16:17:18:19[3]/**Jon**:1:2:3[2]:7:9,10:12/**2**:2:3:6[4]/**3**
:1:3f[3]:4,5:6/**4**:1:2:5:6:7/**Mic1**:1[4]:2:5[2]:6[2]:7:7f:10[2]:
11:11f[2]:11:11f[2]:11:11f[2]:12:13[3]:14f:14[4]:15[2]/**2**:2:4
:5:6:7[2]:8:9:11[2]:13[3]/**3**:1:4:8:9:10:12[2]/**4**:1[2]:2[3]:8:10[2]
:12:13[4]/**5**:1:2:3[2]:4[3]:6[2]:7[2]:11/**6**:4[2]:5[4]:6:7[4]:9:10[3]:
11:16[4]/**7**:4[3]:9:10:11:12:13f:13:14:15:18:19/**Nah**
1:1:3:4[2]:9:10:11:12:13:15/**2**:1f[2]:2[2]:7:9:11[2]:13/**3**:
1[2]:2:3[2]:4[2]:5:9:10:12:13:15:17/**Hab1**:6f[2]:9:11f:12[2]
/**2**:9:11:14[2]:17[2]/**3**:1:2:3:4:7[2]:8,9:11:13:16:18:19/
Zep1:1[7]:3:4[2]:7[3]:8[2]:9:10[4]:11:15[5]:18[5]/**2**:2[2]:3:5f[3]:5[2]
:6:7[2]:8[2]:9[4]:10[3]:11:13:14[2]:15[2]:15f[2]/**3**:1:2:3:8[2]:9:9f
:10:11:12:13:14[2]:15[3]:20[2]/**Hag1**:1[6]:7:12[3]:14,15[2]/
2:1:2:4:6:7:7f:7:8,9[3]:10[2]:12:18,19:18,19f:18,19:
21:22[2]:23/**Zec1**:1[5]:2:7[4]:10:11:12[3]:13:14:16:17[2]:
21/**2**:4:5[2]:6,7:8:8f:9:11,12/**3**:1[2]:2f:2:3:5,6,7[3]:8:9[2]
:10[3]/**4**:3:6f:6[2]:7:9[2]:10[3]:11:14/**5**:3:4[2]:9:11f[2]/**6**:1:5
:10,11[5]:12[2]:14:15[4]/**7**:1[3]:2[4]:3[2]:5:6[2]:12/**8**:2[2]:3[2]:4:9[2]
:11:12:13:14,15:17:18:19:22:23/**9**:1:1f[2]:6[2]:7[2]:10[2]
:10f[2]:11:12[2]:13[3]:16,17/**10**:2:3[2]:7:10:11:11f[3]:11/
11:2[2]:3:4:6:8:11:12f:14:15/**12**:1[3]:2:3:4[2]:5[3]:6:7[3]:8[2]
:10[2]:11f[2]:11:12,13,14/**13**:1:2[4]:3:4:6:6f:7:8[2]/**14**:1[2]
:4[3]:5f[2]:5[2]:10[4]:14[2]:16:16f:16:17:20:21[5]/**Mal1**:2,3:
4[2]:8:9:10[2]:11[2]:13:14/**2**:1[2]:3:4:5[2]:6:7[3]:8[2]:9:10[2]:11
:15[2]:16[2]/**3**:1[2]:3[2]:4:5:7:8:9:10:11:12[2]:16[3]:17:18/**4**
:1[2]:2:3/**Mt1**:1[3]:2[3]:3[3]:4[3]:5[3]:6[3]:7[3]:8[3]:9[3]:10[3]:11[2]:12[2]
:13[3]:14[3]:15[3]:16[3]:17:18:19:20f:20/**2**:1[2]:2:4:6:13:
17[2]:18:18f:19:23/**3**:2:5:7f:7[2]:9:9f:10:11:16[3]/**4**:3[2]:
4:5:6:8[2]:10:12,13:15,16[3]:17:18:19:23[2]:24[2]/**5**:3:9:
10:17[2]:19[2]:20[2]:21:22[4]:22f:27:29[2]:31[3]:33:35:38[2]:
45/**6**:2:30:34/**7**:3:4[2]:5:9:10:12[2]:15:17:20/**8**:4:8,9
:10:11:12:17:18:19:20f:20:21:26:28[2]:29:30:31:32
:33/**9**:3:5,6f:8:13[2]:14:18:20:26:27:29:35[3]:38/**10**:
1:2,3,4[2]:6:7:14:15:20:22:23f:25:26:28:30:37[2]:38:
41[2]:42/**11**:9:11[2]:12:12f[2]:19f:19:20:25:29/**12**:1[2]:5
:7:8f:8:10:11:17:21:23f:24:27:28[2]:31,32f:34:38:
39,40f:39,40:41:42[2]/**13**:5:11:14:18:19[2]:20:21:22:
23:24:27:31,32[4]:33[3]:34,35:36:37f:38:39:40:41f:
41:42:44:45:46:47,48[2]:49:50:52f[2]:58/**14**:1f:3:3f:
5:9[2]:14:17:22:29:31:33:35:36/**15**:2:3:5,6,7:9:11f:
20:21:21f:24:29:31:34:35/**16**:1f:1,2,3[2]:6[2]:8:11[2]:
12:13f:14:16:17:18:19[2]:21:21f:23:24:26:27[2]:28/
17:1:12f:13:14:20:21:21f:22,23:25:26,27[2]/**18**:1[2]:
3:4:5:6[2]:7f[2]:8:10:11f:14:19:23:24/**19**:7:8:12[2]:14[2]:
20:23:24[2]:27:28f:28/**20**:1[3]:3:4:11,12:13:18f:20[2]:
28f:29/**21**:1[3]:8:9f:10:12:13[2]:15:21:31[2]:34:36:39:
42f:43[2]:44:46[2]/**22**:1[2]:6:8:13:15:16[2]:23:25[2]:26[2]:
28[2]:29[2]:31:32[3]:32f[2]:34,35[2]:36:40:42:43/**23**:3:5:8
:13,14:15:22:25:26:27[2]:28[2]:29,30:31[2]:32:33[2]:34:
35[3]:36[2]:39f/**24**:1:2:3[3]:6:7:8:10:12:15f:22:27f:29:
29f:30:30f[3]:30[2]:31[2]:31f:37,38:45[2]:47:51[2]/**25**:1[2]:
2,3,4:13:14[2]:24,25:30:31f:31:34[2]:45/**26**:2f:3:4:6:
7:8,9:13:14:17:20,21:24f:26:27:28:30:31:38:45f:
45:47:51[2]:53:56:57:58:60,61:63[2]:64f:64[2]:69:73/
27:5:8:9[3]:11f:18[2]:21:24[3]:29:37:38:40:41,42,43:
47:48:56[3]:57:62[2]/**28**:2:9:11,12,13:17:19f:19[3]:20[2]
/**Mk1**:1[2]:3f[2]:4:4f[2]:7:10[2]:16[2]:17:21[2]:24[2]:25:27:28[2]
:32,33[2]:34[2]:39[2]:40/**2**:1:4:6:9,10,11f:14:15:16:16f
:16:18:19:21[2]:23:24:25,26:28f/**3**:3:6f:10:11[2]:
14,15:16-19[6]:20:21:22[2]:28:30/**4**:2[2]:4:8[2]:11,12:15[3]
:16:18:19[3]:20:21:26:30:31,32[4]:35:37:38/**5**:1:5:
7,8:9:11:13:20:21:22:23:33:34/**6**:1:2,3:5:8,9[2]:15:
21:22,23:25:26:27:38:39,40:41:43,44:47:53:55:
56/**7**:2:4[3]:6,7:9:12,13:14:15,16f[2]:19:21[2]:24[2]:31[2]/
8:1:3:5:10:11:13:14:15[3]:19[2]:23:27:28:31f:33:34:
35:38[2]:38f:38[2]/**9**:1[2]:2:5:9f:11:12,13f:14:17:18:25[2]
:30,31f:34:35:38[2]:39f:41:42:43,44f:43,44:45:46f:
47[2]/**10**:1:2:4:14:20:23:24f:24:25[2]:29:33f:35:38[2]:
42:44[2]:45f:46:47:48[2]:49f/**11**:1[3]:9[3]:10[2]:15[2]:16:17[2]
:18[2]:22,23/**12**:1:2[2]:4:8:12:14[2]:18:20,21,22:23[2]:
24:26[4]:27[2]:28[3]:32:33[2]:34:35:37:38[4]:39:40[3]:43,44
:43,44f/**13**:1:3,4[3]:7:8:9:19[2]:20[2]:22f:26f:27:30:30f
:34f:34/**14**:3[2]:4,5:8:10:12:13[2]:18[2]:20:21f[2]:23:24f:
25:26:27:32:34:41f:41:43:45:53:54:61:62f:62[2]:65
:66,67:68:68f:69:70/**15**:1:2:3,4:7:9:11[2]:15:16,17[2]
:18:20:21[2]:26:27:28f:32:35:38f[2]:39:40[2]:42,43[2]:46[2]
:47/**16**:1:7/**Lk1**:1,2,3f:4[2]:5[6]:6:10:11,12[2]:15:17[4]:
17f[2]:19:23:25:27:32[2]:35[2]:39,40:41:43:48[2]:58:63:
65:66:68:69:74:76:77:78:79/**2**:2:4[2]:4:8:9:11f:13[2]:
15:20:22[2]:24:25f:32:34,35[2]:36,37[4]:38:38f:39[2]:
46,47/**3**:1[3]:3:3f[2]:4:7[2]:8[2]:9:14:15:16:16f[2]:19,20:
22:23-38/**4**:1[2]:3:5[2]:9,10,11[2]:14:16:17:18,19:
18,19f:22:25,26[3]:27:29:32[2]:34:37:40:41:43[2]/**5**:1[2]
:3:4:7:8:9:10[2]:12[3]:13:15[2]:17:18,19:21:23,24f:27:
29[2]:30:33[2]:36/**6**:1:5f:5:7:9:11:13[2]:14,15,16[3]:
17,18[3]:20:22f[2]:25:27:28:35:39:42[3]:44:49/**7**:1:2:
6,7,8[2]:11:12:16:17[2]:18[2]:19:20,21,22:24:27:28[2]:
29:30:32:33:34:34f:35f:36:37:39:42:45:46/**8**:1[4]:3[2]
:5:6:10[2]:12[2]:13[2]:14:16:19:21:22:25:27[2]:28:29:30f[2]
:30:32:37[2]:40:41:43,44f:43,44:56/**9**:2[2]:5:6:7:10:
11:12:13[2]:14:17:19:20:21:22f:22:26f:26[4]:27[2]:29f:
31:43[2]:44f:46:48[2]:53:53f:54:55f:58f:60[2]:61:62/
10:2:4:6:7:8,9:11[3]:13[2]:13f:15:18:19:20:21[2]:22:24
:29[2]:30:31:34f:35f:35:36/**11**:1:5,6f:5,6[2]:8:12:15:
16:16f:17[2]:20[2]:22:24:28:29,30[2]:31:31f:31:32[2]:
37,38:39:42[2]:43:44:46:49:50[3]:51[2]:53,54/**12**:1:4:6[3]
:7[2]:8:8f:10f:23:25[2]:26:31:33:39:40f:42,43,44[2]:
46[2]:50:52:53/**13**:4:8:12:14[2]:18:24,25:28[2]:30:31:
32:33:35/**14**:1[2]:5:7:9:10:14:15:19:21:24[2]:28:29:
30:31[2]:32/**15**:3,4:8:10[2]:12[2]:17:19:21:24:26:30/
16:4[2]:5,6:7:8:8f:9f[2]:11:12:15:16[3]:22:24:28/**17**:6:
7,8,9:10:15:16:20[2]:21[2]:22f:26:28:30/**18**:3:8f:9:12
:16,17[2]:21:24:25[2]:29[2]:31:36:38:39[2]/**19**:1[2]:7:9,10[2]
:9,10f:11:12[2]:14[2]:17:27:28:29[2]:35:36,37[2]:39:46[2]:
47:48/**20**:1:10[2]:15:21[2]:27:28:29[2]:31:33:34,35:36:
37,38[6]:39:41:42,43:46[2]:47/**21**:3:4:5[2]:6[2]:7:9:12:
15:16:18:20:21:22:22f:22:24[2]:26[3]:27:27f:31:32:
34,35[2]:37,38/**22**:3:4:5:7:10:16:17:18:19[2]:20[2]:22f
:22:23:30:32:39:41,42:44[2]:47:50:52:58:59:62:
63,64:65:66:69f:70/**23**:3f:14:26:28:36:37:38:39:
47:50,51,52[4]:53:54/**24**:6,7f:6,7:10:13[3]:14:18:
22,23:24:26:27[2]:28:30:33,34:35:40:42:47[2]:49f:50
f/**Jn1**:1f[3]:11,12:13f:13:14f[3]:14[4]:18[2]:23:28:29:31:
32:34:35:36:40:45:47:49[2]:51:51f/**2**:1:7,8:9[2]:11:
16:23/**3**:1[3]:3:5:5f:5:13f:14:16f:18f:18:23,24:26[2]:
31[2]:33,34:36/**4**:3:5,6[2]:15:20:21-24:27:34:35[2]:36:
39:40,41:42[2]:43,44:45:46,47[3]:48:51/**5**:1:3[2]:4:4
5:7[2]:18:22:24:25[2]:27[2]:28:30:32,33f:45[2]/**6**:1[2]:2
2-5f:2-5:8,9:10[2]:26:27f:29:34:35:38:39[2]:42:45:
48-51[2]:53:53f:57[3]:62f:64:66:69:70:71[3]/**7**:1:2:7
:10:12:13:16:17:19[2]:20:21,22,23[2]:25:28:35:37:
:39:40:41,42[2]:48/**8**:1:3:4:9:10:12[2]:20:23:24:28
30,31:33:34[2]:37[2]:38:41:44[4]:46[2]:47:52/**9**:2[2]:3:4
11:16[2]:22,23:28:32:35f/**10**:4:9:20:21:22,23f[2]:
22,23:25:26:34,35:36[3]:37/**11**:4[3]:5:9[2]:10[2]:18:19
27:42[2]:45:49:51:52:54[2]/**12**:3[2]:4:6:9[2]:11[2]:12:13
15[2]:16[2]:23,24[3]:29:31:31f:31:36:36f:37:38f:40f:
:42[2]:43[2]:48/**13**:1:4f:10:11:17:18[2]:21[2]:23f[2]:26f:
:28:31[2]/**14**:6:11:12,13:26[2]:27:30:31/**15**:3:5:11,
19:21:24:26/**16**:5[2]:5f:7:8[4]:8f:11:17,18:21:22:24
25:26f:33/**17**:1:8:10[2]:12[2]:15:16:17:20[2]:21[2]:22/
18:1:3:4,5:7:9:10:13:15:17:21:22:25[2]:26[3]:28[2]:2
:29:32:33:34f[3]:36:38:39[2]/**19**:2:3:5:6:7:12:14:17
19[2]:21[2]:23,24:29:31:32:34:36,37[2]:38[3]:39:40
41[2]:42/**20**:1f:2:12[2]:19:24:30,31/**21**:1:2:2f:6[4]:8:
10:12[2]:15:16[2]:17:19:20:21:24/**Act1**:1f:3:4[2]:8:1
12:13:14[4]:17:19[3]:20[2]:21,22:24,25/**2**:1:2:3:8:9f:
10:11:14[2]:15:19:20:22[2]:24:27:30:32:33:34[2]:37:
38[3]:39:40:42f:43/**3**:6[2]:12:13[2]:14:15[2]:17:19[2]:
21,22:25:26[2]/**4**:1[2]:1f[2]:4[3]:5:6:8:10[2]:11[2]:11f:13:1
19:22:24[2]:25,26[2]:27:30:32:33:36[3]:37/**5**:2:9[2]:9f:
14:15:16:19[2]:24f:30:31:32:34:35:37[2]:39:40/**6**:1
:3[3]:5[2]:7[2]:8:8f:9[3]:10:13:14[2]/**7**:4[2]:5[2]:6:7:8[6]:9:10[5]
16[2]:20:22:23:24:26:29:30:31:32[2]:34:36[2]:37:38[2]
40[2]:42:45:46[2]:48,49:52:53:55[2]:56f:58[2]/**8**:1[3]:5:6
9,10,11[2]:9,10,11f:12:14:16[2]:23f:26:27[2]:28:31:3
33[2]:33f:36:37:39[2]/**9**:2:7:11[2]:12:15:20:24:25:26
27:29:31[2]:32:35:36/**10**:1:2:3:7[2]:9,10:12:13:22:2
:30:32:36,37[2]:38:39:42[2]:45:48/**11**:6:12:16:18:2
21:24[2]:26:28[4]:30/**12**:1:4:7:10:12[2]:15:17:20:22[2]
23[2]/**13**:1[2]:5:6,7:10[4]:11:12:13:14:15[3]:16[2]:17[2]:18
21[3]:22:23[2]:26[3]:36:37:41:44:46:47:50[2]:51[2]/**14**:2
:5,6[3]:11:13[4]:15:19:22:23:27/**15**:1:3[2]:5:11:15:1
:20:22:26:27,28,29[3]:30:36f:40,41/**16**:2:3:6:7[3]:8
10f:14[3]:16:17:18[2]:19:26:40/**17**:1:3:4[2]:4f[2]:5:6[2]:7
8,9:11:12:18:22:23:24:26[2]:27[2]:28[2]:29:32[2]:34/**1**
2,3:5:8:11:12:13:15[3]:16:17:18:19:21f:22:25,26[2]
25,26f:27/**19**:5:8f:9:10:12:13[2]:14:16[2]:17[2]:18,19
24:25:27[6]:28:31[3]:32:35[3]:40/**20**:4[2]:7f:
10,11,12:16:17:19:21:24:25:30:32:34[2]:35:38/**2**
2:3[2]:5:8[2]:9:10[2]:11:12:13:14:16[2]:18:20:21[2]:24:
26,27f:28:30[2]:31:37,38/**22**:5:8:12[2]:14:16:17,18
23/**23**:3:5[2]:6[3]:8:9:12,13:16:17:23,24:29:30/**24**:
5:7:8:10:12:13:14[4]:15:16:22:23/**25**:2:10,11[2]:14
15:16:20:23:25/**26**:5:6:7:8:9[2]:10:12:18[2]:25:31/
27:1[2]:2f[2]:4:4f:5[3]:7,8:7,8f:7,8[2]:9f:10:11:12,14,15
17[2]:22:23:24:27:28:30:34:37:41[2]:42/**28**:1[2]:3:4:7
10:11:17:20f[2]:23[3]:28,29f:31/**Rom1**:4[2]:5:8[2]:10:1
f:11,12:15:16[2]:17f:20:21:23:24:25:26:27:28:29[3]:
30[3]:32/**2**:5[3]:7:8:16[2]:19[2]:20[2]:23:24[2]:28[2]:29/**3**:1:2
3:4[2]:6:8:13:14:18:19[3]:20:21,22f:23:24:25:26/**4**:1
:6[2]:7:10:11[2]:12:15:16[2]:17[2]:19:22:24/**5**:1:2[2]:4:6:
9:10:11[2]:13[3]:16:17[4]:20/**6**:2,3[3]:5:5f:6:13[4]:15:17:
19[2]:20:21:22[2]:23[2]/**7**:2:5:6[2]:7[2]:8:10:11[2]:21/**8**:2[2]:
:8:9[2]:10:10f:11[2]:13:14[2]:15:19f[2]:22:23:27:34:36:
38:39/**9**:1:4:5[2]:8[3]:10-13[3]:14:17[5]:21[2]:23,24:25:2
:27f:27:29[2]:32:33[2]/**10**:1:2:3:4:8[2]:10:13:15[3]:18:1
/**11**:1[2]:5:7[3]:8:9:11:12[3]:14:15:16:17[3]:18:24:25[3]:2
:28[4]:34/**12**:1:2:3[2]:4,5[2]:6:7[2]:8[2]:9:13:16[2]:20[2]/**13**:2
4:8[2]:10:11:12,13[3]/**14**:1f:2[2]:3:5:10[2]:12[2]:14:20[2]:2
/**15**:1[4]:3[2]:5:6[2]:12:13:15,16:17:19:20:21[2]:23:27:
27f:28:30:32/**16**:1:3:8:10:19:20:24:25,26,27[2]/
1Co1:2:3[2]:5:7[2]:10[2]:11[2]:12[3]:13:14:15:16:17[3]:18:
19[3]:20:24[3]:25[2]:26:27:29:30:31[2]/**2**:2:4:6[2]:7[2]:8[2]:10
12:15:16[3]/**3**:3:5[2]:8:12:13[2]:15:16[3]:19[2]:20:21[2]:22
/**4**:5:6[2]:9[2]:10[2]:11:17[2]:18:20/**5**:3,4[3]:5:5f:6:8:12:1
/**6**:1[2]:6:9,10,11[3]:12f:12:13[2]:15[2]:16[2]:19:20/**7**:5[4]:
:12:14[2]:18:19:21:22[2]:23f:27[2]:31:34:39/**8**:6f:7:13
/**9**:1:2:4:7[5]:8:10[2]:12:13[3]:15:17:19:20:21:25f[2]/**10**
1[2]:2:3,4f:3,4:5:7:8:10:14:16[4]:17[3]:19:20:24[2]:28[2]:
31/**11**:5:7:8:10f:12:14,15:17:25[2]:26:27[3]:29[2]:30:
32/**12**:1:2:3[3]:4[2]:5:6:7[2]:10:11:12:13[4]:15[2]:16[2]:22:
23:24:27[4]:28[3]:29:30[3]:31[2]/**13**:1[2]:2[2]:3:7:9:11:13/
14:1[2]:2[2]:3:5[3]:6:7:10:11:12:13[2]:18[2]:20[3]:22:24:31:
32f:36:37/**15**:1:2:5:6:8:9[2]:12:13:15:19[2]:20:20f:2
:22[2]:24:27:28:32:34:34f:35:37[2]:38[2]:39[2]:40[2]:41:
43[2]:47:48[2]:49:50[2]:52:57/**16**:2:8:18:21:23:24/
2Co1:1:2:3,4[2]:9:13,14[2]:15,16:17:18:19:20[2]:22[2]/
:5,6:12:15:16:17[3]/**3**:1[2]:3:4:5:6:7[2]:10:11[2]:14[2]:17:
18[2]/**4**:1:2:4[3]:4f:5[2]:6[2]:10:11:12:15[2]:17[2]/**5**:2:4:10:
11[2]:12:13,14:16:18:21f/**6**:1:2:4[2]:5:6:7[3]:10:12[2]:14
:16[2]/**7**:1[2]:2[3]:4:5:6:7:9[2]:10[2]:11:14/**8**:2:3:4:5:6:7:9
11:13[2]:18:23/**9**:2[2]:4:5:12:13:14[2]/**10**:1:2[2]:7:13/
11:2:3:10:12:14:15:19,20:22:26:28:31/**12**:6:9[2]:1
:17[2]:18:21[2]/**13**:4[2]:11:14/**Gal1**:1:5:13:14[3]:17[2]:20
24/**2**:2:6:7,8,9:12[2]:14[3]:16:18:20[2]:21/**3**:1[2]:2:5[3]:7[2]
:10[2]:12[3]:13:14:16[2]:18:19[3]:21,22[4]:26:29[2]/**4**:4:6[2]:9

Con't)
:19:23[2]:24,25[5]:29[2]:31[2]/5:1:5:11[2]:15[2]:17:20:
22:25/6:1:4:5[3]:6:7:8[3]:9[2]:12[2]:14[3]:16:17:18/
1:3:7:8:11[2]:13[2]:15[2]:16,17:18:20:21:22:23/2:
:6:7:8:8f:8:9:11[2]:12:13:14[2]:15[2]:16[2]:17:18[2]:19[2]
21:22[2]/3:1[3]:2,3[3]:6[2]:7[2]:8[2]:9:10:12:14,15[5]:16[2]:
8,19:20:21[2]/4:1:2:4:6:7[3]:9[2]:11[3]:12[2]:13:15,16[2]
18[2]:22:25:28:30f:31/5:2[2]:3:4:5[4]:6:8[2]:9:11:12:
15,16:20:23[3]:25:26f:28:29,30:32[3]:33/6:2:3:
10:11[2]:12[4]:13:14[2]:15:17[3]:18/Php1:1[2]:2:3:4:5
:11:14[3]:15[2]:20:24:28:29[2]:30/2:3:7:7f:8f:9[2]:10
15[3]:16:17:18:21:26:27:30[2]/3:1:3[2]:5[2]:8:9:11[2]:
:15:18[2]:19[2]:21/4:3[2]:4:9:12:13:17:19:23/Col1
:5:11[2]:12:13[3]:15:15f:18[3]:19:22[2]:23[3]:24[2]:
27[2]:28[2]/2:2[3]:3:5:8:9:11[2]:12[2]:13:14[2]:15:17[2]:19
20f:23/3:1[2]:5:7:8:9:10[2]:12[2]:14:15[2]:17[2]:22:24
3:4:5:9:10:12/1Th1:1:3:4:5[2]:6:8:10[2]/2:4:6:10:
16/3:2,3[2]:4:5:7/4:1[2]:3,4[2]:5:7:8[2]:13:15:16[2]/5
:4:5[2]:8[2]:10:12:13:14:22:23:27/2Th1:1:3[2]:4:5:
:11:12[4]/2:1[3]:3[4]:4[2]:7:7f:7:8:9[2]:12:13:14/3:1:2[2]
[3]:6[2]:8:11:12:13[2]:14:15:16:17:18/1Ti1:1[2]:2[2]:
:7[2]:10,11:12:13:14[2]:15:17[2]:20[2]/2:2:7:9,10/3:
7:8:9[2]:10:15[3]/4:1:5:7:12:14/5:3:9:10[2]:11:14:
16[2]:18:20:21[3]:22/6:1[2]:3:4:5:9:10[3]:15[2]:20[3]:21
i1:6f:7:10[4]:12[2]:13:16[2]:18/2:3[2]:9:13:14[2]:16[2]:
18[3]:20:21[2]:22:24:26[2]/3:3:5f:7:9:10:11:12:14:
4:2:5:8:10:15:17f[2]:19/Tit1:1[3]:3:4:5[2]:6:7:11:
:14:15/2:3[2]:7[3]:8:11:13/3:2:3:4:5[2]:6:7[2]:9[2]:11:
15/Phm1:1:5:6:7:8,9[4]:11[3]:15:25/Heb:3[3]:4[2]:
:7[2]:8:10/2:4:6[2]:8[2]:9:10:12:14[3]:15:17/3:1:6:
:10:11[2]:12:13[2]:15:16[2]/4:1[3]:2:3:4:8[2]:9:11[2]:12:
14:15:16[2]/5:1[2]:5:5f:7:7f[3]:7:9:14/6:1[2]:2f:2:4:5[2]
:12[2]:14[2]:19[2]:20/7:1[3]:2[5]:3f[2]:3[4]:4[2]:9[2]:11[3]:
13,14[3]:15:16[3]:17[2]:18:21[2]:22[2]:26[2]:27[2]/8:1:2:4:
8[2]:9[2]:10:13[4]/9:1[2]:3:4[2]:5[3]:6:7:8:9:11[2]:12[3]:13[2]:
:15:16:17[2]:18:19[4]:20:22[2]:23[2]:24[2]:25:26[2]:28/
1[2]:2:3[2]:4:4f[3]:5[2]:9:12:14:16:18:19[3]:20:21:25:
:27:29:31/11:2[2]:7[5]:11[2]:12[2]:13:15:17:18:21[2]:
:24,25[3]:26:27[2]:28[2]:29:30[2]:32[2]:33:37,38:39[2]/
1[2]:2[3]:4:7:14:15:17:22[2]:23[3]:24[2]:25/13:3:5:6:7[2]
[3]:13:15[3]:20,21[3]:23/Jas1:1[2]:2:4:5:6:12:14:17:
:18:21[2]:27[2]/2:1:3:5:6:8:9:10:14[2]:15:21:23:25[2]
1f:1:3:6[4]:7[2]:10:11:13:14:15:16:17[3]:18[2]/4:1:4[4]:
11:14/5:1[2]:3[2]:4[4]:8:10:11[2]:12:14:16:20/1Pe1:
:3[4]:4[2]:7[2]:9:11:12[2]:13:17:19[2]:21:25/2:1[2]:2,3f:
:4:5:6:7:9[2]:10:11:12:13[3]:14:20:21:23:24:25/3:
[2]:6:7[2]:8[2]:10:16:18[2]:20[2]:21:22[2]/4:2[2]:3[2]:4:5:7[2]:
10[2]:13:14:14f[2]:15:16/5:1:2[2]:5[2]:6:10:12[2]:14[2]/
e1:1[5]:2:9:11[2]:12:16:19/2:2:3:5[3]:6[3]:7,8[2]:9:10f:
12[2]:14[2]:15:17[2]:20:21/3:1[2]:3:4[2]:5,6:10:13:
16[4]:17[2]/1Jn1:1:2:4:7[2]/2:8:9:12[2]:17:18:19[2]:26
1:2:4:5:8[2]:9:10[2]:23/4:3:6:7:15:17:18[3]:19:20/5
4:5:6,7,8f:6,7,8[2]:13:14:17[2]:17f[2]:18[2]:19[2]/2Jn1:
4:5:7:8:9:13[2]/3Jn:3[2]:5:6:8:9:10[2]:12:15/Jud:1[3]
3:4[2]:5[4]:6[3]:7[4]:9[2]:11:12:13:14:15:17:19:20[2]:23[2]:
,25/Rev:1[2]:1f:2:4f:6:7f[2]:8f:8:9[2]:12:13:13f:14:
:17,18:20[2]/2:1[2]:2:5:6:6f:7[3]:8:9[3]:10[3]:12:13:14:
[2]:15f:16:17:18[3]:19:22[2]:23:24,25[3]:27[2]/3:1:1f:1:
5:7[2]:9:10f:10:12[2]:14[3]:16:19/4:2:3:5:5f:5:7[4]:8[2]:
/5:1:5[4]:6:6f:6[2]:7:8:10:11[2]/6:1:2:5:6[2]:6f[2]:8[2]:9[2]:
:11[2]:13:13f:15[2]:16[2]:17/7:1:2:3[2]:4-8[2]:9:13:14[2]:
:17:17f[2]:17[2]/8:3[2]:4:7[2]:8,9[3]:10:11:12[2]:13[2]/9:1f
5:8:9[2]:11:13[2]:15:16:16f[2]:16:17,18:19:20/10:3/
:1[2]:1f:4:5:6:7[2]:8,9:10:11:13[2]:15:19[2]/12:1:2:4:6
10[2]:11:12[2]:14:15[2]:17/13:1:3:8:8f[4]:8:10:11[2]:12
4[2]:17[3]:18/14:2[3]:3[2]:8[2]:10[4]:11[2]:13f:14:14f:14:18[2]
9/15:2[2]:3,4[4]:3,4f:5[2]:7[3]/16:1[2]:2:3:5:6:7:9[2]:10:
[2]:13:14[2]:16[2]:17:17f:18:19[7]:21/17:1[2]:2[3]:4[2]:5[2]:6[2]
[3]:11:14:15[2]:17:18/18:2[3]:2f:3[2]:6:8:11:12:13:17[2]
0:22[3]:23:24/19:1:2f:2:5:6[3]:7:8[2]:9:9f:10[4]:10f[2]:
:13f:14:15[3]:16[2]:17:18[3]:19:20[2]:21[2]/20:4[2]:5:6[2]:
8:9[2]:10:12:14[2]:15[2]/21:2:3:4:6[2]:9:10:11:12[2]:14[2]
6:17:17f[2]:18,19,20[2]:21:23[3]:24[2]:26:27/22:1[3]:2[2]:
:2[2]:3[2]:9:10:14[2]:17:19

22862

FF

Gen9:4/14:11/17:14:23/21:16:28,29/22:3/25:
29:26/31:42/37:23/39:12/40:18,19[2]/45:18:
/49:17/Ex3:5/4:25,26/14:25/19:23/22:6/24
29:17:21/32:12/Lev1:15,16,17/4:31/7:20:21/
3:33/14:8/16:23/19:27/20:3:5:6:17/Num5:23
15:30:31f/17:10/22:21:22,23/Deu2:27/6:15/
:5/22:8/23:1/25:10:12/Jos5:15/7:10,11/8:24
15:18,19/Ju1:4,5,6/11:3/14:8/16:19/21:6:23/
u1:11f/2:16/3:4:6,7/4:7:8/1Sa5:4/17:20:
3,39:46:50,51/19:24/24:4:11/25:13/30:2/31:9[2]
2Sa2:26/4:6,7:12/10:4[2]/12:20/13:31/16:9/18:
5:21/19:7/20:12:22/1Ki13:24,25/15:17/18:35
20:41/2Ki1:2/11:9/12:18/15:19,20/17:21:23/
8:16/1Ch10:9[2]/19:4/2Ch14:13/21:10/23:4:8/
5:13:24/26:21/32:4/Ez8:31/Neh4:23/Est8:2/
Job1:17/3:6/10:16[2]/14:20,21/15:27,28:33f/16:
4/18:16/24:24/27:8/30:11/31:7,8/35:2,3/40:24
/Ps3:7/30:6,7/37:8:38/44:23/55:7/58:6/60:
9,10/68:2/75:10/88:16/89:38/94:23/104/105:
16/109:15:22,23/118:11/119:10:67:87:119/129
:2/143:12/Pro2:22f/3:23/6:4:35/10:19/26:6/
Ecc4:2/6:3/8:12/Sol5:7/Is1:4:25/3:1/5:29/7:
20/10:10:13:27/11:1/13:17/14:22/15:2/18:5/
20:2/27:11/28:19/30:28/32:11[2]/39:6/40:4:12:
24/47:2/49:23/52:2/55:7/57:13/59:2/Jer2:20/
3:20/5:23,24/9:21/12:3/13:24,25/19:8/20:5/22
:22:24,25/28:3:10/30:24/34:16/36:10:23/40:4:
10/41:5/43:2,3:5:12/44:17/48:2,3,4:25:32/52:
17/Lam3:66/4:9/Eze7:25/10:9-13/13:9:20:21/
14:13/17:3,4:9/20:17/21:26/23:17:25/24:5/25:
7:8/29:19/31:13/34:26:27/35:7/36:14/44:19:20
/47:4/Dan4:14[2]/7:4/8:7:22:25/11:30,31/Hos1:
7f:7/4:18/5:14/8:4:10/9:3:6/Joe3:5/Amo2:9/3:
14/5:5/Ob1:10:11/Jon2:6/Mic1:14/2:8/3:6/7:
3/Nah1:15/3:10/Zep:6/Zec5:7:9/6:7/9:14/11:
16/13:8/Mal2:12/3:14,15/Mt4:6/5:30/10:14:
15/11:1:22:24/12:1:43,44,45/14:13/18:8/24:51
/26/27:31:64/Mk2:23/3:9/4:4/5:20/6:11:27:
43,44/9:45,46/10:50/11:4,5:13/14:47:51,52/15
:20/Lk4:9,10,11/5:18,19:36/6:1[2]/7:38/9:16/10:
12/11:22:26/17:2,3/22:13:50/Jn1:45/6:22,23/
9:11/13:4/15:2/18:10:26/Act7:33:58/9:8,9/10:
8/12:7/13:51/16:26/18:6/27:32:35:40/28:5/
Rom2:25:27/11:17:18:19:20:22/15:24/1Co8:8[2]
/10:16/11:6/2Co12:9/Gal4:1:17/5:12/Eph4:22
/Col3:8/Heb6:8/7:23/12:1/2Pe2:6:15:20/Rev
14:18/18:10:17

376

OH

Gen18:32/19:2:18,19,20/27:36/44:16/Ex12:32
/16:3/32:31/Num11:4,5[2]/12:11/14:9:17,18:19/
23:7-10/24:3-9/Deu5:29/9:7:27/28:67[2]/30:19/
32:29[3]/Ru1:13/2/1Sa1:15,16:18/10:15/15:25:
30/24:21/2Sa7:19/13:12/14:9/1Ki1:31/3:26/
13:6/18:9/20:32/22:8/2Ki3:10/4:40/6:5:21/8:5
/19:4/1Ch4:10/16:8:19:34:35/2Ch6:42/14:11/
18:6,7/Neh1:8/Job3:16:20,21/5:17/6:2:8,9:11/
7:4:16/9:34/10:9:20,21/11:5:6/13:3:5/14:13/17
:3,4/19:21:23,24/23:3/29:2/30/31:35/Ps1:1/2:
12/6:3/7:17/9:11/14:7/18:3:13[2]/20:9/25:11:17
:20/27:9/28:2:6/30:4:8:10/31:19:23/34:8/43:3/
51:2:6:14,15/53:6/54:2/55:6/56:10,11/61:4:7/
64:1/68:4/77:1/78:40/79:8:9/81:13[2]/85:6/88:2
/89:47/95:1:7/107:8:15:21:31/108:12/118:1:29
/119:5:8:8f:97:107:156/134:1/135:20/136:1:26
/Pro5:12:13/8:33/Ecc5:9/Sol2:5/5:1/7:6/8:1/
Is1:4:5,6:16/10:3/12/17:6/21:2/22:5/30:9/36:
7/37:4/38:16/40:1/42:18/43:26/44:22/48:18/
53:1/58:2/64:1:9[2]/Jer8:19/9:1:2/13:15/15:10/
20:17/41:6/48:9/50:45[2]/Lam3:19:50/Eze:23/
18:30/Dan4:19/Hos6:3/11:8/12:6/Jon1:9,10/
Mic6:6/Mal1:10:13/Mt6:23/17:17/18:26/Mk
9:19:22:24/10:39/14:21[2]/Lk1:46/5:8/6:24/8:
28/12:49/22:22/Jn16:12/Act13:40/16:37/Rom
7:23,24,25/9:1[2]/11:33/1Co1:16/10:12/2Co2:4/
6:11/10:12/Gal3:1/4:19/1Ti1:14/6:11:20/2Ti2:
1/1Jn3:7/Rev4:2

230

ON

Gen1:7,8:13:14,15:19/2:2/3:14:15[2]:20f/4:12[2]:
15:25/6:9,10/7:23/8:5f:7f[2]:20/9:16,17/11:6f/12
:2f:8[2]:10:17/14:11/15:6/17:12/18:16:22,23:27:
33/19:2:17:22/21:23:31/22:1:4:6:8:9:13/24:7:
15,16:29,30/25:26:34/26:24/27:13:15:26/28:4:
13:20/29:1:9:12,13/31:17-20:29:34:54/32:1:6:
16:21:31/33:3:14:19/34:9,10:17:22:23:28/35:1:
2:3:5:12:16:21/37:19,20:31:34/38:9:9f:14:30/39
:10/40:4:14:16:18,19/41:1:5:6:13:22:41,42/42:
19:33/43:8/44:3:12:17/45:23/46:28[2]/47:26/48:
17[2]:18[2]/49:13/50:4/Ex3:2:5/4:3:20/9:10/11:1/
12:2:3,4[2]:6:7[2]:11:13:16[3]:23:34:37:39:40,41/13:
6,7/14:5:16:21:22:26:29[2]:30/15:17:19[2]:22:26/
16:1[2]:5:14:22:25:26:28,29:30/17:12[2]/19:4:16:22
:24/20:10:20/21:2f:24/22:30/23:1:2,3[2]:5/24:12:
17/25:12:16:30:40/26:1:4,5:14:17:20:22:25:
26,27:35[3]:37/27:8:9,10:11:14,15:19/28:9:10:
13,14:25:26:29:30,31f:32:36/29:5:6:9:12:13:25:
35/30:4:7:8/31:12,13:14,15[2]:17:18[2]/32:7:15:16:
26:30:34/33:21/34:1:2:3:21:23:28[2]:34:35/35:2:
35/36:4-7:11,12:20:23:25,26:30/37:20,21:27/38
:21/39:15-18:19:20:30:41/40:2:4:17:19:20:24/
Lev1:11:12[2]:15,16,17/2:12f:15/3:3,4,5:9,10,11:
15,16/4:8:9:10:11,12:35/5:11:12/6:2:4,5[2]:10:12[3]
:19,20:21:22,23/7:17,18:36:38[2]/8:8:9:10:13:
15,16:26/9:1:24/10:1:12:19/11:27/12:3/13:5:6:
29,30:32:33:34:35:51:53/14:23:25[2]/15:4[2]:6:8:9:
14:17:20[2]:26:27:29/16:4:18:24:29,30:29,30f:32/
18:16f/19:7:8:27/21:12/22:3/23:5f:7:8[2]:9,10,11:
25:26,27f:32[2]:33,34:33,34f:35:36:40/25:1:9:36:
46/26:30:46/27:27:33:34/Num1:1:1f:1:17,18,19
:17,18,19f/2:3-31[3]/3:1:7,8,9:31-35:38/4:8:12/7:
1:10:11:18-23:24-29[2]:30-35[2]:36-41:48-53[2]:60-65
:66-71[2]:72-77:78-83/8:4/9:1:2,3:4,5:10:11:13:15
:17:20,21/10:5,6,7[2]:11:29/11:11:17/12:3,4/13:
23/14:1:5:40/15:32/16:1:17:18:28:46:47/17:1:5
/18:22/19:12:19/20:16:17[2]:19:26:28[2]/21:11:
17,18:27-30/22:5,6:13:31:34:35:36/23:2:3,4:7-
7-10:14:18-24:30/27:8:21/28:1:9,10:11:15:16:17
:18[2]:24:25:26[3]/29:1[2]:2:7f:8:11:12f:12:17:20:23:
26,27:29:32:35/30:5:7:12/31:1:12:16:19:24/32:
5:9:12:19[3]:22:32/33:3,4:3,4f:8:14:47:49/34:4:
7,8,9:10,11:14,15/35:1:13,14/36:13/Deu1:1[2]:
19,20,21:40:41:43/2:27[2]:29:32/3:10:12:17:21/4:
5:13:21,22:43/5:5[2]:22/6:8[2]:9/7:6/9:1:9:10,11/
10:1:2[2]:3:4[2]:10/12:16:20-23/14:2/15/16:6:8:16
/17:6:9/18:10:16/19:9:15:17:20/21:22:23[2]/22:6
:12/23:7:19/26:2,3:11/27:1f:2,3,4:5,6/28:14:15-
15-19/29:1/30:14:15/31:22/32:2:22:36:40,41:
46/33:17:29/34:8/Jos1:12,13:14:15:17,18/2:1:
15:16/3:2,3,4:15,16:17/4:5:19:22/5:10:11,12[2]/6
:3,4:6-9/7:2:6:7:23/8:8:11,12,13:19:29:31/9:
3,4,5/10:5:19:24:26:28:32:33:34,35/11:1[2]:10:13:
15/12:1:2:5[2]:7/13:2-7:8:9:16:17:19/14:3,4:11/
15:2,3,4:7[2]:8:10,11:47[2]/16:1[2]:5,6[2]/17:1:2:7:8:13
/18:7:17/19:10:24,25,26:34/20:8/22:4:7,8:19:
22,23/23:11/24:8:27:30[2]/Ju1:8:9/2:2/3:16:
17,18,19:25/4:14:15:24/5:10[2]:21:23/6:5:10:11:
16f:26[2]:28:32:37/7:18/8:27f:34/9:29:38[2]:45:49:
53[2]/10:4:9/11:16:34/12:14/14:5:15:17/15:1:15
/16:3:4:27f/18:7:9,10:13:21/19:1:5[2]:9:12,13:14:
16:18[2]:27:28/20:30:35-39[2]:40,41/21:4/Ru1:14:
21/2:16/3:2:3[2]:15-18[2]/4:5:10/1Sa1:3:4:19,20f:
21,22/2:15:22:34/3:4,5:6:21,4:1/4:6:12:17/5:5/
6:8:15/8:11/9:12,13[2]:16:19[2]:25:26,27[2]/10:1:3:7[2]
/11:2/12:20/14:1:5:10:12[2]:13:24,25[2]:43:45/15:
12:18/16:5/17:3:14,15[2]:35:38,39:47:48,49/18:9[2]
:25/19:13:23/20:21/21:2:5[3]:10:13/22:8:18/23:
14,15:19:20:21:24,25:26/24:7,8/25:13:19:20/26
:1:20[2]:25/28:9:23/29:11/30:14:17:20:21:25/31:
1:2:7:8/2Sa1:1:4:6:9:21/2:13:19:21/3:6:16:
24,25/4:11/5:12/7:18:29[2]/9:10,11/10:9:18/11:
2:19,20,21:24/12:10:16:18:29,30/13:19:25:27:
29,30[2]:34/14:4:14:31/15:19,20[2]:35,36/16:2:13[2]:
22/17:19:21:22:28,29/18:9[2]:18/19:4:8,9,10:40/
20:1:13/21:12,13,14:16:20,21[2]/22:11/23:2:
18,19:20[2]/24:18:20:22/1Ki1:33:38:41:44,45:
46,47:53/2:2[2]:17:36,37:44/3:2:19/5:2,3:4/6:6:
10:29:35/7:16-22[2]:24:25:27-30:31:32:36:38:39[3]:
41-46:49[2]/8:12,13:27/9:25:26/10:5:6:9:19:20/
11:7:29:37/12:10:11:28[2]:31:32,33:32,33f:32,33/
13:2:3:9:16,17:24,25:33/14:12:21:23/15:14/16:
15,16:23:24:29/17:19/18:5:10:23[3]:26:27[2]:33:42
/19:4:6:11:20/20:23:29:30:31/21:1:3:12:27/22:
10[2]:19:24:35:43/2Ki1:4,5:6:9:14/2:1:4:6,7:8:9:
16/3:25/4:7:10:20:31/5:17:17f:18/6:24/7:9:17:
18/8:1/9:17:26[2]:27:32:33/10:6/11:5[2]:9[2]/12:3:7[2]
:9:17:20/13:25/14:4:5:9:13:20/15:4:34,35/16:4:
5:14/17:17:29:31:32:34/18:4:9:20,21:25:26:27:
28:36/19:1:15:28/20:7:9:11:11f/21:6:22/22:8/
23:5:6:8[2]:12:13:19/25:1:3:8:27/1Ch4:9f/5:10:19
/6:32:44-47/7:28[3]/9:22:33,34/10:1/11:22/12:
15:18:40/13:7/14:8/15:15:28/16:34:39/17:11/
18:8:10/20:2:6,7[2]/21:26:29/24:1/26:16:31,32/
27:2,3:4:5,6:7:8:9:10:11:13:14:15:26:29/28:5:13:
16/29:15:21/2Ch1:15/2:4/3:2:7:11,12,13:16:17[4]
/4:3:8:12-16[3]/6:1:12,13/7:3:9:10/8:12:13[2]/10:
2,3:4:8,9:10:11[2]/11:15/14:3/15:5[2]/16:1:8:9:
13,14/17:6:10/18:9:29/20:1[2]:20:24:26:33/22:4/
23:2,3:4:5,6:12/24:4:11/25:17:18:25:28/26:6:10[2]
/27:3:4/28:6:15:19/29:6:17:21:22/30:15/31:16/
32:18:23/33:15:17:19/34:3:9/35:1:20[2]/36:15[2]/
Ez3:3:6:10/4:4,5/5:4:16/6:6:11:19/8:33/10:1:9:
16-19/Neh2:7:11,12[2]/3:8:19:25/4:15:16:20,21:
22/5:1:16[2]/6:7/7:3[2]/8:1:9:16[2]:18[2]/9:1:4:11/10:
28:31[2]/12:37:39[2]:43:44/13:1:15[2]:16:19[3]:21/Est
1:6:8:10/2:17:21:22:23f/3:5,6:12f:13:14/4:1/5:
10:14[2]/6:4:9:11[2]/7:9/8:1:9,10:15/9:1:5:17:18:
19:21:24,25:27/10:1/Job1:4:19/2:12/4:15/6:
25,26/7:2:15[2]/8:2:9:14:15/12:14/13:7:27,28/15
:4,5:7,8:10:32/16:16:18:19/17:8/19:10:27:28/
21:2,3:7/22:14/24:20/25:3/28:3,4/31:2,3:25:40
/32:1:18/33:15[2]:28/34:21/35:14,15/36:2/39:14
:15/40:1:10:20/41:33/42:8:9/Ps1:2:5/3:6/4:1/7
/9:4f:7,8:10:13:15/11:4:6/12:8/14:2/15:1/18:5:
10:18:22:28/19:2/21:4[2]/22:2:8/25:10/27:5/30:
12/31:9,10:24/32:4[2]/33:2:3/34:8/35:1[2]:2/36:1:
10/37:32/39:4/40:2/41:13/42:4,5/43:3/45:4:16

(ON Con't)
/48:2f/49:10:11/50:2:10,11/51:16/53:3:5/55:14/56:1/58:11/60:3/62:3,4:9/66:6:11:17/68:22:34/69:13/70:2,3/71:14/72:16/73:11:18:24:25/74:2:7/75:6,7/76:8/77:9/78:7:17:32:49/79:4:6[2]:12/80:3:7:13:19/81:5/82:1:2/84:9/85:1:5[2]:7:12/87:1/88:5:7:13/89:3,4:14,15:17:35,36:46/91:12:13:15/92:1/93:4/98:7/100:5[2]/102:7:13:26[2]/104:21:27/105:4:16:33/106:1/108:8/109:28/112:6/113:5/115:17/116:9/118:7/119:19:44,45,46:55:132:151/123:3,4/124:1[2]/128[2]/132:7:11[2]/133:3[3]/135:14/137:7/139:5/145:6:18:21/148:7/Pro1:10:14:22:30/2:20/3:7,8:18:24,25,26:33[2]/6:28:34/7:14f:18:19/9:1/10:8:16:17:26/11:4:24,25:31/13:14:18/15:3:14:21/16:9:15/17:10/19:3:12:17/20:3/22:17,18,19:26,27/23:1:9:13,14:19,20,21:23/24:25/25:2,3:19/26:27/27:15/28:10/29:12:13:26/31:27/Ecc3:18/4:1:11/5:1:13,14:19,20/7:3:15-17[3]/8:9,10:16,17/9:5f[2]:6:10f:13/11:6/12:9:12/Sol1:6:12/2:17/3:11/5:7/8:5/Is1:15:20:24:31/2:12/3:5:9:11:16:25,26/4:5/5:1:6:8:11:18:24:25/6:1/7:11:17[3]:20:21,22/8:1:2:16/9:1:2:11,12[2]/10:27:32/11:14[2]/12:1/13:2:4:18/14:1:13:13f:17:22:25/16:4,5/17:6[2]:11/18:4:6/19:1:14/20:5,6/21:6,7[2]:6,7f[2]:8,9[2]/23:8:10/24:21[2]/25:6/26:9:10:16/27:10:11/28:16:19:20:27[2]:28/29:14:15/30:3:6:17:33/31:2:4,5/32:15/33:8:16:23/34:10/36:5:6:8,9:11:13/37:34/38:8:20/39:2/40:15:20:24/41:3:7:18:19:25:27/42:25[2]/44:3:4:12:20/45:14:23/46:1:7/47:12/48:1:15/49:8,9:22/51:5/52:1/53:3:6/54:2:8:9:11:15/55:2/56:12[2]/57:7,8:10:17/58:3:4:5:13/59:4:17[2]/60:10/62:1:2:6,7/64:5:6/65:3:7:21,22/66:2:3[2]:12[2]:17:20[2]/Jer2:3:8:9:15:17:20:28:32/3:4,5:6:21:23[2]:24/4:6:8:10:17:21:30/5:9:15f:29/6:1:9:11:26/7:11:20:24:25/8:2:4,5[2]/9:9/10:25/11:7:19:21,22/12:4[2]:5:15/13:2:13[2]:27/14:17/15:11:17,18/16:1:4:16/17:1:6:8:18:21,22:24:25:27[2]/18:15:17/20:3:4:10[2]:12/21:1:6/22:2:4:7:18:19:24,25/23:10/25:2,3:30:33/26:10/27:2[2]:13:15/28:1:4:9:13:14/29:16,17[3]/30:8:24/31:6:20:29f:30:33f:38,39:40/33:17[2]:20,21:25,26/36:6[2]:9:30f/38:11:24/39:5/40:2,3/42:5:13,14:15:17:18:22/44:5:12:17f:19:28/46:3:4:5/47:7/48:8:15:21:37:38/49:3/50:19/51:6:11[2]:12:27:60/52:4:6:12:17:23[2]:31/Lam1:6:22/2:7/3:3/4:20/Eze1:10[2]:11:15:27,28/2:2:3:9,10/3:17:19:23:24/4:1:4,5:6/6:12:13/7:3:12:14:16/8:9[2]/9:4:8:10/11:13:23/12:3[2]:7[2]/13:14:18/16:5:24:31/17:22,23/18:2f:7:11:15/20:27,28:30:39:47/21:7:19,20/22:6/23:12:14,15[2]:24:37:38:40:41:42/24:3:5:9:10:11:25:26[2]:27/26:1:15:16/27:11:27:31:35/28:2,3[2]:8:13:23/29:6:7/30:4:8/31:12/32:4:10:17f/33:30:32/34:14:22/36:3:12:25/37:6:16[2]/38:19/39:6[3]:13:20/40:2:7-12[2]:14:19:21:22:31:34:37:39:40:43:48,49/41:8:9:10:12:19,20[2]:25:26[2]/42:3[2]:9,10[2]:14:16-20/43:13:14[2]:17[2]:20[2]:27[3]/44:17:19/45:7:18:19:20:21:22:23/46:1[2]:3[2]:4:10:12/47:1:2:5:7:15:15f:16[2]:17:20/48:1[2]:3:5,6,7:21,22[2]:27,28:30,31:32:34/Dan1:18,19/2:21:41,42/3:1:5/4:29/5:5:7:15/6:8:23/7:2:4[2]:6:9:13/8:3:18:25/11:19:30,31f:38:40f:41/12:5:13/Hos1:7:13:21,22/4:12f[2]:13/5:8/6:2:3/7:2:5/9:1:3:5[2]/10:1/12:11/13:10/Joe1:12:15/2:3:29/3:4:12/Amo1:1:2/3:5:9:14/4:7[2]:9/5:15:19/6:4:12:13/8:4:11/9:6/Ob1:1f/Jon:3:6/2:8:10/3:4,5[2]:6/4:5:8/Mic1:3:11/2:6:7:13/3:8/5:1:10/7:19/Nah1:2/2:8/3:9:13/Hab1:6:15/2:2:2f:7:16/Zep1:5:8:17/2:5:15f/3:11:16/Zec1:8:10:21/3:5,6:9/4:3:11/5:7/6:10,11/7:12/8:4:9:13:20,21/9:1:4:9/10:4/12:10[2]/13:6/14:1:5f:10:12:20[2]/Mal1:7:8[2]:9:12/2:1:3:6/3:14,15/4:4/Mt2:16:22/4:6:17/5:14:39:45[2]/6:5:10:17:19/7:24:25:26/8:13:28/9:2:5,6[2]:9:27/11:3:22/12:1:2:5[2]:10:11:12:36/13:2,3:5:8:45/14:3f:8:11:19[2]:23,24:25:28:29/15:22:35/16:4:19[2]:21:23/17:15:22,23:24/18:18[2]:19:33[2]/19:13:15:28/20:7:17:21:23:30/21:1:5:7:9:28:33:38:44:44f:44/22:5:20:26/23:2f:5:7:8:9:18:19:20:29,30/24:1:2:3:17:20:20f:46/25:15:41/26:12:16:17:36:39:45:64/27:25[2]:28:29:30[2]:31:32:38:40:48:62f/28:1:2:11/Mk1:4:8f[2]:10:14:15:21:38:45/2:3:4:9,10,11[2]:23:24:28/3:4/4:1:4:5,6:21:38/5:6:11:21:23:32:37/6:5:25:28:33:34:39,40:47:48:53:55:56/7:29:32/8:6:14:35/9:1:22:33/10:16:17:30:32:34:37:40:47:48:49/11:1[2]:7:13:21:27,28/12:7:16:20,21,22:33/13:1:3,4:15,16:33:34/14:12:16:22:35:41:65/15:16,17:19[3]:20:27:32:36/16:3:5:9:18/Lk1:3:8,9:23:50/2:14:15:40/3:3:4/4:6,7:16:29/5:1[2]:7:10:18,19[3]:23,24[2]:27:36/6:2:6:9:17,18:22f:28:29:37[2]:44[2]:47,48/7:19:38/8:4:5[3]:6:8:23:32:40:43,44/9:14:24:56/10:1:12:13:14:25:30:32:34:38:39/11:9[4]:31:33:53,54/12:7:8:21:37:52:58/13:4:6:14[2]:15[2]:32/14:3:5:12/15:2:5:13:19:22:26:30[2]/17:13:16/18:4,5:20:38:39/19:8[2]:23:28:29:35:43:48/20:1:14:18:24:28:34,35/21:5:6:25:37,38/22:30:47/23:11:14:30:32,33[2]:54/24:1:27:28:30:33,34:46:50f:51/Jn1:9[2]:11,12f:14:28/2:11f/3:8:12:14:19:26/4:4:5,6:43,44:51/5:3:8:9:10:45/6:2-5:10:22,23:40/7:8:19:21,22,23[4]:30:31:37/8:15:17:33:42/9:6:14:14f:16:17/10:12:42f/11:1:19:24:45:53/12:12:14:15:32/13:1[2]:12:19:23f[2]/14:7/16:13:33/17:4:8:26/19:2:13:18:27:29:36,37/20:1f:6:10:22/21:4:6:7/Act1:3:15[2]:24,25/2:3:19:30:33:43/3:24/5:9:15:28:30:34:38/6:6/7:33:38:44/8:19:39/9:3:12:17[2]:27/10:9,10:39/11:15[2]:17:25/12:7:8[2]:21[2]/13:3[2]:14[2]:51/14:13:25:27/15:3:4:21:22:25:27,28,29:34,35/16:1:3:8:10f:11:13:18:31/17:11:14:15:23/18:6:22/19:4:6:10:13:15:16:17:21:22/20:5:7:7f:9[3]:13/21:3:4:8:12:16:40/22:6:16:19/23:2:9:15:30:32/24:12/25:7:20/26:3:12:13/27:1:2:4:7,8f:10:19:26:27[2]:44/28:1[2]:3:8:10:14:15:23[2]/Rom1:10/2:9/3:12:26:27[2]/4:11/6:1[2]:2,3:15[2]/7:4/8:8:13:20,21:31/9:15:16:32/10:20:21/11:9:12:13:22:23:29/12:9:20/13:6:12,13/14:3:5:10:14/15:12:24:28/1Co1:8:25/2:2:5:6/3:2:10[2]:12:14/4:3:5:7:8[2]:9/5:6[2]:13/6:3:12/7:20/8:1:5/9:9/10:27/11:5:7:10:10f:17:18:23[2]/13:8/14:25/15:3:17:46/16:2[2]:6:7:12/2Co1:3,4:12:13,14:15,16[2]/2:5,6:13/3:3/4:8/5:2:12[2]:16:21f/6:2:3:12/7:5:11/8:3/9:5:10/10:6:11/11:1[2]:7:19,20/12:1:10/13:4:5/Gal1:8:11/2:4:7,8,9/3:1[2]:10:13/4:4:10:24,25/5:2:4:5/6:17[2]/Eph1:9:10/2:20/3:14,15[2]/4:30/6:4:11:15:20/Php1:6[2]:9:19:25:27/2:3:8:10:27[3]/3:9[3]:13:15[2]:19/4:8[2]:12:15/Col1:9:20[2]:22/2:7:8[2]:20:23/3:1:12/4:8:16/1Th2:9/3:10[2]:13/4:12:17/5:6:17/2Th1:8:11/2:7:10:15/3:8/1Ti1:13:16/2:5[2]/4:16/6:12/2Ti2:2:19/3:14/4:6:8/Tit1:5:14/3:8/Heb1:4:9/2:3/3:5:9/4:1:4/5:7:7f:12,13/6:1:2f:3:8:11:18/7:5:8:16:18:23:27/8:4:5:6:9/9:1:4[2]:7:12:21[2]:23:25/10:4f:32:36:39/11:6:12:13:17:21:27:28:29/12:2[2]:9:12/13:17/Jas2:1:2:3:6:12:21/3:5:6/5:3:5:13:14/1Pe1:7:17:23/2:24[2]/3:3:18/4:10:19/5:1/2Pe1:8:12:13,14:17,18/2:3:10:13:21/3:10:12/1Jn1:5:6:9/2:4:24/3:2:4:6:8:9:19:23/4:20/5:18/3Jn1:6/Jud:8:12/Rev1:9:17,18/2:8f:12f:17:18f:26/3:1f[2]:7f:12:14f:21[2]/4:2:4:8:9/5:1[3]:2:6:13/6:10:11:16[2]/7:15/8:7:11/9:4:7/10:2[2]:5/11:11:16/12:1:3:17/13:1:16[2]/14:1[2]:4:6:9:14:15:16:19/15:2/16:14/17:3:5:9:15/18:19/19:6:11:12[2]:14:16:19/20:4[2]:9[2]/21:5:12:13:14:18,19,20/22:2:4:11

3167

ONE

Gen1:4,5f:16[2]/2:11,12:21:24:24f/3:20/4:8:23:25/7:4:10,11,12/9:5,6:20,21/10:8/14:5,6:13/15:4/16:9-12:14/17:2,3,4/18:1/19:18,19,20:31/20:1/22:2/24:3:14[2]:21:37:44:63/25:18:23:25:29/26:22:26/27:1:36:38:45:46/28:1:2:9/29:15/30:2:14:31,32/31:4:17-20:34:38:53/32:8:28/33:10f/34:1:16:22[2]/35:10/36:20,21/37:3:5:12/39:7:11[2]/40:5:8/41:1:5:8:11:22:24:49/42:1:13:16:19:27:32[2]:33/43:3,4,5:29/44:9[2]:10:18:20:28/48:1:18/49:4:24/Ex2:5[2]:6:7:11[2]:12:13:21/3:1:12/6:25[2]/8:2:10:31,32/9:6/10:15:19/11:1/12:21:30:46/14:28/17:5,6/18:21/19:13/21:18:36/22:1[2]:2:6:9/23:29/24:7/25:19[2]:31:34,35[3]:36/26:3:9:10,11:21/28:22,23,24/29:15,16:23[3]:39:40/32:27/34:3[2]:15:20:24/36:16:33/37:8:17:22:25/38:2/Lev2:2/4:22[2]:27/5:7/6:4,5/7:14:17,18/8:26[2]/12:8/13:1/14:4:5:10:12:21:22:31:50/15:15:30/16:22:32/22:10[2]:11:13/23:18:19/24:10[2]/25:26:29:32:34:48/26:17:26:36/27:6[2]:29:29f/Num3:14,15:47,48/6:11:19[2]/7:3:13:84,85,86/8:12/9:10:14/10:4:29/11:19,20:28:31/12:1:12/13:2/14:22:29:34,35/15:3,4:15,16:23,24[2]:32[2]/16:1:6,7f:15:22:40/18:4:16/19:1:8:10/21:8/25:6/26:5-11:64,65/27:1:3,4:12:21/28:4:11:15:19:27:30/29:2[2]:8[2]:11:34:36[2]:38/31:28:48,49/32:10,11/34:16-28/35:30[2]/36:1:9/Deu1:12:23:24,25:34,35/2:35,36/3:11/4:32:35/5:22/7:14:24/10:21/11:1:25/12:14/13:1:12,13,14[2]/15:4,5/17:6/19:2,3:5:6,7:11:15/20:16/21:1:15/22:6:19:25,26,27/25:11/27:20/28:26:31:56,57:64:68/29:19/30:12:13/32:30:39/34:6/Jos1:5:7/2:11:12,13:19/3:12/4:2,3:5:8/6:1:5/7:14[2]:15:18/8:22/10:8:14:21:28:37:42/11:4:8:10/15:17/17:14/18/20:3/21:44/22:14:20/23:9:10/24:17/Ju2:1/3:29/4:4:6:16:20/6:11:16f:31:33:39/7:12,13:14:22/8:10:23,24/9:1:2:5:18:26/12:7/13:2,3/14:1:3[2]/16:1:28[2]/17:2:4,5:7,8:10,11/18:19:25:28/19:6:15:18:29/20:1:4:8,9,10[2]/21:3:8,9/Ru2:2:13:20:20f/3:1:12/1Sa1:5:9/2:2:7:9:10:20:27:32/3:2,3/8:7/9:3/10:12/11:2[2]:7:13/12:4/13:1:17/14:3:5:24,25:36:39:42:45/15:1/16:6:7:9:12:18/17:17:25/18:15,16:17:25:25f/19:9,10/21:1:5:11/22:5:8:20/23:1:14,15/24:14,15/25:14:17:18:21:22:34/26:5,6,7:22/27:5[2]:9:1/28:7,8/29:3/30:17/2Sa1:10:15/2:12:16/3:7:1/4:5/7:9:12:13/8:4/9:1:2:10,11/10:6/11:2:25:2f:27/12:1:6/13:4:13:21-24:28:29,30/14:5,6[2]:7:8:12:18:25[2]:27/15:12:16/16:1[2]/17:12:19/18:10:26/19:7:14:42/20:11/23:3:7:8:9:13:18,19:23[2]:24-39/24:2:17/1Ki1:3,4:20:24:48/2:4:13:20:45/3:1:4:13:17,18:22[2]/4:7[2]/5:6/6:36/7:2:3,4:8:16-16-22[2]:35:41-46/8:19:25:37:56:65/9:5:16/10:20/11:12,13:19:23:29:32:34:36/12:20f:29/14:2/15:29/16:9/17:17/18:3,4:5:13:23:25:26:31:40/19:14/20:20:25:30:35:41/21:2:21:25/22:8:9:11:21:31:43/2Ki3:11/4:1[2]:5:8:18:19:22:38:39:42:43/5:3:18/6:1[2]:5:12:14:26-30[2]/7:5:8:10:13:16/8:5:6:18:26/9:1:5:10:11:36/10:2,3:5:11:18,19:20,21:22:25/12:4,5/14:8:11:26/15:14:19,20/16:11,12/17:27,28[2]/18:19:22:31,32/19:22/21:6:16/22:8/23:10/24:16/1Ch1:46/2:34,35/4:10:19/5:1/7:12:28/9:4/10:6/11:2:20/15:2/16:20:23/17:11:12:20/19:10/20:4/21:8:12:17/23:27/24:6/25:6,7/26:10/27:1/2Ch1:10/3:8:11,12,13f:17[3]/4:3/5:6:13,14/6:9:30:42/7:8:12/14:5:11:13/18:6,7:8:10:29:33/20:14[2]:23:24/21:6[2]:7/22:2/23:10/28:24/29:2/30:26/31:19/32:12:14:19/34:14/35:16:18/36:5/Ez2:61/8:15/9:7:11/Neh1:2/2:1/3:28:31/5:18/6:2:8/7:63/11:15,16,17/12:8/13:15:28/Est1:8:18/2:21/4:2:5/6:9/7/9:1/Job1:6:14,15/2:13/4:21/5:1:4/6:14:22/9:3:17/10:4-7/14:4:5/17:3,4/18:17/19:7/21:30-32[2]/23:2/24:14,15[2]:20/27:15/29:12:25/30:13:24/31:37/32:11,12/33:6/36:18:26/40:24/41:10[2]:11:31,32/42:2/Ps2:7/5:9/7:2/14:3[2]/16:10/18:2:22:41/22:8:9,10,11:20f:23/24:2/27:4/34:19/35:17/39:9/40:5/44:1/45:3/49:4:7:8,9/50:22/53:2:3[2]/56:8:9/58:1/59:7/61:6/62:12/69:20[2]:26[2]/71:11:22/72:12/73:17:20:25/75:6,7/76:5/77:9:19/78:41:44/79:3/84:9/85:2/86:9/87:4/89:8:14,15:18:34:38:51/102:26/104:27/105:13:14:31/106:11:16f:23/109:12,13[2]:21/118:26[2]/119:162/132:2-5/141:6,7f/142:4[4]/143:2/144:10/Pro7:6/8:36/14:10/17:14f:22/21:30/22:9/23:26,27,28:29,30/24:15,16/25:14/26:12/28:1/29:4/Ecc1:8-11:12-15/2:13,14/3:9:20:22/4:1:9:10:11:12/5:18/7:1:14:27,28[3]/8:4:8[2]/9:1:2,3:15:18/Sol1:7:13/2:10:13/3:1:3:8/4:2:9[2]:12/5:2:8:9:10/6:1:6:9[2]/7:10/8:1:11/Is1:4:24:31/5:1:19:24/6:6/7:24:25/9:14,15/10:8:14:17:20:27f:34/12:6/13:8/14:10:16:17/15:1:8/17:2:7/19:15:18/22:9,10,11:18/24:15,16/27:12[2]/28:15/29:11:19:23/30:5:10,11:12:13:15:17/31:1:4,5:7/32:6/33:14/34:10:15:16[2]/36:7:17:20[2]/37:23:30:38/38:12:19/40:22:25:28/41:2:14:20:26[2]:28[2]/42:1:5:19:22:23/43:3:12:13:14:15/44:10:25/45:3:6:11:19:21/47:4:9[2]:10/48:14:17/49:7[3]:26/50:3:10/51:1:13:16:18/52:14,15/53:6:12/54:5/56/57:1[2]:15[2]/59:4:16[2]/60:9:14:16/63:1:3:5:11/64:4:7/65:5:12:17:25/66:7,8:13/Jer2:6:36/3:10:14/4:4/5:1[2]:23,24/7:19:33/8:10/9:4:11:12:22/10:20/11:23/12:11:12/14:8:16/16:4:7/17:9:27/18:13/20:11/21:13/22:8:20/23:18[2]:23:33[2]/24:2/25:26:33[2]/26:2:9[2]:15/30:10:13/31:30:32:34/32:23:39/35:2:4/36:2:24,25:30/38:14/41:1:9/42:10:17/44:7:10:11:14:30f/46:18/48:2,3,4:33/49:4:7:18:19:22:26:33/50:3:29:32:40[2]/51:3:5:43/52:24,25/Lam1:7:9:17:21/3:38/4:3,4:8:12/5:8/Eze1:1:11:15/4:6:8:10:11:17/7:5,6:10,11:13:14/9:2[2]/10:6:7,8:9-13/11:19/12:23/14:9/15:7/16:4:5[2]:33,34:57/18:20[2]:25/19:3/21:19,20/22:28:30/24:1:23/30:22[2]:24/33:21:24:28/34:6:23:28/37:17:18,19,20:22[2]/38:2,3f:17/39:7:26/40:15:23:27:44[2]/41:6:7:11:19,20[2]/42:3:5/45:7:12:14:15:24/46:5:6[2]:7f:7:7f:11[2]:16:17/48:30,31[4]/Dan2:1:11:25:44/3:15:29/4:5:13:13f:18:35/5:31f/6:2:13:17/7:1:16:19:20:28/8:2f:3:4:5:7:9:13:23f/9:25:26:27/10:4:13:18/11:1:5:13:45/12:1:6:11f/Hos1:1:6:11:10/4:2/7:1:7/8:5:9/10:3:15/11:7:9:12/12:9/Joe2:3/Amo1:2/4:7[2]:13/5:2/6:9:10[2]/7:14/9:9/Ob1:8:11/Jon:7/3/Mic4:2/7:1/Nah1:9/3:7:19/Hab1:2:7:12/Zep2:5/3:2:5:13/Hag2:8,9:12/Zec:8f/3:5,6/4:3/6:6/7:14/8:23/9:9/11:7/13:4[2]/14:9:10/Mal1:10:14/2:15/3:1/Mt:14/4:18/5:1:36:38:39/6:13:18:24:34/7:29/8:8,9:19:28/9:14:38/10:2,3,4:23:29/11:3:14/12:1:6:11:13:18:29:31,32:38/13:2,3:25:34,35/14:1f/16:1:14/17:4[3]:22,23/18:6:9:10:12[2]:14:16:24/19:5,6[2]:20:26/20:1:7:11,12:13/21:24:35[2]/22:5:34,35:46/23:10:15:39/24:2:31f:36:40:41/25:15/26:14:20,21:22[2]:23:24:25:27:40:47:48:51:73/27:15:38:48:57/Mk1:9:16/2:18/4:2:31,32[2]/5:3,4/6:10:27/7:1:4:12,13/8:1:14/9:2:5:17:38[3]:39:42:

NE Con't)
0:20:21:29:37/11:29/12:2:6:28:29^2:32:34/13
:21:32/14:10:18^2:19^3:20:37:43:44:66,67:70/
6:7:9:36/16:4:13/Lk1:1f:8,9:15:36:49:61/3:
21/4:32:40/5:1:3:12:17:27:36^2:37:39/6:1:10^2
:29:39/7:19f:23:27:28:36:39:41:43:47/8:4:8:
25/9:1:4:18:19:33^3:35:52/10:4f:7:22^2:25:37:
/11:1^2:31:33:37,38/12:6:53/13:8:10/14:1:18:
33/15:3,4^2:7:8:10:16:26:29/16:5,6^3:7:13^2:20:
/17:1:5:15:20:34:35,36/18:1:10:15:19:21:22/
:1:9,10:44/20:1:10:31/21:6^2/22:3:26:36^2:47:
58:59/23:14f:17,f:18:35:39:40,41/24:18/Jn1:
5:18:30:31:33^3:40/2:24,25/3:1:5:25:26:33,34
:25:37:52/5:1:5:7:38/6:29:33:35:39:44:64:65:
:71/7:2:13:18:27:28:33:44:48/8:9^2:10:12:18:
:26:34:46^2:50f:51/9:4/10:16^2:18:28:29:30:32:
:35,36:41/11:25:27:49:50/12:4^2:45/13:10:16:
^{2}:21:23f:26/14:6:21^2/16:5:22:32/17:2:3:12:21
:23/18:8:9:14^2:17:22:25:26/19:18:23,24:34:
:37/20:24/21:20/Act1:4:17:20/2:30:38:39/3:
:14/4:11:12:32^2:36:37/5:16:23:34/6:9/7:5:23
^{2}/8:31/9:5:7:39/10:3:7/11:5:28^2/13:2:23:27:
/16:14:16/17:23:26:27:28/18:9:10/19:4:32/
:21/21:7:8:16:34/22:8:14f:17,18:22/23:17/24
:21:21f/26:13:15/27:21:22/28:17:31/Rom1:
:10/2:6/3:10^2:11:12^3:19:20/4:10:19/5:15^2:16
7^2/6:16/7:4/8:33:34/9:5:20:21:25/10:11/11:
:4/12:4,5:13/13:1:9/14:3/15:6/16:4:8:17:22/
Co1:9:10:15:29:30/2:11^2:16/3:3:7:11^2:21f/4:5^2
:15:17/5:6/6:16:17:18/8:1:3:4:6^2/9:1:15:20:24
0:8:17/11:3:21/12:2^2:3^2:8:11:12:13^3:14:17:19:
:26^2:27^2/14:3:4:7:11:27:28:29,30^2:31:33/15:6:
:41/2Co1:2:3,4:19/3:3:6/4:3/6^2:15/7:2^3/8:8:
/9:7/10:16/11:2^2:4:8,9:29/Gal1:7:8:9:12:14/
16:21/3:2:10:11:12:15:28/4:22^2:24,25/5:8:9:
/6:1:12/Eph1:14/2:14f:15/3:2,3:8/4:3:4:5^3:
^{2}:30:32/5:3:28:29,30:31^2/Php1:10:27/2:2:15:
/3:5:9:11:13/4:8/Col1:7:8:28/3:24/4:9/1Th2
:10/4:9/5:2:15:28/2Th1:5/2:7:8/1Ti1:12:17/2
/3:2:3:12/5:9:14:20/6:14/2Ti1:12/2:4:15:21/
16/Tit1:6:12:16/2:15/3:12/Phm1:17/Heb:3/
10/5:4:7/6:13/7:3f:5:9:24/8:8:9:11:13^2/9:1:16
7/10:2:9:12:14/11:7:12/12:14:15:16/13:22/
as1:27/2:10:19/3:5/4:11/5:16:17/1Pe1:23/3:8^2
3/2Pe2:5/1Jn1:2/2:1:2:7:8:13:18:22/3:11:15:
3/4:3:21/5:16^2:17:18/2Jn1:1:5/Jud:5:9/Rev:8
1:13:17,18/2:4:17^3:26/3:1:7^3:8:11:12:14:15:21
4:5f:8:9:10/5:1:3:4^2:5:6f:7:13/6:1:16/7:13:15:
7f/9:1:12/11:8,9/12:9/13:1:3:11:17/14:3:14f:
6/15:7:8/16:5/17:1:11:12/18:10:11:17/19:11^2:
9:21/20:11/21:5:9:27/22:17

2121

R

Gen1:1f:2f^4:4,5f:7,8f:13f:19f:23f:31f/2:5:7f^3:25
3:2,3^2:9f/4:18f^4:26f/5:3,4,5f^2/9:26,27f/10:8f:9f^2
3,14f:23f:26-30f/11:12,13f/12:2f:3f/13:9:10/
5:2,3f/17:23:24-27/18:21/19:12:15:17:33/20:
1,12/21:9f^2:12:16:23^2/24:49^3:55/26:11/27:18/
0:1:31,32:33/31:39:39f:50/34:12/37:3f:32/41:
4,35f:45f^2/42:16:34/44:8:19/Ex3:14f^2:15f/4:
1^3/5:3:7,8:14:17/12:3,4:5:9:21:23f:32f:45:51f/
3:6,7:9:13:21/14:14f/16:4:24/17:7/18:5,6f:22/
9:12:13^2:24/20:4:4f^2:5:7f:10^4:11f:16f:17^3:19:23^3
25:26/21:4:10^2:15:16:17^2:18:20:26:28:31:32:33
22:1^2:4^3:5^2:6:7:8:9:10^3:12:14^2:22/23:4:13f:14f/
25:17f/28:30,31f:43/29:28:34:37f^2/30:9:20^2:29f^2
33/32:18:32f/33:13f^2/34:3:7/35:5-9:23/38:
5,26/Lev1:10:14/2:8:11/3:1:6^4/4:10/5:2^2:3:4:6
7:11^2:16/6:2^4:3:18f:28/7:9:10:16:21:23:24:
6,27/8:8f/10:1f:8,9/11:4-7:8:9:11:12:26:29,30:
32^2:36:40:46/12:6^2:8/13:1^4:19:24:28:29,30^2:38:
7,48^4:49:52^2:55f^3:56^2:59^3/14:22:30:37:47:55:
56^3:57/15:10:14:17:20:21,22,23:25:27:29:32/16:
f:10f:26f:29,30:31f/17:3,4:8,9^2:10:13^2:15^2/18:3
4,5f:9^3:10:17:28/19:3:4:6:15:17:26:27/20:1:9:17
19:25:27^2/21:2,3:5:11:18^4:19^2:20^6/22:3:4^2:5^3:8:
13:17,18^2:19^2:21^3:22^3:23^2:24:26,27:28/23:33,34
f/25:10:14,15,16:20:40:43:47:49:53/26:1:14:27/
27:10:20:26:27:28^2:30:31:33/Num1:17,18,19/3:
38/4:27/5:1:5,6:15^2:18:29:30/6:1:3,4^4:6,7:10/7:
9/9:10^2:20,21:22:23/11:8:19,20^4:23:31:37/12:1
f/13:3-15f:18^2:19^2:20:22f/14:2:42/15:3,4^5:11,12
:15,16:22:30/16:29^2/18:2,3:17:31/19:16^3:18^4/
21:22^2/24:3-9/26:2/28:26/29:39^2/30:1:3:5:6:8:
9:13/31:19:20:22/35:17:20:21:22,23:24^2/Deu2:
6/3:17:23,24,25/4:2:7:18:19:48/5:8:14^2/6:7/7:2
:14:25^2/8:2:4/9:28/11:2:26/12:2:32/13:1:3:6,7^2
/14:7:21:26:27:29^2/15:7:12:21^2:22/16:2/17:12:
2,3^2:5:6:8:12/18:3:10^2:11^3:16:21/21:14:18/22:1:
3:4:6^2/23:1:3:6:17,18^2:19/24:3:7:14,15/25:18/
26:11:13/27:15:16:22/28:39:50/29:4^2:6:18^2/30:
15:19^2/32:13f/Jos1:5/2:19/5:13/6:1/7:3:12f/8:
1:17:22/10:25/13:13/15:21-32:48-62^2/18:21-28
/22:22,23^2:28:29^2/23:7/24:12:15/Ju1:30:31,32:
33/2:22/4:5f/5:8:30/6:32f/8:26^2/9:2/11:27:39f
/13:4:7:13,14^4/14:6:15:16/18:5:7/19:12,13/20:
27,28/Ru1:4,5/4:6f/1Sa2:16/4:9:20/12:3:4/13:
20:22/14:1:9:41/15:6:9/16:7/17:34:38,39/20:8:
10:12:27/21:3:8/22:2/24:14/25:8:21/26:10^2:12
/28:5,6^2:15/30:11,12:15/2Sa3:29^4/12:31f/13:
21-24/14:14f/15:14:21/17:9/19:24,25:42/24:13^2
/1Ki1:10/2:42/3:11^2:12/5:4/6:7/7:24/8:22,23:
29:32:37^6:46/9:6/10:12/13:8:9:16,17/17:1/18:
27^3:44/20:18:40/21:2:6:7/22:6:15/2Ki2:16:21/
3:9/4:13:40/5:17/7:1/9:17:18:19:32/12:4,5:
13,14/13:19/17:34:35,36/18:5:12/20:9:11f/23:
10:18/1Ch1:1f^2:24-27f:38,39f/3:10-14f^2:15f:16f
/4:32,33/6:39-43f/7:34f/8^2/9:40f^2/11:4/12:3-7
/15:21f/18:16f/20:3f/21:12^2/23:3:10,11f:24:29
/24:31/25:8/27:23/28:12f/29:22f/2Ch6:23:28^5:
31f:36/7:13^2/15^2/18:3,4,5:14/19:10/20:9:17/
25:8/30:5f/32:7:15/35:21/Ez2:62,63/3:8/7:20:
24:26/8:31f/10:13/Neh2:16^3/4:18/5:2,3,4:14/6
:15f/7:64,65^2/8:16^4/9:3:5:20:31:34/10:31^2:35/
13:20/Est2:12,13,14:19f/3:12/4:11:16^2/5:9/
Job1:22/3:16:20,21/4:3,4^3/6:27/8:11-13/9:13f:
14:22/12:7,8,9^2/13:9:15f:22/14:20,21/15:29/19
:26f/24:7:9/26:13f/27:10:14/28:15:16^2:18/29:
25/30:24/31:7,8^3:9:16:17:19,20^2:21:26^2:31:33:
38,39^2/32:11,12/33:19:23,24f/34:12:26:32/35:7
:8:12f/36:9:23:31/37:8:13/38:16:19:20:22,23:31
:32:36f:39,40/39:15:19:21-23/40:2:24/41:1:2:3:
5:7:13/Ps4:4f/7:4/8:5f/10:12/11:7f/16:4:8/19:
3,4:5:9f/22:1/26:9,10/28:5^2/29:9f/32:9/35:14/
38:8f/40:4/55:19:22/58:7f/62:9/68:4f/69:15:28
f:31/72:15f/73:4f:24f/78:22/83:9/85:4f:5:13f/
87:4^2/90:2/91:10:13/96:9f/102:6/106:15f:28f/
109:18^2:19/115:5:7/119:113/121:3,4/123:2/
136:6f/138:1f/139:2/140:10^2/143:7/144:3f/
Pro1:12/2:3,4,5/3:24,25,26/4:12/5:9f/6:5/7:22
/8:10:19:30f:34/9:14/10:22f:26/11:9f:30f/14:9f:
10/16:29f/17:7:20f/19:10:26/20:15:20/21:29f:
30/22:16/25:2,3:16:17:18^2:19:20:26/26:1:2:4,5/
27:10:16/28:15/30:32/31:1f/Ecc1:1f:8-11:16-
16-18f/2:19:24-26/3:14/4:8/5:12/6:5/7:12:15-
15-17/8:4/9:1:2,3^3:10^3:12/11:3/12:14/Sol2:9:
17/6:11/8:14/Is1:8:15:30/3:7/5:6:9:12:18f:27/
6:10^3/7:11:11f:15,16f/8:4:9,10f:20/9:11,12f/10:
4:14:26/11:3:9/13:10^2:17:18^2/14:13f/17:6^2/18:
4/19:9:15/24:13f/27:11/29:22/30:10,11:14/37:
12^2/38:18f/40:13^2:26:28/41:10f:22:23/42:4f:6f/
44:5^2:19/45:9/47:7/49:3f/51:7:18/52:14,15f/55
:5/57:1/60:19/61:10:11/62:1:4/63:9f/64:4:7/65
:16:25/66:3^2:7,8:19f/Jer1:17/2:6:22/3:16/4:4/5
:23,24/7:13,14:26:32/10:14/11:19/13:23/14:13
:14^2/15:12,13/16:4:5:7:16/17:1^2:2,3:11:23/18:7
/19:6/21:7:8:9/22:11f:30/23:5,6f:33^2:38,39f/28
:4f/30:13/31:22f:40/32:23:33/33:15f:25,26^2/34
:18,19/35:7^2:8^2:9^2:14:15:17/36:23:24,25/37:18^2
/38:2:16/42:6:12/43:2,3/44:7:10:28:30f/46:18/
48:8/50:20/Lam2:9:18:22/5/Eze1:13:24^2/2:1f:
5:7/3:9:11/4:14^2/5:9/7:2:12/13:19/14:6,7:17/
16:5/17:9/18:8f:10:13f:17f:25:30/20:31/21:21/
22:10f:24/24:22:23/26:20/27:17f:19f/28:16f/32
:2f:9f/33:32/34:6/38:2,3f/39:10:26/40:7-12f^2:
43/43:7:22:25/44:17:22:25:31^2/45:11f:13:20/46
:12/47:22/48:14^2/Dan1:8f:13/2:27/3:7:12:14:
18:28:29/4:35/5:8:12:17:19/6:7:8:12^2:13/7/8:4:
12f:15/9:24f:25f/11:30,31f:33/Hos1:7:9/3:4^2/4
:12f/6:2:3/9:11^2:17/11:3/12:11f/13:7/Joe1:15f
/2:5/3:2f/Amo4:8/5:5:6:18:19/8:6^2:11/Ob1:5/
Jon4:11f/Mic2:2/5:7/Hab2:4f/3/Zep2:5f:15/3
:11/Hag1:6/2:7f:12^2/Zec4:7f^2/6:6f/8:13/9:1f:
10f/10:11f/14:14f:16f/Mal2:6:12:17/3:3:5^2/Mt
2:18f/3:2f:11f^2/4:17f^2:24^3/5:36:37/6:13f:19:24:
26^2/7:16:20/8:8,9:21f/9:36/10:5:7f^2:10:11:14:
37^2/11:3:8:9/12:20:25:31,32^2:37/13:21:23:23f:
39f:40f:49f/15:32/16:14/17:4f:15:25/18:8:16:20
/19:12f:29/20:2f/21:19f:25/22:16:17/23:19/24:
20:23^2:26:34f/25:13:32f:37:38^2:39:44^5/26:62/
27:17:45f:54f/28:20f/Mk1:8f^2/3:4^2/4:8:11,12^2:
20:21/5:20f/6:8,9:11:39,40/7:10/8:28/9:18f:22
/10:29:38/11:30/12:5:14/13:15,16:21:32:
35,36,37/14:2/15:33f/Lk1:8,9f:15/2:24/3:3f:15
/4:27/6:9^2:13:17,18:37^2:38:44/7:6,7,8^3:19/8:2/
9:8:13:19^2:60f/10:4^2/12:22:24^2:33:38:41:52/14:
3:26:31/15:8/16:8f:13/17:7,8,9:21:21f:22f:23^2:
30f/18:29/20:4:22:37,38/21:23f:24:29:32f:36f/
22:35:67,68^2/23:44f/24:50f/Jn1:13:14f:24,25^2:
26f:31f:33f/3:5f:8:16f:18f:33,34/4:11:21-24:27/
5:2:3:14:37:41,42/6:18,19/7:17:35:48/9:2:21:25
/10:20/12:40f/13:29/14:11:18:26f:27/16:3/18:
34:34f^2/19:10/Act1:5f^2:26f/2:3:27/4:7:34,35/5:
4/7:44/8:2f:7:34:37f/11:16f^2/12:9/13:27:45f:48
f^2/15:32f/17:18:29^2/19:5f:12/20:7f:20:22f:33/
21:34f/22:5/23:8^2:9:12,13:29/24:12:23/25:6:8^2
/26:29:31/28:6:21:30f/Rom1:10f:20f:21^2:31f/2:
4:10:12-15:17f:28/3:9:11:17:21,22:30/4:9^2:16/6
/7:23,24,25f/8:10f:35^5:39^2/9:10-13:16:23,24/12
:13/13:9^5:12,13^3/14:2:4:7:8:10:17:21^3/15:19f/
1Co1:2f:12:18f^2:26^2:30f^2/2:9:11:13f:16^2:16f/3:7:
12:13/4:3:5:19:21/5:10:11^5/6:4f:9,10^3/7:7:11:
12:15^2:17:19:30^2/8:8/9:4:25:26/10:25:27:32^2:33
/11:4:5:16/12:3:10:17/13:4^2:5^3/14:7:23:24:26^3:
27:29,30^2:32:37:38f/15:11:34f:37/16:11/2Co1:1
f:17/3:6/4:4/5:9:10:16/6:3:8^2/7:1:3:12/11:4^2/
12:2,3:4/13:1:5/Gal1:11/2:4/3:17:20:28^5/4:9:
10^4:14/5:3:6^3:12f/6:15/Eph1:10:21^4/2:3:8f:18/
3:18,19^2:20^2/4:14/5:3:5:10f:27^2/6:8/Php1:20:
22:27/3:9/4:11:12^3/Col2:16^4:21/3:11^3:17/1Th2
:3:6/5:10/2Th2:1:13f/1Ti2:9,10^2:12/3:1f:3/5:4:
19:21/6:1/2Ti1:8/2:5:20/Tit1:6:7^3/3:12/Phm1:
18/Heb2:1/6:10:16/7:3:3f^3/8:11^2/9:14/10:28/
11:34/12:1:16/13:4:6/Jas1:17:24/2:3:12:16:18/
3:7^2:12:16/4:5:11:12^2:13:15/5:12^3/1Pe1:7:18/3:
3^2:21f/4:8f:9:12:14f:15^3/2Pe1:9:10/2:10f/3:8/
1Jn2:2f:5:19/3:6:20f/5:17f/Jud1:6f:9/Rev:1f:8f:
14/2:5:16/3:10f^2:11f:14^2:15/4:3/5^2:9f:11f:12f/6
:6^2/9:1f:4^2/11:8,9:15f/12:9/13:8f:10f:16:17^2/14
:2:9:11/18:4/19:6^2/20:4^2/21:23:27/22:5:6,7f:12
f

1873

OTHER

Gen1:20/4:22/8:5/9:23/10:22/14:8,9:16:17/15:
2,3/17:23:24-27/18:22,23/19:9:25/20:17/22:24
/25:22:23:26/30:13/31:50/32:8/34:18,19/37:3/
38:29/39:14,15:22/41:3:19:56,57/42:28/45:23/
46:34/48:6:20/49:16/Ex4:27/8:2/9:14/14:7:26
/16:15/18:11:13/20:3:5/21:1:18/22:9:10:20/23:
13:24/24:6/25:20/26:4,5:9:35/28:25:27/29:17:
19,20:39:41/32:27/33:16/34:14:16/35:26/36:1:
11,12:18:29:33/37:9/39:20/Lev4:35/5:7:12/7:
10:24/8:22/11:10:23/12:8/14:6:22:31:42/15:15
:30/16:10/17:8,9/18:8/19:34/20:5:12:24:26/22:
5:17,18:22/25:33/26:37/27:32/Num4:14:34/6:
11/8:5,6:12:13/13:31/15:3,4:33:39/18:11:13:20
:22/19:16/20:17/23:7-10/28:4/31:12:27/32:2:5
:19/35:3:6/36:7/Deu1:18/3:20:21/4:2:6:7:19:32
:38:39/5:13/7:7/8:19:20/9:1:4:5/10:15/11:16:
28/12:6:11/13:2/14:10/16:15/17:2,3:14/18:1^3:
20/19:19/21:15/22:4:9:22:30f/24:5/25:11/26:
19/27:2,3,4/28:14:64/29:18:26/30:17/31:18:20
/32:31/Jos1:14^2/2:1/4:12,13/6:23/7:7:9/9:
14,15/10:3/11:12:18f/12:7/13:8:17:21:33/15:
37-44/19:12/21:5:20,21,22/22:4:7,8/23:15,16/
24:2:8:16:18:20:31/Ju2:17/6:1:3,4:27:33/7:1:
12,13:14:19,20:22^2/9:9:11:13:44/10:13:18/11:1
/13:11/16:31/Ru2:8,9:22/4:7/1Sa2:2:20:29/6:
18/8:5:8/12:19:21/13:2/14:20/17:3:21:55f/19:
20:21/20:23:41f:42/21:6/22:1:11,12/30:9,10/
31:7/2Sa2:13:17:26/3:18/6:5/7:14:22^2:23/10:
15,16/11:9:17/12:3/13:16:21-24:29,30/14:7/17
:22/18:20/22:1:32/24:2:4/1Ki1:3,4:9/3:22:23:
26/6:7:17:23-28/7:3,4^2/8:60:65/9:1:6:9/10:15:
20/11:1:9,10:32:36/12:18:29/14:9^2:19:29/16:21
:30:33^2/18:5:23/19:19:21/20:12:29/22:13/2Ki2
:9/3:23/5:17/7:3:9/8:1:18/9:5:7/10:15:20,21/
11:6,7,8/12:7:11,12/13:13:18/14:16:29/15:38/
17:1:7:9:24:37:38:40/18:33/19:12/21:16/22:17
/23:1:8:9:25:31,32:36,37/25:9:14,15:28/1Ch3:
6-8/6:48^2:60/8:13/9:15,16:30:33,34/11:26-47/
12:24-37/16:26/17:20:21/19:11/21:2/22:19/24
:20/26:11:12:20,21,22:26/27:16-22/28:1^2:12f:
16/29:2:21/2Ch1:12/2:4:5/3:17/5:4,5:13,14/7:
8:22/8:6/9:13,14:19:22:28/10:18/11:13,14:15:
21:23/12:13/13:9/17:2/19:7:10/20:22:23/21:2:
3,4/23:10/26:6:17,18:22/27:7/28:26/31:1:3:4:
17,18:19/32:13:17:33/33:7/34:9:13/35:26/36:7
/Ez1:7/2:1:70/3:1:5:12/4:2:3:8,9:10/5:6/7:7:
19:24:25/8:2-14^{12}:24:25:33/9:11/Neh3:1:12:18:
32/4:16:19/5:14:17/6:14/7:71/9:26/10:31^2:33:
37/11:1:20/12:38^2/Est2:8:15:17:19f/3:8/4:13:
14/8:8f/9:16:19/Job2:11/18:19/31:7,8/34:37/
40:20/42:15/Ps10:16/13:1/16:2:4/31:11/44:1:
24/51:13/64:5/69:33/73:27/77:13/78:18:58/81
:3:9/87:1/88:14/89:8:14,15/96:5/97:8,9/105:31^2
/119:37:128/126:2/135:5/147:20/Pro3:27,28/
9:10/12:4:12/18:17/30:4/31:23/Ecc4:10:11/7:
14:15-17/8:9,10/Sol1:1/2:2:3/3:6/4:13,14^2/5:9
/6:5:8/Is1:21/6:12/11:13/15:8/19:2/22:25/26:
13/32:12/34:14/35:9/36:18/41:26/43:10:11/44
:6:8^2/45:5:6:18:21:22/46:9/53:3/57:7,8/65:4/
Jer1:3:15:16/2:25/3:2:6^2:8/4:16/5:19/7:18/9:5

(OTHER Con't)
/10:11/11:15/12:12/13:14/16:11/17:19:27/22:
24,25f/23:30,31:35/24:2/25:8,9:23:26:33/26:22
/27:19,20,21/28:4/29:25/32:29/35:1f:15/36:2/
40:11:12:13,14/42:21/43:2,3:5/44:2,3/46:12:25
/50:37/51:46/52:18:24,25:32/Lam1:2f/3:30/
Eze1:11:13/3/4:8/6:9/9:5/16:23:32:33,34:38:
40,41:43/18:24/21:19,20:29/23:4,5:30:40/24:6
/25:8/28:24/29:12:15/30:7/31:5:8:9:14:16:18/
32:18:30/34:28/36:13/37:7:16:23/40:15:19:
29,30f:33:42/41:6:11:19,20^2/42:3:9,10:11:14/43
:3:7/44:12:19:31/45:17/46:2/48:12/Dan1:8f:8:
10:13/2:43/3:5f:7f:10f:29/6:3:4/7:3:7:12:24/8:3
:13:14/11:27^2:37:42/Hos1:2^2:4:5:18/3:1:3/4:10:
12/6:10/7/9:1:10/13:4/Joe2:8/Amo9:7:9/Mic3
:4/4:3/Hag1:11/2:12:22/Zec1:8:11/2:4/3:8/7:
10/8:20,21/9:10f/11:7:14/14:13:15:18:19/Mal
2:10/3:16/Mt4:21/5:20:39/6:24^2/7:22/8:18:28
/12:13:31,32:43,44,45/13:7/14:22/15:1/16:14/
20:18:24/21:15:23:45/22:1:4:40/23:13,14:23/
24:7:10:31f:40:41/25:2,3,4:11/26:3:35:60,61:
65,66/27:3:12:61/28:1/Mk1:38/2:15/4:7:10:35
:36/5:1:21/6:53/7:22/8:13:16:28:31/9:14:50/10
:28:37:41/11:18:27,28/12:13:31:32:38/13:8:12/
14:1:17:43:53:56/15:41/Lk1:1,2:42/2:15:44/3:
19,20/4:4:43/5:7:29/6:39/7:41/8:4:6:7:8:22:26:
37:40/9:8:19/10:1:31/11:26:42/12:1:42,43,44:
52:53/13:2/14:10/15:1/16:12:13^3/17:34:35,36/
18:10/19:47/20:1:31/21:29/22:2:49:65:71/23:
10:13:40,41:50,51,52/24:32:33,34/Jn1:28/3:26
/4:33/5:44/6:52/7:35/8:18/9:8/10:16/11:47:56
/12:19/13:22:34:35/14:22/15:12:17/18:14:15:
16/20:2f:3,4f^2:30,31/21:2:25/Act1:26/2:4f:12:
37:42:44/4:12:16:23/5:13/9:30:39/10:23/11:1/
14:22/16:25/17:6/19:39/24:9/25:2:15/26:16/
27:1/28:4:9:20f/Rom1:11,12:13:26:27^2/9:7:25/
10:15/11:9:23/12:4,5:10^2:20/14:13:19/15:1:5^2:
7:32/16:14:16/1Co3:11/6:1:18/7:5:15:25:34:35
/8:4/9:5/10:8:24/11:11:33:34/12:25/13:1/14:
17:21:23:31:33:37/15:10:21:41/16:20/2Co8:14:
19:23/9:5/10:12^2:16/11:8,9:18/12:11:13:14:18:
20^3:21/13:12/Gal1:1:7:8^2:9:19/2:12:13:17/3:
21,22/5:3:13:15:17/6:13/Eph1:21/2:15:16:19:
22/4:2:15,16:25^3:32/5:4:19:21:27/Php1:23/2:1:
2^2:9/4:15:22/Col2:1:10/3:9:16/1Th1:7/3:12/4:
18/5:11^2:15/2Th1:3:4/2/1Ti:5/3:10/5:13:24/
2Ti1:4/2:16/3:6/Heb:13/5:1^2/6:3/7:11:21:27/
10:24^2:25/11:32/12:8:15/13:1:24,25/Jas3:1:16
/4:11/5:9:16/1Pe1:22/3:8/4:3:8:10:15/5:5:9:14
/2Pe1:4:7/3:15,16/1Jn1:7/3:14/4:7:11:12/5:
6,7,8f/2Jn1:6/Jud:7/Rev3:15/6:11/11:10/21:
16

1099

OTHER'S

Gen11:7/31:49/46:29/Ex18:7/1Sa20:42/2Sa2:
16/Pro12:12/Jn13:14/Rom1:24/2Co12:18:20/
Gal6:2/Eph4:2/1Pe:8f

14

OTHERS

Gen12:2:2f/23:10^2/27:38f/37:26,27/42:5/43:34
/Ex28:3/35:23:24:34/36:1:10:16/Lev20:5/25:
10/Num2:3-31/3:49/7:60-65:72-77:78-83/17:9
/27:1/Jos7:5/10:10/11:19/24:11/Ju7:5,6:7/9:
37/18:14/21:16/1Sa2:7/8:12/9:24/14:41/17:
26:30/22:2/2Sa15:12/19:43/23:24-39/1Ki11:
16,17,18/20:20/22:12/2Ki1:14/9:6/13:7/1Ch9:
29/12:3-7:16/16:41/28:21/2Ch5:6:11,12/18:11
/26:20/28:13/34/Ez3:12/4:8,9/10:3/Neh2:
11,12/7:7/10:1/11:19/Est1:16/2:6/3:3,4/Job:
20,21/4:13/5:5/8:10:19/24:24/31:34/32:4/34:
24/36:17:18/Ps7:16/9:15/10:2/15:3/34:5/37:3:
26/49:10/71:17:24/105:44/106:3/107:2:17:39/
109:8:16:17^2/119:79/131:1/Pro11:24,25/12:15
/16:29/17:4:5/19:25/20:18/21:10/22:17,18,19:
20,21/26:27/27:2/Ecc2:7,8:18/6:2/7:21,22/Sol
5:10/Is:8/6:2/32:8/33:1/43:4/56:8/Jer1:3:10/
7:5/8:10/24:8/36:12/39:3/44:14/50:29/Lam1:
3/Eze:23/10:22/18:8/19:11/20:38/31:10:16/
32:29/38:6/40:24:25^2:29,30^2:31:32:35:36/48:14
/Dan2:10:13:18:21/7:7:19:20^2:23/11:2:4/12:5f/
Hos1:2/9:1/Amo6:10/Mic2:4:5/Hab:2/Zep1:8
/Zec3:4/6:15/8:17/Mt5:19/7:2:12:22:29f/11:1f
/13:11:12,13f:23:47,48/14:33/15:30/16:20/18:
12:13:16:33/20:7/21:8:41/22:6:40/23:11:13,14:
34/25:7,8:9/26:50/27:41,42,43/Mk1:22:36,37/
4:13:14/6:15^2/7:12,13:22/8:28/10:29:45/11:8/
12:5:9:31:33/14:29:31:69:70/15:7:31:40/16:13/
Lk2:13:34,35/3:19,20/4:32/5:9/6:4:22:31:37/8:
3:4:15/9:8:32:48/11:16:16f:49:52/15:3,4:7/19:
21:24/20:16:21/22:14/23:32,33:35/24:10:49/
Jn4:38/7:12:41,42^2/9:8:16/10:8:21/12:29/13:
28/15:6/18:8/19:18/20:24/21:15:18/Act2:13/4
:6:34,35/5:11:36/8:35/9:36/10:27/11:18/12:6:
17/13:16/15:34,35/17:32:34/18:8/19:25/20:24
/21:26,27/26:30/28:15/Rom1:9:32/2:3:21^2/3:9
:13f/9:23,24/10:9:10:19/11:4:7/12:4,5:7:8^2:9:15
/13:8/14:1f:2:5:18:22/15:1:14:18/1Co1:12/2:14
/4:15/6:8/7:7/9:2:6:12:27/10:13/11:21/12:10^2:
23:28^2/13:1:2:3:5/14:2:3:29,30/15:8/16:11:12:
16:19/2Co1:3,4/2:14/3:6/4:1/5:11:19/6:8:10/8
:2:8/9:13/12:4/13:2/Gal2:14/5:9:14/Eph1:13/
2:2:10/4:11^2:28:31/5:2/6:19/Php1:7:9:14:15/2:
3^2:4/3/4:3:8/Col1:8:10:23/2:8/3:12:13/4:5/
1Th1:8/4:12/5:6/1Ti1:10,11:16/2:1:2/3:13/4:6:
16/6:11:18/2Ti1:8/2:2^3/3:3/4:5:21/Tit1:9/2:3:
14/3:3^2/Phm1:6/Heb5:12,13/6:11/7:23/10:33
/11:31:34:35:36:37,38/13:15/Jas2:14/3:1^2:17/
4:2:12/1Pe2:1:4:9/3/4:10:11/5:13f/2Pe3:15,16
/1Jn:14/4:6/3Jn1:10/Jud:12:16:23/Rev:5f/9:
17,18/18:6

454

OUR

Gen1:26f^2/13:8^2/19:31^2:32:34/23:5,6/24:60/26
:20^2/29:26/31:1^2:14:15:16^2:51,52/33:14/34:
9,10^2:17:21:31/37:8:21,22:26,27/38:8:23/41:12
/42:8,9:13^4:32/43:7^2:8^2:18^2:20:21:22/44:8:16^2:
24:26:30:31/45:13/46:34^2/47:3:4:15:18^3:19:25/
Ex1:10/2:14/5:3:16/8:10:26:27/10:9:25^2:26/12
:27/13:14/16:23/17:3/34:9^2/Num9:2,3f/10:29/
11:6:22/14:3:17,18/16:13/20:3:4:14:15/27:3,4^3
/31:50^2/32:3,4:5:16^2:17:26:32/36:1:3/Deu1:6:
19,20,21:24,25:28:32:41/2:8:29^2:33,34:35,36^2:
37/4:5:7/5:2,3:24/6:4:20:22:23:25/21:7^2/26:2,3
:6,7:15/29:18:29/32:27:31/Jos2:15/4:23^2/6:17/
8:5/9:11^3:13^2:20:23:24/14:8/17:4/21:2^2/22:4:
17,18:19^3:24,25^2:26,27^3:28^2:29:34/24:17^3:18/Ju
1:1/4:18/5:8/6:13/7:12,13^2:18/8:22^2/9:10:14:
28^2:38/10:10:15:18^2/11:1:8:13:21,22:24/12:2/
13:23/15:11/16:23,24^4/18:5/19:19/20:22,23,24
:27,28/21:3:5:7:18/Ru2:20:20f/4:3:12/1Sa2:2/
4:3/5:7/6:9/9:7/10:12f/11:3:12:14/12:10:19/14
:30/17:9/20:3:23:23f/25:14:17/30:14/2Sa1:4/2
:14:26/5:2^2/7:24:29/10:12^2/11:24/14:14:15,16/
19:8,9,10^3:42:43/20:1/22:32:32f/1Ki1:11:43/8:
21:53:57^2:58:59:61/11:11/12:2,3,4/15:19/20:31
/22:3/2Ki2:16:19/6:1^2:8:16/10:5/18:25/19:19/
22:12,13/1Ch11:2/12:17/13:2^2:3/16:14:35/19:
13^2/28:2:8/29:10:13:15^2:16:18/2Ch2:4/6:26^3:
28:31f/10:4:16/13:10^2:11:12/14:7:11/20:6:7:10:
12/23:2,3/28:13/29:6^2:9^2/32:8^2:11/34:21/Ez4:
14/5:5:12/7:27/8:21^3:22:28:33:35/9:6^3:7^3:8^2:9:
12^3:13^2:15/10:2^2:3^4:14^2:16-19/Neh2:17:19/4:9:
11^2:12:15^2:23^2/5:5^4:8:9:10/6:1:9:16^2/9:9:12:16:
18:32:34:36:37^3:38^2/10:30^2:31:32:35:36^3:37^5:
39,40/13:18/Est7:6/Job8:9/15:10:17-19/22:20
/31:18^2/Ps8:1:9/12:3,4^3/18:31/20:7^2:9^2/21:13/
22:3,4:30/33:4:22/35:21:25/36:9/40:3/44:1:5:9:
10^3:17:18:20:22:24/45:12/46:1:4:8/47:6,7^3/48:
8:14^2/59:11/60:1:9,10:11:12/65:1:3:5/66:9^2:11:
12:12f/67:6,7/68:19^2:30/74:9,10:22/76:3:5/78:
2,3:5/79:8^2:9^2/80:4:10:12:14:16/83:12/84:9^2:11^2
/85:9/89:17:18^2/90:1:8^2:9:12:14^2:15:16:17/94:
12,13:23/95:1:6:7^2/96:5/97:12/99:5:8:9/102:28
/103:10:12:15/105:5,6:7/106:6:28/108:11:12:
13/118:15,16:27,28/123:2:3,4/124:1^2:2,3:7:8/
126:4f/130:3,4/132:9/136:23:24/137:2:3,4^2/
140:11/141:6,7f/144:12-15^2/147:7/Pro7:14:18
/10:22^2/16:1/20:24/21:2^2/Ecc6:12/Sol2:12f/7:
13/Is3:6/4:1/7:6/8:9,10/9:8,9,10/10:13^2:14/16
:3:4,5^2/25:9/26:1:8:13:15^2:18/30:16/33:2^2:22^3/
35:2/36:7/37:20/40:8:16/47:4/52:10:13f/53:2:
3:4^2:5:6/55:7/58:3^2/59:13^3:14/61:6/63:16^3:17:
18/64:3:5:6^2:7:8:9:11^2/Jer3:22:23:24^2:25^2/8:14^3
/9:19/10:12/14:8:19:20^2:22/16:10^2:19/17:12/
18:18/20:10/23:5,6/26:16/28:6/29:28/31:6/32:
23:25/33:16/34:5:18,19/35:6^2:7:8^2:10/42:6^2/43
:2,3/44:17^2:19^2:26/51:10:34,35^4/Lam2:16/3:39:
41:44:46/4:2:7:17:18^3:19:20^4/5:2^2:3^2:4:5^2:7:8^2:
10:12:15^2:16^3:17^2:21/Eze4:14/11:3/33:10:21/
40:1/Dan3:17/6:5/9:3^2:6:7:8^2:9:10:12:13^2:15:16
:17:18^2/Hos1:23/6:2/8/10:3/14:2:3^2/Joe1:16^3/
2:17/Amo5:18/7:10/Jon1:14/Mic2:4:6/4:5/5^3:
6/7:17:19:20/Hab1:12^2/3:2/Hag2:18,19f/Zec
13:9/Mal1:5/2:10/3:14,15/Mt6:9:11:12/8:17^2/
9:33/15:2/23:29,30/26:18/27:6:25/Mk2:24/7:5
/9:38/11:3:10/12:29/14:14:15/Lk1:55:71:72,73
:74:78/3:12/9:49/10:11/11:3:4/13:26/18:28/19
:33/20:14:33/22:11/23:2^2:40,41/24:20:22,23:24
/Jn4:12:20:21-24/6:30,31:34/7:15:26:36/8:39:
41:53/9:20/11:11/13:6/19:7/Act1:21,22/2:11:
39/3:12:13/4:8:25,26/5:30/6:2:4/7:2:11:12f:19:
39:44/10:14/11:8/13:17:32,33^2/15:10:19:25^2:
26/16:20,21/17:6/19:25:26:27/20:21/21:3:5:1
:15:21^2:24:28/22:3:14/24:4:8:14/26:6/27:1:6:2
/28:12:17/Rom1:3:6,7^2:17/3:5^3:21,22:24:25^2:2
/4:1:24:25:25f/5:1:2:4:5^2:11^3:20:21/6:11:15:23
7:23,24,25f:23,24,25/8:3:16:23:26^3:28:31:38^2:3
/10:8/11/12:4,5/13:11f:12,13f/14:7:9/15:6:33
16:9:18:20:24:25,26,27/1Co1:2:3:7:9:30/2:7^2/
5/4:11:12^2/5:5:12^2/6:11:13^2:14/7:26:29^2/9:1:6
12^2/10:1:16/12:6:12:18/13:9/15:3:14:30:42:53
55,56^2:57/2Co1:1:2:3,4^3:6,7^2:11:12^2:13,14:22/
15/3:4:5:11:18/4:7^2:11^2:12:16^2/5:2:4:6^2:9:10:1
:13,14^2:21:21f/6:6^3:10:13/7:5:10/8:5:9:19/10:
13^2:15/11:3:31/12:18/13:4:7:8:9:14/Gal1:4^2:1
23/2:7,8,9^2:16^2:17/3:13:24^2/4:6^2:26:31/5:5:17
22:25/6:2:10:14:18/Eph1:2^2:3:7:14:16,17/2:3^3
:14:16/3:11:20/4:13^2:14/5:20^2/6:24/Php1:2:1
/3:3^2:20^2/4:23/Col1:2:3:7:14^2/2:19/3:4/4:7/
1Th1:1^2:3^2:5^2:6^2:10/2:4:8:9:10:13:17:19^2:20/3:
2,3:5:6:7:9:11^2:12:13^2/5:8:9:23:28/2Th1:1:3:8:
11:12/2:1^2:13:14:15:16^2/3:6:7:18/1Ti1:1^3:2^2:
10,11:12:14/2:2:3/4:9,10/6:14:17/2Ti1:2:8:10/
2:12/3:16/Tit1:3:4/2:10:13:14/3:3:4:5:6:14/
Phm1:1^2:3:25/Heb:1:3/2:17/3:1:6^3:7,8/4:11:12
13:14:15:16/6:1:19:20f:20/8:1/9:12:14^2:24:28/
10:11:12:22:25:39^4/12:1:2:9:10^2:25:29/13:12:14
:15:18:20,21/Jas1:18:21^2/2:8:9:21/3:1:6:9/1Pe
1:3:24^2/2/3:21^2/5:10/2Pe1:1^2:8:11:16/2:20/3:
:15,16:18/1Jn1:9:9f:9/2:2^2:8:12:13:19/3:1:5:16
:18:19^2:20f^2:21/4:10^2:13:14:17:19/5:6,7,8:9:15/
2Jn1:2/Jud:4:17:20:21:24,25/Rev:5/5:10/6/7:
12/11:15/12:10^2/19:1:5:6

128

OURS

Gen31:16/34:23/Deu21:20/Jos22:24,25:26,27/
Ju8:2,3/18:9,10/1Sa4:9/2Sa12:26,27/Ps115:1/
116:5/Is8:9,10/64:4/Mic2:4/Mk12:7/Lk20:14
/Act15:9/Rom8:3^2:17:37/1Co3:9^2/15:40^2:50/
2Co4:10:15:17/5:1/6:7/Php3:21/Heb4:15/5:7f
/10:21:23/1Pe2:24/1Jn:2/2Jn1:7

39

OUT

Gen2:23/3:14:23/4:7:8:16/6:7/7:23/8:8:9:15,16
/12:20/13:7/14:17/15:7/18:19/19:2:5:10:12:14
:15:27:28/21:14/22:2/24:13:29,30:43:53:63/25:
11/26:8:27/27:2,3,4:8,9,10:13/29:12,13/30:16:
31,32:35,36:39,40/31:4:17-20^2:23:24:36,37:49/
32:25/34:1:5/37:7:21,22:28:29/38:21:24:25:29/
39:10/40:13:14/41:2:3:18:20:23:30:46/42:16^2:
33:35/43:23:30:31/44:4/45:1^2/46/47:15:30/48:
14/50:24/Ex1:10^3/2:10f:10^2:11:13/3:1:3,4:8:10:
12:21/4:6:7:25,26/5:1:7,8:20/6:1:26/7:4:5:14:
17/8:3,4:12:20:25:30/9:7:9:10:19:21:23:29:32:
33/10:6:11:12:15:18:19:28/11:1:8f/12:17:33:39:
42:51/13:3:14:16:19:22/14:10:11:16:25:26/15:
12:22/16:4:6:10:17:27:28,29/17:3^2:5,6^3:10:14/
18:1:7:9:18/19:17/21:4:24^2:27/22:6:24/23:26:
28:30:31/25:20:32,33/27:21/28:35/29:46/30:
34/32:4:8:10:23:24:32:33/33:2:7/34:11:24:28:
34/37:2/Lev1:15,16,17/4:7:18:25:30:34/5:9:12
/6:10:12:13:15:16:28/8:15,16/9:9:22:23/10:5/
11:36:45/13:20:25:39:42:45:56/14:3:45/15:1f:
16/16:10:15:17:18:24:26/17:7:13/18:4,5:24:25:
25f:28^2:28f^2/20:14:22:22f:23/24:10:23/25:38/
26:13:26:33:45/Num3:10/4:17,18,19:37/5:15/8
:19/10:35/11:1:15:32/12:11:13/13:17:21/14:3/
15:22:34:41/16:6,7:13:27:39:40:46/17:9:10/19:
16:19/20:8:11:16:18:20/21:5:7:31,32/22:5,6:19:
36:41/23:18-24/24:1:11/26:2/27:14/28:7/31:
4,5:13:28:48,49/32:8:21:39/33:1:52:55/35:20/
Deu1:22:28:44/2:12/3:27/4:9:37/5:15:22:32/6:
7:10,11,12:19:21:23/7:2:7:8:19:20:22/8:2:14^2/9:
3:5:7:12:13,14:21/10:3/11:19:23/12:16:24,25:
26,27/13:3:5^2/15:9:23/16:1:12/19:11:19/20:1:3
/22:25,26,27^2/23:4/24:11:14,15/25:4/26:8/27:
2,3,4/28:2-6:7:15-19:25:51/29:5:7:20:21:25:28/
30:3/31:2f:9:17/32:49:52/33:21:22:27/34:1^2/
Jos2:1:19/3:6:10:13,14/4:2,3:5^2:10:11:18/6:1:
15/7:7:9:14^2:17/8:5:14:16:22:25/9:13:16:17/10:
20:22,23/13:2-7:12:13/14:7:12/15:14:63/16:10
/17:12:15:16,17,18/18:3:8/23:4,5:9:15,16/24:5:
7:12:18/Ju1:3:20:24:27:31,32:33/2:1:12-14^2:15:
20:21:23/3:8:9:21:22,23:25/4:18:22/5:4^2/6:6,7:
8:9:13:19:22:27:30:38/8:1:25/9:29:32:33:38:41:
42:43/10:12/11:1:7:30,31:34:35/13:22/14:14^2/
15:4:19/16:3^2:5:21:25,26/18:1:2:11:18/19:22:24
:25/20:21:22,23,24:27,28:30:31:42/21:3:21^2/Ru
1:21/2:2:17/3:2/1Sa1:15,16/2:13,14:32/3:4,5/
4:7/5:10/6:20/7:6/9:9,10,11:14/10:23/11:2:10/
12:6:8:19/13:1f:10/14:11:15:17:20:23:34:38:47/
15:6^2:12:13/16:10,11/17:4-7:22:23:41,42:48,49^2
:55:56/18:5:6:17:27/19:2:3^2:8:9,10:11:14:16/20:

JT Con't)
20:35:41/22:9,10/24:7,8/25:28:33:34/26:3,4
:19:20/28:13:24:25/29:2/30:9,10:16/31:8/
1:7:9/2:13:20:23:24/3:27/5:6:12:18:19:20:
23/6:6:7:20/7:2:6/10:3:5:9:11/11:2:3:11:23/
9:15:17,18^2/14:4:5,6:14/15:2:14:16:23/16:5:
/17:1:9:21/18:13:28/19:7:8,9,10^2:11,12/20:1
:8,9,10:13:16:22/21:2:17^2/22:14:17/23:16/
4/1Ki2:30/3:26/5:2,3/6:6/8:7:8:21:22,23:44:
52:53:54,55/9:7:9:20,21/11:16,17,18/13:5:6:
25/14:6:10:24/16:2/17:20:21/18:16:27:28:
/19:11:13/20:16:26:31:39/21:10:25:26/22:
33:34/2Ki2:3:12:13,14:21:24/3:10:11:24/4:
37:39:40/5:5:10:11/6:13:15:19:32/7:4:5:6:8:
12^2:13:14:16:17/9:8:17^2:18^2:19:21:26:32:33:
/10:9,10:12:14:25:26/11:12:15/14:8:27/16:6
7:7:8:11:35,36/18:4:18/19:14/20:5/21:1/23:
/24:3,4/25:4,5^2:7/1Ch5:20/8:13/9:28/10:4:6
/11:8:18,19/12:17:19/13:9:10/14:11/16:35/
1:2:5:21/19:2,3:5:9^2/21:26/24:19/27:24/28:
4:15:16:17:18/2Ch3:15/4:5/5:4,5:11,12/6:
13:16:34/7:22/8:7,8/12:7/13:1:13,14/14:11:
/15:2:14/16:6:13,14/17:7,8,9/18:24:31:33/
2:4:10/20:7:9:11:17:19:20:24:25/21:19/22:7^2
3:2,3:11:13,14:15,16,17:19/24:6/25:18/26:10
,18^2:20^3/28:3^2:9/29:7:16^2/30:2,3/31:1:5,6/
20:31/33:12/34:4:14:21:25/35:13:23:24,25/
2:62,63/4:22/6:3/9:6/10:13/Neh1:5/2:11,12
3:16/4:1:5:12:19/5:2,3,4:7:12:13f/6:1/7:64,65
1:16:17/9:5:18:21/13:8:21:25:28:30/Est1:18
:11/3:15/4:1:5^2:6:11/5:2/6:5:7,8/7:7/8:4:5:
:15/9:1/Job2:7/3:24/4:2:16:21/6:25,26/7:11
:8/10:17/11:13,14/13:9:10:17:23/15:22/16:9:
/17:8:13,14/18:5:18^2/20:25/22:15,16/24:4:
^{2}/26:7/29:6:7:17/30:3:8:24/31:7,8:12:22:34/
:5:19/35:12:14,15/36:9:18/37:3:18/38:25-27:
/39:12/Ps3:4/6:6/9:5:11/15:4/18:6f:16:48/
:3,4:5/22:14/25:4/27:6/28:4:7/30:9/31:3/34:
16:17:21/35:17/36:10/40:2^2/41:1:8/42/43:3/
:1/47:6,7/49:8,9/50:2f/55:23/58:1f:6/59:3:
,13^2/62:8/68:11,12,13:31/69:14:24:28f/73:14
4:8/75/78:55/79:6/81:10:16f/83:4/85:1:7/88
:8/90/94:1/96:2/97:4/98:8,9/101:8/102:9,10
103:20/104:1:3:20/105:37:39:41/106:29/107:
109:12,13/110:2f/118:10/119:147/126:6/
36:11,12/138:8/139:24/140:4/141:9/142:1:7/
43:6:11/144:12-15/147:7/Pro1:21:23/4:13/6:
5/7:6:25/9:3/10:14/15:28/17:14f/18:19/20:3:
20:26/21:10:23/22:10:15/23:13,14:29,30/24:
5,16:19,20/26:13:20/27:11/30:2:17/31:16/
cc8:2,3/Sol1:6/2:13/3:2:11/5:2/6:11/7:12/8:
1/Is1:9:15:18:24:31/3:8:24/5:2:25/6:6/7:3/8:
9^2:22/9:8,9,10/10:30/11:8/14:10:19:30/16:8:
0/17:6/21:5f:6,7:8,9/22:19:25^2/23:11^2/24:1:
0/28:13/29:10:18/30:5:22:28^2/32:4:17/36:3:
6/37:14:32:36/40:4:22:29/42:5:16:25/43:17/
4:3:13:19:22:24/45:5:8:12/46:1:7/47:12/48:9:
3:21/49:8,9/50:3:6/51:17:20/53:12/54:1:2:9/
5:8:11/57:4/58:10/60:18/62:1:10^3/63:2:5:9f:
1^2/65:1:2:4:5:6/66:5:15:24/Jer1:12:14:17/2:6:
6,27:28/4:4:14/5:6:18/6:11:25:29/7:20:22:27/
2^2/9:5/10:12:25/11:4:7/13:4:6:7:24,25^2/14:14
16^2:18/15:1/16:13:14,15/17:4:19:27/18:4:21:
3/19:1:13/20/21:9:12/22:7^2:19:26/23:2:20:
8,39/26:2^2:3/27:10/28:11/29:14/31:6:7:32:40
32:10:21:29/36:30:31/37:10:11/38:8:10:13:
1,22:23:27/39:4:7:14/40:12/41:2:3:6:12/42:6:
8^2/44:19:25:28/45:4/46:14/48:11:12:21/49:3:
7/50:25:29/51:12:15:26:27:34,35^2:48:54/52:7:
1:31/Lam1:9:17/2:4:8:11:14:19/3:2:46/4:11/
Eze1:11^2:22:23/2:9,10/3:22/4:10:16^2/5:4/7:8,9
19/8:3:7/9:8^2/10:5:7,8^2/11:1:7:7f:9:13/12:5:7:
1:12:12f:13f:18:22/13:9:12:17:23/14:19/16:5/
17:7:9^2:16/18:6:13/19:4:14f/20:5,6:8:9,10:13:14
21:22:27,28:34:35,36:38:46:48/21:24:31:32/22:
5:31/23:8:45:46/24:6/25:9,10:13:14:15:16/27:
:29/28:16:16f/29:4:7/30:15^2/32:3:7:15/35:7:
5/36:18:20:26/39:9:29/40:7-12f:18/41:8:9/42:
:14:15/43:1:11:17/45:9/46:8:9^3:12:21,22/48:
24/Dan2:12/3:4:12:15:17:22:26^2/4:10,11:14:32^2
/5:7f:21/6:14:19:20/7:3:7:8:24/8:4/9:27/11:3:
24:40:45/12:8/Hos1:13/3:3/7:7/9:4/10:9:11/
11:1:8/12:13/13:4/14:6/Joe2:28^2:29/Amo:10/4
:3/5:6:8/7:12/8:3:5/9:3:7^2:8/Ob1:7/Jon:12:14/
2:6/4:5/Mic2:1:9:10:13/5:9:15/6:4:9:15/7:9:15:
17/Nah1:15/2:7/Hab1:12:15/2:11:19/3:10:13:
14/Zep1:15:17/2:4:11/3:3:8/Zec1:14/3:2f:2:7/
4:7/5:3/6:5/7:7/9:14/10:11f/11:12/12:1:10/13:
2/14:3:8/Mal2:3/3:10/4:2/Mt2:7:9/3:1:3:5:16/
4:1:10:18:19/5:13:29:38^3/7:4:22/8:31:32:34/9:
24:33:34/10:1:5:8:13:16/11:7:20/12:13:24:26:
27^2:28:29/13:7:21:22:23:28:30:41:47,48:52f/14:
14:23,24:31/15:11f:17/16:4:6/17:4:19/18:9:12/
19:27/20:1:2:7/21:8:12:23:28:39/22:7:9:13/23:
24/24:26/25:5,6:7,8:30/26:28:30:51:71/27:5:18
:27:31:33:50/28:1/Mk1:3^2:5:10:17:25:34:35:
36,37:45/2:13:22/3:5:14,15^2:21:23:27:31,32/4:
19:21:36/5:1:6:7,8:13:14:30/6:6:7^2:12:13:24:38:
45:47:48:54:56/7:15,16f:21/8:1:23:27/9:7:18:25
:28:33:38:47:48/10:17:47/11:8:11:15:27,28/12:
1:8:40:43,44f/13:7:9:15,16:27:34/14:24:26:43/
15:16,17:34/16:1^2:9:17/Lk1:22:66:80/2:40/3:1:
5/4:1:35:41:42/5:3:4:13/6:10:12:17,18:19/7:12:
17:20,21,22:24:25/8:2^2:5:7:14:22:27:29:35:46/9:
1:11:31:33:38:40:42:49/10:2:3:10/11:1:14:15:18
:19:20:24:27:34:35^2/13:15:31:32/14:5:16:19:23^2
:29:30:34f:35/15:28/16:3/17:13:23:37f/18:4,5/
19:15:36,37:45/20:2:9:15:47/21:13f:30:34,35/
22:20:20f:27:35:62/23:32,33/24:13:24:40:50/Jn
1:15:31/2:3:7,8:10:15^2:16:18/4:15:40,41/5:24:
32,33/6:11:17:18,19:20:48-51/7:1:10:13:20:28/
8:3:20:41/9:4:34/10:3:9/11:43/12:18:31:35/13:
1:26f:30/15:19/17:15/18:9:26:29:38/19:4:5:13:
17:34/20:2/21:6:11:18/Act1:18/2:17/3:11/4:15
/5:6:9:10:15:19:25/6:14/7:3:10:31:36:40:57:58/
8:3:7:39/12:15:16:17/13:44:46:50/14:14:19/15:
3/16:18:30:39/17:6:23:31/18:9:16/19:4:9:12:13^2
:16/20:31/21:30:32:34/22:24:30/23:21:28/24:8
:21/25:16/27:14,15:19:29:30/28:3/Rom1:1:5^2/
2:8:19/4:7/9:21:27/10:5:21/11:7:20:26/12:13/
13:11/16:13/1Co1:5/2:10/4:19/5:5:13/9:9:17/
10:27/11:8:12/13:6/14:5:28/15:10:37/2Co1:20
/2:3:9:17^2/3:7/5:19/6:12/8:11/9:3:11/10:2/11:
12/Gal3:10:13:21,22^2/4:15:21/5:15/Eph1:6/2:
3/3:16/4:7/5:17/6:20/Php1:7:12:19:20/2:15:16
:17:23/3:2:10/Col1:6:13/2:12:14/3:16/1Th1:8/
2:15/3:5/5:9/2Th2:7/3:2/1Ti1:1/5:18/6:20/
2Ti1:1/2:13/3:16/4:2:6:17f/Tit3:6:9/Heb1:3:9:
11:14/2:8/3:16/5:7f/7:17/8:9:13/9:5:6:8/10:4f/
11:22/12:13:14:15:16:24:27/13:13:23/Jas1:4/2:
13/3:8:9:10:11/1Pe1:1/2:9/5:2:8/2Pe1:17,18/2
:7,8:11/3:15,16:17/1Jn2:7/4:2/5/2Jn1:7/3Jn:
10/Jud:5:12/Rev:5:16f/2:2/3:12:16/4:6:7/5:2:6
/6:2:4^2/7:2:4-8:14/8:4/9:2:17,18/11:7/12:15:17
/13:1:11/14:10:15:20/15:2:6:8/16:1:2^2:3:4:6^2:8:
10:12:17:20/17:1:8:17/18:10:16/19:5/20:7:8/
21:2:10:17/22:1

2075

OVER

Gen1:2:2f^3:16:18:31/9:14:23/11:3,4:8/13:9^2/14:
5,6:19,20/19:4:18,19,20/20:15/21:12/22:9/24:
17/26:20:21/27:22:25:26/28:18/29:3:4:10:27/
31:5/32:10f/34:27/35:13,14/37/38:12/39:6:22
/41:3:44:56,57/43:19/45:4:26/48:8:9:18/50:1:4
/Ex1:11/3:3,4/4:18/5:6/9:9/10:12:22/12:13:21
:23:27^3/14:4:16:21:26^2/16:18/18:25^2/26:14/28:
29:30,31^2/29:2:19,20/32:26/34:25:31:33/38:28
/39:9/40:19/Lev7:17,18/10:5/13:12/14:50:
51,52/16:10:21/26:37/27:7:8/Num3:31-35/4:7:
8:11:14/6:12/7:89/8:21/10:10/15:22/16:25/19:
15/20:8/21:31,32/24:20:21,22/28:16/32:10,11:
17:27:29/35:24/Deu1:36:38/2:7/3:14:23,24,25:
26/4:21,22:49/7:2/8:1/15:6/19:12/21:6/24:20/
25:8:9/28:63/29:23/30:9^2/31:5/32:11/Jos2:24/
4:11/5:13/7:7/8:29/10:12^2/16:1/18:15/Ju3:20:
22,23/6:20^2/8:9/9:12:36:37/11:21,22:36/16:4/
18:15,16/Ru2:4,5:7:8,9/4:1/1Sa1:8:9/4:3:6:14/
10:1/12:12:13/13:1f:14/14:4:14:33:40^2/15:32/
17:4-7:30:38,39:44:50,51/20:19/22:23/26:5,6,7:
22/2Sa6:19/8:9:15/10:5/11:2:27/15:2/16:9/17
:19/18:1:17:33/20:12:16:21/22:30/24:13/1Ki1:
39/2:11:22/3:19/4:8-19:24/5:13/6:18/8:7:29:
60/9:2,3/12:5:6/13:29/14:14/15:9:25/16:18:23
/18:30:33/19:19/20:38/22:24:36,37:41:51/2Ki3
:1:18/4:43/5:11/8:15:19/9:3:6:29/11:18/13:1:
14:16,17/14:1:23/16:13:15/17:24/19:14/21/23:
17/25:22:28/1Ch17:11:14^2/18/21:12/22:10/27
:16-22^{13}/28:4:18/2Ch1:9/5:7,8/6:16/7:8/9:9:26
:30/11:16/15:3:17/20:24/21:6:13/23:5,6:12^2:
15,16,17/25:12/28:2:14/31:10/34:4/35:18/Ez1
:11/7:18/8:15/Neh2:13/3:27/4:14/6:7/8:13/9:
22:25:32:37/13:26/Est1:5/2:1/7:8/Job13:3:19:
24/16:11/26:7/34:13/Ps1:6/3:5/17:8/23:5f/25
:2/30:1/31:8/32:1/33:18,19/35:24/41:11/42:7/
44:7/54/60:8/61:7/66:12f/68:11,12,13/73:18/
78:50/85:2/97:8,9/103:19/104:26/108:9/110:2
/118:18/133:2/140:5/142:4/Pro19:10/20:14/
25:14/Ecc1:12-15/3:19/5:8f:9/6:6/Sol2:8:11/
Is1:8:18/4:1:5/5:30^2/6:6/10:26:28,29/11:15/16
:3/19:4/22:9,10,11:22/23:11/24:1/25:7/28:10^2:
13^3/31:4,5/36:18/37:1:14/38:21/41:2:7:25/46:
1/62:5/64:7/Jer1:12f:13/4:20/6:11:17/7:2/8:
20/10:4/11:7^2/12:4/13:21/15:3/20:4/22:1/26:
10:24/27:6/29:20:21:29/31:10:12/34:17/35:3/
36:1f:6:9/38:19/40:7/43:10/44:4^2:27:30^2/48:34
/49:1:19/50:44/52:15:32/Lam2:17/3:51/Eze1:
25f/4:6:8:12/6:2/10:4/11:1:9:23/16:61/17:20/
18:28/23:12:28/25:16/26:2/28:22/30:25/34:6:
23/37:8/38:15,16/40:6:20:28/41:25:26/Dan1:1
:11/2:37:48^2/5:10:21/6:3:17/7:1:6:11:14/11:6:7
:21f:21:32/12:1/Hos5:8/7:12/10:5/Amo6:2:8/8
:5/Jon1:4/4:6/Mic:1/5:5/7:1/Nah1:2/3:3/Hab
2:15/3:19/Zep:15:17,18^2/Hag1:7/Zec2:3/5/9:
6/10:4:11/12:4/14:9:10/Mt2:9:9f/3:5/4:25/6:
7,8^2/8:4:8,9:11:32/9:31/12:9/14:1f:20:28:29/15
:37,38/16:9/17:5:7/18:2:13^2/20:19:25/21:7:12:
19:21:25/24:9/25:23/26:7:69:73/27:7:19/Mk1:
5:29,30:32,33/3:1:7,8/4:21/5:41,42/8:8,9:23:25
:34/10:30:33:35:42/11:2:13:15:31/12:41/13:27
/14:3:19:44:68/15:15:33f/Lk1:33:57/2:43/3:1^4:
9/4:29/5:26^2/6:17,18:38/7:6,7,8:14:23f/8:24:33
:37/9:1:8:18:42:43/10:19:32:40:41/12:4:14:26/
13:12:29/14:9/15:7^2:14/16:24:26/17:6/18:11:
16,17:30:32:40/19:3:19/20:5:18/22:4:47/23:1:5
:25/24:20:30/Jn2:9:15^2:16/3:26/4:46,47/6:1:
22,23/9:6:11:15/10:1/11:48/13:10/14:30/16:20
:26/17:2/19:11:19/20:14/21:9/Act4:1/5:20/7:
10:27:35:57/8:1:26:29:30/9:11:17/10:19/14:23
/15:39/16:9^2:35/17:13/18:19/20:1:31/21:11/
22:27/23:18/25:1:10,11/26:31/28:17/Rom5:17:
21/6:2,3:7:9/7:4/8:3/9:5:32:33/11:12/13:7/15:
12:19/16:11/1Co3:19/4:3/10:27/15:24:27^2:28/
2Co2:4:14/3:13:18/4/8:15/9:8/10:14/Gal1:16/
5:17/Eph4:6:8:19:26/6:1:13/Php1:13/2:17/4:
16/Col1:6:23/2:10/1Ti1:20/2:2:12/4:7/6:4/2Ti
2:7:14/Tit3:9/Heb5:12,13/6:1/7:27/9:5:10:19^2
/10:4f:21/11:37,38/13:17/Jas2:3^2:9:13/3:1/4:5
/5:14/1Pe2:8/5:11/2Jn1:12/3Jn:9/Jud:8:12/
Rev2:26/10:1/11:2/13:7/14:16:18f/15:2/16/17
:1:3:14:18/18:20

778

SAID

Gen1:3:6:9,10:11,12:14,15:20:21,22:24:26/2:18/
3:14:16:17:20:22/4:1:10:23/5:28-31/6:3:7:12,13
/7:1/8:21f:21/9:26,27/11:3,4:6/12:7/13:8:14/
16:2,3:5/17:17:18:19/18:3,4:5^2:6:10:13:22,23:28
:31^2:32^2/19:2^2:15:21:31:34/20:4:5:11,12:16/21:
1:16:22/22:12/23:3:7:11:14,15/24:2:18:19:21:
29,30:33^2:45:54:57/26:7:16:20:22:24:28/27:6,7:
41:43:46/28:1:13/29:4:15:21:32:33:34:35/30:6:
8:13:15:16:18:20:23,24^2:25:34/31:8^2:12:31:
47,48:49/32:8:9:26:30/33:10:12:15/34:14:21:30
/35:1:10:11/37:21,22:26,27/38:8:26/40:9,10:12
:16/41:9:13:17:38:39:52/42:1:8,9:13:14f:18:21:
31:37/43:2:3,4,5:8:11:16:18:20:31/44:4:16:17:
18:20:21:22:24:25:27/45:3:4^2:17:28/46:30:31/
47:5,6:15:18:23:25:29/48:3:4:9:11:18:19:21/49:
1/50:6:11:15:18/Ex1:22/2:6:13:22/3:16/4:1:7:8
:13:14:18:19:27:28:30/5:21/6:8,9^2:26:28,29/7:1:
8:15/8:1:5:9:10^2:16:24:25:29/9:8:13:22/10:1:8:
12:16:21:24:25/11:1/12:21:31^2:33:35:43/13:3/
14:12:15:26/15:9/16:4:11,12:16:25/17:5,6:
15,16/18:3:4:10:14/19:2,3:7:9:24:25/20:19/24:
7:8:12/25:1/30:11,12:17,18:26,27/31:1/32:8:9:
23:30:31/33:1^2:12:12f:15/34:5,6:9:27/35:4/40:1
/Lev4:13/5:14/6:1:8:19,20:24/7:22:28/8:1:5:31:
35/9:4/10:3^2:6:12:19/11:1/13/14:33,34/16:1/
21:1:16,17/22:17,18:26,27/23:1/24:13,14/27:1
/Num1:47,48,49/3:5:11,12:40:44/4:1:17,18,19:
21,22,23/5:5,6:11,12/6:22,23/7:11/8:1:5,6/9:8/
10:1:29:36/11:11:16:21:23/12:2:6:14/13:30:31/
14:7:10,11:17,18:20,21:31:40:41/15:17,18:35:
37,38/16:3:5:13f:15:16:20:23,24:28:36,37:43,44:
46/17:1/18:25,26/19:1/20:7:10:12:12f:18:23/
22:8:19:37/23:1:3,4:15:17:18-24^2:27:30/24:13/
25:10,11:16,17/26:1:64,65/27:3,4:12:15/31:1:3:
21:25:48,49/32:2:20^2:23:24:27:31/34:13:16-28/
35:1:9,10/Deu1:19,20,21:27:29:32:37:39:42/2:2
:13:16,17:24:27:31/3:21/5:1:5:28^2/10:2:10:11/
13:12,13,14/18:17/23:23/31:1:7:14:16:23/32:
20:48/33:7:8:12:13:18:20:22:23/34:5/Jos1:1:3/
2:17,18:24/3:5:9/4:1:21/5:8,9:14/6:2:22/7:
10,11^2:19:22:25/8:1:18:31/10:8:25/11:6/13:1/
14:6/15:16/17:16,17,18/19:50/20:1/21:2/22:15
:34/23:2/24:22:23:27^2/Ju1:3:7/2:1/3:20/4:6:14
:18:19:22/5:23/6:12:14:16:20:36:39/7:2:8,9/8:5
:9:15:21:22/9:10:12:36:37:38:54/10:15/11:1:7:
13:36:38/12:6/13:2,3:15:17:23/14:12:15:16/15:
12,13:18/16:10:11:13:18:25,26:28/17:2:10,11/
18:5:19/19:9:11:12,13:20:28:30/20:22,23,24:
27,28/21:5/Ru1:8:10:15/2:2^2:4,5:8,9:21:22/3:1:
14:15-18/4:3:8:9:14:16,17/1Sa1:17:19,20/2:34/
3:4,5:6:9:11:15:16,17:18/4:3/7:[illegible]/8:10:19:21/9

(SAID Con't)
:6:8:17:24/10:1:9:16:18,19:24/11:2:12:14/12:1:
12/13:11[2]:12/14:1:6:33:36[2]:38:41:42:44/15:1:
10:12:13:16:19:28:32:33/16:1:7:8:9:10,11:12:
15,16:17:18/17:17:34:37:55:58/18:8:17:21[2]/19:
15:24f/20:3:18:33:42/21:14,15/22:9,10:18/23:3
:10:11:19:21/24:4:6:9,10:17/25:12:19:24:25:39/
26:9:17,18:25/27:5/28:1:11:13:17:21/30:7:23/
2Sa1:13:15:16/3:18:31:38/5:1:2/7:4:17/9:7:9/
10:2/11:23:25/12:7:18:22/13:4:5:10:21-24:26:
32,33:35/14:11:12:15,16:22:30:33/15:7,8:19,20:
25,26/16:3:10/17:1:5:6:14:15:20:28,29/18:3:14:
18:19:21:23:27:28:31/19:5:30:33/20:3:6:8,9,10/
21:1:5,6/23:3/24:2:10:11:17:18:24/1Ki1:14:27:
28:33:42:53/2:15:20:26:30[2]/3:22:23:25:26:27/5:
4:7/8:12,13:15:16:18:22,23/9:2,3/11:11:31:41/
12:16,17/13:5:7:8:11:13:15:18:27:31/14:12/15:
29/16:2/17:8,9:12:13:15/18:1:5:15:25:31f:33[2]:
41:43/19:7:9:13:20/20:22:23:31:37:39:42/21:15
:17/22:3:6:12:17:19:20:21:22:28[2]:30:38/2Ki1:6:
9:15/2:1:4:6,7:9:16[2]:17:20:22/3:12/4:1[2]:6:7:9:
11,12:13:19:23:24:25:27:28[2]:29:30:36[2]:38:41[2]:
43:44/5:3:4:6:7:11:13:15:17:19:20:22/6:3:7:8:
26-30:32/7:2:9:16:19/8:8,9[2]/9:5:6:12[2]:25:26:34:
36/10:4:8:15[2]:16:17:30/12:4,5/14:27/16:15/17:
38/18:26:37/19:27/20:8:16/21:7/23:27[2]/1Ch
11:5,6:10:18,19/12:17:23/17:1:3:15:16/21:8:9:
17:22:23/22:1:5:8/23:25/27:23f/28:8/29:1:20/
2Ch6:1:4:8:20,21/8:11/10:4/18:15:16:19,20[2]:21
:27:29/20:20/24/29:31/30:6:17,18,19/33:4,5/
34:17/Ez6:2/10:5:12[2]/Neh1:8/2:16:19/4:14/5:
12/6:5,6[2]:10:19/8:6:9:15/13:1:21/Est2:10/4:15
/5:5:6/6:10[2]:13/7:9/8:5:7/9:13/Job1:5:21/2:9:
10/3:2,3/13:7/16:3/22:17/26:3/29:11/32:6:7/
33:8[2]/34:5:9/38:11/40:5/42:4:7[2]/Ps2:7/16:2/
25:20/30:6,7/31:14,15:22/32:5/39:1/40:7/69:
19/73:15/74:8/77:10/81:5:7/83:12/89:19:34/
105:12/110:1/116:10,11f/119:106:116:170/126
:2/132:14/Pro1:4/4:5/7:13/25:8,9,10/Ecc1:8-
8-11:16-18/2:1/3:17/5:16/7:27,28/10:20/Sol2:
10/3:3/5:2:3/7:8/Is6:5:7:8:9:11/7:3:4:11:12:13
/8:3:5:11/14:13/16:13,14/20:3/21:10/25:1/30:
18/34:16/36:10:11/37:30/38:3/39:5/41:9:26/
43:9/45:21/46:11/47:10/48:3/49:5/53:7/62:11
/63:8/Jer1:4:6:9:11:14/2:1/4:10[2]/5:4:12/6:6:9:
12:17/7:1/8:8/11:1:6:7:9:19/12:7/13:1:3:6:8,9/
14:13:14/15:1:10/16:1/17:19/18:5:10:13:18/19
:1:3:14/20:3:7/22:1/23:17:37/24:3:4,5/25:2,3:
15/26:11:12:16:17:18/27:12/28:1:5:11:15/29:3:
26/30:2/31:3:26/32:8[2]:13:24/33:23/34:9/35:6:
18,19/36:5:16:19:27:29/37:2:14:17/38:4:5:9:14:
15:17:19:21,22:24:27/39:11,12/40:2,3[2]:9:16/41:
6/42:2:5:9:19:20:21/43:2,3:8/44:20:24:25/45:3/
48:8:12:30/49:31/50:7/51:12:61,62[2]/Lam2:14[2]
/Eze:1:3/3:1:3:4:16:22:24/4:14:15/8:5:6:8:9:12
/9:4:7:9:11/10:2/11:1/12:2/13:6:7/16:2:6,7/17:
24/20:7:18:21:29:49/21:18/22:1:14:17/24:2:19
/25:1:8/27:1/29:3:10/32:17/33:1:13/35:1:10/
36:20/37:3:11/38/40:4:45/43:7:18/44:2:5/46:
24/Dan1:3,4:10/2:1:4:7:16:24:25:26:47/3:9:24:
28/4:9:19/5:10/6:12:15:16:22/7:17/8:13:17:19/
9:22/10:2:11:12:16:19[2]/12:8[2]:9[2]/Hos1:2:4,5:6:9
:5/3:1:3/Amo4:3/7:2:5:6:8/8:2/9:12/Ob1:1/
Jon1:9,10:12/2:4/3:1/4:4:8:9[2]:10/Hab2:2/Zep:
15/Hag:14/Zec1:4:5,6:14/2:2:4/3:2:4[2]:5,6[2]/4:5
:6:8:13/5:5:8/6:7:8:9/8:14,15/11:4:12:16/Mal3:
13:14,15/Mt1:20/2:5:13/3:7:14:15:17/4:3:6:9/
5:27/8:7:8,9:10:13:19:20:21/9:2:9:18:22:24:29:
34/11:14/12:3:13:24:49/13:34,35:37:51/14:2:
15:18:27:29:31/15:10:15:23:24:26:32/16:17:22:
23:24/17:5[2]:7:14:26,27/18:3:26:32/19:10:11:13:
14:23:26:27/20:25:32,33/21:2:6:19:25[2]:27:30:38
/22:1:8:13:21:24:29:31:32f:43:44/23:1/25:23:
24,25/26:8,9:10:20,21:26:27:31:35:45:49:50:
60,61:62:63:64:69:71:72:73:74:75/27:6:14:49:63
/28:5:6:9:10:15:16/Mk1:3f:3:11:41/2:5:6:8:16:
24/3:5:21:22:34/4:35:39:41/5:7,8:19:23:31:34:
36:41,42/6:2,3:10:16:30:35,36:37:50/7:6,7:10:
14:29:37/8:1:11:12:15:17:19:20:24:26:33/9:6:7:
17:19:25:35:36:39/10:4[2]:14:23:24:27:28:35:37:
39[2]:42:49[2]:51:52/11:6:14:21:22,23:33/12:7:14:
15:17:26:27:34:36[3]/13:1:5/14:2:6:16:18:22:24:
29:30:34:36:37:41:57:62:63,64:68:71/15:5:28:31
:36/16:6:20/Lk1:13:18:19:28:38[2]:45:60:62f/2:
10:14f:15:17:23:29,30,31:33:34,35:48/3:22/4:3:
9,10,11:23:32/5:4:8:12:13:14:20:27/6:2:8:9:10:
20/7:4:9:13:14:33:39:40:44:48:49:50/8:8:24:25:
32:38:45:48:50:52:55/9:9:12:22:23:35:41:43:48:
49:50:54:55f:57:59f:61/10:16:21:23:35:37:40:41
/11:1:15:17:39:45[2]:46/12:3:20:22:54/13:7:12:31
/14:3:12:18:19:21:23/15:17:21:22:31/16:2:7:15:
19:25:27:29:31/17:1:5:14:19:22/18:2:4,5:6:
16,17:22:24:28:34:40:42/19:5:8:19:20:25:30:32:
39:48/20:14:17:21:23:25:39:41:42,43:45/21:6/
22:13:15:17:33:34:36:38:46:47:48:51:57:58:60[2]:
61/23:4:7:28:34:35:42:47/24:17:19:24:25:27:44:
46/Jn1:15:20:29:30:33:39:42:47/2:4:7,8:10/3:1:
26[2]/4:11:14:15:17,18:19:25:32:42/5:7:10:12/6:
25:32:34:53:60:61:65:70/7:12[2]:25:31:41,42/8:4:
7:10:11[2]:12:21:23:24:28:30,31:33:49:52:55/9:9[3]:
16[2]:22,23:28:35:37:38/10:7:19:20:21:32/11:4:7:
8:11:12,13:16:21:24:36:37,38:39:41:42:49/12:4:
14:19:21:33:39:49/13:6:11:31:36/14:5:8:22/15:
25/16:19:29/17:1/18:4,5:6:8:11:17:20:21:28:37
/19:4:5:6:11:14:21[2]:23,24:26:27:28:30/20:2:9:15
:16:21:27:28/21:3[2]:6:7:10:12:15:16[2]:17[2]:19:23[2]/
Act1:11:24,25/2:13:17:34:37/3:4:6:12:17:21,22
/4:8:23/5:3:9/6:2/7:26:33/8:26:29:36/9:11:15:
17:27:34:40/10:3:13:19:21:26/11:5:16:18/12:7:
11:15:17/13:2:8:9:16:22:40:45:47/15:13/16:7:
15:18/17:19:32/18:6:14:18:21:25,26/19:4:21:35
:36/20:1:10,11,12:38/21:5:11:13:14:20:37,38/
22:3:9:10:13:21:25/23:3:4:11:17/24:9:21/25:8:
22:24/26:1:22:32/27:10:21:24:25:31:33/28:4:25
:28,29f/Rom4:7/7:5:7/9:10-13:15:26:33/10:16:
19:20/11:4:9:10:26/12:19/15:3:12/1Co4:13/5:9
:10/6:12/7:10:16/9:9[2]:10/11:23:24/14:13/15:3:
15/2Co2:1:13/4:6:13/6:16:17/7:3/12:9:19/13:
11/Gal2:14/3:8,9:11/Col2:8/4:10/1Th1:5/2:13
/5:21/2Th2:10/1Ti1:3,4/6:1/2Ti2:17/4:15/Tit
1:12/Heb:5,6[4]:10/2:13/4:3:5/5:6:7f/7:21[2]/8:8/
9:20/10:5:7[2]:8:15:30[2]/11:5:11/12:5/13:22/Jas2
:11[2]/1Pe1:16/2Pe:19/1Jn2:27/4:21/5:6,7,8:10:
11/Jud1:9:14:15/Rev:17,18/4:1/5:4:5:9f:11f:12
f/6:1:6:10/7:12:14/10:4:9:10/17:1/19:4:5:10/
21:5[2]:9/22:6,7:9

2095

SAW
Gen6:5:12,13/9:22/12:15/15:17/16:13/19:1:28
/21:19/22:4/24:29,30:63/26:8/28:12/29:2/31:
10/32:1:25/33:1/34:2/37:18/39:13/40:8:9,10:
16/41:5/42:21/43:16:18/45:27/48:17/49:15/
Ex2:1:11[2]:13/3:2/5:19/8:15/9:34/14:10:30:31/
16:15/18:14/20:18/24:10:11:17/32:5:19:25/
Lev9:24/Num12:10/13:22:28:33/22:22,23:25:
31:33/25:7/Deu1:30/5:23/6:22/7:19/26:6,7/32
:19/Jos7:21/8:19:20,21/24:7/Ju3:24/9:36:46:
55/11:35/13:21/16:23,24/18:18:26/19:17/Ru1:
18/1Sa4:5/5:10/6:13/9:9,10,11:14:17/10:10/
13:6:11/14:16:22:52/15:35/16:21/17:23:24:
50,51/18:15,16/19:20/21:1/22:9,10:22/25:23/
28:5,6:12:21/31:5/2Sa1:6:7/2:20/6:16/10:14:
19/12/13:34/17:18/18:10:11:24:26/20:12/24:
17:20/1Ki3:21/10:4:5/11:27,28/13:24,25/16:18
/17:10/18:7:17:39:44/19:6/22:17:19:32,33/2Ki
2:12:15/3:26/4:25/5:21/6/9:17:32/11:13,14/13
:4/14:26/16:10f/23:29/1Ch6:49/15:29/19:15/
20:3f/21:16:19,20:21:28/2Ch9:4[2]:6/12:7/15:9/
18:16:18:31/26:20/31:7,8/Neh9:9/13:15/Est2:
15/5:2:9/Job2:13/29:8:11:16/32:5/Ps35:21/51
:4/73:21:22/77:16/78:59/114:3/139:16/Pro7:7
/24:30,31/Ecc3:22/9:11/Sol6:9/Is1:1/6/10:15
/59:16/Jer3:7:8/4:24/22:16/24:2/41:13,14/44:
2,3/52:3/Eze1:1:4:15:27,28/2:9,10[2]/3:23/8:2/
11:1/13:7:23/16:4:6,7:8/19:5/20:14/23:11:13:
14,15:16/40:2:3:7-12/44:4/46:19,20:21,22/47:1
:2/Dan2:31:41,42/3:27/4:10,11:13:20:23/5:5[2]/
7:1:2:13/8:3:20:22/9:23/10:7[2]:8/12:5/Amo1:2/
9:1/Jon3:10/Hab:8,9/Zec1:8:18/2:1/5:9/6:1/
Mt1:20/2:7/3:16/4:18:21/9:2:8:9:23/12:2/14:
13/20:3:6/21:15:32:38/22:18/27:3:24/28:4/Mk
1:10:16:19/2:5:14:16/5:15:16:38/6:33:48:49:50
/8:25/9:20:25:38/10:14/11:20/12:7:15/14:69/
15:39/16:4:9/Lk5:12:27/7:13:39/8:28:35/9:32:
43:49/10:18:31:33/13:11/15:20/16:23/18:43/
19:41/20:14:23/22:49/23:47:48:55/24:12/Jn1:
29:34:38/2:14/5:6/6:2-5:15:18,19:24/8:38/9:1/
11:31:33:45/15:24/19:26:33:35/20:5:8:12:14:20
:30,31/21:4:9:20:24/Act3:2:9:12:15/4:13:20/6:
15/7:24:26:31:55/8:18:39/9:7:35:40/10:3:11/
11:5:23/12:3/13:12:37f:45/14:11:14/16:9/17:
16:23/21:26,27:32/22:9:17,18/24:18/28:4:15/
1Co1:21/15:7:8/2Co1:9/Gal2:7,8,9:14/Php4:9/
2Th3:7/Heb11:13:23/1Pe5:1/2Pe2:7,8/Rev1:2:
7f:17,18:20/4:1:2/5:1:6/6:5:8:9/7:1:2:9/8:2:13/
9:1:17,18/10:1/12/13:3:11/14:1:6:14/15:1:5/16
:13/17:3:18/18:1/19:11:17:19/20:1:4[2]:11:12/21
:1:2/22:8

456

SAY
Gen12:11,12,13[2]/14:23/18:13/24:43:50/26:3:9
/31:24/37:4:17:35/41:40/42:34/43:7/44:16:18/
45:3:11,12/Ex3:14/4:1:12:16:28/7:2:16/8:20
12:32f/13:16/30:31/32:12/33/Num5:19:21,2
14:15/18:6/22:8:20:35[2]:38[2]/23:12:16:26/24:
/Deu1:28/9:4:5:6:28/18:18/20:2/21:7/25:9/
2,3:5/28:67[3]/31:17/32:1/Jos1:3/8:6/22:24,2
26,27:28/24:22/Ju12:6/16:15/Ru3:5/4:1/1S
16:36/3:9:16,17/8:7:22/9:9,10,11[2]/10:15/11:
14:9:10:19/16:2/18:22/20:9:26/24:9,10/25:2
28:22/29:6/2Sa7:20/14:2,3:19/15:3/16:10/1
12/19:11,12/1Ki1:12/2:38:42/17:1:24/18:11
/19:20/20:35/22:8:13:14/2Ki2:16/18:22:36/
1Ch16:31/17:18:24/2Ch11:3/18:6,7:13/32:1
Ez5:14[2]/9:10/Neh1:6,7/5:8/9:5/Est4:10:14/
Job1:18/4:2/9:15/10:2/12:12/13:14:17/15:4,
13/16:8/17:12/21:19[2]:27/22:18:20/24:14,15/
28:14/31/33:1:10:11:31:32/35:13:14,15/36:2
40:8/42:5/Ps2:3/3:2/4:6/10:11/12:3,4/13:4/
:23/27:8/32:6/35:3:21:25/36:3/38:13,14/41:
/52:4:6/53:1[2]/56:5/64/74:9,10/83:4/88/92:1
94:6,7/106:48/107:1/115:2/116:10,11/119:6
106/139:4[2]/Pro1:11/3:27,28/4:10:20/5:7:12/
6,7/15:23/17:15/20:9/23:33:35/24:28,29/30:
/Ecc5:5[2]/6:3:12/Is2:3/3:6:11/4:1/5:9:19:20/
5:9/8:4/10:9/12:1:4/14/19:25/20:5,6/22:13:
15,16/28:9:15[2]/29:13:15:16/30:9:10,11:16:21
22/33:24/36:4:7:21/38:15/39:3/40:27/41:7:1
44:5:25:26[2]:27:28[2]/45:14/46:10/47:8/48:5:7:
/49:14:20/50:4/55:1/56:4:12/57:14/58:3/65:
8/Jer1:7:17/2:23[2]:25:31:35[2]/3:4,5:12/5:13:19
6:5/7:4:23:28/8:6:8:14/10:11/11:6/12:2:4/13
18/14:15/15:2/17:15:20/19:11/20:9:10[2]/22:1
:14/23:7:8:16:21:25:26:30,31/26:9/27/28:6/2
15:22:24/31:6:23/32:25/34:5/35:13/36:29/38
21,22:26/42:13,14/43:2,3/46:16/48:2,3,4/50:
51:34,35:61,62:64/Lam2:15:16/3:62/Eze2:8/
27/6:3:11/8:12/9:9/11:3:5/12:19:27:28/13:15
14:10/16:44/18:25/20:3:14:47:49/22:24/24:
20,21/27:3/28:2,3:21/30:2,3/32:2/33:7:8[2]:18:
32/34:2/36:6:14:22:35/37:4:9:11/39:17/44:6/
Dan6:6/10:11/Hos1:23/5:15/8:12/10:3/13:2/
14:2/Joe2:17/Amo5:18/7:16/9:10/Mic2:6[2]/3
11/4:2/6:11/Hab1:16/2:11/Zec1:17/7:5/8:13
20,21:23/11:5/12/13:6:9[2]/Mal1:4[2]:5:6:7:13/3
:13/Mt4:10/5:18:22f:28:32:34[2]:35:37:39:44/7:
/8:8,9[2]/9:5,6/10:19/11:16[2]:18/12:10/15:5,6:8
10:11:31/16:11:14/17:20/18:16/19:7:24/20:2
21:3:13:16:21:25/22:23/23:3:18:29,30/24:48/
25:34:41/26:62:65,66/27:41,42,43/28:12,13/
Mk1:25/2:9,10,11/7:11:15,16/8:28:32/9:1:6:
30,31:41/10:3:5/11:3:14:22,23:31:32/12:18/1
11[2]/14:40:58:60/15:2:3,4/Lk4:9,10,11:12/5:5:
23,24:39/7:6,7,8[3]:27:31:34:40/9:44/10:8,9:10:
15:26:36/11:18/12:11:19:54:55/13:26:35/14:9
10/15:18/17:21/18:20:26/19:31/20:5:6:19:
37,38/22:11:71/23:3/Jn1:22/4:20:43,44/5:24
6:30,31/7:26:40/8:17:26:30,31:48:52/9:17/11:
51/12:50[2]/13:13/14:10/16:15/18:34f/Act4:20
6:14/7:3/8:6/9:15/11:7:9/19:40/20:26/23:5:8
26:7/28:26/Rom1:8/2:1:22[2]:24/3:5:8:10:13:26
4:9:17/8:31/9:1:7:20[2]:30/10:15/11:2,3:8:17/13
9/14:5/16:8:12:17:23/1Co1:12:23/2:9/4:10/6:
18/7:8:40/9:22/10:15:19/11:16:22/12:3:16:21
27/14:39/15:33:34/16:20/2Co1:12:19/3:4[2]/4:
13/5:13,14/8:15:23[2]/9:9/10:10:12:17/11:1:21:
22:23/12:7:19/Gal1:9:12/2:17/3:16:17/4:9:30/
5:3:11/Eph3:4/4:17,18:29/5:33/Php3:2:12:18/
4:4:8:21/Col2:18[2]/3:17/4/1Th:9/5:1/2Th1:7/2
3:17/3:13:14/1Ti4:3/5:8:14:18/2Ti2:15:23/4:6
19/Tit1:10/2:8:15/3/Heb1:13/5:11/7:9/9:22/
11:32/13:6:17/Jas2:3:16:18[2]:23/4:4:13:15/5:1
/1Pe2:8/3:9/2Pe2:19/1Jn1:3:4:6:8/2:4:14/5:
6,7,8/2Jn1:12[2]/3Jn:12:13/Jud:4/Rev:11/2:2:9
/3:9f:17/6:3:5:7/16/18:19/22:17

72

SAYING
[2]Gen12:19/48:20/Ex5:17/17:7/Num11:13/14:
26,27/16:4:41/24:23,24/32:28/Deu20:9/22:
13,14/Jos9:22/Ju7:11:12,13/9:30/21:6/1Sa15:
11/25:21/2Sa5:8/19:27/20:18/1Ki1:46,47:48/
8:47/13:4/22:13/2Ki6:33/8:4/16:7f/2Ch10:16
16:10/18:12/Neh6:7/Job12:3/13:1:15/27:12/
36:2/Ps78:1/85:8/107:43/129:8/Pro5:1/18:21
/24:11,12/Is1:2/36:18/37:15/45:9/48:15/49:
8,9/Jer4:3/6:14:27/11:7/16:19/18:11/20:1/23:
17:18:34:35/26:7,8:19:21/27:4/29:28/31:15/33
:24[2]/44:26/Eze11:5:15/12:23/13:10/18:29/22:
23/23:1/24:15/26:2/33:10:17:20:24:30[2]/35:2:
12:13/36/37:15/38:17/Dan2:20/4:23:30:35/7:
/Hos1:10/Amo:5f/3:9/7:10/9:1/Jon3:6/Mic6:
1:11/Hab2:6/Hag1:2/Mal:12/2:17[2]/Mt5:43/9
3:18/16:7:13/19:3/21:15/22/23:31/26:44:68/

(SAYING Con't)
27:24:39/Mk2:17/3:30/6:14:17,18/7:19/8:27/
12:13:32/14:70/Lk3:16/6:42/9:7:18:33:34/11:
53,54/18:19/19:39:46/21:8/22:19:20/Jn2:22/6
:42:43/8:6:43:54/9:22,23:40/11:32/12:28:34:36
/13:18/16:17,18/17:1/18:34f/Act2:15:25:31/4:
25,26/9:4/10:43:44/13:35/14:2/16:14/17:20/
22:7:17,18/Rom1:20f/2:1/4:14/8:27/11:19/
1Co1:12/4:6/7:35/10:19:20/11:25/12:10:30/14
:5:14:16:26^2:27:37/15:12/2Co7:3/8:8/10:1/12:
16:19:20/Gal1:20:23/Col2:4/1Th3:5/5:3/1Ti3:
1/Heb4:7/6:9/8:1:11/Jas2:14/2Pe1:17,18/2:22
/1Jn:13/3:18/3Jn1:10/Jud:4/Rev:11/2:7:11:17
:22/3:6:13:22/4:8/5:9f:11f:12f:14/9/11:16/14:8
:13/16:17/18:18/21:3
241

SAYINGS
Pro31:1
1

SAYS
Gen3:1:2,3/11:32f/21:12/24:14/27:38/41:45f/
45:9/Ex4:22/5:1/7:17/8:1:20/9:13/11:4/20:19
/32:27/Num22:11/23:3,4/24:3-9^2:13/30:4:7:14
/Deu5:26,27/10:12,13/13:2/15:16/31:23:29/
Jos7:13/24:2/Ju4:7/1Sa9:6/20:7/24:13/2Sa12
:7/1Ki2:30:31/3:23/11:31/13:2:21,22/17:14/20
:42/22:27/2Ki1:4,5:11/3:1f:16/4:43/5:13/7:1/9
:6/10:9,10/18:19/19:3:5,6:10:20/20:1/1Ch17:7
/2Ch11:4/12:5/18:10:13:26/20:15/21:12/34:21
:23:26^2:27/Job9:20/28:28/33:23,24:23,24f/34:5
:18/Ps12:6/14:1/32:8/50:16/60:6,7/68:22/75:
10/89:3,4/91:14/95:10/108:8/Pro8:1/10:11/20
:14/22:13/24:24/26:13:18,19/28:24/31:26/Ecc
7:27,28/8:5:16,17/9:16/12:8/Is1:18:24/7:7/8:
16:20/9:8,9,10/10:1:15:24/14:22:23/16:13,14/
19:4/21:16/22:19:22/23:12/28:16/29:11:12:13:
22/30:1:10,11:15/31:9/33:10/36:4/37:6:18:21:
22:34/38:6/39:8/40:1:6/41:21/42:5/43:1:10:14
/44:2:6^2:17:24/45:11:14:18/48:17:22/49:7:8,9:
22:25/51:16:22/52:3/54:8:10:17/56:1:8/57:15:
21/59/65:1:7:8:13:25/66:12:17:20:21/Jer1:19/
2:2:4,5:19:22:29/3:1:10:16/4:9:17:27/5:11:14:
15:18/6:22/7:3:13,14:20:21:30:32/8:1:3/9:6:7:
15:17,18:22:23:25,26/10:17/11:5:11/12:14:17/
13:11:12:14/14:15/15:2:3:20/16:9:14,15^2/17:5:
21,22:24/18:12/19:3:6:15/20:3:4/21:3,4:8:10:
11:14/22:3:5:11:30/23:5,6:11:15:16:32/25:8,9:
27:28/26:4/27:15:16:19,20,21/28:4:13:14:16/
29:8:9:11:14:21:23:25:31/30:2:8:9:11:18/31:1:7:
14:16:17:23:27:31:32:34:35:38,39/32:14:15:36/
33:2:14/34:2:4:5:13:17/35:13:17:18,19/36:29/
37:7/38:17/39:16/42:4:5:15:18:20/43:10/44:
2,3:11:25:26/45:2:4/46:5:18:25:28/47:2/48:15:
35:40:43:47/49:2:5:6:7:12:13:15:16:18:26:29:30:
35:37:38:39/50:10:18:20:33:35/51:1:20:24:33:
39:48:52:53:57/Eze3:11:27/5:5,6,7:8/6:11/7:
5,6/11:5:7:8:16:21/12:10:19:23:25:28/13:8:13:
16:18:20/14:4:6,7:11:14:20:21/15:5,6:8/16:3:14
:23:30:36:43:48:58:59,60:63/17:16:19:22,23/18:
3:9:32/20:3:5,6:27;28:31:39:40/21:3:7:24:26/22
:12:18,19,20:31/23:22:28:34:46/24:3:6:24/25:3:
6:8:12:15/26:3:5:7:14:19:21/28:2,3:6:10:12:22/
29:3:8:13:19:20/30:2,3:6:10:22/31:10:15:18/32:
3:11:14:16:31/33:11:25:27/34:2:8:11:15,16:17:
20:30:31/35:3:6:11/36:4:6:13:14:15:22:33:37,38
/37:5:9:12:18,19,20:21/38:2,3:14:17:21/39:5:13
:20:25:29/43:18:27/44:6:9:12:15:27/45:9:15:18
/46:1:16/47:13/48:29/Hos1:13:16:21,22/8:2/
Joe2:12/3:1/Amo1:3:6:9:11:13/2:1:4:6/3:10:11:
12:13/4:6:8:9:11/5:3:4:16:25,26,27/6:14/7:11/8
/9:15/Ob1:4:8/Mic2:3/4:6/5:10/Nah1:14/3:5/
Zep1:2/2:9/3:8:20/Hag1:7:8/2:4:6:7:8,9:16,17:
23/Zec1:16/2:6,7^2:10/4:6/5:3:4/6:12/8:2:6:9:
11:17/10:12/11:6/12:4/13:7/Mal1:2,3:10:11:14
/2:4:8:16/3:1:5:7:11:13:17/4:3/Mt:7/5:31:33:
38/8:3:4/12:43,44,45/15:18/26/27:9/Mk12:29
/Lk4:17/10:27/11:49/20:17/22:11/Jn5:32,33/
7:46/8:5/10:34,35,36^2/19:23,24:35f:36,37/Act1
:20/7:48,49/10:15/13:32,33:34/15:16:18/17:28
/Rom1:17/3:4:21,22/9:25^2:29/10:6/14:1f:11/
15:21/16:23:25,26,27/1Co1:9:19:31/3:19/9:8/
10:13/12:15/2Co1:17:19/6:2/Gal3:11:12/Eph4
:8:9/5:14:31/1Ti6:4/2Ti2:15/4:4/Heb1:8/2:6:
12/3:10/4:12/7:17/8:10/10:23/12:26/Jas1:25:
26/4:5:6/1Jn1:10/2:6:9:22/3:23:24/4:1:15:20/
5:6,7,8/Rev1:3:8/2:1:29/14:13
679

SEE
Gen2:19,20/3:10/8:8/9:16,17/11:5:29f:32f/12:
11,12,13/13:14/16:6/18:14:21/19:18,19,20^2/22
:8/24:7:13:21/26:28/27:46/30:38/31:30:35f:
36,37:49:50/33:10:13/37:13,14:19,20/39:14,15
/41:41,42/42:8,9:12/44:21:34/45:28/46:3,4/47:
1:23/48:10:11^2/50:23/Ex2:4/3:21/4:11^2:23/5:1
/6:20f/7:1:10/9:7:27/10:4,5:10:28:29/12:13/14^2
:17/16:4:7,8,9:32/19:10:21/20:26/23:5:8:20/31:
1/33:18:19f:20^2:23/34:10:28f:33f^2:35/40:38/
Lev9:15f/13:9,10:36/18:16f/20:21f/Num11:23/
12:7,8/13:3-15f:18^2:20:27/14:14:23/19:12f/22:
41/23:3,4:7-10:13/24:3-9:15-19:25f/28:1/32:
10,11/Deu1:34,35/3:23,24,25:27:28/4:12:15:28
:32:36/9:16/11:3:4:5/13:12,13,14/14:19,20f/18
:16/20:1/21:11/22:1^2:4/23:14/26:10/27:8f/28:
10:34:66/29:4:22:23/31:7/32:20:36:39:50:52/
Jos2:14/3:2,3,4/6:26f/8:31f/9:12/11:4/14:10/
15:37-44f/17:4f/20:2f/22:10/Ju2:22/3:4/5:22/
6:16f/9:29:37/11:23/16:19/19:3/20:27,28/Ru1:
11f:15/2:2f/3:3/1Sa5:3/9:8/10:2:3/11/14:9:29
/15:28/17:18:28:38,39/18:21/19:18:24f/21:1/
24:11/25:25/26:16/28:2:5,6f:13^2/2Sa1:10f/3:
15f/8:18f/13:5:6:35/14:1:8:24:32/15:3:25,26/
16:12:16:22/20:8,9,10/21:4:19f/24:3/1Ki1:
22,23:48/2:13:27f/9:11,12/14:4/15:15f/16:34f/
17:23/18:5^2:43/20:13^2:31/21:29/22:6f:23/2Ki2
:10:19/3:17/4:26/5:3/6:1:10:17^2:20/7:2:13:14:
19/8:3:6/10:16:18,19/15:12f:15f/19:7:16/22:20
/23:16f:18f/1Ch3:15f/7^2/10:13f/12:17:23/20:2
f/21:19,20/28:20/29:17:18/2Ch7:18/10:10:15f
/13:12/16:3/18:22:31/20:10:11:17/22:2f/23:12
/24:22:27/29:8/32:31/34:15,16/35:20f/Ez4:14
/Neh1:6,7/2:13/8:1/Est2:1:3/3:3,4/4:16/5:13/
8:6/Job1:11/3:9^2/4:16/5:14/7:8/8/9:11/10:
20,21/11:6/17:2:8/19:26:26f:27/20:9/21:6:8/
22:13:14:19:20/24:14,15/26:13f/28:7/31:35/35
:14,15/36:30/40:16/42:4:16/Ps8:3/9:13/10:5:
14/11:7/14:2/17:15/18:14/21:12/22:8:17:27/
25:18:19/26:2/27:13/34:8^2/37:34/40:7f:7/46:8
/48:2^2:8:11/49:8,9f/50:18/51:7f/52:6:7/53:2/
58:8/59:4:10/63:2/64:8/66:5/68:11,12,13/69:
19:32/74:3:18/80:2:14/81:10/83:2/86:17/89:50
/90:8:16^2/91:8/94:4:5/104:26/107:42/109:25:
27/112:6:10/115:5/116:15f/118:23/119:18:27:
82:159/143:8/Pro10:5/13:19/14:15/23:33/26:
24,25,26/27:1/29:16/31:9/Ecc1:8-11/2:24-26/
3:11:18/5:8/7:13/8:16,17/Sol1:6/2:4:14/3:11^2/
6:11^2:13/7:12/Is1:7:11:16/3:12:17/4:2,3,4f/5:
19/6:10/9:2/10:17f:27f/12:2/13:9/14/17:12/
21:2^2/22:9,10,11/24:1/26:11/28:16:26/29:15:
18:23/30:6:16:20:27/31:9/32:6/33:17:20/34:16
/37:16,17/38:11^2:17/40:10:26:27/41:2f:11:20:
29/42:1:3:18:20:23/43:8:19^2/44:9:18/49:12:16:
18:22/50:9:11/51:4:22/52:8:10:13:14:15^3/55:3f
/57:13/58:3:14/60:1:3:4/62:2:3:11/63:3:15/64:
9/65:1f^2:6:15f:17/66:14^2:15:18^2/Jer1:8:9:11^2:
13^2:18/2:10,11^2:15:16:19:22/4:21:23/5:1:15:21
/6:4:22/7:11:12:17/8:12/9:7/10:20/11:16:20/
12:14:13:20/16:17/18:19/19:9/20:4:12/22:10:
12:13f:20:22/23:12:19:20:23/24:3:6/25:32/26:
24f/29:32/31:16:32f/32:24/33:9:12/34:22/35:3
/36/37:12:12f/39:11,12/40:4:8/41:6:9f/42:18/
44:17f:27/48:17:39:44/49:5:20/50:9:31:34:41/
51:18:20f:25:37/Lam1:9:11:12:18:20:21/2:11:21
/3:63/5:1/Eze1:8/3/4:14f/5:15/8:6^2:9:12/9:4:9
/10:14f/12:3:12:12f:13:13f:24/13:7:9/14:22/15:
7/16:36:37:40,41/18:23/20:25f:41:48/23/24:7/
28:22/36:9:34/37:5:18,19,20/38:2,3f/39:15,16:
21/40:5f:6f:28f/43:13f/44:24/47:13f/48:8f/
Dan1:3,4f:13/2:8,9:16:24/3:25/4:20/5:13:23/7:
23f/8:9f:10f^2/9:7:18:24f:25f/11:37f/Hos1:4,5f:
11f:10:23f/5:10f:13/7:2/9:9f:10f/Joe2:19:28/
Amo1:5f/2:8f:11f/5:24/6:2/7:7:8/8:2/9:4/Ob1:
10/Jon:6:7/2:4/4:5/Mic1:14f:16/4:2/6:14f:16/
7:9:10^2:17/Nah1:15/2:3^2/3:5:7:10/Hab1:3:5/2:
1/3:3:7/Zep2:15/3:9f/Zec2:2/3:4:8:9f/4:2^2:3:6f
:10^3/5:2:7/9:5/10:7/11:12f/13:6f/Mal1:5:8/3:
18/4:5/Mt2:7/5:8:14:15,16/6:5/7:4:5/8:4f:34/
9:28:30/10:25f/11:7:8/12:18:22/13:12,13:14:16^2
:17/15/16:28/20:32,33:34/21:2:19/22:9/23:39/
24:15:17f:21:25:29f:30:33/25:37:39:44/26:18:58
:64/27:49/28:6/Mk1:5/3:7,8:31,32/4:11,12/5:
14:32/7:18/8:23:24^2/9:1:47/10:51:52/11:2:13/
12:11/13:14:26:29/14:13:14:62/15:36/16:7/Lk
2:15/3:6/4:18,19/6:7:8:42^2/7:20,21,22:24:44/8:
16f:17f:19:20:35/9/9:31/10:13f:23:24/11:31f/12
:54:57/13:6:28:35/14:1:28:30/18:4,5:41:43/19:
3/21:20:26:27:31/22:10/23:8^2:35:48/24:24:39^2:
40/Jn1:14f:21f:33:36:39:46:48:50:51/3:21:36/4:
30:40,41:45f/5:32,33f/6:22,23:62:63f/7:3:24:52
/8:56/9:10:11:15:19:21:25:39/11:1f:28:34:36:40
:56/12:9^2:31f:40:45/14:9/16:10:16^2:20:22/17:
24/18:26/19:23,24:39f/20:3,4:25/21:4:15f/Act
1:1f/2:6:16:17:23f/4:13/6:8f/7:31:56/8:23/9:12
:18/10:12f:19:34/12:20/13:13f/15:15f:16f:36/
16:27/17:11/20:25:38/21:8f/22:14/23:9/27:
2f/28:26:27/Rom1:10:13/2:4/3:5:20^2/4:11:12/
5:20^3/7:12:13:23,24,25/9:18:23,24/11:10:24/12
:8:17/14:13/15:21:26:28/16:1/1Co1:24/3:13^2/4
:5/8:10^2/9:23/10:15/13:12^3/14:18f:22/2Co1:11
:15,16/3:2:3:13:14/4:4:7:18/7:11/8:17/9:5/10:
10/12:6/Gal1:10/2:4/3:1:7/6:11/Eph1:16,17:
18/3:18,19/5:13:33/Php1:10:27:28/2:19:24:28/
3:15/4:1:5/Col1:16/2:7:12/4:8/1Th2:3:17/3:6^2:
10/5:15/2Th1:9:12/2Ti:4/Tit3:13/Phm1:6/
Heb2:9:13/3:9/7:4:15/10:7/11:1:27/12:11:14:
25/13:23/Jas1:24/2:17:18:22:24/4:14/5:9:11/
1Pe1:5:7:22/2:6/4:6f/1Jn2:10:11/3:1/4:10:19/
5:6,7,8f:16/2Jn1:4:8:12/3Jn:14/Jud:14/Rev:4f^2
:7^2:11:12/2:6f:8f:12f:18f:19/3:1f^2:7f:14f/4:5f/5:
6f/9:20/17:6/18:9/19:20f/21:5/22:4:12
1082

SEEING
Gen44:30/Jos8:14/Ju9:36/1Sa26:12/1Ch10:5/
Est2:12,13,14/Ps17:15/Pro21:11/Ecc6:5/Eze
13:23/18:32/Lk5:20/18:42/24:37/Jn1:32/9:7/
11:57/12:45/Act1:3/2:33/5:10/1Co:2/16:11:12
/2Co5:7/Tit1:16/1Pe:8/1Jn3:2/Rev1:13f
29

SEEN
Gen6:11/9:14/31:12:42/32:30/33:10f/37:16/41
:19/44:28/46:30/Ex3:7:9:16/4:31/19:4/32:9/
Num14:22/16:42/23:18-24/24:3-9/25:18/27:13
/Deu1:28/3:21/4:3:9/10:21/11:2:7/19:16/21:1:
7/29:2,3:17/34:4/Jos5:11,12/8:29/23:3/Ju2:7-
7-9/6:22/13/16:2/18:9,10/Ru4:9/1Sa6:18/17:
25/23:22/24:9,10/2Sa14:28/17:17:20/18:21/
1Ki8:8/10:7/2Ki19:35/20:5:15/1Ch16:14/2Ch
5:9/30:26/Job3:16/7:10/13:1/31:7,8:19,20/36:
25/38:22,23/39:1/42:5/Ps17:3/18:43,44,45/31
:7/35:21/37:25^2:35,36/48:6/55:9f/56:8/92:11/
95:9/98:2,3/105:7/Pro7:11,12/16:31/Ecc4:3/5
:13,14/6:1/7:15-17/8:9,10/10:5:6:7/Sol3:3/Is
21:5f/39:4/40:5/42:16/43:12/48:6/57:18/64:4/
66:7,8:19/Jer3:6:24/14:14/23:11/29:23/Lam1:
8:10/2:16/3:1:59:60/Eze8:4:12:15:17/10:15,16:
20:22/20/26:16/32:9/40:4/43:3/47:6/Dan4:
10,11/7:15:21:28/8:17:19/9:21/Hos5:3/6:10/9:
13/Joe2:2/Nah1:15/Zec2:8f/Mal:14/Mt:2/4:
15,16/8:10/9:33/11:4/13:17/17:9/24:21/Mk2:
12/4:21/5:6/9:9/16:10,11:14/Lk1:22/2:20:26:
29,30,31^2/5:26/7:16:20,21,22/8:16:36/9:27:36/
10:23:24/24:22,23:48/Jn1:14:18:50/3:10,11:32
/4:45/6:36:46/7:11/8:57/9:37/12:17:41/14:7:9^2
:11/19:35f/20:18:25:29^2/Act3:10/7:34/9:27/13
:31/19:26/21:29/22:15/Rom1:20/1Co2:9/9:1/
12:23:24/15:5:6/2Co4:6:18/13:1/Eph3:10/Php
1:30/Col2:18/1Ti6:16/Tit2:13/Heb:8/11:3/
1Pe1:8/3:5/4:14f/2Pe1:16:19/1Jn:1:2:3/4:12:
14:20/Rev1:19/11/18:23/21:22
233

SEES
Gen4:14/16/33:10f/44:31/Ex12:23/Lev13:12:
20:21:26:56/14:3:44/Num24:15-19/2Sa15:
25,26/22:25/1Ki14:13/1Ch28:9/Job11:11/31:4
/34:21/41:34/Ps16:6/22:7/58:10f/97:4:6/Pro1
:17/Ecc2:13,14/Is21:6,7^2:6,7f/29:23f/32:6/38:
5/47:10/53:11/Jer51:26f/Eze18:14/33:3:6/39:
15,16/Lk14:10/Jn5:19/6:40:46/10:12/1Co13:
12/Tit1:15^2/1Jn3:17
50

SHALL
Gen1:14,15/3:14:15:16^3:18:20/9:5,6/16:2,3/17:
2,3,4:6:7,8^2:9,10:11:12:14:16:19:20/18:18/20:7/
21:6/24:5/25:23^2/26:4:11:22/27:39,40/28:22/
30:34/32:28/34:9,10/35:10:11/37:10:30/41:44/
42:19:34:38/44:16:17:29:32:34/45:10:18/46:3,4
/48:6^2:19^2/49:4:8^3:10^2:13^2:16:17:19^2:20:26/Ex2
:7/3:12:13/6:1:7:8,9/7:1/8:10/10:26:28/11:5:7^2
/12:3,4:5:6:7:8:11:14:15^2:19:22:43:46^2:47:48^2/
13:6,7^2:12:13:14:16/14:4:16:18/15/16:11,12/17
:4/19:5:6:12:13^2/20:4:7:10/21:2:3^2:4^2:5:6^2:7:8:
12:15:17:20:21:22^2:23:26:27:28^2:29^2:30f:32^2:34^2
:35^2:36^2/22:1^3:4:6:7:8:9^2:11:13^2:17:18:19:20:20f
:24:28/23:17:18^2:19:19f:23:25:27/24:2/25:9:15:
16f:19:20^2:21:31/26:15,16/27:21/28:4^2:5,6:8:10
:13,14:17:29:30,31^2:32:33,34:35:37,38/29:2:9:10
:11:15,16^2:19,20:21:29:30:32:33^2:34:35^2:36:37^2:
37f:42:43:46/30:1:7:8^2:10f:10:11,12:13:14:15^2:
19:29:29f:31:32^2:33:35:38/31:14,15/32:10:13:
34/33:23/34:3:10:20:23/40:9:10:15^2/Lev1:5:6,7
f:13^2:15,16,17^3/2:2f:5:7:8:16/3:2^2:3,4,5:7,8^2:
9,10,11:13^2:14:17/4:4^2:5:6:7^2:8:10:11,12:14:15:
16:17:18^2:19:20^2:21:24:25^2:26^3:29:30^2:31^4:33:34^2
:35^4/5:5:6^2:7^2:8:9^2:10^3:11:12^3:13^3:15:16^4:17,18^2

(SHALL Con't)
/**6**:4,5:6^2:7^2:9:10:11:12:14:15:16:18f:19,20:21:
22,23^3:25:26:28/**7**:2^2:4:7:8:9:12:13:14^2:17,18^2:
19:20:21:25:26,27:30:31^2:32,33/**10**:15^2/**11**:24:
27:28:31:32:33:39:40:41,42/**12**:2:5^2:5f/**13**:3f:4:6
:8:13:14,15:20:21:23:26:28:31:33^2:34^2:37:43:54:
55:56/**14**:3:4^2:5:6:7^3:8:9^2:10:11:12:13^2:14:15:17:
18^2:19:20:21:22:23:24:25:26:29:31:35:36:38:40:
41:42:44:45^2:46:47:49:50:51,52^2:53/**15**:10:13:14
:15^2:16:19^2:20:21,22,23:24:27^2:29:30:31/**16**:5:6:
7:9:10^3:12:13:14:16:17:18:20:21:22^2:23:24:25:26
:27:28:31:32^2:34/**17**:3,4:7:8,9:15:16/**18**:4,5:4,5f^2
:6:10:18:21:23:29,30/**19**:8:13^2:16f:20:21^2:22^2:23
f:24^2:28:32/**20**:1:9:10:12:14:15:16f:17^2:18:19:20:
21:25^2:26:27/**21**:5:6^2:7^2:9:12:22:23/**22**:3:6^2:7:14
:24:26,27:28/**23**:7^2:7f:8^2:9,10,11:12:13:15,16:17:
18:19:20:21:26,27:29:32/**24**:3,4:5-8^3:9:15,16:18:
18f:20:22/**25**:6,7^2:10^3:11:12:13^2:14,15,16:20:28:
40:46:50:51:54/**26**:4,5:12:16^2:20^2:29:32:33:36:
37:38:39:40,41:43^2/**27**:1:3:4:5:6:7:8^4:10:11,12^2:
13:14,15:17:18:19:20:21^2:23^2:24:25:25f^2:27:28:
29:33^3/**Num1**:51:52:53/**3**:10:31-35:41:45/**4**:8:
10^2:13:15:16:17,18,19/**5**:9,10:15:16:18^2:19^2:
21,22^2:23:25:26:27:28:30^2:31/**6**:9:11:16:18^3:19:
20:27:27f/**8**:10:11:12:14:15/**9**:13:14/**10**:4:5,6,7f ^{2}
:5,6,7^2/**11**:17:18^2:23/**12**:7,8/**14**:20,21:23:24:30:
31:32:34,35/**15**:10:15,16:15,16f:25^2:26:27:28^2:
30:31f^2:35/**16**:28:38^2/**18**:4:7^2:14,15:17:18:21:22
:23^3:24:28,29^2:30/**19**:1^2:4:5:6:8:9^2:11:13:14:16:
18:19:20:21:22/**20**:12:24:26^2/**21**:8/**22**:38/**23**:18-
18-24^3/**24**:3-9^6:14:15-19^6:21,22^2:23,24^2/**25**:
12,13/**26**:64,65/**27**:8:9:10:11:13:21/**28**:3^2:4:5:7:
11:13:14:15:16:17:18^2:19:20,21^3:23:24:25:27^2:
28,29/**29**:1^2:2:3,4:5:7:8:12^2:13:17/**30**:4:7:11:15^2
/**31**:23^2/**32**:22:26:32/**35**:4:6:7:8:11:17:19:21:24:
25^2:30:34/**36**:9/**Deu1**:37:38/**2**:18:31/**3**:27:28/**4**:
26:29/**5**:9,10:14:16:31/**7**:10:14/**8**:19/**11**:15:29/
12:6:7^2:12:18:20-23/**13**:9:16/**14**:23/**15**:2:6^3:17:
19:20:21/**16**:2:4^2:6:8^2:10:15:16/**17**:5^2:7^2:8:15:17
:19/**18**:4:8:18:20:21/**19**:12^2:17:19:21/**20**:2:5:11/
21:2:3:5:6:19:21^2:23/**22**:9:15:16:17,18^2:19:21^2:
23,24:25,26,27:28,29f:30/**23**:1:11:12:15,16/**24**:5
:16^2/**25**:1:6:7:9^2:10:12/**26**:5:13/**27**:12:13:14:15:
16:17:18:19:20:21:22:23:24:25:26/**28**:10:12^2:13:
15-19:22:24:29^2:31:36:42:43:44^3:45:46:47,48:60:
63:65/**29**:19:20:22/**30**:5:6:18/**31**:2:3:5:7:16:17/
32:2:25:40,41/**33**:10^2:19:29^2/**Jos1**:6:17,18/**7**:15
/**8**:2/**9**:23/**14**:9:12/**17**:16,17,18/**23**:4,5/**Ju1**:12/
2:3/**5**/**6**:16:23/**7**:4^2/**8**:22:23,24/**9**:13/**10**:18/**13**:
5/**20**:18^2:22,23,24:27,28^2/**21**:7:16:18/**Ru1**:16^2/
1Sa1:11/**2**:9^2:10:31:33:35:36/**3**:14/**6**:2^2:4,5/**8**:
17/**14**:37:39:45/**15**:33/**19**:6/**22**:16/**23**:2/**24**:20/
25:26:29/**26**:25/**28**:2/**30**:8/**2Sa2**:1^2/**4**:11^2/**5**:19
/**7**:5f:10,11:13:14:15:16/**9**:7/**12**:6:10:14:23^2/**14**:
11/**16**:20/**19**:21:38/**22**:44:45:46/**23**:3:4:7/**1Ki1**:
30^2:52/**2**:4/**5**:5/**8**:19:25:41,42/**9**:5/**11**:36:38/**13**:
2^3:21,22:32/**14**:11^2/**18**:31f/**19**:17^2/**20**:14:28:36:
42/**21**:19:23:24^2/**22**:6:15/**2Ki1**:16/**2**:9:21/**3**:10/
4:2:15,16/**5**:27/**6**:15:21^2/**9**:10/**11**:6,7,8/**14**:6/**19**
:30^2:31:32^2:33/**20**:17^2/**22**:12,13/**1Ch11**:2^2:5,6/
13:12/**17**:13:24/**22**:9:10^2/**28**:6/**2Ch6**:16/**7**:20/
10:6:8,9/**16**:9/**18**:3,4,5:14/**20**:20/**23**:2,3/**25**:4:9/
Ez6:5:11^2/**7**:24:26/**Neh9**:29f/**Est1**:13-15/**2**:4/**5**
:7,8/**Job1**:21/**2**:10/**4**:11^2/**5**:22:24:25^2:26/**7**:9:21
/**8**:22/**11**:20/**14**:11,12:14/**15**:30^3:33f/**16**:22/**17**:
5:8:9^2:16/**18**:4:5:13:14^2:15:16/**19**:26:26f:27/**20**:
7:10^2:11:17:18:21:22^2/**22**:19^2:25/**24**:20^2:24/**27**:
4^2:15:17^2:22/**29**:18/**32**:16/**34**:20/**36**:12/**38**:11^2/
Ps1:3^2:5/**6**:5f:10/**9**:17:18^2/**10**:16/**11**:7/**13**:2:5/
14:5/**15**/**16**:4/**22**:26^4:27^2:29:30^2:31/**23**:6/**25**:3:
13^2/**27**:1:3/**32**:6f/**34**:1f/**35**:9/**37**^{2}:10:11^2:17:20:
22^2:28:29:38^2/**42**:4,5^2:11/**43**:5/**45**:16/**49**:14f/**51**
:7^2/**58**:10^2/**60**:6,7:8:12/**61**:4:7/**63**:5:9:11/**64**:9:
10/**65**:8/**66**:4:15/**69**:32^2:35:36^2/**72**:9^2:15:15f/**75**
:9/**80**:3:7:19/**81**:9f/**89**:1:5:14,15:22^2:37/**92**:9:12
/**94**:3/**101**:6/**102**:18^2:26/**108**:13/**109**:28/**110**:3^2:
7/**112**:2:3:9/**116**/**118**:12:17:27,28/**119**:27:144/
120:3:4/**121**:1/**125**:3/**126**:5/**127**/**128**:2:3/**130**:8
/**132**:12:14:16:17:18/**137**:8/**138**:4^2:5/**140**:13/
143:7/**145**:6:10/**Pro1**:33/**2**:21f:22f:22/**5**:23/**6**:
29/**8**:17/**10**:30^2/**11**:5:24,25:29:31/**12**:7^2:11f/**14**:
19:22^2/**16**:5/**17**:11/**19**:9^2:29/**22**:8:16:29/**24**:24:
25/**28**:10/**29**:14/**30**:17/**31**:30:31/**Ecc5**:10/**8**:13/
11:4f^2/**Sol1**:11/**5**:3/**8**:8:12/**Is1**:26:27:28/**2**:2f:13
:16/**3**:11:18:20:25,26^2/**5**:14:15^2/**6**:8/**7**:14^2:15,16
f/**8**:18/**9**:1:2:6/**10**:15/**11**:2:6:9/**13**/**14**:2:25:30^2:
32/**16**:9:13,14/**17**:3/**19**:20:23/**22**:21/**26**:19^3/**29**:
2:19/**30**:30^2:31/**33**:16/**34**:17/**37**:32:33/**40**:5:6:8:
30:31^4/**41**:15:16^5:18/**42**:6/**44**:4:26:27/**45**:1^4:13:
14^4:16:17^2:23^2:24^2:25/**47**:3:9:11:15/**49**:3:6:7^2:10
:11:12:17:18:19^2:20:22:23^5:25:26^2/**50**:9^2/**51**:5:6^3
:8^3:11:14:22/**52**:6:10:12:13^2:14,15^5:14,15f/**53**:
10^2:10f:10:11^3/**54**:10:13^2:14:17/**55**:11/**56**:7/**57**:
2:13/**58**:10/**59**:21^2/**60**:2:7:12:16:17:20^2:22^2/**61**:
4:5^2:6^3:7:9^2:11/**62**:2^2:4:6,7:8:9^2:12^2/**65**:10^2:12:
13^5:14:15:16:18:19:23:25^3:25f:25/**66**:5:7,8:9:12^2
:16:18:19:20:22^3:23:24^4/**Jer4**:13:28^2/**5**:6^3:9^2:17^2
:19/**6**:3^2:9^3:12:15^2:21^2/**7**:23^2:33^2:34/**8**:1:2^2:3:17
/**9**:9:11:16:22/**10**:10^2:11:18:22/**11**:11:21,22^3:23
/**12**:12:13:16/**13**:10:12f:17^2:19/**14**:15^2:16^2:17/
15:8:14/**16**:4^5:6^2:7/**17**:4:13:25^4:26:27^2/**18**:16/
19:6:11^2/**20**:4:5:6:11^3/**21**:6:10^2/**22**:4:5:12:19:26:
30/**23**:3:4^2:5,6^2:17:33:40/**24**:7^2:9/**25**:10^2:11^2:14:
16:29:32^2:33^3:34/**26**:18^2/**27**:7^2/**29**:22:32/**30**:3:5
:8:9:10^2:16^4:20^2:21:22:23/**31**:1^2:6:9^2:12^4:16f:21:
22:22f^2:23:24:29:30:33^2:34:38,39:40^3/**32**:5:24:
28:29:38:40:44/**33**:15:16:17:18:20,21/**34**:2:3^4:20
/**35**:18,19/**36**:30^2/**37**:7:8:17/**38**:18/**39**:17/**43**:10
:11^2:12^2:13/**44**:7:12^3:14:27:28^2/**46**:5:10:14:19:
26:27^2/**48**:1:7^2:8:9:11:13:18:26:42:43:44^2/**49**:2^4:
3:5^2:12:13^2:19:26:27:32:33^3:36/**50**:3^4:4:5:9:10:
12^2:13^3:20:35^2:36^2:37^3:39^4:45:46^2/**51**:2^2:3^3:4:14 ^{2}
:18:26^3:37:44:47:48^2:53:57:58^3:64/**Lam2**:20^2/
Eze3:20:21:27/**4**:13/**5**:4/**7**:10,11:17:18^3:21:
26,27/**12**:11:12:13^2:15:16:19:20^2/**13**:9^3:14:21:23
/**14**:8/**15**:7/**17**:9:16^2:17:18:20:22,23:24/**18**:9:13 ^{2}
:17^2:18:19:20:21:22:24:27:28^2/**20**:11:21:31:38:
40:48/**21**:5:12^2:30/**22**:16:24/**23**:29/**24**:14:23^2:
27/**25**:7:11:14:17/**26**:2:5^2:6^2:16:17:19/**28**:7:8:22
:23:24:26/**29**:6:9:21/**30**:4^2:5:6^3:7^2:9:11:13:14:17:
19:24:25:26/**32**:7:10^4:11:15:32/**33**:15^2:16^2:18:19
:27^3:28^2:29/**34**:23:24:26:27:28^2/**35**:4,5:9:10:12/
36:11:23:28^2/**37**:6:14:22^2:23^2:24^2:25^3:27:28/**38**:
5:6:20^4/**39**:6:7:21:27/**42**:13/**43**:7:20:22:24:25/
44:2^4:3:9:13:15^2:16^2:23:24^2:28:29^2:30^2/**45**:1^3:2:3
:4:5:7:8^3:11^2:12^3:16:17^2:19:21^2:22:23:24:25/**46**:1
:2^3:3:4:5^2:6:7f:8:10:11:12^4:14,15/**47**:9:13:14/**48**:
17:21,22/**Dan2**:44/**3**:29/**6**:7:25,26^3/**7**:14:18:27^3
/**8**:23:24:25/**9**:27/**11**:30,31f:32:43/**12**:3:4:10^2/
Hos1:10:21,22/**3**:5/**4**:10:19^2/**5**:5/**6**:4/**8**:13/**9**:14
:16/**10**:7:14:15/**11**:5:7:10^3/**13**:3:14^2/**Joe2**:20:27:
31/**3**:17^2:18/**Amo1**:5:7/**2**:2/**5**:5/**8**:14/**9**^{2}:15/**Ob**
1:19^3:20^2:21/**Jon2**:4/**Mic1**:7f/**4**:3:7/**5**:1:4^2/**6**:6:
11/**Hab2**:4f/**Zep**:11/**3**:8/**Hag2**:7/**Zec**:11,12^3/**5**:
4/**8**:3/**9**:4:10^2:14^3:16,17^2/**10**:7^4:11/**11**:6/**12**:5/
14:5f:5:9^2:11:21/**Mal1**:11/**3**:14,15^2:17/**Mt1**:21:
23^3/**2**:6:23/**3**:11/**5**:4:6:7:8:9:19^2:27:33/**8**:11:12/
10:21^3:22^2/**11**:3:16:23:29,30/**12**:21:31,32:39,40:
41:42/**13**:28:40:42:43:50/**15**:13,14/**16**:18:19^2:25^2
:27/**17**:12:17/**18**:35/**19**:5,6:28^2:29^2/**20**:16:23/
21:16:43:44/**23**:12^2:33:36/**24**:10:13:24:27:29f^2:
31^2:34f:39/**25**:29^3:30:31^2:32:34:46/**26**:2:17/**27**:
21:22/**Mk4**:25^2:30/**9**:49f/**10**:21:30:31:39/**11**:14
/**13**:13:31/**14**:25/**15**:12/**16**:17^2/**Lk1**:32^3:33^2:35^2
:37:48:76/**2**:23:34,35^3/**3**:6:12/**4**:4f:18,19^3/**6**:21:
37f/**7**:19:31/**8**:17:18^2/**9**:54/**10**:15^2:19:28/**11**:31:
32/**12**:3^2:10/**14**:11^2/**16**:9:9f/**17**:33^2/**18**:14^2:18/
19:17/**20**:13:18:28/**21**:10:13f:24:27:33/**22**:20:49
:69/**Jn1**:42/**3**:16:36/**5**:25^2:28:29/**6**:45:48-51:57:
58:68/**7**:33:38/**8**:51/**10**:28^2/**11**:25:26/**12**:27:31/
13:8:26f:31:32/**14**:12,13:17/**15**:5/**16**:10:13:14:
20:26f/**18**:11/**19**:36,37^2/**Act1**:5/**2**:17^2:18^2:20:21^2
:38/**3**:23/**4**:16/**11**/**21**:11/**22**:10/**23**:3/**25**:12:22:
26/**26**:16/**27**:34/**Rom6**:1:5/**8**:13/**9**:26:30/**10**:14
/**11**:26^2/**14**:11/**15**:12/**1Co4**:21^2/**14**:15/**15**:42:49
:51^2:52/**2Co1**:13,14/**3**:8/**5**:2^2:3/**6**:16/**10**:8/**Eph**
5:14:31/**Php2**:10:11/**2Th3**:10/**Tit2**:13/**Heb4**:5/
8:10/**Jas4**:15/**Jud1**:24,25/**Rev**:7:9/**2**:11:17:23/**3**
:4:14/**5**:10/**11**:15:15f/**14**:13/**15**:3,4/**18**:8^2:15:21 ^{2}
/**20**:6/**21**:4:26/**22**:3:4^2:5:18:19

2575

SHE

Gen2:23^2/**3**:6:13:20/**4**:1^2/**8**:12/**11**:29:30/**12**:
11,12,13:15:18:19/**16**:4^4:6:13/**18**:11:12:13:15^2/
19:26:34/**20**:5^2:11,12/**21**:10:14:15:16:19^2/**23**:1/
24:14:18:19:20:21^2:24:36:40:44:45:46^2:47:55:57:
58:65^2:67^2/**25**:1:21^2:22^2:24/**26**:7^3:9^2/**27**:6,7:14:
15:16:17:42:43/**29**:9:10:12,13:32:33^2:34^2:35^3/**30**
:1^2:4:5:6:8:9^2:13:16:17:18^2:19:20^2:21:23,24^4/**31**:
34:35f/**35**:18^2/**36**:2,3/**38**:14^2:15:16^2:17:18^3:19:
25:26:27:29/**39**:10:12^2:13^2:14,15^3:16:17/**Ex2**:1:
3^2:5^2:6^2:9:10^3/**21**:7:8:11:22^2:23/**Lev12**:4^2:5^2:6^2:
7:8^3/**15**:19:20:21,22,23:26^2:27:28:29:33/**18**:10:
12:13:16/**19**:20/**20**:21f/**21**:2,3:14,15/**22**:12:13^2:
28/**Num5**:15:19:24:27^2:28^2:30:31/**12**:1f^3:14^2:15
/**22**:22,23:25:27:28/**26**:58,59/**30**:3:4:5:6:9:10^2:
15/**Deu21**:12:13^2/**22**:13,14:17,18^2:19:20:21:
23,24^2:25,26,27:30/**24**:2:4/**25**:6:7:9/**27**:20:22:23
f/**28**:56,57^3/**32**:11/**Jos2**:3:4^2:6:9:15:16:21^2/**6**:17
:25/**15**:18,19^4/**Ju1**:14f:14^2:15/**4**:5:6:9^2:18:19:21
/**5**:24:25:26^2:29/**11**:36:38:39^2/**13**:2,3:9^2:10:
13,14/**14**:3:17^3/**15**:2/**16**:5:6:8:9^2:14:15:16,17:18 ^{2}
:19^2:20/**17**:3/**19**:2:3:26:28/**20**:5/**Ru1**:6,7^2:8:9:18
:20/**2**:3^2:4,5:7^3:10,11^2:13:14^2:15:17^3:18/**3**:6,7:9:
14:15-18^4/**4**:3:5:10/**1Sa1**:5:7:10^2:11:12,13^2:
15,16:18:19,20^2:21,22:23:28/**2**:5:19/**4**:20^2:21,22 ^{2}
/**19**:12:13:14/**25**:19^3:20^2:23:24:36^3:41:42^2/**28**:
12:13:21:24:25/**2Sa4**:4^2/**6**:16/**11**:3^2:4^3:5^2:26:27^2
/**12**:24/**13**:2f:5:8^2:9:11:12:14:16:17,18:19/**14**:4:
5,6:9:11:12:13:18/**17**:20^2/**20**:18/**21**:8:11/**1Ki1**:2
:3,4:17:22,23:28/**2**:13:14:16:19^3:20:21/**3**:19:20:
27/**9**:16/**10**:1:2^2:4^3:5:6:10:13^2/**11**:20/**14**:17/**15**:
13/**17**:11:12:15^2:18:24/**19**:2/**21**:8:9:15/**2Ki4**:1^2:
2:5^2:6:7:9:11,12:13^2:14:15,16^3:21:22:23:24:25:
26:27^2:28:36:37/**6**:26-30^2/**8**:3:4:6^2/**9**:30:31:33:
34/**11**:1:2,3^2:13,14^2/**14**:26/**22**:14:15,16/**1Ch2**:
21:24/**4**:9:17:18/**7**:16:24/**15**:29/**2Ch8**:11^2/**9**:1:3
:4^2:5:9:12^3/**11**:18:20/**15**:16/**22**:10:11/**23**:12/**34**:
23/**Est1**:11:12:19/**2**:10:12,13,14^4:15:20^3/**4**:4:8/
5:12/**8**:4/**Job3**:12/**39**:14:15:16:18^2:28:29:30/**Ps**
45:14/**113**:9/**Pro1**:21:22/**4**:6^2:8,9^3/**5**:4f:5:6^2/**7**:
10:11,12:13^2:14f^3:21:25^2:26/**8**:1^2:4,5/**9**:3:14:16/
18:22/**23**:26,27,28/**30**:21,22,23/**31**:10:11:12:13:
14:15:16^2:17:18:19,20:21^2:22:24:25:26^2:27:31/
Sol8:9:9f:9/**Is7**:14/**8**:3/**21**:2/**23**:15,16:17^3/**36**:6
/**54**:1^2/**62**/**Jer2**:14/**3**:1:7^2:8^3:9^2/**6**:6:7/**7**:28/**15**:
9/**17**:11/**31**:15/**48**:9:11^2:26:39:42/**49**:2:9,10/**50**:
9:14:15^2:29^2/**51**:8:34,35^3:42:43:49:53^2/**Lam1**:1^2
:2:3^3:4:7^3:8^2:9^3:10^2:11/**Eze5**:5,6,7/**16**:50/**17**:15/
19:5/**23**:7:8^2:9:10:11:12:13:14,15^3:16^3:17:18:
19,20^3:32/**24**:7^2:16/**25**:3/**26**:2^2/**27**:18/**29**:14:15 ^{2}
:16^2:19/**30**:7/**31**:10:15/**32**^{2}:20:21^2/**38**:13/**Dan5**:
10/**11**:6:17/**Hos1**:3:8:2:3^2:5^2:7^4:8^3:12:13^2:15:16
/**3**:1^2/**4**:17/**5**:5:11/**7**:12/**8**:4:8:9^3:10^2/**9**:6:16^2/**10**
:1^2:11/**12**:1^2/**13**:16/**14**:5/**Amo1**:6/**5**:2/**Mic1**:14^2
/**5**:3f:9/**Nah2**:8^2/**3**:9/**Zep2**:15/**3**:2^3/**Zec2**:4/**5**:8:
11^2/**9**:4:7/**Mt1**:18^2:21:23:25/**5**:32/**8**:15/**9**:21:24
:25/**12**:42/**13**:33/**14**:7/**15**:23:25:27/**20**:21/**22**:26
:27:28^2/**26**:8,9:10:12:13^2/**Mk1**:31/**5**:23:26:27^2:
28:29^3:33:39:40:41,42^2/**6**:19:24:25:28/**7**:25^2:26:
28:30/**10**:12/**12**:23^2:43,44/**14**:3:4,5:8^2:66,67/**16**
:10,11^2/**Lk1**:25:41:42/**2**:7^2:36,37^3:38^2/**4**:39/**7**:
38^2:44:45:46:47/**8**:43,44^4:47^3:52^2:53:55/**10**:40^2/
11:31/**13**:13^2/**15**:8^2:9/**18**:4,5^3/**20**:33/**21**:4^3/**22**:
56/**Jn4**:9:11/**8**:7:11/**11**:20:27:28:31:32/**12**:7/**18**
:16/**19**:27/**20**:2:11^2:13:14^2:15^2:16^2:18/**Act5**:8:
10^2/**9**:37:40^3/**12**:14^3:15/**16**:14^3:15^3:17/**25**:13f/
Rom7:2:3^2/**16**:1^2/**1Co6**:16/**7**:11:12:13:34^2:39^2:
40^2/**9**:5/**11**:6^3:10/**Gal4**:26/**Eph5**:33/**1Ti**:10^6/
Heb11:11^2:31^2/**Jas2**:25^3/**1Pe5**:13f^2:13/**Rev2**:20
:21/**12**:2:4:5:14^2/**14**:8/**16**:19/**17**:6^2:7^2/**18**:2:6^2:7 ^{2}
:8:12:19:21:23:24/**19**:8

990

SHOULD

Gen4:7:9:24/**16**:9-12/**17**:1/**18**:17:25/**24**:49/**27**:
45/**30**:30/**31**:12/**32**:18/**34**:31/**41**:38/**42**/**47**:15:
19:26/**Ex3**:15f/**5**:2/**6**:30/**Lev**:21/**10**:18/**22**:14/
Num9:23/**23**:18-24/**27**:3,4^2/**35**:28/**Deu1**:22/**5**:
15/**8**:5/**10**:2/**11**:8/**19**:6,7/**Jos18**:10/**Ju1**:1/**6**:31
/**9**:9:11:28^3:38/**11**:23/**13**:12/**14**:16/**Ru1**:15:21/
4:4/**1Sa10**:7/**12**:23/**18**:18:22/**19**:5/**20**:3:16:32/
21:14,15/**22**:9,10/**23**:9/**24**:14/**25**:11/**26**:20/**28**:
5,6/**29**:6/**2Sa3**:33,34/**5**:2/**9**:8/**11**:11/**12**:5:23/
13:4/**15**:19,20/**16**:9/**17**:6:11/**19**:42/**20**:3:19/**21**:
17/**1Ki2**:26/**5**:5/**8**:35,36/**12**:6:9/**22**:5/**2Ki5**:13/
6:33/**10**:5/**13**:19/**17**:27,28/**1Ch11**:18,19/**13**:2/
16:25/**17**:6/**29**:14/**2Ch10**:8,9/**19**:2/**20**:3:21/**32**:
4/**Ez1**:4/**5**:13/**7**:23/**10**:7,8/**Neh2**:4:9/**5**/**6**:3:11/
8:14:15/**9**:29/**10**:31:34/**13**:1/**Est1**:8:22^2/**4**:8/**6**:6
/**Job3**:20,21/**4**:6/**6**:14/**7**:17/**9**:14/**11**:3/**12**:13/
15:6/**21**:15:19/**22**:18/**29**:25/**31**:11/**32**:21,22/**33**:
13/**34**:4:36/**37**:19,20/**41**:12/**42**:8/**Ps2**:1/**25**:4/
27:10/**32**:6/**48**:1/**49**:8,9f/**62**:2:6/**76**:11/**79**:10/
90:11:12/**101**:2/**111**:1/**119**:7/**131**:3/**Pro5**:16/
14:3/**16**:9/**27**:18/**31**:8/**Ecc3**:13:14:22/**7**:15-17/
8:15/**Sol5**:3/**6**:13/**Is37**:26/**44**:19:25/**48**:17/**49**:
15/**50**:4/**Jer3**:9/**5**:29/**7**:16/**8**:14/**9**:9/**18**:20/**25**:
29/**26**:11/**27**:13/**29**:28^2/**30**:15/**32**:24/**34**:9/**35**:6
/**40**:15^2/**42**:5/**Lam3**:39/**Eze13**:19^2/**14**:3/**16**:20/
18:24/**33**:26/**Dan6**:7/**Hos4**:14/**10**:5/**Amo1**:5f/**6**
:11:12/**Ob1**:12^4/**Jon**:11/**Hab**:13/**Zep2**:15f/**Mal**
1:4:9:13/**2**:7^2/**Mt7**:4/**9**:15/**10**:10/**18**:14:17:21/
19:5,6/**20**:15/**22**:24/**23**:3:9:23/**24**:18/**25**:27/**Mk**
1:4/**2**:19/**7**:27/**12**:19/**Lk1**:43/**2**:1/**3**:3/**9**:41/**11**:
42^2/**16**:12/**17**:10/**22**:32/**24**:47/**Jn4**:21-24/**6**:28:
39^2:40^2/**7**:21,22,23^2/**11**:50:51/**12**:5/**16**:30f/**18**:
14:23/**Act2**:37/**6**:2/**8**:27/**10**:28/**13**:46/**15**:19:20
/**17**:21:26:27/**19**:36/**25**:5/**27**:2:17f:21/**Rom2**:1/
6:2,3/**8**:15^2:26^2:29/**9**:20/**12**:8/**13**:4:5:12,13:14/
14:4:5/**1Co3**:5/**4**:1/**6**:3:4f:13:15/**7**:3^2:5:15:20:25
:29:30:31/**8**:4/**9**:10^2:12:14:27/**10**:23:25/**11**:1:6^2:
7:10:14,15:16:28:34/**12**:11:23/**14**:6:13:27:29,30:
34:37/**15**:30/**16**:2/**2Co2**:5,6/**5**:13,14/**7**:10/**8**:11:

SHOULD Con't)
4:15:20/9:7/10:8/11:2/12:6/Gal2:3:17/4:9/6:
:6:10:14/Eph1:12/2:10/3:13:18,19/4:31/5:8:9:
0f:28/6:20/Php1:7:27/2:5:18/3:12:13:19/Col2
18/3:3:12/4:4/1Th2:12/4:9:11/2Th3:9/1Ti1:
5/2:9,10^2:11/3:10:12^2:15/4:9,10/5:3:4^2:5:7:9:
1:17^2:20:23/6:1:2:8:17:18^2/2Ti2:19/Tit:3:8/3:
0/Heb2:10/5:7f/8:11/12:9/Jas1:9:10,11/3:1f:
/5:13^2:14^2/1Pe2:15/3:7:8:14/5:12:13f/2Pe3:9:
11:12/1Jn2:6/3:11/5:16/2Jn1:4:5/3Jn:8/Rev
10:6

437

SHOULDN'T

1Sa11:12/24:6/2Sa16:19/2Ki5:20/Neh2:3/Job
1:9/4:6/11:2:3/Ps139:21^2/Jer5:29/Eze34:2/
Jon4:11/Mal3:13/Mt18:33/23:23/Mk2:24/8:
32/Lk9:50/Jn6:27/13:6/Act7:26/17:29/19:36/
24:21/Rom14:14:23/1Co7:18^2/9:12/15:9

32

SO

Gen1:4,5:7,8:9,10^2:11,12^2:14,15:21,22:24:27/2:
2:19,20/3:1:6^2:7:10:14:16:23/4:6:16:17/5:3,4,5f
/6:4/7:5/8:3,4:9:11:17:18,19/11:3,4:7:8:12,13f:
32f/12:2f:4:10/13:1:7:11:16/14:23/15:18/16:1:
4:6:15/18:12:19:20:22,23/19:5:11:14:18,19,20:
29:32:33:34:35:36/20:4:17/21:14:16:19:31/22:2
:6:13:19/23:5,6:8:16:19,20/24:5:9:20:21:27:32:
35:46^2:47:49:50:55:58:59:61:65/25:22:25^2:26:34
/26:1:6:15:17:20:21:22:24:30:33/27:5:14:19:20:
31:41/28:1:5:9:10/29:7^2:18:20^2:21:22:28:30:32:
33/30:4:16:35,36:38:39,40:42/31:4:16:17-20:21:
30:34:38:43:45:49:53/32:1^2:21/33:11:14:16/34:
5:20:23:24:30/35:2:4:5:19:27/37:1:3:8:13,14:17:
23:28/38:7:8:9:10^2:11:16:17:18:21:22/39:2:4:6:
22:23/40:1^2:11/41:17:28:30:31:36:45:49:53:
56,57/42:3:5:14:17:26:29/43:7:11:12:14^2:15:17/
44:2:4:6:21:24/45:3:4:7:10:21:24/46:1:5:15:26:
33/47:11:13:17:20^2:26:27:28/48:1:10^2:14:17:20
/49:17:28/50:7:9:12,13:16,17:20:22:26/Ex1:5:7:
9:11:19:20/2:8:9:18/3:20:21/4:3:11:15:17:20:21
:27:29/5:2:10,11:12/6:8,9/7:4:6:10:18:20:21:22
/8:5:9:12:17:24:30:31,32/9:7:10:12:17^2:23:33:35
/10:1:3^2:4,5:8:13:15:18:19:22:27/11:1:10^2/12:
17:21:22:28:36:42:50/13:10:15:17,18:21/14:4:6:
20:22:25:26/15:11/16:10:17:21:23:28,29:30:32:
35/17:2:10:12/19:9:14:20:25/20:11:20/21:12:
18:22:24/22:6:23:24/24:12:13/25:37/26:6:25/
27:18:21/28:3:10:32:35:37,38/29:37:46/30:
11,12:20:30/31:6:10/32:2,3:6:11:12:14:22:24:28
:31/33:6:13^2/34:4:33f/35:20:29/36:1:4-7:18:30/
37:8:25/38:21/39:23:32:42/40:16:30:33:38/Lev
4:3/5:10:17,18/7:38/8:4:21:36/9:5:8/10:2:5:13/
12:8/14:21:36/15:5:26/16:13:22/18:3^2:12:17:
29,30/19:5/20:7:22/21:24/23:44/24:23/25:42:
46/26:22:26/Num1:17,18,19f:54/2:3-31^4:34/3:
16-24:39:42:49/4:17,18,19:34/5:3:21,22/7:6:12:
84,85,86^3/8:2:3:20/9:4,5:6,7:16:19:23/10:12/11
:1:4,5:17:24:32:34/12:1f:3,4:15/13:21:23:32:33/
14:22:25/15:15,16f:36/16:15:18:21:25:27:33:39:
45:50/17:6:11/18:14,15:24/19:13:20/20:2:9:15:
27/21:6:9:25,26:35/22:4:5,6:8:14:19:21:22,23:
25:26:27:35:37/23:3,4:14:17:28/24:1:15-19:25/
25:4:5:8:10,11/26:3,4:51:63:64,65f/27:5:17:20:
22/28:1/29:40/30:13/31:4,5:31:36-40:50/32:2:
14:28:31:33:40/35:20:21/36:6:8:11,12/Deu1:13
:23:41:46/2:1:4:8:14,15:29:30/3:3:29/4:10^2:
16,17:35:40^2/5:16:32/6:3^2:23:24/7:13:15:17/8:
5:15:16^2:17/9:3:4:20/10:3:15/11:8:18:21/12:14
/14:2:7:24:29/16:12:15/17:19/18:1/19:2,3:6,7/
20:5:6/24:12,13/25:6:13,14,15/26:12/27:10/28
:33:56,57^3:60:63/29:6:9:24:27/30:6:12:13:14:16^2
/31:12:13:14:17:22:28:30/32:26/33:28/34:5:9/
Jos1:8:14:17,18/2:4:7/3:2,3,4:6:7/4:4:6:8:17:24^2
/5:1:7:8,9:11,12/6:6-9:20:27/7:4:16:21:22:26/8:
9:16:20,21:22:25:28/9:11:21:24:26/10:3:5:7:10:
13:20:40/11:8:15:16:20:23^2/12:8-24/13:2-7/14:
5:12:13,14/15:13:17:20:63/16:10/17:2:5,6/18:4
:8/19:9:35-39:47,48:49/20:9/21:3:8:19:26:33:40
:43/22:4:6:9:17,18:26,27/23:11/24:1:10:11:14:
25:27/Ju1:3:4,5,6:15:17:20:21:25:27:31,32:33/2
:5:12-14:15:18:23/3:5:7:10:12:17,18,19:30/4:2,3
:9:14:18:19:21:22:23/5:9:28/6:2:6,7:27:40/7:3:
5,6:8,9:11:19,20/8:2,3:21f:21:27/9:2f:3:34:39:43
:49^2:54:56,57/10:7,8:13/11:3:11:17:20:21,22:23:
32:38:39/12:3:6/13:1:2,3:10:12/14:7:16:17:18:
20/15:2:4:6:8:11:12,13:19/16:2:5^2:6^2:8:9^2:12:14:
15:18^2:21:23,24:25,26^2:28:30/17:3:4,5:6:12/18:
2:7:8:11:15,16:26:27:31/19:4:8:10:14:15:21:22:
28/20:6:11:13:19,20:22,23,24:29:31:32:35-39:42
:46,47/21:10,11,12:17:23:24/Ru1:4,5:19/2:3:
10,11:13:14:17:19^3:23/3:2:6,7:10:14/4:1^2:4:5:8:
10:13:15/1Sa1:5:7:23:24:28/2:3:11:15:17:29:31:
36/3:4,5:8:9^2:14:18/4:4:5:10/5:8:10:11/6:3:10:
14:21/7:1:4:6^2:9:13/8:10:19:21:22/9:3:9,10,11:
12,13:14:24^2:26,27/10:12:14:18,19:20:22:23/11:
5:9:11:15/12:9:17:18/13:3,4:5:12:20:22/14:1:13
:23:24,25:27:34:37:45/15:4:6:11:31/16:4:12:13:
19/17:3:20:50,51:55f/18:5:9:26:27:30/19:12:15:
18/20:1:2:3:9:13:16:19:24,25:26:28,29:31:33:36^2
:38:42/21:5:6:13/22:1:5:18/23:5:8:13^2:18:24,25:
28/24:2:22/25:12:21:36:42/26:2:5,6,7:12:15:19
/27:2,3:4:6/28:7,8:15:18:22:24/29:6:11/30:7:
9,10:11,12:16:22/31:3,4:6/2Sa1:10:15/2:2:5:15:
16:23/3:15:16:21^2:30/4:12/5:3:4,5:9:10:12:20^2:
25/6:7:10:13:15:21:23/7:9:17:29/8:6:13:14/9:3:
5,6:7/10:2^2:4:6:15,16/11:6:10:12:13:16:19,20,21
:22/12:1:14:18:28:29,30/13:2:4^2:6:8^2:9:10:17,18
:20^2:29,30/14:14f:21:30:33/15:6:9:12:16:22:29:
37/16:13:14:22/17:11:12:14:17:19:22:23/18:4:6
:30/19:8,9,10:15:26:27:28:39:43/20:2:3:5:7:
8,9,10:16:18/21:2:9:12,13,14/22:25:39/23:16/
24:2:4:13:15:19:21:24/1Ki1:3,4:5:6:15:28:38:53
/2:3:19^2:25:27:30:34:38:46/3:8:9:11:22:24/5:1:5
:10:12:14/6:6:7:23-28^2:38/7:14/8:7:8:59:64/9:
17,18/10:20:23/11:11:12,13:14:22:36/12:2,3,4:
5:12:15:23,24:28/13:6:10:12:19:29/14:2:4:6:17/
15:19:28:29/16:3:17:22:26/17:5:10:15/18:2:6:
16:17:20:26:28:37:40:42:46/19:3:6:8:19/20:9^2:
15:25:32:43/21:2:4:5:8:16:20:25/22:6:9:29:30:
32,33:40:43:52,53/2Ki1:4,5:11:15:17/2:1:4:6,7:
20/3:6,7,8:9:11:12:27/4:5:20:22:24:30/5:1:5:8:9
:12:13:14:19:21/6:14:17:23:26-30^2/7:4^2:5:7:10:
12:16:18/8:2:6:8,9:22:29/9:4:6:12:18:19:20:26:
27:33:36/10:5:16:25/11:9:16:20/12:3:7:8:18/13
:3:5:18:20,21^2/14:4:11:27/15:5:12:18:19,20:25/
16:9:15/17:3:4^2:11:17:20:23:24:27,28/18:7:35/
19:22:26/20:4:11:11f/21:6/22:5,6:14:20/23:1^2:
10:18^2:25/24:14:20/25:16:21/1Ch1:24-27/2:3:4
/4:40,41/5:1:20:22:26/7:17/10:4:6:9:14/11:3:
5,6^2/12:18/13:5^2:10/14:2:8:11:16/15:12:14:28/
16:1:19/17:15:21/18:6/19:2,3^2:4:14/20:4/21:3:
6:14:19,20:21:25/22:3:5^2:8:11:14:16/23:1/24:5/
28:8:10/29:15:19:23/2Ch1:8:12/2:7:15/4:11/5:
1:9:13,14^2/7:1:3:10:11:13/9:22:30/10:12:15:16/
11:4:17/12:5:9/13:12:13,14:18,19/14:7:13/15:
19/16:3:9:10:13,14/17:5^2:10:12/18:3,4,5:8:22:
28:29^2:31/19:4/20:3:6^2:10:24:25:30:37/22:9/23
:8:15,16,17:21/24:5:6^2:7,8:13:16:17,18/25:10:12
/26:4:15:21/27:2:5/28:14:19f:21:24/29:10:17:
22:31:34:35:36/30:5:6:8:10:13:15:21:22:23/31:4
:16/32:21:25:26:27/33:11/34:18:22:28:33/35:
18:22:24,25/36:12:13/Ez2:62,63:64,65:70/3:13
/4:24/5:1:10:16/6:1:6:14/8:16:21:23:30:32/9:2/
10:5:13:16-19/Neh1:5/2:1:5,6:14,15:18/4:1:10:
13:19^2:22/5:7:12/6:3/7:64,65/8:1^2:12:16/9:11:
12:18:25:27:30:33:36/10:32:39,40/11:25-30/12:
47/13:10:15:19^2:25:26:28:30/Est1:11:21/2:2:8:
16:17/3:2:14/4:6:9:12:17/5:2:5/6:6:7,8:11/7:1:
10/8:4:8:13:14/9:1:14:19:23:28:32/Job1:9:
12,13:19/2:7:10:12/5:16:19/6:3:15-18:19-21:29
/7:3:9:20:21/8:9:16/9:4^2:7:29:31:34/10:4-7:9:12
/12:7,8,9:11/14:3:5:6:11,12:14:16:18,19/15:3/
16:3:13:22/19:3:5/21:4:34/22:12:14/23:15/24:
14,15/25:5/27:14/28:3,4/30:6/31:34/32:6:10:
20/33:10:20:30/34:23/36:24:26/37:7:19,20:23/
38:4:21:25-27/39:11/40:8:19/41:15-17:33/42:3:
9:12/Ps3:1^3:2/7:17/9:14/10:4:18/13:6/16:8/17
:13,14/18:24:36:42/26:2/27:13/28:3:4/29^2/30:
12/31:16:24/32:11/37:27/39:7/41:6:10/42:1/
43:5/45:3^2/46:2/48:13/49:8,9f:16/50:14,15/55:
18/56:1:13/57:3/62:3,4/68:2/69:5:16^3:19:32/
71:7/73:2:6:10:16:22^2:23/77:2:9:11/78:4:6:32:
33:44:53/81:12/82:5^2/85:3:4/86:5^3:13^2:16/89:
38/92:4/94:12,13/95:9/102:18:21,22/104:5:9/
105:43/106:6:8:15:23:29:44:47/107:1^2/109:21:
27/113:9/116:5/118:1:21:29/119:11:17:133:
140:149:157:159:166/125:2/127/132:1/135:3:
18/138:6/139:14/142:7/Pro1:24:28/3:11,12/5:
13/6:21:29:31/7:21/8:32:34/9:7,8/10:19:24:27/
12:28/17:14/19:24/21:1:6/22:7/23:1:24,25/24:
13,14/25:8,9,10:27/26:9:11:24,25,26/27:23,24/
30:33/31:28/Ecc1:16-18/2:3^2:9^2:11:15^2:17^2:20-
20-23^2:24-26^2/3:11:12:18^2:19:22^2/4:2:5,6:8^2:16
/5:1^2:4:8:11/6:2:3:10:11/7:14:15-17/9:2,3:7:15:
17/10:15/11:10/Sol1:6/2:2/3:3/4:7/6:10:13/7:
5/Is1:2:22/3:6/4:1^2/5:8^2:13:25/7:15,16/8:2:12:
19/10:2:11:19/11:9/13:19/16:6:9/17:3:9:11/19:
14/21:4:8,9:12/22:17:25/28:11:13:17^2:18:22:28
/29:8:11:13/30:8:18:26/33:4/36:1:12/37:5:20:
27/38:4:8/39:1f/40:7:21^2:26/41:7/42:19/43:20
/44:9^2:13:18/45:19/47:4:11/48:5:6:8:16/50:4/
51:1:12/52:14,15^2:14,15f/53:7/54:9/55:11/57:
13/58:2^2/60:15/63:2:5:14:17/64:3:9/65:8:17/
66:18:22/Jer2:10,11:21:23/3:4,5:6:9^2/5:6^2:18:
22:25:31/6:9/7:20:31:32/8:9:11/9:12/10:4:24/
11:5^2:19:21,22/12:1^2:8/13:2:5:11:15:16:23/15:4
:12,13/17:2,3:10:11/18:4:6:16/19:3:8:11^2:12/22
:15:24,25/23:30,31/25:7:17:18:19,20:29/27:6/
28:9/29:7:22/30:10:14^2:15^2/31:33:33f:40/32:8:
9:31:35:42/33:20,21^2:22/34:6/35:3/36:4:18/37:
4:21/38:5:11:16:27/39:13:17/40:6/42:2:8:12:18
/43:2,3:4:7/44:6/50:29:31/51:49:57:61,62:64/
52:3:27/Lam1:8/2:14:17/3:44/5:20/Eze1:
19,20,21/2:1f/3:2:9:25:26/4:8/5:14/6:12/7:23:
24/8:3:5:10:11/9:6:10/10:2:17/11:8:15:20:24/
12:3^2:4:7/13:20:22/14:11^2/15:4:5,6/16:13^2:29:
31:33,34:52/17:10^2:14/18/19:9/20:9,10:11:21:
29/21:27/22:26:31/23:7:9^2:16:27:31/24:6:27/
25:12/26:14/28:2,3/29:18f:20f/30:19/31:10/33
:7:8:22:24:28:31/34:5:22:25:29f:29:31/35:6/36:
18:27/37:7:10:18,19,20/38:6:15,16/39:14:15,16^2
/40:4:17:29,30:41/41:15,16:19,20/43:10/44:2:
30/45:20/47:5:15f:17/Dan1:16:18,19/2:6:15:16
:18/3:7:21:23:26:30/4:20:36/5:10:13:24,25/6:2:
4:5:8:9:16:17:22:28/7:4:13:14:16:19/8:3:5:12f:
17:25^2:26/9:3:5:11:13:14:15:18/10:11:13/11:6f:
17/12:4:8/Hos1:2:3:6:16f/3:2/4:5/6:11/7:4/9:7
/11:4^2:7/12:8/13:7/Joe1:11/2:14/Amo1:4:7:10:
12:14/2:5/3:12/5:25,26,27/6:1/7:2:3:5/8/9:12/
Ob1:15/Jon:6/3:3^2/4:5:7/Mic2:7/6:12/Hab2:2
:13/Zep1:4/2:13:15f^3/3:7:9/Hag1:9:11:14,15/2
:5:13:15:16,17/Zec1:16:21/2:4/3:5,6/6:7^2:15/7:
3:13/8:4:11:13/9:3:7/11:9:12:13/12:7/13:2/14:
19/Mal2:7/3:3:9:10^2/Mt1:17f/2:8:21:22/3:11:
15/4:15,16:24/5:15,16:19:23:29/6:16:18:25:30:
31,32:34/7:19/8:26:28:31/9:1:5,6:33:36:37^2:38/
10:31/11:2:17:25:28/12:1:10:22:39,40:43,44,45^2
/13:6:12,13:16:34,35:40:56:58/14:7:10:14:15:29
/15:5,6:13,14/16:8/17:2:16:26,27/18:8:14:25:
35/20:4:10:16/21:20:27:32:39/22:4:10:25:26:28
:32/23:2:25:35/24:14:15:24:26:27:33:39:42:44/
25:5,6:13:21:23:24,25:27/26:19:44:49/27:21:40:
41,42,43:64:66/28:15/Mk1:4:7:34:39:43,44/2:2
:4:9,10,11:15/3:20/4:1:7:19:36:40/5:18:20:30/6
:12:14:20^2:25:27:31:32:34/7:4:5:12,13:29/8:6:7:
13:32/9:10:18:20:33:41:50/10:1f:8:24:42:46:49/
11:6:7:11:13:18:25:33/12:8:12:20,21,22^2:28/13:
5/14:11:16:45:51,52/15:28:29,30:36:44/16:5:6/
Lk1:21:35:62/2:27:52/4:8:44/5:3:5:6:18,19:
23,24:28:33/6:8:33:46/7:4:6,7,8:42/8:14:18:24:
26:29:33:37:39:45/9:6:9:15:39:47:53f/10:2^2:29:
41/11:9:17^2:26:35/12:32:40/14:23:33/15:3,4:16
:20:24/16:2:5,6:8:8f:9f:18:25/17:10:35,36/18:20
:38/19:4:22:23:35/20:15:19:31:37,38/21:28/22:
6:32:54/23:3:4:24:35:39:53:56/24:3:4:17:25:29:
50f/Jn1:22:39/3:5:7:8:14:15:16^2:26:28/4:21-24:
30/5:10:16:23:28:34:40:41,42:46/6:2-5:12:15:24
:27:53/7:4:9:15:16:19:21,22,23:28:43:47/8:7:12:
19:28:36:42:43:45:53/9:7:15:16:19:24/10:7:12:
29:34,35,36/11:3:27:29:31^2:41:42:45:53:55:57/
12:18:40:46:50/13:4:18:19:25:32:34/14:2,3^2:5:9:
27:29:31/15:11:16:19:20/16:1:4:12:19:33/17:1:
10:11:12:13:21:23:24:26/18:12:15:29:39/19:11:
17:20:25:29:31:32:33:35:38:42/20:21:30,31/21:
6^2:11:23/Act1:12:21,22/3:7,8:10:12:19/4:4:7:15
:18/5:15:22:31:32:38/6:2:8:11/7:4:8:10:12:15:
24:35:40:41:43:51/8:8:19:27:32:35/9:2:12:17^2:
21:25/10:21:23:27:29:33^2:48/11:21:29/12:9:10:
14:23/13:3:16:49/14:8:10:18/15:6:7:17:19:25:
39/16:3:5:8:24:36:37:39/17:11:22/18:11:21:
25,26/19:9:10:12:16:26/20:3:10,11,12/21:11:15
:26,27:35:40/22:5:24^2:27/23:6:9:11:18:31/24:26
/25:21:23:26/26:1:11:18^2:19:22/27:1:4:7,8:13:
14,15:17:25:32:43:44/28:13:20:23:28,29/Rom1:
5:11,12:13:15:20:24:25:26:27:28/2:5:19:23:27/3
:2:19:28/4:1:11:14:16:18/5:1:12:14:18:20/6:1:5^2
:6:11:19/7:4^2:9:10:13:18:22:23,24,25/8:1:4:12:
15:29/9:4^2:5:16:17:18:23,24:31/11:7:8^2:10:14:
17:19:24:25:32/12:1:4,5^2:6:8/13:2:3:6:12,13^2/
14:6:9:13:18:23/15:4^2:7:13:14:15,16:17:22/16:4:
6:12:23:25,26,27/1Co1:10:13:14:20:23:29/2:13/
3:13:21/4:1:5^2:7^2:16/5:1:2^2:7:8/6:2:3:15:20/7:5^3
:8:23:24:25:29:33:38/8:4:7:11:13/9:19:20:21:22:
24:26/10:11:12:13^2:14:32:33/11:2:10:19:21:27:
32:33:34/12:12:20:24:25/13:2:9^2/14:4:5:12:13:
15:22:23:39^2/15:28:39:49:58/16:9:17:19/2Co1:
3,4^2:12:15,16^3/2:3^2:7:9:13:14/3:11:13/4:1:2:10:
18/5:4:9:11:13,14:15:16/6:3/7:4:9:12:15^2/8:4:6:
7^6:9^3:11:15/9:4:5:8:10:11:12/10:9/11:4:8,9:15:
18:19,20:22^2:33/12:1:4:7^2/Gal1:6:16/2:2:7,8,9:
14:16/3:4:8,9:23/4:5:6:17^2:29/5:1:7/6:2:12/
Eph1:7:18/2:4^2:9:16/3:13:18,19^2/4:3:15,16^2:28
/5:15,16:24:27:31:33/6:11:13/Php1:25:27:30/2:

(SO Con't)
12:15:16:17:28/3:5:6^2:7:11/4:14/Col1:9:10:11:18:21:28/2:5:10:16:18/3:1:13:21/4:10:14/1Th1:6:9/2:3:5:8:9:16/3:7:13/4:3,4:10:13:18/5:6:10:11/2Th1:7:11/2/1Ti1:16^2/2:2:8:15/3:6:7:15/4:2:8:15/5:7:12:14:20:23/6:8:14:16/2Ti1:6/2:15:21/4:1:21/Tit1:1:5:9:13:16/2:5:8:14:15/3:7:8/Phm1:7:15:24/Heb:9/2:1:6^2:17/3:7,8:13/4:5:9:16/5:7f:11/6:17/7:2:15:23:24/8:4:9:10^2/9:15:28/10:1:5:15:16^2:19/11:12^2:17:22:28/12:1:9:12:13:15:17:19:21:25:27/13:9:13:19/Jas1:4:10,11:16:21:22/2:11:12:17:19:22:23:24:26/3:5:10:13/4:2^2:7:12/5:16/1Pe1:3:6:7:12:13:17:22/2:1:5:8:9:24/3:4/4:6:11:19/5:13f:13/2Pe1:6:9:10:15:19/2:9:10:12:19/3:4:11:14:17/1Jn1:3:4:6/2:1:11:14:21:24:27^2:28/3:5:6:9:10:13:16:24/4:2:5:17:19/5:2:6,7,8^2:9:12:13/2Jn1:1:8/3Jn:8:15/Rev:7/3:11:18:19/7:1/8:7:12/10:9:10/11:6:10/14:16:19/16:2:12:19/17:3:7:17/18:14^2:15:16/20:3/22:15

3350

SOME

Gen3:6^2:12/5:1/6:1f/8:20/14:10/15:2,3/18:6:6f/24:43/27:2,3,4:17:38f/30:14^2:16/33:13:15/34:1/37:2:26,27:29/40:1:4:14/41:10/42:2:4:27/44:28/Ex9:20/16:27/18:21/22:13/24:5/28:30,31f/29:19,20:21^2/30:36^2/35:24:26/Lev4:7:25:30:34/5:2:9:17,18/8:15,16:23:24:30^2/13:24/14:4^2:14:17:25:27:28:33,34/15:25/16:14/19:16/25:25/Num9:6,7/11:4,5:25:27/13:20:23:27:33/16:29/19:4:9/21:1/22:7/25:1/31:3/32:37,38/Deu1:13:15:36/13:12,13,14/14:26^2/15:11/Jos7:1:2:21:22/11/15:13:18,19/16:9/19:47,48/21:3:4/Ju4:19^2/6:17:19:37/9:4/14:8:9^2/16:25,26/17:4,5/18:14:22/21:17/Ru2:2:16/3:3^2/1Sa1:2:15,16:24/2:7/8:12/9:9,10,11/10:27/11:3/13:7/16:15,16/17:26:30/24:3:9,10/26:10/27:1/29:6/30:11,12:22/2Sa2:12:14/3:8:22/6:19/10:1/11:24/13:5:7:8^2/16:7,8/17:9:13/18:9:20/23:15:22/1Ki2:2/8:46/10:1:16,17/11:15/13:7:19^2/14:3/15:20/18:5/19:6:7/20:17/22:11/2Ki2:16^2:23/4:1:38:39:41:43/5:13/7:9/8:1:4/12:4,5/13:15:20,21/17:1:25/19:2/20:7:18/25:23/1Ch4:32,33:34-39/9:3:28:32/11:10:18,19/12:19/16:3/17:1/26:11/2Ch1:14/6:36/8:2/9:15/12:7/13:18,19/17:11/18:6,7:10/19:3/21:3,4/23:1/28:12/29:30/30:11/32:1:21/33:25/36:7/Ez2:68:70/4:20/6:21,22/7:28/9:1:2:13/10:16-19/Neh1:2/4:10/5:1:2,3,4:5/7:70/9:4/11:2:25-30:36/13:15:16:19:23/Est4:14/6:7,8/Job2:10/7:12/18:2/26:14/33:7:17,18/34:23/35:7/38:3/Ps19:13/20:7/35:15/37:21/45:16/55:8/69:20/90:10/Pro1:4:26/3:27,28/5:2/12:18/13:7^2/19:24/20:17/24:21,22/25:6,7/30:18,19f/Ecc5:8/6:2/7:15-17^2/8:14^2/Sol2:14/8:11/Is3:6/4:2,3,4f/8:16/9:11,12f/10:27f:28,29/22:9,10,11/39:7/41:23/43:21/45:19/56:12/65:1f^2:8/66:21/Jer1:10/4:17/9:2/15:19/19:1^2/24:3^2/26:17/27:1f/31:32f/32:44/33:3/38:11/40:5/52:8:15:16/Eze3:5/4:4,5f/10:6:7,8/14:1/20/28:12f^2/33:21f:30/39:15,16/40:28f/43:20/45:19/Dan1:1:3,4/2:1:41,42^2/3:8^2:12:20/6:4:14/7:7/8:10/11:34:35/12:2^2/Hos1:2/4:18/Joe2:32^2/Amo1:2/4:11/Hab3:1f/Hag2:12/Zec:4/6:15/14:18/Mt2:1/6:13f/9:2:3/12:1:2:38^2/13:4:5:8:19/14:15/15:1/16:4:14^3:28/18:11f/19:3:9f:12^3:30/20:3:6/21:8:33/22:6:15:16:23/23:34/25:9:27/26:55:67/27:47/28:11:17/Mk1:3f/2:6:16:18:20:24/4:3:4:5,6:8^2:11,12:15^2/5:10/6:35,36:41/7:1:2:28/8:3:22:28^2/9:1:14:29f:43,44f:45,46f/10:2:13:24f:48/11:4,5/12:1:38:41/13:3,4/14:4,5:24f:48:57:65:68f/15:28f:35:40/16:17f/Lk1:28f:66/2:8/3:14/4:41/5:17:18,19^2/6:1:2:7:39/7:3:6,7,8/8:2:5:12:43,44f/9:7:8:27:59f/10:29:37/11:5,6f:15:29,30:49/13:1:30^2:31/16:9f:24/18:9:15/19:14:23:35:39:47/20:9:27:37,38:39/21:5:16/23:17,f/24:22,23^2:24/Jn1:14/2:7,8:15/3:5f/4:8:10:15:32:45:51/6:37:64/7:12:25:40:44/8:8:37/9:9^2:16/10:20/11:37,38:46/12:20:29/13:7:29^2/14:17/16:17,18/18:21/21:10:12/Act1:11/2:15/3:3/4:1/5:15:36:37/6:9:11/7:12/8:2/9:25:29/10:5,6:23:32/11:20^2:27/12:1/14:4^2:19/15:1:2:5:24:33f/16:13^2/17:4:4f:5:6:18^2:20:32/18:14:23/19:9:31:32^2:33/20:30/21:16:23:26,27:34^2/23:9:12,13:20/24:1:18/27:30:35/28:14:24^2:28,29f/Rom1:11,12f/3:3:5^2:8/9:18^2/11:14:17^2:25:31/14:5/15:15,16:27/1Co1:11:12^2/3^2/4:18/6:2:11:12f:12:13/7:7:12/8:5:7:9/9:7^2:10:13/10:8:10:19/11:24f:30/12:10:13^4:22:23:28/14:5:6:9:26^2/15:6:12:20:29:34^2:34f:49/2Co1:13,14/5:12/8:14/9:4/10:1:2:10/11:3/12:16^2/Gal1:11/2:4:12/3:16/5:11/6:1:5/Eph3:14,15^2/4:11^2/5:13/Php1:15:16,17/3:15/1Th2:6:16/2Th3:11/1Ti1:19/4:1/5:15:24:25/6:3:10:21/2Ti2:12:18:20/3:9/4:1/Heb1:12/4:1:6/5:7f/9:4/10:25/11:34^2:35:36:37,38^3/13:2/Jas2:19/5:15/1Pe2:8/4:10/5:8/2Pe3:15,16^2/2Jn1:4/3Jn:3:10/Jud:3:4:23/Rev:1:20f/2:10:14:15/3:4/9:2:17,18/13:18f/15:3,4f/21:3f

743

THAN

Gen4:13/19:9/25:23/27:46/29:19:30/37:3/38:26/39:9/41:38/49:12^2/Ex14:12/18:11/20:3/22:20/36:4-7/Lev13:3:4:21:25:26:32:34/17:8,9/20:5/25:53/27:13/Num14:3:12/16:3^2/18:22/22:15/24:3-9/26:64,65f/30:15/31:51,52/35:30/Deu4:38:39/7:1:7:17/9:1:13,14/11:23/14:2/15:18/17:20/20:1/25/26:19/30:5/Jos7:3:21/10:2:11/Ju2:19/8:2,3:2,3f/9:13/11:25/14:18^2/15:2/16:30/Ru2:14:22/3:10:12/4:15/1Sa1:8/2:29/9:2:5:9,10,11/15:22^2:28/18:13:17:30/24:17/29:4/2Sa1:23^2:26/6:22/13:14:15:16/17:14/18:8/19:7/20:5:6/21:16/24:14/1Ki1:37:46,47^2/2:32/3:12/4:31/6:17/9:27,28/10:7:23:27/12:2,3,4:32,33f/13:33/14:9:22/16:25:30^2:33/18:27/19:4f/20:10/2Ki5:12/6:16/7:13/14:17/18:20,21^2/21:9:11/1Ch2:34,35f/4:9:27/12:3-7/21:13/29:25/2Ch2:5/9:6:22/10:4:8,9:10/11:21/12:8/19:7/21:13/24:13/25:9/29:34/30:2,3/32:7/33:9/Ez9:6:13/10:10/Neh7:2/9:5/Est1:8:19/2:17/4:11/6:6/Job4:17^2/5:14/6:3/7:15/9:31/11:6:9^2/12:3/15:9:10/22:12^2/23:2:12/25:5/28:17/30:1^2/31:23^2/32:4/33:12/34:19/35:2,3:11/42:12/Ps4:7/8:5:5f/19:10^2/37:16/38:3,4/39:5,6/40:12/45:7/49:10/51:7/52:3^2/57:10/58:9/62/63:3/69:31/71:21/78:18/84:10^2/87:1/93:4/97:8,9/105:24/108:5/113:4/118:8:9/119:14:20:37:71,72:98:99:100:102,103:127/130:6/131:1/135:5/137:5,6/148:13/Pro3:13,14,15^2/8:10:19/11:15/12:9/15:16:17/16:8:16^2:19:32^2/17:1:10:12/18:19:24/19:1:22/20:15/21:3:9:19/22:1^2/24:5^2/25:6,7:24/26:1:2:9:10:12:16:17/27:3:4:5:6:16/28:6:23:24/29:20/31:10/Ecc1:16-18/2:7,8:9:13,14^2:24-26/3:12:18:22/4:2:5,6:9:13/5:5/6/7:1^2:2:3:5:8^2:10:19:26/8:15/9:4:16:17:18/Sol1:1:2:4/4:10^2/5:9:10/Is8:20/9:8,9,10/10:10:15^2/13:12/14:29/23:17/29:16/30:10,11:26/32:10/40:17/41:24/44:25/49:6/54:1/55:9^3/56:5/57:7,8:11/65:1f^2:5/66:3/Jer3:11/4:13/7:26/8:3/16:12/20:7/31:33f/33:10,11:25,26/42:21/48:32/Lam4:6:7f^3:9:19/Eze3:7/4:11/5:5,6,7:9/8:6:13:15/16:3:13:31:51:54/21:9,10,11/22:26/23:11:14,15/24:6/25:8/28:2,3/31:8:14/36:11/38:2,3f/41:7/43:14/Dan1:15:20/2:30/3:19:28/4:36/6:3/7:7:20:23:24/8:3/11:2:13:36:37/12:1/Hos1:7/4:18/Amo6:2:12:13/9:7/Jon4:3:8/Mic7:4:11/Nah3:8/Hab1:8^2:13/Zep2:15f/Hag:8,9/Zec12:11/Mt3:11/5:20:29:30/6:25:26/8:24/10:15:24:31:37^2/11:9:11^2:22:24/12:6:7:12:41:42:43,44,45^2/13:23f/18:8:9:13/19:24/27:64/Mk1:7/2:21:22/6:2,3/8:37/9:3:43,44:45,46:47/10:25/12:31:33:43,44/Lk3:13:16/4:4:27/6:40/7:26:28^2/10:12:14:35/11:26^2:31:32/12:1:6:7:23:24/13:2/14:8:10:26^2/15:7/16:8/17:2,3/18:25/21:3/Jn1:15:30:50/3:19:31/4:1:12^2/5:20:36/7:21,22,23/8:53^2/10:29/12:43/13:16^2/14:28/15:20/17:16/19:8/21:15:15f/Act5:29/15:27,28,29/17:11/20:35/23:21/24:11/26:13/27:11/Rom2:25:27/3:9/7:17/13:11/14:2/15:20/1Co1:25^2/3:4:11:18/4:6/6:13/7:9/8/9:15/10:22/11:16:17/12:31/14:5:7:18:19:27/15:6:10:45/2Co2:5,6/7:12:15/9:7/10:8/11:4^2:5/12:6/Gal1:7:8:9:12/3:18/4:1:27/Eph1:21/3:20/5:5/Php1:23/2:3/3:8/4:7:18/1Ti5:8/2Ti1:18/2:10/Heb1:4^2:9/2:7:9/3:3^2/4:12/6:16/7:7/8:4:6/11:4:26:35/Jas3:1/1Pe1:7/2:10/3:1:17/5:10/2Pe1:5/2:11:12:20:21/1Jn3:12:20f/4:4/3Jn1:4/Rev:5

615

THAT

Gen1:9,10:11,12:23:31/2:1:19,20:24/3:2,3:5:8:20f:22/4:24:26/6:1:1f:5:7:9,10:12,13:21/7:8,9:13:22/8:7:11:13:17:20/9:9,10,11:15/10:32/11:1:7:8^2:9^2:10,11:12,13f:12,13:14,15:20,21:32f^2/12:2f:4:6:8:10:11,12,13/13:1:9:11:16/14:3:8,9:14:15:16:23/15:5:8:12:14:17:18/16:14/17:5:7,8:9,10:11:19:22:23:24-27/18:14:19:20:19^2:25^2/19:1:11:18,19,20:21:22^2:27:29:31:32:33:34:35^2:36/20:2:3^2:6^2:9,10^2:13:17/21:4,5:7:10:22:23^2:28,29:30:31^2/22:11:12:14:16:20-23/23:5,6:14,15/24:3:6^2:7^2:9f:14:21:28f:35:44:46:49:65/25:16:25:30:33/26:12:22:24:28:29:32:33^2/27:2,3,4:11:12:19:27,28,29:31:42/28:6,7,8^4:11:12/29:3:12,13:21:23:33/30:9:14f:16:27^2:31,32:33:35,36^3:38^2/31:1:10:12:12f:12:24:26:32:35f:38^2:42:43:49:51,52/32:5:6:9:11:17:21:25:32/33:16:17/34:22:23:30/35:5:7:22/36:20,21:31-39/37:19,20^2:21,22/38:8:11:13:14:16:17:24:26/39:2:3:7:13^2:16:17:22:23^2/40:1:6:9,10,16/41:1:15^2:20:26:27:30:31:32:33:36:44:49:51/42:1:2:5:6:14:15:16:19:23:28:29/43:6:7:12:14:16:21:25/44:7^2:9:10:21:27:28:30:31:32/45:5:7:10^2:27/46:3,4:28:31^2/47:13:22:26:28:29:31/48:1:2:10:11:14:17:20^2:22/49:7f:9:17^2:27:28/50:5^2:15:20:25/Ex1:6:7:19/2:1:12:13:14^2:25/3:2^2:10:11:12:13:16:19:21^2/4:5^2:11:17:21:31^2/5:2^2:6:9:16:19/6:6:7:11:13:26:30/7:2:5:9^2:14^2:15:16:17:18:21/8:5:9:10:15:22:24:26:29:31,32/9:1:5:7^2:10:12:14:26:29:30/10:1:2:4,5^2:7:11^2:13:15:19^2:23/11:1^2:7:10/12:7:8:10:13:15:17:19^2:21:22:23f:23:25:29:36:37:40,41:51/13:15^2:16:17,18:19/14:4:5:18:20:21:25:26:28:30/15:23:25/16:3^2:6:11,12:13:26:28,29^3:32/17:7:14/18:8:11:22^2/19:9:10/20:12:20:22:25/21:2f:6:12:18:19:20:22:29/22:6:11:24:31/23:4:11:15:33^2/24:12/25:1:26,27:37:40/26:6:25/27:21/28:2:3^2:10:21:30,31f:32:35:37,38/29:13:22:23:33:37:46^2/30:2:6:11,12:30/31:6:10:12,13:14,15/32:4:7:8:12:25:28:34/33:6:12:13^2:16^2/34:1:7:9:18:19f:27f:27:28^2:29:33f/35:2:3/36:4-7:18/37:8:9:25/38:4:21/39:23/40:15:30:38/Lev3:3,4,5:17/4:2:6:13:31/5:3:10:17,18/6:3:11:17:21:25:30/7:3:15:16^2:19^3:21:24:29:36:38/8:21^2:30:31:34^2:36/10:12:15^2:16:20/11:2,3:4-7:12:21,22:23:26:27:32:36:41,42^3:44/12:8/13:5:12:20:21:22:23:25:26:28:31^2:37:39:43:55:56/14:3:21:35:36^2:42:44:51,52:57/15:10:11:19:20:26^2:31/16:13:35/17:11:12^2:14:15^2/18:6f:25^2:28f:28/19:5:10:34/20:3:5:6:20:22:22f:23/21:11f:16,17/22:6^2:8:11:17,18:20:21:22:24/23:1:12:21^2:28:30,31:35:39:40:43/24:3,4:5-8:15,16:18/25:4:5:6,7^2:12^2:20:21,22:24:29:41:50:54/26:10:13:22:26:34,35:46/27:1:9:11,12:13:14,15:16:23:27/Num1:1/4:8:17,18,19:26:36:46,47,48/5:1:3:5,6:11,12:18:19^2/6:3,4:5^2:11:12:20^2:22,23/7:87/8:2^2:22/9:4,5:6,7:11:15^2:22:23/10:3:28/11:4,5:12:17:25:29^2:31:32:34:35/12:1f:7,8:14/13:16:20:23:24/14:14^3:15:17,18^2:20,21^2:22:26,27:40:44/15:7:17,18^2:19,20,21:31f:39/16:3:8,9:10:11,12^3:13^2:21:26:28^2:30^2:34:40:45/17:1:8/18:7:14,15:16:18:20:23:32/19:1:19/20:2:3:8/21:1:2^2:14:17,18:24f:34:35/22:5,6^2:9:11^2:19:20:26:28:36:38/23:7-10:13:18-24:26/24:1:3-9^2:13^2:15-19:25f/25:4:12,13/26:5-11:64,65f/27:3,4:6,7:8:17:20/28:1:18:25:26^2:27:31/29:1:2:6:8:11:12:13:35/30:1^2:4:5/31:16:22:23:30/32:7:10,11:13:23/33:3,4:40^2:49:50,51/35:9,10:21:25/36:8/Deu1:6:9:18:24,25:28^2:34,35^2/2:4:7:8:10:14,15:20:30/3:12:18^2:23,24,25/4:10^2:14^2:15:18:21,22:26^2:28:34:35^2:37:40^3:47/5:11:14:22^2:24:26,27:29/6:3^2:23:24/7:4:8:9:13:17/8:3^2:5:11^2:14^2:15:16^2:17^3:18:20/9:3:4:5^2:9:13,14:19:21:23:25/10:1:2^2:8:9:15/11:8:12:13:14:16:21/12:16:31^2/13:8,12,13,14^5:15:16:18/14:6:21:24^2:29/15:4,5^2:11:15^2:17:18/16:1:3^3:8:10:20/17:5:8:15:16:19^2:20/18:1:2:12:16:20/19:2,3:6,7:14/20:20/21:3^2:13^2/22:17,18:25,26,27/23:4:21/24:1:12,13:18^3:22^2/25:6:13,14,15:18/26:2,3:12^2:17:18^2/27:11/28:2-6:10:13:47,48:52:53:56,57:61:63:64:66:67^2/29:1:2,3:4^3:6^2:9:11:13:18^3:20:21^2:22:23:27^2/30:2:6:7,8:12:13:14:16^2:18:19^3/31:2:7:10,11:12:13:17:22:24:28:29/32:22:26:29^3:39:40,41:48/33:1:13/34:4:9/Jos1:2:8/2:2^2:3:6:9:11:12,13:14:19:23/3:1:2,3,4:7^2:10^2:15,16/4:6:7:19:22^2:24^3/5:1:2,3:4,5^3:6^2:8,9:11,12/6:11:24:26/7:1:8:12^2:13:14:15:17:21:26/8:9:11,12,13:14:20,21:25:31:34/9:9:19:22:24^2/10:10:11:17:18^2:20:21:26:27:28/11:8/13:32^2/14:10:11:12^2:15/15:2,3,4:7:16/17:4/18:7^3/19:50/20:6:8:9^2/22:17,18^3:20:22,23^2:24,25:26,27:28:29:31:34/23:3:7:13:14/24:3:12:25:26/Ju1:4,5,6:16:24:31,32/2:1:5:10:15:18/3:1f:10:12:17,18,19:24^2:30/4:4:9:12:20:23:24/5:31/6:2:10^2:16f:17^3:20:22:25^2:28:29:38:40/7:1:2:12,13:19,20/8:2,3:10^2:14:15:19:27:28/9:3:9:13:16^2:19:24:25:26:27:36^2:38:54:55/10:7,8:12:17/11:4:9:13:26:29:30,31:39:40/12:3:4:5:6/13:4:7:13,14^2:16:17:21^3/14:2:4^2:6:12/15:11:12,13^2:15/16:2:5^2:12:14:18:19:20:28/17:2:7,8/18:1:4:26/19:9/20:5:12:13:21:25:27,28:31:32:35-39:40,41^2:44:46,47/21:3:5^2:7,8,9:17:18:19/Ru1:4,5,6,7:12:13^2:18/2:4,5,6:19:20^2/3:1:2,6:7:10:12:14:15-18/4:4^2:5:6f:9:10^2/1Sa1:3:15,16:17:26/2:13,14:15:22:30^3:31:34:36/3:14:20/4:1:5:10:12f:19^2:20^2/5:5/6:3:4,5:7^2:9^2:15:16:18:21/7:2:3:6:7:13/8:5/9:20:23/10:2^2:5:6:7:9:12:16:18,19/11:8:9:11:12/12:5:10:12:17^2:20^2:22:23/13:3,4^2:5:11^3:15:22/14:1:3:10^2:17:18:22:23:28^2:29^2:32:33^2:34:39:45/15:1:9:11^2:12:15:21:35/16:2^2:13:14:19/17:26:28:43:46:47:50,51:55f^2/18:9:18:22^2:25^2/19:8:15:16:18^2:19/20:3:6:7^2:9:12:21^2:22:26^4:28,29:30:31:33^2:34

THAT Con't)
/21:6:7:8:9/22:8:8^2/23:1:7:10:13:14,15:22:24,25
7:28/24:1:9,10^2:11^2:13:20:21^2/25:4:7:11:17:21^2
26:34:36:37,38:39/26:1:8:11:16^2:17,18:19/27:4:
2/28:1:7,8,9:10:14:23/30:1:8:15:17:24/31:5:6:
^{2}:12/2Sa1:12:16:17,18/2:4:7:16:20:27:29:30/3:
:17:23:24,25^2:28:35,36:37/4:6,7:10^2/5:2:8:17^2:
1:24/6:13/7:4:9:27^2/8:14/9:7:9:10,11^2/10:9:
5,16:19^2/11:3:5:9:11^2:13:16:26/12:5:7:8:11:21:
8:31/13:2:6:8:20/14:7^2:8:10:11^2:14:14f:17:20:
2:30:32/15:3^2:7,8:10:19,20:21:30:31:35,36/16:
:12:21/17:9:11^3:12:14:21/18:3:7:11f:19:20:32/
9:1:2:7:8,9,10:20:22:26:27^2:29:34/20:3:4:6:
,9,10:12:20/21:1:8:17/22:25^2:39/23:6:9:15:
8,19:20:22/24:2:3:5:12:15:18:21:24/1Ki1:5:9:
1^2:13:17:30:51/2:3:4:5^2:9:15:19:41/3:2:3:5:8:9:
0:21:23/4:30/5:1:5:14/6:1:23-28/7:32:51/8:7:
:9:12,13:21:25:27:31:33,34:43:51:53:59:60^2:66/
:9/10:4:20/11:21:36/12:13,14:16,17:23,24:
2,33^2/13:2:3:4^2:5:21,22/14:2^2:5:11:22/15:14:
9:29:34/16:4-7:15,16:18:31:34/17:12:13:14:24 ^{2}
'18:1^2:5:9:10^2:14^2:15:16:27:36^3:37^2:46/19:1:2:4:
1/20:4:7:13:23:25:27:28:29:31/21:3:14:20f:23/
2:3:8:11:14:22:23:28:46:47:49:51/2Ki1:3^2:4,5:
1/2:1:3:4:5:6,7/3:2:14:19:25:26/4:8:13:15,16:
2:25:30:39/5:7:8:15:16:22:26/6:17:20:23:26-30^2
'7:1:2:5:12:16^2:18:19/8:1:5:6^3:7:10:13^2:14:19:22
'9:3:11:12:14:18:30:36^4/10:5:8:9,10^3:18,19:22:
3:31:32,33/11:1:10:17/12:1:8:16:18/13:16,17:
5/14:6:27:28/15:8:12:13:24:29:34,35/16:6:10f
'17:9:22:27,28:35,36/18:1:4:9:11^2:18:20,21:22:
1,32/19:7:8:9:10^2:17:18:19:25:29:32:35/20:5:8 ^{2}
11f:12/21:1:12/22:5,6:15,16^2:18,19/23:1:10:17 ^{2}
22:24:27:35/24:2:3,4:7:18,19/25:4,5^2:23:24/
1Ch1:1f:5-9f:19/2:3/3:17,18/4:10^2:14/6:49/9:4:
21/10:5:7^2/11^2:18,19/12:19:24-37/13:2:5:11/
14:8^2:11:15/15:12/16:7:23:40/17:3:6^2:10:16:18:
21:22:23:24/18:4:9/19:2,3^2:10:15/20:3f^2/21:15:
24:28/22:3:14/24:5/26:30/28:2:4:8:20/29:4,5:
12:14:16:17:18:19:30/2Ch1:7:17/2:1:11:17/4:19
/5:6:9:13,14^2/6:1^2:5,6^2:9:16:19^2:20,21:33:37,38
/7:1:6:7:13:18:22/8:3:7,8/9:13,14/13:5^2:8^2:17/
14:4:5:13:14/15:9:13/16:3^2:7:9:10^2:13,14/17:2:
10/18:6,7:12:13:29^2:31:34/19:3:4:6/20:2:3:9^2:
16:19:21:23:24:25:27:29:33/21:8:12:14:18/22:7
/23:2,3:8:15,16,17:18:19/24:5:6^2:7,8:9:22:24/25
:4:5,6,9:12:13:16/26:17,18^2/27:5/28:3:5:16:23^2:
24/29:10:24:35/30:6:8:13/31:4/32:2:11:12:13:
22:24/33:4,5:13^2:14:15:16/34:5:15,16:21^3:30/
35:1^2:16:22^2/36:10:21/Ez1:1f:2/2:59/3:6:13/4:
1:12:13:15:16:19:20:21/5:1:8:10:11:13^2:17/6:1:8
:12:20/7:13:18:24/8:15:21^2:22^2/9:1:7:11:12^2/10
:5^2:7,8^3:13^2:16-19/Neh1:6,7/2:10/3:15:32/4:1:7^2
:10^2:15^2:19:22/5:2,3,4^2:12:14^2:15:17:19/6:1:5,6^4
:7^4:12,13:16/7:3^a:7:61:66/8:1:7,8:14^3:15/9:12:
21:33/10:31:32:38/12:24:43:44:46/13:1^2:5:7:9:
10:14:15:18:19^2:21:23:24:25:27:30/Est1:8:11:19^4
:22/2:1:3:4:10:12,13,14:17:19:23f/3:9:13:14/4:5
:8:11:14/5:7,8^2/6:1/7:4:7/8:1^2:8:8f:13^2/9:5:11:
12:19:24,25:26:28/10:3/Job1:2,3:19/2:3:11:12:
13/3:4:6:7/4:6:7,8/5:19:27/6:2:3:8,9:10:27/7:1:
4:12:17/8:10:19/9:2:14:16:26:28:34:35/10:4-7:9
:15:20,21/11:5:6/12:7,8,9^3/13:5:7:9:13:16:18:25
/14:13:14/15:9/16:3:5:13:21:22/17:12/18:5:21/
19:6:23,24:25^2:26/20:4/21:7:14:16:19:30-32/22
:4:10,11:13:14:15,16:18^3:21:29/23:3^2/24:6:10:
25/25:4:5/27:3:5:14:17:19/28:3,4:7:11f/29:16:
24/30:13:23/31:2,3:6:7,8:11:12:23^2:28:34:35^2:
40/32:2:5:8,9:11,12^2:13:14:21,22/33:12:16:20:
30/34:10:34,35/35:6:14,15/36:9:19:21:23:26/
37:7:23/38:25-27/39:15:27/40:8:14^2/41:8:20:34
/42:2^2:16/Ps2:1/3:2/4:6/6:5f/9:4:14^2/10:4:4f:6
:13:18/11:4/12:3,4:7/13:4/14:1^2:7^2/16:5:6/17:3^2
:13,14/18:5:36/20:5/25:9:20/26:2:11/27:3:13/
30:12/31:19:21/32:6:9/35:3:15:21:26/39:4/40:
9/41:6:8/42:10:11^2/44:5:22/46:5:8:10/48:11:13
/49:7:8,9f/50:6:9/51:19/52:4/53:6/54:4f/56:13
/58:4,5:8:11^2/59:6:12,13/60:4,5f/66:6:15/68:
11,12,13/69:4:15:31/71:8:16:18/72:6:16/73:15:
20/74:2:9,10/75:1:8/76:11/77:1:10:10f:20/78:4
:6:25:35^2:39:44/79:6^2/81:5:13^2/83:14:18/85:3:4
/87/89:35,36:49/90:5,6/91:2/92:7/95:11/96:2:
7:10/97:8,9/98:4/102:13:18^3:19:21,22/103:15/
104:5:9:10/105:24:25/106:19,20:26:40:41,42/
107:8:12:15:21:30:31/109:27:28/110:3:4/111:9
/112:7:8/113:9/114:1:5/119:11:17f:17:38:69:
71,72:75,76,77^3:116:133:140:152/127:5/128:4/
129:3,4/130:5/132:1:2-5:7:11:12/133:2/135:5:
17/137:3,4:7/139:17,18:24/141:6,7/142:7/144:
3:3f/Pro1:15:31/3:7,8:13,14,15f:21/4:11:12/5:
22/6:5/7:14f:22/8:34:36/9:5:18/10:14:26/11:

21^2:30:30f/12:3:20^2/13:19/14:12:29/15:9,10/
16:2:17/17:15/19:27/20:2:21:24:30/22:28/23:
19,20,21:33/24:15,16:30,31:34/25:2,3/26:9:12:
17/27:8:17/28:24/30:20:21,22,23:24-28/31:9:
27/Ecc1:8-11:12-15:16-18/2:1:3:9:13,14^3:15:18:
24-26^2/3:12:13:14^2:16:18^4:21:22^3/4:2:4:5,6:15/
5:4:6,7^3:10:13,14:19,20^2/6:2:3^2:5/7:9:14^3:15-17:
18:25:26:29/8:8^2:9,10:12:15^3:16,17/9:1,2,3^2:5:
11^2:13:16/10:15/11:4f^2:8^2:9:10/12:11/Sol1:10/
2:7:7f/3:4:6/4:1:12/5:8:9^2/6:13/8/Is1:1:31/2:
12:16/3:9:15:16:24/4:1^3:2,3,4f/5:2:7:11:13:15:
20^2:25^2/7:3:11:12:14f^3:18:20:23/8:2:4:6f:18/9:1
:2:3^2:4^2:5:8,9,10^2:17^2:19,20/10:2^2:3:7:8:17:19:22
:27:32:33/11:6:10:11:15/12:1:4/14:3:26:28:29^2:
32^2/16:4,5:13,14/17:6:8:11^2/18:2:7^2/19:14:16:
18:21:23/21:6,7f:10:12/22:14:25^2/23:1:14/24:
21:23/25:4:7^2:9/26:1/27:2:12:13/28:12:16:19:
22/29:18:22/30:8:9:13:24:25/32:12/33:13/34:4
:11:16/35:8:10/36:4:6^2:8,9^2:12^2:22/37:6:7:8,9:
10:18:20^2:26^3:30:36/38:1:5:8:22/39:1/40:2:6^2:
20^2:26:27:28:31/41:9:20:23:26/42:8:21:23:25^2/
43:4:9:10:12:14:18:20:28/44:8^2:9:10:11^2:13:18:
20/45:3:19:20^2:21^2:23/46:1^2:11^2/47:10:11^2/48:
5^2:7:13:16:17:18:20/49:8,9:15:18:24:26/50:1:2^2:
4:7/51:4:23/52:6^2:7/53:4:5:8^3:11/54:3:9^2:14:16:
17/55:2^3:3:7/56:3:4:5/57:1:11^2:13:15:16/58:6:
13:14/59:2:9:16/60:7:12f:16/61:2:9/62:4:5/63:
10:19/64:1:9/65:16:17:20/66:1:6:17:19:22/Jer1
:6:7:12:18/2:4,5:6:10,11:13:22:23^3:26,27:32:37/
3:1:3:4,5:7:8:9:13^2:18:19/4:9:11,12:16:24:31/5:5
:6:7:17:19:21^2:22^2/6:1:16:24:27/7:4:7:8:9:16:19:
22:27:28:32^3/8:11:12^2/9:1:2:12:24^3/10:4:7:9:13:
14/11:1:4:5^2:6:12:17:19^2:20/13:8,9:12f:15:16:19
f:22:24,25/14:13^3:18:20/15:4^2:7:10:15/16:14,15^2
:21^2/17:2,3:4:11/18:4:7:8:9:10^2:16:18/19:3:4:8^2:
9:11/20:6:9:14:15:16:17^2/21:14/22:5:15:16:18:
21/23:5,6:7:12:15:29:32:36:38,39/24:6:7/25:11:
18^2:19,20:31:33/26:12:15^2:18/27:4:8:13:16:18^2/
28:1:3:9^2:11^3:13/29:8:22:28^3:31/30:2:3:7:8:15^2:
16/31:1:7:33:33f:34/32:3:4:8:22^2:23:36/33:
10,11:15:16:17:20,21^2:24^2:25,26/34:1:2:5:8:9:12
:14:15:22/35:6:7:10:15:18,19/36:6:9:18/37:7:9:
19:20:21^2/38:2:3:4:7:16:21:22,25:26:28/39:1:4:
11,12/40:2,3:4:7:9:11^3:13,14/41:18/42:12:17:22
/43:2,3:10/44:2,3:12:15:19:20:21:22:25:26:27:
29^2/45:4/46:8/48:9:10:11:14:20:28:44/49:13:22
:27:31^2/50:2:3:5:11:21:25:29:32:34:40:44/51:1:
29:61,62^2/52:3^2:17:27:30:31/Lam1:6:9:13/2:14
/3:1:22:44:50/4:6:11:20/5:1:7:21/Eze1:4^2:5:6:
13:27,28/2:9,10/3:26/4:4,5:8:11:14^2/5:13/6:9:
10^3:13/7:8,9:19:26,27/8:3:17/9:10/10:14:17f/
11:5^2:15:16^2:20/12:6:11:12f^2:13f^2:19:22/13:7^2:
10:11:12:23/14:2:6,7:9:11:16:17:18:20:23^2/15:7
/16:5:20:28:29:31:37:40,41:44:47:52:55:63/17:6
:9:14:15:21:24^3/18:4:9:10:13:14^2/19:5:9/20:3:
5,6:12^2:14^2:15:20:21:23,24:26^2:27,28:29:38:48/
21:5:7:12:17:27^2:29/22:14:22:30/23:19,20:22:29
:31:32:34:39^2:44:49/24:6:24:26:27/25:8/26:17/
28:6:15:26/29:3:9:11:13:15:16/30:5:9^2:22/31:9:
17/32:13:15:24:31/33:2:8^2:11:22:28:30f/34:5:12
:18^2:19:25:29:30^2/35:10:12:13/36:7:13:19:21:23
:27:32^2:34:36:37,38/37:1:3:9:14:28/38:2,3f:2,3:8
:10:12:15,16^2:17:19:23/39:8:13:14:15,16:21:22/
40:6:7-12:16:19:28:31/41:1:5:8^2:19,20^2/42:7,8:
16-20/43:19/44:4:12:18:24:28:30:31^2/45:20/46:
19,20^2:21,22/47:1:3:5/48:11:24/Dan1:8f:16:20/
2:1:8,9:15:19:30:35^2:36:38:39:41,42:43:44:45^2/3
:10:11:14:18:19:27:29:30/4:2:3:5:9:17^2:18:19:22:
25^2:26^2:32:33/5:2,3,4:6:7:13:14^2:15:16:19:21^2:
23:30/6:2:4:7^2:8^2:12^2:13:17^2:22:23:25,26/7:4:14
:19^2:20:23:24:28/8:3:5:17:19:21:22:25:26/9:2^2:
18:23:26:27/10:3:12:13/11:10,11:17:30,31f:37/
12:1:4:7/Hos1:2:10:11:6:8^2:13:16:18:21,22^2:23/
3:4/4:3/5:7/6:3/7:2:16/8:4:12/9:4:14^2/10:9^2:12
:13:15/11:3:8f/13:3:5/Joe2:12:14:25:27^2/3:1:7:
17/Amo1:2:5:5f^2/2:13:16/3:2:14/4:2:8/5:3^2:18:
19:20/6:6:11:12:14/7:1:6/8:9:10/9:4:8^2:9:11:12:
13:15/Ob1:1:8:14:18/Jon4:2/6/3:1:3:4,5:10/4:
3:7/Mic2:6^2:7:11^2:12/3:7:12/4:6^2/5:10/6:3:5:7^2
:11:12:16/7:10^2/Nah1:2/2:11/3:12:15/Hab1:1:
5:14/2:2:13:18/3:1:8,9f/Zep1:3:4:8:14:18/2:3:
14:15^4:15f^3/3:3:7:9^2:16:17,18:20/Hag1:10/2:5:7
f:12:14:20:23/Zec1:5,6:8:17:19:21/2:4^2:8:11,12
/3:9:10/4:2:7:8:10:12/5:3/6:12/7:7:12^2/8:2:4^2:7
:9:14,15:17^2:18:23/9:3:5:7:16,17/10:2^2:4:8/11:
10:11^2:14:16/12:2:4:6^2:7:9:11/13:1:2^2:6f:9/14:1:
4:5:9:17:20/Mal1:7:8:9:12:14/2:1:3:17^3/3:3:5:6:
10:13:17/Mt2:1:8:14:16:22/3:7:8:9:11:15/4:4:
12,13:24/5:15,16:20:22^2:23:30:32:37:41:45:46^2:
47/6:5:10:16:18:23:30:31,32/7:4:13f:18:22f/8:
8,9:11:13:16:27:28^2:31/9:5,6:11:17:22:31f:32:34

:35:36/10:7:14^2:34/11:19/12:1:4:11:22:36/13:1:
8:11:12,13:27:34,35:49/14:2:6:15:16:21/15:11:
12:15:17:21:27/16:4:10:12:20:21^3/17:2:4:10f:18
:19/18:1:10^2:14:32/19:3:4:5,6:8:9:10/20:6:8:16:
30^2/21:26:43^2:45^2/22:3:12:21:23:24:31:34,35:40
:46/23:4:8:9:16^2:17:18:19:31:35:37/24:14:17f:
20:24:26:32:33/26:3:16:20,21:23f:24:31:34:47:
48:53:54:55:56:59:62:63:68/27:3^2:8:17:18:19:24 ^{2}
:33:38:45:54:63:64/28:7^3:20/Mk1:2^2:3:4^2:7:26:
28:34:38:43,44^2:45^2/2:2:5:9,10,11:13:15^3:18:24:
25,26/3:10:20:22:28/4:7^2:11,12:19:22:38:41/5:
3,4:20:27:30:35:38/6:1:6:11:20:31:38:43,44:48/
7:2:6,7:10:18:19:20:24:29/8:8,9:16:17:21:31^2:32
/9:11:12,13^4:28:30,31:42:45,46/10:4:5:8:15:28:
29:32:46:47/11:2^2:4,5:19:20:22,23:25:31:32/12:
1:17:19:24:27:28:29:32:34:35:43,44/13:1:18:20:
21:22:28:29^3:30:34/14:4,5,9:18:21:25:35:35f:48:
51,52:55:65:69/15:7:10:27:28:33:38f:42,43:44/
16:4:10,11:12:20/Lk1:3:8,9:10:13:22:43:45^2:61/
2:1:8:15:24:25:26:27:32:36,37:38:44:49/3:1:3^2:7 ^{2}
:8^2:9:12/4:1:9,10,11:14:18,19^3:22:23:24:36:38:
40:43/5:3:6:14:17:23,24:33/6:4:7:23^2:24:32:33^2:
34:35:42:49/7:2:6,7,8:17:18:29:30:39:42/8:4:17:
22^2:23:25:29:47^2:49:55:56/9:39:50:59f:60/10:3:
20^2:21:27:35:40/11:13:18:20:25:27:29,30^3:35:46
:48:53,54/12:6:14:16:26:28^2:29:42,43,44:48:49:
59/13:1:2:3:24,25:32^2:34^2/14:7:17:20:23:30^2:34
/15:16:29/16:1:5,6:8:9:9f^2:16:17^2:25/17:6:14:21
:23^3:24:31:34:37f/18:1:3:4,5:6:7:11:26:37/19:
9,10:11:14:21:23:26^2:39:47/20:6:16:18:19^3:25^2:
27^2:28:37,38:37,38f:37,38:40:41/21:15:20:30:31 ^{2}
:32:36/22:5:12:16:22:30:32:34:40:40f:44:46:52:
61:63,64/23:4:12:48^2:56/24:2:6,7^2:13:18:19:21:
22,23^2:25:26:31:38:39^3:44:46:47/Jn1:3:5:6,7:34:
39/2:9:11:22:23/3:1:7:12:15:16^2:19:20:21:25:28 ^{4}
:33,34/4:1:9:13:15:20^2:21-24:25:37:46,47:51:53^2
/5:10:12:23:24:25:32,33:34:36:40:44/6:8,9:12:
15:16:22,23^2:24:26:27:29:34:39^2:40^2:42:43:46:
48-51^2:61:65^2:68/7:24:26^2:31:32:38:41,42/8:17^2
:24^3:27:28^2:29:37:40:41:42:52:58:59/9:8:20:
22,23:39/10:17:20:34,35,36:38:42/11:12,13:17:
20:22:40:42:49:51:52:53:55:57^2/12:5:6:11:12:14:
16:18:23,24^3:27:34:40:42:46/13:1^4:10:11:16:17:
19:26f:29:31:35:38/14:2,3:10:11:20:22:29:31^2/
15:2^2:11:12:15:16:17/16:1^2:4:7^2:15:16:21:22:23:
27:30:30f:30:33/17:1:7:8:11:12:13:21^2:23^2:24:26
/18:4,5:13:14:15:20:22:28:34f:37/19:4:10:13f:20
:23,24:25:28:31:33:35:35f:36,37/20:1:7:8:9:11:
17:19:30,31^3/21:7f:7:9:20:22:23^4:24^2:25/Act1:3:
9/2:1:5:15:20:30:31:32:36/3:7,8:11:17:18:25/4:
1f:2^2:4:5:10^2:13:16:17:27:28:32/5:9:10:15:21:25:
31:34:36:41:42/6:1^2:13:14/7:3:5:6:7:8:10:12:20:
25:28:40:60/8:1:8:9,10,11f:12:14:18:19:23:24:26
:37/9:2:8,9^2:12:14:17:20:21:22:24:28:38/10:28:
34:36,37:38:42:43:45:46,47/11:1:21:26:28/12:1:
14^2:19:23/13:10:27:32,33^2:34:41:42:46:49/14:1:
8:12^2:15:19:22/15:1:3:5:7^2:8:10:11:17:18:19^2:20:
24:31:36:38:39/16:3:6:9:10^2:14:15:20,21:33/17:
3:10:13:21:22:27:33/18:5:7:13:18:20:25,26^2:28/
19:4^2:10:12:16:21:23:26:27^2:35/20:18:23^2:25:26:
28:29:34:38/21:14:20:21^2:22:24^2:29^2:31:35:
37,38/22:5:13:19:22/23:3:4:9:10:11:27:31/24:8:
9:10:11^2:12:14^2:15:21^2:26/25:4:16/26:5:8:9:11:
18^2:19:20:22:23:29/27:2:4:4f:16:37/28:1:11:20^2:
22:23:28,29/Rom1:5:8:10:10f:11,12:11,12f:
11,12:13^2:17:21:26^2:28/2:2:3:4:7:17:19:20:24:29
/3:2:3:4:5:8^2:9:20^2:26:28:31/4:1:3:9:10:11^4:12^2:
13:14^2:17^2:18:19^2:21:23:24/5:2:3:5^2:7:9:10:13^2:
18:20/6:1:6^3:8:15:16:17:19/7:1:3:4^2:7^3:8:9^2:13^3:
16^2:17^2:21:23,24,25^3/8:3:5:9^2:16:19:20,21^2:22:
23^2:24:25:26:28^2:29^2:36:38/9:1^3:7^2:8-10-13^2:17:
17f:20:23,24:25:27:29:30/10:1:3^2:4^2:5:6:8:9^2:10:
11:15:19^2:20/11:1:2,3:6:8^2:10:11:14^2:15:18^2:20:
24:25^2:27:32/12:7:8:9:14:17:19^2/13:1:4:6:8:
12,13/14:1f:2^2:5^2:6:9:13:14^2:16^2:21:22:23^2/15:1:
4^2:8^2:9^3:13^2:14^3:15,16:21:22:27^2:29:31^2/16:17:
19:25,26,27/1Co1:4:8^2:10:12^2:14:15:18:21:22:
24:26:29:30/2:4:6^2:9^2:11:12:13:15/3:3:5:11:12 ^{2}
:13:16^2:17:20/4:2:4:5^2:6:7:8^2:15:17:18^2/5:1^2:2:5:
6^2:7:10^2:11/6:1:2:3:7:9,10:11:12:13^2:15:16^2:18:
19^2/7:1:3:5^2:15:16:17:19:21:22^2:25:28:29^2:29f:
33:37/8:1^2:4^3:6:7:8/9:5f^2:9:10:12:13^2:14:15:17:
19:20:21:22^2:25:25f:25:27/10:1:3,4:3,4f:6:10:11:
12:13^3:16^2:17:18:19^2:20^2:23^2:25:28:33^2/11:2:3:4
:5:10:11:14,15:16^2:18:19:21^2:23:25:26:28:30:32:
34/12:2:13:15:16:18:22:23^2:24^3:25^2:30:31/13:2:
12:13/14:2^2:5^2:6^3:8:10:12:13:15^2:18:19:21:22:24
:25:26:32:36:37:39:40/15:2:3:4^2:6:11:12^2:15^2:18:
20:20f:21:24:28:29:31^2:32:45^2:52:53^2:55,56:58/
16:6:12:17:22/2Co1:3,4:5:9:12^3:13,14:15,16^3:18:
22^2:23/2:3^4:4^2:5,6:7:8:9:10:14/3:2:3:4:6:7^3:9^2:10

(THAT Con't)
:12:13:15:18/**4**:2:4:5:6[2]:7[3]:10:14:16/**5**:1[2]:2:4:6:
11[3]:12:13,14[2]:15:16:21f/**6**:3[2]:4:17/**7**:7:8[2]:9:11:
12:16/**8**:3:6:8[2]:9:10:13:15[2]:16[2]:17:20:21:23[2]:24/
9:1:2[2]:3[2]:4:5:8:10:11:13/**10**:3:5:7:9:10:12[2]:15[2]:
16[2]/**11**:2:3:5:8,9[2]:10:12:16:21[2]:22[2]:30/**12**:2,3:4:
5:9:11:12:13:15:16[2]:19[2]:20[2]:21/**13**:1:2:3:6[2]:7[2]:7f
:7:9:10/**Gal1**:6:10:11:16:18:19:23/**2**:2[2]:3:4:5:10[2]
:12:14:16[2]:17[4]:19[3]:19f/**3**:3:7:10:11[2]:12:13:16[2]:
18:25:29/**4**:1[2]:3:5:7:8:9[3]:11:15[2]:15f:15:17:22:
24,25[2]:27:28:30/**5**:1:10:11[6]:12f:17[2]:20[2]:21[3]/**6**:1:
4:7:12[2]:13[2]:14[2]:17/**Eph1**:6:7:10:11:12:14[4]:15:
16,17:18[3]:19[2]:20:21/**2**:3:5:10:11[2]:12:14:15[2]/**3**:1:
2,3[2]:6:9:16:17:18,19/**4**:8:9[2]:10:10f:12[2]:15,16:20:
22:30/**5**:14:18:27:28:31[2]:33/**6**:2:3:10:11:15:19:
20/**Php1**:2:6[2]:7:9:11:12:13:16,17[2]:18:19:20[4]:24:
27[2]:28[2]/**2**:1:5:9:10:11:12[3]:15:16:17:24:26:28/**3**:3[3]
:4:5:6:7[2]:8:10:12[2]:15:21/**4**:5[2]:8:10:11:18/**Col1**:6[2]
:10[2]:11[2]:12:17:18[2]:20:22:23[3]:26,27/**2**:2[2]:4:7:17/
3:5:9[2]:10:18:20:21:24:25/**4**:1:3:4:13:17/**1Th1**:4:
5:9/**2**:1:3:5:8:9:10:12:13:19/**3**:2,3:4:5[2]:6[2]:7:8:13[2]
/**4**:1[2]:3,4:6:9:13:14[2]:15/**5**:1:2[2]:4:10:12:15:21:23/
2Th1:11:12/**2**:1[2]:3:4:5:15/**3**:1:2:4[2]:5:7:8:9:11:14:
17/**1Ti1**:3,4:5[3]:10,11:13:15[2]:16[3]:18:19[2]/**2**:2:5/**3**:
1:7:15:16/**4**:1:2:8:9,10:15/**5**:4:7:15:16:20:22:24/
6:1:2:9:14[2]:16:20/**2Ti1**:6[2]:8:9:12[3]:13f/**2**:8[3]:9:10:
11[2]:12[2]:17[2]:18:19:21:22[3]/**3**:1:5:7:10[2]:11:14:15/**4**
:5:8[2]:16/**Tit1**:1[2]:5:8:9:10/**2**:1:5:7:8:12:13:14:15/
3:7:8:10:13:14/**Phm1**:1:6[2]:10:15[2]:21:22/**Heb**:3:
4:5,6[2]/**2**:3:4:6:10:11:15:17/**3**:5:11:12:13:14:18/**4**
:1:2:3:4[2]:7:8[2]:11:13/**5**:1:4:5:7f[7]:9:10/**6**:7:9[2]:11[2]:
12:14:17:18/**7**:3f[2]:3:8:9:12,13,14:15:16:20:21:23
:24:25/**8**:9:10[2]/**9**:1:4[2]:8:10:11:12:15[2]:16:18:20:
22:23:24[2]:26:27[2]/**10**:5:7:11:14:15:16[2]:23[2]:25:34[2]
:36/**11**:1[2]:3[3]:4[2]:5:6[2]:10:11:12:13[3]:14:19[2]:20:22[2]:
23[2]:24,25:26[2]:27:28[2]:30:35:39:40/**12**:1[3]:6:8[2]:9:
10[2]:13:15[2]:16:19:20:21:25:27[2]/**13**:6[2]:7:12:13:18:
19:20,21:23/**Jas1**:6[2]:7,8:10,11[2]:12:19:20:21/**2**:1:
4:5:6:14[2]:16:17[2]:18[2]:19[3]:20[2]:21:22:23:26/**3**:1:7:
13:14:17/**4**:2:4[2]:5:15:17/**5**:3[2]:12:16:17:18:20/
1Pe1:3[2]:5[2]:8:12[2]:17:22:24:25/**2**:2,3:5:7:8[3]:9[2]:15:
16:24/**3**:3:5:7:18:19:20:21[2]/**4**:5:6[2]:11[2]:12:13:14/
5:7:9/**2Pe1**:1:4:5:6:9[2]:10:13,14:15:17,18:19[2]/**2**:2
:5:9:13:21:22[2]/**3**:3:5,6:7:8:9[3]:12:14:17/**1Jn1**:2:3:
5:8/**2**:1[2]:3:5:11:15[2]:16[2]:18:19:20:22:27:28[2]:29[2]/
3:1:2:5[3]:8:10:11:12:14:15:19:20:22/**4**:2:6[2]:7[2]:8:
11:13:14:15:16:18[2]:21/**5**:1[2]:3:5:6,7,8:9:10:11[3]:13
:14:15:16[4]:17[2]:19[2]:20:21/**2Jn1**:1:4:5:7:8[2]/**3Jn**:2[2]
:3[2]:8:11[3]/**Jud**:4:5:7:13:18:21:23/**Rev**:10:20f/**2**:6:
9:13:17:20[3]:23:26:27/**3**:5:8:9:11:14:17/**4**:1/**5**:6/
6:1/**7**:15/**8**:2:7:12:13/**9**:9:13:15:19/**10**:6[2]:7/**11**:1
f:6:13/**12**:12:17/**13**:3:6:8f:15:17:18/**14**:8:17/**15**:
5/**16**:12:14/**17**:3:6:11:15:17[2]:18/**18**:10:14:16:19:
21/**19**:5:20[2]/**20**:2:3/**21**:4:8:10:17f/**22**:9:11
6406

THE

Gen1:1f:1[2]:2[3]:2f[3]:4,5[5]:6:6f:6[2]:7,8[4]:9,10[5]:11,12[3]:
13:14,15[7]:16[9]:17[2]:18[3]:19:20[2]:21,22[3]:23:24:26[4]:
28[3]:29[3]:30[2]:31/**2**:1:2:3[2]:4[4]:5[3]:6[2]:7[4]:7f:7:8[4]:9[7]:10[3]
:11,12[3]:11,12f:13[4]:14[6]:15[3]:16,17[4]:18:19,20[4]:21[3]:
22[2]:24:25/**3**:1[8]:2,3[5]:4:5:6[2]:7:8[4]:9:11[2]:12:13[3]:14[5]:
15[3]:16:17[2]:19[3]:20:20f:20[2]:21:22[4]:23[3]:24[4]/**4**:3:4[3]:
6:8:9:10[2]:12:13:15[2]:16[3]:18:18f:18:18f:18:18f:18:
18f:20[2]:21[2]:21f[2]:21:22:22f:25:26:26f[2]/**5**:1f:1[2]:1f:
1:2:3,4,5f:3,4,5[2]:6,7,8:9,10,11:12,13,14:15,16,17
:18,19,20:25,26,27:28-31[2]/**6**:1[2]:1f[5]:1:4[2]:5[3]:7[5]:8[2]:
9,10[2]:11[4]:12,13[2]:14:16[5]:17[2]:18:19,20[2]:21[2]/**7**:1[5]:
2:3f:3:4:5:6:7[2]:8,9[3]:10,11,12[4]:13:14,15:16[2]:17[4]:
18[3]:19[3]:20:21:23[2]:24[2]/**8**:1[4]:2[2]:3,4[3]:5f[2]:5:7f[3]:7:9[4]:
10:11[2]:12:13f[4]:13[2]:14:17:18,19[3]:20:21f:21[2]:22/**9**
:1:7:9,10,11[2]:13[3]:14[3]:15:16,17[3]:18[3]:18f[2]:19[2]:22:
23[2]:24,25f:24,25[3]:26,27f[2]:26,27:28/**10**:1[3]:2:3:4:5
:6:7[2]:8:8f:8[2]:9f[2]:10[2]:11,12[2]:13,14[3]:15-19[4]:20:21:
25[2]:26-30[3]:31:32[3]/**11**:2[2]:2f[3]:3,4[3]:5[2]:6f[4]:8[3]:9[3]:
10,11:12,13f[3]:24,25:26:28[2]:29:31[3]:32:32f[2]/**12**:1[2]
:2:3:3f:4:5:6:8[4]:9:10:11,12,13[3]:15[2]:15f:17:20/**13**:
1:3,4[3]:6[2]:7[4]:9[5]:10[4]:10f:10:11[2]:12[4]:13:14:17:18/
14:1:2:3[2]:4:5,6[10]:7[2]:8,9[3]:10[6]:11:13[4]:14[2]:15:16[2]:
17[3]:18[2]:19,20[3]:21[2]:22:24/**15**:5[3]:7[2]:10[3]:11[2]:12:14[2]
:16[2]:17[3]:18:18f:18/**16**:2,3[2]:5[2]:5f:6:7[3]:8:9-12[3]:13:
14[2]/**17**:1:2,3,4[2]:7,8:9,10:11[2]:12:16:17:22:24-27[3]
/**18**:1[4]:3,4:6[2]:7:8[3]:9:10[2]:11:16[2]:18[2]:20[2]:22,23[2]:
24:25[5]:26:27:28:31[2]:32[3]:33/**19**:1[3]:2[2]:3:4[5]:6:9:10[2]
:11[2]:12[2]:13[3]:14[3]:15[4]:16[4]:17[3]:18,19,20[3]:21:23[2]:
24:25[2]:27[2]:28[2]:29[2]:30[2]:31:33:34:35:37[4]:38[5]/**20**:1[2]
:5:6:8[4]:9,10:11,12:13:15[2]:17[3]:18/**21**:1:8[2]:9[2]:9f:
12[2]:13[2]:14[3]:15[2]:17[4]:18:19[2]:20,21[2]:25[2]:26[2]:27:
28,29:31[3]:33[4]:34/**22**:2[2]:3[3]:4[4]:5[3]:6[5]:7[5]:9[5]:10:11:
12[3]:13[2]:14:15:16:17[4]:18[2]:20-23[3]/**23**:1:3:5,6[2]:8:9[3]
:10[4]:11[3]:12:13[2]:14,15:16:17,18[9]:19,20[2]/**24**:3:5:7:
9:9f:10:11[4]:12[2]:13[2]:14:15,16[3]:17:18:20[4]:21[3]:22:
23:24[2]:25:26:27:28:29,30[4]:31[2]:32[3]:33:35:37:37f:
42[2]:44[2]:45[2]:46:47[3]:48[3]:50:51:54[3]:56:57:59:60:61
:62:63[2]:65[2]:66[2]:67/**25**:4f[2]:6[2]:7,8:9,10[4]:11:12-15[4]
:16:17:18[4]:19:20[2]:22:23[4]:25:25f:26[2]:27:28:29:34[2]
/**26**:1[3]:4[3]:7:8:12:14:15:16:18[4]:20[3]:21:22[3]:24[2]:29[2]
:30:31:32:33[4]:34[3]/**27**:2,3,4[3]:5[3]:8,9,10:13:14:15:
16[3]:17:18[2]:19:22[2]:23:25[2]:26:27,28,29[4]:30:31:36/
28:2:4:5[2]:6,7,8:9[2]:12:13[5]:14[3]:16,17:18:19[3]:19f/
29:1[2]:2[3]:3[6]:4:5:6:7[2]:8[3]:10[4]:16:19:20:21:22[2]:25:27
:30/**30**:2:6f[6]:13:14:14f:15:16:23,24:25:27:31,32[2]:
35,36[3]:38[2]:39,40[4]:41[2]:42[3]/**31**:3:4[2]:5:8[4]:10[3]:11:
12:12f:12:13[4]:16:17-20[2]:21[2]:25[2]:29:33[2]:34[3]:35f[2]:
39[3]:40[3]:41:42[3]:46:47,48:49[2]:53[3]:54[4]:55/**32**:1[2]:3:
6[3]:7:8:9:10:11:12[2]:13,14,15:17[2]:19[2]:20:21[2]:
22,23,24[4]:25[3]:26:27[2]:28:29:30[2]:31:32[3]/**33**:1:2:5:
6:8:10f:12:13[2]:17:18:19[2]:20[2]/**34**:1:2:5:6,7[2]:12:
18,19[3]:20:20f:21:22:23:24:25:27:28[3]:29:30[2]/**35**:
1:2:3[2]:4:5[2]:7[2]:7f:8[3]:11:12:13,14[2]:15:17:19:21:22[2]
:23:24:25:26:28,29/**36**:1:2,3[2]:2,3f:2,3:5:6,7,8[2]:9[2]:
13,14f:15,16[11]:17[6]:18,19[5]:20,21[12]:22[2]:23:24[3]:25:
26:27:28,29,30f:28,29,30:31-39[9]:40-43[17]/**37**:1:2[2]
:5:7:8:9:13,14[2]:15:17:18:25:26,27:28[2]:29[2]:30:31:
32[2]:36[5]/**38**:2:7:9[2]:9f:10:12[4]:13:14[4]:20[3]:21[6]:22[2]:
23[2]:25[2]:26:27:28[3]:29[2]:30[2]/**39**:1[5]:2[2]:3:4:5:6[3]:8:11[2]
:12:12f:12:14,15[2]:16:20:21[2]:22[3]:23[2]/**40**:1[6]:6:7[2]:
9,10:11[2]:12[2]:15:16[2]:17[2]:18,19[2]:20:21:22/**41**:1[2]:2[2]
:3[2]:4[2]:6[2]:7:8[2]:9:10[4]:11:12[3]:13:14:17[3]:18[2]:19[2]:20:
23:24[3]:25[2]:26[2]:27[3]:29[2]:30[2]:31[3]:32:33:34,35f:
34,35[4]:36:38[2]:39[4]:40:41,42[2]:43[2]:44[2]:45:45f:45:
46[4]:47:48[2]:49[2]:50[5]:51[2]:52:53:54[3]:55:56,57[3]/**42**:5
:6[3]:7:8,9[2]:13:15[2]:16:18:19:20:24:25[2]:26:27[4]:29:
30:32[2]:33[2]:35[4]/**43**:1[2]:2:3,4,5:7:8:9:11[3]:12:14[2]:15
:16:17:18:19[2]:21[3]:22:23[2]:24:27:29:32:33[3]:34[3]/**44**
:1[2]:2[3]:3:4:6:7:8[2]:9:10[3]:11:12[4]:13[2]:14:16:17[3]:22:
30[2]:31[2]:32[2]:33[2]:34/**45**:2[2]:8:9:10:15:16:18[4]:20[2]:
21:23:24:25:26:27/**46**:1:2:3,4[2]:5:6:8-14[2]:18[2]:19-
19-22[3]:23,24,25[2]:26[2]:28:31:34/**47**:1:4[2]:5,6[2]:11[2]:
12:13[2]:14[2]:15:17:18:19:20[4]:21:22[2]:23[2]:25:26[5]:27[2]
:28:29/**48**:2:3:5:7:8[2]:10:12,13[3]:14[5]:15[2]:16[2]:18[2]:
20[2]:21:22[2]/**49**:1:3[3]:4[2]:7f:10:11:13[2]:14:15[3]:17[3]:
22:24[3]:25[5]:26[5]:27[3]:28:29,30[5]:32[2]:33/**50**:2:3:4:5:
7[2]:8:10f:10:11[3]:12,13[5]:14:15:16,17[3]:20:23[2]:24[2]:
26/**Ex1**:1[2]:5:7:8[2]:10:11[2]:12[5]:13,14[2]:15,16[3]:17[3]:
18[2]:19[2]:20[2]:21:22[3]/**2**:1[2]:3[3]:4:5[5]:6:7[4]:8[2]:9[2]:10:10f
:10:11[2]:12[2]:13[4]:14:15:16[2]:17[3]:18:19[2]:21:23[3]:24:
25/**3**:1[5]:2[2]:6[2]:7[2]:8[3]:9[4]:11:12[3]:13:14:14f:14:15f:
15:16:17[3]:18[6]:19:20:21:22[2]/**4**:2:3[2]:4[2]:5[2]:8[3]:9[2]:11
:14:14f:16:17:20[2]:21[2]:24:25,26:27[2]:28:29[2]:30:31
/**5**:1[3]:3[3]:4,5:6[2]:7,8[2]:10,11[2]:12:13:14:16:18:19:20:
22/**6**:1:2,3:4:5[3]:6:7:8,9[3]:8,9f:10:11:13[3]:14[5]:15[3]:
16[5]:17:18:19[4]:20:21:22:23:24[3]:25[7]:26[3]:27[2]:28,29[2]
:30/**7**:1:2:3:5:6:8:10:11[2]:13:14[2]:15[5]:16[3]:17[4]:18[3]:
19[4]:20[5]:21[4]:22[2]:24[3]:25/**8**:1:2:3,4:5[4]:6:7[3]:8[2]:9[3]:10
:11[2]:12[3]:13[3]:14:15[3]:16[3]:17[2]:18[2]:19[2]:20[3]:21:22[4]:
25[2]:26:27:29[2]:30[2]:31,32[3]/**9**:1[3]:3:4[3]:5[3]:6[4]:7[2]:8[2]:9[2]
:10[2]:11[3]:12:13[4]:14[2]:16:18:19[3]:20[2]:21[2]:22[2]:23:24:
25[3]:26[3]:29[4]:31[3]:32[3]:33[4]:35[2]/**10**:1:2[2]:3[2]:4,5[3]:6[3]:7[2]
:9:10:12[4]:13[2]:14[3]:15[7]:18:19[3]:20[2]:21:22:23[2]:26:
27:28/**11**:1[2]:2:3[4]:5[5]:6[2]:7:8:9[2]:10[3]/**12**:1:2[2]:3,4[2]:
3,4f:3,4[4]:6[2]:7[6]:9[2]:10:11:12[4]:13[4]:15[3]:16[5]:17[2]:18[6]:
19[2]:21[4]:22[6]:23[7]:23f[2]:23:25[3]:27[5]:28:29[7]:30[3]:31:
33[3]:34:35[2]:36[4]:37[2]:38f:39[3]:40,41[4]:42[5]:43[4]:47[2]:
48[3]:49:50:51[4]:51f[2]/**13**:1[2]:1f:3[4]:4,5:4,5f:4,5[3]:6,7[3]:
8:10:11[3]:12:13[2]:14:15[5]:16:17,18[8]:19[2]:20[2]:21[2]:22
/**14**:2[3]:3[2]:4[2]:5[2]:6:7:8[2]:9[4]:10[4]:11:12[2]:13[4]:14:15[2]:
16[3]:17[3]:19[3]:20[6]:21[4]:22[2]:23[4]:24[4]:25[2]:26[6]:27[5]:28[5]:
29[2]:30[4]:31[5]/**15**:1[4]:2:3:4[3]:5[2]:6:7:8[3]:9[2]:10[2]:11[2]:12:
13:14[2]:15[3]:17:19[5]:20[3]:21[3]:22[3]:23[2]:24:25[6]:26[5]:27
/**16**:1[3]:2:3:4:5:6[3]:7,8,9[4]:10[3]:11,12[2]:13[4]:14[3]:15[2]:
16f:17:21[4]:22[3]:23[2]:24[2]:25[2]:26[2]:27[2]:28,29[5]:30[2]:
31:32[4]:34[3]:35[3]:36[3]/**17**:1[2]:2:5,6[6]:7[2]:8[2]:9[5]:10:10f[2]:
10[2]:11[2]:12:13[2]:14:15,16[3]/**18**:1[3]:4[2]:5,6:5,6f:8[5]:9:
10[2]:11[2]:12[3]:13[2]:15,16[2]:18:19,20:21:22[3]:23[3]:25:
26[2]/**19**:1[3]:2,3[4]:4:5[3]:7[4]:8[3]:9[2]:10:11[2]:12[2]:13[3]:14:
16[4]:17[3]:18[4]:19:20[4]:21[3]:22:22f:23[3]:24[3]:25/**20**:4f:
5[3]:7:7f[2]:8:10[2]:11[4]:12[2]:18[6]:21[3]:22[3]:24:25:26[2]/**21**:
2f:2:3:4[2]:5:6:7[2]:8:18:19[2]:20:21[3]:22[4]:23:26[3]:27:28[2]
:29[6]:30[3]:30f:31[2]:32[3]:34[5]:35[4]:36[6]/**22**:1:2[2]:3[2]:4:5[3]:
6[6]:7:8[2]:9[5]:11[2]:12[3]:13[2]:14[3]:15[2]:16:16f:17:21:25:
29[2]:30[4]:31/**23**:1:2,3[3]:7f:8[2]:9:11[7]:12[2]:13:15[4]:16[5]:
17:18:19[2]:19f:19:20:23[2]:24[2]:25:26[2]:27[3]:28:29[2]:
30:31[6]/**24**:1[2]:2[3]:3[3]:4[5]:5[3]:6[3]:7[5]:8[5]:9[2]:10[2]:11[2]:12[4]:
13:14:15[3]:16[5]:17[6]:18/**25**:1[6]:8:9[2]:12:13,14[4]:15:16[3]
:16f[2]:17:18[3]:19:20[4]:21[4]:22[5]:25[3]:26,27[6]:28:30[3]:31[2]
:32,33:34,35[3]:36:37:38:39f:39:40[2]/**26**:1:3:4,5:6[3]:
7,8[2]:9[4]:10,11[2]:12[2]:13:14:15,16[2]:17:18,19[4]:20:22:
24:25[2]:26,27[4]:28[4]:29[3]:30[2]:31[3]:32:33[7]:34[4]:35[9]:36[2]
/**27**:2[2]:3:5[3]:6:7[3]:8[2]:9,10[5]:11[3]:12[2]:13:14,15:16[2]:
17[3]:18:19[5]:20[3]:21[3]/**28**:3[2]:4:4f[2]:5,6[3]:7:8[2]:9[2]:10[2]:
11[2]:12[5]:13,14[2]:15[3]:17:18:19:20:21[2]:22,23,24[5]:25[7]
:26[2]:27[3]:28[6]:29[4]:30,31[3]:30,31f:30,31[3]:32:33,34[2]:
35[6]:37,38[7]:39:41:43[3]/**29**:1[2]:2:3,4[6]:5:6[2]:7:10[2]:11[3]
:12[5]:13[5]:14[4]:15,16[3]:17[6]:18[2]:19,20[8]:21[4]:22[10]:23[2]:
24[2]:25:26[2]:27[2]:28[2]:29:30[3]:31[3]:32[5]:33:34[2]:35:36:
37[2]:38:39[3]:41[5]:42[3]:43[2]:44[3]:45:46/**30**:2[2]:3[3]:4[2]:5:6
:7[2]:8[3]:10f:10[4]:11,12[3]:13f[3]:15[3]:16[4]:17,18[3]:20[4]:
22,23[2]:22,23f:24:25:26,27[5]:28[2]:31:34[3]:35[2]:36[2]:
37/**31**:1[2]:3[2]:6[2]:7[5]:8[3]:9[2]:10[3]:11[4]:12,13[4]:14,15:16[3]
:17[4]:18[3]/**32**:1[2]:4[4]:5[2]:6[2]:7:9:11:12[4]:13:14:15[2]:16[2]:
17[2]:19[7]:20[5]:21[2]:24:25[2]:26[3]:27[3]:29[3]:30[4]:31:32:33
:34[2]:35[2]/**33**:1[2]:2:3:4:5:7[3]:8[2]:9[3]:10[2]:11[5]:12[2]:13:14
:16[2]:17:19[3]:20:22[2]/**34**:1[4]:2[3]:3[3]:4[3]:5,6[3]:5,6f:5,6:7[2]
:8:9:10[7]:11[2]:12[2]:13:15[2]:15f:18[3]:19f:20:21:22[4]:23
:24[2]:25[3]:26[4]:27:27f:27:28[5]:29[3]:30:31[2]:32[4]:33f[2]:
34[4]:35[2]/**35**:1[2]:2:3:4[2]:5-9[4]:10-19[31]:20:21[2]:22:23:
24[3]:25:26:27[3]:28[3]:29[3]:30,31[3]:34[2]:35[2]/**36**:1[3]:3[2]:
4-7[4]:8,9:11,12[2]:13[4]:14,15:17:18[2]:19[2]:20[2]:21[2]:22:
23:24:25,26[2]:27[2]:29:30:31,32[3]:33[4]:34[2]:35:36:37[2]
:38/**37**:1:2[2]:5[4]:6:7[2]:8:9[2]:11:12[3]:13:14[2]:15,16:17:
18:19:20,21[5]:22:23,24[6]:25[2]:26:27:28:29[5]/**38**:1[2]:2[2]
:3[2]:4:5[2]:6:7[5]:8[5]:9[2]:11:12[2]:13:14,15[2]:16[3]:17[5]:18[7]:
19[2]:20[2]:21[6]:22[2]:23:24[2]:25,26[3]:27[5]:27f:28[3]:29[16]/
39:1[4]:2:3:4,5[3]:6,7[7]:6,7f:6,7:8[3]:10:11:12:13:14[3]:
15-18[6]:19[4]:20[3]:21[8]:22[2]:23[3]:24[2]:25,26[6]:28,29[5]:30[4]
:31[2]:32[2]:33-40[35]:41[4]:42[2]:43/**40**:1:2[3]:3[5]:4[4]:5[6]:6[2]:
7[3]:8[6]:9[3]:10[3]:11:12[2]:13:16:17[4]:18:19[4]:20[7]:21[4]:22[4]
:23[5]:24[4]:25[3]:26[3]:27[2]:28[3]:29[4]:30[4]:32[3]:33[7]:34[4]:35[4]
:36[2]:37:38[5]/**Lev1**:1[2]:2,3[8]:4[6]:5[9]:6,7[3]:8[3]:9[5]:9f:10:
11[6]:12[7]:13[6]:15,16,17[15]:15,16,17f/**2**:1:2:2f[2]:2[2]:3[3]:
4[2]:5[2]:8[3]:9:9f:9[2]:10[3]:11:12f:13f[4]:13:14[3]:15:16[4]/**3**:
1[3]:2[7]:3,4,5[7]:6:7,8[7]:9,10,11[10]:12:13[5]:14[4]:15,16[5]/**4**
:1:2[2]:3[2]:4[2]:5[3]:6[5]:7[12]:8[2]:9[3]:10[2]:11,12[6]:13[2]:14:15[4]:
16[2]:17[3]:18[10]:19[2]:20[3]:21[4]:22:24[3]:25[8]:26[6]:27:29[4]:
30[9]:31[7]:33[2]:34[8]:35[7]/**5**:2[2]:4:6[3]:7[3]:8[2]:9[7]:10[3]:12[3]:
13[6]:14:15f[3]:15:16[2]:16f:16[5]:17,18[2]:19/**6**:1:4,5[4]:6:
7[2]:8:9[5]:10[5]:11[2]:12[6]:13[2]:14[4]:15[7]:16[4]:17[4]:18[2]:
19,20[5]:21:22,23[4]:24:25[5]:26[4]:27:28[2]:29:30[4]/**7**:1[2]:
2[4]:3[5]:4[3]:5[3]:6[2]:7[6]:8[3]:9[6]:10:11[3]:12:14[7]:15[3]:16[4]:
17,18[7]:19:20:21:22:23:24:25:28:29[2]:30[4]:31[4]:
32,33[2]:34[4]:35[2]:36[3]:37[4]:38[3]/**8**:1[8]:4:7[2]:8[3]:8f:9[4]:10[2]
:11[4]:12:13[3]:14[2]:15,16[15]:17[4]:18[3]:19[2]:20[4]:21[6]:22[2]:
23[3]:24[6]:24f[2]:25[7]:26[2]:27[3]:28[2]:28f:28[2]:29[5]:30[4]:31[5]
:32:33:34:35[3]:36/**9**:1[3]:2[2]:3:4[2]:5[4]:6:7[5]:8[2]:9[6]:10[3]:
11[2]:12[3]:13[3]:14[3]:15[4]:16[2]:17[3]:18[4]:19[7]:20[3]:21[2]:22[2]:
23[5]:24[6]/**10**:1[5]:2[2]:3[2]:4[4]:6[6]:7[2]:8,9[2]:10[2]:11:12[7]:13[2]:
14[6]:15[7]:16[3]:17[5]:18:19[3]/**11**:1:2,3[2]:4-7[9]:9:13-19[22]:
21,22:24:26:27:28:29,30[10]:32:33[2]:34[3]:35:36[2]:37[2]
:38[3]:39:44[2]:45[2]:46[3]:47[2]/**12**:1[2]:2[2]:3:4[2]:5[2]:6[4]:7[3]:8[2]
/**13**:1[2]:3[4]:4[6]:5[6]:6[6]:7[4]:8[3]:9,10[4]:11[2]:12[2]:13:14,15[2]:
16,17[5]:18:19[2]:20[7]:21[5]:22[2]:23[4]:24:25[7]:26[5]:27[4]:28[4]
:29,30[6]:31[3]:32[4]:33[4]:34[4]:36:37[3]:38:39:41[2]:42:43:
44:46[2]:49:50:51[2]:52:53[2]:54[2]:55[2]:55f[3]:56[4]:59/**14**:
1:3[4]:4[2]:5[2]:6[5]:7[6]:8[2]:9[2]:10[2]:11[5]:12[6]:13[5]:14[7]:15[3]:16:
17[8]:18[5]:19[6]:20[3]:21[4]:22[2]:23[5]:24[6]:25[8]:26[3]:27:28[7]:
29[4]:30:31[6]:32[3]:33,34[2]:35[3]:36[3]:37[4]:38:39[3]:40[5]:41[4]
:42:43:44[3]:45[3]:46:47:48[5]:49:50:51,52[7]:53[4]:54[2]/
15:1[2]:3:5:6:7:11:12:13:14[5]:15[5]:16:17:18[3]:25[4]:28:
29[4]:30[3]:31:32[2]/**16**:1[9]:3:4:5:6[2]:7[4]:8:9[2]:10[4]:11:12[3]:
13[7]:14[4]:15[5]:16[4]:17[3]:18[7]:19[2]:20[5]:21[6]:22[5]:23[4]:24[2]:
25[3]:26[4]:27[6]:28[2]:29,30:29,30f[3]:29,30[6]:31:32[3]:33[5]:
34:35/**17**:1[3]:3,4:5[8]:6[8]:7[2]:8,9[3]:11[7]:12[2]:13:14[4]:15:
16/**18**:1[2]:3[2]:4,5[2]:6f:6:9[2]:10:14:16f[3]:21:24[3]:25[2]:
25f:26:27[3]:28:28f:28:29,30[2]/**19**:1[4]:5:6[4]:7:8[2]:9[2]:
10[5]:12:14:16f:21[5]:22[4]:23[2]:23f:24[4]:25[2]:27[2]:28:29:
30:32[2]:34:35,36/**20**:1[2]:4[3]:7:8:10:11[2]:13:15:16[2]:
17[2]:19:22f:23[3]:24[2]:25[2]:26/**21**:1[2]:4:5:6:8[3]:9:10[3]:
11:11f[2]:12[3]:14,15:16,17[2]:21[2]:22[4]:23[3]:24/**22**:1[2]:3[4]
:4:6:7[2]:9[2]:10[2]:11:12[2]:12f[2]:13:14[3]:15[3]:16[2]:17,18[3]:
19:21[2]:22[3]:23[2]:24:25:26,27[3]:28:29,30[6]:31:32,33/
23:1[3]:3[3]:4:5[3]:5f[3]:6[3]:7[2]:8[5]:9,10,11[9]:12:13:14:
15,16[3]:17[3]:17f:18[3]:18f:20[6]:21:22[4]:23,24:23,24f[3]:
23,24:25[3]:26,27:26,27f[3]:26,27[3]:28:29:32[2]:33,34[2]
:33,34f[3]:33,34[2]:35[2]:36[6]:37[2]:38[2]:39[5]:40[4]:43[2]:44[2]/
24:1[2]:3,4[5]:5-8[5]:9[3]:10[2]:11[2]:11f[2]:11:12:13,14[3]:
15,16[6]:19[2]:22[3]:23[2]/**25**:1[5]:4[3]:5[3]:9:9f[3]:9[2]:10[5]:12[2]:
13:14,15,16[10]:17,18:19:20:21,22[4]:23:24[2]:27[5]:28[4]
:29:30[4]:31[2]:32[2]:33[5]:34[2]:36:38[3]:40:42:44:45[2]:46:
47[2]:49:50[3]:51[2]:52[3]:53:54[2]:55[3]/**26**:1:2:4,5[3]:4,5f:
4,5:6:10:13[3]:25:26:30[2]:33:34,35[5]:36[2]:38:39:
40,41[2]:42:43:45:46[2]/**27**:1[3]:3:3f[2]:4:8[4]:9:10[6]:11,12[4]
:13[4]:14,15[4]:16[2]:17[2]:18[4]:19[4]:20[4]:21[3]:22:23[4]:24[3]:
25:25f[3]:26[2]:27[7]:28[2]:29:29f:30[3]:32:33[6]:34[3]/**Num**
1:1:1f[3]:1[8]:2-15[2]:16[2]:17,18,19:17,18,19f[3]:
17,18,19[3]:17,18,19f[2]:20-46[2]:47,48,49[5]:50[4]:51[2]:
53[3]:54/**2**:1[3]:3-31[22]:32,33[2]:34[3]/**3**:1[2]:2f:3:4[2]:5:6:
7,8,9[6]:10[2]:11,12[5]:13[5]:14,15[3]:25-30[14]:31-35[14]:
36,37[10]:38[7]:39[3]:40[2]:41[5]:42[3]:43:44:45[8]:46[2]:47,48
f[4]:49[5]:50:50f[2]:51/**4**:1[3]:3:5[4]:6[4]:7[6]:8[3]:9[3]:10:11[3]:12[3]
:13[3]:14[4]:15[8]:16[7]:17,18,19[3]:20[2]:21,22,23[7]:25[6]:26[11]
:27:28:29[4]:30,31[5]:32[2]:33:34[2]:35[2]:36:37:38-41:
42-45:46,47,48[4]:49/**5**:1[3]:3:5,6[3]:7:8[3]:9,10[3]:11,12[2]
:15[3]:16[2]:17[2]:18[3]:19[2]:21,22:23[2]:24[2]:25[4]:26[4]:27:

(THE Con't)
30:30[2]/**6**:1[4]:3,4[3]:5:6,7[2]:8[2]:9[2]:10[5]:11[3]:12:13[5]:14:
15:16[4]:17[4]:18[7]:19[7]:20[6]:21[3]:22,23[2]:24,25,26[2]:27f:
27/**7**:1[3]:2[5]:3[2]:4,5[4]:6[3]:7:8[2]:9[3]:10[4]:11[3]:12[3]:17:18-
18-23[5]:18-23f[3]:24-29[5]:24-29f[3]:30-35[5]:30-35f[3]:
36-41[4]:36-41f[3]:42-47[3]:42-47f[3]:48-53[5]:48-53f[3]:
54-59[3]:54-59f[3]:60-65[5]:60-65f[3]:66-71[6]:66-71f[3]:
72-77[4]:72-77f[3]:78-83[3]:78-83f[3]:84,85,86[8]:87[2]:88:
89[6]/**8**:1:2[2]:4[5]:5,6[3]:9[4]:10[2]:11[5]:12[6]:13[3]:14[4]:15:16[4]:
17[4]:18[2]:19[9]:20[2]:21[3]:22[2]:23,24[5]:25,26/**9**:1[5]:2,3[3]:
2,3f[3]:2,3:4,5[5]:6,7[5]:8:10[3]:11[4]:12[3]:13[4]:14[2]:15[6]:16[2]:
17[2]:18[3]:19:20,21[4]:22[3]:23[3]/**10**:1[3]:3[3]:4[2]:5,6,7[2]:
5,6,7f[2]:5,6,7[7]:8[2]:9[2]:10[2]:11[5]:12[4]:13:14[4]:15[2]:16[2]:
17[6]:18[3]:19[2]:20[2]:21[5]:22[2]:23[2]:24[2]:25[5]:26[2]:27[2]:28[2]:
29[3]:31[2]:31f:32[2]:33f:33[3]:34:35:36[2]/**11**:1[6]:2:3[4]:4,5[6]
:7[3]:8[2]:9[3]:10[3]:11[2]:12[2]:14:16[3]:17[4]:18[2]:19,20:21:22:
23:24[4]:25[6]:26[3]:28:29[2]:30[2]:31[4]:31f:32[5]:33[4]:34[4]/
12:1f[6]:2[2]:3,4[3]:5[4]:6:7,8:9[2]:10[2]:13:14[2]:15[2]:16/**13**:2[2]
:3-15[17]:16f[2]:17[2]:18[2]:19:20[4]:21[3]:22[3]:23[2]:24[3]:26[3]:
27:28:29[8]:30:31:32[4]:33[2]/**14**:1:2:4[2]:5[2]:6[3]:7:8[2]:9[4]:
10,11[6]:13[3]:14[2]:15:16[3]:17,18[4]:19[2]:20,21[4]:22[3]:23:
24:25[7]:26,27:28:30:31[3]:33[3]:34,35[4]:36,37,38[6]:39[2]
:40[4]:41[2]:42:43[3]:44[4]:45[3]/**15**:1[3]:3,4[2]:6:7:8,9[2]:10[2]:
11,12:13,14:15,16[2]:15,16f:17,18[3]:19,20,21[4]:22[2]:
23,24[3]:25[3]:26[3]:27:28[2]:30:31[2]:32[3]:33:33f:34:35[4]:
36[2]:37,38[4]:39[4]:41[2]/**16**:1[3]:2:3[2]:4:5[2]:6,7[2]:6,7f:6,7:
8,9[4]:10:11,12:14:15:16:18[3]:19[3]:22[4]:23,24[3]:25[2]:
26[2]:27[3]:30[3]:31[2]:32:33:34[2]:35:36,37[6]:38[7]:39[3]:40[4]
:41[3]:42[4]:43,44[3]:45[2]:46[3]:47[3]:48[3]:49:50[3]/**17**:1[4]:4[3]:
5:6[3]:7[3]:8[2]:9:10[4]:11:12,13[3]/**18**:1[2]:2,3[6]:4:5[6]:6[4]:7[5]:
8[8]:9[6]:11[4]:12[5]:13:14,15[4]:16[2]:17[4]:18[5]:19[3]:21[3]:22[2]:
23[3]:24[5]:25,26[8]:27:28,29[5]:31:32[5]/**19**:1[4]:4[2]:5:6:7[2]:
8[2]:9[5]:10[5]:12[5]:13[5]:14[3]:15:16:17:17f:18[6]:19[3]:20[3]:
21[3]/**20**:1[2]:1f:2:3:5[2]:6[4]:8f:8[2]:9[3]:10[2]:11[3]:12:12f[2]:
12[3]:13:14[2]:14f[2]:15:16[2]:17[2]:18:19[2]:20[2]:23[3]:24[5]:
27[3]:28[4]:29/**21**:1[5]:2[4]:3[5]:4[5]:5:6:7[3]:8[2]:9[2]:11:12[2]:13[8]
:14[5]:15[2]:16[3]:17,18[4]:20[4]:21:22:23:24[5]:24f[5]:25,26[3]
:27-30[7]:31,32[4]:33:34[4]:35/**22**:1[3]:2,3[2]:4:5,6[3]:7[2]:8[2]:
11[2]:13[3]:15:18[2]:19:21:22,23[6]:24[3]:25[3]:26[4]:27:28[2]:
30:31[4]:32:33:35[2]:36[4]:39:40:41[3]/**23**:1:3,4[3]:5:6[3]:7-
7-10[4]:13:14[2]:15[2]:16:17[3]:18-24[3]:25:27:28[2]:29[2]:30
/**24**:1[2]:2[2]:3-9[10]:13:14:15-19[8]:20[4]:21,22[5]:23,24:
25f/**25**:1[2]:2[4]:3[4]:4[4]:5:6[6]:7:8[6]:10,11[2]:12,13:14[4]:15:
16,17[2]:18/**26**:1[2]:2:3,4[6]:5-11[14]:12-14[7]:15-18[10]:
19-22[10]:23-25[7]:26,27[6]:28-37[25]:38-41[10]:42,43[4]:
44-47[9]:48-50[7]:51[2]:52,53[4]:54[2]:55,56[6]:57[6]:58,59[9]:
61:62[8]:63[4]:64,65f[2]:64,65[5]/**27**:1[6]:3,4[3]:5:6,7[3]:11:
12[4]:14[6]:15:16[3]:17[2]:18[2]:19[4]:20:21[8]:22[2]:23/**28**:1[4]:
4[3]:6[2]:7[3]:8[4]:9,10[3]:11[2]:12:13:14[2]:15[3]:16[6]:17:18[3]:
19:20,21[2]:23:24[3]:25[2]:26[7]:27:28,29[2]:31[2]/**29**:1[2]:1f[3]
:1:2:3,4[3]:6:6f:6[3]:7f[3]:7[2]:8:9,10[3]:11[3]:12f[3]:12[3]:13:14[3]
:15:16:17:18:19:20[2]:21:22:23[2]:25[2]:26,27[3]:28[2]:29[2]
:31[2]:32[2]:34[2]:35[2]:36:37:38[2]:39:40/**30**:1[6]:3:5[3]:7:9:
10:11:12:15:16[2]/**31**:1[2]:3:4,5:6[2]:6f[2]:8[2]:9,10,11[4]:
12[6]:13[4]:14:15:16[4]:17[2]:18:19[2]:21[4]:23[2]:24[2]:25:26[5]
:27[4]:28[3]:29[4]:30[5]:31[2]:32-35[3]:36-40[6]:36-40f:41[3]:
42-46[5]:47[2]:48,49[2]:50[2]:51,52[2]:53:54[4]/**32**:1[2]:2[2]:
3,4[2]:5[3]:6:7[4]:8[2]:9[3]:10,11[2]:12[5]:13[2]:14:15[2]:17[3]:18:
19[3]:21[2]:22[8]:23:25:26:27:28:29[5]:30[2]:31[2]:32[2]:33[5]:
34,35,36:37,38[4]:39[3]:40:41[4]:42/**33**:1[3]:2:3,4[2]:3,4f[3]
:3,4[8]:5,6[2]:7:8[3]:10:11:14:15-37[5]:38,39[7]:38,39f[3]:40[4]
:41:44:47:48[2]:49[2]:50,51[4]:52[3]:53:54[5]:55/**34**:1[4]:3[6]:
4:5[2]:5f:5:6[2]:7,8,9:10,11[4]:12[2]:13[2]:14,15[4]:16-28[6]:
29[5]/**35**:1[3]:2[2]:3:4:5[3]:6[2]:7[2]:8[4]:9,10[3]:12[2]:13,14[3]:15:
16:17[2]:18:19[2]:21[2]:22,23:24[4]:25[7]:26[2]:27:28[7]:32[2]:
33[4]:34/**36**:1[10]:3[2]:4:5[3]:6[2]:7[3]:8[3]:10[2]:13[5]/**Deu1**:1[7]:
1f[3]:1:1f[2]:1[3]:7[10]:8[2]:9:10:15:17:19,20,21[7]:22:24,25[4]
:26[2]:27:28[7]:30:31:32:33[3]:34,35[2]:36[3]:37[2]:38[3]:39[3]:
40[3]:41[3]:42:43[2]:44:45/**2**:1[4]:2:4[5]:5:7[2]:8[2]:9[3]:10[2]:11[4]
:12[5]:13:14,15[4]:16,17:18:19[3]:20[2]:21[3]:22[3]:23[3]:24[4]:
25:26:27[2]:29[5]:30:31[2]:33,34[2]:35,36[8]:37[4]/**3**:1[3]:3:4:
5:6[2]:7:8[7]:9[2]:10[3]:11[4]:12[6]:13[6]:14[5]:15:16[7]:17[6]:18[8]:
19[2]:20[5]:21[5]:22[2]:23,24,25[5]:26:27[4]:28[3]:29/**4**:1[2]:2:
3:4:5[3]:6:7:9:10[3]:11[4]:12[2]:13[2]:14[3]:15[2]:18:19[3]:20:
21,22[3]:23[3]:25[3]:26[2]:27:30[2]:31[2]:32[4]:33:34:36[3]:39[2]
:40[2]:41[2]:43[5]:44,45,46[7]:47:48[3]:49[4]/**5**:1:2,3:4[3]:5[2]:
9,10[4]:11f[2]:12:13:14[3]:15[2]:16[2]:22[5]:23[5]:24[3]:26,27[4]:
28[2]:29:31[2]:32[4]:33/**6**:1[2]:2[2]:3:7[2]:9:10,11,12[5]:14[2]:
15[2]:18[3]:19[2]:20[3]:21:25[2]/**7**:1[10]:2:4[2]:5[4]:6[4]:7:9[2]:12[2]:
13:14[2]:15[2]:16[2]:18[2]:19[6]:20:21:22:24[2]:25[2]/**8**:1[3]:2[2]:
5:6[2]:7:9:10[2]:11[2]:14[3]:15[4]:16:18:19:20[3]/**9**:1[4]:3:4[4]:
5[3]:7[3]:9[5]:10,11[7]:12[2]:13,14:15[3]:16[2]:17[2]:18[2]:19:20[2]
:21[3]:22:23[2]:24[2]:25:27[2]:28[4]/**10**:1[3]:2[4]:3[3]:4[5]:5[3]:6[2]:8[4]
:9[3]:10[5]:11[2]:12,13[2]:14:17[2]:18:19:20:21:22[3]/**11**:1:
2:3:4[3]:5[3]:6[2]:8[2]:9[3]:10[2]:12[2]:13:14:17[5]:20:21[4]:22[2]:
23[2]:24[4]:25:26:27[2]:28:29[2]:30[4]:31[3]:32/**12**:1[3]:2[4]:3[4]:
4,5:6[4]:7:9[2]:10[3]:11:12[2]:14[4]:15[2]:16[3]:17[6]:18[4]:19[2]:
20-23[8]:24,25[2]:26,27[8]:28[2]:29[2]:31[2]:32/**13**:1:2[2]:3:5[4]
:8:9[3]:10[3]:12,13,14[6]:15:16[5]:17[2]:18[3]/**14**:1[3]:2[3]:
3,4,5[11]:6:7[5]:8[2]:11-18[21]:21:23[4]:24[2]:25[3]:26[2]:27:29
/**15**:1:2:4,5[5]:7[2]:9[4]:10:12[2]:14:15[2]:17[2]:18[2]:19[3]:20:
22:23[2]/**16**:1[2]:1f[2]:2:3[4]:4[2]:5:6[4]:7[2]:8[4]:9:10[3]:11[4]:13[5]:
14:15[4]:16[6]:17:18[3]:19[2]:20[3]:21[2]:22/**17**:1:2,3:4:5:6:
7[3]:8[3]:9[4]:10:11:12[4]:13[2]:14[3]:15[2]:16:17:18[2]:19[2]:20[2]
/**18**:1[10]:2:3[4]:4[8]:5[4]:6,7[5]:8:9[3]:10:11[2]:12[3]:13:14[2]:16[5]
:17:18:21[2]:22[4]/**19**:1[2]:2,3[2]:4:5[4]:6,7[3]:8[2]:9:10:11:12[2]
:14[3]:15:17[3]:18:19[2]:20/**20**:1[2]:2[2]:4[2]:5[4]:7:8:9[3]:11:
13[2]:14:15:15f:16[3]:17[8]:18[4]:19[3]:20/**21**:1[2]:2[3]:3:5[2]:6
:8:9[2]:10:11:15[3]:16[2]:17[5]:19[2]:21[3]:23[4]/**22**:2[2]:3:4:5:
6[5]:7[2]:8[3]:9[4]:9f[2]:12:15[3]:17,18[5]:19f:19:20:21[5]:22:
23,24[6]:25,26,27[4]:28,29[2]:30f/**23**:1:2:3[2]:4[2]:5[3]:6[2]:7[4]
:8[4]:9,10[4]:11:12[2]:13[2]:14[3]:17,18[3]:19:20[2]:21[2]:23[2]:
24:25/**24**:1:3:4[3]:5:7[2]:8[3]:9:11:12,13[3]:14,15:16[3]:18
:19[3]:20[3]:21[3]:22/**25**:1[5]:4:5:6[3]:7[3]:8[2]:9[3]:10[2]:11[3]:
13,14,15[2]:16:17:19[3]/**26**:1:2,3[5]:4[3]:5:6,7[2]:8:10[5]:11
:12:13[5]:14[3]:15:16:18:19/**27**:1[2]:1f:2,3,4[7]:5,6[3]:7:8:
9[3]:11:12[2]:13:14:15[3]:16:17[2]:18:19[4]:20:21:22:23:
24:25:26/**28**:1[4]:2-6[3]:7:8[3]:10[3]:11[2]:12:13[5]:14:15-
15-19[5]:20[2]:21[2]:23[2]:24:25[3]:26:29[2]:30[3]:31:33:34:
35:36:37[2]:38:39[3]:40:42:44[2]:45:47,48:49:52:53[2]:
54:55[4]:56,57[8]:58,59[2]:60[2]:61:62:63[3]:64[4]:65:66:67[3]
:68/**29**:1[4]:2,3[3]:4:5:6[2]:8[2]:9:10[2]:11:16[2]:18[2]:19:20[3]:
21[3]:22[6]:23[2]:24[2]:25[5]:27[2]:28:29/**30**:1[4]:2[2]:3[2]:4[2]:5[2]:
6[2]:7,8[3]:9[2]:10[3]:12:13:16[3]:18:20[4]/**31**:1:2[2]:3[3]:4[5]:5[2]:
6:7[2]:8:9[9]:10,11[7]:12[3]:13[2]:14[4]:15:16[2]:19[2]:20:21[2]:
22[3]:23[4]:24:25[3]:26[3]:27:28:29[2]:30/**32**:2[3]:3[2]:4:6:7[2]:
8[2]:10[2]:11:12:13:14[3]:15:18:21[2]:22[3]:24:25[4]:26:27:
30:31:33:35:36:37:40,41[5]:44,45[2]:46:47[2]:48:49[5]:
50:51[3]:52[2]/**33**:1[3]:2:4:5[3]:7:8:10[3]:11[2]:12:13[3]:14[2]:
15[2]:16[5]:17[4]:18:19[5]:20:21[3]:22:23[5]:24:25:26[2]:27[2]:
28:29/**34**:1[3]:2:3[4]:4[2]:5[4]:6[2]:8[2]:9[4]:10:11,12[2]/**Jos1**:1[3]
:2[3]:3:4[10]:6:7:8:9:10,11[4]:12,13[6]:14[3]:15[3]:17,18/**2**:1[5]
:2[2]:3[2]:4[2]:5[2]:6:7[4]:8[2]:9:10[4]:11:12,13[2]:14:15:16[2]:
17,18[2]:19:21[2]:22[5]:23[3]:24[3]/**3**:1[4]:2,3,4[4]:2,3,4f[3]:
2,3,4:5[3]:6[4]:7:8[4]:9[2]:10[4]:11[3]:13,14[13]:15,16[9]:17[5]/**4**:
1[2]:2,3[5]:4:5[4]:6:7[4]:8[6]:9[4]:10[7]:11[4]:12,13[5]:14[4]:15,16[6]:
17:18[4]:19:19f[3]:19[4]:20[2]:21[3]:22[2]:23[5]:24[3]/**5**:1[7]:2,3[8]
:4,5[5]:6[5]:7:8,9:8,9f:8,9[4]:10[5]:11,12[4]:13:14[3]:15/**6**:1[3]
:2:3,4[5]:5[4]:6-9[5]:10:11[4]:12,13,14[2]:15[2]:16[5]:17:18:
19[3]:20[5]:22[2]:23[2]:24[5]:25[4]:26[3]:26f:27/**7**:1[6]:2:5[5]:6[3]:
7[4]:9[3]:10,11:12:13[2]:14[8]:15[4]:16[4]:17[5]:18:19:20[2]:21[3]
:22[5]:23:24[5]:25[2]:26[4]/**8**:1[3]:2[3]:3,4[2]:5[2]:6[2]:7[2]:8[2]:9[4]:
10[2]:11,12,13[5]:11,12,13f[3]:11,12,13[2]:14[6]:15[2]:16[3]:
17:18[2]:19[2]:20,21[6]:22[5]:23:24[3]:25:26:27[4]:29[4]:30:
31[5]:32[4]:32f:33[8]:34[2]:35[4]/**9**:1[10]:3,4,5:6[2]:7:9[2]:10[2]:
11:12:14,15[4]:16:17[3]:18[6]:19[2]:20:21:23:24:26:27[5]/
10:1[3]:2:4:6[4]:7:8:9:10[5]:11[7]:12[5]:13[7]:14[4]:15:16[2]:17:
18[3]:19[5]:20[3]:21:22,23[4]:24[2]:25:26:27[5]:28[2]:29:30[2]:
32[3]:33[2]:34,35[3]:37:40[8]:42/**11**:1[24]:4[2]:5:6:7:8[5]:9[3]:
10[3]:11:12[2]:13:14[4]:15[3]:16[7]:17[5]:19[3]:20[4]:21[3]:22:23[6]
/**12**:1[11]:2[11]:3[5]:4[2]:5[9]:6[4]:7[6]:8-24[46]/**13**:1:2-7[33]:8[5]:9[6]
:10[3]:11[3]:12[3]:13[4]:14[6]:15[5]:16[7]:17[2]:19[2]:20:21[6]:22[3]:
23[3]:24[3]:25[2]:27,28[8]:29[4]:30[2]:31:32[3]:33[2]/**14**:1[8]:3,4[6]
:5[3]:6[3]:7[3]:8[3]:9:10[2]:12[5]:13,14:15[4]/**15**:1[6]:2,3,4[6]:5[8]:
6:7[6]:8[9]:9[5]:10,11[10]:12[3]:13[3]:14[2]:15[2]:16:17:18,19[2]:
20[2]:21-32[3]:33-36[2]:37-44:45[3]:46[4]:47[7]:48-62f[2]:48-
48-62[2]:63[5]/**16**:1[11]:5,6[6]:7:8[3]:9[3]:10[2]/**17**:1[7]:2[3]:4[4]:
5,6[4]:7[6]:8[4]:9[7]:10[9]:11[4]:12[3]:13[2]:14[2]:15[3]:16,17,18[7]/
18:1[4]:3[3]:4:5,6[2]:7[6]:8[7]:9[4]:10[3]:11[7]:12[4]:13[2]:14[6]:15[3]:
16[7]:17[3]:18[4]:19[4]:20[4]:21-28f:21-28[3]/**19**:1[5]:2-7f:8[2]:
9:10[4]:11[2]:12[3]:14[2]:15,16:17-23[6]:24,25,26[6]:27[2]:29[4]
:32[4]:33[2]:34[7]:35-39[2]:40[3]:41-46[2]:47,48[3]:49[4]:50[2]:
51[9]/**20**:1:2[2]:3[2]:4[2]:5[3]:6[7]:7[4]:8[10]:9/**21**:1[5]:2:3:4[4]:5[4]:
6[4]:7[2]:8[4]:9-16[6]:9-16f:9-16[6]:17,18:19[2]:20,21,22[2]:
20,21,22f[2]:20,21,22:23,24[2]:25[2]:26[3]:27[3]:28,29:
30,31:32:33:34,35[4]:40[2]:41,42[2]:43[2]:44[2]:45/**22**:1[3]:
2,3[3]:4[5]:5[2]:7,8[6]:9[4]:10:11:13[4]:14:15[3]:16[4]:17,18[2]:19[5]
:20[4]:21[3]:22,23[5]:24,25[6]:26,27[3]:28[4]:29[3]:30[3]:31[2]:
32[2]:34[3]/**23**:1[2]:2[2]:3:4,5[8]:6[4]:7[3]:8:10[2]:12:13[2]:14[2]:
15,16[3]/**24**:1[2]:2[3]:3[2]:4:6[2]:7[4]:8[4]:9:11[8]:12[2]:14[3]:15[6]:
16[2]:17[6]:18[5]:19[2]:21[2]:22:23[2]:24[2]:26[5]:27[2]:28[2]:29:
30[3]:31[5]:32[7]:33[3]/**Ju1**:1[4]:3[7]:4,5,6[4]:7:8:9[5]:10[2]:11:
12:13[2]:15[2]:16[6]:17[4]:18[2]:19[6]:20[5]:21[3]:22,23[3]:24[3]:
24f[3]:25:26:27[3]:28[3]:29[2]:30[2]:31,32[5]:33[2]:34[4]:35[2]:
36[4]/**2**:1[3]:2:3[2]:4[2]:5[3]:6[3]:7-9[9]:10[2]:11[2]:12-14[8]:15[3]:
16:17[2]:18[3]:19[5]:20[3]:21:22:23[2]/**3**:1[6]:1f:1[5]:4[3]:5:6[3]:
7[2]:8[2]:9:10[5]:11:12:13[5]:14[2]:15[3]:17,18,19[6]:21[2]:
22,23[7]:24[3]:25[2]:26:27:28[5]:29[2]:30[2]:31/**4**:1[2]:2,3[4]:4[3]
:5[2]:6[3]:7[2]:9:10:11[5]:13[2]:14[3]:15[4]:16[2]:17[4]:20[2]:21[2]:22[3]
:23/**5**:1:2[3]:3[2]:4[3]:5[2]:6[3]:9[2]:11[9]:13,14[3]:15[4]:16[2]:17[2]:
18[2]:19[2]:20:21:22[4]:23[2]:24[2]:26:28[4]:31[3]/**6**:1[3]:2[3]:3,4
:5:6,7[3]:8[3]:9:10[3]:11[7]:12[3]:13[4]:14[2]:15[4]:16:16f[2]:16:
18:19[3]:20[4]:21[4]:22[4]:23:24[4]:25[4]:26[7]:27[4]:28[5]:29:30[2]
:31[3]:33[3]:34[3]:37[4]:38[2]:39[3]:40[3]/**7**:1[4]:2[3]:4[2]:5,6[9]:7[3]:
8,9[6]:10:11[3]:12,13[7]:14[4]:15[4]:16:17[2]:18[2]:19,20[10]:
21:22[7]:23[2]:24[4]:25[6]/**8**:1[2]:2,3[5]:2,3f[2]:4[2]:5[2]:6:7[3]:8:
10[2]:11[2]:12:14[3]:16[2]:16f:17[2]:18:20:21f[2]:21:22:
23,24[3]:25:26[5]:27f:27:28[2]:32[3]:33[2]:34:35/**9**:2:3[2]:4[2]
:5:6[3]:7[2]:8[2]:9[2]:10:11[2]:12:13[3]:14[2]:15[2]:16:17:20:
22,23:24[2]:25[4]:26[2]:27[4]:30[2]:31:32:33[2]:34[2]:35[4]:37[2]
:38[2]:39[2]:40[3]:42[2]:43[3]:44[3]:45[3]:46[4]:49[5]:50:51[5]:53:
54:56,57[2]/**10**:1[4]:4[2]:6[4]:7,8[5]:9[3]:10:11[5]:12[3]:14:16:
17:18[2]/**11**:1[2]:3[2]:4:5:6:8[2]:11[4]:12:13[8]:14,15:16[2]:17[4]
:18[4]:19:21,22[5]:23[3]:25:26[2]:27:28:29[4]:30,31[4]:32[3]:
33[4]:35[2]:36[2]:37:40[2]/**12**:1:3[2]:4[5]:5[7]:6:7:8:11,12:15[2]
/**13**:1[2]:2,3[6]:5[2]:6[3]:7[3]:8[2]:9[3]:10:11[2]:12:13,14[2]:15:16[4]
:17[2]:18:19[2]:20[6]:21[3]:23:24:25[6]/**14**:3[2]:4[4]:5[3]:6[3]:7[2]:
8[4]:9:10,11[4]:12:13:14[2]:15[2]:16:17[6]:18[2]:19[5]:20/**15**:
1:5[8]:6[4]:8:9:10[2]:11[3]:12,13[2]:14[4]:15:16,17[2]:18[2]:19[6]:
20[3]/**16**:1[2]:2[5]:3[6]:4:5[2]:8:9[3]:9f:12[4]:14[2]:18[3]:20[2]:21[2]:
23,24[4]:25,26[9]:27[3]:27f:28[3]:29:30[5]/**17**:1:3[3]:4,5[2]:
7,8:10,11:13/**18**:1[3]:2[4]:3:6[2]:7[4]:8:9,10[4]:11:12:13[2]:
14[2]:15,16[5]:17[5]:18:20[4]:21[2]:23:25:26:27[6]:28[5]:29:
30[2]:31[2]/**19**:1[3]:5[2]:7:8[2]:10:14[2]:15[2]:16[3]:17[2]:18[5]:20[2]
:22[5]:23:25:26[2]:27[3]:28:30[2]/**20**:1[4]:3[5]:5[2]:6[2]:8,9,10[3]:
11:12[2]:13[2]:14,15[2]:17[2]:18[4]:19,20[3]:21[2]:22,23,24[6]:
26[2]:27,28[7]:29[2]:30:31[6]:32[4]:33[2]:34[3]:35-39[16]:42[6]:
43:44:45[5]:46,47[2]:48[4]/**21**:1[2]:2:4:5:6:7[2]:10,11,12[4]:
13[2]:14:15[2]:16[4]:19[4]:20[2]:21:23[3]:24/**Ru1**:1[2]:3:6,7:8
:11f[3]:13:15:17:19[2]:21[2]:22[2]/**2**:2[2]:3:4,5[2]:6[2]:7[3]:8,9[2]:
10,11[2]:12:14f[2]:15:17[2]:18:19[4]:20:21:22:23[3]/**3**:2[2]:
3:4:6,7[2]:11:13[2]:14[2]:15-18[2]/**4**:1:1f[2]:1:2[2]:4[2]:5[2]:6:6f
:7[3]:8:9[3]:10[3]:11[4]:12[3]:13:14[3]:15:16,17[3]:18-22/**1Sa**
1:1[3]:3[5]:4[2]:5:7:8:9[3]:10:15,16:17:19,20[6]:19,20f[2]:
19,20:21,22[5]:23[2]:24[2]:25[2]:26[2]:28[3]/**2**:1[2]:2:3:5:6[2]:8[6]
:9:10[2]:11[3]:12[2]:13,14[5]:15[4]:16[5]:17[5]:18[2]:19:20[2]:21[3]
:22[3]:23,24,25[4]:26:27[2]:28:29[3]:30[2]:32:33:34:36/**3**:
1[2]:2,3[2]:4,5:6:8[4]:10:11:12:14:15[3]:16,17:18[2]:19:20:
21,4:1[3]/**4**:1[3]:2:3[5]:4[5]:5[3]:6[6]:8[3]:10[2]:11:12[3]:13[8]:14[2]:
16:17[3]:18[4]:19:20[2]:21,22[2]/**5**:1[5]:3[4]:4[7]:5[3]:6[3]:7[3]:8[5]:9[3]
:10[4]:11[5]/**6**:1[2]:2[2]:3[2]:4,5[6]:6:7:8[5]:9[2]:10[2]:11[5]:12[4]:13[3]
:14[7]:15[8]:16:17[5]:18[7]:19[6]:20:21[4]/**7**:1[3]:2[2]:3[3]:4:5:6[2]:
7[4]:9[2]:10[4]:11:12[2]:13[3]:14[4]:15:16:17/**8**:3:4[2]:5[2]:6:7[2]:
8:10[2]:12:14:16:18:19:20:21[2]:22[2]/**9**:1[2]:2[2]:4[4]:5[3]:6[3]
:8:9,10,11[6]:12,13[5]:14[3]:15[2]:16[3]:17[2]:18:19[3]:20:21[6]
:22[4]:23[4]:24:25[4]:26,27[6]/**10**:1[3]:2[2]:3[3]:4:5[3]:6[2]:7[2]:10[4]
:12[3]:13[2]:14[3]:16:18,19[4]:20[3]:21[6]:22[3]:24[5]:25[4]:26/
11:1[4]:2:3:4:5[3]:6:7[2]:9[2]:10:11[3]:12:13:14:15[2]/**12**:1:
2:3:5:6[2]:7[2]:8[2]:9[4]:10[2]:11:12[2]:13[2]:14[3]:15:16:17[4]:18[4]
:20:22:23:24[2]/**13**:1f[2]:1:2[4]:3,4[9]:5[2]:6[3]:7[2]:9[2]:11[2]:12[3]
:13[2]:14[3]:15[2]:16[2]:17[3]:18[4]:19[3]:20:21:22:23[2]/**14**:1[3]:
2[2]:3[6]:4:5[3]:6:7:11[2]:12:13[2]:15[3]:16[2]:18[3]:19[5]:20[2]:21[3]
:22[4]:23[2]:24,25[2]:27:30[2]:31:32[3]:33[2]:34[4]:35:36[2]:37[2]
:38:39[4]:40:41[4]:42:43:45[3]:46[2]:47[4]:48:50,51[3]:52[2]/
15:2:3:5[2]:6[5]:7[2]:8[2]:9[4]:10:11:12:13:14:15[4]:16:18[2]:
19[2]:20:21[3]:22[2]:23[2]:24[3]:25:26[3]:28[2]:29:30[2]:32:33[2]
:35/**16**:1[2]:2[2]:3:4[3]:5[3]:6[2]:7[3]:8[2]:9[3]:10,11[4]:12[2]:13[2]:
14[3]:15,16[2]:18[2]:19:21:23[3]/**17**:1:3[2]:4-7[2]:8[2]:10:11f[3]
:11:12[2]:13[2]:14,15[2]:16[2]:18:19[2]:20[7]:21:22:23[3]:24:
25[6]:26[3]:27:28[2]:30[2]:31:33:34:35[2]:36[2]:37[5]:38,39:
43:44:45[4]:46[4]:47:48,49[5]:50,51[2]:52[6]:53[2]:55:55f:
56:57/**18**:1:4:5:6[3]:10[2]:11,12[2]:13[3]:14:17[2]:18:19[2]:
20:21:22[2]:23:25:25f:25:26[2]:28[3]:30[3]/**19**:2:4:5[2]:6:
8:9,10[8]:11:12:14:19:20[2]:21:22:23[2]:24f/**20**:3[2]:5[6]:
11:12[3]:13[2]:14[2]:15:16:18:19[3]:20:21:22:23:23f:
24,25[4]:27:30f:34:35[2]:36[3]:37[3]:38[2]:40[2]:41[2]:42/**21**:
1[2]:2:4[2]:6[6]:7:7f:8:9[6]:9f:9:11[3]/**22**:1:2:3:4[2]:5[4]:6[2]:7:
9,10[5]:11,12:14:15:16:17[2]:18:19[4]:20:22/**23**:1[2]:2[2]:
3:4[3]:5[2]:6[2]:9[3]:11[2]:12:13:14,15[5]:17:18:19[4]:21:23[2]:
24,25[4]:27:28[4]:29/**24**:1[2]:2[2]:3[4]:4[3]:7,8[2]:9,10[4]:11:12
:14:15:18:19[3]:21/**25**:1:2[2]:3:7:9:14:15,16[2]:20:21:
25:26[2]:28:29[3]:30,31[5]:32:33:34[2]:36:37,38:39:40:
42:44/**26**:1[2]:3,4[3]:5,6,7[4]:8:9:11:12[2]:13[2]:15:16[3]:19[3]
:20[3]:23[2]:24/**27**:1:2,3:5[2]:6:7:8[4]:9[2]:10[3]:11:12[2]/**28**:
1:3:4[2]:5,6[4]:5,6f[2]:5,6:7,8:9[2]:11:12:13[2]:15:16:17:
18:19[2]:20:21[2]:22:23[3]:24:25[3]/**29**:1[3]:2[2]:3[2]:4[3]:5[2]:6[2]
:9:10:11[3]/**30**:1[3]:2:3:6:7[2]:8[2]:9,10[3]:11,12:13:14[4]:
15:16[5]:17:18,19:20:21:22[2]:23[2]:24:26[3]:27-31[7]/**31**
:1[3]:2:3,4[3]:7[5]:8[4]:9[2]:10[2]:11[2]:12[2]:13/**2Sa1**:1[3]:3:4[3]:6
:10f[2]:11:12[2]:13[2]:17,18:19:20[3]:21f[2]:21:25[3]:26:27/
2:1[3]:2:4[3]:5:6:7:9[2]:10,11[2]:13[3]:16[3]:17[5]:18:23[4]:24[3]:
25[3]:28:29[3]:30:31/**3**:1[2]:2:3[3]:4:6[2]:9,10[3]:12[2]:14:17:
18[3]:19[3]:21:23:24,25:26:27[2]:28:29[2]:30[2]:31[2]:32[3]:
33,34[3]:35,36[2]:37:39/**4**:2,3[3]:4[8]:6,7[2]:8[4]:9:12/**5**:1:2[2]
:3[2]:4,5[2]:6[2]:7[2]:8[9]:9[5]:10:12[2]:17[2]:18[2]:19[2]:20[2]:21:22[2]
:23[2]:24[4]:25[3]/**6**:1[3]:3[2]:5[2]:6[3]:7[3]:8[3]:9[2]:10[2]:11:12[2]:13
:14:15[2]:16[3]:17[3]:18[3]:20[3]:21[4]:22/**7**:1[3]:2[2]:3:4:6:7:8[3]
:9[2]:10,11[2]:13:17:18[2]:23:27/**8**:1:2:3[2]:4:6[2]:7:9:
11,12[3]:13:14[3]:16:17[2]:18f/**9**:2:3:4[2]:5,6:7[2]:8[3]:9:
10,11:12:13/**10**:1:3:4:5:6[4]:7,8[5]:9[3]:10[3]:11[2]:12[2]:13
:14[3]:15,16[5]:17[2]:18[3]:19[3]/**11**:1[6]:2[3]:3[2]:4:6:7[2]:9[4]:10:
11[3]:12[2]:13[2]:14:15[4]:16[2]:18:19,20,21[4]:22[2]:23[2]:24[3]
:25:25f:25:27[3]/**12**:1[2]:3:4[4]:5:6[2]:7[2]:8:9:12:13[2]:14[2]:
15:16[3]:17[2]:18[4]:19:20[4]:21[2]:22[3]:24[2]:25f:25[3]:25f:
26,27[2]:26,27f:28[5]:29,30:31[7]/**13**:2:3:4[2]:6:9[2]:10:
13[2]:16:17,18[3]:19:20:21-24[2]:25:26:27[2]:28[2]:29,30[4]
:31[2]:32,33:34[6]:35:36:37,38,39/**14**:1:2,3:4[3]:5,6[2]:7[4]
:8:9:10:13:14:15,16:17[2]:18:19:20:21:22[2]:24:28:
32[2]:33[2]/**15**:2[3]:3:4:6[2]:7,8[2]:9:10[2]:12[2]:14[2]:16[2]:
17,18[4]:19,20[4]:23[3]:24[4]:25,26[5]:27[2]:28[3]:29[2]:30[4]:32[4]
:35,36[2]:37/**16**:1[3]:2[6]:3[2]:4:5[2]:6[3]:7,8[2]:9:10[2]:11:12:
13:14[2]:16[3]:17:18[2]:21[2]:21f:22[3]:23/**17**:2,3:4[2]:5:8[2]:
10:11[2]:13[4]:14[4]:15:16[3]:17[2]:19[4]:20:21[3]:22[3]:24[3]:25[3]

(THE Con't)
:26:28,29/**18**:2[4]:3:4[4]:5[3]:6[2]:7:8[3]:9[4]:11f[3]:12[2]:13[3]:
14[2]:16[2]:17[2]:18:19[2]:20:21[2]:23[2]:24[6]:25[3]:26[2]:27[4]:
28[4]:29:29f:30:31[2]:32[2]:33[2]/**19**:1:2[3]:3[2]:4:5[2]:7[2]:
8,9,10[9]:11,12[4]:14[2]:15[3]:16[4]:17[4]:18[2]:19[2]:20[2]:21:
24,25[4]:26:29:31,32[3]:33:35:36[2]:38:39[3]:40:41[3]:42[2]
:43[6]/**20**:2[2]:3:4[2]:5[2]:7:8,9,10[6]:12[3]:13[2]:14:15[2]:16:
17:19:21[4]:22[5]:23[2]:23f:24[3]:25[2]:26/**21**:1[4]:2[3]:4:5,6[5]
:7:8[3]:9[5]:10[3]:10f:10[3]:12,13,14[8]:15[3]:17[3]:18[2]:19[3]:
20,21[3]:22/**22**:1:4:5:7:8[3]:9:10:11[3]:13:14[2]:16[4]:17:
19[2]:21:25:26[2]:28:31[2]:34[2]:36:40:43:44[3]:47[2]:50/
23:1[5]:2[2]:3[2]:4[4]:6[2]:8[5]:9[5]:10[5]:11,12[3]:13[6]:14[3]:15[3]:16[4]
:17:18,19[8]:20f[2]:20[2]:21[2]:22[2]:23[3]:24-39[9]:24-39f[2]/
24:1[2]:2[4]:3:3f:4[3]:5[4]:6:7[3]:8:9[3]:10[2]:11[5]:13:14[3]:15[2]:
16[5]:17[3]:18[3]:19:20[3]:21[2]:22[4]:23:24[4]:25[3]/**1Ki1**:2:
3,4[5]:5:7:8[2]:9[3]:10[2]:11[2]:12:13:15:17[2]:18:19:20[2]:
22,23[3]:24[2]:25[2]:26:27:28:29[2]:30[2]:31f:31:32[3]:34[3]:
35:37:38[2]:39[3]:40:41[2]:42[2]:44,45[8]:46,47[3]:48:49,50[4]
:51:53[2]/**2**:1:3[2]:4[3]:7[3]:8[3]:12:13:15[5]:17:19[2]:22[2]:
23,24[2]:26[4]:27[4]:28[3]:30[3]:31[3]:32[4]:33:34[2]:35:36,37[3]
:40:42:44[2]:46[2]/**3**:1[5]:2[4]:3[2]:4[3]:5:7:9:10:11:13[2]:15[4]:
16:17,18[2]:19:20:21:22[6]:23[5]:24:25:26[5]:27[4]:28[4]/**4**:
1[5]:7[3]:8-19[12]:21[6]:22[2]:23:24[3]:25:27:28[3]:30[2]:31[3]:32
:33[3]/**5**:1:2,3[4]:4:5[2]:6:7[2]:8:9[6]:12:14:15:17[3]:18[4]/**6**:1[5]
:2:3[2]:5[3]:6[9]:7[7]:8[7]:9[2]:10[3]:11,12[2]:13:14:15[2]:16[6]:17[3]:
18[3]:19[4]:21,22[6]:23-28[4]:29[2]:30:31[2]:33[2]:36[2]:37[4]:38[2]
/**7**:2[5]:3,4[2]:5:6:7[3]:8[2]:10:11[2]:12[5]:14[2]:16-22[10]:24[3]:
26[2]:27-30[2]:31[2]:32[3]:33[3]:34[3]:35[2]:36[2]:37[2]:38:39[7]:
40[4]:41-46[9]:47:48[6]:49[5]:50[5]:51[6]/**8**:1[10]:2[3]:3,4[6]:5[2]:6[7]
:7[4]:8[4]:9[5]:10[3]:11[4]:12,13[2]:14[2]:15:17:18:19:20[2]:21[6]:
22,23[3]:25:27[2]:29:30:35,36[3]:37[3]:38:43[3]:51:53[3]:
54,55[2]:56[2]:57:58[2]:60[2]:61:62,63[4]:64[7]:65[3]:66[4]/**9**:1[3]
:2,3[3]:5[2]:7[2]:8:9[5]:10[4]:11,12[5]:13:15[3]:16[4]:19[2]:20,21[5]
:23:24[4]:25[2]:26[2]:27,28/**10**:1[2]:1f[3]:3[2]:3f:4:5[4]:6:7:9[3]:
10[2]:12[3]:13[3]:15[2]:16,17[3]:20:21[2]:22:23[2]:26[2]:27:29[2]
/**11**:1[2]:2[2]:3:4:5[4]:6:7[5]:9,10:11[2]:12,13[3]:14[3]:15[3]:
16,17,18:19:23[2]:24:26[2]:27,28[3]:29[4]:31[4]:32f:32[3]:
33[5]:34[3]:35[2]:36[4]:37:39:40:41[3]:43/**12**:1:2,3,4[4]:5:6:
8[2]:10:12:13,14[3]:15[5]:16,17[3]:18[2]:19:20[5]:21[2]:22:
23,24[5]:25[2]:26:27:28[3]:29:30:31[4]:32,33[2]:32,33f[4]:
32,33[5]/**13**:1[3]:2[7]:3[3]:4[3]:5[5]:6[5]:7[3]:8[2]:9[2]:11[2]:12:13[3]:
14[2]:15[2]:16,17[2]:18[3]:19[2]:20[3]:21,22[4]:23[3]:24,25[8]:26[4]
:28[6]:29[4]:30:31[2]:32[4]:33[4]:34[2]/**14**:2[3]:3:5[3]:6:7[3]:8[2]:9:
11[2]:12[2]:13[4]:14[2]:15[4]:17[2]:18[2]:19[4]:20:21[5]:22[2]:24[4]:
25:26[3]:27:28[5]:29[3]:31[2]/**15**:1[2]:4[2]:5[2]:7[3]:9[2]:10:11:12[2]
:14[2]:14f:15[2]:15f:15:17:18[4]:20[3]:21[2]:22[2]:23[5]:24[2]:
25[3]:27[4]:28[3]:29[4]:30[2]:31[2]:34[4]/**16**:1[2]:2[3]:3:4-7[10]:8[2]:
9[5]:10[3]:11:12[3]:13[3]:14[4]:15,16[4]:17:18[3]:19:20[4]:21[4]:
23:24:25:27[3]:29[2]:31[2]:33[2]:34[4]/**17**:1[4]:2:3[2]:4[2]:5[2]:6[2]
:7[2]:8,9[3]:10[2]:12[4]:14[4]:16[2]:17:19[3]:20[2]:21[2]:22[3]:24/
18:1:2:3,4[3]:5[4]:7:8:10[3]:12[3]:13[2]:14:15[2]:17:18:19[2]:
20[2]:21[2]:22[2]:23[6]:24[5]:25[3]:26[3]:27[2]:28:29[2]:30[3]:31:
31f[3]:32[3]:33[7]:35[3]:36[4]:38[6]:39[2]:40:42:43:44[5]:45:46[3]
/**19**:1:2:4[2]:5:7[2]:8[2]:9:10[3]:11[10]:12[5]:13[2]:14[3]:15[2]:16:
19[3]:20[2]:21[3]/**20**:1:2,3[2]:5,6:7:8:9[7]:10[2]:11:12:13[2]:
14[5]:15[3]:16[3]:19:20[2]:21[3]:22[2]:23[3]:24:25[3]:26[2]:27[4]:
28[7]:29[4]:30[6]:31:32[2]:33[3]:34:35[3]:36[3]:37:38[3]:39[3]:40[2]
:41[4]:42[3]:43/**21**:1[2]:2[3]:4[2]:5[2]:7:8:9:9f:10:11[2]:12:13[2]
:14:15[2]:16:17:19[2]:20:20f[2]:21:22[2]:23[3]:24[3]:25:26[5]
/**22**:2:3:5:6f[2]:7:8:10[4]:11[3]:12[2]:13[3]:14:15[2]:16[2]:17[2]:
19[3]:20:21:22[3]:23[5]:24[3]:25:26[2]:27:27f:28[2]:30:31:
32,33:34[2]:35[4]:36,37[3]:38[4]:39[6]:40:41[3]:42[2]:43[4]:44:
45[4]:46[2]:49:50[2]:51[2]:52,53[3]/**2Ki1**:1:2[3]:3[2]:3f:3[3]:4,5[4]
:6[4]:7:8[2]:9[2]:11[2]:12:13[3]:14:15[3]:16:17[4]:18[4]/**2**:1[3]:3[2]:
4:5[2]:6,7[4]:8[2]:9:12[2]:13,14[5]:15[2]:16[4]:19[2]:19f:21[3]:22:
23[2]:24[3]/**3**:1[2]:1f:2:3[4]:4:5:6,7,8[3]:9[2]:10[3]:11[3]:12:12f[2]
:12:13[3]:14[2]:15[4]:16[2]:18[3]:19[2]:20[4]:21[2]:22[3]:23[2]:24[5]:
25[3]:25f:26[3]:27[5]/**4**:1[3]:2:4[2]:5:6[2]:7[2]:8:10:11,12[2]:13[3]
:15,16:17[2]:18:19:21[3]:22[2]:24[2]:25:26[2]:27[4]:29[3]:30:
31[3]:32[2]:33[2]:34[5]:35[4]:36:37:38[2]:39[2]:40:41:42[2]:43:
44/**5**:1[2]:2:3[2]:4[2]:5[3]:6[3]:7:8[2]:9:10:11[3]:12[2]:13:14[2]:15[2]
:17:18[5]:22:23:24[5]:26:27/**6**:1[2]:4:5:6[6]:8[2]:9[3]:10:11[3]:
12[5]:13[2]:14[2]:15[2]:17[3]:18:19[3]:20[2]:21:23[3]:25:26-30[11]
:31:32[5]:33[4]/**7**:1[2]:2[4]:3:4[3]:5[2]:6[6]:7:8[3]:9[2]:10[5]:11[3]:12[4]
:13[3]:14[2]:15[5]:16[4]:17[6]:18[3]:19[4]:20[2]/**8**:1[2]:2[3]:3[3]:4[2]:5[6]
:6[2]:7[3]:8,9[7]:10:12[7]:13[2]:14:15[2]:16[4]:18:20:21[4]:23[4]:
24,25[3]:24,25f:24,25[4]:26:28[2]/**9**:1:2[2]:3[3]:4:5:6[6]:7[2]:
8:9[2]:10:12:13:14[2]:15:17[2]:18[4]:19[3]:20:21:22:23:24[2]
:25[2]:26[2]:27[3]:28:29[2]:31[2]:32:33[4]:34[2]:36[3]/**10**:1[2]:2,3
:5[4]:6[4]:7:8[5]:9,10[3]:11[3]:11f[2]:12:13[3]:14:15[3]:16:17[4]:
18,19:20,21[2]:22[3]:23[3]:24[2]:25[3]:26[2]:27:29[2]:30[3]:31[2]
:32,33[7]:34[3]:35/**11**:1:2,3[3]:2,3f[2]:4[7]:5[2]:6,7,8[4]:9[3]:10[2]
:11[4]:12[4]:13,14[5]:15[3]:16:17[6]:18[6]:19[8]:20/**12**:1:2:3[3]:
4,5[2]:6[2]:7[3]:8:9[7]:10[3]:11,12[5]:13,14:15:16[3]:18[7]:19[4]:
20:21[5]/**13**:1[3]:2:3:4[4]:5[4]:6[2]:7[3]:8[4]:9,10[3]:11:12[5]:13[2]:
14:14f:16,17[5]:18[4]:19[2]:20,21[4]:22:23[2]:25[2]/**14**:1[2]:2
:3:4[3]:5[2]:6[4]:8[2]:9[4]:11[2]:12:13[3]:14[3]:15[4]:16[2]:18[3]:20[2]:
21[2]:23[2]:24[2]:25[4]:26[2]:27:28[3]:29[2]/**15**:1[3]:3:4[3]:5[3]:6[4]:
7:8:9[3]:10[2]:11[4]:12:13:14[2]:15[2]:16[4]:17:18:19,20[4]:
21[4]:22:23:24:25[4]:26[4]:27:28[2]:29[3]:30[3]:31[4]:32,33:
34,35[7]:36[3]:37:38[4]/**16**:1:2:3[7]:4[4]:6[2]:7:8[4]:9[4]:10f:10:
11,12:13[2]:14[7]:15[12]:16:17[8]:18[4]:18f:19[5]:20[3]/**17**:1[2]
:4[4]:5[2]:6[7]:7[3]:8[3]:9[2]:10:11[6]:12:13:14[2]:15[2]:16[3]:17[2]:
18[2]:19[3]:20[2]:21[3]:22[2]:23[2]:24[5]:25[2]:26[4]:27,28[8]:29[2]:
30:31[4]:32[3]:33[2]:34[3]:35,36[3]:37:38:39:40:41[2]/**18**:1[2]
:4[6]:5[2]:6:7[2]:8:8f[3]:9[4]:10[4]:11[7]:12[4]:13[3]:14[2]:15[3]:16[4]:
17[5]:18:19[2]:20,21:22[3]:23[2]:24[2]:25:26[2]:27[3]:28[4]:30:
31,32:33[3]:34:35:36[3]:37[4]/**19**:1:2[2]:3:4[4]:5,6[2]:7[2]:8:9[2]
:11:12[4]:13[3]:14[4]:15[6]:16:17:19[2]:20:21[2]:22:23[4]:24:
25:26[2]:27:28:29[3]:30[3]:31:32:33:34[2]:35[4]:37[3]/**20**:1[2]
:2:4[2]:5[3]:6[3]:7:8[2]:9[3]:10:11[3]:11f[4]:12:13[2]:16[2]:17[2]:18[2]
:19[2]:20[6]:21/**21**:1[4]:3,4,5[9]:6:7[6]:8[2]:9[5]:10[2]:11[2]:12:13
:16[4]:17[4]:18[2]:19,20[2]:21[2]:22:23:24[2]:25[3]:26[2]/**22**:1[3]:
3,4[8]:5,6[2]:7:8[4]:9,10[6]:11:12,13[4]:14[5]:15,16[2]:17:
18,19[2]:20[4]/**23**:1[9]:3[4]:4[13]:5[5]:6[5]:7[4]:8[10]:9f[2]:9[3]:10[4]:
11[6]:12[8]:13[7]:14[2]:15[3]:16[5]:17[5]:18:19[4]:20[3]:21[5]:22[4]:
23[2]:24[6]:25[3]:26[2]:27[2]:28[4]:29[2]:30[2]:31,32[2]:34:35[3]:
36,37/**24**:1:2[3]:3,4[4]:5[5]:6:7[5]:8,9:10[2]:11:12[3]:13[7]:14[5]
:15:16:17[2]:20[3]/**25**:1[2]:2[2]:3[2]:4,5[8]:6:8[4]:9[3]:10[2]:11[5]:
12[3]:13[5]:14,15[5]:16[4]:17[3]:18[3]:19[4]:20:21:22[2]:23[6]:24[2]
:25[3]:26[3]:27[5]:28:29:30[2]/**1Ch1**:1:1f[3]:5-9:5-9f:5-9[5]:
10:11,12[11]:13-16[2]:17:19[2]:20-23:24-27:24-27f[2]:
24-27[8]:28-31[2]:33[2]:35:36:37:38,39:40:41:42:43[5]:
44[2]:45[3]:46[5]:47[2]:48[2]:49:50[2]:51-54[2]/**2**:1:3[2]:4:5:6:7[2]
:9:10[2]:11[2]:12[2]:16:17:18[2]:21[2]:22[2]:24:25[3]:26:27:
29:34,35:42[3]:43:44[3]:45:47:48,49[2]:50[3]:51[2]:52[2]:53[6]
:54[4]:55[5]/**3**:1:2[5]:3[4]:4:5[2]:9:10-14:15:16:17,18[2]:
19,20/**4**:1:2[3]:3-4[6]:5:8[4]:9f:10[2]:11,12[5]:13:14[4]:15[3]:
17:18[3]:19[5]:20[2]:21-22[7]:23:24:26:31:34-39[4]:40,41[8]
:42:43[2]/**5**:1[3]:2:3:6:7,8[2]:9[4]:10[4]:11[2]:12:13[2]:14[2]:15[3]
:16[3]:17[2]:18[2]:19[4]:20:21:22[7]:23[2]:24[2]:25[3]:26[4]/**6**:1[2]:
4-15[26]:16:17:18:19,20,21[4]:22,23,24:25,26,27[2]:28[4]
:29,30[2]:31[2]:32[2]:33-38[3]:44-47:48[2]:49[8]:50-53:54[3]:
55,56,57[2]:58,59:60[2]:61[3]:62[4]:63[2]:64,65[2]:66-69[3]:
70[4]:71[2]:72:73:74:76:77[2]:78,79[2]:80/**7**:1:2[4]:4:5[4]:6:
7[3]:8:9:10[2]:11[3]:12[2]:13:14[2]:17[3]:19:20,21[2]:
25,26,27[8]:28[2]:29[3]:30:31[2]:35:36,37:38:39:40/**8**:1[6]
:3,4,5:6,7[3]:8,9,10:12:13:15,16:17,18:19,20,21:
22-25:26,27:28[2]:29:30,31,32:33[2]:34[2]:35:36[2]:37:
39[3]:40/**9**:1[4]:2[5]:3:4[2]:5:6:7,8[11]:10,11[4]:12:14:15,16[7]
:17,18[3]:19[5]:20[3]:21[4]:22:23:24:25:26[3]:27[2]:28[2]:29[4]:
30:31[3]:32[3]:33,34[2]:35,36,37:39[3]:40[2]:41:42[3]:43/
10:1[4]:3:4:5:6:7[4]:8[7]:9[2]:10[4]:11[2]:12[3]:13:14[4]/**11**:1:2[3]
:3[2]:4[4]:5,6[8]:7[2]:8[3]:9[2]:10[4]:11[4]:12[4]:13[3]:14[4]:15:15f[3]:
15[3]:16[3]:17[2]:18,19[4]:20[2]:21[4]:22:22f[2]:22:23:24,25[2]:
26-47[7]/**12**:1[2]:1f:2:3-7[2]:8-13[4]:14[2]:15[3]:17:18[2]:19[3]:
20:21:22:23[2]:24-37[22]:38[2]:40[2]/**13**:2[4]:3:5[2]:5f[2]:5:6[3]
:6f:7[2]:8[2]:9[3]:10[3]:11[3]:12:13[3]:14[3]/**14**:2:3:4-7[2]:8[2]:9[2]:
10[3]:11[2]:12[3]:13[2]:14[2]:15[3]:16[4]:17[2]/**15**:1:2[2]:3[3]:4-10[7]
:11[2]:12[6]:13[2]:14[5]:15[3]:16[2]:17[3]:18[2]:19:20f[2]:21:21f[2]:
22[3]:23:24[3]:25[5]:26[2]:27[4]:28[5]:29[3]/**16**:1[3]:2[4]:4[4]:5[3]:6[2]
:7[4]:8[3]:10:11:14[2]:15:18:19:23[2]:24:25:26[3]:28:29[3]:
30[2]:31[4]:32[2]:33[4]:34:35:36[2]:37:37f[3]:38:39[5]:40[3]:41:
42:43[2]/**17**:1[3]:2[2]:5:6[2]:7[2]:8[2]:9:10:12:14:15:16:17[2]:
21[3]:24[2]:25/**18**:1:3[3]:4:5:6[3]:7:8[6]:11[4]:12:13[2]:15[2]:16[2]
:17[2]/**19**:1:2,3[3]:4:7[3]:8:9[6]:10[2]:11[3]:12[2]:13[2]:14[2]:15[3]:
16[2]:17,18[5]:19[2]/**20**:1[5]:2[4]:3[2]:3f:3:4[5]:5[5]:6,7:8/**21**:2[3]
:3:4[2]:5:6[2]:7:8:9:10,11:12[5]:13[3]:14:15[7]:16[5]:17[2]:18[5]
:19,20[2]:21[3]:22[2]:23[5]:24[3]:26[4]:27[2]:28:29[3]:30[3]/**22**:1[4]
:2[2]:3[4]:4:5[5]:6:8[2]:9:11[3]:12[2]:13:14:16:17:18[4]:19[5]/
23:1[2]:2[2]:3[3]:4,5[4]:6[4]:7:8,9[3]:8,9f:10,11:12:13:13f:13[4]
:14,15[2]:17:18:19:20[2]:21[2]:22:24[5]:25:26[2]:27[2]:28[8]:
29[6]:30:31[5]:32[3]/**24**:1[2]:3[2]:4:5[2]:6[10]:7-18[25]:19:20:21
:22:23:24,25:26,27:30[2]:31[5]/**25**:1[4]:2[2]:3[2]:4,5[2]:6,7[5]:
8:9-31[5]/**26**:1[6]:2,3[7]:4,5[9]:10[3]:11[4]:12[5]:13[2]:14,15[5]:
16[3]:17[4]:18[3]:19[2]:20,21,22[7]:23,24[3]:25:26[6]:27[2]:28[8]
:29:30[3]:31,32[8]/**27**:1[3]:2,3[3]:4[3]:5,6[7]:7[4]:8[3]:9[4]:10[3]:11[4]
:12[4]:13[3]:14[3]:15[4]:16-22[5]:23[2]:23f[2]:24[4]:25[4]:26[2]:27[2]
:28[3]:29[3]:30[3]:31[3]:32[3]:33[2]:34[2]/**28**:1[5]:2[4]:4[4]:5[2]:8[4]:9[2]
:10:11[7]:12[6]:12f[3]:13[5]:15[3]:16[7]:17[4]:18[6]:19[2]:20[3]:21[3]
/**29**:1[5]:3[3]:4,5[5]:6,7[6]:8:10[3]:11[2]:12:15:19[2]:20[4]:21[2]:
22[2]:23:24[2]:25[2]:26,27:29[6]:30[2]/**2Ch1**:1[2]:2,3[4]:2,3f[2]
:2,3[2]:4:5,6[3]:8:9:12[2]:13[2]:14[3]:15:17[2]/**2**:1[2]:2:4[2]:4f[2]:
4[3]:6:7:8:9:10:11:12[3]:14[2]:15:16[2]:17/**3**:1[8]:2[3]:3:4[4]:5[2]
:6[5]:7[3]:8[4]:9:10[2]:11,12,13[3]:14:15[3]:16f:16[2]:17[10]/**4**:
2[2]:3[2]:5[3]:6[7]:7:8:9[3]:10[4]:11[3]:12-16[17]:17,18[4]:19[6]:20:
21:22[5]/**5**:1[4]:2[8]:3:4,5[5]:6[2]:7,8[7]:9[4]:10[4]:11,12[12]:
13,14[9]/**6**:1[3]:3[2]:4[3]:5,6[2]:8[3]:9:10[4]:11[4]:12,13[7]:14:18[3]
:20,21:26:27:28[3]:29:30:33[2]:40:41/**7**:1[5]:3[3]:4,5[4]:6[7]
:7[3]:8[5]:9:10[2]:11:12[2]:13[2]:18:19:21:22[4]/**8**:1[2]:2[2]:3:4:
5:6:7,8[4]:9:11[4]:12[4]:13[7]:14[5]:15:16[2]:17,18/**9**:1:3:4[3]:
5:8:9:11[6]:12[2]:13,14[2]:15:16[2]:19:20[2]:21:22:23:25[2]:
26[4]:27:29[8]:31/**10**:1:2,3[3]:6:8,9[2]:12:13[2]:14[2]:15[3]:16[2]
:17[2]:18[2]/**11**:1[3]:2[2]:3:4[2]:11:13,14[3]:15[2]:16:17[2]:17f:
18[2]:20[2]:22:23[2]/**12**:1[3]:2:5[4]:6[3]:7:9[3]:10[2]:11[4]:12[3]:13[4]
:14:15[5]:16/**13**:1[3]:4[3]:5[2]:8[2]:9[4]:10[3]:11[7]:12:13,14[5]:
15,16[4]:18,19:20:22/**14**:1[3]:2:3[4]:4[3]:5[3]:7[2]:9,10[3]:12[4]
:13[3]:14[3]:15[2]/**15**:1:2[2]:3[2]:4:5[2]:7:8[7]:9[4]:10:11[3]:12:15
:16[2]:17[2]:18[3]:19/**16**:1[3]:2[3]:3:4[2]:6[2]:7[5]:8[2]:9[3]:10[2]:11[4]
:12[4]:13,14/**17**:1:2[3]:3[2]:4[4]:5[2]:6[4]:7,8,9[10]:10[3]:11[2]:17
:19[4]/**18**:1:2:3,4,5[2]:6,7[2]:8:9[3]:10[3]:11[2]:12[6]:14[2]:15[2]:
16[2]:17:18:19,20[3]:21[3]:22[3]:23[3]:25:26[2]:27:28[2]:29:
30[2]:31[5]:32:33[7]:34[4]/**19**:2[3]:3[2]:4[3]:5[2]:8:9:10[5]:11[5]/
20:1[4]:2:3[2]:4:5[2]:6[5]:7[2]:10:13[2]:14[5]:15[2]:16[4]:17[2]:18[6]:
19[4]:20[5]:21[5]:22[3]:23:24[5]:25[2]:26[3]:27:28:29[4]:31:32:
33[5]:34[5]:35:37[2]/**21**:1[3]:3,4[4]:6[2]:7[3]:8:9f:10[2]:11[2]:12[4]:
13[3]:14:16[4]:17[2]:18:19[3]:20/**22**:1[2]:3:5[2]:7[2]:8[2]:9[3]:10:
11f:11[3]:12/**23**:1[4]:2,3[7]:4[2]:5,6[6]:7[3]:8[4]:9[2]:10[4]:11[4]:12[11]
:13,14[3]:15,16,17[10]:18[6]:19[2]:20[7]:21[3]/**24**:2[3]:4:5[5]:6[9]
:7,8[6]:9[5]:10[4]:11[9]:12[4]:13[2]:14[7]:16[3]:17,18[4]:19[2]:20[3]:
21[3]:23[4]:24[4]:25[6]:26:27[7]/**25**:3[2]:4[7]:5,6[2]:7[2]:9[3]:11:12[2]
:13[3]:14[2]:15:16[2]:17:18[2]:20:21:23[4]:24[4]:25:26[3]:28/
26:1:2:4[2]:5[2]:6[4]:7[3]:8:9[4]:10[6]:11[3]:13:15[2]:16[4]:17,18[5]
:19:20[2]:21[6]:22[2]:23[2]/**27**:1:2[2]:3[5]:4[2]:5[2]:6[2]:7[3]:9/**28**:
2[3]:3[6]:4[2]:5[3]:6[2]:7[3]:8:9[3]:10:11[2]:12[5]:13[2]:14[3]:15[3]:16[2]:
17,18[3]:19[4]:21[2]:23[3]:24[6]:25[2]:26[3]:27[2]/**29**:1[2]:2:3[4]:
4,5[7]:6[2]:7[3]:8[2]:10:11:12,13,14[8]:15[3]:16[7]:17[4]:18[7]:19[4]
:20[3]:21[6]:22[8]:23[3]:24[7]:25,26[5]:27[7]:28[4]:29[2]:30[4]:31[3]:
34[5]:35[3]:36/**30**:1[2]:2,3[5]:4:5f[3]:6[4]:7:8[2]:9[2]:10[2]:11:12[3]
:13[2]:14[2]:15[4]:16[5]:17,18,19[7]:20:21[4]:22[4]:23[2]:24[2]:
25[5]:26:27[3]/**31**:1[7]:2[3]:3[4]:4[3]:5,6[10]:7,8[3]:9:10[3]:11:
12,13[5]:14,15[7]:16[2]:17,18[6]:19[4]:20[3]:21[2]/**32**:1:3[2]:4[3]:
5[3]:6[2]:7:8:9[2]:11[2]:12[4]:13[2]:16[2]:17[4]:18[6]:19[2]:20:21[3]:
22[2]:23[2]:24[2]:25:26[3]:28,29:30[4]:31:32[8]:33[3]/**33**:2[5]:3[4]
:4,5[5]:6[2]:7[3]:8:9[4]:10:11:13[2]:14[7]:15[8]:16[4]:17[4]:18[4]:19[6]
:20,21:22[2]:25/**34**:2:3[5]:4[5]:5[4]:6[2]:7[4]:8[6]:9[9]:10,11[2]:12[7]
:13[3]:14[5]:15,16[7]:17[5]:18[2]:19:20[2]:21[6]:22[6]:23[2]:24[3]:
26[3]:27:28[3]:29[2]:30[7]:31[3]:33[4]/**35**:1[3]:2[2]:3[4]:4,5[3]:6[4]:7[2]
:8[5]:9[2]:10[3]:11[7]:12[5]:13[4]:14[4]:15[5]:16[4]:17[3]:18[4]:19[2]:
20[2]:21:21f:22[3]:23[2]:24,25[4]:26[3]:27[2]/**36**:1:3:4[3]:6:7[2]
:8[6]:9[2]:10[3]:12[4]:13:14[7]:15:16[4]:17[5]:18[5]:19[4]:20[2]:21[6]:
22,23[11]/**Ez1**:1[3]:1f[2]:1[3]:2[3]:3[2]:4[3]:5[4]:6[2]:7[3]:8[3]:9,10/**2**
:1[3]:2:3-35[35]:36-39[7]:40,41,42[9]:43-54[2]:55,56,57[2]:
58[2]:59:60:61[2]:62,63[4]:68[3]:69[2]:70[8]/**3**:1[6]:3[3]:4[4]:5[6]:6
:6f[3]:6[5]:7[5]:8[8]:9[2]:10[7]:11[3]:12[2]:13[2]/**4**:1[3]:2:3[4]:4,5[2]:6:
7[3]:8,9[3]:10[3]:11[3]:12[3]:13:15[3]:16[2]:17[4]:18:19:20[2]:21[2]
:22:23:24[3]/**5**:1[3]:3[3]:4[3]:5[3]:6[2]:8[5]:9:11[3]:12[2]:13[2]:14[4]:
15[3]:16[3]:17/**6**:1:2[3]:3[6]:4[2]:5[3]:6[4]:7[2]:8:9[2]:10:11:12[2]:
13:14[5]:15:15f[2]:15[2]:16[4]:17[2]:18[3]:19[2]:19f[3]:20:21,22[11]
/**7**:1[18]:6[3]:7,8,9[5]:10[3]:11[2]:12[5]:13:14:15[2]:16[2]:17[2]:
18[2]:19[2]:20[3]:21[6]:23[2]:24:25[4]:26[3]:27[4]:28f[3]:28[3]/**8**:1[3]
:2-14[17]:15[4]:16:17[4]:18:19:20[2]:21:22[4]:24:25[6]:
26,27:28[4]:29[5]:30[3]:31[2]:31f[3]:31:33[5]:34[2]:35[2]:36[6]/**9**
:1[7]:2[4]:4[3]:5[2]:6:7:9[2]:11[5]/**10**:1[2]:2[2]:3[3]:5[4]:6[4]:7,8:9:9f[3]
:9[6]:10:11[2]:12:14[4]:15:16-19[3]:20:21:22:23:24[2]:25[2]:
26:27:28:29:30:31,32:33:34-42:43/**Neh1**:1[5]:2[2]:3[2]
:4[2]:6,7[2]:8:9[3]:10:11[3]/**2**:1:3f:3[2]:4[3]:5,6[2]:7[3]:8[8]:9[5]:10:
11,12[3]:13[4]:14,15[7]:16[3]:17[2]:18[5]:19[2]:20/**3**:1[7]:2[2]:3[6]:
4:5:6[4]:7:8[2]:9[2]:10:11[2]:12[3]:13[6]:14[5]:15[8]:16[5]:16f[2]:17[5]
:18[4]:19[5]:20[4]:21[4]:22[3]:23:24[3]:25[6]:26[4]:27[4]:28[4]:29[3]:
30:31[5]:32[3]/**4**:1[4]:3:6[3]:7[4]:9:10[2]:12[2]:13[2]:14[4]:15:16:
17:18[2]:19[2]:20,21:22[2]:23[2]/**5**:1:2,3,4:5:8[2]:9[2]:10:12
:13:13f:13[3]:14[5]:15[3]:16[2]:17:18[2]/**6**:1[6]:2[2]:4[2]:5,6[3]:7[2]
:8:10[3]:11[2]:12,13:14[3]:15:15f:16[3]:17:18/**7**:1[4]:2[3]:3[5]
:4[3]:5[6]:6[3]:7:8-38[33]:39-42[7]:43,44,45[8]:46-56[2]:
57,58,59:60[2]:61:62:63[2]:64,65[3]:70[3]:71:72[2]:73[8]/**8**:
1[10]:6[5]:7,8[3]:7,8f:7,8[2]:9[6]:10[2]:11[2]:12:13[4]:14[2]:15[6]:
16[7]:17[3]:18[5]/**9**:1f[2]:1[2]:3[2]:4[3]:5[5]:6[5]:7[2]:8[2]:9[2]:10:11[4]:
12:14[2]:15[2]:17:19[5]:21:22[2]:23[2]:24[3]:26:29f:30:32[3]:
35[2]:36:37[3]:38/**10**:1[3]:9-13:14-27:28[10]:29:31[4]:32:
33[9]:34[6]:35[2]:36[4]:37[9]:38[3]:39,40[8]/**11**:1[4]:3[8]:4,5,6[3]:
7,8,9[2]:10-14[7]:15,16,17[4]:20:21:22,23[4]:22,23f:
22,23[2]:25-30[4]:31-35[4]:36[2]/**12**:1:8[3]:9:10,11[5]:12-
12-21[24]:22[5]:23[5]:24[4]:25[3]:26[4]:27[6]:28[4]:29[2]:30[4]:
31,32[9]:35,36[4]:37[6]:38[4]:39[9]:40,41[2]:42[3]:43[3]:44[8]:45[4]
:46[3]:47[8]:47f[2]/**13**:1[4]:2[2]:3[2]:4[2]:5[8]:6[3]:7:8:9[3]:10[3]:11[3]:
12[2]:13[5]:14:15:16[2]:17[2]:18[3]:19[5]:20:21[3]:22[4]:23[2]:24[2]
:26:28[5]:29[3]:30[2]:31[4]/**Est1**:1[6]:4[2]:5[4]:6:7:8[3]:9[3]:10[3]:
11[2]:12[2]:13-15[7]:16[2]:18[3]:19:21:22/**2**:1:2[3]:3[2]:4[4]:5:8[2]
:9[5]:11[2]:12,13,14[12]:15f:15[5]:16[3]:17[3]:18[3]:19:19f[2]:
21[4]:22[3]:23:23f:23[2]/**3**:1[4]:2[2]:3,4[3]:5,6[2]:7[5]:8[5]:9[3]:10:
10f:11:12f[2]:12[4]:13[5]:14[2]:15[5]/**4**:1:2[2]:3[3]:4:5[2]:6[2]:7[5]:
8[2]:11[4]:13:14[2]:16[3]/**5**:1[4]:2[2]:3[2]:5[2]:6[3]:7,8:9[2]:11[4]:12[3]
:13[2]:14[5]/**6**:1[7]:3:4[6]:5[3]:6:7,8[4]:9[6]:10[3]:11[6]:14[2]/**7**:1:2[2]
:3:4:6:7[2]:8[7]:9[4]:10/**8**:1[4]:2:3[2]:4[2]:5[2]:7[3]:8[3]:8f[6]:9,10[15]
:11[3]:12[3]:12f[3]:13[2]:14[4]:15[5]:16:17[5]/**9**:1[9]:3[4]:4[2]:5:7-
7-10[2]:11[2]:12[3]:13[2]:14[3]:15[2]:16[2]:17[3]:18[3]:19[3]:20[2]:
21[2]:22[2]:23:24,25[9]:26:27[3]:28[4]:29-31[8]:32/**10**:1[3]:2[7]
:3[3]/**Job1**:1:2,3:5:6:6f:6[2]:7[2]:8[3]:12,13[2]:14,15[5]:16[2]:
19[3]:20:21[3]/**2**:1[2]:2[2]:3[4]:6:7[2]:8:10:11[4]:12:13/**3**:1:
2,3[2]:5:6[3]:8f[2]:9[3]:12:16:17[2]:19/**4**:1:3,4[2]:6f:7,8:9:16[2]
:20/**5**:3:5:10[3]:11:12:14[2]:15[3]:16[3]:17[3]:20[2]:21/**6**:3:
4:5,6,7[2]:8,9:10[3]:14:15-18:25,26:30/**7**:2[3]:11:18:
21/**8**:1:8:10[3]:16:17[2]:19:22/**9**:2:5:6:7[2]:8[2]:9[4]:13:13
f:17:22:23:24[5]:26:29:31/**10**:3:4-7f:13,14:15:16:
19[2]:20,21[2]:22[2]/**11**:1:4:7[2]:9[2]:10:11:15:16:20/**12**:4[2]
:5:7,8,9[6]:10[3]:15[4]:19:20[3]:21:22[2]:24,25/**13**:3:4:7:8:
13:25:26/**14**:2:8,9[2]:11,12[2]:13:16:18,19[2]:20,21/
15:1[2]:7,8[3]:14:15[2]:17-19[2]:22:25,26:30[2]:31:33:33f:
34:35/**16**:4:11[2]:12:13:15:16:19/**17**:1:6:8[2]:9:11:
12:13,14[2]:16[2]/**18**:1[2]:5:7[2]:14[2]:16:17:18[2]/**19**:1:6[2]:
9:20:21:23,24:25/**20**:1[2]:2:4:5[4]:6[3]:10:11:12:14:15:
17:19:20:22[2]:25[3]:27[2]:28:29/**21**:7[2]:12,13:14:16:

(E Con't)
8:19^2:20^2:22:26^2:29:30-32^2:33/**22**:2:3:6:7^2:8
2^2:13:14:15,16^2:19^3:20^2:23:25:26:28^2:29/**23**:
:16,17/**24**:1^2:3^3:4^2:5^4:6^2:7:8^2:9:11^2:12^4:13^4:
15^3:16^2:17^3:18^2:20^2:21^2:22,23/**25**:1^2:3:4:5/**26**
^{2}:7:8^3:10^3:11:12:13:13f:13:14/**27**:2^2:8:10:13^4
16:17:18:20^2:21/**28**:2:3,4^3:5^2:8:9:10:11:11f^2:
14^2:16:19:21^3:23,24^2:25^3:26^3:28/**29**:2:3^2:4:5:
:8^2:9:10^2:12^2:13:15^2:16:17^2:19/**30**:3:6:7^2:9:
22^2:25:26:28,29:31/**31**:7,8:16:23^2:26^3:28^2:34:
:38,39/**32**:1:2^2:4:8,9^3:13:18/**33**:3:4^3:6:11:15:
18:20:23,24f:28:30^3/**34**:3^2:11:13^2:17:19^2:21:
28^4:33^3:36^2/**35**:5:6:9,10^4:11:12/**36**:2:3:4:6:7:
13:18:20:27:28:29^3:30^3:31:33:33f^2/**37**:2:3:4^3:
5^3:8^2:9^4:10^2:11:12^2:13:14:15^2:16,17^3:18^2:
20:21^3:22:23^2:24/**38**:1^2:4^2:5:6,7^2:8,9^3:12^3:13^4
:15^2:16^3:17,18^4:19^2:22,23^3:24^4:25-27^7:28:29^2:
31:32^5:33^4:34:36f^2:37,38^2:39,40^2:41/**39**:4:5:6
8:9:10:12^2:13:14^2:15:18:19:21-23^3:24^2:25^6:26
^{2}:28:30/**40**:1:2^2:4:6^2:7:11:12^2:13:15:16:17:20^2
^{2}:22^2:23/**41**:2:6:8:11:12:18^2:22:25:29:30:
32^3:34^2/**42**:4:7^2:9^5:10^2:11^2:12^3:13,14:15^2/**Ps**
^{2}:4:5:6^4/**2**:1f:1^2:2^3:6^2:7^2:8^2:10:11:12/**3**:4:5:7/
:3^2:4:5:6:7/**5**:4:9^2:10:12/**6**:1:5f:8/**7**:5^2:6:9f:9^2:
:11:14:16:17^3/**8**:1^3:2:3^4:5:8^3:9^2/**9**:1:4f:5^2:6^2:
^{3}:11^2:12:13^2:14:14f^2:15^3:16^3:16f^2:17^4:18^4:19:
/**10**:1:2^2:3:8:9:10:12:13:14^3:15^2:16:17:18/**11**:1^2
:3f:3:4:5^3:6:7:7f/**12**:1:3,4:5^4:6:7:8/**13**:1:2:6/**14**
6^2:7^2/**15**:4^2:5^2/**16**:3^4:4^2:5:6f:7^2:8:10^2:11^2/**17**:3^2
:11:13,14/**18**:1:2^2:3:4:5:6:7:8:9:10:12^2:13^5:15^4
^{2}:20:24:25f:26:27^2:28:33^4:38:39:41:42^2:
,44,45:46:47^2:49:50/**19**:1^2:3,4^4:5:6^2:9f^3/**20**:1^2:
:6:7/**21**:1:3:4:6:7^4:9,10^2/**22**:3,4:8^4:9,10,11:12:
:16:18:20f^3:21:22^2:23:25^2:26:26f:26:27^3:28^2:
^{2}:31/**23**:1:2,3^3:4^2:5/**24**:1^2:2^2:2f:3^3:6^3:7:8:9^2:10
5:3:4^2:5:8^2:9:11:12^3:13:14:15/**26**:1:5:8:9,10:12
7:1:4^3:7:12:13^3:14/**28**:2f^2:3:4:6:8/**29**:1:2:3^5:
^{2}:7^3:8^2:9^3:9f:9^3:10^2/**30**:3^2:5:6,7:9^2:12^2/**31**:1:4:
1:13^2:17:18:20:21^2:22:23^2:24/**32**:5:6f:8^2:10^2/
:1^3:2^2:3:5:6^2:7:8^2:9:10^2:11:12^2:13,14,15:16,17:
,19^2:20:21/**34**:1:3:6^2:7^2:8^2:9:10:11^2:15^2:16^3:17^2
:19^2:21^2:22/**35**:5^3:6^2:9:10^4:13:16^2:18^2:19f:27/
:1^2:5^2:6:7:9/**37**:1:3^2:4:5:6^2:7:9^2:10:11:12,13^2:
:17^2:17f:18^2:18f^2:21:22^2:23^2:24:25^3:26:28:29^2:
,31:32:33^3:34:34f:34:37^5:39^2:40/**38**:8f:17^2:20/
:1:2,3^5:12/**40**:2^3:3^2:4:6:7:9:10:16^2:17/**41**:1:2:6
3^2/**42**:1:2:3:4,5^2:4,5f:6:7f:8^2/**43**:1:2:4:5f/**44**:1^5:
10:11:13^2:14^2:19:21:24:25/**45**:1^2:2:9:12^2:13:13
4:15:16:17^2/**46**:2^3:3^2:4^3:5:6^2:7^3:8^2:9:10:11^3/
:1:2^4:3:4f:4:6,7^2:8:9^6/**48**:1:2:2f^2:2^4:3:4^3:5:7:8^4:
^{3}:12/**49**:1:4:7:8,9:8,9f:10:13:14^4:15:18:19:20f/
:1^2:2:2f:3:8:10,11^4:12:21:22:23/**51**:1^2:5:6:7:12
6:18f:19:19f:19/**52**:1f:4:5^2:6:8^2/**53**:5:6/**54**:1^2:4
/**55**:7:9f:10^2:11:14^2:15:16:18:22^2:23/**56**:1:3,4:
7:8:9^2:13^3/**57**:1:2:5^2:8:9^2:10^2:11^2/**58**:1^2:1f^2:4,5
:8:9:10^2:10f:10/**59**:1:5:6:11:12,13^2:14,15:16/
:1^3:4,5f:8/**61**:2^3:4:5:6f^2:7/**62**:1:3,4:5:8:9^2:
,11:12/**63**:1:7^2:9:10^2:11f/**64**:1:4^2:6f^2:9^2:10^2/
:4^2:5^3:6:7^2:8^4:9^3:10^4:11,12:13^3/**66**:1^2:2:4:5:6:7
:12:15:16/**67**:2^2:3^2:4:4f:5^2:6,7/**68**:2^3:3:4^2:5^2:6:
8^3:11,12,13^3:11,12,13f:11,12,13^4:14:15,16:17:
:22^2:24^2:25:26^2:27^4:29^2:30f:32^3:33^2:34:35^2/**69**
^{3}:6:10:12^4:13:13f:15^3:24:26^3:28:28f:28^3:32:33^2:
:35:36/**70**:4/**71**:3:15:16^2:17:19:20^2/**72**:1:2:3:4
^{2}:6:6f^2:6^3:7:8^3:9^2:10^3:12:13:15:16^4:17:18:19:20
73:2^2:3^2:9^2:12:13:16:17:18^2:20:24:26:28/**74**:1:2^2
^{3}:5,6^2:7^2:8^2:9,10:12:13,14^3:15^2:16^2:17^2:19:19f:
:22:23/**75**:2^2:3:4^2:4f:8^3:9^2:10^3/**76**:3:4:5^2:8:9^3:
2^2/**77**:1:5^2:6:7:9:10:10f^2:11:14:15:16:17^3:18^4:
9/**78**:4:9^2:11,12:13^2:14:15^2:16:17:21:23^2:26^2:27
8^3:29:30:31^3:32:35:41:43^2:43f:45^2:48:49:50:51:
1f:51:52:53:54:55^2:56:57^2:64:65:67:68:69^2:
1,72/**79**:1:2:3^2:4:6:8:9:10:11^3:13/**80**:1:6^2:8:9^3:
0^2:10f:11^3:13^3:14:17:17f:17:17f:19/**81**:1:2:3^3:4:
f:7:10:15:16^2:16f/**82**:1:1f:2^2:3^4:4^2:5:5f:5:6:8/**83**:
^{2}:4:7:8:8f:9:10:13:18^2/**84**:1:2:3:5:6:7:8:9:10:12/
5:1:1f:2:8:11:12^2:13f/**86**:8:9/**87**:1^2:4:5^2:6:7/**88**:
:10:11:12^2:14/**89**:1^2:2:3,4:5f^2:6f^2:7:7f^2:8:9:11^2:
4,15^5:18^2:19^2:22:25^2:27^2:29:35,36:35,36f:37^2:
8:39:40:47:48^2:49:50:51:52/**90**:1^2:2^2:4f:5,6^3:9:
0:11:14:15:16:17/**91**:1^3:3:5^3:6^2:7:8:9:12^2:14/**92**
:1f:1^2:3:7:8^2:11:12^2:13:15/**93**:1:1f:1:3:4^3:5/**94**:
^{3}:3:6,7:6,7f:10:11^2:14:15:16:17:21,22^3:23/**95**:1^2
3^2:4^4:5^2:6:8:10:11^2/**96**:1^2:3^2:4^2:5^2:7:8:9^2:9f:9:10^2
11^4:12^3:13^3/**97**:1^2:2:4^2:5^3:6:8,9^2:10^3:11^2:12/**98**:
:2,3:4:5:6^3:7^3:8,9^4/**99**:1^3:2:4:5:7:9/**100**:1:3^2:5/
01:3:6^2:8/**102**:6:7:11:13^2:15^2:17^2:18^2:20:21,22^3
25^3:26/**103**:1:2^2:5:7:11^3:12^2:16:17,18^2:19^2:20:
1:22/**104**:1^3:3^6:4:5:6^2:7,8^3:9^2:10^2:11^2:12^4:13^2:
4^2:16^2:17^3:18^3:19^4:20^2:21^2:23:24:25:26^3:30^2:32^2
33:34/**105**:1^3:3:5,6:7^2:10,11^2:13:16:20:21:22^2:
24^2:25^2:27:28:29^2:30:31^2:32:33^2:35:36:38:39:41:
43:44^2/**106**:2:5:7^2:8^2:9:11^2:14:16:16f:17:19,20:
21,22:23^3:24:26:28^2:30:34^2:35:37,38^3:39:41,42:
47:48^3/**107**:1:2:3^3:4:8:9^2:10:11^2:13:14:15:17:19:
20:21:23^4:24:25^2:26^3:28:29^2:31:32^3:34^2:36:40:41
:43^2/**108**:2:3:4^2:5^2:6:7:8^2:9:13/**109**:2:9,10:14:15^2
:18^2:20:22,23:30:31/**110**:1:2f^2:4f:5:6:7/**111**:4:6^2:
10/**112**:1^2:5/**113**:4^2:6^2:7^4:9^2/**114**:1:2:3^2:4^2:7^3/
115:2:3:9:10:12^2:14:16^3:17:18/**116**:1:3:6^3:7:13f^2:
14:15f^4:18,19^5/**117**:1^3:2/**118**:1:2:3:4:5:7:8:9:10^2:
13:14^2:15,16^5:18:19^2:19f:20^4:22^4:22f^2:23:24^2:26^2
:26f^2:26^2:27,28:29/**119**:1:25:35:44,45,46:59,60:
63:64:69:71,72^2:78:83:90,91:95^2:100:101:105:
107:109:110:117:119^2:121:122:127:130:134:139
:147^2:148:155:169/**120**:4f:5,6/**121**:1:2^2/**122**:1^3:
2,3:4^2:5^3:6:8:9^2/**123**:2:3,4^2/**124**:1^2:4,5:7:8/**125**:1
:2^2:3^3:4/**126**:2^2:4/**127**:1^3:5^2:5f/**128**:1:3:5/**129**:
3,4^2:5:6,7^2/**130**:1:6:7/**131**:2^2:3/**132**:2-5^4:6^2:7:8^2:
9^2:10:12^2/**133**:2^2:3^2/**134**:1^2:2:3^2/**135**:4:5^2:6:7^4:8^3
:11^2:15:20:21f:21/**136**:1:2:3:5:6^2:6f^2:7:8^2:9:10^2:
13^2:15:16:17:21:26/**137**:1:2^2:3,4:5,6:7^2:8:9^2/**138**
:1:1f^2:2:3:4:6:8/**139**:3:8^2:9^2:11^2:12:13:17,18:19:
24/**140**:1:5:9:10:12^3:13/**141**:5^2:6,7:6,7f^2/**142**:3:4
:7/**143**:3^3:5:8/**144**:1:3:3f:5^2:7:8:10^2:12-15^4/**145**:
11:12:14^2:15:16:17:19:20:21/**146**:1:5^3:6^3:7^3:8^4:9^4
:10^2/**147**:1:2:3:4:6^4:8^3:9^2:10^2:14:15:16^3:17^2:18^2:
20/**148**:1^2:2:4:7:9^2:10^2:11^2:13:14^3/**149**:1:4,5:6,7:
9/**150**:1^2:1f:3:4:5:6/**Pro1**:1:4:5,6^2:7,8,9^2:13:19:
20:21^3:22:23:29^2:31^3/**2**:3,4,5^2:6:7,8:9:10:
11,12,13:16,17^3:18:19^2:19f:20^3:21:21f:22:22f/**3**:
1:4,5:7,8:9,10^3:11,12:13,14,15:13,14,15f:
13,14,15:18:19^3:20^3:23:24,25,26^2:32^2:33^3:34^2:35
/**4**:1:3:5f:7:11:14:16:18^3:19^2:24:26/**5**:3:4f:6:9^2:9f^2
:16:18:22:23/**6**:3:5:6:8:14:16-19:22^2:23:29:32:34
/**7**:6:8,9^2:11,12^2:14f:22:23:26:27/**8**:1^4:11:14,15:
19:22^2:23:24^3:25^2:26:27,28,29^8:34:35:36/**9**:2:3^2:
5:7,8:9:10:11^2:14^3:17^2/**10**:1^3:3^2:5:6:6f^2:7:8:11^2:
15^2:16^3:17:19:20:22:24^2:25^2:26:27:28^2:29^2:30^2:
31^2:32^2/**11**:1:2:3:5^2:6^2:8:9f:10^2:11^3:18^3:19^2:20^2:
21^3:23^2:24,25:26^2:29^2:31^2/**12**:2^2:3:4:6^2:7^2:10^2:14
:18^2:19:21^2:26^2:27^2:28^2/**13**:2^2:3:4:8:9^2:12:14^2:18
:21:22:25^2:25f/**14**:3:6^2:8^2:9:9f:9:10:11^4:13^2:14^2:
17:18^2:19:20^2:21:25:27:31^2:32^2:33/**15**:3^3:6:7:8^4:
9,10^4:11^2:14:19:21^2:23^2:24^2:25^3:26^3:27:28:29^4:
31,32:33/**16**:1:2:3:4^2:5:10^2:11:11f^3:12f:13:14^2:15
:17^2:20^2:21^2:27:28:30:31:33:33f:33/**17**:4:5^2:9:10:
11:15:24^3:26:27,28/**18**:1:2:5^2:9:10:10f^2:10:11:13
:15:17^2:18f:19:19f:21^2:22^2:23^2/**19**:2:3:4:12^2:14:
16:17^2:20^2:25/**20**:1:2:4^2:5:6:8^2:10:11^2:14^2:17:18:
19:20^2:22^2:23:24^2:25^2:27:29:29f:30/**21**:1^2:4f^2:6:7
:9:11^2:12^2:13^2:16:17:18^2:18f^2:19:20^2:20f^2:20:21:
22^2:25,26^2:27:29f^2:30:31:31f^2/**22**:2^3:3^3:4:5^2:6:7^4:
8:9^3:10:11:12^3:12f:12:13^2:16^2:17,18,19:20,21:
22,23^2:26,27:28/**23**:4,5:6,7,8:9:10,11:12:17,18^2:
23^2:24,25:29,30^3:31^2:32/**24**:3,4:9^3:10:13,14:
15,16:18:19,20^2:21,22^2:23^2:24:30,31:32,33/**25**:1:
2,3^5:4,5^2:6,7^3:8,9,10:13:14:23:25:26:27/**26**:2:7:9:
10:13:27/**27**:12^2:13^2:14:16:17:18:19:20f:21:
23,24^2:25,26,27^3/**28**:1^2:4^2:5^2:7:8^2:9^2:10^2:11:12^2:
14^2:15:20^2:23:27:28^2/**29**:1:2^2:7^3:10:14:16:18:19:
24:26^2:27^6/**30**:1:4^3:13,14:15,16:18,19^3:18,19f^2:
21,22,23:24-28^4:29,30,31^5:33^2/**31**:1:1f:2:3:6,7:9:
15:18:19,20^2:23^2:24:26:29^2:31^3:31f^2/**Ecc1**:1:1f^3:
1:3-7f:3-7^8:8-11:12-15^5:16-18^4/**2**:1^2:3^3:4,5,6:7,8^2
:9:11:12^2:12f^2:13,14^2:15:16^2:17:18:20-23:24-26^3
/**3**:10:11^2:13:14:15:16^2:18:19^2:20:21^2:22/**4**:1^5:2^2
:3^2:4^3:5,6^2:7:8:9:10:11:15:16^3/**5**:1:6,7^2:8^4:9:10:
11^4:12^2:15:16:17:18:19,20^3/**6**:2:5:6:7,8^2:9^3:11^2:
12^2/**7**:1^3:4:7:10:13^2:14:15-17^4:19:20:25^2:26f:
27,28^2/**8**:2,3^2:4:5:8:9,10^5:13:14:15^3:16,17^2/**9**:2,3
:4:5^2:9^3:11^7:15^2:16:17^2/**10**:3^2:4:5:10:11^2:11f:14:
15:15f:16,17^4:18^2:20^2/**11**:2:3^3:4f^2:5^4/**12**:1^2:2:4^2:
5^2:6^6:7^3:8:9^2:10^2:11:13/**Sol1**:1:1f^3:3:4^4:5^3:6^4:7:8^3
:11:12^2:14:16:17/**2**:1^4:2:3^3:4:7^3:8^2:9^2:11^2:12^3:12f^2
:13:13f:13:14:15^3:16:17^3/**3**:1:2^3:3:5^3:6^2:7^2:8:9:10^4
:11/**4**:1:4:5:6^4:8^3:8f^2:8:10^2:11^3:13,14:15^3/**5**:1^2:2^2
:4:5:7^3:8:9:12/**6**:1^2:2:3:4:5^2:7f:9^3:10^4:11^5:12f:12:
13/**7**:1^2:4^2:5^2:8^2:9^3:10:11^2:12^4:13^3/**8**:1:4:5^3:6:7^3:
9f^2:9:11:13:14/**Is1**:1^4:2^2:3^3:4^2:8^3:9:10:11:12,13^3:
14:15:17^2:18^2:20:21:23:24^2:26^2:27:31^3/**2**:1:2^4:2f^2
:2:3^5:4^3:5^2:6^3:8:10^2:11^2:12^3:13^2:14:16^2:17^4:19^6:
20:21^8/**3**:1:5:8:9^2:10:11^2:12:13^2:14^4:15^2:16^5:17:
18:25,26^2/**4**:2,3,4^4:2,3,4f^7:5^3/**5**:1:2^6:3^2:5:6:7^3:7f^2
:8^2:9:11:12^2:13:15^3:16:17:19^2:22:23:24^3:25^5:26^3:
28^2:29:30^3/**6**:1^3:3^2:4^2:5^2:6^2:8:11:12/**7**:1^3:1f^2:1:2^5
:3^6:4^2:5:6:7:8:8f^3:9:10:12^2:13:14^2:14f^5:15,16:
15,16f^2:15,16^2:15,16f:17^3:18^2:18f^2:19^2:20:21,22^2
:23:24:25^2/**8**:1^3:2^4:3:4:5:6:6f:7,8:11^2:13^2:14,15:
16^2:17:18^3:19^4:20:22/**9**:1^4:2^3:3^2:4^4:5^2:6^4:7^4:
8,9,10^2:11,12^6:13:14,15^3:16^2:17^2:18^2:19,20^5/**10**:
1:2^3:4:5,6:7^2:12^3:13^2:15^5:16:17^4:18:20^3:21:22^2:
23:24^3:26^6:27^2:27f^2:28,29^5:30:31^2:32^2:33^4:34^3/
11:1^2:1f^2:1:2^6:3:4^3:6^3:7^2:9^5:10:10f^3:10^3:11^4:12^4:
13:14^4:15^2:15f:15:15f:16/**12**:1:2:3^2:4^2:4f:5^2:6^2/
13:1:2^3:3:4^6:6^3:7:8^2:9^5:10:11^6:12:13^3:14:16^2:17:
18^4:19^2:20^3:21^4:22/**14**:1^3:2^2:3:4:5:6:7^2:8^3:9:11:
12^4:13:13f:13^3:13f^5:14^2:15:16^4:17^2:18^2:19^2:20:21^4
:22:23^4:25:26^2:27^2:28^2:29^2:30^3:31:32^3/**15**:2:3^2:4^3
:5^2:6^2:7^3:8^2:9^2/**16**:1:2^3:3^2:4,5:8^7:9:10^7:12^3:13,14^2
/**17**:2:3^4:4^2:5^2:6^6:7:8^2:9^4:10^2:11:12:13:14^3/**18**:1^2:
1f^3:1:2^2:2f:2:3^3:4^2:5^2:6^4:7^3/**19**:1^4:4:5^4:7:8^2:9^2:11^3
:12:13^2:14:15:16^2:17^2:18^3:18f:18^2:19^3:20^2:21^3:22^3
:23^3:24:25^2/**20**:1^3:2^2:3^3:4^3:5,6:5,6f/**21**:1^2:2^4:3:5:
5f^3:6,7^2:6,7f^5:8,9^4:10^2:11^2:12:13:15:16f^2:16^3:17^2
/**22**:1f:1:2^2:3:5^4:6,7^4:8:9,10,11^5:12:13:14^2:15,16^4
:17:19:20:21:25^4/**23**:1f:1:2,3^4:4f:4:5:7:8:9^3:11^4:
13^3:14:15,16^3:17^2:18^4/**24**:1^4:3^2:4,5^8:6^2:7^4:8^3:9^2:
10:11^2:12:13:13f^2:13^2:14^2:15,16^5:17^2:18^3:19:20^3:
21^5:23^5/**25**:2:4^3:5:6^2:7^3:8^2:9:10:11:12/**26**:1^2:2^2:3
:4^2:5^3:6:7^2:9:10:11:15^2:19:20^2:21^7/**27**:1^5:3^2:6^2:
7,8:10:11^2:12^5:13^2/**28**:1^5:2^3:3^5:5^2:6:9:11:13:14^2:
15:15f:15^2:16:17^3:18^3:19^2:20^2:21:22:23,24:27:29^2
/**29**:1:4:5:6:7:10^2:13:15:16^2:17:18^3:19^4:21^5:22:23^2
:23f:23:24/**30**:1:6^2:7:8:10,11:12^2:14^2:15^2:16^2:17:
18^2:19:20:21:24^3:26^5:27:28:29^5:30:31^3:32:33^4/
31:1:2:3:4,5^5:7:8^3:9^3/**32**:2^3:3:4:5^2:6:7^4:10^2:14^3:
15:16:19/**33**:2:3^3:4^2:5^2:8^3:9:10:12:14^2:16^3:17^2:18
:21:22:23^3:24^2/**34**:1^2:2^2:3^3:4^3:5^2:6^3:7^3:8^2:9^2:10:
11:12:13^2:14^5:15^2:16^3:17/**35**:1^2:2^4:5^4:6^3:7^2:8^3:9:
10^3/**36**:1^2:2^4:3^4:4^3:5:6:7^4:8,9^2:10^2:11f:11^2:13^5:15^3
:16^2:18^3:20:21:22^3/**37**:1^3:2^2:3:4^4:5:6^3:7:8,9^3:10:
11:12^3:13^4:14^2:16,17^4:18^2:19^2:20^2:21^2:22^2:23:24^4
:27^3:28:29^2:30^3:30f:32^3:33:34^2:36^6:38^2/**38**:1^2:2:4
:5:6^2:8^2:10:11^3:12:18f^3:19^3:20^3:21:22/**39**:1^2:1f^2:2^2
:3^2:5:6^2:7^2:8/**40**:2:3^4:4^5:5^3:6^2:7^3:8^3:9^2:10:11^2:12^6
:13^2:15^5:17:20:21^3:22^5:23^2:24:25:26:27:28^5:29^2:
30^2:31/**41**:1^2:2:2f:2^2:3:4^3:5^2:7^7:9^2:10f:13:14^2:16^5
:17:18^3:19:21:22:23:25^2:27^2:29/**42**:1^2:2:3^3:4^2:5^6:
6^2:6f:6:7^2:8:9:10^2:11^2:12^2:13:15^2:16^2:19^3:21^2:22^2
:23^2:24^2:25/**43**:1:2^2:3^2:6^2:9^2:10:11:14^4:15:16^3:17^2
:19^3:20^5:21:23:24:27/**44**:2:5^3:6^4:7:11:12:13^3:14^5:
15^2:16:19^2:20:22:23^2:24^3:25^2:26:27:28/**45**:1^3:2^2:
3^4:4:6:7^2:8^2:9^4:10:11^2:12^3:13f^2:14^2:18^2:20:22:23:
24:25/**46**:1:1f^2:1^5:9^2:11:13/**47**:1^3:2:4^2:5:6:7^2:8^3:9
:12:13^2:14/**48**:1^3:3:7:9:10:11:12^2:13^4:14^4:16:17^4:
19^3:20^4:21^2:22^2/**49**:1^2:2:5^3:6^2:7^7:8,9^4:10^3:11^2:13:
18:19:20:21:22^2:23^3:24^2:25^3:26^3/**50**:1:2^4:3^3:4:5:6^2
:7:9:10^2/**51**:1^3:3^2:5^2:6^6:7:8^2:9^3:9f:10^3:11:12:13^4:
15^4:16^3:17^6:19:20^2:22^3:23^2/**52**:2^2:3:5:6:7^5:8^2:9^2:
10^6:11^4:12^2:13f^7:14,15f^2/**53**:3:6^2:7^2:8:10:11:12^2/
54:3^4:4^2:5^4:6:8:9^3:10^3:11:16^5:17^5/**55**:2:3^2:3f:5^2:6:
7^2:8:9^2:10^6:12^4:13^2/**56**:1:2^2:3^2:4^2:5^2:6^5:8^2:9^3:10^2
/**57**:1^2:2:5^2:6^2:7,8^2:13^3:14^2:15^3:16:20f:20/**58**:1:2^4
:5:6:7:8^2:9^2:10^3:11:12^2:13^4:14^3/**59**:1:2:3:9:10:12:
13:14^2:15^2:17:19:21^3/**60**:1^3:2^4:3^2:5^2:6:7^2:9^2:9f:9^4
:11^4:12:13^2:14^5:15^2:16^3:19^2:20^2:22^3/**61**:1^7:2^2:4:6^3
:8:9:10:11^3/**62**:2:3:4^5:6,7^2:8:9^2:10^4:11^2:12^4/**63**:1^5
:2:3:4^2:6^2:7:9f:9:11^3:12:13^3:14^3:15/**64**:1^2:2^5:3:4:6
:8^2:11/**65**:1:1f^4:3:4:7^3:8:9:10^2:11^2:12:13:15:16^3:
17:19:21,22^2:23^2:25^3:25f:25/**66**:1:2:3^3:4:5^2:6^5:
7,8^3:9^2:12^3:14^2:15^2:16^4:17:19f^6:19^4:20^5:21:24/
Jer1:1^6:3^4:4:5:8^2:10^3:11^2:12:13:14^2:15^6:16:18:19
/**2**:1:2^2:3:3f:4,5:6^3:8:9:10,11^4:12:13:15f:16:17^2:
19^3:21:22:23^2:24:26,27:29:31:32:33:34^3:37^2/**3**:1:
2^4:3:4,5:6^2:7:9:10:13:14:16^4:17^4:18^3:19^2:21^2:22:
23^3:25/**4**:2^3:3^5:4f:4:5^3:6^2:8^2:9^5:10^2:11,12:13:16^3:
17:19^3:20:23:24:25^2:26^4:27^2:28^2:29^6:31/**5**:1:4^2:5^4
:6^4:7:10^4:11^2:14:15:15f^4:16:18:19:21^2:22^4:23,24^2
:27:28^2:29:31/**6**:1^3:3:4:6^3:7:8:9^3:10:11^4:12^2:13^2:
14:15:16^5:17^2:18,19^2:21:22^3:23:24:25^3:26:28^2:29^4
/**7**:1:2^4:3^2:4^2:8:11:12^2:13,14^2:15:17^2:18^4:18f^7:19^2
:20^2:21^2:22:25:28^2:29^2:30^2:31^2:32^6:33^2:34^6/**8**:1^5:
2^4:3:4,5^4:6^2:7^6:9^2:12^2:13:14^3:16^2:16f^3:16^6:19^4:20^2
:21/**9**:1:2:3:6:7:9:10^2:11:12^2:13:14:15^2:16^2:17,18^3
:20:21^4:22^3:23^4:24:25,26^2/**10**:1^2:2,3^2:7^4:8:10^6:11^2
:12^3:13^6:16^3:17:21:22^3:23:25^2/**11**:1^4:4:5^2:6^3:8^2:9^2
:10^2:11:16^2:17^3:18:19:20:21,22^3/**12**:1:3:4^5:5^2:7:8
:9:10:11:12^5:13^2:14^4:17/**13**:1:2:3:4^3:5:6^3:7:8,9^3:
11:12:13^5:14:15:16^2:17:18^2:19^4:19f^2:20^2:22^2:23^2:
24,25^2:27^2/**14**:1^2:2^2:3^4:4^2:5:6^2:7:8^2:10^2:11:13:14^2
:15:16^2:17:18^6:19:21^2/**15**:1:2^3:3^4:4^3:7:8:9:12,13:
17,18^2:19:20/**16**:3:4^2:7:9^5:10^3:11:14,15^6:16^2:19^2:
20/**17**:1:2,3^3:4:5^2:6^4:7^3:8^2:9^2:10:11^2:13^3:15:16^2:
19^5:20^4:21,22^2:24^2:25^2:26^5:27^5/**18**:1:2:3:4:5:6^2:
11^2:13^2:14^4:15^2:17:18:21/**19**:1^7:3^6:4^3:6^3:7:8:9:10
:11^4:13^4:14^3:15^4/**20**:1^3:2^2:3^3:4^4:5^3:7^2:9:11^2:12:13
:14:15^2:16/**21**:1^3:1f^2:3,4^4:7^3:8:9:10^2:11^2:12:14^2/
22:1^2:3^3:5:6^3:7:8^2:9^3:10^2:11:11f:13f:16^2:17^2:18:
19^2:20:23:24,25f:24,25:27:29^2:30^2/**23**:1^4:2:3:5,6^3
:5,6f:5,6:7^3:8^3:9^2:10^5:11^3:13:14^3:15:16:17^2:19:20^3
:20f:25:27^2:29^2:32:33^5:34:37:38,39^2:38,39f^4:40/
24:1^4:2^3:3:4,5^3:8^2:9:10/**25**:1^5:2,3^3:4:5^4:7:8,9^4:11^3

(THE Con't)
:12:12f[3]:12:13[3]:14:15[3]:16:17[3]:18[2]:19,20[7]:21:22[4]:
23:24[3]:25:26[6]:27[2]:28[2]:29[2]:30[5]:31[5]:32[4]:33[5]:34[2]:
36[4]:37[3]:38[2]/**26**:1[3]:2[4]:3:4[2]:5:6[2]:7,8[4]:9[2]:10[4]:11[4]:12
:13[2]:15[2]:16[5]:17[2]:18[7]:19[6]:20[4]:21[2]:24[3]/**27**:1[3]:3:4[2]:
5:7:9:10:11[3]:12:13:14[2]:15:16[5]:17:18[6]:19,20,21[8]/
28:1[4]:2[4]:3:4[4]:5:6[2]:7[2]:8:9:10[2]:11[3]:12:13:14[3]:15[3]:
16[2]/**29**:1[6]:3[2]:4[3]:7:8[4]:9:10[2]:11[2]:14[2]:15[2]:16,17[2]:18
:20:21[2]:22[2]:23:24:24f[4]:25[4]:26[2]:28:29:30:31[3]:32[2]
/**30**:1:2[2]:3[2]:8[2]:9:9f:9:11[2]:17[2]:18[2]:19:21f[3]:23[4]:24[3]
:24f/**31**:1[3]:2:3:4:5:6[3]:7[5]:8:9:10[3]:12[8]:13[2]:14[4]:15:
15f[2]:16[3]:17:18[2]:20:22:23[3]:25[2]:27[4]:28[2]:29:29f[3]:30[2]
:31[3]:32[4]:33:33f[3]:34[2]:35[6]:37[3]:38,39[10]:40[9]/**32**:1[5]:2
:2f[3]:2[2]:3[2]:4:5:6,7[2]:8[7]:9:10:11[2]:13[2]:14[2]:15[2]:16:17
:18[2]:19:20[2]:24[4]:25[2]:27[2]:28:29[4]:31:32[3]:35:36[2]:37:
39:42:43:44[5]/**33**:1:2[2]:4[5]:5[2]:6:7:9[5]:10,11[6]:13[8]:14[3]
:15[2]:15f[5]:16[2]:17[2]:18:19:20,21[3]:22[6]:23:24:25,26[3]
/**34**:1[4]:2[2]:3:5:6:7[2]:8[3]:9:10[4]:11f:12[2]:13[2]:17[3]:18,19[2]
:20:21[3]:22[2]/**35**:1[3]:1f:2[5]:3[2]:4[10]:12:13[3]:15:16:17[3]:
18,19[3]/**36**:1:1f[2]:2[2]:3[2]:4:6[3]:7:8[2]:9[5]:10[7]:11:12[5]:
13[2]:14,15[2]:16[2]:18:19:20[5]:21[4]:22[3]:23[4]:24,25[3]:26[2]
:26f:26:27[3]:29[4]:30:30f[3]:30[2]:31[2]:32/**37**:1:1f[3]:2[3]:3:
5[5]:6:7[4]:8:9:10[2]:11:12[3]:13[4]:14:15,16[3]:17[4]:18[3]:19:
20:21[4]:21f[2]/**38**:1:2:3[2]:4[4]:6[3]:7[2]:8[2]:9[4]:10:11:12:13:
14[4]:15:16:17[4]:18:19[3]:20:21,22[4]:23[2]:26:27[5]:28[3]/
39:1[2]:2[3]:3[4]:4[7]:5[4]:6[2]:7[6]:8[4]:9[2]:10[3]:11[5]:12:13[3]:15[3]:16[3]/**40**
:1[2]:2,3[3]:4:5[2]:6[2]:7[6]:8[4]:9[2]:10[3]:11[5]:12[2]:13,15[2]/
41:1[2]:2:3:4[2]:5[2]:6:7:8:9[4]:9f:10[5]:11[2]:12:13,14:15[2]:
16,17:18[4]/**42**:1[2]:2:3:5:6:7:8[2]:9[2]:10:11:13,14:15[3]:
16:17[2]:18[3]:19[2]:20:21/**43**:1:2,3[3]:4[3]:5[2]:6[4]:7[2]:8:9[3]:
10[3]:11:12[5]:13[4]/**44**:1[4]:2,3[3]:4:6[2]:7[4]:8[4]:9[4]:10:11[2]:
12[2]:14:15[3]:17[3]:18:19[2]:21[4]:22:23[2]:24[3]:25[3]:26[4]:28
:29/**45**:1[3]:2:3:4/**46**:1[2]:2[5]:4:5[3]:6[4]:7[2]:8[2]:9[2]:10[6]:12[2]
:13:14[2]:15:16[2]:17:18[3]:19:20,21[2]:22,23[2]:24[2]:25[3]:
26[4]:28[2]/**47**:1[3]:1f:1:2[5]:3[2]:4[4]:5[3]:6:7[3]/**48**:1[6]:2,3,4,5[2]
:6:8[4]:10:11:12[3]:15[3]:17[2]:18:19:20[2]:21[2]:24[2]:25:26:
28[3]:29:30:31:32:33[3]:34[3]:35:38:39[2]:40[2]:41[2]:42:43
:44[2]:45:46[2]:47[3]/**49**:1[4]:2[3]:3:5:6[4]:7:8[2]:8f:9,10[2]:12[2]:
13:14[2]:15[2]:16[6]:17[2]:18:19[5]:20[2]:21[5]:22[3]:23[2]:26[2]:
27[2]:28f:28[2]:29[2]:30[2]:30f[2]:31[3]:32f:32:33:34[2]:35[2]:
36[3]:37:38:39[3]/**50**:1[4]:2:3:4[2]:5[2]:6[2]:7[3]:8[2]:9[3]:10:12[2]:
13[2]:14[2]:15:16[2]:17[4]:18[4]:19:20[2]:21[3]:22[3]:23[2]:24:25[5]
:27:28:29[3]:30:32[2]:33[2]:34[2]:35[4]:38[2]:39[2]:40:41:42[3]:
43[3]:44[2]:45[6]:46[2]/**51**:1[2]:3[3]:4[2]:5[4]:7[2]:10[2]:11[6]:12:13:
14[2]:15[2]:16[6]:17[2]:18:19[2]:20:21[3]:23[2]:25:26f[3]:27[2]
:28[5]:29:30[3]:31:32[3]:33[4]:34,35:36:38:39[2]:40:41[2]:
42:44[3]:45[2]:46[2]:47[2]:48[2]:49:50[2]:51[2]:52[7]:53:54[3]:55[2]
:56:57[2]:58[3]:59:60[2]:61,62:63[2]:64/**52**:3[4]:4[3]:5:6[6]:7[12]
:8:9[3]:10:11:12[5]:13[3]:14[3]:15[5]:16[2]:17[5]:18[5]:19[2]:20[4]:
21:22:23[2]:24,25[11]:26:27:28[2]:30:31[2]:32:33:34/
Lam1:2:2f:3:4[3]:5[2]:7[2]:9[3]:12:13:15[3]:17:18:19f:19[2]:
20[2]:21/**2**:1[5]:2[2]:3[5]:5:6:7[3]:8[2]:10[3]:11[2]:13:14:15[3]:
17[2]:18[2]:19[3]:20[2]:21[2]:22[3]/**3**:1[3]:11:18:19:22:24:25:
26[2]:28:29:30:31:32:34,35,36[3]:37:38:40:42:45:
48,49:50:51:54[2]:55:59:60:61:64:66[3]/**4**:1[3]:2[3]:3,4[3]:
5:6[2]:7:9:10:11[2]:12[2]:13:14:15[2]:16[2]:17f:17:18:19[3]
:20[2]:21[3]/**5**:4:5:7[2]:9:11[2]:13[2]:14[3]:15:16:18[3]:19:21/
Eze1:1[3]:1f:1:4[2]:5[2]:9:10[5]:11[4]:12f:13:14:15:16:17:
18[2]:19,20,21[10]:22:23:24[3]:25:25f:26:27,28[5]/**2**:1f[6]:
2:3:4[2]/**3**:1:2:4:5:7[2]:11:12[4]:12f:13[4]:14,15[2]:14,15f:
14,15[2]:16[3]:18[2]:20[2]:22[2]:23[3]:24:26:27/**4**:1[3]:3[2]:6:7[2]
:8[2]:9[2]:10:12[2]:13[2]:14[2]:14f:15:16[2]:17/**5**:1:2[4]:3:4:
5,6,7[2]:8[2]:9:10:12[4]:14[2]:15[3]:16:17[3]/**6**:1:2:3[4]:4-7[4]:8[2]
:9:11[2]:12:14[4]/**7**:4:5,6[2]:7[3]:8,9,10,11[2]:12[4]:13:14:
15[2]:16:19:20:22[2]:23:24[2]:25[2]:26,27[5]/**8**:1[4]:3[7]:4[3]:5[4]
:6:7[3]:8:9:10[3]:11:12[3]:14[2]:14f[2]:16[8]:17[2]/**9**:1:2[3]:3[4]:3
f:3[4]:4[4]:5[3]:6[3]:7[3]:8:9[4]:11[3]/**10**:1[3]:2[5]:3[6]:4[12]:5[5]:6[6]:7,8[5]
:9-13[7]:14[5]:15,16[4]:17[3]:17f[4]:17[2]:18[5]:19[5]:20[4]:22[3]/
11:1[8]:3:3f[2]:5[4]:6:7:7f[2]:8[2]:10[3]:11:12[2]:13:14:15[3]:16[5]
:17[2]:21:22[4]:23[5]:24[3]:25[2]/**12**:1:2:3:4[2]:5[2]:6[3]:7[5]:8[2]:9
:10:10f:10:12:12f[2]:13[2]:13f[2]:14[2]:15[2]:16[2]:17:19[3]:
20:21:22:23[2]:24:25[2]:27:28/**13**:2,3:5[2]:8:9[2]:12[3]:13:
14:15[2]:16:17[2]:18[2]:18f:19:20[2]:21[2]:22[2]:23/**14**:1[2]:2
:4[2]:5:6,7[3]:8:9:11[2]:12:13:14[2]:15[2]:16[3]:17[2]:18[2]:19[2]:
20:21/**15**:1:2,5:6,5[3]:7:8[2]/**16**:1:3[2]:3f:5:6,7[2]:9,10:13:
14[3]:15:16:17:18:19:21:23:27[2]:28:29:30:35[2]:36[2]:
40,41:43:46:48:49:52:53:57[3]:58:59,60[2]:61:62:63
/**17**:1:2:3,4[3]:5f[2]:6:9:10[3]:11:12,13[5]:16[4]:17:18:19[2]:
21[5]:22,23[5]:24[6]/**18**:1:2[2]:2f[2]:3:6[3]:7[2]:9:11[2]:12:15[2]:
16[2]:17:19[2]:20[6]:23[2]:25[2]:26:27:29[2]:32/**19**:1:4:5[2]:6:
7[3]:8[2]:9[2]:10:11:12[4]:13[3]:14f:14/**20**:1f:1[2]:2:3[2]:4[2]:
5,6[2]:7[2]:8:9,10[4]:12[2]:13[2]:14[2]:15[3]:17:19:20[2]:21[2]:22:
23,24[3]:25:25f[2]:26[2]:27,28[2]:29f:29:30:31:32:34:
35,36f[3]:35,36[2]:38[4]:39:40[2]:41[2]:42[2]:43:44:45:46[2]:
47[4]:48[3]/**21**:1:2f:3:4[3]:5[2]:6:7[4]:9,10,11:13[2]:14:16[2]:
17:18:19,20[2]:19,20f:19,20[2]:21[3]:21f:22[4]:23[4]:24[2]:
26[4]:27[3]:28:29[3]:31[2]:32[3]/**22**:1:2:4[3]:8:12:14:15[2]:16[2]
:17:18,19,20[9]:21:22:23[2]:24[2]:25[2]:26[2]:28:29[2]:30[3]:
31[3]/**23**:1:4,5[2]:7:8:9[2]:10:11:13:16:16f[2]:17:17f[3]:
19,20:19,20f:22:23[3]:24:27:28:29[2]:30:31:32[3]:33:
34[3]:35:38:42[2]:44:45[2]:46:48:49/**24**:1[2]:2:3[2]:4[2]:5[7]:6[2]
:7:9:10[6]:11[2]:12:13:14:15:17:18[5]:19:20,21[4]:22:23:
24[2]:25[2]:27[2]/**25**:1:2:3:4[3]:5[4]:6[2]:7:8[2]:9,10[6]:11[2]:12[3]:
13:14:15[2]:16[4]:17/**26**:1[4]:2[5]:2f[2]:3:4:5[2]:6[2]:7[3]:10[3]:
11:12:13[2]:14f[4]:14[2]:15[3]:16[2]:17[2]:18:19[3]:20[6]:21/**27**
:1:3[4]:4:6[2]:9:10:11[2]:17[2]:18:19f:21:22:25[2]:26[3]:27[3]:
28[2]:29:32[4]:33[4]:34:35:36[2]/**28**:1:2,3[5]:6:7[2]:8[3]:10[2]:
11:12[3]:13[2]:14[3]:14f:15:16[3]:16f[3]:17[3]:18f[2]:18[2]:20:
21:22[2]:23[2]:25[4]:26[2]/**29**:1[3]:3[3]:4:5[3]:6:7:8:9[3]:10[3]:
12:13[5]:14[2]:15[3]:17[3]:18[4]:18f[3]:19[2]:20:20f[3]:20:21[3]/
30:1:2,3[5]:4[3]:5:6[3]:8:9:10[2]:11[5]:12[3]:13[2]:14[2]:15[2]:17[3]
:18:19:20f:20[2]:21:21f[3]:22[4]:23:24[4]:25[7]:26[3]/**31**:1:1
f[2]:1:2,3:4[2]:5[2]:6[4]:8:9[3]:10[3]:11:12[5]:13[2]:14[3]:15[2]:15f:
15:16[8]:17:18[8]/**32**:1[2]:2[4]:3:4[5]:5[2]:6[4]:7[4]:8:9f:9:10:11[3]
:12[3]:13:14[2]:15:16[3]:17f[3]:17:18[4]:19[2]:20[5]:21[4]:22[3]:
23[3]:24[2]:25[5]:26[3]:27:28[2]:29[4]:30[5]:31:32[3]/**33**:1:2:3[2]:
4[2]:5[3]:6[5]:7:8:11[4]:12[2]:13:14:15[2]:16:17[2]:18:19:20:
21:21f:21:22[5]:24[3]:25[3]:26:27[5]:28[2]:29[2]:30[2]:30f[2]:31
/**34**:1:2[5]:3[2]:4[3]:6[3]:7[2]:8:9,10[2]:11:12:13[4]:14:15,16[4]:
17:18[5]:20:24[2]:25[4]:26:27:29:29f[3]:30[3]:31[2]/**35**:1:2:
3:4,5:6:7:8[2]:9:11:12:13:14:15/**36**:1:4[5]:6[3]:9:10:11[2]
:13[2]:14:15:16:17:18[2]:19:20[3]:21:22[3]:23[3]:24:28:30
:31:33[2]:34[2]:35:36[5]:37,38[4]/**37**:1[5]:3:4[2]:5:6[2]:7[2]:8[3]:9[3]
:10[2]:11[2]:12[2]:13:14:15:16:18,19,20[3]:21[4]:24:25[2]:
28[2]/**38**:1:2,3:2,3f[2]:2,3:6[2]:8[2]:9:12[3]:13:14:15,16[4]:
15,16f[2]:15,16:17[3]:18:19:20:21:22:23[2]/**39**:2[3]:4[2]:5[3]:6[2]
:7[3]:9[2]:10[2]:11[8]:12[2]:13:14[4]:15,16[3]:17[4]:18[6]:19:20:
21[2]:22[2]:23:24:25[2]:26:27[3]:28[2]:29/**40**:1[4]:2:3:4:5[4]:6[6]
:7-12[2]:7-12f[2]:7-12[3]:13[5]:14[2]:15[3]:16[7]:17[5]:18[5]:19[5]:
20[3]:21[5]:22[5]:23[6]:24[4]:25[3]:26:27[6]:28[4]:28f:29,30f[2]:
29,30[3]:31[3]:32[5]:33[4]:34[2]:35[4]:36[3]:37[4]:38[3]:39[5]:40[3]:
41:42:43[5]:44[3]:45[4]:46[7]:47[4]:48,49[5]/**41**:1[4]:2[2]:3[5]:4[2]:
5[3]:6[3]:7[5]:8[3]:9[4]:10[3]:11[3]:12[2]:13[2]:14[3]:15,16[9]:17,18[5]:
19,20[6]:21[3]:22[2]:22f[2]:23[2]:25[4]:26[5]/**42**:1[4]:3[6]:4[5]:5[3]:6[4]
:7,8[7]:9,10[10]:11[7]:12[2]:13[6]:14[9]:15[2]:16-20[3]:16-20f[2]/
43:1[3]:2[6]:3[4]:4[4]:5[5]:6[3]:7[5]:9:10[2]:11[3]:12[6]:13[4]:14[3]:15[3]:
16:17[6]:18[6]:19[2]:20[6]:21[4]:22[3]:23:24[2]:25:26:27[6]/**44**:
1[2]:2[2]:3[6]:4[9]:5[5]:6[2]:7[3]:8:9[3]:10[2]:11[2]:12[2]:13:14[2]:15[6]:
17[4]:19[4]:21:22:23:24[3]:25:27[4]:29[8]:30[8]/**45**:1[3]:2:3[2]:
4[2]:5[4]:6:7[4]:8[3]:9[2]:11f:11[2]:12[2]:13[2]:15[2]:16[2]:17[7]:18:
18f[2]:18:19[10]:20[2]:21[3]:22[3]:23[3]:24[2]:25[3]/**46**:1[6]:2[8]:3[5]
:4[4]:5:6:7[3]:8[4]:9[8]:10[2]:11[5]:12[5]:13:14,15[4]:16[2]:17[4]:18
:19,20[16]:21,22[3]:23:24[4]/**47**:1[5]:2[2]:2f:2[4]:3[2]:4:6:7:8[4]:
9[2]:10[7]:11:12[6]:13[5]:14:15[2]:15f:16[2]:17[5]:18[6]:19[5]:20[5]
:21[2]:22[4]:23/**48**:1[10]:2:3[3]:4:5,6,7[4]:8[6]:10:11[4]:12[4]:13[2]
:14:15[3]:16:17:18[3]:19:20:21,22[5]:23[4]:25:26:27,28[4]
:29[2]:30,31[2]:32[2]:33[3]:34[2]:35[5]:35f/**Dan1**:1[5]:3,4[3]:
3,4f[2]:3,4:5[2]:6[2]:8[2]:8f:8:9:10[2]:11[2]:13[4]:14[2]:15[5]:16[2]:
17[3]:18,19[4]:20[2]:21[3]/**2**:1:4[3]:5[2]:6:7:8,9[4]:10[3]:11[2]:12[2]
:13:14[2]:15[2]:16[2]:18[3]:19[2]:20:23[2]:24[2]:25[2]:26:27:28:
32[2]:34[3]:35[5]:36:37:38:39f[3]:39[3]:40:40f:41,42:44[2]:
45[10]:46:47[3]:48[2]:49[4]/**3**:1[2]:2[3]:3:4:5:5f:5:7:7f:7[2]:8[2]:
10[2]:10f:12:14:15[3]:17:18:19:20:21:22[4]:23:24:25[3]
:25f:26[4]:27[2]:28[2]:29:30[2]/**4**:1[3]:2[2]:6[2]:7[2]:8[5]:9[2]:10,11[2]
:12:14[3]:15[4]:16:17[8]:18[3]:19[4]:20[3]:21:22[2]:23[7]:24:25[3]
:26[3]:27:29[2]:30:32[5]:33:34:34f[2]:34:35[4]:37[3]/**5**:1[2]:
2,3,4[3]:5[6]:7[4]:7f[2]:7:8f[2]:8:9[2]:10[2]:11[4]:11f:11:12[2]:13[3]:
14[2]:15:16[3]:18:19[2]:21[6]:23[3]:26:27:28:29:30:31:31f[2]
:31[2]/**6**:1:2[3]:3[3]:4[3]:6:7[2]:8:9:11:12[4]:13[2]:14[4]:15[4]:16[4]
:17[4]:18:19[2]:20[2]:22:23[2]:24[6]:25,26[2]:27[2]:28[3]/**7**:1[2]:3[2]
:4[2]:5:6:7[2]:8[2]:9[2]:10[2]:11[2]:12:13[2]:14[3]:16[2]:17:18[5]:19[2]
:20[8]:22:23[4]:24f:24:25[2]:25f[3]:26[2]:27:27f[3]:28[2]/**8**:1[3]:
2:2f:2[2]:3[2]:4:5[2]:6:7[5]:8[2]:8f[2]:9[2]:9f[2]:10:10f[2]:11[3]:12:
12f[2]:13[4]:14:15:16[2]:17[3]:18:19[2]:20[3]:21[3]:22[3]:23:23f[2]
:25[2]:26[2]:26f[6]:27[2]/**9**:1[4]:2[2]:3:6[3]:7[2]:9:10[2]:11[3]:13[3]:
14[2]:16:20[2]:21[3]:23[3]:24[5]:25f[6]:25[4]:26[4]:27[4]/**10**:1[4]:4:
5,6:7:9:12[2]:13[2]:13f:13[2]:14[3]:16:18:20,21[5]/**11**:1[3]:2[2]
:3f:4:5:5f:6:6f[3]:6[5]:7f[3]:7:8:9:10,11:13:13f[2]:13:14:
14f:15[2]:16[2]:17[2]:18:19:20f:20:21f:21:22:22f:23:24[5]
:27:28:29:30,31[2]:30,31f:30,31[2]:30,31f:32:32f[2]:32
:32f:35[2]:36[2]:37[2]:38:38f:39[2]:40[2]:40f[4]:40[4]:41[3]:43[2]
:44:45/**12**:1[3]:2[3]:4:6[2]:7[3]:7:9[2]:10:11[3]:12:13:13f[2]/
Hos1:1[4]:2[3]:4,5[4]:4,5f:4,5[3]:4,5f:7:7f:10[2]:11[3]:11f[2]:3
:6:8:9[4]:13[3]:14:16:16f:18:21,22[10]/**3**:1:4[2]:5f:5f:5[2]/
4:1[4]:3[3]:4:5:7[4]:8[3]:9[2]:12f:12:13[3]:14:16:18:18f[2]:19f[2]
/**5**:1[2]:4[2]:5:7[2]:8:10[2]:12:13/**6**:1:2:3[3]:5:9/**7**:3[2]:4:5[2]:
6[2]:8:12:13:16[3]/**8**:1[3]:4:7[2]:8:9:10:13/**9**:2:5:6:7[5]:8[4]:
9[2]:10[2]:10f:11[2]:13[2]:15f[2]:16:17[2]/**10**:1[7]:2:3[2]:4[2]:5[3]:6
:8[3]:9:10[2]:11[2]:12[4]:13:14:15/**11**:2[2]:8f:9[2]:10[3]:11:12
/**12**:1:2:4:5[2]:6:9[4]:11[2]:13:14[2]/**13**:1:2[3]:3:5:7:10[2]:
11f:13:15[4]:16[2]/**14**:1:2[2]:3[2]:5[3]:6:7:8:9[2]/**Joe1**:1:3:4[4]
:5:6:7[2]:9[5]:10[4]:11[2]:12[5]:13:14[4]:15f[2]:15[2]:16:17[5]:18[3]
:19[3]:20[3]/**2**:1[5]:2[4]:3[2]:5[5]:6:7:9[4]:10[4]:11[4]:12:13:14:15[2]
:16[5]:17[7]:18[2]:19:20[7]:22[4]:23[3]:24[2]:25[2]:26[2]:27:30:
31[4]:32[3]/**3**:1[2]:2[4]:4:6[2]:8[5]:10:12[3]:13[4]:14[5]:15:16[3]:
17[2]:18[5]:19:21/**Amo1**:1[3]:2[6]:3[2]:4:5[4]:5f[3]:5:6:7:8[3]:9[2]
:10:11[2]:12:12f[3]:13[2]:14:15/**2**:1[5]:2[2]:3[2]:4[3]:6[3]:7[4]:9[3]:
10[3]:11:12:14[2]:15[4]:16[2]/**3**:1[2]:2[3]:4:6[2]:8[2]:9[3]:10[2]:11:
12[3]:13[2]:14[5]:15[2]/**4**:1[2]:2[4]:3[3]:6:7[2]:8:9[2]:10:11:13[7]/**5**
:2:3[3]:4[2]:5[2]:6[2]:7:8[6]:9:10:11[4]:12[2]:13[2]:14:15[2]:16[3]:
18[3]:25,26,27[6]/**6**:1:2:3:4[3]:5[2]:6:7:8[2]:10[6]:11:12:14[4]
/**7**:1[4]:3[2]:4[3]:6:7:8:9[3]:10[3]:12:13[2]:14:15[2]:16:17[2]/**8**:
1:2:3[4]:4[2]:5[2]:6:7[2]:8[2]:9[3]:11[5]:12[2]:13:14/**9**:1[8]:2:3[5]:
5[3]:6[8]:7[3]:8[3]:9:10:11[2]:12[3]:13:14/**Ob1**:1[3]:1f[2]:
:2:4[2]:5:8f:8[2]:9[2]:12[2]:14[2]:15:16:17:18[2]:19[5]:20[3]:
21/**Jon**:1[2]:2[2]:3[6]:4[4]:5[4]:6:7[3]:9,10[4]:11:12:13[2]:15[2]:
16:17[2]/**2**:1[2]:2[2]:3[2]:5[3]:6[5]:7:8[2]:9:10[3]/**3**:1:3f[4]:4,5[6]:
7[3]/**4**:2:4:5[3]:6[4]:7[4]:8[2]:9:10/**Mic1**:1[5]:2[3]:3:4:5[3]:6[3]:
7f:8:9:10[2]:11:11f[4]:11:11f[4]:11:11f[4]:11:12[2]:13[4]:1
:15/**2**:3:5[2]:6:7[4]:8[2]:9:11[2]:12:13:13f:13[2]/**3**:2[2]:3:4[2]
6[2]:8[2]:11[2]:12[2]/**4**:1[5]:2[6]:3[2]:4:5[2]:6:7:8:10[2]:12[4]:13[3]/
:1[3]:2:3[2]:4[6]:5:6[3]:7[3]:8:10[2]:11:14[2]:15/**6**:1[2]:2[2]:5[2]:6:
:10[2]:12:14:15[3]:16[4]/**7**:1[2]:3[2]:4[2]:6[3]:7:8:9[3]:10:12:1
:13:14:15:16:17:18[2]:19[2]/**Nah1**:1[2]:1f:3[3]:4[3]:5:6:7
9:10:11:12[2]:13:14:15[4]/**2**:1f[4]:1[3]:2[3]:3[2]:4[2]:5[2]:6[3]:7[2]
9[2]:10:11[3]:13[2]/**3**:2[4]:3[5]:4[3]:5[2]:6:8f:8[2]:9:10[2]:12[2]:13
14[5]:15[4]:17[4]:18[2]/**Hab1**:1[2]:4[4]:5:6[2]:6f[3]:6:9:11f:12
13:16/**2**:2f:2[2]:3[2]:4:6:8[2]:9:10:11[4]:13:14[6]:17[2]:19:
20[2]/**3**:1[2]:2:3[4]:6[5]:7:8,9f[4]:8,9[3]:10[4]:11[2]:12[2]:13[2]:15
16[2]:17[6]:18[2]:19[5]/**Zep1**:1[2]:1f[3]:2[2]:3[5]:4:5[2]:6:7[3]:8:8
10[6]:13[4]:15:16:17[3]:18[4]/**2**:2[3]:3:5f[2]:5[4]:6:7[4]:8[2]:9:10
:11[2]:13[2]:14[6]:15[2]:15f/**3**:2[2]:4:5[3]:8[6]:9:9f[2]:9:10:12[4]
15[4]:16:17,18[2]:19:20[3]/**Hag1**:1[3]:1f:1[2]:2[2]:3,4[2]:5:7
8[2]:10:11[3]:12[5]:13[2]:14,15[2]/**2**:1[2]:2[2]:3:4[2]:6[4]:7:7f[4]:7
8,9[4]:10[4]:11[2]:12:13:14:15:16,17[2]:18,19:18,19f:
18,19[4]:20:21[3]:22[3]:23/**Zec1**:1[5]:2:4[2]:5,6:7[6]:8:10[6]
11[4]:12[3]:13[2]:14[2]:15[2]:16[2]:17[3]:19[2]:20:21[3]/**2**:2:3:4[2]
5[3]:6,7[5]:8:8f[2]:8:9:10:11,12[4]:13/**3**:1[5]:2:2f[3]:2[2]:3[2]:4
:5,6[2]:7[2]:8[3]:8f:9[2]:9f:9:10/**4**:1:2[3]:3[2]:5:6f[2]:6:7f[2]:8:9
:10[8]:11[2]:12:14[3]/**5**:1:3[2]:4[2]:5[2]:6[2]:7[3]:8[2]:9[2]:10:11f[2]
6:2[2]:4:5[3]:6[4]:7[3]:8:9:10,11[7]:12[5]:13[2]:14[3]:15[5]/**7**:
:2[5]:3[2]:4:6:7[2]:8,9:12[4]:14[2]/**8**:1:2:3[4]:4:5:6:9[6]:10[2]:1
:12[4]:13[2]:16:17:18:19:20,21[2]:22[2]:23/**9**:1[3]:1f[3]:3[2]:4
:5:6[3]:7[3]:9[2]:10[5]:10f[3]:11:12:13[2]:14[5]:16,17[3]/**10**:1[2]
2:3:4[6]:4f:5[2]:6:7[3]:8:9:11:11f[4]:11[3]:12/**11**:2[3]:3[3]:4[2]:
:6[3]:7[2]:11[2]:12f:13[2]:13f[4]:13:14:15[2]:16[6]:17/**12**:1[6]:2
3[3]:4[3]:5[3]:6:7[4]:8[6]:9:10[2]:11[3]:11f[2]:11:12,13,14/**13**:
1:2[4]:3[2]:4:5:6:6f[3]:7[5]:8:8f:8[3]/**14**:1[10]:3:4[6]:5:5f[2]:5
6:6f:7:8[2]:9[2]:10[11]:12[2]:13:14[2]:15[3]:16[4]:16f:17[3]:19:
20[2]:20f:20[5]:21[3]/**Mal1**:1[2]:2,3[4]:4[3]:5[2]:8[5]:10[2]:11[4]:
13[3]:14[2]/**2**:1[2]:3:4[2]:5:6[2]:7[5]:8[2]:9[3]:10[3]:11:12:13[2]:14
:15[3]:16[2]:17[2]/**3**:1[2]:1f:1[2]:2:3[3]:4[3]:5[2]:6:7:8:9:10[3]:11
12[3]:13,14,15:16[2]:17:18/**4**:1[3]:2:3[2]:4:5f/**Mt1**:1:2[3]
3[3]:4[3]:5[3]:6[3]:7[3]:8[3]:9[3]:10[3]:11[3]:12[3]:13[3]:14[3]:15[3]:16[4]:
17f:17[3]:18[3]:19:20[3]:23:24/**2**:1[2]:2[2]:4[2]:5:7[3]:8:9[2]:9f
11[2]:13[4]:14:15:16[5]:17:18f:19:20[2]:22[2]:23[3]/**3**:1[2]:2:
3[4]:5[2]:6:7f[2]:7:10:11f:11:12[4]:13:14:16[4]/**4**:1[2]:3:4:5[2]
:6[3]:7:8[3]:10[2]:12,13:15,16[8]:17:18[2]:19:21:23[3]:24[2]:
25[2]/**5**:1[2]:3:5[2]:7:9:10:12:13[2]:14[2]:17[3]:18[2]:19[4]:20[2]:
21[2]:22[2]:22f:23[2]:24:26:27:31:33:34:35[4]:38[3]:39:41
:45[4]:47/**6**:1[2]:3[5]:5[3]:6:7,8[2]:13:13f[3]:16[2]:24[2]:26:28:
31,32:34f[2]/**7**:3:4:5:6:7:8:12[2]:12f[2]:13[2]:13f:13:14[2]
16:19[3]:20[2]:21:22:25[3]:27:28:29f/**8**:1:2:3[2]:4[2]:8,9[2]:
10[2]:11[2]:12[2]:13[2]:15:16[2]:17:18[3]:19:20:20f:23:24:
25:26[2]:27[3]:28[4]:29f:30:31:32[4]:33[3]:34/**9**:1:2:3:5,6:
5,6f:5,6[2]:7:8:9:9f:11:12:13[2]:14[3]:15[2]:15f:16[2]:17[4]:
18[2]:19[2]:22:23[3]:24:25[3]:26[2]:28:31:33[3]:34[3]:35[4]:36:
37[2]:38[2]/**10**:2,3,4[4]:5[2]:6:7:8[3]:11:13:14:15:17:18[2]:
19[2]:20[2]:22:23:23f:25[4]:26[2]:27[2]:29:30:34:41/**11**:1:
1f:2[3]:3:4:5[7]:7[3]:10[2]:11[3]:12[3]:12f:13[2]:14[4]:18:19:19f
:19:20:21:22:23:24:25:27[5]/**12**:1[3]:2[2]:4[4]:5[4]:6:7:8:8
f:8:9:10[2]:11:12:13[2]:14:15[2]:16:17:18:20[2]:21[2]:23[2]:
23f:24[2]:27:28[2]:29f:31,32f:31,32[2]:35:38:39,40[3]:
39,40f:39,40[2]:41[2]:42[3]:43,44,45[6]/**13**:1[2]:2,3[2]:4[3]:5[2]
:6:7[2]:11:12,13:12,13f:14:18[3]:19[5]:19f:19:20[3]:21:
22[3]:23[4]:23f:24:25:26[2]:27[2]:28:29:30[5]:31,32[3]:33[3]:
34,35[3]:36[5]:37f:37[2]:38[7]:39[9]:40[3]:41f:41:42:43[2]:44[2]
:45[2]:47,48[6]:49[6]:50[2]:52[2]:52f:53,54:55/**14**:1f[2]:2:3:
5:8[2]:9[2]:10:11:13[2]:14:15:19[8]:20:21[2]:22:23,24[4]:
25[2]:28:29[4]:30:32[2]:33[2]:35[2]:36[2]/**15**:2:3:5,6[2]:10:12
:13,14:17:18:19:20:21[2]:21f:24[4]:26[2]:27[3]:29:31[3]:
32:33[2]:35[2]:36[4]:37,38[2]:39[2]/**16**:1[3]:2,3[3]:4[2]:5[2]:6[2]:9[2]:
10:11[2]:12[2]:13:13f:14[2]:16[4]:18:19[2]:20[2]:21[2]:21f:24:
26[2]:27[2]/**17**:1:2:5:6[2]:9[2]:10[2]:12:12f:13[2]:14[2]:15[2]:18
:19:21f:22,23[3]:24:25:26,27[6]/**18**:1[2]:2:3:4[2]:6:7[3]:11
:11f:11:12[3]:13:17[3]:17f[2]:23:24:25[2]:26[3]:27:28[3]:29:
30[2]:31[2]:32[2]:34[3]/**19**:1:4[2]:5,6:9f:12[3]:13:14[2]:17:18:
20:21[2]:22:23:24[2]:25[2]:28:28f:28:28f:28/**20**:1[2]:2f:
4[2]:5[2]:7:8[3]:9:10,11,12,14:15:16[2]:17[2]:18f:18:19[2]:
20[2]:22:23[2]:24:25:27:28:28f:29[2]:30:31[2]:32,33[2]/
21:1[4]:3:4:6:7[2]:8[3]:9:9f[2]:10:11[2]:12[4]:13:14[2]:15[4]:16:
18:19[2]:20[2]:21:23[4]:25:26:28[2]:30[2]:31[3]:32:33[2]:34[3]:
35:36[2]:37:38[2]:39:40:41[3]:42[4]:42f[2]:42:43[2]:43f:45[2]:
46/**22**:1[2]:3:4[2]:5:7[2]:8[3]:9:10[2]:11[3]:12:13[2]:15:16:16f
:16[2]:17:20:23:24[2]:25[2]:26[3]:28[2]:29:30[2]:31[2]:32[4]:32f
:33:34,35[2]:36[2]:37:38,39[2]:40[4]:41:42[2]:43[2]/**23**:1:2:
5:6[3]:7[2]:8:10:11[3]:13,14[2]:15:16[2]:17[3]:18[3]:19[4]:20:21
:22:23[2]:25[3]:26[3]:29,30[3]:31:32:33:34:35[4]:36[3]:37[2]:
39:39f[2]/**24**:1[2]:3[5]:5:6:7[2]:8[2]:9:12:13:14[4]:15:15f:15
:15f:16:18:20:20f[2]:21:22:22f:23:24f:26[2]:27[3]:27f:
28[2]:29[4]:29f:29[3]:29f[2]:30:30f[2]:30[5]:31[3]:31f[2]:32[2]:33:
36[3]:36f:36:37,38[3]:39:40[2]:41:45[2]:51[2]/**25**:1[3]:2,3,4:
5,6[3]:7,8[3]:9[2]:10[3]:11[2]:13:14[2]:15:16[2]:17:18[4]:20[2]:21:

THE Con't)
2^2:24,25^3:27:28^3:29^2:30:31:31f:31:32^2:32f:32^2:
3^2:34^4:40:41^2:45:46/**26**:2:2f:3^3:5:6^2:8,9^2:11:13^3
14^2:17^4:18^2:19^2:20,21:22:23:23f:24f:24:25:26:28^2
29:30:31^4:34^2:35^2:38:39:40:41^2:44^2:45^2:45f:45:
6:47^2:48^2:49f:50:51^3:54:55^2:56^4:57^4:58^4:59^2:
0,61:62:63^5:64^2:64f:64^2:65,66:69:69f:71:72:73:
4^2:75/**27**:1^2:1f:2:3^2:5^3:6^3:7:8^2:9^4:10^2:11^2:11f:11
12:14:15^2:17:18^2:19:20^2:21^2:24^3:25:26:27^2:29:
0^2:31^2:32^2:34:35^2:37^2:39:40^3:41,42,43^3:44^2:45:
7:49:51^4:53:54^3:56^3:59:60:61:62^4:62f^2:62:64^2:
6f^2:66/**28**:1^3:2^2:4:5^2:7:8^4:9:11^6:12,13^3:14^2:15^3:
6^2:19^5:20^3/**Mk1**:1^3:2^3:3:3f^2:3:3f^2:4^2:4f:5^2:8f^2:9:
0^5:12,13^3:15:16^2:17:19:20^2:21^3:22:22f:24:25^2:
6^2:27:28:29,30:31^2:32,33^4:34:35^2:36,37:39^3:42^2
43,44^3:45^3/**2**:1^2:2^3:4^3:5:6:9,10,11^3:12^3:13^2:14^2:
5:16:16f^2:17^2:18:19^2:21^3:22^3:23^3:24^2:25,26^4:27^2
28:28f/**3**:1:2^2:3^2:5:6:6f^2:6:7,8^3:9:11:13:16-19^5:
0^2:22:29:30:31,32/**4**:1:2:4^2:5,6^3:7:8:10:11,12^2:
3:14:15^3:16^3:18^3:19^3:20^2:21^2:24^2:26:27^2:28^4:29
30:31,32^2:33:35^2:36:37:38^2:39^3:41/**5**:1^3:3,4^3:5^3:
2:7,8^3:9:10:11^2:12:13^6:14^3:15:17:18^3:20^3:21^3:22^2
23:24:25:26:27^2:29:30:33^2:35:37:39^2:40^2:41,42/
:1:2,3^3:6^2:11:12:14^3:15^3:16^2:17,18:21:22,23:24:
5^3:26:27^3:28:30^2:31:33:34^2:35,36^3:39,40^2:41^5:
2:43,44:45^3:46:47^4:48^3:51^2:52^2:53^3:54:55^2:56^4/
2:3^3:3f:4:5^2:6,7^3:9:12,13:14:15,16f^3:17^2:19:20:
4^2:26:27:27f:27^2:28^3:29:30:31^2:32:33^4:35:36^4/**8**
1^2:3:4:6^5:7:8,9^4:10:11^2:13^3:14^2:15^2:16:19:20:23^3
24:25^3:26:27^2:28^2:29:31:31f:31^3:34:35^2:36^2:38:
8f:38^2/**9**:1:2:7^2:9:9f:9:10:11^2:12,13^4:12,13f:14^3:
5:16:17^2:18^4:19:20^5:21:22^2:24:25^2:26^4:27:28:29
30,31:30,31f:33^2:34:35^3:36:42:43,44f:43,44:
5,46f:47^2:48^2/**10**:1^4:6,7:10^2:13:14^2:16:19:20:21^2
22:23^2:24f^2:24:25^2:26^2:28:29:30:31:32^2:33:33f:
3^3:35:37^2:38^2:40:41:42^3:44:45:45f:46^2:48^2:49^2:
1:52^2/**11**:1^2:4,5^3:6:7^2:8^3:9^5:10^3:11^3:12:13:14^2:
5^3:17:18^2:19:20^3:21^3:22,23^3:27,28^4:30:32^2/**12**:1^4
2:3^2:4^2:5:7^3:8:9^2:10^6:11:12^2:14^3:16^2:18:19:
0,21,22^5:23^2:24^2:25^3:26^5:27:28^4:29^3:31:32:33^2:
4:35^3:36:37:38^3:39^3:40^2:41^3/**13**:1^3:3,4^4:7^2:8^2:9^3
10^2:11:13:14^3:15,16^2:19:20^3:21:24^3:25^2:26:26f:
6:27^3:29:30^3:32:32f:32^2:33:34f^2:34/**14**:1^2:2:3^3:
5^3:7:9^2:10:11^2:12^5:13:14^4:16^3:17^2:18:19:21f:21^3
21f:24f:24:25^2:26:27^3:29:30:31^2:32:34:35^2:35f:
7:38^3:41^2:41f:41:43:44f:46:47:48:49^2:51,52^2:53^2
54^3:55^2:60^2:61^3:62f:62^2:63,64^3:65:66,67^3:68^2:68
69^2:70:72^3/**15**:1^4:2^2:3,4:6:7:9^2:10:11^3:14:15:
6,17^4:18:19:20:21^2:25^2:26^3:28f:28:29,30^3:31:
2^2:33:33f:34f^2:35^2:38:38f^5:38:39^2:40^2:42,43^4:44
45^3:46^3:47/**16**:1^5:3^3:4^2:5^3:6^2:8^2:9f:9^2:10,11:12:
3:14^2:15^2:18:19:20^3/**Lk1**:1f:1,2^2:3f:4:5^4:8,9^4:10^3
11,12^3:13:15^2:16:17^5:17f^6:18:19^2:20^2:21:22:23^2:
5:26:27^2:28:28f:29:30:32^3:34:35^5:36:38^2:39,40^2:41^2
43:44:46:49:51:52:53^2:57^2:58^2:59^4:62:65^3:66^2:
7:68^2:69:74:76^4:78:79:80^2/**2**:1^2:4^2:6:7:8^2:9^3:10^2
11^3:11f:13^2:14:15^2:16^3:17^2:18:20^5:21^3:22^5:23:24
25^3:25f:26:27^3:28:29,30,31^2:32^3:34,35^2:36,37^4:
8^2:38f:38:39^2:40:41,42,43^2:44:46,47^2:49/**3**:1^4:3
3f:4^5:5^4:6:7:8:9^2:10:11:13:15^3:16:16f:16:17^2:18^2:
1^2:22^2:23-38/**4**:1^4:4:5^2:6,7:8:9,10,11^4:12^2:13^2:
4:15:16^3:17^3:18,19^6:18,19f^2:20^3:22:25,26^4:27^2:
9^4:30:31:32^4:33:34:35^5:36:37^2:38:39:40^3:41^3:42^3
43^2/**5**:1^2:2^2:3^4:7^2:9^2:10^2:12^2:13^2:14^2:15:16:17^2:
8,19^4:20:21^2:23,24:23,24f:23,24^2:25:27^3:29:30^2
31:33^3:34:35^2:36^2:37^4:39^4/**6**:1^3:2^3:3:4^4:5f:5:6:7^5:
2:9^3:10:11:12:13:14,15,16^2:17,18^4:20:21:22f:23:
4^2:26:28:29:32:34:35^2:37:39^2:41:42^2:44:45:
7,48^3:49/**7**:1:2:3:4^2:5:6,7,8^3:9^2:10^2:11^2:12^4:13:
4^2:15:16^2:17^2:18^2:19:19f:20,21,22^9:23:24^2:25:
7^3:28^2:29:29f^2:30:32f:33:34:36^2:37:38:39:40:41:
2:43^2:44^2:45^2:46:49^2:50/**8**:1^3:3:4:5^3:7:9:10^4:11:
2^5:13^4:14^4:15:16:17:19^2:21:22^3:23^2:24^2:25:26^3:
7^3:28:29^4:30^2:30f:31:32^3:33^5:34^3:35^2:36:37^3:38:
9:40^3:42:43,44f:43,44^3:47:49^4:50:51^3:52^2:54:56
9:2^3:5:6^3:7:7f:7:8^2:10^2:11^2:12^5:13:14:16^3:18:19^3
20^2:22:22f:22^3:25:26:26f:26^3:27^2:28:29f:32^2:35:
6:37^2:38:39:40:42^5:43^3:44:44f:45:46:48:51:53^2:
3f^4:55f:58:58f:59:59f^2:60^3:62^2/**10**:1^2:2^4:4:4f:6^3:
7:8,9^2:11^2:12:13^2:14:16:17^2:19^2:20:21^4:22^6:23:
7:29:30:31^3:33f:34^3:35^2:35f:35^3:36:37^3:38:39:
0^3:41/**11**:2:5,6f:7^2:9:10:13:14:15:16^2:17:20:21f:
4^2:25f:26^2:27^3:28:29,30^5:31^2:31f:31:32^2:33:34:
5:37,38^2:39:40^2:42^3:43^4:44:46:47:48:49:50^3:51^4
52^2:53,54/**12**:1^2:3^4:4:5:6:7:8:8f:8:9:10f:10:11:12^2
13:24:25:26:27:28:31:32:33:36^3:39:40^2:40f:
2,43,44^3:45^2:46^2:49:51:52:53^2:54^2:55:56^3:58^3:
9/**13**:1:4^3:8:14^7:15^3:16^2:17^2:18^2:19:24,25^6:28^2:
9:32:33:34^3:35^2/**14**:1^3:3^3:4^2:5:7^3:8:9^3:10^2:12:13^4
14^2:15^2:17:21^4:23^3:24:28^3:29:31:32^2:34f^2/**15**:2^2:
,4^3:7:8:10^4:12:14^2:16^3:17:22^3:23^2:24:25^3:26:27:

28:30^2/**16**:1:3^2:4:5,6^5:7^3:8^2:8f^2:8^2:8f:9f^4:11:13^3:
14:15^2:16^6:17^2:21^2:22^3:23:24:27:29:30^2:31:31f/
17:1^2:2,3^2:5^2:6^2:11:14:16^2:17:19:20^3:21^2:22:22f:
24^2:26^3:27^3:28^2:29:30:30f:31:34^2:35,36^2:37^3:37f^2
/**18**:1:4,5:6:8^2:8f:10^2:11:13:14^3:15:16,17^5:20:21:
22^2:23:24^2:25^2:29^2:30:31^3:32:33:35:36:39^3:40^2:
41:43/**19**:1^2:3:4:7^2:8^2:9,10^2:9,10f:11^2:12^2:15^2:16^2
:17^2:18^2:20^2:21:22:23^2:24^4:26:29^2:30^2:31:32:33:
34^2:35:36,37^7:38^2:39^2:40^2:41:44^2:45^2:46:47^3:47f^2
:48/**20**:1^3:2^2:6:9:10^3:11:12:13:14^2:15^2:16:17^4:19^3
:21^3:22:24:25:26:27:28^4:29:30:31^2:32:33:34,35:
36:37,38^6:37,38f:39^2:41:42,43^2:44^2:45:46^4/**21**:1^3
:3:5^4:6:8^2:9:11:13:14:15:20:21^3:22^3:23f^2:24^4:25^4:
26^5:27^2:27f:27:29:30:31^3:32:34,35^3:37,38^5/**22**:1^2
:2:3:4^3:6:7^4:10f:10:11^3:12^3:13^2:14^3:16:18:20^2:20f
:21:22f:22:23:24^2:25^2:25f:26:27^3:29:30:32:34:35:
37^2:39^3:44:45:47:47f:48:49^2:50:51^2:52^4:53^2:54:
55^2:56:57:60:61:62:63,64:66^5:67,68:69^2:69f:70/
23:1^2:2:3f^2:4^2:5:7:8:10^2:13^2:14:14f:15^2:17,f:18:
19:22:25^2:26^2:29^2:30^2:31:31f:32,33^3:34:35^3:36:37^2
:38^3:39^2:40,41:44:44f:45^4:46f:47^3:48^2:49^2:
50,51,52^6:53^2:54^2:55^3:56^3/**24**:1^2:2^2:3:5^2:6,7:6,7f:
6,7^2:9f:10^3:11^2:12^2:13:18^2:19^2:20^2:21:24:25^2:26^2
:27^5:28:29:30:32^3:33,34^4:35^3:37:40^3:44^2:46^3:47:
49:49f^3:49^2:50:50f^2:51:53/**Jn1**:1f^3:5^3:6,7^3:8:9^3:
10^2:11,12^3:13:14f^3:14^3:15^3:16:17:18^2:19:19f:19:
20:21:23^3:24,25^3:26:28^2:29^3:30:31^2:32^2:33^6:34:
35:36:39^2:41:42:43:45^4:43:48:49^2:50:51^2:51f/**2**:1:3^3
:5:7,8^3:9^4:10^4:11:12:13:14:15^3:16:17:18:18f:19:
22^2:23^3:24,25/**3**:1^2:3^2:5f:5^2:6:8^2:13:13f:14^2:16:
16f:17:18:18f:19^4:20^2:21:23,24:26^5:28^3:29^5:31^2:
35:36/**4**:1^3:3:4:5,6^5:8^2:9:14:15:17,18^2:19:20:21-
21-24^6:25^3:26:28,29^4:30^2:31:33:34:35^2:36^4:38^2:
39^3:40,41:42^3:43,44^2:45^2:46,47^4:49:50:51:52:53^4
/**5**:1:2^2:3^2:4^3:4f^3:5:7^4:9^3:10^3:11:13^2:14:15^2:18^2:
19^3:20^3:21^2:22:23^3:25^4:26:27^2:28^3:30^2:32,33:
32,33f^2:34:36^3:37:38:39^2:44^2:45/**6**:1^2:2-5:2-5f^3:
2-5^3:10^3:11^4:12:13:14^2:15:16:17^2:18,19^2:21:21f^2:
22,23^4:24^2:26^2:27^2:27f:27:29^2:30,31^3:33^3:35:36:
37:38:39^2:40:41^2:42:44^3:45^3:46:48-51^4:52:53^3:54
:55^2:57^3:58:59:62:62f:63:63f^2:64^2:65:67:68:69:70
:71/**7**:1:2^2:3:4:6:7:8f^2:8:10^2:11^2:12^2:13^2:14^2:15:
18:19:20:21,22,23^6:25^2:26:28^2:30:31^3:32^3:33:35^4
:37^4:38^2:39^2:40^3:41,42^6:43:45^2:47:48:50:52:53/**8**
:1:2^2:3^2:4:6:7^2:8:9^4:12^4:13:15:16:18:20^3:22:24^2:
25:26:27f:28:28f:28:30,31^2:32^2:35:36:38:40:44^3:
45:46:47:48:51:52^3:53:57:58:59^2/**9**:3:4^3:5:6^4:7^3:8
:9^3:10:11^2:13^2:14f:15^2:16:17^3:18:22,23^2:24^3:25:
27:30:32^2:35^2:35f:36:38:39:40/**10**:1^2:2:3^3:7^2:8:9^2
:10:11^3:12^3:13^2:14:15^2:17:18^3:19:21:22,23f^3:
22,23^4:24^2:25^3:30:31:32:34,35,36^6:38^2:40^2:42^2/
11:1:3:4^3:6:7:8:10:12,13:16:18:19:25^2:27^3:28:30^2
:31^2:33:36:37,38:39^3:41:44:45:46:47^2:48^3:50^2:51
:52^2:53:54^3:55^3:56^2:57/**12**:1^2:2:3:4:5^2:6^2:8:9^2:10:
11:12^4:13^3:14:16:17:18:19^2:20:23,24^3:26:27:29^2:
30:31^4:32:34^2:35:36:37^3:38:38f^2:40f:41:42^4:43^2:
44:45:46:47:48^2:49/**13**:1^4:4:4f:5^2:14:16^2:17:18:
20:22:23f^6:23:26^3:26f^3:28^2:29^2:30:31^2:33:35:38/
14:5:6^4:8:9:10^3:11^3:12,13^4:15,16:17^3:18:19:21^2:
22:23:24^2:26^4:27^3:28:30:31^3/**15**:1^3:3:4:5^2:6:9:13:
15^2:16:18:19^2:21^2:25^2:26^4:27/**16**:2^3:3:5^2:5f:7^3:8^2
:8f:9:10:11:13^2:15:17,18:20:21^2:23:25^2:26f^2:26:
27^2:28^4:32^3:33/**17**:1^3:2:3^3:5^2:6:8:9:11:12^2:14:15:
18^2:20^2:21:22^2:23:24^2:25:26/**18**:1:2:3^2:6:8:9:10^2:
11^2:12^2:13^2:14^2:15^3:16^4:17:18^2:19:20^2:22^3:23:24
:25:26^4:28^4:28f:29:30:32:33^3:34^2:34f^3:36^2:37^2:38
:39^2/**19**:2:3:4:5^3:6:7:9:10:11:12:13^2:13f^2:14^2:15:
17^3:19^2:20^3:21^4:23,24^2:25^2:26f:27f:28:31^7:32^3:34
:36,37^2:38:39:40^2:41:42^3/**20**:1f^2:1^3:2f:2^3:3,4f:3,4:
3,4f:5:6:7^2:9:10f:11:12^3:13:15:17:18^2:19^2:21:22:
24^4:25^2:26^2:30,31^3/**21**:1^2:2:2f:4:6^5:7^3:8^4:10:11^2:
12:13:14^2:16:17^2:20^2:23^2:25^3/**Act1**:1f:1:3^3:4^2:5:7
:8^4:9:11:12^3:13:14^4:16^3:18:19^4:20:21,22^3:23:
24,25^2:26/**2**:1:1f:1:2^3:4^2:5:6^4:8^2:10:11:13:14^2:16:
17:18:19^2:20^3:21:23:23f:23:24:25:27:30:31^3:32:
33^5:34^2:36^2:37:38^3:39:40:42^3:42f^2:43:44:46:47/**3**
:1^2:2^5:5:6:7,8^4:9:10^2:11:12:13^2:14:15:17:18^2:19^2:
21,22^2:23f:25^4/**4**:1^5:1f^3:2:4^2:5^3:6^2:7^2:8:9^2:10^4:11^6
:11f^2:13^2:14^3:15:17:20:21:22:23^2:24^2:25,26^7:27^4:
30:31^2:32:33^4:34,35^2:36^5:37^2/**5**:2^2:3^2:4:5:6:9:9f^2:
9:10^2:11:12^4:13^2:14:15:16:17^2:18^2:19^3:20:21^6:22^4
:23^3:24:24f^2:24:25^4:26,27^4:28^2:29:30:31:32:33:
34^3:37^2:40^3:41:42^2/**6**:1^3:2^2:3:5^4:6:7^2:8^3:9^4:12^2:12
f^2:12:13^3:14:15/**7**:1:2:2f:4^3:5:6:7:8^7:10^2:13:16^2:
17,18^2:19:22^2:23:24:26:27^2:29^2:30:31^2:32:33:34:
35:36^2:37:38^7:42^4:43^2:44^5:45^3:46^2:48,49^3:51:52^4
:53:53f:54:55^2:56^2:56f:58^4:59/**8**:1^4:2f:3:4:4f:4:5^2:
6:9,10,11^3:12^3:13:14^2:15:16^2:17:18^2:19:23f:25^2:
26^3:27^4:28^2:29^2:31^2:32^3:33^3:34:36:37^2:38^2:39^4:
40^2/**9**:1:2:4^2:5:6:7^2:8,9:10:11^2:13^2:14:15^3:17^3:19:
20^3:21^2:22^2:23:24^2:25^2:26:27^5:28:29^2:30:31^6:32^2

:35^2:36^2:39^2:40^2:41:42^3:43/**10**:3:4^2:5,6^2:7:9,10^3:
11^2:12^2:12f:15:16^2:17^4:18:19^2:21:22^2:23:24:25:
27:28:30:32^2:33:34:36,37^4:38:40,41^2:42^2:43:44:
45^3:46,47:48^2/**11**:1^2:2:4:5:6:9:10:11:12^4:14:15^3:
16^2:17^2:18^3:19^3:20^2:21:22^2:23^4:24^2:26^2:28^3:28f:
28:29^2:30^2/**12**:1:2:3^2:4^3:5^2:6^2:7^5:8^2:9^3:10^4:11^2:12
:13^2:14:16:17^2:18:19:20^3:21:22:23^3/**13**:1^4:2:3:4:
5^2:6,7^3:8^3:9^2:10^2:12^3:13:14^4:15^4:16f:17:18:19,20:
21^2:24^2:25:27^4:29^2:31^2:32,33:34^2:36:37:39:40:41
:42^3:43^4:44^3:45:45f:45:47^4:48:50^4:51^3:52f:52/**14**:
1:2^3:3:4^4:5,6^2:7:10:11:12^2:13^6:14:15^3:16:17:18:
19^2:20^3:21:22^4:23^2:26:27^3:28/**15**:1^2:2^2:3^7:4^2:5^2:6
:7^3:8^2:10:11^3:12^3:13:14^2:15^2:16^2:16f:17:18^2:19:
22^4:23^3:26:27,28,29:30^3:31:32:36f:36:40,41^3/
16:2:3^2:4^3:5:6^2:7^3:8:9f:10f:10:11:12:13^3:14:15:16^2
:18^2:19^2:20,21^2:22:23^2:24^2:25^2:26^3:27^3:29^2:31:
32^2:35^3:36:38^2:39^2:40^2/**17**:1:2^2:3^4:4:4f^2:5^4:6^4:8,9^3
:10^2:11^3:13:14^2:16^2:17^4:18:19:21^3:22:23:24:26^5:
28:31^2:32:34/**18**:4^2:5^3:6^3:7:8^3:9:11^2:12^2:16:17^4:
18^3:18f^2:19^3:20f:21:21f:22^3:22f^2:23^2:25,26^6:
25,26f:27^2:28^3/**19**:2^2:3:4:5^2:6:7:8:8f:9^2:10^3:11:13^3
:15:17^4:18,19^3:20:21:21f:23:24:26:27^5:28:29^2:30:
31^2:32:33^2:34^3:35^2:35f:35^2:38^4:39:40/**20**:1:2^3:3:
4:6:7f^2:7:8:9:10,11,12^2:15^2:16:17^3:18:19^3:20:21:
22:23:24^4:25:28:30:31:32:34:35^3:38/**21**:1^2:2:3^3
:4^2:5^4:7^2:8^3:9:10:11^4:12:13^2:14^2:16^2:17:18^3:19^2:
20:20f:21^2:24^3:25^2:26,27^4:26,27f:26,27^3:28^3:29^2:
30^4:31^2:32^3:33^2:34^2:35^3:36:37,38^4:40^4/**22**:2:4:5^3:
6:7:8:9^2:10^2:11:12^2:14^2:16^2:17,18^2:20:21:22:23:
24^2:26^2:27:28:29^2:30^5/**23**:1:2^2:3:4:5^2:6^3:7^4:8^2:9^2:
10^4:11^2:12,13^2:14^2:15^3:16:17^2:18^2:19^3:20^2:21:22^2
:23,24:25:27^2:31:32^3:33^2:35^2/**24**:1^3:2^3:5^5:6:7^2:8:
9:10:11:12:13:14^4:15:17:18:21^2:22^4:23:25:27/**25**:
2:5:6:7:8^4:9:10,11:14:15^2:17^3:18:21:22:23^4:24^3:
26:27/**26**:4:5:6^2:7:8^2:9:9f:10^2:12^2:13:14f:15^2:16^2:
17^2:18:20:21^2:22:23^3:27:29:30^3/**27**:1^2:2:2f:3:4^3:4
f^2:5^3:7,8f:7,8^5:9^2:9f^3:9:11^4:12^3:13^2:14,15^4:16:17^5:
17f:17^2:18^4:19^2:20:21^2:22:23:24:27^4:29^2:30^4:31:
32^3:33^2:37:38^3:39^3:40^4:41^6:42^3:44^2/**28**:1^5:3^2:4^3:5^2
:6:7^3:9^2:10^2:11^3:13:15^4:17^4:18^3:19^2:20:20f^3:22:
23^6:25^2:26:28,29f^2:28,29:30:31^2/**Rom1**:2:3:4^3:5^3
:8:9^2:10^2:10f:11,12^3:13:13f:14:15:16:17^2:18:19:
20:21:23:25^3:27^2/**2**:5^2:7^2:8:11:12-15^2:16^2:17f:18:
19:20^2:24^2:25:26^3:28/**3**:1^2:4^2:5:8^3:10^2:13:13f:13:
19^3:20^3:21,22:25^3:26:28:29^2:30:31/**4**:1:3:4,5:6:8:
9^5:10^2:11^3:12:13:15^3:16:17^3:19^2:24^3/**5**:5:6:10:12^2
:12f:13:14:16:17:20^4/**6**:2,3:4:5f:6:9:13:14:15:16:
17:19:21:22:23^2/**7**:1f:1:2^2:4^5:5:6:6f:6^2:7^5:9^3:10^3:
11:12:13:14^2:20:23,24,25^3/**8**:2^3:3:3^2:5:6^2:7:8:9^2:
10f^2:11^2:13^2:14:15:18:19f^2:20,21^4:22:22f:23^2:26^3
:27^2:29^2:33:34^2:36^2:38^2:39^3/**9**:1:6:7^3:8:10-13^6:17^4
:17f:20^2:21:23,24:25:26^2:27^2:27f^2:28^2:29^2:30^2:31
:32^2:33^3/**10**:1^2:2:3:6^2:7:9:11:12^2:13^2:15^3:16^2:17:
18^4:19^2:21^2/**11**:1,2,3^7:4:5^2:6:7^6:11^2:12^4:13:15^3:
16^4:17^2:18:20:21^2:23^4:24^2:25^2:26^2:28^3:30:31^2:34^2
:35/**12**:1:2:4,5:6^2:8^3:9^2:11:13^3:16^2:19:21/**13**:1^2:2^2
:3^2:4:5:8:9:10:11^2:12,13^5:14/**14**:1f^2:2:5:6^5:8:10:
11:14^2:17^2:19:20^2:21:22/**15**:1^5:3^4:4^2:5^2:6^2:7:8:9^3:
10:11:12^3:13:15,16^2:18:19^5:20^2:21^3:22:25:26:27^5
:27f:29:30^2:31^2:32/**16**:1^3:3:4^2:5:7:10^2:11:12^3:13:
14:15:16:20^2:22:23^2:24:25,26,27^6/**1Co1**:2^2:3:4:5:
7:8:9:10^3:12:16:17^4:18:19^2:21^2:22^2:23^2:24^3:25^3:
27^2:28^2:29:30:31^2/**2**:2:4^2:6^3:7^2:8^3:9^2:12^2:13^4:14^4:
15^3:16^3/**3**:1^3:3:4^2:5:6^2:7^3:8:10^2:13:14^2:15:16^2:18:
19^2:20^3:21:22^3/**4**:2:4:5^4:8:9^3:13:15^2:17^3:19:20/**5**:
1^2:3,4^5:5^2:5f^2:5:8^3:12:13^2/**6**:1:2:3:4f^2:5:7:8:9,10:
11^2:12f:13^3:14^2:16^2:17:18:19^2/**7**:3^3:4^2:5^3:7^3:10:
11:12:14^8:15^3:16:17:18:19:20:22^2:24:25^2:26:29^3:
31^3:32:34^4:35:37:38^2:39/**8**:1^2:2:3^2:6:7:10/**9**:1:2:4^2
:5^2:7^3:8:9^2:10^2:13^4:14^3:15:16:17^2:18^2:20^2:21:22:
23^2:25:25f^2:26:27/**10**:1^3:3,4f:3,4^2:3,4f:5:7^3:9:11^2:
13^3:16^7:17^2:18^2:19^2:20^2:21^3:22:24:25^2:26^2:27^2:
28^2:29:30:31:33/**11**:7:8^2:9:10f:10:10f:12:16^3:18^2:
20:21^2:22:23^3:25^3:26^2:27^4:28^2:29^4:32^3:33^2:34/**12**
:1^2:3^5:4^2:5:6^2:7^2:8^3:9^2:10^3:11:12^2:13^3:14:15^3:16^2:
17:18:21^4:22^2:23:24^2:25^3:26:27:28^2:29:30^2:31/
13:1:2^3:3:7^2:8:9:10:11:12:13/**14**:1^4:2^2:3^2:4:5:6^2:7^3
:7f:7^2:8^3:9:10:12^3:13^2:15:16:17:18:21:22^3:24:26^2:
28,29,30^4:31^2:32:32f^3:33:34^3:36:37^4/**15**:1^2:2:3^2:
4^2:5^2:5f:7:8:9^4:10:11^3:12:13:15^2:19:20^3:20f:21^3:
24^3:26:27^2:28^3:29^2:31:32:35:36^2:37^4:38:40:40f:
40^4:41^3:42^2:43:45^2:45f:47^2:48:50:52^4:53:55,56^2:
58^2/**16**:1^6:2^3:7:8:10:11:12^2:13:15:17:18:19^2:20:
22:23^2/**2Co1**:2:3,4^3:5^2:6,7:8:9^2:12^2:13,14:17:19:
21:22:23^2/**2**:2:3:5,6^3:10:12^3:14^2:15^3:17/**3**:2^2:3^2:6^6
:7^2:8:9^2:10^2:11^2:13^2:14^3:15^2:16^2:17^3:18^4/**4**:2^3:3^3:
4^3:4f:6^3:7:10:11^2:13:14^2:15^4:16:18^4/**5**:2:8:10:11:
12:13,14:16^2:17:18:19^2:20:21^2:21f/**6**:2:3^3:6^2:7:8:9
:10^3:14^3:15:16^2:17/**7**:1:4:6:7^2:9^2:10^3:11^4:12^3:13:
14:15/**8**:1:2:4^3:5:6:7:10^2:11^2:15:16:18^2:19^3:20:23^3
/**9**:2:5:7:9^3:10:14/**10**:4:7^3:14^2:15^2:16:17^2:18/**11**:

(THE Con't)
2:3:4[2]:8,9:12[3]:15:17:19,20:24:25[2]:26[6]:28[2]:29:30:
31[2]:32[2]:33/**12**:1[2]:2,3f:10[3]:13:14[2]:15[2]:17:18[2]:20:
21[2]/**13**:1[2]:3:4[2]:5:6:8:8f[2]:10[2]:11:12:13:14[2]/**Gal1**:
1[5]:3[2]:5:6:7[2]:8:9:11:13[2]:14[3]:16[2]:17[2]:19:20:22:23/
2:2[5]:4:6[4]:7,8,9[7]:10[2]:12[3]:13:14[4]:16:17:18:19[2]:19f[2]
:20[2]/**3**:1[2]:2[3]:3[2]:4:5[3]:6:7[2]:8,9[3]:10[3]:11[4]:12:13[3]:14[2]:
16[2]:17:19[5]:21,22[4]:23[2]:24:28:29/**4**:3:4[2]:5:6:7:13:
15f:16:19[2]:21:23[4]:24,25[8]:26:27:28:29[4]:30[4]:31[2]/**5**
:1:2:5[2]:6:7:8:9:10:11[3]:14:16[2]:17[6]:18:20[3]:21:22:25[2]
/**6**:1[2]:4:6:7:8[4]:11:12[2]:13:14[4]:17[2]:18/**Eph1**:1:3:4:
7:8:10:11:12:13[2]:14:15[2]:16,17:18:20[2]:21:22[2]:23/
2:2[7]:3:5:6[2]:9:11[3]:14:15[5]:16[3]:18[2]:20[4]:22/**3**:1:2,3:5
:6[5]:7:8[5]:9[3]:10:11:14,15[3]:16:17:18,19:21/**4**:1:3:4[2]:
6:8:9[3]:10[4]:11[2]:12[2]:13[2]:14[2]:15,16[6]:17,18[3]:20:21:
22:23:25:26:27:30[3]:30f/**5**:2:5[2]:6:8:10:11:12:13:
14[2]:15,16:17:18:19[2]:20:22[2]:23[2]:24:25[2]:26f:29,30
:31[3]:32[2]:33/**6**:1:2:3:4[2]:6,7[2]:8:9:10:12[3]:13:14[2]:15:
16:17[4]:18[2]:19[3]:21:23[2]/**Php1**:1[3]:2:5[2]:6:7[2]:8:9:10:
11:12:13[2]:14:15[2]:16,17[2]:18[2]:19:20:24:27:29:30[2]/
2:1[2]:5:7:7f:8f[2]:9:10[2]:11[2]:12:16:19:22:24:28:29:30[3]
/**3**:1:3[2]:5[4]:6[2]:8:10[2]:11[2]:13:14[3]:16:18[2]:20:21/**4**:1:
2:3[3]:4:5:7:8:9:10[2]:12:13[2]:15:17:18[2]:21[2]:22:23/
Col1:2[2]:3:4:5[2]:6[2]:7:8[3]:10[3]:11[2]:12[3]:13[2]:15[2]:15f:16[4]
:18[4]:18f[3]:20:22[3]:23[7]:24[2]:26,27[2]/**2**:1:2:3:7[2]:10:11
:12[3]:13:14[2]:15[2]:17:19:20:20f[2]:23/**3**:1[3]:5[2]:8:13:14
:15:16:17[3]:18:20:22[2]:23:24[2]/**4**:3:5[2]:6:7:9:11:13:
15:16[3]:17/**1Th1**:1[3]:3:5[3]:6[3]:7:8[2]:9[2]:10/**2**:2[2]:4[2]:13[2]
:14[2]:15:16[2]/**3**:2,3:5[2]:6:7:9:12/**4**:1[4]:5:6:8:9:10:14:
15[2]:16[7]:17[4]/**5**:2[2]:4[2]:5[2]:6:7[2]:8[3]:10:12:19:23:26:27[3]
/**2Th1**:1[2]:2[2]:3[2]:4:5:6:7:9[2]:11:12[5]/**2**:1[3]:3[2]:4:7:7f:7[2]
:8[2]:10:12:13[2]:13f:13[3]:14[2]:15[2]/**3**:1[2]:2[2]:3:4[2]:5[3]:6[2]:
8:9:12[2]:13:16[2]:17:18/**1Ti1**:1:2[2]:3,4:5:7[2]:10,11:12
:13:14:15[2]:16:17[3]:18[2]:20/**2**:2:5[2]:6[3]:7[2]:9,10[3]:14/**3**
:5:6:7:8[3]:9:10:13:15[3]:16[3]/**4**:1[3]:5:6[2]:7:8:9,10[2]:12:
13[2]:14[3]/**5**:1:2[2]:3:4[2]:5[2]:7:8:9:10:11:15:16[3]:18[3]:19:
20:21[5]:23:24[2]:25/**6**:1:2[2]:3[3]:4:5[2]:7:10[2]:12:15[2]:17:
19:21/**2Ti1**:1:2:3:5:6:6f:7:8:9:10[3]:11:12[2]:13[2]:14[2]
:15:16:18[2]/**2**:1:4:5[2]:7:8[3]:9:14[2]:16:18[5]:19:20[3]:21[2]:
22[3]:25:26/**3**:1:6:7:8:9:10:11[2]:12:14:15:16/**4**:1[2]:2[3]
:3:4:5:7:8[2]:10:13[3]:14[2]:16[2]:17[4]:17f[2]:18[2]:19:21:22
/**Tit1**:1[4]:4[3]:5[2]:6[2]:9:10[2]:11:13[2]:14[2]:16/**2**:1:2[2]:3:4:
5:6[2]:7[2]:11:12:13/**3**:1:4[2]:5[2]:7[2]:8:12:13:15/**Phm1**:
1[3]:3:5:6:7:8,9[3]:10:11:13:17[2]:19:20:25/**Heb**:1:2:3[4]
:4[4]:5,6[2]:7:10[4]:14/**2**:1:2:3:4:5:6:7:9[2]:11:12:13:14[3]:
17[2]/**3**:1:6[2]:7,8[3]:10:12:13:14:15[4]:16:17:18/**4**:1:2[2]:
3:4:6[2]:7:8[2]:9:10:11:12:13:14:15:16/**5**:1[5]:4:5:5f[2]:6
:7:7f[7]:9:10:12,13[4]:14/**6**:1[3]:2f:2[2]:3:4[4]:5[3]:6[2]:8:9:10
:12:14:16:18:19:20/**7**:1[2]:2[4]:3:4[3]:5:7[2]:8:9:10[2]:11[4]:
12,13,14[2]:15[2]:16[3]:17[2]:18:21[2]:22:23[3]:26[2]:27[4]:28[2]
/**8**:1:2[3]:4[4]:5[4]:6[2]:7:8[4]:9[4]:10[3]:11:13[3]/**9**:1[3]:3[2]:4[6]:5[5]:
6[2]:7[5]:8[6]:9[3]:10[2]:12[3]:13[3]:14[6]:15[3]:16[2]:17[3]:18:19[5]:
20[4]:21[2]:22[2]:23[3]:24[2]:25[2]:26[4]:28/**10**:1[4]:2:3:4:4f[3]:5[2]
:6:7:8[2]:9:11[3]:12:14:15:16[2]:19[2]:20[3]:23:25:26[2]:27:
28:29[3]:30:31[2]:32:33:35/**11**:1[2]:3[2]:3f:7[5]:9:12[4]:15:
17:21:22[2]:23[2]:24,25[3]:26[3]:27[2]:28[4]:29[3]:30[2]:31[3]:32[3]
:34:37,38:40/**12**:1[2]:2[4]:5[2]:9:10:11:14:16:18:19:20:
21:22[4]:23[3]:24[2]:25[2]:26[3]/**13**:3:5:6:7[3]:8:9:10:11[8]:12
:13[2]:15:17:20,21[5]:24,25[2]/**Jas1**:1:3:6[2]:7,8:9:10,11[2]
:12[2]:14:15:17:18[2]:21:27[5]/**2**:1[2]:2:3[5]:5[2]:6[3]:7:9:10[2]:
11[2]:14:18[2]:19:21:23[3]:25:26[2]/**3**:4[2]:5:6[3]:8:10:14:
15:17/**4**:1:2:4[3]:5[2]:6[3]:7:9:10:12:14[2]:15/**5**:1[2]:3:4[4]:
5:7[2]:8[2]:9:10:11[2]:13:14[3]:15[2]:16:17:18[2]:19[2]:20/
1Pe1:1:2[3]:3[4]:4[2]:6:7[2]:8:9:10:11[2]:12[3]:15:18[2]:19[2]:
20:21:23:25[3]/**2**:2,3f[2]:2,3[2]:4:6[2]:7[5]:8[3]:9[2]:11:13[3]:14
:15:16:17:19:20:21:23:24[2]:25/**3**:1:3:4:5:6[2]:7:12[2]:
18:19[2]:20[2]:21[2]:21f:21:22[3]/**4**:1:2[2]:3[4]:4:5[2]:6[2]:7[2]:9:
11:12:13:14:14f[2]:16:17[2]:18[2]:19/**5**:1[2]:2[2]:4:5:6:9[2]:
12[2]:13:13f[2]:13:14/**2Pe1**:1[2]:4[3]:7:8[2]:9[2]:11[2]:13,14:
16:17,18:19[5]:20,21[2]/**2**:3:4[2]:5[5]:6[5]:7,8[3]:9[4]:10:10f[2]:
11[3]:12[2]:12f:12:12f:13[2]:15[3]:17[2]:20[2]:21:22[2]/**3**:1[2]:3[2]
:4:5,6[5]:7[3]:8:9:10[5]:12[3]:15,16[3]:17/**1Jn1**:1:2:3[3]:5:7[2]
:8/**2**:1[2]:2[3]:5:7:8[2]:9:10:11[2]:12:13[2]:14:16[3]:17:18[5]:
20[2]:21[2]:22[3]:23[2]:24[2]:26:27[2]:28/**3**:4:8[2]:9:11[2]:13:
19:20:20f:21:22:23:24/**4**:2[3]:3[3]:5:6:7:14:15:17/**5**:
1[2]:2:5:6,7,8[5]:6,7,8f[3]:6,7,8[2]:13:17f[3]:18:19[2]:20[2]/
2Jn1:1[3]:2:3:4:5[2]:6:7[2]:8[2]:9[3]:13/**3Jn**:1:3[3]:5:6:7:8:9[3]
:10[3]:12[2]:15/**Jud**:3[3]:4:5[2]:6:7:8:9[3]:11:12[2]:13[4]:14:
15[3]:17:18:19[3]:20[3]:21[2]:23[2]:24,25/**Rev**:1[2]:1f:1:2:3[3]
:4[2]:4f[3]:5:5f[3]:5:7f[2]:7:8[2]:8f[2]:8[4]:9[4]:10:11[2]:11f:11[2]:
13:13f:14f:15[2]:16[2]:17,18[3]:20[8]/**2**:1[3]:1f[2]:2:5:6[2]:6f[2]
:7[5]:8[3]:9[4]:10[2]:11[3]:12[3]:13[2]:14:16:17[6]:18[3]:19:23:
24,25:26[2]:27:28:29[2]/**3**:1[4]:1f:1:2[2]:4:5:6[2]:7[4]:9[2]:10:
10f[4]:10[2]:11:12[4]:13[2]:14[3]:14f:14[2]:15:19:20[2]:22[2]/**4**:
1[2]:2:5[3]:5f[3]:6:7[7]:8[2]:9[3]:10[3]:11[3]/**5**:1[5]:2:3:5[5]:6[5]:6f[4]:6
:7[4]:8[4]:9:10:11[4]:12[9]:13[10]:14[2]/**6**:1[4]:2:3[3]:4[2]:5[2]:6:6f:
7[2]:8:9[3]:10[4]:11:12[3]:13:13f[2]:14:14f:15[4]:16[6]:17/**7**:1[5]
:2[3]:3[2]:4-8:9[2]:10[2]:11[5]:13:14[4]:15[3]:16:17:17f[4]:17[3]/
8:1[2]:2:3[4]:4[4]:5[4]:6[2]:7[5]:8,9[5]:10[2]:11[3]:12[6]:13[5]/**9**:1:1f:
1[2]:2[2]:3[2]:4[2]:5:7:11[3]:13[4]:14[3]:16f:17,18:20/**10**:1:2[2]:
3[2]:4:5[2]:6[2]:7[3]:8[4]:9/**11**:1[4]:1f[2]:2[3]:4[3]:6[3]:7[3]:8,9[3]:10[2]:
11:13[3]:14[2]:15[2]:15f[2]:16:18[3]:19[3]/**12**:1[2]:2:4[4]:6[2]:7[2]:
8[2]:9[5]:10[5]:11[2]:12[2]:13[3]:14[4]:15[2]:16[2]:17[2]/**13**:1:2:3[3]:
4[2]:5[4]:7[2]:8[3]:8f[5]:8:10:11[2]:12[3]:13:14[4]:15:16[2]:17[4]:18[2]
/**14**:2[3]:3[4]:4[4]:6[2]:7[4]:8[4]:9[4]:10[5]:11[3]:12:13[2]:13f:13:14[2]
:15[5]:16[4]:17:18[7]:19[4]:20[3]/**15**:1:2:3,4[4]:3,4f:5[2]:6[3]:7[3]:
8[3]/**16**:1[5]:2[5]:3[4]:4[2]:5:6[2]:7[2]:7f:8[2]:9[2]:10[4]:11:12[4]:13[3]:
14[3]:16[3]:17[4]:18:19[6]:21[3]/**17**:1[5]:2[5]:3[2]:3f[3]:4:5[2]:6[2]:7[2]
:8[4]:8f:10[2]:11[3]:14[3]:15[2]:16[2]:17[2]:18[3]/**18**:1:2:3[4]:8[2]:9[2]
:11[2]:13:14[2]:15:17[4]:18[2]:20[2]:21:22[2]:23[3]:24[3]/**19**:1[2]:
2[2]:2f[3]:2:3[2]:4[3]:5:6[7]:7[3]:8[3]:9:9f:9[2]:9f:10:10f[2]:11[3]:13
:13f[2]:14:15[4]:17[4]:18:19[5]:20[6]:21[5]/**20**:1[2]:2[2]:3[3]:4[4]:5[4]
:6[2]:7:8[3]:9[4]:10[3]:11[2]:12[7]:13[5]:14[3]:15[2]/**21**:1:2[2]:3[2]:5[2]
:6[7]:8[4]:9[5]:10[2]:11:12[3]:14[4]:15[2]:16[2]:17[3]:17f[2]:
18,19,20[14]:21[2]:22[3]:23[3]:24[4]:26[2]:27/**22**:1[2]:2[3]:2f:2[2]
:3[3]:5:6,7[3]:8:9[2]:10:11:12:13[5]:14[5]:15[3]:16[2]:17[5]:18:
19

48721

THEIR

[2]**Gen1**:30/**2**:19,20/**3**:7/**6**:1:4:18/**7**:7:13/**8**:2:
18,19/**9**:4:23[2]/**10**:5:31/**11**:6:29[2]/**12**:15/**13**:6/**14**:
3:11[2]/**17**:23/**18**:16:24:26/**19**:36/**21**:14:27:31/**22**
:17:20-23/**24**:32/**25**:12-15:16/**30**:39,40/**31**:22:
53/**32**:13,14,15/**33**:2:6:7:13/**34**:5:13:20f:20:21:
25[2]:26:27:28/**35**:4[2]/**36**:6,7,8/**37**:4:12:16:32:33/
38:3,4,5/**41**:3/**42**:6:24:25:26:29:35/**43**:2:11:14:
24[2]:25:26:33[2]:34/**44**:1:3[2]:4:11[2]:13/**45**:15:17[2]:19:
25/**46**:5[2]:6[2]:15:19-22:31:32/**47**:1[2]:12:17:20/**48**:
12,13/**49**:6[2]:7[2]:7f:24:28/**50**:8[2]:15:22/**Ex1**:1:7:
15,16:19:21/**2**:16:17[2]:18:20:23[3]:24:25:25f/**3**:7[2]:
13/**4**:5:31[2]/**5**:4,5:7,8[2]:20/**6**:4:7[2]:8,9f:16:16f:17:
19:19f:20:23/**7**:7:11:12[2]:22/**8**:7:17:18:26/**9**:20:
34/**10**:7/**11**:2:7/**12**:27:34[4]:40,41/**13**:17,18/**14**:
25[2]:26/**15**:25/**16**:11,12/**18**:15,16[3]:19,20[2]/**19**:1:
10:14/**20**:5/**23**:24:32:33/**25**:37/**26**:21/**27**:16/**28**:
10:12:41[2]:42[2]/**29**:8:9[2]:10:15,16:19,20[3]:21[2]:25:28[2]
:33[2]:35:45:46[2]/**30**:14:19/**32**:25:32:34/**33**:4:8:10
/**34**:7:12:13[2]:15f:15:16[2]/**35**:10-19[2]:20[2]:21:22[2]:
24:26:29:34/**36**:4-7:38[2]/**38**:21:28/**39**:43/**40**:14:
15[3]:18:31:38/**Lev2**:3:10/**4**:15/**6**:16:22,23[2]:27/**7**:
35:36[2]:38/**8**:1:14:15,16:18:22:24[3]:25:30[2]:33/**9**:3[2]
:16:19/**10**:1:1f[2]:5:19/**11**:8[2]:11[2]:24:31:41,42/**15**:
31/**16**:5[2]:16:21:27:34/**17**:5/**19**:15:23f/**20**:11:16:
16f:19:20[2]:24:27/**21**:5[2]:6[2]/**23**:22:26,27/**24**:13,14
/**25**:10:33:34[2]/**26**:20:37:39[2]:40,41[5]:43:44:45[4]/
Num1:2-15:47,48,49:53/**2**:34/**3**:4:36,37[2]:49/**4**:4
:6:24:32[2]/**7**:2:4,5:7:9[2]:84,85,86/**8**:2:7[2]:10:12:15:
16:21/**9**:6,7[2]/**10**:13:17:34/**11**:1[2]:10:12[2]/**13**:25:
26:27:28/**14**:2:6:24/**15**:3,4[3]:23,24:25[2]:37,38[2]/**16**
:15:18:26:27[2]:32:34:38/**17**:1/**18**:14,15:17[2]:21:24
:31[4]/**20**:8:11:21,22/**21**:3[2]:17,18:24:33/**22**:40/**23**
:17:18-24[2]/**24**:3-9[3]:15-19:25/**25**:2:18/**26**:5-11[4]:
12-14[5]:15-18[7]:19-22[5]:23-25[4]:26,27[3]:28-37[12]:38-
38-41[7]:44-47[5]:48-50[4]:52,53:57[3]/**27**:1[4]:5:6,7[2]/**29**
:9,10:30/**32**:9:17:18:41/**33**:2:3,4:52[3]/**35**:2:3[2]:4/
36:3:6:8[2]:11,12[3]/**Deu1**:8:15:17:27:28[2]:34,35[2]:41
:42/**2**:4:5[2]:9:19:21:29/**3**:14:18/**4**:10:37:38/**5**:29:
30/**7**:3:4:16:19:24[2]:25/**9**:13,14/**10**:9[2]:11:15/**11**:
4:6[2]:9/**12**:4,5:12:30[3]:31[3]/**13**:12,13,14/**14**:1/**16**:
19/**18**:2/**19**:1/**20**:9:18/**21**:6/**22**:30f/**24**:16[2]/**28**:
40/**29**:8[2]:17:25:28/**30**:13/**31**:7:18:20:21/**32**:15[2]:
21:24:30:31:32:35:36:37[2]:38/**33**:3:11:19:29/**34**:4
/**Jos1**:6:12,13:14:16/**2**:10[2]:12,13/**3**:12f:13,14/**5**:
1:7[2]:8,9/**6**:3,4:6-9[2]/**7**:3:6[2]:10,11:12:25/**8**:20,21[2]:
33/**9**:1[2]:3,4,5:11:17:18:21[2]:22/**10**:1:5:6:19:20:21
:24:27:43/**11**:4[2]:5:6[2]:21:23/**12**:8-24/**13**:8:9:16:
30:33/**14**:3,4/**15**:21-32:33-36:37-44:46:48-62/
17:5,6:11/**18**:7:8:21-28/**19**:2-7[2]:15,16:30,31:35-
35-39:47,48/**21**:3:9-16[2]:17,18:25:33:43:44/**22**:
7,8[3]:9:12/**23**:1:3:7/**24**:1:8:12:17[2]:28/**Ju1**:14:16:
18:19:27:30:35/**2**:2:3:6:10:12-14[2]:15:16:17:18[2]:
19:20:22/**3**:1:6[3]:7:12:25:29/**4**:5/**6**:1:3,4[3]:9:35/**7**:
2:5,6[5]:19,20[5]/**8**:12:21:26:27f:34[2]/**9**:3:24:25:35:
42:43:55:56,57/**10**:16[2]/**11**:4:6:16:17:19/**14**:18:
19/**15**:4/**16**:23,24/**18**:7[2]:8:21[2]:29:30/**19**:5:21/
20:1:14,15:30:35-39:40,41/**21**:1:6:8,9:10,11,12:
14:21:22:23[2]:24/**Ru1**:3:8:19:22/**1Sa2**:13,14:
23,24,25:33/**4**:3[2]:5:7:9:10/**5**:1/**6**:2:7:9:10/**7**:4:6:
7:14/**8**:3:7/**9**:16/**10**:3/**11**:4:10:11/**12**:9/**13**:6:16:
19:20/**14**:11:13:14:48/**15**:2/**17**:1:18:18f:50,51/
18:7:8:27/**19**:8/**20**:41/**21**:11/**22**:18/**23**:5:18/**24**:
22/**25**:10:13/**27**:2,3:8:9/**28**:1:4:23/**29**:2:5/**30**:1:3
:6[2]:18,19[2]:22[2]/**31**:7[2]:9[2]:13/**2Sa1**:11:22:27/**2**:3:7:
26/**3**:17:18:21:30:39/**4**:12[2]/**5**:1/**7**:10,11/**8**:1/**10**:
4[2]:5[2]:7,8/**12**:26,27/**13**:29,30:31/**15**:22:30:35,36
/**18**:7:17/**19**:31,32:43/**20**:2:3[2]/**21**:10:12,13,14[2]/
22:28:46:49/**23**:17:18,19/**24**:3:8/**1Ki1**:41:46,47:
49,50/**2**:4[2]:33/**3**:2/**4**:8-19:34/**6**:1:23-28[2]/**8**:7[2]:
22,23:33,34[3]:35,36:38:40:43:44:45:46:47:48:49[2]:
50[2]:52/**9**:9/**10**:13/**11**:2:4:8/**12**:7:16,17:21:23,24:
26:27/**14**:15:22[2]/**16**:4-7:15,16/**18**:23:28:39/**19**:
10:14:21/**20**:1:12:23/**22**:10:17[2]:29/**2Ki3**:9[2]:19:
21:27/**5**:2/**6**:9:20:23/**7**:7:12:15/**8**:12[2]:20:21/**9**:
13:19/**10**:7:25/**11**:5/**12**:8[2]:16/**14**:6[3]/**15**:16/**16**:
15:17/**17**:7[2]:9f:13[2]:14[2]:15[2]:16:17:19:20:29[2]:30[2]:
31[2]:34:41[2]/**18**:12:27[2]:33:37/**19**:1:18/**21**:8:9:14:
15/**22**:7/**23**:20:21/**25**:11:23[2]/**1Ch4**:23:31:32,33[2]
:34-39:42/**5**:10:13:14:20:24:25/**6**:32:48:49:58,59
:70:75:78,79:81/**7**:4:9[2]:11:22:29:30:32:40/**8**:12:
40/**9**:2:19:22[3]:23:25:27:33,34/**10**:7[2]:9:12/**11**:2:
10:18,19/**12**:2[2]:3-7:24-37:39/**14**:8/**15**:4-10[6]:15:
18/**16**:6:38:42:43/**17**:9:22:24/**19**:4[3]:5:16:17,18:
19/**23**:22/**24**:1:19:30:31/**25**:1[2]:6,7[3]:8/**26**:6,7[3]:8:
13:27:31,32/**27**:1:32/**29**:17:18:22[3]:24/**2Ch2**:11/
4:6/**5**:7,8:9:11,12[2]:13,14[3]/**6**:24:25[2]:27:34:35:36:
37,38[2]/**7**:6[2]:14[3]:22/**8**:5:14[3]/**9**:4:12/**10**:6:7:8,9/
11:4:11:13,14:16/**12**:6/**13**:10:18,19[2]/**14**:4/**15**:5:
12:14:15/**16**:8[2]/**17**:5/**18**:16:28:31/**19**:4:11/**20**:
13:23:27:33/**21**:3,4/**22**:1:5:10/**23**:20/**24**:5:17,18
:24/**25**:4:15/**26**:1/**28**:6:11:12:15[2]:17,18/**29**:6:15:
22:23:24:25,26:30:31:34/**30**:7:9:15:16:17,18,19:
22[3]:27/**31**:1:4[2]:5,6[3]:14,15:16:17,18[2]/**32**:13:17/
33:17/**34**:5[2]:25:33[2]/**35**:2[2]:4,5:9:10:15[4]:23/**36**:15
:16:17/**Ez2**:1:59:62,63:69/**3**:1:8[2]:9:10[3]/**4**:7:10:
13:17/**5**:3:10:11/**6**:7:13:14:18:21,22/**7**:16/**9**:2:9:
12[2]/**10**:16-19[2]/**Neh1**:2/**2**:7/**3**:5:23/**4**:3:4[2]:5:15[2]:
18:22/**5**:2,3,4[3]:5:8:11:12[4]:15/**6**:5,6/**7**:7:61[2]:70:
73/**8**:1:6[2]:7,8f:16[2]/**9**:1:3[3]:9:11:12:20:21[2]:23:27[3]:
28:30:35:37/**10**:28/**11**:3:7,8,9:19:20:25-30[2]/**12**:
9:24:27:29:44/**13**:10:11:12:13[3]:15:24:25[2]/**Est1**:
13-15[2]:17:20[2]/**3**:8:13:14/**8**:11[3]:13/**9**:1:5:16[3]:17:
18:22[3]:27:29-31/**Job1**:5:18/**2**:11[2]:12[3]/**3**:14,15/**4**
:11:21/**5**:1:2:4:5[2]:13[2]/**6**:5,6,7:19-21/**7**:10[2]/**11**:20
/**12**:18/**15**:17-19:34:35/**16**:13/**17**:5[2]/**20**:10:19/
21:8[2]:9:10:12,13:19:28/**22**:6:15,16:18/**24**:5[2]:9:
12:14,15:17:18/**27**:15/**29**:9[2]:12:17:24:25/**30**:9/
31:38,39/**33**:15:16:17,18/**34**:24:31/**35**:9,10/**36**:
6:10:11:12/**37**:8/**38**:10:16:39,40:41[2]/**39**:1:2,3[2]:4[2]
:8/**40**:20:22/**42**:9:15[2]/**Ps1**:3/**2**:4:12/**3**:7/**4**[2]/**5**:5:
6:9[4]:10[2]/**7**:7,8:9[2]/**8**:2/**9**:5:9:16:20/**10**:3:5:7[2]:9[2]:
10[2]:17[2]/**11**:2[2]/**14**:7/**16**:4/**17**:7:9:10:12:13,14/**18**
:17:38:43,44,45:48/**19**:3,4/**21**:9,10/**22**:5:13:26/
24:5[3]/**25**:20/**27**:12/**28**:3:4[2]/**31**:17:18/**32**:1[2]/**33**:
13,14,15/**34**:18/**35**:1:6:8:16:20/**36**:2[2]:4:11/**37**:
12,13:15[3]:26[2]:32:38:39[2]/**38**:12:13,14:16/**40**:3:
14,15/**41**:1:2:3/**42**:10/**44**:3/**45**:16/**49**:6:14:14f:
16:17/**50**:5/**52**:1:7[2]/**53**:3/**55**:9:10[2]:15[3]:23/**56**:5:
6/**57**:4/**58**:3:4,5:6:7[2]/**59**:11/**62**:3,4/**64**:3:5:6/**65**:
1/**66**:15/**67**:4[2]/**68**:14:21:23:29/**69**:20:22:22f:22:
25:27:32:36/**71**:18/**72**:4:10:14/**73**:4:6[2]:7:9:12:18
:19:20/**74**:4[3]:5,6/**75**:4[2]:10/**77**:17:20/**78**:5:6:8[2]:9:
11,12:17:24:29:30:33:35[2]:36[2]:37[2]:38:42:44:46[2]:
47[2]:48[2]:53:57:59:63[3]:64[2]:71,72/**79**:10/**81**:6:12[2]:
15/**83**:5[2]:11[2]/**84**:3/**85**:8/**86**/**89**:9:12:17:51/**91**:
12/**94**:4[2]:23/**95**:9/**97**:7/**98**:8,9[2]/**99**:8/**101**/**102**:
15:17/**104**:11:17:21:22:29/**105**:24:33:36:44/**106**
:5:10:11:15[2]:21,22:23:25:27:35:36:37,38:39[2]:
41,42:43[2]:44[2]:46/**107**:13:14:16[2]:17:18:19:22:26:
27:28:36:37[3]/**109**:2:9,10:25:28:31/**110**:6/**112**:10
/**115**:2:2f:4:5:7:8/**119**:44,45,46:70:78:85,86:110:
172/**120**:7/**124**:2,3/**126**:6/**127**:2:5f/**128**:2/**129**:
3,4/**135**:12/**136**:11,12:18/**138**:6/**140**:3:4[2]:9:10/
141:4:5:6,7[2]:9:10/**144**:8/**145**:14:15:19/**146**:3:8/
147:3/**148**:11[2]/**149**:4,5:8:9/**Pro1**:16[2]:18:21/**2**:
7,8[2]:11,12,13:14:16,17:18/**3**:31/**4**:15:16/**6**:6:21[2]
:22[2]:23:24[2]:25[2]/**8**:21:24:27,28,29/**9**:15/**10**:7:26/
11:5[2]:26/**12**:22/**13**:6/**14**:9:24[2]:32/**17**:2/**20**:17:
29[2]/**21**:7/**22**:22,23/**23**:6,7,8[4]:10,11[2]:19,20,21:
26,27,28/**24**:1:2/**28**:3:11:27/**29**:16/**30**:11,12[2]/
31:5:6,7/**Ecc2**:3/**3**:22/**4**:1/**5**:8/**6**:7,8/**8**:9,10[2]:13
/**9**:2,3:5:6/**10**/**12**:3:11/**Sol1**:8/**4**/**7**:13/**Is1**:3:4[3]/
2:4:4f[2]:20/**3**:8:9[3]:14:16:17[2]:18[2]:19:20:21:23:24[2]:
25,26/**4**:2,3,4/**5**:9:18:21:24[2]:27[2]:28[4]:30/**6**:2[3]:10[3]
:10f:11/**7**:6:15,16f/**8**:4:14,15:19:20:21[3]/**9**:17:18:
19,20/**10**:13:14:27:28,29[2]/**11**:14/**13**:2:3:11:14[2]:
16[4]:20:21/**14**:1:2:9:18:25/**15**:2[3]:5/**16**:8:9:10:12[3]
/**17**:7:8[2]:9/**19**:3[2]:6:11[2]:12:13:14:17:21:22:23:24:
25/**20**:4:5,6/**21**:5:16/**23**:18/**24**:4,5/**25**:11[2]/**26**:6:
16:19:21/**27**:2:13/**28**:5:8:12/**29**:13:14:15:18/**30**:
28/**31**:1:2:3:4,5:9/**32**:6[2]:19:20/**33**:1:7:8:15[2]:16:
23[2]:24/**34**:2:3[2]:14/**36**:19[2]:20:22/**37**:12:19:24[2]:
27:33:38/**40**:24:31/**41**:17/**42**:4:15/**43**:4:7:9:17/
44:5:7:9[3]:18[2]/**45**:8:14[2]:17/**46**:1:7/**48**:11/**49**:13:
22[2]:26[2]/**50**:10/**51**:7:13/**52**:8:14,15/**53**:8[2]:11/**54**:
3:13/**55**:7[2]/**56**:11/**57**:1:17:18/**58**:1:2:12/**59**:18:
21[2]/**60**:8:9:16:21/**61**:2:6:8:9/**63**:3:4:8:9:9f:10:11
/**65**:2:3:7[2]:21,22[2]:23[4]:24[2]/**66**:3[3]:24[2]/**Jer1**:15:18
/**2**:8[5]:10,11[2]:16:26,27[2]:32:36:37/**3**:17:18[2]:21/**4**:
11,12:22:23:31/**5**:3:5[2]:6[3]:7:13:16:19:26:27:28/**6**:
3:10:12[3]:18,19:23:24:27:29/**7**:18:19:24:26:30:31
/**8**:2[2]:4,5:6:10[2]:13[2]:16f:19/**9**:3[2]:4:5:8[2]:10:11:14/
10:2,3[2]:5:9:14:15:21[2]/**11**:1:4[2]:10[2]:11:12[2]:18[2]:
21,22[2]:23/**12**:2[3]:4[2]:7:9:16/**13**:19/**14**:3:6:12:13:

EIR Con't)
6:18/15:7:8:11:15:17,18^3:21/16:3:4^2:6^3:7:8/
^{3}:2,3:26^2/18:16^2:17^3:21^6:22:23^2/19:4:5:9:11
:4:10/22:9:10/23:3:8:10:11:12^4:14:21:22:27:
30,31:32:33:34/24:4,5:7:10/25:12:14:18:34^2:
38/26:3^2:11:19/27:3:7:10:11/28:13/29:22:23
:3:6:8^3:9^2:10^2:20^2:21/31:8^2:9:12^2:13^3:17:29:
33:33f^2:33:34:37/32:18:22:30^2:32:33:34:35:
39^2:40/33:5:7:8:13:16:20,21:25,26/34:10:11^2
:13/35:14:16/36:7:31/37:10/38:20/40:8:12
:2:5^2:7:8:12/44:2,3:5^2:14^2:15/47:2:3:4/48:10
:37^2/49:18:23^2:29^4:32:32f/50:4:6^2:7:16:17:28 ^{2}
:34:38:40:42/51:3:5:14:28:30^2:38:39:58/Lam
:14:19:22/2:4:6:7^2:9:10^2:12^2:15:16:17:20^2/3:
30:34,35,36:62:65/4:3,4^3:8^3:10:20/5:12:13^2/
e1:7^2:8:12:18:19,20,21:24^2:25f/2:3:6^2/3:9:13:
19/4:17/5:10^2/6:4-7:9^3:13/7:10,11^2:26,27/8:
12:14:16:17/9:1:8/10:9-13:19:21:22/11:15:
22^2/12:4:11:19^3/13:2,3:11:18:22/14:3:10:11:
14:16:20/16:3f:28:33,34:40,41:45^2:55/18:2/
4:7^3/20:4:8:16^2:18^2:21:23,24:26^2:27,28^3/21:
15:21:28/22:9:10f:10:27/23:6:7:8:10:14,15:
23:30:36:37:39^2:47^3/24:25^5/25:4/26:5:14:16 ^{2}
7:9:10:11:17f:23:30:31:32:35:36/28:7:25^2:26^3
:18/31:15/32:10^2:23^3:24^2:25:26:27^2:27f^2:27^2
3:6^3:29:30:31^2/34:2:9,10^3:13:15,16:20:24:26^2:
:30/35:4,5/36:7:12:17^3:23:37,38/37:21:23^2:
^{2}:25^5:27/38:5:7:13^2:14:15,16/39:10:22:23^2:24
:26^2:27:28/42:14/43:7^2:8^2:9^2:10/44:13:20:24
:29/45:4:9^2:16/46:18/47:22^2/48:11:12/Dan
:7:13/2:21^3:43/3:27^2:28/5:2,3,4:8f/6:24/7:
:27/8:10:23:24/9:25f:27^2/11:6f:8:30,31:32:32
5:39:40/12:10/Hos1:11:5:12:17/3:5^2:5f/4:8:9
:12f^2:15:18^2/5:6:7:15/6:9/7:2:3^2:6^2:7:8:9:13:
^{2}/8:4:7:13^2:14/9:8:10:13:15^3/10:2^2:5^2/11:6^4:
/12:1^2/13:2/Joe2:6:20:22^2/3:3:6:14:15:16:19:
/Amo1:5f:9^2:13^3:14:15/2:3:4^2:6:8^2:9^2:16^2/3:
^{2}:11:15^3/4:8/5:11/6:8/7:17/8:2:6/9:14^3/Ob1
14:20/Jon:5^2/2:8/3:1:10/4:11f^2/Mic1:6^2:11f ^{4}
1:11f^2/2:9^2/3:3/4^2:7^2:13/5:3^3/6:11:12/7:1:3:
:17^2/Nah1:2/2:3^2:5^2:7/3:3:19/Hab1:7:8^3:9:
^{2}:11^3:14:15^2:16:17/2:5^2:6:13:15:19/3:8,9f:14/
ep1:4:5:7:8f^2:9:12/2:7:8:10:14/3:3^2:4^2:6^3:7:10^2
Hag1:12:14,15/2:18,19:22/Zec1:4:5,6/2:4:9^2/
10,11/7:3:11^2:12:14/8:8^2:8f:20,21/9:5:8:15^3:
,17/10:5^3:6^2:7^2:8:9/11:3^2:5:6:8:12:16/12:2:5:
12,13,14/13:1/14:12:14:15^5:21/Mal1:4^2/2:6/3:3:5/
t1:3:21/2:3:10:11:12/3:6:11/4:8:20:21^2:22^2:
/5:41/6:2:20/7:17:29/8:22/9:2:8:29:36/10:21^3
6:41/11:1f:16:21f:21:23f/12:25:41/13:15^3:43:
/14:14:22:35^2/15:5,6:8:9^2:30/17:12:24:25/18
0/19:2:15/20:34/21:7:8/22:5:7:16:24:34,35/
3:2^5:5:5f:5:13,14:32^2/24:17:18^2:41/25:1:2,3,4:
8^2:15:19/26:22:43/27:12:21:39:54/28:15/Mk
4^2:5:18:19:20:34/2:8:18/3:5/4:11,12:14:17:19:
0:31,32/5:36/6:5:8,9:30:47:52f/7:3^2:4:6,7^2/8:
6:35/10:13:16:34/11:7:8:15:18^2/12:6:15:17:18:
0^2:41:43,44:43,44f/13:12^2:17/14:55:59:65^2/15:
^{2}:19:20:27:29,30/16:14^2:18:20/Lk1:1,2:52:77/
:8:16:20:24:34,35:44/3:3:12/4:6,7:18,19:40^2/5:
:6:7:9:15:20:32:33/6:1:8:14,15,16:24:25:34/7:
0,21,22:32/8:3/9:6:45:47:60f/10:13f:13^3:38/
2:24:48/13:15:29/16:14:30/17:14:28:37f/18:1:
:15:16,17/19:14^2:15:35:36,37:45/20:20:23:26:
8:40:47/21:1/22:8:25:63,64/23:2:3^2:10:23:25/
4:17:28:31:32:33,34:35:45/Jn2:14:15/3:19^2:
0/4:40,41/5:18:28/6:2-5:15:22,23/8:17/10:12:
9/11^2/12:11:16:40^2:42:46/13:12:29/15:22/17:
9/18:12:34f^3:35/19:3:31/20:20^2/Act1:10/2:3:
:40:45:46/4:4:17:25,26:29^2/5:16:31:34:38:42/6
1:6/7:11:19:34:35:42:45:54:57^3:58/8:7:17:18/9:
:24/10:43/11:12:18:20:30/12:16:20:25/13:3^2:5
,7:17:19,20:27:51:52/14:3:4:5,6:11:14:16:26:
7/15:4:5^2:9:26:32:39/16:3:23:24:33:38/17:18:
1:26:27/18/19:6:18,19^2:28/20:4/21:21:23:
6,27:35/22:23/23:16:21:28:29:30/24:1:18:20/
25:2:3:14:15:19/26:6:18^3:20^2/27:3:19:42/28:6:
5/Rom1:19:21:26:27:28:29:30:31/2:12-15^2:16:
9/3:13:13f^2:13:14:26^3/5:14^2:20/7:6/8:5:8^2/
11:6:8:9^2:10:16:23:27/12:15/15:12:27f/16:1:4:5:
16:21/1Co1:20:22:24/6:12f/7:5:31/8:7^2/9:13:
21/10:2^3/11:12:14,15/14:35^2/15:40:41/16:15:
16:19^4/2Co3:15/5/6:16:17/8:2^2:5/10:12^2/11:15
19,20:24/12:14^2/13:13/Gal2:4:6:7,8,9/3:8,9/5:
17:24/6:6:13/Eph2:11/3:6/4:11:17,18^2:19/5:13
28/Php1:14:16,17:18:28/3:19^3/4:21/Col2:8^2/
1Th2:14:15:16/4:5:15/2Th2:10:11:12/3/1Ti1:
3,4^2:5^2:6:9:19^2/2:9,10^2:15^2/3:9:10:11:13/4:2:12:
14/5:6^2:11:12:13:14:17:18:25/6:1:2^2:5:10:17^2:18
:20^2/2Ti2:17:25:26/3:2^2:4:6:9/4:4/Tit1:6^3:8:9:
12^2:14/2:4^2:5^3:9^2/3:13:14^2/Phm1:6/Heb2:10:
15/3:10:16/4:12/5:1^3/6:12/7:5^2:11:23:25:27/8:
5:9^2:10^3:12^2/9:5:6/10:1:2:3^2:16^3:17/11:2:13:14:
16:28:33:34:35:36:37,38/12:8:15/13:7:17:24,25
/Jas1:10,11/3:1/5:4^2:15/1Pe1:12/2:1/3:5:7:12
/4:6^2/2Pe1:19/2:1^2:2:3^2:10:13:14:18^2:22/3:4/
1Jn4:2:14/5:10:17f/3Jn1:6:15/Jud:4:6f^2:7:8^2:10
:23^2/Rev2:1:22/3:4/4:8:10/6:9:11:17/7:9:14:17 ^{2}
/8:6:13/9:4:7^2:8^2:9:10^2:11:17,18^3:19^4:20^2:21^3/
10:3:4/11:5:7:8,9^2:12:13:16/12:11^2/14:1:11:13^3
/15:6/16^2:9:10:11^2:12:15/17:12:13:17^2/18:11:
12:19^2/19:3:10:19:21^2/20:4^3/21:3f:4:8:24/22:4:
5:14

3717

THEM

Gen1:17:21,22^3:27:28^2/2:19,20^3:25/4:4/5:2^2/6:
6:7:19,20/7:2:14,15:16:23/9:1:2,3/10:1/11:6:7:
8:9^3/12:20/13:11/14:12:14:15/15:10^2:11:14:
19,20,21/17:7,8/18:2^2:6:8^2:16/19:1^3:3:5:6:8:12:
16:25/20:8:14/21:28,29/22:6/23:7/24:14:28f:
32/25:6/26:4:7:18^2:27:30:31:35/27:8,9,10:15:46
/29:3:4/30:14f:14^2:26^2:31,32:33:35,36^2:37:38:
39,40^3:41/31:5^2:21:23:26:28:32^2:33:34^3:39:41:
54:55/32:1:16:22,23,24/33:4:10:11/34:6,7:21^3/
35:2:3:4/36:6,7,8/37:12:16:17^2:25:26,27:28/38:
3,4,5:18:23:25/39:1/40:4:5:17/41:8^2:24:48:55^2/
42:4:7:8,9:17:18:23^2:24:25:27:35/43:2:11^2:16^2:
17:23^2:32:33^2:34/44:4^4:5:6^2:11:28/45:18:21:22/
46:5:32/47:2:3:5,6^4:12:27/48:5:9^2:10:14/49:6:
19:29,30/50:4:5:12,13:19:21^2:25/Ex1:9:11^3:12:
13,14:18:21/2:1:13:17:21:25/3:8^2:9:13^2:15:16^2:
17^2/4:1:20:30:31^3/5:9^3:20:21^2:22:23^2/6:1^2:2,3:4 ^{2}
:6^2:7^2:8,9/7:5^2:6:10:20/8:3,4^3:9:19:21^2/9:11:21/
10:2:6:17:27/12:21:22^2:33:34^2:36:37:38:39:51:51f
/13:12:14:17,18^2:19^3:21/14:8:10^3:13:19:23:24:
25:27:29:31/15:4:5:7:9^4:10:12:13:16^2:17^3:19:25^2
/16:4^2:5:6:10:11,12:15:19:20^2:22:23:28,29:32^3/
17:7:13/18:1:8:9:15,16,19,20^3:21^2:22:25/19:2,3:
7:10^2:12:14:15:17:22:23:24:25/20:11:20:24:25/
21:35/23:24^2:30:31:32:33/24:3:11:12/25:8:12:
16:18:37/26:1:10,11:14/27:2/28:9:26:29:40:41:
42/29:2:13^2:17:22:24:25^2:33:40:46^2/30:11,12:29^3
:29f:30/32:10^3:12^3:13:14:17:21:24^3:27:32f:34/
33:5/34:1:15^2:31:32:33/35:1:25:29:30,31:35/36:
3:8,9:30/37:4:7:13/39:33-40:43/40:12:14:15:20
/Lev1:9:15,16,17/2:14^2/3:3,4,5:9,10,11:15,16/4
:9:10/6:18f^2/7:5:36^2/8:5:6:10:11:15,16:21:27:28
:33:34:35/9:2:4:6:22/10:1:2:4^2:5^3:10:11:15:17/
12:6:7/14:12^2:23:24/15:14:15:29:31/16:16:23:
24/17:5:12/18:4,5^2:4,5f^2:21:24^2:25/19:10:13:33:
34:37/20:16f:23:25/22:9/23:40/25:55/26:10:16
:36^3:40,41^3:44^2/Num1:17,18,19f:53/3:6:47,48f/
4:14:17,18,19:27/5:3:23/6:19:27/7:3:4,5:10:11:
87/8:2:7^2:8:10:11:12:15^2:16:17:19:21^3/9:18:19/
10:10:33:34:35/11:1^2:2:3:4,5:12:16:17:18:21:24:
25:26:28:29:31:31f:32f:33/12:2:6:9/13:17:23^2:
26:33/14:9^2:10,11^2:12^2:16^4:19:20,21:28:31:45^2/
15:1:17,18:26:32/16:6,7^2:8,9:15^2:17:18^2:21:26^2:
28:30^2:31:32^2:33:34:39:45:46^2:47/17:7:9/18:2,3:
8:11/19:6:9:10:18/20:6:8:10:12^2:13:25:26:27:28
/21:2:3:6^3:16:23:24:25,26:33/22:2,3:5,6^2:11^2:12 ^{2}
:21:35/23:7-10^2:11:18-24^5:25^2:27/24:3-9^4:10/
25:2:4/26:5-11:64,65/27:6,7^2:14:17^2:21/28:3:5:
12:16/29:6/30:1/31:6:18/32:7:8:10,11^2:17^2:29:
42/33:1:56/36:3:5:6/Deu1:1:13:15^2:16:17^2:18:
29:33^3:37:42^2:43:44^3/2:5:6:11:14,15:19:21:22:
35,36/3:3:18^2:19:20/4:1:2:5:6:7:10^2:13/5:1^2:
9,10:22^2:29:30:31^3/6:7^2:8^2:9/7:2^3:3:10:15:18:19:
22:23/9:1:3^3:5:9:17^2:28^7/10:1:2:4^2:9:15:18:22/
11:4^2:6:18^3:19^2:20:28/12:2:3:17:18:19:20-23:32
/15:7:8:11/16:22/18:2:12:18/19:6,7/20:20/21:5
:8/22:16/25:7/27:2,3,4:2,3,4f:14/28:12:22:26:
32^2:39:44:55:56,57^2/29:2,3:7:25^2:27:28^2/30:1:
7,8:12^2:14/31:2:3:5:6:9:12:13:15:16:17^4:18:19:
20:21^2:23:27:28^2/32:8:10:11^2:12:13:14:18^2:19:
20^2:21:23^2:24^4:26^2:30^3:36:38:46:47:50/33:11:19:
27/Jos1:7:8^2:10,11,12,13^2:14:15/2:3:4:5:6^2:7:9:
15:16:22:23/3:2,3,4:9/4:2,3^2:5:6:7:8^2:15,16:22:
23/5:2,3:6/6:2:6-9^2:17:20:23/7:21^2:24:25:26/8:
2:5:6:16:20,21^2:22:33^3:34/9:14,15:19:20:26:27/
10:4:8^3:10^3:11:19^3:26^2:30:32:41/11:6:8:21/13:8:
12^2:33^2/14:1:8:12/17:4/18:1:3:4:7/19:9/20:4:5/
21:9-16:17,18:36,37:38,39:44^3:45/22:2,3:6^2:7,8^2
:31:32:34/23:2:6:7^2/24:2:6:7^2:8:11:13:25^2:32/Ju
1:2:4,5,6:7:12:16:22,23:24:25:28:30:33:34^2:35^2/
2:12-14^2:15:16:18:19:23^2/3:4:6^2:8:9^2:15:28/4:
2,3:5f:6:7^2:10:20/5:21:23/6:1:8:13:21:35/7:1:3:4
:5,6^2:8,9^3:17:23/8:6:7^2:9:12:16:19:20:21:34:35/9
:2:4:5:33:36:41:43:44:49/10:7,8:10:14/11:7:13:
20/13:12/14:9/15:6:8^2:11/16:3^3:8:12:18:25,26/
18:1:4:18^2:20:22:23:26/19:15:17:21:23:24^2:25/
20:13:14,15:31:32^2:40,41:42:43/21:7:14^2:17:18:
21^2:22^4:23^2/Ru1:6,7:9:13:20/2:16:23/4:2/1Sa2:
8:10:20:23,24,25:32/3:13:21,4:1/4:2:3/5:11/6:2
:6:7:12:14:15:21/7:2:3:5:10:11^2:13:14/8:8:9:11:
13:14:22/9:3:4:9,10,11:14:16^2:22^2/10:6:10:14:
18,19:25/11:7^2:8^2:11^2:12^2/12:8:9:20/13:2:7^2:19:
20/14:9:10:11:12:13:34^2:36:37/15:5:6^2:9:15:21/
16:5:10,11:18/17:3:18:23:26:30:38,39:40:52/18:
1:15,16:17:25:30/19:8:14:20/20:23:36:40/21:
14,15/22:18^2/23:2:13:18:24,25/25:7^2:13:14^2:
15,16:18/26:12^2/29:3:4:6:7:9/30:8^3:15:16:17^2:
20^2:21:22^2:26/31:1:7:12^2/2Sa2:5:13:16/3:17:18:
20:22:26:35,36/4:6,7:12/5:7:8:19^3:20^2:23:24/6:
1/7:7:10,11/8:2/9:1/10:3:4:5:7,8:9^2/11:23/12:
11:17:19:31:31f/13:36/14:5,6^2:7/15:35,36/16:5:
6:13:21/17:2,3:10:11:12:16:17:18^2:20/18:3:5:14:
24:26/19:7:13:18/20:3/21:2^2:3:5,6:8^2:9^2:10:
12,13,14^2/22:23:37:38:39:41:43^2/23:6:7:18,19^2/
24:1:2/1Ki1:33/2:4:7:11:40/3:17,18/4:7/5:6:9^3:
14/6:13/7:38/8:14:21:25:33,34^4:35,36^4:39:43:
45:46^2:50:52/9:7^3:9^2:11,12:20,21/10:9:16,17:28
/11:1:2:16,17,18^3:29/12:6:7^3:9:10:13,14:16,17:
23,24:30:32,33/14:15/15:18/16:23/17:4/18:3,4 ^{2}
:13^2:21:22:27:37:40^4/19:21/20:7:13:15:18:20:23
:25^2:30:33/21:8^2/22:6:17:27/2Ki1:3:4,5:10^2:12/
2:3:11^2:24^2/3:21:24:25/4:4:39^2:41/5:16^2:22:23/
6:1:5:18^2:19^2:20:21^3:22^2:23^2:26-30/7:13/9:11:
12:18:19/10:7:8^2:9,10^2:13:14^3:17:18,19^2:24:25^2/
11:4^3:5:10/12:7/13:3:5:11:18^2:23/16:9/17:7:8:9
f:13:18:20^2:21:22:23:24:25^2:27,28:29:34:35,36^2/
18:4:11:12^2:18:26:36/19:12^2/20:7:13^2:15/21:8^2:
9:14/22:15,16/23:1:12:14:16^2:19:20/25:26/1Ch
5:11:20:22:26/6:72:74:76:78,79:80/7:4:22/9:25:
28^2/10:2:7:9:12/11:2:3:5,6:14/12:2:17:18^3:19^3:
24-37/13:2/14:10:11^2:12/15:2:12/16:21^2:22/17
:9^2:10/18:5:10/19:4:5:9/20:1:3:3f^3/22:18/23:
4,5:6/25:6,7/26:8/28:2^2/29:26,27/2Ch1:2,3:10
/2:8:16:17/3:10:16:17/4:7/6:4:25^2:27:31:33:35:
36^3:37,38:39/7:14:20:22^2/8:2:9:10/9:8^2/10:5:6:
7^2:8,9:10^2:13:14/11:11^2:13,14^2:23^2/12:5:7^2:10^2:
11^2/13:7:8:10:13,14^2/14:9,10:13^2/15:3:4:6:15/
16:6:8:9/17:10/18:3,4,5:9:10:12:16:26:27/19:4:
6:9:10^3:11/20:5:10:12:16^2:20:23:25:27^2:29/21:
3,4:11/22:8:10/23:2,3:8:15,16,17/24:5:19:20^2:
22:24/25:7:8:10^2:14^3/26/27:5/28:9^2:15^2:23:24/
29:3:4,5:15:21:23:34/30:14:17,18,19^3:20/31:5,6
/32:1:4:6^2:8:18:26/33:15/34:4:21:25:30:31:32:
33/35:2:13:15/36:7:15:17^4/Ez1:4:6/2:62,63^2:
66,67/3:7/4:4,5^2/5:1^2:12/6:9/7:7,8,9:25/8:17:
26,27:29^2/9:2/10:3:10/Neh2:7:17:18/3:2^2:7:9:
19/4:12:14:16:17:19/5:1:5:7:8^3:11^2:12^2:13:15/6:
2:3/7^2:68,69/8:1^2:9:11:16/9:3:6:10:13^2:14^2:15^3:
17^3:19^3:20^2:21:22:23:24:26:27^4:28^2:29^3:30^3:31^2:
35^3:37/10:36:39,40/11:22,23f/12:8:9:24:31,32:
38:45/13:2:10:11:15:16:21:25^3:29/Est1:1:13-15
/2:2/3:3,4:5,6:8:13/5:11/6:1:11/8:8:11:17/9:1^2:
16:21:24,25^2/10:3/Job1:5^2:6:14,15:19/2:1/3:8f:
18/5:1:4:6^2/8:4:5/9:24:30/11:7/12:24,25/14:3:
17/15:34/17:2:3,4^2/19:15/21:8:9:17/22:6:9:19:
22/23:12/24:14,15:22:23^3/27:15:17^2/29:12:17:
19:22:24:25^2/30:5:9/31:18:27^2/32:11,12/33:16:
17,18^4/34:19:21:25^2:26/35:9,10/36:6:7^2:8:9:10:
13:15:31/38:8,9:10/39:1:4:6^2:7:14:15^3/40:13/
41:15-17:25/42:4:9:11:15/Ps1:2/2:5^2:9^2/3:7^2/4:
2:6/5:10^3:11^2/6:10/7:2:7,8^2:12/9:6:9:15:19:20/
10:5^2:6:12:13:14:15^2:17:18/11:6/12:5/13:4/14:
5:6/17:13,14^2/18:23:37:38:40:41^2:42^3/19:11:13
/21:9,10:12/22:3,4:5/25:2:11:14:17:20/26:5/27:
12/28:3:4^3:5:9^2/29:11/30:1/31:17:19/32:5^2:6/
33:7:18,19/34:5:19:22/35:1:3:4^2:5:6^2:7:8:10:12:
13^2:19^2:25:26^3:27/36:1^2:8^2/37:10:18:19:24:32:
40^2/38:13,14:19/40:14,15^3/41:1:2^3:3:10/42:4,5
/43:3^2/44^2/49:7:11:14:17^2/50:6:8/51:9/53:5^2:6
/54:4f:5/55:9:15^2:19:22/56:7^2:8/58:7:7f:8:9/59:
3:7:8:11^4:12,13^2/64:5:7^2:8/65:3:9/66:6/68:1:2^2:
9,10:11,12,13:23^2:30/69:6:19:24^2:27:28f:28:32:
34:35/70:2,3^4/71:13^2/72:12:13:14/73:18/74:
9,10:11:15/75:3/76:6:8/77:12/78:4:5:11,12:13^3:
14:15:18:21:22:24:25:27:29:31:33:34:38:41^2:42:
49^2:50:52:53^2:54^2:56:66^2:71,72/79:3:11/81:5:12
/83:8:9:13:15:16:17^2/84:7/89:11:30,31:32^2:33:
42/90:8:12/91:13/92:6:7:11/94:5:12,13^2:23^3/
95:10:11/97:10/99:3:6:7:8^2/101:3:6/102:19:20:
26/104:24:27:28:29/105:1:14:14f:25:37:38:39^4:
40^2:44:45/106:5:7:8:10:15^2:15f:23^2:24:26:29:34:
39:40:41,42^2:43:45:46^2/107:7:12^2:13:14:19^2:22:
28:30:32:38:41/109:4^2:14:28:29^2:31/110:1:6/
111:1:6/113:8/114:3^3/115:8/116:1:15/118:10:
11:12/119:5:11:14:15^2:16^2:22:31:40,41,42:48^3:
55:83:93:97^2:129:140:144:167:168:172/124:6/
126:2/127:5/129:8/135:18^3/136:11,12:13:14/
137:2,3,4:9/138:4:7/139:13:21:22/140:6,7,8:9:

(THEM Con't)
11/**141**:6,7,8:10/**144**:6/**145**:15:19/**146**:6/**147**:4/
148:6/**149**:4,5/**Pro1**:2:3:7,8,9:10:12/**2**:3,4,5,7,8:
19/**3**:3:21:24,25,26/**4**:4:13:21/**6**:7/**7**:3:3f:3/**8**:
27,28,29/**10**:7/**11**:13:26/**13**:19/**14**:21:31/**15**:
9,10:18/**17**:5:9/**18**:15/**19**:7:14:16/**20**:1^2:12:19/
21:1:7/**22**:2:3:22,23:24,25/**23**:13,14^3/**24**:11,12:
21,22/**27**:12/**28**:1:8:13:15/**29**:10/**31**:6,7:21:29/
Ecc3:22^2/**4**:1/**5**:8f:9/**6**:2/**8**:1^2/**9**/**10**:20/**12**:9:10:
11:12/**Sol1**:10/**2**:15/**3**:3/**5**/**6**:9/**7**:13/**Is1**:3^2:4:
11:12,13:14^2:23/**2**:3:8^2:9:12/**3**:9:15:24/**4**:1:2,3,4
/**5**:7:18:19:24^2:25^2:29^2/**6**:9:10^2/**7**:25/**8**:6:7,8:
14,15^2:20^2/**9**:4:8,9,10:16:17:21^2/**10**:5,6^3:12:16:
17:18:19:21:22:23:25^2:26/**11**:4:6:11:12:14/**13**:2^2
:4:5:10:17/**14**:1^2:2^2:21:25:32/**16**:4,5:12/**17**:2:13
/**19**:2:3:12:14:17:20^3:21:22:24/**20**:4/**22**/**23**:
15,16/**24**:1:6:15,16/**25**:1^2:11/**26**:1:7^2:10:11^2:14^2
:16:19/**27**:3:4,5:11^3:12^2/**28**:11^2:12:13:15/**29**:6:
11/**30**:6:9:17^2:18:22^2:26:28^4:32/**31**:2:3:8/**32**:4/
33:1:16:24^2/**34**:2^2:11:15/**35**:4:10/**36**:1:4:8,9:12:
19:21/**37**:11:12:19:36/**39**:2^3:4/**40**:22:23:24^2:26/
41:3:12:16^3:17:18^2:21:22:25/**42**:5:6:16^2:17:22:24
:25^2/**43**:7^2:8:19:20:25/**44**:7^2:9:25/**45**:8/**47**:6^3:7:
12:14/**48**:6:11:21^2/**49**:4^2:6:10^2:11:13:21/**50**:8:10^2
/**51**:8^2:20/**52**:3:4:5:6/**55**:7^3/**56**:2:3^2:5^2:7^2/**57**:1:6
:11:13^3:18^4:19^2:21/**58**:2:6^2/**59**:4:21^2/**60**:9:21/**61**
:2:3:4:8/**63**:4:5:6:9f:9^4:10:12:13:14/**65**:2:6:7:8^2:
24/**66**:4^3:19:20/**Jer1**:10^3:17^3/**2**:3^2:4,5^2:6^2:7:25:
26,27:28:30:31/**3**:8/**4**:5:10:11,12/**5**:3^3:5:6^2:9:10:
14:23,24:25^2/**6**:4:6:10^2:11:13:29^2:30^2/**7**:16^2:22:
23:25:26:27^4:28:33/**8**:2:3:4,5^2:8:10:11:12:13/**9**:2
:7^4:8:9:11:14:15^2:16^3:22^2:24/**10**:9:14:20/**11**:4^3:7:
8:11:12^2:14^2:20:23/**12**:2:3^2:6^2:8^2:9:13^2/**13**:12:13
:14:19f/**14**:11:12^2:13^2:14^3:15:16^2:17/**15**:1^3:2:3:8:
11:15^3:17,18:19^2/**16**:4^2:5^2:7:8^3:11^2:14,15:21:21f:
21/**17**:16^2:18:27/**18**:17:20^2:22:23^3/**19**:1:3:5:11:
13/**20**:4^2:7:8:11:12/**21**:7/**22**:9:13f:20^3/**23**:2^3:3^2:
4^2:8:9^2:12:14:15^3:18:20:21:32:34/**24**:6^5:7:8:9^2:10^2
/**25**:2,3:8,9:13:14:16:27:28:30^2:33^2/**26**:2^2:3:4:5^2:
19^2/**27**:15^2:16:17:18:22^2/**28**:14/**29**:1:6:9:15:
16,17:18^2:19:21:28:31/**30**:3:7:9f:9:10:19:20/**31**:
2:8:9:10^2:11:13^3:14:16:23:32^3:32f:33:37/**32**:14^2:
23^2:33:37^3:39:40^3:41^2:42^2:44/**33**:5^3:8:14:24:
25,26/**34**:13:14:16:17/**35**:2^3:5^2:14/**36**:2:3^2:7^2:13
:14,15:17:18^2:24,25:26:31^2/**37**:3:7^2/**38**:19:25/**39**
:10/**40**:9:10:11:13,14/**41**:1:6^2:7:8:10:13,14:16,17
:18/**42**:9/**43**:5:6:10/**44**:2,3,4:8:12:13^2:14:19:20:
24/**45**:1/**46**:4:5:26^2/**47**:2/**48**:10:21/**49**:1^2:19:28:
32/**50**:6^2:7^3:9:16:17:21:27^2:32:33^2:34^2:40:41:44^3
/**51**:17^3:18:39^2:40/**52**:8:17:26:27/**Lam1**:3:21:22
/**2**:4^2:9^3:21^3/**3**:17:34,35,36:64:65:66^2/**4**:3,4:8:15^2
:16^2/**Eze1**:13:15:19,20,21:22:25:26/**2**:4:5:6:7/**3**:
9:10:11:13:14,15:17:18:19:26:27/**4**:13/**5**:4/**6**:2:3
:10^2/**7**:14:22:26,27^2/**8**:11:17:18/**9**:1^2:2:4:5:6:10^3
/**10**:2:7,8^2:9-13:15,16^2:19^2/**11**:4:13:15:21:22^2/
12:3:10:11:14:15:16^2:23:28/**13**:2,3^2:10:17:18^3/
14:2:3:4:6,7^2:13:23/**15**:7/**16**:17:18:19^2:20:28:
33,34^3:37:47:54:61/**17**:12,13/**18**:6:12^2:15:16:31
/**20**:4^3:5,6^3:7:8^2:9,10^2:11^3:12^4:13^3:14^3:15^3:17^2:
21:22^2:23,24^4:25:25f:25:26^2:27,28^4:29:31:38/**21**:
7:9,10,11:13:14:23:28/**22**:26^2:28/**23**:4,5:7:12:16:
17^2:18:23:24:37:40:44:45^2:46^2:47^2/**24**:3:25/**25**:3
:17^2/**26**:10/**27**:33/**28**:25^2:26/**29**:3/**30**:5:9/**31**:16
/**32**:10:18:26:27^2/**33**:3:7:11:27:28:31:32:33^2/**34**:
2:4:6^2:8^3:9,10:12:13^2:14:15,16^4:23^2:25:26:27:28^2
:29f:30/**35**:4,5:10:13/**36**:1:12:18:19^2:20:23:
37,38^3/**37**:1:8:12:17:18,19,20^2:21:22^2:23:25:26^4:
27:28/**38**:9:12:13^2/**39**:9:10^2:14:15,16^4:17:23^2:24
:25:26^2:27^2:28^3:29^2/**40**:4:7-12:48,49/**41**:3/**42**:5:
13/**43**:8:9^2:10:11^2:24^2/**44**:18:19^2/**45**:7:9:15/**47**:
8/**Dan1**:1:3,4:5^2:7:8:13:16:18,19^2/**2**:14:18^2:24:
34:35/**3**:20:21^2:22:27^2/**4**:7:17:32:37/**5**:2,3,4:8:
17:21:23/**6**:2:24^3:27/**7**:7:8:12:16:22:24:27/**8**:13:
22:25^2:26/**11**:5:10,11:14:32:33:34:35^2:37:39^2/**12**
:6:10/**Hos1**:10^2:5:7^3:12:23/**3**:1/**4**:12^3:14:19/**5**:2:
6:10:14:15/**7**:2^3:13^2:14:15^2:16/**8**:9:13/**9**:6:8:9:12
:15^3/**10**:4:6:8^3/**11**:6:7^2:11/**12**:13/**13**:10^2:11/**14**:9
/**Joe1**:4:12:18:20/**2**:2:3^3:5:8:10:11:17^2:20^2/**3**:2:5
:6:7^2:8:12^2/**Amo1**:1:6:9:13/**2**:1:4:6^2:9^2:12^2/**3**:11
/**5**:12:25,26,27^2/**6**:2:9/**7**:2:4:5/**8**:6^2/**9**:2^2:3^4:4:14:
15^2/**Ob1**:11:14/**Jon**:2:4:7:9,10/**2**:8/**3**:1:10/**4**:3/
Mic1:11f^3:12:16/**3**:2:3^3/**4**:7/**6**:2:9:15/**7**:3^4:4:9:
10:14^2:16:19/**Nah1**:2:8/**2**:7:8/**3**:3:4:9:15:17:18/
Hab1:10:14:16:17/**2**:6:19^2/**3**:8,9f:8,9/**Zep1**:4:5:
12/**2**:9:11:15f/**3**:6:7:8:13/**Hag1**:1:3,4:13:14,15/
2:1/**Zec1**:4:5,6^2:10:12:15:21^2/**2**:5:9:11,12/**4**:2/**6**
:10,11^2/**7**:7:8,9:10:12:13^2:14/**8**:8^2:14,15/**9**:8:15/**10**:
2^2:3^2:4:5:6^3:8^2:9:10^3:11f/**11**:2:5^2:6^4:9:10:11:13/
12:4:8^2/**13**:1:9^2/**14**:20:21/**Mal2**:5:7/**3**:3:11:
14,15:17/**Mt2**:7^3:9:9f:12:16^2/**3**:6:7/**4**:15,16:21:
24/**5**:1:3^2:5:17^2:19:33/**6**:5:7,8:14,15:16:20:26:
31,32^2:33/**7**:2:11:12:16:24:26/**8**:15f:15:28:32:34
/**9**:4:15^3:24:28:30/**10**:1:5:7:18:23/**11**:1f:4/**12**:2:3
:15:16:27^2:37:38:41/**13**:6:11:12,13:16:30:34,35:
36:42^2:57/**14**:14:16:18:19:25:27^2:36/**15**:13,14:
18:30^2:31:32:34:36^4/**16**:1:4:6:8:15/**17**:5:7:8:9:14
:20:22,23:26,27^2/**18**:1:2:20/**19**:4:13^2:14:15:20:
26/**20**:2^2:4^3:6:7:8:11:12:13:18:20:22:23:25:31:34
/**21**:1:2^2:3:8:14:21:42:45/**22**:4:6^2:20:22:26:28:
34,35:40:41/**23**:7:34/**24**:2:4:39:43/**25**:2,3,4:7,8:
14:19:40/**26**:1:16:19:27:31:36^2:38:40:42:43^2:48:
53/**27**:17:26:48:56:65/**28**:7^2:8:9:10:11:15:17:19/
Mk1:4:5:17:20:31:38/**2**:2:8:17:19:20/**3**:4:5:12:
13:14,15:16-19:21:23:30:31,32/**4**:2:15:21:34:40/
5:10:13:17:19:26:40:43^2/**6**:4:5^2:7:8,9^2:13:22,23^2:
33^2:34^2:37:45^2:48^2:49:50:56/**7**:9:11:36/**8**:3^3:4:6^4
:7:8,9:13:15:23:24:27:28:30:31:32:34/**9**:7:8:9:
12,13:14:15:30,31^2:33:34:35:36^2/**10**:1:3:11:13^3:
14^2:16:24:27:32:33:42/**11**:2:6:9:17/**12**:9:12:23:
35:38^2/**13**:9:34/**14**:7:10:13^2:19:22:23:24:27:34:
37:40^2:41:44:48:65:70/**15**:12:15/**16**:1:13:14:15:
18^2:19:20/**Lk1**:22:55:68/**2**:7:9:10:17:19:20:
34,35:46,47:51^2/**4**:25,26:28:30:39f:39:40:41^2:42
/**5**:31:35f/**6**:10:13:25:30:31:35^2/**7**:4:6,7,8:29:30:
31:38^3:42^3:44^2/**8**:2:8:13:15^2:23:25:29:30:31:32:
37^2:39/**9**:1^2:2:3:5f:10:11^2:13:14:18:20:21:34^3:46^2
:48:52:53:54:55:55f:61f/**10**:1:2:8,9:18:19:21:34:
38/**11**:2:5,6:15:17:19:29,30^2:49/**12**:1:6:24:33^3:
37^2/**13**:4:15:18/**14**:5:7:17:19:24:25:33/**15**:2:3,4:
10/**16**:15:28:29^2:30^2/**17**:14:15:27:29/**18**:1:8:15:
16,17:31/**19**:13:27^2:46/**20**:9:16:17:19:33:41/**21**:
3:8:29/**22**:4:5;6:19:20:23:25:35:40:45:50:55:58/
23:2:17,f:20:25:28:30^3/**24**:4:5:15^2:16:18:22,23:
25:27:29^2:30:32:33,34:35:36^2:40^2:41:50^2/**Jn1**:
11,12:26:38^2/**2**:7,8:15:16:18:24,25/**3**:18:21:25:
32:36^2/**4**:1:9:14^3:27:40,41:52/**5**:15/**6**:2-5:10:11:
18,19:20^2:29:30,31:32:37:39:61:69/**7**:16:19:33:
40:49/**8**:2:10:14^2:21:23:27:30,31:42:54:59^2/**9**:11
:15:16^2:19/**10**:3:4:7:8:12:16:20:27:28^2:29^2:38:39
/**11**:1:6:14:25:34:39:44:46:49/**12**:3:6:26^2:29:30:
36:40:42/**13**:5:17/**14**:2,3:23^3/**15**:22:24/**17**:6^2:8^2:
10^2:11^2:12:13^2:14^2:15^2:17^2:18:21:22:23^2:24:26^3/
18:4,5:7:18:19:21:28:29:31:38/**19**:13:16:18:
23,24^2/**20**:17:18^2:19^2:20:21:22^2:23:25:26^3/**21**:6:
24/**Act1**:3^2:4^3:5:6:9:10:15/**2**:2:4:8:37:43:47^2/**3**:3
:5:7,8/**4**:1:3^2:7:8:12:13:14:15:17^3:18^2:21^3:23:24:
28:33f:34,35/**5**:13^2:15:16:18:19^2:26,27^3:33:39:
40^3:41/**6**:3:6^2:10/**7**:7:16:25:26:34:36:38:42^3:44^2:
45:53:56:58:60/**8**:3:16:25/**9**:2:21^2:27:32:38:39:
40:41/**10**:8^2:13:20^3:23^3:28:46,47^2:48^2/**11**:3:4:11:
12:15^2:26:28/**12**:10:17^2:21:25/**13**:2:3^2:5:13f:13:
15:16:17^2:18:21:42:43:44:47:50/**14**:2:3:4:5,6:13^2
:15:18:22^2:23^2/**15**:2^2:3:7:8:9:12:14:20:23:30:33:
38/**16**:3:6:14:19:22:24:30^2:34^2:37:39^3:40/**17**:6^2:
7:8,9:12:16:18:22^2:23:33:34/**18**:2,3:16:23^2:27/
19:2:4:6:9:12:16^2:18,19:25:32:35:38^2:41/**20**:1:
10,11,12:17:18:36:38/**21**:4^2:24:25^2:40/**22**:4:5:
17,18:30/**23**:10:14/**24**:24:25/**25**:16/**26**:10:11^2/
27:28:35:40:42^2:43/**28**:14:15:17:19:23^2:31/**Rom**
1:5:18:19:19f:21:23:24:26^3:28:32^2/**2**:3^2:8:12-15^4:
23:26/**3**:1:2:3:4:15:16:18:19:20/**4**:4,5:12:15:16/
5:13^4:21/**6**/**7**:11/**8**:3/**9**:7:16^2:19^2:25^2:27:28:29:
33/**10**:3:12:14^2:15:16:19/**11**:5:8^2:9^3:10:14^2:15:
23^2:32/**12**:1:7:9:13:15/**13**:8/**14**:1f^3:3:4^2/**15**:1:9:
14:19^2:27f:31/**16**:4:7:14:15:18/**1Co1**:18:19:20:
22:23:24/**2**:4:14:16/**6**:12/**7**:5:25:31/**8**/**7**/**9**:12^2:
19:20^3:21^2:22^2:23^2/**10**:1^3:3,4^2:3,4f:3,4:5^2:8:10^2:
11^3:33/**12**:1:4:31/**13**:1/**14**:3:10:26:35/**15**:5f:20f:
33^2/**16**:16^2:20/**2Co1**:3,4:20/**2**:1:17/**3**:1:6^5:7:17/
5:15:16:19^2/**6**:16^2:17^2/**8**:5:14^2:24/**9**:2:3:4:11/**10**
:5^2:6/**12**:4:7/**13**:2^2/**Gal1**:13^2:16/**2**:5:14:16/**3**:3:
10:19/**4**:15:17:24,25/**5**:24/**6**:6/**Eph2**:15/**3**:6^2:8:
14,15/**4**:11^2:29/**5**:6:11:13^2:28/**6**:1:4^2:5^2:9^2:19/
Php1:14/**2**:15:16/**3**:2:7:21/**Col1**:28^3/**2**:20/**3**:7:
12:16^2:19:22^2/**4**:5:16/**1Th1**:8/**2**:16/**4**:10:17/**5**:3:
13^2/**2Th1**:8/**2**:1:10:11:12/**3**/**1Ti1**:13:15:20^2/**2**:1^2
:5^2:7:12^2/**4**:2:11:12^2/**5**:2:3:14:15:22/**6**:1:2:5^2:9^3:
18^2/**2Ti1**:1:7^2:8:11/**2**:2:14:18:23:25:26/**3**:2:6/**4**:
2^2:3/**Tit1**:1^2:9:12:13:14/**2**:5:7:9:15^2/**3**:8:12/**Heb**
1:1:12^2/**2**:1:2:10/**3**:7,8:9^2:10^2:11^2:16/**4**:2:3:8:15/
6:12:18^3/**7**:12,13,14/**8**:9^2:10^3:12/**9**:4:9:10:15^2:
17/**10**:3:4f:16:18:30:38^2/**11**:12:13^2:16:22^2:23:28^2
:29:30^2:33:39^2:40/**12**:18/**13**:3:17^2/**Jas2**:9:25/**3**:
13/**4**:2:8/**1Pe1**:11^2:12/**2**:8:14:15/**3**:1^2:7:9:19:20
/**4**:4:10/**5**:3/**2Pe1**:7^2:12:15^2:20,21/**2**:1:2:3:4:6^2:
12f/**3**:1:15,16/**1Jn2**:5/**3**:18:24/**4**:5/**2Jn1**:7:8/
3Jn1:6:7:8^2:10/**Jud**:5^2:6:8:11:13^3:14:16:19:23^4/
Rev1:13/**2**:14^2:16:19:20:24,25:27^2/**4**:4/**5**:10^2/**6**:
11^2:16/**7**:14:15:17^2/**8**:4/**9**:5^2:10/**11**:1f:5:7^2:8,9^2:
10:11:18/**12**:10:11/**13**:7/**14**:5:8:9:13/**15**:7/**16**:6:
14/**17**/**19**:15:20/**20**:4:6:8:9:10:11f:13^2/**21**:3^2:14:
17/**22**:8:17

THEMSELVES 52

Gen3:7:8/**4**:26/**11**:3,4/**12**:3f/**21**:28,29/**35**:2/**3**
40-43/**42**:21/**Ex18**:22:26/**19**:9:22/**32**:7:8:31/
4/**38**:6/**Lev20**:12:13/**21**:1/**Num4**:17,18,19/**8**:
21/**11**:18/**31**:32-35:53/**Deu3**:14/**9**:12/**Jos1**:1
3:5/**8**:27/**9**:3,4,5/**11**:14/**20**:9/**24**:1:25/**Ju2**:19,
9/**7**:2/**9**:34/**18**:9,10/**20**:30/**21**:5:6/**1Sa16**:9/**2**
1Ki6:6/**18**:28/**20**:16/**2Ki3**:21/**17**:17:32/**19**:2/
:24/**1Ch4**:40,41/**21**:16/**2Ch1**:5,6/**4**:12-16/**5**:
11,12/**6**:24/**7**:14/**12**:7/**20**:22/**29**:15:34/**30**:15
24/**31**:4/**32**:26/**35**:14/**Ez6**:20/**Neh4**:4/**9**:1^2:2
10:28/**12**:30/**13**:22/**Est9**:1:29-31/**Job1**:6/**2**:1
5/**16**:10/**21**:12,13/**24**:17/**39**:2,3/**Ps10**:11/**22**:
/**35**:26/**37**:11/**55**:9/**57**:6/**80**/**83**:5/**119**:118/**P**
1:18/**2**:22/**19**:24/**30**:11,12:24-28/**31**:8/**Ecc3**:
/**10**:16,17/**Is1**:4/**3**:9/**29**:15/**44**:9/**46**:1/**47**:14/
65:21,22/**Jer1**:16/**2**:13/**5**/**7**:19/**9**:5:25,26/**13**:
/**14**:2:15/**16**:6/**41**:5/**Eze6**:9/**20**:26/**25**:12/**34**:
36:5/**37**:23/**44**:24/**Dan2**:43/**Hos8**:4/**9**/**Amo2**
14/**Mic1**:11/**Hab**:6f/**2**:4/**Zec12**:5/**Mt2**:11/**8**:
/**9**:3/**11**:25/**21**:38/**23**:4:12^2/**27**:1f:35/**Mk2**:6/
7,8/**4**:41/**5**:14/**6**:2,3:35,36/**7**:4/**9**:10/**11**:31/**1**
/**14**:4,5/**Lk5**:21:32/**7**:49/**8**:35/**9**:60/**20**:5:19/**2**
8/**22**:23:24/**Jn5**:43/**7**:25/**18**:28/**Act2**:40/**4**:15
16:37/**23**:12,13:21/**28**:25:28,29f/**Rom1**:22:23,
:14/**8**:5^3/**10**:3/**11**:9:11:25/**16**:18/**1Co7**:5/**12**:2
14:28/**2Co3**:1/**5**:15^2/**8**:5/**9**:13/**10**:12^2/**11**:5/**G**
5:12:12f/**Eph2**:11/**4**:19/**5**:28/**1Ti6**:10:19/**2Ti**
2:13/**Tit2**:10/**Heb3**:7,8/**9**:10/**12**:1:13/**Jas5**:6/
1Pe3:16/**2Pe2**:14:19/**Jud1**:12:18/**Rev**:20/**6**:1
9:6/**11**:16/**14**:4f/**18**:3:15

THEN 2

Gen1:3:4,5:9,10^2:14,15:20:26:31/**2**:8:21/**3**:13:
:19:22/**4**:1:15:17/**5**:21-24/**6**:3/**7**:16/**8**:14:15,1
20/**9**:8:23:26,27/**10**:20:31/**11**/**12**:7:11,12,13^2:
:18/**13**:3,4:8:9^2:18/**14**:7:11:19,20^2/**15**:4:5:6:9:
:16/**16**:5/**17**:15:17:23/**18**:6:7:10:13:16:21:22,2
27:29:31^2:32/**19**:24:32/**20**:2:9,10:14:16:17/**21**:
17:19:25:27:32/**22**:5:9:13:15/**23**:3:7:13/**24**:5:8
19:22:33:41:47:48:49:50:53:54:55:66/**25**:7,8:2
26:33:34/**26**:11:20:21:25:31/**27**:8,9,10:15:17:2
33:41:45:46/**28**:16,17:21/**29**:11:12,13:28:35/**3**
3:7:12:19:22:33:37:39,40/**31**:8^2:11:23:33^2:54/**3**
:9:22,23,24:26/**33**:1:3:4:5:6:18/**34**:4:11:13:16:2
:27:30/**35**:5:13,14:21/**36**:6,7,8:40-43/**37**:9:19,2
:25:31:34:35/**38**:8:11:23:30/**39**:11/**40**:21/**41**:3
:6:7:9:19:21:23:41,42:54/**42**:8,9:16^2:25:33:34^2:
36:37/**43**:9:11:14:23:24:25:28:30:31/**44**:18:26:
27/**45**:2:14:17/**46**:30/**47**:7:10:16:19:23/**48**:8:1
21/**49**:1:29,30:33/**50**:4:14:18:25/**Ex1**:8:15,16:2
/**2**:3:7:12:17/**3**:3,4:7:12:20/**4**:4:5:9:14:22,25,26
31/**5**:14:19:22/**6**:13/**7**:1:4^2:8:11:19:22:24/**8**:5:8
10:16:18:29/**9**:7:8:13:22:27/**10**:1:6:12:16:21:24
11:1:7:8^2/**12**:1:21:22:30:43:48^2/**13**:3:6,7/**14**:15
19:23/**15**:1:20:22:24:26/**16**:4:6:22:32/**17**:4:5,6:
14/**18**:2:7/**19**:9^2:11:13/**20**:1:25/**21**:3^2:6:8:9:10:
11:13:21:22:26:30f:35:36/**22**:1:3:8:11:14:15:17
23:16:22:25/**24**:3:5:8:9:15/**25**:18:23:37/**26**:6/**2**
:9,10/**28**:15:26:40:41/**29**:5:7:9:10:13:14:21:22:
26:35/**30**:1:22,23/**31**:12,13:18/**32**:4:7:9:15:21:
29:32:32f/**33**:10:18:23/**34**:5,6,9:11:16:20:34/**3**
4/**36**:4-7:10:13:17:31,32:36:37/**37**:4:6:10:13:17
23,24:29/**38**:3:9/**39**:1:33-40/**40**:8:10:11:14:1
21:25:33:34/**Lev1**:4:5:6,7:9:12:13:15,16,17^2/**2**:
14:16/**3**:2/**4**:1:5:7:8:16:18:21:25:30/**5**:7:9:11:15
/**6**:8:11:15:21:24:28/**7**:6:14:21:22:31/**8**:6:8:10:
12:14:18:21:22:25:28:31:34/**9**:7^2:10:14:17:19:2
24/**10**:3:4:6:12:16/**11**:1/**12**:4:5:7^2:8/**13**:5:6:8:1
16,17:20:21:25:31:36:37:44:54:56:57/**14**:5:7:8:
11:13^2:15:17:19:20:21:25:26:28:30:32:33,34:35
40:41:45:48:53:54/**15**:32/**16**:5:7:9:10:14:15:18:
23:24:26:28/**18**:1:18/**20**:5/**22**:7/**23**:37/**24**:13,1
/**25**:25:27:28:30:52:54/**26**:21:24:28:34,35^2:42:4
/**27**:13:14,15:17:18:27:33/**Num3**:5:40/**4**:1:6:8:
10:11:15:17,18,19/**5**:5,6:19:21,22:23:25:26:29/
:9^2:17:18:20/**7**:2/**8**:5,6:7:9:13:21/**9**:18:19^2/**10**:4
18/**11**:4,5:8:16:23:30/**12**:5:7,8:9/**13**:23/**14**:1:5:
10,11:20,21:26,27:36,37,38:45/**15**:8,9:23,24:27
35/**16**:5:8,9:11,12:15:19:23,24:29:30:35:38:50/
17:1:5:9/**18**:32/**19**:5:7:9:12:18:19/**20**:8:10:11:2
/**21**:2:4:7:8:11:13:16:17,18:20/**22**:26:28:31:34/
23:3,4:5:13:15:27/**24**:2:20:21,22/**25**:10,11:16,1
/**26**:52,53:64,65/**27**:8:10:11:15/**28**:14/**30**:4:5^2:
14:15:16/**31**:1^2:9,10,11^2:19:21:23:24:27:48,49/
32:20:22^2:23:29:30:39/**33**:11:13:14:40:42:43:44
46/**34**:7,8,9,10,11^2:12/**35**:24:25/**36**:1:5/**Deu1**:1
19,20,21^2:41:45/**2**:1:2:9:16,17:24:26:31:32/**3**:15
20:21:28/**4**:26:41/**5**:26,27:29:31:33/**6**:10,11,12:
18/**7**:4:26/**8**:3/**9**:4:18/**10**:5:6:7/**11**:8:14:23/**12**:

HEN Con't)
-23:30/13:9:11:16:17/14:25:29/15:17/16:7/
:5:7:13:18:20/19:9:11:13:20/20:5:11/21:3:5:
:19:21:22/22:2:13,14:15/23:11/24:2:19/25:7:
)/26:4:5:10:13/27:1:2,3,4:9:14/28:15-19:
,59:68/29:22/30:3:18:20/31:7:9:14:17:21:23/
:15:20:27:37/33:8/34:1/Jos1:8:10,11:12,13:
/2:1:15:16:20:23/3:5:9:15,16/4:21:23/5:2,3/6
^{2}:10:22:24:26/7:9:14:17^2:24:25/8:1:7:18:22:30
1:33:34/10:10:19:21:26:29:34,35:38:43/11:9:
/13:27,28/14:11/15:2,3,4:6:8^2:10,11:15:18,19
6:1^3:5,6^2/17:14:16,17,18/18:3:5,6:8:9:12:17:
/19:13:27:29:34/20:6/21:1/22:19:32/23:13/
:1:2:5:7^2:9:11:15:23:27:28/Ju1:3:10/2:5:17:20
:8:11:28:29/4:14:15:21/5:1:26/6:1:6,7:14:17:
:26:32:34:36:39/7:2^2:15:17:19,20:21:23/8:7:8:
:15:16:18:20:21/9:6:10:12:14:19:20:21:38/10:
16/11:12:17:19:23:30,31:39/12:1:4:6:15/13:
3:8:15:17:19:21/14:13:19/15:5:8:14:15:19/16:
9:14:20:27:28:29/18:5:13:17:20:27:28:30/19:3
:16:25:30/20:1:7:12:22,23,24:26:32:35-39:48/
:8,9:13:23/Ru1:9/2:23/3:4:6,7:13:15-18^3/4:2:
6:9/1Sa1:11:19,20:21,22:24/2:16:29:35:36/3:
8:11:15:21,4:1/4:21,22/5:6/6:2:3:4,5:9^2:11/7:
5:12:16^2:17/8:22/9:18:22:23:26,27/10:1:18,19
1:24:25^2/11:6:10:12:14:15/12:1:10:11:14:15/
:3,4:15/14:8:9:10:12:15:20:28:38:40:41:42:46
5:7:10:12:14:16:19:30:32:34/16:3:8:13:22/17:
7:9^2:38,39:40:46:50,51:52:53/18:22/19:3:5:7:
:15:22/20:7^2:10:12:13:18:21^2:22:33:40/21:10
22:2:9,10^2:18:19/23:23^2:27:29/24:4:5:9,10,15/
5:18:35:37,38:39/26:11:14:19^2:21:25/27:1/28:
8:25/30:7:15:25/31:3,4:13/2Sa1:10:13:15:
7,18/2:1:4:14:17:28:32/3:4:12:14:16:19:26:27:
1/4:2,3:6,7/5:1:4,5:9:11:19/6:1:7:18/7/8:4:14/
3:9/10:14/11:4^2:8:15:19,20,21:27/12:7:9:13:
5:18:20^2:24:31/13:8:10:15:21-24:26:28:29,30:
2,33/14:11:23:26:31:32:33/15:1:4:14:22:25,26:
7:33,34/16:20:21/17:10:12:14:15:21/18:14:15:
6:19:21:23:28:31:33/19:5:7:11,12:14:16:23:37:
0/20:1:4:6:22/21:1:4:5,6:10:12,13,14/22:8/24:
:7/1Ki1:9:11:13:31:34:40:49,50:53/2:4:10:21:
3,24:26:32:35:43:46/3:15^2:20:22:23:25:26:27/5
:9:13/6:11,12:21,22:33/7:1:13:23:27-30:38/8:
:6:14:22,23:31:38:62,63/9:5:7:24/10:10:13:29/
1:38:43/12:5:27/13:2:3:7:15:20:27/14:6:12:15:
8/15:18:22:24:27/16:9:10:15,16:24:31:33/17:1
:8,9:12:20:23/18:21^2:22:24:25:26:30:32:38:40:
1:43:44/19:4:5:7:15:16:20:21^2/20:7:10:13^2:15:
2:27:28:36:37:41:42/21:9:10:13:14:28/22:4:17:
9:20:24:26:28/2Ki1:9:10:15/2:4:5:6,7:8:10^2:
3,14:17:21:25/3:11:24:27/4:3:4:6:22:28:29:34:
5:36:37:41/5:15:24/6:17:19:23/7:11:12/8:11:
4,25/9:3:10:16:21:23:24:34/10:1:11:12:15:17:
3:25/11:5:12^2:19/12:17/13:5:16,17^2:19:24/14:
:14:21/15:10:19,20:25:30:38/16:5:14:17/17:4:
1:26:27,28/18:7:14:19:26:28:37/19:2:8:15:19:
0:36/20:3:7:14:16/21:10:14:24/22:9,10/23:1:4
10:12:14:21:34^2/24:1:17/25:1:7:10:22:26/1Ch2
/3/6:32:61:64,65/9:3/10:5:9:12/11:1:4/12:17:
8/13:6:8:10/15:3:11:15:25/16:3:35/17:16/18:
:12/19:2,3:4:15:19/20:3/21:1:9:15:18:21:22:27
22:1:17/23:6/24:3/25:1/28:8:11:17:20/29:1:
,5:6,7:20:22/2Ch1:13:17/3/4:2:7:9/5:1:7,8/6:3
23:25:26:27:31:33:35:39/7:4,5:6:10:14:18:20/8:
2:17,18/9:12:31/12:6:8/13:7:13,14/14:1:12:13
15:1:9:12/16:6:8/17:1:10/18:2:16:23:27/19:11
20:18:19:27:37/21:12:16/22:1/23:9:11:
5,16,17:20/24:9:11:20:21/25:5,6:11:18:23/26:
/27:8/28:7:15^2/29:12,13,14:16:18:23:24:27:30
30:15:17,18,19:25:27/31:1/32:5:9:20:23:33/33
12:14:16/34:5:6:10,11:18:29/35:1:7:11:13/36:3
17:19/Ez1:5/3:1:7:11/4:4,5:13:17/5/6:10:16:
8/8:21:28:35:36/9:4,5/10:2:6:7,8:10:12:14/
Neh2:1:7:14,15:18/3:1^2:11:13:15:17:22:27:31/4:
:10:14:16/5:7:9:12:13f/6:12,13^2:19/7:5/8:6^2:9
9:5:6:11:22/10:34/12:30:37:39^2:40,41/13:9:11:
7:19:22/Est2:12,13,14/3:12f:13:15/4:2:5:15:
6/5:3:12/7:4:6:9/8:1:7:15/9/Job1:8:20/2:8:13
/3/4:16/5:3/6:24/7:4/9:24:28:32,33:35/10:18:
9/11:15:16/12:23^2/13:20/14:20,21^2/16:12/17:
5/19:5:26f:27/21:21/22:23:25:26/26:14/28:20
/31:7,8:10:22:37:40/32:2:16/33:23,24:25:33/36
9:11:27/37:19,20/38:1/39:4/40:2:6:10:14/42:1:
0:11:17/Ps2:5/3/7/18:7:15/19:13/27:6/30:6,7
9:11/34:13/37:3:4:32/39:2,3:8/40:1:7/42:4:5,
50:22/51:13:14,15:19:19f/52:6/55:12/58:11/60
4,5/62:2:6/64:9/65:11,12/69:30/73:17/74:15/
77:6/78:34:35:51:60:65/79:13/80:3:7:19/81:14
/85:6/88:10/89:30,31,32:38/91:10/104:9:21:29
:30/105:17:20:23:30:36:37/106:11:12^2:28/107:2
:13:19:23:28/109^2/114:2/116:4:6/119:27:32:
40,41,42:80:88:117:134/130:3,4/132:2-5:6:12/
141:6,7/142:5/147:18/Pro1:28/2:3,4,5/3:4,5:
7,8/11:4/16:3/19/22:20,21/24:32,33/27:10:
25,26,27/30:20/Ecc2:4,5,6:7,8:15:24-26/3:18/4
:4:16/5:5/6:4/8:8:15/9:16/10:16,17/12:2:4:9/
Sol8:1/Is1:19:26/2:4:20/4:5/5:2/6:5:6:8:11/7:3
:6:13:14/8:3:5/9:11,12/10:3:4:12:20:25:33/11:
13/14:32/16:4,5/17:7/19:20:22/20:3:5,6/21:8,9
:12/22:20/23:15,16/24:23/26:11/28:5:11/29:9:
23/30/32:3:15:16/34:5/36:2:3:11:13:22/37:6:
21:30:30f:37:38/38:3:22/39:3:5/41:7:17/43:9/
44:13:15/46:6/47:11/48:7:18:19/49:21:23/52:6
/53:10/57:12/58:9:10:14/59:19/63:11/64:2/66:
9/Jer1:9:11:13/2:31:36/3:1:10:16/4:2:10/5:4:
19/6:18,19/7:1:7^2:10/8:1:9:14/10:9/11:1:4:5:6:
12:18/12:7:16/13:3:6:8,9:11:13:15:16:17:24,25/
14:13:14/15:1^2:10:15/17:19^2:25:27/18:5:8:10^2:
13:18/19:3/20:7:9:10/21:1/22:4/23:25:38,39/
24:3:4,5/25:5:6:12/26:3:6:11:12:16:17:22/27:3:
7:18:22/28:5:10:15/29:6:10:30/30:6/31:26:33:
34/32:6,7:8:11:16:26/33:9:17:19:20,21:24/35:8:
12:15:18,19/36:3:20:26:32/37:6:18:21/38:10:12
:17:24/39:7:9/40:1:5^2:12:15^2/41:3:7:16,17/42:1
:5:15/43:8/44:15:20:24:25:30f/46:9:13:16/48:
2,3,4:12:13/49:1:2:22/50:4:6:17/51:46:63/52:6:
11:15:29/Lam2:12:18/3:29:39/Eze1:5/2:9,10/3
:1:4:10:11:12:24:27/4:14:15:16/5:4:13/6:4-7:9^2:
14/8:1:7:12:13:16/9:1:5:11/10:2:4:18/11:1^2:5:
13:22:23/12:4:15:17:24:26/13:1:15/14:1:4:6,7:
12:13/15:1:7/16:1:9,10:23:42:52/17:1:11:21/18
:1/19:4:8/20:2:7:8:13:18:21:39:42:43:44:45:49/
21:1:8:14:18/22:14:17/23:4,5:39/24:10:19:24/
25:1:5:7:17/26:6:8:16/27:1/28:9:11:20:22:23:26
/29:16^2:21/30:26/32:15/33:4:13:14:23:29:33/
34:1/35:4,5:9:15/36:11:16:20:25:31:36/37:3:4:8
:9:11:13:14:16:23:28/38:14/39:28/40:4:6:13:14:
19:24:28:32:35:47:48,49/41:3:5:13/42:1:13/43:
3:5:11:21/44:1:4/46:2:12:17:21,22/47:1:2:6:15:
16:19/48:1^2:4:5,6,7^2:26:27,28^2/Dan1:3,4:10:13/
2:4^2:15:17:19:24:25:35:46:48:49/3:2:13:15:18:19
:26:27:28:30/4:13:19:23/5:29/6:11:13:16:18:21:
24/7:3:7:10:19:24:26:27/8:13:18:26:27/9:24^2:27
/10:4:9:12:13:16:18:20,21/11:3:10,11:15:22:25:
28:29:40:44/12:5/Hos1:10:11:7:18:20:21,22/3:
1/5:6/8:10/9:5:10/10:3/12:13/13:6/14:4/Joe1:
4/2:18:20/3:17/Amo2:15/5:14:18/6:2/7:4:5:6:7
:12/8:1:2:3/9:5:11/Ob1:19/Jon:7:9,10:14:15/2:
1:4/3:1/4:4:8:10/Mic1:13/2:4:5/3:4:7/5:3:7/6/
7:9:10/Nah3:4/Hab1:16/2:15/3:6:8,9/Zep1:1f/
2:15f/3:11/Hag1:3,4:8:12:13/2^2:14/Zec1:5,6:
10:11:14:18:20/2:3:9:11,12/3:1:4:5,6^2:7/4:1:6:9:
11:14/5:5:9/6:1:8:10,11:14/7:8,9/11:4:11:14:15
/12:10/13:4^2:6/14:3:10/Mal1:4:5/2:1:4/3:1:4:
16:18/4:3/Mt1:19/2:7^2:11:22/3:13:15/4:1:3:5:
11:17/5:24/6:1/7:5/8:4:8,9:13:19:21:23:26/9:
5,6:13:15:24:29/11:6:13:20/12:9:13:14:22:27:28
:29:29f:37:43,44,45^2:50/13:11:19:36:43:52:57/
14:12:19^2:23,24:28/15:10:12:15:21:23:24:28:32:
35:39/16:4:12:15:20:21,24/17:13:18:25:26,27/
18:16:17^2:21:27:31:34/19:7:10:23:25:27:30^2/20:
7:20:22/21:9:17:19:21:25:27:30:31:33:36:42/22:
7:13:15:21:25:27:32f:41:43/23:1:15:26/24:9:14:
16:23:30:34/25:7,8:15:24,25:31:34:37:41:44/26:
14:31:36:38:40:45:50:55^2:57:62:63:65,66:67:75/
27:2:5:19:22:26:33:36:40:50:64/28:5:10:16:20/
Mk1:9:29,30:43,44/2:9,10,11:12:13:20:25,26/3:
4:14,15/4:21:29:39/5:7,8:10:13:33:37/6:4:6:
22,23:26:31:39,40:51/7:14:17:20:24:31:33:34/8:
6:11:25:29:31:33:34/9:4:8:12,13:15:26:36/10:1:
16:22:23:26:27:28:31:35/11:6:8:11:14:21:31:32:
33/12:1:4:7:12:18:20,21,22:40:41:42/13:11:21:
24:26/14:3:10:13:20:26:37:44:46:54:59:60:61:63,64
:65:66,67:68/15:3,4:15:16,17:18:21:24:34:37/16
:15/Lk1:19:23:38:56:67/2:20:34,35:51/3:3:6:21
/4:1:5:9,10,11:14:21:23:31:35/5:14:18,19:23,24:
35:36/6:9:10:20:25:35:37:42/7:14:15:40:41:44:
49/8:12:16:25:36:54/9:2:16:20:23:26:30:36/10:
16:21:23:32:34:37/11:5,6:26:36:39/12:5:13:16:
18:20:22:36:54/13:6:24,25:30^2/14:5:12:14:22:23
:28:29:32:33/15:5:9/16:4:15:27^2:30/17:29/18:6:
9:16,17:24:41/19:23:24:36,37:45/20:5^2:8:11:14:
17:25:27:29:41:45/21:2:20:21:25:27:29/22:3:14:
17:19:23:35:39:43:52:61:70/23:1:4:5:6:13:42:46:
50,51,52:56/24:5:8:12:25:27:30:35:41:44:45:50:
51/Jn1:21:22:24,25:32:36:37:41:42/2:7,8:10:13:
16:17/4:15:26:27:28,29:34:42:50:53/5:15:18:23
/6:8,9:11:21:41:52:62:67:70/7:10:14:17:30:33:
50:53/8:8:10:19:23:28:30,31:42:54/9:6:10:13:15
:16:17:28:39/10:31:38/11:11:14:28:37,38:41:43:
47:48/12:3:10:16:19:28:30:35:36/13:9:27:33/14
:2,3:7/15:18/16:22:26/17:6/18:10:16:24:31:33:
36:37:38/19:1:5:11:12:16:21:27:31/20:6:8:9:18:
22:27:29/21:6:7:13:15:16:17:19/Act1:24,25:26/
2:3:14:24:38:40/3:4:7,8^2/4:8:21:24/5:19:25:31:
35:40/6:4/7:1:4:14:17,18:42:57/8:13:17:35/9:
19:27:28:29:30:35:40/10:13:15:16:17:22:27:34/
11:4:11:16:25/12:8:10/13:4:9:19,20:21:46:50/
14:24/15:5:22:32:33/16:1:4:7:32:34:40/17:15/
18:1:17:18:22/19:3:4^2:6:8:41/20:10,11,12:38/21
:1:6:8:20:24:33/22:14:16:24/23:6:14:23,24:25:28:
34/24:9:22:27/25:9:12:24:26/26:1:20:30/27:9:
13:17:35:43/28:9:14/Rom1:11,12:23/2:21:22:
25/3:1:5:6:9:27:31/4:1:4,5:9:11:13:14/5:5/6:1/7
:3:4:7:13:14/8:34:35/9:6:19:30/10:5/11:1:6:11:
26/12:2:6/13:5/14:14/15:6:7:32/16:7:10/1Co1:
21/3:14:4:5:19:6:4/7:39/8:10/9:17/10:7:27:28
/11:6^2/12:17/13:10:12/14:15:21/15:1:7:13:14:
16:23:28:29:32:38:46:52:54:55,56^2/16:2:4:6:7/
2Co1:9:17/2:3/3:16/5:8:21/7:6/8:12:14/10:16/
11:28/12:10:20/13:2/Gal1:15:17:21/2:1:13:17:
21/3:3:18:19^2:21,22^2/4:12:15/5:2:16:26/6:4/
Eph1:4/2:15/4:14:17,18:22/6:6,7/Php1:22/2:2:
13:16:17:19/4:15/Col2:12:13/3:5:14/4:6/1Th1:
7/2:14/4:17/5:3:21/2Th1:12/2:3:8/1Ti3:10/5:
14:16:20/2Ti2:4:12:26^2/Tit3:5/Heb1:3/3:11:12
:16/6:6:12:15/7:2:4:11:27/8:11/9:3:7:20:26/10:
7:9:12:17/11:7:37,38/12:8/13:11:17/Jas1:2:4:
7,8^2/2:13:16/3:11:13:17/4:10:17/5:11:18/1Pe1:
11/2:12/3:1:6:16/4:11/2Pe1:2:5:10:19/2:20:21
/3:4:10/1Jn1:2:4:7/3:19/4:2/5:1:15/2Jn1:9:12
/3Jn:14/Jud:5/Rev:1:11/2:8/3:18/4:1/5:4:11:
13/6:1:3:13/7:1:13/8:3:5:6:8,9/9:1:3/10:1:5:7:8:
11/11:12:13:15:19/12:1:7:10:17/13:5:11:14:15/
14:1:8:9:14:15:18/15:1:5:6/16:8:10:17:18/18:4:
21/19:4:6:10:11:17:19/20:1:3:4:10/21:1:5:9:17/
22:6,7:10

3372

THERE

Gen1:2f:3:4,5:4,5f^2:6f:7,8f^2:13f^2:14,15:19f^2:23f^2:
31f^2/2:5^2:9:19,20/4:8/6:17/7:3/8:22/10:11,12/
11:2f:3,4:9:12,13f:31:32/12:7:8:10:17/13:3,4:6:9^2
:11:18/17:24-27/18:24:26:28:29^2:30^3:31/19:1:
18,19,20^2:22:28:30:31:35/21:17:33/22:2/23:1:
5,6:10:19,20/24:4:5:7:8:11:26:54/25:30/26:2:7:
17:21:25:33/27:15:37:44/28:6,7,8:9/29:3:5:6:14
/31:3:17-20:33:54/32:22,23,24:29/33:17:20/34:
25:27/35:1:3:7^2:15:20:22/36:6,7,8/37:12:17:23:
24:26,27:29/38:1:2:11/39:2:6:21/40:4:8:9,10:16
/41:12:22:26:27:30:36:47:49:54^2/42:1:2:13^2:23:
27:35/43:1:21:23:25:30/45:6:11,12^2/46:1:3,4:27
/47:4^2:18:27/49:31^3/50:5:12,13/Ex1:5:7:9:19/2
:1:6:15:20/3:16/4:2:27/5:1:3/7:15^2:21/8:5:10:
22:24:27/9:14:18:24/10:6:14:15:19:22:26/11:6/
12:16:19:22:30^3:37:38/13:6,7/14:2:11/15:22:25:
27^2/16:1:2:3^2:10:18:25:26^2:27:28,29:35/17:1:5,6
:7:15,16/18:8:23/19:2,3:16^2/20:24/21:36/22:10
:14:15/23:14:16:23:26/24:4:10:14:18/25:15:22^2:
34,35/26:4,5:7,8:12:20:22:25/27:5:14,15:20/29:
3,4:43/30:6:11,12:19/32:5/33:7:12/34:5:6,12/
36:23:25,26:30/37:3/38:2:10/39:23:33-40/40:9:
31:35:38/Lev1:5/4:4:11,12:18:21:29:33/7:17,18
/8:1:26/9:5/10:12:18/11:36/13:9,10:14,15:21:
26:31:42:43:49:58/14:13:33,34:35:36^2/15:15/16
:3:13:23/18:19:25:28/22:11/23:35:36/25:6,7:24
:26:32:51/26:25:36/27:33^2/Num4:20/5:8:13^2/8
:10:19^2/9:4,5:14:17:18/11:3:16:17:21:26:31:34/
13:18:19:20:22:28^2:29:33/14:3:39:43/15:15,16/
17:10/18:16:23/20:2:5:8:15:26^2/21:4:5:10:12:24
:31,32/22:2,3:25:34/23:3,4:13:14:27/24:15-19/
27:1/28:11:20,21^3:25:26^2/29:1:5:12:16/31:54/
32:14:39:40/33:8:9^2:14:38,39:45:50,51:52:53:55
/34:10,11/35:5:7:25:30:34/Deu1:28:44:46/2:21:
22/3:27/4:26:28:35:39/5:4/9:9:16/10:7:8:22/11
:3:6:17:21:27/12:6:7:12:14/13:1/14:26/15:1:7:
11/16:3:6:8:10/17:4:6:8:16/18:6,7:9:16/19:15/
21:4^2/22:2:6:25,26,27/26:1/27:5,6:7/28:26:27:
31:40:61:62:64:65:68/29:29/31:3:5/33:26/34:2^3
:3:10/Jos2:1:6:16:22:24/4:8:9:20/6:10/11/7:1:3:
22:26/8:11,12,13f:14:17:29/10:13:14^2:18:27:30/
11:11/12:8-24/13:1:13/14:12:15/15:7:9^2:21-32:
33-36:63/16:5,6/17:11:16,17,18/18:10:13:14:16
/19:11:12:15,16:47,48:50/20:6/21:43/23:4,5^2/
Ju1:7:21:26:27:36/3:11:22,23/4:7:17:22/5:30:
31/6:20:24^2/7:2:4:5,6:11:12,13^2:15/8:8:14/9:2f:
5:37^2:41:51/10:12/11:17/12:6/14:3/15:19/16:2
:23,24:27/18:1:7:14^2:26:27:28^2/19:1:2:12,13:15:
26:27:28:29:30/20:16:43/21:6:10,11,12:14:17:
25/Ru1:3:17/2:1:4,5^2:7:17:22/3:4:6,7:8:12^2/4:
11/1Sa1:21,22:28/2:2/3:21,4:1/4:16:21,22/5:9:
12/7:2:6:14:17^2/9:6:12,13:25/10:5:8:24:27/11:8
:9/13:15:19:22/14:6:15:20:40/15:4:13/16:10,11 ^{2}

(THERE Con't)
:26/17:46/18:1/19:3:5/20:11:21:28,29/21:3:4:6:
7:9:11/22:3:9,10:14:22/23:13:22:24,25/24:9,10
/25:2:10:17/26:5,6,7:15/27:7/29:4/2Sa1:21^2/2:
23:25/3:23/4:4/5:3:6/6:7:11/7:10,11:22/11:9:
15:19,20,21/12:1/13:11:35:37,38,39/14:5,6:32/
15:10:23:28:29:35,36:37/16:14/17:9:13:19/18:7
:11:11f:22:23:29/19:7:8,9,10^2:33:40:43/20:
8,9,10^2:18/21:1:10/23:20^2/24:2:3^2:25/1Ki1:34/
2:31/3:3:4:8/4:7:24/6:8:10:34/7:3,4:7:34:36/8:8
:9^2:22,23:35,36:37:60/9:23/10:3f:5:12:20^2/11:
21:40/12:20:32,33/13:11:24,25:28/14:18:24:30
/15:6:16:32,33/17:1:7:8,9^2:13:14:16/18:25:26:
29:40/19:3:7:11^2:12^2:18:20/22:1:7:36,37:43:47/
2Ki1:3:6:16/2:3/3:1f:9:11:20/4:6:7:31:32:38:43:
44/5:8:15:18:26/6:1:9:15:25/7:3:5^2:10^2/8:29/9:
16^2:22:23:27/10:1:8:13/11:2,3:16/12:3/14:4:19^2
/15:1:8:13:17:23:27:30:32,33/16:1:6:10/17:1/
18:1/19:7/20:19/23:1:6:16:17:22^2:25/1Ch4:14:
43^2/5:9:18/6:32/7:9/9:6:22/11/12:24-37^8/13:4
:10:14/14/16:39/17:1:20^2/18:10/21:26:30/23:
31/24:4:5^2/2Ch1:4:12/2:16:17/4:4/5:9:10/6:11
:14:26:28/7:7:13/8:11:13/9:11:13,14/11:17/12:
15/14:1:9,10/15:5:6:19/16:3/17:14,15/18:6,7^2:
19,20^2/19:3:7/20:14:17:21:24/22:5/23:12/25:
11:27/28:9:17,18:24/29:16:32,33:34:35/30:2,3/
31:16/32:7:11:21:22/34:6:9:15,16:30/35:18:
24,25/36:16/Ez1:11/4:19:20/5:1:15/6:4:21,22/
7:14/8:15:26,27/9:11/10:2:13:24/Neh2:9:16/3:
8/4:10/5:1/6:8/7:63:66/8:18/10:32/11:1:10-14^3
:18:19:22,23f/13:16:26/Est1:7:18/2:5:12,13,14^2
/3:8/4:3:13/5:2:9:13/6:5/7:4/Job1:1/3:17^2:18:
19/4:16/6:5,6,7:15-18^3:19-21/9:32,33/12:14/
13:20/14:7:13:22/15:21/16:19^2/18:6^2:10/22:14
:29/23:3:8:9^2:14/28:5:8/31:23:35/32:15/33:
23,24/34:12:23/35:5/36:16/38:19/39:8:29/40:
22/41:33/42:15/Ps2:10/10:4f:5/12:2/14:1:2/
20:5/22:2/27:5/30/32:3:6/35:15:17/37:29:37/
39:2,3/40:5/41:6/43:4/46/49:5:8,9/53:1:2/55:7
:11^2:15/58:11/59:3/63:1/65:4/66:6/68:9,10/69
:36/71:11:19/72:15:16/74:4:9,10/75:8/76:3/77:
2:13:18:19/78:69/81:7:9f/84:3/86:8:11/88:18/
89:8/92:7:15/95:9/103:19^2/104:11:14:17:18:25:
26/105:18:23:37/107:23:36:38/111:6/118:20/
119:160/122:5:7:9/128:3/139:8^2:10:15/142:4/
Pro4:11/6:16-19/7:23/8:8:27,28,29^3/10:11/11:
14/12:21/13:12/14:4:12/15:6/16:10:25:27f/18:
24^2/19:18/20:13:21/21:20f/23:17,18/24:6:
13,14:17/26:12:13/27:25,26,27/28:2^2/29:18:20
/30:4:11,12:15,16:18,19:20:21,22,23:24-28:
29,30,31/31:29/Ecc1:3-7:12-15/2:7,8:11:13,14:
24-26/3:1:12:22/5:6,7:8f:13,14^2/6:1/7:2:20/8:
6,7:8:14:15/9:2,3:4:10:14:15/10:5:8,9:11f/11:3/
12:2:3^2:12/Sol1:7:8/2:9/5:6/6:11/7:12:13/8:2:5
:11/Is1:8/2:2:3/5:17/7:14f:17:25/8:22/9:5/10:
2:31/11:16/13:20:21^2/14:1:9:16/17:2/19:19/22
:18/23:5/24:23/27:12/29:2/34:6:10:11:14^3:15:
16/35:2^2:7:8:9^2:10/36:17/37:33/39:8/41:17/43:
9:10^2:11/44:6:8^2/45:5:6^2:14:18:21:22/46:7^2:9/
47:11/48:10:19:22/51:3/52:14,15/53:2/55:1/56
:10/57:7,8:12:21/60/61:4/63:3/65:8^3:9:19/66:
13:17:19/Jer1:12f/2:10,11:28:36/3:1:2:14:17/4:
14:27/5:12:28/6:14:16:20:29/7:11:31:32^2/8:14:
15:22^3/9:16/10:5:6:7:20/11:13/14:5:6:16:18^2:
19^2/15:8/16:13:14,15/17:9:25^2/18:2/19:5:11/
20:3:6/22:4/23:28/24:2/25:23/26:2:15/27:22/
29:5:8:20/30:5:6:7:13/31:5:15:17:40/32:3:5:27:
34:35/33:18/36:6:12/37:10:15,16:17^2:20:21/38:
6^2:11:26/39:3:14/42:16:17/44:6:10:11/46^2/48:
2,3,4:11:19:33/49:7:9,10:16:18:33/50:22:34/51:
16:17:19:46/52:9:23^2/Lam1:2:3:7:12:21/2:13/3:
21:29/4:3,4:15:19/5:8/Eze1:4:19,20,21:25:
27,28/3:22:23/4:3:4,5:7/5:2/7:12:15/8:4:9:11^2:
14:16/11:24/12:13:25/13:16/14:20:22/16:6,7:
16:25:28/17:5:20/18:30/19:14/20:11:13:35,36:
40/22:10/23:2,3/24:8:16:17/26:13:20/27:32/28
:8/29:18f:20f/30:13/31:12:16/32:21:22:24:26:
29:30/34:6:14:26/35:10/36:8/37:7:25/39:11:
15,16/40:7-12:16:21:22^2:26:29,30f:33:34^2:35:37:
39:40:41:42:43:44:47/41:21:25:26/42:9,10:11:
12:13/44:3/46:14,15:19,20:21,22:23/47:12^2/48:
30,31:35f/Dan2:10^2:28/3:12^2:30/4:13:19/5:11/
6:11:15/7:13/8:7/9:12/10:5,6:20,21/11:10,11:
36:45^3/12:1:11/Hos1:14:15^2/4:1:2:12f:13/5/6:
11/7:14/8:7/9:3:4^2:15/10:6:9:14/12:4/13/Joe1
:13:14:18:20/2:12/3:2:12/Amo1:14/4:8/5:16:17
/6:2:9/7:2:5:12/8/9:4:13:15/Ob1:18/Jon:3:16/
4:2:5:10/Mic1:11:11f^3:14/4:1:2:3:4:10/5:4:12/6
:5:10/Nah2:9:13/3:15:18:19/Hab1:2:3:4/2:18:
19/3:17/Zep1:17/2:2:7:14:15/3:5:11/Hag1:8/2
:16,17^2/Zec1:11/2:6,7/3:1:4/4:2/6:6:8/8:4:10^2/
9:12/10:2:10/14:7^2:9:21/Mal2:11:16/3:10/Mt2
:13:15/3:13/4:1:15,16/5:1:24:26:43/6:21:22/8:
10:27/9:10^2/11:23f/12:10:46,47/13:5:42:50:
53,54:58/14:15:20:33/15:20:22:29:37,38/16:21:
26/18:20/21:2:3:14:19^2/22:13:23:30:31/24:7:21
:23:28:30:51/25:30/26:5:19:32:59:73/27:16:36:
38:53/28:2:7:9:10:17/Mk1:9:12,13:45/2:2:6:15
/3:1:10:13/4:1:39/5:9:11:15:35/6:10:34:35,36:
38:43,44^2:51:54/7:12,13:24/8:8,9^2/9:2:26/10:1f
:1:31:33:49/11:2:4,5:13/12:6:12:18:20,21,22^2:26
:28:32/13:3,4:8:22/14:2:15:28:49:51,52:69^2/15:
23:32:35:40/16:5:7/Lk1:61/2:4:6:7:16:28:33:
36,37^2:40:45/4:22:25,26^2:31/5:3:12:29/6:20:21^2
/7:28:37/9:12:14^2:25:36/10:31:32:42/11:24:45/
12:12:33:34:37:38:42,43,44:50/13:7:14:28:29/
14:22:30/15:10:13/16:19:21:23:26^2/17:1:6:12:
21/18:2:11:22:31/19:4/20:19:27:37,38:39/21:7:
11:12:23:25/22:11:12:40:53:55/23:9:10:32,33/
24:4:18:22,23:36:41:47/Jn1:1:3:29:36:46/2:6/3:
18:22:23,24^2:26:35/4:46,47/5:5:7/6:24/7:12:25:
48/8:35:44:50f/9:4:16:32:40/10:16:42f/11:8:9:
10:15:54/12:36/13:23f/14:2,3^2:4/16:10:11:12/
18:2:18:22:26/19:18:26:29:31:41:42/20:3,4:5:6:
19:24/21:2:6:9^2:11/Act1:10:14:18/2:2:12/3:7,8:
11/4:6:12^2:14:33:36/5:1:22:23:36:37/6:1/7:6:11
:12/8:5:8:9,10,11:23:31:40/9:2:8,9:10:11:20:33:
36/10:1:36,37:46,47/11:26^2/12:7:19:24/13:5:13
:38/14:3:7:17:21:28/15:2:12:31:34,35:40,41/16:
10:12:26/17:1:2:6:17:25/18:2,3:11:23:25,26:27/
19:9:32:39:40/20:14:22/21:2/22:10:12:20:25/
23:8:9:21^2/24:15:18^2/25:4:14:26/27:4:6:9:10:12
/28:4:13/Rom1:20f/2:5:9:10/3:1^2/4:8/7:7:8^2:14
:23,24,25/8:1:34/9:25:27/11:5:20:21:24:26/12:
4,5/13:1^2/14:2:14:20:22/15:12:24:25:27:31/16:
1:7:10:17/1Co1:10^2:17/3:4:12:13/4:8/5:1:3,4^3/
6:5:11/7:16:24^2/8:4:5:6:10/9:13/10:3,4^2:16:17/
11:3/12:5:6:20/13:1:13/14:10:25/15:13:21:22:
29:32:34f:39^2:40f:44^2:52:58/16:2:3:5:9^2/2Co1:1:
20/2:13:15:17/3:6:17/4:6:15/6:16/7:5/8:7/9:8/
10:10:13:16/12:2,3^2:11:12/13:2/Gal1:7:18/2:2^2:
4:6:21/3:19/4:20:23/5:20:23:24/Eph2:15/3:8/4
:5/5:3/Php2:1:12:20/3:5:18:20/4:21/Col1:22/2
:9/1Th:2:9/3:10/4:9/5:3:26/2Th2:3:4/3:10/1Ti
1:3,4:5/4:13/5:19/2Ti2:20/4:3/Tit1:5:10:13/2:
8/3:12:15/Heb1:2/2:8/3:13/4:1:9:10:16/5:7f:
11/6:4:13^2/7:3f:3:23:25/8:7/9:1^3:3:4:22/10:4f:
18:23^2:26:27:28/11:6:7:12:27/12:19/13:3:13:
24,25/Jas2:3:10:13:19:26/3:16^2/4:1:9^3:13/1Pe
1:5:6/2Pe:17,18/2:1^2:2:22/3:3:13:15,16/1Jn2:1
/3:5/4:1:4:20/5:16^2/2Jn1:7/3Jn:9:15/Jud:7:18
/Rev:9:12/2:4:6/3:4/4:2:5/5:6/6:2:6:8:12/8:1:5
/9:12:16f:16/10:6:8/11:10:13:15:19/12:7/13:4:
14/16:18:21/17:3/18:11:18:22^3/19:11/20:11f/
21:4:10:13:25/22:3^2:5

2283

THERE'S

^{2}Gen31:14/Jos7:3/1Ki20:25/22:8/2Ki4:40/Ps
142:4/Pro29:9/Ecc6:10/Mk14:69/Lk8:49/Jn6
:8,9

11

THESE

Gen1:2f:11,12/2/9:9,10,11:19/10:1:13,14:15-19
:20:26-30:31/14:3:24/15:19,20,21/17:14/18:21
/19:8/22:17/24:3^2:45/25:4f:16:18/26:4/27:46/
28:1:9/30:29:38/31:32:43^3/32:5:11:17:18/33:5/
35:26/36:5:18,19:20,21:31-39:40-43/38:3,4,5/
41:6:7:15:20:34,35/43:16/45:6/46:15:18:19-22:
23,24,25:32/48:5:8:9:15:16/49:26:28/50:11/Ex
1:9/3:1f/4:9/5:15/6:14:16:24:25/11:8:10/12:6:
19^2:43/14:5/16:28,29/18:19,20:21:22/19:2,3/
21:11/23:13:17:24^2/24:6:7:8/25:15:26,27:36/26
:4,5:7,8:9:10,11:14:18,19:20:24/28:11:30,31f:41^2
:43/29:24:29:30:33/30:21:34/31:12,13/32:9:22:
31:34/33:1:4:12/34:13f:22:23:27/35:1:5-9/36:
10:11,12:16:29/39:6,7:15-18:24/Lev4:1:2/5:5/6
:9:14:18:22,23:25/7:36:37:38/8:26/9:5:14:20/
11:13-19:29,30:44^2:46:47/12:1:6:7:8/13:11:39:
59/14:1:32:54:57/15:1/16:35/17:1/18:24^2:26^2:
27:28:29,30^2/20:1:23/21:24/22:9^2:15/23:3:4:20
:37:38:42:44/24:5-8:9/25:1:34/26:46/27:1:34/
Num1:16:54/2:1^2:3-31^2/3:2f:25-30:31-35^2:
36,37/4:4:24:26/5:1:4:23/6:1:16:21^2/7:4,5:
84,85,86/9:1:14/10:9/11:13/13:3-15:17/14:
10,11:26,27/15:1:11,12:13,14:22/16:3:21:26:28:
29:30:38^2:45/17:4:5/18:7:8^2:9:11:13:18:19:24/
19:14/21:8/22:9:16,17:20:28/23:18-24/25:2/26
:57:58,59:63/27:1:21/28:1:23:28,29:31/29:2:6:
39:40/30:16/31:47/32:34,35,36:37,38/34:16-28
:29/35:3:8:12:13,14:15:29/36:5:11,12:13/Deu1:
27/2:7/3:5/4:1:2:5:6:8:35:40:43/5:1:22/6:1:2:3:
6:20:24/7:11:17/8:4/9:27^2/11:7:8:18:28/12:1:9:
18:26,27:28:30:31/13:6,7/14:3,4,5/15:20/16:1
/17:18/18:12^2:14/19:2,3^2:4:6,7:9/20:15:15f/23
4/26:16/27:1:8:10:15:26/28:1:2-6:14:15-19^2:22
45:46/29:18:29/30:1:11:12/31:1:7:10,11:13:16
21/32:38:46:47/33:16/Jos1:8/3:2,3,4/4:10:21:
22/8:11,12,13f:27/9:1:7:13:16/10:5/11:4/12:6,
13:2-7/14:10/15:21-32:33-36:48-62/17:4:5,6/
18:21-28^2/19:2-7:15,16^2:24,25,26/20:3:4:9/21:
:6:17,18/22:7,8:21/24:13/Ju1:33/2:20:22/3:4:
13/6:5:20/7:7/9:24/10:7,8/11:1/13:23/14:3:12
/15:18/20:6:13:16/21:10,11,12:14/Ru1:4,5/4:4
/1Sa2:17/4:8/6:4,5:10/9:24/13:16/16:10,11/
17:17/21:12/22:17/23:12/24:7,8/25:10:30,31/
29:3/30:20/31:3,4/2Sa1:25/3:39/5:14,15,16/7
21:28/8:11,12/10:3:15,16/15:3/16:2:12/21:22,
23:1:8:17:22/24:17/1Ki2:33/3:25/4:8-19^2/6:6:
35/7:9:16-22:27-30^2:34:39:41-46:47:50/8:59/9:
13/10:29/11:8:31/12:28:29/14:27/15:14:22/18
37/20:13/21:27/22:6f:11:23/2Ki1:13/2:21/4:
38/10:6/13:20,21/16:11,12/17:13:25:29:41/19
5,6:25/20:14/21:11/23:9:11:13:14/24:3,4/25:
23^2/1Ch1:1:1f:33/2:18:23:25:55/3:4:10-14:
17,18/4:1:2:21-22:23:31:32,33:34-39:40,41:42/
:7,8:24/6:1:33-38:66-69/7:2:7:17:40/8:8,9,10:2
:30,31,32:40/9:7,8:9/10:4/11:10:18,19^2/12:1:1
:38/14:4-7/15:2:4-10/16:2:4:22/17:19/18:11/
19:2,3:7/20:8/21:17/23:8,9:24/24:6:20:30/25:1
/26:8:20,21,22:27:31,32/27:1:31/28:12:14:21/
29:4,5:19:30/2Ch1:17/2:4/4:9/5/8:15:17,18/9:
7:16/11:5-10/13:9/14:7:14/17:7,8,9:19/18:10:
22:30/19:9/23:2,3:9:10/24:5/25:16/26:12/28:
10:11:12:23/31:7,8^2:10^2:12,13/32:19/34:15,16:
19:21/35:24,25/36:16/Ez1:8/4:21/5:3:14/7:17
/8:1:20:28:29/9:2^2:14/10:2:11:44^2/Neh2:8/5:
2,3,4:5:7:12:19/6:7/7:62/8:17/9:4/10:9-13:28:
38:39,40/11:4,5,6:10-14/12:24:26:44^2/13:5:13:
25/Est1:13-15/2:12,13,14/3:11:12/6:10/9:20:
27:29-31:32/Job1:4:5/5:15/7:3:16/12:3/13:12/
15:13/16:10/26:4:14/27:12/28/30:8:11/31:22/
33:29/36:25/42:13,14/Ps4:2/9:16f/10:2^2:3:4:15
/17:13,14^2/18:48/19:12/21:11/22:17:20:21^2/24
:6/31:18/35:11:17:26/36:11/37:20:33/38:16/40
:14,15^2/42:9/43:1/49:13/53:5/54/55:9/57:3/
58:3:6/59:1:2^2:5:8:14,15/64:1^2/66:15/69:4:14:
28/71:4:13/73:7:12:17/74:18:19:21:22:23/78:4^2
/79:12/81:4/83:2:6:12/90:10/94:4/97:8,9/104:
27:34/105:15/106:18:29/107:8:10:15:21:31/
108:10/110:1f/118:2/119:54^2:85,86:106:126:
150:158/120:5,6^3/124:4,5/136:21/137:7/140:5:
6,7,8/141:6,7/144:11^3/Pro1:1:5,6:18/2:16,17:
19/3:3/4:21/10:1/25/30/31:28:31/Ecc2:9/3:13
/6:12/7:10/8:9,10/9:5f^4:10f^2/Sol3:10/Is1:1^2:16
/7:20/8:16:20/9:1:6:18/10:13/13:3/19:18/21:
6,7f:14/27:4,5/29:11:13:14/31:3/33:16:19/35:
10/36:20/37:36/40:26/41:21/42:22:23/43:21/
44:11^2/45:7:21/47:12/49:21^2/50:4/51:19/57:
7,8:17/58:8/60/Jer1:1^2/2:25:28/3:2/5:14:25^2/
7:5:10:16/8:4,5:9:17/9:25,26/10:9:14:16/11:20:
23/12:5:16/14:15/15:1:11:21/16:8:10/17:15:27
/18:15/19:10/20:4/21:8:12/22:4/23:14:16:17:
18:19:21:27:28:30,31^2/25:12/27:5:12:15/28:7:
13:14/29:23/31:36/32:15:25:29:42/33:25,26/
35:8/36:7:8:17/37:8/38:9:12:21,22/40:2,3:8/43:
10/44:5:23/45:5/46:24/49:32/Lam1:16/2:20/3
/4:14/Eze1:13/7:10,11/8:6:13:15:17/10:9-13:
15,16:20/11:1/12:9:23/13:4:8:10^2:11:18/14:3:
16:18:23/16:22:30:37:39:43/17:12,13:21/23:16:
43:44/24:3:27/27:10f:17f/28:9:12f/31:18/32:23
/33:33/34:20:21/36:5:20:37,38/37:3:7:9:11:16^2:
18,19,20/38:2,3f:11/39:10/40:7-12^2:42/41:6:9/
42:9,10:13^2:14:15/43:13:18/44:6:8:15/45:25/46
:10:19,20:23:24/47:21:23/48:24:29/Dan1:17:20
/2:43:44/4:28:31:35/5:2,3,4:5:23/7:6:16:17/8:3:
9:26/9:24f/10:13:19/11:6f:27:34:38/12:6/Hos1
:1^2:13/7:4/13:2/14:9/Joe1:9/2:2:7:20:26/3:7:
13/Amo4:12/9:10/Jon4:2/Mic1:1/Hab:12:16/
2:3^2:4:5/Zep:4/3:8/Zec1:1:19:21/3:4:7/4:9:10/
6:4:5:15/8:12:20,21/10:3/11:8/13:6:6f:9/14:20
/Mal1:13/2:3:5/3:12/Mt1:1:17:18/3:9:9f/6:9:
31,32/7:29f/9:17f/10:5/11:1:16/12:49/13:10:
12,13:34,35:53,54/14:2/15:8:20:32/18:6:10:14:
16/21:15^2:23f:38/22:25:40^2/23:2^2/24:6:33:34f/
25:37:40:45/26:60,61/27:21/28:20/Mk2:16/3:
16-19:23:34/7:6,7:23/8:1:7:38/9:7:42/10:30/12
:14:25:27:31/13:1:8:9:29:30:32/14:49/15:3,4/
16:12f/Lk1:3/2:19:23:51/3:8/4:6,7:21:28/5:17/
8:10^2/9:8/10:2:8,9:21:24:36:41/11:29,30^2:42/
12:1:4:11/15:29/16:24/17:2,3/18:16,17:21/19:
27/20:36:46:47/21:6:28:32:36:36f/22:28/23:34:
38/24:18f:26:33,34:45:48/Jn1:40/2:16/3:10,11:
12/5:32,33:36/6:2-5/7:49/8:14:20:30,31:54/10:

(THESE Con't)
42/12:26:36:49/13:17:18:33/14:25:29/15:24/
16:1:4:25:26/17:1:6:12:20^2:24:25/18:1:8/19:13/
20:30,31/21:15:15f:24^2/Act1:3:4:24,25/2:7:11:
15:29:34:37/3:18/4:16/5:5:32:35:38/6:6/7:1:6:9
/8:2f:15:17:24/10:44/11:12:17:21/13:2:31/14:
11:15/15:21:25:26/16:17:20,21/17:8,9:30/19:
37/20:34/21:4:24:25:30:37,38f:39/23:8/24:13:
15:20/25:10,11:20/26:22:26^2:28:29/28:22:28,29
f/Rom1:25:26:32/2:1:2/3:19:26/4:9:11:16/7:7:
16:17/8:31/9:6:30/11:9:17/13:6/14:18/15:1^2:4:
14:15,16:23:27/1Co1:20^3/2:10:13:14/4:19/5:12
/6:2:4f:5:12/7:5:12:17:23:26:28/9:5:6/10:11^2:19
:20^2/11:18:22/12:11:31/13:8:10:13/14:11:20:23
:24^2/15:46:50/16:1:18:21/2Co1:6,7/3:4:8/4:10:
15:17/5:1:4^2:6:7:18/7:1/8:24/9:3:4:5/10^2:6:12/
11:5/12:7:11/13/Gal2:12:14/3:10/4:12^2/5:10:
12:17:19/6:11:17/Eph1:12/2:10/3:4/4:1:12/5:4
:6:15,16/Php1:20/3:7:15:21/4:3/Col2:17:18:23
/3:8/4:11/1Th:8/5:3:4/2Th2:15/1Ti1:6:10,11/
3:14/4:2:3:11:15/5:4:14/6:2:3:5:11:20:21/2Ti2:
2:7:9:14:19:21/3:8:15/Tit1:7:12/2:4:15/3:8/
Phm1:13/Heb:2/2:4/3:13:17/5:11/8:10:13/9:9:
10:23/10:30/11:13:33:39/Jas1:15/1Pe:7:12:20/
2:2,3f/4:13/5:9/2Pe1:5:9:12:13,14:20,21/2:3:11^2
:13:17:19/3:14:15,16:17/1Jn2:12:13:15:16^3:17:
19:26/3:8/4:5/5:6,7,8:17/2Jn1:12/Jud:8:10:12:
14:16:18/Rev:1:3:8f/2:15:19/4:7:8/5:9/7:13:14
/9:20/11:4/13:14^2/16/18:15/19:9f/21:7:17/22:
6,7:8:16:19

1548

THEY

Gen1:4,5:11,12:14,15/2:1/3:7^3:8^2/4:15/6:1:21/
7:8,9:16/8:17/9:2,3:23:24,25/11:2f:3,4^2:6^3:7:31
/12:6:11,12,13:14:15/13:1^2:3,4:7:16/14:4^2:5,6:7
:8,9/15:14:16/17:11/18:5:8:9:20/19:1:2:3:4:8:9^2
:11:15:33:35/20:11,12:17/21:30:31/22:8:9:19/
23:17,18/24:19:20:41:54:57:58^2:59:60/25:18:25:
26/26:4:7:15:18:20:24:28:30:31^2:32/27:15:36/
28:6,7,8:14/29:4^2:7:8:20/30:38^2/31:47,48/32:
12:17:18^2/33:8:13^2:18/34:14:21:22^2:23^2:25:26:
28^2:30:31/35:2:4:5^3:6:16/36:17/37:2:4:8:13,14:
17^2:18^2:19,20:23:25^2:28:32/38:3,4,5:21:25:26:28
/40:4:6:8^2:20/41:3^2:21:38:55/42:7:10:13:20:21:
23:26:27:28^2:29:30:35/43:2:7:15:18^4:19^2:24:25^3:
26:27:28^2:34/44:1:4^2:7:11:13:14/45:3:4:25:26:
27/46:6:28^2:29:32^2/47:1:3:15^2:17:18:22:25/48:5
:16/49:5:6:31^2/50:8:10^2:11:15:16,17:25^2:26/Ex
1:7^2:10:15,16:17:19^2/2:11:18:19:22/3:13:17:18/
4:1^2:5^2:8^2:9:18:27:28^3:30:31^2/5:1^2:3:7,8^2:13:14^2:
15:19:20^2:21^2/6:4:7:8,9^2/7:11:22:24/8:3,4^2:7:14
:18:19:26/9:10:32:34/10:3:4,5:6:11:12:15/12:33
:36^3:39^3:48^4/13:1:17,18^2:19:20:21/14:4^2:5:8:9:
10:11:17:31/15:5:8:10:14:16:22:23:24:27^2/16:1:
3:4:15:18:20:21:22:28,29:32:35/17:2:3:4:7:12/
18:5,6:7:12:22:26^2/19:2,3:8:9:14:17:21^2/20:18:
19/21:4:30/22:23/23:27:33/24:10:11/25:18f:19
:37/28:4^2:30,31f:43/29:9:21:33:46/30:2:20^4:30/
31:6:10:11/32:1:2,3:6^2:8:13:17:19^2:22:23:24:28:
35/33:4:6/34:13:15:15f:27/35:22:35/37:8^2/39:
30:33-40:41/40:15:32^2:37/Lev1:9/4:14^2/6:
19,20:22:23:29/7:38/9:5:13:23^2:24/10:5:7:15^2:
19/11:8/15:18:31/17:12/18:17:18:24/19:15:20:
23:34/20:4:12:13:16:17:19^2:20:21:23:27/21:6^2/
22:9/23:1:20:26,27/24:23/25:34:45:46/26:7:36^2
:37:40,41^3:43:44/27:28:32/Num1:50/2:3-31^2/3:
4^2:7,8,9^3:13/4:6:7:8^2:9:11:15^2:17,18,19^2:20^2:25:
26^3:30,31/5:1:3/6:22,23/7:3^2:4,5,9:18-23:78-83:
87^2:88/8:2:15:16:22:25,26/9:6,7^2:10^2:11:12:18:
19^2:22:23^3/10:3:21:33:34^2/11:2:4,5,8:12:13:17:
18:25:26:34:35^2/12:1f:2:3,4,5:15:16/13:18:19:
21:22^2:23^3:24:25:26^3:30:31^2:33/14:1:2:4:9:10,11
:12:13^2:14^3:26,27:31:40^2:44/15:3,4:17,18:
19,20,21:23,24:25^2:34^2:36/16:3:4:11,12:13:18^2:
19:22:30:32:33^2:36,37:38:42/17:9:12,13/18:6:10
:13:17:17f:19:21:22:23^2:24:25,26:31:32/19:9/20
:3^2:6:8:28:29/21:1:2:5^2:11:12:13:17,18:22:24:33
/22:2,3:4^2:5,6:7:8:10:16,17/23:7-10^3:18-24^3/24:
3-9^2:15-19:23,24/25:6:18^3/26:58,59:61:64,65f:
64,65/27:3,4/28:1:9,10:24/29:36/31:16/32:2:9^2
:10,11:12:16:30^2:34,35,36:37,38:40/33:3,4^2:5,6:
7:8:9^2:10:15-37:38,39:45:49:50,51:52/34:1/35:
9,10/36:1:3^2:6:13/Deu1:1:14:15:22:24,25:27:28^2
:32:39:41^2:42:43^2:45:46/2:4:12:21/3:14:17:18:
20/4:2:5:6^2:10^2:44,45,46^2:47/5:29:31/7:25/9:1:
13,14:26:29/10:4:5:7/11:3:4^2:5:6:23/12:12:30:
31/13:12,13,14/14:1:7:8^2:27:29/15:6:8/16:18/
17:13/18:2:17/19:18/20:9:19/21:18/22:17,18/
23:4/24:21/25:18/26:5^2:12/28:7:10:44^2:51:60/
29:23:25:26:28/30:13:14/31:7:16:17^2:20:21/32:
5^2:7:10:12:14:15^2:17:18:19:20:21:29^4:32:33:36:
37:38:47/33:3^2:11:19^2/34:1/Jos1:6:15:16:17,18
/2:1^2:3^2:4:5^2:8:14:17,18:19:24/3:1:2,3,4:6/4:8^3:
14^2:21/5:1:6^2:10^2:11:12^4/6:5:12,13,14^2:15^2:20^2:
21:25/7:3:4:9:10,11^2:12:12f:21:22:23/8:5:6^3:9:
19:20,21^3:24:27/9:1:3,4,5^2:6^2:8:9:13:14,15:21:24
:27/10:4:6:8:17:27:31:34,35:36:38:39^3:40/11:5:6
:9:14:20/13:14:33/16:10/17:1:9:13:16,17,18/18
:7^3:9^2/19:47,48/20:4:8/21:2:3:43/22:10^3:11:12:
13^2:15^2:28:30:34/23:13/24:1:2:6:8:14:22:32/Ju
1:1:3:11:14:16:17:19:20:21:22,23^2:24:25:28:29/2
:3:5:11:12-14^3:17^2:19^2:22/3:4:7:8:15:24:25^3:29/
4:2,3/5:11:13,14:15:23/6:3,4:27:29:30:33/7:2:
5,6:8,9:11:19,20:21:22/8:1:2,3:4:15:18^3:19:25:34
:35/9:2:3^2:4:5:8:10:12:14:20:22,23:25^2:31:55/10
:4:6:10:15:16/11:1^2:8:10:17^2:18^3/12:5:6/13:21:
24/14:3^2:12^3:13:14:15:18^2/15:11^2:12,13^2/16:2:5^2
:8:18:19:23,24^2:31/18:1:2^2:3:5:7^3:8:12:13^2:15,16
:19:21:22:27:28^3:30/19:4:5:6:8^2:10:14^2:15^2:17^2:
21^2:22^2:25^3/20:1:5:8,9,10:16:18:25:31^2:33:35-39
:40,41:42:43:46,47/21:3:4:5:6:8,9,10,11,12^2:14:
20:23^2/Ru1:1f:8:9:10:14:19/4:1:16,17/1Sa1:7:9:
19,20:24:25/2:11:13,14^2:17:20^2:23,24,25:29:36/
4:3:4:6:7^2:8:9/5:3:7:8:10^3:11/6:3:4,5^2:6:8:9^2:12:
13^2:16:19:20:21^2/7:4:6^2:7^2:8:10/8:3^3:5^2:7^3:8^2:9:
12:19:22/9:4:9,10,11^4:12,13:14^3:20:25:26,27/10
:2:4:5:10:11:14:21:22:23:27/11:1:5:7:15^3/12:4:5:
9:10^3:19/13:3,4,5^2:6:20/14:9^2:10:11:12:13:17^2:
22:24,25:26:30:31^2:32:34/15:6:9:15:18:24/16:4:
6:15,16/17:11:24:50,51/18:8:22/19:16^2:20^2:21:
22:24/20:11:18:41:41f:42/21:5^2:11/22:4:11,12:
17^3/23:5:12:19/25:7:8:15,16^2:40/26:12:13^2/27:
7:9^2/28:7,8:25^2/29:4^2/30:1:4^2:9,10:11,12^2:15:16^2
:18,19:20:21:22^2/31:7:8:9:12:13/2Sa1:5:11:12:
20:23^4/2:13^2:23:24:29:32/3:17:21:26:32/4:2,3^3:
6,7^2:8^2:12^3/5:1:3:6^3:17^2/6:6:13/7:10,11^2/8:2:5/
10:6^2:14:15,16^3:19/11:1:19,20,21/12:18:19:21/
13:9:29,30^2:35:36/14:14f:30/15:11:30:32:35,36/
16:14^2:21/17:8:10:17:18:19:20^2:21^2:28,29^2/18:3^2
:17/19:3:14^2:17:18^2/20:3:8,9,10^2:12:15:22^2/21:
1:2:5,6:12,13,14^2/22:19:39:42^2:45:46/23:6:7/24
:5:6:8/1Ki1:3,4^2:7:9:25:32:40:41:44,45:49,50:53
/2:7:39/3:22:28/6:23-28/7:27-30:47/8:8^2:9:14:
22,23:30:33,34:35,36^2:40^2:41,42:44:46:47:48:51:
52:66/9:9:13:20,21:22:27,28/10:8:11:25/11:2:3:
4:16,17,18^2:25/12:2,3,4^2:7:16,17^2:23,24:27^3:28/
13:12:13:19:20:27/14:15:23/16:13:15,16/17:16
/18:6:23:26^3:28:29:30:33:34^2:39:40/19:10:14^2:
21/20:5,6^2:11:12:17:18:23:25:32/21:12:19/22:6:
11:12:32,33^4:48^2/2Ki1:4,5:6:8:9/2:1^2:4:6,7:8:9:
11:12:15^2:16:17:18:19:20:21/3:4:21:23:24^2:25/4
:4:6:39:40/5:15:24/6:4^2:20^3/7:3:4^2:5:6:7:8:9:10^2
:12^2:13:15/9:12:13:21:27:28:33:35^2:36/10:4^2:6:
13:15:20,21:25:27/11:2,3:9:16:17/12:15/13:5:6^2
:7:19:20,21:23/16:5:6:9:17/17:6:8:9:10:11:12:15^2
:16^2:17^2:19:20:23:25:26:29:32^2:33^2:34:35,36^2:41
/18:12^2:17:18:27:34/19:11^2:18^3:26:29:37/20:14:
15/21/22:5,6:7:20/23:3:5^2:8:9:18:19/24:13/25:
14,15:16:21:24^2:26/1Ch2:34,35^2:55/4:23:27:28:
40,41^2:43^2/5:19:20^2:23:25^2:26^2/6:49:61/7:9:11:
20,21:28/8:6,7:13:40/9:17,18:22^2:23:24:26:27^2:
28:33,34^2/10:2:7:8:9^2:10:12/11:3/12:2^2:8-13:15:
19^2:21^2:23:24-37:39/13:5:9/14:8^2/15:2:16:26/
16:5:8:20:40:42/17:6:9^2:24/19:2,3^2:7:15/20:8/
21:3/22^2:16/23:24:28:29^2:30:31:32^2/24:1:31/25
:6,7^2/26:12:13:30/29:8:17:20:21^2:22:22f:22^3/
2Ch3:11,12,13/5:1:10:11,12/6:3:16:20,21:24^2:
31:31f:33^2:34:36:37,38/7:3^2:8^2:21:22/10:4:7:10:
16^3/11:4:16:17f/12:5/13:11^2:12:13,14:15,16:17
/14:7:9,10:13:14^2:15/15:3:4:9:10:11:12:14:15^2/
16:4/17:7,8,9/18:3,4,5:11:22:29:31^2:32^2/20:5:
11^2:21:22^2:23^2:24:26^2:27:28:36/21:17/22:4:9/
23:2,3,5,6:11:15,16,17:18^2/24:22:24:25/25:12:
27:28/26:17,18:20^2/28:6:8:13:23^2/29:6:15:16:
17:18:19:22^2:30/30:5^2:8:9:10:14:15:16:17,18,19^2
/31:4,5,6,7,8,14,15:16:17,18/32:4^2:8/33:11/34:
9:22:28:33/35:12^2:13:14:24,25^2/Ez1:6/2:59^2:
62,63^3:66,67:70/3:4:5:6:7:8:11/4:2:6:10:11:12:
23/5:1:4:13:14^2/6:5:10:14:21,22/7:7,8,9:25/8:2-
2-14:29:36/9:9/10:5^2:9:16-19/Neh1:2:3/2:10:
18:19/3:1:3:6:13:19/4:1^5:4:5:7:8/5:2,3,4:8:12^2:
13:18/6:2^2:4:10:12,13:16^2:19^2/7:3:61:64,65^2:
68,69:73/8:6:9:12:14^2:17/9:1:3:11^2:12:15^2:16:17^2
:18^2:21:22:25^2:26^3:27:29^2:30:35^2:37/10:38/11:2
/12:29:31,32:35,36:37^3:42:45:47/13:2^2:10:15:21
:25^2:29:31/Est1:8:12:13-15^2:17/2:3:15:23f/3:
3,4:8:9:13:14/6:13:14/7:10/8:1f:9,10:17/9:1:6:
7-10^2:12:13:14:15:16:17:19:27^2/Job1:4:5:21/2:
11:12^2:13^2/3:22/4:9:10^2:11:20^2:21/5:1^2:2:13:14^2
/6:3:5,6,7:15-18/8:11-13/12:4:7,8,9:12/13:4/14
:20,21/15:17-19:21:34:35/16:8:10/17:5:6:8:12^2/
19:18/20:17/21:8:11:12,13^3:14:15:17:18^2/22:6:
8^2:17:18:20/24:3:4:5:6^2:7:8:9:10^2:11^2:14,15^4:16^2
:17:18^3:21^2:24^2/26:5,6/27:7:14/28:6:8:10:11:12:
13/29:22:23^2:24:25/30:2^2:3:4:6:7:10:13^2:14^2:15
/32:3:5/33:15/34:20:25:27/36:8:9^2:11^2:12^2:13:
14/37:11/38:8,9:39,40:41/39:2,3^2:7:8:16^2/40:
12/Ps1:2:3^2:4:5^2/2:3/4:7/5:9:10/7:12/9:15^2:20^2
/10:2:3:4:5^2:6:7:8:9^2:11:13:14^2/12:5:8/14:4^2/16:
3:4/17:10:11:12/18:7:14:18:41^2:43,44,45/19:1:2
:7,8:10^2:11/21:9,10:11:12^2/22:3,4,5^2:8:13:16:18:
30/24:5/25:11:19/26:4/27:2:12/28:4:5/29:5,6:9
/31:11:13:17/32:6f/33:13,14,15/34:15/35:7:11:
12:13:15^2:16:20:21^3:26/36:1:2^2:3^2:4:12^2/37:2:14
:19:23:24:28:33:40/38:3,4^2:12:20/40:16/41:3:6^5
:7^2:8/42:3:10/44:3:6/45:5:15:16/48:5:6^2/49:3:6^2
:13^2:14^2:17^2/51:13/52:6^2/53:3:4^2:5:6/55:3:10:
15:19/56:1:5:6^2:7/57:6^2/58:4,5:10/59:3:4:6:7:
12,13:14,15/62:3,4^3:9/63:10/64:3^2:4^2:5^3:6^2:8^2:9
/66:6/68:9,10:21:22/69:4^2:8:9:10:11:19^2:21^2:26:
32/70:2,3/72:12^2:15f/73:4f:4:5:8^2:9:11:12:18:20
/74:4:5,6:8/75/76:5/78:6:8:10^2:11,12:17:18:
19,20^2:22^2:29:30:34^2:35:36:37:39:40:41:42:
43:53:56:57^2:58:63:64/79:4:7/80:6:16/81:4/83:
2:3:4:5:16:17:18/84:6:7/85:8/86:17/88:4:5:8:11
:17/89:9:14,15:16/90:4:10:12/91:4:12/92:13:14
/94:1:6,7^2:14/95:5:9:10^2:11/96:12/99:7:8/102:
20:26^2/104:9:11:16:21:22:28^2:29/105:12:13:18:
24:25:28:30:38:40:44/106:7^2:12:13^2:16:19,20:
21,22:24^2:25:29:37,38:41,42:43/107:4:6:11:12:
13:19:20:24:27:28:38/109:3^2:4:5:9,10:12,13:25^2:
28:29/111:8:9/112:10^2/114:5/115:6/116:10,11^2
/118:11:12^2/119:11:35:43:44,45,46:49,50^3:
71,72:78:87:98^2:100:118:155:157:158:161/120:
7/126:6/127:3:5f/128:3/129:6,7/135:1:17/137:
7/138:5/139:20^2/140:4:5:9:10:12:13/141:4:5/
142:6/143:3^2/144:8/145:11:12:15/147:20/148:
5/149:4,5/Pro1:3:4:11:18^2:19/2:14:15:22^2/3:23
/4:13:16^2:17:22:23/5:22/6:7:8/8:36/9:18/11:7:
26/13:19/14:32:35/15:9,10^3/17:11/18:8/19:7:
24/20:6^2:17:18/21:27/23:4,5:6,7,8^2:13,14:
19,20,21:35/24:2/25:27/29:2/30:13,14^2:24-28^4
/31:5^2:9/Ecc3:18:20^2:22^2/6:2^3:11/7:10/8:9,10:
13:14^2/9:2,3,5^2:6^2/10:16,17/12:11/Sol2:13/3:8
/6:9:10/Is1:3:4^4:7:15:28/2:8:20/3:8:9^3:14^2:18^2/
4:2,3,4/5:7:19^2:20:22:23:24^2:26:27^2:29^2:30/6:2^3:
3:9:11:12/7:5:19:21,22/8:2:12:20:21^2:22^2/9:3:
11,12:17:19,20/10:2:12:13:24:28,29^3/11:13:14^2:
16/13:2:5^2/14:1:10:11:25:30/15:2:3:5:7/16:12/
17:7:8^3:13^2/19:3:11^3:12:13^2:14:20:21^2:23/20:5,6
/21:5^3:15/22:1^2:3^2:6,7:23,24/23:13:18/24:6:22^2
/26:10:11^3:14^2:16^2/27:9:11^2/28^3:12^4:13:15/29:
13^2:15^2:16:23^2/30:6:9^2:10,11^2:16/31:2:3^2:8:9/
32:7:8:20/33:8^2:14:16^2:18:19/34:17/37:3:5:11:
19:27:38/38:18/39:3^2:4/40:15^2:17:24:31^4/41:4:
7^3:12:17:21:29/42:16:17:22:24^2:25/43:8^2:9^2/44:
4:7:9^2:11^2:18:22:25^2:26:27/45:14^2:17:20:21/46:
1^3:6^2:7^2/47:14^2/48:13:21/49:8,9:10:14:18:22:23^2
:26/50:6/51:5:11/52:6^2:8:14,15^5/53:8/55:5/56:
3^2:5:10^2:11^2:12/57:6:13:17:18/58:2^6:3:6/59:19:
21^2/60:12:14^2:21/61:4^2:5:9/62:12/63:8^2:10:11^2:
13:15/64:6/65:2:3:4^2:5^3:7:13^2:14:23:24^2/66:2:3^3
:4^5:5^2:17:18^3:19:20:24^2/Jer1:16:18:19^2/2:4,5:6:
7:13^2:26,27^3:28:30/3:22/4:2:16:17:22^4:24/5:2:3^3
:4^2:5^2:7:8:10:12:13:17^2:22:23,24^2:26:27:28/6:3:5
:10^2:13:15^4:18,19^2:20:23:27^2:28^2:29/7:17:19^2:24^4
:26^2:30:31^2:32/8:2:7^2:9^2:11^2:12^4:17:19^2/9:2:3^3:5^2
:6:8:10:14^2:24/10:2,3:9^2:14:15:21^2:25/11:4^2:6^2:8^2
:10:11^2:12:14:19^2:20:21,22/12:2^4:6^2:11:13^2:16^2/
13:11^2:12:18:19:19f/14:6:12^2:13:14^3:15:16:18/
15:2:7:10:15^2:16^2:17,18:20^2/16:4:10:11^2:19:20:
21/17:13^2:15:23^2/18:12:15^2:19:20^2:22^2/19:4:5^2:
11/20:8:10^2:11^4/22:7:9:10:13f:20/23:1^2:3:4:8:12^2
:13:14^3:16^4:17^2:21^2:22^2:23:25^2:26^3:27:32/24:6:7^2
:9:10/25:14:16:18^2:19,20:28:33:34/26:3:9:10:11:
19:23/27:10:14:15:18/29:3:8:9:11:18:19:23^2/30:
3:5:6:7:9:10:21/31:1:9:12:15:16:23:32:32f:33:33f
:33/32:13:23^2:30:33^2:34:35^2:38:40/33:5:24/34:5^3
:11:11f:20:22/35:6^2:14/36:3:7:16^2:24,25:31/37:
9:10^2:15,16/38:4:6:13:19:21,22:25:27/39:2:4:6:
14/40:8:12^3/41:2:3:5:7:8:12^2:13,14:16,17:18/42
:5/43:6:7^2:9/44:2,3^2:5^2:12^2:28/46:6:20,21/48:
2,3,4:8:20:37:45/49:1:4:5:23:24:31^2:36/50:5^2:6:
7:9:28:34:42^3/51:2:4:14:17:18:24:28:30^2:39^2:57/
52:9:20^2/Lam1:8:11^2:19^2:21/2:10:12:14^2:16:19:
20/3:14:53:59:61:62:63:64/4:3,4:10:14:15:16:19^2
/5:7:11:13/Eze1:9:12:16:17:19,20,21:24^3:25/2:3
:4:5^4:6:7^3/3:6:7^2:8:9:11:13:18:19^2:26:27/6:9^3:10:
13/7:21:22^2:26,27^2/8:6:12:17:18/9:2:4:6:7^2:8:9:
10/10:9-13^2:15,16^2:20:22/11:3:15/12:2^5:3^4:4^2:5:
6:11:15:16^2:22^2:23/13:16:18^2:19:21:22/14:10:14
:18:20:22^2/15:2^2:4^2:5,6,7^2:8/16:20:27:37:39:
40,41:45:47:51:52/18:12/19:7:9/20:8^3:11:12:13^3

(THEY Con't)
:20:21^2:23,24^2:25:25f:26^2:27,28^4:38^2:47:49/**21**:7
:13:14:21^2:21f:22^3:28:29/**22**:5:18,19,20:25^3:26^2:
27:28^2/**23**:4,5:6:10:14,15:17:24^3:26:29:37^3:38:39^3
:40:43:44^2:45^2:47/**24**:27/**25**:4^2:9,10:11:14:17^2/
26:4:6:11:12^2:16:17:18/**27**:5:6:10:16:19f:24:31/
28:8:13:24:26^2/**29**:13:14/**30**:6:8:11:19:26/**31**:14:
17/**32**:4:10^2:24^3:25^4:26:27^3:29^2:30^2/**33**:6:17:29:
30:31^5:32:33^2/**34**:5^2:12:13:14:19:22:27:28:30^2/
35:4,5:12/**36**:8:14:17:18:19:20^2:35/**37**:7:9:10:11:
18,19,20:22:23^2:24:25^2:27/**39**:6:10^4:11:14:18:23:
26/**40**:24:29,30f:46/**41**:1/**42**:11:14^3/**43**:7:8^2:10:
11^2/**44**^{2}:12^2:13^4:14:15:16^2:17^3:18^2:19^4:20^2:24^2:
28/**46**:9^3:19,20^2/**47**:10:11:12:23/**48**:13:34/**Dan**
1:5:13:17:18,19/**2**:1^2:7:10:11:18^2/**3**:3:9:21:22:24
:25:26:27:28:30/**4**:7^2/**5**:2,3,4:5^3:8:8f:15:17:19:26
/**6**:4^3:5:6:12^2:13:16:22:24/**7**:12:27/**8**:23:25/**9**:24
:26/**10**:7/**11**:14:30,31f:33/**12**:7/**Hos1**:11:4^2:23/
3:5^2/**4**:6:7^2:8:10^4:12^2:13^2:18:19^2/**5**:6^3:7^2:13:15^2/
7:4:7:8:9:13:14^2:15:16^2/**8**:1^2:4^2:7^2:11^2:12^2:13:14
/**9**:4:7:9:10:17^2/**10**:2:3:4^2:6/**11**:5:11/**12**:7/**13**:2^2:
3/**14**:7/**Joe1**:7:11/**2**:3:4^2:5:7^2:8:9^3:11:17^2:20/**3**:3^2
:8:19/**Amo1**:3:5f:9^2:13/**2**:1:4^2:6^2:7:8^3/**3**:12/**4**:2/
5:23/**6**:2:9/**7**:2/**8**:3/**9**:1^3:2^2:3^2:4^2:14^2:15/**Ob1**:5:
7:12/**Jon**:8:9,10^2:13:14^2:15/**3**:4,5:10/**Mic1**:4:7f:
15:16^2/**2**:5/**4**:2:3:12/**5**:1:6^2/**7**:1:3^2:9:14:16:17^5/
Nah1:10/**2**:5:8/**3**:2:12/**Hab1**:7^3:8^2:9:10^2:11^2:13^3
:15:16:17/**2**:3:5^2:8:11:13:18:19/**Zep1**:5^2:13^5/**2**:5
f:7:10^2/**3**:3:7^3:12:13^2:20/**Hag1**:1f:12:14,15/**Zec**:
4^2:5,6^3:19:21/**2**:4:11,12/**3**:2:5,6/**4**:14/**5**:9:10/**6**:5
:7:10,11^2/**7**:3^2:11:12:13^2/**8**:7:8:13:19/**9**:2:14:15^3
:16,17^2/**10**:2:5^2:7^2:9^2:11:12^4/**11**:6^2:8:12:13/**12**:3
:6:10^2/**13**:3:9^2/**14**:12:13:19/**Mal1**:11/**3**:3:11:17/
4:1/**Mt2**:5:7:11^2:12^2:13:18:22/**3**:1:6:10/**4**:6:
15,16:18:20:22:24/**5**:4:6:7:8:9:10:15,16/**6**:2^2:5:
16:19:20:25:26^3:28:29:31,32/**7**:6:16:21^2/**8**:27:28^2
:29:32/**9**:4:8^2:24:28^2:30:31:33:36^2/**10**:15:25f:29:
40^2/**11**:1:20/**12**:1:2:4:10^2:15:23:24:27:41:46,47/
13:6^2:11:12,13f:14^2:15:16^3:28:41:51:56:57/**14**:
15:17:23,24:26^2:32:33:34/**15**:2^3:8:9:13,14:23:32:
34/**16**:5:7^2:8:12:14/**17**:2:8:9^2:11:14:16:22,23/**18**
:20/**19**:3:7:13:25/**20**:7:10^3:11,12:18^2:19:22:24:
30^2:31:32,33^2:34/**21**:10:15:16:25^2:27:31:37:38:
39:45:46^2/**22**:10:15:16:18:19:21:22:34,35^2:42:46
/**23**:2:3^3:4^2:5^2:6:7:29,30/**24**:17:22:31/**25**:5,6^2:10
:11:44:46/**26**:5:8,9:10:15:26:30^2:48:60,61:65,66:
67/**27**:1f:2:4:6:7:9:13:15:22:23:27:28:29:30:31:
32^2:33:36:37:41,42,43:53:54:65:66/**28**:4:9^2:
12,13:15:16:17/**Mk1**:5:16:18:20:22:27^2:29,30^2:
34/**2**:4^2:5:6:12^2:15:16:17:19:20:22:24:25,26/**3**:2:
4:11:13:21^2:23:30:31,32/**4**:7:10:11,12^2:17^2:33:33
f:36:38:41/**5**:1:14:15^2:20:38:40/**6**:2,3^2:6:12:13:
29:30^3:31:32:33:34^2:37:38:42:48:49^2:50:51:52^2:
53^2:56/**7**:3:4^3:5:6,7^2:23:36:37^2/**8**:1:3:5:8,9:11^2:
14:15:16:17:19:20:22:24:27^2/**9**:6:8:9^2:10:11:
12,13:14:18:20:28:30,31:32:33^3:34^2/**10**:2:4:8:10:
14:26:32^3:34:35:37:39:41:46^2:49^2/**11**:1:4,5:6:12:
15:18:19:20:27,28:31:33/**12**:6:7:8:12^4:13:16^2:17:
25^2:37:38^2:39:40^3:43,44/**14**:2:4,5^2:7:11:18:19:22
:23:26:32:40^2:45:56:59:65^3/**15**:10:13:14:18:19:
20^2:22:24:29,30^2:31:32:41/**16**:1:3^2:4^2:5:10,11:12
:13^2:14:17:17f:18^3:20/**Lk1**:7^2:10:22:36:59:61:62
/**2**:6:9:14:16:20:39:41,42:43:44^2:45^2:46,47:50/**3**:
3/**4**:6,7:22:29:41:42^2/**5**:6:11^2:18,19^2:22:26:33:35
:39/**6**:1:7:13:17,18^2:19^2:24:25:35:37/**7**:4^3:6,7,8^2:
10:16:18:20,21,22:24:27:29:30:32:36:47/**8**:10:13^2
:14:15:16:19:20:22:23:24^2:25:26:30:31:32:33^2:34
:40:43,44:51:53:56/**9**:6:10:12:13:15:19:31^2:32:36^2
:37:40:43^2:45:53^2:56:57/**10**:17:30:34:38/**11**:13:
19^2:26:29,30:32:44:48:53,54^2/**12**:1^2:3:4^2:24^2:27^2
:37:39^3/**13**:1:2^2:4/**14**:6:12:18:21:30/**16**:9f:28^2:29
:30^2:31^2/**17**:11^2:12:14:27:37/**18**:1:34:35/**19**:7:14
:15:25:29:30^2:32:33^2:35:36,37^2:38:40:41:48^2/**20**:
2:5:6:7:13:14:15:16:19^6:20:21:24:26:34,35:36^3:
40:46^3:47^2/**21**:4^2:7:24:26/**22**:2:5:9:13:24:25f:35:
38:49:54:63,64:65:70:71/**23**:2:5:7:11:18:21:23:
24:25:31:31f:34^2:35:37:48:56^3/**24**:1:3:4:8:11:14^2
:16:17:19:20:22,23:27:28:29:30:31:32:33,34:35^2:
36:37:41:42:43:52/**Jn1**:11,12:21:38:39:47/**2**:6:
20/**3**:19:20^4:21:26/**4**:9:25:27^2:40,41^2:42:45:52/**5**
:10:12:16:23:31:36:39/**6**:14:15:17:18,19^4:21^2:
22,23:24:25^2:28:30,31^2:34:42:45:48-51:52:58/**7**:
3:15^2:25:26:31:32:35:45:46:49:52/**8**:4:6^2:7:19:25
:27:33:39:41/**9**:9:10:11:12:13:18:22,23:24:26:28:
34^2:39^2/**10**:4^2:5^2:12:14:16:27:28:33:39:41/**11**:8:
17^2:31^2:34:36:37,38:41:42:47:55:56^3:57/**12**:9:16:
18:22:26:39:40:43/**14**:29^2/**15**:20^4:21:22^2:24^3:25
/**16**:2:3:4:19/**17**:6^3:7:8^2:9:10^2:11:13:14:16:21^2:
24/**18**:3:4,5:6:7:13:18:21:28^2:30:31:40/**19**:3:7:15
:17:18:23,24^3:25:31:33^3:36,37^2:40:42/**20**:2^2:13^2:
20:23^2:25/**Act1**:3:6:7:10:12^2:13:19:24,25^2:26/**2**:
2:4:6:7:12^2:13:18:37:42:46/**3**:2^2:4:10^2:11/**4**:1:3:
11:13^2:14:15:16^2:17:18:21:23:28:31^2/**5**:9:12:21^2:
22:24:25:26,27^2:38:41:42/**6**:1:2:5:9:11^2:14/**7**:13^2
:21:25:40:41^2:44:52:57/**8**:2f:7:12:14:15^2:16:17:
19:36^2:38:39/**9**:7:21:24:26^2:28:30:35:38^2:39/**10**:
9,10:14:22:24:27:46,47^2/**11**:3:18^2:22:30/**12**:10^2:
15^4:16:25/**13**:4:5:6,7^3:14:27^2:28:29:40:42:45:48:
51/**14**:3:5,6:8^2:11:12:14:21:22^3:23:24:26^2:27:28/
15:1^2:4:7:13:23:24:30:31:33:36^2:39/**16**:1:3:4:6:7:
8:17:19:20,21^2:23^2:31:32:36:37^3:38:39:40/**17**:1:5
:6^3:7^2:8,9:10:11^2:13:19^2:27:32/**18**:2,3^2:13:20:
25,26:27/**19**:2:3:5^2:6:12:13:15:16:28:32:34:39:41
/**20**:4:10,11,12:18:37^2:38/**21**:6:20^2:20f:22:26,27:
29:31:32:35/**22**:2:19:20^2:22:23:25:29/**23**:9:10:
12,13:14^2:15:20:21^2:27:32:33^2/**24**:13:14:19:24/
25:3:7:17:18/**26**:5^2:7:10:18^2:26:31^2/**27**:13:14,15^3
:17f:17:19^2:28^2:29^3:30:39^2:40^2/**28**:6^2:14:18:21:
22:25^2:28,29/**Rom1**:5:20^2:20f:21^3:22:23:24:25^3:
27:28:30:31:32^2/**2**:1:10:12-15^6/**3**:2:3:5:13:15:16^2
:17:18:19:26:30/**4**:4,5:12:17^2/**5**:3^2:14:18/**8**:22/**9**
:7:10-13:16:19:30:32^2/**10**:2:3^2:4^2:12:14^5:15:18^2:
19^2:21/**11**:2,3^2:7:8^2:10:15:20:28:31/**12**:13:15/**13**
:6/**14**:1f:2:4^4/**15**:12:27^6:27f/**16**:3:4:7:18/**1Co1**:
12^2:18:19:22^2/**2**:7:8^2:14/**4**:19/**6**:12/**7**:5^2:12:16:
25:29f/**8**:7^2/**9**:10:20:22^2/**10**:3,4:3,4f:6:7:9:11:32:
33/**12**:3^2:12:25:28/**13**:10/**14**:2:5:8:11:16^2:21:27^2
:28^2:29,30:34^2:34f^2:35/**15**:11:16:35:42:43^4:44^3/
16:15^2:17:18^2/**2Co3**:3:6:14:15^2/**4**:8/**5**:11:12:16/
6:8^2:16/**8**:2^2:3^4:4^2:5:6:14/**9**:11:12:13:14/**10**:12^2/
11:5:8,9:12:13^2:15:16:18:19,20:21:22^6:23^2/**12**:4:
18/**Gal1**:23:24/**2**:2:3^2:4:7,8,9^2:10:13:14^2/**3**:19^2/
4:3:17:18/**6**:12^3:13^2/**Eph2**:3:11^2/**3**:6:13/**4**:17,18^4
:19^2/**5**:13^2/**6**:9/**Php1**:14:15^2:16,17^2:28/**2**:4/**3**:19^3
/**4**:3^2:18/**Col2**:17:18^4:19:23^2/**3**:21:22/**4**:2:11/
1Th1:9:10/**2**:14:15^4/**5**:13/**2Th1**:9:12/**2**:3:10^2/
1Ti1:7^2:9^2:16:19^2:20/**2**:9,10:15/**3**:8:9:10^4:11:12/
4:3/**5**:4:5:6:8:11:12^2:13/**6**:2:3:18:19^2:21/**2Ti2**:7:
18^2:24:25:26^2/**3**:2:3^3:4^2:5^3:6:7:8:9:13:14/**4**:2:3:4:
8:16/**Tit1**:1:6:7^3:8^3:9^3:12:16^4/**2**:2:3^3:9:10/**3**:2:3:
13^2/**Phm1**:6/**Heb**:11^2/**3**:7,8:9:10:12:15:16:18:
19^2/**4**:2^2:5^2:6/**5**:1/**6**:18^2/**8**:9:10^3/**9**:6:15/**10**:1:2:
16^3:38/**11**:3:13^3:14^2:15^2:16^2:22:23^3:29^2:31:33:34^2
:35:37,38^2:39/**12**:9:10:20:25/**13**:3:7:17^2/**Jas1**:
10,11/**2**:7:19/**5**:11^3:14/**1Pe1**:10^2:11^2:12:23/**2**:8^3
:11^2:12^2:18^3/**3**:1^2:14:16/**4**:4^2:5^3:6/**2Pe1**:19/**2**:1:
12^3:12f:12^2:13^4:14^3:15:17^2:18^2:19/**3**:3:5,6:15,16^2
/**1Jn2**:16:19^4/**3**:1:6^3:24/**4**:5:7^2/**5**:6,7,8/**2Jn1**:4^2
/**3Jn**:6:7^2:10:11^2/**Jud**:4:10^3:11^3:12^5:13^2:15^2:16^3:
19^3:24,25^2/**Rev2**:2^2:9^3:22:24,25:27/**3**:4^2:9f:9^2/**4**:
8:11/**5**:9:10:12/**6**:8:10:11:16/**7**:10:12:13:14:15:
16^2/**8**:2/**9**:4:5:6:7:9:10:15^2:16:20:21/**11**:2:6^3:7:
11:12/**12**:11^2:17/**13**:4^3/**14**:4f^2:4:5:10:11^2:12:13^2:
18/**15**:3,4/**16**:3:4:9^2:11:16:21/**17**:10:12:13:14:17
/**18**:9:10:14^2:18:19/**20**:4^2:6:9:10:11/**21**:3:25/**22**:
4:5

6039

THIS

Gen1:7,8:13:19:31/**2**:2:3:16,17:23:24/**3**:14:20f/
4:5:11:26f/**5**:1f:3,4,5f:28-31/**6**:1/**8**:11:12/**9**^{2}/**11**:
3,4:6:6f:32f/**12**:6:7:11,12,13:18/**13**:8:10:13/**14**:
19,20/**15**:1:7:16:18^2/**16**:2,3:5^2:9-12:16/**17**:7,8^2:
9,10:11^2:12^3:21/**18**:1:3,4:32/**19**:9:12:31/**20**:9,10^5
:11,12:16/**21**:6:11:22:26:30/**22**:14:20-23/**23**:4:8:
17,18/**24**:7:8:13:14:15,16:38:42^3:43:49:52:58:60
/**25**:19:22:30/**26**:3^2:5:10:11:20:27:33/**27**:38f:43/
28:4:15:16,17:20^2:22/**29**:9:25^2/**30**:14f/**31**:9:13:
26^2:28:47,48^2:49:51,52^2/**32**:4:10f/**34**:4:18,19:23^2
:30/**35**:8:20/**36**:24/**37**:6:10^2:11:21,22:32/**38**:1:
11:25^2/**39**:1:3:7:9:14,15/**40**:15/**41**:5:22:24:40:49
:50:52/**42**:15^2:20^2:21:28:33/**43**:10:11:16:29/**44**:
4:18:34/**45**:5:8/**46**:27:34/**47**:29/**48**:1:4:14:15:18
:20/**50**:16,17:20:24/**Ex1**:1:8f:10/**2**:1:5:6:9:12/**3**^{2}
:15f:15:16/**5**:1:6:15:22^2/**6**:30/**7**:7:14:17/**8**:18:19:
23:26/**9**:14:18:20:28:29:34/**10**:6:17^2/**11**:9/**12**:2:
3,4^3:5:6:11:14^3:15:17^2:24:26^2:42:47/**13**:2:4,5:9:
14:16/**14**:4:5:12/**15**:1:21/**16**:3:4:6:22:25:32:34/
17:14/**18**^{2}:18:23:24/**20**:1:20/**22**:15/**23**:7:12:15/
24:8/**25**:1:9:17/**26**:12:14:30:32:33:37/**27**:21^2/**28**
:4:16:28:29:32:37,38^2:39:43/**29**:1:22:28:35^2:37:
42/**30**:8:10^2:14:16:25:26,27:31:36/**31**:14,15:16/
32:1:4:8:12:13:23:24/**33**:1:13^2:15:21/**34**:7:10:30
/**35**:4/**36**:38/**37**:1:15,16:27/**38**:2:21/**39**:1:2:6,7:
21:25,26:28,29/**40**:38/**Lev1**:15,16,17/**2**:8/**3**:
15,16:17/**4**:20:21:24:25/**5**:9:12:13^2:17,18/**6**:16:
17^2:22,23^2:25:27:29/**7**:6:9:13:14:34:35/**8**:27:29:
35/**9**/**10**:3:8,9:15:16:19/**11**:4-7:41,42/**13**:3:
21:35:39:40:41/**14**:13:14:51,52:53:57/**15**:3:24:
31:32/**16**:29,30^3:31:32:34/**17**:5:6:7/**18**:14f:23:25
:29,30/**20**:21/**21**:11f:23/**22**:8:10:13:16:25^2/**23**:5:
6:7:13:14^2:17^2:21:30,31:32^2:39^2:41:43/**24**:5-8:
15,16/**25**:14,15,16/**26**:16:23/**27**:8:31/**Num1**:
17,18,19f:47,48,49/**3**:4:10/**4**:3:10:15:17,18,19:
37:49/**5**:3:19:29/**6**:18:22,23:27/**8**:3:7:14:15/**9**:
2,3^2:9:18/**10**:8:11f:13/**11**:4,5:6:11:14:15^2/**12**:11
/**13**:16:27/**14**:3:14^2:19:23:29:32:33:34,35/**15**:7:
10:15,16,17,18:19,20,21:29:37,38:39/**16**:6,7:10:
13:28/**17**:5:10^2/**18**:5:19:23:27:28,29/**19**:10:12:
19:21/**20**:4:5:10:13/**21**:5:14:16:17,18^2:27-30/**22**
:4:15:16,17:30/**23**:7-10/**24**:3-9:15-19^2:21,22:
23,24/**25**:7/**26**:5-11^2:12-14:15-18:19-22^2:23-25:
26,27:38-41:42,43:44-47:48-50:64,65/**27**:8:21/
28:6:13:14:15:24/**29**:7:11:17/**31**:4,5:21:29:30:50
:51,52/**32**:3,4:5:8:14:15^2:19:32/**33**:1:38,39/**34**:
13/**35**:33/**36**:3:6:7:9/**Deu1**:1^2:14:19,20,21:23/**2**:
7:14,15/**3**:23,24,25/**4**:19:20:21,22:23:32:39:
44,45,46/**5**:5:12:14:16:25/**6**:23/**7**:19/**9**:4:6:7:
13,14/**10**:5/**11**:4/**12**:15:18/**13**:11/**14**:23^2/**15**:3:
4,5^2:10:11:15:21/**16**:3:12:14:15/**17**:7:12:20/**18**:
16:22/**19**:9:10:19:21/**20**:5:9:17:18/**21**:7:8:9:20:
21^2/**22**:5:16:22:25,26,27^2/**23**:4/**24**:18:22/**25**:7:9
:19/**26**:2,3:9^2:19/**27**:11/**28**:9:58,59:61:62:67/**29**:
9:14,15:19:20:21^2:24:27^2/**30**:10:18/**31**:13:19:21^2
:24:26:30/**32**:6:44,45/**33**:1:17/**Jos1**:16/**2**:12,13^2
:17,18^2:19:20/**4**:6:7:9:19:22:24/**5**:2,3^2:4,5:8,9:15
/**6**:12,13,14:15:26f/**7**:1:5:12:13:26/**8**:2:5:33/**9**:
12:23:24:27^2/**10**:13:25:42/**11**:6:18:21/**12**:2:7/**13**
:2-7:8:13:25/**15**:2,3,4:18,19,20:63/**16**:1/**18**:14:
20/**19**:35-39:47,48:51/**20**:8/**21**:43/**22**:14:21:28:
30/**23**:1:13:15,16/**24**:15:27:29/**Ju1**:7:24f:25:29/
2:1:2:15^2/**3**:16/**5**:1/**6**:8:13:26:29:37:39/**7**:12,13^2
/**8**:9^2:10:27f/**9**:7:41:47,48/**10**:6:7,8:9/**11**:4:16:26
/**12**:1/**13**:17:23/**14**:14:15/**15**:6/**16**:5:18^2/**17**:
10,11/**18**:23:28:30/**19**:1:8:10:12,13:24^2:30/**20**:
8,9,10:11/**21**:3:18/**Ru1**:11f/**2**:3:7:22/**3**:15-18/**4**:
7:11:12:14:18-22/**1Sa1**:1:11:11f:19,20f:27/**2**:1:
13,14:20:23,24,25:27/**4**:7:12f:21,22/**5**:4:5/**6**:9:
20/**8**:18/**9**:6:12,13:16/**10**:1:12f:18,19:24:27/**11**:
1:7/**12**:8:17/**13**:1:11/**14**:8:29:44/**16**:6:7:8:9:12/
17:8^2:11:17:18:26^2:32:36^2:37:41,42:55:55f^2/**18**:7
:8:10:11,12:15,16:24/**20**:2:5:8:12:17:21:30f:30/
21:5:14,15/**22**:15^2/**24**:9,10:11/**25**:2:5:8:10^2:21:
24/**26**:8:16:19/**27**:6:11/**28**:18/**29**:3:5:8/**30**:24:
25/**2Sa2**:5/**3**:7:8^2:14:28:35,36/**6**:7:8:12:22/**7**:2:8
:10,11:27/**8**:1/**10**:7,8:18/**12**:1:9:10:11f:12:13/**13**
:6:12:12f:17,18:21-24:28:32,33/**14**:9:13:22/**15**:3:
6/**16**:9:11:17/**17**:5:7/**18**:5:14/**19**:5:22:42/**21**:3/
22:1/**23**:17:24-39f/**24**:3f:10:13:14/**1Ki1**:2:27/**2**:
1:4:23,24^3:29:31:45/**3**:17,18/**4**:8-19:20/**5**:6:8:14
/**6**:1:11,12:20^2/**7**:8:48/**8**:2:8:12,13:17:20:26:27:
29^2:30:33,34:35,36:38:40^2:41,42:43:44:48^3:
54,55^2/**9**:2,3:7^2:8^3:9:13:22/**11**:9,10:12,13:
16,17,18:27,28:38/**12**:5:15:19:20f:22:30:32,33f/
13:3^2:4:5:8:34/**14**:7:10:13:15/**15**:18:30/**16**:1:10:
12:26:34/**17**:12:20:21/**18**:17:24:33:36/**19**:2^2/**20**:
2,3:5,6:7:9f:10:12:13:24:26:28^2:33:39/**21**:2:9f:19^2
:29/**22**:14:18:19:27/**2Ki1**:4,5^2:6:7:13:16^2:17/**2**:
19/**3**:1f:6,7,8:16:17:18/**4**:9:15,16:23:35:40:43/**5**:
6:7:8:18:20:26:27/**6**:10:19:26-30^2:31:32:33^2/**7**:1:
9^2:17/**8**:5:6:22/**9**:1:25:34/**10**:2,3:4:5:6^2:9,10:11f:
29:30/**11**:2,3f/**12**:17/**13**:16,17,23/**14**:7/**15**:1:5:
32,33/**16**:1:6/**17**:1:4:7:23:34:41/**18**:1:14:15:19:
25:31,32^2/**19**:2:3:9:15:16:20:21:25:29^2:31:32:34
/**20**:6:11:11f:17:19/**21**:7:8:11/**22**:5,6:12,13:
15,16^2:18,19:20^2/**23**:23/**25**:27/**1Ch3**:9/**5**:26/**6**:
54/**7**:25,26,27/**9**:20/**11**:17/**12**:38/**15**:2/**16**:4:5:7:
38/**17**:4:16:23:24:25:26:27/**18**:13/**19**:8:17,18/
20:3f/**21**:3:8:13:22/**22**:14:17/**23**:1:3:27/**24**:7-18
/**25**:6,7/**28**:8:19/**29**:3:4,5:9:11:16:17/**2Ch1**:9:10
/**2**:2/**3**:8:14/**4**:3:12-16/**5**:3:9/**6**:1:7:12,13:17:18:
20,21^4:22:24:25:26:27:31f:32:33:34^2:37,38^2:40:
41/**7**:4,5:12:15:16:20^2:21^2:22/**8**:3:6/**10**:18:19/
11:17:19/**12**:1:6/**14**:11^2/**15**:8:13:15/**16**:2:10/**17**:
7,8,9/**18**:25:26/**19**:10/**20**:3:5:7^2:8:9^3:12:15:27/
21:10:12:18/**22**:7^2/**23**:4/**24**:11/**25**:7:9:14:15:16:
18:27/**26**:17,18^2/**28**:13:19f:22/**29**:9:17:25,26/**30**
:2,3:4:9:17,18,19:24:26/**31**:9:10:16:20/**32**:1:6:8:
9/**33**:7:8:14:18:19/**34**:5:7:21:24:25:26^2:27:28^2:
32/**35**:3:17:18:19:21:24,25/**36**:22,23^2/**Ez1**:1:3/
2:59:60/**3**:6:7:11/**4**:3:4,5:12:13:14^2:15:16^2:17:23
/**5**:3:9:12:17/**6**:2:3:6:11:12^3/**7**:10:11:21/**9**:3:4:10
:12:14/**10**:1:2:13^2:15:16-19/**Neh1**:4/**2**:7:17:19:
20^2/**4**:1:23/**5**:1:6:7:10:11:13:15:17/**6**:3:5,6/**7**:5/
8:9:11:17/**9**:1:5:18:26:36:37:38^2/**10**:29/**11**:1:2/
12:35,36/**13**:3:4:7:14:18^2:21:22:26:27/**Est1**:1:8:
13-15:18:20:21/**2**:4:7:23/**3**:7^2:9:14/**4**:13:14^2/**5**:
7,8:13:14^2/**6**:3:9:11/**7**:6/**8**:8f:11:12:12f:13/**9**:17:
19:22:23:26:27:29-31/**Job1**:5:14,15:16:17:22/**2**:
9:10/**3**/**4**:6:12:16/**5**:8:27/**6**:10/**7**:15/**8**:2/**10**:19/
11:2^2/**13**:3:11:15:16:18:19/**14**:14/**15**:2:12:17-19^2
:27,28:32/**16**:2/**17**:3,4/**18**:4/**19**:26^2/**20**:29/**21**:
14/**23**:4,5/**27**:13/**28**:28/**30**:12/**31**:28:35/**32**:
11,12/**33**:12:31:32/**34**:12:18/**35**:7:12/**36**:15:19:

(THIS Con't)
1/38/Ps2:3:6:7:7f/4:3/9:17/10:13/17:6/18:1:
24:49/22:8[2]:16/24:8:10/26:2:8/30:6,7/31:3/34:
6:9/38:17/40:7f:10/42:3:6/44:1:17/48:14/49:
20f/50:22:23/51:2:4:6/52:1/53:4/55:8:20/56:9/
57:1/60:2/62:3,4/63:1/68:9,10/69:14/71:18/72
:6:20/73:16:21/74:9,10/77:10/78:7:54:56/79:
10/80:14:15/83:5/85:1/87:5/89:46/91:2/92:6:
15/94:12,13/98:2,3/99:4/100:3/102:2:18/105:
10,11:12:45/106:17:31/109:20/112:10/116:5:7
/118:23:24:27,28[2]/119:40,41,42:56:168/122:6:8
/130:3,4/132:14[2]:15/133:3/137:9f/139:6/143:
11/149:4,5/Pro4:5:11/6:5:29/7:8,9:14f[2]/11:7/
16:11/17:8f/18:19f/19:11/22:17,18,19/24:
15,16:32,33/25:21,22/27:20/29:13/Ecc1:16-18
/2:1:10:18:20-23:24-26/3:10:14[2]/4:4:8/5:9:16/
6:2/7:14:15-17:27,28[2]/8:14:15/9:1/12:13/Sol1:
1/3:3:6/5:9/6:10/8:5/Is1:18/2:1:9/3:6/5:14/6:
7:9/7:7:8f:10[2]:14f[4]:15,16:15,16f:20/8:4[2]:7,8/9:7
:13:18:21/10:5,6/13:1:3[2]/14:8:16:17:21:24:26:
28/16:6:13,14/17:1:14/18:2:4/19:1:20/20:5,6/
21:1:5f:6,7:11:13/22:1:2:9,10,11:14:15,16[2]/23:1:
7:8:11/25:9/26:1:19/27:2/28:9:13/30:8:10,11:
12:15:21/31:4,5/33:14:18/34:10/35:3/36:10:11
f:12[2]:17:18:20/37:3[2]:4:6:8,9[3]:10:14:16,17:21[2]:26[3]
:30[3]:32:34/38:1[3]:2:6:9:11:15:17/39:1f:2:5/41:2:
20:26[2]:28/43:26/44:9:20[2]:23:28f/45:1:3:4/46:8
/48:14:15:16/49:5/51:12:21:22/52:5:13f[2]/54:9:
17[2]/55:8:13/56:3:4:12/57:6:7,8:15/58:4:5[3]/59:9
:21/60/63:1[2]/64:12/65:1f[2]/66:7,8/Jer1:14:16/
2:2:10,11:17:21[3]:25:26,27/3:6:10:19/4:18:21/5:
9[2]:14[2]:19:20:25:29:30/6:1:6:8:11:12:18,19[2]:27/7
:2[2]:7:13,14[4]:20:28:29/8:3:4,5:9/9:7:9[2]:12:15:22:
24[2]/10:11:18:25/11:6[2]:7:14:19/12:1:4:14/13:3:
8,9:10[2]:12:13:22:24,25/14:1:11:17:22/15:12,13:
19/16:3:6:9:11:13:14,15/17:15:20:21,22:25[2]/18:
6/19:3:4[3]:6:11[4]:12:14:15/21:3,4:6:10:13/22:2:4:
5[2]:6:8:11:16:18:26:28:30:30f/23:5,6:15:16:26:
30,31:34:36:38,39f:38,39/24:1:8/25:1[2]:5[2]:8,9:11
:12f:13:15:18:26:27/26:1:6:9:11[2]:12[2]:15:16:18[2]:
19/27:1:4:15:17/28:6:12:14:16/29:3:4:10:21:24:
24f:26:27:30:31/30:1:3:4:21f/31:10:29:33:33f:35
/32:2:6,7:14:15:20:22:23:26:28:31:36:37:41:43/
33:1:2:4:5:9:10,11[2]:12:19:25,26/34:1:2[2]:4:5:7:8:
14:22/35:1:1f:4:11:12/36:1:9:10:29[2]:30:32/37:6:
8:10:18/38:4[2]:18:23:24/39:16[2]/40:2,3[2]:15/42:9:
10:15/43:1:2,3:10/44:1:4:6:10:12:29/45:1:1f:2:4[2]
/46:2:7:10:13:16/47:1/48/49:2:12:14:20:28/50:
1:39/51:11:14:26f:47:59:59f[2]:64/Lam2:15:16:20
:22/3:54/Eze1:4:15/2:3/3:1:11:14,15f/4:7:10/5
:4:5,6,7/6:9:10/7:1/8:15:17/11:1:3f:7:7f:11:13:
18/12:3:6:8:9:17:23[2]:26/13:1:7/14:2:12:13/15:1
:5,6/16:37:58:61/17:1:2:7:9:11:12,13:20/18:2:3:
4:14/19:1:14/20:2:4:29:35,36f:45/21:1:8:
9,10,11:14:18:23[2]:28/22:11:17/23:16f:30/24:2:3
:18:19/25:14:17/26/27:1:2:32/28:11:12f/29:1:
17:18/30:9:20:21f/31:1:8:18/32:1:33/33:23/34:1:
30/36:1:14:16:32[2]:35/37:16[2]:23/38:15,16/39:1:
19/40:5:7-12:13:17:18:19:28:36/41:4:22[2]/42:2:
3/43:7:12[2]:14[2]:15:16:20:23:26/44:2:19/45:1:2:4
:8:13:17:19:20:23/46:3:14,15/47:4:8:9[2]:15f/48:9
:14:21,22[2]/Dan1:13:21/2:11:12:23:26:28:30:39:
41,42:43[2]:45:47/3:4:29[2]/4:1:17[2]:19:25:26:29:30:
31[2]:33/5:10:11:11f:12:22:24,25:26:31f/6:4:8:14[2]
:25,26/7:1:8:21:23:26/8:2:2f:5[2]:9f:12:15:22:26/
9:2f:25f[2]:26:27[2]/10:1:2:7:8:14:15/11:5:6f:10,11:
12:17:18:21f:24:30,31f:35:40f/12:4:8/Hos1:2:6:
8:16f/3:4/4:12f:18f/5:1:9/8:5[2]:6/9:3:4/10:6[3]/
11:9/Joe1:1:15/2:11:17:26:27/3:8:9/Amo1:2[2]/2
:11/3:1:7:13/5:1:16/6:8:11/7:1:2:6:7:10:16:17[2]/
8:2/9:8/Ob1:1/Jon:1:2:5:6:7:8:9,10:12:14[2]/3:7/
4:1:2:4:6:8/Mic1:5/2:8:10/3:5/4:4:10/6:8/Nah
1:1:11:13:15/2:1f/3:4:8f/Hab1:1:3:11f:12:17/2:
4/3:1:2:16:19/Zep1:1f[2]/2:15/Hag1:3,4/2:1:2:7f[2]
:7[2]:8,9:8,9f:10:11:18,19[2]:18,19f:18,19[3]/Zec1:12[2]
:14/2:4:8f/3:2f:9[2]/4:4:6:7:9:10/5:3:4/6:15[2]/7:4:
7:8,9:11/8:6:14,15/9:1/11:5:8:13:15:16[2]:17/12:
1/13:6f[2]:8f/14:15/Mal1:2,3:8:10/2:1:4:12/Mt1
:20:22/2:5:7:9:15:17:23/3:14:17/4:14/7:12:12f/
8:8,9:10:11[2]:17:27/9:3:5,6:8:9f:13:18:26:33/10:
18:25f/11:6:16:25:26/12:7:11:17:31,32:36:41:42
:43,44,45/13:2,3:14:22:33:40:55/14:2:22/15:33
/16:4:7:17[2]:18:22/17:5:6:20:21:21f/18:4:5:11f:
18:19/19:1:9:9f:11:16:22:25/21:4:10:21[2]:28:32:
33:38:44:44f/22:16:20:26:38,39/23:36:39/24:3:
6:8:34:34f:36f/25:21:23:28/26:1:12:13:26:28:29:
34:39:42:56:60,61:71:72/27:9:16:19:24:37:54:66
f/28:15:20/Mk1:3:3f:4:8f[2]:15:27/2:7:8:9,10,11:
12:15:18/3:4:30/4:13:19:24:31,32:41/5:3,4:9:
31:39/6:35,36:37:45/7:4[2]:10:12,13:19/8:1:10:12
:12f:33/9:5:6:7:21:25:29:37:41/10:1f:21:24/11:
22,23[2]:26,f:27,28/12:10:11:12:16:23:34:35:37:
38:40/13:3,4:7:9:21:30f:35,36,37/14:4,5:9[2]:14:
22:24:24f:36:44f:48:58:60:61:68f:71/15:10:11:
12:38f:39:42,43/16:7/Lk1:3:18:19:43:45:66:67:
78/2:1:2:3:5:15[2]:17:34,35[2]:48/3:15:19,20/4:3:
22[2]:36/5:6:14:21[2]:23,24:36/6:4:11/7:6,7,8:9:
20,21,22:24:39[2]:41:44:49/8:4:6:8[2]:11:17:25:29:
43,44f:53/9:7:9:12:13:21:27:33:34:35:38:43:48/
10:13f:25:28/11:2:5,6f:5,6:7:8:19:29,30:31:32[2]:
37,38:49:50/12:8:33/13:1:6:16:17:30/14:7:9:10[2]
:15:16/15:2:3,4:10:13:24:30/16:1:2:8:9:9f[2]:14:28
:31f/17:16:18:21:22:23:25:37f/18:4,5:9:11:14:18
:23:26/19:9,10[3]:28/20:9:14[2]:19:24:28:37,38/21:
3:12:23[2]:29:32:32f:34,35/22:15[2]:17:19:20:20f:21
:25:37:41,42[2]:47:47f:48:53:56:59:66/23:2:14[2]:15
:31:31f:38:40,41:43:47:54/24:21:22,23:28:47:49f
/Jn1:4:13:15:28:34:50[2]/2:7,8:10:11:17:18:19[2]:
20:21:22/3:1:3:5:5f[2]:8:19:23,24:33,34:35/4:9:11[2]
:12:13:15:21-24:28,29:46,47:54/5:9:20:40:45/6:
1:8,9:27:29:39:42:47:48-51[2]:52:53:58:59:60:61:
63[2]:66/7:1:4:8f:19:21,22,23:24:25:27:31:32:35:
40[2]:49f/8:4:14:23:50:51:54/9:2:8:14:16:17:19:
20:22,23:25:29:33/10:6:18:21:22,23f:41/11:4:15
:26:37,38:47:50:51/12:16:18:28:31f:31:33:38:41:
46/13:1:6:18:19:23f:24:32/14:2,3:9:12,13:24:30
/15:8:11:25/16:3:5f:11:15:17,18:24:25:26f:30:31
:33/17:3:16/18:2:9:21:29:32:32f:34f[4]:40/19:8:
12:23,24:35:36,37/20:26:30,31/21:1:14:17:19:
21f/Act1:12:15[2]:16:20:26/2:1f:4:7:12:16:24:36:
38/3:12[2]:13:14:15:16[2]/4:7:10:21:24:27:31/5:2:3
:4:9:20:24[2]:28[2]:33/6:3:5:12:14:15/7:2:7:19:24:
26:29:38:40:41:44:45:60/8:9,10,11f:18[2]:19:21:
22:32:35/9:3:13:21:37:39/10:3:18:28:30:36,37/
11:10:18:21:27:28:30/12:3:10/13:15:17:26:31:
32,33[2]:32,33f:34:36:38:46:47:48/15:2[2]:6:15[2]:22:
23:27,28,29:39/16:3:10f:18/17:19:23:27:29:32/
18:10:14:21f:27/19:5:10:13:14:20:25:26[2]:27[3]:28:
36/20:16/21:11:12:13:23:24:28/22:5:26/23:7:
10:17:18:22:25:27/24:3:4:10:16:21f:27/25:5:20:
24/26:7:16:21:29:31/27:4f:21:29/28:11:20:25:
28,29/Rom1:1:2:8:16[3]:17[2]:17f:19/2:4:16/3:4:8[2]:
21,22:25:26[2]:29[2]:31/4:1:6:9:10[2]:12:15:17:20:23/
5:2:5:9:13:15[2]:17[2]/6:15:19/7:8:23,24,25/8:2:11:
22:37/9:8:10-13[3]:17:20:22:30:33/10:12:17/11:
2,3:7:8[2]:9:11:13:25[2]:26:28/12:1:2/13:9:11/14:2:
5:9:19:22/15:15,16:18:19:27[2]:28[2]/16:17:19:22:
25,26,27[2]/1Co1:7:9[2]:18:20:25/2:5:6:7/3:4:18[2]:
19:21/4:3[2]:11:17/5:2:3,4:5:6:7[2]:10:13/6:18[2]/7:5
:10:17:19:25:27[2]:35:40/8:1:7:10[2]:13/9:3:9:10:12
:15:17:18:19:23:25/10:2:5:6:12:13[2]:16[2]:28:29/
11:10f:13:16[2]:19:22:23:24[3]:25[2]:26[3]:27[2]/12:8:24:
25/13:11/14:20:31/15:1:2:8:12:19:21:26:27:32:
40f:50:51:54[2]:57/16:2:7:21/2Co1:1:3,4[2]:6,7:21:
23/2:10:16/3:12:14/4:1:4:7[2]:11:17/5:1:5:9[2]:11[2]:
12:19/6:1/7:3:11:16/8:6:8:10:11:14:15:19[2]:20:
21:22/9:1:2:3:6:13/10:9:11:13/11:10:16:23:28/
12:1:7:11:13:19[2]/13:1[3]:2:10/Gal1:4:16:20[2]:21/2
:1:20/3:2:7:8,9[2]:12:14[2]:17:18:19[2]/4:1:20[2]:24,25[2]
/5:2:14:22/6:3:16/Eph1:1:5:10:12:14:21/2:17:
22/3:2,3[2]:4:5:6:7:8:18,19/4:8:9:17,18:24/5:5[2]:9:
32/6:1:2:3:12:14:20:22/Php1:11:12:19:28:30/2:
9:18[2]:27/3:1:13:19/4:7:8[2]:15/Col1:7:21:22:23:
26,27[2]:29/2:2:4:14:15:20:23/3:3:7:10:11:12:15/
4:8:16/1Th2:13/3/4:1:6[3]:11:15:18/5:1:18:24:27
/2Th1:5:12/2:1[2]:5:7:8:9/3:1:10:14:17/1Ti1:6:20
/2:2:3:4:6:7[2]/4:6:8:9,10/5:4:7:11:16:21:23/6:1:
19/2Ti1:6:8:10/2:11/3:1:9/4:6:10/Tit1:3[2]:10[2]:
13/2:10:12/3:8:9/Phm1:15:19:20:21/Heb:5,6f/
2:3:6:8:10:13/3:1:11/4:2:7:8:15/5:4:7f:9/6:19/7:1:
3f:4:5:17:22/8:1:9:10:13/9:1[2]:8:9:10:11[2]:15:20:
23:24:28/10:5:8:10:15:16:20:21:26:35/11:5:10:
11:13:15:37,38/12:27/13:2:13:14:17:22/Jas1:
7,8:9/2:19:25/3:10/4:4:11:15/5:18/1Pe1:10:11:
12:20:21:23/2:2,3:8:9:11:21/3:8:21f/4:12/5:1:
12[2]:13f/2Pe1:1:7:8:17,18/2:19/3:1:4:5,6:8/1Jn
1:2:4:5:9/2:1:8:15:16:17:18[2]:25/3:2:3:6:7:9:23:
24/4:4:5:9:10/5:5:6,7,8f[2]:10[2]:11:13:14:17f/2Jn1
:12/3Jn:9:11/Jud:4:5:14/Rev:1:3:7f:9:20:20f/2:
1:6:7:8[2]:12[2]:18[2]:20:24,25/3:1[2]:7[2]:9:10f:14[2]/5:2[2]
/6:4/7:4-8:9/9:1f:16f/11:15:15f/12:9/13:2:3:11:
15:18/14:3[2]:12:13/16:5[2]:9/17:18/18:1:18:21/
19:1:9[2]:16/20:5:14/21:5:8/22:6,7:9:18

3837

THOSE

[2]Gen4:20/6:4/7:2:8,9[2]:23/12:3[2]/19:5:9/26:15/
31:15/34:21/35:2/41:48:56,57/46:26/47/49:23
/Ex4:19/8:11/9:21/12:16:19:20:49/13:8/14:3/
15:7/16:18[2]/20:5:6/23:23/24:17/28:3/29:33:37
f/34:24/35:5-9:21/36:29/38:25,26/39:41/Lev6:
27/10:3/11:21,22:41,42/14:32:42/18:29,30/19:
10/20:25/22/23:42/26:17:36:39[2]/27:27/Num2:
3-31/7:24-29:30-35:48-53:60-65:66-71:78-83/
11:1/16:5:6,7:36,37:49/19:14/22:5,6[2]:32/27:3,4
/31:8/32:10,11/33:55/Deu3:21/4:30/5:9,10[2]:
22/7:9:10:20:21:23/8:2/9:1:10,11/12:15/19:5:
20/20:15/24:21/25:18/28:61:65/29:11:21/30:
7,8/32:38/33:11:20/Jos11:1:10:12:17/17:12/19
:15,16/23:4,5:13/Ju2:7-9:23/3:17,18,19/5:10[2]:
31/7:5,6/9:33/16:30[2]/17:6/20:27,28/21:15:25/
Ru4:7:12/1Sa1:11f/2:4[2]:5[2]:10:30[2]:33/3:1/5:12/
7:14:16/9:9,10,11:20/11:12/12:23/13:7:19/14:
6:48/22:2/25:29/30:5:24[2]/2Sa3:31/5:8/13:
17,18/14:14f:15,16/16:14/17:2,3:28,29/18:31/
19:6[2]:14:28/22:18[2]:27[2]:28:40:48/23:18,19:24-
24-39f/1Ki1:8/4:21:30/9:20,21/10:27/11:2/12:
31/13:24,25/14:10:11[2]:22/16:4-7[2]/19:17/21:24
/2Ki3:19/7:11/10:20,21:23/11:5:9/13:20,21/15
:37/17:30[2]/19:17:25:30/21:9:12:14/23:8:18:29/
1Ch9:22/16:4/26:4,5/27:23:29/28:1/2Ch1:5,6/
2:14/6:20,21/8:7,8/9:20/11:17/13:8/17:19/18:
27/19:2/20:10/23:8/26:6/28:15/29:31/31:1/32
:13/33:25/34:4/36:20/Ez1:4[2]/2:2:55,56,57/3:8
/7:10/8:22[2]/9:12/Neh1:5:11/2:16/4:1/6:17/7:
5/8:10/9:3:10/10:1/11:22,23/12:40,41/Est1:
3:8:13/6:9:11/7:4/9:11:16/Job3:8:20,21/4:3,4:6
:7,8/5:3/7:9/8:11-13:22/12:5[2]/17:9/18:21/19:
15:19/20:7/21:23,24:25/22:15,16/27:7:15/28:8
/29:7:13:23:25/30:1:25/31:2,3/32:7/34:28/35:
13/Ps1:1/2:12/6:5f/7:4:10/9[2]:12:13/10:3:16/
11:5/12:3,4/14:5/15:4/16:17/17:7/18:17:25[2]:26:
43,44,45:47/19:11/20:8/24:4/25:9:14/31:5,6[2]:
14,15:19[2]:23/32:1[2]:10:11[2]/33:18,19/34:10:18[2]:
21:22/35:1:4:10:15:19/36:10[2]/37:9:12,13:14:17:
22[2]/40:4[2]/41:1/42:4,5/44:7/47:4/49:14[2]/50:23
/52:7/58:6/61:5:6/63:9/64:8/65:4/68:18:30f/
69:4:6:14/70:4/72:10/73:1:16:27[2]/77:12/78:40
/79:11/81:15/84:4:5:11:12/85:9/86:17/87:4:6/
88:5:11/89:7:14,15:23/94:5:21,22/97:7:10/98:7
/101:6:7/103:8:11:13:17,18[2]/106:3:30:41,42/
109:16:19/111:5/112:9/115:8/118:7:20/119:21
:40,41,42:53:74:84:113:132:165/125:1:4/126:5/
128:3:4/129:8/135:18/139:21/140:12/143:3:12
/144:12-15/145:14:19:20/146:8/147:11[2]/Pro1:
5,6/3:18/5:17/8:20:21:36/9:15/10:13/11:20/12
:22[2]/13:14/14:21:22[2]:35/15:9,10/16:15:20:22/
17:5:15/18:21/22:14/24:11,12:25/28:3:5:10:26:
27/29:10/30:11,12/31:5:6,7:8/Ecc1:8-11/2:24-
24-26[2]/4:3/8:2,3:5:12/Sol4:1/7:9/8:12/Is1:15:
26:27:29/2:3/3:6/4:2,3,4/5:7f:17:18:21:22:26/7
:4/9:2/10:1:10:17:20/13:8:15/14:2[2]:19/15:9[2]/
17:14/19:8[2]:13:19:20/24:14:15,16/26:3:14:19[2]/
29:15:20:24/30:18/31:1:3/32:4:5:12[2]/33:15/34:
17/35:1:4:6/37:4:18/38:18f/42:3:7:17/44:9/47:
7:9/49:17:23:25/50:6/51:23/52:1:5:7/57:15[2]:20
/58:6:7[2]:10/59:3:8:9:20/61:2/63:11/64:4:5/65:
1f[2]:7:9:21,22:23:25/66:3:17:19:19f:21:24/Jer2:3
/3:16/5:22/7:4:9/8:3/9:25,26/10:11/14:18[2]/15
:2[4]/19:3:9/20:6:10:12/22:3:24,25/23:14:17/24:
8/25:30:33/27:18/29:12/30:16[2]/31:2:8:11/33:
10,11/37:19/38:21,22/39:9:17/41:16,17/43:5:6
:11[2]/44:14:17:28:30/46:26/47:4:7/48:10:18:19[2]
/49:2:9,10:31:32f/50:20:28/51:11/52:15[2]/Lam
1:3/2:12:20/3:6:25[2]:30/4:5[2]:9[2]/Eze1:7/5:10/6:
12[2]/7:13/9:1:7/10:22/11:21/13:15:19[2]/14:5:16
/16:22:27:37[2]:53/17:21/18:7:16/20:27,28:38/
21:9,10,11/23:12[2]:21[2]:22:28/25:16/26:20[3]/28:8
:18/29:20/31:12:17/32:13:22:28/33:21[2]:27[3]/34:
4:15,16:27/35:7[2]:8/36:7:15:36/38:12[2]/39:10/
40:33/42:6/44:7/45:15:21/46:9/48:1/Dan1:3,4
/2:44/4:37/5:16:21:24,25/7:6:16/9:4[2]:9/11:6:
26:29:32:33[2]:35:39/12:2:3[2]:10:12:13/Hos1:23[2]/
4:15/5:10f/7:5/8:9:14[2]/9:7:10/Joe1:6/2:23/3:
19/Amo:11/4:10:11/5:5:13/6:1/8:14/Ob1:3:14:
19:20/Jon2:8/Mic:8/3:5[2]/4:2/6:14:16/7:15/
Nah1:2[2]/3:12/Hab1:13/2:19/3:14/Zep1:4:6[2]:9:
12/2:9:11/3:10:12:19/Zec1:9/5/6:8:14/7:5/8:
13:23/11:5:11/14:3:16/Mal1:4/3:5:14,15[2]:16[2]:
18[2]/Mt2:20/3:1f:11/5:4:6:8:9:10:19:42[2]:44:46/
6:12:14,15/7:11:26/8:12:22/10:10:26:28:40/11:
6:25:27/12:7/13:12,13f:43:52/15:9:30:31[3]/17:
22,23/19:11:13/20:11,12[2]:23:25/21:12:40:44/
23:12[2]:28:37/24:13:16:17:18:19[2]:22:29/25:10:
34:41/26:52:71/Mk3:11:34/4:11,12:15:16:20/5
:12:16/8:35/10:20:24:24f:40/11:15/12:27:43,44
/13:17:19:20/14:4,5/16:14:16[2]:17/Lk1:79/2:14
/3:11/4:23:25,26/5:31:32/6:26:27:28[2]:32:33:34:
35:47,48:49/7:15:20,21,22/8:12:13:14:21:36/9:
11:60:60f:61/10:16[3]:21:22/11:4:13/12:9:10[2]:33:
37:48/13:14:34/14:14:24/17:2,3:31[2]/18:26/19[2]
/20:1:18:34,35/21:16:21[2]:22:23[2]/23:46/Jn1:13:
22:24,25/3:18[2]:21:33,34:36/5:25:29[2]:43/6:35:
37:39:45:57:63/7:16/8:29:50/9:2:31:39[2]/10:6:9:

(THOSE Con't)
17/14:23/15:2/16/17:9:11:12f/18:9:21/19:11/
20:29/Act1:7:14/2:39:41:45/3:25/4:37[2]/5:16/6
:1/7:42/10:35:44/12:20/13:13:15/15:17:33/16:
35/17:11:15/19:4/20:32:34/22:19/23:2:4/25:5:
24/26:20/27:24/28:21/Rom1:6,7/2:7:8:12-15:
27:29[2]/3:8:25[2]/4:4,5:7:9[2]:11[2]:12:14[2]/5:13/6:20:
21/8:1:5[3]:8:29/9:6:8:16:22[2]:33/10:4:12:15[2]/11:
19:20:22:25/12:8:19/13:2:3:7[2]/14:1f:3[4]/15:1:3:
21:26:31/16:5:10:17/1Co1:11:18:21:24:27:28/2:
4:9:14/4:12[2]:17/5:12:13/6:9,10[2]/7:1:8:10:29:29
f:31/9:3:10[2]:13[3]:14[2]:22/10:20/11:22/12:10:23:
24:28[6]:30/13:9:11/14:10:12:16/15:29:32:33/
2Co2:16[2]:17[2]/3:1/5:12/6:14/7:6/8:13:15:23/9:
11:12:13/10:2:4/11:12:13:18:19,20/13:2/Gal1:7
:17/2:21/3:8,9:10:18:25/4:15:17:21:29/5:4:12f:
20:24/6:6:12:13:16/Eph1:19/2:2:12/4:1:28:29/
5:6[2]:12/6/Php1:11/2:21/3:2:11/4:2:22/Col1:12
:18:26,27/3:6/4:15/1Th2:4/3:13/4:15/5:14[3]:20
/2Th1:6:8:10/2/1Ti1:7:8/3:7:13/4:9,10/5:8:10:
17:18/6:17:18:20/2Ti2:2:10:19:22:24:25/3:3:12[2]
:14/4:8:19/Tit1:1:9:10/2:5/Heb1:14/2:3:4:15/3
:5:16:17:18/4:2:3:6/5:9/6:1:12:17:18/8:4:6/9:17
:28/10:1:3:4f:14:29:32:34:38/11:6:7:28/12:1:13:
17:23/13:3[2]:4:9:10:16/Jas1:12/2:5:13:25/3:18/
5:13/1Pe2:5:6:7:13:14[2]:15:16/3:9:12:20/4:6:9:
17/5:5[3]/2Pe1:10/2:1:10[2]:18:22/1Jn:5:21[2]:26:
29/3:4:6:24/4:4:6:7/5:17f/3Jn1:7:11[2]/Jud:6:7:8
:22[2]/Rev:3:7:11/2:2:5:9:22f/3:9:22/6:9:10/7:2/
9:4:6:8/11:18/12:14/13:6:8f:10:11:18/14:3:6:13
f/15:2/16:6/19:9/20:4[2]:6/21:8[2]:27/22:6,7:9:11:
15

1389

THOUGH

Gen8:21[2]/16:5/18:27/19:14/25:22/28:19/31:
30:36,37/33:10/38:14/39:10/44:18/Ex6:2,3/12
:27:48/13:9:17,18/16:27/19:4/24:11/32:29/Lev
4:21/5:2/13:40:55/20:25/25:32:45/26:36:37[2]/
Num14:17,18/16:3/18:27:30:32/Deu1:1/19:6,7
/21:17:18/28:62/29:19/30:4/32:10/Jos3:13,14[2]
:15,16/8:15/9:3,4,5/11:22/17:9:16,17,18/22:2,3
/24:13:20/Ju1:19/8:34/13:2,3/14:6/19:16:19/
Ru3:10/1Sa1:24/2:18/14:24,25:39/20:20/24:
11/25:29/2Sa3:39/4:2,3:6,7/9:10,11/13:25/14:
2,3/16:23/17:10/19:3:5/20:8,9,10/23:18,19/
1Ki2:28/11:2:39/16:31/22:6f:27f/2Ki13:7/14:3
/18:4/21:9/23/1Ch17:17/26:10/2Ch1:14/7:20
/9:27/26:23/28:21/30:17,18,19[2]/32:19/36:13/
Ez5:16/9:13/Neh1:9/6:1/9:18:29/11:3/13:6/
Est4:16/7:4/9:1:15/Job4:10:12/5:18/8:7/13:15
f/14:8,9/19:28/20:6:11:20/24:22,23:24/28:12/
30:17/33:19/34:6[2]/39:16[2]:21-23/Ps4:8/27:3/
35:7:14/38:19/49:5:7:11:13:18/55:10:18/61:2/
65:3/69:4:7/75:3/78:9:15:23:56:65/80:8/91:7[2]/
95:9/105:8,9/111:6/118:10/119:95:161/129:
3,4/138:6:7/Pro1:28/6:7:31/20:5/23:1:4,5/24:
15,16/25:6,7/26:24,25,26/27:22/30:24-28/Ecc
2:20-23/3:11/4:14/6:4:6/7:29/8:6,7:12:14[2]/9:
16/Is1:15/6:9[2]:13/8:17/9:1:8,9,10/10:22/14:12
/17:10:11:13/18:5/27:7,8/30:4:20/31:6/34/40:
15/41:3:14/42:25/45:5/58:2[2]/59:10/60:15/61:
4/63:19[2]/65:2/66:3/Jer2:10,11/3:1:8/5:22:
23,24:29/8:4,5/11:11/12:8/14:15/17:1[2]/29:19/
30:14[2]/31:32f/32:25/33:4:12/34:21/36:7/37/
45:5/46:11/49:16/50:11/51:53[2]/Lam2:4:6/3:8:
52/Eze1:22/2:6/3:9/8:18/12:3:18/13:22/14:20
/17:8:10/20:13:31/28:2,3:24/31:14/33:31/36:
25/Dan5:11/6:10/8:24:25/9:15/Hos3:1[2]/4:10:
15/8:10/Amo9:1:2[2]:3[2]:4/Ob1:4/Jon4:10/Mic2:
2/4:5/6:14/7:8/Nah1:12/3:15/Hab:17[2]/Hag1:
6/Zec4:1:6/9:2:3/10:6:9/11:1/12:3/Mal3:7/
Mt7:25/11:23/26:60,61/Mk4:11,12:17:31,32:
36/12:27/14:38:51,52/Lk8:43,44/11:8:36:42/
12:47/16:31/21:33/24:31/Jn2:9/4:1/5:34:37:
43/6:36:58/7:10/8:14:50/11:25/12:21f/13:33/
Act3:12/5:13/7:5:53/9:18/13:27/17/27:22:30/
28:4:16:17/Rom2:12-15/3:4:21,22:25/4:17:18/
5:7/6:17/8:10/9:7:25:27:30/14:1:16/1Co2:7/3:
1:8/4:7[2]/5:3,4/7:29f/9:20:22/14:24/15:6:8/2Co
1:13,14/2:5,6/3:7:14/4:16/5:20/7:8/8:2:9/10:
15/12:11:15/Gal2:3:13:14/3:1/4:13:14[2]:27/
Eph2:5:11:13/3:8[2]:18,19/5:8/6:6,7/Php2:6/4:
17/Col2:5:18/3:23/1Th2:2:17/1Ti1:13/3:14/4:
3/5:1/2Ti1:8/2:9/Heb:7/3:9/4:3:15/5:1:8/6:9/
7:8/10:16:29:32/11:1:4:7:27:29:39/12:9:13:17/
13:3/Jas2:11/3:4/5:11/1Pe1:6:8[2]:10/2:4/3:18:
20/4:11/2Pe1:12/2:13/3:9/1Jn4:12/3Jn1:7/
Rev1:17,18/4:7/6:14/9:2:17,18

464

THROUGH

Gen1:16/2:10/6:19,20/10:32/12:6/20:8/21:12/
24:65/28:14/30:29/31:36,37:40[2]/35:5/42:23/
Ex11:4/12:12:23/13:17,18[3]/14:16:21:22:28:29/
15:19[2]/34:10/39:23/Lev10:11/13:55[2]/19:10/
26:46/Num11:32/12:2[2]/13:22/15/19:12/20:17[3]
:19:21,22/21:17,18:22/25:8/27:21/31:23/33:8/
34:7,8,9/36:13/Deu1:19,20,21/2:4:8:27:28:29/8
:2:15/11:5/24:12,13/29:5:16/32:47/Jos2:10/3:
2,3,4/15:7:8/16:1/17:5,6/18:12/24:3:17[2]/Ju1:
24/3:4/4:21:22/5:11:26:28/6:8/7:11/9:34/11:
17:18:19/15:5:18/17:7,8/Ru2:22/3:15-18/1Sa9
:4/19:12/26:8/31:3,4/2Sa1:15/2:23[2]/5:8:20/12
:25/15:25,26/17:28,29/21:10/23:16/24:8/1Ki1:
46,47/12:15/13:5/14:17:18/15:29/16:12/17:16
/22:28:36,37/2Ki1:17/3:9:26/6:26-30/8:21/10:
9,10/11:6,7,8/12:8/14:6:25/17:13/21:8:10/24:2
/25:4,5/1Ch5:23/6:33-38:39-43:44-47/9:19/11:
18,19/14:11[2]/21:4/22:13/24:19/26:25/2Ch18:
27/32:4:30/33:18/35:6/36:21/Neh1:6,7/2:7:13:
14,15/9:11:14:19:32/Est1:13-15/3:8/6:9:11/8:
15/Job22:13/29:3/41:2/Ps18:12/22:9,10,11/
23:4/25:6,7[2]/29:3:7:8/39:12/42:8/44:5/46:4/
49:18/53:3[2]/56:8/63:7/66:6:12/68:7/73:4:9/74
:3:8/77:19/78:13:52/84:6/90:1/100:4/102:24/
105:14:28:41/107:39/119:54:148/136:14:16/
138:7/Pro7:23/13:6/15:19/24:3,4/26:2/30:
18,19/Ecc5:11/9:9/Is11:15/15:3:9/27:10/30:6
/32:16/35:8/40:3[2]/42:21/43:2[3]:16[2]:19/45:17/
46:4/48:8[2]:21/49:8,9/51:10:15/59:16/60:10/63
:9:11:13[2]/Jer1:8:10/2:2:6/5:1/6:6[2]/9:12:21/14:
8:17:18/17:27/23:40/25:4/27:3/29:19/32:36/
37:2:13/39:4/51:52/Lam1:2:13:19/3:44/4:12:
14/Eze9:4:5:7/12:5[2]:7:12/20:25/22:10f[2]/26:10
/33:28/34:6/36:34/38:17/39:27/40:6:7-12:16:
17:20:23[2]:27[2]/42:15/43:1:4:7/44:2:3:4/45:20/
46:9[2]:19,20[3]/47:2:8:15/Dan2:43/9:6:10/10:13/
11:28/Hos4:12/7:6/9:10/11:6[2]/Joe2:9/3:17/
Amo2:10/3:7/4:3:5/5:6:17/Jon3:10/4:7/Mic2:
3:13/6:5:12/Nah2:4/3:2/Hag1:13/2:1:8,9f:10/
Zec4:2:12/5:1:5/7:12:14/8:4/10:11:11f/11:1:11
:17/13:9/14:5/Mal1:1/2:14/4:4/Mt1:22/2:12/
4:15,16:23/7:13/8:28/9:8:35/10:20/12:1:
43,44,45f/15:17:20/19:24/Mk1:28/2:1:4[2]:12:23
/4:28/5:5:26:27/7:19/9:26:30,31/10:25/11:
27,28/12:36:38/14:27:72/16:9f/Lk1:65:70:77/4
:30/5:18,19/6:1/8:13:39:42/10:34/11:43/16:3:9
/18:25/19:1/20:23/21:36f/24:27/Jn1:5/4:4:21-
21-24:46,47/6:30,31/7:14:24/8:12/10:1:2:22,23
/11:55/12:12/14:10/17:17/Act1:16/2:22/3:25/
4:25,26/7:36[2]:44:48,49/8:26/9:25:42/10:36,37[2]
:43/12:10/13:18:49/14:22:24/15:4:9:12/16:6:8/
17:1/18:23/19:1:17:38/20:2:10,11,12:21/21:4:
19/26:20/28:25/Rom1:5:8:17/2:28/3:8/4:9:10:
11:23/5:12f:15[2]:21/6:2,3:11:23/7:18[2]:23,24,25f
/8:2:13:37/10:6/12:17/15:13:17:19:23:26/16:
25,26,27/1Co1:21:30/3:13:15/7:18:19/9:2/10:1
/12:6:7:10/15:57/2Co1:8[2]/2:14/3:4/5:18/6:5/8
:2:5:11/9:14/13:3/Gal1:5:6/2:19:19f/3:8,9:11:
14:17:21,22:24:26/5:6:11/Eph1:4:7/2:8:11/3:6:
11:21[2]/4:6:22[2]/Php1:20/3:5/Col1:20:22/2:10/
1Th3:2,3/5:9/2Th1:4:8/2:14[2]/1Ti1:18/2:7/4:14
/2Ti1:1:9:10/4:7/Phm1:13/Heb:1:2[2]/2:15:18/4
:7/7:9:25/11:18:29:34:35/13:3:20,21/Jas1:18/
1Pe3:21f/4:11[2]:12/5:9:10:12/2Pe1:3/1Jn4:9/
3Jn1:5/Jud:3:24,25/Rev3:10f/8:13/10:7/14:6:8
/19:2f/22:14

598

THUS

Gen3:24/7:3/8:7f/11:9/12/13:11/17:13/25:34f
/30:39,40/41:45f/47:21/49:4/Ex8:22/14:30/21
:2f/26:10,11/28:29:30,31:37,38:41/29:9/36:13/
Lev4:26:31/8:12:15,16:30/9:16/14:18/15:15/
16:13:16:19/18:23/19:12/20:3/21:9/Num4:
46,47,48/16:40/35:5/Deu9:18/20/28:58,59/
Jos6:25/Ju7:24/9:56,57/11:33/2Sa3:37/1Ki11:
6/2Ki5:17f/10:28/17:7/2Ch8:16/28:25/29:4,5/
32:16/36:14:21/Neh4:11/Job34:29,30/38:11/
Ps65:1/78:6:8/106:10:21,22/Pro30:9/Is:1/63:
14/Lam4:10/Eze21:29/22:28/23:21:48/25:11/
38:23/39:7:21/40:48,49/43:22:26/44:7/Dan2:
45/11:14/Hos4:9/7:8/Lk3:19,20/14:10/20:26/
Jn13:26f/Act21:26,27/27:17/Rom15:1/Eph2:
15/1Ti5:6/6:20/Heb1:4/4:11

98

TO

Gen1:2f:6f:6:14,15[3]:16[3]:17:18[2]:21,22:26:30/2:5:
8:10:14:15:16,17[2]:18[2]:19,20[2]:21:22:24/3:1:2,3:5:
6:7:9:10:14[2]:16:17[4]:19[3]:20f:23:24[2]/4:1:4:7[3]:8:9:
10:12:13:14:15[2]:20:22:23[2]:25:26:26f/6:1f[2]:1:3:8:
9,10[2]:11:12,13[2]:17:18:19,20/7:1[2]:7/8:1[2]:3,4:5:7f
:8:9[2]:11:13:21/9:1[2]:2,3[2]:5,6[2]:9,10,11:13[2]:15[2]:
16,17:23:24,25/10:1:11,12:15-19[2]:25:26-30:31/
11:3,4[4]:5:6[2]:12,13f:31[2]/12:1[2]:2[2]:2f:6:7[4]:8[3]:9:10[2]:
11,12,13:15:18:19/13:3,4:8[2]:9[2]:11:14:15[2]:16:18[2]
/14:4:7:10:13:15:17:19,20:24/15:1:4:5:7:8:9:10[4]:
16:18[2]:19,20,21/16:2,3[2]:5[2]:6:7:9-12[2]:13[2]/17:1:
2,3,4:7,8:9,10:12[3]:17:18:19:20[2]:21:23/18:1:2:3,4
:5[2]:6[2]:7[2]:12:13:14:19:21:25:27:31[2]:33/19:1[2]:2:4:
5[2]:6[2]:8[2]:9[2]:13[2]:14[2]:15:16:17:18,19,20[2]:27:28:30:
31:32:34/20:1:2:3:7[3]:9,10[3]:11,12[2]:13:14[2]:15:16[3]:
17:18/21:8:10:14:16:17:22[2]:23:24:25:27[2]:30:33[2]
/22:2[2]:3[2]:7:8:9:10[2]:11:14:15:18:19[2]/23:3:4:5,6:8
:9:11[3]:12:13:19,20/24:2:4[2]:5:7[4]:8:9f:9:10[2]:11:12
:13:15,16:17:18:20[2]:21:23:27[2]:28:28f:29,30[2]:32[2]:
33:36:37:38[5]:41:42[2]:43[2]:44:45[2]:48:49[2]:52:53:54:
56[2]:58:62:65:67/25:5:6:11:17f:18[2]:21:27:33[2]:34:
34f/26:1:2[2]:3[2]:4[2]:7:9:16:17:23:24[2]:28:29:31:32:
33/27:2,3,4[3]:5:6,7:8,9,10[2]:15:19:20:21:22[2]:25:31
:33:34:37:41[2]:42:43[2]:46/28:1:2[2]:4[4]:5[2]:6,7,8[2]:9:
11[2]:12:13[2]:14[2]:15:16,17:20:21/29:2:4:7:10:12,13
:15[2]:19[2]:20[2]:21[2]:22:23:24[2]:26:27:28:29[2]/30:1:4:
9[2]:14[3]:15:16:17:18:21:23,24:25[3]:26:28[2]:31,32[2]:
35,36[2]:38:39,40:41/31:1:3[3]:4[2]:5[2]:7:11:12:13[2]:14:
15:16[2]:17-20[2]:24[2]:27:28:29[2]:31:33:36,37[2]:39[2]:41
:42[2]:46:49:50:51,52[2]:53[2]:54[2]/32:1:3:5[2]:6:9[2]:11:
12[3]:16:18:19:20[3]:22,23,24:30:32/33:4:8:10:11:
15:16:20/34:1:3:4[2]:6,7[2]:8:9,10[2]:11:13[2]:14:16:
18,19:21[2]:23:25:26:30/35:1[4]:2[3]:3[2]:7[2]:9:10:11[4]:
12[4]:13,14[2]:15:19:20:26:27/36:5:6,7,8[2]:9:
10,11,12[2]:13,14:17:40-43/37:2[2]:3:4:5:6:8:9[2]:11:
12[2]:13,14:17[2]:18:21,22[3]:25:26,27[2]:28[2]:29:30:32[2]
:35:36/38:1:3,4,5:6:8:9[3]:10[2]:11[8]:12[2]:14[5]:16:18:
20[3]:22:23:25[2]:26[3]:29/39:5:6[2]:10:14,15[5]:17:21:22[2]
/40:4:8:9,10:11[2]:13:14[2]:15:16:20:21:22/41:8:12:
13:24:25:28:32[2]:34,35f:36:39[3]:40:44:49:50:51[2]:
53:55[3]:56,57[4]/42:1:2:3[2]:4[2]:5:6[2]:7:8,9[2]:10:12:15:
18[3]:19:20[2]:21:22[2]:23:25[2]:27[2]:28[3]:29:30:33:34[3]:
36:37[2]:38/43:2:6:7[2]:8:9:11[2]:15:16:17:18[2]:19[2]:20[3]
:22:23:24:29:30:33[3]:34[3]/44:1[3]:2:4[2]:6:9:12:13:14:
15:16[2]:17:18:21:22:24:27:28:30:31:32:34[3]/45:1:
2:3:5[2]:6:7:8:9[2]:11,12:13:16:17[3]:18[4]:19[3]:22:23:25[2]
:26/46:1[2]:2:3,4[3]:5:6:8-14:15:18:23,24,25:26:28:
29[2]:30:31[3]/47:1[2]:2:4[2]:5,6[2]:7:11:12:14:15:17:19:
22[2]:23:24[2]:27:29[3]:31/48:1[2]:2:3[2]:4[3]:5:6:7:9:10:11
:12,13[2]:14:16[2]:17:21[3]:22[2]/49:1[3]:2[2]:6:9:10f:11:13
:15:26:33/50:2:4[2]:5[5]:12,13:14[2]:15:16,17[4]:19:20:
21:22:23:24[2]:25/Ex1:1:8[2]:9:10[2]:11:12:13,14[2]:
15,16[2]:20[2]:22/2:1:4[2]:5[3]:7:10:10f:10:11[2]:12:13:
14:16:17:18:21[2]:24[2]/3:2:3,4[2]:6:8[2]:9:10[3]:13:15[2]:
16[3]:17[3]:18[4]:21/4:1[2]:5:6:9:10:12[2]:14:15[3]:16[3]:17:
18:19[4]:20[2]:21[2]:22:23:24[2]:25,26:27[3]:28:29[2]:30:31
/5:1[3]:2:3:4,5:6:7,8[2]:9[2]:10,11:12:15:16:17:18:21:
22[3]:23/6:1[2]:2,3[2]:4:5:6:8,9[3]:10:11:12[2]:13[4]:16f:19:
19f:20:26:27[3]:28,29:30/7:1[2]:2[3]:3:4:5:8:9[2]:10:11:
14[3]:15[3]:16[3]:17[3]:18:19[2]:20:22:23:24/8:1[2]:2:5[2]:7:8[2]
:9[2]:15:16[2]:18:19[2]:20[3]:25:26:27:29[4]:30:31,32/9:1[3]
:3:7[2]:8:9:10:12[2]:13[2]:14[5]:16[3]:17:22[2]:28:29[2]:33[2]:
34:35[2]/10:1:2:3[2]:4,5:7[2]:8[2]:12[2]:13:14:16:17[3]:21[2]:
25/11:1[2]:2[2]:3[2]:4:5[2]:8:9/12:1:3,4[2]:14:15:17:19[2]:
21:23f:23:27:29:32f:33:39[4]:42:43:48[2]:49[2]:50/13:
1:3[3]:6,7:8:10f:11:12[2]:13:15:17,18[3]/14:2[2]:4:5[3]:10[2]
:11:12[3]:14:15:20[3]:24:26:27[2]/15:1[2]:6:8:13:17:19:
21:25[4]:26:27/16:3[2]:4[3]:5:7,8,9[2]:11,12:15:16:21:
23[2]:25:27:28,29[2]:32[2]:33[3]:35:36/17:1:2[2]:3:4:5,6[2]:
7[4]:8:9[4]:10[2]:12[2]:13:14[2]/18:2:5,6:7[2]:8[3]:12[2]:13[2]:14[2]
:15,16[3]:18[4]:19,20:22[2]:23:24:26[2]:27/19:2,3[4]:4[2]:6:
8:9[3]:13:14:17:20[2]:21[3]:22f:23[3]:24[2]:25/20:5:7f:7[2]:
8:10:17[2]:19[2]:20[2]:22[4]:24[2]/21:2:4:8[2]:10:12:14:15:
17:18:19:20:23:27:28:29:34[2]:36/22:1[2]:3:5:7[2]:8[2]:
9[2]:10[3]:13[2]:16:16f:17:18:20:23:25[2]:27[2]:30[2]:31/23
:4:5:7:9:11[2]:12:13:15[2]:16:19:20[2]:22[2]:23:24:28:29
:30:31[2]:32:33/24:1:2[2]:3:5[2]:7[2]:10:12[2]:16/25:1[3]:8:
12:13,14:15:26,27[2]:36:38/26:3:4,5[2]:6:7,8:9:
10,11:17:18,19:26,27:28:29:32/27:3:7:8:9,10[2]:16[2]
:17:20[3]/28:1[3]:2[3]:3[3]:4f:13,14:15:16:17:22,23,24[2]:
25:28:29:30,31f:30,31:35[2]:36:37,38[2]:40:41:42[3]:
43[2]/29:3,4:10:18[2]:21:24[2]:25:28[2]:29:30:35:36:37:
41/30:2[2]:4:5:8:10:11,12[2]:13f:15[2]:16[3]:17,18:20[3]:
21[2]:22,23:25:26,27:29:30[2]:31:34/31:1:6[3]:11:
12,13[3]:16/32:1[3]:5:6[2]:8:11:12[2]:13[3]:17:19:21[3]:23[3]:
24:25:27:30[3]:31:33:34[2]/33:1[3]:2:3:5[2]:7:8:10:11[4]:
12[2]:13:17:18:19[3]/34:2[2]:3:4:5,6:7[2]:9:10:11:12:15[3]
:17:18:20:22:24:25:26:27:30:31:32:34[2]:35/35:2[2]:
4:5-9[3]:10-19[3]:20[2]:22:24:26:27:29[4]:32:34/36:1[3]:
4-7[2]:10:13[2]:16[2]:18[2]:22:24:29:31,32:33:36:37:38/
37:5:14[2]:15,16:27/38:3:5:8:10:17:18:21:28:29/
39:1[2]:3:6,7[2]:6,7f:6,7:9:15-18[3]:19:20:21[2]:23:24:
25,26:30[2]:31:32:33-40:41[2]:42/40:1:3:8:9:12:13[2]:
15[2]:16:20:21:24:26:32:35/Lev1:1:2,3[5]:4:4f:9:13[2]
:14:15,16,17/2:1[4]:2[3]:3[3]:4:8[5]:9:10[2]:11:14/3:1[4]:6:
9,10,11[2]:12:14:15,16/4:1:3:4:6:7:11,12:13:14:18:
23:24:28[2]:29:32:33:35/5:1:6:7[2]:8:11:12[2]:13:14:
15:16:17,18/6:1:2[3]:4,5[2]:6:8:11:14:16:17[2]:18:

(TO Con't)
19,20^2:21:24:30/**7**:5:7^2:9:11:14^2:15^5:16:17,18^3:
22:23:25:28:29:30^2:31:32,33:34:35^6:36:38^5/**8**:1^3:
5^2:8f:11^2:15,16:18:21:27^2:28:29:30:31^2:33:34:35
/**9**:2^2:3:4^3:5:6:7^3:8:13:16:17:18:21:23/**10**:1:3:5:6:
7:8,9^3:10^2:11:12^3:13^3:14^3:15^2:17^3/**11**:1:9:10:12:
23:27:28:34:37:39:45/**12**:1^2:6^2:8/**13**:1^4:3^2:4:7^3:
9,10^3:11:12:16,17^3:19:20:21:25:26:29,30:31:32:
34:35:36:45:49^2:54:59/**14**:3:4:8:12:13:18:21^2:22:
23:24:27:29:30:31:32:33,34:35^2:36:37:39:42:45:
48/**15**:1:7:14:29/**16**:1^2:6:8^2:9:17:18:27:28:32:34:
35/**17**:1:5^5:6^2:7^2:8,9:11:12:14/**18**:1:3:12:16f^3:17:
18:20:21:23^2:24:26^2:29,30/**19**:1:5:7:10:12:20^2:21
:24^3:32/**20**:1:3^2:4^2:5:9:10:13:14:20:21:24^2:25^2:26^2
:27/**21**:1^2:6^2:8:11f^2:16,17^3:21^2:22:24^2/**22**:1^2:3:9:
13^2:14:15:17,18^3:19:21^2:22:23:24:25:26,27^2:
32,33^2/**23**:1^3:3^2:4:5:6:8:9,10,11:12:13^3:15,16:17^2
:17f:18^2:18f:20^2:21^2:23,24^2:25:26,27^2:30,31^2:
33,34:36^3:37^2:38^3:39:41:42:43^2:44/**24**:1^2:3,4:5-8
:9:11:12:13,14^3:15,16^2:19:20^2:21/**25**:1:4:6,7^2:10^4
:13:14,15,16:17,18:20:26:27^2:28^2:29^2:30^2:31:33:
34^2:35^2:37:38^2:39:41:46^2:47^2:50^2:53/**26**:6:10:14:
16:21:22:23:25:26^2:27:30:31:32:34,35:36^2:37:42:
45^2:46/**27**:1^3:3:4:5:6:8^2:9^2:10^2:11,12^4:13:14,15^2:
16^3:18:19^2:20^5:21^3:22:23:24:25f:26:27^2:28^2:29^2:
29f^2:31^2:33^2:34/**Num1**:1:2-15^3:17,18,19:
47,48,49:50:51:53:54/**2**:1:3-31^9:32,33:34/**3**:1:3:
4:5:6:7,8,9:10:11,12:14,15^2:38:40:43:44:46:
47,48:49:50:51/**4**:1:3^2:12:13:14^2:15:17,18,19^2:
21,22,23:26^2:27:28:29:30,31:32:33:35:37^2:
46,47,48:49^2/**5**:1:3:5,6:7:8^2:9,10^2:11,12:15^3:18:
19^2:21,22:24:25:26:30^2:31/**6**:1:3,4:5:8:10:11:13^2:
14:21^2:22,23^3:24,25,26/**7**:3:4,5:6:7:8:9^2:11:18-
18-23f:24-29f:30-35f:36-41f:42-47f:48-53f:54-59
f:60-65f:66-71f:72-77f:78-83:78-83f:89^2/**8**:1:2:4:
5,6:9:11:12:13^4:15:19:20:21^2:22:23,24^2/**9**:1:2,3f:
2,3:6,7^2:10:11:13^3:14^2:15:16:17:18/**10**:1^3:3:4:
5,6,7^3:5,6,7f:8^3:9:10:13:29^3:30:31:31f:33^2:36/**11**:
2:4,5^2:6:11^2:12:13^2:15:16^3:18^3:22^2:23:24:30:32f:
35/**12**:1f^3:3,4:6:7,8^2:11^2:13:14/**13**:2:16:21:23^2:
26:27:30/**14**:3:4^2:7:8:9:10,11^2:14^2:16^3:17,18:22:
23:26,27^2:28^2:30:34,35:39:40:41^2:45/**15**:1^3:3,4^2:
7:10:11,12:13,14^3:15,16:17,18^2:19,20,21^3:22:29:
31:33f:35^2:37,38^5:39^3:40^2/**16**:2:3^2:4:5^2:6,7f:8,9^7:
10^2:11,12:13^2:14^2:15:16:17:19^2:20:22:23,24^2:25:
26:28:30:36,37^3:38:39:40^6:43,44:45:46:47:49:50
/**17**:1^3:5:6:9:10^4:12,13/**18**:1:2,3:5:6:7:8^4:9:10:11:
12:14,15:16:17^3:18:19^2:24^2:25,26^5:27:28,29:30:
32/**19**:1^3:7:12:17^3:20/**20**:2:4:5^2:6^2:7:8^2:10^2:12:
12f^2:13:14:14f:15:16:17:18:19:20:21,22^3:23:24/
21:2:4^3:5^5:6:7^3:8:10:11:12:13:16:20:21:24:24f:
27-30^3:31,32:33:34^3/**22**:1:2,3:5,6^2:7^2:8:9:11:12:
16,17^2:18^2:19:20^2:22,23^2:28:32:34:35:36:38^2:39:
40:41/**23**:1:3,4^3:7-10:11^2:12:13:15^2:16:17:18-24^2
:25^2:26:27^3:28:29^2/**24**:1^2:3-9:10:11^2:14^3:15-19:
25/**25**:1:2^2:4:5:10,11:16,17:18/**26**:1^2:2^3:3,4:5-11
:52,53^2:54:58,59:60/**27**:1^3:6,7^2:8:9:10:11:12^3:14^3
:15:19:21^5:22:23/**28**:1^4:6^2:8:9,10^2:11:15^2:19:22:
23:24:26^4:27:30:31/**29**:5:6^3:8^2:9,10:11^3:13:16:19^2
:22:23:25:28:31:34:35:36:38:39:40/**30**:1^3:3:5^2:8:
12:14:15^2/**31**:1:3^2:4,5:12^2:13:16:20:21:23:25:26:
27^2:29^3:30^2:36-40^5:41:42-46^3:47:48,49^2:50^2:
51,52/**32**:2:3,4:6:7^2:8:10,11^2:12:15:17^3:22^2:27:
28:33:39:40:41:42/**33**:9:14^2:15-37^{23}:38,39:45:46
:48:50,51:53:54^2:55:56/**34**:1:4^2:5:7,8,9^3:10,11^2:
13^2:16-28^2:29/**35**:1:2^2:7:8:9,10:11:12:13,14:16:
22,23:24^2:25:28:29:32^2:34/**36**:1^4:3:6:7^2:9:11,12:
13/**Deu1**:1^6:7:8^2:9:12:14:15:16^2:17:19,20,21^3:22^2
:24,25^2:26:27:29:32:33:34,35:37:38:39:41^2:42^2:
43:44/**2**:4:8:9:10:11:12:14,15^2:16,17:19:20:24:26
:28:29:31^3:35,36^2:37/**3**:1^3:8:12^2:14:15:16:17:18:
20^2:21^3:23,24,25^2:27:28^2/**4**:1^2:3:4:5^4:9:10^2:12:14
:15:16,17:19^2:20:29:30^2:31:32^3:33:37:41:
44,45,46:48:49/**5**:1^3:4:5^3:9,10^2:11^2:11f:22^2:23:
24:25:26,27:28^3:29:30^2:31^2:33/**6**:1^2:2^2:3^2:7:13^5:
18:19^2:20:23:24^2/**7**:2^2:4:6^2:8:13^3:15:17:18^2:19:
20:24:25^2/**8**:1:2:3^2:5:11^2:12,13:14:18^3:20/**9**:1^2:3:
4:5:8:12:17:18:19^2:23^2:25:26:27:28^3/**10**:1^5:3:4:5:
6:7^2:8^4:10:11^3:12,13^6:14:15:18:20/**11**:2:3:4^2:8^3:9^2
:10:13:14:15^2:16:18^4:19:22:24^2:25:29:31/**12**:3:
4,5^2:6^2:9:11:12^2:13:14:15:16:17^3:18:19:20-23:
26,27^2:28:32/**13**:1:3^2:4:5^2:6,7^2:9^2:10^2:12,13,14:
16^2:17:18^2/**14**:2^2:3,4,5^2:19,20:21^2:23^4:24^2:25:26^3
:27:28:29^3/**15**:1:3:6^2:9^2:11:16:19/**16**:1:2:3^2:5:7:
10^2:11^4:12:14:15:16:19:21/**17**:1:5:6:8^2:9:10^2:11:
12:13^2:14^2:16^3:19/**18**:1^3:2:3:4:5^3:6,7^2:10^3:12:14:
15:16^2:17:18^2:19:20:22^2/**19**:2,3^2:5^2:6,7^3:9:10:12^2
:20:21/**20**:1:3^2:9:10:11:13:15^2:16:18:19:20/**21**:2:
4:5^2:10^2:16:17:21/**22**:1:2^2:3:4:5:8^2:15:16^2:17,18:
19^2:21^2:23,24:25,26,27:28,29:30/**23**:4^2:5:6:14^4:
15,16:17,18^2:19:21:23^2/**24**:5^2:6:7:8^2:9:10^2:11:
12,13^2:14,15:16:17:19/**25**:1^3:6:7^6:9^3:10:11:16:17
:19/**26**:2,3^4:5:6,7:9:12^2:13:14:17^3:19^3/**27**:1:5,6^2:
10:11:12:13:14:19:20:23f:25/**28**:1:9^2:10:12^3:15-
15-19:21:25^3:26^2:31^3:32:33:35:36^2:40:44^2:45^2:
47,48^2:52^2:55:56,57^2:58,59^2:62:64:66:68^5/**29**:6:8^2
:12:13^2:18^2:21:22:24:29^2/**30**:1:2^3:5:7,8:10:12^2:16^4
:17:18^2:19:20^5/**31**:1:2:2f:5:7^3:9^3:10,11:12^2:13:14
:15:16:19^2:21:22:23^2:26^2:28^2:29:30/**32**:1:16:17^2:
20:21:22:24:26^2:30:31:37:38:40,41:44,45:46:47:
48:49^3/**33**:1:2:8:10:17:19:26/**34**:1^2:2:4:9:10^2/
Jos1:1^2:3^2:4^2:5^2:6:7^4:8:10,11^4:14:16^2/**2**:1^2:3^3:5:6
:7:8^2:9^2:10:12,13:14:16:17,18^2:22:23^2:24/**3**:5:8:9
:10:13,14:15,16^2/**4**:1:2,3^2:5:6:7^2:8:9:10:12,13:
15,16^2:22/**5**:2,3^3:4,5:6^2:7:8,9^2:8,9f:11,12:13:14/
6:1:2^2:3,4^2:5:10:11:12,13,14:16:18:19:22:23:25/
7:1:2:3:7^2:8:9:10,11^2:14:15:18:19^2:22^2:23:24:25^2:
26/**8**:1^4:2^2:3,4:5^2:7:11,12,13:11,12,13f^2:16:18:
20,21:23:30:31:33:34/**9**:1^2:3,4,5^4:6:7:10:11^2:
14,15:17:22:23:24:26:27/**10**:3:6:7:8^5:10:11^2:15:
17:18:19^2:20:21^2:22,23^2:24:25^3:29:31:32:33^2:36:
38:41^2:43/**11**:1:4:6:8:15^2:17:18:20:23/**12**:1:2:5^3:
6:7/**13**:1^2:2-7^8:8:9:13:14^3:15^2:15f:15:16:24^3:24f:
26^2:29^3:29f:31:33^2/**14**:1^3:3,4^2:5:6^3:7:9/**15**:1:
2,3,4^2:5:6^2:7^3:8^2:9^3:10,11^6:13^3:16:18,19^3:20:33-
33-36:46:47:48-62f:63/**16**:1^6:5,6^3:7:8/**17**:1:2:4^3:
5,6^2:7^2:8^2:9^2:10^2:11:13:14:15:16,17,18/**18**:1:3^2:4
:5,6^2:8^4:9:11^3:13^2:15:16^2:17^3:20:21-28^2/**19**:1^2:8:
9:10^2:11:12^2:17-23^2:24,25,26^3:27:29:32^2:33:34:
40^2:47,48:49:51/**20**:1:2:3^2:4:5^2:6^2:9/**21**:1^2:2^2:4^2:
8:9-16^2:19:26:33:41,42^2:43^2/**22**:4:5^3:7,8^2:9:10:
12^2:13:15:16:19:20:21:22,23:24,25^2:26,27^4:29^2:
31:32/**23**:1:2:4,5^2:6:9:10:11:12:13:14^2/**24**:1:4:5:
7:9:10:11:12:15:19:22:24:25:27^2:28:32:33/**Ju1**:1^4
:3:7:13:14f:14^3:15:19:20:21:24:25:26:27:28^2:33:
36/**2**:1^2:2:3^2:5:7-9:12-14:15:16:17^2:18:19^3:22^2/**3**
:1^5:4^3:9^2:12^2:14^2:15^3:17,18,19^2:20^3:26:27:28/**4**:4
:5^2:5f^3:6^3:7^2:9^3:10:13:14:17:18^2:21:22:23/**5**:7:11:
18:23:30/**6**:1:2:3,4:5:6,7^3:8:9:10:11:12:13:14:16:
16f:17^3:19^2:20:22:25^3:26:28:30:31^2:34^2:36^3:37^2:
39/**7**:2^2:3:4:5,6^3:8,9^2:10:11^3:12,13^2:14:15^3:19,20
:22^4:23:25/**8**:1:7:8:9:15^2:16:17:20^3:21:22:25:33:
35/**9**:2^2:3:4^3:5:7^2:8:9^2:10:11:12:13:14:18:20:25:
26:29:31^3:36:40:42:43:44:45:46:47,48:49:51^2:52:
54:55/**10**:7,8:9:10^2:12:13^2:14:17/**11**:6:7^2:9:12^2:
13^2:17^2:19^4:21,22^2:23^2:25:26^2:27:28:30,31^3:33:
34:35^2:39:39f:40/**12**:1^3:2^2:3^3:5:9,10^2/**13**:2,3^2:5:6^2
:7^5:8^2:9:11:15^2:16^3:17^2:19:20:22:23^2:25/**14**:2:5:7
:8:9:12:13:14:15^3:16^2:17:18:19^4:20/**15**:1^2:2:5:6:8
:10^3:11^3:12,13^2:18^2:19/**16**:1:2^2:3^2:5^2:6:10:12:
16,17:19^2:20:21^2:22:23,24^3:25,26^3:28:31/**17**:2:3^3
:4,5:6:7,8^2:9:10,11/**18**:1^3:2^2:7^2:8:9,10^2:14:15,16^2
:19^4:20:23:25:26:27:28^2/**19**:1:2:3^5:4:5:6:9:11^2:
12,13:14:22^3:23^2:24^2:25^2:27:29:30^2/**20**:1:5:
8,9,10:12:14,15:18^2:19,20^3:22,23,24:26:27,28:31^2
:32:35-39^2:40,41:46,47/**21**:1:5:6:8,9^3:10,11,12^2:
13:14^2:17:19:21:22^2:23:24/**Ru1**:1:6,7^2:8^4:10^2:11^3
:11f^2:12^2:13:14:15^3:16^2:17^3:19/**2**:2^2:3:4,5:8,9^6:
10,11^2:12:13:14:15^2:16^3:17:18:19:20^2:21/**3**:1^2:2^2
:3:4^2:6,7^2:9:10:12:13:14:15-18^2/**4**:1^4:2:3^2:4:4f:4:
5^3:6:7^2:8:9^2:10^2:14:15/**1Sa1**:3^4:4:5^2:7:9:10:11:11
f:15,16:18:19,20^4:19,20f:21,22^2:24:25:26:27:28^2
/**2**:7^2:10^2:11:13,14^4:16:17:19:20^3:22:23,24,25^3:
27:28^5:29:30:31^2:34^2:35^2:36/**3**:2,3:4,5^2:6^2:8^2:9^2:
11^2:12:15^2:16,17:19:20^2:21,4:1^3/**4**:3:7:10:13:14:
18/**5**:1:3^2:5:6:8^4:10^2:11^2/**6**:2:7:8:9:10:14:15:16:
17:18:20:21/**7**:1^2:3^4:5^2:8:9^2:11:14:16:17^2/**8**:4:6:7
:9:12^2:13:14:15:19^2:20^2/**9**:3:5:7^2:8:9,10,11:12,13
:14:16:19:23:25^2:26,27^3/**10**:1:2:3^2:4:5:8^2:9:10:12
f:13:14^3:24:26:27/**11**:3^2:4:5:7^6:8:9^2:10^2:12:14^2:
15^2/**12**:8^2:10:11:12^2:14:15^2:17:18:19^2:22:23:25/
13:1f:2:3,4^2:6:7:8:9:10^2:12^2:13:15:18:20^3/**14**:1^2:
4^2:6^3:12^3:16:18:19:20:30:31:33:34^3:35:38:45/**15**:
1^2:2^4:4:6^3:7:9:10:11^2:12^5:15^2:16^2:19:20:21^2:22^2:
25:27^3:28^2:30:32:34^2/**16**:1^3:2^2:3^2:4^2:5^3:7:8:9:
10,11:13:15,16:19:22/**17**:4-7:8^3:9:13:14,15^2:17^2:
18:22^2:23:24:25:26^4:28^2:30:35:36^2:38,39:40:44:
45^2:46:47^3:48,49^2:52:54:55:55f^2:57/**18**:1:6^2:8:10^2
:11,12^2:13:14:17^4:19:21^3:22^2:23:24:26:27^2:29/**19**
:1:3^2:4^2:5^2:7:8:9,10^2:11:12:14^2:15:16:17^2:18^4:20^2
:22:23^2/**20**:1:2:3:6^2:7:8:9:11:12:13:14:15:16^2:17:
21:23:24,25:28,29^3:30:32:33:34:35:38:40^3:42^2/
21:1^2:2^2:3:9:10:12:13:14,15/**22**:1:3^4:5^3:8:9,10^2:
11,12:13^3:15:17:18:19:20:23/**23**:1:3^3:4:5:6^2:7:8^2:
9^2:10:11:12:14,15^2:16:17^2:19^2:22:23:24,25:26^2:
28:29/**24**:2:3^2:4^2:6^2:7,8:9,10^4:11:12^2:14:15^2:17:
18:20^2:21:22/**25**:1:5^2:8:9:11:11f:13:14^2:15,16^2:
17^2:19:21^2:24^2:25:27:32^2:34:35:39^3:41:42:44/**26**:
1^3:2:3,4:5,6,7^4:8^3:11:14:15:16:19:20;21:23:25/**27**
:1^2:2,3:4:5:6^2:8:9:11^2:12/**28**:1:2:5,6:7,8^6:9:11:15^2
:17:22:23:25/**29**:4:8:9:11/**30**:1:3:7:9,10:11,12^2:
15^2:16:21:22:24^2:26:27-31/**31**:3,4^2:8:9^2:10:12^2/
2Sa1:1^2:7^2:10^2:13:15/**2**:1^2:3:4:5:6^2:7:8^2:12:13:14
:15:17:20:22^2:23^3:26^2:30:32/**3**:2^2:3^2:4^2:5:8^3:9,10^3
:12^4:14:19^3:24,25^3:26^2:27:31^3:35,36^2:38/**4**:2,3^2:
6,7:8^2:11:12/**5**:1:6^2:11:12:13:17:19:23:25/**6**:1^2:6:
8:10:12:17:19:20^3:21^2:22/**7**:2:4:5:5f:7:8^2:10,11^2:
14:17:19:21^2:23^3:24:27^2/**8**:2:3:5:7:8:10:11,12:14^2
:15/**9**:1^2:3^2:7^4:8^2:9:10,11^2:13^2/**10**:2^4:3^2:5:7,8:9^2:
10^2:12:13:14:17:19^2/**11**:1^2:2:3:5:6:8^2:10:11:12:
13^2:14^3:15^2:16^2:18:19,20,21:22:23:25:27^2/**12**:1:3
:5:6:7:11^3:12:13:14^2:15:16:17:18^2:20:21:22:23^2:
24:26,27:29,30^2:31/**13**:2:2f^3:4:5^4:6^3:7^3:9:10^3:11:
12:12f:13:14:15:16^3:20:21-24^5:29,30:31:
37,38,39^2/**14**:1:2,3^3:5,6:7^2:8:10:11:13^2:14:14f:
15,16^3:18:19:20:22:23^2:24^2:26:29^3:30^3:31:32^2/
15:1:2^3:3:4:5^2:7,8^7:9:10^2:13:14:16:17,18^2:19,20^6:
25,26^2:27:30:33,34:35,36^2:37/**16**:2^3:3:7,8:10^2:11^2
:16:17:20:21:22:23/**17**:1:2,3:8:14:15:16:17^5:18^3:
19:20:21:23:28,29/**18**:2:3^2:12:13:17:18^2:19:20:
21:22:24:25:28^3:29:29f:33/**19**:5^2:6^2:8,9,10^2:
11,12^3:13:14^2:15^3:16:17^2:20:22:23:24,25:27:30:
31,32:33:35:36:37:37f:37:40^2:41:43^2/**20**:1:2:3^2:4^2
:5:6^2:8,9,10^6:11:12:13:14:15:16^3:18^2:19:21^2:22^3/
21:2^2:3^4:4:5,6:10:12,13,14^4:16:17^2/**22**:1:4:9:10:
26^2:27:34:35:37:40:42^2:45:47:50^2:51^3/**23**:1:3:5f:
6:7:10^2:13:16^2:18,19:24-39f^2/**24**:1:2^2:3^2:4:6^3:7^2:
9:10^2:11^2:13^6:14:16^2:17:18^3:19:21^2:22:23:24^3:25
/**1Ki1**:1:2^2:3,4^4:5^2:7:8^2:9^2:11:12:13:17:20^2:22,23
:24^2:25:27^2:30:31f:33^3:34:38:40:42:44,45:48^2:53
/**2**:1:2:4:5:6:7:8^2:9:13^2:14:15^2:16:17^2:19^2:20:22:
25:26^2:27:28:29:30^3:32:34:39:40^3:41:42:44/**3**:1^2:
3^2:5^3:6^4:8:9:15^2:16^2:20:21:23:24:25:27^2/**4**:8-19^2:
21^4:23:24:33:34/**5**:1:2,3^4:4:5:6^3:7:8:9^3:12:14/**6**:6
:8^2:10:11,12^2:15:16:21,22^2:23-28^2:31:33:34:38/**7**
:1:3,4:7^2:9:10:11:13:14:16-22f:23:25:32:33:40:
41-46:47:50/**8**:1^2:3,4:8:11:12,13:16^2:17:18^2:
22,23^2:24:25^2:29^2:30^2:33,34^3:35,36:40^2:41,42:44^2
:46:47^3:48:49:50:52^2:53:56:58^2:62,63:64:65:66^2/
9:2,3^2:5:7:8:11,12^2:14:15:16:19:20,21:24:27,28^3/
10:1:3f:5:6:8:9:11:12:13:21:24^2:28:29^2/**11**:2:4:6:
8^2:9,10^2:11^2:14:15:16,17,18^4:21^2:22:23:24:29^2:
31^2:32f:35:36^3:38^2:40^2/**12**:2,3,4^3:5:7^2:15^3:16,17^2
:18^3:19:20:21^2:22:23,24^3:27^3:28^3:32,33^3/**13**:1^3:2:
3:4:6^3:7^2:8:9^3:11:15:16,17^3:18^2:20:21,22^2:26:27:
29^2:31:32:33^3/**14**:2:4:5^3:6:8^4:9:12:13:17:21^2:24:
28^2/**15**:17:18^4:21:22^3:27/**16**:1:2:4-7:10:17:19:21
:33/**17**:2:3:4:5:8,9:10:11^2:12:13:15:18^2:19^2:20:21^2
:23/**18**:1:2:3,4:5^4:7:9^2:10^4:13:15:16^2:18:19:20:21^2
:24^4:25^2:26^2:27^4:30:31:31f:32:36:37:39:40^2:41:
42:43^2:44^2:46^3/**19**:2^2:3:4:5:8^2:9:10:14:15^2:16^2:18
:19:20^2:21^4/**20**:2,3:5,6:7:9:10^4:12:13^2:17:23:27:
28:31^3:32:33^2:35^2:36:37:38:39:40:43/**21**:2^2:4^4:6^2
:8:9f:13:14:15:16^2:17:18^2:20^3:20f:21^2:22:25^2:26:
28:29/**22**:3:4^3:5^2:7:8:9:12:13^2:14:15:16^2:17:18:
19:20:24:25:26^2:27^2:28:29:30:31:32,33^2:34:
36,37:48^2:49:51/**2Ki1**:1^2:2^2:3^2:4,5:6^4:9^3:11:13:
15^2:16^3:17/**2**:1^7:3^2:4^4:5^2:6,7^3:9:13,14:15:18:19:
20:21:23:25^2/**3**:2:3:6,7,8^2:10:11:12:13^2:15^2:16^2:
25:26^2:27^3/**4**:1^2:5:6^2:7^2:8^2:9^2:10:11,12^3:13^5:
15,16^2:18:19^2:21:22^2:24^2:25:27^3:28^2:29^2:30:31:
33:34:37:38^2:39:42^2/**5**:1:2:3^2:5^2:6^2:7^3:8^2:10^2:11^2:
13^3:14^2:15:16:17^2:18:20:21:22^3:23^2:25:26^2/**6**:1:6
:7:8:9:10:13:14:15:19^2:21:23:26-30^3:32^3/**7**:2:4:5:
6:9:10^2:11:13^2:14:15:17^2:19:20/**8**:1^2:3^2:5^2:6^3:7:
8,9^5:12:13:15:21:22:26:27:29^3/**9**:1^2:3:7:11:15^5:
16^3:18^3:19^2:21:23:25^2:27^3:28:30:35/**10**:1^2:2,3^2:4:
5:6^2:7:8^2:9,10^3:11:13^2:14^2:15^4:17^3:18,19^5:20,21:
23^2:30^3:31:32,33/**11**:2,3:4:5:6,7,8:9:10:13,14:15^3
:16:18/**12**:4,5^3:8^2:11,12^4:13,14^2:16:17^2:18:20/**13**
:2:3:4:5:6^2:7:9,10:11:16,17:20,21^2:23:25/**14**:7^2:8^2
:9:10:11:13:14:19:22:26:27/**15**:12:14:16:29:37/
16:3:6^2:7^2:8:10^3:15^2:18/**17**:3^2:4^3:6:9:11:13^4:14:
17^2:19:20:23^2:25:26^2:27,28^3:32^2:33:34^2:35,36^3:
37:40:41/**18**:1:4^3:5:6:7:8f:11:12^5:14:15:16:18^2:
19:20,21:22^2:24:26:27^5:28^2:29:30:31,32^4:34:35:
36:37/**19**:1:2^3:3^2:5,6:7^2:8:9^3:13^2:14:16:19:20:21:
28:31^2:36/**20**:1^2:2:3^2:4:5:6:7^2:8^5:9:11^2:12:14:16^2:
17/**21**:1:3,4,5^2:7:9^2:13^2:14:16^2:22^2/**22**:3,4^5:5,6^3:
7:8^3:9,10^2:12,13:14^2:15,16^2:18,19:20/**23**:1^3:3^3:4^2
:5^2:6^2:8:10^3:11^2:12:15:16^4:20^2:21:24:25:29:30:33
:34^3:35/**24**:2:3,4:7:12:15:17^2/**25**:1:6:7^2:11^2:12:
13:14,15:16:18:20:21:24^2:25:26^2:29/**1Ch1**:1f:47
/**2**:24:34,35/**3**:1:4^2:17,18/**4**:10:21-22:34-39:
40,41:42/**5**:1:9^2:20^2:23:25:26^3/**6**:31:48:49^3:54:
55,56,57:60:61^2:64,65:66-69:70:71:77/**7**:14:
20,21:22/**8**:1:6,7/**9**:1:2:5:19:21:24:25^2:28^2/**10**:4^2
:8^2:10^2:11:12:13:14/**11**:1:2:4^2:5,6^3:10:13:15:17:
18,19^5:23^2/**12**:8-13:16:17^4:18:19^2:20^2:23:24-37^3
:38:40/**13**:2^2:5f:6^2:9:11:13^3/**14**:1:2^2:3:4-7:8:11:
14:15:16:17/**15**:1:2^3:3^2:12:16:19:20f:21f^2:24:25^3:
28/**16**:3f:4^2:7^2:8^2:9:15:16:17:20^2:21:23:24:25:28:
29:33:34:35:37^2:39^3:40:41^2:42^2:43^2/**17**:1:3:4:5:6^2

(TO Con't)
:9:10:17^2:18:19^2:22:24:25^3:26/**18**:2:3:5:6:7:10^2:
11:13^2/**19**:2,3^5:4^2:5^2:6:9:10:13:15:19/**20**:1:3:3f^2:
3/**21**:1:2f:3^3:4:5:8^2:9:12^3:13:15:16:17:18^3:19,20:
21:22^2:23^2:24:26^3:27:28:30^2/**22**:2:3:4:6:7:8^2:9:10
:11:12:13:14:16:17:19/**23**:3:4,5:13:22:24:26^2:28:
30^2/**24**:1:3:5:6:31^2/**25**:1^2:6,7^2:8^2/**26**:12:13:14,15^3
:16:17^4:18^3:20,21,22:26^2:27:28^2:31,32/**27**:23f:32
/**28**:1:2^2:3:4:5:7:8^5:9:10:13^2:14:15:19:20^2/**29**:1^2:
3^3:4,5^2:10:14^2:16^2:17:18^2:19^2:20^2:21:23:24:30^3/
2Ch1:2,3^3:5,6:7^2:8:9:10^2:11^3:13^2:14:16^2:17/**2**:1:
3^2:4^2:5:6^3:6f:7^2:8:9:10:11:12^2:16^3/**3**:1:6^2:
11,12,13^2:14:15:16/**4**:2:4:6^3:11:17,18:22/**5**:1:2^2:
6:11,12:13,14/**6**:1:3^2:4^3:7:8^2:9:14^2:15:16:19^2:
20,21^3:22^2:24^2:25^2:27:29:31:31f:32^2:34:36:37,38^2
:40^2:42/**7**:4,5:6:7:8:10^2:11:12^3:13:15:16:18:21^2:
22/**8**:2^2:6:11:12:13:14^3:17,18^5/**9**:1^2:2:5:7^2:8^2:11^2
:12^2:13,14:15:20:21^2:23^2:25:26:28/**10**:1:2,3^2:5:7^2
:11:12:13:15^3:16:17:18^3:19^2/**11**:1:3^2:4:5-10:12:
13,14^2:15^3:16^2:17:22:23/**12**:5^2:6:7^2:8^3:10:11^2:14
/**13**:4:6:7:11^2:13,14^2:15,16^2/**14**:2:6:7^2:9,10^2:11^2:
15/**15**:2^2:3:4:10:11:12:13:14:18/**16**:1^2:2^3:3^2:4^2:5:
6^2:7:8:12^2/**17**:7,8,9^3:19/**18**:2^3:3,4,5,6,7^2:10:11^2:
12:14:15^2:17:18:19,20^2:23:25^2:26:27:28:29:30:
31^2:33:34/**19**:2:3^2:4^4:7^2:9^2:10^3:11^3/**20**:3:4^2:7:9^2:
11:12^3:15:17:18^2:19:20^2:22^3:25^2:27:28:32:33:34:
36^2/**21**:3,4:5:7^2:9:10:11:16^2:20/**22**:2:4:5:6^3:7^4:9^2
/**23**:2,3^5:5,6:8:9^2:10:12^3:13,14^2:15,16,17^2:18^2:20
/**24**:2:4:5:7,8^2:9^3:11^3:12^3:14^2:15:17,18^3:19^2:20^2:
21:23:25:27/**25**:5,6^3:8^3:9:10:11:12:14:15:16:18:
19:20:23^2:24:27:28/**26**:2:5:8^2:11:14:15:17,18^3:19
:20^2:22/**27**:6:8/**28**:3^4:5^2:8:9:10:11^2:13:14^3:15^3:
16:19f:19:23^2:24^2/**29**:4,5^2:8:10:11^3:15:16:17:18^2
:20:21:24:27^2:30:31:34^3:35/**30**:1^2:2,3^2:5:6^2:8^2:9^5:
10:11^2:12:14:17,18,19^4:20:22^2:23/**31**:1^3:2^3:4^3:
5,6^5:7,8:11:14,15^3:17,18^2:19^3:21/**32**:1^2:2:3:4^2:5:
6:8:9:11^3:12^2:13^3:14:15:17:18^2:20:21:24:27:30:
31^4/**33**:2:7:8:9:11:12^2:13^2:14:17:18:20,21:22:25/
34:3^2:4^2:6^2:7^2:8:9:10,11^2:13:14^2:15,16^3:17:18:21:
22:26^2:28:30^3:31^3:32^2:33/**35**:2:3^4:4,5:6:8:9:11:12^2
:13^2:15^2:21^3:22^2:23:24,25^2/**36**:2:4^2:6:10^2:12:13:
15:17:20^2:21^2:22,23^4/**Ez1**:1f:1:3^2:5^5:6:8^3:11^3/**2**:
1^3:59:61:62,63^4:64,65^2:68:69:70/**3**:1^2:3^2:6:7:8:9:
10:11/**4**:2:4,5^3:6:7^2:11:12:13^4:14^3:15^2:16^2:17^2:18
:22:23^3/**5**:1^2:3:5:6:7:8^2:9:12:15^3:17/**6**:3^2:5:6:8:9:
10^3:11^2:18:21,22^3/**7**:1:6^4:10^3:11:12:13:14^3:15^3:
16:17:21^2:22:24:25^4:26:27:28^3/**8**:17^3:20:22^3:23:
25^2:26,27^2:28^2:29^2:30:31:35:36/**9**:1:5^2:6^2:8^2:9^3:
11:12^4/**10**:2:3^2:4:7,8:11:16-19/**Neh1**:2^3:4^2:5,6,7:
9^4:11^3/**2**:4^3:7^4:8^3:9^2:13^2:14,15^2:16^3:18/**3**:2:7:8:
10:11:13:15:16:19:20:21:23:24:25:27:29:30:31:
32/**4**:6:8^2:9^2:10:11:12^2:14:15:18^2:19^2:20,21:22/**5**
:2,3,4^4:5^4:7:8^2:9:10:11:12^3:13:14:15:16^2:18/**6**:2^2:
3^2:5,6^2:7^3:8:9:10^2:12,13^4:14:18^2:19/**7**:2^2:3^4:5^2:6:
57,58,59:61:64,65^3:66:73^2/**8**:1^7:9:10^3:12^3:13:14:
15^5:16/**9**:3:5^2:8^3:14:15^2:16^2:17^5:19:20:23:26^2:27^2
:28^3:29^2:30^2:32:34:35:36:37:38^2/**10**:28^2:29^2:30^2:
31^4:32^2:33:34:35^2:36^3:37^3:38:39,40^3/**11**:1:2:3^2:
25-30:36/**12**:23:27^3:28:31,32^3:37^2:38^2:39^3:40,41
:44^3:46^2:47:47f/**13**:1:2^2:5:6^3:10^2:11:12:13^2:16:18
:19:21:22^3:30/**Est1**:1^2:6:8^2:11^2:12^2:13-15:17:18:
19:22/**2**:2:3:6:8:9:10:11^4:12,13:14^4:15^3:16:18^3:
19f:21:22/**3**:1:2:3,4^2:5,6^2:8^2:10:12^2:13:14^2/**4**:2:4^2
:5^2:6:7:8^5:9:10^2:11^3:12:13:16:17/**5**:2:3:4^2:5^3:6^2
:7,8^2:11^2:12:13^2:14^2/**6**:1^2:4^2:5:6^4:9^2:10^2:12:13^2:
14^2/**7**:1:2:4^5:7^3:9/**8**:1:2^2:3:4:5:6:7^2:8^2:9,10^3:11^4:
13^2:17^2/**9**:1^5:7-10:12:19^2:20:21:22^2:24,25^3:27^5:
28:29-31^2/**10**:3/**Job1**:4:5:6:8:11:12,13:14,15:16:
17:18:19:21/**2**:1:3:4,5^2:7:8:9^3:11:12/**3**:4:6:8f:10^3:
16^2:18:20,21:23^2:25/**4**:1:3,4^2:18,19/**5**:1:4:6:8^2:8f
:8:10:11^2:21:27/**6**:8,9:14:15-18^2:19-21:25,26^2:28
/**7**:2^2:3:4:10:11:13,14:19:20/**8**:1:10:11-13^3:19^2/**9**
:3:6:10:12^2:14:22:27^2:30^2:31:32,33:35/**10**:2:3^4:9:
10:12:13,14^3:16:19:20,21/**11**:1:7^2:10^2:12^2:13,14^2
:15^2:19:20/**12**:4:5:18:23/**13**:3^3:6^3:8:10^2:11:13:15^2
:16:17^2:20^3:22^3:23:24:27,28/**14**:13:18,19/**15**:2:3:
4,5:14:17-19^2:29^2:32:33:35/**16**:5:6:8:9:10:11:12:
19:20:21/**17**:1^2:5:16/**18**:2^2:3:4:12:14:21^2/**19**:2^2:
3:4:8:12:15:17:18/**20**:2:3:16:17:23/**21**:2,3,7:8^2:
12,13:16^2:21:27:28:30-32/**22**:2^2:3^2:6^3:7^2:17:19:
22:23:26:27^2/**23**:3^2:4,5:10:13:14/**24**:1:3:5^2:10:11^2
:12:14,15:21:22,23/**25**:3:4:5/**27**:9:10:12^2:14:15^2:
19^2:22/**28**:1:2:3,4:5:6:9^2:11f:12:13^2:18:23,24:27:
28^3/**29**:6:7:12:13^2:16^2:21:23/**30**:8:13^2:20^2:24:26:
28,29^3:31/**31**:1:12:13:16:17:19,20:27:29:32:33:
34^2:35^3:37:38,39/**32**:1^2:2^2:3:4:6:7:10:11,12:16:
19:20/**33**:1^2:2:5:6^2:7:10^3:13:17,18:22:23,24^2:26^2:
27:31:32^3:33/**34**:2:3^2:4:9:10:14:15:16:17:18^2:19^2
:22:23:28^2:29,30:31:33^3:37/**35**:2,3,7:9,10:12:13:
14,15/**36**:9^2:10:12:13:15:16^2:19:21:26^2/**37**:2:6:
13:15:19,20^3/**38**:2:3^2:12^2:13^3:15:17,18:20:24:25-
25-27:30:34:35:36f:37,38:39,40:41^2/**39**:1:2,3^2:4:
6:10:11:12:14:18:20^2:21:23:26:27/**40**:2^2:6:8:11:
19:20/**41**:3^2:4:5^2:6:9^3:10^2:27,28/**42**:1:4:7:8^2:16/
Ps1:2^2:6/**2**:1^2:2:3:7/**3**:1:4:7:8/**4**:3^2/**5**:1^2:3:8^2:9^2/
7:1:2:5^2:14:17^2/**8**:2:4^2/**9**:7,8:9:11:12^3:17/**10**:4:9:
11:13:14/**11**:1:5/**12**:3,4:5/**13**:6/**14**:1:2^2:7/**15**:3^2:
5/**16**:1:2:7:8^2:10/**17**:1:10:11^2:12:15/**18**:3^2:5:6:8:
9:10:19:23:25:26^2:28:34:38:41^3:42:50^2/**19**:3,4:5^2
:6:11:13:14/**20**:5:8:9/**21**:3:13/**22**:1^3:15:19:22:24:
27:29/**24**:1:2:6/**25**:1:4:8^2:9^2:12:15:17:21:22/**26**:
1:5:6:11/**27**:2:7:9:11:13^2/**28**:1^2:2^2:3^2:4^2:5:6:7:8/
29:9f:9:10/**30**:1:4^2:8:9:11:12/**31**:2:7:8^2:17:19:22:
23/**32**:5^4:6^2:9^2:10:11/**33**:1^2:3:16,17:20/**34**:2:4:6:
8:9:14:15:16:17:18:21/**35**:4:10:11:12:13^2:17:19:
24f:26:27/**36**:1^2:4^2:10^2/**37**:3:5^2:6:7:8:14^2:16^2:26^2
:32:34:34f/**38**:3,4:12:13,14^2:16:17f:19^2/**39**:1^2:
2,3:4^2:5,6^2:9:12/**40**:1:3^2:4:5:6:7f:8:10:12^3:14,15:
16/**41**:1:6:12/**42**:2:4,5:6:7f:8:11^2/**43**:3:4/**44**:1^2:
17/**45**:1:4^2:10,11:14:17/**46**:7:9:11/**47**:1:6,7^2/**48**:
2:4:11/**49**:1:4:5:8,9^3:10:14f/**50**:1:4^2:5:8:12:14,15
:16/**51**:1:12^2:13^2:14,15:19/**52**:1:4^2:7/**53**:1:2:4^2/
54:1^2:2:5^2:6/**55**:1^2:2:3^2:6:7:8:9:14:15:16:19:22^2:
23^2/**56**:1^2:3,4:5:6^2:7^2:10,11/**57**:2:3/**58**:4,5/**59**:1^2
:4:6:11^2:17/**60**:1:2^2:4,5^4:6,7^2:9,10/**61**:1:2^2:4:5:6f:
7/**62**:1:3,4^3:5:12/**63**:1:2:3:4:9^2:10^2/**64**:1:5^2/**65**:1:
4^2:9:10/**66**:1:5:9:12:12f:13^2:17:19/**67**:4:5/**68**:4^2:
5^2:6:9,10:11,12,13:15,16:17:21:22:24:29:31:32^2:
33:34:35/**69**:3:4:6^2:11:13^2:22/**70**:1:5/**71**:2:3^2:11:
14:17:18:19:20:22:24^2/**72**:1^2:2^3:4^2:6f^2:7:8^2:12^2:
14:15/**73**:1^2:2:12:13:15:16:17:18:19:20:22:27:28
/**74**:3:4:5,6:7:9,10^2:13,14^2:15:16:21/**75**:4^2:5:8/
76:9^2:11:12/**77**:1^2:2:4:9^2:10:16/**78**:1^2:2,3:4^2:5^3:6
:7^2:8^3:10:15:22:23:28^2:32:41:45:46:50^2:54^2:56:
58:61:62:63:66:71,72/**79**:3:6:8:10:11^2:13/**80**:2:3:
3f:7:7f:11:18:19/**81**:1:3:7:8:12:13/**82**:1:2^2:3:5:8/
83:3:5:9^3:10/**84**:2^3:3:5:7/**85**:4:4f:5:8^2:9:13/**86**:2:
3:5:6:7:11^2:12:14:16/**87**:5/**88**:2:5:6:8:9:15/**89**:
3,4:10:12:19:19f^2:19:25:26:28:35,36^2:43:49^2/**90**:
3:4:10:12^2:14:15:16/**91**:5:9:11:12/**92**:1^5/**94**^{2}:3:
20^2:21,22:23/**95**:1:7:10/**96**:1:4:8:13/**97**:1:7:12f/
98:1:2,3^3:4:7:8,9/**99**:4:6:7/**100**:3:4:5/**101**:2^2:3^3:6
:7:8/**102**:1:5:12:13:17^2:21,22^3:24/**103**:6:7:8:13^2:
17,18^5/**104**:3:7,8:11:14^2:15^2:19^2:22:23:26:27:28:
29:30:33^2:35/**105**:1:13:14:14f:17^2:27:31:39^2:41:
42:45^2/**106**:3^2:5:7:8^2:9:13:14:15f:18:19,20:23:24^2
:27:28:28f:30:34:36:37,38:43:44:45:46:48/**107**:1:
7^2:13:19:25:26^2:28:36:37:40:43/**108**:1:7:8^2:10/
109:3:4:6:8:12,13:16^2:17:19:22,23:25:28:30^2:31/
110:1:1f:2:3:5/**111**:1^2:5:6:9^2:10/**112**:9/**113**:3:6:9
/**114**:3:5:8/**115**:1:16^2:17/**116**:15:18,19/**118**:5:6:
8^2:9:13:17:18:23:27,28:29/**119**:4:5:10:17:18:
29,30^2:31:32:33,34:36^2:40,41,42^2:44,45,46:48^2:
49,50:51:52:56^2:57:59,60:61^2:62^2:67:70:71,72^4:
73:80^2:82:83:85,86:87:88:90,91:93:94^2:95:101^2:
105:107:109:112:113:115:116:117:119:121:122:
123^2:124:125^2:126:144:148:149:150:157:161:
168:169:173^2/**120**:1/**121**/**122**^{2}:4^2:9/**123**:1:2/
125:3:4:5/**126**:1/**127**:2^3:4^2/**128**:6/**129**:2:3,4,5:8/
130:3,4,5:7:8/**131**:1/**132**:2-5^2:7/**135**:3:7:12:13/
136:1:2:3:8:10:11,12^2:13:15:18:19:20:21^2:22:25:
26/**137**:5,6,7/**138**:2/**139**:3:4:6:7:8^2:9:11:12^2:14:
16:17,18:17,18f/**140**:5^3/**141**:1:2:3:4:6,7^2:8/**142**:
3^2:4^2:5/**143**:1:2:3^2:8^2:9^2:10:11^2:12^2/**144**:2:8:10:
12-15/**145**:8:9:15:18:21/**146**:3:7^2/**147**:1:7^2:9:10:
11:15:19/**148**:5:14/**149**:6,7/**150**:6/**Pro1**:2^3:3:4^2:
5,6:7,8,9^3:21^3:23:29^2:32:33/**2**:1:7,8:9:11,12,13^3:
18:19f:21/**3**:3:11,12:18:22f:32^2:35^2/**4**:1^2:4:5:6:7:
8,9:10:13:16:18:20:25:26/**5**:1:4:5:6:7^2:9^2:9f^2:15:
23/**6**:3:7:12,13:16-19:21:23^2:26:31:35/**7**:1:5:8,9:
11,12:14:15:21:22:23:24:27^2/**8**:1:6,7:9:12:18:
27,28,29:32:33:34/**9**:3:5:6^2:7,8:10:15^2/**10**:3:5:6:
7:8:10^2:14:17^2:18^4:20:22:26:27/**11**:11:12:13:16^2:
23:24,25^2:26:29/**12**:1^3:9^3:12:14:15:18:28/**13**:2:5:
10:18:19^2:22:24^2:25^2/**14**:2^3:6:8:15:21^2:25:31^2:34
/**15**:9,10:11:12:15:17:18:23^2:27:31,32^3/**16**:3:7^2:9
:10:12^2:22:26:32^3/**17**:8f:10:12:14:16^2:17:18^2:19:
21:23^2:25^2:26^2:27,28^2/**18**:2:5:9:10:13:15:19^2:20:
21:22:24/**19**:2:10^2:11:13:17:19:22:27/**20**:1^2:2^2:3:
7:12:13:16^2:17:18:19^2:22:24:25^2/**21**:1:9:10:13:15
:17:19:21:25,26^3:27/**22**:1:4:6:7:13:17,18,19^2:
24,25/**23**:1^2:4,5,6,7,8^2:12:13,14,15,16,17,18:
19,20,21:22:23:26,27,28:34/**24**:6:8:11,12^3:15,16^2
:21,22:23:24:26:28,29:32,33/**25**:2,3^2:6,7^3:8,9,10:
12:19:21,22:24:25:27^2/**26**:3:4,5f:6^2:8:11:14^2:15^2:
18,19:21f^2:21:24,25,26^3/**27**:7:10^2:11^2:12:13:14:
20f:21:22/**28**:4^4:6:7:9:10:11:13:15:20^2:21:22^2:25
:26:27^2/**29**:1:4:8:10:14:15^3:16:18:21:25/**30**:1:2^2:
4:5:6:8^2:10:18,19:24-28:33/**31**:1:2:3:4:5^2:6,7:15:
16:19,20:24^2/**Ecc1**:3:7^3:8-11:12-15^2:16-18^2:16-
16-18f:16-18/**2**:1^3:3^2:4,5,6^3:12:13,14:16:18:19:
20-23^2:24-26^3/**3**:2^4:3^4:4^4:5^2:6^2:7^4:10:11:12^2:15^2:
16:17:20^2:22^2/**4**:5,6^2:8^2:13^2:15^2/**5**:1^2:4^3:5^2:6,7^2:
8:9:11^2:13,14^2:15:18,19,20^4/**6**:2^2:3:5:7,8:11/**7**:2^3
:5^2:6:11:23:24:25^3:27,28^2:29/**8**:1^4:2,3^2:5:6,7:8^2:
11:14:15^2/**9**:2,3^2:4:7:11:12:15^2/**10**:1:2^2:11:12,13^3
:14:15f:16,17^2:18/**11**:1:2f^2:7:8:9^3/**12**:1:2^3:3:7^2:
10:11:12/**Sol1**:6^2:8:9f^2/**2**:3:4:10:14:17/**3**:1:2:3:5:
8/**4**:6^2:16/**5**:2:4:5:6^2/**6**:2^4:8:11^3:12:12f:13/**7**:9:
12/**8**:2^2:4:5:7:8:11:12:13/**Is1**:1^3:2:4:5,6^2:9:10:11
:12,13:15:17^3:20^2:26:27:28^2:29^2:31/**2**:1:2:3:5:12:
19:20:21^4/**3**:6:9:10:11:12:14:16:17^2:24/**4**:2,3,4:
2,3,4f^4/**5**:1:5^2:6:7:8:11^3:15:18:19^2:21:22^2:23:25:
26^2:29/**6**:4:6:8:10^6:11:12:13/**7**:2:3^4:4:8f:9^2:10:11
:13:14:14f^2:15,16f^3:18f:18^3:19:20^2:21,22:25/**8**:1:
2:4:5:6^2:7,8:9,10:11^2:12:16^4:17:19^2/**9**:1:7^3:11,12^3
:13:17:19,20:21/**10**:1^2:3:4:7:12:14:21:22^2:23:25:
26:27f:30:31/**11**:3:10^2:11:12^2:14:15/**12**:2:5/**13**:2^2
:3^2:6:14:16:21/**14**:1:2^2:4:7:9^2:12:13^2:14:15^2:24:
25^2:28:29^2/**15**:1:2^2:5^3:8/**16**:3^2:4,5:8:12^3/**17**:1:2/
18:2^2:6:7^2/**19**:2:3^4:4^2:5:11:12^3:17:18:19^2:20^2:21^3
:22^2:24/**20**:2^2:4:5,6/**21**:2:3:5:6,7:6,7f:11^2:12:14:
16f/**22**:1:4^2:8:9,10,11:12^4:14:15,16:17:20:21:22:
23,24^2:25^3/**23**:1:6:7:9:11:12:13^2:15,16^2:17:18/
24:10:15,16^2:23/**25**:2:4:10:12/**26**:1:2:3:5:6:8^2:9:
10:11:18:19:21/**27**:3:9^2:11:12:13^3/**28**:1^2:2:3:5:6^3
:9^3:11:12:15:16:17:20^2:21^2:22:23,24:26/**29**:1:1f:
3:8:11^2:12:13:15^4:16:21^2:24/**30**:1^3:2^2:3:4:5:6^2:14
:15:16^2:18^5:19:20:22^2:25:26^2:28^2:29^2:30/**31**:1^3:3:
4,5:6/**32**:3^2:6:7:8:9/**33**:1^3:2:11:12:13:15^4:16:18:
21/**34**:2:8:10:14:17^2/**35**:3:4^2:10/**36**:1:2:3:4^3:6:
8,9^2:10^2:11^2:12^2:13:16^2:17^3:19:21:22^2/**37**:1^2:2:3:
5:7:8,9^3:13^3:14:21^2:22:24:25:26:29:30^2:32^3:34:
36:37^2/**38**:1^2:2:3^2:4:16:17:19:22/**39**:2:3:5^2:6/**40**:
2:9:10:14:16^4:17:20^2:21:22:23:26:29^2/**41**:2^3:7:13^2
:15:17:22:24:27/**42**:1:3^2:5^2:6^3:8:10:14:19:21:22^3:
24:25/**43**:3:4:6:8:10^3:13:14:17:18^2:19^2:28/**44**:1:7
:12:13:14:15^4:16^2:17:19^2:20:21:22^2:25^2:27:28f/
45:1^3:5:6:9:10^2:11^2:13f^2:13:14^2:18^2:19^2:20:22:23^2
:24/**46**:3:6:7:9:10^2:12:13/**47**:2f:2:6:8:10:11:12:13
:14^2:15/**48**:1:3:5^2:6:12:14^2:18:19:20:21/**49**:1:3:5^4
:6^4:7:8,9^3:18:21:22^2:23/**50**:1:2^2:4^2:5:6^2:7:8/**51**:1:
4:5:7:8:11:12:16:17:18^2:19^2:21:23/**52**:6^2:11/**53**:1
:2:6:7:8:10:11/**54**:9:15^2/**55**:2:3^3:5:7^2:10^3:11/**56**:
1^2:2:4^2:7:10^4:11/**57**:1^2:9^4:11:13^2:15:18^2:19/**58**:2^3
:7:9^3:14^2/**59**:1:7^2:8:11:15:16:19:20:21/**60**:1:3^2:4:
5:6^2:8^2:9:11^2:12:13:16:19:22/**61**:1^6:2^3:3/**62**:1^3:3:
6,7:8^2:10:11^2/**63**:1:3:4^2:5:6:7:11:15:17/**64**:7:12/
65:1f^4:2:3:4:5:9:10:12^2:23:24^2/**66**:3^3:4^2:5^3:9:12:
15:17:19f:19^4:20^4:21:23^3:24/**Jer1**:1^2:4:5:7:10:11
:12f:15^2:17:18^2/**2**:1:2:7:9^3:10,11^4:15:16:17:19:24
:26,27^2:29:31^4:32:33:35:36/**3**:1^3:4,5:6^2:7:8^3:9:10:
12^2:13:14:17:18:19^3:20:22/**4**:1:2^3:3:4^2:5^4:10:22^2:
29:31/**5**:3^4:5^2:7^2:10:14:15f:19^3:20^2:22:28^2/**6**:1:6^2
:9:10:13:16:18,19^4:25^2:27:29/**7**:1:2^4:4:5:6:7^2:10^2:
12^2:13,14^4:18^2:18f^2:18:19:24:26^2:27^3:28^4:31^3:32^2
:33/**8**:3:4,5:6^2:8:10^2:12^2:14^3:19/**9**:3^2:6^2:8^2:10:12^3
:14:15:16:20^2:24/**10**:2,3:7:9:11:13:17:20:23/**11**:1
:5:6:7:8^2:9:10^3:11^2:12:13^2:14^2:15^2:16^3:17:19^2:20:
21,22^2/**12**:1:2:3:5:6^2:7:9:12:14:15^2:16:17/**13**:1:3:
4:5:6:10^2:11^4:12:13:15:16^2:17:18:19:20:22:23:26
:27/**14**:1:2^2:6^2:8:9:10^2:11:12:14:16^2:18:21:22/**15**
:1:2^6:3^3:5:6:7^2:8^3:10^2:11:12,13:14:15:16^3:19^2:20/
16:1:4:8:10:12^3:14,15^2:16^3:17:19:21f/**17**:1,2,3^2:4
:10^2:19:20:21,22:23:24:26:27^5/**18**:1:2^2:6^2:7:10^2:
12^2:13:15:17:19^2:20^3:21:22/**19**:1:3^2:4:5:7:8:9^3:11^2
:13^2:14:15^2/**20**:3:4^2:5:6:7:8:12:13/**21**:4:3,4:7:9:
10:11:12^2/**22**:1^2:2:4^2:5^2:6:7^2:8:10:13:13f^2:16^2:20
:23:24,25^3:27:28:30/**23**:1:2^3:4^2:5,6:8^2:12:15:16^3:
17^3:18^3:19:21:22:25^2:27^3:29:37:38,39^3/**24**:1:2:3:
4,5:7^2:8:9^2:10^2/**25**:1,2,3:4:5^3:6:8,9:14:15^3:17:18^2
:19,20:28:29:32:33^2:34:35^2:36^2/**26**:1:2^3:3:4:5^3:
7,8:9:10:11:12:15:16:17:19^2:21^2:22^2:23:24^3/**27**:
1:3:5^2:6^2:8^2:9:10^3:11^2:12^3:13^2:14:15:16^2:17^2:18^2:
19,20,21:22^2/**28**:3:4:5:7^2:9:11^2:12:14:15/**29**:1:3^2
:4^2:5:8:11:14:16,17^2:19^3:20:21^3:22:24:24f:25^3:26^5
:28^4:29^2:30:31^2:32/**30**:1:2:3^2:13^2:15:21f^2:21^2/**31**:
2:3^2:6^2:8:9:10:14:15:16:17:18:20:21^2:22:25^2:32^2:
33:33f^2:34^2:35^2:36^2:38,39^2:40^3/**32**:1:3:5:6,7^5:8:
12:13:14:16:18:19^2:20^2:23^3:25^2:26:28^2:29^4:31:33
:35^3:36:37:39:40^3:41:44/**33**:3:4:5:9^2:10,11:15:18^2
:19:20,21:22:23:24/**34**:1:2:3:4:6:8:9:11f:12:17^2:
18,19:20^2:21:22/**35**:1f:2^2:3:4^2:5:7^3:11^2:12:13:14^2
:15^4:16^2:17:18,19/**36**:1:3:5:7:8^2:9:10^2:12^2:13:
14,15^3:17:18:19:20^2:21:24,25^2:26:27:29:30^2:31:
32/**37**:1:1f:2:3^2:5^2:6:7^5:8:10:11:12^4:13:17^2:18:20
:21/**38**:2:4:6:8:10:11^3:12^2:13:14^3:15:16:17^2:18:
19^4:21,22^3:23:24:26^2:27^2:28/**39**:5:7^2:9^2:11,12:13
:14^3:15:16^2/**40**:1^2:4^4:5^3:6:7:8:9^2:10:12^5:13,14^3:
15^2:16/**41**:1:5:6^2:8:9:12:13,14:16,17^3/**42**:1:2:3^3:
5^2:6:7:9^2:10^2:11^2:12:13,14^2:15:17:19:20/**43**:1:2,3^6
:4:6:8:10:12/**44**:1:2,3^2:4^3:5:8^3:10^2:12^2:14:15:16:
17^4:18:19:20:21:23:24^2:25^2:26^2:27:28^2:29:30f:30^2

(TO Con't)
/**45**:1:2/**46**:1:3:4:11:13:16:19:27:28[2]/**47**:1:2:5/
48:1:2,3,4:7:10:11:12[2]:15[2]:16:19[2]:34[4]:35[2]:39:44:
45[3]:46/**49**:1:8:9,10:12:14[2]:19:20[2]:24:28[2]:30:31:
32:34:36[2]:37/**50**:5[2]:6[2]:7:9[2]:14:15:16:19[3]:25:27[2]:
28[2]:29[4]:33:34:44[2]:45/**51**:2:4:9:11:14[2]:16:17:20f:
20[2]:24:26f:27:31[2]:34,35:37:39[3]:40:50:58:59[4]:
61,62[3]:63:64/**52**:3[2]:5:9:11:14:15[2]:16:17:26:28:31
32:34/**Lam1**:2f:2:3:4[2]:6:7:9[3]:10:11:12[2]:14[3]:15:
18:19f:21[4]/**2**:1:2:4:7[2]:8:9[2]:11:13:14[2]:17:19[3]:20/**3**
10:15:18:19:25[2]:26:27:28:29:30:32:34,35,36:40:
41:50:51:56:57:59[2]/**4**:3,4:5:8:11:15:16:17f:17[2]:
18:19/**5**:4[2]:8:9:13:15:15f:19:21[2]/**Eze1**:1:9:11[2]:
14:15:17:23:26:27,28[4]/**2**:1[2]:3[2]:4:8[2]:9,10/**3**:1[2]:4:5
6:7[3]:10:11:12:14,15:16:17:18[2]:19:20:22[2]:23:24:
26:27[3]/**4**:3[2]:4,5:6:7:8:10[2]:13:14f:17[3]/**5**:1[2]:2:5,6,7
12:15[3]:16/**6**:3[2]:8:10:11:13:14/**7**:1:10,11:12:14:
15:20[2]:21[2]:24[2]:26,27[2]/**8**:2:3[4]:5:6:7:8:12:14:14f:
16:17/**9**:1[2]:2:3[2]:4:8:9:11/**10**:2:4:6:19:22/**11**:1[2]:3[2]
5[2]:8:9:10:11:13[2]:16:24[3]/**12**:1:2[2]:3:4:6[2]:8:10:10f:
10:11[2]:12:12f[2]:13:13f[2]:14:16[2]:17:19:21:23[2]:28/
13:1:2,3:5:6:7[2]:18[2]:19[3]/**14**:1:2[3]:4:5:6,7[2]:11[3]:12:
13:15:17:21:22[2]:23/**15**:1:3:7[2]/**16**:1:2:3f:5:8:15:
16:17:18[2]:19:20[2]:23:25:26:30:33,34[3]:36:37:39[2]:
40,41[2]:43:47:54:57:59,60[2]:61:63/**17**:1:2:3,4:8:9:
11:12,13[2]:15[3]:17[2]:18:20:21/**18**:1:4:6[2]:7[4]:11:12:
15:16:21:23[2]:24[2]:25:28:30/**19**:3:4:5:6:12/**20**:1:3[2]
:5,6[3]:7:9,10:12:14:15:18:20:22:23,24:25f:26:
27,28[3]:29:29f:30[2]:31[6]:32:35,36f:39:40:41:42:45:
47/**21**:1:4:5:8:9,10,11[2]:13:14[2]:16[2]:18:19,20[3]:21[3]:
22[2]:23:27[2]:28:30/**22**:4:7:9:13:18,19,20[2]:23:24:26
:28/**23**:1:4,5[2]:10:11:12f:16[6]:17f:18:19,20:21:24:
27:28[2]:29:34[2]:37:39:40[3]:44[2]:45:46:48[2]/**24**:1:3[2]:6
:7[3]:8[2]:9:11:13:14:15:16:17:18[2]:19:20,21[2]:22:23:
24:26[3]:27/**25**:1:3:4:7:9,10:13:17/**26**:1[2]:5:14f[2]:14:
19:20[2]:21[2]/**27**:1:5:9:10:12:15:16:18:24:25:29/**28**
:1:2,3[2]:4:8:9:11:12f[4]:13:14[2]:17:18:20:21:23/**29**:1
:4:5[2]:10:12:13:14:17:18f[4]:19:20f[4]:21/**30**:6:9[2]:11:
12[2]:16:18:20f:20:21f[2]:21[2]:22:23:25/**31**:1:4:6:7:8[2]
:10:11:15:16[2]:17:18/**32**:1:2:3:4:6:10:17:18:20:21:
26:27:29:30:31:32/**33**:1:3:4:7:8:9:12:13:16:18:21
:23:24:28:31:32[2]:33/**34**:1:2[3]:5:6:8:9,10[3]:13:15,16
:18:19:23/**35**:7:11:12/**36**:1[2]:3:4[2]:5:6:7:8:12:16:
17:19:22[2]:24:26f:30:33:34:37,38[2]/**37**:1:3[2]:4[3]:5:7[3]
:9[2]:10:12[2]:14:15:18,19,20:21:22/**38**:1:2,3f[3]:4:8:
10:12:13:14:18:20/**39**:4[2]:9[2]:11:12:14:15,16[2]:17[2]:
23:24:27:28/**40**:2[2]:4[5]:5:6:14:15:17:19:20:21:22[2]:
23[2]:24:26:27[2]:28:29,30:31:32:34:35:37:38:39:40:
43:45:46[3]:47:48,49[3]/**41**:3:6:7[2]:9:11:21/**42**:1[2]:7,8[2]
:9,10:13:14[2]:15:16-20/**43**:1[2]:3:6:7:10:11[2]:17:18[2]:
19:25:26/**44**:1:2:3:4[2]:5[4]:6:7:8:10:11:12[2]:13:14[2]:
15:16[3]:17:18:19[2]:21:24[2]:26:27:28:29[2]:30[2]/**45**:1:2
:5:6[2]:8[2]:9:13:15:16:17[2]:18:23:24/**46**:2[2]:4:5[2]:7[4]:9:
11[2]:12[3]:13:14,15:16[2]:17[3]:18[2]:19,20[2]:21,22[2]/**47**:1[2]
:2:3[2]:4[2]:5[4]:6:7:8:10:13:14[2]:15:16[2]:17[3]:18[3]:19[2]:20
:22:23[2]/**48**:1[6]:5,6,7:10:12:14:16:18:19:21,22[3]:23[2]
:24:27,28[2]:29[2]/**Dan1**:1[2]:3,4[3]:5:8[3]:8f[2]:11:13:14:
17[2]:18,19[2]/**2**:1:4:8,9[2]:10:11:12:13:14:16:18:22:
24[4]:25:26:29:30:34:39[4]:43:45:46[2]:48:49/**3**:2[3]:5[2]:
6:7[2]:8[2]:9:10:12[2]:13:14[2]:16:17:20:24:26:28[2]:30/**4**:
1:2[2]:6:9:12:17[2]:19[4]:20:21:22[2]:25:27[2]:28:32[3]:34:
35:36[2]:37/**5**:1:2,3,4[3]:10[2]:11:13:15:17:21:24,25:
28:31f/**6**:2:3:4[2]:6[2]:7:10:11:12[3]:13:14[3]:15:16[2]:18[2]
:19:20:22:24:25,26/**7**:4:5[2]:6:7:8:9:10[2]:11:12:13[2]:
16:19:23f:25:25f[2]:26:27/**8**:1:3:7:11:13:15:17[2]:18:
19[3]:23:23f:25:26/**9**:3[2]:4:6[4]:7:11:12:13:15:18:19:
21:22[2]:23[2]:24:25:26:27/**10**:1:2:7:9[2]:10:11[4]:12[2]:
13[2]:14[2]:15:16:17:18:19:20,21[3]/**11**:1:2:3:4:6f:6:6f[2]
:7f:8:9:10,11:14f:15[2]:16:18[2]:20f:21[2]:21f:25:27:
30,31[2]:32f:32:34[2]:36:39[3]:40:44:45/**12**:2[2]:3:7:7f:9
:10:11:13/**Hos1**:1:2[3]:4,5[2]:4,5f:4,5:6[2]:8:10[2]:2[3]:3:4[3]
:5:6:7:9:10[2]:11:13:14:15[2]:16f[2]:17:18:19:20:21,22[2]
:23/**3**:1[3]:3:5[2]:5f:5[2]/**4**:3:4[2]:6[3]:10:12[3]:12f[2]:13[3]:14:
16:17:18:19/**5**:1:2:4:6[2]:8:11:13[2]:15[2]/**6**:1:2:3[2]:5:6
:9:11/**7**:1:2:4:7:10[2]:11[2]:13[2]:16[3]/**8**:6:10:11:12:13[2]
/**9**:1:3:4[4]:5:6:8:10[2]:13[2]:15/**10**:4:6[3]:8[3]:10:11[2]:12:
14/**11**:2[3]:3:5[2]:7[2]:8:9[2]:12/**12**:1[2]:4[2]:6:7:9:10:11:12
:14/**13**:1:2[2]:8:11f:16/**14**:1:2[2]:8/**Joe1**:1:2:3[2]:6:9[2]:
20/**2**:3:5:12:13[2]:14[2]:17:19:31:32/**3**:3:4[3]:5:6:7:8[2]:
12[2]:13:16[2]:18/**Amo1**:2[3]:4:5:5f[3]:7:9:10:12:13:14/
2:4:8f:10:11:12[2]:15/**3**:4:8:9:10:12:13:14/**4**:1[3]:4:6
:8[2]:9:10[2]:11:12:13/**5**:2:3:4:5[2]:7:12:13:16[2]:23[2]:24:
25,26,27[2]/**6**:1:2[3]:5[2]:7:8:10[2]:11:12:14[2]/**7**:1[2]:4:7:8
:10[3]:12[2]:15:16[2]/**8**:3:5[2]:10:12/**9**:2:3:4[2]:6:7:11:12:
13/**Ob1**:1[2]:2:5:7:9:10[2]:11[2]:12:14[2]:15[2]:20:21/
Jon1:1:2[3]:3[4]:4[2]:5[2]:6:7[2]:8:11[2]:13[2]:14:16[2]:17/**2**:1:
2:6:7[2]:10/**3**:1[3]:3[2]:3f:4,5[2]:8:9:10[2]/**4**:2[4]:4:5[3]:6[2]:8[2]:
9[4]:10/**Mic1**:1[3]:3:7:7f:9[2]:10:11f[6]:13[2]:15[2]:16/**2**:1[2]:
4:7[4]:8:11:13/**3**:1:2:4:5[2]:9:11/**4**:2[2]:3:4:8:9:11:13[2]
/**5**:1:3:5[2]:9:12[2]:15/**6**:1[3]:2[2]:4:5:6:8[2]:9[2]:10:11:12:
14[3]:15[2]/**7**:1[2]:3:7[2]:9:12[3]:13:16:17:18/**Nah1**:1:7:9[2]
:11:13:14[2]/**2**:1:5[2]:7[2]:9:12/**3**:1:3:4[2]:10[2]:13:14:18:
19/**Hab1**:1:2[2]:3[2]:5[4]:6f:8:12[2]:14[2]/**2**:1[2]:2[2]:3:9[2]:12:
13:15:18:19[5]/**3**:1f[2]:2[3]:8,9f:10:11:13[2]:16:19[2]/**Zep**
1:1:2:4:5:6:9:12[2]:13:18/**2**:3[2]:5:5f:7:11:14:15[2]/**3**:1
:2:4:6[2]:7[4]:8:9:9f:10:11:16:17,18:19/**Hag1**:1[4]:1f:
3,4[2]:6[2]:11[3]:12:14,15/**2**:6:7:8,9:8,9f:12[2]:14:15:
16,17[3]:18,19f:18,19:20:21:22/**Zec1**:1:3:4[2]:7:10:
11:12:14:16:21[3]/**2**:2[2]:3[2]:6,7[3]:8f:10:11,12[3]:13/**3**:2[4]
:4[2]:5,6:7[2]:8[2]/**4**:6:10[2]/**5**:2:3:11/**6**:5:7[2]:13:14:15/**7**
:1:2[2]:3:5[3]:6:7:8,9[5]:10[2]:11[2]:12[2]:13[2]/**8**:1:2:3[2]:6:8:
12:13[2]:14,15[2]:17:18:19:20,21[5]:22[2]/**9**:1f:3[2]:4:8:
10[2]:10f:12/**10**:2[2]:3:8[2]:9[2]:11f/**11**:1:3:4:7:10:12[2]:
13f:14:15[2]:16:17/**12**:2[2]:3:5:7:9:12,13,14/**13**:1[2]:4[2]
:6f/**14**:1:3:4[2]:5:10[4]:11:16[3]:17[3]:18:19:20f:21[3]/
Mal1:1:2,3[3]:4:5:7[2]:8:9:10:12[3]:13[3]:14[3]/**2**:1[4]:4[2]:5[2]
:6:7:8[2]:10:13:14[2]:15/**3**:1[3]:4:7:8:10[2]:14,15[4]:16[2]/**4**
:2:4/**Mt1**:11:17[3]:18[2]:19[3]:20:23:24/**2**:2:6:7[3]:8:9:
12[4]:13[5]:16[3]:19:20[2]:21:22[4]/**3**:2:5[2]:7:9:9f:10:11:13[2]
:14[2]:15f:16/**4**:1:3:4:5[2]:6:7[2]:8:9:12,13[3]:17[2]:19:21[2]
:24/**5**:3:5:6:13[2]:14:15,16:17[3]:19:22:23:24[2]:25:29[3]
:30:31:32:33:34[2]:37:40:42[2]:45:47:48/**6**:1:2[3]:3:6:
14,15:16:25:26[3]:27:33[2]/**7**:5:6[2]:11[3]:12:13:13f:14:
20:21[2]:22[2]:24:29f/**8**:2:3:4[5]:5,6[2]:8,9[7]:10:13:16:18[3]
:19:20:25:29:29f:33:34[2]/**9**:1:2:3:5,6[3]:8:9:13[3]:14:
15[2]:17[2]:18:19:22:30:36[2]:38[2]/**10**:1[3]:5:6:7:12:13:
18[3]:19:21:22[2]:23:29:31:34[2]:35:38:39:42/**11**:1[2]:1f[2]
:2:4:5[2]:7[3]:8:10[3]:13:14:15:16:20[2]:21[2]:23:25:26:27[2]
:28/**12**:3:4:7:9:10:11:12:13:14:22[2]:31,32:38[2]:
39,40:41[3]:42[2]:43,44,45:46,47:49/**13**:1:11[2]:12,13:
12,13f[2]:16:17:23:26:30:33:34,35[2]:36[2]:38:44[2]:46:
53,54/**14**:2[2]:4:7:9:11[2]:12:13[2]:15[3]:19[3]:22[3]:23,24:
25:27:28[3]:30:35[2]:36/**15**:1:5,6:5,6f:5,6:10[3]:15:21:
22:23[2]:24[2]:26[2]:27:29:31:32[3]:33:35:36[3]:39/**16**:1[2]:
4:5:7:13:17:21[5]:22[3]:23:24[2]:27:28/**17**:1:4:6:9:16:
17:20:22,23[2]:24:25[3]:26,27[3]/**18**:1[2]:2:3:6:6f:6[2]:7[2]:
8[3]:9[3]:10:11:12:15:16:17[2]:17f:21:23[3]:28:29:31:32:
34:35[2]/**19**:1:3[2]:5,6:10[2]:12[2]:13:14:16[2]:17[2]:21[2]:23[2]
:24[2]:27[2]:29/**20**:1:2:2f:2:8:10:13:14:15[2]:17:18[4]:19[2]
:20:21:22[3]:23[2]:26:27:28[3]:31:32,33[3]/**21**:4:5:7[2]:14:
17:18:19[2]:21:23[3]:32[3]:33[3]:34[2]:36:38:40:41[2]:43:46[2]
/**22**:1:3[2]:4:5[2]:8:9:11:13:15[3]:16[2]:17[2]:18:21[2]:23:26
:31[2]:34,35:44/**23**:1[2]:3[2]:4:6:7:11[2]:13,14[2]:15[2]:16[2]:
18[2]:23:25[2]:27:28:29,30[2]:34:35:37[2]:38:39[2]/**24**:1:5
:8:13:15:17:18:19[2]:26:27:29:31f:32:33:34:39:45:
48:51/**25**:1:2,3,4:5,6:7,8:9:10:14:15[4]:16:17:19[2]:
20:21:22:28:34:37:40[2]:41:42:45[2]/**26**:4:6[2]:8,9:10:
12:14:15:16[2]:17[2]:24:26:27:28:30:31:32[2]:36[3]:37:
38:40:43:44:45:48:49:53:55[2]:56:57:58[5]:59:60,61[2]
:62:63[2]:68:69:71:73:74/**27**:1[4]:1f[2]:2:3[2]:6:7[2]:14:15
:17:20:21:26[3]:31:32[2]:33:34:35:48[2]:51:52:53:55:
58[3]:62:63:64[2]:66/**28**:1:5:6:7[3]:8[2]:9:10[3]:11:12,13[2]:
15[2]:16:20[2]/**Mk1**:2[2]:3:4:5:7:7f:12,13[2]:14[2]:17:22[2]:
24:25[2]:29,30:31[2]:32,33[2]:34[3]:35:36,37:38[2]:40[2]:41
:43,44[2]:45[3]/**2**:1:2:4:5:6:8:9,10,11[3]:13[2]:14:15:16[2]:
17[2]:18:19:22:24[2]:25,26:27[2]:28/**3**:1:2:3:4[4]:5[2]:6:
7,8[2]:9[3]:10:12:13:14,15[4]:20[3]:21[2]:31,32[2]/**4**:2:3:
11,12[3]:13:14[2]:15[2]:18:21[2]:22:24:25:30:31,32:33[2]:
33f:34:35[2]:37[2]:38:39/**5**:3,4:6:7,8[3]:10[2]:14[2]:17:18:
19:20:20f:20:21:23:28:31:32:33:34:35:36:37:39:
40:41,42:43[3]/**6**:1:2,3[2]:5:7:8,9:10:11[2]:12:14:15:
17,18[2]:20[2]:22,23:25:26:27[3]:28[2]:30[2]:31:34:35,36[4]
:37:38:39,40:41[3]:45[2]:46:48:50:51:52:55[2]:56/**7**:1:
2:3:3f:4:6,7:11[3]:12,13:14[3]:15,16f:17:22:24[2]:25:
26:27[2]:31[2]:32[2]:34:36/**8**:1[2]:4:6[2]:7:10:11:11f:13:
14:15:16:17:18:22[2]:26[2]:27:28:30:31:32f:33:34[2]:
35/**9**:1[3]:2[2]:6[2]:7:9:10:15:17:18[2]:19[2]:20:22:24:25:
26:27:30,31[5]:32:33:34:35:36:38[2]:39f:42:45,46/
10:1f:1:2:4:5:6,7[2]:11:13[3]:14[3]:15[2]:17[3]:21:23[2]:24:
25[2]:28[2]:29:30:31:32[3]:33[3]:34:35:35f:35:37[2]:38[2]:
40[2]:42:43:44:45[3]:47:49:50:51[2]:52/**11**:1:6:7[2]:9:10
:11:13:14:15[3]:17:18:21:22,23[2]:24:27,28[2]:33/**12**:1[3]
:2:9:11:12[2]:13[2]:14[2]:16:17[3]:23:26[2]:28:33[3]:34:36:
37:38[3]:39:40[2]:41:43,44/**13**:3,4[2]:6:9[2]:11[2]:12[2]:13:
14:17[2]:27:28:34[3]:35,36,37[2]/**14**:1[2]:4,5:7:10[4]:11:
12[2]:13:14:15:22:23[2]:24:26:28[2]:29:31:32:33:34[2]:
35:37:40[2]:41:44:44f:45:48[2]:49:51,52:53:55[3]:57:
60[2]:61:62:65[2]:68:70:71:72/**15**:1[3]:5:6:8[2]:11:15[3]:
19:20:21:22:23:26:36:38f:38:41[2]:42,43/**16**:1:6:7[2]
:8:9:12:13[2]:14[2]:15[2]:16:17:18[2]/**Lk1**:3[5]:4:6:8,9[2]:
11,12:13[2]:16[2]:17[2]:17f[3]:18:19:20[2]:21:22:25:26:27[3]
:28:29:30:31:35:38:39,40[3]:42:49:50[2]:54:55[2]:56:
57:58[2]:62:63:66:68:71:72,73[3]:75:77:78:79[4]:80/**2**:
3[2]:4[2]:6:7:14:15[3]:16[2]:17:20:22[3]:23:25:26:27[5]:
29,30,31:34,35[2]:39:41,42:43:44:45[2]:48[3]:49:51[2]/
3:1:3[4]:4:7[4]:9:10:11[2]:12[2]:13:15[2]:18:19,20/**4**:3:5:
6,7[2]:9,10,11[5]:12:14:16[3]:17[2]:18,19[7]:18,19f:20:24:
25,26[2]:28:29[2]:31:34[2]:35:38:39[2]:40:41:42[2]:44/**5**:1[2]
:3[2]:4:6:8[2]:12[2]:14[2]:15[2]:16:18,19[2]:20:23,24[3]:25:27:
30:32[3]:35:36:39/**6**:2:7[3]:8:9[5]:10:11:12:13:17,18[2]:
19:20:21:27:30:31:33:34[2]:35[4]:36:38[5]:39:42[2]/**7**:3[2]
:4:5:6,7,8[5]:9:10:11:14[2]:15[3]:16:17:19[2]:20,21,22[2]:
24[2]:27[2]:32:33:36[3]:39:40[3]:41[3]:44[4]:46:48:49:50/**8**:
1:3:4[2]:5[2]:6:10:11:13[2]:14[2]:15[3]:16:17[2]:18:19:20:22
:23[2]:24:25:27:28:29:31:32:34:35:37[3]:38:39:41:
43,44:47[2]:48:49:50:55/**9**:1[2]:2[2]:5:7:9:10:12[4]:13:
14:16:21[2]:22:23[3]:28:29:31[2]:33:35:38:40:41:42[3]:
43:44[2]:45:46:48:49[3]:51:52:53[2]:54[2]:55f[3]:56:57:58[2]
:59[3]:59f:60[2]/**10**:1[2]:2[3]:6:7[2]:11:13:15[2]:16:17:19[2]:
21:22[2]:23[2]:24:25[3]:29:29f:30:31:33f:34:35:36:38[2]:
39:40[3]:41/**11**:1[3]:4:5,6[5]:7:10:13:14:16[2]:18:24[2]:
29,30[3]:31[2]:33[2]:37,38:39:42[2]:43:46:47:49:51:52[2]:
53,54/**12**:1[2]:3:4:5[2]:7:11[2]:13:14:15:17:19[2]:20:22[3]:
24[2]:25:29:31:32:33:36:41[2]:42,43,44:45[4]:46:47:
48:49[2]:51[2]:54[2]:56:57:58[3]/**13**:3:6:7:11:12:14[3]:16:
22[2]:24,25[3]:29:31[2]:33:34[2]:35/**14**:1:3[2]:4:5[2]:7[2]:8:9[2]
:11:12:15:17[2]:18[2]:19:21[3]:23:26:26f:28[2]:31[2]:32:
34f/**15**:1[2]:3,4:6:7:9:10:12:13:14:15[2]:16:17[3]:18:
20:21:22:24:27:29[2]:31:32[2]/**16**:1[2]:2:3[3]:4:5,6[2]:8:9[2]
:9f[4]:13:15:16:22:24:25:26[3]:27:28:29:30[2]:31:31f[2]/
17:1[3]:2,3:5[2]:6:7,8,9:14:15[2]:18[2]:19:21:22:23:26:
27:30:31[2]:32:33:37f[2]/**18**:1[2]:3[2]:4,5[2]:7:9:10[2]:12:13[2]
:15[3]:16,17[4]:18[2]:20:22:24[2]:25[2]:30:31:32[2]:34:39:
41/**19**:3[2]:4:5:6:7:8:9,10[3]:11:12[2]:13:15[2]:17:21:24[2]
:29:30[3]:35[2]:36,37:38:41[2]:44:45:46:47[2]:48/**20**:2:9[4]
:10[2]:16:18:19[3]:20:21:22[2]:25:26:28[3]:33:34,35:
37,38[3]:41:42,43:45:46[3]:47/**21**:14:15:16:21[3]:23:
24:28:32:36:36f:37,38[4]/**22**:2[2]:4[4]:5[2]:6[2]:8[2]:9:11[2]:
12:13:15[2]:19:20[2]:24[2]:25:28:30:31[2]:32:33[3]:35:37:
39:44:45[2]:47:47f:49:52:54:67,68[2]/**23**:1:2[3]:4[2]:5:7[3]
:8[2]:11:14:15[2]:17,f:18:20:22[2]:24:25[2]:26[2]:28:30[2]:
31[2]:32,33:37:38:40,41:46:48:50,51,52:56/**24**:1:4[2]
:6,7:9[2]:10:11:12[2]:13:17:19:20[3]:21:24:25[2]:26:29:
30[2]:33,34[2]:35:40:41:45:47[2]:49f:50[2]:51:52/**Jn1**:1
f:4:6,7:8:9:11,12[5]:11,12f:14f:15:16:19[2]:22[2]:24,25
:27:31[2]:33:34:39:41:42:43[2]:45:51/**2**:3:4f:5:6:7,8[3]
:13:16:18[2]:20:22[2]:24,25[2]/**3**:1:13[2]:17[2]:18:20:21[3]:
26[2]:28[3]:29:31:36/**4**:1[4]:3:4:5,6[2]:7:8:9[2]:15:17,18:
21-24[3]:25:27[2]:28,29:30:31:33:38:40,41[3]:42:
43,44:46,47[3]:52/**5**:1:4[2]:6:7[2]:10[2]:11:14:15:18[2]:21:
22:23[2]:24:26:27:29[2]:30:32,33f:32,33[2]:36:37[2]:38[3]
:39:40:41,42:43[2]:45:46[3]/**6**:2-5[4]:6:7[2]:10:11[2]:15:
16[2]:20[2]:21:22,23:24[2]:26:28:30,31:32:33:35:37:
38[2]:39:41[2]:44[3]:45[2]:48-51[2]:52:60:61:62:63:65[2]:67
:68/**7**:1[3]:3[2]:4:6:11:13:14:15:17:18:20:25:26:29:
30:31:32:33[2]:34:35[2]:36[2]:37[2]:39[2]:45[2]:50:51/**8**:1:2
:4:5:6:10:12:21:23:25:26:27:29:30,31[3]:33:37:40:
42:44:47:50:56:59/**9**:3:4:11[2]:13:21[2]:24[2]:27[2]:29:
31[2]:34:36:37:39[3]:41/**10**:1:3:7:8:10[2]:18[3]:20:21:24
:29:31:32:33:34,35,36:39:40:41:42/**11**:3:6[2]:7[2]:8:
11:15[2]:16:19[2]:20:21:22[2]:23:28[2]:29:31[3]:35:37,38:
41:46[2]:47[2]:51:54[2]:56/**12**:1:5:9[3]:10:12:13[2]:15:16:
17:18:19:20[2]:21[2]:22:23,24[2]:26[2]:28:29:32:33[2]:35[2]
:38f:40[2]:41:42[2]:44:46:47[2]:49:50[2]/**13**:1[5]:5[2]:6[2]:10[2]
:13:14:15[2]:18:20[2]:23f[3]:23:24[2]:25f:26:29[3]:31:33:
34:35:37/**14**:2,3:4:6:9:12,13[2]:18:20:21:22[4]:23[2]:
24:28[2]:30[2]/**15**:4:8:13:16[2]:19[2]:20[2]:21:22:26/**16**:4:
5:7:10:12:13:17,18:19:20[3]:21:23[2]:26[2]:28:30:32/
17:1[2]:2:3[2]:4[2]:6[2]:8[2]:9:10[2]:11:13:15[2]:19:20:26/**18**:
3:4,5[3]:6:9:11:13:16:22:24:28[2]:29:31f[2]:33[2]:34f:37[2]
:38:39[2]/**19**:4[3]:7:10[3]:11[2]:12:13:14:16[2]:17:21[2]:
23,24:26:27:27f:28:29:31[2]:33:38[2]:39/**20**:1:3,4[2]:9
:11:17[2]:21:23:27/**21**:1:7[2]:8:14:15:18[3]:19[2]:20:22[2]:
23[2]/**Act1**:1:3[4]:4:6[2]:7:8[3]:11:12:16[2]:17:20[2]:21,22[2]:
24,25[3]/**2**:6[2]:14:23[2]:24:29:33[2]:34[2]:36[2]:37[2]:38:39[3]
:40:47[2]/**3**:1[2]:7,8:11[2]:13[3]:15:17:19[2]:20:21,22:23:
25[3]:26[3]/**4**:1[2]:8:9:10[3]:11:12[2]:18:19:21:25,26:29:
34,35[3]:37[2]/**5**:2:3:4[5]:5:9[2]:9f:10:14:20:21:22:25:28[2]
:30:31[2]:32:33:35[2]:36:39:40:41:42/**6**:5[2]:6:10:11:
12/**7**:2[2]:3[5]:4:5:7:9:12:13[2]:14[2]:15:16:17,18[2]:19:21
:23:25:26:27:28:30:31[2]:33:34[2]:35:38:39[2]:40:41:
42:44:54:58:60/**8**:3:5:6[2]:15:18:24:25[3]:26[2]:27[2]:29
:31[2]:32:33f:35:36:40/**9**:1[2]:2[2]:4[2]:8,9:10:11[2]:13:14
:15[3]:17:20[2]:21[2]:23:24:26:27[3]:29:30[2]:31:32[3]:34:
35:38[3]:40[2]:41/**10**:2:5,6[3]:8:9,10:11:12:13:16:17:
19[2]:22[3]:24:25:28:32:33[3]:35:40,41[4]:42[3]:45:46,47:
48/**11**:6:11[2]:12[2]:13[4]:17:18[2]:19:20[2]:22[2]:23[2]:24:25[2]
:26:27:28:29[2]:30[3]/**12**:4[2]:5:6:7:10[3]:11[3]:12:13:14:
17:18:19[2]:20:21:23:25/**13**:4:5:6,7[4]:8[3]:10:11:13:
14:16:24[2]:28[2]:30:31[2]:32,33[3]:34[3]:36[2]:37[2]:40:42[2]:
43:44:46[2]:47[3]:48f[2]:51/**14**:1:3:5,6[3]:9:10[2]:13[2]:15[4]:
16:18:21:22[2]:23:24:25:26[2]:27/**15**:1[2]:2[3]:3[3]:5[2]:6:7[2]
:8:10[2]:13:14[3]:15:19:20[3]:22[3]:23:25[3]:27,28,29[5]:30:
32:33[2]:34,35:36[3]:37:40,41/**16**:1[2]:3[2]:4:6:8:10[2]:11[2]
:13[2]:14:15[2]:16:17[2]:18[2]:20,21:25:26:27[2]:28:29:30
:35:36:37:38:39[3]:40[2]/**17**:1:2[2]:3:5[3]:10[3]:11[3]:14:15[3]
:17[3]:19:20:21:23[2]:25[2]:30:31:32/**18**:1:2,3:4:5:6:7:
9:10:13[2]:14[4]:18[2]:18f[2]:19:20[2]:20f:21[2]:22f[2]:22:
25,26[2]:25,26f:27[4]/**19**:4[5]:8[2]:9[2]:11:13[3]:17:21[4]:22:
24:29[2]:30:31[2]:33:35[3]:40[2]/**20**:1:2:3[3]:4:7f:9:13:14:
16[2]:17[4]:21:22:27:30:32[3]:34[2]:35[3]:38/**21**:1[2]:4[2]:5[2]:
8:11:12[2]:13[2]:18:20:23:24[2]:25[6]:26,27[3]:28:34[2]:35[2]
:37,38[2]:39[2]:40[2]/**22**:1:3[3]:4[2]:5[4]:7[2]:8:11:13:14[2]:15:

(TO Con't)
17,18:21[2]:22[2]:24[2]:25[3]:26:29:30[2]/**23**:2[2]:3[2]:4[3]:9[2]:
10[2]:12,13:14:15[3]:16:17[2]:18[3]:19:20[3]:21[4]:23,24[3]:
25:26:27:28[3]:30[4]:31:32[3]:33/**24**:1:2[2]:3:5[2]:6:10:11:
14:16:17[4]:19:21:22:23[4]:25:26:27/**25**:1:3[3]:6:9[3]:
10,11[5]:12[2]:15:16[3]:20[3]:21[4]:22:25[2]:26[2]:27[2]/**26**:1:2[2]
:5[2]:6[2]:7:8[3]:9[3]:10:11[3]:12:14:14f:16[4]:17[2]:18[2]:19:20[3]
:21:22[2]:23[3]:26:28:29:32[2]/**27**:1[2]:2:3[2]:4[2]:7,8:9:11[2]:
12[4]:13:14,15[3]:17[2]:21:23:27:30[2]:31:33[2]:35:40:41[2]
:42:43[2]:44/**28**:1[2]:3:4[2]:6[2]:7:10:13:14[2]:15:16[2]:17[2]:
18:19[2]:20:20f:22:23:26:27[3]:28,29[2]:31/**Rom1**:1[2]:
4:5:6,7:9:10[2]:11,12[5]:13[2]:14[4]:15[4]:16[4]:17[2]:17f:19:
21[2]:22:23:24:25[2]:28:30:31:32/**2**:4[4]:5[2]:7:12-15[2]:
17:19[3]:21:22[2]:26/**3**:3:5:6:7:8:11:15:17:19:20:
21,22[4]:25[2]:25f:25:26:27:29/**4**:1:4,5[4]:7:9[2]:10[2]:11:
13[3]:14[2]:15[4]:16[3]:18:19[2]:21:25/**5**:2[2]:3:5[2]:7:8:9:10:
12:13[2]:14:15[2]:16:17:18:19[3]:20:21/**6**:2,3[2]:4[2]:5:6[4]:
7:10:11[3]:12:13[4]:14:16:17[2]:18:19[4]:21[2]:22/**7**:2[3]:3:
4[5]:5[2]:8:9:10:11:13:15[2]:18:19[2]:20:21[2]:22:
23,24,25[6]/**8**:1:3:5:6[2]:12[3]:15:16:17[2]:18:23:24[2]:25:
26:28:29:30[2]:31:34[2]:36:37:39/**9**:1[3]:4[3]:6[3]:7:8:10-
10-13[3]:15[4]:16[3]:18[3]:20[2]:21[4]:22:23,24[3]:30:31:32/
10:3[3]:4[2]:6[3]:7[3]:12:14:17:18:19[4]:21[2]/**11**:2,3[2]:4:8[3]:
9:11[3]:12:13:15[4]:18[2]:19:22[2]:23[2]:24[3]:25[2]:28[3]:30:
32:33:34:35[3]:36/**12**:1[3]:4,5[4]:6[3]:8[2]:13:16[2]:19:20[2]/
13:2[2]:3:4:5:6:7[3]:9[2]:10:14[2]/**14**:1[2]:1f:2[2]:3[2]:4[3]:5[4]:6[4]
:7:10:11[2]:12:13:14:19:20:21[2]:22:23/**15**:1[2]:4[3]:5:6:
8[3]:9[3]:14:15,16[4]:17:18[2]:20:22:23:24[2]:25[3]:27[4]:27f[3]
:28[2]:30:31:32[2]/**16**:1:4:5[3]:6[2]:8:10:11[2]:12[2]:13[2]:14:
15[2]:17[2]:19[2]:23[2]:25,26,27[3]/**1Co1**:1:2[4]:8:10[2]:15:
17[2]:18[2]:19:20:21:22[3]:23:24[3]:27[2]:28[2]:30:30f:30:
30f[2]:31/**2**:1[2]:3:4:5:6[2]:7:10:12:13[2]:14:16[3]/**3**:1[3]:2[2]:
3:6[2]:10:12:13[2]:19[2]:22:23/**4**:2:5[5]:6:8:9[2]:11[2]:12:13
:14[2]:15[3]:16:17[2]:18[2]/**5**:2:3,4[2]:5:6:9[2]:11[2]:12[2]/**6**:1[4]:
2:3:4:4f:5[2]:7[3]:12[4]:13[2]:14:15:16:17:18:19:20[2]/**7**:2
:4[4]:5[5]:7:8[3]:9[2]:11:12[3]:13:14:15[2]:16[2]:21:23:24:25[4]:
26[2]:28[2]:29:31:32[2]:33[2]:34:35[5]:36:37[2]/**8**:1[2]:3:4:5:6
:7[3]:9[3]:10[2]:11[2]:12[2]:13[4]/**9**:1:2[2]:3:5f[2]:7[3]:8:9[2]:10:11:
12[4]:13[3]:15[3]:16[2]:18:19[2]:20[3]:22[2]:23[3]:24:25[3]:25f:
26[2]:27[3]/**10**:1:2:3,4[2]:7[2]:10:11[3]:12:13[2]:15:16:19[2]:
20[5]:22:23[4]:24:25:26[2]:27[3]:28:32:33/**11**:3[4]:4:5:6[2]:
7:10f:10:13:14,15:16:17:20:21[2]:22[3]:23:24[3]:31:34
/**12**:1[2]:2:3:5:8[2]:9[3]:10[7]:21[2]:23:24:27:28:29:30:31/
13:1:2[2]:3:7:8:10:12[2]/**14**:1:2[5]:5[2]:6[3]:8:9[2]:11[4]:12[2]:
20:21[2]:22[3]:23[2]:26:27:28[2]:32:32f:33:34[2]:34f[3]:35[2]:
37[2]:39[2]/**15**:1:3[2]:5f:10:11:12:15:17[2]:19:20:22[2]:24
:27[2]:29:33:34:35:38:40f:42:43:44:50/**16**:1[3]:2:3[2]:
4:5[2]:6:7[2]:9:11[2]:12[2]:13:15:16:17:18[2]:20[2]:24[2]/**2Co**
1:1[2]:3,4:6,7[3]:8:9[2]:10:11[2]:13,14[3]:15,16[4]:19:20:21:
22[2]:23[3]:24[4]/**2**:1:2[2]:3:4[4]:5,6[3]:7[2]:9:10:11[2]:12:13[5]:
14[3]:15:16[2]:17/**3**:1[2]:4[3]:6[2]:7[3]:9:15:16:17/**4**:1:2[3]:3[2]
:4[2]:10:11[2]:13:14[2]:15[2]:18[2]/**5**:2:4[2]:6:8:9:10:11:12:
13,14[5]:15[2]:16:18[3]:19[2]:20[3]/**6**:1:2[3]:3:4:5:6:8:9[2]:10:
12:13[2]:18/**7**:1:2:3:7:8[2]:9[3]:10:11[4]:12[2]:13:14:15/**8**:
1:2:3:4:5[4]:6[2]:7:8:9:10[4]:11:12[3]:16:17[2]:19[4]:21:22[3]:
23:24/**9**:1[2]:2[4]:3[2]:4:5[3]:7[3]:8[4]:9[2]:10[4]:11[2]:12:13[2]/**10**
:1:2[3]:3:4:5[3]:6:8[3]:11:13[2]:14[2]:15:16[2]:17/**11**:3:4:7:
12:16[2]:17:19,20:21:23:26:27:29:31:32/**12**:2,3:4[3]:
5[3]:6[2]:7:8:9[2]:11:12:13[5]:14[2]:15:16:17:18:19[4]:20[2]/
13:1:2:4:5:6:7:8[2]:9:10[5]:11/**Gal1**:1[2]:5:6[3]:8:10[3]:11:
12:13:14:15:16[3]:17[3]:18:20[2]:21:23:24/**2**:1:2[3]:4[3]:5[2]
:6[4]:7,8,9[3]:10:11[2]:14[2]:16:17[3]:18:19[3]:21/**3**:1:2[2]:3[2]:
4:5:8,9:10:11:14:15[2]:16[3]:17[2]:19[7]:20:21,22[3]:23:
24:25[2]:29[2]/**4**:2[2]:3:5[2]:7:8:9[4]:10:12[2]:14:15:15f:17[4]
:18:19:20[2]:21[3]:24,25[5]:26:27:29:30:31[2]/**5**:1:2[2]:3:4[2]
:5:6[2]:7:8:9:10[2]:11:12:13[2]:16[4]:17[4]:18:20:24[2]:26[2]/
6:3[2]:4:8:10[2]:11:12[2]:13[3]/**Eph1**:1[3]:2:3:4[2]:5[3]:6[3]:10:
11[2]:12[2]:13[3]:14[3]:16,17[2]:18[3]:19[2]:21/**2**:3:7:13[2]:14:
15[3]:16:17[2]:18:19[2]/**3**:2,3:4[2]:5:6[3]:7:8[2]:9[2]:10[3]:13:
14,15:18,19[2]:20[3]/**4**:1:3:4:7:8[2]:9[2]:10:11[4]:12[3]:13:
14:19:25[2]:27:28:29[2]:30:32[2]/**5**:2[3]:3:5:6:12:17[2]:19:
20:21:22[2]:23:25[2]:26:27:31:32:33/**6**:1:4:5:9[2]:10:
11:13:14:15:16:19[2]:22[2]:23/**Php1**:1:3:10[3]:11:12[2]:
14:16,17[4]:19[2]:20[3]:21:22[3]:23[2]:24:25:26[2]:27[3]:29/**2**
:1[3]:3:6:8:9:11:12[2]:13:15:16:17[4]:19:21:22:23[4]:24:
25[3]:27:28[3]:30/**3**:1:2:3:4:5:6[2]:9:10[7]:12[2]:13[2]:14[2]:
15:17:20:21/**4**:1[2]:2:3[2]:6:10:11:12:13:15:21:22[2]/
Col1:1:2:3:5[2]:6[2]:7:9[3]:10:12[3]:19:20[2]:23[3]:24[2]:25[3]:
26,27[2]:28[4]/**2**:6:11:14:15[2]:18[2]:19[2]:20:22:23/**3**:1:5
:7:8:9:10:11:12[2]:13:16[2]:17:18:19:22[2]:24/**4**:1:2:3[2]
:4:5:8[2]:12[2]:15[3]:16[2]:17[2]/**1Th1**:1[3]:3[2]:5[2]:7:8[2]:9:10[2]
/**2**:2[3]:4[2]:5[2]:6:9[3]:11[2]:12[2]:13:16[3]:17[2]:18/**3**:1:2,3[3]:5
:6[2]:7:10[2]:11:12[3]:13/**4**:1[2]:3,4[2]:7[2]:8[2]:9[2]:10:11:12[2]:
13[2]:14:15:16[2]:17/**5**:1[2]:3[2]:5:9[2]:11:13:15[3]:18:21:
23:24:27[2]/**2Th1**:1:3[3]:4:5:7:8[3]:9:10:11:12/**2**:1[2]:10[3]
:11:13[2]:13f[2]:14/**3**:1[3]:7:8[2]:9[3]:11:12[3]:13:14:15[3]/
1Ti1:2[2]:3,4[3]:7:10,11:12[3]:13:14:15:16:17:18:19:
20[5]/**2**:1:4[2]:5:6:7[3]:8[2]:15/**3**:1:7:10:14[2]:16[3]/**4**:3[4]:5:
6:13:14:15:16[2]/**5**:1[3]:3:5:8:9:10[3]:11[2]:13[2]:14[2]:16[3]:
19[2]:21:23/**6**:2:4:5[2]:6:9[4]:11[2]:12:13:14:17[2]:18[4]:20[2]
/**2Ti1**:1:2:3[2]:4:6[2]:7[3]:8[3]:9[2]:10:11[3]:12:13:17[2]/**2**:2[2]:
7[2]:10[2]:12:13[3]:14:15[2]:17:20:22[2]:25[3]:26[3]/**3**:1[2]:2[2]:3[2]
:4:5:9:11:12:15:16[3]:17[2]/**4**:1:2[2]:3[3]:4:5[2]:6[2]:7[2]:8[3]:
10[3]:12:13:16:17[3]:18:19:21/**Tit1**:1[4]:3[3]:4:5[2]:6:9[2]:
10[2]:12:13[2]:14[2]/**2**:2:3:4[2]:5[2]:6:7:8[2]:9[3]:10[2]:11:12[2]:
13:15[2]/**3**:1[2]:2:3:4:5:7:8:9:10:12[4]:13:14:15/**Phm1**
:1[4]:8,9[3]:10[2]:11[3]:12:13:14[4]:16[2]:17:22/**Heb**:1[2]:2[2]:
3:4:5,6[2]:13[2]:14[2]/**2**:1:3[2]:4[2]:6:10[3]:11:12:15:17[3]:18
/**3**:1:2:5:6:7,8[4]:9:10[2]:11:13:14[2]:15:16:18[2]/**4**:1[2]:2[3]
:4:6:7:8:11[3]:12:13[2]:14[2]:15:16[4]/**5**:1[4]:4[3]:5[2]:5f:6[2]:7:
7f[4]:7:8[2]:9:10:11[3]:12,13[3]:14/**6**:1[4]:3:4[2]:5:6[4]:9:10:
12:13[2]:16[4]:17[2]:18[3]:20/**7**:2:3f:5[2]:7:9:10:11[2]:
12,13,14[2]:16:19[2]:21:23:24:25[3]:26:27/**8**:1:3:4:5[3]:
6:7:9[3]:10[2]:11[2]:12/**9**:6:7[2]:8[2]:9:10[3]:14[4]:15:16[2]:17:
19:20:23:24:26[2]:28[2]/**10**:4:4f:5:7[2]:9:12:13:16:18[2]:
20:22[3]:23:24[2]:26:27[2]:28[2]:29:30:31:36[2]/**11**:1:3f:5
:6[2]:7[2]:8[3]:9:10[2]:11:12[2]:14:15[2]:16[2]:17:18[2]:19[2]:20:
22:24,25[2]:26[3]:28[2]:31[2]:32[2]:35[3]:40/**12**:2:3[2]:5[2]:9[2]:
14[2]:15:18[2]:19:22[2]:23[3]:24[2]:25[7]/**13**:1:2[2]:6:7:10:13[3]
:14:15:16[3]:17[4]:18:19:20,21[2]:22:23[2]:24,25[2]/**Jas1**:
1:3:4:5[4]:6:7,8:9:10,11:13[3]:15[2]:17:19:21:22[3]:27/**2**
:1[2]:3:5[3]:12:13:16:17[2]:18:20:21[2]:22[2]/**3**:1:4:8:17[2]/
4:2[2]:4:6[2]:7:8[4]:11[2]:12[2]:13:14:15[2]:17/**5**:1:3:6:7:11[2]
:13[2]:14:16:18:20/**1Pe1**:1:2:3:5[2]:7[3]:10:11[3]:12[4]:13[2]
:15:17[2]:18[3]:20:22[2]:23[2]:25/**2**:1:2,3[2]:4[2]:5[3]:6:7[2]:8:9
:11:14[2]:16[2]:23:25/**3**:1[3]:4:6:8:9[2]:11[2]:12:13:14:15[2]
:17[2]:18:19:20[2]:21f:21[2]:22/**4**:1:2:6:8:9:10[3]:11[3]:12[2]
:16:19[2]/**5**:1[2]:2:5:8:11:12[2]:13f[2]:14/**2Pe1**:1[4]:2:4[2]:5[4]
:6:7[3]:8:9[2]:10:11:12:13,14[3]:15:16:19[3]/**2**:3:6:9:10:
12:14:16:17:19[2]:21[2]:22[3]/**3**:1[2]:3:4:5,6:8:9:11:12:
13:14[3]:15,16[4]:18/**1Jn1**:1:2[2]:5[2]:8:9[5]/**2**:1:3[3]:4[3]:5[3]:
7:8:12:13[4]:14[2]:16[2]:19:21[3]:26:27[2]:28/**3**:1:2:3:6[2]:8[3]
:10:11:12[2]:15:16:17[2]:21/**4**:1:2[2]:3:4:5[2]:6[3]:7:9[2]:10:
11:13:14:18[2]/**5**:3:4:13:14:15:16:20/**2Jn1**:1[2]:4[2]:5:
6[2]:7:8[2]:9:10:12[4]/**3Jn**:1:4:7:9[4]:10[3]:13[2]:14[2]/**Jud**:1:
3[4]:5:6:7[2]:9:12:15[2]:16:18:20:21:22[2]:23[3]:24,25[3]/
Rev1:1[4]:3[2]:4[2]:4f:5[3]:5f[2]:5:6:8f:9:11[2]:12:19:20f/**2**:
1[3]:5:6f[2]:7[3]:8[2]:10[2]:11[2]:12:13[2]:14[3]:16:17[3]:18:19[2]:
20[4]:21:22[2]:23:24,25:26[2]:27:29[2]/**3**:1[2]:3[3]:6[2]:7[4]:8[2]:
9[2]:10f:10:11:13[2]:14:18[5]:22[2]/**4**:1:8:9:11/**5**:2[2]:3:5[3]
:9:12:13[2]/**6**:1:2:3:4[2]:8:10[2]:11[2]:13[2]:13f:16[2]/**7**:2[2]:9
:12:17f:17/**8**:3[3]:4:6:8,9:13/**9**:1f:1[3]:3:4[2]:5[2]:6[3]:9:
10[2]:14:15:19:20/**10**:4[3]:5:8:9/**11**:1[2]:2:3[2]:5:6[4]:8,9[2]
:10[2]:12:13:15[2]:15f:17:18[3]/**12**:1:4[4]:5[4]:6:12[2]:13[2]:
14[2]:15:17[2]/**13**:4:5[2]:7:7f:7[2]:12:13:14[3]:15[3]:16:18[2]/
14:4:6[3]:12[3]:13[2]:15[3]:18[3]/**15**:1[3]:2:6/**16**:1:8:9:11:
14:15:17f:19/**17**:1[2]:8:8f:10:11:11f:12[3]:13:17[2]/**18**
:5:6[3]:11:15/**19**:1:8:9[2]:10[2]:13f:15:17:19/**20**:1:4[2]:5
:8:11:12[2]:13/**21**:5:6:8:9:10:15:17[2]:23:24/**22**:1:2:
6,7[2]:8[2]:12[2]:14[3]:15:16[2]:17:18

21366

TOO

[3]**Gen3**:6/**6**:7/**7**:2/**8**:9/**12**:4/**13**:5:6/**15**:5/**18**:14/
19:31/**21**:11:13/**24**:14:19:44:46/**26**:16/**27**:34:38
/**29**:27:28:30/**30**:15/**31**:29/**32**:12/**33**:13/**34**:6,7/
35:27/**38**:10:11/**39**:21/**40**:16/**41**:54/**42**:36/**45**:
14/**46**:6/**47**:5,6/**48**:11:19/**Ex1**:17/**6**:8,9/**7**:12:22
/**8**:7:28/**9**:11/**16**:2/**17**:3:12/**18**:18:22/**23**:29/**28**:
39/**31**:5/**38**:23/**39**:2/**Lev1**:10/**2**:7/**5**:11/**10**:6/**12**
:8/**19**:34/**27**:8/**Num7**:42-47/**10**:10/**11**:14:32/**12**
:2/**14**:41/**16**:16:34/**19**:8/**20**:3/**24**:23,24/**28**:8/**30**
:5/**Deu1**:17/**2**:20:35,36/**3**:20/**7**:22/**8**:20/**9**:19/
10:19/**12**:15:20-23/**17**:8:17/**25**:1/**Jos10**:30:32/
15:18,19/**17**:16,17,18[2]/**19**:9/**22**:22,23:26,27:34/
Ju1:15:26/**6**:5/**7**:2:4:12,13/**13**:6/**18**:26:28/**19**:
11:20/**Ru1**:12/**2**:23/**4**:6/**1Sa2**:26/**4**:17/**5**:10/**7**:
17/**10**:10:12/**16**:5/**17**:36/**18**:11,12/**19**:21:23:24/
25:26/**30**:9,10:21/**2Sa2**:6:30/**4**:1/**10**:11:14/**11**:
19,20,21:24/**13**:25/**14**:26/**15**:14/**18**:22/**19**:34/
22:18/**23**:10/**1Ki2**:22:26/**3**:8:17,18/**7**:34:47/**8**:
26:64/**10**:3/**12**:28/**13**:18/**16**:19/**17**:11/**19**:10:14
/**21**:19/**22**:7:49/**2Ki5**:18/**6**:1/**9**:16:27/**10**:4/**15**:
28/**17**:19/**18**:27/**1Ch5**:23/**17**:17/**18**:6/**19**:12[2]/
21:7:23/**22**:3:8/**26**:9/**2Ch3**:8/**4**:17,18/**6**:17:33/**7**
:7/**8**:3/**9**:20/**11**:16/**14**:14/**18**:6,7/**19**:8/**21**:10/**22**
:3/**28**:23/**29**:31:34/**32**:17:23/**33**:6/**36**:12/**Ez2**:
62,63/**Neh3**:8/**5**:5/**8**:11/**11**:1/**12**:43/**Est8**:8f/
Job2:13/**9**:10/**15**:11[2]/**21**:8/**23**:9/**31**:15:28/**32**:
17/**33**:7/**35**:4/**36**:17/**37**:19,20/**40**:5:15/**41**:12/
42:3:16/**Ps8**:7/**22**:30/**26**:2/**31**:22/**34**:5:19/**38**:
3,4/**40**:12[2]/**49**:8,9/**59**:8:12,13/**71**:18/**74**:17/**77**:
4/**78**:6/**83**:8/**88**:10/**95**:5/**102**:17/**103**:22/**106**:4:
16:32/**107**:24/**119**:74/**121**:2/**131**:3/**139**:6[2]:22/
142:6/**Pro1**:28/**4**:3/**11**:24,25/**12**:9/**15**:22/**19**:28
/**23**:19,20,21/**24**:7/**25**:16:17:27/**26**:15/**27**:14/**29**
:16/**30**:2:9:18,19:20/**Ecc2**:1:24-26/**4**:4/**5**:1/**7**:
15-17[3]/**9**:1/**10**:11/**12**:2:3[2]/**Sol8**:8:13/**Is1**:4/**3**:
11/**7**:8:18/**9**/**10**:12/**17**:3/**22**/**26**:18/**28**:20[2]/**31**:2
/**33**:1/**34**:7/**37**:30/**39**:2/**40**:20/**42**:11/**43**:20/**48**:
19/**49**:6/**50**:2/**56**:3[2]:8/**57**:11/**58**/**59**:1/**60**:6/**65**:
5:7:23/**Jer1**:6/**3**:8/**5**:5/**9**:20/**13**:16/**14**:20/**18**:10
:13/**19**:12/**22**:2/**24**:8[2]/**25**:19,20/**27**:15/**29**:16,17
/**31**:11/**32**:17:27:44/**33**:4/**36**:7:14,15/**38**:4/**43**:6
/**46**:25/**48**:18:21/**49**:9,10/**50**:27:35/**51**:8:22/
Lam1:6/**3**:32/**4**:21/**5**:6/**Eze1**:19,20,21[2]/**2**:8/**3**:
21/**10**:22/**13**:17/**16**:28:45:49:53:55/**19**:6/**20**:21/
21:28/**30**:18/**31**:17/**32**:29/**38**:5/**39**:7/**40**:21:26:
32/**44**:20:30/**47**:5/**Dan4**:9/**5**/**7**:7:20/**8**:17/**11**:25
/**Hos1**:10/**4**:5:9/**5**:5:6/**7**:1/**8**:3/**9**:7/**10**:5:15/**12**:
2:11/**Joe1**:4:6:11/**3**:19/**Amo**:12:15/**5**:16/**6**:9/**7**:
6/**9**:7/**Ob1**:16/**Jon**:13/**Mic**:9/**Nah2**:6/**3**:11:19/
Hab2:8/**Zep1**:5/**2**:4:5:12/**Hag1**:11/**2**:6:12/**Zec**:
11,12/**3**:1/**9**:2/**10**:6:7/**11**:8/**Mal1**:13/**Mt2**:8/**4**:
21/**5**:12:25:39:40:45/**6**:21:34/**12**:4/**13**:26:44/**20**
:10/**25**:12:17/**26**:25/**Mk1**:20:38/**2**:18:25,26/**4**:
19/**5**:35/**8**:7:17/**10**:12/**11**:13:25/**12**:20,21,22[2]/
14:70/**16**:8/**Lk4**:32:43/**5**:8:10/**6**:23:29/**8**:38/**11**:
32:36:45/**13**:5:24,25/**16**:3/**18**:43/**19**:3:42/**20**:12
:30/**23**:36:39/**Jn2**:2/**3**:26/**4**:17,18/**5**:32,33/**6**:67
/**7**:10:21,22,23:52/**8**:19/**9**:27/**10**:16/**11**:22/**12**:
10:35/**14**:19:21:23/**19**:39/**20**:8/**21**:3/**Act2**:15/**5**:
9/**6**:7/**8**:19:25/**10**:45/**11**:18/**14**:27/**15**:3:17/**21**:
24/**22**:28/**27**:7,8/**28**:27:28,29/**Rom1**:5:6,7:11,12
:32/**2**:3/**3**:29/**4**:19[2]:24/**5**:3/**8**:17:23/**9**:7/**11**:2,3:
12:16[2]:17:22:31/**12**:1/**13**:6/**14**/**16**:22/**1Co4**:8/**7**:
4/**8**:10/**9**:11:21/**10**:12:21:24:33/**11**:21/**14**:5/**15**:
8[2]:26:52/**16**:4:18/**2Co1**:6,7:11/**2**:5,6:10[2]/**3**:14/**5**
:11/**6**:12/**8**:21/**9**:15/**10**:14/**11**:15:21:22/**12**:11/
13:4/**Gal2**:1:10:13:16/**3**:14/**6**:3/**Eph1**:13/**2**:8:11
/**3**:2,3:9/**5**:18/**6**:19[2]/**Php2**:4:18:27/**4**:3:21/**Col1**:
11:26,27/**2**:6/**4**:1:3/**1Th2**:8/**2Th3**:2/**1Ti1**:16/**4**:
8/**2Ti2**:13/**3**:1/**4**:12/**Tit3**:3/**Phm1**:6:16/**Heb2**:
14/**3**:12/**4**:11/**5**:1[2]/**8**:3:11/**11**:5:11:12:23:32:
37,38/**12**:17:26/**13**:17/**Jas2**:7:18:19/**3**:1/**4**:17/
1Pe4:1/**5**[2]:9/**2Pe2**:1/**3**:17/**1Jn1**:4/**2**:13/**4**:11:17
:21/**5**:1:6,7,8/**2Jn1**:9/**Rev**:9/**6**:3/**7**:9/**17**:11/**22**:
9

652

UNDER

Gen7:19/**12**:20/**19**:8/**24**:6:8:9f:41/**31**:35f/**40**:4/
43:31/**Ex1**:11/**2**/**3**:1f:19/**6**:4/**18**:21[2]/**21**:29:36/
24:10/**26**:18,19:21:25/**39**:19/**Lev10**:7/**12**:2:5/
13:20/**24**:9/**27**:29f/**Num2**:3-31:34/**6**:18/**7**:8/**10**:
25/**19**:19/**26**:64,65f/**Deu4**:44,45,46/**9**:13,14/**12**
:2/**16**:21/**25**:19/**29**:20/**Ju1**:7/**2**:18/**3**:8:11:27/**4**:
7/**9**:6/**Ru2**:12/**1Sa10**:7/**22**:3/**27**:2,3/**2Sa10**:9:
15,16/**12**:11f/**18**:2[2]/**1Ki8**:6/**12**:20/**13**:14/**14**:23
/**18**[2]:25/**19**:4/**22**:27f/**2Ki8**:21/**17**:10/**1Ch3**:
17,18/**4**:31/**6**:4-15/**12**:24-37/**19**:11:15/**23**:24/
25:2:3:4,5:6,7/**26**:31,32/**27**:31/**2Ch4**:12-16/**11**:
11/**14**:9,10/**17**:14,15:17/**26**:11/**28**:4/**31**:17,18/
32:1/**34**:12/**Ez3**:8/**10**:10/**Neh3**:17/**11**:10-14[3]/
12:12-21:42/**Est2**:12,13,14/**Job28**:23,24/**40**:21
/**41**:11/**Ps8**:6/**92**:13/**94**:20/**144**:2/**Ecc4**:11/**5**:8:
17/**Sol2**:6/**4**:11/**8**:3:5/**Is**:11/**9**:1/**28**:15/**36**:12/
54:14/**57**:5/**Jer2**:20/**3**:13/**5**:2/**7**:5/**25**:8,9/**27**:8/
30:21f/**36**:30f/**37**:15,16/**38**:12/**41**:10/**Lam3**:27/
4:20/**Eze3**:18/**6**:13/**10**:21/**17**:22,23/**20**:27,28/
Dan2:21:38/**3**:18/**4**:14/**5**:7f/**6**:1:7/**7**:27/**Hos5**:5
/**10**:11/**Amo2**:3:8f/**Zep1**:1f/**Zec10**:12/**13**:8f/
Mt2:16/**5**:21/**8**:8,9/**22**:43/**Mk6**:20/**7**:9:28/**15**:1
/**Lk7**:6,7,8/**8**:29/**13**:34/**20**:4/**23**:7/**Jn1**:48:50/
18:32f/**Act4**:12/**8**:27/**12**:4/**22**:3/**23**:21/**27**:4f/
Rom4:15/**6**:6:14/**8**:8/**15**:3/**16**:20/**1Co4**:13/**9**:18
/**11**:10/**15**:17:28/**2Co4**:11/**9**:5/**11**:12:32/**Gal3**:
10:13/**Eph1**:22/**2**:1:3/**4**:15,16/**Php2**:10/**Tit**:14/
Heb5:7f/**7**:23:28/**8**:6/**9**:8:9:13:15:22/**10**:1[2]:8:10:
11:13/**12**:20/**13**:11/**1Pe5**:6/**1Jn**:19/**Jud1**:11/
Rev12:7

221

UNTIL

Gen3:19/**7**/**8**:3,4:7/**9**:13/**15**:16/**19**:3:22/**24**:19:
20:33/**27**:44/**28**:15/**29**:3:8:27/**32**:4:12:22,23,24:
26/**34**:5/**38**:11/**42**:15/**49**:10/**Ex10**:26/**12**:18/**16**
:20:35/**17**:12/**19**:13/**21**:19/**23**:18:30/**24**:12:14/
29:34/**33**:5:8:22/**34**:25:34:35/**40**:37/**Lev7**:17,18
/**11**:24:25:27:28:31:32:39:40/**14**:46/**15**:5:6:8:10:
11:16:17:18:19:21,22,23:27/**16**:17/**17**:15/**19**:6/
22:4:6[2]/**23**:14:32/**24**:12:23/**25**:14,15,16:21,22:
27:28:40:51:52/**26**:4,5f/**27**:18:23/**Num9**:12/**10**/
11:12:19,20/**12**:15/**14**:19:33/**15**:34/**19**:7:8:10:
21:22/**20**:17/**21**:22/**23**:18-24/**32**:13:17:18:21/
34:10,11/**35**:25:28/**Deu2**:14,15[2]/**3**:18:20/**6**:
10,11,12:24/**9**:7/**11**:4:5/**12**:9/**16**:4/**22**:2/**23**:11/
28:20:21:22:45:47,48:51:61/**Jos1**:15/**2**:16:22/**3**:
15,16/**4**:10:23/**5**:6:8,9/**6**:10/**7**:6:13/**8**:6:26:29/
10:13:26/**14**:10/**15**:2,3,4/**19**:11/**20**:6[2]/**23**:8/**Ju4**
:16:24/**5**:7/**6**:5:18[2]/**11**/**13**:7:15/**16**:3:16,17/**18**:
30/**19**:7:25:26/**20**:5:8,9,10:22,23,24:26/**21**:2/**Ru**
2:21:23/**3**:3:13:14:15-18[2]/**1Sa1**:21,22:23/**3**:15/
6:6/**9**:12,13/**15**:18/**16**:10,11/**20**:5:41:41f/**21**:
14,15/**22**:2:3/**25**:36/**26**:13/**27**:1/**28**:23/**30**:4:17/
2Sa2:29/**3**:35,36/**10**:5/**13**:27:28/**15**:24/**17**:13/

NTIL Con't)
10f/23:10^2/1Ki3:1/10:7/11:40/17:1:14/18:
29/22:11:21:27/2Ki2:17/7:3:9/8:11:15/10:8
:19/15:5/17:18:20:23/18:31,32/22:20/1Ch4
/5:22/12/19:5/28:7/2Ch9:6/15:19/18:26/
10/26:15:21/29:34^2/31:7,8/34:28/36:16:20/
2:62,63/4:4,5:21:24/9:4:14/Neh2:1/5:14/7:3
,65/8:1/9:32/13:19/Job5:26/14:11,12:13/16
/27:5/29:21/32:4/Ps9:20/10:15/18:37/28:7
2:5/48:14/57:1/69:3/77:2:4/83:16:18/89:3,4
94:23/105:19:24/106:30/119:67:112/127:2/
o4:16/6:4/7:18:21/18:17/20:18/Sol2:7f/3:4/
/8:4/Is6:11/13:14/22/24:22/26:20/28:19/
8:17/32:15/36:12:17/42:4f:4^2/62:1:6,7/Jer1
4:20:22/5:7/6:4/7:25/9:16/11:7/19:9/23:20
4:10/25:2,3,18:27/27:7:8:22/30:24/31:37/32:
1/36:23/37:10/38:28/44:6:10:27/46:10/50/
39/52:3:34/Lam2:11/Eze:3/4:8:14/5:16/20:
21:5:27:31/24:5:13/28:15/32:4/34:21/39:19^2
6:2:17/Dan1:21/2:8,9/4:10,11:25:32/5:21/7:
26/8:13^2:17/9:25/11:27:35:36/12:4:6:7:9:12
Hos5:15/Amo9:1/Jon4:8/Mic3:11/5:3:3f/
p1:10/2:5/Zec1:12/Mt:25/2:9f:13:15/5:18:
:26/10:11/11:12/13:30:33/14:20/15:37,38/
9/18:30:34/22:26:44/23:39/24/25:5,6/26:29
2/27:45:64/Mk4:37/6:42/7:3/8:8,9/9:9:19/
1f/12:5:20,21,22:36/14:25/15:33/Lk1:20:80
:26/9:27:36:59/11:22/12:1:50:59/13:20,21:
/14:28/15:3,4:8:12/16:16/17:29/18:1/20:31:
,43/21:24/22:16:18/23:44/24:49f:49/Jn1:39
:35/5:17f/6:11/8:7:9/9:18/20:9/21:22:23/
ct1:4:21,22/2:35/3:21,22/7:4:45/13:6,7/16:15
3/20:7:18/22:22/23:12,13/25:21/27:20/Rom
1/5:4:13/8:22f/11:25/1Co:26/15:25/16:2:8/
al1:18/3:19:23^2:24/4:1:2/Eph:13/Php1:5:6:10
Th5:23/2Th2:3:7/1Ti1:20/4:13/5:25/6:14/
Ti1:12/Heb:13/5:7f:14/6:15/9:10:16/10:4f/12
/Jas5:7/1Pe1:17/2Pe2:4:9/Rev:24,25/6:11/7
/15:8/20:3:5

525

NTO

ev1:9f:15,16,17f/7:20f/21:6/1Ch12:18/Ps16:6
51:18f/73:24f/Is9:6^2/42/53:12/Eze21:29/30:
/46:7f/Mt1:17f/3:9f/6:34f/8:15f/Lk4:39f/21
3f/23:17,f/Jn7:8f/Act3:21,22f/7:37f/Rom10:
9f/11:32f/1Co9:16/Gal2:19f^2/Eph4:30f/Php2
f/4:20/1Ti6:16/Heb5:7f/Rev1:13f

36

P

en2:5:6:21/4:26/12:6/15:5/18:2:6:16/19:1:2:
7:33/20:8/21:14:20,21/22:3:10/23/24:23:63/
6:15:31:33/27:19:31/28:12:16,17:18/31:23:25:
5:45:55/32:22,23,24/35:20/37:7/38:6:20/41:2
:4:7^2:9:18:19:20:21:24:51:56,57/42:26/44:3:6:
0/48:2/Ex2:11/3:2/8:7:20/9:13/12:30/14:16:
1:29:30/15:9/16:28,29/17:11:12^2/19:2,3:12:20
1:23:24/20:26/23:11/24:1:2:9:12:13:15/26:28
0:37/27:9,10^2:11:14,15/29:17/32:6/34:2:4:24:
8/36:33/38:4:16:17/39:33-40/40:5:21:33/Lev
22,23/9:8/14:38/19:9:10:14/23:22/25:5:29/
6:34,35^2/Num1:51/2:3-31:34/7:1/13:30/14:40
16:19:30:32:35/19:9:10/20:25:27/21:12:17,18:
1,32/22:20/23:3,4:14:18-24^2/24:3-9/25:4:7/
7:12/32:23/33:38,39/34:13:16-28/Deu1:43/4:
9/5:5/7/10:3/11:6/12:2/16:22/17:16/18:15:
8:22/25:1/32:8/Jos2:5:6:8:22/3:6:13,14:15,16^2
4:2,3:11:15,16:20:23/5:1:7:13/6:26/7:10,11:13
8:7:19/10:8/14:1/15:2,3,4:8:18/18:1/Ju2:16/3:20
4:21/6:38/7:8,9:12,13:15/8:8/9:22,23:29:43/
1:1:37/13:20:24/14:17/15:15/16:9:14:20/18:
3:30/19:5:8:9/20:13:26:33/21:4/Ru1:11:13:18
2:7/3:8:14:15-18/1Sa1:17:19,20/2:7:13,14:21:
35/3:4,5:6:8/5:3/6:10:14/7:16/9:12,13:14:19:25
26,27^3/13:16/14:10:12:13/15:6/17:40/20:38:
42/22:9,10/26:12:14:19/27:1/28:4:7,8:11:13:23
29:10/30:20/2Sa3:26/5:8/12:17:18:20/13:31/
4:14/15:2:30/16:1/17:6/18:33/21:8/22:9/1Ki
:49,50/2:19:27/3:15:20/6:8/8:35,36/10:26/11:
20/12:8/13:1/14:14/16:34/17:7/18:36:38/19:5:
7:8/20:7:26:27:33/21:7/22:35/2Ki1:6:12/2:
3,14/3:25/4:21:37/5:21:23/6:15/9:19:32/12:8
/13:5:18^2/18:4/20:11f/21:7/25:13:24/1Ch10:2
/11:23/14:12/21:26/27:1/2Ch1:2,3:14/3:17/7:
1:13^2/10:8,9/13:7/15/16:5/18:11:23:34/19:8/
20:16/21/23:1:11:15,16,17^2/25:14/29:15:16:17
/31:5,6/32:16:30/33:19/34:3:8:9/35:12/36:21:
22,23/Ez3:8/7:22/9:1:6/10:5:12:14/Neh3:6/8:
1/9:5/12:37/Est5:9/7:7/9:14/Job1:5:20/4:
15/8:19/10:16/12:23/13:26/15:16:30/16:12/18
:16/22:14:24:26:29/27:19/28:11/29:8/30:28,29
/32:18/35:5/36:27/38:25-27:41/39:4:18/40:7/
41:10:25/Ps3:5/8:3/15:1/18:37/22:15:22/24:7/
28:1/31:19:24/33:1/34:16/35:23/39:5,6/40:12^2
/44:26/46:2/63:4/71:20/75:4f/76:9/77:18/78:
13:65/82:1:8/86:3/97/104:6:14:29/105:35:41/
107:33/108:2/114:3/119:69:109:147/139:8/
140:2:5/141:2/145:15/147:3/Pro6:9:14:22/13:
19:22/21:16/23:35/24:15,16/28:8/30:4:24-28/
31:9:15/Ecc3:7/4:8:10:16/5:8^2:11/8:1/Sol2:7f:
10:12/3:1/5:5/7:8:12:13/8:5/Is2:3:19^2/3:13/5:
8:11:14:19/8:16/9:3:18^2/10:14/13:12:17/15:6/
21:5/22:6,7:18/24:10:22/25:8/26:11/27:4,5:10/
28:4/29:8:21/30:1:10,11/32:20/33:3:6:10/34/
35:6/37:33/38:14/39:6/40:15:26:30:31/41:2:18
:25/42:15:23/43:2/45:8^2:13:13f/50:9/51:10:17^2
/52:1^2/55:2:13/57:7,8:10:20/59:5:12/60:4/61:
11/63:9:12/Jer1:17/2:9:10,11/4:3:28/5:1:7:14/
6:1:3/7:13,14:30/8:2:4,5:8/11:16/12:4/15:3/16:
18/18:7:14/21/23:10:16/24:6/25:33/27:7/30:9
f:9:13/31:6:21:28/32:32/40:5/41:2:12/44:25/
46:11:19/49:1:27/50:9:17:21:32/51:1:11^2:36:57
/Lam2:19/3:9f/4:5/Eze1:13:19,20,21:27,28/2:1
/3:12:14,15/5:3/8:2:3/13:12/15:3/16:6,7/18:15
/20:27,28/25:4:9,10/26:9/29:18f:20f/30:12/31:
2,3/33:16/34:4:29/37:10/39:9:15,16/40:22:26:
31:34:37:40:41:48,49^2/41:7/42:13/43:2:5:15/46
:12/47:3:4:5/Dan1:8/2:13:44/3:1:5:12:14:19:24
/4:22:34/7:3:5:7:20/8:27/10:5,6:11^2/11:25:
30,31f:36/12:1:2:4:11/Hos1:7/4:8:13:18/5:2/6:
1/7:8/9:6:16/10:4:8/11/12/13:15/Joe1:5:17:19
/2:9/3:2:3/Amo2:12/4:4/7:1:4:17/8:8/9:2:8:15
/Ob1:3/Jon:6:15/2:10/4:6/Mic1:6/2:10/3:3/5:
9/6:1:6:14/Nah2:5/3:14:15:17/Hab1:10:13:15/
2:6:7/Zep1:5/3:8:16/Hag1:8/Zec:5,6/5:1:5/6:1
:12:12f/12:4:6/14:16/Mal1:13/3:10:16:17/4:1/
Mt2:13:20/3:9f:16/4:21/5:1:12/6:19:26/8:15:
24:26/9:2:5,6:7:9:20:25/10:38:39/13:5:47,48/
14:19:20:23,24/15:13,14:37,38/16:24/17:7/18:
23/19:29/21:11:19:23/22:6:34,35^2/23:2:32/25:
7,8/26:46:62/27:6:35:48/28:14/Mk1:10:19:31^2:
35/2:9,10,11:12:14/3:13:27/4:5,6:7/5:27:41,42^2
/6:41:43,44:46/7:34/8:8,9:14:19/9:17:27/10:1f:
10:28:29:35f:48:50/11:2:22,23:27,28/12:3:40:
43,44/14:15:42:45:57:60/15:11:36:38f:41/16:4:
19/Lk1:80/2:44/3:5:17/4:5:16:29:39/5:17:
18,19:23,24:25:28/7:15:40/8:16:24:43,44:54:55
/9:16:17:32:33:41:54/10:30/11:5,6:7:8:34/12:
50/13:7/14:8/16:5,6/17:19:27:30/19:5:43/20:
10:11:36/21:26:28/22:32:45:46/23:46f/Jn2:19/
3:14^2/5:8^2:9/6:2-5:8,9/7:8f:14:50:53/8:7:10:28f:
59/10:31/11:41:44/12:32/13:4/14:2,3:24/16:33
/17:1/18:34f/19:23,24:29/20:7/Act1:15/3:7,8:
21,22/5:26,27:34/7:37:42/8:31:39/9:6:8,9:34:
40^2:41/10:9,10:16:26:27/11:28/12:5:7/13:50/
14:2:10:20/16:34/17:11:13/19:16:34/21:14/22:
10:23/23:9/26:16/27:12:13:14,15:22:39/Rom1:
21:28^2/2:5/3:7/4:15/8:11:32/9:10-13/10:19/11
:32:32f/13:9:11/14:17:19/15:1:15,16:26/1Co1:8
/3:3:15/4:7:13/6:14/10:7:13^2/12:12/14:26^2/15:
37:54/16:17/2Co1:17/2:3/4:1:8:9:16/5:4/7:11/
9:2:7:8/10:13/11:8,9/12:2,3:7:9:19/13:5/Gal1:
17/2:4^2/4:1/5:14/6:9/Eph2:6/3:18,19/4:10:12/
5:13:14/6:4:13/Php2:1:9:17:19/3:10:14:17/Col
1:18:24/2:7:12:22/1Th:16/3:10/4:17/5:11/2Th
2:8/3:6/1Ti1:3,4^2/2:8/3:16/5:10:18:23/6:4:19/
2Ti1:6f:8/2:4:12:25/3:4/4:1/Tit2:1/Heb1:12/3:
6:10/6:6:7/10:20/11:1:17:24,25/12:1:15:22/Jas
4:10:13/5:3/1Pe2:2,3:12/4:8/5:6:10/2Pe1:
20,21/2:5:20/3:10:17/Jud1:6:19:20/Rev3:2/4:1
/6:14/8:4/11:11:12/12:5/13:1:11/16:12/17:8/
18:21/20:9:13/22:10

1105

UPON

Gen1:16:26/3:17/4:12/6:1^2/7:10,11,12:18:21:
22/8:3,4:7f/9:24,25/11:6f/12:17/14:19,20/15:
11:12/16:13/19:24/21:10:33/22:2:3:6/23:9/24:
45/25:11/28:12/31:32:35f^2:53/34:18,19/35:5:9:
20/41:17/47:1/48:14^3/49:19:26/50:1/Ex2:25/3
:12/4:9/8:7/9:9:11:22/10:1:21/12:12:21:22:23:
33/13:9:16/14:24/16:21/17:1/19:11:16:18:20/
20:5:6:24/21:30f^2/23:4:27/24:16/25:20:21/26:
32/27:5/28:12:21:36:37,38/29:7:10:12:13:15,16^2
:18:19,20^3:21^2:36:38/30:10:32:33/31:7/32:20:
21:35/33:16/34:1:30:32/36:8,9/37:9:15,16/38:
4/39:6,7/40:9^2:10:14:23:27:29:38/Lev1:4:5:6,7:
8:9:11:13:15,16,17/2:6f/3:2:7,8:9,10,11:13:
14/4:3:4:7:15:18:19:24:25:26:29:30:31:33:34/6:
9:13:15/7:2:3:5:31/8:10:12:14:15,16^2:18:19:21:
22:23^2:24^5:24f:25:28:28f:30^5/9:9:10:12:13:14:17
:18:20^2:24/10:6:7/11:29,30:32:38:41,42:44:46:
47/14:7:14^3:17:20:25^2:28^3:29/15:6:21,22,23:24:
26/16:13:14:15:19:21^2:25/17:6:11/18:21/19:12:
28/20:12:13:16f/21:12/24:5-8:13,14/26:34,35/
Num4:7:10:14/5:26/6:27f:27/7:9/8:7:10:12/10:
17/11:25^3:26:29/15:31f/16:6,7:33/17:1/18:5:9:
17/19:4:13:18^3:20/24:2:3-9/27:23/29:1f/30:15/
Deu4:7:9:30:32:36:39/5:9,10/7:7:19/9:9/11:12:
20^2/12:24,25:26,27^2/13:9:17/15:23/16:10/17:
18:20/24:4/27:7:8:12:13:15/28:2-6:15-19^3:20:
27:28:49:50:58,59^2:60:61/29:2,3:20:21:22:27/30
:1:3/31:17:21/32:2^2:11:23:24:40,41:46/33:2:16:
20/34:9/Jos6:5:18:26/7:3:15:25^2:26/8:20,21:32
/9:20:23/23:15,16/24:5:7:20/Ju5:17:18/6:20:
34/7:12,13/8:27f/9:5:8:18:35:47,48/11:29/14:6
:7:19/15:14:16,17/16:30/1Sa1:11/2:28/4:7/6:3
:9:11/10:6:10/11:2:6/12:15^2/14:24,25:28:32/16
:13^2/19:20:23/28:18:20/31:3,4:5/2Sa1:6:10f:19
:21:25/4:8^2/6:3:8/7:1:12/15:32/17:2,3:14/18:9
/21:10/22:4:5:7:10:11:19:34/23:4/24:15/1Ki1:1
:13:17:24:30:35:48/2:45:46/5:5/6:34/7:2/8:25:
35,36:54,55/9:5:9:25/12:2,3,4:32,33^2/13:2^2:29/
14:10/16:34/17:21/18:17:33:39/21:20/22:17:
23/2Ki2:15/3:27/4:29:31:32:34^4:35/5:11:27^2/6:
17:18/7:9/9:36/10:2,3/11:12:19/13:16,17^2/16:
11,12:13:17/17:7/21:12:24/22:20/23:16:20^2/
1Ch12:8-13:18/15:16/16:4:40/17:11:27/20:2/
21:1:14:26/27:24/2Ch1:5,6/6:18:20,21^2:27/11:
1/12:7/13:11:18,19/14:14/15:1/17:10/18:16:18
/19:2:10/20:14:29/21:7/23:11:20/24:9:17,18:
20^2:24:27/25:12/26:16/28:11/29:8:22:23:24:27
/32:12:25^2:26/33:16:17/34:5:21:25:28/35:3:11:
16/36:17/Ez1:3/3:1/7:17/Neh2:4/4:11/5:13/9
:32^2:35/13:18^3:22/Est1:11^2/5:1/7:8/8:7/9:13:
29-31/10:1/Job1:20/2:13/4:3,4/5:6:10/7:8/9:
26:28/10:16:17/12:21/14:16/16:9:14/18:12/19:
25/20:4:23:25/21:5:6/22:28/26:7/27:9/28:8/29
:9:19/30:14:27/31:1/35:6/36:7:8/37:6:10:22/38
:25-27/39:27:28/40:4:23/41:8/42:11/Ps2:6f/4:
4:6/7:2:16/8:5/9:7,8/10:2:9/11:7f/17:11/18:33:
38/21:3:7/22:9,10,11/24:2f/31:16/33:2:
13,14,15:18,19:20/38:17/40:8/41:6/42:7:8/44:
3/46:8/48:1:9/50:5:10,11/51:1:19/54:5/55:16/
57:3/59:10/65:5/68:4:9,10:17:30f:33/69:24/72:
6/75:8/76:2/77:6/78:43:53/79:6^2/80:3f:7f/81:
14/94:23/99:1/104:3:13/105:27/106:29/107:
40/108:9f/109:20/118:27,28/119:15:78:95:135:
153/121:8/123:2/129:8/137:2:5,6/140:10/144:
6/147:16:17/149:4:5,6,7/Pro1:23/4:8,9/6:11/7:
3f/11:7/16:12/17:13/22:6/24:34/25:20f/28:27
/30:18,19/Ecc8:6,7:14/Sol1:10:16/2:8/3/4:16/
6:13f/8:9:14/Is1:4/5:29/6:5/7:18/9:6:17:21/10
:3,5:6,12/11:2/13:8/14:13f/16:9/17:13/18:3/19
/20/21:1:3/22:9,10,11/24:6:18/25:10/26:19/28
:2/29:6:10/30:13^2:28:30/31:4,5/32:14/34:5/35:
8/37:8,9:27/40:31/42:1/44:5/45:12/47:3:8:9/
49:13:16/50:10/51:20:23/52:7/54:10/55:6:7:10
/58:8/60:3:6/61:1/63:3/64:7/65/66:4:6:14^2/
Jer1:14/3:21/4:11,12:13^2:18:20:23/5:6^2:12:13/
6:11^2:18,19:26/7:29/8:2/9:6^2/10:13/11:11:23/
12:9:13/13:16^2:27/14:6:16/15:6:8/17:1:18/18:
22/19:3:7:13:15/20:11/21:12/22:30/23:1:2:5,6:
12:40/25:7:13:16:27:34/26:3:15^3:19/27:8/29:
16,17/30:18:23/31:5:12:33:33f/32:23:33:42/33:
20,21:22/35:17/36:7:18:30:31^3/39:5/42:17:18/
43:10/44:6/45:5/46:10/48:21/49:5:11:32:37/50
:3:25:28:44^2/51:33:42:55:64/52:9/Lam2:4:10^2:
12:18:20:22/3:55/5:16/Eze1:26/3:14,15:25f/4:
8f/6:3/7:26,27^3/8:1/11:5/12:6/13:2,3/14:8/16:
23/19:9/20:8:13:21/21:12:31^2/22:21:22:31^2/23
:8:30:32^2:35:41:42/24:6f:7:13/25:7:9,10^2:11:12:
17/27:10:11^2:29:30/28:18:22/30:15/32:4:11:27f
:32/33:10:22/34:13:15,16/36:12:18:20/37:1:9/
38:9:23/39:4:5:25:29/40:1/43:18:24/44/45:19^2
/Dan2:12/6:24/7:9/9:17:24:27/Hos1:6:11/5:10
/8:1:14/9:2/10:7:8:12/13:7:15/Joe2:1:9^2:20:28:
32/Amo:2/4:12/5:2:8/9:1:6:13:15/Ob1:15^2:16/
Jon1:8:14/4:8/Mic3:6:11/4:12/5:15/7:20/Nah
1:14/Hab:8/3:8,9f:8,9:16/Zep:8/Hag1:2:23
/Zec1:12/4:3/5:4/13:9/14:4/Mal2:1/4:3/Mt:
15,16/12:18/16/18:7:10/19:28/23:15:16:23:36/
25:31/Mk8:23/13:2/Lk1:35:65:66:78/2:32/3:
22/4:18,19/5:17/6:47,48/7:38/11:29,30:36/12:
1/18:13:32/19:15:44/21:23:23f^2:23:26/24:49/
Jn1:16^2:32:33/3:14:33,34:36/6:18,19/7:49/Act
1:4:8/2:17:18/4:12:33f/8:16:17:18/9:3:26/10:
44/11:28:28f/12:20/13:11^2/14:8:27/18:6:27/19
:6:12/27:17f:20f/Rom1:5/2:8:17f/3:19/6:11/9:
28/10:13/11:9:31:32/16:20/1Co1:2/2:5/4:1/5:
8^2/10:16/11:29:34/15:1:10/16:23/2Co1:12:22:
23/2:17/4:4:17/Gal1:9/3:1:2:13^2/6:16^2/Eph1:6
:8:14/5:6:13/6:24/Php4:23/Col3:6/1Th1:5/5:3:
9/2Th3:18/1Ti2:1/4:14/6:21/2Ti1:6/Tit3:6/
Phm1:25/Heb:9/6:7^2:16/7:6/9:1/10:5/Jas5:14

(UPON Con't)
/1Pe4:14/2Pe1:15/2:6/1Jn:2:20/Jud1:11:20/Rev2:22/3:3:10:12/4:4/5:7:10/6:2/7:3:10/8:3:5:7:10/10:8/11:6:18/13:1/14:14/16:1:3:4:6:8:10:12/17:1/18:7/19:4/20:11

1188

US

Gen1:26:26f/5:28-31/11:3,4^2:7/17:2,3,4:7,8/19:5:9^2:13:31/20:9,10/23:5,6/24:23:31:33:65/26:10:16:22^2:28:29/31:14^3:15^2:36,37:47,48^2:51,52:53/32:5:18:20/33:14/34:9,10^3:21:22:23:30/39:14,15/40:8/41:10:12/42:2:13:28:30^2:33/43:2:3,4,5:7^2:18^2/44:7:9^2:16:19:21:23:25:26:27:30:31/45:11,12/47:15:19/50:15:16,17^3/Ex1:9:10/2:19^2/3:18^3/5:3:15:17:21^2/8:26:27:29/10:7:9/12:27^2:31/13:14:15:16/14:11^3:12:25/15:16/16:3^3:7,8,9/17:2:3^2:7^2/19:8/20:19^3/24:14/32:1^3:23^3/33:15^2:16/34:9^2/35:10-19/Num10:29:31^2:31f:32/11:13/12:2:11/13:27:30:31/14:3^2:4:8^3:9^2:14^2:17,18^2:40/16:3:13^2:14^2/20:4^2:5^3:16^2:17/21:5:22/22:4:16,17/31:16:48,49/32:5:13:27/Deu1:6:19,20,21^3:24,25^2:27^2:28:41/2:9:14,15:27:29^2:32:35,36^2:37/3:1:3:23,24,25^2/4:7/5:24:25^2:26,27/6:20:21:23^2:24^2:25/9:4/13:2/17:14/20:8/21/26:6,7^2:8:9^2:15/29:7:29^2/31:17/33:2^2/Jos1:10,11/2:3:14:20^2:24^2/3:6/4:7/6:16/7:3^2:7^2:9^3:25/8:6/9:11:20:22^2:23:25/10:6/14:7:8:11/15:18,19/17:14^2:16,17,18/21:2/22:4:17,18^2:19^2:22,23:28:29:31^2:34/24:17/Ju1:3^2:15/5:4:8/6:13^5/8:1:6:7:15:22/9:12:37/10:15^2/11:13:24:27/12:1:2:3/13:8^3:12:23^3/14:15/15:10:11/16:5:23,24^2/18:9,10:19^2:23/19:18/20:8,9,10^3:18/21:22/Ru1:17/2:8,9:14:20/3:2/4:3/1Sa:3^3:7:8/5:10/6:9/7:8:12/8:5:20^3/9:5:6/10:22:27/11:1:3^2:10:14/12:4:10:19/13:12/14:6:9:10:12:29:37:41/17:18:47/20:23/24:12:15^2/25:7:8:15,16^4:21/28:1:15/29:4^3:6/30:22:23^2/2Sa3:24,25^2/11:23:24/14:14:15,16:17/15:19,20:22/18:3^3/19:5:6:8,9,10:14:42^2:43/20:6/21:3:5,6^2/1Ki3:17,18:26/8:57^2:58/12:2,3,4/15:19/18:26/20:25:31/22:5/2Ki1:6^2:9:14^2/3:10^2:11:13/4/5:7/6:1:3:12/7:4^2:6:9:12^2:13/9:5:12:22/10:5/17:26^2/18:22:25^2/19:4:19/22:12,13/1Ch13:2^2:3/15:13/16:35^2/19:13/21:3:23:25/29:15/2Ch6:20,21:26/10:4/12:6/13:10:12^2/14:7^2:11^3/16:3/20:9^3:11^3/29:8^2:10/30:6/32:7 8:11:14/34:21/Ez4:2^2/5:5^2:17/8:18:21^2:22^2:23:31^2/9:8^2:9^4:11:12^2:13:14:15/10:4:13:14^2/Neh1:6,7:11/2:17:20/4:1^2:4:5:11^2:19:23^2/5:8:9^2:10/6:9:10/9:18:32^2:33^2:37/12:43/13:18/Est1:18^2/2:2/5:12/7:4/Job1:14,15/9:32,33^2/15:2:17-19/18:2/21:15/22:14:17/24:2/31:15/34:32/35:11/36:33f/37:19,20:22:23/Ps2:3/4:6^2/12:3,4/17:15/19:7,8^3:11/22:30:31/25:10/33:20^3:22/34:3:10/40:5/44:1^2:7^2:9^2:10^2:11^2:12^2:13:19^2:26^2/46:7^2:11^2/47:3:9/57:8/59:5:7/60:1^3:3^2:4,5^2:6,7:9,10^2:11/62:12/65:4:5:5f:5/66:10:11:12/67:1^2:2:6,7/68:11,12,13:18:19:20^2:28/72:16/74:1^2/76:5^2/77:15/78:2,3:19,20/79:4^2:5:6:8:9^3/80:2:3^2:3f:5:6:7^2:7f:8^2:12:13^2:14:18:19^2/81:1:4/83:1^2:4:12/84:11/85:4:4f:4:6:7^2:13f/89:18/90:10:11:12^2:13^2:14^2:15:16:17^2/94:12,13^4/95:1:2/100:3/103:10:12:13/105:5,6/106:1:47^2/108:7:11:12/115^2/117:2/118:25^3/119:4/123:3,4/124:6/130:7/136:24/137:8/Pro1:10:14/16:9/Ecc7:3/12:14/Sol5:9/6:13/7:11:12/Is1:9/2:3^2:5/4:1^2/5:19/7:2:14f:14/8:9,10^3:17/9:6^2/10:9:14/14:8/16:3^3:4,5/22:13/26:12/28:9:10:15/29:16/30:9:10,11^3:16/32:15/33:2:14:21:22^2/36:11/37:4:20/41:22:23/49:14^2/53:2:6/63:15^2:16:17^2:19/64:5:6:7^2:9:12^2/Jer4:13^2/5:12^2:13:19/6:5:24/8:14^2:19/9/12:4/13:12/14:7:8:9^3:19:21^2:22^2/16:10/18:18^2/21:1^3:13/26:16:19^2/29:28/31:6:35/35:6:7:10/36:17/42:2:3:5:6:20/43:2,3^2/44:17:19:26/46:16/50:5/51:10^2:34,35^4/Lam3:22:40:41:43^2:45:46/4:17^2:19^2/5:1:4:8:16:20^2:21^3:22^2/Eze8:12/11:3:15/13:12/20:20/24:19/33:10:30:30f/35:12/Dan2:4:7/3:16:17^2/9:3:7^4:10:11:12^2:13:14/Hos6:1^4:2:3^2/8:2/14^2:3/Joe1:19/Amo3:3/5:18/7:13/9:10/Ob1:3/Jon:6^2:8:14^2/3:9^2/Mic2:4/3:11^2/4:2^2:5/5^2:6/7:19:20^2/Hab1:12^2:13:16/3:2^3:16/Zec1:5,6/5:9/8:20,21^2/Mal1:6:9^2/2:14:17/Mt1:23/2:4/4/6/6:11:12^2:13^2/8:25:29^2:29f:31^2/9:27/15:23/17:26,27/20:7:11,12:30/22:17:25/25:11/26:53:63:68/27:25/Mk1:24^2/5:9:12/6:2,3/8:11/9:22:40^2/10:35/12:14:19/14:14^2/Lk1:1,2:3f:69:71^2:74:75:78:79/2:15:48/3:10:14^2/4:34/5:8/7:5:16/9:13^2/10:17/11:1:3:4^2/12:41/13:24,25/16:26^2/17:5:13/19:38/20:6:22/22:9:11:12:21:38/23:15:18:39/Jn1:14^2:16^2:17^2:18:22^2/2:18/3:1:26/4:21-24:25:35:42/6:30,31^3:34:52/7:48/8:25/9:4^2:34/10:21:24^2/11:48/12:38/14:8:22/15:24/17:21/18:31f/21:2:8:12:13:14:20/Act1:6:17:21,22^4:24,25/2:29/3:12:16/4:19/5:4:28/7:27:35:40^3/10:33:40,41:42/11:13:15:17/13:15:17/15:8:9:24:25:27,28,29/16:9:10:14:15^2:17:37^4/17:19:27/18:19/19:35/20:5:14/21:5:11:12:16:17:18/23:8/24:2^2:7/26:1/27:2:6:16:20f:22:37/28:1^2:7^2:14:15^2/Rom1:5^2:11,12:17^4/3:5:20:21,22^3:24:25^2:30/4:3:16^2:24^3:25^2/5:1:2^2:3^2:4^2:5^3:6:7:8^2:9^4:10^2:11:20:21/6:1:2,3/8:3^2:4:7:16^2:18:20,21:23^3:25:26^2:27:28:30^6:31:32^3:33^3:34^4:35^3:36:37^2:38:39^2/9:23,24/10:8:11/11:33:34/12:4,5:6/14:10:12:17/15:4^2:6/16/1Co1:30^3:30f^2/2:7:10^2:12^3:13:14:16/3:5:8/4:5:8:9:10:11:12^2:13/5:7:8^3/6:13:16/8:1:6^2/9:10^2/10:7:8:11^2:17/11:14,15/12:4:6:7:11:13^3:18:30/15:19:22:32:43:45:46:49:57/2Co1:3,4^2:5:6,7:9:10^2:11^2:21:22^3/2:14^2:15^2:17/3:1:3:4:6:18/4:1:2:5:6:7:9:10:11:13:14^2:17:18/5:1:4:5^2:10:12:13,14^2:18^2:19:20:21/6:3:7:8^5:9:12:13/7:1:2^2:5^3:6:10:12:13:16/8:4:5^2:7/10:13:15/12:16^3/13:1/Gal1:4/2^2:7,8,9^2:17^2/3:13:14:18:21,22:24:25^2:29/4:3^2:5^2:7:29/5:1:5:17^4:22:25/6:5^2:9/Eph1:3:4^3:5^2:6^2:7:8^3:9:10:12:13:14^6/2:3^3:4:5:5f:6:7^2:9:10^2:14^2:14f:14:15^2:16:17:18^2/3:20/4:5:6^3:7^2:11:12:14^2/Php2:5/3:3^2:9:14^2/4:19/Col1:7:8:12:13^2:14/2:19/4:3^2/1Th1:8:9^2/2:2:5:15^2:16:18:19^2/3:2,3:6:9:10:11/4:7/5:8:9^2:10:25/2Th1:7/2:14^2:16^2/3:1:7:9/1Ti1:7:9:18/2:2/4:1/6:7:17/2Ti1:9^3:10^2/2:12:13^4/3:14:16^5:17/Tit2:12:14^2/3:3:5^2:6:7^2/Phm1:11/Heb1:2:3/2^2:4^2:9:11:17^2:18/3:6:7,8/4:2^2:11:12^2:13:14^2:16^2/6:1^2:18:19:20/7:11:19/8:6/9:8:9:14^2:26/10:1:10:20^2:22^3:23:24^2:25/11:1:40/12:1^2:9:10^2:24:25:28/13:13:18/Jas1:17:18f:18:20/4:5^2:6:12^2:15/1Pe1:3:12^2/3:9:18^2:21/2Pe1:1^2:3:4^4:19/2:9/3:1:11:15,16/1Jn1:2^2:5:7:9^3/2:2:3:18:19^3:25/3:1^2:11:16:18^2:20f:24^2/4:6:7:9^2:10:11:12^2:13^2:16^3:17:18^5:19/5:3:11:14:15:19:20/2Jn1:3:5:6^2/Jud1:3:7:24,25/Rev:5^4:6^2/5:4/6:10:16^2/18:19/19:7

1737

VERY

Gen3:5/4/5:3,4,5/7:13/12:11,12,13/13:1:5/16:4/17:23/18:11/19:3/21:11/24:1:36:67/26:7:32/28:18/29:14/30:35,36:43/33:11/34:18,19^2/35:17/37:13,14/38:10/39:3:6/41:3:8:19/42:30/44:20/45:16:18/47:4/50:9:10:11:21/Ex1:7/4:14/8:22/9:5/10:19:29/11:3^2/12:51/16:20/18:9/20:5/22:27^2/29:18/30:36/34:12^2/Lev3:15,16/6:21/8:21/10:16/18:29,30/22:1/23:13:18/Num12:7,8/13:22:28/14:8/16:15:41/18:17/21:4/26:5-5-11/28:13:24:27/29:8:36/31:14:16/Deu1:34,35/2:10/4:9:25:34/8:12,13/11:4/12:19/17:4/18:9/24:8/26:18/30:14/31:22:29/32:16:21/Jos7:1/9:9/10:2/22:30/23:1:6:11:14/Ju3:7:17,18,19/4:19/5:20/8:4/10:7,8/15:18/19:4/Ru2:1/3:6,7/1Sa1:5:15,16/2:17:22/3:1/8:3/11:6:15/12:18/14:33/16:22/17:45/18:8:10:30/23:22/24:9,10/25:3:15,16/26:21^2/2Sa3:6/8:8:13/10:5/11:27/12:1:3/13:21-24/14:27/15:9f:12/17:28,29/19:20^2:31,32^2:43/24:10/1Ki1:6/2:23,24:42/3:26/5:7:17/11:9,10:16,17,18:27,28/13:4/14:1:5/16:13:26/18:2/19:10:14/20:31/21:22/22:52,53/2Ki3:2/6:31/8:5^2/9:11/13:3/14:10/17:11^2:17/18:5:22/19:35/21:3,4,5:6:7/22:12,13:17/23:19/1Ch4:21-22/5:23/11:18,19:24,25/17:17/21:13/26:6,7/28:10/2Ch9:1/11:23/13:21/14:7/16:13,14/17:5^2:12/19:7/20:35/24:15/25:10:15:19/26:8:15^2/27:2/28:19/29:3:36/30:13:22/31:21^2/32:12:27/33:4,5:6:7:14/34:25/Ez4:20/8:16:18/Neh2:10/4:1/5:6:9:11/6:7/7:2/13:8/Est1:7:11/2:4:9/7:8/10:3/Job24:24/32:11,12/33:12/38:21/39:29/Ps35:3/47:4/56:9/60:3/73:9/76:1/83:4/89:8/105:12/116:15/117:2/119:53:167/138:5/140:9/142:6/Pro2:10/6:26/11:21^2/12:25/Ecc4:16/5:6,7:16:19,20/6:1:2:3/7:24/8:9,10:12:14/9:15/11:8/12:12/Sol8:6/Is3:9/5:1:7f/9:1/10:25/16:11/17:4:6:11/24:20/26:15/29:17/33:5/36:17/39:1/43:23:27/55:7:13/57:16/60:9/63:8/65:12/Jer2:21/5:6/7:30/16:9/21:5/22:23/23:1/24:3^2/28:16/31:26:33f/32:20:37/38:9/39:10/44:10:23/48:29/52:6/Eze2:3/9:9/16:17:47/19:11/20:26/21:21f:26/23:22:34/28:5^2/33:31:32/37:10/Dan2:48/4:10,11:33/5:30/6:4:14:19/8:4:5:9/9:23:26/10:12^2:19/11:20:29/Hos5:5/Joe3:16/Jon2:5/3:3:4,5/4:1:6/Mic1:11/2:8/3:2/6:10/Hab1:11f/2:11/Zep1:10:13/3:20/Zec1:2:15/3:5,6/14:4/Mal1:2,3^2:7/Mt4:2:8/5:3:12/10:30/13:21/19:22/21:32/22:16/23:36/26:3:7:34:47/27:18/28:15/Mk4:17/5:43/7:6^2/8:8,9:15:24:33/9:21/10:6,7:14:22:41/12:27/13:29/14:40/16:4/Lk1:7:19:31:32:78/2:25:36,37/4:1:38/6:35^2/9:32/10:8,9/13:14/15:31/18:2:23/19:1/21:26/24:1/Jn1:45/4:11:46,47/6:18,19:27:60/8:4/9:30/11:3^2:5/12:8:27:40f/13:32/14:28/16:25/19 31/Act4:2/5:34/7:9/8:9,10,11/10:17:34/13:48 17:22/21:20/22:3^2:6:13/24:3^2/25:10,11:12:17/27:3/28:1/Rom1:6,7/2:1/3:19/8:15:29/9:4:17:23,24/11:2,3:8:22^2:24/13:4/14:9/15:3:22:27/1 :5:13:19^2/1Co1:18^2/2:4:13:16/3:7:10/4:9:11:1 /6:3/7:29/13:4/14:12:17/15:37/2Co1:13,14/2 3:4:8/3:7/4:17/6:9:13/7:8:11/8:9^2:17/9:4/Gal 20:23/2:11:16/3:10/4:5/6:4/Eph1:4/2:7^2:13:1 :19/3:9/4:10^2/5:23/6:5/Php1:7/3:6:7/Col1:6:22/2:13:18/1Th1:5/2:13:17:18/4:9/2Th2:13/1Ti5:4/2Ti2:21/3:1/4:6^2/Tit2:14/Phm1:19/Heb2:1/3:10/4:16/5:1:12,13^2/10:19/13:16/1P 1:18/2:4:7:9:10^2:11/4:4/5:12/2Pe1:9/2:11:19/1Jn3:1:12/2Jn1:1:6/3Jn:3/Jud:23/Rev2:15:26 11:8,9

60

WAS

Gen1:2:4,5^2:4,5f^2:7,8f^2:9,10^2:11,12^2:13f^2:14,15:18:19f^2:23f^2:24:25:31:31f^2/2:3:5:11,12:19,20^2:23:25/3:1:6^2:12/4:2^2:18^4:20:21:21f:22:22f:26:2 f/5:1:3,4,5:3,4,5f:3,4,5^2:3,4,5f:6,7,8^2:9,10,11^2:12,13,14^2:15,16,17^2:18,19,20^2:21-24^3:25,26,27^2 28-31^2:32/6:1:6:8:9,10,11^2:12,13^2/7:6:10,11,12 23/8:7f:7:9:11:13:14:18,19:21/9:18f^2:20,21:29/10:8:9:13,14:15-19^2:24^2:26-30/11:2^2:5:6f:9^2:10,11:12,13:12,13f:12,13:14,15^2:16,17^2:18,19^2:20,21^2:22,23^2:24,25:26:28^2:29:30:32f/12:4:6:10 11,12,13^2:15:18:19/13:1:5:10^2:14/14:10:13:18/15:12:17/16:4:13:14:16/17:1:17:24-27^2/18:1^2:10:11:15/19:1:3:16:22:23:26:27:33:35:36:37:38 20:2:8/21:4,5^2:8:11:15:31^2/23:1:10/24:1:2:11:15,16^2:21:29,30:33:36:45^2:62:63:67/25:1:9,10:12-15:17f:20:25^2:26^2:27:28^2:29/26:7^3:9:13:21:3 /27:1:18:33:35:42^2/28:9:19/29:3^3:9^2:10:12,13:17:18:20:23:25:31^2:33:35/30:1:6f:16:30/31:4:17-20:24:25:31:34^2:35f^2:49:55/32:6:7:13,14,15:20:22,23,24:27:31/33:10/34:6,7:18,19^2/35:3:5:8^2:19:22^2/36:2,3:6,7,8:24:31-39^2/37:2^2:3:21,22 24:29:35:36/38:3,4,5:7:9:10^2:11:12:14^2:15^2:16:21:24:29^2:30^2/39:1^2:3:4:6:11^2:12:14,15:18:19:2 :23/40:1^2:11:15/41:1:7:12:13^2:14:17:25:46:49:51:52:54/42:1:5^3:6^2:23:27:35/43:1:2:7^2:12^2:16:17:21:30:34/44:2^2:12:14:16/45:1:2:8:16:24:26/46:8-14:19-22:26/47:20:22:27:28/48:1:10:14^2:17/49:15:26/50:4:15:22:26/Ex1:5^2:7/2:1^2:6^2:1(:12:13:14^2:15/3:1:2:6:14/4:6:7/6:15:25/7:7:13:21/8:19/9:6:7^2:18:24:25:26:31^2/10:13:14:15:22 /11:3^2/12:30^3:39:40,41:42^2/13:17,18^2:19/14:9:19/15:23:25/16:6:13:18:20^2:24:27:31:34/17:1:5,6:7:10f^2:11/18:3:4:5,6:9:14/19:16^2:18/20:21/21:3:4:29^2:36/22:13:15^2/24:18/27:8/29:23/31:17/34:4:18:28/36:14,15:19:21:24:27^2:33:35:36:37:38/37:1^2:2:6:8:11:12:19:20,21:25^3/38:1^2:2:7:9:11:12:13:18^2:19:21^2:22:23:24:25,26:28:29/39:1:2:3:4,5^2:6,7:8:9:15-18:21^2:22:23:25,26:28,29:31:32:43/40:17:35^2:38/Lev2:13f/5:13/8:17:21^2:27:28:29/9:20/10:3:15^3:16:18:20/13:6/14:51,52 /15:10/16:27/18:16f/20:21f/24:10^2:11^2:12/25:1/26:40,41/27:24/Num1:1^2/2:3-31^6/3:25-30:31-35:36,37:38^3/4:36:37:46,47,48:49/7:8:9:10:42-47:60-65:66-71:84,85,86^4/8:4^2:22/9:9:15:16 23/10:11f:13:14:17:19:21:22:28:34:35:36/11:3:7 :10:25:27:31f:32:34/12:1:1f^4:3,4:15^2/13:16:22:22f^2:27:32/14:10,11:39/15:25:32:33/16:15:42:48:50/17:8:10/19:13/20:1:2:9:13^2:14:14f:20/21 3:17,18:24f:31,32:34:35/22:5,6:22,23:22,23f:36/23:6:7-10/24:10:20/25:1:3^2:8:10,11:14^2:15/26:3,4:5-11^2:28-37^3:42,43:51:58,59^2:62^2/27:1^4:3,4^2 14/31:4,5:7:8:14:32-35:41:54/32:1:10,11/33:12:14:38,39^3:40:50,51/35:1:17:24:25/36:7/Deu1:1:1f:6:24,25^2:34,35:37/2:14,15:35,36/3:11:16:18:26/4:14:21,22:37:44,45,46^2/7:8/8:15:16:17/9:8:9^2:19:20^2:25/10:6:8/16:1:3/21:13^2/22:13,14:17,18:20:25,26,27:30f/23:23/26:14^2/29:1:24:27/32:9:12:15:16^2:18:27/34:7^3:9/Jos1:5:17,18/2 :1:15/3:7:13,14^2:15,16^2/4:11:14:15,16/5:2,3^3:4,5:8,9^2:11,12:13/6:1:11:26:27/7:1^4:5:10,11:16:17^2:18^2:26/8:14:16:17:20,21:23:25:26:29:33:35/9:12/10:2^2:11:14:17:27^2:28:30:32:37:42^2/11:11^2 :19:22/12:7/13:1:12:21^2:23:27,28:31:32:33^2/14:1:5:7^2:11:15/15:12:13:17:18,19:20/16:9/17:1:2:10^3:11/18:14:17:20^2/19:10:17-23:24,25,26:32:40:49:51/20:5:6/21:8:9-16^3:26:40/22:7,8:17,18:20:21/23:1/24:12:18:26:30:32:33/Ju1:7:20:22,23:29/2:5:7-9:18/3:6:11:15^2:17,18,19:20:24:30^2:31/4:2,3:4^2:12:16^2:17:21/5:31/6:1:5:6,7:8:11:19:21:28^2:29:32:40/7:12,13^3:15:19,20:25/8:10^2:20^2:26:27f^2:28^2:32:33/9:2f:3:6:30^2:38:40:41:46:51:52:55/10:1^2:2^2:3:5:16/11:1^3:4:11^2:12:13:

AS Con't)
17:23:39/12:5:6:7[2]:8:9,10:11,12[2]:13:14:15/
5[2]:9[3]:16:21[2]:24/14:1:4[2]:10,11[2]:14:17:19:20/
3:6:14:15:18:19:20/16:9:19:21:25,26[2]:27:31/
2:4,5:7,8/18:1[2]:4:7:15,16:20:28:29:30/19:1:2:
0:14:16[3]:22:26:28[2]:30/20:5:12:27,28[2]:31:35-
39:40,41/21:5[2]:6:15:25[2]/Ru1:3:4,5:19:22/2:
4,5:18:19[2]/3:8:14[2]/4:7:16,17/1Sa1:1[4]:7:9:10[2]
f:12,13:15,16:19,20[2]:19,20f:23:24/2:1:13,14[3]:
17:18:22[3]:23,24,25:26[4]/3:1:2,3[2]:8:15:19:20/4
3:5:6:8:10:11:12f:13:15[2]:16:18[2]:19:20[2]/5:4:7:
11:12/6:9[3]/7:2:6:10:13:14:17/8:6/9:1[2]:2[2]:
0,11:24/10:12f:20:21/11:5:9:11/12:2:6:12:15
1f:2:10:13:21:22/14:1:3[2]:5[2]:15:18:19:20:28:
38:39:42:43:47[2]:50,51[2]/15:9:11[2]:14:16:21:24:
16:12:18[2]/17:4-7:11f[3]:14,15[2]:20:23:28:29:31
38,39:50,51:55:55f/18:1:5[2]:6:7:8:10:11,12[2]:
15,16:20:25:26:28[2]:30/19:2:7:9,10:14:16:19/
9:24,25[2]:26:27:34:41/21:6[2]:7:10:12/22:2:3:4:
10[2]:15:17/23:7:14,15:24,25:26:28/24:1:4/25
[4]:4:13:15,16:19:20:21:36:37,38:39/26:1:3,4:
27:11[2]/28:3:5,6:14:18:20:21/30:6:8:13/31:
5:10[2]/2Sa1:1:6:10f:26/2:10,11[2]:24/3:1:2[2]:3[2]
5:8:11:23:37/4:1:2,3,4[4]:5:10/5:2:10:12:17/6:
4:5:8:9:14:14f:16:17:19:21:23/7:1/8:14:15:16[2]
:18/9:1:13/10:2:10:17/11:3[3]:7:17:18:
20,21:26:27[2]/12:3:5:18:21:22/13:2f:11:14:
18[2]:21-24:32,33[2]:37,38,39f/14:1:5,6[2]:25:26:
15:7,8:9f[2]:10:12:14:23:30:31/16:1[2]:3f:5:22:
17:14:23:24:25[4]:27/18:7:11f:24:29[2]:29f/19:1
8,9,10[3]:18:31,32:37f/20:1:8,9,10:12:23[2]:24[2]:
26/21:1:2:7:16[2]:19/22:6:13:16:19:20:24/23:2
9[2]:10[2]:11,12:13:14:15:18,19[3]:20[2]:21:23[2]:24-
39/24:1:10:11:16[4]:25/1Ki1:1[2]:3,4,5:6[2]:15[2]:
23:42:51/2:5[2]:8:10:15[2]:32:34/3:4:6:10[2]:17,18[2]
21:22:24:26/4:1[7]:8-19[11]:24:31[2]:32:33/5:1:7:
/6:1[2]:2:3:5:7:8:10[2]:11,12:14:15:16:17:18:19[2]:
23-28[2]:30:31:34:37:38/7:2[2]:6[3]:7[2]:13:14:16-
22[2]:26:31[2]:35:36:37:38:39:47:48:50:51/8:9:
24:57:64/9:16[2]:25:27,28/10:3:3f:4:5:10:20:
22:23:27[2]/11:6:9,10[2]:14:16,17,18:20:23:26[2]:
28[3]:29:43/12:1:2,3,4[3]:10:11:15:16,17:18:20[2]:
30:32,33f:32,33/13:3:4:5:11:18:24,25:34/14:
6:8:18:21[4]:22:24:30:31[2]/15:1:3[4]:6:8:10:14f:16:
26:27:29:30:32,33/16:1:4-7[2]:9:12:13:15,16:
22:25:26:28:30[2]:34[2]/17:7:11:12:15:16/18:1:
4[2]:5:10:13:26:28:29:45:46/19:5:11[4]:12[3]:19[2]/
21:39:40/21:9f:13:14:25:26/22:1:2:36,37[2]:40
2[2]:47:50:51:52,53/2Ki1:2:7:8[2]/2:11:17:18:22:
/3:1f[2]:1:2:9:11:15:20[3]:25:27/4:1[2]:6:11,12:17:
[2]:19:28:31:32:38[2]:44/5:1[2]:2:11:14:26/6:5[2]:8:
11:25:26-30[2]:32:33/7:5:10[2]:16:17/8:4:5:6[2]:
18:21:24,25:26[2]:27[2]:28:29/9:4:11:16[2]:18:27:
36/10:11:11f:13:15:18,19:29:35/11:1:2,3[3]:
3f[2]:11:13,14[2]:20:21/12:1[2]:2:6:13,14:15:16[3]:21
3:2:3:4:9,10:11:13:14:19:20,21:23[2]:25/14:2[2]:3[2]
2:13:16:19:20[2]:24:29/15:3:5:7:9:18:24:28:29:
35[3]:38/16:3:9:10:10f:15[2]:20/17:4:5:11:17:23:
/18:4:5:7:9[2]:11:17/19:9:37/20:19/21:6[2]:16:
26/22:11:14[2]/23:16:22:23[2]:25:27:30/24:12[2]/
3:6[2]:7[2]:16:17:21:25:27:29/1Ch1:10:13-16:18[2]
9:24-27[9]:38,39:41:50/2:3:7[2]:8:10[2]:11[2]:12[2]:13[3]:
[2]:15[2]:17:20[2]:21:22:26:31[2]:36[2]:37[2]:38[2]:39[2]:40[2]
1[2]:42[4]:44[3]:45:48,49:50/3:1[4]:2[3]:3[2]:5:17,18:
20,21:22[5]/4:2:3-4:8[2]:9:10:11,12[3]:14[2]:17:18[2]:
[3]:21-22:25[3]:27:40,41/5:1[2]:2:5[3]:6[3]:9:12[2]:15:22
5:25,26,27:33-38[2]:39-43[2]:44-47[2]/7:2:3:10:12:
[3]:16:17:24/8:29:30,31,32[2]:33[2]:34[2]:36[3]:37/9:1[2]
10,11:12[2]:14[2]:15,16[2]:20[2]:31:35,36,37:39[3]:40[2]:
42[3]:43/10:4:5:6/11:2:5,6,9:11:12:13[2]:15:16:
21[2]:22[2]:23[2]:24,25[2]:26-47[2]/12:1:3-7:8-13[11]:14[2]
9:20[2]:24-37:38/13:4:5:7:11:12/14:2:8/15:22[2]/
6:1:7:19/18:14:15[2]:16:17/20:1:2:3:4:5:6,7[2]/21:
6:7:8:15:19,20:30/22:3/23:1:3:10,11[2]:12:13:17
9[3]:20:27:28/24:4:7-18:24,25:26,27:29:31/25:
7/26:1:10:13:23,24[2]/27:1:2,3:4[2]:5,6[3]:7[2]:8:9:10
1:12:13:14:15:24:25[2]:26:27:28:29:32[2]:33[2]:34[2]/
8:2:13:19/29:9[2]:26,27/2Ch1:1:2,3:4:15/2:3/3:
3:4:5:6:8[2]/4:2:3:10:19/5:1:10:11,12:13,14/6:8:
2:12,13[2]/7:4,5:9/8:1:3:11[2]/9:2:3:13,14:20:22:
7:31/10:2,3[2]:4[2]:8,9:10:16/11:17:18:22/12:1:12
3:14:16/13:1:6:7:13,14/14:1[2]:2:8:9,10:13/15:2
[2]:6:9:11:17:19/16:2:3:5:10:13,14[2]/17:3:13:
4,15:16:18/18:12:31:32/19:11/20:3:14:30:31[2]:
2[2]:35/21:1:3,4:5:6[2]:7:18:19:20[2]/22:2[2]:4:5[2]:7:8:
11[4]:12/23:2,3:8:12:19:21[2]/24:1[2]:9:10:13:14[3]:
6:22:24:26[2]/25:1[2]:2:3:5,6:20:22/26:3:4[2]:5[3]:8:
0:11:15:19[2]:20:21:23[2]/27:1[2]:3:5:6:8:9/28:1[2]:3:
[2]:16:27/29:1[2]:2:15:17:25,26:34:35[3]/30:13:
7,18,19:23/31:1:5,6:12,13:14,15[2]:17,18:19:20:
1/32:2[2]:3:5:14:22:25:27:31:33/33:1:2:13:14[2]:
19:20,21[2]:22/34:1:2:3:9[2]:14:15,16:22:30:31/35:
10:16:17:22:24,25/36:1:2:3:4[2]:5[2]:9[3]:10:11:12[2]:
13[2]:16/Ez3:3[2]:6[2]:8:9/4:7:15:23/5:5:11[2]/6:2:14:
15:16:19:21,22/7:1[15]:6[2]:10:28[2]/8:18[2]:22:34[2]/9:
11/10:6:7,8:16-19[2]:24/Neh1:1:11/2:1[3]:5,6:8:10[2]
:11,12/3:2:3:6:8[2]:9:10:12:14:16:17:20:24:25:29:
30/4:1:3:6:7:10/5:1:2,3,4[2]:6:14:15/6:8:10[2]:15:
18[2]:19/7:1:4[2]:5:66/8:7,8:12:17:18/9:8:28/10:38[2]
/11:7,8,9[2]:10-14:15,16,17:20:22,23[2]:22,23f/12:8
:10,11[5]:22:26[2]:38:43:46/13:3:4:6:8:10:13:15:21:
26[2]:28/Est1:1[2]:5:7[2]:8:10:11:12/2:5:6:8:9[2]:10:11:
12,13,14[3]:15:15f:16:17:20[2]:21:23[2]/3:1:3,4:5,6:7[3]
/4:2:3:4:5[2]:8:13/5:1:9[2]/6:4/7:7:8[2]:10/8:1[2]:8f:
9,10[2]:12:12f[2]:14/9:4[2]:11:14:17:22:32/10:3[3]/Job
1:2,3[2]:5:16:18/2:12:13/3:2,3:26/4:7,8:12/10:
13,14/15:17-19/16:12/19:4/20:20/29:4:5:14[2]:
16/32:3/36:21/38/41:31,32/42:3:7/Ps3:5/18:1:
7:9:17:18/30:6,7[2]/31:13:14,15/32:3[2]:4/34:5/35:
14/37:35,36/40:7f/41:12/49:20f/51:5/55:12:13
:20:21/60:1[2]/63/66:6:14:20/73:2:3/77:18:19/
78:18:21:30:35[2]:36:38:46:51:59:62/81:7:10/83:5
/87:4/89:19f/90:2/94:18/95:9/105:21:38[2]:45/
106:39/107:18/111:6/116:3:6/119:40,41,42:
59,60:71,72:75,76,77:147/122:1/126/132:6/
133:2/139:15:16[2]/Pro4:3/5:13/7:6:11,12:14f:15
:23/8:26:27,28,29[3]:30[2]:31/24:30,31/26:18,19/
Ecc1:12-15:16-18/2:1:10:11[2]:13,14:24-26/3:15/
5:6,7/6:10/8:15:16,17/9:14:15[2]/12:7:9:10/Sol1:
1/3:4/5:2[2]:4:6[2]/6:12/8:1/Is1:1/6[2]:4[2]:10f/7:1[2]:
14f[4]/8:2/12:1/14:4:29/18:1f/20:2/21:5f/23:1f:
2,3:4f:7:17/26:16/27:9/30:2f/36:3:11f/37:8,9[2]:
23:26[2]:38/38:1:9:13:17:18f/39:1f[2]:1/41:8:26:27
/43:10/44:28f/46:9/47:6/48:3:5:13/50:1:2/51:1
/52:13f:14,15/53:2[2]:3:4:5[3]:7[3]:8[3]:9:10:12/54:1/
57:17/59:15:16/63:3:5:9/64:3/Jer1:3/2:6/3:9[2]:
10/4:23:25/5:7/7:18f:22:23/8:15/13:7[2]/14:1:18
/18:4/20:1:14:15:18/21:1f/22:11:13f:15:30f/25:
1:5/26:10:20[2]:21/29:24f/30:18/31:19[2]:33f/32:1
:2[2]:8:12:31/33:1:15f/34:7:10:11f:14:15/35:1:3:4[2]
/36:5:10:12:13:22:22f:22:23/37:10:13[3]:15,16:17
:21[2]/38:6[2]:7:8:11:12:28/39:1:3:4:5:15/40:11/41
:1:9/44:15:22:30f[2]/45:1/46:2/47:1/48:13/49:8f[2]
/51:20f:26f:59/52:1[2]:2:6:7:8:9[2]:11:20:24,25:27[2]:
28:31:34/Lam1:7:9/2:14/4:20/5:10/Eze1:1[2]:4:
13:16:19,20,21:22:26:27,28[2]/2:9,10/3:13:14,15:
22/4:14/8:1:2[2]:3:4:11/9:8/10:4[2]:5:9-13:14:17f:
17:19/11:13/12:7:11:12f:13f/14:22/16:4:14[2]:15
:47/17:8/19:2:9:10:11:12[2]/20:1:14/23:4,5[2]:8:10
:13:14,15:19,20:32/25:3[2]/26:1/27:17:32/28:13:
15:17/29:18f[3]:20:20f[3]/30:22/31:1f:2,3:7:8:9/33:
24/34:6/36:17:21/37:1[2]:7/38:2,3f/39:23[2]/40:1[2]
:5:6:7-12[4]:13:15:18:19[2]:23:25:27:29,30:31:33:38:
43:47:48,49[2]/41:2[2]:3:4:5[2]:6:7:8:9:10:11:13:14:
15,16:17,18:19,20:21[2]:22:25/42:2:6:7,8:9,10[2]:11
:12:16-20/43:2:3:6:22/44:1/45:11f:18f/46:21,22
/47:2f:3:4:5[2]:15f/Dan1:3,4:3,4f:7[4]:8f:10:11:
18,19/2:1:5:6:7:12:26:28:29:32:34:36:39f/3:19:
24:27/4:3:4:12:18:19f:29:31:33[3]:36/5:2,3,4[2]:7f[2]:
8f:10:11[2]:13:21[2]:29[3]:30/6:2:4[2]:14:16:17:20:21:
23[2]/7:4[3]:6:7:8:9:11:13:14:15:20:28[3]/8:2:2f:3[2]:5:
7[3]:8:9f:12:15[2]:17:27[3]/9:1[2]:20:23[2]/10:4:5,6:8:12[2]
:13:15/11:1:7f:13f:21f:30,31f/12:6/Hos1:7f:3:7:
8:16f/3:5f/8:6/9:10:15f/10:9/11:1:3/12/13:1:
15/Amo1:1:2[2]:5f:11:12f/2:8f/3:12/4:7:10/6:5/7
:1:4:7[2]:10/Ob1:1f:8f[2]/Jon:3:4:5:9,10:11:13:17[2]
:3:5:6/3:3:3f:6/4:2:8/Nah1:1f/3:8f/Hab2:18/3:
8,9f[3]:8,9/Zep1:1f/Hag:1/2:3[2]/Zec1:2:8:10:15/
2:3:9:11,12/3:1:3/4:6f:7/5/6:2/7:4:7/8:10[2]/11:
11[2]:14:15/12:11/Mal1:2,3/2:4:5/Mt1:2[3]:3[4]:4[3]:
5[5]:6[3]:7[3]:8[3]:9[3]:10[3]:11:12[2]:13[3]:14[3]:15[3]:16[2]:18[2]:25
/2:1:3[2]:9f:16:22[3]/3:1:4[2]/4:1:18/5:21/6:29/8:5,6
:12:13:14:18:24:26:30/9:9:12:18:22:25[3]:27:28:32
/11:1f:2[2]/12:1[2]:4:11:22[2]:23:39,40:46,47/13:2,3:
5:8/14:1f:4:5[2]:9:10:11:13:14:26:30/15:22:24:28:
31/16:7:10:11:20/17:4f:8:12:13:14:18/18:24:27
/19:8:22/20:3:4:6:17:30:34/21:4:10:18[2]:23:25:
26:31:45/22:3[2]:10:26:28:31:32f/24:1:37,38:39/
25:5,6:10:14:24,25:24,25f:35[2]:42/26:7:17:24:47:
55:58[2]:69:71/27:1:7:9:11:15:16:19:24:32:45:47:
51:54:66f/28:1:2:3:5:6:9:12,13[2]:17/Mk1:4:9:
12,13:14:16:22:23:32,33:34:35:42[2]:45/2:2[2]:14:
25,26[2]:27/3:2:5[2]:9:20[2]:21:30:31,32[2]/4:1:2:10:20
:34:36:37:38:39/5:1:3,4[3]:6:11:15:22:25:26[2]:29:
32:35[4]:38:40:41,42/6:2,3:14:15[2]:17,18:19:20[2]:21
:26[2]:34:47:49:52/7:6,7:24:25:26:30[2]:32/8:20:25
/9:2:7:8:21:25:27:28:34/10:1f:4:5:10:14[2]:17:22:
32[2]:46[3]:47/11:7:9:11:13:18:20:27,28:30:32/12:4
:5:6:12:18:27:28:35:36/13:1:34/14:1:3:43:47f:49
:51,52:53:63,64:66,67/15:1:6:7:10:21[2]:23:25:26:
28[2]:34f:35:38f:38:39:41:42,43:44:47/16:4[2]:6[2]:9[2]:
10,11:13:19:20/Lk1:5[3]:7:8,9[2]:10:11,12[2]:19:21:
41:57[2]:59:62f:67/2:2[2]:3:4:5:7:13:16:21[2]:24:25[2]:
28:33:36,37[3]:38:40:41,42:43:44:46,47:51:52/3:1[2]
:4:15[4]:21[2]:23-38[78]/4:1:17:25,26:29:33:41:43/5:1
:9:12[2]:17[2]:26:27:33/6:4[2]:6[3]:7:19/7:2:4:9:12[2]:18:
20,21,22[2]:37:39[2]/8:3[2]:4:5:8:19:23:24:27:29:30:
32:35:42:46:47:49[2]:52:53/9:7:11:18:29:33:34:36:
42:43/10:21:30:33f:36:40[3]/11:14:26:27:37,38:
45:48/12:27:39/13:1:6:10:11:14/14:1[3]:17[2]:21:
22:30/15:2:3,4:6:14:16:20[2]:24[2]:25:26:27:28:32[2]/
16:1:7:19[2]:20:22[2]/17:16:28/18:2:10:21:23:35:36
:37[2]/19:1:3:9,10:11:12:13:21:42:48/20:1[2]:4[2]:5:6[2]
:11:12[2]:17:19/21:1/22[2]:3:5:7:44:49:53:56:66/23
:7:8:9:17,f:19:26[2]:35:38:44:45:47[2]:48:50,51,52:
54:55:56/24:3:19[2]:21:22,23:24:29:30:31:35:36:
37:44:46:50f/Jn1:1:8[2]:11,12[2]:14:15:28:30:31:33:
35:39:40:44/2:1:7,8:9:11[2]:13:23/3:23,24[3]:25:26
/4:5,6:8:9:39:46,47[4]:51[2]:53[2]:54/5:2:4:9[3]:10:11:
15/6:2-5f:6[2]:10:21:21f:71/7:2:12:27:28:29:30:39
:41,42:43:50/8:2:3:4:9:20:27:38:44:56[2]:58[2]:59/9
:1:2[2]:7:14f:15:16:19:20:22,23:25/10:22,23:22,23
f:22,23[2]:40:42/11:1:5:6:12,13:18:20:31:32:33:
37,38[2]:49:51:52:55/12:1:2:3:5:6:11:12:16:18:21f[2]
:21:29:30:33:36:37:41/13:1:12:21:23f:23:23f[2]:24
:26f:29[2]/16:4/17:13/18:4,5:14:15[2]:18:25[2]:28:28
f:34f[2]:36:37:40/19:8:14:17:20[3]:23,24:28:29[2]:31[2]:
33:41[2]:42/20:1[2]:7[2]:11:14:15:19:20:24:26[2]/21:4:
7:9[2]:12:14:17/Act1:3:9:16[2]:17:21,22[2]:26/2:1f:2:
4:6:16:29:30:31:32:34:43:47/3:2:10:11:16:17:18
/4:3:5:6:9:10:14:21:32[2]:33:33f:36[2]:37/5:1:2:3:4[2]:
5:10:16:23:33:36[2]:37/6:7:13/7:2:8[3]:9:11[2]:12:
17,18:20:23:31:35:38:42:43:44:45:47:53f/8:1:3:8
:9,10,11:12:13[2]:18:28:30:32[2]:33:34/9:3:8,9[2]:10:
18[2]:19:22:24:26:28:34:36[2]:38:39/10:2[3]:3:7:9,10[3]
:16[2]:17[2]:18:19:24:29:30[2]:38[2]:39:44/11:5:11:15:
17[2]:23[2]:24:26:28[2]/12:4:5[2]:6[2]:7:9[2]:14[2]:18:20[2]:21:
23:24/13:12:25:29:31:36[2]:37[2]:43:46/14:3:9:12[3]:
14/15:12:31:39/16:1:2:3:10:14[3]:15:16:22:23:26[2]
/17:1:2:13:16[2]:18:23:34/18:2,3:18f:22:22f:25,26[3]
:27/19:1:4:13:17:20:29:32:33:34:35/20:1:3[2]:7:8:
10,11,12[2]:13:16:31:35/21:7:14:30[2]:31:33:37,38/
22:2:6:9:11:17,18:20[2]:29[2]:30/23:5:9:27[2]:29:30:
34/24:2:6:9:10:11:18[2]:25:27/25:3:4[2]:13f:14:15:
19:20/26:4:11:12:19/27:2[2]:3:7,8f:9[2]:9f:12[2]:16:
20:27:39:41/28:5:6:7:8:11[2]:12:16:17:23:25/Rom
1:2:4:13:16:21[2]:25:28/3:25[2]/4:1[2]:9:10:11[2]:12:13
:19[3]:21[2]:23:24/5:13:14[2]/6:2,3[2]:4:6:21/7:3:5:7:9:
10[2]:12:13[2]/9:5:10-13[4]:14:17:26/11:2,3[2]:11:24:
30/16:5/1Co1:30/2:4[3]:7[2]/3:6[3]:13/4:15/5:11/6/
7:20/9:9:10/10:3,4f:3,4:25/11:9[2]/13:11/15:4:5:
5f:6:32[2]:45:45f:45:47/16:12/2Co1:9:15,16[2]/2:3:
4:13/3:7:9:11:14/5:19/6:2/7:5[2]:7:8:9:12/8:5:9[2]:
19/9:2:3/11:8,9[3]:25[4]:33/12:2,3[3]:7[2]:12[2]:13/13:2:
4/Gal1:1f:1:13:14:15:17:18:19:23/2:2[2]:3:6:10[2]:
11[2]:12[2]:14:19:21/3:13:19[3]/4:3:11:13:14:15f:23[2]:
24,25:28:29/6:14/Eph1:10:12/2:15/3:8/4:22/5:
2[2]:8/Php1:7[2]/2:5:6:7f:9:12:16:26:27:30/3:5[5]/4:
11:16/Col1:5:7:17:20/2:12:22/3:7:9/1Th1:5[2]/2:
1:13/3:5[3]/2Th2:5/1Ti1:13:14:15:19/2:14[3]/3:16[5]
/2Ti1:9:16/2:8[2]/3:9:11[2]:16/4[2]:17f/Tit1:5/Phm:
17/Heb:4/2:9:10[2]:17/3:2:5[2]:7,8:9:10:17:18[2]/4:2
/5:5:7:7f[6]:8[2]:9/6:13[2]/7:1[2]:3f:3:6:10:18[2]/8:5/9:1[2]
:3[2]:6:12:18:22:24[2]/10:28:34/11:4:5[2]:7[3]:8:10:11:
12:13:17[2]:19[2]:20:21:22[2]:24,25:26[2]:27:28:30/12:
2:7:17:19:21/13:10/Jas1:18/2:21[2]:22[3]:23:25/5:
15:17/1Pe1:10:11:12:18:20:23:25/2:7/3:5:18:19
:20/4:6/5:13f/2Pe1:17,18:20,21[2]/2:7,8:16:20/3
:4/1Jn1:1:2[2]/3:12/5:6,7,8[2]/Jud1:4:9/Rev:1:4:5:
8:9:10[2]:12:13:14f:14/2:8:13/3:14/4:2:6:7:8/5:1:
2:3:4:12/6:2[2]:4:7:8[2]:12[2]/7:4-8/8:1:3:5:7:8,9:11:
12[2]/9:1[2]:8:10:19/10:3:4:7:10/11:1:2:8,9:17:19[3]/
12:2:4[2]:5[2]:7:8:9:14[2]/13:3:7f:13:14[3]:15:17/14:2:
14:16/15:2:5:8/16:2:5:9:10:18:19:21/17:5:6:8:8f
/18:12:24/19:4:11:12:13[2]:16:20[2]:21/20:11f:13:
15[2]/21:2:11:16[4]:17f:18,19,20[3]:21

5018

WASN'T
Gen30:9:15/37:29/43:3,4,5/Ex16:27/Lev5:2/
Num14:16[2]/Deu9:28/2Sa11:19,20,21/1Ki3:21/
9:11,12/10:21[2]/2Ch18:6,7/30:2,3/Neh13:18:26
/Job30:25/Jer7:22/38:27/Eze6:10/13:12/16:
20/Amo4:8/Mt17:12/22:11/27:24/Mk2:2/Lk
24:26/Jn6:24/11:15/Act2:29/12:19/Rom4:11:
23/1Co5:10/9/15/2Co2:13/2Th3:9/Heb7:10/
11:27

43

WE
Gen3:2,3[4]:22/12:11,12,13/13:8[2]:9/19:5:9:13:32
/20:11,12:13/22:7/24:25:31:50:55/26:10:22:28:
29[2]:32/28:4/29:5:8:15/31:44:49[2]/34:9,10[2]:14:
16:17:21:23:30[2]/35:3/37:7:32/38:23/40:8/41:
12/42:2:7:10:11[2]:12:21[3]:22[3]:31[2]:32/43:3,4,5:7[3]:

(WE Con't)
8[2]:10:18:21[4]:22:23/44:7:8[3]:16[5]:19:20[2]:22:24:26[3]
:31/46:34/47:3:4[2]:15:19[4]:25/48:7/50:15:16,17[2]:
18/Ex1:10:19/5:1:3[3]:16[2]/8:26:27/10:9[3]:25:26[3]/
12:33/13:15/14:5:12[3]/15:24/16:3[2]:7,8,9:23/19:
8/20:19/24:3:7:14/25:18f/33:16/35:35/36:4-7/
Lev25:20[2]/Num10:29[2]:31f/11:4,5[2]:6:12:22[2]/12:
11/13:27[2]:28:30:33[2]/14:2[2]:19:40[4]/16:3[2]:6,7:14/
17:12,13[2]/20:3:10:14:16[2]:17[3]:19[3]/21:5:7[2]:22[3]/
27:3,4[2]/31:48,49:50/32:16:17[3]:18:19[2]:25:31:32/
Deu1:19,20,21[2]:22:28:41[2]/2:1[2]:8:13:27[2]:28[5]:29:
33,34[2]:35,36[3]:37/3:1:3:4:5:6[2]:7:8:10:29/4:7/5:
24[2]:25:26,27[2]/6:21:22:25/7:17[2]/9:4/17:14/18:
21/26:6,7/29:7[2]:16[3]/Jos1:10,11:17,18[2]/2:9:10[2]:
11:17,18:19[2]/3:2,3,4/4:6:23/7:7[3]/8:5:6/9:7[2]:8:9[2]
:12:19[3]:20[2]:24[4]:25/14:6:12/17:4/22:17,18:19:
22,23[4]:24,25[3]:26,27[2]:31[2]/24:15:16:17[2]:18:21:22:
24/Ju1:3/5:28/7:17:18/8:5:6:15/9:28/10:10:15
/11:8[2]:10[2]:23:24/12:1/13:12:15:17:22[2]/14:15/
15:12,13[2]/16:25,26/18:9,10:14/19:9:12,13[2]:19/
20:4:8,9,10:13:22,23,24:27,28[2]/21:5:7[3]:16:18[2]:
22[3]/Ru1:10/3:15-18/4:11/1Sa:3:7:9/5:7[2]/6:2[3]:
4,5:9:20/8:19:20/9:7[2]:8:9,10,11/10:14[3]:18,19/
11:1:3[2]:9:10[2]:12/12:10:19[2]/14:9:10:30:37:38:45
/15:15/16:10,11/17:8:9:58/20:42/21:4:14,15/
22:15/23:3:19:20/25:7:8:15,16:21/27:5/28:2/
30:14:24/2Sa2:27/5:1/7:22/10:12[2]/11:23/12:
18:21/13:25[2]/15:14[3]:15/17:6:12[2]:13/18:3[2]:12:
22/19:5[2]:6:8,9,10[2]:42:43[2]/20:1:6:18:21[2]/21:4:
5,6:17/22:32/1Ki3:17,18/5:9[2]/8:47[2]/11:22/12:
2,3,4/18:5[3]/20:14:23:25[2]:31/22:5:15/2Ki2:19/3
:10:11:12/4:10:13[2]:14/6:1:8:15:22:26-30[3]/7:3:4[6]
:9[2]:12[2]/9:15/10:4:5[2]:13[2]:18,19/17:26[2]/18:25:26
/19:19/22:12,13[3]/1Ch11:1/12:17:18[2]/13:3/15:
2:13/16:35/17:20/29:11:13:14[3]:15:16/2Ch2:16
/6:26/10:4/13:10:11/14[3]/18:3,4,5:14/20:9[2]:10:
12[3]/24:5/28:13/29:18:19/31:10/32:8:13/Ez4:2[2]
:13:14[3]:15:16:22/5:8[2]:9:10[2]:11[2]:17/7:15[2]:19:23/
8:15:21[4]:22:23:31:32/9:7[3]:8:9:10[2]:11:12[2]:13[2]:14:
15[2]/10:2[2]:3[3]:4:10[2]:12:13:16-19/Neh1:6,7:10/2:
13:14,15[2]:20/4:1:4:9:10:15[2]:19:20,21:23/5:5[4]:8[2]
:9:18/6:1[2]:7:15/7:1/9:5:32:33[2]:36:37:38[2]/10:29[2]
:30:31[3]:32:33[2]:34:35:36[2]:37:39,40/12:38:39/13:
27/Est1:13-15:19/2:3/5:12/6:3/7:4[2]/Job2:10/
8:9/9:32,33/12:13/15:9[2]/17:16/18:3:4/21:15/
28:20/31:18/34:3[4]:4[2]:31[2]:32[3]/36:26:33/37:5:
19,20[3]:21:22:23/Ps11:3/12:3,4:7/13:4/20:5:8/
21:13/22:8/25:10/33:20:21[3]/35:25/40:5/41:9/
44:1:5:17:18:19[2]:20:22[2]:23:25/46:2/48:1:8[2]:9:14
/55[2]/60:12/62/65:1/66:12/68:35/71:11/74:2:8
:9,10/75:1/79:8:13/80:3:7:8:9:10:14:16:18:19/
81:5/83:1:4/90:5,6[2]:7[2]:10:12/91:1/95:7/100:3/
103:10:14/106:6:47/108:2:13/115:18[2]/118:24:
26/119:79/122:2,3/123:2:3,4/124:2,3:4,5:7[2]/
126:2:4/129:8/132:6f:7:7f[2]:9/137:1:2:3,4[2]/Pro
10:7/16:1:2[2]:9:33/21:2:3[2]/Ecc1:8-11[6]/2:24-26/
12:14/Sol1:4:11/4:8/6:1:13/8:8[2]:9[2]/Is1:9/2:3/
4:1[2]/5:19/7:6:14f/9:8,9,10[2]/10:9[4]:10:11[2]:13[3]:14
/14:8:10:32/16:6/20:5,6/22:13/25:9[2]/26:1:8:12
:13[2]:14:17[2]:18:19/28:9:15/30:10,11:16/33:2:24
/36:7:11/40:18[2]/41:7/43:26/48:7/49:20/53:3[3]:
4:5[2]:6[2]/58:3[2]/59:12[2]:13[6]/63:17:18:19[2]/64:5[3]:6[4]
:8[2]:9/Jer2:31[2]/3:22:23:24:25[3]/4:13/5:4/6:16:17
:24[2]:25/8:8:14:15[2]:20/9:19[2]/13:12/14:7:9[2]:19:
20:22/15:2/16:10/18:12[3]:18[2]/20:10[2]/21:13/26:
19/29:28[3]/30:5/35:6[2]:7[2]:8[2]:9:10:11[2]/36:16/38:
4:25/40:15/42:2[2]:5[2]:6[4]:13,14:20/43:2,3/44:16:
17[7]:18[2]:19/46:16/48:2,3,4:14:29[2]/49/50:7/51:9[2]
:51/Lam1:16:18/2:12:16[2]/3:39[2]:42[2]:47[2]/4:17[3]:
18[2]:19[2]:20[2]/5:1:3:4:5:6:7:9:21/Eze6:11/11:3f/
33:10[2]:24[2]/35:10[2]/37:11/40:6:17/Dan2:4:7/3:
16:17:18:24[2]/6:7:8/9:5[2]:6:7:8:10[2]:11:13:14:15:
18[2]/Hos6:3/10[2]/14:2:3[2]/Amo3:3/Jon1:11/Mic
2:4/4:2:5/6:6[2]/Nah1:15/Hab:13:14[2]:15/Zec:
5,6[2]:11/Mal:4:6:7/2:10[2]:17/3:7:8:13[2]/Mt2:2/3:
9[2]/4:4/6:9:10:12/7:22/9:14:28:33/11:3[2]:17[2]/13
:28:51:55/14:17/15:33/17:4:19:26,27/19:27[2]/
20:22:32,33/21:25[2]:26:27/22:16:25/23:29,30/
25:9:37:39:44/26:17:65,66:73[2]/27:6:64[2]/Mk1:
38/4/6:2,3:38/8:4:11:21/9:5:28:38[2]/10:33:35:
37:39/11:31:32:33[2]/12:14:23/14:2:14:42:58:
63,64/Lk3:12[2]/4:8:34/5:5:26/7:16:19:32[2]:32f[2]/
8:24/9:13:49[2]:54/10:11:17/11:4:7/12:15/13:7:9
:26/14:10/15:23[2]:27:30/17:5/18:28:31[2]/20:5[2]:6
:7:21:29/22:38:49[2]:71[2]/23:40,41/24:21/Jn1:16:
22:41:45/3:1:8/4:20:21-24[7]:42[2]/6:2-5:14:28:42:
68:69/7:27/8:33:41:48:52/9:20:21:24:28:29[2]:40
/11:27:47:48/12:21:34/14:5[3]:8:23/16:17,18:30[2]
/17:5:11:22/18:30:31/19:15/20:3,4:9:10:25/21:
3[2]:4:5:6:9[2]:12:24/Act1:17:21,22/2:8[2]:9:11:32:37
/3:6:12:15/4:16[2]:17:20[2]/5:8:23:28:29:32/6:2:3:
4:14/7:2f:40[2]/9:14:21/10:33:39:46,47/11:6:12:
17/13:46/14:15[2]/15:10:19:20:24:26:36f/16:10[2]:
11:13[3]:15:16[2]:28:37/17:20:28[2]:29:32/18:21/19:
2:40/20:6[2]:7:8:13:14:15[3]:17/21:1[2]:2:3:4:5[2]:6:7:8
:14:15:16:23[2]:25[2]/23:9:15/24:3:5:6[2]/26:14/27:2
:3:4[2]:4f:7,8[3]:9:10:16[2]:26:27:37/28:1[2]:7:10[2]:11:
12:13[2]:14[2]:15:16:20:21[2]:22[2]/Rom1:17/2:2/3:5:
8:9[2]:20[3]:21,22[4]:24:27:28[2]:31[4]/4:9:11:15[4]:16[3]:24
/5:1[2]:2[2]:3[3]:4:5[3]:6:7[2]:8:10[3]:11:13:20[2]/6:1:2,3[3]:8:
15/7:6f/8:3[2]:4[2]:15[2]:16:17[4]:18:22:23[3]:24[2]:25:26[3]:
28[2]:30:31:35[3]:36[2]:39/9:23,24:30/10:8/11[2]:17:
33/12:4,5[3]/13:11:12,13/14:7[2]:8[2]:9[2]:17/15:1[4]:4:
24:32/1Co1:18:23/2:10:13[3]:16/3:5:6:9:11:20/4:
5:8:10[2]:11[2]:12[3]:13[2]/6:2:3:13[2]/7:7:26/8:4[2]:6:8[4]/
9:5f[2]:11:12[4]:25/10:1:6[2]:11:16[3]:17[2]/11:16:32[2]/
12:5:13:23[2]/13:9:10:12[3]/14:21:38/15:11:12:15[2]:
19:30:32[4]:42[2]:43[3]:46:49:51[2]:52:53:57/16:4:24/
2Co1:1:3,4[2]:5:6,7:8[3]:9[4]:10:12[4]:20:22/2:11:14:16[2]
:17/3:1[2]:2:4[2]:5[2]:6[2]:8:12[2]:18[3]/4:1:2[7]:3:4:5[3]:8[4]:9[3]:
11[2]:12:13[2]:14:16:18[4]/5:1[4]:2[4]:3:4[2]:6[2]:7:8[2]:9[2]:10:
11:12[2]:13,14[7]:20[2]:21f/6:1:3[2]:4[4]:5:6[3]:7[2]:8[2]:9[4]:10[5]
/7:2:5:10:13/8:6:20[3]:21[2]:22/9:11/10:13[2]:14[3]:15[2]
:16/11:4:6:12/12:18/13:4[2]:7f:7[3]:8f:9/Gal1:4:7:8
/2:4[2]:5[2]:10:16[5]:17[4]:18[2]:21/3:11:21,22[2]:23[2]:25:
26:27:28[4]:29[2]/4:3[2]:6[2]:7[2]:15:29:31/5:5:6[4]:17[2]:25:
26/6:9[2]:10[2]:15[2]/Eph1:3[2]:4:6:7:10:11[2]:12:18/2:3
:5[2]:6:9:10[2]:21/3:12[2]:20/4:4[3]:6:13:14[2]:15,16:25[3]
/5:29,30:32/6:12:22/Php1:7:30/2:1/3:3[2]:20/
Col1:3[2]:4:9[2]:11:16[2]:28[4]/2:19[3]/1Th1:2:3[2]:4:5[3]:8[3]
/2:2[4]:3[2]:4[3]:5[2]:6[2]:7:8[2]:9[3]:10:11:13[4]:17[2]:18:19[2]/3:
4[2]:6:7[2]:8[2]:9:10/4:1[3]:6:10:11:14[2]:15:17/5:10[2]/
2Th1:4:10:11/2:13:15[2]:16/3:2:4[2]:6:8[4]:9[2]:10[2]:11:
12[2]:14/1Ti2:2/4:4[2]:5:9,10/6:7[4]:8[2]:17/2Ti1:4:9/
2:11[2]:12[4]:13/4:15/Tit3:3[3]:5:7[2]/Heb2:1[3]:3[2]:5:8:
9:11:12:14:16:18/3:6[2]:14[4]/4:1:3:4:12:13[2]:15/6:1
:3:11:18/7:8:12,13,14:15:19[2]:26/8:1[2]/9:11:22/
10:10:19:22:23[2]:30:39/11:1[3]:3:4/12:1:9[3]:10:11:
25:28/13:6:10:14:15:18/Jas1:18:20:21/3:1[2]:3[2]/
4:13:15/5:11[2]:17/1Pe1:3[2]/2:24/3:9:21[3]/4:17/
2Pe1:16[2]:19/3:11:13/1Jn1:2[2]:3[3]:4:6[3]:7[2]:8[3]:9:9f:
10[4]/2:3[3]:8:29[2]/3:1[2]:2[4]:6[2]:10:11:12:14[2]:16[2]:18:
19[3]:20[3]:21:22[2]:23:24/4:6:10:11:12[2]:13:14:16[3]:17[3]
:18[3]/5:6,7,8[2]:9[2]:14[2]:15[3]:19[2]:20[3]/2Jn1:6[2]:12/
3Jn1:8[2]:14/Jud:4[3]/Rev:9/7:3/11:17

2200

WE'LL

Gen13:9/19:2:9/24:57/33:14:15/34/37:19,20:
21,22/42:16/Jos2:14:15/Ju14:15/16:2/1Sa9:19
/14:8:9:12/16:15,16/26:11/2Ki3:6,7,8/6:13/18:
23/2Ch10:16/23:4/Ps22:8/Pro1:11:12:13:14/
Is7:6/56:12/Mt21:26/27:41,42,43:64/28:14/
Mk15:32/Lk5:5/9:33/Jn21:3/Act4:17

42

WENT

[2]Gen4:16/8:14/9:22/12:4:10/13:11/14/15:17/
18:16:22,23:29:33/19:3:30:33:35/21:8:16/22:6:
8/24:32:45:61/25:34/26:23/28:5:9/29:4:10/30:
16:35,36/31:33[2]/33:3:17/34:1:6,7:27/38:9:11:
12:15/41:3:43:46/42:3/43:15:19/44:28/46:8-14[2]
/47:1/48/50:7/Ex1:5/2:11/3:3,4/5:1:15:22/6:
27/7:10/8:12:30/9:10:33/10:18/11:8f/12:38/
15:5/16:17:27/17:10[2]/18:7[2]/19:14:25/24:9:13:
15/32:1:15/33:4:7:8/34:34/35:20/Lev9:8:23/10
:5/16:23/Num7:89/8:22/14:44/16:3:33/17:8/
20:6:15:27/21:11/22:7:22,23f:24:35:36/23:3,4/
24:1/31:13:36-40:48,49/32:39/33:8:15-37:45/
Deu1:43/10:22/26:5/Jos2:5:7:8:22/3:2,3,4/4:7
/6:12,13,14:15/8:14:24/9:14,15/10:7:29:31:36/
14:8/15:7:10,11/16:1:8/17:7:10/18:8:12:13:17:
18/19:12:24,25,26/21:43/22:10:32/24:4/Ju1:1:
3/2:15/3:16/4:9:18[2]:22/5:15/7:1/8:8:17/9:3:42
:43:45/10:9/11:18:40/12:3/14:9:19[2]/15:4:8:11/
16:1:3:5/18:7:13:15,16:27/19:3:14:15/20:18:
22,23,24:26:30/Ru1:21/2:8,9:15/3:6,7[2]/4:1/
1Sa1:7:9:18:19,20:21,22/3:9/5:3/6:12[2]:13/7:6/
8:6/9:14/10[2]/11:15/13:10:15:17:18/15:12:31:
34/17:14,15/18:27/19:18:22/20:11:35/21:1:10/
22:3:5:19/23:5:6:16:19:24,25:29/24:2:3:22[2]/25:
1:14/26:2:5,6,7:25/28:7,8:25/29:11/30:15/31:8
/2Sa1:4/2:23/3:6:16:19/5:17:20/7:17:18/8:14/
11:2/12:16:20/13:8:19/14:23/15:2:9:22:23:30/
16:13:16:22/17:23/18:9[2]:33[2]/19:5:8,9,10[2]:40/
20:5:13:22/23:13:20/24:4:6:19/1Ki1:9:11:15/2:
19:30:40/3:4:15/10:16,17/11:16,17,18/12:
23,24/13:10:11:19/14:4:28/16:18/17:10/18:2:
16[2]/19:3:4:13:19[2]:21/20:28:32:43/21:4[2]:16:27/
22:13:30:35/2Ki1:15/2:1:4:6,7:8:13,14:15:21:23
:25/3:12:24/4:8:18:31:33:35:37:39/5:12:14:15:
25/6:15:19/7:5:8:10/8:3:7:14:29/9:6:11:34:35/
10:9,10:23:25[2]/11:18/12:17/16:10/18:37/19:1:
14/20:1:14/22:8:14/23:29/25:25/1Ch4:42/6:4-
15/9:19/10:8:12/11:1:4:15:23/12:8-13:17/1
6/15:25/17:16/18:3:6/19:9/21:19,20/26:14,1
25/2Ch1:13/8:17,18[2]/12:11/14:7/15:2/16:6/
18:2:12:31:34/19:2:4/20:10:20:25:35/22:6:7/
:11/24:13/25:27/26:17,18/28:3:9/29:12,13,1
18:20/30:10/31:1/34:4:6:22/Ez4:4,5/5:8/8:1
10:6/Neh2:13:14,15/4:12/6:10:17/8:7,8:12:1
12:8:31,32[2]:37[2]:38:39/Est3:15/4:1:6/5:10/7:7
8:14:15/9:5:18/Job1:12,13/2:7/29/40:1/Ps3
14/66:6:12/73:17/74:8/99/Ecc12:9/Sol3:2/6
11/Is36:3:22/37:1:8,9:14:36/38:1/53:3/57:10
17/Jer7:24/22:16/25:18:19,20/29:3/35/36:1
12:20/38:4:11/40:12/41:3:6[2]:16,17/Lam5:9/
Eze1:12[2]:19,20,21[3]/3:14,15:14,15f:23/8:10/9:
7/10:3:4:6:7,8/12:7/23:11:44/31:4:7:16:17/40
20/41:3/47/Dan2:16:17:24/3:8/6:10:18/10:3
Hos1:4,5f:13/Amo7:1/Ob1:13/Jon:3[2]:6/2:7/
3/4:5/Hab3:13/Hag2:15/Zec:3/6:8/Mt2:9f:2
/3:5:13/4:11:20:22:25/5:1/8:25/9:1:9:25:28:3
11:1:7/12:4:9/13:1:36/14:13:23,24:29/17:25/
18:28:31/19:22/20:1/21:12:19:29:33/22:5:22/
25:1:10:17/26:14:30:36:39:44:58:75/27:5:33:5
58:62/28:1:11/Mk1:14:18:20:21:29,30:31:35:
36,37:45/2:13:14:18:25,26/3:1:6:13/4:2:27[2]/5
24:39:40/6:2,3:6:12:24:46:56/7:17:24:31/8:27
9:1/10:1f:1:22/11:4,5:11[2]:13:15/12:12:41/13:
/14:10:16:26:35:39/15:19:42,43/16:1:20/Lk1:
24:56/2:20:45/3:3/4:13:16:38:40:42/5:11:18,1
:25:28/6:4:12:19/7:1:6,7,8:11:24/8:2:5:33:39:4
:43,44/9:56/10:32/11:5,6:31/13:22[2]/16:1:23/
17:27:28/18:10:23/19:28/20:9:31/21:37,38/2
4:13:39/23:48:50,51,52:56/24:3:10:12:29:51/J
1:39:41:45/2:13/4:28,29:43,44:46,47/5:15/6:2
2-5[2]:15:16:24/7:1:10:14:53/9:7/10:40/11:20:2
46:54/12:13:18:22:36/18:29:33:38/19:4/20:6:
10/21:11:13/Act1:11:15/3:1:7,8/5:15:26,27/7
13/8:4:5:13:38:39/9:1:17:20/10:9,10:21:23:27
38/11:20:25/12:12:16/13:4:5[2]:14[2]:51/14:1:20
25/15:3:30/16:1:4:8:11:13:18/17:2:10:13:15:1
/18:1:19/19:8:10/20:9:10,11,12[2]:13:25/21:1:4
:8:26,27/22:26:27/23:14/24:27/28:8:14:23/
Rom1:32/4:10/1Co12:2/2Co1:8/2:13/7:11/8:
/Gal1:13:17:18:21/2:1:2/Eph:2/4:10/Php3:5/
:15/2Ti:10/Heb9:6:7:11/11:8:29:37,38

84

WERE

Gen2:1:5:25/3:7:11:19/4:8/6:4:5/7:8,9[2]:14,15/
9:18:24,25f/10:1[2]:2:6:7[2]:20:23:25[2]:31/12:19/1
6:13/14:5,6:8,9:21/17:24-27/18:11/19:4/22:3
20-23/24:11/25:3[2]:4:4f:18[2]:22:26/26:12:31:35
27:15:20/29:3:10/30:35,36[2]:39,40:42[2]/31:1:8:
10:16:36,37:39/32:21/33:4:8/34:5:24:25/35:5:
16:26/36:5:10,11,12:13,14:15,16:17:22:40-43/
37:2:7:11:17:25/38:3,4,5:25:26:28/39:20:22/40
9,10:16:17:20/41:3:6:10:21:22[2]:37:47:49:50:54
42:28/43:18[2]:21:24[2]:25:32/44:1:3:4:15:18/45:
16/46:8-14:15:16,17[2]:18:19-22[2]:23,24,25:28:34
47:13:15:17:22/48:7/49:7f[2]:24/50:15/Ex1:7:
15,16[2]/2:1:5:11:16:23/4:24:28/5:13:19:22/6:4:
8,9:17:20:23/7:11/8:14:15:24/9:7:25[2]:31:32[2]/
10:8:11/12:33:36:37:38:39/13:16:22/14:4:5:9:
10:11:12:26:31/15:22:27/16:3:32:35/17:11/18
5,6:26/22:8:21/24:4/28:30,31f[2]/30:34/31:18/
32:5:6/33:5/34:1:13f:30/35:21:22/36:3:4-7[2]:10
11,12:13:18:23:25,26:29:30:34[2]:38[2]/37:3:8[2]:17:
22:27:28/38:2:5:6:7:8:10:12:14,15:16:17[3]:19:20
25,26/39:6,7[3]:10[2]:11:12:14:19:20:24[2]:25,26:27:
28,29/Lev4:21:26/7:37:38/8:21/10:12/19:34/
26:40,41:46/Num1:16:17,18,19:54/2:3-31[2]:
32,33/3:2:3:39:49[2]/4:35:46,47,48[2]/5:4/6:12:20
7:7:8:9:18-23:30-35[2]:66-71:78-83:84,85,86/9:1
6,7/10:17:25/11:1:26:29:31:32/12:1:1f[2]:7,8:11
13:3-15:20:33/14:34,35:36,37,38:40/15:32/16:
:3:4:5:32:35:38:40/17:10/18:27:30:32/20:14f[2]:
29/21:1[2]:4:6:24/22:2,3[2]:7:18:22,23:34/23:2:17
24:3-9:15-19/25:2:6/26:5-11[4]:12-14:15-18:19-
19-22:23-25:26,27:38-41[2]:44-47[2]:48-50:58,59:
60:62[2]:64,65f[3]:64,65/27:1[2]/31:4,5:8:9,10,11:12
:21:27:36-40[3]:36-40f/32:12:34,35,36:39/33:3,4
38,39:40:50,51/36:11,12:13/Deu1:1:19,20,21/
:12:14,15[2]:21:22/3:5/4:4:43:44,45,46[2]:47/5:5:
15:22/6:21/7:7[2]/10:2:4:19:22/11:4:5/15:15/16
12/24:9:18:22/25:18/26:5[2]/27:23f/28:62:67[2]/
32:10:19[2]:29/Jos2:1:2:4[2]:5:6:7:22/3:13,14:17/4
1:8:9:10:20:23/5:1:6:10/6:1[2]:23[2]:24:25:26/7:4[2]
5:17/8:11,12,13f[2]:16:17:20,21[2]:22[2]:27/9:1:13:
16:17:18[2]:22:24/10:1:2:12/11:14:19:20/12:1:8-
8-24[2]/13:14:27,28:31:32/14:1:3,4:6:9/15:21-32
:33-36[2]/16:10/17:1:3:4:5,6:9:11/18:9:21-28[2]/1
:8:15,16:35-39/20:7:8:9/21:3:4:5:6:8:9-16[2]:19:
23,24:33:34,35/22:10:14:30/24:4:32/Ju1:4,5,6:

ERE Con't)
:28:31,32/2:7-9:12-14^2:15/3:4:7:8:13:14:
,18,19:24/4:11:12:24/5:6/6:2:9:11/7:1:3:
,13^2:25/8:1:2,3:4:10:15:18^2/9:24:25:40:49/10
/11:33/12:4/13:20:23/14:4:5:6:7:14:15/16:2:
:12:16,17:27^2:30/17:2/18:7^3:8:22:26:28:31/
:5:6:8:9:17^2:22/20:12:16^2:33:35-39:40,41^2:45
1:4:10,11,12^4:14^2:23/Ru1:1f:1:12/4:1f/1Sa1:
:11f/2:4^2:5^2:12:22:27/3:1/4:6:11:17:19:20:
,22/5:4:12/6:3:4,5:6:10^3:11:13:15:17:18/7:7^2:
:13:14:16/8:3^3:5/9:9,10,11^2:14:20:26,27/10:
:18,19:25:27/11:8:11:15/12:8:12:18/13:3,4:5:
8:11^2:15^2:19/14:2:14:17:22:31:33:41^2:50,51^2/
:4:5:6/16:9/17:11:19:25:52/18:6/19:4:5:22:
/20:19:20/22:2/23:1:5:26:27/24:3/25:15,16^3:
/26:5,6,7:13/28:4:5,6f^2:23/29:2:4/30:5:9,10:
:16:27-31/31:1:7/2Sa1:23^4/2:15:18:30^2:31/3:
31:33,34^3/4:1:2,3^2:4/5:2:6:14,15,16:17/6:5:13
:8/8:2^2:10:17:18:18f/9:10,11/10:5:15,16^2:19/
:7:16:24/12:1:18:21:26,27:29,30/13:2:21-24:
,30/15:4:30^2/16:14^2/17:17:19:20:22:28,29/
:2:7:8/19:3:17:40:43^2/20:3:25/21:2^2:8:
,13,14:15^2:20,21:22^2/22:9f:12:18:21:38/23:13
2:24-39:24-39f/1Ki1:1:8:39:41:49,50/2:22:32:
/3:6:28/4:1^2:7:8-19^2:20:22/6:4:6^3:7:8:15:20:
-28^2:29:32:34:35/7:3,4:9:10:11^2:24^2:26:27-30^4
1:32^2:33^2:34^2:36:37^2:39:41-46^2:47:48/8:8/9:
^{2}/10:20:21:28:29^2/11:1:21:25:29:32f/12:20f:
/13:20:28/15:14^2:19/16:21:31/19:11/20:12:
:21:33/22:6f^2:10^2:13:20:27f:38:48/2Ki2:11/3:
4:39/6:15:20/7:3:10^2:14:16/8:27/9:7:15:19:
/10:1:4:6:7^2:11/11:2,3:9^2/12:15:21/13:7:19:
,21:23/15:25/17:6^2:9:14:20:31:35,36^2:37/18:
/19:18^2:26:35/20:11f/21:1:3,4,5:11/22:7^2:
8,19/23:8:24/24:14:16/25:7^2:11:12:14,15:16:
9:20:21:26:28/1Ch1:1f:5-9^3:11,12:13-16:19:28-
8-31:32:33:40:42:51-54/2:1:5:6:9:16:28^2:29:30:
0:53:54/3:4:15:17,18:19,20:21,22/4:2:11,12:13^2
6:17:18:23:31:32,33:42/5:3:4:7,8:9:11:13:14:
7:18:20:23:24:25/6:2:3:4-15:16:17:18:19,20,21^2
8:29,30:48:49^2:50-53:54:55,56,57:60:61:64,65:
0:71/7:3:6:7^3:8:9^2:10:11:12:13:14:17:19:20,21:
1:32:33:34:35:36,37:38:39:40^2/8:1:3,4,5:6,7^2:
2:13:15,16:19,20,21:22-25:26,27:28:37:40^3/9:2
:6:7,8:9:10,11:17,18:19:22^3:23:24:25:26^2:28:29
2:33,34^4/10:1:7/11:2:15f:15:26-47/12:2^2:3-7:
-13^2:14:19:21:23:24-37^{11}:40/14:8:9/15:4-10:13
7:18:19:21:21f:23:24:26:27/16:5:21:41:42/17:
7/18:6:16:17/19:7:9:10:15/20:8^2/21:3:29/23:3
7:8,9:10,11^2:13:14,15:16:18:19:20:21^2:22:23:24^3
31^2:32/24:1^3:4:5^2:6:20:28:30^2:31/25:1:2:3:4,5:
,7^2:8/26:1:2,3:4,5:6,7^3:8^2:9:11:12^2:13:14,15:17:
8:19:20,21,22:26:28:29:30^2:31,32^2/27:1:2,3:4:
,6:16-22:31^2/28:18/29:8:15/2Ch1:14^2:15:17/2
7:17/3:6:7:9^2:15/4:3:4:5:17,18:22^2/5:1:9:10:
1,12^3:13,14/7:6^2:7/8:1:6:10:13/9:20^2:27:28/11
12:19:20/12:15/14:8:14^2/15:6:15:17/17:14,15:
9/18:9^2:12:19,20:31/19:9/20:24/21:2:6:13/22:
/23:8^2:9/24:10:14:22:26/25:12^2/26:11:20/28:
:12:15:17,18:23/29:32,33^2:34^3:36/30:2,3:4:7:8:
0:17,18,19^2:22:25/31:1:12,13^2:14,15:16^2:17,18^3
32:19/33:10:15/34:4:9:12^3/35:1:10^2:15^2:16:
4,25/36:10:20/Ez1:11/2:2:43-54:59:62,63:68/
:3:5:7:8^3:9:12/4:1:8,9/5:1:4:14/6:1:5^2:14:17^2:
8/8:16:20^2:21:26,27^2:33^2:36/9:2^2:7^2:9/10^2:10:
6-19:23:25/Neh1:2/2:10:11,12/3:4:5^2:7^2:8:18:
9/4:1:7:10:11:20,21:23/5:1:18^2/6:2:16/7:3:4:7^2
43,44,45:46-56:62:63:64,65^2/8:1^2:9/9:3:4^2:5:10
15^2:16:24:25:26:29:30:33/10:1^2:9-13:28:37:
39,40/11:1^2:2^2:4,5,6:10-14^3:15,16,17^2:18:19:21:
25-30:36/12:8:12-21:22:23:24:25:26^2:35,36:
40,41:43:44^2/13:1:3:5:10:16/Est1:6:7:10:13-15^3
/2:7:12,13,14:21:23f/3:12:13/6:14/7:4/8:1f:
9,10:16:17/9:1^2:22:24,25:29-31/Job1:12,13:
14,15:18:21/2:11/6:2/7:4/8:6:9/9:15:16:20:30:
32,33/10:12/15:7,8^2/16:4^2/19:28/22:3:21/29:5:
7:13:20^2:21:24/30:17/31:35/32:4/33:6/34:14/
38:4:5:21/42:13,14f:13,14:15/Ps7:3:4/14:7/18:
8f:15:37:38/22:5/31:13/33:6/34:5/35:13:14:15
/39:12/44:20/50:12/55:21^3/68:9,10:18/73:2:20
/77:6/78:8:37:39:48:53:63^2:64/80:8:10^2/81:5/
83:8f/87:6/90:2/95:10^2/102:20:21,22/105:12^2:
13^2:24:30:33:37:38/106:16:36:41,42:43/107:4:
17:18:20/114:5/136:18/139:15/Pro3:20/7:14f/
8:24:25/24:30,31/25:1:6,7/Ecc2:7,8^2/4:1:2/7:
10/8:9,10:14^2/Sol1:6/6:9:11^2/8:1/Is1:4:9/5:2/
6:2/10:10/13:19/14:6:12/21:6,7f/23:2,3/28:12/
36:21/37:27^2/42:22/44:24/45/46:3/47:2f/48:3:
21/49^2/51:1^2/52:4/53:5/55:13/57:11/59:10/63
:19/66:19f^2/Jer1:3:5^2/2:2:3/4:23:26^2/5:7/6:15/
7:26/9:1/11:19/13:11:15/16:12/17:1/20:10/21:
1f/22:16:21:24,25/23:1:13:14:22/24:2^2/29:
16,17/30:14^2:21f/31:15f:33f/34:9/35:11/36:12:
16/37:2:15,16/38:16/39:14/40:1:7:8:11/41:2:3:
5:7:18/42:2:18:20/43:6/44:1:17:19:21:22/46:2:
16/48:27/50:11/52:3^2:10:11:15:21:23^2/Lam1:
19/2:4:6/3:52/4:7:7f/Eze1:1:7^2:9:13:16:18:22/8
:10:11:16/9:7:8/10:3:15,16:20^2:22/11:15/12:12f
:13f:18/13:16/14:14:16:18:20/16:3f:4:5^2:6,7^2:8:
13^3:22:49:59,60/19:2:5:7:12/20:5,6:16:23,24:25:
29f/21:30/23:2,3:6:14,15/27:10f:17f/28:12:13^3:
15^2/29:14:18^2/31:15f/32:27:29/34:5:8:12:13/
35:4,5/36:17:20^2:34/37:1/40:7-12:16^3:17:21^2:
22^2:24:26:28f:29,30f^2:29,30^2:33^2:34^2:35:36:37:
39^2:40:41^2:42^3:43:44/41:1:6:12:15,16^2:17,18:21:
22:25:26/42:3^2:5:6^2:7,8:11/46:24/47:5:7/Dan1:
6:18,19/2:13:32:35/3:3:27:28/4:12^2:26:33/5:5:9
:11:20/6:2/7:4:8:9:10:12^2/8:8f:12f/9:24f/10:5,6:
7/11:32f/Hos4:12f/7:1:7f/9:10/10:9:14/13:6/
Amo1:2:5f/5:18:25,26,27/6:2/Ob1:5:11/Jon:
9,10/3:3f/4:2/Mic1:1:13/3:7/Nah:9:10^3/Hab2:
18/3:8,9f^2:8,9^2/Zep2:5f/3:19/Hag1:1f:6/2:14:
16,17^2/Zec1:1:4:8/6:7/7:5:7/8:10/10:11f/11:11
/Mal2:15/Mt:11:13:20/3:1:16/4:18:24^3/5:1:12
/7:28/8:16^2:28/9:4:10^2:11:17f:19:36^2/11:1:8:15
/12:1:3:10:15:46,47^2/13:11^2:12,13f^2/14:20^2:21:
23,24^2:35:36/15:31^3:37,38^2/16:8/17:3:9:22,23^2
/19:13/20:9:10:24:30:32,33/21:1:15:19^2:20:36:
45:46/22:3:16f:18:32f:33/23:2/24:17f:20f:24/25
:2,3,4^2:5,6:7,8:10^2:24,25:40:45/26:3:8,9:10:26:
43:48:57:60,61:69/27:32:38:54:55:56:61:64/28:
9:11:15/Mk1:6^2:16:22/2:15:17:23^2:25,26^2/3:6f:
10:30/4:33:33f:40:41/5:15:16:20/6:2,3^2:14^2:31:
34:38:39,40:43,44^2:47:48:52f:56/7:37/8:7:8,9^4:
15:17:27/9:6:8:32:33^3:34:42^2/10:1:2:13:26:32^3:
41/11:4,5^2:13:18/12:5:12^2:20,21,22^3:27:41/14:1
:4,5:11:12:18:22:35:40:51,52:55^2:65:66,67/15:27
:31:40:41:47/16:3:5:12:14/Lk1:4:6:7:21/2:6:8:9
/3:1/4:22^2:25,26:32:40:41/5:6:7:9:17:22:29:33/
6:1^2:3:7:11:13:17,18:19:23/7:12:20,21,22:29^2/8:
2:3:4:7:20:22:23:25:30f:56/9:7:8:11:14:17:31^2:
33:43:45:53^2:57/10:2:11:33f/11:53,54/12:1:17:
49/13:1:2:4/14:1:7:25/15:27/16:16/17:2,3:6:14:
16f:26/19:7:15:30:33:47/20:19^2:26:33:39/22:2:5
:35/23:32,33^2:56/24:4:5:10:13:14:22,23:28:31:
33,34:35:36:37:53/Jn1:24,25:39/2:2:6^2:23/3:19
/4:27:31/5:18/6:2-5:13:15:18,19^2:21^2:22,23:61/
7:1:15:21,22,23:32:35/8:6:16:39:41:42:48/9:33:
34f:40:41/10:8:19/11:8:17:31:36:45/12:17/17:6^2
/18:18:34f:36/19:11:25/20:19:26^2/21:2:6:9:11:
12:18^2:25/Act1:3:10^2:12:13:14^2:15:17/2:2:5:6:8:
13:41:47/3:3:7,8:10/4:1:1f:2:7:13^2:23:31^2:32/5:
3:12:14:15:23^2:24:25:26,27:36/6:1^3:6:7:9:10/7:9
:13:16:29:42:54/8:2f^2:7^3:12/9:21:24:26:39/10:
9,10:12:17:27:38:45/11:1:6:18:24:26/12:11:12:
20:24/13:1:2:19,20:45:48:48f:52/14:4:8:17/15:1
:3:4:10:22:34,35:36/16:16:19:23:25^2:33:34:36:38
/17:4:5:8,9:11^2/18:2,3:8^2:14:18f:22f:25,26/19:5:
7:12^2:13:14:32^2/20:4^3:5:34/21:16:19:26,27:30:
31/23:6^3:10:27/24:18/26:10:26/27:1^2:17^2:27:30
/28:1^2:9:10:15/Rom1:30:31f:31:32/2:28/3:3/4:
1:17/5:6:7:8:10^2:13:20/6:2,3:4:6:20/7:4:5:8/9:5:
10-13:32/11:2,3:17^2:18:19:20:24^2:30/15:3:4:27/
16:7/1Co1:13/3:1/4:8/5:3,4/6:11:12f:13/9:5:17
/10:11/12:17^2/13:3:12/14:5^2/15:58/16:15:18/
2Co1:8:9^2/3:14/5:4:20/6:2:13/7:5:7^2:13/8:6:10
/9:2:5/10:14:15/12:7/Gal1:10:17:23/2:6:7,8,9/
3:16^2:19^2:23:24/4:3:5:8:14/5:7/Eph1:11:12:13/
2:1:2:3:5:11^4:12^3:13:17^2/4:30f/Php2:12:30/Col
1:16:21^3/2:7:13^2:15:17^2:20/3:23/1Th1:5/2:2:3^2:
5:7/3:2,3:4/2Th2:15/3:10/1Ti1:9/5:1/2Ti3:15^2
/Tit:3^3:5/Phm1:17/Heb3:10:16^2/4:8/7:3f:5^2:28
/8:4/9:1^2:4^2:5:8:9:21:23/10:1:6:28:29:33:34^2/11
:2:3^2:13^2:14:16:23:29^2:33:34^2:35:36^2:37,38^3:40/
13:3:11/Jas1:18/1Pe:12/2:10/3:20/4:6^2:11/
2Pe2:1:13:21/1Jn:19/Jud1:6:7/Rev:12/3:15/4:
4:5^2:8:11/5:6:9^2/6:8:11^2/7:4-8:10:11/8:2:7^2:8,9
/9:2:3:4:5:8:15:16f:16:17,18:19/11:15:18/12:17
/13:1:8:8f/14:1:20/15:1:2:3,4:6/16:19/18:23/
19:12^2:20:21/20:3:4:12^2:14/21:12^2:13:14:21/22:
2
2749

WHAT
Gen1:25/2:19,20/3:22/4:7:10/9:24,25^2/11:6/
12:18/13:9:11/14:23:24/15:1:2,3/17:5:19/19:9:
12/20:8:9,10^2:16/23:14,15/24:49^2:50:57/25:32
/27:6,7:11,12:13:37:41:42:43:45/29:25^2/30:13:
30:31,32/31:15:24:26:36,37^2/32:27:29/33:8:9:
10/34:5:12:13:15/37:10:11:19,20/38:17:18:22/
39:6:14,15/40:7:8^2:12/41:8^2:12:15:16:25:28:32:
40:51/42:14:21:28:33:34/43:12/44:5^2:7^2:15:16:
24:34/47:3/48:19/49:1/50:20/Ex2:4:5:13/3:14f^2
:16/4:1:2:12:15^2:16:25,26:28^2:30/6:1:8,9^2/9:34/
10:2^2:11:26/12:10:26^2/13:8:14/14:5:12/15:14:
26/16:15:23:31/17:4/18:8:18/19:4:7:25/20:19/
22:10/23:8:9/25:18f/28:30,31f/30:29f/32:9:21:
22/33:5:17:19f/35:4:10-19/Lev5:1:4:15/6:4,5/7
:20:21/8:5:35/10:1:3:10^4/11:47^2/20:4:11:20:21/
24:12/25:11:14,15,16:20:37/26:10:16:32/Num4
:17,18,19^2/5:7/11:27/12:10/13:18^2:19:23/14:
13:28:31:34,35:39/15:11,12/16:3:4:11,12^2/21:
17,18/22:2,3:5,6:7:19:20:28:35:38^2/23:3,4:7-10:
11:12:16:17:18-24^3/24:3-9:13:14:15-19/25:
12,13^2/32:1:10,11:20/36:6/Deu1:12:28/3:21:
23,24,25^2/4:3:6:7:8:9:20:30:34/5:5:26,27:28/6:
18:20/7:18/9/10:12,13/11:4/12:28/15:10/17:
13/18:2:16:18/21:21/24:9/25:17/31:21:29/32:1
:19:20:29/33:14:29/Jos1:3/2:10:17,18/3:9/4:6:
21/7:7:8:9:19/9:1:3,4,5:10/11:1/14:6:7/15:
18,19^2/19:9/20:4/22:11:24,25:32/24:7/Ju1:14/
6:27:31/7:11/8:2,3:18/9:29:30:46/11:16/14:7:
18^2/15:11^2/16:5:15/18:3:8^2:14:18:23:24^2/20:3/
21:15:16/Ru2:18/3:3:4:11:15-18^2/1Sa2:3:22:
23,24,25:30:34/3:4,5^2:6:8:15:16,17:18^2/4:13:14^2
:18/5:7/6:2^2:4,5/8:9:10:21/9:8:19/10:11:15:25/
11:7:9/13:7:11/14:8:19:33:34:38:39:41:43/15:9:
11:14:16^2:19:20:24/16:4/17:26:28^3:29:31:38,39:
55/18:25/19:2:7:21:24/20:1:4:32:39/21:3:12/
22:3:9,10:11,12:21/23:9/24:11:12/25:19:24:25:
37,38/26:11:17,18^2/28:2:5,6:7,8:13:14:15:22/29
:3:8/30:3/31:11/2Sa1:4/2:6/3:24,25^2/5:23/6:8
/7:3:20^2:23/10:5:17/11:10:27/12:11:18:19/13:5
:12:21-24^2/14:2,3:19:33/15:19,20:21:25,26:28:
35,36/16:2:20/17:5:6^2:10:11:15^2/18:11:21:29^2:
29f:32/19:27/20:19/21:2:3:4:11/24:10:13:16:17
:19/1Ki1:16:44,45/2:6:14:16:20:44/3:9^2:12:13/
6:11,12/8:15:20:32/9:13/11:6:22:33:38:41/12:6
:9:16,17:23,24/13:11^2:26/14:5/16:12/17:4:18/
18:9/19:1:9/20:7/21:5^2:29/22:5:13:14:16:28/
2Ki1:7/2:9:15/3:6,7,8:10:11/4:2:7:13:14:26:27:
43/5:4/6:15:26-30/7:10:12:17/8:14/9:11^2:12:15
:18:19:36/10:4/12:2:18/18:12:23:34:35^2:37/19:
11:13^2/20:14:15:19/22:11:12,13/23:17^2/25:26/
1Ch7:23/10:11/13/14:14/17:16:17:18:21:24/19
:5:13/21:6:12:17:24/22:11/26:4,5/29:14/2Ch6:
10:27:33/7:11/9:7/10:6:8,9:10:16/16:5:8:9/18:
6,7:12^2:13:15:18:22:27:29/19:2:7/20:10:12/23/
24:22/25:2:9/28:10:14/29:36/31:20/32:14:31/
34:10,11:15,16:19:31/Ez4:15/6:2/9:10:15/10:
11:12/Neh1:6,7:8/2:4:19/4:1/5:2,3,4:7:9/6:5,6^2
:19/7:5/9:8:31:33/12:47/13:10:21/Est1:13-15^2:
17:18/2:11/4:1:5:8/5:3^2:6:7,8:9/6:3:6:13/7:2^2:5
/8:17/9:12^2:28/Job2:10/3:22:25/6:24/7:17/9:
12:21/11:5:8/12:13:14/13:1:4:6:9:14:17:23/15:
3:4,5:9^2:12:14/16:2:3/18:21/19:27/20:29/21:15
:27:30-32/22:13:17/23:4,5:10/24:6/26:2:3/27:8
/28:28/29:11:25/31:7,8:14:23:37/32:6/33:1:13:
23,24/34:4^2:25:32/35:6:14,15/36:2:9:23/38:6,7
/42:7/Ps1:4/2:1/3:8/5/10:14^2/11:3/14:7/16:6:
7/17:1/18:24:30/19:12/23:2,3/26:11/27/28:5^2
/30:9/31:1:17/32:1^3:3/34:1:5/37:21:37/38:18/
41:7/45^2:15/48:2:6/50:14,15/52:7:9/55:14^2/56:
3,4:5:12/59:4/62:3,4/64:9/65:4/66:5:6:16/68:
19:35/69:4:19/70:4/73:11:18:21/74:3/78:1:29/
80:15/83:2/87:3/88:10/89:6:17:34/92:5/94:10/
100:3/104:24/105:44/107:30:43/111:9/112:7/
114:5/116:12/118:6/119:27:33,34:56:102,103:
121/120:3/126:2:3^2/130:3,4/137:7/139:4/141/
142:4/144:3:8/145:4/Pro1:7,8,9/4:20/5:1:7:20/
6:35/8:1:31/10:5:11:32/14:15:35/18:8:11:13:14
/19:27/20:1:6:11/22:20,21/23:24,25/25:8,9,10/
27:1:19/29:18/30:4/Ecc1:3-7:8-11^3:12-15^2/2:1:
12f:15:20-23/3:9:15:15f:19:22^2/5:11/6:10:12/8:
5:6,7/9:15:16/10:14:20/12:10:11/Sol1:6:9:16/5
:9/8:8/Is1:1:2:3:4:10/3:9:10:12/5:4:19:20^2/6:9/
7:9/10:3:30/14:4:32/17:8/19:3^2:11:12^2/20:5,6/
21:2:3:6,7:11^2/22:1^2:5^2:9,10,11/23:7/25:9/26/
28:26/29:15^2/30:1:12/33:13/34:8/36:5:19^2/37:
11:13/38:15:22/39:3/40:6:14:18/41:21:22^2:23/
42:20:22/43:13:18/44:7:9:20:25^2:26/45:11^2:19^2:
20:21/46:5:9:10/47:13/48:3^2:5:8:16/50:4/51:12
:18:22/52:5:14,15/53:11/55:8/57:18/58:4:5^2:6:
13/59:8^2:12:13/65:12/66:1:4:6^2:18^2/Jer1:11:13
/2:4,5:18:19:32/3:6/4:10/5:4:14/6:9:27^2/7:12:
17:23/8:6^2:10:17/9:7:15/10:14/11:15/12:5/14:
12:22/15:10:15:16/16:10^2/17:15/18:11:12:19/
20:1/21:12/22:3/23:18:20:23:33^2:35^2:36:37^2/24
:3/25:19,20/26:9^2:10:11:19:21/29:3/30:24/32:
35/33:3:24/34:15/36:24,25/37:2:7:18^3/38:1:19:
25:27/40:15/41:4:6:11:18/42:2:3:4:15:20:21/44
:2,3/45:4/46:7/48:19/49:1:20/50:44/51:61,62/
Lam1:21/2:11:13/3:17:51/5:1/Eze1:26/2:8^2/3:
1:11/4:3/5:5,6,7:13:15/8:2:3:6^2:12/10:7,8:21/

(WHAT Con't)
12:3/12:9:11^2:12:22:24:25/13:5/15:2:5,6/16:30:
37:44/17:12,13/18:5:12:19^2:21/19:2/20:29:32/
21:13/23:10:11:44:45/24:19^2:26/25:3:17/26:14f
:16/27:17/29:18f:20f/30:21f/32:19/33:7:8:14:
15:30:30f:31:32/34:9,10:19/35:10:11/37:14:
18,19,20/38:23/40:2/41:21/43:11/44:23^4:23f/
47:6/Dan2:1^2:4:5^2:6^2:7^2:10:15:16:19:23:24:26^2:
28:45/3:15:16:29/4:9:18:19:27:35/5:7:8:10:12:
15:17:26/7:1:28/8:5:19^2/9:12:23/10:1:11:14:
20,21/11:2/12:8^2:9:10/Hos1:11/4:12/5:2/6:4/
9:5:9:14/Joe2:2/Amo1:2/3:10/5:18/6:2:12/7:1:
2:5:8:10/8:2/9:12/Ob1:10/Jon:6:8^4:11/3:6/4:2
/Mic1:5/2:4/4:2/5:13/6:1:3:5:6:8:14/7:16:17/
Nah1:9/Hab:5/2:1:11:18^4:19/3:3/Zep2:3/3:6/
Hag1:7/Zec:5,6^2:9:14:19:21/4:2:4^2/5:2:6/6:1:4
/8:14,15/10:2/11:11/13:6/14:1/Mal1:5:13/2:
15/3:8:13^2:14,15/Mt2:5/4:4/5:13:46/6:3:7,8:25
:26/7:7:12:18/8:13:29:33/9:4:36^2/10:19:27^2:29/
11:7:14:16/12:3:15:27:34:39,40/13:17^2/14:12:
17/15:10:11:11f:15:20:31/16:8:21:26^2/17:4f:9:
25/18:12:31/19:5,6:8:16:20:27/20:18:21:22:24:
32,33/21:3:15:23f:25:28:40:42:43/22:1:18:42/
23:3^2/24:15:39:42/25:24,25:29^2/26:8,9:10:13:
50:54:58:62:65,66^2:70:75/27:3:13:22:23/28:11:
15/Mk1:22:27^2:28/2:7:17:21:28/3:21/4:10:13:
24^2:25:26:30/5:7,8:9:16:19:33^2:43/6:29:30:37/7
:11:15,16^2:15,16f:17:18:22:23/8:16:17:19:27:35
/9:6:9:10:12,13:19:32:33/10:3:9:14:17:36:38:41:
51/11:3:4,5:6:18:21:30/12:9^2:14:23/13:1:11^2/
14:8:29:40:60:63,64^2:68/15:3,4:12:14/16:20/Lk
1:29:43:45:61:62f:65:66/2:17^2:33:48:50/3:10:14 ^{2}
/4:36:37:40/5:8:14:22/6:3:20:21^2:22:26:30:34:
38:39/7:4:17:31^2:34:39^2/8:9:18:28:30:35:39:50:
56/9:10:25:33:36:44:45:54:55f/10:13:15:23:24:
25:26/11:13:18:19:45:48:49/12:3:6:11:15:25:29:
33:57/13:4:18/14:15:21:24:31:34/15:26/16:3/
17:7,8,9:16:32/18:18:19:20:27:36:41/19:15^2:21:
31:33/20:2:13:15:17:21^2/21:4/22:16:49:60:61:
71/23:22:31:31f:34:47/24:4:6,7:9:12:17:19:27^2/
Jn1:22:24,25:38:48/2:4f:18:20:22/3:4:5:9:10,11:
12:21:32^2/4:10:27:36:42/5:19:47/6:6:8,9:14:28:
42^2:52:60:62:65/7:31:36:49/8:5:22:26:28:33:38:
43/9:10:21:26:35:41/10:6/11:47:56/12:27:34:
38:49/13:11:12:28/14:12,13:28:31/15:16:20:25
/16:13:15:17,18^2:19:20:23:30f/18:19:20:21:29^2:
35:38/19:15:22:25:35f/21:19:21^2:21f:22:23^2/
Act2:3:6:9f:12:16:37/3:12:17:24/4:7:13:16:23:
27:32/5:7:9:11:24:35:38/7:31:40:48,49/8:6:30/
9:15:27/10:4:8:17^2:21:22:29:33/11:22/12:11^2:
17^2:18/13:8:12:32,33/14:11:14:15/15:4:15:18:
26/16:30/18:25,26^2/19:2^2:3^2:8:17:26:36:40/20:
10,11,12:22/21:33/22:9:10^2:15:26:30/23:3:14:
19:28/24:6:20/25:18:26^2/26:22/27:4f/28:22/
Rom1:21^2:25/2:1:12-15^2:18/3:4:6:8:12:17:18:20
:21,22:27^2/4:1:8:9:17/5:1:5:10:11:13:14:15/6:21
/7:9:13:15^3:16:20:21^2:23,24,25/8:12:18:26:27:
31/9:4:10-13^3:19:25:30/10:2:8:15:18/11:2,3:8^2:
14:26:33/12:1:9:20/13:9/14:1:15:16:17:22^2:23/
15:1:9/16:17:19/1Co1:6:9:20:22^2:31/2:9^2:11^2:
14/3:13^2/4:2:3^3:5:6:7^2:17/5:3,4:6:11/6/7:10:25^2
/8:1:4:10/9:7^2:8^2:18:21:27^2/10:1:8:13:15:19:20:
22:24:25:29:33^3/11:13:22^2:23:29/12:10:16:19:
27:30/13:2^2:7/14:5:6^4:9:13:14:15:16:22:26^2:27:
37/15:1:3:12:21^2:29:32^2:35:36/16:2/2Co1:3,4:
19/2:4:11:13:14/3:4/4:2:5:13:18/5:5:16^2:18/6:6
:14:15:16/7:7:11/8:1:3:10:12^2:15/10:12:17/11:1
:6:8,9:33/12:6:20/13:7:11/Gal1:1f:12:13:15:20^2:
22:23/2:2:4:6:11:12:14^2:17/3:1:17/4:2:10:17:20:
21:27/5:16/6:9:15/Eph1:4:8:11:13/2:6:10:13:18
:20/3:6:13/4:14:29^2/5:9:10/Php1:28/2:4:13:23
/3:3:4:10:13:14:19/4:8:10:17:19/Col1:9:11:20:
28/2:2:8:16/3:10:11:16:18/4:11/1Th1:5^2/2:13:
14:19/4:13/5:18/2Th1:10/2:1:3:6/3:14:16/1Ti1
:5:7:13:19^2/3:15/4:16/5:7/6:11/2Ti2:15:25/3:
10^2:16^3/4:3:4/Tit2:15/3:6/Phm1:21/Heb2:3:6:
18/4:8:12/5:8/6:9:12:16/8:1:10/9/10:23:35/11:
1^2:11:19:33/12:7/13:3:5:16:17:22/Jas1:5:24:25
/2:12^3:16:20:21:22:24^2:25/3:5/4:1:2^3:3:5:12:14:
15:17/5:3/1Pe1:10:11/2:15/3:6:16^2:21/4:17:18:
19/5:2:12/2Pe1:5:19/2:22/3:11:15,16/1Jn1:3/
2:3:4:5:24:27/3:2:7:16:23:24/4:10:18^2/5:3:10:11
:17f/2Jn1:10/3Jn:10^2:11^2/Jud:17/Rev:3:9:19^2/
2:7:10:11:17:22:24,25:29/3:2^2:3:6:7^2:13:22/4:1/
5:4/6:10/8:1:8,9/9:7/10:4/15:2/17:1:7/19:6/21
:5/22:6,7:10:18

2218

WHAT'S
Gen17:5/21:17/28:15/Num13:28/16:14/Deu24
:21/1Sa1:8/4:6^2/11:5/16:18/18:8/28:19/2Sa11
:10/13:4/14:5,6/1Ki1:41/2Ki6:26-30/8:12/2Ch
21:11/29:19/Est4:14/Job9:29/Ps114:5/Pro28:
24/30:20/Ecc6:6/Is22:2:13/36:10/44:17/56:1/
Jer15:3/Eze33:19/Hos10:3/Joe1:4/Hab2:5/
Mk9:16/11:27,28/Lk12:25:26/16:2/Act27:24/
Rom3:1/1Co15:32/Gal3:8,9/Php:5/Jas2:14/
1Pe2:5

49

WHEN
Gen1:1/2:3:7/3:17/4:26/5:3,4,5:3,4,5f:6,7,8:
9,10,11:12,13,14:15,16,17:18,19,20:21-24^2:
25,26,27:28-31/6:4:5/7:1:6:10,11,12/9:14:24,25
/11:5:6:10,11:12,13:14,15:16,17:18,19:20,21:
22,23:32f/12:11,12,13:14:15/14:14/15:2,3:11/
16:4/17:1/18:10f:11:33/19:1:16/20:1:13/21:9:
15:28,29/22:9/23:1/24:14:22:29,30:31:36:42:49
/25:20:26:29:32/26:7:18:23/27:1:5/28:11/29:
23/30:9:30:38^2/31:8:49/32:1:10:17:25/34:2:25/
35:1:7/36:31-39/37:18:23:28:29^2/38:6:13/39:1:
13:14,15^2:16:19/40:14:15:16/41:2:10:18:36/42:
1:27/43:2:3,4,5:16:18:26/44:1:4^2:14:25:31/45:
27^2/46:33:34/47:15:24:30/48:2:7:17/49:15:33/
50:4:10:16,17:22:25/Ex2:1:3:6:10:11:14:15:18/3
:2:12:21/4:6:7:14:21:31/5:20/7:5:9/8:15/9:7:34
/10:13/12^2:17:23:25^2:39/13:4,5:8:11:14:19/14:
5:26:31/16:14:15:18:20:21:23:32/18:3:14/19:9/
20:5/23:2,3:15:16/25/28:11:29:30,31^2:37,38/30
:7:8:11,12:20^2/32:1:5:17:19:20:25:34/33:4:22/
34:24:33/35:10-19/39:3:25,26:41/Lev1:2,3/3:1
/4:14/5:4/7:8/8:11/9:6:23:24/10:3:8,9:15:20/
12:2:5:6/13:9,10:53/14:33,34:48/15:13/16:17:
20:23/18:16f/19:5:9:23/21:12/22:7:26,27:29,30
/23:1:9,10,11:22:37/25:1:10:19:51:52/26:4,5:10
:17:34,35:36:40,41/27:1:21/Num2:3-31/3:1:4/4
:5:15:17,18,19:30,31/5:5,6:9,10:24/6:1/7:89/8:
2/9:17:20,21/10:3:5,6,7f:5,6,7:9^2:34:36/11:2:23:
25:26/12:10/14:13:19:39/15:1:17,18:23,24/16:
4:22:31/17:8:9/18:16/19:14/20:16:28:29/21:1/
22:2,3^2:25:36:37/23:6/24:23,24/25:7/26:61:62:
64,65/27:14/28:3:16/30:1:10/32:1:9:22:29/33:
38,39:50,51/34:1/35:9,10:19/Deu1:1:17/2:23:
31/3:20/4:5:6:14:25:29:30:32:44,45,46/5:23/6:
7:10,11,12^3:13:16:20:25/7:1:2:13/8:10:12,13^2/9
:4:23:25/10:22/11:6:19^2:29/12:1:10:20-23:29/
14:1:26/15:7:18/16:1/17:8:14:18/18:9/19:1^2:14
:16/20:1:9:13:19/21:1:10:13/22:4:13,14:17,18/
23:4:9,10:20:21/24:19:20/25:19/26:1/27:2,3,4:
12/28:2-6^2:8:15-19^2/29:7:19:25/30:1/31:10,11:
14:20^2:24/32:8:12:36:44,45/34:7/Jos2:10:12,13
/3:2,3,4:13,14/4:1:6:7:11:21/5:1:4,5:6/6:5:20:26^2
/7:9:10,11/8:5:19:20,21^2:24/9:1:3,4,5:6:12:22/
10:1:14:17/11:1/13:2-7/14:6:11/17:13:14/20:4
/22:11:15:20:30/23:1^2/24:6:14:17:32/Ju1:14f:
16:28:35/2:6:15^2:19:21/3:9:10:11:15:24:25^2:27/
4:10:12:22/5:4:8/6:3,4:13:20:22:38/7:15:17:
19,20/8:1:7:9:15/9:7:30:33:36:43:47,48:55/10:2
:5:12/11:1:7^2:13:16:30,31:34:35/13:17:24/14:1:
2:8:12/16:2:9f:15/18:18:22:26/19:3:17:27:29/
20:31:33:35-39/21:5:21:22^2/Ru1:1:18:21/2:8,9:
15:17/3:15-18/4:13/1Sa1:9:19,20/2:13,14:19:
27/4:5:6:8:18:19/5:3:7:9:10/6:2:13/7:7^2/9:17:
25:26,27/10:2:3:8:10:11:13:21:26/11:4:5:9/12:8
:12/13:1f:6:8:11:15/14:9:11:17:22:27/15:2:6:11:
13:17:21/16:4:6/17:11:28:31:34:50,51/18:6:
15,16:19:20:24:28/19:11:14:16:19:20:21/20:18:
24,25:27:33:37/21:1:5/22:4:7:9,10:11,12:21:22/
23:24,25/24:4:7,8:18:19:21/25:4:23:29:30,31^2:
36:37,38:39:40/26:15:23/28:5,6:12:18:21/30:1:
9,10:21:24:26/31:5:7:8:11/2Sa1:7:11/2:4:20:23:
30/3:7:21:23:27:28/4:1:4:10/5:2:8:17:23:24/6:6
:12:19/7:1:8:10,11:12:26/8:5:9/10:5:7,8:9:13:14
:15,16:17:19/11:1:4:5:7:10:18:26:27/12:18:19:
23:24/13:5:6:9:21-24^2/14:1:4/15:2:5:31/16:1:16
/17:6:9:12:20:23:27/18:24:29/19:15:19/20:3:12
:15/21:11:15:20,21/22:45/23:4:9:11,12:13/24:3
:17:20/1Ki1:32:35:51/2:7:8:28:29:39:40:41/3:
17,18:19:21^2/5:1/7:51/8:16:30:33,34:35,36^2:38:
41,42:44:53/9:1:5/10:1:5:11/11:15:21:24:27,28
/12:12:16,17:18:20:21:27/13:13:26:31/14:6:12:
20:21:31/15:8:21:24:29/16:15,16:18:23:28:29:
34^2/17:14/18:3,4:10:12:13:17:39/19:1:13:15/20
:33/21:15:27/22:15:24:25:32,33^2:38:42:50/2Ki1
:4,5/2:9:10:15:18/3:20:21:24:26/4:1:7:11,12^2:
15,16:18:27:32:36/5:7:8:13:18^2:21:24:25:26/6:4:
8:15:21:26-30^2:32^2/7:8:17/8:5:8,9:14:17:26/9:4:
25:30:31:35:36/10:7:8:17:35/11:1:13,14:21/13:
14/14:16:29/15:7:22:32,33:38/16:3:20/17:11:
25/18:31,32/19:1:3:7:10/20:17:21/21:7:9:18/
22:3,4:9,10:11:18,19/23:15:29:31,32:36,37/24:6
:18,19/25:23/1Ch1:44:45:46:47:48:49:50/6:4-
4-15:32/10:3:7:8:11/11:2:17:22/12:17:21/13:5/
14:8:15/15:2/16:19:20:29/17:10:11:21:27/18:5:
9/19:1:2,3:5:6:8:10:15:17,18/20:1:2/21:16:28
22:12/27:23/2Ch1:4/2:3/5:10:11,12/6:20,21
26:32/7:6/9:1:3:4/10:12:16:18^2/12:1:7:12:16,
13:4/15:8:9/18:14:22:23:24:31/20:7:10:23:24
29:31/21:1:3,4:5:20/22:2:10/23:12/24:1:14:2
25:27/25:1:3:14:16/26:20:23/27:8:9/28:1:20:
/29:1:19/31:7,8/32:2:14:21:31:33/33:1:2:9:
20,21^2/34:1:3:14:19:22:27/35:10/36:2:5:9:11:
/Ez3:10/4:1:6:23/7:17/9:3/Neh1:1:4/2:1:5,6
10:19/4:1:7:19/5:6/6:1:16/8:9/9:8:15^2:28:32/
10:34/12:26^2:37/13:3:7/Est1:5:10:12:17:20/2
:15^2:19f/4:1:4:13/5:2:9:13:14/6:13/9:11:19:22
24,25^2/Job1:4:5:9:12,13:14,15:19:21/2:9:11/3
2,3:22/4:5/5:17/6:5,6,7^4:15-18:19-21/7:4:13,
:21/8:18/9:12:23/11:3/12:11:14/13:7/14:10/
:8/19:18/21:6:17:21:34/23:10:15/24:14,15:
22,23/27:8:9/29:2:3:4:5:6:7:24/30:14/31/32:
16/33:15:26/34:29,30/35:12/36:13/37:16,17:
21/38:4:8,9:22,23:37,38:41/39:21-23:24:25/4
23/41:18:25/42:10/Ps3:1/4:2:3/8/9:12/10:1/
11:1/13/14:6:7/17:15/18:1:18/20:5/21:9,10:
/22:5:8:24/23:4/25:10/27:2:5:9/31:2:11:17:22
32:1:3:3f:6:6f/33:9/34:15:17/35:13/37:19:33:
35,36:39/38:16/39:1:11/41:3:6^2:7/42:4,5/46:
49:5:14:16:17/51:19/53:6/55:1/56:3,4/58:10f
60:1/61:2/62:3,4:6/63:1/66:14:20/68:7:9,10/
:10:11/71:9:15/72:12/73:21/74:9,10/75:2/76
/77:16/78:9:31:34:59/81:7/83:1/84:6/86:17/
:4:6/88:10/89:9/91:15/94:19^2/99:6:8/102:1/
104:20:29/105:12:31:38/109:7:25/112:4:10/
114:1/116:10,11/119:7f:82/126:1/127:5:5f/1
:6,7/132:1/133/137:7/138:3/139:2^2:17,18/14
1:6,7:6,7f/Pro1:17:27^2/3:7,8:11,12/5:11/6:9:2
30/8:27,28,29^3/9:7,8/10:20/11:7:9f:17^2/12:16
13:12:19:22^2/14:13:32/15:15^2/16:7:13/17:14f
27,28/18:14/19:17/21:3^2/22:6/23:1:33:35/24
13,14:17^2/25:4,5^2/26:20/27:17/28:1:2:3:12^2:2
/29:16/30:21,22,23/31:26/Ecc4:5,6:10/5:4/7:
14/8:2,3/9:12/10:8,9:11/11:3^2/12:1:2:3:4/Sol
9/Is1:8^2:12,13:15/2:11:19:21/5:22/7:2:21,22/
12/9:3:4/10:3^2:11:18:24:26/11:16/13:12:19/1
3:25:27/16:4,5/17:4:6:9/18:3^2:7/19:20/20:1/2
:3:5f:6,7:6,7f/23:5:18/24/26:9:11:16/27:6:12/
28:18/29:8:11:12:23:23f/30:25:26:29^2:32/31:3
4,5:7:9/32:6/33:3:18/34:5/35/37:1:3:36/38:2:
12/39:6/40:24/41:17^2:28/43:2^3:8/44:26:27:28
45:4/46:7^2/48:1:3:21/49:7/50:2/51:1^2:9:11/5
3:14,15/53:3:10:11/56:3:10/57:13/58:4:9/59:
9:10/60:22/63:11:12/64:3:6/65:12^2:16:20:21,2
/66:3^2:4^2:14/Jer1:3/2:17:21:28/3:16^2/5:19/6:
10:14:15:17/7:22:32/8:4,5^2:8:11/9:25,26/10:1
/11:7:14/12:1/13:16:21/14:12^2/16:10:14,15:2
/19:6/20:1:3:6:7/22:18:21/23:5,6:7:12:16:20:3
:38,39/26:7,8:10:18:21/27:19,20,21/28:9/29:3
12:13:31/30:3:7:18/31:2:6:23:27:31:32:38,39/
33:5:6:14/34:1:11f:13:18,19/35:1:11:17/36:3:5
11:13/37:5:11/38:1:7:12/39:4/40:7:11/41:6:7:
10:11:13,14:18/42:20/43:1:11/46:2/47:4:6:7/
48:12/49:8/50:43/51:6:16:17:18:46:47:61,62:6
/52:1:6/Lam1:21/3:39/Eze1:1:19,20,21^3:24:
27,28/3:3:18:22/5:15/6:9:10:13/7:22/10:3:5:6
9-13:15,16:17/11:18/12:4:15/13:2,3:6:7:10:12:
16:22/14:13:15:17:19:23/16:4^2:5:6,7:8:9,10:22:
59,60:61:63/17:7:10:17/18:8:26/19:5:7/20:5,6
27,28:31:38:41:42:44/21:7^2:29/22:18,19,20:28
23:8^2:11:12f:16:16f:19,20:21:39/24:24/25:3^2:1
/28:15:22:26/29:6:21/30:8:18:21f:25/31:15/32
9:9f:10:15:31/33:2:3:8:14:18:29:33/34:27/35:
4,5^2:14/36:17:20:33:35/37:28/38:14:18/39:13:
27/42:14:15/43:3:18:23/44:7:10:15:17:19/45:1
/46:9:17/48:11:12/Dan1:1:5:18,19/2:14/3:3:5:
:10:15:28/4:5:7:26:35:36/5:2,3,4:8:10:20/7:28/
8:22:23/10:2:8:20,21/11:7:8:21f:30,31/12:4:7f/
Hos1:10:11:5:7:13/4:12f/5:9:13/8:6/9:10:12/
10:6/11:1/12:3^2/13:1:6/Joe3:1:17/Amo:4:12/
2/6:10:12:13/7:10/8:11/9:13/Ob1:11:12/Jon:
9,10/2:7/3:4,5:6:10/4:2:3:6:8:10/Mic2:12/4/5
5:6/7:1:8:15/Nah1:3:7/2:1f/3:17/Hab2:3:6:14
3:16:19/Zep1:1:14/3:8:20/Hag1:1:3,4:9/2:5:
16,17^2:23/Zec:1/6:15/7:5^2:7:13/8:9:14,15:17/
10:8:11f/Mal1:2,3:6:7^2:9/2:15/3:2:8:17/Mt1:2
/2:7:8:12:16:19/3:6:7/4:12,13/5:11/6:2:3:5:6:1
:17/7:3:4:27/8:5,6:14:15:16:18:21:28/9:2:15:23
25/10:12:19:23:26:27:40/11:1:7^2/12:3:24:27:4
46,47/13:21:26:34,35:47,48:53,54/14:1:14:20:
30:32/15:15:37,38/16:13/17:8:14/18:28/19:17
22:28/20:9:10:18:24:30:32,33/21:15:23:32:38:
40:45/22:3:11:31:34,35/23:20:21:22/24:3:6:15:
27:32:33:36/25:5,6^2:11:31:37:39:40:44:45/26:1
17:30/27:1:3:12:21:24:34:57/28:4:12,13/Mk1:
/2:16:17/3:20:21/4:10:21:34/5:1:6:21:38/6:29:

/HEN Con't)
/7:4:6,7:30/8:8,9:11:12:20:22:38/9:12,13:20:
:28:33/10:10:11:13:14:32:33:41:47:49/11:15:
:25/12:7^2:9:16:19:25:36/13:3,4:9:11:14:28:29:
:33:34f:35,36,37/14:1:11:41:44:51,52/15:20:
:39:41/16:1:4:9:13:19/Lk1:5:10:11,12:22:44:
:80/2:2:15:22:27:39:41,42:44:45/3:23-38/4:
:16:42/5:4:8:12:35/6:3:17,18:19:21:22:23:30:
:42:46:47,48:49/7:1:3:10:13:18:20,21,22:27:
:44/8:13:19:20:29:47:50:51/9:5:7:25:26:54:59
9f/10:7:17^2:31:33/11:1:14:21:24:37,38/12:1:
:39:40:54:55/13:4:24,25/14:4:7:10:12:17:34f/
:6:10:12:17:25:30/16:4:9f^2:28/17:7,8,9:20:22:
:26:27/18:8:19:23:31:36:40/19:5/20:1:10:14^2:
:34,35:37,38/21:6:7:9:20:28:30:31:32/22:1:6:
17:19:32:34:35:46:49:53:69/23:7:29:31f^2:
,41:42:47:48/24:15:31:44/Jn1:10:15:30:33/2:
8:9:10/3:12/4:1:21-24:25:40,41:52/5:6:9:25:
:31/6:2-5:14:18,19:24:25:48-51:65/7:4:8:15^2:
:32:40/8:28:28f:38:41:44:45/9:14f:15:35/10:
:18:19:34,35,36/11:4:17:20:24:31:32:33/12:9:
:31:32:41:45/13:6:11:19:26/14:2,3:20:26:29/
:4:10:13/16:2:4:8:13:15:20:21:25:32/17:1/18:
5/19:8:23,24:26:30:33/20:19:25/21:9:18^2/Act
6:8:12:15/2:1f:6:29/3:9/4:11:13:14/5:3:22:23:
4/7:8:11:17,18:21:45/8:14:18^2:19:31:39/9:30:
5:38:40/10:30/11:2:9:16:17:18:22:23:26/12:3:
:14:15:16:19:21/13:12:29:32,33:41:45:47:48/
4:5,6:11:14/15:13/16:38/17:13:18:26:32/18:6:
2/19:2:6:12:15:34/20:1:3:10,11,12:17:18:36/
:5:14:26,27:32:34/22:2:17,18:20:29/23:27:30:
3:35/24:2:6:21:25/25:15:17/26:5:10:13:16/27:
:39/28:6:10:15:16:19:25:28,29f/Rom1:17:20:
8/2:1:3:5:12-15:16/3:5^2:25:31/4:10:15:16:17:
8:24/5:3:5:6:10:12:14/6:2,3^2:4^2:5:7:20/7:1:2:4:
:9:19^2:21/8:19:23:30:35^2:39/9:1:10-13:21:33/
0:15:16/11:6:8^2:9:12^2:15^3:30/12:1:13:15/13:11
14:1f:9/15:4:9:24:29/1Co1:8:18:23/2:1:6/3:3/
:5:8:13:15/5:5:9:10/6:1:11:12:18/7:20:24:40/8
/9:9^2:20^2:21:22:23/10:8:16^2:20/11:7:16:17:20:
3:24:32:33:34/12:13/13:5:10:11^2/14:16:20:26/
5:23:24:28:36:37:42:43^2:44:52:54/16:3:12:20/
Co1:3,4:6,7:13,14:15,16:17:19:24/2:3:10:12/3:
:14:15/4:13/5:1^2:2:17/6:2^2/7:5:7:13:15/8:14/9
11/10:1^2:2:9:10:14:18^2/11:8,9:19,20/12:10:12:
8:20:21/13:2:5:10/Gal1:13:16/2:7,8,9:11:12^2:
4/3:5:8,9^2:17:20/4:4:12:13:18^2:19:24,25:27/5:
7:18:19:22/Eph1:10/2:5/3:6:10:12:14,15/4:8:
5:27:30/5:13^2:25:28:31/6:6,7^2:13/Php1:4:6:7^2:
6/2:12:16:19/3:5:8:12:21/4:15:16:18/Col2:10:
1:17:18:23/3:1:4:7:22/4:2/1Th1:5/2:13^2:19/3:
:5:13/4^2:14:15/5:1:3^2:4:7:23/2Th1:7:10/2:5:6:
8/3:1/1Ti1:3,4:7:8/2:15/4:14/5:8:18/6:7^2/
2Ti1:6:17/2:11:12:13:15:25/3:15/4:1:2^3:3:11:13
Tit2:13:15/3:4/Phm1:4/Heb:5,6:10/2:18/3:14
15:18/4:7/5:8:12,13/6:7:16:18/7:1:10:12,13,14
:17:23:27/8:5:8:9/9:6:16/10:18:32:34/11:7:8:9:
4:21:22:23:24,25:29:31/12:5^2:6^2:8:17:18:25:26
/Jas1:3:4:6:12:13:18/2:8:9:20:21:25:26/3:1/4:3:
5:8:10/5:17/1Pe1:11:13:17:22:24/2:12:23^2:24/
3:1:6/4:1:4:12:13:14/5:1:4:9/2Pe1:16:17,18:19
/2:16:20/3:7:12:14/1Jn1:1/2:15:19:28/3:2:19/
4:10:12:16/5:6,7,8:15/3Jn1:6:10^2/Jud:9:12:16/
Rev1:3:7:10:12:17,18/2:6f:10:13:14/3:21/4:9/6:
5:7:9:10/8:1:13/9:2/10:4:7:9:10/11:7/12:13/14:
7/19:20/20:7/21:16/22:11

2811

WHERE

Gen2:11,12/3:9f/4:9^2/11:28/13:3,4^2/16:8^2/18:
9/19:27/20:15/21:31/22:3:7:9/24:29,30/25:
9,10/26:1/27:18/28:4/29/31:13/32:13,14,15:17
:32/35:13,14:27/37:1:30/38:21:29/39:20/40:1/
42:7:24/43:18:33/Ex2:20/3:8/6:4/8:22/9:26/
12:30/13:11/14:4:13/15:27/16:35/20:21:24/21:
13/25:8/29:42/30:36/34:12/39:20/Lev1:2,3/4:
11,12:15:24:29:33/6:25/7:2/11:36/14:13:54/16
:1:22/17:8,9/18:3^2:27:29,30/26:30/Num4:7/5:3
/9:18/11:13:35/13:23/17:4/19:9/20:1:5:6:9:13^2
/21:14:16/22:24:40/23:17/25:8/33:7:9:14:52/
35:6:34/Deu2:8/3:27/4:3:5:34:42/6:1/8:9^2:15/
10:5:6/11:10^2:30^2/12:18^2:29/18:6,7/21:4/22:21
/29:28/30:1:3/31:14/32:37:38/Jos2:5/3:1:2,3,4
:15,16/4:2,3^2:5:8:9/5:2,3:8,9/9:8:27/10/12:5/
13:32/15:5:7:8:10,11:48-62f/17:11:15/18:7:16:
18:21-28f/19:2-7f/21:9-16f:20,21,22f/22:19/24:
13/Ju2:5/6:11:13/9:38:47,48,49/13:6/14:9/16:
21:31/17:9/19:12,13:17^2/20:33:46,47/Ru1:17/
2:3:19/3:4/4:1f/1Sa6:20/9:6:9,10,11:18/10:5:
14^2:22/11:12/14:9/19:22/20:6:19:41/21:2/22:1
/23:19:22:28/24:3/25:11f/26:3,4:15:16/27:10:
11/30:13:15:27-31/31:12/2Sa1:3:13/2:23/4:2,3
/7:10,11/9:4/10:17/11:16/13:13/15:19,20:32/
16:3:22/17:18/19:37/20:6/21:12,13,14/1Ki1:9/
2:2:39/6:19/7:7:48/8:7:30:49/9:26/10:28/11:1:
16,17,18:24/12:2,3,4/13:24,25:31/17:3:19/18:
12/19:9/21:8/22:38/2Ki2:13,14/5:24:25/6:1:6:
13/7:14/8:7/9:27:28/10:6/15:4:34,35/17:23/18
:17/19:27/20:14/23:7:8:34/25:6:21/1Ch3:4^2/5:
26/11:4/12:24-37/19:7/22:1/2Ch1:14/2:4/3:1^2
/6:5,6:20,21:30:31:33:39:41/7:12/8:6/10:2,3/11
:16/18:33/24:11/27:3/31:9/33:4,5:7:14:15:19/
35:24,25/Ez6:1:3/8:29/Neh2:3/3:19/4/11:25-
25-30/Est2:12,13,14/5:1/7:8/Job1:7/2:2/10:22^2
/14:10/17:15/18:6/20:7/23:3/26:5,6/28:12:20^2
:23,24:27/35:9,10/38:4:19^2:22,23:24^2:28/39:11
/40:12/Ps12:1/18:2^3/19:3,4/24:3/25:4:12/26:8
/33:13,14,15/35:10/42:2:3:6^2:10/61:3/62:7/63:
1/68:15,16/71:3:19/74:8/77:13/78:60/79:10/
81:5:7/84:6/86:8^2:11/89:8:49^2/94:21,22/101:2/
115:2f/132:7:14/139:3^2/143:8/144:12-15/Pro5
:6/7:25/8:12/14:15/24:21,22/29:18/Ecc5:15/8:
9,10^2/9:10/Sol1:7^2/4:8/6:1/8:5/Is7:18f:25/9:1
/10:3/11:10/18:1:7/19:12/22:1/23:2,3/29:4/30
:6/32:14/33:20/35:7/36:2:17:19/37:7/39:3/42:
24/43:9/44:13/47:11/50:8/55:2:13^2/57:15/63:
11^2:12:15^2/64:11/66:18/Jer2:6/3:2/6:16/8:3:
4,5:19/9:11:12/13:7:20/15:2:14/16:13:14,15:16
/17:19/18:2/19:14/26:18/29:14:18/30:5:11/32:
29:37:43/35:2/36:12:19/37/38:8:11:13/39:5/40
:4:5:8/41:9/42:3:13,14:22/43:5/46:16/49:7/51:
43/52:27/Lam4:6/Eze3:5/6:13/8:3:7/9:3/11:1:
17/17:5:10:16/19:13/20:29f:29:34:38/21:30/25
:5/27:32/28:25/29:14/34:13^2/37:25/40:2:38:39
:41:42/43:7:12/46:19,20:24/47:2:8:18:20:23/48
:12:19/Dan5:1/Hos9:15f^2/10:8/13:10^2/Joe2:17
:20/3:2/Amo7:13/Jon1:3/Mic2:5/3:12/4:9^2/5:
14/7:10:18/Nah2:11^2/3:19/Zep1:10/Zec2:2/3:
10/5:11^2/6:10,11/Mt2:2:4:9f:11/3:3/4:15,16/6:
5:19:20/8:19/9:25:28:36/10:25f/11:1:1f:20/13:
2,3:5:19:27:31,32/14:13/15:33/18:20/20:32,33
/21:17/22:13/25:24,25f^2/26:17:57/27:7:34/28:
6:16/Mk1:21:29,30/2:2/3:20:31,32/4:15:31,32
/5:15:40/6:45/9:30,31:33:48:49/13:14f/14:12:
14:53/16:6/Lk1:39,40/4:1:17:38/5:4/6:8/7:
6,7,8/8:12:16:19:25:33/9:11:57/10:34:38/14:9/
17:17:37^2/19:36,37/20:17/22:9:11:51/24:33,34
/Jn1:28:38:39/2:9/3:8^2:29/4:11:20:21-24:38:
46,47/6:2-5:21/7:1:3:27^2:28:34:35:36:41,42/8:
10:14^2:19:21:22/9:7:12/10:40/11:6:30:32:34/12
:1:26:35/13:36/14:2,3^2:4:5/19:9:20:41/20:2:12:
13:15/21:18/Act1:13:20/2:2:8/3:11/4:31/5:24/
7:15:29/9:39/10:18:27:39/11:11/12:12/13:6,7/
14:22:26^2/15:30:36/16:1:13:40/17:1/18:22/19:
1/20:6:8/21:3:5:7/23:34/25:2/27:16:41f/28:7:
12:14/Rom5:2/6:14/7:20/8:39/15:20^2:21/1Co
12:18/15:55,56^2/2Co2:13/3:17/10:16/Gal4:15/
5:16/Eph2:6/Php3:20/Col2:15/3:1/Tit1:9/
Heb5:12,13/6:20/10:19/11:8/12:5/13:10^2:12/
2Pe3:4:13/1Jn2:11/Jud1:21/Rev:4f/2:13/4:5f/
5:6f/7:13/8:4/11:1:8,9/12:6:14/13:4/17:9/18:
18/20:10

771

WHETHER

Gen17:24-27/18:21/21:9f/24:21:49/31:39/42:
16:20:34/43:7/Ex4:18/9:7/12:3,4/16:4/19:13/
20:10/21:16:20:26:32/22:8/29:28/Lev2:8/5:4/7
:9:10:21:23:26,27/11:9/12:6/13:55f^2:59/14:57/
16:29,30/17:8,9:10:13/18:9^2/19:15/20:1:17:19:
27/22:17,18:21:28/27:30:33/Num5:15:18:30/
11:23/12:1f/13:18:19^2:20^2/15:3,4:30/22:19/35:
24^2/Deu4:16,17/5:8/7:14/8:2/13:3/15:12/17:
2,3:8^2/18:21/19:9/23:19/24:14,15/27:15:22/30
:15/Ju2:22/3:4/9:2/11:39f/18:5/1Sa9:9,10,11/
20:10/25:8/2Sa15:21/1Ki1:20/8:29:32:46/14:3
/20:18/2Ki1:2:3/6:1/8:8,9^2/9:18:19/12:4,5/
1Ch20:3f/2Ch15:13/19:10/Ez2:62,63/5:17/
Neh7:64,65/10:35/Est3:3,4/4:11/Ps49:20f/
119:113/Pro20:11/Ecc2:19/5:12/7:10/9:1:2,3/
11:3/Sol6:11/7:12^3/Is66:19f/Jer34:18,19/42:6
/48:8/Eze2:5:7/3:11/14:6,7/20:30/21:21/47:
22/Dan1:13/Zec2:2/7:3/Mal2:12/Mt7:21/22:
31/26:63/27:49/Mk12:26/Lk3:15/6:7/8:30f/
12:22/14:31/20:37,38/22:67,68/Jn1:19/4:21-
21-24/7:17/9:25/18:34f/Act4:19/8:2f^2/10:18/
25:20/26:29/27:39/Rom2:10/3:9:30/4:16/9:
23,24/14:2:4/15:1/1Co3:4:13/4:5:19^2/7^2/8:8/
10:15:25:27:32/12:3^2:10^2/2Co5:9/6:8^2/7:1/12:
2,3/Gal2:4/5:6^2/6:15^2/Eph2:18/6:8/Php1:20^2:
27/4:11:12/Col3:11/1Th:5/5:10/1Ti:21/Heb6:
17/7:3f/Jas2:12:18/4:11/1Pe1:7/1Jn2:5/4:6/5
:17f/Rev3:10f/9:1f

223

WHICH

^{2}Gen2:4:14:21/3:19:23/4:11/5:28-31/6:17/8:7f
/10:11,12/11:6f/22:2/25:18:25f:30/27:14/31:
35f/38:9:14/41:4/44:5/45:6/46:28/48:22/49:
10f:32/Ex3:13/22:9/25:16f/31:18/36:27/38:24:
25,26:29/Lev1:9/3:14/6:28/7:30/8:26:33/10:14
/11:2,3^2:29,30:32:34:39/12:5/13:18:19/14:
33,34:37/16:8^2/18:16f:24/20:25/22:22/23:3:4:
36/24:3,4/27:22/Num6:18/7:8:14/10:28/11:17
/12:1f/15:22/18:8/21:20:25,26/22:41/24:2/28:
1/29:2:6:13/30:15/31:32-35:36-40^3/34:4/35:
22,23^2/36:3:13/Deu1:19,20,21:22/2:35,36/3:16
/6:1:18:20/7:12:16:19/9:9:10,11:29/11:27/12:1
/13:18^2/16:15:20/17:2,3/20:15f/21:13/24:6/26
:16/28:21:27:60/29:1:21:27:29/32:21/34:11,12
/Jos1:10,11/4:10/5:11,12/6:11/7:1:12f:14:15/8
:29/9:18/10:39/12:2^2:7/13:2-7/14:1^2:3,4:12/15
:9:13:21-32/17:7:11/18:3:5,6:10:17:19/22:17,18
:28/23:13:15,16/24:14:31:32^2:33/Ju1:2:11/7:
4^2/9/10/11:27/15:14/16:11/18:12/20:18/1Sa2
:23,24,25:29/6:17/7:14/10:4/12:23/13:1f/14:4/
16:3/18:5/21:4/24:15/27:6/28:5,6f/2Sa2:1/5:
21/6:8:17/7:10,11:27/8:7/17:14/1Ki1:27/4:33/
7:1:6:8:24:32:40/8:3,4:9:21:33,34:35,36^2:40:44:
48^3/9:2,3:7^2:10:19:27,28/10:3f/11:32/12:32,33f
/13:12/14:13:21:24/15:13/16:15,16:23/18:30/
21:20f/2Ki6:11/9:5/10:27/11:11/14:28/15:5/
16:3/17:8:11:13:33/18:9:20,21/19:28/21:3,4,5^2:
7:16^2/22:20/23:1:12^2:15:24/24:13/1Ch1:19/21:
5:10,11/22:13:14/28:2:13:16/29:8:19/2Ch5:10/
6:18:27:31f:34^2/7:20/8:2:7,8/11:15/15:18/20:
11:34/25:10/26:11/28:8/29:17:30/30:8/33/34:
14/35:21f/Ez1:7/2:1:70/5:6:14/6:5:11/7:6:15:
17/8:25:26,27:28/Neh1:9/2:11,12:18/8:1:15/9:
29f:36/12:31,32:37:38/13:1:15/Est1:1/3:3,4/8:
2:13/Job16:22/32:8,9/36:24:28/38:16/40:20/
Ps5:8/31/40:6/58:1/71:7/78:68/90:11/119:
59,60/140:10/142:3/Ecc1:12-15/3:20^2/6:1/8:
15/11:5:6/Sol3:11/8/Is7:3/8:1/16:6/31:7/33:
14/36:20/43:9^2/48:14/51:1^2/57:12:20/59:5/63:
7/Jer7:13,14:18f/8:17/13:24,25^2/17:11/20:16/
21:13/23:8/24:10/25:5/27:13/29:24f/32:1/36:
22f/37:15,16/38:11/40:12/46:28/49/51:7/52:
17/Eze2:1f/4:13/16:17/20:25:25f/21:21f/23:22
:32/29:13/34:22^2/36:28/38:15,16f/40:5:19/41:
11:22f/42:7,8:14/45:3/46:2:4:14,15/47:16/Dan
4:1/7:20/8:5:26f/Hos1:11/10:14/Amo7:1/9:11
/Jon1:7/3:3f^2/Mic1:11f^3:11/Hag2:7f/Zec10:4:
11f/Mal3:16/Mt18:1/19:18/21:31/22:15:36/
23:17:19/24:17f/27:9^2:17:21:46:62f/Mk9:34:
43,44f:45,46f/11:33/12:28/14:44/Lk1:28f/2:15
:41,42/4:29/7:42/9:46/10:29:36/11:27:53,54/
13:16:20,21/14:5/22:23/24:21/Jn4:12/8:46/10
:32:34,35,36/18:32f/19:31/21:20/Act1:24,25/4
:11/8:9,10,11f/11:6/15:16f/17:26/20:32/21:39
/24:14/25:7/27:2/Rom2:16:20/6:17/7:10:18/8:
20,21/9:8/10/1Co1:21/2:9:14/4:21/6:1/11:24/
12:2:6:11:28/15:42:55,56/2Co4:18/5:2:11/12:7
/13:10/Gal1:4:6:11/3:12/5:26/6:8/Eph1:23/2:
15/5:12:29,30:31/6:17/Php1:11:22/2:9:17/3:14
/4:7/Col1:8:18/2:14:19/3:15/4:3/1Th2:13/2Th
:16/3:17/1Ti2:6/3:15/6:4:12^2:17/2Ti2:16:23:26
/4:8/Tit1:1:9/Heb:4/7:2:10:12,13,14/8:6/9:7:
11:23/10:4f:20:27/11:7:8/12:24/13:9/1Pe1:11:
18/2:4/3:21f/2Pe1:7/2:12/1Jn5:16/Jud1:3:5:7
/Rev3:10/5:6/9:20/12:4/13:17/17:16/20:3/22

575

WHILE

Gen3:15/4:2:8/11:29/13:12/18:1:3,4:22,23/19:
15/22:6/24:45/25:27/29:31/31:17-20/35:16:22
/36:17:24/46:8-14:29/Ex1:11/14:12/15:19/18:
5,6/21:4/24:14/33:9/39:1:41/Lev7:32,33/12:4/
14:46/15:3:6:33/18:14f/21:11f/25:1/Num9:1/
13:29/15:32/20:14:14f/21:31,32/23:15/25:1/
26:58,59/32:6/33:38,39:49:50,51/35:1:8/36:13
/Deu3:9/9:10,11/22:21:30f/26:14^2/28:36:43/
31:27/33:28/Jos5:10/7:5/22:10/24:4/Ju6:39/9
:25:44/16:8:14/19:21/Ru2:4,5/1Sa:13,14/8:12/
13:2/14:19/23:18/25:7/27:11/29/2Sa3:1:2/7/
10:7,8/12:21:22/15:7,8:10:12/17:2,3/1Ki1:14:
22,23:42:48/3:20/6:23-28/11:12,13/13:9:20/15
:27/18:5/20:40/22:2/2Ki6:25:33/8:29/10:13/
11:2,3/16:10/1Ch3:5/11:8:15/12:1/17/25:3/27
:28/29:10/2Ch1:2,3/5:11,12/14:7:14/22:8:12/
26:5/32:8:9:11/34:12/Ez3:12/5:5/8:15:21/Neh
4:16/7:3/8:7,8f/Est6:14/Job1:16/5:24/11:3/24
:10/27:3/28:5/Ps2:10/27:12/28:3/32:6/37:10/
38:1/41:6/42:3/62:3,4/63:11/81:8/89:41/92:9/
94:12,13/102:12/106:4/107:42/109:2:4/119:
127/139:15/141:10/Pro4:19/10:5/11:8:13:23/
12:12:27/13:4:6:21:25/14:1:20/15:14/19:18/21

(WHILE Con't)
:8/29:23/Ecc2:3:13,14/4:1/7:2:4/10:7/11:5/12:
4:6/Sol3:4/Is1:7/10:25/18:5/26:20/27:7,8/33:
1/37:38/54:8/55:6^2/58:3/65:13:14:24/Jer4:14/
5:19/9:8/15:9/28:1/32:2/33:1/34:21/39:15/41:
2/48:5/51:33:39:50/52:10/Lam1:19/Eze4:12/5
:8/9/10:2/11:13/12:5:7/16:49/18:30/20:8:
23,24/27:14:20/30:25/32:24:25:27/44:17:19/
46:2/48:27,28/Dan4:31/5:2,3,4:23/8:5/9:20/11
:24:45/Hos7:4/8:10/Joe2:12/Amo1:2/4:7/5:
25,26,27/Ob1:7/Mic6:11/7:9/Hab1:13^2:15/2:7
/Zep:2/Hag:6/Zec6:6/12/Mt1:18/3:1/9:15/12
:43,44,45/13:2,3:21/14:22/17:22,23/21:32/23:
13,14/24:48/25:2,3,4:10:14/26:7:36:47:73/Mk
2:19/3:1/5:35/6:10:31/9:7/11:8/12:43,44/13:
34/14:32:43/Lk2:6/4:13:20/5:2:17:34/7:
20,21,22/8:4:23:49/10:40/12:10/14:32/15:20/
18:4,5/19:13/20:47/22:58/23:39/Jn1:17/3:22/
4:20:21-24:46,47:51/5:7:35/6:30,31/7:12/8:20/
9:5/12:29:35^2:36/14:19:25/16:4:16^2/17:13/18:
16/20:1:7/Act4:1/5:34/9:23/10:3:9,10:27/11:5
/12:19:20/14:8:28/15:1:40,41/17:14:16/18:19:
25,26/19:1:22/22:17,18/27:41/Rom5:8:16/7:3:
6/14:9/15:20:24/1Co4:10/9:6/11:4:14,15:21/
12:24/14:19:29,30^2/15:41/16:5/2Co2:16/7:8/
11:8,9:16/Gal2:7,8,9/6:9/Php1:20/2:30/4:10/
Col1:10/1Th2:17/3:4/2Th1:6/3:10/2Ti:11/
Phm1:10:13:15/Heb2:7/3:7,8:13/5:7/9:15:17/
11:17/12:11/1Pe1:6/3:20/5:10/2Pe2:13/3:14/
2Jn1:9/Jud:23/Rev3:9/13:13/20:3
417

WHO

Gen3:11:12/4:14:15:23:24/5:1/9:5,6/10:1:8/11:
3,4:29/12:3^2/14:12:13^2:18:19,20:21/15:7/16:13^2
:14/17:6:14:21/18:19/19:9:15/20:9,10/21:6:7:
26/22:3/24:2:5:39:43:59:65/25:12-15:27/26:24
/27:18:27,28,29^2:32:33^2/30:2/31:32:34:53/32:9
:28/33:5/35:1:3:7:10/36:24/37:15:25:29/38:
3,4,5:9:21:25:28/40:1/41:12:38^3:56,57/44:10:15
:17/45:8:15/46:8-14/48:15:16/49:9:23:26/50:
14:23/Ex1:1:5:8:8f/2:1:14:16/3:3,4:12/4:11^2:19
/5:2:4,5/6:2,3:7:27:30/9:21/10:8/12:15:19^2:44:
46/14:19/15:7:11^3:26/16:6:7,8,9:18^2/18:15,16^2:
21/19:22f/20:2:5:6/21:8:12:15:17:19:22/22:2:3:
6:9:14:16/23:8/25:1/29:29:37f:44/30:11,12:14:
33^2/31:6:12,13:14,15^2/32:1:23:26/33:7:11:16/
34:14:16/35:5-9:10-19:22:29/36:1/38:8:25,26/
Lev1:4:11/2:1/3:2:7,8/4:2/5:17,18/6:26:27/7:7:
8:9:14:17,18^3:19:20:21:25:26,27:35/10:3:12/11:
36:45/13:18:45/14:4:8:11:20:32:47/15:1:32:33/
16:26/17:3,4:8,9:10:13:14:15/18:19:26/19:17:
20:35,36/20:1:5:6:8:9:24/21:8:9:14,15:16,17:23
/22:3:4^4:5^3:9:13:16^2/23:22:29:30,31:42/24:
13,14:15,16^2:18/25:49/26:13:17:36/27:29f/
Num1:2-15:17,18,19/2:32,33/3:10:38^2:40:49/4:
3:21,22,23:29:35:46,47,48^2/5:1^2/7:2/9:13^2/11:
4,5:19,20:34/13:18/14:14:22:29:34,35:36,37,38:
45/15:13,14:29:30:41/16:5^3:32:35:38:40:49/17:
12,13/18:4:7/19:8:9:10:11:13:14^2:16^2:18^3:20:21
/20:16/21:8:9/22:5,6:9/24:3-9^3:23,24/25:5:14/
26:2:5-11^2:19-22:64,65f:64,65/27:1:3,4:17:18/
30:16/31:12:16:17:19:21:27:48,49/32:1:27:29:
39/33:3,4:40:55/35:6:12/36:8/Deu1:13:28:33:
36:44/2:4:14,15:22/4:4:42/5:2,3:6:9,10^2/6:
10,11,12:15/7:9^3:10:20/8:14:15:18/10:17:21/11
:2/12:15:20-23/13:1:5^2:10/14:29/15:7:11/17:13
/18:6,7:10:19:20^2:22/19:2,3:20/20:1:19/21:17^2:
18/22:2:23,24^2:28,29/23:8:9,10/25:9:10:16:18/
26:5/27:15:16:17:18:19:20:21:22:23:24:25:26/
28:50:54:56,57/29:6:11:21/30:7,8/31:9:13:25/
32:18^2:27/33:11:16:20:27:29/Jos1:17,18/2:1:2:
16:22/3:8:10:11:13,14^2:17/4:10:15,16/5:1:4,5:6:
7/6:23:25:26/7:15/8:20,21^2:22:23:35/9:8/10:6/
11:8:15:21/12:2:4:8-24/13:10:12:13:21:31/14:8
/15:16:17:63/17:1:12/18:17/20:3:6^2:9/21:9-16/
22:20/24:17^2:18:31/Ju1:12:19:24:31,32/2:7-9:
12-14/3:1:15:17,18,19^2/4:2,3:4:6/5:9:10^2:24:31
/6:9:10:16f:17:19:27:29:31^2/7:3^2:5,6^2:24/8:31/9
:4:5:24:25:28:33:38^3/10:3:18/11:19:23:25:39/12
:8:14/13:1:2,3:11/14:4:19:20/15:6:19/16:23,24:
25,26:27/19:1:3:22/20:16:34:40,41:42:46,47/21
:5:7:8,9:18:20:23/Ru1:11/2:1:6/3:9:12/4:3:11:
14:15^2/1Sa1:1:11f:26/2:4^2:5^2:10:12:22:30^2:33:
35/3:8/4:4:8^2:19:20/5:12/6:9:20/9:6/10:3:27/
11:7:12/12:2:6/13:7:14:15/14:17:21:24,25:28:
39:41:45:48/15:28:29/16:18/17:10:12:25:26:37
/18:10:18/22:2:9,10:14/23:22/24:9,10:14^2:19/
25:3:10^3:11:11f:29:30,31:32:34/26:9:14/27:8/28
:23/30:5:13:17:21:24^2/2Sa1:8:12:13/2:7:30/3:4:
31/4:2,3^2:4:8:9:11/5:6:14,15,16/6:5:10:13:21^2/
7:13/9:2:10,11:13/10:10/11:3:19,20,21/12:5/
13:28/14:2,3:15,16:27/15:12:17,18:19,20:30/16
:2:6:10:14:18:21f/17:2,3:8:25:28,29/18:13:28^2:
31/19:6^2:14:28:31,32/20:21:24/21:5,6:7:8:16/
22:3:4:18^2:27^2:31:32f:40:48^2/23:3^2:9:17:21:24-
24-39f/24:11:17/1Ki1:8:29:48/2:23,24:32/3:7:9
:26^2:27/4:8-19^2/8:15:19:24:39:46:56/9:9:20,21:
23/10:5:9:26/11:9,10:15:16,17,18:20:23:24:26:
29:34/12:2,3,4:6:16,17:18:31/13:2:14:24,25:26:
33/14:2:10^2:11^2:13:14/16:4-7^2:9/17:8,9/18:3,4:
12:17:19:22:24/19:17^2:18:19/21:10:13:24^2/22:
10:13:20:52,53/2Ki1:7/3:3:13:21:27/4:1:9:18:
28/5:2/6:11/9:7:8:11:15:16:31:32/10:11^2:13:15:
18,19:20,21:23^2/11:2,3^2:5:6,7,8:9^2:15/13:2:
20,21/14:5:24/15:1:8:13:17:23:24:27:28:30:
32,33/16:1:11,12/17:1:7:35,36/18:1:23/19:4:25
:30/20:18/21:11:12:14/22:15,16/23:5:8:17:25:
31,32/25:11:25:28/1Ch1:10:43^2:46/2:7:19:22:
42^2:44:50:55/3:1:2:17,18/4:3-4:10:18:21-22^2:
34-39/5:11/6:4-15:44-47/7:14:15^2/8:12:
30,31,32:40/9:7,8:10,11:14^2:15,16^4/10:1/11:2:
10:18,19:23/12:1:18:20:23:24-37/15:22:26/16:
10:21:23:31:41/17:12:16/21:8:12:17:19,20:26/
22:9/23:3:24/24:3^2:28/25:3/26:8:28/27:2,3:4:7:
11:12:15/29:4,5^2:14^2/2Ch1:10/2:6^2:7:12^2/5:
11,12/6:4:14^3:36:39/7:21:22/8:10/10:6:8,9/11:
15/13:9/15:13/18:12:19,20/19:2/20:6:7:14:35/
21:6:13/22:5:9^2:11/23:2,3:4:13,14/24:12^2/25:3:
15/26:5:10:17,18/27:2/28:15^2:23/29:15:23:
25,26:31/30:6:7:17,18,19/31:1^2:5,6:14,15/32:7:
12:18:21/33:25/34:4:12:13:23:26/35:4,5:6:11/
36:3:12:20:22,23/Ez1:2:3:4^2:6/2:1:2:40,41,42:
55,56,57/3:1:8^2:12/4:8,9:15:20/5:1:3:4:9/6:11:
12:21,22/7:1:27/8:1:15:16:22^2/9:1:4:14/10:3:
7,8:14:16-19:23:25/Neh1:2^2:5^2:11/2:10:16/3:7:
11:17:20:24:27:30/4:3:5:12:14:23/5:1:2,3,4:8:9:
13:15^2/6:10:14/7:2:3:5:6:7:57,58,59:66/8:1:9/9:
7:26:27:32/10:1:9-13:14-27:28^2:36/11:2:3:4,5,6:
7,8,9:10-14:15,16,17^2:22,23:36/12:1:8^2:12-21:
25:26:35,36:45/13:4^2:10:26/Est1:8:10:13-15^2/2
:4:9:15f^2:21:22/3:13/4:5:11:14/6:1:4:6:9:10/7:4:
5:9/9:1:13:16:27/Job1:1:8/2:3/3:8:8f^2:20,21^2/4
:2:3,4:6:7,8^3:18,19/5:3/7:9/8:11-13:22/9:4:12^2:
14:17:24/11:8:10/12:3:4:7,8,9/13:4:19/15:16:
17-19/18:2/20:7/21:15:19:22:23,24:25:28:29/
22:29/23:13/24:14,15:21:25/25:3:4:6/26:14/27
:2^2:7:15/28:27/29:11:12:13:25^2/30:24/31:2,3:
35/32:7/34:7,8:18:29,30/35:9,10/36:18:22:23/
37:19,20/38:5:6,7:8,9^2:25-27^2:29:36:36f:37,38^2:
41/39:5/41:10:13^2/42:3^2/Ps1:1^2/2:12/5:11^2/6:
5f^2/7:9:11:17/9:9:10^2:11:12^2:13/10:2:16:18/12:
3,4^3/14:1^2:2^2:5/15:1:2:3/16:7/18:17^2:25^2:26:30:
31^2:40:43,44,45:46:47^2/19:11/21:7:8/22:7:8^2:23
:25:26:29/24:2:3^2:4:6:8:10/25:3^2:5:8:9:12:14/26
:9,10/28:3/31:1:5,6^2:14,15:18:19^2:23^3/32:1:10:
11^2:11f/33:10:18,19^2/34:2:7:8:9:10:15:18:21:22^2
/35:4:10^2:14:15:19:20:26^2:27^2/36:10^2/37:7:9:11
:12,13:14:25:28/38:13,14:16/40:4^3:5:14,15:16/
41:1:13/42:8/44:7/49:14^2/50:5:5f:22:23/52:1:7
/53:2/54:3/55:12:20/57:2:3/58:8^2:11/59:1/60:
4,5:9,10^3/61:5/63:11/64:8/65:5/66:16:20/68:4:
18:19:26:30f^2:30:33/69:4^2:6:14:32:36/70:4/71:
24/72:18/73:16/74:9,10/76:7/77:15/78:17:51/
80:1/81:10:15/83:2:12/84:4:5^2:11:12/85:9/86:5
:17/87:6/89:7:14,15:19f:23:41:48/90:11/91:1/
92:1/94:9:16^2:21,22/97:7^2:10:12/101:5:6:7/103
:6:8:11:13:17,18^2:20:21/104:35/105:14/106:2^2:
3:21,22:41,42:46/107:10^2:11:41/108:10^2/109:
20:21/111:1:4:5/112:1^2:5:6/113:5/115:8:13:15/
118:7:26/119:1:2:21:40,41,42:53:63:74:79:84:
85,86:113:118:132:162:165/120:5,6/121:2/122:
6:8/124:6:8/125:1:4/126:5/127/128:1^2:4/129:5
/130:3,4/131:2/134:1:3/135:18^2:20/136:4:5:6:6
f:7:10:13:16:17:18/137:8:9:9f/139:21/140:2/
143:12/144:1:10/145:18:19:20/146:5:6^2/147:11^2
:17/Pro1:19:19f:33/2:1:11,12,13^2:19/3:
13,14,15^2:18^2/6:29:32/8:14,15^2:17^2:21:32:34:36^2
/10:5/11:20:26^2:29:30/12:11f:22^2/14:17:21:22^2:
25:31^2:35^2/15:9,10/16:15:17:20^2:33/17:4:5^2:15:
16/18:21:22:24^2/19:6:8:26/20:9:12:20/21:13:16
:17:21/22:2:5:9:11:16/23:29,30^3/24:11,12^2:
21,22:24:25/25:14/26:12:18,19:27/27:7:8:13:18
/28:5:7^2:8:9:10^2:13:14^2:20^2:24:26:27/29:1:3:4:
10:14:24/30:4^3:5:11,12:17:21,22,23^3:21,22,23f:
24-28/31:5:8:30/Ecc2:12f:19:20-23:24-26^3/3:21
/4:3:8:13/5:1:9:10:12:15:19,20/6:7,8:12^3/7:20/
8:2,3:5:12:13:16,17/10:14/12:7:11/Sol3:6/6:10
/7:9/8:1:5:12/Is1:12,13:27^2/2:6/3:16/5:11:18:
21:22/6:8/9:2^2:8,9,10/10:1:7:15^2:17/11:4:8:10/
12:6/13:15/14:16:17:27^2:29/15:9^2/16:3/17:6:
10^2:14/19:8^2:20/20:3:5,6/22:9,10,11^2:15,16:17:
18/23:8:13:15,16/24:14/25:4/26:2:3:17:19^2/27:
11/28:5:6:9:11:15:16/29:11:15^2:21^4:22/30:7f:
:31/31:1/32:4:9/33:1:15^7/35:4:6/36:3:6/37:4:
8,9:11:23:26^2:30:31/38:18f/40:12^2:13:22^2:25:2
/41:2^2:4:20:24:26^2/42:3:5^2:7:10^2:17:19^3:22:24,
43:1:7:16:25/44:2^2:6:7:9^2:10:11:24:25/45:3:7:9
10:11:16:20:21:24/46:3:5:10:13/47:4:7:13/48:
17/49:5^3:7:19:21^3:23:24^2:25/50:3:6:8^2:9:10:11
51:1^2:7:10:12^2:13:15:16:19^2:22:23/52:1:5:6:7:1
/53:1:6^2:8:12/54:1:10:16/56:2^2:4:6:8:11/57:2:
13:15:20/58:6:7^3:12/59:8:9:15:20/60:8^2/61:2:
62:5:6,7^2/63:1^4:11^2:13:17/64:4^2:5^2/65:1^2:10:1
/66:2^2:3:5:7,8:10^2:17:19f:19:24/Jer1:1/2:3^2:4,
6:24/3:1:6:15:20:21/4:22/5:6:23,24:26/6:9:10:
17/7:2:4:18f/8:3/9:12:20:25,26/10:2,3:7:8:9:1
:25/11:1:17/13:23/14:8:15^2:22/15:2^2:5^3/17:7:
11:13:18/18:16/19:3/20:10:12^2:15/22:11:18:
24,25/23:5,6:7:8:14:17^2:18:23:27:30,31^2:34/24
8/25:30/26:2:19:23/27:6:9:14:16/28:8:9/29:8:
16,17^2:21:26/30:16^2:20:21/31:2:8:10:11:15f:35
/32:12^2/33:22/35:3:4:18,19/37:1f:2:7:19/38:1
19^2/39:5:9:14/40:1:5:7:8:10:15/41:1:3:10/42:1
/43:5/44:1:7:14:15:20:24:26:28^4:30f^2:30/46:9:
18:22,23:25:26:27/48:19:44^2/49:1:2:9,10:11:17
19^3:22:32f/50:7:13:28:44^3/51:11:50/52:9:15^3:
24,25:31/Lam1:4:8:12:16/2:7:13:15:17/3:1:25
30:37:38/4:5:9:13:16/Eze1:1:26/3:27^2/5:10/6
12/7:16/9:4/10:7,8/11:1:9:12:21/12:2/13:2,3:
15:17:18:19^2/14:4:5:6,7:10/16:3f:15:25:27:32:
57/17:16:24/18:10^2:11:14:16:20^2:25:29/20:9,1
:12:14:22:38/21:27/22:6:10:27:30^2/23:2,3:10:4
:43:44/26:2:20^2/27:35/28:19:22/30:24/31:12/
32:23:26:27:28:29:30:32/33:4:21:32/34:2:4:
15,16:27/35:7^2:15/36:34/38:2,3f:12:13/39:6:1
/40:45/42:13/43:6:19/44:5^2:7:10/45:4:5:15:20
47:22/48:11/Dan1:3,4^2:11:13:15/2:10^2:24:25:
28:29/3:6:11:12:29/4:34:37/5:7f:11:18:19:23/
7:24:27/7:17/8:23f:24/9:4^2:9/10:13:18:20,21/
11:2f:3:7f:13f:20:21f:30,31:32:32f^2:32:35:39/12
1:3^2:6:7:10:12/Hos1:2:8:23^2/4:15/5:10f/6:1/7
/9:4:6:7/10:14f/11:3/12:9^2:11:13/13:9/Joe2:1
:14:17:26:32/3:6/Amo2:6/4:1^2:13/5:8^3:10:13:1
:19^2/8:4:5:6:14/9:7:10:12/Ob1:3:19/Jon:8:9,1
/2:8/3:9/4:11f/Mic1:1/2:8^2:13f/3:2:5^4:9:11^2/5
2:3f:15/6:14:16/7:18/Nah1:1:2:6:7:11^2/3:4f:7:
10:12:19^2/Hab1:3:6f:6:12:13^2:16/2:12:19^2/3:1
:16/Zep1:4:6^2:9^2:12/2:3^2:9/3:3:10:12:19^2/Hag
:1:1f/2:3:8,9f/Zec1:13/2:3:8:9:11,12/3:2f/4:1:
:14/5:3:4/6:5:8:12:14:15^2/11:5^2:11^2:16:17/12:
8:10:11/13:6f:7/14:12:16:21/Mal1:6:10:14/2:4
11:12:14/3:2^2:5^2:14,15^2:16^2:18^2/4:2/Mt1:16/2
20/3:7f:7:11:14/4:15,16/5:4:6:9:10:19:28:32^2:3
:42^2:44:46/6:4:5:6:7,8:12:14,15:16:18/7:8^2:11:
13:15:21:24^2:26^2:29/8:4:5,6:22:27/9:9f:12^2:16:
17:20:32/10:2,3,4:22:26:28^2:40^2/11:2:5:6:16:25
28/12:6:7:30:48^2:50/13:12,13^2:12,13f:19:20:22
23:37:39:41:52/14:11:36/15:4:18:22:30:31^2:36/
16:13:15:25^2/17:22,23/18:4:5:6:7:21:23:24:28/
19:9:9f:12:13:25:29:30^2/20:11,12:23/21:9f:10:
41:44/22:1:11:18:23/23:12^2:21/25:1:7,8:10:14:
16:18:22:29^2/26:46:59:60,61^2:68:73/27:3:7:17f
52:55/28:5:11/Mk1:7:24:34:43,44/3:16-19:22:
33^2:35/4:14:15:16:18:20:25^2:41/5:16:18:25:30:
31:32^2/6:24:52/7:10/8:27:29:35:38/9:1:37^3:40:
42/10:15:24:24f:26:30:31^2:33/11:4,5:9:26,f:
27,28/12:4:18:27:28:41/13:13:22:34/14:18:65:
66,67/15:21:34f:41:42,43/16:6:9:12:13:14:16^2:
17/Lk1:1:1f:5:19:50:66:71:79/2:5:18:38/3:11:
16/4:18,19:22:27:32:34:40/5:14:21^2:31:32/6:
14,15,16:17,18:20:21^2:27:28^2:30:32:33:34:35:
47,48^2:49^2/7:12:19f:20,21,22:23:23f:24:25:29:3
:39:43:47:49/8:3:12:13:14:15:16:21:25:27:35:36
38:43,44:45:46/9:9:11:18:20:23:26:27:48^2:50:60
f:62/10:16^4:21:37/11:4:10^3:11:13:14:23:28:33:
45:47:51/12:4:5:9:10^2:14:20:21:37:38:48/13:4:
11:30^2:35/14:1^2:7:11^2:14:26:27:28:31/15:7^2/16
5,6:11:14:18^2:19/17:1:2,3/18:2:3:7:8:9:16,17^2:
26:29:43/19:24:26^2:27/20:34,35:39/22:3:11:21
22:24:26:52:63,64/23:14f:26:29:49:50,51,52/24
5:10:18:19:22,23:47/Jn1:9:11,12:13:15:21:22^2:
24,25:27:29:30:33/3:15:16:18^2:33,34:36^2/4:10:
28,29:33:34:46,47/5:10:11:12:15:24^2:25:29^2:30:
43:45/6:38:40:44:45:47:48-51:54:56:57^2:58:60:
63f:64^2:71/7:16:18:25:33:38:39:40:45:48:50/8:7
:16:18:19^2:25:26:29:30,31:50:50f:51:53^3:54/9:4:
8:17^3:21:22,23:24:31:32:36:39^2:40/10:1:6:8:9/
11:1^2:25^2:31:45:49/12:4:9:17:20:21:38^2:45:46:4
/13:10:11:16:18:20:24^2:25/14:7^2:9^2:10:17:21^2:
23:24^2:28/15:21/16:2:5:13/17:20/18:14:15:21:
37/19:11:12:23,24:35f:38:39/20:3,4f:29/21:4:20
/Act1:1:14:16:21,22:24,25/2:21:39:41:47/3:13:
21,22:23/4:4:22:34,35:37/5:1:9:11:32^2:36/6:1^2:

(WHO Con't)
5:6/7:17,18:27:35:38:40:47:52/8:2f:4:7:27:33:33
f^2/9:5:17:21^2:36:39/10:5,6:32:35:36,37:38:40,41
:43:45/11:11:12:17^2:19:20/13:16:21:23:26:31:39
:43/14:2:8:15/15:5:8:18:19:26:33:34,35/16:13:
16:38/17:4:17:23:32/18:2,3:7/19:13:15:18,19:
24:37/20:4:32:34/21:9:10:23:28:33:37,38/22:8:
19:25/24:5:19:22/25:19/26:15:18/27:43/28:30/
Rom1:3:16:17:18:25/2:2:7:7f:8:9:10:10f:12-15:
19:27:29/3:4:8:15:21,22:24:25:26/4:4,5:6:9^2:11^2
:12:14^2:17^2:18:24/5:6:14:17/7:1f:4:23,24,25/8:1
:5^2:8:10f:11:14:24:27:29^2:31:33^2:34^2:35:37/9:5:6
:8:20^2:22:23,24:25:31:33/10:4:11:12^2:13:15^2:16^2
:20/11:2,3:4:17:22:24^2:25:34^2:35/12:8:19/13:1:
2:3:12,13/14:1:3^4:6^2:22^2:23/15:1:3:5:13:21:26:
31:33/16:4:5:6:7:12:13:14:15:17:22:25,26,27^2/
1Co1:9:11:18^2:21:26:30/2:4:6:9:14^2:15:16f/3:1^2:
3:5^2:6:7^2:10:14/4:1:4:12^2:15/5:1:10:11:12^2/6:4:
5:8:9,10^2:12f/7:4:8:10:12:13:14^2:15:18:25:29:29f
:34^2:38^2/8:3^2:6^2:10/9:1:3:7:10:12:13:14^2:20/10:
16:18:20:27:28/11:5:19:22/12:3:4:6^2:10^3:11:28^6:
30/14:3:4:10:16:23:24:26:28:29,30:31:32:33:37/
15:11:18:20:22:27:28:29:33:34f:48:52^2:57/16:11
:16:19/2Co1:3,4:9:11:17:21/2:2:3:5,6:16^3:17/3:
1:6:13:17/4:1:2:3:4^2:4f:6:10:14:15/5:12:15^2:18:
21f/6:14:15/7:6^2:10:11:12/8:6:13:18:23^2/9:6:10
:11/10:2:6:12/11:2:12:13:26:29^4:31/12:21/13:2
/Gal1:1:6:7:8:12:17/2:4:6:7,8,9:12^2:20:21/3:7:
8,9^2:10^2:11:13:19:21,22:27/4:5:17:21:24,25:29^2/
5:7:8^2:10:12:24/6:1^2:6:12:13:16^2/Eph1:3:4:12:
13^2:16,17:18:19/2:2^2:10:17^2:21/3:9:20/4:1:6:10 ^{2}
:15,16:30/5:2:5:6^2/6:12:21:24/Php1:6/2:15/3:2
:5:11^2:15:17:18^2/4:13:19:22/Col1:7:8:12^2:14:16:
18:21:26,27:28/2:1:12:19/3:4:6:10:12:24:25/4:1
:10:15/1Th1:1/2:4^2:12/3:13/4:8:12:13:14:15^2:
16:17/5:8:12:14^3:18:20:24/2Th1:6:7:8^2/2:7:10:
16/3:6:10:14:15/1Ti1:3,4:9:10,11^2:17/2:2:14/3:
3:4:7:9:13:16/4:6:9,10^2/5:4:5:8:9:10:16:17^2:18/
6:4:9:13^2:16^2:17^2:20/2Ti1:9:10:14:15/2:2:4:6:13
:15:18:19^2:22:24:25/3:3:6:12^2:14/4:1:3/Tit1:4:5
:9:10^2:14:15/2:5:8:15/3:14/Phm1:1:17:23/Heb:
3:14/2:3:4:6:9:10:11:14:15:17/3:1^2:2:3:16^3:17^3:
18/4:2:3^2:6:14/5:7:9:12,13/6:12:18/7:3f:7:9:15:
23:25:28^2/8:6/9:9:15:16:17:28/10:1:28:29^2:30^2/
11:6^2:7:11:12/12:7:13:14:23:24:25^2/13:2:4:7:9:
10:20,21^2:24,25/Jas1:5:9:12^2:13:26:27^3/2:2:5:6:
7:10^2:11^2:13:15:19/3:1:9:18/4:4:12:13/5:6:7^2:11
:13:20/1Pe1:12:15:21/2:4^2:5:6:7^2:14^2:15:16:21:
23:25/3:5:9:12:20/4:6:9:17^2:19/5:5^3:10:12:13f:
14/2Pe1:1:9:20,21/2:1:4:5^2:10^2:11:15:18:19:22/
3:1:3:15,16/1Jn1:2^2/2:1^2:2:5:6:9:11:13:14^2:18^2:
21^2:22^2:23^2:26:29/3:3:4:6:8:9:10^2:12:14:15:17:
24/4:3^2:4^2:6:7:15:16:18:20/5:1:5:6,7,8f:9:10:13:
17f:18:20/2Jn1:7/3Jn:5:7:9:11^2/Jud:5:6:6f:11:
14:22^2:24,25^2/Rev:3:4:5^3:7:8^2:8f^2:9:12:13^2:17,18^3
/2:1:1f:2:6f:7^2:8^2:9:11^2:12:14:17^2:20:22f:23:
24,25:26^2:29/3:1:5:6:7:12:13:14:21:22/4:8:9/5:1
:2:12/6:9:17/7:2:13^2/9:1:4/10:6^2/11:7:10:17:18 ^{2}
/12:5:13:17/13:4:9:10:14:18/14:1:3:7:12:13f:14^2
:18:18f/15:2:3,4:6:7/16:2:5:6:9:15^2/17:1^2:7:8f:
12:16/18:8:9:15/19:2:4:5:9:10:11:20^3/20:4^3:6:
10:11/21:7:8^2:9/22:6,7^2:8:9:11:14:15^2:17^2:18

4026

WHOEVER
Ex19:12/29:30/32:33/Lev6:18f^2/18:29,30/24:
21^2/Ju1:12/10:18/Ru2:19/Job40:19/Pro8:35/
17:8/Dan5:7/Hos14:9^2/Mk10:43:44/Lk8:18^2/
9:24^2:48/17:33^2/20:18/Jn15:5/Rom2:29/1Co1:
2/Gal5:10/Heb12:7/1Jn2:10:17/3:10/5:12

37

WHOM
^{2}Gen6:4/10:13,14/21:12/22:2/45:4/48:9/49:10
f:10/Ex6:26:28,29/15:16/22:8:9/28:3/32:11/33
:12/Lev21:2,3/27:24/Num5:8/16:5:6,7:6,7f:14/
22:5,6^2/31:36-40/Deu9:1/18:15^2/21:8/28:36/
32:38/Jos24:4:15/Ru4:11/1Sa6:19/17:45/28:
11/2Sa3:18/6:22/19:8,9,10/23:1/1Ki5:5/11:23
/12:8/17:1:20/18:31f/21:26/2Ki10:1/19:22^2/
24:16/25:19/1Ch2:34,35:53/5:25/6:54/7:2:7:16
:23/15:24/26:31,32/29:1/2Ch22:7/Ez3:9/5:14/
8:33/Neh7:43,44,45/9:37/12:22/Est2:7/6:6/
Job5:17/15:17-19/Ps17:13,14/27:1/73:25/88:5
/94:1/Pro31:2/Ecc4:8/Is6:8/10:3/25:9^2/37:23 ^{2}
/40:25/41:2/42:1^2/45/46:5/51:1/53/Jer8:2/12
:16/14/20:6/22:13f:24,25/25:15/29:22/30:9f:9
/31:2/42:6/43/Lam2:20/3:52/4:20/Eze9:1/23:
37/32:29/38:13/Dan3:12/4:8/6:16:20/9:6:21/
Mic7:3/Zec3:8/Mal1:4/Mt8:12/11:27/12:18/
19:11/25:20/26:24/Mk14:21/16:9/Lk7:27/8:2 ^{2}
/9:9/10:22/12:5:48/16:31f/19:15/20:18/Jn3:8
/5:23/6:68/10:34,35,36/12:38f/13:22:26f/17:
12f/18:4,5:7/19:26f:36,37/20:2f:15/21:7f/Act3:
13/7:52/9:29/13:22/14:23/19:13/20:25/27:23^2
/Rom6:16/8:33/9:26/11:2,3/13:7/14:15/16:8:
10:13/1Co8:6f:11/10:19/15:6/2Co7:12/8:22/
Gal3:19/5:6/Eph1:7/4:30f/1Th1:10/2Th2:8/
1Ti1:9/2Ti:12/Tit3:6/Phm1:10/Heb:2^2/3:1:18
/4:13/10:14/11:7:9:18/Jas4:5/5:4/1Pe1:11:17/
5:13f/1Jn4:20/2Jn1:1/3Jn:1/Rev13:12

211

WHOSE
Gen24:23:40:47:62/31:36,37/32:17^2/44:16/Ex6
:15/23:27/35:21/Lev14:1:25/24:10^2/Num12:12
/20:14f/24:3-9:15-19/Deu2:12:29/4:44,45,46/
28:49/Jos1:1/12/17:3/Ju11:1/Ru2:12/1Sa10:
26/12:3/17:55f/2Sa20:1/21:16:19/1Ki4:8-19^{12}
/18:15/21:9f/2Ki8:1/9:36/17:34/18:22/1Ch2:
17:48,49/3:1/4:11,12/6:39-43/7:3/8:37/9:
35,36,37/11:22:23/24:29/28:18/2Ch16:9/23:8/
24:26^2/Neh7:64,65/11:21:22,23/Est2:7/Job3:
14,15/30:1/Ps7:10/10:3/17:13,14/32:1/33:12^2
/34:18/57:4/68:33/73:1/83:10/95/106:30/125:
4/144:12-15/146:5/Pro23:29,30/25:20/Ecc7:
26f/10:16,17^4/Is4:2,3,4/6:13/10:10/18:2:2f:7/
26:3/54:1/63:12/Jer5:15/9:24/31:30/Eze7:13/
9:5/17:16/23:9/31:16/40:3/Dan2:39f/4:19f:34:
37/6:25,26^2/9:26/12:1:2/Hos4:12f/13:8/Joe1:
8/Zep:13^2/Zec6:12/Mt5:8/21:23/22:20^2:28:42
/Mk1:7f/5:22/7:25/12:16:23/Lk6:6/8:14/11:
29,30/12:42,43,44/20:24^2:33/Jn4:46,47/5:45/6
:42/8:47/18:26/Act4:7/13:37/16:1/19:35/22:3
/25:14:24/26:18/Rom2:29/4:7:8/14:1f/1Co3:
14/8:9/9:22/2Co2:17/10:5/Php4:3/1Ti1:10,11
/3:2/5:3/2Ti4:8/Tit1:15/Phm:11/Heb8:1/10:
38/11:10/Jas2:7/Jud1:18/Rev2:18^2/6:8/9:11/
13:8:8f:12/17:8/20:11/21:27

192

WHY
Gen2:24/3:9/4:6^2/11:9/12:18:19/18:13^2:25/20:
6^2/21:26:28,29/24:31:33/26:9:27/27:32:45/29:
7/31:27:28:30:42/32:32/33:17/37:26,27/41:15/
42:1/43:6^2/44:4:8/47:15:19/Ex1:18/5:14:22/6:
30/13:8:15/14:11/15:23/16:22/17:3^2/18:14/32
:11/Lev10:17/14:57/17:14/18:25/Num6:5/11:
11:12/12:7,8/16:11,12/20:5^2/21/22:32:37/27:
3,4/31:15/Deu5:15/7:8/9:25/10:9/15:11:15/24
:18:22/29:24^2:27/Jos4:21/7:7^3:12^2:25/9:22:24/
17:14/22:16/Ju2:2/5:16:17^3:28^2/6:13/8:1/9:28 ^{2}
:38/11:7^2:12:23:26/12:1/14:3^2:16/15:10/16:6/
18:3/21/Ru1:8:21/2:20/1Sa1:8^2/2:29^2/4:3/5:5
/11/14:41/15:19^2/16:4/19:5:17/20:1:3:27:32/
21:1^2:2/22:8:13^3:14/24:9,10/25:40/26:15:17,18
:20/28:15:16/29:8/2Sa1:14/5:12/7:7:18:27/11:
10:19,20,21/12:9:23/13:4:26/14:13:31:32/16:9:
17:19/19:8,9,10:11,12:20:24,25:42^2:43/21:17/
22:25/24:3f:21/1Ki1:13:41/2:43/8:27/9:8:9/11:
22/14:6/17:20/19:13:20/20:23/21:5/22:15/2Ki
1:3:4,5:6:16/4:23/5:8/6:33/7:3/12:7/14:10/19:
11:25/1Ch11:7/14:2^2:11/21:3^2/2Ch6:18/7:21:
22/14:5/18:3,4,5/24:6:20/25:15/28:5/32:4/Ez
7:23/9:7/Neh2:1:3:16/6:3:5,6/13:11:17/Est3:
3,4/4:5/9:26/Job1:9/3:11:12^2:20,21:23/6:3:11:
22/7:19:20:21/10:2:18^2/13:24^2/15:6:15/19:3:
22^2/21:15/22:10,11:13/24:1^2:10/31:37/33:13/
34:9:31/37:16,17/38:2/Ps2:1f/10:1^2:13/17:6/
22:1^2/42:4,5^2:9^2/43:2^2:5/44:24^2/53:1/62:2:6/
66:15/73:13/74:1^2:11^2/78:19,20/79:10/88:14^2/
89:38^2/98:4/106:40:41,42/107:12/112:8/114:5:
6^2/115:2/119:140/130:5/144:3/Pro1:31/5:13^2:
16:17:20/12:28/13:19/20:24/21:6/22:26,27/23:
4,5/24:28,29/30:18,19f/Ecc4:8/6:11/7:15-17^2/
9:2,3/Sol6:13/Is1:5,6/5:4:25^2/8:19^2/9:17^2/17:
10/22:1/27:9/29:22/37:27/42:18^2:25^2/43:28/
44:19/45:4:10/47:11/48:5/50:1:2/52:5/55:2^2/
57:1:11/58:3^4/59:9/63:2:10:17:19/Jer2:4,5:14^2:
21:25:28:31/3:3/4:30/5:19/6:29/8:12:14:19:22^2
/9:12/12:1^2/13:22^2/14:1:8/16:10/17:15/20:18/
22:8^2:15^2/27:13^2/29:27/30:6:15/32:5:23/34:12
/35:11/38:27/40:2,3:15^2/44:7/46:15/49:1^2/50:
38/Lam1:3/3:39/5:20^2/Eze13:12^2/18:2:31/21:
7/33:11/34:22/39:23/Dan2:15/10:20,21/Hos4:
3:14/13:10/Joe2:12/Amo3:2/Ob1:10/Jon:9,10
/4:2:11/Mic1:5/6:3/Nah1:2/Hag:2:9:10/Zec7:
12/Mal1:9/2:14^2/3:6/Mt5:17/6:28:31,32/7:3/
8:26/9:4:11:14/13:10:12,13/14:2:31/15:2:3/16:
8/17:10:19/19:7/20:6/21:25/22:43/26:8,9:10/
27:8:23:46/Mk1:24:27:38/2:8:18/3:22/4:40/5:
27:39/7:5/8:12f:18^2/9:28/10:5^2:18/11:31/12:
35/14:4,5:6:11:49:63,64/15:3,4:14:34/Lk1:21:
45/2:48:49/3:7/4:23:43/5:22:33/6:41:46/8:47/
9:13/12:57/13:2:7/16:12/19:23:33/20:5:37,38:
41/22:53/23:22/24:5:38^2/Jn4:20:27/6:42/7:19 ^{2}
:21,22,23:45/8:24:43:46/9:2:27:30/10:20/11:
37,38:50/12:18:27:34/13:7:37/14:9:22/16:5/18
:21:35/20:13:15/Act1:11/3:12/4:25,26/8:36/9:
4/19:8:32/21:13/22:7:16:24/26:14/Rom1:26/2:
21/3:27/4:3/7:9/8:8/9:19:20:32/13:10/15:27/
1Co3:5/4:7:17/5:2/6:4:7:18/10:10:29:30:31/11:
4:5:28:30/15:12:29:30/2Co1:3,4:17/2:3/4:8:16/
5:2/6:17/8:21/11:11/Gal2:14/3:3:19/4:21/6:10
/Eph1:15/4:12/5:14/Col2:20/1Ti:13/2Ti1:12/
Heb2:11/3:19/5:5/7:11/9:18:23/10:5/11/13:6:
12/1Pe3:15/4:6/2Pe3:4:15,16/1Jn:12/4:6/Rev
7:15/17:7

638

WILL
Gen1:9,10:11,12/2:16,17^2:18/3:2,3:5^3:15^4:17:18
:19^3/4:7:12^2:14:15:24/5:28-31/6:3:7:9,10:12,13:
17:21/7:3:4^2/8:17:21^2:22/9:2,3:9,10,11:14:15^2:
16,17/11:3,4:6^2/12:1:2^3:2f^2:3^2:3f:11,12,13^2/13:
9/14:23/15:1^2:2,3:4^2:5:8:13:14^2:15:16^2/16:9-12^6
/17:2,3,4:5:6^2:7,8^3:11:13:16^2:19:20^2:21/18:10:
14:18:21:22,23:24:26:28^2:32/19:13:15:17:
18,19,20:31:32^2:34/20:4:7:11,12^2/21:12:13:18:
23/22:5:8:17^2/23:5,6:9^2:11:13/24:3:5:7^2:14^2:39:
40^2:43:44:46:49:58/25:23/26:3^2:4^2:5:24^3:29/27:
2,3,4:8,9,10:19:25:39,40^3:41^2:45/28:13:14^3:15^3:
20:21^2:22/29:32:34:35/30:3:13:15^2:20:31,32:33
/31:3:14:44^2:47,48:50:51,52^2/32:5:20:26/33:12:
13/34:9,10:11:12:15:16:17:22:23^3:30^2/35:3:11:
12^2/37:19,20:35/38:8:16:17^2/40:18,19^2/41:16:
27:29:30^3:31^2:36^2:40/42:15:20^2:33:34/43:8^2:14:
16/44:9:10:31^2/45:6^2:7:11,12^2:18:28/46:3,4^3:32
:34/47:5,6:16:19^3:25:29:31/48:4^2:5^2:9:21^2/49:1:
7:9:29,30/50:5:15:21:24^2/Ex1:10/2:9/3:12:13:
14f^2:18:19:20^3:21^2:22^2/4:5^2:8:9:12^2:14:15^3:16^2:
18:21^2:23/5:2:9:18/6:1^3:6:7:8,9/7:2:3^2:4:5:9^2:17
:18^3:19/8:2:3,4^5:5:8:9^2:10:11:16:21^3:22^3:23^2:26:
29/9:3:4^2:9:14:18:19:28:29^3:30/10:3:4,5^2:6^2:9^2:
10:12:14:21:26:29/11:1^4:4:6^2:7:8^2:9/12:2:12:13^3
:16:17:21:22:23^2:23f:25:27/13:9/14:3:4^2:13^3:14:
14f:16:17^4:26/15:1:2^2:9^2:16:17:26^2/16:4^2:6:7,8,9^2
:11,12^2:25:26:28,29^2/17:5,6^2:9:14:15,16/18:18:
19,20^2:21^3:22^2:23^2/19:5:8:9:11:21:24/20:5:7:12:
19^2:20:22:24/21:6:13:19:30:36/22:23:24^2:27/23
:7:7f:21:22:23:25^2:26^2:27:28:29:30:31^3:33/24:3/
25:9:16:22^3:26,27:32,33:34,35^2:39/26:9:12:
18,19:20:22:24:25:33:35/27:9,10^2:11:12:13:
14,15:16:18:19/28:2:3:7:12:18:19:20:21^2:28:29:
32:35^2:37,38^2/29:9:42:43:44:45/30:6:11,12:20/
32:5:10:13^2:29:30^2:32:33:34/33:1:2:3:12:13:14:
16:17:19^2:19f^3:22:23/34:1:10^2:11:12:24^2/35:32:
35/Lev1:2,3:4:5:6,7:9^2:9f:11^2:12^2:15,16,17^3:
15,16,17f/2:2:9/3:3,4,5/4:20:31/5:17,18/6:15:
16/7:3:5:17,18^3/8:8f:35/9:4:6/10:3^2:6^2:10/12:5:
7^2:8^3/13:5:6^2:16,17^2:50/14:36:48:57/16:13^2/17:
5:6^2:8,9:10^2/18:18:25:28^2/19:5:7:17/20:3:5:6^2:
22:22f:24/21:6/22:8:17,18:19:20:21:23/23:1:
9,10,11^2:13:20:30,31:35:36/24:3,4:5-8/25:11:
14,15,16^3:19:20:21,22^2:30:33^2:46:52/26:4,5^4:6^3:
7^2:8^2:9:10:11:12:13:14:16^4:17^4:18:19:21^2:22^2:23:
24^2:25^4:26^3:28:30^3:31^2:32:33:34,35^4:36^3:42^2:44:
45/27:14,15^2:19/Num2:1^2/3:7,8,9/4:3:5:6:8:14:
16:17,18,19:24:25:26:28:33/5:3:21,22:27^3:28/6:
9:27/8:2:11:14:19^4:25,26/10:3:5,6,7:9:10:29:31:
31f:32/11:15:17^4:19,20/14:3^2:8:10,11^2:12^2:13:
15:20,21:24:26,27:29:31:33:34,35:42:43/15:7:
23,24:40/16:5:6,7:16:17:30/17:5^3/18:1:5:27:32/
19:12^2:19/20:8:17^2:18:19^2/21:16:22:34/22:4:19:
34/23:3,4^3:13:18-24:27^2/24:3-9/25:4/27:17^2:20
:21^3/28:13:14:17:24/29:2:7:8:13/30:5^2:8:12/31:
22/32:14:15^2:16:17^2:18:20:22:23^2:25:27:31:32/
33:54^3:55:56/34:3^2:4^3:5:6:7,8,9^2:10,11^2/35:5:8^2:
12:22,23:33:34/36:3^2:4:7/Deu1:13:17:30:39:41:
42^2/2:4^2:5:9:19:25:27:28^2/3:1:21:22:27:28/4:5:6^2
:10^2:23:26^3:27^2:28:29:30:31:34:40^3/5:9,10^2:11:
25^2:26,27:31^2:33/6:1^2:2:3^3:18^3:19/7:1^2:10:12:13^3
:14:15^3:16:17:19:20:22^2:23^2:24^3:25/8:1^3:20/9:3^2
:5^2:13,14^2:28/11:9:13^3:14^2:15:17^4:21:23:24:25^2:
27/12:4,5:8:9:11:14^2:18:24,25:26,27^2:28:29/13:
5:11^2:17:18/14:29/15:4,5^2:6^2:7:9:10:11:18/16:
14:15^3:18:20/17:7:9:13^2:14:19:20^4/18:1:12:14:
15:17:18^2:19^2/19:1:6,7^2:10^2:13:19:20/20:4^2:9/
21:9:18:21^2/22:7:22:25,26,27/24:11:12,13:19/
25:6:8:13,14,15/26:4:12:19/28:1:2-6:7^2:8:9^2:10:
11:12^2:13^2:20^2:21:22^2:23^2:24:25^3:26^2:27^2:28:29^2
:30^3:31^4:32^3:33^3:34:35:36^2:37^2:38^2:39^2:40^2:41:
47,48^3:49:50:51^2:52^2:53:54:55:56,57^3:58,59:60:
61:62:63:64^2:65:66^4:67^3:68^3/29:9:18^2:20^3:21:22:
23:24:25/30:1^2:3^3:4:5:6^2:7,8:9^2:10:16^2:18:20/31:
3^2:4:5:6^2:8^3:12^2:13:16^2:17^4:18:21^2:23:27:29^3/32:
3:7:20:21:23:24^3:27:36^3:37:40,41^2:47:52^2/34:4/
Jos1:3:5^3:6:7:8^2:10,11:17,18/2:12,13:19:20:24/3

(WILL Con't)
:5:7[2]:10[2]:11:13,14[2]/4:6:7:24[2]/6:5:18:19/7:9[2]:12:
14[2]:25/8:5[2]:6[2]:7[2]:18/9:8:19:20/10:8:19/11:6/14
:12/17:16,17,18/18:4:5,6[3]/20:4/22:17,18:19:
24,25:26,27/23:4,5[2]:13[3]:14:15,16[4]/24:15[3]:19:20
:24:27/Ju1:2:3:12/2:3:21:22[2]/4:7[2]:9:18:22/5:30[2]
/6:14:16f[2]:16:37/7:2:5,6[2]:8,9:11/8:7:9:23,24/10
:18/11:8[2]:24:27/13:2,3:5:7:17:22/15:7/16:5:11:
20/17:10,11:13/18:5/19:9:12,13/20:8,9,10[3]:
27,28/21:7:17:22/Ru2:22/3:2:4:13[2]/4:4:12/1Sa
1:11[2]:21,22:23/2:3:9:30[2]:31[3]:32[4]:33:34[2]:35[3]:36[2]
/3:18/4:3[2]:9/5:5:7/6:3[2]:4,5:9[2]/7:3:5/8:9:11:12[3]:
13:14:15:16[2]:17:18[2]:20/9:5:16[2]:17:19/10:2[2]:3[4]:4
:5[2]:6[3]:7:8[2]/11:1:2:3[2]:7:9:10:12:13/12:3:10[2]:14[2]:
15:17[2]:22:23:25/13:14/14:6:9:10[3]:12:37:40:45/
15:29/16:2:3:10,11:15,16/17:8[2]:9:10:25[2]:26:37:
46[4]:47[2]/18:21/20:10:12:18:19:20:21:22/22:23/
23:4:11[3]:12[2]:17[2]:20[2]/24:4:9,10:12[3]:15:21/25:8:
19:28[2]/26:10[2]/27:1:12/28:2:5,6f:7,8:19[2]/30:8[2]:
15[2]:24/2Sa2:6:26/3:13:18:21[2]/5:19[2]:24[2]/6:22/
7:9[2]:10,11[3]:12[2]:13:14[2]:27/9:7:10,11[2]/10:11:12/
11:11/12[3]:12:18:22:28/13:13/14:7[2]:10:14[2]:14f:
15,16:17/15:10:14[2]:21:25,26:28:33,34[2]:35,36/
16:3:7,8:12[2]:19:21[2]:21f/17:2,3[4]:9[2]:10:11:13:16/
18:3[2]:26/19:7[2]:29:33:38/20:21[3]/21:4:5,6[2]/22:3:
4[2]:28/23:5:5f/24:2:3[2]:12:13:21:23:24[2]/1Ki1:2:
21:52/2:3:4[2]:6:9:17:31:32:36,37:42/3:12[2]:13[2]:14
:26/5:5:6[2]:8:9[3]/6:11,12:13/8:22,23:25:40:43[2]:58
/9:2,3:5:7[4]:8[3]:9/11:11:12,13[2]:31:32:34[2]:35:36:
37:38:39/12:26:27[2]:28/13:3[2]/14:2:3:10[3]:12:13[2]:
14[2]:15[2]:16/15:19/16:3:4-7[2]/17:8,9:13:14/18:1:5
:12[2]:15:23:24:37/20:5,6[2]:9:13[2]:14:25[2]:28:31:34/
21:10:18:21:29[3]/22:4:6:11:12:14:15[2]:20:22[3]:25:
28/2Ki1:3:4,5[2]:6[2]:16/2:5:10:16/3:6,7,8[2]:16:17[2]:
18:19/4:7:10:43[2]/5:5:8:16:17:20/6:3:8:19:32/7:
1:2:4[2]:9:12[2]:19/8:1:8,9[2]:10:12[2]/9:7:9:10:26/10:
5:18,19:30/13:16,17:19/16:15/17:39/18:14[2]:
20,21[2]:24:26:29:31,32/19:4:7[3]:19:29[3]:34/20:5[2]:
6[2]:8[2]:9:17[2]:18[2]:19/21:7:8[2]:12[2]:13[2]:14[2]/22:18,19
:20[3]/23:27[2]/1Ch14:10[2]:15/16:18:35/17:2:8:9[3]:
10[2]:11[2]:12:13[2]:14[2]:23:24/21:10,11:22[2]:24[2]/22:5
:9[4]:10[2]:13:19/23:4,5[3]:25:26/28:4:6:7:9[2]:20[2]:21[2]
/29:1:4,5[3]:19[2]/2Ch1:7:12/2:4:6:8:9[2]:10:14:16/6
:5,6:14:16:18:19:20,21:31[2]:33[3]/7:14[2]:15:18[2]:20[2]:
21[2]:22/10:4:7:14[2]/12:7[3]:8/13:12[2]/15:2[3]:7/16:3
/18:3,4,5:10:11:12:13:14:21[2]:29/19:6:10/20:9:
16:17[2]:20/21:14[2]:15[2]/23:2,3:4:5,6[2]/25:8/28:13[2]
/29:10/30:6:8:9[3]/32:11:17/33:7:8/34:24[2]:28/35
:4,5:21/Ez3:11/4:13[2]:16/6:3[2]:4[2]:10:11:12/7:17:
18/9:14/10:3[2]:4:12:14[4]/Neh1:8:9/2:5,6[2]:20[2]/4:
19/13:21:27/Est1:17:18[3]:20/2:3[2]/3:9:14/4:13:
14[2]:16[2]/5:3:6:7,8/6:13[2]/7:2:4:8/8:8f/9:12[2]:29-
29-31/Job1:8/2:4,5[2]/4:2:6/5:19:20:21:22:23/6:
24/8:2:10[2]:14:20:21/9:18:23:28:29/10:1:2:9/11:
7:16:17[2]:18[3]:19[2]/12:2:6:7,8,9/13:10:14:15f[2]:16:
20:22:25/15:17-19:21:29:31:32[2]:33/16:21/17:
3,4:16/18:6:7[2]:8,9:16:17[2]:18:19:20/19:25:27/20
:7:8:9:15:17:18:19:23:24:26[2]:27[2]:28/21:15:19:21
:28/22:20:21[3]:23:25:26:27[3]:28[2]:29[3]/23:10:14/
24:9:14,15[2]:20/27:5[2]:9:11:14:23/28:27/31:35/
32:17/33:3:25:26:27:28:33/34:31:32:34,35/35:4
:6:14,15/36:2:3:11:19[2]/38:22,23/39:9[2]:10:11[2]/
40:2/41:3:4:7:8[2]/42:4:8[2]:15/Ps2:7:8:12/3:2:7[2]/
4:2:3:6:8[2]/5:1:3:5:6:7[2]:8/6:9:10/7:12:17/9:1:2[2]:
3:6[2]:10/10:13:17:18[2]/11:6/12:3,4[3]:5[2]:7/13:1[2]:5:
6/16:4:7:10[2]/17:6:15[2]/18:49:50/20:8[2]/21:7:8:
9,10[2]:12:13/22:21:22[2]:23:25[2]/23:4:6/24:5/25:3:
9:12/27:2:3:5[2]:6:13:14[2]/28:5/29:11[2]/30:1:9:12/
31:19/32:5:6:8[2]/33:18,19/34:1[2]:2:10:21:22[2]/35:
3:9:17:18:25:28[2]/36:10:12/37:3:4:5:6[2]:10:15[2]:19
:20:28[2]:33:34[2]/39:4:8:9/40:3:8/41:7/42:6:11/43
:4:5/45:1:12:16:17[2]/46:5:10/47:4/48:11:14/49:
4:13:14:15[2]:17/50:6:23/51:13[2]:14,15[3]:17:19:19f
/52:4:5:6[3]:9[2]/53:5[2]/54:6/55:16[2]:17[2]:18:19:22[2]:
23[2]/56:3,4[2]:12/57:1:2:3[2]:9[2]/58[2]:11/59:7:9:10[2]:
12,13:16/60:4,5:8:9,10[2]:12/61:2:6:8/63:4:5:11/
64:5:7[2]:8[2]:9/65:1:5:5f:9/66:7:16/67:3:4[2]:6,7[2]/
68:18:21:22f:23:31[2]/69:30[2]:31:32:35/71:14:15:
20:21:22:23:24/72:10:11[2]:12:13:14:15[3]:17[4]/73:
18:20:24:24f:27:28/74:9,10[3]/75:2:10/76[2]/77:7/
78:2,3:4:57/79:5[2]:6:13/80:4:18/81:6[2]:8:10/82:2[2]
:7/83:4/84:6:7:11/85:4:5:8:9/86:7[2]:9:11:12[2]:17/
87:5[2]:6/88:10:13/89:1:5:21:23:24[2]:25:26:27:28[2]:
29[2]:30,31,32:33:34[2]:35,36[2]:46[3]:48/90:13/91:4[2]:
7:8[2]:12:14[2]:15[2]:16/92:14/94:15[2]:16[2]:20:23[2]/96:
10:13/101:1[2]:2:4:5[2]:6:7:8/102:12:13:16[2]:17:18:
26[2]:28[2]/103:2:7/104:33[2]:35/105:10,11/106:31/
107:42/108:1:2:3:9/109:27:28:30/110:1:2f:4:5:6[2]
/112:3:4:6[2]:7:9:10[2]/115:12[2]:15/116:2:10,11:13:
14:16:17:18,19/118:7:10:11:19:24/119:2:6[2]:7:8:
15:16:23:32[3]:33,34:40,41,42:44,45,46[3]:48:62:74:
78:79:80:82:93:95:101:106:109:110:133:145:152
:157:164:172:173:175[2]/121:3,4/127:2/132:7[2]:7f[2]
:9:11:12:15:16/135:14/138:1:7[3]:8/139:10[2]:19/
140:12[2]/141:5:6,7/142:4:7/143:10:11/144:9:10
/145:1:5:6:7:10:11:12:21/146:2:10/148:6/149:
4,5/Pro1:4:7,8,9[2]:19:22[2]:26:28[2]:32/2:1:3,4,5[2]:
10:11,12,13:19/3:6:7,8:9,10/4:4:6[2]:8,9[3]:10:13:
22/5:23/6:9:15:22:24:26:34[2]/8:13/9:7,8[4]:9[2]:11/
10:3[2]:9:24[2]/11:21[2]:27[2]:29/12:13/13:18:24/14:9
:11[2]:33/15:9,10[2]:27f:31,32:33/16:3:10:14/17:2:
5:8:11f/18:16:21/19:8:18:25[2]/20:5:6:13[2]:17/21:
6:13:16:18[2]:29/22:5:6:8:10:15:17,18,19:22,23/
23:6,7,8[2]:9:10,11:13,14:15,16[2]:33[2]:34:35/24:
11,12:15,16:19,20:21,22[2]:34/25:4,5:15:16:17:
21,22[2]/26:2:4,5:8:9[2]:24,25,26:27[2]/27:11[2]:14:
25,26,27/28:8:16[2]:17:18[2]:20[2]:27/29:1:12:16:17:
21/30:18,19f/31:11:12/Ecc1:8-11/2:15[2]:16:19[2]
/3:17:18:22/4:8/5:4:5:19,20/6:12/7:14:23/8:5[2]:
12:13/9:1[2]:5:16[2]/10:1:4:8,9:20/11:1:4:6[2]/12:2:3[5]
:4[2]:5:14/Sol1:4:7[2]/4:6:8/6:1/7:8:12/8:9[2]:12/Is
1:5,6:15:19[3]:20:24:25:26:29[2]:30:31[2]/2:2[2]:3[4]:4[4]:9
:11[2]:12:17[3]:18:19:20/3:1:2:4:5:6:7:8[2]:14:15:16:
17[2]:18:24[3]/4:1[3]:2,3,4[3]:5/5:1:5:6:9:10[2]:13[3]:17[2]:
24[3]:25[2]:26[2]/6:8:11:13[2]/7:3:6:7:8[3]:9:11:14:15,16:
15,16f:17[3]:18:19:20:21,22[5]:23:24:25[3]/8:1[2]:1f:4:
7,8[3]:9,10[2]:14,15:17:18[2]:21[2]:22[2]/9:1[2]:2:3:4:5[2]:6:7[3]
:8,9,10[2]:11,12[3]:13:14,15:18[2]:19,20[2]/10:3[3]:4[4]:5,6
:7[2]:8[2]:9[4]:11:12:16:17[3]:18[2]:19:20:21:22:25[3]:26:27[2]
:34/11:1[2]:3[2]:4[2]:5:6[3]:7[3]:8[2]:9:10[3]:11:12[2]:13[2]:14[2]:
15:16/12:1:2:4/13:5:10[2]:11[2]:12[2]:13[2]:14:15:16[2]:
17[2]:18:19:20[4]:21[4]:22[2]/14:1[3]:2[3]:4:8:13[3]:13f:14:
15:16:20[2]:22:23[2]:26:29[2]:30[2]:32/15:1:5:9[2]/16:4,5[3]
:7:10:11[2]:12[4]:13,14/17:3[2]:4:5:6[2]:7:8[3]:9:11[3]:13[2]/
18:4:5[2]:6[3]:7[2]/19:2:4:5[2]:7[3]:8[2]:9[2]:10:11[2]:16:17:18[3]
:19:20[2]:21[3]:22[3]:23[2]:24[3]:25[2]/20:3:4:5,6[2]/21:2[3]:
13:16:17/22:9,10,11:14:17:18[2]:19:20:21:22[3]:
23,24[3]:25[3]/23:5:12[3]:13[2]:15,16[3]:17[3]:18[3]/24:2:3:6
:7[4]:14[2]:15,16:18[2]:20:21:22:23[3]/25:1:2:3[2]:5:6:7:8[3]
:9:10[2]:11[2]:12/26:1:3:8:9:11[2]:14:19:21[2]/27:1:3:
4,5:6[2]:9:10:11:12[2]:13[2]/28:2[2]:3:4:5:6:11[2]:13[2]:15:
17[4]:18[2]:19[2]:21/29:2[2]:3[2]:4:5:6:7:8:14:16:17[2]:18[2]:
19:20[3]:22:23:24[2]/30:3:5:6:8:9:13:14[3]:15:16[2]:17[3]:
18:19[2]:20[2]:21:22:23:24:25:26[2]:28:29[2]:32:33/31:
2[3]:3[2]:4,5[4]:7[2]:8[4]:9/32:2[2]:3[2]:4[2]:5[2]:6[3]:7[2]:8[2]:9:10[2]:
12:13[2]:14[2]:15:16:17:18:19:20[3]/33:1:4:5:10:11[2]:
12:15:16[3]:17:18[2]:19[2]:20:21:22:23[2]:24[2]/34:2:3[3]:4[2]
:5:6:7[2]:9[2]:10[4]:11[3]:12[2]:13[3]:14[4]:15[2]:16[4]/35:1[2]:2[3]:5
:6[3]:7[2]:8[3]:9[3]:10[3]/36:4:6:8,9:11:12[2]:14:16:18/37:4
:7[3]:10:11:20:30[4]:31:32:34[2]:35/38:1:5:6[2]:8:11[2]:20
:21:22[2]/39:6[2]:7:8/40:2:5:10:11[2]:20:25:30/41:9:
10[3]:11:12[2]:14:17[2]:18[3]:19:20:23:25[3]/42:1:2[2]:3[3]:4
f:6:6f:7:8[2]:9[2]:13[2]:14[2]:15[2]:16[3]:17[2]:25/43:2[4]:5:6:7:
10:14[3]:19:20:21:25/44:2:3[2]:11[2]:21:26:28[2]/45:2:
3[2]:5:6:13:23/46:4[3]:6:10:11[3]:13/47:1:3[2]:4:5:11/
48:6:9:11[2]:14[2]:15/49:2:6:8,9[3]:10[2]:11:13:15:18:
21:22:25[2]:26/50:4:7[3]:8:11/51:3[3]:4:5:6:11[3]:13:23
/52:1:6[2]:12[2]/53:1[2]:12/54:3[2]:4[2]:5:7:8:9:10:11:12:
14[3]:15[2]:17/55:5[2]:7:12[2]:13[3]/56:3:5[3]:7[2]:8:12/57:
14:16:18[2]:19/58:4:8[5]:9[2]:10:11[2]:12[2]:14[2]/59:2:18:
19[2]:20/60:2:3[2]:5[3]:6:7:10[3]:11[2]:12f:12:13[2]:14[3]:15[2]
:16:17:18[3]:19[3]:20[2]:21[4]:22/61:3:8:11[2]/62:1:2:3:4[2]
:5[2]:8:11/63:7[3]:8/64:12/65:6[3]:7:8[3]:9[2]:12:15:16[2]:
17:18:19:20[3]:21,22[6]:23[2]:24[2]/66:2:3:4:12[2]:13:14[3]
:15:16:17:18:19[2]:20:21/Jer1:7:8:10:12:14:16:17:
18:19[3]/2:9[3]:19[2]:30:32:35:36:37[2]/3:4,5:12:14:15[2]
:16[3]:17[3]:18:22[2]/4:1:2[3]:3:4[2]:7:9[2]:11,12[2]:27:28:30[2]
/5:3:5:6:12[2]:13:15:18/6:8:10:11:12:16:17:18,19[3]
:21:26/7:3:4:7:8:13,14[2]:15:16:20[2]:23:27:32[3]:34/
8:3:9:10:12[2]:13[3]:14:17[2]/9:7[2]:11:15:16:22:25,26/
10:15:17:20:21/11:8:11:12:14:19:21,22:23/12:5[2]
:9:14[2]:15[2]:17/13:8,9:12[3]:13:14[2]:16:17:21[2]:24,25:
26:27/14:10[2]:12[3]:13[3]:15:16[2]:19[3]:22/15:3:4[2]:5[3]:6
:7[2]:8[2]:12,13[2]:14:17,18:19:20[2]:21/16:9:13[2]:14,15[5]
:16:18:19:21:21f/17:2,3:4[2]:11[2]:27[2]/18:2:8:9:10:
12:16:17[2]/19:3[2]:7[2]:8[2]:9:11:12[3]:13:15/20:4[3]:5:10[3]
:13/21:1:3,4[2]:5:6:7:10:13:14[3]/22:4:6:7[2]:8:9:10:
14:18[2]:22:23:24,25f:26:27:28:30/23:1:2:3:4:5,6[3]:
7:8:12[3]:15:20[2]:26:34:38,39[2]:40/24:6[4]:7[2]:8:9:10/
25:8,9[3]:10:11:12[2]:13:14:29:30[2]:31[2]:35:37/26:3:4
:5:6[2]:9:13:15[2]:19/27:8[2]:9:10:11:13:14:16:17:18:
22[3]/28:3:4[2]:6:11:14:16/29:5:7:10[2]:12:13:14[2]:
16,17:18[2]:22:28[2]:32/30:3[2]:7:8:9:10:11[4]:17:18[2]:
19[2]:20:21[3]:22:24[2]/31:2:4[2]:5:6:7:8[2]:9:10:11:13[5]:
14[2]:16[2]:17:20:22[2]:27[2]:28:31[2]:33[3]:34[2]:37/32:6,7:
15[3]:25:28:36:37[3]:38:39:40[2]:41[2]:42:43:44/33:3:5[2]
:6[2]:7:8:9[4]:10,11[3]:12:13:14[2]:15:16:20,21:22:25,26[3]
/34:2:5[3]:17[3]:18,19[2]:20[2]:21:22[3]/35:17:18,19/36:
3[2]:6:7:31[2]/38:4:9:15:17[2]:18:19[2]:20[3]:21,22[2]:23[4]/
39:16[2]:17:18/40:4:9:10[2]:15/42:4[3]:6[2]:10[2]:12[3]:
13,14[2]:16[2]:17[3]:18[4]:20[2]:21:22/43:2,3:10[2]:12/44:
11:12[2]:13:16:17[2]:25:26:27[2]:28:29[2]:30/45:4[2]:5[2]/
46:6:8:10:12:16:25[2]:26:27:28[3]/47:2[3]:4:5[2]:6/48:
2,3,4[4]:5:12:38:44:47/49:2:4:5:6:8:9,10[4]:11:15:16
:17[2]:18[2]:19[3]:20[3]:22[4]:27:28:29[3]:32[2]:35:36:37[2]:38[2]
:39/50:2[2]:5[2]:9:18:19:20:21:25:28[2]:30[2]:32[4]:34:38:
40[2]:44[4]/51:1:6:12:18:20:21:24:25:29:33:36[4]:39:
40:44:46[2]:47:52:57:61,62[3]/Lam1:21[2]/3:8:20:24:
31:32/4:15:21:22/Eze2:1:5/3:11:18[3]:19:20:22:
25:26:27/4:3:4,5:6:7:8:8f:16[4]:17/5:2:5,6,7:8:9[2]:
10[3]:11:12[3]:13[2]:14:15:16[2]:17[4]/6:3:4-7[4]:8:9[4]:10:
12[4]:13:14[2]/7:3:4[2]:5,6:8,9[3]:10,11[2]:12:13[3]:15:16:
19[2]:20:21:22[3]:23:24:25:26,27[5]/8:6:13:15:18[3]/9:
8:10[2]/11:3:7[3]:7f:8:9[2]:10[2]:11[2]:12:16:17:18:19[2]:20
:21/12:3[2]:6:13:14:16[2]:23[2]:24:25[2]:28/13:8:9[2]:10:
11[3]:12:13[2]:14[2]:15[2]:16:18f:19:20[2]:21[2]:23[3]/14:4:5
:6,7:8:9[2]:10:11:13:22[2]:23/15:7[2]:8/16:37[2]:38:39[2]:
40,41[2]:42[3]:43:44:53:54[2]:55[2]:59,60[3]:61[3]:62[2]:63[2]/
17:9[3]:10[2]:12,13:15[2]:16:19:20[2]:21[3]:22,23[4]:24/18:
3:4:20:22:24:30:31/20:3:8:13:21:31:32:33:34:
35,36[2]:37:38[3]:40:41[2]:42:43:44:47[4]:48/21:3:4[2]:5:
7[5]:9,10,11:13:16:17:21[3]:22[3]:23[2]:27[3]:29[2]:30:31[2]:
32[2]/22:4:5:14[2]:15:16:18,19,20:21:22[2]:31[2]/23:22
:23:24[3]:25[4]:26:27[2]:28:29:31:32[2]:33:34[2]:43:45[2]:
47[2]:48[2]:49[3]/24:9:14:16:20,21[2]:22:23:24[2]:26:27[2]
/25:4[3]:5[2]:7[3]:9,10[4]:11:13[2]:14:16[2]:17/26:3:4[2]:7:8[2]
:9:10[2]:11[3]:12[2]:13[2]:14[2]:15[2]:19[2]:20[3]:21[2]/28:8:9[2]:
10:22:23[2]:25[3]:26/29:4:5:8:9:10:11[2]:12[3]:13[2]:14[2]:
15[3]:16[3]:19[2]:21[3]/30:8:9[2]:10:12[2]:13[2]:15[2]:16[4]:17:
18[3]:19:22[2]:23:24[2]:25:26/31:11[2]:12[3]:13[2]:14:18[2]/
32:3[2]:4[2]:5:6:7[3]:8[2]:9:12[3]:13[2]:14:19:20[2]:21:28:31/
33:6[2]:8[3]:9[2]:11:12[2]:13[3]:14:20:28[2]:33[2]/34:9,10[3]:
11:12[2]:13[2]:14[2]:15,16[5]:17:20:22[3]:23:24:25:26[2]:27[2]
:28:29:29f:29:30/35:3:4,5:6:7:8[2]:9[3]:10:11[3]:14:15[3]
/36:8[3]:9:10[2]:11[3]:12[3]:14[3]:15[2]:23[2]:24:25[3]:26[3]:27[2]:
28:29[2]:30[2]:31:32:33:34:35:36[2]:37,38[3]/37:6[2]:12:
13:14[2]:18,19,20:23:26[2]:27[2]/38:4[2]:8[3]:9:10:11[2]:12[2]
:13:14:15,16[5]:18:21[2]:22:23[2]/39:2[2]:3:4[2]:5[2]:6:7[2]:8[2]
:9:10[3]:11[4]:12:13[2]:14[2]:15,16[3]:21:22:23:25:26[2]:27[2]
:28[2]:29[2]/43:7:9:10:20:27[2]/44:24:30/45:4:6:20:
21:23[2]/46:16/47:8:9[3]:10[3]:11[2]:12[5]:14:15:17:18[2]:
19:20/48:9:12:13:30,31[2]:32:33:34:35/Dan1:10[2]
/2:6:16:24:25:28:39[3]:40:41,42[2]:43[2]:44[4]:45/3:6:
11:15[2]:16:17:18/4:24:25[3]:26:27:32/5:7:12:16:17
:28/6:8:12/7:14:17:23[3]:24[3]:25[2]:26/8:13:17:22:
24[3]:25[5]:26/9:24[4]:25[2]:26[4]:27[3]/10:14:20,21[2]/11:2[3]
:3[2]:4[2]:5[2]:6[4]:7:8[2]:9[2]:10,11[3]:12[2]:13:14[3]:15[2]:16[3]:17[3]
:18[2]:19[2]:20[2]:21[2]:22:23[3]:24[4]:25[3]:26[2]:27[2]:28:29[2]:
30,31[4]:32:33[2]:34[2]:35[2]:36:37[2]:38:39[2]:40[3]:41[2]:42:
43:44[2]:45[3]/12:1[3]:2:3:4:6:7:8:10[2]:11:13/Hos1:2[2]:
4,5:6:7[2]:10[3]:11[5]:3:4:6:7[3]:9[2]:10[2]:11:12[2]:13:14:15[2]
:16:16f:17[2]:18[4]:19:20[2]:21,22:23[4]/3:3:4:5/4[3]:6:9:
10/5:2:5:6[3]:7:9:10:11:12[2]:13:14[2]:15[2]/6:1[2]:2:3:5/
7:12:16[2]/8:3:5:6:7[2]:10[2]:13:14/9:2[2]:3:5:6[5]:7:9:11:
12[2]:14:15[2]:16:17[3]/10:2:3:4:6[3]:8[3]:10[2]:11:12:14:
15/11:6[2]:9[2]:11[2]/12:2:9:14/13:7:8[2]:14:15[3]:16/14
:2:3:4[3]:5[2]:6:7[2]:9/Joe1:4[2]:16[2]/2:2:14[2]:17[2]:18:19[2]:
20[4]:22[3]:23:24:25:26[2]:27:28[3]:29:31:32[2]/3:2:4:7[2]:
8[2]:12:15:16:17[2]:18[3]:19:20[2]:21[2]/Amo1:3[2]:4:5:6[2]:
7:8[2]:9[2]:10[2]:11[2]:12[2]:13[2]:14[3]:15/2:1[2]:2[2]:3:4[2]:5:6[2]:
13:14[2]:15:16/3:11:12[2]:14[2]:15/4:2[3]:3:12/5:2:3[2]:5
:6:11:13:14:15:16:17[2]:18[3]:19:20:22[2]:23:25,26,27
/6:7[2]:8:9:10[4]:14[2]/7:8[2]:9[2]:10:11[2]:17[4]/8:2:3[3]:8[3]:9:
10[4]:11:12[2]:13/9:1[2]:2[2]:3[2]:4[2]:8[2]:9:10[2]:11:12:13[4]:
14:15/Ob1:2:4:6:7[4]:8[2]:9:10[2]:15[3]:16:17[2]:18[2]:21/
Jon1:6:12/2:9[2]/3:4,5:9[2]/Mic1:6[2]:7[2]:8[2]:15[2]:16/2
:3[2]:4:5[2]:6:10:12[2]:13[2]/3:4:5:6[4]:7:12[2]/4:1[2]:2[5]:3[5]:4[2]
:5:6:8:10[2]:12[2]:13[3]/5:2:3[2]:4:5[2]:6[2]:7:8[2]:9[2]:10:12[2]:
13:14:15/6:2:13[2]:14[3]:15[3]:16[4]/7:4:6:7:8[2]:9[4]:10:
11:12:13f:15:16[3]:17[4]:19[3]:20[2]/Nah1:9:12:13:14[3]:
15[2]/2:2:13[2]/3:5:6:7:11:12[2]:13[2]:15[3]:17:19/Hab1:
2:5[2]:6:13:16:17[2]/2:1[2]:3[3]:6[2]:7:8:13:14:16:17[2]/3:
16:18[2]:19/Zep1:2[2]:3[3]:4[3]:5:6:8:9:10:11:12[2]:13[4]:
14:17[3]:18[3]/2:3:4:5:6:7[3]:9[2]:10:11[2]:12:13[2]:14[6]:15/
3:7[2]:8:9:9f:10:11[4]:12[2]:13[3]:15[3]:16:17,18[3]:19[3]:20[2]
/Hag1:8:13/2:6:7:7f[2]:7:8,9[2]:12:18,19[2]:22[2]:23/
Zec1:3:12:16[2]:17[2]/2:4[3]:5[2]:6,7:9[3]:11,12[3]/3:7[3]:8:9[2]
:9f:9:10[2]/4:6:7[2]:7f:9[2]/5:11/6:6[2]:6f:6:10,11[2]:12[2]:
12f:12:13:15[3]/8:3:4[2]:5:7:8[3]:8f:12[4]:14,15:19:
20,21[2]:22:23/9:4:5[6]:6:7[3]:8[3]:10:12:13:15[4]:16,17[3]
/10:1[2]:3[2]:4:5:6[4]:8:9[2]:10[2]:11[3]:12[3]/11:1:5:6[3]:16[3]:
17[2]/12:2:3[2]:4[2]:6[2]:7:8[3]:10[2]:11:12,13,14[3]/13:1:2[3]:
3[2]:4[2]:5:6:7[2]:8[2]:9[5]/14:1[4]:3:4[3]:5[3]:6:7[3]:8:9:10[2]:12[4]:
13[2]:14[2]:15:16:17:18:19:20[2]:21/Mal1:4[3]:5:10:11[2]
/2:1[2]:3[2]:4:7/3:1[2]:3[3]:4:5[2]:7:8:10[2]:11[2]:12[2]:17:18/
4:1[2]:2[2]:3:5/Mt1:21[2]:22/3:3:10:12/4:3:6[2]:9:19/5
:13[2]:15,16:18:26:37:45/6:1:2:4:5:6:10[2]:14,15[2]:16[2]
:18[2]:20:21:22:24:27:33:34/7:2:6:7[3]:8[2]:9:10:15:22
:23:27/8:7:8,9[3]:19:21/9:15:18:21:29/10:15:17:
18:19:20:23:25:26[2]:32:33:36:39[2]:41[2]:42/11:11:
22:24:28/12:18[2]:20:29f:37[2]:39,40:43,44,45/13:
12,13[4]:30:34,35[2]:41[2]:49[2]/15:13,14:32/16:4:18:
19:28/17:22,23[2]:26,27/18:3:12:13:14:18:19:20:

(WILL Con't)
29/**19**:21:27:30^2/**20**:18^2:19^3:21:23/**21**:2:3:21:25:
30:31:40:41^2:43:44/**22**:28:40/**23**:26:34^2:35:39/
24:2:3^2:5^2:7^2:8:9:11:12^2:14^3:20:21^2:22^2:24:28:29^4
:30^3:34:35:36:37,38:40^2:41^2:47:50:51/**25**:21:23:
32:37:40:41:44:45/**26**:11:13^2:15:18:20,21:29:31^3
:32:34:39:41:42:52:64:75/**27**:49:63/**28**:14/**Mk1**:
3^2:8:17:43,44/**2**:20^2/**3**:24:35/**4**:11,12:13:22:24/
5:28/**6**:22,23/**7**:3/**8**:11:35^2:38/**9**:1:5:30,31:39:39
f/**10**:15:30:31:33^2:34^2/**11**:2:3:22,23:25:26,f:31:
32/**12**:7^2:9^2:23:25:26:40/**13**:2:3,4:6^2:7:8^2:9^2:11^2:
12^3:13:18:19^2:20^2:22^2:24^2:25^2:26:27:30:32:33:34
f:35,36,37/**14**:2:9:13:14:15:18:27^3:28:29:30:36:
44:58^2:62:72/**15**:36/**16**:7:16^2:17f:18^2/**Lk1**:13:14^2
:15^2:16:17^4:20:31:35:66:76:77:78/**2**:12^2:32^2:
34,35/**3**:9:16:17/**4**:6,7^2:9,10,11:23/**5**:4:12:13:14:
35^2:36^2/**6**:21:23^2:34:35^2:37^2:38^3:39/**7**:6,7,8^2/**9**:
22:24^2:26:27:51:57:61/**10**:6^2:12:14:15/**11**:8:9^3:
13:29,30^2:36:49^2:50:51/**12**:2:8:9:12:20:25:28:29:
31^2:33^2:34:36:37^2:38:40:42,43,44^2:46:47:48:52:
53^3:55/**13**:3:5:23:24,25^3:26:27:28:29:30^2:32^2:35
/**14**:9^2:10^2:12:14:23:24:32/**15**:7:18/**16**:9:9f:11:
13^2:30/**17**:1:20:22:23:24^2:26:28:30:34^2:35,36^3:
37:37f/**18**:7:8^2:16,17:22:30:31:32:33/**19**:8^2:40:
43:44/**20**:5:6:13:14^2:15:16:18:28:33/**21**:6^3:7:8:8f
:11:12^2:13:15^2:16^2:17:18:19:20:22^2:23:24:25^2:26^2
/**22**:10:12:18:21:26:30:34:37^2:40:41,42:46:61/**23**
:16:22:29:30:31:31f:43/**24**:49/**Jn1**:13:27:50:51/
2:17:19^2/**3**:8^2:13:15:28:29^2/**4**:21-24:25^2:34:35:
36^2/**5**:20:21:23:24:30:34:45^2/**6**:29:35^2:37^2:38:39
:40:44:45:54:62:63/**7**:6:17^2:24:27^2:34:40:41,42^2:
52/**8**:12:21:24^2:28:32^2:36:52/**9**:31/**10**:5:9^2:12^2:
16^2:38/**11**:4:11:15:22^2:23:39:40:42:48^2:56/**12**:15
:23,24^2:25^2:26:28:32:34:35^2:36:38^2:46:48/**13**:7:
18^2:19:21:31:35:36:38/**14**:2,3:8:12,13^3:14:15,16^3
:18^2:19^4:20:21^3:23^2:26:28^2:29:31^2/**15**:7:11^2:16:
20:21:26^3/**16**:2^2:4:7^2:8:8f:13^3:15:16^3:20^2:21:22^2:
23:24^2:25^3:26:28:32^2:33^2/**17**:11:20:21^3:23^2:26/
20:15:30,31^2/**21**:18^2:20:21/**Act1**:8:11/**2**:17:19:
26:27:28/**3**:21,22^2:23/**4**:28/**5**:9:38:39/**6**:3:14/**7**:
7^2:34:37:40:43/**8**:19:22:33f/**9**:16/**10**:43/**11**:14/
13:10:11:22:34:35:36:46/**15**:16:17:26/**16**:31/**18**:
6/**19**:27^2/**20**:25:29:30/**21**:14:22:24/**22**:10:14:21
/**23**:15:30:35/**24**:12:15:21/**26**:17/**27**:22^2:24^2:25:
26:31/**28**:4:26:28,29/**Rom1**:5:10f:10:10f:11,12^2:
17:20/**2**:2:3:5:6:7^2:8^2:9:10:12-15^3:16^2:27:27f:29/
3:2:3:4:5:21,22/**4**:17:24/**5**:9^2:17/**6**:8:9:14f:16^2/**7**
:22:23,24,25:23,24,25f/**8**:7:10^2:10f:11:13:17:18:
19:20,21^3:23^3:24:27:33:34^2:39/**9**:4:9:15^2:25^2:28:
33^2/**10**:9:11:13:15/**11**:12:15^2:16^2:22:23:24:25^3:
26:27:29:31/**12**:2^2:14:19:20^2/**13**:2:3^2:4:8:9:12,13
/**14**:2:10:12:13:16:18^2/**15**:4^2:7:9:12^2:13^2:21:24:
28:29:30:31^2:32^2/**16**:1:20:25,26,27/**1Co1**:7:8:9:
19/**3**:8:13:14:15^2:17/**4**:5^3:8:17:18:19^2/**5**:3,4^2:5:6
/**6**:3:9,10^2:13/**7**:16:25^2:28:31:35:40/**8**:10^2:11/**9**:
17:20:22/**10**:13^2/**11**:19:31:32/**12**:2/**13**:5:7^2:8^2:
10^2:12/**14**:2^3:6:7:8:9:11^2:12:15^3:17:24^2:25^2:26^2:
31:36:38/**15**:12:20:22:23:24^2:25:28^2:29^2:32:33:
35^2:36:42:43^2:44:48:52^4:53:54:55,56^2/**16**:3^2:5:6:
7:8:12^2:21/**2Co1**:5:6,7^2:11:13,14/**2**:3^2/**3**:4:12/**4**:
2:14:17:18^2/**5**:1^2:4:8:10/**6**:3:16^2:17:18/**8**:14:19:
20/**9**:6^3:8:9:10^2:11^2:13^2:14/**10**:1:6:9:10:13:15^2:
16^2/**11**:1:2:3:8,9,10:12:15/**12**:7:20^2:21^2/**13**:2:3:7^2
:9/**Gal1**:9/**2**:16/**3**:3:8,9:11/**4**:17:19/**5**:10:16:19:
20:21:22/**6**:4:7:8^3:9:11/**Eph1**:10:14:18:19/**3**:6:
16:17:18,19^2/**4**:12:14:15,16:29:30/**5**:5/**6**:3:6,7:8:
11:13:14:16:17:20:21/**Php1**:6:9:11:16,17:20^4:
22:25:26:27:28^2/**2**:16:17^2:19:28^2/**3**:11:12:15^2:21^2
/**4**:7^2:9:17:19/**Col1**:10^2:11:28/**2**:2^2/**3**:4:14:25/**4**:
3:4:6:7:9:12:16/**1Th2**:13:19/**3**:13/**4**:3,4,6^2:12^2:
13:14:15:16^2:17/**5**:2:3^3:18:24/**2Th1**:7:9:10:11^2:
12^2/**2**:3^3:4^2:7^2:8^2:9^3:10:11:12/**3**:1:2:3:4/**1Ti1**:5^2:
16/**2**:15/**3**:13:15/**4**:1:2:3:6:8:9,10:16/**5**:7:12:14:
20:22:24/**6**:15:16:17:19^2/**2Ti1**:8^4/**2**:2:10:11:13^2:
17^2:21:26^2/**3**:2^2:3^4:4^2:5:9:12:13/**4**:1:3^2:4:6:8:14:
16:18^2/**Tit1**:9/**2**:8:10/**3**:8:14/**Phm1**:6:16:19:20:
21:22/**Heb**:8:11^3:12^3/**2**:5:12^2:13/**3**:14/**4**:3/**5**:7f:
14/**6**:3:11:12:18/**7**:21:25^2/**8**:8^2:9:10^6:11^2:12^2/**9**:
14:16^2:17:28^2/**10**:7:16^6:17:23:27^2:29:30^2:36:37:
38/**12**:13:14:15:26:27^2/**13**:4:5:15:17^2:20,21:23/
Jas1:4:5^2:6:7,8:10,11^2:12:18f:25^3/**2**:12:13^2:14:
20/**3**:1:13^2:16:18/**4**:3:7:8:10:11:16/**5**:3:12:15^3:
20/**1Pe1**:5^2:7:9:17:23^2:24:25/**2**:6:8^5:12:15:16/**3**:
1^2:6^2:7:9:13:14:16/**4**:2^2:4^2:5:11:13^3:14:18:19^2/**5**:
1:2:4:6^2:10^2/**2Pe1**:3:6:7^2:8:10:11:15:19^3/**2**:1^3:2^2:
3:12:12f:13/**3**:1:3^2:4:7:10^3:12^3:13:14/**1Jn1**:4^2/**2**:
1:5:17^3:24:28^2/**3**:2:3:4:5:19^2:20:20f/**4**:6:17/**5**:14^2
:15:16/**2Jn1**:3:6:9^3:11/**3Jn**:10:14/**Jud**:11^2:15/
Rev1:3^3:7:19/**2**:5:7:10^3:16:17^2:22:23^2:24,25:26:
27^2:28/**3**:3:5^3:9:10:10f:10:11:12^6:16:18:20:21/**4**:
1:11/**6**:10^2/**7**:15:16^2:17^2/**8**:13/**9**:6^4/**10**:9^2/**11**:2:
3:5:6:7:8,9^3:10^2:11^3:12^2:13^2/**13**:10^2:10f^2/**14**:7:10
:11/**15**:1:3,4/**16**:15^2/**17**:1:8^2:8f:10:11:12:13:14^2:
16^2:17^4/**18**:4:7:9:10:11:14:17:19:22^3:23^2/**20**:6:7:
8:9^2:10^2/**21**:3^3:4:6:7^3:9:24^2:27/**22**:3^2:5^2:6,7:11
8005

WITH
^{4}**Gen1**:2:4,5:11,12^2:20^2:21,22:25/**2**:1/**3**:21:24/**4**:
1^2:5:6:7:11:17/**5**:21-24^2/**6**:4:12,13:14:17:18:
19,20/**7**:1:7:8,9:13:14,15:23/**8**:11:18,19:21/**9**:
9,10,11:12/**10**:5:20/**11**:3,4:6f:20,21:22,23:32f/
13:1:5:6:8:11/**14**:12:19,20/**15**:14:18/**16**:2,3:4/
17:2,3,4:19^2:21:24-27/**18**:12:16:22,23:25:29:33/
19:3^2:8:9^2:25:30:32^2:33:34^3:35/**20**:4:7:18/**21**:6:
10:14:20,21:23/**22**:2:3:5:17/**23**:4/**24**:10^2:15,16:
26:31:32:35:40:45:54:58:60:61:65/**25**:18:21:25:
26/**26**:3:8:15:20:24:26/**27**:17:19:25:31:33^2:34:
39,40:44/**28**:6,7,8:15^2/**29**:6:9:18:21:22:23:30/**30**
:3:4:5:8:10:15:16^2:19:26:35,36:39,40:42:43/**31**:3:
4:5:7:10:12:14:16:21^2:23^2:25:27:35f:38:54/**32**:4^2
:6^2:7^2:13,14,15:19:20:22,23,24:28^3/**33**:1:2:5:6:7:
12:17/**34**:3:6,7:8:16^2:18,19:21/**35**:2:3:10:13,14:
18:22/**37**:2:13,14/**38**:1:9:14:16:18:30/**39**:3:4:6:7
:8:10:12:21^2:23/**40**:1:9,10/**41**:5:10:38:55:56,57/
42:4:5:6:13:19:25:26:28:32:33:38/**43**:3,4,5^2:8:11:
16^2:18:22:30:32/**44**:1:2:3:6:9:18:23:26:29:30:31^2
:33:34/**45**:1:3:5:10:11,12:14:15:23:27/**46**:1:3,4^2:
5:8-14:27:32/**47**:1:2:12/**48**:1:10:15:20:21:22^2/
49:4:13:15:25:28:29,30/**50**:3:10:14:25^2/**Ex1**:1:5
/**2**:3:21/**3**:6:8:9:12:17:18^2:20:21:22/**4**:6:18^3/**5**:3:
9:10,11:15:20/**6**:4:30/**7**:4:7:11:17:20/**8**:3,4^2:7:8:
12:16:18:21^2:28/**10**:3:4,5:9^2:24/**11**:8^2/**12**:3,4:8:
11:17:20:34:36:38:39:48^3/**13**:3:4,5:14:16:19^2/**14**
:8:14f:21/**15**:9^2:10:15:25/**16**:3:11,12:13:20:32/
17:2:3:4:5,6^3:9:15,16/**18**:3:14:15,16:22^2/**19**:2,3:
5:9:13:15:18^2:24/**20**:5:17:18:25/**21**:3:6:10:18^2:
19:19f/**22**:16:19:24:25:30/**23**:1:7:15:18:25^2:32^2:
33/**24**:1:4:8:14/**25**:11^2:13,14:16:19:22^2:24:28:
32,33:34,35/**26**:1:10,11:17:18,19:21:24:25:29^2:
31:32^2:33:37^2/**27**:2:4:6:9,10^2:11:12:18/**28**:32:
33,34^2:37,38:41:43/**29**:1:2^3:3,4:6:9:12:17:21:40^2:
41:42^2:43/**30**:2:3:5:6:17,18^2:28:35:36/**31**:3:7:8:9
:18^2/**32**:11/**33**:3:5:7^2:9:12^2:14:15:16^2:17:22/**34**:
3:5,6:9:10:12:15^3:17:25:27^2:28:29:31:33:34:35/
35:5-9:10-19^2:21:35/**36**:1:4-7:8,9:24:25,26:30:34
:35:36:37:38/**37**:2:4:9:11^2:12:19:20,21:25:26/**38**:
2^2:3:6:7:10^2:11^2:12:14,15:17:18:19^2/**39**:1:6:7^2:14
:21:24:25,26,28,29:30:31:33-40^2/**40**:7:12:13:20:
30/**Lev1**:2,3:9:12:13:15,16,17/**2**:4^2:5:7:11:13:16
/**3**:9,10,11/**4**:25:30:34/**5**:11:13:16:17,18/**6**:9:15^2
:30/**7**:10:12f:12^4:13:19:29/**8**:1:6:7^2:9:13:15,16:
17:21:25:26:28:31/**9**:4:16:22/**10**:15:16:19/**11**:
2,3:20:21,22:26:41,42/**12**:8/**13**:1:9,10/**14**:6:10:
16:17:20:21:27:28:31/**15**:24:33/**16**:12:14:15:19/
17:13/**18**:6f:19:20^2:23^2:25:29,30/**19**:10:17:19^2:
22:26:28/**20**:5:10:11:12:14^2:15:16:17:18:20:24:
25/**21**:10:22/**22**:11:14:26,27/**23**:13:18:20:32:40^2
/**24**:3,4:5-8:10:12/**25**:21,22:29:35:36:41/**26**:4,5:
9:10:13^2:16^2:33:36:37:44/**27**:8/**Num1**:50:52/**2**:1
:3-31/**3**:31-35/**4**:5:6^2:9:10:11:12:13:17,18,19:25:
32^2/**5**:8:15^2:19/**6**:12:15^2:17^2:24,25,26/**7**:13^2:24-
24-29:36-41:54-59:60-65:78-83:87:89/**8**:8^2:11:
25,26/**9**:11/**10**:9:10:18:29:31:33:34/**11**:4,5:9:16:
17^2:25:30:31f:33/**12**:6:7,8^2:10/**13**:17:26:27/**14**:8
:9:12:13:14^2:19:20,21:42^2/**15**:3,4^2:6:8,9:13,14:
23,24:25:37,38/**16**:1:3:5:6,7:11,12:16:17^2:18^2:22
:26:27:32^2:49/**17**:1:4/**18**:21/**19**:12/**20**:3:4:18:20
/**21**:17,18:20:31,32:33/**22**:4:7:16,17^2:18:20:21:
22,23:27:29:31:35^2/**23**:6:13:18-24/**24**:3-9^2:10:13
/**25**:1:14:18/**26**:5-11/**27**:3,4:6,7:19:21/**28**:5^2:7^2:
8:9,10:12^4:13:14^2:20,21^4:28,29^4/**29**:3,4^4:6:9,10^4:
14:16:19:21:22:24:25:28:30:33:34:38:39/**30**:4/
31:6f:6:14:23:47/**32**:29:34,35,36/**33**:41/**35**:5:
7:8:17:18:21:30/**36**:1:3/**Deu1**:24,25:28:30:37:42
/**2**:25:26:35,36/**3**:5:23,24,25:26/**4**:11:19:21,22:
23:29:37:40/**5**:2,3^3:4:15:21:29^2/**6**:3^2:5:21:22^2:25
/**7**:3:8:10:12:19/**8**:3:15:16/**9**:9^2:15:20/**10**:12,13/
11:6:9:11:13/**12**:12^2:15:19:20-23^2:24,25:28/**13**:3
:12,13,14/**14**:9:19,20:26:27/**15**:14:16:17:21/**16**:
3:8:11:14:15/**17**:2,3/**18**:19/**19**:2,3:5:13/**20**:1:4:
12/**21**:8:12/**22**:6^2:10:13,14^2:21:30/**23**:4:8:13:25
/**24**:5/**25**:1:5:8:16:18^2/**26**:8:9:11^2:15/**27**:2,3,4^2:
2,3,4f:7:20:21:22:23/**28**:8:22:32:35:56,57/**29**:1:
2,3:11:12^2:14,15^2:25/**30**:6:10:12/**31**:6:8:16:20:
23:27/**32**:5:23:24^2:32:40,41^2/**33**:2:7:12:13:14:15
:16^2:17:19:20:23:25/**Jos1**:5^2:9:12,13:15:17,18^3/
2:5:12,13:15/**3**:2,3,4:7^2:13,14/**5**:1:6:13/**6**:3,4:22:
23^2:25:27/**7**:1:5:6:7:12:13:15^2:21:22/**8**:20,21:33^2
/**9**:3,4,5:6:7:14,15:18:23:25/**10**:1:4:6:11:26:33:
39/**11**:4/**13**:11:21/**14**:5:8:12/**15**:18,19:21-32:33-
33-36:37-44:46:47^2:48-62/**17**:5,6:11/**19**:2-7:17-
17-23:34^3:35-39:49/**20**:4/**21**:1^2:3:9-16:25:33:
38,39/**22**:7,8:17,18:19:26,27:28/**23**:7:12/**24**:1:6:
25:32/**Ju1**:3:18:21:22,23:27/**2**:1:2:17:20/**3**:6:13:
17,18,19:21:31/**4**:7:8:9^2:10:18:22/**5**:11:15:17:21
/**6**:12:13:16f:16:21:24:26:28:39:40/**7**:4:5,6^2:7:8,9^2
:16:19,20/**8**:1:2,3:4:7:10:16:27f:31/**9**:3:26:28:32:
33^2:35:39:54/**10**:7,8:15/**11**:10:33:37:38/**12**:1/**13**
:9:11/**14**:7:9:15:17:18:19/**15**:1:4:5:8:12,13:14^2:
15:16,17^2/**16**:1:3^2:4:7:8:11:12:18:19:21:25,26:27
:29:30/**17**:3:10,11/**18**:4:7:14:15,16:19:20:27:28/
19:2:6:21:22:27/**20**:1/**21**:18:21/**Ru1**:1:3:6,7:8:9:
10:14/**2**:4,5:6:8,9:14^2:18:22:23/**4**:4:10:13:18-22/
1Sa1:19,20:24/**2**:5:17:19/**3**:2,3:13:19/**4**:1:3:8:12
/**5**:3:6:7:9/**6**:2:3:6:13/**7**:8:9:10/**8**:4/**9**:7:24:25/**10**
:6:12/**12**:20/**13**:2^2:7^2:15/**14**:7:21:52/**15**:2:6:25:
30:31/**16**:2:5:12:14:18/**17**:2:3:4-7^2:10:14,15:20^3:
22:23:33:35:37:40:41,42:43:45:50,51^2:57/**18**:1:6:
8^2:10:11,12:14:20:28^2:29/**19**:1:3:13^2:18:24/**20**:5:
11:13^2:16^2:30:35/**21**:1:4:6/**22**:9,10:16:17:23^2/**23**
:6^2:23/**24**:1:4/**25**:13:15,16:28:33:36/**26**:5,6,7^3:8:
19/**27**:2,3:5/**28**:1:5,6:15:18:19:20^2:23/**29**:2:3:4^2:
6:9/**30**:16:22/**31**:3,4:5/**2Sa1**:1^2:6:15:24/**2**:6:23:
30/**3**:7:8:13:14:17:19:20:22:26^2:27:31:39/**4**:1:6,7
/**5**:3:10:20/**6**:12:14:14f:15:16/**7**:1:3^2:9/**8**:2:11,12
:15/**9**:10,11^2/**11**:4:9:10:11:17:27/**12**:11:17^2:24:
29,30:31:31f/**13**:1:4:11:17,18:19:21-24:36:
37,38,39/**14**:2,3:8:14:15,16:17:32/**15**:4:11:15:
17,18:19,20^3:22:25,26:27:30:32:33,34/**16**:1^2:2:
13:14:17:21:21f:22/**17**:2,3:10:16:19:22:28,29/**18**
:5:19:22:27:28/**19**:4:14:16:17:24,25:26:33:36:37:
38:39:40/**20**:1:2:3:7:8,9,10^4:13^2:22/**21**:15:18:
20,21/**22**:13/**23**:5:9:21^3/**24**:11:20/**1Ki1**:3,4:14:
25:27:37^2:40:44,45/**2**:8:23,24:25:26/**3**:1:10/**4**:8-
8-19:29:33/**5**:2,3:6:7:9/**6**:15:16:18:20:21,22:23-
23-28:30:32^2:35/**7**:6:7:11:12:15:16-22:24:27-30^4
:31:34:35^2/**8**:3,4:9:21:22,23:46:54,55:57^2:59/**9**:8
:11,12:17,18/**10**:1^2:2:10:15:18:19:22:26^2/**11**:
9,10:15:20:24/**12**:6:8:16,17:27/**13**:4:7:15:18:
24,25/**14**:9:16:22/**15**:3:15:17:18:19:27/**16**:12:19
/**17**:20/**18**:3,4:13:19:23:28:33:42:45/**19**:10:19^2:
20:21/**20**:1:5,6:24:28:35:37/**21**:4:8/**22**:4:11:27:
35:44:50/**2Ki1**:8:9^2:11:13:15/**2**:8:13,14:20/**3**:11:
12f:14:16:17:19/**4**:4:18:30:39:43/**5**:9:13:17:21:
23/**6**:3:8:14:32/**7**:9:13/**8**:4/**9**:1:5:13:14:15:24/**10**
:5:6:16^2:24^2:31/**11**:6,7,8:11/**12**:18/**13**:3:13:19:
23/**14**:10:15:16:29/**15**:5:7:17:19,20:23:25:27:30:
38/**16**:10^2:11,12/**17**:5:15:35,36^2:38/**18**:7:16:17:
23:24^2:27:31,32:37/**19**:2:19:32/**20**:12/**21**:16/**22**:
8:12,13/**23**:1:9/**24**:3,4/**25**:7:14,15:17:25/**1Ch2**:
19:21/**4**:10/**5**:1/**6**:58,59:60:66-69:75:76:78,79:
81/**8**:40/**9**:20:31:38/**10**:1:2:3:4/**11**:3:9:11:13:14:
20:23/**12**:8-13:18:19^2:24-37^4:38:39/**13**:1:4:8:14/
14:1/**15**:4-10^6:12:15:21f:25:28/**16**:16:17:29:42/
17:8/**18**:10/**20**:2:3:3f:3:5:6,7/**21**:7:16/**22**:8:9:11:
14:16:18^2:19/**23**:4,5:14,15:29/**24**:3^2/**25**:4,5:9-31
/**26**:4,5/**27**:1:8:10:13:14/**28**:9:20:21/**29**:8:9:17:
22:22f:25/**2Ch2**:14^2/**3**:4^2:5^3:7^2:8:9:10:11,12,13:
14:16/**4**:9:11/**5**:4,5:10:13,14/**6**:18:20,21:36:
37,38^2:41/**7**:8/**8**:13:17,18/**9**:1:6:17:19/**10**:6:7:
8,9:14^2/**11**:5-10:11^2:21/**12**:3:5:10/**13**:8^2:9:12:
13,14/**14**:7^3:8^2:9,10/**15**:2^2:6:9:14:15^2/**16**:2:3:8:
10:12:13,14/**17**:3:14,15:16:17:18/**18**:1:2:3,4,5^3:
10:12:26/**19**:8:9:11/**20**:4:9:13:17:18:19:21:25:27
:33:35:37/**21**:7:9^2:14:15:18/**22**:5^2:7^2/**23**:12:18/
25:7^2:8:14:16:18:19/**26**:7^3:17,18/**28**:9:13:17,18/
29:10:20:22:24:25,26:35/**30**:10:21^2:25^2/**31**:5,6/
32:6:7:9:21:23:24:25:28,29/**33**:11^2/**34**:15,16:21:
25:31:32/**35**:12:18:21^2:21f:21^2:23/**36**:18^2:22,23/
Ez1:4/**2**:66,67/**3**:1:7/**4**:2/**5**:8^2/**6**:4:12:13:16:
21,22/**7**:7,8,9:13:15:19:25:28^2/**8**:18:19/**9**:4:11:
14/**10**:1:3:14/**Neh1**:2/**2**:1^2:4^2:5,6:11,12:18/**4**:17
:18^2:23^2/**5**:7/**6**:3:5,6:7:16/**7**:5:68,69/**8**:6:10:13:
17/**9**:1:4:8:13:25:30/**10**:28:32:38/**11**:15,16,17:
36/**12**:8:27:40,41/**13**:15:22:25^2:26:27:31/**Est1**:1
:6:6f:11/**2**:6:8:9:12,13,14^3:15:17:22/**3**:3,4:11:12/
4:1:9/**5**:7,8:14/**6**/**7**:6/**8**:3:8:8f:9,10:15^2:17/**9**:18:
22:29-31/**10**:3/**Job1**:4:6:8:12,13:14,15^2:16/**2**:1:
4,5:6:7:11:13/**3**:14,15^2:18/**4**:14:20/**5**:4:23/**6**:4/**7**
:5:13,14/**8**:6:7^2:21^2:22/**9**:3:14^2:18:25:30^2/**10**:15
/**12**:2:16:22/**13**:3:10:15:19:21/**14**:3:13/**15**:12:15
:25,26:34/**16**:9:16/**17**:7:9:16/**19**:2:3:22:23,24/
20:6/**21**:16:17/**22**:18:21^2/**23**:3:6^2:7:14f:16,17/
24:8:13:16:17/**26**:9/**27**:15:16/**29**:5:23/**30**:3:17:
21:30/**31**:1^2:21/**32**:3:14^2:15/**33**:3:26/**34**:7,8:10:
34,35/**36**:6:11:17:20:32/**37**:11:16,17:19,20/**38**:
8,9:25-27:32/**39**:10:18:19/**40**:2:12:14/**41**:1^2:5:
7:30:31,32/**42**:7^3:11:15/**Ps1**:1/**2**:5:9:11^2/**5**:7:9^2:
11:12/**6**:3^2:6^2:7/**7**:2:11:13:14/**8**:4/**9**:1:2/**10**:13:
18/**11**:6/**12**:3,4/**14**:3:5/**15**/**16**:4:9/**17**:4:9:13,14/
18:4:10:11^2:24:25f:32:37:39/**20**:1:3:5/**21**:3:5:
6/**22**:13:26/**23**:5f:6^2/**24**:4:5f/**25**:10:14^2/**26**:4/**27**
:6:8/**28**:1:3/**29**:11/**30**:2/**31**:7:9,10^3/**32**:3:7/**33**:5:

(WITH Con't)
14/35:6:13:15:16:19f:21:27/36:6:8/37:4:6:21:24
:26:34/38:5,6^2:7:19/39:2,3:13/40:5:12:14,15/41
:11/42:4,5/43:4/45:1:2:8:12:13/47:5^2:9/48:6:7:
10f/49:3:12:14:17:20/50:3:5f:6:18/51:1:7:7f:10/
52:4/53:1:3/54:1^2/55:3^2:9:17:20/56:7/57:8/59:
11/60:1^2:12/62:2:6/63:5/64:3:6/65:1:4:5:10:
11,12^2:13^3/66:10:13:17/67:1:2/68:6:11,12,13:
15,16:23:30f/69:3:13:24:28:30/70:4/71:6:13:22
/72:7:16:19/73:5:24/74:5,6:9,10:13,14/76:4/77:
3:6:20/78:17:36^2:47:71,72^2/79:5/80:10:19/81:
16^2/83:8:15/84:2:7/85:9/86:12/88:8:9/89:3,4:6
:20:24:28:38:39:49/90:9:14:15/91:4:12:15:16:16
f/92:10f/95:2/96:9:12:13/98:7:8,9/100:1:2:4^2/
102:1:25/103:1:4:5/104:1^2:6:13:25:28/105:8,9:
10,11^2:18:23:26:37:44/106:29:37,38/107:9:12/
108:2:6:13/109:20:21:29/110:6/111:1/113:5/
118:2:11/119:3:17:28^3:44,45,46:53:58:65:69:
75,76,77:78:82:83:123:124:132:133:145/120:1:4^2
:4f/124:7/125:4/127:5:5f/128:5^2/129:2:3,4^2/
130:7/132:1:8:12:15:16:18/135:8:16/136:11,12
/138:1/139:21/140:5/141:4/142:1:7/143:2:4/
144:3:8:9:12-15^2/145:9/146:2/147:8:14:20/148:
11/149:3:8/150:1:3^2:4^2:5/Pro1:14^2/2:10/3:4,5:
6:9,10^2:13,14,15:22:24,25,26^2/4:7/5:16:17:19:
20/6:12,13:24:29^2/7:13:16,17^2:20:21:23/8:9:11:
16:31:34/9:7,8:16/10:1:6:11:13/11:12^2:14/12:5^2
:8^2/13:15:20^2/14:6:14:16:18^2:35/15:16^2:17^2:22/
16:7:30/17:1:4/18:8:23/20:17:18:19f:21/21:9:
19/22:15:20,21/23:1:6,7,8:19,20,21^2:29,30^2/24:
18:21,22^2:30,31^2/25:6,7,8,9,10:18^3:19:24:26:28/
26:1^3:3^3:4,5^2:22:24,25,26/27:16/28:2:24/29:2^2:
3:9/30:13,14:18,19f:20:32/31:3:16:22:23:28/
Ecc2:9/3:10/5:8:15:19,20/6:10/8:15^2/9:8:9:14^2
/10:4:12,13/11:10/12:3:4^2/Sol1:4:6:10^2/2:2:3:5
:6/3:7:10^2:11/4:4:8:13,14/5:1^3:2:5^2:8:14^2/6:4f:
10f:12/7:2^2/8:6:7:9/Is1:5,6:12,13:15^2:22/2:6:19
/3:14:16:18/5:2:6:9:18f:24:29/6:1:2^3:3:4:6:7:10f
/7:2^2:12:14:17/8:3:7,8:9,10:11/9:1:3:7:8,9,10:
11,12/10:11/11:5^2/12:1:6/13:5:7:8:9/14:6:10:
11:19:23:30/15:9^2/16:1/17:2/18:5/19:1:3:6:8:
13:25/21:3^2:5/22:23,24:25/24:15,16^2/25:3:6:11
/27:6:10/28:8:15:18:27^2/29:2:6:19:22/30:1:2f:6:
20^2:23^3:27^2:30^2:32:33/31:9/32:1:13/33:6:14:19:
23/34:3:6^2:7^2:9^2:14:15/35:1:3:7:8/36:2^2:3:8,9^2:
22/37:4:8,9:24:25:38/38:3:18/40:7:10^3:11:12:15
:18:19^3:25:26:31/41:10^2:10f/42:6:6f:8:22/43:2:5
:12:17:23:24^3/44:11:12:17/45:9^3:12:14:17:24/
46:4:5:6^3/47/48:10:16/49:3:4:13:19:26^2/50:2/
51:9:11^2/52:1:8/53:3:10:12/54:7:8/55:3^2:3f/56:
4/57:5:15^2/58:1:4:5:7:11:13/59:3:6:10:11:17/60
:5:9:16:21/61:6:8:10^2/62:5^2:8/63:1:7:11/64:6:7:
9/65:10/66:2:10^2:15^3:22/Jer1:8:10:19/2:9:15:
18^2:22:25:31:34:37/3:2:12:15:16/4:8:9:28:30/5:
3:13:21/6:7:16:24/7:12:21/8:12:19:21/9:5^2:7:11
:15/10:4^2/11:1:5:6:10/12:4:5/13:12f:13:17/14^2
/15:1:11:17,18^2:20/16:7:8:18^2/17:1:6:8:11:26/
18:23/19:1:4:8:10:12/20:5:16/22:9:13f:13:14^2:
17:22/23:5,6:9:15:16/24:1:7/25:15:19,20/26:11
:14:22:23:24/27:2:18:19,20,21/28:6/29:3:23/30
:11:19:23/31:3^2:4:7^2:8:9:13:14^2:31:32:33:36/32:
21:22:30:40:41/33:9:20,21^4/34:13/35:1f/36:2:
12:24,25/37:15,16/38:10:21,22:25^2/40:1:4:5:6:
10:12:15/41:2:3:10:12:13,14:15:16,17/42:6:9:11
:18^2/43:5:6^2/44:4:5:8:19/46:10:12:17^2:28/48:7:
33:41:45/49:3:16:21:23:29/50:3:5:10:12:14:38/
51:5:14^2:16:21:34,35:39:59/52:4:6:15:21:24,25/
Lam1:1^2:4:9/2:2:16:19/3:5:7:9f:9:11:15:
34,35,36:44:47:48,49:53:63/4:14:16/5:2:12:22/
Eze1:1:4^2:10:16:18:19,20,21/2:9,10/3:4:6/4:7:
16^2/5:2^2:11:16/6:11/7:5,6:13:18:23:26,27/8:1:
10:11:14f:16:18/9:1:2:3:6:7/10:4^2:9-13:15,16:19
:21/11:6:22/12:7^2:12^2:12f:13f:19/13:10:13^3:18:
20/14:4:11:13:22/16:4:6,7,8:13:22:26:27:28:32:
33,34:36:37:38:40,41:42:46:51:52:59,60:61:62/
17:3,4^2:8,12,13:20/18:6/19:7:10/20:5,6:7:16:18:
26:33^2:34/21:6:7:12:15:17:22:24:29:30/22:9:10f
:10^2:11:18,19,20:28:31/23:7:14,15^2:17^2:19,20:23
:24^3:25:29:30:31:40:43:44:47/24:4:6^2:27/25:6:
13/26:7:9:10:15:16:17:20/27:7:9:17:17f:17:22:
24:28:31:34:35/28:8:12f:13:16:17:18:24:26/29:4
:7/30:5:11:16/31:2,3:14^2:16^3:17^2:18/32:3:5^2:6:7
:10:12:20:21:24:27^2:29^2:30:3:6:7:10:20:25:31:
32/34:4:18:25:30/35:3:8^2:11/36:5:7^2:10:11:18^2:
35/37:6:23:26/38:5:12^2:13:15,16:22/39:19:26/
40:5:7-12^2:16:36:48,49/41:3:5:6:15,16:17,18^3:24
:25/42:4:6:16-20/43:2:3:8:13:15:17/44:4:19/45:
7:17:18:24/46:5^2:7^4:10:11^4:14,15^2:23/47:10:14:
17:22/48:3:4:5,6,7:8:15:25:27,28:30,31:32/Dan
1:1:10:11:13:18,19/2:1:13:14:18:43^2/3:19^2:21/4
:12:15^2:21^3:23^3:25:32:33:36/5:6:7:12:14:16:21:
31f^2/6:10:14:17:23:24/7:2:5:7:19^2:20:25:28/8:3:
9f:17:18:22:23:24f/9:3^2:6:7:8:14:17:20:26:27/10
:5,6:7^2:8:11/11:8^2:12:13:17:21f:23:24:28:32f:33:
40^2/12:7/Hos1:2:3:6:7^2:15:19/3:3/4:2:3:14:15/
5:1:2:6:8/6:4:5^2:8/7:4:5:6:8:14/8:2:3:4:7/9/10:1
:6/11:4:8f:12/12:3^2:4:10/13:1:2:16/Joe1:6:8:12:
18/2:6:11:12:24^2/3:13:18:21/Amo1:3:9:11:13/2
:1:5:8:13/3:3/4:2:13/5:9:13:16:21:23:25,26,27/
6:4:6/7:7^2:8:13/Ob1:1:8/Jon3:3/4:11:11f/Mic1
:7:11f^6/2:3^2:10/3:4:6:8^2:10:12/5:1:6/6:8:11/7:3:
10:18/Nah1:8:9:14:15/2:7:12/3:1:4:4f:6:16/
Hab1:17/2:6:8:12:14:19/3:8,9f^2:8,9:14:16/Zep1
:4:9:12:18/2:5f:15f^3/3:8:10:14:19/Hag1:6:8:13/
2:4:7f:7:8,9f:14:16,17/Zec1:2:4:5,6:8:15^2:16:17/
2:4:9/3:7:9f/4:1:7:7f/5:6:9^2/6:13/7:3:7:14/8:5:9
:12^2:13:16:20,21:23/9:5^2:7^2:9:11^2:15:16,17/10:1
:5:7:9:12/11:8/12:7:12,13,14/14:5:13:18/Mal2:
1:6:7:13:15:17/3:3:12/4:2^2/Mt1:23/2:3:3f:13:
14:21/3:11^3:12:17/4:18:19:20:21:22/5:1:18:22f:
25:28^2:37:38/6:23/7:16^2:27/8:4:5,6^2:11:14:23:
24:28:29:33/9:9:11:15:16:17:20/10:5:9:10/11:
19/12:1:10:15:20:35:46,47/13:20:22:43:53,54:
57/15:23:31:32/16:9:22:26:27/17:3:5:8:17:
22,23/18:8:9^2:15:16:26:27/19:16:26/20:8:34/21
:2:28:33/22:10:16:18:34,35:37/23:4:5:13,14:25:
28:34/24:2:19:30:31/25:2,3,4:7,8:10:16:17:22:
24,25:28:31:41/26:1:7:17:18:20,21:23f:29:37^2:
38^2:40:47^2:51:55^2:58:69:69f:71:72/27:18:22:30:
45:48:55:66f/28:4:8:20/Mk1:8^2:16:18:20^2:29,30
:32,33:41/2:2:14:16^2:19:21/3:1:6:21:25:31,32/4:
5,6:10^2:16:29:31,32:34:38:41/5:5:17:23:24:25:35
:37:38/6:1:7:8,9:13:20:37/7:3f:19:26:32:33:37/8
:10:11:18:19:20:32:38/9:2:4:8:12,13:14:19^2:28:
30,31:43,44f:43,44^2:45,46f:49:49f:50/10:10:14:
27:30:32:34:38^2:39/11:9:11/12:13:30:33:37/13:
3,4:26:34/14:1:3:17:18:20:31:33^2:34:37:38:43^2:
45:58:65:66,67/15:7:12:15:19:23:32:34:36:41/
16:10,11:18:19:20/Lk1:5:14:15:19:28:41:53:56:
67/2:5:9:25:38:44:46,47^2:51/3:14:16^3:17/4:34:
38/5:7:9:11:12:26:27:28:29:30:32:34:36/6:4:8:
11:17,18:21:39:42/7:4^2:6,7,8:9:11^2:12:13:16:31:
37:38^2:44^2:46/8:1:6:25:28:29:30:32:40:41:42:49:
52:56/9:10:18:23:28:29:30:31:32^2:36:41:51:53:
59:60/10:2:4:21:27^4:30:34/11:9:17^2:29,30:36^2:
44:48:53,54/12:13/13:7:26/14:15:16:31/15:2^2:6
:9:20:23:29/16:7:10:11:12^2:22:23/17:2,3:20:22^2:
35,36/18:4,5:7/19:15:17:20:21:30/20:28:41:45:
47/21:23:27:34,35/22:7:11:15^2:20:28f:33^2:44:48
:52:56:63,64/23:13:16:18:20:25:32,33:38:43:46:
47:50,51,52/24:22,23:27:29^2:32:33,34:41:44:49:
52/Jn1:1:17:26:31:33:35:39^2:43/2:3:4f:7,8:12/3
:1:3:8:25:29^2/4:14:17,18:45:46,47:51/5:2:3:18:
38/6:2-5:8,9^2:11:13:26:52:53:63/7:29/8:6:9^2:16:
29:38:51/10:16/11:1^2:16:33^2:37,38^2:45:54/12:2:
3^3:8/13:5:18:36/14:2,3:9:12,13:17:19:22:23:25:
27/15:6:11:27/16:4:6:32/17:10:11:13^2:14:24/18
:1:2:3:12:15^2:18:22:26/19:1:3:15^2:18^2:32:34:40/
20:24:26/Act1:4:5^2:8:18:20:21,22^2:26/2:4:14:25
:26^2:30:33:42:44:45:46/3:7,8^2/4:8:13:16:31/5:1:
6:17:25:26,27:28:31:34/6:1:9/7:32:44^3:45:57:60^2
/8:1:2:20:31:35:37/9:1:7^2:14:17:19:26:28:29:38:
39:43/10:5,6:20:23:36,37^2:38^3:40,41:45:48/11:2
:3^2:11:12:15:16^2:23/12:6:20^3:21:23^2:25/13:5:9:
11:13:16f:16:22:25:52^2/14:1:4:8:20:23:28/15:2:
4:10:15:16:17:22:23:25:39:40,41/16:9:15:22:23:
29:39:40/17:15^2:17:18:33/18:2,3^3:7:10:18:19:
25,26/19:24:25:29/20:4:7:8:19:28:31:34:36/21:
4:5:11:18^2:24^2:26,27^2:29:33:36^2:37,38^2/22:5:9:
22^2:24:30/23:9:32/24:1:16:17:24:25:26:27/25:5^2
:12:13^2:14:16:23/26:1:12:18:28:28f/27:2:3:7,8:
12:16:17:24:39/28:8:10:14:19:20:25:31/Rom1:4
:9:11,12:24:26:27^4/2:4:29^2/3:2:5:8:13:15/4:12:
17:25^2/5:1:5:6:11:18:21/6:4^2:5:5f:6:8:10:16^2:17:
20/7:4:6:14^2:16:23,24,25/8:26^2:27:29:30^2:33:35
/9:4:22:31/10:3:9:10^2:15/11:10/12:1:2:4,5:8^2:
10:15:18^2/13:9/14:2:3:14:20:22/15:5^2:6:10:13:
23:30:32:33/16:7:14:15:16:24/1Co1:9:10:17:22/
2:4:6:16/3:1:2^2:5^2:8:12:14/4:8:12^2:18:21^2/5:1:
3,4^2:8:9:10:11^2:12:13/6^2:20/7:9:12:13:14^2:17:20
:31:34:35/8:11/9:1:20^2:21^2:22^2:26/10:3,4:8:10:
20^2:22/11:14,15:17:21:29:32/12:12:26/13:9/14:
16^2:36/15:52/16:3:6:11^2:12:14:16:21/2Co1:5:12
:23/2:1:3:17^2/3:1:3:7^2:9:10:12/4:14^2/5:6^2:8:9:20
/6:3:6:7:11:14^3:15/7:3:7^2:9:15/8:2:14^2:15:18:19:
20/9:3:4:12:14/10:1:7:12:13:14/11:1^2:2:6,8,9:10
:25:27^2/12:9:18:19:20^2/13:3:4:11^2:14/Gal1:16:
17:18^2/2:1:2^2:7,8,9^3:12^3:16:19:20/3:1:14:24:27/
4:3:10:18^2:19:20^2:27:30/5:2:3:5:7:10:17:23/6:4:
7:17:18/Eph1:3:4:10:18:23/2:2:3:6^2:13:18:19:21
:22^2/3:5:6:12:18,19/4:2:3:10:13:24:26/5:7:18:19
:26f/6:2:4^2:6,7^2:15:18^2:23/Php1:8:9:23:27:28^2/
2:2^2:12^2:17:18:29/3:3:8:9^2:10:15:18/4:2^2:3^2:9:12
:13:18:21/Col1:2^2:11:14:16:20:22/2:2:4:5:6:7:8:
10^3:12^3:20/3:3:4:5^2:9:16:17:25/4:5:7:10:11:13/
1Th1:5:6/2:3:5:11:16/3:4:6:13:13f/4:14:16^2:17^2:
18/5:10:14:26:28/2Th1:7^2:11/2:5:8:9:11:15^2:17
/3:10:16:17/1Ti1:3,4:5:16/2:8/3:4:7:14/4:1:2/5
:1/6:7:10:12:14:18:20/2Ti1:2:7:8/2:1:11:12^2:16:
19:25/3:4:6:9/4:2:11^2:13:17:22/Tit1:9/2:1:2:12:
14/3:6:10:13:15/Phm1:6:12:13:19:20/Heb:3:
5,6/2:7:9:13:17/3:9:10:11:16:18/4:1:2:12/5:1^3:6
:7^2:10/6:9:12:17:19:20/7:11^2:15:17:19:21:25/8:
5:6:8^2:10/9:1:4^3:5:7:10^2:12:15:19^2:20:22:23^2:28/
10:6:8:16:22^3:32:33:34/11:5:12:22:24,25:27:31:
36:37,38/12:1:12:18:19:21:28^2/13:1:3:5:13:15:
16:17:20,21^2:23:24,25^2/Jas1:7,8:10,11:27/2:2/3
:11^2/4:4:5:8/5:1/1Pe1:2:8:17:19:22/2:1:24/3:1:
4:5:8:22/4:6:9:11:13:14/5:1:5/2Pe1:3:6:17,18^2/
2:2:5:12:12f:15:16:20:22/3:5:6:10:14^2:18/1Jn1:
1^2:2:3^2:7/2:2:13:14:17:19:24:28/3:21:24^2/4:2:4:
6:13^2:14:15:16:17^2/5:6,7,8:14/2Jn1:3^2:7:11/
3Jn1:2:6:8/Jud:9:14:24,25/Rev:7f:13f:13/2:16:
22:22f^2:22:27/3:4^2:17:20^2:21/4:4^2:5f:6:7:8/5:1^2:
2:4:6f:8^2:9/6:1:5:8/7:9:10/8:3^2:4:5:6:7/9:5:19/
10:1^2/11:18^2/12:1^2:3:5:9/13:11:16/14:1:4f:10:
11:14:18^2/15:6:7:8/16:14/17:1^2:2:3:6:12:16/18:
1^2:3f:3:4:7^2:10:16:23/19:2:13:15:20^2:21^2/20:1:4:
6:8:10/21:1:3:8^2:9:11:12:18,19,20^{13}/22:2:12
5329

WITHIN
Gen18:24/40:13/Ex6:24:25/13:6,7/16:10/25:
21/40:3/Lev13:55f/16:15/25:30/Num5:24:27/
18:5:7/36:6:8/Deu14:29/20:16/22:23,24/32:34
/Jos19:41-46/Ju20:16/1Sa25:37,38f/26:8/2Sa
20:4/1Ki6:23-28/2Ch3:8:10/Ez10:7,8:9/Neh4:
17/Job6:4/20:14/28:8/32:18/36:29/41:13/Ps7
:9/25:13/28:2f/39:2,3/40:12/45:13/55:4/65/68
:22/69:9:20/74:17/91:1/119:44,45,46/122:7/
136:6/Pro3:3/4:21/7:3/20:5/28:2/Ecc2:7,8/Is
7:8/8:4/13:22/14:32/16:13,14/21:16f/32:2/49:
1/51:16/56:5:7/62:9/Jer1:5/4:18:19/10:23/20:
17/28:3:11/Lam1:13/2:20/3:13:55/Eze1:16f/
10:9-13/11:7:11/19:14/22:6:15/36:26:27/43:6/
45:3/47:21/Dan3:15/5:11:14/11:17/Hos5:4/11
:8/Zep3:5/Zec8:3/12:1/Mt1:20/12:35/15:22/
Mk4:14/5:7,8:9/7:21:23/Lk1:41/11:36/13:28/
14:3/17:21/18:16,17/19:42:44/24:33,34/Jn4:
14/5:4f:41,42/6:53:61/8:37/15:9/17:12/Act2:
24/16:18/18:20f/19:12/23:8/Rom1:27/2:12-15
/5:5:10/7:5:8:23,24,25^2/8:4:7:10:11:23/9:1/10:
8/15:13/1Co2:14:16/6:19/2Co2:15/3:18/4:7^2:
10:11/5/7:5/10:15/13:3:5/Gal1:16/2:20/5:17/
Eph1:14/2:3/3:17:20/5:9/6:10/Php1:6^2/2:13/
Col1:29/3:5:10/2Ti1:14/Jas4:1:5/1Pe1:11/2Pe
:20,21/1Jn2:3:27/3:15:17/4:12/Jud1:21/Rev2:
23
191

WITHOUT
Gen15:2,3/23:11/29:15/31:17-20:32:42/34:25/
37:21,22:33/Ex9:26/10:21/12:5:15:18:34/13:
6,7/15:22/16:24/21:11/22:27/29:2/34:20/Lev1
:10/2:4^2:5/3:1/4:3:13:22:23:28:32/5:15:17,18^3/
6:6:16:17/8:1/9:2:3/13:36:55f/14:10^2/15:11/20
:1/22:14:19/23:12:18/25:31/26:6/Num5:15/6:
14^3:15:17:19^2/19:1:15/22:14/23:18-24/27:17/
28:3:9,10:11:19:31/29:2:8:13:17:20:23:26,27:29:
32:36/35:22,23^3/Deu13:15/17:10/25:5:12/29:
23^2/32:4:12:28/Jos2:22/3:10/10:21/Ju12:3/21
:22/Ru1:4,5/2:15/3:15-18/1Sa1:21,22/2:11/7:
6/8:12/13/17:47/21:8/25:35/26:12/2Sa12:16/
17:20/1Ki6:7/16:22/18:23/22:3:17/2Ki4:30:39
/5:20/1Ch2:30:32/23:22:29/24:31/25:8/26:13/
29:15/2Ch2:8/5:11,12/11:17/15:3/18:16/20:3/
28:9/Ez6:8:9/8:29/Neh5:10:12/Est1:13-15/4:
11/8:8f/Job2:3/5:9/6:13:14/8:11-13^2:14/9:17:
35/11:11:15^2/12:24,25/19:26f/22:9/24:7:10:11
/32:19/34:24/Ps1:3/19:3,4/26:1/35:19/49:20f
/69:4/80:12/90:2/Pro3:24,25,26/9:4/10:13/11:
14/15:28/20:18/24:6/25:14:28/30:9/Ecc4:8/6:
4/12:5/Sol4:2/6:9/Is1:30/5:27/6:11/16:13,14/
22:3/30:2/34:16/36:10/47:2f/48:1/49:4/50:10/
52:4:5/Jer2:34/4:7/9:10/10:14^2/20:16/21:7/34
:22/38:27/44:2,3:19:22/46:5:19/47:3/48:9/49:
31/51:29:37/Lam2:2:9^2:17:21/3:37:43/4:6:18/
Eze1:9:12:17/14:23/16:15/18:8:8f/22:24/34:5/
43:22^2/45:21:23/46:6/47:12/Dan1:16/2:45/6:
18/8:25/10:3/11:24/Hos1:7/3:4^2/6:5/7:1/Zep
3:6/Zec11:5/Mal2:9/Mt9:15:36/10:29/11:5:18
/12:29/13:12,13f:34,35/15:20/17:21/19:12/22:
16:24:25:26/Mk2:18:21/4:27/6:19:34/7:5/8:3/
10:27/12:19:20,21,22/13:13/14:58/Lk3:7/4:35
/5:14:33/6:49/7:20,21,22:33/9:60/10:7/11:

(WITHOUT Con't)
46/14:28:31/18:12/20:11:28:29/21:30:36/22:1:2:35/Jn3:33,34/5:30/8:15/10:18/15:25/Act2:23f/4:21/5:26,27/9:8,9/14:17/16:37/17:23/25:27/Rom1:22:31/2:4/4:11/14:2/1Co4:11[2]/5:10/7:7:31/9:12:15:18/11:5:13:21/13:1:2/15:10/2Co5:3/6:5/11:7:8,9:23:27[2]:29[2]/Gal2:17/3:12:20/Eph1:4/2:12[2]/5:27[2]/6:12/2Th3:8/1Ti:7/6:8/Phm1:14/Heb6:18/8:10/9:14:22/10:28/11:5:6[2]:13/12:27/13:2:6/Jas1:17:27/2:18:20/1Pe:15/2Pe2:10/3:14/1Jn2:10/Jud1:3:4:12[3]/Rev2:3/13:17/16:12/22:17

391

WOULD
Gen2:19,20/3:6/8:7f/10:9/18:10f:25/19:31/20:9,10[2]/21:7[2]/24:21[2]:23/25:25/26:7:9[2]:10/30:14f:38/31:8:42/32:9/34:14/37:35/38:9[2]:11/39:9/42:38/43:25/44:8:15:22:32:34/46:28/48:11/50:25/Ex2:4/7:14/9:5/10:27/13:19[2]/14:12/20:25/21:5/23:29[2]:33/28:36/33:3:5:8:9:11/34:16[2]:33f:34:35[2]/39:23/Lev7:38/8:33/10:19/15:26/21:23/24:12/25:50/Num8:19/9:4,5:8/11:22:29/12:6:14/13:31/14:16:31/16:34/17:10/20:3/21:2[2]/22:29:33:37/24:13/27:6,7/30:5/32:10,11:19/Deu1:34,35:36:39:41/2:12/3:26/4:35/5:29[2]/7:4[3]:22/8:2[2]:16[2]:17/9:23/10:2/19:19/20:5:6:7/24:4:14,15/27:23f/28:56,57:68/29:6/30:19/31:10,11/32:26:29/34:4/Jos6:6-9[2]:26[2]/9:27/13:33/14:1/15:16[2]/22:4/24:16/Ju1:24/2:1:2:15:17:20/3:4/5:8/6:27/8:15/9:3/11:30,31[2]/14:12[2]/16:5:7:16,17[2]/20:32/Ru1:13/4:6:6f/1Sa1:4:8/2:13,14:15[2]:16:20/7:17[2]/9:9,10,11[2]/12:22/13:11/14:39/16:23[3]/18:25/22:22/24:19/25:34:35/27:5:10[2]/28:17/2Sa1:10f/2:27/3:35,36/10:9/11:19,20,21/12:5:8/13:13:25/14:15,16/15:3:4:7,8[2]/18:11:13[2]/19:6:35:38/20:3/1Ki1:13[2]:17[2]/2:22[2]/3:5/6:11,12/8:7:12,13:27/11:2/12:32,33/13:5:8/14:2:5/15:29/18:32f/22:18:38/2Ki1:2/4:1/5:3[2]:10:11:22/7:4:18/8:13:14:19/9:36[3]/10:9,10/11:17/12:8/13:19/14:27/15:12/17:23/19:11/22:18,19/23:16:17/24:2:3,4/25:24[3]:26/1Ch4:10/11/12:19:23/21:3/24:5/27:23f/28:16/2Ch2:6/6:1:20,21/12:11/13:5/18:12/23:15,16,17/28:23/33:4,5/34:5/35:1/Ez1:1f/2:62,63/8:21[2]:22/9:11/10:5:7,8/Neh2:16/4:3/5:12:14/6:11:12,13/10:31:32:38/13:25/Est2:1:12,13,14/6:6/7:4:5/8:13/9:27:28[2]/Job1:4:5/3:13/5:8f[2]/6:8,9:27:28:30/7:15/8:6:7/9:15:20:28:31[2]/10:19[2]/11:5:6/13:5:19:25/14:13:15[3]/16:4:5[3]:21/22:3/23:4,5:6[2]/24:22,23/31:12:28:35:36:37/32:14/34:15[2]/37:19,20/41:21:31,32/Ps5:8/7:2:3:5/14:7/17:8/27:10/35/44:21/50:12/51:16/53:1:6/55:7:8/66:18/69:20[2]/72:1/73:15/77:1/81:13[2]:14[2]:15[2]:16[2]/84:10/94:17/95:7:11/102:21,22/104:5:9/105:14/106:23:26/107:8:15:21:31/116:14/119:11:92:170/124:2,3:4,5/132:2-5:11/Pro2:3,4,5/4:1:11/23:33/Ecc2:12/5:6,7/6:3:4:10/8:15/Sol3:4/8:1:2[3]:3[2]/Is1:9/7:14f:18f/28:12/37:30f/41:26/42:24/44:8:10/45:21[2]/46:11/47:7/48:16:18:19[2]/52:14,15/54:9/55:8/56:5/57:16/58:2/63:16[2]/64:1[2]:2[3]/66:4/Jer2:20/3:7:19[2]/9:1[2]/10:7:24/11:4[3]:5:6/13:15/18:10/20:6/22:24,25/23:22/26:5/27:2/30:21/32:3:4:8:33/33:25,26[2]/34:15/35:7:15/36:23:29/37:10:19/38:2[2]:3:16:26/40:2,3:9/41:18/43:7/51:9:12/Lam4:12/Eze3:6/4:12/6:10/12:2/14:14[2]:16[4]:18:20/17:5:14:24/20:5,6:8:13:14:15:23,24:26:35,36f/22:30/33:5/38:17/44:18/Dan1:3,4f:8f/2:10:18/4:19/9:12:14/Hos1:4/7:13/11:4/Amo1:12f/3:4/4:6:8/5:18/Ob1:5[3]/Jon3:3/4:5/Mic6:7[4]/Nah3:10/Hab:14/Hag2:5/Zec1:5,6/7:7:11/8:10:14,15/9:5/Mal1:10/2:1/Mt2:4/9:16[2]:17[3]/11:14:21:23/12:7:10:11[2]:39,40/13:34,35/14:5/15:33/16:21[4]/17:20[2]/18:1:6:30/19:3/20:4:10:18/21:37/22:24:32f/23:2:29,30/24:24/25:24,25:26/26:5:35:48:53:54:59[2]/28:6:16/Mk1:2[2]/2:5:22[2]/3:2:11:26/4:34/5:5/6:37:45[2]/8:31[3]/9:12,13:30,31:42/12:6:27/13:22/14:55/Lk1:3:8,9f:45:59/2:26:29,30,31:49/6:7/7:39/9:46/10:13:36/11:5,6:7:46:48/12:39[2]/14:1:15:28:29:30:31:35/15:5:6/16:9f[2]:16:21/17:2,3:6[2]/19:11:14:21:30/20:16:19:37,38f/22:23:24/23:25/24:6,7:26:28/Jn1:11,12/3:20[2]/4:9:10:11/5:6/6:7:64:71/7:39/8:16:19:39:42:55/9:22,23/11:32:52/12:4:34:37:42/13:1[2]:4f:11:24/14:2,3:7/15:19:20:22:24/17:13/18:28:34f[2]:36/19:11/20:9/21:19/Act2:30:31[2]/5:15:24[2]:26,27:31/7:3:5:6:17,18:25:48,49/10:45/16:10/18:14/19:4/20:38/23:10/24:6:22:26/25:18:20/26:5:23:29/27:21:29/28:10/Rom1:28/3:6:25/4:1:18[2]/7:3:7:8/8:29[2]/9:1[2]:4:10-13:17:27[2]:29/10:19[2]:20/11:6:11/1Co1:21/2:2:8/3:1/6:7/7:5/9:15[2]:16:17:25/10:12/12:16[2]:17:19/13:1:2[2]:3/14:6:19:21[2]/15:3:58/2Co1:8/2:3:9/7:8:14/8:17:24/9:3:4[2]/10:1/11:30/12:6/Gal2:2:12/3:8,9:16:18:21,22/4:15[2]:23/5:11:12:12f[2]/6:12/Eph1:4/3:20/5:12/6:5/Php3:4/1Th2:5:9/3:4/2Th1:7/3:8:15/1Ti1:18/5:1/2Ti1:4/Tit:5/Phm:13:17/Heb2:17/3:5:11/4:8/5:7:11/6:14:17/7:5:20/8:7/9:26/10:1:2[3]:7:34/11:11:19:20:23:26:28:32:35:37,38/12:2/Jas3:1/5:17:18/1Pe1:2:11:12[2]/2Pe:19/2:21/1Jn:19:26/2Jn1:12/Jud:18/Rev9:20/10:7/20:3

895

WOULDN'T
Gen18:25[3]/42:4:21:22/Ex5:7,8:17/6:8,9/7:13:16:22/8:19/11:10/13:15/16:20/Deu1:43:45/9:23/23:5/Jos5:6/24:10/Ju1:34/8:19/9:41/13:23[2]/14:18/15:1/19:25/20:13/1Sa2:23,24,25/6:6/13:19/18:4/20:2:9/28:10/2Sa2:19/13:14:16:25/14:29/15:5/18:12:20/1Ki2:8/13/21:15/2Ki3:14/5:13/17:14/2Ch20:10/24:19/25:20/31:4/35:22/Neh9:29:30/Job:15/Ps10:4/14/32:3/106:13:24/Pro5:13/Is28:12/65/Jer7:24:26/11:8/15:1/35:15/36:24,25:31/37:14/40:13,14/44:5[2]/Eze33:5/47/Amo4:8:9/Zec1:4/Mt18:30/21:32/23:37/24:39/25:42[2]:43/Mk3:4/5:37/6:6/Lk8:51/13:33:34/15:3,4:28/Jn4:9/8:40/9:18:41/11:21/12:42/18:28[2]:30/21:23/Act19:30/21:14/Rom1:21:25/4:4,5/5:7/2Co:4/10:12/Gal2:4:12:17/Heb8:4

121

YE
Ps4:4f

1

YOU
Gen1:28:29/2:16,17[4]/3:1:5[3]:9:9f:10[2]:11[4]:12:13:14[3]:15[4]:16[2]:17[3]:18[2]:19[5]/4:6:7[6]:10:11[2]:12[3]:14[2]:15/6:18:19,20:21/7:1/8:15,16/9:2,3:9,10,11[3]:13:15/12:1[2]:2[4]:3[3]:3f:11,12,13[5]:18[2]:19/13:9[4]:14:15:16:17/14:19,20[2]:23[2]/15:1[2]:4[2]:5:7[2]:8:15/16:2,3:5:5f:6[2]:8[2]:9-12[4]/17:1:2,3,4[2]:5:6:7,8:9,10[2]:11:16:19[2]:20:21/18:5[2]:10:14:22,23:24[2]:25[3]:28/19:2[2]:8[2]:9[3]:12:15[2]:17:18,19,20:22:34/20:3[2]:4:6[2]:7[4]:9,10[2]:13:15/21:22[2]:23[3]:26:28,29:30/22:2[3]:12:16:17[2]:18/23:5,6[3]:11[2]:13/24:3:6:7[2]:8[3]:14:23:27[2]:31:33:40:41[2]:42:44:47:49[3]:50:58:60/26:3[4]:9:10:16:24[3]:27[2]:28:29[5]/27:2,3,4[2]:8,9,10[2]:13:19[3]:20:21:24:25:27,28,29[4]:31:36:39,40[3]:45[3]/28:2[3]:4[2]:13[2]:14[2]:15[6]:22[2]/29:5:7[2]:15[2]:18:19:25:27[2]/30:15[2]:16[2]:26[3]:28[2]:29[2]:30[2]:31,32[3]:33[3]:34/31:3:6:12:13[2]:16[2]:24:26[2]:27:28:29:30[3]:32[2]:36,37[3]:38:39[3]:40:41:42[2]:43:44:50:51,52[2]/32:5[2]:9:10:12:17[2]:26[2]:28[2]:29/33:5:9:10:12:13:14[2]:15[2]/34:9,10[3]:11:12:14:15[2]:16[2]:30/35:1[2]:10:11:12[2]/37:8[2]:10:15:16/38:8[2]:16:17[3]:18:25:29/39:9[2]/40:8:13[2]:14/41:10:15[2]:16:25:28:32:33:39[2]:40[3]:41,42:44:55/42:1:7:8,9[2]:12[2]:14f:14:15:16[4]:18:19:19f:19[2]:20[3]:22[2]:33[2]:34[6]:36[2]:37:38/43:3,4,5[2]:6[3]:8:9:10:12:14:27:29[3]/44:5[2]:7[3]:9:10:15[2]:17:18[3]:19:21:22:23[2]:24:26:27:29:32/45:1:4:5[2]:7[2]:8:10[3]:11,12[3]:18[2]/46:3,4[3]:30[2]:31[2]:33[2]:34[2]/47:5,6:8:16:23:24[2]:25:29:31/48:4[2]:6[2]:11:20:21[2]:22/49:1[2]:3[2]:4[4]:8[3]:25:29,30/50:6:16,17[3]:19:20:21:24[3]/Ex1:18/2:7:9:13:14[5]:18:20/3:5:10[2]:12[4]:13:15:16[2]:18:19:20:21[3]:22/4:1:2:5[2]:9:10:12[3]:14[2]:15[3]:16:17[2]:19:21[3]:22:23[2]/5:1:4,5[2]:10,11[3]:14:17[2]:18[2]:21:22[3]:23/6:1:28,29/7:1:2:4:9[2]:16[2]:17/8:2:3,4:9[2]:10[2]:21:22:29[2]/9:1:2:14[2]:15:16:17[3]:28:29:30[2]/10:2[2]:3:4,5[2]:7[2]:8:10:11[2]:16:17:24[2]:28[3]:29/11:1[3]:7:8/12:13[3]:14[2]:15:17[3]:19:20:21[2]:22:24:25[3]:27:31[2]:32:46[3]:48[4]:49/13:3[2]:4,5:6,7:8[4]:9:11:12:13[2]:14[2]:16/14:4:11[2]:12:13[5]:14[2]:14f:16:17[2]/15:7[3]:12:13[3]:16:17[2]:26[3]/16:3:6[2]:7,8,9[3]:11,12[3]:15:23:26:28,29/17:2[2]:3[2]:5,6[3]/18:10:14:18[2]:19,20[3]:22[3]:23[2]/19:4[2]:5[3]:6:9[3]:13:23[2]:24/20:2:3:4:5:7[3]:10:12[2]:13:14:15:16:16f:17:19:20[2]:22[2]:23:24[3]:25[2]/21:1:2:2f/22:21[2]:22:23:24[2]:25[2]:26[2]:27:28:29:31/23:1:4[2]:5[2]:8[2]:9:14:14f:15[3]:16:19:19f:20[3]:22:23[3]:24[3]:25[3]:26:27[2]:28:31[3]:32:33[3]/24:1:8[2]:12[2]/25:9:16:16f:21:22[3]:39:40[2]/26:30/27:8:20/28:15:36/29:9:11:35:36:42[2]/30:6:11,12[2]:16[2]:32[2]:36:37/31:6:11:12,13[3]/32:4:7:8:10:11:12[2]:13:21[2]:22:26:29[3]:30[2]:32[2]:34[3]/33:1:2:3[3]:5[4]:12[5]:12f[2]:12:13[3]:14[2]:15:16[2]:17[3]:17f:19[2]:19f:20:22[2]:23/34:1:3:10[2]:11:12[3]:13:14:15[3]:16:17:18[2]:20:22:24[2]:25:26[2]:27[2]/35:1:5-9:10-19/40:15/Lev1:2,3/2:8:12:14/3:17/5:15/6:6/8:31:35[2]/9:6[2]/10[2]:7[2]:8,9[2]:13[2]:14:15:17[2]:18[2]/11:8[2]:9:10:11:12:13-19:23:26:27:28:33:39:45[2]/14:33,34[2]:57/15:31/16:29,30[3]:31[2]:34/17:7:8,9:10:11:13/18:3[2]:4,5[4]:6:10:11:15:17:18:21:24:26[4]:27:28:28f:29,30/19:1[2]:5:6:8[4]:9:11:12:13[2]:14:16f:17:23:23f:26:27:28:32:34:35,36[2]:37/20:1:8[2]:14:22[2]:22f[2]:23[3]:24[3]:25[4]:26[2]/21:8/22:17,18:25:28:29,30[2]:31:32,33[3]/23:7:7f:8[2]:9,10,11[2]:12:14:15,16:18:19:22[3]:32:36:42:43[2]/24:1:22/25:1[3]:3:6,7[2]:11:12:14,15,16[2]:17,18[2]:19[2]:20:21,22[2]:23[2]:35[2]:36[2]:38[2]:39[2]:40:42[3]:44[2]:45[2]:46[2]:47/26:1[2]:2:3:4,5[2]:6[2]:7:8[3]:9[3]:10[2]:11[2]:12[2]:13[3]:13f:14:16[3]:17[6]:18[2]:21[2]:23[2]:24:25[4]:26[2]:27:28:29:30[2]:32:33[3]:34,35[4]:38/27:26/Num1:2-15/4:17,18,19/5:3:19:20:21,22/6:24,25,26[5]/8:14:15/9:14/10:4:5,6,7f[2]:9[4]:10:29:31:31f[2]:32[2]:35/11:12[2]:15:16:17[4]:18[3]:19,20[5]:21:23:29/12:3,4:7,8:13/13:20:27/14:12:13:14[3]:15:17,18[3]:19[2]:20,21:25:28[2]:29[2]:31[2]:32:33[3]:34,35[3]:41:42[2]:43[3]/15:13,14:15,16f:22[2]:29:39[4]:40:41/16:3[4]:5:6,7[4]:8,9[3]:10[3]:11,12[3]:13[2]:14[3]:22:26:28:30:41/17:1:4:5/18:1:2,3[2]:4:5:6:7:8:11:16:19[3]:20[2]:23:28,29:30:32[4]/19:1/20:4:5[2]:8[2]:10[2]:12[2]:14:18[2]:19:24:26/21:5:7:27-30/22:5,6[2]:8:12:16,17[3]:20:29[2]:32[3]:33:34[2]:35:37[3]/23:3,4:11[3]:13:18-24:25:26:27[2]/24:3-9[2]:10[2]:11[2]:13:14:21,22[2]/25:18[4]/27:8:13[2]:14[2]/28:1[2]:3[2]:15:16:19:22:25:26:31/29:2:5:8:11:17:19:23:29:35:39/31:1[2]:3:15:18:19:24[2]:26/32:6[2]:7:14[2]:15[2]:20[2]:22[2]:23[5]:24:27:29[2]:30/33:50,51:52:53:54:55:56[2]/34:1:13/35:6:34[2]/36:1/Deu1:6:8:9:10:11[2]:17[2]:30[2]:31[2]:37:40/2:3:5:6:7[4]:9:19:25:31[2]/3:1[2]:19:20[2]:21[2]:22:23,24,25[2]:26:27[3]:28[2]/4:1[3]:3[2]:4:5[4]:6[2]:8:9[2]:10:11:12[2]:13:14[2]:15[2]:19:20[2]:21,22[2]:23[4]:25[2]:26[3]:27[2]:28:29[3]:30[3]:31[2]:32:33:34[2]:35:36[4]:37:38[2]:40[5]/5:1:2,3[2]:4:5[3]:6:9,10:11[2]:11f:14[3]:15[3]:16[3]:17:18:19:20:21:22[2]:23:26,27:28:31[3]:32[2]:33[2]/6:1[4]:2[5]:3[5]:5:6[2]:7[2]:10,11,12[9]:13:14:15[3]:16[3]:17:18[4]:19[2]:20:21/7:1[2]:2:4[2]:5:6[2]:7[4]:8[2]:11:13[7]:14[2]:15[2]:16[3]:17:19[3]:20:21:23:24[2]:25/8:1[5]:2[6]:3[5]:5[3]:7:10[2]:11:12,13:14[2]:15[3]:16[3]:17[2]:18:19[2]:20/9:1[2]:3[2]:4:5[2]:6[4]:7[4]:8[3]:9:13,14:16[2]:18:19[2]:21:22:23[5]:24[2]:25:28:29/10:4[2]:10:12,13[3]:15:19[2]:20:21:22/11:1:4[2]:5[2]:7:8[4]:9[3]:10[2]:13[3]:15[2]:17[4]:18:19[2]:21[3]:22[2]:23:24:25[3]:26:27[2]:28:29:31[2]:32[2]/12:1[3]:2[2]:3:4,5[2]:6:7[2]:8[2]:9[2]:10[3]:11:12[2]:13:14[2]:15[5]:16:17:18[3]:20-23[3]:24,25[2]:26,27[2]:28[2]:29:31:32/13:1:3[2]:4:5[4]:6,7:10[2]:11:12,13,14[4]:15:16:17[3]:18[3]/14:1:2[2]:3,4,5[2]:7:8:11-18:19,20:21[4]:22:23:25:26:27:28:29[2]/15:4,5[5]:6[4]:7[4]:8:9[2]:10[3]:11[2]:12[3]:14:15[3]:16[2]:18[5]:19:20:21/16:1:3[4]:3f:8:10:11:12:15:17[2]:18:20[2]:21/17:7[2]:8[2]:14[2]:15:16/18:9[3]:13:14[2]:15[3]:16[4]:18:21:22/19:1[2]:2,3:8:9[2]:10[2]:13:14[3]:19[2]:21/20:1[4]:2:3[2]:4[3]:5:6:7:8[2]:10:11:12[2]:13:14:16:18:19[2]:20/21:1:8:9[2]:10[2]:11[2]:12:13:14[5]:21[2]:23[2]/22:1[2]:2:3:4:6:7:9:12:21:25,26,27[2]/23:4[3]:5[2]:6[2]:7:8:9,10:14[4]:15,16[2]:17,18:19:20[4]:21[4]:22:23[4]:24:25/24:4:7:8:9:10[2]:11:12,13[4]:14,15[2]:17:18[3]:19[2]:20:22[2]/25:13,14,15[3]:17[3]:18:19[2]/26:1:2,3:5:10[2]:11[2]:12:13[2]:14:15[2]:16[2]:17[3]:18[2]:19[4]/27:1f:2,3,4:9:10[2]:12/28:1[3]:2-6[3]:7[3]:8[4]:9[2]:10:11:12[4]:13[4]:14[2]:15-15-19[5]:20[4]:21[3]:22[2]:23:24:25[3]:27:28:29[5]:30[2]:31[4]:32[2]:33[3]:34[3]:35:36[4]:37[2]:38:39[2]:41:43[2]:44[3]:45[3]:46:47,48[5]:49[3]:51:52[2]:53:54:56,57:58,59[2]:60[2]:61[2]:62[3]:63[5]:64[3]:65[2]:66[2]:67[4]:68[4]/29:2,3:4:5:6[3]:9[2]:10:11:12[2]:13:14,15[2]:16:17:18/30:1[4]:2[3]:3[4]:4[3]:5[3]:6:7,8[4]:9[3]:10[2]:12[2]:13:14:15[2]:16[4]:17[2]:18[4]:19[4]:20/31:2:3[2]:5[3]:6[3]:7:8[3]:12[2]:13:14:16[2]:23[2]:27[4]:29[3]/32:2:6[4]:7:39:46:47[2]:50[2]:51:52[3]/33:3:8:10:11:18[2]:23:25:26:27:29[2]/34:4[2]/Jos1:2:3[2]:5[5]:6:7[5]:8[3]:9[2]:12,13:15:17,18[2]/2:5[2]:9[2]:10[4]:11:12,13[2]:14[2]:15:16:17,18:20/3:2,3,4[5]:7[2]:10[3]:11/4:2,3:5:7:21:22:24/5:13/6:2:3,4:10[2]/7:7[2]:12[2]:13[3]:14:19:25[2]/8:1:2[3]:7[2]:8:18/9:6:7[3]:8[2]:10:12:22[3]:23[2]:24:25[2]/10:8[2]:19/13:1:2-7[2]/14:6:9[2]:10:12[2]/15:18,19[2]/17:14:15[3]:16,17,18[4]/18:3[2]:4/22:2,3[4]:4:5:16:17,18[3]:19[2]:20:24,25[2]:26,27:31[2]/23:3[4]:4,5[4]:7:8:9[2]:10[2]:12[3]:13[3]:14[2]:15,16[8]/24:7:8[3]:9:10:11[3]:12[2]:13[6]:15[2]:19:20[4]:22[2]:23[3]:27[2]/Ju1:3:14:15/2:1[2]:2[3]:3[2]/3:17,18,19/4:6:7:8:9[3]:18:22[2]/5:3:4:16/6:8:9[4]:10[4]:12:14[2]:16f:16[2]:17:18[2]:23:31:36[2]:37/7:2[2]:4[2]:8,9:10[2]:11:15:18/8:1[2]:2,3:6[3]:15[2]:18[2]:19[2]:21:22[2]/9:7:10:12:14:15[2]:16[2]:17[2]:18[2]:19[3]:20:31:33[3]:38/10:10[2]:11:12[2]:13[2]:14[2]:15/11:1:7[2]:8[3]:9:23[2]:24[2]:25[3]:26[2]:27[2]:35:36[3]/12:1[3]:2[3]:3[2]:5/13:2,3[2]:7:8:11:12:15:16:17/14:3[3]:12[2]:13[2]:15:16[4]:18[2]/15:2:3:10:11[2]:12,13[3]:18/16:5:6[2]:10[3]:12:13[3]:15[5]:20/17:2[4]:3:9:10,11[2]/18:3[2]:6:8:18:19:23:24:25[2]/19:9:20:24[2]/20:12[2]:27,28/21:21:22/Ru1:8[2]:9:10:11:13[3]:15:16[3]:17:21/2:8,9[2]:10,11[4]:12[2]:13[2]:19[2]:22/3:1[2]:3[2]:4:5:9[2]:10[4]:11:12:13/4:1:3:4[4]:4f:4[2]:6:8:9:11:12:14:15[3]/1Sa1:8:11[2]:14:17:18:23:26/2:3:16:23,24,25:28:29[3]:30:32[2]/3:4,5[2]:6[2]:8:16,17[3]/4:9/6:3[2]:4,5[2]:9/7:3[2]:5[2]/8:7:8:11:13:17:18[3]/9:12,13:16[2]:17:18:19[3]:20:21:24:26,27[2]/10:1:2[4]:3[3]:4[3]:5[3]:6[3]:7:8:14:18,19[5]/11:2:9:10[3]/12:1[2]:3[2]:4[2]:5[2]:7[2]:10[3]:11[2]:12[4]:13[2]:14[2]:15[2]:17[2]:20[3]:21:22:23[2]:24:25[2]/13:11[4]:12:13[3]:14/14:7[3]:9[2]:12:36:37:40:41:44[2]/15:1[2]:2:6:17[2]:18[2]:19[2]:23[2]:26[2]:28[2]/16:1:2[2]:3:4:7:15,16[3]/17:8[3]:9:25[2]:28[3]:33[2]:37:43:45[3]:46[2]:47/18:17[2]:21[2]/19:2:3[2]:4[2]:5[3]:11:17/20:3:9:12[3]:13[4]:14:18:19[2]:21[2]:22[2]:30[3]:36:37/21:1[2]:3:4:9[2]:14,15/22:7[2]:8[2]:11,12:13[3]:15[2]:16:18:

(YOU Con't)
23/23:4:12:17[3]:20:23/24:4:9,10[6]:11[5]:12[3]:13:15:
17[2]:18[2]:19[2]:20:21/25:6[2]:7:8[2]:25:26:27:28[3]:29[3]:
30,31[4]:32:33:34[2]/26:5,6,7:11:15[2]:16:17,18[2]:19[3]:
21[2]:23[2]:25[2]/27:5:10/28:2[4]:7,8:9[3]:11:12:13:15[3]:
16:17:18[2]:19:22/29:6[2]:9/30:8[2]:13[2]:15[4]:24[3]:26/
2Sa1:3:5:8:10:13:14:16[3]:21:24:26[2]/2:5:6[4]:7:20:
22:26:27/3:8[2]:9,10:13[2]:21:24,25[3]:33,34/4:8[2]/5:
2[2]:6:8:19[2]:24[2]/6:22/7:3[2]:5f:7:8[2]:9[3]:10,11:12:18:
19:20:21[3]:22[2]:23[2]:24[2]:25:26[3]:27:28[2]:29[3]/9:2:7[4]:
10,11[2]/10:11[2]/11:10[2]:12/12:7[3]:8[2]:9[2]:10:11[2]:12[2]
:13[2]:14:21[3]:28/13:5[5]:12:13[2]:16:20:25:26/14:2,3[2]
:9[2]:10:11:12:13[4]:14[2]:15,16:17[2]:19:20[3]:22[2]:32/15
:3:10[2]:13:15[2]:19,20[6]:21:28:33,34[4]/16:2:4[3]:7,8[6]:
17:19:21[2]:21f/17:2,3:8:11[3]:13:28,29/18:3[4]:4:11[3]
:11f:12:13:20:21:22:28:31[2]:33/19:5:6[5]:7[3]:11,12[3]:
13[2]:14:19:20:24,25:26:27[2]:28[2]:29[2]:30:33:36:37[2]:
38:42:43[2]/20:1:8,9,10:11:16:17:18:19[2]:21[2]/21:3[2]
:4:17/22:3:26[2]:27[2]:28[3]:29[2]:36:37:40:41:44[2]:49[2]:
50/24:3[2]:13:21:22[2]:23/1Ki1:2:11:12:13:14:16:
17:18:20[2]:21[2]:22,23:24[2]:27[2]:30:31:35:37:42[2]:
46,47[2]/2:2:3[3]:4:5:6:8:9[3]:13:14:16:17:20[4]:22:26[3]:
36,37[2]:38:42[3]:43:44[2]/3:6[3]:7:11:12[3]:13[3]:14[2]:23/5
:6[3]:8:9[3]/6:11,12[2]/8:12,13[2]:18:22,23[3]:24:27:28:
29:30[2]:33,34[3]:35,36[2]:39:40[2]:41,42:44[2]:46[2]:47[2]:
48[3]:49:51:52:53[3]:61[3]/9:2,3:4:6/10:9[4]/11:11[2]:
12,13:22[2]:31:35:37[2]:38[3]/12:2,3,4[2]:6:7[2]:9:10[2]:11:
28/13:2[2]:7[2]:8:14:18[3]:21,22[2]/14:2:6[2]:7[2]:8[2]:9[4]:12
/15:19/16:2[4]:3/17:4[2]:8,9:13:18[2]:20:24[2]/18:5:7:
9[2]:10:11:12[3]:13:14:17:18:21:25[2]:36:37[2]/19:2[2]:7:
9:10:13:15:16:20/20:5,6:9[2]:10:13[3]:25:28[2]:31:34:
36[3]:39:42[2]/21:5[2]:7[2]:15[3]:19[2]:20[2]:20f[2]:21[2]:22:29/
22:3:4[2]:6:11:12:15[2]:16[2]:18:22:23[2]:24:25[2]:28:30/
2Ki1:3:4,5:6[5]:9:10:11:12:14:16[4]/2:1:3[2]:4:5[2]:6,7:
9[2]:10[5]:18:19/3:6,7,8:13:14:17[2]:18:19/4:2:4:7:
15,16:24:28[2]:30/5:5:6:8:13[3]:22:25:26[2]:27[2]/6:1:
11:12:19:26-30[2]/7:2[2]:19[2]/8:8,9:12[2]:13:14[2]/9:1:5[2]
:6:7[2]:11:15:18[3]:19:22:25:31[3]/10:2,3:5[2]:6:9,10:13
:15[2]:24:30/12:7/13:14:16,17:19[3]/14:10[2]/17:38[2]
:39[2]/18:14[2]:19:20,21[4]:22[2]:23[2]:24[2]:25:26:27[2]:29[2]
:30[2]:31,32[4]:35/19:10:11[2]:15[2]:19[2]:20:21[2]:22[2]:23:
25[2]:26[2]:27[3]:28[2]:30[2]/20:1:3[2]:9[2]/22:12,13:15,16[2]:
18,19[3]:20[2]/23:17/1Ch4:10/11:2[4]/12:17[3]:18[3]/
13:2/14:10:15[2]/15:12[2]:13/16:18/17:4:7[3]:8:10:
11:16:17[4]:18[2]:19[2]:20[2]:21[3]:22[3]:24[2]:25[2]:27/19:12[2]
/21:3[2]:10,11[2]:12:22:23[2]/22:8[3]:9:11[4]:12[2]:13[2]:15:
16:18[2]:19/28:3[2]:8[2]:9[4]:10:20[2]/29:11:12[2]:13:14[3]:
16[2]:17[2]:18[2]:19/2Ch1:7:8[2]:9:11[3]:12[4]/2:11:13:15:
16[3]/6:1:14[3]:15:16:18:19[2]:20,21[5]:24[3]:25:26[2]:27:
30[2]:31[2]:31f:33[3]:34:36[3]:37,38[3]:39[2]:40/7:12:13:17
:18:19[3]/9:5:7:8/10:4:7[2]:8,9:10[2]:11[2]:14[4]/12:5[3]:7[2]
:8[2]/13:5:8[6]:9[2]:11:12[3]/14:11[2]/15:2[6]:7[2]/16:3:7[2]:8[2]
:9[2]/18:3,4,5[2]:10:11:12:15[2]:17:22[2]:23[2]:24:27:29/
19:2[3]:3[3]:6[4]:7:9:10[5]:11/20:2:6[2]:7[2]:8:9[4]:10:11:12[2]:
15[2]:16:17[3]:20:37/21:12:13[3]:14[2]:15/23:4:7/24:6:
20[5]:27/25:8[3]:9:15[2]:16[3]:19[2]/26:17,18[3]/28:9[2]:10:
11:13[2]/29:4,5:8:11/30:8:9[3]/32:10[2]:11:12:13:14:
15/33:8[2]/34:23:26:27[3]/35:3:21[2]/36:22,23[2]/Ez1
:3/4:2[2]:3:13[2]:14[3]:15:16[2]:18/5:3:8:9:10:17/6:8/7:
13:14:15[2]:16:17:18:19[2]:20[2]:21[2]:25[3]/9:6:8[2]:9[2]:10:
12[2]:13:15[3]/10:10[2]:11:12/Neh1:6,7[2]:8[4]:9[3]:10:11
/2:1[3]:4:5,6[2]:17:19:20/4:5:19[2]/5:7[2]:8:9[2]:10:13/6:
3:5,6[2]:7[5]:8[2]:10/8/9:6[4]:7:8[5]:9[2]:10[3]:11[2]:12:13:14:
15[3]:17[3]:19:20[2]:21:22[2]:23[2]:24:26[2]:27[4]:28[4]:29:30[3]
:31[2]:32[2]:33[3]:35[4]:36:37/13:17:18:21[3]:27[2]/Est1:
19[2]/2:4/3:3,4:11[2]/4:13[2]:14[3]/5:3[2]:4[2]:6[2]:7,8[2]:14[2]
/6:10[2]:13/7:2[2]:5[2]/8:7:8/9:12[2]/Job1:7:8:9:10[3]:
11:12,13[2]:16:17:19/2:2:3[3]:4,5:6:9[2]:10/4:2:3,4:5:
6:7,8/5:8:17:19[2]:20:21:22[2]:23:24[2]:26/6:14:15-
15-18:19-21[2]:22[2]:25,26/7:8:12:13,14:17:18:19:
20[2]:21/8:2:5:6[3]:7[2]:10[3]:22/9:12:28:31[2]:32,33[2]/
10:2:3[2]:4-7:4-7f:4-7[3]:8[2]:9:10:11:12:16:17:18[2]:
20,21/11:3[3]:4[2]:5:6[3]:7[3]:8[2]:13,14[2]:15[2]:16:18[3]:19[2]/
12:2[2]:3:7,8,9[2]:12/13:1[2]:2:4[2]:7[2]:8:9[3]:10[2]:11:12:19
:20[2]:22[2]:24:25[2]:26:27,28/14:3:4:5[2]:6:13:15[2]:16:
17:20,21[2]/15:2[3]:4,5:6:7,8[5]:9[2]:11:12:13:14:16:17-
17-19/16:2:3[2]:4[5]:5:8/17:3,4:10[3]/18:2[2]:3:4:5[2]/19
:2:3[2]:4:5:22[2]:28:29[2]/20:2:3[2]:4/21:19:27:28:29:
34/22:3[2]:4[2]:6[3]:7:8:9:10,11:13:15,16:17:21[4]:23[2]:
24:26:27[3]:28[2]:29[3]/26:2[2]:3[2]:4/27:5:11:12[2]/30:20[4]
:21:22/32:6[2]:15:16/33:5:6[2]:7[2]:8:10[2]:11:12:13[2]:
32[2]:33/34:2:10:17:18[2]:33:34,35:36[2]:37/35:2,3[2]:
4:5:6[2]:7:14,15[2]:16/36:2:3:4:16[2]:17:18[3]:19[2]:21/
37:15:16,17[3]:18:19,20[2]/38:2:3[2]:4[2]:5:11:12:13:14
:16:17,18[3]:19:20:21[3]:22,23:31[2]:32:33:34:35[2]:
39,40/39:1[2]:2,3:10[2]:11[2]:12:19:20:26/40:2[3]:7:8[3]:
9[2]:14[3]:15/41:1:2:3[2]:4:5:8[3]/42:2[2]:3:4[3]:5[2]:7[3]:8[2]/
Ps2:7:7f:7:8:12[2]/3:3[2]/4:1[2]:2:7:8/5:1:3[2]:4:5:6[2]:7:
8[2]:10:11[3]:12[2]/6:5[2]:5f:8/7:1:5:7,8:9/8:2[2]:3:4:5:6[2]
/9:1[2]:2:4[2]:4f:5:6:10[3]:14[2]:19/10:1[3]:13:14[5]:17[2]:18
/11:1/12:7/13:1[2]:5/16:1:2:10[2]:11/17:1:2:3[2]:6:8[2]
:13,14:15[2]/18:1[2]:25[2]:25f:26:27:28:35:36:39:40:
43,44,45:49:50[3]/19:14/20:1[2]:2:3:4:5/21:2[2]:3[2]:4:
5[2]:6[2]:8:9,10:11/22:1[2]:3,4[3]:5:9,10,11[4]:15:22[2]:23[2]:
23f:25:25f/23:4:5[2]:5f:6/25:1:2:5[2]:20:21/26:1/27
:8:9[2]:10:14[2]/28:1[3]/29/30[3]:2[2]:3:4:6,7:8:9[2]:12/31:
1[2]:2:3:4:4f:5,6[3]:7:8:14,15[2]:16:17:19[3]:22:23:24/
32:5[2]:7[3]:8[3]:11f/33:22/34:9:11:12/35:3[2]:17:18:
22:24:28[2]/36:6:6f:8:9:10/37:3:4:5[2]:6:10:27:34[2]/
38:1:9[2]:15/39:5,6:7:9[2]:9f:11/40:5[2]:6[2]:6f:9[2]:17[2]/
41:3f:10:11[2]:12[2]/42:1:4,5[3]:9/43:2[2]/44:1[2]:3:4:7:8
:9:10:11:12[2]:13:14:17:18:22:24[2]/45:2[2]:5:7[2]:9:
10,11:12:17/48:10[2]:11:13/49:10[3]:11[2]/50:7:8[2]:9:
12:14,15[4]:17:18:19:20:21[2]:22[3]/51:4[3]:6:8:12:13:
14,15[2]:16[4]:17[2]:19:19f/52:1[3]:2:3:4[2]:5[3]:9:9f:9/54:
5:6/55:1:11:13:23/56:3,4:8[3]:12:13/57:1:9/58:1[3]
:1f/59:9:16:17[2]/60:1[2]:2[2]:3:4,5[2]/61:2:3:5[4]:6:8/63
:1[3]:3:4[2]:5:6:7:8/65:1[3]:3:4[2]:5[2]/66:4:10:11:12:12f:
12:14:15[2]:16[2]/67:1:4:5/68:7:8:9,10[2]:15,16:28/
69:5[2]:6:9:13[4]:19[2]:26[2]/70:5/71:1:2:3:5[2]:6[2]:7:8[2]:
14[2]:15[2]:16:17[2]:19[2]:20[2]:21:22/72:1:5/73:22:23[2]:
24:24f:25[2]/74:1:2[2]:8:9,10[2]:11:12:13,14[3]:15:16[2]:
17:18:22/75:1[2]/76:4:6:7:8[2]:9:10[2]:11/77:4:13:14[2]
:15:16:20/78:2,3:4[2]/79:5:12:13/80:2:4:5:8:9:12:
14:15[2]:17:17f:18[2]/81:7[3]:8[2]:9:9f:10[3]:16[2]/82:2[2]:5[2]
:6:7[2]:8/83:2[2]:9[2]:10:18/84:9:12/85:1[2]:4:5:6/86:2[2]
:3:4:5:7[2]:8:9[2]:10[2]:11:12:13[3]:15:17/87:3/88:1:6:8
:9:10:14[2]/89:5:8:9[2]:10:11:12:14,15:17:19:26:38:
39[2]:40:42:43:44:45:46:47[2]:49[2]:51/90:1:2:3:4:8[2]:
11:13:16/91:3[2]:4[2]:5:11[2]:12[2]:13/92:1:2:4:5:10/
93:1:4/94:5:10[2]:20:21,22/95:7[2]/97:8,9/99:8/
102:9,10:12:13[2]:24:25:26[2]:27[2]/103:20:21/104:1[3]
:5:6:7,8[2]:9:24[2]:26:27:28[2]:29[2]:30/105:10,11/106:
1[2]:4:5:7:8:9:10:47/107:1:2[2]:22:43/108:1[2]:3:8:11[2]
/109:17[2]:21:26:27:28/110:1:3:4:5[2]/114:6/115:
11:14:15/116:16[2]:17[2]/118:13:21:26:27,28[2]/119:
4:7[2]:10:17:21:22:26[2]:27:32:37:38:44,45,46:52:55
:58:59,60:62:65:67[2]:68:70:71,72:73:74:75,76,77:
79:81:82:84:85,86:88:90,91:93:102,103:107:112:
113:114:115:116:118:119:120:123:126:132:134:
137:147:149:151:154:159:164:168[2]:169:170[2]:
171:175[2]/120:4/121:5:6:7:8[3]/123:1/127:2[2]/128
:5:6/129:8[2]/130:3,4[2]/131:3/132:1:10:11[2]:12:13:
14/134:1:3/135:20/137:5,6:8[3]/138:1:2:2f:3:4:7[2]
:8/139:1:2[2]:3[2]:4:5:8[2]:12[2]:13:14:15:16:17,18[2]:19:
20:21:24[2]/140:13/141:1:2:8[2]/142:3:5[2]:7/143:1:
2:5:6[2]:8:9:10:11:12/144:3:3f:9:10[2]/145:1:7:10[2]:
13:15[2]:16/148:3:7/150:6/Pro1:7,8,9[3]:10:14:22[3]:
23[2]:24[2]:25:26[2]:27[2]:28:29:30:31[2]:32[2]/2:3,4,5[4]:
11,12,13[2]/3:1[2]:4,5:6[2]:7,8[2]:11,12[2]:22:23:24,25,26[4]
:27,28:29/4:1:4[2]:6[2]:8,9[3]:10:11:12[2]:13:22:24f/5:2
:4:5:9:10:11:12:16:19[2]:21[2]/6:1[3]:2:3:4:5[2]:6:9[3]:11[4]
:12,13:21:22[4]:23[2]:24:25:34:35[2]/7:5:15[2]:25[2]:27/8
:1:4,5[3]:6,7/9:4:7,8[5]:12[2]/10:19/11:4:15[2]:17[2]:21[2]:
27[4]:28/12:1/13:18[4]:24[4]/14:7/15:17[2]:27f:31,32[2]:
33/16:26/17:13/18:16:19/19:17[2]:18[2]:19[3]:20:27
/20:4[2]:6:12[2]:13[2]:19/22:1:10:17,18,19[2]:20,21:
22,23[2]:24,25:26,27[2]:29/23:1:6,7,8[2]:10,11:12:
13,14:15,16:17,18[3]:23:31:33[3]:34:35/24:10[2]:
11,12[2]:13,14[2]:15,16[3]:18:21,22:24:34/25:2,3:4,5[3]
:6,7:8,9,10[5]:15:16[2]:17:21,22/26:4,5:24,25,26:27
/27:10:11:14:16[2]:22[2]/28:27/29:17:21:26/30:4:6[2]
:7:10:32/31:8:10:29/Ecc1:8-11[2]/5:1[4]:4[2]:5:6,7:8:
11[2]/6/7:2:10:12:14:15-17:18[2]:21,22[4]:26/8:2,3/9
:9[2]:10[2]/10:3:4:8,9/11:1:2:4[2]:6:9[3]/12:1:4[2]:5:6/
Sol1:3:4[2]:6:7[3]:8:9f:9:11:15:16/2:7[2]:7f/3:3:5/4:1:
7[2]:9:13,14:15/5:8[2]:9/6:1:4[2]:4f:9[3]:13[3]/7:6:7:12/8
:1[2]:2[3]:4:5:12/Is1:5,6[5]:7:8:10[4]:12,13[2]:15[2]:16:18[3]:
19[4]:20[2]:24:25:26[2]:29[3]:30:31/2:6[2]:8:9/3:6[2]:10:11
:12[2]:15/4:1/5:3[2]:7:8[2]:11[2]:12[2]:13[3]:19/6:7:9[4]/7:3[2]
:5:9[4]:11:13[2]:15,16:17:18[2]:20[4]/8:1:9,10[3]:12[3]:13[2]:
19/9:11,12[3]:13/10:3[4]:4[3]:24:25:30/12:1:4:6/13:5
:6:8[2]/14:4[5]:6[2]:9[3]:10:11:12[3]:13:15:16:20[3]:29[3]:30[2]
:31[2]/16:4,5[4]:7/17:10[4]:11[2]/18:2[2]:5[2]/19:12:13/21
:1:2:5:10:11:12:13/22:8:9,10,11[5]:12:13[2]:14[2]:
15,16[2]:17[3]:18[4]:19[2]:20/23:1:2,3:4:6:7:12[4]:14/24:
18[6]/25:1[5]:2:3:4:5/26:9[2]:11[2]:12:13:14:16/28:2[3]:
14:15[3]:17[2]:18:19[2]:20[2]:22/29:1:2:4:9[4]:10:11:12:
16[2]/30:1[3]:2:3[2]:6:9[2]:12[2]:13:14:15:16[3]:17[4]:18[4]:19[3]
:20[4]:21[3]:22[2]:23:25/31:6:7[2]/32:9[2]/33:1[6]:2:3:11[2]:
13:15:19:20/35:4:8/36:4[2]:5:6:7:8,9[5]:10:12[2]:14[2]:
15[3]:16[2]:17:18[2]:19:20/37:10[2]:11[2]:16,17[2]:20[2]:22[2]:
23[3]:24[2]:25[2]:26[3]:27[2]:28[3]:29[2]:30[3]:31/38:1[2]:3[4]:5[2]:6[2]
:17[2]:18:18f:19/39:6/40:21[3]:25:27:28[2]/41:8[3]:9[4]:
10[4]:11:12:13[3]:14[2]:15:16[3]:23:24[2]:26[2]:28/42:6[3]:6f
:6:7:9:10[2]:11[2]:18[3]:20[3]:23[2]/43:1[4]:2[7]:4[3]:5[2]:10:12[5]:
19:22[2]:23[3]:24[2]:26/44:2[2]:3:7[2]:8[2]:17:21[3]:22:24/45
:2:3[3]:4[3]:5[3]:9:10[2]:11[2]:14[4]:15:20:21/46:3[3]:4[3]:5:6:9
:10:12:13[2]/47:1:3[2]:5:6[2]:7[2]:8:9:10[4]:11[2]:12:13[2]:14
/48:1[2]:3:4[2]:5[2]:6[4]:7:8[2]:9:10[3]:11[2]:14[2]:16[2]:17[3]:18[2]:
19:20/49:1:3[2]:6[2]:7[3]:8,9[4]:15:17:19:21:22:23[3]:25/
50:1[3]:2:10:11[2]/51:1[4]:7:9:10:12[3]:13[3]:14:15:16[2]:
17[2]:19:22:23/52:3[2]:11[4]:12[3]/54:3:4:6:7[2]:8:9:10[3]:
11:14[2]:15[2]:15f:17[3]/55:1:2[3]:3[2]:5[2]:6:8:12[2]/56:1/
57:3[3]:4[2]:5:6:7,8[4]:9[2]:10[3]:11[3]:12:13[3]:16/58:3[9]:4[2]:5
:6[2]:7:8[6]:9[2]:10:11[4]:12:13[2]:14/59:1[3]:2[2]:3:4:5:6[2]:7[2]:
8[3]:9[5]:10[2]:11[4]:12:16[2]/60:1:2:3:4:5[2]:6:7:9:10[3]:11:
12f:14:15[2]:16[2]:19[2]/61:6[2]:7:10/62:2:3:4[3]:5[2]:6,7:8
:9[4]:11[2]/63:3:15:16[2]:17[4]:19[2]/64:1:2:3[2]:5:7[2]:8[2]:11
:12[2]/65:5:11:12[5]:13[3]:14:15:16/66:1:5[3]:10[2]:13:14
:22/Jer1:5[5]:7[3]:8[2]:11:13:17[2]:18[4]:19[2]/2:2[2]:9[2]:
10,11[2]:17[3]:18:19[2]:20[2]:21[2]:22[2]:23[4]:24[3]:25[2]:28[4]:
29:30:32:33[2]:34:35[3]:36[2]:37[3]/3:1[2]:2[4]:3:4,5[6]:6:12:
13[2]:14[2]:15[2]:16[2]:17:19[3]:20[3]:22[2]/4:1:2[2]:4:6:10[2]:14
:18:30[4]/5:1[2]:3[4]:7:15[2]:17:18:19[3]:21:22[2]/6:2:3:8:9
:14:16[4]:17[4]:22:26:27[2]/7:2:3[2]:4:5[2]:6:7:8[2]:9[2]:13,14[5]
:15:17:23/8:8:17[5]/9:25,26[2]/10:5:6[2]:7[3]:18[2]:24/
11:5[3]:13:15[2]:16[3]:20[2]:21,22[2]/12:1[3]:2[2]:3[3]:5[4]:6[2]:14
:15[2]/13:12:15[2]:16[4]:17:20:21[3]:22[2]:23:24,25[4]:26:
27[2]/14:7:8:9[3]:10[3]:13[2]:19[2]:22[2]/15:2:4:5[3]:6[4]:7[3]:11[3]
:14[3]:15:17,18[2]:19[4]:20[4]:21[2]/16:2:8:10:12[2]:13[6]:
14,15[3]:16[6]:17[2]:18[2]:19/17:2,3:4[3]:13:14[3]:15:17:20
:24:27[3]/18:2:6[2]:11:20:23[2]/19:1[2]:7:10[2]:11:15/20:
3:4[2]:6[5]:7[3]:8:10:12/21:3,4:5:12[4]:14/22:4[2]:5:6[3]:7:
13[3]:14:17[3]:20:21[5]:22:23:24,25[6]:26[2]:27/23:2[3]:16[2]
:17:18:20:33[4]:35:36[2]:37[2]:38,39[6]:40/24:3/25:2,3[2]
:4[2]:5[4]:6[2]:7[3]:8,9[4]:11:15:27[2]:28[2]:29[2]:35/26:4[2]:5[3]:9[2]
:11:13[2]:14:15[4]/27:2:4:9:10[3]:12:13[3]:14[2]:15[4]:16:
18/28:6:7:8:13:15:16[2]/29:5:7:8[2]:10[3]:11[2]:12:13[3]:
14[4]:15[2]:20:21:22:25:26[2]:27:31[2]:32/30:2:10:11[6]:
13:14[3]:15[2]:16[3]:17[2]:18:22:24[2]/31:3[2]:4:5:10:16[2]:
18[3]:21[2]:22:23/32:5[4]:6,7[2]:8:17[2]:18[2]:19[2]:20[3]:21:
22[2]:23[3]:24[2]:25/33:3:4:20,21:24/34:3[4]:4:5[2]:15[4]:
16:17[3]:18,19[7]:20[2]/35:13:14[2]:15[6]:16:17:18,19/36
:6:17[2]:19[2]:28:29:30/37:7[2]:10[2]:17:18:19:20/38:5[2]
:12:14:15[3]:17[2]:18[2]:20[3]:21,22[5]:23[2]:24:25[3]:26[3]/39
:17[3]:18/40:4[6]:5[3]:9:10[2]:15:16[2]/42:2:4[2]:6:9:10[4]:11[3]
:12[4]:13,14[3]:15:16[3]:17[4]:18[5]:19:20[4]:21[3]:22[2]/43:
2,3[3]:9/44:2,3[2]:7[4]:8[4]:9:10[2]:11:19:21[2]:22:23[2]:24:
25[3]:26[2]:27[4]:29[3]/45:2:3:5[3]/46:3:9:11[2]:14:19:27[2]:
28[5]/47:5:6/48:7[2]:14:27:32[2]:44:46/49:1[3]:2[2]:4[3]:5[2]
:8:12[3]:16[3]:25:30[2]/50:11:12:14:21:24[3]:31:32[2]:42/
51:6[2]:20f:20:21:25[4]:26[2]:36:46:50[2]:61,62[3]:63/
Lam1:10:12[2]:21[4]:22/2:13[2]:14:16:18:20:21[2]:22/3
:17:19:34,35,36[2]:37:43:44:45:56[3]:57:58[2]:59:60:
61/4:15:21[2]/5:19:20[2]:21:22[2]/Eze2:1:3:4:7:8[3]/3:
1:4:5[2]:7[2]:8:17:18[4]:19[4]:20[3]:21[2]:22:25f:25[2]:26:27[3]
/4:1:3[2]:4,5:8f:8[3]:10:12:15/5:8[2]:9[2]:11[4]:12[2]:14:15:
16[2]:17[3]/6:3[2]:4-7:11:12:13:14[2]/7:2:3:4[2]:5,6:8,9[3]:
15[4]:18[3]:19:20[3]:24:25[2]:26,27[3]/8:6[3]:12:13:15[2]:17/
9:7:11/11:5[2]:6:7[3]:7f:8[2]:9[3]:10[2]:11[3]:12[3]:13:16[3]:17[3]
:18[2]:19[3]:20/12:2:3:11:18:20:24/13:5:6[4]:7[5]:8:9[4]:
12[2]:14[3]:18f:19[3]:20[2]:21[2]:22:23[5]/14:6,7:8:22[3]:23[2]
/15:7/16:3:4[4]:5[5]:6,7[5]:8[5]:9,10:11:13[4]:14:15[4]:16[2]:
17[2]:18[2]:19[3]:20[3]:21:22[2]:23:24:25:26:27[4]:28[3]:29[2]:
30[2]:31[2]:32:33,34[6]:37[5]:38:39[3]:40,41[2]:42[3]:43[4]:44:
45[2]:46:47[3]:48:51[2]:52:56:57:59,60[5]:61[7]:62[2]:63[5]/
17:12,13[2]:21/18:3:19:23:25[2]:29:30:31[2]:32/20:3[2]
:20:21:29:30:31[6]:32[2]:33:34[2]:35,36[3]:37:38[2]:39:40[2]
:41[2]:42[2]:43[2]:44[2]:47/21:3:7:9,10,11[2]:16[2]:17:24[3]:
28:29[3]:30[3]:31[2]:32[2]/22:4[3]:5:7:10f:12:14:15[2]:16[2]:
18,19,20[3]:21:22[3]:24:25:30:31[3]/23:21[2]:22[2]:24[4]:
25[2]:26:27:28[2]:29[4]:30:31[2]:32[2]:33:34:35[2]:36:40[3]:
41[2]:49[3]/24:6:13[3]:16:17[2]:19:22[3]:23[3]:24[3]:26[2]:27[3]/
25:3:4[2]:5:6:7[5]/26:3[2]:13:14:17[2]:19[2]:20[2]:21[2]/27:3:
4[2]:5[2]:7:10:15:18:21:26:31:33:34[2]:36/28:2,3[7]:4:5:
6[2]:8[2]:9[2]:10:12:13[3]:14[3]:15[4]:16[4]:16f:17[3]:18:18f:18[2]
:19[3]:22[3]:23:24/29:3:4:5[3]:6[2]:7[2]:8:10[2]/31:2,3:18[4]/
32:2[2]:3[2]:4[3]:7[2]:8:9:9f:9:10:11:12:19[3]:28/33:7[2]:8[3]:
9[2]:10:11:20[2]:25[6]:26:30[2]:31:32[2]/34:2:3[2]:4[2]:8[4]:17:
18[3]:31[2]/35:3[3]:4,5[4]:6[2]:9[3]:10:11[2]:12[2]:13:14:15[3]/
36:2:3[3]:6:9[3]:11[3]:12[3]:13:15:22[3]:23[2]:24:25[2]:26[4]:27[2]
:28[2]:30:31[2]:32:33[2]:35/37:3:5:6[4]:12:13:14[4]:
18,19,20/38:2,3:4[2]:5:7:8[2]:9:11:13:14:15,16[2]:17[2]:
18:21[2]:22/39:1:2[3]:2f:3:4[3]:5[2]:19[3]/40:4[5]/43:10:20
:23:27/44:5:6:7[2]:8[3]:9/45:1[2]:10:13[2]:21/47:14:22
/Dan1:10/2:4:5[3]:6[2]:7[2]:8,9[2]:11:16:23[2]:25:26:28:
29[2]:31:34:37[2]:38[2]:41,42:47/3:5:10:12[3]:14:15[5]:18
/4:2:9[2]:18[2]:19:20:22[2]:23:25[3]:26[2]:27[2]:31[2]:32[2]:35
/5:12:13:14[3]:16[4]:17:18:22[3]:23[4]:27/6:7[2]:12[2]:13:
15[2]:16[2]:20[2]:22/8:17[2]:19[2]:20:22:26/9:4[3]:5:6:7[4]:
10[2]:11:12[3]:15:16:18:22:23[4]/10:11[2]:12[2]:14:17:19[3]
:20,21[2]/11:2/12:1:13/Hos1:2:10[2]:11:17:18[2]:19:
20[3]:23[2]/3:1:3[2]/4:1:2:4:5:6[4]:14[2]/5:1[4]:2:3[2]:4[3]:9/6:
4:5[4]:6:7[2]:11[2]/8:2:5[3]:6[2]/9:1:3[2]:4:5:6:10[3]:12[2]/10:
9:10[3]:12[2]:13[2]:15/11:8[4]:9[2]/12[3]:10/13:4[2]:5:6[2]:7:8[2]
:9[2]:10[3]:11/14:1:2:3:4:8[3]/Joe1:2[3]:5:11[2]:13:20/2:
13:14[4]:17:19[2]:20:21:25[2]:26[3]:27:28/3:4[3]:5:6:7[3]:
17/Amo2:10[2]:11:12[2]:13/3:2[2]:4:7/4:1[3]:2[3]:3:5:6[2]:
8:9:10[2]:11:12:13/5:1:7[2]:10[2]:11[4]:12[3]:14:16:18[4]:
19:20:25,26,27[4]/6:2:3[3]:4:5:6:7:10:12[2]:13[2]:14[2]/7:
2:5:8:11:12[2]:16[2]:17/8:2:4:5[2]:6:10/9:7[2]/Ob1:1:2[2]
:3[3]:4[2]:5[2]:7[3]:10[2]:11[3]:12[4]:13[2]:14[2]:15[2]:16/Jon:2:6:

(YOU Con't)
8^2:9,10:11:14/**2**:2:3:4:6:7:9^3/**3**:1/**4**:2^3:9:10^2/**Mic**
1:2:13:15:16/**2**:1^4:2^2:3^2:4:7^4:8^2:9:10^2:11^2:12^2:13^3
/**3**:1^2:2^2:3:4^2:5^5:6^3:7:9:11^3:12/**4**:8:9^3:10^4:11^2:13^3
/**5**:2^2:10:13^2:14/**6**:3:4^3:5^6:6^2:7^2:8:9:13:14^4:15^3:
16^6/**7**:12:15^2:16:18^3:19^3:20^4/**Nah1**:9^2:12:13:14^2:
15/**2**:1^2:12:13^3/**3**:5:6^2:7:8:15^4/**Hab1**:2^2:5^2:12^2:
13^2:17/**2**:6^3:7^3:8^4:9:10^2:11:12:15:17^5:18^2/**3**:2^3:
8,9f^4:8,9^3:12:13^2:14/**Zep1**:11:17^2:18^2/**2**:1:3^2:5^4:
12/**3**:11^3:15^2:17,18^6:19:20^4/**Hag1**:3,4:6^4:7:9^3:10
:11^2:13^2/**2**:3:4:5^2:12:14^2:15^2:16,17^3:18,19^5:23^3/
Zec1:3^2:9:12:14/**2**:2:6,7^2:8^2:9:10:11,12^2/**3**:2f^2:2:
4:7^5:8^3:10^3/**4**:2:5:6^2:9:13/**5**:2/**6**:12:15^2/**7**:5^3:6/**8** ^{2}
:7:9^4:10^2:12:13^2:14,15^3:19^2:23/**9**:11^2:12^2:13^3/**11**
:1:2^2:9^3:12^2:13/**13**:3^2/**14**:5^2/**Mal1**:2,3^3:4:5:6^3:7^2:
8^2:9^3:10^2:12:13^3/**2**:1^7:3^2:4^2:8^3:9^3:13^2:14^4:15^3:17^2
/**3**:1^2:6:7^4:8^4:9:10^4:12^2:13^2:14,15:18/**4**:2^2:3:5/
Mt1:21/**2**:6^2:8:13/**3**:7^2:8:9:11:14/**4**:3:6^3:9^2:19/**5**
:11^2:12:13^3:14:20^2:21^2:22^7:23^2:25^2:26^2:27:29^3:
30:33:35:36:39:40^2:41:44:45:46^2:47^2:48/**6**:1:2^2:3
:4:5:6^3:7,8^2:14,15^5:16:17:18^2:23:24^2:25:26:30:
31,32:33^3/**7**:1:2^2:3:4^3:5:6:7^3:8:11:12^2:15:16^3:22:
23:23f/**8**:2^2:4f:4:8,9^4:11:13:19^2:21:26^2:29^2:29f:
31/**9**:4:5,6^2:13:18^2:22:28^2/**10**:8:9:10^2:11^2:12:14^2
:16:17:18^2:19^2:20^2:22^3:23^2:25:26:27:31:37^5:38^2:
39^4:40:41^4:42^2/**11**:3:7^2:8:10f:14:15:17^2:18:19^2:
21^2:22:23:24:25:26:28^2:29,30^3/**12**:3:5:7^3:11^3:27:
28:34^2:36^3:37^2:41^2:42/**13**:9:10:17^2:27:29:51/**14**:
16:28^2:31:33/**15**:5,6^3:7^2:11^3:12:16:17^2:34/**16**:2,3^2
:8:9^2:10:11:15:17^2:18:19^3:22:23^3:26:28/**17**:4^2:17 ^{2}
:20^2:21:25:26,27^2/**18**:3^2:5^2:6^2:8:9:10^2:15^2:16^2:17
:17f:18^3:19^4:32^3:33^2:35^2/**19**:3:4:9:17^4:21^3:27:28/
20:6:13^2:15:21:22^3:23:26^2:27^2:32,33^2/**21**:2^2:3^2:
13:15:16:21^3:22^3:23f:24^2:28:30:31:32^5:40:42:43/
22:9:12:16:18^2:31^3:38,39:40^3/**23**:2:3^2:4:8^2:11:
13,14^5:15^3:16^2:18:20^2:21^2:22^2:23^5:24:25^3:27^3:28
:29,30^3:31:32:33:34^2:35^2:37:38:39^4/**24**:4:6:9^2:10:
15^2:23:25:26:32:33^2:42:44:45^2:46^2:48:51^2/**25**:12
f:13:21^3:22:23^3:24,25^2:24,25f^2:26:27:34:35^3:36^2:
37^3:38^2:39^2:40^2:41^2:42^2:43^3:44^2:45^2/**26**:2:10:11^3
:15:20,21:29:31:32:33:34:40:41:50:53:55^4:62^2:63^2
:64:65,66:68^2:69^2:70:73:75/**27**:11:13:17:21:40^3:
41,42,43^3:46:64/**28**:5:14:20^2/**Mk1**:8^2:11^2:17:24^3
:36,37:40^2:43,44/**2**:8:9,10,11^2:22:25,26/**3**:11:
31,32/**4**:9:11,12:13^2:23:24^4:38:40^2/**5**:7,8^2:19:31^3
:34/**6**:10:11^4:22,23^2:37/**7**:6,7^2:8:9:10:11^3:12,13:
14:15,16^2:18^3:23^2:29/**8**:5:11:12:17:18^3:19:21:21f
:23:28^2:29^2:32:33:34^2:35^2/**9**:1:5:17:19^4:22:23:25:
33:41^2:45,46^2/**10**:2:5:15:18:19:21^3:28:29:35:38^3:
39:40:42:43^2:49^2:51^2:52/**11**:2^2:3^2:4,5:14:17:21:
22,23^3:24^3:25^3:26,f:27,28:29^2:31/**12**:9:10:14^2:15
:24:26:27:30:31:32:34/**13**:5:9^2:11^3:13^2:14^2:15,16 ^{2}
:21:23:28:29^2:33:34f:35,36,37^3/**14**:7^4:9:13^3:14:
15:18^2:20:27:28:29:30:31^2:36:37:38:44^2:48:49:
60^2:61:62:63,64:65^2:66,67:70^2:71:72/**15**:2^2:3,4^2:
9^2:12:29,30^2:32^2:34/**16**:6:7^3:15/**Lk1**:3:4^2:13^3:14 ^{2}
:19:20^2:28:28f:30:31^2:35^3:38:42:44:45^2:76^2:77/**2**
:10:12^2:29,30,31^2:48^2:49^2/**3**:7^3:8^4:9^2:10:11^2:12:
13^2:14:16:22/**4**:3:6,7^2:9,10,11^3:23^3:24:34^3:41/**5**:
4:5:8:12^2:14:23,24^2/**6**:3^2:9:20:21^4:22^4:23^3:27^2:28^2
:29:30^3:31^2:32^3:33^2:34^2:35:37^2:37f:38^5:42^4:46^2/
7:6,7,8^2:19:20,21,22:24^2:25:26:27^2:32^2:32f^3:33:
34:35:40:42:44:45:46:50/**8**:10:18:28^2:39:48/**9**:5^3
:13^2:20:27^2:33:41^2:50^3:55f:57^2/**10**:2:3:4:5:6:7^2:
8,9^4:10:11:13^3:14:15^4:16^2:19^2:20:21^3:23^2:24:27^3:
28:36:40:41/**11**:5,6^2:7:8^4:9^2:11^3:12:13:18:19^2:27 ^{2}
:34:36^2:39^2:42^5:43^3:44^3:45^2:46^3:47^2:48^2:49^3:50:
51:52^4/**12**:3f:3:4:5:7:8^3:11:12^2:14:15:19^2:20:22:
24:28^3:29:31^3:32:33:36:41:51:54^3:55:56^3:57:58^2:
59/**13**:2:3^3:5^2:12:15^3:24,25^2:26^3:27^4:28:31^2:34:
35^2/**14**:5^2:8^2:9^2:10^3:12:14^2:23:28:35/**15**:3,4^3:5:6 ^{3}
:12:18:21:29^3:30:31/**16**:2:5,6^2:7:8f:9:9f^4:10^4:11^2:
12^2:13^4:15^2:25^3:26/**17**:2,3:4:10^3:14:19:21^2:21f:
22^2:23:24/**18**:7:14:19^3:20:22^3:28:29:31:41:42/**19**
:17^4:19:21^2:22^3:23:31^2:33^2:42:43^2:44^4:46/**20**:3:5:
15:16:21^2/**21**:6:8:9:12:13f:14:15:16^4:17^2:19^2:20^2
:30:31^2:32:34,35^2:36/**22**:9:10^2:11:12:15:16:19:20
:20f:26^2:28:28f:29:30:31^2:32^2:33^2:34^3:35^3:36^2:40
:40f:41,42:46^2:48:52:53:58:60:61:63,64:67,68^2:
70^2/**23**:3:3f:3:14:31:37:39:40,41^2:42:43:46/**24**:5:
6,7^2:17^2:18:25^2:38^2:39^2:41:44^3:48:49^2/**Jn1**:21^3:
22^2:24,25^2:26:27:33^2:38^2:42^2:48^3:49:50^4:51/**2**:4:
4f:5:10:18^2:19:20/**3**:1:3^3:4:5:5f:7:8:9:10,11^4:12^4:
26^2:28^2/**4**:10^3:11^2:12^2:17,18^2:19:20:21-24:32:35 ^{2}
:38^3:42:48/**5**:6:10:14^3:23^3:32,33^2:34^2:35:37^2:38^3:
39^3:40^2:41,42^2:43^3:44^3:45^2:46^3:47^2/**6**:25:26^3:27^2
:29:30,31^3:32:36^3:47:53^4:61:62^2:63:64:67:68:69:
70/**7**:4^2:6:7:8:16:17^2:19:20:21,22,23^5:24:28^2:29:
31:34^2:36:45:47:52/**8**:10:12^2:13:14:15^2:19^4:21^2:
22:23^2:24^3:25:26^2:28:28f:28^2:30,31^3:32^2:33:34^2:
36^2:37^2:38^2:39:40^2:41^2:42^2:43^2:44^2:45:46^3:47^2:
48^2:49:51:52^3:53^3:54:55^2:57/**9**:17:26:27^4:28:30:
34:34f:34^2:35:37^2:40:41^4/**10**:24^2:25^2:26^2:32:33:
34,35,36:38^2/**11**:1:8^2:15:21:22:26:27:28:32:40^3:
41:42^2:49:56/**12**:8^2:15:25^4:34^2:35^4:36:44^2:45^2:49^2
/**13**:6:7^2:8^2:10:11:12:13^2:14:15^2:17:18^2:19^2:21:
33^3:34^2:35:36^3:37:38^2/**14**:1:2,3^3:4:5:7^3:9^3:10:11:
12,13^3:15,16^3:17^3:18^3:19^2:20^3:22:25^2:26^3:27:28^4
:29^2:30/**15**:3^3:4^2:5^2:7^3:9:10^2:11^2:12^2:14^2:15^3:16^5:
17:18^2:19^5:20^4:21^2:26^3:27^2/**16**:1^2:2^2:4^5:5:5f:6:7^2:
10:12^2:13^3:14:15:16^2:19:20^2:22^4:23^5:24^2:25:26:
26f:26:27^2:29:30^2:30f:30:31:32:33^3/**17**:1:2^2:3^2:4^2
:6^4:7:8^3:9^2:10^2:11^2:12f:12:13:15:18:21^4:22:23^4:
24^2:25^2:26^3/**18**:4,5:7:8^2:9:17:21^2:23:25:26:29:33:
34:34f^2:35^2:37:39^2/**19**:4:6:9:10^4:11^3:12^2:35:35f/
20:13:15^4:21:23^2:29^2:30,31^2/**21**:15^2:16^2:17^3:18^9:
20:22^2:23/**Act1**:1:5^2:6:7:8^2:11:24,25^2/**2**:14:15:
16:22:23:27:28:33:36:38^2:39/**3**:6^3:13:14^2:15^2:16:
17:19:20:21,22^2:25^2:26^3/**4**:7:9:10^2:19^2:25,26:28/
5:3^2:4^3:8:9^2:28^2:30:35:39^2/**7**:26:27:28^2:33:34:35:
42:43^2:48,49:51^3:52:53^2/**8**:20:21:30:37^2/**9**:4:5:
17^2:34/**10**:4:5,6:13:19:21:28:29:33^3:36,37:38/**11**
:3:7:14^2:16/**13**:10^2:11^2:15:25:26^2:32,33^2:32,33f:
34:40:41^3:46^2:47/**14**:15^3:17^2/**15**:7^2:10:11:14:24:
25:27,28,29^2/**16**:15:17:18:31/**17**:20:22:23^2/**18**:
10^2:14^2:15/**19**:2^3:3:13:15:26:36:37/**20**:18:20:25:
27:28^2:29^2:30:31^3:32^2:34:35/**21**:13:20:21^2:22:24 ^{2}
:37,38^3/**22**:3:7:8:10^2:12:14:15^2:17,18^2:19:21:25:
26:27/**23**:3^2:3f:3:11^2:15:18^2:19:20:21:22:30^2/**24**:
2:3:4:8:10:11:12:25/**25**:9:10,11^2:12^2:22:26^2/**26**:2
:3:8:14^2:14f:15^2:16^4:17^2:24:27^2:28:29/**27**:21^2:24 ^{2}
:31:33/**28**:20^2:21:22:26:27^3:28,29/**Rom1**:6,7^2:8^2
:9^2:10:11,12^3:13^2:14:15/**2**:1^6:3^3:4^7:5^2:17^2:17f:17 ^{2}
:18^3:19^3:20^3:21^4:22^3:22f:23^2:24:25^3:27f:27:28^3:
29/**3**:4:8^2:20/**4**:14^2/**6**:4:5^3:6:7^3:8:13^3:14^3:16^6:17 ^{3}
:18^2:19^2:20^2:21^2:22^2/**7**:1:4^7:5^2:6^3:7:12:13:
23,24,25/**8**:9^4:10:10f^3:11^3:12^2:13^4/**9**:1^3:4^{11}:5:9:
18:20^2:26/**10**:6^2:7:9^2/**11**:2,3:4^3:13^2:14:17^2:18^4:
19:20^2:21:22^4:24^3:25^4:26:28^2:30^2:31/**12**:1^3:2^3:3^2:
6^2:7:8^4:9:12:13:14^2:16:17:20^2/**13**:3^2:4^4:5^2:6:7:8^2:
9^5:10:11:12,13:14^2/**14**:1:2:3:4:6^3:10:13^2:15^3:16^2:
18:22^2/**15**:5:7:9:10:11:13^6:14^3:15,16^5:22:24:26:
28:29:30^2:32:33/**16**:1^2:16:17:19^2:20:21:23^2:24:
25,26,27^4/**1Co1**:3:4^2:5^2:6^2:7:8:9^2:10^2:12:13^2:14:
26:30/**2**:1^2:3:13/**3**:1^3:2^3:3^4:4^2:4f:5:9^2:16^3:17:18^3:
21^2:22^3:23/**4**:3:6^2:7^6:8^7:10^4:14^2:15^5:16:17^2:18^2:
21/**5**:1^2:2^2:3,4^4:6^3:7^2:9:10:11:13/**6**:1^3:2^2:3^2:4f:5:
7:8:9,10:11^4:15:16:17^2:18:19^4:20/**7**:1^2:2:6^3:8:9:
16^2:17^2:21^3:22^6:23^2:25:27^2:28^2:32^2:35^4:40/**8**:9:
10^3:11^2/**9**:2^2:6:7:8:9^2:12^5:13:15^2:25^2/**10**:10:12^3:
13^5:15:20^2:21^2:22^3:23^3:25^2:27^4:28^2:29:31^2/**11**:1:
2^2:3:13:17^2:18:19^2:20^2:22^3:23:24:25^2:26^3:30:31^2:
33:34^2/**12**:1:2^3:3^2:16^2:17^2:21^2:27^2:31/**13**:7^3/**14**:
2^4:5^4:6^6:9^3:12:16^5:17:18:22:23^2:24:25:26:36^4:37:
39/**15**:1^3:2^3:3:11^2:12^2:17^3:29:33^2:34:36^2:37^3:50:
51:58^2/**16**:1:2^3:3:5:6^2:11:12^2:14:15:16:17:18^2:19 ^{2}
:20^2:23:24/**2Co1**:1:2^2:5:6,7^6:8:11^2:12:13,14^5:
15,16^3:17:19:21:23^2:24/**2**:2^4:3^2:4^5:5,6:8:9^2:10/**3**:
1^5:2^2:3/**4**:12:14:15/**5**:11:12^3:20^4/**6**:1:2^3:11^2:13^2:
16^2:17:18^2/**7**:2^2:3^3:4^4:7^3:8^3:9^4:11^7:12:13^2:14^3:15 ^{2}
:16/**8**:1:6^2:7^3:8^2:9^3:10^3:11^3:12^5:14^4:15^2:16:17^2:
22:23^2:24/**9**:1:2^2:3^3:4^2:5:6^2:8^3:10^2:11^2:13:14^2/**10**
:1^2:2^2:6^2:7^3:8^3:9^2:10^2:11:12:13:14^2:15^2:16/**11**:1:2
:3:4^6:6:7^3:8,9^4:11:13:16:18:19,20^8/**12**:9^2:11^2:12^3:
13^3:14^4:15^3:16:17^2:18:19^4:20^3:21^3/**13**:1:3^4:4:5^6:6
:7^2:9^2:10^3:11:13:14/**Gal1**:6^3:7^2:8:9:10^2:13:20^2/**2**:
5:14^3:15/**3**:1^4:2^5:3^4:4^2:5^4:7:8,9/**4**:8^2:9^3:10^2:11^2:
12^3:13:14^3:15:16:17^2:18^2:19^3:20^2:21^3:27^4:28/**5**:1
:2^3:4^3:7^3:8:9:10^2:12^3:12f:13:14:15:16^4:18^2:19:21
/**6**:1^2:7:12:13^2:16:18/**Eph1**:1:2:13:15:16,17^4:18^3
:19/**2**:1:2:8:11^2:12^4:13^4:14:17:19^3:20:22/**3**:1^2:2,3^2
:4:13^2:16:17^2:18,19^3/**4**:1:20:21:22:24:26^2:27^2:29:
30^2:30f:32^2/**5**:1:2^2:3^2:4:5:9^2:10:13:14:15,16^2:17:
22^2:24:25/**6**:1:3:4:5:8^3:9^4:10^2:11:13:14:15^2:16^2:
17:21:22^2:23/**Php1**:2^2:3:4:5:6^3:7^2:8:9^2:10^2:11^2:
12:19:24:25:26^3:27^2:28^3:29:30^2/**2**:1^2:12^3:13^3:14:
15^2:16:17^2:18^2:19^3:20:22:23:24:25^2:26^2:28^2:30^2/
3:1^2:2:15^3:16^2:18/**4**:1^3:3:5^2:7^3:8:9^2:10^4:14:15^3:16
:17:18:22/**Col1**:2^2:3:4^2:5^2:6^2:7:8:9^4:10^3:11^2:21^3:
22^4:23^4:24:25:26,27/**2**:1^2:2^3:4:5^3:6^2:7^2:10^3:11^2:
12^3:13^2:14^2:15:16^2:18^4:20^3/**3**:1:3:4:5:7:10^2:12^4:
13^2:16:17:18^2:19:20:22^3:23^2:24^3:25^3/**4**:1^3:6:7:8^2:
9:10:12^5:13^2:16^2:17^2:18/**1Th1**:1:2^2:3:4:5^8:6^3:7:8:
9^2:10/**2**:1:2^3:3:5^3:6^2:7:8^2:9^3:10^2:11^4:12:13^4:14:17^4
:19^2:20/**3**:2,3^5:4^2:5:6^2:7:8:9^3:10^2:11:12:13/**4**:1^6:
3,4^2:6^3:8:9:10:11:12^2:13^2:15/**5**:2:4^2:5:11:12^2:13:
18:23:24^2:27:28/**2Th1**:2:3:4:5:6:7^2:10^3:11^5:12^3/
2:1:5^3:6:13^2:13f:13:14^2:15^2:17^2/**3**:1^2:3^2:4^3:5:6:7^3:
8:9^3:10^2:11:13:15:16^2:18/**1Ti1**:2^3:18^2:19/**3**:14^2:
15^2/**4**:6^3:8^2:12^3:14:16^3/**5**:1:16:21:22^3:23^3:24/**6**:6^3
:11:12^2:13:14^3:20:21/**2Ti1**:2:3^3:4:5^2:6^4:7:8^4:13^2:
14^2:15:18^2/**2**:1:2^2:4^2:7^2:15:21^3:22^2:25^2/**3**:1:10^5:
11^2:14^6:15^4/**4**:1:2:5:6:9:11^2:13:21/**Tit1**:4:5^4:6/**2**:
1:7^3:8:15^2/**3**:8:10:12^2:13:15/**Phm1**:3:4:6^2:8,9^5:
10:11:12:13:14^3:15^2:16:17:18^2:19^2:21^2:22:23/
Heb1:5,6^2:5,6f:9^2:10:11:12^2/**2**:6^2:7^2:8/**3**:1^2:12^2:
13:15^2/**4**:1:7/**5**:5f:5:6:11^2:12,13^6:14^2/**6**:2:4^2:6^2:9 ^{2}
:10:11^2:12^3/**7**:17:21/**8**:11/**9**:20^2/**10**:5^2:6^2:32^2:33 ^{2}
:34^5:36^3/**11**:6/**12**:3:4^2:5^5:6^4:7:8^4:13:15^2:18:22:25^2
/**13**:3^2:5^3:7:16:17^2:19:20,21^4:23^2:24,25^2/**Jas1**:4:
5^3:6^3:7,8^4/**2**:1^3:3^3:4:6^4:7:8^3:9^2:11^4:12^5:13^3:14^2:
15:16^2:17^3:18^3:19:20^2:21:22:24/**3**:1f:12^2:13^3:14/
4:1^2:2^8:3^4:4^4:5:7:8^3:9:10^3:11^2:12:13:14^2:15:16/**5**:
1^2:3^2:4:5:6^2:7:9:12:13:16/**1Pe1**:2^6:4:5^2:7:8^4:13^2:
14^2:15^2:16:17^4:18^2:19:20:22^4:23^3:25/**2**:2,3f:2,3^2:
5^3:7:9^7:10^3:11^3:12^3:16^2:18^2:19:20^3:21^2:25^3/**3**:1:6 ^{3}
:7^4:8^2:9:10:11:13:14^2:15^2:16^4:17:21f/**4**:1^2:2:3:4^2:
10:11^3:12^2:13^2:14^2:14f:19^3/**5**:1^2:2^2:5^2:6^2:7^2:10^5:
12^5:13f:13:14/**2Pe1**:1:2:3^3:5^4:6^2:7^2:8^2:10^2:11:12^2
:13,14:15^2:16^2:19^2/**2**:1:3:9:13^2:19^3/**3**:1^6:3:12:14^2
:17^3/**1Jn1**:3^2:4^2:5/**2**:1^4:5:7^3:8:12:13^7:14^2:15^4:16:
18:20^3:21^2:24^3:26^2:27^6:28/**3**:5:7^3:8^2:13:15/**4**:1:3:
4:19/**5**:1^2:2^3:13^3:16^2/**2Jn1**:5:8^2:9^5:10:11^2:12/
3Jn1:2:3:5:6:10:11:12:14/**Jud**:2:3^2:4:5:6:9:12^2:
17:20:21^2:22:23:24,25^2/**Rev**:3^2:4:9:11:19^2:20/**2**:
1^2:2^4:3:4:5:6^2:9^3:10^5:13^3:14^3:15^2:16:20^2:23^2:
24,25^3:27:28/**3**:1^2:3^4:7:8^3:8f:8:9:10^2:10f:11:15^3:
16^2:17^3:18^4:19^2/**4**:1:11^2/**5**:9^2:10/**6**^{2}/**7**:13/**10**:9:
11/**11**:17:18/**12**:12^3/**13**:10f^2/**14**:15/**15**:3,4^2/**16**:
5:6/**17**:1:7^2:18/**18**:4:6:14^2:20^3/**19**:5:10^2/**21**:5:9/
22:6,7:9:10:16

13945

YOUR

Gen1:21,22:29/**2**:16,17/**3**:5:14^2:15^3:16^2:17^2:19^2
/**4**:6:9:10:11:15/**6**:18^2/**7**:1/**9**:2,3:9,10,11:9,10,11
f/**12**:1^2:2:2f:7:18:19/**13**:9:15/**14**:19,20/**15**:2,3:4:
5:13:18/**16**:5^2:9-12^3/**17**:5:6:7,8^4:9,10^2:12^2:13:15
:16/**18**:3,4:5:6:9/**19**:2:15^2:17:21/**20**:7:16/**21**:10:
12/**22**:2:12^2:16:17/**23**:8:11:14,15/**24**:5:14:19:23:
33:40:41:44:46:51:60^2/**25**:23:31/**26**:3^2:4:9^2:24/
27:2,3,4:8,9,10^2:19^2:20:27,28,29^4:31:32:35^2:37:
39,40^3:43:44/**28**:2:2f:2^2:2f:4:13^2:14/**30**:2:27:29:
30:31,32/**31**:3^2:5:6:9:13:24:29:30:32:36,37:38:39
:41:42/**32**:10:18:27:29/**33**:8:10:10f:15/**34**:8:9,10^3
/**35**:1:11:12/**37**:7:10:13,14:17/**38**:8:18^2/**40**:13:
18,19^3/**42**:15:16^2:19:20:33^2:34^2/**43**:3,4,5:7:11:
12:13:23^3:27:29/**44**:8:9:16:17:23/**45**:4:5:7:9:10^3:
11,12:17:18^2:19^2:20/**46**:3,4^3:33/**47**:3:16:23:24/
48:4:6:7:11:18^2:21:22^2/**49**:2:8^3:18:25/**50**:6:16,17^2
:18:21/**Ex2**:13/**3**:5:6:15:18^2:22/**4**:2:6^3:14:14f:16:
17:18:23/**5**:4,5:13:14:16:22:23/**7**:1^2:15/**8**:2:3,4^6:
21:23:25:29/**9**:3:14:19:22:30/**10**:1:2:6^2:8:10^2:12:
16:17:21:24^2/**11**:8/**12**:11^4:13:19:21:23:24:26:32
/**13**:3^2:4,5^2:6,7^2:8:9^2:11:13:14:16/**14**:26/**15**:6:7^2:
8:12:13^2:16^2:17^2:26/**16**:7,8,9^2:11,12:25:28,29/
17:5,6/**18**^{3}:14/**19**:5:15/**20**:2^2:5^2:7:7f:9^2:10^4:12^2:
17:24^2:26^2/**21**:2f/**22**:24^2:27:28^2:29^3/**23**:2,3^2:5:9:
10:11^2:12^3:16:19^2:21:22:25:26^2:30:31/**25**:17/**28**:
1/**29**:12/**32**:2,3:7:8:11^2:12^2:13^5:24:27^2:29/**33**:1:
5:13f^2:13/**34**:9^2:11:16^2:20:24^3:25:26/**35**:3/**Lev1**:
2,3^3/**2**:7:11:14/**3**:17/**10**:6^3:8,9^2:10:13:14^3:15/**11**
:29,30:44:45/**16**:1:29,30/**17**:11/**18**:1:4,5:10^3:10f:
11:12^3:13^3:14^2:15^2:16^2:18:21^2:29,30/**19**:1^3:3,4:9 ^{2}
:10^2:12:13:14:16:16f:17:18:19^2:26:27^3:29:31:33:
34:35,36/**20**:7:22:24/**21**:8/**23**:3:9,10,11^2:14:
15,16:17^2:20:22^2:28:32:38^3:39:40:43/**24**:22/**25**:3^3
:4^2:6,7^2:12:17,18:19:35^2:36^2:37:38^2:43:45:46^2:55
/**26**:1:4,5:7^2:8:12:13^2:16^4:17:18:19^3:20^3:21:22^4:
24^2:25^2:26^2:28:29:30^4:31^3:32^2:33^2:38/**27**:25f:32
/**Num5**:19:21,22^3/**10**:9^2:10^3:35/**11**:18:19,20:22/
14:13:15^2:17,18^2:19:31:32:33:34,35:42^2/**15**:1:
19,20,21:39^2:40:41^2/**16**:3:16:17/**18**:1^3:2,3^3:6^2:7^2
:8:11^2:13:19^2:21:27^2:30/**20**:14:16:17^5:19/**21**:22^5
/**22**:16,17:28:32/**23**:3,4:7-10:15/**24**:12:14:21,22
/**27**:13:20/**28**:28,29/**29**:13:39/**31**:19:20:24/**32**:6
:8:21:22^2:23:24^2:25/**33**:54:55^2/**34**:1:6:7,8,9/**Deu**
1:8:12:13:17:30:38/**2**:7:25:27:30/**3**:19^2:20^2:21:
22/**4**:1:2:4:9^3:21,22:23^2:25^3:26:29^2:30:31^2:34^2:
37:39:40^2/**5**:2,3:6:9,10:11f:14^3:15:16^2:23:28:32/
6:1:2^3:3:5:7:8^2:9:10,11,12^2:13:15:18:19:20/**7**:2:3:
4:6:8:9:12^3:13^3:14:15^2:16^2:18:19^2:20:21:24:25:
26^2/**8**:1:3:4^2:6:7:10^2:11^2:12,13^2:14^2:16:17:18^2:19
:20^2/**9**:3:5:6:7:16^2:17:21:26^3:27^2:29^4/**10**:12,13^3:
14:15:16^2:17:20:21^2:22^2/**11**:1:2:5:9:12:13^2:14:15
:16:18^3:19:20^2:21:21f:22:23:24:25:27:29/**12**:1:
4,5:6^8:7^2:8:10:11:12:13:14^2:17^3:18^3:20-23^3:24,25
:26,27^4:28^2:31/**13**:3:5:6,7:9:10:16:17:18/**14**:1:2:
21:22:23^4:24:25:26^2:27^2:28:29^3/**15**:4,5:7:14^4:15:
16^2:17^2:18:19^4:20^2:22/**16**:1:2^2:3:4:5:7:8:10^2:11:
14^2:16:18:20:21/**17**:1:2,3^2:8:14:15/**18**:5:12:13:
14/**19**:1:8^2:9^2:14:21/**20**:1:4^2:7:11:13:17:18/**21**:5:
8:10^2:11:13:23/**22**:2:5:9:12/**23**:7:14:17,18:20:21:
23^2:24/**24**:4:9:12,13:14,15:18:19^2:20:21/**25**:1^2:

(YOUR Con't)
13,14,15:16:19^2/**26**:4:5:10:11:12:13^2:15^2:16:17:19/**27**:5,6^2:7:9/**28**:1:7:8:13:14:15-19^4:22:25^2:26:30:31^5:32^2:36:38:41:42:45:46:47,48^4:51^2:52^2:53:55:56,57^2:58,59^2:62:64:66:68/**29**:2,3,5^2:6:10^4:11^4:12:13^2:22:29/**30**:1:2^2:3^2:5^2:6^5:7,8^2:9^2:10^2:11:14^2:16^2:17:19:20^4/**31**:3:6:12:13^2:16:28/**32**:6:7:46:47:50^2/**33**:3:4:8^2:9:18:23:25^2:27^2:29^4/**Jos1**:9:12,13:14^2:17,18^2/**2**:9:11:12,13:14:16:17,18^2:21/**3**:9/**4**:5:6:21/**5**:8,9:14:15/**6**:3,4:22/**7**:9:10,11:12:13^2:19/**8**:7:8:18/**9**:8:9:25/**10**:6:25/**14**:9/**18**:3/**22**:2,3^2:5:19:24,25^3:26,27^2/**23**:3^2:4,5:8:10:13^5/**24**:2:3:12:14:15:19:27/**Ju2**:1:2:3^2/**3**:28^2/**4**:14/**5**:12:16:31/**6**:9:10:26:30:31/**7**:3:8,9:10:14/**8**:2,3:6f:7:22^2:23,24^3/**9**:2:16:18^2:29/**10**:14/**11**:21,22^2:24:36/**12**:1/**13**:5:13,14/**14**:15^2/**15**:2/**16**:13/**17**:3:10,11/**19**:9/**20**:7^2/**21**:21:22^2/**Ru1**:8^3:10:11^2:12:15:16^2/**2**:10,11^4:13:20/**3**:9:10:15-18/**4**:5^2:11:15^3/**1Sa1**:14:17/**2**:3:28:29:30:31:32:34:36/**6**:4,5/**7**:3^2/**8**:11:13:14:15:16^3:17/**9**:19:26,27/**10**:2:7:24/**11**:1:3/**12**:6:7:12^3:13:14^2:15:17:20:25/**13**:13^2:14/**15**:15:22^4:24:30:33^2/**17**:9^2:17:44:46^2:58/**18**:17/**20**:1:3^2:5:6:8:10:15:18:30^2/**21**:4/**22**:14^4:16:22/**23**:20/**24**:4^2:11:13:15:18/**25**:6:7^2:8:13:26^3:27:28^2:29^3:33/**26**:8^2:15:16:22^2/**27**:10/**28**:16:17:19:21:22/**29**:8/**30**:20/**31**:3,4/**2Sa1**:19:21:26/**2**:5:22:26/**3**:8:33,34^2/**4**:8:11/**5**:1/**6**:21/**7**:8:9^2:10,11:12^2:15:16:18:23^3:24:26:27:28/**9**:7^2:9:10,11/**10**:3/**11**:10/**12**:11^2:14:21/**13**:5:29,30:32,33:35/**14**:2,3:11:13:14:31/**15**:9:19,20^3:21:27:33,34/**16**:2:7,8^2:17:19:21/**17**:6:8^2:9^3:10:13:28,29/**18**:28:32/**19**:5^4:7:23:28/**22**:26:30^2:36^2:50/**24**:3:13:17:21:23/**1Ki1**:2^2:12^2:13:17^2:19:20:24:25:27^2:30/**2**:7:21:26:36,37:43/**3**:6^2:8:9:11:13:14/**5**:5^2:6^2:8/**6**:11,12/**8**:19:22,23^3:24^2:25^3:31:33,34:35,36^2:41,42^2:43^3:44^3:48:50:51^2:52^2:53^2/**9**:2,3,4:5^3:6:10:7:8^3:9^2/**11**:11:12,13^2:38/**12**:2,3,4:28^2/**13**:6:8:21,22^2/**14**:7:9:10^3:11:13/**15**:19/**16**:3:4-7/**17**:12:13:14/**18**:18:24:25:27:31f:36^2/**19**:10^2:14^2/**20**:2,3^3:5,6^3:9:11:32:33:34:35:37:40:42/**21**:3:19:21:22:23:24/**22**:4^2:25:30/**2Ki1**:10:12:13:16/**2**:5:10:16/**3**:6,7,8:13:17/**4**:3:4^3:7^2:36/**5**:27^2/**6**:12:26-30/**8**:1:8,9/**9**:3:22/**10**:2,3:5:6:15:24:30^3/**12**:7/**14**:9:10/**16**:7f^2/**17**:39/**18**:20,21^3:27:31,32/**19**:4:5,6:15:16:25:27:28^3/**20**:1:15:17:18/**22**:12,13:18,19^2/**1Ch10**:4/**11**:1:1f:2/**12**:18^2/**13**:2/**14**:15/**15**:12/**16**:18:35^2/**17**:2:8^2:10^2:11^3:19:21^2:22:23:24/**19**:2,3/**21**:17/**22**:18:19^2/**28**:6:8:9:21/**29**:10:11:12^2:16:18:19:20/**2Ch1**:9:11^3/**2**:8:10:14^2/**6**:15:15f:16^2:20,21^2:24^2:27^2:28:32^2:33^2:34^3:37,38:39:41^4:42^4/**7**:12:13:17:18/**9**:6:8/**10**:4/**11**:13:6:8^2:12/**14**:11/**16**:3^2:7^2:8/**18**:3,4,5:29/**19**:6:10:11/**20**:7^2:8:11:17:20:37/**21**:12^2:13:14^3:15/**25**:8:16:18:19/**28**:9:10^2/**29**:4,5:11:31/**30**:7:8:9^3/**32**:14:15/**33**:8/**34**:27:28/**35**:3^2:4,5/**Ez4**:2:11:13:16/**5**:17/**6**:8/**7**:17:18^2:19:25:26/**9**:9:10:14^2/**10**:3:11^2/**Neh1**:6,7^2:10^2/**2**:4^2/**4**:5:14^3/**5**:11:13/**8**:9:10/**9**:5:8:11:14:16:19:20:22:25^2:26:28^3:29:30:31:32:34^2/**13**:18:22:31/**Est1**:16:18^2:19^2:20/**3**:8:14/**4**/**5**:3:4:7,8:14/**6**:13/**7**:2:3^2/**8**:5/**9**:13/**Job1**:11:14,15:16:17^2:18/**2**:4,5/**4**:6:6f^2/**5**:8:24^2:25^2:27/**6**:23:25,26:28/**7**:17:20/**8**:4:6:21^2/**10**:4-7^2:12:13,14/**11^2**:16:17:18/**12**:6/**13**:5:8:11:12:21/**14**:6:13^2/**15**:4,5^3:6:10:12/**16**:3:5/**18**:4:5/**19**:2:29/**21**:5^2:34/**22**:5^2:22:23:24^2:25^2:27:30/**30**:23/**32**:11,12/**34**:33^2:37/**35**:4:8^2/**36**:17:18^2:19/**37**:19,20/**38**:2:11/**39**:9^2:27/**40**:10^2:11:14/**41**:3:4:5:8/**42**:3:7:8^3/**Ps2**:7^2/**4**:1:4:5:6/**5**:5:7^3:11:12/**6**:1:4/**8**:1:2:3:9/**9**:2:3:4:6:10:11/**10**:5/**12**:7/**13**:5^2/**15**:1^2/**16**:10:11/**17**:1:4:5:7^2:8^2:13,14/**18**:15^2:26:29:35^3/**20**:1:3:4^2:5^2/**21**:1^2:6:8^2:9,10:12:13^2/**22**:2:3,4:5:25/**23**:4f^2:5:6^2/**25**:11:16/**26**:1:3^2:6:7:8^2/**27**:9/**28**:2f:2:9^3/**30**:6,7^2:9/**31**:3:5,6:7:14,15:16^2:19:20^3/**32**:4:8^2/**33**:22/**34**:13^2:14/**35**:2^2:3:24f/**36**:5^2:6^2:7^2:8^2:9:10^2:10f:10/**37**:4:6:8^2:27/**38**:2^2:3,4/**39**:10:12/**40**:5^2:6^2:8^2:9f:10f:10:11^2/**41**:12/**42**:6:7:7f/**43**:3^4/**44**:4:5^2:17:18:19:26/**45**:2:4:5^2:6^2:7:8^3:9:10,11^5:12:16:17/**47**:6,7^2/**48**:9^3:10:10f:13/**49**:10:11^2/**50**:7:13:14,15^3:18:19:20:21/**51**:4:9:11^2:12:13:14,15:18:18f:19/**52**:2:5:9^2/**53**:5/**54**:1f:1:6/**55**:22/**56**:8^2:12/**57**:1:5:7:9:10^2:11/**58**:1:1f/**59**:9:11:16/**60**:1:3:4,5^2/**61**:4^2:5:7:8/**62**/**63**:2^2:3:7:8/**66**:3^3:4:7:11:13/**67**:1:2^2/**68**:1:4:7:9,10^2:23:28^2:29/**69**:7:9f:9^2:13f:16^2:17f:24^2/**70**:4/**71**:2:15:18:19:22^2:23:24^2/**72**:2/**73**:15:24/**74**:1^2:2^3:3:7:9,10^2:11^2:13,14:15^2:17:18:19^2:20:21^2:22/**75**:1/**76**:11^2/**77**:13:14:15:17:19:20/**78**:1:4/**79**:1^2:2:5:6^2:7:8:9:10:11:13^3/**80**:1^2:2:3f:7f:8:14:16:17f:17:19/**81**:6^2:7:9:10^2/**82**:8/**83**:2:3^2:10:15:16/**84**:1:2:3:4^2:5:9:9f:10/**85**:2:3^2:4:6:7^2/**86**:2:5:9:11:12:16:17/**88**:5:7:9:10:11^2:12^2:14:15:16^2/**89**:1:2^2:5^2:8:10^2:12:13^3:14,15^3:16^2:17:19:19f:39:46:49:51/**90**:7^2:9:11:13:14:16/**91**:4:13/**92**:2:5:10/**93**:1f:3:5^2/**94**:1:5:20/**95**:8:9/**96**:8/**97**:8,9/**98**:5/**99**:3/**101**:1^3:2/**102**:9,10^2:12:14:25:27:28/**104**:7,8:24:28^2:30/**105**:10,11/**106**:1:4:5:7^2:8^2:47/**107**:2/**108**:4^2:6/**109**:21^2/**110**:1:2:2f:2:3^2/**114**:5/**115**:1^3:9^2:10^2:11^2:14/**118**:13/**119**:4:7f:9:10:11:12:13:18:19:20:21:23:24:25:26:27:28:29,30:31:32^2:38:39:40,41,42^4:43:44,45,46:47^2:49,50^2:52:53:58:61:62:64^2:65:66:68:69:71,72:73:74:75,76,77^5:78:79:80:81^2:82^2:83:85,86:87:88:89:90,91^3:92:93:94:95:96:99:101:102,103:104:105:108:109:110:111:113:114:117:118:119:120:123:124:125^2:126:127:129:130:131:132:133:135:136:137:138:139:140:141:142^2:143:144:145:148:151:152:153:155:156:157:158:159:160^2:161:162:163:164:165:166^2:167:171:173:174^2:175:176/**120**:3/**121**:5:5f^2:7/**122^2**/**128**:3^2:6/**130**:1/**132**:8^2:10^2:12:13/**134**:2/**135**:13^2/**137**:9:9f/**138**:1:2^5:2f^2:4:7^2:8/**139**:5:7:10^2:14:16:17,18:17,18f:20:22/**140**:13/**142**:7/**143**:1:8:10^2:11^2:12/**144**:5:6^3:10/**145**:1:5:6^2:7:10:11^2:12^2:13/**146**:10/**147**:7:12:13^2:14^2/**149**:2^2/**Pro1**:7,8,9:10:14:28:29:30:31:32/**2**:10^2/**3**:3:6:7,8^2:9,10^3:22:22f:27,28:29/**4**:1:7:8,9:21:23^2:25:26:27/**5**:9^2:10:11:15^2:17^2:18^2/**6**:2:3^2:20^2:21:23/**7**:2:3f:3:4:25/**9**:6:11^2/**10**:19^2/**11**:4:17:28/**12**:9/**13**:24/**15**:31,32/**16**:3/**17**:13/**19**:16:17:18:20/**20**:2:18:19/**21**:23/**22**:24,25:26,27/**23**:1:4,5:6,7,8^2:9:13,14:15,16:22:24,25/**24**:17:21,22:27^2/**25**:8,9,10:17^2:21,22/**26**:6:17/**27**:1:10^2:23,24^3:25,26,27/**28**:27/**29**:17:30/**30**:10:32^2/**31**:3/**Ecc5**:1^3:4:6,7^2:11^2:19,20^2/**6**:10/**7**:2:15-17:21,22/**8**:2,3/**9**:9^2/**10**:8,9:20/**11**:1:2:6/**12**:1^2:2^2:3^3:4^2:6/**Sol1**:2:3^2:4:7^2:8:10^3:15/**2**:5^3:14^2/**4**:1^3:2:3^4:3f:4:5:9^2:10^2:11^3:13,14f/**5**:9/**6**:1:5^3:6:7^2/**7**:1^2:2^2:3:4^3:5^3:7:8^2:9/**8**:5^2:6:13^2/**Is1**:7^2:11^3:12,13^5:15^3:16:18:20^2:23:25:26:29:31/**2**:11:22/**3**:11^3:12/**4**:1/**5**:8:9:12:13/**6**:7^2/**7**:3:11:17^2:19:20^3/**8**:1:7,8,9,10^4:12:14,15:18:19/**9**:11,12^2/**10**:3^2:16^2/**13**:5:7:8/**14**:5^2:6:8:11^4:19:20^3:31/**15**:1:2/**16**:4,5/**17**:11/**18**:4:5:6/**19**:12/**21**:5:12/**22**:3:6,7^2:8:9,10,11:12^3:18:19:21/**23**:1:2,3:7:9:10:14/**24**:17/**25**:1:3/**26**:4:8^2:10^2:11^3:16:17:20/**28**:6^3:18:22/**29**:1:3:4:5:8:10/**30**:1:2:5:10,11^2:15:16:19:20^2:22:23:25/**31**:7/**32**:9:11^3:12:13^2/**33**:3:7:8:11^2:12:17:18^4/**35**:4^2/**36**:6:7:8,9:16/**37**:4:21:23:24:27:28:29^4:30:31/**38**:1:5^2:16:19/**39**:6:7/**40**:1:9:27/**41**:1^2:10:11:13^2:14:21:28:29/**43**:3^4:12:14^2:15:24:25:26^2:27^2:28/**44**:3^3:22:24/**45**:3:14:21^2/**46**:4^4:6/**47**:1:2^2:6:7:8:9^2:10^2:11:13:15/**48**:4:14:17^3:19:20/**49**:8,9^2:16:17:18^2:19^3:22^2:23^2:25^2:26^2/**50**:1^4:11^2/**51**:1:5:7:10:13:14:15:16:19:20:22^2:23^2/**52**:1^2:2:3:11:12/**54**:2^2:3:4:5^3:6:8:11:12^2:13:14:15/**55**:1:2:3^2:5^2/**57**:4:5^2:6^2:7,8^2:9:10:12^2:13/**58**:3:7^3:8:10:12^2:13^2:14^3/**59**:2:3^2:4^2:5:6:7^2:12/**60**:1:3:4^2:5^2:10:11:12:14:16^2:17^5:18^3:19^3:20^3:21/**61**:5^4/**62**:2^2:4:5:6,7:8^2:11/**63**:1:2^3:15^4:17f:19/**64**:1:2^3:5:7:8:9:10/**65**:12:15/**66**:5:9:14:20/**Jer1**:5:9:10^2/**2**:4,5,9:17:18:19^2:24:25:30:32:33:34:36:37^2/**3**:2^3:13^2:14:16:19:22/**4**:1:3:4f:4^3:5:7^2:14^2:15:18^3:30^3/**5**:7:14:17^5:19^2:31/**6**:1:3:8:16:20^2/**7**:3^2:5:6^2:7:11:13,14:15:21:22:23:25:27:29/**8**:8/**9**:4^2:17,18^2:20^2:21^3:25,26^2/**10**:6:11:17:24:25/**11**:6:7:8:13^2:15:16/**12**:6^2:14:15/**13**:12:16:17:18^3:20^2:21^2:22:24,25^3:27^3/**14**:7:9^2:10:21^3/**15**:4:6:7:12,13^2:14:15^2:16^2:17,18/**16**:9^2:11:12^2:13^2:14,15:18^3/**17**:2,3^3:4^2:12:16:21,22/**18**:11:12:20:23/**19**:7:9:13/**20**:3:4:5^2:6:7^2:12/**21**:3,4^2:8:9:14/**22**:2^2:3:7:13:15:20:22^3:26:27/**23**:36:38,39:40/**25**:5:7^2:10^5/**26**:11:13^2:14/**27**:2:4:6^2:8:9:10:13:16/**28**:2:4:6:14:15:16/**29**:14^3:16,17:21:26/**30**:10:12:13:14^4:15^4:16:17^2:18^2:22/**31**:4:5^2:16:16f:17^2:21^2/**32**:6,7:17:19:20:23/**34**:5^3:13:15:16:18,19^2:20^2/**35**:15^2:18,19/**37**:18/**38**:12:17:20:21,22^2:23/**39**:16:18/**40**:2,3:4/**42**:2:3:9:12:18:20/**44**:2,3:9^3:10:16:21^2:22:25^4/**45**:5/**46**:3:4^3:10:11:12^3:15^2:22,23:27^2/**47**:6/**48**:7^2:10:18:28:29^3:32^2:43:44:46/**49**:2:3:4^2:5^3:7:11^2:16^2:18:26^3:30/**50**:12:31/**51**:9:12^2:13^2:14:24:25:26:36^2/**Lam2**:13^2:14^2:16:19^4:20:21:22/**3**:34,35,36:43:55/**5**:19/**Eze2**:8/**3**:9:10:11:18^2:21:24:26^2:27/**4**:4,5,6:7^2:8/**5**:1:2^3:3:14:17^2/**6**:3:4-7^2:11^2:11f^2:13^2:14/**7**:2:3:5,6,7:8,9,10,11^3:18:19^3:24^4/**9**:8/**11**:5:6:7^2:15:19:20/**12**:3^2:4^2:5:6^3:18^3:20^2:25/**13**:4:6:9^2:14:18f:20:21:22:23^2/**14**:6,7^2:22/**16**:3^2:4:6,7^3:12^3:13:14^2:15^2:16:18:20:23:24:25:26^2:27:28^2:31^3:36^6:37:39^3:40,41^4:43^3:45^4:46^2:48:49:51^2:52^2:54:55:56:57:58^2:59,60^2:61^2:63/**18**:30^2/**19**:2:10/**20**:7:18:19:20:27,28:30:31:39^2:40^2:41:42:43:44/**21**:3:4:6:7:12:14:24^2:25:26:29^3:30:32^3/**22**:4^2:6:7:13:15:26:27:28:31/**23**:21:25^3:26:27:28:29:31:32:33:35^2:40^2:42^3:49^2/**24**:13^2:16:17:20,21^2:23^2:27/**25**:4^3/**26**:8^2:9^2:10^2:11^2:12^5:13:14:15:17:18:20/**27**:4^2:6^2:7:8^2:9:10^3:11^3:12:15:16:19f:25^2:26^3:27^4:28:29:33:34^2:36/**28**:2,3:4:5:7^2:8:13:16:17^4:18:18f:18:19:22:23/**29**:3^2:4^2:6:10/**32**:5^2:6:8:10:13:19/**33**:2:11:17:30^2/**34**:3:18:31/**35**:4,5:6:8^4:9:11^2/**36**:2^2:9:10:11:14^2:25^2:26:28^2:29:30^2:31:32:33:34/**37**:12:14:17/**38**:4^3:9:10:15,16^2/**39**:2:3^2:4:6:9/**45**:5:7:30/**45**:11:14:15/**47**:14:20:22/**Dan1**:10/**2**:5:8,9^2:11:25:28^2:30^2:37^2:38:39^2:45:47/**3**:9:12:17^2:18:24/**4**:19:22^3:24:25^4:26/**5**:10:11^2:11f:16:17:18:23^2:26:28/**6**:7:8^2:13:15:16:20:21/**8**:17:26/**9**:4^2:5:6^2:10:11^2:15^2:16^5:17^4:18^3:19^4:24/**10**:12:14:16:20,21:20,21f/**11**:14/**12**:1^2:13^3/**Hos1**:11^3:2:17/**3**:1/**4**:3:4:5^3:6^2:13^2:14/**5**:3:4:9/**6**:4:5:6^3/**9**:1:2^2:6^2:10:11:12:14/**10**:10^2:12:14^2:15^2/**12**:6:11/**13**:4:10:14^2/**14**:1^2:2/**Joe1**:2^2:3:4:5:14/**2**:12:13^4:14:17:19:23:27:28^3:29/**3**:4:5:8:9^2:10^2:11:17/**Amo2**:11:12:14:16/**3**:1:2:3:5:6:8:9/**4**:1:2:3:4^2:5:7:9^3:10^2:11:12:13/**5**:11:12:13:14:15:21^3:22^2:23^2:25,26,27^4/**6**:3:6^2:7:13^2:14^2/**7**:2:10:12:13:17^4/**8**:5:6:7:10^4/**9**:15/**Ob1**:4:5:7^5:10^2:15^2/**Jon**:2:6:8^2:14/**2**:3:4:7/**4**:2:10/**Mic1**:10:13^2:15:16^2/**2**:1:3:4^2:5:7:10:13^3/**3**:6^2:7^2/**4**:8:9^2:10^2:11/**5^2**:13:14/**6**:1^2:3:4:7^2:8:10:11:12^2:13^2:14:15/**7**:4^2:5^2:11:14^2:18:19:20/**Nah1**:13:14^4/**2**:1:2:4:12^5:13^3/**3**:5:7:12:13^2:14:15:16^2:17:18^2:19^3/**Hab1**:5:12/**2**:6^2:7:10^2:11:15:16^2:17:18/**3**:2^3:8,9f^4:8,9^3:11^2:12:13:15/**Zep1**:2:11^2:17^2:18/**2**:2/**3**:11:14:15^2:17,18^3:20^2/**Hag1**:6:9^2:11^2/**2**:14^2:16,17:18,19/**Zec1**:2:4:5,6:12/**3**:2:4:10^2/**6**:7:15/**7**:5^3:6:11/**8**:12:14,15:16/**9**:9:12/**10**:3^2/**11**:1^2:9/**13**:6^2/**14**:5/**Mal1**:2,3:5:6^2:8:10:13/**2**:1:3^2:4:8:9:13^2:14^2:15^4:16^2:17/**3**:1^2:13/**Mt1**:20/**3**:2/**4**:7/**5**:13:15,16^3:20:22:22f:22:24^2:25:29^2:29f:30^2:33:37^2:40^2:43^2:44:45:47:48/**6**:1^2:3^2:4:6^3:7,8:9:10^2:14,15:16:18:21^2:22^2:23:26:27^2:28:31,32:33:34/**7**:3:4^2:5:11^2:22:23/**8**:4/**9**:2:5,6:11:13^2:14:22:29/**10**:13:14:19:20:27:28^2:29:30:37^2:38:39/**11**:10f:19:21:29,30/**12**:2:7:13:27^2:37^2/**13**:16^2/**15**:2:3:4:5,6^3:28^2/**17**:16:20:24/**18**:3:6:8:9:17:35/**19**:8:17:19^2/**20**:21^2:26:28/**21**:27/**22**:18:29^2:37^2:38,39:44^2/**23**:8:10:11:13,14:16:23:29,30:34:37:38/**24**:3:20:42:46:49:50/**25**:24,25:26:35/**26**:15:18:39:42:45:52:65,66:73/**27**:4:17:22:65/**Mk1**:15/**2**:5:9,10,11/**3**:5:31,32/**4**:10/**5**:9:19:23:34^2/**6**:11/**7**:5:8:9:10,12,13:15,16:18:19:29/**8**:17:18^2:34^2:35/**9**:18:38:43,44:45,46:47:50/**10**:5:19^2:37^3:43:52f:52/**11**:22,23:25^2:26,f^2:33/**12**:24:30:35:36^2/**13**:6:9:11:15,16^2:18/**14**:7:36:41:63,64/**15**:12/**Lk1**:13^2:36:42:44:61/**2**:32:34,35:48/**3**:9:13:14/**4**:6,7:12:23/**5**:4:20:23,24/**6**:2:10:22:27:29^2:35^2:36:38:41:42/**7**:4:35:44:48:50/**8**:25:30:39:48/**9**:5:40:48^2:49:55f:60/**10**:5:11^2:17:20:27^6/**11**:2^2:8:11:13:19:27:34^3:36:42:47:48/**12**:4:7:8:11:25:30^2:31:32:33^2:34^2:36:58/**13**:3:12:15:34:35/**14**:5:10/**15**:5:6^2:12:19:21:27^2:30:32/**16**:2^2:7:9:9f:12:15^2:16:25:29/**17**:2,3:6^2:10:19/**18**:20^2:42/**19**:5:17:39:42:43^2:44^2/**20**:8:37,38:42,43^2/**21**:15:16:18:19:28/**22**:20:26:27:32^2:36^2:41,42:53/**23**:28:42/**Jn3**:1/**4**:16:50:53/**5**:8:41,42:45/**6**:27:48-51:58/**7**:3:20:21,22,23/**8**:10:12:17:19:21:24^2:37:38:41:44:54:56/**9**:17:19:41/**10**:34,35,36/**11**:3:15:23/**12**:15:25^2:28:30:35/**13**:14:35/**14**:1:2,3:24/**15**:11/**16**:20:24:26/**17**:1:5:11:12:12f:14:17/**18**:11:29:31^2:35/**19**:14:15:26:27/**20**:17^2:27^2/**21**:6:15:16:18/**Act2**:17^3:27:28:35:38:39/**3**:17:19^2:20:25:26/**4**:25,26:27^2:28,29:30^2/**5**:3:8:9^2:28/**7**:32:33:37:43^2:51:52/**8**:20:21:22:23:37/**9**:17:34/**10**:4:31^2/**11**:14/**12**:8^2:15/**13**:10:38:41/**15**:24:24f:26/**16**:17:31/**17**:23:28/**18**:6^2:15/**19**:3/**20**:20:32/**21**:24/**22**:13:16:20/**23**:5:35^2/**24**:2:4/**26**:1:17:24^2/**27**:34^2/**28**:27^3/**Rom1**:8:9:11,12^2/**2**:4:5^2:17f:22/**6**:2,3:4:6^2:8:11:12:13:14f:14:16^2:17:18^2/**7**:4^2:5:6:7/**8**:9:10^2:11:12/**9**:5/**10**:9^3/**12**:1:2:3^2:6^2:7:8:11:19:20/**13**:6:7:8:9^2:12,13^2/**14**:10:13:15^2:21:22/**15**:9:30/**16**:1:20/**1Co1**:5:11:13:30/**2**:5/**3**:1:3^2:6^2:22^2/**4**:7:8^2:15/**5**:1:2:6:13/**6**:3:8:11:15:18:19^2:20/**7**:1:16^2:25:35/**8**:1:9:12/**9**:1:4:11:12:24:25/**10**:13:25:31/**11**:17:21:22/**12**:17:31/**13**:7/**14**:1:2:20/**15**:1:14:17:31:34^2:36:55,56^2/**16**:3:13:16/**2Co1**:11:15,16:24^2/**2**:3:5,6:10/**3**:2/**4**:5:15/**5**:13,14/**6**:2:12:13/**7**:2:7:11:13/**8**:6^2:8:11^2:13^2:22:24/**9**:3:8:10:11^2:12:13^3/**10**:15/**11**:2:3/**12**:14:15:19:21/**Gal3**:5/**4**:15:16:17^2/**5**:4:16:19^2:20/**Eph1**:15:18/**2**:1/**3**:17^2/**4**:2:22^2:23:26:31/**5**:2:8^2:10f:19:22:24:25/**6**:1:2:3:4:5^2:6,7^2:9:10:16:18/**Php1**:2^5:5:25:28/**2**:1:4:5:17:29/**3**:17/**4**:6:7^2:8:17^2:19:23/**Col1**:7:21:26,27^2/**2**:5:7^2:8:10:11^2:12:13^2:15/**3**:1:2^2:3:7:9:14:15^2:16:17:18:19:20:21:22^2:23:24:25/**4**:1:5^2:6:9:10:12/**1Th1**:1:3^2:8^2:9^2/**2**:5:12:13:14/**3**:2,3:5:6:10:12:13/**4**:1:10^2:11^3:12/**5**:6:12:13:23/**2Th1**:3^2:4:5:11:12/**2**:13:17/**3**:9:11/**1Ti1**:19^2/**2**:12/**4**:6:7:12^3:14:15^2/**5**:1:2:7:23/**2Ti1**:4:5^2:6:8/**2**:3:14:15/**4**:2:22/**Tit1**:11/**2**:7:8:15/**3**:1/**Phm1**:1:5:6:7^2:14:16:17:19:22:25/**Heb**:8:9:10:12:13^2/**3**:12:15/**4**:7/

UR Con't)
2:11/10:5:7:35/12:2:12²:13/13:4:7:9:17²:19:
:5/Jas1:2:3:4²:21/2:2:8/4:3:4:8²:10:11:14:16
2:3²:5³:16/1Pe1:2:7³:9²:14:17:18:21²:22²:23
:2,3:10:11²:12²:13:15:18:21:25²/3:1³:4:6:7³:
15/4:1:2:4:8:9:15/5:3:4:7:8:13f:13/2Pe1:6:
/2:3:13/1Jn:12:13:14²:27/4:4²/5:1:2:21/2Jn
8:10:13/3Jn:2²:3:6²/Jud:20/Rev:9:11/2:2³:
:16:19⁵/3:1:2:9:11:18²:19/4:11/5:9/10/11:
8³/13:10/14:18/15:3,4⁴/16:1:6:7/17:18/19:
22:9

5594

URS
9:2,3/16:9-12/21:13/22:17/27:39,40/28:13
:38/45:20/47:18/48:5/Ex11:8/Lev19:25/
n18:9:12:14,15:18/Deu3:1/11:24/20:1/33:
Jos8:1/23:4,5/Ju1:3/7:18/9:38/1Sa1:11/2:
24,25/15:28/24:20/26:24/30:20/1Ki1:37:
47/3:22:26/20:4/22/2Ki3:6,7,8/18:24/1Ch
18/21:3:24/29:11²:14/2Ch1:10/6:33:41/9:7
:9/18:22/20:15/28:11/Job33:6/Ps16:2/42:
)/49:11/52:1/74:23/89:11/119:37:54:94:
/Pro5:20/24:11,12/27:10/Is10:30/23:7/32:
36:20/43:4/45:14/55:8:9²/60:13/66:14/Jer
/8/12:4/13:18/17:15:16/48:14/49:32/Eze
4/16:37/35:15/Dan2:39/9:18/Mic7:4:10/
h1:11/Mt6:13f/20:21/23:28/27:24/Mk10:
11:24/Lk5:33/6:20:42/15:30:31/19:21/Jn
6:10/Act5:4²/Rom1:6,7:11,12/14:1:4/1Co1:
:22/8:9/10:26:29/2Co3:1/5:12/9:2/13:14/
1:3/6:12/Eph1:2/6:3/Col1:6/1Ti5:21/Phm
5/Heb10:34/1Pe1:5:12/Rev18:14

135

URSELF
n14:21/27:37/39:9/Ex18:18²/29:26/34:2/
v18:20/19:18:34/25:5²/Num16:13/Deu7:17/
21/Jos1:8/Ru2:8,9/4:8/1Sa15:17/18/20:8:
/2Sa1:16/14:13/18/22:27/1Ki3:11/14:2/18:
37/21:20:20f/22:25/2Ki14:10/22:18,19/1Ch
21/19:2,3/2Ch7:17/20:37/34:27/Neh6:7/
b11:6/22:26/40:7/Ps18:25f/27:9/34:8/44:23
5:3/52:1/55/57:8/80:2:3:7:15²:17f:19/89:46/
2:27/109/114:5/119:122/Pro3:4,5/5:2:20/6:
/7:25/9:12/13:13/15:31,32/23:1:4,5/27:2/
c2:1/5:6,7/7:15-17:21,22/11:2/12:4/Is14:13
2:15,16/47:2:10/49:21/51:9²/57:10/Jer3:20/
:22/14:21/45:5/Lam3:44/Eze:10:24/4:10/16
/23:30²:40/24:22/28:2,3/32:2/38:14/Dan5:
/10:19/Amo7:17/Jon4:10/Mic6:15/Mt5:30/
/19:19/22:38,39/24:48/Mk12:31/14:60/15:
,30/Lk4:23/7:6,7,8/10:27/23:37:39/Jn1:22:
/7:52/10:33/14:22/18:34f/Act21:24/23:3/24
/26:14/Rom6:16/13:9²/14:16:22/1Co3:18/6:
/10:24/Gal5:14:18:20/Eph4:24/Php2:3/1Ti4
15/5:22/2Ti2:4/Tit:7/Heb1:12/6:4:6/13:3/
s2:8/1Pe3:15/4:19

159

URSELVES
n42:18/45:5/47:24²/Ex20:4/22:21:31/30:15:
:37/32:29/Lev11:43:44²/18:24:29,30/19:28²:
/20:7:25²/22/23:14/Num16:3/28:22:30/31:
:19/32:20/34:13/Deu4:16,17:25/9:4/10:19:
/11:15/14:1/18:16/20:14/28:40:68/31:29/
s7:12/8:2/24:22/Ju9:15/15:12,13/1Sa10:
,19/16:5/2Ki3:17/1Ch15:12/2Ch12:7/29:4,5
0:8/35:4,5:6/Ez10:11/Job19:5:29/27:12/42:
Ps49:11/Is1:16/28:15/30:1/33/50:11/52:1:
/58:5/62:9/Jer2:17:30/4:4f/5:19/7:8/25:7/
:9/44:7/51:6:45/Lam2:18/Eze7:18/20:7:18:
:43/22:10f/34:8:18²/36:31/38:21/39:19/47:
/Hos4:6/9:10/Joe1:13/Amo4:5/6:6:13/Ob1:
13²/Hab2:16:18/Zep1:18/3:11/Zec11:9/Mt5
3/23:13,14:15:31/25:9/26:55/Lk11:13:46:48:
2/12:57/16:9f/17:10/22:17/23:28/Jn3:28/6:
3/16:19/18:31/Act5:39/6:3/13:46/14:15/20:
)/Rom2:1:5:17:19:21/6:13:19/12:3:19/1Co1:
):26/3:18/5:13/6:2:7:8:9,10/7:9/9:25/10:15/
1:13:31/16:3/2Co3:2/6:17/10:6/13:5/Gal5:12
5/Eph2:8f:8/3:18,19/6:9/Col3:18/1Th1:7/2:
10/5:13/Jas1:22/4:7/5:3:9/1Pe:6/2Pe3:17/
ud1:23

$20 in modern times, or *. Mt 20:2f
e agreed to pay them * a day Mt 20:2
quivalent to * in modern times, Mt 20:2f
ere paid, each received *. Mt 20:9
ut they, too, were paid *. Mt 20:10
ou agree to work all day for *? Mt 20:13
af of bread for *, or three Rev 6:6
0
r *, delivered at Jerusalem. 2Ch 1:17
od and wine and * a day in cash, Neh 5:15
0
e horses were valued at * each. 1Ki 10:29
0
, and a bar of gold worth $500. Jos 7:21
r * from the sons of Hamor. Jos 24:32
0
Jerusalem cost *, and the horses 1Ki 10:29
hariots sold for * each and horses 2Ch 1:17
0
200, and a bar of gold worth *. Jos 7:21
one and * to the other. Lk 7:41
00
pproximately *. Mt 18:28f
000
another, and * to the Mt 25:15
But the man who received the * Mt 25:18
Then the man with the * came Mt 25:24,25
365
ollected came to a total of *. Num 3:50
800
hields (* worth of gold in each). 1Ki 10:16,17
000
ou must die, or else pay me *!' 1Ki 20:40
nd he would like * in silver and 2Ki 5:22
in the form of a special tax. 2Ki 15:19,20
e went to a man who owed him * Mt 18:28
'He gave $5,000 to one, * to Mt 25:15
'he man with * went right to Mt 25:17
vork, too, and earned another *. Mt 25:17
ad received the *, with the Mt 25:22
to use, and I have doubled it.' Mt 25:22
to invest while he was gone. Lk 19:13
,000
wner, Shemer, for * and built a 1Ki 16:24
'Take *," Naaman insisted. 2Ki 5:23
,300
So David paid Ornan * in gold, 1Ch 21:25
,000
gold bowls worth a total of *. Ez 8:26,27
The governor gave * in gold, 50 Neh 7:70
'He gave * to one, $2,000 to Mt 25:15
The man who received the * began Mt 25:16
with it and soon earned another *. Mt 25:16
he * brought him $10,000. Mt 25:20
o one and $500 to the other. Lk 7:41
,000
armor (gold worth * went into each 1Ki 10:16,17
0,000
the $5,000 brought him *. Mt 25:20
and give it to the man with the *. Mt 25:28
the value of the books at *. Act 19:18,19
0,000
taking gifts of * in silver, 2Ki 5:5
5,000
Their value was estimated at *, Ju 8:26
0,000
Rabbah's crown—a * treasure made 2Sa 12:29,30
in gold; * in foreign currency; 1Ch 29:6,7
0,000
$20,000 in silver, * in gold, and 2Ki 5:5
0,000
$100,000 in gold, * in silver, and Neh 7:72
7,000
$100,000 in gold and * in silver; Neh 7:71
00,000
* in gold and $77,000 in silver; Neh 7:71
and the common people gave * in Neh 7:72
40,000
300 smaller shields, each worth *. 2Ch 9:16
70,000
$300,000 of gold, * of silver, and Ez 2:69
200,000
He also paid * to hire 100,000 2Ch 25:5,6
annual tribute of * in silver, 2Ch 27:5
of heaven), up to * in silver; Ez 7:22
in silver; * in silver utensils; Ez 8:26,27
230,000
a tax against Judah totaling *. 2Ki 23:33
250,000
an annual tribute from Judah of *. 2Ch 36:3
280,000
each worth *, and 300 smaller 2Ch 9:15
300,000
its total value to be more than *. Num 31:51,52
gifts amounted to * of gold, Ez 2:69
1,300,000
and found it to total * in silver; Ez 8:26,27
1,500,000
then demanded a settlement of *. 2Ki 18:14

$2,000,000
off with a gift of *, so he turned 2Ki 15:19,20
realized his mistake he sent * 1Ch 19:6
gold bullion, * worth of silver, 1Ch 22:14
$3,000,000
$200,000 in silver utensils; * in Ez 8:26,27
Approximately *. Mt 18:24f
$3,500,000
sent gold to Solomon valued at *! 1Ki 9:14
the king a gift of * in gold, along 1Ki 10:10
$10,000,000
was brought in who owed him *! Mt 18:24
$12,000,000
value of which was more than *. 1Ki 9:27,28
$13,000,000
back * worth of gold to him! 2Ch 8:17,18
$18,000,000
with the finest gold, valued at *. 2Ch 3:8
$20,000,000
gold worth about *, besides sales 1Ki 10:14
from Ophir and * worth of purest 1Ch 29:4,5
and I will pay * into the royal Est 3:9
and about the * Haman had Est 4:7
$30,000,000
$50,000 in foreign currency; * in 1Ch 29:6,7
$85,000,000
consist of * worth of gold from 1Ch 29:4,5
1
of Caleb (* Chronicles 2:18,19). Ex 17:10f
* feet wide, and 2¼ feet high. Ex 25:23
There will be a * length of this Ex 26:12
and a * length at the front. Ex 26:13
myrrh; and * gallons of olive oil. Ex 30:24
* feet wide and 2¼ feet high. Ex 37:10
* applied to ordinary priests. Lev 21:11f
Deuel in chapter *. Num 2:3-31f
See * Kings 16:34 for the Jos 6:26f
See Numbers 35 and * Chronicles 6. Jos 20:2f
In Group * will be all the men Ju 7:5,6
(See * Samuel 10:10–12. 1Sa 19:24f
He was evidently lying. See * 2Sa 1:10f
See * Samuel 25:44. 2Sa 3:15f
See * Chronicles 18:17. 2Sa 8:18f
(See * Chronicles 20:5. 2Sa 21:19f
See * Samuel 2:31–35. 1Ki 2:27f
was a round piece * feet high. 1Ki 7:31
See * Kings 14:27. 1Ki 15:15f
slain. See * Kings 18:19 and 40. 1Ki 22:6f
Chapter *, verse 17, says King 2Ki 3:1f
Length of reign: * month 2Ki 15:13
See * Kings 13:2. 2Ki 23:16f
See * Kings 13:31, 32. 2Ki 23:18f
The remainder of * Chronicles 1Ch 10:1
See * Samuel 28. 1Ch 10:13f
Implied; see * Kings 11:5. 1Ch 20:2f
See * Kings 11:30, 31. 2Ch 10:15f
his enemy Doeg (* Samuel 22), who Ps 52:1
and kill him. * Samuel 19:11 Ps 59:1
* Kings 4:32. Pro 25:1f
See * Kings 15:22. Jer 41:9f
See Diagrams *, 2, 3, pages 000, Eze 40:5f
2⅝ feet square and * feet high. Eze 40:42
miles by * Eze 45:6
gallons to go with each bushel. Eze 45:24
And he shall bring * gallons of Eze 46:5
With each bushel he is to bring * Eze 46:7
* gallons of oil with each bushel. Eze 46:11
miles long by * Eze 48:15
The city itself is to be * miles Eze 48:16
On the north side, with its * Eze 48:30,31
On the east side, with its * Eze 48:32
on the * miles of the west side, Eze 48:34
* Kings 21:21 and 2 Kings 10:11. Hos 1:4,5f
See chapter *, verses 6, 9, and Hos 1:23f
was instituted (* Samuel 11:15). Hos 9:15f
See verse * of chapter 1. Mic 1:14f
See verse 1 of chapter *. Mic 1:14f
Implied in verse * and 3:18. Nah 1:11f
Implied in verse * and 3:18. Nah 1:13f
false prophets. See * Kings 18:28. Zec 13:6f
(1)* whatever is set Lk 10:8,9
See * Kings, chapter 10. Lk 11:31f
see footnote chapter *, verse 1. Act 1:1f
see footnote chapter 1, verse *. Act 1:1f
* Kings 19:18. Rom 11:4f
to pray and prophesy (* Cor. 1Co 14:34f
but not to teach men (* Tim. 1Co 14:34f
Implied in * Timothy 4:12. 1Co 16:11f
Implied. See * Peter 3:19, 20. 1Pe 4:6f
8:14, * Corinthians 9:5, etc. 1Pe 5:13f
ends in physical death (* Cor. 1Jn 5:17f
1:1
See Haggai *; Zec 4:6f
as in John *—the ultimate method of Rev 19:13f
1–4
See verses *. Deu 27:8f
for it by the prophet Hosea (*). 2Ki 10:11f
See note on *. Rev 3:1f
1:6
See Haggai *. Mic 6:14f
1:9
Isaiah *. Rom 9:29f

1:10
See Ezekiel *. Eze 10:14f
1:13
See John *. Jn 6:63f
1:20
Literally, "angel," as in *. Rev 2:1f
See note on *. Rev 2:8f
See note on *. Rev 2:12f
See note on *. Rev 2:18f
See note on *. Rev 3:1f
See note on *. Rev 3:7f
See note on *. Rev 3:14f
1:23
However, the Gospel of Matthew (* Is 7:14f
2¼
* feet wide, and 2¼ feet high. Ex 25:10
long, 2¼ feet wide, and * high. Ex 25:10
3¾ feet long and * feet wide. Ex 25:17
1½ feet wide, and * feet high. Ex 25:23
feet high and * feet wide, standing Ex 26:15,16
flour mixed with * pints of oil, Ex 29:40
* pints of wine, as a libation. Ex 29:40
fade. See * Corinthians 3:13. Ex 34:33f
fifteen feet and the width * feet. Ex 36:21
* feet wide, and 2¼ feet high. Ex 37:1
2¼ feet wide, and * feet high. Ex 37:1
it was 3¾ feet long and * feet Ex 37:6
1½ feet wide and * feet high. Ex 37:10
Implied in chapter *, verse 22; Ju 3:1f
Implied in chapter *, verse 22; Ju 3:1f
In Group * will be those who Ju 7:5,6
Its center was concave, * feet 1Ki 7:31
Implied in * Kings 8:25. 2Ki 9:29f
See * Kings 10:30. 2Ki 15:12f
been the king there for * years 2Ki 15:32,33
Length of his reign: * years, in 2Ki 21:19,20
Or, "Jehoahaz" (see * Kings 1Ch 3:15f
Implied in * Samuel 23:30. 1Ch 11:26-47f
but see * Kings 8:26. 2Ch 22:2f
Implied. See * Kings 23:29. 2Ch 35:20f
* Kings 16:7–8. Is 7:20f
See * Kings 19:35 and Isaiah Is 10:17f
* Kings 19:35. Is 33:4f
* Kings 18:14–17. Is 33:8f
See * Samuel 7 for the terms of Is 55:3f
Implied. See * Kings 22:12. Jer 26:24f
II (* Kings 16:7, 8). Eze 23:12f
See Diagrams 1, *, 3, pages 000, Eze 40:5f
These tables were about * feet Eze 40:42
See * Kings 20:17, 18. Dan 1:3,4f
of * Thessalonians 2:3, 4. Dan 7:24f
See 1 Kings 21:21 and * Kings Hos 1:4,5f
see 2:23.▮ * Hos 1:11
Implied in * Chronicles 35:24, 25. Zec 12:11f
Isaiah 9:1, *. Mt 4:15,16f
(2)* the sick Lk 10:8,9
See * Corinthians 4:4, and Jn 12:31f
2:2
4:4, and Ephesians * and 6:12. Jn 12:31f
2:3
of 2 Thessalonians *, 4. Dan 7:24f
2–4
Implied in verses * and 6. Ps 82:1f
Habakkuk *. Rom 1:17f
2–7
explained in chapter 4, verses *. Jos 3:12f
also see Revelation *. Rev 1:4f
2:12
See Romans *. Act 2:23f
but not to teach men (1 Tim. *). 1Co 14:34f
2:14
(See Revelation * and Numbers Rev 2:6f
2:19
Deuteronomy * indicates that Num 21:24f
2:21
daughter of Reuel (Exodus *); Num 12:1f
Genesis *. 1Co 11:8f
2:23
of Jezreel ('God sows')"; see *. Hos 1:11f
See Haggai 1:1; *, etc. Zec 4:6f
See John *. Jn 4:45f
Hosea *. Rom 9:26f
2:24
Implied in *. 1Ch 2:50f
2:31–35
See 1 Samuel *. 1Ki 2:27f
2:40
be a revived Roman Empire. See *. Dan 7:23f
2:18,19
house of Caleb (1 Chronicles *). Ex 17:10f
3
godly in character (verse *). Gen 6:1f
wood, make an Ark * feet long, 2¼ Ex 25:10
"And make a lid of pure gold, * Ex 25:17
wood and was * feet long, 2¼ feet Ex 37:1
it was * feet long and 2¼ feet Ex 37:6
and chapter *, verse 4. Ju 3:1f
and chapter *, verse 4. Ju 3:1f
Length of reign: * years, in 2Ki 15:23
been the king there for * years 2Ki 18:1
Length of his reign: * months, in 2Ki 23:31,32

(3 Con't)
Length of his reign: * months, in 2Ki 24:8,9
See Diagrams 1, 2, *, pages 000, Eze 40:5f
a 14-foot hall with * columns. Eze 40:7-12
and found them to be * feet thick; Eze 41:3
This altar was * feet square, Eze 41:22
is a stone platform * feet high. Eze 43:14
miles long and * Eze 45:3
miles long and * Eze 45:5
miles long by * Eze 48:10
From verse *. Lk 1:1f
See chapter *. Jn 19:39f
* years, as in Daniel 12:7. Rev 11:2f
* years, as in Daniel 12:7. Rev 11:3f

3:1
of Isaiah, appears in Malachi *. Mk 1:3f

3:8
(Jeremiah 23:5, Zechariah *). Is 4:2,3,4f

3:13
See 2 Corinthians *. Ex 34:33f

3:14
See Exodus *. Ex 33:19f
name is used here as in Exodus *. Ju 6:16f

3:16
See Matthew *, 17; 1Jn 5:6,7,8f

3:18
Implied in verse 1 and *. Nah 1:11f
Implied in verse 1 and *. Nah 1:13f

3:19
See 1 Peter *, 20. 1Pe 4:6f

3:29
death (Mark *) but can a Christian 1Jn 5:17f

3:32
Implied in Mark *. Mt 12:46,47f

4½
at the top, and * feet high. Ex 38:1
in chapter *, verses 2–7. Jos 3:12f
and chapter 3, verse *. Ju 3:1f
and chapter 3, verse *. Ju 3:1f
See 1 Samuel 31:3, * for the true 2Sa 1:10f
6 feet square and * feet high. 1Ki 7:27-30
decorating the * capitals at the 2Ki 25:17
7½ feet square and * feet high. 2Ch 6:12,13
to talk (verse *) the two invading Is 7:14f
See Diagram *, page 000. Eze 40:6f
of 2 Thessalonians 2:3, *. Dan 7:24f
Zechariah 4:3, *, 11. Rev 11:4f

4:2–6
and Zechariah *, giving probability Rev 1:4f
But see Zechariah *, where the Rev 4:5f
but see Zechariah *, 10, where Rev 5:6f

4:3
Zechariah *, 4, 11. Rev 11:4f

4:4
See 2 Corinthians *, and Jn 12:31f

4:8
Implied in Ephesians *. Ps 68:18f

4:9
of discrimination (cf. John *). Lk 9:53f

4:12
Implied in 1 Timothy *. 1Co 16:11f

4:15
Baal-worship flourished (Hosea *; Hos 9:15f

4:32
1 Kings *. Pro 25:1f

4:34
See John *. Ps 40:7f

5
of the names listed in verse *. Gen 36:13,14f
Note: This was approximately May * Num 10:11f
Implied in verse *. Sol 1:6f
in Daniel, chapter *, as this Is 21:5f
A papyrus dating from the * Jer 7:18f
is further described in Daniel *. Jer 25:12f
See Diagram *, page 000. Eze 40:28f
was 24½ feet wide with * walls. Eze 40:48,49
3½ feet square, and * feet high; Eze 41:22
See verse *. Act 6:8f

5:1
Implied in *. 1Ch 5:7,8f

5:2
Micah *. Mt 2:5f

5:13
Matthew *. Lk 14:34f
Compare Joshua *. Dan 8:11f

5:16
See Matthew *. Lk 8:16f
See Matthew *. Lk 8:17f

5:19
Chapter *; Jn 10:25f

6
So also in verses *, 9, 12, 15, Gen 5:3,4,5f
Totaled from verses * and 7 of the Jos 19:2-7f
See Numbers 35 and 1 Chronicles *. Jos 20:2f
7½ feet high, and * feet wide. 1Ki 7:16-22
* feet square and 4½ feet high. 1Ki 7:27-30
Length of reign: * months 2Ki 15:8
Implied in verses 2–4 and *. Ps 82:1f
See Diagram *, page 000. Eze 43:13f
miles long and * Eze 45:1
about 220 litres, or * bushels. Eze 45:11f

miles long and * Eze 48:9
miles by * Eze 48:13
See chapter 1, verses *, 9, and Hos 1:23f
See Numbers, chapter *. Amo 2:11f

6:1
Implied in *. 1Ch 6:16f

6:2–6
implying jealousy, as in Mark *. Mk 6:52f

6:4–8
And Hebrews * speaks of the 1Jn 5:17f

6:5
See Acts *; Act 21:8f

6:6
Hosea *. Mt 9:13f

6:9
Isaiah *, 10. Act 28:27f
Prayer as recorded in Matthew *. Lk 11:5,6f

6:10
or paraphrase, of Isaiah *. Jn 12:40f

6:12
See Ephesians *. Mt 24:29f
4:4, and Ephesians 2:2 and *. Jn 12:31f

6:15
All include this in Matthew *. Mk 11:26,f

6:26
See Joshua *. 1Ki 16:34f

7½
* feet wide, and three feet high. Ex 27:1
with curtain walls * feet high, Ex 27:18
it was * feet square at the top, Ex 38:1
It was thirty feet long and * feet Ex 38:18
More literally, verse * reads: Num 10:5,6,7f
Totaled from verses 6 and * of the Jos 19:2-7f
lower floor being * feet wide, the 1Ki 6:6
Each story of the annex was * 1Ki 6:10
each wing was * feet long, so 1Ki 6:23-28
each * feet high, and 6 feet wide. 1Ki 7:16-22
round bronze tank, * feet high and 1Ki 7:23
the same Shime-i as in verse *. 1Ch 23:8,9f
* capital flaring out to the roof. 2Ch 3:15
The rim stood * feet above the 2Ch 4:2
* feet square and 4½ feet high. 2Ch 6:12,13
Then, on October *, he sent the 2Ch 7:10
Implied in verse *. Job 29:12f
See 2 Samuel * for the terms of Is 55:3f
see note on chapter *, verse 18. Jer 44:17f
The top * feet of each column Jer 52:22
See Diagram *, page 000. Eze 47:13f
See Diagram *, page 000. Eze 48:8f
Three and a half years (verse *) Dan 12:11f
Implied in verses *, 10. 1Co 11:5f

7:4
See also Acts *. Gen 11:32f

7:13
In Daniel *, the corresponding Eze 2:1f

7:25
Judges *. Ps 83:11f
Judges *. Ps 83:11f

7:53–8:11
ancient manuscripts omit John *. Jn 7:53f

8
of his reign: * years old 2Ki 22:1
Implied in verse *. Ps 61:5f
II (2 Kings 16:7, *). Eze 23:12f
with a distance of * feet along the Eze 40:7-12
were 37½ feet by * feet broad." Eze 40:28f
37½ feet long and * feet broad." Eze 40:29,30f
each of them * feet thick. Eze 40:48,49
was 17½ feet wide and * feet deep. Eze 41:2
of these rooms was * feet thick, Eze 41:9
a free space of * feet out to the Eze 41:9
yard, which was * feet wide; Eze 41:11
Its walls were * feet thick. Eze 41:12
This piece shall be * Eze 45:1
built within the area which is * Eze 45:3
"The strip next to it, * Eze 45:5
the holy lands will be a section * Eze 45:6
This Temple area will be * Eze 48:9
"A strip of land measuring * Eze 48:10
Together they measure * Eze 48:13
"The strip of land * Eze 48:15
sacred lands and city lands—is * Eze 48:20
to Judah and Benjamin, is * Eze 48:21,22
prohibited in verses * and 9. 1Co 6:12f

8:1–4
and her newborn son (Isaiah *). Is 7:14f
See Acts 6:5; *. Act 21:8f

8:3
Deuteronomy *. Lk 4:4f

8:9B
See Hebrews *. Jer 31:32f

8–11
See verses *. Lev 9:15f

8:14
Matthew *, 1 Corinthians 9:5, etc. 1Pe 5:13f

8:21
Judges *. Ps 83:11f
Judges *. Ps 83:11f

8:24
See *. Dan 8:10f
See *. Dan 8:10f

8:25
Implied in 2 Kings *. 2Ki 9:2

8:26
but see 2 Kings *. 2Ch 22:

8:30–31
Shechem (Judges *), so Abimelech Ju 9:

8:36
Chapter 5:19; *, 56, 58, etc. Jn 10:2

9
So also in verses 6, *, 12, 15, Gen 5:3,4,
the second floor * feet wide, and 1Ki 6
Length of his reign: * years, in 2Ki 17
with events preceding chapter *. 1Ch 10
Implied in verse *. Is 21:
See chapter 1, verses 6, *, and Hos 1:2
Verses * through 20 are not found Mk 16:
People don't get drunk by * A.M. Act 2:1
prohibited in verses 8 and *. 1Co 6:1
described in 12:3, * and 13:1. Rev 17:

9:1
Isaiah *, 2. Mt 4:15,1

9:5
8:14, 1 Corinthians *, etc. 1Pe 5:1

9:7
Kir and now were free. (See *). Amo 1:

9:11
Revelation *. Rev 11:
See Amos *. Act 15:1
See Amos *. Act 15:1

9:18–22
See Exodus 12:22, Hebrews *. Ps 51:

9:27
Daniel *, 11:31, 12:11. Mt 24:1

9:31
See Matthew 3:16, 17; Luke *, 1Jn 5:6,7,

9:34
See Matthew *, where they called Mt 10:2

10
colts,40 cows,* bulls,20 female Gen 32:13,14,1
female donkeys,* male donkeys. Gen 32:13,14,1
bushels of meal, * oxen from the 1Ki 4:2
and the upper floor * feet wide. 1Ki 6
See verse *. 2Ki 15:1
Length of reign: * years, in 2Ki 15:1
ON OCTOBER * Neh 9:
stick, which was * feet long. Eze 40:
He told me, "This wall is * feet Eze 40:
10½ feet high and * feet wide." Eze 40:
it was * feet wide. Eze 40:
each of these rooms was * feet Eze 40:7-1
Beyond the guardrooms was a * Eze 40:7-1
They were * feet square. Eze 41:
its doorway was * feet wide, with Eze 41:
found that it was * feet thick, Eze 41:
out * feet onto the terrace. Eze 41:
with a * curb around the edges. Eze 43:1
See chapter 1, verses 6, 9, and *. Hos 1:23
See 1 Kings, chapter *. Lk 11:3
Isaiah 6:9, *. Act 28:27
Implied in verses 7, *. 1Co 11:5
but see Zechariah 4:2–6, *, where Rev 5:6

10:1
Luke * remarks, "The Lord Mt 11:1
See Exodus 34:1, Deuteronomy *. Ex 34:28

10:9
See Acts *. Mt 24:17

10:10–12
(See 1 Samuel *. 1Sa 19:24

10:11
See 1 Kings 21:21 and 2 Kings *. Hos 1:4,5

10–14
is frequent word play in verses *. Mic 1:11
is frequent word play in verses *. Mic 1:11
is frequent word play in verses *. Mic 1:11

10:20–21
But see Romans *. Is 65:1
But see Romans *. Is 65:1

10:22
Isaiah *; Rom 9:28

10:30
See 2 Kings *. 2Ki 15:12

11
Length of his reign: * years, in 2Ki 23:36,3
Length of his reign: * years, in 2Ki 24:18,1
King Jehoram's daughter, verse * 2Ch 22:11
See verse *. Job 26:13
(almond) in verse * and shoqedh Jer 1:12
here refers to, in Leviticus *. Eze 4:14
In contrast, see verse *. Eze 20:25
see Leviticus * for the forbidden Act 10:12
Zechariah 4:3, 4, *. Rev 11:4

11:1
Hosea *. Mt 2:15

11:2
But see Isaiah *, where various Rev 1:4

11:5
see 1 Kings *. 1Ch 20:2
prophesy (1 Cor. *), apparently in 1Co 14:34

11:15
God, was instituted (1 Samuel *). Hos 9:15

11–16
See chapter 13, verses *. Rev 19:20

1–19
In this passage (verses *) some Eze 28:12f
1:20–23
See Leviticus *. Deu 14:19,20f
1:26
with Genesis * and 12:4. Gen 11:32f
See Acts *. Is 65:15f
1:30
See 1 Kings *, 31. 2Ch 10:15f
ends in physical death (1 Cor. *). 1Jn 5:17f
1:31
Daniel 9:27, *, 12:11. Mt 24:15f
2
So also in verses 6, 9, *, 15, Gen 5:3,4,5f
* silver platters (each weighing Num 7:84,85,86
* silver bowls (each weighing Num 7:84,85,86
* golden trays (the trays weighing Num 7:84,85,86
* bulls, 12 rams, Num 7:87
12 bulls, * rams, Num 7:87
* yearling male goats (with the Num 7:87
* male goats. Num 7:87
been the king there for * years 2Ki 17:1
See verse *. 1Ch 7:15f
in verse *: "For I am watching Jer 1:12f
Certain aspects of verses * and 14 Eze 26:14f
a hallway * feet deep behind it. Eze 41:3
Verse * implies death from Rev 14:13f
2:3
See John *. Jn 11:1f
also described in *, 9 and 13:1. Rev 17:3f
2:4
with Genesis 11:26 and *. Gen 11:32f
2:7
3½ years, as in Daniel *. Rev 11:2f
3½ years, as in Daniel *. Rev 11:3f
2:11
(Hosea 4:15; *), and where the Hos 9:15f
Daniel 9:27, 11:31, *. Mt 24:15f
2:22
See Exodus *, Hebrews 9:18–22. Ps 51:7f
nor with the one in Nehemiah *. Dan 5:31f
2–26
the preceding laws in verses *. Ex 34:27f
2:27
Luke 9:31, 35; John *, 28, 32, 1Jn 5:6,7,8f
3
recorded in verses * to 17. Num 7:18-23f
recorded in verses * to 17. Num 7:24-29f
recorded in verses * to 17. Num 7:30-35f
recorded in verses * to 17. Num 7:36-41f
recorded in verses * to 17. Num 7:42-47f
recorded in verses * to 17. Num 7:48-53f
recorded in verses * to 17. Num 7:54-59f
recorded in verses * to 17. Num 7:60-65f
recorded in verses * to 17. Num 7:66-71f
recorded in verses * to 17. Num 7:72-77f
recorded in verses * to 17. Num 7:78-83f
mind: see verse *) will now do it Ju 6:16f
Literally, "Then, on the * day of Est 3:12f
end of a * siege (587–574 B.C.). Eze 29:18f
end of a * siege (587–574 B.C.). Eze 29:20f
See chapter *, verses 11–16. Rev 19:20f
3:1
also described in 12:3, 9 and *. Rev 17:3f
3:2
See 1 Kings *. 2Ki 23:16f
3:7
Zechariah *. Mt 26:31f
13:11–15
Described in * and 19:20. Rev 16:13f
13:31
See 1 Kings *, 32. 2Ki 23:18f
13:36
asked before (John *, 14:5), but Jn 16:5f
14
Verse * is a repetition of the Gen 36:13,14f
Note: The * day of the first month Num 9:2,3f
evening of the * day of the month. Jos 5:10
Implied in verse *. Ju 16:8f
in verse *, as otherwise the Is 7:14f
Certain aspects of verses 12 and * Eze 26:14f
a * hall with 3½-foot columns. Eze 40:7-12
Verse * is the basis for the Dan 8:26f
14:3
Psalm *. Rom 3:10f
14:5
(John 13:36, *), but apparently not Jn 16:5f
14:27
See 1 Kings *. 1Ki 15:15f
14:29
See Mark *. Jn 21:15f
15
So also in verses 6, 9, 12, *, Gen 5:3,4,5f
See Leviticus *. Gen 31:35f
The date of his death was July *, Num 33:38,39
speech was given on February *, Deu 1:1
high and * feet from brim to brim; 1Ki 7:23
we began our work on December *, Ez 10:16-19
15, and finished by March *. Ez 10:16-19
See chapter *, verse 38. Act 13:13f
15:22
See 1 Kings *. Jer 41:9f
16
See verse *. Num 13:3-15f
Implied in verse *, where a Jos 21:9-16f
of his reign: * years old 2Ki 15:1
Duration of his reign: * years, in 2Ki 15:32,33
Duration of reign: * years, in 2Ki 16:1
Verse * is omitted in many of the Mk 7:15,16f
2:14 and Numbers 31:15, *. Rev 2:6f
16:7
Tiglath-pileser II (2 Kings *, 8). Eze 23:12f
2 Kings *. Is 7:20f
16:14
the year of a hireling," like *. Is 21:16f
16:34
See 1 Kings * for the fulfillment Jos 6:26f
17
recorded in verses 13 to *. Num 7:18-23f
recorded in verses 13 to *. Num 7:24-29f
recorded in verses 13 to *. Num 7:30-35f
recorded in verses 13 to *. Num 7:36-41f
recorded in verses 13 to *. Num 7:42-47f
recorded in verses 13 to *. Num 7:48-53f
recorded in verses 13 to *. Num 7:54-59f
recorded in verses 13 to *. Num 7:60-65f
recorded in verses 13 to *. Num 7:66-71f
recorded in verses 13 to *. Num 7:72-77f
recorded in verses 13 to *. Num 7:78-83f
See verse *. Num 19:12f
expected from Bethel (verse *). Jos 8:11,12,13f
Chapter 1, verse *, says King 2Ki 3:1f
been the king there for * years 2Ki 16:1
22¾ feet wide and * feet long. Eze 40:7-12
The entrance hall was * feet Eze 41:2
on the other. A * walk ran between Eze 42:4
see verses *, 19, 23. Dan 8:9f
add verse *, "For it was necessary Lk 23:17,f
See Matthew 3:16, *; 1Jn 5:6,7,8f
17:1
In Jeremiah * their sin was Jer 31:33f
17:2
See Matthew *. Jn 1:14f
17:7
Exodus *. Ps 95:8f
17:17
Genesis *. Rom 4:19f
18
6, 9, 12, 15, *, 21, 25, 28, 32. Gen 5:3,4,5f
See verse *. Ex 6:20f
of his reign: * years old 2Ki 24:8,9
The completion date was February * Ez 6:15
See verse *. Jer 22:13f
see note on chapter 7, verse *. Jer 44:17f
pagan customs of verses * and 26. Eze 20:25f
See 2 Kings 20:17, *. Dan 1:3,4f
Compare verse *. Dan 11:13f
Implied in verse *. Rev 17:9f
18:10
It was Peter. John *. Mk 14:47f
18:14
See Ezekiel *. Dan 11:37f
2 Kings *. Is 33:8f
18:15
See Deuteronomy *. Jn 1:21f
18:17
See 1 Chronicles *. 2Sa 8:18f
18:19
See 1 Kings * and 40. 1Ki 22:6f
Implied from Luke *. Mt 19:17f
18:28
See 1 Kings *. Zec 13:6f
18:29
but included in Luke *. Mt 19:29f
19
Also called Pul, in verse * above. 2Ki 15:29f
was 35 feet wide and * feet long. Eze 40:48,49
see verses 17, *, 23. Dan 8:9f
Judges, chapters * and 20. Hos 10:9f
See verses * and 28. 1Co 14:18f
19:9
See Leviticus * and Deuteronomy Ru 2:2f
19:11
1 Samuel * Ps 59:1
19:14
See Deuteronomy *; Hos 5:10f
See Judges *. Hos 9:9f
19:18
See Isaiah *. Zep 3:9f
1 Kings *. Rom 11:4f
19:20
Described in 13:11–15 and *. Rev 16:13f
19:29
See Acts *, 20:4, Philemon 24. Act 27:2f
19:35
See 2 Kings * and Isaiah 37:36. Is 10:17f
2 Kings *. Is 33:4f
20
Implied in verses * and 26. Gen 25:21f
nanny goats,* billy goats,200 Gen 32:13,14,15
goats,200 ewes,* rams,30 milk Gen 32:13,14,15
female donkeys,10 male donkeys. Gen 32:13,14,15
the names listed in verses *, 21. Gen 36:28,29,30f
fattening pens, * pasture-fed 1Ki 4:23
Length of reign: * years, in 2Ki 15:27
been the king there for * years 2Ki 15:30
Age: * years old 2Ki 16:1
Judges, chapters 19 and *. Hos 10:9f
Verses 9 through * are not found Mk 16:9f
See 1 Peter 3:19, *. 1Pe 4:6f
20:3
Revelation *. Rev 20:10f
20:4
See Acts 19:29, *, Philemon 24. Act 27:2f
20:5
(See 1 Chronicles *. 2Sa 21:19f
20:7–9
See also Revelation *. Eze 38:2,3f
20:12
See Genesis *. Gen 11:29f
20:17
See 2 Kings *, 18. Dan 1:3,4f
20:19
in Matthew *, which indicates his Jn 18:32f
21
6, 9, 12, 15, 18, *, 25, 28, 32. Gen 5:3,4,5f
the names listed in verses 20, *. Gen 36:28,29,30f
Implied in verse *. 2Ki 2:19f
His age when he became king: * 2Ki 24:18,19
21:6
Implied in *. 2Ch 18:1f
Implied in *. 2Ch 18:1f
21:21
See 1 Kings * and 2 Kings 10:11. Hos 1:4,5f
21:32
See Exodus * and Matthew 27:3–9. Zec 11:12f
22½
there will be * feet of curtain, Ex 27:14,15
the entrance were * feet wide, each Ex 38:14,15
Implied in verse *, where the Jos 21:20,21,22f
Implied in chapter 2, verse *; Ju 3:1f
Implied in chapter 2, verse *; Ju 3:1f
of his reign: * years old 2Ki 21:19,20
Babylon on July * of the nineteenth 2Ki 25:8
Doeg (1 Samuel *), who later Ps 52:1
* feet wide and 17½ feet long. Eze 40:7-12
Implied in verse *. Dan 7:26f
22:12
See 2 Kings *. Jer 26:24f
22:18
Psalm *. Jn 19:23,24f
22:26
See Exodus *. Amo 2:8f
22:41–45
In Matthew *, Jesus applies these Ps 110:1f
23
His age when he became king: * 2Ki 23:31,32
in—it was now the * day of the Est 8:9,10
see verses 17, 19, *. Dan 8:9f
See Numbers, chapter *. Hos 9:10f
23:3–5
Deuteronomy *. Neh 13:1f
23:5
(Jeremiah *, Zechariah 3:8). Is 4:2,3,4f
23:16
See Leviticus *. Act 2:1f
23:29
See 2 Kings *. 2Ch 35:20f
23:30
Or, "Jehoahaz" (see 2 Kings * 1Ch 3:15f
Implied in 2 Samuel *. 1Ch 11:26-47f
23:31
Implied in * and 24:18. 2Ki 24:17f
24
* young bulls, Num 7:88
Implied in verses * and 28, where Jos 18:21-28f
was eaten on July *, and that 2Ki 25:3
The entrance was * feet wide with Eze 40:48,49
The platform beneath it is * Eze 43:17
mentioned in verse *, leaving seven Dan 9:25f
today, this * day of the month, Hag 2:18,19
"The * day of Kislev." Hag 2:18,19f
See Acts 19:29, 20:4, Philemon *. Act 27:2f
Press Release, April *, 1964). Rev 9:16f
24:1–4
Deuteronomy *. Jer 3:1f
24:18
Implied in 23:31 and *. 2Ki 24:17f
24:19
Leviticus 19:9 and Deuteronomy *. Ru 2:2f
25
6, 9, 12, 15, 18, 21, *, 28, 32. Gen 5:3,4,5f
This miracle occurred on the * Jos 4:19
His age when he became king: * 2Ki 15:32,33
of his reign: * years old 2Ki 18:1
His age when he became king: * 2Ki 23:36,37
arriving on March * of the ninth 2Ki 25:1
where the powerful * Ethiopian Is 7:18f
* Egyptian Dynasty (730–660 B.C.). Is 18:1f
On February *, of the 37th year Jer 52:31
Implied in 2 Chronicles 35:24, *. Zec 12:11f
December * was the usual date for Jn 10:22,23f
25:1–3
situation described in Numbers *. Num 24:25f

25:5
See Deuteronomy *. Lev 18:16f
See Deuteronomy *. Lev 20:21f
See Deuteronomy *. Ru 1:11f
25:11–12
Jeremiah *; Dan 9:2f
25:12
(in Jeremiah * and 29:10) that the Ez 1:1f
25–27
See verses *. Dan 9:24f
25:44
See 1 Samuel *. 2Sa 3:15f
26
Implied in verses 20 and *. Gen 25:21f
pagan customs of verses 18 and *. Eze 20:25f
add verse *, "but if you do not Mk 11:26,f
26-28
event, see Ezekiel, chapters *. Lk 10:13f
26:33
See Numbers *. 1Ch 7:15f
27
been the king there for * years. 2Ki 15:1
see verse * and the Revelation. Dan 9:25f
27:2–8
See Deuteronomy *. Jos 8:31f
27:3–9
See Exodus 21:32 and Matthew *. Zec 11:12f
27:5–7
See Numbers *. Jos 17:4f
27:17
See Deuteronomy 19:14; *. Hos 5:10f
28
6, 9, 12, 15, 18, 21, 25, *, 32. Gen 5:3,4,5f
Implied in verses 24 and *, where Jos 18:21-28f
See 1 Samuel *. 1Ch 10:13f
(son of Bebai), and * other men; Ez 8:2-14
be killed on the * day of February Est 3:13
was the * day of February! Est 8:12
SO ON THE * day of February, the Est 9:1
was done on the * day of February, Est 9:17
Verse * is omitted in some of the Mk 15:28f
See verses 19 and *. 1Co 14:18f
John 12:27, *, 32, 33. 1Jn 5:6,7,8f
28:16
Isaiah *. Rom 9:33f
28:22
Isaiah 10:22; *. Rom 9:28f
28:30
See Exodus *. 1Sa 28:5,6f
29
Verses * and 30 repeat the names Gen 36:28,29,30f
Length of his reign: * years, in 2Ki 18:1
* censers, Ez 1:9,10
29:10
Jeremiah 25:12 and *) that the Jews Ez 1:1f
Jeremiah 25:11–12; *. Dan 9:2f
29:13
Isaiah *. Mt 15:9f
29:23
and Gomorrah (Deuteronomy *). Hos 11:8f
30
ewes,20 rams,* milk camels, with Gen 32:13,14,15
Verses 29 and * repeat the names Gen 36:28,29,30f
Literally, verse * reads: "But if Ex 21:30f
For sharpening an axe, *Ç 1Sa 13:21
For sharpening a sickle, *Ç 1Sa 13:21
For sharpening an ox goad, *Ç) 1Sa 13:21
* bowls of solid gold, Ez 1:9,10
rendering of verse * could be, Ps 68:30f
Verse *, omitted in the Septuagint Eze 40:29,30f
31
Implied in verse *. 1Ki 7:27-30f
Duration of his reign: * years in 2Ki 22:1
different Sheshan than in verse *. 1Ch 2:34,35f
See 1 Kings 11:30, *. 2Ch 10:15f
Implied in verse *. Act 2:29f
Implied in verse *. Act 2:30f
Implied in verse *. Act 2:34f
31:3
See 1 Samuel *, 4 for the true 2Sa 1:10f
31:1,2
grandfather of Bezalel (Exodus *). Ex 17:10f
31:15
Jeremiah *. Mt 2:17f
Revelation 2:14 and Numbers *, 16. Rev 2:6f
31:16
See Numbers *. Num 24:25f
32
6, 9, 12, 15, 18, 21, 25, 28, *. Gen 5:3,4,5f
16,000 girls (of whom * went to Num 31:36-40
See 1 Kings 13:31, *. 2Ki 23:18f
John 12:27, 28, *, 33. 1Jn 5:6,7,8f
32:1–2
Psalm *. Rom 4:8f
32:6–15
See chapter *. Jer 37:12f
33
Implied in verse *. Lk 14:28f
John 12:27, 28, 32, *. 1Jn 5:6,7,8f
34:1
See Exodus *, Deuteronomy 10:1–4. Ex 34:28f

35
See Numbers * and 1 Chronicles 6. Jos 20:2f
Thus the entry hall was * feet Eze 40:48,49
side, and having a * strip of inner Eze 42:3
Luke 9:31, *; 1Jn 5:6,7,8f
35:24
Implied in 2 Chronicles *, 25. Zec 12:11f
36
point of time, follows chapter *. Jer 45:1f
36–37
the days of Hezekiah (Isaiah *). Jer 21:1f
of God's angel (Isaiah *). Hos 1:7f
37TH
On February 25, of the * year of Jer 52:31
it were * feet by 8¾ feet broad." Eze 40:28f
* feet long and 8¾ feet broad." Eze 40:29,30f
See verse *. Jn 5:32,33f
omit verse * wholly or in part. Act 8:37f
37:6–11
lifted (Jeremiah *) they became Jer 34:11f
37:36
See 2 Kings 19:35 and Isaiah *. Is 10:17f
38
been the king there for * years 2Ki 15:8
See chapter 15, verse *. Act 13:13f
38–39
Babylon (Isaiah *), also during the Eze 23:16f
39
been the king there for * years 2Ki 15:13
been the king there for * years 2Ki 15:17
(Events told about in chapter *. Jer 52:1
40
with their colts,* cows,10 bulls,20 Gen 32:13,14,15
See 1 Kings 18:19 and *. 1Ki 22:6f
40:3
Isaiah *. Mt 3:3f
41
See verses * and 44. Jos 15:37-44f
Not Cyrus, as in chapter *, but Is 42:1f
42
From the subclan of Azmaveth, *; Ez 2:3-35
the subclan of Beth-azmaveth, *; Neh 7:8-38
as in verse * which appears in all Lk 1:28f
42:1–4
Isaiah *. Mt 12:21f
43¾
this distance was * feet. Eze 40:13
feet long and * feet from side to Eze 40:21
was 87½ feet long and * feet wide. Eze 40:25
was 87½ feet long by * feet wide. Eze 40:29,30
and it was 87½ feet long by * Eze 40:33
of 87½ feet and a width of * feet. Eze 40:36
44
See verses 41 and *. Jos 15:37-44f
to worship her (chapter *). Jer 7:18f
Verses * and 46 (which are Mk 9:43,44f
Verses * and 46 (which are Mk 9:45,46f
44:28
See Isaiah *. Is 41:2f
See also, Isaiah *; Jer 51:20f
45
75 feet wide, and * feet high. Gen 6:15
75 feet wide, and * feet high. 1Ki 7:2
to brim; * feet in circumference. 1Ki 7:23
45:1
See also, Isaiah 44:28; *. Jer 51:20f
46
Verses 44 and * (which are Mk 9:43,44f
Verses 44 and * (which are Mk 9:45,46f
47
relates this to verse *. Lk 24:49f
48
with verse *) are omitted in some Mk 9:43,44f
with verse *) are omitted in some Mk 9:45,46f
48:2
sides of the north" (Psalm *); Is 14:13f
50
been the king there for * years 2Ki 15:23
of Jonathan), and * other men; Ez 8:2-14
$5,000 in gold, * golden bowls, and Neh 7:70
51
Implied in verses *, 54, 57, 59, Jos 15:48-62f
51:4
Psalm *. Rom 3:4f
52
Length of his reign: * years, in 2Ki 15:1
been the king there for * years 2Ki 15:27
were two pillars * feet high, 2Ch 3:15
From the subclan of Nebo, *; Ez 2:3-35
From the subclan of Nebo, *; Neh 7:8-38
by * feet wide, enclosed by walls. Eze 46:21,22
52:7
Isaiah *. Rom 10:15f
52:11
was taken to Babylon, Jeremiah *. Eze 12:12f
was taken to Babylon, Jeremiah *. Eze 12:13f
53:1
Isaiah *. Jn 12:38f
Isaiah *. Rom 10:16f
53:4
Isaiah *. Mt 8:17f

53:12
The quotation is from Isaiah *. Mk 15:
54
Implied in verses 51, *, 57, 59, Jos 15:48-
55
Length of his reign: * years, in 2Ki 2
Later manuscripts add to verses * Lk 9:
56
From the subclan of Netophah, *; Ez 2:3
to verses 55 and *, "And Jesus Lk 9:
8:36, *, 58, etc. Jn 10:
57
Implied in verses 51, 54, *, 59, Jos 15:48-
57:1,2
Isaiah * may indicate that Old Ps 6
those who trust in God (Isaiah *). Is 38:
58
8:36, 56, *, etc. Jn 10:
59
Implied in verses 51, 54, 57, *, Jos 15:48-
60
* rams, 60 male goats, Num 7
60 rams, * male goats, Num 7
* male lambs a year old. Num 7
51, 54, 57, 59, *, and 62, where Jos 15:48-
For sharpening a plow point, *Ç 1Sa 13
For sharpening a disc, *Ç 1Sa 13
Shemaiah, and * other men (they Ez 8:2-
61
30,500 donkeys (of which * were Num 31:36-
62
57, 59, 60, and *, where the Jos 15:48-
65:1
Isaiah *. Rom 10:
69:25
Psalm *. Act 1:
70
In all, there were * young bulls 2Ch 29:32,
of Athaliah), and * other men; Ez 8:2-
Zaccur, and * other men. Ez 8:2-
there was a room * feet long by 52½ Eze 46:21,
Jerusalem in A.D. * by Titus and Dan 9:
Take 200 spearmen and * mounted Act 23:23,
72
36,000 oxen (of which * were given Num 31:36-
74
of the subclan of Hodaviah, *; Ez 2:40,41,
Hodevah of the clan of Jeshua, *; Neh 7:43,44,
75
Make it 450 feet long, * feet Gen 6:
150 feet long, and * feet wide, Ex 27:
* feet wide, and 45 feet high. 1Ki 7
"get ready a * gallows, and in the Est 5:
has just ordered a * gallows Est 7
78:2
Psalm *. Mt 13:34,3
80
* from the subclan of Hebron; 1Ch 15:4-
(son of Michael), and * other men; Ez 8:2-
85
And I will destroy * percent Eze 39
87½
* feet from one end to the other. Eze 40:
east passageway—* feet long and 43¾ Eze 40:
And like the others, it was * Eze 40:
And, like the others, it was * Eze 40:29,
and it was * feet long by 43¾ Eze 40:
of * feet and a width of 43¾ feet. Eze 40:
was 175 feet long by * feet wide. Eze 42
outer court, were * feet long—only Eze 42:7
An additional * strip all around Eze 45
90
And Sarah, to have a baby at *?" Gen 17:
of Moses, the man of God. * Ps 90
95
From the subclan of Gibbar, *; Ez 2:3-
From the subclan of Gibeon, *; Neh 7:8-
96
and * gallons of pure olive oil. 1Ki 5:
98
(the descendants of Hezekiah), *; Ez 2:3-
of the subclan of Ater, *; Neh 7:8-
00
See Diagrams 1, 2, 3, pages *, Eze 40:
See Diagrams 1, 2, 3, pages 000, * Eze 40:
1, 2, 3, pages 000, 000, and *. Eze 40:
See Diagram 4, page *. Eze 40:
See Diagram 5, page *. Eze 40:2
See Diagram 6, page *. Eze 43:1
See Diagram 7, page *. Eze 47:1
See Diagram 7, page *. Eze 48:
100
flood when Shem was * years old; Gen 11:10,
he said in amusement. "Me—* Gen 17:
(Abraham was * years old at that Gen 21:4
times the grain he sowed. Gen 26:
father, for * pieces of silver. Gen 33:
The least anyone gathered was * Num 11:3
cattle, * sheep, and, from time to 1Ki 4:2
the pillars, with * pomegranates 2Ch 3:1
And he molded * solid gold bowls. 2Ch 4:

00 Con't)
offerings, * rams, and 200 lambs. 2Ch 29:32,33
and * robes for the priests. Ez 2:69
celebration * young bulls, 200 Ez 6:17
will men be considered old at *! Is 65:20
the porch to be about * feet high. Eze 40:14
around with walls * feet high and Zep 2:15f

2
when overwhelmed with trouble.▮ * Ps 102:1

5
Seth: Seth was * years old when Gen 5:6,7,8

7
You will need about * Ex 25:39
The entire lampstand weighed * Ex 37:23,24

9:8
Psalm *. Act 1:20f

0
Joseph was * years old when he Gen 50:22
So Joseph died at the age of *, Gen 50:26
this he died at the age of *. Jos 24:29
died at the age of *, and was Ju 2:7-9
of Hakkatan), and * other men; Ez 8:2-14

12
* from the subclan of Uzziel; 1Ch 15:4-10
From the subclan of Jorah, *; Ez 2:3-35
From the subclan of Hariph, *; Neh 7:8-38

9
He lived * years afterwards, and Gen 11:24,25

20
I will give him * years to mend Gen 6:3
told them, "I am now * years old! Deu 31:2
Moses was * years old when he Deu 34:7
* from the clan of Kohath; 1Ch 15:4-10
The choir was accompanied by * 2Ch 5:11,12
DARIUS DIVIDED THE kingdom into * Dan 6:1
a day when about * people were Act 1:15
They sounded, and found * feet Act 27:28

22
From the subclan of Michmas, *; Ez 2:3-35
From the subclan of Michmas, *; Neh 7:8-38
* feet wide by 157½ feet long. Eze 41:12

23
when he was * years old. Num 33:38,39
From the subclan of Bethlehem, *; Ez 2:3-35
the subclans of Bethel and Ai, *; Neh 7:8-38

27
WHEN SARAH WAS * years old, she Gen 23:1
with its * provinces stretching Est 1:1
from India to Ethiopia, * in all; Est 8:9,10
throughout the * provinces of the Est 9:29-31

28
From the subclan of Anathoth, *; Ez 2:3-35
members from the clan of Asaph, *; Ez 2:40,41,42
From the subclan of Anathoth, *; Neh 7:8-38
There were also * stalwart men Neh 11:10-14

30
Adam: Adam was * years old when Gen 5:3,4,5
Jacob replied, "I have lived * Gen 47:9
* from the clan of Gershom; 1Ch 15:4-10
very old age, finally dying at *. 2Ch 24:15

33
(Kohath lived * years. Ex 6:18

37
of *, and joined his ancestors. Gen 25:17
(Levi lived * years. Ex 6:16
Amram lived to the age of *. Ex 6:20

38
(all of whom were gatekeepers), *. Neh 7:43,44,45

39
Akkub, Hatita, and Shobai), *. Ez 2:40,41,42

40
Job lived * years after that, Job 42:16

44
Literally, "* cubits by human Rev 21:17f

45
died when he was * years old, so Gen 11:32f

47
so that he was * years old at the Gen 47:28

48
members from the clan of Asaph, *; Neh 7:43,44,45

50
water covered the earth * days. Gen 7:24
receded until, * days after it Gen 8:3,4
will stretch for * feet, and be Ex 27:9,10
side of the court—* feet of Ex 27:11
So the entire court will be * Ex 27:18
The south wall was * feet long; Ex 38:9
The north wall was also * feet Ex 38:11
It was huge—measuring * feet 1Ki 7:2
These men had * sons and 1Ch 8:40
Parosh—Zechariah, and * other men; Ez 8:2-14
I regularly fed * Jewish officials Neh 5:17

153
By his count there were * large Jn 21:11

156
From the subclan of Magbish, *; Ez 2:3-35

157½
122½ feet wide by * feet long. Eze 41:12

160
of Josiphiah), and * other men; Ez 8:2-14

162
Jared: Jared was * years old when Gen 5:18,19,20

168–167
This event was fulfilled in * Dan 11:30,31f

172
There were also * gatekeepers, Neh 11:19

175
ripe old age of *, and his sons Gen 25:7,8
that the distance was * feet. Eze 40:19
the two passageways was * feet. Eze 40:23
the passageways was * feet. Eze 40:27
and found it to be * feet Eze 40:47
The area was * feet square. Eze 41:13
Temple was also * feet wide, and Eze 41:14
This group of structures was * Eze 42:2
court, which was * feet long. Eze 42:7,8

180
at the ripe old age of *. Gen 35:28,29
The roof was * feet high. 2Ch 3:4

182
Lamech: Lamech was * years old Gen 5:28-31

187
Methuselah: Methuselah was * Gen 5:25,26,27

188
of Bethlehem and Netophah, *; Neh 7:8-38

190
Some versions read, "* days." Eze 4:4,5f

195
the palace were * bushels of fine 1Ki 4:22

200
He lived * years afterwards, with Gen 11:22,23
his brother Esau:* nanny goats,20 Gen 32:13,14,15
billy goats,* ewes,20 rams,30 milk Gen 32:13,14,15
there were * leaders of the tribe 1Ch 12:24-37
* from the subclan of Elizaphan; 1Ch 15:4-10
the gold to make * large shields, 2Ch 9:15
offerings, 100 rams, and * lambs. 2Ch 29:32,33
in addition to 7,337 slaves and * Ez 2:64,65
100 young bulls, * rams, and 400 Ez 6:17
of Zerahiah), and * other men; Ez 8:2-14
Hezekiah lived * years after Pro 25:1f
from each * sheep in all your Eze 45:15
Literally, "* denarii," a year's Mk 6:37f
Literally, * denarii, a denarius Jn 6:7f
and ordered, "Get * soldiers ready Act 23:23,24
* spearmen and 70 mounted cavalry. Act 23:23,24
out in a stream * miles long and as Rev 14:20

205
there Terah died at the age of *. Gen 11:32

207
He lived * years after that, with Gen 11:20,21

209
He lived another * years Gen 11:18,19

212
There were * doorkeepers in 1Ch 9:22

216
found them to be * feet across (the Rev 21:17

218
(son of Jehiel), and * other men; Ez 8:2-14

220
* from the clan of Merari; 1Ch 15:4-10
and * Temple attendants. Ez 8:20
These * men were all listed by Ez 8:20
The homer was about * litres, or Eze 45:11f

223
From the subclan of Hashum, *; Ez 2:3-35
the subclans of Bethel and Ai, *; Ez 2:3-35

232
the provinces, * of them, then the 1Ki 20:15

240
and contained * gallons of water. 1Ki 7:38

242
And there were * priests under Neh 11:10-14

245
them 736 horses, * mules, 435 Ez 2:66,67
also, 7,337 slaves and * choir Neh 7:67
them 736 horses, * mules, 435 Neh 7:68,69

250
a censer for each man, * in all; Num 16:17
closely by the * Israeli leaders. Num 16:25
* men who were offering incense. Num 16:35
So Eleazar the priest took the * Num 16:39
them; and * men were destroyed by Num 26:5-11

252
In * B.C. Ptolemy II of Egypt gave Dan 11:6f

273
To redeem the * eldest sons in Num 3:46
money for the * eldest sons of Num 3:49

284
In all, there were * Levites in Neh 11:18

288
each one—* of them in all—was a 1Ch 25:6,7

300
Afterwards he lived another * Gen 5:21-24
He once killed * men with his 1Ch 11:11
* men at one time with his spear. 1Ch 11:20
$280,000, and * smaller shields, 2Ch 9:16
from Ethiopia with * chariots, 2Ch 14:9,10
and * oxen as Passover offerings. 2Ch 35:8
son of Jahaziel, and * other men; Ez 8:2-14
also and killed * more men, though Est 9:15
to the beach, about * feet away. Jn 21:8

318
his household, * of them in all, Gen 14:14

320
From the subclan of Harim, *; Ez 2:3-35
From the subclan of Harim, *; Neh 7:8-38

323
From the subclan of Bezai, *; Ez 2:3-35

324
From the subclan of Bezai, *; Neh 7:8-38

328
From the subclan of Hashum, *; Neh 7:8-38

345
From the subclan of Jericho, *; Ez 2:3-35
From the subclan of Jericho, *; Neh 7:8-38

350
Noah lived another * years after Gen 9:28

365
then, when he was *, and in Gen 5:21-24

372
From the subclan of Shephatiah, *; Ez 2:3-35
From the subclan of Shephatiah, *; Neh 7:8-38

390
of fine flour, * bushels of meal, 1Ki 4:22
"Now lie on your left side for * Eze 4:4,5
for * years by captivity and doom. Eze 4:4,5
"During the first * days eat Eze 4:9

392
of Solomon's officers numbered *. Ez 2:58
Solomon's officers numbered *." Neh 7:60

400
in a foreign land for * years. Gen 15:13
"Well, the land is worth * Gen 23:14,15
he had suggested—* pieces of Gen 23:16
meet Jacob—with an army of * men! Gen 32:6
saw Esau coming with his * men. Gen 33:1
of Baal and the * prophets of 1Ki 18:19
These were evidently the * 1Ki 22:6f
The * pomegranates hanging from 2Ch 4:12-16
So King Ahab summoned * of his 2Ch 18:3,4,5
rams, and * lambs were sacrificed; Ez 6:17
About * others joined him, but he Act 5:36
there become slaves for * years. Act 7:6

403
he lived another * years, and had Gen 11:12,13
was born, living * years after Gen 11:14,15

430
He lived another * years Gen 11:16,17
had lived in Egypt * years, and it Ex 12:40,41
last day of the * year that all of Ex 12:40,41

434
be forty-nine years plus * years Dan 9:25
"After this period of * years, Dan 9:26

435
* camels, and 6,720 donkeys. Ez 2:66,67
* camels, and 6,720 donkeys. Neh 7:68,69

437½
Literally, "* feet" in every Eze 48:17f

450
Make it * feet long, 75 feet Gen 6:15
Carmel, with all * prophets of Baal 1Ki 18:19
them, "but Baal has * prophets. 1Ki 18:22
the * prophets of Baal were slain. 1Ki 22:6f
Judges ruled for about * years, Act 13:19,20

454
From the subclan of Adin, *; Ez 2:3-35

468
These were the * stalwart Neh 11:4,5,6

480
(This was * years after the 1Ki 6:1

483
This totals * years, instead of Dan 9:25f

486–465
Perhaps Xerxes (*) who launched an Dan 11:2f

490
"The Lord has commanded * years Dan 9:24
instead of the * years mentioned in Dan 9:25f

500
Noah: Noah was * years old and Gen 5:32
after that he lived another * Gen 11:10,11
Moses had built the Tabernacle * 2Ch 1:2,3f
and goats and * oxen to the Levites 2Ch 35:9
They even killed * men in Est 9:6
"The Jews have killed * men in Est 9:12
3,000 camels, * teams of oxen, 500 Job 1:2,3
500 teams of oxen, * female Job 1:2,3
Christ who, * years later, came Hag 2:8,9f

530
golden bowls, and * sets of Neh 7:70

539
Great entered Babylon in * B.C. Jer 25:12f

550
And there were * men of Israel 1Ki 9:23

568
ruled Egypt from 588 to * B.C. Jer 44:30f

587
Late in July, * B.C. Jer 52:12f
* B.C., the year Jerusalem fell to Eze 30:20f
It was the year * B.C. Eze 31:1f

587–574
end of a 13-year siege (* B.C.). Eze 29:18f
end of a 13-year siege (* B.C.). Eze 29:20f

588
ruled Egypt from * to 568 B.C. Jer 44:30f

(588 Con't)
Jerusalem in *, Nebuchadnezzar Eze 30:21f
595
Afterwards Lamech lived * Gen 5:28-31
597
ruler before the exile of * B.C. Jer 21:1f
600
He was * years old when the Gen 7:6
One week later, when Noah was * Gen 7:10,11,12
chariot corps—* chariots in all—and Ex 14:7
In addition, * oxen and 3,000 2Ch 29:32,33
601ST
Literally, "in the * year, in the Gen 8:13f
605
Probably in the summer of * B.C. Jer 36:1f
609
brief months in the year * B.C. Jer 22:11f
In * B.C., the year King Josiah Jer 47:1f
609–598
He ruled from * B.C. Jer 22:13f
612
the events of the year * B.C. Nah 2:1f
616
Some manuscripts read "*." Rev 13:18f
621
the subclans of Ramah and Geba, *; Ez 2:3-35
the subclans of Ramah and Geba, *; Neh 7:8-38
623
From the subclan of Bebai, *; Ez 2:3-35
626
in Jeremiah's time (around * B.C. Jer 5:15f
628
From the subclan of Bebai, *; Neh 7:8-38
630
the Assyrians around * B.C. Hab 1:6f
642
From the subclan of Bani, *; Ez 2:3-35
Tobiah, and Nekoda—a total of *. Neh 7:62
648
From the subclan of Binnui, *; Neh 7:8-38
652
Tobiah, and Nekoda—a total of *. Ez 2:60
From the subclan of Arah, *; Neh 7:8-38
655
From the subclan of Adin, *; Neh 7:8-38
666
From the subclan of Adonikam, *; Ez 2:3-35
the letters in his name add to *! Rev 13:18
667
From the subclan of Adonikam, *; Neh 7:8-38
675
337,500 sheep (of which * were Num 31:36-40
690
Jeuel and his relatives: * in all. 1Ch 9:6
700
been lost, he led * of his 2Ki 3:26
721
of Lod, Hadid, and Ono, *; Neh 7:8-38
722
to the Assyrian armies in * B.C. Is 7:8f
725
of Lod, Hadid, and Ono, *; Ez 2:3-35
730–660
25th Egyptian Dynasty (* B.C.). Is 18:1f
736
They took with them * horses, Ez 2:66,67
They took with them * horses, Neh 7:68,69
740
who invaded Gilead around * B.C. Hos 10:14f
743
Chephirah, and Be-eroth, *; Ez 2:3-35
Chephirah, and Be-eroth, *; Neh 7:8-38
745
guard, and took *—a total of 4,600 Jer 52:30
760
From the subclan of Zaccai, *; Ez 2:3-35
From the subclan of Zaccai, *; Neh 7:8-38
775
From the subclan of Arah, *; Ez 2:3-35
777
and died at the age of *. Gen 5:28-31
782
afterwards he lived another * Gen 5:25,26,27
800
Adam lived another * years, Gen 5:3,4,5
Afterwards he lived another * Gen 5:18,19,20
$30,000,000 in silver; * tons of 1Ch 29:6,7
it with one for only * bushels!' Lk 16:7
807
Afterwards he lived another * Gen 5:6,7,8
815
Afterwards he lived another * Gen 5:9,10,11
822
In all, there were * priests doing Neh 11:10-14
830
Afterwards he lived * years, Gen 5:15,16,17
832
years later, he took * more; Jer 52:29
840
Afterwards he lived another * Gen 5:12,13,14
845
From the subclan of Zattu, *; Neh 7:8-38
850
'My debt is * gallons of olive Lk 16:5,6
875
form of a square, * feet long on Eze 42:16-20
"A section of this land, * feet Eze 45:2
895
and died at the age of *. Gen 5:15,16,17
905
and died at the age of *. Gen 5:9,10,11
910
and died at the age of *. Gen 5:12,13,14
912
and died at the age of *. Gen 5:6,7,8
930
and died at the age of *. Gen 5:3,4,5
945
From the subclan of Zattu, *; Ez 2:3-35
950
and was * years old at his death. Gen 9:29
956
A total of * Benjaminites 1Ch 9:9
962
and died at the age of *. Gen 5:18,19,20
968
The * descendants of Gabbai and Neh 11:7,8,9
969
and died at the age of *. Gen 5:25,26,27
973
of the subclan of Jeshua, *; Ez 2:36-39
of the subclan of Jedaiah, *; Neh 7:39-42
990
1,225 bushels of wheat; * gallons Ez 7:22
1000
one judge for each * people; Ex 18:21
Conscript * men from each Num 31:4,5
From Naphtali there were * 1Ch 12:24-37
it * burnt offerings to the Lord. 2Ch 1:5,6
King Hezekiah gave the people * 2Ch 30:24
and the princes donated * young 2Ch 30:24
* gold trays, Ez 1:9,10
* silver trays, Ez 1:9,10
* miscellaneous items. Ez 1:9,10
6,000 camels, * teams of oxen, and Job 42:12
of oxen, and * female donkeys. Job 42:12
him in chains for * years, and Rev 20:2
1,005
3,000 proverbs and wrote * songs. 1Ki 4:32
1,017
From the subclan of Harim, *. Ez 2:36-39
From the subclan of Harim, *. Neh 7:39-42
1,052
From the subclan of Immer, *; Ez 2:36-39
From the subclan of Immer, *; Neh 7:39-42
1200
coast of Palestine around * B.C. Zep 2:5f
1,222
From the subclan of Azgad, *; Ez 2:3-35
1,225
in silver; * bushels of wheat; Ez 7:22
1,247
From the subclan of Pashhur, *; Ez 2:36-39
From the subclan of Pashhur, *; Neh 7:39-42
1,254
From the subclan of Elam, *; Ez 2:3-35
From the subclan of Elam, *; Ez 2:3-35
From the subclan of Elam, *; Neh 7:8-38
From the subclan of Elam, *; Neh 7:8-38
1,260
two witnesses to prophesy * days Rev 11:3
to take care of her for * days. Rev 12:6
1,290
worshiped, there will be * days. Dan 12:11
1335TH
wait and remain until the * day! Dan 12:12
1,365
Literally, "* shekels after the Num 3:50f
1,400
and cavalry—* chariots in all, and 1Ki 10:26
He built up a huge force of * 2Ch 1:14
1500
for * feet in each direction. Num 35:4
then they repaired the * feet of Neh 3:13
went, he took me * feet east along Eze 47:3
He measured off another * feet Eze 47:4
Another * feet and it had become Eze 47:5
on them, and with * towers, should Zep 2:15f
other dimensions—* miles each way. Rev 21:16
1550
from about 1900 B.C. to * B.C. Jer 5:15f
1,700
Hashabiah and * of his clansmen 1Ch 26:30
1720
times) was founded about * B.C. Num 13:22f
1,760
In all, * priests returned. 1Ch 9:13
1900
Empire lasted from about * B.C. Jer 5:15f
1961
In China alone, in *, there were Rev 9:16f
1964
Press Release, April 24, *). Rev 9:16f
2,000
* donkeys, and 100,000 captives. 1Ch 5
—that you don't have * men left in Is 36:
If you do, he will give you * Is 36:
2,056
From the subclan of Bigvai, *; Ez 2:3
2,067
From the subclan of Bigvai, *; Neh 7:8-
2,172
From the subclan of Parosh, *; Ez 2:3-
From the subclan of Parosh, *; Neh 7:8-
2,322
From the subclan of Azgad, *; Neh 7:8-
2,410
* silver bowls (of various Ez 1:9,
2,600
gave the priests * sheep and goats, 2Ch 3
2,630
of the Gershon division totaled *. Num 4:38-
2,750
found that the total number was *. Num 4:
2,812
of Jeshua and Joab), *; Ez 2:3-
2,818
of the subclan of Pahath-moab, *; Neh 7:8-
3000
Thus there will be * feet Num 3
He was the author of * proverbs 1Ki 4:
tribe Saul was from, there were *. 1Ch 12:24-
It held * barrels of water. 2Ch 4
Samaria, killing * people and 2Ch 25:
In addition, 600 oxen and * sheep 2Ch 29:32,
offerings, and * young bulls. 2Ch 3
for he owned 7,000 sheep, * Job 1:2
Babylonian soil as early as * B.C. Jer 5:1
were baptized—about * in all! Act 2:
3,023
of Nebuchadnezzar's reign was *. Jer 52:
3,140
The people brought gifts of * Ex 38:
3,200
And of the Merari division, *. Num 4:42-
3,500
Approximately * *. Act 19:18,1
3,600
in the hills, and * foremen. 2Ch 2
as loggers and * as foremen. 2Ch 2:
3,630
From the subclan of Senaah, *. Ez 2:3-
3,700
Aaron—there were * troops under 1Ch 12:24-
3,930
From the subclan of Sanaah, *. Neh 7:8-
4,000
In addition, Solomon had * stalls 2Ch 9:2
And everyone ate until full—* Mt 15:37,
Don't you remember the * I fed, Mt 16:
There were about * people in the Mk 8:8
"And when I fed the * with seven Mk 8:2
and took * members of the Act 21:37,
4,600
From the Levites, *. 1Ch 12:24-3
800 tons of bronze; and * tons of 1Ch 29:6
745—a total of * captives in all. Jer 52:3
5,000
and Jozabad—gave * sheep and goats 2Ch 35
(About * men were in the crowd Mt 14:2
Don't you remember at all the * I Mt 16
There were about * men there for Mk 6:43,4
"What about the * men I fed with Mk 8:1
For there were about * men Lk 9:1
*—sat down on the grassy slopes. Jn 6:1
reached a new high of about * men! Act 4:
5,469
In all there were * gold and Ez 1:1
6,000
For now he had 14,000 sheep, * Job 42:1
a legion consisted of * troops. Lk 8:3
6,200
* Num 3:31-3
6,720
mules, 435 camels, and * donkeys. Ez 2:66,6
mules, 435 camels, and * donkeys. Neh 7:68,6
6,800
From Judah, * troops armed with 1Ch 12:24-3
7,000
And incidentally, there are * 1Ki 19:1
the rest of his army of * men. 1Ki 20:1
bulls for offerings, and * sheep; 2Ch 30:2
for he owned * sheep, 3,000 Job 1:2,
tenth of the city, leaving * dead. Rev 11:1
7,100
From the tribe of Simeon, * 1Ch 12:24-3
7,337
in addition to * slaves and 200 Ez 2:64,6
also, * slaves and 245 choir Neh 7:6
7,500
* Num 3:16-2
7,540
The people brought * pounds of Ex 38:2
7,700
* rams and 7,700 male goats. 2Ch 17:1

(7,700 Con't)
7,700 rams and * male goats. 2Ch 17:11
8,580
service and transportation, was *. Num 4:46,47,48
8,600
* Num 3:25-30
9,500
the veil required * pounds of Ex 38:27
9,575
The amount of silver used was * Ex 38:25,26
10,000
and there killed * men from Seir. 2Ch 25:11
Another * were taken alive to 2Ch 25:12
in silver, * sacks of wheat, and 2Ch 27:5
of wheat, and * sacks of barley. 2Ch 27:5
1,000 young bulls and * sheep. 2Ch 30:24
Literally, "* talents." Mt 18:24f
his army of * is strong enough to Lk 14:31
12,000
of Israel, * armed men were sent to Num 31:4,5
in all, and * cavalrymen who lived 1Ki 10:26
and recruited * cavalry to guard 2Ch 1:14
and chariots, and * cavalrymen 2Ch 9:25
slaughtered * men of Edom in the Ps 60:1
Judah * Rev 7:4-8
Reuben * Rev 7:4-8
Gad * Rev 7:4-8
Asher * Rev 7:4-8
Naphtali * Rev 7:4-8
Manasseh * Rev 7:4-8
Simeon * Rev 7:4-8
Levi * Rev 7:4-8
Issachar * Rev 7:4-8
Zebulum * Rev 7:4-8
Joseph * Rev 7:4-8
Benjamin * Rev 7:4-8
14,000
For now he had * sheep, 6,000 Job 42:12
14,700
but not before * people had died Num 16:49
16,000
* girls (of whom 32 went to the Num 31:36-40
oxen,30,500 donkeys, and* girls Num 31:42-46
17,200
included * warriors at the time of 1Ch 7:11
18,000
From the half-tribe of Manasseh, * 1Ch 12:24-37
20,000
will pay your men * sacks of 2Ch 2:10
of crushed wheat, * barrels of 2Ch 2:10
barrels of barley, * barrels of 2Ch 2:10
and * barrels of olive oil." 2Ch 2:10
to defeat the * men who are Lk 14:31
20,800
From the tribe of Ephraim, * 1Ch 12:24-37
22,000
* males a month old and older. Num 3:39
Lord—a total of * oxen and 120,000 1Ki 8:62,63
was * oxen and 120,000 sheep. 2Ch 7:4,5
22,034
the leaders of * troops (all of 1Ch 7:7
22,200
The tribe of Simeon: *. Num 26:12-14
At the time of David there were * 1Ch 7:9
22,273
a month old and older to be *. Num 3:43
22,600
war from these families totaled *. 1Ch 7:2
23,000
in the census was *, counting all Num 26:62
wives, and * fell dead in one day. 1Co 10:8
24,000
after * people had already died. Num 25:9
each with * troops, including 1Ch 27:1
He had charge of * troops who 1Ch 27:2,3
He had charge of * troops who 1Ch 27:4
was Benaiah. His * men were on duty 1Ch 27:5,6
He had * men on duty the fourth 1Ch 27:7
from Izrah, with * men on duty the 1Ch 27:8
he had * men on duty the sixth 1Ch 27:9
in Ephraim, with * men on duty the 1Ch 27:10
Zerah, who had * men on duty the 1Ch 27:11
who commanded * troops during the 1Ch 27:12
in Zerah, with * men on duty the 1Ch 27:13
in Ephraim, with * men on duty 1Ch 27:14
who commanded * men on duty during 1Ch 27:15
25,100
army killed * men of Benjamin that Ju 20:35-39
27,000
fell on them and killed another *. 1Ki 20:30
28,600
From the tribe of Dan there were * 1Ch 12:24-37
30,000
Then the king contributed * lambs 2Ch 35:7
30,500
* donkeys (of which 61 were given Num 31:36-40
oxen,* donkeys, and16,000 girls Num 31:42-46
32,000
61,000 donkeys; and * young Num 31:32-35
32,200
Joseph -* Num 1:20-46
census: 40,500 * Num 2:3-31
32,500
The tribe of Joseph: * in the Num 26:28-37
The * registered in the half-tribe Num 26:28-37
35,400
Benjamin Num 1:20-46
Census: 40,500 32,200 * Num 2:3-31
36,000
* oxen (of which 72 were given to Num 31:36-40
to:337,500 sheep,* oxen,30,500 Num 31:42-46
of King David, numbered * troops; 1Ch 7:4
genealogy numbered * men of war. 1Ch 7:40
37,000
1,000 officers and * troops 1Ch 12:24-37
38,000
The total came to *. 1Ch 23:3
40,000
were * trained and ready troops. 1Ch 12:24-37
40,500
Joseph -* Num 1:20-46
census: * Num 2:3-31
The tribe of Gad: *. Num 26:15-18
41500
Asher -* Num 1:20-46
census: 62,700 * Num 2:3-31
42,360
So a total of * persons returned Ez 2:64,65
There was a total of * citizens Neh 7:66
43,730
The tribe of Reuben: *. Num 26:5-11
44,760
There were * armed, trained, and 1Ch 5:18
45,400
The tribe of Naphtali: *. Num 26:48-50
45,600
The tribe of Benjamin: *. Num 26:38-41
45,650
Gad -* Num 1:20-46
* Num 2:3-31
46,500
son of Jacob) -* Num 1:20-46
Census: * Num 2:3-31
50,000
The booty included * camels, 1Ch 5:21
there were * trained warriors; 1Ch 12:24-37
52,750
* in the half-tribe of Manasseh. Num 26:28-37
53,400
Naphtali -* Num 1:20-46
census: 62,700 41,500 * Num 2:3-31
The tribe of Asher: *. Num 26:44-47
54,400
Issachar -* Num 1:20-46
Census; 74,600 * 57,400 Num 2:3-31
57,400
Zebuluh -* Num 1:20-46
Census: 74,600 54,400 * Num 2:3-31
59,300
Simeon -* Num 1:20-46
* Num 2:3-31
60,500
The tribe of Zebulun: *. Num 26:26,27
61,000
72,000 oxen; * donkeys; Num 31:32-35
62,700
Dan -* Num 1:20-46
census: * Num 2:3-31
64,300
The tribe of Issachar: *. Num 26:23-25
64,400
The tribe of Dan: *. Num 26:42,43
70,000
Israel and * men died as a result. 1Ch 21:14
This required a force of * 2Ch 2:2
He indentured * as common 2Ch 2:18
72,000
was 675,000 sheep; * oxen; Num 31:32-35
74,600
Judah -* Num 1:20-46
Census: * Num 2:3-31
75,000
killing * of those who hated them; Est 9:16
76,500
The tribe of Judah: *. Num 26:19-22
80,000
70,000 laborers, * stonecutters in 2Ch 2:2
* as loggers and 3,600 as foremen. 2Ch 2:18
87,000
Issachar numbered * stouthearted 1Ch 7:5
100,000
And the Israelis killed * Syrian 1Ki 20:29
annual tribute of * lambs and the 2Ki 3:4
lambs and the wool of * rams; 2Ki 3:4
2,000 donkeys, and * captives. 1Ch 5:21
He also paid $200,000 to hire * 2Ch 25:5,6
108,100
of the camp was *, and they were Num 2:3-31
120,000
22,000 oxen and * sheep and goats! 1Ki 8:62,63
lived—there were * troops equipped 1Ch 12:24-37
was 22,000 oxen and * sheep. 2Ch 7:4,5
Remaliah, killed * of his bravest 2Ch 28:6
Nineveh with its * people in utter Jon 4:11
Or, "with its * children who Jon 4:11f
125,000
annual payment of * bushels of 1Ki 5:11
144,000
I heard the number—it was *, out Rev 7:4-8
and with him were * who had his Rev 14:1
This tremendous choir—* Rev 14:3
song except those * who had been Rev 14:3
151,450
the Reuben side of the camp was *. Num 2:3-31
153,600
found that there were * of them. 2Ch 2:17
157,600
on Dan's side of the camp was *. Num 2:3-31
175,000
of about * persons—and the Jon 3:3f
180,000
and Benjamin: * special troops—to 1Ki 12:21
and Benjamin, * strong, and 2Ch 11:1
was Jehozabad, with * trained men. 2Ch 17:18
185,000
of the Lord killed * Assyrian 2Ki 19:35
Assyrians and killed * soldiers; Is 37:36
186,400
on Judah's side of the camp was *. Num 2:3-31
200,000
of unusual piety, with * troops. 2Ch 17:16
Benjamin supplied * men equipped 2Ch 17:17
also captured * Judean women and 2Ch 28:8
250,000
50,000 camels, * sheep, 2,000 1Ch 5:21
280,000
numbered *, armed with large 2Ch 14:8
Jeho-hanan with an army of * men. 2Ch 17:14,15
300,000
King Asa's Judean army was * 2Ch 14:8
he had an army of * men twenty 2Ch 25:5,6
307,500
The army consisted of * men, all 2Ch 26:13
337,500
* sheep (of which 675 were given Num 31:36-40
to:* sheep,36,000 oxen,30,500 Num 31:42-46
400,000
men of Benjamin, numbered * men. Ju 20:17
Abijah, fielded * seasoned warriors 2Ch 13:3
450,000
their leaders and * troops to Ju 20:1
470,000
age in Israel and * in Judah. 1Ch 21:5
500,000
age in Israel, and * in Judah. 2Sa 24:9
* elite troops of Israel that day. 2Ch 13:17
600,000
But Moses said, "There are * men Num 11:21
601,730
men throughout Israel was *. Num 26:51
603,550
old or older, a total of * men. Ex 38:25,26
Grand Total: * Num 1:20-46
of Israel totaled * (not including Num 2:32,33
675,000
kept for themselves) was * sheep; Num 31:32-35
800,000
people to the king—* men of 2Sa 24:9
approximately * pounds sterling at 1Ch 19:6f
1,000,000
by an army of * troops from 2Ch 14:9,10
slaughter of * Jews during the Dan 9:25f
1,100,000
he gave came to * men of military 1Ch 21:5
$3,000,000,000
"By hard work I have collected * 1Ch 22:14
6,000,000,000
of * in the near future. Rev 9:16f
$145,000,000
of the king pledged * in gold; 1Ch 29:6,7
200,000,000
They led an army of * Rev 9:16
an "estimated * armed and Rev 9:16f